2004

75TH EDITION

INTERNATIONAL MOTION PICTURE ALMANAC

Editor
EILEEN S. QUIGLEY

Associate Editor & Operations Manager
AARON DIOR PINKHAM

Contributing Editor
DEE QUIGLEY

R 791.43
In61

Quigley Publishing Company, A Division of QP Media, Inc.
Publishers of the International Motion Picture Almanac (Annual)
& The International Television & Video Almanac (Annual)
(800) 231-8239, www.quigleypublishing.com

2004 75th Edition
INTERNATIONAL MOTION PICTURE ALMANAC

ISSN: 0074-7084
ISBN: 0-900610-73-5

PRINTED IN THE UNITED STATES OF AMERICA

TABLE OF CONTENTS

DIGITAL

EXHIBITION

PROFESSIONAL ORGANIZATIONS AND GOVERNMENT OFFICES

THE WORLD MARKET

INDEX

MOTION PICTURE YEAR IN REVIEW

BY WILLIAM J. QUIGLEY

THE INDUSTRY

In a year like 2003, where there were major concerns about terrorism, war, the economy and SARS, it is quite remarkable that the motion picture industry had such a successful year. It is really a testament to the power and desirability of motion pictures that people the world over, particularly in troubled times, want to suspend disbelief and be entertained out of their homes, no matter what other concerns they may have. Whether people go to theatres to laugh, to cry, to be challenged or stimulated, to be amused or to learn, this industry and art form is unmatched in its power to reach, excite and delight people globally.

However, there is a major problem upon the industry that the Studios and other media conglomerates spent an extraordinary amount of effort fighting this year: digital media. While most companies view digital technology as ultimately an opportunity for new revenue streams and new financial models, it is clear that the uncompensated sharing or trading of digital media files is any film producer or distributor's worst nightmare. The industry is panicked by the thought that the Kazas, Gnutellas, Napsters and other digital file sharers that have hurt the recording industry will do the same thing to the motion picture industry. Piracy is estimated to cause $10 billion of losses each year and it will get worse as broadband becomes more pervasive. Symptomatic of the problem is Jack Valenti's move this year to ban "screeners," that are used by distributors to promote films for Academy Awards, which the MPAA says is an important source of digital piracy. First run films that have been recorded in theatres, digitized and then uploaded are available worldwide, often before the theatrical release. This is also reflected in the slow and careful progress of the studios' digital cinema standards group, DCI, which can work out the controversy between 2K and 4K but can't yet agree on the proper protection of digital assets in transmission and storage.

The industry has been working on a number of levels to try to stem the tide of theft of intellectual property and filmed content with an effort to educate the public about copyright, enforce global anti-piracy regulations and technological research to develop and propagate standards to protect motion pictures throughout all the distribution channels. The good news is that Apple Computer's music downloads subsidiary, iTunes, demonstrated that the consumers are willing to pay for digital content if there is ease of use and the pricing is right. When the motion picture industry figures out how to deliver what audiences want at a price they are willing to pay, then digital distribution through the Internet or Video on Demand will become just another profit center in the distribution chain for motion pictures. This in turn, much as television, pay per view, cable, satellite, home video and DVDs already do, will stimulate the production of more product to feed all these outlets, especially the first release in motion picture theatres.

THE STUDIOS

Disney has had incredible success at the boxoffice for the last decade doing over $1 billion theatrically in eight of the last ten years. That streak continued in 2003 and became the record-setting year in the history of the company. "Finding Nemo," from Pixar's animation studio, was the monster film of the summer, grossed over $400 million domestically and became the eighth biggest film of all time. Earlier in the year both "Shanghai Knights" and "The Recruit" delivered over $50 million and 'The Lizzie McGuire Movie" exceeded $40 million. Jerry Bruckheimer found treasure with the number two film of the summer, "Pirates of the Caribbean: The Curse of the Black Pearl" and "Freaky Friday" and Kevin Costner's, "Open Range" performed well. "Under the Tuscan Sun" did good business with discerning audiences in the fall and Cate Blanchett starred in the true-life story of an Irish journalist "Veronica Guerin" during the same period. The family animated film, "Brother Bear," opened nationally in November, as did the Eddie Murphy film based on the Disney theme ride, "Haunted Mansion." The two holiday offerings were "Calendar Girls" about the English women in a small town who bared all for charity, starring Julie Walters and Helen Mirren and "The Alamo" which features Billy Bob Thornton and Dennis Quaid. Dreamworks had a strong start to the

year with Steven Spielberg's "Catch Me If You Can," which starred Leonardo DiCaprio and Tom Hanks, opened Christmas of 2002 and did over $100 million in 2003. "Old School" performed well with $75 million but Chris Rock's "Head of State," "Biker Boyz" and "Sinbad: Legend of the Seven Seas" less so. Dreamworks closed the year with "House of Sand and Fog" which stars Jennifer Connelly and Ben Kingsley. Scheduled for spring 2004 is the romantic comedy, "Win a Date With Tad Hamilton" and a Barry Levinson directed comedy starring Ben Stiller called "Envy." The summer of 2004 will bring two potential blockbusters; "Shrek 2" with the vocal talents of Eddie Murphy, Cameron Diaz and Mike Meyers reprising their roles and the Steven Spielberg directed "The Terminal" which stars Tom Hanks and Catherine Zeta-Jones. "Collateral" starring Tom Cruise and "Anchorman" with Will Ferrell will open during the summer. The year will be rounded out with the computer animated "Shark Tale, " the sequel to last year's hit, "The Ring 2" and "Surviving Christmas."

Fox started well out of the gates with "Just Married" which generated over $56 million, two $100 million plus films, "Daredevil" with Ben Affleck and the monstrous $215 million gross of "X2." Both " The League of Extraordinary Gentlemen" and "Phone Booth" attracted a significant number of patrons later in the summer. Fall brought Gene Hackman and Dustin Hoffman in John Grisham's "Runaway Jury" and "Master And Commander: The Far Side Of The World," based on one of the best selling Jack Aubrey novels by Patrick O'Brian, directed by Peter Weir and starring Russell Crowe. December's offerings were the Farrelly brother's comedy, "Stuck On You" and Steve Martin and Bonnie Hunt in a remake of "Cheaper By The Dozen." In 2004 Denzel Washington will be in "Man On Fire" and Roland Emerich's "The Day After Tomorrow" will star Dennis Quaid and Jake Gyllenhaal. "Garfield," a live action, CGI picture opens during the summer of 2004 as will "I, Robert" with Will Smith and "Alien Versus Predator" and Wayne Wang's "Because Of Winn-Dixie."

MGM and United Artists had a much better year than in the recent past. "Agent Cody Banks" opened in March and did a very respectable $50 million. During the summer months "Jeepers Creepers II" and "Uptown Girls" did well and Reese Witherspoon in "Legally Blonde 2: Bigger, Bolder, Blonder" generated over $90 million. Fall brought the thriller "Out of Time" starring Denzel Washington, Jim Henson Pictures' comedy, "Good Boy" and from United Artists, "Pieces of April" with Katie Holmes and Oliver Platt. MGM starts 2004 with "Barbershop 2" featuring Ice Cube and Cedric the Entertainer and United Artists opens "Osama" and the high school comedy, "Saved." "Agent Cody Banks 2," "Walking Tall" and "Soul Plane" round out the spring. "De-lovely," the story of Cole Porter is directed by Irwin Winkler and stars Ashley Judd, Kevin Kline and Jonathan Pryce. Other titles for 2004 are Michael Winterbottom's "Code 46," "The Undertow" and " The Woods."

Miramax and Dimension Films continue their extremely successful mix of quality and critically acclaimed specialized fare and pictures aimed at broad commercial release. This company is quite unique in the fact that the Weinstein brothers have been able to develop and fine-tune their acquisition and production models to win simultaneously at the boxoffice and among the critics and award programs. They have been doing it for the last twenty years and are likely to do it long into the future. Dimension had another $100 million franchise hit with "Spy Kids 3-D: Game Over" and Miramax had its two holdovers from 2002, "Chicago" and Martin Scorsese's "Gangs of New York" which did $170 million and $45 million respectively. Quentin Tarantino's first installment of "Kill Bill Volume 1" starring Uma Thurman opened in the fall with "Kill Bill Volume 2" set to open in February 2004. Another successful franchise, "Scary Movie 3" opened in autumn spoofing "The Matrix," "The Ring," "The Others," "Signs" and other films. "Bad Santa" with Billy Bob Thornton was released in late November. The traditional "Academy" release for Miramax at Christmas was Anthony Minghella's, "Cold Mountain" which features Jude Law and Nicole Kidman. The spring of 2004 will bring "Jersey Girl" with Ben Affleck, Liv Tyler and Jennifer Lopez and the family film, "Ella Enchanted" with Cary Elwes, Vivica A. Fox and Minnie Driver. Also in 2004, Johnny Depp will star with Kate Winslet in "J. M. Barrie's Neverland," which co-stars Dustin Hoffman. New Line started the year with a bang with the smash holdover of the second installment of co-writer, director, producer Peter Jackson's "The Lord of the Rings" trilogy, "The Two Towers," which has now achieved the fourth highest gross of all time: $921 million worldwide. 2002's "About Schmidt" continued to do business through the Academy Awards. "Final Destination 2" reached $47 million and "Freddy Vs. Jason" scared up over $80 million during the summer months. October brought a remake of the classic, "Texas Chainsaw Massacre" produced by Michael Bay and November brought the Will Ferrell comedy, "Elf." Christmas brought the extraordinary conclusion to Tolkein's Middle Earth trilogy with the ascendancy of Aragorn in, "The Lord of the Rings: The Return of the King."

Paramount built on the success of 2002's "Narc" and Nicole Kidman's Best Actress Academy Award for "The Hours" in the first months of the year. The Kate Hudson and Matthew McConaughey hit, "How to Lose a Guy in 10 Days" and "The Italian Job" starring Mark Wahlberg, Edward Norton, Charlize Theron and a bunch of Mini Coopers both exceeded $100 million domestically. "Lara Croft Tomb Raider: The Cradle of Life" did fine as did "Rugrats Go Wild!" and "The Fighting Temptations." The surprise hit of the fall starred Jack Black in "The School of Rock." November brought "Tupac: Resurrection" and the film based on Michael Crichton's novel, "Timeline." John Woo's "Paycheck" with Ben Affleck and Uma Thurmond opened on Christmas Day. The New Year will bring many features including; "The Perfect Score" about the SAT exams, Meg Ryan as a neophyte boxing manager in "Against the Ropes," "Twisted" starring Ashley Judd and Samuel L. Jackson and "The World of Tomorrow" with Jude Law, Gwyneth Paltrow and Angelina Jolie. Paramount's "Tent Pole" pictures for the summer of 2004 are "Sahara" based on the Clive Cussler bestseller with Matthew McConaughey, Denzel Washington and Meryl Streep in Jonathan Demme's "The Manchurian Candidate" and the remake of "The Stepford Wives" with an all star cast including Nicole Kidman, Matthew Broderick, Bette Midler and Glenn Close. For the 4th Quarter Paramount will have a Jim Carrey movie, "A Series of Unfortunate Events" and Ben Kingsley in "Suspect Zero" and "Elizabethtown" written and directed by Cameron Crowe.

Sony Pictures had another resoundingly successful year with "Darkness Falls," "Anger Management" with Jack Nicholson and Adam Sandler, "Identity," "Charlie's Angels: Full Throttle," "Bad Boys II," "S.W.A.T" and "Once Upon A Time In Mexico" with Antonio Banderas, Salma Hayeck and Johnny Depp, which all did in excess of $100 million in North America. "Underworld" and Jane Campion's film starring Meg Ryan, "In The Cut" came from Screen Gems and opened in the fall, as did Ron Howard's "The Missing" with Tommy Lee Jones and Cate Blanchett. The three holiday pictures were: Tim Burton's unusual "Big Fish," "Something's Gotta Give" starring Jack Nicholson, Diane Keaton, Frances McDormand and Keanu Reeves and "Mona Lisa Smile" with Julia Roberts. Sony will release two interesting films in the spring of 2004; "50 First Kisses" featuring Adam Sandler and Drew Barrymore and "Hellboy" which is based on the Dark Horse comic book series. Summer will bring "13 Going on 30" starring Jennifer Garner, a Wayans brothers comedy, "White Chicks," "The Forgotten" with Julianne Moore and "Spider-Man 2."

Universal had a sensational year capped by a record-breaking summer that had five films with boxoffice over $100 million and three over $50 million. "2 Fast 2 Furious," "American Wedding," "Hulk" and "Seabiscuit" were all terrific and Jim Carrey playing "Bruce Almighty" was exceptional, grossing over $240 million. Good performers in the fall were "The Rundown" with The Rock and Christopher Walken, George Clooney and Catherine Zeta-Jones in "Intolerable Cruelty" and Jessica Alba in "Honey." Thanksgiving brought Mike Myers in "Dr Seuss' The Cat in the Hat" and "Love Actually" with Hugh Grant, Liam Neeson, Colin Firth and Emma Thompson. "Peter Pan" opened on Christmas Day and was a co-production with Columbia Pictures and Revolution Studios.

Warner Bros. has been a powerhouse supplier of commercial product for the last few years and shows no sign of stopping anytime soon. Starting out the year playing off the second picture in what may come to be the most successful series of films ever, "Harry Potter and the Chamber of Secrets" and continuing with "Kangaroo Jack," "The Matrix Reloaded" at $281 million, "Terminator 3: Rise of the Machines," at $150 million, "Two Weeks Notice" and "What a Girl Wants." In the fall the powerful drama, "Mystic River" produced and directed by Clint Eastwood, was released, as was the creepy "Gothica," starring Halle Berry and Penelope Cruz. The conclusion of the Matrix trilogy, "The Matrix Revolutions" opened in early November and "Looney Tunes: Back in Action" was the Thanksgiving release. Tom Cruise starred in "The Last Samurai" at year end and "Love Don't Cost a Thing" opened in early December. The company has

a slew of releases for 1st and 2nd Quarter 2004 with "Torque," "The Big Bounce," "Exorcist: The Beginning," "Taking Lives" with Ethan Hawke, Angelina Jolie and Kiefer Sutherland, and Ben Stiller in the comedy, "Starsky & Hutch," are already scheduled. The summer season starts early with Brad Pitt in "Troy," directed by Wolfgang Petersen. The rest of the summer will bring the third installment of the series, "Harry Potter and the Prisoner of Azkaban," Hilary Duff in "A Cinderella Story" and Halle Berry as "Catwoman." The extraordinary parade of product will continue in the fall with Keanu Reeves in "Constantine" and Colin Farrell, Anthony Hopkins and Angelina Jolie in "Alexander" directed by Oliver Stone. Tom Hanks starts "The Polar Express" for Christmas and "Ocean's Twelve" will return with the same cast, as "Ocean's Eleven," directed by Steven Soderbergh. To round out what will be an extraordinary year for Warner Bros., Martin Scorsese's Howard Hughes story, "The Aviator," will take flight and Joel Schumacher will bring "The Phantom of the Opera" to the silver screen.

STUDIO RELATED DISTRIBUTORS

Fine Line Features seemed to be on hiatus during much of 2003 as topper Mark Ordesky paid most of his attention to "The Lord of the Rings" trilogy for parent New Line. A Sundance acquisition, "American Splendor" has done over $6.0mm this year and their Palme d'Or winner which opened in October, "Elephant," directed by Gus Van Sant, has been well received. Coming up in 2004 will be "M'Lady" produced and directed by Eric La Salle and "I Was Amelia Earhart," directed by Jean-Jacques Beineix. Later on in the year an adaptation of Umberto Ecco's, "Foucault's Pendulum," and a remake of "The Women" are scheduled.

Focus Features had a great year in 2003 highlighted by the three Academy Awards for "The Pianist," including Best Director and Best Actor and the critically acclaimed "Far From Heaven," which also opened in late 2002 and played well into the next year. "Deliver Us from Eva" was released in February and did over $17 million and Francois Ozon's "Swimming Pool" exceeded $10 million. The fall saw the opening of Sophia Coppola's " Lost in Translation," which featured Bill Murray. Gwyneth Paltrow opened in "Sylvia" this October, acting in a story based on the life of the poet, Sylvia Plath. "21 Grams" by Alejandro Gonzalez Inarritu, opened in November and starred Sean Penn, Naomi Watts and Benecio Del Toro. Focus will release a film written by Charles Kaufman and starring Jim Carrey in early 2004 called, "Eternal Sunshine of the Spotless Mind." Other 2004 titles will be the story of the famous Australian outlaw, "Ned Kelly" with Naomi Watts and Geoffrey Rush, Reese Witherspoon in "Vanity" and "Door In The Floor" starring Jeff Bridges and Kim Basinger.

Fox Searchlight also had a terrific year in 2003 with "28 Days Later" which did over $45 million and "Bend It Like Beckham" and "Antwone Fisher" which were released through the studios' Twentieth Century Fox Film Distribution in the latter part of 2002 and played well into the next year. "Thirteen" performed well in limited release and "Le Divorce" garnered over $9 million. 2004 will bring some important films from Searchlight including, Bernardo Bertulucci's "The Dreamers" and "The Clearing" which has Robert Redford, Willem Dafoe and Helen Mirren. Also, 2004 will see the release of "Never Die Alone" with DMX and David Arquette, "Broken Lizard's Club Dread," Cedric the Entertainer in "Johnson Family Vacation," the Farrelly Brothers' "The Ringer," a film about Alfred Kinsey called "Kinsey," with Liam Neesson, Chris O'Donnell and Laura Linney and a new Woody Allen film.

Paramount Classics had two art house successes in the first part of 2003; Patrice Leconte's "Man On The Train" grossed $2.5 million and "Norfolk," which did $1.5 million. In the fall the company released "The Singing Detective" with Robert Downey Jr., Mel Gibson, Adrien Brody and Robin Wright Penn. Their first picture for 2004 will be a British gangster film, "I'll Sleep When I'm Dead," with Charlotte Rampling and Malcolm McDowell and the second out of the gates will be "The United States of Leland" featuring Kevin Spacey and Don Cheadle. In June, they will open "The Reckoning," with Willem Dafoe.

Sony Pictures Classics had a fairly quiet year with "Winged Migration" achieving north of $10 million at the boxoffice. "My Life Without Me," was a fall offering, and Sony Pictures Classics first animated film, "The Triplets of Belleville" was released in November. Errol Morris' latest documentary, a film about Robert McNamara, "The Fog Of War," opened in December, along with Norman Jewison's, "The Statement" with Michael Caine and Robert Altman's, "The Company," which features Neve Campbell. 2004 looks to be very promising and will bring films by directors Ingmar Bergman, Pedro Almodovar and Hector Babenco.

Warner Bros. finally formed the much awaited, Warner Independent Pictures, with the hiring of ex-Miramax marketing, acquisition and production maven, Mark Gill. They plan to acquire foreign and domestic films initially to feed their distribution setup and start production with Warner Bros. based entities such as Killer Films and Section Eight with budgets approaching $20 million.

INDEPENDENTS

Artisan was on the block this year as a number of interested buyers kicked the tires with most of the interest being in the company's library. In that kind of environment it is difficult to focus on production and distribution. Two films that opened in 2002 and continued to play off and do well in 2003 were 'Confessions of a Dangerous Mind" and "Boat Trip". "House of the Dead," based on the Sega video game, opened in October. 2004 starts out with "I Am David," based on Anne Holms novel of the same title and February brings a co-production with Miramax, 'Dirty Dancing: Havana Nights." "Eulogy" with Ray Romano and Debra Winger will open in the spring as will, "The Punisher," which is part of Artisan's deal with Marvel. "Compleat Female Stage Beauty" with Rupert Everett, Claire Danes and Billy Crudup is the summer picture and another Marvel title, "Iron Fist" will come out at year's end.

Goldwyn has struggled since the collapse of Fireworks Pictures and Stratosphere Entertainment who were partners with Goldwyn in the IDP alliance that started in 2000. Goldwyn did have a good size art house hit in 2003 with "Mambo Italiano" which did $5.5 million. "Japanese Story" opened at year-end.

It is tough for any Independent the year following a hit the scale of "My Big Fat Greek Wedding" and IFC had its share of boxoffice disappointments in 2003. "A Decade Under the Influence," received good critical office but little boxoffice. John Sayles "Casa de los Babys" with Daryl Hannah, Mary Steenburgen, Maggie Gyllenhaal and Rita Moreno opened in the fall as did, the drag, gender-bending comedy, "Girls Will Be Girls." IFC will start 2004 with two documentaries, "Touching the Void" and "This So Called Disaster," with Sam Shepard, Nick Nolte and Sean Penn. "InterMission," starring Colin Farrell will open in the spring and so will "The Intended" starring Olympia Dukakis and Brenda Fricker.

Coming on the heels of last year's $20 million success, "Cabin Fever," Lions Gate followed up with two films that did over $12 million each, "Confidence" and "House of 1000 Corpses." Rounding out the year were "Shattered Glass" directed by Billy Ray, "Wayne Kramer's, "The Cooler," and "Girl With A Pearl Earring" directed by Peter Webber. Coming up for 2004 are: "Godsend" a Lars Von Trier film called "Dogville," "Danny Deckchair" and "Final Cut."

Newmarket Films, with Bill Berney's extraordinary proven film picking and marketing abilities, had a $20 million hit with "Whale Rider" in their first year in business. The company worked with Loews Theatres and Sundance Films to expand the releases of "In This World," "Dopamine" and "Die Mommie Die" in the fall. "Monster" with Charlize Theron and Christina Ricci open for Academy consideration at year end. The only film in the pipeline so far for 2004 is the black comedy, "The Green Butchers" but Newmarket is clearly an independent in ascendancy.

Exhibitors are excited by the product and the business that the Independents bring to their theatres all year long. Some of the smaller distributors that really produced this year were: Zeitgeist with "Nowhere in Africa" which grossed $6 million, Thinkfilm's, "Spellbound" which conjured $4.6 million and Magnolia's "Capturing the Friedmans" with $2.5 million. Other distributors that brought interesting and unusual films to theatres this year include: First Run, First Look, Indican, New Yorker Films, Strand, Castle Hill, Wellspring Media, Palm, Cowboy Pictures, Rialto Pictures and many others.

EXHIBITORS

This year it has become clear that Exhibition has stabilized from the bankruptcies of the previous years and with careful building and renovations planned and executed, the industry is well on its way back to fiscal health. Gone is the reckless and relentless overbuilding of the 1990s that practically wrecked this segment of the business. Hopefully, overbuilding will be permanently relegated to the past. Although the pace of building has slowed substantially and theatres are still being closed, it has been interesting to see that the screen count has not declined as substantially as many industry observers thought it would. According to NATO,

screen count in the US as of July 2003 stood at 35,400 versus 37,700 in July of 2002, which in turn is some 2,000 screen less than what it was in the high water mark year of 2000. The large circuits have been aggressive about divestitures but as quickly as some of the larger circuits closed under-performing and non-profitable theatres during bankruptcies, other companies came along to snap them up. Apparently, some smaller circuits and individual operators see opportunity in the theatres no longer in the strategic plans of the major circuits.

2003 saw a continuation of the ongoing trend towards consolidation among theatre operators. The aggregation of Regal, United Artists Theatre Circuit and Edwards, which is operated now as Regal Entertainment Group, swallowed the best theatres from Hoyts and established a major presence in the Northeast, the only region where they were underrepresented. An interesting question is to speculate about how much of that acquisition was driven by cash flow and operational synergies, versus how much the advertising section of the company, Regal CineMedia, needed venues in the Northeast to make them a true national media outlet. Onex announced that it would spin out Loews Cineplex Entertainment Corporation as a Canadian income trust. Essentially, in Canada the income generated by one of these trusts is passed along to unit holders without being taxed on the corporate level. The attraction of this is that the underlying U.S. Company characterizes most of its payments as to that entity as tax-deductible interest. It will be interesting to see what the IRS makes of this.

There continues to be fundamental concerns about distribution patterns and the way that so many films, especially during the summer of 2003 were, "one week wonders," in that they first opened to huge grosses, followed by precipitous drops in boxoffice by the next week. This kind of fast burn rate creates quick playoffs and ultimately drives up film rental for the exhibitors. One way that exhibitors and distributors are trying to grapple with the speed at which films pass through the multiplexes is by looking at "aggregate film rental" and trying to make a more equitable distribution of the boxoffice. One of the biggest bones of contention between exhibitors and distributors may be an element in a partial solution to this problem. Practically all distributors will balk at the very concept of paying for trailers that theatre owners have historically played without compensation. There is some evidence that certain distributors are willing to reduce film rental or make other concessions for better trailer placement and playoff. As more exhibitors embrace onscreen advertising, the economic value of the limited screen time is readily apparent and quantifiable. It will be interesting to see how this pans out in the coming year.

On the technology front, there is now a clear trend towards self-ticketing kiosks in theatre lobbies and Internet ticketing is fairly common, but mostly restricted to holidays and Friday and Saturday nights. Competition for boxoffice data collection finally happened with Rentrak collecting and disseminating boxoffice data in competition with AC Nielsen EDI. The much-anticipated conversion to digital cinema is proceeding slowly although the studios have taken the important step of setting up the Digital Cinema Initiative consortium that will set the standards for digital cinema from the film producer's and distributor's point of view. Business models and financial plans are being aired and the technology is pretty much in place. There is a lot of discussion of 2K versus 4K, but the major reason why the Studios are in the go-slow mode is fear of piracy. Regal CineMedia, AMC and others are being very aggressive with their screen advertising programs and many exhibitors are exploring the delivery of alternative content such as sports, prerecorded music concerts and corporate meetings.

DOLBY DIGITAL

www.dolby.com

MOTION PICTURE STATISTICS

EXHIBITION

GROSSES AND ADMISSIONS

Domestic theatrical grosses were reported at $9,519 million in 2002. Total U.S. theatre admissions in 2002 were 1,639 3 million

	Gross ($ millions)	Admissions (millions)	Per week (millions)
2002	9,519.0	1,639.3	31.5
2001	8,412.5	1,487.3	28.6
2000	7,661.0	1,420.8	27.3
1999	7,448.0	1,465.2	28.2
1998	6,949.0	1,480.7	28.5
1997	6,365.9	1,387.7	26.7
1996	5,911.5	1,338.6	25.7
1995	5,493.5	1,262.6	24.3
1994	5,396.2	1,291.7	24.8
1993	5,154.2	1,244.0	23.9
1992	4,871.0	1,173.2	22.6
1991	4,803.2	1,140.6	21.9
1990	5,021.8	1,188.6	22.9
1989	5,033.4	1,262.8	24.3
1988	4,458.4	1,084.8	20.9
1987	4,252.9	1,088.5	20.9
1986	3,778.0	1,017.2	19.6
1985	3,749.4	1,056.1	20.3
1984	4,030.6	1,199.1	23.1
1983	3,766.0	1,196.9	23.0
1982	3,452.7	1,175.4	22.6
1981	2,965.6	1,067.0	20.5
1980	2,748.5	1,021.5	19.6
1979	2,821.3	1,120.9	21.6
1978	2,643.4	1,128.2	21.7
1977	2,372.3	1,063.2	20.4
1976	2,036.4	957.1	18.4
1975	2,114.8	1,032.8	19.9
1974	1,908.5	1,010.7	19.4
1973	1,523.5	864.6	16.6
1972	1,583.1	934.1	18.0
1971	1,349.5	820.3	15.8
1970	1,429.2	920.6	17.7
1969	1,294.0	911.9	17.5
1968	1,282.0	978.6	18.8
1967	1,110.0	926.5	17.8
1966	1,067.1	975.4	18.8
1965	1,041.8	1,031.5	19.8
1964	947.6	1,024.4	19.7
1963	925.0	1,093.4	21.0
1962	874.9	1,080.1	20.8
1961	945.5	1,224.7	23.6
1960	984.4	1,304.5	25.1
1959	1,006.0	1,488.2	28.6
1958	1,010.0	1,553.8	29.9
1957	1,078.0	1,727.6	33.2
1956	1,125.0	1,893.9	36.4
1955	1,204.0	2,072.3	39.9
1954	1,251.0	2,270.4	43.7
1953	1,339.0	2,630.6	50.6
1952	1,325.0	2,777.7	53.4
1951	1,332.0	2,840.1	54.6
1950	1,379.0	3,017.5	58.0
1949	1,448.0	3,168.5	60.9
1948	1,506.0	3,422.7	65.8
1947	1,594.0	3,664.4	70.5
1946	1,692.0	4,067.3	78.2

Source: MPAA

ADMISSIONS PER CAPITA

	Admissions Per Capita	Yearly Change (%)	2002 Versus (%)
2002	5.6	5.7	
2001	5.3	1.9	5.7
2000	5.2	-3.8	7.7
1999	5.4	-1.9	3.7
1998	5.5	5.8	3.6
1997	5.2	2.7	7.7
1996	5.0	5.1	12.0
1995	4.8	-3.2	16.6
1994	5.0	2.8	12.0

ADMISSION PRICES

Average admission prices increased in 2001-2002 to $5.81, an increase of 7.8% vs. 2000. Since 1980, admission prices have risen by 116% (from $2.69, dollars not adjusted).

	Average Admission Price ($)	Annual change (%)	2002 Versus (%)
2002	5.811	2.7	
2001	5.660	4.9	2.7
2000	5.390	6.1	7.8
1999	5.080	8.3	14.4
1998	4.690	1.6	23.9
1997	4.587	3.9	26.7
1996	4.416	1.5	31.6
1995	4.351	4.1	33.6
1994	4.178	0.8	39.1
1993	4.143	-0.2	40.3
1992	4.152	-1.4	40.0
1991	4.211	-0.3	38.0
1990	4.225	6.0	37.5
1989	3.986	-0.6	45.8
1988	4.110	5.2	41.4
1987	3.907	5.2	48.7
1986	3.714	4.6	56.5
1985	3.550	5.6	63.7
1984	3.361	6.8	72.9
1983	3.146	7.1	84.7
1982	2.937	5.7	92.7

ADMISSION DEMOGRAPHICS

The following admission demographics are compiled from the Motion Picture Association of America. These definitions apply with respect to frequency data: "Frequent" means "at least once per month," "Occasional" means "once in two to six months," "Infrequent" means "less than once in six months."

ATTENDANCE BY AGE GROUP

Age	% Resident Civilian Population as of 1/02	% of Total Annual Admissions		
		2002	2001	2000
12-15	7	10	12	10
16-20	9	17	16	17
21-24	7	12	10	11
25-29	8	11	9	12
30-39	18	17	19	18
40-49	19	15	17	14
50-59	14	8	9	10
60 +	19	9	8	8

FREQUENCY OF ATTENDANCE BY AGE GROUP, 2002

Age	Frequent %	Occasional %	Infrequent %	Never %
12-17	46	42	9	2
18 and over	25	34	11	29

FREQUENCY OF ATTENDANCE BY GENDER AND AGE, 2002

Gender and Age	Frequent %	Occasional %	Infrequent %	Never %
Males 12 and older	29	34	11	25
Females 12 and older	26	35	11	27
Males 18 and older	27	30	12	30
Females 18 and older	20s	32	12	35

FREQUENCY OF ATTENDANCE BY MARITAL STATUS, 2002

Marital Status	Frequent %	Occasional %	Infrequent %	Never %
Married	23	36	12	29
Single	28	32	11	29

FREQUENCY OF ATTENDANCE BY FAMILY COMPOSITION, 2002

Family Type	Frequent %	Occasional %	Infrequent %	Never %
Adults with children under 18	29	41	11	18
Adults without children	24	31	11	34
Adults with teens, 12-17	30	38	9	21

FREQUENCY OF ATTENDANCE BY EDUCATIONAL BACKGROUND, 2002

Education	Frequent %	Occasional %	Infrequent %	Never %
Did not complete high school	16	28	7	47
Completed high school	21	31	11	37
At least some college	29	36	12	22

U.S. THEATRE AND SCREEN STATISTICS

Year	Total Screens	2002 Versus (%)	Indoor Screens	2002 Versus (%)	Drive-In Screens	2002 Versus (%)
2002	36,672	--	36,038	--	634	--
2001	36,764	-.2	36,110	-.2	654	-3.2
2000	37,396	-2.0	36,679	-2.0	717	-13.1
1999	37,185	-1.4	36,448	-1.4	737	-16.2
1998	34,186	.7.3	33,440	.7.8	746	-17.7
1997	31,640	.15.9	30,825	.16.9	815	-28.5
1996	29,690	.23.5	28,864	.24.9	826	-30.3
1995	27,805	.31.2	26,958	.33.7	847	-33.6
1994	26,586	.37.9	25,701	.40.2	885	-39.6
1993	25,737	.42.5	24,887	.44.8	850	-34.1
1990	23,689	.54.8	22,774	.58.2	915	-44.3
1985	21,147	.73.4	18,327	.96.6	2,820	-344.8

THE TOP 10 U.S. THEATRE CIRCUITS, 2002

Circuit	U.S. Theatres	U.S. Screens	% of All U.S. Screens	% of Top 10
Regal Entertainment Group	563	6,124	16.69	31.5
AMC Entertainment, Inc.	225	3,280	8.94	16.8
Cinemark USA, Inc.	194	2,265	6.18	11.6
Carmike Cinemas, Inc.	304	2,233	6.09	11.5
Loews Cineplex Entertainment Corp.	223	2,143	5.84	11.0
National Amusements, Inc.	92	1,059	2.89	5.5
Century Theatres.	76	856	2.33	4.4
Kerasotes Theatres.	77	532	1.45	2.7
Marcus Theatres Corp.	46	488	1.33	2.5
Wallace Theatres Hollywood	57	467	1.27	2.4

PRODUCTION

NUMBER OF FILMS RATES & RELEASED, INCLUDING REISSUES

	Films Rated	Films Released
2002	786	467
2001	739	482
2000	762	478
1999	677	461
1998	661	509
1997	679	510
1996	713	471
1995	697	411

HIGH GROSSING FEATURES (FILM RENTALS)

	Films Grossing > 10 million	Films Grossing > 20 million
2002	151	113
2001	90	50
2000	90	49
1999	71	42
1998	69	37
1997	66	39
1996	69	31
1995	75	36
1994	57	33
1993	64	28
1992	57	36
1991	68	30
1990	59	30
1985	42	13

AVERAGE COSTS OF NEW FEATURES: PRODUCTION, ADVERTISING AND PRINTS*

	Production costs ($ millions)	Advertising ($ millions)	Print ($ millions)	Total ($ millions)
2002	58.80	27.3	3.3	89.4
2001	47.70	27.2	3.7	78.7
2000	54.80	24.0	3.3	82.1
1999	51.50	21.4	3.1	76.0
1998	52.70	22.1	3.2	78.0
1997	53.42	19.2	3.0	75.7
1996	39.84	17.2	2.6	59.6
1995	36.37	15.4	2.3	54.0
1994	34.29	13.9	2.2	50.4
1993	29.91	12.1	1.9	44.0
1992	28.86	11.5	1.9	42.3
1991	26.14	10.4	1.6	38.2
1990	26.78	10.2	1.7	38.8

*All figures in this table are for MPAA member companies

INDUSTRY FILM RATING SYSTEM (CARA RATINGS)

In the first three columns of the following table, "#" is the number of films released in the given year that received the corresponding rating, and "%" is the percentage of the total number of films released in the given year that received the corresponding rating. In the fourth (rightmost) column, "#" and "%" represent cumulative figures for the range 1968-2001.

	2002 #	2002 %	2001 #	2001 %	2000 #	2000 %	1968-2001 #	1968-2001 %
G	55	.7	30	.4	36	.5	1,338	.7.2
PG	173	.22	55	.7	51	.7	4,159	.22.5
PG-13	86	.11	163	.22	146	.19	2,025	.10.9
R	456	.58	490	.67	528	.69	10,547	.57.0
NC-17/X	16	.2	0	.0	0	.0	434	.2.4
Totals	786	.100.0	738	.100.0	761	.100.0	18,503	.100.0

EMPLOYMENT

	Total (millions)	Production & Services (millions)	Exhibition (millions)	Video Tape Rental (millions)	Other (millions)
2002	582.9	259.2	142.0	163.6	18.1
2001	583.0	264.8	137.7	163.7	16.8
2000	590.3	270.1	138.6	164.7	16.9
1999	598.8	270.9	140.4	170.3	17.2
1998	576.0	255.4	136.8	166.7	17.1
1997	550.4	237.4	133.0	160.9	19.1
1996	524.7	222.5	123.9	155.1	23.2
1995	487.6	200.7	118.7	146.1	22.1
1994	441.2	169.9	113.4	138.8	19.4
1993	412.0	152.7	110.6	132.4	16.3
1992	400.9	148.8	110.2	127.1	14.8

Sources: MPAA, Quigley Publishing Company

TOP GROSSING FILMS 1991-2003

The ten top-grossing films each year from 1991-2003, as selected by Quigley Publishing. Some films may have been held over from the previous year. The 2003 films are for the year as of October 31, 2003.

2003

Finding Nemo (BV) 1
Pirates of the Caribbean: The Curse of the Black Pearl (BV) 2
The Matrix Reloaded (WB) 3
Bruce Almighty (Univ) 4
X2 (20th) 5
Chicago (Miramax 2002) 6
Terminator 3: Rise of the Machines (WB) 7
Bad Boys II Sony) 8
Anger Management (Sony) 9
Bringing Down the House (BV) 10

2002

Spider-Man (Sony) 1
Star Wars: Episode II–Attack of the Clones (20th) 2
Signs (BV) 3
Austin Powers in Goldmember (New Line) 4
Men in Black II (Sony) 5
My Big Fat Greek Wedding (IFC) 6
Ice Age (20th) 7
Scooby-Doo (WB) 8
Lilo & Stitch (BV) 9
XXX (Sony) 10

2001

Harry Potter and the Sorcerer's Stone (WB) 1
Shrek (DrmWks) 2
Rush Hour 2 (New Line) 3
Pearl Harbor (BV) 4
Jurassic Park III (Univ) 5
Planet of the Apes (20th) 6
American Pie 2 (Univ) 7
The Fast and the Furious (Univ) 8
Dr. Dolittle 2 (20th) 9
Legally Blonde (MGM) 10

2000

Mission Impossible 2 (Par) 1
Gladiator (DrmWks) 2
The Perfect Storm (WB) 3
X-Men (Fox) 4
Scary Movie (Mir) 5
What Lies Beneath (DrmWks) 6
Dinosaur (BV) 7
Nutty Professor II: The Klumps (Uni) 8
Big Momma's House (20th/New Regency) 9
The Patriot (Sony) 10

1999

Star Wars: Episode 1 (20th Fox) 1
The Matrix (WB) 2
The Mummy (Univ) 3
Notting Hill (Univ) 4
The Sixth Sense (BV) 5
Austin Powers: The Spy Who Shagged Me (New Line) 6
Tarzan (BV) 7
Runaway Bride (Par) 8
Wild Wild West (WB) 9
Big Daddy (Sony) 10

1998

Saving Private Ryan (DrmWks) 1
Armageddon (BV) 2
There's Something About Mary (Fox) 3
A Bug's Life (BV) 4
The Waterboy (BV) 5
Doctor Dolittle (Fox) 6
Rush Hour (New Line) 7
Deep Impact (Par) 8
Good Will Hunting (Mir) 9
Patch Adams (Uni) 10

1997

1996

1995

1994

1993

1992

1991

TOP 50 GROSSING FILMS BY DOMESTIC BOX OFFICE

Movie	Year Released	Domestic B.O. (millions)	Budget (millions)	World B.O. (millions)
Titanic (Par)	1997	600.8	200	1835.4
Star Wars (Fox)	1977	460.9	11	797.9
Star Wars: Episode I -- The Phantom Menace (Fox)	1999	431.1	110	925.5
Spider-Man (Sony)	2002	405.8	139	791.4
E.T. (Univ)	1982	399.8	11	757.0
Jurassic Park (Univ)	1993	357.1	63	920.0
Finding Nemo (BV)	2003	339.0	94	473.0
The Lord of the Rings: The Two Towers (NL)	2001	313.4	109	860.3
Forrest Gump (Par)	1994	329.7	55	680.0
Harry Potter and the Sorcerer's Stone (WB)	2001	317.6	130	922.0
The Lord of the Rings: The Fellowship of the Ring (NL)	2001	313.4	109	860.3
The Lion King (BV)	1994	312.9	79	771.9
Star Wars: Episode II -- Attack of the Clones (Fox)	2002	310.7	120	626.2
Return of the Jedi (Fox)	1983	309.1	33	573.0
Independence Day (Fox)	1996	306.1	75	813.1
Pirates of the Caribbean: Curse of Black Pearl (BV)	2003	301.0	125	630.8
The Sixth Sense (BV)	1999	293.5	40	661.5
The Empire Strikes Back (Fox)	1980	290.0	18	533.9
Home Alone (Fox	1990	285.8	15	533.8
The Matrix Reloaded (WB)	2003	271.9	127	815.8
Shrek (BV)	2001	267.7	60	469.7
Harry Potter and the Chamber of Secrets (WB)	2002	261.9	100	866.3
Jaws (Univ)	1975	260.0	12	471.0
Dr. Seuss' How the Grinch Stole Christmas (Univ)	2000	260.0	123	340.0
Monsters, Inc. (BV)	2001	255.9	115	524.2
Batman (WB)	1989	251.2	25	413.0
Men In Black (Sony)	1997	250.1	90	587.2
Toy Story 2 (BV)	1999	245.8	90	485.7
Bruce Almighty (Univ)	2003	243.7	81	460.1
Raiders of the Lost Ark (Par)	1981	242.4	20	384.0
Twister (WB)	1996	241.7	92	495.0
My Big Fat Greek Wedding (IFC)	2002	241.4	5	356.5
Ghostbusters (Col)	1984	238.6	30	291.6
Beverly Hills Cop (Par)	1984	234.8	25	316.4
Cast Away (Fox)	2000	233.6	90	424.3
The Lost World: Jurassic Park (Univ)	1997	229.1	73	614.4
Rush Hour 2 (NL)	2001	226.2	90	329.1
Signs (BV)	2002	225.6	62	376.2
Mrs. Doubtfire (Fox)	1993	219.2	--	423.2
Ghost (Par)	1990	217.6	22	517.6
Aladdin (BV)	1992	217.4	28	502.4
Saving Private Ryan (Dream)	1998	216.3	70	479.3
Mission: Impossible 2 (Par)	2000	215.4	125	545.4
X2 (Fox)	2003	215.2	110	406.7
Austin Powers in Goldmember (NL)	2002	212.9	63	287.7
Back to the Future (Univ)	1985	210.6	19	350.6
Grease (Par)	1978	210.0	6	228.5
Austin Powers: The Spy Who Shagged Me (NL)	1999	206.0	33	310.3
Terminator 2: Judgment Day (Tri)	1991	204.8	100	516.8
The Exorcist (WB)	1973	204.7	12	357.5

TOP 50 GROSSING FILMS BY DOMESTIC BOX OFFICE, ADJUSTED FOR INFLATION

Movie	Year Released	Domestic B.O. (millions)	Budget (millions)	World B.O. (millions)	Adjusted B.O. (millions)
Gone With the Wind	1939	198.7	3	390.5	1187.7
Star Wars	1977	460.9	11	797.9	1026.7
The Sound of Music	1965	163.2	8.2	163.2	824.1
E.T.	1982	434.9	10.5	757.0	815.0
The Ten Commandments	1956	80.0	14	80.0	758.1
Titanic	1997	600.8	200	1835.0	747.4
Jaws	1975	260.0	12	471.0	741.1
Doctor Zhivago	1965	111.7	11	111.7	700.7
The Jungle Book	1967	141.8	--	205.8	626.8
Snow White and the Seven Dwarfs	1937	184.9	1	184.9	615.2
Ben-Hur	1959	70.0	15	70.0	607.9
One Hundred and One Dalmatians	1961	152.6	4	215.0	593.9
The Exorcist	1973	204.7	12	357.5	582.3
The Empire Strikes Back	1980	290.2	18	533.9	555.7
Return of the Jedi	1983	309.1	33	573.0	533.2
The Sting	1973	159.6	6	159.6	514.8
Mary Poppins	1964	102.3	--	102.3	493.9
Raiders of the Lost Ark	1981	242.4	20	384.0	492.1
Jurassic Park	1993	357.1	63	920.0	486.6
Star Wars: Episode I–The Phantom Menace	1999	431.1	110	925.5	484.5
The Graduate	1967	104.4	--	104.4	482.9
Fantasia	1940	76.4	2	76.4	468.7
The Godfather	1972	134.6	6	134.8	448.5
Forrest Gump	1994	329.7	55	680.0	445.2
Close Encounters of the Third Kind	1977	128.3	20	300.0	440.5
The Lion King	1994	312.9	79	771.9	422.5
Sleeping Beauty	1959	51.6	6	51.6	410.2
Grease	1978	181.5	6	379.8	404.6
Spider-Man	2002	403.7	139	791.4	403.7
Butch Cassidy and the Sundance Kid	1969	102.3	--	102.3	398.2
Bambi	1942	102.8	--	268.0	397.4
Independence Day	1996	306.1	75	813.1	395.4
Love Story	1970	106.4	--	106.4	395.1
Beverly Hills Cop	1984	234.8	15	316.4	394.3
Pinocchio	1940	84.3	3	84.3	380.5
Home Alone	1990	285.8	15	533.8	380.3
Cleopatra	1963	57.8	44	57.8	379.2
Airport	1970	100.5	10	100.5	373.2
American Graffiti	1973	115.0	1	115.0	371.0
Ghostbusters	1984	238.6	30	291.6	371.0
The Robe	1953	36.0	5	36.0	369.4
Around the World in 80 Days	1956	42.0	6	42.0	364.8
Blazing Saddles	1974	119.5	--	119.5	356.9
Batman	1989	251.2	35	413.0	355.3
The Bells of St. Mary's	1945	21.3	--	21.3	354.2
The Towering Inferno	1974	116.0	14	116.0	346.4
National Lampoon's Animal House	1978	141.6	--	141.6	341.5
The Greatest Show on Earth	1952	36.0	4	36.0	338.7
My Fair Lady	1964	72.0	17	72.0	338.7
Let's Make Love	1960	44.8	--	44.8	337.5

TOP 50 GROSSING
FILMS WORLDWIDE

Movie	Year Released	Domestic B.O. (millions)	Budget (millions)	World B.O. (millions)
Titanic	1997	600.8	200	1,835.00
Harry Potter and the Sorcerer's Stone	2001	317.6	130	968.70
Star Wars: Episode I–The Phantom Menace	1999	431.1	110	925.50
Jurassic Park	1993	357.1	63	920.00
The Lord of the Rings: The Two Towers	2002	313.4	109	918.60
Harry Potter and the Chamber of Sevrets	2002	261.9	100	866.30
The Lord of the Rings: The Fellowship of the Ring	2001	313.4	109	860.30
The Matrix Reloaded	2003	271.9	127	815.80
Independence Day	1996	306.1	75	813.10
Star Wars	1977	460.9	11	797.90
Spider-Man	2002	403.7	139	791.40
The Lion King	1994	312.9	79	771.90
E.T.	1982	434.9	11	757.00
Forrest Gump	1994	329.7	55	680.00
The Sixth Sense	1999	293.5	40	661.50
Pirates of the Caribbean: Curse of the Black Pearl	2003	301.0	125	630.80
Star Wars: Episode II–Attack of the Clones	2002	302.2	120	626.20
The Lost World	1997	229.1	73	614.40
Men In Black	1997	250.1	90	587.20
Star Wars:Return of the Jedi	1983	309.1	33	573.00
Armageddon	1998	201.6	140	554.60
Mission: Impossible 2	2000	215.4	125	545.40
Star Wars: The Empire Strikes Back	1980	290.2	18	533.90
Home Alone	1990	285.8	18	533.80
Monsters, Inc.	2001	255.9	115	524.20
Ghost	1990	217.6	22	517.60
Terminator 2: Judgment Day	1991	204.8	100	516.80
Aladdin	1992	217.4	28	502.40
Twister	1996	241.7	92	495.00
Indiana Jones and the Last Crusade	1989	197.2	39	494.80
Toy Story 2	1999	245.8	90	485.70
Saving Private Ryan	1998	216.3	70	479.30
Finding Nemo	2003	339.0	94	473.00
Jaws	1975	260.0	12	471.00
Shrek	2001	267.7	60	469.70
Mission: Impossible	1996	181.0	75	467.00
Pretty Woman	1990	178.4	14	463.40
Bruce Almighty	2003	243.7	81	460.10
The Matrix	1999	171.5	63	456.50
Gladiator	2000	187.7	103	456.30
Pearl Harbor	2001	198.5	153	450.40
Ocean's Eleven	2001	183.4	85	444.30
Tarzan	1999	171.1	150	435.30
The Mummy Returns	2001	202.0	98	429.50
Men in Black II	2002	190.4	97	425.60
Cast Away	2000	233.6	90	424.30
Dances With Wolves	1990	184.2	19	424.20
Mrs. Doubtfire	1993	219.2	--	423.20
Terminator 3: The Rise of the Machines	2003	150.0	150	418.20
X2	2003	215.2	110	406.70

QP Top Ten Money-Makers Poll

QP Top Ten Poll of Money-Making Stars

In the 70th annual poll of circuit exhibitors and independent theatre owners in the United States conducted by Quigley Publishing, these stars were voted the top ten money-makers of 2002:

Tom Hanks	1
Tom Cruise	2
Mike Myers	3
Reese Witherspoon	4
Leonardo Di Caprio	5
Nicole Kidman	6
Catherine Zeta-Jones	7
Denzel Washington	8
Mel Gibson	9
Vin Diesel	10

QP Stars of Tomorrow

Major and independent exhibitors were asked to name those stars they thought would be top money-makers within the next 5-10 years. The overwhelming choices were:

Eminem	1
Jennifer Garner	2

QP Money-Making Stars of 1933-2001

2001: (1) Tom Cruise; (2) George Clooney; (3) Julia Roberts; (4) Russell Crowe; (5) Nicole Kidman; (6) Denzel Washington; (7) Will Smith; (8) Brad Pitt; (9) Ben Affleck; (10) Jackie Chan.

2000: (1) Tom Cruise; (2) Julia Roberts; (3) George Clooney; (4) Eddie Murphy; (5) Russell Crowe; (6) Mel Gibson; (7) Martin Lawrence; (8) Tom Hanks; (9) Jim Carrey; (10) Harrison Ford.

1999: (1) Julia Roberts; (2) Tom Hanks; (3) Adam Sandler; (4) Bruce Willis; (5) Mike Ryan; (6) Tom Cruise; (7) Will Smith; (8) Mel Gibson; (9) Meg Ryan; (10) Sandra Bullock.

1998: (1) Tom Hanks; (2) Jim Carrey; (3) Leonardo DiCaprio; (4) Robin Williams; (5) Meg Ryan; (6) Mel Gibson; (7) Adam Sandler; (8) Eddie Murphy; (9) Cameron Diaz; (10) Julia Roberts.

1997: (1) Harrison Ford; (2) Julia Roberts; (3) Leonardo DiCaprio; (4) Will Smith; (5) Tom Cruise; (6) Jack Nicholson; (7) Jim Carrey; (8) John Travolta; (9) Robin Williams; (10) Tommy Lee Jones.

1996: (1) Tom Cruise & Mel Gibson; (3) John Travolta; (4) Arnold Schwarzenegger; (5) Sandra Bullock; (6) Robin Williamsl (7) Sean Connery; (8) Harrison Ford; (9) Kevin Costner; (10) Michelle Pfeiffer.

1995: (1) Tom Hanks; (2) Jim Carrey; (3) Brad Pitt; (4) Harrison Ford; (5) Robin Williams; (6) Sandra Bullock; (7) Mel Gibson; (8) Demi Moore; (9) John Travolta; (10) Kevin Costner & Michael Douglas.

1994: (1) Tom Hanks; (2) Jim Carrey (3) Arnold Schwarzenegger; (4) Tom Cruise; (5) Harrison Ford; (6) Tim Allen; (7) Mel Gibson; (8) Jodie Foster; (9) Michael Douglas; (10) Tommy Lee Jones.

1993: (1) Clint Eastwood; (2) Tom Cruise; (3) Robin Williams; (4) Kevin Costner; (5) Harrison Ford; (6) Julia Roberts; (7) Tom Hanks; (8) Mel Gibson; (9) Whoopi Goldberg; (10) Sylvester Stallone.

1992: (1) Tom Cruise; (2) Mel Gibson; (3) Kevin Costner; (4) Jack Nicholson; (5) Macaulay Culkin; (6) Whoopi Goldberg; (7) Michael Douglas; (8) Clint Eastwood; (9) Steven Seagal; (10) Robin Williams.

1991: (1) Kevin Costner; (2) Arnold Schwarzenegger; (3) Robin Williams; (4) Julia Roberts; (5) Macaulay Culkin; (6) Jodie Foster; (7) Billy Crystal; (8) Dustin Hoffman; (9) Robert De Niro; (10) Mel Gibson.

1990: (1) Arnold Schwarzenegger; (2) Julia Roberts; (3) Bruce Willis; (4) Tom Cruise; (5) Mel Gibson; (6) Kevin Costner; (7) Patrick Swayze; (8) Sean Connery; (9) Harrison Ford; (10) Richard Gere.

1989: (1) Jack Nicholson; (2) Tom Cruise; (3) Robin Williams; (4) Michael Douglas; (5) Tom Hanks; (6) Michael J. Fox; (7) Eddie Murphy; (8) Mel Gibson; (9) Sean Connery; (10) Kathleen Turner.

1988: (1) Tom Cruise; (2) Eddie Murphy; (3) Tom Hanks; (4) Arnold Schwarzenegger; (5) Paul Hogan; (6) Danny De Vito; (7) Bette Midler; (8) Robin Williams; (9) Tom Selleck; (10) Dustin Hoffman.

1987: (1) Eddie Murphy; (2) Michael Douglas; (3) Michael J. Fox; (4) Arnold Schwarzenegger; (5) Paul Hogan; (6) Tom Cruise; (7) Glenn Close; (8) Sylvester Stallone; (9) Cher; (10) Mel Gibson.

1986: (1) Tom Cruise; (2) Eddie Murphy; (3) Paul Hogan; (4) Rodney Dangerfield; (5) Bette Midler; (6) Sylvester Stallone; (7) Clint Eastwood; (8) Whoopi Goldberg; (9) Kathleen Turner; (10) Paul Newman.

1985: (1) Sylvester Stallone; (2) Eddie Murphy; (3) Clint Eastwood; (4) Michael J. Fox; (5) Chevy Chase; (6) Arnold Schwarzenegger; (7) Chuck Norris; (8) Harrison Ford; (9) Michael Douglas; (10) Meryl Streep.

1984: (1) Clint Eastwood; (2) Bill Murray; (3) Harrison Ford; (4)Eddie Murphy; (5) Sally Field; (6) Burt Reynolds; (7) Robert Redford; (8) Prince; (9) Dan Aykroyd; (10) Meryl Streep.

1983: (1) Clint Eastwood; (2) Eddie Murphy; (3) Sylvester Stallone; (4) Burt Reynolds; (5) John Travolta; (6) Dustin Hoffman; (7)Harrison Ford; (8) Richard Gere; (9) Chevy Chase; (10) Tom Cruise.

1982: (1) Burt Reynolds; (2) Clint Eastwood; (3) Sylvester Stallone; (4) Dudley Moore; (5) Richard Pryor; (6) Dolly Parton; (7) Jane Fonda; (8) Richard Gere; (9) Paul Newman; (10) Harrison Ford.

1981: (1) Burt Reynolds; (2) Clint Eastwood; (3) Dudley Moore; (4)Dolly Parton; (5) Jane Fonda; (6) Harrison Ford; (7) Alan Alda; (8) Bo Derek; (9) Goldie Hawn; (10) Bill Murray.

1980: (1) Burt Reynolds; (2) Robert Redford; (3) Clint Eastwood; (4) Jane Fonda; (5) Dustin Hoffman; (6) John Travolta; (7) Sally Field; (8) Sissy Spacek; (9) Barbra Streisand; (10) Steve Martin.

1979: (1) Burt Reynolds; (2) Clint Eastwood; (3) Jane Fonda; (4) Woody Allen; (5) Barbra Streisand; (6) Sylvester Stallone; (7) John Travolta; (8) Jill Clayburgh; (9) Roger Moore; (10) Mel Brooks.

1978: (1) Burt Reynolds; (2) John Travolta; (3) Richard Dreyfuss; (4) Warren Beatty; (5) Clint Eastwood; (6) Woody Allen; (7) Diane Keaton; (8) Jane Fonda; (9) Peter Sellers; (10) Barbra Streisand.

1977: (1) Sylvester Stallone; (2) Barbra Streisand; (3) Clint Eastwood; (4) Burt Reynolds; (5) Robert Redford; (6) Woody Allen; (7) Mel Brooks; (8) Al Pacino; (9) Diane Keaton; (10) Robert De Niro.

1976: (1) Robert Redford; (2) Jack Nicholson; (3) Dustin Hoffman; (4) Clint Eastwood; (5) Mel Brooks; (6) Burt Reynolds; (7) Al Pacino; (8) Tatum O'Neal; (9) Woody Allen; (10) Charles Bronson.

1975: (1) Robert Redford; (2) Barbra Streisand; (3) Al Pacino; (4)Charles Bronson; (5) Paul Newman; (6) Clint Eastwood; (7) Burt Reynolds; (8) Woody Allen; (9) Steve McQueen; (10) Gene Hackman.

1974: (1) Robert Redford; (2) Clint Eastwood; (3) Paul Newman; (4) Barbra Streisand; (5) Steve McQueen; (6) Burt Reynolds; (7) Charles Bronson; (8) Jack Nicholson; (9) Al Pacino; (10) John Wayne.

1973: (1) Clint Eastwood; (2) Ryan O'Neal; (3) Steve McQueen; (4) Burt Reynolds; (5) Robert Redford; (6) Barbra Streisand; (7) Paul Newman; (8) Charles Bronson; (9) John Wayne; (10) Marlon Brando.

1972: (1) Clint Eastwood; (2) George C. Scott; (3) Gene Hackman; (4) John Wayne; (5) Barbra Streisand; (6) Marlon Brando; (7) Paul Newman; (8) Steve McQueen; (9) Dustin Hoffman; (10) Goldie Hawn.

1971: (1) John Wayne; (2) Clint Eastwood; (3) Paul Newman; (4) Steve McQueen; (5) George C. Scott; (6) Dustin Hoffman; (7) Walter Matthau; (8) Ali MacGraw; (9) Sean Connery; (10) Lee Marvin.

1970: (1) Paul Newman; (2) Clint Eastwood; (3) Steve McQueen; (4) John Wayne; (5) Elliott Gould; (6) Dustin Hoffman; (7) Lee Marvin; (8) Jack Lemmon; (9) Barbra Streisand; (10) Walter Matthau.

1969: (1) Paul Newman; (2) John Wayne; (3) Steve McQueen; (4) Dustin Hoffman; (5) Clint Eastwood; (6) Sidney Poitier; (7) Lee Marvin; (8) Jack Lemmon; (9) Katharine Hepburn; (10) Barbra Streisand.

1968: (1) Sidney Poitier; (2) Paul Newman; (3) Julie Andrews; (4) John Wayne; (5) Clint Eastwood; (6) Dean Martin; (7) Steve McQueen; (8) Jack Lemmon; (9) Lee Marvin; (10) Elizabeth Taylor.

1967: (1) Julie Andrews; (2) Lee Marvin; (3) Paul Newman; (4) Dean Martin; (5) Sean Connery; (6) Elizabeth Taylor; (7) Sidney Poitier; (8) John Wayne; (9) Richard Burton; (10) Steve McQueen.

1966: (1) Julie Andrews; (2) Sean Connery; (3) Elizabeth Taylor; (4) Jack Lemmon; (5) Richard Burton; (6) Cary Grant; (7) John Wayne; (8) Doris Day; (9) Paul Newman; (10) Elvis Presley.

1965: (1) Sean Connery; (2) John Wayne; (3) Doris Day; (4) Julie Andrews; (5) Jack Lemmon; (6) Elvis Presley; (7) Cary Grant; (8) James Stewart; (9) Elizabeth Taylor; (10) Richard Burton.

1964: (1) Doris Day; (2) Jack Lemmon; (3) Rock Hudson; (4) John Wayne; (5) Cary Grant; (6) Elvis Presley; (7) Shirley MacLaine; (8) Ann-Margret; (9) Paul Newman; (10) Jerry Lewis.

1963: (1) Doris Day; (2) John Wayne; (3) Rock Hudson; (4) Jack Lemmon; (5) Cary Grant; (6) Elizabeth Taylor; (7) Elvis Presley; (8) Sandra Dee; (9) Paul Newman; (10) Jerry Lewis.

1962: (1) Doris Day; (2) Rock Hudson; (3) Cary Grant; (4) John Wayne; (5) Elvis Presley; (6) Elizabeth Taylor; (7) Jerry Lewis; (8)Frank Sinatra; (9) Sandra Dee; (10) Burt Lancaster.

1961: (1) Elizabeth Taylor; (2) Rock Hudson; (3) Doris Day; (4) John Wayne; (5) Cary Grant; (6) Sandra Dee; (7) Jerry Lewis; (8)William Holden; (9) Tony Curtis; (10) Elvis Presley.

1960: (1) Doris Day; (2) Rock Hudson; (3) Cary Grant; (4) Elizabeth Taylor; (5) Debbie Reynolds; (6) Tony Curtis; (7) Sandra Dee; (8) Frank Sinatra; (9) Jack Lemmon; (10) John Wayne.

1959: (1) Rock Hudson; (2) Cary Grant; (3) James Stewart; (4) Doris Day; (5) Debbie Reynolds; (6) Glenn Ford; (7) Frank Sinatra; (8) John Wayne; (9) Jerry Lewis; (10) Susan Hayward.

1958: (1) Glenn Ford; (2) Elizabeth Taylor; (3) Jerry Lewis; (4) Marlon Brando; (5) Rock Hudson; (6) William Holden; (7) Brigitte Bardot; (8) Yul Brynner; (9) James Stewart; (10) Frank Sinatra.

1957: (1) Rock Hudson; (2) John Wayne; (3) Pat Boone; (4) Elvis Presley; (5) Frank Sinatra; (6) Gary Cooper; (7) William Holden; (8) James Stewart; (9) Jerry Lewis; (10) Yul Brynner.

1956: (1) William Holden; (2) John Wayne; (3) James Stewart; (4) Burt Lancaster; (5) Glenn Ford; (6) Dean Martin & Jerry Lewis; (7) Gary Cooper; (8) Marilyn Monroe; (9) Kim Novak; (10) Frank Sinatra.

1955: (1) James Stewart; (2) Grace Kelly; (3) John Wayne; (4) William Holden; (5) Gary Cooper; (6) Marlon Brando; (7) Dean Martin & Jerry Lewis; (8) Humphrey Bogart; (9) June Allyson; (10) Clark Gable.

1954: (1) John Wayne; (2) Martin & Lewis; (3) Gary Cooper; (4) James Stewart; (5) Marilyn Monroe; (6) Alan Ladd; (7) William Holden; (8) Bing Crosby; (9) Jane Wyman; (10) Marlon Brando.

1953: (1) Gary Cooper; (2) Martin & Lewis; (3) John Wayne; (4) Alan Ladd; (5) Bing Crosby; (6) Marilyn Monroe; (7) James Stewart; (8) Bob Hope; (9) Susan Hayward; (10) Randolph Scott.

1952: (1) Martin & Lewis; (2) Gary Cooper; (3) John Wayne; (4) Bing Crosby; (5) Bob Hope; (6) James Stewart; (7) Doris Day; (8) Gregory Peck; (9) Susan Hayward; (10) Randolph Scott.

1951: (1) John Wayne; (2) Martin & Lewis; (3) Betty Grable; (4) Abbott & Costello; (5) Bing Crosby; (6) Bob Hope; (7) Randolph Scott; (8) Gary Cooper; (9) Doris Day; (10) Spencer Tracy.

1950: (1) John Wayne; (2) Bob Hope; (3) Bing Crosby; (4) Betty Grable; (5) James Stewart; (6) Abbott & Costello; (7) Clifton Webb; (8) Esther Williams; (9) Spencer Tracy; (10) Randolph Scott.

1949: (1) Bob Hope; (2) Bing Crosby; (3) Abbott & Costello; (4) John Wayne; (5) Gary Cooper; (6) Cary Grant; (7) Betty Grable; (8) Esther Williams; (9) Humphrey Bogart; (10) Clark Gable.

1948: (1) Bing Crosby; (2) Betty Grable; (3) Abbott & Costello; (4) Gary Cooper; (5) Bob Hope; (6) Humphrey Bogart; (7) Clark Gable; (8) Cary Grant; (9) Spencer Tracy; (10) Ingrid Bergman.

1947: (1) Bing Crosby; (2) Betty Grable; (3) Ingrid Bergman; (4) Gary Cooper; (5) Humphrey Bogart; (6) Bob Hope; (7) Clark Gable; (8) Gregory Peck; (9) Claudette Colbert; (10) Alan Ladd.

1946: (1) Bing Crosby; (2) Ingrid Bergman; (3) Van Johnson; (4) Gary Cooper; (5) Bob Hope; (6) Humphrey Bogart; (7) Greer Garson; (8) Margaret O'Brien; (9) Betty Grable; (10) Roy Rogers.

1945: (1) Bing Crosby; (2) Van Johnson; (3) Greer Garson; (4) Betty Grable; (5) Spencer Tracy; (6) Humphrey Bogart, Gary Cooper; (7) Bob Hope; (8) Judy Garland; (9) Margaret O'Brien; (10) Roy Rogers.

1944: (1) Bing Crosby; (2) Gary Cooper; (3) Bob Hope; (4) Betty Grable; (5) Spencer Tracy; (6) Greer Garson; (7) Humphrey Bogart; (8) Abbott & Costello; (9) Cary Grant; (10) Bette Davis.

1943: (1) Betty Grable; (2) Bob Hope; (3) Abbott & Costello; (4) Bing Crosby; (5) Gary Cooper; (6) Greer Garson; (7) Humphrey Bogart; (8) James Cagney; (9) Mickey Rooney; (10) Clark Gable.

1942: (1) Abbott & Costello; (2) Clark Gable; (3) Gary Cooper; (4) Mickey Rooney; (5) Bob Hope; (6) James Cagney; (7) Gene Autry; (8) Betty Grable; (9) Greer Garson; (10) Spencer Tracy.

1941: (1) Mickey Rooney; (2) Clark Gable; (3) Abbott & Costello; (4) Bob Hope; (5) Spencer Tracy; (6) Gene Autry; (7) Gary Cooper; (8) Bette Davis; (9) James Cagney; (10) Judy Garland.

1940: (1) Mickey Rooney; (2) Spencer Tracy; (3) Clark Gable; (4) Gene Autry; (5) Tyrone Power; (6) James Cagney; (7) Bing Crosby; (8) Wallace Beery; (9) Bette Davis; (10) Judy Garland.

1939: (1) Mickey Rooney; (2) Tyrone Power; (3) Spencer Tracy; (4) Clark Gable; (5) Shirley Temple; (6) Bette Davis; (7) Alice Faye; (8) Errol Flynn; (9) James Cagney; (10) Sonja Henie.

1938: (1) Shirley Temple; (2) Clark Gable; (3) Sonja Henie; (4) Mickey Rooney; (5) Spencer Tracy; (6) Robert Taylor; (7) Myrna Loy; (8) Jane Withers; (9) Alice Faye; (10) Tyrone Power.

1937: (1) Shirley Temple; (2) Clark Gable; (3) Robert Taylor; (4) Bing Crosby; (5) William Powell; (6) Jane Withers; (7) Fred Astaire and Ginger Rogers; (8) Sonja Henie; (9) Gary Cooper; (10)Myrna Loy.

1936: (1) Shirley Temple; (2) Clark Gable; (3) Fred Astaire and Ginger Rogers; (4) Robert Taylor; (5) Joe E. Brown; (6) Dick Powell; (7) Joan Crawford; (8) Claudette Colbert; (9) Jeanette MacDonald; (10) Gary Cooper.

1935: (1) Shirley Temple; (2) Will Rogers; (3) Clark Gable; (4) Fred Astaire and Ginger Rogers; (5) Joan Crawford; (6) Claudette Colbert; (7) Dick Powell; (8) Wallace Beery; (9) Joe E. Brown; (10) James Cagney.

1934: (1) Will Rogers; (2) Clark Gable; (3) Janet Gaynor; (4) Wallace Beery; (5) Mae West; (6) Joan Crawford; (7) Bing Crosby; (8) Shirley Temple; (9) Marie Dressler; (10) Norma Shearer.

1933: (1) Marie Dressler; (2) Will Rogers; (3) Janet Gaynor; (4)Eddie Cantor; (5) Wallace Beery; (6) Jean Harlow; (7) Clark Gable; (8) Mae West; (9) Norma Shearer; (10) Joan Crawford.

1932: (1) Marie Dressler; (2) Janet Gaynor; (3) Joan Crawford; (4) Charles Farrell; (5) Greta Garbo; (6) Norma Shearer; (7) Wallace Beery; (8) Clark Gable; (9) Will Rogers; (10) Joe E. Brown.

NATIONAL & INTERNATIONAL AWARDS

ACADEMY AWARD WINNERS 2002

The 75th annual Academy Awards were presented on March 23, 2003 by the Academy of Motion Picture Arts and Sciences.

PICTURE
Chicago. A Producer Circle Co. Production, A Zadam/Meron Production; Martin Richards, Producer. Miramax Films.
ACTOR
Adrien Brody, The Pianist, Focus Features.
ACTRESS
Nicole Kidman, The Hours, Paramount
SUPORTING ACTOR
Chris Cooper, Adaptation, Sony Pictures.
SUPPORTING ACTRESS
Catherine Zeta-Jones, Chicago, Miramax.
DIRECTOR
Roman Polanski, The Pianist, Focus Features.
FOREIGN LANGUAGE FILM
Nowhere in Africa, Caroline Link, MTM Medien & Television Munchen Production (germany), Zeitgeist Films.
ORIGINAL SCREENPLAY
Pedro Almodovar, Talk to Her, Sony Pictures Classics.
ADAPTED SCREENPLAY
Ronald Harwood, The Pianist, Focus Features.
CINEMATOGRAPHER
Conrad L. Hall, Road to Perdition, Dreamworks.
ART DIRECTION
John Myrhe and Gordon Sim, Chicago, Miramax.
COSTUME DESIGN
Colleen Atwood, Chicago, Miramax.
FILM EDITING
Martin Walsh, Chicago, Miramax.
ORIGINAL SCORE
Elliot Goldenthal, Frida, Miramax.
ORIGINAL SONG
Eminem, Jeff Bass & Luis Resto, Music, Eminem, Lyrics for 8 Mile, Universal.
SHORT SUBJECT—ANIMATED
The Chubbchubbs!, Eric Amstrong, Sony.
SHORT SUBJECT—LIVE ACTION
Der er en yndig mand, An M&M Productions for Novellefilm Production, Martin Strange-Hansen and Mie Andreasen.
SOUND
Mike Minkler, Dominic Tavella, David Lee for Chicago, Miramax.
SOUND EFFECTS EDITING
Ethan Van der Ryn, Mike Hopkins for The Lord of the Rings: The Two Towers, New Line.
MAKE-UP
John E. Jackson, Beatrice De Alba, Frida, Miramax.
VISUAL EFFECTS
Jim Rygiel, Randall William Cook, Joe Letteri, Alex Funke, The Lord of the Rings: The Two Towers, New Line.
DOCUMENTARY—FEATURE
Bowling for Columbine, Michael Moore, Michael Donovan, United Artists and Alliance Atlantis
DOCUMENTARY—SHORT SUBJECT
Twin Towers, A Wolf Films/Shape Pictures/Universal/Mopo Entertainment Production, Bill Guttentag, Robert David Port
HONORARY AWARD
Peter O'Toole

ACADEMY AWARD WINNERS 1996-2001

Productions, players, directors and craftspersons named for superior merit by the Academy of Motion Picture Arts and Sciences, from 1996-2001. For a complete list of winners from the inception of the awards, please see Vols. 1995 and earlier.

2001

PICTURE
A Beautiful Mind, A Universal Pictures & Imagine Entertainment Production; Brian Grazer and Ron Howard, Producers.
ACTOR
Denzell Washington, Training Day, Warner Bros.
ACTRESS
Halle Berry, Monster's Ball, Lion's Gate.
SUPORTING ACTOR
Jim Broadbent, Iris, Miramax.
SUPPORTING ACTRESS
Jennifer Connolly, A Beautiful Mind, Universal & DreamWorks.
DIRECTOR
Ron Howard, A Beautiful Mind, Universal & DreamWorks.
FOREIGN LANGUAGE FILM
No Man's Land, A Noé, Productions/Fabrica Cinema/Man's Films/Counihan Villiers Productions/Studio Maj/Casablanca Production; Bosnia & Herzegovina.
ORIGINAL SCREENPLAY
Julian Fellowes, Gosford Park, USA Films.
ADAPTED SCREENPLAY
Akiva Goldsman, A Beautiful Mind, Universal & DreamWorks.
CINEMATOGRAPHER
Andrew Lesnie, The Lord of the Rings: The Fellowship of the Ring, New Line.
ART DIRECTION
Catherine Martin and Brigitte Broch, Moulin Rouge, 20th Century Fox.
COSTUME DESIGN
Catherine Martin and Angus Strathie, Moulin Rouge, 20th Century Fox.
FILM EDITING
Pietro Scalia, Black Hawk Down, Sony.
ORIGINAL SCORE
Howard Shore, The Lord of the Rings: The Fellowship of the Ring, New Line.
ORIGINAL SONG
Randy Newman, "If I Didn't Have You" from Monsters Inc., Buena Vista.
SHORT SUBJECT—ANIMATED
For the Birds, A Pixar Animation Studios Production; Ralph Eggleston, executive producer.
SHORT SUBJECT—LIVE ACTION
The Accountant, A Ginny Mule Pictures Production; Ray McKinnon and Lisa Blount, executive producers.
SOUND
Mike Minkler, Myron Nettinga and Chris Munro, Black Hawk Down, Sony.
SOUND EFFECTS EDITING
George Watters II and Christopher Boyes, Pearl Harbor, Buena Vista.
MAKE-UP
Peter Owen and Richard Taylor, The Lord of the Rings: The Fellowship of the Ring, New Line.
VISUAL EFFECTS
Jim Rygiel, Randall William Cook, Richard Taylor and Mark Stetson, The Lord of the Rings: The Fellowship of the Ring, New Line.
DOCUMENTARY—FEATURE
Murder on a Sunday Morning, A Maha Productions/Pathé Doc/France 2/HBO Production; Jean-Xavier de Lestrade and Denis Poncet, producers.
DOCUMENTARY—SHORT SUBJECT
Thoth, An Amateur Rabbit Production; Sarah Kernochan and Lynn Appelle, producers.
THE JEAN HERSHOLT HUMANITARIAN AWARD
Arthur Hiller
THE GORDON E. SAWYER AWARD
Edmund M. Di Giulio
HONORARY AWARD
Sydney Poitier
HONORARY AWARD
Robert Redford

2000

PICTURE
Gladiator, A Douglas Wick in association with Scott Free production; Douglas Wick, David Franzoni and Branko Lustig, producers. DreamWorks and Universal.
ACTOR
Russell Crowe, Gladiatior, DreamWorks and Universal.

ACTRESS
Julia Roberts, Erin Brokovich, Universal and Columbia.
SUPORTING ACTOR
Benicio Del Toro, Traffic, USA Films.
SUPPORTING ACTRESS
Marcia Gay Harden, Pollock, Sony Pictures Classics.
DIRECTOR
Steven Soderbergh, Traffic, USA Films.
FOREIGN LANGUAGE FILM
Crouching Tiger, Hidden Dragon, A Zoom Hunt International production; Bill Kong, Hsu Li Kong and Ang Lee, producers; Taiwan.
ORIGINAL SCREENPLAY
Cameron Crowe, Almost Famous.
ADAPTED SCREENPLAY
Stephen Gagnon, Traffic.
CINEMATOGRAPHER
Peter Pau, Crouching Tiger, Hidden Dragon.
ART DIRECTION
Tim Yip, Crouching Tiger, Hidden Dragon.
COSTUME DESIGN
Janty Yates, Gladiator.
FILM EDITING
Stephen Mirrione, Traffic.
ORIGINAL SCORE
Tan Dun, Crouching Tiger, Hidden Dragon.
ORIGINAL SONG
Bob Dylan, "Things Have Changed" from Wonder Boys.
SHORT SUBJECT—ANIMATED
Father and Daughter, A CineTe Filmproductie BV/Cloudrunner Ltd. production; Michael Dudok de Wit, producer.
SHORT SUBJECT—LIVE ACTION
Quiero Ser (I Want to Be...), A Mondragon Films production; Florian Gallenberger, producer.
SOUND
Scott Millan, Bob Beemer and Ken Weston, Gladiator.
SOUND EFFECTS EDITING
Jon Johnson, U-571.
MAKE-UP
Rick Baker and Gail Ryan, Dr. Seuss' How the Grinch Stole Christmas.
VISUAL EFFECTS
John Nelson, Neil Corbould, Tim Burke and Rob Harvey, Gladiator.
DOCUMENTARY—FEATURE
Into the Arms of Strangers: Stories From the Kindertransport, A Sabine Films production; Mark Jonathan Harris and Deborah Oppenheimer, producers.
DOCUMENTARY—SHORT SUBJECT
Big Mama, A Birthmark production; Tracy Seretean, producer.
THE IRVING G. THALBERG AWARD
Dino de Laurentiis.
HONORARY AWARD, CINEMATOGRAPHY
Jack Cardiff.
HONORARY AWARD, WRITING
Ernest Lehman.

1999

PICTURE
American Beauty, A Jinks/Cohen Co. production; Bruce Cohen and Dan Jinks, producers. DreamWorks.
ACTOR
Kevin Spacey, American Beauty, DreamWorks.
ACTRESS
Hilary Swank, Boys Don't Cry, Fox Searchlight.
SUPPORTING ACTOR
Michael Caine, The Cider House Rules, Miramax.
SUPPORTING ACTRESS
Angelina Jolie, Girl Interrupted, Sony.
DIRECTOR
Sam Mendes, American Beauty, DreamWorks.
FOREIGN LANGUAGE FILM
All About My Mother, An El Desea SA/Renn/France 2 Cine production, Spain.
ORIGINAL SCREENPLAY
Alan Ball, American Beauty.
ADAPTED SCREENPLAY
John Irving, The Cider House Rules.
CINEMATOGRAPHER
Conrad Hall, American Beauty.

ART DIRECTION
Rich Heinrichs (art direction), Peter Young (set decoration), Sleepy Hollow.
COSTUME DESIGN
Lindy Heming, Topsy-Turvy.
FILM EDITING
Zach Staenberg, The Matrix.
ORIGINAL SCORE
John Corigliano, The Red Violin.
ORIGINAL SONG
Phil Collins, "You'll Be in My Heart" from Tarzan.
SHORT SUBJECT—ANIMATED
The Old Man and the Sea, A Productions Pascal Blais/ Imagica Corp./Dentsu Tech./NHK Enterprise 21/ Panorama Studio of Yaroslvl production; Alexandre Petrov, producer.
SHORT SUBJECT—LIVE ACTION
My Mother Dreams the Satan's Disciples in New York, A Kickstart production; Barbara Schock and Tamara Tiehel, producers.
SOUND
John Reitz, Gregg Rudloff, David Campbell and David Lee, The Matrix.
SOUND EFFECTS EDITING
Dane A. Davis, The Matrix
MAKE-UP
Christine Blundell and Trefor Proud, Topsy-Turvy.
VISUAL EFFECTS
John Gaeta, Janek Sirrs, Steve Courtley and Jon Thum, The Matrix.
DOCUMENTARY—FEATURE
One Day in September, An Arthur Cohn Production; Arthur Cohn and Kevin Macdonald.
DOCUMENTARY—SHORT SUBJECT
King Gimp, A Whiteford-Hadary/University of Maryland/ Tapestry International Production; Susan Hannah Hadary and William A. Whiteford.
THE IRVING G. THALBERG AWARD
Warren Beatty.
THE GORDON E. SAWYER AWARD
Dr. Roderick T. Ryan.
THE JOHN A. BONNER MEDAL OF COMMENDATION
Edmund M. DiGiulio and Takuo Miyagishima.

1998

PICTURE
Shakespeare In Love, A Miramax Films, Universal Pictures, Bedford Falls Co. production, David Parfitt, Donna Gigliotti, Harvey Weinstein, Edward Zwick and Marc Norman, producers.
ACTOR
Roberto Benigni, Life Is Beautiful, Miramax.
ACTRESS
Gwyneth Paltrow, Shakespeare In Love, Miramax.
SUPPORTING ACTOR
James Coburn, Affliction, Lions Gate.
SUPPORTING ACTRESS
Judi Dench, Shakespeare In Love, Miramax.
DIRECTOR
Steven Spielberg, Saving Private Ryan, DreamWorks.
FOREIGN LANGUAGE FILM
Life Is Beautiful, A Melampo Cinematografica production, Italy.
ORIGINAL SCREENPLAY
Shakespeare In Love, Marc Norman and Tom Stoppard.
ADAPTED SCREENPLAY
Gods and Monsters,written for the screen by Bill Condon.
CINEMATOGRAPHER
Saving Private Ryan, Janusz Kaminski.
ART DIRECTION
Martin Childs (art direction), Jill Qiertier (set decoration), Shakespeare In Love.
COSTUME DESIGN
Sandy Powell, Shakespeare In Love.
FILM EDITING
Michael Kahn, Saving Private Ryan.
ORIGINAL DRAMATIC SCORE
Nicola Piovani, Life Is Beautiful.
ORIGINAL MUSICAL OR COMEDY SCORE
Stephen Warbeck, Shakespeare In love.
ORIGINAL SONG
"When You Believe," from The Prince of Egypt; music and lyrics by Stephen Schwartz.
SHORT SUBJECT—ANIMATED
Bunny, A Blue Sky Studios, Inc. production; Chris Wedge, producer.

SHORT SUBJECT—LIVE ACTION
Election Night, An M&M production; Kim Magnusson and Anders Thomas Jensen, producers.
SOUND
Gary Rydstrom, Gary Summers, Andy Nelson and Ronald Judkins, Saving Private Ryan.
SOUND EFFECTS EDITING
Gary Rydstrom and Richard Hymns, Saving Private Ryan.
MAKE-UP
Jenny Shircore, Elizabeth.
VISUAL EFFECTS
Joel Hynk, Nicholas Brooks, Stuart Robertson and Kevin Mack, What Dreams May Come.
DOCUMENTARY—FEATURE
The Last Days, A Survivors of the Shoah Visual History Foundation production, James Moll and Ken Lipper.
DOCUMENTARY—SHORT SUBJECT
The Personals: Improvisations on Romance in the Golden Years, A Keiko Ibi Film, Keiko Ibi.
THE IRVING G. THALBERG AWARD
Norman Jewison.
HONORARY AWARD
Elia Kazan.

1997

PICTURE
Titanic, A 20th Century Fox and Paramount production, Jon Landau and James Cameron, producers.
ACTOR
Jack Nicholson, As Good As It Gets, a TriStar production.
ACTRESS
Helen Hunt, As Good As It Gets, a TriStar production.
SUPPORTING ACTOR
Robin Williams, Good Will Hunting, a Miramax production.
SUPPORTING ACTRESS
Kim Basinger, L.A. Confidential, Warner Bros.
DIRECTOR
James Cameron, Titanic.
FOREIGN LANGUAGE FILM
Character, A First Floor Features Production (The Netherlands).
ORIGINAL SCREENPLAY
Ben Affleck and Matt Damon, Good Will Hunting.
ADAPTED SCREENPLAY
Brian Helgeland and Curtis Hanson, L.A. Confidential, Warner Bros.
CINEMATOGRAPHER
Russell Carpenter, Titanic.
ART DIRECTION
Peter Lamont (art direction), **Michael Ford** (set decoration), Titanic.
COSTUME DESIGN
Deborah L. Scott, Titanic.
FILM EDITING
Conrad Buff, James Cameron and Richard A. Harris, Titanic.
ORIGINAL DRAMATIC SCORE
James Horner, Titanic.
ORIGINAL MUSICAL OR COMEDY SCORE
Anne Dudley, The Full Monty, a Fox Searchlight production.
ORIGINAL SONG
"My Heart Will Go On," from Titanic; Music by James Horner, lyric by Will Jennings.
SHORT SUBJECT—ANIMATED
Geri's Game, A Pixar Animation Studios production, produced by Jan Pinkava.
SHORT SUBJECT—LIVE ACTION
Visas and Virtue, A Cedar Grove production, produced by Chris Tashima and Chris Donahue
SOUND
Gary Rydstrom, Tom Johnson, Gary Sumers and Mark Ulano, Titanic.
SOUND EFFECTS EDITING
Tom Bellfort and Christopher Boyes, Titanic.
MAKE-UP
Rick Baker and David LeRoy Anderson, Men In Black, Columbia Pictures.
VISUAL EFFECTS
Robert Legato, Mark Lasoff, Thomas L. Fisher and Michael Kanfer, Titanic.
DOCUMENTARY—FEATURE
The Long Way Home, A Moriah Films production at the Simon Wiesenthal Center, produced by Rabbi Marvin Hier and Richard Trank.
DOCUMENTARY—SHORT SUBJECT
A Story of Healing, A Dewey-Obenchain Films production, produced by Donna Dewey and Carol Pasternak.

HONORARY AWARD
Stanley Donen, in appreciation of a body of work marked by grace, elegance, wit and visual innovation.

1996

PICTURE
The English Patient, A Tiger Moth production, Saul Zaentz, producer.
ACTOR
Geoffrey Rush, Shine, Momentum Films, Fine Line Features.
ACTRESS
Frances McDormand, Fargo, a Working Title production.
SUPPORTING ACTOR
Cuba Gooding, Jr., Jerry Maguire, a TriStar Pictures production, Sony Pictures Entertainment.
SUPPORTING ACTRESS
Juliette Binoche, The English Patient.
DIRECTOR
Anthony Minghella, The English Patient.
FOREIGN LANGUAGE FILM
Kolya, Biograf Jan Sverak/Portobello Pictures/Ceska Televize/Pandora Cinema production Miramax (Czech Republic).
ORIGINAL SCREENPLAY
Ethan Coen & Joel Coen, Fargo.
ADAPTED SCREENPLAY
Billy Bob Thornton, Slingblade, A Shooting Gallery production, Miramax.
CINEMATOGRAPHER
John Seale, The English Patient.
ART DIRECTION
Stuart Craig (art direction), **Stephanie McMillan** (set decoration), The English Patient.
COSTUME DESIGN
Ann Roth, The English Patient.
FILM EDITING
Walter Murch, The English Patient.
ORIGINAL DRAMATIC SCORE
Gabriel Yared, The English Patient.
ORIGINAL MUSICAL OR COMEDY SCORE
Rachel Portman, Emma, a Matchmaker Films production in association with Haft Entertainment, Miramax.
ORIGINAL SONG
"You Must Love Me," from Evita; Music by Andrew Lloyd Webber, lyric by Tim Rice.
SHORT SUBJECT—ANIMATED
Quest, A Thomas Stellmach Animation production; Stellmach, Tyron Montgomery, producers.
SHORT SUBJECT—LIVE ACTION
Dear Diary, A Dreamworks production; David Frankel, Barry Jossen, producers.
SOUND
Walter Murch, Mark Berger, David Parker, Chris Newman, The English Patient.
SOUND EFFECTS EDITING
Bruce Stambler, The Ghost and the Darkness, a Douglas/Reuther production, Paramount.
MAKE-UP
Rick Baker, David Leroy Anderson, The Nutty Professor, an Imagine Entertainment production, Universal.
VISUAL EFFECTS
Voker Engel, Douglas Smith, Clay Pinney, Joseph Viskocil, Independence Day, a Centropolis Entertainment production, 20th Century Fox.
DOCUMENTARY—FEATURE
When We Were Kings, UFA Non-Fiction/USA, Gramercy, DASFilms Ltd; Leon Gast, David Sonenberg, producers.
DOCUMENTARY—SHORT SUBJECT
Breathing Lessons: The Life and Work of Mark O'Brien, an Inscrutable Films/Pacific News Service production; Jessica Yu, producer.
IRVING G. THALBERG MEMORIAL AWARD
Saul Zaentz
CAREER ACHIEVEMENT AWARD
Michael Kidd

American Film Institute Awards

AFI MOVIES OF THE YEAR–OFFICIAL SELECTIONS 2002

About A Boy
About Schmidt
Adaptation
Antwone Fisher
Chicago
Frida
Gangs of New York
The Hours
The Lord of the Rings: The Two Towers
The Quiet American

LIFETIME ACHIEVEMENT

2003 RECIPIENT
Robert De Niro

PAST RECIPIENTS

Tom Hanks	2002
Barbra Streisand	2001
Harrison Ford	2000
Dustin Hoffman	1999
Robert Wise	1998
Martin Scorcese	1997
Clint Eastwood	1996
Steven Spielberg	1995
Jack Nicholson	1994
Elizabeth Taylor	1993
Sidney Poitier	1992
Kirk Douglas	1991
Sir David Lean	1990
Gregory Peck	1989
Jack Lemmon	1988
Barbara Stanwyck	1987
Billy Wilder	1986
Gene Kelly	1985
Lillian Gish	1984
John Huston	1983
Frank Capra	1982
Fred Astaire	1981
James Stewart	1980
Alfred Hitchcock	1979
Henry Fonda	1978
Bette Davis	1977
William Wyler	1976
Orson Welles	1975
James Cagney	1974
John Ford	1973

American Society of Cinematographers Awards

BEST CINEMATOGRAPHY
Conrad L. Hall, Road to Perdition.

British Academy of Film & Television Arts (BAFTA) Awards

BEST FILM
The Pianist.

THE DAVID LEAN AWARD FOR BEST ACHIEVEMENT IN DIRECTION
Roman Polanski, The Pianist.

BEST ORIGINAL SCREENPLAY
The Magdalene Sisters, Peter Mullan.

BEST ADAPTED SCREENPLAY
Adaptation, Charlie Kaufman, Donald Kaufman.

BEST ACTRESS
Nicole Kidman, The Hours.

BEST ACTOR
Daniel Day-Lewis, Gangs of New York.

BEST SUPPORTING ACTRESS
Catherine Zeta-Jones, Chicago.

BEST SUPPORTING ACTOR
Chistopher Walken, Catch Me If You Can.

BEST FILM NOT IN THE ENGLISH LANGUAGE
Talk To Her (Hable con Ella), Pedro Almodovar.

BEST CINEMATOGRAPHY
Conrad L. Hall, Road to Pedfition.

BEST PRODUCTION DESIGN
Dennis Gassner, Road to Perdition.

BEST COSTUME DESIGN
Ngila Dickson, Richard Taylor, The Lord of the Rings: The Two Towers.

BEST EDITING
Daniel Rezende, City of God (Cidade de Deus).

BEST SOUND
Micael Minkle, Dominick Tavella, David Lee, Maurice Schell, Chicago.

ACHIEVEMENT IN SPECIAL VISUAL EFFECTS
Jim Rygiel, Joe Letteri, Randall William Cook, Alex Funke, The Lord of the Rings: The Two Towers.

BEST MAKE-UP/HAIR
Judy Chin, Beatrice De Alba, John Jackson, ReginaReynes, Frida.

BEST SHORT FILM
My Wrongs 8245-8249 And 117, Mark Herbert, Chris Morris.

BEST SHORT ANIMATION
Fish Never Sleep, Gaelle Denis.

THE FELLOWSHIP
Saul Zaentz

THE ANTHONY ASQUITH AWARD FOR ACHIEVEMENT IN FILM MUSIC
Phillip Glass, The Hours.

THE ALEXANDER KORDA AWARD FOR THE OUTSTANDING BRITISH FILM OF THE YEAR
The Warrior, Bertrand Faivre, Asif Kapadia.

THE MICHAEL BALCON AWARD FOR OUTSTANDING BRITISH CONTRIBUTION TO CINEMA
David Tomblin, Michael Stevenson.

THE CARL FOREMAN AWARD FOR THE MOST PROMISING NEWCOMER IN BRITISH FILM
Asif Kapadia, The Warrior.

THE ORANGE AUDIENCE AWARD
The Lord of the Rings: The Two Towers.

Broadcast Film Critics Association

BEST PICTURE:
Chicago

BEST ACTOR
(tie):Daniel Day-Lewis, Gangs of New York and **Jack Nicholson**, About Schmidt

BEST ACTRESS:
Julianne Moore, Far from Heaven

BEST SUPPORTING ACTOR:
Chris Cooper, Adaptation

BEST SUPPORTING ACTRESS:
Catherine Zeta-Jones, Chicago

BEST ACTING ENSEMBLE:
Chicago

BEST DIRECTOR:
Steven Spielberg, Catch Me If You Can and Minority Report

BEST WRITER:
Charlie Kaufman, Adaptation and Confessions of a Dangerous Mind

BEST DIGITAL ACTING PERFORMANCE:
Gollum, The Lord of the Rings: The Two Towers

BEST YOUNG ACTOR/ACTRESS:
Kieran Culkin, Igby Goes Down

BEST ANIMATED FEATURE:
Spirited Away

BEST FAMILY FILM (LIVE ACTION):
Harry Potter and the Chamber of Secrets

BEST PICTURE MADE FOR TELEVISION:
Door to Door

BEST DOCUMENTARY:
Bowling for Columbine

BEST FOREIGN LANGUAGE FILM:
Y Tu Mama Tambien

BEST SONG:
"Lose Yourself," Eminem, 8 Mile

BEST COMPOSER:
John Williams, Catch Me If You Can, Harry Potter and the Chamber of Secrets, and Minority Report
FREEDOM AWARD:
Antwone Fisher

CANNES FILM FESTIVAL AWARDS

PALME D'OR
Elephant, Gus Van Sant, United States.
GRAND PRIZE
Uzak, Nuri Bilge Ceylan, Turkey.
BEST ACTRESS
Marie Josee Croze, Barbarian Invasion, Canada
BEST ACTOR
tie Muzzaffer Ozdemir, Mehmet Emin Toprak, Uzak, Turkey..
BEST DIRECTOR (TIE)
Gus Van Sant, Elephant
JURY PRIZE
Panj e Asr, Five in the afternoon, Samira Makhmalbaf, Iran.
SCREENPLAY
Denys Arcand, Barbarian Invasion, Canada
CAMERA D'OR
Christoffer Boe, Reconstruction, Denmark.

DIRECTORS GUILD OF AMERICA AWARD

FILM DIRECTOR'S AWARD
Rob Marshall, Chicago
DOCUMENTARY AWARD
Tasha Oldham, The Smith Family
LIFETIME ACHIEVEMENT AWARD
Martin Scorsese

GOLDEN GLOBE AWARDS

BEST PICTURE—DRAMA
The Hours.
BEST ACTOR—DRAMA
Jack Nicholson, About Schmidt.
BEST ACTRESS—DRAMA
Nichole Kidman, The Hours.
BEST PICTURE—COMEDY OR MUSICAL
Chicago.
BEST ACTOR—COMEDY OR MUSICAL
Richard Gere, Chicago.
BEST ACTRESS—COMEDY OR MUSICAL
Renee Zellweger, Chicago.
BEST SUPPORTING ACTOR
Chris Cooper, Adaptation.
BEST SUPPORTING ACTRESS
Meryl Streep, Adaptation.
BEST DIRECTOR
Martin Scorsese, Gangs of Neew York.
BEST SCREENPLAY
Alexander Payne & Jim Taylor, About Schmidt.
BEST ORIGINAL SCORE
Elliot Goldenthal, Frida.
BEST ORIGINAL SONG
U2, The Hand s That Built America, Gangs of New York.
BEST FOREIGN FILM
Talk to Her
CECIL B. DEMILLE AWARD
Gene Hackman.

INDEPENDENT SPIRIT AWARDS

BEST FEATURE
Far From Heaven.
BEST DIRECTOR
Todd Haynes, Far From Heaven.
BEST SCREENPLAY
Mike White, The Good Girl.

BEST FIRST SCREENPLAY
Erin Cressida Wilson, Secretary.
BEST CINEMATOGRAPHY
Edward Lachman, Far From Heaven.
BEST FOREIGN FILM
Alfonso Cuaron, Y Tu Mama Tambien.
BEST DEBUT PERFORMANCE
Nia Vardalos, My Big Fat Greek Wedding.
BEST ACTRESS
Julianne Moore, Far From Heaven.
BEST ACTOR
Derek Luke, Antwone Fisher.
BEST SUPPORTING ACTRESS
Emily Mortimer, Lovely & Amazing
BEST SUPPORTING ACTOR
Dennis Quaid, Far From Heaven
BEST DOCUMENTARY
Bowling For Columbine, Michael Moore.

LOS ANGELES FILM CRITICS AWARDS

BEST PICTURE
About Schmidt.
BEST ACTOR
tie Daniel Day-Lewis, Gangs of New York & Jack Nicholson, About Schmidt.
BEST ACTRESS
Julianne Moore, Far From Heaven, The Hours.
BEST SUPPORTING ACTOR
Chris Cooper, Adaptation.
BEST SUPPORTING ACTRESS
Edie Falco, Sunshine State.
BEST DIRECTOR
Pedro Almodovar, Talk to Her.
BEST SCREENPLAY
About Schmidt, Alexander Payne, Jim Taylor.
BEST FOREIGN LANGUAGE FILM
Y Tu Mama Tambien.
BEST CINEMATOGRAPHY
Far From Heaven, Edward Lachman.
BEST ANIMATED FILM
Spirited Away.
BEST MUSICAL SCORE
Far From Heaven, Elmer Bernstein.
BEST DOCUMENTARY
The Cockettes.
CAREER ACHIEVEMENT
Arthur Penns.

NATIONAL BOARD OF REVIEW

BEST PICTURE
The Hours.
BEST DIRECTOR
Phillip Noyce, The Quiet American & Rabbit Proof Fence.
BEST ACTOR
Campbell Scott, Roger Dodger.
BEST ACTRESS
Julianne Moore, Far From Heaven.
BEST SUPPORTING ACTOR
Chris Cooper, Adaptation.
BEST SUPPORTING ACTRESS
Kathy Bates, About Schmidt.
BREAKTHROUGH PERFORMANCES
Derek Luke, Antwone Fisher & Magiie Gyllenhal, Secretary.

NATIONAL SOCIETY OF FILM CRITICS AWARDS

BEST PICTURE
The Pianist
BEST DIRECTOR
Roman Polanski, The Pianist.
BEST ACTOR
Adrien Brody, The Pianist.

BEST ACTRESS
Diane Lane, Unfaithful.
BEST SUPPORTING ACTOR
Christopher Walken, Catch Me If You Can.
BEST SUPPORTING ACTRESS
Patricia Clarkson, Far From Heaven.
BEST CINEMATOGRAPHY
Edward Lachman, Far From Heaven.
BEST FOREIGN FILM
Y Tu Mama Tambien, Alfonso Cuaron
BEST SCREENPLAY
Ronald Harwood, The Pianist.

New York Film Critics Circle Awards

BEST PICTURE
Far From Heaven
.BEST DIRECTOR
Todd Haynes, Far From Heaven.
BEST ACTOR
Daniel Day-Lewis, Gangs of New York.
BEST ACTRESS
Diane Lane, Unfaithful.
BEST SUPPORTING ACTOR
Dennis Quaid, Far From Heaven.
BEST SUPPORTING ACTRESS
Patricia Clarkson, Far From Heaven.
BEST SCREENPLAY
Adaptation, Charlie Kaufman & Donald Kaufman.
BEST FOREIGN FILM
In the Mood for Love, Kar-wai Wong.
BEST CINEMATOGRAPHY
Edward Lachman, Far From Heaven.

BEST FIRST FEATURE FILM
Roger Dodger, Dylan Kidd, Artisan Entertainment.
BEST ANIMATED FEATURE
Spirited Away, Hayao Miyazaki, Buena Vista.
BEST NON-FICTION FEATURE
Standing in the Shadows of Motown, Paul Justman.

Screen Actors Guild Awards

BEST ACTOR
Daniel Day-Lewis, Gangs of New York.
BEST ACTRESS
Renee Zellweger, Chicago.
BEST SUPPORTING ACTOR
Christopher Walken, Catch Me If You Can.
BEST SUPPORTING ACTRESS
Catherine Zeta-Jones, Chicago.
BEST ENSEMBLE CAST
Chicago.
LIFETIME ACHIEVEMENT AWARD
Clint Eastwood.

Writers Guild Awards

BEST SCREENPLAY
Bowling For Columbine, Michael Moore.
BEST ADAPTED SCREENPLAY
The Hours, David Hare.

INTERNATIONAL FILM FESTIVALS AND MARKETS

JANUARY

BRUSSELS INTERNATIONAL FILM FESTIVAL
(32) 2-227-3980. FAX: (32) 2-218-1860.
email: infoffb@netcity.be
GENERAL DELEGATE
Christian Thomas

CINEMART
c/o International Film Festival Rotterdam, P.O. Box 21696, AR
Rotterdam, 3001, The Netherlands. (31) 10-890-9090. FAX:
(31) 10-890-9091. www.iffrotterdam.nl
email: cinemart@iffrotterdam.nl
COORDINATOR
Ido Abram

FESTIVAL INTERNATIONAL DE PROGRAMMES AUDIOVISUELS
(33) 1-4489-9999. FAX: (33) 1-4489-9960.
www.persa.wonadoo.fr/fipa email: fipa@wanadoo.fr
PRESIDENT
Marie-France Pisier

FILMFESTIVAL MAX OPHULS PREIS
Mainzertstr. 8, Saarbrucken, 66111, Germany. (49) 681-936-
7421. FAX: (49) 681-936-7429.
www.saarbruecken.de/filmhaus.htm email: filmfestsb@aol.com
DIRECTOR
Christel Drawer

GOTEBORG FILM FESTIVAL
(46) 31-410-546. FAX: (46) 31-410-063.
www.goteborg.filmfestival.org email: goteborg@filmfestival.org
DIRECTOR
Gunnar Bergdahlm

INTERNATIONAL FILM FESTIVAL ROTTERDAM
(31) 10-890-9090. FAX: (31) 10-890-9091.
www.iffrotterdam.nl email: tiger@iffrotterdam.nl
DIRECTOR
Simon Field

KIDFILM/USA FILM FESTIVAL/ DALLAS
6116 N. Central Expwy., Ste. 105, Dallas, TX 75206. (214) 821-
6300. FAX: (214) 821-6364. www.usafilmfestival.com

THE NEW YORK FESTIVALS
186 5th Ave., 7th Flr., New York, NY 10010. (914) 238-4481.
FAX: (914) 238-5040. www.nyfests.com

NORTEL PALM SPRINGS INTERNATIONAL FILM FESTIVAL
(760) 322-2930. FAX: (760) 322-4087. www.psfilmfest.org
email: cprater@psfilmfest.org
EXECUTIVE DIRECTOR
Craig Prater (January)

PREMIERS PLANS-FESTIVAL D'ANGERS
(European Films Only)
(33)1-4271-5370. FAX: (33)1-4271-0111.
www.anjou.com/premiersplans
FESTIVAL DIRECTOR
Claude-Eric Poiroux

SLAMDANCE FILM FESTIVAL
(323) 466-1786. FAX: (323) 466 1784.
www.slamdance.com email: mail@slamdance.com
FESTIVAL DIRECTOR
Gianna Chachere

SOLOTHURN FILM FESTIVAL
(41) 32-625-8080. FAX: (41) 32-623-6410.
www.filmtage-solothurn.ch email: filmtage@cuenet.ch
DIRECTOR
Kummer Ivo

SUNDANCE FILM FESTIVAL
Park City, UT. (801) 328-FILM. FAX: (801) 575-5175.
www.sundance.org email: institute@sundance.org
V.P.
Nicole Guillemet

FEBRUARY

AMERICAN FILM MARKET (AFM)
(310) 446-1000. FAX: (310) 446-1600. www.afma.com
email: info@afma.com
E.V.P.
Jonathan Wolf

BERLIN INTERNATIONAL FILM FESTIVAL
(49) 30-2592-0202. FAX: (49) 30-2592-0299. www.berlinale.de
email: info@berlinale.de

CINEQUEST THE SAN JOSE FILM FESTIVAL
(408) 995-6305. FAX: (408) 995-5713. www.cinequest.org
email: sjfilmfest@aol.com
PROGRAMMING DIRECTOR
Mike Rabehl

CLERMONT FERRAND SHORT FILM FESTIVAL
(33) 47-391-6573. FAX: (33) 47-392-1193.
www.clermont-filmfest.com
CO-DIRECTOR
Roger Gonin

FANTASPORTO-OPORTO INTERNATIONAL FILM FESTIVAL
(351) 2-507-3880. FAX: (351) 2-550-8210.
www.caleida.pt/fantasporto email: fantas@caleida.pt
DIRECTOR
Mario Dorminsky

FILM ALTERNATIVE/BIG MUDDY FILM FESTIVAL
(618) 453-1482. FAX: (618) 453-2264.
email: bigmuddy@siu.edu

FILM SOCIETY OF MIAMI
(305) 377-3456. FAX: (305) 577-9768.
www.filmsocietyofmiami.com
FESTIVAL DIRECTOR
Nat Chediak

FRIENDS OF THE GERMAN FILM ARCHIVE & INTERNATIONAL FORUM OF NEW CINEMA
(49) 30-2548-9246. FAX: (49) 30-261-5025. www.fdk-berlin.de
email: forum@fdk-berlin.de
DIRECTOR
Ulrich Gregor

PORTLAND INTERNATIONAL FILM FESTIVAL
(503) 221-1156. FAX: (503) 294-0874. www.nwfilm.org
email: info@nwfilm.org

SANTA BARBARA INTERNATIONAL FILM FESTIVAL
(805) 963-0023. FAX: (805) 962-2524. www.sbfilmfestival.org
email: info@sbfilmfestival.org
MGR./DIRECTOR
Rhea A Lewis-Woodson

SMPTE ADVANCED MOTION IMAGING CONFERENCE
(914) 761-1100. FAX: (914) 761-3115. www.smpte.org
email: mktg@smpte.org
MARKETING COORDINATOR
Linda Alexander

UCLA ENTERTAINMENT SYMPOSIUM
(310) 825-0971, (310) 206-1121. FAX: (310) 825-1372.
www.law.ucla.edu

U.S. COMEDY ARTS FESTIVAL
(310) 201-9595. FAX: (310) 201-9505.
www.hbocomedyfestival.com
PROGRAMMER/CONTACT
Kevin Haasarud

MARCH

ANN ARBOR FILM FESTIVAL
(734) 995-5356. FAX: (734) 995-5396. www.aafilmfest.org
email: vicki@honeyman.org
DIRECTOR
Vicki Honeyman

BRADFORD FILM FESTIVAL
(44) 127-420-3345. FAX: (44) 127-477-0217.
www.nmsi.ac.uk/nmpft email: w.lawrence@nmsi.ac.uk
HEAD OF CINEMA
Bill Lawrence

BRUSSELS INTERNATIONAL FESTIVAL OF FANTASY, THRILLER & SCIENCE-FICTION FILMS
(32) 2-201-1713. FAX: (32) 2-201-1469. www.bifff.org
email: peymey@skypro.be
CONTACT
Bozzo Freddy

CHICAGO LATINO CINEMA
(312) 431-1330. FAX: (312) 344-8030.

CINEMA DU REEL
(33) 1-4478-4421, (33) 1-4478-4516. FAX: (33) 1-4478-1224.
www.bpi.fr email: cinereel@bpi.fr
CONTACT
Suzette Glenadel

CINEMATECA URUGUAYA
(598) 408-2460. FAX: (598) 409-4572. www.cinemateca.org.uy
email: cinemuy@chasque.apc.org
DIRECTOR
Manuel Carril

CLEVELAND INTERNATIONAL FILM FESTIVAL
(216) 623-3456. FAX: (216) 623-0103. www.clevelandfilm.org
email: cfs@clevelandfilm.org
EXECUTIVE DIRECTOR
David W. Wittkowsky

FESTIVAL DE FILMS DE FRIBOURG
(41) 26-322-2232. FAX: (41) 26-322-7950. www.fiff.ch
email: info@fiff.ch
DIRECTOR
Knaebel Martial

LAON INTERNATIONAL FILM FESTIVAL FOR YOUNG PEOPLE
(33) 3-2379-3937. FAX: (33) 3-2379-3932.
email: festival.cinema.laon@wanadoo.fr
ADMINISTRATOR
Fabienne Pechard

LONDON LESBIAN & GAY FILM FESTIVAL
(44) 207-815-1323. FAX: (44) 207-633-0786.
email: carol.coombes@bfi.org.uk
EXECUTIVE DIRECTOR
Adrian Wootton

SAN FRANCISCO INTERNATIONAL ASIAN AMERICAN FILM FESTIVAL
(415) 863-0814. FAX: (415) 863-7428.
www.naatanet.org/festival email: festival@naatanet.org
FESTIVAL DIRECTOR
Brian Lau

SANTA BARBARA INTERNATIONAL FILM FESTIVAL
(805) 963-0023. FAX: (805) 962-2524. www.sbfilmfestival.com
email: info@sbfilmfestival.com
PROGRAMMER
Cynthia Felando

SANTA CLARITA INTERNATIONAL FILM FESTIVAL
(805) 257-3131. FAX: (805) 257-8989. www.sciff.org
email: pattemitch@col.com
EXECUTIVE DIRECTOR
Chris Shoemaker

SEDONA INTERNATIONAL FILM FESTIVAL WORKSHOP
P.O. Box 2515, Sedona, AZ 86339. (800) 780-ARTS.
(520) 282-0747. FAX: (520) 282-5358.
www.sedona.net/scp/festival email: scp@sedona.net

SHOWEST
(310) 657-7724. FAX: (310) 657-4758. www.showest.com
email: showest@aol.com
CHAIRMAN
Milton Moritz

U.S. INTERNATIONAL FILM & VIDEO FESTIVAL
(630) 834-7773, (630) 834-7774. FAX: (630) 834-5565.
www.filmfestawards.com
email: filmfestinfo@filmfestawards.com
CHAIRMAN
J. W. Anderson

VIEWPOINT 99, INTERNATIONAL DOCUMENTARY FILM FESTIVAL
(32) 9-225-0845. FAX: (32) 9-233-7522.
www.cinebel.com/studioskoop email: studio.skoop@net7.be
PROGRAMMER
Cis Bierinckx

WOMEN IN THE DIRECTOR'S CHAIR INTERNATIONAL FILM & VIDEO FESTIVAL
941 W. Lawrence Ave., Ste. 500, Chicago, IL 60640. (773) 907-0610. FAX: (773) 907-0381. www.widc.org email: widc@widc.org

APRIL

ASPEN SHORTSFEST
(970) 925-6882. FAX: (970) 925-1967. www.aspenfilm.org
email: shortsfest@aspenfilm.org
GENERAL MANAGER
Jennifer Swanson

BAC FILM & VIDEO FESTIVAL
(718) 625-0080. FAX: (718) 625-3294.
email: baca195@aol.com

DUBLIN FILM FESTIVAL
(353) 1-679-2937. FAX: (353) 1-679-2939. www.iol.ie/dff
email: dff@iol.ie

HONG KONG INTERNATIONAL FILM FESTIVAL (HKIFF)
(852) 2734-2903. FAX: (852) 2366-5206.

HUMBOLDT INTERNATIONAL FILM FESTIVAL
(707) 826-4113. FAX: (707) 826-4112.
www.humboldt.edu/~theatre/ filmfest.html
email: filmfest@axe.humboldt.edu
CONTACT
Marcelle Pecot

THE INTERNATIONAL COMMUNICATIONS FILM & VIDEO COMPETITION
(312) 425-9400. FAX: (312) 425-0944.
www.chicago.ddbn.com/filmfest email: filmfest@wwa.com
DIRECTOR
Michael Kutza

MIP-DOC
(44) 207-528-0086. FAX: (44) 207-895-0949.

MINNEAPOLIS/ST. PAUL INTERNATIONAL FILM FESTIVAL
(612) 627-4431, (612) 627-4432. FAX: (612) 627-4111.
www.ufilm.org email: filmsoc@tc.umn.edu
DIRECTOR
Al Milgrom

NEW ENGLAND FILM & VIDEO FESTIVAL
(Open to New England Residents Only)
(617) 536-1540. FAX: (617) 536-3576. www.bfvf.org
email: info@bfvf.org
FESTIVAL CO-DIRECTOR
Devon Damonte

PHILADELPHIA FESTIVAL OF WORLD CINEMA
(215) 895-6593. FAX: (215) 895-6562. www.libertynet.org/pfwc

SAN FRANCISCO INTERNATIONAL FILM FESTIVAL
(415) 929-5000. FAX: (415) 921-5032. www.sfiff.org
email: sfiff@sfiff.org
ARTISTIC DIRECTOR
Peter Scarlet

SINGAPORE INTERNATIONAL FILM FESTIVAL
(65) 738-7567. FAX: (65) 738-7578. www.filmfest.org.sg
email: filmfest@pacific.net.sg
FESTIVAL PROGRAMMER
Philip Cheah

TURIN INTERNATIONAL GAY & LESBIAN FILM FESTIVAL
(39) 011-534-888. FAX: (39) 011-535-796.
www.space.tin.it/cinema/gminerba
email: glfilmfest@assioma.com
DIRECTOR
Giovanni Minerba

USA FILM FESTIVAL/DALLAS
6116 N. Central Expwy., Ste., 105, Dallas, TX 75206. (214) 821-6300. FAX: (214) 821-6364. www.usafilmfestival.com

WORLDFEST-HOUSTON INTERNATIONAL FILM FESTIVAL
(713) 965-9955. FAX: (713) 965-9960. www.worldfest.org

YOSEMITE FILM FESTIVAL
40637 Hwy. 41, Oakhurst, CA 93644. (559) 683-4636.
www.yosemitefilm.com
CONTACT
Peggy Kukulus

MAY

FESTIVAL INTERNATIONAL DU FILM (CANNES)
(33) 1-4561-6605. FAX: (33) 14561-9494. (212) 832-8860. FAX:
(212) 755-0629. email: gilles.jacob@festival-cannes.fr.
GENERAL DELEGATE
Gilles Jacob

MAUI FILM FESTIVAL

P.O. Box 669, Paia, HI 96779. (808) 579-9996. FAX: (808) 579-9552. www.mauifilmfestival.com
email: mauifilmfestival@mauifilmfestival.com
CONTACT
Donne Dawson

MUNICH INTERNATIONAL DOCUMENTARY FILM FESTIVAL

(49) 89-470-3237. FAX: (49) 89-470-6611.

PRO VISION INTERNATIONAL, INC.

213 Congress Ave., Ste., 282, Austin, TX 78701. (512) 476-8999. FAX: (512) 476-2441. email: pvi100@yahoo.com
CEO
Frances Jones

QUINZAINE DES REALISATEURS (DIRECTOR'S FORTNIGHT)

(Independent Section of the Cannes Film Festival)
(33) 1-4489-9999. FAX: (33) 1-4489-9960.
email: quinzain@club-internet.fr
GENERAL DELEGATE, DIRECTOR'S FORTNIGHT
Marie Pierre Mascia

SAGUARO FILM FESTIVAL

(602) 970-8711. FAX: (480) 945-3339.
www.extracheese.com/afs email: afs@extra_cheese.com
FESTIVAL DIRECTOR
Durrie Parks

SEATTLE INTERNATIONAL FILM FESTIVAL

(206) 464-5830. FAX: (206) 264-7919. www.seattlefilm.com
email: mail@seattlefilm.com
FESTIVAL DIRECTOR
Darryl Macdonald

TRIBECA FILM FESTIVAL

(212) 941-2400. FAX: (212) 941-3939
www.tribecafilmfestival.org
email: festival@tribecafilmfestival.org
PROGRAMMERS:
David Kwok, Nancy Schafer

YORKTON SHORT FILM & VIDEO FESTIVAL

(306) 782-7077. FAX: (306) 782-1550.
www.yorktonshortfilm.org email: info@yorktonshortfilm.org

JUNE

ADRIATICOCINEMA

(39) 0541-26-399. FAX: (39) 0541-24-227.
email: adriaticocinema@comune.rimini.it

ANNECY INTERNATIONAL ANIMATED FILM FESTIVAL

(33) 4-5010-0900. FAX: (33) 4-5010-0970. www.annecy.org
email: info@annecy.org
PRESIDENT
Dominique Puthod

BITE THE MANGO FILM FESTIVAL

(44) 127-420-3300. FAX: (44) 127-477-0217.
www.bitethemango.ac.uk email: filmfest@nmsi.ac.uk
HEAD OF CINEMA
Bill Lawrence

BRADFORD ANIMATION FESTIVAL

c/o National Museum of Photography, Film & Television,
Pictureville Cinema, Bradford, BD1 1NQ, England. (44) 127-420-3345. FAX: (44) 127-477-0217. www.nmsi.ac.uk
email: filmfest@nmsi.ac.uk
HEAD OF CINEMA
Bill Larwence

BUREAU OF THE INTERNATIONAL FILM FESTIVALS/ "FESTIVAL OF FESTIVALS"

(812) 237-0304. FAX: (812) 394-5870.
DIRECTOR
Alexander Momontov

CHICAGO ALT.FILM FILM FESTIVAL

3430 N. Lake Shore Dr., Ste. 19N, Chicago, IL 60657. (773) 525-4559. FAX: (773) 327-8669.
FOUNDER & DIRECTOR
Dennis Neal Vaughn

CINEMA EXPO INTERNATIONAL

(212) 246-6460. FAX: (212) 265-6428. www.cinemaexpo.com
email: sunshine@maestro.com
CONVENTION MANAGER
Andrew Sunshine

CINEVISION INTERNATIONAL FILM FESTIVAL

(43) 512-580-723. FAX: (43) 512-581-762.
www.pirolkultur.at/cinema

FLORIDA FILM FESTIVAL

(407) 629-1088. FAX: (407) 629-6870.
www.floridafilmfestival.com email: filmfest@gate.net
DIRECTOR OF PROGRAMMING
Matthew Curtis

HONG KONG INTERNATIONAL FILM & TV MARKET (FILMART 2000)

(852) 2584-4333. FAX: (852) 2824-0249.
www.hkfilmart.tdc.org.hk email: hktdc@tdc.org.hk
MANAGER
Johnson Yip

THE HUDSON VALLEY FILM FESTIVAL

40 Garden St., Poughkeepsie, NY 12601. (914) 473-0318.
FAX: (914) 473-0082. www.sandbook.com/hvfo
email: hvfo@vh.net
FESTIVAL DIRECTOR
Aslihan Coker

INDEPENDENT FEATURE PROJECT

104 W. 29th St., 12th Flr., New York, NY 10001. (212) 465-8200. FAX: (212) 465-8525. www.ifp.org email: ifpny@ifp.org

INFOCOMM INTERNATIONAL

11242 Waples Mill Rd., Ste. 200, Fairfax, VA 22030. (703) 273-7200. FAX: (703) 278-8082. www.infocomm.org
CONTACT
Bob Brown

IFP- LOS ANGELES FILM FESTIVAL

(INDEPENDENT FEATURE PROJECT)
(310) 432-1200/(310) 951-7090. FAX: (310) 432-1203.
www.lafilmfest.com email: lafilmfest@ifp.org
DIRECTOR
Richard Raddon

MARIN COUNTY NATIONAL SHORT FILM FESTIVAL

(415) 499-6400. FAX: (415) 499-3700.
MANAGER
Jim Farley

MUNICH FILM FESTIVAL

(49) 89-381-9040. FAX: (49) 89-381-9047.
CONTACT
Eberhard Huwff

NANTUCKET FILM FESTIVAL

(212) 708-1278. FAX: (212) 654-4784.
www.nantucketfilmfestival.org email: ackfest@aol.com
DIRECTOR
Jill Goode

SAN FRANCISCO INTERNATIONAL LESBIAN & GAY FILM FESTIVAL

(415) 703-8650. FAX: (415) 861-1404. www.frameline.org
email: info@frameline.org
CONTACT
Michael Lumpkin

SHOWBIZ WEST EXPO REED EXHIBITION COMPANIES

(203) 840-5556, (203) 840-5688. FAX: (203) 840-9556, (203) 840-9688.

SYDNEY FILM FESTIVAL

(61) 2-9660-3844. FAX: (61) 2-9692-8793.
www.sydfilm-fest.com.au email: info@sydfilm-fest.com.au

JULY

BRISBANE INTERNATIONAL FILM FESTIVAL

c/o Pacific Film & Television Commission, III George St.,Level 15, Brisbane, Queensland 4000, Australia. (61) 7-3220-0333.
FAX: (61) 7-3220-0400. www.pftc.com.au
EXECUTIVE ASSISTANT
Megan Rowe

JUST FOR LAUGHS! THE MONTREAL INTERNATIONAL COMEDY FESTIVAL

(514) 845-3155. FAX: (514) 845-4140. www.hahaha.com

PALM SPRINGS INTERNATIONAL SHORT FILM FESTIVAL

(760) 322-2930. FAX: (760) 322-4087. www.psfilmfest.org
email: cprater@psfilmfest.org
EXECUTIVE DIRECTOR
Craig Prater

WINE COUNTRY FILM FESTIVAL

(707) 996-2536. FAX: (707) 996-6964.
www.winecountryfilmfest.com email: wcfilmfest@aol.com
DIRECTOR
Stephen Ashton

AUGUST

LOCARNO INTERNATIONAL FILM FESTIVAL
41-91-756-2121 FAX: 41-91-756-2149.
www.pardo.ch email: info@pardo.ch
DIRECTOR
Irene Bignardi

MONTREAL WORLD FILM FESTIVAL
(514) 848-3883. FAX: (514) 848-3886.
www.ffm-montreal.org

ODENSE INTERNATIONAL FILM FESTIVAL
(45) 66-131-372. FAX: (45) 65-914-318. www.filmfestival.dk
email: filmfestival@post.odkomm.dk

SEPTEMBER

A.J. PRODUCTIONS
(New York Independent Film Festival)
1335 N. La Brea Ave.,Ste. 2197, Hollywood, CA 90028. (323)
876-0975. FAX: (323) 876-0975.
www.hollywoodindependents.com email: jaa@simplyweb.net
PROGRAMMING DIRECTOR
John Greenlow

ASPEN FILMFEST
(970) 925-6882. FAX: (970) 925-1967. www.aspenfilm.org
email: filmfest@aspenfilm.org
GENERAL MANAGER
Jennifer Swunson

FILMMAKERS SYMPOSIUM
(732) 528-6660. Direct line: (800) 222-7719.
email: filmrose@aol.com
EXECUTIVE DIRECTOR
Chuck Rose

HOLLYWOOD INDEPENDENT FILM FESTIVAL
c/o Hollywood Independents, 1335 N. La Brea Ave., Ste. 2197,
Hollywood, CA 90028. (323) 876-0975. FAX: (323) 876-0975.
www.hollywoodindependents.com email: jaa@simplyweb.net
PRESIDENT
Jorge Ameer

INDEPENDENT FEATURE FILM MARKET
(212) 465-8200. FAX: (212) 465-8525. www.ifp.org

INFOCOMM ASIA
(Fall 2001, takes place every 2 years)
II242 Waples Mill Rd., Ste. 200 Fairfax, VA 22030.
(703) 273-7200, (800) 659-7469. FAX: (703) 273-5924.
www.infocomm.org

L.A. INTERNATIONAL SHORT FILM FESTIVAL
(213) 427-8016. www.lashortsfest.com
email: info@lashortsfest.com
FOUNDER & FESTIVAL DIRECTOR
Robert Arentz

LAGUNA BEACH FILM FESTIVAL
P.O. Box 4444, Laguna Beach, CA 92652. (949) 494-1313.
www.lagunafilmfestival.org email: info@lagunafilmfestival.org

NEW YORK FILM FESTIVAL
THE FILM SOCIETY OF LINCOLN CENTER
(212) 875-5638. FAX: (212) 875-5636. www.filmlinc.com
email: sbensman@filmlinc.com

POST/LA EXPO
(323) 654-6530. FAX: (323) 654-2954. www.postlaexpo.com

TELLURIDE FILM FESTIVAL
(603) 433-9202. FAX: (603) 433-9206.
www.telluridefilmfestival.com email: Tellufilm@aol.com
CONTACT
Stella Pence

TEMECULA VALLEY INTERNATIONAL FILM FESTIVAL
(909) 699-6267. FAX: (909) 308-1414. www.tviff.com

TORONTO INTERNATIONAL FILM FESTIVAL
(416) 967-7371. FAX: (416) 967-9477. www.bell.ca/filmfest

VANCOUVER INTERNATIONAL FILM FESTIVAL
(604) 685-0260. FAX: (604) 688-8221. www.viff.org
email: viff@viff.org
FESTIVAL DIRECTOR
Alan Franey

OCTOBER

AFI/LOS ANGELES INTERNATIONAL FILM FESTIVAL
(323) 856-7707. FAX: (323) 462-4049. www.afifest.com
email: afifest@afionline.org

CHICAGO INTERNATIONAL CHILDREN'S FILM FESTIVAL
(773) 281-9075. FAX: (773) 929-5437. www.facets.org
email: kidsfesf@facets.org

CHICAGO INTERNATIONAL FILM FESTIVAL
(312) 425-9400. FAX: (312) 425-0944.
www.chicago.ddbn.com/filmfest email: filmfest@com
FOUNDER & ARTISTIC DIRECTOR
Michael Kutza

DENVER INTERNATIONAL FILM FESTIVAL
(303) 595-3456. FAX: (303) 595-0956. www.denverfilm.org
email: dfs@denverfilm.org
DIRECTOR
Ron Henderson

FILMFESTIVAL MANNHEIM- HEIDELBERG
Collini Center Galerye, Mannheim, 68161, Germany. (49) 621-
102-943. FAX: (49) 621-291-564.

FORT LAUDERDALE INTERNATIONAL FILM FESTIVAL
(954) 760-9898. FAX: (954) 760-9099.
www.ftlaudfilmfestival.com email: brofilm@aol.com
CONTACT
Gregory Von Hausch

THE HAMPTONS INTERNATIONAL FILM FESTIVAL
(516) 324-4600. FAX: (516) 324-5116. www.hamptonsfest.org
EXECUTIVE DIRECTOR
Denise Kasell

HEARTLAND FILM FESTIVAL
(317) 464-9405. FAX: (317) 635-4201.
www.heartlandfilmfest.org email: hff@pop.iquest.net
ARTISTIC DIRECTOR
Jeff Sparks

HOT SPRINGS DOCUMENTARY FILM FESTIVAL
(501) 321-4747. FAX: (501) 321-0211. www.DocuFilmInst.org
email: hsdff@docufilminst.org
CONTACT
Gretchen Taylor

INDEPENDENT FILMMAKERS COMPETITION
(323) 737-3292. FAX: (323) 737-2842. www.wsbrec.org

MILL VALLEY FILM FESTIVAL
THE FILM INSTITUTE OF NORTHERN CALIFORNIA
(415) 383-5256. FAX: (415) 383-8606. www.finc.org
email: finc@well.com
EXECUTIVE DIRECTOR
Mark Fishkin

MIPCOM
c/o Reed Midem Organization Ltd., 125 Park Ave, 24th Flr.,
New York, NY 10017. (212) 370-7470. FAX: (212) 370-7471.
c/o Reed Midem Organisation Ltd., Walmar House, 296 Regent
St., London W1R 6AB, UK. (44) 207-528-0086. FAX: (44) 207-
895-0949. www.midem.com

MIPCOM JR.
c/o Reed Midem Organization Ltd., 125 Park Ave, 24th Flr.,
New York, NY 10017. (212) 370-7470. FAX: (212) 370-7471.
c/o Reed Midem Organisation Ltd., Walmar House, 296 Regent
St., London W1R 6AB, UK. (44) 207-528-0086. FAX: (44) 207-
895-0949. www.midem.com

THE MURPHY'S CORK FILM FESTIVAL
(353) 21-271-711. FAX: (353) 21-275-945. www.corkfilmfest.org
email: ciff@indigo.ie
FESTIVAL DIRECTOR
Mick Hannigan

NEW ORLEANS FILM & VIDEO FESTIVAL
225 Baronne St., Ste. 1712, New Orleans, LA 70112. (504)
523-3818. FAX: (504) 529-2430.www.neworleansfilmfest.com
email: neworleansfilmfest@worldnet.att.net
EXECUTIVE DIRECTOR
Carol Gniady

SHOWBIZ EAST EXPO REED EXHIBITION COMPANIES
383 Main Ave., Norwalk, CT 06851. (203) 840-5556. FAX:
(203) 840-9556.
CONTACT
Steven Kalman

SHOWEAST
(212) 246-6460. FAX: (212) 265-6428. www.showeast.com
email: sunshine@maestro.com
CONVENTION MANAGER
Mitch Neuhauser

VERMONT INTERNATIONAL FILM FESTIVAL
(802) 660-2600. FAX: (802) 860-9555. www.vtiff.org
email: viff@together.net
EVENTS COORDINATOR
Jennie Bedusa

YAMAGATA INTL. DOCUMENTARY FILM FESTIVAL
(81) 3-3266-9704. FAX: (81) 3-3266-9700.
www.city.yamagata.yamagata.jp/yidff
DIRECTOR
Yano Kazuyuki

NOVEMBER

BRITISH FILM FESTIVAL
2775 Market St.,Ste. 303, San Francisco, CA 94114-1825.
(415) 437-6789. FAX: (415) 487-9750.
www.grin.net/~britfilms
email: britfilms@grin.net
MANAGING DIRECTOR
Simon Overton

THE CHICAGO LESBIAN & GAY INTERNATIONAL FILM FESTIVAL
(773) 293-1447. FAX: (773) 293-0575.
www.chicagofilmmakers.org/reeling
email: reeling@chicagofilmmakers.org
EXECUTIVE DIRECTOR
Brenda Webb

HAWAII INTERNATIONAL FILM FESTIVAL
(808) 528-3456. FAX: (808) 528-1410.
www.hiff.org
email: hiffinfo@hiff.org
FESTIVAL DIRECTOR & DIRECTOR OF PROGRAMMING
Christian Gaines

LONDON FILM FESTIVAL
(44) 207-815-1323. FAX: (44) 207-633-0786.
email: sarahlutton@bfi.org.uk
FESTIVAL DIRECTOR
Adrian Wootton

NORTHWEST FILM & VIDEO FESTIVAL
(503) 221-1156. FAX: (503) 294-0874. www.nwfilm.org
email: info@nwfilm.org

THE OJAI FILM SOCIETY
10942 Encino Dr., Oak View, CA 93022. (805) 649-4000.
www.ojai.net/film email: stevo@ix.netcom.com
FESTIVAL CO-CHAIR & ARTISTIC DIRECTOR
Steve Grumette

WORLDFEST-FLAGSTAFF INTERNATIONAL FILM FESTIVAL
2700 Post Oak Blvd., Ste. 1798, Houston, TX 77056. (713)
965-9955. FAX: (713) 965-9960. www.worldfest.org

DECEMBER

CINE VEGAS INTERNATIONAL FILM FESTIVAL
c/o Blo Towers Plaza, 3745 Las Vegas Blvd., Ste. 204, Las
Vegas, NV 89109. (704) 477-7530. FAX: (704) 477-7533.
www.cinevegas.com email: cinevegas@aol.com
FESTIVAL COORDINATOR
Amy Carrelli

CINEASIA
(212) 246-6460. FAX: (212) 265-6428. www.cineasia.com
email: sunshine@maestro.com

BIOGRAPHIES

■

WHO'S WHO

IN THE ENTERTAINMENT WORLD

A

AARON, PAUL
Director, Producer, Writer.
THEATRE: *B'way*: Salvation, Paris Is Out, '70 Girls '70, Love Me Love My Children, That's Entertainment, The Burnt Flowerbed.
PICTURES: A Different Story, A Force of One, The Octagon (co-s.p.), Imperial Navy, Deadly Force, Maxie, Morgan Stewart's Coming Home (director, as Alan Smithee) Home Front, Bill & Ted's Bogus Journey (co-prod.), In Too Deep (prod., s.p.).
TELEVISION: *Movies*: The Miracle Worker, Thin Ice, Maid in America, When She Says No, Casebusters (exec. prod.), Save the Dog!, In Love and War, Laurel Avenue (creator, co-writer, exec. prod.),Untamed Love, Grand Avenue (creator, exec. prod.). *Series*: Under One Roof (creator, co-writer, exec. prod.)

AARON, ROY H.
Executive, Entertainment Industry Consultant. b. Los Angeles, CA, April 8, 1929. e. UC Berkeley, BA; USC, LLB. Attorney in L.A. law firm of Pacht, Ross, Warne, Bernhard & Sears (1957-78). Joined Plitt Companies in 1978 as sr. v.p. & gen. counsel. In 1980 was named pres. & CEO of Plitt Theatres, Inc. and related Plitt companies. 1985-93, pres. & CEO of Showscan Corp. 1993, business consultant, pres. of Plitt Entertainment Group Inc. & chmn. of Pacific Leisure Entertainment Group, L.L.C. Chmn. & CEO Intra-Asia Ent. Corp., 1997.

ABARBANEL, SAM X.
Producer, Writer, Publicist. b. Jersey City, NJ, March 27, 1914. e. Cornell U., U. of Illinois, B.S. 1935. Newspaperman in Chicago before joining NY exploitation dept. of Republic, then to studio as asst. publicity director. WWII in Europe with 103rd Div. After war became independent publicist and producer. Formed own co. in Spain, 1966. A founder of the Publicists Guild in Hollywood.
PICTURES: *Producer/Co-Prod./Exec. Prod./Assoc. Prod.*: Argyle Secrets, Prehistoric Women (also co-s.p.), Golden Mistress, Gunfighters of Casa Grande, The Sound of Horror (s.p.) Son of Gunfighter, Narco Men, The Last Day of War (also s.p.), Summertime Killer (s.p.).

ABEND, SHELDON
Executive. b. New York, NY, June 13, 1929. Maritime Labor-Rel. Negotiator, 1954-56; chmn., Maritime Union, 1954-56. Head, exec. dir. Authors' Research Co. (est. 1957) representing estates of deceased authors. Ind't literary negotiator: CC films, A.A.P., RKO General Inc., David O. Selznick, 7 Arts, Warner Bros., 1959-65. Pres. American Play Co. Inc. & Century Play Co. Inc., 1961-present. Est. Million Dollar Movie Play Library, 1962. Pres. Amer. Literary Consultants, est. 1965. Exec. v.p. Chantec Enterprises Inc. 1969-72. Mktg. literary cons. for Damon Runyon Estate. Copyright analyst and literary rights negotiator, United Artists Corp. Founder and chmn., Guild for Author's Heirs, 1970-72. Literary negotiator and prod. cons. for Robert Fryer, 1972. Founder, Copyright Royalty Co. for Authors' Heirs, 1974. Copyright consultant, Films, Inc. 1975; literary agent for B'way. play, Chicago, 1975. Owner of 53 classic RKO motion pictures for the non-theatrical markets, distributed by Films, Inc. Revived publishing of Damon Runyon stories in quality paperback. Published Cornell Woolrich mystery stories--all prod. by Alfred Hitchcock for TV & motion pictures, 1976. Assoc. prod. of film, Why Would I Lie?, 1978. Originator of Million Dollar Movie Book Theatre and Million Dollar Movie Sound Track Co., 1980. Assoc. prod. of B'way revival, Shanghai Gesture, 1981. Publ. 5 Cornell Woolrich books owned by S. Abend, 1982-83. Co-authored, The Guardians, 1985 and Romance of the Forties by Damon Runyon, 1986. Founder and pres. American Concerts, Inc. and American Theatre Collections, Inc., 1985. Published Into the Night by Cornell Woolrich. Packaged m.p. Bloodhounds of Broadway, 1988; co-author s.p. Ultimate Deman; stage adapt. of Bloodhounds of Broadway, Madam La Gimp, 1990. Exec. prod. adaptation of Cornell Woolrich stories for TV and movies. Won landmark copyright case before U.S. Supreme Court protecting Woolrich estate, also affecting other deceased authors, songwriters and their copyright renewals of their work, 1990. Acquired Damon Runyon copyrights, 1992. Guys & Dolls handbook published by Viking, 1993. Produced "Rear Window" remake for tv, 1998; exec. prod. film "Original Sin" 2001.
(d. Aug. 24, 2003)

ABRAHAM, F. MURRAY
Actor. r.n. Fahrid Murray Abraham. b. Pittsburgh, PA, Oct. 24, 1939. e. U. of Texas, 1959-61; trained for stage at Herbert Berghof Studios with Uta Hagen. First NY acting job was as Macy's Santa Claus. Stage debut in Los Angeles in The Wonderful Ice Cream Suit, 1965. New York debut in The Fantasticks, 1966. Full professor of theatre at CUNY Brooklyn College. Honorary Doctorate, Ryder College.
THEATRE: Antigone (NYSF, 1982), Uncle Vanya (Obie, LaMamma, etc.), The Golem (NYSF), Madwoman of Chaillot, Othello, Cyrano, A Life in the Theatre, Sexual Perversity in Chicago, Duck Variations, The David Show, Adaptation/Next, Don't Drink the Water, And Miss Reardon Drinks a Little, Where Has Tommy Flowers Gone?, A Christmas Carol, The Seagull, Landscape of the Body, 6 Rms Riv Vu, Survival of St. Joan, Scuba Duba, Teibele & Her Demon, The Ritz, Legend, Bad Habits, Frankie & Johnnie in the Claire De Lune, Twelfth Night, Macbeth, A Midsummer's Night Dream, Waiting for Godot, King Lear, Angels in America: Millenium Aproaches/Perestroika, Little Murders, A Month in the Country; also 5 Children's musicals, Theatreworks. A Christmas Carol (2002).
PICTURES: They Might Be Giants (debut, 1971), Serpico, The Prisoner of 2nd Avenue, The Sunshine Boys, All the President's Men, The Ritz, Madman, The Big Fix, Scarface, Amadeus (Academy Award, 1984), The Name of the Rose, Slipstream, The Favorite, Russicum (The Third Solution), An Innocent Man, Beyond the Stars, Eye of the Widow, The Bonfire of the Vanities, Cadence, Mobsters, National Lampoon's Loaded Weapon 1, By the Sword, Last Action Hero, Sweet Killing, The Final Card, Surviving the Game, Nostradamus, The Case, Jamila, Quiet Flows the Dawn, Money, Dillinger and Capone, Mighty Aphrodite., Baby Face Nelson, Looking for Richard, Children of the Revolution, Eruption, Mimic, Star Trek: Insurrection, All New Adventures of Laurel and Hardy: For Love or Mummy, Muppets from Space, Excellent Cadavers, Finding Forrester, The Knights of the Quest, I Cavalieri che fecero l'impressa, 13 Ghosts, Joshua, Papa Rua Alguem 5555.
TELEVISION: *Movies*: Sex and the Married Woman, Galileo Galilei, Vaclav Havel's 'Largo Desolato', A Season of Giants, - The First Circle, Journey to the Center of the Earth, Il Caso Dozier, Color of Justice, Esther, Noah's Ark, The Darkling, Un Dono semplice. *Series*: Love of Life, How to Survive a Marriage. *Mini-Series*: Dead Man's Walk, I Promessi sposi, Dream West, Marco Polo. *Guest*: Kojak, All in the Family.

ABRAHAMS, JIM
Producer, Writer, Director. b. Shorewood, WI, May 10, 1944. e. U. of Wisconsin. Former private investigator. 1971, with friends David and Jerry Zucker, opened the Kentucky Fried Theatre in Madison, WI, a multimedia show specializing in live improvisational skits mixed with videotaped and film routines and sketches, with the threesome writing and appearing in most. Opened new theatre in Los Angeles in 1972 and developed large following. Co-wrote, co-dir., and co-exec. prod. TV series Police Squad!
PICTURES: *With Zuckers*: The Kentucky Fried Movie (co-s.p.), Airplane! (co-dir., co-exec. prod., co-s.p.), Top Secret! (co-dir., co-s.p.,co-exec. prod.), Ruthless People (co-dir.). *Also*: Big Business (dir.), The Naked Gun (exec. prod., co-s.p.), Cry-Baby (co-exec. prod.), Welcome Home Roxy Carmichael (dir.), The Naked Gun 2-1/2 (co-exec. prod.), Hot Shots! (dir., co-s.p.), Hot Shots Part Deux! (dir., co-s.p.), Naked Gun 33 1/3: The Final Insult (co-exec. prod.), Jane Austen's Mafia (dir., s.p.).
TELEVISION: *Movies*: First Do No Harm (dir, prod.). *Series*: Police Squad (s.p.) *Guest*: The Directors.

ABRAHAMS, MORT
Producer, Writer. Actor. b. New York, NY, March 26, 1916. Dir. programming, prod., NTA, 1958-60. Exec. prod. Cooga Mooga Prod. Inc., 1960-61. Prod.: Target, The Corruptors 1961, Route 66, 1962-63; writer TV shows, 1963-64. Prod., Kraft Suspense Theatre, 1965; prod., Man from U.N.C.L.E., 1965-66; exec. v.p., APJAC Prod., 1966; v.p. in charge of prod., Rastar Prods., 1969; exec. prod. American Film Theatre & v.p. Ely Landau Organization, in charge of West Coast prod., 1971-74. Member of Faculty and prod.-in-residence, Center for Advanced Film and TV Studies of A.F.I. Vice-pres. Alph Productions, 1993-present.
PICTURES: *Assoc. Prod.*: Doctor Dolittle, Planet of the Apes, The Chairman, Goodbye Mr. Chips, Beneath the Planet of the Apes (also s.p.). *Exec. Prod.*: Luther, Homecoming, The Man in the Glass Booth, The Greek Tycoon, Hopscotch, The Chosen (exec. in charge of prod.), Beatlemania (exec. in charge of prod.), The Deadly Game, Arch of Triumph, The Holcroft Covenant, Seven

Hours to Judgment. TELEVISION: *Movies: The House on Garibaldi Street. Series: The Man from U.N.C.L.E.* (prod., prod. exec.) *Tales of Tomorrow* (prod.) *Tom Corbett, Space Cadet* (prod.) *TV Documentary:* Behind the Planet of the Apes (himself), *Video:* The Mercurian Invasion (prod. supervisor.

ACKERMAN, ANDY
Director, Producer, Editor.
PICTURES: Dead and Buried (1981. second asst. dir.)
TELEVISION: *Movies:* Cheers: 200th Anniversary Special (co-prod., editor) *Series:* WKRP in Cincinnati (Emmy for editing, 1981) Dir: Cheers (also co-prod., editor, Emmy Award, 1988, 1991), Wings, Seinfeld (also prod., Directors' Guild Award, 1997-98), Frasier, Almost Perfect, Suddenly Susan, Public Morals, Jenny, LateLine (also prod.), Becker (also prod.), It's Like, You Know...., The Trouble with Normal (also prod.), Curb Your Enthusiasm, Raising Dad, The Ellen Show (also prod.), Andy Richter Controls the Universe (also exec. prod.) The O'Keefes.

ACKERMAN, BETTYE
Actress. r.n. Bettye Louise Ackermann. b. Cottageville, SC, Feb. 28, 1928. e. Columbia U., 1948-52. Taught dancing, 1950-54.
THEATRE: No Count Boy, 1954; Tartuffe, Sophocles' Antigone and Oedipus at Colonus, The Merchant of Venice.
PICTURES: Face of Fire, Rascal, Ted & Venus Prehysteria! 2.
TELEVISION: *Movies:* Companions in Nightmare, Colombo: Blueprint for Murder, Heat of Anger, Murder of Mercy, Never Con a Killer, Doctors' Private Lives, A Day for Thanks on Walton's Mountain, Confessions of a Married Man, Trouble in High Timber Country. *Series:* Ben Casey, Return to Peyton Place. *Guest:* Alcoa Premiere, Alfred Hitchcock Presents, Perry Mason, Breaking Point, Hope-Chrysler Theatre, Bonanza, FBI Story, Mannix, Ironside, Medical Center, Columbo, Sixth Sense, Heat of Anger,The Rookies, Barnaby Jones, Police Story, Gunsmoke, Harry O, Streets of San Francisco, S.W.A.T., Petrocelli, Wonder Woman, Police Woman, Chips, 240-Robert, The Waltons, Dynasty, Falcon Crest, Me and Mom, Trapper John M.D., St. Elsewhere.

ACKLAND, JOSS
Actor. b. North Kensington, London, England, Feb. 29, 1928. e. Central Sch. of Speech Training & Dramatic Art. Spent time in Central Africa as a tea planter. Over 400 TV appearances. Autobiography, I Must Be in There Somewhere. Awarded C.B.E. (Commander of the British Empire).
THEATRE: The Old Vic (3 yrs.), Mermaid Theatre (artistic dir., 3 yrs.); Hotel in Amsterdam, Jorrocks Come as You Are, The Collaborators, A Streetcar Named Desire, The Madras House, Captain Brassbound's Conversion, Never the Sinner, Henry IV Parts I & II, Peter Pan (dramatic & musical versions), A Little Night Music, Evita, The Visit, etc.
PICTURES: Seven Days to Noon, Crescendo, Trecolonne in Cronaca, The House That Dripped Blood, The Happiness Cage, Villain, England Made Me, The Black Windmill, S.P.Y.S, The Little Prince, Royal Flash, Operation Daybreak, Who Is Killing the Great Chefs of Europe, Saint Jack, The Apple, Rough Cut, Lady Jane, A Zed and Two Noughts, The Sicilian, White Mischief, To Kill a Priest, It Couldn't Happen Here, Lethal Weapon 2, The Hunt for Red October, Object of Beauty, Bill and Ted's Bogus Journey, The Palermo Connection, The Mighty Ducks, Nowhere to Run, Mother's Boys, The Princess and the Goblin (voice), Miracle on 34th Street, Giorgino, Mad Dogs and Englishmen, A Kid in the Court of King Arthur, Occhio Pinocchio, Daisies in December, To the Ends of Time, Mighty Ducks 3, Surviving Picasso, Deadly Voyage, Firelight, Milk, Passion of Mind, Mumbo Jumbo, Lounge Act (voice), Painting Faces, K-19: The Widowmaker, No Good Deed, I'll Be There.
TELEVISION: *Movies since 1980:*The Love Tapes, the Barretts of Wimpole Street, The Tragedy of Coriolanus, Shadowlands, Queenie, When We Are Married, Codename: Kyril, First and Last, Jekyll & Hyde, The Secret Life of Ian Fleming, They Do It With Mirrors, A Murder of Quality, Voices in the Garden, Jacob, Citizen X, Daisies in December, Hidden in Silence, Deadly Voyage, To the Ends of Time, Gioco di specchi, Othello. *Mini-Series:* Tinker, Tailor, Soldier, Spy, Bekenntnisse des Hochstaplers Felix Krull, Shroud of a Nightingale, The Man Who Lived at the Ritz, A Woman Named Jackie, Ashenden, Il Figlio di Sandokan.

ADAM, KEN
Art Director, Prod. Designer. b. Berlin, Germany, Feb. 5, 1921. e. St. Pauls Sch., London, England; London U., student of architecture. 6 years war service as RAF pilot. In 1947 entered motion picture industry as draughtsman for movie, This Was a Woman. Appeared in numerous documentaries about Stanley Kubrick and also has appeared in numerous documentaries about designing various James Bond movies.
PICTURES: *Art Dir.:* The Devil's Pass, Soho Incident, Around the World in 80 Days. *Prod. Designer:* Spin a Dark Web, Night of the Demon, Gideon's Day, The Angry Hills, Beyond This Place, The Rough and the Smooth, In the Nick, Let's Get Married, Trials of Oscar Wilde, Dr. No, Sodom and Gomorrah, In the Cool of the Day, Dr. Strangelove, Goldfinger, Woman of Straw, Thunderball, The Ipcress File, Funeral in Berlin, You Only Live Twice, Chitty Chitty Bang Bang, Goodbye Mr. Chips, The Owl and the Pussycat, Diamonds Are Forever, Sleuth, The Last of Sheila, Barry Lyndon (Acad. Award, 1975), Madam Kitty, The Seven Percent Solution, The Spy Who Loved Me, Moonraker, Pennies From Heaven (visual consult., assoc. prod.), King David, Agnes

of God, Crimes of the Heart, The Deceivers, Dead-Bang, The Freshman, The Doctor, Company Business, Undercover Blues, Addams Family Values, The Madness of King George (Acad. Award, 1994), Boys on the Side, Bogus, In & Out, The Out of Towners, The White Hotel, Taking Sides.

ADAMS, BROOKE
Actress. b. New York, NY, Feb. 8, 1949. e. H.S. of Performing Arts; Inst. of American Ballet. Studied with Lee Strasberg. Made professional debut at six in Finian's Rainbow. Worked steadily in summer stock and TV until age 18. After hiatus resumed acting career.
THEATRE: Petrified Forest, Split, Key Exchange, Linda Her, Over Mother's Dead Body, Old Neighborhood, Heidi Chronicles, Lost in Yonkers. *Director:* Two Faced. Helps run small summer theatre in upstate NY.
PICTURES: Shock Waves (Death Corps), Car Wash, Days of Heaven, Invasion of the Body Snatchers, Cuba, The Great Train Robbery, A Man a Woman and a Bank, Tell Me a Riddle, Utilities, The Dead Zone, Almost You, Key Exchange, The Stuff, Man on Fire, The Unborn, Gas Food Lodging, Sleepless, The Fire This Time, The Baby Sitter's Club, Made-Up.
TELEVISION: *Movies:* F. Scott Fitzgerald and "The Last of the Belles," The Daughters of Joshua Cabe Return, James Dean, Who is the Black Dahlia?, Murder on Flight 502, Lace, Haunted, Special People, Lace II, The Lion of Africa, Bridesmaids, Sometimes They Come Back, The Last Hit, Gun, Song of the Succubus, Picture Windows. *Specials:* Paul Reiser: Out on a Whim. *Series:* O.K. Crackerby. *Pilot:* A Girl's Life, Nero Wolfe, The Lords of Flatbush. *Guest:* Kojack, Family, Police Woman, Moonlighting, Tony Randall Show, Bob Newhart Show, thirtysomething, Frasier, Wings, Gun, Monk.

ADAMS, CATLIN
Actress, Director, Producer. b. Los Angeles, CA, Oct. 11, 1950. Began career as actress then studied directing at American Film Institute. Made directorial debut with, Wanted: The Perfect Guy. Also directed Little Shiny Shoes (short, written and prod. with Melanie Mayron), Stolen: One Husband (TV), Toothless (TV).
THEATRE: Safe House, Scandalous Memories, Dream of a Blacklisted Actor, The Candy Store, Ruby Ruby Sam Sam, Bermuda Avenue Triangle (dir.)
PICTURES: *Actress:* The Jerk, The Jazz Singer. *Director:* Sticky Fingers (also dir., co-s.p., co-prod.).
TELEVISION: *Movies:* Panic in Echo Park, Wanted: The Perfect Guy (dir. won DGA award), Stolen: One Husband (dir.) Freaky Friday, Toothless. *Series:* Square Pegs, Beverly Hills 90210 (dir. only). *Specials:* How to Survive the 70's and Maybe Even Bump into a Little Happiness, She Loves Me She Loves Me Not. *Guest:* thirtysomething, Nash Bridges, Providence.

ADAMS, DON
Actor. r.n. Donald James Yarmy. b. New York, NY, April 13, 1926. Won Arthur Godfrey talent contest. Was nightclub impressionist before starting in TV.
PICTURES: The Nude Bomb, Jimmy the Kid, Back to the Beach, Inspector Gadget (voice).
TELEVISION: *Movies:* Joys, The Love Boat, Murder Can Hurt You, Get Smart Again! NBC 75th Anniversary Celebration. *Series:* Perry Como's Kraft Music Hall, The Bill Dana Show, Tennessee Tuxedo (voice), The Hollywood Palace, Get Smart (3 Emmy Awards, 2 Clio Awards), The Partners, Don Adams' Screen Test, Three Times Daley, Inspector Gadget (voice), Check It Out!, Get Smart (1995), Gadget Boy and Heather (voice), Pepper Ann (voice) Gadget Boy's Adventures In History (voice). *Guest:* The Andy Williams Show, Hollywood Squares, Rowan & Martin's Laugh-In, Wait til Your Father Gets Home, The Love Boat, Fantasy Island, The New Scooby-Doo Movies, The Fall Guy, Inspector Gadget, Empty Nest.

ADAMS, EDIE
Actress, Singer. r.n. Elizabeth Edith Enke. b. Kingston, PA, April 16, 1931. e. Juilliard Sch. of Music, Columbia Sch. of Drama.
THEATRE: *NY:* Wonderful Town, Lil Abner (Tony Award), Mame.
PICTURES: The Apartment, Lover Come Back, Call Me Bwana, It's a Mad Mad Mad Mad World, Under the Yum Yum Tree, Love With the Proper Stranger, The Best Man, Made in Paris, The Oscar, The Honeypot, Up in Smoke, Racquet, The Happy Hooker Goes Hollywood, Boxoffice, Adventures Beyond Belief, Broadway the Golden Age, by the Legends Who Were There.
TELEVISION: *Movies:* Cinderella, Evil Roy Slade, Cop on the Beat, Return of Joe Forrester, Superdome, Kate Loves a Mystery, Fast Friends, Make Me an Offer, Portrait of an Escort, A Cry for Love, The Haunting of Harrington House, Shooting Stars, Ernie Kovacs' Between the Laughter. Adventures Beyond Belief, Jake Spanner, Private Eye *Series:* Ernie in Kovacsland, The Ernie Kovacs Show (1952-54, 1955-56), The Chevy Show, Take a Good Look (panelist), Here's Edie, The Edie Adams Show, *Mini-series:* The Seekers, Tales of the City. *Guest:* Suspense, I've Got a Secret, What's My Line?, The Lucy-Desi Comedy Hour, The Hollywood Squares, Jack Paar, Ed Sullivan Show, Perry Como Show, Pat Boone Show, G.E. Theatre, Colgate Comedy House, Dinah Shore Show, Palace, Bob Hope Show, The Lucille Ball Show, The Carol Burnett Show, Love, American Style, Harry O, The Love Boat, Kate Loves a Mystery, Bosom Buddies, Vegas, Murder, She Wrote, Designing Women, Biography.

ADAMS, JOEY LAUREN
Actress. b. Little Rock, AR, Jan. 6, 1971.
PICTURES: Exorcist II: The Heretic (as Joey Adams), Coneheads, Dazed and Confused, The Program, Sleep with Me, S.F.W., The Pros & Cons of Breathing, Mallrats, Bio-Dome (as Joey Adams), Michael, Drawing Flies (as Lauren Lyle), Chasing Amy (Chicago Film Critics. Award, Most Promising New Actress, 1997, Sierra Award, Las Vegas Film Critics Society), A Cool Dry Place, Big Daddy, Reaching Normal,The Dress Code, Beautiful, Harvard Man, Dr. Dolittle 2 (voice), In the Shadows, Jay and Silent Bob Strike Back, Beeper, A Promise Kept, The Big Empty, Jersey Girl.
TELEVISION: Series: Top of the Heap, Vinnie & Bobby, Second Noah. Guest: Married...with Children, Double Rush, Disney's Hercules (voice), Dinner for Five.

ADAMS, JULIE
Actress. r.n. Betty May Adams. b. Waterloo, IA, Oct. 17, 1928. e. jr. coll., Little Rock, AK. Coll. dramatics. In addition to film credits, has made nearly 100 television guest appearances.
PICTURES: Red Hot and Blue (debut, 1949), The Dalton Gang, Crooked River, Hostile Country, West of the Brazos, Colorado Ranger, Fast on the Draw, Marshal of Heldorado. As Julie Adams: Hollywood Story, Finders Keepers, Bend of the River, Bright Victory, Treasure of Lost Canyon, Horizons West, Lawless Breed, Mississippi Gambler, Man From the Alamo, The Stand of Apache River, Wings of the Hawk, The Creature From the Black Lagoon, Francis Joins the WACS, The Looters, One Desire, The Private War of Major Benson, Six Bridges to Cross, Away All Boats, Four Girls in Town, Slim Carter, Slaughter on 10th Avenue, Tarawa Beachhead, Gunfight at Dodge City, Raymie, Underwater City, Tickle Me, Valley of Mystery, The Last Movie, McQ, Psychic Killer, The Wild McCullochs, Killer Inside Me, Goodbye Franklin High, The Fifth Floor, Black Roses, Catchfire, Back to the Black Lagoon.TELEVISION: Movies: The Trackers, Go Ask Alice, Code Red, Backtrack, The Conviction of Kitty Dodds. Series: Yancy Derringer, General Hospital, The Jimmy Stewart Show, Code Red, Capitol. Guest appearances since 1980: Quincy, Trapper John, M.D., Vega$, Too Close For Comfort, Cagney & Lacey, Beverly Hills, 90210, Diagnosis Murder, Melrose Place, Sliders, Family Law.

ADAMS, MASON
Actor. b. New York, NY, Feb. 26, 1919. e. U. Wisconsin. B.A., 1940; M.A., 1941. Trained for stage at Neighborhood Playhouse. Began radio in 1946 for nearly two decades in starring role of Pepper Young's Family. Made Broadway. debut in Get Away Old Man, 1943.
THEATRE: Career Angel, Public Relations, Violet, Shadow of My Enemy, Inquest, The Sign in Sidney Brustein's Window, Tall Story, The Trial of the Catonsville Nine, Foxfire, Checking Out, Danger Memory, The Day Room, The Rose Quartet.
PICTURES: Dream No More (narrator), The Happy Hooker, God Told Me To, Raggedy Ann and Andy (voice), Northstar, The Final Conflict, Annie, F/X, Toy Soldiers, Son-in-Law, Houseguest, Not of This Earth, Life Among the Cannibals, Touch, Hudson River Blues, The Lesser Evil.
TELEVISION: Movies/Specials: The Deadliest Season, And Baby Makes Six, The Shining Season, Flamingo Road, Murder Can Hurt You, The Revenge of the Stepford Wives, Peking Encounter, The Kid with the Broken Halo, Adam, Passions, Solomon Northrup's Odyssey, Under Siege, , Northstar, The Night They Saved Christmas, Who is Julia?, Rage of Angels: The Story Continues, Perry Mason: The Case of the Maligned Mobster, Jonathan: The Boy Nobody Wanted, Assault at West Point, Series: Another World, Lou Grant, Morningstar/Eveningstar, Knight and Daye. Mini-series: ,Freedom to Speak, Murder One: Diary of a Serial Killer, From the Earth to the Moon. Guest: Robert Montgomer Presents, The Love Boat, Family Ties, Matlock, Murder, She Wrote, Monsters, Family Matters, Civil Wars, Murder One, The West Wing, Oz.

ADAMS, MAUD
Actress. r.n. Maud Wikstrum. b. Lulea, Sweden, Feb. 12, 1945. Formerly a model. Acting debut in The Boys in the Band. Known for work in James Bond movies and has appeared in several documentaries about the Bond films. Nearly 70 television guest appearances since 1971.
PICTURES: The Boys in the Band, The Christian Licorice Store, U-Turn, Mahoney's Estate, The Man With the Golden Gun, Rollerball, Killer Force, The Merciless Man, Tattoo, Octopussy, Target Eagle, Jane and the Lost City, The Women's Club, A Man of Passion, The Favorite, Soda Cracker, Deadly Intent, Angel III, The Kill Reflex, Forbidden Sun, Favorite, Ringer.
TELEVISION:Movies: Big Bob Johnson and His Fantastic Speed Circus, The Hostage Tower, Playing for Time, Nairobi Affair, Blacke's Magic, A Perry Mason Mystery: The Case of the Wicked Wives Series: Hawaii Five-O, , Chicago Story, Emerald Point, N.A.S., Walker, Texas Ranger, Radioskugga, Vita logner.

ADAMS, TONY
Producer. b. Dublin, Ireland, Feb. 15, 1953. Began career as asst. to dir. John Boorman and was associated with Burt Reynolds prior to joining Blake Edwards as a prod., 1971. Then president, The Blake Edwards Entertainment; Pres. & CEO, The Blake Edwards Company, 1988.
PICTURES: Assoc. Prod.: Return of the Pink Panther, The Pink Panther Strikes Again. Exec. Prod.: Revenge of the Pink Panther. Prod.: ``10'', S.O.B., Victor/Victoria, Trail of the Pink Panther, Curse of the Pink Panther, The Man Who Loved Women, Micki & Maude, That's Life, A Fine Mess, Blind Date, Sunset, Skin Deep,

Switch, Son of the Pink Panther.
TELEVISION: Movies: Justin Case, Peter Gunn, The Leading Ladies (exec. prod.), My Favorite Broadway: The Love Songs.

ADEFARASIN, REMI
Cinematographer. Received best cinematography recognition for Elizabeth from BAFTA and the British Society of Cinematographers in 1999. Has more than 30 television movie cinematography/camera credits since 1973 debut.
PICTURES: Dead Lucky, Truly Madly Deeply, The Hummingbird Tree, Captives, Hollow Reed, The English Patient (dir. of photog.), Sliding Doors, Elizabeth (Acad. Award nom.), Onegin, The House of Mirth, Unconditional Love, The One and Only, Who Shot Victor Fox, About a Boy, Johnny English, The Haunted Mansion.
TELEVISION: Movies since1980: Grown-Ups, Home Sweet Home, The Files on Jill Hatch, Stan's Last Game, The Case of the Frightened Lady, Amy, Four Days in July, Shoot for the Sun, Sweet As You Are, Christabel, Testimony of a Child, Dream Baby, News Hounds, The Land of Dreams, Children Crossing, The Lost Language of Cranes, Memento Mori, Hot Millions, Great Moments in Aviation, Wide-Eyed and Legless, Midnight Movie, Human Bomb, Emma, Arabian Nights. Mini-series: Summer's Lease, Sleepers, The Buccaneers, Into the Fire, Cold Lazarus, Band of Brothers.

ADELMAN, GARY
Executive. Producer. b. Los Angeles, CA, March 16, 1944. e. California State U., Long Beach State Coll. Assisted Winston Hock in development of 3-D process, 1975. Pres. & COO of Monarch Prods, 1976-Present. Post-prod. consultant for Jerry Gross Organization. Founder and partial owner of New Image Releasing Inc., a prod. & dist. co., 1983. Had post of secty./treas. then named v.p., chg. prod., All-American Group, 1987. Now is pres. of Monarch Productions, which produces theatrical feature films, trailers, commercials and industrial films.
PICTURES: Incubus (1965-Restoration Consultant) The Candy Snatchers (assoc. prod.), The Severed Arm, Nobody's Perfect (assoc. prod.), Heartwood (post-prod. supervisor), The Month of August (post-prod.supervisor), Sex and the Teenage Mind (co-prod.)
TELEVISION: Movies: Hope Ranch (line prod.)

ADELMAN, JOSEPH A.
Executive. b. Winnipeg, Manitoba, Canada, Dec. 27, 1933. e. NYU, B.A., 1954; Harvard Law Sch., J.D., graduated cum laude, 1957. Attorney, United Artists Corp., New York, 1958; named west coast counsel, Hollywood, 1964; named exec. asst. to the v.p. in charge of prod. 1968; named v.p., west coast business and legal affairs, 1972. Appointed exec. v.p., Association of Motion Pictures and Television Producers, 1977. Appointed v.p. in chg. of business affairs, Paramount Pictures Corp., 1979. Co-founder Kidpix, Inc., 1984. Founder and CEO of Kidpix Theaters Corp. 1985. Appointed sr. v.p. for business/legal affairs, Color Systems Technology, Inc. 1986. Named pres. of CST Entertainment, 1987. Appointed mng. dir., Broadway Video Entertainment, 1990. CEO, Intl. Entertainment Enterprises 1991. Admitted to NY, California and U.S. Supreme Court bars. Member: Phi Beta Kappa, American Bar Association, Los Angeles Copyright Society, Academy of Motion Picture Arts and Sciences, National Assn. of Television Programming Executives. On bd. of dirs., AMPTP, 1969-1979; bd. of trustees, Theatre Authority, 1970-79. Recipient of Alumni Achievement Award, NYU, 1982.

ADELSON, GARY
Producer. b. 1954. e. UCLA, B.A. Son of Merv Adelson. Joined Lorimar Prods. 1970 as prod. asst. on TV movie Helter Skelter. In 1989, formed Adelson/Baumgarten Prods. with Craig Baumgarten. In 1993, founded Interactive Cable Systems which was acquired by MCI. Currently, Partner with EastWest Venture Group.
PICTURES: The Last Starfighter, The Boy Who Could Fly, In The Mood, Tap, Hard to Kill (also s.p.), Hook, Universal Soldier, Nowhere to Run, Blank Check, It Could Happen to You, Jade, Hidden Assassin,Rolling Thunder, The Shooter.
TELEVISION: Helter Skelter (asst. prod.), The Blue Knight (prod.). Exec. prod.: Too Good To Be True, Our Family Business, Cass Malloy, The Winter of Our Discontent, Lace, Lace II, Glitz, Detective in the House, Lace II, , Everything to Gain, Critical Choices, The Hunchback, Love in Another Town Series: Eight is Enough (supervising prod.), Sybil (assoc. prod.)Flatbush (exec. prod.), Spies, Studio 5-B (exec. prod.).

ADELSON, MERV
Producer, Executive. b. Los Angeles, CA, Oct. 23, 1929. e. UCLA. Pres., Markettown Builders Emporium, Las Vegas, 1953-63. Managing partner Paradise Dev., 1958-. Pres. Realty Holdings, 1962-. Bd. chmn., Lorimar Inc., 1969-86. Bd. dirs. chmn. & CEO, Lorimar Telepictures, 1986-1990. Developed Lorimar's advertising arm in Bozell, full service agency. Merged Lorimar with Warner Communications; became vice-chmn., Time Warner. Currently, chmn. finance committee for Time Warner; founding partner EastWest Venture Group. Bd. of Trustees, AFI and Aspen Institute.
PICTURES: Twilight's Last Gleaming, The Choirboys, Who Is Killing the Great Chefs of Europe?, Avalanche Express, The Big Red One.
TELEVISION: Movies/Mini-Dir.: Sybil, A Man Called Intrepid, The Blue Knight, Helter-Skelter. Series: The Waltons, Eight Is Enough, Dallas, Kaz, The Waverly Wonders, Knots Landing.

ADJANI, ISABELLE
Actress, Producer. b. Gennevilliers, France, June 27, 1955. Recipient of Super-Cesar award in 1990.
PICTURES: Le Petit Bougnat, Faustine and the Beautiful Summer, The Slap, The Story of Adele H. (Acad. Award nom.), The Tenant, Barocco, Violette and Francois, The Driver, Nosferatu—The Vampire, The Bronte Sisters, Clara et les Chics Types, Possession, L'Annee prochaine..si tout va bien, Quartet, Next Year If All Goes Well, One Deadly Summer, Antonieta, Deadly Circuit, Subway, Ishtar, Camille Claudel (also co-prod.; Acad. Award nom.), Toxic Affair, Queen Margot, Diabolique, Paparazzi, The Repentant, Adolphe, Bon Voyage.

ADLER, ALLEN
Writer, Producer. b. New York, NY, 1946. e. Princeton U., B.A.; Harvard Business Sch., M.B.A. Started with Standard & Poor's Inter-Capital then joined Alan Hirschfield at American Diversified Enterprises. Moved to Columbia Pictures as corporate officer, 1973; named sr. v.p., Columbia, 1979. Teamed with Daniel Melnick in IndieProd Co., 1981. Writer: The Giant Behemoth, Making Love (prod.), Parasite, The Concrete Jungle, Metalstorm: The Destruction of Jared-Syn (writer, prod.), The Alchemist, Toys (toy consultant).

ADLER, GILBERT
Producer, Director.
PICTURES: The Maestro (prod.as Gil Adler), Certain Fury, Basic Training, Children of the Corn 2: The Final Sacrifice (s.p. only), Demon Knight, Bordello of Blood (also s.p.), Double Tap, House on Haunted Hall, Thir13en Ghosts, Ghost Ship, Stalag 17.
TELEVISION: Movies: W.E.I.R.D. World. Series.: Freddy's Nightmares, Tales from the Crypt, Perversions of Science, Fantasy Island, Charmed. The Strip (co-exec. prod).

ADLON, PERCY
Director, Writer, Producer. b. Munich, Germany, June 1, 1935. e. Munich Univ. m. Eleonore Adlon, with whom he has worked on several film projects. Created more than 40 tv documentaries.
PICTURES: Celeste, The Last Five Days (dir. only), The Swing, Sugarbaby, Bagdad Cafe, Rosalie Goes Shopping, Salmonberries, Younger and Younger, Eat Your Heart Out (prod. only), Forever Flirt, Hawaiian Gardens.
TELEVISION: Movies: Herr Kischott, Herschel und die Musik der Sterne, Babycakes.The Guardian and His Poet (Adolf Grimme Award), Hotel Adlon.

AFFLECK, BEN
Actor, Writer, Director. b. Berkeley, CA, Aug. 15, 1972. Began acting at age 8.
PICTURES: The Dark End of the Street, School Ties, Buffy the Vampire Slayer, Dazed and Confused, I Killed My Lesbian Wife Hung Her on a Meat Hook, and Now I Have a Three-Picture Deal at Disney (dir. only), Mallrats, Glory Daze, Going All the Way, Office Killer, Chasing Amy, , Good Will Hunting (also s.p., Acad. Award, Golden Globe Award, Best Screenplay, 1997), Phantoms, Armageddon, Shakespeare in Love, 200 Cigarettes, Forces of Nature, Dogma, Boiler Room, Reindeer Games, Bounce, The Third Wheel (also prod.), Daddy and Them, Pearl Harbor, Jay and Silent Bob Strike Back, Changing Lanes, Stolen Summer (prod. only) Crossing Cords (exec. prod. only), The Sum of All Fears, The Third Wheel (also exec. prod.), Speak Easy (exec. prod.) Daredevil, Tough Love, Jersey Girl, Paycheck, The Battle of Shaker Heights (prod. & exec. prod.), Surviving Christmas.
TELEVISION: Movies: Wanted: The Perfect Guy, Hands of a Stranger, Daddy, SNL Fanatic. Specials: A People's History of the United States (prod. only). Series: Voyage of the Mimi, Against the Grain, Lifestories: Families in Crisis, Project Greenlight. Guest: Almost Home.

AGOGLIA, JOHN J.
Executive. Worked for 14 years for CBS Entertainment in New York, becoming v.p. business affairs. Joined NBC in 1979 as v.p., program and talent negotiations; named sr. v.p. business affairs NBC, 1980; exec. v.p. NBC Prods., 1984; exec. v.p., business affairs NBC-TV Network, 1986; in charge of foreign marketing relating to NBC Productions products, 1987; pres. of NBC Enterprises, 1990; pres. of NBC Prods., 1993-1998. After leaving NBC, formed GII Media, Inc., a consulting co. and Canan Filmworks LLC which produces family-oriented programming. Consultant with ExperTelligence, Inc. Bd. of directors, KCET; pres. Bd. of Airport Commissioners.

AGUTTER, JENNY
Actress. b. Taunton, Devonshire, England, Dec. 20, 1952. e. Elmhurst Ballet Sch. Received Variety Club of Great Britain Most Promising Artiste Award, 1971.
THEATRE: School for Scandal, Rooted, Arms and the Man, The Ride Across Lake Constance, The Tempest, Spring Awakening, Hedda, Betrayal. Member, Royal Shakespeare Co.-King Lear, Arden of Taversham, The Body. Breaking the Silence, Shrew (Los Angeles), Love's Labour's Lost, Mothers and Daughters.
PICTURES: East of Sudan (debut, 1964), Ballerina (tv in U.S.), A Man Could Get Killed, Vrata raja, Star!, I Start Counting, The Railway Children, Walkabout, Shelley, Logan's Run, The Eagle Has Landed, Equus (BAFTA Award, 1977), Dominique, China 9 Liberty 37, The Riddle of the Sands, Sweet William, , Amy, An American Werewolf in London, The Survivor, Miss Right, Secret Places, Amazon Women on the Moon, Dark Tower, King

of the Wind, Darkman, Child's Play 2, Freddie as F.R.O. 7 (voice), Blue Juice, The Parole Officer, At Dawning, Number One Longing Number Two Regret.
TELEVISION: Movies: Long After Summer, The Great Mr. Dickens, The Wild Duck, The Cherry Orchard, The Snow Goose (Emmy Award, 1972), A War of Children, The Savage Curse, The Man in the Iron Mask, School Play, Mayflower: The Pilgrams' Adventure, This Office Life, Silas Marner: The Weaver of Raveloe, Love's Labour's Lost, The Grand Knockout Tournament, Not a Penny More Not a Penny Less, Romeo and Juliet, September, Bramwell: Our Brave Boys, Bramwell: Loose Women, The Railway Children. Mini-series: Beulah Land, The Buccaneers, A Respectable Trade. Series: The Railway Children, TECX, The All New Alexei Sayle Show, And the Beat Goes On, Spooks. Guest: Numerous guest appearances since 1977.

AIELLO, DANNY
Actor. b. New York, NY, June 20, 1936.
THEATRE: Lampost Reunion (Theatre World Award), Wheelbarrow Closers, Gemini (Obie Award), Knockout, The Floating Light Bulb, Hurlyburly (LA Drama Critics Award), The House of Blue Leaves.
PICTURES: Bang the Drum Slowly (debut, 1973), The Godmothers, The Godfather Part II, The Front, Hooch, Fingers, Blood Brothers, Hide in Plain Sight, Defiance, Fort Apache the Bronx, Chu Chu and the Philly Flash, Once Upon a Time in America, Old Enough, Deathmask, The Purple Rose of Cairo, Key Exchange, The Protector, The Stuff, Radio Days, Man On Fire, The Pick-Up Artist, Moonstruck, The January Man, Do the Right Thing (LA, Chicago & Boston Film Critics Awards; Acad. Award nom.), Russicum (The Third Solution), Harlem Nights, Jacob's Ladder, The Closer, Once Around, Hudson Hawk, 29th Street, Shocktroop, Ruby, Mistress, The Cemetery Club, The Pickle, Me and the Kid, The Professional, Ready to Wear (Pret-a-Porter), Power of Attorney, City Hall, Two Much, 2 Days in the Valley, Mojave Moon, Bring Me The Head of Mavis Davis, A Brooklyn State of Mind, Wilbur Falls, Prince of Central Park, Off Key, Marcus Timberwolf, The Last Request, Mail Order Bride.
TELEVISION: Movies: The Last Tenant, Lovey: A Circle of Children Part 2, A Family of Strangers (Emmy Award),A Question of Honor, Blood Feud, Lady Blue, Alone in the Neon Jungle, The Preppie Murder, Brothers' Destiny, The Last Laugh. Mini-Series: The Last Don, The Last Don II Series: Lady Blue, Dellaventura (also prod). Specials: Lieberman in Love.

AIMEE, ANOUK
Actress. r.n. Francoise Sorya Dreyfus. b. Paris, France, April 27, 1932. Studied dancing at Marseilles Opera, acting at Bauer-Therond dramatic school, Paris. Started in films as teenager billed as Anouk.
PICTURES: La Maison Sous la Mer (debut, 1946), La Fleur de l'age, Les Amants De Verone, The Golden Salamander, Noche de Tormenta, Le Rideau Cramoisi, The Man Who Watched the Trains Go By (Paris Express), Contraband Spain, Forever My Heart, Les Mauvaises Rencontres, Ich Suche Dich, Nina, Stresemann, Pot Bouille, Montparnasse 19, Tous Peuvent Me Tuer, Le Tete Contre Les Murs, The Journey, Les Dragueurs, La Dolce Vita, Le Farceur, Lola, L'Imprevu, Quai Notre-Dame, Il Giudizio Universale, Sodom and Gomorrah, Les Grand Chemins, 8 1/2, Il Terrorista, Il Successo, Lola, Le Voci Bianche, La Fuga, La Stagione del Nostro Amore, A Man and a Woman (Acad. Award nom.), Lo Sacandalo, Il Morbidonne, Un Soir Un Train, The Model Shop, Justine, The Appointment, Si C'Etait d Refaire, Mon Premier Amour, Salto nel Vuoto (Leap Into the Void), Tragedy of a Ridiculous Man, What Makes David Run?, Le General de l'Armee Morte, Success is the Best Revenge, Viva la Vie, A Man and A Woman: 20 Years Later, Arrivederci e Grazie, La Table Tournante, The House of the Lord, Dr. Bethune, Rabbit Face, Ready to Wear (Pret-a-Porter), A Hundred and One Nights, Ruptures, Marmottes, Men, Women: A Users Manual, LA Without a Map, Riches, Belles, One 4 All, 1999 Madeline, Festival in Cannes, The Birch-Tree Meadow.
TELEVISION: Movies: Une page d'amour, Fernanda, Voices in the Garden, Solomon, L'Ile bleueu. Mini-series: Mon dernier reve sera pour vous, Victoire, u la douleur de femmes, Napoleon.

ALBERGHETTI, ANNA MARIA
Singer, Actress. b. Pesaro, Italy, May 15, 1936. d. Daniele Alberghetti, cellist. Concert debut in 1948 in Pesaro, then toured Italy, Scandinavia, Spain; Am. debut Carnegie Hall, 1950, sang with NY Philharmonic Society, Phila. Symphony, on television. Made B'way debut in Carnival, 1962 (Tony Award).
PICTURES: The Medium (debut, 1951), Here Comes the Groom, The Stars Are Singing, San Antonio de Bexar, Duel at Apache Wells,The Last Command, Ten Thousand Bedrooms, Cinderella, The Whole Shebang, Friends and Family.
TELEVISION: Movies: Kismet. Guest: Toast of the Town, Cavalcade of Stars, Arthur Murray Show, Bob Hope, Eddie Fisher, Red Skelton, Dinah Shore, Desilu Playhouse, G.E. Theatre, Chevy Show, Dupont Show, Voice of Firestone, Colgate Hour, Climax, Loretta Young, Ford Jubilee, Perry Como.

ALBERT, EDDIE
Actor. r.n. Edward Albert Heimberger. b. Rock Island, IL, April 22, 1908. e. U. of Minnesota. Son is actor Edward Albert. Performer on Radio NBC.THEATRE: B'way: Brother Rat, Say

Darling, The Music Man, Room Service, The Boys from Syracuse, Seven Year Itch, Our Town, No Hard Feelings, Reuben Reuben, Miss Liberty, You Can't Take It With You.
PICTURES: Brother Rat (debut, 1938), On Your Toes, Four Wives, Brother Rat and a Baby, Angel from Texas, My Love Came Back, Dispatch from Reuter's, Four Mothers, The Wagons Roll at Night, Out of the Fog, Thieves Fall Out, The Great Mr. Nobody, Treat 'em Rough, Eagle Squadron, Ladies' Day, Lady Bodyguard, Bombadier, Strange Voyage, Rendezvous With Annie, Perfect Marriage, Smash-Up, Time Out of Mind, Hit Parade of 1947, Dude Goes West, You Gotta Stay Happy, Fuller Brush Girl, You're in the Navy Now,Meet Me After the Show, Carrie, Actors and Sin, Roman Holiday (Acad. Award nom.), Girl Rush, I'll Cry Tomorrow, Oklahoma!, Attack, Teahouse of the August Moon, The Sun Also Rises, The Joker is Wild, Orders to Kill, Gun Runners, The Roots of Heaven, Beloved Infidel, The Young Doctors, Two Little Bears, Madison Avenue, Who's Got the Action?, The Longest Day, Captain Newman M.D., Miracle of the White Stallions, The Party's Over, Seven Women, The Heartbreak Kid (Acad. Award nom.), McQ, The Take, The Longest Yard, Escape to Witch Mountain, The Devil's Rain, Hustle, Whiffs, Birch Interval, Moving Violations, Yesterday, The Concorde — Airport 79, Foolin' Around, How to Beat the High Cost of Living, Take This Job and Shove It, Yes Giorgio, Dreamscape, Head Office, Stitches, Turnaround, Brenda Starr, The Big Picture, Death Valley Memories, TELEVISION: Movies/Specials: The Yeagers, Benjamin Franklin, The Borrowers, Killer Bees, Nutcracker, Anything Goes, Crash, The Word, Evening in Byzantium, Pirates Key, Living in Paradise, Oklahoma Dolls, The Plan, Peter and Paul, Goliath Awaits, Concord, Beyond Witch Mountain, Rooster, Demon Murder Case, Coalfire, In Like Flynn, Dress Gray, Mercy or Murder?, War and Remembrance, Return to Green Acres, The Girl from Mars, The Barefoot Executive, The Rodgers & Hart Story:Thou Swell, Thou Witty. Series: Leave It To Larry, The Eddie Albert Show, On Your Account, Nothing But the Best, Saturday Night Revue, Green Acres, Petticoat Junction, Switch!, Falcon Crest, General Hospital, Spider Man (voice). Guest: More than 80 guest appearances since 1948, including: The Fall Guy, Love Boat, Highway to Heaven, Falcon Crest, Murder She Wrote, thirtysomething,Twilight Zone, Dr. Quinn–Medicine Woman.

ALBERT, EDWARD
Actor. b. Los Angeles, CA, Feb. 20, 1951. e. UCLA. Son of actor Eddie Albert and late actress Margo. Was prod. asst. on Patton in Spain. Has appeared with father on radio and TV shows. Is photographer and has exhibited work in L.A.
THEATRE: Room Service, Our Town, The Glass Menagerie, Hamlet.
PICTURES: The Fool Killer (debut, 1965), Wild Country, Butterflies Are Free, Forty Carats, Midway, The Domino Principle, The Purple Taxi, The Greek Tycoon, When Time Ran Out, The Squeeze, Galaxy of Terror, Butterfly, The House Where Evil Dwells, A Time to Die, Ellie, Getting Even, Distortions, Terminal Entry, The Rescue, Mind Games, Sight Unseen, Fist Fighter, Shootfighter:Fight to the Death, Red Sun Rising, The Ice Runner, Broken Trust, Guarding Tess, Sorceress, Sexual Malice, Enter Deliah, Demon Keeper, The Royal Affair, The Secret Agent Club, Space Marines, The Man in the Iron Mask, Unbowed, Stagehoot, Ablaze, Extreme Honor, Night Class, A Light in the Forest, Fighting Words.
TELEVISION: Movies: Killer Bees, Death Cruise, The Millionaire, Silent Victory: The Kitty O'Neil Story, Blood Feud, The Girl from Mars, Body Language, Star Witness, USMA West Point. Miniseries: Black Beauty, The Last Convertible, Series: The Yellow Rose, Falcon Crest, Beauty and the Beast, The Fantastic Four (voice), Spider-Man (voice), California, Port Charles, Invasion America, Power Rangers Time Force. Host: Viva, Different Point of View, On Call Specials: Daddy Can't Read, Orson Welles' Great Mysteries (BBC). Guest: More than 45 guest appearances, including Profiler, Dr. Quinn, Medicine Woman, Nash Bridges, Martial Law, Chicken Soup for the Soul, Sabrina the Teenage Witch, The Sentinel.

ALBRIGHT, LOLA
Actress. b. Akron, OH, July 20, 1925. e. Studied piano 12 years. Switchboard operator and NBC stenographer; stenographer with WHAM and bit player; photographers' model. Made screen debut in The Pirate, 1947.
PICTURES: The Pirate (debut, 1947), Easter Parade, Julia Misbehaves, Champion, Tulsa, The Girl From Jones Beach, Bodyhold, Beauty on Parade, The Good Humor Man, When You're Smiling, Sierra Passage, The Killer That Stalked New York, Arctic Flight, The Silver Whip, The Treasure of Ruby Hills, The Magnificent Matador, The Tender Trap, The Monolith Monsters, Pawnee, Oregon Passage, Seven Guns to Mesa, A Cold Wind in August, Kid Galahad, Joy House, Lord Love a Duck, The Way West, Where Were You When the Lights Went Out?, The Impossible Years, The Money Jungle.
TELEVISION: Movies: How I Spent My Summer Vacation, Helicopter Spies, The Nurse Killer, Columbo: Fade in to Murder, Delta County USA, Terraces. Series: Peter Gunn, Peyton Place. Guest: More than 40 appearances, including, Medical Center, Police Story, Starsky and Hutch, The Incredible Hulk, Airwolf.

ALCAINE, JOSE LUIS
Cinematographer. b. Tangier, Algeria, Dec. 26, 1938. e. Spanish Cinema Sch., Madrid. After graduation joined Madrid's Studio Moros doing commercials. Cinematographer on more than 115

projects.
PICTURES: El Hueso (debut 1967) More than 95 cinematography credits. Since 1994, credits include: La Pasion turca, Dile a Laura que la quiero, Two Much, Freedomfighters, In Praise of Older Women, La Pistols de mi hermano, Mas alla del jardin, Don Juan, Il Mio West, Blast from the Past, Celos, L'Amante perduto, Antonio Rapaz de Lisboa, I Know Who You Are, Sound of the Sea, Chica do Rio, The Dancer Upstairs, Don Quixote-Knight Errant, Nobody's Life, South from Granada.

ALDA, ALAN
Actor, Writer, Director. r.n. Alphonso D'Abruzzo b. New York, NY, Jan. 28, 1936. e. Fordham U., 1956. Son of actor Robert Alda. Studied at Cleveland Playhouse on Ford Foundation Grant; performed with Second City, then on TV in That Was The Week That Was. for work as director, writer and actor on M*A*S*H won 5 Emmys, 2 Writers Guild Awards, 3 Directors Guild Awards, 6 Golden Globes, 7 People's Choice Awards, Humanitas Award (for Writing). Has appeared in a dozen documentaries/specials, including Keepers of the Frame (1999) and TV Guide 50 Best Shows of All Time: A 50th Anniversary Celebration (2002).
THEATRE: B'way: Only in America, The Owl and The Pussycat, Purlie Victorious, Fair Game For Lovers (Theatre World Award), The Apple Tree (Tony nom.), Jake's Women (Tony Award nom.). London: Our Town.
PICTURES: Gone Are The Days (debut, 1963), Paper Lion, The Extraordinary Seaman, Jenny, The Moonshine War, The Mephisto Waltz, To Kill a Clown, Same Time Next Year, California Suite, The Seduction of Joe Tynan (also s.p.), The Four Seasons (also dir., s.p.), Sweet Liberty (also dir., s.p.), A New Life (also dir. s.p.), Crimes and Misdemeanors (D.W. Griffith Award, NY Film Critics Award), Betsy's Wedding (also dir., s.p.), Whispers in the Dark, Manhattan Murder Mystery, Canadian Bacon, Flirting With Disaster, Everyone Says I Love You, Murder at 1600, Mad City, The Object of My Affection, Keepers of the Frame, What Women Want.
TELEVISION: Movies: The Glass House, Playmates, Isn't It Shocking?, Kill Me If You Can (Emmy nom.), Free to Be...You & Me (voice), The Caryl Chessman Story, M*A*S*H: Goodbye Farewell and Amen, And the Band Played On, White Mile, Jake's Women, , Attika, Club Land, The Killing Yard. Series: Secret File USA, That Was the Week That Was, What's My Line? M*A*S*H (11 years; also wrote, dir. and creative consultant), Scientific American Frontiers (PBS, host), We'll Get By, The Four Seasons (creator, exec. prod.), Influences. Guest: Phil Silvers Show, The Nurses, Route 66, East Side/West Side, Trials of O'Brien, Coronet Blue, To Tell the Truth, Carol Burnet Show. Pilots: Where's Everett, Higher and Higher.

ALDREDGE, THEONI V.
Costume Designer. b. Salonika, Greece, Aug. 22, 1932. m. actor Tom Aldredge. e. American School, Athens; Goodman Theatre School, Chicago, 1949-52. Costume designer on 45 pictures. Best-known for The Great Gatsby (Acad. Award, 1974), Eyes of Laura Mars (Sci Fi. Acad. Honor), Network, Ghostbusters, and Moonstruck.
THEATRE: B'way.: Sweet Bird of Youth, That Championship Season, Sticks and Bones, Two Gentlemen of Verona, A Chorus Line, Annie (Tony Award), Ballroom, Much Ado About Nothing, Barnum (Tony Award), Dream Girls, Woman of the Year, Onward Victoria, La Cage aux Folles (Tony Award), 42nd Street, Merlin, Private Lives, The Corn is Green, The Rink, Blithe Spirit, Chess, Gypsy, Oh Kay!, The Secret Garden, High Rollers.
PICTURES: Stella (debut 1955) Since 1994 work includes: Milk Money, The First Wives Club, Mrs. Winterbourne, The Mirror Has Two Faces, The Rage: Carrie 2.

ALEANDRO, NORMA
Actress. b. Buenos Aires, Argentina, May 2, 1936. Sister is actress Maria Vaner. As child, performed with parents in theatre troupe. In Argentina performed in every theatrical genre and epoch and also directed. Has written & published short stories (1986), poems and the screenplay for Argentinian film, Los Herederos. Was in exile in Uruguay (18 months) and Spain 1976-82 because of the military junta in Argentina. Before exile had made 12 films; after return in 1982 starred in theatre and 7 films. Industry recognition for: The Official Story (Cannes Film Festival Award, 1985, Silver Condor from Argentinian Film Critics Assn., 1986,) Gaby: A True Story (Golden Globe nom., Acad. Award nom, 1988), Foolish Heart (Havana Film Festival award, 1998), Son of the Bride (won Silver Condor, Argentinian Film Critics Assn, Golden Kikito from Gramado Film Festival, 2002)
THEATRE: U.S.: About Love and Other Stories (one-woman show, toured South America, then at La Mama and later off-B'way at Public Theater 1986); The Senorita of Tacna (written for her by Mario Vargas-Llosa, 1987).
PICTURES: La Muerte en las Calles (debut 1952). Since 1994: Facundo: The Tiger's Shadow, Carlos Monzon-el segundo juicio, Autumn Sun, Foolish Heart, Prohibido, The Lighthouse, A Night with Sabrina Love, La Fuga, Son of the Bride, Every Stewardess Goes to Heaven, Desire, Cleopatra.
TELEVISION: Movies: Dark Holiday, One Man's War, Guest: Tiempofinal, Primicias.

ALEXANDER, JANE
Actress. r.n. Jane Quigley. b. Boston, MA, Oct. 28, 1939. e. Sarah Lawrence Coll., U. of Edinburgh. m. director Edwin Sherin. Mother of actor Jace Alexander. Stage career includes

appearances on B'way; at Arena Stage, Washington D.C.; Kennedy Center, D.C.; Music Center, L.A.; and Shakespeare Festival at Stamford, Conn. Appointed chair of the National Endowment for the Arts, 1993.
THEATRE: *NY*: The Great White Hope (Tony & Theatre World Awards, 1969), 6 Rms Riv Vu, Find Your Way Home, Hamlet, The Heiress, First Monday in October, Goodbye Fidel, Losing Time, Monday After the Miracle, Old Times, Night of the Iguana, Approaching Zanzibar, Shadowlands, The Visit, The Sisters Rosensweig.
PICTURES: The Great White Hope (debut, 1970), A Gunfight, The New Centurions, All the President's Men, The Betsy, Kramer vs. Kramer, Brubaker, Night Crossing, Testament, City Heat, Square Dance, Sweet Country, Glory, The Cider House Rules, Sunshine State, The Ring.
TELEVISION: *Movies*: Welcome Home Johnny Bristol, Miracle on 34th St., This is the West That Was, Death Be Not Proud, Eleanor and Franklin, Eleanor and Franklin: The White House Years, A Circle of Children, Lovey: A Circle of Children Part II, A Question of Love, Playing for Time (Emmy Award), In the Custody of Strangers, When She Says No, Calamity Jane (also prod.), Malice in Wonderland, Blood & Orchids, In Love and War, Open Admissions, A Friendship in Vienna, Daughter of the Streets, Stay the Night, Yesterday's Children, Bitter Winter. *Guest*: Law and Order, Law and Order:Special Victims Unit. *Specials*: Mountain View, A Marriage: Georgia O'Keeffe and Alfred Stieglitz. *Pilot*: New Year.

ALEXANDER, JASON
Actor, producer. r.n. Jay Scott Greenspan. b. Newark, NJ, Sept. 23, 1959. e. Boston Univ. Received an honorary doctorate from Boston University.
THEATRE: *NY*: Merrily We Roll Along, Forbidden Broadway, The Rink, Personals, Stop the World, Light Up the Sky, Broadway Bound, Jerome Robbins' Broadway (Tony, Drama Desk & Outer Critics' Circle Awards, 1989), Accomplice. *Regional*: Give 'em Hell Harry.
PICTURES: The Burning (debut, 1981), Brighton Beach Memoirs, The Mosquito Coast, Pretty Woman, White Palace, Jacob's Ladder, I Don't Buy Kisses Anymore, The Return of Jafar (voice), Down on the Waterfront, Coneheads, Sexual Healing, For Goodness Sake, The Paper, North, Blankman, The Last Supper, For Better or Worse (also dir.), , Dunston Checks In, The Hunchback of Notre Dame (voice), Love! Valour! Compassion!, Denial, Love and Action in Chicago, The Adventures of Rocky and Bullwinkle, Just Looking (also dir.), The Trumpet of the Swan (voice), Odessa Or Bust, On Edge, Hunchback of Notre Dame II, Shallow Hal, How to Go Out On a Date in Queens, Agent Cody Banks (exec. prod.), Madagascar.
TELEVISION: *Movies*: Senior Trip, Rockabye, Favorite Son, Bye Bye Birdie, Cinderella, Larry David: Curb Your Enthusiasm, Jingle Bells (actor narrator), Get Into My Shorts, Stage on Screen: The Women, The Man Who Saved Christmas.. *Series*: E/R, Everything's Relative, Seinfeld, Duckman (voice), Aladdin (voice), Disney's Hercules (voice), Dilbert (voice), House of Mouse (voice), Bob Patterson. *Guest*: More than 30 appearances, including Newhart, Dream On, The Larry Sanders Show, Remember WENN,.Reading Rainbow, Friends, Walker Texas Ranger, Curb Your Enthusiasm, Son of the Beach, The Twilight Zone.

ALEXANDER, RALPH
Executive. Began career with Universal Pictures in sales, 1949. Had various sls. jobs with 20th Century Fox and Lorimar. Appointed v.p., theatrical foreign sls., Filmway Pictures, 1981-82. Appoined v.p., sls. for Latin America & Southeast Asia, Embassy Pictures Intl., 1982-84. Named exec. v.p., multi-media foreign sls. for Robert Meyers Intl., 1984. Joined Dino De Laurentiis Corp. as intl. sls. dir. in chg. all foreign sls. theatrical and ancillary rights except tv., 1985. Promoted to v.p., intl. sls., DEG, 1986. Appointed pres. mktg. and sales, Kings Road Intl., 1989. Joined Scotti Bros. Pictures as pres. intl. sales and mktg., 1989.

ALLEN, COREY
Director, Actor. r.n. Alan Cohen. b. Cleveland, OH, June 29, 1934. e. UCLA, 1951-54; UCLA law sch. 1954-55. Actor turned dir. starred in Oscar-winning UCLA student film, A Time Out of War, which also won best short film at the Cannes and Venice Film Festival. Appeared in 20 plays at Players Ring, Players Gallery and other L.A. theatres. Turned to directing in the 1970s.
PICTURES: *Actor*: Rebel Without a Cause, Shadow on the Window, The Big Caper, Juvenile Jungle, Darby's Rangers, Party Girl, Key Witness, Private Property, Sweet Bird of Youth, The Chapman Report.. *Director*: The Erotic Adventures of Pinocchio (also s.p.), Thunder and Lightning, Avalanche, Lost (prod.).
TELEVISION: *Movies*: (All as dir.) See the Man Run, Cry Rape!, Yesterday's Child, Stone (pilot), Man in the Santa Claus Suit, The Return of Frank Cannon, Code Name: Foxfire (pilot), Brass, Beverly Hills Cowgirl Blues, I-Man, The Last Fling, Destination America, Star Trek: The Next Generation-Encounter at Farpoint, Ann Jillian Story, Moment of Truth:Stalking Back, the Search, Men Who Hate Women & the Women Who Love Them.
Series Dir: More than 40 series dir. credits. Best known for Hill Street Blues (Emmy, 1984), Star Trek: The Next Generation, The Rockford Files and the Paper Chase. With partner John Herman Shaner, prod. Freeway Circuit Theatre. Led Actors Workshop with actor Guy Stockwell for over 10 years.

ALLEN, DAYTON
Performer. b. New York, NY, Sept. 24, 1919. e. Mt. Vernon H.S. Motion picture road shows, 1936-40. Disc jockey, WINS, N.Y., 1940-41. Writer, vaudeville comedy bits, 1941-45, then radio

comic, puppeteer and voices. In television since 1948, film commercials and shows. Primarily cartoon voice credits among his more than 120 appearances.
PICTURES: The Cotton Club (actor), Appointment with Fear.
TELEVISION: (voices): Terrytoons, Deputy Dwag, Heckle & Jeckle, Lancelot Link: Secret Chimp, Lariat Sam, Oaky Doky, Bonny Maid Varieties, Howdy Doody, Jack Barry's Winky Dink, The Steve Allen Show. 130 Dayton Allen 5 min. shows (synd.).

ALLEN, DEBBIE
Actress, Choreographer, Director. b. Houston, TX, Jan. 16, 1950. e. Howard U. Sister is actress Phylicia Rashad.
THEATRE: Ti-Jean and His Brothers (debut, 1972), Purlie, Raisin, Ain't Misbehavin', West Side Story (revival), Sweet Charity (revival, Tony Award, 1986), Carrie (choreographer).
PICTURES: The Fish That Saved Pittsburgh (1979), Fame, Ragtime, Jo Jo Dancer Your Life is Calling, Blank Check, Mona Must Die, Forget Paris (choreographer), Out of Sync (dir.), Amistad (prod. composer-song), Everything's Jake, All About You, The Painting (also exec. prod.).
TELEVISION: *Movies*: The Greatest Thing That Almost Happened, Ebony—Ivory and Jade, Women of San Quentin, Polly (dir., choreographer), Polly-Comin' Home! (dir., choreographer), Stompin' at the Savoy (also dir.), American Hero: The Michael Jordan Story, Cool Women (dir.), The Old Settler (also dir., exec. prod.) *Series*: The Jim Stafford Show, 3 Girls 3, Drawing Power, Fame (series; 3 Emmys as choreographer, 1 nom. as actress, also dir., co-exec. prod.), Family Ties (dir.), A Different World (dir.,prod.), The Fresh Prince of Bel-Air (dir.), The Sinbad Show (dir.), In the House, , C. Bear and Jamal (voice and voice dir.), The Jamie Foxx Show (dir.), Between Brothers (dir.), Linc's (dir.) Healthy Kids, The Twilight Zone (dir.). *Mini-Series*: Roots-The Next Generation, Celebrity. *Specials*: Ben Vereen-His Roots, Loretta Lynn in Big Apple Country, Texaco Star Theater—Opening Night, The Kids from Fame, John Schneider's Christmas Holiday, A Tribute to Martin Luther King Jr.—A Celebration of Life, Motown Returns to the Apollo, The Debbie Allen Special (also dir., chor.), Academy Awards (choreographer: 1993, 1995, 1999). *Guest*: More than 17 appearances, including the Cosby Show, A Different World, Touched by an Angel, Heart of the City. Documentaries: Disneyland's 30th Anniversary Celebration, 50 Years of Funny Females, 3 Intimate Portrait documentaries...Phylicia Rashad, Harriet Tubman and Jasmine Guy, Living Positive, Inside TV Land: African Americans in Television.

ALLEN, DEDE
Film Editor. r.n. Dorothea Carothers Allen b. Cleveland, OH, Dec. 3, 1925. Started as messenger at Columbia Pictures, moved to editing dept., then to commercials and features. Theatrical Production v.p. then pres. at Warner Brothers, 1992-1997. A.C.E. Honorary Lifetime Achievement Award, 1994.
PICTURES: Because of Eve (1948), Terror from the Year 5000, Odds Against Tomorrow, The Hustler, America America, Bonnie and Clyde, Rachel Rachel, Alice's Restaurant, Little Big Man, Slaughterhouse 5, Serpico, Night Moves, Dog Day Afternoon (Acad. award nom.), The Missouri Breaks, Slap Shot, The Wiz, Reds (also exec. prod. Acad. award nom.), Harry and Son, Mike's Murder, The Breakfast Club, Off Beat, The Milagro Beanfield War (co-ed.), Let It Ride (co-ed.), Henry and June, The Addams Family, Wonder Boys, John Q.

ALLEN, IOAN
Executive. b. Stafford, England, Oct. 25, 1938. e. Rossall School and Dartmouth Naval College, England. Artist mgmt. and record prod., 1964-1969. Responsible for origination and devt. of Dolby Stereo film program, after joining Dolby in 1969. Fellow of Society of Motion Picture & Television Engineers, Audio Engineering Society and the British Kinematograhic Sound & Television Society. Past Pres., Intl. Theatre Equipment Assn. U.S. correspondent on the Intl. Standards Org. cinematographic subcommittee. Adjunct prof., USC School of Cinema-Television. Vice pres., Dolby Laboratories. Recipient: Acad. Scientific & Technical Awards, 1979 & 1987. Acad. award for work in Dolby Laboratories film program, 1989; Samuel L. Warner Award for contribution to motion picture sound, 1985. Academy Commendation for work on TASA Trailer Loudness Standard, 2001.

ALLEN, JAY PRESSON
Writer, Producer. r.n. Jacqueline Presson. b. Fort Worth, TX, March 3, 1922. m. prod. Lewis M. Allen.
THEATRE: *Writer*:The First Wife, The Prime of Miss Jean Brodie, Forty Carats, Tru (also dir.), The Big Love (also dir.).
PICTURES: *Writer*: Marnie, The Prime of Miss Jean Brodie, Cabaret, Travels with My Aunt, 40 Carats, Funny Lady, Just Tell Me What You Want (also prod.), It's My Turn (exec. prod. only), Prince of the City (also exec. prod.), Deathtrap (also exec. prod.), The Celluloid Closet (act. only).
TELEVISION: *Movies*: The Borrowers. *Series*: Family (creator), Hot House (also exec. prod.).

ALLEN, JOAN
Actress. b. Rochelle, IL, Aug. 20, 1956. Founding member of Steppenwolf Theatre Co., in Chicago where she performed in over 20 shows.
THEATRE: *Chicago*: A Lesson from Aloes, Three Sisters, The Miss Firecracker Contest, Cloud 9, Balm in Gilead, Fifth of July, Reckless, Earthly Possessions. *Off B'way*: And a Nightingale Sang (Clarence Derwent, Drama Desk, Outer Critics' Circle and

Theatre World Awards). *B'way.*: Burn This (debut, 1987; Tony Award), The Heidi Chronicles.
PICTURES: Compromising Positions (debut, 1985), Manhunter, Peggy Sue Got Married, Tucker: The Man and His Dream, In Country, Ethan Frome, Searching for Bobby Fischer, Josh and S.A.M., Mad Love, Nixon, The Crucible, The Ice Storm, Face/Off, Pleasantville, All The Rage, When the Sky Falls, The Contender, Off the Map, The Notebook.
TELEVISION: *Movies*: Say Goodnight, Gracie, All My Sons,The Room Upstairs, Without Warning: The James Brady Story. *Mini-Series*: Evergreen, The Mists of Avalon. *Guest*: The Twilight Zone, Frasier. *Documentaries*: The Big Show, New York: A Documentary Film, War Letters.

ALLEN, KAREN

Actress. b. Carrollton, IL, Oct. 5, 1951. e. George Washington U., U. of Maryland. Auditioned for theatrical company in Washington, D.C., and won a role in Saint, touring with it for 7 months. Spent several years with Washington Theatre Laboratory Co. Moved to NY, acted in student films at NYU and studied acting at Theatre Institute with Lee Strasberg.
THEATRE: *NY*: Monday After the Miracle (B'way debut, 1982; Theatre World Award), Extremities, The Miracle Worker, The Country Girl. *Williamstown (MA) Theatre*: Tennessee Williams–A Celebration, The Glass Menagerie.
PICTURES: National Lampoon's Animal House (debut, 1978), Manhattan, The Wanderers, Cruising, A Small Circle of Friends, Raiders of the Lost Ark, Shoot the Moon, Split Image, Until September, Starman, Terminus, The Glass Menagerie, Backfire, Scrooged, Animal Behavior, Sweet Talker, Malcolm X, The Sandlot, King of the Hill, Ghost in the Machine, The Turning, 'Til There Was You, Wind River, Falling Sky, The Basket, The Perfect Storm, In the Bedroom, World Traveler, Shallow End, The Root..
TELEVISION: *Movies*: Lovey: A Circle of Children Part II, Challenger, Secret Weapon, Voyage, Rapture, Hostile Advances: The Kerry Ellison Story, All the Winters That Have Been. My Horrible Year! *Mini-Series*: East of Eden, Shaka Zulu: The Citadel. *Series*: The Road Home. *Guest*: Knots Landing, Alfred Hitchcock Presents (1986), Law & Order, Law & Order: Special Victims Unit.

ALLEN, LEWIS M.

Producer. b. Berryville, VA, June 27, 1922. e. Univ. of VA. m. writer-producer Jay Presson Allen.
PICTURES: *Prod./Exec. prod./Co-prod.*:The Connection, The Balcony, Lord of the Flies, Fahrenheit 451, The Queen, Fortune and Men's Eyes, Never Cry Wolf, 1918, Valentine's Day, Swimming to Cambodia, O.C. & Stiggs, End of the Line, Miss Firecracker.

ALLEN, NANCY

Actress. b. New York, NY, June 24, 1950. e. H.S. Perf. Arts, N.Y.
PICTURES: Money in My Pocket (debut 1962), The Last Detail, The Last Entry, Carrie, I Wanna Hold Your Hand, 1941, The Maestro, Home Movies, Dressed to Kill, Blow Out, Strange Invaders, The Buddy System, The Philadelphia Experiment, The Last Victim, Not for Publication, Terror in the Aisles, Robocop, Sweet Revenge, Poltergeist III, Limit Up, Robocop 2, Robocop 3, The Patriots, Dusting Cliff 7, Against the Law, Secret of the Andes, The Pass, Out of Sight, Children of the Corn 666: Isaac's Return, Secret of the Andes, Kiss Toledo Goodbye, For What It's Worth, Quality Time, Circuit.
TELEVISION: *Movies*: The Gladiator, Memories of Murder, Acting on Impulse, Eyes of a Stranger, The Man Who Wouldn't Die. *Guest*: Touched by an Angel,.The Outer Limits, The Commish,

ALLEN, TIM

Actor. r.n. Timothy Allen Dick. b. Denver, CO, June 13, 1953. e. W. Michigan Univ., Univ. of Detroit, studied acting. Worked as creative dir. for adv. agency before becoming stand up comedian. Made stand up tv debut on Showtime Comedy Club All-Stars, 1988. Author: Don't Stand Close to a Naked Man (1994).
PICTURES: Comedy's Dirtiest Dozen, The Santa Clause, Toy Story (voice), Meet Wally Sparks, Jungle2Jungle, For Richer or Poorer, Toy Story 2 (voice), Galaxy Quest, The Cat in the Hat, Who is Cletis Tout? Joe Somebody, Big Trouble, Buzz Lightyear of Star Command: The Adventure Begins, The Santa Clause 2, Doin' the Splits
TELEVISION: *Movies*: Tim Allen: Men Are Pigs (also writer, exec. prod.), Tim Allen Rewires America, AFI's 100 Years,100 Laughs: America's Funniest Movies, The Beatles Revolution. *Series*: Home Improvement.

ALLEN, WILLIAM

Executive. e. USC Cinema/TV Sch., Pepperdine Univ. 1979. Exec. trainee in CBS Entertainment division, eventually serving as assoc. program exec. in the Comedy Series Programming Dept.; mngr./dir. of the CBS Comedy Program Development. Dept. Joined MTM as sr. v.p., Comedy Programming, 1986-87; sr. v.p. creative affairs, 1987-88; exec. v.p. MTM Television, 1989-1991. pres., MTM Television, 1992. Currently, pres. & ceo of non-profit, the Economic Alliance.

ALLEN, WOODY

Actor, Director, Writer. r.n. Allan Stewart Konigsberg. b. New York, NY, Dec. 1, 1935. e. NYU, 1953; City Coll. NY, 1953. Began writing comedy at age 17, contributing to various magazines (Playboy, New Yorker) and top TV comedy shows incl. Sid Caesar (1957), Art

Carney (1958-59), Herb Shriner (1953). Appeared in nightclubs starting in 1961 as stand-up comic; later performed as a jazz musician at Michael's Pub, NY. Special Award, Berlin Film Fest., 1975.
AUTHOR: Getting Even, Without Feathers, Side Effects.
THEATRE: *Author*: Play It Again Sam (also actor), Don't Drink The Water, The Floating Lightbulb, Central Park West (from Death Defying Acts).
PICTURES: *Actor-Screenplay*: What's New Pussycat?, What's Up Tiger Lily? (also dubbed and compiled footage; assoc. prod.), Casino Royale (actor only). *Director/Screenplay/Actor*: Take the Money and Run, Bananas, Play It Again Sam. Everything You Always Wanted to Know About Sex But Were Afraid to Ask, Sleeper, Love and Death, The Front (actor only), Annie Hall (Acad. Awards for Best Director and Original Screenplay, 1977), Interiors (dir., s.p. only), Manhattan, Stardust Memories, A Midsummer Night's Sex Comedy, Zelig, Broadway Danny Rose, The Purple Rose of Cairo (dir., s.p. only), Hannah and Her Sisters (Acad. Award for Best Original Screenplay, 1986), Radio Days (dir., s.p., narrator only), King Lear (actor only), September (dir., s.p. only), Another Woman (dir., s.p. only), New York Stories (Oedipus Wrecks segment), Crimes and Misdemeanors, Alice (dir., s.p. only), Scenes From a Mall (actor only), Shadows and Fog, Husbands and Wives, Manhattan Murder Mystery, Bullets Over Broadway (dir., s.p. only), Mighty Aphrodite, Everyone Says I Love You (dir. & actor), Deconstructing Harry, The Imposters (actor only), Antz (voice), Wild Man Blues, Sweet and Lowdown,Company Man (actor only), Picking Up the Pieces (actor only),The Curse of the Jade Scorpion, Small Time Crooks, Count Mercury Goes to the Suburbs (writer only), Light Keeps Me Company (actor only), Hail Sid Caesar! The Golden Age of Comedy (actor only), Stanley Kubrick: A Life in Pictures (actor only), Hollywood Ending, Anything Else, Why Men Shouldn't Marry.
TELEVISION: *Movies*: Don't Drink the Water (also dir., writer), The Sunshine Boys, Woody Allen: A Life in Film, Last Laugh. *Guest*: More than 25 appearances, including That Was the Week That Was, Hullabaloo, Andy Williams, Hippodrome, Just Shoot Me.

ALLEY, KIRSTIE

Actress. b. Wichita, KS, Jan. 12, 1955. e. KS State U., U. of Kansas. On L.A. stage in Cat on a Hot Tin Roof.
PICTURES: Star Trek II: The Wrath of Khan (debut, 1982), Champions, Runaway, Blind Date, Summer School, Shoot to Kill, Loverboy, Look Who's Talking, Madhouse, Sibling Rivalry, Look Who's Talking Too, Look Who's Talking Now, Village of the Damned, It Takes Two, Sticks and Stones, Nevada (also co-prod.), Deconstructing Harry, For Richer or Poorer, The Mao Game, Drop Dead Gorgeous, Back by Midnight.
TELEVISION: *Movies*: Sins of the Past, A Bunny's Tale, Stark: Mirror Image, Prince of Bel Air, Infidelity, David's Mother (Emmy Award, 1994), Radiant City, Peter and the Wolf, Toothless, Profoundly Normal (also exec. prod.) *Mini-Series*: North and South, North and South Book II, The Last Don, The Last Don II, Blonde, Salem Witch Trials,.*Series*: Masquerade, Cheers (Emmy Award, 1991), Veronica's Closet (also prod.). *Guest*: More than 12 appearances, including The Hitchhiker, Wings, The Roseanne Show and Dharma and Greg.

ALLYSON, JUNE

Actress. r.n. Ella Geisman. b. Westchester, NY, Oct. 7, 1917. Started as chorus girl. Voted one of ten top money-making stars in Motion Picture Herald-Fame poll, 1955.
THEATRE: *B'way*: Sing Out the News, Panama Hattie, Best Foot Forward, 40 Carats. *Tour*: No No Nanette.
PICTURES: Nearly 40 picture credits since 1943 debut in Best Foot Foward. Best known for Little Women, Executive Suite and The Glenn Miller Story (1954).
TELEVISION: *Movies*: See the Man Run, Letters from Three Lovers, Curse of the Black Widow, Three on a Date, The Kid With the Broken Halo. *Series*: DuPont Show With June Allyson. *Guest*: Nearly 30 appearances, including Murder She Wrote, Misfits of Science, Crazy Like a Fox, Biography and Larry King Live.

ALMODOVAR, PEDRO

Director, Writer. b. La Mancha, Spain, Sept. 25, 1951. r.n.Pedro Almodovar Cabellero. Grew up in Calzada de Calatrava. At 17 moved to Madrid where worked 10 years for telephone co. while writing comic strips and articles for underground newspapers and working as actor with independent theatre co., Los Goliardos. Upon the end of Francoist repression in 1975, made Super-8 experimental films starring friends. Wrote fiction, sang with rock band and created character of porn star, Patty Diphusa, whose fictionalized confessions he published in the magazine La Luna. Received 49 awards and 26 nom., including Acad. Award in 2003 for Talk to Her.
PICTURES: Folle...folle...Folleme Tim! (debut 1978) Pepi Lucy Bom and Other Girls on the Heap, Labyrinth of Passion (also prod.), Entre tinieblas, Dark Habits, What Have I Done to Deserve This?, The Bullfighter, Law of Desire, Women on the Verge of a Nervous Breakdown (also prod.), Tie Me Up! Tie Me Down!, Madonna:Truth or Dare (actor only), High Heels, Accion mutante, Kika, The Flower of My Secret, Mi nombre es sombra, Shampoo Horns, Live Flesh, All About My Mother (Cannes Film Fest. best dir., 1999; BAFTA best film not in Eng. and dir. award, 2000), The Devil's Backbone (prod.), The Paperboy, Talk to Her (Acad. award, best writing, and nom.for Best Achiev. in Dir., 2003. BAFTA award best film not in Eng. and best screenplay, 2003) La Mala educacion.

ALONSO, MARIA CONCHITA
Actress, Singer. b. Cienfuegos, Cuba, June 29, 1957. Family moved to Venezuela when she was five. 1971, named Miss Teenager of the World. 1975, Miss Venezuela. 6th runner up, Miss World. Appeared in four feature films and 10 soap operas before coming to U.S. Recorded several albums as singer: 5 gold albums, 1 platinum, 3 Grammy noms.
THEATRE: Aurora. B'way: Kiss of the Spider Woman.
PICTURES 30 film appearances, including Solon (debut 1979), Scarface (singer), Fear City, Moscow on the Hudson, Extreme Prejudice, The Running Man,, Touch and Go, A Fine Mess, Colors, Vampire's Kiss, Predator 2, McBain, The House of the Spirits, Roosters, For Which He Stands, Caught, El Crito en el Cieto, Catherine's Grove, Acts of Betrayal, Knockout, Expose, Blackheart, Chain of Command, The Code Conspiracy, Blind Heat, Babylon Revisited, Homeroom, Heart of America, Chasing Papi.
TELEVISION: Movies: Cuerpos clandestinos, Teamster Boss: The Jackie Presser Story, MacShayne: The Final Roll of the Dice, Texas, The Gun, Sudden Terror: Hijacking of School Bus #17, Latino Laugh Festival, Al dia con Maria Conchita, Fx, My Husband's Secret Life, A Vision of Murder: The Story of Donielle, Best Actress, High Noon, The Princess and the Barrio Boy.. Guest: Eight appearances, including One of the Boys, Chicago Hope, The Outer Limits, Touched by an Angel, Resurrection Blvd and Robbery Homicide Division.

ALTERMAN, JOSEPH GEORGE
Executive. b. New Haven, CT., Dec. 17, 1919. e. Wesleyan U., B.A., 1942; Inst. for Organization Management, Yale U., 1957-59. Exec. assist., SoundScriber Corp., 1945-48. District mgr., Industrial Luncheon Service, 1948-55. Asst. secretary and admin. secretary, Theatre Owners of America, 1955; exec. dir. and vice pres., Natl. Assn. of Theatre Owners, 1966. Exec. v.p. COMPO., 1970. Retired 1988 from NATO. Consultant m.p. industry, conventions and meetings. Chmn., bd. govs., Institute for Learning in Retirement, Albertus Magnus College.

ALTMAN, ROBERT
Director, Writer, Producer. b. Kansas City, MO, Feb. 20, 1925. e. U. of Missouri. Early film writer credits: Bodyguard (co-story), Corn's-a-Poppin (co-s.p.). Made industrial films and documentaries for the Calvin Company in Kansas City, before dir. first indept. feature in 1957. Received D.W. Griffith Lifetime Achievement Award from Directors Guild of America, 1994. Received lifetime achievement from the Gotham Awards, which cover the East Coast's independent film scene, (2000).
More than 100 credits to his name, 20+ awards and 45+ nom. Most recently, work for Gosford Park received the AFI Film Award, Golden Globe for best dir.-motion picture, BAFTA for best brit. film, Eve. Standard Brit. Film Award for best film, Nat'l. Soc.of Film Critics Award for best dir., and Acad. Award nom., 2002. Also NY Film Critics Circle Award, 2001.).
THEATRE: NY: Two By South, Come Back to the Five and Dime Jimmy Dean Jimmy Dean. Operas: The Rake's Progress, McTeague.
PICTURES: Director: The Delinquents (also s.p., prod.), The James Dean Story (also co-prod., edit.), Countdown, That Cold Day in the Park, M*A*S*H (Cannes Film Fest. Golden Palm Award, 1970; Acad. Award nom.), Brewster McCloud, McCabe & Mrs. Miller (also co-s.p.), Images (also s.p.), The Long Goodbye, Thieves Like Us (also co-s.p.), California Split (also co-prod.), Nashville (also prod.; NY Film Critics, Natl. Society of Film Critics & Natl. Board of Review Awards for Best Director & Picture, 1975; Acad. Award noms. for dir. & picture), Buffalo Bill and the Indians: Or Sitting Bull's History Lesson (also co-s.p., prod.), Three Women (also s.p., prod.), A Wedding (also co-s.p., prod., co-story), Quintet (also co-s.p., prod., co-story), A Perfect Couple (also co-s.p., prod.), Health (also co-s.p., prod.), Popeye, Come Back to the Five and Dime Jimmy Dean Jimmy Dean, Streamers (also co-prod.), Secret Honor (also prod.), Fool for Love, Beyond Therapy (also co-s.p.), O.C. and Stiggs (also co-prod.), Aria (dir. Les Boreades sequence; also s.p.), Vincent & Theo, The Player (BAFTA & Cannes Film Fest. Awards for Best Director, 1991; Acad. Award nom.), Short Cuts (also co-s.p.; Acad. Award nom. for dir.), Ready to Wear/Pret-a-Porter (also co-s.p., prod.), Jazz '34, Kansas City (also s.p., prod.), Cookie's Fortune (also s.p., prod.), Dr. T and the Women, Another City,Not My Own. Producer: The Late Show, Welcome to L.A., Remember My Name, Rich Kids (exec.), Mrs. Parker and the Vicious Circle, Trixie, Dr. T and the Women, Roads and Bridges (exec. prod.), Gosford Park (see awards above, including Academy Award nom.), Voltage, The Company.
TELEVISION: Movies: Nightmare in Chicago, Rattlesnake in a Cooler (also exec. prod.), Peking Encounter, Two by South, The Laundromat, The Dumb Waiter, Best of Friends, The Caine Mutiny Court-Martial, McTeague (also opera dir.), Black and Blue, The Real McTeague (also creative supervisor).Series: Director/Writer and/or Producer: For 22 series, including The Millionaire, Alfred Hitchcock Presents, Maverick, U.S. Marshall, The Lawman, Peter Gunn, Bonanza, Route 66, Bus Stop, , Kraft Mystery Theatre, Tanner '88 (also co-exec. prod.; Emmy Award for dir. episode The Boiler Room, 1989), Gun (also exec. prod.)

ALVARADO, TRINI
Actress. b. New York, NY, Jan. 10, 1967. e. Fordham U. m. actor Robert McNeill. Prof. acting debut at 9 in stage musical Becca.
THEATRE: Runaways, Reds, The Magic Show, Godspell.
PICTURES: Rich Kids (debut, 1989), Times Square, Mrs. Soffel, Sweet Lorraine, Satisfaction, The Chair, Stella, American Blue Note, The Babe, American Friends, Little Women, The Perez Family, The Frighteners, Paulie.
TELEVISION: Movies: A Movie Star's Daughter, Private Contentment, Dreams Don't Die, Prisoner Without a Name, Frank Nitti, Sensibility and Sense, The Christmas Tree, The Last Dance, Bitter Winter. Guest: Kate and Allie, Spenser: For Hire.

ALVIN, JOHN
Actor. r.n. John Alvin Hoffstadt. b. Chicago, IL, Oct. 24, 1917. e. Pasadena Playhouse, CA. Attended Morgan Park Military Acad. On radio Chicago & Detroit; on N.Y. stage Leaning on Letty, Life of the Party. Screen debut 1943 in Destination Tokyo.
PICTURES: Among his 52 picture credits are: Destination Tokyo, Objective Burma, San Antonio, The Beast With Five Fingers, Night and Day, Cheyenne, Missing Women, Two Guys From Texas, Bold Frontiersman, Train to Alcatraz, Shanghai Chest, Carrie, April In Paris, Roughly Speaking, The Very Thought of You, Shadow of a Woman, Three Strangers, Romance on the High Seas, Torpedo Alley, Irma La Douce, Marnie, Inside Daisy Clover, The Legend of Lylah Clare, They Shoot Horses Don't They?,They Call Me Mr. Tibbs, Somewhere in Time, Beethoven's 2nd, Milk Money.
TELEVISION: Movies: The Magnetic Moon, Sweet Sweet Rachel, The Legend of Lizzie Borden, The Quest: The Longest Drive, Passions, Dennis the Menace. Series: The Beverly Hillbillies. Guest: More than 45 appearances, including Meet Millie, Burns and Allen, Dragnet, Jack Benny Show, My Three Sons, The Texan, Rifleman, Alfred Hitchcock, Mannix, I Spy, All in the Family, Family Affair, Get Smart, The Incredible Hulk, The Lucy Show, Ironside, Nightstalker, M*A*S*H, Lou Grant Show, Hart to Hart, Yellow Rose, Murder She Wrote, General Hospital, Starsky & Hutch, Policewoman, Amazing Stories, Capitol, Passions, The Quest, Visions/KCET, Swallows Came Back, Return to Green Acres, Moving Target, From Out of the Night, The Walkers, The Bold and the Beautiful.

AMATEAU, ROD
Director, writer. b. New York, NY, Dec. 20, 1923. U.S. Army, 1941. 20th Century-Fox, 2nd unit dir.
PICTURES: Monsoon, Hook Line and Sinker (s.p. only), Pussycat Pussycat I Love You, The Statue, Where Does It Hurt?, The Wilby Conspiracy, The Money, Drive-In, Hitler's Son, The Seniors, The Osterman Weekend (2nd unit dir.), Lovelines, Thunder Run, Garbage Pail Kids (also s.p., prod.), Sunset (story only).
TELEVISION: Movies: Uncommon Valor, High School U.S.A., Swimsuit (prod.). Series: Schlitz Playhouse of Stars, Four Star Playhouse, General Electric Theatre, Private Secretary, Dennis Day Show, Lassie, Ray Milland Show, Bob Cummings Show, Burns & Allen Show (also prod.), Dobie Gillis, Mister Ed, Gilligan's Island, The Dukes of Hazzard, Supertrain, Enos.

AMENABAR, ALEJANDRO
Director, Writer. b. Santiago, Chile, March 31, 1972. Was raised and educated in Madrid. Wrote, directed and produced first short, La Cabeza, at age 19. Also composer with credits in eight pictures.
PICTURES: Himenoptero, Luna, Tesis, Open Your Eyes, The Others, Vanilla Sky (s.p.).

AMES, LOUIS B.
Executive. b. St. Louis, MO, Aug. 9, 1918. e. Washington U., St. Louis. m. Jetti Ames. Began as music consultant and staff dir. of musical programs for NBC; appt. music dir., WPIX, 1948; program mgr., WPIX, 1951. Assoc. prod., Today, NBC TV, 1954. Feature editor Home, 1957. Adm.-prod. NBC Opera, 1958. Dir. cultural prog. N.Y. World's Fair, 1960-63; dir. RCA Pavillion, N.Y. World's Fair, 1963-65; dir., Nighttime, TV, 1966; dir. of programming N.W. Ayer & Sons, Inc., 1969. Mgr. Station Services, Television Information Office. NY, 1973.

AMIEL, JON
Director, Producer. b. London, England, May 20, 1948. e. Cambridge. Was in charge of the Oxford & Cambridge Shakespeare Co., then literary mgr. for Hamptead Theatre Club where he started directing. Became story editor for BBC, then director.
PICTURES: Silent Twins, Queen of Hearts, Tune in Tomorrow, Sommersby, Copycat, The Man Who Knew Too Little, Entrapment, Simply Irresistible (prod. only), The Core.
TELEVISION: Movies: Dear Janet Rosenberg-Dear Mister Kooning, A Sudden Wrench, Gates of Gold, Busted. Mini-Series: The Singing Detective. Series: Tandoori Nights.

AMIN, MARK
Producer, Executive. b. Rafsanjan, Iran, 1950. e. M.B.A., marketing, John Anderson School of Business (UCLA), 1975. Began career in business ventures, 1975-81; co-founder, 20/20 Video, 1981-87; founder, Vidmark (now Trimark), 1984. Currently chairman & CEO, Trimark Holdings, Inc. (parent company of Trimark Pictures).
PICTURES: Exec. prod.: Demon Warp, The Sleeping Car, Whore, Servants of Twilight, Into the Sun, Interceptor, Leprechaun, Philadelphia Experiment II, Extreme Justice, Deadfall, Love and a .45, Curse of the Starving Class, Night of the Running Man, A Million to Juan, Frank and Jesse, Dangerous Touch, A Kid in King Arthur's Court, Kicking and Screaming, Separate Lives, True Crime, The Maddening, Leprechaun 3, Iron Eagle IV, Evolver, Aurora: Operation Intercept, Never Ever, The Dentist, Underworld, Sometimes They Come Back...Again,

Pinocchio's Revenge, Leprechaun 4: In Space, Crossworlds, Spring, Eve's Bayou, A Kid in Aladdin's Palace, Standoff, Chairman of the Board, Carnival of Souls, Ground Control, Trance, The Dentist II, Held Up, Diplomatic Siege, Let the Devil Wear Black, Cord, Skipped Parts, The Bogus Witch Project, Attraction, Krocodylus, X Change, Fear of Flying, Pursuit, After the Storm, Frida., The Prince & the Freshman.
TELEVISION: *Exec. prod.:* The Simple Life of Noah Dearborn, The Bogus Witch Project.

AMIS, SUZY

Actress. b. Oklahoma City, OK, Jan. 5, 1962. e. Heritage Hall, Oklahoma City. At 16 was introduced on the Merv Griffin Show by Eileen Ford whose modeling agency she worked for, as "The Face of the Eighties." After modeling and living in Europe, made film debut in Fandango (1985). Off-B'way debut: Fresh Horses (Theatre World Award).
PICTURES: Fandango, The Big Town, Plain Clothes, Rocket Gibraltar, Twister, Where the Heart Is, Rich in Love, Watch It, The Ballad of Little Jo, Two Small Bodies, Blown Away, The Usual Suspects, Nadja, One Good Turn, Titanic, The Ex, Cadillac Ranch, Firestorm, Judgment Day.
TELEVISION: *Movies:* The Beneficiary, Dead by Midnight, Last Stand at Saber River.

AMOS, JOHN

Actor. b. Newark, NJ, Dec. 27, 1941. e. East Orange H.S., Colorado State U, Long Beach City Col. Inducted as honorary Master Chief Petty Officer in U.S. Navy 1993. Worked as professional football player, social worker (heading the Vera Institute of Justice in NY), and advertising copywriter before writing television comedy material (for the Leslie Uggams Show) and performing as stand-up comedian in Greenwich Village. Has also dir. theatre with Bahamian Rep. Co. Artistic dir., John Harms Theatre, Englewood, NJ.
THEATRE: *L.A.:* Norman Is That You?, Master Harold...And the Boys, Split Second, The Emperor Jones. *B'way:* Tough to Get Help. NYSF: Twelfth Night. *Off-B'way:* The Past is the Past. Regional: Fences, Halley's Comet (also writer). *Foreign:* Life and Death of a Buffalo Soldier.
PICTURES: Vanishing Point (debut, 1971), Sweet Sweetback's Baadasssss Song, The World's Greatest Athlete, Let's Do It Again, Touched By Love, The Beastmaster, Dance of the Dwarfs, American Flyers, Coming to America, Lock Up, Die Hard 2, Ricochet, Two Evil Eyes (The Black Cat), Mac, Night Trap (Mardi Gras for the Devil), Hologram Man, For Better or Worse, A Woman Like That, The Player's Club, All Over Again, Ralph Ellison: An American Journey.
TELEVISION: *Movies:* The President's Plane is Missing, Future Cop, Cops and Robin, Willa, Alcatraz-The Whole Shocking Story, Bonanza-the Next Generation, The Rockford Files: Murder and Misdemeanors, Something to Sing About, Disappearing Acts. *Mini-Series:* Roots. *Series:* Mary Tyler Moore, The Funny Side, Maude, Good Times, Hunter, South by Southwest, 704 Hauser, The Fresh Prince of Bel-Air, The West Wing, The District. Guest: More than 50 appearances, including Bill Cosby Show, Love American Style, Sanford and Son, The Love Boat, Martin, Walker Texas Ranger, The Outer Limits, In the House, King of the Hill.

ANDERS, ALLISON

Director, Writer. b. Ashland, KY, Nov. 16, 1954. e. UCLA; Los Angeles. NY Film Critics Circle Award for Gas Food Lodging, (1992).
PICTURES: Border Radio (debut, 1987), Gas Food Lodging, Mi vida loca, Four Rooms (The Missing Ingredient segment), Grace of My Heart, Lover Girl (exec. prod. only), Sugar Town, Things Behind the Sun.
TELEVISION: Sex and the City, Grosse Pointe.

ANDERSON, DAVID LEROY

Special Effects/Makeup.
PICTURES: (As Dave Anderson:The Serpent and the Rainbow, Alien Nation, Never on Tuesday, Pet Sematary) As David Leroy Anderson: Shocker, Cadence, Beyond the Law, Alien 3, Death Becomes Her (prosthetic makeup), Loaded Weapon 1, The Chase, The Nutty Professor, Men in Black (Acad. Award, Best Makeup, 1997), Jane Austen's Mafia, Krippendorf's Tribe, The Nutty Professor II: The Klumps, The Brightness You Keep.
TELEVISION: Tuesdays With Morrie.

ANDERSON, GERRY

Hon. F.B.K.S., Producer, Director, Writer. b. London, England, April 14, 1929. Entered industry in 1946. Chmn./man. dir. Gerry Anderson Productions, Ltd. Over 320 pictures produced for TV worldwide. Co-founded Anderson Burr Pictures, 1981. Prod. Terrahawks in association with London Weekend Television, 1982; second series, Terrahawks, 1984. Space Police pilot for series in assoc. with TVS, 1985-6. Dick Spanner stop motion series for Channel Four, 1987. Entered commercials as a dir.: numerous commercials incl. Royal Bank of Scotland, Children's World, Domestos, Shout, Scotch Tape, etc. Anglo Russian Cartoon Series Astro Force and lecture tour An Evening with Garry Anderson, 1992.
PICTURES: Producer: Crossroads to Crime (also dir.), Thunderbirds Are Go (s.p. only), Thunderbird 6 (also s.p.), Journey to the Far Side of the Sun (also story), Invasion UFO (exec. prod., s.p. and creator, dir.) Invaders from the Deep, The Thunderbirds (writer-characters).
TELEVISION: *Movies:* Journey Through the Black Sun, Into Infinity, Destination Moonbase Alpha (exec. prod., s.p.), Cosmic

Princess (creator), Alien Attack, (also s.p. and creator), I Love Christmas. *Series:* The Adventures of Twizzle, Torchy the Battery Boy, Four Feather Falls, Supercar, Fireball XL5, Stingray, Thunderbirds 2086, Captain Scarlet vs. the Mysterons (writer/creator only), Joe 90, The Secret Service, The Protectors, UFO, Space 1999, Terrahawks, Dick Spanner, Space Precinct, Lavender Castle.

ANDERSON, GILLIAN

Actress. b. Chicago, IL, Aug. 9, 1968. e. Cornell University, NY; DePaul University, Chicago.
PICTURES: The Turning, Three at Once, A Matter of Choice, The Mighty, Chicago Cab, The X-Files: Fight the Future, Playing by Heart, The House of Mirth.
TELEVISION: Movies: Why Planes Go Down (narrator) Series: The X-Files, Future Fantastic. *Guest:* Class of '96, The Simpsons (voice), Frasier (voice), Harsh Realm (voice), The Martin Short Show, V. Graham Norton, Parkinson.

ANDERSON, HARRY

Actor. b. Newport, RI, Oct. 14, 1952. m. actress-magician Leslie Pollack. Performed magic show prior to plays at Oregon Shakespeare Festival. Also opening act for Kenny Rogers, Debbie Reynolds and Roger Miller in Las Vegas. Owner of magic shop in Ashland, OR. Received Stage Magician of Year Award, National Acad. of Magician Arts and Sciences.
PICTURES: The Escape Artist, The Best of the Big Laff Off, Explore Our World.
TELEVISION: *Movies:* Spies Lies and Naked Thighs; The Absent-Minded Professor, Magic in the Magic Kingdom, Mother Goose Rock 'n' Rhyme, It, Circus of the Stars and Sideshow, Circus of the Stars Goes to Disneyland, Harvey. *Series:* Night Court (Emmy nom. also writer, dir.), Our Time, Dave's World, The Science of Magic. *Guest:* Cheers, The Tonight Show, David Letterman, Saturday Night Live, Wil Shriner, Tales from the Crypt, Parker Lewis Can't Lose, Hearts Afire, Night Stand, The John Larroquette Show, Lois & Clark: New Adventures of Superman, Penn & Teller's Sin City Spectacular, Noddy, Son of the Beach.

ANDERSON, J. WAYNE

Executive. b. Clifton Forge, VA, Feb. 19, 1947. e. USA Signal School (1965-67); USN Service Schools (1967). USMC, 1965-69; opened and operated 1st military 35mm m.p. theatre, DaNang, Vietnam, 1967-69. R/C Theatres, dist. mgr., 1971-75; v.p., 1976-83; pres./COO, 1983-present. Bd. of dirs., Maryland Permanent Bank & Trust co., 1988-present; chmn., 1992-present. Member of NATO, bd. of dirs., 1987-present; technical advancement committee, 1981-present; chmn., 1991-present. Inter-Society for the Enhancement of Theatrical Presenation, 1986-present. Huntsman bd. of dirs., 1979-83; pres., 1982-83. Member: NRA, 1970-life; Will Rogers Inst., 1988-present; Presidential Task Force, 1990-life.

ANDERSON, KEVIN

Actor. b. Gurnee, Illinois, Jan. 13, 1960. e. Goodman School. Member of Chicago's Steppenwolf Theatre where he starred in Orphans. Moved with the play to New York (1985) and later starred in the London production, as well as the film version.
THEATRE: *NY:* Orphans (Theatre World Award), Moonchildren, Brilliant Tracers, Orpheus Descending. *London:* Sunset Boulevard.
PICTURES: Risky Business (debut, 1983), Pink Nights, Orphans, A Walk on the Moon, Miles From Home, In Country, Sleeping With the Enemy, Liebestraum, Hoffa, The Night We Never Met, Rising Sun, A Thousand Acres, Eye of God, Firelight, A Thousand Acres, Gregory's Two Girls, Rapid Transit (stunts), Shearer's Breakfast, Doe Boy, When Strangers Appear.
TELEVISION: *Movies:* Orpheus Descending, Hale the Hero, The Wrong Man, The Hunt for the Unicorn Killer, Ruby's Bucket of Blood, Monday Night Mayhem, Power and Beauty. *Series:* Nothing Sacred. *Special:* Hale the Hero.

ANDERSON, LONI

Actress. b. St. Paul, MN, Aug. 5, 1946. e. U. of Minnesota. Taught school before acting.
PICTURES: Stroker Ace, The Lonely Guy (cameo), All Dogs Go to Heaven (voice), Munchie, A Night at the Roxbury, 3 Ninjas: High Noon at Mega Mountain.
TELEVISION: *Movies:* The Magnificent Magnet of Santa Mesa, Three on a Date, The Jayne Mansfield Story, Sizzle, Night of 100 Stars, Country Gold, My Mother's Secret Life, A Letter to Three Wives, Stranded, Blondie and Dagwood (voice), Necessity, A Whisper Kills, Too Good to Be True, Sorry Wrong Number, Coins in the Fountain, White Hot: The Mysterious Murder of Thelma Todd, The Price She Paid, Gambler V: Playing for Keeps, Without Warning, Deadly Family Secrets. *Series:* WKRP in Cincinnati, Partners in Crime, Easy Street, Nurses.

ANDERSON, MELISSA SUE

Actress. b. Berkeley, CA, Sept. 26, 1962. Took up acting at suggestion of a dancing teacher. Did series of commercials; gained role in episode of Brady Bunch; episode of Shaft. Gained fame as Mary Ingalls on Little House on the Prairie series (Emmy nom.).
PICTURES: Skatetown USA, Happy Birthday to Me, Chattanooga Choo Choo, Far North, Looking Your Best, Dead Men Don't Die.
TELEVISION: *Movies:* More than 20 movies, including The Loneliest Runner, James at 15, Where Have All the Children Gone, Forbidden Nights, Earthquake in NY. *Series:* The Little House on the Prairie. Guest: More than 25 appearances incl. Bewitched, Brady Bunch.

ANDERSON, MICHAEL
Director. b. London, England, Jan. 30, 1920. e. France, Germany. Ent. motion picture industry as actor, 1936. Son is actor Michael Anderson, Jr.
PICTURES: More than 35 dir. picture credits, including Private Angelo (debut, 1949; co-dir. with Peter Ustinov), Waterfront Women, Hell Is Sold Out, Night Was Our Friend, 1984, Around the World in Eighty Days, The Shoes of the Fisherman, Logan's Run, Murder by Phone, Millennium, Summer of the Monkeys, The New Adventures of Pinnocchio.
TELEVISION: Movies: Sword of Gideon, Young Catherine, The Sea Wolf, Rugged Gold, Captains Courageous, 20,000 Leagues Under the Sea. Mini-series: The Martian Chronicles. Series: Scales of Justice.

ANDERSON, MICHAEL, JR.
Actor. b. London, England, Aug. 6, 1943. Father is director Michael Anderson. Ent. films as child actor, 1954.
PICTURES: More than 15 picture credits, incl. The Moonraker (1958), The Greatest Story Ever Told, The Sons of Katie Elder, Logan's Run, Nightkill, Sunset Grill, Terminal Rush.
TELEVISION: Movies: More than 12 tv movie credits, incl. The Day Before Sunday, The House That Would Not Die, Rent-A-Kid, Elvis Meets Nixon.Mini-series: Washington: Behind Closed Doors, Martian Chronicles. Series: The Monroes, Capitol.Guest: More than 35 appearances incl. Sir Francis Drake, Police Story, Highlander, Kung Fu: The Legend Continues, Psi-Factor.

ANDERSON, PAUL THOMAS
Director, Writer, b. Sudio City, CA, Jan. 1, 1970. LA Film Crits. Award, New Generation, 1997. BSFC Award for Best New Filmmaker for Boogie Nights in 1997. Garnered Best Screenplay Acad. Award nominations for Boogie Nights and Magnolia. Won the Golden Berlin Bear award for Magnolia as best picture at Berlin Int'l. Film Fest. (insert year here.)
PICTURES: The Dirk Diggler Story (short), Cigarettes and Coffee(short), Sydney (aka Hard Eight), Boogie Nights (also prod., Acad. Award nom.), Flagpole Special (short), Magnolia (Acad. Award nom.), Punch Drunk Love (Cannes Golden Palm Award), A Decade Under the Influence (documentary).
TELEVISION: Movies: SNL Fanatic.

ANDERSON, RICHARD
Actor. b. Long Branch, NJ, Aug. 8, 1926. e. University H.S. W. Los Angeles. Served in U.A. Army, WWII. Began acting career in summer theatre in Santa Barbara and Laguna Playhouse where spotted by MGM executives, who signed him to six-year contract. Appeared in 26 films for MGM before leaving studio. More than 100 credits to his name since 1949.
PICTURES: More than 50 picture credits, including Twelve O'Clock High (1949), The Long Hot Summer, Ride to Hangman's Tree, Tora! Tora! Tora!, The Retrievers, The Player Gettysburg, The Johnny Johnson Trial.
TELEVISION: Movies: Neary 30 credits since 1970, including Along Came A Spider, The Stepford Children, Hoover vs. the Kennedys: The Second Civil War, In the Lake of the Woods. Series: Bus Stop, The Lieutenant, Perry Mason, Dan August, The Six Million Dollar Man, The Bionic Woman, Cover Up, Dynasty, Kung Fu: The Legend Continues.Guest: More than 110 appearances, including Ironside, The Big Valley, Mannix, The Mod Squad, The FBI, Gunsmoke, Unhappily Ever After.

ANDERSON, RICHARD DEAN
Actor. b. Minneapolis, MN. Jan. 23, 1950. Planned to become professional hockey player. Became a street mime and jester. Performed with his own rock band, Ricky Dean and Dante.
PICTURES: Young Doctors In Love, Summer Jobs, Ordinary Heroes, Fallout (voice).
TELEVISION: Movies: MacGyver, In the Eyes of a Stranger, Through the Eyes of a Killer, Past the Bleachers, Pandora's Clock, Stargate SG-1: Children of the Gods, Firehouse. Series: General Hospital, Seven Brides for Seven Brothers, Emerald Point N.A.S., MacGyver, Legend, Stargate SG-1.(also exec. prod.).

ANDERSON, SARAH PIA
Director.
TELEVISION: Movies: A Woman Calling, Prime Suspect 4: Inner Circles. Mini-series: The Modern World: Ten Great Writers, Plastic Man. Series: Doctor Finlay, Alleyn Mysteries, ER, Profiler, Leaving L.A., Ally McBeal, Nothing Sacred, Strong Medicine, James Cameron's Dark Angel, Gilmore Girls, The District, Level 9, Heart of the City.

ANDERSON, SHERYL J.
Writer.
TELEVISION: Series: Parker Lewis Can't Lose, Charmed, (also co-exec. prod.)

ANDERSON, SYLVIA
Producer. Writer (Pinewood Studios). r. n. Sylvia Thamm. b. London, England. e. London U. Entered m. p. ind. 1960. First pub. novel, Love and Hisses. UK rep for Home Box Office of America.
PICTURES: Thunderbirds Are Go, Thunderbird Six (prod.), Journey to the Far Side of the Sun, Invaders from the Deep (prod. only), The Thunderbirds (only writing/characters).
TELEVISION: Creator &/or Prod.: Space 1999, UFO, Thunderbirds, Journey Through the Black Sun, Destination Moonbase Alpha, Alien Attack, I Love Christmas.

ANDERSON, WES
Director, Writer. b. Houston, TX, May 1, 1969. e. U. of Texas, BA.
PICTURES: Bottle Rocket, Rushmore (also exec. prod.; Independent Spirit Award, best dir., New Generation Award, L.A. Film Critics), The Royal Tenenbaums (also prod.; Acad. Award nom., BAFTA nom. WGA nom. for screenplay).

ANDERSSON, BIBI
Actress. b. Stockholm, Sweden, Nov. 11, 1935. e. Royal Dramatic Theatre School (Kungliga Dramatiska Teatern).
PICTURES: Featured in 70 pictures, incl. Dum-Bom (debut, 1953), Sir Arne's Treasure, Smiles of a Summer Night, The Seventh Seal, Wild Strawberries, The Magician, Brink of Life, The Face, The Devil's Eye, Square of Violence, Pleasure Garden, The Swedish Mistress, Not to Mention These Women, My Sister My Love, Persona, Duel at Diablo, A Question of Rape, The Passion of Anna, The Kremlin Letter, The Touch, I Never Promised You a Rose Garden, An Enemy of the People, The Concorde: Airport '79, Prosperous Times, The Marmalade Revolution, Black Crows, Exposed, Manika, A Passing Season, The Butterfly's Dream, Little Big Sister, Light Keeps Me Company, Shit Happens, Anna, Elina: As If I Wasn't Here..
TELEVISION: Movies: Among 17 appearances are Rabies, Wallenberg—A Hero's Story, Till Julia, The Lost Prince.

ANDRESS, URSULA
Actress. b. Bern, Switzerland, Mar. 19, 1936. To Rome as teen where she landed roles in Italian Films.
PICTURES: Sins of Casanova (debut, 1954), An American in Rome, The Tempest Has Gone, La Catena dell'Odio, Anyone Can Play, Dr. No, Four For Texas, Fun in Acapulco, Nightmare in the Sun, She, The Tenth Victim, What's New Pussycat?, Up to His Ears, Once Before I Die, The Blue Max, Casino Royale, The Southern Star, Perfect Friday, Red Sun, Africa Express, Scaramouche, The Sensuous Nurse, Slave of the Cannibal God, Tigers in Lipstick, The Fifth Musketeer, Primitive Desires, Four Tigers in Lipstick, Clash of the Titans, Reporters, Mexico in Flames, Liberte/Egalite/Choucroute, Class Reunion, Cremaster 5.
TELEVISION: Movies: Man Against the Mob: The Chinatown Murders, Cave of the Golden Rose III, Cave of the Golden Rose IV, In 80 Jahren um die Welt. Mini-Series: Peter the Great. Series: Falcon Crest.

ANDREWS, ANTHONY
Actor, Producer. b. London, England, Dec. 1, 1948. e. Royal Masonic Sch., Herts. Regional stage debut, 1967.
PICTURES: Take Me High/Hot Property (debut, 1973), Operation Daybreak, Under the Volcano, The Holcroft Covenant, The Second Victory, The Lighthorsemen, Hanna's War, Lost in Siberia, The Law Lord, Haunted (also co-prod.).
TELEVISION: A Beast With Two Backs, Upstairs Downstairs, A War of Children, Romeo and Juliet, QB VII, Ivanhoe, The Scarlet Pimpernel, Danger UXB, Brideshead Revisited, Sparkling Cyanide, A.D., Bluegrass, Suspicion, The Woman He Loved, Columbo Goes to the Guillotine, Danielle Steel's Jewels, Strange Case of Dr. Jekyll and Mr. Hyde, Hands of a Murderer, Heartstones, Mothertime, David Copperfield, Love in a Cold Climate.

ANDREWS, JULIE
Actress, Singer. r.n. Julia Wells. b. Walton-on-Thames, England. Oct. 1, 1935. m. dir./writer Blake Edwards. Debut, England Starlight Roof Revue London Hippodrome, 1948. Author of Mandy, Last of the Really Great Whangdoodles, 1973.
THEATRE: NY: The Boy Friend, My Fair Lady, Camelot, Putting It Together, Victor/Victoria.
PICTURES: Mary Poppins (debut, 1964; Acad. Award), The Americanization of Emily, The Sound of Music (Acad. Award nom.), Hawaii, Torn Curtain, Thoroughly Modern Millie, Star!, Darling Lili, The Tamarind Seed, 10, S.O.B, Victor/Victoria (Acad. Award nom.), The Man Who Loved Women, That's Life, Duet For One, A Fine Romance, Relative Values, The Princess Diaries, Who Shot Victor Fox, Shrek 2.
TELEVISION: Movies: Our Sons, One Special Night, On Golden Pond, Eloise at the Plaza, Eloise at Christmastime. Series: The Julie Andrews Hour (1972-73), Julie. Specials: Appeared in more than 15 specials, incl. Julie and Carol at Carnegie Hall, The World of Walt Disney, Julie and Carol at Lincoln Center, Julie on Sesame Street, Julie Andrews' Christmas Special, Julie Andrews: My Favorite Things, Julie Andrews:The Sound of Christmas, Julie and Carol: Together Again.

ANDREWS, NAVEEN
Actor. b. England, 1971. e. Guildhall School of Music and Drama.
PICTURES: London Kills Me, Wild West, Kama Sutra: A Tale of Love, The English Patient, True Love and Chaos, Mighty Joe Young, Drowning on Dry Land, Blessed Art Thou, Rollerball, The Ground Beneath Her Feet.TELEVISION: Movies: Double Vision, My Own Country, The Peacock Spring, The Chippendales Murder. Series: The Beast.

ANGELOPOULOS, THEO
Director, Writer, Producer, Actor. b. Athens, Greece, April 17, 1935.
PICTURES: Reconstruction, Days of 36, The Travelling Players, The Hunters, Alexander the Great, Voyage to Kythera (Cannes Film Fest. Award, Best Screenplay, 1984), The Beekeeper, Landscape in the Mist, The Suspended Step of the Stork, The

Gaze of Odysseus (Cannes Film Fest. Award, Jury Prize, 1995), Lumiere and Company, Eternity and a Day.

ANGERS, AVRIL
Actress, Comedienne, Singer. b. Liverpool, England, April 18, 1922. Stage debut at age of 14; screen debut in 1947 in Lucky Mascot (The Brass Monkey).
THEATRE: The Mating Game, Cockie, Murder at the Vicarage, Little Me, Norman, Is That You?, Blithe Spirit, Oklahoma!, Gigi, The Killing of Sister George, Cards on the Table, When We Are Married, Cinderella, Easy Virtue, Post Mortem, Crazy for You.
PICTURES: Miss Pilgrim's Progress, Don't Blame the Stork, Women Without Men, Green Man, Devils of Darkness, Be My Guest, Three Bites of the Apple, The Family Way, Two a Penny, The Best House in London, Staircase, There's a Girl in My Soup, Forbush and the Penguins, Gollocks, Confessions of a Driving Instructor, Dangerous Davies.
TELEVISION: Movies: The Millionairess. Series: How Do You View, All Aboard, The More We are Together, Odd Man Out, No Appointment Necessary, Just Liz, Common As Muck.

ANISTON, JENNIFER
Actress. b. Sherman Oaks, CA, Feb. 11, 1969. e. NY High School of the Performing Arts. Daughter of actor John Aniston. m. Brad Pitt. Started training as a drama student in high school. In 1987, after graduation, appeared in For Dear Life and Dancing on Checker's Grave (off B'way.) Won People's Choice Awards, USA, favorite female TV performer, 2001, 2002, 2003.
PICTURES: Leprechaun, Waiting for Woody, She's the One, 'Til There Was You, Picture Perfect, The Object of My Affection, Dream for an Insomniac The Thin Pink Line, Office Space, The Iron Giant (voice), Time of our Lives, Rock Star, The Good Girl, Bruce Almighty.
TELEVISION: Movies: How I Spent My Summer, Camp Cucamonga. Series: Molloy (debut, 1989), Ferris Bueller, The Edge, Muddling Through, Friends (TV Guide Award, 2000, Emmy Award, 2002, Golden Globe, best perf. by actress in tv series, 2003). Guest: Quantum Leap, Herman's Head, The Larry Sanders Show, Burke's Law, Partners, Ellen, Hercules (voice), South Park (voice). Special: Friends: The Stuff You've Never Seen, Bad Hair Days

ANN-MARGRET
Actress, Singer, Dancer. r.n. Ann-Margret Olsson. b. Valsjobyn, Sweden, April 28, 1941. e. New Trier H.S., Winnetka, IL; Northwestern U. m. Roger Smith, actor, dir., prod. Radio shows, toured with band; worked with George Burns in Las Vegas. TV debut, Jack Benny Show, 1961.
PICTURES: Pocketful of Miracles (debut, 1961), State Fair, Bye Bye Birdie, Viva Las Vegas, Kitten With a Whip, The Pleasure Seekers, Bus Riley's Back in Town, Once A Thief, The Cincinnati Kid, Made in Paris, Stagecoach, The Swinger, Murderer's Row, The Prophet, The Tiger and the Pussycat, Rebus, Criminal Affair, RPM, C. C. & Company, Carnal Knowledge (Acad. Award nom.), The Outside Man, The Train Robbers, Tommy (Acad. Award nom.), The Last Remake of Beau Geste, The Twist, Joseph Andrews, The Cheap Detective, Magic, The Villain, Middle Age Crazy, I Ought To Be in Pictures, Lookin' to Get Out, The Return of the Soldier, Twice in a Lifetime, 52 Pick-up, A Tiger's Tail, A New Life, Newsies, Grumpy Old Men, Grumpier Old Men, The Limey, The Last Producer, Any Given Sunday, A Woman's A Helluva Thing, The 10th Kingdom: The Making of an Epic, Interstate 60.
TELEVISION: Movies: Who Will Love My Children?, A Streetcar Named Desire, The Two Mrs. Grenvilles, Our Sons, Nobody's Children, Following Her Heart, Blue Rodeo, Life of the Party: The Pamela Harriman Story, Happy Face Murders. Mini-Series: Queen, Scarlett, Perfect Murder Perfect Town, The 10th Kingdom, Blonde. Series: Four Corners.

ANNAUD, JEAN-JACQUES
Writer, Director. b. Draveil, France, Oct. 1, 1943. Began career as film dir. in French army, making educational pictures. Also directed 500 commercials. Received 1989 cinema prize from French Acad. for career's work. Directed IMAX film Wings of Courage.
PICTURES: Black and White in Color (winner of Best Foreign Language Film Oscar, 1978), Too Shy to Try (writer only), Coup de Tete (Hothead), Quest for Fire (Cesar Award for best dir., 1982), The Name of the Rose, The Bear (Cesar Award for best dir., 1989), The Lover, Wings of Courage, Seven Years In Tibet, Running Free (s.p. and prod.) Enemy at the Gates (also prod.), Two Brothers (also prod., exec. prod.).

ANSARA, MICHAEL
Actor. b. Syria, April 15, 1922. e. Pasadena Playhouse. Served in U.S. Army; then summer stock, road shows.
PICTURES: Appeared in more than 70 pictures, incl. Soldiers Three, Only the Valiant, Julius Caesar, Mohammad Messenger of God, The Manitou, Gas, Access Code, Knights of the City, Assasination, Lethal (KGB: The Secret War), Border Shootout., Johnny Mysto: Boy Wizard, The Long Road Home.
TELEVISION: Movies: How I Spent My Summer Vacation, Powderkeg, Call to Danger, Ordeal, Shootout in a One-Dog Town, Barbary Coast, The Fantastic World of D.C. Collins, Batman Beyond: The Movie. Series: Broken Arrow, Law of the Plainsman, I Dream of Jeannie (dir.), Buck Rogers in the 25th Century, Rambo (voice), Batman: The Animated Series (voice), The New Batman/Superman Adventures (voice). Mini-Series:: Centennial.

ANSCHUTZ, PHILIP
Executive, Producer. b. 1939, Russell, KS. e. U. of Kansas, 1961. Entered U. of Virgina law school but returned to help with family oil wildcatting business. On first discovery of oil in 1967, Anschutz bought up surrounding oil leases on credit. When a spark ignited the entire field, threatening to bankrupt him he called in the famed firefighter, "Red" Adair, who was reluctant to cap the blazing well without assurance of compensation. Anschutz contacted Universal Studios, who were filming a story on Adair at the time, and sold them rights to film his fire, for $100,000, enough to assure payment to Adair and continued operations. In 1982, Anshutz sold land to Mobil for $500 million and 17% royalties. In 1984, he bought the small Denver & Rio Grande Western Railroad. In 1988, he took control of the Southern Pacific Railroad. Developed a fiber-optics network along the railroad right-of-way. In 1996, the Southern Pacific was sold to the Union Pacific Railroad for $5.4 billion. Anshutz retained a 5.4% stake in the combined company. In addition, he retained the telecomm company and the fiber-optics network it was based on along the railroad right-of-way. 1997, this company, now called Qwest Communications, was taken public. As a public company, Anshutz still owns 18%. Now focusing on entertainment: bought stakes in troubled United Artists, Edwards and Regal theatres comprising 20% of U.S. movie screens. Founded companies Crusader, Walden Media to develop films with family-friendly bent. Trustee, Kansas University Endowment, John F. Kennedy Center for the Performing Arts; hon. board member, Museum of Natural History, New York and the National Associates Board of the Smithsonian Institute, Washington, D.C. Director, The Anschutz Foundation
PICTURES: Producer: A Sound of Thunder.

ANSPACH, SUSAN
Actress. b. New York, NY, Nov. 23, 1945. e. Catholic U., Washington, DC. After school returned to NY and in 3 years had performed in 11 B'way and off-B'way prods. Moved to Los Angeles and entered films.
PICTURES: The Landlord (debut, 1970), Five Easy Pieces, Play It Again Sam, Blume in Love, The Big Fix, Running, The Devil and Max Devlin, Gas, Montenegro, Misunderstood, Blue Monkey, Into the Fire, Blood Red, Back to Back, Candle Smoke, Alien X Factor.
TELEVISION: Movies: I Want to Keep My Baby, The Secret Life of John Chapman, Rosetti & Ryan, Mad Bull, The Last Giraffe, Portrait of an Escort, The First Time, Deadly Encounter, Cagney & Lacey: The Return, Dancing at the Harvest Moon. Series: The Yellow Rose, The Slap Maxwell Story. Mini-Series: Space.

ANSPAUGH, DAVID
Director, Producer. b. Decatur, IN, Sept. 24, 1946. e. Indiana U., 1965-70; USC, 1974-76. School teacher, Aspen, CO, 1970-74.
PICTURES: Director: Hoosiers (debut, 1986), Fresh Horses, Rudy, Moonlight and Valentino, Wise Girls, The Game of Their Lives..
TELEVISION: Movies: Deadly Care, In the Company of Darkness, Swing Vote, Two Against Time. Series: Hill St. Blues (assoc. prod. 1980-81; prod.-dir. 1981-82; prod.-dir. 1983-84, dir. 1985. DGA Award: 1983, 2 Emmy Awards for producing: 1982, 1983), St. Elsewhere (dir.), Miami Vice (dir.).

ANTHONY, LYSETTE
Actress. r.n. Lysette Chodzko. b. London, England, 1963. Stage work incl. Bristol Old Vic, 1988-90.
PICTURES: Krull, Night Train to Murder, L'Etincelle, Dombey & Son, A Drop in the Ocean, Looking for Eileen, The Emperor's New Clothes, Without A Clue, Switch, The Pleasure Principle, Husbands and Wives, The Hour of the Pig, Look Who's Talking Now, Save Me, Face the Music, The Hard Truth, A Brilliant Disguise, Affair Play, Dr. Jekyll and Ms. Hyde, Dracula: Dead and Loving It, Dead Cold, Robison Crusoe, Prince of Lies, Man of Her Dreams, Misbegotten, Tale of the Mummy, Beneath Loch Ness, Farewell to Harry.
TELEVISION: Movies: Ivanhoe, Oliver Twist, Frost in May, Princess Daisy, Jack the Ripper, The Lady and the Highwayman, A Ghost in Monte Carlo, Target of Suspicion, Trilogy of Terror II, Hotel!. Mini-Series: Oliver Twist, The Bretts. Series: Crossroads, Auf Wiedersehen Pet, Three Up Two Down (BBC), Dark Shadows, Cluedo, Night & Day.

ANTON, SUSAN
Actress. b. Oak Glen, CA, Oct. 12, 1950. Concert & night club singer. Country album & single Killin' Time went top 10 on Country charts. Made B'way debut in Hurlyburly, 1985. Also in The Will Rogers Follies. Off-B'way in X-mas a Go-Go. 1992, hon. chmn. of Amer. Cancer Soc., Calif. Special Olympics, & hon. capt. U.S. Woman's Olympic Volleyball Team.
PICTURES: Goldengirl, Spring Fever, Cannonball Run II, Making Mr. Right, Lena's Holiday.
TELEVISION: Movies: The Great American Beauty Contest, Baywatch: River of No Return. Series: Baywatch. Guest: Quantum Leap, Blossom, Murder She Wrote, Night Court, The Famous Teddy Z, Circus of the Stars, The Ben Stiller Show, The Larry Sanders Show. City Guys.

ANTONIO, LOU
Director, Actor, Writer, Producer, b. Oklahoma City, OK, January 23, 1934. e. U. of OK. Two Emmy Noms for TV Movies.
THEATRE: Actor: The Buffalo Skinner (Theatre World Award), various other productions.
PICTURES: Actor: America America, Hawaii, Cool Hand Luke, The Phynx. Dir.: The Gypsy Warriors.
TELEVISION: Movies: Director: More than 35 dir. credits, incl. Lanigan's Rabbi, Someone I Touched, Something for Joey, The

Critical List, Silent Victory-The Kitty O'Neil Story, A Real American Hero, We're Fighting Back, Something So Right, A Good Sport, Threesome, Rearview Mirror, Face to Face, The Outside Woman (also prod.), Dark Holiday (also exec. prod.), Between Friends, Mayflower Madam, Pals, 13 at Dinner, This Gun for Hire, Lies Before Kisses, The Last Prostitute, The Rape of Dr. Willis, A Taste for Killing, Nightmare in the Daylight, The Contender, *Director: Mini-Series:* Rich Man, Poor Man (co-dir.), Breaking Up Is Hard to Do, The Star Maker. *Series:* Dir. for 34 series, incl. The Flying Nun (1967), Banacek, Rich Man Poor Man Book II, Party of Five, Chicago Hope, American Gothic, Dark Skies, Dawson's Creek, Vengeance Unlimited, Get Real, The West Wing, C.S.I.: Crime Scene Investigation, First Monday.

ANTONIONI, MICHELANGELO
Director, Writer. b. Ferrara, Italy, Sept. 29, 1912. e. Centro Spiremintale di Cinematografia; degree in economics. Film critic on local newspaper; film critic with Corriere Padano, 1936-40; script writer for Un Pilota Ritorna, I due Foscari and asst. dir. for Les Visiteurs du Soir, 1942; with Italia Libera and on edit. staff of Cinema, 1944-45. First films as dir. were short documentaries including: Gente del Po (1943-47), N.U., L'Amorosa Menzogna, Superstizione, Sette canne un vestito, followed by latter works La Villa dei Mostri, La Funivia del Faloria, Kumbha Mela, Roma, Noto—Mandorli—Vulcano—Stromboli—Carnevale. Recipient of: Palme d'Or, 1987; Prix Lumiere, 1990; h.c. degree, Univ. of Berkeley, 1993; honorary Academy Award, 1995; Legion d'Honneur, Paris 1996 and many others. Prof. at Cornell Univ., NY.
PICTURES: *Director/Writer:* Story of a Love Affair (feature debut as dir., 1950), The Vanquished, Lady Without Camelias, Love in the City (segment: When Love Fails), The Girl Friends, The Outcry, I Am a Camera, L'Avventura, The Night, Eclipse, Red Desert, I Tre Volti/Three Faces of a Woman (dir. only; segment: Prefazione), Blow-Up (Acad. Award nom. for dir.), Zabriskie Point, Chung Kuo (documentary), The Passenger, The Oberwald Mystery, Identification of a Woman, The Crew, Beyond the Clouds (co-dir., co-s.p., with Wim Wenders), Just to Be Together, Destinazione Verna.

ANTONOWSKY, MARVIN
Executive. b. New York, NY, Jan. 31, 1929. e. City Coll. of New York, B.A., M.B.A. Joined Kenyon and Eckhart in 1957 for which was media research dir. then mktg. v.p. With Norman, Craig, & Kummel as v.p., mktg. svcs. Became v.p. in charge of media research and spot buying at J. Walter Thompson, 1965. Joined ABC-TV as v.p. in charge of research, 1969. Left to become v.p. in charge of programming at NBC-TV. Became sr. v.p., Universal-TV, 1976. Joined Columbia Pictures as pres., mktg. & research, 1979. Rejoined MCA/Universal Pictures as pres, mktg., 1983. Formed Marvin Antonowsky & Assoc., mktg. consultancy firm, 1989. Rejoined Columbia Pictures in 1990 as exec. v.p. and asst. to chmn. Joined Price Entertainment as exec. v.p., 1993. Marketing consultant to movie distributors.

ANWAR, GABRIELLE
Actress. b. Laleham, England, Feb. 4,1970.
PICTURES: Manifesto (debut, 1989), If Looks Could Kill, Wild Hearts Can't Be Broken, Scent of a Woman, For Love or Money, The Three Musketeers, Body Snatchers, Things to Do in Denver When You're Dead, Innocent Lies, The Grave, Nevada (also co-prod.), Kimberly, The Guilty, The Manor, If You Only Knew, North Beach, Without Malice, Flying Virus, Mob Dot Com.
TELEVISION: *Movies:* Prince Caspian and the Voyage of the Dawn Treader, In Pursuit of Honor, The Ripper, My Little Assassin, How to Marry a Billionaire: A Christmas Tale, Without Malice, Case of Evil. *Mini-Series:* First Born. *Series:* Press Gang, Fallen Angels, John Doe. *Guest:* The Practice, Beverly Hills 90210, The Storyteller.

APATOW, JUDD
Producer, Writer. b. 1968
PICTURES: Crossing the Bridge (assoc. prod. only), Heavyweights (exec. prod. and actor), Happy Gilmore (s.p. only), Celtic Pride (s.p., exec. prod.), The Cable Guy (s.p., exec. prod.), The Wedding Singer (s.p. only), The Whistlebowner, Action News (prod. only).
TELEVISION: *Movies:* The TV Wheel (writer only), Life on Parole.*Series:* The Larry Sanders Show (dir. only), The Ben Stiller Show (actor only), Freaks and Geeks (exec. prod, dir., writer), Undeclared (writer, exec. prod., dir.).

APPLEGATE, CHRISTINA
Actress. b. Hollywood, CA Nov. 25, 1972. m. actor Johnathon Schaech.
PICTURES: Jaws of Satan (debut, 1980), Streets, Don't Tell Mom the Babysitter's Dead, Across the Moon, Wild Bill, Mars Attacks!, Nowhere, The Big Hit, Jane Austen's Mafia, The Giving Tree, Out in Fifty, Just Visiting, The Sweetest Thing, A View From the Top, Wonderland, Grand Theft Parsons, Surviving Christmas.
TELEVISION: *Movies:* Grace Kelly, Dance 'til Dawn, Prince Charming. *Series:* Washington, Heart of the City, Married...With Children, Jesse. *Guest:* Charles in Charge, Amazing Stories, 21 Jump Street, Top of the Heap, Friends.

APTED, MICHAEL
Director, Producer. b. Aylesbury, England, Feb. 10, 1941. e. Cambridge. Broke into industry at Granada TV in England in early 1960s as trainee, researcher and finally director. By 1965, was prod.-dir. for local programs and current affairs then staff

drama dir. for TV series, plays and serials. In late 1960s left Granada to freelance.
PICTURES: *Director:* Triple Echo, Stardust, The Squeeze, Agatha, Coal Miner's Daughter, Continental Divide, Gorky Park, The River Rat (exec. prod. only), Firstborn, Critical Condition, Gorillas in the Mist: The Story of Dian Fossey, Class Action, Thunderheart, Dracula (exec. prod. only), Blink, Nell, Extreme Measures, The World Is Not Enough, Enigma, Enough, Tell No One.
TELEVISION: *Movies: Director:* Another Sunday and Sweet F.A., The Reporters, Play for Today: Kisses at Fifty, Joy, High Kampf, Jack Point, The Collection, Stronger Than the Sun, P'tang Yang Kipperbang, The Long Way Home, Always Outnumbered, Nathan Dixon. *Series:* Haunted, Big Breadwinner Hog, The Lovers, My Life and Times, New York News.

ARAKI, GREGG
Director. Editor, Producer, Writer. b. Los Angeles, CA, Dec. 17, 1959.
PICTURES: Three Bewildered People in the Night (1987), The Long Weekend (O'Despair), The Living End, Totally F***ed Up, The Doom Generation, Nowhere, Splendor.
TELEVISION: *Movies:* This Is How the World Ends.

ARAU, ALFONSO
Director, Actor. b. Mexico City, Mexico, Jan. 11, 1932. e. Univ. of Mexico. Studied drama there and with Saki Sano in Mexico; UCLA film school; studied pantomime in Paris.
PICTURES: *Actor:* Pedro Paramo, The Wild Bunch, Scandalous John, Run Cougar Run, Nest of Virgins, Inspector Calzonzin (also dir.), Tivoli, Posse, Used Cars, Romancing the Stone, Three Amigos!, Walker, Committed, Pickiing Up the Pieces (also dir., exec. prod.). *Director:* Mojado Power (also acting, prod.), Tacos de oro (also s.p.) Como aqua para chocolate, A Walk in the Clouds, Zapata.
TELEVISION: *Movies: Actor:* Stones for Ibarra, Where the Hell's That Gold?!. *Director:* Catch a Falling Star, The Magnificient Amberson, A Painted House. *Series:* E! Show de Arau. *Guest:* Marshal Dillon, Bonanza.

ARCAND, DENYS
Director. b. Deschambault, Quebec, Canada, June 25, 1941. e. U. of Montreal, 1963. While still history student, co-prod. Seul ou avec D'Autres (1962). Joined National Film Board of Canada, where he began making documentary shorts (Champlain, Les Montrealistes and La Route de l'ouest) forming a trilogy dealin with colonial Quebec. In 1970, socio-politicial doc. about Quebec textile workers, On Est au Coton, generated controversy resulting in the NFB banning film until 1976.
PICTURES: Un Maudite Galette (1st fiction feature, 1971), Dir. &/or writer: Seoul ou Avec D'autres, Entre la Mer et L'eau Douce, Quebec: Duplessis et Apres...(doc.), Dirty Money, Rejeanne Padovani, Gina, Comfort and Indifference, Le Crime d'Ovide Plouffe, The Decline of the American Empire, Night Zoo (actor only), Jesus of Montreal (Cannes Film Fest. jury prize, 1989), Leolo (actor only), Montreal Sextet (also actor), Love and Human Remains, Poverty and other Delights, 15 moments, Joyeaux Calvaire, Stardom, Les Invasions barbares.
TELEVISION: Mini-Series: Duplessis (writer), Murder in the family.

ARCHER, ANNE
Actress. b. Los Angeles, CA, Aug. 25, 1947. Daughter of actress Marjorie Lord and actor John Archer. m. Terry Jastrow, TV network sports prod.-dir. and pres. Jack Nicklaus Prods.
THEATRE: A Coupla White Chicks Sitting Around Talking (off B'way, 1981), Les Liaison Dangereuses (Williamstown Film Fest., 1988).
PICTURES: The Honkers (debut, 1972), Cancel My Reservation, The All-American Boy, Trackdown, Lifeguard, Paradise Alley, Good Guys Wear Black, Hero at Large, Raise the Titanic, Green Ice, Waltz Across Texas (also co-story), The Naked Face, Too Scared to Scream, The Check Is in the Mail, Fatal Attraction (Acad. Award nom.), Love at Large, Narrow Margin, Eminent Domain, Patriot Games, Body of Evidence, Family Prayers, Short Cuts, Clear and Present Danger, There Goes My Baby (narrator), Mojave Moon, Nico the Unicorn, Whispers (voice), Dark Summer, Rules of Engagement, The Art of War, Uncle Nino, The Gray in Between.
TELEVISION: *Movies:* The Blue Knight, The Mark of Zorro, The Log of the Black Pearl, A Matter of Wife...and Death, The Dark Side of Innocence, Harold Robbins' The Pirate, The Sky's No Limit, A Different Affair, A Leap of Faith, The Last of His Tribe, Nails, Jane's House, Because Mommy Works (also co-prod.), The Man in the Attic, Jake's Women, Almost Forever, Indiscretion of an American Wife, My Husband's Secret Life, Night of the Wolf, 2004: A Light Knight's Odyssey. *Mini-Series:* Seventh Avenue, Camino de Santiago. *Series:* Bob and Carol and Ted and Alice, The Family Tree, Falcon Crest.

ARCHERD, ARMY
Columnist, TV commentator. r.n. Armand Archerd. b. New York, NY, Jan. 13, 1922. e. UCLA, grad. '41, U.S. Naval Academy Post Graduate Sch., 1943. m. actress Selma Archerd. Started as usher at Criterion Theatre, N.Y., while in high school. After grad. UCLA, worked at Paramount studios before entering Navy. Joined AP Hollywood bureau 1945, Herald-Express, Daily Variety as columnist, 1953. M.C. Hollywood premieres, Emmys and Academy Awards. Pres., found., Hollywood Press Club. Awards from Masquers, L.A. Press Club, Hollywood Foreign Press Club, and Newsman of the Year award from Publicists Guild, 1970; Movie Game. Co-host on TV series, People's Choice. Received

Hollywood Women's Press Club Man of the Year Award, 1987. Appeared in numerous movies and tv series and specials as himself. Continues as columnist reporting on ent.industry for Daily Variety, with columns also appearing online at variety.com.

ARDANT, FANNY
Actress. b. Monte Carlo, March 22, 1949. Majored in political science in college. Served a 5-year apprenticeship in the French theatre acting in Polyeucte, Esther, The Mayor of Santiago, Electra and Tete d'Or. TV debut in Les Dames de la Cote.
PICTURES: Les Chiens (debut, 1979), Les uns et les Autres, The Woman Next Door, The Ins and Outs, Life Is a Novel, Confidentially Yours, Benevenuta, Desire, Swann in Love, Love Unto Death, Les Enrages, L'Ete Prochaine, Family Business, Affabulazione, Melo, The Family, La Paltoquet, Three Sisters, Australia, Pleure pas My Love, Adventure of Catherine C., Afraid of the Dark, Rien Que des Mensonges, La Femme du Deserteur, Amok, Colonel Chabert, Beyond the Clouds, Sabrina, Pedale douce (France's Cesar Award, best actress, 1997), Desire, Ridicule, Elizabeth, La Cena, Augustin roi du Kung Fu, La Debandade, Le Fils du Francais, Le Libertin, Sin Noticias de Dios, Change My Life, 8 Women (Silver Berliln Bear, Berlin Int'l. Film Fest., outstanding artistic achievement, shared with ensemble cast, 2002, European Film Award, best actress, shared with ensemble cast, 2002), Callas Forever.
TELEVISION: Movies: The Fall of the House of Usher, Mademoiselle Julie, Balzac. Mini-series: Les Mutants, Les Dames de la Cote, Le Chef de famille, Les Uns et les Autres, La Grande cabriole. Special: Vivement Truffaut.

ARGENTO, DARIO
Director, Writer. b. Rome, Italy, Sept. 7, 1940. Son of prod. Salvatore Argento.
PICTURES: Writer/Co-s.p.: Today It's Me...Tomorrow It's You, Cemetery Without Crosses, Once Upon a Time in the West, Commandos, Zero Probability, The Five Man Army, One Night at Dinner, Sexual Revoultion, Legion of the Damned, Seasons of Love. Also Dir./Prod./Co-Prod.: Bird With the Crystal Plumage, Cat O'Nine Tails (also story), Four Flies on Grey Velvet, The Five Days of Milan, Deep Red, Suspiria (also music), Dawn of the Dead (prod., also music), Inferno (also story), Tenebrae Unsane (also story), Creepers, Demons, Demons 2: The Nightmare is Back, Opera (Terror at the Opera), The Church (also story), Two Evil Eyes (episode: The Black Cat), Devil's Daughter, Innocent Blood (actor only), Trauma, Stendhal's Syndrome, The Wax Mask, Phantom of the Opera, Sleepless (also dir., prod.), Il Cartaio (dir. only).
TELEVISION: Movies: Il Tram (also prod.), La Bambola (prod.), Masters of Horror (interviewee). Series: Door Into Darkness.

ARKIN, ADAM
Actor. b. Brooklyn, NY, Aug. 19, 1956. Father is actor Alan Arkin. Made acting debut in short film prod. by father, People Soup.
THEATRE: I Hate Hamlet (Theatre World Award), Four Dogs and a Bone.
PICTURES: Made for Each Other, Baby Blue Marine, Improper Channels (s.p.), Under the Rainbow, Chu Chu and the Philly Flash, Full Moon High, The Doctor, With Friends Like These, Halloween: H20, With Friends Like These, Lake Placid, East of A, Hanging Up, Mission, Dropping Out, Stark Raving Mad.
TELEVISION: Movies: It Couldn't Happen to a Nicer Guy, All Together Now, In the Line of Duty: Hunt for Justice, Not in This Town, Thirst, A Slight Case of Murder, My Louisiana Sky (dir. only), Off Season, Roughing It, Damaged Care. Specials: Mark Twain's America: Tom Edison, The Fourth Wise Man, Baseball (voice). Series: Busting Loose, Teachers Only, Tough Cookies, A Year in the Life, Northern Exposure (dir.), Big Wave Dave's, Chicago Hope, Baby Bob, Monk (dir.). Mini-Series: Pearl, Lewis & Clark: The Journey of the Corps of Discovery (voice), Not for Ourselves Alone: The Story of Elizabeth Cady Stanton & Susan B. Anthony. Guest: St. Elsewhere, West Wing, Law & Order, Picket Fences,.Monk.

ARKIN, ALAN
Actor, Director, b. New York, NY, March 26, 1934. e. Los Angeles City Col., Los Angeles State Col., Bennington (VT) Col. m. Barbara Dana, actress-author. Father of actor Adam Arkin. Was member of folk singing group The Tarriers, then one of the original members of Chicago's Second City improvisational group. Directed short films T.G.I.F., People Soup (Acad. Award nom.). Author: Tony's Hard Work Day, The Lemming Condition, Halfway Through the Door, The Clearing, Some Fine Grandpa.
THEATRE: B'way: Enter Laughing (Tony & Theatre World Awards, 1963), Luv. Off-B'way: Second City, Man Out Loud, From the Second City. Director: Eh?, Little Murders, White House Murder Case (Obie Award), Joan of Lorraine, Rubbers and Yanks Three, The Sunshine Boys, The Sorrows of Stephen, Room Service.
PICTURES: 50 credits, incl. Calypso Heat Wave (debut, 1957), The Russians Are Coming The Russians Are Coming (Golden Globe Award, Acad. Award nom.), Woman Times Seven, Wait Until Dark, Inspector Clouseau, The Heart Is a Lonely Hunter (NY Film Critics Award, Acad. Award nom.), Catch-22, Little Murders (also dir.), Deadhead Miles, Last of the Red Hot Lovers, Freebie and the Bean, Hearts of the West (NY Film Critics Award), The 7 Per Cent Solution, Fire Sale (also dir.), The In-Laws (also exec. prod.), Simon, Improper Channels, Chu Chu and the Philly Flash, Full Moon High, The Last Unicorn (voice), Joshua Then and Now, Bad Medicine, Big Trouble, Coupe de Ville, Edward Scissorhands, Havana, The Rocketeer, Glengarry Glen Ross, Indian Summer, So I Married an Axe Murderer, North, The Jerky Boys, Steal Big Steal Little, Mother Night, Grosse Point

Blank, Gattaca, The Slums of Beverly Hills, Jakob the Liar, Arigo (also dir. & s.p.), America's Sweethearts, 13 Conversations About One Thing, Don't You Cry For Me, Counting Sheep.
TELEVISION: Movies: The Defection of Simas Kurdirka, The Other Side of Hell, A Deadly Business, Escape from Sobibor, Cooperstown, Taking the Heat, Doomsday Gun, Blood Money, Varian's War, The Pentagon Papers,. Specials: The Love Song of Barney Kempinski, The Fourth Wise Man, A Matter of Principle, Fay (pilot; dir.), Twigs (dir.), The Emperor's New Clothes (Faerie Tale Theatre), The Visit (Trying Times; dir.), The Boss (Trying Times; dir.), Necessary Parties (also co-s.p., co-prod.). Series: Sesame Street, Fay (dir.), Harry, 100 Centre Street. Guest: Chicago Hope, St. Elsewhere, East Side/West Side.

ARKUSH, ALLAN
Director. b. Jersey City, NJ, April 30, 1948. e. Franklin & Marshall, NYU, Film Sch. With New World Pictures as film, music and trailer editor, 1974-79. Co-dir. Hollywood Boulevard and Death Sport and was 2nd unit dir. of Grand Theft Auto before directing on own. Dir. rock videos with Bette Midler and Mick Jagger, Elvis Costello, Christine McVie.
PICTURES: Hollywood Boulevard (co-dir., co-edit.), Deathsport (co-dir.), Rock 'n' Roll High School (also story), Heartbeeps, Get Crazy, Caddyshack II.
TELEVISION: Movies: XXX & OOOs (co-exec. prod.), Shake Rattle and Rock,.Young at Heart, Desert Breeze (co-exec. prod.), Elvis Meets Nixon, The Temptations, Prince Charming. Mini-Series: The Temptations. Series: More than 30 series dir. credits, incl. Fame, St. Elsewhere, L.A. Law, Moonlighting (Emmy nom.), Shannon's Deal (spv. prod.), Tattinger's, The Twilight Zone, Mann & Machine, Central Park West (co-exec. prod.), The Practice, Snoops, Ally, Bull, Tucker (also exec. prod.), Crossing Jordan (also co-exec. prod., prod.). Pilots: The Bronx Zoo, Capital News (prod.), Parenthood (co-exec. prod.), Bodies of Evidence, Moon Over Miami (exec. prod.).

ARLEDGE, ROONE
Executive. b. Forest Hills, NY, July 8, 1931. e. Columbia U. Entered industry with Dumont Network in 1952. Joined U.S. Army, 1953, serving at Aberdeen Proving Ground in Maryland, prod. and dir. radio programs. Joined NBC, held various production positions, 1954. Went to ABC TV, 1960; named v.p. in charge of ABC Sports, 1964; created tv mainstays "Monday Night Football," "Nightline," and "ABC's Wide World of Sports." Named pres. of ABC Sports, 1968-1986; pres. of ABC News, 1977-1998 and Chairman, ABC News, 1999. Recipient of four George Foster Peabody Awards for sports reporting; 19 Emmy awards. Director of the boards of the Council on Foreign Relations, Arts and Entertainment Television Networks, The History Channel and ESPN. Former member of the President's Council, Memorial Sloan-Kettering Cancer Center and former member of the Dean's Council at the Harvard University John F. Kennedy School of Government.
(d. Dec. 5, 2002)

ARMSTRONG, BESS
Actress. b. Baltimore, MD, Dec. 11, 1953. e. Brown U m. producer John Fiedler.
PICTURES: The Four Seasons, Jekyll and Hyde—Together Again, High Road to China, Jaws 3-D, The House of God, Nothing in Common, Second Sight, Mother Mother (short), The Skateboard Kid, Serial Mom, Dream Lover, That Darn Cat, Pecker, Diamond Men.
TELEVISION: Movies: Getting Married, How to Pick Up Girls, Walking Through the Fire, Lakeside Killer, Barefoot in the Park, This Girl for Hire, Lace, Take Me Home Again, She Stood Alone: The Tailhook Scandal, Mixed Blessings, Stolen Innocence, Forgotten Sins, She Cried No, Christmas Every Day, Forever Love, Her Best Friend's Husband. Series: On Our Own, All is Forgiven, Married People, My So-Called Life, That Was Then.

ARMSTRONG, GILLIAN
Director. b. Melbourne, Australia, Dec. 18, 1950. e. Swinburne Coll. Among 1st class in dirs. course at National Aust. Film & TV School, Sydney. Worked as art dir. on a number of films. Dir. numerous shorts (One Hundred a Day, The Singer and the Dancer) and documentaries (A Busy Kind of Bloke, Bingo Bridesmaids and Braces) before turning to features.
PICTURES: My Brilliant Career (Australian Film Inst. Award), Starstruck, Mrs. Soffel, High Tide, Little Havana, The Last Days of Chez Nous, Little Women, Not Fourteen Again, Oscar & Lucinda, Charlotte Gray.

ARMSTRONG, GORDON
Executive, b. East Orange, NJ, Nov. 26, 1937. e. Arizona State U., graduate studies at NYU. Joined 20th Century-Fox as nat. pub. dir., 1970. Was appointed dir. of adv.-pub.-promo. for Dino De Laurentiis Corp., 1975; became vice pres., worldwide marketing for the company, 1978. Named v.p., adv.-pub.-prom., Universal Pictures, 1970; exec. v.p., mktg. MCA Recreation, 1984; pres. mktg., Morgan Creek Prods., 1991. Pres., Entertainment Marketing Group, 1993. V.p., sales and mktg., ATTICA Cybernetics ,1995; v.p., sales and mktg., Doubleclick Network, 1996.

ARNAZ, JR., DESI
Actor, Singer. b. Los Angeles, CA, Jan. 19, 1953. e. Beverly Hills H.S. Son of Lucille Ball and Desi Arnaz. Sister is actress Lucie Arnaz. Gained fame as rock singer and musician with the

Dino, Desi and Billy group. Video: A Day at the Zoo. Regional theatre includes Sunday in New York, Grease, Promises Promises, Alone Together, I Love My Wife, Is There Life After High School?, Love Letters, The Boys Next Door.
PICTURES: Red Sky at Morning (debut, 1971), Marco, Billy Two Hats, Joyride, A Wedding, Fake-Out, House of the Long Shadows, The Mambo Kings.
TELEVISION: Movies: Mr. & Mrs. Bo Jo Jones, Voyage of the Yes, She Lives, Giving Birth, Flight to Holocaust, Black Market Baby, To Kill a Cop, The Courage and the Passion, How to Pick Up Girls, Crisis in Mid-Air, Gridlock, Advice to the Lovelorn, The Night the Bridge Fell Down, I Love Liberty, TV Road Trip. Series: Here's Lucy, Automan. Guest: The Love Boat, Fantasy Island, Paul Reiser: Out on a Whim, Matlock. Special: I Love Lucy's 50th Anniversary Special.

ARNAZ, LUCIE
Actress. b. Los Angeles, CA, July 17, 1951. Daughter of Lucille Ball and Desi Arnaz. m. actor Laurence Luckinbill. Brother is actor Desi Arnaz Jr. B'way: They're Playing Our Song (Theatre World Award), Lost in Yonkers. National touring companies: Whose Life is It Anyway?, Educating Rita, My One and Only, Social Security. Nightclubs: Lucie Arnaz-Latin Roots, Irving Berlin in Concert-In Sicily.
PICTURES: Billy Jack Goes to Washington, The Jazz Singer, Second Thoughts, Down to You.
TELEVISION: Movies: Who is the Black Dahlia, The Mating Season, The Washington Mistress, Who Gets the Friends?, Abduction of Innocence, TV Road Trip. Series: Here's Lucy, The Lucy Arnaz Show, Sons and Daughters. Pilot: One More Try. Specials: Lucy & Desi: A Home Movie (host, co-exec. prod., co-dir.), The Wizard of Oz in Concert: Dreams Come True, I Love Lucy's 50th Anniversary Special.

ARNESS, JAMES
Actor. r.n. James Aurness. b. Minneapolis, MN, May 26, 1923. e. Beloit Coll. Brother of actor Peter Graves. Served in U.S. Army; worked in advertising, real estate. Started in films in late 1940's appearing under his real name.
PICTURES: The Farmer's Daughter (debut 1947), Roses Are Red, The Man From Texas, Battleground, Sierra, Two Lost Worlds, Wyoming Mail, Wagon Master, Double Crossbones, Stars in My Crown (1st billing as James Arness), Cavalry Scout, Belle le Grand, Iron Man, The People Against O'Hara, The Girl in White, The Thing, Carbine Williams, Hellgate, Big Jim McLain, Horizons West, Lone Hand, Ride the Man Down, Island in the Sky, Veils of Bagdad, Hondo, Her Twelve Men, Them!, Many Rivers to Cross, Flame of the Islands, The Sea Chase, The First Travelling Saleslady, Gun the Man Down, Alias Jesse James (cameo).
TELEVISION: Movies: The Macahans, The Alamo: 13 Days to Glory, Gunsmoke: Return to Dodge, Red River, Gunsmoke: The Last Apache, Gunsmoke: To the Last Man, Gunsmoke: The Long Ride (also exec. prod.), Gunsmoke: One Man's Justice (also exec. prod.). Series: Gunsmoke (20 years), How the West Was Won, McClain's Law. Mini-Series: How the West Was Won.

ARNOLD, EDDY
Singer. b. Henderson, TN, May 15, 1918. Radio performer, Nashville, TN. Recording star since 1946; records include That's How Much I Love You, Anytime, Bouquet of Roses (on the Country Music charts longer than any record in the history of country music), Make the World Go Away. Holds the record for most Country Records on the charts. Elected to Country Music Hall of Fame, 1966; Entertainer of the Year, 1967; Pioneer Award from Acad. of Country Music, 1984; President's Award from Songwriter's Guild, 1987.
TELEVISION: Series: Eddy Arnold Show (1952-3), Eddy Arnold Time, Eddy Arnold Show (1956), The Kraft Music Hall (1967-71). Hosted Music from the Land, Tonight Show, more than 20 specials.

ARNOLD, TOM
Actor. b. Ottumwa, IA, June 3, 1959.
PICTURES: Has more than 25 picture credits, incl. Freddy's Dead: The Final Nightmare, Hero, Undercover Blues, True Lies, Nine Months, Big Bully, Carpool, McHale's Navy (also co-prod.), Golf Punks, Blue Ridge Fall, Ablaze, Exit Wounds, Just Sue Me, Animal Factory, We Married Margo, Lloyd, Children On Their Birthdays, True Lies 2, G-S.P.O.T, Just For Kicks, Hansel and Gretel, After School Special, Manhood, Cradle 2 the Grave.
TELEVISION: Movies: Backfield in Motion, Body Bags, The Woman Who Loved Elvis, Jackie's Back!, Shriek If You Know What I Did Last Friday the 13th, Romantic Comedy 101, Dennis the Menace in Cruise Control. Series: Roseanne (also exec. prod., writer) The Jackie Thomas Show (also creator, exec. prod.), Tom, The Tom Show (also creator, exec. prod.), Disney's Hercules (voice), THe Best Damn Sports Show Period (himself). Guest: The Ben Stiller Show, Saturday Night Live, The Larry Sanders Show, High Society, The Naked Truth, L.A. Doctors, The Norm Show, Veronica's Closet, Baywatch, Arli$$, King of the Hill (voice), Late Show with Craig Kilborn.

ARONOFSKY, DARREN
Director, Writer. b. Brooklyn, New York, Feb. 12, 1969. e. Harvard U.
PICTURES: Protozoa, Pi (Independent Spirit Award, best first screenplay; Sundance Festival, director's award), Requiem for a Dream, Batman: Year One, Below (writer, exec. prod.), The Fountain.

ARQUETTE, DAVID
Actor. b. Sept. 8, 1971. m. actress Courtney Cox. Brother of actresses Patricia and Rosanna Arquette and actors Richmond and Alexis Arquette.
PICTURES: Has appeared in 35 pictures, incl. Where the Day Takes You, Buffy the Vampire Slayer, The Killing Box, Airheads, Fall Time, Wild Bill, Beautiful Girls, Johns, Scream, Life During Wartime, Dream with the Fishes (also co-prod.), Scream 2, Ravenous, Never Been Kissed, Muppets From Space, Scream 3, Ready to Rumble, The Shrink Is In, 3000 Miles to Graceland, See Spot Run, The Grey Zone, Happy Here And Now, Eight Legged Freaks, Stealing Sinatra, A Foreign Affair, Never Die Alone.
TELEVISION: Movies: Cruel Doubt, Roadracers, It's a Very Merry Muppet Christmas Movie. Mini-Series: Dead Man's Walk. Series: The Outsiders, Parenthood, Double Rush, Pelswick (voice). Guest: Blossom, Beverly Hills 90210, Friends, Son of the Beach, The Hughleys, Penn & Teller's Sin City Spectacular.

ARQUETTE, PATRICIA
Actress. b. Chicago, IL, April 8, 1968. Sister of actress Rosanna Arquette and actors Richmond, Alexis and David Arquette. Prof. debut in children's version of Story Theatre. Studied acting with Milton Katselis.
PICTURES: A Nightmare on Elm Street 3: Dream Warriors (debut, 1987), Pretty Smart, Time Out, Far North, Prayer of the Rollerboys, The Indian Runner, Ethan Frome, Trouble Bound, Inside Monkey Zetterland, True Romance, Holy Matrimony, Ed Wood, Beyond Rangoon, Infinity, Flirting With Disaster, The Secret Agent, Nightwatch, Lost Highway, The Hi-Lo Country, Goodbye Lover, Stigmata, Bringing Out the Dead, Little Nicky, Human Nature, Holes.
TELEVISION: Movies: Daddy, Dillinger, Wildflower, Betrayed by Love, The Badge. Special: The Girl With the Crazy Brother. Guest: The Edge (Indian Poker), thirtysomething, Tales From the Crypt.

ARQUETTE, ROSANNA
Actress. b. New York, NY, Aug. 10, 1959. Granddaughter of humorist Cliff Arquette (Charlie Weaver). Daughter of actor-producer Lewis Arquette. Sister of actress Patricia Arquette and actors Richmond, Alexis and David Arquette. Prof. debut in children's version of Story Theatre. Started acting in San Francisco. Role in LA play led to bit parts on tv then regular role as Shirley Jones' teenage daughter on series Shirley (1979).
PICTURES: 50 picture credits, incl. More American Graffiti (debut, 1979), Gorp, S.O.B., Desperately Seeking Susan, Silverado, After Hours, 8 Million Ways To Die, Nobody's Fool, Amazon Women on the Moon, The Big Blue, The Linguini Incident, Fathers and Sons, Nowhere to Run, Pulp Fiction, Search and Destroy, Crash, Do Me a Favor, I'm Losing You, Hell's Kitchen NYC, Buffalo '66, Palmer's Pick Up, The Whole Nine Yards, Pigeon Holed, Interview With A Dead Man, Too Much Flesh, Things Behind the Sun, Good Advice, Diary of a Sex Addict, Saving Grace.
TELEVISION: Movies: Having Babies II, The Dark Secret of Harvest Home, Zuma Beach, The Ordeal of Patty Hearst, A Long Way Home, The Wall, The Executioner's Song, Johnny Belinda, One Cooks the Other Doesn't, The Parade, Survival Guide, Promised a Miracle, Sweet Revenge, Separation, Son of the Morning Star, Black Rainbow, In the Deep Woods, The Wrong Man, Nowhere to Hide, I Know What You Did, Switched at Birth, Poison, Rush of Fear. Mini-Series: The Dark Secret of Harvest Home. Series: Shirley Guest: Eight is Enough, Homicide: Life on the Street.

ARTHUR, BEATRICE
Actress. r.n. Bernice Frankel. b. New York, NY, May 13, 1926. Franklin Inst. of Sciences & Art. Studied with Erwin Piscator at New School for Social Research; first stage role as Lysistrata; professional stage debut in Dog Beneath the Skin, 1947.
THEATRE: Gas, Yerma, No Exit, Six Characters in Search of an Author, The Taming of the Shrew, (1948) The Owl and the Pussycat, The Threepenny Opera (1953 revival), The ShoeString Revue, What's the Rush?, Nature's Way, Ulysses in Nighttown, Gay Divorcee, Fiddler on the Roof, Mame (Tony Award, 1966), The Floating Light Bulb.
PICTURES: That Kind of Woman, Lovers and Other Strangers, Mame, History of the World Part I, For Better or Worse, Enemies of Laughter, Broadway the Golden Age: By The Legends Who Were There.
TELEVISION: Movies: The Star Wars Holiday Special, The Beatrice Arthur Special, Family Comedy Hour (as herself), My First Love, Broadway at the Hollywood Bowl (as herself). Series: Caesar's Hour, All in the Family, Maude (Emmy Award, 1977), Amanda's by the Sea, The Golden Girls (Emmy Award, 1988), Dave's World. Numerous guest appearances.

ARTHUR, KAREN
Director, Actress. b. Omaha, NB, Aug. 24, 1941. Ballet dancer, choreographer and musical comedy singer, dancer and actress, 1950-68; actress, film, tv and theatre, 1968-75; film, tv director, 1970-.
PICTURES: Actress: A Guide for the Married Man, Winning, Like It Is... Director: Legacy (also prod.), Int'l Film Critics & Josef Von Sternberg Awards, 1975), The Mafu Cage, Lady Beware.
TELEVISION: Movies: Charleston, Victims for Victims: The Theresa Saldana Story (Christopher Award), A Bunny's Tale, The Rape of Richard Beck, Evil in Clear River (Christopher

47

Award), Cracked Up, Bridge to Silence, Fall from Grace, Blue Bayou, Bump in the Night, Shadow of a Doubt, The Secret, The Disappearance of Christina, Against Their Will: Women in Prison, Journey of the Heart, The Staircase, Labor of Love, The Lost Child, The Song of the Lark, Passion and Prejudice (also prod.), The Locket. Mini-Series: Love and Betrayal: The Mia Farrow Story, Crossings, Return to Eden, The Jacksons: An American Dream, Dead by Sunset, A Will of Their Own, True Women. Series: Hart to Hart, Rich Man Poor Man Book II, Cagney & Lacey (Emmy Award, 1985), Remington Steele, . Emerald Point, New York News.

ARTZ, BOB
Theatre executive. b. Spokane, WA, Aug 21, 1946. e., B.T.A. Pasadena Playhouse College of Theatre Arts. Began in 1968 as doorman, became asst. mgr. to mgr. with National General Theatre Corporation. Joined Plitt Theatres in 1978 as dist. mgr. and ad/pub. dir., West Coast. Joined General Cinema Theatres in 1986 as reg. mktg. dir., Western region. Became dir., film mktg. in 1993. National dir., Entertainment Mktg. & Operations in 1996. Dir. client svc's., Global Cinema Network, 1998. Member: Variety Club, Film Information Council, Pasadena PlayHouse Alumni & Assoc (life mem.).

ASH, RENE
Producer, executive. b. Brussels, Belgium, March 14, 1939. e. U. of Omaha. Employed with I.A.T.S.E. 1968-1979, prior to which was assoc. editor, Greater Amusements. Eastern v.p. of Pub. Guild, 1973-1981; editor-in-chief, Backstage, 1979-80; pres., Cinereal Pictures, 1984-85; co-pres., Eagle Films Corp., 1985-94; pres. Rea Film Prods. Author of various articles published in foreign film magazines and The Film Editor in Motion Pictures & Television. Member of the Pub. Guild since 1968.

ASHER, JANE
Actress. b. London, England, April 5, 1946.
PICTURES: Mandy (Crash of Silence; debut, 1952), Third Party Risk, Dance Little Lady, Adventure in the Hopfields, Charley Moon, Greengage Summer (Loss of Innocence), The Model Murder Case, The Masque of the Red Death, Alfie, The Winter's Tale, Deep End, The Buttercup Chain, Henry VIII and His Six Wives (from the BBC series the Six Wives of Henry VIII), Runners, Success Is the Best Revenge, Dream Child, Paris By Night, Closing Numbers.
TELEVISION: Movies/Specials: The Stone Tape, East Lynne, Voyage 'Round My Father, Bright Smiler,. The Volunteer. Mini-series: Brideshead Revisited, Wish Me Luck, The Choir. Series: The Mistress, Good Living (as herself), Crossroads. Numerous guest appearances, incl. Journey to the Unkown, Hazell, French and Saunders, This Morning, Today with Des & Mel.

ASHLEY, ELIZABETH
Actress. b. Ocala, FL, Aug. 30, 1939. e. Studied ballet LA State U., 1957-58; grad. Neighborhood Playhouse, 1961. Author: Postcards From the Road.
THEATRE: Take Her She's Mine (1962 Tony & Theatre World Awards), The Highest Tree, Barefoot in the Park, Ring 'Round the Bathtub, The Skin of Our Teeth, Legend, Cat on a Hot Tin Roof (B'way revival), Caesar and Cleopatra, Agnes of God, The Milk Train Doesn't Stop Here Anymore, When She Danced.
PICTURES: The Carpetbaggers (debut, 1964), Ship of Fools, The Third Day, The Marriage of a Young Stockbroker, Paperback Hero, Golden Needles, Rancho DeLuxe, 92 in the Shade, The Great Scout and Cathouse Thursday, Coma, Windows, Paternity, Split Image, Dragnet, Vampire's Kiss, Dangerous Curves, Lost Memories, Sleeping Together, Happiness, Just the Ticket, Hey Arnold! The Movie (voice). TELEVISION: Movies: Harpy, The Face of Fear, When Michael Calls, Second Chance, The Heist, Your Money or Your Wife, The Magician, One of My Wives is Missing, The War Between the Tates, Tom and Joann (Pilot), A Fire in the Sky, Svengali, He's Fired She's Hired, Stagecoach, Warm Hearts Cold Feet, The Two Mrs. Grenvilles, Blue Bayou, Reason for Living: The Jill Ireland Story, Love and Curses... and All That Jazz, In the Best Interest of the Children, Harnessing Peacocks, May and June. Mini-Series: Freedom to Speak, The Buccaneers, Series: Evening Shade, Another World, Guest: Miami Vice, Hunter, Murder She Wrote, Caroline in the City, Hey Arnold! (voice), Homicide: Life on the Street, Law & Order: Special Victims Unit.

ASHTON, JOHN
Actor. b. Springfield, MA, Feb. 22, 1948. e. USC, BA in theatre.
THEATRE: The Last Meeting of the Knights of the White Magnolia (L.A. Drama Critics Circle Award), True West (Drama-Logue Award), A Flea in Her Ear (L.A. Drama Critics Circle Award).
PICTURES: Breaking Away, Borderline, Honky Tonk Freeway, The Adventures of Buckaroo Banzai Across the 8th Dimension, Beverly Hills Cop, The Last Resort, King Kong Lives, Some Kind of Wonderful, Beverly Hills Cop II, She's Having a Baby, Midnight Run, I Want to Go Home, Curly Sue, Little Big League, Trapped in Paradise, Hidden Assassin, Fast Money, Meet the Deedles, Instinct, Avalanche, Bill's Gun Shop.
TELEVISION: Movies: Elvis and the Beauty Queen, A Death in California, The Deliberate Stranger, I Know My First Name is Steven, Dirty Work, Stephen King's The Tommyknockers, Little Girls in Pretty Boxes, The Day Lincoln Was Shot. Mini-Series: The Rhinemann Exchange.Series: Dallas, Breaking Away, Hardball. Guest: M*A*S*H*, Police Squad!, JAG, King of the Hill

(voice), Fantasy Island, Judging Amy, Body and Soul.

ASNER, EDWARD
Actor. r.n. Isaac Edward Asner. b. Kansas City, MO, Nov. 15, 1929. e. U. of Chicago, where affiliated with campus acting group. Served two years with U.S. Army in France. Returned to Chicago to join Playwright's Theatre Club. Moved to NY and joined NY Shakespeare Festival, 1960 and American Shakespeare Festival, 1961. In 1961, moved to Hollywood to become active in films and tv. National pres. Screen Actors Guild, 1981-85. Involved in more than 13 documentaries, incl. Earth and the American Dream, The Long Way Home, 187: Documented. Prod. tv & feature projects through his company, Quince. Winner of numerous humanitarian awards.
THEATRE: B'way: Face of a Hero, Born Yesterday (debut, 1989). Off-B'way: Ivanov, Threepenny Opera, Legend of Lovers, The Tempest, Venice Preserved.
PICTURES:The Murder Men (debut 1961), Kid Gallahad, The Slender Thread, The Satan Bug, The Venetian Affair, El Dorado, Gunn, Change of Habit, They Call Me Mister Tibbs, Halls of Anger, Do Not Throw Cushions Into The Ring, The Todd Killings, Skin Game, The Wrestler, Gus, Fort Apache-The Bronx, O'Hara's Wife, Daniel, Pinocchio and the Emperor of the Night (voice), Moon Over Parador, JFK, Happily Ever After (voice), Cat's Don't Dance (voice), Goldilocks and the Three Bears, The Fanatics, A Christmas Carol (voice), Basil, Hard Rain, The Bachelor, Above Suspicion, Perfect Game, Mars and Beyond, Bring Him Home, The Animal, Island Prey, Donzi: The Legend, Academy Boyz, The Confidence Game, The Commission, Elf, Missing Brendan.
TELEVISION: Movies: Nearly 50 tv movie credits, incl. The Doomsday Flight, Daughter of the Mind, The House on Greenapple Road, The Old Man Who Cried Wolf, The Last Child, They Call It Murder, The Police Story, The Imposter, Death Scream, Hey I'm Alive, Life and Assassination of the Kingfish, The Gathering, The Family Man, A Small Killing, A Case of Libel, Anatomy of an Illness, Vital Signs, Kate's Secret, The Christmas Star, Cracked Up, A Friendship in Vienna, Not a Penny More Not a Penny Less, Good Cops Bad Cops, Switched at Birth, Silent Motive, Yes Virginia There Is a Santa Claus, Cruel Doubt, Gypsy, Heads, Higher Education, Gone in the Night, The Story of Santa Claus, Payback (also prod.), Common Ground, Becoming Dick, Papa Giovanni-Ioannes XXIII, The King and Queen of Moonlight Bay.. Mini-Series: Rich Man Poor Man (Emmy Award, 1976), Roots (Emmy Award, 1977), Tender Is the Night, More Tales of the City. Series: Has appeared in 22 series, incl. Slattery's People, The Mary Tyler Moore Show (3 Emmy Awards: 1971, 1972, 1975), Lou Grant (2 Emmy Awards: 1978, 1980), Off the Rack, The Bronx Zoo, The Trials of Rosie O'Neill, Fish Police (voice), Hearts Afire, The Magic School Bus (voice), Gargoyles (voice), Thunder Alley, Spider-Man (voice), Freakazoid (voice), Bruno the Kid (voice), Batman: Ask Harriet, The Closer, Max Steel.. Guest: Numerous appearances, incl. Gunsmoke, Hawaii Five-O, Roseanne, Mad About You, The Practice, The X-Files, Touched By An Angel, Arli$$, The Ellen Show, ER.

ASPEL, SIR MICHAEL
Radio/TV Presenter. b. London, England, Jan. 12, 1933. Entered industry in 1954 as actor/presenter for BBC Radio, and announcer/newsreader for BBC TV. Presentations incl: Miss World, Crackerjack, Give Us A Clue, Ask Aspel, Family Favourites, Child's Play, ITV Telethon 1988, 1990 & 1992, Aspel and Company, This Is Your Life, BAFTA Awards, Strange ... But True?, Caught on Camera, Light Camera Action, ITN's V.E. Day Programme 1995, Blockbusters. Received OBE in 1993. Most recently a presenter on the Antiques Roadshow.

ASSANTE, ARMAND
Actor. b. New York, NY, Oct. 4, 1949. e. American Acad. of Dramatic Arts. Appeared with regional theatre groups incl. Arena Stage, DC; Long Wharf, New Haven; Actor's Theatre of Louisville.
THEATRE: B'way: Boccaccio, Comedians, Romeo and Juliet, Kingdoms. Off-B'way: Why I Went Crazy, Rubbers, The Beauty Part, Lake of the Woods, Yankees 3 Detroit 0.
PICTURES: Paradise Alley, Prophecy, Little Darlings, Private Benjamin, Love and Money, I the Jury, Unfaithfully Yours, Belizaire the Cajun, The Penitent, Animal Behavior, Q & A, Eternity, The Marrying Man, The Mambo Kings, 1492: Conquest of Paradise, Hoffa, Fatal Instinct, Trial by Jury, Blind Justice, Judge Dredd, Striptease, Looking for an Echo, Hunt for the Devil, The Road to El Dorado (voice), After the Storm, Last Run, Federal Protection, Partners in Action, Consequence, Citizen Verdict.
TELEVISION: Movies: Human Feelings, Lady of the House, Sophia Loren-Her Own Story, Rage of Angels, Why Me?, A Deadly Business, Stranger in My Bed, Hands of a Stranger, Jack the Ripper, Passion and Paradise, Fever, Kidnapped, Gotti (Emmy Award, 1997), The Odyssey, C.S.S. Hunley, On The Beach. Mini-Series: Evergreen, Napoleon and Josephine: A Love Story. Series: How to Survive a Marriage, The Doctors, Push Nevada.

ASSEYEV, TAMARA
Producer. e. Marymont College; UCLA, MA, theatre arts. Began career as asst. to Roger Corman, working on 8 films with him. In 1967 started to produce films independently. Then co-produced films with Alex Rose, starting with Drive-In. In 1966 at 24, became youngest member of Producers Guild of Amer. Member: Costume Council, LA City Museum; founding member, LA

Museum of Contemporary Art.
PICTURES: The Wild Racers (assoc. prod.), Paddy, A Kiss from Eddie (aka Sweet Kill), Drive-In, I Wanna Hold Your Hand, Big Wednesday (exec. prod.), The History of Atlantic Records, Norma Rae (nom. for Acad. Award, best pic., shared with Alexandra Rose, 1980) A Month by the Lake. (Assoc. prod.)
TELEVISION: Movies: A Shadow on the Sun, The Secret Life of Kathy McCormick (also co-exec. prod.), The Hijacking of the Achille Lauro (exec. prod.), Murder By Moonlight (exec. prod.).

ASTIN, JOHN
Actor. b. Baltimore, MD, March 30, 1930. e. Washington and Jefferson Coll., Washington Drama Sch., Johns Hopkins U., grad. BA, U. of Minnesota Graduate School. Father of actors Sean and Mackenzie Astin. Theatre debut on Off-B'way stage, Threepenny Opera. B'way debut, Major Barbara. Dir., co-prod., A Sleep of Prisoners, Phoenix Theatre. Did voices in cartoons, commercials, 1955-59. Prod. & dir. short subject Prelude.
THEATRE: The Cave Dwellers, Ulysses in Nighttown, Tall Story, Lend Me a Tenor, H.M.S. Pinafore.
PICTURES: That Touch of Mink, Period Of Adjustment, Move Over Darling, The Wheeler Dealers, The Spirit is Willing, Candy, Viva Max!, Bunny O'Hare, Get to Know Your Rabbit, Every Little Crook and Nanny, The Brothers O'Toole, Freaky Friday, National Lampoon's European Vacation, Body Slam, Teen Wolf Too, Return of the Killer Tomatoes, Night Life, Gremlins 2, Killer Tomatoes Eat France, Stepmonster, The Silence of the Hams, Frighteners, Betaville, School of Life.
TELEVISION: Movies: Two on a Bench, Evil Roy Slade, Skyway to Death, Only with Married Men, The Dream Makers, Operation Petticoat (also dir.), Rossetti and Ryan: Men Who Love Women (dir. only), Operation Petticoat, Halloween with the New Addams Family, Mr. Boogedy. Series: I'm Dickens He's Fenster, The Addams Family, The Pruitts of Southampton, McMillan and Wife, Operation Petticoat, Mary, The Attack of the Killer Tomatoes (voice), Taz-Mania (voice), The Addams Family (voice for animated series), The Adventures of Brisco County Jr., Aladdin (voice), Twisted Adventures of Felix the Cat (voice), The New Addams Family. Guest: Numerous appearances, incl. The Flying Nun, Partridge Family, Police Woman, Love Boat, Night Court, Duckman, The Nanny, The Hughleys, The Strip, Becker.

ASTIN, MACKENZIE
Actor. b. Los Angeles, CA, May 12, 1973. Parents are actors John Astin and Patty Duke. Brother is actor Sean Astin.
PICTURES: The Garbage Pail Kids Movie, Widow's Kiss, Iron Will, Wyatt Earp, In Love and War, The Last Days of Disco, Dream for an Insomniac, The Evening Star, Mating Habits of the Earthbound Human, Stranger than Fiction, Off the Lip, The Zeros, The Month of August, Two Days, How to Deal.
TELEVISION: Movies: Lois Gibbs and the Love Canal, I Dream of Jeannie: 15 Years Later, The Facts of Life Down Under, A Child Lost Forever, Widow's Kiss, The Long Island Incident, Selma Lord Selma, Laughter on the 23rd Floor. Series: The Facts of Life, First Years. Guest: Brooklyn Bridge, Outer Limits, Without A Trace.

ASTIN, SEAN
Actor. b. Santa Monica, Feb. 25, 1971. Parents are actors John Astin and Patty Duke. Brother is actor Mackenzie Astin. First acting job at 7 opposite mother in Afterschool Special, Please Don't Hit Me Mom. Dir. short films On My Honor, Kangaroo Court (Acad. Award nom.). On LA stage in Lone Star.
PICTURES: The Goonies (debut, 1985), White Water Summer, Like Father Like Son, Staying Together, The War of the Roses, Memphis Belle, The Willies, Toy Soldiers, Encino Man, Where the Day Takes You, Rudy, Safe Passage, The Low Life, Courage Under Fire, The Long Way Home (voice), Bulworth, , Bulworth, Boy Meets Girl, Kimberly, Deterrence, Icebreaker, The Last Producer, The Sky is Falling, Lord of the Rings: The Fellowship of the Ring, Lord of the Rings: The Two Towers, Lord of the Rings: The Return of the King, The Riding of the Laddie.
TELEVISION: Movies: The Rules of Marriage, The B.R.A.T. Patrol, Harrison Bergeron. Pilot: Just Our Luck. Series: Jeremiah, Party Wagon (voice).

ATHERTON, WILLIAM
Actor. r.n. William Knight. b. New Haven, CT, June 30, 1947. While in high school became youngest member of Long Wharf Theatre Co. Given scholarship to Pasadena Playhouse; then switched to Carnegie Tech Sch. of Drama in 1965. In college years toured with USO prods in Europe and in stock and industrial shows. Came to NY where first prof. job was in nat'l co. of Little Murders.
THEATRE: The House of Blue Leaves, The Basic Training of Pavlo Hummel, The Sign in Sidney Brustein's Window, Suggs (Theatre World Award, Outer Circle Critics Award, Drama Desk Award), Rich and Famous, Passing Game, Happy New Year, The American Clock, Three Acts of Recognition, The Caine Mutiny Court-Martial, Child's Play, Loco Motives.
PICTURES: The New Centurions (debut, 1972), Class of '44, The Sugarland Express, The Day of the Locust, The Hindenburg, Looking for Mr. Goodbar, Ghostbusters, Number One, No Mercy, Die Hard, Die Hard 2, Grim Prairie Tales, Oscar, The Pelican Brief, Saints and Sinners, Frank and Jesse, Bio-Dome, Hoodlum, Executive Power, Mad City, Michael Kael in Katango, The Crow: Salvation, Bread and Roses, Race to Space, Who's Your Daddy.
TELEVISION: Movies: House of Mirth, Tomorrow's Child, Malibu, A Fight for Jenny, Intrigue, Buried Alive, Diagnosis Murder, Chrome Soldiers, Robin Cook's Virus, Broken Trust, Raven Hawk, Introducing Dorothy Dandridge. Mini-Series:

Centennial. Guest: Murder She Wrote, Nash Bridges, The Practice, The Outer Limits, Night Visions, Law & Order.

ATKINS, CHRISTOPHER
Actor. b. Rye, NY, Feb. 21, 1961. e. Dennison U., Ohio. Early modeling jobs before being hired for theatrical film debut in The Blue Lagoon (1980). PICTURES: The Blue Lagoon, The Pirate Movie, A Night in Heaven, Beaks, Mortuary Academy, Listen to Me, Shakma, King's Ransom, Outrage, Dracula Rising, Die Watching, Exchange Lifeguards, A Bullet Down Under, Trigger Fast, Project Shadowchaser III, It's My Party, Mutual Needs, Breaking the Silence, Beings (writer only), Deadly Delusions, The Day October Died, Civility, Stageghost, Title to Murder, The 13th Child: Legend of the Jersey Devil, Tequila Express, The Stoneman, Mending Fences, The Employee of the Month, The Color of Water, Quigley, True Legends of the West.
TELEVISION: Movies: Child Bride of Short Creek, Secret Weapons, Fatal Charm, Miami Killer, Bandit Goes Country, Guns of Honor, Deadman's Island, Angel Flight Down. Series: Dallas. Guest: Streets of San Francisco, Silk Stalkings, Suddenly Susan.

ATKINSON, ROWAN
Actor, Writer. b. England, Jan. 6, 1955. e. Newcastle U., Oxford.
THEATRE: Rowan Atkinson in Revue (also writer), Not in Front of an Audience, The Nerd, Rowan Atkinson at the Atkinson (also writer; NY), Mime Gala, The Sneeze.
PICTURES: The Secret Policeman's Ball (documentary, also co-s.p.),Dead on Time, Never Say Never Again, The Appointments of Dennis Jennings, The Tall Guy, The Witches, Hot Shots Part Deux, Four Weddings and a Funeral, The Lion King (voice), Mr. Bean (also exec. prod.), Black Adder Back and Forth, Maybe Baby, Rat Race, Scooby Doo, Johnny English.
TELEVISION: Movies: Peter Cook & Co., The Grand Knockout Tournament, Blackadder's Christmas Carol, Hysteria 2!, Bernard and the Genie, Full Throttle, Reflections of Mr. Bean (himself). Series: Not the Nine O'Clock News (also writer; BAFTA Award for acting), Black Adder (also writer), Blackadder II, Blackadder the Third, Mr Bean (also writer), Blackadder Goes Forth, The Thin Blue Line, Mr. Bean (voice).

ATTENBOROUGH, BARON RICHARD (SAMUEL)
Actor, Producer, Director. b. Cambridge, England, Aug. 29, 1923. e. Wyggeston Grammar Sch., Leicester; Leverhulme Scholarship to Royal Acad. of Dramatic Art, 1941 (Bancroft Medal). m. Sheila Beryl Grant Sim, 1945. Stage debut in Ah Wilderness (Palmers Green, 1941). West End debut in Awake and Sing (1942), then The Little Foxes, Brighton Rock. Joined RAF, 1943; seconded to RAF Film Unit, and appeared in training film Journey Together, 1945; demobilized, 1946. Returned to stage, 1949, in The Way Back (Home of the Brave), To Dorothy a Son, Sweet Madness, The Mousetrap (original cast: 1952-54), Double Image, The Rape of the Belt. Formed Beaver Films with Bryan Forbes, 1959; formed Allied Film Makers, 1960. Life Peer of Richmond Upon Thames; CBE 1967; Kt 1976.
PICTURES: Actor: More than 70 credits, incl. In Which We Serve (debut, 1942), The Hundred Pound Window, Journey Together, Stairway to Heaven, Secret Flight, The Smugglers, Dancing With Crime, Young Scarface, Dulcimer Street, The Guinea Pig, The Lost People, Boys in Brown, Operation Disaster, Hell Is Sold Out, The Magic Box, Glory at Sea, Father's Doing Fine, Eight O'Clock Walk, The Ship That Died of Shame, Private's Progress, The Baby and the Battleship, Strange Affection, Brothers in Law, Dunkirk, Desert Patrol, The Man Upstairs, SOS Pacific, The League of Gentlemen, Jet Storm, I'm All Right Jack, Breakout, The Angry Silence (also co-prod.), All Night Long, Only Two Can Play, Trial & Error, The Great Escape, The Third Secret, Seance on a Wet Afternoon (also prod.; San Sebastian Film Fest. & Brit. Acad. Awards for Best Actor), Guns at Batasi (Brit. Acad. Award), The Flight of the Phoenix, The Sand Pebbles (Golden Globe Award), Dr. Dolittle (Golden Globe Award), Only When I Larf, The Bliss of Mrs Blossom, The Magic Christian, The Last Grenade, A Severed Head, Loot, 10 Rillington Place, Ten Little Indians, Rosebud, Brannigan, Conduct Unbecoming, Shatranj Ke Khiladi, Magic, The Human Factor, Jurassic Park, Miracle on 34th Street, Hamlet, E=MC², The Lost World: Jurassic Park, Elizabeth. Producer: Whistle Down the Wind, The L-Shaped Room. Director: Oh! What a Lovely War (also prod.; 16 Intl. Awards incl. Golden Globe and BAFTA UN Award), Young Winston (Golden Globe), A Bridge Too Far (Evening News Best Drama Award, 1977), Magic, Gandhi (also prod.; 8 Oscars, 5 BAFTA Awards, 5 Golden Globes, DGA Award, 1982), A Chorus Line, Cry Freedom (also prod.; Berlinale Kamera, 1987; BFI Award for Tech. Achievement), Chaplin (also prod.), Shadowlands (also prod.; BAFTA Award for Best British Film of 1993), In Love and War (also prod.), Grey Owl (also prod.), Puckoon (also writer).
TELEVISION: Movies: David Copperfield, Diana: Queen of Hearts (himself), The Railway Children, Mini-Series: Jack and the Beanstalk: The Real Story.

ATTENBOROUGH, SIR DAVID
Broadcaster. b. London, England, May 8, 1926. Brother of Baron Richard Attenborough. e. Wyggeston Sch., Leicester; Clare Coll., Cambridge. Early career, editor in educational publishing house. Ent. BBC-TV, 1952. Prod. Zoo Quest series, Travellers Tales, Eastward with Attenborough, The Tribal Eye, Life on Earth. Controller BBC-2, 1965-68; Dir. of Prog. BBC-TV, 1969-72. Received Desmond Davis Award, 1970 and a Fellowship, 1979.
PICTURES: A Zed and Two Noughts (narrator).

TELEVISION: Narrator &/or actor in several programs about nature &/or travel, incl. The Living Planet, Wilderness Men, Ultimate Wild Paradises: The Top Ten Destinations, The Blue Planet, Cities of the Wild (also writer), Survival Island (also writer) and several others.

AUBERJONOIS, RENE
Actor. b. New York, NY, June 1, 1940. e. attended Carnegie Mellon U.
THEATRE: Dark of the Moon, Beyond the Fringe, Tartuffe, King Lear, Fire, Julius Caesar, Charley's Aunt, Coco (Tony Award, 1970), Tricks, The Ruling Class, Twelfth Night, The Good Doctor (Tony nom.), Break a Leg, The New York Idea, Every Good Boy Deserves Favor, Richard III, The Misanthrope, Flea in Her Ear, Big River (Tony nom.), Metamorphosis, City of Angels (Tony nom.).
PICTURES: Lilith (debut, 1964), Petulia, M*A*S*H*, Brewster McCloud, McCabe and Mrs. Miller, Pete 'n Tillie, Images, Hindenberg, The Big Bus, King Kong, Eyes of Laura Mars, Where the Buffalo Roam, The Last Unicorn (voice), 3:15, Walker, Police Academy 5: Assignment Miami Beach, My Best Friend is a Vampire, The Little Mermaid (voice), The Feud, The Player (himself), Little Nemo (voice), The Ballad of Little Jo, Batman Forever, Cats Don't Dance (voice), Los Locos, Inspector Gadget, The Patriot, Burning Down the House, We All Fall Down, The Princess Diaries, Snide and Prejudice, The Last Unicorn.
TELEVISION: Movies: Once Upoon A Dead Man, The Birdmen, Shirts/Skins, King Lear, Panache, Kate Loves a Mystery, The Wild Wild West Revisited, Once Upon A Midnight Dreary, More Wild Wild West, The Kid from Nowhere, The Christmas Star, Longarm, Scooby Doo and the Ghoul School (voice), A Connecticut Yankee in King Arthur's Court, Absolute Strangers, Ned Blessing: The True Story of My Life, Wild Card, Sally Hemmings: An American Scandal, Gepetto. Mini-Series: The Rhineman Exchange, Dark Secret of Harvest Home, Series: Work on 23 series, many featuring voice work for animated programs incl. Xyber 9: New Dawn, House of Mouse, The Legend of Tarzan, Benson (actor, Emmy nom.). Star Trek: Deep Space Nine (dir.)Specials: Faerie Tale Theatre (The Frog Prince, Sleeping Beauty), King Lear, Legend of Sleepy Hollow (Emmy nom.), Fort Necessity, Incident at Vichy, The Booth, The Cask of Amontillado, Ashenden (BBC), The Lost Language of Cranes (BBC).

AUDRAN, STEPHANE
Actress. b. Versailles, France, Nov. 8, 1938. r.n. Collette Suzanne Dacheville. Former wife of French star Jean-Louis Trintignant and director Claude Chabrol.
PICTURES: Has appeared in 84 pictures, incl. Les Cousins (debut under direction of Chabrol, 1959), Les Bonnes Femmes, Bluebeard, The Third Lover, Six in Paris, The Champagne Murders, Les Biches, La Femme Infidele, The Lady in the Car, Le Boucher, Without Apparent Motive, La Rupture, Just Before Nightfall, The Discreet Charm of the Bourgeoisie, Blood Wedding, The Devil's Advocate, Le Cri de Couer, Vincent Francois Paul and the Others, The Black Bird (U.S. film debut), Ten Little Indians, The Silver Bears, Eagle's Wing, The Big Red One, Coup de Torchon, La Cage aux Folles III: The Wedding, Cop au Vin, Babette's Feast, Seasons of Pleasure, Faceless, Body-To-Body, Sons, Manika: The Girl Who Lived Twice, Quiet Days in Clichy, Mass in C Minor, Betty, Poulet au Vinaigre, Au Petit Marguery, Arlette, Maximum Risk, Arlette, Madeline, Belle Maman, Lulu Kreutz's Picnic, Speaking of Bunuel, J'a Faim!!!, My Wife's Name Is Maurice.
TELEVISION: Movies: Tatort, Les Affinites electives, La Marseillaise, Poor Little Rich Girl: The Barbara Hutton Story, Champagne Charlie, Weep No More My Lady, Petit, Un printemps de chien. Mini-Series: Orient-Express, Brideshead Revisited, The Sun also Rises, Mistral's Daughter, La Bicyclette bleu. Series: TECX.

AUERBACH, NORBERT T.
Executive. b. Vienna, Austria, Nov. 4, 1922. e. UCLA, business administration. Served with U.S. Army Intelligence in Europe during WWII. Entered motion picture industry after grad., 1946. First asst. dir. at Service Studios in CA. Moved to N.Y. to join domestic sales dept. of Film Classics. Joined Columbia Pictures in foreign dept. In 1950 assigned to Paris office, where remained for over decade, except for 18 mos. in Portugal as mgr. Returned to Paris in 1953 and filled number of exec. sls. positions for Columbia, ultimately rising to continental mgr. Left Columbia to produce films in France, 1961. Resumed career in dist. as continental mgr. at Paris office of United Artists. Returned to prod. to make The Thief of Paris, 1966. Joined Seven Arts Prods. heading theatrical and TV sls. operations in Paris, 1967. When Seven Arts acquired Warner Bros., he became continental sls. mgr. for Warners in Paris. Set up European prod. and dist. org. for CBS Cinema Center Films, operating from London, 1968. Moved to L.A. as v.p., foreign mgr. for CCF, 1972. Returned to London to be consultant in prod. and dist., 1973. Rejoined UA as sls. mgr. for Europe and the Middle East, 1977; named sr. v.p. & foreign mgr., 1978; named pres. & COO, Jan. 1981; pres. & CEO, Feb. 1981. Co-pres., United Int'l Pictures, London, until 1982. Acting pres. and chief exec. officer of Almi Distribution Corp., 1982. Formed packaging and financing Co., Eliktra, Inc., 1983. Now Almi consultant, exec. v.p. American Screen Co.

AUGUST, BILLE
Director. b. Brede, Denmark, Nov. 9, 1948. e. trained in advertising photography, Danish Film School, grad. 1971, cinematography. As cinematographer shot: Christiania, Homeward in the

Night, Man kan inte valdtas (Men Can't Be Raped), Karleken, The Grass is Singing. Became dir. 1978 with short Kim G. and dramas for Danish TV. Won Norway's Amanda Award for Lifetime Achievement in 1993.
PICTURES: Honning Maane (also sp.), Zappa (also s.p.), Buster's World, Twist and Shout (also s.p.), Pelle the Conquerer (also s.p.), The Best Intentions (Cannes Film Festival Palm d'Or Award, 1992), The House of the Spirits (also s.p.), Jerusalem (also s.p.), Smilla's Sense of Snow, Les Miserables, A Song for Martin.
TELEVISION: Movies: Maj. Mini-Series: Den Goda viljan, Busters verden.

AUSTIN, RAY
Baron Devere-Austin of Delvin, Lord of Bradwell. Producer, Director, Writer. b. London, England, Dec. 5, 1932. Has written, produced and directed many TV series, specials and movies. Lecturer, film & tv techniques, etc., 1978-93. Lecturer U. of VA.
PICTURES: Fun and Games, Virgin Witch, Curse of the Dead, Master Ninja I.
TELEVISION: Series: Dir.: Avengers, The Champions, Department S, Randall & Hopkirk, Ugliest Girl in Town, Journey into the Unknown, Magnum P.I., Simon and Simon, House Calls, Kings Crossing, Fall Guy, Lime Street (pilot), Spencer for Hire, Heaven Help Us, JAG. It's the Only Way to Go, Fun and Games, Space 1999, New Avengers, Hawaii Five-O, Sword of Justice, Webb, Barnaby Jones, Hardy Boys, Wonder Woman, Salvage, B.J. and the Bear, Hart to Hart, The Yeagers, Man Called Sloane, From Here to Eternity, Bad Cats, Westworld, Tales of the Gold Monkey (2-hr. pilot), The Return of the Man from U.N.C.L.E. Dir./Writer: Randall & Hopkirk, Black Beauty, Zany Adventures of Robin Hood, The Master, V, Air Wolf, Lime Street (pilot and episodes), Magnum P.I. (season premiere 2-hr. episode); Return of the Six Million Dollar Man (pilot); Our House (episodes), Dirty Dozen, Alfred Hitchcock Presents, A Fine Romance, Zorro, Boys of Twilight, Crossroads, Highlander, Heaven Help Us, JAG, CI5: The New Professionals.

AUTEUIL, DANIEL
Actor. b. Algeria, Jan. 24, 1950. Parents were lyric opera singers in roving troupe. Lived in Avignon. Performed in Amer. prod. in Paris of Godspell. Then did musical comedy for 2 years. Provided voice of baby for French print of U.S. film Look Who's Talking.
PICTURES: L'Aggression, Attention Les Yeaux, La Nuit de Saint-Germain des Pres, Monsieuer Papa, L'Amour Viole (Rape of Love), Heroes Are Not Wet Behind the Ears, Us Two, Les Sous-Doues, The Woman Banker, Clara et les Chic Types, Men Prefer Fat Girls, Pour 100 Briques t'as Plus Rien Maintentant, Que les Gros Salaires Levent le Doigt!!!, L'Indic, P'tit Con, The Beast, L'Arbalete, Palace, L'Amour en Douce, Jean de Florette, Manon of the Spring, Romuald and Juliette, A Few Days With Me, My Life is Hell, L'Elegant Criminel, Un Coeur en Hiver (A Heart in Winter), Ma Saison Preferee (My Favorite Season), Queen Margot, The Separation, Un Femme Francais, According to Pereira, The Eighth Day (Best actor, Cannes 1996), Thieves, Death in Therapy, Lucie Aubrac, On Guard, The Wrong Blonde, An Interesting State, The Lost Son, The Widow of Saint-Pierre, Sade, Le Placard, Vajont, L'Adversaire, Small Cuts.

AVALON, FRANKIE
Singer, Actor. r.n. Francis Thomas Avalone. b. Philadelphia, PA, Sept 18, 1940. e. South Philadelphia H.S. Trumpet prodigy age 9 yrs. Recording contract, Chancellor Records, Inc., 1957; Gold Record: Venus 1959; Gold Album: Swingin' on a Rainbow, 1959.
PICTURES: Jamboree (debut, 1957), Guns of the Timberland, The Alamo, Alakazam the Great (voice), Voyage to the Bottom of the Sea, Sail a Crooked Ship, Panic in the Year Zero, The Castilian, Operation Bikini, Drums of Africa, Beach Party, Muscle Beach Party, Bikini Beach, Pajama Party, Beach Blanket Bingo, I'll Take Sweden, Ski Party, How to Stuff a Wild Bikini, Sgt. Deadhead, Dr. Goldfoot and the Bikini Machine, Fireball 500, The Million Eyes of Sumuru, Skidoo, Horror House, The Take, Grease, Blood Song, Back to the Beach (also co-exec. prod.), Troop Beverly Hills, The Stoned Age, Casino
TELEVISION: Movies: A Dream Is A Wish Your Heart Makes: The Annette Funicello Story. Series: Easy Does It... Starring Frankie Avalon. Guest: Numerous appearances incl. Ed Sullivan, Perry Como, Pat Boone, Dick Clark Shows, Milton Berle, Steve Allen Show, The Patty Duke Show, Happy Days, Our Time, Full House, Sabrina the Teenage Witch.

AVEDON, DOE
Actress, b. Old Westbury, NY, April 7, 1928.
THEATRE: Young and the Fair, My Name Is Aquilon.
PICTURES: The High and the Mighty, Deep in My Heart, The Boss, Love Streams.
TELEVISION: Series: Big Town.

AVILDSEN, JOHN G.
Director, Cinematographer, Editor. b. Chicago, IL, Dec. 21, 1935. m. actress Tracy Brooks Swope. e. NYU. After service in Army made film with friend, Greenwich Village Story, then joined ad agency to write, direct, photograph & edit industrial films. Entered motion picture industry as ass't cameraman on Below the Hill, followed with prod. mgr. job on two Italian films

made in U.S. Afterwards, made first theatrical short, Smiles. Asst. dir., Black Like Me; prod. mgr., Mickey One, Una Moglie Americana; 2nd unit dir., Hurry Sundown. Produced, photographed & edited a short, Light—Sound—Diffuse. Returned to industry to make industrial films for ad agencies before resuming theatrical career. In 1977 won Acad. Award, best dir. for Rocky.
PICTURES: *Dir./photo./edit.*: Turn on to Love (debut), Out of It (assoc. prod., dir. of photog.), Sweet Dreams (aka Okay, Bill), Guess What We Learned in School Today?, Joe, Cry Uncle, The Stoolie, Save the Tiger, W. W. and the Dixie Dancekings, Foreplay, Rocky (Acad. Award, 1976), Slow Dancing in the Big City (also prod.), The Formula, Neighbors (also supv. edit.), Traveling Hopefully (documentary; Acad. Award nom.), A Night in Heaven, The Karate Kid, The Karate Kid: Part II, Happy New Year, For Keeps, Lean On Me (also exec. prod.), The Karate Kid Part III (also co-edit.), Rocky V (also co-edit.), The Power of One, Steal This Video Abbie Hoffman (documentary), 8 Seconds, Save The Everglades (documentary), A Fine and Private Place, Coyote Moon.
TELEVISION: From No House to Options House (2 On the Town, Emmy Award) Series: Murder Ink.

AVNET, JON
Producer, Director. b. Brooklyn, NY, Nov. 17, 1949. e. U. of PA, Sarah Lawrence Coll. Began career as director of off-B'way prods. Produced and directed low-budget film, Confusion's Circle, which brought a directing fellowship at American Film Institute. Joined Weintraub/Heller Prods. as assoc. prod., where met Steve Tisch, with whom formed Tisch/Avnet Prods. Formed Avnet/Kerner Co., 1986.
PICTURES: Checkered Flag or Crash (assoc. prod.), Outlaw Blues (assoc. prod.). *Producer:* Coast to Coast, Risky Business, Deal of the Century (exec. prod.), Less Than Zero, Tango & Cash, Men Don't Leave, Funny About Love, Fried Green Tomatoes (also dir., co-s.p.), The Mighty Ducks, The Mighty Ducks II, The Mighty Ducks III, The Three Musketeers (co-exec. prod.), When a Man Loves a Woman, The War (also dir.), Miami Rhapsody (co-exec. prod.), Up Close and Personal (also dir.), Red Corner (also dir.), George of the Jungle, Inspector Gadget (exec. prod.) Steal This Move (exec. prod.), The World of Tomorrow.
TELEVISION: Movies: *Producer:* No Other Love, Homeward Bound, Prime Suspect, Something So Right, Silence of the Heart, Calendar Girl Murders, Call to Glory (pilot and series), The Burning Bed, In Love and War (also exec. prod.), Between Two Women (also dir., co-s.p.), My Last Love. *Exec. Prod.*: Side By Side, My First Love, Breaking Point, Heatwave, Backfield in Motion, The Nightman, The Switch, Naomi and Wynona: Love Can Build a Bridge, Poodle Springs, Mama Flora's Family, My Last Love (exec. prod.) Parting the Waters (mini-series),A House Divided (exec. prod.), Uprising.

AXEL, GABRIEL
Director. b. Denmark, April 18, 1918. e. France, then studied acting at Danish National Conservatory. Returned to France where joined the Paris theatre co. of Louis Jouvet as stagehand. Worked as actor in Copenhagen Boulevard theatre where made directing debut. Went on to dir. Danish TV, mostly classic plays.
PICTURES: Golden Mountains (debut, 1957), Crazy Paradise, The Red Mantle, Danish Blue, Babette's Feast (also s.p.; Acad. Award for Best Foreign-Language Feature, 1988), Christian (also s.p.), Prince of Jutland (Royal Deceit; also s.p.), Lumiere & Company. *Actor:* The Reluctant Sadist, Love Me Darling, and numerous other Danish films. *Writer:* Crazy Paradise, The Red Mantle, Det Kaere Iegetoj, Babette's Feast, Christian, Prince of Jutland, Lumiere and Company, Leila.

AXELMAN, ARTHUR
Executive, Producer.. b. Philadelphia, PA, Dec. 10, 1944. e. Florida Atlantic U., B.A., 1969. Entered NY offices of William Morris Agency, June 1972; transferred to Bev. Hills offices, 1976, as literary agent. Founded company's original TV Movie dept., 1977; appointed v.p. in 1980; sr. v.p. in 1991. Among clients represented while overseeing network sales, negotiation, packaging, development, etc. of some 100 TV movies have been EMI TV, Bob Banner, Edward S. Feldman, Lee Grant, Thom Mount, Edward Anhalt, Zev Braun, Marvin Worth, Gilbert Cates, Jerry London, Jeremy Kagan, Dick Berg, Patty Duke, Finnegan-Pinchuk Prods.
TELEVISION: Movies: Family Blessings (exec. prod., 1996), The Alibi.

AXELROD, GEORGE
Writer, Producer, Director. b. New York, NY, June 9, 1922. Stage mgr., actor, summer stock, 1940-41; radio writer, 1941-52. AUTHOR: Novels: Beggar's Choice, Blackmailer; co-writer, night-club musical: All About Love, 1951. Memoirs: Where Am I Now When I Need Me?
THEATRE: B'way: The Seven Year Itch, Will Success Spoil Rock Hunter?, Visit to a Small Planet, Once More with Feeling, Goodbye Charlie (also dir.).
PICTURES: *Writer*: Phffft, The Seven Year Itch, Bus Stop, Breakfast at Tiffany's (Writer's Guild of Amer. Award, best-written Amer. comedy, 1962), The Manchurian Candidate (also co-prod.), Paris When It Sizzles (also co-prod.), How to Murder Your Wife, Lord Love a Duck (also dir., prod.), The Secret Life of an American Wife (also dir., prod.), The Lady Vanishes, The Holocroft Covenant, The Fourth Protocol, The Next Best Thing (acting only).

AXELROD, JONATHAN
Writer, Producer. b. New York, NY, July 9, 1952. Stepson of writer George Axelrod. Started as on-set "gofer" before writing screenplays. V.p. primetime drama dev., ABC Entertainment,1978-80; v.p. exec. dir. in charge dev. ABC Ent., 1980-82. Exec. v.p., Columbia Pictures TV, 1983-85. Pres. New World Pictures, 1985-87. Co-owner, Camden Artists, 1987-. Exec. v.p. Ventura Entertainment Group, 1989. Pres. & CEO Producers Entertainment Group, 1990-93. Formed Axelrod Woddoes Productions, 1994.
PICTURES: Every Little Crook and Nanny (writer).
TELEVISION: *Exec. Prod.*: Dave's World, Can't Hurry Love, A Day With, Manhattan Match, Late Bloomer, Brother's Keeper, The Price She Paid, Against the Wall (documentary), Movie Stars, Some of My Best Friends. *Writer:* Every Little Crook and Nanny.

AYKROYD, DAN
Actor, Writer. b. Ottawa, Canada, July 1, 1952. m. actress Donna Dixon. Member of Toronto Co. of Second City Theater. Worked as mgr. of Club 505, after-hours Toronto nightclub 1970-73. Performed and recorded (Briefcase Full of Blues, Made in America) with John Belushi as the Blues Brothers. Co-owner, Hard Rock Cafe.
PICTURES: Has appeared in nearly 60 pictures since debut in 1977 with Love at First Sight (also co-s.p.). Pictures incl. Mr. Mike's Mondo Video, 1941, The Blues Brothers (also co-s.p.), Neighbors, Trading Places, Twilight Zone—The Movie, Doctor Detroit, ndiana Jones and the Temple of Doom (cameo), Ghostbusters (also co-s.p.) It Came From Hollywood, Nothing Lasts Forever, Into the Night, Spies Like Us (also co-s.p.), Dragnet (also co-s.p.), The Couch Trip, The Great Outdoors, Caddyshack II, My Stepmother Is an Alien, Ghostbusters II (also co-s.p.), Driving Miss Daisy (Acad. Award nom.), Loose Cannons, Nothing But Trouble (also dir., s.p.), Masters of Menace, My Girl, This Is My Life, Sneakers, Chaplin, Coneheads (also co-s.p.), My Girl 2, North, Exit to Eden, Tommy Boy, Casper (cameo), The Random Factor (voice), Rainbow, Sgt. Bilko, Getting Away With Murder, Celtic Pride, Feeling Minnesota, My Fellow Americans, Grosse Pointe Blank, Susan's Plan, Antz (voice), Blues Brothers 2000 (also prod., s.p.), The House of Mirth, Stardom, Loser, On the Nose, Hitting the Wall, Pearl Harbor, Evolution, The Curse of the Jade Scorpion, The Devil and Daniel Webster, Crossroads, Unconditional Love, Bright Young Things.
TELEVISION: *Movies:* Things We Did Last Summer, All You Need Is Cash, The Arrow, Earth vs. the Spider. *Series:* Coming Up Rosie (Canada), Saturday Night Live 1975-79 (writer and performer; Emmy Award for writing: 1977). Steve Martin's Best Show Ever (performer, writer), Soul Man (also sup. prod.), Extreme Ghostbusters (writer only).

AZARIA, HANK
Actor. b. Forest Hills, NY, April 25, 1964. e. Tufts Univ.
PICTURES: Pretty Woman, Quiz Show, Now and Then, Heat, The Birdcage (Screen Actors Guild Award, outstanding performance by a Cast, 1997), Grosse Pointe Blank, Anastasia (voice), Mystery Alaska, Homegrown, Celebrity, Godzilla, Great Expectations, The Cradle Will Rock, Mystery Men, Cyber World (voice), America's Sweethearts, Bark.
TELEVISION: *Movies:* Tuesdays With Morrie (Emmy Award), Bartok the Magnificent, Cool Blue, Fail Safe, Uprising. *Series:* The Simpsons (voice, 2 Emmy Awards, 1998, 2001), Herman's Head, If Not for You, Mad About You, Stressed Eric (voice), The Hank Azaria Show, Imagine That. *Guest:* Fresh Prince of Bel-Air, Growing Pains, Friends.

AZNAVOUR, CHARLES
Actor, Singer, Songwriter. b. Paris, France, May 22, 1924. r.n. Shahnour Varenagh Aznavourian. Studied dance and drama as a child and was performing at the age of 10. Encouraged by Edith Piaf, became one of France's leading performers by the mid-1950s and an international concert star by the 1970s. Has also composed music for film.
PICTURES: Has appeared in 87 pictures acting &/or composing songs. Work includes Adieu Cherie (1947), C'est arrive a 36 Chandelles, Les Dragueurs, Shoot the Piano Player, Le testament d'Orphee, Le Passage du Rhin, Un taxi pour Tobrouk, Horace 62, Tempo di Roma, Les Quatres Verites, Le Rat'd Amerique, Pourquoi Paris?, Paris in August, Candy, The Games, The Adventurers, The Blockhouse, Ten Little Indians, The Twist, Sky Riders, Ciao Les Mecs, The Tin Drum, The Magic Mountain, Hatter's Ghosts, What Makes David Run?, Edith and Marcel, Long Live Life!, Mangeclous, Friend to Friend, Il Maestro, Double Game, The Country Years, Ararat, The Truth About Charlie.
TELEVISION: *Movies*: Sans Ceremonie, Un Alibi En Or, Laura, Les Momes, Judicael, Angelina, Passage du bac.. *Series:* Baldi.

B

BABENCO, HECTOR
Director. b. Buenos Aires, Argentina, Feb. 7, 1946. Early years spent in Mar del Plata. Left home at 17 and traveled throughout Europe for 8 years working as a writer, house-painter, salesman, and, in Rome, as an extra at Cinecitta. Moved to Sao Paulo, Brazil where he made several short documentaries, before turning to features in 1975.
PICTURES: Rei Da Noite (King of the Night; debut, 1975), Lucio

Flavio—Passageiro da Agonia, Pixote (also co-s.p.), Kiss of the Spider Woman, Ironweed, Besame Mucho (prod.), At Play in the Fields of the Lord (also co-s.p.), Foolish Heart (also prod. and s.p.), The Venice Project (additional dir.), Before Night Falls (acting only), Carandiru.

BACALL, LAUREN
Actress. r.n. Betty Joan Perske. b. New York, NY, Sept. 16, 1924. e. American Acad. Dram. Arts. Was m. Jason Robards, late Humphrey Bogart. *Autobiographies*: By Myself (1979), Now (1994).
THEATRE: *B'way*: Cactus Flower, Goodbye Charlie, Applause (Tony Award), Woman of the Year (Tony Award). *Foreign*: Sweet Bird of Youth. *Tour*: Wonderful Town.
PICTURES: To Have and Have Not (debut, 1944), Two Guys From Milwaukee (cameo), Confidential Agent, The Big Sleep, Dark Passage, Key Largo, Young Man With a Horn, Bright Leaf, How to Marry a Millionaire, A Woman's World, Cobweb, Blood Alley, Written on the Wind, Designing Woman, Gift of Love, Flame Over India, Shock Treatment, Sex and the Single Girl, Harper, Murder on the Orient Express, The Shootist, Health, The Fan, Appointment With Death, Mr. North, Innocent Victim, Misery, A Star for Two, All I Want for Christmas, Le Jour et La Nuit, Ready to Wear (Pret-a-Porter), The Mirror Has Two Faces (Golden Globe Award, 1997; Screen Actors Guild Award), My Fellow Americans, Day and Night, Madeline: Lost in Paris (voice), Diamonds, The Venice Project, Presence of Mind, Dogville, The Limit, Birth.
TELEVISION: *Movies*: Blithe Spirit, Applause, Perfect Gentlemen, Dinner at Eight, A Little Piece of Sunshine (BBC), The Portrait, From the Mixed Up Files of Mrs. Basil E. Frankweiler. *Mini-Series*: Too Rich: The Secret Life of Doris Duke. Guest: The Rockford Files, Inside Actors Studio, Chicago Hope, So Graham Norton.

BACH, CATHERINE
Actress. r.n. Catherine Bachman. b. Warren, Ohio, March 1, 1954. PICTURES: The Midnight Man (debut 1974), Thunderbolt and Lightfoot, Hustle, Widow's Revenge, Cannonball Run II, Street Justice, .Driving Force, Tunnels (Criminal Act), Music City Blues, Masters of Menace, The Nutt House, Rage and Honor.
TELEVISION: Movies: Matt Helm, Strange New World, Murder in Peyton Place, White Water Rebels, The Dukes of Hazzard: Reunion!, The Dukes of Hazzard: Hazzard in Hollywood, TV Road Trip. *Series*: The Dukes of Hazzard (1979-85), The Dukes (cartoon, voice), African Skies. Guest on many specials.

BACHARACH, BURT
Composer, Conductor, Arranger, Actor.. b. Kansas City, MO, May 12, 1928. e. McGraw U., Mannes Sch. of Music, Music Acad. of the West. Studied with composers Darius Milhaud, Henry Cowell, and Bohuslav Martinu. Conducted for Marlene Dietrich, Vic Damone. As a performer albums include: Burt Bacharach; Futures, Man! His Songs. Book: The Bacharach-David Song Book (1978).
THEATRE: Promises Promises (Tony Award, 1969).
PICTURES: Composer: Lizzie, The Sad Sack, The Blob, Country Music Holiday, Love in a Goldfish Bowl, Wives and Lovers, Who's Been Sleeping in My Bed?, Send Me No Flowers, A House Is Not a Home, What's New Pussycat?, Alfie, Made in Paris, After the Fox, Promise Her Anything, Casino Royale, The April Fools, Butch Cassidy and the Sundance Kid (2 Acad. Awards: Best Original Score & Best Song: Raindrops Keep Fallin' on My Head; 1970), Something Big, Lost Horizon, Together?, Arthur (Acad. Award for Best Song: Arthur's Theme; 1982), Night Shift, Best Defense, Tough Guys, Baby Boom, Arthur 2 on the Rocks, Love Hurts, Grace of My Heart, Austin Powers—International Man of Mystery (actor only), Austin Powers: The Spy Who Shagged Me (actor only), Isn't She Great, Bandits, Austin Powers in Goldmember.
TELEVISION: *Series*: Mont-Joye, Any Day Now.

BACON, KEVIN
Actor. b. Philadelphia, PA, July 8, 1958. m. actress Kyra Sedgwick. Studied at Manning St. Actor's Theatre. Apprentice at Circle-in-the-Square in N.Y. B'way debut in Slab Boys with Sean Penn. Narrated short film, A Little Vicious.
THEATRE: *B'way*: Slab Boys. *Off-B'way*: Getting Out (debut), Album, Forty Deuce (Obie Award), Poor Little Lambs, Flux, Men Without Dates, The Author's Voice, Loot, Road, Spike Heels.
PICTURES: National Lampoon's Animal House (debut, 1978), Starting Over, Hero at Large, Friday the 13th, Only When I Laugh, Forty Deuce, Diner, Enormous Changes at the Last Minute, Footloose, Quicksilver, White Water Summer, Planes Trains and Automobiles, She's Having a Baby, End of the Line, Criminal Law, The Big Picture, Tremors, Flatliners, Queens Logic, He Said/She Said, Pyrates, JFK, A Few Good Men, The Air Up There, The River Wild, Murder in the First, Apollo 13, Balto (voice), Sleepers, Picture Perfect, Telling Lies in America, Elizabeth Jane, Digging to China, Wild Things (also exec. prod.), My Dog Skip, Stir of Echoes, Hollow Man, Novocaine, We Married Margo, Trapped, Dolan's Cadillac, Mystic River, In the Cut, Cavedweller.
TELEVISION: Movies: The Gift, The Demon Murder Case, The Tender Age (The Little Sister), Lemon Sky, Losing Chase (dir. only). *Specials*: Mr. Roberts. *Series*: Search for Tomorrow, The Guiding Light. Guest: Mad About You, Frasier (voice), Will & Grace.

BADALAMENTI, ANGELO
Composer, orchestrator. b. New York, NY, March 22, 1937. PICTURES: Gordon's War (debut 1973), Law and Disorder,

Blue Velvet, Weeds, A Nightmare on Elm Street 3: Dream Warriors, Tough Guys Don't Dance, Wait Until Spring Bandini, Parents, National Lampoon's Christmas Vacation, Cousins, The Comfort of Strangers, Wild at Heart, Twin Peaks: Fire Walk with Me, Naked in New York, The City of Lost Children, The Blood Oranges, Lost Highway, Story of a Bad Boy, Arlington Road, The Straight Story (Golden Globe nom., best orig. score, 2000), Holy Smoke, Forever Mine, The Beach, A Piece of Eden, Mulholland Drive (Golden Globe nom. for best orig. score, 2002), Cet amour-la, Suspended Animation, Secretary, The Adversary Mysteries of Love, Autofocus, Cabin Fever, Rabbits, Resistance.
TELEVISION: *Movies/Specials*: Industrial Symphony No. 1: The Dream of the Broken Hearted, The Last Don. *Series*: Twin Peaks, On the Air, Hotel Room, Inside the Actors Studio (main theme), Cracker, Profiler (main title theme).

BADER, DIEDRICH
Actor. b. Alexandria, VA, Dec. 24, 1966.
PICTURES: The Beverly Hillbillies (debut 1993), Teresa's Tattoo, Office Space, Certain Guys, Couple Days...A Period Piece, Recess: School's Out (voice), Jay and Silent Bob Strike Back, Ice Age (voice), The Country Bears, Evil Alien Conquerors, Dead & Breakfast.
TELEVISION: *Movies*: Desert Rats, The Preppie Murder, The Assassination File, Olive the Other Reindeer (voice), Rock & Roll Back to School Special. *Series*: Danger Theatre, The Drew Carey Show, Disney's Hercules (voice), Baby Blues (voice), Buzz Lightyear of Star Command (voice), The Zeta Project (voice), Lloyd in Space (voice). *Guest*: Numerous appearances incl. 21 Jump Street, Star Trek: The Next Generation,Cheers, Quantum Leap, Frasier, Gargoyles (voice),

BADHAM, JOHN
Director, Producer.. b. Luton, England, Aug. 25, 1939. Raised in Alabama. e. Yale U., B.A.; Yale Drama School, M.F.A. Sister is actress Mary Badham. Landed first job at Universal Studio mailroom; later was Universal tour guide, a casting dir. and assoc. prod. to William Sackheim. Twice nominated for Emmy Awards for TV movies. Recipient of George Pal Award.
PICTURES: The Bingo Long Traveling All-Stars and Motor Kings (debut 1976), Saturday Night Fever, Dracula (Best Horror Film award, Science Fiction/Fantasy Academy), Whose Life Is It Anyway? (San Rafael Grand Prize), Blue Thunder, War Games (Best Directing award, Science Fiction/Fantasy Academy), American Flyers, Short Circuit, Stakeout (also exec. prod.), Disorganized Crime (exec. prod. only), Bird on a Wire, The Hard Way, Point of No Return, Dragon: The Bruce Lee Story (Exec. prod. only), Another Stakeout (also exec. prod.), Drop Zone (also exec. prod.), Nick of Time (also prod.), Incognito, Floating Away, Ocean Warrior.
TELEVISION: *Movies*: Night Gallery (assoc. prod. only), Neon Ceiling (assoc. prod. only), The Impatient Heart, Isn't It Shocking?, The Law, The Gun, Reflections of Murder, The Godchild, The Keegans, Relentless: Mind of a Killer (co-exec. prod. only), Rebound: The Legend of Earl "The Goat" Manigault (exec. prod. only), The Jack Bull, The Last Debate, My Brother's Keeper, Obsessed.. *Series episodes*: The Senator (also assoc. prod.), Night Gallery, Streets of San Francisco, The Doctors, Owen Marshall - Counsellor at Law, Sunshine, Nichols, Cannon, Sarge, The Sixth Sense, Cool Million, Police Story, The Shield.

BAILEY, JOHN
Cinematographer. b. Moberly, MO, Aug. 10, 1942. m. film editor Carol Littleton. e. U. of Santa Clara, Loyola U., U.S.C., U. of Vienna. Lecturer, American Film Institute, 1982, 1984, 1994.
PICTURES: Premonition, End of August, Legacy, The Mafu Cage (visual consult.), Boulevard Nights, Winter Kills (add. photog.), American Gigolo, Ordinary People, Honky Tonk Freeway, Continental Divide, Cat People, That Championship Season, Without a Trace, The Big Chill, Racing With the Moon, The Pope of Greenwich Village, Mishima: A Life In Four Chapters (Cannes Film Fest. Award, best artistic contrib., 1985), Silverado, Crossroads, Brighton Beach Memoirs, Light of Day, Swimming to Cambodia, Tough Guys Don't Dance (visual consult.), Vibes, The Accidental Tourist, My Blue Heaven, The Search for Signs of Intelligent Life in the Universe (also dir.), A Brief History of Time, Groundhog Day, In the Line of Fire, China Moon (dir. only), Nobody's Fool, Mariette in Ecstasy (dir. only), Extreme Measures, As Good As It Gets, Living Out Loud, Forever Mine, The Out-of-Towners, For Love of the Game, Michael Jordan to the Max, Via Dolorosa, Anti-Trust, The Anniversary Party, N'Sync: Bigger Than Life, The Kid Stays in the Picture, The Divine Secrets of the Ya-Ya Sisterhood, Naqoyqatsi, The Fig Rig, How to Lose a Guy in 10 Days,
TELEVISION: *Movies*: Battered, City in Fear, Always Outnumbered, Searching for Michael Cimino (documentary).

BAIO, SCOTT
Actor. b. New York, NY, Sept. 22, 1961. Started career at 9 doing commercials and voiceovers.
PICTURES: Bugsy Malone (debut 1976), Skatetown USA, Foxes, Zapped!, I Love New York, Detonator, Very Mean Men, The Bread My Sweet, Face Value, Face to Face (also s.p.), Dumb Luck, Baby Geniuses 2: Superbabies.
TELEVISION: *Movies*: Luke Was There, The Boy Who Drank Too Much, Senior Trip, Stoned, All the Kids Do It, Alice in Wonderland, The Truth About Alex, Perry Mason: The Case of the Fatal Fashion, Mixed Blessings, Bar Hopping. *Series*: Blansky's Beauties, Happy Days, Who's Watching the Kids?, Joanie Loves Chachi, Charles in Charge (also dir.), Baby Talk, Diagnosis Murder, Before They Were

Stars (host). *Series/Director*: The New Lassie, Out of This World, First Time Out, Harry and the Hendersons, Wayans Brothers, Jamie Foxx Show, Nick Freno: Licensed Teacher, Kirk, The Parkers. *Guest*: Hotel, The Fall Guy, Full House, Can't Hurry Love.

BAKER, BLANCHE
Actress. r.n. Blanche Garfein. b. New York, NY, Dec. 20, 1956. Daughter of actress Carroll Baker and dir. Jack Garfein. e. Wellesley, Coll., studied acting with Uta Hagen. Acting debut, White Marriage, Yale Repertory Co. (1978), Regional Theater. B'way debut in Lolita (1981).
PICTURES: The Seduction of Joe Tynan (debut, 1979), French Postcards, Sixteen Candles, Raw Deal, Cold Feet, Nobody's Child, Shakedown, The Handmaid's Tale, Livin' Large, Bum Rap, Dead Funny.
TELEVISION: *Movies*: Mary and Joseph, The Day the Bubble Burst, The Awakening of Candra, Day the Bubble Burst, Embassy, Nobody's Child. *Mini-Series*: Holocaust (Emmy Award, 1978). *Specials*: Romeo & Juliet. *Guest*: The Equalizer, Spenser: For Hire, Law & Order, In the Heat of the Night.

BAKER, CARROLL
Actress. b. Johnstown, PA, May 28, 1931. e. PA schools and St. Petersburg (FL) Junior Coll. Career started as dancer in night-clubs. Actors' Studio N.Y. Made stage debut in Escapade, then acted in All Summer Long. *Autobiography*: Baby Doll.
PICTURES: Easy to Love (debut, 1953), Giant, Baby Doll, The Big Country, But Not for Me, The Miracle, Bridge to the Sun, Something Wild, How the West Was Won, The Carpetbaggers, Station Six Sahara, Cheyenne Autumn, The Greatest Story Ever Told, Sylvia, Mister Moses, Harlow, Jack of Diamonds, The Sweet Body of Deborah, Paranoia, A Quiet Place to Kill, Captain Apache, The Harem, Honeymoon, My Father's Wife, Bloodbath (The Sky Is Falling), Andy Warhol's Bad, The World is Full of Married Men, Watcher in the Woods, Star 80, The Secret Diary of Sigmund Freud, Native Son, Ironweed, Red Monarch, Kindergarten Cop, Blonde Fist, Cybereden, Undercurrent, Skeletons, Just Your Luck, The Game, Nowhere to Go, Cinerama Adventure (documentary).
TELEVISION: *Movies*: Hitler's SS: Portrait in Evil, On Fire, Judgment Day: The John List Story, Men Don't Tell, A Kiss to Die For, North Shore Fish, Heart Full of Rain, Big Guns Talk: The Story of the Western, Another Woman's Husband. *Guest*: Tales from the Crypt, L.A. Law, Chicago Hope.

BAKER, DIANE
Actress. b. Hollywood, CA, Feb. 25, 1938. e. USC.
PICTURES: The Diary of Anne Frank (debut, 1959), The Best of Everything, Journey to the Center of the Earth, Tess of the Storm Country, The Wizard of Baghdad, Hemingway's Adventures of a Young Man, The Prize, Straight Jacket, Marnie, Mirage, Sands of Beersheba, The Horse in the Grey Flannel Suit, Baker's Hawk, The Pilot, The Silence of the Lambs, The Closer, The Joy Luck Club, Twenty Bucks, Imaginary Crimes, The Net, The Cable Guy, Murder at 1600, Harrison's Flowers, On the Roof, The Keeper.
TELEVISION: *Movies*: Dangerous Days of Kiowa Jones, Trial Run, The D.A.: Murder One, The Old Man Who Cried Wolf, Do You Take This Stranger?, Sarge: The Badge or the Cross, Congratulations It's a Boy!, A Little Game, Killer By Night, Police Story (pilot), A Tree Grows in Brooklyn, The Dream Makers, The Last Survivors, Fugitive Family, The Haunted, Perry Mason: The Case of the Heartbroken Bride, About Sarah, The Trouble With Marnie, *Mini-Series*: The Blue and the Gray, A Woman of Substance (also prod.), Jackie Bouvier Kennedy Onassis. *Series*: Here We Go Again, Crazy Love.

BAKER, DYLAN
Actor. b. Syracuse, NY Oct. 7, 1959. e. Southern Methodist Univ. (BFA), Yale Sch. of Drama (MFA).
THEATRE: *B'way*: Eastern Standard (Theatre World Award), La Bete (Tony nom.). *Off-B'way*: Not About Heroes (Obie Award). In 1999 received the Gotham Awards "Breakthrough Award."
PICTURES: Planes Trains & Automobiles (debut, 1987), The Wizard of Loneliness, The Long Walk Home, Delirious, Passed Away, Love Potion No. 9, The Last of the Mohicans, Life With Mikey, Radioland Murders, Disclosure, The Stars Fell on Henrietta, True Blue, Happiness (Ft. Lauderdale Int'l. Film Fest. Critic's Choice Award, best actor, 1998), Oxygen, Simply Irresistible, Random Hearts, Committed, Requiem for a Dream, The Cell, Thirteen Days Which Shocked the World, The Tailor of Panama, Along Came a Spider, A Gentleman's Game, The Laramie Project, Changing Lanes, Road to Perdition, Grasp (short), Head of State, The Amazing Spider-Man.
TELEVISION: *Movies*: A Case of Deadly Force, Judgment, Love Honor and Obey: The Last Mafia Marriage, Forbidden Territory: Stanley's Search for Livingstone, The Invisible Man, The Big Time. *Mini-Series*: Return to Lonesome Dove, From the Earth to the Moon. *Series*: Murder One, Feds, The Pitts.

BAKER, GEORGE
Actor. b. Varna, Bulgaria, April 1, 1931. e. Lancing College, Sussex. Stage debut Deal Repertory Theatre, 1946. AUTHOR: The Fatal Spring, Imaginary Friends, Going for Broke, The Marches of Wales, The Hopkins, Just a Hunch, Sister, Dear Sister, From Doom With Death, Talking About Mira Beau, The Last Silence.
PICTURES: The Intruder (debut, 1953), The Dam Busters, The Ship That Died of Shame, Woman for Joe, The Extra Day, The Feminine Touch, A Hill in Korea, No Time for Tears, These Dangerous Years, The Moonraker, Tread Softly Stranger, Lancelot and Guinevere, Curse of the Fly, Mister Ten Per Cent,

Goodbye Mr. Chips, Justine, The Executioners, On Her Majesty's Secret Service, A Warm December, The Fire Fighters, The Spy Who Loved Me, Thirty-Nine Steps, A Nightingale Sang in Berkeley Square, Hopscotch, North Sea Hijack, For Queen and Country, Back to the Secret Garden.
TELEVISION: *Movies*: Has appeared in more than 35 tv movies, 23 in the role of Detective Chief Inspector Reg Wexford--Hake Hands Forever (1988), It Shouldn't Happen to a TV actor (2003). Other tv movies incl. Alice, The Bonegrinder, Fatal Spring (writer only), The Secret Adversary, The Canterville Ghost, Coast to Coast, At Bertram's Hotel. *Mini-Series*: I Claudius, A Woman of Substance, Goodbye Mr. Chips, Dead Head, If Tomorrow Comes, Little Lord Fauntleroy, Ruth Rendell: The Strawberry Tree (writer only). *Series*: The Truth About Melandrinos, Nick of the River, Bowler, Triangle, No Job for a Lady, Johnny and the Dead.

BAKER, JOE DON
Actor. b. Groesbeck, TX, Feb. 12, 1936. e. North Texas State Coll., B.B.A., 1958. Began career on N.Y. stage, in Marathon 33 and Blues for Mr. Charlie. L.A. stage in The Caine Mutiny Court Martial.
PICTURES: Cool Hand Luke (debut, 1967), Guns of the Magnificent Seven, Adam at Six A.M., Wild Rovers, Five Days Home, Junior Bonner, Walking Tall, Charley Varrick, The Outfit, Golden Needles, Mitchell, Framed, Checkered Flag or Crash, Speedtrap, The Pack, Wacko, Joysticks, The Natural, Fletch, Getting Even, The Living Daylights, The Killing Time, Leonard Part 6, Criminal Law, The Children, Cape Fear, The Distinguished Gentleman, Reality Bites, Panther, The Underneath, Congo, Grass Harp, Goldeneye, Mars Attacks!, Tomorrow Never Dies, Vegas City of Dreams, The Commission
TELEVISION: *Movies*: Mongo's Back in Town, That Certain Summer, To Kill a Cop, Power, The Abduction of Kari Swenson, Edge of Darkness (BBC mini-series), Defrosting the Fridge (BBC), Citizen Cohn, Complex of Fear, Ruby Ridge: An American Tragedy, To Dance with Olivia, George Wallace, Poodle Springs, Too Rich: The Secret Life of Doris Duke. *Series*: Eischeid, In the Heat of the Night. *Guest*: In the Heat of the Night, Gunsmoke, Mission: Impossible, The Streets of San Francisco.

BAKER, KATHY
Actress. B. Midland, TX, June 8, 1950. Raised in Albuquerque, NM. e. U of C-Berkeley. Stage debut in San Francisco premiere of Fool for Love (won Obie and Theatre World Awards for New York debut in same). Also appeared in Desire Under the Elms, Aunt Dan and Lemon.
PICTURES: The Right Stuff (debut, 1983), Street Smart (Natl. Society of Film Critics Award), Permanent Record, A Killing Affair, Clean and Sober, Jacknife, Dad, Mr. Frost, Edward Scissorhands, Article 99, Jennifer Eight, Mad Dog and Glory, To Gillian on Her 37th Birthday, Inventing the Abbotts, The Cider House Rules, Things You Can Tell Just by Looking at Her, A Little Inside, Ten Tiny Love Stories, The Glass House, Assasination Tango, Cold Mountain, 13 Going on 30..
TELEVISION: *Movies*: Nobody's Child, The Image, One Special Victory, Lush Life, Not In This Town, Weapons of Mass Destruction, Oklahoma City: A Survivor's Story, A Season for Miracles, Ratz, Sanctuary, A Family's Decision, Door to Door. *Series*: Picket Fences (2 Emmy Awards: 1993, 1995), Boston Public, Murphy's Dozen. *Mini-series*: Shake Rattle and Roll: An American Love Story. *Guest*: Gun, Ally McBeal, The Practice, The Guardian.

BAKER, RICK
Makeup Artist, Performer. b. Binghamton, NY, Dec. 8, 1950. Started as assist. to makeup artist Dick Smith before creating his own designs in 1972. Frequent film appearances in makeup, usu-ally as gorillas. Worked on Michael Jackson's video Thriller. Winner of 6 Academy Awards.
PICTURES: *Actor*: The Thing With Two Heads, King Kong, The Kentucky Fried Movie, The Incredible Shrinking Woman, Into the Night. *Makeup Design*: Shlock, Zebra Force, It's Alive, The Incredible Melting Man, Star Wars (2nd unit; also actor), It Lives Again, The Howling (consultant), Funhouse, An American Werewolf in London (Acad. Award, 1981), Videodrome, Greystoke: The Legend of Tarzan Lord of the Apes (also cos-tume design; Acad. Award nom.), Ratboy, Harry and the Hendersons (Acad. Award, 1987), Coming to America (Acad. Award nom.), Gorillas in the Mist (also assoc. prod.), Missing Link, Wolf, Ed Wood (Acad. Award, 1994), Batman and Robin, Mighty Joe Young, Batman Forever (also designed monster bat), Escape From L.A. The Nutty Professor (Acad. Award, 1996), Men in Black (Acad. Award, Best Makeup, 1997), A Thousand Acres, The Devil's Advocate, Critical Care, Psycho, Mighty Joe Young, Life, Nutty Professor II: The Klumps, How the Grinch Stole Christmas (Acad. Award, 2001), Planet of the Apes, Ring, Hellboy, The Hulk, The Cat in the Hat, The Haunted Mansion, Cursed, Hellboy.. *Other*: Tanya's Island (beast design), Starman (transformation scenes), Cocoon (consultant), My Science Project (Tyrannosaurus Rex sequences consultant), Max My Love (chimpanzee consultant), Gremlins 2: The New Batch (co-prod., f/x supervisor), Baby's Day Out (baby f/x), Just Cause (special bodies), Little Panda (panda suits).
TELEVISION: *Movies*: The Autobiography of Miss Jane Pittman (Emmy Award), An American Christmas Carol, Something Is Out There. *Makeup Design*: *Series*: Werewolf, Beauty and the Beast, Harry and the Hendersons.

BAKER, ROY WARD
Director, Producer. b. London, England, Dec. 19, 1916. e. Lycaee Corneille, Rouen; City of London School. Ass't dir. with Gainsborough 1934-40; served in Army 1940-46.

PICTURES: Has 32 picture credits, incl. The October Man, Operation Disaster, Don't Bother to Knock, Inferno, One That Got Away, A Night to Remember, The Singer Not the Song (also prod.), Flame in the Streets (also prod.), The Anniversary, Vampire Lovers, Dr. Jekyll and Sister Hyde, Asylum (Paris Grand Prize), Seven Brothers Meet Dracula, The Monster Club.
TELEVISION: Movies: The Spy Killer, Foreign Exchange, Sherlock Holmes and the Masks of Death, Minder: An Officer and a Car Salesman. Mini-Series: The Flame Trees of Thika. Series: Dir. credits on 21 series, incl. The Avengers, Return of the Saint, Fairly Secret Army, The Good Guys.

BAKER, DR. WILLIAM F.
Executive. b. 1944. e. Case Western Reserve U., B.A., M.A., Ph.D. Began broadcasting career in Cleveland while still a student. Joined Scripps-Howard Broadcasting, 1971. Joined Group W as v.p. and general mgr., WJZ-TV, 1978; served as pres. and CEO, Group W Productions; pres. of Group W. Television, 1979; chmn., Group W Satellite Communications, 1981. Carried Explorers Club flag to top of world, becoming one of few in history to visit both North and South Poles, 1983. Appointed pres. and CEO, WNET/Thirteen, NY PBS station, 1987 - present. Pres., NY Chapter, Natl. Acad. Television Arts & Sciences, 1998-2001. Recipient of 4 Emmy Awards, 2 Columbia Dupont Journalism Awards. Author of, Down the Tube, 1998.

BAKER, WILLIAM M.
Executive. b. Newark, NJ, Dec. 26, 1939. e. University of Virginia 1961. Joined FBI in 1965. From 1987 to 1989, took a haitus from the FBI to serve as dir. of Public Affairs for the CIA. Retired from position as asst. dir., Criminal Investigative Division of FBI in 1991. Pres. and COO Motion Picture Assoc. and exec. v.p., Motion Picture Assoc. of America.

BAKSHI, RALPH
Animator, Writer, Director. b. Haifa, Israel, Oct. 29, 1938. Began career at Terrytoons at age 18 as cell painter and animator, then creative dir. 1965, headed Paramount Cartoons, 1967. Pres., Bakshi Prods. Inc., 1973-.
PICTURES: Dir./S.P./Writer: Fritz the Cat, Heavy Traffic, Coonskin. Also Prod/Co-prod.: Wizards (also prod.), The Lord of the Rings, American Pop, Hey Good Lookin', Fire and Ice, Cannonball Run II (animator), Cool World, Malcolm and Melving, Babe He Calls Me.
TELEVISION: Movies: Imaging America (dir. only), Cool and the Crazy. Series: Matty's Funday Funnies, Hector Heathcote Show (animator), The Mighty Heroes (dir. only), Spider-Man (also prod.), Mighty Mouse: The New Adventures, Tattertown (writer and prod.), Spicy City (also exec. prod.).

BAKULA, SCOTT
Actor. b. St. Louis, MO, Oct. 9, 1955. e. Kansas Univ.
THEATRE: NY: Marilyn: An American Fable, Three Guys Naked from the Waist Down, Romance/Romance (Tony nom.).
LA: Nite Club Confidential.
PICTURES: Sibling Rivalry, Necessary Roughness, Color of Night, A Passion to Kill, My Family, Lord of Illusions, Cats Don't Dance (voice), Major League: Back to the Minors, Luminarias, American Beauty, Above Suspicion, Life As A House, Role of a Lifetime.
TELEVISION: Movies: I-Man, The Last Fling, An Eye for an Eye, Quantum Leap: Genesis, In the Shadow of a Killer, Mercy Mission: The Rescue of Flight 771, Nowhere to Hide, The Bachelor's Baby (also exec. prod.), Mean Streak, NetForce, In the Name of the People, Papa's Angels, The Trial of Old Drum, Star Trek Enterprise: Broken Bow, What Girls Learn. Miniseries: The Invaders, A Girl Thing. Series: Gung Ho, Designing Women, Eisenhower & Lutz, Quantum Leap (Emmy noms.), Golden Globe Award, also dir.), Murphy Brown, Mr. & Mrs. Smith, Enterprise. Guest: Matlock, My Sister Sam.

BALABAN, BOB
Actor, Director. b. Chicago, IL, Aug. 16, 1945. Began studying with Second City troupe while still in high school. Attended Colgate U. and NYU while appearing on Broadway in Plaza Suite.
THEATRE: You're a Good Man Charlie Brown, The Inspector General, Who Wants to Be the Lone Ranger?, The Basic Training of Pavlo Hummel, The Children, The White House Murder Case, Some of My Best Friends, The Three Sisters, The Boys Next Door, Speed-the-Plow, Some Americans Abroad.
PICTURES: Actor: Midnight Cowboy (debut, 1969), Me Natalie, The Strawberry Statement, Catch-22, Making It, Bank Shot, Report to the Commissioner, Close Encounters of the Third Kind, Girlfriends, Altered States, Prince of the City, Absence of Malice, Whose Life Is It Anyway?, 2010, In Our Hands (doc.), End of the Line, Dead-Bang, Alice, Little Man Tate, Bob Roberts, For Love or Money, Greedy, Pie in the Sky, Deconstructing Harry, Waiting For Guffman, Conversation with the Beast, The Definite Maybe (also prod.), Clockwatchers, Natural Selection, The Cradle Will Rock, Jakob the Liar, Three to Tango, Best in Show, Tex: The Passive Aggressive Gunslinger, The Mexican, Plan B, Ghost World, Gosford Park (also idea, prod.), The Majestic, Voltage, The Tuxedo, A Mighty Wind, 5-25-77.. Director: My Boyfriend's Back, The Last Good Time (also prod, co-s.p.).
TELEVISION: Movies: Marriage: Year One, The Face of Fear, Unnatural Pursuits, The Late Shift, Giving Up the Ghost, Swing Vote. Series: Director: Tales From the Darkside, Amazing Stories, Eerie Indiana, Subway Stories: Tales from the Underground, Legend, Oz, Strangers with Candy, Now and Again, Deadline, The Twilight Zone.

BALDWIN, ADAM
Actor. b. Chicago, IL, Feb. 27, 1962. While in high school in Winnetka, was chosen by dir. Tony Bill for role in My Bodyguard. Made stage debut in Album, Chicago.
PICTURES: My Bodyguard (debut, 1980), Ordinary People, D.C. Cab, Reckless, Hadley's Rebellion, Bad Guys, 3:15, Full Metal Jacket, The Chocolate War, Cohen and Tate, Next of Kin, Predator 2, Guilty By Suspicion, Radio Flyer, Where the Day Takes You, Deadbolt, Bitter Harvest, Eight Hundred Leagues Down the Amazon, Wyatt Earp, How to Make an American Quilt, Independence Day, Lover's Knot, Starquest II, The Patriot, The Right Temptaions, Pursiot of Happiness, Jackpot, The Keyman, Double Bang, Betrayal, The Crawl Space.
TELEVISION: Movies: Off Sides, Poison Ivy, Welcome Home Bobby, Murder in High Places, Cruel Doubt, Cold Sweat, Sawbones, Smoke Jumpers, The Cape, Indiscreet, From the Earth to the Moon, Gargantua, Dr. Jekyll & Mr. Hyde, Control Factor. Special: The Last Shot. Series: The Cape, Firefly. Guest: The Visitor, VR5, The X-Files, C.S.I.: Miami.

BALDWIN, ALEC
Actor. r.n. Alexander Rae Baldwin III. b. Massapequa, NY, April 3, 1958. e. George Washington U., NYU. Brother of actors Stephen, William and Daniel Baldwin. Trained at Lee Strasberg Theatre Inst. and with Mira Rostova, Elaine Aiken. Started career in daytime TV on serial, The Doctors. Member, The Creative Coalition.
THEATRE: A Midsummer Night's Dream, The Wager, Summertree, A Life in the Theatre (Hartman), Study in Scarlet (Williamstown). NY: Loot (B'way debut); Theatre World Award, 1986), Serious Money, Prelude to a Kiss, A Streetcar Named Desire.
PICTURES: Forever Lulu (debut, 1987), She's Having a Baby, Beetlejuice, Married to the Mob, Working Girl, Talk Radio, Great Balls of Fire!, The Hunt for Red October, Miami Blues, Alice, The Marrying Man, Prelude to a Kiss, Glengarry Glen Ross, Malice, The Getaway, The Shadow, Heaven's Prisoners (also exec. prod.), The Juror, Looking For Richard, Ghosts of Mississippi, The Edge, Mercury Rising, Thick as Thieves, Notting Hill, The Confession (also prod.), Outside Providence, Thomas and the Magic Railroad, State and Main, The Acting Class, Pearl Harbor, Cats & Dogs, Final Fantasy: The Spirits Within (voice), The Royal Tenenbaums (narrator), The Devil and Daniel Webster, Broadway: The Golden Age by the Legends Who Were There, The Cooler, The Playmakers of New Orleans, The Cat in the Hat, The Last Shot, The Aviator.
TELEVISION: Movies: Sweet Revenge, Love on the Run, Dress Gray, The Alamo: 13 Days to Glory, A Streetcar Named Desire, Path to War, Second Nature. Series: The Doctors (1980-82), Cutter to Houston, Knots Landing, Thomas the Tank Engine & Friends (narrator), Clerks (voice). Guest: Hotel, Saturday Night Live, The Simpsons, Friends.

BALDWIN, DANIEL
Actor. b. Long Island, NY, Oct. 5, 1960. e. Nassau Comm. Col., Ball St. Univ. Brother of actors Alec, William and Stephen Baldwin.
PICTURES: Born on the Fourth of July, Harley Davidson and the Marlboro Man, Knight Moves, Car 54 Where Are You?, Bodily Harm, Yesterday's Target, Trees Lounge, Lone Justice, Mullholland Drive, The Invader, The Treat, Phoenix, The Pandora Project, On the Border, Love Kills, John Carpenter's Vampires, Water Damage, Net Worth, In Pursuit, Fall, Silver Man, Irish Eyes, Ancient Warriors., Dynamite, Water's Edge, King of the Ants.
TELEVISION: Movies: Too Good to Be True, L.A. Takedown, The Heroes of Desert Storm, Ned Blessing: The True Story of My Life, Attack of the 50 Foot Woman, Family of Cops, Twisted Desire, Wild Grizzly, Homicide: The Movie, Killing Moon, Open House. Series: Sydney, Homicide: Life on the Street. Guest: Family Ties, The Larry Sanders Show, Dead Man's Gun, The Outer Limits, NYPD Blue, Touched By An Angel.

BALDWIN, STEPHEN
Actor. b. Long Island, NY, May 12, 1966. Brother of actors Alec, William and Daniel Baldwin. Stage debut in Off-B'way prod., Out of America.
PICTURES: The Beast of War, Born on the Fourth of July, Last Exit to Brooklyn, Crossing the Bridge, Bitter Harvest, Posse, New Eden, 8 Seconds, Threesome, A Simple Twist of Fate, Mrs. Parker and the Vicious Circle, Fall Time, The Usual Suspects, Under the Hula Moon, Bio-Dome, Fled, Sub Down, Scar City, One Tough Cop, Half Baked, The Sex Monster, The Flintstones in Viva Rock Vegas, Friends & Lovers, The Sex Monster, Mercy, Cutaway, Xchange, Table One, Dead Awake, Greenmail, Protection, Slap Shot 2: Breaking the Ice, Deadrockstar, Fly Boys, Firefight, Six: The Mark Unleashed, Shelter Island.
TELEVISION: Movies: Jury Duty, Dead Weekend, Mr. Murder, Absence of the Good, Zebra Lounge. Specials: In a New Light: Sex Unplugged (co-host). Series: The Young Riders. Guest: Family Ties, China Beach,Night Visions, Fear Factor.

BALDWIN, WILLIAM
Actor. b. Massapequa, NY, Feb. 21, 1963. e. SUNY/Binghamton. Degree in political science; worked in Washington on staff of rep. Thomas J. Downey. Brother of actors Alec, Stephen and Daniel Baldwin. With Ford Model agency, appearing in tv ads while studying acting. Member, The Creative Coalition.
PICTURES: Born on the Fourth of July (debut, 1989), Internal

Affairs, Flatliners, Backdraft, Three of Hearts, Sliver, A Pyromaniac's Love Story, Fair Game, Curdled, Shattered Image, Virus, Primary Suspect, Relative Values, One Eyed King, Double Bang, Say Nothing, You Stupid Man, Red Rover.
TELEVISION: *Movie*: The Preppie Murder, Brotherhood of Murder. *Series*: VH1 Legends (narrator).

BALE, CHRISTIAN
Actor. b. Pembrokeshire, Wales, Jan. 30, 1974. Acting debut at age 9 in U.S. Pac-Man commercial. London stage debut following year in The Nerd.
PICTURES: Empire of the Sun, Henry V, Newsies, Swing Kids, Royal Deceit, Little Women, Pocahontas (voice), The Secret Agent, The Portrait of a Lady, Metroland, Velvet Goldmine, All the Little Animals, A Midsummer Night's Dream, American Psycho, Shaft, Reign of Fire, Captain Corelli's Mandolin, Laurel Canyon, Reign of Fire, Equilibrium, The Machinist.TELEVISION: *Specials/Movies*: Heart of the Country (BBC), Anastasia: The Mystery of Anna, Treasure Island (released theatrically in U.K.), A Murder of Quality, Mary Mother of Jesus.

BALK, FAIRUZA
Actress. b. Point Reyes, CA, May 21, 1974.
PICTURES: Return to Oz, Discovery, The Outside Chance of Maximilian Glick, Valmont, Gas Food Lodging, Tollbooth, Imaginary Crimes, Things to Do in Denver When You're Dead, The Craft, The Island of Dr. Moreau, The Maker, American Perfekt, What Is It? (voice), American History X, The Waterboy, There's No Fish Food In Heaven, Red Letters, Great Sex, Deuces Wild, Personal Velocity: Three Portraits.
TELEVISION: *Movies/Specials*: Best Christmas Pageant Ever, Deceptions, The Worst Witch, Poor Little Rich Girl: The Barbara Hutton Story, Deadly Intentions...Again?, Shame, The Danger of Love, Murder in the Heartland, The Witching Hour (doc. short), Shadow of a Doubt, *Series*: Family Guy. The Sopranos.

BALL, ALAN
Writer, Producer. b. Atlanta, GA, 1957. e. Florida State University School of Theatre.
PICTURES: American Beauty (s.p., co-prod. Won Acad. Award, best writing, s.p., 2000, Golden Globe, best s.p., 2000, London Critics Circle Film Award, screenwriter of year, 2000), The Parlor (exec. prod.).
TELEVISION: *Series*: Grace Under Fire (writer), Cybill (exec. prod., writer), Oh Grow Up (writer/creator &prod.), Six Feet Under (creator, dir. & exec. prod.; won Emmy, outstanding dir./drama series, for pilot, 2002).

BALLARD, CARROLL
Director. b. Los Angeles, Oct. 14, 1937. e. UCLA. Prod. of 1967 film Harvest. Camera operator on Star Wars.
PICTURES: The Black Stallion (debut, 1979), Never Cry Wolf, Nutcracker: The Motion Picture, Wind, Fly Away Home, The Cruelest Winter, How It Was with Dooms.

BALLARD, KAYE
Actress. r.n. Catherine Gloria Balotta. b. Cleveland, OH, Nov. 20, 1926. Began career as impressionist-singer-actress, toured vaudeville. 17 recordings incl.: The Fanny Brice Story, Peanuts, Oklahoma (w/ Nelson Eddy), Unsung Sondheim, Then & Again. Appeared in short film Walking to Waldheim.
THEATRE: Three to Make Ready, Carnival, Molly, The Pirates of Penzance, Hey Ma It's Me, Working 42nd Street at Last, Chicago, Touch & Go (London), Nymph Errant (concert version), Hello Dolly, She Stoops to Conquer, Funny Girl, High Spirits, Crazy Words Crazy Times: The Cole Porter-Irving Berlin Revue, Beloved Enemies.
PICTURES: The Girl Most Likely (debut 1957), A House is Not a Home, Which Way to the Front?, The Ritz, Freaky Friday, Falling in Love Again, Pandemonium, Tiger Warsaw, Modern Love, Eternity, Ava's Magical Adventure, Anna Petrovic: You Rock!, Fortune Hunters, Baby Geniuses, The Million Dollar Kid, Little Insects (voice), Broadway: The Golden Age by the Legends Who Were There.
TELEVISION: *Movies*: The Dream Merchants, Alice in Wonderland, Due South. *Series*: Henry Morgan's Great Talent Hunt, The Perry Como Show, The Mothers-in-Law, The Doris Day Show, The Steve Allen Comedy Hour, What a Dummy. *Pilot*: Makin' Out. Guest appearances incl. over 100 spots on The Tonight Show.

BALLHAUS, MICHAEL
Cinematographer. b. Berlin, Germany, Aug. 5, 1935.
PICTURES: Deine Zartlichkeiten, We Two, Whity, Beware of a Holy Whore, Tschetan, The Indian Boy, The Bitter Tears of Petra von Kant, Fox and His Friends, Mother Kusters Goes to Heaven, Summer Guests, Satan's Brew, I Only Want You To Love Me, Adolf and Marlene, Chinese Roulette, Bolweiser (The Stationmaster's Wife), Willie and the Chinese Cat, Women in New York, Despair, The Marriage of Maria Braun, Germany in Autumn, German Spring, The Uprising, Big and Little, Malou, Looping, Baby It's You, Friends and Husbands, Dear Mr. Wonderful, Magic Mountain, Edith's Diary, Aus der Familie der Panzereschen, The Autograph, Heartbreakers, Old Enough, Reckless, After Hours, Under the Cherry Moon, The Color of Money, The Glass Menagerie, Broadcast News, The House on Carroll Street,The Last Temptation of Christ, Working Girl, Dirty Rotten Scoundrels, The Fabulous Baker Boys, GoodFellas, Postcards from the Edge, Guilty by Suspicion, What About Bob?,

The Mambo Kings, Bram Stoker's Dracula, The Age of Innocence, Quiz Show, Outbreak, Sleepers, Air Force One, Primary Colors, Wild, Wild West, The Thirteenth Floor (exec. prod. only), What Planet Are You From?, The Legend of Bagger Vance, Gone Underground, The Gangs of New York, Mummy, Uptown Girls.
TELEVISION: More than 15 tv movie credits, incl. Martha, German Spring, Death of a Salesman, Baja Oklahoma.

BANCROFT, ANNE
Actress. r.n. Anna Maria Italiano. b. New York, NY, Sept. 17, 1931. m. dir-comedian Mel Brooks. e. American Acad. of Dramatic Arts. Acting debut on TV, Studio One as Anne Marno in Torrents of Spring.
THEATRE: Two For the Seesaw (Tony Award, Theatre World Award: 1958), The Miracle Worker (Tony Award, 1960), Mother Courage, The Devils, A Cry of Players, Golda, Duet For One, Mystery of the Rose Bouquet, The Little Foxes.
PICTURES: Don't Bother to Knock (debut, 1952), Tonight We Sing, Treasure of the Golden Condor, The Kid from Left Field, Gorilla at Large, Demetrius and the Gladiators, The Raid, New York Confidential, Life in the Balance, The Last Frontier, Walk the Proud Land, Nightfall, The Restless Breed, Black Stockings, The Miracle Worker (Acad. Award for Best Actress, 1962), The Pumpkin Eater, The Slender Thread, Seven Women, The Graduate, Young Winston, The Prisoner of Second Avenue, The Hindenburg, Lipstick, Silent Movie, The Turning Point, Fatso (also dir., s.p.), The Elephant Man, To Be or Not to Be, Garbo Talks, Agnes of God, 'Night Mother, 84 Charing Cross Road, Torch Song Trilogy, Bert Rigby You're a Fool, Honeymoon in Vegas, Love Potion No. 9, Point of No Return, Malice, Mr. Jones, How to Make an American Quilt, Home for the Holidays, Dracula–Dead & Loving It, The Sunchaser, Great Expectations, Critical Care, G.I. Jane, Antz (voice), Mark Twain's America in 3D (voice), Keeping the Faith, Up at the Villa, In Search of Peace (voice), Heartbreakers.
TELEVISION: *Movies*: Broadway Bound, Oldest Living Confederate Widow Tells All, Homecoming, Deep in My Heart, The Roman Spring of Mrs Stone. *Mini-Series*: Jesus of Nazareth, Marco Polo. *Specials*: The Women in the Life of a Man (also dir.; Emmy Award for Best Variety Special, 1970), *Guest*: The Simpsons, Exhale with Candice Bergen.

BAND, ALBERT
Producer, Director. b. Paris, France, May 7, 1924. e. Lyceum Louis le Grand, won French-English Lit. Prize 1938. Entered m.p. industry as cutter Pathe Lab.; prod. ass't to John Huston at MGM. First screen credit adaptation Red Badge of Courage novel; first direction, The Young Guns. Formed Maxim Prods., Inc., Sept. 1956.
PICTURES: The Young Guns, I Bury the Living, Face of Fire, The Avenger, Grand Canyon Massacre, The Tramplers, The Hellbenders (prod. only), A Minute to Pray a Second to Die, Little Cigars, Mansion of the Doomed, Dracula's Dog, She Came to the Valley, Metalstorm: The Destruction of Jared-Syn, Swordkill, Buy and Cell (exec. prod. only), Troll, Terrorvision, Ghoulies II, Robot Jox, Trancers III; Honey, I Blew Up the Kid, Pet Shop, Oblivion, Oblivion 2: Backlash, Zarkorr! The Invader, Prehysteria, Prehysteria 2.
(d. June 14, 2002, in Los Angeles, CA)

BAND, CHARLES
Producer, Director. b. Los Angeles, CA, Dec. 27, 1951. e. Overseas Sch. of Rome. Son of Albert Band. Formed Media Home Ent., 1978; formed Empire Ent., 1983; formed Full Moon Ent., 1988; formed Moonbeam Productions, 1993.
PICTURES: More than 135 picture credits as prod., exec. prod. &/or dir. *Prod.*: Prod.: Mansion of the Doomed, Cinderella, End of the World, Laserblast, Fairy Tales, Swordkill, Dungeonmaster, Puppet Master 4, Eliminators, Pet Shop. *Dir./Prod.*: Crash, Parasite, Metalstorm, Trancers, Trancers II, Dr. Mordrid, Dollman vs. Demonic Toys, Hideous, The Creeps. *Exec. Prod.*: Tourist Trap, Day Time Ended, Ghoulies, Zone Troopers, Troll, Terrorvision, The Caller, Spellcaster, Cellar Dweller, Ghoulies II, Enemy Territory, Deadly Weapon, Robot Jox, Prison, Buy & Cell, Ghost Town, Catacombs, Arena, Puppet Master, Shadowzone, Puppet Master II, The Pit and the Pendulum, Subspecies, Puppet Master III, Arcade, Dollman, Netherworld, Bad Channels, Trancers III, Shrunken Heads, Oblivion, Seed People, Bad Channels, Robot Wars, Subspecies II, Prehysteria, Remote, Dragonworld, Beanstalk, Prehysteria II, Curse IV: The Ultimate Sacrifice, Bloodstone: Subspecies III, Puppet Master 5, Oblivion 2: Backlash, Magic in the Mirror, Kraa! The Sea Monster, Curse of the Puppet Master, Subspecies 4: Planet Patrol, The Dead Hate the Living, Voodoo Academy, Demonicus, Groom Lake, Pulse Pounders (also prod. dir.), Subspecies 5, numerous others.

BANDERAS, ANTONIO
Actor. r.n. Jose Antonio Dominguez Banderas. b. Malaga, Spain, Aug. 10, 1960. e. School of Dramatic Art, Malaga. m. actress Melanie Griffith. Moved to Madrid in 1981 where he made his stage debut in Los Tarantos. Other theatre incl.: The City and the Dogs, Daughter of the Air, The Tragedy of Edward II of England.
PICTURES: More than 50 picture credits since Labyrinth of Passion debut in 1982. Other incl. Pestanas Postizas, Y del Seguro... Libranos Senor!, El Senor Galindez, El Caso Almeria, Los Zancos, La Corte de Faraon, Requiem por un Campesino Espanol, 27 Horas, Puzzle, Matador, Asi Como Habian Sido, Law of Desire, The Pleasure of Killing, Baton Rouge, Bajarse al Moro,

Women on the Verge of a Nervous Breakdown, Si te Dicen que Cai, Tie Me Up! Tie Me Down!, Contra el Viento, La Blanca Paloma, Truth or Dare, The Mambo Kings, Philadelphia, Dispara!, Of Love and Shadows, The House of the Spirits, Interview With the Vampire, Miami Rhapsody, Desperado, Four Rooms, Never Talk to Strangers, Two Much, Assassins, Evita, The Mask of Zorro, White River Kid (also prod.), The Thirteenth Warrior (won ALMA Award, outstanding actor, 2000), Play it to the Bone, Original Sin, The Body, Spy Kids, Frida, Ecks vs. Sever, Spykids 2: The Island of Lost Dreams, Femme Fatale, Imagining Argentina, Spy Kids 3-D: Game Over, Once Upon a Time in Mexico, *Director:* Crazy in Alabama (Won ALMA Award, Outstanding Dir.).
TELEVISION: Movies: La Mujer de Tu Vida, La Otra historia de Rosendo Juarez, And Starring Pancho Villa as Himself. *Special:* I Love Lucy's 50th Anniversary Special.

BANDY, MARY LEA
Director, b. Evanston, IL, June 16, 1943. e. Stanford U., B.A., 1965. Asst. editor, Harry Abrams and Museum of Modern Art dir., 1980-93; chief Curator 1993-. Dept. of Film, Museum of Modern Art in NY. Editor of MOMA film publications incl.: Rediscovering French Film (1983). Member: Advisory Bd., AFI's National Center for Preservation of Film and Video; Film Advisory Comm., American Federation of Arts; Advisory Comm. on Film, Japan Society; Advisory Comm., NY State Motion Picture and Television. Co-pres., National Alliance of Media Arts Center, 1986-88. Bd. mem.: Intl. Film Seminars; MacDowell Colony; Natl. Film Preservation Bd.; Library of Congress; Advisory Board, Film Foundation; Bd. of Directors., Third World Newsreel. Appeared in the following documentaries: The Race to Save 100 Years, Without Lying Down: Frances Marion and the Power of Women in Hollywood.

BANERJEE, VICTOR
Actor. b. Calcutta, India, Oct. 15, 1946. Helped form the first Screen Extras Union in India. Won int'l recognition for A Passage to India. On stage in: Pirates of Penzance, An August Requiem (dir.), Desert Song, Godspell.
PICTURES: The Chess Players (debut 1977), Kalyug, Jaipur Junction (German), An August Requiem (dir. only), Arohan, A Passage to India (Won Nat'l. Board of Review Award, best actor, 1984; won Evening Standard British Film Awards, best actor, 1986), Ghare-Baire, Foreign Body, Mahaprithivi, Bitter Moon, Bhoot.
TELEVISION: Movies: Hullabaloo Over Georgie and Bonnie's Pictures, Dadah Is Death, NY Spice. *Series:* True Adventures of Christopher Columbus.

BANNER, BOB
Producer, Director. b. Ennis, TX, Aug. 15, 1921. e. Southern Methodist U., B.A., 1939-43; Northwestern U., M.A., 1946-48. U.S. Naval Reserve 1943-46. Faculty, Northwestern U., 1948-50. Staff dir., NBC-TV in Chicago, 1949-50. Pres., Bob Banner Assocs. Visiting Prof.: Southern Methodist U.
PICTURES: Warning Shot (1967).
TELEVISION: Movies: Mongo's Back in Town, The Last Survivors, Journey From Darkness, My Sweet Charlie, Bud and Lou, Yes Virginia There is a Santa Claus, Crash Landing, With Murder in Mind, The Sea Wolf, Angel Flight Down. Specials: Garroway at Large (dir.), Fred Waring Show (prod., dir.), Omnibus (dir.), Nothing But the Best (prod. dir.), Dave Garroway Show (prod. dir.), Dinah Shore Show, Candid Camera TV Show (exec. prod.), Carnegie Hall Salutes Jack Benny (exec. prod.), Julie & Carol at Carnegie Hall, Carol & Co., Jimmy Dean Show, Calamity Jane, The Entertainers, Carol & Co., Ice Follies, Carol Burnett Show, John Davidson at Notre Dame, Here's Peggy Fleming, Peggy Fleming at Sun Valley, The American West of John Ford, Love! Love! Love!—Hallmark Hall of Fame, To Europe with Love, Peggy Fleming Visits the Soviet Union, Perry Como's Lake Tahoe Holiday, Perry Como's Christmas In Mexico, Perry Como's Hawaiian Holiday, Perry Como's Spring In New Orleans, Don Ho Show, Perry Como Las Vegas Style, Perry Como's Christmas in Austria, All-Star Anything Goes, Peggy Fleming and Holiday on Ice at Madison Square Garden, Julie Andrews, One Step Into Spring, Leapin' Lizards, It's Liberace, Ford Motor Company's 75th Anniversary; Gift of Music, specials starring Bob Hope, Julie Andrews, Andy Williams, Los Angeles Music Center 25th Anniversay, Amazing Music Series, Happy Birthday George Gershwin. *Series:* Almost Anything Goes, Solid Gold, Star Search, It's Showtime at the Apollo, Uptown Comedy Club.

BAR, JACQUES JEAN LOUIS
Executive, Producer, Exhibitor. b. Chateauroux, France, Sept. 12, 1921. e. Lycees Lakanal and Saint Louis, France. Formed Citae-Films S.A., 1947; CIPRA in assoc. with MGM, 1961; S.C.B., Bourges, 8 cinemas; S.C.M., Le Mans, 9 cinemas. Hollywood films incl.: Bridge to the Sun, Once A Thief, Guns for San Sebastian. Prod. 57 films in France, Spain, Italy, Switzerland, Japan and Brazil 1948-89.
PICTURES: Where the Hot Wind Blows, Bridge to the Sun, Rififi in Tokyo, A Very Private Affair, Swordsmen of Siena, Monkey in Winter, The Turfist, Any Number Can Win, The Day and the Hour, Joy House, Guns for San Sebastian, Last Known Address, The Homecoming, Dancing Machine, The Candidate, Once a Thief, My Father the Hero, Bridge Between Two Shores.
TELEVISION: Mini-series: The Count of Monte Cristo.

BARANSKI, CHRISTINE
Actress. b. Buffalo, NY, May 2, 1952. e. Juilliard Sch. of Music & Dramatic Arts.
THEATRE: NY: Private Lives, One Crack Out, Says I Says He, Shadow of a Gunman, Hide and Seek (B'way debut, 1980), Company, Coming Attractions, Operation Midnight Climax, A Midsummer Night's Dream (Obie Award, 1982), Sally and Marsha, The Real Thing (Tony Award, 1984), Hurlyburly, It's Only a Play, The House of Blue Leaves, Rumors (Tony Award, 1989), Elliot Loves, Nick and Nora, Lips Together Teeth Apart, The Loman Family Picnic.
PICTURES: Soup for One (debut, 1982), Lovesick, Crackers, 9-1/2 Weeks, Legal Eagles, The Pick-Up Artist, Reversal of Fortune, The Night We Never Met, Life With Mikey, Addams Family Values, New Jersey Drive, The Ref, Jeffrey, The Birdcage, The Odd Couple II, Bulworth, Cruel Intentions, Bowfinger, How the Grinch Stole Christmas, Marci X, The Guru, Chicago: The Musical, Marci X.
TELEVISION: Movies: Playing for Time, A Midsummer's Night Dream, House of Blue Leaves, To Dance With the White Dog, Eloise at the Plaza, Eloise at Christmastime. Special: The Addams Chronicles. Series: Another World, All My Children, Cybill (Emmy Award, 1995), Welcome to New York (also exec. prod.). Happy Family. Guest: Law & Order, Frasier, 3rd Rock from the Sun, Now and Again (voice).

BARATTA, DANA
Writer, Producer.
PICTURES: Andre (co-prod.).
TELEVISION: Series.: Dawson's Creek, Providence, Pasadena, Kate Brasher.

BARBEAU, ADRIENNE
Actress. b. Sacramento, CA, June 11, 1947. e. Foothill Col.
THEATRE: B'way: Fiddler on the Roof, Grease (Tony nom., Theatre World Award). L.A.: Women Behind Bars, Strange Snow, Pump Boys & Dinettes, Drop Dead. Canadian Premiere: Lost in Yonkers. Regional: Love Letters, Best Little Whorehouse in Texas.
PICTURES: The Fog, Cannonball Run, Escape From New York, Swamp Thing, Creepshow, The Next One, Back to School, Open House, Two Evil Eyes, Jungle Heat, Two Evil Eyes, Father Hood, Silk Degrees, Bimbo Movie Bash, A Wake in Providence, The Convent, Across the Line, No Place Like Home, The Reckoning.
TELEVISION: Movies: The Great Houdini, Giving Birth, Red Alert, Return to Fantasy Island, Crash, Someone's Watching Me!, The Darker Side of Terror, The Top of the Hill, Valentine Magic on Love Island, Tourist, Charlie and the Great Balloon Chase, Seduced, Bridge Across Time, Blood River, Doublecrossed, The Burden of Proof, The Parsley Garden, Jailbreakers, Bram Stoker's Burial of the Rats, A Champion's Fight, Scooby Doo on Zombie Island (voice), A Champion's Fight, Spring Break Lawyer, The Santa Trap. Series: Maude, Head of the Class, Batman (voice), Gotham Girls (voice), Carnivale.. Guest: Quincy, 8 Is Enough, Tony Orlando and Dawn, The David Frost Special, Bobby Vinton Show, FBI, Love Boat, Hotel, Twlight Zone, Murder She Wrote, Dream On, Daddy Dearest, The Carlin Show, Babylon 5, The Drew Carey Show, Love Boat: The Next Wave, Star Trek: Deep Space Nine.

BARBER, FRANCES
Actress. b. Wolverhampton, England, May 13, 1957. e. Bangor U.; grad. studies in theatre, Cardiff U. Stage experience with fringe theaters including improvisational troupe Hull Truck Theatre Company, Glasgow Citizens and Tricycle Theatre (Killburn) before joining Royal Shakespeare Co. (Camille, Hamlet).
PICTURES: The Missionary (debut, 1982), A Zed and Two Noughts, White City, Castaway, Prick Up Your Ears, Sammy and Rosie Get Laid, We Think the World of You, The Grasscutter, Young Soul Rebels, Secret Friends, Soft Top Hard Shoulder, Germaine and Benjamin, Giorgino, Photographing Fairies, Still Crazy, Mauvaise passe, Esther Kahn, Toy Boys, Shiner, Superstition, La Sirene Rouge, 24 Hours in the Life of a Woman, Flyfishing, Boudica.
TELEVISION: Clem, Jackie's Story, Home Sweet Home, Flame to the Phoenix, Reilly, Ace of Spies, Those Glory Glory Days; Hard Feelings, Behaving Badly, The Nightmare Years, The Leaving of Liverpool, Three Steps to Heaven, A Royal Scandal, The Ice House, Rules of Engagement, Real Women, Dalziel and Pascoe: The Wood Beyond, The Gentleman Thief. Mini-Series: Rhodes, Plastic Man, .Love in a Cold Climate.

BARBER, GARY
Executive Producer. COO, Morgan Creek Prod.; former pres. Morgan Creek Int'l. Current pres., Spyglass Entertainment.
PICTURES: Midnight Crossing, Communion, Young Guns II, Pacific Heights, Robin Hood: Prince of Thieves, Freejack, White Sands, Stay Tuned, The Crush, True Romance, Ace Ventura: Pet Detective, Chasers, Silent Fall, Trial by Jury, Imaginary Crimes, Ace Ventura: When Nature Calls, Two if by Sea, Big Bully, Diabolique, Bad Moon, Wild America, Incognito, Major League: Back to the Minors, Wrongfully Accused, Keeping the Faith, Shanghai Noon, Unbreakable, Out Cold, The Count of Monte Cristo (prod.), Dragonfly (prod.), Abandon (prod.), The Recruit (prod.), Reign of Fire (prod), Shanghai Knights (prod.), Bruce Almighty, Seabiscuit, One Love, Mr. 3000, Connie and Carla (prod.).

BARBERA, JOSEPH R.
Executive. b. New York, NY, Mar. 24, 1911. e. NYU, American Institute of Banking. After schooling joined Irving Trust Co. in N.Y.; started submitting cartoon drawings to leading magazines selling one to Collier's. Joined Van Buren Assocs. as sketch artist, later going to work in animation dept. of MGM Studios. At MGM met William Hanna, who became his lifelong business associate. Made first animated short together in 1937, starting the famous Tom & Jerry series which they produced for 20 years. Left MGM in 1957 to form Hanna-Barbera Productions to make cartoons for TV. Hanna-Barbera became a subsidiary of Taft Ent. Co. in 1968 with both men operating the studio under long-term agreements with Taft. Taft and the studio were sold to Great American Broadcasting, 1988. Hanna-Barbera Prods. acquired by Turner Bdcstg. System, 1991; Barbera is co-founder, chmn. Team received Governor's Award from the Acad. of Television Arts & Sciences, 1988.
PICTURES: Hey There It's Yogi Bear, The Man Called Flintstone, Charlotte's Web, Mother Jugs & Speed (exec. prod.), C.H.O.M.P.S., Heidi's Song, Jetsons: The Movie, The Flintstones (exec. prod. of live action film; also cameo appearance), GoBots: War of the Rock Lords (exec. prod.) Top Cat and the Beverly Hills Cats (exec. prod.), The Flintstones (exec. prod.), Flintstones in Viva Rock Vegas (exec. prod, writer), Scooby-Doo (exec. prod., writer), Hong Kong Phooey (writer), Scooby 2 (writer). .
TELEVISION: Specials/Movies: The Gathering (Emmy Award), I Yabba Dabba Do!, Hollyrock-a-Bye Baby. Series: Work on 108 series, incl. The Huckleberry Hound Show (Emmy Award), Quick Draw McGraw, Yogi Bear, The Flintstones, The Jetsons, Top Cat, Jonny Quest, Scooby-Doo, The Smurfs, Droopy: Master Detective, Johnny Bravo, Harvey Birdman-Attorney at Law.

BARBOUR, MALCOLM
Executive. b. London, England, May 3, 1934. e. Radley Coll., Oxford, England, A.B., Columbia Coll. At National Broadcasting Co., was press info. asst., 1958-59; asst. magazine ed., 1959-62; assoc. mag. ed., 1962-64; sr. mag. ed., 1964-65; mgr. of magazine pub., 1965-67. Pub. mgr., Buena Vista, 1967-68; relations, Buena Vista, 1969. Eastern story ed., Walt Disney Prod., 1968-69; dir. of adv. & pub. Partner, Producers Creative Services, 1976-79. Pres., The International Picture Show, 1980-81 (Tim Conway comedies The Billion Dollar Hobo and They Went That-A-Way & That-A-Way; Slayer. Distributor: Soldier of Orange, The Magic of Lassie, The Visitor, etc.). Pres., Barbour/Langley Productions, 1982-present.
PICTURES: Behind Enemy Lines (writer), Deadly Sins (writer, prod.), Dog Watch (exec. prod.), Cocaine Blues (documentary, dir.)
TELEVISION: Movies: Cops Files (prod.), Prod., Geraldo Rivera specials: American Vice, Innocence Lost, Sons of Scarface, Murder: Live from Death Row, Satan Worship. Prod., Jack Anderson specials. Writer, P.O.W. The Escape.

BARCLAY, PARIS
Director. b. June 1956.
PICTURES: Don't Be a Menace to South Central While Drinking Your Juice in the Hood.
TELEVISION: Movies: America's Dream, The Cherokee Kid (also actor), The Big Time (also co-exec. prod.). Series: NYPD Blue (Emmy Award, 1998), Diagnosis: Murder, ER, Sliders, Clueless, Brooklyn South, The West Wing, City of Angels (also co-exec. prod.), Fastlane, The Street Lawyer (dir. pilot).

BARDOT, BRIGITTE
Actress. b. Paris, France, Sept. 28, 1934. e. Paris Conservatory. Studied ballet, before becoming model. Studied acting with Rene Simon. On stage in L'Invitation au Chateau. Awarded French Legion of Honor, 1985. Active in the movement to preserve endangered animals. Created the Brigitte Bardot Foundation for animal protection, April 1986.
PICTURES: Le Trou Normand (debut, 1952), Nanina la Fille san Voiles, Les Dents Longues, Act of Love, Le Portrait de Son Pere, Royal Affairs in Versailles, Tradita, Le Fils de Caroline Cherie, Helen of Troy, En Effeuillant la Marguerite, The Bride is Much Too Beautiful, And God Created Woman, Une Parisienne, The Night Heaven Fell, En Cas de Malheur, Le Femme et le Pantin, Babette Goes to War, Come Dance With Me, La Verite, La Bride sur le Cou, Les Amours Celebres, A Very Private Affair, Love on a Pillow, Contempt, Dear Brigitte, Viva Maria, Masculine-Feminine, Two Weeks in September, Spirits of the Dead, Shalako, Les Femmes, L'Ours et la Poupee, Les Novices, Boulevard du Rhum, Les Petroleuses, Don Juan 73, L'Historie Tres Bonne et Tres Joyeuse de Colinot Troussechemise, Tykho Moon (singer).

BARE, RICHARD L.
Producer, Director. b. Turlock, CA, 1925. Started as dir. for Warners. SDG Best Dir. TV award, 1959. Author of The Film Director (Macmillan, 1971). Writer/director for 60+ film shorts from 1942-1956. Pres., United National Film Corp.
PICTURES: Director: Smart Girls Don't Talk, Flaxy Martin, This Side of the Law, House Across The Street, This Rebel Breed, Return of Frontiersman, Prisoners of the Casbah, Hurricane at Pilgrim Hill, The Outlanders, Border Showdown, The Travellers, 77 Sunset Strip, The Black Rebels, I Sailed to Tahiti with an All-Girl Crew (also writer), Dir./Prod./Writer: Wicked Wicked, Story of Chang & Eng, City of Shame, Sudden Target, Purple Moon.
TELEVISION: Maverick, So This is Hollywood, The Islanders,

Dangerous Robin, This Rebel Breed, Twilight Zone, Bus Stop, Adventures in Paradise, The Virginian, Kraft Theatre, Petticoat Junction, Green Acres, Nanny and the Professor, Faraday and Company.

BAREN, HARVEY M.
Executive. b. New York, NY, Nov. 25, 1931. e. State U. of New York. Served in U.S. Army, 1952-54. United Artists Corp., 1954-59 (contract dept., print dept., booker—NY branch). Asst. to general sls. mgr., Magna Pictures Corp., 1959-61. Road show mgr., nat'l. sls. coordinator, 20th Century-Fox, 1961-71. Asst. general sls. manager, Allied Artists Pictures, 1971-79. V.p., gen. sls. mgr., Nat'l. Screen Service, 1978-79. V.p., gen. sls. mgr., Cannon Pictures, 1979-80. Pres. of Summit Feature Distributors, 1980. Exec. v.p., dir., MGM/UA Classics, 1983. Joined New Century/Vista as v.p., sls. admin, 1986. Pres., Sea Movies Inc., 1991-present.

BARENHOLTZ, BEN
Executive. b. Kovel, Poland, Oct. 5, 1935. Asst. theatre mngr., RKO Bushwick, Brooklyn, 1959-60. Mngr., Village Theatre, NY, 1966-68. Owner, operator, Elgin Cinema, 1968-75; originated Midnight Movie concept with El Topo. Pres., owner, Libra Film Corp., 1972-84. V.p & partner, Circle Releasing (which launched and distributed The Family Game, Therese, Blood Simple and prod. Raising Arizona) 1984-1992. Pres., Barenholtz Prods. Inc.
PICTURES: Exec. Prod.: Miller's Crossing, Barton Fink, Cheat, White Man's Burden, Georgia, Requiem for a Dream (co-exec. prod.). Prod.: The Naked Man, Bruiser, Rabbit.

BARISH, KEITH
Producer. b. Los Angeles, CA, Nov. 11, 1944. Background in finance. Founded Keith Barish Prods., 1979. In partnership with Taft Broadcasting Co., Entertainment Div., 1984-88. Founder and chmn. of Planet Hollywood. Appeared in film Last Action Hero.
PICTURES: Sophie's Choice, Light of Day, Ironweed, Her Alibi. Exec. prod.: Endless Love, Prisoners, Misunderstood, Nine 1/2 Weeks, Big Trouble in Little China, The Running Man, The Monster Squad, Firebirds, The Fugitive, U.S. Marshals.
TELEVISION: Movie: A Streetcar Named Desire (exec. prod.).

BARKER, BOB
TV host. b. Darrington, WA, Dec. 12. e. Springfield Central H.S., Drury Coll. News writer, announcer, disc jockey KTTS until 1949. News editor, staff announcer, Station WWPG. Pres. Bob Barker Prod., Inc. Started as M.C. for both Miss USA Pageant and Miss Universe Pageant, 1966. First time as M.C. of both Rose Bowl Parade and Pillsbury Bakeoff. Series, 1970. Host of The Price Is Right, the longest-running game show in tv history, which debuted in 1972.
PICTURES: Happy Gilmore.
TELEVISION: Emcee or host: The End of the Rainbow, Truth or Consequences (daytime: 1956-65; nighttime synd: 1966-74), Lucky Pair (prod.), That's My Line (1980-1), The Price Is Right (exec. prod. & m.c.; 1972-; received several Emmy Awards as host). Narrator: 500 Festival Parade, Indianapolis 1969-81. Specials: The Price Is Right Primetime Special. Movies: The Price Is Right: Showdown in Vegas.

BARKER, CLIVE
Writer, Producer, Director. b. Liverpool, England, Oct. 5, 1952. e. Liverpool Univ. Moved to London at twenty-one, forming theatre company. Began writing short stories which were subsequently published as Books of Blood (Vols. 1-3 & Vols. 4-6). Author of: Novels: Damnation Game, Weaveworld, The Great and Secret Show, Imajica, The Thief of Always, Everville, Sacrament. Books: Clive Barker: Illustrator, The Art of Clive Barker, Incarnations. Plays: History of the Devil, Colossus, Frankenstein In Love. Painter with exhibitions in NY, California.
PICTURES: Underworld, Rawhead Rex (from his story), Hellraiser (dir., s.p.; from his novella The Hellbound Heart), Hellbound: Hellraiser II (co-exec. prod.; writer), Nightbreed (dir., s.p.; from his novel Cabal), Sleepwalkers (actor), Hellraiser III: Hell on Earth (exec. prod.; from his story), Candyman (exec. prod.; from his story The Forbidden), The Forbidden (short), Clive Barker's Freaks (himself), Candyman: Farewell to the Flesh (exec. prod.; from his story), Lord of Illusions (dir., s.p., co-prod.; from his story The Last Illusion), Gods and Monsters (exec. prod.), Tortured Souls: Animae Damnatae (writer from novella Tortured Souls, prod. dir.).
TELEVISION: Movies: Quicksilver Highway (actor, writer from The Body Politic), Saint Sinner (writer, exec. prod.).

BARKER, MICHAEL W.
Executive. b. Nuremberg, Germany, Jan. 9, 1954. e. U. of Texas at Austin, B.S. in International Communications, 1976. Joined Films Inc. 1979-80; then United Artists 1980-83, first as non-theatrical sls. mngr., then as nat'l. sls. mngr. of UA Classics. Co-founder and v.p., sls. & mktg. for Orion Classics, a div. of Orion, 1983-1992. Co-founder and co-pres., Sony Pictures Classics, 1992-present. Member bd. of dirs. of BAFTA NY, and Independent Features Project. Recipient of Independent Feature Project's Industry's Lifetime Achievement Award.

BARKETT, STEVE
Actor, Director, Producer, Film Editor, Writer. b. Oklahoma City, OK, Jan. 1, 1950. Exhibited and scored over 52 feature length classic silent films 1966-1968 as dir. of two film series at the Oklahoma Art Center and Science and Arts Foundation, prior to coming to LA in 1970. Toured in stage prod. 1971-72: Pajama

Tops, Winnie the Pooh. Exec. in several non-theatrical releasing cos., incl. Independent Film Associates and Thunderbird Films. Active in film preservation and restoration work on early silent and sound films, 1968-1974. Founded The Hollywood Book and Poster Company, 1978; est. The Nautilus Film Co., 1978. Founded and operated Capt. Nemo's Video, 1985-87; co-wrote and performed 42 episodes of Capt. Nemo's Video Review for radio.
PICTURES: *Actor*: The Egyptians are Coming, Corpse Grinders, Dillinger, Night Caller, Cruise Missile, Beverly Hills Vampire, Wizard of the Demon Sword, Bikini Drive-In, Cyber Zone, Hard Bounty, Masseuse, Star Hunter, Rapid Assault. *Prod./Dir./S.P./ Edit.*: Collecting, Empire of the Dark, Angels of Death. *Also Actor*: The Movie People, Cassavetes, The Aftermath, Angels of Death, Empire of the Dark. *Actor/FX*: Dark Universe, Dinosaur Island, Attack of the 60's Centerfold, Invisible Mom. *FX Only*: Warlords, Sorceress. *Editor only*: Hurricane Express.

BARKIN, ELLEN
Actress. b. Bronx, NY, Apr. 16, 1954. e. Hunter Coll.; Actors Studio.
THEATRE: Irish Coffee (debut, Ensemble Studio Theatre), Shout Across the River, Killings Across the Last, Tobacco Road, Extremities, Eden Court.
PICTURES: Diner (debut, 1982), Tender Mercies, Daniel, Enormous Changes at the Last Minute, Eddie and the Cruisers, Harry and Son, The Adventures of Buckaroo Banzai Across the Eighth Dimension, Terminal Choice, Desert Bloom, Down by Law, The Big Easy, Siesta, Made in Heaven, Sea of Love, Johnny Handsome, Switch, Man Trouble, Mac, This Boy's Life, Into the West, Bad Company, Wild Bill, Mad Dog Time, Fear and Loathing in Las Vegas, Drop Dead Gorgeous, The White River Kid, Crime and Punishment in Suburbia, Mercy, In the Boom Boom Room, Someone Like You, Buckaroo Banzai Declassified (video short).
TELEVISION: *Movies*: We're Fighting Back, Parole, Terrible Joe Moran, Act of Vengeance, Clinton and Nadine, Before Women Had Wings (Emmy Award, 1998). *Series*: Search for Tomorrow.

BARNHOLTZ, BARRY
Executive, Producer.. b. St. Louis, MO, Oct. 12, 1945. e. California State U., Northridge; USC; UCLA; WLAU, studied law. Concert promotions in So. Calif. 1963-71. With Medallion TV as v.p. in chg. sls. Barnholtz Organization, representing ind't. prod. cos. for feature films for cable. Founder, sr. v.p. of Vidmark Inc., and Trimark Films. Pres., Barnholtz Entertainment.
PICTURES: Leprechaun (assoc. prod.), Deadfall (assoc. prod.), *Exec.prod.*:All American Murder, Trigger Fast, Jailbait, Proteus, Sometimes They Come Back 2, Crimetime, Public Enemies, Another Nine & a Half Weeks, Fall: Price of Silence. *Prod.*: Backyard Dogs, Hunt for the Devil.
TELEVISION: *Movies*: The Mangler.

BARONE, TRACY
Producer. b. Hartford, CT, Nov. 1, 1962. m. actor Paul Michael Glaser.
PICTURES: *Exec. Prod*: Money Train, My Fellow Americans, Rosewood, Cops and Robbersons (assoc. prod.)
TELEVISION: *Movies*: Writer's Block (writer).

BARR, ANTHONY
Producer, Director, Actor. b. St. Louis, MO, March 14, 1921. r.n. Morris Yaffe. e. Washington U., B.S. 1942. Actor, asst. stage mgr., 1944-46; stage mgr., Katharine Dunham Dancers, 1946-47. Teacher, actor, dir. in chg. Film Actors' Workshop, Professional Theatre Workshop, Hollywood. v.p. prime time series, ABC-TV. V.p., dramatic program production, CBS-TV; v.p., CBS Entertainment Prods. Author of Acting for the Camera, 1982.
THEATRE: Jacobowsky and the Colonel, Winters' Tale, Embezzled Heaven.
PICTURES: *Actor*: People Against O'Hara, Border Incident, The Hollywood Story, The Mozart Story, Murder in the First. *Co-prod.*: Dime with a Halo.
TELEVISION: *Director*: Art Linkletter's Houseparty, About Faces. *Assoc. dir.*: Climax, Shower of Stars. *Producer.*: Climax, Summer Studio One. *Assoc. prod.*: Climax, Playhouse 90, Pursuit, G.E. Theatre, The Law and Mr. Jones, Four-Star.

BARR, JULIA
Actress. b. Ft. Wayne, IN, Feb. 8, 1949.
PICTURES: I, the Jury.
TELEVISION: *Series*: All My Children (Emmy Awards, 1990, 1998), Ryan's Hope.

BARRAULT, MARIE-CHRISTINE
Actress. b. Paris, France, March 21, 1944. m. dir. Roger Vadim.
PICTURES: My Night at Maud's, Le Distrait, Lancelot of the Lake, The Aspern Papers, Les Intrus, La Famille Grossfeld, Chloe in the Afternoon, John Glueckstadt, Cousin Cousine (Acad. Award nom.), By the Tennis Courts, Perceval, The Medusa Touch, Tout est a nous, Femme Entre Chien et Loup, Ma Cherie, Stardust Memories, Table for Five, Josephs Tochter, A Love in Germany, Les Mots Pour le Dire, Swann in Love, Grand Piano, Prisonnieres, Un Etae de orages, Savage State, Necessary Love, Next Time the Fire, Bonsoir, Obsession, C'est la tangente que je préfère, La Dilettante, Azzurro
TELEVISION: *Movies*: Mon pere avait raison, Les Braconniers de Belledombre, Maison de famille, Le Vieil ours et l'enfant, Le Le Don fait à Catchaires, La Deuxième vérité, Rêves en France.

BARRETT, RONA
News Correspondent b. New York, NY, Oct. 8, 1936. e. NYU (communications major). Created the column, Rona Barrett's Young Hollywood, which led to featured column in 1960 in Motion Picture Magazine and a nationally syndicated column distributed to 125 newspapers by the North American Newspaper Alliance. Turned to TV; initial appearances on ABC-owned stations in 5 cities, providing two-minute reports for local newscasts. Resulted in Dateline Hollywood a network morning prog., co-hosted by Joanna Barnes. In 1969, created first daily syndicated TV news segment for Metromedia. In 1975, became arts and entertainment editor for ABC's Good Morning America. In 1980, joined NBC News. Publ. and exec. editor, newsletter, The Rona Barrett Report. Became pres., Rona Barrett Enterprises, Inc. in 1985 and also sr. corresp., Entertainment Tonight; Mutual Radio Network. In 1988, creator of original novels for television, for NBC prods. Appeared in films Sextette, An Almost Perfect Affair.

BARRIE, BARBARA
Actress. b. Chicago, IL, May 23, 1931. e. U. of TX, B.F.A., 1953. Trained for stage at Herbert Berghof Studio. NY stage debut, The Wooden Dish, 1955. Author of, Lone Star (1990), Adam Zigzag (1994), Second Act (1997).
THEATRE: The Crucible, The Beaux Stratagem, The Taming of the Shrew, Conversations in the Dark, All's Well That Ends Well, Happily Never After, Horseman Pass By, Company, The Selling of the President, The Prisoner of Second Avenue, The Killdeer, California Suite, Big and Little, Isn't It Romantic, Torch Song Trilogy, Fugue, After-play.
PICTURES: Giant (debut, 1956), The Caretakers, One Potato Two Potato (best actress, Cannes Film Fest, 1964), The Bell Jar, Breaking Away (Acad. Award nom.), Private Benjamin, Real Men, End of the Line, Hercules (voice), $pent, Second Best.
TELEVISION: *Movies*: More than 20 tv movie credits, incl. Tell Me My Name, Summer of My German Soldier, To Race the Wind, The Children Nobody Wanted, Barefoot in the Park, Not Just Another Affair, Two of a Kind, The Execution, Vital Signs, Winnie, My First Love, Guess Who's Coming for Christmas?, The Odd Couple: Together Again, My Breast, A Chance of Snow. *Mini-Series*: 79 Park Avenue, Backstairs at the White House, Roots: The Next Generations, Scarlett. *Series*: Love of Life, Diana, Barney Miller, Breaking Away, Tucker's Witch, Reggie, Double Trouble, Suddenly Susan, Disney's Hercules (voice).. *Guest*: Numerous appearances, incl. Kraft Television Theatre, Dr. Kildare, Ironside, Mary Tyler Moore Show, Lou Grant, Kate & Allie, Family Ties, Babes, thirtysomething, Law & Order, The Commish, Once and Again.

BARRON, ARTHUR RAY
Executive. b. Mt. Lake, MN, July 12, 1934. e. San Diego State U. 1956-60, B.S. Accounting. Certified public acc't, Calif., 1960. Coopers & Lybrand, 1960-63; Desilu Productions, Inc., 1963-67. V.p. finance and admin., Paramount TV, 1967-70; v.p. finance, Paramount Pictures Corp., 1970; s.v.p. finance and admin., 1971; exec. v.p., finance & admin., 1974; exec. v.p. 1980. Exec. v.p., Gulf & Western Industries, entertainment & comm. group, 1983; promoted to pres., 1984-88. Became chmn, Time Warner Enterprises, 1990 and also served as chmn. of Time Warner International until 1995. In 1998, he received hon. doctor of humane letters from the Calif. State Univ. system.

BARRY, GENE
Actor. b. New York, June 14, 1921. r.n. Eugene Klass.
PICTURES: Los Alamos (debut, 1949), The Girls of Pleasure Island, The War of the Worlds, Those Redheads from Seattle, Alaska Seas, Red Garters, Naked Alibi, Soldier of Fortune, The Purple Mask, The Houston Story, Back From Eternity, China Gate, The 27th Day, Forty Guns, Thunder Road, Hong Kong Confidential, Maroc 7, Subterfuge, The Second Coming of Suzanne, Guyana: Cult of the Damned.
TELEVISION: *Movies*: Prescription Murder, Istanbul Express, The Name of the Game,Do You Take This Stranger?, The Devil and Miss Sarah, Ransom for Alice!, A Cry for Love, The Girl-The Gold Watch & Dynamite, Amazing Nellie Bly, Perry Mason: The Case of the Lost Love, Turn Back the Clock, These Old Broads. *Mini-Series*: Aspen. *Series*: Our Miss Brooks, Bat Masterson, Burke's Law (1963-66, Won Golden Globe, best male TV Star, 1963), The Name of the Game, The Adventurer, Burke's Law (1994-95).

BARRY, JOHN
Composer, Arranger, Conductor. r.n. John Barry Prendergast. b. York, England, Nov. 3, 1933. Started as rock 'n' roll trumpeter. Artist and prod., CBS Records.
PICTURES: Composer for music in more than 100 pictures, incl. Never Let Go, The L-Shaped Room, The Amorous Mr. Prawn, From Russia With Love, Seance on a Wet Afternoon, Zulu, Goldfinger, The Knack, King Rat, Mister Moses, Thunderball, The Chase, Born Free (2 Acad. Awards: Best Music Scoring and Best Song: title song, 1966), The Wrong Box, The Whisperers, Deadfall, You Only Live Twice, Petulia, The Lion in Winter (Acad. Award, 1968), Midnight Cowboy, The Appointment, On Her Majesty's Secret Service, Monte Walsh, The Last Valley, They Might Be Giants, Murphy's War, Walkabout, Diamonds Are Forever, Mary Queen of Scots, Alice's Adventures in Wonderland, The Public Eye, A Doll's House, The Tamarind Seed, The Dove, The Man With the Golden Gun, The Day of the Locust, Robin and Marian, King Kong, The Deep, The Betsy, Hanover Street, Moonraker, Game of Death, Raise the Titanic, Somewhere in Time, Inside Moves, Touched By Love, Body Heat, The Legend of

the Lone Ranger, Frances, Hammett, High Road to China, Octopussy, The Golden Seal, Until September, The Cotton Club, A View to a Kill, Jagged Edge, Out of Africa (Acad. Award, 1985), Howard the Duck, Peggy Sue Got Married, The Living Daylights, Hearts of Fire, Masquerade, A Killing Affair, Dances With Wolves (Acad. Award, 1990), Chaplin, Indecent Proposal, Deception, My Life, The Specialist, Cry the Beloved Country, The Scarlett Letter, Swept from the Sea, Playing by Heart, Mercury Rising, Enigma, The Incredibles.
TELEVISION: Movies: Sophia Loren in Rome, The Glass Menagerie, Love Among the Ruins, Eleanor and Franklin, War Between the Tates, The Corn is Green, Willa, Svengali.

BARRYMORE, DREW
Actress. b. Los Angeles, CA, Feb. 22, 1975. Father is actor John Barrymore, Jr. (John Drew Barrymore). At 11 months appeared in first commercial. Author of Little Girl Lost (1990).PICTURES: Altered States (debut, 1980), E.T.: The Extra Terrestrial, Firestarter, Irreconcilable Differences, Cat's Eye, See You in the Morning, Far From Home, Motorama, Poison Ivy, Waxwork II, Guncrazy, No Place To Hide, Doppelganger, Wayne's World 2, Bad Girls, Inside the Goldmine, Boys on the Side, Mad Love, Batman Forever, Everyone Says I Love You, Scream, Best Men, Wishful Thinking, The Wedding Singer, Ever After: A Cinderella Story, Home Fries, Never Been Kissed (also exec. prod.), Titan A.E. (voice), Charlie's Angels (also prod.), Donnie Darko (also exec. prod.), Riding in Cars With Boys, Confessions of a Dangerous Mind, Duplex (also prod.), Charlie's Angels 2, So Love Returns (also prod.), 50 First Kisses, A Confederacy of Dunces (also prod.).
TELEVISION: Movies: Suddenly Love, Bogie, The Adventures of Con Sawyer and Hucklemary Finn, Babes in Toyland, Conspiracy of Love, 15 and Getting Straight, The Sketch Artist, The Amy Fisher Story, Olive-the Other Reindeer (voice) Series: 2000 Malibu Road, Disney's Hercules (voice).

BARRYMORE, JOHN DREW
Actor. r.n. John Blythe Barrymore Jr. b. Beverly Hills, CA, June 4, 1932. e. St. John's Military Acad., various public and private schools. Son of actors John Barrymore and Delores Costello. Daughter is actress Drew Barrymore. Started acting at age 18 under the name John Barrymore Jr.
PICTURES: Sundowners (debut, 1950), High Lonesome, Quebec, The Big Night, Thunderbirds, While the City Sleeps, Shadow on the Window, Never Love a Stranger, High School Confidential, Night of the Quarter Moon, The Cossacks, The Boatmen, The Night They Killed Rasputin, The Pharaoh's Woman, The Trojan Horse, The Centurion, Pontious Pilate, Invasion 1700, The Christine Keeler Story, War of the Zombies, The Clones.
TELEVISION: Movies: Winchester 73, This Savage Land.

BART, PETER
Executive, Producer.. b. Martha's Vineyard, MA, July 24, 1932. e. Swarthmore Coll. and The London School of Economics. New York Times correspondent for eight years, with work also appearing in magazines such as Harper's, The Atlantic, Saturday Review, GQ, etc. Joined Paramount Pictures in 1965. Named exec. ass't. to Robert Evans, in charge of world-wide prod. Appointed v.p. prod. Resigned 1973 to develop and produce own films for Paramount. Appointed pres. Lorimar Films, 1978. Resigned, 1979, to be independent. prod. 1983, joined MGM as sr. v.p., prod., m.p. div. Resigned, 1985, to be independent prod. Current v.p., editor -in-chief, Variety. Author of novels: Thy Kingdom Come (1983), Destinies (1979), Fade Out, Who Killed Hollywood? (1999), The Gross: The Hits, the Flops-the Summer That Ate Hollywood (1999).
PICTURES: Producer: Islands in the Stream, Fun with Dick and Jane, Youngblood, Revenge of the Nerds (exec. prod.), , Revenge of the Nerds II. Actor: An Alan Smithee Film: Burn Hollywood Burn, Junket Whore, The Young and the Dead. Writer: Making It (1971). Actor: An Alan Smithee Film: Burn Hollywood Burn (1997 as himself), Junket Whore (documentary, as himself), The Young and the Dead (documentary, as himself), former Paramount exec.).
TELEVISION: Marlon Brando: The Wild One (documentary, as himself), Steve McQueen: The King of Cool (documentary, as himself), Hollywood, D.C. (documentary, as himself), Easy Riders Raging Bulls (documentary, as himself).

BARTEK, STEVE
Composer, orchestrator. b. Jan. 30, 1952. Co-founded musical group Oingo Boingo with composer Danny Elfman.
PICTURES: Composer: Guilty as Charged (1991), Past Midnight, Cabin Boy, Senior Trip, Coldblooded, Romy and Michele's High School Reunion, Meet the Deedles (also act.), Snow Day, An Extremely Goofy Movie, Coyote Ugly, The Crew, Get Over It (also orchestrator), Novocaine. Orchestrator: Forbidden Zone, Pee-Wee's Big Adventure, Summer School, Beetlejuice, Midnight Run, Batman, Strike It Rich, Nightbreed, Bird on a Wire, Darkman, Edward Scissorhands, Article 99, Batman Returns (also music prod.), Sommersby, The Nightmare Before Christmas, Black Beauty, Dolores Claiborne, Dead Presidents, To Die For, The Frighteners, Extreme Measures, Good Will Hunting (also score prod.), A Simple Plan, Psycho, A Civil Action, Sleepy Hollow. Also songs: Sommersby, Dolores Claiborne, Black Beauty , To Die For.
TELEVISION: Series: Dilbert (music producer/arranger).

BARTKOWIAK, ANDRZEJ
Cinematographer. b. Lodz, Poland, 1950. Attended Polish Film School. Moved to U.S. in 1972, gaining experience in TV commercials and low-budget features. Protege of Sidney Lumet, for whom did several pictures.
PICTURES: Deadly Hero (1976), Prince of the City, Deathtrap, The Verdict, Daniel, Terms of Endearment, Garbo Talks, Prizzi's Honor, The Morning After, Power, Nuts, Twins, Family Business, Q&A, Hard Promises, A Stranger Among Us, Falling Down, Turkey Cake (short), Guilty As Sin, Speed, A Good Man in Africa, Losing Isaiah, Species, Jade, The Mirror Has Two Faces, Dante's Peak, The Devil's Advocate, U.S. Marshals, Lethal Weapon 4, Gossip, Thirteen Days Which Shocked the World. Director: Romeo Must Die (2000), Exit Wounds, Cradle 2 the Grave.
TELEVISION: Director: HRT(2001).

BARUCH, RALPH M.
Executive. b. Frankfurt, Germany, Aug. 5, 1923. e. The Sorbonne. m. Jean Ursell de Mountford. Administrative aide, SESAC, Inc. 1944-48. Account exec., DuMont Television Network, 1950-54. Account exec., CBS Films, 1954; account supr., 1957; dir. int'l sales, 1959; CBS Group President 1961-70. Pres. and CEO Viacom International, 1971-1983; chmn. 1983-87. Currently a consultant to Viacom International. Trustee of Lenox Hill Hospital. Chmn. Emeritus of the Nat'l Academy of Cable Programming and recipient of the Academy's first Governor's Award. Past-pres., the International Radio & Television Society and was honored by an IRTS gold medal award. Founder and fellow of the International Council of the Nat'l Academy of Television Arts & Sciences. Recipient of an Emmy Award. Former dir., Exec. Committee of the Nat'l Cable Television Assoc. Co-founder of C-Span. Recipient of the Vanguard Award, three NCTA President's Awards and NCTA Chmn. of the Year Award. Chmn. of the USIA's Television Communications Board of Advisors under Pres. Reagan. Elected to the Broadcasting/Cable Hall of Fame in 1992. Appointed to New York City Cultural Affairs Advisory Comm., Recipient of International Emmy Directorate Award for outstanding contrib. to int'l. tv, 1999.

BARWOOD, HAL
Writer, Producer, Director. b. Hanover, NH. e. U. of Southern California Sch. of Cinema. Has written scripts in collaboration with Matthew Robbins. Barwood branched out into producing with Corvette Summer, 1978 and directing with Warning Sign, 1985. Since the 1990s, has been involved with designing and supervising video games for LucasFilm Games. Most recent vid. game: Indiana Jones and the Emperor's Tomb (2003).
PICTURES: Screenplays (all with Robbins): The Sugarland Express, The Bingo Long Traveling All-Stars and Motor Kings, Close Encounters of the Third Kind (uncredited), MacArthur, Corvette Summer (also prod.), Dragonslayer (also prod.), Warning Sign (also dir.).

BARYSHNIKOV, MIKHAIL
Dancer, Actor. b. Riga, Latvia, Jan. 27, 1948. Joined Kirov Ballet, Leningrad, 1969-74; defected to U.S. With American Ballet Theatre 1974-78; New York City Ballet Company 1978-79; named dir. of the American Ballet Theatre. B'way stage debut, Metamorphosis (1989).
PICTURES: The Turning Point (debut, 1977; Acad. Award nom.), That's Dancing! (documentary), White Nights (also co-choreog.), Dancers (also choreog.), Company Business, The Cabinet of Dr. Ramirez.
TELEVISION: The Nutcracker, Baryshnikov at the White House (Emmy Award, 1979), Bob Hope on the Road to China, Baryshnikov on Broadway (Emmy Award, 1980), AFI Salute to Fred Astaire, Baryshnikov in Hollywood, AFI Salute to Gene Kelly, David Gordon's Made in USA, All Star Gala at Ford's Theater, Dance in America: Baryshnikov Dances Balanchine (Emmy Award, 1989), Bourne to Dance (documentary). Series: Stories from My Childhood (prod.)

BASCH, BUDDY
Print Media Syndicater, Publicist, Producer. b. South Orange, NJ, June 28, 1922. e. Columbia U. Began career as youngest radio editor in U.S. at 15. Has since written for nat'l mags, syndicates, wire services, and newspapers. Edit. & pub. Top Hit Club News for 7 yrs. Joined Donahue and Coe 1940 on m.p. accounts, U.S. Army in Europe 1942-45. 1945-67, own publicity and promotion office, working on m.p. company accounts and stars such as Burl Ives, Dinah Shore, Tony Martin, Danny Kaye, Peter Lorre, Tony Bennett, McGuire Sisters, Rhonda Fleming, Sammy Davis, Jr., Polly Bergen, Meyer Davis, The Beatles, Glenn Miller and Tommy Dorsey Orchestras. Produced many shows for radio, TV and stage in New York, Newark, Chicago, Hartford. Asst. to publisher, The Brooklyn Eagle 1962. 1966, formed Buddy Basch Feature Syndicate, covering assignments on show business, travel, health, medicine, food, human interest and general subjects for such publications as N.Y. Daily News, A.P., Grit Magazine, Travel/Holiday, Frontier Magazine, Womens' News Service, Today Magazine, Christian Science Monitor, New York Post, Deseret News, California Canadian and Diversion. Provided Associated Press with worldwide exclusives on a number of national and intl. events. Member: Friars Club since 1959; Admission Comm. and House Comm. Organized & appointed permanent chmn. of VIP Reception and Security for Friars luncheons and dinners since 1970. Served as chmn. of Elections (6 times). Contributing ed. Friars Epistle.

BASINGER, KIM
Actress. b. Athens, GA, Dec. 8, 1953. e. Neighborhood Playhouse. Began career as Ford model in New York.
PICTURES: Hard Country (debut, 1981), Mother Lode, Never Say Never Again, The Man Who Loved Women, The Natural, Fool for Love, 9-1/2 Weeks, No Mercy, Blind Date, Nadine, My Stepmother is an Alien, Batman, The Marrying Man, Final Analysis, Cool World, The Real McCoy, Wayne's World 2, Prêt-à-Porter, The Getaway, L.A. Confidential (Acad. Award, Golden Globe Award, Best Supporting Actress, 1998), I Dreamed of Africa, Bless the Child, People I Know, 8 Mile, Aurora Island, The Door in the Floor.
TELEVISION: Movies: Dog and Cat (pilot), The Ghost of Flight 401, Katie: Portrait of a Centerfold, Killjoy. Series: From Here to Eternity, Dog and Cat, Guest: Charlie's Angels, The Simpsons,

BASS, RONALD
Writer. b. Los Angeles, CA. e. Yale, Harvard Law School. Entered industry as entertainment lawyer, while writing novels: The Perfect Thief, Lime's Crisis, The Emerald Illusion.
PICTURES: Code Name: Emerald, Black Widow, Gardens of Stone, Rain Man (Academy Award, 1988), Sleeping With the Enemy, The Joy Luck Club (also prod.), When a Man Loves a Woman (also exec. prod), Dangerous Minds, Waiting to Exhale (exec. prod.), My Best Friend's Wedding (prod.), How Stella Got Her Groove Back (also exec. prod.), What Dreams May Come (also exec. prod.), Stepmom (also exec. prod.), Entrapment (also exec. prod.), Snow Falling on Cedars (also prod.), Passion of Mind (also prod.), The Memoirs of Elizabeth Frankenstein.
TELEVISION: Movies: The Enemy Within, Reunion, Border Line, Invisible Child, Swing Vote.

BASSETT, ANGELA
Actress. b. New York, NY, Aug. 16, 1958. Moved to St. Petersburg, FL, at 5 yrs. old. e. Yale.
THEATRE: B'way: Ma Rainey's Black Bottom, Joe Turner's Come and Gone. Off-B'way: Colored People's Time, Antigone, Black Girl, Henry IV Part 1. Regional: Beef No Chicken.
PICTURES: F/X (debut, 1986), Kindergarten Cop, Boyz N the Hood, City of Hope, Innocent Blood, Malcolm X, Passion Fish, What's Love Got to Do With It (Acad. Award nom.; Golden Globe Award), Strange Days, Waiting to Exhale, Vampire in Brooklyn, Panther, Contact, How Stella Got Her Groove Back, Supernova, Boesman and Lena, The Score, Our America (exec. prod. only), Sunshine State, Masked & Anonymous, Mr. 3000.
TELEVISION: Movies/Specials: Liberty, Family of Spies, Challenger, Perry Mason: Case of the Silenced Singer, In the Best Interest of the Child, Line of Fire: The Morris Dees Story, The Heroes of Desert Storm, Locked Up: A Mother's Rage, One Special Victory, The Jacksons: An American Dream, Ruby's Bucket of Blood, The Rosa Parks Story (also exec. prod.). Mini-series: Africans in America: America's Journey Through Slavery (narrator), Unchained Memories: Readings from the Slave Narratives.. Guest: Cosby Show, thirtysomething, Tour of Duty, Equal Justice, The Flash, Nightmare Cafe.

BATEMAN, JASON
Actor. b. Rye, NY, Jan. 14, 1969. Brother of actress Justine Bateman. Son of prod.-theatrical mgr. Kent Bateman. Started in commercials until cast in Little House on the Prairie at 12 (1981).
PICTURES: Teen Wolf Too, Necessary Roughness, Breaking the Rules, Love Stinks, Sol Goode, The Sweetest Thing, One Way Out.
TELEVISION: Movies: Fantastic World of D.C. Collins, The Thanksgiving Promise, Can You Feel Me Dancing, Bates Motel, Moving Target, Crossing the Mob, A Taste for Killing, Confessions: Two Faces of Evil, This Can't Be Love, Black Sheep, Hart to Hart: Secrets of the Hart. Mini-Series: Robert Kennedy and His Times. Series: Little House on the Prairie, Silver Spoons, It's Your Move, Valerie, The Hogan Family, Simon, Chicago Sons, George & Leo, For Your Love (dir. only), Some of My Best Friends.

BATEMAN, JUSTINE
Actress. b. Rye, NY, Feb. 19, 1966. Brother is actor Jason Bateman.
THEATRE: Lulu, Self-Storage, The Crucible, Love Letters, Carnal Knowledge, Speed-the-Plow.
PICTURES: Satisfaction, The Closer, Primary Motive, The Night We Never Met, God's Lonely Man, Highball, Say You'll Be Mine, Kiss & Tell
TELEVISION: Movies: First the Egg, Family Ties Vacation, Right to Kill?, Can You Feel Me Dancing?, The Fatal Image, In the Eyes of a Stranger, Deadbolt, Terror in the Night, Another Woman, Bucket of Blood. Mini-series: A Century of Women. Series: Family Ties, Men Behaving Badly, Out of Order. Guest: Tales from the Dark Side, One to Grow On, It's Your Move, Lois & Clark.

BATES, ALAN
Actor. b. Allestree, Derbyshire, England, Feb. 17, 1934. e. Herbert Strutt Grammar Sch.; after natl. service with the RAF studied at RADA with Albert Finney, Peter O'Toole and Tom Courtenay. Professional stage debut 1955 with the Midland Theatre Co. in You and Your Wife. Queen Elizabeth bestowed knighthood on Bates in Dec. 2002.
THEATRE: London: The Mulberry Tree, Look Back in Anger (also NY, Moscow), Long Day's Journey Into Night, Poor Richard, Richard III, In Celebration, Hamlet, Butley (also NY; Tony Award, 1973), The Taming of the Shrew, Life Class, Otherwise Engaged, The Seagull, Stage Struck, A Patriot for Me, One for the Road, Victoria Station, Dance of Death, Yonadab, Melon, Much Ado

About Nothing, Ivanov, Stages, The Showman, Simply Disconnected, Fortune's Fool, Life Support.
PICTURES: It's Never Too Late (debut, 1956), The Entertainer, Whistle Down the Wind, A Kind of Loving, The Guest, The Running Man, Nothing But the Best, Zorba the Greek, Georgy Girl, King of Hearts, Far From the Madding Crowd, The Fixer (Acad. Award nom.), Women in Love, Three Sisters, The Go-Between, A Day in the Death of Joe Egg, Story of a Love Story, Butley, In Celebration, Royal Flash, An Unmarried Woman, The Shout, The Rose, Nijinsky, Quartet, The Return of the Soldier, Britannia Hospital, The Wicked Lady, Duet for One, A Prayer for the Dying, We Think the World of You, Mr. Frost, Hamlet, Force Majeure, Shuttlecock, Secret Friends, Silent Tongue, Gentlemen Don't Eat Poets, The Grotesque, Varya, Gosford Park, The Mothman Prophecies, The Sum of All Fears, Evelyn, Hollywood North.
TELEVISION: Movies: Plaintiffs and Defendants, Two Sundays, The Collection, The Trespasser, Voyage Round My Father, Separate Tables, An Englishman Abroad, Dr. Fischer of Geneva, Pack of Lies, 102 Boulevard Haussmann, Hard Times, Nicholas' Gift, St. Patrick: the Irish Legend, Arabian Nights, The Prince and the Pauper, Bertie and Elizabeth. Mini-series: The Mayor of Casterbridge, Oliver's Travels, In the Beginning, Love in a Cold Climate, Salem Witch Trials.

BATES, KATHY
Actress. b. Memphis, TN, June 28, 1948. e. S. Methodist U. Regional Theatre incl. D.C. and Actor's Theatre in Louisville. Has garnered more than 40 ent. industry wins and/or nominations for various roles throughout career, with more than eight wins and/or award nominations in 2003 for her role in About Schmidt.
THEATRE: Vanities (Off-B'way debut, 1976), Semmelweiss, Crimes of the Heart, The Art of Dining, Goodbye Fidel (B'way debut, 1980), Chocolate Cake and Final Placement, Fifth of July, Come Back to the 5 & Dime Jimmy Dean Jimmy Dean, 'night Mother (Tony nom., Outer Critics Circle Award), Two Masters: The Rain of Terror, Curse of the Starving Class, Frankie and Johnny in the Clair de Lune (Obie, L.A. Drama Critics Award), The Road to Mecca.
PICTURES: Taking Off (debut, 1971), Straight Time, Come Back to the Five & Dime Jimmy Dean Jimmy Dean, Two of a Kind, Summer Heat, My Best Friend is a Vampire, Arthur 2: On the Rocks, Signs of Life, High Stakes, Men Don't Leave, Dick Tracy, White Palace, Misery (Acad. Award, Golden Globe & Chicago Film Critics Awards, Best Actress 1991), At Play in the Fields of the Lord, Fried Green Tomatoes, Shadows and Fog, Prelude to a Kiss, Used People, Road to Mecca, A Home of Our Own, North, Curse of the Starving Class, Dolores Claiborne, Angus, Diabolique, The War at Home, Titanic, Swept from the Sea, Primary Colors (Acad. Award nom., 1999), The Waterboy, The Dress Code, Dragonfly, American Outlaws, Love Liza, About Schmidt (Acad. Award nom. 2003), Unconditional Love, Around the World in 80 Days.
TELEVISION: Movies: Johnny Bull, Murder Ordained, Hostages, The West Side Waltz, The Late Shift (Golden Globe, 1997), Annie (American Comedy Award, funniest female perf., 2000), My Sister's Keeper. Series: All My Children (1984). Dir./episodes: Homicide: Life on the Street, NYPD Blue, Oz, Everwood. Guest: The Love Boat, St. Elsewhere, Cagney and Lacey, L.A. Law, China Beach, Six Feet Under (in recurring role).

BATTY, PETER
Producer, Director, Writer. b. Sunderland, England, June 18, 1931. e. Bede Grammar Sch. and Queen's Coll., Oxford. Feature-writer both sides Atlantic 1954-58. Joined BBC TV 1958 dir. short films. Edited Tonight programme 1963-4. Exec. prod. ATV 1964-68. Awarded Grand Prix for doc. at 1965 Venice and Leipzig festivals. Official entries 1970 and 1971 San Francisco and Melbourne festivals. Nominated Int'l. Emmy, 1986. Own company since 1968 prod. TV specials, series, commercials.
TELEVISION: Includes: The Quiet Revolution, The Big Freeze, The Katanga Affair, Sons of the Navy Man, The Road to Suez, The Suez Affair, Battle for the Desert, Vietnam Fly-In, The Plutocrats, The Aristocrats, Battle for the Bulge, Birth of the Bomb, Search for the Super, Farouk: Last of the Pharaohs, Superspy, Spy Extraordinary, Sunderland's Pride and Passion, A Rothschild and His Red Gold, The Story of Wine, The Rise and Rise of Laura Ashley, Battle for Warsaw, Battle for Dien Bien Phu, Nuclear Nightmares. Swindle!, The Algerian War, Fonteyn and Nureyev: The Perfect Partnership, The Divided Union, A Time for Remembrance, Swastika Over British Soil. Contributed 6 episodes to Emmy-winning World at War series.

BAUER, STEVEN
Actor. r.n. Rocky Echavarria. b. Havana, Cuba, Dec. 2, 1956. Moved with family to Miami at age 3. e. Miami Dade Jr. Coll. where studied acting. Breakthrough came with selection for role in Que Pasa U.S.A.? for Public TV. Signed by Columbia TV and moved to California.
PICTURES: Scarface (debut, 1983), Thief of Hearts, Running Scared, The Beast, Wildfire, Gleaming the Cube, Raising Cain, Woman of Desire, Improper Conduct, Stranger by Night, Wild Side, Primal Fear, Navajo Blues, Plato's Run, Kickboxing Academy, The Versace Murder, Star Portal, Rave, Naked Lies, Forever Lulu, Traffic, Glory Glory, Rave, El Grito, The Learning Curve, Speed Limit, Nola..
TELEVISION: Movies: She's in the Army Now, An Innocent Love, Sword of Gideon, Sweet Poison, False Arrest, Drive Like Lightning, Sisters and Other Strangers, Boss of Bosses, King of Texas. Mini-Series: Drug Wars: The Camarena Story. Series: ¿Qué pasa, U.S.A.?, From Here To Eternity, Wiseguy, UC:

Undercover. *Guest:* The Rockford Files, One Day at a Time, Hill Street Blues, Outer Limits, Relic Hunter, Nash Bridges.

BAUM, MARTIN
Executive, Producer.. b. New York, NY, March 2, 1924. 1968-1971, Pres. of Theatrical Motion Pictures for ABC Pictures. Previously partner Baum & Newborn Theatrical Agency. Head of West Coast, General Artists Corp. Head of m.p. dept., Ashley Famous Agency. Pres., Martin Baum Agency. Sr. exec. v.p. Creative Management Assoc. Pres., Optimus Productions, Inc. Partner with Michael Ovitz, Ron Meyer, Rowland Perkins, Bill Haber in Creative Artists Agency, Inc.
PICTURES: *Producer:* The Last Valley (exec.prod.) Bring Me the Head of Alfredo Garcia, The Wilby Conspiracy, The Killer Elite, They Shoot Horses Don't They?, Lovers and Other Strangers, Straw Dogs, Kotch, Cabaret.

BAUMGARTEN, CRAIG
Executive, Producer. b. Aug. 27, 1949. Partner in independent prod. co., New America Cinema. Joined Paramount Pictures as prod. exec.; named v.p., prod. In 1980 went to Keith Barish Prods., of which was pres. three years. In 1983 appt. exec. v.p. & exec. asst. to the pres. & CEO, Columbia Pictures; resigned 1985. Joined Lorimar Motion Pictures as pres. Joined 20th Century Fox m.p. div. as exec. v.p. of prod., 1987; resigned. Formed Adelson/Baumgarten Prods. with Gary Adelson, 1989. Formed Baumgarten/Prophet Entertainment Inc., 1994.
PICTURES: *Exec. prod./prod.:*Prisoners, Misunderstood, Hook (co-prod.), Universal Soldier, Nowhere to Run, Blank Check, It Could Happen to You (exec. prod.), Jade, Hidden Assassin, Cold Around the Heart, Universal Soldier: The Return, Love Stinks, The Order, Shattered Glass.
TELEVISION: Movies(All exec. prod): Streetcar Named Desire, The Hunchback, The Devil's Child, Lathe of Heaven.Series: Michael Hayes (exec. prod.)

BAXTER, BILLY
Executive. b. New York, NY, Feb. 8, 1926. e. Holy Cross, 1948. Mgr., Ambassador Brokerage Group, Albany, 1957-58. Bill Doll & Co., 1959-63. Organ., prod., radio show, Earl Wilson Celebrity Column, 1962; prod. B'way show, Mandingo, with Franchot Tone, 1962. Dir. of promotion, spec. events, Rumrill Ad Agency, 1963-64; dir. of promotion, exploitation, Landau Co., 1964-65; dir. of adv. and pub., Rizzoli Co., 1965-86. Consultant on special events to the Philip Morris Corp. and American Express.
PICTURES: *Co-prod.:* Love and Anarchy, Daughters-Daughters, Outrageous, One Man, Dawn of the Dead. *Prod.:* Diary of the Cannes Film Festival with Rex Reed, 1980. *Prod./dir.:* documentaries: Artists of the Old West, Remington & Russell, Buffalo Bill Cody (1988).

BAXTER, KEITH
Actor. b. Monmouthshire, Wales, April 29, 1933. e. Wales, entered Royal Acad. of Dramatic Art in 1951. 1952-55 in national service; returned to RADA. Did years of repertory work in Dublin, Croydon, Chichester, London's West End, and New York. Biggest stage hit in Sleuth, both London and NY. Later in Corpse (London, NY).
PICTURES: The Barretts of Wimpole Street, Peeping Tom, Chimes at Midnight, With Love in Mind, Ash Wednesday, Golden Rendezvous, Berlin Blues, Killing Time.
TELEVISION: For Tea on Sunday, Hold My Hand Soldier, Saint Joan, *Mini-Series:* Melody of Hate, Merlin. *Special:* Cleopatra: The Film that Changed Hollywood (2001). *Series:* Life of Shakespeare.

BAXTER, MEREDITH
Actress. b. Los Angeles, CA, June 21, 1947. e. Interlochen Arts Academy. On stage in Guys and Dolls, Butterflies Are Free, Vanities, Country Wife, Talley's Folly, Love Letters, Diaries of Adam & Eve. Has appeared in more than 45 TV movies since 1973.
PICTURES: Ben, Stand Up and Be Counted, Bittersweet Love, All the President's Men, Jezebel's Kiss, Heaven's Pond.
TELEVISION: Movies: Cat Creature, The Stranger Who Looks Like Me, Target Risk, The Imposter, Night That Panicked America, Little Women (1978 version), The Family Man, Two Lives of Carol Letner, Take Your Best Shot, The Rape of Richard Beck, Kate's Secret, The Long Journey Home, Winnie, Diaries of Adam and Eve, She Knows Too Much, The Kissing Place, Burning Bridges, Bump in the Night, A Mother's Justice, A Woman Scorned: The Betty Broderick Story, Her Final Fury: Betty Broderick—The Last Chapter, Darkness Before Dawn (also co-exec. prod.), For the Love of Aaron, One More Mountain, My Breast (also co-exec. prod.), Betrayed: A Story of Three Women (also co-exec. prod.),.Inheritance, Miracle in the Woods, Let Me Call You Sweetheart, Holy Joe, Down Will Come Baby, Miracle on the 17th Green, Wednesday Woman, Murder on the Orient Express, A Mother's Fight for Justice, Aftermath, A Christmas Visitor. *Mini-series:* Beulah Land. *Series:* Bridget Loves Bernie, Family, Family Ties, The Faculty.

BAXTER, STANLEY
Actor. b. Glasgow, Scotland, May, 1926. e. Hillhead H.S., Glasgow. Principal comedian in Howard & Wyndham pantomimes. Summer revues. Televised regularly on BBC-TV, and also frequent broadcaster. M.P debut in Geordie, 1955.
THEATRE: The Amorous Prawn, On the Brighter Side, Chase Me Comrade (Australia), Cinderella, What the Butler Saw, Phil The Fluter, Mother Goose Pantomime seasons 1970-74. Jack &

The Beanstalk, Cinderella, Mother Goose, Aladdin, Cinderella.
PICTURES: Geordie, Very Important Person, Crooks Anonymous, The Fast Lady, Father Came Too, Joey Boy, Arabian Knight (voice).
TELEVISION: Baxter on (series) 1964; The Confidence Course, The World of Stanley Baxter, Stanley Baxter Show, Time for Baxter, The Stanley Baxter Big Picture Show, The Stanley Baxter Moving Picture Show, Part III, Stanley Baxter's Christmas Box, Bing Crosby's Merrie Olde Christmas, Stanley Baxter's Greatest Hits, Baxter on Television, Stanley Baxter Series, The Stanley Baxter Hour, Children's Royal, Stanley Baxter's Christmas Hamper, Stanley Baxter's Picture Annual 1986; Mr. Majeika (series, 1988-89), Fitby, Stanley Baxter Is Back, Stanley Baxter in Reel Terms, The Sketch Show Story.

BAY, MICHAEL
Director. b. Los Angeles, CA, Feb. 17, 1965. e. Wesleyan U.; Pasadena's Art Center College of Design. Worked on advertisements and created music videos for artists such as Tina Turner, Meatloaf, Lionel Richie and Wilson Phillips. Recipient of the Gold Lion for The Best Beer campaign for Miller Lite; Silver Lion & Grand Prix Clio for Commercial of the Year, for the Got Milk/AaronBurr commercial; Commercial Dir. of the Year, Directors Guild of America, 1995.
PICTURES: Bad Boys, The Rock, Armageddon (also prod.), Mystery Men (actor), Coyote Ugly (actor), Pearl Harbor (also prod.), Bad Boys 2, The Texas Chainsaw Massacre (prod.).

BEACHAM, STEPHANIE
Actress. b. Casablanca, Morocco, Feb. 28, 1947. e. RADA. On London stage in The Basement, On Approval, London Cuckolds, etc.
PICTURES: The Games, Tam Lin, The Nightcomers, Dracula A.D., And Now the Screaming Starts!, Schizo, The Confessional, Horror Planet, The Wolves of Willoughby Chase, Troop Beverly Hills, Wedding Bell Blues, Saving Grace, Relative Values, Would I Lie to You?
TELEVISION: *Movies/Specials:* Napoleon & Josephine: A Love Story, Lucky/Chances, Secrets, To Be the Best, Foreign Affairs, Jane Eyre, A Change of Place. When Shoulder Pads Ruled the World. *Series:* Tenko (PBS), Connie, The Colbys, Dynasty, Sister Kate, Cluedo, Beverly Hills 90210, SeaQuest DSV, Bad Girls. *Guest:*So Graham Norton, Charmed, Breakfast.

BEALS, JENNIFER
Actress. b. Chicago, IL, Dec. 19, 1963. Started as fashion model before making film debut in small role in My Bodyguard, 1980.
PICTURES: My Bodyguard, Flashdance, The Bride, Split Decisions, Vampire's Kiss, Sons and Blood and Concrete, In the Soup, The Gamble, Caro Diario, Mrs. Parker and the Vicious Circle, Arabian Knight (voice), Devil in a Blue Dress, Let It Be Me, Four Rooms, The Search for One-Eye Jimmy, Wishful Thinking, Body and Soul, Something More, Militia, Fear of Flying, Out of Line, The Anniversary Party, After the Storm, Rodger Dodger, 13 Moons, Mission Without Permission, The Runaway Jury, Break a Leg.
TELEVISION: *Movies:* Terror Stalks the Class Reunion, Indecency, Night Owl, Twilight of the Golds, The Spree, A House Divided, Being Brewster, The Shoot Divas, Don't They? *Mini-series:* Feast of All Saints. *Series:* 2000 Malibu Road, Nothing Sacred, Earthlings.

BEAN, ORSON
Actor. r.n. Dallas Frederick Burrows. b. Burlington, VT, July 22, 1928. Performed in nightclubs as comic and on Broadway (Never Too Late, Will Success Spoil Rock Hunter?, Subways Are for Sleeping, Roar of the Grease Paint, the Smell of the Crowd, Ilya Darling.) Author of Me and the Orgone. Founder, administrator, dir. 15th St. School, NY.
PICTURES: How to Be Very Very Popular (debut, 1955), Anatomy of a Murder, Lola, Forty Deuce, Innerspace, Instant Karma, Final Judgement, One of Those Nights, Being John Malkovich, Unbowed, Frank McKlusky CI.
TELEVISION: *Movies/Specials:* Arsenic and Old Lace, Chance of a Lifetime, Just My Imagination, Dr. Quinn Medicine Woman: The Movie. *Series:* The Blue Angel (host), I've Got a Secret (panelist), Keep Talking, To Tell the Truth (panelist),Match Game (panelist), Mary Hartman Mary Hartman, Dr. Quinn: Medicine Woman, Normal Ohio. *Guest:* Has appeared on more than 30 shows since 1952, including: Diagnosis Murder, Ellen, Ally McBeal, The King of Queens, Family Law and Will & Grace.

BEAN, SEAN
Actor. b. Sheffield, Yorkshire, England, Apr. 17, 1958.
THEATRE: Romeo and Juliet, Fair Maid of the West, Midsummer Night's Dream, Who Knew Mackenzie and Gone, Deathwatch, Last Days of Mankind.
PICTURES: Winter Flight, Caravaggio, Stormy Monday, War Requeim, The Field, Patriot Games. Shopping, Black Beauty, Goldeneye, When Saturday Comes, Leo Tolstoy's Anna Karenina, Ronin, Bravo Two Zero, Airborne, The Canterbury Tales (voice), The Book That Wrote Itself, Essex Boys, Don't Say a Word, Lord of the Rings: Fellowship of the Ring, Equilibrium, Tom and Thomas, The Big Empty, Troy.
TELEVISION: Troubles, Small Zones, 15 Street, My Kingdom for a Horse, Winter Flight, Samson & Delilah, The True Bride, Prince, Tell Me That You Love Me, Clarissa, Scarlett, Jacob, The "Sharpe" teleplays, The Lord of the Piercing (tv short).

BEART, EMMANUELLE
Actress. b. Gassin, France, Aug. 14, 1965. Moved to Montreal at age 15. Returned to France and enrolled in drama school.
THEATRE: La Repetition ou l'Amour Puni, La Double Inconstance.
PICTURES: Premiers Desirs, L'Enfant Trouve, L'Amour en Douce, Manon of the Spring, Date With an Angel, A Gauche en Sortant de L'Ascenseur, Les Enfants du Desordre, Capitaine Fracasse, La Belle Noiseuse, J'Embrasse Pas, Un Coeur en Hiver, Ruptures, Divertimento, L'Enfer, Une Femme Francaise, Nelly & Mr. Arnaud, Mission: Impossible, Voleur de Vie, Le Temps Retrouve, Don Juan, Elephant Juice, Season's Beatings, Replay, Voyance et manigance, 8 femmes, Strayed, Nathalie X, Marie et Julien.
TELEVISION: Zacharius, Raison Perdue.

BEATTY, NED
Actor. b. Lexington, KY, July 6, 1937. Worked at Barter Theatre in Virginia appearing in over 70 plays, 1957-66; with Arena Stage, Washington D.C. 1963-71. Made B'way debut in The Great White Hope.
PICTURES: Deliverance (debut, 1972), The Life and Times of Judge Roy Bean, The Thief Who Came to Dinner, The Last American Hero, White Lightning, Nashville, All the President's Men, The Big Bus, Network (nom., Acad. Award, best actor in supporting role, 1977), Mikey and Nicky, Silver Streak, Exorcist II: The Heretic, Gray Lady Down, Superman, Alambrista!, Promises in the Dark, 1941, Wise Blood, American Success Company, Hopscotch, The Incredible Shrinking Woman, Superman II, The Toy, Touched, Stroker Ace, Back to School, The Big Easy, The Fourth Protocol, The Trouble With Spies, Switching Channels, Rolling Vengeance, The Unholy, Midnight Crossing, After the Rain, Physical Evidence, Time Trackers, Big Bad John, Chattahoochee, A Cry in the Wild, Repossessed, Blind Vision, Going Under, Hear My Song (nom. for Golden Globe, 1992), Prelude to a Kiss, Ed and His Dead Mother, Rudy, Black Water, Radioland Murders, Just Cause, The Curse of Inferno, He Got Game, Life, Cookie's Fortune, Spring Forward, Where the Red Fern Grows, Thunderpants.
TELEVISION: Movies: Has appeared in approx. 50 tv movies/mini-series, incl.: Footsteps, Marcus-Nelson Murders, Dying Room Only, The Execution of Private Slovik, Attack on Terror: The FBI vs. the Ku Klux Klan, A Question of Love, Friendly Fire, Guyana Tragedy, The Violation of Sarah McDavid, Splendor in the Grass, A Woman Called Golda, Kentucky Woman, Hostage Flight, Spy, Last Train Home, The Inside Story, T Bone N Weasel, Gulliver's Travels, Roughing It. Mini-Series: The Last Days of Pompeii, Robert Kennedy and His Times, Streets of Laredo. Series: Szysznyk, The Boys, Homicide: Life on the Street, The Great War (voice). Guest: Murder She Wrote, M*A*S*H, Rockford Files, Highway to Heaven, B.L. Stryker.

BEATTY, WARREN
Actor., Producer, Director, Writer. r.n. Henry Warren Beaty. b. Richmond, VA, March 30, 1937. e. Northwestern U. Sister is actress Shirley MacLaine. m. actress Annette Bening. Studied with Stella Adler. Small roles on television; on stage in Compulsion (winter stock, North Jersey Playhouse); B'way debut: A Loss of Roses (Theatre World Award).
PICTURES: Splendor in the Grass (debut, 1961), The Roman Spring of Mrs. Stone, All Fall Down, Lilith, Mickey One, Promise Her Anything, Kaleidoscope, Bonnie and Clyde (also prod.), The Only Game in Town, McCabe and Mrs. Miller, $ (Dollars), The Parallax View, Shampoo (also prod., co-s.p.), The Fortune, Heaven Can Wait (also prod., co-dir., co-s.p.), Reds (also prod., dir., co-s.p.; Acad. Award for Best dir., 1981), Ishtar (also prod.), Dick Tracy (also prod., dir.), Bugsy (also co-prod.), Love Affair (also prod., co-s.p.), Bulworth (also prod., dir., s.p.; Acad. Award nom.), Forever Hollywood, Down to Earth (s.p. 1978 s.p. Heaven Can Wait), Town and Country.
TELEVISION: Series: The Many Loves of Dobie Gillis (1959-60). Guest: Kraft Television Theatre, Studio One, Howard Stern Show, Mad TV, Seitenblicke.

BECK, ALEXANDER J.
Executive. b. Ung. Brod, Czechoslovakia, Nov. 5, 1926. e. Charles U., Prague; NYU. Owns 500 features and westerns for foreign distribution and library of 1400 shorts, importer and exporter. Pres., chmn. of bd. Alexander Beck Films, 1955. Formed Albex Films and A.B. Enterprises, 1959; formed & pres., Beckman Film Corp., 1960; formed Alexander Beck Productions, 1964. In 1969 formed Screencom Int'l Corp., 1986, formed Beck Int'l Corp., 1987; formed Challenger Pictures Corp., 1988.

BECK, MICHAEL
Actor. r.n. Michael Beck Tucker. b. Memphis, TN, Feb. 4, 1949. e. Millsaps Coll. on football scholarship (quarterback). Became active in college theatre. In 1971 attended Central Sch. of Speech & Drama, London; studied 3 years, following which toured England with repertory companies for 2 years. Returned to U.S.; cast as lead in independent film, Madman (shot in Israel in 1977).
PICTURES: Madman, The Warriors, Xanadu, Megaforce, War Lords of the 21st Century, The Golden Seal, Triumphs of a Man Called Horse, Final Judgment, Forest Warrior, Jungle Book: Lost Treasure (voice), Yerba City.
TELEVISION: Movies: Mayflower: the Pilgrim's Adventure, Alcatraz: The Whole Shocking Story, Fly Away Home, The Last Ninja, Rearview Mirror, Chiller, Blackout, Only One Survived, Houston: Legend of Texas, Deadly Game, Stranger at My Door,

Fade to Black. Mini-series: Holocaust, Celebrity. Series: Houston Knights. Guest: Murder She Wrote, Robin's Hoods, Babylon 5, Walker Texas Ranger, Diagnosis Murder, Crusade, Nash Bridges.

BECKER, HAROLD
Director. b. New York, NY, 1950. Dir. documentaries, Eugene Atget Interview with Bruce Gordon, Blind Gary Davis, Signet, Ivanhoe Donaldson.
PICTURES: The Ragman's Daughter (debut, 1972), The Onion Field, The Black Marble, Taps, Vision Quest, The Boost, Sea of Love, Malice (also co-prod.), City Hall (also co-prod.), Mercury Rising, Domestic Disturbance (also prod.).

BECKINSALE, KATE
Actress. b. London, England, July 26, 1973.
PICTURES: Prince of Jutland, Uncovered, Marie-Louise ou la permission, Haunted, Shooting Fish, The Last Days of Disco, Brokedown Palace, The Golden Bowl, Pearl Harbor, Serendipity, Laurel Canyon, Underworld, Van Helsing.
TELEVISION: Movies: One Against the Wind, Rachel's Dream, Cold Comfort Farm, Emma, Alice Through The Looking Glass. Mini-Series: Devices and Desires Series: Hercules (voice). Guest: Anna Lee, So Graham Norton, The Big Breakfast.

BEDELIA, BONNIE
Actress. r.n. Bonnie Bedelia Culkin. b. New York, NY, March 25, 1946. e. Hunter Coll.
THEATRE: Enter Laughing, The Playroom, My Sweet Charlie (Theatre World Award).
PICTURES: The Gypsy Moths (debut, 1969), They Shoot Horses Don't They?, Lovers and Other Strangers, The Strange Vengeance of Rosalie, Between Friends, The Big Fix, Heart Like a Wheel, Death of an Angel, Violets Are Blue, The Boy Who Could Fly, The Stranger, Die Hard, The Prince of Pennsylvania, Fat Man and Little Boy, Die Hard 2, Presumed Innocent, Needful Things, Speechless, Judicial Consent, Homecoming, Bad Manners, Gloria, Sordid Lives, Manhood.
TELEVISION: Movies, incl.: Then Came Bronson, Sandcastles, A Time for Love, Hawkins on Murder, Message to My Daughter, Heatwave!, Question of Love, Walking Through the Fire, Salem's Lot, Tourist, Fighting Back, Million Dollar Infield, Memorial Day, Alex: The Life of a Child, The Lady from Yesterday, Somebody Has to Shoot the Picture, Switched at Birth, A Mother's Right: The Elizabeth Morgan Story, The Fire Next Time, Legacy of Sin: The William Coit Story, Shadow of a Doubt, Her Costly Affair, Any Mother's Son, To Live Again, Locked in Silence, Flowers for Algernon, Picnic.Series: Love of Life, The New Land, Fallen Angels, Partners, Heart of the City. Guest: Bonanza, The Outer Limits, Love Story, Doogie Howser M.D., The Division.

BEGLEY, ED, JR.
Actor. b. Los Angeles, CA, Sept. 16, 1949. Son of late actor Ed Begley. Debut in a guest appearance on My Three Sons at 17. On NY stage in The Cryptogram.
PICTURES: Now You See Him Now You Don't (debut, 1972), Showdown, Superdad, Cockfighter, Stay Hungry, Blue Collar, The One and Only, Goin' South, Hardcore, The In-Laws, The Concorde: Airport '79, Private Lessons, Cat People, Eating Raoul, This Is Spinal Tap, Streets of Fire, Protocol, Transylvania 6-5000, Waiting to Act, Amazon Women on the Moon, The Accidental Tourist, Scenes from the Class Struggle in Beverly Hills, She-Devil, Meet the Applegates, Dark Horse, Greedy, Even Cowgirls Get the Blues, Renaissance Man, The Pagemaster, Sensation, Batman Forever, Rave Review, Storybook Hourglass, The Crazysitter, Santa With Muscles, Lay of the Land, Ms. Bear, Joey, I'm Losing You, Best In Show, Get Over It, Anthrax, Diary of a Sex Addict, Bug, Auto Focus, Back By Midnight, Net Games, Bathroom Boy, A Mighty Wind, Going Down, Stateside.
TELEVISION: Movies: Family Flight, Amateur Night at the Dixie Bar and Grill, Elvis, Hot Rod, A Shining Season, Rascals and Robbers - Secret Adventures of Tom Sawyer and Huck Finn, Tales of the Apple Dumpling Gang, Not Just Another Affair, Still the Beaver, An Uncommon Love, Roman Holiday, Spies Lies & Naked Thighs, Not a Penny More Not a Penny Less, In the Best Interest of the Child, Chance of a Lifetime, The Story Lady, In the Line of Duty: Siege at Marion, Exclusive, Running Mates,. Cooperstown, Columbo: Undercover, Incident at Deception Ridge, The Shaggy Dog, Murder She Purred: A Mrs. Murphy Mystery, Homicide: The Movie, Hounded. Series: Roll Out, St. Elsewhere (1982-88), Parenthood, Winnetka Road, Meego, Providence, Six Feet Under. Guest: Room 222, Love American Style, Happy Days, Columbo, M*A*S*H, Barnaby Jones, Mary Hartman Mary Hartman, Ellen, The Simpsons, The Drew Carey Show, The Larry Sanders Show, Family Law, 7th Heaven, The Agency, Dharma & Greg, Scrubs.

BEHRING, JOHN
Director.
TELEVISION: Movies: My Indian Summer. Series.: Charmed, Roswell.

BEINEIX, JEAN-JACQUES
Director, Writer, Producer. b. Paris France, October, 8, 1946. Various films as second unit director or assistant director.
PICTURES:Diva (also writer), Moon in the Gutter (also writer), Betty Blue (also writer, prod.), Roselyne et les lions (also writer), IP5: Island of the Pachyderms (also writer, prod.), Mortal Transfer (also writer)
TELEVISION: Loft Paradoxe (documentary, 2002).

BELAFONTE, HARRY
Actor, Singer, Producer. r.n. Harold George Belafonte, b. New York, NY, March 1, 1927. Trained for stage at the Actors Studio, New Sch. for Social Research and American Negro Theatre. Professional debut, Royal Roost nightclub, N.Y., Village Vanguard, 1950. Broadway debut: John Murray Anderson's Almanac, 1953. Recording, concert artist. Emmy Award for Tonight With Harry Belafonte, 1961.
THEATRE: Juno and the Paycock, John Murray Anderson's Almanac. (Tony Award, 1953), Three for Tonight, A Night With Belafonte, To Be Young Gifted and Black (prod.), Asinamali (co-prod.).
PICTURES: Bright Road (debut, 1953), Carmen Jones, Island in the Sun, Odds Against Tomorrow, The World the Flesh and the Devil, Angel Levine, Buck and the Preacher, Uptown Saturday Night, Beat Street (prod., composer), The Player, Prêt-à-Porter, White Man's Burden, Kansas City (NY Society of Film Critics Award, 1997), Jazz '34,
TELEVISION: Movies: Grambling's White Tiger, Swing Vote, The Nightclub Years. Many variety specials and more than 12 documentaries. Series: Sugar Hill Times. Guest: Rowan & Martin's Laugh-In, Sesame Street, PB&J Otter (voice).

BELAFONTE, SHARI
Actress. b. New York, NY, Sept. 22, 1954. e. Carnegie-Mellon U., BFA, 1976. Daughter of actor-singer Harry Belafonte. Worked as publicist's asst. at Hanna Barbera Prods. before becoming successful model (appearing on more than 200 magazine covers and in numerous TV commercials).
PICTURES: If You Could See What I Hear, Time Walker, Speed Zone!, Feuer Eis & Dynamit, Murder by Numbers, The Player, Mars, Loving Evangeline.
TELEVISION: Movies: Hotel, The Midnight Hour, Kate's Secret, Perry Mason: The Case of the All-Star Assassin, French Silk, Heidi Chronicles, Thirdspace. Host: Big Hex of Little Lulu, AM Los Angeles, Living the Dream: a Tribute to Dr. Martin Luther King Jr., Lifestyles with Robin Leach and Shari Belafonte, First Edition, The Caribbean with Shari Belafonte. Series: Hotel, Pilot: Velvet, Beyond Reality. Guest: Hart to Hart, Code Red, The Love Boat, Matt Houston, Hey Arnold!, The District.

BELFER, HAL B.
Executive Producer, Director, Choreographer. b. Los Angeles, CA, Feb. 16. e. USC; U. of CA (writing). Head of choreography dept. at both 20th Century-Fox and Universal Studios. Dir. of entertainment, in Las Vegas, Riviera and Flamingo Hotels. Prod., musical shows for Mexico City, Aruba, Puerto Rico, Montreal, Las Vegas. Dir., TV commercials and industrials. H.R. Pufnstuf TV series. Prod., dir., choreographer, Premore, Inc. Develop TV specials and sitcom, tape and film. Exec. prod.: Once Upon a Tour and Dora's World, Rose on Broadway, Secret Sleuth, Inn by the Side of the Road, Imagine That! Special staging Tony The Pony Series and prod., segment of What a Way to Run a Railroad TV specials. Talent dev't. programs, Universal Studios, 20th Century-Fox. Personal mgr. and show packager. 1982, exec. prod.: Enchanted Inn (TV Special), Cameo Music Hall I; stage mgr.: Promises, Promises, A Chorus Line (Sahara Hotel, Las Vegas). Created: Hal Belfer Associates Talent and Production Consultant; Convention Destination & Services Consultant.

BEL GEDDES, BARBARA
Actress. r.n. Barbara Geddes Lewis. b. New York, NY, Oct 31, 1922. Father was Norman Bel Geddes, scenic designer. B'way debut in Out of the Frying Pan. Toured USO camps in Junior Miss, 1941; voted Star of Tomorrow, 1949. Author-illustrator children's books: I Like to Be Me (1963), So Do I (1972). Also designer of greeting cards for George Caspari Co.
THEATRE: Out of the Frying Pan, Deep Are the Roots, Burning Bright, The Moon Is Blue, Living Room, Cat on a Hot Tin Roof, The Sleeping Prince, Silent Night Holy Night, Mary Mary, Everything in the Garden, Finishing Touches.
PICTURES: The Long Night (debut, 1947), I Remember Mama (Acad Award nom.), Blood on the Moon, Caught, Panic in the Streets, Fourteen Hours, Vertigo, The Five Pennies, Five Branded Women, By Love Possessed, Summertree, The Todd Killings.
TELEVISION: Movies: Our Town, Live TV in 1950s: Robert Montgomery Presents (The Philadelphia Story), Schlitz Playhouse of the Stars; several Alfred Hitchcock Presents episodes (incl. Lamb to the Slaughter). Series: Dallas (Emmy Award, 1980). Guest: Dr. Kildare, Daniel Boone, Spencer's Pilots.

BELL, TOM
Actor. b. Liverpool, England, Aug. 2, 1933. Early career in repertory and on West End stage. First TV appearance in Promenade.
PICTURES: The Concrete Jungle (debut, 1960), Echo of Barbara, The Kitchen, Damn the Defiant!, A Prize of Arms, The L-Shaped Room, Blues for Lovers, He Who Rides a Tiger, Sands of Beersheba, In Enemy Country, The Long Day's Dying, Lock Up Your Daughters!, All the Right Noises, The Violent Enemy, Quest for Love, Straight on Till Morning, Royal Flash, The Sailor's Return, Summer Lightning, Wish You Were Here, Resurrected, The Magic Toy Shop, The Krays, Let Him Have It, Angels, Seconds Out, Feast of July, Swept from the Sea, Preaching to the Perverted, The Boxer, Swing, My Kingdom, The Last Minute, Long Time Dead, Lava, Oh Marbella!, Devil's Gate.
TELEVISION: Movies: No Trams to Lime Street, Angels Are So Few, Stronger than the Sun, The Rainbow, Words of Love, Red King White Knight, The Cinder Path, The Great Kandinsky,

Dalziel and Pascoe: Recalled to Life, Tube Tales, Pollyanna. Miniseries:Holocaust, Out, Sons & Lovers, Reilly: Ace of Spies, The Detective, Prime Suspect 3, No Bananas, Four Fathers. Series: King's Royal, Chancer, Hope It Rains.

BELLAMY, EARL
Producer, Director. b. Minneapolis, MN, March 11, 1917. e. Los Angeles City Coll. President, The Bellamy Productions Co.
PICTURES: Dir. more than 60 pictures, incl.: Seminole Uprising (debut, 1955), Blackjack Ketchum: Desperado, Toughest Gun in Tombstone, Stagecoach to Dancers' Rock (also prod.), Fluffy, Gunpoint, Munster Go Home!, Incident at Phantom Hill, Three Guns for Texas, Sidecar Racers, Seven Alone, Part 2: Walking Tall, Against a Crooked Sky, Sidewinder 1, Speedtrap, Magnum Thrust.
TELEVISION: Dir. work on more than 70 series/tv movies, incl.: Bachelor Father, Wells Fargo, Lone Ranger, Alcoa Premiere, Arrest and Trial, The Virginian, The Crusaders, Schlitz Playhouse, Rawhide, The Donna Reed Show, Andy Griffith Show, Wagon Train, Laramie, Laredo, I Spy, Mod Squad, Medical Center, To Rome With Love, My Friend Tony, The Partners, The Partridge Family, The Rookies, The Sixth Sense, MASH, The Six Million Dollar Man, S.W.A.T., Matt Helm, Starsky and Hutch, Isis, Eight is Enough, Future Cop, Fantasy Island, The Love Boat, Trapper John MD, Hart to Hart, Code Red, Blue Thunder, V.

BELLFORT, TOM
Sound.
PICTURES: Sound work in 40 pictures, incl. Rumble Fish, The Cotton Club, The Journey of Natty Gann, Seize the Day, Tucker: The Man and His Dream, The Godfather: Part III, Bingo!, The Last Supper, Mission: Impossible, One Fine Day, Volcano, Campfire Tales, Titanic (Acad. Award, Best Sound Editing, 1998), 54, Star Wars: Episode I-The Phantom Menace (nom. BAFTA, Acad. Award), Fight Club, Frequency, Hart's War, Panic Room, Adventures of Pluto Nash, The Recruit.
TELEVISION: Series: Tales from the Crypt, The Young Indiana Jones Chronicles.

BELLOCCHIO, MARCO
Director, Writer. b. Piacenza, Italy, Nov. 9, 1939. e. Academy of Cinematografia, Rome (studying acting, then film directing); Slade School of Fine Arts, London 1959-63.
PICTURES: Fist in His Pocket (debut, 1965), China Is Near, Amore e Rabbia (segment: Discutiamo Discutiamo), Nel Nome del Padre, Slap the Monster on the Front Page (also co-s.p.), Madmen to Be Released, Triumphal March, Il Gabbiano, The Film Machine, Leap Into the Void, The Eyes and the Mouth, Henry IV, Devil in the Flesh, The Sabba's Vision, The Conviction, The Butterfly's Dream, Broken Dreams, The Prince of Homburg, The Nanny, Another World Is Possible The Religion Hour (My Mother's Smile) (also co-prod.).

BELMONDO, JEAN-PAUL
Actor. b. Neuilly-sur-Seine, France, April 9, 1933. e. private drama school of Raymond Girard, and the Conservatoire d'Art Dramatique. Formed a theatre group with Annie Girardot and Guy Bedos.
THEATRE: (Jean Marais' production) Caesar and Cleopatra, Treasure Party, Oscar, Kean, Cyrano de Bergerac, Tailleur pour Dames, La Puce a L'Oreille.
PICTURES: A Pied a Cheval et En Voiture (By Foot Horse and Car), Look Pretty and Shut Up, Drole de Dimanche, Les Tricheurs, Les Copains du Dimanche, Charlotte et Son Jules, A Double Tour, Breathless, Classe Tous Risques, Moderato Cantabile, La Francaise et l'Amour, Les Distractions, Mademoiselle Ange, La Novice, Two Women, La Viaccia, Une Femme Est une Femme, Leon Morin Pretre, Les Amours Celebres, Un Singe en Hiver, Le Doulos, L'Aine des Ferchaux, La Mer A Boire, Banana Peel, That Man From Rio, Cent Mille Dollars au Soleil, Echappement Libre, La Chasse a l'Homme, Dieu a Choisi Paris, Weekend a Zuydcocte, Par Un Beau Matin d'Ete, Up to His Ears, Is Paris Burning?, Casino Royale, The Thief of Paris, Pierrot le Fou, The Brain, Love Is a Funny Thing, Mississippi Mermaid, Borsalino, A Man I Like, The Burglars, Tender Scoundrel, Inheritor, Stavisky, Fear Over the City, L'Animal, The Professional, Ace of Aces, The Vultures, Happy Easter, Hold Up, Le Solitaire, Itinerary of a Spoiled Child (also prod., Cesar Award), L'Inconnu dans la Maison, Les Miserables, Les Cent et une Nuits, Desire, Une chance sur deux, Peut-etre, Les Acteurs, Amazone.
TELEVISION: Les Trois mousquetaires, Belmondo le maqnifique, L'Aine des Ferchaux.

BELSON, JERRY
Producer, Director, Writer. With Garry Marshall, writer of The Dick Van Dyke Show, prod. of The Odd Couple. Co-authoring the Broadway play The Roast (1980).
PICTURES: How Sweet It Is (prod., s.p.), The Grasshopper (s.p., prod.), Smile (s.p.), Fun With Dick and Jane (s.p.), Smokey and the Bandit II (s.p.), Student Bodies (exec. prod.), The End (s.p.), Jekyll and Hyde Together Again (s.p., dir.), Surrender (dir., s.p.),The Couch Trip (actor), For Keeps (prod.), Always (co-s.p.).
TELEVISION: Special: Billy Crystal: Midnight Train to Moscow (co-writer; Emmy Award). Series: The Dick Van Dyke Show, The Odd Couple, The Tracey Ullman Show (co-creator, co-exec. prod.; Emmy Awards), Tracey Takes On..., The Norm Show (consulting prod.).

BELUSHI, JAMES
Actor. b. Chicago, IL, June 15, 1954. e. DuPage Coll., Southern Illinois U. Brother was late actor John Belushi. Began at Chicago's Second City Theatre.
THEATRE: Sexual Perversity in Chicago, The Pirates of Penzance, True West, Conversations With My Father, Baal.
PICTURES: Thief (debut, 1981), Trading Places, The Man with One Red Shoe, Salvador, About Last Night, Jumpin' Jack Flash, Little Shop of Horrors, Number One With a Bullet (co-s.p. only), The Principal, Real Men, Red Heat, Who's Harry Crumb?, K-9, Homer and Eddie, Wedding Band, Taking Care of Business, Mr. Destiny, The Palermo Connection, Only the Lonely, Masters of Menace (cameo), Curly Sue, Once Upon a Crime, Diary of a Hitman (cameo), Traces of Red, Last Action Hero (cameo), Destiny Turns on the Radio, Separate Lives, Canadian Bacon, Race the Sun, Jingle All the Way, Gold in the Streets, Retroactive, Living in Peril, Gang Related, Wag the Dog, The Florentine, Angel's Dance, Made Men, Return to Me, Joe Somebody, Snow Dogs, One Way Out, K-9: P.I., Pinocchio (voice), Easy Six.
TELEVISION: Movies: Royce, Parallel Lives, Sahara, Who Killed Atlanta's Children? Mini-Series: Wild Palms. Series: Who's Watching the Kids?, Working Stiffs, Saturday Night Live, Mighty Ducks (voice), It's Good to Be King, Total Security, According to Jim.

BELZER, RICHARD
Actor, Comedian. b. Bridgeport, CT, Aug. 4, 1944.
PICTURES: The Groove Tube (debut, 1974), Fame, Author Author, Night Shift, Scarface, America, Flicks, The Wrong Guys, Freeway, Fletch Lives, The Big Picture, The Bonfire of the Vanities, Off and Running, Mad Dog and Glory, Girl 6, A Very Brady Sequel, Get on the Bus, Species II, Man on the Moon, Jump, Bitter Jester (also exec. prod.).
TELEVISION: Movies: The Flash, Bandit: Bandit Bandit, Hart to Hart: Crimes of the Hart, Prince for a Day, Deadly Pursuits, Homicide: The Movie. Mini-series: The Invaders. Specials: On Location: Richard Belzer in Concert (also writer), Belzer on Broadway (also writer, exec. prod.), Comic Relief. Series: Homicide: Life on the Street, Crime Stories (host), Law & Order: Special Victims Unit. Guest: The X-Files, Law & Order, Mad About You, The Beat, 3rd Rock From the Sun (as himself).

BENBEN, BRIAN
Actor. b. Winchester, VA, June 18, 1956. Raised in Marlboro, NY. m. actress Madeleine Stowe. In regional and alternative theatre before making B'way debut in Slab Boys.
PICTURES: Gangster Wars, Clean and Sober, I Come in Peace, God's Payroll, Radioland Murders.
TELEVISION: Movies/Specials: Family Business, Conspiracy: The Trial of the Chicago 8, Comfort Texas, The Flamingo Rising, Sister Mary Explains It All. Mini-series: The Gangster Chronicles, Kingpin. Series: Kay O'Brien, Dream On (Cable ACE Award, 1992), The Brian Benben Show (also co-exec. prod.) Guest: Tales from the Darkside, Matlock.

BENDICK, ROBERT
Indep. documentary prod., dir. b. New York, NY, Feb. 8, 1917. e. NYU, White School Photography. U.S. Air Force, W.W.II. Documentary and still cameraman before joining CBS Television as cameraman and dir.; 1940; rejoined CBS Television as dir. special events, 1946; promoted dir. news & special events; acting program dir. 1947; resigned 1951. Collaborated with Jeanne Bendick on: Making the Movies, Electronics for Young People, Television Works Like This, Filming Works Like This, 1971. Prod. Peabody Award-winning U.N. show The U.N. in Action. V.p., Cinerama Prod. Co-prod., This Is Cinerama; co-dir., Cinerama Holiday; prod., Dave Garroway Show Today and Wide Wide World, 1955-56. NBC prod. dir. C.V. Whitney Pict., 1956; Merian C. Cooper Ent., 1957; prod. NBC, 1958. Prod.: Garroway Today Show, Bob Hope 25 Yrs. of Life Show, 1961; Bell Telephone Threshold Science Series, Groucho Marx, Merrily We Roll Along, U.S. Steel Opening New York World's Fair, 1964; First Look Series 1965 (Ohio St. Award); also dir. American Sportsman, ABC; prod., pilot, Great American Dream Machine (NET) (Emmy Award, 1971 and 1972); co-exec. prod., Dick Cavett—Feeling Good, 1975. Pres. Bendick Assoc. Inc.; prod. of education audio-visual systems. Bd. of Govs., NY Academy of TV Arts and Sciences. 1976, co-author with Jeanne Bendick, TV Reporting. Consultant, Warner Qube Cable Co. Prod., dir., Fight for Food (PBS), 1978. Program consultant to Times-Mirror Cable Co., L.A. Prod. segment ABC 20/20. Member awards committee, National TV Acad. Arts & Science. Co-author with Jeanne Bendick of Eureka It's Television (1993). Inducted into Natl. TV Academy Arts & Science, NY chapter, Silver Circle, 1994. Co-author with Jeanne Bendick of Markets—From Barter to Bar Codes, 1998.

BENDER, LAWRENCE
Producer. b. The Bronx, NY, 1958. Together with Quentin Tarantino, founded record company called A Band Apart Records. It focuses on film soundtracks. Trademark includes small acting roles in pictures he produces.
PICTURES: Intruder (also story), Tale of Two Sisters, Reservoir Dogs, Fresh, Killing Zoe (exec. prod.), Pulp Fiction, Four Rooms, White Man's Burden, From Dusk Till Dawn (exec. prod.), Snakeland (exec. prod.), Good Will Hunting, Jackie Brown, A Price Above Rubies, Anna and the King, The Mexican,

Knockaround Guys, Stark Raving Mad (exec. prod), Kill Bill, Havana Nights: Dirty Dancing 2, The Great Raid..
TELEVISION: Movies: Anatomy of a Hate Crime (exec. prod.), Nancy Drew (exec. prod.), Series: Lost in Oz.

BENEDICT, DIRK
Actor. r.n. Dirk Niewoehner. b. Helena, MT, March 1, 1945. e. Whitman Coll., Walla Walla, WA. Enrolled in John Fernald Academy of Dramatic Arts, Rochester, MI, after which had season with Seattle Repertory Theatre; also in summer stock at Ann Arbor, MI. Made B'way debut in Abelard and Heloise, 1970. Author: Confessions of a Kamikaze Cowboy, And Then We Went Fishing.
PICTURES: Georgia Georgia (debut, 1972), Sssssss, W, Scavenger Hunt, Ruckus, Underground Aces, Body Slam, Blue Tornado, Shadow Force, Official Denial, The Feminine Touch, Demon Keeper, Christine's Dream (dir. only), Alaska, Steel Stomachs (host), Adventures of Young Brave, Cahoots.
TELEVISION: Movies: Journey from Darkness, Voyage Into Evil, Battlestar Gallactica, Mission Galactica: The Cylon Attack, The Georgia Peaches, Scruples, Family in Blue, Mark of the Devil, Trenchcoat in Paradise, Bejewelled, Abduction of Innocence. Series: Chopper One, Battlestar Galactica, The A Team. Guest: Love Boat, Murder She Wrote, Hawaii Five-O, Baywatch.

BENEDICT, PAUL
Actor, Director. b. Silver City, NM, Sept. 17, 1938. Acted with the Theatre Company of Boston, Arena Stage, D.C.; Trinity Rep., Providence; Playhouse in the Park, Cincinnati; Center Stage, Baltimore; A.R.T., Cambridge.
THEATRE: NY: Little Murders, The White House Murder Case, Bad Habits, It's Only a Play, Richard III, The Play's the Thing. LA: The Unvarnished Truth, It's Only a Play. Director: Frankie & Johnnie in the Clair de Lune, Bad Habits, The Kathy and Mo Show, Beyond Therapy, Geniuses, Any Given Day.
PICTURES: The Virgin President, Taking Off, They Might Be Giants, The Gang that Couldn't Shoot Straight, Up the Sandbox, Deadhead Miles, Jeremiah Johnson, The Front Page, Mandingo, The Goodbye Girl (also dir.), Billy in the Lowlands, The Man With Two Brains, This Is Spinal Tap, Arthur 2 on the Rocks, Cocktail, The Chair, The Freshman, Sibling Rivalry, The Addams Family, Waiting for Guffman, Who Was That Man, A Fish in the Bathtub, Isn't She Great, A Mighty Wind.
TELEVISION: Movies: Hustling, The Electric Grandmother, Baby Cakes, Attack of the 50 Ft. Woman. Mini-Series: The Blue and the Gray. Series: Sesame Street (1969-74), The Jeffersons, Mama Malone, One Life To Live, Guiding Light. Guest: Kojak, Maude, All in the Family, Harry-O, Seinfeld, Drew Carey Show.

BENIGNI, ROBERTO
Actor, Writer, Director, Producer. b. Misericordia, Arezzo, Italy, Oct. 27, 1952. Has 38 ent. industry award wins and 18 nom. Won Best Actor and Best Foreign Film Oscar for Life is Beautiful, 1999.
PICTURES: Berlinguer ti voglio bene (also s.p.), Giorni cantati, Chiedo asilo (also s.p.), Clair de femme, La Luna, In the Pope's Eye, Il Minestrone, Tu mi turbi (also s.p., dir.), F.F.S.S. cioe che mi hai portato a fare sopra Posillipo se non mi vuoi piu bene, Nothing Left to Do But Cry (also s.p., dir.), Coffee and Cigarettes, Down by Law, The Little Devil (also s.p., dir.), The Voice of the Moon, Johnny Toothpick (also s.p., dir.), Night on Earth, Son of the Pink Panther, The Monster (also s.p., dir., prod.), Life Is Beautiful (also s.p., dir.; Acad. Award for Best Actor/Leading Role, nom. for dir., s.p.), Asterix and Obelix vs. Caesar, Fellini: Je suis un grand menteur, Pinocchio (s.p., dir.).
TELEVISION: Movies: L'Ultimo del paradiso (host), Who is Alan Smithee? (documentary).

BENING, ANNETTE
Actress. b. Topeka, KS, May 29, 1958. Raised in San Diego. e. San Francisco St. Univ. m. actor Warren Beatty. Acted with San Francisco's American Conservatory Theatre. Voted Star of the Year, 2000 at ShoWest.
THEATRE: Coastal Disturbances (Tony Award nom., Theatre World & Clarence Derwent Awards), Spoils of War.
PICTURES: The Great Outdoors (debut, 1988), Valmont, Postcards from the Edge, The Grifters (Natl. Society of Film Critics Award, Acad. Award nom., 1990), Guilty by Suspicion, Regarding Henry, Bugsy, Love Affair, The American President, Richard III, Mars Attacks!, The Seige, In Dreams, American Beauty (SAG, BAFTA awards), Forever Hollywood (documentary), What Planet Are You From?, Open Range, Being Julia.
TELEVISION: Movies: Manhunt for Claude Dallas, Hostage. Guest: Miami Vice, Wiseguy. Pilot: It Had to Be You. Series: Liberty's Kids (voice).

BENJAMIN, RICHARD
Actor, Director. b. New York, NY, May 22, 1938. e. Northwestern U. m. actress Paula Prentiss.
THEATRE: (Central Park productions) The Taming of the Shrew, As You Like It; toured in Tchin Tchin, A Thousand Clowns, Barefoot in the Park, The Odd Couple. Star Spangled Girl (B'way debut; Theatre World Award, 1966). Also: The Little Black Book, The Norman Conquests, Barefoot in the Park (dir. only; London prod).
PICTURES: Actor: Goodbye Columbus, Catch-22, Diary of a Mad Housewife, The Steagle, The Marriage of a Young Stockbroker, Portnoy's Complaint, The Last of Sheila, Westworld, The Sunshine Boys (Golden Globe Award), House

Calls, Love at First Bite, Scavenger Hunt, The Last Married Couple in America, Witches' Brew, How to Beat the High Cost of Living, First Family, Saturday the 14th, Lift, Deconstructing Harry, Marci X. *Director:* My Favorite Year, Racing with the Moon, City Heat, The Money Pit, Little Nikita, My Stepmother Is an Alien, Downtown, Mermaids, Made in America, Milk Money, Mrs. Winterbourne, The Shrink is In, Marci X.
TELEVISION: *Movies:*Fame, No Room to Run, Packin' It In, The Pentagon Wars (also dir.) Tourist Trap (dir. only), The Sports Pages (dir. only), Laughter on the 23rd Floor (dir. only) *Series:* He and She (with Paula Prentiss, 1967), Quark, Semi-Tough (dir. only). *Guest:* Saturday Night Live (host), Ink, Mad About You, Titus.

BENNETT, ALAN
Author, Actor. b. Leeds, England, May 9, 1934. e. Oxford U. With Jonathan Miller, Dudley Moore and Peter Cook co-authored and starred in satirical revue Beyond the Fringe in London (1961) and on B'way (special Tony Award, 1963).
THEATRE: Forty Years On (actor, author), Getting On, Habeas Corpus (also actor), The Old Country, Enjoy, Kafka's Dick, Single Spies (also dir.), The Madness of George III.
PICTURES: *Actor:* Long Shot, Dream Child (voice), Little Dorrit, The Wind in the Willows (voice), In Love And War. *Writer:* A Private Function, Prick Up Your Ears, The Madness of King George (also actor). The End of the Affair (prod. asst.)
TELEVISION: *Movies:* Writer: Beyond the Fringe, A Day Out, Sunset Across the Bay, Me! I'm Afraid of Virginia Woolf, Doris and Doreen, The Old Crowd, Afternoon Off (also acting), One Fine Day, All Day on the Sands, Intensive Care (also acting), Our Winnie, A Woman of No Importance, Rolling Home, Marks, Say Something Happened, An Englishman Abroad, The Insurance Man, 102 Boulevard Haussmann, A Question of Attribution, Talking Heads (6 TV monologues). Acting: Alice in Wonderland, The Merry Wives of Windsor, Westminster Abbey (host), The Wind in the Willows (voice). *Mini-Series:*Talking Heads (also acting, dir.), Fortunies of War (acting only), Selling Hitler (acting only), A Dance to the Music of Time (acting), Talking Heads 2 (writer), Changing Stages (as himself).

BENNETT, BRUCE
Actor. r.n. Herman Brix. b. Tacoma, WA, May 19, 1909. e. U. of W.
PICTURES: Has appeared in 109 pictures, incl. Student Tour, The New Adventures of Tarzan, My Son Is Guilty, Lone Wolf Keeps a Date, Atlantic Convoy, Sabotage, Underground Agent, The More the Merrier, Sahara, Mildred Pierce, The Man I Love, A Stolen Life, Nora Prentiss, Cheyenne, Dark Passage, Treasure of the Sierra Madre, Smart Girls Don't Talk, Task Force, The Second Face, The Great Missouri Raid, Angels in the Outfield, Sudden Fear, Dream Wife, Dragonfly Squadron, Robber's Roost, Big Tipoff, Hidden Guns, Bottom of the Bottle, Strategic Air Command, Danger Signal, Silver River, Younger Brothers, Without Honor, Mystery Street, The Last Outpost, Three Violent People, The Outsider, Deadhead Miles, The Clones, Laat de dokter maar schuiven(1980).

BENNETT, HARVE
Producer. r.n. Harve Fischman. b. Chicago, IL, Aug. 17, 1930. e. UCLA. Quiz Kids radio show, 5 yrs.; newspaper columnist, drama critic; freelance writer; Assoc. prod., CBS-TV; freelance TV writer; prod. of special events. CBS-TV; dir., Television film commercials; program exec., ABC, vice pres., programs west coast, ABC-TV. Pres., Bennett-Katleman. Productions at Columbia Studios.
PICTURES: Star Trek II: The Wrath of Khan (exec. prod., co-story), Star Trek IV: The Voyage Home (also co-s.p.), Star Trek V: The Final Frontier (also co-story).
TELEVISION: *Movies:* A Woman Named Golda (exec. prod.; Emmy Award), The Jesse Owens Story (exec. prod.), Crash Landing: The Rescue of Flight 232 (writer). *Mini-Series:* Rich Man Poor Man. *Series:* Mod Squad (prod., writer), The Young Rebels (creator-writer), Six Million Dollar Man (exec. prod.), Bionic Woman (exec. prod.), American Girls (exec. prod.), From Here to Eternity, Salvage 1, Time Trax (exec. prod.), Invasion America (also developer).

BENNETT, HYWEL
Actor, Director. b. Garnant, South Wales, Apr. 8, 1944. Early career National Youth Theatre where he played many leading Shakespearean roles followed by extensive work in British theatre. 1971-81: directed numerous stage productions.
PICTURES: The Family Way (debut, 1967), Drop Dead My Love, Twisted Nerve, The Virgin Soldiers, The Buttercup Chain, Loot, Percy, Endless Night, Alice's Adventures in Wonderland, The Love Ban, Murder Elite, Witness in the War Zone, Deadly Advice, Married 2 Malcolm, Misery Harbour, Nasty Neighbours, Vatel.
TELEVISION: *Movies:* Where The Buffalo Roam, Romeo and Juliet, Malice Aforethought, Artemis 81, The Critic, Frankie and Johnnie, Absent Friends, Trust Me, The Other Side of Paradise, Hospital!, Harper and Iles, Mary Mother of Jesus, Lloyd and Hill, The Quest. *Mini-series:* Pennies from Heaven, Tinker Tailor Soldier Spy, The Modern World: 10 Great Writers, NeverWhere, Karaoke. *Series:* Shelley, The Return of Shelley, EastEnders. *Guest:*Twilight Zone, Boon, The Bill .

BENNIS, JEFFREY D.
Executive. e. State U. and U. Conn., MBA. Started with Clairol, Inc., Hair and Skin Care Divs. as marketing dir. VP Marketing/Programming of Rifkin & Assocs., 1991-94. Elected

to bds. of Nat'l Cable TV Assoc. and C-SPAN in 1995. Pres. and COO, Rifkin & Assocs., 1994-2001. Principal of 5280 Partners, L.P., in Denver, CO. 5280 is a venture capital firm investing in media & communications, software applications, outsourced business services.

BENSON, ROBBY
Actor, Writer, Director. r.n. Robert Segal. b. Dallas, TX, Jan. 21, 1956. m. actress Karla DeVito. Father is Jerry Segal, novelist and screenwriter, mother is Ann Benson, veteran of Dallas stage and nat'l summer stock and nat'l spokesperson for Merrill Lynch. Appeared in commercials and summer stock at age 5. B'way debut at age 12 in Zelda. Made dir. debut with White Hot (a.k.a. Crack in the Mirror), 1989. Composed music for Diana Ross, Karla DeVito and soundtrack of film The Breakfast Club.
THEATRE: *NY:* Zelda, The Rothschilds, Dude, The Pirates of Penzance. *Regional:* Oliver!, Evita, The King and I, King of Hearts, Do Black Patent Leather Shoes Really Reflect Up?
PICTURES: Jory (debut, 1973), Jeremy, Lucky Lady, Ode to Billy Joe, One on One (also co-s.p. with father), The End, Ice Castles, Walk Proud (also co-composer with father), Die Laughing (also prod., Tribute, National Lampoon Goes to the Movies, The Chosen, Running Brave, Harry and Son, City Limits, Rent-a-Cop, White Hot (also dir.), Modern Love (also dir., s.p., composed songs), Beauty and the Beast (voice), Betrayal of the Dove (s.p. only), The Webbers, Deadly Exposure, Belle's Magical World (voice), Beauty and the Beast: The Enchanted Christmas (voice), Just A Dream.
TELEVISION: *Movies:* Remember When, All the Kind Strangers, Virginia Hill Story, Death Be Not Proud, The Last of Mrs. Lincoln, The Death of Richie, Our Town, Two of a Kind, California Girls, Invasion of Privacy, Precious Victims. *Series:* Search for Tomorrow, Tough Cookies, Sabrina The Teenage Witch, . *Guest:* One Day at a Time, House of Mouse (voice), American Dreams. *Episode dir.:* True Confessions, Thunder Alley, Evening Shade, Good Advice, Muddling Through, Monty, Dream On, Friends, Family Album, Ellen, House Rules, Jesse, Brother's Keeper, Reunited. *Pilot dir.:* Bringing Up Jack, George Wendt Show, Game Nigh, Commonlaw, Family Beat, Style & Substance, Sabrina the Teenage Witch (also episodes), The Naked Truth.

BENTON, ROBERT
Writer, Director. b. Waxahachie, TX, Sept. 29, 1932. e. U. of Texas, B.A. Was art dir. and later consulting ed. at Esquire Magazine where he met David Newman, a writer-editor, and formed writing partnership. Together, wrote monthly column for Mademoiselle (10 years). Made dir. debut with Bad Company, 1972. Winner of three Acad. Awards and 18 other ind. awards; 19 19 add'l. award nominations.
THEATRE: It's a Bird... It's a Plane... It's Superman (libretto), Oh! Calcutta (one sketch).
PICTURES: Bonnie and Clyde, There Was a Crooked Man, What's Up, Doc?, Oh! Calcutta (writing contrib.), Superman (with Mario Puzo and Tom Mankiewicz). *Dir./Writer:* Bad Company, The Late Show, Kramer vs. Kramer (Acad. Awards for Best Dir. and Adapted Screenplay, Golden Globe, 1979), Still of the Night, Places in the Heart (Acad. Award for Best Original Screenplay, 1985), Nadine, The House on Carroll Street (co-exec. prod. only), Billy Bathgate (dir. only), Nobody's Fool, Twilight, The Human Stain.

BERENGER, TOM
Actor. r.n. Thomas Michael Moore. b. Chicago, IL, May 31, 1950. e. U. of Missouri (drama). Studied acting at H.B. Studios. Acted in regional theatres and off-off-Broadway. Plays include Death Story, The Country Girl, National Anthems, The Rose Tattoo, Electra, Streetcar Named Desire, End as a Man (Circle Rep.).
PICTURES: Rush It, The Sentinel, Looking for Mr. Goodbar, In Praise of Older Women, Butch and Sundance: The Early Days, The Dogs of War, Beyond the Door, The Big Chill, Eddie and the Cruisers, Fear City, Rustler's Rhapsody, Platoon (Acad. Award nom.), Someone to Watch Over Me, Shoot to Kill, Betrayed, Last Rites, Major League, Born on the Fourth of July, Love at Large, The Field, Shattered, At Play in the Fields of the Lord, Sniper, Sliver, Gettysburg, Major League 2, Chasers, Last of the Dogmen, The Substitute, An Occasional Hell (also exec. prod.), Shadow of a Doubt, The Gingerbread Man, Takedown, One Man's Hero (also prod.), Diplomatic Siege, Fear of Flying, Cutaway, Training Day, The Hollywood Sign, True Blue, Watchtower, D-Tox,
TELEVISION: *Movies:* Johnny We Hardly Knew Ye, Flesh & Blood, The Avenging Angel, Body Language, Rough Riders (also prod.), In the Company of Spies, The Junction Boys, Peacemakers (also prod.). *Mini-Series:* If Tomorrow Comes, Johnson County War. *Series:* One Life to Live (1975-76). *Guest:* Dream On, Cheers, Law & Order, Ally McBeal, Third Watch.

BERENSON, MARISA
Actress. b. New York, NY, Feb. 15, 1947. Granddaughter of haute couture fashion designer Schiaparelli. Great niece of art critic and historian Bernard Berenson. Former model.
PICTURES: Death in Venice (debut, 1971), Cabaret, Barry Lyndon, Casanova & Co., Killer Fish, S.O.B., The Secret Diary of Sigmund Freud, La Tete Dans Le Sac, L'Arbalete, Desire, Quel Treno da Vienna, Il Giardino Dei Cigliegi, Winds of the South, White Hunter Black Heart, Night of the Cyclone, The Cherry Orchard, Flagrant Desire, Tonka, Rich ladies etc., The Photographer, Retour a la vie, Primetime Murder, Lonesome, Lisa.
TELEVISION: *Movies:* Tourist, Playing for Time, Notorious, Maintenant et pour toujours, Fashion Victim: The Killing of Gianni

Versace (narrator/voice). *Mini-Series*: Sins, Hemingway, Lo Scialo, Blue Blood, Have a Nice Night, L'Enfant Des Loups, Oceano, Hollywood Detective, Bel Ami, *Guest*: Murder She Wrote.

BERESFORD, BRUCE
Director, Writer. b. Sydney, Australia, Aug. 16, 1940. e. U. of Sydney, B.A. 1962. Worked as teacher in London, 1961. Film editor, East Nigerian Film Unit, 1966; sect. and head of prod., British Film Inst. Production Board, 1966-71.
PICTURES: The Adventures of Barry McKenzie (also co-s.p.), Barry McKenzie Holds His Own (also prod., co-s.p.), Don's Party, The Getting of Wisdom, Money Movers, Breaker Morant (also s.p.), The Club, Puberty Blues, Tender Mercies, King David, The Fringe Dwellers (also s.p.), Crimes of the Heart, Aria (sequence), Her Alibi, Driving Miss Daisy, Mister Johnson (also co-s.p.), Black Robe, Rich in Love, A Good Man in Africa, (also prod.) Silent Fall, The Last Dance, Paradise Road (also s.p.), Sydney: A Story of a City, Double Jeopardy, Bride of the Wind, Evelyn.
TELEVISION: *Movie*: Curse of the Starving Class (writer, exec. prod.) And Starring Pancho Villa as Himself (2002).

BERG, DICK
Writer, Producer. b. New York, NY. e. Lehigh U. 1942; Harvard Business Sch. 1943. Prior to 1960 writer for TV shows Playhouse 90 Studio One, Robert Montgomery Presents, Kraft Television Playhouse. Prod., writer for Universal Studios, 1961-69: exec. prod., The Chrysler Theatre, Alcoa Premiere, Checkmate. Created and wrote Staccato (series). Prod., writer of over 50 TV movies via his Stonehenge Prods, 1971-85. TV films won 15 Emmies, 23 nominations. Twice elected pres. National Acad. of Television Arts and Sciences.
PICTURES: *Prod.*: Banning, Counterpoint, House of Cards, Banning Shoot (also s.p.), Fresh Horses, Rated X (exec. prod).
TELEVISION: *Prod. and/or writer: Movies*: Thief, Firehouse, American Geisha, Class of '63, Louis Armstrong-Chicago Style, Bloodlines: Murder in the Family (exec. prod.), For the Love of My Child: The Anissa Ayala Story (exec. prod.), Sin & Redemption (exec. prod.), White Mile, Pronto, The Wednesday Woman. *Mini-Series*: A Rumor of War, The Martian Chronicles, The Word, Space.

BERG, JEFF
Executive. b. Los Angeles, CA, May 26, 1947. e. U. of California, Berkeley, B.A., 1969. V.P., head lit. div., Creative Mgt. Associates, Los Angeles, 1969-75; v.p., m.p. dept., International Creative Associates, 1975-80; pres., 1980-. Dir., Joseph Intl. Industries. Named chmn. ICM.

BERG, PETER
Actor. b. New York, NY, 1964. e. Malcalester Col., St. Paul, MN.
PICTURES: Miracle Mile, Heart of Dixie, Race for Glory, Shocker, Genuine Risk, Crooked Hearts, Late for Dinner, A Midnight Clear, Aspen Extreme, Fire in the Sky, Girl 6, The Great White Hype, Cop Land, Dill Scallion, Very Bad Things (writer, dir. only), Corky Romano.
TELEVISION: *Movies*: Rise and Walk: The Dennis Byrd Story, The Last Seduction (also released theatrically). *Series*: Chicago Hope, Wonderland (dir. only).

BERGEN, CANDICE
Actress. b. Beverly Hills, CA, May 9, 1946. e. U. of PA. m. late dir. Louis Malle. Father was late ventriloquist Edgar Bergen. Modeled during college; freelance photo-journalist. Autobiography: Knock Wood (1984). B'way debut in Hurlyburly.
PICTURES: The Group (debut, 1966), The Sand Pebbles, The Day the Fish Came Out, Live for Life, The Magus, The Adventurers, Getting Straight, Soldier Blue, Carnal Knowledge, The Hunting Party, T. R. Baskin, 11 Harrowhouse, The Wind and the Lion, Bite the Bullet, The Domino Principle, A Night Full of Rain, Oliver's Story, Starting Over (Acad. Award nom.), Rich and Famous, Gandhi, Stick, Belly Talkers, Miss Congeniality, A View From the Top, Sweet Home Alabama.
TELEVISION: *Movies*: Arthur the King, Murder: By Reason of Insanity, Mayflower Madam, Mary & Tim (also co-exec. prod.). *Mini-Series*: Hollywood Wives. *Specials*: Woody Allen Special, Moving Day, A Century of Women (voice), AFI's 100 Years...100 Movies. *Series*: Murphy Brown (5 Emmy Awards: 1989, 1990, 1992, 1994, 1995), Exhale with Candice Bergen (talk show).

BERGEN, POLLY
Singer, Actress. r.n. Nellie Burgin b. Bluegrass, TN, July 14, 1930. e. Compton Jr. Coll., CA. Prof. debut radio at 14; in light opera, summer stock; sang with orchestra and appeared in night clubs; Columbia recording star. Bd. chmn. Polly Bergen Co.; chmn. Culinary Co., Inc.; co-chmn. Natl. Business Council for Equal Rights Amendment. Humanitarian Award: Asthmatic Research Inst. & Hosp., 1971; Outstanding Mother's Award, 1984.
THEATRE:*B'way*.:John Murray Anderson's Almanac, Champagne Complex, First Impressions, Top Man, Plaza Suit, Love Letters.
PICTURES: At War With the Army (debut, 1950), That's My Boy, Warpath, The Stooge, Half a Hero, Cry of the Hunted, Arena, Fast Company, Escape from Fort Bravo, Belle Sommers, Cape Fear, The Caretakers, Move Over Darling, Kisses for My President, A Guide for the Married Man, Making Mr. Right, Mother Mother, Cry-Baby, Dr. Jekyll and Ms. Hyde, Once Upon a Time... When We Were Colored.
TELEVISION: *Movies*: Death Cruise, Murder on Flight 502,

Telethon, How to Pick Up Girls, The Million Dollar Face, Born Beautiful, Velvet, Addicted to His Love, She Was Marked For Murder, The Haunting of Sarah Hardy, My Brother's Wife, Lightning Field, Lady Against the Odds, Perry Mason: The Case of the Skin-Deep Scandal, Leave of Absence, Hand In the Glove, In the Blink Of an Eye, The Surrogate, For Hope. *Mini-Series*: 79 Park Avenue, Playhouse (host 1954-1955), to tell the Truth (panelist), The Polly Bergen Show, Baby Talk. Guest: G.E. Theatre, Schlitz Playhouse, Playhouse 90, Studio One, Perry Como, Ed Sullivan Show, Bob Hope Show, Wonderful World of Entertainment, Dinah Shore Show, Dean Martin Show.

BERGER, HELMUT
Actor. r.n. Helmut Steinberger. b. Salzburg, Austria, May 29, 1943. e. Feldkirk College and U. of Perugia. First film, small role in Luchino Visconti's The Witches (Le Streghe) in 1966.
PICTURES: The Witches, I Giovani tigri, The Damned, The Garden of the Finzi-Continis, Love Me Strangely, Dorian Gray, Ludwig, Les Voraces, Ash Wednesday, Merry-Go-Round, Conversation Piece, Order to Assassinate, The Romantic Englishwoman, Madam Kitty, The Human Beast, The Biggest Battle, Die Jäger, Heroin, Femmes, Veliki transport, Victoria! La gran aventura d'un poble, Code Name: Emerald, Faceless, The Godfather: Part III, Ludwig 1881, Under the Palms, Honey Baby (2003).
TELEVISION:*Movies*:Abgründe, Victory at Entebbe, Fantômas: Le tramway fantôme, Boomtown, L'Affaire Dreyfus, Rosa Roth-Die Abrechnung, Schneemann, sucht Schneefrau. *Mini-series:* I Promessi sposi. *Series:* Dynasty. *Guest:* Die Harald Schmidt Show.

BERGER, RICHARD L.
Executive. b. Tarrytown, NY, Oct. 25, 1939. e. Cornell U., UCLA, 1963, B.S. In 1964 joined acct. dept., 205h Century Fox; promoted to exec. position in Fox-TV: was dir. of programming, then v.p. of programs; asst. v.p. prod. 205h-Fox. Left in 1975 to join CBS-TV as v.p. dramatic development. Returned to 20th-Fox in 1977 as v.p., domestic prod., 20th Century-Fox Pictures. Joined Disney as pres. Walt Disney Pictures; resigned 1984. Named sr. v.p., United Artists Corp., promoted pres. MGM/UA Film Group, 1988. Joined Iwerks Entertainment. Currently is an entertainment consultant and producer. Board member, Children's Institute Int'l.

BERGER, SENTA
Actress. b. Vienna, Austria, May 13, 1941. Studied ballet, then acting at Vienna's Reinhardt Seminar. Debuted in German films as a teen.
PICTURES: Die Lindenwirtin vom Donanstrand (debut 1957), The Journey, Katia, The Good Soldier Schweik, The Secret Ways, Sherlock Holmes and the Deadly Necklace, The Testament of Dr. Mabuse, The Victors, Major Dundee, The Glory Guys, Cast a Giant Shadow, Bang! Bang! You're Dead, The Poppy Is Also a Flower, The Quiller Memorandum, To Commit a Murder, The Treasure of San Gennaro, The Ambushers, Diabolically Yours, If It's Tuesday This Must Be Belgium, De Sade, When Women Had Tails, Percy, The Scarlet Letter, Merry-Go-Round, White Mafia, The Swiss Conspiracy, Cross of Iron, Nest of Nipers, The Two Lives of Mattia Pascal, The Flying Devils, Swiss Cheese, Am I Beautiful?
TELEVISION: Numerous German and Austrian television movies.

BERGERAC, JACQUES
Actor. b. Biarritz, France, May 26, 1927. Career includes Five Minutes With Jacques Bergerac on radio; in the theatre, on tour in Once More with Feeling; on most major network TV shows. Won the Foreign Newcomer Golden Globe award in 1957.
PICTURES: Twist of Fate, The Time is Now, Strange Intruder, Come Away With Me, Les Girls, Gigi, Man and His Past, Thunder in the Sun, Hypnotic Eye, A Sunday in Summer, Fear No More, Achille, A Global Affair, Taffy and the Jungle Hunter, The Emergency Operation: Lady Chaplin, The Unkissed Bride.

BERGIN, PATRICK
Actor. b. Ireland, Feb. 4, 1951
PICTURES: Taffin, The Courier, Mountains of the Moon, Sleeping with the Enemy, Love Crimes, Highway to Hell, Patriot Games, The Hummingbird Tree, Map of the Human Heart, Soft Deceit, Double Cross, Lawnmower Man2: Beyond Cyberspace, Angela Mooney, The Proposition, The Island on Bird Street, Suspicious Minds, The Lost World, Escape Velocity, One Man's Hero, Eye of the Beholder, Treasure Island, Press Run, Merlin: The Return, Africa, When the Sky Falls, High Explosive, Cause of Death, The Invisible Circus, Amazons and Gladiators, Gas Station Jesus, Devil's Prey, Beneath Loch Ness, Ella Enchanted, Bl,.m (2004).
TELEVISION: *Movies:* Act of Betrayal, Morphine and Dolly Mixtures, Robin Hood, Frankenstein, Children of the Mist, Triplecross, The Witch's Daughter, Apocalypse Watch, Stolen Women, Captured Hearts, The Ripper, Durango, St. Patrick: The Irish Legend, Jewel, King of Texas, Brush with Fate. *Mini-series:* The Real Charlotte, Dracula, The Secret World of Spying (tv documentary).

BERGMAN, ALAN
Songwriter. b. Brooklyn, NY. e. U. of North Carolina, UCLA. m. Marilyn Bergman with whom he collaborates.
THEATRE: Ballroom, Something More, The Lady and the Clarinet.

PICTURES: Lyrics: Harlow, Harper, In the Heat of the Night, Fitzwilly, The Thomas Crown Affair (Acad. Award for Best Song: The Windmills of Your Mind, 1968), John and Mary, The Happy Ending, Gaily Gaily, The Magic Garden of Stanley Sweetheart, Move, Pieces of Dreams, Wuthering Heights, Doctor's Wives, Sometimes a Great Notion, Pete 'n' Tillie, The Life and Times of Judge Roy Bean, Breezy, 40 Carats, The Way We Were, (Acad. Award for title song, 1973) Summer Wishes Winter Dreams, Harry and Walter Go To New York, Ode to Billy Joe, A Star Is Born, Same Time Next Year, The Promise, And Justice For All, A Change of Seasons, Back Roads, Author Author, Yes Giorgio, Best Friends, Tootsie, Never Say Never Again, Yently (Acad. Award for song score, 1983), The Man Who Loved Women, Micki and Maude, The January Man, Major League, Shirley Valentine, Welcome Home, Switch, For the Boys, Sabrina, Bogus.
TELEVISION: Queen of the Stardust Ballroom (Emmy Award), Hollow Image, Sybil (Emmy Award). Themes: Bracken's World, Maude, The Sandy Duncan Show, Good Times, Alice, The Dumplings, Nancy Walker Show, The Powers That Be, Brooklyn Bridge, etc.

BERGMAN, ANDREW
Writer, Director, Producer. b. Queens, NY, Feb. 20, 1945. e. Harpur Coll., magna cum laude; U. of Wis., Ph. D., history, 1970. Worked as publicist at United Artists. Author: We're in the Money, a study of Depression-era films, and the mysteries: The Big Kiss-Off of 1944, Hollywood and Levine, Sleepless Nights. Also wrote Broadway comedy, Social Security.
PICTURES: Writer: Blazing Saddles, The In Laws, So Fine (also dir.), Oh God You Devil, Fletch, The Freshman (also dir.), Soapdish, Honeymoon in Vegas (also dir.), The Scout, Striptease (also dir.), Isn't She Great? Director: It Could Happen To You. Exec. Prod.: Chances Are, Undercover Blues, Little Big League.

BERGMAN, INGMAR
Writer, Director. b. Uppsala, Sweden, July 14, 1918. e. Stockholm U. Directed university play prods.; wrote and dir. Death of Punch, 1940; first theatrical success, dir. Macbeth, 1940; writer-dir., Svensk Film-Industri, 1942-. first s.p., Frenzy, 1943; first directorial assignment, Crisis, 1945; chief prod., Civic Malmo, 1956-1960. Directed Swedish prod. Hamlet for stage at Brooklyn Acad. of Music, 1988.
PICTURES: Writer/dir. for more than 55 pictures, incl. Torment (1944, writer/asst. dir.), Crisis (also dir.), Port of Call (also dir.), Eva, The Devil's Wanton (also dir.), A Lesson in Love (also dir.), Smiles of a Summer Night (also dir.), Last Pair Out, Wild Strawberries (also dir.), The Passion of Anna (also dir.), The Touch (Also dir., prod.), Scenes from a Marriage (also dir.), The Magic Flute (also dir.), Face to Face (also dir.), A Little Night Music, Fanny and Alexander (also dir.), Den Goda viljan, Sunday's Children, Trolösa (2000).
TELEVISION: Movies: Has written and/or dir. more than 20 tv movies, incl. Riten, The Lie, After the Rehearsal, Markisinnan de Sade, Private Confessions, Larmar och gor sig till, Bildmakarna, Saraband (2003).

BERGMAN, MARILYN
Songwriter. b. Brooklyn, NY, Nov. 10, 1929. e. NYU. m. Alan Bergman, with whom she collaborates. Became pres. of ASCAP, 1994.
THEATRE: Ballroom, Something More, The Lady and the Clarinet.
PICTURES: Lyrics: Harlow, Harper, In the Heat of the Night, The Thousand Bedrooms, The Right Approach, Fitzwilly, The Thomas Crown Affair, Charro!, A Man Called Gannon, Stiletto, John and Mary, The Happy Ending, Gaily Gaily, Pieces of Dreams, Move, The Magic Garden of Stanley Sweetheart, Doctors' Wives, Sometimes A Great Notion, The Life and Times of Judge Roy Bean, Molly and Lawless John, 40 Carats, The Way We Were (Acad. Award for title song, 1973), 99 and 44/100% Dead, Ode to Billy Joe, Harry and Walter Go to New York, From Noon Till Three, A Star Is Born, The One and Only, Same Time Next Year, ...And Justice For All, The Promise, A Change of Seasons, Bolero, Author! Author!, Yes Giorgio, Tootsie, Never Say Never Again, Yentl (Acad. Award for song score, 1983), The man Who Loved Women, Shirley Valentine, Sabrina, Bogus.
TELEVISION: Queen of the Stardust Ballroom, Sybil (Emmy Award), Having Babies III, Hollow Image, Barbra Streisand: The Concert. Series/Themes: The Gale Storm Show, The Nat King Cole Show, Bracken's World, Maude, Good Times, Alice, The Nancy Walker Show, All That Glitters, Co-ed Fever, Brooklyn Bridge.

BERKOFF, STEVEN
Actor, Director, Writer. b. London, England, Aug. 3, 1937. e. studied drama in London and Paris Founder of London Theatre Group. Author of plays; East, West, Greek Decadence, Sink the Belgrano, Kvetch (London, NY). Staged, adapted and toured with: Kafka's In the Penal Colony, The Trial and Metamorphosis; Agamemnon, the Fall of the House of Usher. Starried in Hamlet and Macbeth. NY theatre: Dir.:Kvetch (also writer, actor), Coriolanus, Metamorphosis (starring Baryshnikov). Also dir. Roman Polanski in Metamorphosis in Paris.
PICTURES: Actor: Nicholas and Alexandra, A Clockwork Orange, Barry Lyndon, The Passenger, Outland, McVicar, Octopussy, Beverly Hills Cop, Rambo: First Blood II, Revolution, Underworld, Absolute Beginners, Under the Cherry Moon, The Krays, Decadence (also dir., s.p.), Fair Game, Flynn, Doppelganger (voice), Love in Paris, Rancid Aluminium, Stanley Kubrick: A Life in Pictures, Riders, Bockshu the Myth, Charlie, Headrush.

TELEVISION: Movies: Beloved Enemy, Coming Out of the Ice, Metamorphosis (also writer), A Season of Giants, Intruders, Hans Christian Andersen: My Life as a Fairy Tale, NCS II. Mini-series: Sins, War and Remembrance, In the Beginning, Changing Stages, Attila, Children of Dune. Series: Silent Night.

BERLINGER, WARREN
Actor. b. Brooklyn, NY, Aug. 31, 1937. e. Columbia U.
THEATRE: Annie Get Your Gun, The Happy Time, Bernardine, Take A Giant Step, Anniversary Waltz, Roomful of Roses, Blue Denim (Theatre World Award), Come Blow Your Horn, How To Succeed in Business Without Really Trying, (London) Who's Happy Now?, California Suite (1977-78 tour).
PICTURES: Teenage Rebel, Three Brave Men, Blue Denim, Because They're Young, Platinum High School, The Wackiest Ship in the Army, All Hands on Deck, Billie, Spinout, Thunder Alley, Lepke, The Four Deuces, I Will I Will... for Now, Harry and Walter Go to New York, The Shaggy D.A., The Magician of Lublin, The Cannonball Run, The World According to Garp, Going Bananas, Outlaw Force, Ten Little Indians, Hero, Crime and Punishment, Feminine Touch, That Thing You Do!
TELEVISION: Movies: The Girl Most Likely To..., The Red Badge of Courage, Ellery Queen, Wanted: The Sundance Woman, Sex and the Single Parent, The Other Woman, Trial By Jury, Death Hits the Jackpot, Justice. Series: Secret Storm (serial), The Joey Bishop Show, The Funny Side, A Touch of Grace, Operation Petticoat, Small & Frye, Shades of L.A. Guest: Alcoa, Goodyear, Armstrong, Matinee Theatre, The London Palladium, Kilroy, Bracken's World, Columbo, Friends.

BERMAN, BRUCE
Executive, Producer. b. New York, NY, April 25, 1952. e. California Inst. of the Arts Film School; UCLA, magna cum laude, history degree 1975; Georgetown Law School and California Bar, 1978. Entered motion picture industry while in law school, as assistant to Jack Valenti, MPAA. Assistant to Peter Guber, Casablanca Filmworks, 1979. Assistant to Sean Daniel & Joel Silver, Universal Pictures, 1979; v.p. prod., Universal, 1982. V.p prod., Warner Bros., 1984; sr. v.p., prod.,1988; pres., Theatrical Prod.,1989; pres., Worldwide Prod., 1991-96. Founded Plan B Ent., an independent motion picture prod. co., funded by Warner Bros., Inc., 1996. The company has since been acquired by Village Roadshow Pictures, where Berman now holds the post of chmn. and CEO.
PICTURES: (Exec. Prod.): Practical Magic (1998), Analzye This, The Matrix, Deep Blue Sea, Three Kings, Three to Tango, Gossip, Red Planet (prod.), Miss Congeniality, Valentine, Saving Silverman, See Spot Run, Exit Wounds, Angel Eyes, Swordfish, Cats & Dogs, Training Day, Hearts in Atlantis, Don't Say a Word, Ocean's Eleven, Queen of the Damned, Showtime, Eight Legged Freaks (prod.), The Adventures of Pluto Nash, Ghost Ship, Analyze That, Two Weeks Notice, Dreamcatcher, The Matrix Reloaded, Mystic River, The Matrix Revolutions, Torque, Cats # Dogs 2, Troy, Taking Lives (2004).

BERMAN, JOEL P.
Executive. b. Forest Hills, NY, Dec. 3, 1951. e. Ohio University, BS communications, 1973. Acct. exec., Petry Television, NY, 1976-79. In radio: ITF ad. sales, Westwood One, NY, 1979-80. East. div. mgr., Paramount Pictures Domestic Television, NY, 1981-84, VP. East. reg. mgr., 1985-87. Sr. VP/sales mgr., GTG Marketing, NY, 1987-89, where he helped launch USA Today: The TV Show. Back to Paramount Pics. Domestic TV, VP, off-network and features, 1989-90, Sr. VP/nat'l sales mgr., 1990-92, Exec. VP/sales and mktng., LA. 1992-94, pres. of distribution, 1994-97, co-pres., 1997-present.

BERMAN, RICK
Writer, Producer. r.n. Richard Keith Berman. b. Dec. 25, 1944. e. Univ. of Wisconsin-Madison, BA in speech, 1963-67. Heads the Star Trek franchise.
PICTURES: Star Trek: Generations (also prod.), Star Trek: First Contact (also prod.), Star Trek: The Experience, Star Trek: Insurrection (also prod.), Star Trek: 3D (also story), Star Trek: Nemesis (also prod.)
TELEVISION: Movies: Star Trek: Deep Space Nine: Emissary (writer), Star Trek: Deep Space Nine-Behind the Scenes (writer), Caretaker (writer/creator), Star Trek Enterprise: Broken Bow (writer/creator and exec. prod.) Series: Star Trek: The Next Generation, Star Trek: Deep Space Nine, Star Trek: Voyager., Enterprise (2001).

BERMAN, STEVEN H.
Executive. b. Middletown, OH, March 22, 1952. e. Ohio U., B.F.A. in playwriting, 1974; USC, Annenberg Sch. of Communication studied management, 1977. Special research projects Paramount and ABC TV, 1977. Account exec., Gardner Advertising, 1978. Devt. exec., CBS Television, 1979-82; dir. of comedy devt., CBS Television, 1982-84; five years at CBS in series devt., comedy and drama. Vice pres., dramatic devt., Columbia Pictures TV, 1984-85; sr. v.p., Creative Affairs, Columbia Pictures TV, 1985-87; exec. v.p., Columbia TV, div. of Columbia Entertainment TV, 1987-90; ind. prod., Columbia Pictures TV in 1990s. Joined BulkRegister.com, a leading domain name registrar, as sr. v.p., corp. comm. in June 2000.

BERNARD, MARVIN A.
Executive. b. New York, NY, Oct. 1, 1934. e. NYU. Lab technician to v.p. in charge of sales, Rapid Film Technique, Inc., 1949-63; developed technological advances in film rejuvenation and

preservation, responsible for public underwriting; real estate sales & investments in Bahamas, then with Tishman Realty (commercial leasing div.), 1964-69; est. B-I-G Capital Properties; v.p. and operating head of International Filmtreat 1970-1973; authored Film Damaged Control Chart, a critical analysis of film care and repair, 1971; founded Filmlife Inc. with latest chemical/mechanical and technical advancement in field of film rejuvenation and preservation. Bd. chmn. and chief executive officer of Filmlife Inc., m. p. film rejuvenation, storage and distribution company, 1973-75. Elected president in addition to remaining bd. chairman, Feb. 1975. Consultant to National Archives of U.S. on m.p. preservation, 1979. Dev. m.p. rejuvenation and preservation for 8mm and S8mm, 1981. Introduced this technology to private home movie use before and after transfer to videotape, 1986. Active mem. of awards comm. for tech. achievements, National Acad. TV Arts & Sciences, 1987. Recognition as leading authority and m.p. conservator from Intl. Communications Industries Assn. (ICIA), 1988. Filmlife became 1st national film to video transfer lab in U.S., 1989. Elected to Princeton Film Preservation Group. Established Film/Video Hospital, repairing broken tapes & videocassettes, 1990.

BERNARD, TOM
Executive. e. University of Maryland at College Park, BA in Radio/Film/TV. Held positions in theatrical sales at New Line Cinema. In 1980, established specialized distribution company, United Artists Classics; 1983, co-founded Orion Classics. Is a founding partner and co-president of Sony Pictures Classics (1992-present), with Michael Barker and Marcie Bloom. Member of the A.M.P.A.S., Sundance Institute Advisory Board. Chairman of the Board of Advisors for the Independent Feature Project/West. Recipient of Independent Feature Project's Industry's Lifetime Achievement Award for consistent support of new work from filmmakers around the world.

BERNHARD, HARVEY
Producer. b. Seattle, WA, March 5, 1924. e. Stanford U. In real estate in Seattle, 1947-50; started live lounge entertainment at the Last Frontier Hotel, Las Vegas, 1950. Partner with Sandy Howard, 1958-60; v.p. in chg. prod., David L. Wolper Prods., dividing time between TV and feature films, 1961-68; with MPC, v.p., chg. prod., 1968-70. Now pres. of Harvey Bernhard Ent., Inc.
PICTURES: The Mack (1973), The Omen, Damien: Omen II, Omen III: The Final Conflict, The Beast Within, Ladyhawke (exec. prod.), The Goonies, The Lost Boys, Mackin' Ain't Easy (video short, 2002).
TELEVISION: Movies: Omen IV: The Awakening, The Omen Legacy (TV documentary).

BERNHARD, SANDRA
Actress, Comedian, Singer. b. Flint, MI, June 6, 1955. Moved to Scottsdale, AZ at 10. Began career in Los Angeles 1974 as stand-up comedian while supporting herself as manicurist in Beverly Hills. Has written articles for Vanity Fair, Interview, Spin, recorded and written lyrics for debut album I'm Your Woman (1985) and starred in one-woman off-B'way show Without You I'm Nothing (1988). Published collection of essays, short stories and memoirs, Confessions of a Pretty Lady (1988). Frequent guest on Late Night with David Letterman and Robin Byrd Show.
PICTURES: Cheech and Chong's Nice Dreams (debut, 1981), The King of Comedy, Sesame Street Presents: Follow That Bird, The Whoopee Boys, Track 29, Heavy Petting, Without You I'm Nothing, Hudson Hawk, Inside Monkey Zetterland, Dallas Doll, Madonna: Truth or Dare, Unzipped, The Reggae Movie, Plump Fiction, Lover Girl, The Apocalypse, An Alan Smithee Film: Burn Hollywood Burn, Somewhere in the City, I Woke Up Early the Day I Died, Wrongfully Accused, Expose, Dinner Rush, Playing Mona Lisa, Zoolander, Shot at the Top (video documentary), The Third Date (2003).
TELEVISION: Movies: Freaky Friday, The Late Shift, Hercules Zero to Hero, Sandra Bernhard: I'm Still Here Damn It! Series: The Richard Pryor Show, Roseanne, Hercules, The Sandra Bernhard Experience.

BERNSEN, CORBIN
Actor. b. North Hollywood, CA, Sept. 7, 1954. e. UCLA, B.A. theater arts; M.F.A playwriting. m. actress Amanda Pays. Son of actress Jeanne Cooper. Teaching asst. at UCLA while working on playwriting degree. 1981 studied acting in NY while supporting self as carpenter and model (Winston cigarettes). Built own theatre in loft. Formed theatre co. Theatre of the Night.
PICTURES: Three the Hard Way (debut, 1974), Eat My Dust!, King Kong, S.O.B., Hello Again, Bert Rigby You're a Fool, Major League, Disorganized Crime, Shattered, Frozen Assets, The Killing Box, Fatal Inheritance, Major League 2, Trigger Fast, A Brilliant Disguise, The New Age, Radioland Murders, Tales From the Hood, The Great White Hype, The Dentist, Menno's Mind, Circuit Breaker, Recipe for Revenge, Drop Dead, Beings, Major League: Back to the Minors, The Dentist II (also assoc. prod.), The Misadventures of Margaret, Beings, Kiss of a Stranger, Final Payback, Rubbernecking, Killer Instinct, Delicate Instruments, Borderline Normal, Quiet Kill, The Tomorrow Man, I Saw Mommy Kissing Santa Claus, Fangs, Apocalypse IV: Judgment, The Commission, Bellacam (prod. only).
TELEVISION: Movies: Breaking Point, Line of Fire: The Morris Dees Story, Dead on the Money, Grass Roots, Love Can Be Murder, Beyond Suspicion, I Know My Son is Alive, Where Are My Children?, Voice From Within, Dangerous Intentions, In the Heat of the Night: By Duty Bound, Bloodhounds, The Cape,

Tidalwave: No Escape, Loyal Opposition: Terror in the White House, Nightworld: Riddler's Moon, Recipe for Revenge, Young Hearts Unlimited, Two of Hearts, A Place Apart, L.A. Law: Return to Justice, Atomic Twister, The Santa Trap, Gentle Ben 2: Danger on the Mountain, Love Comes Softly (2003). Series: Ryan's Hope, L.A. Law, A Whole New Ballgame, The Cape. Guest: Anything But Love, Roc, Love and War, The Nanny, Night Watch, Seinfeld, Dear John, JAG (recurring role), Presidio Med, Dragnet (2003).

BERNSEN, HARRY
Producer, Executive. b. Chicago, IL, June 14, 1935. Served in U.S. Marine Corp., 1953-55. Had own agency, Continental Management, 1956-70. Became prod., 1970.
THEATRE: Producer: Beyond the Rainbow, The Boys in Autumn.
PICTURES: Producer/Assoc. prod.: Fool's Parade, Something Big, Three the Hard Way, Take a Hard Ride, Fatal Inheritance.
TELEVISION: Movies: Exec. prod.: The Awakening Land, Mighty Moose and the Quarterback Kid (prod.) ABC After School Specials.

BERNSTEIN, ARMYAN
Producer, Director, Writer. Chairman of Beacon Pictures; co-founder with Marc Abraham.
PICTURES: Prod: One From the Heart (prod.), Satisfaction (exec. prod.), The Commitments (exec. prod.), A Midnight Clear (exec. prod.), Princess Caraboo (exec. prod.), The Road to Wellville, The Baby-Sitters Club (exec. prod.), 364 Girls a Year, Air Force One, A Thousand Acres (exec. prod.) Disturbing Behavior, For Love of the Game, The Hurricane (also s.p.), End of Days, Bring It On (exec. prod.), The Family Man (exec. prod.), Thirteen Days Which Shocked the World, Spy Game (exec. prod.), Tuck Everlasting (exec. prod.), The Emperor's Club (exec. prod.), Open Range (exec. prod.), Ladder 49 (exec. prod.), She's Gone (also s.p.), Dawn of the Dead (2004). Writer: Thank God It's Friday, One from the Heart, Windy City (also dir.), Cross My Heart (also dir.)

BERNSTEIN, BOB
Executive. Began public relations career 1952 at DuMont TV Network, followed by 2 yrs. as press agent for Liberace. With Billboard Magazine as review editor 3 yrs. Joined Westinghouse Bdg. Co. as p.r. dir., 1959. In 1963 named p.r. dir. for Triangle Publications, serving in various capacities to 1971. Joined Viacom Intl. as dir. of information services. In 1975 formed own co., March Five Inc., p.r. and promotion firm.

BERNSTEIN, ELMER
Composer, Conductor. b. New York, NY, April 4, 1922. e. Scholarship, Juilliard; Walden Sch., NYU., U.S. Army Air Force radio unit. After war 3 yrs. recitals, musical shows, United Nations radio dept. Pres., Young Musicians Found. 1st v.p. Academy of Motion Picture Arts & Sciences; co-chmn. music branch. Music dir. Valley Symphony. Recording artist, United Artists. Composer featured in more than 165 films and music/themes for 16 tv series. Pres. of Composers & Lyricists Guild of America. Among his numerous ind. recognitions, Bernstein received the ASCAP Film and Television Music Awards Lifetime Achievement Award (1990), ASCAP Award for Top Box Office Films for Wild Wild West (1999), and the ASCAP Founders Award in 2001. Won Acad. Award in 1968 for best orig. music. score for Thoroughly Modern Millie.
THEATRE: How Now Dow Jones?
PICTURES: Never Wave at a WAC, Sudden Fear, Robot Monster, Cat Women of the Moon, It's a Dog's Life, Man With the Golden Arm, Storm Fear, The View From Pompey's Head, The Ten Commandments, Fear Strikes Out, Desire Under the Elms, Drango, The Naked Eye, Sweet Smell of Success, The Tin Star, Anna Lucasta, The Buccaneer, God's Little Acre, Kings Go Forth, Some Came Running, The Miracle, The Story on Page One, From the Terrace, The Magnificent Seven, The Rat Race, By Love Possessed, The Commancheros, Summer and Smoke, The Young Doctors, Birdman of Alcatraz, Walk on the Wild Side, A Girl Named Tamiko, To Kill a Mockingbird, The Great Escape, The Caretakers, Hud, Kings of the Sun, Rampage, Love With the Proper Stranger, The Carpetbaggers, Four Days in November, The World of Henry Orient, The Hallelujah Trail, The Reward, Seven Women, Cast a Giant Shadow, Hawaii, Thoroughly Modern Millie (Acad. Award, 1967), I Love You Alice B. Toklas, The Scalphunters, True Grit, The Gypsy Moths, Midas Run, Where's Jack?, Cannon for Cordoba, The Liberation of L.B. Jones, A Walk in the Spring Rain, Doctor's Wives, See No Evil, Big Jake, The Magnificent Seven Ride, Cahill U.S. Marshall, McQ., Gold, The Trial of Billy Jack, Report to the Commissioner, From Noon Till Three, The Incredible Sarah, The Shootist, Slap Shot, National Lampoon's Animal House, Bloodbrothers, Meatballs, The Great Santini, Saturn 3, The Blues Brothers, Airplane!, Zulu Dawn, Going Ape, Stripes, An American Werewolf in London, Honky Tonk Freeway, The Chosen, Five Days One Summer, Airplane II: The Sequel, Spacehunter, Trading Places, Class, Bolero, Ghostbusters, The Black Cauldron, Spies Like Us, Legal Eagles, Three Amigos, Amazing Grace and Chuck, Leonard Part 6, Da, Funny Farm, The Good Mother, Slipstream, My Left Foot, The Grifters, The Field, Oscar, A Rage in Harlem, Rambling Rose, Cape Fear (adapt.), The Babe, The Cemetery Club, Mad Dog and Glory, Lost in Yonkers, The Age of Innocence, The Good Son, I Love Trouble, Roommates, Canadian Bacon, Devil in a Blue Dress, Buddy, Hoodlums, The Rainmaker, Twilight, The Deep End of the Ocean, Wild Wild West, Bringing Out the Dead, Keeping the Faith, Chinese Coffee, Far From Heaven.
TELEVISION: Movies: Gulag, Guyana Tragedy, Today's FBI,

Rough Riders, Introducing Dorothy Dandridge, A Storm in Summer (2000). *Specials*: Hollywood: The Golden Years, The Race for Space: Parts I & II, D-Day, The Making of the President—1960 (Emmy Award), Hollywood and the Stars, Voyage of the Brigantine Yankee, Crucifiction of Jesus, NBC Best Sellers Theme (1976). *Mini-series*: A Personal Journey with Martin Scorcese Through American Movies. *Series*: The Beachcomber, Hollywood and the Stars, The Big Valley, Julia, Owen Marshall, Appointment with Destiny, The Rookies, Arthur of the Britons, Ellery Queen, Serpico, Delta House, The Magnificent Seven.

BERNSTEIN, FRED
Executive. Was sr. v.p. of business affairs and pres. of worldwide prod. for Columbia Pictures in 1980's before serving as sr. v.p. of MCA Inc.'s Motion Picture Group, 1987-94. Former pres. of Coumbia TriStar Motion Pictures.

BERNSTEIN, JACK B.
Executive. b. New York, NY, May 6, 1937. e. City U. of New York, B.A., sociology. U.S. Army-Europe, 1956-58; research bacteriologist, 1959-61. Entered industry in 1962 with S.I.B. Prods., Paramount, as v.p. gen. mgr.; 1964-66, v.p. gen. mgr. C.P.I. Prods.; 1966-73, prod. mgr. asst. dir., free lance. 1973-1982, assoc. prod. exec. prod. at several studios. 1983-86, v.p. worldwide prod., Walt Disney Pictures; 1987, sr. v.p., worldwide prod., United Artists Pictures; 1988-90, sr. v.p. worldwide prod., MGM Pictures. Member: DGA, Friars, Academy of MP Arts & Sciences, Academy of TV Arts & Sciences, AFI.
PICTURES: *Asst. dir:* Hearts of the West. *Prod. mgr.*: Silver Streak. *Assoc. prod.*: The Other Side of Midnight, The Fury, Butch and Sundance: The Early Days, Six Pack, Unfaithfully Yours. *Exec. prod.*: North Dallas Forty, Monsignor, The Beast Within. *Co-prod.*: The Mambo Kings, Under Siege.
TELEVISION: Series: Deadly Games (supervising prod.), She Spies (co-exec. prod., 2002).

BERNSTEIN, JAY
Producer, Personal manager. b. Oklahoma City, OK. e. Pomona Coll. 1963-76, pres. of Jay Bernstein Public Relations, representing over 600 clients. Formed Jay Bernstein Enterprises, acting as personal manager for Farrah Fawcett, Suzanne Somers, Kristy McNichol, Susan Hayward, Donald Sutherland, Robert Blake, William Shatner, Linda Evans, Cicely Tyson, etc. Past pres., Bernstein Thompson Entertainment Complex, entertainment and personal mgt. firm. Currently runs Jay Bernstein Productions. Others he has managed, publicized or produced incl.: Drew Barrymore, Sharon Stone, Brooke Shields, Sela Ward, Steve Guttenberg, Ray Liotta and Jim Carrey.
PICTURES: *Exec. prod.*: Sunburn, Nothing Personal.
TELEVISION: *Exec. prod. Movies*: The Return of Mike Hammer, Mickey Spillane's Margin for Murder, Wild—West Revisited, More Wild—Wild West, Murder Me Murder You, More Than Murder, The Return of Mike Hammer, Murder Takes All, The Diamond Trap, Final Notice, Double Jeopardy, Come Die with Me: A Mickey Spillane's Mike Hammer Mystery, Headliners & Legends: Farrah Fawcett (tv documentary) *Series*: Bring 'Em Back Alive, Mike Hammer, Houston Knights.

BERNSTEIN, WALTER
Writer, Director. b. New York, NY. Aug. 20, 1919. e. Dartmouth. Wrote for NY Magazine; in W.W.II was roving correspondent for Yank Magazine. Returned to NY after war. Wrote TV scripts; published Keep Your Head Down (collection of articles).
PICTURES: *Writer*: Kiss the Blood Off My Hands (co-s.p.), That Kind of Woman, Heller in Pink Tights, A Breath of Scandal (co-s.p.), Paris Blues, The Magnificent Seven (uncredited), Fail Safe, The Money Trap, The Train, The Molly Maguires, The Front, Semi-Tough, The Betsy (co-s.p.), An Almost Perfect Affair, Yanks, Little Miss Marker (dir. debut), The House on Carroll Street.
TELEVISION: Women & Men 2: In Love There Are No Rules (also dir.), Doomsday Gun, The Affair (story), Miss Evers' Boys, Durango, Fail Safe, American Masters: On Cukor (tv documentary, as himself), Marilyn Monroe: The Final Days (tv documentary).

BERNSTEIN, WILLIAM
Executive. b. New York, NY, Aug. 30, 1933. e. New York U., B.A. 1954; Yale U., L.L.B. 1959. Joined United Artists as an attorney in 1959; v.p., business affairs, 1967-72; promoted to sr. v.p. Executive v.p., Orion Pictures, 1978-91. Pres. and CEO Orion Pictures, 1991-92. Exec. v.p., Paramount Pictures. Member, A.B.A., A.M.P.A.S.

BERRI, CLAUDE
Director, Actor, Producer. r.n. Claude Langmann. b. Paris, France, July 1, 1934. Started as actor, playing roles in French films and on stage in the 1950s. Began dir. career with short film Jeanine, followed by Le Poulet (The Chicken; also prod.; Acad. Award for best live action short subject, 1965). 1963, created Renn Productions. 1973, became partner in AMLF distribution co.
PICTURES: *Director*: The Two of Us (feature debut, 1967), Marry Me Marry Me (also s.p., actor), Le Pistonne (The Man with Connections), Le Cinema de Papa (also prod.), Le Sex Shop (also s.p.), Male of the Century (also s.p., actor), The First Time (also s.p.), Tess (prod.), Inspecteur la Bavure (prod.), Je Vous Aime (prod., s.p.), In a Wild Moment, Je Vous Aime, Le Maitre d' Ecole (also prod., s.p.), A Quarter to Two Before Jesus Christ (prod.), L'Africain (prod.), Banzai (prod.), L'Homme Blesse (prod.), Tchao Pantin (also prod., s.p.), Jean la Florette, Manon of the Spring, The Bear (exec. prod.), Valmont (exec. prod.), Uranus (also s.p., prod.), Germinal (also prod., co-s.p.), Queen Margot (prod.), La

Separation (prod.), French Twist (exec. prod.), Les Trois Freres (prod., actor), Arlette (prod.), The Ogre (prod.), Didier (Prod.), Le Pari (exec. prod.), Lucie Aubrac (s.p.), Asterix and Obelix vs. Ceasar (prod.), Amen, A Housekeeper (also dir., writer), Le Bison (et sa voisine Dorine) (prod. only), Les Sentiments (prod. only, 2003).

BERRIDGE, ELIZABETH
Actress. b. New Rochelle, NY, May 2, 1962. Studied acting at Lee Strasberg Inst., Warren Robertson Theatre Workshop.
THEATRE: NY: The Vampires, The Incredibly Famous Willy Rivers, Outside Waco, Ground Zero Club, Cruise Control, Sorrows and Sons, Crackwalker, Coyote Ugly, Briar Patch. *Regional*: Tuesday's Child, Hedda Gabler, Lulu, Venus and Thumbtacks.
PICTURES: Natural Enemies (debut, 1979), The Funhouse, Amadeus, Smooth Talk, Five Corners, When the Party's Over, Payback, Broke Even, Hidalgo, Break a Leg.
TELEVISION: *Movies*: Silence of the Heart, Home Fires Burning, Montana, When Billie Beat Bobby. *Series*: Another World: Texas, One of the Boys, The Powers That Be, The John Larroquette Show. *Guest*: Miami Vice, Touched By An Angel, Still Standing.

BERRY, HALLE
Actress. b. Cleveland, OH, Aug. 14, 1968. Named Miss Teen Ohio, Miss Teen All-American, runner up to Miss U.S.A.
PICTURES: Jungle Fever, Strictly Business, The Last Boy Scout, Boomerang, Father Hood, The Program, The Flintstones, Losing Isaiah, Race the Sun, Girl 6, Executive Decision, Rich Man's Wife, B.A.P.S., Bulworth, Why Do Fools Fall in Love, X-Men, Swordfish, Monster's Ball (Acad. Award for best actress, 2002), Die Another Day, X2, Gothika, Catwoman.
TELEVISION: *Movie*: Solomon and Sheba, The Wedding, Introducing Dorothy Dandridge (also exec. prod. Emmy Award, Golden Globe, 2000). *Mini-Series*: Queen. *Series*: Living Dolls, Knot's Landing. *Guest*: A Different World, Frasier (voice).

BERRY, KEN
Actor. b. Moline, IL, Nov. 3, 1933.
PICTURES: Two for the Seesaw, Hello Down There, Herbie Rides Again, The Cat from Outer Space.
TELEVISION: *Movies*: Wake Me When the War Is Over, The Reluctant Heroes, Every Man Needs One, Letters from Three Lovers, Love Boat II, The Legend of Forrest Tucker. *Series*: The Ann Sothern Show, Bob Newhart Show (1962), F Troop, Mayberry RFD, Ken Berry Wow Show, Mama's Family. *Guest*: Dick Van Dyke Show, Hazel, Lucy Show, Carol Burnett, Sonny & Cher.

BERSTEIN, WILLIAM
Executive. e. Yale Law School and New York U. Joined United Artists Corp. as a member of its legal dept. in 1959, then moved to senior v.p. of business affairs and became a member of its board of directors. Exec. v.p. and member of the board of directors, Orion Pictures Corp., 1978-91; named president and CEO of Orion in 1991. Currently exec. v.p., Paramount Pictures (since 1992), where he oversees business affairs, legal, finance, and gov't. operations and studio administration depts.

BERTINELLI, VALERIE
Actress. b. Wilmington, DE, April 23, 1960. Dramatic training at Tami Lynn Academy of Artists in California. Made early TV appearances in the series, Apple's Way, in commercials, and in public service announcements. Started own prod. company to acquire properties for self.
PICTURE: C.H.O.M.P.S., Ordinary Heroes, Number One with a Bullet, Saved.
TELEVISION: *Movies*: Young Love First Love, The Promise of Love, The Princess and the Cabbie, I Was a Mail Order Bride, The Seduction of Gina, Shattered Vows, Silent Witness, Rockabye, Pancho Barnes, In a Child's Name, What She Doesn't Know, Murder of Innocence, The Haunting of Helen Walker, Two Mothers for Zachary, A Case for Life, Personally Yours, John Christmas (2003). *Mini-Series*: I'll Take Manhattan, Night Sins. *Specials*: The Secret of Charles Dickens, The Magic of David Copperfield. *Series*: One Day at a Time, Sydney, Cafe Americain, Touched By An Angel.

BERTOLUCCI, BERNARDO
Director, Writer, b. Parma, Italy, May 16, 1940. e. Rome U. Son of Attilio Bertolucci, poet and film critic. At age 20 worked as asst. dir. to Pier Paolo Pasolini on latter's first film, Accatone. Made debut film, The Grim Reaper, from script by Pasolini, 1962; published poetry book, In Cerca del Mistero, 1962. Directed and wrote 3-part TV documentary, La vie del Petrolio for Ital. Oil co. in Iran, 1965-66. Collaborated on s.p. for Ballata de un Milliardo, Sergio Leone's Once Upon a Time in the West, L'inchiesta. Prod.: Sconcerto Rock, Lo Con Te Non Ci Sto Piu, Lost and Found.
PICTURES: The Grim Reaper, Before the Revolution, Love and Rage (episode: Agony), Partner, The Spider's Strategem, The Conformist, Last Tango in Paris, 1900, Luna, Tragedy of a Ridiculous Man, The Last Emperor (Acad. Awards for Best Dir. & Screenplay, 1987), The Sheltering Sky, Little Buddha, Stealing Beauty, L'Assedio, Paradiso e Inferno, Heaven and Hell, Ten Minutes Older, The Dreamers.

BESSON, LUC
Producer, Writer, Director. b. Paris, France, March 18, 1959. Formed Les Films de Loups, which later changed name to Les Films de Dauphins.

PICTURES: Le Dernier Combat, Le Grand Carnaval (2nd unit dir.), Subway, Kamikaze (prod., s.p.), Taxi Boy (tech. advis.), The Big Blue (also lyrics, camera op.), La Femme Nikita (also song), The Professional, The Fifth Element (dir.), Taxi (s.p., prod.), Joan of Arc (dir.), Nil by Mouth (prod., BAFTA Award, Outstanding Brit. Film, 1997), The Dancer (prod & writer), Kiss of the Dragon (writer, prod.), Wasai (writer, prod.), The Transporter, (writer, prod.), Taxi 3 (writer, prod.), Peau d'ange (prod.), La felicita non costa niente (co-prod.), A ton image, Special police, Moi Cesar, Michel Vaillant (writer, prod.), Fanfan la tulipe (writer, prod.), Les Côtelettes, À ton image, Michel Vaillant (exec. prod, prod. & writer), Vice & Versa, Taxi (writer also), Special police, Crimson Rivers 2: Angels of the Apocalypse (co-prod. & writer), Miss June, Cheeky, Danny the Dog (prod. & writer), Arthur (prod. & writer, 2004)
TELEVISION: Series: La Femme Nikita (writer, Nikita character).

BEST, BARBARA
Publicist. b. San Diego, CA, Dec. 2, 1921. e. U. of Southern California, AB, 1943. Radio. 20th Century-Fox, 1943-49; reporter, San Diego Journal, 1950 Stanley Kramer Co. 1950-53; own agency, Barbara Best & Associates, 1953-66; exec. v.p. Barbara Best Inc. publ. rel. 1975-85; Barbara Best Personal Management, 1997. Retired, 1998.

BEST, JAMES
Actor. r.n. Jules Guy. b. Corydon, IN, July 26, 1926. Magazine model; on stage in European roadshow cast of My Sister Eileen. Served as M.P with USAAF, WWII.
PICTURES: One Way Street (debut, 1950), Commanche Territory, Winchester 73, Peggy, Kansas Raiders, Air Cadet, Cimarron Kid, Target Unknown, Apache Drums, Ma & Pa Kettle at the Fair, Steel Town, Francis Goes to West Point, Battle at Apache Pass, Flat Top, About Face, The Beast from 20000 Fathoms, Seminole, The President's Lady, City of Bad Men, Column South, Riders to the Stars, The Raid, The Caine Mutiny, Return from the Sea, They Rode West, Seven Angry Men, The Eternal Sea, A Man Called Peter, Forbidden Planet, Calling Homicide, When Gangland Strikes, Come Next Spring, Gaby, The Rack, Man on the Prowl, Hot Summer Night, Last of the Badmen, Verboten!, The Naked and the Dead, The Left Handed Gun, Cole Younger—Gunfighter, The Killer Shrews, Ride Lonesome, Cast a Long Shadow, The Mountain Road, Shock Corridor, Black Gold, The Quick Gun, Black Spurs, Shenandoah, Three on a Couch, First to Fight, Firecreek, The Brain Machine, Sounder, Ode to Billy Joe, Gator (also assoc. prod.), Nickelodeon, Rolling Thunder, The End (also assoc. prod.), Hooper, Death Mask.
TELEVISION: Movies: Run Simon Run, Savages, The Runaway Barge, The Savage Bees, The Dukes of Hazzard: Reunion!, TV Road Trip. Mini-Series: Centennial. Series: Dukes of Hazzard, Dukes of Hazzard 2000. Guest: Alfred Hitchcock Presents, Twilight Zone, The Andy Griffith Show, Hawkins, Enos, In the Heat of the Night.

BETHUNE, ZINA
Actress, Dancer, Singer. b. New York, NY, Feb. 17, 1950. New York City Ballet (Balanchine), Zina Bethune & Company Dance Theatre, Bethune Theatredanse. Special performance at the White House and Kennedy Center.
THEATRE: B'way: Most Happy Fella, Grand Hotel. National tours: Sweet Charity, Carnival, Oklahoma!, Damn Yankees, Member of the Wedding, The Owl and The Pussycat, Nutcracker.
PICTURES: Sunrise At Campobello, Who's That Knocking at My Door, The Boost.
TELEVISION: Movies: Party of Five, Nutcracker: Money Madness Murder (also choreographer). Specials: The Gymnast (An ABC Afterschool Special), Heart Dancing, From the Heart. Series: The Nurses, The Guiding Light, Love of Life. Guest: Lancer, Cains Hundred, Naked City, Route 66, Little Women, Santa Barbara, Judy Garland Show, Jackie Gleason Show, Gunsmoke, Dr. Kildare, Emergency, Planet of The Apes, Police Story, Chips, Hardy Boys.

BETTGER, LYLE
Actor. b. Philadelphia, PA, Feb. 13, 1915. e. Haverford School, Philadelphia, American Acad. of Dramatic Art, N.Y. m. Mary Rolfe, actress. Started in summer stock; in road cos. of Brother Rat, Man Who Came to Dinner.
THEATRE: John Loves Mary, Love Life, Eve of St. Mark, The Male Animal, Sailor Beware, The Moon is Down.
PICTURES: No Man of Her Own, Union Station, First Legion, Greatest Show on Earth, The Denver & Rio Grande, Vanquished, Forbidden, The Great Sioux Uprising, All I Desire, Drums Across the River, Destry, Carnival Story, Sea Chase, Showdown at Abilene, Gunfight at OK Corral, Town Tamer, Johnny Reno, Nevada Smith, Return of The Gunfighter, Impasse, The Hawaiians, The Seven Minutes.
TELEVISION: Court of Last Resort, Grand Jury, Hawaii 5-0, Police Story, Bonanza, Combat, Gunsmoke.

BEVILLE, HUGH M., JR.
Executive; b. April 18, 1908. e. Syracuse U., NYU (MBA). To NBC 1930 statistician, chief statistician; research mgr., dir., research. U.S. Army 1942-46. Dir. of research and planning for NBC then v.p., planning and research, 1956; v.p., planning, 1964; consultant, 1968. Professor Business Admin., Southampton Coll., 1968. Exec.

dir., Broadcast Rating Council, 1971-82. Author, cons., contributing ed., TV/Radio Age, 1982-85. Author of Audience Ratings; Radio, Television, Cable, 1985, Elected mbr., Research Hall of Fame, 1986.

BEY, TURHAN
Actor. b. Vienna, Austria, March 30, 1922. Came to U.S. in 1930's studying acting at Ben Bard's School of Dramatic Arts, sadena Playhouse.
PICTURES: Footsteps in the Dark (debut, 1941), Burma Convoy, Raiders of the Desert, Shadows on the Stairs, The Gay Falcon, Junior G-Men of the Air (serial), The Falcon Takes Over, A Yank on the Burma Road, Bombay Clipper, Drums of the Congo, Destination Unknown, Arabian Nights, The Unseen Enemy, The Mummy's Tomb, Danger in the Pacific, Adventures of Smilin' Jack (serial), White Savage, The Mad Ghoul, Background to Danger, Follow the Boys, The Climax, Dragon Seed, Bowery to Broadway, Ali Baba and the 40 Thieves, Frisco Sal, Sudan, Night in Paradise, Out of the Blue, The Amazing Mr. X, Adventures of Casanova, Parole Inc., Song of India, Prisoners of the Casbah, Stolen Identity (prod. only), Healer, Possessed by the Night, The Skateboard Kid II, Virtual Combat.
TELEVISION: Movie: Universal Horror. Guest: Seaquest, Murder She Wrote, Babylon 5.

BEYMER, RICHARD
Actor. r.n. George Richard Beymer, Jr., b. Avoca, IA, Feb. 21, 1939. e. N. Hollywood H.S., Actors Studio. Performer, KTLA, Sandy Dreams, Fantastic Studios, Inc., 1949, Playhouse 90.
PICTURES: Indiscretion of an American Wife (debut, 1953), So Big, Johnny Tremain, The Diary of Anne Frank, High Time, West Side Story, Bachelor Flat, Five Finger Exercise, Hemingway's Adventures of a Young Man, The Longest Day, The Stripper, Grass (Scream Free!), Cross Country, Silent Night Deadly Night 3: Better Watch Out, My Girl 2, The Little Death, Foxfire, The Disappearance of Kevin Johnson, Playing Patti, Home the Horror Story, West Side Memories (video documentary, 2003).
TELEVISION: Movies: Generation, With a Vengeance, A Face to Die For, Elvis Meets Nixon. Series: Paper Dolls, Twin Peaks. Guest: The Virginian, Walt Disney (Boston Tea Party), Dr. Kildare, Man from U.N.C.L.E., Moonlighting, Murder She Wrote, The Bronx Zoo.

BIALIK, MAYIM
Actress. b. San Diego, CA, Dec. 12, 1976.
PICTURES: Pumpkinhead (debut, 1988), Beaches.
TELEVISION: Movies: Blossom in Paris, Don't Drink the Water. Specials: Earth Day Special, Sea World Mother Earth Celebration (host), Surviving a Break-Up, The Kingdom Chums: Original Top Ten (voice), I Hate the Way I Look, For Our Children: The Concert (host), Recess (voice). Series: Blossom, Hey Arnold (voice), The Adventures of Hyperman Pilot: Molly. Guest: Webster, The Facts of Life, MacGyver, Empty Nest, The John Larroquette Show.

BICK, JERRY
Producer. b. New York, NY, April 26, 1923. e. Columbia U., Sorbonne. Taught English at U. of Georgia, before entering film industry in pub. dept. of MGM, N.Y. Opened own literary agency in Hollywood after stint with MCA. Began career as producer in London; debut film, Michael Kohlhaas, 1969. 1986-89, exec. v.p. worldwide prod., Heritage Entertainment.
PICTURES: The Long Goodbye, Thieves Like Us, Russian Roulette, The Big Sleep, Against All Odds (exec. prod.), Swing Shift.

BIEHN, MICHAEL
Actor. b. Anniston, AL, July 31, 1956. Raised in Lincoln, NB, and Lake Havisu, AZ. At 18 years moved to Los Angeles and studied acting with Vincent Chase. First professional job in 1977 in TV pilot for Logan's Run.
PICTURES: Grease (debut, 1978), Coach, Hog Wild, The Fan, The Lords of Discipline, The Terminator, Aliens, The Seventh Sign, Rampage, In a Shallow Grave, The Abyss, Navy Seals, Time Bomb, K2, DeadFall, Tombstone, Deep Red, Jade, The Rock, Mojave Moon, The Ride, American Dragon, Dead Men Can't Dance, Susan's Plan, Wonderland, Silver Wolf, Cherry Falls, The Art of War, Meggido: The Omega Code 2, Clockstoppers, Borderline (2002).
TELEVISION:. Movies: Zuma Beach, A Fire in the Sky, China Rose, Deadly Intentions, A Taste for Killing, Strapped, Conundrum, Asteroid, Alien Evolution, When Muscles Ruled the World (tv documentary), The Legend of Butch & Sundance (2003). Series: The Runaways, The Magnificent Seven. Guest: Logan's Run, Hill Street Blues, Police Story, Family Pilots: James at 15, The Paradise Connection.

BIGELOW, KATHRYN
Director, Writer. b. San Carlos, CA, Nov. 27, 1951. e. SF Art Inst., Columbia. Studied to be painter before turning to film with short Set-Up, 1978. Was script supervisor on Union City; appeared in film Born in Flames.
PICTURES: The Loveless (feature debut as co-dir. with Monty Montgomery, 1981; also co-s.p.), Near Dark (also co-s.p.), Blue Steel (also co-s.p.), Point Break, Strange Days, Undertow (s.p.), The Weight of Water, K19 The Widowmaker (also prod.), Living in Darkness (documentary, appearing as herself)
TELEVISION: Mini-Series: Wild Palms (co-dir.).

BIGGS, JASON
Actor. b. Pompton Plains, NJ, May 12, 1978. Began acting at age 5 in national commericials. Starred opposite Judd Hirsch on B'way in Conversations With My Father.
PICTURES: Camp Stories, American Pie, Boys and Girls, Loser, Prozac Nation, Saving Silverman, American Pie II, Jay and Silent Bob Strike Back, American Wedding, Jersey Girl (2003).
TELEVISION: Series: Drexel's Class, As The World Turns. Guest: Total Security, The Andy Dick Show, Off Centre.

BIKEL, THEODORE
Actor. b. Vienna, Austria, May 2, 1924. Moved to Palestine (Israel) as teen where he made stage debut in Tevye the Milkman. Studied acting at Royal Academy of Dramatic Arts in London. London stage debut in 1948. Autobiography: Theo (1995).
THEATRE: Tonight in Samarkland, The Lark, The Rope Dancers, The Sound of Music, Cafe Crown, Fiddler on the Roof.
PICTURES: The African Queen, Melba, Desperate Moment, The Divided Heart, The Little Kidnappers, The Vintage, The Pride and the Passion, The Enemy Below, Fraulein, The Defiant Ones (Acad. Award nom.), I Want to Live, The Angry Hills, The Blue Angel, A Dog of Flanders, My Fair Lady, Sands of the Kalahari, The Russians Are Coming, the Russians Are Coming, Sweet November, My Side of the Mountain, Darker Than Amber, 200 Motels, The Little Ark, Prince Jack, Dark Tower, See You in the Morning, Shattered, Crisis in the Kremlin, My Family Treasure, Benefit of the Doubt, Shadow Conspiracy, Trickle, Second Chances, Crime and Punishment, The Lost Wooden Synagogues of Eastern Europe (narr.).
TELEVISION: Movies: The Eternal Light, Look Up and Live, Who Has Seen the Wind?, The Diary of Anne Frank, Killer by Night, Murder on Flight 502, Victory at Entebbe, Christine Cromwell: Things That Go Bump in the Night, The Final Days, Babylon 5: In the Beginning, H.U.D. Mini-series: Testimony of Two Men, Loose Change.

BILL, TONY
Director, Producer, Actor. b. San Diego, CA, Aug. 23, 1940. e. Notre Dame U. Founded Bill/Phillips Prods. with Julia and Michael Phillips, 1971-73; Tony Bill Prods. 1973-92; Barnstorm Films, 1993-. Acad. of M.P. Arts & Sciences, bd. of govs., bd of trustees, chmn. prods. branch.
PICTURES: Director: My Bodyguard (debut, 1980), Six Weeks, Five Corners (also co-prod.), Crazy People, Untamed Heart (also co-prod.), A Home of Our Own. Prod.: Hearts of the West (exec. prod.), Harry and Walter Go to New York, Boulevard Nights (exec. prod.), Going in Style, Little Dragons (also actor). Co-producer: Deadhead Miles, Steelyard Blues, The Sting (Acad. Award for Best Picture, 1973), Taxi Driver. Actor: Come Blow Your Horn (debut, 1963), Soldier in the Rain, Marriage on the Rocks, None But the Brave, You're a Big Boy Now, Ice Station Zebra, Never a Dull Moment, Castle Keep, Flap, Shampoo, Heartbeat, Pee-wee's Big Adventure, Less Than Zero, Barb Wire, Lying In Wait.
TELEVISION: Director: Dirty Dancing (pilot), Love Thy Neighbor, Next Door, One Christmas, Oliver Twist, Harlan County War, In the Time of the Butterflies (prod. only), Whitewash: The Clarence Brandley Story, Fitzgerald (exec. prod. only) Actor: Movies: Haunts of the Very Rich, Having Babies II, The Initiation of Sarah, With This Ring, Are You in the House Alone?, Portrait of an Escort, Freedom, Washington Mistress, Running Out, The Killing Mind, Naked City: Justice with a Bullet, The Fixer (also prod.), A Chance of Snow, Mini-Series: Washington Behind Closed Doors. Series: What Really Happened to the Class of '65? Guest: Alfred Hitchcock Presents (Night Caller, 1985). Special: Lee Oswald - Assassin (BBC).

BILLS, ELMER E.
Executive. b. Salisbury, MO, July 12, 1936. e. University of Missouri, B.S. Partner B & B Theatres, Inc.

BILSON, BRUCE
Director. b. Brooklyn, NY, May 19, 1928. e. UCLA, BA, Theater Arts, 1950. m. actress Renne Jarrett. Father was prod. George Bilson, son is prod.-dir. Danny Bilson, daughter is prod. Julie Ahlberg. Asst. film ed. 1951-55; USAF photo unit 1952-53; asst. dir. 1955-65. Dir. since 1965 of more than 390 TV shows.
PICTURES: The North Avenue Irregulars, Chattanooga Choo Choo.
TELEVISION: Movies/pilots: The Odd Couple, The Dallas Cowboys Cheerleaders, BJ and the Bear, The Misadventures of Sheriff Lobo, Half Nelson, Finder of Lost Loves, The Girl Who Came Gift Wrapped, The Ghosts of Buxley Hall, The New Gidget, Barefoot in the Park, The Bad News Bears, Harper Valley PTA, Deadly Games. Series: The Sentinel, Touched by an Angel, Viper, The Flash, Dinosaurs, Barney Miller, Get Smart (Emmy Award, 1968), Andy Griffith Show (asst. dir.), Route 66 (asst. dir.), The Baileys of Balboa (also assoc. prod.), Hogan's Heroes, House Calls, Alice, Private Benjamin, Life With Lucy, Spenser: For Hire, Hotel, Dallas, Hawaii Five-O, Dynasty, The Fall Guy, Nightingales, The Love Boat: The Next Wave.

BINDER, STEVE
Producer, Director, Writer. b. Los Angeles, CA, Dec. 12. e. Univ. of Southern California. 1960-61, announcer in Austria and Germany with AFN, Europe. Prof. of Cinema, Univ. Southern CA. Mem.: DGA, Producers Guild of America, Writers Guild of America, NARAS, ATAS.
PICTURES: Director: The T.A.M.I. Show, Give 'Em Hell Harry!, Melissa, Father Guido Sarducci Goes to College.

TELEVISION:Prod./Dir.: Soupy Sales Show, Jazz Scene U.S.A., Hullaballoo, The Danny Kaye Show, Hallelujah Leslie!, TJ's, Petula, America, A Funny Thing Happened on the Way to the White House, Comedy of the 60's, Don Kirshner's Rock Concert, Olivia Newton-John, Norman Corwin Theater, Mac Davis Series, The Big Show, Primetime Emmy's, Motown Revue, Peggy Fleming Special, Dorothy Hammil Special, Shields & Yarnell Series (also writer) The Magic Castle Special, Star Wars Holiday Special, Father Guido Sarducci at UCSB, A Tribute to Sam Kinison, Smhatar, Jane Fonda In Search of the Missing Smhatar, Steve Allen Show (1963-65, 1973), Elvis Presley Comeback Special, Barry Manilow Special (also exec. prod., writer, Emmy Award, 1977), Diana Ross '81, Ringling Bros & Barnum Bailey Circus (also writer), Pee-wee's Playhouse (exec. prod., writer), Barry Manilow Big Fun on Swing Street, Pee-wee's Playhouse Christmas Special, A Tribute to Sam Kinison, Diana Ross at Wembley, Diana Ross Sings Jazzy Blues, Diana Ross—World Tour, Diana Ross in Central Park (Cable Ace Award, also writer), Diana Ross (also writer), The International Special Olmpics, 65th Anniversary of the Grand Ole Opry, The First Annual ESPY Awards, Liza Minneli, Lucy in London, Fiesta Texas, Eddie Rabbit Special, One Night With You, Disney's First Lady of Magic (exec. prod.). Exec. Prod./Writer.: Soul Train Music Awards, Zoobilee Zoo, Disney's Greatest Hits on Ice, Disney's Aladdin on Ice, Disney's Beauty and the Beast on Ice, Innocent Love (MOW), The Chevy Chase Show, SK8 TV, On the Television Series, Tales From the Whoop, The Beach Boys Summer Series, Television's Greatest Performances.

BINOCHE, JULIETTE
Actress. b. Paris, France, March 9, 1964. e. Natl Schl. of Dramatic Art, Paris. Began acting career while in school, performing on stage. In 1984, after some small roles in films and TV prods., appeared in Jean-Luc Godard's, Je Vous Salue Marie. In 1985, gained recognition at the Cannes Film Festival for her role in Andre Techine's Rendez-Vous.
PICTURES: Liberty Bell, Le Meilleur de la Vie, Adieu Blaireau, La Vie de la Familie, Je Vous Salue Marie, Les Nanas, Rendez-Vous, Mauvais Sang, Mon Beau-Frere a Tue Ma Soeur, The Unbearable Lightness of Being, Un Tour de Manege, Les Amants du Pont-Neuf, Mara, Wuthering Heights, Damage, Red, White, Blue, Le Hussard Sur le Toit, The English Patient (Acad. Award, 1996; BAFTA), A Couch in New York, Alice et Martin, Les Enfants du Siecle, La Veuve de Saint-Pierre, Code Unknown: Incomplete Tales of Several Journeys, Chocolat, Decolage horaire, Picasso at the Lapin Agile, Country of My Skull, The Assumption.
TELEVISION: Movies: Women & Men 2: In Love There Are No Rules.

BIONDI, JR. FRANK J.
Executive. b. Jan. 9, 1945. e. Princeton U.; Harvard U., MBA (1968). Various investment banking positions, 1968-74. Asst. treas. Children's TV Workshop 1974-78. V.p. programming HBO 1978-82; pres. HBO 1983, then chmn. & chief exec. off. Joined Coca-Cola Co. as exec. v.p., entertainment business arm, 1984. Resigned 1987 to join Viacom International as pres. and CEO. Pres., MCA, 1996. Resigned, 1998. Currently Managing Director, WaterView Advisors, LLC, a private equity fund specializing in media. Biondi is a director of The Bank of New York, Amgen, Inc.; Hasbro, Inc.; Vail Resorts, Inc.; The Museum of Television and Radio; and the Int'l. Tennis Hall of Fame. Founding member of USC's Board of Councilors of the School of Cinema-Television and is on the bd. of advisors for The Annenberg School for Comm. at USC.

BIRCH, THORA
Actress. b. Los Angeles, CA, March 11, 1982. Began acting at age 4. First appeared in commericals.
PICTURES: Paradise, All I Want for Christmas, Patriot Games, Hocus Pocus, Monkey Trouble, Clear and Present Danger, Now and Then, Alaska, American Beauty, Anywhere But Here, The Smokers, Dungeons & Dragons, Ghost World, After The Hole, Silence Becomes You (2003).
TELEVISION: Movies: Night Ride Home, Shadow Realm, Homeless to Harvard: The Liz Murray Story (2003). Series: Parenthood, Day by Day. Guest: Amen, Doogie Howser M.D., Outer Limits, Promised Land, Touched By An Angel, Night Visions.

BIRKIN, JANE
Actress. b. London, England, Dec. 14, 1946. Daughter is actress Charlotte Gainsbourg. Sister of dir.-writer Andrew Birkin. Was subject of Agnes Vardas' 1988 documentary Jane B. par Agnes V.
PICTURES: The Knack...and How to Get It, Blow-Up, Kaleidoscope, Wonderwall, Les Chemins de Katmandou, La Piscine, Cannabis, Romance of a Horse Thief, Trop jolies pour etre honnetes, Dark Places, Projection Privee, La Moutarde me monte au nex, Le Mouton Enrage, 7 Morts sur Ordonnance, Catherine et Cie, La Course a l'echalote, Je T'Aime Moi Non Plus, Seriex comme tel plaisir, Le Diable au Coeur, L'Animal, Death on the Nile, Au bout du bout du banc, Melancolie Baby, La Miel, La Fille Prodigue, Evil Under the Sun, L'Ami de Vincent, Circulez u'a rien a voir, Love on the Ground, le Garde du Corps, The Pirate, Beethoven's Nephew, Dust, Leave All Fair, la Femme de ma vie, Comedie!, Kung Fu Master (also story), Soigne ta droite, Daddy Nostalgia, Between the Devil and the Deep Blue Sea (voice), A Soldier's Daughter Never Cries, The Last September, This Is My Body, A Hell of a Day, Merci Docteur Rey.
TELEVISION: Cinderella.

BIRNBAUM, ROGER
Producer, Executive. b. Teaneck, NJ. e. Univ. of Denver. Was v.p. of both A&M Records and Arista records before becoming m.p. prod.. Headed Guber/Peters Company, then named pres. of worldwide prod., United Artists; pres. of worldwide prod. and exec. v.p. of 20th Century Fox. Left Fox in 1993 to become co-founder of Caravan Pictures.
PICTURES: *Prod./Exec. Prod.:* The Sure Thing, Young Sherlock Homes, Who's That Girl, The Three Musketeers, Angie, Angels in the Outfield, A Low Down Dirty Shame, Houseguest, Tall Tale, While You Were Sleeping, Dead Presidents, Powder, Celtic Pride, The Beautician and the Beast, G.I. Jane, Gone Fishin', Grosse Pointe Blank, Washington Square, Metro, Rocket Man, A Small Miracle, Holy Man, Six Days Seven Nights, Simon Birch, Rush Hour, Stretch Armstrong (exec. prod.), A Course in Miracles, Inspector Gadget, Shanghai Noon, The Hitchhiker's Guide to the Galaxy, Keeping the Faith, Unbreakable, Rush Hour 2, Out Cold, The Count of Monte Cristo, Dragonfly, Abandon, Reign of Fire, Shanghai Knights, Bruce Almighty, Seabiscuit, One Love, The Perfect Score (2004), Mr. 3000 (2004), Connie and Carla (2004).
TELEVISION: *Movies:* Flash (exec. prod.), Angels in the Endzone, Angels in the Infield. *Series:* exec. prod.: The Ranch, Miracles.

BIRNEY, DAVID
Actor. b. Washington, DC, April 23, 1939. e. Dartmouth Coll., B.A., UCLA, M.A. Phd. Southern Utah St. (hon.). Following grad. sch. and the Army spent 2 yrs. in regional theatre, Amer. Shakespeare Festival, Lincoln Center Repertory Theatre, Great Lakes Theatre Festival, Mark Taper Forum, Shakespeare Theatre Washington DC, Hartford Stage Co., Barter Theatre, to N.Y. where appeared in Lincoln Center prod. of Summertree (Theatre World Award). Appeared for two yrs. on TV daytime series, Love Is a Many Splendored Thing, doing other stage roles in same period. Theatre panelist, Natl. Endowment for the Arts; bd. mem., Hopkins Center, Dartmouth College; bd. of Foundation for Biomedical Research.
THEATRE: Comedy of Errors (NY debut; NY Shakespeare Fest). *NY & Regional:* Amadeus, Benefactors, Anthony & Cleopatra, Man and Superman, Macbeth, Hamlet, Richard II, III, Romeo & Juliet, Much Ado About Nothing, King John, Titus Andronicus, Major Barbara, Biko Inquest, Playboy of the Western World, The Miser, Antigone, My Fair Lady, Camelot, Love Letters, Present Laughter, Twelfth Night, Talley's Folley, Rumors, Social Security, Enemy of the People, Mark Twain's The Diaries of Adam & Eve.
PICTURES: Caravan to Vaccares, Trial by Combat, Oh God Book II, Prettykill, Nightfall, Touch and Die, The Naked Truth, Comedy of Errors.
TELEVISION: *Movies:* Murder or Mercy, Bronk, Serpico: The Deadly Game, Someone's Watching Me!, High Midnight, Only With Married Men, OHMS, Mom The Wolfman & Me, The Five of Me, The Long Journey Home (also co-exec. prod.), Love and Betrayal, Always Remember I Love You, Keeping Secrets. *Mini-Series:* Night of the Fox, Seal Morning, Adam's Chronicles, Testimony of Two Men, Master of the Game, Valley of the Dolls, The Bible. *Specials:* Missing: Have You Seen This Person? Drop Everything and Read, 15 and Getting Straight, Mark Twain's The Diaries of Adam and Eve (co-prod.), St. Joan. *Series:* Love Is A Many Splendored Thing, A World Apart, Bridget Loves Bernie, Serpico, St. Elsewhere, Glitter, Live Shot, Beyond 2000 (host), Raising Kids (host), Great American TV Poll (host), The Perfect Pitch (tv documentary). Guest in series & anthology shows.

BISHOP, LARRY
Actor.
MOVIES: Wild in the Street, The Savage Seven, The Devil's Eight, Angel Unchained, Chrome and Hot Leather, Shanks, How Come Nobody's on Our Side?, The Big Fix, Hey Good Lookin' (voice), The Sting II, Mad Dog Time (also dir., prod., s.p.), Underworld (also s.p.)

BISSET, JACQUELINE
Actress. r.n. Winnifred Jacqueline Fraser-Bisset, b. Weybridge, England, September 13, 1944. e. French Lycaee, London. After photographic modeling made debut in the Knack, 1965.
PICTURES: The Knack... and How to Get It (debut, 1965), Cul de Sac, Two For The Road, Casino Royale, The Cape Town Affair, The Sweet Ride, The Detective, Bullitt, The First Time, Secret World, Airport, The Grasshopper, The Mephisto Waltz, Believe in Me, Stand Up and Be Counted, The Life & Times of Judge Roy Bean, The Thief Who Came to Dinner, Day for Night, Le Manifique, Murder on the Orient Express, End of the Game, The Spiral Staircase, St. Ives, Sunday Woman, The Deep, The Greek Tycoon, Secrets, Who Is Killing the Great Chefs of Europe?, Together?, When Time Ran Out, Rich and Famous, Inchon, Class, Under the Volcano, High Season, Scenes From the Class Struggle in Beverly Hills, La Maison de Jade, Wild Orchid, The Maid, A Judgment in Stone, Dangerous Beauty, Let the Devil Wear Black, Les gens qui s'aiment, New Year's Day,The Sleepy Time Gal, Fascination, Swing, Latter Days, Joan of Arc: The Virgin Warrior.
TELEVISION: *Movies:* Anna Karenina, Choices, Leave of Absence, End of Summer, September, Witch Hunt, Britannic, Sex and Mrs X, Dancing at the Harvest Moon, America's Prince: The John F. Kennedy Jr. Story. *Mini-Series:* Napoleon and Josephine: A Love Story, Joan of Arc, Jesus, In the Beginning.

BJÖRK
Actress, Composer. b. Reykjavik, Iceland, November 21, 1965. Winner of best actress award for Dancer in the Dark at Cannes. Solo recording artist. Former member of pop band The Sugarcubes.

PICTURES: Juniper Tree (act. only), The Young Americans (comp. only) Pret A Porter (act. only), Anton (comp. only), Dancer in the Dark (Academy Award nom.), Von Trier's 100 Eyes.
TELEVISION: Movies: Bjork at the Royal Opera House (2002).

BLACK, KAREN
Actress. b. Park Ridge, IL, July 1, 1942. r.n. Karen Ziegler. e. Northwestern U. Left school for NY to join the Hecscher House, appearing in several Shakespearean plays. In 1965 starred in Playroom, which ran only 1 month but won her NY Drama Critic nom. as best actress.
THEATRE: Happily Never After, Keep It in the Family, Come Back to the Five and Dime Jimmy Dean Jimmy Dean.
PICTURES: Appeared in more than 115 pictures, incl.: You're a Big Boy Now (debut, 1966), Hard Contact, Easy Rider, Five Easy Pieces (Acad. Award nom.), Drive He Said, A Gunfight, Born To Win, Cisco Pike, Portnoy's Complaint, The Pyx, Little Laura and Big John, Rhinoceros, The Outfit, The Great Gatsby, Airport 1975, Law and Disorder, Day of the Locust, Crime and Passion, Burnt Offerings, Capricorn One, In Praise of Older Women, The Squeeze, The Last Word, Chanel Solitaire, Come Back to the Five and Dime Jimmy Dean Jimmy Dean, Killing Heat, Can She Bake a Cherry Pie?, Martin's Day, Bad Manners, Cut and Run, Invaders from Mars, Hostage, Eternal Evil, The Invisible Kid, Out of the Dark, Homer and Eddie, Night Angel, Miss Right, Dixie Lanes, Twisted Justice, Over Exposure, The Children, Mirror Mirror, Haunting Fear, Quiet Fire, Children of the Night, Hotel Oklahoma, Killer's Edge, Moon Over Miami, Final Judgment, Caged Fear, Bound & Gagged: A Love Story, The Player, Rubin & Ed, The Trust, The Double O Kid, Sister Island, Plan 10 From Outer Space, Odyssey, Every Minute Is Goodbye, A Thousand Stars, I Woke Up Early the Day I Died, Felons, Fallen Arches, Bury the Evidence, Spoken in Silence, Mascara, The Underground Comedy Movie, Sugar: The Fall of the West, Karen Black: Actress At Work, The Independent, Red Dirt, Oliver Twisted, The Donor, Gypsy 83, Soulkeeper, A Light in the Darkness, Hard Luck, Don't Try This At Home, House of 1000 Corpses, Paris, Max and Grace, The Last Patient, Firecracker.
TELEVISION: *Movies:* Trilogy of Terror, The Strange Possession of Mrs. Oliver, Mr. Horn, Power, Where the Ladies Go, Because He's My Friend, Full Circle Again (Canadian TV), My Neighbor's Daughter, The Big Show. *Guest:* In the Heat of the Night, Moon Over Miami, Murder She Wrote.

BLACK, NOEL
Director. b. Chicago, IL, June 30, 1937. e. UCLA, B.A., 1959; M.A. 1964. Made short film Skaterdater and won numerous awards including the Cannes' Grand Prix for Best Short Film.
PICTURES: Pretty Poison (debut, 1968), Cover Me Babe, Jennifer on My Mind, Marianne, A Man a Woman and a Bank, Private School, Mischief (s.p., exec. prod.), The Gladys Milton Story.
TELEVISION: *Movies:* Mulligan's Stew, The Other Victim, Prime Suspect, Happy Endings, Quarterback Princess, Promises to Keep, A Time to Triumph, My Two Loves, Conspiracy of Love, The Town Bully, Trilogy: The American Boy; The World Beyond; I'm a Fool, The Golden Honeymoon, The Electric Grandmother, The Doctors Wilde, Meet the Munceys, Eyes of the Panther, The Hollow Boy. *Series:* One Life To Live, Hawaii Five-O, McCloud, Kojak, Switch, Quincy, The Hardy Boys/Nancy Drew Mysteries, Big Hawaii, The Twilight Zone, Dolphin Cove, Over My Dead Body, The Baby-Sitters Club, Swans Crossing.

BLACK, STANLEY
Composer, Conductor, Musical director. OBE. b. June 14, 1913, London, Eng. Resident conductor, BBC, 1944-52. Musical director 105 feature films and Pathe Newsreel music: Music dir. Associated British Film Studios 1958-64. Guest conductor, Royal Philharmonic Orchestra and London Symphony. Orchestra: many overseas conducting engagements including (1977) Boston Pops and Winnipeg Symphony. Associated conductor Osaka Philharmonic Orchestra. Exclusive recording contract with Decca Record Co. since 1944.
PICTURES: Crossplot, The Long the Short and The Tall, Rattle of a Simple Man, The Young Ones, Hell Is a City, Top Secret, Valentino, Day of Redemption (asst. camera).
(d. Nov. 26, 2002)

BLACKMAN, HONOR
Actress. b. London, England, Aug. 22, 1926. Stage debut. The Gleam 1946.
PICTURES: Fame Is the Spur (debut, 1947), Quartet, Daughter of Darkness, A Boy A Girl and a Bike, Diamond City, Conspirator, So Long at the Fair, Set a Murderer, Green Grow the Rushes, Come Die My Love, Rainbow Jacket, Outsiders, Delavine Affair, Three Musketeers, Breakaway, Homecoming, Suspended Alibi, Dangerous Drugs, A Night to Remember, The Square Peg, A Matter of Who, Present Laughter, The Recount, Serena, Jason & the Golden Fleece, Goldfinger, The Secret of My Success, Moment to Moment, Life at the Top, A Twist of Sand, Shalako, Struggle for Rome, Twinky, The Last Grenade, The Virgin and the Gypsy, Fright, Something Big, Out Damned Spot, Summer, Cat and the Canary, Russell Mulcahy's Talos the Mummy, To Walk with Lions, Bridget Jones's Diary, Jack Brown and the Curse of the Crown.
TELEVISION: African Patrol, The Witness, Top Secret, Ghost Squad, Invisible Man, The Secret Adversary, Lace, The First Olympics: Athens 1896, Minder on the Orient Express, Voice of

the Heart, The Secret Garden (voice), The James Bond Story, Blondes: Diana Dors, Jack and the Beanstalk: The Real Story, The Sight (2000). *Series:* Four Just Men, The Avengers, Probation Officer, Never the Twain, The Upper Hand.

BLADES, RUBEN
Actor, Composer, Singer, Writer. b. Panama City, Panama, July 16, 1948. e. U. of Panama (law and political science, 1974), Harvard U., L.L.M., 1985. Has recorded more than 14 albums, winning 3 Grammy Awards (1986, 1988, 1997). With his band Seis del Solar has toured U.S., Central America and Europe. President of Panama's Papa Egoro political party.
PICTURES: *Actor:* The Last Fight (debut, 1982), Crossover Dreams (also co-s.p.), Critical Condition, The Milagro Beanfield War, Fatal Beauty, Homeboy, Disorganized Crime, The Lemon Sisters, Mo' Better Blues, The Two Jakes, Predator 2, Homeboy, The Super, Life With Mikey, A Million to Juan, Color of Night. *Music:* Beat Street, Oliver & Company, Caminos Verdes (Venezuela), Q&A (also composer), Scorpion Spring, The Devil's Own, The Chinese Box, The Cradle Will Rock, All the Pretty Horses, Assassination Tango, Empire (Composer only), Once Upon a Time in Mexico, Spin.
TELEVISION: *Movies:* Dead Man Out (ACE Award), One Man's War, The Josephine Baker Story (Emmy nom.), Crazy from the Heart (Emmy nom.), The Heart of the Deal, Miracle on I-880, The Maldonado Miracle. *Guest:* Sesame Street, The X-Files.

BLAIR, JANET
Actress. r.n. Martha Janet Lafferty. b. Altoona, PA, April 23, 1921. With Hal Kemp's Orchestra; toured in South Pacific, 1950-52.
PICTURES: Three Girls About Town (debut, 1941), Blondie Goes to College, Two Yanks in Trinidad, Broadway, My Sister Eileen, Something to Shout About, Once Upon a Time, Tonight and Every Night, Tars and Spars, Gallant Journey, The Fabulous Dorseys, I Love Trouble, The Black Arrow, Fuller Brush Man, Public Pigeon No. 1, Boys Night Out, Burn Witch Burn, The One and Only Genuine Original Family Band, Won Ton Ton the Dog Who Saved Hollywood.
TELEVISION: *Special:* Arabian Nights, Tom Sawyer. *Series:* Leave it to the Girls (panelist), Caesar's Hour, The Chevy Show, The Smith Family. *Guest:* Bell Telephone Hour, Ed Sullivan, Murder She Wrote.

BLAIR, LINDA
Actress. b. St. Louis, MO, Jan. 22, 1959. Model and actress on TV commercials before going into films.
PICTURES: The Sporting Club (debut, 1971), The Exorcist, Airport '75, Exorcist II: The Heretic, Roller Boogie, Wild Horse Hank, Hell Night, Ruckus, Chained Heat, Savage Streets, Savage Island, Red Heat, Night Patrol, Night Force, Silent Assassins, Grotesque (also prod.), Witchery, The Chilling, Bad Blood, Moving Target, Up Your Alley, Repossessed, Aunt Millie's Will, Zapped Again, Dead Sleep, Double Blast, Temptress, Prey of the Jaguar, Scream.
TELEVISION: *Movies:* Born Innocent, Sarah T.: Portrait of a Teenage Alcoholic, Sweet Hostage, Victory at Entebbe, Stranger in Our House, Calendar Girl Cop Killer? The Bambi Bembenek Story, Perry Mason: The Case of the Heartbroken Bride, Fear of God: The Making of the Exorcist, Monster Makers. *Guest:* Fantasy Island, Murder She Wrote. *Series:* Walking After Midnight, S Club 7 in L.A., The Scariest Places on Earth (Host). *Special:* Linda Blair: The E! True Hollywood Story.

BLAIR, STEWART
Executive. b. Scotland. e. Univ. of Glasgow. Was v.p. of Chase Manhattan Bank N.A. in NY, before joining Tele-Communications Inc. in 1981. Served as vice-chmn. & CEO of United Artists Entertainment Co. 1992, appointed chmn. and CEO of United Artists Theatre Circuit Inc.; removed, 1996. Since then, formed Spean Bridge, a London-based cinema circuit, along with several other cinema ind. players. Also bd. member of Foundation of Motion Picture Pioneers, exec. v.p., Will Rogers Memorial Fund.

BLAKE, JEFF
Executive. e. B.A., economics, Northwestern U. and J.D., Whittier College of Law. Began career as sales broker and mgr., Paramount Pictures, 1974-78; asst. gen. sales mgr., Buena Vista Distribution (Walt Disney Co.) 1980. mgr., Western Div., Paramount, 1981; v.p., theatrical distribution, Paramount, 1984-1987; exec. v.p. & gen. sales mgr., Columbia Pictures (Sony Pictures Entertainment-SPE); 1987-92; president, domestic distribution, SPE, 1992-94; president, Sony Pictures Releasing, 1994-99. Became a vice chmn. of SPE in Oct. '02. Also is pres. of Columbia TriStar Motion Picture Group, Worldwide Marketing & Distribution. Responsible for mktg. & dist. of all Columbia, TriStar, Revolution and Screen Gems releases worldwide. Member, Calif. Bar Assn., v.p. of the Motion Picture Pioneers Foundation, member of Academy of Motion Picture Arts & Sciences, member of Variety Club Children's Charities, L.A. chapter.

BLAKE, ROBERT
Actor. r.n. Michael Gubitosi. b. Nutley, NJ, Sept. 18, 1933. Started as a child actor in Our Gang comedies as Mickey Gubitosi, also appeared as Little Beaver in Red Ryder series. Later was Hollywood stunt man in Rumble on the Docks and The Tijuana Story. First adult acting job was at the Gallery Theater in Hatful of Rain.
PICTURES: I Love You Again (debut, 1940, as Bobby Blake), Andy Hardy's Double Life, China Girl, Mokey, Salute to the Marines, Slightly Dangerous, The Big Noise, Lost Angel, Red

Ryder series (as Little Beaver), Meet the People, Dakota, The Horn Blows at Midnight, Pillow to Post, The Woman in the Window, A Guy Could Change, Home on the Range, Humoresque, In Old Sacramento, Out California Way, The Last Round-Up, Treasure of the Sierra Madre, The Black Rose, Blackout (also co-prod.), Apache War Smoke, Treasure of the Golden Condor, Screaming Eagles, Pork Chop Hill, The Purple Gang, Town Without Pity, PT 109, The Greatest Story Ever Told, The Connection, In Cold Blood, Tell Them Willie Boy is Here, Ripped-Off, Corky, Electra Glide in Blue, Busting, Coast to Coast, Second-Hand Hearts, Money Train, Lost Highway.
TELEVISION: *Movies:* The Big Black Pill (also creator & exec. prod.), The Monkey Mission (also creator & exec. prod.), Of Mice and Men (also exec. prod.), Blood Feud, Murder 1--Dancer 3 (also exec. prod.), Heart of a Champion: The Ray Mancini Story, Judgment Day: The John List Story. *Series:* The Richard Boone Show, Barretta (Emmy Award, 1975), Hell Town (also exec. prod.). *Guest:* One Step Beyond, Have Gun Will Travel, Bat Masterson.

BLAKE, TONY
Writer, Producer.
TELEVISION: *Movies:* Magical Make-Over. *Series:*: Renegade, Lois & Clark: The New Adventures of Superman (also super-visiing prod.), Sliders (co-exec. prod.), The Pretender, Charmed (also consulting prod.), Sheena, Mutant X.

BLAKELY, SUSAN
Actress. b. Frankfurt, Germany, Sept. 7, 1952, where father was stationed in Army. Studied at U. of Texas. m. prod., media consultant Steve Jaffe. Became top magazine and TV commercial model in N.Y.
PICTURES: Savages (debut, 1972), The Way We Were, The Lords of Flatbush, The Towering Inferno, Report to the Commissioner, Shampoo, Capone, Dreamer, The Concorde—Airport '79, Over the Top, Dream a Little Dream, My Mom's a Werewolf, Russian Holiday, Seven Sundays, Gut Feeling, Chain of Command, The Perfect Nanny, Crash Point Zero, Hungry Hearts, L.A. Twister.
TELEVISION: *Movies:* Secrets, Make Me an Offer, A Cry For Love, The Bunker, The Oklahoma City Dolls, Will There Really Be A Morning?, The Ted Kennedy Jr. Story, Blood & Orchids, April Morning, Fatal Confession: A Father Dowling Mystery, Broken Angel, Hiroshima Maiden, Ladykillers, Sight Unseen, The Incident, End Run, Dead Reckoning, Murder Times Seven, And the Sea Will Tell, Sight Unseen, Blackmail, Wildflower, Against Her Will: An Incident in Baltimore, Intruders, No Child of Mine, Honor Thy Father and Mother: The True Story of the Menendez Murders, Color Me Perfect, Co-ed Call Girl, Race Against Fear, Her Married Lover, A Mother's Testimony. *Special:* Torn Between Two Fathers. *Mini-Series:* Rich Man Poor Man. *Series:* Falcon Crest, The George Carlin Show. *Guest:* Step by Step, Murder She Wrote, Father Dowling Mysteries, Diagnosis Murder. *Pilot:* Dad's a Dog.

BLAKLEY, RONEE
Actress. Singer. b. Stanley, ID, Aug. 24, 1945. Wrote and performed songs for 1972 film Welcome Home Soldier Boys.
PICTURES: Nashville (debut, 1975; Acad. Award nom.), The Private Files of J. Edgar Hoover, The Driver, Renaldo and Clara, Good Luck Miss Wyckoff (Secret Yearnings/The Sin), The Baltimore Bullet, A Nightmare on Elm Street, Return to Salem's Lot, Student Confidential, Someone to Love, Murder by Numbers.

BLANC, MICHEL
Actor. b. France, June 16, 1952.
PICTURES: Que la Fete Commence, The Tenant, Les Bronzes, The Adolescent, Les Bronzes font du Ski, Le Cheval d'Orgueil, Walk in the Shadow, Les Fugitives, Evening Dress, Menage, I Hate Actors!, Story of Women, Monsieur Hire, Chambre a Part, Strike It Rich, Uranus, Merci la Vie, Prospero's Books, The Favor the Watch and the Very Big Fish, Ready to Wear (Pret-a-Porter), Grosse Fatigue (also dir., s.p.), The Monster, The Grand Dukes, Embrassez qui vous voulez (also dir., s.p.), See How They Run (also writer, dir.).
TELEVISION: Movies: Soeur Thérèse.com (writer), Les Bronzés, le père Noël, papy et les autres (tv documentary).

BLANCHETT, CATE
Actress. b. Melbourne, Australia, May 14, 1969. e. National Institute of Dramatic Art, Australia.
THEATRE: Top Girls, Kafka Dances, Oleanna, Hamlet, Sweet Phoebe, The Tempest, The Blind Giant is Dancing.
PICTURES: Police Rescue, Parklands, Paradise Road, Thank God He Met Lizzie, Oscar and Lucinda, Pushing Tin, Elizabeth (BAFTA Award, Golden Globe Award, Acad. Award nom., AFI nom.), The Talented Mr. Ripley (BAFTA nom.), An Ideal Husband, The Man Who Cried, The Gift, Bandits (AFI nom.), Golden Globe nom., SAG nom.), Lord of the Rings: The Fellowship of the Ring (SAG nom.), Heaven, The Shipping News, Charlotte Gray, The Lord of the Rings: The Two Towers, The Lord of the Rings: The Return of the King, Veronica Guerin, The Missing, The Aviator.
TELEVISION: *Movies:* Heartland, Bordertown. *Guest:* G.P., Police Rescue.

BLANCO, RICHARD M.
Executive. b. Brooklyn, NY. e. electrical engineering, Wentworth Institute. J.C., 1925-27; bus. admin., U. of CA, 1939-40; U.S. Govt. Coll., 1942. Superv. Technicolor Corp., 1931-56; organ. and operator Consumer Products, Kodachrome film process., Technicolor, 1956-62; dir. of MP Govt. and theatre sales, NY & DC, 1963-65; gen. mgr. of Technicolor Florida photo optns. at

Kennedy Space Center.; prod. doc. & educ. films for NASA, 1965; v.p. of tv div., Technicolor Corp. of America; 1967 elected corporate v.p. Technicolor, Inc.; 1971 pres., Technicolor Graphic Services, Inc.; 1974, elected chmn. of bd. of Technicolor Graphic Services; 1977, elected to bd. of dirs. of Technicolor Inc.

BLANK, MIKE
Executive. e. U. Michigan, 1933. Began career as poster clerk for Pathe, 1927. Head of const., maint., concessions, Central States Theatres, 1933. U.S. Navy, 1942, in charge of visual ed. for 7th Naval Dist. in Miami. Pres., CEO, chmn., Central States 1950. B. V. Sturdivant Award, NATO/ShoWest, 1990.

BLANK, MYRON
Circuit executive. b. Des Moines, IA, Aug. 30, 1911. e. U. of Michigan. Son of A. H. Blank, circuit operator. On leaving coll. joined father in operating Tri-States and Central States circuits. On leave 1943-46 in U.S. Navy, officer in charge visual educ. Now pres. Central States Theatre Corp.; pres. TOA, 1955; chmn. bd. TOA Inc. 1956-57; exec. chmn. of NATO. Pres. of Greater Des Moines Comm. Built Anne Blank Child Guidance Center-Raymond Blank Hospital for Children. Endowed chair for gifted and talented children at Univ. of Iowa; permanent scholarship at Wertzman Inst., Israel. Sturdevant Award from NATO, Humanitarian Award from Variety Club in 1980. Partial scholarship for 80 students annually for 3-week seminar at Univ. of Iowa.

BLATT, DANIEL H.
Producer. e. Philips Andover Acad., Duke U., Northwestern U. Sch. of Law. Indepentent prod. since 1976; prior posts: resident counsel, ABC Pictures; exec. v.p. Palomar Pictures.
PICTURES: I Never Promised You a Rose Garden, Winter Kills, The American Success Company, The Howling, Independence Day, Cujo, Restless, The Boost.
TELEVISION: Movies: Circle of Children, Zuma Beach, The Children Nobody Wanted, Sadat, V: The Final Battle, Badge of the Assassin, Raid on Entebbe, Sacred Vows, A Winner Never Quits, Sworn to Silence, Common Ground, Beyond Betrayal (exec. prod.), Kissinger and Nixon (exec. prod.), It Was Him or Us (exec. prod.), Sins of Silence (exec. prod.), Childhood Sweethearts? (exec. prod.), Dead by Midnight (exec. prod.), Miracle on the 17th Green (exec. prod.), The Virginian (exec. prod.), Murder on the Orient Express (exec. prod.), A Town Without Christmas (exec. prod.). Series: V, Against the Law.

BLATTY, WILLIAM PETER
Writer, Director, Producer. b. New York, NY, Jan. 7, 1928. e. George Washington U., Seattle U. Worked as editor for U.S. Information Bureau, publicity dir. for USC and Loyola U. before becoming novelist and screenwriter. Novels include: John Goldfarb Please Come Home (filmed), Twinkle Twinkle Killer Kane, The Exorcist, Legion (filmed as Exorcist III).
PICTURES: The Man From the Diner's Club, A Shot in the Dark, Promise Her Anything, What Did You Do in the War Daddy?, Gunn, The Great Bank Robbery, Darling Lili, The Exorcist (also prod.; Academy Award for Best Adapted Screenplay, 1973), The Ninth Configuration (also dir., prod.), The Exorcist III (also dir.).
TELEVISION: Linda Blair: The E! True Hollywood Story.

BLAY, ANDRE
Executive. In 1979, sold Magnetic Video to 20th Century Fox, named pres., CEO, 20th Century Fox Home Video; 1981, formed The Blay Corporation; 1982, joined with Norman Lear and Jerry Perenchio, founders of Embassy Communications, as chairman and CEO of Embassy Home Entertainment; 1986, when Embassy sold to Nelson Group, left to form Palisades Entertainment Group with Elliott Kastner.
PICTURES: Exec. Prod.: Prince of Darkness, They Live, Jack's Back, Homeboy, Braindamage, The Blob, A Chorus of Disapproval, Village of the Damned (prod.), Mosquito.

BLECKNER, JEFF
Director, Producer. b. Brooklyn, NY, Aug. 12, 1943. e. Amherst College, BA., 1965; Yale Sch. of Drama, MFA 1968. Taught drama at Yale, also participated in the theatre co. 1965-68. 1968-75 theatre dir. NY Shakespeare Fest. Public Theatre (2 Drama Desk Awards, Tony nom. for Sticks and Bones); Basic Training of Pavlo Hummel (Obie Award, 1971), The Unseen Hand (Obie Award). Began TV career directing The Guiding Light, 1975.
PICTURES: Dir: White Water Summer, Hostile Witness, IN the Hands of the Enemy, The Beast.
TELEVISION: Dir./Prod. more than 25 tv movies, incl.: Henry Winkler Meets William Shakespeare (1979), On Seventh Ave., Concealed Enemies (Emmy Award, 1984), Daddy, I'm Their Momma Now (Emmy nom.), Do You Remember Love (Christopher, Humanitas, Peabody Awards, Emmy nom.), Serving In Silence (Emmy nom.), Rear Window, Runaway Virus, Flowers for Algernon, The Music Man (2003). Series: Dir: Welcome Back Kotter, Knots Landing, Dynasty, Hill Street Blues (Emmy Award, DGA Award, 1983), Bret Maverick, King's Crossing, Ryan's Four, Me and Mom, Mancuso FBI, The Round Table, Any Day Now, The Fugitive (2000).

BLEDEL, ALEXIS
Actress. b. Houston, Texas, Sept. 16, 1981. Began career as a model before acting in Gilmore Girls.
PICTURES: Tuck Everlasting, DysEnchanted (short, 2003).
TELEVISION: Series.: Gilmore Girls.

BLEES, ROBERT
Writer, Producer. b. Lathrop, MO, June 9, 1925. e. Dartmouth, Phi Beta Kappa. Writer/photographer, Time and Life Magazines. Fiction: Cosmopolitan, etc. Exec. boards of WGA, Producers Guild. Executive consultant, QM Prods.; BBC (England). Trustee, Motion Picture & TV Fund. Expert witness, copyright and literary litigation, U.S. Federal Court, California Superior Court.
PICTURES: Writer: Sweater Girl (1942), Magnificent Obsession, Autumn Leaves, Savage Harvest.
TELEVISION: Movies: Writer: Curse of the Black Widow, Columbo: Make Me a Perfect Murder, Gidget's Summer Reunion. Producer: Combat!, Bonanza, Bus Stop, Kraft Theater. Writer: Alfred Hitchcock, Cannon, Barnaby Jones, Harry O, Airwolf. Co-creator: The New Gidget.

BLEIER, EDWARD
Executive. b. New York, NY, October 16, 1929. e. Syracuse U., 1951, C.U.N.Y., grad. courses. Reporter/sportscaster: Syracuse and NY newspapers/stations: 1947-50. Prog. service mgr., DuMont Television Network, 1951; v.p., radio-television-film, Tex McCrary, Inc. 1958. American Broadcasting Company, 1952\-57; 1959-68 v.p. in chg. pub. relations (marketing, advertising, publicity), & planning, broadcast div.; v.p. in chg. of daytime sales & programming; v.p./gen. sales mgr., ABC-TV Network. U.S. Army Psy. War School; Ex-chmn., TV Committee, NASL; Trustee, NATAS; founder-dir. & vice-chmn., International TV Council (NATAS); past-pres., IRTS; trustee, Keystone Center for Scientific & Environmental Policy, ATAS; AMPAS; guest lecturer at universities. Through 2000, pres. of Warner Bros. Inc., Pay-TV, cable & network features. In 2001, became sr. advisor of Warner Bros. Chmn., Steering comm. for Aspen Institute's B'dcaster's Conference; chair for the Center for Comm. and the Academy of the Arts Guild Hall, trustee of the Dana Foundation and the Martha Graham Dance Center; a director of RealNetworks, Inc. since 1999; member of the Council on Foreign Relations.

BLETHYN, BRENDA
Actress. b. Ramsgate, Kent, England, Feb. 20, 1946.
PICTURES: The Witches, A River Runs Through It, Secrets & Lies (Acad. Award. nom.; Golden Globe Award, 1997; L.A. Film Critics Award; BAFTA Award), Remember Me?, Girls Night, Music From Another Room, In the Winter Dark, Little Voice (Acad. Award nom.), Keeping Time, Saving Grace, On the Nose, Daddy and Them, The Sleeping Dictionary, The Wild Thornberrys (voice), Pumpkin, Sonny, Plots With A View, Blizzard.
TELEVISION: Movies: Grown-Ups, King Lear, Henry VI (Part One), Floating Off, The Bullion Boys, RKO 281, Anne Frank: The Whole Story, Between the Sheets. Mini-series: The Buddha of Suburbia. Series: Chance In a Million, The Labours of Erica, Outside Edge. Guest: Yes Minister, Alas Smith & Jones, So Graham Norton.

BLIER, BERTRAND
Writer, Director. b. Paris, France, March 14, 1939. Son of late actor Bernard Blier. Served as asst. dir. to Georges Lautner, John Berry, Christian-Jaque, Denys de la Paatelliere and Jean Delannoy for two years before dir. debut.
PICTURES: Hitler Connais Pas (debut, 1963), If I Were A Spy, Take It Easy It's A Waltz, Going Places, Calmos, Get Out Your Handkerchiefs (Academy Award for Best Foreign-Language Film, 1978), La Femme de mon pote, Menage, Merci la vie, Un deux trois soleil, Mon Homme, Actors, Les Côtelettes.

BLOCK, BILL H.
Executive. Began career as a talent agent at ICM, then began his own agency, InterTalent, 1988, which later merged with ICM, where he served as head of West Coast operations, representing a spectrum of top-level talent in motion picture production and entertainment. President, Artisan Entertainment 1998-2001. Resigned to pursue entertainment financing and M&A.

BLOCK, WILLARD
Executive. b. New York, NY, March 18, 1930.; e. Columbia Coll., Columbia U. Law Sch., 1952. Counter-Intelligence Corps., U.S. Army, 1952-54, account exec., Plus Marketing, Inc. 1954-55; joined sales staff, NBC Television Network, 1955-57; sales staff, CBS Enterprises, Inc., 1957; intl. sales mgr, 1960; dir., intl. sales, 1965; v.p., 1967; v.p., Viacom Enterprises, 1971; pres., 1972; v.p. MCA-TV, 1973; v.p., gen. mgr., Taft, H-B International, Inc.; pres. Willard Block, Ltd.; 1979, named pres., Viacom Enterprises; 1982-89, pres. Viacom Worldwide Ltd.; 1989, retired. Currently consultant to Sumitomo Corp., TCI, Int'l. Telecommunications, Jupiter Telecommunications, Ltd. Past consultant & mem. bd. dirs, Starsight Telecast.

BLOODWORTH-THOMASON, LINDA
Producer, Writer. b. Poplar Bluff, MO, April 15, 1947. With husband Harry Thomason co-owner of Mozark Productions.
TELEVISION: Movies: The Man From Hope (prod.), A Place Called America (prod.), Legacy: Bill Clinton Retrospective (prod.). Series: M*A*S*H (writer), Rhoda (writer), Filthy Rich (writer, exec. prod.), Designing Women (co-exec. prod., creator, writer), Evening Shade (co-exec. prod., writer), Women of the House (prod., writer), Emeril (prod., writer). Pilots: Dribble (prod.), Over and Out (writer), London and Davis in New York (prod.).

BLOOM, CLAIRE
Actress. r.n. Patricia Claire Blume. b. London, England, Feb. 15, 1931.e. Guildhall School of Music & Drama, Central Sch. To U.S. in 1940 during London evacuation. Returned to England in 1943. Stage debut with Oxford Rep 1946 in It Depends What You Mean. Author: Limelight and After: The Education of an Actress (1982).
THEATRE: The White Devil (London debut), The Lady's Not for Burning, Ring Round the Moon, A Streetcar Named Desire; at Stratford-on-Avon, Old Vic seasons, etc. B'way: Rashomon, A Doll's House, Hedda Gabler, Vivat Vivat Regina, Cherry Orchard, Long Day's Journey Into Night.
PICTURES: The Blind Goddess (debut, 1948), Limelight, Innocents in Paris, The Man Between, Richard III, Alexander the Great, The Brothers Karamazov, The Buccaneer, Look Back in Anger, The Royal Game, The Wonderful World of the Brothers Grimm, The Chapman Report, The Haunting, 80000 Suspects, High Infidelity, The Outrage, The Spy Who Came in From the Cold, Charly, The Illustrated Man, Three Into Two Won't Go, A Red Sky at Morning, A Doll's House, Islands in the Stream, Clash of the Titans, Deja Vu, Crimes and Misdemeanors, The Ae of Innocence, The Princess and the Goblin (voice), Mighty Aphrodite, Daylight, Wrestling With Alligators, The Book of Eve, The Republic of Love.
TELEVISION: Specials/Movies (U.S./UK): Cyrano de Bergerac, Caesar and Cleopatra, Misalliance, Anna Karenina, Wuthering Heights, Ivanov, Wessex Tales, An Imaginative Woman, A Legacy, In Praise of Love, Henry VIII, Backstairs at the White House, Brideshead Revisited, Hamlet, King John, Ann and Debbie, Ellis Island, Separate Tables, Florence Nightingale, The Ghost Writer, Time and the Conways, Shadowlands, Liberty, Promises to Keep, Hold the Dream, Anastasia, Queenie, Intimate Contact, Oedipus the King, The Lady and the Highwayman, The Mirror Crack'd, It's Nothing Personal, Remember, Imogen's Face, The Lady in Question, Love and Murder, Yesterday's Children, On Cukor. Series: As The World Turns, Family Money.

BLOOM, VERNA
Actress. b. Lynn, MA, Aug. 7, 1939. e. Boston U. Studied drama at Uta Hagen-Herbert Berghof School. Performed with small theatre groups all over country; then started repertory theatre in Denver.
THEATRE: B'way: Marat/Sade, Brighton Beach Memoirs. Off B'way.: Messiah, Bits and Pieces, The Cherry Orchard.
PICTURES: Medium Cool (debut, 1969), The Hired Hand, High Plains Drifter, Badge 373, National Lampoon's Animal House, Honkytonk Man, After Hours, The Journey of Natty Gann, The Last Temptation of Christ.
TELEVISION: Movies: Where Have All the People Gone?, Sarah T.: Portrait of a Teenage Alcoholic, The Blue Knight, Contract on Cherry Street, Playing for Time, Rivkin–Bounty Hunter, Gibbsville, Dr. Quinn Medicine Woman.

BLOUNT, LISA
Actress. b. Fayetteville, AK, July 1, 1957. e. Univ. of AK. Auditioned for role as extra in film September 30, 1955 and was chosen as the female lead.
PICTURES: 9/30/55, Dead and Buried, An Officer and a Gentleman, Cease Fire, What Waits Below, Radioactive Dreams, Prince of Darkness, Nightflyers, South of Reno, Out Cold, Great Balls of Fire, Blind Fury, Femme Fatale, Needful Things, Stalked, Box of Moonlight, If...Dog...Rabbit, Birdseye, Chrystal (also prod., 2004).
TELEVISION: Movies: Murder Me Murder You, Stormin' Home, The Annihilator, Unholy Matrimony, In Sickness and in Health, An American Story, Murder Between Friends, Get to the Heart: The Barbara Mandrell Story. Series: Sons and Daughters, Profit. Pilot: Off Duty. Series: Sons and Daughters, Profit, Trash. Guest: Moonlighting, Magnum P.I., Starman, Murder She Wrote, Hitchhiker, Picket Fences.

BLUM, HARRY N.
Executive. b. Cleveland, OH, Oct. 3, 1932. e. U. of Michigan, B.B.A., LL.B. Toy & hobby industry exec., gen. mngr. Lionel division of General Mills, mngt. consultant, and venture capital mngr. before entering industry. Now heads The Blum Group, entertainment financing, packaging, production, licensing, and worldwide distrib. of motion pictures, documentaries, and television programming.
PICTURES: Executive Action (assoc. prod.), The Land That Time Forgot (assoc. prod.), At the Earth's Core (exec. prod.), Drive-In (assoc. prod.), Diamonds (exec. prod.), The Bluebird (prod.), Obsession (prod.), Skateboard (prod.), The Magician of Lublin (exec. prod.), Duran Duran—Arena (exec. prod.), Young Lady Chatterly II (exec. prod.), Eminent Domain (exec. prod.).

BLUM, MARK
Actor. b. Newark, NJ, May 14, 1950. Studied drama at U. of Minnesota and U. of Pennsylvania. Also studied acting with Andre Gregory, Aaron Frankel and Daniel Seltzer. Extensive Off-B'way work after debut in The Cherry Orchard (1976).
THEATRE: NY: Green Julia, Say Goodnight Gracie, Table Settings, Key Exchange, Loving Reno, Messiah, It's Only a Play, Little Footsteps, Cave of Life, Gus & Al (Obie Award), Lost in Yonkers (Broadway). Regional: Brothers (New Brunswick, NJ), Close Ties (Long Wharf), The Cherry Orchard (Long Wharf), Iago in Othello (Dallas). Mark Taper Forum: American Clock, Wild Oats, Moby Dick Rehearsed and An American Comedy.
PICTURES: Lovesick, Desperately Seeking Susan, Just Between Friends, Crocodile Dundee, Blind Date, The Presidio, Worth Winning, Emma & Elvis, The Low Life, Miami Rhapsody, Denise

Calls Up, Sudden Manhattan, Stag, You Can Thank Me Later, Getting to Know All About You, Down to You, Shattered Glass.
TELEVISION: Movies: Condition: Critical, Indictment: The McMartin Trial, The Judge. Series: Sweet Surrender, Capitol News. Guest: St. Elsewhere, Roseanne, The Practice, TheSopranos, The West Wing, Ed, NYPD Blue.

BLUMOFE, ROBERT F.
Producer. b. New York, NY, Sept. 23, 1909. e. Columbia Coll., AB, Columbia U. Sch. of Law, JD. v.p., West Coast oper., U.A., 1953-66; indept. prod., pres. RFB Enterprises, Inc; American Film Institute, dir., AFI—West, 1977-81. Became independent producer: Yours Mine and Ours, Pieces of Dreams, Bound for Glory.

BLUNDELL, CHRISTINE
Make-Up.
PICTURES: Life is Sweet, Naked, I.D., Hackers, Secrets and Lies, Carla's Song, Career Girls, The Full Monty, Seven Years in Tibet, Martha, Meet Frank, Daniel and Laurence, Topsy-Turvey (Acad. Award), Sorted, New Year's Day, Me Without You,All or Nothing, To Kill a King, J. M. Barrie's Neverland.
TELEVISION: Lady Chatterly, Bertie and Elizabeth.

BLUTH, DON
Animator, Director, Producer, Writer. b. El Paso, TX, Sept. 13, 1937.e. Brigham Young U. Animator with Walt Disney Studios 1956 and 1971-79; animator with Filmation 1967; Co-founder and dir. with Gary Goldman and John Pomery, Don Bluth Productions, 1979-85; animator, Sullivan Studios, 1986. Joined Fox Animation as dir./prod., 1995.
PICTURES: Animation director: Robin Hood, The Rescuers, Pete's Dragon, Xanadu. Director/Co-Producer: The Secret of NIMH (also co-s.p.), An American Tail, The Land Before Time, All Dogs Go to Heaven (also co-story), Rock-a-Doodle, Hans Christian Andersen's Thumbelina (also s.p.), A Troll in Central Park, The Pebble and the Penguin, Anastasia, Bartok the Magnificent, Titan A.E..
TELEVISION: Banjo the Woodpile Cat (prod., dir., story, music and lyrics).

BLYTH, ANN
Actress. b. Mt. Kisco, NY, Aug. 16, 1928. e. New Wayburn's Dramatic Sch. On radio in childhood; with San Carlos Opera Co. 3 years; Broadway debut in Watch on the Rhine.
PICTURES: Chip Off the Old Block (debut, 1944), The Merry Monahans, Babes on Swing Street, Bowery to Broadway, Mildred Pierce (Acad. Award nom.), Swell Guy, Brute Force, Killer McCoy, A Woman's Vengeance, Another Part of the Forest, Mr. Peabody and the Mermaid, Red Canyon, Once More My Darling, Free for All, Top o' the Morning, Our Very Own, The Great Caruso, Katie Did It, Thunder on the Hill, I'll Never Forget You, Golden Horde, One Minute to Zero, The World in His Arms, Sally and Saint Anne, All the Brothers Were Valiant, Rose Marie, The Student Prince, King's Thief, Kismet, Slander, The Buster Keaton Story, The Helen Morgan Story.
TELEVISION: Guest: Lux Video Theatre (A Place in the Sun).

BOCHCO, STEVEN
Producer, Writer. b. New York, NY, Dec. 16, 1943. m. actress Barbara Bosson. e. Carnegie Tech, MFA. Won MCA fellowship in college, joined Universal-TV as apprentice. 1978, moved to MTM Enterprises. Went on to create shows for NBC and in 1987, sealed deal with ABC to create 10 series pilots over 10 years. Awards incl. 8 Emmys, Humanitas, NAACP Image, Writers Guild, George Foster Peabody, & Edgar Allen Poe Awards.
PICTURES: Silent Running (writer).
TELEVISION: Movies: More than 20, incl.: The Counterfeit Killer, Double Indemnity, Vampire, Operating Room, Name of the Game, Columbo (9 tv movies), L.A. Law: The Movie. Series: 22 titles, incl.: Griff (prod.), The Invisible Man (prod.), Delvecchio (prod.), Paris (exec. prod.), Hill Street Blues (writer, exec. prod.), Emmys 1981, 1982, 1983, 1984), Bay City Blues (prod.), L.A. Law (creator, writer, exec. prod., Emmys 1987, 1989), Hooperman (writer, prod.), Doogie Howser M.D. (writer, prod.), Cop Rock (creator, writer, prod.), Capitol Critters (prod.), NYPD Blue (creator, writer, prod., Emmy 1995), The Byrds of Paradise (prod.), Murder One (writer, exec. prod.), Exec. Prod.: Public Morals, Brooklyn South, Total Security, City of Angels, Philly (also writer), Boston Public (co-creator).

BOCHNER, HART
Actor, Director. b. Toronto, Canada, Oct. 3, 1956. Son of actor Lloyd Bochner. e. U. of. San Diego. Wrote, prod., dir. short film The Buzz (1992) starring Jon Lovitz.
PICTURES: Islands in the Stream (debut, 1977), Breaking Away, Terror Train, Rich and Famous, The Wild Life, Supergirl, Making Mr. Right, Die Hard, Apartment Zero, Mr. Destiny, Mad at the Moon, The Innocent, Break Up, Anywhere But Here, Urban Legends: Final Cut, Say Nothing, Speaking of Sex, Liberty Stands Still. Dir.: High School High, PCU.
TELEVISION: Movies: Having It All, Complex of Fear, Children of the Dust, Once Around the Park. Mini-Series: Haywire, East of Eden, The Sun Also Rises, War and Remembrance. Special: Teach 109. Series: Callahan.

BOCHNER, LLOYD
Actor. b. Toronto, Canada, July 29, 1924. Father of actor Hart Bochner.
PICTURES: Drums of Africa, The Night Walker, Sylvia, Tony Rome, Point Blank, The Detective, The Horse in the Gray Flannel Suit, Tiger By the Tail, Ulzana's Raid, The Man in the Glass Booth, The Lonely Lady, It Seemed Like A G ood Idea At The Time, Millenium, The Naked Gun 2 1/2, Hot Touch, The Crystal Heart, Landslide, Legend of the Mummy, The Commission.
TELEVISION: Movies: Nearly 30 titles, incl.: King Lear, The Nurse Killer, The Immigrants, Fine Gold, Morning Glory, Loyal Opposition: Terror in the White House, Before I Say Goodbye. Series: One Man's Family, Hong Kong, Dynasty, Batman: Animated Series (voice). Guest: Fantasy Island, Masquerade, The A-Team, Hotel, Murder She Wrote, Designing Women, Hart To Hart, Who's The Boss, Golden Girls, Dr. Quinn Medicine Woman.

BOGART, PAUL
Director. b. New York, NY, Nov. 21, 1919. Puppeteer-actor with Berkeley Marionettes 1946-48; TV stage mgr., assoc. dir. NBC 1950-52. Won numerous Christopher Awards; recipient homage from French Festival Internationale Programmes Audiovisuelle, Cannes '91.
PICTURES: Marlowe (debut, 1969), Halls of Anger, Skin Game, Cancel My Reservation, Class of '44 (also prod.), Mr. Ricco, Oh God! You Devil, Torch Song Trilogy.
TELEVISION: Series: U.S. Steel Hour, Kraft Theatre, Armstrong Circle Theatre, Goodyear Playhouse, The Defenders (Emmy Award, 1965), All in the Family (Emmy Award, 1978), The Golden Girls (Emmy Award, 1986). Specials: Ages of Man, Mark Twain Tonight, The Final War of Ollie Winter, Dear Friends (Emmy Award, 1968). Secrets, Shadow Game (Emmy Award, 1970), The House Without a Christmas Tree, Look Homeward Angel, The Country Girl, Double Solitaire, The War Widow, The Thanksgiving Treasure, The Adams Chronicles, Natica Jackson. Movies: In Search of America, Tell Me Where It Hurts, Winner Take All, Nutcracker: Money, Madness and Murder, Broadway Bound, The Gift of Love, The Heidi Chronicles.

BOGDANOVICH, PETER
Director, Producer, Writer, Actor. b. Kingston, NY, July 30, 1939. e. Collegiate Sch., Stella Adler Theatre Sch., N.Y. 1954-58. Stage debut, Amer. Shakespeare Festival, Stratford, CT, followed by N.Y. Shakespeare Festival, 1958. Off-B'way: dir./prod.: The Big Knife, Camino Real, Ten Little Indians, Rocket to the Moon, Once in a Lifetime. Film critic and feature writer, Esquire, New York Times, Village Voice, Cahiers du Cinema, Los Angeles Times, New York Magazine, Vogue, Variety, etc. 1961–. Owner: The Holly Moon Company Inc. (L.A.), 1992-present. LA Film Crits. Career Achievement Award, 1997.
PICTURES: Voyage to the Planet of the Prehistoric Women (dir., s.p., narrator; billed as Derek Thomas), The Wild Angels (2nd unit dir., co-s.p., actor). Director: Targets (also prod., co-s.p., actor), The Last Picture Show (also co-s.p.; N.Y. Film Critics' Award, best s.p., British Academy Award, best s.p. 1971), Directed by John Ford (also s.p., interviewer), What's Up Doc? (also prod., co-s.p.; Writer's Guild of America Award, best s.p., 1972), Paper Moon (also prod.; Silver Shell, Mar del Plata, Spain 1973), Daisy Miller (also prod.; Best Director, Brussels Festival, 1974), At Long Last Love (also prod., s.p.), Nickelodeon (also co-s.p.), Saint Jack (also co-s.p., actor; Pasinetti Award, Critics Prize, Venice Festival, 1979), Opening Night (actor only), They All Laughed (also co-s.p.), Mask, Illegally Yours (also prod.), Texasville (also co-prod., s.p.), Noises Off (also co-exec. prod.), The Thing Called Love, The Cat's Meow. Actor: Jean Renior, The Battle Over Citizen Kane, Ben Johnson: Third Cowboy on the Right, Mr. Jealousy, The Shore Store, Clarie Makes it Big, Rated X, The Independent, An American Dream, Festival in Cannes, John Ford Goes to War (as himself), The Definition of Insanity (as himself).
TELEVISION: Movies: Dir.: To Sir with Love 2, The Price of Heaven, Rescuers; Stories of Courage/2 Women, Naked City: A Killer Christmas, A Saintly Switch. Acting: Bella Mafia, I Love New York. Series: CBS This Morning (weekly commentary; 1987-89), Out of Order (actor), The Sopranos (actor). Guest: Northern Exposure (actor), Moonlighting (actor).

BOGOSIAN, ERIC
Actor, Writer. b. Woburn, MA, Apr. 24, 1953. e. studied 2 years at U. of Chicago, then Oberlin, theatre degree, 1976. In high school, acted in plays with Fred Zollo (now prod.) and Nick Paleologus (now MA congressman). Moved to NY and worked briefly as gofer at Chelsea Westside Theater. Then joined down-town performance space, the Kitchen, first acting in others pieces, then creating his own, incl. character Ricky Paul, a stand-up comedian in punk clubs. Theatre pieces include: The New World, Men Inside, Voices of America, FunHouse, Drinking in America (Drama Desk and Obie Awards), Talk Radio, Sex Drugs Rock & Roll, Pounding Nails in the Floor With My Forehead (Obie Award), Suburbia (author only).
PICTURES: Special Effects, Talk Radio (also s.p.; Silver Bear Award 1988 Berlin Film Fest.), Sex Drugs Rock & Roll (also s.p.), Naked in New York, Dolores Claiborne, Under Siege 2: Dark Territory, SubUrbia (s.p., lyricist), Deconstructing Harry, Gossip, In the Weeds, Wake Up and Smell the Coffee, Ararat, Igby Goes Down, Wonderland, The Pursuit of Happiness.
TELEVISION: Movies: Crime Story, The Caine Mutiny Court Martial, Last Flight Out, Witch Hunt, A Bright Shining Lie, Shot in the Heart. Special: Drinking in America. Guest: Miami Vice, Twilight Zone, Law & Order, The Larry Sanders Show, Third Watch.

BOLAM, JAMES
Actor. b. Sunderland, England, June 16, 1938. Entered industry in 1960.
PICTURES: The Kitchen, A Kind of Loving, Loneliness of the Long Distance Runner, Murder Most Foul, In Celebration, Clockwork Mice, Stella Does Tricks, Island on Bird Street, The End of the Affair, It Was an Accident, To Kill a King.
TELEVISION: Movies: The Four Seasons of Rosie Carr, Macbeth, The Maze, The Beiderbecke Tapes, The Stalker's Apprentice, Dirty Tricks, Shipman, Dalziel and Pascoe: Sins of the Fathers, New Tricks. Series: Likely Lads, When the Boat Comes In, Only When I Laugh, Father Matthew's Daughter, Andy Capp, Second Thoughts, Close & True, Born and Bred.

BOLOGNA, JOSEPH
Actor, Writer. b. Brooklyn, NY., Dec. 30, 1938. e. Brown U. m. actress-writer Renee Taylor. Service in Marine Corps and on dis-charge joined ad agency, becoming dir.-prod. of TV commercials. Collaborated with wife on short film, 2, shown at 1966 N.Y. Film Festival. Together they wrote Lovers and Other Strangers, B'way play, in which both also acted; wrote s.p. for film version. Both wrote and starred in Made for Each Other, and created and wrote TV series, Calucci's Dept.
PICTURES: Lovers and Other Strangers (co-s.p. only), Made for Each Other (also co.-s.p.), Cops and Robbers, Mixed Company, The Big Bus , Chapter Two, My Favorite Year, Blame It on Rio , The Woman in Red, Transylvania 6-5000, It Had to Be You (also co-dir., co-s.p.), Coupe de Ville, Jersey Girl, Alligator II: The Mutation, Love Is All There Is (dir., s.p.), Heaven Before I Die, Big Daddy, Blink of an Eye, Returning Mickey Stern, Squint, Pledge of Allegiance.
TELEVISION: Movies: Honor Thy Father, Woman of the Year (also co-writer), Torn Between Two Lovers, One Cooks The Other Doesn't, Copacabana, A Time To Triumph, Prime Target, Thanksgiving Day, Citizen Cohn, Revenge of the Nerds IV: Nerds in Love, The Don's Analyst, The Batman/Superman Movie (voice). Special: Acts of Love and Other Comedies (Emmy Award, 1974). Mini-Series: Sins. Series: Calucci's Dept. (creator, co-writer only), Rags to Riches, Top of the Heap. Guest: Arli$$.

BONANNO, LOUIE
Actor. a.k.a. Louix Dor Dempriey. b. Somerville, MA, Dec. 17, 1961. e. Bentley Coll., Waltham, MA, BS-economics, finance; AS accountancy, 1983. In Who's Who Among Students in American Univ. & Colleges; Who's Who Among Rising Young Americans. Moved to NY, 1983 to study at Amer. Acad. of Dramatic Arts. Toured U.S. 1985-86 as Dangermouse for MTV/Nickelodeon. Stand-up comedian 1987-89. Stage debut in The Head, 1990.
PICTURES: Sex Appeal (debut, 1986), Wimps, Student Affairs, Cool as Ice, Auntie Lee's Meat Pies.
TELEVISION: Series: Eisenhower & Lutz, 227, Tour of Duty, TV 101, Santa Barbara, New York Story.

BONET, LISA
Actress. b. Los Angeles, CA, Nov. 16, 1967. First gained recog-nition on The Cosby Show as Denise Huxtable at the age of 15.
PICTURES: Angel Heart, Dead Connection, Bank Robber, New Eden, Serpent's Lair, Enemy of the State, High Fidelity, Biker Boyz.
TELEVISION: Movies: New Eden, Lathe of Heaven. Special: Don't Touch. Series: The Cosby Show, A Different World. Guest: Tales From the Dark Side, St. Elsewhere.

BONET, NAI
Actress, Producer. Worked in entertainment field since age of 13, including opera, films, TV, stage, night clubs and records.
PICTURES: Actress: The Soul Hustlers, The Seventh Veil, Fairy Tales, The Soul of Nigger Charlie, The Spy with the Cold Nose, John Goldfarb Please Come Home, Nocturna (also s.p.), Hoodlums, (also s.p.).
TELEVISION: Johnny Carson Show, Merv Griffin Show, Joe Franklin Show, Beverly Hillbillies, Tom Snyder Show.

BONHAM CARTER, HELENA
Actress. b. London, England, May 26, 1966. Great granddaugh-ter of Liberal Prime Minister Lord Asquith. e. Westminster. Appeared on BBC in A Pattern of Roses; seen by dir. Trevor Nunn who cast her in Lady Jane, 1986, theatrical film debut. On London stage in Trelawny of the Wells.
PICTURES: Lady Jane, A Room with a View, Maurice (cameo), Francesco, La Mascheral (The Mask), Getting It Right, Hamlet, Where Angles Fear to Tread, Howards End, Mary Shelley's Frankenstein, Mighty Aphrodite, Margaret's Museum, Twelfth Night, Shadow Play, The Wings of the Dove (LA Film Crits. Award, Best Actress, 1997), Keep the Aspidistra Flying, The Theory of Flight, The Revengers of Comedy, Fight Club, Women Talking Dirty, Carnivale, Novcaine, Planet of the Apes, Till · Human Voices Wake Us, The Heart of Me, Big Fish.
TELEVISION: Movies: A Hazard of Hearts (U.S.), Fatal Deception: Mrs. Lee Harvey Oswald, Dancing Queen, Merlin, Live From Baghdad. Guest: Miami Vice, Absolutely Fabulous, So Graham Norton.

BOOKMAN, ROBERT
Executive. b. Los Angeles, CA, Jan. 29, 1947. e. U. of California, Yale Law Sch. Motion picture literary agent: IFA 1972-74, ICM 1974-79. 1979-84, ABC Motion Pictures v.p., worldwide produc-tion; 1984-6, Columbia Pictures, exec. v.p., world-wide prod. 1986, Creative Artists Agency, as motion picture literary and directors' agent.

BOONE, PAT
Singer, Actor. r.n. Charles Eugene Boone. b. Jacksonville, FL, June 1, 1934. e. David Lipscomb Coll., North Texas State Coll., grad. magna cum laude, Columbia U. Winner of Ted Mack's Amateur Hour TV show; joined Arthur Godfrey TV show, 1955. Most promising new male star, Motion Picture Daily-Fame Poll 1957. One of top ten moneymaking stars, M.P. Herald-Fame Poll, 1957. Daughter is singer Debby Boone. Author: Twixt Twelve and Twenty, Between You & Me and the Gatepost, The Real Christmas, A New Song, others.
RECORDINGS: Ain't That a Shame, I Almost Lost My Mind, Friendly Persuasion, Love Letters in the Sand, April Love, Tutti Frutti, many others.
PICTURES: Bernardine (debut, 1957), April Love, Mardi Gras, Journey to the Center of the Earth, All Hands on Deck, State Fair, The Main Attraction, The Yellow Canary, The Horror of It All, Never Put It in Writing, Goodbye Charlie, The Greatest Story Ever Told, The Perils of Pauline, The Cross and the Switchblade, Roger and Me, In a Metal Mood, The Eyes of Tammy Faye.TELEVISION: Movie: The Pigeon. Series: Arthur Godfrey and His Friends, The Pat Boone-Chevy Showroom (1957-60), The Pat Boone Show (1966-68).

BOORMAN, JOHN
Director, Producer, Writer. b. London, England, Jan. 18, 1933. Wrote film criticism at age of 17 for British publications incl. Manchester Guardian; founder TV Mag. Day By Day; served in National Service in Army; Broadcaster and BBC radio film critic 1950-54; film editor Independent Television News; prod. documentaries for Southern Television; joined BBC, headed BBC Documentary Film Unit 1960-64, indep. doc. about D.W. Griffith; chmn. Natl. Film Studios of Ireland 1975-85; governor Brit. Film Inst. 1985-.
PICTURES: Director: Catch Us If You Can (debut, 1965), Point Blank, Hell in the Pacific, Leo the Last (also co-s.p., Cannes Film Fest. Award, Best Director 1970), Deliverance (also prod.; 2 Acad. Award noms.), Zardoz (also prod., s.p.), Exorcist II: The Heretic (also co-prod.), Excalibur (also exec. prod., co-s.p., Cannes Film Fest. Award, Best Art. Contribution, 1981), Danny Boy (exec. prod. only), The Emerald Forest (also prod.), Hope and Glory (also prod., s.p., actor; 3 Acad. Award noms., Nat'l Film Critics Awards for dir., s.p.; L.A. Film Critics Awards for picture, s.p., dir.; U.K. Critics Awards for picture), Where the Heart Is (also prod., co-s.p.), I Dreamt I Woke Up (also s.p., actor), Two Nudes Bathing (also s.p., prod.), Beyond Rangoon (also co-prod.), The General (also s.p., prod.), The Tailor of Panama (also prod., s.p.), Country Of My Skull (dir., prod.)
TELEVISION: Movies: The Hard Way, Lee Marvin: A Personal Portrait by John Boorman. Series: Citizen '63 (dir.), The Newcomers (dir.).

BOOTH, MARGARET
Film editor. b. Los Angeles, CA, 1898. Awarded honorary Oscar, 1977.
PICTURES: Why Men Leave Home, Husbands and Lovers, Bridge of San Luis Rey, New Moon, Susan Lenox, Strange Interlude, Smilin' Through, Romeo and Juliet, Barretts of Wimpole Street, Mutiny on the Bounty, Camille, etc. Supervising editor on Owl and the Pussycat, The Way We Were, Funny Lady, Murder by Death, The Goodbye Girl, California Suite, The Cheap Detective (also assoc. prod.), Chapter Two (also assoc. prod.), The Toy (assoc. prod. only), Annie, The Slugger's Wife (exec. prod. only).
(d. Oct. 28, 2002)

BOOTHE, POWERS
Actor. b. Snyder, TX, June 1, 1949. e. Southern Methodist U. On B'way in Lone Star.
PICTURES: The Goodbye Girl, Cruising, Southern Comfort, A Breed Apart, Red Dawn, The Emerald Forest, Extreme Prejudice, Stalingrad, Rapid Fire, Tombstone, Blue Sky, Sudden Death, Nixon, U-Turn, Men of Honor, Frailty.
TELEVISION: Movies: Skag, Plutonium Incident, Guyana Tragedy—The Story of Jim Jones (Emmy Award, 1980), A Cry for Love, Into the Homeland, Family of Spies, By Dawn's Early Light, Wild Card, Marked for Murder, Web of Deception, The Spree, A Crime of Passion. Mini-Series: True Women, Joan of Arc, Attila. Series: Skag, Philip Marlowe Private Eye.

BORGNINE, ERNEST
Actor. r.n. Ermes Effron Borgnino. b. Hamden, CT, Jan. 24, 1917. e. Randall Sch. of Dramatic Art, Hartford, CT. Joined Barter Theatre in Virginia. Served in U.S. Navy; then little theatre work, stock companies; on Broadway in Harvey, Mrs. McThing; many TV appearances. Honors: 33rd Degree of the Masonic Order, Order of the Grand Cross, from same. Named honorary Mayor of Universal City Studios.
PICTURES: Has appeared in more than 100 pictures, incl.: China Corsair (debut, 1951), The Mob, Whistle at Eaton Falls, From Here to Eternity, The Stranger Wore a Gun, Demetrius & the Gladiators, Bounty Hunter, Vera Cruz, Bad Day at Black Rock, Marty (Acad. Award for Best Actor, 1955), Run for Cover, Last Command, Square Jungle, Catered Affair, Best Things in Life are Free, Three Brave Men, The Vikings, Badlanders, Torpedo Run, Season of Passion, Pay or Die, Go Naked in the World, Barabbas, McHale's Navy, Flight of the Phoenix, The Oscar, The Dirty Dozen, Ice Station Zebra, The Split, The Wild Bunch, The Adventurers, Suppose They Gave a War and Nobody Came?, A Bullet for Sandoval, Willard, Rain for a Dusty Summer, Hannie Caulder, The Revengers, Ripped Off, The Poseidon

Adventure, Emperor of the North Pole, The Neptune Factor, Law and Disorder, The Devil's Rain, Shoot, Love By Appointment, The Greatest, Strike Force, Diary of Madam X, The Black Hole, When Time Ran Out, High Risk, Escape from New York, Spike of Bensonhurst, The Opponent, Any Man's Death, Laser Mission, Turnaround, Captain Henkel, Moving Target, The Last Match, Mistress, McHale's Navy, Gattaca, BASEketball, All Dogs Christmas Carol, 12 Bucks, Mel, The Last Great Ride, Abilene, Castlerock, The Long Ride Home, Crimebusters (also exec. prod.), Muraya (l'expérience secrète de Mike Blueberry).
TELEVISION: Movies: Sam Hill: Who Killed the Mysterious Mr. Foster?, The Trackers, Twice in a Lifetime, Future Cop, Jesus of Nazareth, Fire!, The Ghost of Flight 401, Cops and Robin, All Quiet on the Western Front, Blood Feud, Carpool, Love Leads the Way, Last Days of Pompeii, The Dirty Dozen: The Next Mission, Alice in Wonderland, The Dirty Dozen: The Deadly Mission, The Dirty Dozen: The Fatal Mission, Jake Spanner-Private Eye. Specials: Billy the Kid, Legend in Granite: The Vince Lombardi Story, Big Guns Talk: The Story of the Western, AFI's 100 Years 100 Thrills: America's Most Heart Pounding Movies. Series: McHale's Navy, Future Cop, Air Wolf, The Single Guy, All dogs Go to Heaven: the Series (voice), SpongeBob SquarePants (voice). Guest: Philco Playhouse, G.E. Theater, Wagon Train, Little House on the Prairie, Murder She Wrote, Home Improvement, The Simpsons (voice), Pinky and the Brain (voice).

BORIS, ROBERT
Writer, Director. b. NY, NY, Oct. 12, 1945. Screenwriter before also turning to direction with Oxford Blues, 1984.
PICTURES: Electra Glide in Blue, Some Kind of Hero, Doctor Detroit, Oxford Blues (also dir.), Buy and Cell (dir.), Steele Justice (dir.), Extreme Justice, Diplomatic Siege, Backyard Dogs, Deep Freeze.
TELEVISION: Birds of Prey, Blood Feud, Deadly Encounter, Izzy and Moe, Frank and Jesse (also dir.), Marilyn and Me.

BORNSTEIN, STEVEN M.
Executive. e. Univ. of Wisconsin, 1974. Began his career in entertainment spending three years at WOSU-TV in Columbus, Ohio, his last two years serving as executive producer. Joined ESPN in 1980 as manager of programming. From 1990 to 1999, Bornstein served as president and CEO of ESPN. In 1993 he also was named vice president of Capital Cities/ABC, Inc. In 1996, he was given the additional title of president, ABC Sports. Chairman of Walt Disney Internet Group, September 1999. Became Pres., ABC Television, Inc., May 2001. Resigned, April 2002.

BORODINSKY, SAMUEL
Executive. b. Brooklyn, NY, Oct. 25, 1941. e. Industrial Sch. of Arts & Photography. Expert in film care and rejuvenation. Exec. v.p., Filmtreat International Corp. Previously with Modern Film Corp. (technician) and Comprehensive Filmtreat, Inc. & International Filmtreat (service manager). 1998 Emmy Award for pioneering development of scratch removal systems.

BOSCO, PHILIP
Actor. b. Jersey City, NJ, Sept. 26, 1930. e. Catholic U., Washington, DC, BA. drama, 1957. Studied for stage with James Marr, Josephine Callan and Leo Brady. Consummate stage actor (in over 100 plays, 61 in NY) whose career spans the classics (with NY Shakespeare Fest. and American Shakespeare Fest, CT.), 20 plays with Arena Stage 1957-60, to modern classics as a resident actor with Lincoln Center Rep. Co. in the 1960s, winning Tony and Drama Desk Awards for the farce Lend Me a Tenor, 1988. Recipient: Clarence Derwent Award for General Excellence, Outer Critics Circle Award & Obie for Lifetime Achievement.
THEATRE: Auntie Mame (B'way debut, City Center revival, 1958), Measure for Measure, The Rape of the Belt (Tony nom.), Donnybrook, Richard III, The Alchemist, The East Wind, The Ticket of Leave Man, Galileo, Saint Joan, Tiger at the Gates, Cyrano de Bergerac, Be Happy for Me, King Lear, The Miser, The Time of Your Life, Camino Real, Operation Sidewinder, Amphitryon, In the Matter of J. Robert Oppenheimer, The Good Woman of Setzuan, The Playboy of the Western World, An Enemy of the People, Antigone, Mary Stuart, The Crucible, Enemies, Mrs. Warren's Profession, Henry V, The Threepenny Opera, Streamers, Stages, The Biko Inquest, Whose Life Is It Anyway? A Month in the Country, Don Juan in Hell, Inadmissible Evidence, Ah! Wilderness, Man and Superman, Major Barbara, The Caine Mutiny Court Martial, Heartbreak House (Tony nom.), Come Back Little Sheba, Loves of Anatol, Be Happy for Me, Master Class, You Never Can Tell, A Man for All Seasons, Devil's Disciple, Lend Me a Tenor (Tony Award, 1989), The Miser, Breaking Legs, An Inspector Calls, The Heiress, Moon Over Buffalo.
PICTURES: Requiem for a Heavyweight, A Lovely Way to Die, Trading Places, The Pope of Greenwich Village, Walls of Glass, Heaven Help Us, Flanagan, The Money Pit, Children of a Lesser God, Suspect, Three Men and a Baby, Another Woman, Working Girl, The Luckiest Man in the World, Dream Team, Blue Steel, Quick Change, True Colors, FX2, Shadows and Fog, Straight Talk, Angie, Milk Money, Nobody's Fool, Safe Passage, It Takes Two, My Best Friend's Wedding, Critical Care, Frank Lloyd Wright (voice), Wonder Boys, Shaft, Brooklyn Sonnet, Kate & Leopold, Abandon.
TELEVISION: Movies: Echoes in the Darkness, Second Effort, Internal Affairs, Murder in Black and White, The Return of Eliot Ness, Against the Wall, The Forget-Me-Not Murders,

Janek: A Silent Betrayal, Young at Heart, Carriers, Twelfth Night, Bonanno: A Godfather's Story, Cupid & Cate, After Amy. *Miniseries*: LIBERTY!: The American Revolution, Mark Twain (voice). *Specials*: Prisoner of Zenda, An Enemy of the People, A Nice Place to Visit, Read Between the Lines (Emmy Award), New York: A Documentary Film (voice), The Birth of Ohio Stadium (voice). *Series*: The Guiding Light, TriBeCa, As The World Turns, All My Children. *Guest*: Nurses, Trials of O'Brien, Law & Order, Spenser: For Hire, The Equalizer, Against the Law, Janek, Spin City, Ed, Law & Order: Special Victims Unit.

BOSLEY, TOM
Actor. b. Chicago, IL, Oct. 1, 1927. e. DePaul U. Had roles on radio in Chicago and in stock productions before moving to New York. Appeared off-Broadway and on road before signed to play lead in Fiorello! for George Abbott on Broadway. First actor to win Tony, Drama Critics, ANTA and Newspaper Guild awards in one season for that role.
PICTURES: Love with the Proper Stranger, The World of Henry Orient, Divorce American Style, Yours Mine and Ours, The Secret War of Harry Frigg, To Find a Man, Mixed Company, Gus, O'Hara's Wife, Million Dollar Mystery, Wicked Stepmother, Little Bigfoot II: The Journey Home, The Tangerine Bear, Returning Mickey Stern, The Chocolate Fairy.
TELEVISION: *Movies*: Marcus Welby M.D.: A Matter of Humanities (pilot), Night Gallery, A Step Out of Line, Vanished, Congratulations It's a Boy!, Mr. & Mrs. Bo Jo Jones, Streets of San Francisco (pilot), No Place to Run, Miracle on 34th Street, The Girl Who Came Gift Wrapped, Death Cruise, Who Is the Black Dahlia?, Last Survivors, The Night That Panicked America, Love Boat, Testimony of 2 Men, Black Market Baby, With This Ring, The Castaways on Gilligan's Island, The Rebels, For the Love of It, Jesse Owens Story, Fatal Confession: A Father Dowling Mystery, The Love Boat: A Valentine Voyage, Legend of the Candy Cane, Mary Christmas.
Specials: Alice in Wonderland (1953), Arsenic and Old Lace, The Drunkard, Profiles in Courage. *Guest*: Focus, Naked City, The Right Man, The Nurses, Route 66, The Perry Como Show, The Drew Carey Show. *Series*: That Was the Week That Was, The Debbie Reynolds Show, The Dean Martin Show, Sandy Duncan Show, Wait Til Your Father Gets Home (voice), Happy Days, That's Hollywood (narrator), Murder She Wrote, Father Dowling Mysteries, Port Charles.

BOSTWICK, BARRY
Actor. b. San Mateo, CA, Feb. 24, 1946. e. USIU Sch. of Performing Arts, San Diego, BFA in acting; NYU Grad. Sch. of the Arts. Made prof. stage debut while in coll. working with Walter Pidgeon in Take Her She's Mine. Joined APA Phoenix Rep. Co. making his B'way debut in Cock-A-Doodle Dandy.
THEATRE: Salvation, House of Leather, Soon, The Screens, Colette, Grease (created role of Danny Zuko, 1972), They Knew What They Wanted, The Robber Bridegroom (Tony Award, 1977), She Loves Me, L'Histoire du Soldat, Nick and Nora.
PICTURES: The Rocky Horror Picture Show, Movie Movie, Megaforce, Eight Hundred Leagues Down the Amazon, Weekend at Bernie's 2, Spy Hard, The Secret Agent Club, Swing.
TELEVISION: *Movies*: The Chadwick Family, The Quinns, Murder By Natural Causes, Once Upon a Family, Moviola—The Silent Lovers, Summer Girl, An Uncommon Love, Deceptions, Betrayed by Innocence, Body of Evidence, Addicted to His Love, Parent Trap III, Challenger, Captive, Between Love and Hate, Praying Mantis, Once in a Lifetime, The Return of Hunter, The Secretary, National Lampoon's Men in White. *Mini-Series*: George Washington, I'll Take Manhattan, War and Remembrance. *Specials*: A Woman of Substance, You Can't Take It With You, Working. *Series*: Foul Play, Dads, Spin City.

BOSUSTOW, NICK
Producer. b. Los Angeles, CA, March 28, 1940. e. Menlo Coll., administration. MCA, intl. sales, 1963. Pres., Stephen Bosustow Productions, 1967. Pres., ASIFA-West. Pres., Bosustow Entertainment Inc., 1973. Founded Animation Consultants International, 1995.
PICTURES: Is It Always Right to Be Right?(Acad. award, 1971) The Legend of John Henry (Acad. award nom.).
TELEVISION: *Specials*: The Incredible Book Escape, Misunderstood Monsters, A Tale of Four Wishes, Wrong Way Kid (Emmy, 1984). *Series*: The Hayley Mills Story Book.

BOSWALL, JEFFERY
Producer, Director, Writer. b. Brighton, England, 1931. e. Taunton House School, Montpelier Coll., Brighton. Started career as an ornithologist for the Royal Society for the Protection of Birds. Joined BBC in 1958 as radio prod., moving to TV 1964 making films in diverse locations (Ethiopia and Antarctica). Contributed to 50 films as wildlife cameraman. Co-founder of British Library of Wildlife Sounds. 1987: returned to RSPB. Head of Film and Video Unit, 1987. 1992, sr. lecturer in Biological Film & Video, Derby Univ. Chairmanship BKSTS Intl Wildlife Filmmakers' Symposium. AUTHOR: Birds for All Seasons. Ed. Look and Private Lives. Contrib.: Times, Countryman, the Field, Wildlife and Country-side, BBC Wildlife, Scientific Film, Journal of the Society of Film and TV Arts, Image Technology. Has written for scientific journals and writes annual update for Encyclopedia Britannica on ornithology.
TELEVISION: 18 films in the Private Lives series of which 4 (about the Kingfisher, Cuckoo, Starling and Jackass Penguin) won intl awards. Animal Olympians, Birds For All Seasons, Where the Parrots Speak Mandarin, Wildlife Safari to Ethiopia.

BOTTOMS, JOSEPH
Actor. b. Santa Barbara, CA, April 22, 1954. Brother of Sam and Timothy Bottoms. Did plays in jr. high school in Santa Barbara and then with community theatre.
PICTURES: The Dove (debut, 1974), Crime and Passion, The Black Hole, Cloud Dancer, King of the Mountain, Blind Date, Open House, Born to Race, Inner Sanctum, Snide and Prejudice, Joseph's Gift.
TELEVISION: *Movies*: Trouble Comes to Town, Unwed Father, Stalk the Wild Child, The Intruder Within, Side By Side: The True Story of the Osmond Family, I Married Wyatt Earp, The Sins of Dorian Gray, Time Bomb, Braker, Island Sons, Cop Killer, Gunsmoke: To the Last Man, Treacherous Crossing, Liar's Edge. *Mini-Series*: Holocaust, Celebrity. *Special*: Winesburg Ohio. *Series*: The Net. *Guest*: Owen Marshall, Murder She Wrote.

BOTTOMS, SAM
Actor. b. Santa Barbara, CA, Oct. 17, 1955. Brother of Timothy, Joseph and Ben Bottoms. Co-prod. documentary Picture This. Appeared in documentary Hearts of Darkness.
PICTURES: The Last Picture Show (debut, 1971), Class of '44, Zandy's Bride, Up From the Depths, The Outlaw Josey Wales, Apocalypse Now, Bronco Billy, Hunter's Blood, Gardens of Stone, After School, Hearts of Darkness: A Filmmaker's Apocalypse, Picture This--The Times of Peter Bogdanovich in Archer City Texas, Ragin' Cajun, Dolly Dearest, In 'n Out, North of Chiang Mai, Prime Risk, The Trust, Sugar Hill, Sunny Side Up, Project Showchaser 3000, Angel Blue, Snide and Prejudice, Joseph's Gift, The Unsaid, Shadow Fury, Looking Through Lilian, True Files, Seabiscuit.
TELEVISION: *Movies*: Savages, Cage Without a Key, Desperate Lives, Island Sons, The Witching of Ben Wagner, Zooman, My Neighbor's Daughter. *Mini-Series*: East of Eden, Return to Eden. *Guest*: Greatest Heroes of the Bible, Murder She Wrote, Marcus Welby M.D., Doc Elliot, Eddie Capra, Lucas Tanner, 21 Jump Street, X Files. *Series*: Santa Barbara.

BOTTOMS, TIMOTHY
Actor. b. Santa Barbara, CA, Aug. 30, 1951. Brother of actors Joseph and Sam Bottoms. Early interest in acting; was member of S.B. Madrigal Society, touring Europe in 1967. Sang and danced in West Side Story local prod. With brother Sam co-prod. documentary Picture This about making of the Last Picture Show and Texasville.
PICTURES: Has appeared in more than 60 pictures, incl.: Johnny Got His Gun (debut, 1971), The Last Picture Show, The Paper Chase, The White Dawn, Operation Daybreak, A Small Town in Texas, Rollercoaster, The Other Side of the Mountain: Part 2, Hurricane, The High Country, Tin Man, The Census Taker, In the Shadow of Kilimanjaro, The Sea Serpent, The Fantasist, Invaders from Mars, The Drifter, Return to the River Kwai, A Case of Law, Texasville, Istanbul, I'll Met By Moonlight, Uncle Sam, Ringer, Fox Hunt, Mr. Atlas, Absolute Force, Mixed Blessings, The Man in the Iron Mask, The Prince and the Surfer, X-Ray Boy, A Smaller Place, Held for Ransom, Murder Seen, The Entrepreneurs, Elephant, Paradise.
TELEVISION: *Movies*: The Story of David, The Gift of Love, A Shining Season, Escape, Island Sons, , Mortal Challenge, DC 9/11, The Big Dance. *Special*: Look Homeward Angel. *Mini-Series*: The Money Changers, East of Eden. *Series*: Land of the Lost, The Great War (voice), That's My Bush! *Guest*: Gideon's Crossing, That '70s Show.

BOUCHEZ, ÉLODIE
Actress. b. France, April 5, 1973.
PICTURES: Stan the Flasher, The Stolen Diary, Tango, Good Old Daze, Les mots de l'amour, The Wild Reeds, Those Were the Days, Clubbed to Death, Mademoiselle Personne, Full Speed, The Proprietor, Fire in Paradise, La divine poursuite, Le ciel est a nous, The Dreamlife of Angels (Cannes Film Fest. Award, Best Actress, 1998), Louise, J'aimerais pas crever un dimanche, Zonzon, Les Kidnappeurs, Shooting Vegetarians, Lovers, Meurtre d'une petite grue, Blame it on Voltaire, Too Much Flesh, The Beat Nicks, CQ, Tom Thumb, Being Light, Le Merveilleuse odysee de l'idiot Toboggan, La guerre a Paris, Noces indiennes, Dreams of Trespass, Le Pacte du silence, Stormy Weather.

BOUQUET, CAROLE
Actress. b. Neuilly-sur-Seine, France, Aug. 18, 1957. e. Sorbonne, Paris, Paris Conservatoire. Also model for Chanel No. 5 perfume.
PICTURES: That Obscure Object of Desire (debut, 1977), Buffet Froid, Il Cappotto di Astrakan, For Your Eyes Only, Bingo Bongo, Mystere, Nemo, Le Bon Roi Dagobert, Rive Droite Rive Gauche, Special Police, Double Messieurs, Le Mal d'aimer, Jenatsch, Bunker Palace Hotel, New York Stories, Too Beautiful for You, Against Oblivion, Tango, Women in Skirts, Grosse Fatigue, A Business Affair, Lucie Aubrac, In All Innocence, Un Pont Entre Deux Rives, Lulu Kreutz's Picnic, Speaking of Bunuel, Wasabi, Embrassez qui vous voulez, Blanche, Bienvenue chez les Rozes.
TELEVISION: *Mini-Series*: Le Rouge et le Noir. *Movies*: Berenice, Madame de.

BOUTSIKARIS, DENNIS
Actor. b. Newark, NJ, Dec. 21, 1952. e. Hampshire Col.
THEATER: *Off-B'way*: Another Language (debut, 1975), Funeral March for a One Man Band, All's Well That Ends Well, Nest of the Wood Grouse, Cheapside, Rum and Coke, The Boys Next

Door, Sight Unseen. B'way: Filomena, Bent, Amadeus.
PICTURES: The Exterminator, Very Close Quarters, Batteries Not Included, Crocodile Dundee II, The Dream Team, Talent for the Game, The Boy Who Cried Bitch, Boys on the Side, Chasing the Dragon, Surviving Picasso, Blue Vision, In Dreams, Taken, Custody of the Heart, Crawlers.
TELEVISION: Series: Nurse, Stat, The Jackie Thomas Show, Misery Loves Company. Movies: Rappaccini's Daughter, Internal Affairs, Thunderboat Row, The Keys, Love Lies and Murder, The Hit Man, Victim of Love: The Shannon Mohr Story, The Yarn Princess, Tonya & Nancy: The Inside Story, Beyond Betrayal, Love and Betrayal: The Mia Farrow Story, The Three Lives of Karen, Survival on the Mountain, Perfect Murder Perfect Town. Mini-Series: The Last Don. Guest: Murphy Brown, Law & Order, The Burning Zone, ER.

BOWIE, DAVID
Actor, Composer, Singer. r.n. David Robert Jones. b. Brixton, South London, England, Jan. 8, 1947. m. model-actress Iman. Broadway debut: The Elephant Man (1980).
PICTURES: The Virgin Soldiers (debut, 1969), Ziggy Stardust and the Spiders from Mars (1973; U.S. release 1983), The Man Who Fell to Earth, Just a Gigolo, Radio On, Cat People (lyricist, performed song), The Hunger, Yellowbeard, Merry Christmas Mr. Lawrence, Into the Night, Absolute Beginners (also songs), Labyrinth (also songs), The Last Temptation of Christ, Linguini Incident, Twin Peaks: Fire Walk With Me, Inspirations, Mr. Rice's Secret, Il Mio West, Lou Reed: Rock and Roll Heart, Everybody Loves Sunshine, Zoolander, Mayor of Sunset Strip. Composer/Songs: Boy Meets Girl, The Falcon and the Snowman, Bad Blood, Pretty Woman, Lost Highway, The Saint, Grosse Point Blank, Almost Famous, Moulin Rouge!, The Banger Sisters, Dogville.
TELEVISION: Specials: Christmas With Bing Crosby, The Midnight Special, Glass Spider Tour, Closure, Saturday Night Live: 25th Anniversary Special, The Beatles Revolution, Bowie at the BBC, The Old Grey Whistle Test at 30, Bad Hair Days, Concert for New York City, I Love Christmas. Series: The Hunger.

BOWSER, EILEEN
Curator, Film Archivist, Historian. b. Ohio, Jan. 18, 1928. e. Marietta Coll., B.A., 1950; U. of North Carolina, M.A., history of art, 1953. Joined Dept. of Film, Museum of Modern Art, 1954. Curator, Dept. of Film (1976-1993). Organized major exhib. of the films of D.W. Griffith, Carl-Theodor Dreyer, Art of the Twenties, recent acquisitions and touring shows. On exec. comm. of Federation Internationale des Archives du Film 1969-91, v.p. FIAF 1977-85; pres. FIAF Documentation Commission 1972-81. Film Archives Advisory Comm. since 1971. Assoc. of Univ. Seminars on Cinema and Interdisciplinary Interpretation. Publications: The Transformation of Cinema: 1907-15, Vol II, History of the American Film Series, The Movies, David Wark Griffith, Biograph Bulletins 1908-1912. A Handbook for Film Archives. Has written numerous articles on film history. Received career recognition award from Assn. of Moving Image Archivists in 1994.

BOXLEITNER, BRUCE
Actor. b. Elgin, IL, May 12, 1950. m. actress Melissa Gilbert. After high school enrolled in Chicago's Goodman Theatre, staging productions and working with lighting and set design in addition to acting.
PICTURES: Six-Pack Annie, The Baltimore Bullet, Tron, The Crystal Eye, Breakaway, Diplomatic Immunity, Kuffs, The Babe, Wyatt Earp: Return to Tombstone, Perilous, The Perfect Nanny, Life in the Balance, Contagion, Silence, Gods and Generals, Tron Killer App (voice).
TELEVISION: Movies: The Chadwick Family, A Cry for Help, The Macahans, Kiss Me—Kill Me, Murder at the World Series, Happily Ever After, Wild Times, Bare Essence, I Married Wyatt Earp, Passion Flower, Angel in Green, The Gamble (I, II, III, & V), Red River, The Road Raiders, Murderous Vision, The Secret, Perfect Family, Double Jeopardy, House of Secrets, Zoya, Babylon 5: In the Beginning, Babylon 5: Thirdspace, Babylon 5: A Call to Arms, Freefall, Hope Ranch, Killer Flood. Mini-Series: How the West Was Won, East of Eden, The Last Convertible. Series: How the West Was Won, Bring 'Em Back Alive, Scarecrow and Mrs. King, Babylon 5. Guest: Tales from the Crypt, Touched By An Angel, Outer Limits.

BOYER, PHIL
TV Executive. b. Portland, OR, Dec. 13, 1940. e. Sacramento State U. Began broadcasting career as 12-year-old in Portland, establishing nation's first youth radio facility—a 5-watt facility in the basement of his home. At 16 began working at KPDQ, Portland; two years later joined KPTV, Portland, as announcer. In 1960 joined KEZI-TV, Eugene, OR, heading prod. and prog. depts. In 1965 named staff prod.-dir. for KCRA, TV, Sacramento, CA, becoming prod. mgr. in 1967 and prog. mgr. in 1969. In 1972 joined KNBC-TV, Los Angeles, as prog. dir. In 1974 named v.p., programming, of ABC Owned TV Stations; 1977, v.p.-gen. mgr., WLS-TV, Chicago; 1979, v.p.-gen. mgr. of WABC-TV, NY, 1981; v.p., gen mgr., ABC-owned TV station div.; 1984, joined ABC Video Enterprises as v.p. intl. dev.; 1986-97 sr. v.p., intl and prog. dev., CC/ABC Video Ent.

BOYES, CHRISTOPHER
Sound.
PICTURES: Rush, Terminator 2: Judgment Day, Bingo!, Single White Female, Jurassic Park, Under Siege 2: Dark Territory, The Rock, Broken Arrow, Eraser, Titanic (Acad. Award, Best Sound Effects Editing, 1997), Volcano, The Lost World: Jurassic Park, Con Air, Big Daddy, The 13th Warrior, Dinosaur, Titan A.E., Space Cowboys, Pearl Harbor (Acad. Award), Jurassic Park 3, The Lord of the Rings: Fellowship of the Ring (Acad. Award nom.), Lilo & Stitch, Minority Report, Blood Work, The Lord of the Rings: The Two Towers.

BOYETT, ROBERT LEE
Producer. e. Duke U., B.A.; Col. U., M.A., marketing. Began career in media and mkt. research at Grey Advertising, Inc. Was program development consultant for PBS. In 1973 joined ABC as dir. of prime time series TV, East Coast. In 1975 named ABC TV v.p. & asst. to v.p. programs for West Coast. In 1977 joined Paramount Pictures in newly created position of v.p., exec. asst. to pres. & chief operating officer. 1979, joined Miller-Milkis-Boyett Productions to produce for Paramount Television.
TELEVISION: Exec. prod.: Laverne and Shirley, Happy Days, Bosom Buddies, Mork and Mindy, Valerie, Perfect Strangers, Family Matters, Meego, Step By Step, Full House, Family Matters, Going Places, The Family Man, Getting By, On Our Own, Two-N-Two Together, Hogan Family, Two of a Kind.

BOYLE, BARBARA D.
Executive. b. New York, NY. e. U. of California, Berkeley, B.A., 1957; UCLA, J.D., 1960. Named to bar: California, 1961; New York, 1964; Supreme Court, 1964. Atty. in busn. affairs dept. & corp. asst. secty., American Intl. Pictures, Los Angeles, 1965-67; partner in entertainment law firm, Cohen & Boyle, L.A., 1967-74; exec. v.p. & gen. counsel, COO, New World Pictures, L.A., 1974-82. Sr. v.p. worldwide prod., Orion Pictures, L.A., 1982-86; exec. v.p., prod., RKO Pictures, L.A., 1986-87. President, Sovereign Pictures, L.A., 1988-92; Partner in Boyle-Taylor Prods., 1993-Present. Co-chmn. 1979-80, Entertainment Law Symposium Advisory Committee, UCLA Law Sch. Member, AMPAS, Women in Film (pres., 1977-78, mem. of bd., chairperson 1981-84), Women Entertainment Lawyers Assn., California Bar Assn., N.Y. State Bar Assn., Beverly Hills Bar Assn., Hollywood Women's Political Committee, American Film Institute. Bd. mem.: Women Director's Workshop, Independent Feature Project/West (pres. 1994-), Los Angeles Women's Campaign Fund. Founding mem. UCLA Sch. of Law's Entertainment Advisory Council (& co-chairperson 1979 & 80).
PICTURES: Exec. prod: Desperately Seeking Susan, The Terminator, Platoon, Breaker Morant, Tin Drum, My Left Foot, Bottle Rocket, Phenomenon, Instinct.

BOYLE, LARA FLYNN
Actress. b. Davenport, IA, Mar. 24, 1970. e. Chicago Academy for the Visual and Performing Arts. First studied acting at the Piven Theatre. Professional debut at age 15 in tv mini-series Amerika.
PICTURES: Poltergeist III (debut, 1988), How I Got Into College, Dead Poets Society, May Wine, The Rookie, The Dark Backward, Mobsters, Wayne's World, Where the Day Takes You, The Temp, Eye of the Storm, Equinox, Red Rock West, Threesome, Baby's Day Out, The Road to Wellville, Farmer & Chase, Cafe Society, The Big Squeeze, Afterglow, Red Meat, Susan's Plan, Happiness, Chain of Fools, Speaking of Sex, Men In Black 2.
TELEVISION: Movies: Terror on Highway 91, Gang of Four, The Preppie Murder, Past Tense, Jacob, Since You've Been Gone. Series: Twin Peaks, The Practice. Guest: Ally McBeal Mini-Series: Amerika.

BOYLE, PETER
Actor. b. Philadelphia, PA, Oct. 18, 1935. e. LaSalle Coll. Was monk in Christian Bros. order before leaving in early 60s to come to N.Y. Acted in off-Broadway shows and joined The Second City in Chicago. Also did TV commercials.
THEATRE: NY: Shadow of Heroes, Paul Sills' Story Theatre, The Roast, True West, Snow Orchid.
PICTURES: Appeared in 55+ pictures, incl.: The Virgin President (debut, 1968), The Monitors, Medium Cool, Joe, Diary of a Mad Housewife, The Candidate, Steelyard Blues, Slither, Kid Blue, Crazy Joe, Young Frankenstein, Taxi Driver, Swashbuckler, F.I.S.T., The Brink's Job, Hardcore, Beyond the Poseidon Adventure, Where the Buffalo Roam, In God We Trust, Outland, Yellowbeard, Johnny Dangerously, Turk 182, Surrender, Walker, The In Crowd, Red Heat, The Dream Team, Speed Zone, Men of Respect, Solar Crisis, Kickboxer 2, Honeymoon in Vegas, Nervous Ticks, Malcolm X, The Shadow, The Santa Clause, Bulletproof Heart, Born to Be Wild, While You Were Sleeping, Doctor Doolittle, Monster's Ball, Pluto Nash, Final Guardian, Santa Claus 2: The Mrs. Claus, Scary Movie 3, The Blackout Murders.
TELEVISION: Movies: The Man Who Could Talk to Kids, Tail Gunner Joe, Echoes in the Darkness, Disaster at Silo 7, Guts and Glory: The Rise and Fall of Oliver North, Challenger, In the Line of Duty: Street War, Taking the Heat, Royce, In the Lake of the Woods, A Deadly Vision. Specials: 27 Wagons Full of Cotton. Series: Comedy Tonight, Joe Bash, Everybody Loves Raymond, Hollywood Squares. Mini-Series: From Here to Eternity. Guest: Cagney & Lacey, Midnight Caller, X-Files (Emmy Award, 1996), NYPD Blue.

BRABOURNE, LORD JOHN
Producer. b. London, England, Nov. 9, 1924.
PICTURES: Harry Black and the Tiger, Sink the Bismarck, H.M.S. Defiant (Damn the Defiant!), Othello, The Mikado, Up the Junction, Romeo and Juliet, Dance of Death, Peter Rabbit and Tales of Beatrix Potter, Murder on the Orient Express, Death on the Nile, Stories from a Flying Trunk, The Mirror Crack'd, Evil Under the Sun, A Passage to India, Little Dorrit.

BRACCO, LORRAINE
Actress. b. Brooklyn, NY, Oct. 2, 1955. m. actor Edward James Olmos. At 16 began modeling for Wilhelmina Agency appearing in Mademoiselle, Seventeen, Teen magazine. Moved to Paris where modeling career continued and led to TV commercials. After making her film debut in Duo sur Canape became a disc jockey on Radio Luxembourg, Paris. 1983 produced a TV special on fashion and music. In Lincoln Center workshop performance of David Rabe's Goose and Tom Tom, 1986.
PICTURES: Cormorra, The Pick-up Artist, Someone to Watch Over Me, Sing, The Dream Team, On a Moonlit Night, Good Fellas (Acad. Award nom.), Talent for the Game, Switch, Medicine Man, Radio Flyer, Traces of Red, Being Human, The Basketball Diaries, Hackers, The Liars, Ladies Room, Custody of the Heart, Riding in Cars With Boys, Tangled, Max and Grace.
TELEVISION: *Movies:* Scam, Getting Gotti, Lifeline, The Taking of Pelham One-Two-Three, Sex In Our Century. *Series:* The Sopranos. *Guest:* Crime Story.

BRACKEN, EDDIE
Actor. b. New York, NY, Feb. 7, 1915. e. Prof. Children's Sch. for Actors, N.Y. m. Connie Nickerson, actress. Vaudeville & night club singer: stage debut in Lottery, 1930.
THEATRE: Lady Refuses, Iron Men, So Proudly We Hail, Brother Rat, What A Life, Too Many Girls, Seven Year Itch, Shinbone Alley, Teahouse of the August Moon, You Know I Can't Hear You When The Water's Running, The Odd Couple, Never Too Late, Sunshine Boys, Hello Dolly, Sugar Babies, Show Boat, The Wizard of Oz, No No Nanette.
PICTURES: Too Many Girls (debut, 1940), Life With Henry, Reaching for the Sun, Caught in the Draft, The Fleet's In, Sweater Girl, Star Spangled Rhythm, Happy Go Lucky, Young and Willing, The Miracle of Morgan's Creek, Hail the Conquering Hero, Rainbow Island, Bring on the Girls, Duffy's Tavern, Hold That Blonde, Out of This World, Ladies' Man, Fun on a Weekend, The Girl From Jones Beach, Summer Stock, Two Tickets to Broadway, About Face, We're Not Married, Slight Case of Larceny, Wild Wild World (narrator), Shinbone Alley (voice), National Lampoon's Vacation, Preston Sturges: The Rise and Fall of an American Dreamer, Oscar, Home Alone 2: Lost in New York, Rookie of the Year, Baby's Day Out, The Brave Little Toaster (voice).
TELEVISION: *Series:* I've Got a Secret (panelist), Make the Connection (panelist), Masquerade Party (host, 1957), Winnetka Road. *Guest:* Goodyear Playhouse, Studio One, Climax, Murder She Wrote, Blacke's Magic, Amazing Stories, Tales of the Dark Side, Golden Girls, Wise Guy, Empty Nest, Monsters. *Movies:* The American Clock, Assault at West Point. *Specials:* The Rodgers and Hart Story: Thou Swell Thou Witty, AFI's 100 Years 100 Laughs: America's Funniest Movies, The Ryan Interview. (d. Nov. 14, 2002)

BRADEN, WILLIAM
Executive, Producer. b. Alberta, Canada. e. U.S., Canada, and abroad. Began career as stuntman in Hollywood, and has worked in all aspects of industry Worked for Elliott Kastner as prod. exec. and with Jeffrey Bloom, of Feature Films, Inc., as prod. exec and v.p. in chg. of prod. Also with Dunatai Corp., as head of film and TV prod. With Completion Bond Co. one yr. as prod. exec., Australia then with Filmaker Completion as pres. 4 years. Now indep. prod.
PICTURES: Pyramid (assoc. prod., prod. supv.), Russian Roulette (prod. exec.), 92 in the Shade (prod. exec.), Breakheart Pass (prod. exec.), Dogpound Shuffle (asst. dir.), Dublin Murders (supvr. re-edit), He Wants Her Back (prod.), Goldengirl (prod. exec.), Running Scared (prod.), Death Valley (asst. dir.), The Seduction (prod. exec.), Slapstick of Another Kind (prod. exec.).
TELEVISION: Requiem for a Planet (series, prod./creator) *Specials:* Nothing Great is Easy (exec. prod.), King of the Channel (exec. prod.), I Believe (prod.), If My People... (prod.), America: Life in the Family (dir./prod.). Also various Movies of the Week for networks and many industrial and doc. films.

BRADFORD, JESSE
Actor. b. May 28, 1979. Made first appearance as infant in Q-tip commercial.
PICTURES: Falling in Love (debut, 1984), Prancer, Presmued Innocent, My Blue Heaven, The Boy Who Cried Bitch, King of the Hill, Far From Home: The Adventures of Yello Dog, Hackers, Romeo & Juliet, A Soldier's Daughter Never Cries, Speedway Junky, Cherry Falls, Bring It On, Dancing at the Blue Iguana, According to Spencer, Clockstoppers, Swimfan.
TELEVISION: *Movie:* The Boys. *Special:* Classified Love. *Guest:* Tribeca.

BRADLEY, ED
Newscaster. b. Philadelphia, Pa., June 22, 1941. e. Cheyney State Coll, B.S. Worked way up through the ranks as local radio reporter in Philadelphia 1963-67 and NY 1967-71. Joined CBS News as stringer in Paris bureau, 1971; then Saigon bureau. Named CBS news correspondent, 1973. Became CBS News White House corr. and anchor of CBS Sunday Night News, 1976-

81; principal corr. and anchor, CBS Reports, 1978-81; co-editor and reporter 60 Minutes since 1981-82 season. Recipient: Alfred I. duPont-Columbia University and Overseas Press Club Awards, George Foster Peabody and Ohio State Awards, George Polk Award.
TELEVISION: *Special reports:* What's Happened to Cambodia, The Boat People, Blacks in America—With All Deliberate Speed, Return of the CIA, Miami. The Trial That Sparked the Riot (Emmy Award), The Saudis, Too Little Too Late (Emmy Award), Murder—Teenage Style (Emmy Award, 1981), In the Belly of the Beast (Emmy Award, 1982), Lena (Emmy Award, 1982), In the Killing Fields of America (Awarded Robert F. Kennedy Journalism Grand Prize for documentary, 1995).

BRAEDEN, ERIC
Actor. r.n. Hans Gudegast. b. Kiel, Germany, Apr. 3, 1941. Awarded Federal Medal of Honor by pres. of Germany for pro-moting positive, realistic image of Germans in America.
PICTURES: Morituri, Dayton's Devils, 100 Rifles, Colossus: The Forbin Project, Escape from the Planet of the Apes, Lady Ice, The Adulteress, The Ultimate Thrill, Herbie Goes to Monte Carlo, The Ambulance, Titanic, Meet the Deedles.
TELEVISION: *Series:* The Rat Patrol, The Young and the Restless (People's Choice Award, Soap Opera Award, 2 Emmy noms., Emmy Award, 1998). *Movies:* Honeymoon With a Stranger, The Mask of Sheba, The Judge and Jake Wyler, Death Race, Death Scream, The New Original Wonder Woman (pilot), Code Name: Diamond Head, Happily Ever After, The Power Within, The Aliens Are Coming, The Case of the Wicked Wives. *Mini-series:* Jackie Collins' Lucky Chances.

BRAGA, SONIA
Actress. b. Maringa, Parana, Brazil, June 8, 1950. Began act-ing at 14 on live children's program on Brazilian TV, Gardin Encantado. Stage debut at 17 in Moliere's Jorge Dandin, then in Hair! Starred in many Brazilian soap operas including Gabriella, as well as a prod. of Sesame Street in Sao Paulo.
PICTURES: The Main Road, A Moreninha, Captain Bandeira Vs. Dr. Moura Brasil, Mestica, The Indomitable Slave, The Couple, Dona Flor and Her Two Husbands, Gabriella, I Love You, A Lady in the Bus, Kiss of the Spider Woman, The Milagro Beanfield War, Moon Over Parador, The Rookie, Roosters, Two Deaths, Tieta do Agreste (also co-prod.), Memorias Postumas, In the Shadow of Hollywood, Perfume, Angel Eyes, Empire, Constellation.
TELEVISION: *Movies:* The Man Who Broke 1000 Chains, The Last Prostitute, The Burning Season, Money Plays, Streets of Laredo, A Will of Their Own, The Judge. *Series:* Four Corners, Forca de Um Desejo, American Family. *Guest:* The Cosby Show, Tales From the Crypt, Family Law, Sex and the City.

BRANAGH, KENNETH
Actor, Director, Producer, Author. b. Belfast, Northern Ireland, Dec. 10, 1960. Moved to Reading, England at age 9. e. RADA. Went from drama school into West End hit Another Country, fol-lowed by Gamblers, The Madness, Francis. Royal Shakespeare Co.: Love Labors Lost, Hamlet, Henry V. Left Royal Shakespeare Company to form his own Renaissance Theater Co. with actor David Parfitt for which he wrote a play Public Enemy (also pro-duced Off-B'way), wrote-directed Tell Me Honestly, directed Twelfth Night, produced-directed-starred in Romeo & Juliet, and played Hamlet, Benedick and Touchstone in a sold-out nationwide tour and London season. L.A.: King Lear, A Midsummer Night's Dream. Author: Beginning (1990). Received BAFTA's Michael Balcon Award for Outstanding Contribution to Cinema (1993). Made short film Swan Song (Acad. Award nom.).
PICTURES: High Season (debut, 1987), A Month in the Country, Henry V (also dir., adapt.; BAFTA & Natl. Board of Review Awards for Best Dir., 1989), Dead Again (also dir.), Peter's Friends (also dir., prod.), Swing Kids, Much Ado About Nothing (also dir., adapt.), Mary Shelley's Frankenstein (also dir., co-prod.), In the Bleak Mid-Winter (dir., s.p. only), Anne Frank Remembered (nar-rator), Othello, Looking for Richard, Hamlet (also dir., prod.), The Theory of Flight, Celebrity, The Gingerbread Man, The Proposition, The Dance of Shiva, Love's Labour's Lost (also, dir., s.p.),The Betty Schimmel Story (dir. only), Wild Wild West, Galapagos: The Enchanted Voyage (voice), Love's LaEdurls Lost, The Road to El Dorado (voice), How to Kill Your Neighbor's Dog, Alien Love Triangle, Rabbit Proof Fence, Harry Potter and the Chamber of Secrets.
TELEVISION: *Movies:* The Billy Plays, Maybury, To the Lighthouse, Ghosts, Strange Interlude, Look Back in Anger, Conspiracy, Shackleton. *Mini-series:* The Lady's Not For Burning, Fortunes of War. *Specials:* Cold War (voice), Great Composers (narr.), Walking with Dinosaurs (narr.), Galapagos: The Enchanted Voyage (narr.), Lon Chaney: A Thousand Faces (narr.), *Series:* Thompson.

BRANDAUER, KLAUS MARIA
Actor, Director. r.n. Klaus Maria Steng. b. Bad Ausse, Steiermark, Austria, June 22, 1944. m. film and TV dir-screen-writer Karin Mueller. e. Acad. of Music and Dramatic Arts, Stuttgart, W. Germany. Was established in the German and Austrian theatre before film debut.
PICTURES: The Salzburg Connection (debut, 1972), Mephisto (Cannes Film Fest. Award, 1981), Never Say Never Again, Colonel Redl, Out of Africa, The Lightship, Streets of Gold, Burning Secret, Hanussen, Hitlerjunge Salomon, Das Spinnennetz (The Spider's Web) The French Revolution, The Russia House, White Fang, The Resurrected, Seven Minutes

(also dir.), Becoming Colette, Felidae (voice), Marco and the Magician (also dir.), Die Wand (dir. only), Rembrandt, Klaus Maria Brandauer: Speer in London, Dykaren, Belief Hope and Blood, Druids, Everyman's Feast, Between Strangers, Daddy.
TELEVISION: Quo Vadis?, Jeremiah, Introducing Dorothy Dandridge, Cyrano von Bergerac, Perlasca un eroe italiano.

BRANDIS, BERNARDINE
Executive. e. B.A., (magna cum laude) UCLA, 1975. J.D., UCLA, 1978. Began career as private practice attorney. senior dist & mktg./prod. counsel, 20th Century Fox Film Corp.; dir., business affairs, Universal Pictures, 1983-85; v.p., business affairs, Walt Disney Pictures, 1985-89; senior v.p., business and legal affairs, Hollywood Pictures, 1989-present. Currently exec. v.p., business affiars, The Walt Disney Motion Pictures Group, overseeing all aspects of business and legal affairs for the motion pictures division, studio administration, and theme park film productions.

BRANDIS, JONATHAN
Actor. b. Danbury, CT, April 13, 1976. Started as print model at age 4; followed by several tv commercials.
PICTURES: Fatal Attraction, Stepfather 2, Never Ending Story II: The Next Chapter, Ladybugs, Sidekicks, Ride with the Devil, Outside Providence, Ride With the Devil, A Fate Totally Worse than Death, Hart's War, The Year that Trembled, Puerto Vallarta Squeeze.
TELEVISION: Movies: Poor Little Rich Girl, Stephen King's IT, SeaQuest DSV, Good King Wenceslas, Born Free: A New Adventure, Her Last Chance, Fall Into Darkness, Two Came Back, 111 Gramercy Park. Guest: Murder, She Wrote, L.A. Law, The Wonder Years, Alien Nation, The Flash, Saved by the Bell: The College Years. Series: SeaQuest DSV, Aladdin (voice).

BRANDO, MARLON
Actor. b. Omaha, NB, April 3, 1924. Sister is actress Jocelyn Brando. e. Shattuck Military Acad., Faribault, MN. Studied acting at New School's Dramatic Workshop, NY, with Stella Adler; played stock in Sayville, Long Island. Broadway debut: I Remember Mama, followed by Truckline Cafe, Candida, A Flag Is Born, A Streetcar Named Desire. Voted one of top ten Money-Making Stars, M.P. Herald-Fame poll, 1954-55. Autobiography: Brando: Songs My Mother Taught Me (1994).
PICTURES: The Men (debut, 1950), A Streetcar Named Desire, Viva Zapata!, Julius Caesar, The Wild One, On the Waterfront (Academy Award, 1954), Desiree, Guys and Dolls, The Teahouse of the August Moon, Sayonara, The Young Lions, The Fugitive Kind, One-Eyed Jacks (also dir.), Mutiny on the Bounty, The Ugly American, Bedtime Story, The Saboteur—Code Name: Morituri, The Chase, The Appaloosa, A Countess From Hong Kong, Reflections in a Golden Eye, Candy, The Night of the Following Day, Burn!, The Nightcomers, The Godfather (Academy Award, 1972), Last Tango in Paris, The Missouri Breaks, Superman, Apocalypse Now, The Formula, A Dry White Season, The Freshman, Christopher Columbus: The Discovery, Don Juan DeMarco, Divine Rapture, The Island of Dr. Moreau, The Brave, Free Money, The Score.
TELEVISION: Mini-Series: Roots: The Next Generations (Emmy Award, 1979). Movies: Larry and Vivien: The Oliviers in Love, The Huey P. Newton Story.

BRANDON, MICHAEL
Actor. r.n. Michael Feldman. b. Brooklyn, NY, April 20, 1945. e. AADA. Appeared on B'way in Does Tiger Wear a Necktie?
PICTURES: Lovers and Other Strangers, Jennifer on My Mind, Four Flies on Grey Velvet, Heavy Traffic (voice), FM, Promises in the Dark, A Change of Seasons, Rich and Famous, Deja Vu, The Contaminated Man.
TELEVISION: Movies: Appeared in 30+ tv movies, incl.: The Impatient Heart, The Strangers in 7A, The Third Girl From the Left, Hitchhike!, The Red Badge of Courage, Queen of the Stardust Ballroom, Cage Without a Key, James Dean, Scott Free, Red Alert, The Comedy Company, A Vacation in Hell, A Perfect Match, Between Two Brothers, The Seduction of Gina, Deadly Messages, Not in My Family, Moment of Truth: Murder or Memory?, The Apocalypse Watch, The Lost Battalion. Series: Emerald Point, Dempsey & Makepeace, Home Fires, Dinotopia.

BRANDT, RICHARD PAUL
Executive. b. New York, NY, Dec. 6, 1927. e. Yale U., BS, Phi Beta Kappa. Chmn. Trans Lux Corp.; chmn., Brandt Theatres; dir., Presidential Realty Corp.; chmn. emeritus & trustee, American Film Institute; trustee, American Theatre Wing; vice-chmn. & trustee, College of Santa Fe; board member for Taos Talking Pictures Festival.

BRAUGHER, ANDRE
Actor. b. Chicago, IL, July 1, 1962.
PICTURES: Glory, Striking Distance, Primal Fear, Get on the Bus, Thick as Thieves, City of Angels, All the Rage, Frequency, Duets, A Better Way to Die.
TELEVISION: Movies: Kojak: Fatal Flaw, Kojak: Ariana, Kojak: None So Blind, Murder in Mississippi, Somebody Has to Shoot the Picture, The Court-Martial of Jackie Robinson, Simple Justice, The Tuskegee Airmen, Passing Glory, Love Songs (also dir.), 10,000 Black Men Named George, A Soldier's Girl, Salem's Lot. Series: Kojak, Homicide: Life in the Street (Emmy Award, 1998), City of Angels, Gideon's Crossing, Hack. Guest: Law & Order, The Practice.

BRAUNSTEIN, GEORGE GREGORY
Producer. b. New York, NY, May 23, 1947. e. Culver Military Acad., U. of California, B.A., biology, chemistry, 1970. U. W.L.A. Law School, J.D. 1987. Father is Jacques Braunstein (Screen Televideo Prods. At War with the Army, Young Lions.).
PICTURES: Train Ride to Hollywood, Fade to Black, Surf II, And God Created Woman, Out Cold, Don't Tell Her It's Me, Red Scorpion 2, Uncle Sam.

BRAVERMAN, CHARLES
Director, Producer. b. Los Angeles, CA, March 3, 1944. e. Los Angeles City Coll., USC, B.A. m. Kendall Carly Browne, actress. Child actor, 1950-57. Two-time Emmy winner.
PICTURES:Hit and Run (prod./dir.), The Best of the Big Laff Off (dir.), Peanuts to the Presidency: The Jimmy Carter Campaign (prod., documentary), Rocky and Rolanda (documentary), Bottom of the Ninth (documentary).
TELEVISION: Movies: Dir: The Richard Lewis "I'm In Pain" Concert (also prod.), Prince of Bel Air, Brotherhood of Justice, Final Shot: The Hank Gathers Story, High School Boot Camp. Series: Dir: St. Elsewhere, Crazy Like A Fox, Shadow Chasers, The Wizard, The New Mike Hammer, Sledge Hammer!, Rags to Riches, The Making of Beatlemania (tv documentary), Freddy's Nightmares, Gabriel's Fire, Beverly Hills 90210 (9 episodes, 1991), Melrose Place, Hercules: The Legendary Journeys.

BRECHER, IRVING
Writer. b. New York, NY, Jan. 17, 1914. e. Roosevelt H.S. in Yonkers. Yonkers Herald reporter; network programs writer for Milton Berle, Willie Howard, Al Jolson, etc., m.p. writer since 1937. On B'way in Sweet Charity, 1942.
PICTURES: At the Circus, Go West, Du Barry Was a Lady, Shadow of the Thin Man, Best Foot Forward, Meet Me in St. Louis, Summer Holiday, Yolanda and the Thief, Life of Riley (also dir.), Somebody Loves Me (also dir.), Cry for Happy, Sail a Crooked Ship (also dir.), Bye Bye Birdie.
TELEVISION: The People's Choice, The Life of Riley.

BREGMAN, MARTIN
Producer, Writer. b. New York, NY, May 18, 1931. m. actress Cornelia Sharpe. e. Indiana U., NYU. Began career as business and personal mgr. to Barbra Streisand, Faye Dunaway, Candice Bergen, Al Pacino. Chairman NY Advisory Council for Motion Pictures, Radio and TV (co-founder, 1974).
PICTURES: Serpico, Dog Day Afternoon, The Next Man, The Seduction of Joe Tynan, Simon, The Four Seasons, Eddie Macon's Run, Venom, Scarface, Sweet Liberty, Real Men, A New Life, Sea of Love, Nesting, Betsy's Wedding, Whispers in the Dark, The Real McCoy, Carlito's Way, The Shadow, Gold Diggers: The Secret of Bear Mountain, Matilda (exec. prod.), Nothing to Lose, The Bone Collector, The Adventures of Pluto Nash, Carolina.
TELEVISION: S*H*E (movie), The Four Seasons (series).

BREMNER, EWEN
Actor. b. Edinburgh, Scotland, UK
PICTURES: The Gospel According to Vic, As You Like It, Naked, Royal Deceit, Judge Dredd, Ruffian Hearts, Dead London (short), The Name of this Film is Dogme95 (documentary), The Phoenix and the Magic Carpet, Trainspotting, Rhinoceros Hunting in Budapest, Mojo, The Life of Stuff, The Acid House, Julien Donkey-Boy, Paranoid, Snatch: Pigs and Diamonds, Pearl Harbor, Black Hawk Down, The Reckoning, Fancy Dancing, Skagerrak, The Rundown.
TELEVISION: -Movies: A Girl Named Scooner, Love Story (tv short), Deacon Brodie, Surrealissimo: The Trial of Salvador Dali. Mini-Series: The Secret World of Michael Fry. Guest: A Touch of Frost, Shooting Stars, Langt fra Las Vegas.

BRENNAN, EILEEN
Actress. b. Los Angeles, CA, Sept. 3, 1938. e. Georgetown U., American Acad. of Dramatic Arts, N.Y. Daughter of silent film actress Jean Manahan. Big break came with lead in off-Broadway musical, Little Mary Sunshine (Obie & Theatre World Awards, 1960).
THEATRE: The Miracle Worker (tour), Hello Dolly! (Broadway), and revivals of The King and I, Guys and Dolls, Camelot, Bells Are Ringing; also An Evening with Eileen Brennan, A Couple of White Chicks Sitting Around Talking.
PICTURES: Divorce American Style (debut, 1967), The Last Picture Show (BAFTA nom.), Scarecrow, The Sting, Daisy Miller, At Long Last Love, Hustle, Murder by Death, FM, The Cheap Detective, The Last of the Cowboys (The Great Smokey Roadblock), Private Benjamin (Acad. Award nom.), Pandemonium, The Funny Farm, Clue, Sticky Fingers, Rented Lips, The New Adventures of Pippi Longstocking, It Had to Be You, Stella, Texasville, White Palace, I Don't Buy Kisses Anymore, Reckless, Pants on Fire, Changing Habits, Boy's Life 2, The Last Great Ride, Moonglow, Jeepers Creepers, Dumb Luck, Comic Book Villains, The Hollow (2004).
TELEVISION: Movies: Appeared in more than 30 tv movies, incl.: Playmates, My Father's House, The Night That Panicked America, The Death of Richie, When She Was Bad..., My Old Man, When the Circus Came to Town, Incident at Crestridge, My Name Is Kate, Take Me Home Again, Freaky Friday, Trail of Tears, Toothless. Mini-Series: Black Beauty. Series: Rowan & Martin's Laugh-In, All That Glitters, 13 Queens Boulevard, A New Kind of Family, Private Benjamin (Emmy Award, 1981), Off the Rack, 7th Heaven (recurring guest role), Bonkers (voice) . Specials: Working, In Search of Dr. Seuss. Guest: Taxi, Magnum

P.I., Newhart, All in the Family, Murder She Wrote, Blossom, Mad About You, Veronica's Closet, ER, McMillian and Wife, Will & Grace. Lizzie McGuire.

BRENNEMAN, AMY
Actress. b. Glastonbury, Connecticut, June 22, 1964.
PICTURES: Bye Bye Love, Casper, Heat, Fear, Daylight, Nevada (also co-prod.), Lesser Prophets, Your Friends & Neighbors, The Suburbans, Things You Can Tell Just By Looking At Her, Off the Map.
TELEVISION: *Movies:* A.T.F., Mary Cassatt: An American Impressionist. *Series::* Middle Ages, NYPD Blue, Judging Amy (also exec. prod, writer/creator). *Guest:* Frasier, Murder She Wrote.

BREST, MARTIN
Director, Producer. b. Bronx, NY, Aug. 8, 1951. e. NYU Sch. of Film. m. prod. Lisa Weinstein. Made award-winning short subject, Hot Dogs for Gauguin (featuring Danny DeVito). Accepted into fellowship program at American Film Institute, making first feature, Hot Tomorrows (dir., prod., s.p.), as AFI project. Appeared in Fast Times at Ridgemont High, Spies Like Us. Produced film: Josh and S.A.M.
PICTURES: Hot Tomorrows (appearing in Style (also s.p.), Beverly Hills Cop, Midnight Run (also prod.), Scent of a Woman (also prod.), Meet Joe Black (also prod.), Gigli (also prod., writer).

BRIALY, JEAN-CLAUDE
Actor. b. Aumale, Algeria, March 30, 1933. e. Strasbourg U. (philosophy) also attended drama classes at Strasbourg Conservatoire. Made several short films with Jacques Rivette and Jean-Luc Godard. Appeared in several French TV movies.
PICTURES: Has appeared in more than 140 pictures, incl.: Paris Does Strange Things, Elevator to the Gallows, Les Cousins, Three Faces of Sin, A Woman Is a Woman, Seven Capitol Sins, The Devil and Ten Commandments, Two Are Guilty, Nutty Naughty Chateau, Carless Love, Male Hunt, Circle of Love, King of Hearts, The Oldest Profession, Shock Troops, The Bride Wore Black, Claire's Knee, A Murder is a Murder, The Phantom of Liberty, Catherine et Cie, The Accuser, Les Violets Clos, Bobo Jacco, La Banquiere, La Nuit de Varennes, Cap Canaille, Le Demon Dan L'Isle, Edith and Marcel, Sarah, Stella, The Crime, Papy Fait de la Resistance, Pinot, Comedie d'été, My New Partner 2, No Fear-No Die, August, The Monster, Queen Margot, A French Woman, A Hundred and One Nights, Shadow Play, Beaumarchais the Scoundrel, The Unpredictable Nature of the River, Man of My Life, Kennedy and I, In Extremis, Unfair Competition, Special Delivery, Aimez-moi les uns les autres (2004).
TELEVISION: *Movies:* Has appeared in more than 20 tv movies, incl.: Lucas, Nos Jolies Colonies de Vacances, Elisabeth, Les Filles a Papa, Nana, On ne choisit pas sa famille (2001). *Mini-series:* Arsène Lupin joue et perd, Mozart, Quelques hommes de bonne volonté, Les Uns et les Autres, Die Schöne Wilhelmine, C'est quoi ce petit boulot?, Sandra princesse rebelle, The Count of Monte Cristo, The Blue Bicycle. *Series:* Ferbac.

BRICK, RICHARD A.
Producer. b. New York, NY, Sept. 20, 1945. e. New York University, B.A.; Columbia University, M.F.A. Chair, Columbia Univ., graduate film division, School of the Arts, 1992-94; Comm. of New York City Mayor's Office of Film, Theatre and Broadcasting, 1992-1994. Presently, ADJ Prof., Columbia Univ.; Board of Dir. for the Independent Feature Project, 1985-2001; chair 1995-96. Chairman/Founder Advisory Board for the Geri Ashur Screenwriting Award of the New York Foundation for the Arts, 1985-present. Member DGA 1981-present, Eastern AD/UPM/TC Council 2002-2004; Delegate to annual convention in 2003. PGA 1998-present. President, Silo Cinema, Inc., 1970-present.
PICTURES: Ragtime (unit mgr.), Part of the Family (prod. mgr), Andrea Doria: The Final Chapter (UPM, assoc. prod.), The Trials of Alger Hiss (UPM, assoc. prod.), Pilgrim...Farewell (prod. mgr.), Little Gloria...Happy at Last (unit prod. mgr.), Silkwood (unit. prod. mgr.), Places in the Heart (unit prod. mgr.), Arizona Dream (co-prod.), Deconstructing Harry (co-prod.), Celebrity (co-prod.), Sweet and Lowdown (co-prod., UPM), Hangin' with the Homeboys (prod.), Caught (prod.).

BRICKMAN, MARSHALL
Writer, Director. b. Rio de Janeiro, Brazil, Aug. 25, 1941. e. U. of Wisconsin. Banjoist, singer, writer with folk groups The Tarriers and The Journeymen before starting to write for TV. Appeared in films Funny and That's Adequate.
PICTURES: *Co-writer* (with Woody Allen): Sleeper, Annie Hall (Acad. Award, 1977), Manhattan, Manhattan Murder Mystery. *Dir./Writer:* Simon (dir. debut, 1980), Lovesick, The Manhattan Project (also prod.). *Co-Writer:* For the Boys, Intersection.
TELEVISION: *Writer:* Candid Camera 1966, The Tonight Show 1966-70. *Specials:* Johnny Carson's Repertory Co. in an Evening of Comedy (1969), Woody Allen Special, Woody Allen Looks at 1967. *Prod.:* Dick Cavett Show (1970-72, Emmy Award).

BRICKMAN, PAUL
Writer, Director. b. Chicago, IL, April 23, 1949. e. Claremont Men's Coll. Worked as camera asst., then story analyst at Paramount, Columbia, and Universal.
PICTURES: Handle With Care (assoc. prod., s.p.), The Bad News Bears in Breaking Training (s.p.), Risky Business, Deal of the Century (also co-exec. prod.), Men Don't Leave (co-s.p.

only), True Crime (s.p.).
TELEVISION: *Movie:* Uprising (writer).

BRIDGES, ALAN
Director. b. England, Sept. 28, 1927. Started dir. for the BBC before moving into feature films.
PICTURES: An Act of Murder (debut, 1965), Invasion, Shelley, The Hireling, Out of Season, Summer Rain, Age of Innocence, Little Girl in Blue Velvet (also writer), The Return of the Soldier, The Shooting Party, Fire Princess, Secret Places of the Heart.
TELEVISION: Movies: Miss Julie, The Lie, The Wild Duck, Brief Encounter, Saturday-Sunday-Monday, Rain on the Roof, Pudd'nhead Wilson, Displaced Person. Series: Out of the Unknown, Great Expectations.

BRIDGES, BEAU
Actor, Director, Producer. r.n. Lloyd Vernet Bridges III. b. Hollywood, CA, Dec. 9, 1941. e. UCLA; U. of Hawaii. Father was late actor Lloyd Bridges; brother is actor Jeff Bridges.
PICTURES: Has appreared in more than 45 pictures, incl.: Force of Evil (debut, 1948), No Minor Vices, The Red Pony, Zamba, The Explosive Generation, Village of the Giants, The Incident, For Love of Ivy, Gaily Gaily, The Landlord, Adam's Woman, The Christian Licorice Store, Hammersmith Is Out, Child's Play, Your Three Minutes Are Up, Lovin' Molly, The Other Side of the Mountain, Dragonfly (One Summer Love), Swashbuckler, Two-Minute Warning, Greased Lightning, Norma Rae, The Fifth Musketeer, The Runner Stumbles, Silver Dream Racer, Honky Tonk Freeway, Night Crossing, Love Child, Heart Like a Wheel, The Hotel New Hampshire, The Killing Time, The Wild Pair (also dir.), Seven Hours to Judgment (also dir.), The Iron Triangle, Signs of Life, The Fabulous Baker Boys, The Wizard, Daddy's Dyin'...Who's Got the Will?, Married to It, Sidekicks, Jerry Maguire, Rocket Man, Meeting Daddy, The White River Kid, Sordid Lives.
TELEVISION: *Movies:* Has appeared in more than 50 tv movies, incl.: The Man Without a Country, The Stranger Who Looks Like Me, Medical Story, The Four Feathers, Shimmering Light, The President's Mistress, The Child Stealer, The Kid from Nowhere (also dir.), Outrage!, Fighting Choice, The Thanksgiving Promise (also dir., co-prod.), Everybody's Baby: The Rescue of Jessica McClure, Just Another Secret, Guess Who's Coming for Christmas?, Without Warning: The James Brady Story (Emmy Award, 1992), Wildflower, Elvis and the Colonel, The Positively True Adventures of the Alleged Texas Cheerleader-Murdering Mom (Emmy Award, 1993), Secret Sins of the Fathers (also dir.), Kissinger and Nixon, Losing Chase, The Defenders: Choice of Evils, The Defenders: Taking the First, Inherit the Wind, Common Ground, Songs in Ordinary Time, The Christmas Secret, Sightings: Heartland Ghost, We Were the Mulvaneys, Change of Heart. *Series:* Ensign O'Toole, United States, Harts of the West, Maximum Bob, The Agency. *Mini-series:* Benjamin Franklin, Space, The Second Civil War (Emmy Award, 1997), P.T. Barnum, Voyage of the Unicorn. *Guest:* Sea Hunt, Ben Casey, Dr. Kildare, Mr. Novak, Combat, Eleventh Hour, Cimarron Strip, Amazing Stories, The Outer Limits, Will & Grace, The District.

BRIDGES, JEFF
Actor, Producer. b. Los Angeles, CA, Dec. 4, 1949. Appeared as infant in 1950 film The Company She Keeps. Made acting debut at eight in the TV series Sea Hunt starring his father, Lloyd Bridges. Studied acting at Herbert Berghof Studio, NY. Mil. service in Coast Guard reserves. Brother is actor-dir-prod. Beau Bridges. Composed and performed song for film John and Mary. Named Male Star of the Year (1990) by NATO.
PICTURES: Halls of Anger (debut, 1970), The Yin and Yang of Mr. Go, The Last Picture Show (Acad. Award nom.), Fat City, Bad Company, The Iceman Cometh, The Last American Hero, Lolly-Madonna XXX, Thunderbolt and Lightfoot (Acad. Award nom.), Hearts of the West, Rancho Deluxe, Stay Hungry, King Kong, Somebody Killed Her Husband, The American Success Company, Winter Kills, Heaven's Gate, Cutter's Way, Tron, Kiss Me Goodbye, Against All Odds, Starman (Acad. Award nom.), Jagged Edge, 8 Million Ways to Die, The Morning After, Nadine, Tucker: The Man and His Dream, See You in the Morning, Cold Feet, The Fabulous Baker Boys, Texasville, The Fisher King, The Vanishing, American Heart (also co-prod.), Fearless, Blown Away, Wild Bill, White Squall, The Mirror Has Two Faces, The Big Lebowski, Arlington Road, A Soldier's Daughter Never Cries, The Muse, Simpatico, The Contender, K-PAX, Scenes of the Crime, Masked & Anonymous, Seabiscuit, The Door in the Floor.
TELEVISION: *Movies:* Silent Night-Lonely Night, In Search of America, Hidden in America, Raising the Mammoth (narrator, tv documentary). *Special:* Faerie Tale Theatre (Rapunzel). *Guest:* Sea Hunt, Lloyd Bridges Show, The F.B.I., Parkinson (as himself, 2002).

BRIGHT, KEVIN
Producer, Director.
TELEVISION: *Movie:* Couples (exec. prod.). *Series:* Dream On (prod. only), Friends (exec. prod., dir.), Veronica's Closet (exec. prod., dir.), Jesse (exec. prod., dir.). *Special:* Young Comedians All-Star Reunion (prod.). *Guest:* Friends (acting).

BRIGHT, RICHARD
Actor. b. Brooklyn, NY, June 28, 1937. e. trained for stage with Frank Corsaro, John Lehne and Paul Mann.
THEATRE: The Balcony (1959), The Beard, The Salvation of St. Joan, Gogol, The Basic Training of Pavlo Hummel, Richard III, Kid Twist, Short Eyes as well as regional theatre.

PICTURES: Odds Against Tomorrow, Lion's Love, Panic in Needle Park, The Getaway, Pat Garrett and Billy the Kid, The Godfather, The Godfather II, Rancho Deluxe, Marathon Man, Citizens Band, Looking For Mr. Goodbar, On the Yard, Hair, The Idolmaker, Vigilante, Two of a Kind, Once Upon a Time in America, Crackers, Crimewave, Cut and Run, Brighton Beach Memoirs, 52-Pick-up, Time Out, Red Head, The Godfather III, Who's the Man, The Ref, Sweet Nothing, Ripper, Jaded, Beautiful Girls, Night Falls of Manhattan, OK Garage, Anima, Joe the King, The Photographer, Getting to Know You, Broke Even, Trigger Happy.
TELEVISION: Movies: A Death of Innocence, The Connection, The Gun, Cops and Robin, Sizzle, Brass, There Must Be A Pony, Penalty Phase, Witness to the Mob. Mini-series: From Here to Eternity, Series: Somerset. Guest: Skag, Hill Street Blues, Houston Knights, Third Watch, The Sopranos, Law & Order.

BRIGHT, RICHARD S.
Executive. b. New Rochelle, NY, Feb. 28, 1936. e. Hotchkiss Sch., 1953-54; Wharton Sch. of Finance, U. of Pennsylvania, 1954-58. With U.S. Army Finance Corp., 1959-60. Was corporate exec. prior to founding Persky-Bright Organization in 1973, private investment group to finance films.
THEATRE: A History of the American Film, Album (co-prod.).
PICTURES: Last Detail, Golden Voyage of Sinbad, For Pete's Sake, California Split, The Man Who Would Be King, Funny Lady, The Front, and Equus. Financing/production services for: Hard Times, Taxi Driver, Missouri Breaks, Bound for Glory, Sinbad and the Eye of the Tiger, Hair, Body Heat, Still of the Night. Exec. prod.: Tribute.
TELEVISION: The President's Mistress (co-prod.).

BRILLSTEIN, BERNIE
Producer, Talent Manager. b. New York, NY, April 26, 1931. e. NYU, B.S. advertising. Manager whose clients have incl. Lorne Michaels, John Belushi, Jim Henson and the Muppets. Chairman and chief exec. officer, Lorimar Film Entertainment. Founder, chmn., pres., The Brillstein Company. Former co-partner of Brillstein-Grey Entertainment and Brillstein-Grey Communications.
PICTURES: Exec. Prod.: The Blues Brothers, Up the Academy, Continental Divide, Neighbors, Doctor Detroit, Ghostbusters, Spies Like Us, Summer Rental, Armed and Dangerous, Dragnet, Ghostbusters II, Hexed, The Celluloid Closet (documentary), Cat and Mouse, Happy Gilmore, The Cable Guy, Bulletproof, Dirty Work, The Replacement Killers, What Planet Are You From? Run Ronnie Run!, La La Wood (prod.).
TELEVISION: Movies: Don't Try This At Home (exec. prod.) Series: Exec. prod.: Burns and Schreiber Comedy Hour, ALF, The Real Ghostbusters (exec. consultant), It's Garry Shandling's Show, The Days and Nights of Molly Dodd, The "Slap" Maxwell Show, The Boys (pilot), The Larry Sanders Show, Newsradio, Def Comedy Jam—Prime Time, Hightower 411, The Naked Truth, The Steve Harvey Show, Mr. Show, Just Shoot Me, The Martin Short Show, Primetime Glick, The Wayne Brady Show.

BRIMLEY, WILFORD
Actor. b. Salt Lake City, UT, Sept. 27, 1934. Formerly a blacksmith, ranch hand and racehorse trainer; began in films as an extra and stuntman. Also acted as A. Wilford Brimley. Original member of L.A. Actors Theatre.
PICTURES: True Grit, Lawman, The China Syndrome, The Electric Horseman, Brubaker, Borderline, Absence of Malice, Death Valley, The Thing, Tender Mercies, Tough Enough, High Road to China, 10 to Midnight, Hotel New Hampshire, Harry and Son, The Stone Boy, The Natural, Country, Cocoon, Remo Williams: The Adventure Begins, American Justice, End of the Line, Cocoon: The Return, Eternity, The Firm, Hard Target, Last of the Dogmen, My Fellow Americans, In & Out, Summer of the Monkeys, All My Friends are Cowboys, Progeny, Comanche, Brigham City, The Hound and Round, The Road Home.
TELEVISION: Movies: The Oregon Trail, The Wild Wild West Revisited, Amber Waves, Roughnecks, Rodeo Girl, The Big Black Pill, Ewoks: The Battle for Endor, Murder in Space, Thompson's Last Run, Act of Vengeance, Gore Vidal's Billy the Kid, Blood River, Tom Clancy's Op Center, Crossfire Trail, The Ballad of Lucy Whipple. Series: Our House, Boys of Twilight. Guest: The Waltons, Homicide: Life on the Street, Seinfeld.

BRINKLEY, DAVID
TV news correspondent. b. Wilmington, NC, July 10, 1920. e. U. of North Carolina; Vanderbilt U. Started writing for hometown newspaper. Joined United Press before entering Army, WWII. After discharge in 1943, joined NBC News in Washington as White House corr. In 1956, first teamed with the late Chet Huntley to cover political conventions for NBC and then appeared together for years in "The Huntley-Brinkley Report" on NBC Nightly News. Then began David Brinkley's Journal. Moved to ABC in 1981 to host "This Week with David Brinkley," the top Sunday public affairs program for many years. Brinkley won 10 Emmys, three George Foster Peabody Awards and the Presidential Medal of Freedom, the nation's highest civilian honor.
(d. June 11, 2003)

BRITTANY, MORGAN
Actress. r.n. Suzanne Cupito. b. Hollywood, CA, Dec. 5, 1951.
PICTURES: Gypsy, The Birds, Marnie, Yours Mine and Ours, Gable and Lombard, Sundown: The Vampire in Retreat, The Prodigal, Last Action Hero, The Saint, Riders in the Storm, The Protector,

Legend of the Spirit Dog, The Chocolate Fairy, The Biggest Fan.
TELEVISION: Movies: Amazing Howard Hughes, Delta County U.S.A., The Initiation of Sarah, Samurai, Fantastic Seven, Death Car on the Freeway, The Dream Merchants, Moviola: The Scarlett O'Hara War, The Wild Women of Chastity Gulch, LBJ: The Early Years, Perry Mason: The Case of the Scandalous Scoundrel, Favorite Deadly Sins. Series: Dallas, Glitter. Guest: B. L. Stryker, L.A. Law, Buck Rogers in the 25th Century, The Nanny, Melrose Place, Sabrina the Teenage Witch, Son of the Beach.

BROADBENT, JIM
Actor, Writer. b. Lincolnshire, England, May 24, 1949. Member of the National Theatre and the Royal Shakespeare Company. Wrote and starred in short film, A Sense of History (Clermont-Ferrand Intl. Film Fest. Award).
THEATRE: The Recruiting Officer, A Winter's Tale, The Government Inspector, A Flea in Her Ear, Goose Pimples.
PICTURES: The Shout (debut, 1978), The Passage, Breaking Glass, The Dogs of War, Time Bandits, Brazil, The Good Father, Superman IV: The Quest for Peace, Life Is Sweet, Enchanted April, The Crying Game, Widow's Peak, Princess Caraboo, Bullets Over Broadway, Rough Magic, The Secret Agent, Richard III, The Borrowers, Little Voice, The Avengers, Topsy Turvey, Bridget Jones's Diary, Moulin Rouge (BAFTA Award for best actor/supp. role, 2002), Iris (Acad. Award/Golden Globe, best actor/supp. role, 2002), Gangs of New York, Nicholas Nickleby, Bright Young Things, Around the World in 80 Days, Tooth (voice).
TELEVISION: Movies: Bird of Prey, Birth Of A Nation, Silas Marner: The Weaver of Raveloe, Blackadder's Christmas Carol, Work!, Wide-Eyed and Legless, The Last Englishman, The Gathering Storm. Series: Only Fools and Horses, Gone to Seed, The Boss. Guest: Victoria Wood Show, Inspector Morse, The Comic Strip Presents.

BROADHEAD, PAUL E.
Executive. e. Univ. of MS. Founder of Paul Broadhead & Assocs. real estate development. 1984, sold his interests in that company. Became chmn. of bd. of Theatre Properties, Cinemark USA.

BROCKMAN, MICHAEL
Executive. b. Brooklyn, NY, Nov. 19, 1938. e. Ithaca Coll. Became v.p., daytime programming, ABC Entertainment, 1974; later v.p., tape prod. operations and admin. Left to become v.p., daytime programs, NBC Entertainment, 1977-1980. Became v.p. programs, Lorimar Prods. 1980-82; v.p. daytime and children's prog. CBS Entertainment, 1982-89. 1986, title changed to v.p. daytime, children's and late night. Became pres. ABC daytime, children's & late night entertainment 1989-90. Joined Mark Goodson Prods. as v.p. 1991. Became sr. v.p. in 1993. Pres., M. Brockman Broadcast Inc., 1995-Present. Appointed by Ca. gov. to the Ca. Lottery Commission in 2001, with term expiring Nov. 2003. He is a member of the National Academy of Television Arts and Sciences and the Pacific Pioneer Broadcasters.

BRODERICK, MATTHEW
Actor, Producer, Director. b. New York, NY, Mar. 21, 1962. Son of late actor James Broderick and writer-dir./artist Patricia Broderick. m. actress Sarah Jesicah Parker. Acted in a workshop prod. of Horton Foote's Valentine's Day with his father (1979).
THEATRE: NY: Torch Song Trilogy, Brighton Beach Memoirs (Tony & Theatre World Awards, 1983), Biloxi Blues, The Widow Claire, How to Succeed in Business Without Really Trying (Tony Award, 1995), The Producers.
PICTURES: Max Dugan Returns (debut, 1983), WarGames, Ladyhawke, 1918, On Valentine's Day, Ferris Bueller's Day Off, Project X, Biloxi Blues, Torch Song Trilogy, Glory, Family Business, The Freshman, Out on a Limb, The Night We Never Met, The Lion King (voice), The Road to Wellville, Mrs. Parker and the Vicious Circle, Infinity (also dir., co-prod.), The Cable Guy, Infinity (also dir., prod.), Addicted to Love, Lion King II: Simba's Pride (voice), Godzilla, Election, Inspector Gadget, Walking to the Waterline, You Can Count On Me, Good Boy!, Providence.
TELEVISION: Movies: Master Harold... and the Boys, A Life in the Theater, The Music Man, Shelley Duvall's Faerie Tale Theatre: Cinderella. Guest: Lou Grant, Frasier. Mini-series: Jazz (voice).

BRODSKY, JACK
Producer. b. Brooklyn, NY, July 3, 1932. e. George Washington H.S. Writer for N.Y. Times. Joined 20th-Fox publicity in N.Y. in 1956. Left in 1961 to head national ad-pub for Filmays. Joined Rastar Productions to work on Funny Girl; later named v.p. in charge of prod. In 1976 named v.p. in chg. film prod. prom., Rogers & Cowan; 1978, Columbia Pictures v.p. of adv., pub., promo.; 1979, named exec. v.p. of Michael Douglas' Big Stick Productions; 1983 joined 20th-Fox as exec. v.p., worldwide adv., pub., exploit. Resigned 1985 to resume career as prod.
PICTURES: Harry & Walter Go to New York (actor only), Two Minute Warning (actor only), Little Murders, Everything You Always Wanted To Know About Sex But Were Afraid to Ask (exec. prod.), Summer Wishes Winter Dreams, The Jewel of the Nile, Dancers (co-exec. prod., actor), King Ralph, Scenes From a Mall (actor), Rookie of the Year (co-exec. prod.), Black Knight, Daddy Day Care (co-prod.).
AUTHOR: The Cleopatra Papers, with Nat Weiss.
(d. Feb. 17, 2003)

BRODY, ADRIEN
Actor. b. New York, NY, April 14, 1973 e. American Academy of Dramatic Arts and High School for the Performing Arts.
PICTURES: New York Stories, King of the Hill, Angels in the Outfield, Solo, Bullet, The Last Time I Committed Suicide, The Undertaker's Wedding, Six Ways to Sunday, Restaurant, The Thin Red Line, Summer of Sam, Oxygen, Liberty Heights, Bread and Roses, Harrison's Flowers, Love the Hard Way, The Affair of the Necklace, Dummy, The Pianist (Acad. Award, best actor/leading role, 2003), The Singing Detective.
TELEVISION: Movies: Home at Last, Jailbreakers. Series: Annie McGuire.

BROKAW, CARY
Executive, Producer. b. Los Angeles, CA, June 21, 1951. e. Univ. of CA/Berkeley, UCLA Grad. Sch. Worked at several positions at 20th Century Fox before serving as exec. v.p. for Cineplex Odeon Corp. 1983 became co-chmn., pres. of Island Alive; 1985, became co-chmn., pres. & CEO of Island Pictures. 1987, formed Avenue Pictures; In 1991, he founded Avenue Entertainment Group, which includes Avenue Pictures, an independent motion picture prod. company, Avenue Pictures Television, a producer of made-for-tv movies, mini-series and movies for cable tv, and Wombat Productions, a producer of Hollywood Star profile programs. Brokaw currently is chairman of Avenue Pictures.
PICTURES: Executive Producer: Trouble in Mind, Down by Law, Nobody's Fool, Slamdance, Pascali's Island, Signs of Life, Cold Feet, Drugstore Cowboy, After Dark My Sweet, The Object of Beauty, Sex Drugs Rock & Roll, The Player, American Heart, Stained Glass, Normal. Producer: Short Cuts, Restoration, Voices From a Locked Room, Finding Graceland, Stand by Your Man, Wayward Son, Mindhunters.
TELEVISION: Movies: In the Eyes of a Stranger, Amelia Earhart: The Final Flight, See Jane Run, Stranger in Town, Two Mothers for Zachary. Tell Me No Secrets, The Almost Perfect Bank Robbery, Path to Paradise: Untold Story of the WTC Bombing, Thrill Seekers, Wit, Path to War. Mini-series: Angels in America.

BROKAW, NORMAN R.
Executive. b. New York, NY, April 21, 1927. Joined William Morris Agency as trainee in 1943; junior agent, 1948; sr. agent, company exec. in m.p. and TV, 1951; 1974, v.p., William Morris Agency, World Wide all areas. 1981, named exec. v.p. & mem. of bd., William Morris Agency, worldwide; 1986, named co-chmn. of bd., WMA, worldwide. 1989, named pres. & CEO, William Morris Inc. worldwide. 1991, named Chmn. of Board of CEO. Member Acad. of TV Arts & Sciences, AMPAS. Member bd. of dir. of Cedars-Sinai Medical Center, Los Angeles; pres., The Betty Ford Cancer Center.

BROKAW, TOM
TV Newsman, Anchorman, Host. b. Yankton, S.D., Feb. 6, 1940, e. U. of South Dakota. Newscaster, weatherman, staff announcer KTIV, Sioux City, IA, 1960-62. Joined KMTV, NBC affiliate in Omaha, in 1962; 1965, joined WSB-TV, Atlanta. Worked in L.A. bureau of NBC News, anchored local news shows for KNBC, NBC station (1966-73). In 1973 named NBC News' White House correspondent; was anchor of NBC Saturday Night News. Named host of Today Show in August, 1976. In 1982 co-anchor, NBC Nightly News; sole anchor since 1983. Anchor of "The Brokaw Report," a series of prime-time specials, 1992-1993. Co-anchor NBC newsmagazine series, "Now With Tom Brokaw & Katie Couric," 1993-94. Earned the Alfred I. DuPont-Columbia U. award for excellence in broadcast journalism for Dateline NBC Special Report examining racial separation in U.S. suburbs, 1997. Recipient of numerous awards, including seven Emmy awards; inducted into Broadcasting & Cable's TV Hall of Fame, 1997. Also an accomplished writer, his work has appeared in The New York Times, The Washington Post, The Los Angeles Times, Newsweek, Life, among others. Book Author: The Greatest Generation, The Greatest Generation Speaks.

BROLIN, JAMES
Actor, Producer, Director. b. Los Angeles, CA, July 18, 1940. r.n. James Bruderlin. e. UCLA. Son is actor Josh Brolin. m. Barbra Streisand. Debut in Bus Stop (TV series); named most promising actor of 1970 by Fame and Photoplay magazines. Winner, Emmy and Golden Globe Awards.
PICTURES: Take Her She's Mine (debut, 1963), John Goldfarb Please Come Home, Goodbye Charlie, Dear Brigitte, Von Ryan's Express, Morituri, Fantastic Voyage, Way ... Way Out, The Cape Town Affair, Our Man Flint, The Boston Strangler, Skyjacked, Westworld, Gable and Lombard, The Car, Capricorn One, The Amityville Horror, Night of the Juggler, High Risk, Pee-wee's Big Adventure, Bad Jim, Super High Score, Ted & Venus, Gas Food Lodging, Cheatin' Hearts (also exec. prod.), Back Stab, Savate, Relative Fear, Parallel Lives, Indecent Behavior, The Expert, Tracks of a Killer, Lewis and Clark and George, Blood Money, My Brother's War, Haunted Sea, Goodbye America, Lewis & Clark & George, My Brother's War (also dir.), Haunted Sea, Traffic, Master of Disguise, , Catch Me If You Can, A Guy Thing.
TELEVISION: Movies: Marcus Welby M.D., Short Walk to Daylight, Class of '63, Trapped, Steel Cowboys, The Ambush Murders, Mae West, White Water Rebels, Cowboy, Beverly Hills Cowgirl Blues, Hold the Dream, Intimate Encounters, Voice of

the Heart, Finish Line, Nightmare on the 13th Floor, And the Sea Will Tell, Deep Dark Secrets, The Sands of Time, Visions of Murder, Gunsmoke: The Long Ride, The Calling, Parallel Lives, A Perry Mason Mystery: The Case of the Grimacing Governor, Terminal Virus, A Marriage of Convenience, To Love Honor and Betray, Children of Fortune. Special: City Boy (PBS), Body Human 2000: Love Sex & the Miracle of Birth. Director: Hotel (12 episodes), The Young Riders, Hijacked: Flight 285, Pensacola Wings of Gold (also exec. prod.), Beyond Belief, Fact or Fiction. Series: Marcus Welby M.D. (Emmy Award, 1970), Hotel, Angel Falls, Extreme, World of Discovery, Pensacola: Wings of Gold (also dir., exec. prod.), Beyond Belief: Fact or Fiction (host). Guest: Roseanne, Batman, The West Wing.

BRON, ELEANOR
Actress, Writer. b. Stanmore, Middlesex, England, March 14, 1934. Started career in Establishment Club, London, and on American tour. Leading lady on British TV show Not So Much a Programme—More a Way of Life. Author of Double Take, The Pillowbook of Eleanor Bron, Life and Other Punctures. Translator of Desdemona—If You Had Only Spoken, by Christine Bruckner.
THEATRE: The Doctor's Dilemma, Howards End, The Prime of Miss Jean Brodie, Hedda Gabler, The Duchess of Malfi, The Madwoman of Chaillot, Uncle Vanya, A Delicate Balance, A Perfect Ganesh, The Cherry Orchard, A Month In the Country.
PICTURES: Help!, Alfie, Two for the Road, Bedazzled, The Turtle Diary, Thank You All Very Much, Women in Love, The Millstone, Little Dorrit, Black Beauty, A Little Princess, Saint-Ex, Deadly Advice, Black Beauty, A Little Princess, Saint-Ex, The House of Mirth, Iris, The Heart of Me.
TELEVISION: Movies: The Day Christ Died, The Attic: The Hiding of Anne Frank, Intrigue, Friends in Space, Micky Love, The Blue Boy. Series: Where Was Spring? (also co-wrote), Beyond A Joke (also writer), Fat Friends, Gypsy Girl, Ted and Alice. Guest: Rumpole of the Bailey, Yes Minister, Absolutely Fabulous.

BRONDFIELD, JEROME
Writer. b. Cleveland, OH, Dec. 9, 1913. e. Ohio State U., 1936. Reporter, ed. on Columbus Dispatch, Associated Press, story ed., script head, RKO Pathe, Oct., 1944; writer, dir. & supvr. of many doc. shorts incl. This Is America series; TV writer; short story writer; collab. s.p., Below the Sahara; s.p. Louisiana Territory; doc. film writer. Author: Woody Hayes, The 100-Yard War, Knute Rockne, The Man and the Legend. Sr. editor, Scholastic, Inc.

BRONFMAN, EDGAR, JR.
Executive. b. May 16, 1955.
Joined Seagram 1982 as asst. to office of the pres.; served as mng. dir. of Seagram Europe until he was appointed pres. of The House of Seagram, 1984-88; became pres. & COO in 1989. June 1994 named pres. & CEO of The Seagram Company Ltd. Upon acquisition of MCA Inc. was named acting chairman, 1995. Remained President & CEO of Seagram after the merger with Vivendi until he resigned in Dec., 2001 shortly before Vivendi Universal merged with USA TV. Bronfman is currently vice chairman of the board of Vivendi Universal; co-chmn. of A&G Group Limited (parent of Asprey and Garrard); a member of the boards of Fandango Inc., USA Interactive; Equitant Inc., NYU Medical Center; and on the bd. of governors of the Joseph H. Lauder Institute of Mgt and Int'l. Studies at the U. of Pa. Currently, is CEO of Lexa Partners, L.L.C., a privately held mgt. and venture capital group based in New York City.

BRONSON, CHARLES
Actor. r.n. Charles Buchinsky. b. Ehrenfeld, PA, Nov. 3, 1921. Worked as a coal miner. Served in Air Force (1943-46) as tail gunner on B29s in Pacific. Studied acting at Pasadena Playhouse. Started in films billed under real name. Guest in numerous TV shows in addition to those below.
PICTURES: You're in the Navy Now (debut, 1951), The People Against O'Hara, The Mob, Red Skies of Montana, My Six Convicts, The Marrying Kind, Pat and Mike, Diplomatic Courier, Bloodhounds of Broadway, House of Wax, The Clown, Miss Sadie Thompson, Crime Wave, Tennessee Champ, Riding Shotgun, Apache, Drum Beat (lst billing as Charles Bronson), Vera Cruz, Big House U.S.A., Target Zero, Jubal, Run of the Arrow, Machine Gun Kelly, Gang War, Showdown at Boot Hill, When Hell Broke Loose, Ten North Frederick, Never So Few, The Magnificent Seven, Master of the World, A Thunder of Drums, X-15, Kid Galahad, The Great Escape, Four for Texas, The Sandpiper, The Battle of the Bulge, This Property Is Condemned, The Dirty Dozen, Villa Rides, Guns for San Sebastian, Farewell Friend, Once Upon a Time in the West, Rider on the Rain, You Can't Win Em All, The Family, Cold Sweat, Twinky (Lola), Someone Behind the Door, Red Sun, Chato's Land, The Mechanic, The Valachi Papers, The Stone Killer, Chino, Mr. Majestyk, Death Wish, Breakout, Hard Times, Breakheart Pass, From Noon Till Three, St. Ives, The White Buffalo, Telefon, Love and Bullets, Caboblanco, Borderline, Death Hunt, Death Wish II, Ten to Midnight, The Evil That Men Do, Death Wish 3, Murphy's Law, Assassination, Death Wish 4: The Crackdown, Messenger of Death, Kinjite: Forbidden Subjects, The Indian Runner, Death Wish V: The Face of Death, Family of Cops II & III.
TELEVISION: Movies: Raid on Entebbe, Act of Vengeance, Yes Virginia There Is a Santa Claus, The Sea Wolf, Donato and Daughter, A Family of Cops. Series: Man With a Camera, Empire, Travels of Jamie McPheeters. Guest: Philco Playhouse (Adventure in Java), Medic, A Bell for Adano,

Gunsmoke, Have Gun Will Travel, Meet McGraw, The FBI, The Fugitive, The Virginian.
(d. Aug. 30, 2003)

BROOK, PETER
Director. b. London, England, March 21, 1925. e. Magdalen Coll., Oxford. To London 1943 to dir. his first play, Doctor Faustus; other stage incl. Man and Superman, Marat/Sade, A Midsummer Night's Dream, etc.
PICTURES: The Beggar's Opera (debut, 1953), Moderato Cantabile (also co-s.p.), Lord of the Flies (also s.p., edit), The Persecution and Assassination of Jean-Paul Marat as Performed by the Inmates of the Asylum of Charenton Under the Direction of the Marquis de Sade, Tell Me Lies (also prod.), King Lear (also s.p.), Meetings With Remarkable Men (also s.p.), The Tragedy of Carmen, Swann in Love (s.p. only).
TELEVISION: Movies: Don Giovanni (opera dir.). Mini-series: The Mahabharata (also writer).

BROOKS, ALBERT
Director, Writer, Actor. r.n. Albert Einstein. b. Los Angeles, CA, July 22, 1947. e. Carnegie Tech. Son of late comedian Harry Einstein (Parkyakarkus). Brother is performer Bob Einstein. Sports writer KMPC, L.A. 1962-63. Recordings: Comedy Minus One, A Star is Bought (Grammy nom.).
PICTURES: Taxi Driver, Real Life (also dir., co-s.p.), Private Benjamin, Modern Romance (also dir.; co-s.p.), Twilight Zone—The Movie, Terms of Endearment (voice), Unfaithfully Yours, Lost in America (also dir., co-s.p.), Broadcast News (Acad. Award nom.), Defending Your Life (also dir., s.p.), I'll Do Anything, The Scout (also co-s.p.), Mother (also dir.; NY Society of Film Critics Award, Natl Society of Film Critics Award for best s.p., 1997), Doctor Dolittle (voice), Out of Sight, The Muse, My First Mister (actor), Til Death Do Us Part, Finding Nemo (voice), The In-Laws.
TELEVISION: Series: Dean Martin Presents the Golddiggers, Saturday Night Live (writer, 1975), Hot Wheels (voices), The Associates (wrote theme song). Specials: Milton Berle's Mad Mad Mad World of Comedy, General Electric's All-Star Anniversary. Guest: Love American Style, The Odd Couple, Ed Sullivan Show, Tonight Show, The Simpsons (voice).

BROOKS, JAMES L.
Director, Producer, Writer. b. North Bergen, NJ, May 9, 1940. e. NYU. Copyboy for CBS News, N.Y.; promoted to newswriter. 1965 moved to L.A. to work for David Wolper's documentary prod. co. In 1969 conceived idea for series, Room 222; formed partnership with fellow writer Allan Burns. Together they created Mary Tyler Moore Show in 1970. 1977, established prod. co. on Paramount lot with other writers, producing and creating the series, The Associates and Taxi. Formed Gracie Films. Directed play Brooklyn Laundry in L.A.
PICTURES: Real Life (actor), Starting Over (s.p., co-prod.), Modern Romance (actor), Terms of Endearment (dir., prod., s.p.; Acad. Awards for Best Picture, Dir. and Screenplay, 1983), Broadcast News (dir., prod., s.p.), Big (co-prod.), Say Anything... (exec. prod.), The War of the Roses (co-prod.), I'll Do Anything (dir., prod., s.p.), Bottle Rocket, Jerry Maguire, As Good As It Gets (dir., s.p.), The Simpsons Movie (exec. prod.), Riding in Cars with Boys.
TELEVISION: Movie: Thursday's Game (writer, prod., 1971). Series: The Mary Tyler Moore Show (co-creator, writer, exec. prod.; 2 Emmy Awards for writing: 1971, 1977; 3 Emmy Awards as exec. prod.: 1975, 1976, 1977), Rhoda (writer, prod.), The New Lorenzo Music Show (writer), Lou Grant (co-exec. prod.). Series (co-creator, and/or exec. prod.): Taxi (3 Emmy Awards as exec. prod.: 1979, 1980, 1981), Cindy, The Associates, Cheers, Tracey Ullman Show (Emmy Award as exec. prod., 1989), The Simpsons (2 Emmy Awards as exec. prod.: 1990, 1991), Phenom (exec. prod.), The Critic (exec. prod.), What About Joan (exec. prod.).

BROOKS, JOSEPH
Producer, Director, Writer, Composer, Conductor. Well-known for composing music for TV commercials before turning to producing, directing, writing and scoring theatrical feature, You Light Up My Life, in 1977. Winner of 21 Clio Awards (advertising industry), Grammy, Golden Globe, People's Choice, Amer. Music Awards; created music for 100 commercials. Has also composed for theatrical films. Winner of Cannes Film Festival Advertising Award.
PICTURES: Scores: The Garden of the Finzi-Continis, Marjoe, Jeremy, The Lords of Flatbush. Prod.-Dir.-Writer-Composer: You Light Up My Life (Academy Award for Best Song: title song, 1977), If Ever I See You Again (also actor), Headin' for Broadway, Eddie and the Cruisers, Invitation to the Wedding (composer, prod., dir.)

BROOKS, MEL
Writer, Director, Actor. r.n. Melvin Kaminsky. b. Brooklyn, NY, June 28, 1926. m. actress Anne Bancroft. e. VA Military Inst. 1944. U.S. Army combat engineer 1944-46. As child, did impressions and was amateur drummer and pianist. First legitimate job as actor in play Separate Rooms in Red Bank, NJ. Was also social dir. of Grossinger's Resort in the Catskills. Became writer for Sid Caesar on TV's Broadway Review and Your Show of Shows. Teamed with Carl Reiner for comedy record albums: The 2000 Year Old Man, The 2000 and 13 Year Old Man. Founded Brooksfilms Ltd., 1981. Won Academy Award for Best Short

Subject (animated): The Critic (dir., s.p., narrator). Co-writer of Shinbone Alley.
THEATRE: Writer: New Faces of 1952 (sketches), Shinbone Alley (book), All-American (book), The Producers.
PICTURES: New Faces (co-s.p.), The Producers (dir., s.p.; Academy Award for Best Original Screenplay, 1968), The Twelve Chairs (dir., s.p., actor), Blazing Saddles (dir., co-s.p., actor), Young Frankenstein (dir., co-s.p.; Acad. Award nom. for s.p.), Silent Movie (dir., co-s.p., actor), Frances (exec.-prod), High Anxiety (dir., prod., co-s.p., actor), The Muppet Movie (actor), History of the World Part 1 (dir., prod., s.p., actor, lyrics), To Be or Not To Be (exec-prod., actor), Spaceballs (dir., prod., co-s.p., actor), , Look Who's Talking Too (voice), Life Stinks (dir., prod., co-s.p., actor), Robin Hood: Men in Tights (dir., prod., co-s.p., actor), The Silence of the Hams (actor), The Little Rascals (actor), Dracula: Dead and Loving It (dir., prod., co-s.p., actor), The Prince of Egypt (voice), Svitati (actor, s.p.), Screwloose. Exec. Prod.: The Elephant Man, My Favorite Year, The Doctor and the Devils, The Fly, 84 Charing Cross Road, Solarbabies, The Vagrant, The Fly II, Hail Sid Caesar.
TELEVISION: Specials: The Sid Caesar-Imogene Coca-Carl Reiner-Howard Morris Special (co-writer; Emmy Award, 1967), I am Your Child, Pretty As A Picture: The Art of David Lynch, Intimate Portrait: Madeline Kahn, AFI's 100 Years 100 Laughs: America's Funniest Movies. Series: Get Smart (co-creator, co-writer), When Things Were Rotten (co-creator, co- writer, prod.), The Nutt House (prod., co-writer) Get Smart (1995, writer/characters). Guest: Mad About You (Emmy Award, 1997), The Simpsons (voice), Frasier.

BROSNAN, PIERCE
Actor. b. Navan, County Meath, Ireland, May 16, 1953. Left County Meath, Ireland for London at 11. Worked as commercial illustrator, then joined experimental theater workshop and studied at the Drama Center. On London stage (Wait Until Dark, The Red Devil Battery Sign, Filumenia, etc.)
PICTURES: The Mirror Crack'd (debut, 1980), The Long Good Friday, Nomads, The Fourth Protocol, Taffin, The Deceivers, Mister Johnson, The Lawnmower Man, Entangled, Mrs. Doubtfire, Love Affair, Goldeneye, Mars Attacks, The Mirror Has Two Faces, Dante's Peak, Tomorrow Never Dies, Quest for Camelot (voice), The Nephew (also prod.), Grey Owl, The Thomas Crown Affair (also prod.), The World is Not Enough, Dolphins, The Tailor of Panama, Blood and Champagne, Die Another Day, Evelyn, (also prod.).
TELEVISION: Movies/Specials: The Heist, Murder 101, Victim of Love, Robin Hood: Myth-Man-Movie (narrator), Death Train, The Broken Chain, Don't Talk to Strangers, Night Watch. Mini-series: The Manions of America, Nancy Astor, Noble House, Around the World in 80 Days. Series: Remington Steele.

BROUGH, WALTER
Writer, Producer. b. Phila. PA, Dec. 19, 1935. e. La Salle U. (B.A.), USC (M.A.). Began career with Stage Society Theatre, LA. Currently CEO, Orb Enterprises, Inc.
PICTURES: Gabriella, A New Life, No Place to Hide, Run Wild Run Free, The Desperados, Funeral for an Assassin (also prod.), On a Dead Man's Chest (also prod.), Jed and Sonny (also prod.), Jamaican Gold.
TELEVISION: Series: Doctor Kildare, The Fugitive, Branded, Name of the Game, Mannix, Mission Impossible, The Magician, Man From Atlantis, Police Story, Wildside, Heart of the City (also prod.), Thunder Guys (pilot), Spencer for Hire (also co-prod.), Law & Harry McGraw, New Mission Impossible (also co-prod.), Over My Dead Body, Hunter, Tequila & Bonetti.

BROUGHTON, BRUCE
Composer. b. Los Angeles, CA , March 8, 1945. e. U. of Southern California, B.M., 1967. Music supvr., CBS-TV, 1967-77. Since then has been freelance composer for TV and films. Member of Academy of TV Arts & Sciences Society of Composers & Lyricists (past pres.), AMPAS (governor). Nominated 17 times for Emmy. Nominated for Grammy for Young Sherlock Holmes.
PICTURES: The Prodigal, The Ice Pirates, Silverado (Acad. Award nom.), Young Sherlock Holmes, Sweet Liberty, The Boy Who Could Fly, Square Dance, Harry and the Hendersons, Monster Squad, Big Shots, Cross My Heart, The Rescue, The Presidio, Last Rites, Moonwalker, Jacknife, Betsy's Wedding, Narrow Margin, The Rescuers Down Under, All I Want for Christmas, Honey I Blew Up the Kid, Stay Tuned, Homeward Bound: The Incredible Journey, So I Married an Axe Murderer, For Love or Money, Tombstone (and score prod.), Holy Matrimony, Baby's Day Out, Miracle on 34th Street, Infinity, Carried Away, House Arrest, Homeward Bound II: Lost in San Francisco, The Shadow Conspiracy, A Simple Wish, One Tough Cop, Krippendorf's Tribe, Lost in Space, Fantasia 2000 (conductor Rhapsody in Blue), Last Flight Out.
TELEVISION: Movies: The Paradise Connection, Desperate Voyage, The Return of Frank Cannon, Killjoy, The Master of Ballantrae, MADD, The Candy Lightner Story, Cowboy, A Thanksgiving Promise, The Old Man and the Sea, O Pioneers! (Emmy Award), Night Ride Home, The Ballad of Lucy Whipple, Roughing It, Bobbie's Girl, Eloise at the Plaza. Mini-Series: The Blue and the Gray, The First Olympics—Athens: 1896 (Emmy Award), George Washington II, True Women. Series: Hawaii Five-0, Gunsmoke, Quincy, How the West Was Won, Logan's Run, The Oregon Trail, Buck Rogers (Emmy Award), Dallas (Emmy Award), Dinosaurs (theme), Capitol Critters (theme), Tiny Toon Adventures (Emmy Award), JAG (theme), First Monday.

BROUMAS, JOHN G.
Executive. b. Youngstown, OH, Oct. 12, 1917. e. Youngstown. Usher, Altoona Publix Theatres, 1933, usher to asst. mgr., Warner Thea. 1934-39; mgr. Grand 1939-40; mgr. Orpheum 1940-41. WWII active, Officer Chemical Corps, commanding officer 453rd Chem. Battalion (Reserve); Life member Reserve Officers Assoc.; Gen. mgr. Pitts & Roth Theatres 1946-54; pres., Broumas Theatres; v.p. NATO, 1969; bd. of dir. of NATO of VA, MD, D.C.; pres., Broumas Theatre Service 1954-82; bd. chmn., Showcase Theatres 1965-82; past pres. & bd. chmn. Maryland Theatre Owners; v.p. & bd. of dir., Virginia Theatre Owners; bd. of dir. NATO of D.C.; pres. B.C. Theatres; Past dir. and mem. Motion Picture Pioneers; Advisory Council; Will Rogers Memorial Hospital; Washington, D.C. Variety Club, Tent No. 11, bd. of gov. 1959, 1st asst. chief. barker, 1964 & 71, chief barker 1965-66, 1972, and 1978-79, and bd. chmn., 1980; lecturer, Georgetown Univ., 1972-; Life Patron, Variety Clubs Int'l, 1978 Life Liner, Variety Clubs Intl.; member: Screen Actors Guild. 1994.

BROWN, BLAIR
Actress. b. Washington, DC, April 23, 1946.. e. National Theatre Sch. of Canada.
THEATRE: NY: The Threepenny Opera (NY Shakespeare Fest), Comedy of Errors, The Secret Rapture, Arcadia. Acted with Old Globe, San Diego; Stratford, Ont. Shakespeare Fest.; Guthrie Theatre MN; Arena Stage, Wash.; Long Wharf, New Haven; Shaw Festival.
PICTURES: The Paper Chase, The Choirboys, One-Trick Pony, Altered States, Continental Divide, A Flash of Green, Stealing Home, Strapless, Passed Away, The Good Policeman, The Astronaut's Wife, Random Hearts, Space Cowboys, Grasp, Dogville.
TELEVISION: Movies: The 3,000 Mile Chase, And I Alone Survived, The Child Stealer, The Bad Seed, Hands of a Stranger, Eleanor and Franklin: The White House Years, Extreme Close-Up, Those Secrets, Majority Rule, Rio Shannon (pilot), The Day My Parents Ran Away, Moment of Truth: To Walk Again, The Gift of Love, The Ultimate Lie, Convictions, In His Life: The John Lennon Story, Following the Stars Home, The Perfect Pitch (tv documentary). Mini-series: Captains and the Kings, James Michener's Space, Arthur Hailey's Wheels, Kennedy, A Season in Purgatory, Benjamin Franklin (tv documentary). Specials: School for Scandal, The Skin of Your Teeth, Lethal Innocence, Oregon Trail, The Quinns, Space. Series: The Days and Nights of Molly Dodd, Talk It Over, Feds.

BROWN, BRYAN
Actor. b. Sydney, Australia, June 23, 1947. m. actress Rachel Ward. Began acting professionally in Sydney. Worked in repertory theatres in England with the National Theatre of Great Britain. Returned to Australia to work in films while continuing stage work with Theatre Australia.
PICTURES: Love Letters From Teralba Road (debut, 1977), The Irishman, Weekend of Shadows, Newsfront, Third Person Plural, Money Movers, Palm Beach, Cathy's Child, The Odd Angry Shot, Breaker Morant, Blood Money, Stir, Winter of Our Dreams, Far East, Give My Regards to Broad Street, Parker (Bones), The Empty Beach, F/X, Tai-Pan, Rebel, The Good Wife, Cocktail, Gorillas in the Mist, Shall We Dance, FX2 (also co-exec. prod.), Sweet Talker (also co-wrote story), Prisoners of the Sun, Blame It on the Bellboy, The Chart of Jimmy Balcksmith, Age of Treason, Dead Heart, On the Border, Dear Claudia, Two Hands, Grizzly Falls, Risk, Mullet (voice), Styx, Dirty Deeds (also prod.), Captured (short).
TELEVISION: Movies: The Shiralee (Aust.), Dead in the Water, Devlin, The Last Hit, Eureka Stockade, Full Body Massage, Twisted Tales, 20,000 Leagues Under the Sea, Dogboys, Journey to the Center of the Earth, On the Beach, Footsteps. Mini-Series: Against the Wind, A Town Like Alice, The Thorn Birds, Eureka Stockade, The Shiralee. Series: The Wanderer.

BROWN, CLANCY
Actor. b. Ohio, Jan. 5, 1959. e. Northwestern Univ.
PICTURES: Bad Boys (debut, 1983), The Adventures of Buckaroo Banzai, The Bride, Thunder Alley, Highlander, Extreme Prejudice, Shoot to Kill, Blue Steel, Waiting for the Light, Ambition, Past Midnight, Pet Sematary II, The Shawshank Redemption, Dead Man Walking, Female Perversions, Starship Troopers, Flubber, The Hurricane, Claire Makes It Big, Chump Change, Recess: School's Out (voice), The Laramie Project, Normal, The Making of Daniel Boone (exec. prod.)
TELEVISION: Movies: Johnny Ryan, Love Lies & Murder, Cast a Deadly Spell, Desperate Rescue: The Cathy Mahone Story, Bloodlines, Last Light, The Patron Saint of Liars, The Batman/Superman Movie (voice), In the Company of Spies, Vendetta, The Night of the Headless Horseman, Boss of Bosses, Yesterday's Children, Show White. Series: Earth 2, ER, Voltron: The Third Dimension (voice), SpongBob SquarePants (voice), Roughnecks: The Starship Trooper Chronicles, Big Buy and Rusty the Boy Robot (voice), Jackie Chan Adventures (voice), Lloyd In Space, Breaking News, Heavy Gear: The Animated Series (voice), Carnivále, Battle Force: Andromeda.

BROWN, DAVID
Executive, Producer. b. New York, NY, July 28, 1916. m. writer-editor Helen Gurley Brown. e. Stanford U., A.B., 1936; Columbia U. Sch. of Journalism, M.S., 1937. Apprentice reporter, copy-editing, San Francisco News & Wall Street Journal, 1936; night ed. asst. drama critic, Fairchild Publications, N.Y., 1937-39; edit. dir. Milk Research Council, N.Y., 1939-40; assoc. ed., Street & Smith

Publ., N.Y., 1940-43; assoc. ed., exec. ed., then ed.-in-chief, Liberty Mag., N.Y., 1943-49; edit. dir., nat'l education campaign, Amer. Medical Assn., 1949; assoc. ed., mng. ed., Cosmopolitan Mag., N.Y., 1949-52; contrib. stories & articles to many nat'l mags.; man. ed., story dept., 20th-Fox, L.A., Jan., 1952; story ed. & head of scenario dept., 1953-56; appt'd. member of exec. staff of Darryl F. Zanuck, 1956; mem. of exec. staff, 20th-Fox studios, and exec. studio story editor, 1956-60; Prod. 20th-Fox Studios, Sept. 1960-62; Editorial v.p. New American Library of World Literature, Inc., 1963-64; exec. story opers., 20th Century-Fox, 1964-67; vp. dir. of story operations, 1967; exec. v.p., creative optns. and mem. bd. of dir., 1969-71. Exec. v.p., mem. bd. of directors Warner Bros., 1971-72; partner and dir., The Zanuck/Brown Co., 1972-88. Pres., Manhattan Project Ltd., 1988; mem., bd. of trustees, American Film Institute, 1972-80. Recipient with Richard D. Zanuck of the Mo. Pic. Acad. of Arts & Sciences' Irving G. Thalberg Memorial Award. Books: Brown's Guide to Growing Gray, Delacorte, Let Me Entertain You, Morrow, The Rest of Your Life is the Best of Your Life, Barricade.
PICTURES: Prod/Exec.Prod.: Ssssss, The Sting (Academy Award for Best Picture, 1973), Sugarland Express, Black Windmill, Willie Dynamite, The Girl from Petrovka, The Eiger Sanction, Jaws, MacArthur, Jaws 2, The Island, Neighbors, The Verdict, Cocoon, Target, Cocoon: The Return, Driving Miss Daisy, The Player, A Few Good Men, The Cemetery Club, Watch It, Canadian Bacon, The Saint, Kiss the Girls, Deep Impact, Angela's Ashes, Chocolat, Enigma (co-prod.), Along Came a Spider.
TELEVISION: Movies: Women & Men 2: In Love There Are No Rules (prod.), A Season in Purgatory (exec. prod.), Framed (exec. prod.).

BROWN, GEORG STANFORD
Actor, Director. b. Havana, Cuba, June 24, 1943. Acted on stage with the New York Shakespeare Fest. in the 1960s. Gained fame as one of the rookie cops in the 1970s TV series, The Rookies, before turning to TV directing.
THEATRE: All's Well That Ends Well, Measure for Measure, Macbeth, Murderous Angels, Hamlet, Detective Story.
PICTURES: The Comedians, Dayton's Devils, Bullitt, Colossus: The Forbin Project, Wild in the Sky, The Man, Stir Crazy, House Party 2, Dreaming of Julia.
TELEVISION: Movies: The Young Lawyers, Ritual of Evil, The Rookies (pilot), Dawn: Portrait of a Teenage Runaway, The Night the City Screamed, The Kid With the Broken Halo, In Defense of Kids, The Jesse Owens Story, Murder Without Motive. Dir. of movies: Grambling's White Tiger, Kids Like These, Alone in the Neon Jungle, Stuck With Each Other (also exec. prod.), Father & Son: Dangerous Relations. Series: Actor: The Rookies (also dir.), Linc's, Freedom. Series: Dir.: Starsky and Hutch, Family, Charlie's Angels, Fantasy Island, The Paper Chase, Tenspeed and Brown Shoe, Palmerstown USA, Dynasty, Hill Street Blues, The Greatest American Hero, The Fall Guy, Fame, Cagney & Lacey (Emmy Award, 1986), The Mississippi, Hotel, Miami Vice, Finder of Lost Loves, Viper.

BROWN, HIMAN
Producer, Director. b. New York, NY, July 21, 1910. e. City Coll. of New York, St. Lawrence U. Radio & TV package prod. since 1927 include: Inner Sanctum, Thin Man, Bulldog Drummond, Dick Tracy, Terry and the Pirates, Joyce Jordan MD, Grand Central Station, CBS Radio Mystery Theatre, pres. Production Center, Inc.
PICTURES: The Thin Man, Nero Wolfe, Bulldog, Drummond, That Night, Violators, The Stars Salute, The Price of Silence, The Road Ahead.

BROWN, JIM
Actor. b. St. Simons Island, GA, Feb. 17, 1936. e. Manhasset H.S., Syracuse U. For nine years played football with Cleveland Browns; in 1964 won Hickock Belt as Professional Athlete of the year. Founder, Black Economic Union.
PICTURES: Rio Conchos (debut, 1964), The Dirty Dozen, Ice Station Zebra, The Split, Riot, Dark Of The Sun, 100 Rifles, Kenner, El Condor, The Phynx, ... tick ... tick ... tick ..., The Grasshopper, Slaughter, Black Gunn, I Escaped from Devil's Island, The Slams, Slaughter's Big Rip-Off, Three the Hard Way, Take a Hard Ride, Adios Amigo, Mean Johnny Barrows, Kid Vengeance, Fingers, One Down Two to Go (also exec. prod.), Richard Pryor: Here and Now (exec. prod. only), Pacific Inferno (also exec. prod.), Abducted, The Running Man, I'm Gonna Git You Sucka, L.A. Heat, Crack House, Twisted Justice, The Divine Enforcer, Original Gangstas, Mars Attacks!, He Got Game, Small Soldiers (voice), Any Given Sunday, Jim Brown: All American (documentary),Playmakers of New Orleans.
TELEVISION: Movies: Lady Blue, Hammer-Slammer & Slade, Muhammad Ali: The Whole Story (as himself), Unitas (tv documentary, as himself), Keeping the Music Alive (dir.). Guest: Knight Rider, The A-Team, Highway to Heaven, Living Single, Between Brothers, Arli$$.

BROWNE, ROSCOE LEE
Actor, Director, Writer. b. Woodbury, NJ, May 2, 1925. e. Lincoln U., PA; postgraduate studies in comparative literature and French at Middlebury Coll., VT, Columbia U., N.Y. Taught French and lit. at Lincoln U. until 1952. National sales rep. for Schenley Import Corp. 1946-56; United States' intl. track star and a member of ten A.A.U. teams. Twice American champion in the 1000-yard indoor competition, twice all-American and, in 1951 in Paris, ran the fastest 800 meters in the world for that year. Professional acting debut, 1956, in Julius Caesar at the NY Shakespeare Fest.; published poet and short story writer.

Trustee: Millay Colony Arts, NY; Los Angeles Free Public Theatre.
THEATRE: *NY*: The Ballad of the Sad Cafe, The Cool World, General Seeger, Tiger Tiger Burning Bright!, The Old Glory, A Hand Is on the Gate (dir., actor), My One and Only. Off-Broadway: The Connection, The Blacks, Aria da Capo, Benito Cereno (Obie Award), Joe Turner's Come and Gone (L.A., S.F., Pittsburgh), Two Trains Running.
PICTURES: The Connection (debut, 1961), Black Like Me, The Comedians, Uptight, Topaz, The Liberation of L. B. Jones, Cisco Pike, The Cowboys, The World's Greatest Athlete, Superfly T.N.T., The Ra Expeditions (narrator), Uptown Saturday Night, Logan's Run, Twilight's Last Gleaming, Nothing Personal, Legal Eagles, Jumpin' Jack Flash, Oliver & Company (voice), Moon 44, The Mambo Kings, Naked in New York, Brother Minister: The Assassination of Malcolm X (narrator), Babe (voice), The Pompatus of Love, Last Summer in the Hamptons, Dear God, Forest Warrior, Juda Kiss, Babe: Pig in the City (voice), Morgan's Ferry, Treasure Planet (voice).
TELEVISION: *Movies*: The Big Ripoff, Dr. Scorpion, Lady in a Corner, Columbo: Rest in Peace Mrs. Columbo, Meeting of Minds (Peabody Award), A Connecticut Yankee in King Arthur's Court (Peabody Award), Hard Time, The Premonition, Hamlet. *Mini-Series*: King, Space. *Series*: McCoy, Miss Winslow and Son, Soap, Falcon Crest. *Guest*: All in the Family, Maude, Barney Miller, Soap, Head of the Class, The Cosby Show (Emmy Award, 1986), Falcon Crest, ER, The Shield.

BROWNING, KIRK
Director. b. New York, NY, March 28, 1921. e. Brooks School, Andover, MA, Avon Old Farms, Avon, CT., and Cornell U. 1940. Reporter for News-Tribune in Waco, TX; with American Field Service, 1942-45; adv. copywriter for Franklin Spier, 1945-48; became floor mgr. NBC-TV 1949; app't asst. dir. NBC-TV Opera Theatre in 1951 directing NBC Opera Theatre, TV Recital Hall, and Toscanini Simulcasts.
TELEVISION: Trial of Mary Lincoln, Jascha Heifetz Special, Harry and Lena, NBC Opera Theatre, Producers Showcase, Evening with Toscanini, Bell Telephone, The Flood, Beauty and the Beast, Lizzie Borden, World of Carl Sandburg, La Gioconda (Emmy Award, 1980), Big Blonde, Working, Ian McKellan Acting Shakespeare, Fifth of July, Alice in Wonderland, You Can't Take it with You, The House of Blue Leaves, O Pioneers!, Live From the Met—Centennial, many others. Most recently, directed tv movie, Death of a Salesman (2000).

BROWNLOW, KEVIN
Film Historian, Writer, Director, Film Editor. b. Crowborough, England, June 2, 1938. e. University College Sch. Asst. ed./editor, World Wide Pictures, London, 1955-61; film editor, Samaritan Films, 1961-65; film editor, Woodfall Films, 1965-68. Dir., Thames Television 1975-90. Dir., Photoplay Productions 1990-present.
PICTURES: It Happened Here (dir. with Andrew Mollo) 1964, Charge of the Light Brigade (editor), Winstanley (with Andrew Mollo), Napoleon (restoration of 1927 film, re-released 1980), The Tramp and the Dictator.
TELEVISION: Charm of Dynamite (dir., ed.), All with David Gill; Hollywood (dir., writer), Unknown Chaplin (dir., prod.; Emmy Award), Buster Keaton: A Hard Act to Follow (prod.; 2 Emmy Awards), Harold Lloyd—The Third Genius, D.W. Griffith: Father of Film, Cinema Europe—The Other Hollywood, Universal Horror, Lon Chaney: A Thousand Faces.
AUTHOR: How It Happened Here (1968), The Parade's Gone By... (1968), Adventures with D.W. Griffith (editor, 1973), The War, the West and the Wilderness (1979), Hollywood: The Pioneers (1980), Napoleon: Abel Gance's Classic Film (1983), Behind the Mask of Innocence (1990), David Lean—A Biography (1996).

BRUBAKER, JAMES D.
Producer. b. Hollywood, CA, March 30, 1937. e. Eagle Rock H.S. Transportation coordinator for 15 years before becoming unit prod. mgr., 1978-84. Then assoc. prod., exec. prod. & prod. Prod. tv movie, Runnng Mates.
PICTURES: *Assoc. Prod.*: True Confessions (also prod. mgr.), Rocky III (also prod. mgr.), Rhinestone (also prod. mgr.). *Unit Prod. Mgr.*: New York New York, Comes a Horseman, Uncle Joe Shannon, Rocky II, Raging Bull, Staying Alive, K-9, Problem Child, Mr. Baseball. *Prod./Exec. Prod.*: The Right Stuff, Beer, Rocky IV, Cobra, Over the Top, Problem Child (also prod. mgr.), Brain Donors (also prod. mgr.), A Walk in the Clouds, Liar Liar, The Nutty Professor (co-prod.) Life (and unit prod. mgr.), The Nutty Professor II: The Klumps, Her Majesty, Dragonfly, Bruce Almighty (prod.).
TELEVISION: The Gifted One (Unit prod. mgr.) Running Mates, Gia (prod. and unit prod. mgr.).

BRUCKHEIMER, BONNIE
Producer. b. Brooklyn, NY. Started in advertising and public relations eventually working for treasurer of Columbia Pictures. Later worked as asst. to Arthur Penn and Ross Hunter. Became partner with Bette Midler in All Girl Productions, 1985.
PICTURES: Big Business (assoc. prod.), Beaches, Stella, For the Boys, Hocus Pocus, Man of the House, That Old Feeling, Divine Secrets of the Ya-Ya Sisterhood, Aurora Island.
TELEVISION: *Movie*: Bette Midler in Concert: Diva Las Vegas (exec. prod.), Gypsy (exec. prod.).*Series*: Bette, Some of My Best Friends.

BRUCKHEIMER, JERRY
Producer. b. Detroit, MI, Sept. 21, 1945. e. U. of Arizona. Was art dir./prod. of TV commercials before becoming prod. of films. 1983, formed Don Simpson/Jerry Bruckheimer Prods. with the late Don Simpson and entered into deal with Paramount Pictures to produce; company moved over to Walt Disney in early 1990's. Formed Jerry Bruckheimer Films in 1997.
PICTURES: *Assoc. Prod.*: The Culpepper Cattle Company, Rafferty and the Gold Dust Twins. *Prod.*: Farewell My Lovely, March or Die, Defiance, American Gigolo, Thief, Cat People (exec. prod.), Young Doctors in Love, Flashdance, Thief of Hearts, Beverly Hills Cop, Top Gun, Beverly Hills Cop II, Days of Thunder, The Ref, Bad Boys, Crimson Tide, Dangerous Minds, The Rock, Con Air, Enemy of the State, Armageddon, Gone in 60 Seconds, Coyote Ugly, Remember the Titans, Bad Boys 2, Pearl Harbor, Black Hawk Down, Bad Company, Kangaroo Jack, Veronica Guerin, King Arthur.
TELEVISION: *Movies:Exec Prod*: Max Q: Emergency Landing, Swing Vote, Skin, *Series:Exec. Prod.*: Soldier of Fortune Inc., CSI: Crime Scene Investigation, The Amazing Race, CSI: Miami, Without a Trace, Skin (writer/creator), Fearless (also co-prod.), Cold Case (prod.).

BRYAN, DORA
Actress. r.n. Dora Broadbent. b. Southport, Lancashire, England, Feb. 7, 1924. e. Council Sch. Stage debut 1935.
PICTURES: Once Upon a Dream, (debut, 1947), The Fallen Idol, No Room at the Inn, Blue Lamp, Cure for Love, Now Barabas, The Ringer, Women of Twilight, The Quiet Woman, The Intruder, You Know What Sailors Are, Mad About Men, See How They Run, Cockleshell Heroes, Child in the House, Green Man, Carry on Sergeant, Operation Bullshine, Desert Mice, The Night We Got the Bird, A Taste of Honey, Two a Penny, Up the Front, Screamtime, Apartment Zero, An Angel for May.
TELEVISION: *Movies*: Bed. *Series*: My Wife's Sister, Both Ends Meet, On the Up, Mother's Ruin, Las of the Summer Wine.

BUCHHOLZ, HORST
Actor. r.n. Henry Bookholt. b. Berlin, Germany, Dec. 4, 1933. e. high school. In radio and stage plays. Started in films dubbing foreign movies. Work with Berlin's Schiller Theatre result in film debut in French film.
PICTURES: Marianne (debut, 1955), Emil and the Detectives, Himmel Ohne Sterne (Sky Without Stars), Regine, Teenage Wolfpack, The King in Shadow, The Confessions of Felix Krull, The Legend of Robinson Crusoe, Mompti, Endstation Liebe, Nasser Asphalt, Resurrection, Das Totenschiff, Tiger Bay (English-language debut, 1959), The Magnificent Seven, Fanny, One Two Three, Nine Hours to Rama, The Empty Canvas, Andorra, Marco the Magnificent, That Man in Istanbul, Johnny Banco, Cervantes (The Young Rebel), L'Astragale, How When and With Whom, La Sauveur, La Columba non deve Volare, The Great Waltz, The Catamount Killing, Women in Hospital, The Amazing Captain Nemo, From Hell to Victory, Avalanche Express, Aphrodite, Sahara, Fear of Falling, Code Name: Emerald, And the Violins Stopped Playing, Escape From Paradise, Aces: Iron Eagle III, Far Away So Close, Ptak Ohnivak, Life is Beautiful, Mulan (voice), Minefield, Brighter Than the Moon, The Enemy.
TELEVISION: *Movies*: The Savage Bees, Raid on Entebbe, Return to Fantasy Island, Berlin Tunnel 21, Family Affairs, The Lion of Granada, Come Back to Kampen, Cave of the Golden Rose IV, Voyage of Terror, Dunckel, Kidnapped in Rio, Der Club der grunen Witwen, Traumfrau mit Verspatung, Detective Lovelorn und die Rache des Pharao, In der Mitte eines Lebens. *Mini-Series*: The French Atlantic Affair, Clan der Anna Voss. (d. March 3, 2003)

BUCKLEY, BETTY
Actress. b. Fort Worth, TX, July 3, 1947. e. Texas Christian U., BA. Studied acting with Stella Adler. NY Stage debut: 1776 (1969); London debut: Promises Promises. Appeared in interactive short film Race for Your Life.
THEATRE: Johnny Pott, What's a Nice Country Like You Doing in a State Like This?, Pippin, I'm Getting My Act Together and Taking It on the Road, Cats (Tony Award, 1983), Juno's Swans, The Mystery of Edwin Drood, Song and Dance, Carrie, The Fourth Wall, The Perfectionist, Sunset Boulevard (London/ B'way; Olivier Award nom.).
PICTURES: Carrie (debut, 1976), Tender Mercies, Wild Thing, Frantic, Another Woman, Rain Without Thunder, Wyatt Earp, Simply Irresistible, Last Time Out, The Keyman (co-prod. only), A Promis Kept (prod. only), Broadway: The Golden Age by the Legends Who Were There, Mummy an' the Armadillo.
TELEVISION: *Movies*: The Ordeal of Bill Carney, Roses Are for the Rich, The Three Wishes of Billy Grier, Babycakes, Bonnie & Clyde: The True Story (Emmy nom.), Betrayal of Trust, Critical Choices. *Specials*: Bobby and Sarah, Salute to Lady Liberty, Taking a Stand (Afterschool Special; Emmy nom.), Stephen Sondheim Carnegie Hall Gala, Eight is Enough: The E! True Hollywood Story. *Mini-Series*: Evergreen, Tribeca. *Series*: Eight is Enough, Oz.

BUCKLEY, DONALD
Executive. b. New York, NY, June 28, 1955. e. C.W. Post Coll, NY, Sch. of Visual Arts. Ad. mgr., United Artists Theatres, 1975-78. Acct. exec., Grey Advertising, 1978-80. Joined Warner Bros. in 1980 as NY adv. mgr.; 1986; promoted to east. dir. of adv./promo. for WB; 1988, named eastern dir. of adv. and publicity; 1991, promoted to v.p., East Coast Adv. & Publicity; 1996,

promoted to v.p., Adv. & Publicity, v.p., WB On-Line; 1997, promoted to senior v.p., Theatrical Marketing & New Media.

BUFF, CONRAD
Editor.
PICTURES: The Empires Strikes Back (effects ed.), Raiders of the Lost Ark (effects ed.), Poltergeist (effects ed.), E.T.: The Extra-Terrestrial (effects ed. superv.), Return of the Jedi (asst. ed.), Jagged Edge, Solarbabies, Spaceballs, Short Circuit 2, The Abyss, Side Out, Terminator 2: Judgment Day, Jennifer Eight, The Getaway, True Lies, Species, Titanic (Acad. Award, 1998), Dante's Peak, Switchback, Arlington Road, Mystery Men, Thirteen Days, Training Day, The Antwone Fisher Story, Tears of the Sun.

BUJOLD, GENEVIEVE
Actress. b. Montreal, Canada, July 1, 1942. e. Montreal Conservatory of Drama. Worked in a Montreal cinema as an usher; American TV debut: St. Joan.
THEATRE: The Barber of Seville, A Midsummer Night's Dream, A House...A Day.
PICTURES: La Guerre est Finie, La Fleur de L'Age, Entre La Mer et L'eau Douce, King of Hearts, The Thief of Paris, Isabel, Anne of the Thousand Days, Act of the Heart, The Trojan Women, The Journey, Kamouraska, Earthquake, Swashbuckler, Obsession, Alex and the Gypsy, Another Man Another Chance, Coma, Murder by Decree, Final Assignment, The Last Flight of Noah's Ark, Monsignor, Tightrope, Choose Me, Trouble in Mind, The Moderns, Dead Ringers, False Identity, Secret Places of the Heart, A Paper Wedding, An Ambush of Ghosts, Mon Amie Max, Dead Innocent, The Adventures of Pinocchio, The House of Yes, You Can Thank Me Later, Last Night, Eye of the Beholder, Alex in Wonder, La Turbulence des fluides, Finding Home, Downtown: A Street Tale, Jericho Mansions, Finding Home.
TELEVISION: Movies: Antigone, Mistress of Paradise, Les Noces de papier, The Bookfair Murders, Children of My Heart. Specials: Saint Joan, Antony and Cleopatra.

BULLOCK, SANDRA
Actress. b. Arlington, VA, July 26, 1964. e. East Carolina Univ., drama major. Raised in Germany; studied piano in Europe. First prof. acting job in NY in Off-B'way prod. No Time Flat.
PICTURES: Who Shot Patakango?, Love Potion No. 9, When the Party's Over, The Vanishing, The Thing Called Love, Demolition Man, Speed, Me and the Mob, While You Were Sleeping, The Net, Two If by Sea, A Time to Kill, In Love and War, Speed 2 Cruise Control, The Prince of Egypt (voice), Making Sandwiches (also dir., s.p.), Hope Floats, Practical Magic, Forces of Nature, 28 Days, Welcome to Hollywood, Gun Shy, Famous, Miss Congeniality, Divine Secrets of the Ya Ya Sisterhood, Murder By Numbers (also exec. prod.), Two Weeks Notice (also prod.), Exactly 3:30 (also prod.).
TELEVISION: Series: Working Girl, George Lopez (only exec. prod.) Movies: The Preppie Murder, Bionic Showdown: The Six Million Dollar Man and the Bionic Woman, Jackie Collins' Lucky/Chances.

BURGHOFF, GARY
Actor. b. Bristol, CT, May 24, 1943. Winner of Student Hallmark Award while in high school, 1961. Also wildlife artist, with work exhibited in many U.S. galleries.
THEATRE: NY: You're a Good Man Charlie Brown, The Nerd. Also: Finian's Rainbow, Bells Are Ringing, Sound of Music, The Boy Friend, Romanoff and Juliet, Whose Life Is It Anyway?
PICTURES: M*A*S*H*, B.S. I Love You, Small Kill (also co-dir.), Behind the Waterfall.
TELEVISION: Series: The Don Knotts Show, M*A*S*H (Emmy Award, 1977), Pets: Part of the Family. Guest: Good Guys, Name of the Game, Love American Style, Fernwood 2-Night, Sweepstakes, Love Boat, Fantasy Island. Movies: The Man in the Santa Claus Suit, Casino. Special: Twigs, M*A*S*H 30th Anniversary Reunion (tv documentary, 2002).

BURKE, ALFRED
Actor. b. London, England, February 28, 1918.
PICTURES: Touch and Go, The Man Upstairs, The Angry Silence, Moment of Danger, The Man Inside, No Time To Die, Children of the Damned, The Nanny, One Day in the Life of Ivan Denisovitch, Law and Disorder, Yangtse Incident, Interpol, Bitter Victory, Guns in the Heather, One Day in the Life of Ivan Denisovich, A Midsummer Night's Dream, Harry Potter and the Chamber of Secrets.
TELEVISION: Movies: The Lady of teh Camellias, The House on Garibaldi Street, Pope John Paul II, Kim, Bewitched (1985), Longitude. Mini-series: The Brontes of Haworth, The Borgias. Series: Public Eye, Enemy at the Door, Sophia and Constance.

BURKE, DELTA
Actress. b. Orlando, FL, July 30, 1956. e. LAMDA. m. actor Gerald McRaney. Competed in Miss America contest as Miss Florida, prior to studying acting in England.
PICTURES: Maternal Instincts (also exec. prod.), Sordid Lives, What Women Want, Hansel and Gretel, Good Boy!
TELEVISION: Movies: Charleston, A Last Cry for Help, Mickey Spillane's Mike Hammer: Murder Me Murder You, A Bunny's Tale, Where the Hell's That Gold?!!? Love and Curses... And All That Jazz (also co-exec. prod.), Day-O, Simon & Simon: In Trouble Again, A Promise to Carolyn, Melanie Darrow (also prod.), Dangerous Child. Special: Intimate Portrait: Dixie Carter. Series: The Chisholms, Filthy Rich, 1st & Ten, Designing Women, Delta

(also co-exec. prod.), Women of the House (also exec. prod.), Any Day Now, DAG, Popular, St. Sass. Guest: The Love Boat, The Fall Guy, Nero Wolfe, Fantasy Island, Remington Steele, numerous others.

BURNETT, CAROL
Actress, Singer, Producer, Director. b. San Antonio, TX, April 26, 1933. e. Hollywood H.S., UCLA. Daughter was actress Carrie Hamilton (d. Jan. 20, 2002). Introduced comedy song "I Made a Fool of Myself Over John Foster Dulles," 1957; regular performer Garry Moore Show, 1959-62. Recipient outstanding commedienne award Am. Guild Variety Artists, 5 times; TV Guide award for outstanding female performer 1961, 62, 63; Peabody Award, 1963; 5 Golden Globe awards for outstanding comedienne of year; Woman of Year award Acad. TV Arts and Scis. Voted one of the world's 20 most admired women in 1977 Gallup Poll. First Annual National Television Critics Award for Outstanding Performance, 1977. Best Actress Award at San Sebastian Film Fest. for film A Wedding, 1978. Inducted Acad. of Television Arts and Sciences Hall of Fame, 1985. Author: Once Upon a Time (1986).
THEATRE: NY: Once Upon a Mattress (debut, 1959; Theatre World Award), Fade Out-Fade In, Moon Over Buffalo. Regional: Calamity Jane, Plaza Suite, I Do I Do, Same Time Next Year.
PICTURES: Who's Been Sleeping in My Bed? (debut, 1963), Pete 'n' Tillie, The Front Page, A Wedding, H.E.A.L.T.H., The Four Seasons, Chu Chu and the Philly Flash, Annie, Noises Off, Get Bruce (documentary), The Trumpet of the Swan (voice) Broadway: The Golden Age by the Legends Who Were There (documentary).
TELEVISION: Movies: The Grass Is Always Greener Over the Septic Tank, Friendly Fire, The Tenth Month, Life of the Party: The Story of Beatrice, Between Friends, Hostage, Seasons of the Heart, Grace, Happy Birthday Elizabeth, The Marriage Fool. Series: Stanley, Pantomime Quiz, The Garry Moore Show (Emmy Award, 1962), The Entertainers, The Carol Burnett Show (1967-78; in syndication as Carol Burnett & Friends), Carol Burnett & Company, Carol & Company, The Carol Burnett Show (1991), Mama's Family, Mad About You (Emmy Award, 1997). Mini-Series: Fresno. Specials: Julie & Carol at Carnegie Hall, Carol and Company (Emmy Award for previous 2 specials, 1963), An Evening with Carol Burnett, Calamity Jane, Once Upon a Mattress, Carol + 2, Julie & Carol at Lincoln Center, 6 Rms Riv Vu, Twigs, Sills & Burnett at the Met, Dolly & Carol in Nashville, All-Star Party for Carol Burnett, Burnett Discovers Domingo, The Laundromat, Carol Carl Whoopi & Robin, Julie & Carol—Together Again, The Carol Burnett Show: A Reunion (also co-exec. prod.), Men Movies & Carol, CBS: The First 50 Years, Carol Burnett: Show Stoppers. Guest: Twilight Zone, The Jack Benny Program, Get Smart, The Lucy Show, Fame, Magnum P.I.

BURNETT, CHARLES
Director, Writer, Cinematographer. b. Vicksburg, MI, April 13, 1944. e. LA Community Col., UCLA.
PICTURES: Director: Several Friends, Killer of Sheep (also prod., s.p., photog., edit.), My Brother's Wedding (also prod., s.p., photog.), To Sleep With Anger (also s.p.), America Becoming (also writer), The Johnny Johnson Trial (also s.p.), The Annihilation of Fish, Olivia's Story (documentary, also editor). Cinematographer: Bush Mama, Bless Their Little Hearts (also s.p.), Guest of Hotel Astoria.
TELEVISION: Movies: Dir: Nightjohn, The Wedding, Finding Buck McHenry, Selma Lord Selma. Mini-series: The Blues.

BURNS, EDWARD J.
Actor, Director, Producer. b. Valley Stream, NY, Jan. 29, 1968. Has production co. with brother Brian Burns, Irish Twins.
PICTURES: Actor, dir. s.p.: The Brothers McMullen (Sundance award), She's the One (also prod.), No Looking Back, Sidewalks of New York, Ash Wednesday. Actor: Saving Private Ryan (SAG nom.) 15 Minutes, Life or Something Like It, Confidence, The Breakup Artist, A Sound of Thunder.
TELEVISION: Series: Entertainment Tonight (prod. asst.), The Fighting Fitzgeralds (exec. prod. and writer only). New York at the Movies (tv documentary)

BURNS, KEN
Producer, Director, Cinematographer, Writer. b. July 29, 1953. e. Hampshire Col. Co-author: Shakers: Hands to Work Hearts to God: The History and Visions of the United Society of Believers in Christ's Second Appearance from 1774 to Present, The Civil War: An Illustrated History, Baseball: An Illustrated History. Appeared in film Gettysburg.
TELEVISION: Prod. and dir. of the following documentaries: Brooklyn Bridge (also photog., edit.; Acad. Award nom.), The Shakers: Hands to Work Hearts to God (also co-writer), The Statue of Liberty (also photog.; Acad. Award nom.), Huey Long (also co-writer), Thomas Hart Benton (also photog.), The Congress, The Civil War (also photog., co-writer; numerous awards incl. Peabody and Emmy), Lindbergh (co-prod. only), Empire of the Air: The Men Who Made Radio (also photog., music dir.), Baseball (co- writer, prod., dir.), Lewis & Clark: The Journey of the Corps of Discovery (also photog.), Frank Lloyd Wright (also photog.), The West (exec. prod only), Thomas Jefferson (prod. only), Not for Ourselves Alone: The Story of Elizabeth Cady Stanton & Susan B. Anthony, Frank Lloyd Wright, Jazz, Mark Twain.

BURRILL, TIMOTHY
Producer, Executive. b. North Wales, June 8, 1931. e. Eton Coll., Sorbonne U., Paris. Grenadier Guards 2 yrs, then London

Shipping Co. Ent. m.p. ind. as resident prod. mgr. Samaritan Films working on shorts, commercials, documentaries, 1954. Ass't. dir.: The Criminal, The Valiant Years (TV series), On The Fiddle, Reach for Glory, War Lover, Prod. mgr: The Cracksman, Night Must Fall, Lord Jim, Yellow Rolls Royce, The Heroes of Telemark, Resident prod. with World Film Services. 1970 prod. two films on pop music for Anglo-EMI. 1972 first prod. administrator National Film School in U.K. 1974 Post prod. administrator The Three Musketeers. Prod. TV Special The Canterville Ghost; assoc. prod, That Lucky Touch; UK Administrator, The Prince and the Pauper; North American Prod. controller, Superman; 1974-1983 council member of BAFTA; mng. dir., Allied Stars (Breaking Glass, Chariots of Fire); 1979-80 V. chmn. Film BAFTA; 1980-83 chmn. BAFTA; 1981-92, Gov. National Film School, executive BFTPA mem. Cinematograph Films Council. 1982-88 Gov Royal National Theatre; 1987-93, chmn., Film Asset Developments, Formed Burrill Prods, 1979-; chmn. First Film Foundation. Exec. member PACT, 1991. Vice-chmn. (film) PACT, 1993.
PICTURES: Privilege, Oedipus the King, A Severed Head, Three Sisters, Macbeth (assoc. prod.), Alpha Beta, Tess (co-prod.), Pirates of Penzance (co-prod.), Supergirl, The Fourth Protocol, To Kill a Priest (co-prod.), Return of the Musketeers (tv in U.S.), Valmont, The Rainbow Thief, The Lover, Bitter Moon, Sweet Killing, Vatel, The Pianist, Swimming Pool (co-prod.).

BURROWS, JAMES
Director, Producer. b. Los Angeles, CA, Dec. 30, 1940. e. Oberlin, B.A.; Yale, M.F.A. Son of late Abe Burrows, composer, writer, dir. Directed off-B'way.
PICTURE: Partners.
TELEVISION: Movies: More Than Friends, Every Stray Dog and Kid, Dexter Prep Pilot.
Series: Has dir./exec.prod. 51 series since 1970, incl.: Mary Tyler Moore, Bob Newhart, Laverne and Shirley, Rhoda, Phyllis, Tony Randall Show, Betty White Show, Fay, Taxi (2 Emmy Awards: 1980, 1981), Lou Grant, Cheers (also prod.; 4 Emmy Awards as prod.: 1983, 1984, 1989, 1991; 2 Emmy Awards as dir.: 1983, 1991), Dear John, Night Court, All is Forgiven (also exec. prod.), The Fanelli Boys, Frasier (Emmy Award, 1994), Friends, NewsRadio, Men Behaving Badly, Chicago Sons, 3rd Rock from the Sun, Pearl, Fired Up (pilot), George & Leo, Dharma & Greg, Veronica's Closet, Union Square, Will & Grace (also exec. prod.), Conrad Bloom, Jesse, The Secret Lives of Men, Ladies Man, Stark Raving Mad, Madigan Men, Cursed, Good Morning Miami, Bram and Alice.

BURROWS, ROBERTA
Executive. e. Brandeis U; Academia, Florence, Italy. Career includes freelance writing for natl. magazines: GQ, Italian Bazaar, U.S., Family Circle. Dir. of pub. for Howard Stein Enterprises and with Rogers & Cowan and Billings Associates. Joined Warner Bros. as sr. publicist 1979; named dir. east coast publicity, 1986. Resigned 1989 to dev. novelty products. Proj. coordinator at Orion Pictures in NY for The Silence of the Lambs, Little Man Tate, Married to It, Bill & Ted's Bogus Journey.

BURSTYN, ELLEN
Actress. r.n. Edna Rae Gilhooley. b. Detroit, MI, Dec. 7, 1932. Majored in art; was fashion model in Texas at 18. Moved to Montreal as dancer; then N.Y. to do TV commercials (under the name of Ellen McRae), appearing for a year on the Jackie Gleason show (1956-57). In 1957 turned to dramatics and won lead in B'way show, Fair Game. Then went to Hollywood to do TV and films. Returned to N.Y. to study acting with Lee Strasberg; worked in TV serial, The Doctors. Co-artistic dir. of Actor's Studio. 1982-88. Pres. Actors Equity Assn. 1982-85. On 2 panels of Natl. Endowment of the Arts and Theatre Advisory Council (NY).
THEATRE: NY: Same Time Next Year (Tony Award, 1975), 84 Charing Cross Road, Shirley Valentine, Shimada. L.A.: Love Letters. Regional: The Trip to Bountiful.
PICTURES: As Ellen McRae: For Those Who Think Young (debut, 1964), Goodbye Charlie, Pit Stop. As Ellen Burstyn: Tropic of Cancer, Alex in Wonderland, The Last Picture Show, The King of Marvin Gardens, The Exorcist, Harry and Tonto, Alice Doesn't Live Here Anymore (Academy Award, 1974), Providence, A Dream of Passion, Same Time Next Year, Resurrection, Silence of the North, The Ambassador, In Our Hands (doc.), Twice in a Lifetime, Hanna's War, Dying Young, The Color of Evening, The Cemetery Club, When a Man Loves a Woman, Roommates, The Baby-sitters Club, How to Make an American Quilt, The Spitfire Grill, Liar, You Can Thank Me Later, Playing by Heart, The Yards, Requiem for a Dream (Acad. Award nom.), Divine Secrets of the Ya-Ya Sisterhood, Cross the Line.
TELEVISION: Movies: Thursday's Game, The People Vs. Jean Harris, Surviving, Act of Vengeance, Into Thin Air, Something in Common, Pack of Lies, When You Remember Me, Mrs. Lambert Remembers Love, Taking Back My Life: The Nancy Ziegenmeyer Story, Grand Isle, Shattered Trust: The Shari Karney Story, Getting Out, Getting Gotti, Trick of the Eye, My Brother's Keeper, Follow the River, A Deadly Vision, Flash, The Patron Saint of Liars, A Will of Their Own, Night Ride Home, Mermaid (Emmy nom.), Dodson's Journey, Within These Walls, Brush With Fate. Special: Dear America: Letters Home From Vietnam (reader). Series: The Doctors, The Ellen Burstyn Show, That's Life. Guest: Cheyenne, Dr. Kildare, 77 Sunset Strip, Perry Mason, The Iron Horse.

BURTON, KATE
Actress. b. Geneva, Switzerland, Sept. 10, 1957. e. Brown Univ. (B.A.), Yale Drama Sch. Daughter of late Richard Burton. m. stage manager Michael Ritchie. Worked at Yale Repertory Theatre, Hartford, Stage Co., the Hartman, Huntington Theatre, Williamstown, Berkshire Theatre festivals, The O'Neil Playwright's Conference, Pray Street Theatre.
THEATRE: Present Laughter (debut, 1982; Theatre World Award), Alice in Wonderland, Winners, The Accrington Pals, Doonesbury, The Playboy of the Western World, Wild Honey, Measure For Measure, Some Americans Abroad (Drama Desk nom.), Jake's Women, London Suite, Company.
PICTURES: Big Trouble in Little China (debut, 1986), Life With Mikey, August, First Wives Club, Looking for Richard, The Ice Storm, Celebrity, The Opportunists, Unfaithful, Swimfan.
TELEVISION: Mini-Series: Ellis Island, Evergreen. Movies: Alice in Wonderland, Uncle Tom's Cabin, Love Matters, Mistrial, Notes For My Daughter, Ellen Foster, Obsessed, The Diary of Ellen Rimbauer. Series: Home Fires, Monty.

BURTON, LEVAR
Actor, Director. b. Landstuhl, W. Germany, Feb. 16, 1957. e. U. of Southern California. Signed to play role of Kunta Kinte in TV mini-series, Roots, while still in school. Has hosted Public TV children's shows, Rebop, and Reading Rainbow.
PICTURES: Looking for Mr. Goodbar, The Hunter, The Supernaturals, Star Trek: Generations, Star Trek: First Contact, Yesterday's Target, Star Trek: Insurrection, Dancing in September, Ali, Star Trek: Nemesis, Blizzard (dir. only).
TELEVISION: Movies: Billy: Portrait of a Street Kid, Battered, One in a Million: The Ron Leflore Story, Dummy, Guyana Tragedy: The Story of Jim Jones, The Acorn People, Grambling's White Tiger, Emergency Room, The Jesse Owens Story, A Special Friendship, Roots: The Gift, Firestorm: 72 Hours in Oakland, Parallel Lives, The Tiger Woods Story (dir. only), Smart House (dir. only) Mini-Series: Roots. Specials: Almos' a Man, Roots: Celebrating 25 Years. Series: Rebop (host), Reading Rainbow (PBS; host, co-exec. prod.), Star Trek: The Next Generation (acting and dir.), Captain Planet and the Planeteers (voice), Star Trek: Deep Space Nine (episode dir.), Star Trek: Voyager (episode dir.), Christy (acting only), Soul Food (dir. only), Enterprise (episode dir.). Guest: Trapper John M.D., Houston Knights Voyager, Becker, Weakest Link.

BURTON, STEVE
Actor. b. Indianapolis, IN, June 28, 1970.
PICTURES: Red Sun Rising, CyberTracker CyberTracker 2, The Last Castle.
TELEVISION: Series: Out of This World, Days of Our Lives, General Hospital (Emmy Award, 1998). Mini-series: Taken.

BURTON, TIM
Director, Producer. b. Burbank, CA, Aug. 25, 1958. Cartoonist since grade school in suburban Burbank. Won Disney fellowship to study animation at California Institute of the Arts. At 20 went to Burbank to work as apprentice animator on Disney lot, working on such features as The Fox and the Hound, The Black Cauldron. Made Vincent, 6-minute stop-motion animation short on his own which was released commercially in 1982 and won several film fest. awards. Also made Frankenweenie, 29 minute live-action film. Appeared in film Singles. Wrote and illustrated children's book based on The Nightmare Before Christmas.
PICTURES: Director: Pee-wee's Big Adventure, Beetlejuice, Batman, Edward Scissorhands (also co-story, prod.), Batman Returns (also co-prod.), The Nightmare Before Christmas (also story, prod. design, co-prod.), Ed Wood (also co-prod.), Mars Attacks! (also prod, s.p.), Sleepy Hollow, Planet of the Apes, Big Fish. Co-Prod.: Cabin Boy, James and the Giant Peach, Batman Forever.
TELEVISION: Episode Director: Aladdin (Faerie Tale Theatre), Alfred Hitchcock Presents, Amazing Stories (Family Dog). Exec. Prod.: Beetlejuice, Family Dog, Lost in Oz (also creator, writer). Writer: Point Blank.

BURWELL, LOIS
Make-Up.
PICTURES: Gregory's Girl, The Draughtsman's Contract, Legend, No Surrender, Highlander, Mona Lisa, The Princess Bride, The Lonely Passion of Judith Hearne, Without A Clue, Dirty Rotten Scoundrels, Shirley Valentine, Air America, Hamlet, Blue Ice, The Muppet Christmas Carol, Widows' Peak, Braveheart (Acad. Award), Mission: Impossible, The Fifth Element, The Rainmaker, Saving Private Ryan (Acad. Award nom.), Hilary and Jackie, The Green Mile, Magnolia, Almost Famous, Captaon Corelli's Mandolin.
TELEVISION: Movies: Jack the Ripper, Charles and Diana: Unhappily Ever After, Jekyll & Hyde. Mini-Series: Master of the Game.

BUSCEMI, STEVE
Actor. b. Brooklyn, NY, 1957. Started as standup comedian in New York City, also wrote and acted in numerous one-act plays in collaboration with Mark Boone Jr. Acted in many plays by John Jesurun and worked briefly with the Wooster Group; worked as fireman. Studied acting at Lee Strasberg Inst. in NY.
PICTURES: The Way It Is/Eurydice in the Avenue, No Picnic, Parting Glances, Sleepwalk, Heart, Kiss Daddy Good Night, Call Me, Force of Circumstance, Vibes, Heart of Midnight, Bloodhounds of Broadway, Borders, New York Stories (Life

Lessons), Slaves of New York, Mystery Train, Tales from the Dark Side, Miller's Crossing, King of New York, Zandalee, Barton Fink, Billy Bathgate, Crisscross, In the Soup, Reservoir Dogs, Trusting Beatrice, Rising Sun, Twenty Bucks, Ed and His Dead Mother, The Hudsucker Proxy, Floundering, Airheads, Me and the Mob, Pulp Fiction, Billy Madison, Desperado, Somebody to Love, The Search for One-Eye Jimmy, Living in Oblivion, Things to Do in Denver When You're Dead, Pistolero, Fargo, Kansas City, Trees Lounge (also dir., s.p.), John Carpenter's Escape From L.A., Con Air, The Impostors, The Big Lebowski, The Wedding Singer, Armageddon, Louis & Frank, Big Daddy, 28 Days, Final Fantasy (voice), Ghost World (Golden Globe nom., AFI nom.), Monsters,Inc. (voice), The Grey Zone, Double Whammy, The Animal Factory (also dir.), The End of Love, Domestic Disturbance, the Laramie Project, Love in the Time of Money, Mr. Deeds, Spy Kids 2: Island of Lost Dreams, Deadrockstar, 13 Moons, The Sky Is Green, Minnesota Nice (video short, himself), Big Fish.
TELEVISION: *Mini-Series*: Lonesome Dove. *Movie*: The Last Outlaw. *Guest*: Miami Vice, The Equalizer, L.A. Law, Mad About You, The Drew Carey Show. *Director*: Homicide: Life on the Street (DGA award nom.,) The Sopranos (DGA award nom., Emmy nom.), Baseball Wives (dir.)

BUSCH, H. DONALD
Exhibitor. b. Philadelphia, PA, Sept. 21, 1935. e. U. of Pennsylvania, physics, math, 1956; law school, 1959. Practiced law, anti-trust & entertainment, 1960-87. 1984, pres., Budco Theatres, Inc. 1975-87. Pres., Busch, Grafman & Von Dreusche, P.C. 1987. Pres. & CEO, AMC Philadelphia, Inc., 1986-96. NATO chmn.,1990-91; chmn. emeritus, 1992. ShowEast, gen. chmn., 1990-91. Will Rogers Memorial Fund, dir. Pres. of NATO of Pennsylvania, 1988. Motion Picture Pioneers, Inc., dir., 1995.

BUSEY, GARY
Actor, Musician. b. Goose Creek, TX, June 29, 1944. e. Coffeyville Jr. Coll. A.B., 1963; attended Kansas State Coll, Okla. State U. Played drums with the Rubber Band 1963-70. Also drummer with Leon Russell, Willie Nelson (as Teddy Jack Eddy).
PICTURES: Angels Hard as They Come (debut, 1971), Didn't You Hear?, Dirty Little Billy, The Magnificent Seven Ride, The Last American Hero, Lolly Madonna XXX, Hex, Thunderbolt and Lightfoot, The Gumball Rally, A Star Is Born, Straight Time, Big Wednesday, The Buddy Holly Story (Natl. Society of Film Critics Award; Acad. Award nom., 1978), Foolin' Around, Carny, Barbarosa, D.C. Cab, The Bear, Insignificance, Stephen King's Silver Bullet, Let's Get Harry, Eye of the Tiger, Lethal Weapon, Bulletproof, Act of Piracy, Predator 2, My Heroes Have Always Been Cowboys, Hider in the House, Point Break, The Player, Under Siege, South Beach, The Firm, Rookie of the Year. Surviving the Game, Chasers, Breaking Point, Drop Zone, Man With a Gun, Black Sheep, Carried Away, 18 Suspicious Minds, Rough Draft, The Rage, Plato's Run, Livers Ain't Cheap, Lost Highway, Lethal Tender, Steel Sharks, Deadly Current, Warriors, Fear and Loathing in Las Vegas, Detour, Soldier, Jacob Two Two Meets the Hooded Fang, Apocalypse III: Tribulation, G-Men from Hell, Glory Glory, Down and Dirty, A Crack in the Floor, Joe Dirt, Frost: Portrait of a Vampire, Two Faced, Sam and Janet, Quigley, Skin Deep, El Padrino, Latin Dragon, The Reckoning.
TELEVISION: *Movies*: Bloodsport, The Execution of Private Slovik, The Law, Wild Texas Wind, Chrome Soldiers, Universal Soldier II: Brothers in Arms, Rough Riders, The Girl Next Door. *Mini-Series*: A Dangerous Life, The Neon Empire. *Series*: The Texas Wheelers, Howie, Fallen Angels, A Force of One. *Guest*: High Chaparral (debut, 1970), Gunsmoke, Saturday Night Live, The Hitchhiker (ACE Award), Law & Order, The Man Show.

BUSFIELD, TIMOTHY
Actor, Director. b. Lansing, MI, June 12, 1957. e. East Tennessee State U; Actor's Theatre of Louisville (as apprentice and resident). Founded Fantasy Theatre in Sacramento, 1986, a professional acting co., which performs in Northern CA schools, providing workshops on playwriting for children and sponsors annual Young Playwrights contest.
THEATRE: Richard II, Young Playwrights Festival (Circle Rep.), A Tale Told, Getting Out (European tour), Green Mountain Guild's Children Theatre, Mass Appeal, The Tempest, A Few Good Men (B'way). Founded & co-prod. The "B" Theatre, 1992, prods. Mass Appeal, Hidden in This Picture.
PICTURES: Stripes, Revenge of the Nerds, Revenge of the Nerds II, Field of Dreams, Sneakers, The Skateboard Kid, Striking Distance, Little Big League, Quiz Show, First Kid, The Souler Opposite, Erasable You, Wanted, Time at the Top, Wanted, Terminal Error, National Security.
TELEVISION: *Movies*: Strays, Calendar Girl-Cop-Killer?: The Bambi Bembenek Story, Murder Between Friends, In the Shadow of Evil, In the Line of Duty: Kidnapped, When Secrets Kill, Buffalo Soldiers, Trucks, Dreamhouse, Carson's Vertical Suburbia, The Darklings, Dead in a Heartbeat. *Series*: *Actor*: Reggie, Trapper John M.D., thirtysomething (Emmy Award, 1991; also dir. 3 episodes), Byrds of Paradise, Champs, The West Wing. Dir: Rude Awakening, Sports Night, Cover me: Based on the True Life of an FBI Family, That's Life, Ed (also co-exec. prod., supervising prod.) Lizzie McGuire, First Years, Danny. *Guest*: Family Ties, Matlock, Paper Chase, Love American Style, After M.A.S.H, Hotel, Tracey Takes On, Ed.

BUTTONS, RED
Actor. r.n. Aaron Chwatt. b. New York, NY, Feb. 5, 1919. Attended Evander Child H.S. in the Bronx. Singer at the age of 13; comic, Minsky's. Served in U.S. Army, during WWII; in Army stage prod. and film version of Winged Victory. Received Golden Globe Award noms. for Harlow and They Shoot Horses Don't They?; Best Comedian Award for The Red Buttons Show. Performed in most major Variety nightclubs shows.
PICTURES: Winged Victory (1944, debut), 13 Rue Madeleine, Footlight Varieties of 1951, Sayonara (Acad. Award for Best Supporting Actor, 1957; also Golden Globe Award), Imitation General, The Big Circus, One Two Three, The Longest Day, Gay Purr-ee (voice), Five Weeks in a Balloon, Hatari!, A Ticklish Affair, Your Cheatin' Heart, Harlow, Up From the Beach, Stagecoach, They Shoot Horses Don't They?, Who Killed Mary What's 'er Name?, The Poseidon Adventure, Gable and Lombard, Viva Knievel!, Pete's Dragon, Movie Movie, C.H.O.M.P.S., When Time Ran Out..., 18 Again!, The Ambulance, It Could Happen to You, The Story of Us, Let Me In I Hear Laughter, Odessa Or Bust.
TELEVISION: *Series*: The Red Buttons Show (1952-55), The Double Life of Henry Phyfe, Knots Landing, Rosanne, Bill Cosby, E.R., Street Time. *Movies*: Breakout, The New Original Wonder Woman, Louis Armstrong: Chicago Style, Telethon, Vega$, The Users, Power, The Dream Merchants, Leave 'Em Laughing, Reunion at Fairborough, Alice in Wonderland, Hansel & Gretel. Barefoot Boy With Cheek, Hold It, The Admiral Had a Wife, Winged Victory, Tender Trap, Play It Again Sam, The Teahouse of the August Moon, Red Buttons on Broadway, Finian's Rainbow, Off Your Rocker.

BUZZI, RUTH
Actress. b. Westerly, RI, July 24, 1936. e. Pasadena Playhouse Col. of Theatre Arts. On Country Music charts with You Oughta Hear the Song. Has received 5 Emmy nominations; Golden Globe winner, AGVA Variety Artist of the Year, 1977, Rhode Island Hall of Fame, Presidential commendation for outstanding artist in the field of entertainment, 1980, NAACP Image Award.
THEATRE: Sweet Charity (Broadway), 4 off-Broadway shows incl. A Man's A Man, Little Mary Sunshine, Cinderella, Wally's Cafe, 18 musical revues and Las Vegas club act.
PICTURES: Record City, Freaky Friday, The Apple Dumpling Gang Rides Again, The North Avenue Irregulars, The Villain, Surf Two, Skatetown USA, Chu Chu and the Philly Flash, The Being, The Bad Guys, Dixie Lanes, Up Your Alley, Diggin' Up Business, My Mom's a Werewolf, It's Your Life Michael Angelo, The Trouble Makers, Boys Will Be Boys, The Adventures of Elmo in Grouchland, Nothing But the Truth, Adventures in Home Schooling.
TELEVISION: *Series*: Rowan & Martin's Laugh-In, The Steve Allen Comedy Hour, Donny & Marie, The Lost Saucer, Betsy Lee's Ghost Town Jamboree, Carol Burnett's The Entertainers, Days of Our Lives, Sesame Street, Cro (voice), The Savage Dragon (voice), Sheep In the Big City (voice); semi-regular on 12 other series including Flip, Tony Orlando & Dawn, That Girl, Glen Campbell's Goodtime Hour, Leslie Uggums Show, The Dean Martin Variety Hour. *Guest*: Medical Center, Adam 12, Trapper John M.D., Love Boat, They Came from Outer Space, Major Dad, Alice, Here's Lucy, Saved by the Bell. *Movie*: In Name Only. Many cartoon voice-over series and over 150 on-camera commercials.

BYGRAVES, MAX
Comedian, Actor. b. London, England, October 16, 1922. e. St. Joseph's R.C. School, Rotherhithe. After RAF service, touring revues and London stage. TV debut in 1953, with own show. Autobiography: I Wanna Tell You A Story, 1976. Novel: The Milkman's on His Way, 1977. Received O.B.E., New Year's Honours 1983.
PICTURES: Skimpy in the Navy (debut, 1949), Bless 'em All, Nitwits on Parade, Tom Brown's Schooldays, Charley Moon, A Cry from the Streets, Bobbikins, Spare the Rod, The Alf Garnett Saga.
TELEVISION: *Series*: Roamin' Holiday, Max, Max Bygraves Side by Side, Family Fortunes. *Movies*: Family Misfortunes, Drake's Progress (tv documentary), The Showbiz Set (tv documentary, as himself).

BYRD, CARUTH C.
Production Executive. b. Dallas, TX, March 25, 1941. e. Trinity U, San Antonio. Multi-millionaire businessman, chmn. of Caruth C. Byrd Enterprises, Inc., who entered entertainment industry forming Communications Network Inc. in 1972. Was principal investor in film Santee (1972) and in 1973 formed Caruth C. Byrd Prods. to make theatrical features. 1983, chmn., Lone Star Pictures. 1987, formed Caruth C. Byrd Television. Formed Caruth C. Byrd Entertainment Inc. May, 1989. Concerts incl. Tom Jones, Natalie Cole, B.J. Thomas, Tammy Wynette, Seals & Croft, Eddie Rabbit, Helen Reddy, Jim Stafford, Tanya Tucker and many more.
PICTURES: Murph the Surf, The Monkeys of Bandapur (both exec. prod.), Santee, Sudden Death, Hollywood High II, Lone Star Country, Trick or Treats.
TELEVISION: Fishing Fever, Kids Are People Too, Tribute to Mom and Dad, Back to School, Texas 150: A Celebration Special.

BYRNE, DAVID
Composer, Actor, Singer, Director. b. Dumbarton, Scotland, May 14, 1952. Moved to Baltimore at 7. e. Rhode Island Sch. of Design studying photography, performance and video, and

Maryland Inst. Coll. of Art 1971-72. Prod. and dir. music videos. Awarded MTV's Video Vanguard Award, 1985. Best known as the lead singer and chief songwriter of Talking Heads. Composed and performed original score for choreographer Twyla Tharp's The Catherine Wheel (B'way). Wrote music for Robert Wilson's The Knee Plays.
PICTURES: Stop Making Sense (conceived and stars in concert film), True Stories (dir., s.p., narrator), The Last Emperor (music, Academy Award, 1988), Married to the Mob (music), Heavy Petting, Between the Teeth (also co-dir.), Young Adam (composer). Also contributed music to such films as Times Square, The Animals' Film, King of Comedy, America is Waiting, Revenge of the Nerds, Down and Out in Beverly Hills, Dead End Kids, Cross My Heart, Somebody's Waiting, The Book of Life, The Bachelor, The Family Man, Someone Like You, The Banger Sisters.
TELEVISION: A Family Tree, Alive From Off-Center (also composed theme), Survival Guides; Rolling Stone Magazine's 20 Years of Rock and Roll, The Catherine Wheel (composer).

BYRNE, GABRIEL
Actor. b. Dublin, Ireland, May 12, 1950. e. University Coll., Ireland. Worked as archaeologist, then taught Spanish at girls' school. Participated in amateur theatre before acting with Ireland's Focus Theatre, an experimental rep. co. and joining Dublin's Abbey Theatre Co. Cast in long-running TV series the Riordans. Also worked with National Theater in London. Author: Pictures in My Head (1994).
PICTURES: On a Paving Stone Mounted, The Outsider, Excalibur, Hanna K, The Keep, Defence of the Realm, Gothic, Lionheart, Siesta, Hello Again, Julia and Julia, A Soldier's Tale, The Courier, Miller's Crossing, Shipwrecked, Dark Obsession, Cool World, Point of No Return, Into the West (also assoc. prod.), A Dangerous Woman, In the Name of the Father (prod. only), Prince of Jutland, A Simple Twist of Fate, Trial by Jury, Little Women, The Usual Suspects, Frankie Starlight, Dead Man, Last of the High Kings (also co-s.p.), Mad Dog Time, Somebody Is Waiting (also prod.), The End of Violence, Toby's Story, Polish Wedding, This Is the Sea, The Man in the Iron Mask, Quest for Camelot (voice), The Brylcreem Boys (also prod.), Stigmata, End of Days, Mad About Mambo (exec. prod.), Canone inverso - Making Love, When Brendan Met Trudy, Spider, Emmett's Mark, Virginia's Run, Ghost Ship, Shade, Vanity Fair, The Bridge of San Luis Rey.
TELEVISION: Movies/Specials: Wagner, The Search for Alexander the Great, Treatment, Joyce in June, Mussolini, Christopher Columbus, Lark in the Clear Air (also dir., writer), Buffalo Girls, Weapons of Mass Destruction. Series: The Riordan's, Bracken, Madigan Men (also co-exec. prod.).

BYRNES, EDD
Actor. r.n. Edward Byrne Breitenberger. b. New York, NY, July 30, 1933. e. Harren H.S. Prof. debut, Joe E. Brown's Circus Show. Author of Edd Byrnes: Kookie No More.
THEATRE: Tea and Sympathy, Picnic, Golden Boy, Bus Stop, Ready When You Are C.B., Storm in Summer.
PICTURES: Reform School Girl, Darby's Rangers, Up Periscope, Marjorie Morningstar, Yellowstone Kelly, Girl on the Run, The Secret Invasion, Wicked Wicked, Grease, Stardust, Go Kill and Come Back, Payment in Blood, Troop Beverly Hills.
TELEVISION: Series: 77 Sunset Strip, Sweepstake$. Has appeared in over 300 TV shows incl.: Matinee Theatre, Crossroads, Jim Bowie, Wire Service, Navy Log, Oh Susanna!, Throb, Rags to Riches, Murder She Wrote. Movies: The Silent Gun, Mobile Two, Telethon, Vega$, Twirl. Mini-series: Shake Rattle and Roll: An American Love Story.

BYRON, KATHLEEN
Actress. b. London, England, Jan. 11, 1923. e. London U., Old Vic. co. student, 1942. Screen debut in Young Mr. Pitt, 1943.
PICTURES: Silver Fleet, Black Narcissus, Matter of Life and Death, Small Back Room, Madness of the Heart, Reluctant Widow, Prelude to Fame, Scarlet Thread, Tom Brown's Schooldays, Four Days, Hell Is Sold Out, I'll Never Forget You, Gambler and the Lady, Young Bess, Night of the Silvery Moon, Profile, Secret Venture, Hand in Hand, Night of the Eagle, Hammerhead, Wolfshead, Private Road, Twins of Evil, Craze, Abdication, One of Our Dinosaurs Is Missing, The Elephant Man, From a Far Country, Emma, Remembering Sister Ruth (documentary), The Frighteners, Saving Private Ryan, Diary, A Profile of Black Narcissus (short).
TELEVISION: The Lonely World of Harry Braintree, All My Own Work, Emergency Ward 10, Probation Officer, Design for Murder, Sergeant Cork, Oxbridge 2000, The Navigators, The Worker, Hereward the Wake, Breaking Point, Vendetta, Play To Win, Who Is Sylvia, Portrait of a Lady, Callan, You're Wrecking My Marriage, Take Three Girls, The Confession of Mariona Evans, Paul Temple, The Worker, The Moonstone, The Challengers, The Golden Bowl, The Edwardians, The New Life, Menace, The Rivals of Sherlock Holmes, The Brontes, On Call, Edward VII, Sutherland's Law, Crown Court, Anne of Avonlea, Heidi, Notorious Woman, General Hospital, North & South, Angelo, Within these Walls, Jubilee, Z Cars, Tales from the Supernatural, Secret Army, An Englishman's Castle, The Professionals, Forty Weeks, Emmerdale Farm, Blake Seven, The Minders, Together, Hedda Gabler, Nancy Astor, God Speed Co-operation, Take Three Women, Reilly, Memoirs of Sherlock Holmes, Moon And Son, The Bill, Casualty, Portrait of a Marriage, Gentlemen & Players, Dalziel and Pascoe: Cunning Old Foxes, In A Land of Plenty, Perfect Strangers.

BYRUM, JOHN
Writer, Director. b. Winnetka, IL, March 14, 1947. e. New York U. Film School. First job as gofer on industrial films and cutting dailies for underground filmmakers. Went to England where wrote 1st s.p., Comeback. From 1970-73, was in NY writing and re-writing scripts for low-budget films.
PICTURES: Writer: Mahogany, Inserts (also dir.) Harry and Walter Go to New York, Heart Beat (also dir), Sphinx, Scandalous, The Razor's Edge (also dir.), The Whoopee Boys (also dir.), The War at Home (also dir.), Duets (also prod.).
TELEVISION: Movie: Murder in High Places (dir., writer). Series: Alfred Hitchcock Presents (1985), Middle Ages (creator, writer, exec. prod.), South of Sunset (creator, writer, exec. prod.), Winnetka Road (creator, writer, exec. prod.).

C

CAAN, JAMES
Actor. b. Bronx, NY, March 26, 1939. e. Hofstra U. Studied with Sanford Meisner at the Neighborhood Playhouse. Appeared off-B'way in La Ronde, 1961. Also on B'way in Mandingo, Blood Sweat and Stanley Poole.
PICTURES: Irma La Douce (debut, 1963), Lady in a Cage, The Glory Guys, Red Line 7000, El Dorado, Games, Countdown, Journey to Shiloh, Submarine X-1, The Rain People, Rabbit Run, T.R. Baskin, The Godfather (Acad. Award nom.), Slither, Cinderella Liberty, The Gambler, Freebie and the Bean, The Godfather Part II, Funny Lady, Rollerball, The Killer Elite, Harry and Walter Go to New York, Silent Movie, A Bridge Too Far, Another Man Another Chance, Comes a Horseman, Chapter Two, Hide in Plain Sight (also dir.), Thief, Bolero, Kiss Me Goodbye, Gardens of Stone, Alien Nation, Dick Tracy, Misery, The Dark Backward, For the Boys, Honeymoon in Vegas, The Program, Flesh & Bone, A Boy Called Hate, Bottle Rocket, Eraser, Bulletproof, This is My Father, The Yards, Mickey Blue Eyes, Luckytown, Way of the Gun, Viva Las Nowhere, In the Shadows, Night at the Golden Eagle, Dogville, City of Ghosts, This Thing of Ours, Elf, Jericho Mansions, The Incredible Mrs. Ritchie, Dallas 362, Castle of Lies.
TELEVISION: Much series guest work (Naked City, Route 66, Wagon Train, Ben Casey, Alfred Hitchcock Presents, NewsRadio, etc.). Movies: Brian's Song (Emmy nom.), Poodle Springs, Warden of Red Rock, A Glimpse of Hell, Lathe of Heaven, Blood Crime. Mini-series: Les Uns et les autres, Naked Hollywood (as himself). Specials: AFI's 100 Year 100 Stars, Playboy: The Party Continues. Series: Las Vegas.

CACOYANNIS, MICHAEL
Producer, Director, Writer. b. Limassoc, Cyprus, June 11, 1922. Studied law in London, admitted to bar at age 21. Became a producer of BBC's wartime Greek programs while attending dramatic school. After acting on the stage in England, left in 1952 for Greece, where he made his first film, Windfall in Athens, with his own script. While directing Greek classical plays, he continued making films.
PICTURES: Director/Writer: Windfall in Athens (Sunday Awakening; debut, 1954), Stella, Girl in Black, A Matter of Dignity (The Final Lie), Our Last Spring (Eroica), The Wastrel, Electra, Zorba the Greek, The Day the Fish Came Out, The Trojan Women, Attila '74, Iphigenia, Sweet Country, Up Down and Sideways, Varya, The Cherry Orchard (also prod.)
TELEVISION: Movies: The Story of Jacob and Joseph (dir.)

CAESAR, SID
Actor. b. Yonkers, NY, Sept. 8, 1922. Studied saxophone at Juilliard School; then appeared in service revue Tars and Spars. Cast by prod. Max Liebman in B'way revue Make Mine Manhattan in 1948. Voted best comedian in M.P. Daily's TV poll, 1951, 1952. Best Comedy Team (with Imogene Coca) in 1953. Received Sylvania Award, 1958. Formed Shelbrick Corp. TV, 1959. Appeared in B'way musical Little Me (1962), Off-B'way & B'way revue Sid Caesar & Company (1989). Author: Where Have I Been? (autobiography, 1982).
PICTURES: Tars and Spars (debut, 1945), The Guilt of Janet Ames, It's a Mad Mad Mad Mad World, The Spirit Is Willing, The Busy Body, A Guide for the Married Man, Airport 1975, Silent Movie, Fire Sale, Grease, The Cheap Detective, The Fiendish Plot of Dr. Fu Manchu, History of the World Part 1, Grease 2, Over the Brooklyn Bridge, Cannonball Run II, Stoogemania, The Emperor's New Clothes, Vegas Vacation, The Wonderful Ice Cream Suit, Let Me In I Hear Laughter, Hail Sid Caesar: The Golden Age of Comedy.
TELEVISION: Series: Admiral Broadway Revue, Your Show of Shows (Emmy Award for Best Actor, 1952), Caesar's Hour (Emmy Award for Best Comedian, 1956), Sid Caesar Invites You (1958), As Caesar Sees It, The Sid Caesar Show. Movies: Flight to Holocaust, Curse of the Black Widow, The Munsters' Revenge, Found Money, Love Is Never Silent, Alice in Wonderland, Freedom Fighter, Side By Side, The Great Mom Swap. Guest: G.E. Theatre, The Ed Sullivan Show, Carol Burnett Show, Lucy Show, That's Life, Love American Style, The Love Boat, Amazing Stories, Mad About You. Specials: Tiptoe Through TV, Variety—World of Show Biz, Sid Caesar and Edie Adams Together, The Sid Caesar Imogene Coca Carl Reiner Howard Morris Special, Christmas Snow, Added Attractions:The Hollywood Shorts Story. Appeared in numerous video documentaries featuring his comedy favorites, such as The Sid Caesar Collection: The Fan Favorites.

CAGE, NICOLAS
Actor. b. Long Beach, CA, Jan. 7, 1964. r.n. Nicholas Coppola. Nephew of dir. Francis Ford Coppola. Joined San Francisco's American Conservatory Theatre at age 15. While attending Beverly Hills High School won role on tv pilot Best of Times.
PICTURES: Fast Times at Ridgemont High (debut, 1982; billed as Nicholas Coppola), Valley Girl, Rumble Fish, Racing with the Moon, The Cotton Club, Birdy, The Boy in Blue, Peggy Sue Got Married, Raising Arizona, Moonstruck, Vampire's Kiss, Fire Birds, Wild at Heart, Tempo di Mecidere (Time to Kill), Zandalee, Honeymoon in Vegas, Amos & Andrew, DeadFall, Red Rock West, Guarding Tess, It Could Happen to You, Trapped in Paradise, Kiss of Death, Leaving Las Vegas (Academy Award, Chicago Film Critics Award, Nat'l Society of Film Critics Award; Golden Globe Award), The Rock, Con Air, Face/Off, Tom Slick: Monster Hunter, 8mm, City of Angels, Snake Eyes, Bringing Out the Dead, Gone in Sixty Seconds, Captain Corelli's Mandolin, Christmas Carol: The Movie (voice), Windtalkers, Sonny ((also prod.., dir.), Adaptation, The Life of David Gale (prod. only), Matchstick Men, Ghost Rider.

CAINE, MICHAEL
Actor. r.n. Maurice Micklewhite. b. London, England, March 14, 1933. Asst. stage mgr. Westminster Rep. (Sussex, UK 1953); Lowestoft Rep. 1953-55. London stage: The Room, The Dumbwaiter, Next Time I'll Sing For You (1963). Author: Michael Caine's Moving Picture Show or: Not Many People Know This Is the Movies, Acting on Film, What's It All About? (autobiography, 1993). Awarded C.B.E., 1992. Video: Michael Caine—Acting on Film.
PICTURES: Has appeared in 98 pictures, incl.: A Hill in Korea (debut, 1956; aka Hell in Korea), How to Murder A Rich Uncle, The Key, Two-Headed Spy, Blind Spot, Breakout (Danger Within), Foxhole in Cairo, Bulldog Breed, The Day the Earth Caught Fire, Solo for Sparrow, Zulu, The Ipcress File, Alfie (Acad. Award nom.), The Wrong Box, Gambit, Funeral in Berlin, Hurry Sundown, Woman Times Seven, Billion Dollar Brain, Deadfall, The Magus, Play Dirty, The Italian Job, The Battle of Britain, Too Late the Hero, The Last Valley, Get Carter, Kidnapped, X Y & Zee, Pulp, Sleuth (Acad. Award nom.), The Black Windmill, The Marseille Contract, The Wilby Conspiracy, Peeper, The Romantic Englishwoman, The Man Who Would Be King, Harry and Walter Go to New York, The Eagle Has Landed, A Bridge Too Far, Ashanti, Beyond the Poseidon Adventure, The Island, Dressed to Kill, Victory, Deathtrap, Educating Rita (Acad. Award nom.), Beyond the Limit, Blame It on Rio, The Jigsaw Man, The Holcroft Covenant, Hannah and Her Sisters (Academy Award for Best Supporting Actor, 1986), Sweet Liberty, Mona Lisa, Half Moon Street, Jaws—The Revenge, The Whistle Blower, The Fourth Protocol (also exec. prod.), Surrender, Without a Clue, Mr. Destiny, Bullseye!, The Muppet Christmas Carol, On Deadly Ground, Bullet in Beijing, Blood & Wine, Shadow Run, Little Voice, Curtain Call, The Cider House Rules, Quills, Shiner, Get Carter, Miss Congeniality, The Quiet American, Last Orders, Quicksand, Austin Powers in Goldmember, The Actors, Secondhand Lions, The Statement.
TELEVISION: Movies: Jack the Ripper, Jekyll and Hyde, Blue Ice (also prod.), World War II: 20,000 League under the Sea, Mandela and De Klerk. Series: Rickles (1975). In more than 100 British teleplays 1957-63 incl. The Compartment, The Playmates, Hobson's Choice, Funny Noises with Their Mouths, The Way with Reggie, Luck of the Draw, Hamlet, The Other Man.

CALLAN, MICHAEL
Actor, Singer, Dancer. b. Philadelphia, PA, Nov. 22, 1935. Singer, dancer, Philadelphia nightclubs; to New York in musicals including The Boy Friend and West Side Story; dancer at Copacabana nightclub; in short-run plays, Las Vegas: That Certain Girl, Love Letters.
PICTURES: They Came to Cordura (debut, 1958) The Flying Fontaines, Because They're Young, Pepe, Mysterious Island, Gidget Goes Hawaiian, 13 West Street, Bon Voyage, The Interns, The Victors, The New Interns, Cat Ballou, You Must Be Joking!, The Magnificent Seven Ride!, Frasier the Sensuous Lion, Lepke, The Photographer, The Cat and The Canary, Record City, Double Exposure (also prod.), Chained Heat, Freeway, Leprechaun III, Hello Muddah—Hello Fadduh (prod. only), Stuck On You.
TELEVISION: Movies: In Name Only, Donner Pass: The Road to Survival, Last of the Great Survivors, Young Hearts, My Wicked Wicked Ways...Legend of Errol Flynn. Mini-Series: Blind Ambition, Scruples. Series: Occasional Wife, One Life To Live. Guest: Murder She Wrote, Superboy, T.J Hooker, The Fall Guy.

CALLEY, JOHN
Producer, Executive. b. Jersey City, NJ, 1930. Exec., Ted Bates advertising and NBC; exec. v.p., Filmways, Inc., 1961-1968; president, vice chairman, exec. v.p., Warner Bros., Inc., 1968-81; 1989-93 independent prod., president & COO, United Artists (MGM); Pres. & COO of Sony Pictures Entertainment (SPE), 1996; chairman & CEO, SPE, 1998-Oct. 2003, at which time he resigned.
PICTURES: Assoc. prod./Prod. or Exec. Prod.: The Wheeler Dealers, Face in the Rain, The Americanization of Emily, The Sandpiper, The Cincinnati Kid, The Loved One, Eye of the Devil, Don't Make Waves, Castle Keep, Catch-22, Fat Man & Little Boy, Postcards from the Edge, The Remains of the Day, One Night Stand (acting), Stanley Kubrick: A Life in Pictures (documentary, as himself), This Is Gary McFarland (as himself).

CALLOW, SIMON
Actor, Writer, Director. b. London, June 13, 1949. e. Queens, U. of Belfast, The Drama Centre. Originated role of Mozart in London premiere of Amadeus and Burgess/Chubb in Single Spies. Author: Being an Actor, Acting in Restoration Comedy, Charles Laughton: A Difficult Actor, Shooting the Actor, Orson Welles: The Road to Xanadu.
THEATRE: London: Plumber's Progress, The Doctor's Dilemma, Soul of the White Ant, Blood Sports, The Resistible Rise of Arturo Ui, Amadeus, Restoration, The Beastly Beatitudes of Balthazar B, Titus Andronicus (Bristol Old Vic), Faust. Shakespeare's Sonnets. Director: Loving Reno, The Infernal Machine (also translator), Jacques and His Master (also trans.; L.A.), Single Spies, Shades, My Fair Lady (Natl. tour), Shirley Valentine (London, NY), Carmen Jones.
PICTURES: Amadeus, A Room With a View, The Good Father, Maurice, Manifesto, Postcards From the Edge, Mr. and Mrs. Bridge, The Ballad of the Sad Cafe (dir. only), Howards End, Four Weddings and a Funeral, Street Fighter, Jefferson in Paris, Ace Ventura: When Nature Calls, James and the Giant Peach, The Scarlet Tunic, Bedroom and Hallways, Shakespeare in Love, Notting Hill, Junk, No Man's Land, Christmas Carol: The Movie (voice), Thunderpants, George and the Dragon, Sex & Violence, George and the Dragon
TELEVISION: Man of Destiny, La Ronde, All the World's a Stage, Wings of Song, The Dybbuk, Instant Enlightenment, Chance of a Lifetime (series), David Copperfield, Honour, Profit and Pleasure, Old Flames, Revolutionary Witness: Palloy, The Woman in White, Trial & Retribution II, Trial & Retribution III, Deadly Appearances, Robert's Rescue, Don't Eat the Neighbours, Judi Dench: A BAFTA Tribute.

CAMERON, JAMES
Director, Writer, Producer. b. Kapuskasing, Ontario, Canada, Aug. 16, 1954. e. Fullerton Junior Col. (physics). 1990, formed Lightstorm Entertainment.
PICTURES: Piranha II—The Spawning (dir.), The Terminator (dir., s.p.), Rambo: First Blood Part II (co-s.p.), Aliens (dir., s.p.), The Abyss (dir., s.p.), Terminator 2: Judgment Day (dir., co-s.p., prod.), Point Break (exec. prod.), True Lies (dir., co-s.p., prod.), Strange Days (co-prod., co-s.p., story), Titanic (dir., prod., story, Acad. Award, Golden Globe Award, Best Pic., Best Dir., Best Film Edit., 1997), True Lies 2, Ghosts of the Abyss (dir. only) Solaris (prod.) Terminator 3: Rise of the Machines (writer), Actor: Fear City: A Family Style Comedy, Your Studio and You, Titanic, The Muse, High Heels and Low Lifes.
TELEVISION: Movies: Dark Angel (writer, exec. prod.), Earthship TV (dir.), Expedition: Bismarck (prod., dir. and acting/himself). Series: Dark Angel. Actor: Alien Evolution.

CAMERON, JOANNA
Actress, Director. r.n. Patricia Cameron. b. Aspen, CO, Sept. 20, 1951. e. U. of California, Sorbonne, Pasadena Playhouse, 1968. Guinness Record: Most network programmed TV commercials. TV Director: Various commercials, CBS Preview Special, closed circuit program host U.S.N., all TV equipped ships–actress and dir. Documentaries: Razor Sharp (prod., dir.), El Camino Real (dir., prod.).
PICTURES: How To Commit Marriage (debut), I Love My Wife, B.S. I Love You, Pretty Maids All in a Row.
TELEVISION: Movies: The Great American Beauty Contest, A Time for Love, Sorority Kill, Night Games, Columbo: Negative Reaction, It Couldn't Happen to a Nicer Guy, High Risk, Spider Man Strikes Back, Swan Song. Series: Isis. Guest: The Survivors, Love American Style, Daniel Boone, Mission Impossible, The Partners, Search, Medical Center, Name of the Game, The Bold Ones, Marcus Welby, Petrocelli, Columbo, Switch, MacMillan, Spiderman. Specials: Bob Hope Special, Bob Hope 25th NBC Anniversary Special.

CAMERON, KIRK
Actor. b. Canoga Park, CA, Oct. 12, 1970. m. actress Chelsea Noble. Sister is actress Candace Cameron. Started doing TV commercials at age 9.
PICTURES: The Best of Times, Like Father-Like Son, Listen to Me, The Willies.
TELEVISION: Movies: Goliath Awaits, Starflight: The Plane That Couldn't Land, A Little Piece of Heaven, Star Struck, The Computer Wore Tennis Shoes, You Lucky Dog, The Growing Pains Movie, The Miracle of the Cards. Specials: The Woman Who Willed a Miracle, Andrea's Story. Ice Capades with Kirk Cameron. Series: Two Marriages, Growning Pains, Kirk.

CAMP, COLLEEN
Actress, Producer. b. San Francisco, CA, June 7, 1953. Spent 2 years as a bird trainer at Busch Gardens before being noticed by an agent and cast on TV. TV debut on The Dean Martin Show. Assoc. prod. on Martha Coolidge's film The City Girl. Sang several songs in They All Laughed and made Billboard charts with song One Day Since Yesterday.
PICTURES: Battle for the Planet of the Apes (debut, 1973), Swinging Cheerleaders, Death Game (The Seducers), Funny Lady, Smile, The Gumball Rally, Cats in a Cage, Game of Death, Apocalypse Now, Cloud Dancer, They All Laughed, The Seduction, Valley Girl, Smokey and the Bandit III, Rosebud Beach Hotel, The Joy of Sex, Police Academy II, Doin' Time, Eye of the Devil, Walk Like a Man, Illegally Yours, Track 29, Wicked Stepmother, My Blue Heaven, Wayne's World, The Vagrant, Un-Becoming Age, Sliver, Last Action Hero, Greedy, Naked in New York, Die Hard With a Vengeance, The Baby-sitter's Club, Three Wishes, Plump Fiction,

House Arrest, The Ice Storm, Speed 2: Cruise Control, Jazz Night, Election, Love Stinks, Goosed, Loser, Bar Hopping, Someone Like You, An American Rhapsody, Rat Race, Second to Die, Joshua, L.A. Twister, Who's Your Daddy, .
TELEVISION: *Movies*: Amelia Earhart, Lady of the House, Addicted to His Love, Backfield in Motion, For Their Own Good, The Right to Remain Silent, How to Make a Monster (also prod.), The Day the World Ended (prod. only), She Creature (prod. only), Teenage Caveman (prod. only). *Mini-Series*: Rich Man Poor Man Book II. *Series*: Dallas. *Guest*: George Burns Comedy Week, Happy Days, Dukes of Hazzard, WKRP in Cincinnati, Magnum PI, Murder She Wrote, Tales from the Crypt, Roseanne. *Specials*: Going Home Again, Dorothy Stratten: The E! True Hollywood Story.

CAMP, JOE
Producer, Director, Writer. b. St. Louis, MO, Apr. 20, 1939. e. U. of Mississippi, B.B.A. Acct. exec. McCann-Erickson Advt., Houston 1961-62; owner Joe Camp Real Estate 1962-64; acct. exec. Norsworthy-Mercer, Dallas 1964-69; dir. TV commercials; founder and pres. Mulberry Square Prods, 1971-present. Author: Underdog.
PICTURES: *Dir./Prod./Writer*: Benji, Hawmps, For the Love of Benji, The Double McGuffin, Oh Heavenly Dog, Benji the Hunted, Benji Returns: The Promise of Christmas, Benji Returns: Rags to Riches (dir., writer, prod.).
TELEVISION: *Specials*: The Phenomenon of Benji (dir., writer, prod.), Benji's Very Own Christmas Story (dir., prod., writer), Benji at Work (prod., writer), Benji at Marineland (dir., writer), Benji Zax and the Alien Prince (dir.).

CAMPANELLA, TOM
Executive. b. Houston, TX, 1944. e. City U. of NY. Joined Paramount Pictures 1968 as asst. business mgr.; later worked for corporate div. and Motion Picture Group. Named exec. dir., nat'l adv. 1979, made v.p., nat'l adv. 1982, appt. sr. v.p., adv., for M.P. Group of Paramount, 1984. Appointed exec. v.p., adv. & promo., 1990. Presently, exec. v.p. of Worldwide Marketing/Advertising for Paramount Pictures.

CAMPBELL, BRUCE
Actor, Producer. b. Birmingham, MI, June 22, 1958.
PICTURES: The Evil Dead (debut, 1983; also exec. prod.), Crimewave (also co-prod.), Evil Dead 2 (also co-prod.), Maniac Cop, Moontrap, Darkman, Maniac Cop 2, Sundown: The Vampire in Retreat, Mindwarp, Lunatics: A Love Story (also prod.), Waxwork II: Lost in Time, Army of Darkness (also co-prod.), The Hudsucker Proxy, The Demolitionist, Congo, Assault on Dome 4, Menno's Mind, John Carpenter's Escape From L.A., Running Time, McHale's Navy, The Ice Rink, From Dusk Till Dawn 2: Texas Blood Money, Nobody Knows, Hubert's Brain, The Majestic, Spider Man, Bubba Ho-Tep, Serving Sara, Phantasm's End, Spider-Man II.
TELEVISION: *Movies*: Tornado!, Missing Links, The Love Bug, In the Line of Duty: Blaze of Glory, Goldrush: A Real Life Alaskan Adventure, Terminal Invasion, Masters of Horror (host), Man With the Screaming Brain (actor, dir. s.p., prod.) *Series*: Generations, The Adventures of Brisco County Jr., Timecop, Ellen, Jack of All Trades. *Guest*: Xena, Hercules: The Legendary Journeys, The X Files, American Gothic.

CAMPBELL, CHRISTIAN
Actor. b. Toronto, Canada, May 12, 1972. Sister is actress Neve Campbell.
PICTURES: Next Time, Trick, Cold Hearts, Angels, Plead, Who is A.B., Thank You Good Night, The Good Things, Gargoyle.
TELEVISION: *Movies*: School's Out, City Boy, Born to Run, Picture Perfect, Seduced by Madness, I've Been Waiting for You, The Piano Man's Daughter. *Series*: Malibu Shores, The $treet, Max Steel, The Atwood Stories. *Guest*: 7th Heaven, Blue Murder.

CAMPBELL, GLEN
Actor, Singer. b. Delight, AK, April 22, 1936. After forming local band became studio guitarist in Hollywood on records for such per-formers as Frank Sinatra and Elvis Presley. Won two Grammy awards for record By the Time I Get to Phoenix, 1967. Appeared frequently on Shindig on TV.
PICTURES: The Cool Ones, True Grit, Norwood, Any Which Way You Can, Rock a Doodle (voice), Family Prayers, Third World Cop.
TELEVISION: *Series*: The Smothers Brothers Comedy Hour, The Glen Campbell Goodtime Hour, The Glen Campbell Music Show; many specials. *Movie*: Strange Homecoming.

CAMPBELL, MICHAEL L.
Executive. b. Knoxville, TN, Jan. 22, 1954. Worked for White Stores, Inc. in a management position until 1982. Founded first the-atre venture, Premiere Cinemas in 1982. Premiere grew to 150 screens and was sold to Cinemark in 1989. Founded Regal Cinemas in 1989. Chairman, President and CEO Regal Cinemas, Inc. Company is now part of Regal Entertainment Group, which includes Regal Cinemas, United Artists Theatres and Edwards Theatres. Cambell is co-CEO of Regal Entertainment Group. The group operates 5,663 screens in 524 locations in 36 states (2003). Named Coopers & Lybrand regional entreprenuer of the year, 1993. Dir. NATO and serves on NATO executive committee.

CAMPBELL, NEVE
Actress. b. Guelph, Ontario, Canada, Oct. 3, 1973. Brother is actor Christian Campbell.
PICTURES: Paint Cans, The Dark, Love Child, The Craft, Scream, Simba's Pride (voice), Scream 2, Hairshirt (also prod.), Wild Things, 54, Three to Tango, Scream 3, Investigating Sex, Panic, Drowning

Mona, Lost Junction, Blind Horizon, The Remains of the Piano.
TELEVISION: *Movies*: Web of Deceit, Baree, I Know My Son is Alive, The Forget-Me-Not Murders, The Canterville Ghost, Fitzgerald. *Guest*: The Kids in the Hall, Are You Afraid of the Dark?*Series*: Catwalk, Party of Five.

CAMPBELL, WILLIAM
Actor. b. Newark, NJ, Oct. 30, 1926. e. Feagin Sch. of Drama. Appeared in summer stock; B'way before film debut.
PICTURES: The Breaking Point (debut, 1950), Breakthrough, Inside the Walls of Folsom Prison, Operation Pacific, The People Against O'Hara, Holiday for Sinners, Battle Circus, Small Town Girl, Code Two, The Big Leaguer, Escape from Fort Bravo, The High and the Mighty, The Fast and the Furious, Man Without a Star, Cell 2455— Death Row, Battle Cry, Running Wild, Man in the Vault, Backlash, Love Me Tender, Walk the Proud Land, Eighteen and Anxious, The Naked and the Dead, Money Women and Guns, The Sheriff of Fractured Jaw, Natchez Train, Night of Evil, The Young Racers, The Secret Invasion, Dementia 13, Hush Hush Sweet Charlotte, Blood Bath, Track of the Vampire, Pretty Maids All in a Row, Black Gunn.
TELEVISION: *Series*: Cannonball, Dynasty, Crime Story. *Pilot*: Heat: When You Lie Down With Dogs. *Movie*: Return of the Six Million Dollar Man and the Bionic Woman.

CAMPION, JANE
Director, Writer. b. Wellington, New Zealand, April 30, 1954. e. Victoria Univ. of Wellington (BA, anthropology, 1975), Sydney Coll. of Arts (BA, painting, 1979). Attended Australian Sch. of Film & TV in early 1980's, where she debuted as dir. & writer with short film Peel (1982; Palme d'Or at Cannes Film Fest., 1986). Other short films: A Girl's Own Story, Passionless Moments, After Hours, Two Friends, Mishaps of Seduction & Conquest.
PICTURES: *Director/Writer*: Sweetie (feature debut, 1989; Australian Film Awards for Best Director & Film; LA Film Critics New Generation Award, American Indept. Spirit Award), An Angel at My Table (Venice Film Fest. Silver Lion Award, Indept. Spirit Award), The Piano (Academy Award, WGA, LA Film Critics, NY Film Critics, & Natl. Society of Film Critics Awards for best screenplay; LA Film Critics & NY Film Critics Awards for best director; Cannes Film Fest. Award for best film), The Portrait of a Lady, Holy Smoke, Soft Fruit (exec. prod.), In the Cut.
TELEVISION: *Series*: *Episode director*: Dancing Daze.

CANNELL, STEPHEN J.
Writer, Producer, Actor. b. Los Angeles, CA, May 2, 1941 e. U. of Oregon, B.A., 1964. After coll. worked at father's decorating firm for 4 years while writing scripts in evening. Sold 1st script for Adam 12, 1966. Asked to serve as head writer at Universal Studios. Chief exec. officer, Stephen J. Cannell Prods. TV prod. co. he formed 1979. Also formed The Cannell Studios, parent co. 1986. Natl. chmn., Orton Dyslexia Society. Received Mystery Writers award 1975; 4 Writers Guild Awards. Acted in films: Identity Crisis, Posse.
PICTURES: Acting: Identity Crisis, Posse, The Contract, Half Past Dead. Exec. prod.: Dead Above Ground, It Waits. Prod.: Bad Boy.
TELEVISION: The Rockford Files (creator, writer, prod.; Emmy Award), The Jordan Chance, The Duke, Stone, 10 Speed and Brownshoe, Nightside, Midnight Offerings, The Greatest American Hero, The Quest, Them, The Rockford Files: Crime and Punishment, The Rockford Files: Murder and Misdemeanors. *Prod.*: The A-Team, Hardcastle and McCormick, The Rousters, Riptide, Brothers-in-Law, *Creator/Prod.*: Baa Baa Black Sheep, Richie Brockelman, Hunter, Wise Guy, 21 Jump Street, J.J. Starbuck, Sonny Spoon, Sirens (co-exec. prod.), Unsub (exec. prod., writer, pilot), Booker (exec. prod.), Top of the Hill (exec. prod.), Scene of the Crime (exec.-prod., creator), The Commish, The Hat Squad, Traps, Greyhounds (exec. prod., writer), Hawkeye, Marker (exec. prod., creator), Renegade (exec. prod., creator), U.S. Customs Classified (exec. prod., host), Profit (exec. prod.), Rockford Files: Murders and Misdemeanors, Hunter (exec. prod., 2003).

CANNON, DANNY
Director, Producer, Writer. b. London, England, 1968.
PICTURES: Strangers (also s.p.), The Young Americans (also s.p.), Judge Dredd, Phoenix, Boston Kickout (exec prod. only), I Still Know What You Did Last Summer, Bjork: Volumen (music video).
TELEVISION: *Series.*: C.S.I.: Crime Scene Investigation (dir. co-exec. prod.), C.S.I.: Miami (co-exec. prod.

CANNON, DYAN
Actress. r.n. Samille Diane Friesen. b. Tacoma, WA, Jan. 4, 1937. e. U. of Washington. Studied with Sanford Meisner. Modelled before becoming actress. Directed, produced and wrote short film Number One (Acad. Award nom.).
THEATRE: *B'way*: The Fun Couple, Ninety-Day Mistress. *Tour*: How to Succeed in Business Without Really Trying.
PICTURES: The Rise and Fall of Legs Diamond (debut, 1960), This Rebel Breed, Bob & Carol & Ted & Alice (Acad. Award nom.), Doctors' Wives, The Anderson Tapes, The Love Machine, The Burglars, Such Good Friends, Shamus, The Last of Sheila, Child Under a Leaf, Heaven Can Wait (Acad. Award nom.), Revenge of the Pink Panther, Honeysuckle Rose, Coast To Coast, Deathtrap, Author Author, Caddyshack II, The End of Innocence (also dir., prod., s.p.), The Pickle, Out to Sea, That Darn Cat, 8 Heads in a Duffel Bag, The Sender, Allie and Me, Kiss of a Stranger, Kangaroo Jack.
TELEVISION: *Mini-Series*: Master of the Game. *Movies*: The Virginia Hill Story, Lady of the House, Having It All, Arthur the King, Jenny's War, Rock 'n' Roll Mom, Jailbirds, Christmas in Connecticut,

Based on an Untrue Story, A Perry Mason Mystery: The Case of the Jealous Jokester, Black Jaq, Diamond Girl, My Mother the Spy. *Series*: Ally McBeal, Three Sisters. *Guest*: Playhouse 90, Inside the Playboy Mansion (tv documentary, herself).

CANNON, WILLIAM
Writer, Producer, Director. b. Toledo, OH, Feb. 11, 1937. e. Columbia Coll., B.A., 1959; M.B.A., 1962. Wrote, prod., dir., Square Root of Zero, Locarno and San Francisco Film Festivals, 1963-65. Distrib., at Doran Enterprises, Ltd. Publisher of Highlife and Movie Digest, 1978 and The Good Guys, 1987. Co-inventor: Cardz (TM), 1988. Author: Authorship: The Dynamic Principles of Writing Creatively, 1993; The Veteran, (novel) 1974; The Trojan Head (play), 1997.
THEATRE: *Off-B'Way*: Death of a Salesman, Pirates of Penzance, 1960.
PICTURES: *Writer*: Skidoo, Brewster McCloud, Hex.
TELEVISION: *Writer*: Knots Landing, Heaven on Earth.

CANOVA, DIANA
Actress. b. West Palm Beach, FL, June 1, 1953. r.n. Diana Rivero. Daughter of actress Judy Canova and musician Filberto Rivero. NY theatre: They're Playing Our Song (1981). People's Choice award, favorite female performer, 1981. On B'way in, Company.
PICTURE: The First Nudie Musical, One True Thing.
TELEVISION: *Movies*: Medical Story, The Love Boat II, With This Ring, Death of Ocean View Park, Night Partners.
Series: Dinah and Her New Best Friends, Soap, I'm a Big Girl Now, Foot in the Door, Throb, Home Free. *Guest*: Ozzie's Girls (debut), Happy Days, Love Boat, Fantasy Island, Hotel, Chico and the Man, Barney Miller, Murder She Wrote.

CANTON, ARTHUR H.
Motion Picture Producer. b. New York, NY. e. NYU, Columbia U. Capt. USAF. Pres., Canton-Weiner Films, indep. foreign films importers, 1947; Van Gogh (Academy Award for best 2-reel short subject, 1949); MGM Pictures, eastern div. publicity mgr., executive liaison, advertising-publicity, Independent Productions; public relations executive, v.p.; pres., Blowitz, Thomas & Canton Inc., 1964; pres., Arthur H. Canton Co. Inc.; prod. exec., Warner Bros., 1968-70; advertising-publicity v.p., Columbia Pictures, 1971; exec. v.p. of advertising and publicity, Billy Jack Productions, 1974-76. Co-founder of Blowitz & Canton Co. Inc., 1976, chmn of bd. Pres. of Arthur H. Canton Co. Member Academy of Motion Picture Arts and Sciences. Exec. v.p. of Filmroos. Retired.

CANTON, MARK
Executive. b. New York, NY, June 19, 1949. e. UCLA, 1978. v.p., m.p. dev., MGM; 1979, exec. v.p., JP Organization; 1980, v.p. prod., Warner Bros.; named sr. v.p., 1983 and pres. worldwide theatrical prod. div., 1985; v.p. worldwide m.p. production, 1989; appointed chmn. of Columbia Pictures, 1991. Promoted to chmn. of Columbia TriStar Motion Pictures, 1994. Resigned, 1996. In 2002, Canton became chmn. and CEO of Artists Production Group, the moviemaking offshoot of Michael Ovitz's Artists Management Group.

CAPELIER, MARGOT
Casting Director
PICTURES: Behold a Pale Horse, Lady L, The Night of the Generals, The Day of the Jackal, The Destructors, Julia, Moonraker, Le Coup du parapluie, Psy, What Makes David Run?, Five Days One Summer, Hanna K, The Outsider, He Died With His Eyes Open, The Original, Family Business, Vent de panique, Europa, Europa, The Double Life of Veronique, The Favour, the Watch, and the Very Big Fish, Olivier Olivier, Blue, Red, Total Eclipse, Those Who Love Me Can Take the Train, Ronin, Le Poulpe.

CAPRA, JR., FRANK,
Executive. Son of famed director Frank Capra. Served in various creative capacities on TV series (Zane Grey Theatre, Gunsmoke, The Rifleman, etc.). Associate producer on theatrical films (Planet of the Apes, Play It Again Sam, Marooned, etc.). Joined Avco Embassy Pictures, 1981, as v.p., worldwide production. In July, 1981, became pres. of A-E. Resigned May, 1982 to become indep. producer. Now with Pinehurst Industry Studios, NC.
PICTURES: *Producer*: Tom Sawyer (assoc. prod.), Billy Jack Goes to Washington, Born Again, The Black Marble, An Eye for an Eye, Vice Squad, Firestarter, Marie, Waterproof. *Exec. prod.*: Death Before Dishonor.

CAPSHAW, KATE
Actress. r.n. Kathleen Sue Nail. b. Ft. Worth, TX, Nov. 3, 1953. e. U. of Missouri. m. director Steven Spielberg. Taught school before moving to New York to try acting.
PICTURES: A Little Sex (debut, 1982), Indiana Jones and the Temple of Doom, Best Defense, Dreamscape, Windy City, Power, SpaceCamp, Black Rain, Love at Large, My Heroes Have Always Been Cowboys, Love Affair, Just Cause, Duke of Groove (short), How to Make an American Quilt, The Locusts, Life During Wartime, The Love Letter (also prod.).
TELEVISION:*Movies*: Missing Children: A Mother's Story, The Quick and the Dead, Her Secret Life, Internal Affairs, Next Door, Due East. *Mini-series*: A Girl Thing. *Series*: The Edge of Night, Black Tie Affair.

CARA, IRENE
Singer, Actress. b. New York, NY, March 18, 1959. Off-B'way shows include The Me Nobody Knows, Lotta. On B'way in Maggie Flynn, Ain't Misbehavin', Via Galactica. Received Academy Award for co-writing theme song from Flashdance, 1983.
THEATRE: *B'way*.: Maggie Flynn, The Me Nobody Knows, Via Galactica, Got to Go Disco. *Off-B'way*.: Ain't Misbehavin'. *Regional*: Lotta, The Wiz, Jesus Christ Superstar. *Foreign*: Mo' Magic.
PICTURES: Aaron Loves Angela, Sparkle, Fame, D.C. Cab, City Heat, Certain Fury, Killing 'em Softly, Paradiso, Busted Up, Maximum Security, Happily Ever After (voice), The Magic Voyage (voice).
TELEVISION: *Series*: Hearts are Wild, Love of Life, The Electric Company. *Mini-Series*: Roots—The Next Generation. *Movies*: Guyana Tragedy, Sisters, For Us the Living, Gabriel's Fire. *Special*: Tribute to Martin Luther King, Jr., Bob Hope Thanksgiving Special, Tribute to Ray Charles.

CARDIFF, JACK
Cinematographer, Director. b. Yarmouth, Eng., Sept. 18, 1914. Early career as child actor, before becoming cinematographer, then dir. in 1958.
PICTURES: *Cinematographer*: A Matter of Life and Death (Stairway to Heaven), Black Narcissus (Acad. Award, 1947), The Red Shoes, Scott of the Antarctic, Black Rose, Under Capricorn, Pandora and the Flying Dutchman, The African Queen, The Magic Box, The Master of Ballantrae, The Barefoot Contessa, The Brave One, War and Peace, Legend of the Lost, The Prince and the Showgirl, The Vikings, The Journey, Fanny, Scalawag, Crossed Swords (The Prince and the Pauper), Death on the Nile, Avalanche Express, The Fifth Musketeer, A Man a Woman and a Bank, The Awakening, The Dogs of War, Ghost Story, The Wicked Lady, Scandalous, Conan the Destroyer, Cat's Eye, Rambo: First Blood II, Blue Velvet, Tai-Pan, Million Dollar Mystery, Delius, Call from Space, The Magic Balloon, Vivaldi's Four Seasons, The Dance of Shiva, The Suicidal Dog. *Director*: Intent to Kill (debut, 1958), Beyond This Place, Scent of Mystery, Sons and Lovers, My Geisha, The Lion, The Long Ships, Young Cassidy (co-dir.), The Liquidator, Dark of the Sun, Girl on a Motorcycle, Penny Gold, The Mutations, Ride a Wild Pony.
TELEVISION: *Cinematographer*: The Far Pavillions, The Last Days of Pompeii. *Actor*: Larry and Vivien: The Oliviers in Love.

CARDINALE, CLAUDIA
Actress. b. Tunis, Tunisia, April 15, 1938. Raised in Italy. Studied acting at Centro Sperimentale film school in Rome. Debuted 1956 in short French film Anneaux d'Or.
PICTURES: Goha (feature debut, 1957), Big Deal on Madonna Street, The Facts of Murder, Upstairs and Downstairs, The Battle of Austerlitz, Il Bell' Antonio, Rocco and His Brothers, Senilita, Girl With a Suitcase, The Love Makers, Cartouche, The Leopard, 8 1/2, Bebo's Girl, The Pink Panther, Circus World, Time of Indifference, The Magnificent Cuckold, Sandra, Blindfold, Lost Command, The Professionals, Don't Make Waves, Mafia, The Queens, Day of the Owl, The Hell With Heroes, Once Upon a Time in the West, A Fine Pair, The Butterfly Affair, The Red Tent, The Legend of Frenchy King, Conversation Piece, Escape to Athena, The Salamander, Careless, Immortal Bachelor, History, The French Revolution, Hiver '54, L'abbe Pierre, Mother, 588 Rue Paradis, Women Only Have One Thing on Their Minds..., A Summer in La Goulette, Sous les pieds des Femmes, Rich Belles Etc, My Best Friend, Brigands, Luchino Visconte, And Now Ladies and Gentlemen.
TELEVISION: Princess Daisy, Jesus of Nazareth, 10-07: L'affaire Zeus, Nostromo, Deserto di Fuoco, Elisabeth, Visconti (tv documentary).

CAREY, DREW
Comedian, Actor. b. Cleveland, OH, May 23, 1958. First break was as contestant on TV show Star Search.
PICTURES: Coneheads, The Big Tease, Gepetto, Hail Sid Caesar! The Golden Age of Comedy.
TELEVISION: *Specials*: Sex, Drugs, and Freedom of Choice, Rock and Roll Back to School Special, Improv All Stars, Inside the Playboy Mansion (tv documentary, interviewee). *Series*: The Good Life, The Drew Carey Show (also prod., creator), Whose Line Is It Anyway? (also exec. prod.). *Guest*: The Torkelsons, The George Carlin Show, Lois & Clark: The New Adventures of Superman, Home Improvement, Ellen, Sabrina the Teenage Witch, Dharma & Greg.

CAREY, HARRY JR.
Actor. b. Saugus, CA, May 16, 1921. e. Newhall, CA, public school, Black Fox Military Acad., Hollywood. m. Marilyn Fix. Son of silent star Harry Carey. Appeared in Railroads on Parade at 1939-40 NY World's Fair. Summer stock, Skowhegan, ME., with father; page boy, NBC, New York; U.S. Navy 1942-45. Author of Company of Heroes - My Life as an Actor in the John Ford Stock Co.
PICTURES: Rolling Home (debut, 1946), Pursued, Red River, Three Godfathers, She Wore a Yellow Ribbon, Wagonmaster, Rio Grande, Copper Canyon, Warpath, Wild Blue Yonder, Monkey Business, San Antone, Island in the Sky, Gentlemen Prefer Blondes, Beneath the 12-Mile Reef, Silver Lode, The Outcast, Long Gray Line, Mister Roberts, House of Bamboo, The Great Locomotive Chase, The Searchers, The River's Edge, Rio Bravo, The Great Imposter, Two Rode Together, Alvarez Kelly, Bandolero, The Undefeated, Dirty Dingus Magee, Big Jake, Something Big, One More Train To Rob, Cahill: U.S. Marshal, Take a Hard Ride, Nickelodeon, The Long Riders, Endangered

Species, Mask, Crossroads, The Whales of August, Cherry 2000, Illegally Yours, Breaking In, Bad Jim, Back to the Future Part III, The Exorcist III, Tombstone, Wyatt Earp: Return to Tombstone, Ben Johnson: Third Cowboy on the Right, The Sunchaser.
TELEVISION: *Movies*: Black Beauty, The Shadow Riders, Wild Times, Once Upon a Texas Train, Last Stand at Saber River, Dobe and a Company of Heroes (tv documentary, as himself). *Guest*: Gunsmoke, Rifleman, Laramie, Wagon Train, Have Gun Will Travel, John Ford's America, Legends of the American West. Disney *Series*: Spin & Marty. *Special*: Wyatt Earp: Return to Tombstone.

CARIOU, LEN
Actor. b. Winnipeg, Manitoba, Canada, Sept. 30, 1939. e. St. Paul's Col.
THEATRE: *NY stage*: House of Atreus, Henry V, Applause (Theatre World Award), Night Watch, A Sorrow Beyond Dreams, Up from Paradise, A Little Night Music, Cold Storage, Sweeney Todd—The Demon Barber of Fleet Street (Tony Award), Master Class, Dance a Little Closer, Teddy & Alice, Measure for Measure, Mountain, The Speed of Darkness, Papa.
PICTURES: Drying Up the Streets, A Little Night Music, One Man, The Four Seasons, There Were Times Dear, Lady in White, Getting In, Never Talk to Strangers, Executive Decision, Thirteen Days, About Schmidt, The Skulls 3 (video).
TELEVISION: *Movies*: Who'll Save Our Children?, Madame X, The Four Seasons, Louisiana, Surviving, Killer in the Mirror, Miracle on Interstate 880, Class of '61, The Sea Wolf, Witness to the Execution, Love on the Run, The Man in the Attic, A Dream Is a Wish Your Heart Makes: The Annette Funicello Story, Derby, The Summer of Ben Tyler, In the Company of Spies. *Series*: Swift Justice. *Specials*: The Master Builder, Juno and the Paycock, Kurt Vonnegut's Monkey House (All the King's Men). *Mini-series*: Nuremberg.

CARLIN, GEORGE
Actor, Comedian. b. New York, NY, May 12, 1937. Stand-up comedian and recording artist. Recipient of 1972 Grammy Award for Best Comedy Album: FM & AM; 1993 Grammy Award for Best Comedy Album: Jammin'. Has released 15 comedy albums between 1960-90. Guest on many TV shows including Talent Scouts, On B'way Tonight, Merv Griffin Show, Saturday Night Live. *Author*: Sometimes a Little Brain Damage Can Help (1984), Braindroppings (1997).
PICTURES: With Six You Get Eggroll, Car Wash, Americathon (narrator), Outrageous Fortune, Bill & Ted's Excellent Adventure, Bill and Ted's Bogus Journey, The Prince of Tides, Dogma, Jay and Silent Bob Strike Back, Jersey Girl.
TELEVISION: *Series*: Kraft Summer Music Hall, That Girl, Away We Go, Tony Orlando and Dawn, Shining Time Station, The George Carlin Show. *Movies*: Justin Case, Working Trash, Streets of Laredo, George Carlin: Complaints & Grievances (writer, exec. prod., exec. album prod.). *Specials*: George Carlin: Jammin' in New York, also appeared in more than 10 HBO comedy specials. *Guest*: Welcome Back Kotter, The Simpsons.

CARLINER, MARK
Producer.
PICTURES: Viva Max!, Heaven Help Us, Crossroads.
TELEVISION: *Movies*: A Death of Innocence, Revenge, Strangers in 7A, Nightmare, The Phoenix (pilot), Disaster at Silo 7 (also story), Stalin, George Wallace (Emmy Award, 1998), The Diary of Ellen Rimbauer. *Series*: The Phoenix. *Mini-series*: The Shining, Storm of the Century, Rose Red, Kingdom Hospital (2004).

CARLINO, LEWIS JOHN
Writer, Director. b. New York, NY, Jan. 1, 1932. e. U. of Southern California. Early interest in theatre, specializing in writing 1-act plays. Winner of Obie award (off-B'way play). Won Rockefeller Grant for Theatre, the Int'l. Playwriting Competition from British Drama League, Huntington Hartford Fellowship.
THEATRE: Cages, Telemachus Clay, The Exercise, Double Talk, Objective Case, Used Car for Sale, Junk Yard.
PICTURES: *Writer*: Seconds, The Brotherhood, The Fox (co-s.p.), A Reflection of Fear, The Mechanic (also prod.), Crazy Joe, The Sailor Who Fell From Grace With the Sea (also dir.), I Never Promised You a Rose Garden (co-s.p.), The Great Santini (also dir.), Class (dir. only), Haunted Summer.
TELEVISION: Honor Thy Father, In Search of America, Where Have All the People Gone?, Resurrection.

CARLTON, RICHARD
Executive. b. New York, NY, Feb. 9, 1919. e. Columbia U., Pace Inst. Columbia Pictures 1935-41; U.S. Army 1941-45; National Screen Serv. 1945-51; Sterling Television 1951-54; U.M. & M. TV Corp. 1955; v.p. in charge of sales, Trans-Lux Television Corp., 1956; exec. v.p., Television Affiliates Corp., 1961; exec. v.p. Trans-Lux Television Corp.; v.p. Entertainment Div. Trans-Lux Corp., 1966. Pres., Schnur Appel, TV, Inc. 1970; Deputy Director, American Film Institute, 1973. Pres., Carlton Communications Corporation, 1982; exec. dir., International Council, National Academy of Television Arts and Sciences, 1983-93. Became writer/consultant, 1994.

CARLYLE, ROBERT
Actor. b. Glasgow, Scotland, April 14, 1961.
PICTURES: Silent Scream, Riff-Raff, Safe, Being Human, Priest, Go Now, Trainspotting, Carla's Song, Face, The Full Monty (BAFTA Award, Best Actor, 1997), Ravenous, Plunkett & MaCleane, The World is Not Enough, Angela's Ashes, The Beach, There's Only One Jimmy Grimble, To End All Wars, The 51st

State, Once Upon a Time in the Midlands, Light in the Sky, Black and White.
TELEVISION: Movies: Benny Lynch. *Mini-series*: Looking After Jo Jo, Hitler: The Rise of Evil (documentary). *Series*: Hamish Macbeth.

CARMEN, JULIE
Actress. b. New York, NY, Apr. 4, 1960. Studied acting at Neighborhood Playhouse. On NY stage in The Creation of the Universe, Cold Storage, Zoot Suit. Also acted with INTAR and the New Conservatory Theater. Recipient of 1992 National Council of La Raza Pioneer Award.
PICTURES: Night of the Juggler, Gloria, Man on the Wall, Comeback, Blue City, The Penitent, The Milagro Beanfield War, Fright Night 2, Kiss Me a Killer, Paint It Black, Cold Heaven, In the Mouth of Madness, Africa, Everything's George, King of the Jungle.
TELEVISION: *Movies*: Can You Hear the Laughter?: The Story of Freddie Prinze, Three Hundred Miles for Stephanie, She's in the Army Now, Fire on the Mountain, Neon Empire, Manhunt: Search for the Night Stalker, Billy the Kid, Drug Wars: The Cocaine Cartel, Finding the Way Home, Curacao, The Omen, Gargantua, The Expendables. *Mini-Series*: True Women. *Series*: Condo, Falcon Crest.

CARMICHAEL, IAN
Actor. b. Hull, England, June 18, 1920. e. Scarborough Coll., Bromsgrove Sch. Stage debut: R.U.R. 1939. B'way debut: Boeing-Boeing (1965). One of the top ten British money making stars Motion Picture Herald Fame Poll 1957, 1958.
PICTURES: Bond Street (debut, 1948), Trottie True (Gay Lady), Mr. Prohack, Time Gentlemen Please, Ghost Ship!, Miss Robin Hood, Meet Mr. Lucifer, Betrayed, The Colditz Story, Storm Over the Nile, Simon and Laura, Private's Progress, The Big Money, Brothers in Law, Lucky Jim, Happy Is the Bride, Left Right and Center, I'm All Right Jack, School for Scoundrels, Light Up the Sky, Double Bunk, The Amorous Prawn, Hide and Seek, Heavens Above, The Case of the 44's, Smashing Time, The Magnificent Seven Deadly Sins, From Beyond the Grave, The Lady Vanishes, Dark Obsession (Diamond Skulls).
TELEVISION: New Faces, Twice Upon a Time, Passing Show, Tell Her The Truth, Lady Luck, Give My Regards to Leicester Square, Jill Darling, Don't Look Now, Regency Room, Globe Revue, Off the Record, Here and Now, The Girl at the Next Table, Gilt and Gingerbread, The Importance of Being Earnest, Simon and Laura, 90 Years On, The World of Wooster (series), The Last of the Big Spenders, The Coward Revue, Odd Man In, Bachelor Father (series), Lord Peter Wimsey (series), Alma Mater, Comedy Tonight, Song by Song, Country Calendar, Down at the Hydro, Obituaries, Strathblair, The Great Kandinsky, Bramwell, Wives and Daughters, The Royal (series). *Guest*: Under The Hammer, Bramwell.

CARNEY, ART
Actor. r.n. William Matthew Carney. b. Mt. Vernon, NY, Nov. 4, 1918. Started as band singer with the Horace Heidt Orchestra. On many radio shows before and after war. Served in U.S. Army, 1944-45. Regular on Morey Amsterdam's radio show which eventually moved to television.
THEATRE: The Rope Dancers. B'way: Take Her She's Mine, The Odd Couple, Lovers, The Prisoner of Second Avenue.
PICTURES: Pot o' Gold (debut, 1941), The Yellow Rolls Royce, A Guide for the Married Man, Harry and Tonto (Academy Award for Best Actor, 1974), W. W. and the Dixie Dancekings, Won Ton Ton the Dog Who Saved Hollywood, The Late Show, Scott Joplin, House Calls, Movie Movie, Ravagers, Sunburn, Going in Style, Defiance, Roadie, Steel, St. Helens, Take This Job and Shove It, Better Late Than Never, Firestarter, The Naked Face, The Muppets Take Manhattan, Night Friend, Last Action Hero.
TELEVISION: *Series*: The Morey Amsterdam Show, Cavalcade of Stars, Henry Morgan's Great Talent Hunt, The Jackie Gleason Show (1951-55; 2 Emmy Awards: 1953, 1954), The Honeymooners (Emmy Award, 1955), The Jackie Gleason Show (1956-57), The Jackie Gleason Show (1966-70; 2 Emmy Awards: 1967, 1968), Lanigan's Rabbi. Guest: Studio One, Kraft Theatre, Playhouse 90, Alfred Hitchcock Presents (Safety for the Witness), Sid Caesar Show, Twilight Zone (Night of the Meek), Bob Hope Chrysler Theater (Timothy Heist), Danny Kaye Show, Men From Shiloh, Batman, Carol Burnett Show, Jonathan, Winters Show, Faerie Tale Theatre (The Emperor's New Clothes). *Specials*: Peter and the Wolf, Harvey, Our Town, Charley's Aunt, Art Carney Meets the Sorcerer's Apprentice, Very Important People, Jane Powell Special: Young at Heart, Man in the Dog Suit, The Great Santa Claus Switch. Movies: The Snoop Sisters, Death Scream, Katherine, Letters From Frank, Terrible Joe Moran (Emmy Award, 1984), The Night They Saved Christmas, A Doctor's Story, Izzy and Moe, Blue Yonder, Where Pigeons Go to Die.
(d. Nov. 9, 2003)

CARON, GLENN GORDON
Writer, Director, Producer. b. 1954. Started as tv writer for James L. Brooks, Steve Gordon. Formed prod. co., Picturemaker Productions, 1985.
PICTURES: *Director*: Clean and Sober (debut, 1988), Wilder Napalm, Love Affair, Picture Perfect (also s.p.).
TELEVISION: *Series*: Breaking Away (prod.), Moonlighting (creator, prod., writer), Now and Again (writer, dir., exec. prod.). *Movies*: Long Time Gone, The Perfect Pitch (tv documentary).

CARON, LESLIE
Actress, Dancer. b. Paris, France, July 1, 1931. e. Convent of Assumption, Paris; Nat'l Conservatory of Dance, Paris 1947-50; joined Roland Petit's Ballet des Champs Elysees where she was spotted by Gene Kelly who chose her as his co-star in An American in Paris. Also with Ballet de Paris.
THEATRE: Orvet, Ondine, Gigi (London), 13 Rue de l'Amour, The Rehearsal, Women's Games, On Your Toes, One For the Tango.
PICTURES: An American in Paris (debut, 1951), The Man With a Cloak, Glory Alley, The Story of Three Loves, Lili (Acad. Award nom.; BFA Award), The Glass Slipper, Daddy Long Legs, Gaby, Gigi, The Doctor's Dilemma, The Man Who Understood Women, The Subterraneans, Austerlitz, Fanny, Guns of Darkness, Three Fables of Love, The L-Shaped Room (Acad. Award nom.; BFA Award), Father Goose, A Very Special Favor, Promise Her Anything, Is Paris Burning?, Head of the Family, The Beginners, Madron, Chandler, Purple Night, Valentino, The Man Who Loved Women, Golden Girl, Contract, Imperative, The Unapproachable, Dangerous Moves, Warriors and Prisoners, Courage Mountain, Damage, Funny Bones, Let It Be Me, The Reef, From Russia to Hollywood: The 100-Year Odyssey of Chekhov and Shdanoff, Chocolat, Le Divorce.
TELEVISION: *Movies*: The Man Who Lived at the Ritz, The Ring, The Last of the Blonde Bombshells, Murder on the Orient Express. *Mini-Series*: QB VIII, Master of the Game, The Great War. *Series*: The Great War. *Guest*: Love Boat, Tales of the Unexpected, Carola, Falcon Crest. *Specials*: The Sealed Train, Jean Pierre Aumont: charme et fou rires.

CARPENTER, CARLETON
Actor. b. Bennington, VT, July 10, 1926 e. Bennington H.S., Northwestern U. (summer scholarship). Began career with magic act, clubs, camps, hospitals in New Eng.; then toured with carnival; first N.Y. stage appearance in Bright Boy. Appeared in nightclubs, radio; as magazine model. TV debut, Campus Hoopla show. Screen debut Lost Boundaries (also wrote song for film, I Wouldn't Mind). Member: SAG, AFTRA, AEA, ASCAP, Dramatists Guild, Mystery Writers of Amer. (ex.-treas., bd. mem.).
THEATRE: *NY*: Career Angel, Three To Make Ready, The Magic Touch, The Big People, Out of Dust, John Murray Anderson's Almanac, Hotel Paradiso, Box of Watercolors, A Stage Affair, Greatest Fairy Story Ever Told, Something for the Boys, Boys in the Band, Dylan, Hello Dolly!, Light Up the Sky, Murder at Rutherford House, Rocky Road, Apollo of Bellac, Sweet Adaline, Geo. White's Scandals, Life on the L.I.E. Miss Stanwyck is Still in Hiding, Good Ole Fashioned Revue, What is Turning Gilda So Grey?, Crazy for You, Many Thousands Gone.
PICTURES: Lost Boundries (debut, 1949), Summer Stock, Father of the Bride, Three Little Words, Two Weeks With Love, The Whistle at Eaton Falls, Fearless Fagan, Sky Full of Moon, Vengeance Valley, Up Periscope, Take the High Ground, Some of My Best Friends Are..., The Prowler, Simon, Byline, Cauliflower Cupids, The Bar, Carnegie Hall.
TELEVISION: Over 6,000 shows (live & filmed) since 1945.

CARPENTER, CHARISMA
Actress. b. Las Vegas, NV, July 23, 1970. Was cheerleader for NFL's San Diego Chargers before turning to modeling, then acting. PICTURES: Switch, The Twins, The Groomsmen, Change Up (documentary, voiceover).
TELEVISION: *Movies*: Josh Kirby...Time Warrior: The Human Pets, Josh Kirby...Time Warrior: Planet of the Dino-Knights, Josh Kirby...Time Warrior: Last Battle for the Universe. *Series*: Malibu Shores, Buffy the Vampire Slayer, Angel, Buffy The Animated Series (voice). *Guest*: Baywatch, Boy Meets World.

CARPENTER, JOHN
Director, Writer, Composer. b. Carthage, NY, Jan. 16, 1948. e. Western Kentucky U., U. of Southern California. At U.S.C. became involved in film short, Resurrection of Bronco Billy, which won Oscar as best live-action short of 1970. Also at U.S.C. began directing what ultimately became Dark Star, science fiction film that launched his career.
PICTURES: *Director*: Dark Star (also co-s.p., music), Assault on Precinct 13 (also s.p., music), Halloween (also s.p., music), The Fog (also co-s.p., music), Escape from New York (also co-s.p., music), The Thing, Christine (also music), Starman, Big Trouble in Little China (also music), Prince of Darkness (also music, and s.p. as Martin Quatermass), They Live (also music, and s.p. as Frank Armitage), Memoirs of an Invisible Man, In the Mouth of Madness (also co-music), Village of the Damned (also s.p., co-music), Escape From L.A, Meltdown (also s.p., co-story), Eyes of Laura Mars (co-sp., co-story), Halloween II (co- s.p., co-prod., co-music), Halloween III: Season of the Witch (co-prod., co-music), The Philadelphia Experiment (co-exec. prod.), Black Moon Rising (co-s.p., story), The Silence of the Hams (actor), Vampires, (also s.p. and music), Ghosts of Mars, Halloween: Ressurection (music, s.p. only), Tales From the Mist: Inside 'The Fog' (video documentary, composer), Vampires: Los Muertos (exec. prod.)
TELEVISION: *Movies* (director): Elvis, Someone Is Watching Me (also writer), John Carpenter Presents Body Bags (also co-exec. prod., actor). *Movies* (writer): Zuma Beach, El Diablo, Blood River, Silent Predators.

CARPENTER, RUSSELL
Cinematographer, Actor.
PICTURES: The Wizard of Speed and Time (also actor), Lady in White, Critters 2: The Main Course, Cameron's Closet, Solar Crisis, Lionheart, Death Warrant, The Perfect Weapon, The Lawnmower

Man, Pet Sematary II, Hard Target, True Lies, The Indian in the Cupboard, Titanic (Acad. Award, Chicago Film Crits. Award, Best Cinematography, 1998), Ghosts, Money Talks, The Negotiator, Charlie's Angels, Shallow Hal, Charlie's Angels: Full Throttle.
TELEVISION: *Movies*: Attack of the 50 Ft. Woman.

CARR, MARTIN
Producer, Director, Writer. b. New York, NY, Jan. 20, 1932. e. Williams Coll. Recipient of: 5 Emmys, 3 Peabody awards, 2 Du-Pont Col. Journalism awards, Robert F. Kennedy award, Sidney Hillman award, Writers Guild Award.
PICTURES: El Efecto Mariposa (prod. mgr.), The IMAX Nutcracker (prod. mgr.) Command Approved (prod.), Vacuuming Completely Nude in Paradise (prod.), Strumpet (prod.), The Human Body (line prod.)
TELEVISION: PBS Smithsonian World (exec. prod.). For CBS prod., wrote and dir. CBS Reports: Hunger in America, The Search for Ulysses, Gauguin in Tahiti, Five Faces of Tokyo, Dublin Through Different Eyes. For NBC prod., wrote and dir. NBC White Paper: Migrant, NBC White Paper: This Child Is Rated X. Also directed drama, dance, music, opera specials and daytime serial for CBS-TV. ABC Close-Up. The Culture Thieves. PRS Global Paper: Waging Peace, ABC News 20/20; NBC, The Human Animal.

CARRADINE, DAVID
Actor. r.n. John Arthur Carradine. b. Hollywood, CA, Dec. 8, 1936. e. San Francisco State U. Son of late actor John Carradine. Brother of actors Keith and Robert Carradine. Began career in local repertory; first TV on Armstrong Circle Theatre and East Side, West Side; later TV includes Shane series and Kung Fu; N.Y. stage in The Deputy, Royal Hunt of The Sun (Theatre World Award).
PICTURES: Has appeared in 100 pictures, incl.: Taggart, Bus Riley's Back in Town, The Violent Ones, Young Billy Young, The McMasters, Heaven with a Gun, The Good Buys and the Bad Guys, Macho Callahan, Boxcar Bertha, Mean Streets, House of Dracula's Daughter, Death Race 2000, Cannonball, Bound for Glory, Thunder and Lightning, A Look at Liv, The Serpent's Egg, Dray Lady Down, Deathsport, Fast Charlie the Moonbeam Rider, Cloud Dancer, The Long Rides, Americana, Safari 3000, Q, Lone Wolf McQuade, The Warrior and the Sorceress, Rio Abajo, A Distant Scream, Armed Response, P.O.W. the Escape, The Misfit Brigade, Wizards of the Lost Kingdom II, Warlords, Open Fire, Fatal Secret, Crime Zone, Animal Protector, Try This One for Size, Sundown: The Vampire in Retreat, Nowhere to Run, The Mad Bunch, Las Huellas del lince, Crime of Crimes, ThinK Big, Sonny Boy, Night Children, Midnight Fear, Future Zone, Future Force, Evil Toons, Dune Warriors, Bird on a Wire, Karate Cop, Field of Fire, Capital Punishment, Waxwork II: Lost in Time, Night Rhythms, Martial Law, Double Trouble, Distant Justice, Animal Instincts, Roadside Prophets, Kill Zone, Dead Center, The Rage, Macon County Jail, Full Blast, Effects of Magic, Crossroads of Destiny, Light Speed, Drop-Dead, The New Swiss Family Robinson, Sublet, Lovers and Liars, The Defectors, Dangerous Curves, Zoo, Shepherd, The Puzzle in the Air, Natural Selection, Kiss of a Stranger, American Reel, Nightfall, G.O.D., Down 'n Dirty, Wheatfield With Crows, Naked Movie, Kill Bill, Dead & Breakfast.
TELEVISION: *Movies*: Maybe I'll Come Home in the Spring, Kung Fu (1972 pilot), Mr. Horn, Johnny Belinda, Gaugin the Savage, High Noon Part II, Jealousy, The Bad Seed, Kung Fu: The Movie, Oceans of Fire, Six Against the Rock, The Cover Girl & the Cop, I Saw What You Did, Deadly Surveillance, Brotherhood of the Gun, The Gambler Returns: Luck of the Draw, Kung Fu: The Legend Continues, The Eagle and the Horse, Lost Treasure of Dos Santos, Last Stand at Saber River, Out of the Wilderness, Martian Law, By Dawn's Early Light, Largo Winch: The Heir, Warden of Red Rock, Balto II: Wolf Quest, The Outsider. *Mini-series*: North & South Books I & II. *Series*: Shane, Kung Fu, Kung Fu: The Legend Continues, Walking After Midnight. *Guest*: Darkroom, Amazing Stories, Charmed, Matlock.

CARRADINE, KEITH
Actor. b. San Mateo, CA, Aug. 8, 1949. e. Colorado State U. Daughter is actress Martha Plimpton. Son of late actor John Carradine, brother of David and Robert Carradine. First break in rock opera Hair.
THEATRE: Wake Up It's Time to Go to Bed, Foxfire, The Will Rogers Follies.
PICTURES: A Gunfight (debut, 1971), McCabe and Mrs. Miller, Hex, Emperor of the North Pole, Thieves Like Us, Antoine et Sebastien, Run Joe Run, Idaho Transfer, Nashville (also composed songs; Acad. Award for best song: I'm Easy, 1975), You and Me, Lumiere, Welcome to L.A. (also composed songs), The Duellists, Pretty Baby, Sgt. Pepper's Lonely Heart Club Band (cameo), Old Boyfriends, An Almost Perfect Affair, The Long Riders, Southern Comfort, Choose Me, Maria's Lovers (also composed song), Trouble in Mind, The Inquiry (The Investigation), Backfire, The Moderns, Street of No Return, Cold Feet, Daddy's Dyin'...Who's Got the Will?, The Ballad of the Sad Cafe, Crisscross, The Bachelor, Andre, Mrs. Parker and the Vicious Circle, The Tie That Binds, Wild Bill, A Thousand Acres, Standoff, Out of the Cold, The Hunter's Moon, Cahoots, The Angel Doll, Wooly Boys, Falcons, Mending Fences.
TELEVISION: *Movies*: Man on a String, Kung Fu, The Godchild, A Rumor of War, Scorned and Swindled, A Winner Never Quits, Murder Ordained, Eye on the Sparrow, Blackout, Stones for Ibarra, My Father My Son, The Revenge of Al Capone, Judgment, Payoff, In the Best of Families: Marriage Pride & Madness, Is There Life Out There?, Trial by Fire, Hard Time: Hide and Seek, Night Ride Home, Enslavement: The True Story of Fanny Kemble, Baby, The Diamond of Jeru, The Outsider, Monte Walsh. *Mini-Series*: Chiefs.

Series: Outreach, Metropolis, Deadwood. *Guest:* Bonanza, Love American Style, Kung Fu.

CARRADINE, ROBERT
Actor. b. Hollywood, CA, March 24, 1954. Son of late actor John Carradine; brother of Keith and David Carradine.
PICTURES: The Cowboys (debut, 1972), Mean Streets, Aloha Bobby and Rose, Jackson County Jail, The Pom Pom Girls, Cannonball, Massacre at Central High, Joyride, Orca, Blackout, Coming Home, The Long Riders, The Big Red One, Heartaches, Tag: The Assassination Game, Wavelength, Revenge of the Nerds, Just the Way You Are, Number One With a Bullet, Revenge of the Nerds II: Nerds in Paradise, Buy and Cell, All's Fair, Rude Awakening, The Player, Bird of Prey, Escape From L.A., Scorpio One, Lycanthrope (also prod.), Stray Bullet I & II, Gunfighter, Palmer's Pick Up, The Kid With the X-Ray Eyes, The Vegas Connection, 3 Days of Rain, Ghosts of Mars, Max Keeble's Big Move, 3 Days of Rain, The Lizzie McGuire Movie.
TELEVISION: *Movies:* Footsteps, Rolling Man, Go Ask Alice, The Hatfields and the McCoys, The Survival of Dana, The Sun Also Rises, Monte Carlo, The Liberators, I Saw What You Did, The Incident, Clarence, Doublecrossed, Revenge of the Nerds III: The Next Generation, Body Bags, The Disappearance of Christina, Revenge of the Nerds IV: Nerds in Love (also co-prod.), A Part of the Family, The Tommyknockers, Young Hearts Unlimited, Mom's Got A Date With A Vampire. Monte Walsh. *Series:* The Cowboys, Lizzie McGuire, Express Yourself. *Specials:* Disney's Totally Minnie. *Guest:* Alfred Hitchcock Presents (1985), The Hitchhiker, Twilight Zone (1986), ER, Kung Fu: The Legend Continues, The Fall Guy.

CARRERA, BARBARA
Actress. b. Nicaragua, Dec. 31, 1951. Fashion model before film career; had part in film Puzzle of a Downfall Child.
PICTURES: The Master Gunfighter, Embryo, The Island of Dr. Moreau, When Time Ran Out, Condorman, I the Jury, Lone Wolf McQuade, Never Say Never Again, Wild Geese II, The Underachievers, Love at Stake, Wicked Stepmother, Loverboy, Spanish Rose, Night of the Archer, Tryst, Love Is All There Is, Panic, Paradise.
TELEVISION: *Movies:* Sins of the Past, Murder in Paradise, Lakota Moon, Sawbones, The Rockford Files: Godfather Knows Best. *Mini-Series:* Centennial, Masada, Emma: Queen of the South Seas. *Series:* Dallas. *Guest:* Fortune Hunter, JAG, That '70s Show.

CARRERE, TIA
Actress. r.n. Althea Janairo. b. Honolulu, HI, 1967. Was prof. model before turning to acting. Received NATO/ShoWest award for Female Star of 1994.
PICTURES: Zombie Nightmare (debut, 1987), Aloha Summer, Fatal Mission, Instant Karma, Showdown in Little Tokyo, Harley Davidson and the Marlboro Man, Wayne's World, Rising Sun, Wayne's World 2, True Lies, Jury Duty, My Generation, The Immortals, Hollow Point, Bad With Numbers, High School High, Top of the World, Dumped, Kull the Conqueror, Scar City, 20 Dates (also exec. prod), Wayne's World, The Return, Meet Prince Charming, Shi, Lilo & Stitch (voice), Stitch! The Movie (video, voice)..
TELEVISION: *Series:* General Hospital. *Mini-Series:* James Clavell's Noble House. *Movies:* The Road Raiders, Fine Gold, Natural Enemy, Dogboys. Series: The Adventures of Lilo & Stitch (voice). *Guest:* The A-Team, MacGyver, Tales From the Crypt.

CARREY, JIM
Actor. b. Newmarket, Ontario, Canada, Jan. 17, 1962. Began performing act at Toronto comedy clubs while teenager. Moved to LA at 19, performing at the Comedy Store.
PICTURES: Finders Keepers (debut, 1984), Once Bitten, Peggy Sue Got Married, The Dead Pool, Earth Girls Are Easy, Pink Cadillac, High Strung, Ace Ventura: Pet Detective (also co-s.p.), The Mask, Dumb and Dumber, Batman Forever, Ace Ventura: When Nature Calls, The Cable Guy, Liar Liar, The Truman Show, Simon Birch, Man on the Moon, How the Grinch Stole Christmas, The Majestic, Bruce Almighty, Eternal Sunshine of the Spotless Mind, Over the Edge (voice).
TELEVISION: *Series:* The Duck Factory, In Living Color. *Movies:* Mickey Spillane's Mike Hammer—Murder Takes All, Doin' Time on Maple Drive, In My Life. *Specials:* Jim Carrey's Unnatural Act, Comedy Store: The E! True Hollywood Story, Concert for New York City, America: A Tribute to Heroes. *Canadian TV:* Introducing Janet, Copper Mountain: A Club Med Experience.

CARROLL, DIAHANN
Actress, Singer. r.n. Carol Diahann Johnson. b. Bronx, NY, July 17, 1935. m. singer Vic Damone. Started singing as teen, winning 1st place on tv's Chance of a Lifetime talent show resulting in engagement at Latin Quarter nightclub in New York. Autobiography: Diahann! (1986).
THEATRE: B'way: House of Flowers, No Strings (Tony Award, 1962), Agnes of God.
PICTURES: Carmen Jones (debut, 1954), Porgy and Bess, Goodbye Again, Paris Blues, Hurry Sundown, The Split, Claudine (Acad. Award nom.), The Five Heartbeats, Eve's Bayou.
TELEVISION: *Movies:* Death Scream, I Know Why the Caged Bird Sings, From the Dead of Night, Murder in Black and White, A Perry Mason Mystery: The Case of the Lethal Lifestyle. The Sweetest Gift, Having Our Say: The Delany Sisters' First 100 Years, Jackie's Back!, The Courage to Love, Sally Hemmings: An American Scandal, Livin' for Love: The Natalie Cole Story. Inside TV Land: African Americans in Television (tv documentary, as herself). TV Land Awards: A Celebration of Classic TV (tv special documentary). *Mini-Series:* Roots: The Next Generations; many specials;

guest appearances incl. The Naked City, Andy Williams, Judy Garland, Dean Martin Shows, Ellen. *Series:* Julia, The Diahann Carroll Show, Dynasty, Sister Sister, The Court.

CARROLL, GORDON
Producer. b. Baltimore, MD, Feb. 2, 1928. e. Princeton U. Advtg. exec., Foote, Cone & Belding, 1954-58; Ent. industry, Seven Arts Prods., 1958-61; v.p. prod., Jalem Prods., 1966-1969; independent producer to present.
PICTURES: How to Murder Your Wife, Luv, Cool Hand Luke, The April Fools, Pat Garrett and Billy the Kid, Alien, Blue Thunder, The Best of Times, Aliens, Red Heat, Alien 3, Alien: Resurrection.

CARROLL, PAT
Actress. b. Shreveport, LA, May 5, 1927. e. Immaculate Heart Coll., L.A, Catholic U., Washington, DC. Joined U.S. Army in capacity of Civilian Actress Technician. Night club entertainer in N.Y., 1950.
THEATRE: Catch a Star (debut, 1955), Gertrude Stein Gertrude Stein (Drama Desk, Outer Critics Circle, Grammy Awards), Dancing in the End Zone, The Show Off. Shakespeare Theatre at the Folger: Romeo and Juliet (Helen Hayes Award), The Merry Wives of Windsor (Helen Hayes Award), Mother Courage (Helen Hayes Award), H.M.S. Pinafore, Volpone.
PICTURES: With Six You Get Eggroll, The Brothers O'Toole, The Last Resort, The Little Mermaid (voice), Invader, A Goofy Movie, Songcatcher, The Little Mermaid II: Return to the Sea (voice),
TELEVISION: *Series:* Red Buttons Show, Saturday Night Revue, Caesar's Hour (Emmy Award, 1957), Masquerade Party (panelist), Keep Talking, You're in the Picture (panelist), Danny Thomas Show, Getting Together, Busting Loose, The Ted Knight Show, She's the Sheriff, The Little Mermaid (voice), House of Mouse (voice). *Specials:* Cinderella, Gertrude Stein. *Movie:* Second Chance, Just My Imagination.

CARSEY, MARCY
Producer. b. Weymouth, MA, Nov. 21, 1944. e. Univ. NH. Was actress in tv commercials, tour guide at Rockefeller Center. Served as exec. story editor, Tomorrow Ent., 1971-74; sr. v.p. for prime time series, ABC-TV, 1978-81; founded Carsey Prods., 1981; owner, Carsey-Werner-Mandabach Co., 1982-. Member of USC School of Cinema-Television's Television Executive Advisory Council
TELEVISION: *Series:* (exec. prod.): Oh Madeline (co-exec. prod.), The Cosby Show, A Different World, Roseanne, Chicken Soup, Grand, Davis Rules, Frannie's Turn, You Bet Your Life (synd.), Grace Under Fire, Cybill, Cosby (1996), Men Behaving Badly, Townies, Damon, That '70s Show, God the Devil and Bob, Normal Ohio, Grounded for Life, You Don't Know Jack, The Downer Channel, That 80s Show. *Pilots:* Callahan, I Do I Don't. *Special:* Carol Carl Whoopi and Robin. *Movie:* Single Bars Single Women.

CARSON, JEANNIE
Actress. r.n. Jean Shufflebottom. b. Yorkshire, England, May 23, 1928. Became Amer. citizen, 1966. Founded Hyde Park Festival Theatre with husband William "Biff" McGuire, 1979. Has taught a musical drama class at U. of WA. Awards: TV Radio Mirror, 1st Recipient of the Variety Club Theatre Award in England.
THEATRE: *U.K.:* Ace of Clubs, Love From Judy, Starlight Roof, Casino Reviews, Aladdin. *U.S.:* The Sound of Music, Blood Red Roses, Finian's Rainbow (revival). *Tours:* Camelot, 110 in the Shade, Cactus Flower. Also extensive work with the Seattle Repertory Theatre as actress, and dir. with Seattle Bathhouse Theatre.
PICTURES: A Date with a Dream (debut, 1948), Love in Pawn, As Long as They're Happy, An Alligator Named Daisy, Mad Little Island (Rockets Galore), Seven Keys.
TELEVISION: Best Foot Forward, Little Women, Berkeley Square, The Rivals, Frank Sinatra Show, Heidi, What Every Woman Knows, Jimmy Durante Show, Pat Boone Show, A Kiss for Cinderella. Series: Hey Jeannie, Jeannie Carson Show, Search for Tomorrow.

CARSON, JOHNNY
Host, Comedian. b. Corning, IA, Oct. 23, 1925. e. U. of Nebraska, B.A. 1949. U.S. Navy service during WWII; announcer with station KFAB, Lincoln, Neb.; WOW radio-TV, Omaha, 1948; announcer, KNXT-TV, Los Angeles, 1950; then hosted own program, Carson's Cellar (1951-53); latter resulted in job as writer for Red Skelton Show. 1958 guest hosting for Jack Paar on The Tonight Show led to his becoming regular host 4 years later. President, Carson Productions. Recipient: ATAS Governor's Award, 1980. Author: Happiness Is a Dry Martini (1965).
PICTURES: *Movies:* Looking for Love, Cancel My Reservation, The Newton Boys.
TELEVISION: *Movies:* Joys (as himself/masked killer), Comedy in Bloom (as himself), James Stewart: A Wonderful Life, The Positively True Adventures of the Alleged Texas Cheerleader-Murdering Mom, *Series:* Earn Your Vacation (emcee; 1954), The Johnny Carson Show (daytime, 1955; later moved to nighttime, 1955-56), Who Do You Trust? (1957-62); The Tonight Show Starring Johnny Carson (1962-92). *Guest:* Playhouse 90, U.S. Steel Hour, Get Smart, Here's Lucy, The Simpsons, Cheers, Newhart, Night Court. Pilot: Johnny Come Lately.

CARTER, CHRIS
Producer, Composer, Writer, Director. b. Bellflower, CA, Oct. 13, 1956.
PICTURES: The X Files: Fight the Future.
TELEVISION: *Producer/Composer/Writer/Director:* In the Shadow of the Sun, The B.R.A.T. Patrol, Rags to Riches (co-prod. only), Millenium (also creator), The X-Files (also creator), Harsh Realm, The Lone Gunmen.

CARTER, DIXIE
Actress. b. McLemoresville, TN, May 25, 1939. m. actor Hal Holbrook. e. U. of Tennessee, Knoxville, Rhodes Coll.; Memphis, Memphis State U. Off-B'way debut, A Winter's Tale with NY Shakespeare Fest (1963). London debut, Buried Inside Extra (1983). Lincoln Center musicals: The King & I, Carousel, The Merry Widow. Video: Dixie Carter's Unworkout.
THEATRE: Pal Joey (1976 revival), Jesse and the Bandit Queen (Theatre World Award), Fathers and Sons, Taken in Marriage, A Coupla Whice Chicks Sitting Around Talking, Buried Inside Extra, Sextet, Pal Joey.
PICTURE: Going Berserk, The Big Day.
TELEVISION: Movies:: The Killing of Randy Webster, Dazzle, Gambler V: Playing for Keeps, A Perry Mason Mystery: The Case of the Lethal Lifestyle, Gone in the Night, The Life & Adventures of Santa Claus (video).Special: Intimate Portrait: Dixie Carter. Series: The Edge of Night, On Our Own, Out of the Blue, Filthy Rich, Diff'rent Strokes, Designing Women, Family Law, Ladies Man.

CARTER, JACK
Actor, r.n. Jack Chakrin. b. New York, NY, June 24, 1923. e. New Utrecht H.S., Brooklyn Coll., Feagin Sch. of Dramatic Arts. Worked as comm. artist for adv. agencies. Debut B'way in Call Me Mister, 1947; starred in TV Jack Carter Show, NBC Sat. Nite Revue. Hosted first televised Tony Awards. Seen on most major variety, dram. programs, incl. Ed Sullivan Show. Emmy nom. 1962 for Dr. Kildare seg. Played most major nightclubs. On B'way in Top Banana, Mr. Wonderful, Dir. several Lucy Shows. TV incl. specials, Top Banana, Girl Who Couldn't Lose.
PICTURES: Horizontal Lieutenant, Viva Las Vegas, The Extraordinary Seaman, Resurrection of Zachary Wheeler, Red Nights, Hustle, The Amazing Dobermans, Alligator, The Octagon, History of the World Part 1, The Arena, Deadly Embrace, In the Heat of Passion, Social Suicide, The Opposite Sex and How to Live With Them, Pastry Pain and Politics, The Modern Adventures of Tom Sawyer, Play it to the Bone, Let Me In I Hear Laughter.
TELEVISION: Movies: The Lonely Profession, The Family Rico, The Sex Symbol, The Great Houdinis, The Last Hurrah, Human Feelings, Rainbow, The Gossip Columnist, The Hustler of Muscle Beach, For the Love of It, Double Deception. Series: American Minstrels of 1949, Cavalcade of Stars, The Jack Carter Show, Make Me Laugh, Hercules (voice), Driving Me Crazy. Guest: Blossom, Empty Nest, Nurses, Murder She Wrote, Time Trax, Burke's Law, New Adventures of Superman, Sanford and Son.

CARTER, LYNDA
Actress. r.n. Lynda Jean Cordoba. b. Phoenix, AZ, July 24, 1951. e. Arcadia H.S. Wrote songs and sang professionally in Ariz. from age of 15; later toured 4 yrs. with rock 'n roll band. Won beauty contests in Ariz. and became Miss World-USA 1973. Dramatic training with Milton Katselas, Greta Seacat, and Sandra Seacat.
PICTURES: Lightning in a Bottle, Super Troopers, Tattered Angel, Bloodhead.
TELEVISION: Movies: The New Original Wonder Woman, A Matter of Wife...and Death, Baby Brokers, Last Song, Hotline, Rita Hayworth: The Love Goddess, Stillwatch (also exec. prod.), Mickey Spillane's Mike Hammer, Murder Takes All, Danielle Steel's Daddy, Posing: Inspired By 3 Real Stories, She Woke Up Pregnant, A Secret Between Friends, Family Blessings, A Prayer in the Dark, Someone to Love Me. Series: Wonder Woman, Hawkeye. Specials: The New Original Wonder Woman Specials; 5 variety specials, Hawkeye.

CARTER, NELL
Actress. b. Birmingham, AL. Sept. 13, 1948.
THEATRE: Hair, Dude, Don't Bother Me I Can't Cope, Jesus Christ Superstar, Ain't Misbehavin' (Tony & Theatre World Awards, 1978), Ain't Misbehaving (1988 revival), Hello Dolly! (L.A.)
PICTURES: Hair, Quartet, Back Roads, Modern Problems, Bebe's Kids (voice), The Grass Harp, The Crazysitter, The Proprietor, Fakin' Da Funk, Perfect Fit, Special Delivery, Swing.
TELEVISION: Movies: Cindy, Maid for Each Other, Final Shot: The Hank Gathers Story. Series: Lobo, Gimme a Break, You Take the Kids, Hangin' With Mr. Cooper. Specials: Baryshnikov on Broadway, The Big Show, An NBC Family Christmas, Ain't Misbehavin' (Emmy Award), Christmas in Washington, Nell Carter, Never Too Old To Dream, Morton's By the Bay (pilot), My Favorite Broadway: The Leading Ladies, Beyond Tara: The Extraordinary Life of Hattie McDaniel.
(d. Jan. 23, 2003)

CARTLIDGE, WILLIAM
Director, Producer. b. England, June 16, 1942. e. Highgate Sch. Ent. m.p. ind. 1959. Early career in stills dept., Elstree Studio. Later worked as an asst. dir. on The Young Ones, Summer Holiday, The Punch & Judy Man, The Naked Edge. As 1st asst. dir. on such pictures as Born Free, Alfie, You Only Live Twice, The Adventurers, Young Winston, Friends. As assoc. prod., Paul and Michelle, Seven Nights in Japan, The Spy Who Loved Me, Moonraker, An Ideal Husband. Prod.: Educating Rita, Not Quite Paradise, Consuming Passions, Dealers, The Playboys. Producer of Haunted, Incognito, The Scarlet Tunic (exec.), Dinotopia (prod. tv series), The Will to Resist (co-prod.).

CARTWRIGHT, VERONICA
Actress. b. Bristol, Eng., April 20, 1950. m. writer-dir. Richard Compton. Sister is actress Angela Cartwright. Began career as child actress. On stage in, The Hands of Its Enemies (Mark Taper Forum, LA 1984), The Triplet Connection (off-B'way).
PICTURES: In Love and War (debut, 1958), The Children's Hour,

The Birds, Spencer's Mountain, One Man's Way, Inserts, Goin' South, Invasion of the Body Snatchers, Alien, Nightmares, The Right Stuff, My Man Adam, Flight of the Navigator, Wisdom, The Witches of Eastwick, Valentino Returns, False Identity, Man Trouble, Candyman: Farewell to the Flesh, Money Talks, Sparkler, My Engagement Party, A Slipping Down Life, Trash, In the Bedroom, Scary Movie 2, Mackenheim.
TELEVISION: Movies: Guyana Tragedy—The Story of Jim Jones, The Big Black Pill, Prime Suspect, Intimate Encounters, Desperate for Love, A Son's Promise, Hitler's Daughter, Dead in the Water, It's Nothing Personal, My Brother's Keeper, The Lottery, The Rat Pack, The Last Man on Planet Earth, Alien Evolution, Inside the Osmonds. Specials: Who Has Seen the Wind?, Bernice Bobs Her Hair, Tell Me Not the Mournful Numbers (Emmy Award), Joe Dancer, Abby My Love, On Hope. Series: Daniel Boone. Guest: Leave It To Beaver, Twilight Zone, The X-Files. Mini-series: Robert Kennedy and His Times.

CARUSO, DAVID
Actor. b. Queens, NY, Jan. 7, 1956.
PICTURES: Without Warning (debut, 1980), An Officer and a Gentleman, First Blood, Thief of Hearts, Blue City, China Girl, Twins, King of New York, Hudson Hawk, Mad Dog and Glory, Kiss of Death, Jade, Cold Around the Heart, Body Count, Proof of Life, Session 9, Black Point.
TELEVISION: Movies: Crazy Times, The First Olmypics—Athens 1896, Into the Homeland, Rainbow Drive, Mission of the Shark, Judgment Day: The John List Story, Gold Coast, Deadlocked. Series: N.Y.P.D. Blue, Michael Hayes (also exec. prod.), C.S.I.: Miami. Guest: Crime Story, Hill Street Blues.

CARVER, STEVE
Director. b. Brooklyn, NY, April 5, 1945. e. U. of Buffalo; Washington U., MFA. Directing, writing fellow, Film Inst. Center for Advanced Studies, 1970. (Writer, dir. films Patent and the Tell-Tale Heart). Teacher of filmmaking art and photo. Florissant Valley Col., MO 1966-68. News photographer, UPI. Instructor, film and photography, Metropolitan Ed. Council in the Arts; St. Louis Mayor's Council on the Arts, Give a Damn (dir., prod.); asst. dir. Johnny Got His Gun; writer, editor with New World Pictures. Member: Sierra Club, Natl. Rifle Assn.
PICTURES: Arena, Big Bad Mama, Capone, Drum, Fast Charlie, The Moonbeam Rider, Steel, An Eye for an Eye, Lone Wolf McQuade (also prod.), Oceans of Fire, Jocks (also co-s.p.), Bulletproof (also co-s.p.), River of Death, Crazy Joe, The Wolves.

CARVEY, DANA
Actor. b. Missoula, MT, June 2, 1955. e. San Francisco State Coll. Won San Francisco Stand-Up Comedy Competition which led to work as stand-up comedian in local S.F., then L.A. comedy clubs. TV debut as Mickey Rooney's grandson on series, One of the Boys, 1982. Received American Comedy Award (1990, 1991) as TV's Funniest Supporting Male Performer.
PICTURES: Halloween II, Racing With the Moon, This is Spinal Tap, Tough Guys, Moving, Opportunity Knocks, Wayne's World, Wayne's World 2, Clean Slate, The Road to Wellville, Trapped in Paradise, The Shot, Little Nicky, Master of Disguise (also writer), Tusker.
TELEVISION: Series: One of the Boys, Blue Thunder, Saturday Night Live (Emmy Award, 1993), The Dana Carvey Show. Specials: Superman's 50th Anniversary (host), Salute to Improvisation, Wayne & Garth's Saturday Night Live Music a Go-Go, various Satruday Night Live specials. Guest: The Larry Sanders Show, Just Shoot Me, Lateline. Pilots: Alone at Last, Whacked Out.

CASEY, BERNIE
Actor. b. Wyco, WV, June 8, 1939. e. Bowling Green U. Played pro-football with San Francisco 49ers and L.A. Rams.
PICTURES: Guns of the Magnificent Seven (debut, 1969), Tick...Tick...Tick, Boxcar Bertha, Black Gunn, Hit Man, Cleopatra Jones, Maurie, Cornbread Earl and Me, The Man Who Fell to Earth, Dr. Black/Mr. Hyde, Brothers, Sharky's Machine, Never Say Never Again, Revenge of the Nerds, Spies Like Us, Steele Justice, Rent-a-Cop, I'm Gonna Git You Sucka, Backfire, Bill and Ted's Excellent Adventure, Another 48 HRS, Under Siege, The Cemetery Club, Street Knight, The Glass Shield, In the Mouth of Madness, Once Upon a Time...When We Were Colored, The Dinner (also prod., dir., s.p.), Tomcats, Jim Brown: All American (documentary).
TELEVISION: Movies: Brian's Song, Gargoyles, Panic on the 5:22, Mary Jane Harper Cried Last Night, It Happened at Lake Wood Manor, Ring of Passion, Love is Not Enough, Sophisticated Gents, Hear No Evil, The Fantastic World of D.C. Collins, The Simple Life of Noah Dearborn, The Last Brickmaker in America. Mini-Series: Roots—The Next Generations, The Martian Chronicles. Series: Harris and Company, Bay City Blues.

CASSAVETES, NICK
Actor, Director, Writer. b. New York, NY, May 21, 1959. Son of director/actor John Cassavetes and actress Gena Rowlands.
PICTURES: A Woman Under the Influence, Mask, The Wraith, Quiet Cool, Black Moon Rising, Assault of the Killer Bimbos, Blind Fury, Backstreet Dreams, Delta Force 3: The Killing Game, Twogether, Sins of the Night, Sins of Desire, Body of Influence, Class of 1999 II: The Substitute, Mrs. Parker and the Vicious Circle, Just Like Dad, Black Rose of Harlem, Face/Off, Life, The Astronaut's Wife, Panic, The Independent Director: Unhook the Stars (also s.p.), She's So Lovely, John Q, Going After Cacciato, The Notebook. Exec. Prod.: The Sky Is Green, The Incredible Mrs. Ritchie. Writer: Blow. TELEVISION: Movies: Reunion, Shooter.

CASSEL, ALVIN I.
Executive. b. New York , NY, July 26. e. U. of Michigan, B.A., 1938. Capt. in U.S. Army European Theatre, 1941-45. Surveyed Central Africa for MGM, 1946-50, then assumed duties as asst. mgr. for MGM South Africa. Continued with MGM in West Indies, 1950-51 and Philippines, 1951-57. In 1957 joined Universal as mgr./supvr. for Southeast Asia; back to MGM in 1963 as supvr. S.E. Asia; 1967, with CBS Films as Far East supvr. In 1972, established Cassel Films to secure theatrical films for foreign distributors, principally in Far East. 1979, consultant for Toho-Towa and the Toho Co. of Japan and other Far East distributors.

CASSEL, JEAN-PIERRE
Actor. r.n. Jean-Pierre Crochon. b. Paris, France, Oct. 27, 1932. Began as dancer, attracting attention of Gene Kelly at Left Bank nightspot, resulting in film debut. Also appeared in plays before becoming established as leading French screen star.
PICTURES: The Happy Road (debut, 1956), A Pied a Cheval et en Voiture, Le Desorde et la Nuit, Love Is My Profession, The Love Game, The Joker, Candide, The Five-Day Lover, Seven Capital Sins, La Gamberge, The Elusive Corporal, Arsene Lupin contre Arsene Lupin, Cyrano and D'Artagnan, The Beautiful Swindlers, The Male Companion, High Infidelity, La Ronde, Les Fetes Galantes, Those Magnificent Men in Their Flying Machines, Is Paris Burning?,Anyone Can Play, The Killing Game, The Bear and the Doll, Oh! What a Lovely War, The Army of the Shadows, The Break Up, The Boat on the Grass, Baxter!, Malpertuis, The Discreet Charm of the Bourgeoisie, The Three Musketeers, Le Mouton Enrage, Murder on the Orient Express, The Twist, That Lucky Touch, No Time for Breakfast, The Four Musketeers, Les Oeufs Brouilles, The Meetings of Anna, Who Is Killing the Great Chefs of Europe?, Alice, Chouans! Grandeson, From Hell to Victory, La Ville des Silence, The Green Jacket, Ehrengard, La Vie Continue, Portrait of a Nude Woman, The Trout, Vive la Sociale! Tranches de Vie, Mangeclous, The Return of the Musketeers, Mr. Frost, Vincent & Theo, Tha Maid, The Favor the Watch and the Very Big Fish, Lieutenant Lorena, Love and Tiny Toes, Between Heaven and Earth, Coup de Jeune, The Secret Coach of 13, Petain, Blue Helmet, Metisse, Cha Forte Com Limao, L'Enfer, Ready to Wear (Pret-a-Porter), La Ceremonie (A Judgment in Stone), The Ice Rink, Influence Peddling, Speaking of Bunuel, Sade, The Crimson Rivers.
TELEVISION: Movies: La Lune d'Omaha, Liberty, A Matter of Convenience, Sentimental Journey, Tu Crois Pa si Bien Dire, Casanova, The Burning Shore, Warburg, Young Indiana Jones Chronicles, From Earth and Blood, Elissa Rhais, The Fatal Image, The Phantom of the Opera, Cave of the Golden Rose, Notorious, Tatort - Eine Todsichere Falle, La Faux, La Maison du canal. Mini-series: The Secret of the Sahara, La Misere sous Riches, Disperatamente Giulia, Rastignac ou les ambitieux, Mediteranee, La Memoria e il perdona.

CASSEL, SEYMOUR
Actor. b. Detroit, MI, Jan. 22, 1935. As a boy travelled with a troupe of burlesque performers including his mother. After high school appeared in summer stock in Michigan. Studied acting at American Theatre Wing and Actor's Studio. After joining a workshop taught by John Cassavetes, began a long creative association with the director-actor. On B'way in, The World of Suzy Wong, The Disenchanted.
PICTURES: Murder Inc., Shadows, Too Late Blues, Juke Box Racket, The Killers, The Sweet Ride, Coogan's Bluff, Faces (Acad. Award nom.), The Revolutionary, Minnie and Moskowitz, Black Oak Conspiracy, Death Game (The Seducers), The Killing of a Chinese Bookie, The Last Tycoon, Scott Joplin, Opening Night, Valentino, Convoy, California Dreaming, Ravagers, Sunburn, The Mountain Men, King of the Mountain, I'm Almost Not Crazy..., John Cassavetes–The Man and His Work (doc.), Love Streams, Eye of the Tiger, Survival Game, Tin Men, Johnny Be Good, Plain Clothes, Colors, Track 29, Wicked Stepmother, Dick Tracy, White Fang, Cold Dog Soup, Mobsters, Diary of a Hitman, Honeymoon in Vegas, In the Soup, Trouble Bound, Indecent Proposal, Boiling Point, Chain of Desire, Chasers, There Goes My Baby, When Pigs Fly, Hand Gun, It Could Happen to You, Tollbooth, Dark Side of Genius, Imaginary Crimes, Things I Never Told You, Dead Presidents, The Last Home Run, Dream for an Insomniac, Four Rooms, Cameleone, Things I Never Told You, Seed, Motel Blue, This World Then the Fireworks, Obsession, The Treat, Snapped, Rushmore, Me and Will, Kubansch Rauchen, Dream for an Insomniac, Relax...It's Just Sex, Black and White, Ballad of the Nightingale, Getting to Know You, Temps, The Animal Factory, The Crew, Just One Night, Women of the Night, The Cure for Boredom, The Sleepy Time Gal, Bartleby, Manna From Heaven, The Royal Tenenbaums, The Chameleon, Stealing Harvard, Sonny, Passionada, Deadrockstar, The Burial Society, Time & Again, The Biz, Wishing Time, A Good Night To Die, The Bride of the Sea.
TELEVISION: Movies: The Hanged Man, Angel on My Shoulder, Blood Feud, I Want to Live, Beverly Hills Madame, Sweet Bird of Youth, My Shadow, Dead in the Water, Face of a Stranger, The Last Don, Emma's Wish. Pilot: Rose City. Special: Partners. Series: Good Company.

CASSIDY, DAVID
Actor, Singer. b. New York, NY, April 12, 1950. Son of late actor Jack Cassidy; brother of Shaun and Patrick. Composed and performed theme song for The John Larroquette Show.
THEATRE: B'way: The Fig Leaves Are Falling (debut, 1968), Joseph and the Amazing Technicolor Dreamcoat, Blood Brothers. Regional: Little Johnny Jones, Tribute. London: Time.

PICTURES: Instant Karma, The Spirit of '76.
TELEVISION:Movie: The Night the City Screamed, We Are Family (tv documentary, as himself). Series: The Partridge Family, David Cassidy-Man Undercover. Guest: The Mod Squad, Bonanza, Adam-12, Ironside, Marcus Welby M.D., Police Story (Emmy nom.), The Love Boat, Alfred Hitchcock Presents, The Flash, The Ben Stiller Show, The John Larroquette Show. Documentaries: Hearthrobs of the 70s, Intimate Portrait: Shirley Jones, TV Land Awards: A Celebration of Classic TV (as himself).

CASSIDY, JOANNA
Actress. r.n. Joanna Virginia Caskey. b. Camden, NJ, Aug. 2, 1945. e. Syracuse U.
PICTURES: Bullitt (debut, 1968), Fools, The Laughing Policeman, The Outfit, Bank Shot, The Stepford Wives, Stay Hungry, The Late Show, Stunts, The Glove, Our Winning Season, Night Games, Blade Runner, Under Fire, Club Paradise,The Fourth Protocol, Who Framed Roger Rabbit, 1969, The Package, Where the Heart Is, Don't Tell Mom the Babysitter's Dead, All-American Murder, May Wine, Vampire in Brooklyn, Chain Reaction, Loved, Executive Power, Dangerous Beauty, Moonglow, The Right Temptation, Ghosts of Mars.
TELEVISION: Movies: She's Dressed to Kill, Reunion, Invitation to Hell, The Children of Times Square, Pleasures, A Father's Revenge, Nightmare at Bitter Creek, Wheels of Terror, Grass Roots, Taking Back My Life, Live! From Death Row, Perfect Family, Barbarians at the Gate, Stephen King's The Tommyknockers, The Rockford Files: I Still Love L.A. Sleep Baby Sleep, The Second Civil War, Circle of Deceit, Wildfire 7: The Inferno, Martha Inc.: The Story of Martha Stewart. Mini-Series: Hollywood Wives, To Serve and Protect, Tribe. Special: Roger Rabbit and the Secrets of Toontown (host), Other Mothers (Afterschool Special), Tribe. Series: Shields and Yarnell, The Roller Girls, 240-Robert, Family Tree, Buffalo Bill, Code Name: Foxfire, Hotel Malibu, Superman, Six Feet Under. Pilot: Second Stage. Guest: Taxi, Love Boat, Hart to Hart, Charlie's Angels, Lou Grant, Melrose Place.

CASSIDY, PATRICK
Actor. b. Los Angeles, CA, Jan. 4, 1962. Son of late actor Jack Cassidy and actress-singer Shirley Jones.
THEATRE: NY: The Pirates of Penzance, Leader of the Pack, Assassins. Regional: Conrack.
PICTURES: Off the Wall, Just the Way You Are, Fever Pitch, Nickel Mountain, Love at Stake, Longtime Companion, I'll Do Anything, Lord Protector, The Dark Mist, Man of Her Dreams.
TELEVISION: Movies: Angel Dusted, Midnight Offerings, Choices of the Heart, Christmas Eve, Dress Gray, Something in Comon, Follow Your Heart, Three on a Match, How the West Was Fun, Oklahoma City: A Survivor's Story, Newton. Mini-series: Napoleon and Josephine: A Love Story. Pilot: The Six of Us. Series: Bay City Blues, Dirty Dancing, Smallville.

CASTELLANETA, DAN
Actor. b. Chicago, IL, Sept. 10, 1958.
PICTURES: Nothing in Common, The War of the Roses, K-9, Don't Tell Mom the Babysitter's Dead (voice), The Return of Jafar (voice), Super Mario Bros., The Client, Love Affair, Forget Paris, Space Jam, Plump Fiction, Rhapsody in Bloom, My Giant, The Settlement, Rugrats in Paris: The Movie (voice), Recess: School's Out (voice), Don't Try This at Home, Return to Never Land (voice), Hey Arnold! The Movie (voice), Buttleman, Adventures in Home Schooling.
TELEVISION: Movies: Working Tra$h, Lady Against the Odds, The Online Adventures of Ozzie the Elf (voice), The Computer Wore Tennis Shoes (1995), Olive the Other Reindeer, Laughter on the 23rd Floor. Series: The Tracey Ullman Show, The Simpsons (voice), Darkwing Duck (voice), Taz-Mania (voice), Sibs, Back to the Future (voice), Eek! the Cat, Aladdin (voice), The Tick (voice), Earthworm Jim, Hey Arnold (voice), Cow and Chicken (voice). Guest: ALF, Married...with Children, Rugrats (voice), Dream On, L.A. Law, Animaniacs (voice), The Critic (voice), Grace Under Fire, Cybil, Murphy Brown, Friends, NYPD Blue, The Drew Carey Show, Duckman (voice), Everybody Loves Raymond, Futurama (voice), Hercules (voice), House of Mouse (voice). Many guest voices on animated series and voice work for more than seven videos.

CASTLE, NICK
Writer, Director. b. Los Angeles, CA, Sept. 21, 1947. e. Santa Monica Coll., U. of Southern California film sch. Son of late film and TV choreographer Nick Castle Sr. Appeared as child in films Anything Goes, Artists and Models. Worked with John Carpenter and other USC students on Acad. Award-winning short, The Resurrection of Bronco Billy.
PICTURES: Skatedown USA (s.p.), Tag: The Assassination Game (Kiss Me Kill Me; s.p.), Escape from New York (co-s.p.), The Last Starfighter (dir.), The Boy Who Could Fly (dir.), Tap (dir., s.p.), Hook (co-story), Dennis the Menace (dir.), Major Payne (dir.), Mr. Wrong (dir.), Delivering Milo (dir.). Actor: Halloween.
TELEVISION: Twas the Night (dir.).

CATES, GILBERT
Director, Producer. r.n. Gilbert Katz. b. New York, NY, June 6, 1934. e. Syracuse U. Brother is dir.-prod. Joseph Cates. Began TV career as guide at NBC studios in N.Y., working way up to prod. and dir. of game shows (Camouflage, Haggis Baggis, Mother's Day, etc.). Created Hootenanny and packaged and directed many TV specials. Pres. Directors Guild of America

1983-87. Awarded DGA's Robert B. Aldrich award 1989. Dir. short film The Painting.
THEATRE: *Director:* Tricks of the Trade, Voices, The Price (Long Wharf Theatre). *Producer:* Solitaire/Double Solitaire, The Chinese and Mr. Fish, I Never Sang for My Father, You Know I Can't Hear You When the Water's Running.
PICTURES: Rings Around the World (debut, 1966), I Never Sang for My Father (also prod.), Summer Wishes Winter Dreams, One Summer Love (Dragonfly; also prod.), The Promise, The Last Married Couple in America, Oh God!—Book II (also prod.), Backfire, $pent (acting role).
TELEVISION: *Specials: Prod. &/or Dir. unless otherwise noted:* International Showtime (1963-65 exec. prod.), Electric Showcase Specials, Academy Awards (prod. 1990-95, 1997-98; Emmy Award, 1991), After the Fall. Movies: To All My Friends on Shore, The Affair, Johnny, We Hardly Knew Ye, The Kid from Nowhere, Country Gold, Hobson's Choice, Burning Rage, Consenting Adult, Fatal Judgement, My First Love, Do You Know the Muffin Man, Call Me Anna, Absolute Strangers (exec. prod.), In My Daughter's Name (co-exec. prod.), Confessions: Two Faces of Evil, To Life: America Celebrates Israel's 50th, Academy Awards (66th, 67th, 70th and 71st.prod., 73rd, 75th, exec. prod.), A Death in the Family, Collected Stories.

CATES, PHOEBE
Actress. r.n. Phoebe Belle Katz. b. New York, NY, July 16, 1963. e. Juilliard. Daughter of late prod-dir. Joseph Cates. m. actor Kevin Kline. Dance prodigy and fashion model before launching acting career. NY stage debut The Nest of the Wood Grouse (1984).
PICTURES: Paradise (debut, 1982), Fast Times at Ridgemont High, Private School, Gremlins, Date With an Angel, Bright Lights Big City, Shag, Heart of Dixie, I Love You to Death (unbilled), Gremlins 2: The New Batch, Drop Dead Fred, Bodies Rest and Motion, My Life's in Turnaround, Princess Caraboo, Scratch the Surface, The Anniversary Party.
TELEVISION: *Movies:* Baby Sister, Lace, Lace II. *Special:* Largo Desolato.

CATON-JONES, MICHAEL
Director. b. Broxburn, Scotland, 1958.
PICTURES: Scandal (debut, 1989), Memphis Belle, Doc Hollywood (also cameo), This Boy's Life, Rob Roy (also exec. prod.), The Jackal (also exec.), City By the Sea.
TELEVISION: *Series:* Trinity.

CATTRALL, KIM
Actress. b. Liverpool, Eng., Aug. 21, 1956. e. American Acad. of Dramatic Arts, N.Y. Started stage career in Canada's Off-B'way in Vancouver and Toronto; later performed in L.A. in A View from the Bridge, Agnes of God, Three Sisters, etc. On B'way in Wild Honey, Chicago Goodman Theatre in the Misanthrope. Regional: Miss Julie (Princeton).
PICTURES: Rosebud (debut 1975), The Other Side of the Mountain Part II, Tribute, Ticket to Heaven, Porky's, Police Academy, Turk 182, City Limits, Hold-Up, Big Trouble in Little China, Mannequin, Masquerade, Midnight Crossing, Palais Royale, Honeymoon Academy, The Return of the Musketeers, Brown Bread Sandwiches, Bonfire of the Vanities, Star Trek VI: The Undiscovered Country, Split Second, Double Vision, Breaking Point, Unforgettable, Live Nude Girls, Where Truth Lies, Baby Geniuses, Modern Vampires, 15 Minutes, The Devil and Daniel Webster, Not a Girl, Crossroads.
TELEVISION: *Movies:* Good Against Evil, The Bastard, The Night Rider, The Rebels, The Gossip Columnist, Sins of the Past, Miracle in the Wilderness, Running Delilah, Above Suspicion, The Heidi Chronicles, Two Golden Balls, Outer Limits, 36 Hours to Die, Sex and the Matrix, Intimate Portrait: Kim Cattrall (herself). *Mini-Series:* Scruples, Wild Palms, Tom Clancy's Op Center, Invasion, Creature. *Series:* Angel Falls, Sex and the City (Emmy nom., SAG Award).

CAULFIELD, MAXWELL
Actor. b. Glasgow, Scotland, Nov. 23, 1959. m. actress Juliet Mills. First worked as a dancer at a London nightclub. After coming to NY in 1978, ran the concession stand at the Truck and Warehouse Theatre. Won a Theatre World Award for Class Enemy.
THEATRE: Entertaining Mr. Sloane, Salonika, Journey's End, Sleuth, The Elephant Man, An Inspector Calls, Sweet Bird of Youth, The Woman In Black.
PICTURES: Grease 2, Electric Dreams, The Boys Next Door, The Supernaturals, Sundown: The Vampire in Retreat, Mind Games, Alien Intruder, Midnight Witness, Ipi/Tombi, In a Moment of Passion, Calendar Girl, Gettysburg, Inevitable Grace, Empire Records, Prey of the Jaguar, Oblivion 2: Backlash, The Real Blonde, The Man Who Knew Too Little, Divine Lovers, Smut, More to Love, Dazzle, The Perfect Tenant, Submerged, Overnight Sensation, Facing the Enemy, The Hit.
TELEVISION: *Movies:* The Parade, Till We Meet Again, Blue Bayou, Dynasty: The Reunion, Missing Pieces. *Series:* Dynasty, The Colbys, All My Children, Spider Man (voice), Strip Mall.

CAVANI, LILIANA
Director. b. near Modena, in Emilia, Italy, Jan. 12, 1933. e. U. of Bologna, diploma in classic literature, 1960; Ph.D. in linguistics. In 1960 took courses at Centro Sperimentale di Cinematografia in Rome where made short films Incontro Notturno and L'Evento. 1961 winner of RAI sponsored contest and started working for the new second Italian TV channel, 1962-66 directing progs. of

serious political and social nature incl. History of 3rd Reich, Women in the Resistance, Age of Stalin, Philippe Petain–Trial at Vichy (Golden Lion Venice Fest.), Jesus My Brother, Day of Peace, Francis of Assisi. Has also directed operas Wozzeck, Iphigenia in Tauris and Medea on stage.
PICTURES: Galileo, I Cannibali, Francesco d'Assissi, L'Ospite, Milarepa, Night Porter, Beyond Good and Evil, The Skin, Oltre la Porta, The Berlin Affair, Francesco, Where Are You I'm Here, Sans Pouvoir le Dire, Dissociated States, Ripley's Game.
TELEVISION: La Traviata, Manon Lescaut, La Cavalleria rusticana.

CAVETT, DICK
Actor, Writer. b. Kearny, NE, Nov. 19, 1936. e. Yale U. Acted in TV dramas and Army training films. Was writer for Jack Paar and his successors on the Tonight Show. Also wrote comedy for Merv Griffin, Jerry Lewis, Johnny Carson. In 1967 began performing own comedy material in night clubs. On TV starred in specials Where It's At (ABC Stage 67) and What's In. Author of, Cavett (with Christopher Porter) 1974.
THEATRE: *B'way:* Otherwise Engaged, Into the Woods.
PICTURES: Annie Hall, Power Play, Health, Simon, A Nightmare on Elm Street 3, Beetlejuice, Moon Over Parador, After School, Funny, Year of the Gun, Forrest Gump, Frequency.
TELEVISION: *Movie:* Elvis Meets Nixon (narr.).
Series: This Morning (ABC daytime talk show, 1968), The Dick Cavett Show (ABC primetime talk show, summer 1969), The Dick Cavett Show (ABC late night talk show, 1969-72: Emmy Award, 1972), ABC Late Night (talk show, 1973-74: Emmy Award, 1974), The Dick Cavett Show (CBS primetime variety: 1975), Dick Cavett Show (talk show: PBS, 1977-82; USA, 1985-86; CBS, 1986), The Edge of Night (1983), The Dick Cavett Show (CNBC talk show: 1989). *Guest:* The Simpsons, Cheers.

CAZENOVE, CHRISTOPHER
Actor. b. Winchester, Eng., Dec. 17, 1945. m. Angharad Rees. e. Eton, Oxford U., trained at Bristol Old Vic Theatre School.
THEATRE: Hamlet (1969), The Lionel Touch, My Darling Daisy, The Winslow Boy, Joking Apart, In Praise of Rattigan, The Life and Poetry of T.S. Eliot, The Sound of Music, Goodbye Fidel (B'way debut, 1980).
PICTURES: There's a Girl in My Soup, Royal Flash, East of Elephant Rock, The Girl in Blue Velvet, Zulu Dawn, Eye of the Needle, From a Far Country, Heat and Dust, Until September, Mata Hari, The Fantastist, Hold My Hand I'm Dying, Three Men and a Little Lady, Aces: Iron Eagle III, The Proprietor, Shadow Run, The Contaminated Man, Beginner's Luck, A Knight's Tale.
TELEVISION: *Specials/Movies:* The Rivals of Sherlock Holmes (1971), Affairs of the Heart, Jennie: Lady Randolph Churchill, The Darkwater Hall Mystery, Ladykillers—A Smile Is Sometimes Worth a Million, The Red Signal, Lou Grant, The Letter, Jenny's War, Lace 2, Kane and Abel, Windmills of the Gods, Shades of Love, Souvenir, The Lady and the Highwayman, Tears in the Rain, Ticket to Ride (A Fine Romance), To Be the Best, The Way to Dusty Death, Dead Man's Island, Home Song, Judge John Deed, Trance. *Mini-series:* Johnson County War, La Femme Musketeer. *Series:* The Regiment, The Duchess of Duke Street, Dynasty, A Fine Romance, Tales From the Crypt, Johnson County War, Fun at the Funeral Parlour.

CELENTINO, LUCIANO
Producer, Director, Writer. b. Naples, Italy, 1940. e. Rome, Paris, London. Entered. ind. 1959. Wrote, prod., dir. many plays incl: Infamita di Questa Terra, Black Destiny, Honour, Stranger's Heart, Youth's Sin, Wanda Lontano Amore. Stage musicals such as Songs...Dots...And Fantasies, Night Club's Appointment, Filumena, Serenada, Mamma. Since 1964, film critic of Il Meridionale Italiano. From 1962, co-writer and first asst. director to Luigi Capuano and Vittorio De Sica. In 1972, formed own company, Anglo-Fortunato Films. Honorary President Accademia Di Arte Drammatica Eduardo de Filippo teaching film acting, writing, directing.
PICTURES: Blood Money, Bandito (dir. only), Toujours (dir., s.p.), Parole (dir.,s.p.), Jackpot (dir., s.p.), Panache (dir.only), Was There a Way Out? (dir. only), Hobo, Gallan (dir. only), The Pinch.

CELLAN-JONES, JAMES
Director. b. Swansea, Wales, July 13, 1931. e. St. John's Coll., Cambridge. Best known for his adaptations of classic novels for the BBC and PBS (shown on Masterpiece Theatre). Won Nymphe d'Or at Monaco Festival.
PICTURE: The Nelson Affair, Chou Chou, Une Vie de Debussy, Married 2 Malcolm.
TELEVISION: The Scarlet and the Black, The Forsythe Saga, Portrait of a Lady, The Way We Live Now, Solo, The Roads to Freedom, Eyeless In Gaza, The Golden Bowl, Jennie (DGA series award), Caesar and Cleopatra, The Adams Chronicles, The Day Christ Died, The Ambassadors, Unity Mitford, Oxbridge Blues (also prod.), Sleeps Six (also prod.), The Comedy of Errors, Fortunes of War, You Never Can Tell, Arms and the Man, A Little Piece of Sunshine, A Perfect Hero (also prod.), The Gravy Train Goes East, Maigret, Harnessing Peacocks, Brighton Belles, The Vacillations of Poppy Carew, La Musique de l'Amour, McLibel, May and June.

CHABROL, CLAUDE
Director. b. Paris, France, June 24, 1930. Worked as newsman for Fox, then writer for Cahiers du Cinema. A founding director of the French New Wave.
PICTURES: Le Beau Serge, The Cousins, A Double Tour, Les Bonnes Femmes, Les Godelureaux, The Third Lover, Seven

CHA-CHA

Capital Sins, Ophelia, Landru, Le Tigre Aime la Chair Fraiche, Marie-Chantal Contre le Docteur Kah, Le Tigre Se Parfume a la Dunamite, Paris vu par... Chabrol, La Ligne de Demarcation, The Champagne Murders, The Route to Corinth, Les Biches, Le Femme Infidele, This Man Must Die, Le Boucher, La Rapture, Ten Days' Wonder, Just Before Nightfall, Dr. Popaul, Les Noces Rouges, Nada, The Blood of Others, The Horse of Pride, Alouette je te plumera, Poulet au Vinaigre, Inspector Lavardin, Masques, Le Cri du Hibou, Story of Women, Clichy Days (Quiet Days in Clichy), The Lark (actor only), Doctor M (Club Extinction), Madame Bovary, Betty, Through the Eyes of Vichy. L'Enfer (Hell; also s.p.), A Judgment in Stone (also co-s.p.), Rien Ne Va Plus, The Color of Lies (also s.p.), Nightcap (also s.p.), Unfaithful (writer only), The Flower of Evil (dir., writer).
TELEVISION:*Movies:* La Deuxième vérité.*Series:* Les Redoutables.

CHAKERES, MICHAEL H.
Executive. b. Ohio. e. Wittenberg U, 1935. Pres. and chmn. of bd. of Chakeres Theates Inc. of Ohio and Kentucky. U.S. Army AF 1942-45. Bd. of Dir.: National NATO, NATO of Ohio, Will Rogers Hospital, Motion Picture Pioneers, Society National Bank, Wittenberg U., Springfield Foundation, Variety Club of Palm Beach, Tent No. 65. Member: Masonic Temple, Scottish Rite, I.O.O.F., AHEPA, Leadership 100, ARCHON-Order of St. Andrew, Rotary Club, City of Hope, University Club.
(d. Dec. 7, 2002 at age 90.)

CHAKIRIS, GEORGE
Actor. b. Norwood, OH, Sept. 16, 1934. Entered m.p. industry as chorus dancer.
PICTURES: Song of Love (debut, 1947), The Great Caruso, The 5000 Fingers of Dr. T, Give a Girl a Break, Gentlemen Prefer Blondes, There's No Business Like Show Business, White Christmas, Brigadoon, The Girl Rush, Meet Me in Las Vegas, Under Fire (1st acting role), West Side Story (Academy Award for Best Supporting Actor, 1961), Two and Two Make Six, Diamond Head, Bebo's Girl, Kings of the Sun, Flight From Ashiya, 633 Squadron, McGuire Go Home! (The High Bright Sun), Is Paris Burning?, The Young Girls of Rochefort, The Big Cube, The Day the Hot Line Got Hot, Why Not Stay for Breakfast?, Jekyll and Hyde... Together Again, Pale Blood.
TELEVISION:*Movie:* Return to Fantasy Island. *Specials:* You're the Top, Highways of Melody, Kismet, Notorious Woman (PBS), Bourne to Dance. *Mini-series:* Les Filles du Lido. *Series:* Dallas (1985-86), Superboy, Santa Barbara.. *Guest:* Fantasy Island, CHiPs, Matt Houston, Scarecrow and Mrs. King, Hell Town, Murder She Wrote.

CHAMBERLAIN, RICHARD
Actor. r.n. George Richard Chamberlain. b. Los Angeles, CA, March 31, 1935. Studied voice, LA Conservatory of Music 1958; acting with Jeff Corey. Founding mem. City of Angels, LA Theater Company. Became TV star in Dr. Kildare series, 1961-66. Founded prod. co. Cham Enterprises. Had hit record Three Stars Will Shine Tonight (theme from Dr. Kildare) in 1962.
THEATRE: Breakfast at Tiffany's, Night of the Iguana, Fathers & Sons, Blithe Spirit.
PICTURES: The Secret of the Purple Reef (debut, 1960), A Thunder of Drums, Twilight of Honor, Joy in the Morning, Petulia, The Madwoman of Chaillot, Julius Caesar, The Music Lovers, Lady Caroline Lamb, The Three Musketeers, The Towering Inferno, The Four Musketeers, The Slipper and the Rose, The Swarm, The Last Wave, Murder by Phone (Bells), King Solomon's Mines, Alan Quartermain and the Lost City of Gold, The Return of the Musketeers (tv in U.S.), Bird of Prey, Pavillion.
TELEVISION: *Movies:* F. Scott Fitzgerald and the Last of the Belles, The Count of Monte Cristo, The Man in the Iron Mask, Cook and Perry: The Race to the Pole, Wallenberg: A Hero's Story, Casanova, Aftermath: A Test of Love, The Night of the Hunter, Ordeal in the Arctic, The Thorn Birds: The Missing Year, All the Winters that Have Been. *Mini-Series:* Centennial, Shogun, The Thorn Birds, Dream West, The Bourne Identity, Too Rich: The Secret Life of Doris Duke. *Specials:* Hamlet, Portrait of a Lady, The Woman I Love, The Lady's Not for Burning. *Series:* Dr. Kildare, Island Son (also co-exec. prod.) *Host:* The Astronomers. *Guest:* Gunsmoke, Thriller, The Deputy, Alfred Hitchcock Presents, The Lost Daughter.

CHAMBERS, EVERETT
Producer, Writer, Director. b. Montrose, CA; Aug. 19, 1926. e. New School For Social Research, Dramatic Workshop, N.Y. Entered industry as actor; worked with Fred Coe as casting dir. and dir., NBC, 1952-57; Author: Producing TV Movies.
PICTURES: *Actor:* Too Late Blues. *Writer:* Tess of the Storm Country, Run Across the River, The Kiss (short; dir.: Acad. Award nom.), The Lollipop Cover (also prod., dir.; Acad. award, Chicago Film Fest.), Private Duty Nurses, A Girl to Kill For.
TELEVISION: *Movies:* Beverly Hills Madam, A Matter of Sex (exec. prod., 1985 Christopher & A.W.R.T. Awards), Will There Really Be a Morning?, Berlin Tunnel 21 (sprv. prod.), Night Slaves (also writer), Moon of the Wolf, Trouble Comes to Town, The Great American Beauty Contest, Can Ellen Be Saved? (also writer), Jigsaw John, Street Killing, Nero Wolfe, Twin Detectives (also writer), The Girl Most Likely to..., Sacrifice the Queen, Paris Conspiracy, Family Secret, Incident in a Small Town (spv. prod.). *Co-writer:* The Perfect Town for Murder, Last Chance (pilot). *Series: Producer:* Johnny Staccato (also writer), Target the Corrupters, The Dick Powell Theatre, The Lloyd Bridges Show (also writer), Peyton Place, Columbo, Future Cop, Timeslip (exec. prod., writer), Lucan (also writer), Airwolf, Partners in

Crime, Rin Tin Tin K-9 Cop (also creative consultant).

CHAMPION, MARGE
Dancer, Actress, Choreographer. r.n. Marjorie Celeste Belcher. b. Los Angeles, CA, Sept. 2, 1919. e. Los Angeles public schools. Father was Ernest Belcher, ballet master. Was model for Snow White for Disney's animated feature. Debuted in films as Marjorie Bell. Made debut in 1947, with former husband Gower Champion as dancing team; team was signed by MGM; voted Star of Tomorrow, 1952. Received Lifetime Achievement award from the American Dance Foundation, 1997.
THEATRE: Blossom Time, Student Prince (LA Civic Opera), Dark of the Moon. Beggar's Holiday (NY), 3 for Tonight (NY), Invitation to a March (tour). Director: Stepping Out, Lute Song (Berkshire Theatre Fest, 1989), She Loves Me, No No Nanette.
PICTURES: Honor of the West (debut, 1939), The Story of Vernon and Irene Castle, Sorority House, Mr. Music, Show Boat, Lovely to Look At, Everything I Have Is Yours, Give a Girl a Break, Three for the Show, Jupiter's Darling, The Swimmer, The Party, The Cockeyed Cowboys of Calico County. *Choreographer only:* The Day of the Locust, Whose Life Is It Anyway?.
TELEVISION: *Movie:* Queen of the Stardust Ballroom (choreographer; Emmy Award, 1975). *Mini-series:* Ike(choreographer, UK). *Series:* Admiral Broadway Revue, Marge and Gower Champion Show. *Guest:* GE Theatre, Chevy Show, Bell Telephone Hour, Ed Sullivan, Shower of Stars, Fame.

CHAN, JACKIE
Actor, Director, Writer. r.n. Chan Kwong-Sang. b. Hong Kong, Apr. 7, 1954. Trained in acrobatics, mime and martial arts at Peking Opera Sch. Was child actor in several films; later became stuntman before being launched as action star by prod.-dir. Lo Wei.
PICTURES: Little Tiger From Canton, New Fist of Fury, Shaolin Wooden Men, To Kill With Intrigue, Snake in the Eagle's Shadow, Snake & Crane Arts of Shaolin, Magnificent Bodyguards, Drunken Master (Drunk Monkey in the Tiger's Eyes), Spiritual Kung Fu, The Fearless Hyena, Dragon Fist, The Young Master (also dir., co-s.p.), Half a Loaf of Kung Fu, The Big Brawl, The Cannonball Run, Dragon Lord (also dir., co-s.p.), Winners and Sinners, The Fearless Hyena Part 2, Cannonball Run II, Project A (also co-dir., co-s.p.), Wheels on Meals, My Lucky Stars, The Protector, Twinkle Twinkle Lucky Stars, Heart of the Dragon (First Mission), Police Story (also dir., co-s.p.), Armour of God (also dir., co-s.p.), Project A Part 2 (also dir., co-s.p.), Dragons Forever, Police Story II (also dir., co-s.p.), Mr. Canton and Lady Rose (Miracle; also dir., co-s.p.), Armour of God II: Operation Condor (also dir., co-s.p.), Island of Fire, Twin Dragons, Police Story III: Super Cop (also dir., co-s.p.), City Hunter, Crime Story, Project S, Drunken Master II, Rumble in the Bronx, Thunderbolt, First Strike, Burn Hollywood Burn, Mr. Nice Guy, Rush Hour, Who Am I? (also dir., s.p.), Gorgeous (also exec. prod.), Shanghai Noon (also prod.), The Accidental Spy, Rush Hour 2, The Tuxedo, Shanghai Knights, Chin gei bin, The Medallion, Around the World in 80 Days (also prod.), Rush Hour 3.

CHANNING, CAROL
Actress. b. Seattle, WA, Jan. 31, 1921. e. Bennington Coll.
THEATRE: B'way: Gentlemen Prefer Blondes, Lend an Ear (Theatre World Award), Hello Dolly! (Tony Award, 1964), Show Girl, Lorelei. Tour: Legends.
PICTURES: Paid in Full (debut, 1950), The First Traveling Saleslady, Thoroughly Modern Millie (Acad. Award nom.), Skidoo, Shinbone Alley (voice), Sgt. Pepper's Lonely Hearts Club Band (cameo), Happily Ever After (voice), Hans Christian Andersen's Thumbelina (voice), Edie & Pen, The Line King: Al Hirschfeld, Homo Heights, The Brave Little Toaster Goes to Mars (voice), Broadway: The Golden Age by the Legends Who Were There (documentary, as herself).
TELEVISION: *Movies:* Free to Be...You & Me (voice), Alice in Wonderland, JFK: The Day the Nation Cried (tv documentary) *Series:* Where's Waldo? (voice), The Addams Family (voice, 1992). *Specials:* Svengali and the Blonde, Three Men on a Horse, Crescendo, The Carol Channing Special. *Guest:* Omnibus, George Burns Show, Lucy Show, Carol Burnett Show, The Love Boat, The Drew Carey Show, Hollywood Squares.

CHANNING, STOCKARD
Actress. r.n. Susan Williams Antonia Stockard. b. New York, NY, Feb. 13, 1944. e. Radcliffe Coll., B.A., 1965. With Theatre Co. of Boston, experimental drama company, 1967.
THEATRE: Two Gentlemen of Verona, No Hard Feelings, Vanities (Mark Taper Forum, LA), They're Playing Our Song, The Lady and the Clarinet, Golden Age, The Rink, Joe Egg (Tony Award, 1985), Love Letters, Woman in Mind, House of Blue Leaves, Six Degrees of Separation, Four Baboons Adoring the Sun.
PICTURES: The Hospital (debut, 1971), Up the Sandbox, The Fortune, The Big Bus, Sweet Revenge, Grease, The Cheap Detective, The Fish That Saved Pittsburgh, Safari 3000, Without a Trace, Heartburn, The Men's Club, A Time of Destiny, Staying Together, Meet the Applegates, Married to It, Six Degrees of Separation (Acad. Award nom.), Bitter Moon, Smoke, To Wong Foo—Thanks for Everything—Julie Newmar, Up Close and Personal, Moll Flanders, Edie and Pen, The First Wives Club, Practical Magic, Baby Dance, Twilight, Lulu on the Bridge (voice), Practical Magic, Isn't She Great, The Venice Project, Where the Heart Is, The Business of Strangers, Life or Something Like It, Behind the Red Door, Le Divorce.
TELEVISION: *Movies:* The Girl Most Likely To..., Lucan, Silent Victory: The Kitty O'Neil Story, Not My Kid, The Room Upstairs, Echoes in the Darkness, The Perfect Witness, David's Mother,

101

An Unexpected Family, Lily Dale, The Prosecutors, An Unexpected Life, The Baby Dance, The Truth About Jane, The Piano Man's Daughter, The Confessions of an Ugly Stepsister, The Matthew Shepard Story. Mini-series: A Girl Thing. Guest: Medical Center, Trying Times (The Sad Professor), King of the Hill (voice). Special: Tidy Endings. Series: Stockard Channing in Just Friends, The Stockard Channing Show, Batman Beyond (voice), It's A Girl Thing. The West Wing, Walking With Beasts (voice).

CHAPIN, DOUG
Producer. Began career as actor; then switched to film production, making debut with When a Stranger Calls, 1979.
PICTURES: Pandemonium, American Dreamer, What's Love Got to Do With It, Love! Valour! Compassion!, The Passion of Ayn Rand (co-exec.).
TELEVISION: Movies: All Lies End in Murder, Belle Starr, Missing Pieces, Second Sight, When A Stranger Calls Back, Jackie's Back (exec.). Series: Tim Conway's Funny America.

CHAPLIN, GERALDINE
Actress. b. Santa Monica, CA, July 31, 1944. e. Royal Ballet School, London. Father was actor-director Charles Chaplin. Starred in over 20 European productions, including seven with Spanish filmmaker, Carlos Saura. On NY stage in The Little Foxes.
PICTURES: Limelight (debut, 1952), Par un Beau Matin d'Ete, Doctor Zhivago, Andremo in Citta, A Countess from Hong Kong, Stranger in the House (Cop-Out), I Killed Rasputin, Peppermint Frappe, Stres es Tres Tres, Honeycomb, Garden of Delights, The Hawaiians, Sur un Arbre Perche, Z.P.G. (Zero Population Growth), Innocent Bystanders, La Casa sin Fronteras, Ana and the Wolves, The Three Musketeers, Le Marriage a la Mode, The Four Musketeers, Summer of Silence, Nashville, Elisa My Love, Noroit, Buffalo Bill and the Indians or Sitting Bull's History Lesson, Welcome to L.A., Cria, In Memorium, Une Page d'Amour, Roseland, Remember My Name, Los Ojos Vendados, The Masked Bride, L'Adoption, A Wedding, The Mirror Crack'd, Le Voyage en Douce, Bolero, Life Is a Bed of Roses, Love on the Ground, The Moderns, White Mischief, Mama Turns 100, The Return of the Musketeers (tv in U.S.), I Want to Go Home, The Children, Buster's Bedroom, Chaplin, The Age of Innocence, Words Upon the Window Pane, Home for the Holidays, Jane Eyre, Crimetime, The Eyes of Asia, Mother Theresa: The Last Days of Switzerland, Just Run, Faces of the Moon, The City of No Limits, Talk to Her.
TELEVISION: Specials: The Corsican Brothers, My Cousin Rachel, The House of Mirth, A Foreign Field. Mini-Series: The World, The Odyssey, In the Beginning, Dinotopia. Movie: Duel of Hearts, Gulliver's Travels.

CHAPMAN, MICHAEL
Cinematographer, Director. b. New York, NY, Nov. 21, 1935. m. writer-dir. Amy Jones. Early career in N.Y. area working on documentaries before becoming camera operator for cinematographer Gordon Willis on The Godfather, Klute, End of the Road, The Landlord. Also camera operator on Jaws.
PICTURES: Cinematographer: The Last Detail, White Dawn, Taxi Driver, The Front, The Next Man, Fingers, The Last Waltz, Invasion of the Body Snatchers, Hardcore, The Wanderers, Raging Bull, Dead Men Don't Wear Plaid, Personal Best, The Man With Two Brains, Shoot to Kill, Scrooged, Ghostbusters II, Quick Change, Kindergarten Cop, Whispers in the Dark, Rising Sun, The Lost Boys, The Fugitive, Primal Fear, Space Jam, Six Days Seven Nights, The Story of Us, The White River Kid, The Watcher, Evolution, Eulogy, Suspect Zero. Director: All the Right Moves, The Clan of the Cave Bear, The Viking Sagas (also s.p.). TELEVISION: Death Be Not Proud, King, Gotham. Dir.: The Annihilator (pilot).

CHARBONNEAU, PATRICIA
Actress. b. Valley Stream, Long Island, NY, 1959. Stage appearances with Actors Theatre of Louisville, KY. Also in NY in My Sister in This House.
PICTURES: Desert Hearts, Manhunter, Stalking Danger, Call Me, Shakedown, Brain Dead, Captive, The Owl, K2, Portraits of a Killer, Kiss the Sky, She's All That.
TELEVISION: Series: Crime Story. Pilots: C.A.T. Squad, Dakota's Way. Guest: Spenser: For Hire, The Equalizer, Wiseguy, UNSUB, Matlock. Movies: Disaster at Silo 7, Desperado: Badlands Justice, One Special Night.

CHAREST, MICHELINE
Producer.
PICTURES: Bonjour Timothy, The Whole of the Moon, The Sleep Room.
TELEVISION: Movie: Revenge of the Land (exec. prod.). Mini-series: Million Dollar Babies. Series: The Wonderful Wizard of Oz, Arthur (Emmy Award, 1998), Lassie, The Country Mouse and the City Mouse Adventures, Emily of the New Moon, Mona the Vampire (exec. prod.)

CHARISSE, CYD
Dancer, Actress. r.n. Tula Ellice Finklea. b. Amarillo, TX, March 8, 1921. e. Hollywood Prof. Sch. m. Tony Martin, singer. Toured U.S. & Europe with Ballet Russe starting at age 13. Began in films as bit player using the name Lily Norwood. Signed contract with MGM in 1946. Named Star of Tomorrow 1948.
PICTURES: Something to Shout About (debut, 1943; billed as Lily Norwood), Mission to Moscow; Ziegfeld Follies (1st film billed as Cyd Charisse), The Harvey Girls, Three Wise Fools, Till the Clouds Roll By, Fiesta, Unfinished Dance, On an Island with You, Words and Music, Kissing Bandit, Tension, East Side West Side, Mark of the Renegade, Wild North, Singin' in the Rain, Sombrero, The Band Wagon, Brigadoon, Deep in My Heart, It's Always Fair Weather, Meet Me in Las Vegas, Silk Stockings, Twilight for the Gods, Party Girl, Five Golden Hours, Black Tights, Two Weeks in Another Town, The Silencers, Maroc 7, Won Ton Ton the Dog Who Saved Hollywood, Warlords of Atlantis, That's Entertainment III, Satin and Silk (video short)
TELEVISION: Movies: Portrait of an Escort, Swimsuit, Cinderella Summer. Special: Marilyn Monroe: The Final Days, Gene Kelly: Anatomy of a Dancer (tv documentary).

CHARLES, MARIA
Actress. b. London, England, Sept. 22, 1929. Trained at RADA. London stage debut 1946 in Pick Up Girl.
THEATRE: London: Women of Twilight, The Boy Friend, Divorce Me Darling!, Enter A Free Man, They Don't Grow on Trees, Winnie the Pooh, Jack the Ripper, The Matchmaker, Measure for Measure, Annie (1979-80), Fiddler on the Roof, Steaming, Peer Gynt, The Lower Depths, When We Are Married, Follies, Party Piece, School for Scandal, Driving Miss Daisy, Hay Fever, Blithe Spirit. Dir.: Owl and the Pussycat. Dir./prod.: The Boy Friend, 40, Starting Here Starting Now.
PICTURES: Folly To Be Wise, The Deadly Affair, Eye of the Devil, Great Expectations, The Return of the Pink Panther, Cuba, Victor/Victoria, Savage Hearts, The Fool.
TELEVISION: The Likes of 'Er, The Moon and the Yellow River, Down Our Street, Easter Passion, Nicholas Nickleby, The Voice of the Turtle, The Fourth Wall, The Good Old Days, Turn Out the Lights, Angel Pavement, The Ugliest Girl in Town, Other Peoples Houses, Rogues Gallery, The Prince and the Pauper, Crown Court, Bar Mitzvah Boy, Secret Army, Agony, Never the Twain, La Ronde, Shine of Harvey Moon, Sheppey, La Ronde, Brideshead Revisited, A Perfect Spy, Casualty, The Fallout Guy, Lovejoy, Anna, Agony Again, Oliver Twist, Crime and Punishment, The 10th Kingdom, Cor Blimey.

CHARTOFF, ROBERT
Producer. b. New York, NY., Aug. 26, 1933. e. Union College, A.B.; Columbia U., LL.B. Met Irwin Winkler through mutual client at William Morris Agency (N.M.) and established Chartoff-Winkler Prods. Currently pres., Chartoff Prods., Inc.
PICTURES: Double Trouble, Point Blank, The Split, They Shoot Horses Don't They?, The Strawberry Statement, Leo the Last, Believe in Me, The Gang That Couldn't Shoot Straight, The New Centurions, Up the Sandbox, The Mechanic, Thumb Tripping, Busting, The Gambler, S*P*Y*S, Breakout, Nickelodeon, Rocky, New York New York, Valentino, Comes a Horseman, Uncle Joe Shannon, Rocky II, Raging Bull, True Confessions, Rocky III, The Right Stuff, Rocky IV, Beer, Rocky V, Straight Talk, Country of My Skull.

CHASE, BRANDON
Producer, Director. President MPA Feature Films, Inc.; newscaster-news director NBC-TV 1952-57. Executive director Mardi Gras Productions, Inc. and member of Board of Directors. Now pres., Group I Films, Ltd., and V.I. Prods., Ltd.
PICTURES: The Dead One, The Sinner and the Slave Girl, Bourbon Street Shadows, Verdict Homicide, Face of Fire, Four for the Morgue, Mission To Hell, The Wanton, Harlow, Girl In Trouble, Threesome, Wild Cargo, Alice in Wonderland, The Models, The Four of Us, Against All Odds, The Giant Spider Invasion, House of 1000 Pleasures, The Rogue, Eyes of Dr. Chaney, Alligator, Crash!, Take All of Me, The Psychic, UFOs Are Real, The Actresses, The Sword and the Sorcerer, Alligator II: The Mutation.
TELEVISION: Wild Cargo (series prod.-dir.); This Strange and Wondrous World (prod.-dir.), Linda Evans: Secrets to Stay Young Forever.

CHASE, CHEVY
Actor. r.n. Cornelius Crane Chase. b. New York, NY, Oct. 8, 1943. e. Bard Coll.; B.A. Studied audio research at CCS Institute. Worked as writer for Mad Magazine, 1969. Teamed with Kenny Shapiro and Lane Sarasohn while still in school to collaborate on material for underground TV, which ultimately became off-off-Broadway show and later movie called Groove Tube. Co-wrote and starred in Saturday Night Live on TV, winning 2 Emmys as continuing single performance by a supporting actor and as writer for show. Wrote Paul Simon Special (Emmy Award, 1977).
PICTURES: The Groove Tube (debut, 1974), Tunnelvision, Foul Play, Caddyshack, Oh Heavenly Dog, Seems Like Old Times, Under the Rainbow, Modern Problems, National Lampoon's Vacation, Deal of the Century, Fletch, National Lampoon's European Vacation, Sesame Street Presents Follow That Bird (cameo), Spies Like Us, Three Amigos!, The Couch Trip (cameo), Funny Farm, Caddyshack II, Fletch Lives, National Lampoon's Christmas Vacation, L.A. Story (cameo), Nothing But Trouble, Memoirs of an Invisible Man, Hero (unbilled), Last Action Hero (cameo), Cops and Robbersons, Man of the House, Vegas Vacation, Dirty Work, Snow Day, Unleashed, Vacuums, Orange County, Pete's a Pizza, The Karate Dog (voice), The Great Goose Caper, Bad Meat.
TELEVISION: Mini-series: The Hamptons. Series: Saturday Night Live, The Chevy Chase Show. Special: Added Attractions: The Hollywood Shorts Story (voice).

CHASE, STANLEY
Producer. b. Brooklyn, NY, May 3. e. NYU, B.A.; Columbia U, postgraduate. m. actress/artist Dorothy Rice. Began career as assoc. prod. of TV show Star Time; story dept., CBS-TV; then produced plays Off-B'way and on B'way, winner Tony and Obie awards for The Threepenny Opera. Joined ABC-TV as dir. in chg. programming; prod., Universal Pictures & TV; exec. consultant, Metromedia Producers Org.; prod. & exec. Alan Landsburg Productions. Formed Stanley Chase Productions, Inc. in 1975, which heads as president.
THEATRE: *B'way Producer*: The Potting Shed, The Cave Dwellers, A Moon for the Misbegotten, European Tour: Free and Easy. *Off-B'way*: The Threepenny Opera.
PICTURES: The Hell with Heroes, Colossus: The Forbin Project, Welcome to Blood City, High-Ballin', Fish Hawk, The Guardian, Mack the Knife.
TELEVISION: Inside Danny Baker (pilot), Al Capp special (prod., writer), Happily Ever After (pilot; prod., writer), Bob Hope Presents the Chrysler Theatre series, Jigsaw (pilot), Fear on Trial (Emmy nom.), Courage of Kavik: The Wolf Dog (exec. prod.), An American Christmas Carol, Grace Kelly.

CHASMAN, DAVID
Executive. b. New York, NY, Sept. 28, 1925. e. Sch. of Industrial Art, 1940-43; Academie De La Grande-Chaumiere, 1949-50. Monroe Greenthal Co., Inc. 1950-53; Grey Advertising Agency, Inc., 1953-60. Freelance consultant to industry 1950-60; worked on pictures for UA, 20th-Fox, Columbia, Samuel Goldwyn, City Film; Adv. mgr. United Artists, 1960; exec. dir. adv., United Artists, 1962; exec. production, United Artists, London, 1964; v.p. in prod. United Artists, 1969; v.p. of west coast operations, U.A. 1970; sr. v.p. in charge of prod., U.A. 1972; president, Convivium Productions Inc., 1974. Joined Columbia 1977, named exec. v.p. worldwide theatrical prod. 1979. Joined MGM 1980; named exec. v.p.-worldwide theatrical prod. Retired.
PICTURES: *Exec. prod.*: Brighton Beach Memoirs, The Secret of My Success.

CHAUDHRI, AMIN QAMAR
Director, Producer, Cinematographer, Editor. b. Punjab, India, April 18, 1942. e. Hampstead Polytechnic, London, City U. of New York. Pres., Filmart Enterprises Ltd. & Filmart Int'l Ltd., Pres./CEO, Continental Film Group Ltd. Pres./CEO, Continental Entertainment Group, Ltd., Heron Int'l Pictures, Ltd.
PICTURES: *Director*: Kashish, Khajuraho, Eternal, Urvasi, Konarak, The Land of Buddha. *Producer*: Night Visitors, Diary of a Hit Man, The Master Mechanic. *Producer/Director*: Once Again, An Unremarkable Life, Tiger Warsaw, The Last Day of School, Gunga Din, Golden Chute, Wings of Grey, Call It Sleep, The Bookie. *Cinematography*: Right On, Sweet Vengeance, The Hopefuls, The Wicked Die Slow, Who Says I Can't Ride a Rainbow, Black Rodeo, Medium Is the Message, Death of a Dunbar Girl, Kashish, The Last Day of School. *Writer*: Seventh Veil (2000).
TELEVISION: Reflections of India (prod.-dir.), Wild Wild East (camera), Nehru (edit.), Medium is the Message (photog.), America... Amerika (prod., dir.).

CHAYKIN, MAURY
Actor. b. Brooklyn, NY, July 27, 1949. e. Univ. of Buffalo. Formed theatre co. Swamp Fox; later acted with Buffalo rep. co., Public Theatre in NY. Moved to Toronto in 1980.
PICTURES: The Kidnapping of the President, Death Hunt, Soup for One, Of Unknown Origin, Harry and Son, Highpoint, Mrs. Soffel, Turk 182!, Meatballs III, The Bedroom Window, Wild Thing, Stars and Bars, Caribe, Iron Eagle II, Twins, Millenium, Breaking In, Where the Heart Is, Mr. Destiny, Dances With Wolves, George's Island, My Cousin Vinny, Leaving Normal, The Adjuster, Hero, Sommersby, Money for Nothing, Josh and S.A.M., Beethoven's 2nd, Camilla, Whale Music (Genie Award), Unstrung Heroes, Devil in a Blue Dress, Cutthroat Island, Love and Death on Long Island, Pale Saints, Strip Search, The Sweet Hereafter, A Life Less Ordinary, Mouse Hunt, Jerry & Tom, Mystery Alaska, Shegalla, Jacob Two Two Meets the Hooded Fang, Entrapment, Touched, Let the Devil Wear Black, What's Cooking, The Art of War, Bartleby, Plan B, On Their Knees, Past Perfect, Owning Mahoney, Whitecoats.
TELEVISION: *Movies*: If Looks Could Kill, Northern Lights, Joan of Arc, Golden Spiders: A Nero Wolfe Mystery, Varian's War, Bleacher Bums, Crossed Over, Ruby Romaine Trailer Tales. *Special*: Canada's Sweetheart: The Saga of Hal Banks (Nellie Award). *Series*: Emily of New Moon, A Nero Wolfe Mystery.

CHEADLE, DON
Actor. b. Kansas City, Missouri, November 29, 1964.
PICTURES: Moving Violations, Hamburger Hill, Colors, Roadside Prophets, The Meteor Man, Devil a Blue Dress, Things to Do in Denver When You're Dead, Rosewood, Volcano, Boogie Nights, Bulworth, Out of Sight, Wings Against the Wind, Mission to Mars, The Family Man, Traffic, Things Behind the Sun, Manic, Swordfish, Rush Hour 2, Ocean's Eleven, The United States of Leland, Tishomongo Blues (also dir.), The Assassination of Richard Nixon.
TELEVISION: *Movies*: Rebound: The Legend of Earl "The Goat" Manigault, Lush Life, A Lesson Before Dying, Fail Safe. *Series*: The Golden Palace, Picket Fences. *Guest*: Fame, LA Law, Hill Street Blues, The Bronx Zoo, Hooperman, Night Court, Booker, China Beach, The Fresh Prince of Bel Air, Hangin' With Mr. Cooper, The Simpsons (voice).

CHELSOM, PETER
Director, Writer. b. Blackpool, England, April 20, 1956. Studied acting at London's Central School of Drama. Acted with Royal Shakespeare Co., Royal Natl. Theatre, Royal Court Theatre. Dir. at Central School of Drama, taught acting at Actors Ints. and at Cornell Univ. Wrote and directed short film Treacle for Channel 4/British Screen. Director of many tv commercials in U.K. and U.S.
PICTURES: Hear My Song (dir., story, co-s.p.), Funny Bones (dir., co-prod., co-s.p.), The Mighty, Town and Country, Serendipity (dir.), Shall We Dance? (dir.).
TELEVISION: Movies/Actor: Cream in My Coffee, Intensive Care, An Englishman Abroad, Star Quality. Mini-series: A Woman of Substance, Sorrell & Son.

CHEN, JOAN
Actress, Director. r.n. Chen Chung. b. Shanghai, China, April 26, 1961. Studied acting with actress Zhang Rei Fang at Shanghai Film Studio. Debuted as teenager in Chinese films. Moved to U.S. in 1981.
PICTURES: Little Flower, Awakening, Dim Sum: A Little Bit of Heart, Tai-Pain, The Last Emperor, Turtle Beach, When Sleeping Dogs Lie, Night Stalker, Heaven and Earth, Golden Gate, On Deadly Ground, Deadlock, The Hunted, Red Rose/White Rose, Judge Dredd, Precious Find (also assoc. prod.), Precious Find, Purple Storm, What's Cooking, Avatar, . *Director/Writer*: Xiu Xiu: The Sent Down Girl (also exec. prod.), Autumn in New York (dir.).
TELEVISION: Movies: Twin Peaks, Wedlock, Steel Justice Shadow of a Stranger, In a Class of His Own. *Series*: Twin Peaks, Children of the Dragon. *Guest*: Miami Vice, MacGyver, Wiseguy, Homicide: Life on the Street., The Outer Limits.

CHER
Singer, Actress. r.n. Cherilyn Sarkisian. b. El Centro, CA, May 20, 1946. Began singing as backup singer for Crystals and Ronettes, then with former husband, the late Sonny Bono in 1965; first hit record I Got You Babe, sold 3 million copies. Made two films and then debuted nightclub musical-comedy act in 1969. CBS comedy-variety series started as summer show in 1971; became regular series the following December. NY stage debut: Come Back to the Five and Dime Jimmy Dean Jimmy Dean (1982).
PICTURES: Wild on the Beach (debut, 1965), Good Times, Chastity, Come Back to the Five and Dime Jimmy Dean Jimmy Dean, Silkwood, Mask (Cannes award), The Witches of Eastwick, Suspect, Moonstruck (Academy Award), Mermaids, The Player, Ready to Wear (Prêt-à-Porter), Faithful, Tea with Mussolini, Detroit Rock City, Mayor of Sunset Strip (documentary), Stuck on You (as herself).
TELEVISION: *Movie*: If These Walls Could Talk (also dir.). *Series*: Sonny & Cher Comedy Hour (1971-74), Cher, The Sonny and Cher Show (1976-77). *Specials*: Cher, Cher... Special, Cher and Other Fantasies, Cher: A Celebration at Caesar's Palace, Cher at the Mirage, The Grand Opening of Euro Disney, Comic Relief: Behind the Nose, Happy Birthday Elizabeth: A Celebration of Life, AFI's 100 Years...100 Movies, 26th Annual American Music Awards, VH1 Divas Live, AFI's 100 Years...100 Stars, I Love Lucy's 50th Anniversary Special, The Royal Variety Performance 2001, National Lottery Christmas Cracker, Judi Dench: A BAFTA Tribute. *Guest*: Shindig, Hullabaloo, Hollywood Palace, The Man from U.N.C.L.E., Laugh-In, Will & Grace, VH1's Behind the Music.

CHERMAK, CY
Producer, Writer. b. Bayonne, NJ, Sept. 20, 1929. e. Brooklyn Coll., Ithaca Coll.
PICTURES: 4D Man (s.p.).
TELEVISION: *Movie*: Murder at the World Series (prod., s.p.), Rescuers: Stories of Courage/Two Couples (s.p.). *Series: Writer, prod., exec. prod.*: Ironside, The Virginian, The New Doctors, Amy Prentiss, Kolchak: The Night Stalker, Barbary Coast, CHiPS.

CHERNIN, PETER
Executive. Began career as assoc. publicity director, St. Martin's Press; editor, Warner Books. v.p. of development & prod., David Gerber Co.; exec. v.p., programming & mktg., Showtime/The Movie Channel, Inc.; president & COO, Lorimar Film Entertainment; President of Fox from 1989-1992. Chmn. of Twentieth Century Fox Film Corporation from 1992-1994. Chmn. & CEO, Fox Filmed Entertainment, 1994-96. Since 1996, director, president and COO of The News Corporation Limited, Rupert Murdoch's global media and entertainment organization; also CEO of NAI since '96. Since 1998, a director, president and COO of Fox Entertainment Group, Inc. A director for the following organizations: TV Guide, Inc, from 1999-2000; Gemstar since April 2002; E*TRADE since 1999. Member of advisory bd. of PUMA AG since 1999.

CHETWYND, LIONEL
Executive, Writer, Director. b. London, England. m. actress Gloria Carlin. Emigrated to Canada, 1948. e. Sir George Williams U., Montreal, BA, economics; BCL-McGill U., Montreal. Graduate Work-Law, Trinity Coll. Oxford. Admitted to bar, Province of Quebec, 1968. C.B.C., TV-Public Affairs and Talks, 1961-1965. CTV network 1965-67. Controller commercial TV and film rights, Expo '67. Freelance writer and consultant 1961-68. Asst. mng. dir. Columbia Pictures (U.K.) Ltd. London 1968-72.Asst. mng. dir. Columbia-Warner UK, 1971. Story and book for musical Maybe That's Your Problem, 1971-1973. Then Bleeding Great Orchids (staged London, and Off-B'way). Also wrote The American 1776, official U.S. Bi-centennial film and We

the People/200 Constitutional Foundation. Former mem. of NYU grad. film sch. faculty, lecturer on screenwriting at Frederick Douglass Ctr. Harlem. Mem of Canadian Bar Assc. Served on bd. of gov., Commission on Battered Children, and the Little League.

PICTURES: Director and/or Writer: The Apprenticeship of Duddy Kravitz (Acad. Award nom.), Morning Comes, Two Solitudes (also prod., Grand Award Salonika), Quintet, The Hanoi Hilton, Redline, The Hot Touch, Darkness at High Noon: The Carl Foreman Documents.

TELEVISION: Producer and/or Writer: Johnny We Hardly Knew Ye (George Washington Honor Medal, Freedom Fdn.), It Happened One Christmas, Goldenrod, A Whale for the Killing , Miracle on Ice (Christopher Award), Escape From Iran: The Canadian Caper, Sadat (NAACP Image Award), Children in the Crossfire, To Heal a Nation (also exec. prod.), Evil in Clear River (exec. prod. only, Christopher Award), So Proudly We Hail (also exec. prod.), The Godfather Wars, The Heroes of Desert Storm, Reverse Angle (also exec. prod.), Doom's Day Gun, The Bible... Moses, The Bible... Jacob, The Bible... Joseph (Emmy award), Falling From the Sky: Flight 174, The Man Who Captured Eichmann, Kissinger & Nixon (also exec. prod.), Human Bomb, The Color of Justice, Ruby Ridge An American Tragedy, National Desk, Net Force, P.T. Barnum, Varian's War.

CHEUNG, MAGGIE
Actress. b. Hong Kong, Sept. 20, 1964. Extensive work in Hong Kong. Cinema.

PICTURES: Jackie Chan's Police Story, Happy Ghost 3, Kino Countdown (cameo), The Game They Call Sex, Police Story 2, Song of Exile, The Dragon from Russia, Heart Against Hearts (cameo), The Banquet, Days of Being Wild, The Actress, Dragon Inn, The Heroic Trio, Double Dragon, Police Story 3: Supercop, Family Happiness, Chasing Boys, Moon Warriors, Heroic Trio 2: Executioners, Seven Maidens, The Eagle Shooting Heroes, Green Snake, Ashes of Time, Comrades: Almost a Love Story, Irma Vep, Chinese Box, The Soong Sisters, Augustin: King of Kung-Fu, Love at First Sight, In the Mood for Love, Chin hei man bo, Hero.

CHINICH, MICHAEL
Producer. b. New York, NY. e. Boston U. Began career as casting agent in N.Y.; moved to L.A. to join MCA-Universal Pictures as executive in casting. Named head of feature film casting; then prod. v.p.

PICTURES: Casting dir.: Dog Day Afternoon, Coal Miner's Daughter, Animal House, Melvin and Howard, The Blues Brothers, Mask, Midnight Run, Twins, Ghostbusters II, Kindergarten Cop, Dave, Junior, The Late Shift, Father's Day, Six Days Seven Nights. Exec. Prod.: Pretty in Pink, Ferris Bueller's Day Off, Some Kind of Wonderful, Planes Trains and Automobiles (co-exec. prod.), Commandments (prod.), Killing Me Softly (prod.).

CHOMSKY, MARVIN J.
Director, Producer. b. Bronx, NY, May 23, 1929. e. Syracuse U., B.S.; Stanford U., M.A. Started in theatre business at early age as art dir. with such TV credits as U.S. Steel Hour, Playhouse 90, Studio One, etc. Later worked with Herbert Brodkin who advanced him to assoc. prod. with such TV shows as The Doctors and The Nurses. Brought to Hollywood in 1965 as assoc. prod. for Talent Associates, producing series of TV pilots. Art dir.: The Bubble.

PICTURES: Evel Knievel, Murph the Surf, Mackintosh and T.J., Good Luck Miss Wycoff, Tank.

TELEVISION: Series: The Wild Wild West, Gunsmoke, Star Trek, Then Came Bronson. Movies: Assault on the Wayne, Mongo's Back in Town, Family Flight, Fireball Forward, Female Artillery, The Magician, The F.B.I. Story: The F.B.I. Vs. Alvin Karpas, Mrs. Sundance, Attack on Terror: The F.B.I. Vs. the Ku Klux Klan, Kate McShane, Brink's: The Great Robbery, Law and Order, A Matter of Wife and Death, Victory at Entebbe, Little Ladies of the Night, Roots (co-dir.), Danger in Paradise, Holocaust (Emmy Award, 1978), Hollow Image, King Crab, Attica (Emmy Award, 1980), Inside the Third Reich (Emmy Award, 1982), My Body My Child, The Nairobi Affair, I Was a Mail Order Bride, Robert Kennedy and His Times, Evita Peron (also prod.), Peter the Great (also prod.; Emmy Award as prod., 1986), The Deliberate Stranger (also prod.), Anastasia: The Mystery of Anna (also prod.), Billionaire Boys Club (also spv. prod.), Angel in Green, I'll Be Home for Christmas (also prod.), Brotherhood of the Rose (also prod.), Telling Secrets, Strauss Dynasty (also prod.), Hurricane Andrew (also prod.), Catherine the Great (also prod.).

CHONG, RAE DAWN
Actress, Director, Producer.. b. Edmonton Alta, Canada, Feb. 28, 1961. Father is director-comedian Tommy Chong. Debut at 12 in The Whiz Kid of Riverton (TV). B'way debut 1991 in Oh Kay!

PICTURES: Stony Island (debut, 1978), Quest for Fire, Beat Street, The Corsican Brothers, Choose Me, Fear City, City Limits, American Flyers, Commando, The Color Purple, Soul Man, The Squeeze, The Principal, Walking After Midnight, Tales From the Darkside, Far Out Man, The Borrower, Amazon, Chaindance, Time Runner, When the Party's Over, In Exile, Boulevard, Boca, Hideaway, The Break, Starlight, Mask of Death, Waiting for the Man, Goodbye America, Highball, Small Time, Valentine's Day, Dangerous Attraction, The Visit, Cursed Part 3 (dir., exec. prod., writer).

TELEVISION: Movies: The Top of the Hill, Badge of the

Assassin, Curiosity Kills, Prison Stories: Women on the Inside, Father & Son: Dangerous Relations, Thing I Forgot to Remember, The Alibi, Valentine's Day, For Hope. Series: Nitecap, Mysterious Ways, Wild Card.

CHONG, TOMMY
Actor, Writer, Director. b. Edmonton, Alta., Canada, May 24, 1938. Daughter is actress Rae Dawn Chong. Was guitar player with various Canadian rhythm and blues combinations, before teaming with Richard (Cheech) Marin in improvisational group. Has made comedy recordings.

PICTURES: Up in Smoke, Cheech and Chong's Next Movie (also dir., co-s.p.), Cheech and Chong's Nice Dreams (also dir., co-s.p.), Things Are Tough All Over, It Came from Hollywood, Still Smokin', Yellowbeard, The Corsican Brothers (also dir., s.p.), After Hours, Tripwire (cameo), Far Out Man (also dir., s.p.), The Spirit of 76, FernGully (voice), National Lampoon's Senior Trip, McHale's Navy, Best Buds (also s.p., exec. prod.), Half Baked (actor only), Secret Agent 420, The Wash, High Times Potluck, You'll Never Wiez In This Town Again, Best Buds (also writer, exec. prod.)

TELEVISION: Trial and Error (co-exec. prod.), That 70s Show.

CHOW, RAYMOND
O.B.E. Producer. b. Hong Kong, 1927. e. St. John's U., Shanghai. Worked for Hong Kong Standard; then joined the Hong Kong office of the U.S. Information Service. In 1959 joined Shaw Brothers as head of publicity, became head of production before leaving in 1970 to start Golden Harvest to produce Chinese-language films in Hong Kong. Kung-fu films featuring Bruce Lee put Harvest into int'l market. Started English-language films in 1977, beginning with The Amsterdam Kill and The Boys in Company C. Named Showman of the Year 1984 by NATO. Awarded O.B.E. in 1988.

PICTURES: Armour of God, The Big Boss (and subsequent Bruce Lee films), The Cannonball Run (and Part II), High Road to China, Lassiter, Miracles, Mr. Boo (a.k.a. The Private Eyes; and many subsequent Michael Hui films), Painted Faces, Police Story (and Part II), Project A (and Part II), Rouge, The Story of the Flying Fox, Love on the Rooftops, A Show of Force, China O'Brien (and Part II), Teenage Mutant Ninja Turtles (and Part II), Lord of East China Sea, The Reincarnation of Golden Lotus, Summer Snow, Rumble in the Bronx, Lost & Found, Viva Erotica, The Stunt Woman, Hold You Tight, The Soong Sisters, Kitchen, Portland Street Blues, Gorgeous, Man Called Hero, Fly Me to Polaris, Tokyo Raiders, Born to Be King, Skyline Cruisers, The Accidental Spy, You Shoot I Shoot.

CHRISTIANSEN, ROBERT W.
Producer. b. Porterville, CA. e. Bakersfield Coll. Spent 3 years in Marine Corps. Worked on Hollywood Reporter in circulation and advertising. Joined Cinema Center Films; P.A. on Monte Walsh and Hail Hero. Co-produced first feature in 1970, Adam at Six A.M., with Rick Rosenberg, with whom co-produced all credits listed.

PICTURES: Adam at Six A.M., Hide in Plain Sight, Death Benefit, Down in the Delta.

TELEVISION: Movies: Suddenly Single, The Glass House, Gargoyles, A Brand New Life, The Man Who Could Talk to Kids, The Autobiography of Miss Jane Pittman, I Love You...Goodbye, Queen of the Stardust Ballroom, Born Innocent, A Death in Canaan, Strangers, Robert Kennedy and His Times, Kids Don't Tell, As Summers Die, Gore Vidal's Lincoln, Red Earth, White Earth, The Heist, A House of Secrets and Lies, The Last Hit, Heart of Darkness, Tad, Kingfish: A Story of Huey P. Long, Redwood Curtain, Sudden Terror: The Hijacking of Schoolbus # 17, Beyond the Call, Lost Treasure of Dos Santos, The Long Island Incident, Twice Upon a Time, Home Invasion, The Crossing.

CHRISTIE, JULIE
Actress. b. Chukua, Assam, India, April 14, 1941. Father had tea plantation in India. e. in Britian, at 16 studied art in France, then attended Central Sch. of Music & Drama in London. 3 yrs. with Frinton-on-Sea Rep., before TV debut in A for Andromeda. Birmingham Rep.; Royal Shakespeare Co.; East European and American tour. NY stage: Uncle Vanya. London stage: Old Times.PICTURES: Crooks Anonymous (debut, 1962), Fast Lady, Billy Liar, Young Cassidy, Darling (Academy Award & BFA Award, 1965), Dr. Zhivago, Farenheit 451, Far From the Madding Crowd, Petulia, In Search of Gregory, The Go-Between, McCabe and Mrs. Miller, Don't Look Now, Shampoo, Nashville (cameo), Demon Seed, Heaven Can Wait, Memoirs of a Survivor, The Return of the Soldier, Heat and Dust, Golddiggers, Power, Miss Mary, La Memoire tatouree (Secret Obsession), Fools of Fortune, Dragonheart, Hamlet, Afterglow (NY Film Crits. Circle Award, Best Actress, 1997; Academy Award nom.), Belphegor, Hermit of Amsterdam, No Such Thing, I'm With Lucy, J. M. Barrie's Neverland, Harry Potter and the Prisoner of Azkaban, Troy.

TELEVISION: Debut: A is for Andromeda (UK series, 1962), Sins of the Fathers (Italian TV), Separate Tables, Dadah Is Death (Amer. TV debut, 1988), The Railway Station Man.

CHRISTOPHER, DENNIS
Actor. r.n. Dennis Carelli. b. Philadelphia, PA, Dec. 2, 1955. e. Temple U. NY stage debut, Yentl the Yeshiva Boy (1974). Other NY theater: Dr. Needle and the Infectious Laughter Epidemic, The Little Foxes, Brothers, Exmass, A Pound on Demand, Advice

from a Caterpillar. Regional theater incl. Balm in Gilead, American Buffalo. Appeared in 1991 short The Disco Years.
PICTURES: Blood and Lace, Didn't You Hear?, The Young Graduates, Fellini's Roma, Salome, 3 Women, September 30, 1955, A Wedding, California Dreaming, The Last Word, Breaking Away, Fade to Black, Chariots of Fire, Don't Cry It's Only Thunder, Alien Predator, Flight of the Spruce Goose, Jake Speed, Friends, A Sinful Life, Circuitry Man, Dead Women in Lingerie, Doppelganger, Circuitry Man II: Plughead Rewired, Skeletons, The Silencers, It's My Party, Skeletons, The Silencers, Mind Lies, Nine Lives..
TELEVISION: Movies: The Oregon Trail, Stephen King's IT, False Arrest, Willing to Kill: The Texas Cheerleader Story, Curacao, Deadly Invasion: The Killer Bee Nightmare, The Ballad of Lucy Whipple. Specials: Bernice Bobs Her Hair, Jack and the Beanstalk (Faerie Tale Theatre), Cristabel. Series: Profiler, Freaky Links. Guest: Trapper John M.D., Tales of the Unexpected, Stingray, Cagney & Lacey, Moonlighting, Hooperman, The Equalizer, Matlock, Murder She Wrote, Monsters, Civil Wars, Dark Justice, The Watcher, The Cosby Mysteries.

CHRISTOPHER, JORDAN
Actor, Musician. b. Youngstown, OH. Oct. 23, 1942. e. Kent State U. Led rock 'n' roll group, The Wild Ones.
PICTURES: Return of the Seven, The Fat Spy, The Tree, Angel Angel Down We Go, Pigeons, Brainstorm, Star 80, That's Life!
TELEVISION: Series: Secrets of Midland Heights.

CHUNG, CONNIE
TV News Anchor. r.n. Constance Yu-Hwa Chung. m. anchor Maury Povich. b. Washington, D.C., Aug. 20, 1946. e. U. of Maryland, B.S. Entered field 1969 as copy person, writer then on-camera reporter for WTTG-TV, Washington; 1971, named Washington corr., CBS News; 1976, anchor KNXT, Los Angeles; 1983, anchor, NBC News at Sunrise; anchor, NBC Saturday Nightly News and news specials; 1989 moved to CBS as anchor, Sunday Night Evening News; anchor and reporter, Saturday Night with Connie Chung (later Face to Face With Connie Chung), 1989-90. Received Emmy Award for Shot in Hollywood (1987), Interview With Marlon Brando (1989); 2 additional Emmy Awards: 1986, 1990. Became co-anchor, with Dan Rather, of CBS Evening News, 1993-95. Prime time series: Eye to Eye With Connie Chung, 1993; Connie Chung Tonight on CNN (canceled March 2003). Many other awards incl. Peabody, 2 LA Emmy Awards, Golden Mike, Women in Business Award, etc.

CHURCH, THOMAS HADEN
Actor. b.El Paso, TX, June 17, 1961.
PICTURES: Tombstone, Tales From the Crypt Presents: Demon Knight, George of the Jungle, One Night, Free Money, Scotch and Milk (prod.), The Specials, 3000 Miles To Graceland, Rolling Kansas, George of the Jungle II (video).
TELEVISION: Movies: Fugitive Nights: Danger in the Desert, The Badge. Series: Wings, Ned and Stacey. Guest: China Beach, Cheers, Booker, 21 Jump Street, Flying Blind, Partners. Mini-series: Mr. Murder.

CILENTO, DIANE
Actress. b. Queensland, Australia, October 5, 1933.. e. Toowoomba. Went to New York and finished schooling and then American Acad. of Dramatic Art. First theatre job at 16; toured U.S. with Barter Co.; returned to London and joined Royal Acad. of Dramatic Art; several small parts and later repertory at Manchester's Library Theatre.
THEATRE: London stage: Tiger at the Gates (also NY: Theatre World Award), The Third Secret, The Four Seasons, The Bonne Soup, Heartbreak House. NY: The Big Knife, Orpheus, Altona, Castle in Sweden, Naked, Marys, I've Seen You Cut Lemons.
PICTURES: Wings of Danger (debut on Course; debut, 1952), Moulin Rouge, Meet Mr. Lucifer, All Halloween, The Angel Who Pawned Her Harp, The Passing Stranger, Passage Home, The Woman for Joe, The Admirable (Paradise Lagoon), The Truth About Women, Jet Storm, Stop Me Before I Kill! (The Full Treatment), I Thank a Fool, The Naked Edge, Tom Jones (Acad. Award nom.), Rattle of a Simple Man, The Third Secret, The Agony and the Ecstasy, Hombre, Negatives, Z.P.G. (Zero Population Growth), Hitler: The Last Ten Days, The Wicker Man, The Tiger Lily, The Boy Who Had Everything, Duet for Four.
TELEVISION: La Belle France (series), Court Martial, Blackmail, Dial M for Murder, Rogues Gallery, Rain, Lysistrata, The Kiss of Blood, For the Term of His Natural Life.

CIMINO, MICHAEL
Writer, Director. b. New York, NY, Nov. 16, 1943. e. Yale U. BFA, MFA. Was tv commecial director before becoming screen writer.
PICTURES: Silent Running (co-s.p.), Magnum Force (co-s.p.). Director: Thunderbolt and Lightfoot (also s.p.), The Deer Hunter (also co-wrote story, co-prod.; Academy Awards for Best Picture and Director, 1978.), Heaven's Gate (also s.p.), Year of the Dragon (also co-s.p.), The Sicilian (also co-prod.), Desperate Hours (also co-prod.), The Sunchaser (also co-s.p.).

CIPES, ARIANNE ULMER
Executive. b. New York, NY, July 25, 1937. e. Royal Acad. of Dramatic Art, London, U. of London. Daughter of film dir. Edgar G. Ulmer. Actress, then production and dubbing, Paris; CDC, Rome; Titra, New York; 1975-77, v.p., Best Intl Films (intl film distributor), Los Angeles; 1977 co-founder and sr. v.p./sales & services of Producers Sales Organization; 1981, named exec. v.p.,

American Film Marketing Assn.; 1982, founded AUC Films, consulting and intl. and domestic sales-prods. rep.; Pres. of the Edgar G. Ulmer Preservation Corp.-committed to the preservation and propagation of the work of independent, pioneering filmmakers.

CIPES, JAY H.
Executive. b. Mt. Vernon, NY, Dec. 14, 1928. e. Cornell U. 1960-66, indt producer-packager-distributor European features for U.S. TV sales; 1967, prod., 20th Century-Fox TV; 1971, prod., Four Star TV; 1971, mktg. exec. Technicolor, Inc.; 1973, v.p., mktg. Technicolor, Inc.; 1979 sr. v.p., dir. worldwide mktg, Technicolor, Inc. Professional Film Division. 1992, indt. consultant to prod. & post-prod. facilities.

CLAPP, GORDON
Actor. b. North Conway, NH, Sept. 24, 1948.
PICTURES: Running, Return of the Secaucus 7, Matewan, Eight Men Out, Termini Station, Gross Anatomy, April One, The Rage: Carrie 2, Splendor Falls, The Rules of Engagement, Skeletons in the Closet, Sunshine State, Moonlight Mile, The Sure Hand of God.
TELEVISION: Movies: The Other Kingdom, Letting Go, The Right of the People, Hands of a Stranger, Small Sacrifices, Family of Spies, Blind Faith, The Secret Life of Archie's Wife, Fever, Mission of the Shark: The Saga of the U.S.S. Indianapolis, Bonds of Love, Kiss of a Killer, Family of Strangers, In the Line of Duty: Ambush in Waco, Her Hidden Truth, Abandoned and Deceived, The Morrison Murders, Badge of Betrayal. Mini-series: Evergreen. Series: Check It Out, NYPD Blue (Emmy Award, 1998).

CLARK, BILL
Producer.
TELEVISION: Series: NYPD Blue (WGA Award, 1993; Emmy Award, 1998), Brooklyn South. Special: America: A Tribute to Heroes.

CLARK, BOB
Director, Writer, Producer. r.n. Benjamin Clark. b. New Orleans, LA, Aug. 5, 1941.
PICTURES: Director: The She Man, The Emperor's New Clothes, Children Shouldn't Play with Dead Things (credited as Benjamin Clark), Deathdream (Dead of Night), Deranged (prod. only), Black Christmas (Silent Night Evil Night), Breaking Point, Murder by Decree, Tribute, Porky's (also s.p., prod.), Porky's II— The Next Day (also s.p., prod.), A Christmas Story (also s.p., prod.), Rhinestone, Turk 182, From the Hip (also co-s.p.), Loose Cannons (also co-s.p.), It Runs in the Family (also s.p.), Baby Geniuses, I'll Remember April, Unleashed, Now & Forever, The Karate Dog, Baby Geniuses 2: Superbabies.
TELEVISION: Movies: The American Clock, Stolen Memories, Secrets from the Rose Garden, Fudge-A-Mania, Derby, Ransom of the Red Chief, Catch a Falling Star, Maniac Magee. Series episode: Amazing Stories (Remote Control Man).

CLARK, CANDY
Actress. b. Norman, OK, June 20, 1947. Was successful model in N.Y. before landing role in Fat City, 1972. Off-B'way debut 1981: A Couple of White Chicks Sitting Around Talking; followed by It's Raining on Hope Street. Appeared in short Blind Curve.
PICTURES: Fat City (debut, 1972), American Graffiti (Acad. Award nom.), I Will I Will... For Now, The Man Who Fell To Earth, Citizens Band (Handle With Care), The Big Sleep, When You Comin' Back Red Ryder, More American Graffiti, National Lampoon Goes to the Movies, Q, Blue Thunder, Amityville 3-D, Hambone and Hillie, Cat's Eye, At Close Range, The Blob, Original Intent, Deuce Coupe, Cool as Ice, Buffy the Vampire Slayer, Radioland Murders, Cherry Falls, The Month of August.
TELEVISION: Movies: James Dean, Amateur Night at the Dixie Bar and Grill, Where the Ladies Go, Rodeo Girl, Johnny Belinda, Cocaine and Blue Eyes, The Price She Paid. Series: Movie Lover's Road Trip (as herself).

CLARK, DICK
Performer; Chairman, CEO, Dick Clark Prods., Inc. b. Mt. Vernon, NY, Nov. 30, 1929. e. Syracuse U. graduated 1951, summer announcer WRUN, Utica 1949, staff announcer WOLF, Syracuse 1950. After grad. 1951, took regular job with WOLF. Rejoined WRUN, Utica, then joined WKTV, Utica. Announcer WFIL Philadelphia 1952. Formed Dick Clark productions 1956, TV and motion picture production with in-person concert division, cable TV programing dept. Host of two weekly synd. radio programs: U.S. Music Survey and Rock Roll & Remember. Founder and principal owner of Unistar Communications Group. Took company public in January, 1987 (NASDAQ: DCPI), serves as chmn. & CEO. Received Emmy Lifetime Achievement Award, 1994.
PICTURES: Actor: Because They're Young (debut, 1960), Jamboree, The Young Doctors, Killers Three, The Phynx, Forrest Gump, The Suburbans, Spy Kids, Confessions of a Dangerous Mind (as himself). Producer: Psychout, The Savage Seven, Remo Williams: The Adventure Begins, Catchfire.
TELEVISION: Movies/Prod. or Exec. Prod.: Werewolf of Woodstock, Elvis, The Man in the Santa Claus Suit, Murder in Texas, The Demon Murder Case, The Woman Who Willed a Miracle, Cocacabana, A Friendly Quiet Little Town, Death Dreams, Caught in the Act, Secret Sins of the Father, The Making of a Hollywood Madam, Deep Family Secrets, ABC 50th Anniversary Blooper Celebration.

Specials: Live Aid—An All-Star Concert for African Relief, Farm Aid III, Super Bloopers & New Practical Jokes, American Bandstand's 33 1/3 Celebration, America Picks the No. 1 Songs, You Are the Jury, Thanks for Caring, Supermodel of the World, Freedom Festival '89, What About Me I'm Only Three, 1992 USA Music Challenge, The Good Doctor, TV Censored Bloopers '98, Motown 40: The Music Is Forever. American Music Awards, Academy of Country Music Awards, Dick Clark's New Year's Rockin' Eve, ACE Awards, Daytime Emmy Awards, Golden Globe Awards, Soap Opera Awards, Superstars and Their Moms, Caught in the Act (pilot), 30th Annual American Music Awards (2003).*Series/Himself or Host:* American Bandstand (also exec. prod.; Emmy Award as exec. prod., 1982-83), The Dick Clark Beechnut Show, Dick Clark's World of Talent, Record Years, Years of Rock. $25,000 Pyramid (3 Emmy Awards as host: 1979, 1985, 1986), $100,000 Pyramid, TV Teen Club, The Dick Clark Show, Missing Links, The Object Is, The Krypton Factor, Inside America, TV's Bloopers & Practical Jokes (also exec. prod.), The Challengers, Scattegories, Winning Lines (also exec. prod.), The Other Half. *Producer:* The Guns of Will Sonnett, Live Wednesday, TV Censored Bloopers 1998, Who Wants to be a Millionaire, Swinging Country, Happening, Get It Together, Shebang, Record Years, Years of Rock. *Executive Producer:* It's Happening, Where The Action Is, TV's Bloopers & Practical Jokes (also host), Rock'n'Roll Summer Action, Puttin' On the Hits, Keep On Cruisin', Trial By Jury, The Weird Al Show, Donny & Marie (1998), Your Big Break, Greed: The Multi-Million Dollar Challenge, Winning Lines (also host), The Chamber, American Dreams. WRITER: Your Happiest Years, 1959; Rock, Roll & Remember, 1976; To Goof or Not to Goof, 1963; Dick Clark's Easygoing Guide to Good Grooming, 1986; The History of American Bandstand, 1986, Dick Clark's American Bandstand, 1997.

CLARK, DUNCAN C.
Executive. b. Sutton, Surrey, England. Entered industry in 1972. Appointed dir. of publicity and adv., CIC, Jan. 1979, taking up similar post in 1981 for United Artists. On formation of U.I.P. in 1982, appt. dir., pub. and adv., & deputy mng. dir., 1983. 1987 appt. v.p. adv. & pub., Columbia Pictures Intl (NY). In 1987, sr. v.p. intl marketing for Columbia (Burbank); appt. sr. v.p., Columbia Tri-Star Film Distribs., Inc., (NY). Relocated to corp. headquarters in Culver City, 1991. Appointed exec. v.p. Worldwide Marketing, 1994. In 1996, appointed president Columbia TriStar Film Distributors Intl.

CLARK, GREYDON
Producer, Director, Writer. b. Niles, MI, Feb. 7, 1943. e. Western Michigan U., B.A., theatre arts, 1963. Heads own company, World Amusement Corp., Sherman Oaks, CA.
PICTURES: *Director:* Danse Macabre, Satan's Sadists (actor only), Hell's Bloody Devils (actor only), The Blood Seekers (actor only), The Bad Bunch (also writer, actor), Black Shampoo (also writer), Satan's Cheerleaders, Hi-Riders (also writer), Angels' Revenge (also prod., writer), Without Warning (also prod.), The Return, Wacko (also prod.), Joysticks, Final Justice, Uninvited, Skinheads (also prod., writer), Out of Sight Out of Mind, The Forbidden Dance, Killer Instinct, Dark Future (also prod.), Stargames (also s.p.).
TELEVISION: *Series:* Star Games.

CLARK, MATT
Actor, Director. b. Washington, DC, Nov. 25, 1936.
THEATRE: *NY:* A Portrait of the Artist as a Young Man, The Subject Was Roses, The Trial of the Catonsville Nine; Regional: One Flew Over the Cuckoo's Nest, Tonight We Improvise.
PICTURES: Black Like Me (debut, 1964), In the Heat of the Night, Will Penny, The Bridge at Remagen, Macho Callahan, Homer (co-s.p. only), Monte Walsh, The Beguiled, The Grissom Gang, The Cowboys, The Culpepper Cattle Company, The Great Northfield Minnesota Raid, Jeremiah Johnson, The Life and Times of Judge Roy Bean, Emperor of the North Pole, The Laughing Policeman, Pat Garrett and Billy the Kid, White Lightning, The Terminal Man, Hearts of the West, Outlaw Blues,Kid Vengeance, The Driver, Dreamer, Brubaker, An Eye for an Eye, Legend of the Lone Ranger, Ruckus, Some Kind of Hero, Honkytonk Man, Love Letters, The Adventures of Buckaroo Banzai, Country, Tuff Turf, Return to Oz, Let's Get Harry, Da (dir. only), The Horror Show, Back to the Future Part III, Cadence, Class Action, Frozen Assets, Fortunes of War, The Harvest, Candyman: Farewell to the Flesh, Mother, Hacks, Claudine's Return, Homegrown, Five Aces, South of Heaven West of Hell.
TELEVISION: *Series:* Dog and Cat, The Jeff Foxworthy Show. *Mini-Series:* The Winds of War, War and Remembrance, Trilogy of Special Terror II. *Movies:* The Execution of Private Slovik, The Great Ice Rip-Off, Melvin Purvis: G-Man, This is the West That Was, The Kansas City Massacre, Dog and Cat (pilot), Lacy and the Mississippi Queen, The Last Ride of the Dalton Gang, The Children Nobody Wanted, In the Custody of Strangers, Love Mary, Out of the Darkness, The Quick and the Dead, The Gambler III: The Legend Continues, Terror on Highway 91, Blind Witness, Deceptions, Dead Before Dawn, Barbarians at the Gate, A Season of Hope, Raven Hawk. *Specials:* Shadow of Fear, Andrea's Story. *Pilots:* The Big Easy, Highway Honeys, Traveling Man. Guest: Hardcastle and McCormick, Midnight Caller, Bodies of Evidence. *Director:* Midnight Caller, My Dissident Mom (Schoolbreak Special).

CLARK, PETULA
Actress, Singer. b. Ewell, Surrey, England, Nov. 15, 1932. On British stage in The Sound of Music, Candida, Someone Like You (also composer, co-writer). B'way debut in Blood Brothers (1993). Starred in own BBC TV series 1967-8. Winner of two Grammy Awards,1964 (Best Rock and Roll Recording: Downtown), 1965 (Best Contemporary R & R Vocal Performance Female: I Know a Place).
PICTURES: Medal for the General (debut, 1944), Strawberry Roan, Murder in Reverse, I Know Where I'm Going, London Town (My Heart Goes Crazy), Vice Versa, Easy Money, Here Come the Huggets, Vote for Hugget, Don't Ever Leave Me, The Huggets Abroad, The Romantic Age (Naughty Arlette), Dance Hall, White Corridors, Madame Louise, The Card (The Promoter), Made In Heaven, The Gay Dog, The Runaway Bus, The Happiness of Three Women, Track the Man Down, That Woman Opposite (City After Midnight), Six-Five Special, A Couteaux Tires (Daggers Drawn), Questi Pazzi Pazzi Italiani, The Big T.N.T. Show, Finian's Rainbow, Goodbye Mr. Chips, Never Never Land.
TELEVISION: Petula, Alma Coogan: The Girl with the Giggle in Her Voice, I Know Where I'm Going Revisited, Petula Clark: A Sign of the Times.

CLARK, SUSAN
Actress. r.n. Nora Golding. b. Sarnid, Ontario, Canada, March 8, 1940. Trained at Royal Acad. of Dramatic Art, London and Stella Adler Academy.
PICTURES: Banning (debut, 1967), Coogan's Bluff, Madigan, Tell Them Willie Boy Is Here, Colossus: The Forbin Project, Skullduggery, Skin Game, Valdez Is Coming, Showdown, The Midnight Man, Airport 1975, Night Moves, The Apple Dumpling Gang, The North Avenue Irregulars, Murder by Decree, City on Fire, Promises in the Dark, Double Negative, Nobody's Perfekt, Porky's, Butterbox Babies.
TELEVISION: *Movies:* Something for a Lonely Man, The Challengers, The Astronaut, Trapped, Babe (Emmy Award, 1976), McNaughton's Daughter, Amelia Earhart, Jimmy B. and Andre (also co-prod.), The Choice, Maid in America (also co-prod.), Snowbound: The Jim and Jennifer Stolpa Story, Tonya and Nancy: The Inside Story, Butterbox Babies. *Specials:* Hedda Gabler, Double Solitaire.*Series:* Webster, Emily of New Moon.

CLAYBURGH, JILL
Actress. b. New York, NY, April 30, 1944. m. playwright David Rabe. e. Sarah Lawrence Coll. 1966. Former member of Charles Playhouse, Boston.
THEATRE: The Nest (*off-B'way*), The Rothschilds, Jumpers, Pippin, In the Boom Boom Room, Design For Living.
PICTURES: The Wedding Party (debut, 1969), The Telephone Book, Portnoy's Complaint, The Thief Who Came to Dinner, Terminal Man, Gable and Lombard, Silver Streak, Semi-Tough, An Unmarried Woman (Acad. Award nom.), Luna, Starting Over (Acad. Award nom.), It's My Turn, First Monday in October, I'm Dancing as Fast as I Can, Hannah K, Where Are The Children?, Shy People, Beyond the Ocean, Whispers in the Dark, Rich in Love, Day of Atonement, Naked in New York, Going All the Way, Fools Rush In, Never Again, Falling.
TELEVISION: *Movies:* The Snoop Sisters, Miles To Go, Hustling, The Art of Crime, Griffin and Phoenix, Who Gets the Friends?, Fear Stalk, Unspeakable Acts, Reason for Living: The Jill Ireland Story, Trial: The Price of Passion, Firestorm: 72 Hours in Oakland, Honor Thy Father and Mother: The True Story of the Menedez Murders, For the Love of Nancy, The Face on the Milk Carton, Crowned & Dangerous, Sins of the Mind, My Little Assassin,Phenomenon. *Series:* Search For Tomorrow, Trinity, Everything's Relative, Leap of Faith. *Guest:* Medical Center, Rockford Files, Frasier (voice).

CLEESE, JOHN
Actor, Writer. b. Weston-Super-Mare, England, Oct. 27, 1939. e. Clifton Coll., Cambridge U. Began acting with Cambridge University Footlights revue. With classmate Graham Chapman wrote for British TV. Co-creator of Monty Python's Flying Circus.Co-author (with psychiatrist Robin Skynner): Families and How to Survive Them (1983), Life and How to Survive It (1995).
PICTURES: Interlude (debut, 1968), The Bliss of Mrs. Blossom, The Best House in London, The Rise and Rise of Michael Rimmer (also co-s.p.), The Magic Christian (also co-s.p.), The Statue, And Now for Something Completely Different (also co-s.p.), Monty Python and the Holy Grail (also co-s.p.), The Life of Brian (also co-s.p.), The Great Muppet Caper, Time Bandits, The Secret Policeman's Other Ball, Monty Python Live at the Hollywood Bowl (also co-s.p.), Monty Python's The Meaning of Life (also co-s.p.), Yellowbeard, Privates on Parade, Silverado, Clockwise, A Fish Called Wanda (also co-s.p., exec. prod.), BAFTA Award, Writer's Guild of America nom., Oscar nom.), The Big Picture (cameo), Erik the Viking, An American Tail: Fievel Goes West (voice), Splitting Heirs, Mary Shelley's Frankenstein, The Swan Princess (voice), Rudyard Kipling's The Jungle Book, George of the Jungle, Fierce Creatures, Parting Shots, The Out-of-Towners, Isn't She Great, The World is Not Enough, Rat Race, Harry Potter and the Sorcerer's Stone, Taking the Wheel, Harry Potter and the Chamber of Secrets, Die Another Day, Charlie's Angels: Full Throttle, Harry Potter & the Prisoner of Azkaban, Shrek 2 (voice).
TELEVISION: *Special:* Taming of the Shrew, Funny Women, Laughter in the House: The Story of British Sitcom, The Sketch Show Story. *Series:* The Frost Report, At Last the 1948 Show, Monty Python's Flying Circus, Fawlty Towers, Look at the State

We're In!, Wednesday 9:30 (8:30 Central) *Guest*: Cheers (Emmy Award, 1987), Third Rock from the Sun.

CLEMENS, BRIAN
Writer, Producer, Director. b. Croydon, England, 1931. Early career in advertising then wrote BBC TV play. Later TV filmed series as writer, script editor and features. Script editor Danger Man; Won Edgar Allen Poe Award for Best TV Thriller of 1962 (Scene of the Crime for U.S. Steel Hour). Various plays for Armchair Theatre; ATV Drama 70; Love Story. Winner two Edgar Allan Poe Awards, Cinema Fantastique Award for best s.p.
PICTURES: The Tell-Tale Heart, Station Six-Sahara, The Peking Medallion, And Soon The Darkness, The Major, When The Wind Blows, See No Evil, Dr. Jekyll and Sister Hyde, Golden Voyage of Sinbad, Watcher in the Woods, Stiff, Highlander 2, Justine (France).
TELEVISION: *Writer/Prod.*: The Avengers (2 Emmy noms.), New Avengers, The Professionals, Escapade (U.S.), Perry Mason, Loose Cannon, Father Dowling, Bugs (writer, creator, UK), CI5: The New Professionals (writer, exec. prod).

CLENNON, DAVID
Actor. b. Waukegan, IL, May 10, 1943. e. Univ. of Notre Dame, Yale Drama School.
THEATRE: *Off-B'way*.: The Unseen Hand, Forensic and the Navigators, As You Like It, Little Eyolf, Welcome to Andromeda, Medal of Honor Rag, The Cherry Orchard. *Regional*: Saved, Blood Knot, Loot, Marat/Sade, Beyond Therapy, others.
PICTURES: The Paper Chase, Bound for Glory, The Greatest, Coming Home, Gray Lady Down, Go Tell the Spartans, On the Yard, Being There, Hide in Plain Sight, Missing, The Escape Artist, The Thing, Ladies and Gentlemen the Fabulous Stains, The Right Stuff, Hannah K., Star 80, Falling in Love, Sweet Dreams, Legal Eagles, He's My Girl, The Couch Trip, Betrayed, Downtown, Man Trouble, Light Sleeper, Matinee, Two Crimes (Dos Crimenes), Grace of My Heart, Mad City, Playing by Heart, The Visit, The Heart of the Possible.
TELEVISION: *Movies*: The Migrants, Crime Club, Helter Skelter, Gideon's Trumpet, Marriage is Alive and Well, Reward, Special Bulletin, Best Kept Secrets, Blood and Orchids, Conspiracy: The Trial of the Chicago 8, Nurses on the Line: The Crash of Flight 7, Black Widow Murders, Original Sins, Tecumseh: The Last Warrior, From the Earth to the Moon, The Staircase, The Agency. *Series*: Rafferty, Park Place, thirtysomething, Almost Perfect, Once and Again, The Agency. *Guest*: Alfred Hitchcock Presents, Murder She Wrote, Barney Miller, Dream On (Emmy Award, 1993), Just Shoot Me, NewsRadio. *Special*: The Seagull.

CLIFFORD, GRAEME
Director. b. Sydney, New South Wales, Australia, 1942. Worked as film editor on such films as Don't Look Now, The Rocky Horror Picture Show, The Man Who Fell to Earth, F.I.S.T., The Postman Always Rings Twice, before turning to directing.
PICTURES: Frances, Burke & Wills, Gleaming the Cube, Deception.
TELEVISION: *Movies*: Nightmare Classics, The Turn of the Screw, Past Tense, A Loss of Innocence. My Husband's Secret Life, The Last Witness, See You in My Dreams, Redeemer, Crossing the Line, Losing It, Profoundly Normal (also prod.). Mini-series: The Last Don, The Last Don II. Series: Barnaby Jones, The New Avengers, Twin Peaks, The Guardian.

CLOONEY, GEORGE
Actor. b. Lexington, KY, May 6, 1961. Father is tv newscaster-host Nick Clooney. Aunt is singer Rosemary Clooney. e. Northern KY Univ.
PICTURES: Return to Horror High, Return of the Killer Tomatoes, Red Surf, Unbecoming Age, The Harvest, One Fine Day, Full Tilt Boogie, From Dusk Till Dawn, Batman and Robin, The Peacemaker, The Thin Red Line, Out of Sight, South Park: Bigger Longer and Uncut (voice), Three Kings, The Perfect Storm, O Brother-Where Art Thou, Spy Kids, Welcome to Collinwood, Ocean's Eleven, Confessions of a Dangerous Mind, Solaris, Intolerable Cruelty.
TELEVISION: *Movies*: Playmate Pajama Party, Fail Safe. *Special*: America: A Tribute to Heroes. *Series*: The Facts of Life, Roseanne, Sunset Beat, Baby Talk, Sisters, Bodies of Evidence, ER, K Street (exec. prod. only). *Guest*: Hunter, Murder She Wrote, The Golden Girls, The Building, Friends, South Park (voice).

CLOSE, GLENN
Actress. b. Greenwich, CT, Mar. 19, 1947. e. Coll. of William and Mary. Began performing with a repertory group Fingernails, then toured country with folk-singing group Up With People. Professional debut at Phoenix Theatre, New York. Also accomplished musical performer (lyric soprano).
THEATRE: *NY*: Love for Love, Rules of the Game, Member of the Wedding, Rex, Uncommon Women and Others, The Crucifer of Blood, Wine Untouched, The Winter Dancers, Barnum, Singular Life of Albert Nobbs (Obie Award), The Real Thing (Tony Award, 1984), Childhood, Joan of Arc at the Stake, Benefactors, Death and the Maiden (Tony Award, 1992), Sunset Boulevard (Tony Award, 1995). *Regional*: King Lear, Uncle Vanya, The Rose Tattoo, A Streetcar Named Desire, Brooklyn Laundry, Sunset Boulevard.
PICTURES: The World According to Garp (debut, 1982), The Big Chill, The Natural, The Stone Boy, Greystoke: The Legend of Tarzan Lord of the Apes (dubbed voice), Jagged Edge, Maxie, Fatal Attraction, Light Years (voice), Dangerous Liaisons,

Immediate Family, Reversal of Fortune, Hamlet, Meeting Venus, Hook (cameo), The Paper, The House of the Spirits, Anne Frank Remembered (voice), Mary Reilly, Mars Attacks!, 101 Dalmatians, Paradise Road, In the Gloaming, Airforce One, In & Out, Cookie's Fortune, Tarzan (voice), Cast and Crew, Things You Can Tell Just By Looking At Her, 102 Dalmatians, The Safety of Objects, Le Divorce, Anything Else.
TELEVISION: *Movies*: Too Far To Go, The Orphan Train, Something About Amelia, Stones for Ibarra, Sarah: Plain and Tall, Skylark (also co-exec. prod.), Serving in Silence: The Margarethe Cammermeyer Story (Emmy Award, 1995; also co-exec. prod.), South Pacific, Brush with Fate, The Lion in Winter. *Specials*: The Elephant Man, Broken Hearts Broken Homes (host, co-exec. prod.). *Guest*: The Simpsons, Ellen.

COATES, ANNE V.
Film editor, Producer. b. Reigate, Surrey, Eng., 1925. e. Bartrum Gables Coll. m. late dir. Douglas Hickox. Worked as nurse at East Grinstead Plastic Surgery Hospital. Recipient of 1995 A.C.E. Career Achievement award.
PICTURES: Pickwick Papers, Grand National Night, Forbidden Cargo, To Paris With Love, The Truth About Women, The Horse's Mouth, Tunes of Glory, Don't Bother to Knock, Lawrence of Arabia (Academy Award, 1962; also ACE nom.), Becket (Acad. Award & ACE noms.), Young Cassidy, Those Magnificent Men in Their Flying Machines (co-ed.), Hotel Paridiso, Great Catherine, The Bofors Guns, The Adventurers, Friends, The Public Eye, The Nelson Affair, 11 Harrowhouse, Murder on the Orient Express (BAFTA nom.), Man Friday, Aces High, The Eagle Has Landed, The Medusa Touch (prod. & sprv. ed.), The Legacy, The Elephant Man (Acad. Award nom., BAFTA nom.), The Bushido Blade, Ragtime (co-ed.), The Pirates of Penzance, Greystoke: The Legend of Tarzan Lord of the Apes, Lady Jane, Raw Deal, Masters of the Universe, Farewell to the King (co-ed.), Listen to Me, I Love You to Death, What About Bob?, Chaplin, In the Line of Fire (Acad. Award nom., A.C.E. nom., BAFTA nom.), G.B.F.E. award), Pontiac Moon, Congo, Striptease, Out to Sea, Out of Sight, Passion of Mind, Erin Brokovich, Sweet November, Unfaithful, In and Out of Focus (documentary, as herself).

COBE, SANDY
Executive, Producer, Distributor. b. New York, NY, Nov. 30, 1928. e. Tulane U., B.A., fine arts. U.S. Army WWII & Korea, combat photographer; produced 11 features for Artmark Pictures, N.Y. General Studios, exec. v.p.; distribution; First Cinema Releasing Corp., pres. Formed Sandy Cobe Productions, Inc., producer, packager, European features for U.S. theatrical & television. 1974 pres., Intercontinental Releasing Corporation, domestic and foreign distribution of theatrical features; 1989, named chmn. of bd. and CEO. Member, dir. of bd., American Film Marketing Assn., Dir. of bd., Scitech Corp. USA, 14 year mem., Academy of Television Arts and Sciences, 32nd degree Mason, Shriner, Variety Club Int'l. Special commendations from: Mayor of Los Angeles, California State Senate, City and County of L.A., California Assembly and Senate, and Governor of CA.
PICTURES: Terror on Tour (prod.), Access Code (exec. prod.), A.R.C.A.D.E. (prod.), Terminal Entry (exec. prod.), Open House (prod.).

COBE, SHARYON REIS
Executive, Producer. b. Honolulu, HI, e. U. of Hawaii, Loyola Marymount U. Dancer Fitzgerald, & Sample, N.Y. United Air Lines, N.Y.; v.p., story editor, Gotham Publishing N.Y.; v.p., distribution-foreign sales, World Wide Film Distributors, L.A.; pres. and chief operating officer, Intercontinental Releasing Corp., L.A. Member of Variety Clubs Intl., Industry Rltns. Com., Amer. Film Mktg. Assoc., Indpt. Feature Projects West. (tent 25), Women in Film.
PICTURES: Home Sweet Home (prod. mgr.), To All a Good Night (assoc. prod.), Access Code (co-prod.), Terminal Entry (prod.), Open House (exec. in chg. of prod.).

COBLENZ, WALTER
Producer.
PICTURES: The Candidate, All the President's Men, The Onion Field, The Legend of the Lone Ranger, Strange Invaders, Sister Sister, 18 Again!, For Keeps, The Babe, Money Talks, Her Majesty.
TELEVISION: *Movie*: Jack Reed: Badge of Honor, House of Secrets, Not Our Son, A Dream for Christmas. *Series*: Apples Way. *Mini-Series*: The Blue Knight.

COBURN, JAMES
Actor. b. Laurel, Neb., Aug. 31, 1928. e. Los Angeles City Coll., where he studied drama. Also studied with Stella Adler in NY for 5 years. Served in U.S. Army. First acting role in coast production of Billy Budd. Later to New York, where he worked on TV commercials, then on live teleplays on Studio One, GE Theatre, Robert Montgomery Presents. Summer stock in Detroit before returning to Hollywood. Commercial: Remington Rand.
PICTURES: Ride Lonesome (debut, 1959), Face of a Fugitive, The Magnificent Seven, Hell Is for Heroes, The Great Escape, Charade, The Americanization of Emily, The Loved One, Major Dundee, A High Wind in Jamaica, Our Man Flint, What Did You Do in the War Daddy?, Dead Heat on a Merry-Go-Round, In Like Flint, Waterhole No. 3, The President's Analyst, Duffy, Candy, Hard Contract, Last of the Mobile Hot-Shots, The Carey Treatment, The Honkers, Duck You Sucker, Pat Garrett and Billy the Kid, The Last of Sheila, Harry in Your Pocket, A Reason to Live—A Reason to Die, The Internecine Project, Bite the Bullet,

Hard Times, Sky Riders, The Last Hard Men, Midway, Cross of Iron, California Suite (cameo), The Muppet Movie, Goldengirl, Firepower, The Baltimore Bullet, Loving Couples, Mr. Patman, High Risk, Looker, Martin's Day, Death of a Soldier, Phoenix Fire, Walking After Midnight, Train to Heaven, Young Guns II, Hudson Hawk, The Player, Hugh Hefner: Once Upon a Time (narrator), Deadfall, Sister Act 2: Back in the Habit, Maverick, Skeletons, The Nutty Professor, Eraser, Keys to Tulsa, Affliction (Acad. Award for Support. Actor), Payback, Intrepid, The Good Doctor, Proximity, The Man From Elysian Fields, Monsters Inc., Kurosawa, Yellow Bird, Texas Rangers, American Gun, Snow Dogs.
TELEVISION: Series: Klondike, Acapulco, Darkroom (host), Hollywood Stuntmakers (host), Fifth Corner, World's Scariest Ghosts: Caught on Tape. Movies: Draw!, Sins of the Fathers, Malibu, The Dain Curse, Valley of the Dolls, Crash Landing: The Rescue of Flight 232, The Hit List, Greyhounds, The Avenging Angel, Ray Alexander: A Menu for Murder, The Set Up, The Disappearance of Kevin Johnson, Ben Johnson: Third Cowboy on the Right, The Cherokee Kid, The Second Civil War, Mr. Murder, Atticus, Noah's Ark, Walter and Henry. Mini-series: Shake Rattle and Roll: An American Love Story. Specials: Pinocchio (Faerie Tale Theater), Mastergate, Marilyn Monroe: The Final Days. Pilot: Silver Fox.
(d. Nov. 18, 2002)

COCHRAN, BARBARA
Executive, Writer. b. Akron, OH, June 16 1945. e. Swarthmore, BA English Lit., 1967. Columbia U., MA journalism, 1968. Various positions and finally managing ed., Washington Times, 1968-79. VP news, NPR, 1979-83. Political ed., NBC, 1983-85. Exec. prod., NBC's Meet the Press, 1985-89. VP news/Wash. bureau chief, CBS news, 1989-95. Exec. prod. for political coverage, CBS, 1996. Pres., Radio-Television News Directors Assoc., 1997-.present. On boards of: International Women's Media Foundation and the National Press Foundation; and is on Board of Visitors of the University of Maryland College of Journalism and Advisory Board of the Columbia Journalism Review.

COEN, ETHAN
Producer, Writer. b. St. Louis Park, MN, Sep. 21, 1957. e. Princeton U. Co-wrote s.p. with brother, Joel, XYZ Murders (renamed Crimewave).
PICTURES: Producer/Co-Writer: Blood Simple (also co-edited under pseudonym Roderick James), Raising Arizona, Miller's Crossing, Barton Fink, The Hudsucker Proxy, Fargo (original s.p. Acad. Award, 1996; Chicago Film Critics Award for s.p.; LA Film Critics Award for s.p.), The Naked Man, The Big Lebowski, O Brother-Where Art Thou?, The Man Who Wasn't There, Intolerable Cruelty, Bad Santa.

COEN, GUIDO
Producer, Executive. In 1959 became production exec. Twickenham Studios, 1963 Appt. a dir. there, then producer and executive prod. series pictures for Fortress Films and Kenilworth Films.PICTURES: One Jump Ahead, Golden Link, The Hornet's Nest, Behind the Headlines, Murder Reported, There's Always a Thursday, Date with Disaster, The End of the Line, The Man Without a Body, Woman Eater, Kill Her Gently, Naked Fury, Operation Cupid, Strictly Confidential, Dangerous Afternoon, Jungle Street, Strongroom, Penthouse, Baby Love, One Brief Summer, Burke and Hare, Au Pair Girls, Intimate Games.

COEN, JOEL
Director, Writer. b. St. Louis Park, MN, Nov. 29, 1954. e. Simon's Rock College, MA; studied film at NYU. m. actress Frances McDormand. Was asst. editor on Fear No Evil and Evil Dead. Co-wrote with brother, Ethan, s.p. for XYZ Murders (renamed Crime Wave.) Cameo role in film Spies Like Us, 1985.
PICTURES: Director/Co-Writer: Blood Simple (also co-editor, under pseudonym Roderick Jaynes), Raising Arizona, Miller's Crossing, Barton Fink (also co-editor, as Roderick Jaynes), The Hudsucker Proxy, Fargo (Best director, Cannes 1996; original s.p. Acad. Award, 1997; Chicago Film Critics Award for s.p. and dir.; LA Film Critics Award for s.p.; BAFTA for achievement in dir.), The Big Lebowski, O Brother, Where Art Thou?, The Man Who Wasn't There, Intolerable Cruelty, Bad Santa (s.p. and exec. prod.).

COHEN, ARTHUR
Executive. President, Bloomingdale's, 1975-78. Founder & president, Lansdowne Advertising, a division of J. Walter Thompson, 1978-82, creating billings to $14 million in four years. President, Tele1st, a division of ABC Video Enterprises, 1982-85; partner with Robert Nederlander, 1985-86; exec. v.p., advertising, Revlon, 1986-89, during which time Revlon restored its consumer image to record highs. Currently president, Worldwide Mktg., Paramount Pictures Motion Picture Grp. (since 1989), where he is responsible for marketing, advertising, publicity, and promotion of all feature films.

COHEN, ELLIS A.
Producer, Writer. b. Baltimore, MD, Sept. 15, 1945. e. Baltimore Jr. Coll., A.A. 1967, Univ. of W. LA, mini-law sch., 1992. 1963, talent coord., Cerebral Palsy Telethon, WBAL-TV, Baltimore; 1964, p.r. asst. Campbell-Ewald Adv. Agency, L.A.; 1966, retail mgr.; 1968-69, talent booking; 1968, journalist & ed.; 1969-72, p.r. & adv. Camera Mart, NY; 1972-74, creator & ed.-in-chief, TV/NY Magazine; 1974-76 dir., worldwide pub./adv., William

Morris Agency. 1973-74, prod., NY Emmy Awards Telecast; WOR-TV (prod.), chmn., exec. prod. of TV Academy Celebrity drop-in luncheon series; 1972, talent coordinator Bob Hope's Celebrity Flood Relief Telethon; 1976, exec. prod., Democratic Nat'l Conv. Gala. 1978, acc. exec., Solters & Roskin P.R., L.A.; 1978, dir. of TV Network Boxing Events, Don King Prod., NY; 1979, prod., Henry Jaffe Ent., Inc.; 1980, prod.-writer, CBS Entertainment & pres. Ellis A. Cohen Prods. Since 1983, pres., Hennessey Ent., Ltd. Author: Avenue of the Stars, (novel 1990), Dangerous Evidence (1995). Member: WGA, Producers Guild of America, World Affairs Council, Friars Club, Amer. Newspaper Guild, Intl. Press Corp., Israeli Press Corp., Acad. of TV Arts & Sciences, SAG. Comm. Public Interest for NYC; Natl. Writers Union, and many others.
TELEVISION: Movies: Producer: Aunt Mary (also story); First Steps, Love Mary, Dangerous Evidence: The Lori Jackson Story (also story). Specials: NY Area Emmy Awards (1973-74).

COHEN, IRWIN R.
Exhibition Executive. b. Baltimore, MD, Sept. 4, 1924. e. U. of Baltimore, (LLB) 1948, admitted to Maryland and U.S. Bar same year. Active limited practice. R/C Theatres outgrowth of family business started in 1932. One of founders of Key Bank and Trust, chairman of board Loan Comm., director and member of exec. comm. Pres. NATO of Virginia 1976-78, chairman 1978-80. Director, member of exec. comm., treasurer, former chairman of finance comm. National NATO. Member of Motion Picture Pioneers, Will Rogers Hospital, and various other orgs.

COHEN, LARRY
Director, Producer, Writer. b. New York, NY, July 15, 1946. e. CCNY. Started as writer for TV series incl. Kraft Mystery Theatre, The Defenders, Arrest and Trial. Creator of series Branded, The Invaders, Cool Million, Blue Light, Cop Talk.
PICTURES: Dir./prod./s.p.: Daddy's Gone A-Hunting (co-s.p.), El Condor, Bone, Black Caesar, It's Alive, Demon, The Private Files of J. Edgar Hoover, It Lives Again, Success (story), Full Moon High, Q, I The Jury, Perfect Strangers, The Man Who Wasn't There (story), Special Effects, Scandalous (story), The Stuff (exec. prod.), Spies Like Us (actor), It's Alive III: Island of the Alive (exec. prod.), Return to Salem's Lot (exec. prod.), Best Seller, Deadly Illusion, Maniac Cop, Wicked Stepmother (exec. prod.), Maniac Cop II, The Ambulance, The Apparatus, Guilty As Sin, Original Gangstas, Invasion of Privacy (writer), The Ex, Misbegotten, Uncle Sam, Phone Booth, Captivity, Air Force One: The Final Mission (documentary, dir., prod.)
TELEVISION: Movies: Writer: Cool Million, Man on the Outside, Shootout in a One Dog Town (co-writer, story) Desperado: Avalanche at Devil's Ridge, As Good as Dead (also dir., prod.), 87th Precinct–Ice, Defenders: Choice of Evil. Series: Writer: NYPD Blue, 87th Precinct Heatwave.

COHEN, PAUL E.
Executive. b. New York, NY, Apr. 16, 1948. e. Hofstra U.; New School for Social Research; Jungian Inst. NY. Started in industry as exec. prod., distributor, screenwriter, producer for Masada Prods. Served as v.p. of Grand Slam Prods., exec. prod. for Moonbeam Assocs. Head of Analysis Films, 1976-84. Founded Aries Film Releasing, 1989, becoming pres. & CEO. Professor, Florida State Univ., 1995-97. Pres., Stratosphere Entertainment; oversaw Stratosphere's acquisition of The Thief, One Tough Cop, Bandits, Six Ways to Sunday, Divine Trash, The Last Big Thing, The Inheritors. Pres. & CEO, Manhattan Pictures International. Co-exec. producer One-Eyed King, Eloge de L'Amour, Enigma.
PICTURES: Caligula, My Brilliant Career, Maniac, Basket Case, The Chosen, Butterfly, The Innocent, Mephisto, The Icicle Thief, My Twentieth Century, Superstar: The Life and Times of Andy Warhol, Overseas, The Story of Boys and Girls, Thank You and Goodnight, Lovers, Bad Lieutenant.

COHEN, ROB
Producer, Director. b. Cornwall-on-the-Hudson, NY, March 12, 1949. e. Harvard U. BA. Formerly exec. v.p. in chg of m.p. and TV for Motown. Started as dir. of m.p. for TV at 20th Century-Fox. Joined Motown at age of 24 to produce films. Headed own production co. 1985, appt. pres., Keith Barish Prods.
PICTURES: Mahogany (prod.), The Bingo Long Traveling All-Stars (prod.), Scott Joplin (prod.), Almost Summer (prod.), Thank God It's Friday (prod.), The Wiz (prod.), A Small Circle of Friends (dir.), Scandalous (dir., co-s.p.), The Razor's Edge (prod.), The Legend of Billie Jean (prod.), Light of Day (co-prod.), The Witches of Eastwick (co-exec. prod.), The Monster Squad (co-exec. prod.), Ironweed (co-exec. prod.), The Running Man (co-exec. prod.), The Serpent and the Rainbow (exec. prod.), Disorganized Crime (exec. prod.), Bird on a Wire (prod.), The Hard Way (prod.), Dragon: The Bruce Lee Story (dir., co-s.p., actor), Dragonheart, Daylight, The Rat Pack, The Skulls, The Fast and the Furious, XXX.
TELEVISION: Miami Vice (dir.), Cuba and Claude (exec. prod.), Vanishing Son (exec. prod.), The Vanishing Son I-IV.

COHEN, ROBERT B.
Executive. e. George Washington U., B.A., Southern Texas Sch. of Law. 1980-84. Atty. for Pillsbury Madison's Sutro and for Greenberg, Glusker, Fields, Clamans and Machtinger (L.A.). Was asst. gen. counsel for Columbia Pictures. Joined Paramount 1985 as sr. atty. for M.P. Group. to oversee legal functions for assigned feature films; 1988 named v.p. in charge of legal affairs, Motion Picture Group of Paramount; 1990, named sr. v.p. legal

affairs, motion picture group, Paramount. Currently, exec. v.p. legal affairs, Fox.

COHEN, SID
Executive. e. Univ. of RI Col. of Business. Served as western div. mngr. for WB tv distrib. in 1970's. 1979-84, v.p. feature planning & sls. develop. for domestic tv distrib. div. of Paramount Pictures Corp. There he created the first satellite- delivered feature-film package for free over-the-air tv on a regularly scheduled natl. basis. 1985-91, pres. of domestic tv distrib. at King World Prods. Sept. 1991-Aug. 1999 pres. of MGM Domestic TV Distribution. Now serves MGM unit in consulting role.

COLBY, RONALD
Producer, Director, Writer. b. New York, NY. e. Hofstra U., NYU. Began career as playwright at Cafe La Mama and Caffe Cino; performed in off-B'way shows; spent year as actor-writer in residence at Pittsburgh Playhouse. Served as dialogue coach and asst. to Francis Coppola; was v.p. of Zoetrope Studios. Directed several documentaries and short films.
PICTURES: Finian's Rainbow (act. only), The Rain People (prod.), Hammett (prod.), Some Kind of Wonderful (exec. prod.), She's Having a Baby (exec. prod.), Jailbait (co-prod.), Harvest of Fire, Moonbase (1st asst. dir.), Brint It On Again (video, unit production mgr.).
TELEVISION: Movies: Margaret Bourke-White (co-prod.), Lush Life (co-prod.), Cora Unashamed (co-prod.), The Ponder Heart (sup. prod.), Almost a Woman, A Death in the Family (co-prod.). Series: Eye to Eye, Nightmare Cafe.

COLE, GARY
Actor. b. Park Ridge, IL, Sept. 20, 1956. e. Illinois State, theatre major. Dropped out of coll. after 3 years and moved to Chicago where he tended bar, painted houses and worked with Steppenwolf Theatre group. In 1979 helped to form Remains Theatre, left in 1986 to become ensemble member of Steppenwolf.
PICTURES: Lucas, In the Line of Fire, The Brady Bunch Movie, A Very Brady Sequel, Gang Related, Santa Fe, Cyclops Baby, A Simple Plan, I'll Be Home for Christmas, Kiss the Sky, Office Space, The Gift, The Rising Place, One Hour Photo, I Spy, .
TELEVISION: Movies: Heart of Steel, Fatal Vision, Vital Signs, Those She Left Behind, The Old Man and the Sea, Son of the Morning Star, The Switch, When Love Kills: The Seduction of John Hearn, A Time to Heal, Fall from Grace, For My Daughter's Honor, Lies He Told, American Adventure, Cadet Kelly, Brady Bunch in the Whitehouse. Mini-Series: Echoes in the Darkness, From the Earth to the Moon. Series: Midnight Caller, American Gothic, Justice League, Crusade, Harvey Birdman Attorney at Law, Kim Possible (voice). Guest: Karen Sisco, The West Wing..

COLE, GEORGE
Actor. b. London, Eng., Apr. 22, 1925. e. secondary sch. Surrey. Stage debut in White Horse Inn, 1939; motion picture debut in Cottage to Let, 1941.PICTURES: Henry V, Quartet, My Brother's Keeper, Laughter in Paradise, Scrooge, Lady Godiva Rides Again, Who Goes There (Passionate Sentry), Morning Departure (Operation Disaster), Top Secret (Mr. Potts Goes to Moscow), Happy Family, Will Any Gentleman, Apes of the Rock, The Intruder, Happy Ever After (Tonight's the Night), Our Girl Friday (Adventures of Sadie), Belles of St. Trinian's, Prize of Gold, Where There's a Will, Constant Husband, Quentin Durward, The Weapon, It's a Wonderful Life, Green Man, Bridal Path, Too Many Crooks, Blue Murder at St. Trinians, Don't Panic Chaps, Dr. Syn, One Way Pendulum, Legend of Young Dick Turpin, The Great St. Trinian's Train Robbery, Cleopatra, The Green Shoes, Vampire Lovers, Fright, The Bluebird, Mary Reilly, The Ghost of Greville Lodge.
TELEVISION: Movies: The Legend of Young Dick Turpin, The Last Lonely Man, Minder on the Orient Express, Minder: An Officer and a Car Salesman, The Sleeper, Station Jim. Series: A Life of Bliss, A Man of Our Times, Menace, Minder, Don't Forget To Write, The Good Life, The Bounder, Root Into Europe, An Independent Man, The Sleeper, Station Jim. Mini-series: Blott on the Landscape. Series: Dad, My Good Friend.

COLEMAN, DABNEY
Actor. b. Austin, TX, Jan. 3, 1932. e. VA Military Inst. 1949-51; U. Texas 1951-57; Neighborhood Playhouse School Theater 1958-60.
PICTURES: The Slender Thread (debut, 1965), This Property Is Condemned, The Scalphunters, The Trouble With Girls, Downhill Racer, I Love My Wife, Cinderella Liberty, The Dove, The Towering Inferno, The Other Side of the Mountain, Bite the Bullet, The Black Streetfighter, Midway, Rolling Thunder, Viva Knievel, North Dallas Forty, Nothing Personal, How to Beat the High Cost of Living, Melvin and Howard, Nine to Five, On Golden Pond, Modern Problems, Young Doctors in Love, Tootsie, WarGames, The Muppets Take Manhattan, Cloak and Dagger, The Man with One Red Shoe, Dragnet, Hot to Trot, Where the Heart Is, Short Time, Meet the Applegates, There Goes the Neighborhood, Amos & Andrew, The Beverly Hillbillies, Clifford, You've Got Mail, Inspector Gadget, Stuart Little, Taken, Where the Red Fern Grows, Recess: School's Out (voice), The Climb, Moonlight Mile.
TELEVISION: Movies: Brotherhood of the Bell, Savage, Dying Room Only, The President's Plane is Missing, Bad Ronald, Attack on Terror: The FBI Versus the Ku Klux Klan, Returning

Home, Kiss Me Kill Me, Maneaters Are Loose!, More Than Friends, Apple Pie, When She Was Bad, Murrow, Guilty of Innocence, Sworn To Silence (Emmy Award, 1987), Baby M, Maybe Baby, Never Forget, Columbo and the Murder of a Rock Star, Judicial Consent, In the Line of Duty: Kidnapped, Devil's Food, Target Earth, My Date with the President's Daughter, Exiled, Must Be Santa, Kiss My Act. Mini-Series: Fresno, Idols of the Game (host). Series: That Girl, Bright Promise, Mary Hartman Mary Hartman, Apple Pie, Forever Fernwood, Buffalo Bill, Drexell's Class, Madman of the People, The Slap Maxwell Story, Recess (voice), The Guardian. Special: Plaza Suite, Texan, The Perfect Pitch (tv documentary as himself).

COLEMAN, GARY
Actor. b. Zion, IL, Feb. 8, 1968. Gained fame as star of TV's Diff'rent Strokes.
PICTURES: The Fish That Saved Pittsburgh, On the Right Track, Jimmy the Kid, S.F.W., Party, Dirty Work, Off the Menu: The Last Days at Chasens, Shafted, The Flunky.
TELEVISION:Movies: Actor/Producer: The Kid from Left Field, Scout's Honor, The Kid With the Broken Halo; The Kid with the 200 I.Q., The Fantastic World of D.C. Collins, Playing With Fire, Like Father Like Santa. Series: Diff'rent Strokes. Guest: America 2-Night, Good Times, The Jeffersons, The Big Show, Martin, Married... With Children, Fresh Prince of Bel-Air.

COLEMAN, THOMAS J.
Executive. b. Connecticut, Apr. 13, 1950. e. Boston U. Pres., Twalzo Music Corp., 1972-73; v.p., natl. sls. mgr., United Intl. Pictures, 1973-74; founded Atlantic Releasing Corp., 1974; Atlantic Television, Inc., 1981. All Atlantic corps. consolidated into Atlantic Entertainment Group, 1986. Co. has distributed over 100 films and produced 30 features and TV movies. Sold Atlantic, March, 1989. Formed Independent Entertainment Group, named chmn. Feb., 1992 formed Rocket Pictures.
PICTURES: Producer or Exec. Prod.: Valley Girl, Alphabet City, Roadhouse, Night of the Comet, Starchaser, Teen Wolf, Extremities, The Men's Club, Modern Girls, Nutcracker, Teen Wolf Too, Cop, Patty Hearst, 1969, Bad Golf Made Easier, Fluke, A New York Minute, Cannes Man, The Love Master.

COLER, JOEL H.
Executive. b. Bronx, NY, July 27, 1931. e. Syracuse U., B.A., journalism. Worked as adv. asst. NBC; acct. exec. Grey advertising. Joined 20th Century-Fox 1964 as adv. coordinator Fox Intl.; 1967, named intl. adv./pub. mgr. 1974, named v.p. dir., intl. adv./pub. Nov. 1990, named v.p. publicity/promotions Fox Intl. 1991, v.p. Worldwide Distrib. Services. 1984, memb. L.A. Olympic Org. Com. Left Fox in 1992 to form Joel Coler & Friends intl. mktg. consultants. Memb. L.A. Philarmonic Business & Professional Comm.

COLIN, MARGARET
Actress. b. Brooklyn, NY, May 26, 1957. Raised on Long Island. Studied acting at Stella Adler Conservatory, Juilliard, Hofstra U. Left Hofstra to pursue acting career in Manhattan where she was cast in daytime TV series The Edge of Night. NY Theatre incl. work at Ensemble Studio, Geva Theatre and Manhattan Theatre Club (Aristocrats, Sight Unseen).
PICTURES: Pretty in Pink, Something Wild, Like Father Like Son, Three Men and a Baby, True Believer, Martians Go Home, The Butcher's Wife, Amos & Andrew, Terminal Velocity, Independence Day, The Devil's Own, Time to Say Goodbye, Milk and Money, The Adventures of Sebastian Cole, Blue Car, Unfaithful.
TELEVISION: Movies: Warm Hearts Cold Feet, The Return of Sherlock Holmes, The Traveling Man, Good Night Sweet Wife: A Murder in Boston, In the Shadow of Evil, Hit and Run, Swing Vote, Private Lies, The Familiar Stranger, The Wedding Dress. Series: The Edge of Night, As the World Turns, Foley Square, Leg Work, Sibs, Chicago Hope, The Wright Verdicts, Now and Again, Madigan Men.

COLLET, CHRISTOPHER
Actor. b. New York, NY, March 13, 1968. Started acting in commercials as teenager.
THEATRE: NY: Off-B'way: Coming of Age in SoHo, An Imaginary Life, Unfinished Stories. B'way: Torch Song Trilogy, Spoils of War. Regional: The Lion in Winter, The Old Boy, Pterodactyls.
PICTURES: Sleepaway Camp (debut, 1983), Firstborn, The Manhattan Project, Prayer of the Rollerboys.
TELEVISION: Movies: Right to Kill?, Stephen King's The Langoliers. Specials: Pigeon Feathers, First Love and Other Sorrows, Welcome Home Jelly Bean. Guest: The Equalizer, The Cosby Show. Series: Central Park West.

COLLETTE, TONI
Actress. b. Sydney, Australia, November 1, 1972. Was nominated for Best Supporting Actress Oscar for The Sixth Sense.
THEATRE: The Wild Party (Tony Award nom.).
PICTURES: Spotswood, Muriel's Wedding (Golden Globe nom.), This Marching Girl Thing, Arabian Knight, Lilian's Story, Cosi, The Pallbearer, Emma, Clockwatchers, The James Gang, Dianna & Me, The Boys, Velvet Goldmine, 8 1/2 Women, The Sixth Sense (Acad. Award nom.), Shaft, Hotel Splendide, The Magic Pudding, Changing Lanes, The Hours, About a Boy, Dirty Deeds, Japanese Story, Providence, Connie & Carla.
TELEVISION: Movie: Dinner with Friends.

COLLINS, GARY
Actor. b. Boston, MA, Apr. 30, 1938.
PICTURES: The Pigeon That Took Rome, The Longest Day, Cleopatra, Stranded, Angel in My Pocket, Airport, Killer Fish, Hangar 18, Watchers Reborn, Jungle Book: Lost Treasure (voice), Beautiful.
TELEVISION: Movies: Quarantined, Getting Away from It All, Houston We've Got a Problem, The Night They Took Miss Beautiful, The Kid From Left Field, Jacqueline Susann's Valley of the Dolls, Danielle Steel's Secrets, Bandit: Bandit Bandit. Mini-Series: Roots. Series: The Wackiest Ship in the Army, The Iron Horse, Sixth Sense, Born Free, Hour Magazine (host), Home, Home Show.

COLLINS, JOAN
Actress. b. London, Eng., May 23, 1933. e. Francis Holland Sch., London. Sister is writer Jackie Collins. Made stage debut in A Doll's House, Arts Theatre 1946. Author: Past Imperfect (autobiography, 1978), Katy, A Fight For Life, Joan Collins Beauty Book, Prime Time, Love & Desire & Hate, My Secrets, Too Damn Famous. On London, LA and NY stage in Private Lives. Video: Secrets of Fitness and Beauty (also exec. prod.)
PICTURES: I Believe in You (debut, 1951), Lady Godiva Rides Again, Judgment Deferred, Decameron Nights, Cosh Boy, The Square Ring, Turn the Key Softly, Our Girl Friday (Adventures of Sadie), The Good Die Young, Land of the Pharaohs, Virgin Queen, Girl in the Red Velvet Swing, Opposite Sex, Sea Wife, Island in the Sun, Wayward Bus, Stopover Tokyo, The Bravados, Rally Round the Flag Boys, Seven Thieves, Esther and the King, Road to Hong Kong, Warning Shot, Can Hieronymus Merkin Ever Forget Mercy Humppe and Find True Happiness?, If It's Tuesday This Must Be Belgium, Subterfuge, The Executioner, Up in the Cellar, Quest for Love, Inn of the Frightened People, Fear in the Night, Tales from the Crypt, Tales That Witness Madness, Dark Places, Alfie Darling, The Devil Within Her, The Bawdy Adventures of Tom Jones, Empire of the Ants, The Big Sleep, The Stud, Zero to Sixty, The Bitch, Game of Vultures, Sunburn, Homework, Nutcracker, Decadence, In the Bleak Mid-Winter, Decadence, In The Bleak Midwinter, Annie: A Royal Adventure, The Line King: Al Hirschfield, The Clandestine Marriage, The Flintstones in Viva Rock Vegas, Ozzie.
TELEVISION: Movies: The Cartier Affair, The Making of a Male Model, Her Life as a Man, Paper Dolls, The Wild Women of Chastity Gulch, Drive Hard Drive Fast, Dynasty: The Reunion, Annie: A Royal Adventure, Hart to Hart: Two Harts in Three Quarters Time, Sweet Deception, These Old Broads. Specials: Hansel and Gretel (Faerie Tale Theater), Mama's Back, Hidden Hollywood: Treasures from the 20th Century Fox Film Vaults (Host), Star Trek: Thirty Years and Beyond, The 100 Greatest TV Ads, Elizabeth Taylor: A Musical Celebration, Cleopatra: The Film That Changed Hollywood.Intimate Portrait: Joan Collins (tv documentary. Mini-Series: The Moneychangers, Sins, Monte Carlo (also exec. prod.) Series: Dynasty, Pacific Palisades, Guiding Light.

COLLINS, PAULINE
Actress. b. Exmouth, Devon, Eng., Sept. 3, 1940. m. actor John Alderton (Thomas on Upstairs, Downstairs). e. Central School of Speech and Drama. Stage debut A Gazelle in Park Lane (Windsor, 1962). Best known to U.S. audiences as Sarah in Upstairs, Downstairs.
THEATRE: Passion Flower Hotel (London debut, 1965), The Erpingham Camp, The Happy Apple, The Importance of Being Earnest, The Night I Chased the Women with an Eel, Come as You Are, Judies, Engaged, Confusions, Romantic Comedy, Woman in Mind, Shirley Valentine (in London won Olivier Award as best actress, in NY won Tony, Drama Desk and Outer Critics Circle Awards.)
PICTURES: Secrets of a Windmill Girl, Shirley Valentine, City of Joy, My Mother's Courage, Paradise Road, Mrs. Caldicot's Cabbage War.
TELEVISION: Upstairs Downstairs, Thomas and Sarah, Forever Green, No—Honestly (all with husband), Tales of the Unexpected, Knockback, Flowers of the Forrest, The Ambassador, Man and Boy .

COLLINS, STEPHEN
Actor. b. Des Moines, IA, Oct. 1, 1947. Appeared off-B'way in several Joseph Papp productions before B'way debut in Moonchildren, followed by No Sex We're British, The Ritz, Loves of Anatol, Censored Scenes from King Kong. Off-B'way: Twelfth Night, The Play's the Thing, Beyond Therapy, One of the Guys, The Old Boy, Putting It Together. Author of play Super Sunday (Williamstown Fest.), and novel Eye Contact (1994).
PICTURES: All the President's Men, Between the Lines, The Promise, Fedora, Star Trek: The Motion Picture, Loving Couples, Brewster's Millions, Jumpin' Jack Flash, Choke Canyon, The Big Picture, Stella, My New Gun, The First Wives Club, An Unexpected Life, Drive Me Crazy, The Commission.
TELEVISION: Movies: Brink's, The Great Robbery, The Henderson Monster, Dark Mirror, Threesome, Weekend War, A Woman Scorned: The Betty Broderick Story, Her Final Fury: Betty Broderick-The Last Chapter, The Disappearance of Nora, Barbara Taylor Bradford's Remember, A Family Divided, On Seventh Avenue, The Babysitter's Seduction, As Time Runs Out. Mini-Series: The Rhinemann Exchange, Hold the Dream, Inside the Third Reich, Chiefs, The Two Mrs. Grenvilles, A Woman Named Jackie, Scarlett. Series: Tales of the Gold Monkey, Tattinger's (revamped as Nick & Hillary), Working it Out, 7th Heaven.

COLT, MARSHALL
Actor, Writer. b. New Orleans, LA, Oct. 26, 1948. e. Tulane U., B.S. Physics; Pepperdine U., M.A. Clinical Psychology; Fielding Inst., PhD. candidate student, Clinical Psychology. Combat tour in Southeast Asia during Vietnam War. Captain, U.S. Naval Reserve. Stage productions: (Hotel Universe, Who's Afraid of Virginia Woolf?, Zoo Story, Killer's Head, etc.).
PICTURES: Bimbo (short), North Dallas Forty, Those Lips, Those Eyes, Jagged Edge, Flowers in the Attic, Illegally Yours.
TELEVISION: Movies: Colorado C-1, Sharon: Portrait of a Mistress, Once an Eagle, To Heal a Nation, Mercy or Murder, Guilty of Innocence, Deceptions. Series: McClain's Law, Lottery! Guest: Family, Paper Chase, Streets of San Francisco, Barnaby Jones, Murder She Wrote.

COLTRANE, ROBBIE
Actor. b. Glasgow, Scotland, 1950. Ent. ind. 1977.
THEATRE: San Quentin theatre workshop, Oxford Theatre Group, Citizens Theatre, Traverse Theatre, Borderline Theatre, Hampstead Theatre, Bush Theatre; one man shows: Your Obedient Servant, Mistero Buffo.
PICTURES: Bad Business (dir.); Flash Gordon, Death Watch, Subway Riders, Britannia Hospital, Scrubbers, Ghost Dance, Krull, National Lampoon's European Vacation, Caravaggio, Defence of the Realm, The Supergrass, Mona Lisa, Eat the Rich, Bert Rigby You're a Fool, Wonderland (The Fruit Machine), Let It Ride, Henry V, Slipstream, Nuns on the Run, Perfectly Normal, The Pope Must Die, Triple Bogey on a Par 5 Hole, Oh What a Night, The Adventures of Huck Finn, Goldeneye, Buddy, Montana, Frogs for Snakes, The World Is Not Enough, On the Nose, Delaney's Flutter, Harry Potter and the Sorcerer's Stone, From Hell, Harry Potter and the Chamber of Secrets, Harry Potter and the Prisoner of Azkaban.
TELEVISION: 1981 Take Two, Seven Deadly Sins, Keep It in the Family, Kick Up The Eighties, The Green Door, The Sheep Stealer, House With Green Shutters, The Lost Tribe, Alfresco, Laugh? I Nearly Paid My Licence Fee, Comic Strip Presents Five Go Mad in Dorset, Beat Generation, Susie, Gino, The Bullshitters, Miner's Strike, Tutti Frutti, Danny the Champion of the World (theatrical release in Europe), Jealousy (also dir., co-writer), Space Sluts From Planet Sex, French and Aunders, The Lenny Henry Show, Robbie Coltrane Special, Mistero Buffo (series), Alive & Kicking, The Secret Ingredients, The Bogie Man, Rednose of Courage, A Tour of the Western Isles, Coltrane in a Cadillac (also co-writer), Cracker (BAFTA & Cable ACE Awards), The Planman (also exec. prod).

COLUMBUS, CHRIS
Director, Writer: b. Spangler, PA, 1959. Grew up in Ohio. Started making short super 8 films in high school, studied screenwriting at New York U. Film Sch., graduated 1980. Sold first s.p., Jocks, while at college. Wrote for and developed TV cartoon series, Galaxy High School.
PICTURES: Writer: Reckless, Gremlins, The Goonies, Young Sherlock Holmes, Little Nemo: Adventures in Slumberland (co-s.p.). Fantastic Four (also prod.). Director: Adventures in Babysitting (debut, 1987), Heartbreak Hotel (also s.p.), Home Alone, Only the Lonely (also s.p.), Home Alone 2: Lost in New York, Mrs. Doubtfire, Nine Months (also co-prod.), Jingle All the Way, (prod. only), Stepmom, Bicentennial Man, Harry Potter and the Sorcerer's Stone, Harry Potter and the Chamber of Secrets, Harry Potter and the Prisoner of Azkaban, Cheaper by the Dozen.
TELEVISION: Amazing Stories, Twilight Zone, Alfred Hitchcock Presents.

COMBS, HOLLY MARIE
Actress. b. San Diego, California, December 3, 1973.
PICTURES: Walls of Glass, Sweet Hearts Dance, New York Stories, Born on the Fourth of July, Simple Men, Dr. Giggles, A Chain of Desire, A Reason to Believe, Vector, Ocean's Eleven.
TELEVISION: Movies: A Perfect Stranger, Sins of Silence, Love's Deadly Triangle : The Texas Cadet Murder, Daughters, See Jane Date. Series: Picket Fences, Charmed.

COMDEN, BETTY
Writer. b. Brooklyn, NY, May 3, 1919. e. Erasmus Hall, NYU sch. of ed., B.S. Nightclub performer and writer with The Revuers, 1939-44. NY City Mayor's Award Art and Culture, 1978. Named to Songwriters Hall of Fame, 1980. NYU Alumnae Assn.'s Woman of Achievement award, 1987. Kennedy Center Honors for Life Achievement, 1991.
THEATRE: With Adolph Green: writer book, sketches & lyrics for B'way shows: On the Town (book, lyrics, actress, 1944); Billion Dollar Baby (bk., Lyrics), Bonanza Bound! (bk., lyrics), Two on the Aisle (sketches and lyrics), Wonderful Town (lyrics; Tony Award, 1953), Peter Pan (lyrics), Bells Are Ringing (bk., lyrics), Say Darling (lyrics), A Party With Comden and Green (bk., lyrics, star; 1959 and 1977); Do Re Mi (lyrics), Subways Are For Sleeping (bk., lyrics), Fade Out-Fade In (bk., lyrics), Leonard Bernstein's Theatre Songs, Hallelujah, Baby (lyrics; Tony Award, 1968), Applause (book; Tony Award, 1970), Lorelei (revision to book), By Bernstein (book and some lyrics), On the Twentieth Century (2 Tony Awards, book and lyrics, 1978); A Doll's Life (bk., lyrics), The Will Rogers Follies (Tony Award, 1991). Actress only: Isn't It Romantic.
PICTURES: Writer with Adolph Green: Good News, Take Me Out to the Ballgame (lyrics), On the Town, Barkleys of Broadway, Singin' in the Rain, The Band Wagon, It's Always Fair Weather (also lyrics), Auntie Mame, Bells Are Ringing (also lyrics), What

a Way to Go, The Addams Family (lyrics), Peter Pan. *Actress*: Greenwich Village, Garbo Talks, Slaves of New York.

CONAWAY, JEFF
Actor. b. New York, NY, Oct. 5, 1950. Started in show business at the age of 10 when he appeared in B'way production, All the Way Home. Later toured in Critics Choice before turning to fashion modeling. Toured with musical group, 3 1/2, as lead singer and guitarist. Entered theatre arts program at NYU. Film debut at 19 in Jennifer on My Mind.
THEATRE: Grease, The News.
PICTURES: Jennifer on My Mind (debut, 1971), The Eagle Has Landed, Pete's Dragon, I Never Promised You a Rose Garden, Grease, The Patriot, Elvira: Mistress of the Dark, Cover Girl, Tale of Two Sisters, The Banker, The Sleeping Car, A Time to Die, Total Exposure, Mirror Images, Sunset Strip, Bikini Summer II, Almost Pregnant, L.A. Goddess, In a Moment of Passion, Alien Intruder, 2002: The Rape of Eden, Jawbreaker, Man on the Moon, Do You Wanna Know a Secret, Dating Service, Y.M.I, Curse of the Forty-Niner, The Biz.
TELEVISION: *Series*: Taxi, Wizards and Warriors, Berrenger's, The Bold and the Beautiful, Babylon 5, Crusade: The Babylon Project. *Guest*: From Sea to Shining Sea (1974), Joe Forrester, The Mary Tyler Moore Show, Happy Days, Movin' On, Barnaby Jones, Kojak, Mickey Spillane's Mike Hammer. *Movies*: Having Babies, Delta County, U.S.A., Breaking Up Is Hard to Do, For the Love of It, Nashville Grab, The Making of a Male Model, Bay Coven, The Dirty Dozen: The Fatal Mission, Ghost Writer, Eye of the Storm, Babylon 5: Thirdspace, Babylon 5: The River of Souls, Babylon 5: A Call to Arms.

CONDON, BILL
Director, Writer.
PICTURES: Dead Kids (s.p. only), Strange Invaders (s.p. only), Sister Sister, F/X 2 (s.p. only), Candyman: Farewell to the Flesh (dir. only), Gods and Monsters (Acad. Award for s.p. adapt.), The Devil and Daniel Webster (s.p. only), Chicago: The Musical (s.p. only), Kinsey (dir., s.p.)
TELEVISION: *Movies*: Murder 101, White Lie, Dead in the Water, Deadly Relations, The Man Who Wouldn't Die (also co-exec. prod.)

CONDON, CHRIS J.
Producer, Director, Motion Equipment Designer. b. Chicago, IL, Dec. 7, 1922. e. Davidson Inst., U. of Southern California. U.S. Air Force 1943-46. Founded Century Precision Optics, 1948. Designed Athenar telephoto lenses, Century Super wide-angle lenses and Duplikins. Co-founded StereoVision International, Inc. 1969 specializing in films produced in new 3-D process. Member SMPTE. Lecturer and consultant on motion picture optics and 3-D motion picture technology.
PICTURES: The Wild Ride, The Surfer, Girls, Airline, The New Dimensions.

CONNELLY, JENNIFER
Actress. b. New York, NY, Dec. 12, 1970. e. Yale, Stamford U.
PICTURES: Once Upon a Time in America (debut, 1983), Creepers, Labyrinth, Seven Minutes in Heaven, Etoile, Some Girls, The Hot Spot, Career Opportunities, The Rocketeer, Of Love and Shadows, Higher Learning, Mulholland Falls, Far Harbor, Inventing the Abbotts, Dark City, Waking the Dead, Requiem for a Dream, Pollock, A Beautiful Mind (Academy Award, BAFTA Award, Golden Globe Award, SAG nom.), The Hulk, House of Sand & Fog.
TELEVISION: *Movie*: The Heart of Justice. *Series*: The Street.

CONNERY, SEAN
Actor. r.n. Thomas Sean Connery. b. Edinburgh, Scotland, Aug. 25, 1930. Worked as a lifeguard and a model before landing role in chorus of London prod. of South Pacific, 1953. Prod. dir., The Bowler and the Bonnet (film doc.), I've Seen You Cut Lemons (London stage). Director of Tantallon Films Ltd. (First production: Something Like the Truth). Recipient of Golden Globe Cecil B. Demille Award, 1996.
PICTURES: No Road Back (debut, 1957), Time Lock, Hell Drivers, Action of the Tiger, Another Time Another Place, Darby O'Gill and the Little People, Tarzan's Greatest Adventure, Frightened City, On the Fiddle, The Longest Day, Dr. No, From Russia With Love, Marnie, Woman of Straw, Goldfinger, The Hill, Thunderball, A Fine Madness, You Only Live Twice, Shalako, The Molly Maguires, The Red Tent, The Anderson Tapes, Diamonds Are Forever, The Offence, Zardoz, Murder on the Orient Express, The Terrorists, The Wind and the Lion, The Man Who Would Be King, Robin and Marian, The Next Man, A Bridge Too Far, The Great Train Robbery, Meteor, Cuba, Outland, Time Bandits, Wrong Is Right, Five Days One Summer, Sword of the Valiant, Never Say Never Again, Highlander, The Name of the Rose, The Untouchables (Academy Award, best supporting actor, 1987), The Presidio, Memories of Me (cameo), Indiana Jones and the Last Crusade, Family Business, The Hunt for Red October, The Russia House, Robin Hood: Prince of Thieves (cameo), Highlander 2: The Quickening, Medicine Man (also exec. prod.), Rising Sun (also exec. prod.), A Good Man in Africa, Just Cause (also exec. prod.), First Knight, Dragonheart (voice), The Rock (also exec. prod.), Playing by Heart, The Avengers, Entrapment (also exec. prod.), Finding Forrester, The League of Extraordinary Gentlemen (also exec. prod).
TELEVISION: Requiem for a Heavyweight, Anna Christie, Boy with the Meataxe, Women in Love, The Crucible, Riders to the Sea, Colombe, Adventure Story, Anna Karenina.

CONNICK, HARRY, JR.
Musician, Actor. b. New Orleans, LA, Sept. 11, 1967. Began performing with Bourbon Street jazz combos at age 6. Studied classical piano. Albums: Harry Connick, 20, When Harry Met Sally..., Lofty's Roach Souffle, We Are in Love (Grammy Award, 1991), Blue Light Red Light, 25, Eleven, When My Heart Finds Christmas, She, Star Turtle. Acting debut in Memphis Belle (1990). B'way debut 1990 in An Evening with Harry Connick Jr.
PICTURES: When Harry Met Sally... (special musical performances and arrangements), Memphis Belle, The Godfather Part III (performed theme song), Little Man Tate, Sleepless in Seattle (performed song), Copycat, Independence Day, Excess Baggage, Hope Floats, The Iron Giant (voice), Wayward Son, My Dog Skip (voice), The Simian Line, Life Without Dick, Mickey, Basic.
TELEVISION: *Movies*: South Pacific. *Specials*: Swingin' Out Live, The New York Big Band Concert, The Harry Connick Jr. Christmas Special, Pistol Pete: The Life and Times of Pete Maravich. *Guest*: Cheers, Mad TV. *Mini-series*: Jazz (voice). Series: Will and Grace.

CONNORS, MIKE
Actor. r.n. Krekor Ohanian. b. Fresno, CA, Aug. 15, 1925. e. UCLA. Film debut in Sudden Fear (1952) as Touch Connors.
PICTURES: Sudden Fear (debut, 1952), Sky Commando, 49th Man, Island in the Sky, Day of Triumph, Five Guns West, The Twinkle in God's Eye, Oklahoma Woman, Swamp Woman, The Day the World Ended, The Ten Commandments, Flesh and Spur, Shake Rattle and Rock, Voodoo Woman, Live Fast Die Young, Suicide Battalion, Panic Button, Seed of Violence, Good Neighbor Sam, Where Love Has Gone, Harlow, Situation Hopeless—But Not Serious, Stagecoach, Kiss the Girls and Make Them Die, Avalanche Express, Nightkill, Too Scared to Scream, Fist Fighter, Friend to Friend, Public Enemy #2, Ciudad Baja, Wild Bill: Hollywood Maverick, James Dean: Race With Destiny, Gideon.
TELEVISION: *Movies*: High Midnight, Beg Borrow or Steal, The Killer Who Wouldn't Die, Revenge for a Rape, Long Journey Back, The Death of Ocean View Park, Casino, Hart to Hart Returns. *Mini-Series*: War and Remembrance. *Series*: Tightrope, Mannix (Golden Globe Award), Today's FBI, Crimes of the Century (host), Disney's Hercules.

CONRAD, ROBERT
Actor, Director. r.n. Conrad Robert Falk. b. Chicago, IL, March 1, 1935. e. public schools, Northwestern U. Prof. debut, nightclub singer. Formed Robert Conrad Productions, 1966 (later A Shane Productions, then Black Sheep Productions).
PICTURES: Thundering Jets (debut, 1958), Palm Springs Weekend, Young Dillinger, The Bandits (also dir.), Murph the Surf (Live a Little Steal a Lot), The Lady in Red, Wrong Is Right, Moving Violations, Uncommon Courage, Jingle All the Way, New Jersey Turnpikes, Jingle All the Way, Garbage Day (short).
TELEVISION: *Movies*: Weekend of Terror, The D.A.: Conspiracy to Kill, Five Desperate Women, Adventures of Nick Carter, The Last Day, Smash-Up on Interstate 5, Wild Wild West Revisited, Breaking Up Is Hard To Do, More Wild Wild West, Coach of the Year, Will: G. Gordon Liddy, Confessions of a Married Man, Hard Knox, Two Fathers' Justice, Assassin, Charley Hannah, The Fifth Missile, One Police Plaza, High Mountain Rangers (also dir., co-story), Glory Days (also dir.), Anything to Survive, Mario and the Mob, Sworn to Vengeance, Two Fathers: Justice for the Innocent, Search and Rescue. *Series*: Hawaiian Eye, Wild Wild West, The D.A., Assignment Vienna, Baa Baa Black Sheep, The Duke, A Man Called Sloane, High Mountain Rangers, Jesse Hawkes, Search and Rescue. *Guest*: Lawman, Maverick, 77 Sunset Strip. *Mini-Series*: Centennial.

CONSTANTINE, MICHAEL
Actor. b. Reading, PA, May 22, 1927.
PICTURES: The Hustler, Hawaii, Skidoo, Justine, If It's Tuesday This Must Be Belgium, Peeper, Voyage of the Damned, The North Avenue Irregulars, Pray for Death, In the Mood, Prancer, Dead Fall, My Life, The Juror, Stephen King's Thinner, My Big Fat Greek Wedding.
TELEVISION: *Movies*: Suddenly Single, Deadly Harvest, Say Goodbye Maggie Cole, The Bait, Death Cruise, The Night That Panicked America, Conspiracy of Terror, Wanted: The Sundance Woman, The Pirate, Crisis in Mid-Air, The Love Tapes, Evita Peron, My Palikari, Finder of Lost Loves, Leap of Faith, Because Mommy Works, WW3. *Mini-Series*: 79 Park Avenue, Roots: The Next Generations. *Series*: Hey Landlord, Room 222 (Emmy Award, 1970), Sirota's Court, My Big Fat Greek Wedding (the series). Numerous guest appearances.

CONTE, JOHN
Actor, Singer. b. Palmer, MA, Sept. 15, 1915. e. Lincoln H.S., Los Angeles. Actor. Pasadena Playhouse; radio anncr., m.c.; Armed Forces, WWII. Pres. KMIR-TV, Channel 36, Desert Empire Television Corp., Palm Springs, NBC Affiliate.
THEATRE: On B'way in Windy City, Allegro, Carousel, Arms and the Girl.
PICTURES: Thousands Cheer, Lost in a Harem, Trauma, Man With the Golden Arm, The Carpetbaggers.
TELEVISION: *Series*: Van Camp's Little Show (1950-52), Mantovani. *Specials*: Max Liebman Spectaculars and dramatic shows, host and star of NBC Matinee Theatre, TV Hour of Stars.

CONTI, BILL
Composer. b. Providence, RI, April 13, 1942. Studied piano at age 7, forming first band at age 15. e. Louisiana State U., Juilliard School of Music. Moved to Italy with jazz trio where scored first film, Candidate for a Killing. Was music supvr. on Blume in Love for Paul Mazursky.
PICTURES: Harry and Tonto, Next Stop Greenwich Village, Rocky, Handle With Care, Slow Dancing in the Big City, An Unmarried Woman, F.I.S.T., The Big Fix, Paradise Alley, Uncle Joe Shannon, Rocky II, A Man a Woman and A Bank, Goldengirl, The Seduction of Joe Tynan, The Formula, Gloria, Private Benjamin, Carbon Copy, Victory, For Your Eyes Only, I The Jury, Rocky III, Neighbors, Split Image, Bad Boys, That Championship Season, Unfaithfully Yours, The Right Stuff (Academy Award, 1983), Mass Appeal, The Karate Kid, The Bear, Big Trouble, Gotcha, Beer, Nomads, F/X, The Karate Kid II, A Prayer for the Dying, Masters of the Universe, Baby Boom, Broadcast News, For Keeps, A Night in the Life of Jimmy Reardon, Betrayed, Cohen and Tate, Big Blue, Lean On Me, The Karate Kid Part III, Lock Up, The Fourth War, Backstreet Dreams, Rocky V, Necessary Roughness, Year of the Gun, A Captive in the Land, The Adventures of Huck Finn, Bound By Honor, By the Sword, Rookie of the Year, Yellowstone, 8 Seconds, The Next Karate Kid, Bushwhacked, The Scout, Spy Hard, Wrongfully Accused, The Real Macaw, The Thomas Crown Affair, Sugihara: Conspiracy of Goodness, Tortilla Soup, Boys on the Run, G, Avenging Angelo, 2 Birds with 1 Stallone.
TELEVISION: Kill Me If You Can, Stark, North and South, The Pirate, Smashup on Interstate 5, Papa & Me, Napoleon and Josephine, Murderers Among Us: The Simon Wiesenthal Story, American Tragedy. Series themes: Cagney and Lacy, Dynasty, Falcon Crest, The Colbys, Kenya, Heartbeat, Lifestyles of the Rich and Famous, Emerald Point N.A.S., Dolphin Cove, The Elite, Instant Recall, Inside Edition.

CONTI, TOM
Actor. b. Paisley, Scotland, Nov. 22, 1941. Trained at Royal Scottish Academy of Music, Glasgow. Did repertory work in Scotland before London stage debut appearing with Paul Scofield in Savages, 1973.
THEATRE: London: Devil's Disciple, Whose Life Is It Anyway?, They're Playing Our Song, Romantic Comedy, Two Into One, Italian Straw Hat, Jeffrey Bernard is Unwell, Present Laughter. Director: Before the Party, The Housekeeper. NY: Whose Life Is It Anyway? (Tony Award, 1979), Last Licks (dir.), Present Laughter (dir.), Chapter Two.
PICTURES: Galileo (debut, 1975), Eclipse, The Duellists, The Haunting of Julia (Full Circle), Merry Christmas Mr. Lawrence, Reuben Reuben (Acad. Award nom.), American Dreamer, Miracles, Saving Grace, Beyond Therapy, The Gospel According to Vic, That Summer of White Roses, Shirley Valentine, Someone Else's America, Subdown, Something to Believe In, Out of Control, Don't Go Breaking My Heart, The Enemy.
TELEVISION: Mother of Men (1959), The Glittering Prizes, Madame Bovery, Treats, The Norman Conquests, The Wall, Nazi Hunter, The Quick and the Dead, Roman Holiday, The Dumb Waiter, Faerie Tale Theater (The Princess and the Pea), Fatal Judgement, Blade on the Feather, Voices Within: The Lives of Truddi Chase, The Wright Verdicts (series), Deadline (series), I Was A Rat, Andy Pandy (narrator).

CONVERSE, FRANK
Actor. b. St. Louis, MO, May 22, 1938. e. Carnegie-Mellon. Early training on stage in New York. Active in repertory theatres. Two seasons with Amer. Shakespeare Fest.
THEATRE: The Seagull, Death of a Salesman, Night of the Iguana, A Man for All Seasons, The House of Blue Leaves, First One Asleep Whistle, Arturo Ui, The Philadelphia Story (1980 revival), Brothers, A Streetcar Named Desire (1988 revival), Design for Living, The Crucible, Hobson's Choice, The Ride Down Mount Morgan, etc.
PICTURES: Hurry Sundown, Hour of the Gun, The Rowdyman, The Pilot, The Bushido Blade, Spring Fever, Everybody Wins, Primary Motive.
TELEVISION: Movies: Dr. Cook's Garden, A Tattered Web, In Tandem, Killer on Board, Cruise Into Terror, Sgt. Matlovich Vs. the U.S. Air Force, Marilyn: The Untold Story, The Miracle of Kathy Miller, Anne of Green Gables—The Sequel, Alone in the Neon Jungle, Our Town. Series: As the World Turns, All My Children. Guest: Mod Squad, Medical Center, Wonderworks, Guests of the Nation. Series: Coronet Blue, N.Y.P.D., Movin' On, The Family Tree, Dolphin Cove, One Life to Live.

CONWAY, GARY
Actor. r.n. Gareth Carmody. b. Boston, MA, Feb. 4, 1936. e. UCLA. As college senior was chosen for title role in Teen-Age Frankenstein. After graduating served in military at Ford Ord, CA. In 1960 began contract with Warner Bros., appearing in films and TV. Has also appeared on stage. Has had several one-man shows as painter and is represented in public and private collections.
PICTURES: I Was a Teenage Frankenstein, Young Guns of Texas, Once Is Not Enough, The Farmer (also prod.), Meet Me Halfway (writer), American Ninja (also s.p.), Over The Top, American Ninja III: Blood Hunt (s.p.), Liberty & Bash.
TELEVISION: Series: Burke's Law, Land of the Giants. Movie: The Judge and Jake Wyler. Guest: 77 Sunset Strip, Columbo, Police Story, Love Boat.

CONWAY, KEVIN
Actor. b. New York, NY, May 29, 1942.
THEATRE: Actor: One Flew Over the Cuckoo's Nest, When You

Comin' Back Red Ryder? (Obie & Drama Desk Awards), Of Mice and Men, Moonchildren, Life Class, Saved, The Elephant Man, Other Places, King John (NYSF), Other People's Money (Outer Critics Circle Award; also L.A. prod.), The Man Who Fell in Love with His Wife, Ten Below, On the Waterfront. Director: Mecca, Short Eyes (revival), One Act Play Fest (Lincoln Center), The Milk Train Doesn't Stop Here Anymore (revival), The Elephant Man (tour), Other People's Money (Chicago, L.A. & S.F.).
PICTURES: Believe in Me, Portnoy's Complaint, Slaughterhouse Five, Shamus, F.I.S.T., Paradise Alley, The Fun House, Flashpoint, Homeboy, The Sun and the Moon (dir., prod.), Funny Farm, One Good Cop, Rambling Rose, Jennifer Eight, Gettysburg, The Quick and the Dead, Lawnmower Man II, Looking for Richard, The Stupids, Mercury Rising, The Confession, Two Family House, Thirteen Days, Joan of Arc: Virgin Warrior, Black Knight, Gods and Generals.
TELEVISION: Series: All My Children. Movies: Johnny We Hardly Knew Ye, The Deadliest Season, Rage of Angels, The Lathe of Heaven, Attack on Fear, Something About Amelia, Jesse, When Will I Be Loved?, Breaking the Silence, The Whipping Boy, Net Worth, Ronnie and Julie, Calm at Sunset, Sally Hemmings: An American Scandal, . Specials: The Scarlet Letter, The Elephant Man, Calm at Sunset. Mini-Series: Streets of Laredo, Mark Twain.

CONWAY, TIM
Actor. b. Willoughby, OH, Dec. 15, 1933. e. Bowling Green State U. After 2 yrs. Army service joined KYW-TV in Cleveland as writer-director and occasional performer. Comedienne Rose Marie discovered him and arranged audition for the Steve Allen Show on which he became regular. In 1962 signed for McHale's Navy, series. Also has done night club appearances.
PICTURES: McHale's Navy (debut, 1964), McHale's Navy Joins the Air Force, The World's Greatest Athlete, The Apple Dumpling Gang, Gus, The Shaggy D.A., Billion Dollar Hobo, The Apple Dumpling Gang Rides Again, The Prize Fighter, The Private Eyes (also co-s.p.), Cannonball Run II, The Longshot, Dear God, Speed 2: Cruise Control, Air Bud: Golden Receiver, View From the Swing.
TELEVISION: Movies: Roll Freddy Roll, Hermie: A Common Caterpillar. Series: The Steve Allen Show, McHale's Navy, Rango, The Tim Conway Show (1970), The Tim Conway Comedy Hour, The Carol Burnett Show (3 Emmy Awards as actor: 1973, 1977, 1978; Emmy Award as writer: 1976), The Tim Conway Show (1980-81), Ace Crawford: Private Eye, Tim Conway's Funny America, The College of Comedy with Alan King, Hercules (voice), SpongeBob SquarePants, On the Spot. Guest: Hollywood Palace, and shows starring Garry Moore, Carol Burnett, Red Skelton, Danny Kaye, Dean Martin, Cher, Doris Day, Coach (Emmy Award, 1996), The Simpsons (voice), The Drew Carey Show.

COOGAN, KEITH
Actor. b. Palm Springs, CA, Jan. 13, 1970. e. Santa Monica City Col. Grandson of late actor Jackie Coogan. Formerly acted as Keith Mitchell. Appeared in shorts All Summer in a Day and The Great O'Grady.
PICTURES: The Fox and the Hound (voice), Adventures in Babysitting, Hiding Out, Under the Boardwalk, Cousins, Cheetah, Book of Love, Toy Soldiers, Don't Tell Mom the Babysitter's Dead, Forever, In the Army Now, Life 101, The Power Within, A Reason to Believe, Downhill Willy, Ivory Tower, Dreamers, Python, ...Or Forever Hold Your Peace, Soulkeeper.
TELEVISION: Series: The MacKenzies of Paradise Cove, The Waltons, Gun Shy. Movies: A Question of Love, Million Dollar Infield, Kid With the Broken Halo, Battered, Memorial Day, Spooner. Specials: Wrong Way Kid, The Treasure of Alpheus T. Winterborn, Rascal, Over the Limit, A Town's Revenge. Guest: Growing Pains, Silver Spoons, Fame, CHips, The Love Boat, Mork and Mindy, 21 Jump Street, 8 is Enough, Fantasy Island, Just the Ten of Us, Sibs, Tales From the Crypt, others. Pilots: Norma Rae, Apple Dumpling Gang, Wonderland Cove.

COOK, FIELDER
Director, Producer. b. Atlanta, GA, March 9, 1923. e. Washington & Lee U., B.A.; U. of Birmingham, Eng., post grad. Served with 7th Amphibious Force, WWII.
PICTURES: Patterns (debut, 1956), Home Is the Hero, A Big Hand for the Little Lady (also prod.), How to Save a Marriage and Ruin Your Life, Prudence and the Pill, Eagle in a Cage, From the Mixed Up Files of Mrs. Basil E. Frankweiler, Seize the Day.
TELEVISION: Movies: Sam Hill: Who Killed the Mysterious Mr. Foster?, Goodbye Raggedy Ann (also exec. prod.), The Homecoming, Miracle on 34th Street, This is the West That Was, Miles to Go Before I Sleep, Judge Horton and the Scottsboro Boys, Beauty and the Beast, A Love Affair: The Eleanor and Lou Gehrig Story, Too Far to Go (also released theatrically), I Know Why the Caged Bird Sings, Gaugin the Savage, Family Reunion, Will There Really Be a Morning?, Why Me?, A Special Friendship, The Member of the Wedding. Mini-Series: Evergreen. Specials: The Hands of Carmac Joyce, Teacher Teacher, The Rivalry, Valley Forge, The Price (Emmy Award), Harvey, Brigadoon (also prod.; 2 Emmy Awards), Seize the Day, Third and Oak: The Pool Hall, A Member of the Wedding. Pilots: Ben Casey, The 11th Hour, The Waltons.

COOK, RACHAEL LEIGH
Actress. b. Minneapolis, MN, Oct. 4, 1979.
PICTURES: The Baby-Sitters Club, Tom and Huck, 26 Summer Street, Carpool, The House of Yes, The Eighteenth Angel, Strike,

The Naked Man, Living Out Loud, The Hi-Line, The Bumblebee Flies Anyway, She's All That, Texas Rangers, Anti-Trust, Tangled, Josie and the Pussycats, Get Carter, Blow Dry, Texas Rangers, Sally, 29 Palms, Scorched, Tempo, Bookies, Stateside, The Big Empty.
TELEVISION: Movies: The Defenders: Payback, Country Justice, True Women. Series: Fearless. Guest: The Outer Limits, Dawson's Creek, Batman Beyond (voice).

COOK, RICHARD
Executive. b. Bakersfield, CA, Aug. 20, 1950.e. USC. Began career as a ride operator at Disneyland, 1970. Disneyland sales rep. & manager of sales, 1971-76; manager, pay TV and non-theatrical releases, The Disney Channel, 1977-80; asst. domestic sales mgr., v.p. & general sales mgr., senior v.p., domestic dist., Buena Vista Pictures, 1980-87; president and head of dist. & mktg., Buena Vista Pictures Distribution, 1988-present; established Buena Vista as a pioneer in new methods of film delivery, helped prohibit paid screen advertising in theaters exhibiting products from any of the Disney Studios' banners; promoted restoration of the classic movie palace and award-winning landmark, the El Capitan, 1989-91; noted for spectacular showmanship in launching new films with live stage shows, parades and gala outdoor premieres; member, Academy of Motion Picture Arts & Sciences; member of the board of trustees, The Chandler School; recipient of the George Washington Medal of Freedom, Freedom Found. of Valley Forge. Currently chairman, The Walt Disney Motion Pictures Group and head of production for Walt Disney, Touchstone, and Hollywood Pictures. Oversees worldwide home video operations and is directly responsible for domestic theatrical mktg. & dist., intl., mktg. & dist. and feature film acquisitions.

COOKE, ALISTAIR
Journalist, Broadcaster. b. Manchester, Eng., Nov. 20, 1908. e. Jesus Coll., Cambridge U.; Yale U.; Harvard U. Film crit. of BBC 1934-37. London corr. NBC 1936-37. BBC commentator in U.S. since 1937. Weekly 15 min. talk on radio show, Letter From America, starting in 1946. Chief Amer. corr., Manchester Guardian, 1948-72; English narrator, The March of Time, 1938-39. Became U.S. citizen in 1941. Peabody award winner for International reporting, 1952, 1973-83. Hon. Knighthood, KBE, 1973.
AUTHOR: Douglas Fairbanks, Garbo & The Night Watchmen, A Generation on Trial, One Man's America, Christmas Eve, The Vintage Mencken, etc. America, 1973; Six Men, 1977; Talk About America, 1968; The Americans, 1979; Above London (with Robert Cameron), 1980; Masterpieces, 1981; The Patient Has the Floor, 1986, America Observed, 1988; Fun and Games with Alistair Cooke, 1995, Alistair Cooke A Biography.
PICTURES: Narrator: Sorrowful Jones, The Three Faces of Eve, Hitler—The Last Ten Days.
TELEVISION: Series: Omnibus (host; 1952-61), m.c. prod. U.N.'s International Zone (host, prod.; Emmy Award, 1958); Masterpiece Theatre (host, 1971-92). Special doc.: America: A Personal History of The United States (writer and narrator; 5 Emmy Awards, 1973; Franklin Medal, Royal Society of Arts, 1973).

COOLIDGE, MARTHA
Director, Writer, Producer. b. New Haven, CT, Aug. 17, 1946. e. Rhode Island Sch. of Design. NYU Inst. of Film and TV grad. sch. m. writer Michael Backes. Dir. short films while in school. Wrote and prod. daily children's tv show Magic Tom in Canada Worked on commercials and political doc. film crews. Prod., dir. and writer of docs. which have won festival awards, including Passing Quietly Through; David: Off and On (American Film Fest.), Old Fashioned Woman (CINE Golden Eagle Award, Blue Ribbon Award, American film festival), Bimbo (short), Magic Tom in Canada. First feature film Not a Pretty Picture (won Blue Ribbon Award, Amer. Film Fest.) Helped start assn. of Indep. Video and Filmmakers, Inc. As an AFI/Academy Intern worked with Robert Wise on his film Audrey Rose, 1976. Wrote orig. story that was filmed as the The Omega Connection. DGA, member of bd. of dirs.; WIF, member bd. of dirs. Acted in film Beverly Hills Cop III.
PICTURES: Not a Pretty Picture, The City Girl, Valley Girl, Joy of Sex, Real Genius, Plain Clothes, Rambling Rose (IFP Spirit Award, 1991), Lost in Yonkers, Angie, Three Wishes, Out to Sea, Aurora Island.
TELEVISION: Movies: Trenchcoat in Paradise, Bare Essentials, Crazy in Love, Introducing Dorothy Dandridge, If These Walls Could Talk 2, The Flamingo Rising, The Ponder Heart. Series: The Twilight Zone, Sledge Hammer (pilot), House and Home (pilot), Leap Years.

COONEY, JOAN GANZ
Executive, Producer. b. Phoenix, AZ, Nov. 30, 1929. e. U. of Arizona. After working as a reporter in Phoenix, moved to NY in 1953 where she wrote soap-opera summaries at NBC. Then was publicist for U.S. Steel Hour. Became producer of live weekly political TV show Court of Reason (Emmy Award) and documentaries (Poverty, Anti-Poverty and the Poor) before founding Children's Television Workshop and Sesame Street in 1969. Currently chmn., exec. committee, CTW. On board of Johnson & Johnson, The Metropolitan Life Ins. Co., the Museum of Television and Radio & the New York and Presbyterian Hospital, Inc. She is a Life Trustee of the National Child Labor Committee and of WNET, Channel 13.

COOPER, BEN
Actor. b. Hartford, CT, Sept. 30, 1933. e. Columbia U. On stage in Life with Father (1942); over 3200 radio, TV appearances

starting from 1945.
PICTURES: Side Street (debut, 1950), Thunderbirds, The Woman They Almost Lynched, A Perilous Journey, Sea of Lost Ships, Flight Nurse, The Outcast, Johnny Guitar, Jubilee Trail, Hell's Outpost, The Eternal Sea, The Last Command, Headline Hunters, The Rose Tattoo, Rebel in Town, A Strange Adventure, Duel at Apache Wells, Outlaw's Son, The Raiders, Gunfight at Comanche Creek, Arizona Raiders, Waco, The Fastest Gun Alive, Red Tomahawk, One More Train to Rob, Support Your Local Gunfighter, Lightning Jack.

COOPER, HAL
Director, Performer. b. New York, NY, Feb. 22, 1923. e. U. of Michigan. m. Marta Salcido; child actor in various radio prog. starting in 1932; featured Bob Emery's Rainbow House, Mutual, 1936-46; asst. dir. Dock St. Theatre, Charleston, SC, 1946-48.
TELEVISION: Your School Reporter, TV Baby Sitter, The Magic Cottage (writer, prod.). Director: Valiant Lady, Search for Tomorrow, Portia Faces Life, Kitty Foyle (also assoc. prod.), Indictment (also prod.), The Happy Time (also assoc. prod.), For Better or Worse (also prod.), The Clear Horizon, Surprise Package (also assoc. prod.), Dick Van Dyke Show, The Art Linkletter Show (also prod.), The Object Is, Death Valley Days, I Dream of Jeannie, That Girl, I Spy, Hazel, Gidget, Gilligan's Island, NYPD, Mayberry, Courtship of Eddie's Father, My World and Welcome to It, The Brady Bunch, The Odd Couple, Mary Tyler Moore, All in the Family. Exec. prod./Director: Maude, Phyl and Mikky, Love, Sidney, Gimme a Break, Empty Nest, Dear John, The Powers That Be, Too Something, Something So Right.

COOPER, JACKIE
Actor, Director, Producer. b. Los Angeles, CA, Sept. 15, 1922. Began theatrical career at age of 3 as m.p. actor; was member of Our Gang comedies (first short was Boxing Gloves in 1929). First starring role in 1931 in Skippy. Worked at every major studio, always with star billing. At 20 enlisted in Navy. After three-yr. tour of duty went to N.Y. to work in live TV. Appeared in 3 plays on B'way stage and in Mr. Roberts on natl. tour and in London. Directed as well as acted in live and filmed TV. Served as v.p. in chg. of TV prod., for Screen Gems, 1964-69, when resigned to return to acting, directing, producing. 2 Emmy Awards for directing M*A*S*H and The White Shadow.
PICTURES: Fox Movietone Follies (feature debut, 1929), Sunny Side Up, Skippy (Acad. Award nom.), Young Donovan's Kid, Sooky, The Champ, When a Feller Needs a Friend, Divorce in the Family, Broadway to Hollywood, The Bowery, Lone Cowboy, Treasure Island, Peck's Bad Boy, Dinky, O'Shaughnessy's Boy, Tough Guy, The Devil Is a Sissy, Boy of the Streets, White Banners, Gangster's Boy, That Certain Age, Newsboys' Home, Scouts to the Rescue (serial), Spirit of Culver, Streets of New York, What a Life, Two Bright Boys, The Big Guy, The Return of Frank James, Seventeen, Gallant Sons, Life With Henry, Ziegfeld Girl, Glamour Boy, Her First Beau, Syncopation, Men of Texas, The Navy Comes Through, Where Are Your Children?, Stork Bites Man, Kilroy Was Here, French Leave, Everything's Ducky, The Love Machine, Stand Up and Be Counted (dir. only), Chosen Survivors, Superman, Superman II, Superman III, Superman IV: The Quest for Peace, Surrender, Going Hollywood: The War Years, Hollywood Chronicles.
TELEVISION: Series: People's Choice (also directed 71 episodes), Hennesey (also dir. 91 epsiodes), Dean Martin Comedy World (host), Mobile One. Movies: Shadow on the Land, Maybe I'll Come Home in the Spring, The Astronaut, The Day the Earth Moved, The Invisible Man, Mobile Two, Operation Petticoat. Director: Having Babies III, Rainbow, White Mama, Rodeo Girl, Sex and the Single Parent, The Ladies, Deacon Street Deer, Perfect Gentlemen, Marathon, Leave 'Em Laughing, Rosie (also prod.), Glitter, The Night They Saved Christmas, Izzy and Moe. Has appeared in 7 tv documentaries since 1990.

COOPER, JEANNE
Actress. r.n. Wilma Jean Cooper. b. Taft, CA, Oct. 25, 1928. e. College of the Pacific, Pasadena Playhouse. Son is actor Corbin Bernsen. Recipient: 3 Soap Opera Update MVP Awards, Soap Opera Digest, Pasadena Playhouse Woman of the Year and Hollywood Entertainment Museum Award.
THEATRE: The Miracle Worker, Plain and Fancy, Picnic, On the Town, The Big Knife, Tonight at 8:30, Dark Side of the Moon, Plaza Suite.
PICTURES: Man From the Alamo, The Redhead From Wyoming, The Houston Story, Red Nightmare, Plunder Road, 5 Steps to Danger, The Intruder, House of Women, 13 West Street, Let No Man Write My Epitaph, The Glory Guys, Tony Rome, The Boston Strangler, There Was a Crooked Man, Kansas City Bomber, All-American Boy, Frozen Assets, The Tomorrow Man.
TELEVISION: Movies: Sweet Hostage, Beyond Suspicion, Gentle Ben, Gentle Ben 2. Series: Bracken's World, The Young and the Restless (1973-). Guest: Perry Mason, The Twilight Zone, Wanted: Dead or Alive, Gunsmoke, The Big Valley, L.A. Law.

COOPERMAN, ALVIN
Producer. b. Brooklyn, NY. Prod., Untouchables, 1961-63; exec. dir., Shubert Theatre Ent. 1963; v.p., special programs, NBC, 1967-68; exec. v.p., Madison Square Garden Center, 1968-72; pres., Madison Square Garden Center, Inc.; founder , Madison Sq. Garden Prods. and Network; chmn. of the board, Athena Communications Corp.; pres., NY Television Academy, 1987-89.
TELEVISION: Producer: Romeo and Juliet (Emmy nom.), Pele's Last Game, The Fourth King, Amahl and the Night Visitors, Live

from Studio 8H—A Tribute to Toscanini (Emmy Award), Live from Studio 8H—An Evening with Jerome Robbins and the New York City Ballet (Emmy Award), Live from Studio 8H—Caruso Remembered, Ain't Misbehavin' (Emmy nom., NAACP Image Award), Pope John Paul II, My Two Loves, Safe Passage, Family Album, U.S.A. (26 half hrs.), Witness to Survival (26 half hrs.), Mobs and Mobsters, Follow The River, Susan B. Anthony Slept Here (documentary).

COPELAND, STEWART
Composer. b. Alexandria, Egypt, July 16, 1952. Drummer and singer for The Police. Member of pop group, Animal Logic.
PICTURES: Rumble Fish, Out of Bounds, Wall Street, Talk Radio, She's Having a Baby, See No Evil Hear No Evil, Riff-Raff, Hidden Agenda, The First Power, Men at Work, Highlander II: The Quickening, Taking Care of Business, Wide Sargasso Sea, Bank Robber, Airborne, Raining Stones, Surviving the Game, Decadence, Fresh, Rapa Nui, Silent Fall, The Girl You Want, The Pallbearer, Boys, The Leopard Son, O Que E Isso Companheiro?, Little Boy Blue, Gridlock'd, Good Burger, Welcome to Woop-Woop, Very Bad Things, Pecker, She's All That, Made Men, Simpatico, Skipped Parts, Boys and Girls, Sunset Strip, On the Line, Deuces Wild, Me and Daphne (short). Actor: Urgh! A Music War, South Park: Bigger Longer and Uncut.
TELEVISION: Movies: White Dwarf, Tyson The Taking of Pelham One Two Three, Futuresport, Legalese. Series: The Equalizer, TV 101, Afterburn, Babylon 5, The Amanda Show, Brutally Normal, Beyond the Glory, Breaking News, Dead Like Me.

COPPOLA, FRANCIS FORD
Director, Writer, Producer. b. Detroit, MI, April 7, 1939. Raised in NYC. Son of late composer Carmine Coppola. Sister is actress Talia Shire. e. Hofstra U, B.A., 1958; UCLA, 1958-68, M.F.A., cinema. While at UCLA was hired as asst. to Roger Corman as dialogue dir., sound man and assoc. prod. 1969; est. American Zoetrope, (later Zoetrope Studios), a prod. center in San Francisco. Publisher, City (magazine, 1975-6). Appeared in documentary Hearts of Darkness: A Filmmaker's Apocalypse.
PICTURES: Tonight for Sure (dir., prod.), The Playgirls and the Bellboy (co-dir., co-s.p. of addtl. sequences for U.S. version), Premature Burial (asst. dir.), Tower of London (dialog. dir.), Battle Beyond the Sun (adapt.), The Young Races (sound, 2nd unit dir.), The Terror (assoc. prod., 2nd unit dir.), Dementia 13 (dir., s.p.), Is Paris Burning? (co-s.p.), This Property Is Condemned (co-s.p.), You're a Big Boy Now (dir., s.p.), The Wild Races (2nd unit dir.), Reflections in a Golden Eye (s.p.), Finian's Rainbow (dir.), The Rain People (dir., s.p.), Patton (co-s.p.; Academy Award, 1970), THX 1138 (exec. prod.), The Godfather (dir., co-s.p.; Academy Award for Best Screenplay, 1972), American Graffiti (exec. prod.), The Great Gatsby (s.p.), The Conversation (dir., co-prod., s.p.), The Godfather Part II (dir., co-s.p., prod.; Academy Awards for Best Picture, Director & Screenplay, 1974), Apocalypse Now (dir., prod., co-s.p., cameo), The Black Stallion (exec. prod.), Kagemusha (co-exec. prod.), One From the Heart (dir., co-s.p.), Hammett (exec. prod.), The Escape Artist (co-exec. prod.), The Black Stallion Returns (exec. prod.), The Outsiders (dir.), Rumble Fish (dir., exec. prod., co-s.p.), The Cotton Club (dir., co-s.p.), Mishima (co-exec. prod.), Peggy Sue Got Married (dir.), Gardens of Stone (dir., co-prod.), Tough Guys Don't Dance (co-exec. prod.), Lionheart (exec. prod.), Tucker: The Man and His Dream (dir.), New York Stories (Life Without Zoe; dir., co-s.p.), The Godfather Part III (dir., co-s.p., prod.), Wind (co-exec. prod.), Bram Stoker's Dracula (dir., co-prod.), The Secret Garden (exec. prod.), Mary Shelley's Frankenstein (prod.), Don Juan DeMarco (exec. prod.), My Family/Mi Familia (exec. prod.), Haunted (co-exec. prod.), Jack, Buddy (exec. prod.), Lanai-Loa (prod.), The Rainmaker (dir., s.p.), The Third Miracle (exec. prod.), Grapefruit Miracle (prod.), Goosed (exec. prod.), The Florentine (prod.), Sleepy Hollow (exec. prod.), Grapefruit Moon (prod.), Monster (exec. prod.), Jeepers Creepers, C.Q. (exec prod.), The Two Fridas, No Such Thing (exec prod.), Pumpkin (exec prod.), Assassination Tango (prod. only), Supernova, Megalopolis, My Dark Places: An L.A. Crime Memoir (exec. prod.), Jeepers Creepers II (exec. prod.), On the Road (prod.).
TELEVISION: Movies: The People (exec. prod.), White Dwarf (co-prod.), Tecumseh: The Last Warrior (co-exec. prod.), Dark Angel (exec. prod.), The Odyssey (exec. prod.), Outrage (exec. prod.), Moby Dick (exec. prod.), The Third Miracle (exec. prod.), Special: Rip Van Winkle (Faerie Tale Theatre; dir.). Series: The Outsiders (exec. prod.), First Wave (exec. prod.), Platinum (exec. prod.)

CORBIN, BARRY
Actor. b. Dawson County, TX, Oct. 16, 1940. e. Texas Tech. U.
PICTURES: Urban Cowboy, Stir Crazy, Any Which Way You Can, Dead and Buried, The Night the Lights Went Out in Georgia, The Best Little Whorehouse in Texas, Six Pack, Honkytonk Man, The Ballad of Gregorio Cortez, WarGames, The Man Who Loved Women, Hard Traveling, What Comes Around, My Science Project, Nothing in Common, Under Cover, Off the Mark, Permanent Record, Critters 2: The Main Course, It Takes Two, Who is Harry Crumb?, Short Time, Ghost Dad, The Hot Spot, Career Opportunities, Solo, Kiss and Tell, Curdled, Judgment Day: The Ellie Nesler Story, Held Up, Race to Space, Nobody Knows, The Journeyman, Drive-In Movie Memories, No One Can Hear You, Dunsmore, Clover Bend, Waitin' to Live, Tin Can Shinny.
TELEVISION: Movies: Rage, This House Possessed, The Killing of Randy Webster, Murder in Texas, Bitter Harvest, A Few Days in Weasel Creek, Fantasies, Prime Suspect, Travis McGee, Flight #90: Disaster on the Potomac, The Jesse Owens Story, Fatal

Vision, I Know My First Name is Steven, Last Flight Out, The Chase, Conagher, Siringo, The Keys, Robin Cook's Virus, Moon Shot, Deadly Family Secrets, My Son Is Easy, Columbo: A Trace of Murder, The Hired Heart, A Face to Kill For, Sealed with a Kiss, Hope Ranch, Monte Walsh. Mini-Series: The Thorn Birds, Lonesome Dove. Series: Boone, Spies, Northern Exposure, The Big Easy, One Tree Hill. Guest: Mash, Murder She Wrote, Hill Street Blues, Murphy Brown, Ellen, The Drew Carey Show.

CORD, ALEX
Actor. r.n. Alexander Viespi. b. Floral Park, NY, May 3, 1933. Early career in rodeo; left to become actor. Studied at Shakespeare Academy (Stratford, Conn.) and Actor's Studio (N.Y.). Spent two yrs. in summer stock; in 1961 went on tour with Stratford Shakespeare Co. Author of novel Sandsong. Co-founder of Chuckers for Charity polo team which has raised more than $2 million for various charities. Champion rodeo team roper and cutting horse rider.
PICTURES: Synanon (debut, 1965), Stagecoach, A Minute to Pray A Second to Die, The Brotherhood, Stiletto, The Last Grenade, The Dead Are Alive, Chosen Survivors, Inn of the Damned, Sidewinder One, Grayeagle, Jungle Warriors, Street Asylum, A Girl to Kill For, Naked Force, THe Naked Truth, CIA Code Name: Alexa, To Be the Best, Hologram Man.
TELEVISION: Movies: The Scorpio Letters, Hunter's Man; Genesis II, Fire !, Beggerman Thief, Goliath Awaits, The Dirty Dozen: The Fatal Mission, University Blues, Dobe and a Company of Heroes (tv documentary, narrator). Series: W.E.B., Cassie & Company, Airwolf, Wild West Showdown (host).

CORDAY, BARBARA
Executive. b. New York, NY, Oct. 15, 1944. Began career as publicist in N.Y. and L.A. Turned to writing for TV; named v.p., ABC-TV, in chg. of comedy series development. 1982-84, headed own production co. in association with Columbia Pictures TV; June, 1984-87 pres., Columbia Pictures TV; CBS Entertainment, exec. v.p. primetime programs, 1988-1990. Producer, Knots Landing tv series, 1992; pres., New World Television, 1993-1994. Member: Caucus of Writers, Producers & Directors; Hollywood Women's Coalition.
TELEVISION: Writer: American Dream (pilot), Turnabout, Cagney and Lacey (also co-creator).

COREY, JEFF
Actor. b. New York, NY, Aug. 10, 1914. e. Feagin Sch. of Dram. Art. On stage in Leslie Howard prod. of Hamlet, 1936; Life and Death of an American, In the Matter of J. Robert Oppenheimer, Hamlet-Mark Taper Forum, King Lear, Love Suicide at Schofield Barracks.
PICTURES: All That Money Can Buy, Syncopation, The Killers, Ramrod, Joan of Arc, Roughshod, Black Shadows, Bagdad, Outriders, The Devil and Daniel Webster, My Friend Flicka, Canyon City, Singing Guns, Seconds, In Cold Blood, Golden Bullet, Boston Strangler, True Grit, Butch Cassidy and The Sundance Kid, Beneath the Planet of the Apes, Getting Straight, Little Big Man, They Call Me Mister Tibbs, Clear and Present Danger, High Flying Lowe, Catlow, Something Evil, Premonition, Shine, Rooster, Oh God!, Butch and Sundance: The Early Days, Up River, Conan the Destroyer, Cognac, Messenger of Death, Bird on a Wire, The Judas Project, Deception, Beethoven's 2nd, Surviving the Game, Color of Night, Home of the Brave, Ted.
TELEVISION: Guest: The Untouchables, The Beachcomber,. Outer Limits, Channing, The Doctors and the Nurses, Perry Mason, Gomer Pyle, Wild Wild West, Run for Your Life, Bonanza, Iron Horse, Judd for Defense, Garrisons Gorillas, Gunsmoke, Hawaii Five O, Star Trek, The Psychiatrist, Night Gallery, Alias Smith and Jones, Sixth Sense, Hawkins, Owen Marshall, Police Story, Bob Newhart Show, Six Million Dollar Man, Doctors Hospital, Starsky and Hutch, Land of the Free, Kojak, McCloud, Captains Courageous, Bionic Woman, Barney Miller, One Day at a Time, The Pirate, Lou Grant, The Powers of Jonathan Starr, Cry for the Strangers, Today's FBI, Knots Landing, Archie Bunker's Place, Faerie Tale Theatre, Night Court, Helltown, Morning Star/Evening Star, New Love American Style, Starman, The A Team, Roseanne, Wolf, Jake and the Fatman, Rose and the Jackal, To My Daughter, Payoff, Sinatra, The Marshal, Home Court, Picket Fences, Murphy Brown, Nothing Sacred. Movies: A Deadly Silence, The Balcony, Yellow Canary, Lady in a Cage.

CORMAN, GENE
Producer. r.n. Eugene H. Corman. b. Detroit, MI, Sept. 24, 1927. e. Stanford U. Went to work for MCA as agent 1950-57; left to produce his first feature film, Hot Car Girl. Partner with brother Roger in Corman Company and New World Distributors. Vice pres. 20th Century Fox Television, 1983-87; exec. v.p. worldwide production, 21st Century Film Corp.
PICTURES: Attack of the Giant Leeches, Not of This Earth, Blood and Steel, Valley of the Redwoods, Secret of the Purple Reef, Beast from Haunted Cave, Cat Burglar, The Intruder, Tobruk, You Can't Win Em All, Cool Breeze, Hit Man, The Slams, Von Richthofen and Brown, I Escaped from Devil's Island, Secret Invasion, Vigilante Force, F.I.S.T. (exec. prod.), The Big Red One, If You Could See What I Hear, Paradise, A Man Called Sarge, Harold Robbins' Body Parts.
TELEVISION: What's In It For Harry, A Woman Called Golda (Emmy and Christopher Awards as prod.), Mary and Joseph, a Love Story, Blood Ties.

CORMAN, ROGER WILLIAM
Executive, Director, Producer, Writer, Distributor. b. Detroit, MI, April 5, 1921. e. Stanford U. 1947; Oxford U., England 1950. U.S. Navy 1944; 20th Century-Fox, production dept., 1948, story analyst 1948-49; Literary agent, 1951-52; story, s.p., assoc. prod., Highway Dragnet. Formed Roger Corman Prod. and Filmgroup. Prod. over 200 feature films and dir. over 60 of them. Formed production-releasing company, org., New World Pictures, Inc., 1970. Formed prod. co., Concorde, 1984; distribution co., New Horizons, 1985. On TV acted in film Body Bags. Recipient of LA Film Critics Award for Career Achievement, 1997. Has more than 400 project credits to his name.
PICTURES: *Director:* Five Guns West (dir. debut, 1955), Apache Woman, Swamp Women, The Day the World Ended, The Oklahoma Woman, The Gunslinger, It Conquered the World, Not of This Earth, Naked Paradise (Thunder Over Hawaii), Attack of the Crab Monsters, Rock All Night, Teenage Doll, Carnival Rock, Sorority Girl, Saga of the Viking Women and Their Voyage to the Waters of the Great Sea Serpent, The Undead, War of the Satellites, She Gods of Shark Reef, Machine Gun Kelly, Teenage Caveman, I Mobster, A Bucket of Blood, The Wasp Woman, Ski Troop Attack, House of Usher, The Little Shop of Horrors, The Last Woman on Earth, Creature From the Haunted Sea, Atlas, The Pit and the Pendulum, The Intruder, The Premature Burial, Tales of Terror, Tower of London, The Raven, The Terror, X—The Man With the X Ray Eyes, The Haunted Palace, The Young Racers, The Secret Invasion, The Masque of the Red Death, Tomb of Ligeia, The Wild Angels, The St. Valentine's Day Massacre, The Trip, Target: Harry (credited as Henry Neill), Bloody Mama, Gas-s-s-s, Von Richtofen and Brown, Frankenstein Unbound (also s.p.). *Producer:* Boxcar Bertha, Big Bad Mama, Death Race 2000, Eat My Dust, Capone, Jackson County Jail, Fighting Mad, Thunder & Lightning, Grand Theft Auto, I Never Promised You A Rose Garden, Deathsport, Avalanche, Battle Beyond the Stars, St. Jack, Love Letters, Smokey Bites the Dust, Galaxy of Terror, Slumber Party Massacre Part II, Death Stalker, Barbarian Queen, Munchies, Stripped to Kill, Big Bad Mama II, Daddy's Boys, Lords of the Deep (also actor), The Terror Within, Two to Tango, Time Trackers, Heroes Stand Alone, Bloodfist, Silk 2, Edgar Allan Poe's The Masque of Red Death, Haunted Symphony, Midnight Tease. *Exec. Prod.:* Black Scorpion, Black Scorpion 2, Not of This Earth, Not Like Us, Sweet Revenge (co-exec. prod.), The Drifter, Singles, Crime Zone, Watcher, The Lawless Land, Stripped to Kill 2, Hollywood Boulevard II, Rock and Roll High School Forever, Bloodfist II (prod.), One Night Stand, Haunted Sea, Future Fear, Falling fire, Eruption, Don't Sleep Alone, Detonator, Criminal Affairs, Club Vampire, Circuit Breaker, Born Bad, Alien Avengers II, Spacejacked, The Protector, Urban Justice, Striptease II, Termination Man, Starquest II, Shadowdancer, The Sea Wolf, Overdrive, My Brother's War, Macon County Jail, Knocking On Death's Door, Haunted Sea, Future Fear, Falling Fire, Eruption, Don't Sleep Alone, Criminal Fears, Club Vampire, Circuit Breaker, Born Bad, Black Thunder, Detonator, Watchers Reborn, A Very Unlucky Leprechaun, Vatican Air Two, Stray Bullet, Star Portal, Running Woman, Desert Thunder, The Haunting of Hell House, Shadow, The Protector, The Suicide Club, The Doorway, Avalanche Alley, The Arena, Raptor, Hard As Nails, Escape from Afghanistan (video), Sting of the Black Scorpion (video), Wolfhound (video), Slaughter Studios (video), Shakedown (video, Barbarian (video), Firefight, . *Actor:* The Godfather Part II, Cannonball, The Howling, The State of Things, Swing Shift, The Silence of the Lambs, Philadelphia., Apollo 13, Some Nudity Required, Scream 3, The Independent, A Galaxy Far Far Away.
TELEVISION: *Movie Series:* Roger Corman Presents (exec. prod.). *Movie:* The Second Civil War, various others.
AUTHOR: How I Made a Hundred Movies in Hollywood and Never Lost a Dime.

CORNELL, JOHN
Producer, Director, Writer. b. Kalgoorlie, Western Australia, 1941. m. actress Delvene Delancy. Grew up Bunbury. e. studied pharmacy for two years in Perth. Won internship at Western Australian Newspapers at 19, becoming columnist then London editor at 26. As Melbourne prod. of TV show, A Current Affair, discovered bridge rigger Paul Hogan. Put him on show, became his manager and formed JP Productions with him in 1972. Prod. and appeared on The Paul Hogan Show. Formed movie co. with Hogan, Rimfire Films.
PICTURES: Crocodile Dundee (prod., co-s.p.), Crocodile Dundee II (prod., dir., editor), Almost an Angel (dir., prod.).

CORNFELD, STUART
Producer. b. Los Angeles, CA. e. U. of California, Berkeley. Entered America Film Institute's Center for Advanced Film Studies as producing fellow, 1975. Joined Brooksfilm as asst. to Mel Brooks on High Anxiety. Assoc. prod., History of the World Part I.
PICTURES: Fatso, The Elephant Man, (exec. prod.), Fast Times at Richmont High (actor only), National Lampoon's European Vacation (co-prod.), Girls Just Want to Have Fun (exec. prod.), The Fly, Moving, The Fly II (prod.), Hider in the House (co-prod.), Darkman (actor only), Kafka, Wilder Napalm, Mimic (co-exec. prod.), Zoolander, Duplex, What Makes Sammy Run.

CORRI, ADRIENNE
Actress. r.n. Adrienne Riccoboni. b. Glasgow, Scotland, Nov. 13, 1933. e. RADA at 13; parts in several stage plays including The Human Touch. Numerous TV appearances.
PICTURES: The Romantic Age (Naughty Arlette; debut, 1949), The River, Quo Vadis, The Little Kidnappers, The Sinners, Devil Girl From Mars, Meet Mr. Callaghan, Lease of Life, Make Me an Offer, Triple Blackmail, The Feminine Touch, Behind the Headlines, The Shield of Faith, Three Men in a Boat, Second Fiddle, The Surgeon's Knife, The Big Chance, Corridors of Blood, The Rough and the Smooth (Portrait of a Sinner), The Tell-Tale Heart, Sword of Freedom, The Hellfire, Dynamite Jack, Sword of Lancelot, A Study in Terror, Bunny Lake Is Missing, Doctor Zhivago, Woman Times Seven, The Viking Queen, Africa—Texas Style!, The File of the Golden Goose, Cry Wolf, Moon Zero Two, Vampire Circus, A Clockwork Orange, Madhouse, Rosebud, Revenge of the Pink Panther, The Human Factor.

CORT, BUD
Actor. r.n. Walter Edward Cox. b. New Rochelle, NY, March 29, 1950. e. NYU School of the Arts. Stage debut in Wise Child, B'way. L.A. theatre includes Forget-Me-Not Lane, August 11 1947, Endgame (Dramalogue Award), Demon Wine, The Seagull, He Who Gets Slapped. Founding member of L.A. Classical Theatre. Theatrical film debut as extra in Up the Down Staircase 1967. Television debut in The Doctors.
PICTURES: Sweet Charity, M*A*S*H, Gas-s-s-s, The Traveling Executioner, Brewster McCloud, Harold and Maude, Die Laughing, Why Shoot the Teacher?, She Dances Alone, Hysterical, Electric Dreams (voice), Love Letters, The Secret Diary of Sigmund Freud, Maria's Lovers, Invaders from Mars, Love at Stake, The Chocolate War, Out of the Dark, Brain Dead, Going Under, Ted and Venus (also dir., co-s.p.), Girl in the Cadillac, Heat, Theodore Rex, Sweet Jane, I Woke Up Early One Day I Died, Dogma, But I'm a Cheerleader, South of Heaven West of Hell, The Million Dollar Hotel, Coyote Ugly, Pollock, Made, The Big Empty.
TELEVISION: *Special:* Bernice Bobs Her Hair. *Guest:* Faerie Tale Theatre (The Nightingale), The Hitchhiker (Made for Each Other), The New Twilight Zone, Midnight Caller, Gun. *Movies:* Brave New World, The Bates Motel, And the Band Played On, Jitters.

CORT, ROBERT W.
Executive. e. U. of Pennsylvania (Phi Beta Kappa). Moved into feature prod. after having worked primarily in marketing/advertising. Joined Columbia Pictures as v.p., 1976; elevated to v.p., adv./pub./promo. Named exec. v.p. of mktg. for 20th-Fox, 1980. Moved into feature prod. as senior v.p., 1981. In 1983 named exec. v.p., prod., 20th-Fox Prods. 1985, joined Interscope Comm. as pres. Partner in Cort/Madden Prods. In 2001 formed Robert Cort Productions.
PICTURES: *Prod.:* Critical Condition, Outrageous Fortune, Revenge of the Nerds II, Three Men and a Baby, The Seventh Sign, Cocktail, Bill & Ted's Excellent Adventure (exec. prod.), Renegades (exec. prod.), Blind Fury (exec. prod.), An Innocent Man, The First Power (exec. prod.), Bird on a Wire, Arachnophobia, Three Man and a Little Lady, Eve of Destruction, Class Action, Bill & Ted's Bogus Journey, Paradise, The Hand That Rocks the Cradle, The Cutting Edge, FernGully, The Gun in Betty Lou's Handbag, Out on a Limb, Jersey Girl, Holy Matrimony, Imaginary Crimes, Operation Dumbo Drop, The Tie That Binds, Mr. Holland's Opus, The Associate (exec. prod.), Snow White (exec.), The Odd Couple II, The Out-Of-Towners, Runaway Bride, Save the Last Dance, The Colony, Against the Ropes.
TELEVISION: *Movies (co-exec. prod.):* A Mother's Courage (Emmy Award), A Part of the Family, Body Language, In the Company of Spies, Harlan County War, The Rats.

CORTESE, VALENTINA
Actress. b. Milan, Italy, Jan. 1, 1924. Started career at 15 in Orizzonte Dipinto while studying at Rome Acad. of Dramatic Art. Following several appearances in European films brought to Hollywood by 20th Century-Fox, 1949; billed in U.S. films as Valentina Cortesa. Experience on dramatic stage in variety of roles inc. Shakespeare, O'Neill, Shaw.
PICTURES: Orrizonte Dipinto (debut, 1940), Primo Amore, A Yank in Rome, A Bullet for Strefano, Les Miserables, The Glass Mountain (English-language debut, 1950), Black Magic, Malaya, Thieves Highway, Shadow of the Eagle, The House on Telegraph Hill, Secret People, Lulu, Forbidden Women (Angels of Darkness), The Barefoot Contessa, Le Amiche, Magic Fire, Calabuch, Barabbas, The Evil Eye, The Visit, The Possessed, Juliet of the Spirits, Black Sun, The Legend of Lylah Clare, The Secret of Santa Vittoria, First Love, Give Her the Moon, The Assassination of Trotsky, Brother Sun Sister Moon, Day for Night (Acad. Award nom.), Tendre Dracula, Widow's Nest, When Time Ran Out, La Ferdinanda, Blue Tango, The Adventures of Baron Munchausen, The Betrothed, Young Toscanini, Buster's Bedroom, Sparrow.

CORWIN, BRUCE CONRAD
Exhibitor. b. Los Angeles, CA, June 11, 1940. e. Wesleyan U. CEO, Metropolitan Theatres Corp.; Past pres., Variety Children's Charities Tent 25; Board of Trustees U.C.S.B. Foundation; pres. emeritus, L.A. Children's Museum; chmn., Coro Natl. Board of Governors; Past President of the Foundation of Motion Picture Pioneers and Pioneer of the Year, 1977.

CORWIN, NORMAN
Writer, Producer, Director. b. Boston, MA, May 3, 1910. Sports ed. Greenfield, Mass. Daily Recorder, 1926-29; radio ed., news commentator, Springfield Republican & Daily News, 1929-36; prog. dir., CBS, 1938. Author of Thirteen by Corwin, More by

Corwin, Untitled & Other Plays, The Plot to Overthrow Christmas, Dog in the Sky, Overkill and Megalove, Prayer for the 70's, Holes in a Stained Glass Window, Trivializing America; taught courses at UCLA, USC, San Diego State U. Faculty, U.S.C. Sch. of Journalism, 1980-; sec., M.P. Academy Foundation, 1985. First v.p., Motion Picture Acad., 1989. Inducted into Radio Hall of Fame, Chicago Museum, 1993. Writer-host Academy Leaders (PBS). Chmn. Doc. Award Com., Motion Picture Acad. 1965-91; elected to bd. of gov., 1980; first v.p., 1988-89; chmn., writers' exec. comm., M.P. Academy; co-chmn. scholarship com., M.P. Academy; mem.: Film Advisory Bd.; bd. of trustees, Advisory Board, Filmex; bd. of dirs., WGA. Books incl. Directors Guild Oral History, Years of the Electric Ear, Norman Corwin's Letters.
THEATRE: The Rivalry, The World of Carl Sandburg, The Hyphen, Overkill and Megalove, Cervantes. Together Tonight: Jefferson Hamilton and Burr.
PICTURES: Once Upon a Time, The Blue Veil, The Grand Design, Scandal in Scourie, Lust for Life (Acad. Award nom. best adapt. s.p.), The Story of Ruth, Madison Avenue, .
TELEVISION: Inside the Movie Kingdom, The FDR series, The Plot to Overthrow Christmas, Norman Corwin Presents, The Court Martial of General Yamashita, The World at War (miniseries documentary, 1974), Network at 50.

COSBY, BILL
Actor, Comedian. b. Philadelphia, PA, July 12, 1938. e. Temple U., U. of Mass., Ed.D. Served in United States Navy Medical Corps. Started as night club entertainer.
AUTHOR: The Wit and Wisdom of Fat Albert, Bill Cosby's Personal Guide to Power Tennis, Fatherhood, Time Flies.
COMEDY ALBUMS: Bill Cosby Is a Very Funny Fellow... Right! (Grammy Award, 1964), I Started Out As a Child (Grammy Award, 1965), Why Is There Air? (Grammy Award, 1966), Wonderfulness (Grammy Award, 1967), Revenge (Grammy Award, 1967), To Russell My Brother Whom I Slept With (Grammy Award, 1969), Bill Cosby Is Not Himself These Days, Rat Own Rat Own Rat Own, My Father Confused Me... What Must I Do? What Must I Do?, Disco Bill, Bill's Best Friend, Cosby and the Kids, It's True It's True, Bill Cosby - Himself, 200 MPH, Silverthroat, Hooray for the Salvation Army Band, 8:15 12:15, For Adults Only, Bill Cosby Talks to Kids About Drugs, Inside the Mind of Bill Cosby.
RADIO: The Bill Cosby Radio Program.
PICTURES: Hickey and Boggs (debut, 1972), Man and Boy, Uptown Saturday Night, Let's Do It Again, Mother Jugs and Speed, A Piece of the Action, California Suite, The Devil and Max Devlin, Bill Cosby Himself, Leonard Part VI (also co-prod., story), Ghost Dad, The Meteor Man, Jack, 4 Little Girls, Comedian (documentary).
TELEVISION: Series: I Spy (3 Emmy Awards for Best Actor: 1966, 1967, 1968), The Bill Cosby Show (1969-71), The New Bill Cosby Show (1972-73), Fat Albert and the Cosby Kids, Cos, The New Fat Albert Show (Emmy Award, 1981), The Cosby Show (1984-92), A Different World (exec. prod. only), You Bet Your Life, Here and Now (exec. prod. only), The Cosby Mysteries, Cosby (also prod., 1996-), Kids Say the Darndest Things. Specials: The Bill Cosby Special, The Second Bill Cosby Special, Fat Albert Easter Special (voice), Cosby Salutes Alvin Ailey, The Kennedy Center Honors, Intimate Portrait: Phylicia Rashad, Starz 10th Anniversary. Movies: To All My Friends on Shore (also exec. prod., story, music), Top Secret, I Spy Returns (also co-exec. prod.), The Cosby Show Reunion: A Look Back.

COSMATOS, GEORGE PAN
Director, Producer, Writer. b. Tuscany, Italy, Jan. 4, 1947. e. London U., London Film School. Asst. on such films as Exodus, Zorba the Greek.
PICTURES: Director: Restless (also co-prod., s.p.), Massacre in Rome (also co-s.p.), The Cassandra Crossing (also co-s.p.), Escape to Athena (also co-s.p.), Of Unknown Origin, Rambo: First Blood Part II, Cobra, Leviathan, Tombstone, Shadow Conspiracy, We Get To Win This Time (video short).

COSTA-GAVRAS (CONSTANTIN)
Director, Writer. r.n. Konstaninos Gavras. b. Athens, Greece, Feb. 13, 1933. French citizen. e. Studied at the Sorbonne; Hautes Études Cinematographique, (IDHEC). Was leading ballet dancer in Greece before the age of 20. Worked as second, then first assistant to Marcel Ophuls, Rene Clair, Rene Clement and Jacques Demy. Pres. of the Cinematheque Francaise, 1982-87. Appeared as actor in film Madame Rosa.
PICTURES: Director: The Sleeping Car Murders (also s.p.; debut, 1965), Un Homme De Trop/Shock Troops (also s.p.), Z (also co-s.p.; 2 Acad. Award noms.), The Confession, State of Siege (also co- s.p.), Special Section (also co-s.p.), Clair de Femme (also s.p.), Missing (also co-s.p.; Acad. Award for Best Adapted s.p., 1982; Palm d'Or at Cannes Film Fest.), Hannah K. (also prod.), Spies Like Us (actor only), Family Business (also s.p.), Betrayed, Music Box (Golden Bear, Berlin Festival, 1989), The Little Apocalypse, Lumiere & Company, Mad City, Amen.

COSTNER, KEVIN
Actor. b. Lynwood, CA, Jan. 18, 1955. e. CA. State U, Fullerton majored in marketing. Acted with South Coast Actors' Co-op, community theater gp. while at coll. After grad. took marketing job which lasted 30 days. Early film work in low budget exploitation film, Sizzle Beach, 1974. Then one line as Luther Adler in Frances. Role in The Big Chill was edited from final print. 1989, set up own prod. co. Tig Prods. at Raleigh Studios.
PICTURES: Sizzle Beach U.S.A., Shadows Run Black, Night

Shift, Chasing Dreams, Table for Five, Testament, Stacy's Knights, The Gunrunner, Fandango, Silverado, American Flyers, The Untouchables, No Way Out, Bull Durham, Field of Dreams, Revenge (also exec. prod.), Dances With Wolves (also dir., co-prod.; Academy Awards for Best Picture & Director, 1990), Robin Hood: Prince of Thieves, JFK, The Bodyguard (also co-prod.), A Perfect World, Wyatt Earp (also co-prod.), Rapa Nui (co-prod. only), The War, Waterworld (also co-prod.), Tin Cup, The Postman (also dir., co-prod.), For Love of the Game, Message in a Bottle (also prod.), Play it to the Bone, Thirteen Days, 3000 Miles to Graceland, Dragonfly, Open Range.
TELEVISION: Special: 500 Nations (co-exec. prod., host).

COUNTER, J. NICHOLAS, III
Executive. e. Univ. of Colorado, B.S., Stanford, J.D.
Law partner at Mitchell, Silberberg & Knupp until he joined the Alliance of Motion Picture and Television Producers in 1982. Has been pres. of AMPTP from 1982-present. In that position, he represents the major studios and major independent producers of television and theatrical motion pictures in industry-wide labor negotiation, including contracts with SAG, AFTRA and WGA. Member, Natl Film Preservation Board, Ent. Industry Development Corp. Trustee for over 14 industry health and pension plans.

COURIC, KATIE
Newcaster. b. Arlington, VA, Jan. 7, 1957. e. Univ. of VA. Started as desk asst. at ABC News, then assignment editor for CNN, reporter for WTVJ, NBC affiliate in Miami. Moved to NBC's Washington D.C. station WRC. Became natl. correspondent for The Today Show, 1989, then co-host in 1991. Served as co-host of Macy's Thanksgiving Day Parade, 1991-present. Regular on Dateline NBC, host of XIX Winter Olympics Opening Ceremony. Appears in the film Austin Powers in Goldmember. TV series documentary host of Freedom: A History of Us.

COURTENAY, TOM
Actor. b. Hull, England, Feb. 25, 1937. e. University Coll., London, Royal Acad. of Dramatic Art, 1960-61; Old Vic.
THEATRE: Billy Liar, Andorra, Hamlet, She Stoops to Conquer, Otherwise Engaged (N.Y. debut), The Dresser, Poison Pen, Uncle Vanya, Moscow Stations, etc.
PICTURES: The Loneliness of the Long Distance Runner (debut, 1962), Private Potter, Billy Liar, King and Country, Operation Crossbow, King Rat, Doctor Zhivago (Acad. Award nom.), The Night of the Generals, The Day the Fish Came Out, A Dandy in Aspic, Otley, One Day in the Life of Ivan Denisovich, Catch Me a Spy, The Dresser (Acad. Award nom.), Happy New Year, Leonard Part VI, Let Him Have It, The Last Butterfly, The Boy From Mercury, Whatever Happened to Harold Smith, Last Orders, Nicholas Nickleby.
TELEVISION: Series: The Lads, Ghosts, Private Potter. Movies/Specials: I Heard the Owl Call My Name, Jesus of Nazareth, Absent Friends, Chekhov in Yalta, Redemption, The Old Curiosity Shop, A Very English Marriage, The John Thaw Story.

COURTLAND, JEROME
Actor, Producer, Director. b. Knoxville, TN, Dec. 27, 1926. Began career in 40s as actor, then turned to directing and producing.
PICTURES: Actor: Kiss and Tell, Man from Colorado, Battleground, The Barefoot Mailman, The Bamboo Prison, Tonka, Black Spurs. Director: Run, Cougar, Run, Diamond on Wheels. Producer: Escape to Witch Mountain, Ride a Wild Pony, Return from Witch Mountain, Pete's Dragon, The Devil & Max Devlin, Amy.
TELEVISION: Actor: The Saga of Andy Burnett, Tonka. Director: Hog Wild (also co-prod.), Harness Fever, Knots Landing, Dynasty, Hotel, Love Boat, Fantasy Island. Director: Falcon Crest, Matt Houston, Hotel, The Colbys, Island Son.

COUTARD, RAOUL
Cinematographer. b. Paris, France, Sept. 16, 1924. Spent 4 years in Vietnam working for French Military Info. Service, later a civilian photographer for Time and Paris-Match. During WWII worked in photo labs. After war returned to France and formed prod. co. making documentaries. Joined Jean-Luc Godard as his cinematographer on Breathless (1960). His use of hand-held camera and natural light established him as a seminal cameraman of the French New Wave, working with Godard, Truffaut and later with Costa Gavras. Director: Hoa Binh (1971).
PICTURES: Breathless, Shoot the Piano Player, Lola, Jules and Jim, The Army Game, My Life to Live, Love at Twenty (segment), Les Carabiniers, Contempt, Alphaville, The Soft Skin, Male Companion, Pierrot le Fou, Made in USA, Weekend, Sailor From Gibraltar, The Bride Wore Black, Z, The Confession, Le Crabe Tambour, Passion, First Name: Carmen, Dangerous Moves, Salt on the Skin, La Garce, Max My Love, Burning Beds, Let Sleeping Cops Lie, Bethune: The Making of a Hero, Punctured Life, The Birth of Love, Happiness Is No Joke, The Phantom Heart, Wild Innocence.

COWAN, WARREN J.
Publicist. b. New York, NY, Mar. 13. e. Townsend Harris H.S., UCLA, graduated 1941. Entered public relations, 1941, with Alan Gordon & Associates; three yrs. Air Force; joined Henry C. Rogers office in 1945; became partner, 1949, and changed name to Rogers & Cowan Public Relations; advisor, Rogers & Cowan, Inc., 1960; pres., Rogers & Cowan, Inc., 1964; named bd. chmn.,

1983. Retired as Rogers & Cowan chmn. in 1992. 1994, started new P.R. company, Warren Cowan & Assocs. Served as natl. communications chmn. for United Way of America. On advisory bd. of the Natl. Assoc. of Film Commissioners; 2nd Decade Council of American Film Inst. On bd. L.A. County High School for the Arts, Scott Newman Center, Young Musicians Foundation.

COX, ALEX
Director, Writer. b. Liverpool, England, Dec. 15, 1954. Studied law at Oxford U. where he dir. and acted in plays for school drama society. Studied film prod. Bristol U. Received Fulbright Scholarship to study at UCLA film school, 1981.
PICTURES: Repo Man (also s.p.), Sid and Nancy (also co-s.p.), Straight to Hell (also co-s.p.), Walker (also co-editor), Highway Patrolman, Floundering (actor only), Dead Beat (actor only), The Queen of the Night (actor only), The Winner (also actor), Death and the Compass (also actor), Perdita Durango (actor only), Waldo's Hawaiian Holiday, Fear and Loathing in Las Vegas (s.p. only), Three Businessmen (also dir.), Kurosawa: The Last Emperor, Revengers Tragedy, Herod's Law, Stanley Kubrick: A Life in Pictures (documentary), A Revenger's Tragedy (acting, dir.).
TELEVISION: Movies: Mike Hama-Private Detective: Mike Hama Must Die! (dir., s.p.), The Inspector Lynley Mysteries: Playing for the Ashes (location mgr.) In His Life: The John Lennon Story, A Hard Look.

COX, BRIAN
Actor. b. Dundee, Scotland, June 1, 1946. e. London Acad. of Music & Dramatic Art. Acted with Royal Lyceum Edinburgh and Birmingham Rep. Theatre; also season with Royal Shakespeare Company. Video: Acting and Tragedy. Author: The Lear Diaries, Salem in Moscow.
THEATRE: The Master Builder, King Lear, Richard III, Fashion, Rat in the Skull (Olivier Award; also B'way), Titus Andronicus (Olivier Award), Penny for a Song, St. Nicholas, Skylight.
PICTURES: Nicholas and Alexandra, In Celebration, Manhunter, Shoot for the Sun, Hidden Agenda, Prince of Jutland, Iron Will, Rob Roy, Braveheart, Chain Reaction, The Boxer, The Long Kiss Goodnight, Kiss the Girls, Rushmore, Desperate Measures, The Minus Man, The Corruptor, For Love of the Game, Longitude, The Invention of Dr. Morel, Complicity, Mad About Mambo, Whipped, A Shot at Glory, Saltwater, Super Troopers, L.I.E., Cocozza's Way, The Affair of the Necklace, The Reckoning, Murder By Numbers, Bug, The Rookie, The Bourne Identity, Adaptation, The Ring, X2, Sin. Director/Writer: Scorpion Spring.
TELEVISION: Inspector Morse, Therese Raquin, Pope John Paul II, Florence Nightingale, Beryl Markham: A Shadow on the Sun, Murder by Moonlight, Six Characters in Search of an Author, Picasso, The Negotiator, The Big Battalions, Bach, Bothwell, Churchill's People, Master of Ballantrae, Lost Language of Cranes, The Changeling, Secret Weapon, Witness Against Hitler, Poodle Springs, Smallpox 2002: Silent Weapon (narrator).

COX ARQUETTE, COURTENEY
Actress. b. Birmingham, AL, June 15, 1964. m. actor David Arquette. Left AL to pursue modeling career in NY. Dir. Brian DePalma selected her to be the young woman who jumps out of audience and dances with Bruce Springsteen in his music video Dancing in the Dark. This break led to featured role in short-lived TV series Misfits of Science (1985-86).
PICTURES: Masters of the Universe, Down Twisted, Cocoon: The Return, Mr. Destiny, Blue Desert, Shaking the Tree, The Opposite Sex, Ace Ventura—Pet Detective, Scream, Commandments, Scream 2, The Runner, Scream 3, The Shrink is In (also exec. prod.), Alien Love Triangle, 3000 Miles to Graceland, Get Well Soon, Alien Love Triangle (short), November.
TELEVISION: Movies: I'll Be Home for Christmas, Roxanne: The Prize Pulitzer, Till We Meet Again, Curiosity Kills, Battling for Baby, Topper, Sketch Artist II: Hands That See. Series: Misfits of Science, Family Ties, The Trouble With Larry, Friends.

COX, RONNY
Actor. b. Cloudcroft, NM, July 23, 1938. e. Eastern New Mexico Univ.
PICTURES: The Happiness Cage (debut, 1972), Deliverance, Hugo the Hippo (voice), Bound for Glory, The Car, Gray Lady Down, Harper Valley P.T.A., The Onion Field, Taps, The Beast Within, Some Kind of Hero, Courage (Raw Courage), Beverly Hills Cop, Vision Quest, Hollywood Vice Squad, Steele Justice, Beverly Hills Cop II, Robocop, One Man Force, Loose Cannons, Martians Go Home!, Total Recall, Scissors, Captain America, Past Midnight, Murder at 1600, Frog and Wombat, Forces of Nature, Deep Blue Sea, The Boys of Sunset Ridge, American Outlaws, Losing Grace, Crazy As Hell.
TELEVISION: Movies: The Connection, A Case of Rape, Who Is the Black Dahlia?, Having Babies, Corey: For the People, The Girl Called Hatter Fox, Lovey: A Circle of Children Part II, Transplant, When Hell Was in Session, Fugitive Family, Courage of Kavik: The Wolf Dog, The Last Song, Alcatraz—The Whole Shocking Story, Fallen Angel, Two of a Kind, The Jesse Owens Story, The Abduction of Kari Swenson, Baby Girl Scott, In the Line of Duty: The FBI Murders, The Comeback, When We Were Young, Murder in Mind, Perry Mason: The Case of the Heartbroken Bride, A Part of the Family, Rebound: The Legend of Earl 'The Goat' Manigault, Never Give Up: The Jimmy V Story, Childhood Sweethearts, Y2K, Secret of Giving, Love Lessons, Point of Origin. Mini-Series: Favorite Son, From the Earth to the Moon, Perfect Murder Perfect Town. Specials: Our Town, Chicago 7 Trial.

Series: Apple's Way, Spencer, St. Elsewhere, Cop Rock, Sweet Justice, Spawn (voice), The Agency.

COYOTE, PETER
Actor. r.n. Peter Cohon. b. New York, NY, 1942. Studied with San Francisco Actors Workshop. Theatre includes The Minstrel Show (dir.), Olive Pits (also co-writer), The Red Snake, True West, The Abduction of Kari Swenson, Baby Girl Scott.
PICTURES: Die Laughing (debut, 1980), Tell Me a Riddle, Southern Comfort, The Pursuit of D.B. Cooper, E.T.: The Extra Terrestrial, Endangered Species, Timerider, Cross Creek, Slayground, Stranger's Kiss, Heartbreakers, The Legend of Billie Jean, Jagged Edge, Outrageous Fortune, A Man in Love, Stacking, Heart of Midnight, The Man Inside, Crooked Hearts, Exposure, Bitter Moon, Kika, That Eye The Sky, Moonlight and Valentino, Unforgettable, Sphere, Patch Adams, The Basket, Last Call, Random Hearts, Erin Brokovich, Red Letters, More Dogs Than Bones, A Time For Dancing, Jack the Dog, Suddenly Naked, Purpose, A Walk to Remember, Femme Fatale, Written in Blood, Northfork, The Hebrew Hammer, Bon voyage.
TELEVISION: Movies: Alcatraz: The Whole Shocking Story, The People vs. Jean Harris, Isabel's Choice, Best Kept Secrets, Scorned and Swindled, Time Flyer, Child's Cry, Sworn to Silence, Echoes in the Darkness, Unconquered, A Seduction in Travis County, Living a Lie, Keeper of the City, Breach of Conduct, Buffalo Girls, Execution of Justice, Founding Fathers (voice), Midwives, Founding Brothers (tv documentary, voice), Seth Eastman: Painting the Dakota (tv documentary, narrator).

CRAIG, MICHAEL
Actor. r.n. Michael Gregson. b. Poona, India, Jan. 27, 1929. At 16 joined Merchant Navy. 1949, returned to England and made stage debut in repertory. Entered industry as extra in 1949.
PICTURES: Passport to Pimlico (debut, 1949), The Magic Box, The Cruel Sea, Malta Story, The Love Lottery, Passage Home, The Black Tent, Yield to the Night, Eye-Witness, House of Secrets, High Tide At Noon, Sea of Sand, Sapphire, Upstairs and Downstairs, The Angry Silence, Cone of Silence, Doctor In Love, Mysterious Island, Payroll, No My Darling Daughter, A Pair of Briefs, A Life for Ruth, The Iron Maiden, Captive City, Summer Flight, Stolen Flight, Of a Thousand Delights, Life at the Top, Modesty Blaise, Star!, Twinky, The Royal Hunt of the Sun, Brotherly Love (Country Dance), A Town Called Bastard, The Fourth Mrs. Anderson, Vault of Horror, Inn of the Damned, Ride a Wild Pony, The Irishman, Turkey Shoot, Stanley, Appointment With Death, Hot Resort.
TELEVISION: Movie: Spoiled, Tartuffe. Series: G.P., Grass Roots. Guest: Doctor Who, The Professionals, Shoestring. Mini-Series: The Timeless Land.

CRAIN, JEANNE
Actress. b. Barstow, CA, May 25, 1925. Model; crowned Miss Long Beach of 1941: Camera Girl of 1942.
PICTURES: The Gang's All Here (debut, 1943), Home in Indiana, In the Meantime Darling, Winged Victory, State Fair, Leave Her to Heaven, Margie, Centennial Summer, You Were Meant for Me, Apartment for Peggy, Letter to Three Wives, The Fan, Pinky, Cheaper by the Dozen, I'll Get By (cameo), Take Care of My Little Girl, People Will Talk, Model and the Marriage Broker, Belles on Their Toes, O. Henry's Full House, City of Bad Men, Dangerous Crossing, Vicki, Duel in the Jungle, Man Without a Star, The Second Greatest Sex, Gentlemen Marry Brunettes, Fastest Gun Alive, Tattered Dress, The Joker is Wild, Guns of the Timberland, Queen of the Nile, Twenty Plus Two, Madison Avenue, Pontius Pilate, Hot Rods to Hell, The Night God Screamed, Skyjacked.

CRAMER, DOUGLAS S.
Executive. e. Northwestern U., Sorbonne, U. of Cincinnati, B.A.; Columbia U.M.F.A. m. Joyce Haber, columnist. Taught at Carnegie Inst. of Tech., 1954-55; Production asst. Radio City Music Hall 1950-51; MGM Script Dept. 1952; Manag. Dir. Cincinnati Summer Playhouse 1953-54. TV supvr. Procter and Gamble 1956-59; Broadcast supvr. 1959-62; v.p. program dev. ABC-TV 1962-66; v.p. program dev. 20 Cent.-Fox TV 1966; exec. v.p. in chg. of prod., Paramount TV, 1968-71; exec. v.p. Aaron Spelling Prods. 1976-89; pres. Douglas S. Cramer Co, 1989-. Now on East Coast working as theatrical producer for works such as "The Tales of the Allergist's Wife."
THEATRE: Call of Duty, Love is a Smoke, Whose Baby Are You, Last Great Dish.
PICTURES: Exec. prod.: Sleeping Together.
TELEVISION: Exec. prod.: Bridget Loves Bernie, QB VII, Dawn: Portrait of a Teenage Runaway, Nightmare in Badham County, Sex Symbol, Danielle Steel's Fine Things, Kaleidoscope, Changes, Message from Nam, Daddy, Palamino, Once in a Lifetime, The Ring, Zoya: Trade Winds, Lake Success, Wonder Woman, Family of Cops. Co-exec. prod.: Love Boat (1977-86), Vegas (1978-81), Dynasty, Matt Houston, Hotel, Colbys, Family of Cops III.

CRANE, DAVID
Producer. b. 1957.
TELEVISION: Movies: Ngaio Marsh's Alleyn Mysteries: Death at the Bar (s.p. editor). Series: Dream On (creator), Ngaio Marsh's Alleyn Mysteries (s.p. editor), Friends (co-exec., co-creator), Veronica's Closet (co-exec., co-creator), Jesse (co-exec.).

CRAVEN, GEMMA
Actress. b. Dublin, Ireland, June 1, 1950. e. Loretto Coll. Studied acting at Bush Davies School. London stage debut, Fiddler on the Roof (1970).
THEATRE: *London*: Audrey, Trelawny, Dandy Dick, They're Playing Our Song, Song and Dance, Loot, A Chorus of Disapproval, Three Men on a Horse, Jacobowsky and the Colonel, The Magistrate, South Pacific, The London Vertigo, Private Lives, Present Laughter.
PICTURES: Kingdom of Gifts, Why Not Stay for Breakfast, The Slipper and the Rose, Wagner, Double X: The Name of the Game, Words Upon the Windowpane, The Last Bus Home, After the Hole.
TELEVISION: Pennies From Heaven, Must Wear Tights, She Loves Me, Song by Song by Noel Coward, Song by Song by Alan Jay Lerner, East Lynne, Robin of Sherwood, Treasure Hunt, Gemma Girls and Gershwin, Boon, The Bill, The Marshal, The Cazelets (series).

CRAVEN, WES
Director, Writer. b. Cleveland, OH, Aug. 2, 1939. e. Wheaton Coll., B.A.; Johns Hopkins, M.A., philosophy. Worked as humanities prof. prior to film.
PICTURES: The Last House on the Left (also s.p., ed.), The Hills Have Eyes (also s.p., ed.), Deadly Blessing, Swamp Thing (also s.p.), A Nightmare on Elm Street (also s.p.), The Hills Have Eyes Part II (also s.p.), Deadly Friend, A Nightmare on Elm Street III: Dream Warriors (co-s.p., co-exec. prod. only), The Serpent and the Rainbow, Shocker (also exec. prod., s.p.), The People Under the Stairs (also s.p., co-exec. prod.), Wes Craven's New Nightmare (also actor, s.p.), Vampire in Brooklyn, The Fear (actor only), Scream, Wishmaster (prod. only), Scream 2, Music of the Heart, Scream 3, Jay and Silent Bob Strike Back (actor only), Carnival of Souls (exec. prod. only), Dracula 2000 (prod. only), Freddy v. Jason (writer), Cursed (dir. only).
TELEVISION:*Movies*: A Stranger in Our House, Invitation to Hell, Chiller, Casebusters, Night Visions (also exec. prod., co-writer), Laurel Canyon (exec. prod. only), Body Bags (actor only). *Series*: Twilight Zone (1985, 7 episodes: Word Play, A Little Peace and Quiet, Shatterday, Chameleon, Dealer's Choice, The Road Less Traveled, Pilgrim Soul). The People Next Door (exec. prod.), Kamelot (exec. prod.)

CRAWFORD, MICHAEL
O.B.E. Actor. r.n. Michael Dumbell-Smith. b. Salisbury, England, Jan.19, 1942. Early career as boy actor in children's films, as a boy soprano in Benjamin Britten's Let's Make an Opera and on radio. Later star of TV's Not So Much a Programme, More a Way of Life. Solo albums: Songs from the Stage and Screen, With Love, Performs Andrew Lloyd Weber, A Touch of Music in the Night. Appeared for MGM Grand in production EFX.
THEATRE: Come Blow Your Horn, Traveling Light, The Anniversary, White Lies and Black Comedy (N.Y.), No Sex Please We're British, Billy, Same Time Next Year, Flowers for Algernon, Barnum, The Phantom of the Opera (London: Laurence Olivier Award; New York: Tony, Drama Desk, Drama League & Outer Critics Awards, 1988; also L.A.), The Music of Andrew Lloyd Weber (U.S., Canada, U.K. & Australia).
PICTURES: Soap Box Derby (debut, 1957), Blow Your Own Trumpet, A French Mistress, Two Living One Dead, Two Left Feet, The War Lover, The Knack... and How to Get It, A Funny Thing Happened on the Way to the Forum, The Jokers, How I Won the War, Hello Dolly!, The Games, Hello-Goodbye, Alice's Adventures in Wonderland, Condorman, Once Upon a Forest (voice).
TELEVISION: Still Life, Destiny, Byron, Move After Checkmate, Three Barrelled Shotgun, Home Sweet Honeycomb, Some Mothers Do 'ave 'em, Chalk and Cheese, BBC Play for Today, Private View, Barnum, The Ghosts of Christmas Eve, My Favorite Broadway: The Love Songs, The 100 Greatest TV Characters, I Love Christmas.

CRENNA, RICHARD
Actor. b. Los Angeles, CA, Nov. 30, 1927. e. Belmont H.S., USC.
RADIO: Boy Scout Jamboree, A Date With Judy, The Hardy Family, The Great Gildersleeve, Burns & Allen, Our Miss Brooks.
PICTURES: Red Skies of Montana (debut, 1951), Pride of St. Louis, It Grows on Trees, Our Miss Brooks, Over-Exposed, John Goldfarb Please Come Home, Made in Paris, The Sand Pebbles, Wait Until Dark, Star!, Midas Run, Marooned, The Deserter, Doctors' Wives, Red Sky at Morning, Catlow, A Man Called Noon, Dirty Money (Un Flic), Jonathan Livingston Seagull (voice), Breakheart Pass, The Evil, Wild Horse Hank, Death Ship, Stone Cold Dead, Body Heat, First Blood, Table for Five, The Flamingo Kid, Rambo: First Blood Part II, Summer Rental, Rambo III, Leviathan, Hot Shots! Part Deux, A Pyromaniac's Love Story (unbilled), Jade, Sabrina, Wrongfully Accused, The Real McCoys Reunion, Darkness at High Noon: The Carl Foreman Documents, Drawing First Blood (video documentary), Guts & Glory (video short), Afghanistan: Land in Crisis (video documentary short).
TELEVISION: *Movies*: Footsteps, Thief, Passions, A Case of Deadly Force, The Day the Bubble Burst, Centennial, The Rape of Richard Beck (Emmy Award, 1985), Doubletake, The Price of Passion, Police Story: The Freeway Killings, Plaza Suite, Kids Like These, On Wings of Eagles, Internal Affairs, Blood Brothers: The Case of the Hillside Stranglers, Murder in Black and White, Stuck with Each Other, Montana, Last Flight Out, Murder Times Seven, And the Sea Will Tell, Intruders, Terror on Track 9, A Place to Be Loved, The Forget-Me-Not Murders, Jonathan Stone:

Threat of Innocence, Janek: A Silent Betrayal, In the Name of Love: A Texas Tragedy, Texas Graces, Race Against Time: The Search for Sarah, Heart Full of Rain, Cold Case, 20,000 Leagues Under the Sea, To Serve and Protect, By Dawn's Early Light, The Day Reagan Was Shot. *Series*: Our Miss Brooks, The Real McCoys, Slattery's People, All's Fair, It Takes Two, Pros & Cons.

CRICHTON, MICHAEL
Writer, Director. r.n. John Michael Crichton. b. Chicago, IL, Oct. 23, 1942. e. Harvard U. Medical School (M.D.), 1969. Postdoctoral fellow, Salk Inst. for Biological Sciences, La Jolla, 1969-70. Visiting writer, MIT, 1988. Recipient Edgar Award, Mystery Writers Amer.: A Case of Need (1968), The Great Train Robbery (1980). Named medical writer of year, Assn. of Amer. Med. Writers: Five Patients (1970). Received Scientific and Technical Achievement Academy Award, 1995.
AUTHOR: *Novels*: (as John Lange): Odds On, Scratch One, Easy Go (The Last Tomb), The Venom Business, Zero Cool, Grave Descend, Drug of Choice, Binary. (as Jeffery Hudson): A Case of Need (filmed as The Carey Treatment). (as Michael Douglas, with brother Douglas Crichton): Dealing or the Berkeley-to-Boston Forty-Brick Lost-Bag Blues (filmed). (as Michael Crichton): The Andromeda Strain (filmed), The Terminal Man (filmed), The Great Train Robbery, Eaters of the Dead, Congo, Sphere, Jurassic Park, Rising Son, Disclosure, The Lost World, Airframe (filmed), The Lost World (filmed). *Non-Fiction* (as Michael Crichton): Five Patients, Jasper Johns, Electronic Life, Travels, Spare, The 13th Warrior.
PICTURES: Westworld (dir., s.p.), Coma (dir., s.p.), The Great Train Robbery (dir., s.p.), Looker (dir., s.p.), Runaway (dir., s.p.), Physical Evidence (dir.), Jurassic Park (co-s.p.), Rising Sun (co-s.p.), Disclosure (co-exec. prod.), Congo (co-s.p.), Twister (co-s.p., co-prod.), The Lost World: Jurassic Park (s.p.), Sphere (s.p., prod.), Airframe, The 13th Warrior (s.p., dir., prod.), Jurassic Park III, Timeline (story, novel).
TELEVISION: *Movie*: Pursuit (dir.; based on Binary). *Series*: ER (creator, co-exec. prod.; Emmy Award, 1996). *Pilot*: ER (Writers Guild Award, 1996).

CRIST, JUDITH
Journalist, Critic. b. New York, NY, May 22, 1922. e. Hunter College, Columbia U. School of Journalism. Joined NY Herald Tribune, serving as reporter, arts editor, assoc. drama critic, film critic. Contributing editor Columbia Magazine. Continued as film critic for NY World Journal Tribune, NBC-TV Today Show, New York Magazine, NY Post, Saturday Review, TV Guide, WWOR-TV. Teaches at Col. Grad. School of Journalism.
AUTHOR: The Private Eye the Cowboy and the Very Naked Girl, Judith Crist's TV Guide to the Movies, Take 22: Moviemakers on Moviemaking.

CROMWELL, JAMES
Actor. b. Los Angeles, CA, Jan. 27, 1940. e. Carnegie Mellon Univ. Father was director John Cromwell, mother was actress Kate Johnson.
PICTURES: Murder by Death, The Cheap Detective, The Man With Two Brains, House of God, Tank, Revenge of the Nerds, Oh God You Devil, Explorers, A Fine Mess, Revenge of the Nerds II: Nerds in Paradise, The Rescue, Pink Cadillac, The Runnin' Kind, The Babe, Romeo Is Bleeding, Babe, Eraser, The People vs. Larry Flynt, Star Trek: First Contact, L.A. Confidential, The Education of Little Tree, Deep Impact, Babe: Pig in the City,.Species 2, Snow Falling on Cedars, The Green Mile, The General's Daughter, The Bachelor, Space Cowboys, Spirit: Stallion of the Cimarron, The Sum of All Fears, Twist of Fate, Blackball, The Snow Walker, Before the Devil Knows You're Dead.
TELEVISION: *Movies*: The Girl in the Empty Grave, Deadly Game, A Christmas Without Snow, The Wall, Spraggue, The Shaggy Dog, A Slight Case of Murder, Fail Safe, Enterprise: Broken Bow, Great Bear Rainforest, Door to Door, A Death in the Family, The Magnificent Ambersons. *Mini-Series*: Once an Eagle. *Series*: All in the Family, Hot L Baltimore, The Nancy Walker Show, The Last Precinct, Easy Street, Mama's Boy, Walking After Midnight, Citizen Baines. *Guest*: M*A*S*H, Dallas, L.A. Law, Star Trek: The Next Generation, Hill Street Blues, ER.

CRONENBERG, DAVID
Writer, Director. b. Toronto, Ont., May 15, 1943. e. U. of Toronto. In college produced two short movies on 16mm. 1971, to Europe on a Canadian Council grant where in 1975 he shot his first feature, They Came From Within (Shivers).
PICTURES: *Director*: Transfer (prod, s.p. and edit.), From the Drain (also s.p. and edit.), Stereo, Crimes of the Future, Jim Ritche Sculptor, They Came From Within (Shivers; also s.p.), Rabid (also s.p.), Fast Company, The Brood (also s.p.), Scanners (also s.p.), Videodrome, The Dead Zone, The Fly (also co-s.p., cameo), Dead Ringers (also co-prod., co-s.p.), Naked Lunch (also s.p.), M. Butterfly, Crash, eXistenZ (also s.p. and prod.), Camera, Spider (also prod.). *Actor*: Into the Night, Nightbreed, Trial by Jury, Blue, Henry & Verlin, Trial By Jury, To Die For, Blood and Donuts, The Stupids, Extreme Measures, The Grace of God, Last Night, Resurrection, The American Nightmare, Jason X.
TELEVISION: *Movie*: Moonshine Highway.

CRONKITE, WALTER
Correspondent. b. St. Joseph, MO, Nov. 4, 1916. e. U. of Texas. Reporter and editor Scripps-Howard News Service, TX; radio reporter; U.P. correspondent. WW II corres. British Isles, N. Africa. Foreign Correspondent, France, Belgium, Netherlands, Soviet Union. Joined CBS as Washington news correspondent, 1950; anchorman and mng. editor, CBS Evening News, 1962-81; special correspondent, CBS News, 1981-present. Many TV shows including You Are There, Twentieth Century, Eyewitness to History: CBS Reports: 21st Century, Walter Cronkite's Universe. Past nat'l pres. & mem. bd. Trustees, Acad. TV Arts & Sciences. Mng. editor of CBS Evening News 1963-81. Special correspondent, Children of Apartheid, Walter Cronkite at Large, Cronkite Remembers. Chairman, Cronkite Ward & Company, which has produced more than 25 award winning documentary hours for the Discovery Channel, PBS and others, 1993-98. Host/commentator of The Cronkite Reports, on the Discovery Channel which investigates current, global news issues. Other Cronkite Ward & Co. productions: Great Books series for the Learning Channel and Understanding: Science programs for the Discovery Channel. Supplied voice for 1995 B'way revival of How to Succeed in Business Without Really Trying. Autobiography, A Reporter's Life, 1996.

CRONYN, HUME
Actor, Writer, Director. b. London, Ont., Canada, July 18, 1911. Was married to late actress Jessica Tandy. e. Ridley Coll., McGill U., Amer. Acad. of Dramatic Art.
THEATRE: N.Y.: Actor: High Tor, Escape This Night, Three Men on a Horse, Boy Meets Girl, Three Sisters, Mr. Big, The Survivors, Now I Lay Me Down to Sleep (dir.), Hilda Crane (dir.), The Fourposter (dir.), Madam Will You Walk, The Honeys, A Day by the Sea, The Man in the Dog Suit, The Egghead (dir.), Triple Play (dir. and toured with wife), Big Fish Little Fish (also in London), The Miser, The Three Sisters, Hamlet, The Physicists, Slow Dance on the Killing Ground (prod.), appeared at the White House, Hear America Speaking, Richard III, The Miser, A Delicate Balance (1966 and tour, 1967), Hadrian VII (tour), Caine Mutiny Court Martial, Promenade All, Krapp's Last Tape, Happy Days, Act Without Words, Many Faces Of Love (concert recital), Noel Coward in Two Keys (National tour), Merchant of Venice and A Midsummer Night's Dream (Stratford Festival Theatre). Canada: The Gin Game (with Miss Tandy; later tour). New Haven, B'way, 1977, co-prod. with Mike Nichols; also toured U.S., Toronto, London, U.S.S.R., 1978-79). Also: Foxfire (co-author, actor, at Stratford, 1980, Minneapolis, 1981 and N.Y., 1982-83); Traveler in the Dark (Amer. Repertory Theatre, Cambridge, MA), Foxfire (Ahmanson, LA 1985-86), The Petition (NY 1986).
PICTURES: Shadow of a Doubt (debut, 1943), Phantom of the Opera, The Cross of Lorraine, Lifeboat, The Seventh Cross (Acad. Award nom.), Main Street After Dark, The Sailor Takes a Wife, A Letter for Evie, The Green Years, The Postman Always Rings Twice, Ziegfeld Follies, The Secret Heart (narrator), The Beginning or the End, Brute Force, Rope (adapt. only), The Bride Goes Wild, Top o' the Morning, Under Capricorn (adapt. only), People Will Talk, Crowded Paradise, Sunrise at Campobello, Cleopatra, Hamlet, Gaily Gaily, The Arrangement, There Was a Crooked Man, Conrack, The Parallax View, Honky Tonk Freeway, Rollover, The World According to Garp, Impulse, Brewster's Millions, Cocoon, Batteries Not Included, Cocoon: The Return, The Pelican Brief, Camilla, Marvin's Room.
TELEVISION: Movies: The Dollmaker (co-writer only), Foxfire (also co-writer), Day One, Age-old Friends, Christmas on Division Street, Broadway Bound (Emmy Award, 1992), To Dance With the White Dog (Emmy Award, 1994), Alone, Twelve Angry Men (Emmy nom., 1997), Seasons of Love, Sea People, Santa and Pete, Yesterday's Children, Cleopatra: The Film That Changed Hollywood, Off Season. Series: The Marriage.
(d. June 15, 2003)

CROSBY, CATHY LEE
Actress. b. Los Angeles, CA, Dec. 2, 1944. e. Grad. of U. of Southern California. Studied with Lee Strasberg. author of The Magic Begin.
THEATRE: Downside Risk, Almost Perfect (Off-B'way debut), Jellyroll Shoes, They Shoot Horses, Don't They? (wrote, dir. starred in 1st theatrical adapt. Hollywood Amer. Legion), Zoot Suit—The Real Story (writer, dir., actress, adapt., Beverly Hills).
PICTURES: The Laughing Policeman (debut, 1973), Trackdown, The Dark, Coach, Training Camp (s.p.), San Sebastian (s.p.), Call Me By My Rightful Name, The Player, The Big Tease, Ablaze.
TELEVISION: Movies: Wonder Woman, Keefer, Roughnecks, World War III, Intimate Strangers, One Child, North & South III: Heaven and Hell, Untamed Love (also co-exec. prod.), When the Cradle Falls, Treasure of Dos Santos, A Memory in My Heart, Final Run, Son of Mistletoe, That's Incredible Special!, Dancing at the Harvest Moon. Series: That's Incredible. Specials: A Spectacular Evening in Egypt, Battle of the Network Stars, Circus of the Stars, Bob Hope Specials, Get High on Yourself, Bob Hope: USO Tour of Lebanon & the Mediterranean.

CROSBY, KATHRYN
Actress. b. Nov. 25, 1933 r.n. Olive Kathryn Grandstaff. b. Houston, TX. e. U. of Texas, Queen of Angels Sch. of Nursing, Immaculate Heart Col. m. late actor-singer Bing Crosby. Author: Bing and Other Things, My Life With Bing. Also credited as Kathryn Grant.
THEATRE: Mama's Baby Boy, The Enchanted, Sunday in New York, Sabrina Fair, The Guardsman, Guys and Dolls, Same Time

Next Year, The Crucible, Cyrano de Bergerac, Tonight at 8:30, The Cocktail Hour, Oh Coward, I Do I Do, The Heiress, The Seagull, Hello Dolly, State Fair, The Music Man, Lion In Winter, and many others.
PICTURES: Forever Female, Rear Window, Living It Up, Sabrina, Arrowhead, Casanova's Big Night, Unchained, Cell 2455 Death Row, Tight Spot, Five Against the House, Reprisal, Guns of Fort Petticoat, The Phenix City Story, Wild Party, Mister Cory, Gunman's Walk, The Librarian, Anatomy of a Murder, The Brothers Rico, Operation Mad Ball, The Seventh Voyage of Sinbad, The Big Circus, The Wild Party.
TELEVISION: Special: Happy Birthday Bob (herself). Guest: Bob Hope Chrysler Theatre, Bing Crosby Christmas Specials, Suspense Theatre, Ben Casey, The Kathryn Crosby Show. Movie: The Initiation of Sarah.

CROSBY, MARY
Actress. b. Los Angeles, CA, Sept. 14, 1959. e. U. TX; American Conservatory Theatre. Daughter of performers Kathryn Crosby and the late Bing Crosby. Formerly acted as Mary Frances Crosby. Appeared from an early age in several TV variety specials with her parents. On stage in: Romeo & Juliet, A Gentleman of Verona (L.A.), As You Like It (L.A.), The Seagull (L.A.).
PICTURES: The Last Plane Out, The Ice Pirates, Tapeheads, Body Chemistry, Corporate Affairs, Eating, The Berlin Conspiracy, Desperate Motive (Distant Cousins).
TELEVISION: Movies: With This Ring, A Guide for the Married Woman, Midnight Lace, Golden Gate, Confessions of a Married Man, Final Jeopardy, Stagecoach, Johnann Strauss: The King Without a Crown, Sharing the Secret, When Shoulderpads Ruled the World. Mini-Series: Pearl, Hollywood Wives, North and South Book II. Pilot: Golden Gate, The Big Easy, Cover Up. Specials: Goldilocks, Bing Crosby's Christmas Show (1970-73, 1976-77), Battle of the Network Stars, The 21st Annual Academy of Country Music Awards, Crazy Dan, Tube Test Two, Best Sellers: Men Who Hate Women and the Wome Who Love Them. Series: Brothers and Sisters, Dallas, Freddy's Nightmares, Sharing the Secret. Guest: Knots Landing, The Love Boat, The Fall Guy, Hotel, Murder She Wrote, Beverly Hills 90210, many others.

CROSS, BEN
Actor. r.n. Bernard Cross. b. London, England, Dec. 16, 1947. e. Royal Acad. of Dramatic Art. Worked as stagehand, prop-master, and master carpenter with Welsh Natl. Opera as set builder, Wimbledon Theatre.
THEATRE: The Importance of Being Earnest (Lancaster, debut, 1972), I Love My Wife, Privates on Parade, Chicago, Lydie Breeze (NY debut, 1982), Caine Mutiny Court Martial.
PICTURES: A Bridge Too Far (debut, 1977), Chariots of Fire, The Unholy, The Goldsmith's Shop, Paperhouse, The House of the Lord, Eye of the Widow, Haunted Symphony, The Ascent, First Knight, Turbulence, The Corporate Ladder, The Invader, The Venice Project, Young Blades, The Order, She Me and Her.
TELEVISION: Movies/Specials: Melancholy Hussar of the German Legion (1973, BBC), The Flame Trees of Thika, The Citadel, The Far Pavilions, Coming Out of the Ice, The Assisi Underground, Arthur Hailey's Strong Medicine, Steal the Sky, Pursuit, Twist of Fate, Nightlife, She Stood Alone, Diamond Fleece, Live Wire, Deep Trouble, Cold Sweat, The House That Mary Bought, Hellfire, 20,000 Leagues Under the Sea, The Sands of Time, The Potato Factory, The Red Phone. Series: Dark Shadows (1991).

CROUSE, LINDSAY
Actress. b. New York, NY, May 12, 1948. Daughter of playwright Russel Crouse. e. Radcliffe.
THEATRE: With Circle Repertory Co. N.Y.: Hamlet, Twelfth Night, Richard II, Childe Byron, Reunion (Obie Award). NY: Serenading Louie, The Shawl, The Stick Wife, The Homecoming (B'way debut; Theatre World Award). With L.A. Matrix Theatre Co.: The Tavern, Habeus Corpus.
PICTURES: All the President's Men (debut, 1976), Slap Shot, Between the Lines, Prince of the City, The Verdict, Daniel, Iceman, Places in the Heart (Acad. award nom.), House of Games, Communion, Desperate Hours, Being Human, Bye Bye Love, The Indian in the Cupboard, The Arrival, The Juror, Prefontaine, Progeny, The Insider, Stranger in My House, Almost Salinas, Imposter, Cherish.
TELEVISION: Movies: Eleanor and Franklin, Chantilly Lace, Final Appeal, Out of Darkness, Parallel Lives, Between Mother and Daughter, Norma Jean and Marilyn, If These Walls Could Talk, Beyond the Prairie: The True Story of Laura Ingalls Wilder, The Warden. Mini-Series: The Kennedys of Massachusetts. Specials: Kennedy's Children, Lemon Sky, Between Mother and Daughter, If These Walls Could Talk. Series: American Nuclear (pilot), NYPD Blue, Traps, Millenium, Buffy the Vampire Slayer. Guest: Colombo, Murder She Wrote, LA Law, Hill Street Blues, Civil Wars, Law and Order, E.R.

CROWE, CAMERON
Writer, Director. b. Palm Springs, CA, July 13, 1957. e. Calif. St. Univ., San Diego. Began career as journalist and editor for Rolling Stone. Adapted his book Fast Times at Ridgemont High into Writers Guild Award-nominated screenplay for 1982 film.
PICTURES: American Hot Wax (actor). Fast Times at Ridgemont High (s.p. only), The Wild Life (s.p.,co-prod.), Say Anything..., Singles, Jerry Maguire (dir. & prod. only), Almost Famous, Vanilla Sky (also prod).
TELEVISION: Series: Fast Times (creative consultant).

CROWE, KEN
Executive. b. Sewickley, PA, Sept. 3, 1939. e. San Diego U. CPA, public accounting, Coopers & Lybrand, 1968-77. Mann Theatres, treas./CFO, 1977-86; Paramount Mann Theatres, sr. v.p./CFO, 1986-88. Cinamerica Theatres, exec. v.p./CFO, 1988-1997. Retired. Member of Motion Picture Pioneers, AICPA, FEI, Variety Club of So. Calif and Sertoma.

CROWE, RUSSELL
Actor. b. New Zealand, April 7, 1964. Raised in Australia. Worked as musician while appearing on Australian stage in Bad Boy Johnny and the Profits of Doom, Blood Brothers, Rocky Horror Show.
PICTURES: For the Moment, The Silver Brumby, Hammers Over the Anvil, Prisoners of the Sun, Love in Limbo, For the Moment, Proof (Australian Film Inst. Award), The Efficiency Expert, Romper Stomper (Australian Film Inst. Award), The Quick and the Dead, The Sum of Us, Virtuosity, Rough Magic, No Way Back, Breaking Up, L.A. Confidential, Heaven's Burning, Breaking Up, Mystery Alaska, The Insider, Gladiator (Academy Award), Proof of Life, A Beautiful Mind (Academy Award nom.), Texas, Master and Commander.

CROWN, DANIEL
Executive. Pres. and CEO, Crown Theatres, S. Norwalk, CT., 1990-. Bd. or dirs., NY Yankees, 1985-. Other bds.: Lenox Hill Hosp., Mt. Sinai Children's Ctr. Fdn., Jerusalem Fdn., Jewish Nat'l. Fund, New York, NY. Member NATO, 1991-.

CRUEA, EDMOND D.
Executive. b. Jersey City, NJ, June 3. Joined Grand Natl. Pictures, LA, 1935; Monogram Pictures, 1938-41, LA & Seattle; U.S. Army Signal Corps., 1942-46; Monogram Pictures, Seattle, 1946; branch mgr. & district mgr. Allied Artists, 1950-65 (Seattle, Portland, San Francisco, LA); v.p. & gen. sls. mgr., Allied Artists, 1965-71; dir. distbn., Abkco Films div. of Abkco Industries Inc., 1971-73; pres. Royal Dist. Corp, 1974; joined Film Ventures Intl. 1976 as exec. v.p. succeeding to pres. & COO in 1976. Co-founded New Image Releasing Inc., 1982, as pres. & CEO. 1985, v.p. theatrical, Cinetel Films; V.P. Distrib. Jerry Gross Org.; 1987 the atrical distbn. cons., Sony Pictures (NY), Sony Video Softwear plus and Shining Armour Commun (London). Acquisitions & distbn. cons. to Columbia TriStar Home Video, Triumph Pictures and Healing Arts Documentary Prods.; 1995, chmn. and CEO Global International Films Inc.; 1996, pres. Capstone films; consultant to Intic Productions. Theatrical consult to Croatian Embassy, NY.

CRUISE, TOM
Actor. r.n. Thomas Cruise Mapother IV. b. Syracuse, NY, July 3, 1962. Acted in high school plays; secured role in dinner theatre version of Godspell. Studied acting at Neighborhood Playhouse, before landing small part in Endless Love. Received American Cinema Award for Distinguished Achievement in Film, 1991. Top winning star of all time with six number ones on Quigley's Top Ten MoneyMakers Poll, est. 1932.
PICTURES: Endless Love (debut, 1981), Taps, Losin' It, The Outsiders, Risky Business, All the Right Moves, Legend, Top Gun, The Color of Money, Cocktail, Rain Man, Born on the 4th of July (Golden Globe Award; Acad. Award nom., 1989), Days of Thunder (also co-wrote story), Far and Away, A Few Good Men, The Firm, Interview With the Vampire, Mission: Impossible, Jerry Macguire (Golden Globe Award, 1997), Eyes Wide Shut, Magnolia, Mission Impossible 2 (also prod.), Without Limits (prod. only) Vanilla Sky, Minority Report, Space Station (voice), Dolan's Cadillac (prod. only), Shattered Glass (exec. prod. only), The Last Samurai (also prod.), Suspect Zero (prod. only.)
TELEVISION: Director: The Frightening Framis (episode of series Fallen Angels).

CRUZ, PENELOPE
Actress. b. Madrid, Spain, April 28, 1974.
PICTURES: The Greek Labyrinth, The Age of Beauty, Salami, Salami, The Rebel, For Love, Only For Love, Alegre ma non troppo, Life's a Bitch, Entre rojas, Brujas, La Celestina, Not Love, Just Frenzy, Love Can Seriously Damage Your Health, A Corner of Paradise, Live Flesh, Open Your Eyes, Don Juan, Twice Upon A Yesterday, Talk of Angels, The Girl of Your Dreams, The Hi-Lo Country, Nada en la Nevera, All About My Mother, Volavérunt, Blow, All the Pretty Horses, Captain Corelli's Mandolin, No News From God, Vanilla Sky, The Diary of a Young London Physician, Masked & Anonymous, Fanfan la tulipe, Gothika, Head in the Clouds.

CRYER, JON
Actor. b. New York, NY, Apr. 16, 1965. Son of actor David Cryer and songwriter-actress Gretchen Cryer. On B'way stage in Brighton Beach Memoirs.
PICTURES: No Small Affair (debut, 1984), Pretty in Pink, Morgan Stewart's Coming Home, O.C. and Stiggs, Superman IV: The Quest for Peace, Hiding Out, Dudes, Penn and Teller Get Killed, Hot Shots!, The Pompatus of Love, Plan B, Went to Coney Island on a Mission from God...Back By 5, Die Wholesale, Holy Man.
TELEVISION: Movie: Heads. Series: The Famous Teddy Z, Partners, It's Good to Be King, Getting Personal, The Trouble With Normal, Two and a Half Men.

CRYSTAL, BILLY
Actor, Writer, Producer, Director. b. Long Island, NY, Mar. 14, 1947. e. Marshall U., Nassau Commun. Col., NYU (BFA in tv &

ilm direction). Father, Jack, produced jazz concerts; family owned Commodore jazz record label. Worked with Alumni Theatre Group at Nassau Commun. College. Later teamed with two friends (billed as We the People, Comedy Jam, 3's Company) and toured coffee houses and colleges. Became stand-up comedian on own, appearing at Catch a Rising Star, The Comedy Story and on TV. Album: Mahvelous!. Book: Absolutely Mahvelous!
PICTURES: Rabbit Test (debut, 1978), Animalympics (voice), This Is Spinal Tap, Running Scared, The Princess Bride, Throw Mama From the Train, Memories of Me (also co-prod., co-s.p.), When Harry Met Sally..., City Slickers (also exec. prn, od.), Mr. Saturday Night (also dir., prod., co-s.p.), City Slickers II: The Legend of Curly's Gold (also prod., co-s.p.), Forget Paris (also dir., prod., co-s.p.), Hamlet, Father's Day, Deconstructing Harry, My Giant, Analyze This, Monsters, Inc. (voice), America's Sweethearts, Analyze That.
TELEVISION: Movies: SST—Death Flight, Human Feelings, Breaking Up Is Hard to Do, Enola Gay: The Men the Mission and the Atomic Bomb, 61. Host: Grammy Awards (Emmy Awards for hosting, 1988, 1989), Academy Awards (Emmy Award for hosting, 1991, 1997; Emmy Award for co-writing, 1992). Series: Soap, The Billy Crystal Comedy Hour (also writer), Saturday Night Live (also writer), Sessions (creator, exec. prod. only). Guest: Saturday Night Live with Howard Cosell, Tonight Show, Dinah, Mike Douglas Show, That Was the Year That Was, All in the Family, Love Boat. Specials include: Battle of the Network Stars, Billy Crystal: A Comic's Line (also writer), A Comedy Salute to Baseball (also writer), On Location: Billy Crystal - Don't Get Me Started (also dir., writer), The Three Little Pigs (Faerie Tale Theatre), The Lost Minutes of Billy Crystal, Midnight Train to Moscow (also exec. prod., co-writer; Emmy Award 1990).

CULBERG, PAUL S.
Executive. b. Chicago, IL, June 14, 1942. Began career in record industry, holding positions with Elektra Records & Wherehouse Record; 1977-80; v.p. sls. mktg., Cream Records.; 1980-82, dir. sls. Paramount Home Video; 1982, v.p. sls. mktg., Media Home Entertainment; 1984-89, pres., New World Video; 1989-present, COO, RCA Columbia/TriStar Home Video.

CULKIN, KIERAN
Actor. b. New York, NY, Sept. 30, 1982. Began working in 1990, making debut with his brother, Macauley Culkin in Home Alone.
PICTURES: Home Alone, Only the Lonely, Father of the Bride, Home Alone 2: Lost in New York, Nowhere to Run, It Runs in the Family, Father of the Bride Part II, Amanda, The Mighty, She's All That, Music of the Heart, The Cider House Rules, The Dangerous Lives of Altar Boys, Igby Goes Down.
TELEVISION: Series Go Fish. Mini-series: The Magical Legend of the Leprechauns.

CULKIN, MACAULAY
Actor. b. New York, NY, Aug. 26, 1980. Acting debut at 4 yrs. old in Bach Babies at NY's Symphony Space. Appeared in several TV commercials. Studied ballet at George Ballanchine's School of American Ballet and danced in NY productions of H.M.S. Pinafore and The Nutcracker. Received Comedy Award and Youth in Film Award for role in Home Alone. Appeared in Michael Jackson video Black and White.
THEATRE: NY: Afterschool Special, Mr. Softee, Buster B. and Olivia.
PICTURES: Rocket Gibraltar (debut, 1988), See You in the Morning, Uncle Buck, Jacob's Ladder, Home Alone, Only the Lonely, My Girl, Home Alone 2: Lost in New York, The Good Son, George Balanchine's The Nutcracker, Getting Even With Dad, The Pagemaster, Richie Rich, Party Monster, Saved.
TELEVISION: Guest: The Equalizer, Saturday Night Live, Bob Hope Christmas Special.

CULLUM, JOHN
Actor. b. Knoxville, TN, Mar. 2, 1930. e. Univ. of TN. Son is actor John David (J.D.) Cullum.
THEATRE: NY: Camelot, On a Clear Day You Can See Forever (Theatre World Award, Tony nom.), Hamlet, Man of La Mancha, 1776, Shenandoah (Tony Award, Drama Desk & Outer Circle Critics Awards, 1975), The Trip Back Down, On the Twentieth Century (Tony Award, 1978), Deathtrap, Private Lives, Doubles, The Boys in Autumn, Aspects of Love, Showboat.
PICTURES: All the Way Home, 1776, The Prodigal, The Act, Marie, Sweet Country, The Secret Life of Algernon, Ricochet River, Held Up.
TELEVISION: Movies: The Man Without a Country, The Day After, Shoot Down, With a Vengeance, Inherit the Wind. Series: Buck James, Northern Exposure, To Have and to Hold, ER. Guest: Quantum Leap (also dir.).

CULP, ROBERT
Actor, Writer, Director. b. Berkeley, CA, Aug. 16, 1930. e. Stockton, College of the Pacific, Washington U., San Francisco State. To N.Y. to study with Herbert Berghof (played Potzo in 1st U.S. prod. of Waiting for Godot. Starred in off-B'way play. He Who Gets Slapped. Best Actor of the Year in an off-B'way Play; motion picture debut, 1962; P.T. 109. Television guest appearances in Rawhide, Wagon Train, Bob Hope Presents the Chrysler Theatre; wrote and acted in Rifleman, Cain's Hundred, The Dick Powell Show.
THEATRE: B'way: The Prescott Proposals, A Clearing in the Woods, Diary of a Scoundrel.
PICTURES: PT 109 (debut, 1963), Sunday in New York, Rhino!,

Bob & Carol & Ted & Alice, The Grove, Hannie Caulder, Hickey & Boggs (also dir., uncredited co-s.p.), A Name for Evil, The Castaway Cowboy, Inside Out (Golden Heist), Sky Riders, Breaking Point, The Great Scout and Cathouse Thursday, Goldengirl, National Lampoon Goes to the Movies, Turk 182!, Big Bad Mama II, Silent Night Deadly Night 3: Better Watch Out, Pucker Up and Bark Like a Dog, Timebomb, The Pelican Brief, Panther, Xtro 3: Watch the Skies, Favorite Deadly Sins, Spy Hard, Most Wanted, Wanted, Unconditional Love, Farewell My Love, Dark Summer, NewsBreak, Hunger.
TELEVISION: Movies: Sammy The Way Out Seal, The Raiders, The Hanged Man, See the Man Run, A Cold Night's Death, Outrage!, Houston We've Got a Problem, Strange Homecoming, A Cry for Help, Flood, Spectre, Last of the Good Guys, Women in White, Hot Rod, The Dream Merchants, The Night the City Screamed, Killjoy, Thou Shalt Not Kill, Her Life as a Man, The Calendar Girl Murders, Brothers-in-Law, The Blue Lightning, The Gladiator, The Key to Rebecca, Combat High, Voyage of Terror: The Achille Lauro Affair, Columbo Goes to College, I Spy Returns. Series: Trackdown, I Spy (also wrote pilot and 6 shows; Emmy noms. as writer and actor), The Greatest American Hero (also wrote 2 shows). Guest: The Cosby Show.

CUMMING, ALAN
Actor. b. Perthshire, Scotland, Jan. 27, 1965.
PICTURES: Prague, Second Best, Black Beauty (voice), Circle of Friends, GoldenEye, Burn Your Phone, Emma, Spice World, For My Baby, Romy and Michele's High School Reunion, Buddy, The Flintstones in Viva Rock Vegas, Eyes Wide Shut, Plunkett & MaCleane, Titus, Urbania, Company Man, Spy Kids, Josie and the Pussycats, The Anniversary Party (also dir.), Cinemagique, Nicholas Nickleby, Zero Effect, Spy Kids 3-D: Game Over.
TELEVISION: Movies: Bernard and the Genie, The Airzone Solution, Micky Love, That Sunday, Annie. Guest: Mr. Bean.

CUMMINS, PEGGY
Actress. b. Prestatyn, North Wales, Dec. 18, 1925. e. Alexandra Sch., Dublin, Gate Theatre, Dublin. Starred in Let's Pretend in London Stage 1938, followed by Junior Miss, Alice in Wonderland, Peter Pan.
PICTURES: Dr. O'Dowd (debut, 1939), Salute John Citizen, Old Mother Riley—Detective, Welcome Mr. Washington, English Without Tears (Her Man Gilbey), The Late George Apley, Moss Rose, Green Grass of Wyoming, Escape, That Dangerous Age (If This Be Sin), Gun Crazy, My Daughter Joy (Operation X), Who Goes There (Passionate Sentry), Street Corner (Both Sides of the Law), Meet Mr. Lucifer, Always a Bride, The Love Lottery, To Dorothy a Son (Cash on Delivery), The March Hare, Carry on Admiral, Night of the Demon, Hell Drivers, The Captain's Table, Your Money or Your Wife, Dentist in the Chair, In the Doghouse.
TELEVISION: The Human Jungle, Looks Familiar.

CUNNINGHAM, SEAN S.
Producer, Director. b. New York, NY, Dec. 31 1941. e. Franklin & Marshall, B.A.; Stanford U., M.F.A. Worked briefly as actor, moving into stage-managing. Became producer of Mineola Theatre (Long Island, NY) and took several productions to B'way. Formed Sean S. Cunningham Films, Ltd., 1971. Produces commercials, industrial film, documentaries, features.
PICTURES: Together (prod., dir.), Last House on the Left (prod.), The Case of the Full Moon Murders (prod.), Here Come the Tigers (prod., dir.), Kick (prod., dir.), Friday the 13th (prod., dir.), A Stranger Is Watching (prod., dir.), Spring Break (prod., dir.), The New Kids (prod., dir.), House (prod.), House II: The Second Story (prod.), Deepstar Six (prod., dir.), The Horror Show (House III), House IV (prod.), My Boyfriend's Back (prod.), Jason Goes to Hell: The Final Friday (prod.), XCU: Extreme Close Up, Jason X, The Many Lives of Jason Voorhees (video short), Celluloid Crime of the Century (video documentary short), Freddy v. Jason (prod. only).

CURLEY, JOHN J
Executive. b. Dec. 31, 1938. e. Dickinson Coll., BA, 1960; Columbia U., MS, 1963. Reporter, editor Associated Press, 1961-66. With Gannett Co., Inc., 1969-; pres. mid-Atlantic newspaper group Gannett Co., Inc., 1980-82; sr. v.p., Gannett Co., Inc, 1983-84; pres., 1984-; COO, 1984-86; CEO, 1986-1997; chmn., and bd. dirs., 1989-.1997.

CURRY, TIM
Actor. b. Cheshire, England, Apr. 19, 1946. e. Birmingham U. Albums: Read My Lips, Fearless, Simplicity.
THEATRE: Hair, A Midsummer Night's Dream, The Rocky Horror Show, Travesties, Amadeus (Tony nom.), The Pirates of Penzance, Me and My Girl (U.S. tour), The Art of Success, My Favorite Year (Tony nom.).
PICTURES: The Rocky Horror Picture Show (debut, 1975), The Shout, Times Square, Annie, The Ploughman's Lunch, Blue Money, Clue, Legend, Pass the Ammo, The Hunt for Red October, Oscar, FernGully... The Last Rainforest (voice), Passed Away, Home Alone 2: Lost in New York, National Lampoon's Loaded Weapon 1, The Three Musketeers, The Shadow, Lovers' Knot, The Pebble and the Penguin (voice), Congo, The Muppet Treasure Island, Lover's Knot, McHale's Navy, The Rugrats Movie (voice), The Titanic Chronicles, Pirates of Plain, Four Dogs Playing Poker, Sorted, Charlie's Angels, Rugrats in Paris: The Movie (voice), Lion of Oz, Scary Movie 2, Ritual, The Scoundrel's Wife, The Wild Thornberrys I Crocodile (narrator), Rescue Me (voice), Rugrats Go Wild (voice).
TELEVISION: Movies: Oliver Twist, Stephen King's IT, Jackie's Back, Attila, Barbie in the Nutcracker (voice). Voice

work—series: Peter Pan and the Pirates (Emmy Award, 1991), Captain Planet and the Planeteers, Fish Police, Over the Top, The Net, The Wild Thornberrys, Voltron: The Third Dimension, Mattimeo: A Tale of Redwall. Specials: The Life of Shakespeare, Three Men in a Boat, Rock Follies, City Sugar.

CURTIN, JANE
Actress. b. Cambridge, MA, Sept. 6, 1947. e. Northeastern U. On stage in Proposition, Last of the Red Hot Lovers, Candida. Author, actress off-B'way musical revue Pretzel 1974-75.
PICTURES: Mr. Mike's Mondo Video, How to Beat the High Cost of Living, O.C. and Stiggs, Coneheads, Antz (voice).
TELEVISION: Movies: What Really Happened to the Class of '65, Divorce Wars—A Love Story, Suspicion, Maybe Baby, Common Ground, Tad, Christmas in Washington, Catch a Falling Star. Our Town. Special: Candida. Series: Saturday Night Live (1974-79), Kate & Allie (Emmy Awards: 1984, 1985), Working It Out, 3rd Rock from the Sun, Recess (voice), Hercules (voice).

CURTIS, DAN
Producer, Director. b. Bridgeport, CT, Aug. 12, 1928. e. U. of Bridgeport, Syracuse U., B.A. Was sales exec. for NBC and MCA before forming own company, Dan Curtis Productions, which he now heads. Producer/owner of CBS Golf Classic (1963-73).
PICTURES: Dir./Prod.: House of Dark Shadows, Night of Dark Shadows, Burnt Offerings (also co-s.p.), Me and the Kid.
TELEVISION: Movies: Director: The Night Stalker, Frankenstein, The Picture of Dorian Gray, The Last Ride of the Dalton Gang, The Long Days of Summer, Mrs. R's Daughter, Intruders (also co-exec. prod.). Trilogy of Terror II (also writer). Prod./Dir.: The Night Strangler, The Norliss Tapes, Scream of the Wolf, Dracula, Melvin Purvis: G-Man, The Turn of the Screw, The Great Ice-Rip Off, Trilogy of Terror, Kansas City Massacre, Curse of the Black Widow, When Every Day Was the Fourth of July (also co-story), The Love Letter. Mini-Series (prod./dir.): The Winds of War, War and Remembrance (also co-writer). Series: Producer: Dark Shadows (ABC daytime serial, 1966-71), Dark Shadows (prime time series, 1991).

CURTIS, JAMIE LEE
Actress. b. Los Angeles, CA, Nov. 22, 1958. e. Choat Rosemary Hall, CT; Univ. of the Pacific. m. actor-director Christopher Guest. Daughter of Janet Leigh and Tony Curtis. While in school won contract with Universal Studios appearing in small parts in several tv shows.
PICTURES: Halloween (debut, 1978), The Fog, Prom Night, Terror Train, Halloween II, Roadgames, Trading Places, Love Letters, Grandview USA, Perfect, Amazing Grace and Chuck, A Man in Love, Dominick and Eugene, A Fish Called Wanda, Blue Steel, Queens Logic, My Girl, Forever Young, My Girl 2, Mother's Boys, True Lies, House Arrest, Fierce Creatures, Halloween H2O: Twenty Years Later, Homegrown, Virus, Drowning Mona, The Tailor of Panama, Daddy and Them, Marlene Dietrich: Her Own Song, Doin' the Splits, Halloween: Resurrection, Freaky Friday.
TELEVISION: Movies: Operation Petticoat (pilot), She's in the Army Now, Death of a Centerfold: The Dorothy Stratten Story, Money on the Side, As Summers Die, The Heidi Chronicles, Nicholas' Gift. Pilot: Callahan. Series: Operation Petticoat (1977-78), Anything But Love (also, dir., Golden Globe Award), Pigs Next Door. Guest: Quincy, Nancy Drew Mysteries, The Love Boat, The Drew Carey Show, Buck Rogers in the 25th Century. Special: Tall Tales (Annie Oakley).

CURTIS, TONY
Actor. r.n. Bernard Schwartz. b. New York, NY, June 3, 1925. e. Seward Park H.S. Daughter is actress Jamie Lee Curtis. In U.S. Navy, amateur dramatics, N.Y., started Empire Players Theatre, Newark, NJ. With Dramatic Workshop, Cherry Lane Theatre, Junior Drama workshop of Walt Whitman School. First prod. work with Stanley Woolf Players. Made m.p. debut unbilled in Criss-Cross; signed with U.-I. Star of Tomorrow, 1953. Author: Tony Curtis: The Autobiography (1993).
PICTURES: Criss Cross (debut, 1948), City Across the River, The Lady Gambles, Johnny Stool Pigeon, Francis, Sierra, I Was a Shoplifter, Winchester 73, Sierra, Kansas Raiders, Prince Who Was a Thief, Flesh and Fury, Son of Ali Baba, No Room for the Groom, Houdini, All American, Forbidden, Beachhead, Johnny Dark, Black Shield of Falworth, 6 Bridges to Cross, So This Is Paris, Purple Mask, Square Jungle, Rawhide Years, Trapeze, Mister Cory, Midnight Story, Sweet Smell of Success, The Vikings, Kings Go Forth, The Defiant Ones (Acad. Award nom.), The Perfect Furlough, Some Like It Hot, Operation Petticoat, Who Was That Lady?, The Rat Race, Spartacus, Pepe (cameo), The Great Impostor, The Outsider, Taras Bulba, 40 Pounds of Trouble, The List of Adrian Messenger, Captain Newman, M.D., Paris When it Sizzles, Wild and Wonderful, Sex and the Single Girl, Goodbye Charlie, The Great Race, Boeing-Boeing, Chamber of Horrors (cameo), Not With My Wife You Don't!, Arrivederci Baby!, Don't Make Waves, On My Way to the Crusades I Met a Girl Who—(The Chastity Belt), The Boston Strangler, Rosemary's Baby (voice), Those Daring Young Men in Their Jaunty Jalopies (Monte Carlo or Bust), Suppose They Gave a War and Nobody Came, You Can't Win 'Em All, Lepke, The Last Tycoon, Casanova & Co., The Manitou, The Bad News Bears Go to Japan, Sextette, Little Miss Marker, The Mirror Crack'd, Brainwaves, King of the City, Insignificance, Club Life, The Last of Philip Banter, Balboa, Midnight, Lobster Man From Mars, The High-Flying Mermaid, Prime Target, Center of the Web, Naked in New York, The Reptile Man, The Immortals, The Celluloid Closet, Hardball, Brittle Glory, Star Games, Play It to

the Bone, Reflections of Evil (documentary).
TELEVISION: *Movies:* The Third Girl from the Left, The Count of Monte Cristo, Vega$, The Users, Moviola: The Scarlett O'Hara War, Inmates: A Love Story, Harry's Back, The Million Dollar Face, Mafia Princess, Murder in Three Acts, Portrait of a Showgirl, Tarzan in Manhattan, Thanksgiving Day, Christmas in Connecticut, A Perry Mason Mystery: The Case of the Grimacing Governor, Elvis Meets Nixon. *Series:* The Persuaders, McCoy, Vega$, Hollywood Babylon (host).

CUSACK, JOAN
Actress. b. Evanston, IL, Oct. 11, 1962. Brother is actor John Cusack. e. U. of Wisconsin, Madison. Studied acting at Piven Theatre Workshop, Evanston, IL. While in coll. joined The Ark, local improvisational comedy group.
THEATRE: Road, Brilliant Traces (Theatre World Award for both), Cymbeline, The Celestial Alphabet Event, 'Tis Pity She's a Whore, A Midsummer Night's Dream.
PICTURES: My Bodyguard (debut, 1980), Class, Sixteen Candles, Grandview U.S.A., The Allnighter, Broadcast News, Stars and Bars, Married to the Mob, Working Girl (Acad. Award nom.), Say Anything..., Men Don't Leave, My Blue Heaven, The Cabinet of Dr. Ramirez, Hero, Toys, Addams Family Values, Corrina Corrina, Nine Months, Mr. Wrong, Grosse Pointe Blank, A Smile Like Yours, In & Out (NY Film Crits. Circle Award, Best Supporting Actress, 1997), Runaway Bride, The Cradle Will Rock, Arlington Road, Toy Story 2 (voice), High Fidelity, Where the Heart Is, The School of Rock, Looney Tunes: Back in Action.
TELEVISION: Movies: It's a Very Merry Muppet Christmas Movie. *Special:* The Mother.*Series:* Saturday Night Live (1985-86), What About Joan.

CUSACK, JOHN
Actor. b. Evanston, IL, June 28, 1966. Sister is actress Joan Cusack. Member of Piven Theatre Workshop in Evanston for 10 years beginning when he was 9 years old. Appeared on several tv commercials as teen. Formed Chicago theatrical company, New Criminals.
PICTURES: Class (debut, 1983), Sixteen Candles, Grandview U.S.A., The Sure Thing, The Journey of Natty Gann, Better Off Dead, Stand By Me, One Crazy Summer, Hot Pursuit, Eight Men Out, Tapeheads, Say Anything..., Fat Man and Little Boy, The Grifters, True Colors, Shadows and Fog, Roadside Prophets, The Player, Bob Roberts, Map of the Human Heart, Money for Nothing, Bullets Over Broadway, The Road to Wellville, Floundering, City Hall, Grosse Pointe Blank (also co-prod. & s.p.), Con Air, Midnight in the Garden of Good and Evil, Anastasia (voice), This Is My Father, The Thin Red Line, Pushing Tin, Chicago Cab, Arigo (also prod.), High Fidelity (also s.p.), Cradle Will Rock, Being John Malkovich, White Jazz, Life of the Party, Arigo, Serendipity, Never Got Outta the Boat (exec prod. only), 2.2 (prod. only), Adaptation, Hoffman, I.D., The Runaway Jury.
TELEVISION: *Movies:* Eastwood on Eastwood. *Mini-Series:* Baseball (voice).

CZERNY, HENRY
Actor. b. Toronto, Canada, 1959. Began acting career performing in musicals at Humberside collegiate in Toronto.
PICTURES: I Love a Man in Uniform, Cold Sweat, Buried on Sunday, Anchor Zone, Clear and Present Danger, Notes From Underground, The Michelle Apartments, The Interview, When Night Is Falling, Mission Impossible, Promise the Moon, Kayla, The Ice Storm, Kayla, External Affairs, Cement, After Alice, Klepto, The Limit, The Failures.
TELEVISION: *Movies:* Deadly Matrimony, A Town Torn Apart, Lifeline to Victory, The Boys of St. Vincent, Ultimate Betrayal, Choices of the Heart, The Margaret Sanger Story, For Hope, Glory and Honor, My Father's Shadow: The Sam Sheppard Story, P.T. Barnum, The Girl Next Door, Possessed, Range of Motion, Haven, Further Tales of the City, Salem Witch Trials. *Guest:* Street Legal, Counterstrike, Kung Fu: The Legend Continues.

D

D'ABO, OLIVIA
Actress. b. England. Jan. 1967. Parents, singer Michael d'Abo, actress Maggie London.
PICTURES: Conan the Destroyer, Bolero, Bullies, Into the Fire, Beyond the Stars, The Spirit of 76, Point of No Return, Wayne's World 2, Bank Robber, Greedy, Clean Slate, The Last Good Time, The Big Green, Kicking and Screaming, Live Nude Girls, Hacks, The Velocity of Gary, It Had To Be You, Texas Funeral, Seven Girlfriends, The Enemy, Jonni Nitro, Tarzan & Jane (video, voice), The Animatrix (video, voice).
TELEVISION: *Movies:* Not My Kid, Crash Course, Midnight's Child, Dad's Week Off, The Triangle. *Series:* The Wonder Years, The Single Guy, Mortal Kombat: The Animated Series (voice), The Legend of Tarzan (voice), Justice League. *Guest:* Party of Five.

DAFOE, WILLEM
Actor. r.n. William Dafoe. b. Appleton, WI, July 22, 1955. Worked with experimental group Theatre X on the road before coming to New York. Built sets and debuted with the Wooster Group at the Performing Garage playing (literally) a chicken heart in Elizabeth Le Compte's Nayatt School. Current member of the Wooster

Group, performing with them frequently in U.S. and Europe. For them appeared in independent film The Communists Are Comfortable.
PICTURES: Heaven's Gate (debut, 1980), The Loveless, The Hunger, Streets of Fire, Roadhouse 66, To Live and Die in L.A., Platoon (Acad. Award nom.), Off Limits, The Last Temptation of Christ, Mississippi Burning, Triumph of the Spirit, Born on the Fourth of July, Cry-Baby, Wild at Heart, Flight of the Intruder, White Sands, Light Sleeper, Body of Evidence, Faraway So Close!, Clear and Present Danger, Tom and Viv, The Night and the Moment, Basquiat, The English Patient, Speed 2: Cruise Control, Affliction, Lulu on the Bridge, New Rose Hotel, eXistenZ, Bullfighter, Boondock Saints, American Psycho, The Animal Factory, Morality Play, Edges of the Lord, Bullfighter, Spider Man, Once Upon a Time in Mexico, Auto Focus, The Clearing.

DAHL, ARLENE
Actress, Writer, Designer. b. Minneapolis, MN, Aug. 11, 1928. e. MN Business Coll.; U. of Minnesota, summers 1941-44; Minneapolis. Coll. of Music. m. Marc A. Rosen. Mother of actor Lorenzo Lamas. At age 8, played heroine of children's adventure serials on radio. Internationally syndicated beauty columnist, Chgo. Tribune-N.Y. News Syndicate, 1951-71; Pres. Arlene Dahl Enterprises, 1951-75; Sleepwear Designer, A.N. Saab & Co., 1952-57; Natl. Beauty Advisor, Sears Roebuck & Co., 1970-75; v.p. Kenyon & Eckhart Advg. Agcy., pres., Women's World Div., Kenyon-Eckhart, 1967-72; Fashion Consultant, O.M.A. 1975-78, Int'l. Director of S.M.E.I., 1973-76, Designer, Vogue Patterns 1978-85. Pres., Dahlia Parfums Inc., 1975-80, pres., Dahlia Prods., 1978-81: pres. Dahlmark Prods. 1981-. Honrs. include: 8 Motion Picture Laurel Awards, 1948-63; Hds. of Fame Award, 1971, Woman of the Year, N.Y. Adv. Council, 1969. Mother of Year, 1979; Coup de Chapeau, Deauville Film Fest 1983. Received star on Hollywood Walk of Fame. Lifetime Achievement Award Filmfest 1994.
THEATRE: *B'way:* Mr. Strauss Goes to Boston (debut, 1946), Cyrano de Bergerac, Applause. *Major U.S. tours include:* Questionable Ladies, The King and I, One Touch of Venus, I Married an Angel, Mame, Pal Joey, Bell Book and Candle, The Camel Bell, Life With Father, A Little Night Music, Liliom, Marriage Go Round, Blithe Spirit, Forty Carats, Dear Liar, Murder Among Friends.
PICTURES: My Wild Irish Rose (debut, 1947), The Bride Goes Wild, A Southern Yankee, Ambush, Reign of Terror (The Black Book), Scene of the Crime, The Outriders, Three Little Words, Watch the Birdie, Inside Straight, No Questions Asked, Caribbean, Jamaica Run, Desert Legion, Here Come the Girls, Sangaree, The Diamond Queen, Wicked as They Come, Fortune is a Woman, Bengal Brigade, Woman's World, Slightly Scarlet, She Played With Fire, Journey to the Center of the Earth, Kisses for My President, Les Ponyettes, DuBle en Liasse, Le Chemin du Katmandu, The Landraiders, A Place to Hide, Night of the Warrior, Broadway: The Golden Age by the Legends Who Were There.
TELEVISION: Max Factor Playhouse, Lux Television Theater, Pepsi Cola Playhouse, Opening Night, Arlene Dahl's Beauty Spot, Hostess, Model of the Year Show, Arlene Dahl's Starscope, Arlene Dahl's Lovescopes, One Life to Live (1981-84), Night of One Hundred Stars, Happy Birthday Hollywood, Who Killed Max Thorn?, Love Boat, Love American Style, Fantasy Island, Burke's Law, Renegade, Glorious Technicolor.
WRITER: Always Ask a Man, 1965, Your Beautyscope, 1969, Secrets of Hair Care, 1971, Secrets of Skin Care, 1973, Your Beautyscope 1977-78, Beyond Beauty, 1980, Lovescopes, 1983.

DAHL, JOHN
Director, Writer. b. Montana, 1956. e. Univ. of MT, Montana St. In collaboration with David Warfield made 30 minute rock musical, Here Come the Pugs and indept. feature, The Death Mutants.
PICTURES: Private Investigations (co-s.p.), Kill Me Again (dir., co-s.p.), Red Rock West (dir., co-s.p.), The Last Seduction (dir.), Unforgettable (dir., co-s.p.), Striking Back: A Jewish Commando's War Against the Nazis (dir., prod.), Rounders (dir.), Joy Ride (dir.), The Great Raid (dir.).

DALE, JIM
Actor. b. Rothwell, Northhamptonshire, England, Aug. 15, 1935. Debut as solo comedian at the Savoy, 1951. Joined National Theatre Co. in 1969 playing in Love's Labour's Lost, The Merchant of Venice, The National Health, The Card. Has written songs and music for films: Twinky, Shalako, Joseph Andrews, Georgy Girl (Acad. Award nom.). Many TV appearances. Director: Asprin and Elephants. In TV movie, American Clock.
THEATRE: *U.S.:* Mark Taper Forum: Comedians, Scapino. *N.Y.:* Theater: Taming of the Shrew, Scapino, Barnum (Tony and Drama Desk Awards, 1980), Joe Egg (Tony Award nom.), Me and My Girl, Privates on Parade, Travels With My Aunt.
PICTURES: Six-Five Special (debut, 1958), Raising the Wind, Nurse on Wheels, The Iron Maiden, Carry on Cabby, Carry on Jack, Carry on Spying, Carry on Cleo, The Big Job, Carry on Cowboy, Carry on Screaming, Don't Lose Your Head, The Winter's Tale, The Plank, Follow That Camel, Carry on Doctor, Lock Up Your Daughters, Carry on Again Doctor, The National Health, Digby—The Biggest Dog in the World, Joseph Andrews, Pete's Dragon, Hot Lead Cold Feet, Unidentified Flying Oddball, Scandalous, Carry on Columbus.

DALEY, ROBERT
Producer. e. UCLA. Began career in pictures at Universal International and TV at Desilu.
PICTURES: Play Misty For Me, Dirty Harry (exec. prod.), Joe Kidd, High Plains Drifter, Breezy, Magnum Force, Thunderbolt and Lightfoot, The Eiger Sanction, The Outlaw Josey Wales, The Enforcer, The Gauntlet, Every Which Way But Loose, Escape from Alcatraz (exec. prod.), Any Which Way You Can (exec. prod.), Bronco Billy (exec. prod.), Stick (exec. prod.), Real Genius (exec. prod.).
TELEVISION: The Untouchables, Ben Casey, The FBI, 12 O'Clock High, The Invaders, etc.

DALSIMER, SUSAN
Executive. Editor for E.P. Dutton before joining Lorimar Prods., as v.p. of east coast development. Left to become consultant for original programming at Home Box Office. 1987, named v.p., creative affairs, east coast, for Warner Bros. 1994, v.p., publishing for Miramax Films.

DALTON, TIMOTHY
Actor. b. Colwyn Bay, No. Wales, March 21, 1946. Started acting at Natl. Youth Theatre, then studied at RADA. Prof. stage debut in Richard III and As You Like It at Birmingham Rep.
THEATRE: Coriolanus, The Merchant of Venice, Richard III, The Doctor's Dilemma, St. Joan, Macbeth, Henry IV, Henry V, The Samarian, Black Comedy, White Liars, Lunatic Lover and Poet, Love Letters (1991).
PICTURES: The Lion in Winter, Cromwell, The Voyeur, Wuthering Heights, Mary Queen of Scots, Permission to Kill, Sextette, Agatha, Flash Gordon, El Hombre Que Supo Amar, Anthony and Cleopatra, Chanel Solitaire, The Doctor and the Devils, The Living Daylights, Brenda Starr, Hawks, Licence to Kill, The King's Whore, The Rocketeer, Naked in New York, Saltwater Moose, The Reef, The Informant, The Beautician and the Beast, Made Men, Time Share, American Outlaws, Looney Tunes: Back in Action.
TELEVISION: Mini-Series: Centennial, Mistral's Daughter, Sins, Scarlett. Movies: The Master of Ballantrae, Lie Down With Lions, Field of Blood, Framed, Cleopatra, The James Bond Story, Possessed. Specials: The Three Princes, Five Finger Exercise, Candida, Faerie Tale Theater: The Emperor's New Clothes (narr.), Nature: In The Company of Wolves (docu.) Series: Sat'day While Sunday, Judge Dee, Hooked International, Charlie's Angels: Fallen Angel, Tales From the Crypt: Werewolf Concerto, Survival Factor Series (narr.).

DALTREY, ROGER
Singer, Actor. b. London, England, March 1, 1944. Lead vocalist with The Who.
PICTURES: Woodstock, Tommy, Lisztomania, The Legacy, The Kids Are Alright, McVicar (also prod.), Mack the Knife, The Teddy Bear Habit, Father Jim, If It Looks Could Kill, Buddy's Song, Lightning Jack, Bad English 1: Tales of a Son of a Brit, Rolling Stone's Rock and Roll Circus, Message to Love: The Isle of Wight Festival, Legends: The Who, The Fifth Freedom, Like It Is, Pixelon's iBash, The Messiah XXI, Chasing Destiny, .com for Murder, The Chemical Wedding.
TELEVISION: Movie: Forgotten Prisoners: The Amnesty Files, Dark Prince: The True Story of Dracula, Piped Dreams. Miniseries: Pirate Tales, The Magical Legend of the Leprechauns. Specials: numerous performances with The Who.

DALY, JIM
Executive Director. b. 1938. Managing director of Film and Television division which includes: Pinewood Studios, Rank Film Laboratories, Odeon Cinemas, Rank Film Distributors, Deluxe Hollywood, Deluxe Toronto, Rank Advertising Films, Rank Theatres, Rank Video Services, Rank Video Services America, Rank Video Services Europe, Film House Company, Rank Brimar, Rank Cintel, Strand Lighting, Rank Taylor Hobson. Appt. exec. dir., Rank Org., 1982 to present.

DALY, JOHN
Executive. b. London, England, July 16, 1937. After working in journalism joined Royal Navy. On leaving Service after three years, trained as underwriter with an Assurance Company. In 1966 became David Hemmings manager and in 1967 formed the Hemdale Company with Hemmings (who later sold interest) Chmn. Hemdale Holdings Ltd.
PICTURES: Images, Sunburn (co-prod., co-s.p.), High Risk, Going Ape, Deadly Force, Carbon Copy, Yellowbeard, The Terminator, The Falcon and the Snowman, Salvador, River's Edge, At Close Range, Hoosiers, Platoon, Best Seller, Shag (exec. prod.), Vampire's Kiss (exec. prod.), Miracle Mile (prod.), Criminal Law (co-exec. prod.), War Party (prod.), The Boost, Out Cold (exec. prod.), Staying Together (exec. prod.), Chattahoochee (exec. prod.), War Party (exec. prod.), Hidden Agenda (exec. prod.), Don't Tell Her It's Me (exec. prod.), Bright Angel (exec. prod.), Alec to the Rescue (exec. prod.), Gunga Din, A Beautiful Day (exec. prod.).

DALY, ROBERT A.
Executive. b. New York, NY, Dec. 8, 1936. e. Brooklyn Coll., Hunter Coll. Joined CBS-TV in 1955; dir. of program acct.; dir. of research and cost planning; dir. of business affairs. Later named v.p., business affairs, NY; exec. v.p. of network on April 1976. Named president, CBS Entertainment. Oct. 1977. In Oct. 1979 became responsible for CBS Theatrical Films as well as the TV operation. In 1981, appointed chmn. of bd. and co-CEO of Warner Bros.; 1982, named chmn. of bd. and CEO; 1994, named chmn.

of bd. and co-CEO, sharing office with Terry Semel; 1995, also named chmn. and co-CEO of the Warner Bros. Music Group. Currently pres. and CEO, Los Angeles Dodgers baseball team.

DALY, TIM
Actor. b. New York, NY, March 1, 1956. m. actress Amy Van Nostrand. Son of late actor James Daly, brother of actress Tyne Daly. e. Bennington Coll., B.A. Acted in summer stock while in college. Moved to NY where had own rock and roll band. Has performed in cabaret at Williamstown Theater Festival.
THEATRE: Fables for Friends, Oliver Oliver, Mass Appeal, Bus Stop, Coastal Disturbances (Theatre World Award).
PICTURES: Diner, Just the Way You Are, Made in Heaven, Spellbinder, Love or Money, Year of the Comet, Caroline at Midnight, Dr. Jekyll and Ms. Hyde, Denise Calls Up, The Associate, The Object of My Affection, Seven Girlfriends, Basic, Against the Ropes.
TELEVISION: Movies: I Married a Centerfold, Mirrors, Red Earth White Earth, In the Line of Duty: Ambush in Waco, Dangerous Heart, Execution of Justice, A House Divided. Special: The Rise and Rise of Daniel Rocket. Mini-Series: I'll Take Manhattan, Queen, From the Earth to the Moon, Storm of the Century. Series: Ryan's Four, Almost Grown, Wings, Superman (voice), The New Batman/Superman Adventures (voice), Invasion America, The Fugitive. Guest: Midnight Caller, Hill Street Blues, Alfred Hitchcock Presents.

DALY, TYNE
Actress. r.n. Ellen Tyne Daly. b. Madison, WI, Feb. 21, 1946. Daughter of late actor James Daly and actress Hope Newell; brother is actor Timothy Daly.
THEATRE: The Butter and Egg Man, That Summer That Fall, Skirmishes, The Black Angel, Rimers of Eldritch, Ashes, Three Sisters, Come Back Little Sheba (L.A., 1987), Gypsy (Tony Award, 1990), Queen of the Stardust Ballroom, The Seagull, On the Town, Call Me Madam (in concert).
PICTURES: John and Mary, Angel Unchained, Play It As It Lays, The Adulteress, The Enforcer, Telefon, Speedtrap, Zoot Suit, The Aviator, Movers & Shakers, The Lay of the Land, Vig, Autumn Heart, The Simian Line, A Piece of Eden.
TELEVISION: Movies: In Search of America, A Howling in the Woods, Heat of Anger, The Man Who Could Talk to Kids, Larry, The Entertainer, Better Late Than Never, Intimate Strangers, The Women's Room, A Matter of Life or Death, Your Place or Mine, Kids Like These, Stuck With Each Other, The Last to Go, Face of a Stranger, Columbo: A Bird in the Hand, Scattered Dreams: The Kathryn Messenger Story, The Forget-Me-Not Murders, Columbo: Undercover, Cagney & Lacey: The Return, Cagney & Lacey: Together Again, Bye Bye Birdie, Cagney & Lacey: True Convictions, Cagney & Lacey: The View Through the Glass Ceiling, Tricks, The Perfect Mother, Three Secrets, Execution of Justice, Absence of the Good, The Wedding Dress. Series: Cagney & Lacey (4 Emmy Awards), Christy (Emmy Award, 1996), Judging Amy (Emmy Award nom.). Guest: Medical Center, Columbo, Ray Bradbury Theatre, Wings.

DAMON, MARK
Executive, Actor. b. Chicago, IL, April 22, 1933. e. UCLA, B.A. literature, M.A. business administration. Actor: 1958 under contract to 20th Century Fox, 1960 winner Golden Globe Award-Newcomer of the Year; early career includes The Fall of The House of Usher, The Longest Day; 1961 moved to Italy, stayed 16 years appearing in leading roles in 50 films; 1974 head of foreign dept. for PAC, a leading film distributor in Italy; 1976 returned to the U.S. as exec. prod. of The Choirboys and in charge of its foreign distribution; 1979 founder and pres. of Producers Sales Organization, intl. distribution org. 1987 formed Vision Int'l.; 1993, formed MDP Worlwide, intl. prod. & distrib. co. and is currently chmn. & CEO. He is a director of the American Film Marketing Assoc. (AFMA).
PICTURES: Exec. prod. or prod.: The Arena, The Choirboys, The Neverending Story, Das Boot, Nine 1/2 Weeks, Short Circuit, Flight of the Navigator, Lost Boys, High Spirits, Bat 21 (co-prod.), Diary of a Hit Man, Wild Orchid, Wild Orchid II: Two Shades of Blue, Stalingrad, The Jungle Book, The Jungle Book 2, The Blackout, The Winner, Orgazmo, Loved, Deceiver (also actor), Eye of the Beholder. Actor: Inside Detroit, Screaming Eagles, Between Heaven and Hell, Young and Dangerous, The Party Crashers, Life Begins at 17, House of Usher, This Rebel Breed, The Reluctant Saint, The Longest Day (uncredited), Beauty and the Beast, The Young Racers, Black Christmas, Pedro el Cruel, Son of Cleopatra, Hundred Horsemen, Ringo and His Golden Pistol, Agente segreto 777 operzione Mistero, Dio—come ti amo, One for All, Train for Durango, Death Does Not Count the Dollars, Johnny Yuma, Morti non si contano I, Kill and Pray, School Girl Killer, Anzio, Long Live Robin Hood, The Norman Swordsman, La Spada Normanna, Posate le pistole reverendo, Leoni di Petersburgo, Monta in sella figlio di...!, The Devil's Wedding Night, Little Mother, Crypt of the Living Death, Byleth, There Is No 13, Lo matas tu o lo mato yo, Do I Kill You or Do You Kill Me?, Stuck on You, Deceiver, Monster, The I Inside, 11:14.

DAMON, MATT
Actor, Writer. b. Cambridge, MA, Oct. 8, 1970. Chicago Film Crits. Award, Most Promising New Actor, 1997.
PICTURES: Actor: Mystic Pizza (debut, 1988), School Ties, Geronimo: An American Legend, Courage Under Fire, Glory Daze, Chasing Amy, The Rainmaker, Good Will Hunting (also s.p., Acad. Award, Golden Globe Award, Best Screenplay, 1997), Rounders, Saving Private Ryan, The Talented Mr. Ripley, Dogma,

All the Pretty Horses, Titan A.E. (voice), The Legend of Bagger Vance, All the Pretty Horses, Ocean's Eleven, The Majestic (voice), The Third Wheel, Spirit: Stallion of the Cimarron (voice), Gerry, The Bourne Identity, Confessions of a Dangerous Mind. Exec. prod.: Speakeasy, The Battle of Shaker Heights.
TELEVISION: *Movies:* Rising Son, The Good Old Boys. Series: Project Greenlight 2 (as himself).

DAMONE, VIC
Singer, Actor. r.n. Vito Farinola. b. Brooklyn, NY, June 12, 1928. m. actress-singer Diahann Carroll. e. Lafayette H.S., Brooklyn. Winner Arthur Godfrey talent show, 1947; then night clubs, radio, theatres. U.S. Army, 1951-53.
PICTURES: Rich Young and Pretty (debut, 1951), The Strip, Athena, Deep in My Heart, Hit the Deck, Kismet, Hell to Eternity.
TELEVISION: *Series:* The Vic Damone Show (1956-57), Lively Ones (1962-63), The Vic Damone Show (1967).

DAMSKI, MEL
Director. b. New York, NY, July 21, 1946. e. Colgate U., AFI. Worked as reporter, journalism professor. USC Cinema instructor.
PICTURES: Yellowbeard, Mischief, Happy Together.
TELEVISION: *Movies:* The Long Journey Back, The Child Stealer, A Perfect Match, Word of Honor, American Dream, For Ladies Only, The Legend of Walks Far Woman, Making the Grade, An Invasion of Privacy, Badge of the Assassin, A Winner Never Quits, Attack on Fear, Hero in the Family, Murder by the Book, The Three Kings, Everybody's Baby: The Rescue of Jessica McClure, A Connecticut Yankee in King Arthur's Court, The Girl Who Came Between Them, Blood River, Shoot First: A Cop's Vengeance, Wife Mother Murderer, Back to the Streets of San Francisco, Wild Card, The Care and Handling of Roses, Their Second Chance, Still Kicking: The Fabulous Palm Spring Follies. *Series:* M*A*S*H, Barnaby Jones, The Bionic Woman, Lou Grant, Picket Fences, Lois and Clark: The New Adventures of Superman, Harts of the West, Chicago Hope, Nowhere Man, American Gothic, Early Edition, The Practice, Ally McBeal, Any Day Now, The Love Boat: The Next Wave, Vengeance Unlimited, Charmed, Hack & Jill, Ally, Young Americans, Boston Public, The Tick.

DANA, BILL
Actor, Writer. b. Quincy, MA, Oct. 5, 1924. Night clubs and TV.
PICTURES: The Busy Body, The Barefoot Executive, The Nude Bomb (also s.p.), The Right Stuff, Lena's Holiday.
TELEVISION: *Movies:* The Snoop Sisters, Rosetti & Ryan: Men Who Love Women, A Guide for the Married Woman, Murder in Texas. *Actor:* Facts of Life, Too Close for Comfort, Golden Girls, Hollywood Palace, St. Elsewhere. *Series:* The Steve Allen Show (performer, head writer, 1961), The Bill Dana Jose Jimenez Show (star, writer), Spike Jones Show (prod., writer, performer), Milton Berle Show (prod., writer, performer), No Soap Radio, Zorro and Son, All in the Family (writer).

DANCE, CHARLES
Actor. b. Worcestershire, England, Oct. 10, 1946. e. Plymouth Coll. Art., Leicester Coll. of Art (graphic design degree). After first working as a West End theatre stagehand, made acting debut in 1970 in a touring company of It's a Two-Foot-Six-Inches-above-the Ground World. Worked in provincial repertory theaters. Joined the Royal Shakespeare Company 1975-80: Hamlet, Richard III, As You Like It. Lead in Henry V (1975, N.Y.), Coriolanus (Paris, London, Stratford).
THEATRE: Plenty, McGuffin, revival of Irma La Douce (West End), Turning Over (London's Bush Theatre).
PICTURES: The Spy Who Loved Me (debut, 1977), For Your Eyes Only, Plenty, The Golden Child, Good Morning Babylon, White Mischief, The Hidden City, Pascali's Island, Alien 3, The Valley of Stone, Last Action Hero, China Moon, Century, Kabloonak, Exquisite Tenderness, Shortcut to Paradise, Undertow, Michael Collins, Space Truckers, What Rats Won't Do, Hilary & Jackie, Don't Go Breaking My Heart, Chrono-Perambulator, Dark Blue World, Gosford Park, Ali G Indahouse, Black and White, Swimming Pool, City and Crimes.
TELEVISION: Very Like a Whale, The McGuffin, The Jewel in the Crown, Lightning Always Strikes Twice, Edward VII, The Fatal Spring, Little Eyolf, Frost in May, Nancy Astor, Saigon—The Last Day, Out On a Limb, BBC's The Secret Servant, Rainy Day Woman, Out of the Shadows, First Born, Goldeneye, Rebecca, Phantom of the Opera (mini-series), Darling of the Gods, In the Presence of Mine Enemies, Justice in Wonderland, Murder Rooms, The Life and Adventures of Nicholas Nickleby, Alien Evolution.

D'ANGELO, BEVERLY
Actress. b. Columbus, OH, Nov. 15, 1954. Studied visual arts and was exchange student in Italy before working as cartoonist for Hanna-Barbera Studios in Hollywood. Toured Canada's coffeehouse circuit as singer and appeared with rock band called Elephant. Joined Charlotte Town Festival Company. B'way debut in rock musical, Rockabye Hamlet. Off-B'way: Simpatico (Theatre World Award).
PICTURES: The Sentinel (debut 1977), Annie Hall, First Love, Every Which Way But Loose, Hair, Highpoint, Coal Miner's Daughter, Honky Tonk Freeway, Paternity, National Lampoon's Vacation, Finders Keepers, National Lampoon's European Vacation, Big Trouble, Maid to Order, In the Mood, Aria, Trading Hearts, High Spirits, National Lampoon's Christmas Vacation, Daddy's Dyin', The Miracle, The Pope Must Die, Man Trouble,

Lonely Hearts, Lightning Jack, Eye for an Eye, Edie and Pen, Pterodactyl Woman from Beverly Hills, Vegas Vacation, A Ratls Take, Nowhere, Love Always, With Friends Like These, Illuminata, American History X, Sugar Town, Jazz Night, High Fidelity, Happy Birthday, Women in Film, Summer Catch, Where's Angelo?, The Pursuit of Happiness.
TELEVISION: *Movies:* A Streetcar Named Desire, Doubletake, Slow Burn, Hands of a Stranger, Trial: The Price of Passion, A Child Lost Forever, The Switch, Judgment Day: The John List Story, Jonathan Stone: Threat of Innocence, Menendez: A Killing in Beverly Hills, Lansky, Talk to Me, On the Edge. *Mini-Series:* Captains and the Kings. *Special:* Sleeping Beauty (Faerie Tale Theater). *Guest:* The Simpsons.

DANES, CLAIRE
Actress. b. New York, NY, April 12, 1979. e. Professional Performing Arts School, NY; Lee Strasberg Studio. Acting career began with off-off-B'way appearances in Happiness, Punk Ballet and Kids on Stage.
PICTURES: Dreams of Love (debut), Thirty (short), The Pesky Suitor (short), Little Women, How to Make an American Quilt, Home for the Holidays, I Love You I Love You Not, Romeo + Juliet, To Gillian on Her 37th Birthday, Polish Wedding, U-Turn, The Rainmaker, Polish Wedding, Les Miserables, The Mod Squad, Brokedown Palace, Igby Goes Down, The Hours, It's All About Love, Flora Plum, Terminator 3: Rise of the Machines.
TELEVISION: *Movies:* No Room for Opal, The Coming Out of Heidi Leiter. *Series:* My So Called Life. *Guest:* Law and Order.

DANGERFIELD, RODNEY
Actor, Comedian. r.n. Jacob Cohen. b. Babylon, NY, Nov. 22, 1921. Performer in nightclubs as Jack Roy 1941-51. Worked as businessman 1951-63, before becoming stand-up comedian. Founder Dangerfields' Nightclub, 1969.
PICTURES: The Projectionist, Caddyshack, Easy Money (also co-s.p.), Back to School, Moving, Rover Dangerfield (voice, exec. prod., s.p., co-story, co-wrote songs), Ladybugs, Natural Born Killers, Casper (cameo), Meet Wally Sparks (also co-s.p.), The Godson, Everything's George, Porn Star: The Legend of Ron Jeremy, The 4th Tenor, Back by Midnight.
TELEVISION: *Movies:* Benny and Barney: Las Vegas Undercover. *Series:* The Dean Martin Show. *Guest:* The Simpsons.

DANIEL, SEAN
Executive. b. Aug. 15, 1951. e. California Inst. of Arts film school. BFA, 1973. Was journalist for Village Voice before starting m.p. career as documentary filmmaker and asst. dir. for New World Pictures. In 1976 joined Universal Pictures as prod. exec.; 1979, named v.p., then pres., production. Resigned March, 1989 to become pres., The Geffen Co., film div.; resigned from Geffen, Nov. 1989. 1990, with Jim Jacks started own prod. co. Alphaville, Inc., in partnership with Universal Pictures, and is pres. of co.
PICTURES: *Prod./Exec. prod.:* Pure Luck, American Me, CB4, Hard Target, Heart and Souls, Dazed and Confused, Tombstone, Village of the Damned, Michael, Mallrats, The Jackal, The Mummy, Lucky Numbers, The Gift, Down to Earth, The Mummy Returns, Pootie Tang, Rat Race, The Scorpion King, Dark Blue, The Hunted, Intolerable Cruelty.
TELEVISION: *Prod./Exec. prod.:* Don't Look Back, Freedom Song, Attila.

DANIELS, JEFF
Actor. b. Athens, Georgia. Feb. 19, 1955. e. Central Michigan U. Apprentice with Circle Repertory Theatre, New York. Established Purple Rose Theatre Co. in Chelsea, Michigan. Playwright: The Kingdom's Coming, The Vast Difference.
THEATRE: Brontosaurus, Short-Changed Review, The Farm, Fifth of July, Johnny Got His Gun (Obie Award), Lemon Sky, The Three Sisters, The Golden Age, Redwood Curtain.
PICTURES: Ragtime (debut, 1981), Terms of Endearment, The Purple Rose of Cairo, Marie, Heartburn, Something Wild, Radio Days, The House on Carroll Street, Sweet Hearts Dance, Checking Out, Arachnophobia, Welcome Home Roxy Carmichael, Love Hurts, The Butcher's Wife, There Goes the Neighborhood, Rain Without Thunder, Gettysburg, Speed, Terminal Velocity, Dumb & Dumber, 2 Days in the Valley, Fly Away Home, 101 Dalmations, Trial and Error, Pleasantville, All the Rage, My Favorite Martian, The Crossing, Cheaters, Chasing Sleep, Escanabia in da Moonlight (also dir.), Super Sucker (also dir.), Gods and Generals, Blood Work, I Witness.
TELEVISION: *Movies:* A Rumor of War, Invasion of Privacy, The Caine Mutiny Court Martial, No Place Like Home, Disaster in Time, Teamster Boss: The Jackie Presser Story, Redwood Curtain, The Crossing. *Specials:* Fifth of July, The Visit (Trying Times). *Guest:* Breaking Away (pilot), Hawaii 5-0.

DANIELS, PAUL
TV performer, Magician. b. South Bank, England, April 6, 1938. Early career starring in British and overseas theatres. 1983, Magician Of The Year Award by Hollywood's Academy of Magical Arts. 1985, his BBC TV special awarded Golden Rose of Montreux trophy. Presenter of Every Second Counts and Paul Daniels Magic Show. Devised children's TV series, Wizbit and radio series Dealing With Daniels, Secret Magic and Game Show Wipeout. Paul Daniels in a Black Hole (tv movie). Various TV specials and series in U.K.

DANIELS, WILLIAM
Actor. b. Brooklyn, NY, Mar 31, 1927. e. Northwestern U. m. actress Bonnie Bartlett. Traveled around NY as part of The Daniels Family song and dance troupe. Appeared with family on experimental TV in 1941. Stage debut in Life with Father. Brought to national attention in A Thousand Clowns in original B'way play and film version.
THEATRE: The Zoo Story, On a Clear Day You Can See Forever, 1776, Dear Me, The Sky Is Falling, A Little Night Music.
PICTURES: Ladybug Ladybug, A Thousand Clowns, Two for the Road, The Graduate, The President's Analyst, Marlowe, 1776, The Parallax View, Black Sunday, Oh God!, The One and Only, Sunburn, The Blue Lagoon, All Night Long, Reds, Blind Date, Her Alibi, Magic Kid, Super Knight Rider.
TELEVISION: Movies: Rooster, Rehearsal for a Murder, Murdock's Gang, A Case of Rape, Sarah T.—Portrait of a Teenage Alcoholic, One of Our Own, Francis Gary Powers, Killer on Board, The Bastard, Big Bob Johnson and His Fantastic Speed Circus, Sgt. Matlovich Vs. the U.S. Air Force, The Rebels, City in Fear, Damien: The Leper Priest, Million Dollar Face, Drop Out Father, The Little Match Girl, Knight Rider 2000 (voice), Back to the Streets of San Francisco. Mini-series: Blind Ambition, The Adams Chronicles, The Lottery. Series: Captain Nice, The Nancy Walker Show, Freebie and the Bean, Knight Rider (voice), St. Elsewhere (Emmy Awards, 1985, 1986), Boy Meets World. Guest: East Side/West Side, For the People, Toma, The Rockford Files.

DANNER, BLYTHE
Actress. b. Philadelphia, PA, Feb. 3, 1943. e. Bard Coll. m. the late writer-prod. Bruce Paltrow. Daughter is actress Gwyneth Paltrow. Appeared in repertory cos. in U.S. before Lincoln Center productions of Cyrano de Bergerac, Summertree, and The Miser (Theatre World Award for last).
THEATRE: NY: Butterflies Are Free (Tony Award, 1971), Major Barbara, Twelfth Night, The Seagull, Ring Around The Moon, Betrayal, Blithe Spirit, A Streetcar Named Desire, Much Ado About Nothing, Sylvia. Williamstown: Picnic.
PICTURES: To Kill a Clown (debut, 1972), 1776, Lovin' Molly, Hearts of the West, Futureworld, The Great Santini, Man Woman and Child, Brighton Beach Memoirs, Another Woman, Mr. and Mrs. Bridge, Alice, The Prince of Tides, Husbands and Wives, To Wong Foo—Thanks for Everything—Julie Newmar, Homage, The Myth of Fingerprints, Mad City, The Farmhouse, The Proposition, No Looking Back, The X Files: Fight the Future, Invisible Circus, Forces of Nature, The Love Letter, Meet the Parents, 3 Days of Rain, The Invisible Circus, The Quality of Light, Sylvia, Hating Her.
TELEVISION: Movies: Dr. Cook's Garden, F. Scott Fitzgerald and The Last of the Belles, Sidekicks, A Love Affair: The Eleanor and Lou Gehrig Story, Too Far to Go, Eccentricities of a Nightingale, Are You in the House Alone?, Inside the Third Reich, In Defense of Kids, Helen Keller: The Miracle Continues, Guilty Conscience, Money Power Murder, Judgment, Never Forget, Cruel Doubt, Getting Up and Going Home, Oldest Living Confederate Widow Tells All, Leave of Absence, A Call to Remember, Saint Maybe, Murder She Purred: A Mrs. Murphy Mystery (voice), We Were the Mulvaneys, Change of Heart. Mini-series: Mark Twain. Series: Adam's Rib, Tattingers (revamped as Nick & Hillary), Presidio Med. Specials: To Confuse the Angel, George M, To Be Young Gifted and Black, The Scarecrow., Kiss Kiss Dahlings.

DANSON, TED
Actor, Producer. b. San Diego, CA, Dec. 29, 1947. e. Kent Sch., Stanford U., Carnegie-Mellon U, 1972. m. actress Mary Steenburgen. Studied at Actors Inst. New York stage debut, The Real Inspector Hound, 1972; mgr. and teacher, Actors Inst., L.A., 1978. Tv debut, The Doctors. Founded Amer. Oceans Campaign; bd. mem. Futures for Children.
PICTURES: The Onion Field (debut, 1979), Body Heat, Creepshow, Little Treasure, Just Between Friends, A Fine Mess, Three Men and a Baby, Cousins, Dad, Three Men and a Little Lady, Made in America, Getting Even With Dad, Pontiac Moon (also co-exec. prod.), Loch Ness, Jerry and Tom, Homegrown, Saving Private Ryan, Mumford, Scene Smoking: Cigarettes Cinema & The Myth of Cool (documentary).
TELEVISION: Movies: The Women's Room, Once Upon a Spy, Our Family Business, Cowboy, Something About Amelia, When the Bough Breaks (also prod.), We Are the Children, Mercy Mission: The Rescue of Flight 771, On Promised Land, Fight For Justice, The Canterville Ghost, Gulliver's Travels, Thanks of a Grateful Nation, Surviving Love. Guest: Laverne & Shirley, Magnum P.I., Taxi, The Simpsons, Frasier. Specials: Monty Python's Flying Circus Live at Aspen, Intimate Portrait: Christine Lahti, Cheers: The E! True Hollywood Story. Mini-series: Living With the Dead.Series: Somerset, Cheers (2 Emmy Awards: 1990, 1993), Ink (also co-exec. prod.), Becker.

DANTE, JOE
Director. b. Morristown, NJ, Nov. 28, 1946. Managing editor for Film Bulletin before going to Hollywood to work in advertising, creating campaigns for many films. Became protege of Roger Corman, co-directing Hollywood Boulevard. Edited film Grand Theft Auto; co-wrote story for Rock 'n' Roll High School.
PICTURES: Director: Piranha (also co-editor), The Howling (also co-editor), Twilight Zone-The Movie (dir. segment), Gremlins, Innerspace, Amazon Women on the Moon (co-dir.), The 'burbs, Gremlins II: The New Batch (also cameo), Matinee, Cat and Mouse, Small Soldiers, Haunted Lighthouse, Looney Tunes: Back in Action. Actor: Cannonball, Slumber Party Massacre, Eating

Raoul, Sleepwalkers, Beverly Hills Cop III, The Silence of the Hams, Hollywood Rated 'R', She's Alive: Creating the Bride of Frankenstein, Cinerama Adventure.
TELEVISION: Movies: Runaway Daughters, The Second Civil War. Amazing Stories, Eerie Indiana, The Warlord: Battle for the Galaxy. Series: Jeremiah (exec. prod.)

D'ANTONI, PHILIP
Producer. Director. b. New York, NY, Feb. 19, 1929. e. Fordham U., business administration. Joined CBS in mailroom, advanced into prod., sales development, prog. analysis, mkt. rsrch. Became indep. radio-TV repr. in 1954 for two years; then joined Mutual Broadcasting as sales manager; later, exec. v.p. Resigned in 1962 to form own prod. co. Made theatrical film debut with Bullitt as prod.; directing debut with The Seven Ups. Heads D'Antoni Prods.
PICTURES: Producer: Bullitt, The French Connection (Acad. Award for Best Picture, 1971). Prod.-Dir.: The Seven Ups.
TELEVISION: Movies: Mr. Inside/Mr. Outside, The Connection, Strike Force, In Tandem, Rubber Gun Squad, Cabo, Shark Kill. Movin' On (series) Elizabeth Taylor in London, Sophia Loren in Rome, Melina Mercouri in Greece, Jack Jones Special, This Proud Land.

DANZ, FREDRIC A.
Executive. b. Seattle, WA, Feb. 28, 1918. Chmn. of Sterling Recreation Organization Co., Seattle. Member, Foundation of Motion Picture Pioneers; v.p., Variety Club Intl.

DANZA, TONY
Actor, Producer. b. Brooklyn, NY, April 21, 1951. e. U. of Dubuque, IA on a wrestling scholarship. After grad. professional boxer before tested for role in TV pilot (Fast Lane Blues) which he won. Back to New York and fighting until called to coast to appear as Tony Banta in Taxi series. On L.A. & NY Stage: Wrong Turn at Lungfish.
PICTURES: Hollywood Knights, Going Ape, Cannonball Run II, She's Out of Control, Mob Justice, Angels in the Outfield, The Jerky Boys (co-exec. prod. only), Mamamia (dir. only), The Whisper.
TELEVISION: Movies: Murder Can Hurt You!, Doing Life (also exec. prod.), Single Bars Single Women, Freedom Fighter (also co-exec. prod.), The Whereabouts of Jenny (also co-exec. prod.), Dead and Alive (also co-exec. prod.), Deadly Whispers, Garbage Picking Field Goal Kicking etc., 12 Angry Men, The Girl Gets Moe, A Brooklyn State of Mind, Noah, Out of Time (exec. prod. only). Series: Taxi, Who's the Boss, Baby Talk (voice), The Mighty Jungle (voice), George (co-exec. prod. only), Hudson Street (also co-exec. prod.), The Tony Danza Show (also prod.), Family Law, Hollywood P.I.

DARABONT, FRANK
Writer, Director. b. January 28, 1959.
PICTURES: Writer: A Nightmare on Elm Street 3: Dream Warriors, The Blob, The Fly II, Frankenstein, The Shawshank Redemption, Eraser, The Fan, Saving Private Ryan, The Green Mile, Collateral Damage, Minority Report. Director: The Woman in the Room, The Shawshank Redemption (Acad. Award nom.), Frankenstein (s.p. only), The Green Mile (also prod.; Acad. Award nom.), The Majestic (also prod.), The Salton Sea (prod. only).
TELEVISION: Two-Fisted Tales (s.p.), The Young Indiana Jones Chronicles (s.p.), Young Indiana Jones Travels with Father (s.p.), Buried Alive (dir.), Till Death Us Do Part (dir.), Black Cat Run (s.p. and dir.), The Adventures of Young Indiana Jones in the Secret Service (s.p.)

D'ARBANVILLE-QUINN, PATTI
Actress. b. New York, NY, May 25, 1951. Grew up in Greenwich Village. Landed first job as baby in Ivory Soap commercials. In early teens worked as disc jockey where discovered by Andy Warhol and cast in small role in Flesh. Moved to Paris at 15 where she became successful model and was featured in book Scavullo on Beauty. Made film debut in Gerard Brach's 1969 film La Maison. Fluent in French, worked in French films until 1973 when moved to Los Angeles. Won Dramalogue Award for John Patrick Shanley's Italian-American Reconciliation (L.A., 1987).
PICTURES: La Maison, La Saigne, The Crazy American Girl, Rancho DeLuxe, Bilitis, Big Wednesday, The Main Event, Time After Time, The Fifth Floor, Hog Wild, Modern Problems, Contract: Kill, The Boys Next Door, Real Genius, Call Me, Fresh Horses, Wired, Frame-Up II: The Cover Up, The Fan, Father's Day, I Know What You Did Last Summer, Celebrity, Archibald the Rainbow Painter, Celebrity, Personal Velocity: Three Portraits, A Tale of Two Pizzas..
TELEVISION: Movies: Crossing the Mob, Blind Spot, Bad to the Bone. Mini-Series: Once an Eagle. Series: New York Undercover, Another World, South Beach, The Guiding Light. Guest: Crime Story, R.E.L.A.X., Tough Cookies, Charlie's Angels, Barnaby Jones, Miami Vice, Murder She Wrote, My So-Called Life.

DARBY, KIM
Actress. r.n. Deborah Zerby. b. Hollywood, CA, July 8, 1948. e. Swanson's Ranch Sch., Van Nuys H.S. Studied at the Desilu Workshop in Hollywood. Professional debut on the Mr. Novak TV series; screen debut as extra in Bye Bye Birdie.
PICTURES: Bus Riley's Back in Town, The Restless Ones, True Grit, Generation, Norwood, The Strawberry Statement, The Grissom Gang, The One and Only, Better Off Dead, Teen Wolf Too, Halloween: The Curse of Michael Myers, The Last Best

Sunday, NewsBreak, Mockingbird Don't Sing.
TELEVISION: *Movies*: The Karate Killers, Ironside (pilot), The People, Streets of San Francisco (pilot), Don't Be Afraid of the Dark, Story of Pretty Boy Floyd, This Was the West That Was, Flatbed Annie & Sweetiepie: Lady Truckers, Enola Gay, Embassy. *Mini-Series*: Rich Man Poor Man, The Last Convertible. *Guest*: Eleventh Hour, Gunsmoke. *Specials*: Flesh and Blood, Leslie Ann Warren: A Cinderella Story.

DARK, JOHN
Producer. Pres. of J.D.Y.T. Producciones S.L., Coin Film City.
PICTURES: Light Up the Sky, Wind of Change, Loss of Innocence (Greengage Summer), The 7th Dawn, Casino Royale, Half a Sixpence, Bachelor of Arts, There's a Girl in My Soup, From Beyond the Grave, Madhouse, Land That Time Forgot, At the Earth's Core, The People That Time Forgot, Warlords of Atlantis, Arabian Adventure, Slayground, Shirley Valentine, Stepping Out.
TELEVISION: *Series*: Eldorado.

DARREN, JAMES
Actor. b. Philadelphia, PA, June 8, 1936. e. Thomas Jefferson h.s., S. Philadelphia h.s. Studied acting with Stella Adler, NYC.
PICTURES: Rumble on the Docks (debut, 1956), The Brothers Rico, The Tijuana Story, Operation Mad Ball, Gunman's Walk, Gidget, The Gene Krupa Story, Because They're Young, All the Young Men, Let No Man Write My Epitaph, Guns of Navarone, Gidget Goes Hawaiian, Diamond Head, Gidget Goes to Rome, For Those Who Think Young, The Lively Set, Venus in Furs, The Boss' Son, Random Acts.
TELEVISION: *Movies*: City Beneath the Sea, Police Story, The Lives of Jenny Dolan, Turnover Smith, Scruples. *Episode Director*: T.J. Hooker, The A Team, Stingray, Werewolf, Hardball, Hunter, Tequila and Bonetti, Raven, Silk Stalkings, Walker: Texas Ranger, Renegade, Nowhere Man, Beverly Hills 90210, Savannah, Melrose Place. *Series*: The Time Tunnel, T.J. Hooker, Hollywood Squares, Melrose Place. *Guest*: Police Story, Hawaii Five-0, Vega$, Baa Baa Blacksheep, One Day at a Time.

DARRIEUX, DANIELLE
Actress. b. Bordeaux, France, May 1, 1917. e. Lycee LaTour, Conservatoire de Musique.
THEATRE: Coco, The Ambassador (B'way).
PICTURES: Le Bal (debut, 1932), La Crise Est Finis, Mayerling, Tarass Boulba, Port Arthur, Un Mauvais Garcon, Club de Femmes, Abus de Confiance, Mademoiselle ma Mere, The Rage of Paris, Katia, Retour a l'Aube, Battlement de Coeur, Premier Rendezvous, Caprices, Adieu Cherie, Au Petit Bonheur, Bethsabee, Ruy Blas, Jean de la reine, Occupe-toi d'Amelie, La Ronde, Rich Young and Pretty, Five Fingers, Le Plaisir, La Verite sur Bebe Donge, Adorable Creatures, Le Bon Dieu sans Confession, The Earrings of Madame De, Le Rouge et le Noir, Bonnes a Tuer, Napoleon, Alexander the Great, A Friend of the Family, Loss of Innocence (Greengage Summer), Les Lions sont Laches, Les Bras de lat Nuit, Bluebeard (Landru), Patate, Le Coup de Grace, L'Or du Duc, Le Dimanche de la Vie, The Young Girls of Rochefort, La Maison de Campagne, Scene of the Crime, A Few Days With me, Epiphany Sunday, Headstrong, Les Mamies, The Young Girls Turn 25, L'Univers de Jacques Demy, Tomorrow's Another Day, Emilie est Partie, 8 Women.
TELEVISION: Marie-Marie, Miss, L'Age vermeil, La Petite fille modele, Tu crois pas si bien dire, Bonjour maitre, Le Front dans les nuages, La Misere des riches, In the Face of Truth, Jalna, Un et font six, Que reste-t-il. Mini-series: Les Liaisons dangereuses.

DARTNALL, GARY
Executive. b. Whitchurch, England, May 9, 1937. e. Kings Col., Taunton. Overseas div., Associate British Pathe. European rep., 1958-60; Middle & Far East rep., Lion Intl. Films; U.S. rep., 1962; pres. Lion Intl. 1963; U.S. rep., Alliance Intl. Films Distributors Ltd., and London Indept. Prods. Ltd.; pres. Alliance Intl. Films Corp. and Dartnall Films Ltd., 1966; mng. dir., Overseas div. Walter Reade Org., 1969; pres. EMI Film Distribs., 1971; vice chmn. EMI TV Programs Inc., 1976; pres. EMI Videograms Inc., 1979; pres. VHD Programs Inc. & VHD Disc Mfg. Co, 1980; chmn. Thorn EMI Cinemas; CEO, Thorn EMI Screen Entertainment Ltd. 1987; acquired Southbrook Intl. TV and formed Palladium Inc., chmn. & CEO. 1993 formed The Douris Corporation to acquire and distribute the 700 title Rohauer Collection of classic titles, and serves as president.

DASSIN, JULES
Director, Writer, Actor. b. Middletown, CT, Dec. 18, 1911. Was married to late actress Melina Mercouri. Actor on dramatic stage several years; radio writer. Joined MGM, 1940, as dir. short subjects; later dir. features.
THEATRE: Ilya Darling, Medicine Show, Joy to the World, Isle of Children, Two's Company, Heartbreak House, Sweet Bird of Youth, A Month in the Country, Who's Afraid of Virginia Wolf?, The Road to Mecca, Death of a Salesman.
PICTURES: *Director*: Nazi Agent, Affairs of Martha, Reunion in France, Young Ideas, The Canterville Ghost, A Letter for Evie, Two Smart People, Brute Force, The Naked City, Thieves' Highway, Night and the City, Rififi (also co-s.p., actor), He Who Must Die (also co-s.p.), Where the Hot Wind Blows (also co-s.p.), Never on Sunday (also actor, prod., s.p.), Phaedra (also prod., co-s.p., actor), Topkapi (also prod.), 10:30 p.m. Summer (also prod., co-s.p.), Survival (also co-prod.), Uptight (also prod., co-s.p.), Promise at Dawn (also actor, prod., s.p.), The Rehearsal, A Dream of Passion (also s.p., prod.), Circle of Two.

DAVENPORT, NIGEL
Actor. b. Cambridge, England, May 23, 1928. e. Trinity Coll., Oxford. Began acting after stint in British military at 18 years. First 10 years of professional career in theatre. Majority of screen work in British films in 1960s and 70s.
PICTURES: Look Back in Anger (debut, 1959), Desert Mice, Peeping Tom, The Entertainer, Lunch Hour, In the Cool of the Day, Operation Snatch, Return to Sender, Ladies Who Do, The Third Secret, Sands of the Kalahari, A High Wind in Jamaica, Where the Spies Are, Life at the Top, A Man for All Seasons, Sebastian, The Strange Affair, Play Dirty, Sinful Davey, The Virgin Soldiers, The Royal Hunt of the Sun, The Mind of Mr. Soames, The Last Valley, No Blade of Grass, Villain, Mary Queen of Scots, L'Attentat, Living Free, Charley-One-Eye, Phase IV, La Regenta, Stand Up Virgin Soldiers, The Island of Dr. Moreau, Zulu Dawn, The Omega Connection, Nighthawks, Chariots of Fire, Greystoke: The Legend of Tarzan Lord of the Apes, Caravaggio, Without a Clue, The Circus Trap, El Coyote, The Mumbo Jumbo.
TELEVISION: To Bury Caesar, The Boneyard, Murphy's Law, The Curse of the Donkins, The News-Benders, To See How Far It Is, From Chekhov With Love, The Year of the Crow, An Affair of Honour, Conan Doyle, The Edwardians, On Such a Night, The Picture of Dorian Gray, Dracula, South Riding, The Applecart, Oil Strike North, Moths, Much Ado About Nothing, Prince Regent, The Ordeal of Dr. Mudd, Masada, A Midsummer Night's Dream, A Christmas Carol, The Biko Inquest, Ladies in Charge, Lord Mountbatten: The Last Viceroy, Howard's Way, Treasure Seekers, Shanghai, David Copperfield, Drake's Progress.

DAVIAU, ALLEN
Cinematographer. b. New Orleans, LA, June 14, 1942. Started as still photographer and stage lighting designer. Received Gold Clio Award for Tackle (Levi's 501).
PICTURES: Harry Tracy, E.T.: The Extra-Terrestrial (Acad. Award nom.), Twilight Zone: The Movie (co-photog.), Indiana Jones and the Temple of Doom (Calif. unit), The Falcon and the Snowman, The Color Purple (Acad. Award nom.), Harry and the Hendersons, Empire of the Sun (Acad. Award nom.; BAFTA & ASC Awards), Avalon (Acad. Award nom.; ASC Award), Defending Your Life, Bugsy (Acad. Award nom.; ASC Award), Fearless, Congo, The Astronaut's Wife, Sweet, The Translator, Hearts in Atlantis, Van Helsing.
TELEVISION: *Movies*: Streets of L.A., Rage, Legs. *Specials*: The Boy Who Drank Too Much. *Series*: Amazing Stories (pilot).

DAVID, KEITH
Actor. b. New York, NY, June 4, 1954. e. Juilliard.
THEATRE: *NY*: The Pirates of Penzance, A Midsummer Night's Dream, Waiting for Godot, Miss Waters to You, La Boheme, Coriolanus, Titus Andronicus, A Map of the World, The Haggadah, Alec Wilder: Clues to a Life, Boesman & Lena, Jelly's Last Jam, Hedda Gabler, Seven Guitars.
PICTURES: The Thing, Platoon, Hot Pursuit, Braddock: Missing in Action III, Off Limits, Stars and Bars, Bird, They Live, Road House, Always, Men at Work, Marked for Death, Final Analysis, Article 99, Reality Bites, The Puppet Masters, The Quick and the Dead, Clockers, Dead Presidents, Johns, Dead Cold (prod.), Marked Man (prod.), Daddy's Girl (prod.), The Dentist (prod.), The Nurse (prod.), The Stranger In The House (prod.), Voodoo (exec. prod.), Serial Killer (prod./dir.), Flipping, Larger than Life, Eye for an Eye, Johns, Hercules (voice), Fallout (voice), Executive Target, Volcano, Armageddon, There's Something About Mary, Where the Heart Is., Requiem for a Dream, The Replacements, Home Invaders, G Spots, Final Fantasy: The Spirits Within (voice), Novocaine, Pretty When You Cry, 29 Palms, Barbershop, Hung-Up, Agent Cody Banks, Head of State, Kaena: The Prophecy (voice), Hollywood Homicide.
TELEVISION: *Movies*: Ladykillers, Murder in Black and White, There Are No Children Here, Vanishing Point, Murder She Wrote: South by Southwest, Don King: Only in America, The Tiger Woods Story. *Series*: Spawn, Hercules (voice), House of Mouse (voice). *Mini-Series*: Roots: The Next Generations, Jazz, Mark Twain. *Special*: Hallelujah. *Guest*: The Equalizer, A Man Called Hawk, New York Undercover.

DAVID, PIERRE
Executive, Producer. b. Montreal, Canada, May 17, 1944. e. U. of Montreal. Joined radio station CJMS 1966 as pub. rel. & spec. events dir., 1969, while running Mutual Broadcasting Network of Canada's live entertainment div., created new film dist. co. Mutual Films. 1972 added prod. unit and as prod. or exec. prod., prod. and dist. 19 French language. Canadian films. With filmmaker Roger Corman est. Mutual Pictures of Canada, Ltd to dist. films in English Canada; 1978 teamed Mutual Films with Victor Solnicki and Claude Heroux to prod. English language films. Pioneered 3-picture concept for Canadian m.p. investors. Moved to L.A. 1983 where became pres., Film Packages Intl. where prod. exec. on Platoon. Then joined Larry Thompson Org. as partner involved in dev. and/or prod. of m.p., Jan., 1987, named chmn. of bd. and chief exec. officer, Image Org., Inc. intl. dist. co. formed by David and Rene Malo. Also pres. Lance Entertainment, prod. co. Sold Image Organization in 1997 and is currently Chairman of WIN Ventures, LLC. Also Chairman of AFMA's producers committee.
PICTURES: *Prod.*: The Brood, Hog Wild, Scanners, Dirty Tricks, Gas, The Funny Farm, Visiting Hours, Videodrome, Going Berserk, Of Unknown Origin, Covergirl, Breaking All the Rules, For Those I Loved, Blind-Fear (co-prod.), The Perfect Bride, Hot Pursuit, The Perfect Weapon, Bounty Tracker, Distant Cousins,

Deep Cover, Marital Outlaw, Stalked, Open Fire, The Force, The Secretary, Scanner Cop 2, The Wrong Woman, Scenes from the Goldmine, My Demon Lover, The Great Land of Small, Voodoo, Marked Man, Dead Cold, The Nurse, Man of Her Dreams, Daddy's Girl, The Dentist, Kid Cop, Stranger in the House, The Night Caller, Never Too Late, Little Men, Cupid, Wishmaster, Catured, The Dentist 2, The Landlady, Wanted, Rites of Passage, A Clean Kill, Someone is Watching, Dead Simple. *Exec. Prod.*: Quiet Cool, Scanners II: The New Order, Desire and Hell at Sunset Motel, Martial Law, Scanners III, Dolly Dearest, Mission of Justice, Deadbolt, Internal Affairs, Twin Sisters, Pin, The Neighbor, The Paperboy. *Prod., Dir.*: Scanner Cop, Serial Killer. Numerous others.

DAVIDOVICH, LOLITA
Actress. b. Ontario, Canada, July 15, 1961. Also acted under the name Lolita David.
PICTURES: Class, Adventures in Babysitting, The Big Town, Blaze, The Object of Beauty, JFK, The Inner Circle, Raising Cain, Leap of Faith, Boiling Point, Younger and Younger, Cobb, For Better or Worse, Now and Then, Jungle 2 Jungle, Touch, Gods and Monsters, Mystery Alaska, Play It to the Bone, Forever Flirt, Dark Blue, Hollywood Homicide.
TELEVISION: *Movies*: Two Fathers' Justice, Prison Stories: Women on the Inside (Parole Board), Keep the Change, Indictment: The McMartin Trial, McMartin Trial, Dead Silence, The Judge, Snow in August, The Kid (voice).

DAVIDSON, JOHN
Actor, Singer. b. Pittsburgh, PA, Dec. 13, 1941. e. Denison U. In numerous school stage prods. before coming to N.Y. in 1964 to co-star with Bert Lahr in B'way show, Foxy. Signed as regular on The Entertainers with Carol Burnett.
PICTURES: The Happiest Millionaire, The One and Only Genuine Original Family Band, The Concorde—Airport '79, The Squeeze, Edward Scissorhands.
TELEVISION: *Movies*: Coffee Tea or Me?, Shell Game, Roger & Harry: The Mitera Target, Dallas Cowboys Cheerleaders II. *Special*: The Fantasticks. *Guest*: The FBI, The Interns, Owen Marshall, The Tonight Show, (also frequent guest host). *Series*: The Entertainers, Kraft Summer Music Hall, The John Davidson Show (1969), The Girl With Something Extra, The John Davidson Show (1976), The John Davidson Talk Show (1980), That's Incredible, New Hollywood Squares, Time Machine (game show), Incredible Sunday, The $100,000 Pyramid.

DAVIDSON, MARTIN
Director, Writer. b. New York, NY, Nov. 7, 1939.
PICTURES: The Lords of Flatbush, Almost Summer, Hero at Large, Eddie and the Cruisers, Heart of Dixie (also exec. prod.), Hard Promises, Looking for an Echo.
TELEVISION: *Movies*: Long Gone, A Murderous Affair: The Carolyn Warmus Story, Follow the River. *Series*: Our Family Honor, Call to Glory, Law and Order, My Life and Times, Picket Fences, Chicago Hope, Judging Amy, Girls Club.

DAVIDTZ, EMBETH
Actress. b. Trenton, New Jersey, Jan. 1, 1966.
PICTURES: Sweet Murder, Mutator, Schindler's List, Army of Darkness, Murder in the First, Feast of July, Matilda, Fallen, The Gingerbread Man, Bicentennial Man, Bridget Jones's Diary, The Hole, Thir13en Ghosts, The Emperor's Club.
TELEVISION: A Private Life, 'Till Death Us Do Part, Deadly Matrimony, The Garden of Redemption, Citizen Baines, Shackleton.

DAVIES, JOHN HOWARD
Producer, Director. b. London, England, March 9, 1939. e. Haileybory, IS.C. and Grenoble Univ. Former child actor played leading roles in Oliver Twist, The Rocking Horse Winner, Tom Brown's Schooldays.
TELEVISION: *Prod./Dir.*: Monty Python's Flying Circus, Steptoe and Son, Fawlty Towers, The Good Life, The Goodies, The Other One, No Job for a Lady, Mr. Bean. *Special*: It's Black Entertainment (writer).

DAVIS, ANDREW
Director. b. Chicago, IL, 1947. e. Univ. of IL. Former journalist and photographer before landing job as asst. cameraman on 1969 film Medium Cool. Was dir. of photog. on several TV commercials and documentaries.
PICTURES: Lepke (dir. of photog.), Stony Island (dir., prod., co-s.p.), Over the Edge (dir. of photog.), Angel (dir. of photog.), Beat Street (co-s.p.). *Director*: The Final Terror, Code of Silence, Above the Law (also co-prod., co-story), The Package, Under Siege, The Fugitive, Steal Big Steal Little (also co-prod., co-s.p., co-story), Chain Reaction, A Perfect Murder, Collateral Damage, Holes (also prod.).

DAVIS, CARL
Composer. b. New York, NY, Oct. 28, 1936. e. Queens Coll., Bard Coll. and New England Coll. of Music. Worked as pianist with Robert Shaw Chorale and wrote music for revue Diversions (1958) and Twists (London), Moved to England 1961 writing incidental music for Joan Littlewood's Theatre Workshop Co., Royal Shakespeare Co. and National Theatre. Other theater music includes Jonathan Miller's Tempest, Forty Years On, and the musical The Vackees. Best known for composing new scores for silent classics (Napoleon, The Crowd, Greed, Intolerance, etc.) for screenings at which he conducts and for Thames TV The

Silents series. Concert work: Paul McCartney's Liverpool Oratorio.
PICTURES: The Bofors Gun, Up Pompeii, Rentadick, Man Friday, The Sailor's Return, Birth of the Beatles, The French Lieutenant's Woman, Praying Mantis, The Aerodrome, Champions, Weather in the Streets, George Stevens: A Filmmaker's Journey, King David, The Rainbow, Scandal, Girl in a Swing, Fragments of Isabella, Frankenstein Unbound, Diary of a Madman, Raft of the Medusa, The Voyage, Liberation, Widow's Peak, Anne Frank Remembered, Tje Raft of Medusa, Topsey-Turvy, The Book of Eve.
TELEVISION: That Was the Week That Was, Hollywood, The Pioneers, World at War, Mayor of Casterbridge, Lorna Doone, Unknown Chaplin, Buster Keaton—A Hard Act to Follow, Treasure Island, The Snow Goose, Our Mutual Friend, Naked Civil Servant, Silas Marner, The Accountant, Secret Life of Ian Fleming, Why Lockerbie?, Buried Mirro, A Christmas Carol, Royal Collection, Hotel du Lac, Black Velvet Gown, Lie Down With Lions, The Return of the Native, Seesaw, Goodnight Mister Tom, Great Gatsby, Back Home. *Mini-series*: Pride & Prejudice, Oliver's Travels, Cinema Europe: The Other Hollywood, Real Women, The Buried Mirror, A Dance to the Music of Time, The Face of Russia, Cold War.

DAVIS, GEENA
Actress. r.n. Virginia Elizabeth Davis. b. Wareham, MA, Jan. 21, 1957. e. Boston U. Acted with Mount Washington Repertory Theatre Co., NH. Was NY model before role in Tootsie, 1982.
PICTURES: Tootsie (debut, 1982), Fletch, Transylvania 6-5000, The Fly, Beetlejuice, The Accidental Tourist (Acad. Award, supporting actress, 1988), Earth Girls Are Easy, Quick Change, Thelma & Louise, A League of Their Own, Hero, Angie, Speechless (also prod.), Cutthroat Island, The Long Kiss Goodnight (also prod.), Stuart Little, Stuart Little 2.
TELEVISION: *Movie*: Secret Weapons. *Series*: Buffalo Bill (also wrote one episode), Sara, The Geena Davis Show. *Guest*: Family Ties, Riptide, Remington Steele, Trying Times.

DAVIS, JOHN
Executive, Producer. e. Bowdoin Col., Harvard Bus. Sch. Served as v.p. at 20th Century Fox before forming Davis Entertainment Company, where he is chairman.
PICTURES: Predator, Three O'Clock High, License to Drive, Little Monsters, The Last of the Finest, Shattered, Storyville, The Firm, The Thing Called Love, Fortress, Gunmen, Grumpy Old Men, Richie Rich, The Hunted, Waterworld, The Grass Harp, Courage Under Fire, Daylight, Out to Sea, Lewis & Clark & George, Bad Manners, Digging to China, Doctor Dolittle, Dudley Doright, Partners in Crime, Heartbreakers, Dr. Dolittle 2, Behind Enemy Lines, Pursuit, Happy Hour, 29 Palms, Life or Something Like It, Daddy Day Care, Paycheck, Heaven's Pond.
TELEVISION: *Movies*: Tears and Laughter: The Joan and Melissa Rivers Story, The Last Outlaw, This Can't Be Love, One Christmas, Kidnapped, Asteroid, Volcano: Fire on the Mountain, Miracle at Midnight, The Jesse Ventura Story, Little Richard, David Copperfield, Bobbie's Girl.
Mini-series: The Old Curiosity Shop, 20,000 Leagues Under the Sea.

DAVIS, JUDY
Actress. b. Perth, Australia, April 23, 1955. m. actor Colin Friels. Left convent school as teenager to become a singer in a rock band. Studied at West Australia Inst. of Technology and National Inst. of Dramatic Art, Sydney. Worked with theatre companies in Adelaide and Sydney and at Royal Court Theatre, London. Los Angeles stage debut Hapgood.
PICTURES: High Rolling (debut, 1977), My Brilliant Career, Hoodwink, Heatwave, Winter of Our Dreams, The Final Option, A Passage to India (Acad. Award nom.), Kangaroo, High Tide, Georgia, Alice, Impromtu, Barton Fink, Naked Lunch, Where Angels Fear to Tread, Husbands and Wives (Acad. Award nom.), On My Own (Australian Film Inst. Award), The Ref, The New Age, Absolute Power, Deconstructing Harry, Blood and Wine, Celebrity, Absolute Power, A Cooler Climate, Gaudi Afternoon, The Man Who Sued God, Swimming Upstream.
TELEVISION: Rocket to the Moon, A Woman Called Golda, One Against the Wind, Serving in Silence: The Margarethe Cammermeyer Story (Emmy Award, 1995), The Echo of Thunder, Dash and Lilly, Rosamunde Pilcher - Zerrissene Herzen, Life With Judy Garland: Me & My Shadows, Coast to Coast.

DAVIS, LUTHER
Writer, Producer. b. New York, NY, Aug. 29, 1921. e. Yale, B.A.
THEATRE: *Writer*: Kiss Them for Me, Kismet (Tony Award), Timbuktu! (also prod.), Grand Hotel (Tony nom.). Co-Prod.: Eden Court, Not About Heroes.
PICTURES: *Writer*: The Hucksters, B.F.'s Daughter, Black Hand, A Lion Is in the Streets, The Gift of Love, Holiday for Lovers, The Wonders of Aladdin, Lady in a Cage (also prod.), Across 110th Street.
TELEVISION: *Writer/Prod.*: Kraft Suspense Theatre and many pilots for series (Run for Your Life, The Silent Force, Eastside, Westside, etc.). *Specials*: Arsenic and Old Lace, The People Trap (prod.). *Movies*: Daughter of the Mind, The Old Man Who Cried Wolf.

DAVIS, MAC
Singer, Songwriter, Actor. b. Lubbock, TX, Jan 21, 1942. e. Emory U., Georgia State Coll. Employed as ditch digger, service station attendant, laborer, probation officer and record company salesman before gaining fame as entertainer-singer in 1969.

Recording artist and composer of many popular songs. On B'way 1992 in The Will Rogers Follies.
PICTURES: North Dallas Forty, Cheaper to Keep Her, The Sting II, Possums, Angels Dance, Where the Red Fern Grows, True Vinyl, Jackpot.
TELEVISION: *Movies:* Brothers-In-Law, What Price Victory?, Blackmail, For My Daughter's Honor, Dolly Parton: Treasures, Still Holding On: The Legend of Cadillac Jack, Murder She Wrote: The Last Free Man. *Series:* The Mac Davis Show.

DAVIS, OSSIE
Actor, Writer, Director. b. Cogdell, GA, Dec. 18, 1917. e. Howard U., Washington, DC. m. actress Ruby Dee. Studied acting in N.Y. with Rose McLendon Players, leading to Broadway debut in 1946 in Jeb. For years thereafter was one of best-known black actors on B'way stage in: Anna Lucasta, Jamaica, The Green Pastures, Wisteria Tree, A Raisin in the Sun, I'm Not Rappaport. Wrote and starred in Purlie Victorious, repeating role for film version. Directed and appeared with Ms. Dee in her musical Take It From the Top. Co-hosted Ossie Davis and Ruby Dee Story Hour on radio (3 years). Published plays: Purlie Victorious, Langston, Escape to Freedom, Curtain Call, Mr. Aldredge, Sir.
PICTURES: *Actor:* No Way Out, Fourteen Hours, The Joe Louis Story, Gone Are the Days, The Cardinal, Shock Treatment, The Hill, Man Called Adam, The Scalphunters, Sam Whiskey, Slaves, Let's Do It Again, Hot Stuff, House of God, Harry and Son, Avenging Angel, School Daze, Do the Right Thing, Joe Versus the Volcano, Jungle Fever, Gladiator, Malcolm X (voice), Grumpy Old Men, The Client, I'm Not Rappaport, Get on the Bus. *Director:* Cotton Comes to Harlem (also co-s.p.), Black Girl, Gordon's War, Countdown at Kusini (also actor, prod.), Get on the Bus, Doctor Dolittle, Scandalize My Name: Stories From the Blacklist, Alyson's Closet, The Unfinished Journey, Dinosaur (voice), Here's to Life, Voice of the Voiceless, Bubba Ho-Tep, Gettin' the Man's Foot Outta Your Ass and Other Life Lessons.
TELEVISION: *Movies:* All God's Children, Don't Look Back, Roots: The Next Generations, King, Teacher Teacher, The Ernest Green Story, Ray Alexander: A Taste for Justice, Ray Alexander: A Menu for Murder, The Android Affair, Ray Alexander: A Menu For Murder, Home of the Brave, 12 Angry Men, The Secret Path, Miss Evers' Boys, Paul Robeson: Here I Stand, The Soul Collector, A Vow to Cherish, The Ghosts of Christmas Eve, Finding Buck McHenry. *Series:* B.L. Stryker, Evening Shade, John Grisham's The Client. *Mini-Series:* Queen, Stephen King's The Stand, Thomas Jefferson, Jazz, Christianity: The First Two Thousand Years, Feast of All Saints. *Writer:* East Side/West Side, The Eleventh Hour. *Guest:* Name of the Game, Night Gallery, Bonanza, etc. *Specials:* Martin Luther King: The Dream and the Drum, With Ossie and Ruby (also co-prod.), Today is Ours (writer, dir.).

DAVIS, PETER
Author, Filmmaker. b. Santa Monica, CA, Jan. 2, 1937. e. Harvard Coll., 1955-57. Parents were screenwriter Frank Davis, and novelist-screenwriter Tess Slesinger. Writer-interviewer, Sextant Prods., FDR Series, 1964-65. Host: The Comers, PBS 1964-65. Author: Hometown (1982), Where Is Nicaragua? (1987), If You Came This Way (1995), articles for Esquire, NY Times Mag., The Nation, NY Woman, TV Guide.
PICTURES: Hearts and Minds (prod., dir.; Acad. Award, best documentary, 1975; Prix Sadoul, 1974), Jack (writer/prod.).
TELEVISION: *Writer-prod.:* Hunger in America (assoc. prod., WGA Award, 1968), The Heritage of Slavery, The Battle of East St. Louis, (Saturday Review Award, 1970; 2 Emmy nom.), The Selling of the Pentagon (WGA, Emmy, Peabody, George Polk, Ohio State, Sat. Review Awards, 1971), 60 Minutes (segment prod.), Middletown (series, prod., Dupont Citation, Emmy noms. 1983), The Best Hotel on Skidrow (ACE Award noms., 1992).

DAVIS, PRESTON A.
Executive. b. Norfolk, VA. Served in U.S. Army. 1976, joined ABC as engineer in Washington DC, later becoming sprv. of Electronic News Gathering; 1979, became tech. mngr. of ENG; 1983, named tech. mngr. then manager of ENG for southeast region, Atlanta; 1986, promoted to gen. mngr. ENG Operations, New York; 1988, named v.p. TV Operations, Broadcast Operations & Engineering, East Coast; In 1993, named to his current position of pres. of Broadcast Operations and Engineering for ABC Television Network Group.

DAVIS, SAMMI
Actress. b. Kidderminster, Worcestershire, England, June 21, 1964. Convent-educated before taking drama course. Performed in stage prods. with local drama society in Midlands, then Birmingham Rep. and Big Brum Theatre Co. Plays include The Home Front, The Apple Club, Nine Days, Databased, Choosey Susie. London stage debut: A Collier's Friday.
PICTURES: Mona Lisa, Lionheart, Hope and Glory, A Prayer for the Dying, Consuming Passions, The Lair of the White Worm, The Rainbow, The Horseplayer, Shadow of China, Four Rooms, Death Do Us Part, Assignment Berlin, Woundings, Soft Toilet Seats.
TELEVISION: Auf Wiedersehn Pet, The Day After the Fair, Pack of Lies, Chernobyl: The Final Warning, The Perfect Bride, Indecency, Spring Awakening. *Series:* Homefront.

DAVIS, WARWICK
Actor. b. 1970
PICTURES: Star Wars: Episode VI-Return of the Jedi, Labyrinth, Willow, Leprechaun, Leprechaun 2, Leprechaun 3, Leprechaun 4: In Space, Prince Valiant, A Very Unlucky Leprechaun, The

Bacchae, Star Wars: Episode I-The Phantom Menace, The New Adventures of Pinocchio, The White Pony, Harry Potter and the Sorcerer's Stone, Harry Potter and the Chamber of Secrets, Skinned Deep., Leprechaun: Back in Da Hood, Harry Potter and the Prisoner of Azkaban.
TELEVISION: *Movies:* The Ewok Adventure, Ewoks: The Battle for Endor, Prince Caspian and the Voyage of the Dawn Treader, The Silver Chair, Gulliver's Travels, Murder Rooms: The Kingdom of Bones, Snow White. *Mini-series:* The 10th Kingdom. *Guest:* Seinfeld.

DAVISON, BRUCE
Actor. b. Philadelphia, PA, June 28, 1946. e. Pennsylvania State U., NYU. debut, Lincoln Center Repertory prod. of Tiger at the Gates, 1967.
THEATRE: NY: King Lear (Lincoln Center), The Elephant Man, Richard III (NY Shakespeare Fest.), The Glass Menagerie, The Cocktail Hour. *Regional:* Streamers (LA Critics Award), The Caine Mutiny Court-Martial, The Normal Heart, To Kill a Mockingbird, A Life in the Theatre, The Front Page, Downside, Breaking the Silence.
PICTURES: Last Summer (debut, 1969), The Strawberry Statement, Willard, Been Down So Long It Looks Like Up To Me, The Jerusalem File, Ulzana's Raid, Mame, Mother Jugs and Speed, Grand Jury, Short Eyes, Brass Target, French Quarter, High Risk, A Texas Legend, Lies, Crimes of Passion, Spies Like Us, The Ladies Club, The Misfit Brigade, Longtime Companion (NY Film Critics, Natl. Society of Film Critics, & Golden Globe Awards, 1990; Acad. Award nom.), Steel and Lace, Short Cuts, An Ambush of Ghosts, Six Degrees of Separation, Far From Home: The Adventures of Yellow Dog, The Cure, The Baby-sitters Club, Homage, Grace of My Heart, The Crucible, Lovelife, Apt Pupil, Paulie, Vendetta, At First Sight, X-Men, The Other Side, Summer Catch, At Seventeen, March, Mind Is A Place of Its Own, High Crimes, Dahmer, X2, Runaway Jury.
TELEVISION: *Movies:* Owen Marshall: Counsellor at Law (A Pattern of Morality), The Affair, The Last Survivors, Deadman's Curve, Summer of My German Soldier, Mind Over Murder, The Gathering, Tomorrow's Child, Ghost Dancing, Poor Little Rich Girl: The Barbara Hutton Story, Lady in a Corner, Stolen: One Husband, Live! From Death Row, Desperate Choices: To Save My Child, A Mother's Revenge, Someone Else's Child, Down Out and Dangerous, The Color of Justice, Hidden in Silence, Little Girl Fly Away, A Memory in My Heart, Off Season, Lathe of Heaven.(co-prod. only). *Specials:* Taming of the Shrew, The Wave. *Guest:* Medical Center, Marcus Welby, Love American Style, Police Story, Lou Grant, Murder She Wrote, Alfred Hitchcock Presents (1985), Amazing Stories. *Series:* Hunter, Harry and the Hendersons.

DAVISON, DALE
Executive. b. North Hollywood, CA, March 21, 1955. e. U.C.L.A., B.A., 1978. Entered the motion picture industry in 1973 with Pacific Theatres. Employed with Great Western Theatres 1974-77 as manager, dir. of concessions, and asst. vice pres. Partner with Great Western Theatres, 1978-1984. Founder and CEO, CinemaCal Enterprises, Inc., from 1985-1999. Director of corporate development, Krikorian Premiere Theatres, 2000-01. VP of special projects, Century Theatres, 2001-present. NATO bd. of directors, 1994-2000. NATO of Ca. exec. comm. 1996-2000. Chief Barker, Variety Club of Northern Ca, 1997-1999.

DAVISON, JON
Producer. b. Haddonfield, NJ, July 21, 1949. e. NYU Film School. 1972, joined New World Pictures as natl. dir. of publ./adv.; 1972, named in charge of prod.; 1980, became indep. prod.
PICTURES: Hollywood Boulevard, Grand Theft Auto, Piranha, Airplane!, White Dog, Twilight Zone—The Movie (episode), Top Secret! Robocop, Robocop 2, Trapped in Paradise, Starship Troopers, The 6th Day, Starship Troopers 2.

DAWBER, PAM
Actress, Singer. b. Detroit, MI, Oct. 18, 1954. m. actor Mark Harmon. e. Farmington H.S., Oakland Community Coll. Worked as model and did commercials. First professional performance as singer in Sweet Adeleine at Goodspeed Opera House, East Haddam, CT.
THEATRE: *Regional:* My Fair Lady, The Pirates of Penzance, The Music Man, She Loves Me, Love Letters.
PICTURES: A Wedding, Stay Tuned, I'll Remember April.
TELEVISION: *Movies:* The Girl the Gold Watch and Everything, Remembrance of Love, Through Naked Eyes, Last of the Great Survivors, This Wife For Hire, Wild Horses, Quiet Victory: The Charlie Wedemeyer Story, Do You Know the Muffin Man, The Face of Fear, The Man With Three Wives, Web of Deception, Trail of Tears, A Child's Cry for Help, Don't Look Behind You. *Series:* Mork and Mindy, My Sister Sam, 101 Dalmations: The Series (voice), Life...and Stuff. *Specials:* Kennedy Center Honors, Salute to Andy Gibb, Night of the 100 Stars, 3rd Annual TV Guide Special.

DAY, DORIS
Singer, Actress. r.n. Doris Kappelhoff. b. Cincinnati, OH, April 3, 1924. e. dancing, singing. Toured as dancer; radio and band singer; screen debut in Romance on the High Seas, 1948. Voted one of Top Ten Money-Making Stars in Motion Picture Herald-Fame poll, 1951-52. Best female vocalist. M. P. Daily radio poll, 1952.
PICTURES: Romance on the High Seas (debut, 1948), My Dream is Yours, It's a Great Feeling, Young Man With a Horn, Tea for Two, Storm Warning, West Point Story, Lullaby of Broadway, On Moonlight Bay, I'll See You in My Dreams, Starlift,

The Winning Team, April in Paris, By the Light of the Silvery Moon, Calamity Jane, Lucky Me, Young at Heart, Love Me or Leave Me, The Man Who Knew Too Much, Julie, The Pajama Game, Teacher's Pet, Tunnel of Love, It Happened to Jane, Pillow Talk (Acad. Award nom.), Please Don't Eat the Daisies, Midnight Lace, Lover Come Back, That Touch of Mink, Bill Rose's Jumbo, The Thrill of It All, Move Over Darling, Send Me No Flowers, Do Not Disturb, Glass Bottom Boat, Caprice, The Ballad of Josie, Where Were You When the Lights Went Out?, With Six You Get Eggroll, Rowan & Martin at the Movies, That's Entertainment Part II, That's Dancing, Antz (singer "High Hopes").
TELEVISION: Movie: Homeward Bound. Series: The Doris Day Show (1968-73), Doris Day's Best Friends (educational cable show; 1985-86).

DAY, LARAINE
Actress. r.n. Laraine Johnson. b. Roosevelt, UT, Oct. 13, 1920. e. Long Beach Polytechic H.S., Paramount Studio School. In school dramatics; with Players Guild, Long Beach, Calif.; toured in church prod. Conflict; Professionally on stage in Lost Horizon, The Women, Time of the Cuckoo, Angel Street.
PICTURES: Stella Dallas (debut, 1937 as Laraine Johnson), Scandal Sheet, Border G-Man, Young Dr. Kildare (and subsequent series), And One Was Beautiful, My Son My Son, Foreign Correspondent, The Trial of Mary Dugan, The Bad Man, Unholy Partners, Fingers at the Window, Journey for Margaret, Mr. Lucky, The Story of Dr. Wassell, Bride by Mistake, Those Endearing Young Charms, Keep Your Powder Dry, The Locket, Tycoon, My Dear Secretary, I Married a Communist (Woman on Pier 13), Without Honor, The High and the Mighty, Toy Tiger, Three for Jamie Dawn, The Third Voice, Painted Desert, Sergeant Madden, Arizona Legion, Tarzan Finds A Son, I Take This Woman, Kathleen, Yank On the Burma Road.
TELEVISION: Appearances include Climax, Playhouse 90, Alfred Hitchcock, Wagon Train, Let Freedom Ring, Name of the Game, FBI, Sixth Sense, Medical Center, Murder on Flight 504 (movie), Fantasy Island, Love Boat, Lou Grant, Airwolf, Hotel, Murder She Wrote.

DAY, ROBERT
Director. b. England, Sept. 11, 1922. Started as cinematographer before turning to direction.
PICTURES: Director: The Green Man (debut, 1956), Stranger's Meeting, Grip of the Strangler (The Haunted Strangler), First Man Into Space, Bobbikins, Two-Way Stretch, Tarzan the Magnificent (also co-s.p.), The Rebel (Call Me Genius), Corridors of Blood, Operation Snatch, Tarzan's Three Challenges (also co-s.p.), She, Tarzan and the Valley of Gold, Tarzan and the Great River, Tarzan and the Jungle Boy (prod. only), The Man with Bogart's Face.
TELEVISION: Pilots include: Banion, Kodiak, Dan August, Sunshine, Switch, Logan's Run, Kingston, Dallas, Matlock. Movies include: Ritual of Evil, The House of Greenapple Road, In Broad Daylight, Having Babies, The Grass Is Always Greener Over the Septic Tank, Peter and Paul, Running Out, Scruples, Cook and Peary—The Race to the Pole, Hollywood Wives, The Lady from Yesterday, Diary of a Perfect Murder, Celebration, Higher Ground, Walking Through the Fire.

DAY-LEWIS, DANIEL
Actor. b. London, England, April 29, 1957. Son of late C. Day-Lewis, poet laureate of Eng., and actress Jill Balcon. Grandson of late Sir Malcolm Balcon who prod. Hitchcock's Brit. films. e. Bristol Old Vic. Theatre School. First professional job at 12 as ruffian scratching cars with broken bottle in film, Sunday Bloody Sunday. Then acted with Bristol Old Vic and Royal Shakespeare Co.
THEATRE: London: Dracula, Funny Peculiar, Troilus & Cressida, A Midsummer Night's Dream, Class Enemy, Edward II, Look Back in Anger, Another Country, Romeo and Juliet The Futurists Hamlet.
PICTURES: Gandhi, The Bounty, A Room With a View, My Beautiful Laundrette, The Unbearable Lightness of Being, Stars and Bars, Nanou, Ever Smile New Jersey, My Left Foot (Acad. Award, 1989; also BAFTA, NY Film Critics, L.A. Film Critics, Natl. Society of Film Critics Awards), The Last of the Mohicans, The Age of Innocence, In the Name of the Father, The Crucible, The Boxer, Gangs of New York, Rose and the Snake.
TELEVISION: BBC Movies/Specials: Eddie Shoestring, Artemis 81, The Lost Traveller, The Sugar House, Beyond the Glass, Dangerous Corner, A Frost in May, How Many Miles to Babylon?, My Brother Jonathan, The Insurance Man, History of Hamlet (host).

DEAKINS, ROGER
Cinematographer. b. Devon, England, May 24, 1949. Accepted into National Film School in 1972. Working as professional filmmaker from 1975 directing and photographing documentary films including Around the World With Ridgeway, Zimbabwe, Eritrea—Behind the Lines, When the World Changed, Worlds Apart S.E. Nuba, Worlds Apart Rajgonds. Photographed first feature, Another Time Another Place in 1982.
PICTURES: 1984, The Innocent, Sid & Nancy, Shadey, Defense of the Realm, White Mischief, Personal Services, Stormy Monday, Pascali's Island, The Kitchen Toto, Mountains of the Moon, Air America, The Long Walk Home, Barton Fink, Homicide, Thunderheart, Passion Fish, The Secret Garden, The Hudsucker Proxy, The Shawshank Redemption (Acad. Award nom.; ASC Award), Rob Roy, Dead Man Walking, Fargo, Courage Under Fire, Kundun, Martial Law, The Big Lebowski,

The Siege, Anywhere But Here, O Brother, Where Art Thou?, Thirteen Days, The Man Who Wasn't There, A Beautiful Mind, Levity, Intolerable Cruelty, House of Sand & Fog.
TELEVISION: Dinner With Friends.

DEAN, JIMMY
Actor, Composer. b. Plainview, TX, Aug. 10, 1928. Country singer and creator of Jimmy Dean Products (food).
SONGS: Composer: Big Bad John, Little Black Book, I.O.U., To a Sleeping Beauty, PT-109, Dear Ivan.
PICTURES: Diamonds Are Forever, Big Bad John.
TELEVISION: Movies: The Ballad of Andy Crocker, Rolling Man, The City. Series: The Jimmy Dean Show (1957; 1963-66), Daniel Boone, J.J. Starbuck. Specials: Sunday Night at the Palladium (London), Celebrities Offstage.

DEAN, MORTON
Television Newsman. b. Fall River, MA, Aug. 22, 1935. e. Emerson Coll. News dir., N.Y. Herald Tribune Net, 1957; corr. WBZ, 1960, corr. WCBS-TV, 1964; anchor, WCBW-TV News, 1967; corr., CBS News, 1967; anchor, CBS Sunday Night News, 1975; anchor, Sunday edition CBS Evening News, 1976; co-anchor, Independent Network News, 1985. Narrator of Traitors Within, tv documentary.

DEARDEN, JAMES
Writer, Director. b. London, England, Sept. 14, 1949. Son of late British director Basil Dearden. e. New Coll., Oxford U. Entered film industry in 1967 as production runner. After editing commercials and documentaries, and working as asst. dir., wrote, prod. and dir. first short film, The Contraption (Silver Bear Award, 1978 Berlin Film Fest.). 1978, began dir. commercials and made short, Panic (Cert. of Merit, 1980 Chicago Film Fest.). 1979, made 45-min Diversion, which became basis for Fatal Attraction (Gold Plaque, best short drama, 1980 Chicago Film Fest.).
PICTURES: Fatal Attraction (s.p.), Pascali's Island (dir., s.p.), A Kiss Before Dying (dir., s.p.), Rogue Trader (dir., s.p., prod.).
TELEVISION: The Cold Room (dir., writer, Special Jury Prize, dir., 1985 Fest. Intl. d'Avoriaz du Film Fantastique).

De BONT, JAN
Cinematographer, Director. b. Holland, Oct. 22, 1943. Trained at Amsterdam Film Acad. Recipient of Kodak Camera Award and Rembrandt Award.
PICTURES: Cinematographer: Turkish Delight, Keetje Tippel, Max Heuelaar, Soldier of Orange, Private Lessons (U.S. debut, 1981), Roar, I'm Dancing as Fast as I Can, Cujo, All the Right Moves, Bad Manners, The Fourth Man, Mischief, The Jewel of the Nile, Flesh + Blood, The Clan of the Cave Bear, Ruthless People, Who's That Girl, Leonard Part 6, Die Hard, Bert Rigby You're a Fool, Black Rain, The Hunt for Red October, Flatliners, Shining Through, Basic Instinct, Lethal Weapon 3. Director: Speed (debut, 1994), Twister, Speed 2: Cruise Control (also s.p., story), The Haunting (also prod.), Cosm (also s.p., prod.). Producer: S.L.C. Punk!, Zero Hour, Like a Hole in the Head, The Haunting, Equilibrium, Minority Report, Lara Croft Tomb Raider: The Cradle of Life (dir.), Thought Crimes (exec. prod.).
TELEVISION: (Photography): Movie: The Ray Mancini Story. Episode: Tales From the Crypt (Split Personality).

De BROCA, PHILIPPE
Director, Writer. b. Paris, France, March 15, 1933. e. Paris Technical School of Photography and Cinematography.
PICTURES: Director/Writer: Les Jeux de l'Amour (The Love Game), The Joker, The Five Day Lovers, Seven Capital Sins (dir. segment only), Cartouche (also actor), Les Veinards (segment), That Man from Rio, Male Companion (Un Monsieur de Compagnie), Les Tribulations d'un Chinois en Chine (Up to His Ears), King of Hearts (also prod.), Devil by the Tail, Give Her the Moon, Chère Louise, Le Magnifique, Dear Inspector (also s.p.), The Skirt Chaser, Someone's Stolen the Thigh of Jupiter, The African, , The Gypsy, Chouans! (dir., co-s.p.), Scheherazade, The Keys to Paradise, On Guard, Amazon.
TELEVISION: Movies: Le Veilleur de nuit, Madame Sans-Gêne, Y aura pas école demain, Louisiana (TV in U.S.).

De CAPRIO, AL
Producer, Director. e. Brooklyn Tech., NYU. Started as radio engineer, cameraman, tech. dir., prod. & dir. CBS; dir. series episodes of Sgt. Bilko, Car 54 Where Are You?, Musical specials for ABC, CBS, NBC; v.p. exec. prod. dir., MPO Videotronics, Pres. World Wide Videotape; Retired.

De CARLO, YVONNE
Actress. b. Vancouver, B.C., Sept. 1, 1922. e. June Roper School of Dance, British Columbia; Fanchon & Marco, Hollywood. Specialty dancing at Florentine Gardens, Earl Carroll's; motion picture debut in This Gun for Hire, 1942. One-woman club act and 7-person club act. Autobiography, Yvonne (1987).
PICTURES: This Gun for Hire (debut, 1942), Harvard Here I Come, Youth on Parade, Road to Morocco, Let's Face It, The Crystal Ball, Salute for Three, For Whom the Bell Tolls, True to Life, So Proudly We Hail, The Deerslayer, Practically Yours, Salome Where She Danced, Frontier Gal, Brute Force, Song of Scheherazade, Slave Girl, Black Bart, Casbah, River Lady, Criss Cross, Gal Who Took the West, Calamity Jane and Sam Bass, Buccaneer's Girl, The Desert Hawk, Tomahawk, Hotel Sahara, Silver City, Scarlet Angel, San Francisco Story, Hurricane Smith, Sombrero, Sea Devils, Fort Algiers, Captain's Paradise, Border

River, Passion, Tonight's the Night, Shotgun, Magic Fire, Flame of the Islands, Ten Commandments, Raw Edge, Death of a Scoundrel, Band of Angels, Timbuktu, McLintock!, A Global Affair, Law of the Lawless, Munster Go Home, Hostile Guns, The Power, Arizona Bushwhackers, The Seven Minutes, Play Dead, It Seemed Like a Good Idea at the Time, Won Ton Ton the Dog Who Saved Hollywood, Blazing Stewardesses, Satan's Cheerleaders, Nocturna, Silent Scream, Guyana Cult of the Damned, The Man With Bogart's Face, Liar's Moon, American Gothic, Cellar Dweller, Mirror Mirror, Oscar, The Naked Truth, Desert Kickboxer, The Sorority House Murders, Seasons of the Heart.
TELEVISION: *Movies*: The Girl on the Late Late Show, The Mark of Zorro, The Munsters' Revenge, A Masterpiece of Murder, Here Come the Munsters, The Barefoot Executive. *Series*: The Munsters. *Guest*: Bonanza, Man From U.N.C.L.E., Murder She Wrote, Hollywood Sign (special), Johnny Carson, Merv Griffin, Steve Allen, David Frost, Perry Como, Tales from the Crypt, Dream On.

DeCUIR, JR., JOHN F.
Art Director, Production Designer. b. Burbank, CA, Aug. 4, 1941. e. U. of Southern California, bachelor of architecture, 1965. Son of John F. De Cuir, Sr. 1966-68, U.S. Coast Guard (holds commission with rank of Lt. Commander, USCGR). 1968-72, project designer, Walt Disney World, Walt Disney Prods. 1972-74, dir. of design, Six Flags Corp. 1974-9, project designer, EPCOT, Walt Disney Prods. 1980-86, pres., John F. De Cuir, Jr. Design Consultants, Inc.; 1987-pres., Cinematix Inc.
PICTURES: *Illustrator*: Cleopatra, The Honey Pot. Design Concepts: The Agony and the Ecstasy. *Art Director*: Raise the Titanic, Ghosbusters. *Special Effects Consultant*: Dead Men Don't Wear Plaid, Monsignor. *Producer*: Jazz Club, The Baltimore Clipper, The Building Puzzle. Prod. *Designer*: Fright Night, Top Gun, Apt Pupil, Elvira Mistress of the Dark, Turner & Hooch, True Identity, Sleepwalkers, Sister Act 2: Back in the Habit, Puppies for Sale, The Land of the Free, The Nephew, Running Red, Slow Burn.
TELEVISION: *Art Director*: Frank Sinatra Special—Old Blue Eyes Is Back, Annual Academy Awards Presentation 1971, Double Agent. *Production Design*: Double Switch, Earth * Star Voyager, Providence, Inherit the Wind, That Championship Season.

DEE, RUBY
Actress. b. Cleveland, OH, Oct. 27, 1924. r.n. Ruby Ann Wallace. e. Hunter Coll. m. actor-dir.-writer Ossie Davis. Worked as apprentice at Amer. Negro Theatre, 1941-44, studied at Actor's Workshop. Stage appearances include Jeb, Anna Lucasta, The World of Sholom Aleichem, A Raisin in the Sun, Purlie Victorious, Wedding Band, Boseman and Lena, Hamlet, Checkmates.
PICTURES: No Way Out, The Jackie Robinson Story, The Tall Target, Go Man Go!, Edge of the City, St. Louis Blues, Take a Giant Step, Virgin Island, A Raisin in the Sun, Gone Are the Days, The Balcony, The Incident, Up Tight, Buck and the Preacher, Black Girl, Countdown at Kusini, Cat People, Do the Right Thing, Love at Large, Jungle Fever, Cop and a Half, Just Cause, A Simple Wish, The Wall, A Time to Dance: The Life and Work of Norma Canner, Baby Geniuses, The Unfinished Journey, Unchained Memories: Readings from the Slave Narratives (reader).
TELEVISION: *Movies*: Deadlock, The Sheriff, It's Good to Be Alive, I Know Why the Caged Bird Sings, All God's Children, The Atlanta Child Murders, Go Tell it on the Mountain, Windmills of the Gods, The Court-Martial of Jackie Robinson, Decoration Day (Emmy Award, 1991), The Ernest Green Story, Homeward Bound, Edgar Allen Poe: Terror of the Soul, Captive Heart: The James Mink Story, Mr. & Mrs. Loving, Passing Glory, Having Our Say: The Delaney Sisters First 100 Years, A Storm in Summer, Finding Buck McHenry, Taking Back Our Town. *Specials*: Actor's Choice, Seven Times Monday, Go Down Moses, Twin-Bit Gardens, Wedding Band, To Be Young Gifted and Black, Long Day's Journey into Night, Edgar Allan Poe: Terror of the Soul (narrator), Porgy & Bess: An American Story. *Mini-Series*: Roots: The Next Generation, Gore Vidal's Lincoln, The Stand, Christianity: The First Two Thousand Years, Feast of All Saints. *Series*: Peyton Place, With Ossie and Ruby, Middle Ages.

DEE, SANDRA
Actress. r.n. Alexandra Zuck. b. Bayonne, NJ, April 23, 1942. Modeled, Harry Conover and Huntington Hartford Agencies, N.Y., 1954-56; signed long term exclusive contract, U-I, 1957.
PICTURES: Until They Sail (debut, 1957), The Reluctant Debutante, The Restless Years, Stranger in My Arms, Imitation of Life, Gidget, The Wild and the Innocent, A Summer Place, The Snow Queen (voice), Portrait in Black, Romanoff and Juliet, Come September, Tammy Tell Me True, If a Man Answers, Tammy and the Doctor, Take Her She's Mine, I'd Rather Be Rich, That Funny Feeling, A Man Could Get Killed, Doctor You've Got to Be Kidding!, Rosie, The Dunwich Horror, Ad est di Marsa Matruh, Lost.
TELEVISION: *Movies*: The Daughters of Joshua Cabe, Houston We've Got a Problem, The Manhunter, Fantasy Island (pilot). *Guest*: Steve Allen Show, Night Gallery, Love American Style, Police Woman. *Series*: Unseen Hollywood.

DEELEY, MICHAEL
Producer. b. London, England, August 6, 1932. Ent. m.p. ind. 1951 and TV, 1967, as alt. dir. Harlech Television Ltd. Film editor, 1951-58. MCA-TV 1958-61, later with Woodfall as prod. and assoc. prod. Assoc. prod. The Knack, The White Bus, Ride of the Valkyrie. Great Western Investments Ltd.; 1972; Great Western

Festivals Ltd.; 1973, mng. dir. British Lion Films Ltd. 1975, purchased BLF, Ltd. Appt. Jnt. man. dir. EMI Films Ltd., 1977; pres., EMI Films, 1978, Member Film Industry Interim Action Committee, 1977-82; Deputy Chairman, British Screen Advisory Council, 1985. Appt. Chief Executive Officer, Consolidated Television Production & Distribution Inc., 1984.
PICTURES: *Prod.*: One Way Pendulum, Robbery, The Italian Job, Long Days Dying (exec. prod.), Where's Jack, Sleep Is Lovely, Murphy's War, The Great Western Express, Conduct Unbecoming, The Man Who Fell to Earth, Convoy, The Deer Hunter (Acad. Award for Best Picture, 1978), Blade Runner.
TELEVISION: *Movies*: A Gathering of Old Men (exec. prod.), Finnegan Begin Again, The Secret Life of Archie's Wife.

DE FINA, BARBARA
Producer. Started as prod. asst. before working at various jobs for such filmmakers as Woody Allen and Sidney Lumet. Became assoc. prod. of development for King/Hitzig Prods., working on Happy Birthday Gemini, Cattle Annie and Little Britches. Was unit mgr./assoc. prod. on Prince of the City. First worked with Martin Scorsese on The King of Comedy as unit mgr. Produced music video Bad.
PICTURES: *Producer*: The Color of Money, The Last Temptation of Christ, New York Stories (segment: Life Lessons), GoodFellas (exec. prod.), The Grifters (exec. prod.), Cape Fear, Mad Dog and Glory, The Age of Innocence, Casino, Kicked in the Head, Kundun, The Hi-Lo Country, Bringing Out the Dead, Dino, You Can Count On Me, The Mesmerist, .45.

DEGENERES, ELLEN
Actress. b. New Orleans, LA, Jan 26, 1958.
PICTURES: Wisecracks, Coneheads, Mr. Wrong, Doctor Dolittle (voice), Edtv, Goodbye Lover, The Love Letter, Trevor, Reaching Normal, You'll Never Wiez in This Town Again, Finding Nemo (voice).
TELEVISION: *Series*: Open House, Laurie Hill, Ellen (also prod.). *Special*: If These Walls Could Talk 2, The Ellen Show, Ellen DeGeneres: Here & Now (tv documentary, exec. prod.)

De HAVILLAND, OLIVIA
Actress b. Tokyo, Japan, July 1, 1916. e. California schools and Notre Dame Convent, Belmont. Acting debut, Max Reinhardt's stage prod., A Midsummer Night's Dream; going to Warner Bros. for film debut in m.p. version, 1935. Recipient: The Snake Pit (NY Film Critics & Look Awards), The Heiress (NY Film Critics, Women's Natl. Press Club & Look Awards). Autobiography: Every Frenchman Has One (1962).
THEATRE: A Midsummer Night's Dream (Hollywood Bowl). B'way: Romeo and Juliet (1951), A Gift of Time. U.S. Tour: Candida (1951-52).
PICTURES: A Midsummer Night's Dream (debut, 1935), Alibi Ike, The Irish in Us, Captain Blood, Anthony Adverse, The Charge of the Light Brigade, Call It a Day, It's Love I'm After, The Great Garrick, Gold is Where You Find It, The Adventures of Robin Hood, Four's a Crowd, Hard to Get, Wings of the Navy, Dodge City, The Private Lives of Elizabeth and Essex, Gone With the Wind, Raffles, My Love Came Back, Santa Fe Trail, Strawberry Blonde, Hold Back the Dawn, They Died With Their Boots On, The Male Animal, In This Our Life, Princess O'Rourke, Thank Your Lucky Stars, Government Girl, The Well Groomed Bride, To Each His Own (Acad. Award, 1946), Devotion, Dark Mirror, The Snake Pit, The Heiress (Acad. Award, 1949), My Cousin Rachel, That Lady, Not as a Stranger, Ambassador's Daughter, Proud Rebel, Libel, Light in the Piazza, Lady in a Cage, Hush ... Hush Sweet Charlotte, The Adventurers, Pope Joan, Airport '77, The Swarm, The Fifth Musketeer.
TELEVISION: *Special*: Noon Wine (Stage 67). *Movies & Mini-series*: The Screaming Woman, Roots: The Next Generations, Murder is Easy, Charles & Diana: A Royal Romance, North & South Book II, Anastasia, The Woman He Loved.

DELANY, DANA
Actress. b. New York, NY, March 13, 1956. e. Phillips Acad., Wesleyan U.
THEATRE: B'way: Translations, A Life. Off-B'way: Blood Moon.
PICTURES: Almost You, Where the River Runs Black, Masquerade, Moon Over Parador, Patty Hearst, Housesitter, Light Sleeper, Batman: Mask of the Phantasm (voice), Tombstone, Exit to Eden, Live Nude Girls, Fly Away Home, Wide Awake, Looking for Lulu, The Curve, The Outfitters, Mother Ghost, Spin.
TELEVISION: *Movies*: A Promise to Keep, Donato and Daughter, The Enemy Within, Choices of the Heart: The Margaret Sanger Story, For Hope, The Patron St. of Liars, Resurrection, Sirens, Final Jeopardy, Conviction, Open House (co-exec. prod. only). *Mini-Series*: Wild Palms, True Women. *Specials*: Texan, Fallen Angels (Good Housekeeping), The Rescuers. *Series*: Love of Life, As the World Turns, Sweet Surrender, China Beach (2 Emmy Awards: 1989, 1992), Pasadena, Presidio Med. *Guest*: Moonlighting, Magnum P.I.

De LAURENTIIS, DINO
Producer, Executive. b. Torre Annunziata, Italy, Aug. 8, 1919. Took part in Rome Experimental Film Center; dir., prod. chmn. of the bd. and CEO, De Laurentiis Entertainment Group Inc.; founded in 1984 the DEG Film Studios in Wilmington, NC. Resigned 1988. Started Dino De Laurentiis Communications, 1990.
PICTURES: L'amore Canta, Il Bandito, La Figlia del Capitano, Riso Amaro, La Lupa, Anna, Ulysses, Mambo, La Strada, Gold of Naples, War and Peace, Nights of Cabiria, The Tempest, Great War, Five Branded Women, Everybody Go Home, Under Ten

Flags, The Best of Enemies, The Unfaithfuls, Barabbas, The Bible, Operation Paradise, The Witches, The Stranger, Diabolik, Anzio, Barbarella, Waterloo, The Valachi Papers, The Stone Killer, Serpico, Death Wish, Mandingo, Three Days of the Condor, Drum, Face to Face, Buffalo Bill and the Indians, King Kong, The Shootist, Orca, White Buffalo, The Serpent's Egg, King of the Gypsies, The Brink's Job, Hurricane, Flash Gordon, Halloween II, Ragtime, Conan the Barbarian, Fighting Back, Amityville II: The Possession, Halloween III: Season of the Witch, The Dead Zone, Amityville 3-D, Firestarter, The Bounty, Conan the Destroyer, Stephen King's Cat's Eye, Red Sonja, Year of the Dragon, Marie, Stephen King's Silver Bullet, Raw Deal, Maximum Overdrive, Tai-Pan, Blue Velvet, The Bedroom Window, Crimes of the Heart, King Kong Lives, Million Dollar Mystery, Weeds, Desperate Hours, Kuffs, Once Upon a Crime, Body of Evidence, Army of Darkness, Unforgettable, Assassins, Breakdown, U-571, Hannibal, Red Dragon.
TELEVISION: Sometimes They Come Back, Slave of Dreams, Solomon & Sheba.

De LAURENTIIS, RAFFAELLA
Producer. Daughter of Dino De Laurentiis. Began career as prod. asst. on father's film Hurricane. Independent prod.
PICTURES: Beyond the Reef, Conan the Barbarian, Conan the Destroyer, Dune, Tai-Pan, Prancer, Dragon: The Bruce Lee Story, Trading Mom, Dragonheart, Backdraft (exec. prod.), Timebomb, Daylight (exec. prod.), Krull the Conqueror, Black Dog, Prancer Returns (video, exec. prod.), The World of Tomorrow (exec. prod.).
TELEVISION: Movie: Uprising. Series: Vanishing Son, The Guardian.

DEL BELSO, RICHARD
Marketing Executive. b. Albany, NY, Aug. 9, 1939. e. Fordham U., 1961, NYU, 1965. Began career in adv./research dept. at Benton & Bowles Advertising, NY. Served as research dept. group head for Kenyon and Eckhart; group head for Grudin/Appell/Haley Research Co. (now known as A/H/F/ Marketing Research, Inc.). Two years as assoc. dir. of mktg., research for Grey Advertising (N.Y.). Joined MCA/Universal in 1976 as assoc. dir., mktg. research. In 1980 named v.p. & dir. of mktg. research for Warner Bros; became worldwide v.p. of mktg. research, 1984; named sr. v.p. worldwide theatrical film market research, 1990. In 1998, promoted to sr. v.p. market strategy, Worldwide Theatrical Films.

DELON, ALAIN
Actor. b. Sceaux, France, Nov. 8, 1935. Discovered by Yves Allegret. Served in French Navy as a Marine.
PICTURES: When a Woman Gets Involved (debut, 1957), Be Beautiful and Keep Quiet, 3 Murderesses, Christine, Le Chemin Des Ecoliers, Plein Soleil (Purple Noon), Quelle Joie de Vivre!, Rocco and His Brothers, Famous Loves, Eclipse, The Leopard, The Devil and the 10 Commandments, Any Number Can Win, The Black Tulip, The Felines (Joy House), L'Insoumis (also prod., co-s.p.), The Yellow Rolls Royce, Once a Thief, Lost Command, Is Paris Burning?, Texas Across the River, The Adventurers, Spirits of the Dead, Samaurai, Diabolically Yours, Girl on a Motorcycle, Goodbye Friend, The Swimming Pool, Jeff (also prod.), The Sicilian Clan, Borsalino, The Red Circle, Madly (also prod.), Doucement Les Basses, Red Sun, The Widow Cuderc, Assassination of Trotsky, Dirty Money, The Teacher, Scorpio, Shock Treatment, The Burning Barn, Big Guns, Two Men in the City, La Race des Seigneurs, Les Seins de Glace, Borsalino & Company (also prod.), Zorro, Police Story, The Gypsy, Mr. Klein (also prod.), Like a Boomerang (also prod., s.p.), The Gang (also exec. prod.), Armageddon, L'Homme Presse, Mort d'un Pourri (also s.p.), Attention Les Enfants Regardent, The Concorde - Airport 79, The Doctor, Teheran 43, Three Men to Destroy (also prod.), For a Cop's Honor (also dir, s.p., prod.), The Shock (also s.p.), The Cache (also prod., dir., s.p.), Swann in Love, Our Story, Military Police (also exec. prod., s.p.), The Passage (also prod.), Let Sleeping Cops Lie (also prod., co-s.p.), New Wave, Dancing Machine, The Return of Casanova, Un Crime... L'Ours en Peluche, A Hundred and One Nights, Day and Night, Half a Chance, Luchino Visconti, Actors.
TELEVISION: Belmondo Le Magnifique, Cannes...les 400 coups, Fabio Montale, Le Lion.

DELPY, JULIE
Actress. b. Paris, France, 1970. Made acting debut as teenager for dir. Jean-Luc Godard.
PICTURES: Detective (debut, 1985) Bad Blood, King Lear, Beatrice, The Dark Night, Europa Europa, Voyager, The Three Musketeers, White, Killing Zoe, Younger and Younger, Before Sunrise, An American Werewolf in Paris, Tykho Moon, The Treat, LA Without a Map, The Treat, The Passion of Ayn Rand, But I'm A Cheerleader, Villa des roses, Tell Me (also s.p.), Sand, Investigating Sex, Villa des roses, Cinemagique.
TELEVISION: Movies: The Passion of Ayn Rand, Crime and Punishment. Series: ER.

DEL ROSSI, PAUL R.
Executive. b. Winchester, MA, Oct. 19, 1942. e. Harvard Coll, 1964; Harvard Business Sch., 1967. Sr. v.p., The Boston Co., 1977-1980; sr. consultant, Arthur D. Little, Inc.; pres. & CEO, General Cinema Theatres. 1998, chmn. General Cinema from 1998 until 2002 when the co. was acquired by AMC. Currently a director of The DeWolfe Companies, Inc. and Charlotte Russe Holdings, Inc.

DELORA, JENNIFER
Actress, Writer, Producer. b. Kingston, NY, March 2, 1962. e. Amer. Acad. Dramatic Arts. 1982. Antioch U., BA, 1993. CA Coast U., MA, 1995; PhD, 1997. Artistic Dir., LA Bridges Theatre Co. of the Deaf, 1993-present. Top industry technical advisor for projects involving deafness, 1995-present. Member AFTRA, SAG, ATAS, Amer. Bd. of Disability Analysts, Nat'l Assoc. of the Deaf, Deaf Artists of Amer., Deaf Entertainment Guild, Amer. Psych. Assoc.
PICTURES: Actor: Bad Girls' Dormitory, Young Nurses in Love, Robot Holocaust, New York's Finest, Deranged, Sexpot, Cleo/Leo, Frankenhooker, Deadly Manor, Bedroom Eyes II, Suburban Commando.
TELEVISION: Movies: Breaking Through, Blue Rodeo. Tech. Advisor: 7th Heaven.

DEL TORO, BENICIO
Actor. b. San German, Puerto Rico, February 19, 1967.
PICTURES: Big Top Pee Wee, Licence to Kill, The Indian Runner, China Moon, Christopher Columbus: The Discovery, Golden Balls, Money for Nothing, Fearless, Swimming With Sharks, The Usual Suspects, Submission (prod. & dir.), Basquiat, The Fan, The Funeral, Joyride, Cannes Man, Excess Baggage, Fear and Loathing in Las Vegas, Bread and Roses, Snatch, The Way of the Gun, The Pledge, Traffic, The Hunted, 21 Grams.
TELEVISION: Mini-Series: Drug Wars: The Camarena Story.

DeLUCA, MICHAEL
Executive, Writer. b. Brooklyn, Aug., 1965. Left NYU to take intern job at New Line Cinema; became story editor before becoming production exec. in 1989. 1993 named pres. of production of New Line. Resigned, 2000. Currently, head of production, Dreamworks SKG.
PICTURES: Writer: Freddy's Dead: The Final Nightmare, In the Mouth of Madness, Judge Dredd (story), Exec. Prod.: B.A.P.S., One Night Stand, Wag the Dog, Dark City, Lost in Space, Blade, Pleasantville, Austin Powers: The Spy Who Shagged Me, Body Shots, The Bachelor, Magnolia, Lost Souls, Little Nicky, Blow, Rush Hour 2, Life as a House, I Am Sam, Highway, Run Ronnie Run!, John Q, Blade II, Unconditional Love, S1mOne, A Man Apart.

De LUISE, DOM
Comedian, Actor. b. Brooklyn, NY, Aug. 1, 1933. e. Tufts Coll. m. actress Carol Arthur. Sons: Peter, Michael, David. Spent two seasons with Cleveland Playhouse. Launched TV career on The Garry Moore Show with character, Dominick the Great.
THEATRE: Little Mary Sunshine, Another Evening With Harry Stoones, All in Love, Half-Past Wednesday, Too Much Johnson, The Student Gypsy, Last of the Red Hot Lovers, Here's Love, Little Shop of Horrors, Die Fledermus (NY Met. Opera: 2 seasons), Peter and the Wolf.
PICTURES: Fail Safe (debut, 1964), Diary of a Bachelor, The Glass Bottom Boat, The Busy Body, What's So Bad About Feeling Good?, Norwood, The Twelve Chairs, Who Is Harry Kellerman...?, Every Little Crook and Nanny, Blazing Saddles, The Adventure of Sherlock Holmes' Smarter Brother, Silent Movie, The World's Greatest Lover, The End, The Cheap Detective, Sextette, The Muppet Movie, Hot Stuff (also dir.), The Last Married Couple in America, Fatso, Wholly Moses, Smokey and the Bandit II, History of the World Part I, The Cannonball Run, The Best Little Whorehouse in Texas, The Secret of NIMH (voice), Cannonball Run II, Johnny Dangerously, Haunted Honeymoon, An American Tail (voice), Spaceballs (voice), A Taxi Driver in New York, Going Bananas, Oliver & Company (voice), All Dogs Go To Heaven (voice), Loose Cannons, Driving Me Crazy, Fievel Goes West (voice), Munchie (voice), The Skateboard Kid (voice), Happily Ever After (voice), Robin Hood: Men in Tights, The Silence of the Hams, A Troll in Central Park (voice), All Dogs Go to Heaven 2 (voice), Boys Will Be Boys, The Good Bad Guys, The Godson, An All Dogs Christmas Carol, Wedding Band, Baby Geniuses, Remembering Mario (voice), The Brainiacs.com, The Lion of Oz (voice), My Ex-Girlfriend's Wedding Reception, Always Greener.
TELEVISION: Movies: Evil Roy Slade, Only With Married Men, Happy (also exec. prod.), Don't Drink the Water, The Tin Soldier. Series: The Entertainers, The Dean Martin Summer Show, Dom DeLuise Show, The Barrum-Bump Show, The Glenn Campbell Goodtime Hour, The Dean Martin Show, Lotsa Luck, Dom DeLuise Show (synd.), The New Candid Camera, Fievel's American Tails (voice), All Dogs Go To Heaven: The Series, Burke's Law, Walking After Midnight. Guest: The Munsters, Medical Center, Amazing Stories, Easy Street, B.L. Stryker, Burke's Law, Murphy Brown, Beverly Hills 90210.

DEMME, JONATHAN
Director, Writer, Producer. b. Rockville Centre, NY, Feb. 22, 1944. e. U. of Florida. First job in industry as usher; was film critic for college paper, The Florida Alligator and the Coral Gable Times. Did publicity work for United Artists, Avco Embassy; sold films for Pathe Contemporary Films; wrote for trade paper, Film Daily, 1966-68. Moved to England in 1969; musical co-ordinator on Irving Allen's EyeWitness in 1970. In 1972 co-prod and co-wrote first film, Angels Hard As They Come. Appeared in film Into the Night.
PICTURES: Hot Box (prod., co-s.p.), Black Mama White Mama (story). Director: Caged Heat (also s.p.), Crazy Mama (also s.p.), Fighting Mad (also s.p.), Citizen's Band (Handle With Care), Last Embrace, Melvin and Howard, Swing Shift, Stop Making Sense, Something Wild (also co-prod.), Swimming to Cambodia, Married to the Mob, Miami Blues (prod. only), The Silence of the Lambs (Acad. Award, 1991), Cousin Bobby, Philadelphia (also co-prod.), Devil in a Blue Dress (exec. prod. only), That Thing

You Do! (prod. only), Beloved (also prod.), The Truth About Charlie (also prod., s.p.), Adaptation (prod. only), Beah: A Black Woman Speaks (documentary, prod.)
TELEVISION: *Movies:* Women & Men 2 (A Domestic Dilemma; prod. only), Subway Stories: Tales from the Underground. *Specials:* Who Am I This Time?, Accumation With Talking plus Water Motor, Survival Guides, A Family Tree (Trying Times series, PBS), Haiti: Dreams of Democracy.

DE MORNAY, REBECCA
Actress. b. Santa Rosa, CA, Aug. 29, 1962. Spent childhood in Europe, graduating from high school in Austria. Returned to America, enrolling at Lee Strasberg's Los Angeles Institute; apprenticed at Zoetrope Studios.
THEATRE: Born Yesterday (Pasadena Playhouse), Marat/Sade (Williamstown Fest.).
PICTURES: Risky Business, Testament, The Slugger's Wife, Runaway Train, The Trip to Bountiful, Beauty and the Beast, And God Created Woman, Feds, Dealers, Backdraft, The Hand That Rocks the Cradle, Guilty as Sin, The Three Musketeers, Never Talk to Strangers (also exec. prod.), The Winner (also exec. prod.), Thick As Thieves, A Table for One, The Right Temptation, Salem Witch Trials, Identity.
TELEVISION: *Movies:* The Murders in the Rue Morgue, By Dawn's Early Light, An Inconvenient Woman, Blindside, Getting Out, The Shining, The Con, Night Ride Home, Range of Motion, A Girl Thing (mini). *Guest:* Boomtown, ER, The Outer Limits.

DEMPSEY, PATRICK
Actor. b. Lewiston, ME, Jan. 13, 1966. e. St. Dominic Regional h.s. in Lewiston where he became state downhill skiing champion. Juggling, magic and puppetry led to performances before Elks clubs and community orgs. Cast by Maine Acting Co. in On Golden Pond. In 1983 acted in Torch Song Trilogy in San Francisco and toured in Brighton Beach Memoirs. NY Theatre debut, 1991 in The Subject Was Roses.
PICTURES: Heaven Help Us (debut, 1985), Meatballs III, Can't Buy Me Love, In the Mood, In a Shallow Grave, Some Girls, Loverboy, Coupe de Ville, Happy Together, Run, Mobsters, For Better and For Worse, Face the Music, Bank Robber, With Honors, Outbreak, Hugo Pool, The Treat, There 's No Fish Food in Heaven, Me and Will, Denial, Scream 3, Sweet Home Alabama, The Emperor's Club, Rebellion.
TELEVISION: *Movies:* A Fighting Choice, JFK: Reckless Youth, Bloodknot, Jeremiah, Crime and Punishment, 2000 Leagues Under the Sea (mini), The Escape, Blonde, Chestnut Hill, Lucky 7. *Series:* Fast Times at Ridgemont High, Once and Again, Rosebud, Corsairs, About a Boy. *Special:* Merry Christmas Baby.

De MUNN, JEFFREY
Actor. b. Buffalo, NY, April 25, 1947. e. Union Col. Studied acting at Old Vic Theatre in Bristol, Eng.
THEATRE: *NY:* Comedians, A Prayer for My Daughter, Modigliani, Augusta, Hands of Its Enemy, Chekhov Sketchbook, A Midsummer Night's Dream, Total Abandon, Country Girl, Bent, K-2, Sleight of Hand, Spoils of War, One Shoe Off, Hedda Gabler, Gunshy.
PICTURES: You Better Watch Out (Christmas Evil), The First Deadly Sin, Resurrection, Ragtime, I'm Dancing as Fast as I Can, Frances, Windy City, Enormous Changes at the Last Minute, Warning Sign, The Hitcher, The Blob, Betrayed, Blaze, Newsies, Eyes of an Angel, The Shawshank Redemption, Safe Passage, Killer, Phenomenon, Turbulence, Rocket Man, Harvest, The X-Files, Harvest, The Green Mile, The Majestic, The Lucky Ones.
TELEVISION: *Movies:* The Last Tenant, Sanctuary of Fear, King Crab, Word of Honor, I Married Wyatt Earp, The Face of Rage, Sessions, When She Says No, Windmills of the Gods, Lincoln, Doubletake, A Time to Live, Who Is Julia?, Young Harry Houdini, Price of Justice, Switch, Elysian Fields, The Haunted, Treacherous Crossing, Jonathan: The Boy Nobody Wanted, Barbarians at the Gate, Crash: The Fate of Flight 1502, Settle the Score, Under the Influence, Betrayal of Trust, Citizen X, Down Came a Blackbird, Hiroshima, Almost Golden: The Jessica Savitch Story, A Christmas Memory, Path to Paradise, Black Cat Run, Storm of the Century, Noriega: God's Favorite, The impressionists, Our Town. *Specials:* Mourning Becomes Electra, Peacemaker (Triple Play II), Sensibly and Sense, The Joy That Kills, Teacher, Pigeon Feathers, Many Mansions, Wild Jackasses, Ebbie. *Mini-series:* Night Sins, Liberty! The American Revolution.

DENCH, DAME JUDI
Actress. b. York, England, Dec. 9, 1934. Studied for stage at Central Sch. of Speech and Drama. Theatre debut Old Vic, 1957. Created a Dame in 1988 Honours List. Recent Theatre: Cymbeline, Juno and the Paycock, A Kind of Alaska, The Cherry Orchard, The Plough and the Stars, Importance of Being Earnest, Pack of Lies, Mr. and Mrs. Nobody, Antony and Cleopatra, The Sea, Coriolanus, The Gift of the Gorgon, The Seagull. Director: Much Ado About Nothing, Look Back in Anger, Boys from Syracuse, Romeo and Juliet, Absolute Hell, A Little Night Music. PICTURES: The Third Secret (debut, 1964), He Who Rides a Tiger, A Study in Terror, Four in the Morning, A Midsummer Night's Dream (RSC Prod.), Luther, Dead Cert, Wetherby, A Room With a View, 84 Charing Cross Road, A Handful of Dust, Henry V, Jack and Sarah, Goldeneye, Hamlet, Mrs. Brown (BAFTA Award, Golden Globe Award, Chicago Film Crits. Award, Best Actress, 1997), Tomorrow Never Dies, Shakespeare in Love (Acad. Award Best Supp. Actress), Tea with Mussolini, The World is Not Enough, Into the Arms of Strangers: Stories of the Kindertransport, Chocolat, Therese Raquin, Iris

(Acad. Award nom.), The Importance of Being Earnest, Die Another Day, Sweating Bullets.
TELEVISION: Major Barbara, Pink String and Sealing Wax, Talking to a Stranger, The Funambulists, Age of Kings, Jackanory, Hilda Lessways, Luther, Neighbours, Parade's End, Marching Song, On Approval, Days to Come, Emilie, The Comedy of Errors (RSC Prod.), Macbeth (RSC Prod.), Langrishe Go Down, On Giant's Shoulders, Love in a Cold Climate, Village Wooing, A Fine Romance (series), The Cherry Orchard, Going Gently, Saigon—Year of the Cat, Ghosts, Behaving Badly, Torch, Can You Hear Me Thinking?, Absolute Hell, As Time Goes By (series), The Last of the Blonde Bombshells, Judi Dench: A BAFTA Tribute.

DENEUVE, CATHERINE
Actress. r.n. Catherine Dorleac. b. Paris, France, Oct. 22, 1943. Sister was the late Francoise Dorleac. Made screen debut as teen using adopting mother's maiden name.
PICTURES: Les Collegiennes (debut, 1956), Wild Roots of Love, L'homme a Femmes, The Doors Slam, La Parisiennes (segment: Sophie), Vice and Virtue, Satan Leads the Dance, Vacances Portugaises, Les Plus Belles Escroqueries du Monde, The Umbrellas of Cherbourg (Cannes Film Fest. Award, 1964), Male Hunt (La Chasse a l'Homme), Male Companion, La Costanza della Ragione, Repulsion, Le Chant du Monde, La Vie de Chateau (A Matter of Resistance), Who Wants to Sleep?, Les Creatures, The Young Girls of Rochefort, Belle de Jour (Venice Film Fest. Award, 1967), Benjamin, Manon 70, Mayerling, La Chamade (Heartbeat), The April Fools, Mississippi Mermaid, Don't Be Blue, Tristana, Donkey Skin, Henri Langolis, Liza, It Only Happens to Others, Dirty Money, Melampo, The Slightly Pregnant Man, Touche Pas a la Femme Blanche, La Grande Bourgeoise, Zig-Zag, La Femme aux Bottes Rouges, Hustle, Lovers Like Us, Act of Agression, The Beach Hut, Second Chance, March or Die, Ecoute voir, L'Argent des Autres, When I Was a Kid I Didn't Dare, Anima Persa, An Adventure for Two, Ils Sont Grandes ces Petits, Courage--Let's Run, The Last Metro, Je vous Aime, Choice of Arms, Hotel des Ameriques, Reporters, Daisy Chain, Le Choc, The African, The Hunger, Le Bon Plaisir, Fort Saganne, Love Songs, Let's Hope It's a Girl, Le Mauvaise Herbe, Scene of the Crime, Agent Trouble, A Strange Place to Meet (also prod.), Hotel Panique, The Man Who Loved Zoos, Frequency Murder, Helmut Newton: Frames From the Edge (doc.), The White Queen, Indochine (Acad. Award nom.), Ma Saison Preferee (My Favorite Season), The Chess Game, The Convent, The Child of the Night, Genealogies of a Crime, Place Vendome, Time Regained, The Last Napoleon, East-West, The Letter, Belle Maman, Pola X, Dancer in the Dark, Von Trier's 100 Eyes, Clouds: Letters to My Son, Absolument fabuleux, The Musketeer, Tom Thumb, I'm Going Home, 8 Women, Au plus pres du paradis, Un film parlé.

DENHAM, MAURICE
Actor. O.B.E., 1992: b. Beckenham, Kent, England, Dec. 23, 1909. e. Tonbridge Sch. Started theatrical career with repertory com. 1934. Served in W.W.II. In numerous plays, films & radio shows.
PICTURES: Blanche Fury, London Belongs To Me, It's Not Cricket, Traveller's Joy, Landfall, Spider and the Fly, No Highway in the Sky, The Net, Time Bomb, Street Corner (Both Sides of the Law), Million Pound Note (Man With a Million), Eight O'Clock Walk, Purple Plain, Simon and Laura, 23 Paces to Baker Street, Checkpoint, Carrington V.C. (Court Martial), Doctor at Sea, Night of the Demon, Man With a Dog, Barnacle Bill, The Captain's Table, Our Man in Havana, Sink the Bismark, Two-Way Stretch, Greengage Summer, Invasion, Quartette, The Mark, HMS Defiant, The Very Edge, Paranoiac, The Set Up, Penang, The King's Breakfast, Downfall, Hysteria, The Uncle, Operation Crossbow, Legend of Dick Turpin, The Alphabet Murders, The Night Callers, The Nanny, Those Magnificent Men in Their Flying Machines, Heroes of Telemark, After the Fox, The Torture Garden, The Long Duel, The Eliminator, Danger Route, Attack on the Iron Coast, The Best House in London, Negatives, The Midas Run, Some Girls Do, The Touch of Love, The Virgin and the Gypsy, Bloody Sunday, Countess Dracula, Nicholas and Alexandra, The Day of the Jackal, Luther, Shout at the Devil, Julia, The Recluse, From a Far Country, Mr. Love, The Chain, Monsignor Quixote, Murder on the Orient Express, 84 Charing Cross Road.
TELEVISION: Uncle Harry, Day of the Monkey, Miss Mabel, Angel Pavement, The Paraguayan Harp, The Wild Bird, Soldier Soldier, Changing Values, Maigret, The Assassins, Saturday Spectacular, Vanishing Act, Somerset Maugham, Three of a Kind, Sapper, Pig in the Middle, Their Obedient Servants, Long Past Glory, Devil in the Wind, Any Other Business, The Retired Colourman, Sherlock Holmes (series), Blackmail, Knock on Any Door, Danger Man, Dr. Finley's Casebook, Porridge, For God's Sake, Bosch, Marie Curie, Upchat Line, Secret Army, My Son, My Son, Edward and Mrs. Simpson, Gate of Eden, Potting Shed, Double Dealer, Minder, Agatha Christie Hour, Chinese Detective, The Old Men at the Zoo, The Hope and the Glory, Luther, Love Song, Mr. Palfrey, The Black Tower, Boon, Rumpole, All Passions Spent, Trial of Klaus Barbie, Miss Marple, Tears in the Rain, Behaving Badly, Seeing in the Dark, Inspector Morse: Fat Chance, La Nonna, Lovejoy, Memento Mori, Sherlock Holmes, The Last Vampire, Peak Pratice, Bed, The Bill, Prisoner In Time, Pie In The Sky.
(d. July 24, 2002)

De NIRO, ROBERT
Actor, Producer. b. New York, NY, Aug. 17, 1943. Studied acting with Stella Adler and Lee Strasberg; 1988, formed Tribeca Film Center in NY.
THEATRE: One Night Stand of a Noisy Passenger (Off-B'way), Cuba and His Teddy Bear (Public Theater and B'way; Theatre World Award).
PICTURES: The Wedding Party (debut, 1969), Greetings, Sam's Song (The Swap), Bloody Mama, Hi Mom, Born to Win, Jennifer on My Mind, The Gang That Couldn't Shoot Straight, Bang the Drum Slowly, Mean Streets, The Godfather Part II (Acad. Award, best supporting actor, 1974), Taxi Driver, The Last Tycoon, New York New York, 1900, The Deer Hunter, Raging Bull (Acad. Award, 1980), True Confessions, The King of Comedy, Once Upon a Time in America, Falling in Love, Brazil, The Mission, Angel Heart, The Untouchables, Midnight Run, Jacknife, We're No Angels (also exec. prod.), Stanley and Iris, GoodFellas, Awakenings, Guilty by Suspicion, Backdraft, Cape Fear (also prod.), Thunderheart (prod.), Mistress (also prod.), Night and the City, Mad Dog and Glory, This Boy's Life, A Bronx Tale (also dir., co-prod.), Mary Shelley's Frankenstein (also assoc. prod.), Casino, Heat, Marvin's Room (also exec. prod.), The Fan, Sleepers, Stolen Flower, Cop Land, Jackie Brown, Wag the Dog (also prod.), Great Expectations, Ronin, Analyze This, Flawless (also prod.), Adventures of Rocky and Bullwinkle (also prod.), Men of Honor, Meet the Parents (also prod.), Fifteen Minutes, The Score (also dir.), City by the Sea, Showtime, Scared Guys, Analyze That (also prod.), Godsend.
TELEVISION: Movies: Witness to the Mob (exec. prod. only), Holiday Heart (exec. prod. only). Specials: Night of 100 Stars, Dear America: Letters Home From Vietnam (reader), Lenny Bruce: Swear to Tell the Truth, America: A Tribute to Heroes, The Concert for New York City, Hello, He Lied & Other Truths From the Hollywood Trenches. Series: Tribeca (exec. prod. only).

DENNEHY, BRIAN
Actor. b. Bridgeport, CT, July 9, 1939. e. Columbia U. In Marine Corps five years, including Vietnam. After discharge in 1965 studied with acting coaches in N.Y., while working at part time jobs as a salesman, bartender, truck driver.
THEATRE: Streamers, Galileo (Goodman Th.), The Cherry Orchard, Translations, Death of a Salesman.
PICTURES: Looking for Mr. Goodbar, Semi-Tough, F.I.S.T., Foul Play, 10, Butch and Sundance: The Early Days, Little Miss Marker, Split Image, First Blood, Never Cry Wolf, Gorky Park, Finders Keepers, River Rat, Cocoon, Silverado, Twice in a Lifetime, F/X, Legal Eagles, The Check Is in the Mail, Best Seller, The Belly of an Architect, Return to Snowy River Part II, Miles From Home, Cocoon: The Return, The Last of the Finest, Presumed Innocent, FX2, Gladiator, Seven Minutes, Tommy Boy, The Stars Fell on Henrietta, Midnight Movie, Romeo and Juliet, Dish Dogs, Out of the Cold, Silicon Towers, Summer Catch, Stolen Summer.
TELEVISION: Movies: Johnny We Hardly Knew Ye, It Happened at Lake Wood Manor, Ruby and Oswald, A Death in Canaan, A Real American Hero, Silent Victory: The Kitty O'Neil Story, The Jericho Mile, Dummy, The Seduction of Miss Leona, A Rumor of War, Fly Away Home, Skokie, I Take These Men, Blood Feud, Off Sides, Acceptable Risks, Private Sessions, The Lion of Africa, A Father's Revenge, Day One, Perfect Witness, Pride and Extreme Prejudice, Rising Son, A Killing in a Small Town, In Broad Daylight, The Burden of Proof, To Catch a Killer, Diamond Fleece, Teamster: The Jackie Presser Story, Deadly Matrimony, Foreign Affairs, Murder in the Heartland, Prophet of Evil: The Ervil LeBaron Story, Final Appeal, Jack Reed: Badge of Honor (also co-exec. prod.), Leave of Absence, Jack Reed: Search for Justice (also dir., co-writer), Contagious, Indefensible: The Truth About Edward Brannigan (also dir.), Voyage of Terror, Thanks of a Grateful Nation, NetForce, Sirens, Death of a Salesman (Golden Globe Award, Emmy nom.), The Warden of Redrock, Three Blind Mice, A Season on the Brink, The Roman Spring of Mrs. Stone. Mini-Series: The Crooked E: The Unshredded Truth about Enron Pearl, The Last Place on Earth, Evergreen, Dead Man's Walk, Nostromo, A Season in Purgatory, Founding Fathers, Too Rich: The Secret Life of Doris Duke, Series: Big Shamus Little Shamus, Star of the Family, Birdland, Arrest & Trial, The Fighting Fitzergerralds, Project Greenlight. Guest: M*A*S*H, Lou Grant, Cagney and Lacey, Hunter, Tall Tales (Annie Oakley), Just Shoot Me. Special: Dear America: Letter Home From Vietnam (reader).

DENVER, BOB
Actor. b. New Rochelle, NY, Jan. 9, 1935. e. Loyola U.
PICTURES: A Private's Affair, Take Her She's Mine, For Those Who Think Young, Who's Minding the Mint? The Sweet Ride, Did You Hear the One About the Travelling Saleslady?, Back to the Beach.
TELEVISION: Movies: Rescue from Gilligan's Island, The Castaways on Gilligan's Island, The Harlem Globetrotters on Gilligans Island, The Invisible Woman, High School USA, Bring Me the Head of Dobie Gillis. Also: Far Out Space Nuts, Scamps. Series: The Many Loves of Dobie Gillis, Gilligan's Island, The Good Guys, Dusty's Trail.

De PALMA, BRIAN
Director, Writer, Producer. b. Newark, NJ, Sept. 11, 1940. e. Columbia U.,B.A.; Sarah Lawrence, M.A. While in college made series of shorts, including Wotan's Wake, winner of Rosenthal Foundation Award for best film made by American under 25. Also judged most popular film of Midwest Film Festival (1963); later shown at San Francisco Film Festival. Dir.: The Responsive Eye (doc., 1966).
PICTURES: Director: Murder a La Mod (also s.p., edit.), Greetings (also co-s.p. ed.), The Wedding Party (also co-s.p., co-prod., ed.), Hi Mom (also co-story, s.p.), Dionysus in '69 (also co-prod., co-photog., co-ed.), Get To Know Your Rabbit, Sisters (also co-s.p.), Phantom of the Paradise (also co-s.p.), Obsession (also co-story), Carrie, The Fury, Home Movies (also s.p., co-prod.), Dressed to Kill (also s.p.), Blow Out (also s.p.), Scarface, Body Double (also prod., s.p.), Wiseguys, The Untouchables, Casualties of War, The Bonfire of the Vanities (also prod.), Raising Cain (also s.p.), Carlito's Way, Mission: Impossible, Snake Eyes (also prod., story), Mission to Mars, Femme Fatale (also s.p.).

DEPARDIEU, GÉRARD
Actor. b. Chateauroux, France, Dec. 27, 1948. Studied acting at Theatre National Populaire in Paris. Made film debut at 16 in short by Roger Leenhardt (Le Beatnik et Le Minet). Acted in feature film by Agnès Varda (uncompleted).
PICTURES: Le Cri du Cormoran le Soir au-dessis des Jonques, Nathalie Granger, A Little Sun in Cold Water, Au Renedez-vous de la mort joyeuse, La Scoumone, Rude Journee our la Reine, The Holes, Going Places, Stavisky, Woman of the Granges, Vincent Francois Paul and the Others, The Wonderful Crook, 7 Morts sur ordonnance, Maitresse, Je t'Aime Moi Non Plus, The Last Woman, 1900, Barocco, Rene la Canne, Baxter Vera Baxter, The Truck, Tell Him I Love Him, At Night All Cats Are Gray, Get Out Your Handkerchiefs, The Left-Handed Woman, Bye Bye Monkey, Violanta, Le Sucre, Les Chiens, L'Ingorgo, Buffet Froid, Temporale Rosy, Mon Oncle d'Amerique, Loulou, The Last Metro, Inspector Blunder, I Love You, Choice of Arms, The Woman Next Door, Le Chevre, The Return of Martin Guerre, The Big Brother, Danton, The Moon in the Gutter, Les Comperes (also co-prod.), Fort Saganne, Le Tartuffe (also dir., co-s.p.), Rive Droite Rive Gauche, Police, One Woman or Two, Menage, Ru du depart, Jean De Florette (also co-prod.), Under Satan's Sun (also co-prod.), A Strange Place for an Enounter (also co-prod.), Camille Claudel (also co-prod.), Dreux, Too Beautiful for You (also co-prod.), I Want to Go Home, Cyrano de Bergerac (also co-prod), Green Card, Uranus, Thanks for Life, Mon Pere ce Heros (My Father the Hero), 1492: Conquest of Paradise, All the Mornings of the World, Oh Woe is Me, A Pure Formality, Germinal, My Father the Hero, Colonel Chabert, La Machine, Elisa, Les Anges Gardiens, The Horseman on the Roof, Bogus, Le Garcu, She's So Lovely (exec.prod. only), Hamlet, XXL, The Man in the Iron Mask, La Parola Amore Esiste, Bimboland, Vidocq, Vatel, Mirka, Asterix and Obelix vs. Caesar, Un Pont Entre Deux Rives (also prod., dir.), All the Love There Is, Actors, Envy of the Gods, 102 Dalmatians, In the Shadow of Hollywood, The Closet, Unfair Competition, CQ, Vidocq, Streghe verso nord, Asterix & Obelix: Mission Cleopatre, I Am Dina, Blanche, Crime Spree, City of Ghosts, Between Strangers, Aime ton pere, Tais-toi, Le Pacte du silence, Ruby & Quentin.
TELEVISION: Le Cyborg ou Le voyage vertical, Rendez-vous a Badenberg, Nausicaa, Un monsieur bien range, L'Inconnu, Vivement Truffaut, Cannes...les 400 coups, The Count of Monte Cristo, Berenice, Les Miserables, Balzac, La Femme Musketeer (mini-series).

DEPP, JOHNNY
Actor. b. Owensboro, KY, June 9, 1963. Raised in Miramar, FL. Played lead guitar with band The Kids, with whom he moved to L.A. in 1983. With no prior acting experience made film debut in A Nightmare on Elm Street.
PICTURES: A Nightmare on Elm Street (debut, 1984), Private Resort, Platoon, Cry-Baby, Edward Scissorhands, Freddy's Dead: The Final Nightmare (cameo), Benny & Joon, What's Eating Gilbert Grape?, Ed Wood, Don Juan DeMarco, Dead Man, Nick of Time, Donnie Brasco, The Brave (also dir., s.p.),L.A. Without a Map, Just to Be Together, Fear and Loathing in Las Vegas, The Source, The Libertine, The Ninth Gate, The Astronauts Wife, Sleepy Hollow, The Man Who Cried, Chocolat, Blow, In Bad Taste, From Hell, Pirates of the Caribbean: The Curse of the Black Pearl, Charlie: The Life and Art of Charlie Chaplin, Once Upon a Time in Mexico.
TELEVISION: Movie: Slow Burn. Series: 21 Jump Street. Guest: Lady Blue, Hotel, The Vicar of Dibley, The Fast Show.

DEPREZ, THERESE
Production Designer. b. 1966.
PICTURES: The Refrigerator, Swoon, The Outfit, Postcards from America, Living in Oblivion, Stonewall, The Doom Generation, I Shot Andy Warhol, Box of Moonlight, Grind, Going All the Way, No Looking Back, Happiness, Arlington Road, Summer of Sam, High Fidelity, Hedwig and the Angry Inch, Marci X, How to Lose a Guy in Ten Days, Door in the Floor.
TELEVISION: Movies: Dottie Gets Spanked, Path to Paradise: The Untold Story of the World Trade Center Bombing, American Splendor.

DEREK, BO
Actress. r.n. Mary Cathleen Collins. b. Torrance, CA., Nov. 20, 1956. Discovered by actor-turned-filmmaker John Derek, whom she married.
PICTURES: Orca (debut, 1977), 10, A Change of Seasons, Fantasies (And Once Upon a Time), Tarzan the Ape Man (also prod.), Bolero (also prod.), Ghosts Can't Do It (also prod.), Hot Chocolate, Sognando la California (California Dreaming), Woman of Desire, Tommy Boy, Off the Menu: The Last Days of Chasens, Horror 101, Frozen With Fear, Sunstorm, Life in the Balance, The Master of Disguise, Malibu's Most Wanted.
TELEVISION: Movies: Shattered Image, Murder at the Cannes Film Festival. Series: Hollywood Squares, Wind on Water. Guest: I Love 1970's, 7th Heaven, Lucky.

DERN, BRUCE
Actor. b. Chicago, IL, June 4, 1936. e. U. of Pennsylvania. Daughter is actress Laura Dern. Studied acting with Gordon Phillips, member, Actor's Studio, 1959 After N.Y. debut in Shadow of a Gunman. Broadway: Sweet Bird of Youth, Orpheus Descending, Strangers. Film Awards: Natl. Society of Film Critics (Drive He Said, 1971), People's Choice (Coming Home, 1978), Genie (Middle Age Crazy, 1980), Silver Bear (That Championship Season, 1982).
PICTURES: Wild River (debut, 1960), Marnie, Hush...Hush Sweet Charlotte, The Wild Angels, The St. Valentine's Day Massacre, Waterhole No. 3, The Trip, The War Wagon, Psych-Out, Rebel Rousers, Hang 'Em High, Will Penny, Number One, Castle Keep, Support Your Local Sheriff, They Shoot Horses Don't They?, Cycle Savages, Bloody Mama, The Incredible Two-Headed Transplant, Drive He Said, Silent Running, Thumb Tripping, The Cowboys, The King of Marvin Gardens, The Laughing Policeman, The Great Gatsby, Smile, Posse, Family Plot, Won Ton Ton the Dog Who Saved Hollywood, The Twist (Folies Bourgeoises), Black Sunday, Coming Home (Acad. Award nom.), The Driver, Middle Age Crazy, Tattoo, Harry Tracy: Desperado, That Championship Season, On the Edge, The Big Town, World Gone Wild, 1969, The 'Burbs, After Dark My Sweet, Diggstown, Wild Bill, Down Periscope, Mulholland Falls, Last Man Standing, Small Soldiers (voice), If...Dog...Rabbit, The Haunting, All the Pretty Horses, It Conquered Hollywood! The Story of American International Pictures, The Glass House, Milwaukee Minnesota, Madison, Masked & Anonymous (editor only), Monster.
TELEVISION: Movies: Sam Hill: Who Killed the Mysterious Mr. Foster?, Toughlove, Roses Are for the Rich, Uncle Tom's Cabin, Trenchcoat in Paradise, The Court-Martial of Jackie Robinson, Into the Badlands, Carolina Skeletons, It's Nothing Personal, Deadman's Revenge, Amelia Earhart: The Final Flight, A Mother's Prayer, Comfort Texas, Perfect Prey, Hard Ground. Mini-Series: Space. Series: Stoney Burke. Guest: Naked City, Ben Casey, The Virginian, Twelve O'Clock High, The Big Valley, Gunsmoke, The FBI, Land of the Giants, Fallen Angels.

DERN, LAURA
Actress. b. Los Angeles, CA, Feb. 10, 1967. Daughter of actors Diane Ladd and Bruce Dern. At age 5 appeared with mother on daytime serial The Secret Storm. Was an extra in several of her father's films and her mother's Alice Doesn't Live Here Anymore. Studied acting at RADA appearing on stage in Hamlet, A Midsummer Night's Dream.
THEATRE: NY: The Palace of Amateurs. LA: Brooklyn Laundry.
PICTURES: White Lightning (debut, 1973), Alice Doesn't Live Here Anymore, Foxes, Ladies and Gentlemen: The Fabulous Stains, Teachers, Mask, Smooth Talk, Blue Velvet, Haunted Summer, Fat Man and Little Boy, Wild at Heart, Rambling Rose (Acad. Award nom.), Jurassic Park, A Perfect World, Bastard Out of Carolina, Citizen Ruth, October Sky, Dr. T and the Women, Novocaine, Daddy and Them, Jurassic Park III, Focus, I Am Sam, Searching for Debra Winger.
TELEVISION: Movies: Happy Endings, Three Wishes of Billy Greer, Afterburn (Golden Globe Award), Down Came a Blackbird, Ruby Ridge: An American Tragedy, The Baby Dance, Within These Walls, Damaged Care, Mysteries of Love (documentary). Specials: The Gift (dir, co-story only), AFI's 100 Years 100 Stars. Guest: Fallen Angels, Frasier, Ellen, The Larry Sanders Show, The West Wing.

DE SANTIS, GREGORY JOSEPH
Producer, Writer, Director. b. Los Angeles, CA, July 12, 1955. e. Durham Univ.; Canaan Coll. Pres., Millennium Mulitmedia.
PICTURES: Prod.: The Companion, Car Trouble, Pass the Buck, Die Sister Die!, Diary of a Surfing Film, Firepower, The Forest.
TELEVISION: Prod.: Volleyball: A Sport Come of Age, The Nature Series, Caribou Crossing, California Day, Midnight Son, Lightning, Mysterious River.

DESCHANEL, CALEB
Cinematographer, Director. b. Philadelphia, PA, Sept. 21, 1944. m. actress Mary Jo Deschanel. e. Johns Hopkins U., U. of Southern California Film Sch. Studied at AFI, interned under Gordon Willis then made commercials, short subjects, docs.
PICTURES: Cinematographer: More American Graffiti, Being There, The Black Stallion, Apocalypse Now (2nd unit photog.), The Right Stuff, Let's Spend the Night Together (co-cinematographer), The Natural, The Slugger's Wife, It Could Happen to You, Flying Wild, Fly Away Home, Hope Floats, Message in a Bottle, Anna and the King, The Patriot, The Hunted, Timeline, The Passion. Director: The Escape Artist, Crusoe.

De TOTH, ANDRE
Writer, Director, Producer. b. Hungary. May 15, 1912 Dir.-writer European films, 1931-39; U.S. assoc. Alexander Korda prod., 1940; dir. Columbia, 1943; assoc. David Selznick, 1943; assoc. Hunt Stromberg-UA, 1944-45; staff dir., Enterprise 1946-47; dir., 20th-Fox, 1948-49; collab. story, The Gunfighter; assoc., Sam Spiegel, Horizon Pictures, Columbia, 1962; Harry Saltzman, Lowndes Prod., U.A. 1966-68; National General, 1969-70.
PICTURES: Passport to Suez, None Shall Escape, Pitfall, Slattery's Hurricane, Springfield Rifle, Thunder Over the Plains, House of Wax, The Stranger Wore a Gun, Bounty Hunter, Tanganyika, The Indian Fighter, Monkey on My Back, Two Headed Spy, Day of the Outlaw, Man on a String, Morgan The Pirate, The Mongols, Gold for the Caesars, Billion Dollar Brain (exec. prod. only), Play Dirty (also exec. prod.), El Condor (prod. only), The Dangerous Game, Antychryst (short, writer). (d. Oct. 27, 2002)

DEUTCH, HOWARD
Director. b. New York, NY. e. Ohio State U. m. actress Lea Thompson. Son of music publisher Murray Deutch. Spent 10 yrs. working in various film media, including music videos and film trailer advertising, before feature debut with Pretty in Pink, 1986.
PICTURES: Pretty in Pink, Some Kind of Wonderful, The Great Outdoors, Article 99, Getting Even With Dad, Grumpier Old Men, The Odd Couple II, The Replacements, Family Affair, Electric, The Whole Ten Yards, Wounded (co-prod.).
TELEVISION: Series: Tales from the Crypt (2 episodes; ACE Award for Dead Right), Caroline in the City, Watching Ellie.

DEUTCHMAN, IRA J.
Executive. b. Cherry Point, NC, March 24, 1953. e. Northwestern U., B.S., majoring in film. Began career with Cinema 5, Ltd. serving, 1975-79, as non-theatrical mls. mgr.; dir. theatrical adv./pub./dir. acquisitions. Joined United Artists Classics, 1981 as dir. of adv./pub. 1982, left to become one of the founding partners in Cinecom Intl. Films, where headed mktg./dist. div. from inception. In Jan. 1989 formed the Deutchman Company, Inc., a production company and marketing consultancy firm. Founded and served as pres. of Fine Line Features, a division of New Line Cinema, and sr. v.p. of parent corp, 1991-95. Currenly, pres. of Redeemable Features, a New York-based prod. company. Adjunct prof. Columbia U. film dept. On advisory board Sundance Film Festival.
PICTURES: Exec. Prod.: Swimming to Cambodia, Matewan (assoc. prod.), Miles From Home (co-exec. prod.), Scenes from the Class Struggle in Beverly Hills, Straight Out of Brooklyn, Waterland, The Ballad of Little Jo, Mrs. Parker and the Vicious Circle, Lulu on the Bridge, Twelve, The Center of the World, Laura & Sal, The Lucky Ones, The Brothel. Producer: Kiss Me Guido, 54, The Hairy Bird a.k.a. Strike!, Way Past Cool, Ball in the House, Interstate 60.

DEUTCHMAN, LAWRENCE SCOT
Executive. b. Bronx, NY, Dec. 10, 1960. e. Rutgers U. Wrote, prod. & dir. Mythbusters campaign. 1986-92, various positions: Entertainment Industries Council, Inc.; wrote, prod., co-dir. That's a Wrap campaign. 1986-88, board member, Public Interest Radio & Television Educational Society. 1987-88, wrote, exec. prod., post-prod. sprv., Buckle Up educational & music video (CINE Golden Eagle). 1989: EIC: An Industry in Action (writer, prod., dir.); Campaigns: Natl. Red Ribbon, Office for Substance Abuse Prevention (writer, dir., exec. prod.), Stop the Madness (co-writer, prod.). 1990, developed: Vince & Larry: The Amazing Crash Test Dummies (series, NBC), Drug Proofing Your Kids (TV special); Campaigns: Alcoholism Runs in Families, Texas Prevention Partnership (dir., exec. prod.), They Do as You Do (writer, exec. prod.). 1991: The Inhalant Problem in Texas docum. (co-exec. prod.), Inhalants: The Silent Epidemic award-winning drama (writer, co-exec. prod.), KBVO Fox Kids Club segments (writer, prod., set designer), The Incredible Crash Dummies toy property (co-creator), Ollie Odorfree property (creator). 1992-present: Pres., Dynamic Comm. Intl. Inc.; v.p. prod. & mktg., EIC. 1993: Hollywood Gets M.A.D.D. TV special (co-prod., TBS, TNT, synd.). 1994: Dinorock Time TV series (exec. prod., writer.); 1994-present, s.r., vp. prod. & mktg, EIC (Entertainment Industries Council).

DEUTSCH, STEPHEN
Producer. b. Los Angeles, CA, June 30, 1946. e. UCLA, B.A.; Loyola Law Sch., 1974. Son of late S. Sylvan Simon. Stepson of Armand Deutsch. Private law practice before joining Rastar 1976 as asst. to Ray Stark; 1977, sr. v.p., Rastar; prod. head for SLM Inc. Film Co. entered independent prod. 1978.
PICTURES: Somewhere in Time, All the Right Moves, Russkies (co-exec. prod.), She's Out of Control, Bill & Ted's Excellent Adventure (exec. prod.), Lucky Stiff, Bill and Ted's Bogus Journey (co-exec. prod.), Body of Evidence (exec. prod.), What Dreams May Come, Quantum Project.
TELEVISION: The Linda McCartney Story, Homeless to Harvard: The Liz Murray Story (exec. prod. as Stephen Simon).

DEVANE, WILLIAM
Actor. b. Albany, NY, Sept. 5, 1939. Appeared in some 15 productions with N.Y. Shakespeare Festival, also B'way & off-B'way shows before heading to California for films and TV.
PICTURES: The Pursuit of Happiness (debut, 1970), The 300 Hundred Year Weekend, Lady Liberty, McCabe and Mrs. Miller, Glory Boy (My Old Man's Place), Irish Whiskey Rebellion, Report to the Commissioner, Family Plot, Marathon Man, Bad News Bears in Breaking Training, Rolling Thunder, The Dark, Yanks,

Honky Tonk Freeway, Testament, Hadley's Rebellion, Vital Signs, Exception to the Rule, Payback, Poor White Trash, Space Cowboys, Hollow Man, Race to Space, Threat of Exposure, The Wind Effect.
TELEVISION: *Movies:* Crime Club, The Bait, Fear on Trial, Red Alert, Black Beauty, Red Flag: The Ultimate Game, The Other Victim, Jane Doe, With Intent to Kill, Timestalker, Murder C.O.D., Nightmare in Columbia County, Obsessed, The President's Child, Prophet of Evil: The Ervil LeBaron Story, Rubdown, For the Love of Nancy, Falling From the Sky!: Flight 174, Robin Cook's Virus, Alistair MacLean's Night Watch, Virus, Forgotten Sins, The Absolute Truth, Doomsday Rock, Miracle on the Mountain: The Kincaid Family Story, The Man Who Used to Be Me, The Badge, A Christmas Visitor, Monte Walsh. *Mini-Series:* A Woman Named Jackie, Knot's Landing: Back to the Cul-de-Sac. *Series:* From Here to Eternity, Knots Landing, Phenom, The Monroes, Turks, Titans, The Michael Richards Show. *Special:* The Missiles of October.

De VITO, DANNY
Actor, Director, Producer. b. Asbury Park, NJ, Nov. 17, 1944. m. actress Rhea Perlman. e. Oratory Prep Sch. Studied at American Acad. of Dramatic Arts. Wilfred Acad. of Hair and Beauty Culture. At 18 worked as hair dresser for 1 yr. at his sister's shop. NY stage in The Man With a Flower in His Mouth (debut, 1969), Down the Morning Line, The Line of Least Existence, The Shrinking Bride, Call Me Charlie, Comedy of Errors, Merry Wives of Windsor (NYSF). Three By Pirandello. Performance in One Flew Over the Cuckoo's Nest led to casting in the film version. Prod. short films: The Sound Sleeper (1973), Minestrone (1975).
PICTURES: Lady Liberty (debut, 1971), Hurry Up or I'll Be 30, Scalawag, One Flew Over the Cuckoo's Nest, Deadly Hero, The Van, The World's Greatest Lover, Goin' South, Going Ape, Terms of Endearment, Romancing the Stone, Johnny Dangerously, The Jewel of the Nile, Head Office, Wiseguys, Ruthless People, My Little Pony (voice), Tin Men, Throw Momma from the Train (also dir.), Twins, The War of the Roses (also dir.), Other People's Money, Batman Returns, Hoffa (also dir., co-prod.), Jack the Bear, Last Action Hero (voice), Look Who's Talking Now (voice), Reality Bites (co-prod. only), Renaissance Man, Pulp Fiction (co-exec. prod. only), Junior, Get Shorty (also co-prod.), Sunset Park (prod.), Matilda (also dir., co-prod.), Mars Attacks, Hercules (voice), L.A. Confidential, Space Jam. (voice), The Rainmaker, Living Out Loud, Stretch Armstrong, Foolproof, Out of Sight (prod. only), Gattaca (prod. only), Man on the Moon (also prod.), The Virgin Suicides, Drowning Mona (also prod.), Screwed, What's The Worst That Could Happen?, The Heist, Death to Smoochy, Austin Powers in Goldmember, Anything Else, Duplex (dir. only), The Marx Brothers (prod. only), Captured (prod. only), Big Fish (acting), Catching Kringle (acting).
TELEVISION: *Movies:* Valentine, The Ratings Game (also dir.). *Specials:* All the Kids Do It (Afterschool Special), A Very Special Christmas Party, Two Daddies? (voice), What a Lovely Way to Spend an Evening (dir.), The Selling of Vince DeAngelo (dir.). *Guest:* Police Woman, Amazing Stories (also dir.), The Simpsons (voice). *Series:* Taxi (Emmy & Golden Globe Awards, 1981; also dir. episodes), Mary (dir. only), The Funkhousers (exec. prod. only). *Special:* America: A Tribute to Heroes.

DEVLIN, DEAN
Actor, Writer, Producer. b. Aug. 27, 1962. Began career as an actor, appearing in numerous film and television projects, as well as B'way production of There Must be a Pony. Met Roland Emmerich while acting in Moon 44. Joined Emmerich as a partner at Centropolis Films. Prod. TV series, The Visitor, 1997.
PICTURES: *Actor:* My Bodyguard, The Wild Life, Real Genius, City Limits, Moon 44, Martians Go Home, Total Exposure, Predators From Beyond Nature. *Writer/Producer:* Stargate, Independence Day, Godzilla, The Mark, The Patriot, Eight Legged Freaks. *Writer:* Universal Soldier, Gargoyles.
TELEVISION: *Series creator:* The Visitor. *Series actor:* Hard Copy, Generations.

De WITT, JOYCE
Actress. b. Wheeling, WV, April 23, 1949. e. Ball State U., B.A., theatre; UCLA, MFA in acting. Classically trained, worked in theatre since 13 as actress and dir.
PICTURES: Airplane II: The Sequel, 18.
TELEVISION: *Movies:* With This Ring, Spring Fling. *Specials:* Three's Company: The E! True Hollywood Story, Suzanne Somers: The E! True Hollywood Story. *Series:* Three's Company. *Guest:* Baretta, The Tony Randall Show, Most Wanted, Risko, Finder of Lost Loves.

DEY, SUSAN
Actress. b. Pekin, IL, Dec. 10, 1952. Signed as magazine teen model at age 15. Made professional TV debut at 17, appearing in The Partridge Family, 1970.
PICTURES: Skyjacked (debut, 1972), First Love, Looker, Echo Park, That's Adequate, Rain.
TELEVISION: *Movies:* Terror on the Beach, Cage Without a Key, Mary Jane Harper Cried Last Night, Little Women, The Comeback Kid, The Gift of Life, Malibu, Sunset Limousine, I Love You Perfect, Bed of Lies, Lies and Lullabies (also co-prod.), Whose Child Is This? The War for Baby Jessica, Beyond Betrayal, Deadly Love, Blue River, Bridge of Time, Disappearance, L.A. Law: Return to Justice, L.A. Law: The Movie (2002). *Series:* The Partridge Family, Loves Me Loves Me Not, Emerald Point N.A.S., L.A. Law, Love and War.

DE YOUNG, CLIFF
Actor. b. Inglewood, CA, Feb. 12, 1947. e. California State Coll., Illinois State U. On stage in Hair, Sticks and Bones, Two By South, The Three Sisters, The Orphan.
PICTURES: Harry and Tonto, Blue Collar, Shock Treatment, Independence Day, The Hunger, Reckless, Protocol, Secret Admirer, F/X, Flight of the Navigator, Fear, Pulse, Rude Awakening, Glory, Flashback, Crackdown, Dr. Giggles, Carnosaur II, Final Frontier, The Craft, The Substitute, Suicide Kings, Last Flight Out.
TELEVISION: *Movies:* Sunshine, The 3000 Mile Chase, The Lindbergh Kidnapping Case, Scared Straight: Another Story, Invasion of Privacy, The Seeding of Sarah Burns, The Night That Panicked America, This Girl for Hire, The Awakening of Candra, Deadly Intentions, Sunshine Christmas, Fun and Games, Where Pigeons Go to Die, Fourth Story, Criminal Behavior, Love Can Be Murder, The Tommyknockers, Precious Victims, Heaven & Hell: North and South Book III, JAG, Element of Truth, The Westing Game, Nails, George Wallace, The Westing Game, The Last Man on Planet Earth, Getting Away with Murder: The JonBenet Ramsey Mystery, Deliberate Intent, The Runaway, Path to War, The Secret Life of Zoey. *Series:* Sunshine, Robocop, Relativity. *Special:* Sticks and Bones. *Mini-Series:* Centennial, Master of the Game, Captains and the Kings, King, Robert Kennedy and His Times, Andersonville, Seduced By Madness, The Last Don.

DIAMANT, LINCOLN
Executive, Biographer, Historian. b. New York, NY, Jan. 25, 1923. e. Columbia Coll., A.B. cum laude 1943. Cofounder, Columbia U. radio station. WKCR-FM; served in Wash. as prod., Blue Network (NBC), then in NY as CBS newswriter; 1949 joined World Pub. Co. as adv. and promo. dir.; 1952-69 worked in creative/TV dept. McCann-Erickson, Grey, then Ogilvy & Mather ad agencies (winning 8 Clio Awards). Prod. Lend Us Your Ears (Met. Museum Art broadcast series); founder, pres., Spots Alive, Inc., broadcast adv. consultants, 1969; Author, The Broadcast Communications Dictionary, Anatomy of a Television Commercial, Television's Classic Commercials, biography of Bernard Romans, Chaining the Hudson (Sons of Revolution Book Award), Stamping Our History, Yankee Doodle Days. Contrib., to Effective Advertising, to Messages and Meaning; New Routes to English; columnist Back Stage/Shoot. Member, Broadcast Pioneers, Acad. TV Arts & Sciences; v.p. Broadcast Advertising Producer's Society of America. Adjunct faculty member, Pace U., Hofstra U. Fellow, Royal Society of Arts.

DIAMOND, NEIL
Singer, Songwriter. b. Brooklyn, NY, Jan. 24, 1941.
PICTURES: Jonathan Livingston Seagull (music), Every Which Way But Loose (music), The Last Waltz (actor), The Jazz Singer (actor, music), Switching Channels (title theme), Pulp Fiction (song), Edtv (composer), Saving Silverman (actor, music), Shrek (song), Sorority Boys (song).
TELEVISION: *Specials:* Neil Diamond... Hello Again, I Never Cared for the Sound of Being Alone, I'm Glad You're Here With Me Tonight, Greatest Hits Live, Neil Diamond's Christmas Special, Neil Diamond... Under a Tennessee Moon. *Movies:* Fosse (composer).

DIAZ, CAMERON
Actress. b. Aug. 30, 1972. Began career as model for Elite. Feature debut was in The Mask. Received ShoWest 1996 Female Star of Tomorrow Award.
PICTURES: The Mask, The Last Supper, Keys to Tulsa, Feeling Minnesota, Head Above Water, She's the One, My Best Friend's Wedding, A Life Less Ordinary, There's Something About Mary, Very Bad Things, Invisible Circus, Fear and Loathing in Las Vegas, Being John Malkovich, Any Given Sunday, Things You Can Tell Just By Looking At Her, Invisible Circus, Shrek, Vanilla Sky, The Gangs of New York, The Sweetest Thing, Charlie's Angels 1 & 2, Shrek 2 (voice).

DI BONAVENTURA, LORENZO
Executive. b. New York, NY. e. B.A., intellectual history, Harvard College, M.B.A., Wharton School of Business, U. of Pennsylvania. After running a river-rafting co. following college, held numerous creative, production, and distribution positions at Columbia Pictures, including mgr. Pay Cable & Home Ent. Joined Warner Bros. Pictures as production exec., 1989; promoted to v.p., production, then named sr. v.p., production, 1993; exec. v.p., production, 1995; co-head, theatrical production, 1996. Currently pres., worldwide theatrical production, Warner Bros. Pictures, (since 1998), overseeing the development and production of all feature films, live-action and animation.

DI CAPRIO, LEONARDO
Actor. b. Hollywood, CA, Nov. 11, 1974. Started acting at age 15 in commercials and educational films. Appeared in short film The Foot Shooting Party.
PICTURES: Critters III (debut, 1991), Poison Ivy, This Boy's Life, What's Eating Gilbert Grape? (Natl. Board of Review, Chicago Film Critics & LA Film Critics Awards, Acad. Award nom.), The Quick and the Dead, The Basketball Diaries, Total Eclipse, Marvin's Room, Romeo + Juliet, Titanic, Don's Plum, Celebrity, The Man in the Iron Mask, The Beach, Don's Plum, The Gangs of New York, Catch Me if You Can, The Aviator (also prod.)
TELEVISION: *Series:* Growing Pains, Parenthood.

DICK, ANDY
Actor. b. Charleston, SC, Dec. 21, 1965.
PICTURES: Elvis Stories, Double Dragon, Reality Bites, In the Army Now, Hotel Oasis, The Cable Guy, Best Men, Ted, Bongwater, Picking up the Pieces, Inspector Gadget, Being John Malkovich, Advice From a Caterpillar, The Independent, Road Trip, Loser, Dude Where's My Car?, Scotland PA, Dr. Dolittle 2 (voice), Zoolander, Larceny, Old School, You'll Never Wiez in This Town Again, Naked Movie, The Hebrew Hammer, Scorched, Standing Still.
TELEVISION: Movies: Earth Angel, The Sissy Duckling, Special Delivery, Castaway Dick. Series: The Ben Stiller Show, Get Smart, NewsRadio, The Andy Dick Show, Sammy, Go Fish, Less Than Perfect. Guest: Anything But Love, Talk Soup (host), Flying Blind, The Building, The Nanny, Star Trek: Voyager.

DICKERSON, ERNEST
(A.S.C.): Cinematographer, Director. b. Newark, NJ, 1952. e. Howard U., architecture, NYU, grad. film school. First job, filming surgical procedures for Howard U. medical school. At NYU film school shot classmate Spike Lee's student films Sarah, and Joe's Bed Stuy Barbershop: We Cut Heads. Also shot Nike commercial and several music videos including Bruce Springsteen's Born in the U.S.A., Patti LaBelle's Stir It Up and Miles Davis' Tutu; and Branford Marsalis' Royal Garden Blues directed by Spike Lee. Admitted into Amer. Soc. of Cinematographers in 1989.
PICTURES: Cinematographer: The Brother From Another Planet, She's Gotta Have It (also cameo), Krush Groove, School Daze, Raw, Do the Right Thing, Def By Temptation, The Laser Man, Mo' Better Blues, Jungle Fever, Sex Drugs Rock & Roll, Cousin Bobby (co-photog.), Malcolm X, Our America. Director: Juice (also co-s.p., story), Surviving the Game, Tales From the Crypt Presents Demon Knight, Bulletproood, Blind Faith, Ambushed, Bones, Our America, Never Die Alone.
TELEVISION: Dir: Do it Acapella, FutureSport, Strange Justice, Monday Night Mayhem, Night Visions, Big Shot: Confessions of a Campus Bookie, Good Fences (dir.).

DICKINSON, ANGIE
Actress. r.n. Angeline Brown. b. Kulm, ND, Sept. 30, 1931. e. Immaculate Heart Coll., Glendale Coll., secretarial course. Beauty contest winner.
PICTURES: Lucky Me (debut in bit part, 1954), Man With the Gun, The Return of Jack Slade, Tennessee's Partner, The Black Whip, Hidden Guns, Tension at Table Rock, Gun the Man Down, Calypso Joe, China Gate, Shoot Out at Medicine Bend, Cry Terror, I Married a Woman, Rio Bravo, The Bramble Bush, Ocean's 11, A Fever in the Blood, The Sins of Rachel Cade, Jessica, Rome Adventure, Captain Newman M.D., The Killers, The Art of Love, Cast a Giant Shadow, The Chase, The Poppy is Also a Flower, The Last Challenge, Point Blank, Sam Whiskey, Some Kind of a Nut, Young Billy Young, Pretty Maids All in a Row, The Resurrection of Zachary Wheeler, The Outside Man, Big Bad Mama, Klondike Fever, Dressed to Kill, Charlie Chan and the Curse of the Dragon Queen, Death Hunt, Big Bad Mama II, Even Cowgirls Get the Blues, The Maddening, Sabrina, The Sun The Moon and The Stars, The Last Producer, Duets, Pay it Forward, Ocean's Eleven, Scene Smoking: Cigarettes Cinema & the Myth of Cool, Big Bad Love.
TELEVISION: Movies: The Love War, Thief, See the Man Run, The Norliss Tapes, Pray for the Wildcats, A Sensitive Passionate Man, Overboard, The Suicide's Wife, Dial M for Murder, One Shoe Makes It Murder, Jealousy, A Touch of Scandal, Stillwatch, Police Story: The Freeway Killings, Once Upon a Texas Train, Prime Target, Treacherous Crossing, Danielle Steel's Remembrance, Deep Family Secrets, Sealed with a Kiss. Mini-Series: Pearl, Hollywood Wives, Wild Palms. Special: Ira Geshwin at 100. Series: Police Woman, Cassie & Co.

DICKINSON, WOOD
Executive, Exhibitor. r.n. Glen Wood Dickinson III. b. Fairway, KS, Sept. 14, 1952. e. Texas Christian U (BFA Communications, MA Film). Past Chairman and CEO of Dickinson Theatres, Inc. Currently, he runs a co. called Think!, which consults in creative mgt. He is also CEO of Rolling Thunder Systems, an Int'l. software development company.

DIESEL, VIN
Actor. b. New York, NY, July 18, 1967. e. Hunter College. Began in theatre then wrote a short film based on his experiences as an actor, called Multi-Facial (1994); shot in under three days at a cost of $3,000. Film accepted for the 1995 Cannes Film Festival.
PICTURES: Multi-Facial (also dir.), Strays (also dir.), Saving Private Ryan, The Iron Giant, Boiler Room, Pitch Black, El Diablo, The Fast and the Furious, Knockaround Guys, XXX, The Chronicles of Riddick.

DILLER, BARRY
Executive. b. San Francisco, CA, Feb. 2, 1942. Joined ABC in April, 1966, as asst. to v.p. in chg. programming. In 1968, made exec. asst. to v.p. in chg. programming and dir. of feature films. In 1969, named v.p., feature films and program dev., east coast. In 1971, made v.p., Feature Films and Circle Entertainment, a unit of ABC Entertainment, responsible for selecting, producing and scheduling The Tuesday Movie of the Week, The Wednesday Movie of the Week, and Circle Film original features for airing on ABC-TV, as well as for acquisition and scheduling of theatrical features for telecasting on ABC Sunday Night Movie and ABC Monday Night Movie. In 1973, named v.p. in chg. of prime time TV for ABC Entertainment. In 1974 joined Paramount Pictures as bd. chmn. and chief exec. officer. 1983, named pres. of Gulf & Western Entertainment and Communications Group, while retaining Paramount titles. Resigned from Paramount in 1984 to join 20th Century-Fox as bd. chmn. and chief. exec. officer. Named chmn. & CEO of Fox, Inc. (comprising 20th Fox Film Corp., Fox TV Stations & Fox Bdcstg. Co.), Oct., 1985. Named to bd., News Corp. Ltd., June, 1987. Resigned from Fox in Feb., 1992. Named CEO of QVC Network Inc. Resigned QVC in 1995. CEO and bd. chair, Silver King Communications, Inc, Aug. 1995. Silver King merged with Savoy Pictures and Home Shopping Network in 1996, calling the new company HSN. In 1997 HSN bought Microsoft co-founder Paul Allen's 47% interest in Ticketmaster. Diller followed that up with the $4 billion purchase of USA Networks in 1998. USA Networks bought the remainder of Ticketmaster in 1998, then purchased online entertainment guide publisher CitySearch, merging it with Ticketmaster Online into a new company called Ticketmaster Online-CitySearch. USA Networks then spun-off the new company to the public, retaining a 60% interest (later reduced to about 50%). In 1999 Diller failed in an attempt to merge Ticketmaster Online-CitySearch and Internet portal Lycos (now part of Terra Lycos). Diller then bought parts of PolyGram Filmed Entertainment and independent film companies Gramercy and October from Seagram, renaming them USA Films. USA Networks also bought the Hotel Reservations Network in 1999. In 2000 Diller reorganized the co. into three units: USA Electronic Retailing, USA Entertainment, and USA Information and Services. It also lost World Wrestling Federation programming to Viacom. Later in 2000, when Vivendi bought Seagram, it gained Seagram's 43% stake in USA Networks. USA Networks also agreed to sell its TV stations to Univision for $1.1 billion. Later, Diller announced that his company would buy a 65% stake in Expedia (completed in 2002) and launch a travel venture called USA Travel Group. The group eventually included Hotels.com, a cable travel channel, and USA's minority stake in cruise and vacation package provider National Leisure Group. At the end of 2001, Diller sold USA Networks' entertainment assets to Vivendi Universal for $10.3 billion. The deal was completed in May 2002 and the company changed its name to USA Interactive with Diller retaining his voting control of the firm. Diller is currently chmn, Expedia, Inc.; chmn, USA Networks, Inc., chmn & ceo, InterActiveCorp (IAC, formerly USA Interactive Inc.), dir., The Washington Post Co., and dir., The Coca Cola Co. Diller serves on Board of the Museum of Television and Radio, the New York Public Library, Conservation International and 13/WNET. Member of the Board of Councilors for the University of Southern California's School of Cinema-Television, the New York University Board of Trustees, the Tisch School of the Arts Dean's Council and the Executive Board for the Medical Sciences of the University of California, Los Angeles.

DILLER, PHYLLIS
Comedienne, Actress. b. Lima, OH, July 17, 1917. r.n. Phyllis Ada Driver. e. Sherwood Music Sch., 1935-37; Bluffton Coll., OH, 1938-39. Started as publicist at San Francisco radio station before becoming nightclub comic at the age of 37. Recordings: Phyllis Diller Laughs, Are You Ready for Phyllis Diller?, Great Moments of Comedy, Born to Sing. Performed with many U.S. symphonies, 1971-90.
AUTHOR: Phyllis Diller's Housekeeping Hints, Phyllis Diller's Marriage Manual, Phyllis Diller's The Complete Mother, The Joys of Aging and How to Avoid Them.
THEATRE: Hello Dolly! (B'way), Everybody Loves Opal, Happy Birthday, The Dark at the Top of the Stairs, Subject to Change, The Wizard of Oz, Nunsense, Cinderella.
PICTURES: Splendor in the Grass (debut, 1961), Boy Did I Get a Wrong Number!, The Fat Spy, Mad Monster Party (voice), Eight on the Lam, Did You Hear the One About the Traveling Saleslady?, The Private Navy of Sgt. O'Farrell, The Adding Machine, The Sunshine Boys (cameo), A Pleasure Doing Business, Pink Motel, Pucker Up and Bark Like a Dog, Dr. Hackenstein, Friend to Friend, The Nutcracker Prince (voice), The Boneyard, Wisecracks, Happily Ever After (voice), The Perfect Man, The Silence of the Hams, A Bug's Life (voice), The Debtors, Let Me In I Hear Laughter, Everything's Jake, The Last Place on Earth, Hip! Edgy! Quirky!.
TELEVISION: Series: Showstreet, The Pruitts of Southampton, The Beautiful Phyllis Diller Show. Specials: The Phyllis Diller Special, An Evening With Phyllis Diller, Phyllis Diller's 102nd Birthday Party, Titus. Guest: Laugh In, Love American Style, The Muppet Show, The Love Boat, CHiPs, etc.

DILLMAN, BRADFORD
Actor. b. San Francisco, CA, April 14, 1930. m. actress-model Suzy Parker. e. Yale U., 1951. Studied at Actors Studio. Author: Inside the New York Giants, Are You Anybody?
THEATRE: The Scarecrow (1953), Third Person, Long Day's Journey into Night (premiere; Theatre World Award), The Fun Couple.
PICTURES: A Certain Smile (debut, 1958), In Love and War, Compulsion, Crack in the Mirror, Circle of Deception, Sanctuary, Francis of Assisi, A Rage to Live, The Plainsman, Sergeant Ryker, Helicopter Spies, Jigsaw, The Bridge at Remagen, Suppose They Gave a War and Nobody Came, Brother John, The Mephisto Waltz, Escape from the Planet of the Apes, The Resurrection of Zachary Wheeler, The Iceman Cometh, The Way We Were, Chosen Survivors, 99 and 44/100% Dead, Gold, Bug, Mastermind, The Enforcer, The Lincoln Conspiracy, Amsterdam Kill, The Swarm, Piranha, Love and Bullets, Guyana: Cult of the

Damned, Sudden Impact, Treasure of the Amazon, Man Outside, Lords of the Deep, Heroes Stand Alone.
TELEVISION: *Series:* Court-Martial, King's Crossing, Dynasty. *Movies:* Fear No Evil, Black Water Gold, Longstreet, Five Desperate Women, Revenge, Eyes of Charles Sand, The Delphi Bureau, Moon of the Wolf, Deliver Us From Evil, Murder or Mercy, Disappearance of Flight 412, Adventures of the Queen, Force Five, Widow, Street Killing, Kingston: The Power Play, The Hostage Heart, Jennifer: A Woman's Story, Before and After, The Memory of Eva Ryker, Tourist, The Legend of Walks Far Woman, Covenant, Heart of Justice.

DILLON, KEVIN
Actor. b. Mamaroneck, NY, Aug. 19, 1965. Younger brother of actor Matt Dillon. Stage work includes Dark at the Top of the Stairs, The Indian Wants the Bronx.
PICTURES: No Big Deal, Heaven Help Us, Platoon, Remote Control, The Rescue, The Blob, War Party, Immediate Family, The Doors, A Midnight Clear, No Escape, True Crime, Criminal Hearts, Misbegotten, Stag, Hidden Agenda, Interstate 84, Mob Dot Com.
TELEVISION: *Movie:* When He's Not a Stranger, Frankie's House, The Pathfinder, Gone in the Night, Medusa's Child. *Series:* St. Michael's Crossing. *Special:* Dear America: Letters Home from Vietnam (reader). *Series:* That's Life. *Guest:* Tales From the Crypt, NYPD Blue.

DILLON, MATT
Actor. b. New Rochelle, NY, Feb. 18, 1964. Brother is actor Kevin Dillon. Discovered at age 14 in junior high school by casting dir. who cast him in Over the Edge.
THEATRE: *NY:* The Boys of Winter (B'way debut, 1985).
PICTURES: Over the Edge (debut, 1979), Little Darlings, My Bodyguard, Liar's Moon, Tex, The Outsiders, Rumble Fish, The Flamingo Kid, Target, Rebel, Native Son, The Big Town, Kansas, Bloodhounds of Broadway, Drugstore Cowboy, A Kiss Before Dying, Singles, Mr. Wonderful, The Saint of Fort Washington, Golden Gate, To Die For, Frankie Starlight, Beautiful Girls, Grace of My Heart, Albino Alligator, In & Out, Wild Things, There's Something About Mary, One Night At McCool's, Beyond the Banyan Trees, Deuces Wild, City of Ghosts.
TELEVISION: *Movie:* Women & Men 2: In Love There Are No Rules (Return to Kansas City). *Specials:* The Great American Fourth of July and Other Disasters, Dear America: Letters Home From Vietnam (reader).

DILLON, MELINDA
Actress. b. Hope, AR, Oct. 13, 1939. e. Chicago Sch. of Drama, Art Inst., Goodman Theatre. Launched career on Broadway in original prod. of Who's Afraid of Virginia Woolf? (Theatre World Award, Tony Award nom., Drama Critics Award).
THEATRE: Story Theater, You Know I Can't Hear You When The Water's Running, A Way of Life, Our Town
PICTURES: The April Fools (debut, 1969), Bound for Glory (People's Choice Award), Slap Shot, Close Encounters of the Third Kind (Acad. Award nom.), F.I.S.T., Absence of Malice (Acad. Award nom.), A Christmas Story, Songwriter, Harry and the Hendersons, Staying Together, Spontaneous Combustion, Capt. America, The Prince of Tides, Sioux City, To Fong Woo--Thanks for Everything Julie Newmar, How to Make an American Quilt, Dorothy Day, The Effects of Magic, Magnolia.
TELEVISION: *Movies:* Critical List, Transplant, Marriage is Alive and Well, The Shadow Box, Fallen Angel, Hellinger's Law, Right of Way, Shattered Spirits, Shattered Innocence, Nightbreaker, Judgment Day: The John List Story, State of Emergency, Confessions: Two Faces of Evil, Naomi & Wynonna: Love Can Build a Bridge. *Mini-Series:* Space.*Series:* Paul Sills Story Theatre. *Guest:* Twilight Zone, The Defenders, Bonanza, East Side West Side, The Paul Sand Show, The Jeffersons, Good Morning America, The Today Show, Dick Cavett Show, Dinah Shore Show, Picket Fences, The Client, Texarkana.

DINDAL, MARK
Animator, director. b. Columbus, OH.
PICTURES: The Fox and the Hound, Mickey's Christmas Carol, The Black Cauldron, The Great Mouse Detective, Oliver & Company, The Little Mermaid, The Rocketeer, Cats Don't Dance (voice, dir., writer), The Emperor's New Groove (dir., writer).

Di NOVI, DENISE
Producer. b. Canada. Started as journalist, reporter, film critic in Toronto before entering film industry as unit publicist. 1980, joined Montreal's Film Plan production co. as co-prod., assoc. prod. and exec. in charge of prod. working on such movies as Visiting Hours, Going Berserk, Videodrome. Became exec. v.p. of prod. at New World, then head of Tim Burton Prods., 1989-92.
PICTURES: Heathers, Edward Scissorhands, Meet the Applegates, Batman Returns, The Nightmare Before Christmas, Cabin Boy, Little Women, Ed Wood, James and the Giant Peach, Practical Magic, Almost Heroes, Message in a Bottle, The Second Angel, Happy Campers, Original Sin, Killing Mrs. Duke, A Walk to Remember, What a Girl Wants.
TELEVISION: *Movies:* Eloise at the Plaza, Eloise at Christmastime, Hotel (movie), *Mini-series:* The 70s, *Series:* The District.

Di PIETRA, ROSEMARY
Executive. Joined Paramount Pictures in 1976, rising through ranks to become director-corporate administration. 1985, promoted to exec. dir.-corporate administration.

DISHY, BOB
Actor. b. Brooklyn, NY. e. Syracuse U.
THEATRE: Damn Yankees, From A to Z, Second City, Flora the Red Menace, By Jupiter, Something Different, The Goodbye People, The Good Doctor, The Unknown Soldier at His Wife, The Creation of the World and Other Business, An American Millionaire, Sly Fox, Murder at Howard Johnson's, Grown Ups, Cafe Crown.
PICTURES: The Tiger Makes Out, Lovers and Other Strangers, The Big Bus, I Wonder Who's Killing Her Now?, The Last Married Couple in America, First Family, Author! Author!, Brighton Beach Memoirs, Critical Condition, Stay Tuned, Used People, My Boyfriend's Back, Don Juan DeMarco, Jungle to Jungle, A Fish in the Bathtub, Judy Berlin, Captured.
TELEVISION: *Series:* That Was the Week That Was. *Specials:* Story Theatre (dir.), The Cafeteria. *Guest:* The Comedy Zone. *Movies:* It Couldn't Happen to a Nicer Guy, Thicker Than Blood: The Larry McLinden Story.

DISNEY, ROY E.
Producer, Director, Writer, Cameraman, Film editor. b. Los Angeles, CA, Jan. 10, 1930. e. Pomona Coll., CA. 1951 started as page, NBC-TV. Asst. film editor Dragnet TV series. 1952-78, Walt Disney Prods., Burbank, Calif., various capacities, including head of the animation dept.; vice chmn. of the board, The Walt Disney Co.; bd. chmn., Shamrock Holdings, Inc., bd. dir., Walt Disney Co.
PICTURES: Perri, Mysteries of the Deep, Mustang (dir.), Pacific High, The Fantasy Film Worlds of George Pal (actor), The Wonderful Ice Cream Suit (prod.), Fantasia 2000 (exec. prod.)
TELEVISION: Walt Disney's Wonderful World of Color, The Hound That Thought He Was A Raccoon, Sancho, The Homing Steer, The Silver Fox and Sam Davenport, Wonders of the Water World, Legend of Two Gypsy Dogs, Adventure in Wildwood Heart, The Postponed Wedding, Zorro series, An Otter in the Family, My Family is a Menagerie, Legend of El Blanco, Pancho, The Fastest Paw in the West, The Owl That Didn't Give A Hoot, Varda the Peregrine Falcon, Cristobalito, The Calypso Colt, Three Without Fear, Hamade and the Pirates, Chango, Guardian of the Mayan Treasure, Nosey the Sweetest Skunk in the World, Mustang!, Call It Courage, Ringo the Refugee Raccoon, Shokee the Everglades Panther, Deacon the High-Noon Dog, Wise One, Whale's Tooth, Track of African Bongo, Dorsey the Mail-Carrying Dog.

DIXON, BARBARA
Executive. b. Pasadena CA. e. USC, grad. degree from Johns Hopkins U. Served as staff member of Senate Judiciary Committee and was dir. of legislation for Sen. Birch Bayh, 1974-79. Left to become dir. of Office of Government & Public Affairs of Natl. Transportation Safety Board. Named v.p., Fratelli Group, p.r. firm in Washington; took leave of absence in 1984 to serve as deputy press secty. to Democratic V.P. candidate, Geraldine Ferraro. In 1985 joined Motion Picture Assn. of America as v.p. for public affairs. Moved to Columbia/Tristar.

DIXON, DONNA
Actress. b. Alexandria, VA, July 20, 1957. m. actor-writer Dan Aykroyd. e. Studied anthropology and medicine, Mary Washington U. Left to become a model, both on magazine covers and in TV commercials (Vitalis, Max Factor, Gillette).
PICTURES: Dr. Detroit, Twilight Zone--The Movie, Spies Like Us, The Couch Trip, It Had To Be You, Speed Zone!, Lucky Stiff, Wayne's World, Exit to Eden, Nixon.
TELEVISION: *Movies:* Mickey Spillane's Margin for Murder, No Man's Land, Beverly Hills Madam. *Specials:* Women Who Rate a "10", The Shape of Things, The Rodney Dangerfield Show: I Can't Take it No More. *Series:* Bosom Buddies, Berrenger's.

DIXON, WHEELER WINSTON
Educator, Writer, Filmmaker. b. New Brunswick, NJ, March 12, 1950. e. Rutgers U. In 1960s asst. writer for Time/Life publications; also writer for Interview magazine. 1976, directed TV commercials in NY. One season with TVTV, Los Angeles, as post-prod. suprv. 1978, formed Deliniator Films, Inc., serving as exec. prod./dir. Since 1988 has directed film program at Univ. of Nebraska, where holds rank of tenured full prof. and chair, Film Studies Prog.; received Rockefeller Foundation grant. Prod., dir. with Gwendolyn Audrey-Foster: Women Who Made the Movies (video). 1992, guest prog. at the Brit. Film Inst./ Natl. Film Theatre. 1993, Distinguished Teaching Award. Invited lecturer at Yale, 1995; Series ed. for SUNY Press Cultural Studies in Cinema/Video (20 vol.)
AUTHOR: The 'B' Directors, 1985; The Cinematic Vision of F. Scott Fitzgerald, 1986; PRC: A History of Producer's Releasing Corp., 1986; books on Freddie Francis, Terence Fisher, Reginald Le Borg, 1992-93; The Early Film Criticism of Francois Truffaut; Re-Viewing British Cinema, 1900-92; It Looks at You: The Returned Gaze of Cinema, 1995; The Films of Jean-Luc Godard, 1997; The Exploding Eye: A Revisionary History of 1960s American Experimental Cinema, 1997.
PICTURES: Dir: Quick Constant and Solid Instant, London Clouds, Serial Metaphysics, Waste Motion, Tightrope, Stargrove, Gaze, An Evening with Chris Jangaard, Dana Can Deal, Damage, Un Petit Examen, and Not So Damned Petit Either, or, The Light Shining Over the Dark, Madagascar or Caroline Kennedy's Sinful Life in London, The Diaries, Distance, What Can I Do, Squatters.

DOBSON, KEVIN
Actor. b. New York, NY, March 18, 1943.
PICTURES: Love Story, Bananas, Klute, The Anderson Tapes, The French Connection, Carnal Knowledge, Midway, All Night Long, Mom Can I Keep Her?, Nathan Grimm, Restraining Order, She's No Angel.
TELEVISION: Movies: The Immigrants, Transplant, Orphan Train, Hardhat and Legs, Reunion, Mark I Love You, Mickey Splillane's Margin for Murder, Money Power Murder (also prod.), Casey's Gift: For Love of a Child, Sweet Revenge, Fatal Friendship, Dirty Work, House of Secrets and Lies, The Conviction of Kitty Dodds, If Someone Had Known, Crimes of Passion: Voice from the Grave, Nobody Lives Forever. Mini-series: Knots Landing: Back to the Cul-de-Sac. Series: Kojak, Shannon, Knots Landing (also dir. 9 episodes), F/X: The Series. Guest: The Nurses, The Doctors, Greatest Heroes of the Bible.

DOERFLER, RONALD J.
Executive. e. Fairleigh Dickinson Univ. Became CPA in 1967. 1972, received M.B.A. from Fairleigh Dickinson. Joined Capital Cities 1969 as asst. controller. Became treas. in 1977; v.p. & CFO, 1980. 1983, named sr. v.p., then sr. v.p. & CFO. Currently, sr. v.p. & CFO, The Hearst Corp.

DOHERTY, SHANNEN
Actress. b. Memphis, TN, April 12, 1971. On stage in The Mound Builders.
PICTURES: Night Shift, The Secret of NIMH (voice), Girls Just Want to Have Fun, Heathers, Freeze Frame, Mallrats, Nowhere, Striking Poses, Jay and Silent Bob Strike Back, The Rendering.
TELEVISION: Movies: The Other Lover, Obsessed, Blindfold, Jailbreakers, A Burning Passion: The Margaret Mitchell Story, Gone in the Night, Friends 'Til the End, Sleeping with the Devil, The Ticket, Satan's School for Girls, Another Day. Mini-Series: Robert Kennedy and His Times. Pilot: His and Hers. Series: Little House on the Prairie, Our House, Beverly Hills 90210, Charmed, Scare Tactics (host). Guest: 21 Jump Street, Cagney and Lacey, Highway to Heaven, Life Goes On, The Dennis Miller Show, others.

DOLAN, CHARLES F.
Executive. b. Cleveland, OH, Oct. 16, 1926. e. John Carroll U. Established Teleguide Inc., early 1960s. Found. Sterling Manhattan Cable, mid 1960s. Found. Home Box Office Inc., early 1970s; after sale of HBO to Time Life Inc., organized Cablevision Systems Corp., 1973; presently, chmn. Also, chmn., Natl Acad. of TV Arts & Sci. Bd. govs., Natl Hockey League. Bd. dirs.: Madison Square Garden Prop.; St. Francis Hospital, NY. Mng. dir., Metropolitan Opera of NY. Trustee, Fairfield U, CT.

DOLAN, JAMES L.
Executive. Began working at Cablevision in the 1970s, in construction, field sales & collections depts.; named asst. gen mngr. of Cablevision of Chicago, late 1970's. Early 1980s, as Cablevision v.p., found. & mngd. WKNR-AM, Cleveland; also oversaw weekly TV mag. Total. During the 1980s, corp. dir. advt., at Rainbow & v.p. for advt. sales at Cablevision. CEO, Rainbow Media Holdings, Inc., 1993-1995. Pres. & CEO, Cablevision Systems Corp., 1995-; is chmn. Madison Square Garden, L.P., and chmn. of New York Kickerbockers. also on bd. & exec. com., Natl Cable TV Assn., & chair., music licensing com. On bd. dirs., Hazelden NY & Cable Labs, CO. Hon. co-chair, LI Film & TV Found.

DOLGEN, JONATHAN L.
Executive. b. New York, NY, April 27, 1945. e. Cornell U., NYU Sch. of Law. Began career with Wall Street law firm, Fried, Frank, Harris, Shriver & Jacobson. In 1976 joined Columbia Pictures Industries as asst. gen. counsel and deputy gen. counsel. 1979, named sr. v.p. in chg. of worldwide business affairs; 1980, named exec. v.p. Joined Columbia m.p. div., 1981; named pres. of Columbia Pay-Cable & Home Entertainment Group. Also pres. Columbia Pictures domestic operations, overseeing Music Group. 1985, joined 20th-Fox in newly created position of sr. exec. v.p. for telecommunications. Became pres. of Sony Motion Picture Group, 1991. Appointed chmn. Viacom Entertainment Group, 1994 where he oversees the operations of Paramount Motion Picture Group (Motion Picture Production & Distribution, Famous Music Publishing, Theatrical Exhibition) and Paramount Television Group (prod. & dist. of TV product and ownership of TV stations and interests in the United Paramount Network).

DONAHUE, ELINOR
Actress. b. Tacoma, WA, April 19, 1937.
PICTURES: Mr. Big, Tenth Avenue Angel, Unfinished Dance, Three Daring Daughters, Love is Better Than Ever, Girls Town, Pretty Woman, Freddy's Dead: The Final Nightmare.
TELEVISION: Movies: In Name Only, Gidget Gets Married, Mulligan's Stew (pilot), Doctors' Private Lives, Condominium, High School U.S.A., Going Beserk, Never Say Goodbye, Dr. Quinn Medicine Woman: The Heart Within. Special: Father Knows Best Reunion. Mini-series: The Invaders, Shake Rattle and Roll: An American Love Story. Series: Father Knows Best, The Andy Griffith Show, Many Happy Returns, The Odd Couple, Mulligan's Stew, Please Stand By, Days of Our Lives, The New Adventures of Beans Baxter, Get a Life, Generations, Santa Barbara, Eek the Cat. Guest: One Day at a Time, Sweepstakes$, The Golden Girls.

DONAHUE, PHIL
Television Host. b. Cleveland, OH, Dec. 21, 1935. e. Notre Dame, BBA. m. actress Marlo Thomas. Worked as check sorter, Albuquerque Natl. Bank, 1957, then as announcer at KYW-TV & AM, Cleveland; news dir. WABJ radio, Adrian, MI; morning newscaster WHIO-TV. Interviews with Jimmy Hoffa and Billy Sol Estes picked up nationally by CBS. Host of Conversation Piece, phone-in talk show. Debuted The Phil Donahue Show, daytime talk show in Dayton, Ohio, 1967. Syndicated 2 years later. Moved to Chicago, 1974. Host, Donahue, now in 165 outlets in U.S. In 1979 a mini-version of show became 3-times-a-week segment on NBC's Today Show. Winner of several Emmys. Books: Donahue: My Own Story (1980), The Human Animal (1985).

DONALDSON, ROGER
Director. b. Ballarat, Australia, Nov. 15, 1943. Emigrated to New Zealand at 19. Established still photography business; then began making documentaries. Directed Winners and Losers, a series of short dramas for NZ-TV.
PICTURES: Sleeping Dogs (also prod.), Smash Palace (also s.p. prod.), The Bounty, Marie, No Way Out, Cocktail, Cadillac Man (also prod.), White Sands, The Getaway, Species, Dante's Peak, Thirteen Days, The Recruit.

DONEN, STANLEY
Director, Producer, Choreographer. b. Columbia, SC, April 13, 1924. e. USC. Former dancer, B'way debut 1940 in chorus of Pal Joey starring Gene Kelly. Assisted Kelly as choreog. on stage prod. of Best Foot Forward; hired by MGM to repeat duties in film version. Choreographer on such films as Cover Girl, Holiday in Mexico, This Time for Keeps, A Date With Judy, Take Me Out to the Ballgame (also co-story credit). Honorary Acad. Award, 1997.
PICTURES: Director: On the Town (debut, 1949; co-dir. with Gene Kelly), Royal Wedding, Singin' in the Rain (co-dir., co-choreog. with Gene Kelly), Fearless Fagan, Love Is Better Than Ever, Give a Girl a Break (also co-choreog.), Seven Brides for Seven Brothers, Deep in My Heart (also co-choreog.), It's Always Fair Weather (co-dir., co-choreog. with Gene Kelly), Funny Face, The Pajama Game (co-dir., co-prod. with George Abbott), Kiss Them for Me. Director-Producer: Indiscreet, Damn Yankees (co-dir., co-prod. with George Abbott), Once More With Feeling, Surprise Package, The Grass Is Greener, Charade, Arabesque, Two for the Road, Bedazzled, Staircase, The Little Prince, Lucky Lady (dir. only), Movie Movie, Saturn 3, Blame It on Rio.
TELEVISION: Actor: The Making of Seven Brides for Seven Brothers, The Hollywood Fashion Machine. Dir: Love Letters. Moonlighting.

DONIGER, WALTER
Writer, Director, Producer. b. New York NY. e. Duke U., Harvard U. Graduate Business Sch. Entered m.p. business as writer later writer-prod-dir. Wrote documentaries in Army Air Forces M.P. Unit in W.W.II. WGA award nominee and other awards.
PICTURES: Rope of Sand, Desperate Search, Cease Fire, Safe At Home (dir.), House of Women (dir.), Duffy of San Quentin (dir.), Along the Great Divide, Tokyo Joe, Alaska Seas, Steel Cage (dir.), Steel Jungle (dir.), Hold Back the Night, Guns of Fort Petticoat, Unwed Mother (dir.), Stone Cold (exec. prod., s.p.).
TELEVISION: Series: Delvecchio, Mad Bull, Switch, Moving On, Baa Baa Blacksheep, McCloud, The Man and the City, Sarge, Owen Marshall, Peyton Place, Mr. Novak, The Greatest Show on Earth, Travels of Jaimie McPheeters, Outlaws, Hong Kong, Checkmate, Bat Masterson, The Web, Bold Venture, Tombstone Territory, Maverick, Rough Riders, Lockup, Dick Powell, The Survivors, Bracken's World, Bold Ones, Kung Fu, Barnaby Jones, Marcus Welby, Lucas Tanner.

DONNELLY, DONAL
Actor. b. Bradford, England, July 6, 1931. Studied for theatre at the Dublin Gate Theatre.
THEATRE: NY Theatre: Philadelphia Here I Come (B'way debut, 1966), Joe Egg, Sleuth (NY and U.S. tour), The Elephant Man, The Faith-Healer, The Chalk Garden, My Astonishing Self, Big Maggie, Execution of Justice, Sherlock's Last Case, Ghetto, Dancing at Lughnasa, Translations.
PICTURES: Rising of the Moon (1957), Gideon's Day, Shake Hands With the Devil, Young Cassidy, The Knack, Up Jumped a Swagman, The Mind of Mr. Soames, Waterloo, The Dead, The Godfather Part III, Squanto: A Warrior's Tale, Korea, This Is My Father, Love and Rage.
TELEVISION: Juno and the Paycock (BBC, 1958), Home Is the Hero, The Venetian Twins, The Plough and the Stars, Playboy of the Western World, Sergeant Musgrave's Dance, Yes-Honestly (series).

DONNELLY, RALPH E.
Executive. b. Lynbrook, NY, Jan. 20, 1932. e. Bellmore, NY public school; W. C. Mepham H.S., 1949. Worked for Variety (publication) as writer, 1950; Long Island Press as daily columnist, 1951; joined Associated Independent Theatres, 1953, as gen. mgr.; later film buyer; in 1973 left to become independent buyer and booker for Creative Films; film buyer and v.p., RKO/Stanley Warner Theatres, 1976-79; pres. & gen. mgr. for Cinema 5 Ltd. circuit, N.Y., 1980-87; 1987-93, exec. v.p. City Cinemas, N.Y. Chmn. of Cinema Connection.

DONNER, CLIVE
Director. b. London, England,, Jan 21, 1926. Ent. m.p. ind. 1942. Asst. film ed. Denhem Studios, 1942. Dir. London stage: The

Formation Dancers, The Front Room Boys, Kennedy's Children (also NY). *Film editor:* A Christmas Carol (Scrooge), The Card (The Promoter), Genevieve, Man With a Million (The Million Pound Note), The Purple Plain, I Am a Camera.
PICTURES: The Secret Place (debut, 1957), Heart of a Child, Marriage of Convenience, The Sinister Man, Some People, The Caretaker (The Guest), Nothing But the Best, What's New Pussycat?, Luv, Here We Go Round the Mulberry Bush (also prod.), Alfred the Great, Old Dracula (Vampira), The Nude Bomb, Charlie Chan and the Curse of the Dragon Queen, Stealing Heaven.
TELEVISION: Danger Man, Sir Francis Drake, Mighty and Mystical, British Institutions, Tempo, Spectre, The Thief of Baghdad, Oliver Twist, Rogue Male, The Scarlet Pimpernel, Arthur the King, To Catch a King, Three Hostages, She Fell Among Thieves, A Christmas Carol, Dead Man's Folly, Babes in Toyland, Not a Penny More Not a Penny Less, Coup de Foudre (Love at First Sight), Terror Strikes the Class Reunion (For Better or Worse), Charlemagne.

DONNER, RICHARD
Director. b. New York, NY, 1939. Began career as actor off-B'way. Worked with director Martin Ritt on TV production of Maugham's Of Human Bondage. Moved to California 1958, directing commercials, industrial films and documentaries. First TV drama: Wanted: Dead or Alive.
PICTURES: X-15 (debut, 1961), Salt and Pepper, Twinky (Lola), The Omen, Superman, Inside Moves, The Final Conflict (exec. prod. only), The Toy (also exec. prod.), Ladyhawke (also prod.), The Goonies (also prod.), Lethal Weapon (also prod.), The Lost Boys (exec. prod. only), Scrooged (also prod.), Lethal Weapon 2 (also prod.), Delirious (exec. prod. only), Radio Flyer, Lethal Weapon 3 (also prod.), Free Willy (co-exec. prod. only), Maverick (also prod.), Tales From the Crypt Presents Demon Knight (co-exec. prod. only), Assassins (also prod.), Conspiracy Theory (also prod.), Free Willy 3: The Rescue (exec. prod.), Lethal Weapon 4, Timeline (also prod.).
TELEVISION: *Series episodes:* Have Gun Will Travel, Perry Mason, Cannon, Get Smart, The Fugitive, Kojak, Bronk, Gilligan's Island, Man From U.N.C.L.E., Wild Wild West, Tales From the Crypt, Two Fisted Tales, Twilight Zone, The Banana Splits, Combat. *Movies:* Lucas Tanner (pilot), Sarah T.: Portrait of a Teen-Age Alcoholic, Senior Year, A Shadow in the Streets, Tales From the Crypt (exec. prod.; also dir. episode: Dig That Cat... He's Real Gone).

D'ONOFRIO, VINCENT PHILLIP
Actor. b. Brooklyn, NY, 1960. Studied acting with the American Stanislavsky Theatre in NY, appearing in Of Mice and Men, The Petrified Forest, Sexual Perversity in Chicago, and The Indian Wants the Bronx.
THEATRE: *B'way:* Open Admissions.
PICTURES: The First Turn On! (debut, 1984), Full Metal Jacket, Adventures in Babysitting, Mystic Pizza, Signs of Life, The Blood of Heroes, Crooked Hearts, Dying Young, Fires Within, Naked Tango, JFK, The Player, Desire, Household Saints, Mr. Wonderful, Being Human, Ed Wood, Imaginary Crimes, Stuart Saves His Family, Strange Days, Feeling Minnesota, Men in Black, The Velocity of Gary, The Whole Wide World (also prod.), The Newton Boys, Claire Dolan, Steal This Movie (also exec. prod.), Imposter, The Thirteenth Floor, The Cell, Happy Accidents, Spanish Judges, The Dangerous Lives of Altar Boys, The Salton Sea, Bark, Imposter, Chelsea Walls.
TELEVISION: *Movies:* Taking of Pelham One Two Three, That Championship Season, The Red Sneakers, Case of Evil. *Series:* Homicide: Life on the Street, Law and Order: Criminal Intent.

DONOHOE, AMANDA
Actress. b. London, England, June 29, 1962. e. Francis Holland Sch. for Girls, Central Sch. of Speech & Drama. Member of Royal Exchange Theatre in Manchester. B'way debut 1995 in Uncle Vanya.
PICTURES: Foreign Body (debut, 1986), Castaway, The Lair of the White Worm, The Rainbow, Tank Malling, Diamond Skulls (Dark Obsession), Paper Mask, The Madness of King George, Liar Liar, Writer's Block, I'm Losing You, Stardust, The Real Howard Spitz, Circus, Wild About Harry, Glory Glory, Phoenix Blue.
TELEVISION: *Movies:* Married to Murder, Shame, It's Nothing Personal (also co-exec. prod.), The Substitute, Shame II: The Secret (also co-exec. prod.), A Knight in Camelot, In the Beginning, Rock the Boat, Lucky Day. *Special:* Game Set and Match (Mystery!). *Series:* L.A. Law (Golden Globe Award). *Guest:* The Hidden Room, Murder Most Horrid, Frasier.

DONOVAN, ARLENE
Producer. b. Kentucky. e. Stratford Coll., VA. Worked in publishing before entering industry as asst. to late dir. Robert Rosen on Cocoa Beach, uncompleted at his death. Worked as story editor, Columbia Pictures. 1969-82, literary head of m.p. dept. for ICM; involved in book publishing as well as stage and screen projects.
PICTURES: Still of the Night, Places in the Heart, Nadine, The House on Carroll Street (co-exec. prod.), Billy Bathgate, Nobody's Fool, Twilight.

DONOVAN, TATE
Actor. b. New York, NY, Sept. 25, 1963. Raised in New Jersey. Studied acting at USC. Worked as still photographer for two Mutual of Omaha documentaries.
THEATRE: Ruffian on the Stair, The American Plan, The Rhythm

of Torn Stars, Bent. *B'way:* Picnic.
PICTURES: SpaceCamp, Clean and Sober, Dead Bang, Memphis Belle, Love Potion No. 9, Ethan Frome, Equinox, Holy Matrimony, Murder at 1600, Hercules (voice), Waiting for Woody, The Only Thrill, October 22, Drop Back Ten, 4 a.m.: Open All Night, G-Men From Hell, The Office Party, Jesus and Hutch, Swordfish, Get Well Soon, West of Here, Exposed.
TELEVISION: *Movies:* Not My Kid, Into Thin Air, A Case of Deadly Force, Nutcracker: Money Madness Murder, Rising Son, Tempting Fate. *HBO Special:* Vietnam War Stories. *Series:* Partners, Hercules (voice), Trinity, House of Mouse (voice), Mister Sterling, The O.C. *Guest:* Friends.

DOOHAN, JAMES
Actor. b. Vancouver, B.C., Canada, March 3, 1920. WWII capt. in Royal Canadian Artillery. 1946 won scholarship to Neighborhood Playhouse in NY and later taught there. 1953, returned to Canada to live in Toronto, becoming engaged in acting career on radio, TV and in film. Then to Hollywood and chief fame as Chief Engineer Scott in TV series, Star Trek.
PICTURES: The Wheeler Dealers, The Satan Bug, Bus Riley's Back in Town, Pretty Maids All in a Row, Star Trek—The Motion Picture, Star Trek II: The Wrath of Khan, Star Trek III: The Search for Spock, Star Trek IV: The Voyage Home, Star Trek V: The Final Frontier, Star Trek VI: The Undiscovered Country, Double Trouble, National Lampoon's Loaded Weapon 1, Star Trek: Generations, Storybook, Trekkies, The Duke.
TELEVISION: *Series:* Star Trek. *Guest:* Hazel, Bonanza, The Virginia, Gunsmoke, Peyton Place, The Fugitive, Marcus Welby MD, Ben Casey, Bewitched, Fantasy Island. *Movie:* Scalplock.

DOOLEY, PAUL
Actor. r.n. Paul Brown. b. Parkersburg, WV, Feb. 22, 1928. Began career on NY stage in Threepenny Opera. Later member of Second City. B'way credits include The Odd Couple, Adaptation/Next, The White House Murder Case, Hold Me. Co-creator and writer for The Electric Company on PBS.
PICTURES: What's So Bad About Feeling Good? (debut, 1968), The Out-of-Towners, Death Wish, The Gravy Train, Slap Shot, A Wedding, A Perfect Couple, Breaking Away, Rich Kids, Popeye, Health (also co-s.p.), Paternity, Endangered Species, Kiss Me Goodbye, Strange Brew, Going Berserk, Sixteen Candles, Big Trouble, O.C. and Stiggs, Monster in the Closet, Last Rites, Flashback, Shakes the Clown, The Player, My Boyfriend's Back, A Dangerous Woman, The Underneath, God's Lonely Man, Loved, Clockwatchers, Telling Lies in America, Runaway Bride, I'll Remember April, Guinevere, Happy Texas, A Woman's a Helluva Thing, The Perfect You, Madison, Insomnia, Adventures in Home Schooling, A Mighty Wind, Lake Desire.
TELEVISION: *Movies:* The Murder of Mary Phagan, Lip Service, Guts and Glory: The Rise and Fall of Oliver North, When He's Not a Stranger, The Court Martial of Jackie Robinson, Guess Who's Coming for Christmas?, White Hot: The Mysterious Murder of Thelma Todd, Cooperstown, Mother of the Bride, State of Emergency, The Computer Wore Tennis Shoes, Ruby Roomaine Trailer Tales. *Series:* The Dom DeLuise Show, Coming of Age, Tales of the City, Once and Again. *Specials:* Faerie Tale Theater, The Firm, Traveler's Rest, Sixteen Candles: The E! True Hollywood Story. *Guest:* Dream On, ALF, The Golden Girls, thirtysomething, Mad About You, Evening Shade, Coach, Wonder Years, The Boys, L.A. Law, The Mommies, Star Trek: Deep Space Nine, The Practice, ER, Dharma & Greg, My So-Called Life.

DORAN, LINDSAY
Executive. b. Los Angeles, CA. e. U. of California at Santa Cruz. Moved to London where was contributing author to The Oxford Companion to Film and the World Encyclopedia of Film. Returned to U.S. to write and produce documentaries and children's programs for Pennsylvania public affairs station WPSX-TV. Career in m.p. industry began in story dept. at Embassy Pictures which she joined in 1979; 1982 promoted to dir. of development; then v.p., creative affairs. 1985, joined Paramount Pictures as v.p., production, for MP Group. 1987, promoted to senior v.p., production. 1989. Pres., Mirage Productions. Pres. and COO, United Artists Pictures, 1996-2000. Currently producer with own company, Three Strange Angels.

DORFF, STEPHEN
Actor. b. July 29, 1973. Started acting at age 9.
PICTURES: The Gate (debut, 1987), The Power of One, An Ambush of Ghosts, Judgment Night, Rescue Me, Backbeat, S.F.W., Reckless, Halcyon Days, Innocent Lies, I Shot Andy Warhol, The Audition, Star Truckers, City of Industry, Blade, Entropy, Blood and Wine, Earthly Possessions, Quantum Project, Cecil B. Demented, Deuces Wild, Riders, Fear Dot Com, Den of Lions, Cold Creek Manor.
TELEVISION: *Series:* What a Dummy. *Movies:* I Know My First Name Is Steven, Always Remember I Love You, Do You Know the Muffin Man?, A Son's Promise, Earthly Possessions. *Guest:* Empty Nest, Roseanne, The Outsiders, Married...With Children, Blossom.

DORTORT, DAVID
Executive Producer. b. New York, NY, Oct. 23, 1916. e. City Coll. of New York. Served U.S. Army, 1943-46. Novelist and short story writer, 1943-49. Also TV writer. Now pres. of Xanadu Prods., Aurora Enterprises, Inc., and Bonanza Ventures, Inc. & Pres. TV branch, WGA, West, 1954-55; TV-radio branch, 1955-57; v.p. PGA, 1967; pres. 1968. Chmn., Caucus for Producers, Writers and Directors, 1973-75. Pres., PGA, 1980-81; campaign dir., Permanent Charities Comm., 1980-81; chmn., Interguild Council

1980-81. Received WGA/West noms. for TV work on An Error in Chemistry (Climax), and The Ox-Bow Incident (20th Century Fox Hour). Author: novels include Burial of the Fruit, The Post of Honor.
PICTURES: The Lusty Men, Reprisal, The Big Land, Cry in the Night, Clash by Night, Going Bananas (exec. prod.).
TELEVISION: Creator and exec. prod.: Bonanza, High Chaparral, The Chisholms, Hunter's Moon, Bonanza: Legends of the Ponderosa. Producer: The Restless Gun, The Cowboys. Creator, story and exec. prod.: Bonanza: The Next Generation. Exec. prod.: Bonanza: The Return, Bonanza: Under Attack.

DOUGLAS, ILLEANA
Actress. July 25, 1965. Grandfather was actor Melvyn Douglas. Directed short films The Perfect Woman (Aspen Film Fest. prize, 1994), Boy Crazy—Girl Crazier.
THEATRE: Takes on Women, As Sure as You Live, Black Eagles.
PICTURES: Hello Again, New York Stories, GoodFellas, Guilty By Suspicion, Cape Fear, Alive, Household Saints, Grief, Quiz Show, Search and Destroy, To Die For, Grace of My Heart, Picture Perfect, Hacks, Flypaper, Wedding Bell Blues, Stir of Echoes, Can't Stop Dancing, Message in a Bottle, Happy Texas, The Next Best Thing, Ghost World, Dummy, The Adventures of Pluto Nash, Missing Brendan, The Kiss.
TELEVISION: Movies: Weapons of Mass Distraction, Rough Riders, Bella Mafia. Series: Action.

DOUGLAS, KIRK
Actor, Producer, Director. r.n. Issur Danielovitch (changed to Demsky). b. Amsterdam, NY, Dec. 9, 1916. m. Anne Buydens, pres. of Bryna Prod. Co. Father of Michael, Joel, Peter, Eric. e. St. Lawrence U, B.A, AADA. Stage debut in New York: Spring Again. U.S. Navy during W.W.II; resumed stage work. Did radio soap operas. Signed by Hal B. Wallis for film debut. Autobiography: The Ragman's Son (1988). Novels: Dance With the Devil, The Secret, Last Tango in Brooklyn. Recipient of U.S. Presidential Medal of Freedom, 1981. Career achievement award, National Board of Review, 1989. Received AFI Lifetime Achievement Award, 1991.
THEATRE: Spring Again, Three Sisters, Kiss and Tell, Trio, The Wind is Ninetry, Star in the Window, Man Bites Dog, One Flew Over the Cuckoo's Nest, The Boys of Autumn.
PICTURES: The Strange Love of Martha Ivers (debut, 1946), Out of the Past, I Walk Alone, Mourning Becomes Electra, The Walls of Jericho, My Dear Secretary, Letter to Three Wives, Champion, Young Man with a Horn, The Glass Menagerie, Ace in the Hole (The Big Carnival), Along the Great Divide, Detective Story, The Big Trees, The Big Sky, Bad and the Beautiful, Story of Three Loves, The Juggler, Act of Love, 20,000 Leagues Under the Sea, Ulysses, Man Without a Star, The Racers, The Indian Fighter (also prod.), Lust for Life, Top Secret Affair, Gunfight at the OK Corral, Paths of Glory, The Vikings (also prod.), Last Train from Gun Hill, The Devil's Disciple, Strangers When We Meet, Spartacus (also prod.), The Last Sunset, Town Without Pity, Lonely Are the Brave (also prod.), Two Weeks in Another Town, The Hook, List of Adrian Messenger (also prod.), For Love or Money, Seven Days in May (also prod.), In Harm's Way, The Heroes of Telemark, Cast a Giant Shadow, Is Paris Burning?, The Way West, The War Wagon, A Lovely Way to Die, The Brotherhood (also prod.), The Arrangement, There Was a Crooked Man, A Gunfight, Summertree (prod. only), The Light at the Edge of the World (also prod.), Catch Me a Spy, Scalawag (also dir., prod.), Master Touch, Once is Not Enough, Posse (also dir., prod.), The Chosen, The Fury, The Villain, Saturn III, Home Movies, The Final Countdown, The Man from Snowy River, Eddie Macon's Run, Tough Guys, Oscar, Welcome to Veraz, Greedy, A Century of Cinema, The Films of John Frankenheimer, Diamonds, It Runs In the Family, The Illusion.
TELEVISION: Movies: Mousey, The Money Changers, Draw! (HBO), Victory at Entebbe, Remembrance of Love, Amos, Queenie, Inherit the Wind, The Secret, Take Me Home Again. Guest: The Lucy Show, Tales From the Crypt (Yellow) The Simpsons (voice). Specials: Legend of Silent Night, Dr. Jekyll & Mr. Hyde, AFI's 100 Years, 100 Thrills: America's Most Heart-Pounding Movies, Walt:--The Man Behind the Myth.

DOUGLAS, MICHAEL
Actor, Producer. b. New Brunswick, NJ, Sept 25, 1944. p. Kirk Douglas and Diana Dill. m. actress Catherine Zeta Jones. e. Black Fox Military Acad., Choate, U. of California. Worked as asst. director on Lonely Are the Brave, Heroes of Telemark, Cast a Giant Shadow; after TV debut in The Experiment (CBS Playhouse), appeared off-Broadway in City Scene, Pinkville (Theatre World Award). Produced 1993 Off-B'way show The Best of Friends.
PICTURES: Hail Hero (debut, 1969), Adam at 6 A.M., Summertree, Napoleon and Samantha, One Flew Over the Cuckoo's Nest (co-prod. only; Acad. Award for Best Picture, 1975), Coma, The China Syndrome (also prod.), Running (also exec. prod.), It's My Turn, The Star Chamber, Romancing the Stone (also prod.), Starman (exec. prod. only), A Chorus Line, The Jewel of the Nile (also prod.), Fatal Attraction, Wall Street (Acad. Award; Natl. Board of Review Award, 1987), Black Rain, The War of the Roses, Flatliners (co-exec. prod. only), Shining Through, Radio Flyer (co-exec. prod. only), Basic Instinct, Falling Down, Made in America (co-exec. prod. only), Disclosure, The American President, The Ghost and the Darkness, Face/Off (exec. prod. only), The Game, The Rainmaker (prod. only), A Perfect Murder, Wonder Boys, One Night At McCool's, Traffic, Don't Say A Word, Smoke and Mirrors, It Runs in the Family, The In-Laws, The Husband I Bought (exec. prod.only).

TELEVISION: Movies: Streets of San Francisco (pilot), When Michael Calls. Series: Streets of San Francisco. Guest: The FBI, Medical Center.

DOUGLAS, MIKE
TV host. r.n. Michael Delaney Dowd, Jr. b. Chicago, IL, Aug. 11, 1925. Started career singing with bands in and around Chicago. 1950-54 featured singer with Kay Kyser's band. In 1953 became host of WGN-TV's Hi Ladies in Chicago; also featured on WMAQ-TV, NBC, Chicago, as singer and host. Moved to Hollywood in late '50s, working as piano bar singer. In 1961 hired as host for new show on station KYW-TV in Cleveland, owned by Westinghouse Bdg. Co., featuring celebrity guests. This became the Mike Douglas Show which was later nationally syndicated and moved base of operations to Philadelphia, then Los Angeles. Ran 21 years til Mid-1982. Books: The Mike Douglas Cookbook (1969), Mike Douglas My Story (1978), When the Going Gets Tough.
PICTURES: Gator, Nasty Habits, Birds of Prey, The Incredible Shrinking Woman.

DOUMANIAN, JEAN
Producer.
PICTURES: Oxen, Bullets Over Broadway (exec. prod.), Mighty Aphrodite (exec. prod.), Everyone Says I Love You (exec. prod.), Deconstructing Harry, Story of a Bad Boy, Elements, Wild Man Blues, Deconstructing Harry, The Spanish Prisoner, Celebrity, Into My Heart, Sweet and Lowdown, Sunburn, Women Talking Dirty, Just Looking, Story of a Bad Boy, Small Time Crooks, All the Real Girls.

DOURDAN, GARY
Actor. b. Philadelphia, PA, December 11, 1966.
PICTURES: Weekend at Bernies 2, The Paper, Sunset Park, Playing God, Alien: Resurrection, Get that Number, Fool's Paradise, Thursday, Scar City, The Weekend, Trois, Dancing in September, Imposter.
TELEVISION: Movies: The Good Fight, Laurel Avenue, Keys, Rendezvous, King of the World. Guest: New York Undercover, Lois and Clark: The New Adventures of Superman, Beggars and Choosers, Seven Days, Soul Food. Series: A Different World, The Office, Swift Justice, Lyric Cafe (host), CSI.

DOURIF, BRAD
Actor. b. Huntington, WV, March 18, 1950. Studied with Stanford Meisner. Stage actor, three years with Circle Repertory Co., NY (When You Comin' Back Red Ryder?), before films and TV.
PICTURES: Split, One Flew Over the Cuckoo's Nest (Acad. Award nom., Golden Globe & BAFTA Awards, 1975), Group Portrait with Lady, Eyes of Laura Mars, Wise Blood, Heaven's Gate, Ragtime, Dune, Impure Thoughts, Istanbul, Blue Velvet, Fatal Beauty, Child's Play, Mississippi Burning, Medium Rare, The Exorcist: 1990, Spontaneous Combustion, Grim Prairie Tales, Sonny Boy, Graveyard Shift, Child's Play II, Hidden Agenda, Dead Certain, Jungle Fever, The Horseplayer, Body Parts, Child's Play 3, Common Bonds, Scream of Stone, Critters 4, London Kills Me, Diary of the Hurdy Gurdy Man, Murder Blues, Final Judgment, Amos & Andrew, Trauma, Color of Night, Murder in the First, Alien: Resurrection, Best Men, Brown's Requiem, Bride of Chucky (voice), Senseless, Nightwatch, Urban Legend, The Progeny, Son of Chucky (voice), Silicon Towers, Interceptors, The Hurdy Gurdy Man, Cypress Edge, Shadow Hours, The Ghost, Soul Keeper, The Calling, Lord of the Rings: The Two Towers, Child's Play 5, The Lord of the Rings: The Return of the King, Vlad, El Padrino.
TELEVISION: Movies: Sgt. Matlovitch vs. the U.S. Air Force, Guyana Tragedy—The Story of Jim Jones, I Desire, Vengeance: The Story of Tony Cimo, Rage of Angels: The Story Continues, Desperado: The Outlaw Wars, Class of '61, Escape From Terror: The Teresa Stamper Story, Escape to Witch Mountain. Mini-Series: Studs Lonigan, Wild Palms, Ponderosa. Specials: Mound Builders, The Gardener's Son. Guest: Miami Vice, The Hitchhiker, Spencer for Hire, Tales of the Unexpected, Moonlighting, The Equalizer, Murder She Wrote, Babylon 5, Voyager, The X Files.

DOWN, LESLEY-ANNE
Actress. b. London, England, March 17, 1954. At age of 10 modeled for TV and film commercials, leading to roles in features. Film debut at 14 in The Smashing Bird I Used to Know (billed as Lesley Down).
THEATRE: Great Expectations, Hamlet, etc.
PICTURES: The Smashing Bird I Used to Know (debut, 1969), All the Right Noises, Countess Dracula, Assault, Pope Joan, Scalawag, From Beyond the Grave, Brannigan, The Pink Panther Strikes Again, The Betsy, A Little Night Music, The Great Train Robbery, Hanover Street, Rough Cut, Sphinx, Nomads, Scenes from the Goldmine, Mardi Gras for the Devil, Death Wish V: The Face of Death, Munchie Stikes Back, The Unfaithful, Beastmaster III, The Secret Agent Club, Meet Wally Sparks, The King Guard, The Perfect Wife, The Meeksville Ghost, The 13th Child: Legend of the Jersey Devil.
TELEVISION: Movies: Agatha Christie's Murder is Easy, Hunchback of Notre Dame, The One and Only Phyllis Dixey, Arch of Triumph, Indiscreet, Lady Killers, Night Walk, Family of Cops, Young Hearts Unlimited, You Belong to Me. Mini-Series: North and South Books I & II & III, Last Days of Pompeii. Specials: Unity Mitford, Heartbreak House. Pilots: Shivers, 1775. Series: Upstairs, Downstairs, Dallas, Sunset Beach, The Bold & the Beautiful.

DOWNEY, ROBERT, JR.
Actor. b. New York, NY, April 4, 1965. Father is indep. filmmaker Robert Downey. Film debut at age 5 in his father's film Pound.
PICTURES: Pound, Greaser's Palace, Jive, Up the Academy, Baby Its You, Firstborn, Tuff Turf, Weird Science, To Live and Die in L.A., Back to School, America, The Pick-Up Artist, Less Than Zero, Johnny B. Good, Rented Lips, 1969, True Believer, Chances Are, That's Adequate, Air America, Too Much Sun, Soapdish, Chaplin (Acad. Award nom., BAFTA Award), Hail Caesar, Heart and Souls, The Last Party (also writer), Short Cuts, Natural Born Killers, Only You, Restoration, Danger Zone, Home for the Holidays, Richard III, Two Girls & A Guy, One Night Stand, Hugo Pool, Blue Vision, The Gingerbread Man, U.S. Marshals, Wonder Boys, In Dreams, Friends & Lovers, Bowfinger, Last Party 2000, The Singing Detective, Whatever We Do, Gothika.
TELEVISION: *Movie*: Mr. Willowby's Christmas Tree. *Series*: Saturday Night Live, Ally McBeal. *Mini-Series*: Mussolini: The Untold Story. *Special*: Dear America (reader).

DOWNS, HUGH
Broadcaster. b. Akron, OH, Feb. 14, 1921. e. Bluffton Coll., 1938. Wayne U., 1941. Col. U., N.Y., 1955; Supervisor of Science Programming, NBC's Science Dept. one yr.; science consultant for Westinghouse Labs., Ford Foundation, etc.; chmn. of bd., Raylin Prods., Inc. Today, Chairman, U.S. Committee for UNICEF. Chm. of bd. of governors, National Space Society. Books: Thirty Dirty Lies About Old, Rings Around Tomorrow, School of Stars, Yours Truly Hugh Downs, On Camera: My Ten Thousand Hours on Television, Perspectives, Fifty to Forever.
TELEVISION: *Series*: Kukla Fran & Ollie (announcer), Home, Sid Caesar (announcer), The Jack Paar Show, Concentration, The Tonight Show (announcer, 1962), Today. *Host*: 20/20 (1978-1999), Over-Easy (Emmy Award, 1981), Live From Lincoln Center (Host).
RADIO: NBC's Monitor, ABC's Perspectives.

DOYLE, KEVIN
Executive. b. Sydney, Australia, June 21, 1933. e. N. Sydney Tech. HS., Aust. Jr. exec., asst. adv. & pub. div., 20th Century-Fox, Aust., 1947-59; adv. & pub. dir., Columbia Pictures Aust., 1960-66; international ad/pub. mgr.; Columbia Pictures Int'l, N.Y. 1966; intl. pub./promo. mgr., 1980; 1987, Columbia Int'l. rep., Coca-Cola promotions/mktg. sub-committee; int'l pub./promo. mgr. Columbia Tri-Star Film Distributors Inc., 1988; int'l pub./promo. dir. Columbia/Tri-Star Film distrib. Inc. 1990. Retired 1992.

DOYLE-MURRAY, BRIAN
Actor, Writer. b. Chicago, IL., Oct. 31, 1945. Brother is comedian Bill Murray. Started as member of Chicago's Second City improv. troupe, before joining the Organic Theatre of Chicago and the Boston Shakespeare Co. Appeared Off-B'way in The National Lampoon Show and on radio on weekly National Lampoon Show.
PICTURES: Caddyshack (also s.p.), Modern Problems, National Lampoon's Vacation, Sixteen Candles, The Razor's Edge, Legal Eagles, Club Paradise (also co-s.p.), Scrooged, The Experts, How I Got Into College, Ghostbusters II, National Lampoon's Christmas Vacation, Nothing But Trouble, JFK, Wayne's World, Groundhog Day, Cabin Boy, Jury Duty, Multiplicity, Waiting for Guffman, As Good As It Gets, Casper: A Spirited Beginning, Dennis the Menace 2, Doctor Dolittle (voice), Kill the Man, Stuart Little, Drowning Mona, Bedazzled, Getting Hal, A Gentleman's Game, Snow Dogs, Getting Hal.
TELEVISION: *Movies*: Babe Ruth, My Brother's Keeper, Frosty Returns (voice). *Series*: Saturday Night Live (also writer), Get a Life, Good Sports, Bakersfield P.D., The Martin Short Show, The George Wendt Show, Recess, Love & Money, The Sweet Spot, Teamo Supremo (voice) *Special*: Texan.

DRAGOTI, STAN
Director. b. New York, NY, Oct. 4, 1932. e. Cooper Union and Sch. of Visual Arts. 1959 hired as sketch at ad agency, promoted to sr. art dir., later TV dept. and art dir. of Young & Rubicam. Studied acting HB Studios. Directed Clio awarding-winning TV commercials (including I Love New York campaign).
PICTURES: Dirty Little Billy (debut, 1972; also co-prod., co-s.p.), Love at First Bite, Mr. Mom, The Man With One Red Shoe, She's Out of Control, Necessary Roughness.

DRAI, VICTOR
Producer. b. Casablanca, Morocco, July 25, 1947. e. Lycee de Port Lyautey, 1957-63; clothing designer/mfg. in Paris, France, 1969-76. In Los Angeles real estate, 1976-82; Began producing features in 1984, The Woman in Red.
PICTURES: The Man with One Red Shoe, The Bride, Weekend at Bernie's, Folks!, Weekend at Bernie's II.

DRAZEN, LORI
Executive. Began career as asst. to dir. of adv. for Orion Pictures; creative dept. mgr., Kenyon & Eckhardt; gen. mgr., Seiniger Advertising; joined Warner Bros. 1985 as v.p.; worldwide adv. & pub. services. Spent two years at New Line Cinema as s.v.p., creative marketing, before becoming head of marketing for Franchise Pictures in Feb. 2000.

DREYFUSS, RICHARD
Actor. b. Brooklyn, NY, Oct. 29, 1947. e. Beverly Hills H.S.; San Fernando Valley State Coll. 1965-67. Prof. career began at Gallery Theatre (L.A.) in "In Mama's House." Co-Exec. Prod. of

film Quiz Show.
THEATRE: Journey to the Day, Incident at Vichy, People Need People, Enemy Line, Whose Little Boy Are You, But Seriously, Major Barbara, The Time of Your Life, The Hands of Its Enemy (L.A.), The Normal Heart, Death and the Maiden, others.
PICTURES: The Graduate, Valley of the Dolls, The Young Runaways, Hello Down There, Dillinger, American Graffiti, The Second Coming of Suzanne, The Apprenticeship of Duddy Kravitz, Jaws, Inserts, Close Encounters of the Third Kind, The Goodbye Girl (Acad. Award, 1977), The Big Fix (also co-prod.) The Competition, Whose Life Is It Anyway?, The Buddy System, Down and Out in Beverly Hills, Stand by Me, Tin Men, Stakeout, Nuts, Moon Over Parador, Let It Ride, Always, Postcards from the Edge, Once Around, Rosencrantz and Guildenstern Are Dead, What About Bob?, Lost in Yonkers, Another Stakeout, Silent Fall, The Last Word, The American President, Mr. Holland's Opus, James and the Giant Peach, Night Falls on Manhattan, Mad Dog Time, The Call of the Wild (narr.), A Fine and Private Place, Krippendorf's Tribe, The Crew, The Old Man Who Read Love Stories, In Search of Peace (voice), Who Is Cletis Tout?, Manassas: End of Innocence, Johnstown Flood (documentary)
TELEVISION: *Movies*: Two for the Money, Victory at Entebbe, Prisoner of Honor (also prod.), Lincoln (voice), The Universal Story, Frank Capra's American Dream, Oliver Twist, Lansky, The Day Reagan Was Shot, Coast to Coast. *Series*: Karen, The Education of Max Bickford. *Host*: American Chronicles. *Guest*: Love on a Rooftop, Occasional Wife, The Big Valley, Room 222, Judd for the Defense, Mod Squad, The Bold Ones. *Specials*: Funny You Don't Look 200 (host, co-prod., co-writer), R2-D2: Beneath the Dome, Mr. Dreyfuss Goes to Washington, TR: An American Lion (tv documentary, Theodore Roosevelt voice),

DRESCHER, FRAN
Actress. b. Queens, NY, Sept. 30, 1957. e. Queen's College.
PICTURES: Saturday Night Fever (debut), American Hot Wax, Gorp, The Hollywood Knights, Ragtime, Cadillac Man, Serious Money, UHF, This is Spinal Tap, The Big Picture, Car 54, Where Are You?, Jack, The Beautician and the Beast, Picking up the Pieces, Kid Quick.
TELEVISION: *Movies*: Stranger In Our House, Rock 'n' Roll Mom, Love & Betrayal, Wedding Band, Without Warning: Terror In the Towers. *Series*: Princesses, The Nanny (Golden Globe nom., also co-creator, writer. prod.), Good Morning Miami.

DRIVER, MINNIE
Actress. r. n. Amelia Driver. b. England, Jan. 31, 1970. e. Bedales School, Petersfield, Hants.
PICTURES: Circle of Friends, GoldenEye, Baggage, Big Night, Sleepers, Grosse Pointe Blank, Good Will Hunting, Tarzan (voice), The Governess, Hard Rain, Slow Burn, An Ideal Husband, South Park: Bigger Longer and Uncut (voice), Return to Me, Beautiful, Slow Burn, The Upgrade, High Heels and Lowlifes, Owning Mahowny, Hope Springs, D.C. Smalls, Ella Enchanted.
TELEVISION: *Series*: God on the Rocks, Mr. Wroe's Virgins. *Mini-Series*: The Politician's Wife. *Guest*: Lovejoy. *Movies*: Merry Christmas George Bailey, That Sunday.

DROMGOOLE, PATRICK
Director, Producer, Executive. b. Iqueque, Chile, Aug. 30, 1930; e. Dulwich Coll., University Coll., Oxford. Joined BBC Radio as dir. 1954, later directing TV plays for BBC and ABC, incl. Armchair Theatre, Frontier, Dracula, Mystery Imagination. Joined HTV as West Country Programme Controller, 1968; dir. award-winning dramas; Thick as Thieves, Machine Gunner. Developed Company's drama output and promoted policy of int'l pre-sales with such dramas as Jamaica Inn, Separate Tables, Catholics, Smuggler, Into the Labyrinth, Kidnapped, Robin of Sherwood, Arch of Triumph, Mr. Halpern and Mr. Johnson, Jenny's War, Codename Kyril, The Diamond Trap, Wall of Tyranny, Strange Interlude, The Woman He Loved, Grand Larceny, Suspicion, Maigret, September. Made Fellow of RTS, 1978; chief exec. HTV Group 1988.
THEATRE: *Director*: incl. first plays of Charles Wood, Joe Orton, David Halliwell, Colin Welland; Peter O'Toole in Man and Superman.
PICTURES: Two Vale South, Hidden Face, Dead Man's Chest, Anthony Purdy Esq., Point of Dissent, The Actors, King of the Wind (exec. prod.), Visage du Passe (dir.), Meutres en Douce, The Canterville Ghost, The Little Match Girl (exec. prod.), Sunday Pursuit (exec, prod.), The Last Butterfly (assoc. prod.).
TELEVISION: *Movie*: Machine Gunner, September. *Mini-series*: Kidnapped, Return to Treasure Island. *Series*: Smuggler, Into the Labyrinth, Public Eye.

DRURY, JAMES
Actor. b. New York, NY, April 18, 1934. e. New York U. Acting debut at age 8 in biblical play for children at Greenwich Settlement Playhouse. Performed on stage while youngster. Signed by MGM in 1955, working one day in each of seven movies that year, including Blackboard Jungle. Then got two-year contract at 20th-Fox. Gained fame as hero of TV series, The Virginian, which had nine-year run.
PICTURES: Forbidden Planet, Love Me Tender, Bernardine, Toby Tyler, Pollyana, Ten Who Dared, Ride the High Country, The Young Warriors.
TELEVISION: *Movies*: Breakout, Alias Smith and Jones, The Devil and Miss Sarah, The Gambler Returns: Luck of the Draw, The Virginian (2000). *Series*: The Virginian, Firehouse.

DUBAND, WAYNE
Executive. b. Sydney, Australia, Feb. 13, 1947. Joined Warner Bros. 1969 as mgr. trainee in Australia. 1973, transferred to South Africa as mgr. dir.; 1977 gen. mgr. of CIC/Warner Bros. joint venture, also managing the CIC theatre operation there. 1980, named exec. asst. to Myron D. Karlin, pres. WB Intl., in Burbank. 1981, mgr. dir. of Warner/Columbia joint venture in France. 1985, appt. v.p. of sls. for WB Intl. division. 1987, appt. senior v.p. for Warner Bros. Intl. division. 1992, appt. pres. Intl. Theatrical dist., WB Intl. Resigned 2000.

DUBE, JACKSON E.
Executive. b. New York, NY. e. U. of North Carolina. m. Pat Lavelle, actress. USAF 1942-45 Radar-Gunner, AAF, Italy. Writer: Television and Sponsor Magazine 1947-48; reviews of recorded music. 1947-51, Consol Film Inds. Penthouse Prods. Dist.: E. sales mgr. Atlas Tel. Corp. 1951-54; vp & gen. mgr., Craftsman Film Greatest Fights of the Century 1954; vp, Conquest Prods. CBS Net. Docus. 1954-57. TV and radio dir. Cote Fischer & Rogow Adv., 1957-59; exec. vp, Bon Ami Film; dist.: UA Feats. abroad 1959-63; prod's rep. Le Vien Prods.— Finest Hours King's Story; Eastern sales mgr. Desilu, 1964-67; exec. vp, UCC Films; dist. RKO feature Library abroad, 1969-70; pres. JED Rrns. Corp. Dist. London Films, Rank chidren's features, 1967-88. Consultant: New Century Ent., Windsor Pdns., Rurner Program Services, 1985-88. Agent for Weiss Global, Medallion TV Enterprises, Turner International, Morin International, 1988-92. Agent for Aries S.A. and Sidney Beckerman Prods. Agent for Otto Preminger Films Ltd. 1992, owner of JED Productions Corp., with remake rights to 125 U.S. feature motion pictures.
(d. May 29, 2002)

DUBS, ARTHUR R.
Executive, Producer, Director, Writer, President and Owner of Pacific International Enterprises, b. Medford, OR, Feb. 26, 1930. e. Southern Oregon State Coll. Founded Pacific International Enterprises, 1969.
PICTURES: Producer-Director: American Wilderness, Vanishing Wilderness, Wonder of It All. Exec. Prod.: Challenge to Be Free. Prod.: Adventures of the Wilderness Family, Wilderness Family Part 2 (also s.p.), Mountain Family Robinson (also s.p.), Across the Great Divide, Sacred Ground, Mystery Mansion, Dream Chasers (also co-dir.). Co-Prod.: Windwalker.

DUCHOVNY, DAVID
Actor. b. New York, NY, Aug. 7, 1960. e. Yale. Was teaching asst. at Yale before landing first acting job in beer commercial. m. actress Tea Leoni
PICTURES: Working Girl (debut, 1988), New Year's Day, Bad Influence, Julia Has Two Lovers, Don't Tell Mom the Babysitter's Dead, The Rapture, Ruby, Venice/Venice, Chaplin, Kalifornia, Playing God, The X Files: Fight the Future, Return to Me, Evolution, Zoolander, Full Frontal, My Dark Places: An L.A. Crime Memoir , Connie & Carla.
TELEVISION: Movies: Red Shoe Diaries, Red Shoe Diaries 2: Double Dare, Baby Snatcher, Red Shoe Diaries 3: Another Woman's Lipstick, Red Shoe Diaries 6: How I Met My Husband, Red Shoe Diaries 7: Burning Up, Red Shoe Diaries 8: Night of Abandon. Guest: The Simpsons (voice). Series: Twin Peaks, The X Files (Golden Globe Award, 1997), Eco-Challenge Fiji Islands (series documentary, narrator).

DUDELHEIM, HANS RUDOLF
Communications Executive. b. Berlin, Germany, June 17, 1927. e. Sch. of Photography Berlin, School of Radio & TV NY. Film editor, ABC, 1951-66. Prod/Dir/Edit.: Cinema Arts Assn. 1966-90; served as pres. Founder, 1961, Cinema Arts Film Soc. Editor of documentaries: Saga of Western Man, Comrade Student, Sublimated Birth (also prod.), Kent State, Sigmund Freud, IBM Motivation Project, The Forgotten Pioneers of Hollywood, Painting With Love. Producer: Sesame Street, 60 Minutes: Ranaissance Community, American Dream Machine, Voyage of the Barba Negra. Presently film and video consultant. Instructor at New School For Social Reserach.

DUDLEY, ANNE
Composer. b. Chatham, Kent, England, May 7, 1956.
PICTURES: Hiding Out, Buster, The Misadventures of Mr. Wilt, The Mighty Quinn, Zwei Frauen, Say Anything..., The Pope Must Die, The Miracle, Knight Moves, The Crying Game, Felidae, When Saturday Comes, The Grotesque, Hollow Reed, The Full Monty (Acad. Award, 1997), American History X, Pushing Tin, Monkeybone, Lucky Break, The Human Body, Tabloid, The Gathering, A Man Apart, Bright Young Things.
TELEVISION: Series: Jeeves and Wooster, Ngaio Marsh's Alleyn Mysteries, Anna Lee, Donovan Quick, The 10th Kingdom, The Miracle Maker.

DUDIKOFF, MICHAEL
Actor. b. Torrance, CA, Oct. 8, 1954.
PICTURES: Making Love, I Ought to Be in Pictures, Tron, Bachelor Party, Bloody Birthday, American Ninja, Radioactive Dreams, Avenging Force, American Ninja II: The Confrontation, Platoon Leader, River of Death, American Ninja 4: The Annihilation, Midnight Ride, Human Shield, Rescue Me, Virtual Assassin, Shooter, Executive Command, Bounty Hunters II, Crash Dive, Moving Target, Soldier Boyz, Cyberjack, Chain of Command, Strategic Command, In Her Defense, Freedom Strike, Ringmaster, Muketeers Forever, The Silencer, Ablaze, Stranded, Quicksand.
TELEVISION: Movie: The Woman Who Sinned. Mini-Series:

North and South Book II. Series: Star of the Family, Cobra. Pilot: Sawyer and Finn. Guest: Happy Days, Dallas.

DUFFY, JAMES E.
Executive. b. Decatur, IL, April 2, 1926. e. Beloit Coll. Radio announcer, then reporter; joined publicity dept., ABC in 1949; named dir. of adv. & promo., then account exec. for Central division of ABC Radio Network; dir. of sales ABC Radio, 1957; central div. account exec., ABC TV Network, 1955; natl. dir. of Sales, ABC Radio central division, 1960; v.p., ABC Radio Network, 1961; exec. v.p. & natl. dir. of sales, 1962; v.p. in charge of sales, ABC TV Network, 1963; pres., ABC TV Network, 1970-85; pres., communications, 1985-86; v.p. Capital Cities/ABC, Inc.; pres., communications, ABC Network & Bdgst. Divisions. Retired.

DUFFY, PATRICK
Actor. b. Townsend, MT, March 17, 1949. e. U. of Washington. Became actor-in-residence in state of Washington, where performed with various statefunded groups. Acted off-B'way Taught mime and movement classes in summer camp in Seattle. Moved to L.A. and began TV acting career.
PICTURE: Vamping (also co-exec prod.), Rusty: A Dog's Tale (voice), Perfect Game, The Pirates of Central Park.
TELEVISION: Movies: The Stranger Who Looks Like Me, Hurricane, Man From Atlantis, Enola Gay, Cry for the Strangers, Strong Medicine, Alice in Wonderland, Too Good to Be True, Unholy Matrimony, Murder C.O.D, Children of the Bride, Danielle Steel's Daddy, Texas, Dallas: J.R. Returns, Heart of Fire, Dallas: War of the Ewings, Don't Look Behind You, Doing Dallas. After Dallas. Specials: The Last of Mrs. Lincoln, Freedom Festival '89 (host). Series: Man from Atlantis, Dallas, Step By Step, To Tell the Truth, Dale's All Stars. Guest: Switch, George Burns' Comedy Week.

DUGAN, DENNIS
Actor, Director. b. Wheaton, IL, Sept. 5, 1946. Studied acting at Goodman Theatre School.
THEATRE: NY: A Man's Man, The House of Blue Leaves. LA: Once in a Lifetime, Rainbows for Sales, Estonia, The Dining Room, The Kitchen.
PICTURES: Night Call Nurses, The Day of the Locust, Night Moves, Smile, Harry and Walter Go to New York, Norman ... Is That You?, Unidentified Flying Oddball, The Howling, Water, Can't Buy Me Love, She's Having a Baby, The New Adventures of Pippi Longstocking, Parenthood, Problem Child (also dir.), Brain Donors (also dir.), Happy Gilmore (also dir.), Beverly Hills Ninja (dir. only), Big Daddy (also dir.), Saving Silverman, National Security (dir. only).
TELEVISION: Movies: Death Race, The Girl Most Likely To..., Last of the Good Guys, Country Gold, The Toughest Man in the World, Columbo: Butterfly in Shades of Grey. Mini-Series: Rich Man Poor Man. Series: Richie Brockelman: Private Eye, Empire, Shadow Chasers. Pilots: Alice, Father O Father, Did You Hear About Josh and Kelly?, Full House, Channel 99. Guest: Hooperman, Moonlighting, M*A*S*H, The Rockford Files, Scene of the Crime, Making a Living, Hill Street Blues. Director: Hunter, Sonny Spoon, Wiseguy, Moonlighting, The Shaggy Dog (movie), L.A. Law, Columbo, Picket Fences, NYPD Blue, Chicago Hope, Ally McBeal.

DUGGAN, ERVIN S.
Executive. Started as reporter for the Washington Post in early 1960's. As member of President Lydon Johnson's staff helped define government's role in supporting public broadcasting with the Public Broadcasting Act of 1967. Served as special asst. to Senators Lloyd Bentsen and Adlai Stevenson III, Health Education and Welfare Secretary Joseph Califano; and as member of the State Dept. Policy Planning Staff. 1981-90, managed communications and consulting firm. Served 4 years as Commissioner of the Federal Communications Commission. Feb. 1994 joined PBS as pres. and CEO. Resigned 1999.

DUIGAN, JOHN
Director, Writer.b. Hartley Wintney, Hampshire, England, June 19, 1949. Lived in England and Malaysia before moving to Sydney, Australia. e. Univ. of Melbourne, philosophy, M.A. Taught for several years at Univ. of Melbourne and Latrobe U. before entering films. Directed and wrote experimental short, The Firm Man (1974). Novels: Badge, Players, Room to Move.
PICTURES: Dir.-Writer: Trespassers, Mouth to Mouth, Winter of Our Dreams (Australian Writers Guild Award), Far East, The Year My Voice Broke (Australian Acad. Award for best dir., s.p.) Romero (dir. only), Flirting, Wide Sargasso Sea, Sirens (also actor), The Journey of August King, The Leading Man, Lawn Dogs, Molly, Paranoid, The Parole Officer, Head in the Clouds.
TELEVISION: Mini-Series: Vietnam (co-dir.). Movie: Fragments of War: The Story of Damien Parer.

DUKAKIS, OLYMPIA
Actress. b. Lowell, MA, June 20, 1931. m. actor Louis Zorich. e. Boston U., B.A., M.F.A. Founding mem. of The Charles Playhouse, Boston, establishing summer theatre 1957-60. Taught acting at NYU: 1967-70 as instructor, 1974-83 as master teacher, and at Yale U. 1976. With husband conceived and guided artistic dev. of Whole Theatre of Monclair, NJ, 1977-90; producing artistic dir. Adapted plays for her co. and dir. theater there; also at Williamstown Theatre Fest. and Delaware Summer Fest. Appeared in more than 100 plays on B'way, Off-B'way and in regional and summer theater.
THEATRE: Who's Who in Hell, The Aspern Papers, Night of the Iguana, The Breaking Wall, Curse of the Starving Class, Snow

Orchid, The Marriage of Bette and Boo (Obie Award), Social Security.
PICTURES: Lilith, Twice a Man, John and Mary, Made for Each Other, Death Wish, Rich Kids, The Wanderers, The Idolmaker, National Lampoon Goes to the Movies, Flanagan, Moonstruck (Acad. Award, best supporting actress, 1987), Working Girl, Look Who's Talking, Steel Magnolias, Dad, In the Spirit, Look Who's Talking Too, The Cemetery Club, Over the Hill, Look Who's Talking Now, Naked Gun 33 1/3: The Final Insult (cameo), I Love Trouble, Jeffrey, Mighty Aphrodite, Mr. Holland's Opus, Picture Perfect, Never Too Late, Milk and Money, Better Living, Jane Austen's Mafia, Brooklyn Sonnet, A Life for a Life, Climb Against the Odds, The Papp Project, The Event, Charlie's War, Jesus-Mary & Joey.
TELEVISION: Movies: Nicky's World, The Neighborhood, FDR-The Last Year, King of America, Lucky Day, Fire in the Dark, Sinatra, Young at Heart, A Match Made in Heaven, Scattering Heaven, The Pentagon Wars, Crimes of Honour, The Last of the Blonde Bombshells, And Never Let Her Go, Ladies and the Champ, My Beautiful Son, Babycakes. Mini-Series: Tales of the City, More Tales of the City, Joan of Arc, Further Tales of the City, Guilty Hearts. Specials: The Rehearsal, Sisters, Last Act is a Solo, A Century of Women. Series: Search for Tomorrow, One of the Boys.

DUKE, BILL
Actor, Director. b. Poughkeepsie, NY, Feb. 26, 1943. e. Boston Univ., NY Univ. Sch. of the Arts. Recieved AFI Best Young Director Award for short The Hero (Gold Award, Houston Film Festival). Has written poetry, short stories for children. Member bd. of dirs. American Film Institute.
PICTURES: Actor: Car Wash, American Gigolo, Commando, Predator, No Man's Land, Action Jackson, Bird on a Wire, Street of No Return, Menace II Society, Payback, Foolish, The Limey, Fever, Never Again, Exit Wounds, Red Dragon, National Security, The Blackout Murders. Director: A Rage in Harlem, Deep Cover, The Cemetery Club, Sister Act 2: Back in the Habit, America's Dream, Hoodlum (also exec. prod.).
TELEVISION: Actor: Movies: Love is Not Enough, Sgt. Matlovich Vs. the U.S. Air Force. Series: Palmerstown U.S.A. Director: Series: A Man Called Hawk, Cagney & Lacey, Hill Street Blues, Miami Vice, Dallas. Dir. Movies: The Killing Floor, Johnnie Mae Gibson, A Raisin in the Sun, The Golden Spiders: A Nero Wolfe Mystery, Deacons for Defense.

DUKE, PATTY
Actress. r.n. Anna Marie Duke. b. New York, NY, Dec. 14, 1946. e. Quintano Sch. for Young Professionals. Mother of actors Sean and Mackenzie Astin. Pres., Screen Actors Guild, 1985-88.
Author: Surviving Sexual Assault (1983), Call Me Anna (1987).
THEATRE: The Miracle Worker (Theatre World Award), Isle of Children.
PICTURES: I'll Cry Tomorrow (debut as extra 1955), The Goddess, Happy Anniversary, The 4-D Man, The Miracle Worker (Acad. Award, best supporting actress, 1962), Billie, Valley of the Dolls, Me Natalie, The Swarm, By Design, Something Special, Prelude to a Kiss, Harvest of Fire, Kimberly.
TELEVISION: Series: The Brighter Day, The Patty Duke Show, It Takes Two, Hail to the Chief, Karen's Song, Amazing Grace. Guest: Armstrong Circle Theatre, The SS Andrea Doria, U.S. Steel Hour, All's Fair. Specials: The Prince and the Pauper, Wuthering Heights, Swiss Family Robinson, Meet Me in St. Louis, The Power and the Glory. Movies: My Sweet Charlie (Emmy Award, 1970), Two on a Bench, If Tomorrow Comes, She Waits, Deadly Harvest, Nightmare, Look What's Happened to Rosemary's Baby, Fire!, Rosetti & Ryan: Men Who Love Women, Curse of the Black Widow, Killer on Board, The Storyteller, Having Babies III, A Family Upside Down, Women in White, Hanging by a Thread, Before and After, The Miracle Worker (Emmy Award, 1980), The Women's Room, Mom The Wolfman and Me, The Babysitter, Violation of Sarah McDavid, Something So Right, September Gun, Best Kept Secrets, Fight for Life, Perry Mason: The Case of the Avenging Angel, A Time to Triumph, Fatal Judgment, Everybody's Baby: The Rescue of Jessica McClure, Amityville: The Evil Escapes, Call Me Anna, Always Remember I Love You, Absolute Strangers, Last Wish, Grave Secrets: The Legacy of Hilltop Drive, A Killer Among Friends, Family of Strangers, No Child of Mine, A Matter of Justice, One Woman's Courage, Cries From the Heart, When the Vows Break, Race Against Time: The Search for Sarah, The Disappearing Act, A Christmas Memory, When He Didn't Come Home, A Season for Miracle, Miracle on the Mountain: The Kincaid Family Story, Love Lessons, Little John. Mini-Series: Captains and the Kings (Emmy Award, 1977), George Washington.

DULLEA, KEIR
Actor. b. Cleveland, OH, May 30, 1936. e. Rutgers Univ., San Francisco State Coll., Sanford Meisner's Neighborhood Playhouse. Acted as resident juvenile at the Totem Pole Playhouse in PA. NY theatre debut in the revue Sticks and Stones, 1956; appeared in stock co. prods. at the Berkshire Playhouse and Philadelphia's Hedgerow Theatre, 1959; off-Broadway debut in Season of Choice, 1969. Won San Francisco Film Festival Award for performance in film David and Lisa, 1963.
THEATRE: Dr. Cook's Garden, Butterflies Are Free, Cat on a Hot Tin Roof, P.S. Your Cat is Dead, The Other Side of Paradise.
PICTURES: The Hoodlum Priest (debut, 1961), David and Lisa, The Thin Red Line, Mail Order Bride, The Naked Hours, Bunny Lake is Missing, Madame X, The Fox, 2001: A Space Odyssey,

De Sade, Pope Joan, Paperback Hero, Il Diavolo nel Cervello, Paul and Michelle, Black Christmas (Silent Night Evil Night), Leopard in the Snow, Welcome to Blood City, The Haunting of Julia (Full Circle), Because He's My Friend, The Next One, Brainwaves, Blind Date, 2010, Oh What a Night, The Divine Inspiration, 3 Days of Rain, Stanley Kubrick: A Life in Pictures, Alien Hunter.
TELEVISION: Movies: Black Water Gold, Law and Order, Legend of the Golden Gun, Brave New World, The Hostage Tower, No Place to Hide. Special: Mrs. Miniver. Guest: Law and Order: SVU.

DUNAWAY, FAYE
Actress. b. Bascom, FL, Jan. 14, 1941. e. Texas, Arkansas, Utah, Germany, U. of Florida. Awarded a Fulbright scholarship in theatre. Boston U. of Fine Applied Arts. With Lincoln Center Rep. Co. for 3 years. NY Stage: A Man for All Seasons, After the Fall, Hogan's Goat (Theatre World Award), The Curse of an Aching Heart.
PICTURES: Hurry Sundown (debut, 1967), The Happening, Bonnie and Clyde, The Thomas Crown Affair, The Extraordinary Seaman, A Place for Lovers, The Arrangement, Puzzle of a Downfall Child, Little Big Man, The Deadly Trap, Doc, Oklahoma Crude, The Three Musketeers, Chinatown, The Towering Inferno, The Four Musketeers, Three Days of the Condor, Network (Acad. Award, 1976), Voyage of the Damned, Eyes of Laura Mars, The Champ, The First Deadly Sin, Mommie Dearest, The Wicked Lady, Ordeal by Innocence, Supergirl, Barfly, Midnight Crossing, Burning Secret, The Handmaid's Tale, Wait Until Spring Bandini, The Gamble, On a Moonlit Night, Scorchers, Double Edge, The Temp, Arizona Dream, Don Juan DeMarco, Drunks, Dunston Checks In, Albino Alligator, The Chamber, The Yards, The Thomas Crown Affair, The Messenger: The Story of Joan of Arc, Stanley's Gig, The Yards, Festival in Cannes, The Calling, Yellow Bird, Colored Eggs, The Rules of Attraction, Mid-Century, The Calling, El Padrino, Blind Horizon, The Last Goodbye, Kill Switch, Jennifer's Shadow.
TELEVISION: Movies: The Woman I Love, The Disappearance of Aimee, Evita, Peron, 13 at Dinner, Beverly Hills Madam, The Country Girl, Casanova, The Raspberry Ripple, Cold Sassy Tree, Silhouette, Columbo: It's All in the Game (Emmy Award, 1994), A Family Divided, Rebecca, Gia, Running Mates, The Biographer. Mini-Series: Ellis Island, Christopher Columbus. Specials: Hogan's Goat, After the Fall, Supergirl: The Making of the Movie (host), Inside the Dream Factory (host). Series: It Had to Be You.

DUNCAN, LINDSAY
Actress. b. Edinburgh, Scotland, November 7, 1950. Stage actress with National Theatre, Royal Shakespeare Company.
THEATRE: Plenty, The Provok'd Wife, The Prince of Homburg, Top Girls, Progress, The Merry Wives of Windsor, Les Liaisons Dangereuses (RSC, West End, Broadway; Theatre World Award), Cat On A Hot Tin Roof, Hedda Gabler, A Midsummer Night's Dream, Cryptogram.
PICTURES: Loose Connections, Samson & Delilah, Prick Up Your Ears, Manifesto, The Reflecting Skin, Body Parts, City Hall, A Midsummer Night's Dream, An Ideal Husband, Mansfield Park, Letters to a Street Child.
TELEVISION: Movies: Reilly, Ace of Spies, A Year in Provence, The Rector's Wife, Shooting the Past, Dirty Tricks, Perfect Strangers, Witness of Truth: The Railway Murders, Hamilton Mattress (voice). Mini-series: Dead Head, Traffik, A Year in Provence, G.B.H., Jake's Progress, The History of Tom Jones A Foundling, Oliver Twist. Guest: The Storyteller: Greek Myths, The New Avengers, Colin's Sandwich, Tecx.

DUNCAN, MICHAEL CLARKE
Actor. b. Chicago, IL, December 10, 1957. Worked as a body-guard in Hollywood while taking bit parts.
PICTURES: Back in Business, A Night at the Roxbury, Caught Up, The Players Club, Bulworth, Armageddon, The Green Mile, The Underground Comedy Movie, The Whole Nine Yards, See Spot Run, The Immigrant Garden, Cats & Dogs (voice), Planet of the Apes, Hollywood Digital Diaries, The Scorpion King, Daredevil, George and the Dragon, Brother Bear (voice), Dinotopia: Curse of the Ruby Sunstone (voice), Delgo (voice), D.E.B.S.
TELEVISION: Movie: They Call Me Sirr. Series: The Bold and the Beautiful, Skwids.

DUNCAN, SANDY
Actress. b. Henderson, TX, Feb. 20, 1946. m. singer-dancer Don Correia. e. Len Morris Coll.
THEATRE: The Music Man (NY debut, 1965); The Boyfriend, Ceremony of Innocence (Theatre World Award), Your Own Thing, Canterbury Tales, Peter Pan, Five Six Seven Eight Dance!, My One and Only.
PICTURES: $1,000,000 Duck, Star Spangled Girl, The Cat from Outer Space, Rock a Doodle (voice), The Swan Princess (voice), Never Again, G-Spots.
TELEVISION: Movies: My Boyfriend's Back, Miracle on Interstate 880. Mini-Series: Roots. Specials: Pinocchio, Sandy in Disneyland, The Sandy Duncan Special. Series: Funny Face, The Sandy Duncan Show, Valerie's Family.

DUNLAP, RICHARD D.
Producer, Director. b. Pomona, CA, Jan. 30, 1923. e. Yale U., B.A., 1944; M.F.A., 1948. U.S. Navy 1943-46; Instructor, English dept., Yale U., 1947-48; Prod.-dir., Kraft TV Theatre, 3 years; Dir,

Assoc. Prod., Omnibus, 3 seasons; Dir., 25 half-hr. Dramatic Film Shows. Frank Sinatra Specials, Prod. Dir., 11 Academy Award Shows, 4 Emmy Award Shows.
TELEVISION: *Movies:* Demon, Demon. *Series:* Alfred Hitchcock Presents, Hidden Faces, Sigmund and the Sea Monsters.

DUNNE, DOMINICK

Producer. Writer. b. Hartford, CT, Oct. 29, 1925. e. Canterbury Sch., 1944; Williams Col., 1949. Son is actor-prod. Griffin Dunne. Began career as stage manager at NBC-TV; then produced shows for CBS Studio One. Later exec. prod. at 20th-Fox TV, v.p. at Four Star. Novels: The Winners, The Two Mrs. Grenvilles, People Like Us, An Inconvenient Woman, A Season in Purgatory, Fatal Charms, The Mansions of Limbo. Gossip columnist for Vanity Fair.
PICTURES: The Boys in the Band (exec. prod.), The Panic in Needle Park, Play It as It Lays, Ash Wednesday.
TELEVISION: *Movies:* The Two Mrs. Grenvilles (writer), The Users (prod.), People Like Us (writer), An Inconvenient Woman (writer), 919 Fifth Ave (writer, prod.), A Season in Purgatory (writer). Guilty Pleasure: The Domminick Dunne Story (as himself). *Series:* Adventures in Paradise (prod.), Page to Screen (series documentary, host).

DUNN, KEVIN

Actor. b. Chicago, IL, 1956.
PICTURES: Mississippi Burning, Ghostbusters II (uncredited), Taken Away, Marked for Death, Blue Steel, The Bonfire of the Vanities, Hot Shots!, Only the Lonely, Chaplin, 1492: Conquest of Paradise, Dave, Little Big League, Mad Love, Nixon, Commandments, Chain Reaction, Edwards and Hunt, The Sixth Man, Picture Perfect, Almost Heroes, Godzilla, Snake Eyes, Small Soldiers, Stir of Echoes.
TELEVISION: *Movies:* Night of Courage, Blind Faith, Double Edge, Shadow of a Doubt, The Four Diamonds, Unforgivable, The Second Civil War, On the Edge of Innocence, Beach Boys: An American Family, Gleason. *Series:* Jack & Mike, Arsenio, Bette. *Guest:* Cheers, Roseanne, 21 Jump Street, Seinfeld, Regular Joe (pilot)..

DUNNE, GRIFFIN

Actor, Producer, Director. b. New York, NY, June 8, 1955. Son of prod.-writer Dominick Dunne. Formed Double Play Prods. with Amy Robinson. Studied at Neighborhood Playhouse and with Uta Hagen. On Stage in Album, Marie and Bruce, Coming Attractions, Hotel Play, Search and Destroy (B'way debut; Theatre World Award).
PICTURES: *Actor:* The Other Side of the Mountain (debut, 1975), Chilly Scenes of Winter (also prod.), The Fan, American Werewolf in London, Cold Feet, Almost You, Johnny Dangerously, After Hours (also co-prod.), Golden Globe nom.), Who's That Girl, Amazon Women on the Moon, Big Blue, Me and Him, Once Around (also co-prod.), My Girl, Straight Talk, Big Girls Don't Cry... They Get Even, The Pickle, Naked in New York, Quiz Show, I Like It Like That, Search and Destroy, Famous, Perfume, Pinero, 40 Days and 40 Nights, Cheaters. *Producer only:* Baby It's You, Running on Empty, White Palace, Once Around, Joe's Apartment (exec.). *Director/Writer:* Duke of Groove (short, Oscar nom.), Addicted to Love, Practical Magic, Famous, Nailed Right In.
TELEVISION: *Movies:* The Wall, Secret Weapon, The Android Affair, Love Matters (Ace nom.), Partners, The Android Affair, Sounds From a Town I Love, Warning: Parental Advisory. *Specials:* Lip Service, Trying Times: Hunger Chic, Partners. *Pilot:* Graham. *Guest:* Frasier (Emmy nom.). *Series:* Hotel Room.

DUNST, KIRSTEN

Actress. b. Point Pleasant, NJ, April 30, 1982
PICTURES: New York Stories, The Bonfire of the Vanities, Little Women, High Strung, Greedy, Interview with the Vampire, Jumanji, Mother Night, Anastasia (voice), Wag the Dog, Strike, Small Soldiers, The Virgin Suicides, Drop Dead Gorgeous, Dick, The Crow: Salvation, Luckytown Blues, Bring It On, Deeply, All Forgotten, Get Over It, Crazy/Beautiful, The Cat's Meow, Spider Man, Levity, Kaena: The Prophecy (voice), Eternal Sunshine of the Spotless Mind, Mona Lisa Smile, Spider Man 2.
TELEVISION: *Movies:* Darkness Before Dawn, Children Remember the Holocaust (voice), Ruby Ridge: An American Tragedy, Tower of Terror, Fifteen and Pregnant, The Animated Adventures of Tom Sawyer (voice), Devil's Arithmetic, The Mummy Parody. *Series:* Stories from My Childhood. *Guest:* Sisters, Star Trek: The Next Generation, Touched by an Angel, Gun, ER.

DURNING, CHARLES

Actor. b. Highland Falls, NY, Feb. 28, 1923. e. NYU. Studied acting on the G.I. Bill. Prof. stage debut, 1960. Made several appearances with Joseph Papp's NY Shakespeare Festival.
THEATRE: That Championship Season, Knock Knock, Au Pair Man, In the Boom Boom Room, The Happy Time, Indians, Cat on a Hot Tin Roof (Tony Award, 1990), Queen of the Stardust Ballroom, Inherit the Wind.
PICTURES: Harvey Middleman—Fireman (debut, 1965), I Walk the Line, Hi Mom!, The Pursuit of Happiness, Dealing: or the Berkeley-to- Boston Forty-Brick Lost-Bag Blues, Deadhead Miles, Sisters, The Sting, The Front Page, Dog Day Afternoon, The Hindenburg, Breakheart Pass, Harry and Walter Go to New York, Twilight's Last Gleaming, The Choirboys, An Enemy of the People, The Fury, The Greek Tycoon, Tilt, The Muppet Movie, North Dallas Forty, Starting Over, When a Stranger Calls, Die

Laughing, The Final Countdown, True Confessions, Sharky's Machine, The Best Little Whorehouse in Texas (Acad. Award nom.), Tootsie, To Be or Not to Be (Acad. Award nom.), Two of a Kind, Hadley's Rebellion, Mass Appeal, Stick, The Man With One Red Shoe, Stand Alone, Big Trouble, Tough Guys, Where the River Runs Black, Solarbabies, Happy New Year, The Rosary Murders, A Tiger's Tail, Cop, Far North, Cat Chaser, Dick Tracy, V. I. Warshawski, Brenda Starr, Etolie, Fatal Sky, The Music of Chance, The Hudsucker Proxy, I.Q., Home for the Holidays, The Last Supper, The Grass Harp, Spy Hard, One Fine Day, Shelter, Secret Life of Algernon, Justice, Jerry & Tom, Hi-Life, Hunt for the Devil, O Brother Where Art Thou, Very Mean Men, The Last Producer, State and Main, Never Look Back, Lakeboat, Turn of Faith, LAPD: To Protect & to Serve, Mother Ghost, The Naked Run (short), The Last Man Club, One Last Ride, Death and texas, Jesus-Mary-and-Joey, Duplicity, Broadway: The Golden Age by the Legends Who Were There.
TELEVISION: *Movies:* The Connection, The Trial of Chaplain Jensen, Queen of the Stardust Ballroom, Switch, Special Olympics, Attica, Perfect Match, Crisis at Central High, The Best Little Girl in the World, Dark Night of the Scarecrow, Death of a Salesman, Kenny Rogers as The Gambler III—The Legend Continues, The Man Who Broke 1000 Chains, Case Closed, Unholy Matrimony, Prime Target, It Nearly Wasn't Christmas, Dinner at Eight, The Return of Eliot Ness, The Story Lady, The Water Engine, Roommates, Mrs. Santa Claus, Hard Time: Hostage Hotel, The Judge, Bleacher Bums. *Mini-Series:* Captains and the Kings, Studs Lonigan, The Kennedys of Massachusetts, A Woman of Independent Means, Jazz. *Specials:* The Rivalry, The Dancing Bear, Working, Mr. Roberts, Side by Side (pilot), P.O.P. (pilot), Eye to Eye, Tales from Hollywood, Normandy (narrator), Texan, Leslie's Folly. *Series:* Another World (1972), The Cop and the Kid, Eye to Eye, Evening Shade, First Monday. *Guest:* Madigan, All in the Family, Barnaby Jones, Hawaii Five-O, Amazing Stories, Everybody Loves Raymond.

DURWOOD, RICHARD M.

Executive. b. Kansas City, MO, Aug. 18, 1929. e. Brown U., A.B. Pres. Crown Cinema Corp. Member: Motion Picture Assn. of Kansas City (pres.), United Motion Pictures Assn. (pres. 1972-73), Young NATO (chmn., 1968-69), Past Chief Barker, Tent No. 8. Past mem., exec. comm., National NATO. Sr. v.p., and on bd. of dirs. of American Movie Classics, 1952-1976. 1996, sold Crown Cinema Corp. to Hollywood, Inc.

DUSSAULT, NANCY

Actress. b. Pensacola, FL, Jun. 30, 1936. e. Northwestern U.
THEATRE: *B'way:* Street Scene, The Mikado, The Cradle Will Rock, Do Re Mi (Theatre World Award), Sound of Music, Carousel, Fiorello, The Gershwin Years, Into the Woods. *L.A. stage:* Next in Line.
PICTURE: The In-Laws, The Nurse.
TELEVISION: *Special:* The Beggars Opera. *Host:* Good Morning America. *Series:* The New Dick Van Dyke Show, Too Close for Comfort (The Ted Knight Show), Mad About You.

DUTTON, CHARLES S.

Actor. b. Baltimore, MD, Jan. 30, 1951. e. Towson St., Yale Sch. of Drama.
THEATRE: *Yale Rep:* The Works, Beef No Chicken, Astopovo, Othello. *NY:* Ma Rainey's Black Bottom (Theatre World Award, 1983), Joe Turner's Come and Gone, The Piano Lesson.
PICTURES: No Mercy, Crocodile Dundee II, Jacknife, An Unremarkable Life, Q & A, Mississippi Masala, Alien3, The Distinguished Gentleman, Menace II Society, Rudy, Foreign Student, A Low Down Dirty Shame, Cry the Beloved Country, Nick of Time, Last Dance, A Time to Kill, Get on the Bus, Mimic, Blind Faith, Black Dog, Cookie's Fortune, Random Hearts, D-tox, Against the Ropes, Gothika.
TELEVISION: *Series:* Roc (also prod.). *Guest:* Miami Vice, The Equalizer, Cagney and Lacey, Oz. *Movies:* Apology, The Murder of Mary Phagan, Jack Reed: Search for Justice, The Piano Lesson, Zooman, Aftershock: Earthquake in New York City, Deadlocked, For Love or Country: The Arturo Sandoval Story, 10,000 Black Men Named George, Conviction. *Mini-Series:* The '60s. *Special:* Runaway.

DUVAL, JAMES

Actor. b. Detroit, MI, Sept. 10, 1973.
PICTURES: Totally F***ed Up, An Ambush of Ghosts, Mod F**k Explosion, The Doom Generation, Independence Day, River Made to Drown In, Nowhere, The Clown at Midnight, S.L.C. Punk!, How to Make the Cruelest Month, Go, The Weekend, Gone in Sixty Seconds, Donnie Darko, The Doe Boy, A Galaxy Far Away, Amerikana Comic Book Villains, May, Pledge of Allegiance, Open House, Frog-g-g.
TELEVISION: This is How the World Ends.

DUVALL, ROBERT

Actor. b. San Diego, CA, Jan. 5, 1931. e. Principia College, IL. Studied at the Neighborhood Playhouse, NY.
THEATRE: *Off-B'way:* The Days and Nights of Bee Bee Fenstermaker, Call Me By My Rightful Name, A View From the Bridge (Obie Award, 1965). *B'way:* Wait Until Dark, American Buffalo.
PICTURES: To Kill a Mockingbird (debut, 1962), Captain Newman M.D., Nightmare in the Sun, The Chase, Countdown, The Detective, Bullitt, True Grit, The Rain People, M*A*S*H, The Revolutionary, THX-1138, Lawman, The Godfather, Tomorrow,

The Great Northfield Minnesota Raid, Joe Kidd, Lady Ice, Badge 373, The Outfit, The Conversation, The Godfather Part II, Breakout, The Killer Elite, The Seven Percent Solution, Network, We're Not the Jet Set (dir., co-prod. only), The Eagle Has Landed, The Greatest, The Betsy, Invasion of the Body Snatchers (cameo), Apocalypse Now, The Great Santini, True Confessions, The Pursuit of D.B. Cooper, Tender Mercies (Acad. Award, 1983; also co-prod, songwriter), Angelo My Love (dir., prod., s.p. only), The Stone Boy, The Natural, Bellizaire the Cajun (cameo; also creative consultant), The Lightship, Let's Get Harry, Hotel Colonial, Colors, The Handmaid's Tale, A Show of Force, Days of Thunder, Rambling Rose, Convicts, Newsies, Falling Down, The Plague, Geronimo: An American Legend, Wrestling Ernest Hemingway, The Paper, Something to Talk About, The Stars Fell on Henrietta, The Scarlet Letter, A Family Thing (also co-prod.), Sling Blade, Phenomenon, The Apostle (also s.p., dir., exec. prod., Chicago Film Crits. Award, LA Film Crits. Award, Best Actor, 1997), Deep Impact, The Gingerbread Man, A Civil Action (Acad. Award nom.), Gone in Sixty Seconds, A Shot At Glory (also prod.), The 6th Day, John Q, Gods and Generals, Assassination Tango, Open Range, Secondhand Lions..
TELEVISION: Movies: Fame Is the Name of the Game, The Terry Fox Story, Stalin. Mini-Series: Ike, Lonesome Dove. Guest: Great Ghost Tales, The Outer Limits, Naked City, Route 66, The Defenders, Alfred Hitchcock Presents, Twilight Zone, Combat, Wild Wild West, The FBI, Mod Squad.

DUVALL, SHELLEY
Actress, Producer. b. Houston, TX, July 7, 1949. Founded Think Entertainment, TV prod. co. Appeared in 1984 short film Frankenweenie.
PICTURES: Brewster McCloud (debut, 1970), McCabe and Mrs. Miller, Thieves Like Us, Nashville, Buffalo Bill and the Indians, Three Women (Cannes Fest. Award, 1977), Annie Hall, The Shining, Popeye, Time Bandits, Roxanne, Suburban Commando, The Underneath, Portrait of a Lady, Changing Habits, Rocket Man, Russell Mulcahy's Tale of the Mummy, Home Fries, The 4th Floor, Dreams in the Attic, Stanley Kubrick: A Life in Pictures, Manna From Heaven, Under the Mimosa.
TELEVISION: Actress: Bernice Bobs Her Hair, Lily, Twilight Zone, Mother Goose Rock 'n' Rhyme, Faerie Tale Theatre (Rumpelstiltskin, Rapunzel), Tall Tales and Legends (Darlin' Clementine), Alone. Exec. Producer: Faerie Tale Theatre, Tall Tales and Legends, Nightmare Classics, Dinner at Eight (movie), Mother Goose Rock 'n' Rhyme, Stories from Growing Up, Backfield in Motion (movie), Bedtime Stories, Mrs. Piggle-Wiggle.

DYSART, RICHARD A.
Actor. b. Brighton, MA, March 30, 1929. e. Emerson Coll., B.S., M.S., L.L.D.(honorary). Univ. of Maine, Ph.D. (honorary). Trustee Gallaudet Univ, DC. Bd. of Dir, American Judicature Society.
THEATRE: B'way: in A Man for All Seasons, All in Good Time, The Little Foxes, A Place without Doors, That Championship Season, Another Part of the Forest. Off-B'way: in The Quare Fellow, Our Town, Epitaph for George Dillon, Six Characters in Search of an Author.
PICTURES: Petulia, The Lost Man, The Sporting Club, The Hospital, The Terminal Man, The Crazy World of Julius Vrooder, The Day of the Locust, The Hindenberg, Prophecy, Meteor, Being There, An Enemy of the People, The Thing, The Falcon and the Snowman, Mask, Warning Signs, Pale Rider, Wall Street, Back to the Future Part III, Hard Rain.
TELEVISION: Movies: The Autobiography of Miss Jane Pittman, Gemini Man, It Happened One Christmas, First You Cry, Bogie, The Ordeal of Dr. Mudd, Churchill and the Generals (BBC), People Vs. Jean Harris, Bitter Harvest, Missing, Last Days of Patton, Children--A Mother's Story, Malice in Wonderland, Day One, Bobby and Marilyn: Her Final Affair, Truman, A Child Is Missing, L.A. Law: Return to Justice. Specials: Sandburg's Lincoln, Jay Leno's Family Comedy Hour, Concealed Enemies, Charlie Smith and the Fritter Tree, Moving Target. Mini-Series: War and Remembrance. Series: L.A. Law (Emmy Award, 1992), Spawn (voice).

DZUNDZA, GEORGE
Actor. b. Rosenheim, Germany, July 19, 1945. Spent part of childhood in displaced-persons camps before he was moved to Amsterdam in 1949. Came to NY in 1956 where he attended St. John's U. as speech and theater major.
THEATRE: King Lear (NY Shakespeare Fest., debut, 1973), That Championship Season (tour, 1973), Mert and Phil, The Ritz, Legend, A Prayer for My Daughter.
PICTURES: The Happy Hooker, The Deer Hunter, Honky Tonk Freeway, Streamers, Best Defense, No Mercy, No Way Out, The Beast, Impulse, White Hunter Black Heart, The Butcher's Wife, Basic Instinct, Crimson Tide, Dangerous Minds, That Darn Cat, Species II, Instinct, Above Suspicion, Determination of Death, City by the Sea.
TELEVISION: Movies: The Defection of Simas Kudirka, Salem's Lot, Skokie, A Long Way Home, The Face of Rage, The Last Honor of Kathryn Beck, When She Says No, The Rape of Richard Beck, Brotherly Love, The Execution of Raymond Graham, Something is Out There, The Ryan White Story, Terror on Highway 91, What She Doesn't Know, The Enemy Within, The Babymaker: The Dr. Cecil Jacobson Story, The Limbic Region, The Batman/Superman Movie (voice). Series: Open All Night, Road Rovers (voice), Superman (voice), Law and Order, Batman: Gotham Knights (voice), Jesse, Hack. Guest: Starsky and Hutch, The Waltons.

E

EADS, GEORGE
Actor. b. Fort Worth, Texas, March 1, 1967.
PICTURES: Dust to Dust.
TELEVISION: Movies: The Ulitmate Lie, Crowned and Dangerous, The Spring, Just A Walk in the Park, Second String, Monte Walsh. Guest: Strange Luck, ER. Series: Savannah, Grapevine, C.S.I.

EASTWOOD, ALISON
Actress. b. May 22, 1972. Father is actor-director Clint Eastwood.
PICTURES: Bronco Billy, Tightrope, Absolute Power, Midnight in the Garden of Good and Evil, Suicide: the Comedy, Black & White, Just a Little Harmless Sex, Breakfast of Champions, Friends & Lovers, The Spring, If You Only Knew, How to Go Out on a Date in Queens, Waitin' to Live, The Storyteller.

EASTWOOD, CLINT
Actor, Producer, Director. b. San Francisco, CA, May 31, 1930; e. Oakland Technical H.S., Los Angeles City Coll. Daughter is actress Alison Eastwood. Worked as a lumberjack in Oregon before being drafted into the Army, Special Services 1950-54. Then contract player at Universal Studios. Starred in TV series Rawhide, 1958-65. Formed Malpaso Productions, 1969. Made a Chevalier des Lettres by French gov., 1985. Mayor, Carmel, CA, 1986-88. Best Director for Bird: Hollywood Foreign Press Assoc., Orson Award. Made Commandeur de Ordre des Arts & Lettres by French Government, 1994. Received Irving G. Thalberg Award, 1995. Received American Film Institute Life Achievement Award, 1996.
PICTURES: Revenge of the Creature (debut, 1955), Francis in the Navy, Lady Godiva, Tarantula, Never Say Goodbye, Away All Boats, The First Traveling Saleslady, Star in the Dust, Escapade in Japan, Ambush at Cimarron Pass, Lafayette Escadrille, A Fistful of Dollars, For a Few Dollars More, The Witches, The Good The Bad and The Ugly, Hang 'Em High, Coogan's Bluff, Where Eagles Dare, Paint Your Wagon, Kelly's Heroes, Two Mules For Sister Sara, Beguiled, Play Misty For Me (also dir.), Dirty Harry, Joe Kidd, Breezy (dir. only), High Plains Drifter (also dir.), Magnum Force, Thunderbolt & Lightfoot, The Eiger Sanction (also dir.), The Outlaw Josey Wales (also dir.), The Enforcer, The Gauntlet (also dir.), Every Which Way But Loose, Escape from Alcatraz, Bronco Billy (also dir.), Any Which Way You Can, Firefox (also dir., prod.), Honky Tonk Man (also dir., prod.), Sudden Impact (also dir., prod.), Tightrope (also prod.), City Heat, Pale Rider (also dir., prod.), Heartbreak Ridge (also dir., prod.), The Dead Pool (also prod.), Bird (dir. only), Thelonius Monk: Straight, No Chaser (exec. prod. only), Pink Cadillac, White Hunter Black Heart (also dir., prod.), The Rookie (also dir.), Unforgiven (also dir., prod.; Acad. Awards for Best Picture & Director; L.A. Film Critics Awards for Best Actor, Director & Picture; Natl. Society of Film Critics Awards for Best Director & Picture; Golden Globe Award for Best Director; DGA Award, 1992), In the Line of Fire, A Perfect World (also dir.), Casper (cameo), The Bridges of Madison County (also dir., prod.), The Stars Fell on Henrietta (co-prod. only), Absolute Power (also dir., prod., comp.), Midnight in the Garden of Good &Evil (also dir., prod.), True Crime (also, dir., prod.), Space Cowboys (also dir, prod.), Kurosawa, Blood Work (also dir., prod.), Mystic River (dir., prod., composer).
TELEVISION: Specials: Fame Fortune and Romance, Happy Birthday Hollywood, Clint Eastwood: The Man From Malpaso, Don't Pave Main Street: Carmel's Heritage, Salute to Martin Scorcese, Big Guns Talk: Story of the Western, Eastwood on Eastwood. Dir.: Amazing Stories (Vanessa in the Garden). Mini-series: The Blues (dir. only). Series: Rawhide. Guest: Navy Log, Maverick, Mr. Ed, Danny Kaye Show.

EBERSOL, DICK
Executive. 1968, started at ABC as Olympic Television researcher; 1974, joined NBC as dir. of weekend late- night programming; 1977, became v.p. late night programming; 1981-85, served as exec. prod. of Comedy Variety and Event Programming; 1983, formed his own production company, No Sleep Productions, creating Friday Night Videos, Saturday Night's Main Event, Later With Bob Costas; 1989, named pres. of NBC Sports and also sr. v.p. of NBC News; served as exec. prod. of NBC's coverage of the 1992 Barcelona Summer Olympics, and the 1996 Atlanta Summer Olympics. Appointed chmn. NBC Sports and NBC Olympics in June 1998. Still actively producing, Ebersol has served as exec. prod. of NBC's coverage of the last three Summer Olympic Games and is also co-exec. prod. of the NBA on NBC.

EBERTS, JOHN DAVID (JAKE)
Producer, Financier. b. Montreal, Canada, July 10, 1941. e. McGill Univ., Harvard. President Goldcrest, founder & CEO 1976-83, 1985-6; 1984 joined Embassy Communications Intl. 1985 founded and chief exec. of Allied Filmmakers. Film Prods. Award of Merit 1986; Evening Standard Special Award 1987. Publication: My Indecision Is Final (1990).PICTURES: Prod./Exec. Prod.: Chariots of Fire, Gandhi, Another Country, Local Hero, The Dresser, Cal, The Emerald Forest, The Name of the Rose, Hope and Glory, Cry Freedom, The Adventures of Baron Munchausen, Driving Miss Daisy, Dances With Wolves,

Black Robe, Get Back, City of Joy, A River Runs Through It, Super Mario Bros., No Escape, James and the Giant Peach, The Wind in the Willows, The Education of Little Tree, Grey Owl, Chicken Run, The Legend of Bagger Vance, K-19: Widowmaker. TELEVISION: Snow in August.

EBSEN, BUDDY
Actor. r.n. Christian Ebsen, Jr. b. Belleville, IL, April 2, 1908. e. U. of Florida, Rollins Coll. Won first Broadway role as dancer in Ziegfeld's Whoopee in 1928. Sister, Vilma, became dancing partner. Went to Hollywood and appeared in Broadway Melody of 1936 with Vilma then in many musicals as single. Later became dramatic actor and appeared on TV. Co-wrote title song for film Behave Yourself.
THEATRE: Flying Colors, Yokel Boy, The Male Animal, Ziegfeld Follies, Take Her She's Mine, Our Town, The Best Man.
PICTURES: Broadway Melody of 1936 (debut, 1935), Born to Dance, Captain January, Banjo on My Knee, Yellow Jack, Girl of the Golden West, My Lucky Star, Broadway Melody of 1938, Four Girls in White, Parachute Battalion, They Met in Argentina, Sing Your Worries Away, Thunder in God's Country, Night People, Red Garters, Davy Crockett--King of the Wild Frontier, Davy Crockett and the River Pirates, Between Heaven and Hell, Attack!, Breakfast at Tiffany's, The Interns, Mail Order Bride, The One and Only Genuine Original Family Band, The Beverly Hillbillies.
TELEVISION: Series: Davy Crockett, Northwest Passage, The Beverly Hillbillies, Barnaby Jones, Matt Houston. Guest: Hawaii Five-O, Gunsmoke. Movies: Stone Fox, The Daughters of Joshua Cabe, Horror at 37000 Feet, Smash-Up on Interstate 5, The President's Plane is Missing, Leave Yesterday Behind, The Paradise Connection, Fire on the Mountain, The Return of the Beverly Hillbillies, The Bastard, Tom Sawyer, Stone Fox, Working Trash. Special:s The Legend of the Beverly Hillbillies, The Legend of Oz, Walt: The Man Behind the Myth.
(d. July 6, 2003)

ECKERT, JOHN M.
Producer, Production Executive. b. Chatham, Ontario, Canada, e. Ryerson Poly. Inst., 1968-71 (film major). Member: DGA, DGC.
PICTURES: Power Play (assoc. prod.), Running (co-prod.), Middle Age Crazy (co-prod.), Dead Zone (unit prod. mgr.), Cats Eye (exec. in charge of prod.), Silver Bullet (assoc. prod.), The Incubus, Home Is Where the Heart Is (prod.), Millenium (suprv. prod.), Deep Sleep (prod.), Car 54 Where Are You? (s.p., prod.), Legends of the Fall (unit prod. mngr.), The Scarlet Letter (unit prod. mngr.), Flying Wild (assoc. prod.), Booty Call (co-prod.), The Big Hit (exec. prod), Three to Tango (co-prod.), Gossip (co-prod.), Loser (exec. prod.), Exit Wounds (co-prod.).
TELEVISION: Terry Fox Story (assoc. prod.), Special People (prod., Christopher Award), Danger Bay (series supv. prod., 1985-87), Family Pictures (unit prod. mngr.), Getting Gotti (prod.), Brian's Song (line prod.), The Music Man (prod.)

EDELMAN, RANDY
Composer. b. Patterson, NJ, June 10, 1947.
PICTURES: Feds, Twins, Troop Beverly Hills, Ghostbusters II, Quick Change, Come See the Paradise, Kindergarten Cop, V.I. Warshawski, Drop Dead Fred, Eyes of an Angel, The Distinguished Gentleman, Beethoven, My Cousin Vinny, The Last of the Mohicans (Golden Globe nom.), Gettysburg, Dragon: The Bruce Lee Story, Beethoven's 2nd, Tall Tale, Pontiac Moon, Greedy, Angels in the Outfield, The Mas, Billy Madison, While you Were Sleeping, The Indian in the Cupboard, The Big Green, Down Periscope, Diabolique, The Quest, Dragonheart, Daylight, Anaconda, Gone Fishin', The Chipmunk Adventure, Executive Action, The Big Green, Leave It To Beaver, For Richer or Poorer, Six Days Seven Nights, EdTV, Passion of Mind, The Whole Nine Yards, The Skulls, Shanghai Noon, Head Over Heels, China: The Panda Adventure, Osmosis Jones, Who Is Cletis Tout?, Corky Romano, Black Knight, XXX, Gods and Generals, Shanghai Knights, Frank McCluskey C.I., National Security, Connie & Carla.
TELEVISION: Movies: A Doctor's Story, Dennis the Menace, Citizen X, The Hunley, A Season on the Brink. Series: MacGyver, The Adventures of Brisco County Jr.

EDEN, BARBARA
Actress. b. Tucson, AZ, Aug. 23, 1934. r.n. Barbara Jean Huffman. e. San Francisco Conservatory of Music. Pres. Mi-Bar Productions. Dir. Security National Bank of Chicago.
PICTURES: Back From Eternity (debut, 1956), The Wayward Girl, A Private's Affair, From the Terrace, Twelve Hours to Kill, Flaming Star, All Hands on Deck, Voyage to the Bottom of the Sea, Five Weeks in a Balloon, Swingin' Along (Double Trouble), The Wonderful World of the Brothers Grimm, The Yellow Canary, The Brass Bottle, The New Interns, Ride the Wild Surf, 7 Faces of Dr. Lao, Quick Let's Get Married, The Amazing Dobermans, Harper Valley PTA, Chattanooga Choo Choo, A Very Brady Sequel, Mi Casa Su Casa, Carolina.
TELEVISION: Movies: The Feminist and the Fuzz, A Howling in the Woods, The Woman Hunter, Guess Who's Sleeping in My Bed, The Stranger Within, Let's Switch, How to Break Up a Happy Divorce, Stonestreet: Who Killed the Centerfold Model?, The Girls in the Office, Condominium, Return of the Rebels, I Dream of Jeannie: 15 Years Later, The Stepford Children, The Secret Life of Kathy McCormick (also co-prod.), Your Mother Wears Combat Boots, Opposites Attract, Her Wicked Ways, Hell Hath No Fury, I Still Dream of Jeannie, Visions of Murder I & II, Eyes of Terror, Dean Man's Island (also co-prod.), Nightclub

Confidential, Gentlemen Prefer Blondes. Series: How to Marry a Millionaire, I Dream of Jeannie, Harper Valley P.T.A., A Brand New Life, Dallas.

EDWARDS, ANTHONY
Actor. b. Santa Barbara, CA, July 19, 1962. Grandfather designed Walt Disney Studios in the 1930s and worked for Cecil B. De Mille as conceptual artist. Joined Santa Barbara Youth Theatre; acted in 30 plays from age 12 to 17. At 16 worked professionally in TV commercials. 1980 attended Royal Acad. of Dramatic Arts, London, and studied drama at USC. On NY stage 1993 in Ten Below.
PICTURES: Fast Times at Ridgemont High (debut, 1982), Heart Like a Wheel, Revenge of the Nerds, The Sure Thing, Gotcha!, Top Gun, Summer Heat, Revenge of the Nerds II (cameo), Mr. North, Miracle Mile, How I Got Into College, Hawks, Downtown, Delta Heat, Pet Sematary II, The Client, Charlie's Ghost story, Us Begins with You (also prod.), Playing by Heart, Jackpot, Die-Die-Mommie (prod. only), Northfork, The Thunderbirds.
TELEVISION: Movies: The Killing of Randy Webster, High School U.S.A., Going for the Gold: The Bill Johnson Story, El Diablo, Hometown Boy Makes Good. Series: It Takes Two, Northern Exposure, ER (Emmy Award, 1998), Soul Man, Rock Story. Specials: Unpublished Letters, Sexual Healing.

EDWARDS, BLAKE
Director, Writer, Producer. r.n. William Blake McEdwards. b. Tulsa, OK, July 26, 1922. m. actress Julie Andrews. e. Beverly Hills H.S. Coast Guard during war. Film acting debut, Ten Gentlemen from West Point (1942).
RADIO: Johnny Dollar, Line-up; writer-creator: Richard Diamond.
PICTURES: Writer: Panhandle, Stampede, Sound Off, All Ashore, Cruising Down the River, Rainbow Round My Shoulder, Drive a Crooked Road, The Atomic Kid (story), My Sister Eileen, Operation Mad Ball, Notorious Landlady, Soldier in the Rain. Producer: Waterhole Director: Bring Your Smile Along (also s.p.), He Laughed Last (also s.p.), Mister Cory (also s.p.), This Happy Feeling (also s.p.), The Perfect Furlough (also s.p.), Operation Petticoat, High Time, Breakfast at Tiffany's, Experiment in Terror, Days of Wine and Roses, The Pink Panther (also s.p.), A Shot in the Dark (also s.p., prod.), The Great Race (also s.p., prod.), What Did You Do in the War Daddy? (also s.p., prod.), Gunn (also prod.), The Party (also s.p., prod.), Darling Lili (also s.p., prod.), Wild Rovers (also s.p., prod.), The Carey Treatment (also s.p., prod.), The Tamarind Seed (also s.p.), The Return of the Pink Panther (also s.p., prod.), The Pink Panther Strikes Again (also s.p., prod.), Revenge of the Pink Panther (also s.p., prod.), "10" (also co-prod., s.p.), S.O.B. (also co-prod., s.p.), Victor/Victoria (also co-prod., s.p.), Trail of the Pink Panther (also co-prod., co-s.p.), The Curse of the Pink Panther (also co-prod., s.p.), The Man Who Loved Women (also prod., co-s.p.), Micki and Maude, A Fine Mess (also s.p.), That's Life (also co-prod.), Blind Date, Sunset (also s.p.), Skin Deep (also s.p.), Switch (also s.p.), Son of the Pink Panther (also s.p.).
TELEVISION: Movies: Victor/Victoria. City Detective (prod., 1953), The Dick Powell Show (dir.), Creator: Dante's Inferno, Mr. Lucky, Justin Case (exec. prod., dir., writer), Peter Gunn (exec. prod., dir., writer), Julie (exec. prod., dir.), Specials: Julie! (prod., dir.), Julie on Sesame St. (exec. prod.), Julie and Dick in Covent Garden (dir.).

EDWARDS, JAMES H.
Executive. President & CEO, Storey Theatres, Inc. b. Cedartown, GA, Aug. 14, 1927. e. Georgia State. U.S. Navy, 1948-50. With Ga. Theatre Co., 1950-1952; Storey Theatres, 1952-present. Formerly pres. & chmn., NATO of GA; formerly pres., Variety Club of Atlanta. Former dir. at large, Nat'l. NATO. Director, numerous theatre cos.

EDWARDS, RALPH
Producer, Emcee. b. Merino, CO, June 13, 1913. e. U. of California, Berkeley. Began career in radio in 1929 as writer-actor-prod.-announcer at station KROW, Oakland. Later joined CBS & NBC Radio in New York as announcer. Originated, produced and emceed Truth or Consequences, This Is Your Life and The Ralph Edwards Show for both radio & TV.
PICTURES: Seven Days Leave, Radio Stars on Parade, Bamboo Blonde, Beat the Band, I'll Cry Tomorrow, Manhattan Merry-go-round, The Devil's Bedroom, The Sadistic Lover, Empire of the Air: The Men Who Made Radio, Off the Menu: The Last Days of Chasen's.
TELEVISION: Producer/Creator: It Could Be You, Place the Face, About Faces, Funny Boners, End of the Rainbow, Who in the World, The Woody Woodbury Show, This is Your Life (specials for NBC; host). Producers: Wide Country, Name That Tune, Cross Wits, Knockout, Annabelle's Wish. Producer (with partner, Stu Billett): The People's Court, So You Think You Got Troubles?, Family Medical Center, Love Stories, Superior Court, Bzzz.

EGGAR, SAMANTHA
Actress. b. London, England,, March 5, 1939. e. student Webber-Douglas Dramatic Sch., London; Slade Sch. of Art.
PICTURES: The Wild and the Willing, Dr. Crippen, Doctor in Distress, Psyche '59, The Collector (Acad. Award nom.), Return From the Ashes, Walk Don't Run, Doctor Dolittle, The Molly Maguires, The Lady in the Car With Glasses and a Gun, The Walking Stick, The Grove, The Light at the Edge of the World, The Dead Are Alive, The Seven Percent Solution, The Uncanny, Welcome to Blood City, The Brood, The Exterminator, Demonoid, Why Shoot the Teacher?, Curtains, Hot Touch, Loner, Ragin

Cajun, Dark Horse, Inevitable Grace, The Phantom, Hercules, The Astronaut's Wife.
TELEVISION: *Movies*: Double Indemnity, All The Kind Strangers, The Killer Who Wouldn't Die, Ziegfeld: the Man and His Women, The Hope Diamond, Love Among Thieves, A Ghost in Monte Carlo. A Case for Murder. *Mini-Series*: For the Term of His Natural Life, Davy Crockett, Great Escapes: Secrets of Lake Success. *Series*: Anna and the King, All My Children, Hercules (voice). *Guest*: Columbo, Baretta, Love Story, Kojak, McMillan & Wife, Streets of San Francisco, Starsky and Hutch, Hart to Hart, Murder She Wrote, Stingray, Tales of the Unexpected, Heartbeat, Love Boat, 1st & Ten, Outlaws, Alfred Hitchcock Presents, Matlock, L.A. Law, Star Trek: The Next Generation. *Specials*: Man of Destiny, Hemingway Play.

EGOYAN, ATOM
Director, Writer, Producer, Editor, Actor, Cinematographer.
b. Cairo, Egypt, July 19, 1960. Raised in Victoria, British Columbia, Canada. e. Univ. of Toronto. Made short films, one of which, Open House appeared on TV series Canadian Reflections.
PICTURES: *Various credits*: Howard in Particular, After Grad with Dad, Peep Show, Open House, Next of Kin, Men: A Passion Playground, Family Viewing, Speaking Parts, The Adjuster, Montreal Sextet, Calendar, Exotica, Curtis's Charm, A Portrait of Arshile, The Sweet Hereafter, Vinyl, Bach Cello Suite #4: Sarabande, Felicia's Journey (dir., s.p.), The Line, Ararat, Gambling-God-and LSD (documentary, exec. prod.), Foolproof (exec. prod.)
TELEVISION: *Movies*: In This Corner, Looking for Nothing, Gross Misconduct: The Life of Brian Spencer, Krapp's Last Tape. Escape from the Newsroom (as himself). *Series*: Alfred Hitchcock Presents, Twilight Zone, Friday the 13th.

EICHHORN, LISA
Actress. b. Reading, PA, Feb. 4, 1952. e. Queen's U. Kingston, Canada and Eng. for literature studies at Oxford. Studied at Royal Acad. of Dramatic Art.
THEATRE: The Hasty Heart (debut, LA). NY: The Common Pursuit, The Summer Winds, The Speed of Darkness, Down the Road, Any Given Day.
PICTURES: Yanks, The Europeans, Why Would I Lie?, Cutter and Bone, Weather in the Streets, Wild Rose; Opposing Force, Moon 44, Grim Prairie Tales, The Vanishing, King of the Hill, Sticks and Stones, First Kid, A Modern Affair, Judas Kiss, Goodbye Lover, The Talented Mr. Ripley, Boys and Girls.
TELEVISION: *Movies*: The Wall, Blind Justice, Devlin. *Mini-Series*: A Woman Named Jackie. *Series*: All My Children (1987).

EIKENBERRY, JILL
Actress. b. New Haven, CT, Jan. 21, 1947. e. Yale U. Drama Sch. m. actor Michael Tucker.
THEATRE: B'way: All Over Town, Watch on the Rhine, Onward Victoria, Summer Brave, Moonchildren. Off-B'way: Lemon Sky, Life Under Water, Uncommon Women and Others, Porch, The Primary English Class.
PICTURES: Between the Lines, The End of the World in Our Usual Bed in a Night Full of Rain, An Unmarried Woman, Butch and Sundance: The Early Days, Rich Kids, Hide in Plain Sight, Arthur, The Manhattan Project, Manna From Heaven.
TELEVISION: *Movies*: The Deadliest Season, Orphan Train, Swan Song, Sessions, Kane & Abel, Assault and Matrimony, Family Sins, A Stoning in Fulham Country, My Boyfriend's Back, The Diane Martin Story, The Secret Life of Archie's Wife, An Inconvenient Woman, Living a Lie, A Town Torn Apart, Chantilly Lace, Parallel Lives, Without Consent, Rugged Gold, The Other Woman, Dare to Love, My Very Best Friend, Gone in a Heartbeat, Roughing It, L.A. Law: Return to Justice. *Series*: L.A. Law, The Best of Families (PBS). *Specials*: Uncommon Women & Others, Destined to Live (prod., host), A Family Again, On Hope.

EILBACHER, LISA
Actress. b. Dharan, Saudi Arabia, May 5, 1957. Moved to California at age 7; acted on TV as child.
PICTURES: The War Between Men and Women (debut, 1972), Run for the Roses (Thoroughbred), On the Right Track, An Officer and a Gentleman, Ten to Midnight, Beverly Hills Cop, Deadly Intent, Leviathan, Never Say Die, The Last Samurai, Live Wire, The Skating Rink.
TELEVISION: *Movies*: Bad Ronald, Panache, Spider Man, The Ordeal of Patty Hearst, Love for Rent, To Race the Wind, This House Possessed, Monte Carlo, Deadly Deception, Joshua's Heart, Blind Man's Bluff, Deadly Matrimony, The Return of Hunter: Everyone Walks in L.A., Dazzle, 919 Fifth Avenue. *Mini-Series*: Wheels, The Winds of War. *Series*: The Texas Wheelers, The Hardy Boys Mysteries, Ryan's Four, Me and Mom. *Guest*: Wagon Train, Laredo, My Three Sons, Gunsmoke, Combat.

EISNER, MICHAEL D.
Executive. b. Mt. Kisco, NY, March 7, 1942. e. Denison U., B.A. Started career with programming dept. of CBS TV network. Joined ABC in 1966 as mgr. talent and specials. Dec., 1968 became dir. of program dev.; east coast. 1968, named v.p., daytime programming, ABC-TV. 1975 made v.p.; prog. planning and dev. 1976 named sr. v.p., prime time production and dev., ABC Entertainment. 1976, left ABC to join Paramount Pictures as pres. & chief operating officer. 1984, joined The Walt Disney Company as chmn. & CEO, a position he holds today. Since joining Disney, the company's annual revenues have grown from $1.7 billion to $25. 4 billion. Host of TV series, The Wonderful

World of Disney, 1997; he is the author of: Work in Progress, (co-author with Tony Schwartz). Eisner serves on the boards of CA. Institute of the Arts, Denison Univ., American Hospital of Paris Found., Conservation Int'l., the UCLA Exec. Bd. for Medical Sciences and the National Hockey League. He also has established and funded The Eisner Foundation.

EKBERG, ANITA
Actress. b. Malmo, Sweden, Sept. 29, 1931. Came to U.S. in 1951 as Miss Universe contestant. Worked as model before becoming actress appearing in small roles at Universal.
PICTURES: Mississippi Gambler, Abbott & Costello Go to Mars, Take Me to Town, The Golden Blade, Blood Alley, Artists and Models, Man in the Vault, War and Peace, Back from Eternity, Hollywood or Bust, Zarak, Pickup Alley, Valerie, Paris Holiday, The Man Inside, Screaming Mimi, Sign of the Gladiator, La Dolce Vita, The Dam on the Yellow River (Last Train to Shanghai), Little Girls and High Finance, Behind Locked Doors, The Last Judgment, The Mongols, Boccaccio '70, Call Me Bwana, 4 for Texas, L'Incastro, Who Wants to Sleep?, The Alphabet Murders, Way Way Out, How I Learned to Love Women, Woman Times Seven, The Glass Sphinx, The Cobra, Malenka the Vampire (Fangs of the Living Dead), If It's Tuesday This Must Be Belgium, The Clowns, Valley of the Widows, Killer Nun, Daisy Chain, Intervista, The Seduction of Angela, Quando ancora non c'erano i Beatles, Count Max, Cattive ragazze, Ambrogio, Bambola, The Red Dwarf.
TELEVISION: *Movies*: Gold of the Amazon Women, S*H*E. *Series*: Il Bello delle donne.

EKLAND, BRITT
Actress. b. Stockholm, Sweden, Oct. 6, 1942. Was model before debuting in European films.
PICTURES: Short Is the Summer (debut, 1962), Il Commandante, After the Fox, The Double Man, The Bobo, The Night They Raided Minsky's, Stiletto, Cannibals, Machine Gun McCain, Tintomara, Percy, Get Carter, A Time for Loving, Endless Night, Baxter, Asylum, The Wicker Man, Ultimate Thrill, The Man With the Golden Gun, Royal Flash, Casanova & Co., High Velocity, Slavers, King Solomon's Treasure, The Monster Club, Satan's Mistress (Demon Rage), Hellhole, Fraternity Vacation, Marbella, Moon in Scorpio, Scandal, Beverly Hills Vamp, The Children, Cold Heat, The Victim.
TELEVISION: *England*: Carol for Another Christmas, Too Many Thieves, A Cold Peace. *USA*: *Guest*: Trials of O'Brien, McCloud, Six Million Dollar Man. *Movies*: Ring of Passion, The Great Wallendas, The Hostage Tower, Valley of the Dolls 1981, Dead Wrong.

ELAM, JACK
Actor. b. Miami, AZ, Nov. 13, 1916. e. Santa Monica Jr. Coll., Modesto Jr. Coll. Worked in Los Angeles as bookkeeper and theatre mgr.; civilian employee of Navy in W.W.II; Introduction to show business was as bookkeeper for Sam Goldwyn. Later worked as controller for other film producers. Given first acting job by prod. George Templeton in 1948; has since appeared in over 100 films.
PICTURES: Wild Weed (debut, 1949), Rawhide, Kansas City Confidential, Rancho Notorious, Ride Vaquero, Appointment in Honduras, The Moonlighter, Vera Cruz, Cattle Queen of Montana, The Far Country, Moonfleet, Kiss Me Deadly, Artists and Models, Gunfight at the OK Corral, Baby Face Nelson, Edge of Eternity, Girl in Lovers Lane, The Last Sunset, The Comancheros, The Rare Breed, The Way West, Firecreek, Never a Dull Moment, Once Upon a Time in the West, Support Your Local Sheriff, Rio Lobo, Dirty Dingus Magee, Support Your Local Gunfighter, The Wild Country, Hannie Caulder, Last Rebel, Pat Garrett and Billy the Kid, Hawmps, Grayeagle, Hot Lead Cold Feet, The Norsemen, The Villain, The Apple Dumpling Gang Rides Again, The Cannonball Run, Jinxed, Cannonball Run II, The Aurora Encounter, Big Bad John, Suburban Commando.
TELEVISION: *Movies*: The Over-the-Hill Gang, The Daughters of Joshua Cabe, Black Beauty, Once Upon a Texas Train, Where the Hell's That Gold!!!?, Bonanza: The Return, Bonanza: Under Attack, Bonanza: The Next Generation. *Series*: The Dakotas, Temple Houston, The Texas Wheelers, Struck by Lightning, Detective in the House, Easy Street.
(d. Oct. 20, 2003)

ELEFANTE, TOM
Executive. Began career as usher at Loews Riviera in Coral Gables, FL; progressed through ranks to asst. mgr. & Florida division mgr. 1972, joined Wometco Theatres as gen. mgr. 1975, returned to Loews Theatres as southeast div. mgr.; 1979, named natl. dir. of concessions, moving to h.o. in New York. 1987, appt. sr. v.p. & gen. mgr., Loews. Served as pres. and chmn. of NATO of Florida. 1990, then pres. of NATO of NY. Joined Warner Bros. Int'l Theatres as sr. v.p.; 1992. Founded T.P. Consulting Co., 1997.

ELFAND, MARTIN
Executive. b. Los Angeles, CA, 1937. Was talent agent for 10 yrs. with top agencies; joined Artists Ent. Complex in 1972. First film project as prod.: Kansas City Bomber, first venture of AEC, of which was sr. v.p.; 1977, joined Warner Bros. as production chief.
PICTURES: *Prod.*: Dog Day Afternoon, It's My Turn, An Officer and a Gentleman, King David, Clara's Heart. *Exec. prod.*: Her Alibi, Talent for the Game.

ELFMAN, DANNY
Composer. b. Los Angeles, CA, May 29, 1953. Member of rock band Oingo Boingo, recorded songs for such films as The Tempest, Fast Times at Ridgemont High, 16 Candles, Beverly Hills Cop, Weird Science, Texas Chainsaw Massacre 2, Something Wild. Appeared in Hot Tomorrows, Back to School.
PICTURES: Forbidden Zone, Pee-wee's Big Adventure, Back to School, Wisdom, Summer School, Beetlejuice, Midnight Run, Big Top Pee-wee, Hot to Trot, Scrooged, Batman, Nightbreed, Dick Tracy, Darkman, Edward Scissorhands, Pure Luck, Article 99, Batman Returns, Sommersby, The Nightmare Before Christmas (also vocalist), Black Beauty, Dolores Claiborne, To Die For, Dead Presidents, Mission: Impossible, The Frighteners, Mars Attacks!, Men in Black (Acad. Award nom.), Flubber, Good Will Hunting (Acad. Award nom.), Scream 2, A Simple Plan, A Civil Action, Modern Vampyres, My Favorite Martian, Psycho, Instinct, Anywhere But Here, Sleepy Hollow, Proof of Life, The Family Man, Spy Kids, Heartbreakers, Planet of the Apes, Novocaine, Spider Man, Red Dragon, Men In Black 2, Spy Kids: The Island of Lost Dreams, Undone, Terminator 3: Rise of the Machines, Batman: Year One, , Hulk, Big Fish, Spider Man 2.
TELEVISION: Series: Pee-wee's Playhouse, Sledgehammer, Fast Times, Tales from the Crypt, The Simpsons, The Flash, Beetlejuice, Perversions of Science, Dilbert. Segments of Amazing Stories, Alfred Hitchcock Presents (The Jar).

ELFMAN, JENNA
Actress. b. Los Angeles, CA, Sept. 30, 1971.
PICTURES: Grosse Pointe Blank, Doctor Dolittle (voice) Krippendorf's Tribe, Can't Hardly Wait, Venus, Edtv, Keeping the Faith, CyberWorld (voice), The Tangerine Bear, Town and Country, Looney Tunes: Back in Action..
TELEVISION: Movies: Her Last Chance, Obsessed. Series: Townies, Dharma & Greg. Guest: Roseanne, NYPD Blue, Murder One, Almost Perfect, The Single Guy.

ELG, TAINA
Actress, Dancer. b. Helsinki, Finland, March 9, 1930. Trained and performed with Natl. Opera of Finland. Toured with Swedish Dance Theatre, then Marquis de Cuevas Ballet.
THEATRE: Look to the Lilies, Where's Charley?, The Utter Glory of Morrissey Hall, Strider, Nine, O! Pioneers.
PICTURES: The Prodigal (debut, 1955), Diane, Gaby, Les Girls, Watusi, Imitation General, The 39 Steps, The Bacchae, Liebestraum, The Mirror Has Two Faces, Ça c'est l'amour.
TELEVISION: Movie: The Great Wallendas. Mini-Series: Blood and Honor: Youth Under Hitler (narrator).

ELIZONDO, HECTOR
Actor. b. New York, NY, Dec. 22, 1936. m. actress Carolee Campbell. Studied with Ballet Arts Co. of Carnegie Hall and Actors Studio. Many stage credits in N.Y. and Boston.
THEATRE: The Prisoner of Second Avenue, Dance of Death, Steambath (Obie Award), The Great White Hope, Sly Fox, The Price.
PICTURES: The Fat Black Pussycat, Valdez Is Coming, Born to Win, Pocket Money, Deadhead Miles, Stand Up and Be Counted, The Taking of Pelham One Two Three, Report to the Commissioner, Thieves, Cuba, American Gigolo, The Fan, Young Doctors in Love, The Flamingo Kid, Private Resort, Nothing in Common, Overboard, Beaches, Leviathan, Pretty Woman (Golden Globe nom.), Taking Care of Business, Necessary Roughness, Frankie and Johnny, Final Approach, Samantha, There Goes the Neighborhood, Being Human, Beverly Hills Cop III, Getting Even With Dad, Exit to Eden, Perfect Alibi, Dear God, Turbulence, Entropy, Safe House, The Other Sister, Entropy, The Runaway Bride, Speak Truth to Power, Tortilla Soup, The Princess Diaries, How High, The Zoot Suit Riots (voice), Raising Helen.
TELEVISION: Movies: The Impatient Heart, Wanted: The Sundance Woman, Honeyboy, Women of San Quentin, Courage, Out of the Darkness, Addicted to His Love, Your Mother Wears Combat Boots, Forgotten Prisoners: The Amnesty Files, Finding the Way Home, Chains of Gold, The Burden of Proof, Borrowed Hearts. Mini-Series: The Dain Curse, Fidel. Specials: Medal of Honor Rag, Mrs. Cage, Fidel. Series: Popi (1976), Casablanca, Freebie and the Bean; A.K.A. Pablo (also dir.), Foley Sq, Down and Out in Bevery Hills, Fish Police (voice), Chicago Hope (Emmy Award, 1997), Kate Brasher. Guest: The Wendie Barrie Show (1947), The Impatient Heart, Kojack, the Jackie Gleason Show, All in the Family, The Pirates of Dark Water (voice), Tales from the Crypt, Miracles.

ELKINS, HILLARD
Producer. b. New York, NY, Oct. 18, 1929. e. NYU, B.A., 1951. Exec., William Morris Agy., 1949-51; exec. v.p., Gen. Artists Corp., 1952-53; pres., Hillard Elkins Mgmt., 1953-60; Elkins Prods. Intl. Corp., N.Y., 1960-71; Elkins Prods. Ltd., 1972-; Hillard Elkins Entertainment Corp., 1974; Media Mix Prods., Inc., 1979-82.
MEMBER: Academy of Motion Picture Arts & Sciences, Acad. of TV Arts & Sciences, Dramatists Guild, League of New York Theatres, American Fed. of TV & Radio Artists.
THEATRE: Come On Strong, Golden Boy, Oh Calcutta!, The Rothschilds, A Doll's House, An Evening with Richard Nixon, Sizwe Banzi Is Dead, etc.
PICTURES: Alice's Restaurant, A New Leaf, Oh Calcutta!, A Doll's House, Richard Pryor Live in Concert, Sellers on Sellers, Inside, Stage Kiss, Avenue A.
TELEVISION: The Importance of Being Earnest, The Deadly Game, Princess Daisy, The Meeting (exec. prod.), Father & Son: Dangerous Relationsm A Father for Charlie, In His Father's Shoes.

ELKINS, KEN JOE
Broadcasting Executive. b. Prenter, WV, Oct. 12, 1937. e. Nebraska U., 1966-69. Eng. sta. KETV-TV, NE, 1960-67; asst. chief engr., 1967-70; ops. mgr., nat. sales, gen. sales mgr., 1972-75; gen. mgr., 1975-80. Chief engr. sta. KOUB-TV, IA, 1970-71; gen mgr., 1971-72. Gen. mgr. sta. KSDK-TV, MO, 1980-81. V.P., CEO Pulitzer B'casting Co., St. Louis, 1981-84; pres., CEO, 1984-1999. Currently, a director of Pulitzer, Inc. Bd. Dirs.: Commerce Bank St. Louis; Maximum Svc. Telecasters, WA; BMI; BJC Health Sys. Pres., NE B'casters, 1979-80. Chmn., NBC Affiliate Bd. Govs. With USAF, 1957-61. Inducted into NE Broadcasters Hall of Fame, 1990. Mem.: Nat. Assn. B'casters; Found. B'casters Hall of Fame (bd. dirs., trustee 1990); TV Operators Caucus; Algonquin Club.

ELLIOTT, CHRIS
Actor, Writer. b. New York, NY, May 31, 1960. Father is comedian Bob Elliott. Was performer in improv. theatres, summer stock; also tour guide at Rockefeller Center. Became writer/performer for David Letterman starting in 1982. Author: Daddy's Boy: A Son's Shocking Account of Life With a Famous Father (1989).
PICTURES: Manhunter (debut, 1986), The Abyss, Hyperspace, Groundhog Day, CB4, Cabin Boy (also co-story), Kingpin, The Sky Is Falling, There's Something About Mary, Snow Day, Nutty Professor II: The Klumps, The Sky Is Falling, The Swinger, Scary Movie 2, Osmosis Jones.
TELEVISION: Series: Late Night With David Letterman (also co-writer; 2 Emmy Awards for writing: 1984, 1985), Nick and Hillary, Get a Life (also creator, co-writer, prod.), The Naked Truth, Dilbert (voice), Cursed. Specials: Late Night With David Letterman Anniversary Specials (also co-writer; 2 Emmy Awards for writing: 1986, 1987), Chris Elliott's FDR: One-Man Show (also writer, prod.).

ELLIOTT, LANG
Producer, Director. b. Los Angeles, CA, Oct. 18, 1949. Began acting in films at an early age, influenced by his uncle, the late actor William Elliott (known as Wild Bill Elliott). Employed by, among others the McGowan Brothers. Turned to film production; co-founded distribution co., The International Picture Show Co., serving as exec. v.p. in chg. of financing, production & distribution. In 1976 formed TriStar Pictures, Inc. to finance and distribute product. In 1980 sold TriStar to Columbia, HBO and CBS. 1982, formed Lang Elliott Productions, Inc. Co-founded Longshot Enterprises with actor Tim Conway to prod. films and home videos, 1985. Videos include Dorf on Golf (the first made-for-home-video comedy), 'Scuse Me!, Dorf and the First Olympic Games. Formed Performance Pictures, Inc., in 1989, a prod. & distrib. company. Received Academy Award nom. for Soldier of Orange and The Magic of Lassie.
PICTURES: Prod: Ride the Hot Wind, Where Time Began, The Farmer, The Billion Dollar Hobo, They Went That-a-Way & That-a-Way, The Prize Fighter. Prod.-dir.: The Private Eyes, Cage, Cage II.
TELEVISION: Experiment in Love (prod.), Boys Will Be Boys (writer).

ELLIOTT, SAM
Actor. b. Sacramento, CA, Aug. 9, 1944. m. actress Katharine Ross. e. U. of Oregon.
PICTURES: Butch Cassidy and the Sundance Kid (debut in bit, 1969), The Games, Frogs, Molly and Lawless John, Lifeguard, The Legacy, Mask, Fatal Beauty, Shakedown, Road House, Prancer, Sibling Rivalry, Rush, Gettysburg, Tombstone, The Desperate Trail, The Final Cut, Dog Watch, The Hi-Lo Country, The Big Lebowski, The Contender, Pretty When You Cry, We Were Soldiers, Off the Map, Hulk.
TELEVISION: Movies: The Challenge, Assault on the Wayne, The Blue Knight, I Will Fight No More Forever, The Sacketts, Wild Times, Murder in Texas, Shadow Riders, Travis McGee, A Death in California. The Blue Lightning, Houston: The Legend of Texas, The Quick and the Dead, Conagher (also co-writer, exec. prod.), Fugitive Nights: Danger in the Desert, Buffalo Girls, The Ranger the Cook and a Hole in the Sky, Woman Undone, Rough Riders, You Know My Name, Fail Safe. Series: Mission: Impossible, The Yellow Rose. Mini-Series: Once and Eagle, Aspen (The Innocent and the Damned). Guest: Lancer, The FBI, Gunsmoke, Streets of San Francisco, Hawaii 5-0, Police Woman. Pilot: Evel Knievel.

ELWES, CARY
Actor. b. London, England, Oct. 26, 1962. e. Harrow. Studied for stage with Julie Bovasso at Sarah Lawrence, Bronxville, NY.
PICTURES: Another Country (debut 1984), Oxford Blues, The Bride, Lady Jane, The Princess Bride, Glory, Days of Thunder, Leather Jackets, Hot Shots!, Bram Stoker's Dracula, The Crush, Robin Hood: Men in Tights, Rudyard Kipling's The Jungle Book, Twister, Kiss the Girls, The Informant, Liar Liar, Quest for Camelot (voice), The Cradle Will Rock, Shadow of the Vampire, Wish You Were Dead, Joan of Arc: The Virgin Warrior, The Cat's Meow, Comic Book Villains, American Crime, Ella Enchanted, Neo Ned.
TELEVISION: Movies: The Pentagon Wars, Race Against Time, Uprising. Series: Hercules (voice), The X Files.

EMMERICH, ROLAND
Director, Writer, Exec. Producer. b. Stuttgart, Germany, Nov. 10, 1955. Studied production design in film school in Munich. First film was student production. The Noah's Ark Principle, which opened the 1984 Berlin Film Festival and was sold to more than 20 countries. Formed Centropolis Film Productions. Prod. TV series, The Visitor, 1997.
PICTURES: Co-s.p./Dir.:Making Contact (a.k.a. Joey; dir. only), Ghost Chase, Moon 44, Universal Soldier, Stargate,

Independence Day, Godzilla, The Patriot (also exec. prod.), The Day After Tomorrow (also prod.) *Prod:* Eye of the Storm, The Thirteenth Floor, Eight Legged Freaks.

ENGEL, CHARLES F.
Executive. b. Los Angeles, CA, Aug. 30. e. Michigan State U., UCLA. Son of writer-prod. Samuel G. Engel. Pgm. devel., ABC-TV, 1964-68; v.p. Univ.-TV, 1972; sr. v.p., 1977; exec. v.p., 1980; pres., MCA Pay-TV Programming, 1981. ACE Award, 1988 for outstanding contribution to cable; v.p. Universal TV, exec. in chg. ABC Mystery Movie, 1989. Sr. v.p. 1992 in chg. Columbo, Murder She Wrote, SeaQuest, The Rockford Files. Founding member board of governors, the National Academy of Cable Programming. Member, Television Academy. Exec. v.p. of Programming Universal Television, 1997.
TELEVISION: The Aquarians (exec. prod.), Run a Crooked Mile (exec. prod.), Road Raiders (prod.), ABC Mystery Movie (exec. in chg. of prod.), Murder She Wrote: A Story to Die For, Murder She Wrote: The Last Free Man, Murder She Wrote: The Celtic Riddle (exec. prod.).

ENGELBERG, MORT
Producer. b. Memphis, TN. e. U. of Illinois, U. of Missouri. Taught journalism; worked as reporter for UPI, AP. Worked for U.S. government, including USIA, Peace Corps., Office of Economic Opportunity; President's Task Force on War on Poverty. Left gov. service in 1967 to become film unit publicist, working on three films in Europe: Dirty Dozen, Far From the Madding Crowd, The Comedians. Returned to U.S.; appt. pub. mgr. for United Artists. Sent to Hollywood as asst. to Herb Jaffe, UA head of west coast prod., which post he assumed when Jaffe left. Left to join indep. prod., Ray Stark.
PICTURES: Smokey and the Bandit, Hot Stuff, The Villain, The Hunter, Smokey and the Bandit II, Smokey and the Bandit III, Nobody's Perfekt, The Heavenly Kid, The Big Easy, Maid to Order, Dudes, Three For the Road, Russkies, Pass the Ammo, Trading Hearts, Fright Night Part 2, Rented Lips, Remote Control.

ENGLANDER, MORRIS K.
Executive. b. New York, NY, July 5, 1934. e. Wharton Sch., U. of Pennsylvania. With General Cinema Corp. circuit before joining RKO Century Warner Theatres 1984 as exec. v.p., develp.; later co-vice chmn. of circuit. 1986, sr. real estate advisor, American Multi-Cinema. 1988: v.p. real estate Hoyts Cinemas Corp.; 1990 COO of Hoyts; pres. & COO of Hoyts. 1991. Retired.

ENGLUND, ROBERT
Actor. b. Glendale, CA, June 6, 1949. e. UCLA, RADA. First role was in the Cleveland stage production of Godspell, 1971.
PICTURES: Buster and Billie, Hustle, Stay Hungry, Death Trap (Eaten Alive), The Last of the Cowboys, St. Ives, A Star is Born, Big Wednesday, Bloodbrothers, The Fifth Floor, Dead and Buried, Galaxy of Terror, Don't Cry It's Only Thunder, A Nightmare on Elm Street, A Nightmare on Elm Street Part 2: Freddy's Revenge, Never Too Young to Die, A Nightmare on Elm Street 3: Dream Warriors, A Nightmare on Elm Street 4: The Dream Master, 976-EVIL (dir. only), A Nightmare on Elm Street: The Dream Child, Phantom of the Opera, The Adventures of Ford Fairlane, Danse Macabre, Freddy's Dead: The Final Nightmare, Eugenie, Wes Craven's New Nightmare, The Mangler, The Paper Route, Vampyre Wars, Killer Tongue, Regeneration, Wishmaster, Meet the Deedles, Urban Legend, Strangeland, The Prince and the Surfer, Freddy vs. Jason, Python, Wish You Were Dead, Windfall, Land of Canaan, Il Ritorno di Cagliostro.
TELEVISION: *Series:* Downtown, V, Freddy's Nightmares, Nightmare Cafe, Justice League. *Specials and Movies:* Hobson's Choice, Young Joe: The Forgotten Kennedy, The Ordeal of Patty Hearst, The Courage and the Passion, Mind Over Murder, Thou Shalt Not Kill, The Fighter, Journey's End, Starflight: The Plane That Couldn't Land, I Want to Live, Infidelity, A Perry Mason Mystery: The Case of the Lethal Lifestyle, Robin Cook's Mortal Fear, The Unspoken Truth. *Mini-Series:* V, North and South Book II. *Host:* Horror Hall of Fame, Sci-Fi Channel. *Guest:* The Simpsons (voice).

EPHRON, NORA
Writer, Director. b. New York, NY, May 19, 1941. e. Wellesley Col. Daughter of writers Henry and Phoebe Ephron. m. writer Nicholas Pileggi. *Author:* Heartburn, Crazy Salad, Scribble Scribble. Appeared in Crimes and Misdemeanors, Husbands and Wives.
PICTURES: *Writer:* Silkwood, Heartburn, When Harry Met Sally... (also assoc. prod.), Cookie (also exec. prod.), My Blue Heaven (also exec. prod.), This is My Life (also dir.), Sleepless in Seattle (also dir.), Mixed Nuts (also dir.), Michael (also dir., prod., exec. prod.), You've Got Mail (also prod.), Hanging Up (also prod.), Lucky Numbers (also prod.).
TELEVISION: *Movie (writer):* Perfect Gentlemen, Red Tails in Love: A Wildlife Drama in Central Park (also prod., dir.).

ERICE, VICTOR
Writer, Director. b. San Sebastian, Spain, June 30, 1940.
PICTURES: En la terraza, Paginas de un diario perdido, Los dias perdidos, Entre Vias, Los Desafios, The Spirit of the Beehive, Obscure August Dreams (sp. only), El Proximo otono (s.p. only), The South, The Dream of Light, Ten Minutes Older: The Trumpet.

ERICSON, JOHN
Actor. b. Detroit, MI, Sept. 25, 1926. e. American Acad. of Dramatic Arts. Appeared in stock; then Stalag 17 on Broadway.
PICTURES: Teresa (debut, 1951), Rhapsody, The Student Prince, Green Fire, Bad Day at Black Rock, The Return of Jack Slade, The Cruel Tower, Oregon Passage, Forty Guns, Day of the Bad Man, Pretty Boy Floyd, Under Ten Flags, Slave Queen of Babylon, 7 Faces of Dr. Lao, Operation Atlantis, The Money Jungle, The Destructors, Treasure of Pancho Villa, The Bamboo Saucer (Collision Course), Heads or Tails, Bedknobs and Broomsticks, Hustle Squad, Crash, Final Mission, Alien Zone, Project Saucer, Golden Triangle, Queens Are Wild, Hustler Squad, $10,000 Caper, Primary Target.
TELEVISION: *Series:* Honey West, General Hospital. *Movies:* The Bounty Man, Hog Wild, Hunter's Moon, House on the Rue Riviera, Tenafly. *Mini-Series:* Robert Kennedy and His Times, Space. *Specials:* Saturday's Children, Heritage of Anger, The Innocent Sleep. *Guest:* Marcus Welby, Mannix, Streets of San Francisco, Fantasy Island, Bonanza, Medical Center, Route 66, Murder She Wrote, Police Story, General Hospital, Air Wolf, Gunsmoke, Police Woman, The FBI, One Day at a Time, Magnum P.I.

ERMAN, JOHN
Director. b. Chicago, IL, Aug. 3, 1935. e. U. of California. Debut as TV director, Stoney Burke, 1962.
PICTURES: Making It, Ace Eli and Rodger of the Skies, Stella.
TELEVISION: *Movies:* Letters From Three Lovers, Green Eyes, Alexander the Other Side of Dawn, Just Me and You, My Old Man, Moviola (This Year's Blonde; Scarlett O'Hara War; The Silent Lovers), The Letter, Eleanor: First Lady of the World, Who Will Love My Children? (Emmy Award, 1983), Another Woman's Child, A Streetcar Named Desire, Right to Kill?, The Atlanta Child Murders, An Early Frost, The Two Mrs. Grenvilles (also sprv. prod.), When the Time Comes, The Attic: The Hiding of Anne Frank (also prod.), David (also sprv. prod.), The Last Best Year (also sprv. prod.), The Last to Go (also prod.), Our Sons, Carolina Skeletons, Breathing Lessons (also prod.), The Sunshine Boys (also prod.). *Mini-Series:* Roots: The Next Generations (co-dir.), Queen (also co-prod.), Scarlett (also prod.), The Boys Next Door (also prod.), Ellen Foster, (also prod.), Only Love, Too Rich: The Secret Life of Doris Duke (also prod.), Victoria & Albert.

ESBIN, JERRY
Executive. b. Brooklyn, NY, 1931. Started in mailroom at Columbia at 17 and worked for co. nearly 25 years. Then joined American Multi Cinema. Joined Paramount Pictures in 1975 as mgr. of branch operations; later named v.p., asst. sls. mgr. In 1980 named v.p., gen. sls. mgr. 1981, sr. v.p., domestic sls. & mktg. 1981, joined United Artists as sr. v.p., mktg. & dist.; 1982, named pres., MGM/UA m.p. dist. & mktg. div; 1983, sr. v.p., domestic dist., Tri-Star Pictures; 1985, promoted to exec. v.p.; 1989, joined Loews Theaters as sr. exec. v.p. and chief oper. offi-cer, also in 1989 named pres. as well as chief operating officer, Loews Theater Management Corp. Consultant for Conehco Pictures 1991 to 1992. Consultant for American Multi Cinema 1993 to present.

ESMOND, CARL
Actor. b. Vienna, Austria, June 14, 1906. e. U. of Vienna. On stage Vienna, Berlin, London (Shakespeare, Shaw, German modern classics). Acted in many European films under the name Willy Eichberger. Originated part of Prince Albert in Victoria Regina (London). On screen in Brit. prod. incl. Blossom Time, Even Song, Invitation to the Waltz. To U.S. in 1938. Guest star on many live and filmed TV shows. U.S. stage incl. The Woman I Love, Four Winds. Appeared in Oscar nom. docum. Resisting Enemy Interrogation.
PICTURES: Dawn Patrol, First Comes Courage, Little Men, Sergeant York, Panama Hattie, Seven Sweethearts, Address Unknown, Margin for Error, Master Race, Ministry of Fear, Experiment Perilous, Story of Dr. Wassell, The Catman of Paris, Smash-up, Story of a Woman, Casablanca, Climax, Slave Girl, Walk a Crooked Mile, The Navy Comes Through, Sundown, Lover Come Back, This Love of Ours, Without Love, Mystery Submarine, The Desert Hawk, The World in His Arms, Thunder in the Sun, From the Earth to the Moon, Brushfire, Kiss of Evil, Agent for H.A.R.M., Morituri.
TELEVISION: My Wicked Wicked Ways. *Guest:* The Man From Uncle, Lassie, The Big Valley, Treasury Agent, etc.

ESPOSITO, GIANCARLO
Actor. b. Copenhagen, Denmark, April 26, 1958. Made B'way debut as child in 1968 musical Maggie Flynn.
THEATRE: *B'way:* Maggie Flynn, The Me Nobody Knows, Lost in the Stars, Seesaw, Merrily We Roll Along, Don't Get God Started, Sacrilege. *Off-B'way:* Zooman and the Sign (Theatre World Award, Obie Award), Keyboard, Who Loves the Dancer, House of Ramon Iglesias, Do Lord Remember Me, Balm in Gilead, Anchorman, Distant Fires, Trafficking in Broken Hearts.
PICTURES: Running, Taps, Trading Places, The Cotton Club, Desperately Seeking Susan, Maximum Overdrive, Sweet Lorraine, School Daze, Do the Right Thing, Mo'Better Blues, King of New York, Harley Davidson and the Marlboro Man, Night on Earth, Bob Roberts, Malcolm X, Amos & Andrew, Fresh, Smoke, The Keeper (co-producer only), The Usual Suspects, Kla$h, Blue in the Face, The Keeper, Reckless, Loose Women, Nothing to Lose, The Maze, The People, Trouble on the Corner, Twilight, Phoenix, Stardust, Where's Marlowe?, Big City Blues, Speak

Truth to Power, Josephine, Cadillac Tramps, Monkeybone, Pinero, Ali, Blind Horizon, Ash Tuesday.
TELEVISION: *Series*: Bakersfield P.D, Girls Club. *Movies*: The Gentleman Bandit, Go Tell It on the Mountain, Relentless: Mind of a Killer, The Tomorrow Man, Five Desperate Hours, Thirst, Naked City: Justice With a Bullet, Homicide: The Movie. *Special*: Roanok. *Guest*: Miami Vice, Spencer: For Hire, Legwork, NYPD Blue, Nash Bridges, Living Single, Chicago Hope.

ESSEX, DAVID
Actor, Singer, Composer. b. Plaistow, London, England, July 23, 1947. e. Shipman Sch., Custom House. Started as a singer-drummer in East London band. 1967: Joined touring Repertory Co. in The Fantasticks, Oh, Kay, etc. 1970: West End debut in Ten Years Hard, 1972: Jesus Christ in Godspell, Che in Evita; Lord Byron in Childe Byron, 1983-84: Fletcher Christian in own musical Mutiny! on album and stage. International recording artist. Variety Club of Great Britain show business personality of 1978. Many gold & silver disc intl. awards. 1989, Royal Variety performance. World concerts since 1974.
PICTURES: Assault, All Coppers Are..., That'll Be the Day, Stardust, Silver Dream Racer (also wrote score), Shogun Mayeda.
TELEVISION: Top of the Pops, Own Specials, The River (also composed music), BBC series. U.S.: Merv Griffin, Johnny Carson, Dinah Shore, American Bandstand, Midnight Special, Grammy Awards, Salute To The Beatles, Don Kirshner's Rock Concert, A.M. America, Phil Everly in Session, Paul Ryan Show, The David Essex Showcase, The River, 10 Years of Heartbeat (tv documentary, as himself.).

ESTEVEZ, EMILIO
Actor, Director, Writer. b. New York, NY, May 12, 1962. Father is actor Martin Sheen; brother is actor Charlie Sheen. Made debut at age 20 in TV movie starring his father, In the Custody of Strangers.
PICTURES: Tex (debut, 1982), The Outsiders, Nightmares, Repo Man, The Breakfast Club, St. Elmo's Fire, That Was Then This is Now (also s.p.), Maximum Overdrive, Wisdom (also dir., s.p.), Stakeout, Young Guns, Men at Work (also dir., s.p.), Young Guns II, Freejack, The Mighty Ducks, National Lampoon's Loaded Weapon 1, Another Stakeout, Judgment Night, D2: The Mighty Ducks, The Jerky Boys (co- exec. prod. only), The War at Home (also dir. and prod.), Mighty Ducks 3, Mission: Impossible, The Bang Bang Club (dir., prod. only), Killer's Head, Rated X, Sand.
TELEVISION: *Movies*: In the Custody of Strangers. Nightbreaker, Dollar for the Dead, Late Last Night.

ESTRADA, ERIK
Actor. r.n. Enrique Estrada. m. actress Peggy Rowe. b. New York, NY, March 16, 1949. Began professional career in Mayor John Lindsay's Cultural Program, performing in public parks. Joined American Musical Dramatic Acad. for training. Feature film debut in The Cross and the Switchblade (1970).
PICTURES: The New Centurions, Airport '75, Midway, Trackdown, Where Is Parsifal?, Lightblast, The Repentant, Hour of the Assassin, The Lost Idol, A Show of Force, Night of the Wilding, Twisted Justice, Caged Fury, Guns, Spirits, Do or Die, The Divine Enforcer, Alien Seed, Night of the Wilding, National Lampoon's Loaded Weapon 1, The Last Riders, Gang Justice, Visions, Tom Sawyer, King Cobra, Olver Twisted, UP Michigan, Van Wilder.
TELEVISION: *Movies*: Fire!, Honeyboy, The Dirty Dozen: The Fatal Mission, She Knows Too Much, Earth Angel, Angel Eyes, Panic in the Skies!, We're No Angels, CHiPs '99. *Series*: CHiPS, Walking After Midnight, The Bold and the Beautiful. *Guest*: Hawaii Five-0, Six Million Dollar Man, Police Woman, Kojak, Medical Center, Hunter, Alfred Hitchcock Presents (1988), Cybill, Family Guy (voice), King of the Hill (voice).

ESZTERHAS, JOE
Writer. b. Hungary, Nov. 23, 1944. Author of novel Charlie Simpson's Apocalypse (nom. National Book Award, 1974), Nark!, and novelization of F.I.S.T.,
PICTURES: F.I.S.T., Flashdance, Jagged Edge, Big Shots, Betrayed, Checking Out, Music Box (also co-exec. prod.), Basic Instinct, Nowhere to Run (co-sp., exec. prod.), Sliver (also co-exec. prod.), Jade (writer, exec. prod.), Hearts of Fire, Original Sin, Showgirls, One Night Stand, Telling Lies in America, Male Pattern Baldness, An Alan Smithee Film: Burn Hollywood Burn (also actor), Jackie Chan: My Story (video documentary).

EVANS, HARRY KENT
Executive. b. Long Beach, CA, July 16, 1935. Intl. representative, UAW, 1960-76. Exec. dir., International Photographers Guild, 1976-90. CEO of the ASC, 1990-94. Exec. VP, Meier Entertainment Group, Vancouver, BC, 1994-96. Exec. VP, Meier Worldwide Intermedia, 1996-.

EVANS, LINDA
Actress. b. Hartford, CT, Nov. 18, 1942. e. Hollywood H.S., L.A. TV commercials led to contract with MGM.
PICTURES: Twilight of Honor (debut, 1963), Those Calloways, Beach Blanket Bingo, The Klansman, Mitchell, Avalanche Express, Tom Horn, Trekkies.
TELEVISION: *Movies*: Nakia, Nowhere to Run, Standing Tall, The Last Frontier, I'll Take Romance, Dynasty: The Reunion, The Stepsister. *Mini-Series*: North & South Book II, Dazzle, Bare Essence, The Gambler Returns: Luck of the Draw, Gambler: The Adventure Continues. *Series*: The Big Valley, Hunter, Dynasty.

EVANS, RAY
Songwriter. b. Salamanca, NY, Feb. 4, 1915. e. Wharton Sch. of U. of Pennsylvania. Musician on cruise ships, radio writer spec. material. Hellzapoppin', Sons o' Fun. Member: exec. bd. Songwriters Guild of America, Dramatists Guild, West Coast advisory bd. ASCAP, bd., Myasthenia Gravis Fdn. CA chap., Songwriters Hall of Fame, Motion Picture Acad. Received star on Hollywood Blvd. Walk of Fame. Songs included on Great Composer Series, by Columbia Records.
SONGS: To Each His Own, Golden Earrings, Buttons and Bows (Acad. Award, 1948), Mona Lisa (Acad. Award, 1950), Whatever Will Be Will Be (Acad. Award, 1956), A Thousand Violins, I'll Always Love You, Dreamsville, Love Song from Houseboat, Tammy, Silver Bells, Dear Heart, Angel, Never Let Me Go, Almost in Your Arms, As I Love You, In the Arms of Love, Wish Me a Rainbow.
PICTURES: The Paleface, Sorrowful Jones, Fancy Pants, My Friend Irma, Aaron Slick From Punkin Crick, Son of the Paleface, My Friend Irma Goes West, The Night of Grizzly, Saddle the Wind, Isn't It Romantic, Capt. Carey U.S.A., Off Limits, Here Come the Girls, Red Garters, Man Who Knew Too Much, Stars Are Singing, Tammy, Houseboat, Blue Angel, A Private's Affair, All Hands on Deck, Dear Heart, The Third Day, What Did You Do in the War Daddy?, This Property Is Condemned, Foxtrot, The Godfather Part III, Hudson Hawk, Go, Pushing Tin, Nurse Betty.
TELEVISION THEMES: Bonanza, Mr. Ed, Mr. Lucky, To Rome With Love.

EVANS, ROBERT
Producer. r.n. Robert J. Shapera. b. New York, NY, June 29, 1930. Son is actor Josh Evans. Radio actor at age 11; went on to appear in more than 300 radio prog. (incl. Let's Pretend, Archie Andrews, The Aldrich Family, Gangbusters) on major networks. Also appeared on early TV. At 20 joined brother, Charles, and Joseph Picone, as partner in women's clothing firm of Evan-Picone, Inc., 1952-67. In 1957 signed by Universal to play Irving Thalberg in Man of a Thousand Faces after recommendation by Norma Shearer, Thalberg's widow. Guest columnist NY Journal American, 1958. Independent prod. at 20th Century-Fox. 1966-76, with Paramount Pictures as head of prod., then exec. v.p. worldwide prod. (supervising Barefoot in the Park, Rosemary's Baby, Barbarella, Goodbye Columbus, Love Story, The Godfather I & II, The Great Gatsby, etc.). Resigned to become indep. prod. again; with exclusive contract with Paramount. *Autobiography*: The Kid Stays in the Picture (1994).
PICTURES: *Actor*: Man of a Thousand Faces, The Sun Also Rises, The Fiend Who Walked the West, The Best of Everything. *Producer*: Chinatown, Marathon Man, Black Sunday, Players, Urban Cowboy, Popeye, The Cotton Club, The Two Jakes, Sliver, Jade, The Phantom, The Saint, The Out of Towners, The Kid Stays in the Picture (documentary, as himself, s.p.), How to Lose a Guy in 10 Days.
TELEVISION: *Actor*: Elizabeth and Essex (1947), Young Widow Brown, The Right to Happiness. *Prod.*: Get High on Yourself.

EVERETT, CHAD
Actor. r.n. Raymond Lee Cramton. b. South Bend, IN, June 11, 1937. e. Wayne State U., Detroit. Signed by William T. Orr, head of TV prod. for Warner Bros. to 7-year contract. Appeared in many TV series as well as films. Next became contract player at MGM (1963-67). Received star on Hollywood Walk of Fame.
PICTURES: Claudelle Inglish (debut, 1961), The Chapman Report, Rome Adventure, Get Yourself a College Girl, The Singing Nun, Made in Paris, Johnny Tiger, The Last Challenge, Return of the Gunfighter, First to Fight, The Impossible Years, Firechasers, Airplane II: The Sequel, Fever Pitch, Jigsaw, Heroes Stand Alone, Official Denial, Psycho, Mulholland Dr., A View From the Top, The Distance
TELEVISION: *Movies*: Intruder, The Love Boat, Police Story, Thunderboat Row, Malibu, The French Atlantic Affair, Mistress in Paradise, Journey to the Unknown, In the Glitter Palace, Hard to Forget. *Mini-Series*: Centennial, McKenna, Star Command, When Time Expires. *Series*: The Dakotas, Medical Center, Hagen, The Rousters, McKenna, Dark Skies, Manhattan AZ. *Guest*: Hawaiian Eye, 77 Sunset Strip, Surfside Six, Lawman, Bronco, The Lieutenant, Redigo, Route 66, Ironside, Hotel, Murder She Wrote, Shades of L.A., Cybil.

EVERETT, RUPERT
Actor. b. Norfolk, England, May 29, 1959. e. Ampleforth Central School for Speech & Drama. Apprenticed with Glasgow's Citizen's Theatre. Originated role of Guy Bennett in Another Country on London stage in 1982 and made feature film debut in screen version in 1984. Author: Are You Working Darling?
PICTURES: Another Country, Real Life, Dance with a Stranger, Duet for One, Chronicle of a Death Foretold, The Right Hand Man, Hearts of Fire, The Gold-Rimmed Glasses, Jigsaw, The Comfort of Strangers, Inside Monkey Zetterland, Ready to Wear (Pret-a-Porter), The Madness of King George, Dunston Checks In, Cemetary Man, My Best Friend's Wedding, Shakespeare in Love, B. Monkey, A Midsummer Night's Dream, Inspector Gadget, An Ideal Husband, The Next Best Thing, Who Shot Victor Fox, South Kensington, The Wild Thornberrys, The Importance of Being Earnest, Unconditional Love, To Kill A King, A Different Loyalty.
TELEVISION: Arthur the King, The Far Pavilions, Princess Daisy, One Night with Robbie Williams, Les Liasons Dangereuses.

EVIGAN, GREG

Actor. b. South Amboy, NJ, Oct. 14, 1953. Appeared on NY stage in Jesus Christ Superstar and Grease.
PICTURES: Stripped to Kill, DeepStar Six, House of the Damned, Mel, The Pawn, Pets, Sweet Revenge, Arizona Summer.
TELEVISION: *Series:* A Year at the Top, B.J. and the Bear, Masquerade, My Two Dads, P.S. I Luv U, TekWar, Melrose Place, Pacific Palisades, Family Rules, Big Sound. *Movies:* B.J. and the Bear (pilot), Private Sessions, The Lady Forgets, Lies Before Kisses, TekWar, TekJustice, TekLab, TekLords, One of Her Own, Deadly Family Secrets, Nobody Lives Forever, Survivor, Murder Among Friends, Spirit, He Sees You When You're Sleeping, Straight from the Heart.. *Guest:* One Day at a Time, Barnaby Jones, Murder She Wrote, New Mike Hammer, Matlock.

F

FABARES, SHELLEY

Actress. r.n. Michele Marie Fabares. b. Los Angeles, CA, Jan. 19, 1944. m. actor Mike Farrell. Earned gold record for 1962 single Johnny Angel.
PICTURES: Never Say Goodbye, Rock Pretty Baby, Marjorie Morningstar, Summer Love, Annette, Ride the Wild Surf, Girl Happy, Hold On!, Spinout, Clambake, A Time to Sing, Hot Pursuit, Love or Money.
TELEVISION: *Movies:* U.M.C., Brian's Song, Two for the Money, Sky Heist, Pleasure Cove, Friendships Secrets & Lies, Donovan's Kid, The Great American Traffic Jam (Gridlock), Memorial Day, Run Till You Fall, Class Cruise, Deadly Relations, The Great Mom Swap, Dream Is a Wish Your Heart Makes: The Annette Funicello Story, A Nightmare Come True, Playing to Win: A Moment of Truth Movie. *Series:* Annie Oakley, The Donna Reed Show, The Little People, The Practice, Mary Hartman Mary Hartman, Forever Fernwood, Highcliffe Manor, One Day at a Time, Coach, Superman (voice). *Guest:* Twilight Zone, Mr. Novak, Love American Style, The Rookies, Marcus Welby, Hello Larry.

FAHEY, JEFF

Actor. b. Olean, NY, Nov. 29, 1956. Family moved to Buffalo when he was 10 years old. Was member of Joffrey Ballet for 3 years. Appeared on B'way in Brigadoon (1980), tour of Oklahoma!, Paris prod. of West Side Story, and London prod. of Orphans.
PICTURES: Silverado (debut, 1985), Psycho III, Riot on 42nd Street, The Serpent of Death, Wrangler, Split Decisions, Backfire, Outback, True Blood, Out of Time, Last of the Finest, Impulse, White Hunter Black Heart, Body Parts, Iron Maze, The Lawnmower Man, Woman of Desire, Freefall, Wyatt Earp, Temptation, Quick, The Sweeper (also asst. prod.), Serpent's Liar, Eye of the Wolf, Darkman III: Die Darkman Die, When Justice Fails, Waiting for the Man, Operation Delta Force, Johnny 2.0, Catherine's Grove, Lethal Tender, The Underground (also co-prod), Small Time, Detour, Spoken in Silence, Revelation, Hijack, Dazzle, The Contract, The Sculptress, Epicenter, Spin Cycle, The Newcomers, Blind Heat, Cold Heart, Close Call, Maniacts, Unspeakable, Outlaw, Inferno, Choosing Matthias, Out There, Fallen Angels, Darkhunters, The Reckoning, Day of Redemption. *Producer:* Avenue A.
TELEVISION: *Series:* One Life to Live, The Marshal. *Movies:* Execution of Raymond Graham, Parker Kane, Curiosity Kills, Iran: Days of Crisis, Sketch Artist, In the Company of Darkness, The Hit List, Blindsided, Baree, Sketch Artist II: Hands That See, Virtual Seduction, Every Woman's Dream, On the Line, Wolf Lake.

FAIMAN, PETER

Director. b. Australia. Entered entertainment business through TV, involved early in production-direction of major variety series in Australia. Assoc. prod.-dir. of over 20 programs for The Paul Hogan Show and two Hogan specials filmed in England (1983). Developed Australia's most popular and longest-running national variety program, The Don Lane Show. Responsible for creative development of the TV Week Logie Awards on the Nine Network. For 4 years headed Special Projects Division of the Nine Network Australia. Resigned to establish own prod. co., Peter Faiman Prods. Pty Ltd. 1984. Made m.p. theatrical film debut as director of Crocodile Dundee, followed by Dutch. Also prod., Ferngully: The Last Rainforest and co-exec. prod. tv series Adventure Crazy.

FAIRCHILD, MORGAN

Actress. b. Dallas, TX, Feb. 3, 1950. e. Southern Methodist U.
PICTURES: Bullet for Pretty Boy, The Seduction, Pee-wee's Big Adventure, Red-Headed Stranger, Campus Man, Sleeping Beauty, Midnight Cop, Deadly Illusion, Phantom of the Mall, Body Chemistry 3: Point of Seduction, Freaked, Virgin Hunters, Naked Gun 33 1/3: The Final Insult, Gospa, Venus Rising, Criminal Hearts, Holy Man, Nice Guys Sleep Alone, Held For Ransom, Unshackled, Peril, Call O' The Glen, Jungle Juice, Teddy Bear's Picnic, Arizona Summer.
TELEVISION: *Series:* Search for Tomorrow, Flamingo Road, Paper Dolls, Falcon Crest, Roseanne, The City. *Movies:* The Initiation of Sarah, Murder in Music City, Concrete Cowboys, The Memory of Eva Ryker, Flamingo Road (pilot), The Dream Merchants, The Girl the Gold Watch and Dynamite, Honeyboy, The Zany Adventures of Robin Hood, Time Bomb, Street of Dreams, The Haunting of Sarah Harding, How to Murder a

Millionare, Menu for Murder, Writer's Block. Perry Mason: The Case of the Skin-Deep Scandal, Based on an Untrue Story, Dead Man's Island, Star Command, Into the Arms of Danger, Teenager Confidential, I Was a Teenage Faust. *Mini-Series:* 79 Park Avenue, North and South Book II.

FALK, PETER

Actor. b. New York, NY, Sept. 16, 1927. e. New Sch. for Social Research, B.A., 1951; Syracuse U. M.F.A. Studied with Eva Le Galliene and Sanford Meisner. Worked as efficiency expert for Budget Bureau State of CT.
THEATRE: *Off-B'way:* Don Juan (debut, 1956), The Iceman Cometh, Comic Strip, Purple Dust, Bonds of Interest, The Lady's Not for Burning, Diary of a Scoundrel. *On Broadway:* Saint Joan, The Passion of Josef D., The Prisoner of Second Avenue. *Regional:* Light Up the Sky (L.A.), Glengarry Glen Ross (tour).
PICTURES: Wind Across the Everglades (debut, 1958), The Bloody Brood, Pretty Boy Floyd, The Secret of the Purple Reef, Murder Inc. (Acad. Award nom.), Pocketful of Miracles (Acad. Award nom.), Pressure Point, The Balcony, It's a Mad Mad Mad Mad World, Robin and the 7 Hoods, Italiano Brava Gente (Attack and Retreat), The Great Race, Penelope, Luv, Anzio, Castle Keep, Machine Gun McCann, Operation Snafu, Husbands, A Woman Under the Influence, Murder by Death, Mikey and Nicky, The Cheap Detective, The Brink's Job, Opening Night, The In-Laws, The Great Muppet Caper, All the Marbles, Big Trouble, Happy New Year, The Princess Bride, Wings of Desire, Vibes, Cookie, In the Spirit, Tune in Tomorrow, The Player, Faraway So Close!, Roommates, Cops and Robbers, Anything For John, Enemies of Laughter, Lakeboat, 3 Days of Rain, Hubert's Brain, Made, Corky Romano, Undisputed.
TELEVISION: *Movies:* Prescription: Murder, A Step Out of Line, Ransom for a Dead Man, Griffin and Phoenix: A Love Story, Columbo Goes to College, Caution: Murder Can Be Hazardous to Your Health, Columbo and the Murder of a Rock Star, Death Hits the Jackpot, Columbo: No Time to Die, Columbo: A Bird in the Hand (also exec. prod.), Columbo: It's All in the Game (also writer, exec. prod.), Columbo: Butterfly in Shades of Grey (also exec. prod.), Columbo: Undercover, Columbo: Strange Bedfellows (also exec. prod.), Pronto, Columbo: A Trace of Murder, Columbo: Ashes to Ashes, Vig, Columbo: Murder with Too Many Notes, A Storm in Summer, From Where I Sit, A Town Without Christmas, The Lost Word, Columbo: The Man Who Murdered Himself, Columbo: Columbo Likes the Nightlife, John Christmas. *Specials:* The Sacco-Vanzetti Story, The Million Dollar Incident, Brigadoon, A Hatful of Rain, Clue: Movies Murder and Mystery. *Series:* The Trials of O'Brien, Columbo (1971-77; Emmy Awards: 1972, 1975, 1976), Columbo (1989, also co-exec. prod.; Emmy Award, 1990). *Guest:* Studio One, Kraft Theatre, Alcoa Theatre, N.T.A. Play of the Week, Armstrong Circle Theatre, Omnibus, Robert Montgomery Presents, Brenner, Deadline, Kraft Mystery Theatre, Rendezvous, Sunday Showcase, The Untouchables, Dick Powell Show (The Price of Tomatoes; Emmy Award, 1962), Danny Kaye Show, Edie Adams Show, Bob Hope Chrysler Theatre.

FANGMEIER, STEFEN

Special Visual Effects.
PICTURES: Terminator 2: Judgment Day (comp. graph. super.), Hook (comp. graph. super.), Jurassic Park (lead comp. graph. super.), Casper (dig. char. co-super). *Visual Effects Supervisor:* Twister (Acad. Award nom.), The Trigger Effect, Speed 2: Cruise Control, Small Soldiers, Saving Private Ryan, Galaxy Quest (co-super.), Aizea: City of the Wind, The Perfect Storm (Acad. Award nom.), Signs, The Bourne Identity, Dreamcatcher, Master and Commander: The Far Side of the World.

FARBER, BART

Executive. Joined United Artists Corp. in early 1960s when UA acquired ZIV TV Programs. Served as v.p. United Artists Television and United Artists Broadcasting. 1971 named v.p. in charge of legal affairs of the cos. 1978, named sr. v.p.—TV, video and special markets; indep. consultant, TV, Pay TV, home video. 1982, joined Cable Health Network as v.p., legal & business affairs; 1984, v.p., business & legal affairs, Lifetime Network; 1986, independent communications consultant.

FARENTINO, JAMES

Actor. b. Brooklyn, NY, Feb. 24, 1938. e. American Acad. of Dramatic Arts.
THEATRE: *B'way:* Death of a Salesman, A Streetcar Named Desire (revival, 1973; Theatre World Award). *Off-B'way:* The Days and Nights of Bebe Fenstermaker, In the Summerhouse. *Regional:* One Flew Over the Cuckoo's Nest (Jos. Jefferson, Chas. MacArthur & Chicago Drama Critics League Awards), California Suite, The Best Man, The Big Knife, Good-Bye Charlie, A Thousand Clowns, Love Letters.
PICTURES: Psychomania (Violent Midnight), Engine Pulver, The War Lord, The Pad... And How to Use It (Golden Globe Award, 1966), The Ride to Hangman's Tree, Banning, Rosie!, Me Natalie, The Story of a Woman, The Final Countdown, Dead and Buried, Her Alibi, Bulletproof, Termination Man, Radio Silence, The Last Producer.
TELEVISION: *Movies:* Wings of Fire, The Whole World is Watching, The Sound of Anger, Longest Night, Family Rico, Cool Million, The Elevator, Crossfire, Possessed, Silent Victory: Undercover Cop, The Kitty O'Neil Story, Son Rise: A Miracle of Love, That Secret Sunday, Something So Right (Emmy nom.), The Cradle Will Fall, License to Kill, A Summer to Remember, That Secret Sunday, Family Sins, Naked Lies, The Red Spider,

Who Gets the Friends?, Picking Up the Pieces, In the Line of Duty: A Cop for the Killing, Miles From Nowhere, When No One Would Listen, One Woman's Courage, Honor Thy Father and Mother: The True Story of the Menendez Murders. *Pilot*: American Nuclear. *Series*: The Lawyers (The Bold Ones), Cool Million, Dynasty, Blue Thunder, Mary Tyler Moore, Julie Andrews Show. *Guest*: Naked City, daytime soap operas, Laredo, Route 66, The Alfred Hitchcock Hour, Ben Casey, Twelve O'Clock High, Melrose Place, ER. *Special*: DOS Pasos USA. *Mini-Series*: Sins, Jesus of Nazareth (Emmy nom.), Dazzled, On Common Ground, Death of a Salesman, Vanished, Evita Peron.

FARGAS, ANTONIO
Actor. b. Bronx, NY, Aug. 14, 1946. Studied acting at Negro Ensemble Co. and Actor's Studio.
THEATRE: The Great White Hope, The Glass Menagerie, Mod Hamlet, Romeo and Juliet, The Slave, Toilet, The Amen Corner.
PICTURES: The Cool World (debut, 1964), Putney Swope, Pound, Believe in Me, Shaft, Cisco Pike, Across 110th Street, Cleopatra Jones, Busting, Foxy Brown, Conrack, The Gambler, Cornbread Earl and Me, Next Stop Greenwich Village, Car Wash, Pretty Baby, Up the Academy, Firestarter, Streetwalkin', Night of the Sharks, Shakedown, I'm Gonna Git You Sucka, The Borrower, Howling VI: The Freaks, The Celluloid Closet, Don't Be a Menace to South Central While Drinking Your Juice in the Hood, Gator King, Milo, The Suburbans, Unconditional Love, Three Strikes, The Riff, Osomosis Jones (voice), Extreme Honor.
TELEVISION: *Movies*: Starsky and Hutch (pilot), Huckleberry Finn, Escape, Nurse, The Ambush Murders, A Good Sport, Florida Straits, Maid for Each Other, Percy and Thunder, Soul Survivors, Ali: An American Hero. *Series*: Starsky and Hutch, All My Children. *Guest*: The Bill Cosby Show, Sanford and Son, Police Story, Kolchak The Night Stalker, Miami Vice, Kojak.

FARGO, JAMES
Director. b. Republic, WA, Aug. 14, 1938. e. U. of Washington, B.A.
PICTURES: The Enforcer, Caravans, Every Which Way But Loose, A Game for Vultures, Forced Vengeance, Born to Race, Voyage of the Rock Aliens, Riding the Edge (also actor), Second Chances, Destiny.
TELEVISION: *Movies*: Gus Brown and Midnight Brewster, The Last Electric Knight, Hunter, Snoops, Sky High. *Series*: Tales of the Gold Monkey, Sidekicks.

FARINA, DENNIS
Actor. b. Chicago, IL, Feb. 29, 1944. Served 18 years with Chicago police before being introduced to producer-director Michael Mann who cast him in film Thief. Celebrity Chmn. of Natl. Law Enforcement Officers Memorial in Washington, D.C.
THEATER: A Prayer for My Daughter, Streamers, Tracers, Bleacher Bums, Some Men Need Help, The Time of Your Life.
PICTURES: Thief (debut, 1981), Jo Jo Dancer Your Life Is Calling, Manhunter, Midnight Run, Men of Respect, We're Talkin' Serious Money, Mac, Another Stakeout, Striking Distance, Romeo Is Bleeding, Little Big League, Get Shorty, Eddie, That Old Feeling, Out of Sight, Saving Private Ryan, The Mod Squad, Snatch, Sidewalks of New York, Big Trouble, The Promise, Planet of the Pitts, Stealing Harvard, Poker Night.
TELEVISION: *Series*: Crime Story, Buddy Faro (also co-exec. prod.) In-Laws. *Mini-Series*: Drug Wars: Columbia. *Movies*: Six Against the Rock, Open Admissions, The Hillside Stranglers, People Like Us, Blind Faith, Cruel Doubt, The Disappearance of Nora, One Woman's Courage, The Corpse Had a Familiar Face, Bonanza: Under Attack, Out of Annie's Past, Bella Mafia. *Guest*: Miami Vice, Hunter, Tales from the Crypt. *Special*: The Killing Floor.

FARR, FELICIA
Actress. b. Westchester, NY, Oct. 4, 1932. e. Pennsylvania State Coll. m. Jack Lemmon. Stage debut: Picnic (Players Ring Theatre). In Memorandum for a Spy, 1965 tv movie.
PICTURES: Timetable, Jubal, Reprisal!, The First Texan, The Last Wagon, 3:10 to Yuma, Onionhead, Hell Bent for Leather, Kiss Me Stupid, The Venetian Affair, Kotch, Charley Varrick, That's Life!, The Player.

FARR, JAMIE
Actor. r.n. Jameel Joseph Farah. b. Toledo, OH, July 1, 1934. e. Columbia Coll. Trained for stage at Pasadena Playhouse.
PICTURES: Blackboard Jungle (debut, 1955), The Greatest Story Ever Told, Ride Beyond Vengeance, Who's Minding the Mint?, With Six You Get Eggroll, The Gong Show Movie, Cannonball Run, Cannonball Run II, Happy Hour, Scrooged, Speed Zone!, Curse II: The Bite, Fearless Tiger, You Snooze You Lose, A Month of Sundays.
TELEVISION: *Movies*: The Blue Knight, Amateur Night at the Dixie Bar and Grill, Murder Can Hurt You!, Return of the Rebels, For Love or Money, Run Till You Fall. *Series*: The Chicago Teddy Bears, M*A*S*H (also dir. episodes), The Gong Show (panelist), The $1.98 Beauty Show (panelist), After M*A*S*H (also dir. episodes), Port Charles. *Guest*: Dear Phoebe, The Red Skelton Show, The Dick Van Dyke Show, The Danny Kaye Show, The Love Boat, The New Love American Style, Murder She Wrote.

FARRELL, HENRY
Writer. Author of novels and screenplays
PICTURES: Whatever Happened to Baby Jane? Hush ... Hush Sweet Charlotte, What's the Matter with Helen?, A Gorgeous Bird Like Me.

TELEVISION: *Movies*: How Awful About Allan, The House That Would Not Die, The Eyes of Charles Sand, Whatever Happened to Baby Jane?.

FARRELL, MIKE
Actor, Producer. b. St. Paul, MN, Feb. 6, 1939. m. actress Shelley Fabares. Currently co-chair of Human Rights Watch in CA.; pres. of Death Penalty Focus; member of the adv. bd. of the Natl Coalition to Abolish the Death Penalty; member of the adv. bd. of the Cult Awareness Network; founding bd. member of Peace Studies, ATV, at Augusta Correctional Ctr in Virginia.
PICTURES: Captain Newman M.D., The Americanization of Emily, The Graduate, Targets, The Killers Within, 187: Documented. *Prod.*: Dominick and Eugene, Patch Adams (prod. only).
TELEVISION: *Movies*: The Longest Night, She Cried Murder!, The Questor Tapes, Live Again Die Again, McNaughton's Daughter, Battered, Sex and the Single Parent, Letters from Frank, Damien: The Leper Priest, Prime Suspect, Memorial Day (also prod.), Choices of the Heart, Private Sessions, Vanishing Act, A Deadly Silence, Price of the Bride, Incident at Dark River (also prod.), The Whereabouts of Jenny, Silent Motive (also prod.), Hart Attack, The Enemy Inside, Vows of Seduction, Twisted Path, Hart to Hart: Old Friends Never Die, Superman, Sins of the Mind, The '70s: The Decade that Changed Television (host), The Crooked E: The Unshredded Truth About Enron. *Director*: Run Till You Fall. *Guest*: The Monroes. *Series*: Days of Our Lives, The Interns, The Man and the City, M*A*S*H, Providence. *Specials*: JFK: One Man Show (PBS), The Best of Natl. Geographic Specials (host/narrator), Saving the Wildlife (co-host).

FARRELLY, BOBBY
Writer, Director. b. Cumberland, RI, 1958. Collaborates with brother Peter.
PICTURES: Dumb & Dumber (also prod.), Bushwhacked (co-s.p. only), There's Something About Mary (also co-exec. prod.), Outside Providence (s.p., co-prod. only), Me Myself and Irene (also co-prod.), Osmosis Jones (also prod.), Say It Isn't So (prod. only), Shallow Hal, The Ringer (exec prod.), Dumb & Dumberer: When Harry Met Lloyd (writer/characters), Stuck on You (prod., writer, dir).
TELEVISION: Series: Ozzy & Drix (exec. prod.).

FARRELLY, PETER
Director, Writer, Producer. b. Cumberland, RI, 1957. Collaborates with brother Bobby.
PICTURES: Dumb & Dumber, Bushwhacked (co-s.p. only), Kingpin (dir. only), There's Something About Mary (also co-exec. prod.), Outside Providence (novel, co-prod. only), Me Myself and I (also co-prod.), Say It Isn't So (prod. only), Osmosis Jones (also prod.), Shallow Hal, The Ringer (exec. prod), Dumb & Dumberer: When Harry Met Lloyd (writer/characters), Stuck on You (prod., writer, dir).
TELEVISION: Series: Ozzy & Drix (exec. prod.).

FARROW, MIA
Actress. b. Los Angeles, CA, Feb. 9. 1945. r.n. Maria de Lourdes Villiers Farrow. d. of actress Maureen O'Sullivan and late dir. John Farrow. e. Marymount, Los Angeles, Cygnet House, London.
THEATRE: The Importance of Being Earnest (debut, Madison Ave. Playhouse, NY, 1963); Royal Shakespeare Co. (Twelfth Night, A Midsummer Night's Dream, Ivanov, Three Sisters, The Seagull, A Doll's House), Mary Rose (London), Romantic Comedy (B'way debut, 1979).
PICTURES: Guns at Batasi (debut, 1964), A Dandy in Aspic, Rosemary's Baby, Secret Ceremony, John and Mary, See No Evil, The Public Eye, Dr. Popaul (High Heels), The Great Gatsby, Full Circle (The Haunting of Julia), Avalanche, A Wedding, Death on the Nile, Hurricane, A Midsummer Night's Sex Comedy, The Last Unicorn (voice), Zelig, Broadway Danny Rose, Supergirl, The Purple Rose of Cairo, Hannah and Her Sisters, Radio Days, September, Another Woman, New York Stories (Oedipus Wrecks), Crimes and Misde-meanors, Alice (Natl. Board of Review Award, 1990), Shadows and Fog, Husbands and Wives, Widow's Peak, Miami Rhapsody, Reckless, Redux Riding Hood (voice), Private Parts, Coming Soon, Purpose.
TELEVISION: *Series*: Peyton Place. *Specials*: Johnny Belinda, Peter Pan. *Movies*: Goodbye Raggedy Ann, Miracle at Midnight, The Secret Life of Zoey. *Mini-Series*: A Girl Thing.

FAWCETT, FARRAH
Actress. b. Corpus Christi, TX, Feb. 2, 1947. e. U. of Texas. Picked as one of the ten most beautiful girls while a freshman; went to Hollywood and signed by Screen Gems. Did films, TV shows, and made over 100 TV commercials. Off B'way debut: Extremities (1983).
PICTURES: Love Is a Funny Thing, Myra Breckinridge, Logan's Run, Somebody Killed Her Husband, Sunburn, Saturn 3, Cannonball Run, Extremities, See You in the Morning, Man of the House, The Apostle, Dr. T & the Women, The Flunky.
TELEVISION: *Movies*: Three's a Crowd, The Feminist and the Fuzz, The Great American Beauty Contest, The Girl Who Came Gift-Wrapped, Murder on Flight 502, Murder in Texas, The Burning Bed, Red Light Sting, Between Two Women, Nazi Hunter: The Beate Klarsfeld Story, Poor Little Rich Girl: The Barbara Hutton Story, Margaret Bourke-White, Small Sacrifices, Criminal Behavior, The Substitute Wife, Children of the Dust, Dalva, Silk Hope, Baby, Jewel. *Series*: Charlie's Angels, Good

Sports. *Guest:* Owen Marshall Counselor at Law, The Six Million Dollar Man, Rockford Files, Harry-O, Spin City.

FAVREAU, JON
Actor, Writer, Director. b. Queens, NY, October 19, 1966. Alumnus of Chicago's Improv Olympia improvisational acting troupe.
PICTURES: Folks!, Rudy, Mrs. Parker and the Vicious Circle, PCU, Batman Forever, Notes from Underground, Swingers (also s.p.), Just Your Luck, Persons Unknown, Dogtown, Deep Impact, Very Bad Things, Love & Sex, The Replacements, Made (also dir., s.p., prod.), The First $20 Million (s.p. only), Daredevil, Elf (dir., s.p. only), The Big Empty (also exec. prod.).
TELEVISION: *Movies:* Grandpa's Funeral, Smog (s.p. and dir.), Rocky Marciano, Life on Parole (dir. only). *Guest:* Seinfeld, Chicago Hope, Friends, Dilbert (voice), The Larry Sanders Show, The Sopranos. *Series:* Dinner for Five.

FEINSTEIN, ALAN
Actor. b. New York, NY, Sept. 8, 1941.
THEATRE: *NY:* Malcolm, Zelda, A View from the Bridge (NY Drama Desk Award), As Is, A Streetcar Named Desire.
PICTURE: Looking for Mr. Goodbar.
TELEVISION: *Movies:* Alexander: The Other Side of Dawn, Visions, The Hunted Lady, The Users, The Two Worlds of Jenny Logan, On Fire, Parallel Lives. *Mini-Series:* Masada. *Series:* Edge of Night, Love Of Life, Search for Tomorrow, Jigsaw John, The Runaways, The Family Tree, Berrenger's, General Hospital, Falcon Crest, Santa Barbara.

FEITSHANS, BUZZ
Executive. b. Los Angeles, CA. e. USC. Started in film business as editor. Worked for 10 years at American-International as supvr. of prod. In 1975 formed A-Team Productions with John Milius. With Carolco Pictures: producer, 1981-6; exec. v.p. for mo. pic. production, member bd. dir. 1986-90. 1990-, v.p. for Cinergi Prods.; 1994, pres. of Cinergi.
PICTURES: *Producer:* Dillinger, Act of Vengeance, Foxy Brown, Big Wednesday, Hardcore, 1941, Extreme Prejudice (exec. prod.), Conan the Barbarian, First Blood, Uncommon Valor, Rambo II, Red Dawn, Rambo III, Total Recall, Tombstone (exec. prod.), Color of Night, Shadow Conspiracy (exec. prod.), We Get to Win This Time (video short, himself), Afghanistan: Land in Crisis (documentary short, himself), Joe Killionaire (cinematographer).

FELDMAN, COREY
Actor. b. Reseda, CA, July 16, 1971. Performing since the age of 3 in commercials, television (Love Boat, Father Murphy, Foul Play, Mork and Mindy, Eight Is Enough, Alice, Gloria) and films.
PICTURES: Time After Time, The Fox and the Hound (voice), Friday the 13th—The Final Chapter, Gremlins, Friday the 13th—A New Beginning, The Goonies, Stand by Me, Lost Boys, License to Drive, The 'burbs, Dream a Little Dream, Teenage Mutant Ninja Turtles (voice only), Rock 'n' Roll High School Forever, Edge of Honor, Meatballs 4, Round Trip to Heaven, Stepmonster, Blown Away, National Lampoon's Loaded Weapon 1, Lipstick Camera, National Lampoon's Last Resort, Maverick, Dream a Little Dream 2, A Dangerous Place, Evil Obsession, Tales From the Crypt: Bordello of Blood, Mr. Atlas, Born Bad, The Thief and the Stripper, She's Too Tall (assoc. prod.), The Million Dollar Kid, Citizen Toxie: The Toxic Avenger Part 4, My Life as a Troll, Seance, The Mayor of Sunset Strip, Dickie Roberts: Former Child Star (as himself), Cursed (himself).
TELEVISION: *Movies:* Willa, Father Figure, Kid with a Broken Halo, Still the Beaver, Out of the Blue, When the Whistle Blows, I'm a Big Girl Now, Exile, Legion. *Specials:* 15 & Getting Straight, How to Eat Like a Child. *Series:* The Bad News Bears, Madame's Place, Dweebs.

FELDMAN, EDWARD S.
Producer. b. New York, NY, Sept. 5, 1929. e. Michigan State U. Trade press contact, newspaper and mag. contact, 20th Century Fox, 1950; dir. info. services, Dover Air Force Base. 1954-56; publ. coordinator, The World of Suzie Wong, 1960; joined Embassy, dir. of publicity, 1969; v.p. in chg., adv. & pub, 7 Arts Prods., 1962; v.p. exec. asst. to head prod. Warner-7 Arts Studio 1967; pres., m.p. dept., Filmways, 1970; Formed Edward S. Feldman Co., 1978.
PICTURES: *Prod./exec. prod.:* What's the Matter With Helen?, Fuzz, Save the Tiger, The Other Side of the Mountain, Two-Minute Warning, The Other Side of the Mountain Part 2, The Last Married Couple in America, Six Pack, The Sender, Hot Dog ... The Movie! (co-prod.), Witness, Explorers, The Golden Child, The Hitcher, Near Dark, Wired, Green Card, The Doctor, Honey I Blew Up the Kid, Forever Young, My Father the Hero, The Jungle Book, The Truman Show, 101 Dalmations, 102 Dalmations, K-19: The Widowmaker, The Hitcher-How Do These Movies Get Made?
TELEVISION: *Exec. Prod.:* Moon of the Wolf, My Father's House, Valentine, 300 Miles for Stephanie, Charles and Diana: A Royal Love Story, 21 Hours at Munich, King, Not in Front of the Children, Obsessed with a Married Woman.

FELDON, BARBARA
Actress. b. Pittsburgh, PA, Mar. 12, 1941. e. Carnegie Tech. Former fashion model; also appeared in many commercials. On NY stage in Past Tense, Cut the Ribbons, The Last Request.
PICTURES: Fitzwilly, Smile, No Deposit No Return, The Last Request.

TELEVISION: *Movies:* Getting Away From It All, Playmates, What Are Best Friends For?, Let's Switch, A Guide for the Married Woman, Sooner or Later, A Vacation in Hell, Before and After, Children of Divorce, Get Smart Again! Secrets. *Series:* Get Smart, The Marty Feldman Comedy Machine, The Dean Martin Comedy Hour (host), Special Edition (host), The 80's Woman (synd.; host), Dinosaurs (voice), Get Smart (1995).

FELDSHUH, TOVAH
Actress. b. New York, NY, Dec. 27, 1953. e. Sarah Lawrence Col., Univ. of MN. For humanitarian work received the Israel Peace Medal and the Eleanor Roosevelt Humanitarian Award.
THEATRE: *NY:* Cyrano, Straws in the Wind, Three Sisters, Rodgers and Hart, Yentl (Theatre World Award), Sarava, The Mistress of the Inn, Springtime for Henry, She Stoops to Conquer, Lend Me a Tenor, A Fierce Attachment, Sarah and Abraham, Six Wives, Hello Muddah! Hello Fadduh!
PICTURES: White Lies, Nunzio, The Idolmaker, Cheaper to Keep Her, Daniel, Brewster's Millions, The Blue Iguana, A Day in October, Comfortably Numb, Hudson River Blues, Montana, Charlie Hoboken, A Walk on the Moon, The Corruptor, Happy Accidents, Friends and Family, The Believer, Kissing Jessica Stein, My Angel Is a Centerfold, The 3 Little Wolfs, Broadway: The Golden Age by the Legends Who Were There, The Tollbooth, Death By Committee.
TELEVISION: *Movies:* Scream Pretty Peggy, The Amazing Howard Hughes, Terror Out of the Sky, The Triangle Factory Fire Scandal, Beggarman Thief, The Women's Room, Citizen Cohn, Sexual Considerations. *Specials:* Dosvedanya Mean Goodbye, Saying Kaddish. *Mini-Series:* Holocaust. *Series:* As the World Turns, Mariah. Guest: LA Law, Law and Order, etc.

FELLMAN, DANIEL R.
Executive. b. Cleveland, OH, March 14, 1943. e. Rider Coll., B.S., 1964. Paramount Pictures, 1964-69; Loews Theatres, 1969-71; Cinema National Theatres, 1971-76; 1976-78, pres. American Theatre Mgmt. Joined Warner Bros. in 1978, named exec. v.p. Warner Bros. domestic distribution, Jan. 1993. Named pres. Warner Bros. theatrical distribution, March 1999. Currently, pres., domestic distribution, of Warner Bros. Pictures. President Variety Club Tent 35, 1977-78. Member exec. comm.; Will Rogers Foundation; Past Chmn, Foundation of Motion Picture Pioneers.

FENADY, ANDREW J.
Producer, Writer. b. Toledo, OH, Oct. 4, 1928. e. U. of Toledo, 1946-50. Radio-prod.-actor-writer. *Novels:* The Man With Bogart's Face, The Secret of Sam Marlow, The Claws of the Eagle, The Summer of Jack London, Mulligan, Runaways.
PICTURES: Stakeout on Dope Street, The Young Captives, Ride Beyond Vengeance, Chisum, Terror in the Wax Museum, Arnold, The Man with Bogart's Face.
TELEVISION: *Movies:* The Woman Hunter, Voyage of the Yes, The Stranger, The Hanged Man, Black Noon, Sky Heist, Mayday 40,000 Ft., The Hostage Heart, Mask of Alexander, Masterpiece of Murder, Who Is Julia?, Jake Spanner—Private Eye, The Love She Sought, Yes Virginia There Is a Santa Claus, The Sea Wolf. *Series:* Confidential File, The Rebel, Branded, Hondo.

FENN, SHERILYN
Actress. b. Detroit, MI, Feb. 1, 1965.
PICTURES: The Wild Life (debut, 1984), Just One of the Guys, Out of Control, Thrashin', The Wraith, Zombie High, Two Moon Junction, Crime Zone, True Blood, Meridian: Kiss of the Beast, Wild at Heart, Backstreet Dreams, Ruby, Desire and Hell at Sunset Motel, Diary of a Hit Man, Of Mice and Men, Three of Hearts, Boxing Helena, Fatal Instinct, The Shadow Men, Lovelife, Johnny Hit and Run Pauline, Just Write, Darkness Falls, Outside Ozona, Cement, The United States of Leland, Swindle, A Man Called Rage, Gin and the Rumble Within.
TELEVISION:*Movies:* Silence of the Heart, Dillinger, Spring Awakening, Liz: The Elizabeth Taylor Story, Slave of Dreams, The Assassination File, The Don's Analyst, Nightmare Street, Off Season, Scent o f Danger, Nightwaves. *Guest:* Cheers, 21 Jump Street, Heart of the City, Friends. *Specials:* Tales From the Hollywood Hills (A Table at Ciro's), Divided We Stand, A Family Again. *Mini-series:* A Season in Purgatory. *Series:* Twin Peaks, Rude Awakening, Dawson's Creek, Birds of Prey.

FERRARA, ABEL
Director, Writer. b. Bronx, NY, July 11, 1952. Moved to Peekskill, NY, as teenager where he made short films with future writer Nicholas St. John. Traveled to England, worked for the BBC. Returned to U.S. to attended SUNY/Purchase, making short Could This Be Love, which received some theatrical distribution. Has used the pseudonym Jimmy Laine.
PICTURES: Driller Killer (also actor, s.p. songs), Ms. 45 (also actor), Fear City, China Girl (also songs), Cat Chaser, King of New York, Bad Lieutenant (also co-s.p.), Dangerous Game, Body Snatchers, The Addiction, The Funeral, The Blackout, New Rose Hotel, 'R Xmas, White Boy (prod.).
TELEVISION: Miami Vice, Crime Story(pilot), Subway Stories: Tales from the Underground.

FERRARO, JOHN E.
Executive. b. Greenwich, CT, July 20, 1958. e. Emerson College, B.S. in Mass Communications, 1980. Joined Paramount Pictures Corp. 1980. 1983-84, story analyst, Paramount TV; 1984-85 supervisor, Drama Development; 1985-87 manager, Current Programs & Special Projects; 1987-88, dir. Drama Development.

1988, exec. dir., Acquisitions, Paramount Pictures; 1990, v.p., acquisitions; 1997, sr. v.p., acquisitions & co-productions.

FERRELL, CONCHATA
Actress. b. Charleston, WV, Mar. 28, 1943. e. Marshall Univ.
THEATRE: NY: The Three Sisters, Hot L Baltimore, Battle of Angels, The Sea Horse (Theatre World, Obie & Vernon Rice Drama Desk Awards), Wine Untouched. LA: Getting Out, Picnic.
PICTURES: Deadly Hero, Network, Heartland, Where the River Runs Black, For Keeps?, Mystic Pizza, Edward Scissorhands, Family Prayers, True Romance, Samuari Cowboy, Heaven and Earth, Freeway, My Fellow Americans, Touch, Modern Vampires, Crime and Punishment in Suburbia, Erin Brockovich, K-PAX, Mr. Deeds.
TELEVISION: Series: Hot L Baltimore, B.J. and the Bear, McClain's Law, ER, Peaceable Kingdom, L A Law, Hearts Afire, Townies, Teen Angel, Push Nevada. Movies: The Girl Called Hatter Fox, A Death in Canaan, Who'll Save My Children?, Before and After, The Seduction of Miss Leona, Reunion, Rape and Marriage: The Rideout Case, Life of the Party: The Story of Beatrice, Emergency Room, Nadia, The Three Wishes of Billy Grier, North Beach and Rawhide, Samaritan: The Mitch Snyder Story, Eye on the Sparrow, Your Mother Wears Combat Boots, Goodbye Miss 4th of July, Opposites Attract, Deadly Intentions... Again?, Backfield in Motion, The Buccaneers, Stranger Inside, Amy & Isabelle. Guest: Good Times, Love Boat, Lou Grant, St. Elsewhere, Frank's Place, Murder She Wrote, Who's the Boss?, Matlock, Buffy the Vampire Slayer. Specials: The Great Gilly Hopkins, Portrait of a White Marriage, Runaway Ralph, Picnic.

FERRER, MEL
Actor, Producer, Director. r.n. Melchor Ferrer. b. Elberon, NJ, Aug. 25, 1917. e. Princeton U. During coll. and early career worked summers at Cape Cod Playhouse, Dennis, MA; then writer in Mexico, authored juvenile book, Tito's Hats; later ed. Stephen Daye Press, VT. Left publishing upon reaching leading-man status at Dennis; on B'way as dancer in You Never Know, Everywhere I Roam, others; also in Kind Lady, Cue For Passion; then to radio, serving apprenticeship in small towns; prod.-dir. for NBC Land of the Free, The Hit Parade, and Hildegarde program. Entered m.p. ind., 1945, when signed by Columbia as dial. dir.; then directed The Girl of the Limberlost; later, returned to Broadway, leading role, Strange Fruit; signed by David Selznick as producer-actor, on loan to John Ford as prod. asst. on The Fugitive; then to Howard Hughes-RKO for Vendetta.
THEATRE: Kind Lady, Cue for Passion, Strange Fruit, Ondine, Gore Vidal's "The Best Man" (L.A., 1987,) Cyrano (director).
PICTURES: Actor: Lost Boundaries (debut, 1949), Born to Be Bad, The Brave Bulls, Rancho Notorious, Scaramouche, Lili, Saadia, Knights of the Round Table, Oh Rosalinda!, Proibito (Forbidden), War and Peace, Paris Does Strange Things, The Sun Also Rises, The Vintage, Fraulein, The World the Flesh and the Devil, L'Homme a Femmes, The Hands of Orlac, Blood and Roses, Legge di Guerra, Devil and the 10 Commandments, The Longest Day, The Fall of the Roman Empire, Paris When It Sizzles (cameo), Sex and the Single Girl, El Greco (also prod.), El Senor de la Salle, The Black Pirate, The Girl From the Red Cabaret, Brannigan, The Tempter (The Antichrist), Death Trap (Eaten Alive), Hi-Riders, Pyjama Girl, Island of the Fish Men, The Norsemen, Yesterday's Tomorrow, The Visitor, The Fifth Floor, Nightmare City, Lili Marleen, Deadly Game, Screamers, Mad Dog Anderson, Eye of the Widow. Director: The Girl of the Limberlost (debut, 1945), The Secret Fury, Vendetta (co-dir.), Green Mansions, Cabriola (Every Day Is a Holiday; also exec. prod., co-s.p.). Producer: Wait Until Dark, The Night Visitor, A Time for Loving, Embassy, W.
TELEVISION: Movies: One Shoe Makes It Murder, Seduced, Outrage, Dream West, Peter the Great, Christine Cromwell, A Thanksgiving Promise (prod.), Catherine the Great, Wild Jack. Special: Mayerling. Series: Behind the Screen, Falcon Crest, Stories From My Childhood.

FERRER, MIGUEL
Actor. b. Santa Monica, CA, Feb. 7, 1954. m. actress Leilani Sarelle. Son of actor Jose Ferrer and singer Rosemary Clooney. Began performing as a drummer. With actor Bill Mumy created comic book The Comet Man.
PICTURES: Heartbreaker (debut, 1983), Lovelines, Star Trek III: The Search for Spock, Flashpoint, Robocop, Deepstar Six, Valentino Returns, Revenge, The Guardian, Twin Peaks: Fire Walk With Me, Point of No Return, Hot Shots! Part Deux, Another Stakeout, It's All True (narrator), The Harvest, Blank Check, Death in Granada, Night Flier, Mr. Magoo, Where's Marlowe?, Mulan (voice), Traffic, Sunshine State.
TELEVISION: Movies: Downpayment on Murder, C.A.T. Squad, Guts & Glory: The Rise and Fall of Oliver North, Murder in High Places, In the Shadow of a Killer, Cruel Doubt, Scam, Royce, Incident at Deception Ridge, Jack Reed: Search for Justice, A Promise Kept: The Oksana Baiul Story, The Return of Hunter, In the Line of Duty: Hunt for Justice, Project: ALF, Justice League of America, Brave New World, L.A. Sherriff's Homicide, Heartland Ghost. Pilot: Badlands 2005. Mini-Series: Drug Wars: The Camarena Story, The Stand, The Shining. Series: Twin Peaks, Broken Badges, On the Air, Lateline, Crossing Jordan. Guest: Miami Vice, Hill Street Blues, Cagney & Lacey, Shannon's Deal, Will & Grace.

FERRETTI, DANTE
Production Designer. b. Macerata, Italy, February 26, 1943.
PICTURES: Medea, The Decameron, The Canterbury Tales, Io on vedo, tu non parli, lui non sente, Lulu the Tool, Bawdy Tales, Slap the Monster on Page One, Arabian Nights, How Long Can You Fall?, Salo, or the 120 Days of Sodom, Somewhere Beyond Love, The Beach Hut, La Presidentessa, Il Mostro, Bye Bye Monkey, Orchestra Rehersal, City of Women, The Skin, Il Minestrone, Tales of Ordinary Madness, That Night in Varennes, And the Ship Sails On, The Adventures of Baron von Munchausen, Ginger and Fred, The Name of the Rose, Hamlet, Dr. M, La traviata, The Age of Innocence, Interview with the Vampire, Casino, Kundun, Meet Joe Black, Bringing Out the Dead, Titus, The Gangs of New York, Cold Mountain.
TELEVISION: La Traviata, Cavelleria rusticana, Un ballo in maschera.

FIEDLER, JOHN
Executive. Launched m.p. career in 1975 working in commercials and industrial and ed. films. Joined Rastar 1980 as v.p., prod. dev. and asst. to Guy McElwaine, pres. & CEO. Joined Paramount as v.p. in prod.; then to Tri-Star Pictures in same post. Resigned to join Columbia Pictures as exec. v.p., worldwide prod., 1984, then pres. of prod. 1986. 1987, left to become ind. prod. 1989 named pres. of prod., Rastar Indie Prod. Now works with Polar Ent.
PICTURES: Producer: The Beast, Tune in Tomorrow, Mortal Thoughts, Serial Mom, A Good Man in Africa, Radio Inside, I Love You —I Love You Not, Pecker, Simply Irresistable, Cecil B. Demented. Exec. prod.: Copycat.
TELEVISION: Producer: Beyond the Law.

FIELD, DAVID M.
Executive, Writer. b. Kansas City, MO, Apr. 22, 1944. e. Princeton U. Worked as reporter on city desk at Hartford (CT) Courant. In 1968 with NBC News in N.Y. and Washington, DC. Entered film school at U. of Southern California (L.A.) after which joined Columbia Pictures as west coast story editor. In 1973 went to ABC-TV Network as mgr., movies of the week. 1975, moved to 20th-Fox as v.p., creative affairs. Joined United Artists in 1978; named sr. v.p.—west coast production. Left in 1980 to become 20th-Fox exec. v.p. in chg. of worldwide production 1983, resigned to enter independent production deal with 20th-Fox, Consultant, Tri-Star Pictures. Wrote and produced Amazing Grace and Chuck, 1987.

FIELD, SALLY
Actress. b. Pasadena, CA, Nov. 6, 1946. Daughter of Paramount contract actress Maggie Field Mahoney. Stepdaughter of actor Jock Mahoney. e. Actor's Studio 1973-75. Acting classes at Columbia studios. Picked over 150 finalists to star as lead in TV series, Gidget, 1965.
PICTURES: The Way West (debut, 1967), Stay Hungry, Smokey and the Bandit, Heroes, The End, Hooper, Norma Rae (Academy Award, 1979), Beyond the Poseidon Adventure, Smokey and the Bandit II, Back Roads, Absence of Malice, Kiss Me Goodbye, Places in the Heart (Academy Award, 1984), Murphy's Romance (also exec. prod.), Surrender, Punchline (also prod.), Steel Magnolias, Not Without My Daughter, Soapdish, Dying Young (co-prod. only), Homeward Bound: The Incredible Journey (voice), Mrs. Doubtfire, Forrest Gump, Eye for an Eye, Homeward Bound II: Lost in San Francisco (voice), A Cooler Climate. Beautiful (dir. only), Where the Heart Is, Say It Isn't So, Legally Blonde 2: Red White & Blonde.
TELEVISION: Movies: Maybe I'll Come Home in the Spring, Marriage Year One, Mongo's Back in Town, Home for the Holidays, Hitched, Bridger, Sybil (Emmy Award, 1977), The Christmas Tree (also prod., dir., co-s.p.), Merry Christmas George Bailey, From the Earth to the Moon, David Copperfield. Mini-Series: A Woman of Independent Means (also co-exec. prod.). Host: Barbara Stanwyck: Fire and Desire. Guest: Hey Landlord, Marcus Welby M.D., Bracken's World, King of the Hill (voice). Special: All the Way Home. Series: Gidget, The Flying Nun, Alias Smith and Jones, The Girl With Something Extra, ER, The Court.

FIELD, SHIRLEY-ANNE
Actress. b. London, Eng., June 27, 1938. Ent. films after repertory experience. Under contract to Ealing-M.G.M. 1958.
THEATRE: The Lily White Boys, Kennedy's Children, Wait Until Dark, The Life and Death of Marilyn Monroe, How the Other Half Loves.
PICTURES: It's Never Too Late, The Silken Affair, The Good Companions, Horrors of the Black Museum, Upstairs and Downstairs, Beat Girl, The Entertainer, Man in the Moon, Once More With Feeling, Peeping Tom, Saturday Night and Sunday Morning, These Are the Damned, The War Lover, Kings of the Sun, Alfie, Doctor in Clover, Hell Is Empty, With Love in Mind, House of the Living Dead (Doctor Maniac), My Beautiful Laundrette, Getting It Right, The Rachel Papers, Shag, Hear My Song, At Risk, Taking Liberty, U.F.O., Loving Deadly, Monkey's Tale, The Good Doctor, Christie Malry's Own Double-Entry.
TELEVISION: Movies: Lady Chatterly, Dalziel and Pascoe: Recalled to Life. Series: Bramwell, Santa Barbara, Madson, Where the Heart Is.

FIELD, TED
Producer. r.n. Frederick W. Field. e. U. of Chicago, Pomona Coll. Started career as one of owners of Field Enterprises of Chicago; transferred to west coast, concentrating on movies and records. Founded Interscope Communications, diversified co., which develops and produces theatrical films; Interscope Records, 1990; Radar Pictures, 1999.

PICTURES: Revenge of the Nerds, Turk 182, Critical Condition, Outrageous Fortune, Three Men and a Baby, The Seventh Sign, Cocktail, Bill & Ted's Excellent Adventure (exec.), Renegades (exec.), Innocent Man, The First Power (exec. prod.), Bird on a Wire, Three Men and a Little Lady, Paradise, The Hand That Rocks the Cradle, The Cutting Edge, FernGully, The Gun in Betty Lou's Handbag, Out on a Limb, Jersey Girl, Holy Matrimony, Imaginary Crimes, Operation Dumbo Drop, The Tie That Binds, Jumanji, Mr. Holland's Opus, The Arrival (exec.), Kazaam (exec.), The Associate, Gridlock'd (exec), Snow White (exec.), What Dreams May Come (exec.), Very Bad Things (exec.), Earl Watt, The 59-Story Crisis (exec.), The Proposition, Teaching Mrs. Tingle (exec.), Runaway Bride, They (exec. prod.), Le Divorce (exec. prod.), The Texas Chainsaw Massacre (2003), The Last Samurai (exec. prod.), The Chronicles of Riddick (exec.).
TELEVISION: The Father Clements Story (co-exec.). Everybody's Baby: The Rescue of Jessica McClure (co-exec.). My Boyfriend's Back, A Mother's Courage: The Mary Thomas Story (co-exec.), Crossing the Mob, Murder Ordained, Foreign Affairs (co-exec.), A Part of the Family (co-exec.), Body Language (co-exec.), Pitch Black (exec. prod.)

FIELD, TODD
Actor, Director. r.n. William Todd Field. b. Pomona, CA, Feb. 24, 1964. Extensive behind the scenes work in film. *Dir./Writer:* Too Romantic, When I Was a Boy (also cam. op.), Delivering, Nonnie & Alex (also cam. op.), If...Dog...Rabbit (s.p. only)
PICTURES: Radio Days, The Allnighter, Gross Anatomy (also comp.), Fat Man and Little Boy, Eye of the Eagle 2: Inside the Enemy, Full Fathom Five, Back to Back, Queens Logic, The End of Innocence, The Dog (also dir. comp.), Ruby in Paradise (also comp.), Sleep with Me, When I Was a Boy (dir. only), Delivering (dir. only), Nonnie & Alex (dir. only), Frank and Jesse, Twister, Walking and Talking, Farmer & Chase, Broken Vessels (also co-prod., comp.), Stranger Than Fiction, Net Worth, The Haunting, Eyes Wide Shut, New Port South, Beyond the City Limits., In the Bedroom (dir., s.p., prod., Acad. Award nom., AFI nom.).
TELEVISION: *Movies:* Student Exchange. *Series:* Take Five, Danger Theatre, Once and Again. *Guest:* Roseanne, Tales from the Crypt, Chicago Hope.

FIELDS, FREDDIE
Executive. b. Ferndale, NY, July 12, 1923. Vice-pres., member of bd. of directors, MCA-TV, MCA Canada Ltd., MCA Corp.; mem., Pres. Club, Wash., D.C.; pres., Freddie Fields Associates Ltd.; 1960; founder pres., chief exec. officer Creative Management Assoc. Ltd. Agency, Chicago, Las Vegas, Miami, Paris, Los Angeles, N.Y., London, Rome, 1961. Was exclusive agent of Henry Fonda, Phil Silvers, Judy Garland, Paul Newman, Peter Sellers, Barbra Streisand, Steve McQueen, Woody Allen, Robert Redford, Mick Jagger, Liza Minnelli and others. In 1975 sold interest in CMA (now International Creative Mgt.) but continued as consultant. Produced for Paramount Pictures. 1977: Looking for Mr. Goodbar. American Gigolo, Citizen's Band; Victory. In 1983 named pres. and COO, MGM Film Co. and UA Pictures. Resigned 1985 to become independent producer for MGM/UA. Chairman, The Fields & Hellman Co; dir., Network Event Theater, Inc.; chairman, Net Programming Ltd.; dir., LA Sports and Entertainment Comm.
PICTURES: Lipstick, Looking For Mr. Goodbar, Handle the Care, American Gigolo, Wholly Moses, Victory, Fever Pitch. Poltergeist II, Crimes of the Heart, Millennium, Glory.
TELEVISION: *Exec. Prod.:* The Montel Williams Show.

FIENNES, JOSEPH
Actor. b. Salisbury, England, May 27, 1970. Brother is actor Ralph Fiennes. Worked at Young Vic Youth Theatre, and then went on to train at the Guildhall School of Music and Drama
PICTURES: Stealing Beauty, Shakespeare in Love, Elizabeth, The Very Thought of You, Forever Mine, Rancid Aluminium, Enemy at the Gates, Killing Me Softly, Dust, Leo, Sinbad: Legend of the Seven Seas (voice), Luther, The Great Raid.
TELEVISION: The Vacillations of Poppy Carew, Animated Epics: Beowulf (voice), Judi Dench: A BAFTA Tribute.

FIENNES, RALPH
Actor. b. Suffolk, England, Dec. 22, 1962. e. Chelsea College of Art & Design, RADA. Brother is actor Joseph Fiennes. Stage work with the Royal Shakespeare Co. includes King Lear, Troilus and Cressida, Love's Labour's Lost. B'way debut in Hamlet (Tony & Theatre World Awards, 1995).
PICTURES: Wuthering Heights (tv in U.S.), The Baby of Macon, Schindler's List (Acad. Award nom.; Natl. Society of Film Critics, NY Film Critics & BAFTA Awards), Quiz Show, Strange Days, The English Patient, Oscar and Lucinda, The Avengers, The Prince of Egypt (voice), The Avengers, Onegin (also prod.), The Taste of Sunshine, The End of the Affair, Spider, The Good Thief, Red Dragon, Maid in Manhattan.
TELEVISION: Prime Suspect, A Dangerous Man: Lawrence After Arabia, The Cormorant (theatrical release in U.S.), The Great War (voice), The Miracle Maker (voice), How Proust Can Change Your Life.

FIERSTEIN, HARVEY
Actor, Writer. b. New York, NY, June 6, 1954. e. Pratt Inst.
THEATRE: Actor: Andy Warhol's Pork, The Haunted Host, Pouf Positive. Actor-Writer: Torch Song Trilogy (NY & London; Tony Awards for best actor & play; Theatre World Award), Safe Sex. Writer: Spookhouse, La Cage Aux Folles (Tony Award), Legs Diamond.

PICTURES: Garbo Talks, The Times of Harvey Milk (narrator), Torch Song Trilogy (also s.p.), The Harvest, Mrs. Doubtfire, Bullets Over Broadway, The Celluloid Closet, Dr. Jekyll & Ms. Hyde, Independence Day, Everything Relative, Kull the Conqueror, Mulan (voice), Safe Men, Hookers in a Haunted House, Jump, Playing Mona Lisa, Death to Smoochy.
TELEVISION: *Movies:* The Demon Murder Case (voice), Apology, Double Platinum, The Sissy Duckling, Common Ground. *Series:* Daddy's Girls, Happily Ever After: Fairy Tales for Every Child, Stories From My Childhood, X-Chromosome. *Guest:* Miami Vice, The Simpsons (voice), Cheers, Murder She Wrote. *Specials:* Tidy Endings, In the Shadow of Love.

FIGGIS, MIKE
Director, Writer, Composer. b. Kenya, Feb. 28, 1948. At age 8 family moved to Newcastle, England. Studied music before performing with band Gas Boad; joined experimental theatre group The People Show in early 70's as musician. Began making indept. films including Redheugh, Slow Fade, Animals of the City. Made 1-hr. film The House for U.K.'s Channel 4.
PICTURES: *Director:* Stormy Monday (debut, 1988; also s.p., music), Internal Affairs (also music), Liebestraum (also s.p., music), Mr. Jones, Leaving Las Vegas (also s.p., music; IFP Independent Spirit Award, 1996; Nat'l Society of Film Critics Award), One Night Stand (also s.p., comp., prod., actor), Flamenco Women, Miss Julie (also prod., music), The Loss of Sexual Innocence (also prod., music), Timecode (also. prod., music), Hotel (also prod., music), Agua Dulce (short, exec. prod.), Cold Creek Manor (dir., prod.).

FINCH, JON
Actor. b. London, England, Mar. 2, 1943. Came to acting via backstage activities, working for five years as co. mgr. and dir.
PICTURES: The Vampire Lovers (debut, 1970), The Horror of Frankenstein, Sunday Bloody Sunday, L'affaire Martine Desclos, Macbeth, Frenzy, Lady Caroline Lamb, The Final Programme (The Last Days of Man on Earth), Diagnosis: Murder, Une Femme Fidele, The Man With the Green Cross, El Segundo Poder, Battle Flag, El Mister, Death on the Nile, La Sabina, Gary Cooper Which Art in Heaven, Breaking Glass, The Threat, Giro City (And Nothing But the Truth), Plaza Real, Streets of Yesterday, Game of Seduction, The Voice, Beautiful in the Kingdom, Mirror Mirror, Darklands, Lucan, Bloodlines: Legacy of a Lord, Anazapta.
TELEVISION: The Martian Chronicles (U.S.), Peter and Paul, The Rainbow, Unexplained Laughter, Dangerous Curves, Maigret, Beautiful Lies, Make or Break,Sherlock Homes , Mary Queen of Scots, Riviera, White Men Are Cracking Up, A Love Renewed, Merlin of the Crystal Cave, Richard II, Henry IV, Much Ado About Nothing, South of the Border, Hammer House of Horrors, Polanski y los ojos del mal, New Tricks. Series: Ben Hall, The Oddjob Man, Counterstrike.

FINCHER, DAVID
Director. b. 1963. Ent. ind. at 18, working at Lucas' Industrial Light and Magic for 4 yrs; left to make TV commercials & dir. pop videos for Madonna, Paula Abdul & Aerosmith.
PICTURES: *Dir.:* The Beat of the Live Drum, Alien 3, Se7en, The Game, Fight Club, Panic Room, Mission Impossible 3, Full Frontal, Lords of Dogtown (also prod.). *Exec. prod.:* Ambush, Chosen, The Follow, Star, Powder Keg, The Car Thief and the Hit Men, The Hire: Powder Keg.

FINLAY, FRANK
Actor. C.B.E. b. Farnworth, Eng., Aug. 6, 1926. Rep. in Troon, 1951, Halifax and Sunderland, 1952-3, before winning Sir James Knott Scholarship to RADA. e. Studied acting at RADA. Appeared with Guildford Repertory Theatre Co. 1957. London stage debut: The Queen and the Welshman, 1957. Broadway debut, Epitaph for George Dillon, 1958.
THEATRE: Work with Royal Court, Chichester Fest., National Theatre includes: Sergeant Musgrave's Dance, Chicken Soup with Barley, Roots, Platonov, Chips with Everything, Saint Joan, Hamlet, Othello, Saturday Sunday Monday, Plunder, Watch It Come Down, Weapons of Happiness, Tribute to a Lady, Filumena (and N.Y.), Amadeus, The Cherry Orchard, Mutiny, Beyond Reasonable Doubt, Black Angel, A Slight Ache.
PICTURES: The Loneliness of the Long Distance Runner (debut, 1962), The Longest Day, Life for Ruth (Walk in the Shadow), Private Potter, Doctor in Distress, Underworld Informers, The Comedy Man, Agent 8 3/4 (Hot Enough for June), The Wild Affair, A Study in Terror, Othello (Acad. Award nom.), The Sandwich Man, The Jokers, The Deadly Bees, Robbery, I'll Never Forget What's 'is Name, The Shoes of the Fisherman, Inspector Clouseau, Twisted Nerve, The Molly Maguires, Cromwell, The Body (narrator), Assault (The Devil's Garden), Gumshoe, Danny Jones, Sitting Target, Neither the Sea Nor the Sand, Shaft in Africa, The Three Musketeers, The Four Musketeers, The Wild Geese, Murder by Decree, Enigma, The Ploughman's Lunch, The Return of the Soldier, The Key, 1919, Lifeforce, The Return of the Musketeers (tv in U.S.), King of the Wind, Cthulhu Mansion, Mountain of Diamonds, Sparrow, So This Is Romance?, Limited Edition, Stiff Upper Lips, Dreaming of Joseph Lees, Ghosthunter, For My Baby, The Martins, Silent Cry, The Pianist, Silent Cry, Lighthouse Hill Prime Suspect 6.
TELEVISION: *Movies:* The Adventures of Don Quixote, Casanova, Candide, Julius Caesar, Les Miserables, This Happy Breed, The Lie, The Death of Adolph Hitler, Voltaire, The Merchant of Venice, Bouquet of Barbed Wire, 84 Charing Cross Road, Saturday Sunday Monday, Count Dracula, The Last Campaign, Thief of Bagdad, Betzi, Sakharov, A Christmas Carol,

Arch of Triumph, The Burning Shore, In the Secret State, Verdict of Erebus, Mountain of Diamonds, Encounter, Stalin, An Exchange of Fire, Common As Muck, Charlemagne, A Mind to Murder, How Do You Want Me?, The Magical Legend of the Leprechauns, Longitude, The Sins, Station Jim, The Lost Prince.

FINNEY, ALBERT
Actor. b. Salford, England, May 9, 1936. Studied for stage at Royal Acad. Dramatic Art making his West End debut 1958 in The Party. Appeared at Stratford-Upon-Avon 1959, playing title role in Coriolanus, etc.
THEATRE: The Lily White Boys, Billy Liar, Luther (also NY), Much Ado About Nothing, Armstrong's Last Goodnight, Love for Love, Miss Julie, Black Comedy, A Flea in Her Ear, Joe Egg (NY), Alpha Beta, Krapp's Last Tape, Cromwell, Chez Nous, Hamlet, Tamburlaine, Uncle Vanya, Present Laughter. National Theatre, The Country Wife, The Cherry Orchard, Macbeth, The Biko Inquest, Sergeant Musgrave's Dance (also dir.), Orphans, Another Time (also Chicago), Reflected Glory.
PICTURES: The Entertainer (debut, 1960), Saturday Night and Sunday Morning, Tom Jones, The Victors, Night Must Fall (also co-prod.), Two for the Road, Charlie Bubbles (also dir.), The Picasso Summer (tv in U.K.), Scrooge, Gumshoe, Alpha Beta (tv in U.K.), Murder on the Orient Express, The Adventure of Sherlock Holmes' Smarter Brother (cameo), The Duellists, Wolfen, Looker, Loophole, Shoot the Moon, Annie, The Dresser, Under the Volcano, Orphans, Miller's Crossing, The Playboys, Rich in Love, The Browning Version, A Man of No Importance, The Run of the Country, Washington Square, Breakfast of Champions, Erin Brockovich, Traffic, Joan of Arc: The Virgin Warrior, Delivering Milo, Hemingway: The Hunter of Death, Big Fish.
TELEVISION: The Claverdon Road Job, The Miser, Pope John Paul II, Endless Game, The Image, The Green Man, A Rather English Marriage, The Gathering Storm, My Uncle Silas II.

FIORENTINO, LINDA
Actress. b. Philadelphia, PA, March 9, 1960. e. Rosmont Col. To New York, 1980, studied acting at Circle in the Square Drama School.
PICTURES: Vision Quest (debut, 1985), Gotcha!, After Hours, The Modrens, Queens Logic, Shout, Chain of Desire, The Last Seduction, Bodily Harm, Jade, Unforgettable, Men in Black, Where the Money Is, Killer Kiss, Dogma, Ordinary Decent Criminal, What Planet Are You From?, Where The Money Is, Liberty Stands Still.
TELEVISION: *Movies*: The Neon Empire, Acting on Impulse, The Desperate Trail.

FIRTH, COLIN
Actor. b. Grayshott, Hampshire, Eng., Sept. 10, 1960. Studied acting at the Drama Centre at Chalk Farm. Author of A Month in the Country (screenplay), Making of Pride and Prejudice.
THEATRE: *London*: in Tartuffe, King Lear, Hamlet, Another Country, Doctor's Dilemma, The Lonely Road, Desire Under the Elms, The Caretaker, Chatsky.
PICTURES: Another Country, 1919, A Month in the Country, Apartment Zero, Valmont, Wings of Fame, The Hour of the Pig, The Pleasure Principle, Femme Fatale, Playmaker, The Advocate, Circle of Friends, The English Patient, Fever Pitch, A Thousand Acres, The World of Moss, Shakespeare in Love, The Secret Laughter of Women, My Life So Far, Blackadder Back and Forth, Relative Values, Londinium, Bridget Jones's Diary, The Importance of Being Earnest, Hope Springs, What a Girl Wants, Girl with a Pearl Earring, Love Actually, Trauma.
TELEVISION: *Movies*: Camille, Crown Court, Dutch Girls, Tumbledown, Hostages, Master of the Moor, The Deep Blue Sea, Pride and Prejudice, The Widowing of Mrs. Holroyd, Nostromo, The Turn of the Screw, Donovan Quick, Conspiracy. *Series*: Lost Empires. *Specials*: Tales from the Hollywood Hills (Pat Hobby Teamed with Genius).

FIRTH, PETER
Actor. b. Bradford, Yorkshire, Oct. 27, 1953. Appeared in local TV children's show where casting director spotted him and got him role in series, The Flaxton Boys. Moved to London and worked in TV, first in children's show, later on dramas for BBC. Breakthrough role in Equus at National Theatre, 1973 which he repeated in film.
THEATRE: Equus (Theatre World Award), Romeo and Juliet, Spring Awakening, Amadeus.
PICTURES: Diamonds on Wheels (debut, 1972; tv in U.S.), Brother Sun Sister Moon, Daniel and Maria, Equus (Acad. Award nom.), Joseph Andrews, Aces High, When You Comin' Back Red Ryder, Tess, Lifeforce, Letter to Brezhnev, Trouble in Paradise, White Elephant, A State of Emergency, Born of Fire, The Tree of Hands, Prisoner of Rio, Burndown, The Hunt for Red October, The Rescuers Down Under (voice), The Perfect Husband, White Angel, Shadowlands, An Awfully Big Adventure, The Garden of Redemption, Marco Polo, Amistad, Mighty Joe Young, Chill Factor, Pearl Harbor.
TELEVISION: *Movies and specials*: Here Comes the Doubledeckers, Castlehaven, The Sullen Sisters, The Simple Life, The Magistrate, The Protectors, Black Beauty, Arthur, Her Majesty's Pleasure, the Picture of Dorian Gray, Lady of the Camillias, Blood Royal, Northanger Abbey, The Way, The Truth: the Video, The Incident, Children Crossing, Prisoner of Honor, Married to Murder, The Laughter of God, Murder in Eden, Brighton Boy, The Broker's Man, Holding On, The Magicians, Me & Mrs. Jones. *Series*: The Flaxon Boys, Home and Away, Country Matters, Spooks, That's Life, MI-5.

FISHBURNE, LAURENCE
Actor. b. Augusta, GA, July 30, 1961. Raised in Brooklyn. Landed role on daytime serial One Life to Live at age 11. On NY stage in Short Eyes, Two Trains Running (Tony and Theatre World Awards), Riff Raff (also wrote and directed).
PICTURES: Cornbread Earl and Me (debut, 1975), Fast Break, Apocalypse Now, Willie and Phil, Death Wish II, Rumble Fish, The Cotton Club, The Color Purple, Quicksilver, Band of the Hand, A Nightmare on Elm Street 3: Dream Warriors, Gardens of Stone, School Daze, Red Heat, King of New York, Cadence, Class Action, Boyz N the Hood, Deep Cover, What's Love Got to Do With It (Acad. Award nom.), Searching for Bobby Fischer, Higher Learning, Bad Company, Just Cause, Othello, Fled, Hoodlums (also exec. prod.), Event Horizon, The Matrix, Michael Jordan to the Max (voice), Osmosis Jones (voice), Once in the Life, The Matrix Reloaded, Biker Boyz, Soul of a Man (documentary, narrator), Mystic River, The Matrix Revolutions.
TELEVISION: *Movies*: A Rumor of War, I Take These Men, Decoration Day, The Tuskegee Airmen, Miss Ever's Boys, Always Outnumbered, Sex and the Matrix (short). *Series*: One Life to Live, Pee-wee's Playhouse. *Guest*: M*A*S*H, Trapper John, M.D., Spenser: For Hire, Tribeca (Emmy Award, 1993).

FISHER, CARRIE
Actress, Writer. b. Beverly Hills, CA, Oct. 21, 1956. e. London Central Sch. of Speech & Drama. Daughter of actress Debbie Reynolds and singer Eddie Fisher. On Broadway in the chorus of revival of Irene (1972; with mother); *Author*: Postcards From the Edge (1987), Surrender the Pink, Delusions of Grandma.
PICTURES: Shampoo (debut, 1975), Star Wars, Mr. Mike's Mondo Video, Star Wars: The Empire Strikes Back, The Blues Brothers, Under the Rainbow, Star Wars: Return of the Jedi, Garbo Talks, The Man with One Red Shoe, Hannah and Her Sisters, Hollywood Vice Squad, Amazon Women on the Moon, Appointment with Death, The 'Burbs, Loverboy, She's Back, When Harry Met Sally..., The Time Guardian, Postcards From the Edge (s.p. only), Sibling Rivalry, Drop Dead Fred, Soapdish, This Is My Life, George Lucas: Heroes Myths and Magic, Austin Powers: International Man of Mystery, Scream 3, Famous, Heartbreakers, Jay and Silent Bob Strike Back, A Midsummer Night's Rave, Charlie's Angels: Full Throttle, Wonderland, 5-25-77, Stateside.
TELEVISION: *Movies*: Leave Yesterday Behind, Liberty, Sunday Drive, Sweet Revenge, These Old Broads. *Specials*: Come Back Little Sheba, Classic Creatures: Return of the Jedi, Thumbelina (Faerie Tale Theatre), Paul Reiser: Out on a Whim, Two Daddies? (voice), Trying Times (Hunger Chic), Carrie Fisher: The Hollywood Family (also writer). *Series*: Carrie on Hollywood, "Conversations From the Edge with Carrie Fisher." *Guest*: Laverne and Shirley, George Burns' Comedy Week, Sex in the City.

FISHER, EDDIE
Singer. b. Philadelphia, PA, Aug. 10, 1928. Daughter is actress Carrie Fisher. Band, nightclub singer; discovered by Eddie Cantor, 1949; U.S. Army, 1951-53; hit records include Wish You Were Here, Lady of Spain and Oh My Papa; radio & TV shows, NBC; various tv documentaries.
PICTURES: Bundle of Joy, Butterfield 8, Nothing Lasts Forever, Off the Menu: The Last Days of Chasen's.
TELEVISION: *Series*: Coke Time With Eddie Fisher (1953-57), The Eddie Fisher Show (1957-59).

FISHER, FRANCES
Actress. b. Milford-on-Sea, England, May 11, 1952. Father was intl. construction supervisor. Raised in Colombia, Canada, France, Brazil, Turkey. Made stage debut in Texas in Summer and Smoke.
THEATER: *NY*: Fool for Love, Desire Under the Elms, Cat on a Hot Tin Roof, The Hitch-Hikers, Orpheus Descending, A Midsummer Night's Dream, Jammed.
PICTURES: Can She Bake a Cherry Pie? (debut, 1983), Tough Guys Don't Dance, The Principal, Patty Hearst, Bum Rap, Heavy Petting, Pink Cadillac, Lost Angels, Welcome Home Roxy Carmichael, L.A. Story, Unforgiven, Babyfever, The Stars Fell on Henrietta, Waiting for Guffman, Female Perversion, Wild America, Titanic, True Crime, The Big Tease, Gone in Sixty Seconds, The Rising Place, Blue Car, House of Sand and Fog.
TELEVISION: *Movies*: Broken Vows, Devlin, Lucy & Desi: Before the Laughter, The Other Mother, Traffic, The Audrey Hepburn Story, Jackie Bouvier Kennedy Onassis, Passion and Prejudice. *Pilots*: Elysian Fields. *Series*: The Edge of Night (1976-81), The Guiding Light (1985), Strange Luck, Titus, Glory Days, Becker. *Guest*: The Equalizer, Matlock, Newhart.

FISHER, GEORGE M.C.
Executive. b. Anna, IL. e. Univ. of IL, Brown Univ. Worked in research and devlop. at Bell Labs before joining Motorola in 1976, eventually becoming pres. & CEO in 1988. 1990, elected chmn. & CEO. Named chmn., pres. & CEO of Eastman Kodak Company, Dec. 1993, a position he retired from in Jan. 2001; Currently serves on board of Eli Lilly, Delta Airlines and General Motors Corporation. His affiliations include: chmn., National Acad. of Engineering; mbr., The Business Council and the Int'l. Acad. of Astronautics; fellow of the American Acad. of Arts & Sciences.

FISHER, LUCY
Executive. b. Oct. 2, 1949. e. Harvard U., B.A. Exec. chg. creative affairs, MGM; v.p., creative affairs, 20th Century Fox; v.p., prod., Fox. 1980, head of prod., Zoetrope Studios; 1980-82, v.p., sr. prod. exec., Warner Bros.; 1983, sr. v.p. prod., WB. Joined Columbia TriStar in March, 1996 as vice chmn. Currently, producer with Red Wagon Prods.

FISHER, THOMAS L.
Special Effects.
PICTURES: The Devil's Rain, City on Fire, First Blood, Legal Eagles, Desperate Hours, Terminator 2: Judgment Day, The Taking of Beverly Hills, Under Siege, On Deadly Ground, True Lies, Batman Forever, Titanic (Acad. Award, Best Visual Effects, 1997), Supernova, The 13th Warrior, End of Days, Collateral Damage, Men in Black II, The Cat in the Hat (2003).

FISK, JACK
Director, Production Designer. b. Ipava, IL, Dec. 19, 1945. e. Cooper Union-Pa. Acad. of the Fine Arts. m. actress Sissy Spacek. Began in films as designer; turning to direction with Raggedy Man (1981).
PICTURES: Director: Raggedy Man, Violets Are Blue, Daddy's Dyin', ... Who's Got the Will? Art Director: Badlands, Phantom of the Paradise, Carrie, Days of Heaven. Prod. Designer: Phantom of the Paradise, Heart Beat, The Thin Red Line, The Straight Story, Mulholland Drive.

FITHIAN, JOHN
Executive. e. William and Mary, B.A.; U. of Virgina, J.D. Represented trade associations (including National Assoc. of Theatre Owners), professional athlete unions, telecomm. companies, nonprofits, publishers and advertisers with D.C.-based law firm Patton Boggs LLP. Became president of NATO, Jan. 2000, where he serves as chief public spokesperson for theatre owners before public officials and press.

FITZGERALD, GERALDINE
Actress. b. Dublin, Ireland, Nov. 24, 1914. e. Dublin Art Sch. Mother of director Michael Lindsay-Hogg. On stage Gate Theat., Dublin; then in number of Brit. screen prod. including Turn of the Tide, Mill on the Floss. On N.Y. stage in Heartbreak House. Found. Everyman St. Theatre with brother Jonathan Ringkamp.
THEATRE: Sons and Soldiers, Portrait in Black, The Doctor's Dilemma, King Lear, Hide and Seek, A Long Day's Journey Into Night, (1971), Ah, Wilderness, The Shadow Box, A Touch of the Poet, Songs of the Streets (one woman show), Mass Appeal (dir. only), The Lunch Girls (dir.).
PICTURES: Blind Justice (debut, 1934), Open All Night, The Lad, The Aces of Spades, Three Witnesses, Lieutenant Daring RN, Turn of the Tide, Radio Parade of 1935, Bargain Basement (Department Store), Debt of Honor, Cafe Mascot, The Mill on the Floss, Wuthering Heights (U.S. debut, 1939; Acad. Award nom.), Dark Victory, A Child Is Born, 'Til We Meet Again, Flight from Destiny, Shining Victory, The Gay Sisters, Watch on the Rhine, Ladies Courageous, Wilson, The Strange Affair of Uncle Harry, Three Strangers, O.S.S., Nobody Lives Forever, So Evil My Love, The Late Edwina Black (The Obsessed), 10 North Frederick, The Fiercest Heart, The Pawnbroker, Rachel Rachel, The Last American Hero, Harry and Tonto, Cold Sweat, Echoes of a Summer, The Mango Tree, Bye Bye Monkey, Lovespell (Tristan and Isolde), Arthur, Blood Link, Easy Money, Poltergeist II, Arthur 2: On the Rocks.
TELEVISION: Movies: Yesterday's Child, The Quinns, Dixie: Changing Habits, Do You Remember Love?, Circle of Violence, Night of Courage, Bump in the Night. Mini-Series: Kennedy. Specials: The Moon and Sixpence, Street Songs. Series: Our Private World, The Best of Everything.

FITZGERALD, TARA
Actress. b. England, 1968. e. London's Drama Centre, 1990.
THEATRE: London: Our Song. NY: Hamlet.
PICTURES: Hear My Song (debut, 1991), Sirens, A Man of No Importance, The Englishman Who Went Up a Hill But Came Down a Mountain, Brassed Off!, Conquest, New World Dis Order, Childhood, Rancid Aluminium, Dark Blue World Orchestra, Secret Passage, I Capture the Castle.
TELEVISION: The Black Candle, The Camomille Lawn, Anglo-Saxon Attitudes, Six Characters in Search of an Author, Fall From Grace, The Tenants of Wildfell Hall, The Woman in White, The Student Prince, Little White Lies, Frenchman's Creek, In the Name of Love, Love Again.

FLAGG, FANNIE
Actress, Writer. b. Birmingham, AL, Sept. 21, 1944. e. Univ. of AL. Studied acting at Pittsburgh Playhouse, Town & Gown Theatre. Had her own live 90 minute tv show in Birmingham. To NY where she wrote and appeared in revues for Upstairs at the Downstairs Club. Comedy albums: Rally 'Round the Flagg, My Husband Doesn't Know I'm Making This Phone Call. Author: Coming Attractions: A Wonderful Novel (Daisy Fay and the Miracle Man), Fried Green Tomatoes at the Whistle Stop Cafe.
THEATRE: B'way: Patio Porch, Come Back to the Five and Dime Jimmy Dean Jimmy Dean, The Best Little Whorehouse in Texas. Regional: Private Lives, Gypsy, Mary Mary, Tobacco Road, Old Acquaintance, etc.
PICTURES: Five Easy Pieces (debut, 1970), Some of My Best Friends Are..., Stay Hungry, Grease, Rabbit Test, My Best Friend Is a Vampire, Fried Green Tomatoes (also co-s.p.; Acad. Award nom. for s.p.), Crazy in Alabama.

TELEVISION: Movies: The New Original Wonder Woman, Sex and the Married Woman. Pilots: Comedy News, Home Cookin'. Producer: Morning Show. Series: The New Dick Van Dyke Show, Match Game P.M., Liar's Club, Harper Valley P.T.A.

FLANERY, SEAN PATRICK
Actor. b. Lake Charles, LA, Oct. 11, 1965.
PICTURES: A Tiger's Tale, Frank and Jesse, The Grass Harp, Powder, Raging Angels, Suicide Kings, Eden, Best Men, Run the Wild Fields, Girl, Simply Irresistible, The Boondock Saints, Body Shots, Run the Wild Fields, D-Tox, Con Express, Lone Hero, Kiss the Bride, Borderline, A Promise Kept, Boondock Saints 2.
TELEVISION: Movies: Guinevere, Young Indiana Jones and the Hollywood Follies, Young Indiana Jones and the Attack of the Hawkmen, Young Indiana Jones and the Treasure of the Peacock's Eye, Young Indiana Jones Travels with Father, Just Your Luck, Acceptable Risk, Diamond Hunters (mini), Borderline, Then Came Jones. Series: The Young Indiana Jones Chronicles, The Strip.

FLAXMAN, JOHN P.
Producer. b. New York, NY, March 3, 1934. e. Dartmouth U., B.A. 1956. 1st Lt. U.S. Army, 1956-58. Ent. m.p. industry in executive training program, Columbia Pictures Corp., 1958-63; exec. story consultant, Profiles in Courage, 1964-65; head of Eastern Literary Dept., Universal Pictures, 1965; writer's agent, William Morris Agency, 1966; partner with Harold Prince in Media Productions, Inc. 1967; founded Flaxman Film Corp., 1975. President-Tricorn Productions 1977; pres. Filmworks Capital Corp., 1979-83; Becker/Flaxman & Associates, 1979-83; pres., Cine Communications, 1983-present. Producer Off-Broadway, Yours, Anne (1985). Co-prod. with NY Shakespeare Fest., The Petrified Prince.
PICTURES: Something for Everyone, Jacob Two-Two Meets the Hooded Fang.
TELEVISION: The Caine Mutiny Court-Martial (prod.).

FLEDER, GARY
Director. b. Norfolk, VA, Dec. 19, 1965.
PICTURES: Things to Do in Denver when You're Dead, Kiss the Girls, Don't Say a Word, Imposter, The Runaway Jury.
TELEVISION: Movies: Air Time (also prod.), The Companion. Series: Homicide: Life on the Street, L.A. Doctors, Falcone, The Shield, R.U.S./H. Mini-series: From the Earth to the Moon.

FLEISCHER, RICHARD
Director. b. Brooklyn, NY, Dec. 8, 1916. e. Brown U., B.A.; Yale U., M.F.A. Son of animator Max Fleischer. Stage dir.; joined RKO Pathe 1942. Dir. and wrote This Is America shorts, prod./dir. Flicker Flashbacks. Author: Just Tell Me When to Cry.
PICTURES: Child of Divorce (debut, 1946), Banjo, Design for Death (also co-prod.; Academy Award for Best Feature-Length Documentary, 1948), So This Is New York, Bodyguard, Follow Me Quietly, Make Mine Laughs, The Clay Pigeon, Trapped, Armored Car Robbery, The Narrow Margin, The Happy Time, Arena, 20000 Leagues Under the Sea, Violent Saturday, Girl in the Red Velvet Swing, Bandido, Between Heaven and Hell, The Vikings, These Thousand Hills, Compulsion, Crack in the Mirror, The Big Gamble, Barabbas, Fantastic Voyage, Doctor Dolittle, The Boston Strangler, Che!, Tora! Tora! Tora!, 10 Rillington Place, The Last Run, See No Evil, The New Centurions, Soylent Green, The Don Is Dead, The Spikes Gang, Mr. Majestyk, Mandingo, The Incredible Sarah, Crossed Swords (The Prince and the Paupre), Ashanti, The Jazz Singer, Tough Enough, Amityville 3-D, Conan the Destroyer, Red Sonja, Million Dollar Mystery, Call From Space (Showcan).

FLEMING, RHONDA
Actress. r.n. Marilyn Louis. b. Los Angeles, CA, Aug. 10. m. Ted Mann (Mann Theatres). e. Beverly Hills H.S. Member, several charity orgs. Bd. of Dir. trustee of World Opportunities Intl. (Help the Children). Alzheimer Rsch., Childhelp USA, bd. of trustees of the UCLA Foundation. Opened Rhonda Fleming Mann Resource Center for Women with Cancer at UCLA Medical Center, 1994. Many awards incl. Woman of the Year Award from City of Hope 1986 & 1991; Woman of the World Award from Childhelp USA; Excellence in Media, Gold Angel Award; The Mannequins of Assistance of Southern California, Golden Eve Award. Stage incl. The Women (B'way), Kismet (LA), The Boyfriend (tour), one woman concerts.
PICTURES: Spellbound, Abiline Town, Spiral Staircase, Adventure Island, Out of the Past, A Connecticut Yankee in King Arthur's Court, The Great Lover, The Eagle and the Hawk, The Redhead and the Cowboy, The Last Outpost, Cry Danger, Crosswinds, Little Egypt, Hong Kong, Golden Hawk, Tropic Zone, Pony Express, Serpent of the Nile, Inferno, Those Redheads from Seattle, Jivaro, Yankee Pasha, Tennessee's Partner, While the City Sleeps, Killer Is Loose, Slightly Scarlet, Odongo, Queen of Babylon, Gunfight at the OK Corral, Buster Keaton Story, Gun Glory, Bullwhip, Home Before Dark, Alias Jesse James, The Big Circus, The Crowded Sky, The Patsy (cameo), Won Ton Ton The Dog Who Saved Hollywood, The Nude Bomb, Waiting for the Wind.
TELEVISION: Guest: Wagon Train, Police Woman, Love Boat, McMillian and Wife, Legends of the Screen, Road to Hollywood, Wildest West Show of Stars. Movies: The Last Hours Before Morning, Love for Rent, Waiting for the Wind.

FLENDER, RODMAN
Director, Producer, Actor.
PICTURES: *Director:* The Unborn, In the Heat of Passion (also prod. & s.p.), Leprechaun 2, Idle Hands.. *Producer:* Demon of Paradise, The Terror Within, Watchers 2, The Haunting of Morella, Body Chemistry (exec. prod.), The Unborn, In the Heat of Passion, Concealed Weapon. *Actor:* Carnosaur, Carnosaur 2, Criminal Hearts, Carnosaur 3: Primal Species, Idle Hands. *Writer:* In the Heat of Passion, Dracula Rising.
TELEVISION: *Movies:* Casper Meets Wendy (act. only). *Series dir.:* Tales from the Crypt, Party of Five, Chicago Hope, Dark Skies, Millennium, Arli$$, Dawson's Creek, Gilmore Girls, My Guide to Becoming a Rock Star, Push Nevada.

FLETCHER, LOUISE
Actress. b. Birmingham, AL, July 22, 1934. e. U. of North Carolina, B.A. Came to Hollywood at age 21; studied with Jeff Corey. Worked on TV shows (including Playhouse 90, Maverick). Gave up career to be a mother for 10 yrs.; returned to acting in 1973. Board of Directors: Deafness Research Foundation, 1980- . Honorary Degrees: Doctor of Humane Letters from Gallaudet U. and West Maryland Col. Advisory board: The Caption Center, The Nat'l Institute on Deafness and Other Communication Disorders.
PICTURES: Thieves Like Us, Russian Roulette, One Flew Over the Cuckoo's Nest (Academy Award, 1975), Exorcist II: The Heretic, The Cheap Detective, Natural Enemies, The Magician of Lublin, The Lucky Star, The Lady in Red, Strange Behavior, Mamma Dracula, Brainstorm, Strange Invaders, Firestarter, Once Upon a Time in America, Overnight Sensation, Invaders from Mars, The Boy Who Could Fly, Nobody's Fool, Flowers in the Attic, Two Moon Junction, Best of the Best, Shadow Zone, Blue Steel, Blind Vision, The Player, Georgino, Tollbooth, Return to Two Moon Junction, Virtuosity, High School High, 2 Days in the Valley, Mulholland Falls, Mojave Frankenstein, Edie and Pen, Gone Fishing, High School High, Girl Gets Moe, Love Kills, Cruel Intentions, Time Served, A Map of the World, The Contract, Big Eden, Very Mean Men, More Dogs Than Bones, Silver Man, After Image, Manna From Heaven, Touched By A Killer, Finding Home, Dial 9 For Love, Finding Home, Clipping Adam.
TELEVISION: *Movies:* Can Ellen Be Saved?, Thou Shalt Not Commit Adultery, A Summer to Remember, Island, Second Serve, J. Edgar Hoover, The Karen Carpenter Story, Final Notice, Nightmare on the 13th Floor, In a Child's Name, The Fire Next Time, The Haunting of Seacliff Inn, Someone Else's Child, Stepford Husbands, Twisted Path, Breastmen, Married to a Stranger, Heartless, The Devil's Arithmetic, Turning Homeward. *Series:* Boys of Twilight, Deep Space Nine, Picket Fences, VR 5, Profiler. *Guest:* Twilight Zone, Tales from the Crypt, Civil Wars, Dream On.

FLOCKHART, CALISTA
Actress. b. Freeport, IL, Nov. 11, 1964. e. Rutgers College, NJ.
THEATRE: *B'way:* The Glass Menagerie. *Off B'way:* The Loop, All for One, Sophistry, Wrong Turn at Lungfish, Beside Herself, Bovver Boys. *Regional:* The Three Sisters, Our Town, Death Takes a Holiday, Bash: Latter Day Plays.
PICTURES: Quiz Show, Getting In, Naked in New York, Drunks, The Birdcage, Milk and Money, Telling Lies in America, A Midsummer's Night's Dream, Like A Hole in the Head, Things You Can Tell Just By Looking At Her, Providence.
TELEVISION: *Movie:* Darrow. *Series:* Ally McBeal (Golden Globe Award, 1998), Ally. *Guest:* The Practice. *Special:* Bash: Latterday Plays, America: A Tribute to Heroes.

FLYNN, BEAU
Producer.
PICTURES: I.Q. (asst. prod.), Johns, Life During Wartime (exec. prod), The House of Yes, Dust & Stardust, Little City, Starstruck, Judas Kiss, Coming Soon, The Love Letter, Guinevere, Requiem for a Dream, Tigerland, Bubble Boy, Till Human Voices Wake Us, Slap Her She's French, 11:14.
TELEVISION: *Series:* USA's Connonball Run 2001, An American Town.

FLYNN, JOHN
Director, Writer. b. Chicago IL. e. George Washington U, Stanford, UCLA, B.A. (Eng). Worked in mailroom at MCA then with p.r. firm. Began career as trainee script supvr. for dir. Robert Wise on West Side Story. Soon working as ass't. dir. on MGM-TV shows. Made dir. debut with The Sergeant, 1969.
PICTURES: The Jerusalem File, The Outfit (also s.p.), Rolling Thunder, Defiance, Touched, Out for Justice, Best Seller, Lock Up, Brainscan, Protection.
TELEVISION: Marilyn—The Untold Story (dir.), Nails, Scam, Absence of the Good.

FOCH, NINA
Actress. b. Leyden, Holland, April 20, 1924. Daughter of Consuelo Flowerton, actress, & Dirk Foch, symphony orch. conductor. Adjunct Prof., USC, 1966-67; 1978-80, Adjunct professor, USC Cinema-TV grad. sch. 1986-; sr. faculty, American Film Inst., 1974-77; bd. of Governors, Hollywood Acad. of Television Arts & Sciences, 1976-77; exec. Comm. Foreign Language Film Award, Acad. of Motion Picture Arts & Sciences, 1970-. Cochmn., exec. comm. Foreign Language Film Award 1983-.
PICTURES: The Return of the Vampire (debut, 1943), Nine Girls, Cry of the Werewolf, She's a Soldier Too, She's a Sweetheart, Shadows in the Night, I Love a Mystery, Prison Ship, Song to Remember, My Name is Julia Ross, Boston Blackie's Rendezvous, Escape in the Fog, The Guilt of Jane Ames, Johnny

O'Clock, The Dark Past, Johnny Allegro, Undercover Man, St. Benny the Dip, An American in Paris, Young Man With Ideas, Scaramouche, Sombrero, Fast Company, Executive Suite (Acad. Award nom.), Four Guns to the Border, The Ten Commandments, Illegal, You're Never Too Young, Three Brave Men, Cash McCall, Spartacus, Such Good Friends, Salty, Mahogany, Jennifer, Rich and Famous, Skin Deep, Sliver, Morning Glory, It's My Party, 'Til There Was You, Kilronan, Hush, Shadow of Doubt, Pumpkin, How to Deal.
TELEVISION: *Movies:* Outback Bound, In the Arms of a Killer, The Sands of Time. *Mini-series:* War and Remembrance. *Special:* Tales of the City. Guest star, most major series incl. Studio One, Playhouse 90, U.S. Steel Hour, L.A. Law, Dear John, Hunter; talk shows, specials. *Series:* Q.E.D. (panelist), It's News to Me (panelist), Shadow Chasers, Bull.

FOGARTY, JACK V.
Executive, Producer, Writer. b. Los Angeles, CA. e. UCLA. Management, MGM, 1960-62; exec. prod. mgr., Cinerama, Inc., 1962-64; assoc. prod., The Best of Cinerama, 1963; est. own p.r. firm, 1965; pres., AstroScope, Inc., 1969-74.
TELEVISION: *Writer/prod.:* The Rookies, S.W.A.T., Charlie's Angels, Most Wanted, Barnaby Jones, A Man Called Sloane, Trapper John, T.J. Hooker, Crazy Like a Fox, The Equalizer, Jake and the Fatman, Murder She Wrote, Charlie's Angels (story edit.). *Exec. Story consultant:* Most Wanted, A Man Called Sloane, Sheriff Lobo, T.J. Hooker. *Producer:* T.J. Hooker, Jessie.

FOLEY, DAVE
Actor. b. Toronto, Canada, Jan. 4, 1963.
PICTURES: High Stakes, Three Men and a Baby, It's Pat, Kids in the Hall: Brain Candy, Hacks, A Bug's Life (voice), The Wrong Guy (also s.p.), Dick, Blast from the Past, South Park: Bigger, Longer and Uncut (voice), Toy Story 2 (voice), It's Tough to Be a Bug (voice), Cyberworld (voice), Monkeybone, Kids in the Hall: Same Guys New Dresses, The Frank Truth, On the Line, Stark Raving Mad, Run Ronnie Run!, Fancy Dancing, Swindle, Ham & Cheese, My Boss' Daughter, Whitecoats..
TELEVISION: *Movies/Specials:* Anne of Avonlea, The Lawrenceville Stories, From the Earth to the Moon, It's Tough to Be a Bug (voice). *Series:* The Kids in the Hall (also dir.), NewsRadio (also dir.), The Andy Dick Show.

FOLEY, JAMES
Director. b. New York, NY. E. NYU, USC. While at USC directed two short films, Silent Night and November which brought him attention. Directed two Madonna videos.
PICTURES: Reckless, At Close Range, Who's That Girl, After Dark My Sweet, Glengarry Glen Ross, A Day to Remember, Fear, Two Bits, The Chamber, The Corruptor, Confidence.
TELEVISION: *Series:* Gun.

FOLSEY, GEORGE, JR
Producer, Editor. b. Los Angeles, CA, Jan. 17, 1939. Son of late cinematographer George Folsey Sr. e. Pomona Coll., B.A., 1961. Chairman, Q Sound Labs, Canadian sound localization and Tech. Co., 1988-1992.
PICTURES: *Editor:* Glass Houses, Bone, Hammer, Black Caesar, Schlock, Trader Horn, Bucktown, J.D.'s Revenge, Norman... Is That You?, Tracks, The Chicken Chronicles, The Kentucky Fried Movie, National Lampoon's Animal House, Freedom Road, The Great Santini (addt'l editing), The Blues Brothers (also assoc. prod.), Bullet Proof, Dirty Work, Goosed, Cabin Fever, The Kings of Brooklyn, Basic. *Producer:* An American Werewolf in London, Twilight Zone—The Movie (assoc. prod.); Trading Places (exec. prod. & 2nd unit dir.), Into the Night (co-prod.), Spies Like Us (co-prod.), Clue (co-exec. prod.), Three Amigos, Coming to America (co-prod., co-editor), Greedy (co-exec. prod.), Grumpier Old Men.
VIDEO: Michael Jackson's Thriller (co-prod., editor).

FONDA, BRIDGET
Actress. b. Los Angeles, CA, Jan. 27, 1964. Daughter of actor Peter Fonda. Grew up in Los Angeles and Montana. e. NYU theater prog. Studied acting at Lee Strasberg Inst., and with Harold Guskin. Starred in grad. student film PPT. Workshop stage performances include Confession and Pastels.
PICTURES: Aria (Tristan and Isolde; debut, 1987), You Can't Hurry Love, Light Years (voice), Scandal, Shag, Strapless, Frankenstein Unbound, The Godfather Part III, Drop Dead Fred (unbilled), Doc Hollywood, Leather Jackets, Out of the Rain, Iron Maze, Single White Female, Singles, Army of Darkness, Point of No Return, Bodies Rest and Motion, Little Buddha, It Could Happen to You, The Road to Wellville, Camilla, Rough Magic, Balto (voice), City Hall, Touch, Mr. Jealousy, The Road to Graceland, Jackie Brown, The Break-Up, A Simple Plan, Lake Placid, South of Heaven West of Hell, The Whole Shebang, Delivering Milo, Monkeybone, Kiss of the Dragon.
TELEVISION: *Movies:* After Amy, The Snow Queen. *Specials:* Jacob Have I Loved (Wonderworks), The Edge (The Professional Man), After Amy, The Snow Queen. *Series:* The Chris Isaak Show. *Guest:* 21 Jump Street, In the Gloaming.

FONDA, JANE
Actress. b. New York, NY, Dec. 21, 1937. e. Emma Willard Sch., Troy, NY. Active in dramatics, Vassar. Father was late actor Henry Fonda. Brother is actor Peter Fonda. Appeared with father in summer stock production, The Country Girl, Omaha, NB. Studied painting, languages, Paris. Art Students League, N.Y. Appeared in The Male Animal, Dennis, MA. Modeled, appeared on covers, Esquire, Vogue, The Ladies Home Journal, Glamour, and

McCall's, 1959. Appeared in documentaries: Introduction to the Enemy, No Nukes.
THEATRE: There Was A Little Girl (Theatre World Award), Invitation to a March, The Fun Couple, Strange Interlude.
PICTURES: Tall Story (debut, 1960), Walk on the Wild Side, The Chapman Report, Period of Adjustment, In the Cool of The Day, Sunday in New York, The Love Cage (Joy House), La Ronde (Circle of Love), Cat Ballou, The Chase, La Curee (The Game is Over), Any Wednesday, Hurry Sundown, Barefoot in the Park, Barbarella, Spirits of the Dead, They Shoot Horses Don't They? (Acad. Award nom.), Klute (Academy Award, Best Actress, 1971), F.T.A. (also prod.), Tout va Bien, Steelyard Blues, A Doll's House, The Bluebird, Fun With Dick and Jane, Julia (Acad. Award nom.), Coming Home (Academy Award, Best Actress, 1978), Comes a Horseman, California Suite, The China Syndrome (Acad. Award nom.), The Electric Horseman, Nine To Five, On Golden Pond (Acad. Award nom.), Rollover, Agnes of God, The Morning After (Acad. Award nom.), Leonard Part 6 (cameo), Old Gringo, Stanley and Iris, A Century of Cinema, Cinéma Vérité: Defining the Moment, Searching for Debra Winger.
TELEVISION: Specials: A String of Beads, Lily--Sold Out, The Helen Reddy Special, I Love Liberty, Tell Them I'm a Mermaid, Fonda on Fonda (host), A Century of Women (narrator), AFI's 100 Years, 100 Thrills: America's Most Heart-Pounding Movies, Complicated Women (tv documentary, narrator). Movie: The Dollmaker (Emmy Award, 1984). Series: 9 to 5 (exec. prod. only).

FONDA, PETER
Actor, Director. b. New York, NY, Feb. 23, 1939. e. studied at U. of Omaha. Son of late actor Henry Fonda. Sister is actress Jane Fonda; daughter is actress Bridget Fonda.
PICTURES: Tammy and the Doctor (debut, 1963), The Victors, Lilith, The Young Lovers, The Wild Angels, The Trip, Spirits of the Dead, Easy Rider (also co-s.p., prod.), Idaho Transfer (dir.), The Last Movie, The Hired Hand (also dir.), Two People, Dirty Mary Crazy Larry, Open Season, Race With the Devil, 92 in the Shade, Killer Force, Fighting Mad, Futureworld, Outlaw Blues, High Ballin!, Wanda Nevada (also dir.), Cannonball Run (cameo), Split Image, Certain Fury, Dance of the Dwarfs, Mercenary Fighters, Jungle Heat, Diajobu My Friend, Peppermint Frieden, Spasm, The Rose Garden, Fatal Mission, Family Spirit, Reckless, South Beach, Bodies Rest & Motion, DeadFall, Molly & Gina, Love and a .45, Painted Hero, Nadja, John Carpenter's Escape from L.A., Grace of My Heart, Ulee's Gold (NY Film Crits. Circle Award, Golden Globe Award, Best Actor, 1997), The Passion of Ayn Rand, The Limey, Thomas and the Magic Railroad, Second Skin, Wooly Boys, The Laramie Project.
TELEVISION: Movies: A Reason to Live, The Hostage Tower, A Time of Indifference, Sound, Certain Honorable Men, Montana, The Tempest, Don't Look Back, The Maldonado Miracle.

FONER, NAOMI
Writer, Producer. b. New York, NY. e. Barnard Col., Columbia U. m. dir. Stephen Gyllenhaal. Was media dir. of Eugene McCarthy's 1968 political campaign, then prod. asst. & researcher at PBS. 1968 joined Children's Television Workshop on staff of Sesame Street. Later helped develop series The Electric Company, 3-2-1 Contact. Creator and co-prod. of series The Best of Families. Wrote teleplay Blackout for PBS series Visions.
PICTURES: Writer: Violets Are Blue, Running on Empty (Golden Globe Award, Acad. Award nom.; also exec. prod.), A Dangerous Woman (also prod.), Losing Isaiah (also prod.), Homegrown.

FONTAINE, JOAN
Actress. b. Tokyo, Oct. 22, 1917. r.n. Joan de Beauvoir de Havilland. e. American School in Japan. Sister is actress Olivia de Havilland. Started on stage in L.A., Santa Barbara and San Francisco in Kind Lady; then as Joan Fontaine in Call it a Day (L.A.), where she was spotted and signed to contract by prod. Jesse Lasky. Sold contract to RKO. On B'way in Tea and Sympathy (1954). Author: No Bed of Roses (1978) Appeared in The Lion in Winter at Vienna's English Speaking Theatre 1979.
PICTURES: No More Ladies (debut, 1935), Quality Street, You Can't Beat Love, Music for Madame, Maid's Night Out, A Damsel in Distress, Blonde Cheat, The Man Who Found Himself, The Duke of West Point, Sky Giant, Gunga Din, Man of Conquest, The Women, Rebecca (Acad. Award nom.), Suspicion (Academy Award, 1941), This Above All, The Constant Nymph (Acad. Award nom.), Jane Eyre, Frenchman's Creek, Affairs of Susan, From This Day Forward, Ivy, The Emperor Waltz, Letter From an Unknown Woman, Kiss the Blood Off My Hands, You Gotta Stay Happy, Born to Be Bad, September Affair, Darling How Could You?, Something to Live For, Othello (cameo), Ivanhoe, Decameron Nights, Flight to Tangier, The Bigamist, Casanova's Big Night, Serenade, Beyond a Reasonable Doubt, Island in the Sun, Until They Sail, A Certain Smile, Voyage to the Bottom of the Sea, Tender Is the Night, The Devil's Own, Busby Berkeley, All by Myself, Off the Menu: The Last Days of Chasen's.
TELEVISION: Crossings, Dark Mansions, Cannon, The Users, Bare Essence, Good King Wenceslas.

FOOTE, HORTON
Writer. b. Wharton, TX, March 14, 1916. Actor before becoming playwright.
THEATRE: Only the Heart, The Chase, The Trip to Bountiful, Traveling Lady, Courtship, 1918, The Widow Claire, The Habitation of Dragons, Lily Dale, Valentine's Day, Dividing the Estate, Talking Pictures, The Roads to Home, Night Seasons, The Young Man From Atlanta (Pulitzer prize), Cousins, The

Death of Papa, Convicts, Roots In a Parched Ground, A Coffin In Egypt, Tomorrow, Getting Frankie Married and Afterwards, Laura Dennis, Vernon Early.
PICTURES: Storm Fear, To Kill a Mockingbird (Acad. Award, 1962), Baby the Rain Must Fall, The Chase, Hurry Sundown, Tomorrow, Tender Mercies (Acad. Award, 1983), 1918 (also co-prod.), The Trip to Bountiful (also co-prod.), On Valentine's Day, Convicts, Of Mice and Men.
TELEVISION: Only the Heart, Ludie Brooks, The Travelers, The Old Beginning, Trip to Bountiful, Young Lady of Property, Death of the Old Man, Flight, The Night of the Storm, The Roads to Home, Drugstore: Sunday Night, Member of the Family, Traveling Lady, Old Man (Emmy Award, 1997), Tomorrow, The Shape of the River, The Displaced Person, Barn Burning, The Habitation of Dragons, Lily Dale, Old Man, Alone.

FORBES, BRYAN
Actor, Writer, Producer, Director. b. Stratford (London), July 22, 1926. m. actress Nanette Newman. Former head of prod., man. dir., Associated British Prods. (EMI). Stage debut, The Corn Is Green (London), 1942; screen debut, The Small Back Room, 1948. Pres.: National Youth Theatre of Great Britain, 1985-; Pres.: Writers Guild of Great Britain, 1988-91.
AUTHOR: Short stories: Truth Lies Sleeping. Novels: The Distant Laughter, Familiar Strangers (U.S.: Stranger), The Rewrite Man, The Endless Game, A Song at Twilight (U.S.: A Spy at Twlight), The Twisted Playground, Partly Cloudy, Quicksand. Novelizations: The Slipper and the Rose, International Velvet. Non-Fiction: Ned's Girl (bio. of Dame Edith Evans) That Despicable Race (history of the British acting tradition). Autobiographies: Notes for a Life, A Divided Life.
THEATRE: Director: Macbeth, Star Quality, Killing Jessica, The Living Room.
PICTURES: Actor: Tired Men, The Small Back Room All Over the Town, Dear Mr. Prohack, Green Grow The Rushes, The Million Pound Note (Man With a Million), An Inspector Calls, The Colditz Story, Passage Home, Appointment in London, Sea Devils, The Extra Day, Quatermass II, It's Great To be Young, Satellite in the Sky, The Baby and The Battleship, Yesterday's Enemy, The Guns of Navarone, A Shot in The Dark, Of Human Bondage, Restless Natives. Writer: The Cockleshell Heroes, The Black Tent, Danger Within, I Was Monty's Double (also actor), The League of Gentlemen (also actor), The Angry Silence (also prod., actor), Man in the Moon, Only Two Can Play, Station Six Sahara, Of Human Bondage (also actor), Hopscotch, Chaplin. Director-Writer: Whistle Down the Wind (dir. only), The L-Shaped Room (also actor), Seance on a Wet Afternoon (also prod.), King Rat, The Wrong Box, The Whisperers, Deadfall, The Madwoman of Chaillot (dir. only), The Raging Moon (Long Ago Tomorrow; also actor), The Stepford Wives (dir., actor), The Slipper and the Rose (also actor), International Velvet (also actor), Sunday Lovers (co-dir. only), Better Late Than Never (Menage a Trois), The Naked Face. Exec. Prod.: Hoffman, Forbush and the Penguins, The Railway Children, Peter Rabbit and the Tales of Beatrix Potter, The Go-Between, And Soon The Darkness, On The Buses, Dulcima.
TELEVISION: Actor: Johnnie Was a Hero, The Breadwinner, French Without Tears, Journey's End, The Gift, The Road, The Heiress, December Flower, First Amongst Equals. Writer/Dir.: I Caught Acting Like The Measles (documentary on the life of Dame Edith Evans) Goodbye Norma Jean and Other Things (documentary on the life of Elton John) Jessie, The Endless Game.

FORD, GLENN
Actor. r.n. Gwylin Ford. b. Quebec, Canada, May 1, 1916. Moved to Southern California as child. On stage with various West Coast theatre cos.; featured in The Children's Hour 1935; Broadway in Broom for a Bride, Soliloquy. Signed contract for film career with Columbia Pictures, 1939. Served in U.S. Marine Corps 1942-45.
PICTURES: Heaven With a Barbed Wire Fence (debut, 1940), My Son Is Guilty, Convicted Women, Men Without Souls, Babies for Sale, Blondie Play Cupid, The Lady in Question, So Ends Our Night, Texas, Go West Young Lady, The Adventures of Martin Eden, Flight Lieutenant, Destroyer, The Desperadoes, A Stolen Life, Gilda, Gallant Journey, Framed, The Mating of Millie, The Return of October, The Loves of Carmen, The Man from Colorado, Mr. Soft Touch, The Undercover Man, Lust for Gold, The Doctor and the Girl, The White Tower, Convicted, The Flying Missile, The Redhead and the Cowboy, Follow the Sun, The Secret of Convict Lake, Green Glove, Young Man with Ideas, Affair in Trinidad, Time Bomb (Terror on a Train), The Man from the Alamo, Plunder of the Sun, The Big Heat, Appointment in Honduras, Human Desire, The Americano, The Violent Men, Blackboard Jungle, Interrupted Melody, Trial, Ransom, The Fastest Gun Alive, Jubal, The Teahouse of the August Moon, 3:10 to Yuma, Don't Go Near the Water, Cowboy, The Sheepman, Imitation General, Torpedo Run, It Started With a Kiss, The Gazebo, Cimarron, Cry for Happy, Pocketful or Miracles, The Four Horsemen of The Apocalypse, Experiment in Terror, Love Is a Ball, The Courtship of Eddie's Father, Advance to the Rear, Fate Is the Hunter, Dear Heart, The Rounders, The Money Trap, Is Paris Burning?, Rage, A Time for Killing, The Last Challenge, Day of the Evil Gun, Heaven With a Gun, Smith!, Santee, Midway, Superman, The Visitor, Virus, Happy Birthday to Me, Border Shootout, Raw Nerve, Our Hollywood Education.
TELEVISION: Movies: Brotherhood of the Bell, The Greatest Gift, Punch and Jody, The 3000 Mile Chase, Evening in Byzantium, The Sacketts, Beggarman Thief, The Gift, Final

Verdict. *Mini-Series*: Once an Eagle. *Specials*: 100 Years of the Hollywood Western, AFI's 100 Years, 100 Thrills: America's Most Heart-Pounding Movies. *Series*: Cade's County, Friends of Man (narrator), The Family Holvak, When Havoc Struck (narrator).

FORD, HARRISON
Actor. b. Chicago, IL, July 13, 1942. e. Ripon Coll. Started acting in summer stock at Williams Bay, WI, in Damn Yankees, Little Mary Sunshine. Moved to L.A. where he acted in John Brown's Body. Signed by Columbia Studios under seven-year contract. Took break from acting to undertake carpentry work which included building Sergio Mendes' recording studio. Returned to acting in American Graffiti.
PICTURES: Dead Heat on a Merry-Go-Round (debut, 1966), Luv, A Time for Killing, Journey to Shiloh, Zabriskie Point, Getting Straight, American Graffiti, The Conversation, Star Wars, Heroes, Force 10 from Navarone, Hanover Street, The Frisco Kid, More American Graffiti (cameo), Apocalypse Now, The Empire Strikes Back, Raiders of the Lost Ark, Blade Runner, Return of the Jedi, Indiana Jones and the Temple of Doom, Witness (Acad. Award nom.), The Mosquito Coast, Frantic, Working Girl, Indiana Jones and the Last Crusade, Presumed Innocent, Regarding Henry, Patriot Games, The Fugitive, Jimmy Hollywood (cameo), Clear and Present Danger, Sabrina, The Devil's Own, Air Force One, Six Days Seven Nights, Random Hearts, What Lies Beneath, Lost Worlds (voice), K-19: The Widowmaker, Hollywood Homicide, Indiana Jones 4.
TELEVISION: *Movies*: The Intruders, James A. Michener's Dynasty, The Possessed. *Guest*: The Virginian, Ironside, The FBI, Love American Style, Gunsmoke, The Young Indiana Jones Chronicles. *Specials*: Trial of Lt. Calley, AFI's 100 Years, 100 Thrills: America's Most Heart-Pounding Movies, Concert for New York City.

FORD, MICHAEL
Set decorator, Sound, Actor.
PICTURES: Voyage to the Bottom of the Sea, Don't Worry We'll Think of a Title, Machismo-40 Guns for 40 Guns, The Empire Strikes Back, Raiders of the Lost Ark, Jinxed!, Return of the Jedi, Return of Oz, Empire of the Sun, The Living Daylights, Jaws: The Revenge, Back Street Jane, Licence to Kill, Kill Line, The Taking of Beverly Hills, Nostradamus, GoldenEye, Titanic (Acad. Award, Best Set. Decoration, 1997), Wing Commander.
TELEVISION: *Movies, actor*: Giving Tongue, September.

FORLANI, CLAIR
Actress. b. Twickenham, Middlesex, England, July 1, 1972.
PICTURES: Gypsy Eyes, Police Academy: Mission to Moscow, Mallrats, The Rock, Garage Sale, Basquiat, Basil, The Last Time I Commited Suicide, Meet Joe Black, Into My Heart, Mystery Men, Boys & Girls, Magicians, Anti-Trust, Triggermen, Johnny Domino, Going Greek, Highbinders, Trigger Men, Northfork, The Medallion, The Limit.
TELEVISION: *Movies:* The Pentagon Papers (2003). *Mini-series:* JFK: Reckless Youth.

FORMAN, SIR DENIS
O.B.E., M.A.: Executive. b. Moffat, Dumfriesshire, Scot., Oct. 13, 1917. e. Loretto Sch., Musselburgh, Pembroke Coll., Cambridge. Served in Argyll & Sutherland Highlanders, W.W.II. Entered film business 1946, production staff Central Office of Information, 1947; Chief Production Officer C.O.I. 1948; appointed dir. of the British Film Inst., 1949; joined Granada Television Ltd., 1955. Jnt. Mng. Dir., 1965 chmn., British Film Inst., bd. of Gov., 1971-73. Chmn. Granada T.V. 1975-87. Chmn. Novello & Co. 1972. Fellow, British Acad. Film & TV Arts, 1976. Dep. chmn. Granada Group, 1984-90, consultant, 1990-96. Deputy chmn. Royal Opera House, 1983-92. Film, My Life So Far (1999) based upon his autobiography.

FORMAN, JEROME A.
Executive. b. Hood River, Oregon, June 20, 1934. e. U. Arizona. 1966, became gen. mgr. Forman and United Theatres of the Northwest. 1971, joined Pacific Theatres; 1972, appointed v.p. & gen. mgr.; 1978-87, exec. v.p.; 1987-present, pres. One of the original founders of the ShoWest Convention. Currently chmn. emeritus, NATO of Calif.; 1991, chmn. NATO. 1991 elected chmn. bd. of Will Rogers Memorial Fund. Board member of the Foundation of the Motion Picture Pioneers.

FORMAN, MILOS
Director. b. Caslav, Czechoslovakia, Feb. 18, 1932. Trained as writer at Czech Film Sch. and as director at Laterna Magika. Directed short films Audition (Competition), If There Were No Music. Won Int'l. attention with first feature length film Black Peter, 1964. Emigrated to U.S. after collapse of Dubcek govt. in Czechoslovakia, 1969. Appeared as actor in films Heartburn, New Year's Day.
PICTURES: Peter and Pavla/Black Peter (also co-s.p.; Czech Film Critics & Grand Prix Locarno Awards), Loves of a Blonde (also co- s.p.), The Firemen's Ball (also co-s.p.), Taking Off (U.S. debut, 1971), Visions of Eight (Decathalon segment), One Flew Over the Cuckoo's Nest (Academy Award, 1975), Hair, Ragtime, Amadeus (Acad. Award, 1984), Valmont, The People vs. Larry Flynt (Golden Globe Award, 1997), Man on the Moon, Keeping the Faith (actor only), Milos Forman: Kino ist Wahrheit (actor only), In the Shadow of Hollywood (actor only), Way Past Cool (exec. prod.), AFI's 100 Years...100 Heroes & Villains (himself), The Nomad (exec. prod.), Embers (dir., s.p.)

FORREST, FREDERIC
Actor. b. Waxahachie, TX, Dec. 23, 1936. e. Texas Christian U., U. of Oklahoma, B.A. Studied with Sanford Meisner and Lee Strasberg. Began career off-off B'way at Caffe Cino in The Madness of Lady Bright then off-B'way in Futz, Massachusetts Trust and Tom Paine, all with La Mama Troupe under direction of Tom O'Horgan. Moved to Hollywood in 1970.
PICTURES: Futz (debut, 1969), When the Legends Die, The Don Is Dead, The Conversation, The Gravy Train, Permission to Kill, The Missouri Breaks, It Lives Again!, Apocalypse Now, The Rose (Acad. Award nom.), One From the Heart, Hammett, Valley Girl, The Stone Boy, Return, Where Are the Children?, Stacking, Tucker: The Man and His Dream, Valentino Returns, Music Box, The Two Jakes, Cat Chaser, Rain Without Thunder, Falling Down, Trauma, Chasers, One Night Stand, The Brave, The End of Violence, The Boogie Boy, Point Blank, Black Thunder, Whatever, One of Our Own, Implicated, The First 9 1/2 Weeks, Shadow Hours, Militia, A Piece of Eden, The Spreading Ground, The House Next Door, The Quality of Light.
TELEVISION: *Movies*: Larry, Promise Him Anything, Ruby and Oswald, Calamity Jane, Right to Kill?, The Deliberate Stranger, Quo Vadis, Little Girl Lost, Saigon: Year of the Cat (U.K.), Best Kept Secrets, Who Will Love My Children? A Shadow on the Sun, Margaret Bourke-White, Citizen Cohn, The Habitation of Dragons, Against the Wall, Double Jeopardy, Andersonville, Sweetwater, Shadow Lake, Alone, Path to War. *Mini-Series*: Die Kinder.

FORREST, STEVE
Actor. r.n. William Forrest Andrews. b. Huntsville, TX, Sept. 29, 1925. Brother of late actor Dana Andrews. e. UCLA, 1950. Acted at La Jolla Playhouse; appeared on radio, TV; m.p. debut in Crash Dive billed as William Andrews.
PICTURES: Crash Dive (debut, 1942), The Ghost Ship, Geisha Girl, Sealed Cargo, Last of the Comanches, The Bad and the Beautiful (1st billing as Steve Forrest), Dream Wife, Battle Circus, The Clown, The Band Wagon, So Big, Take the High Ground, Phantom of the Rue Morgue, Prisoner of War, Rogue Cop, Bedevilled, The Living Idol, It Happened to Jane, Heller in Pink Tights, Five Branded Women, Flaming Star, The Second Time Around, The Longest Day, The Yellow Canary, Rascal, The Wild Country, The Late Liz, North Dallas Forty, Mommie Dearest, Sahara, Spies Like Us, Amazon Women on the Moon, Storyville, Killer: A Journal of Murder.
TELEVISION: *Movies*: The Hatfields and the McCoys, Wanted: The Sundance Women, The Last of the Mohicans, Testimony of Two Men, Maneaters are Loose, Hollywood Wives, Gunsmoke: Return to Dodge, Columbo: A Bird in the Hand. *Series*: The Baron, S.W.A.T., Dallas.

FORSTER, ROBERT
Actor. b. Rochester, NY, July 13, 1941. e. Heidelberg Coll., Alfred U., Rochester U., B.S.
THEATRE: Mrs. Dally Has a Lover, A Streetcar Named Desire, The Glass Menagerie, 12 Angry Men, The Sea Horse, One Flew Over the Cuckoo's Nest, The Big Knife, In the Moonlight Eddie.
PICTURES: Reflections in a Golden Eye (debut, 1967), The Stalking Moon, Medium Cool, Justine, Cover Me Babe, Pieces of Dreams, Journey Through Rosebud, The Don is Dead, Stunts, Avalanche, The Black Hole, Lady in Red (unbilled), Crunch, Alligator, Vigilante, Walking the Edge, Hollywood Harry (also prod., dir.), The Delta Force, Committed, Esmeralda Bay, Heat from Another Sun, The Banker, Peacemaker, Diplomatic Immunity, 29th Street, In Between, Maniac Cop 3: Badge of Silence, South Beach, Cover Story, Body Chemistry 3: Point of Seduction, Demo University, American Perfekt, Original Gangstas, Jackie Brown, Outside Ozona, Psycho, Kiss Toledo Goodbye, Night Vision, Family Tree, Great Sex, Supernova, The Magic of Marciano, My Myself & Irene, Lakeboat, It's a Shame About Ray, Finder's Fee, Diamond Men, Mulholland Dr., Human Nature, Strange Hearts, The A-List, Lone Hero, Like Mike, Where's Angelo, Confidence, Charlie's Angels: Full Throttle, Grand Theft Parsons.
TELEVISION: *Series*: Banyon, Nakia, Once a Hero, Spawn (voice). *Movies*: Banyon, The Death Squad, Nakia, The City, Standing Tall, The Darker Side of Terror, Goliath Awaits, In the Shadow of a Killer, Sex Love and Cold Hard Cash, Rear Window, L.A. Sheriff's Homicide, Like Mother, Like Son: The Strange Story of Sante and Kenny Kimes, Due East. *Pilots*: Checkered Flag, Mickie & Frankie.

FORSYTH, BILL
Director. Writer. b. Glasgow, Scotland, July 29, 1946. At 16 joined film co. For next 10 years made industrial films, then documentaries. Joined Glasgow Youth Theater.
PICTURES: *Director-Writer:* That Sinking Feeling (debut, 1979; also prod.), Gregory's Girl, Local Hero, Comfort and Joy, Housekeeping, Breaking In, Rebecca's Daughters, Being Human, Gregory's Two Girls.
TELEVISION: Andrina.

FORSYTHE, JOHN
Actor. b. Penn's Grove, NJ, Jan. 29, 1918. r.n. John Freund. Former commentator for Brooklyn Dodgers, prior to becoming actor. Debuted on tv in 1947.
THEATRE: Mr. Roberts, All My Sons, Yellow Jack, Teahouse of the August Moon and others.
PICTURES: Destination Tokyo (debut, 1943), The Captive City, It Happens Every Thursday, The Glass Web, Escape From Fort Bravo, The Trouble With Harry, The Ambassador's Daughter,

Everything But the Truth, Kitten With a Whip, Madame X, In Cold Blood, The Happy Ending, Topaze, Goodbye and Amen, And Justice for All, Scrooged, Hotel de Love, Charlie's Angels I & II (voice).
TELEVISION: *Series*: Bachelor Father, The John Forsythe Show, To Rome With Love, Charlie's Angels (voice only), Dynasty, The Powers That Be. *Movies*: See How They Run, Shadow on the Land, Murder Once Removed, The Letters, Lisa—Bright and Dark, Cry Panic, Healers, Terror on the 40th Floor, The Deadly Tower, Amelia Earhart, Tail Gunner Joe, Never Con a Killer, Cruise Into Terror, With This Ring, The Users, A Time for Miracles, Sizzle, The Mysterious Two, On Fire, Opposites Attract, Dynasty: The Reunion. *Guest*: Studio One, Kraft Theatre, Robert Montgomery Presents, I Witness Video, Kings of the Court.

FORSYTHE, WILLIAM
Actor. b. Brooklyn, NY.
THEATRE: A Streetcar Named Desire, A Hatful of Rain, Othello, Julius Caesar, 1776, Hair, Godspell, Vox Humana #3, If You Don't Like It—You Can Leave.
PICTURES: King of the Mountain, Smokey Bites the Dust, The Man Who Wasn't There, Sons, Dead Bang, Torrents of Spring, Patty Hearst, Savage Dawn, Cloak and Dagger, The Lightship, Once Upon a Time in America, Raising Arizona, Extreme Prejudice, Weeds, Dick Tracy, Career Opportunities, Out for Justice, Stone Cold, The Waterdance, American Me, The Gun in Betty Lou's Handbag, Relentless 3, Direct Hit, Beyond Desire, The Immortals, Virtuosity, Don't Ask Too Much of love, Things to Do in Denver When You're Dead, The Substitute, The Rock, Palookaville, For Which He Stands, Firestorm, Hell's Kitchen, Row Your Boat, Deuce Bigalow Male Gigalo, Sound Man, Four Days, Blue Streak, Paradise Lost, The Last Marshall, Camouflage, Big City Blues, 18 Shades of Dust, Luck of the Draw, G-Men From Hell, The Librarians, Blue Hill Avenue, Outlaw, Coastlines, City by the Sea, Destiny, The Technical Writer, Scary Movie 3, The Librarians (also writer).
TELEVISION: *Movies*: The Miracle of Kathy Miller, The Long Hot Summer, Baja Oklahoma, Cruel Doubt, A Kiss to Die For, Bedroom Eyes, Willing to Kill: The Texas Cheerleader Story, Peacock Blues, Gotti. *Series*: The Untouchables (1993), UC: Undercover, John Doe. *Guest*: CHiPs, Fame, Hill Street Blues. *Mini-Series*: Blind Faith.

FORTE, FABIAN
Singer, Actor. b. Philadelphia, PA, Feb. 6, 1943. e. South Philadelphia H.S. At 14, signed contract with Chancellor Records. Studied with Carlo Menotti. Formerly billed simply as Fabian.
RECORDS: Turn Me Loose, Tiger, I'm a Man, Hound Dog Man, The Fabulous Fabian (gold album).
PICTURES: Hound Dog Man (debut, 1959), High Time, North to Alaska, Love in a Goldfish Bowl, Five Weeks in a Balloon, Mr. Hobbs Takes a Vacation, The Longest Day, Ride the Wild Surf, Dear Brigitte, Ten Little Indians, Fireball 500, Dr. Goldfoot and the Girl Bombs, Thunder Alley, Maryjane, The Wild Racers, The Devil's Eight, A Bullet for Pretty Boy, Lovin' Man, Little Laura and Big John, Disco Fever, Kiss Daddy Goodbye, Get Crazy, Up Close and Personal.
TELEVISION: *Movies*: Getting Married, Katie: Portrait of a Centerfold, Crisis in Mid-Air. *Guest*: Bus Stop, Love American Style, Laverne & Shirley, The Love Boat. *Special*: Mr. Rock 'n' Roll: The Alan Freed Story.

FOSSEY, BRIGITTE
Actress. b. Tourcoing, France, Mar. 11, 1947. After debut at the age of 5 in Rene Clement's Forbidden Games (1952) returned to school, studying philosophy and translating. Rediscovered by director Jean-Gabriel Albicocco and cast in Le Grand Meaulnes (1967).
PICTURES: Forbidden Games (debut, 1952), The Happy Road, Le Grand Meaulnes (The Wanderer), Adieu l'Ami, M Comme Mathieu, Raphael ou le DeBauche, Going Places, La Brigade, The Blue Country, Femme Fetales, The Good and the Bad, The Man Who Loved Women, The Swiss Affair, Quintet, Mais ou et donc Orincar, The Triple Death of the Third Character, A Bad Son, The Party, Chanel Solitaire, A Bite of Living, Imperativ, The Party-2, Enigma, Au nom de tous les Meins, Scarlet Fever, A Strange Passion, A Case of Irresponsibility, The Future of Emily, The False Confidences, Cinema Paradiso, Dial Code Santa Claus, The Last Butterfly, Shipwrecked Children, A Vampire in Paradise.
TELEVISION: Various European movies and specials.

FOSTER, CHRISTINE
Executive. r.n. Mary Christine Foster. b. Los Angeles, CA, March 19, 1943. e. Immaculate Heart Coll, B.A. 1967. UCLA MJ, 1968. Teacher while member of Immaculate Heart Community, 1962-65. Teacher, Pacific U., Tokyo, 1968; dir., research and dev. Metromedia Producers Corp., 1968-71; dir., dev. & prod. services, Wolper Org. 1971-76; mgr., film progs. NBC TV 1976-77; v.p. movies for TV & mini-series, Columbia Pictures TV, 1977-81; v.p. series programs, Columbia TV, 1981; v.p. prog. dev., Group W. Prods. 1981-87; v.p., The Agency, 1988-90; agent, Shapiro-Lichtman-Stein Talent Agency, 1990-. Member: exec. comm. Humanitas Awards, 1986-; exec. comm. Catholics in Media, 1993-; Activities Committee, Acad. of TV Arts & Sciences, 1989-91; L.A. Roman Catholic Archdiocesan communications Comm., 1986-89; Women in Film, bd. of dirs., 1977-78 teacher at UCLA Extension, 1987-. Foreign and domestic university and public group lecturer and speaker.

FOSTER, DAVID
Producer. b. New York, NY, Nov. 25, 1929. e. Dorsey H.S., U. of Southern California Sch. of Journalism. U.S. Army, 1952-54; entered public relations field in 1952 with Rogers, Cowan & Brenner; Jim Mahoney, 1956; Allan, Foster, Ingersoll & Weber, 1958; left field in 1968 to enter independent m.p. production. Was partner in Turman-Foster Co.
PICTURES: *Producer* (with Mitchell Brower): McCabe and Mrs. Miller, The Getaway. Produced (with Lawrence Turman): The Nickel Ride (exec. prod.), The Drowning Pool, The Legacy, Tribute (exec. prod.), Caveman, The Thing, Second Thoughts, Mass Appeal, The Mean Season, Short Circuit, Running Scared, Full Moon in Blue Water, Short Circuit II, Gleaming the Cube, The Getaway (1993), The River Wild, The Mask of Zorro, Collateral Damage, Hart's War, The Core.
TELEVISION: Jesse (co-exec. prod), Between Two Brothers, Surrogate Mother.

FOSTER, JODIE
Actress. r.n. Alicia Christian Foster. b. Los Angeles, CA, Nov. 19, 1962. e. Yale U. Started acting in commercials including famous Coppertone ad. Acting debut on Mayberry, R.F.D. TV series (1968). Followed with many TV appearances, from series to movies of the week.
PICTURES: Napoleon and Samantha (debut, 1972), Kansas City Bomber, Tom Sawyer, One Little Indian, Alice Doesn't Live Here Anymore, Taxi Driver (Acad. Award nom.), Echoes of a Summer, Bugsy Malone, Freaky Friday, The Little Girl Who Lives Down the Lane, Il Casotto (The Beach Hut), Moi fleur bleue (Stop Calling Me Baby!), Candleshoe, Foxes, Carny, O'Hara's Wife, The Hotel New Hampshire, Mesmerized (also co-prod.), Siesta, Five Corners, Stealing Home, The Accused (Academy Award, 1988), The Silence of the Lambs (Academy Award, 1991), Little Man Tate (also dir.), Shadows and Fog, Sommersby, Maverick, Nell (Acad. Award nom.; also co-prod.), Home for the Holidays (dir., co-prod. only), Contact, Anna and the King, The Dangerous Lives of Altar Boys, Flora Plum (dir. and prod. only), The Panic Room, Tusker.
TELEVISION: *Specials*: Alexander, Rookie of the Year, Menace on the Mountain, The Secret Life of T.K. Dearing, The Fisherman's Wife. *Movies*: Smile Jenny--You're Dead, The Blood of Others, Svengali, Backtrack. *Series*: Bob & Carol & Ted & Alice, Paper Moon. *Guest*: The Courtship of Eddie's Father, Gunsmoke, Julia, Mayberry R.F.D., Ironside, My Three Sons.

FOSTER, JULIA
Actress. b. Lewes, Sussex, England, 1941. First acted with the Brighton Repertory Company, then two years with the Worthing, Harrogate and Richmond companies. 1956, TV debut as Ann Carson in Emergency Ward 10.
THEATRE: The Country Wife, What the Butler Saw.
PICTURES: Term of Trial (debut, 1962), The Loneliness of the Long Distance Runner, Two Left Feet, The Small World of Sammy Lee, The System (The Gir Getters), The Bargee, One Way Pendulum, Alfie, Half a Sixpence, All Coppers Are..., The Great McGonagall.
TELEVISION: *Movies*: A Cosy Little Arrangement, The Planemakers, Love Story, Taxi, Consequences, They Throw It at You, Crime and Punishment, The Image, Henry VI Pt. 1 of 3, Cabbage Patch, The Tragedy of Richard III. Moll Flanders. *Series*: Good Girl, The Wilde Alliance, The Cabbage Patch.

FOSTER, MEG
Actress. b. Reading, PA, May 14, 1948.
PICTURES: Adam at 6 A.M. (debut, 1970), Thumb Tripping, Welcome to Arrow Beach (Tender Flesh), A Different Story, Once in Paris, Carny, Ticket to Heaven, The Osterman Weekend, The Emerald Forest, Masters of the Universe, The Wind, They Live, Leviathan, Relentless, Stepfather 2, Blind Fury, Tripwire, Jezebel's Kiss, Diplomatic Immunity, Dead One: Relentless II, Project Shadowchaser, Immortal Combat, Undercover Heat, The Killers Within, Space Marines, Oblivion 2: Backlash, Spoiler, The Man in the Iron Mask, The Lost Valley, The Minus Man, The Mask of Dumas.
TELEVISION: *Movies*: The Death of Me Yet, Sunshine, Things In This Season, Promise Him Anything, James Dean, Sunshine Christmas, Guyana Tragedy, Legend of Sleepy Hollow, Desperate Intruder, Best Kept Secrets, Desperate, Back Stab, To Catch a Killer. *Series*: Sunshine, Cagney & Lacey. *Guest*: Here Come the Brides, Mod Squad, Men at Law, Hawaii Five-O, Murder She Wrote, Miami Vice. *Mini-Series*: Washington: Behind Closed Doors. *Special*: The Scarlet Letter.

FOWKES, RICHARD O.
Executive. b. Yonkers, NY, April 15, 1946. e. NYU, Geo. Washington U. Staff attorney for The Dramatists Guild, 1973-77; joined Paramount as assoc. counsel, 1977-80; moved to UA (NYC) as prod. attorney from 1980-82; returned to Paramount as v.p., legal & bus. affairs, MoPic division (LA) 1983; promoted to sr. v.p., bus. affairs & acquisitions, 1989; promoted to sr. v.p. in charge of bus. affairs, 1994.

FOWLER, HARRY
Actor. b. London, England, Dec. 10, 1926. e. West Central Sch., London. Stage debut, Nothing Up My Sleeve (London) 1950; Screen debut, 1941.
PICTURES: Demi-Paradise, Don't Take It to Heart, Champaigne Charlie, Painted Boats, Hue and Cry, Now Barabbas, The Dark Man, She Shall Have Murder, The Scarlet Thread, High Treason, The Last Page, I Believe in You, Pickwick Papers, Top of the

Form, Angels One Five, Conflict of Wings (Fuss Over Feathers), A Day to Remember, Blue Peter, Home and Away, Booby Trap, Town on Trial, Lucky Jim, Birthday Present, Idle on Parade, Don't Panic Chaps, Heart of a Man, Crooks Anonymous, The Longest Day, Lawrence of Arabia, Flight from Singapore, The Golliwog, Ladies Who Do, Clash By Night, The Nanny, Life at the Top, Start the Revolution Without Me, The Prince and The Pauper, Fanny Hill, Chicago Joe and the Showgirl.
TELEVISION: Stalingrad, I Remember the Battle, Gideon's Way, That's for Me, Our Man at St. Mark's, Dixon of Dock Green, Dr. Finlay's Case Book, I Was There, Cruffs Dog Show, The Londoners, Jackanory, Get This, Movie Quiz, Get This (series), Going a Bundle, Ask a Silly Answer, London Scene, Flockton Flyer, Sun Trap, The Little World of Don Camillo, World's End, Minder, Dead Ernest, Morecambe Wise Show, Gossip, Entertainment Express, Fresh Fields, Supergram, A Roller Next Year, Harry's Kingdom, Body Contact, Davro's Sketch Pad, The Bill, In Sickness and in Health, Casualty, Leaves on the Line, Young Indiana Jones Chronicles, Southside Party, London Tonight, Alma Cogan: The Girl with the Giggle In Her Voice, Blondes: Diana Dors.

FOX, EDWARD
Actor. b. London, England, April 13, 1937. Comes from theatrical family; father was agent for leading London actors; brother is actor James Fox.
PICTURES: The Mind Benders (debut, 1962), Morgan!, The Frozen Dead, The Long Duel, The Naked Runner, The Jokers, I'll Never Forget What's 'is Name, The Battle of Britain, Oh! What a Lovely War, Skullduggery, The Go-Between, The Day of The Jackal, A Doll's House, Galileo, The Squeeze, A Bridge Too Far, The Duellists, The Big Sleep, Force 10 from Navarone, The Cat and the Canary, Soldier of Orange, The Mirror Crack'd, Gandhi, Never Say Never Again, The Dresser, The Bounty, Wild Geese II, The Shooting Party, Return From the River Kwai, A Feast at Midnight, A Month by the Lake, Prince Valiant, Lost in Space, All the Queen's Men, The Importance of Being Earnest, Nicholas Nickleby, The Republic of Love.
TELEVISION: Edward and Mrs. Simpson, A Hazard of Hearts, Anastasia: The Mystery of Anna, Quartermaine's Terms, They Never Slept, Shaka Zulu, Robin Hood, The Crucifer of Blood, Forbidden Territory, I Was a Rat, Foyle's War, The Maitlands, Gulliver's Travels, September, A Dance to the Music of Time, Daniel Deronda.

FOX, JAMES
Actor. b. London, England, May 19, 1939. Brother is actor Edward Fox. Ent. films as child actor in 1950 as William Fox. Left acting in 1973 to follow spiritual vocation. Returned to mainstream films in 1982. B'way debut 1995 in Uncle Vanya.
PICTURES: The Miniver Story (debut, 1950; as William Fox), The Magnet, One Wild Oat, The Lavender Hill Mob, Timbuktu, The Queen's Guards, The Secret Partner, She Always Gets Their Man, What Every Woman Wants, The Loneliness of the Long-Distance Runner, Tamahine (1st film billed as James Fox), The Servant, Those Magnificent Men in Their Flying Machines, King Rat, The Chase, Thoroughly Modern Millie, Arabella, Duffy, Isadora, Performance, No Longer Alone, Runners, Greystoke: The Legend of Tarzan, A Passage to India, Pavlova, Absolute Beginners, The Whistle Blower, Comrades, High Season, The Mighty Quinn, Farewell to the King, The Boys in the Island, The Russia House, Patriot Games, Afraid of the Dark, The Remains of the Day, Anna Karenina, Up at the Villa, Shadow Run, Mickey Blue Eyes, The Golden Bowl, Sexy Beast, All Forgotten, The Mystic Masseur, Light in the Sky.
TELEVISION: The Door, Espionage, Love Is Old, Love Is New, Nancy Astor, Country, New World, Beryl Markham: A Shadow on the Sun, Sun Child, She's Been Away (BBC; shown theatrically in U.S.), Never Come Back, Slowly Slowly in the Wind, Patricia Highsmith Series, As You Like It, A Question of Attribution, Heart of Darkness, Fall from Grace, Hostage, Doomsday Gun, Headhunters, The Old Curiosity Shop, Fall From Grace, The Choir, Gulliver's Travels, Kings in Grass Castles, Metropolis, Armadillo, The Lost World, Hans Christian Andersen, Shaka Zulu: The Citadel, The Falklands Play, Trial & Retribution VI, Cambridge Spies.

FOX, JORJA
Actress.b. July 7, 1968.
PICTURES: Traveling Companion (comp. only), Kill-Off, Happy Hell Night, Dead Drunk, Dead Funny, The Jerky Boys, Velocity Trap, How to Make the Cruelest Month, The Hungry Bachelors Club, Memento, Forever Fabulous, Down with the Joneses.
TELEVISION: Mini-Series: Summer Stories: The Mall, House of Frankenstein 1997. Series: Missing Persons, ER, The West Wing, CSI. Guest: Law and Order, Moloney, Ellen.

FOX, MICHAEL J.
Actor. b. Edmonton, Alberta, Canada, June 9, 1961. r.n. Michael Andrew Fox. m. actress Tracy Pollan. Appeared in Vancouver TV series Leo and Me, and on stage there in The Shadow Box. Moved to Los Angeles at age 18.
PICTURES: Midnight Madness (debut, 1980), The Class of 1984, Back to the Future, Teen Wolf, Light of Day, The Secret of My Success, Bright Lights Big City, Casualties of War, Back to the Future Part II, Back to the Future Part III, The Hard Way, Doc Hollywood, Homeward Bound: The Incredible Journey (voice), Life With Mikey, For Love or Money, Where the Rivers Flow North, Greedy, Coldblooded (also co-prod.), Blue in the Face, The American President, Homeward Bound II: Lost in San

Francisco (voice), The Frighteners, Mars Attacks!, Stuart Little (voice), Atlantis: The Lost Empire (voice), Interstate 60, Stuart Little 2 (voice).
TELEVISION: Movies: Letters From Frank, High School USA, Poison Ivy, Family Ties Vacation, Don't Drink the Water, I Am Your Child, Hench At Home (writer only), Magic 7 (voice). Series: Palmerston U.S.A., Family Ties (3 Emmy Awards), Spin City (Golden Globe Award, 1998; Emmy award, 2000), Otherwise Engaged (exec. prod. only). Guest: Lou Grant, The Love Boat, Night Court, Trapper John M.D., Tales from the Crypt (The Trap; also dir.). Specials: Teachers Only, Time Travel: Fact Fiction and Fantasy, Dear America: Letters Home From Vietnam (reader), James Cagney: Top of the World (host), The Concert for New York City.Director: Brooklyn Bridge (episode).

FOX, RICHARD
Executive. b. New York, NY, Feb. 24, 1947. Joined Warner Bros. Intl. as mgt. trainee in October 1975, working in Australia and Japan. 1977, named gen. mgr. of Columbia-Warner Dist., New Zealand. Served as gen. mgr. of WB in Tokyo, 1978\-1981. Joined WB in L.A. as exec. asst. to Myron D. Karlin, pres. of WB Intl., 1981; appt. v.p., sls. 1982; 1983, promoted to exec. v.p. of intl. arm; 1985, named pres. of WB Intl., assuming post vacated by Karlin. 1992, promoted to exec. v.p., Intl. Theatrical Enterprises, Warner Bros. Currently, EVP-International at Warner Bros. Entertainment Inc.

FOX, VIVICA A.
Actress. b. July 30, 1964.
PICTURES: Born on the Fourth of July, Don't Be a Menace to South Central While Drinking Your Juice in the Hood, Independence Day, Set It Off, Booty Call, Batman & Robin, Soul Food, Teaching Mrs. Tingle, Why Do Fools Fall in Love?, Idle Hands, Double Take, Kingdome Come, Two Can Play that Game, Juwanna Mann, Boat Trip, Ride or Die, Kill Bill, Ella Enchanted, Motive (also prod.), Blast!
TELEVISION: Series: The Young and the Restless, Generations, Getting Personal, Arsenio. Movies: Out All Night, The Tuskegee Airmen, Solomon, A Saintly Switch, Hendrix. Guest: Who's the Boss, The Fresh Prince of Bel-Air, Beverly Hills 90210.

FOXWORTH, ROBERT
Actor. b. Houston, TX, Nov. 1, 1941. e. Carnegie-Mellon U. Began acting at age 10 at Houston Alley Theatre and stayed with stage part-time while completing formal education. Returned to theatre on full-time basis after graduation. Made TV debut in Sadbird, 1969.
THEATRE: NY: Henry V, Terra Nova, The Crucible (Theatre World Award), Love Letters, Candida. Regional: Antony & Cleopatra, Uncle Vanya, Cyrano de Bergerac, Who's Afraid of Virginia Woolf?, Othello, Habeus Corpus, The Seagull, Macbeth.
PICTURES: Treasure of Matecumbe (debut, 1976), The Astral Factor, Airport '77, Damien: Omen II, Prophecy, The Black Marble, Beyond the Stars.
TELEVISION: Movies: The Devil's Daughter, Frankenstein, Mrs. Sundance, The Questor Tapes (pilot), The FBI Story: The FBI Vs. Alvin Karpis, James Dean, It Happened at Lakewood Manor, Death Moon, The Memory of Eva Ryker, Act of Love, Peter and Paul, The Return of the Desperado, Double Standard, Face to Face, The Price of the Bride, With Murder in Mind, For Love and Glory. Specials: Hogan's Goat, Another Part of the Forest. Series: The Storefront Lawyers, Falcon Crest, 2000 Malibu Road, Real Adventures of Johnny Quest (voice), Lateline, Six Feet Under.

FOXX, JAMIE
Actor. b. Terrell, TX, December 13, 1967.
PICTURES: Toys, The Truth About Cats & Dogs, The Great White Hype, The Player's Club, Booty Call, Any Given Sunday, Bait, Date From Hell, All Jokes Aside, Ali, Shade, Unchain My Heart: The Ray Charles Story.
TELEVISION: Series: In Living Color, The Jamie Foxx Show (also prod.), C Bear and Jamal (voice), It's Black Entertainment. Special: Inside TV Land: African Americans in Television, Jamie Foxx: I Might Need Security.

FRAKER, WILLIAM A.
Cinematographer, Director. b. Los Angeles, CA, Sept. 29, 1923. e. U. of Southern California Film Sch. Worked as camera operator with Conrad Hall; moved to TV before feature films. Photographed and co-prod. doc. Forbid Them Not.
PICTURES: Cinematographer: Games, The Fox, The President's Analyst, Fade In, Rosemary's Baby, Bullitt, Paint Your Wagon, Dusty and Sweets McGee, The Day of the Dolphin, Rancho Deluxe, Aloha Bobby and Rose, Lipstick, The Killer Inside Me, Gator, Exorcist II--The Heretic, Looking for Mr. Goodbar, American Hot Wax, Heaven Can Wait, Old Boyfriends, 1941, The Hollywood Knights, Divine Madness, Sharky's Machine, The Best Little Whorehouse in Texas, WarGames, Irreconcilable Differences, Protocol, Fever Pitch, Murphy's Romance, SpaceCamp, Burglar, Baby Boom, Chances Are, An Innocent Man, The Freshman, Memoirs of an Invisible Man, Honeymoon in Vegas, Tombstone (also co-assoc. prod.), Street Fighter, Father of the Bride II, The Island of Dr. Moreau, Vegas Vacation, Rules of Engagement, Town & Country, Waking Up in Reno. Director: Monte Walsh, Reflection of Fear, Legend of the Lone Ranger.
TELEVISION: Stony Burke, Outer Limits, Ozzie and Harriet, Daktari, B.L. Stryker: The Dancer's Touch (dir.), Walker Texas Ranger (dir.).

FRAKES, JONATHAN
Actor, Director. b. Bethlehem, PA, Aug. 19, 1952. m. Actress Genie Francis.
PICTURES: Gargoyles: The Heroes Awaken (voice), Star Trek: Generations, Star Trek: First Contact (also dir.), Trekkies, Star Trek: Insurrection (also dir.), Star Trek: Nemesis, Director: Clockstoppers, The Thunderbirds.
TELEVISION: Movies: Beach Patrol, The Night the City Screamed, Star Trek: The Next Generation (pilot), The Cover Girl and the Cop, Dying to Live. Series: The Doctors, Bare Essence, Paper Dolls, Star Trek: The Next Generation (also dir.), Gargoyles (voice), University Hospital (dir. only), Gargoyles: The Goliath Chronicles (voice) Beyond Belief: Fact or Fiction, The Lot. Mini-series: Beulah Land, North & South, North & South II, Dream West, Nutcracker: Money—Madness & Murder, North & South III, The Lot. Guest: Voyagers, Remington Steele, Highway to Heaven, Matlock, Married... With Children, The New Twilight Zone, Star Trek: Deep Space Nine (also dir.), Wings, Lois & Clark, Star Trek: Voyager (also dir.), Cybill.

FRANCIOSA, ANTHONY
Actor. b. New York, NY, Oct. 25, 1928. e. Ben Franklin h.s. in NY. Erwin Piscator's Dramatic Workshop (4-year scholarship). First stage part in YWCA play; joined Off-Broadway stage group; stock at Lake Tahoe, CA, Chicago and Boston.
THEATRE: B'way: End as a Man, The Wedding Breakfast, A Hatful of Rain (Theatre World Award, Tony nom.), Rocket to the Moon, Grand Hotel. Tour: Love Letters.
PICTURES: A Face in the Crowd (debut, 1957), This Could Be The Night, A Hatful of Rain (Acad. Award nom.), Wild Is The Wind, The Long Hot Summer, The Naked Maja, Career, The Story on Page One, Go Naked in the World, Senilita (Carless), Period of Adjustment, Rio Conchos, The Pleasure Seekers, A Man Could Get Killed, Assault on a Queen, The Swinger, Fathom, In Enemy Country, The Sweet Ride, A Man Called Gannon, Ghost in the Noonday Sun, Across 110th Street, The Drowning Pool, Firepower, The World is Full of Married Men, Death Wish II, Julie Darling, Ghost in the Noonday Sun, Death Is in Fashion, Tenebrae, Help Me Dream, The Cricket, A Texas Legend, Backstreet Dreams, Death House, Brothers in Arms, Double Threat, City Hall.
TELEVISION: Movies: Fame is the Name of the Game, Deadly Hunt, Earth II, The Catcher, This is the West That Was, Matt Helm, Curse of the Black Widow, Side Show, Till Death Do Us Part, Ghost Writer. Mini-Series: Aspen, Wheels. Guest: Kraft Theatre, Philco Playhouse, Danger, Naked City, Arrest & Trial, Playhouse 90, etc Specials: A Lincoln Portrait, (narrator). Series: Valentine's Day, The Name of the Game, Search, Matt Helm, Finder of Lost Loves.

FRANCIS, ANNE
Actress b. Ossining, NY, Sept. 16, 1932. Child model; radio, TV shows as child & adult; on B'way in Lady in the Dark.
PICTURES: Summer Holiday (debut, 1948), So Young So Bad, Whistle at Eaton Falls, Elopement, Lydia Bailey, Dream Boat, A Lion Is in the Streets, Rocket Man, Susan Slept Here, Rogue Cop, Bad Day at Black Rock, Battle Cry, Blackboard Jungle, The Scarlet Coat, Forbidden Planet, The Rack, The Great American Pastime, The Hired Gun, Don't Go Near the Water, Crowded Sky, Girl of the Night, Satan Bug, Brainstorm, Funny Girl, Hook Line and Sinker, More Dead Than Alive, The Love God?, Impasse, Pancho Villa, Survival, Born Again, The High Fashion Murders, The Return, Little Vegas, The Double-O Kid, Lover's Knot.
TELEVISION: Movies: Wild Women, The Intruders, The Forgotten Man, Fireball Forward, Haunts of the Very Rich, Cry Panic, FBI Vs. Alvin Karpis, The Last Survivors, A Girl Named Sooner, Banjo Hackett, Little Mo, The Rebels, Beggarman Thief, Detour to Terror, Rona Jaffe's Mazes and Monsters, Poor Little Rich Girl: The Barbara Hutton Story, Laguna Heat, My First Love, Love Can Be Murder, Have You Seen My Son? Series: Honey West, My Three Sons, Dallas, Riptide. Guest: Partners in Crime, Crazy Like a Fox, Jake and the Fatman, Twilight Zone, Finder of Lost Loves, Golden Girls, Matlock, Murder She Wrote, Burke's Law.

FRANCIS, CONNIE
Singer. r.n. Constance Franconero. b. Newark, NJ, Dec. 12, 1938. Appeared, Star Time when 12 years old; won Arthur Godfrey's Talent Scout Show, 12 years old. Autobiography: Who's Sorry Now (1984). Regular on series The Jimmie Rodgers Show, 1959. Gold Records: Who's Sorry Now, My Happiness. Numerous vocalist awards.
PICTURES: Where the Boys Are, Follow the Boys, Looking For Love, The Craft (singer, "Fallin"),
TELEVISION: Movies: Connie Francis: A Legend in Concert, Visions of Italy-Northern Style (documentary, singer).

FRANCIS, FREDDIE
Producer, Director, Cinematographer. b. London, Dec. 22, 1917. Joined Gaumont British Studios as apprentice to stills photographer; then clapper boy at B.I.P. Studios, Elstree; camera asst. at British Dominion. After W.W.II returned to Shepperton Studios to work for Korda and with Powell and Pressburger as cameraman.
PICTURES: Director: Two and Two Make Six (A Change of Heart/The Girl Swappers; debut, 1962), Paranoiac, Vengeance, The Evil of Frankenstein, Nightmare, Traitor's Gate, Hysteria, Dr. Terror's House of Horrors, The Skull, The Psychopath, The Deadly Bees, They Came from Beyond Space, Torture Garden, Dracula Has Risen from the Grave, Mumsy Nanny Sonny and Girly, Trog, Tales from the Crypt, The Creeping Flesh, Tales That Witness Madness, Son of Dracula, Craze, The Ghoul, Legend of the Werewolf, The Doctor and the Devils, Dark Tower. Cinematographer: Moby Dick (second unit photo., special effects), A Hill in Korea (Hell in Korea), Time Without Pity, Room at the Top, The Battle of the Sexes, Saturday Night and Sunday Morning, Sons and Lovers (Academy Award, 1960), The Innocents, Night Must Fall, The Elephant Man, The French Lieutenant's Woman, Dune, Memed My Hawk, Clara's Heart, Her Alibi, Brenda Starr, Glory (Academy Award, 1989), Man in the Moon, Cape Fear, School Ties, Princess Caraboo, Rainbow, The Straight Story, Ghosthunter (short).
TELEVISION: Movie: A Life in the Theatre.

FRANCIS, KEVIN
Producer, Executive. b. London, England, 1949. Produced It's Life, Passport, Trouble with Canada, Persecution, The Ghoul, Legend of the Werewolf, etc. Exec. prod.: The Masks of Death, Murder Elite, A One-Way Ticket to Hollywood, etc. 1976, prod. Film Technique Educational course for BFI. 1972-94, CEO Tyburn Prods. Ltd. 1994-present, Arlington Productions Ltd.

FRANK, SCOTT
Writer. b. 1960.
PICTURES: Plain Clothes (story), The Walter Ego, Little Man Tate, Dead Again, Malice, Get Shorty, Heaven's Prisoners, Out of Sight (Acad. Award nom.), Minority Report (also second unit dir.), Dawn of the Dead (s.p.).

FRANKENHEIMER, JOHN
Director. b. Malba, NY, Feb. 19, 1930. e. Williams Coll. Actor, dir., summer stock; radio-TV actor, dir., Washington, DC; then joined CBS network in 1953. Theater: The Midnight Sun (1959).
PICTURES: The Young Stranger (debut, 1957), The Young Savages, Birdman of Alcatraz, All Fall Down, The Manchurian Candidate (also co-prod.), Seven Days in May, The Train, Seconds, Grand Prix, The Fixer, The Extraordinary Seaman, The Gypsy Moths, I Walk the Line, The Horsemen, The Impossible Object (Story of a Love Story), The Iceman Cometh, 99 and 44/100% Dead, French Connection II, Black Sunday, Prophecy, The Challenge, The Holcroft Covenant, 52 Pick-Up, Dead-Bang, The Fourth War, Year of the Gun, The Island of Dr. Moreau, Ronin, Reindeer Games, Ambush.
TELEVISION: Movies: Against the Wall (Emmy Award, 1994), The Burning Season (Emmy Award, 1995; also co-prod.), George Wallace (Emmy Award, 1998; also prod.), Path to War (also exec. prod.) Mini-Series: Andersonville (Emmy Award, 1996). Series dir.: I Remember Mama, You Are There, Danger, Climax, Studio One, Playhouse 90, Du Pont Show of the Month, Ford Startime, Sunday Showcase. Specials: The Comedian, For Whom the Bell Tolls, The Days of Wine and Roses, Old Man, The Turn of the Screw, The Browning Version, The Rainmaker.

FRANKLIN, BONNIE
Actress. b. Santa Monica, CA, Jan. 6, 1944. e. Smith & UCLA.
THEATRE: B'way: Applause (Theatre World Award, Tony nom. Outer Critics Circle award). Off-B'way: Frankie and Johnny in the Claire de Lune. Grace & Glory, Dames at Sea, Your Own Thing.
PICTURES: Broadway: The Golden Age by the Legends Who Were There.
TELEVISION: Series: One Day at a Time, The New Munsters (dir. only). Movies: The Law, A Guide for the Married Woman, Breaking Up Is Hard to Do, Portrait of a Rebel: Margaret Sanger, Your Place or Mine, Sister Margaret and Saturday Night Ladies.

FRANKLIN, CARL
Actor, Director. b. Richmond, CA April 11, 1949.
PICTURES: Actor: Five on the Black Hand Side, Eye of the Eagle 2: Inside the Enemy (also dir, s.p.), Last Stand at Lang Mei (also s.p.), Full Fathom Five (also dir.), In the Heat of Passion. Director: Punk, Nowhere to Run, One False Move, Devil in a Blue Dress (also s.p.), One True Thing, High Crimes, Out of Time.
TELEVISION: Movies: It Couldn't Happen to a Nicer Guy, The Legend of the Golden Gun, One Cooks, The Other Doesn't, Too Good to be True, Laurel Avenue (dir. only). Series: The A-Team, Partners. Guest: Streets of San Francisco, Good Times, Cannon, Trapper John M.D., Lou Grant, MacGyver, Roseanne.

FRANKLIN, PAMELA
Actress. b. Tokyo, Japan, Feb. 4, 1950. Attended Elmshurst Ballet Sch., Camberley, Surrey.
PICTURES: The Innocents (debut, 1961), The Lion, The Third Secret, Flipper's New Adventure, The Nanny, Our Mother's House, The Prime of Miss Jean Brodie, The Night of the Following Day, And Soon the Darkness, Necromancy, Ace Eli and Rodger of the Skies, The Legend of Hell House, The Food of the Gods.
TELEVISION: Movies: The Horse Without a Head (theatrical in U.K.), See How They Run, David Copperfield (theatrical in U.K.), The Letters, Satan's School for Girls, Crossfire, Eleanor and Franklin.

FRANKLIN, RICHARD
Director, Producer, Writer. b. Melbourne, Australia, July 15, 1948. e. USC (Cinema, 1967).
PICTURES: Director: The True Story of Eskimo Nell (also co-prod., co-s.p.), Patrick (also co-prod., co-s.p.), The Blue Lagoon (co-prod. only), Road Games (also prod., co-s.p.), Psycho II, Cloak and Dagger, Into the Night (actor only), Link (also prod.), FX2, Hotel Sorrento (also prod.), Brilliant Lies, Visitors.

TELEVISION: *Pilots:* Beauty and the Beast, A Fine Romance. *Movies:* Running Delilah, One Way Ticket. *Series:* The Lost World, Flatland.

FRANKLIN, ROBERT A.
Executive. b. New York, NY, April 15. e. U. of Miami, B.B.A., 1958; Columbia Pacific U., M.B.A., 1979; Ph.D., 1980 majoring in marketing. Before entering film industry worked with House of Seagram, Canada Dry Corp., J. M. Mathes Adv. 1967, joined 20th Century-Fox as dir. of mkt. planning. Formed RP Marketing Intl. (entertainment consulting firm) in 1976 and World Research Systems (computer software marketer). 1981 joined MPAA; 1983, named v.p., admin. & info. services. 1986, named v.p. worldwide market research. Chmn., MPAA research comm.; member, AMA and ESOMAR.

FRANZ, ARTHUR
Actor. b. Perth Amboy, NJ, Feb. 29, 1920. e. Blue Ridge Coll., MD. U.S. Air Force. Radio, TV shows.
THEATER: A Streetcar Named Desire, Second Threshold.
PICTURES: Jungle Patrol (debut, 1948), Roseanna McCoy, The Red Light, The Doctor and the Girl, Sands of Iwo Jima, Red Stallion in the Rockies, Three Secrets, Tarnished, Abbott and Costello Meet the Invisible Man, Flight to Mars, Submarine Command, Strictly Dishonorable, The Sniper, Rainbow 'Round My Shoulder, The Member of the Wedding, Eight Iron Men, Invaders From Mars, Bad for Each Other, The Eddie Cantor Story, Flight Nurse, The Caine Mutiny, Steel Cage, Battle Taxi, New Orleans Uncensored, Bobby Ware Is Missing, Beyond a Reasonable Doubt, The Wild Party, Running Target, The Devil's Hairpin, Back From the Dead, The Unholy Wife, Hellcats of the Navy, The Young Lions, The Flame Barrier, Monster on the Campus, Atomic Submarine, The Carpetbaggers, Alvarez Kelly, Anzio, The Sweet Ride, The Human Factor, Sister of Death, That Championship Season.
TELEVISION: *Movies:* Murder or Mercy, Jennifer: A Woman's Story, Bogie.

FRANZ, DENNIS
Actor. b. Chicago, IL, Oct. 28, 1944. Started in Chicago Theatre.
PICTURES: Stony Island, Dressed to Kill, Blow Out, Psycho II, Body Double, A Fine Mess, The Package, Die Hard 2, The Player, American Buffalo, City of Angels.
TELEVISION: *Movies:* Chicago Story (pilot), Deadly Messages, Kiss Shot, Moment of Truth: Caught in the Crossfire (also co-prod.), Texas Justice, Bleacher Bums (s.p. only). *Guest:* The Simpsons (voice). *Specials:* Hollywood Salutes Nicolas Cage: An American Cinematheque Tribute, America: A Tribute to Heroes. *Series:* Chicago Story, Bay City Blues, Hill Street Blues, Beverly Hills Buntz, Nasty Boys, N.Y.P.D. Blue (Emmy Award, 1994, 1996, 1997, 1999), Mighty Ducks (voice).

FRASER, BRENDAN
Actor. b. Indianapolis, IN, Dec. 3, 1968. Raised in Holland, Switzerland, Canada. e. Actors' Conservatory, Cornish College of the Arts, Seattle. Member of Laughing Horse Summer Theatre in Ellensberg, WA.
THEATRE: Waiting for Godot, Arms and the Man, Romeo and Juliet, A Midsummer Night's Dream, Moonchildren, Four Dogs and a Bone.
PICTURES: Dogfight (debut, 1991), Encino Man, School Ties, Twenty Bucks, Younger and Younger, With Honors, Airheads, The Scout, Now and Then, The Passion of Darkly Noon, Mrs. Winterbourne, Glory Daze, George of the Jungle, Still Breathing, Gods and Monsters, Dudley Do-Right, Blast from the Past, The Mummy, Bedazzled, Monkeybone, The Mummy Returns, The Quiet American, Looney Tunes: Back in Action.
TELEVSION: *Movie:* Guilty Until Proven Innocent, The Twilight of the Golds. *Pilot:* My Old School. *Guest:* The Simpsons (voice), Scrubs.

FRAZIER, SHEILA E.
Actress, Producer. b. Bronx, NY, Nov. 13, 1948. e. Englewood, NJ. Was exec. sect'y. and high-fashion model. Steered to acting career by friend Richard Roundtree. Studied drama with N.Y. Negro Ensemble Co. and New Federal Theatre, N.Y., also with Bob Hickey at H.B. Studios, N.Y. Currently working as a TV producer.
PICTURES: Super Fly (debut), Superfly T.N.T., The Super Cops, California Suite, What Does It Take?, Three the Hard Way, The Hitter, I'm Gonna Git You Sucker, Two of a Kind, Jim Brown: All American.
TELEVISION: *Movie:* Firehouse. *Mini-Series:* King. *Series:* The Lazarus Syndrome.

FREARS, STEPHEN
Director. b. Leicester, Eng., June 20, 1941. e. Cambridge, B.A in law. Joined Royal Court Theatre, working with Lindsay Anderson on plays. Later assisted Karel Reisz on Morgan: A Suitable Case for Treatment, Albert Finney on Charlie Bubbles, and Lindsay Anderson on If ... Worked afterwards mostly in TV, directing and producing. First directorial credit was 30-minute film The Burning, 1967.
PICTURES: Gumshoe (dir. debut 1971), Bloody Kids, The Hit, My Beautiful Laundrette, Prick Up Your Ears, Sammy and Rosie Get Laid, Dangerous Liaisons, The Grifters, Hero (GB: Accidental Hero), The Snapper, Mary Reilly, The Van, The Hi-Lo Country, High Fidelity, Liam, Dirty Pretty Things.
TELEVISION: A Day Out (1971), England Their England, Match of the Day, Sunset Across the Bay, Three Men in a Boat, Daft as a Brush, Playthings, Early Struggles, Last Summer, 18 Months to Balcomb Street, A Visit from Miss Protheroe, Abel's Will, Cold

Harbour, Song of Experience; series of six Alan Bennett plays; Long Distance Information, Going Gently, Loving Walter, December Flower, Fail Safe.

FREDERICKSON, H. GRAY, JR.
Producer. b. Oklahoma City, OK, July 21, 1937. e. U. of Lausanne, Switzerland, 1958\-59; U. of Oklahoma. B.A., 1960. Worked one yr. with Panero, Weidlinger & Salvatori Engineering Co., Rome Italy. In 1979 named v.p. of feature films, Lorimar Films.
PICTURES: Candy, Inspector Sterling, Gospel 70, An Italian in America, The Man Who Wouldn't Die, The Good, the Bad and the Ugly, Intrigue in Suez, How to Learn to Love Women, God's Own Country, Wedding March, An American Wife, Natika, Echo in the Village, Little Fauss and Big Halsey, Making It, The Godfather (assoc. prod.), The Godfather Part II (co-prod.; Academy Award for Best Picture, 1974), Hit (exec. prod.), Apocalypse Now (co.-prod.; Acad. Award nom.), One From the Heart, The Outsiders, UHF, The Godfather Part III (co-prod.), Ladybugs (exec. prod.), Bad Girls (story), Heaven's Prisoners, South of Heaven West of Hell, My 5 Wives (creative consultant).
TELEVISION: *Producer:* The Return of Mickey Spillane's Mike Hammer, Houston Nights, Staying Afloat.

FREEBORN, STUART
Make-up. London, England, September 5, 1914.
PICTURES: I See A Dark Stranger, Captain Boycott, Oliver Twist, Silent Dust, Obsession, The Man Who Watched The Trains Go By, His MajestyO'Keefe, The Bridge on the River Kwai, The Naked Truth, I Was Monty's Double, Kidnapped, Mr.Topaze, The Hands of Orlac, The Devil's Daffodil, Foxhole in Cairo, Tarzan Goes to India, The Wrong Arm of the Law, Private Potter, Heaven's Above, Dr.Strangelove: Or How I Learned to Stop Worrying and Love the Bomb, Seance on a Wet Afternoon, 2001: A Space Odyssey, Oh! What A Lovely War, 10 Rillington Place, See No Evil, Young Winston, Alice's Adventures in Wonderland, Murder on the Orient Express, The Adventures of Sherlock Holmes' Smarter Brother, The Omen, Star Wars, Superman, The Empire Strikes Back, Superman II, The Great Muppet Caper, Return of the Jedi, Top Secret!, Santa Claus, Haunted Honeymoon.

FREEDMAN, JERROLD
Director, Writer. b. Philadelphia, PA, Oct.29, 1942. e. Univ. of PA. Novel: Against the Wind.
PICTURES: Kansas City Bomber, Borderline, Native Son.
TELEVISION: *Director-Writer:* Blood Sport, Betrayal, Some Kind of Miracle, Legs, This Man Stands Alone. *Director:* The Streets of L.A., The Boy Who Drank Too Much, Victims, The Seduction of Gina, Best Kept Secrets, Seduced, Family Sins, Unholy Matrimony, The Comeback, Night Walk, A Cold Night's Death, The Last Angry Man, Goodnight Sweet Wife: A Murder in Boston, Condition: Critical, The O.J. Simpson Story (dir. as Alan Smithee).

FREEMAN, AL, JR.
Actor. b. San Antonio, TX, March 21, 1934. e. LA City Coll.
THEATRE: The Long Dream (1960), Kicks and Co., Tiger Tiger Burning Bright, Trumpets of the Lord, Blues for Mister Charlie, Conversation at Midnight, Look to the Lilies, Are You Now or Have You Ever Been?, The Poison Tree.
PICTURES: Torpedo Run, Black Like Me, Dutchman, Finian's Rainbow, The Detective, Castle Keep, The Lost Man, A Fable (also dir.), Seven Hours to Judgement, Malcolm X, Once Upon a Time...When We Were Colored, Down in the Delta.
TELEVISION: *Movies:* My Sweet Charlie, Assault at West Point. *Mini-Series:* Roots: The Next Generations, King. *Series:* Hot L Baltimore, One Life to Live (Emmy Award, 1979).

FREEMAN, JOEL
Producer. b. Newark, NJ, June 12, 1922. e. Upsala Coll. Began career at MGM studios, 1941. Air Force Mot. Pic. Unit 1942-46. Became assist. dir. at RKO, 1946. 1948 returned to MGM as asst. dir.; later assoc. prod. 1956 entered indep. field as prod. Supv. on various features and TV series. 1960 to Warner Bros., assoc. producing Sunrise at Campobello, The Music Man and Act One. After such films as Camelot and Finian's Rainbow, became studio exec. at Warners. Former senior v.p. prod., New Century Entertainment Corp. Second Unit dir. or Asst. dir. on over 30 films in the 1940s and '50s.
PICTURES: *Producer:* The Heart Is a Lonely Hunter, Shaft, Trouble Man, Love at First Bite, Octagon, The Kindred, Soapdish (co-prod.).

FREEMAN, MORGAN
Actor. b. Memphis, TN, June 1, 1937. e. LA City Coll. Served in Air Force 1955-59 before studying acting. Worked as dancer at NY's 1964 World's Fair. Broadway debut in Hello Dolly! with Pearl Bailey. Took over lead role in Purlie. Became known nationally when he played Easy Reader on TV's The Electric Company (1971-76).
THEATRE: *NY:* Ostrich Feathers, The Nigger Lovers, Hello Dolly!, Scuba Duba, Purlie, Cockfight, The Last Street Play, The Mighty Gents (Drama Desk & Clarence Derwent Awards), Coriolanus (Obie Award), Julius Caesar, Mother Courage, Buck, Driving Miss Daisy (Obie Award), The Gospel at Colonus (Obie Award), The Taming of the Shrew.
PICTURES: Who Says I Can't Ride a Rainbow? (debut, 1972), Brubaker, Eyewitness, Death of a Prophet, Harry and Son, Teachers, Marie, That Was Then...This Is Now, Street Smart (NY & LA Film Critics & Natl. Board of Review Awards; Acad. Award nom., 1987), Clean and Sober, Lean on Me, Johnny Handsome,

Glory, Driving Miss Daisy (Natl. Board of Review & Golden Globe Awards; Acad. Award nom., 1989), The Bonfire of the Vanities, Robin Hood: Prince of Thieves, The Power of One, Unforgiven, Bopha (dir. only), The Shawshank Redemption (Acad. Award nom.), Outbreak, Seven, Moll Flanders, Chain Reaction, Hurricane (dir., prod., s.p., only), Kiss the Girls, Under Suspicion, Long Walk to Freedom, High Crimes, Along Came a Spider, Sum of All Fears, Tusker, Levity, Bruce Almighty, The Big Bounce.
TELEVISION: Movies: Hollow Image, Attica, The Marva Collins Story, The Atlanta Child Murders, Resting Place, Flight For Life, Roll of Thunder Hear My Cry, Charlie Smith and the Fritter Tree, Clinton and Nadine. Series: The Electric Company, Another World (1982-4). Specials (narrator): The Civil War, Follow the Drinking Gourd, The Promised Land.

FREWER, MATT
Actor. b. Washington, D. C., Jan. 4, 1958. Raised in Victoria, British Columbia. Studied drama at the Bristol Old Vic Theatre, appearing in Romeo and Juliet, Macbeth, Waiting for Godot, Deathtrap.
PICTURES: The Lords of Discipline (debut, 1983), Supergirl, Spies Like Us, Ishtar, The Fourth Protocol, Far From Home, Speed Zone, Honey I Shrunk the Kids, Short Time, The Taking of Beverly Hills, Twenty Bucks, National Lampoon's Senior Trip, Lawnmower Man II, Hercules (voice), Dead Fire, 6ix, Cyberworld (voice), Whitecoats, A Home at the End of the World.
TELEVISION: Movies: The Positively True Adventures of the Alleged Texas Cheerleader-Murdering Mom, The Day My Parents Ran Away, Kissinger and Nixon, Generation X, Apollo 11, Dead Man's Gun, Quicksilver Highway, Desert's Edge, Dead Man's Gun, In the Doghouse, Jailbait, The Hound of the Baskervilles, The Sign of Four, The Royal Scandal, The Case of the Whitechapel Vampire. Mini-Series: The Stand, Taken. BBC: Tender is the Night, Robin of Sherwood; U.S. Series: Max Headroom, Doctor Doctor, Shaky Ground, The Pink Panther (voice), Outer Limits, Aladdin, Iron Man (voice), Dumb and Dumber (voice), The Incredible Hulk (voice), Hercules (voice), Toonsylvania (voice), The House of Mouse (voice). Guest: Miami Vice. Specials: Long Shadows, In Search of Dr. Seuss.

FRICKER, BRENDA
Actress. b. Dublin, Ireland, Feb. 17, 1945. Appeared in short film The Woman Who Married Clark Gable. Theatre work with the RSC, Royal Court Theatre, and The National Theatre.
PICTURES: Quatermass Conclusion, Bloody Kids, Our Exploits at West Poley, My Left Foot (Academy Award, best supporting actress, 1989), The Field, Utz, Home Alone 2: Lost in New York, So I Married an Axe Murderer, Angels in the Outfield, A Man of No Importance, Moll Flanders, A Time to Kill, Swann, Masterminds, Painted Angels, Resurrection Man, Pete's Meteor, The American, The War Bride, The Intended, Veronica Guerin, Conspiracy of Silence.
TELEVISION: Series: Casualty, Cupid & Cate. Specials: Licking Hitler, The House of Bernarda Alba, The Ballroom Romance. Mini-Series: Brides of Christ, A Woman of Independent Means, Relative Strangers, I Was a Rat, No Tears. Movies: Seekers, Durango, Journey, Torso, Watermelon.

FRIEDBERG, A. ALAN
Executive. b. New York, NY, Apr. 13, 1932. e. Columbia Coll., B.A. 1952, Junior Phi Beta Kappa, Summa Cum Laude; Harvard Law School 1955. Past pres. and chmn. of bd. NATO. 1990, named chmn. Loews Theatre Mgmt. Co. Bd. chmn. of National Center of Jewish Film-Brandeis University, Board of Visitor Columbia College, Board of Overseers Boston Symphony Orchestra, Board of Overseers Museum of Fine Arts Boston, Board of Advisors American Repertory Theatre at Harvard University; bd. member of Palace Entertainment. Retired as chmn. of Loews Theatres circuit in 1993.

FRIEDKIN, JOHN
Executive. b. New York, NY, Dec. 9, 1926. e. Columbia Univ. Entered industry in New York as publicist for Columbia Pictures; spent eight years at Young & Rubicam adv. agency. Formed Sumner & Friedkin with Gabe Sumner as partner; left to join Rogers & Cowan, where named v.p. In 1967 resigned to join 20th-Fox, moving to California in 1972 when home offices were transferred. Appointed Fox v.p. worldwide publ. & promo. In 1979 joined Warner Bros. as v.p., adv. pub. for intl. div; 1988, joined Odyssey Distributors Ltd. as sr. v.p., intl. marketing. 1990, formed indept. marketing firm. 1995, rep. for Australia's Kennedy Miller Ent.

FRIEDKIN, WILLIAM
Director, Writer. b. Chicago, IL, Aug. 29, 1939. m. producer Sherry Lansing. Joined WGN-TV, 1957, worked for National Education TV, did TV documentaries before feature films. Dir. B'way play Duet for One.
PICTURES: Director: Good Times (debut, 1967), The Night They Raided Minsky's, The Birthday Party, The Boys in the Band, The French Connection (Academy Award, 1971), The Exorcist, Sorcerer (also prod.), The Brink's Job, Cruising (also s.p.), Deal of the Century, To Live and Die in L.A. (also c-s.p.), Rampage (also s.p.), The Guardian (also co-s.p.), Blue Chips, Jade, Rules of Engagement, The Hunted.
TELEVISION: Movies: C.A.T. Squad (also exec. prod.), C.A.T. Squad: Python Wolf, Jailbreakers, 12 Angry Men. Special: Barbra Streisand: Putting It Together. Series: Tales From the Crypt (On a Dead Man's Chest).

FRIEDMAN, JOSEPH
Executive. b. New York, NY. e. City Coll. of New York, 1940-42, NYU, 1946-47. U.S. Navy 3 yrs. Asst. to nat'l dir. field exploitation, Warner Bros. Pictures, 1946-58; nat'l exploitation mgr., Paramount 1958-60; exec. asst. to dir. of adv., publicity & exploitation, Para., 1961; dir. adv. & pub., Paramount 1964; v.p., Para., 1966; v.p. in charge of mktg., 1968; v.p., adv., and p.r., Avco Embassy, 1969; v.p., p.r. American Film Theatre, 1973; v.p., adv. and p.r., ITC, motion picture div., 1976, pres., Joseph Friedman Mktg. & Adv., Inc., 1977. Exec. dir. New Jersey M.P. & T.V. Commission, 1978; v.p. worldwide adv./pub. /promo., Edie & Ely Landau, Inc., 1980; exec. dir., NJ Motion Picture & Television Commission, 1981-present.

FRIEDMAN, PAUL
Executive. e. Princeton U. Woodrow Wilson Sch. of Public & Intl. Affairs, Columbia Sch. of Journalism. 1967, joined NBC News as newswriter in NY; 1970-75, served as reporter for WRC-TV in D.C., field prod. for The Huntley-Brinkley Report, sr. prod. for NBC Weekend Nightly News, exec. prod. of News 4 New York, sr. prod. NBC Nightly News; 1976-79, was exec. prod. of Today; 1982, joined ABC News as sr. prod. in London; there became dir. of news coverage for Europe, Africa, Middle East; 1988-92, exec. prod. of World News Tonight With Peter Jennings; Jan. 1993 named exec. v.p. and managing editor of ABC TV News.

FRIEDMAN, ROBERT G.
Executive. Began in the mailroom of Warner Bros. and moved up to president of Worldwide Advertising & Publicity. Currently vice chairman, Paramount Pictures Motion Picture Grp., (since 1996) and also COO of Paramount Pictures. Faculty member of the Independent Producers' Program, UCLA Dept. of Theater, Film and Television; member, Next Generation Council for the Motion Picture & Television Fund Found., member of the board of directors, Motion Picture Pioneers, and Southern Calif. Special Olympics.

FRIEDMAN, ROBERT L.
Executive. b. Bronx, NY, March 1, 1930. e. DeWitt Clinton H.S., Bronx. Started as radio announcer and commentator with Armed Forces Radio Service in Europe and U.S. sr. v.p., distrib. & mktg., United Artists Corp.; pres. domestic distribution, Columbia Pictures. 1984, named pres., AMC Entertainment Int'l Inc. 1992, named pres. of AMC Entertainment - the Motion Picture Group. In 2001 became a senior advisor to Chanin Capital Parnters' Entertainment and Media Goup. Member: Exec. div. of the Acad. of Motion Picture Arts & Sciences (bd. of dir.-Center for Motion Picture Study), Variety Club of So. Ca., Motion Picture Pioneers of America, the Will Rogers Hospital, the Motion Picture Associates Found. and on bd. of dir. of the Century City Chamber of Commerce-chmn. of ent. ind. comm.

FRIEDMAN, SEYMOUR MARK
Director. b. Detroit, MI, Aug. 17, 1917. e. Magdalene Coll., Cambridge, B.S. 1936; St. Mary's Hospital Medical Sch., London. Entered m.p. ind. as asst. film ed. 1937; 2nd asst. dir. 1938; 1st asst. dir. 1939, on budget pictures; entered U.S. Army 1942; returned to ind. 1946; dir. Columbia Pictures 1947. Vice president & executive production for Columbia Pictures Television, division of Columbia Pictures Industries, 1955. Member: Screen Directors Guild.
PICTURES: To the Ends of the Earth, Rusty's Birthday, Prison Warden, Her First Romance, Rookie Fireman, Son of Dr. Jekyll, Loan Shark, Flame of Calcutta, I'll Get You, Saint's Girl Friday, Khyber Patrol, African Manhunt, Secret of Treasure Mountain.

FRIELS, COLIN
Actor. b. Scotland, e. Australia Natl. Inst. of Dramatic Art. m. actress Judy Davis. First began acting with the State Theatre Co. of So. Australia and the Sydney Theatre Co. Theatre includes Sweet Bird of Youth and Hedda Gabler. TV includes special Stark.
PICTURES: Buddies, Monkey Grip, For the Term of His Natural Life, Kangaroo, Malcolm, High Tide, Ground Zero, Grievous Bodily Harm, Warm Nights on a Slow Moving Train, Darkman, Class Action, Dingo, A Good Man in Africa, Angel Baby, Back of Beyond, Cosi, Mr. Reliable, Dark City, The Man Who Sued God, Black and White, Max's Dreaming.
TELEVISION: Series: Water Rats. Movies: For the Term of His Natural Life, Stark, Halifax f.p.: Hard Corps, Child Star: The Shirley Temple Story, My Husband My Killer, Black Jack, Temptation. Mini-Series: The Farm, Seven Deadly Sins.

FRIES, CHARLES W.
Executive, Producer. b. Cincinnati, OH. e. Ohio State U., B.S. Exec.-prod., Ziv Television; v.p., prod., Screen Gems; v.p., prod., Columbia Pictures; exec. v.p., prod. and exec. prod., Metromedia Prod. Corp., 1970-74; pres., exec. prod., Alpine Prods. and Charles Fries Prods. 1974-83; chmn. & pres., Fries Entertainment, 1984-1995; pres., Charles Fries Prods., 1996. Nat'l. treas., TV Academy; pres., Alliance TV Film Producers; exec. comm., MPPA. Chmn., Caucus of Producers, Writers and Directors, board of governors and exec. comm. of Academy of TV Arts and Sciences. Bd. trustees, secretary, Exec. committee & vice-chmn., American Film Institute. V.P. & dir. of the Center Theatre Group.
PICTURES: Prod.: Cat People, Flowers in the Attic, Troop Beverly Hills, Screamers.
TELEVISION: Movies: Toughlove, The Right of the People, Intimate Strangers, Bitter Harvest, A Rumor of War, Blood Vows: The Story of a Mafia Wife, The Alamo: 13 Days to Glory, Intimate Betrayal, Drop Out Mother, Crash Course, Supercarrier, Bridge to Silence, The Case of the Hillside Strangler, Deadly Web. Small

Sacrifices, The Martian Chronicles. *Specials:* It's Howdy Doody Time: A 40 Year Celebration.

FRONTIERE, DOMINIC
Executive, Composer. b. New Haven, CT, June 17, 1931. e. Yale School of Music. Studied composing, arranging and conducting; concert accordionist, World's Champion Accordionist, 1943; An Hour with Dominic Frontiere, WNHC-TV, New Haven, 3 years, 1947; exec. vice-pres., musical dir., Daystar Prods. Composer or arranger over 75 films.
PICTURES: Giant, Gentlemen Prefer Blondes, Let's Make Love, High Noon, Meet Me in Las Vegas, 10,000 Bedrooms, Hit the Deck, Marriage-Go-Round, The Right Approach, One Foot in Hell, Hero's Island, Hang 'Em High, Popi, Barquero, Chisum, A for Alpha, Cancel My Reservation, Hammersmith is Out, Freebie and the Bean, Brannigan, The Gumball Rally, Cleopatra Jones and the Casino of Gold, The Stunt Man, Modern Problems, The Aviator, Road, Color of Night, Behind the Badge.
TELEVISION: *Composer-conductor:* The New Breed, Stoney Burke, Bankamericard commercials (Venice Film Fest. Award for best use of original classical music for filmed TV commercials), Outer Limits, Branded, Iron Horse, Rat Patrol, Flying Nun, The Invaders, Name of the Game, That Girl, Twelve O'Clock High, Zig Zag, The Young Rebel, The Immortal, Fugitive, The Love War. *Movie:* Washington Behind Closed Doors.

FUCHS, FRED
Producer.
PICTURES: *Exec. Prod.:* Vietnam War Story: The Last Days, The Spirit of '76, The Godfather: Part III, The Secret Garden, Mary Shelley's Frankenstein, Don Juan DeMarco, Haunted, Jack, Buddy, The Rainmaker. Producer: New York Stories (segment 2), Tucker: The Man and His Dream, Bram Stoker's Dracula, The Secret Garden, Frankenstein, Don Juan deMarco, Haunted, Jack, Buddy, The Rainmaker, The Virgin Suicides, The Third Miracle, Beautiful Joe.
TELEVISION: *Movies:* Dark Angel, Tecumseh: The Last Warrior, Titanic, Riot, The Odyssey, Outrage, Moby Dick. *Series:* Faerie Tale Theater. *Mini-Series:* The Odyssey.

FUCHS, LEO L.
Independent producer. b. Vienna, June 14, 1929. Moved to U.S., 1939. e. Vienna and New York. U.S. Army cameraman 1951-53; int'l. mag. photographer until entered motion pictures as producer with Universal in Hollywood in 1961. Still photographer for several movies in the 1950s.
PICTURES: Gambit, A Fine Pair, Sunday Lovers, Just the Way You Are, Malone.

FUCHS, MICHAEL
Executive. b. New York, NY, March 9, 1946. e. Union Coll., NYU Law School (J.D. degree). Show business lawyer before joining Home Box Office in 1976, developing original and sports programming. Named chmn. and CEO of HBO in 1984. 1982-87, v.p. Time Inc. in NY; 1987-1995, exec. v.p. Time Inc. Currently, chmn. Autobytel and director, IMAX Corporation, and Salon Media Group, Inc.

FUEST, ROBERT
Director. b. London, 1927. Early career as painter, graphic designer. Ent. TV industry as designer with ABC-TV, 1958. 1962: directing doc., commercials. 1966: Wrote and dir. Just Like a Woman, 1967-68; dir. 7 episodes of The Avengers, 1969: wrote and directed 6 episodes of The Optimists.
PICTURES: And Soon the Darkness, Wuthering Heights, Doctor Phibes, Doctor Phibes Rides Again (also s.p.), The Final Programme (also s.p., design), The Devil's Rain, The Geller Effect (s.p. only), The New Avengers, The Gold Bug, Revenge of the Stepford Wives, The Big Stuffed Dog, Mystery on Fire Island, Aphrodite, Worlds Beyond, Cat's Eyes, Avenging the Avengers.

FURIE, SIDNEY J.
Director, Writer, Producer. b. Toronto, Canada, Feb. 28, 1933. Ent. TV and films 1954. Canadian features include: Dangerous Age, A Cool Sound from Hell. Also dir. many Hudson Bay TV series. To England 1960. 1961 appt. exec. dir. Galaworldfilm Productions, Ltd.
PICTURES: The Snake Woman, Doctor Blood's Coffin, Wonderful to Be Young, Night of Passion (also prod., s.p.), The Young Ones, The Leather Boys, Wonderful Life, The Ipcress File, The Appaloosa, The Naked Runner, The Lawyer, Little Fauss and Big Halsy, Lady Sings the Blues, Hit!, Sheila Levine Is Dead and Living in New York, Gable and Lombard, The Boys in Company C, The Entity, Purple Hearts (also prod., s.p.), Iron Eagle, Superman IV: The Quest For Peace, Iron Eagle II (also co-s.p.), The Taking of Beverly Hills, Ladybugs, Hollow Point, Iron Eagle IV, The Rage (also story), Top of the World, The Rage, In Her Defense, The Collectors, Cord, My 5 Wives, Sonic Boom, A Firday Night Date, Going Back, Global Heresy, Donzi: The Legend, The Circle, Partners in Action, Direct Action.
TELEVISION: *Series:* Pensacola: Wings of Gold, V.I.P., 18 Wheels of Justice.

FURLONG, EDWARD
Actor. b. Glendale, CA, Aug. 2, 1977. Discovered by casting agent for Terminator 2, having no previous acting experience. Appeared in Aerosmith video Livin' on the Edge.
PICTURES: Terminator 2: Judgment Day (debut, 1991), Pet Sematary 2, American Heart, A Home of Our Own, Brainscan, Little Odessa, The Grass Harp, Before and After, Pecker,

American History X, Detroit Rock City, The Animal Factory, The Knights of the Quest, Terminator 3, Three Blind Mice, Riders on the Storm, Random Acts of Kindness, The Crow: Wicked Prayer. TELEVISION: *Series:* The Andy Dick Show.

FURMAN, ROY L.
Attorney, Executive. b. New York, NY, April 19, 1939. e. Brooklyn Coll., A.B. 1960; Harvard U., LL.B. 1963. Pres., Furman Selz, and then vice chmn. of ING Barings after it acquired Furman Selz in 1997. In 2001, joined Jefferies & Company, Inc., an institutional brokerage firm & investment bank, as vice chmn. He is also vice chmn. of the Lincoln Center for the Performing Arts and serves on many other charitable, political and philanthropic organizations.

FURST, AUSTIN O.
Executive. e. Lehigh U., B.S. in economics/marketing. Began career in mktg. dept., Proctor and Gamble; 1972, joined Time Inc. as dir., new subscription sales for Time magazine; later joined Time Inc.'s new magazine dev. staff for People magazine; named circulation mgr., People magazine, 1974; 1975 named pres., Time Inc.'s Computer Television Inc., a pay-per-view hotel operation and was responsible for successful turnaround and sale of co.; 1976, v.p., programming, Home Box Office; named exec. v.p. HBO, 1979; appointed pres. and CEO, Time-Life Films, Inc., 1980; 1981 established Vestron after acquiring home video rights to Time/Life Video Library; chmn. and CEO, Vestron, Inc. Currently, chmn., The Natural World

G

GABLER, ELIZABETH
Executive. m. agent/executive Lee Gabler. Began career as literary agent at ICM and creative exec., Columbia Pictures; v.p. of production, United Artists; exec. v.p. of production, Twentieth Century Fox, 1988. President, Fox 2000 Pictures, 1999-present.

GABLER, LEE
Executive. b. New York, NY. m. executive Elizabeth Gabler. Began career in the mailroom of Ashely Steiner Famous Artists in New York (later ICM) where he became an agent in 1964. Promoted to v.p. in 1968. 1970, transferred to ICM in California as exec. v.p. and head of worlwide television. 1983, joined CAA where he is currently partner, co-chmn. and head of television. Serves on bd. of Museum of Television & Radio and bd. of councilors at USC School of Cinema-Television.

GABOR, ZSA ZSA
Actress. r.n. Sari Gabor. b. Hungary, Feb. 6, 1918. e. Lausanne, Switzerland. Stage debut in Europe. *Author:* Zsa Zsa's Complete Guide to Men (1969), How to Get a Man How to Keep a Man and How to Get Rid of a Man (1971), One Lifetime is Not Enough (1991). As accomplished horsewoman has won many prizes in various intl. horse shows. Stage work incl. 40 Carats, Blithe Spirit.
PICTURES: Lovely to Look At, We're Not Married, Moulin Rouge, The Story of Three Loves, Lili, Three Ring Circus, The Most Wanted Man in the World, Death of a Scoundrel, Girl in the Kremlin, The Man Who Wouldn't Talk, Touch of Evil, Queen of Outer Space, Country Music Holiday, For the First Time, Pepe, Boys' Night Out, Picture Mommy Dead, Arrivederci Baby, Jack of Diamonds, Won Ton Ton the Dog Who Saved Hollywood, Frankenstein's Great Aunt Tillie, A Nightmare on Elm Street 3, The Naked Gun 2 1/2: The Smell of Fear, Happily Ever After (voice), The People vs. Zsa Zsa Gabor, The Naked Truth, East & West: Paradise Lost, The Beverl Hillbillies, A Very Brady Sequel.

GAGHAN, STEPHEN
Writer.
PICTURES: Rules of Engagement, Traffic (Academy Award), Abandon (also dir.), Abandon (also dir.), The Alamo, Havoc.
TELEVISION: *Series:* NYPD Blue, American Gothic, Sleepwalkers (prod.), The Practice.

GAIL, MAX
Actor. b. Grosse Ile, MI, Apr. 5, 1943. e. William Coll. B.A. Economics, Univ. of Mich M.B.A.
THEATRE: *NY:* The Babe, One Flew Over the Cuckoo's Nest (also S.F.). *LA:* Visions of Kerouac.
PICTURES: The Organization, Dirty Harry, D.C. Cab, Heartbreakers, Pontiac Moon, Mind Lies, Sodbusters, Ox and the Eye, Forest Warrior, Good Luck, Naturally Native, The Perfect Wife, Mind Lies, Facing the Enemy, Truth and Dare.
TELEVISION: *Series:* Barney Miller, Whiz Kids, Normal Life. *Mini-Series:* Pearl. *Movies:* The Priest Killer, Like Mom Like Me, Desperate Women, The 11th Victim, The Aliens Are Coming, Fun and Games, Letting Go, The Other Lover, Killer in the Mirror, Intimate Strangers, Can You Feel Me Dancing?, Tonight's the Night, Man Against the Mob, The Outside Woman, Ride With the Wind, Robin Cook's Mortal Fear, Naomi & Winona: Love Can Build a Bridge, Secret Agent (prod.), Wrong Side of the Fence (prod.), Tell Me No Secrets, Not in This Town.

GALE, BOB
Writer, Producer. b. St. Louis, MO, May 25, 1951. e. USC Sch. of Cinema. Joined with friend Robert Zemeckis to write screenplays, starting with episode for TV series, McCloud. Also co-wrote story for The Nightstalker series. Turned to feature films,

co-writing with Zemeckis script for I Wanna Hold Your Hand, on which Gale also acted as assoc. producer. Exec. prod. of CBS animated series Back to the Future. Wrote and directed interactive feature Mr. Payback.
PICTURES: I Wanna Hold Your Hand (co-s.p., co-assoc. prod.), 1941 (co-s.p.), Used Cars (prod., co-s.p.), Back to the Future (co.-prod., s.p.), Back to the Future Part II (prod., co-s.p.), Back to the Future Part III (prod., s.p.), Trespass (co-exec. prod., co-s.p.), Tales From the Crypt: Bordello of Blood (co-s.p.), Interstate 60.
TELEVISION: Series: Back to the Future (animated; exec. prod.), Tales From the Crypt (wrote, dir. House of Horror).

GALLAGHER, PETER
Actor. b. New York, NY, Aug. 19, 1955. e. Tufts Univ.
THEATER: NY: Hair (1977 revival), Grease, A Doll's Life (Theatre World Award), The Corn is Green, The Real Thing (Clarence Derwent Award), Long Day's Journey Into Night (Tony Award nom.; also London), Guys & Dolls.
PICTURES: The Idolmaker (debut, 1980), Summer Lovers, Dream Child, My Little Girl, High Spirits, Sex Lies and Videotape, Tune in Tomorrow, Late for Dinner, The Cabinet of Dr. Ramirez, The Player, Bob Roberts, Watch It, Malice, Short Cuts, Mother's Boys, The Hudsucker Proxy, Mrs. Parker and the Vicious Circle, While You Were Sleeping, The Underneath, Cafe Society, The Last Dance, To Gillian on Her 37th Birthday, The Man Who Knew Too Little, Johnny Skidmarks, American Beauty, House on Haunted Hill, Other Voices, Center Stage, Perfume, Lunar Girl, Protection, Mr. Deeds, The Adventures of Tom Thumb and Thumbelina (voice), How to Deal, One Last Chance (line prod.
TELEVISION: Series: Skag, The Secret Lives of Men. Movies: Skag, Terrible Joe Moran, The Caine Mutiny Court-Martial, The Murder of Mary Phagan, I'll Be Home for Christmas, Love and Lies, An Inconvenient Woman, White Mile, Titanic, Path to Paradise, The Frightening Frammis, The Quiet Room, The Cabinet of Dr. Ramirez, Virtual Obsession, Brotherhood of Murder, Cupid & Cate, The Last Debate. Specials: The Big Knife, Long Day's Journey Into Night, Private Contentment, Guys & Dolls: Off the Record. Mini-series: Brave New World, Feast of All Saints.

GALLIGAN, ZACH
Actor. b. New York, NY, Feb. 14, 1964. e. Columbia U.
PICTURES: Gremlins, Nothing Lasts Forever, Waxwork, Mortal Passions, Rising Storm, Gremlins II, Zandalee, Waxwork II: Lost in Time, Round Trip to Heaven, All Tied Up, Warlock: The Armageddon, Ice, Caroline at Midnight, The First to Go, Prince Valiant, Cupid, Storm Troopers, Arthur's Quest, The Storytellers, Raw Nerve, Point Doom, G-Men From Hell, What They Wanted What They Got, Little Insects (voice), Gabriela, The Tomorrow Man, Infested.
TELEVISION: Movies: Jacobo Timerman: Prisoner Without a Name Cell Without a Number, Surviving, Psychic, For Love and Glory, Momentum. Specials: The Prodigious Hickey, The Return of Hickey, The Beginning of the Firm, A Very Delicate Matter, The Hitchhiker: Toxic Shock. Mini-Series: Crossings. Pilot: Interns in Heat. Guest: Tales From the Crypt (Strung Along), Melrose Place, Extreme.

GAMBON, MICHAEL
Actor. b. Dublin, Ireland, Oct. 19, 1940. Ent. ind. 1966. Early experience in theatre. 1985-87 Acting at National Theatre and London's West End. 1988: in Harold Pinter's Mountain Language.
PICTURES: Othello, The Beast Must Die, Turtle Diary, Paris By Night, The Rachel Papers, A Dry White Season, The Cook the Thief His Wife and Her Lover, Mobsters, Toys, Clean Slate, The Browning Version, Squanto: A Warrior's Tale, A Man of No Importance, Midnight in St. Petersberg, Bullet to Beijing, The Innocent Sleep, Nothing Personal, Mary Reilly, The Wings of the Dove, The Gambler, Plunkett & MacLeane, Dancing at Lughnasa, The Last September, The Monkey's Tale, The Insider, Sleepy Hollow, Dead On Time, High Heels and Low Lifes, Gosford Park, Boswell for the Defence, Charlotte Gray, Ali G Indahouse, Standing Room Only, Open Range, The Actors., Sylvia, Harry Potter and the Prisoner of Azkaban.
TELEVISION: Uncle Vanya, Ghosts, Oscar Wilde, The Holy Experiment, Absurd Person Singular, The Singing Detective (serial), The Heat of the Day, The Storyteller, Maigret Sets a Trap, Samson & Delilah, The Wind in the Willows, The Willows in Winter, Wives and Daughters, Perfect Strangers, Larry and Viven: The Oliviers in Love, Path to War.

GAMMON, JAMES
Actor. b. Newman, IL, Apr. 20, 1940. e. Boone H.S., Orlando, FL. Former television cameraman. First acting role was small part on Gunsmoke. Head of Los Angeles' Met Theatre for 10 years.
THEATRE: The Dark at the Top of the Stairs (L.A. Critics Circle Award, best actor), Bus Stop (L.A. Drama Critics award, best director), Curse of the Starving Class (NY, L.A.), A Lie of the Mind (NY, L.A.).
PICTURES: Cool Hand Luke (debut, 1967), Journey to Shiloh, Macho Callahan, A Man Called Horse, Macon County Line, Black Oak Conspiracy, Urban Cowboy, Any Which Way You Can, Smithereens, Vision Quest, Sylvester, Silverado, Silver Bullet, Made in Heaven, Ironweed, The Milagro Beanfield War, Major League, Revenge, Coupe de Ville, I Love You to Death, Leaving Normal, Crisscross, The Painted Desert, Running Cool, Cabin Boy, Vegas Vice, Natural Born Killers, Wild Bill, Traveller, The

Apostle, Point Blank, The Hi-Lo Country, The Man in the Iron Mask, Love From Ground Zero, The Iron Giant (voice), One Man's Hero, The Cell, Life or Something Like It, The Country Bears (voice).
TELEVISION: Movies: Kansas City Massacre, Rage, Women of San Quentin, M.A.D.D.: Mothers Against Drunk Drivers, Hell Town, The Long Hot Summer, Roe vs. Wade, Dead Aim, Conagher, Stranger at My Door, Men Don't Tell, Truman, Two Mothers For Zachary, You Know My Name, Logan's War: Bound by Honor, Monte Walsh. Mini-Series: Lincoln. Series: Bagdad Cafe. Guest: Bonanza, The Wild Wild West, Cagney & Lacey, The Equalizer, Crime Story, Midnight Caller.

GANDOLFINI, JAMES
Actor. b. NJ, 1961. e. Rutgers U.
PICTURES: A Stranger Among Us, True Romance, Mr Wonderful, Money for Nothing, Angie, Terminal Velocity, The New World, Crimson Tide, Get Shorty, The Juror, She's So Lovely, Night Falls on Manhattan, Perdita Durango, The Mighty, A Civil Action, Fallen, 8MM, The Mexican, The Man Who Wasn't There, The Last Castle, Catch Me if You Can, Before the Devil Knows You're Dead, Sharkslayer.
TELEVISION: Movies: 12 Angry Men. Series: The Sopranos.

GANIS, SIDNEY M.
Executive. b. New York, NY, Jan. 8, 1940. e. Brooklyn Coll. Staff writer, newspaper and wire service contact, 20th Century-Fox 1961-62; radio, TV contact and special projects, Columbia Pictures 1963-64. Joined Seven Arts 1965 as publicity mgr.; 1967, appt. prod. publicity mgr. Warner-7 Arts, Ass't prod., There Was a Crooked Man, 1969. Studio publicity dir., Cinema Center Films, 1970. Director of Ad-Pub for Mame, Warner Bros. 1973; Director of Advertising, Warner Bros., 1974; named WB v.p., worldwide adv. & pub., 1977; 1979, sr. v.p., Lucasfilm, Ltd.; 1982 Emmy winner, exec. prod., best documentary, The Making of Raiders of the Lost Ark. 1986, joined Paramount Pictures as pres., worldwide mktg; 1986, named pres., Paramount Motion Picture Group. 1988, elected trustee University Art Museum, Berkeley, CA. 1991, appointed exec. v.p., Sony Pictures Ent. Exec. v.p., pres. mktg. & distrib., Columbia Pictures, 1992. Elected to bd. of govs. AMPAS, 1992. Vice chmn., Columbia Pictures, 1994. Pres., worldwide mktg., Columbia TriStar. Pres.of Out of the Blue...Entertainment, since Sept. 1996. Since 1999, he has also been a dir. of Marvel Enterprises, Inc.

GANZ, BRUNO
Actor. b. Zurich, Switzerland, March 22, 1941. Theatre debut in 1961. Founded the Berlin Theatre troupe, Schaubuehne, with Peter Stein in 1970.
THEATRE: Hamlet (1967), Dans La Jungle Des Villes, Torquato Tasso, La Chevauchee Sur Le Lac de Constance, Peer Gynt.
PICTURES: Der Sanfte Lauf (1967), Sommergaste, The Marquise of O, Lumiere, The Wild Duck, The American Friend, The Lefthanded Woman, The Boys from Brazil, Black and White Like Day and Night, Knife in the Head, Nosferatu the Vampyre, Return of a Good Friend, 5% Risk, An Italian Woman, Polenta, La Provinciale, La Dame Aux Camelias, Der Erfinder, Etwas Wird Sichtbar, Circle of Deceit, Hande Hoch, Logik Der Gerfuhls, War and Peace, In the White City, System Ohne Schatten, Der Pendler, Wings of Desire, Bankomatt, Strapless, The Last Days of Chez Nous, Especially on Sunday, Faraway So Close!, Heller Tag, Lumiere & Company, Saint-Ex, Eternity and a Day, WhoAfraidWolf, Bread and Tulips, Epstein's Night, The Power of the Past, Behind Me-Bruno Ganz (documentary), Luther.
TELEVISION: Father and Son, Todliches Schweigen, Ein Richter In Angst, Tatort — Schattenwelt (German TV), Gegen Ende der Nacht. Mini-series: Grande Fausto II.

GANZ, LOWELL
Writer, Producer, Director. b. New York, NY, Aug. 31, 1948. e. Queens Col. Worked as staff writer on tv series The Odd Couple. Met writing partner Babaloo Mandel at The Comedy Store in the early 1970s. Was co-creator Laverne & Shirley. First teamed with Mandel on script for 1982 comedy Night Shift.
PICTURES: Writer: Night Shift, Splash (Acad. Award nom.; also actor), Spies Likes Us, Gung Ho, Vibes, Parenthood (also actor), City Slickers, A League of Their Own (also actor), Mr. Saturday Night (also actor), Greedy (also actor), City Slickers II: The Legend of Curly's Gold, Forget Paris, Multiplicity, Father's Day, EdTV, Where the Heart Is, Down and Under, Fifty First Kisses.
TELEVISION: Writer-Exec. Prod (series): The Odd Couple, Happy Days, Busting Loose, The Ted Knight Show, Makin' It, Joanie Loves Chachi, Gung Ho, Knight and Dave, Parenthood, Hiller & Diller. Producer: Laverne & Shirley (also writer).

GANZ, TONY
Producer. b. New York, NY. e. studied film at Harvard U. Produced documentaries for PBS in N.Y. Moved to L.A. 1973 where in charge of dev., Charles Fries Productions. Then joined Ron Howard Productions 1980. Left to form own prod. co. with Deborah Blum.
PICTURES: Gung Ho, Clean and Sober, Vibes.
TELEVISION: Series: American Dream Machine, Maximum Security (exec. prod.). Movies: Bitter Harvest, Into Thin Air, The Corpse Had a Familiar Face.

GARCIA, ANDY
Actor. r.n. Andres Arturo Garcia Menendez. b. Havana, Cuba, Apr. 12, 1956. Family moved to Miami Beach in 1961. e. Florida International U, Miami. Spent several years acting with regional theatres in Florida; also part of improv. group. Music producer of album: Cachao Master Sessions Vol. I (Grammy Award), Chachao Master Sessions Vol II (Grammy nom.).
PICTURES: The Mean Season, 8 Million Ways to Die, The Untouchables, Stand and Deliver, American Roulette, Black Rain, Internal Affairs, A Show of Force, The Godfather Part III (Acad. Award nom.), Dead Again, Hero, Jennifer Eight, Cachao... Como Su Ritmo No Hay Dos (Like His Rhythm There Is No Other; also dir., co-prod.), When a Man Loves a Woman, Steal Big Steal Little, Things to Do in Denver When You're Dead, Night Falls on Manhattan, Disappearance of Garcia Lorca, Hoodlum, Desperate Measures, Just the Ticket (also prod.), Sins of the Father, Avenging Angels, Lakeboat, The Unsaid, The Man From Elysian Fields (also prod.), Ocean's Eleven, Just Like Mona, Confidence, Modigliani.
TELEVISION: *Movies:* Clinton and Nadine, Swing Vote, The Arturo Sandoval Story (Emmy nom., Golden Globe nom.).

GARDINER, PETER R.
Executive. b. Santa Monica, CA, Apr. 25, 1949. Independent still photographer and industrial filmmaker before joining Paramount, 1973, in feature post-prod. 1979, joined Warner Bros. as asst. dir., corporate services. 1987, promoted to v.p., opns., WB corporate film-video services. 1993, promoted to v.p Warner Bros. corp. film & video services. Currently the chief media officer for Deutsch, Inc.

GARDNER, ARTHUR
Producer. b. Marinette, WI, June 7. e. Marinette h.s. Entered m.p. ind. as actor, in orig. cast All Quiet on the Western Front, 1929. Juvenile leads in: Waterfront, Heart of the North, Assassin of Youth, Religious Racketeer; production, asst. dir. King Bros. 1941, then asst. prod. U.S. Air Force 1st Motion Picture Unit, 1943-45. Formed Levy-Gardner-Laven Prods. with Jules Levy, Arnold Laven, 1951.
PICTURES: (Asst. dir.): Paper Bullets, I Killed That Man, Rubber Racketeers, Klondike Fury, I Escaped From the Gestapo, Suspense; *Asst. prod.:* Gangster, Dude Goes West, Badmen of Tombstone, Gun Crazy, Mutiny, Southside 1-1000. *Prod.:* Without Warning, Vice Squad, Down Three Dark Streets, Return of Dracula, The Flame Barrier, The Vampire, The Monster that Challenged the World, Geronimo, The Glory Guys, Clambake, Scalphunters, Sam Whiskey, Underground, McKenzie Break, The Honkers, Hunting Party, Kansas City Bomber, White Lightning, McQ, Brannigan, Gator, Safari 3000 (also s.p.).
TELEVISION: The Rifleman, Robert Taylor's Detectives, Law of the Plainsman, The Big Valley.

GARFIELD, ALLEN
Actor. r.n. Allen Goorwitz. b. Newark, NJ, Nov. 22, 1939. e. Upsala Col., Actors Studio. Worked as journalist for Newark Star Ledger and Sydney Morning Herald (Australia) prior to becoming an actor. Has also acted as Allen Goorwitz. Life Member of the Actors Studio, NYC.
PICTURES: Greetings, Putney Swope, Hi Mom!, The Owl and the Pussycat, Bananas, Believe in Me, Roommates, The Organization, Taking Off, Cry Uncle!, You've Got to Walk it Like You Talk It or You'll Lose That Beat, Get to Know Your Rabbit, The Candidate, Top of the Heap, Deadhead Miles, Slither, Busting, The Conversation, The Front Page, Nashville, Gable and Lombard, Mother Jugs & Speed, The Brink's Job, Skateboard, Paco, One-Trick Pony, The Stunt Man, Continental Divide, One from the Heart, The State of Things, The Black Stallion Returns, Get Crazy, Irreconcilable Differences, Teachers, The Cotton Club, Desert Bloom, Beverly Hills Cop II, Rich Boys, Let it Ride, Night Visitor, Dick Tracy, Club Fed, Until the End of the World, Jack and His Friends, Family Prayers, The Patriots, The Glass Shadow, Miracle Beach, Sketches of a Strangler, Destiny Turns on the Radio, Diabolique, Obsession, The Elf Who Didn't Believe, Get a Job, The Ninth Gate, Men Named Milo, Women Named Greta, The Majestic, White Boy.
TELEVISION: *Series:* The Lot. *Movies:* Footsteps, The Marcus-Nelson Murders, The Virginia Hill Story, Serpico: The Deadly Game, The Million Dollar Rip-Off, Nowhere to Run, Ring of Passion, Leave 'Em Laughing, Citizen Cohn, Killer in the Mirror, Incident at Vichy, Judgment: The Trial of Julius and Ethel Rosenberg. *Guest:* Law and Order, Equal Justice, Eddie Dodd, Jack's Place, Taxi.

GARFINKLE, LOUIS
Writer, Director, Producer. b. Seattle, WA, February 11, 1928. e. U. of California, U. of Washington, U. of Southern California (B.A., 1948). Writer KOMO, Seattle, 1945; Executive Research, Inc., 1948; writer, educ. doc. screenplays, Emerson Films, EBF. 1948-50; s.p. You Can Beat the A-Bomb (RKO), 1950; writer-dir. training films, info. films, Signal Photo, 1950-53; copy, Weinberg Adv., 1953; head of doc. research in TV, U. of California, Berkeley, 1954-55; staff, Sheilah Graham Show, 1955; formed Maxim Prod. Inc. with Albert Band, 1956. Co-creator Collaborator Interactive Computer Software to asst. in writing stories for screen & TV, 1990; formed Collaborator Systems Inc. with Cary Brown and Francis X. Feighan, 1991. Received Best Screenwriting Tool Award from Screen Writers Forum, 1991. Member: AMPAS, WGA West, ATAS, Dramatists Guild, Board of Advisers Filmic Writing Major, USC School of Cinema & TV.
PICTURES: *Screenplay:* The Young Guns (also story), I Bury the

Living (also story, co-prod.), Face of Fire (also co-prod.), Hellbenders, A Minute to Pray A Second to Die, The Love Doctors (also story, prod.), Beautiful People, The Models (also story), The Doberman Gang (also story), Little Cigars (also story), The Deer Hunter (story collab.; Acad. Award nom.), Milena.
TELEVISION: *Writer:* 712 teleplays for Day in Court, Morning Court, Accused, 1959-66. *Co-writer-creator:* Direct Line (pilot), June Allyson Show, Threat of Evil, Death Valley Days, Crullers At Sundown, Captain Dick Mine, No. 3 Peanut Place (pilot).

GARFUNKEL, ART
Singer, Actor. b. New York, NY, Nov. 5, 1942. e. Columbia Coll. Began singing at age 4. Long partnership with Paul Simon began in grade school at 13 in Queens, NY; first big success in 1965 with hit single, Sound of Silence. Partnership dissolved in 1970. Winner of 4 Grammy Awards. Composer of songs in a variety of movies.
PICTURES: Catch-22 (debut, 1970), Carnal Knowledge, Bad Timing/A Sensual Obsession, Good to Go, Boxing Helena, 54.

GARLAND, BEVERLY
Actress. r.n. Beverly Fessenden. b. Santa Cruz, CA, Oct. 17, 1930. e. Glendale Coll., 1945-47.
PICTURES: D.O.A., The Glass Web, Miami Story, Bittercreek, Two Guns and a Badge, Killer Leopard, The Rocket Man, Sudden Danger, Desperate Hours, Curucu: Beast of the Amazon, Gunslinger, Swamp Woman, The Steel Jungle, It Conquered the World, Not of This Earth, Naked Paradise, The Joker is Wild, Chicago Confidential, Badlands of Montana, The Saga of Hemp Brown, Alligator People, Stark Fever, Twice Told Tales, Pretty Poison, The Mad Room, Where the Red Fern Grows, Airport 1975, Roller Boogie, It's My Turn, Death Falls, Haunted Symphony, Drive-In Movie Memories, If.
TELEVISION: *Movies:* Cutter's Trail, Say Goodbye Maggie Cole, Weekend Nun, Voyage of the Yes, Unwed Father, Healers, Day the Earth Moved, This Girl for Hire, The World's Oldest Living Bridesmaid, Finding the Way Home. *Series:* Mama Rosa, Pantomime Quiz, The Bing Crosby Show, My Three Sons, Scarecrow & Mrs. King, Decoy, Port Charles. *Guest:* Twilight Zone, Dr. Kildare, Medic (Emmy nom.), Magnum P.I., Remington Steele, Lois and Clark.

GARNER, JAMES
Actor. r.n. James Baumgarner. b. Norman, OK, April 7, 1928. e. Norman H.S. Joined Merchant Marine, U.S. Army, served in Korean War. Prod. Paul Gregory suggested acting career. Studied drama at N.Y. Berghof School. Toured with road companies; Warner Bros. studio contract followed.
PICTURES: Toward the Unknown (debut, 1956), The Girl He Left Behind, Shoot Out at Medicine Bend, Sayonara, Darby's Rangers, Up Periscope, Alias Jesse James (cameo), Cash McCall, The Children's Hour, Boys' Night Out, The Great Escape, The Thrill of It All, The Wheeler Dealers, Move Over Darling, The Americanization of Emily, 36 Hours, The Art of Love, Mister Buddwing, A Man Could Get Killed, Duel at Diablo, Grand Prix, Hour of the Gun, The Pink Jungle, How Sweet It Is, Support Your Local Sheriff, Marlowe, A Man Called Sledge, Support Your Local Gunfighter, Skin Game, They Only Kill Their Masters, One Little Indian, The Castaway Cowboy, Health, The Fan, Victor/Victoria, Tank, Murphy's Romance (Acad. Award nom.), Sunset, The Distinguished Gentleman, Fire in the Sky, Maverick, My Fellow Americans, The Hidden Dimension, Twilight, Space Cowboys, Atlantis: The Lost Empire (voice), Divine Secrets of the Ya-Ya Sisterhood, The Notebook.
TELEVISION: *Movies:* The Rockford Files (pilot), The New Maverick (pilot), The Long Summer of George Adams, The Glitter Dome, Heartsounds, Promise (also exec. prod.), Obsessive Love, My Name Is Bill W. (also exec. prod.), Decoration Day, Barbarians at the Gate, The Rockford Files: I Still Love L.A. (also co-exec. prod.), The Rockford Files: A Blessing in Disguise (also co-exec. prod.), The Rockford Files: Godfather Knows Best, The Rockford Files: Friends and Foul Play, The Rockford Files: Crime and Punishment, Dead Silence, The Rockford Files: Murder and Misdemeanors, Legalese, The Rockford Files: If It Bleeds...It Leads, The Last Debate, Roughing It. *Mini-Series:* Space, Shake Rattle and Roll: An American Love Story. *Specials:* Sixty Years of Seduction, Lily for President. *Series:* Maverick, Nichols, The Rockford Files, Bret Maverick, Man of the People, Chicago Hope, God the Devil and Bob, First Monday.

GAROFALO, JANEANE
Actress. b. Newton, NJ, Sept. 28, 1964. Created I Hate Myself Productions. Began standup comedy career in 1985.
PICTURES: Late for Dinner, Reality Bites, Suspicious, I Shot a Man in Vegas, Bye Bye Love, Coldblooded, Now and Then, Kids in the Hall: Brain Candy, The Truth About Cats and Dogs, The Cable Guy, Larger than Life, Sweethearts, Touch, Romy and Michele's High School Reunion, Cop Land, The Matchmaker, Clay Pigeons, Dog Park, Thick as Thieves, Steal This Movie, 200 Cigarettes, Half Baked, Permanent Midnight, Mystery Men, The Minus Man, Dogma, Can't Stop Dancing, The Bumblebee Flies Anyway, The Adventures of Rocky and Bullwinkle, Titan A.E. (voice), Wet Hot Summer, The Cherry Picker, Nobody Knows Anything, The Search for John Gissing, Big Trouble, Martin and Orloff, Manhood, Wonderland, La La Wood, Ash Tuesday.
TELEVISION: Outlaw Comic: The Censoring of Bill Hicks (narrator), Slice o' Life (exec. prod.). *Mini-series:* Tales of the City.

Guest: Law & Order, Seinfeld, Home Improvement, Felicity (voice), Ellen, NewsRadio, Dr. Katz— Professional Therapist (voice), Mad About You (voice), The Simpsons (voice), Strangers With Candy, The Sopranos, Ed, Primetime Glick.*Series*: Saturday Night Live, The Larry Sanders Show, The Ben Stiller Show, TV Nation, Jimmy Kimmel Live (guest host).

GARR, TERI
Actress. b. Lakewood, OH, Dec. 11, 1949. Began career as dancer, performing S.F. Ballet at 13. Later appeared with L.S. Ballet and in original road show co. of West Side Story. Several film appearances as a dancer incl. Fun in Acapulco, Viva Las Vegas, What a Way to Go, Roustabout, etc. Did commercials; appeared in film Head written by a fellow acting student, Jack Nicholson. Career boosted by appearance on TV as semi-regular on The Sonny and Cher Show.
PICTURES: Maryjane, Head, The Moonshine War, The Conversation, Young Frankenstein, Won Ton Ton the Dog Who Saved Hollywood, Oh God!, Close Encounters of the Third Kind, Mr. Mike's Mondo Video, The Black Stallion, Witches' Brew, Honky Tonk Freeway, One from the Heart, The Escape Artist, Tootsie (Acad. Award nom.), The Sting II, The Black Stallion Returns, Mr. Mom, Firstborn, Miracles, After Hours, Full Moon in Blue Water, Out Cold, Let It Ride, Short Time, Waiting for the Light, The Player, Mom and Dad Save the World, Dumb & Dumber, Ready to Wear (Pret-a-Porter), Michael, A Simple Wish, The Definite Maybe, Changing Habits, The Sky is Falling, Kill the Man, Dick, Ghost World, Life Without Dick, Searching for Debra Winger.
TELEVISION: *Movies*: Law and Order, Doctor Franken, Prime Suspect, Winter of Our Discontent, To Catch a King, Intimate Strangers, Pack of Lies, A Quiet Little Neighborhood A Perfect Little Murder, Stranger in the Family, Deliver Them From Evil: The Taking of Alta View, Fugitive Nights: Danger in the Desert, Murder Live!, Nightscream, Half a Dozen Babies, A Colder Kind of Death. *Specials*: The Frog Prince (Faerie Tale Theatre), Drive She Said (Trying Times), Paul Reiser: Out on a Whim, Mother Goose Rock 'n' Rhyme, The Whole Shebang, Aliens for Breakfast. *Mini-Series*: Fresno. *Guest*: Tales from the Crypt (The Trap), The Larry Sanders Show. *Series regular*: Shindig, The Ken Berry "Wow" Show, (1972), Burns and Schreiber Comedy Hour, Girl With Something Extra, The Sonny and Cher Comedy Hour, The Sonny Comedy Revue, Good and Evil, Good Advice, Women of the House.

GARRETT, BETTY
Singer, Actress. b. St. Joseph, MO, May 23, 1919. e. scholarships: Annie Wright Seminary, Tacoma, WA; Neighborhood Playhouse, N.Y. Sang in night clubs, hotels, Broadway shows: Call Me Mister (Donaldson Award, 1946), Spoon River Anthology, A Girl Could Get Lucky, Meet Me in St. Louis (1989). Motion Picture Herald, Star of Tomorrow, 1949. Starred in one woman show, Betty Garrett and Other Songs, beginning in 1974 and touring through 1993 (Bay Area Critics & LA Drama Critics Awards); also in autobiographical show, No Dogs or Actors Allowed (Pasadena Playhouse, 1989), So There! (with Dale Gonyear; Pasadena Playhouse, 1993). Given Life Achievement Award by Los Angeles Drama Critics Circle, 1995. With Ron Rapaport author of Betty Garrett and Other Songs—A Life on Stage & Screen, 1998.
PICTURES: The Big City (debut, 1948), Words and Music, Take Me Out to the Ball Game, Neptune's Daughter, On the Town, My Sister Eileen, Shadow on the Window, Broadway: The Golden Age By the Legends Who Were There.
TELEVISION: *Movies*: All the Way Home, Who's Happy Now, *Series*: All in the Family, Laverne and Shirley, *Guest*: Love Boat, Black's Magic, Somerset Gardens, Murder She Wrote, Harts of the West, The Good Life, Golden Girls, Townies.

GARY, LORRAINE
Actress. b. New York, NY, Aug. 16, 1937. r.n. Lorraine Gottfried. m. executive Sidney J. Scheinberg. e. Columbia Univ.
PICTURES: Jaws, Car Wash, I Never Promised You a Rose Garden, Jaws 2, Just You and Me Kid, 1941, Jaws-The Revenge.
TELEVISION: *Movies*: The City, The Marcus-Nelson Murders, Partners in Crime, Pray for the Wildcats, Man on the Outside, Lanigan's Rabbi, Crash.

GATES, WILLIAM H.
Executive. b. 1957. Started computer programming at age 13. 1974, developed BASIC for the first microcomputer, MITS Altair. 1975, with Paul Allen formed Microsoft to develop software for personal computers. Chmn. & CEO of Microsoft Corp. leading provider of worldwide software for personal computers.

GATWARD, JAMES
Executive. b. London, England. Ent. Ind. 1957. Early career as freelance drama prod. dir. in Canada, USA, UK (with ITV & BBC). Prod. dir. various intern. co-productions in UK, Ceylond, Australia, Germany. Currently chief executive and Dep. chmn. TVS Television Ltd., chmn. Telso Communications Ltd., dir. of ITN, Channel Four, Super Channel, Oracle Teletext.

GAVIN, JOHN
Executive, Diplomat, Actor. b. Los Angeles, CA, April 8, 1932. m. actress Constance Towers. e. St. John's Military Acad., Villanova Prep at Ojai, Stanford Univ., Naval service: air intelligence officer in Korean War. Broadway stage debut: Seesaw, 1973. 1961-73 public service experience as spec. advisor to Secretary Gen. of OAS, performed gp. task work for Dept. of

State and Exec. Office of the President. Pres. Screen Actors Guild, 1971-73. Named U.S. Ambassador to Mexico, 1981-86. Partner in Gavin & Dailey, a venture capital firm; founder and chmn. Gamma Holdings, an int'l. capital and consulting firm; Member of the Latin America Strategy Bd. of Hicks, Muse, Tate & Furst; a dir. of TCW Convertible Securities Fund, Inc.; TCW Galileo Funds Inc.; and a trustee of TCW Premier Funds. Also a dir. of Claxson Interactive Group, Inc. Consultant to Dept. of State and serves pro-bono on several boards.
PICTURES: Behind the High Wall (debut, 1956), Four Girls in Town, Quantez, A Time to Love and a Time to Die, Imitation of Life, Psycho, Midnight Lace, Spartacus, A Breath of Scandal, Romanoff and Juliet, Tammy Tell Me True, Back Street, Thoroughly Modern Millie, The Madwoman of Chaillot, Pussycat Pussycat I Love You, Keep It in the Family, The House of Shadows, Jennifer, The P.A.C.K., Off the Menu: The Last Days of Chasen's.
TELEVISION: *Movies*: Cutler's Trail, The New Adventures of Heidi, Sophia Loren: Her Own Story. *Series*: Destry, Convoy. *Mini-Series*: Doctors' Private Lives.

GAY, JOHN
Writer. b. Whittier, CA, April 1, 1924. e. LA City Coll.
PICTURES: Run Silent, Run Deep, Separate Tables, The Happy Thieves, Four Horsemen, The Courtship of Eddie's Father, The Hallelujah Trail, The Last Safari, The Power, No Way to Treat a Lady, Soldier Blue, Sometimes a Great Notion, Hennessey, A Matter of Time, Around the World in 80 Days (video, 1999).
TELEVISION: Amazing Howard Hughes, Kill Me If You Can, Captains Courageous, Red Badge of Courage, All My Darling Daughters, Les Miserables, Transplant, A Private Battle, A Tale of Two Cities, The Bunker, Berlin Tunnel 21, Stand By Your Man, Dial "M" For Murder, The Long Summer of George Adams, A Piano for Mrs. Cimino, The Hunchback of Notre Dame, Ivanhoe, Witness for the Prosecution, Samson and Delilah, Fatal Vision, Doubletake, Uncle Tom's Cabin, Outlaw, Six Against the Rock, Blind Faith, Cruel Doubt, Trick of the Eye, Father's Day.

GAYNOR, MITZI
Actress. r.n. Francisca Mitzi Von Gerber. b. Chicago, IL, Sept. 4, 1931. e. Powers Professional H.S., Hollywood. Studied ballet since age four; was in L.A. Light Opera prod. Roberta. Stage: Anything Goes (natl. co., 1989).
OPERA: Fortune Teller, Song of Norway, Louisiana Purchase, Naughty Marietta, The Great Waltz.
PICTURES: My Blue Heaven (debut, 1950), Take Care of My Little Girl, Golden Girl, We're Not Married, Bloodhounds of Broadway, The I Don't Care Girl, Down Among the Sheltering Palms, There's No Business Like Show Business, Three Young Texans, Anything Goes, The Birds and the Bees, The Joker Is Wild, Les Girls, South Pacific, Happy Anniversary, Surprise Package, For Love or Money, Ça c'est l'amour (video short).
TELEVISION: *Specials*: Mitzi, Mitzi's Second Special, The First Time, A Tribute to the American Housewife, Mitzi and a Hundred Guys, Roarin' in the 20s, Mitzi...Zings Into Spring, What's Hot What's Not.

GAZZARA, BEN
Actor. b. New York, NY, Aug. 28, 1930. e. Studied at CCNY 1947-49. Won scholarship to study with Erwin Piscator; joined Actor's Studio, where students improvised a play, End as a Man, which then was performed on Broadway with him in lead. Screen debut (1957) in film version of that play retitled The Strange One.
THEATRE: Jezebel's Husband, End as a Man, Cat on a Hot Tin Roof, A Hatful of Rain, The Night Circus, Epitaph for George Dillon, Two for the Seesaw, Strange Interlude, Traveler Without Luggage, Hughie, Who's Afraid of Virginia Woolf, Dance of Death, Thornhill, Shimada.
PICTURES: The Strange One (debut, 1957), Anatomy of a Murder, The Passionate Thief, The Young Doctors, Convicts Four, Conquered City, A Rage to Live, The Bridge at Remagen, Husbands, The Neptune Factor, Capone, Killing of a Chinese Bookie, Voyage of the Damned, High Velocity, Opening Night, Saint Jack, Bloodline, They All Laughed, Inchon, Tales of Ordinary Madness, Road House, Quicker Than the Eye, Don Bosco, A Lovely Scandal, Girl from Trieste, Il Camorrista, Tattooed Memory, Beyond the Ocean (also dir., s.p.), Forever, Farmer & Chase, The Shadow Conspiracy, The Big Lebowski, The Spanish Prisoner, Buffalo 66, Illuminata, Happiness, The Thomas Crown Affair, Summer of Sam, Believe, Undertakers Paradise, Squirrels to the Nuts, Paradise Cove, Jack of Hearts, Blue Moon, Very Mean Men, The List, Nella terra di nessuno, Home Sweet Hoboken, Believe, Dogville, The Shore.
TELEVISION: *Movies*: When Michael Calls, Maneater, QB VII, The Death of Ritchie, A Question of Honor, An Early Frost, A Letter to Three Wives, Police Story: The Freeway Killings, Downpayment on Murder, People Like Us, Lies Before Kisses, Blindsided, Love Honor & Obey: The Last Mafia Marriage, Parallel Lives, Fatal Vows: The Alexandria O'Hara Story, Valentine's Day, Angelo Nero, Tre Stelle, Un Bacio nel buio, Brian's Song, Hysterical Blindness. *Series*: Arrest and Trial, Run for Your Life.

GEARY, ANTHONY
Actor. b. Coalville, UT, May 29, 1947. e. U. of Utah.
THEATRE: The Inspector General, The Glass Menagerie, The Wild Duck, Barabbas.
PICTURES: Blood Sabbath (debut, 1969), Johnny Got His Gun, Private Investigations, Disorderlies, Penitentiary III, You Can't

Hurry Love, Pass the Ammo, Dangerous Love, It Takes Two, UHF, Night Life, Crack House, Night of the Warrior, Scorchers.
TELEVISION: *Movies*: Intimate Agony, Sins of the Past, The Imposter, Kicks, Perry Mason: The Case of the Murdered Madam, Do You Know the Muffin Man? *Special*: Intimate Portrait: Genie Francis. *Series*: Bright Promise, General Hospital (1978-83; 1990-). *Guest*: The Young and the Restless, Osmond Family Holiday Special, Sunset Beat, Murder She Wrote, Hotel, All in the Family, Streets of San Francisco.

GEDRICK, JASON
Actor. b. Chicago, IL, Feb. 7, 1965.
PICTURES: Massive Retaliation (debut, 1984), The Zoo Gang, The Heavenly Kid, Iron Eagle, Stacking, Promised Land, Rooftops, Born on the Fourth of July, Backdraft, Crossing the Bridge, The Force, Power 98, Silent Cradle, Summer Catch, One Eyed King, Jesus-Mary-And Joey.
TELEVISION: *Movies/Specials*: Dare to Love, EZ Streets (pilot), The Last Don, The Third Twin, The Last Don II, The Partners, A Date with Darkness: The Trial and Capture of Andrew Luster. *Series*: Class of 96, Murder One, Sweet Justice, EZ Streets, Falcone, The Beast, Boomtown..

GEESON, JUDY
Actress. b. Arundel, Sussex, England, Sept. 10, 1948. e. Corona Stage Sch. Began professional career on British TV, 1960.
THEATRE: Othello, Titus Andronicus, Two Gentlemen of Verona, Section Nine, An Ideal Husband.
PICTURES: To Sir with Love, Berserk, Here We Go Round the Mulberry Bush, Prudence and the Pill, Hammerhead, Three into Two Won't Go, The Oblong Box, Two Gentlemen Sharing, The Executioner, Nightmare Hotel, 10 Rillington Place, Doomwatch, Fear in the Night, It's Not the Size That Counts, Brannigan, Diagnosis Murder, The Eagle Has Landed, Carry On England, Dominique, Horror Planet, The Plague Dogs (voice), Young Goodman Brown, The Duke, Everything Put Together, Alien Fury: Countdown to Invasion, Spanish Fly.
TELEVISION: Dance of Death, Lady Windermere's Fan, Room with a View, The Skin Game, Star Maidens, Poldark, She, The Coronation, Murder She Wrote, Astronomy (Triple Play II), The Secret Life of Kathy McCormick, Joan Crawford: The Ultimate Movie Star (documentary).. *Series*: Star Maidens, Mad About You.

GEFFEN, DAVID
Executive, Producer. b. Brooklyn, NY, Feb. 21, 1943. Began in mailroom of William Morris Agency before becoming agent there and later at Ashley Famous. With Elliott Roberts founded own talent management co. for musicians. Founded Asylum Records, 1970. Pres. then chmn. Elektra-Asylum Records 1973-76. Sold co. to Warner Communications for whom he headed film prod. unit. Vice-chmn. Warner Bros. Pictures, 1975; exec. asst. to chmn., Warner Communications, 1977; Member music faculty Yale U., 1978. Formed Geffen Records 1980 and Geffen Film Co. Producer of Broadway shows Master Harold... and the Boys, Cats, Good, Dreamgirls, Social Security, Chess. 1990, sold record co. to MCA, Inc. With Steven Spielberg and Jeffrey Katzenberg formed Dreamworks entertainment company, 1995.
PICTURES: Personal Best, Risky Business, Lost in America, After Hours, Little Shop of Horrors, Beetlejuice (exec. prod.), Men Don't Leave, Defending Your Life, M. Butterfly, Interview With the Vampire.

GELBART, LARRY
Writer. b. Chicago, IL, Feb. 25, 1928. Began at age 16 writing for Danny Thomas on Fanny Brice Show. Followed by Duffy's Tavern, Bob Hope and Jack Paar radio shows. Author of Laughing Matters, 1998.
THEATRE: The Conquering Hero, A Funny Thing Happened on the Way to the Forum (with Burt Shevlove; Tony Award, 1962), Sly Fox, Mastergate, City of Angels (Tony Award, 1990), Power Failure.
PICTURES: The Notorious Landlady, The Thrill of It All, The Wrong Box, Not With My Wife You Don't, The Chastity Belt, A Fine Pair, Oh God!, Movie Movie, Neighbors, Tootsie, Blame It on Rio, Bedazzled, C-Scam.
TELEVISION: *Movies*: Barbarians at the Gate (Cable Ace Award, 1993), Weapons of Mass Distraction, And Starring Pancho Villa as Himself (writer, exec. prod.) *Special*: Mastergate, M*A*S*H: 30th Anniversary Reunion (prod.) *Series*: Caesar's Hour, M*A*S*H (Emmy Award, 1974; also co-prod.), United States, Corsairs (prod.).

GELFAN, GREGORY
Executive. b. Los Angeles, CA, Aug. 7, 1950. Was entertainment atty. with Kaplan, Livingston et. al., and Weissmann, Wolff et. al. before joining Paramount Pictures in 1983 as dir. of business affairs. 1985, named v.p., business affairs, for M.P. Group of Paramount; 1989 promoted to sr. v.p. in chg. of business affairs. 1994, named exec. v.p. in chg. of business & legal affairs, 20th Century Fox. Currently, exec. v.p., Fox Filmed Ent.

GELLAR, SARAH MICHELLE
Actress. b. New York, NY, April 14, 1977.
PICTURES: Over the Brooklyn Bridge, Funny Farm, High Stakes, I Know What You Did Last Summer, Scream 2, Small Soldiers (voice), She's All That (cameo), Simply Irresistible,

Cruel Intentions, The It Girl, Harvard Man, Scooby Doo, Happily N'Ever After (voice), Scooby Doo2: Monsters Unleashed.
TELEVISION: *Movies*: An Invasion of Privacy, A Woman Named Jackie, 2004: A Light Knight's Odyssey (voice). *Series*: Girl Talk, Swans Crossing, All My Children, Buffy the Vampire Slayer, Buffy: The Animated Series (voice). *Guest*: Love Sydney, The Guiding Light, Spenser: For Hire, King of the Hill (voice), Grosse Point, God, the Devil, and Bob (voice), Sex and the City, Angel.

GELLER, BRIAN L.
Executive. b. New York, NY, Feb. 3, 1948. e. Queens Coll. Entered industry with Columbia Pictures as sls. trainee in 1966, leaving in 1968 to go with American Intl. Pictures as asst. branch mgr. In 1969 joined Cinemation Industries as eastern div. sls. mgr.; 1978, left to become gen. sls. mr. of NMD Film Distributing Co. 1982, named dir. of dist., Mature Pictures Corp. 1983, gen. sls. mgr., Export Pix.; with Cinema Group as east. sls. mgr.; joined Scotti Brothers Pictures as national sales, mgr. Joined 20th Century Fox sls. dep't. Member of Motion Picture Bookers Club of N.Y.; Variety Tent 35, Motion Picture Pioneers.

GENDECE, BRIAN
Producer, Executive. b. St. Louis, MO, Dec. 3, 1956. e. Drury Coll., Springfield, MO. 1981-85, Director of Business Affairs, Weinstein/Skyfield Productions and Skyfield Management. 1986-87, dir. of business affairs, Cannon Films; 1987-89, dir. creative affairs, Cannon Films; 1989 co-pres., Sheer Entertainment; indie first look Pictures.; 1991 owner The Gendece Film Co.; 1991-93, prod./dir., 21st Century Film; 1993-96, dir. of mktg., Raleigh Film and Television Studios. 1997-98, pres., G & G Prods. Currently runs Gendece Film, Los Angeles.
THEATRE: Jack Klugman as Lyndon, The Bob Fosse Awards.
PICTURES: Runaway Train, Salsa, Rope Dancin', The Hunters, The American Samurai, Ceremony.
VIDEO: Bad Habits, Shape Up with Arnold, Laura Branigan's Your Love, How to Become a Teenage Ninja, L.A. Raiders' Wild Wild West, The Making of Crime and Punishment.

GEORGE, GEORGE W.
Writer, Producer. b. New York, NY, Feb.8, 1920. e. Williams Coll. U.S. Navy, 1941-44; screen-writer since 1948. President, Jengo Enterprises, dev. theatrical and m.p. projects. Retired.
THEATRE: *Prod.*: Dylan, Any Wednesday, Ben Franklin in Paris, The Great Indoors, Happily Never After, Night Watch, Via Galactica, Bedroom Farce, Program for Murder (also co-author).
PICTURES: *Writer*: Bodyguard, The Nevadan, Woman on Pier 13, Peggy, Mystery Submarine, Red Mountain Experiment, Alcatraz, Fight Town, Smoke Signal, Desert Sands, Uranium Boom, Halliday Brand, Doc, The James Dean Story, The Two Little Bears. *Prod.*: The James Dean Story, A Matter of Innocence, Twisted Nerve, Hello-Goodbye, Night Watch, Rich Kids, My Dinner With Andre.
TELEVISION: Climax, Screen Gems, Loretta Young Show, The Rifleman, Peter Gunn, The Real McCoys, Adventures in Paradise, Hong Kong, Follow the Sun, Bonanza.

GEORGE, LOUIS
Executive. b. Karavas, Kyrenia, Cyprus, June 7, 1935. e. Kyrenia Business Acad., Cyprus (honored 1951). Emigrated to U.S. in 1952. After brief stint in Foreign Exchange Dept. of City National Bank, New York, served in U.S. Army, 1953-55. Entered industry in 1956 as theatre manager with Loew's Theatres in N.Y. metro area, managing Metropolitan, Triboro, New Rochelle, between 1958-66. 1966 joined MGM as dir. of intl. theatre dept. 1969 promoted to dir. of world-wide non-theatrical sales. 1972-74 served as regional dir. of MGM Far East operations. 1974 left MGM to establish Arista Films, Inc., an indep. prod./dist. co. Pres. & CEO, Arista Films, Inc. Sold Arista Films library in 1996 and closed co. Currently, v.p., sales & acquisitions for Four Point Entertainment. Also bd. member, American Film Marketing Assn., chmn. Copyright and Film Security Committee of the assn.
PICTURES: Slaughterhouse Rock, Buying Time, Violent Zone (exec. prod.), Angels Brigade, Final Justice, Surf II, Crackdown, Violent Zone.

GEORGE, SUSAN
Actress, Producer. b. Surrey, England, July 26, 1950. m. actor-prod. Simon MacCorkindale. e. Corona Acad.
PICTURES: Billion Dollar Brain, The Sorcerers, Up the Junction, The Strange Affair, The Looking Glass War, All Neat in Black Stockings, Twinky (Lola), Spring and Port Wine, Eye Witness (Sudden Terror), Die Screaming Marianne, Fright, Straw Dogs, Sonny and Jed, Dirty Mary Crazy Larry, Mandingo, Out of Season, A Small Town in Texas, Tintorera, Tomorrow Never Comes, Enter the Ninja, Venom, The House Where Evil Dwells, Jigsaw Man, Lightning: The White Stallion, Stealing Heaven (exec. prod. only), That Summer of White Roses (also exec. prod.), Diana & Me.
TELEVISION: Swallows and Amazons, Adam's Apple, Weaver's Green, Compensation Alice, The Right Attitude, Dracula, Lamb to the Slaughter, Royal Jelly, Masquerade, Czechmate, Hotel, Blacke's Magic, Jack the Ripper, Castle of Adventure,The House That Mary Bought (also exec. prod.). *Series*: Cluedo, Stay Lucky, EastEnders.

GERALD, HELEN
Actress. b. New York, NY, Aug. 13. e. U. of Southern California, 1948. Stage: Italian Teatro D'Arte, Les Miserables, The Civil Death, Feudalism.
PICTURES: The Gay Cavalier, The Trap, Tarzan and the Leopard Woman, Cigarette Girl, Meet Miss Bobby Socks, G.I. War Brides, Gentleman's Agreement, A Bell for Adano, Tomorrow Is Forever, Janie, Grand Prix, The Sandpiper, Make Mine Mink, Best of Everything, Cock a Doodle Deux.
TELEVISION: Robert Montgomery Presents, Frontiers of Faith, Valiant Lady, Kraft Theatre, Gangbusters, Adventures of The Falcon, Schlitz Playhouse of Stars, This Is the Answer, Man from U.N.C.L.E., Run for Your Life, Perry Mason, Pink Panther Show (voices).

GERARD, GIL
Actor. b. Little Rock, AK, Jan. 23, 1943. e. Arkansas State Teachers Coll. Appeared in over 400 TV commercials. On stage in I Do! I Do!, Music Man, Stalag 17, Applause, etc.
PICTURES: Some of My Best Friends Are (1971), Man on a Swing, Hooch (also co-prod.), Airport '77, Buck Rogers in the 25th Century, Soldier's Fortune, Looking for Bruce, Mom Can I Keep Her?, The Stepdaughter.
TELEVISION: *Movies*: Ransom for Alice, Killing Stone, Help Wanted: Male, Not Just Another Affair, Hear No Evil, Johnny Blue (pilot), For Love or Money, Stormin' Home, International Airport, Final Notice, The Elite, Last Electric Knight. *Series*: The Doctors, Buck Rogers in the 25th Century, Nightingales, Sidekicks, E.A.R.T.H. Force, Fish Police, Code 3 (host).

GERARD, LILLIAN
Publicist, Writer b. New York, NY, Nov. 25, 1914. e. Baruch, CCNY, Columbia U. Publicity, Rialto Theatre, 1936; publicity-adv. Filmarte Theatre, 1938, Gerard Associates, 1938-47; V.P. and managing dir. of Paris Theatre, 1948-62; publicity-adv. dir., Rugoff Theatres, 1962. Film consultant to Times Films, Lopert Films, Landau Co., 1962-65. Adjunct Professor, Film, 1968-70, Columbia U., Sch. of the Arts, Special Projects Co-Ordinator, Museum of Modern Art, 1968-80.
(d. Jan. 27, 2003)

GERBER, DAVID
Executive. b. Brooklyn, NY. e. U. of the Pacific. m. actress Laraine Stephens. Joined Batten, Barton, Durstine and Osborn ad agency in N.Y. as TV supvr. Left to become sr. v.p. of TV at General Artists Corp. 1956, named v.p. in chg. sales at 20th-Fox TV where sold and packaged over 50 prime-time series and specials. Entered indep. prod. with The Ghost and Mrs. Muir, followed by Nanny and the Professor. 1970 was exec. prod. of The Double Deckers, children's series made in England. 1972 joined Columbia Pictures Television as indep. prod.; 1974 was named exec. v.p. worldwide prod. for CPT. 1976 returned to indep. prod. 1985, joined MGM/UA TV broadcasting group in chg. world-wide prod. 1986 named president, MGM/UA Television. 1988-92, chmn & CEO, MGM/UA Television Prods. group. Formed Gerber/ITC Development in 1992. 1995, became pres., All American TV Production. Currently, pres., David Gerber Co.
TELEVISION: *Exec. prod.*: The Ghost & Mrs. Muir, Cade's County, Incident on a Dark Street, Jarrett, Police Story (Emmy, best dramatic series), The Girl on the Late Late Show, Nakia, Born Free, Police Woman, The Lindbergh Kidnapping Case, The Turning Point of Jim Malloy, Cop on the Beat, Joe Forrester, The Quest, Gibbsville, Cover Girls, A Killing Affair, Keefer, Doctors' Private Lives, To Kill a Cop, Power, The Courage and the Passion, David Cassidy: Man Undercover, Pleasure Cove, The Billion Dollar Threat, Eischied, Once Upon a Spy, Beulah Land, Terror Among Us, Walking Tall, Riker, Cry for the Strangers, The Neighborhood, Seven Brides for Seven Brothers, Women of San Quentin, George Washinton, Kessie, Police Story: The Freeway Killings, The Man Who Fell to Earth, Royce, The Price of Love, Nothing Lasts Forever, We the Jury, The Adventures of Sinbad, On the Line, The Sky's on Fire, The Lost Battalion.

GERBER, MICHAEL H.
Executive. b. New York, NY, Feb. 6, 1944. e. St. Johns U., B.A., 1969; St. Johns U. School of Law, J.D., 1969. Atty. for Screen Gems, 1969-71; asst. secy. & asst. to gen. counsel, Columbia Pictures Industries, 1971-74; corporate counsel and secretary, Allied Artists Pictures, 1974, v.p. corporate affairs, Allied Artists, 1978; v.p., business affairs, Viacom Intl. 1980-86; 1986-89, sr. v.p.; 1989-93, pres., first run, intl. distrib. & acquisitions, Viacom Enterprises. He formed Gerber Entertainment Group in 1992 to dev. and package tv programs and feature films. In 1999, he created Victory Entertainment Group (live action and 3-D animation, etc. for Internet and worldwide distribution); he holds the position of company pres. & CEO.

GERE, RICHARD
Actor. b. Philadelphia, PA, Aug. 29, 1949. e. U. of Massachusetts. Started acting in college; later joined Provincetown Playhouse and Seattle Repertory Theatre. Composed music for productions of these groups.
THEATRE: *B'way*: Grease, Soon, Habeas Corpus, Bent (Theatre World Award), A Midsummer Night's Dream (Lincoln Center). *Off-B'way* in Killer's Head. *London*: Taming of the Shrew (with Young Vic).

PICTURES: Report to the Commissioner (debut, 1975), Baby Blue Marine, Looking for Mr. Goodbar, Days of Heaven, Bloodbrothers, Yanks, American Gigolo, An Officer and a Gentleman, Breathless, Beyond the Limit, The Cotton Club, King David, Power, No Mercy, Miles From Home, Internal Affairs, Pretty Woman, Rhapsody in August, Final Analysis (also co-exec. prod.), Sommersby (also co-exec. prod.), Mr. Jones (also co-exec. prod.), Intersection, First Knight, Primal Fear, Runaway Bride, Dr. T and the Women, Steinbeck's Point of View, The Mothman Prophecies, Unfaithful, Chicago: The Musical (Golden Globe, best actor in m.p. musical or comedy, 2003), Shabana! Actor-Activist-Woman (documentary short, as himself).
TELEVISION: *Movies*: Strike Force, And the Band Played On. *Guest*: Kojak. *Pilot*: D.H.P.

GERTZ, IRVING
Composer, Musical director. b. Providence, RI, May 19, 1915. e. Providence Coll. of Music, 1934-37. Assoc. with Providence Symph. Orch., comp. choral works for Catholic Choral Soc.; music dept., Columbia, 1939-41; U.S. Army, 1941-46; then comp. arranger, mus. dir. for many cos. incl. Columbia, Universal International, NBC, 20th Century Fox. Compositions: Leaves of Grass, Serenata for String Quartet, Divertimento for String Orchestra, Tableau for Orchestra.
PICTURES: Bandits of Corsica, Gun Belt, Long Wait, The Fiercest Heart, First Travelling Saleslady, Fluffy, Nobody's Perfect, Marines Let's Go!, It Came from Outer Space, The Man from Bitter Ridge, Posse from Hell, The Creature Walks Among Us, The Incredible Shrinking Man, Hell Bent for Leather, Seven Ways from Sundown, Francis Joins the WACS, Raw Edge, East of Sumatra, A Day of Fury, To Hell and Back, Cult of the Cobra, Plunder Road, Top Gun, Tombstone Express, The Alligator People, Khyber Patrol, The Wizard of Baghdad. Fluffy, Marines-Let's Go!, Daffy Rents (short), Ride to Hangman's Tree, Nobody's Perfect
TELEVISION: *Orig. theme & scores*: America, The Golden Voyage, Across the Seven Seas, The Legend of Jesse James, Daniel Boone, Voyage to the Bottom of the Sea, Peyton Place, Land of the Giants, Lancer, Medical Center, Boutade for Wood-Wind Quartet, Salute to All Nations, A Village Fair, Liberty! Liberte! (for symphony orchestra).

GERTZ, JAMI
Actress. b. Chicago, IL, Oct. 28, 1965. e. NYU. Won a nation-wide talent search competition headed by Norman Lear to cast TV comedy series Square Pegs. Following series studied at NYU drama school. Los Angeles theater includes Out of Gas on Lovers' Leap and Come Back Little Sheba. On NY stage in Wrong Turn at Lungfish. Also appeared in the Julian Lennon music video Stick Around.
PICTURES: Endless Love (debut, 1981), On the Right Track, Alphabet City, Sixteen Candles, Mischief, Quicksilver, Crossroads, Solarbabies, The Lost Boys, Less Than Zero, Listen to Me, Renegades, Silence Like Glass, Don't Tell Her It's Me, Sibling Rivalry, Jersey Girl, Twister, Seven Girlfriends, Lip Service.
TELEVISION: *Movies*: This Can't Be Love, Gilda Radner: It's Always Something, Undercover Christmas. *Series*: Square Pegs, Dreams, Sibs, ER, Still Standing. *Guest*: Diff'rent Strokes, The Facts of Life.

GETTY, BALTHAZAR
Actor. b. California, Jan. 22, 1975. Spotted by talent agent while at Bel Air Prep School, winning lead role in remake of Lord of the Flies.
PICTURES: Lord of the Flies (debut, 1990), Young Guns II, My Heroes Have Always Been Cowboys, The Pope Must Die, December, Where the Day Takes You, Halfway House, Red Hot, Dead Beat, Natural Born Killers, Don't Do It, Terrified, Judge Dredd, City Scrapers, White Squall, Habitat, Lost Highway, Four Dogs Playing Poker, Big City Blues, Center of the World, Macarthur Park, Run for the Money, Sol Goode, In God We Trust, Deuces Wild, Ladder 49.
TELEVISION: *Series*: Pasadena, Rosebud, Corsairs. *Special*: The Turn of the Screw.

GETTY, ESTELLE
Actress. b. New York, NY, July 25, 1923. e. attended New School for Social Research. Trained for stage with Gerald Russak and at Herbert Berghof Studios. Worked as comedienne on Borscht Belt circuit and as actress with Yiddish theatre. Founder Fresh Meadows Community theater. Also worked as acting teacher and coach and secretary. Author, If I Knew What I Know Now... So What? (1988).
THEATRE: The Divorce of Judy and Jane (off-B'way debut, 1971), Widows and Children First, Table Settings, Demolition of Hannah Fay, Never Too Old, A Box of Tears, Hidden Corners, I Don't Know Why I'm Screaming, Under the Bridge There's a Lonely Place, Light Up the Sky, Pocketful of Posies, Fits and Starts, Torch Song Trilogy (off-B'way, B'way and tour, Drama Desk nom.), 1982, Helen Hayes Award, best supp. performer in a touring show).
PICTURES: The Chosen, Tootsie, Protocol, Mask, Mannequin, Stop Or My Mom Will Shoot, Stuart Little, The Million Dollar Kid.
TELEVISION: *Movies*: No Man's Land, Victims for Victims: The Teresa Saldana Story, Copacabana, The Sissy Duckling (voice), Intimate Portrait specials: Rue McClanahan, Betty White, Estelle Getty (2000 & 2001). *Series*: The Golden Girls (Golden Globe Award, Emmy Award, 1988), The Golden Palace, Empty Nest.

Guest: Cagney and Lacey, Nurse, Baker's Dozen, One of the Boys, Fantasy Island, numerous other guest appearances.

GETZ, JOHN
Actor. e. Univ Iowa, Amer. Conservatory Theatre (SF). Appeared on B'way in They're Playing Our Song, M. Butterfly. LA stage: Money & Friends.
PICTURES: Tattoo, Thief of Hearts, Blood Simple, The Fly, The Fly II, Born on the Fourth of July, Men at Work, Don't Tell Mom the Babysitter's Dead, Curly Sue, A Passion to Kill, Painted Hero, Mojave Moon, Some Girl, Requiem for a Dream, Held for Ransom.
TELEVISION: *Movies*: Killer Bees, A Woman Called Moses, Kent State, Rivkin: Bounty Hunter, Muggable Mary: Street Cop, Not in Front of the Children, Concrete Beat, The Execution, In My Daughter's Name, Betrayal of Trust, Untamed Love, Awake to Murder, The Late Shift, Zenon: The Sequel, Hunger Point. *Mini-Series*: Loose Change. *Series*: Rafferty, Suzanne Pleshette is Maggie Briggs, MacGruder & Loud, Mariah, Maggie.

GHOSTLEY, ALICE
Actress. b. Eve, MO, Aug. 14, 1926. e. Univ. of OK.
THEATRE: New Faces of 1952, Sandhog, Trouble in Tahiti, Maybe Tuesday, A Thurber Carnival, The Sign in Sidney Brustein's Window (Tony Award, 1965), Stop Thief Stop, Annie, The Beauty Part, Livin' The Life, Nunsense, Come Blow Your Horn, Bye Bye Birdie, Arsenic and Old Lace, Shangri-La.
PICTURES: New Faces (debut, 1954), To Kill a Mockingbird, My Six Loves, Ace Eli and Rodger of the Skies, Gator, Rabbit Test, Grease, Not for Publication, Viva Ace, The Film Flam Man, With Six You Get Egg Roll, The Graduate, Blue Sunshine, Record City, The Wrong Guys, Odd Couple II, Palmers Pick Up, Whispers: An Elephant's Tale (voice), The Chocolate Fairy.
TELEVISION: *Movies*: Two on a Bench, Perry Mason: The Case of the Silenced Singer. *Specials*: Cinderella, Twelfth Night, Shangri-La, Everybody's Doin' It, Designing Women Reunion (2003). *Series*: The Jackie Gleason Show (1962-64), Captain Nice, The Jonathan Winters Show, Bewitched, Mayberry R.F.D., Nichols, The Julie Andrews Hour, Temperatures Rising, Small Wonder, Designing Women.*Guest*: Please Don't Eat the Daisies, Get Smart, Love American Style, Hogan's Heroes, The Odd Couple, What's Happening!, Good Times, Gimme a Break, The Golden Girls, The Client, Cybill.

GIANNINI, GIANCARLO
Actor. b. Spezia, Italy, Aug. 1, 1942. Acquired degree in electronics but immediately after school enrolled at Acad. for Drama in Rome. Cast by Franco Zeffirelli as Romeo at age of 20. Subsequently appeared in a play also directed by Zeffirelli, Two Plus Two No Longer Make Four, written by Lina Wertmuller.
PICTURES: Rita la Zanzara, Arabella, Anzio, Fraulein Doktor, The Secret of Santa Vittoria, Love and Anarchy, The Seduction of Mimi, Swept Away by an Unusual Destiny in the Blue Sea of August, Seven Beauties, How Funny Can Sex Be?, A Night Full of Rain, The Innocent, Buone Notizie (also prod.), Revenge, Travels with Anita, Lili Marleen, Lovers and Liars, La Vita e Bella, Picone Sent Me, Immortal Bachelor, American Dreamer, Fever Pitch, Saving Grace, New York Stories (Life Without Zoe), I Picari, The Sleazy, Uncle, Snack Bar Budapest, Oh King, Blood Red, Brown Bread Sandwiches, Killing Time, Short Cut, Night Sun, Criminals, Once Upon a Crime, Giovanni Falcone, Colpo di Coda, Celluloide, A Walk in the Clouds, New York Crossing, Come Due Coccodrilli, La Frontiera, Broken Dreams, The Scirocco Room, The Last Target, Blood of a Poet, La Lupa, Heaven Before I Die, Lorca, Mimic, Vuoti o Perdere, Una Vacanza all'inferno, Beyond the Garden, Heaven Before I Die, La Cena, The Room of the Scirocco, No Deposit No Return, Sweet Idleness, Milonga, Terra bruciata, A Night with Sabrina Love, The Whole Shebang, Welcome Albania, Ciao America, Hannibal, A Long Long Long Night of Love, CQ, Francesca and Nunziata, Viper, Joshua, Darkness, Ti voglio bene Eugenio, God's Bankers, The Council of Egypt, A Heart Elsewhere, Piazza delle cinque lune..
TELEVISION: Sins, Jacob, Nessuno Escluso, Voglia Di Volare, World Cup '98, Frank Herbert's Dune, Dracula, Papa Giovanni - Joannes XXIII, My House in Umbria.

GIANNOLI, XAVIER
Director.
PICTURES: J'aime beaucoup ce que vous faites, Dialogue au sommet, L'Interview (Cannes Film Fest. Palme d'Or, 1998), Demonlover (prod. only), Les Corps impatients (also s.p. & cinematographer).

GIANOPULOS, JAMES N. (JIM)
Executive. President of International and Pay Television, Twentieth Century Fox, 1992-1994. Pres., Fox International Theatrical Distribution, 1994-2000. Co-chair, Twentieth Century Fox and Fox Filmed Entertainment, July 2000-present. Shares position with Thomas E. rothman.Board member, USC Entertainment Technology Committee and KCRW for National Public Radio.

GIBBS, DAVID
Executive. b. 1944. Ent. motion picture industry 1961, Kodak research, worked as a photographer for Kodak 1963-66. Left Kodak, 1975, after three years as a market specialist to join Filmatic Laboratories. Appt. asst. man. director, 1977, becoming chmn. and man. director, 1988. Member of RTS, SMPTE and IVCA. Past Chmn. BISFA 1988-90. Past president of the British Kinematograph, Sound and Television Society.

GIBBS, MARLA
Actress. b. Chicago, IL, June 14, 1931. e. Cortez Peters Business School, Chicago. Worked as receptionist, switchboard operator, travel consultant (1963-74) before co-starring as Florence Johnston on the Jeffersons (1974-85). Formed Marla Gibbs Enterprises, Los Angeles, 1978. Member of CA State Assembly, 1980. Image Award NAACP, 1979-83.
PICTURES: Black Belt Jones, Sweet Jesus Preacher Man, The Meteor Man, Border to Border, Foolish, Lost & Found, The Visit, Stanley's Gig, The Brothers.
TELEVISION: *Movies*: The Missing Are Deadly, Tell Me Where It Hurts, Nobody's Child, Menu for Murder, Lily in Winter. *Mini-Series*: The Moneychangers. *Special*: You Can't Take It With You. *Series*: The Jeffersons, Checking In, 227.

GIBSON, DEREK
Executive. b. Huyton, England, July 7, 1945. e. Wigan Col. Head of Prod. at Astral Bellevue Pathe, 1979-80; v.p. Sandy Howard Prods.; Pres. Hemdale Film Group, 1982-1995.
PICTURES: *Prod./Exec.*: Death Ship, Savage Harvest, Triumphs of a Man Called Horse, The Terminator, River's Edge, Platoon, Hoosiers, Salvador, At Close Range, Scenes from a Goldmine, Best Seller, War Party, Vampire's Kiss, Staying Together, Out Cold, Shag, Miracle Mile, Criminal Law, Hidden Agenda, Don't Tell Her It's Me, Bright Angel, Devil's Pact.

GIBSON, HENRY
Actor. b. Germantown, PA, Sept. 21, 1935. e. Catholic U. of America. Appeared as child actor with stock companies, 1943-57; B'way debut in My Mother My Father and Me, 1962.
PICTURES: The Nutty Professor, Kiss Me Stupid, The Outlaws Is Coming, Charlotte's Web (voice), The Long Goodbye, Nashville (Nat'l Soc. Film Critics Award, 1975), The Last Remake of Beau Geste, Kentucky Fried Movie, A Perfect Couple, The Blues Brothers, Tulips, Health, The Incredible Shrinking Woman, Monster in the Closet, Brenda Starr, Inner Space, Switching Channels, The 'Burbs, Night Visitor, Gremlins II, Tune in Tomorrow, Tom and Jerry: The Movie (voice), A Sailor's Tattoo, Biodome, Color of a Brisk and Leaping Day, Mother Night (voice), Asylum, A Stranger in the Kingdom, Magnolia, The Year that Trembled, Teddy Bears' Picnic, No Prom for Cindy (short), The Commission.
TELEVISION: *Series*: Rowan and Martin's Laugh-In (1968-72), Sunset Beach, Rocket Power. *Movies*: Evil Roy Slade, Every Man Needs One, The New Original Wonder Woman (pilot), Escape from Bogen County, The Night They Took Miss Beautiful, Amateur Night at the Dixie Bar & Grill, For the Love of It, Nashville Grab, Long Gone, Slow Burn, Return to Green Acres, Return to Witch Mountain, The Luck of the Irish. *Mini-Series*: Around the World in 80 Days.

GIBSON, MEL
Actor, Producer, Director. b. Peekskill, NY, Jan. 3, 1956. Emigrated in 1968 to Australia with family. Attended Nat'l Inst. of Dramatic Art in Sydney; in 2nd yr. was cast in his first film, Summer City. Graduated from NIDA, 1977. Joined South Australian Theatre Co. in 1978, appearing in Oedipus, Henry IV, Cedoona. Other plays include Romeo and Juliet, No Names No Pack Drill, On Our Selection, Waiting for Godot, Death of a Salesman.
PICTURES: Summer City (Coast of Terror; debut, 1977), Mad Max, Tim, Chain Reaction (unbilled), Attack Force Z, Gallipoli, The Road Warrior (Mad Max II), The Year of Living Dangerously, The Bounty, The River, Mrs. Soffel, Mad Max Beyond Thunderdome, Lethal Weapon, Tequila Sunrise, Lethal Weapon 2, Bird on a Wire, Air America, Hamlet, Lethal Weapon 3, Forever Young, The Man Without a Face (also dir.), Maverick, Braveheart (also dir.,co-prod.; Academy Award, 1996; Golden Globe, 1996), Casper (cameo), Pocahontas (voice), Ransom, Father's Day (cameo), Conspiracy Theory, Lethal Weapon 4, Payback, The Million Dollar Hotel, The Patriot, What Women Want, We Were Soldiers, Signs, The Singing Detective (also prod.). Producer: The Passion (also dir., s.p.), Paparazzi.
TELEVISION: *Movies*: Wallace and Grommmit Go Chicken, Breaking the News. *Series*: The Sullivans, The Oracle, Drama School. *Specials*: The Ultimate Stuntman: A Tribute to Dar Robinson, Australia's Outback: The Vanishing Frontier (host), Wallace and Grommit Go Chicken, Breaking the News (narr.). *Guest*: The Simpsons (voice).

GIBSON, THOMAS
Actor. b. Charleston, SC, July 3, 1962.
PICTURES: Far and Away, Love & Human Remains, The Age of Innocence, Sleep with Me, Men of War, Barcelona, To Love Honor and Obey, The Next Step, The Flintstones in Viva Rock Vegas, Eyes Wide Shut, Psycho Beach Party, The Broken Hearts Club: A Romantic Comedy, Stardom, Jack the Dog, Virginia's Run, Manhood.
TELEVISION: *Movies*: Lincoln, The Kennedys of Massachusetts, Tales of the City, Secrets, Night Visitors, Inheritance, The Devil's Child, Nightmare Street, More Tales of the City, A Will of Their Own, The Lost Empire, Brush with Fate, Evil Never Dies. *Series*: As the World Turns, Another World, Chicago Hope, Dharma & Greg. *Guest*: Leg Work, Caroline in the City.

GIFFORD, KATHIE LEE
Actress. b. Paris, France, August 16, 1953. e. Oral Roberts University.
PICTURES: The First Wives Club, Dudley Do-Right.
TELEVISION: *Movies*: A Musical Christmas at Walt Disney

World, Model Behavior, Spinning Out of Control. *Series*: Name that Tune, Hee Haw Honeys, Good Morning America, Hercules (voice), Hollywood Squares, Happily Ever After: Fairy Tales for Every Child, Live With Regis and Kathie Lee.*Guest:* Seinfeld, Coach, The Cosby Mysteries, Women of the House, Touched by an Angel, Biography, Second Noah, Spin City, numerous others.

GILBERT, ARTHUR N.
Producer. b. Detroit, MI, Oct. 17, 1920. Lt., Enlisted USMC Oct. 1941. In USMC for 37 years and also in reserves. e. U. of Chicago, 1946. Special investigator for Michigan LCC, 1946-53; world sales dir., Gen. Motors, Cadillac Div., 1953-59; investments in mot. pictures and hotel chains, 1957-70; produced motion pictures with associates beginning in 1965: exec. prod., Mondo Hollywood, 1965; exec. prod. Jeannie-Wife Child, 1966; assoc. prod., The Golden Breed, 1967 and many more. 1970-80, exec. prod. Jaguar Pictures Corp; Columbia, 1981-86; Indi Pic. Corp. Also exec. v.p. for Pacific Western Tours. Prod.ucer at Jonte Prods., U.S., France and U.K., 1990-present (2003).
PICTURES: (prod./exec. prod.): The Glory Stompers, Fire Grass, Cycle Savages, Bigfoot, Incredible Two-Headed Transplant, Balance of Evil, The Life and Curious Death of Marilyn Monroe.

GILBERT, BRUCE
Producer. b. Los Angeles, CA, March 28, 1947. e. U. of California. Pursued film interests at Berkeley's Pacific Film Archive; in summer involved in production in film dept. of San Francisco State U. Founded progressive pre-school in Bay Area. Became story editor in feature film division of Cine-Artists; involved in several projects, including Aloha, Bobby and Rose. Formally partnered with Jane Fonda in IPC Films, Inc., then pres., American Filmworks.
PICTURES: Coming Home (assoc. prod.), The China Syndrome (exec. prod.). *Producer:* Nine to Five, On Golden Pond, Rollover, The Morning After, Man Trouble, Jack the Bear.
TELEVISION: *Series:* Nine to Five (exec. prod.). *Movies:* The Dollmaker (exec. prod.), By Dawn's Early Light (writer, exec. prod.), Red Alert (exec. prod.) Glory & Honor (exec. prod).

GILBERT, LEWIS
Producer, Writer, Director, Former Actor. b. London, England, Mar. 6, 1920. In RAF, W.W.II. Screen debut, 1932; asst. dir. (1930-39) with London Films, Assoc. British, Mayflower, RKO-Radio; from 1939-44 attached U.S. Air Corps Film Unit (asst. dir., Target for Today). In 1944 joined G.B.I. as writer and dir. In 1948, Gainsborough Pictures as writer, dir., 1949; Argyle Prod. 1950; under contract Nettlefold Films, Ltd. as dir.
PICTURES: *Actor:* Under One Roof, I Want to Get Married, Haunting Melody. Director: The Little Ballerina, Marry Me (s.p. only), Once a Sinner, Scarlet Thread, There Is Another Sun, Time Gentlemen Please, Emergency Call, Cosh Boy, Johnny on the Run, Albert R.N., The Good Die Young, The Sea Shall Not Have Them, Reach for the Sky, Cast a Dark Shadow, The Admirable Crichton, Carve Her Name with Pride, A Cry from the Street, Ferry to Hong Kong, Sink the Bismarck, Light Up the Sky, The Greengage Summer, H.M.S. Defiant, The Patriots, Spare the Rod, The Seventh Dawn, Alfie, You Only Live Twice, The Adventurers, Friends (also prod., story), Paul & Michelle (also prod., story), Operation Daybreak, Seven Nights in Japan, The Spy Who Loved Me, Moonraker, Educating Rita (also prod.), Not Quite Paradise, Shirley Valentine (also prod.), Stepping Out (also co-prod.), Haunted (also s.p.), Before You Go.

GILBERT, MELISSA
Actress. b. Los Angeles, CA, May 8, 1964. m. actor Bruce Boxleitner. Made debut at age of 3 in TV commercial. Comes from show business family: father, late comedian Paul Gilbert; mother, former dancer-actress Barbara Crane. Grandfather, Harry Crane created The Honeymooners. NY Off-B'way debut A Shayna Madel (1987; Outer Critics Circle & Theatre World Awards). Currently pres., Screen Actors Guild.
PICTURES: Sylvester (debut, 1985), Ice House, Famous.
TELEVISION: *Movies:* Christmas Miracle in Caulfield U.S.A., The Miracle Worker, Splendor in the Grass, Choices of the Heart, Choices, Penalty Phase, Family Secrets, Killer Instincts, Without Her Consent, Forbidden Nights, Blood Vows: The Story of a Mafia Wife, Joshua's Heart, Donor, The Lookalike, With a Vengeance, Family of Strangers, With Hostile Intent, Shattered Trust: The Shari Karney Story, House of Secrets, Dying to Remember, Babymaker: The Dr. Cecil Jacobson Story, Against Her Will: The Carrie Buck Story, Cries From the Heart, A Touch of Truth, Danielle Steel's. Zoya, Seduction in a Small Town, Christmas in My Home Town, Childhood Sweetheart, Me & My Hormones (dir.), Sanctuary. *Series:* Little House on the Prairie, Stand By Your Man, Sweet Justice. *Guest:* Gunsmoke, Emergency, Tenafly, The Hanna-Barbera Happy Hour, Love Boat

GILER, DAVID
Producer, Writer, Director. b. New York, NY. Son of Bernie Giler, screen and TV writer. Began writing in teens; first work an episode for ABC series, The Gallant Men. Feature film career began as writer on Myra Breckenridge (1970).
PICTURES: *Writer:* The Parallax View, Fun with Dick and Jane, The Blackbird (also dir.), Southern Comfort (also prod.). *Prod.:* Aliens (story), Rustlers' Rhapsody, Let It Ride, Alien³ (ex. prod., also writer), Demon Knight, Bordello of Blood, Ritual, Alien:

Resurrection, Undisputed.
TELEVISION: *Writer:* The Kraft Theatre, Burke's Law, The Man from U.N.C.L.E., The Girl from U.N.C.L.E., Tales From the Crypt (exec. prod.).

GILLIAM, TERRY
Writer, Director, Actor, Animator. b. Minneapolis, MN, Nov. 22, 1940. e. Occidental Coll. Freelance writer and illustrator for various magazines and ad agencies before moving to London. Animator for BBC series Do Not Adjust Your Set, We Have Ways of Making You Laugh. Member, Monty Python's Flying Circus (1969-76). Books incl. numerous Monty Python publications. Honorary degrees: DFA Occidental Col. 1987, DFA Royal Col. of Art 1989.
PICTURES: And Now for Something Completely Different (animator, co-s.p., actor), Monty Python and the Holy Grail (co-dir., co-s.p., actor, animator), Jabberwocky (dir., co-s.p.), Life of Brian (actor, co-s.p., animator), The Do It Yourself Animation Film, Time Bandits (prod., dir., co-s.p.), Monty Python Live at the Hollywood Bowl (actor, co-s.p., animator, designer), The Miracle of Flight (animator, s.p.), Monty Python's The Meaning of Life (co-s.p., actor, animator), Spies Like Us (actor), Brazil (co-s.p., dir.), The Adventures of Baron Munchausen (dir., co-s.p.), The Fisher King (dir.), Twelve Monkeys (dir.), Fear and Loathing in Las Vegas (dir., s.p.), Lost in La Mancha (actor only), The Piano Tuner of Earthquakes, Good Omens (dir., s.p.).
TELEVISION: *Series:* Monty Python's Flying Circus (also animator, dir.), Do Not Adjust Your Set, We Have Ways of Making You Laugh, The Mart Feldman Comedy Machine, The Last Machine (1995).

GILMORE, WILLIAM S.
Producer. b. Los Angeles, CA, March 10, 1934. e. U. of California at Berkeley. Started career in film editing before becoming asst. dir. and prod. mgr. at Universal Studios, where worked on 20 feature films. Headed prod. for Mirisch Co. in Europe; then to Zanuck/Brown Co. as exec. in chg. prod. Sr. v.p./prod. of Filmways Pictures, supervising literary development, prod. and post-prod.
PICTURES: Jaws (prod. exec.), The Sugarland Express (prod. exec.), The Last Remake of Beau Geste, Defiance, Deadly Blessing, Tough Enough, Against All Odds, White Nights, Little Shop of Horrors, The Man in the Moon, The Player, A Few Good Men, Watch It, The Sandlot, Curse of the Starving Class, Fire Down Below, A Soldier's Sweetheart, Down, Roper & Goodie.
TELEVISION: Just Me and You, One in a Million--The Ron Leflore Story, The Legend of Walks Far Woman, S.O.S. Titanic, Another Woman's Child, Women and Men, Women and Men 2, Silent Predators (co-exec. prod, s.p.).

GILROY, FRANK D.
Writer, Director. b. New York, NY, Oct. 13, 1925. e. Dartmouth; postgrad. Yale School of Drama. TV writer: Playhouse 90, U.S. Steel Hour, Omnibus, Kraft Theatre, Lux Video Theater, Studio One. B'way playwright.
AUTHOR: *Plays:* Who'll Save the Plowboy? (Obie award, 1962), The Subject Was Roses (Pulitzer Prize & Tony Award, 1965), The Only Game in Town, Present Tense, The Next Contestant, Dreams of Glory, Real to Reel, Match Point, A Way with Words, The Housekeeper, Last Licks, Any Given Day. *Novels:* Private, Little Ego (with Ruth Gilroy), From Noon to 3. *Book:* I Wake Up Screening!: Everything You Need to Know About Making Independent Films Including a Thousand Reasons Not To (1993).
PICTURES: *Writer:* The Fastest Gun Alive, The Gallant Hours, The Subject Was Roses, The Only Game in Town. *Dir.-Writer:* Desperate Characters (also prod.), From Noon Till Three, Once in Paris, The Gig, The Luckiest Man in the World.
TELEVISION: *Writer-Dir.:* The Doorbell Rang, Turning Point of Jim Malloy, Money Plays. *Series:* Burke's Law (writer).

GILULA, STEPHEN
Executive. b. Herrin, IL, Aug. 20, 1950. e. Stanford U. UA Theatre Circuit, film booker for San Francisco area, 1973; Century Cinema Circuit, film buyer, LA, 1974. Co-founder, Landmark Theatre Corp., 1974; serving as pres., 1982-present. Landmark became a subsidiary of Metromedia Intl. Group Inc., in 1996. Chmn. NATO of California/Nevada, 1991-present; also on bd. of dirs. of NATO, 1992-present. Currently, pres. distribution, Fox Searchlight Pictures.

GIMBEL, ROGER
Producer, Executive. b. March 11, 1925. e. Yale. Began tv prod. career as creative chief of RCA Victor TV, then became assoc. prod. of the Tonight Show for NBC; named head of prog. dev. of NBC daytime programming; then prod. of the 90-minute NBC Tonight Specials, including The Jack Paar Show and the Ernie Kovacs Show. Became prod. and co-packager of the Glen Campbell Goodtime Hour for CBS, 1969; v.p. in chg. of prod. for Tomorrow Entertainment, 1971. Formed his own prod. co., Roger Gimbel's Tomorrow Enterprises, Inc., 1975; prod. Minstrel Man. Became U.S. pres. of EMI-TV, 1976. Received special personal Emmy as exec. prod. of War of the Children, 1975. Produced 33 movies for TV under the EMI banner and won 18 Emmys. In 1984, EMI-TV became The Peregrine Producers Group, Inc., of which he was pres. & COO. 1987, spun off Roger Gimbel Prods. as an independent film co; 1988-89, pres./exec.

prod., Carolco/Gimbel Productions, Inc. 1989-1996, pres. & exec. prod. of Roger Gimbel Prods Inc. in association with Multimedia Motion Pictures Inc. 1997, pres. & exec. prod. of Roger Gimbel Prods Inc for independent film production.
TELEVISION: *Movies/Specials:* The Autobiography of Miss Jane Pittman, Born Innocent, Birds of Prey, Brand New Life, Gargoyles, Glass House, In This House of Brede, I Heard the Owl Call My Name, I Love You Goodbye, Larry, Miles to Go Before I Sleep, Queen of the Stardust Ballroom, Tell Me Where It Hurts, The Man Who Could Talk to Kids, Things in Their Season, A War of Children (Emmy Award), The Amazing Howard Hughes, Deadman's Curve, Steel Cowboy, Betrayal, The Cracker Factory, Survival of Diana, Can You Hear the Laughter?, S.O.S. Titanic, Walks-Far Woman, Sophia Loren: Her Own Sotory, Manions of America, A Question of Honor, The Killing of Randy Webster, Broken Promise, A Piano for Mrs. Cimino, Deadly Encounter, Aurora, Rockabye, Blackout, Apology, Montana, Shattered Dreams, Chernobyl: The Final Warning, Desperate Rescue: The Cathy Mahone Story, Murder Between Friends, The Perfect Mother.

GINNA, ROBERT EMMETT, JR.
Producer, Writer. b. New York, NY, Dec. 3, 1925. e. U. of Rochester, Harvard U., M.A. In U.S. Navy, WWII. Journalist for Life, Scientific American, Horizon, 1950-55; 1958-61, contributor to many magazines. Staff writer, producer, director NBC-TV, 1955-58; v.p., Sextant, Inc.; dir., Sextant Films Ltd., 1961-64. Founded Windward Productions, Inc., Windward Film Productions, Ltd., 1965. Active in publishing 1974-82; sr. ed. People; ed. in chief, Little Brown; asst. mgr., Life. Resumed pres., Windward Prods, Inc., 1982; publishing consultant.
PICTURES: Young Cassidy (co-prod.), The Last Challenge (co-s.p.), Before Winter Comes (prod.), Brotherly Love (prod.).

GINNANE, ANTONY I.
Executive, Producer. e. Melbourne U (law), 1976. 1977 formed joint venture with financier William Fayman for Australian film production and distribution. 1981 established company Film and General Holdings Inc. for locating film projects/financing. Currently, pres., Imparato Fay Management in Glendale, CA
PICTURES: *Producer or Exec. Prod:* Sympathy in Summer (debut, 1970; also dir.), Fantasm, Patrick, Snapshot, Thirst, Harlequin, Race for the Yankee Zephyr, Strange Behavior, Turkey Shoot, Prisoners, Second Tim Lucky, Mesmerized, Dark Age, Slate Wyn & Me, Initiation, High Tide, The Lighthorsemen, Time Guardian, Incident at Raven's Gate, The Everlasting Secret Family, The Dreaming, Grievous Bodily Harm, Boundaries of the Heart, Killer Instinct, Savage Justice, Outback, A Case of Honor, Siege of Firebase Gloria, Driving Force, Demonstone, Fatal Sky, No Contest, Screamers, Bonjour Timothy, The Whole of the Moon, Men with Guns, The Truth About Juliet, Sally Marshall Is Not an Alien, Reluctant Angel, Reaper, Captive, Black Light, Blind Heat, Torrent, Sweet Revenge, The Hit.
TELEVISION: Lawless: Dead Evidence, Lawless: Beyond Justice.

GINSBURG, LEWIS S.
Distributor, Importer, Prod. b. New York, NY, May 16, 1914. e. City Coll. of New York, 1931-32. Columbia U., 1932-33. Ent. film industry, tabulating dept., United Artists, 1933; sls. contract dept. 1934; asst. to eastern district mgr., 1938; slsmn., New Haven exch., 1939. Army, 1943. Ret. to U.S., then formed first buying & booking service in Connecticut, 1945-55; in chg., New England Screen Guild Exchanges, 1955; TV film distr., 1957; Formed & org. International Film Assoc., Vid-EX Film Distr. Corp., 1960; TV half-hour series; vice-pres. in chg., dist., Desilu Film Dist. C., 1962; organized Carl Releasing Corp., 1963; Walter Reade-Sterling Inc., 1964-65; formed L.G. Films Corp.; contract and playdate mgr., 20th Fox, 1965-68. Cinerama Releasing Corp. Adm. Ass't to sales mgr., 1968-69; 20th Cent.-Fox. Nat'l sales coordinator, 1969-present. 1970, 20th Century-Fox, Asst. to the Sales Mgr. 1971, Transnational Pictures Corp., v.p. in chg. of dist., pres., Stellar IV Film Corp., 1972.

GIRARDOT, ANNIE
Actress. b. Paris, France, Oct. 25, 1931. Studied nursing. Studied acting at the Paris Conservatory, made her acting debut with the Comedie Franccaise. Has acted on the French stage and in reviews in the Latin Quarter.
PICTURES: Trezie a Table (debut, 1955), Speaking of Murder, Inspector Maigret, Love and the Frenchwoman, Rocco and His Brothers, Le Rendezvous, Crime Does Not Pay, Vice and Virtue, The Organizer, La Bonne Soupe (Careless Love), Male Companion, The Dirty Game, The Witches, Live for Life, Les Galoises Bleues, Dillinger Is Dead, The Seed of Man, Trois Chambres a Manhattan (Venice Film Fest. Award), The Story of a Woman, Love Is a Funny Thing, Shock!, Where THere's Smoke, Juliette et Juliette, The Slap, It Is Raining in Santiago, No Time for Breakfast (Cesar Award), Dear Inspector, The Skirt Chaser, Traffic Jam, Jupiter's Thigh, Five Days in June, La Vie Continue, Prisonniers, Comedie D'Amour, Girls With Guns, Les Miserables, Les Bidochons, When I Will Be Gone, Preference, T'Aime, La Pianiste, This Is My Body, Epstein's Night, Des fleurs pour Irma.
TELEVISION: various European productions.

GISH, ANNABETH
Actress. b. Albuquerque, NM, Mar. 13, 1971. e. Duke U ('93). Started acting at age 8; several TV commercials in Iowa.
PICTURES: Desert Bloom, Hiding Out, Mystic Pizza, Shag, Coupe de Ville, Wyatt Earp, The Red Coat, Nixon, The Last Supper, Beautiful Girls, Steel, S.L.C. Punk!, Double Jeopardy, Race to Space, Morning, Pursuit of Happiness, Buying the Cow, Knots.
TELEVISION: *Series:* Courthouse, The X-Files. *Movies:* Hero in the Family, When He's Not a Stranger, The Last to Go, Lady Against the Odds, Silent Cries, Don't Look Back, to Live Again, God's New Plan, Different, The Way She Moves, Sealed With a Kiss, A Death in the Family, The Way She Moves. *Mini-Series:* Scarlett, True Women.

GIVENS, ROBIN
Actress. b. New York, NY, Nov. 27, 1964. e. Sarah Lawrence Col., Harvard Univ. Graduate Sch. of Arts & Sciences. While at college became model, made appearances on daytime dramas The Guiding Light and Loving.
PICTURES: A Rage in Harlem (debut, 1991), Boomerang, Foreign Student, Blankman, Dangerous Intentions, Secrets, Everything's Jake, Elite, The Expendables, Book of Love, A Cold Day in August, Antibody, Head of State, A Good Night to Die.
TELEVISION: *Movies:* Beverly Hills Madam, The Women of Brewster Place, The Penthouse, Dangerous Intentions, A Face to Die For, Spinning Out of Control. *Series:* Head of the Class, Angel Street, Courthouse, Sparks, Hollywood Squares, Forgive or Forget.

GLASER, PAUL MICHAEL
Actor, Director. b. Cambridge, MA, March 25, 1943. e. Tulane U., Boston U., M.A. Did five seasons in summer stock before starting career in New York, making stage debut in Rockabye Hamlet in 1968. Appeared in numerous off-B'way plays and got early TV training as regular in daytime series, Love of Life and Love Is a Many Splendored Thing.
PICTURES: *Actor:* Fiddler on the Roof, Butterflies Are Free, Phobia. *Director:* Band of the Hand, The Running Man, The Cutting Edge, The Air Up There, Kazaam (also prod., story), F-Stops, Game Theory (video documentary short).
TELEVISION: *Series:* Starsky and Hutch, The Agencey (dir. episodes). *Guest:* Kojak, Toma, The Streets of San Francisco, The Rockford Files, The Sixth Sense, The Waltons. *Movies:* Trapped Beneath the Sea, The Great Houdinis, Wail Till Your Mother Gets Home!, Princess Daisy, Jealousy, Attack on Fear, Single Bars Single Women, Amazons (dir. only), And Never Let Her Go.

GLASS, PHILIP
Composer, Actor, Writer. b. Baltimore, MD, Jan. 31, 1937.
PICTURES: Cenere, Chappaqua, Mark Di Suvero Sculptor, Four American Composers (also actor), Koyaanisqatsi, High Wire, Mishima: A Life in Four Chapters, Dead End Kids, Hamburger Hill, Einstein on the Beach: The Changing Image of Opera, The Thin Blue Line, Powaqqatsi, Le Chiesa, Mindwalk, Closet Land, Anima Mundi, Candyman, A Brief History of Time, Niki de Saint Phalle: Wer ist das Monster-du oder ich?, Jenipapo, Candyman: Farewell to the Flesh, The Secret Agent, Absence Stronger Than Presence, Bent, Kundun (LA Film Critics Award, Best Musical Score, 1997), The Truman Show (actor), The Man in the Bath, The Source, The Eden Myth, Armonie dell'Estasi, Naqoyqatsi, The Baroness & the Pig, Special Delivery, The Hours, Partition, Undertow.

GLAZER, WILLIAM
Executive b. Cambridge, MA. e. State U. of New York, Entered m.p. ind. with Ralph Snider Theatres 1967-69; General Cinema Corp. 1969-71; Loews Theatres 1971-73; Joined Sack Theatres/USA Cinemas 1973 as Dist. mgr.; 1974 Exec. Asst. to Pres.; 1976 Gen. Mgr.; 1980 V.P. Gen. Mgr.; 1982-86 Exec. V.P. Joined Interstated Theatres 1987 (Pres.); Fox Theatres 1993-95. MP industry consultant, 1988-pres. Bd. of Dir. Member of SMPTE; NATO (Exec. Bd.); Theatre Owners of New England (Pres. and Chairman.)

GLEASON, LARRY
Executive. b. Boston, MA, Apr. 30, 1938. e. Boston Coll., M.A., 1960. Held various positions, western div., mgr., General Cinema Corp.; 1963-73; gen. mgr., Gulf States Theatres, New Orleans, 1973-74; pres., Mann Theatres, 1974-85; joined DeLaurentiis Entertainment Group as pres., mktg./dist., 1985. Named sr. v.p., Paramount Pictures Corp, theatrical exhibition group, 1989. Named pres. Paramount Pictures Corp. theatrical exhib. group, 1991. Joined MGM/UA as pres. of Worldwide Distrib., 1994, a position he left in June 2001. Foundation of Motion Picture Pioneers v.p. Member, Variety Club, Will Rogers Foundation.

GLEN, JOHN
Director, Editor. b. Sunbury on Thames, Eng., May 15, 1932. Entered industry in 1947. Second unit dir.: On Her Majesty's Secret Service, The Spy Who Loved Me, Wild Geese, Moonraker (also editor). Editor: The Sea Wolves.
PICTURES: *Dir:* For Your Eyes Only (dir. debut, 1981),

Octopussy, A View to a Kill, The Living Daylights, Licence to Kill, Aces: Iron Eagle III, Christopher Columbus: The Discovery, The Point Men, Checkered Flag. *Editor*: Baby Love, On Her Majesty's Secret Service, Murphy's War, Sitting Target, Pulp, A Doll's House, Gold, Dead Cert, Conduct Unbecoming, The Spy Who Loved Me, The Wild Geese, Moonraker, The Sea Wolves: The Last Charge of the Calcutta Light Horse (editor).
TELEVISION: *Series*: Space Precinct (7 episodes).

GLENN, CHARLES OWEN
Executive. b. Binghamton, NY, March 27, 1938. e. Syracuse U., B.A., U. of PA. Capt., U.S. Army, 1961-63. Asst. to dir. of adv., 20th Cent. Fox, 1966-67; asst. adv. mgr., Paramount, 1967-68; acct. spvsr. & exec., MGM record & m.p. div., 1968-69; nat'l adv. mgr., Paramount, 1969-70; nat'l. dir. of adv., Paramount, 1970-71; v.p. adv.-pub.-prom., 1971-73; v.p. marketing, 1974; v.p. prod. mktg., 1975; joined American Intl. Pictures as v.p. in chg. of adv./creative affairs, 1979. 1980, when Filmways took AIP over he was named their v.p. in chg. worldwide adv./pub./promo.; joined MCA/Universal in 1982 as exec. v.p., adv.-promo.; 1984, appt. Orion Pictures adv.-pub.-promo. exec. v.p.; 1987, appt. Orion mktg. exec. v.p. 1989 recipient Outstanding Performance Award Leukemia Society of Amer. for completing NYC Marathon. 1993, pres. mktg., Bregman/Baer Prods. Currently, v.p. public relations with Univision Communications, Inc. Featured actor in 1993 film Philadelphia.
Member: Acad. of Motion Picture Arts & Sciences, Motion Picture Pioneers & the Screen Actors Guild. Holder of NATO mktg. exec. of year (1983) award, Clio Award for U.S. adv. of Platoon.

GLENN, SCOTT
Actor. b. Pittsburgh, PA, Jan. 26, 1942. e. William & Mary Coll. Worked as U.S. Marine, newspaper reporter before going to New York to study drama at Actors Studio in 1968.
THEATRE: *Off-B'way*: Zoo Story, Fortune in Men's Eyes, Long Day's Jack Street, Journey into Night. *B'way*: The Impossible Years, Burn This, Dark Picture.
PICTURES: The Baby Maker (debut, 1970), Angels Hard as They Come, Hex, Nashville, Fighting Mad, More American Graffiti, Apocalypse Now, Urban Cowboy, Cattle Annie and Little Britches, Personal Best, The Challenge, The Right Stuff, The Keep, The River, Wild Geese II, Silverado, Verne Miller, Man on Fire, Off Limits, Miss Firecracker, The Hunt for Red October, The Silence of the Lambs, My Heroes Have Always Been Cowboys, Backdraft, The Player, Night of the Running Man, Tall Tale, Reckless, Edie and Pen, Courage Under Fire, Carla's Song, Lesser Prophets, Absolute Power, Larga Distancia, Firestorm, The Virgin Suicides, The Last Marshall, Vertical Limit, Training Day, Buffalo Soldiers, The Shipping News, Seabiscuit (documentary, voice), Puerto Vallarta Squeeze.
TELEVISION: *Movies*: Gargoyles, As Summers Die, Intrigue, The Outside Woman, Women & Men 2, Shadowhunter, Slaughter of the Innocents, Past Tense, Naked City: Justice with a Bullet, Naked City: A Killer Christmas, The Seventh Stream, A Painted House, Homeland Security. *Series*: Mobile Suit Gundam.

GLENNON, JAMES M.
Cinematographer. b. Burbank, CA, Aug. 29, 1942. e. UCLA. m. actress Charmaine Glennon. Focus Awards judge 1985-; bd. of dirs., UCLA Theatre Arts Alumni Assoc. 1985-. ASC - member of American Society of Cinematographers, AMPAS.
PICTURES: Return of the Jedi, El Norte, The Wild Life, Smooth Talk, Flight of the Navigator, Time of Destiny, A Show of Force, December, The Gift, Citizen Ruth, Best Men, Election, The Runner, South of Heaven West of Hell, Viva Las Nowhere, Playing Mona Lisa, Madison, Life Without Dick, Local Boys, The United States of Leland, About Schmidt, Good Boy!
TELEVISION: Lemon Sky (American Playhouse), Laurel Ave, DEA (pilot), Bakersfield (pilot), Judicial Consent, Jake's Women, My Very Best Friend, L.A. Johns, Two Voices, Convictions, When He Didn't Come Home, Get to the Heart: The Barbara Mandrell Story, The West Wing, Blonde, Return to the Batcave: Misadventures of Adam and Burt.

GLESS, SHARON
Actress. b. Los Angeles, CA, May 31, 1943. m. producer Barney Rosenzweig. London stage: Misery.
PICTURES: Airport 1975, The Star Chamber, Ayn Rand: A Sense of Life (narr.), Bring Him Home.
TELEVISION: *Movies*: The Longest Night, All My Darling Daughters, My Darling Daughters' Anniversary, Richie Brockelman: Missing 24 Hours, The Flying Misfits, The Islander, Crash, Whisper in the Gloom (Disney), Hardhat and Legs, Moviola: The Scarlett O'Hara War, Revenge of the Stepford Wives, The Miracle of Kathy Miller, Hobson's Choice, The Sky's No Limit, Letting Go, The Outside Woman, Honor Thy Mother, Separated by Murder, Cagney & Lacey: The Return, Cagney & Lacey: Together Again, Cagney & Lacey: True Convictions, Cagney & Lacey: The View Through the Glass Ceiling, The Girl Next Door. *Mini-Series*: Centennial, The Immigrants, The Last Convertible. *Series*: Marcus Welby M.D., Faraday and Co., Switch, Turnabout, House Calls, Cagney and Lacey (2 Emmy Awards, Golden Globe Award), The Trials of Rosie O'Neill (Golden Globe Award), Queer As Folk.

GLICK, PHYLLIS
Executive. b. New York, NY. e. Queens Coll. of C.U.N.Y. Began career with Otto-Windsor Associates, as casting director; left to be independent. 1979, joined ABC-TV as mgr. of comedy series

development; promoted 1980 to director, involved with all comedy series developed for network. 1985, joined Paramount Pictures as exec. dir., production, for M.P. Group; 1989, co-exec. prod., Living Dolls.

GLOBUS, YORAM
Producer. b. Israel, Came to U.S. 1979. Has co-produced many films with cousin and former partner Menahem Golan. Sr. exec. v.p., Cannon Group; Pres. and CEO Cannon Entertainment and Cannon Films; 1989 named chmn. and C.E.O Cannon Entertainment and officer of Cannon Group Inc.; then co-pres. Pathe Communications Corp. and chmn. and C.E.O. Pathe Intl. Left MGM/Pathe in 1991.
PICTURES: All as producer or exec. prod. with Menahem Golan: Sallah; Trunk to Cairo; My Margo; What's Good for the Goose; Escape to the Sun; I Love You, Rosa; The House on Chelouch Street; The Four Deuces; Kazablan; Diamonds; God's Gun; Kid Vengeance, Operation Thunderbolt, The Uranium Conspiracy, Savage Weekend, The Magician of Lublin, The Apple, The Happy Hooker Goes to Hollywood, Dr. Heckyl and Mr. Hype, The Godsend, New Year's Evil, Schizoid, Seed of Innocence, Body and Soul, Death Wish II, Enter the Ninja, Hospital Massacre, The Last American Virgin, Championship Season, Treasure of Four Crowns, 10 to Midnight, Nana, I'm Almost Not Crazy..., John Cassavetes: The Man and His Work, The House of Long Shadows, Revenge of the Ninja, Hercules, The Wicked Lady, Sahara, The Ambassador, Bolero, Exterminator 2, The Naked Face, Missing in Action, Hot Resort, Love Streams, Breakin', Grace Quigley, Making the Grade, Ninja III-The Domination, Breakin' 2: Electric Boogaloo, Lifeforce, Over the Brooklyn Bridge, The Delta Force, The Assisi Underground, Hot Chili, The Berlin Affair, Missing in Action 2-The Beginning, Rappin', Thunder Alley, American Ninja, Mata Hari, Death Wish 3, King Solomon's Mines, Runaway Train, Fool for Love, Invasion U.S.A., Maria's Lovers, Murphy's Law, The Naked Cage, P.O.W.: The Escape, The Texas Chainsaw Massacre, Part 2, Invaders from Mars, 52 Pick-Up, Link, Firewalker, Dumb Dicks, The Nutcracker: The Motion Picture, Avenging Force, Hashigaon Hagadol, Journey to the Center of the Earth, Prom Queen, Salome, Otello, Cobra, America 3000, American Ninja 2: The Confrontation, Allan Quartermain and the Lost City of Gold, Assassination, Beauty and the Beast, Down Twisted, Duet for One, The Emperor's New Clothes, The Hanoi Hilton, The Barbarians, Dutch Treat, Masters of the Universe, Number One with a Bullet, Rumpelstiltskin, Street Smart, UnderCover, The Assault, Hansel and Gretel, Going Bananas, Snow White, Sleeping Beauty, Tough Guys Don't Dance, Shy People, Dancers, Red Riding Hood, King Lear, Braddock: Missing in Action III, Too Much, Die Papierene Brucke, Field of Honor, Barfly (exec. prod.), Surrender (exec. prod.), Death Wish 4: The Crackdown (exec. prod.), Gor (exec. prod.), Business as Usual (exec. prod.), Over the Top, Superman IV: The Quest for Peace. Prod.: Delta Force, Operation Crackdown, Manifesto, Stranglehold, Delta Force II, Cyborg, Step By Step. Exec. prod.: The Kitchen Toto, Doin' Time on Planet Earth, Kickboxer, Kinjite, A Man Called Sarge, The Rose Garden, The Secret of the Ice Cave, Mack the Knife, Journey to the Center of the Earth, Lambada, A Bit of Luck, Licking the Raspberry, Street Knight, Night Terrors, The Mummy Lives, Hellbound, American Cyborg: Steel Warrior, Chain of Command, Delta Force One: The Lost Patrol, Tipul Nimratz (tv series, prod.).

GLOVER, CRISPIN
Actor. b. New York, NY, 1964. e. Mirman School. Trained for stage with Dan Mason and Peggy Feury. Stage debut, as Friedrich Von Trapp, The Sound of Music, Los Angeles, 1977. Wrote books, Rat Catching (1987), Oak Mot (1990), Concrete Inspection (1992), What It Is and How It Is Done (1995). Recorded album The Big Problem Does Not Equal the Solution-The Solution Equals Let it Be.
PICTURES: My Tutor, Racing with the Moon, Friday the 13th-The Final Chapter, Teachers, Back to the Future, At Close Range, River's Edge, Twister, Where the Heart Is, Wild at Heart, The Doors, Little Noises, Rubin and Ed, Thirty Door Key, What's Eating Gilbert Grape, Chasers, Even Cowgirls Get the Blues, Crime and Punishment, Dead Man, What Is It? (dir. and wrote), The People vs. Larry Flynt, Nurse Betty, Charlie's Angels, What Is It?, Crime and Punishment, Beaver Trilogy, Bartleby, Fast Sofa, Like Mike, Willard, Charlie's Angels 2, What is It? (also dir., prod. & s.p.)
TELEVISION: *Movie*: High School U.S.A. *Special*: Hotel Room (Blackout).

GLOVER, DANNY
Actor. b. San Francisco, CA, July 22, 1947. e. San Francisco State U. Trained at Black Actors Workshop of American Conservatory Theatre. Appeared in many stage productions (Island, Macbeth, Sizwe Banzi Is Dead, etc.). On N.Y. stage in Suicide in B Flat, The Blood Knot, Master Harold... and the Boys (Theatre World Award).
PICTURES: Escape from Alcatraz (debut, 1979), Chu Chu and the Philly Flash, Out (Deadly Drifter), Iceman, Places in the Heart, Witness, Silverado, The Color Purple, Lethal Weapon, Bat-21, Lethal Weapon 2, To Sleep with Anger (also co-exec. prod.), Predator 2, Flight of the Intruder, A Rage in Harlem, Pure Luck, Grand Canyon, Lethal Weapon 3, Bopha!, The Saint of Fort Washington, Maverick (cameo), Angels in the Outfield,

Operation Dumbo Drop, Gone Fishin', Wild America (cameo), Switchback, The Rainmaker (cameo), The Prince of Egypt (voice), Beloved, Antz (voice), Lethal Weapon 4, The Monster, Battu, Boesman and Lena, 3 AM, The Royal Tenenbaums, Just A Dream (dir. only).
TELEVISION: *Movies*: Face of Rage, Mandela, Dead Man Out, Buffalo Soldiers (also exec. prod.), Good Fences. *Mini-Series*: Chiefs, Lonesome Dove, Queen. *Series*: Storybook Classics (host), Civil War Journal (host),Courage (exec. prod.). *Specials*: And the Children Shall Lead, How the Leopard Got Its Spots (narrator), A Place at the Table, A Raisin in the Sun, Override (dir. only), Shelley Duvall's Tall Tales and Legends: John Henry, Can't You hear the Wind Howl?: The Life & Music of Robert Johnson (voice), Scared Straight! 20 Years Later (voice). The John Garfield Story (documentary), The Henry Lee Project (acting and prod.). *Guest*: Lou Grant, Palmerstown U.S.A., Gimme a Break, Hill Street Blues, Many Mansions.

GLOVER, JOHN
Actor. b. Kingston, NY, Aug. 7, 1944. e. Towson State Coll., Baltimore.
THEATRE: On regional theatre circuit; Off-B'way in A Scent of Flowers, Subject to Fits, The House of Blue Leaves, The Selling of the President, Love! Valour! Compassion! (also B'way; Tony Award, 1995). With APA Phoenix Co. in Great Odd Brown (Drama Desk Award), The Visit, Don Juan, Chermin de Fer, Holiday. Other NY stage: The Importance of Being Earnest, Hamlet, Frankenstein, Whodunnit, Digby. L.A.: The Traveler (L.A. Drama Critics Award), Lips Together Teeth Apart.
PICTURES: Shamus, Annie Hall, Julia, Somebody Killed Her Husband, Last Embrace, Success, Melvin and Howard, The Mountain Men, The Incredible Shrinking Woman, A Little Sex, The Evil That Men Do, A Flash of Green, 52 Pick-Up, White Nights, Something Special, Masquerade, A Killing Affair, Rocket Gibraltar, The Chocolate War, Scrooged, Meet the Hollowheads, Gremlins 2: The New Batch, Robocop 2, Ed and His Dead Mother, Night of the Running Man, In the Mouth of Madness, Schemes, Automatics, Batman and Robin, Love! Valour! Compassion!, Macbeth in Manhattan, Dead Broke, Payback, On Edge, Sex & Violence, Mid-Century, Sweet Union, Tricks.
TELEVISION: *Movies*: A Rage of Angels, The Face of Rage, Ernie Kovacs-Between the Laughter, An Early Frost (Emmy nom.), Apology, Moving Target, Hot Paint, Nutcracker: Money Madness and Murder (Emmy nom.), David, The Traveling Man (ACE nom.), Twist of Fate, Breaking Point, El Diablo, What Ever Happened to Baby Jane?, Dead on the Money, Drug Wars: The Cocaine Cartel, Grass Roots, Majority Rule, Assault at West Point, Dead by Midnight, The Tempest. *Specials*: An Enemy of the People, Paul Reiser: Out on a Whim, Crime and Punishment (Emmy nom.). *Mini-Series*: Kennedy, George Washington, Medusa's Child. *Series*: South Beach, Brimstone. *Guest*: L.A. Law (Emmy nom.), Frasier (Emmy nom.)

GLYNN, CARLIN
Actress. b. Cleveland, OH, Feb. 19, 1940. m. actor-writer-dir. Peter Masterson. Daughter is actress Mary Stuart Masterson. e. Sophie Newcomb College, 1957-58. Studied acting with Stella Adler, Wynn Handman and Lee Strasberg in NY. Debut, Gigi, Alley Theatre, Houston, TX 1959. Adjunct professor at Columbia U. film sch. Resource advisor at the Sundance Inst.
THEATRE: (NY debut, 1960) Waltz of The Toreadors, The Best Little Whorehouse in Texas (Tony, Eleanora Duse & Olivier Awards), Winterplay, Alterations, Pal Joey (Chicago; Jos. Jefferson Award), The Cover of Life, The Young Man From Atlanta (winner, Pulitzer Prize for Drama, 1995), Amazing Grace.
PICTURES: Three Days of the Condor, Continental Divide, Sixteen Candles, The Trip to Bountiful, Gardens of Stone, Blood Red, Night Game, Convicts, Blessing, Judy Berlin, West of Here, Lost Junction.
TELEVISION: *Series*: Mr. President. *Mini-Series*: A Woman Named Jackie.

GODARD, JEAN-LUC
Writer, Director. b. Paris, France, Dec. 3, 1930. e. Lycee Buffon, Paris. Journalist, film critic Cahiers du Cinema. Acted in and financed experimental film Quadrille by Jacques Rivette, 1951. 1954: dir. first short, Operation Beton, followed by Une Femme Coquette. 1956, was film editor. 1957: worked in publicity dept. 20th Century Fox.
PICTURES: *Director/Writer*: Breathless (A Bout de Souffle; feature debut, 1960), Le Petit Soldat, A Woman Is a Woman, My Life to Live, Les Carabiniers, Contempt, Band of Outsiders, The Married Woman, Alphaville, Pierrot le Fou, Masculine-Feminine, Made in USA, Two or Three Things I Know About Her, La Chinoise, Weekend, Sympathy for the Devil, Le Gai Savoir, Tout a Bien (co-dir.), Numero Deux, Every Man For Himself, First Name Carmen, Hail Mary, Aria (Armide segment), King Lear, Keep Up Your Right (also edit, actor), Nouvelle Vogue (New Wave), Helas Pour Moi (Oh Woe is Me). Germany Year, J.L.G. by J.L.G., The Kids Play Russian, Forever Mozart (also edit.), The Old Place, Eloge de l'Amour, Notre musique.

GOLAN, MENAHEM
Producer, Director, Writer. b. Tiberias, Israel, May 31, 1929. e. NYU. Studied theater dir. at Old Vic Theatre London, m.p. prod. at City Coll, NY. Co-founder and prod. with cousin Yoram Globus, Golan-Globus Prods., Israel, then L.A., 1962. Later Noah Films, Israel, 1963, Ameri-Euro Pictures Corp, before buying controlling share in Cannon Films, 1979. Sr. exec. v.p., Cannon Group; chmn. of bd., Cannon Ent. and Cannon Films.

1988, dir. and sr. exec. v.p. Cannon Group, chmn. and head of creative affairs, Cannon Entertainment when it became div. of Giancarlo Parretti's Pathe Communications Corp. Resigned March, 1989 to form 21st Century Film Corp as chmn. and CEO.
PICTURES: *Director/co-writer*: Kasablan, Diamonds, Entebbe (Operation Thunderbolt), Teyve and His Seven Daughters, What's Good for the Goose? Lepke, The Magician of Lublin, The Goodsend, Happy Hooker Goes to Hollywood, Enter the Ninja. *Producer-Writer-Director*: Mack the Knife, Hanna's War. *Producer-Director*: The Uranium Conspiracy, Delta Force, Over the Brooklyn Bridge, Over the Top, Crime & Punishment, Death Game, Open Heart. *Producer/Exec. prod.*: Sallah, Runaway Train, Sallah, Fool For Love, Maria's Lovers, Cobra, Evil Angels, I Love You Rosa, Body and Soul, also: Deathwish II, The Last American Virgin, That Championship Season, House of Long Shadows, Revenge of the Ninja, Hercules, The Movie Tales (12 children's fairy tales films), The Wicked Lady, Cobra, Barfly (exec. prod.), Breakin', Missing in Action, Dancers (prod.), Surrender (exec. prod.), Death Wish 4: The Crackdown (exec. prod.), King Lear (prod.), Too Much (prod.), Powaqquatsi (exec. prod.), Mercenary Fighters (prod.), Doin' Time on Planet Earth (prod.), Manifesto (prod.), Kinjite (exec. prod.), Messenger of Death (exec. prod.), Alien From L.A. (prod.), Hero and the Terror (exec. prod.), Haunted Summer (exec. prod.), A Cry in the Dark (exec. prod.), Delta Force-Operation Crackdown (prod.), A Man Called Sarge (exec. prod.), Stranglehold: Delta Force II (prod.), Cyborg (prod.), The Rose Garden (exec. prod.), Rope Dancing (exec. prod.), The Phantom of the Opera, Escape to Grizzly Mountain, many others.

GOLCHAN, FREDERIC
Producer. b. Neuilly sur Seine, France, Nov. 20, 1955. e. UCLA Film School, HEC in Paris, NYU Bus.Sch. Journalist/photographer for various European magazines. Worked for American Express, 1979-80. Started indept. investment banking firm, 1980-84. Started own production co., 1985. Directed Victory of the Deaf. V.P. French Hollywood Circle
PICTURES: Flagrant Desire, Quick Change, Intersection, The Associate, Kimberly, All Men Are Mortal.
TELEVISION: Freedom Fighter, Home by Midnight, In The Deep Woods.

GOLDBERG, LEONARD
Executive, Producer. b. Brooklyn, NY, Jan. 24, 1934. e. Wharton ch., U. of Pennsylvania. Began career in ABC-TV research dept.; moved to NBC-TV research div.; 1961 joined BBD&Q ad agency in charge of overall bdcst. coordinator. In 1963 rejoined ABC-TV as mgr. of program devel. 1964-66, v.p., Daytime programs. 1966 named VP in chg of network TV programming. Resigned in 1969 to join Screen Gems as VP in chg. of prod. Left for partnership with Aaron Spelling in Spelling/Goldberg Prods.; later produced TV and theatrical films under own banner, Mandy Prods. 1986, named pres., COO, 20th Century Fox. Resigned, 1989. Currently, a producer with Panda Productions. Elected to the board of Spectradyne Inc.
PICTURES: *Prod.*: All Night Long, WarGames, Space Camp, Sleeping With the Enemy, The Distinguished Gentleman, Aspen Extreme, Double Jeopardy, Charlie's Angels, Charlie's Angels 2.
TELEVISION: *Series*: The Rookies, SWAT, Starsky and Hutch, Charlie's Angels, Family, Hart to Hart, T.J. Hooker, Fantasy Island, Paper Dolls, The Cavanaughs, Class of '96. *Movies*: Brian's Song (Peabody Award, Emmy Awards), Little Ladies of the Night, The Legend of Valentino, The Boy in the Plastic Bubble, Something About Amelia (Emmy Awards, 1984), Alex: The Life of a Child, She Woke Up, Love Letters, Runaway Virus.

GOLDBERG, WHOOPI
Actress. r.n. Caryn Johnson. b. New York, NY, Nov. 13, 1949. e. Sch. for the Performing Arts. Began performing at age 8 in N.Y. with children's program at Hudson Guild and Helena Rubenstein Children's Theatre. Moved to San Diego, CA, 1974, and helped found San Diego Rep. Theatre appearing in Mother Courage, Getting Out. Member: Spontaneous Combustion (improv. group). Joined Blake St. Hawkeyes Theatre in Berkeley, partnering with David Schein. Went solo to create The Spook Show, working in San Francisco and later touring U.S. & Europe. 1983 performance caught attention of Mike Nichols which led to B'way show (for which she received a Theatre World Award) based on it and directed by him. Founding member of Comic Relief benefits. Theatrical film debut in The Color Purple (1985; Image Award NAACP, Golden Globe). Author of Alice.
THEATRE: small roles in B'way prods. of Pippin, Hair, Jesus Christ Superstar. Living on the Edge of Chaos (tour, 1988), A Funny Thing Happened on the Way to the Forum.
PICTURES: The Color Purple (debut, 1985; Acad. Award nom.), Jumpin' Jack Flash, Burglar, Fatal Beauty, The Telephone, Clara's Heart, Beverly Hills Brats (cameo), Homer and Eddie, Ghost (Academy Award, best supporting actress, 1990), The Long Walk Home, Soapdish, House Party 2 (cameo), The Player, Sister Act, Wisecracks, Sarafina!, The Magic World of Chuck Jones, National Lampoon's Loaded Weapon 1 (cameo), Made in America, Sister Act 2: Back in the Habit, Naked in New York (cameo), The Lion King (voice), The Little Rascals, Corrina Corrina, Star Trek: Generations, Theodore Rex, The Pagemaster (voice), Liberation (narrator), Boys on the Side, Moonlight and Valentino, The Celluloid Closet, Bogus, Eddie, The Associate, Ghosts of Mississippi, An Alan Smithee Film: Burn Hollywood Burn, How Stella Got Her Groove Back, The Rugrats Movie (voice), Monkey Bone, Get Bruce, The Deep End of the Ocean, Girl Interrupted, The Adventures of Rocky & Bullwinkle, More

Dogs Than Bones, A Second Chance at Life (narr.), Mary Pickford: A Life on Film, Kingdom Come, Monkeybone, Rat Race, Golden Dreams, Searching for Debra Winger, You'll Never Wiez in This Town Again, Blizzard (voice), Baby Geniuses 2: Superbabies.
TELEVISION: *Movies:* Kiss Shot, In the Gloaming, Cinderella, A Knight in Camelot, Leprechauns, Jackie's Back!, Alice in Wonderland, What Makes a Family, Willie Nelson: Live & Kicking. *Series:* Star Trek: The Next Generation, Bagdad Cafe, The Whoopi Goldberg Show (synd. talk show), Hollywood Squares, Foxbusters, Celebrity Dish, Strong Medicine, Express Yourself, Whoopi. *Specials:* Whoopi Goldberg Direct From Broadway, Comic Relief, Carol Carl Whoopi and Robin, Scared Straight: 10 Years Later, Funny You Don't Look 200, Comedy Tonight (host), My Past is My Own (Schoolbreak Special), Free to Be... a Family, The Debbie Allen Special, Cool Like That Christmas (voice), 34th Annual Grammy Awards (host), A Gala for the President's at Ford's Theatre (host), The 66th Annual Academy Awards (host), The 68th Annual Academy Awards (host), America: A Tribute to Heroes, The 74th Annual Academy Awards (host), Love Lucy's 50th Anniversary Special. *Guest:* Moonlighting (Emmy nom.), A Different World.

GOLDBLUM, JEFF
Actor. b. Pittsburgh, PA, Oct. 22, 1952. Studied at Sanford Meisner's Neighborhood Playhouse in New York. On B'way in Two Gentleman of Verona, The Moony Shapiro Songbook. Off-B'way: El Grande de Coca Cola, City Sugar, Twelfth Night.
PICTURES: Death Wish (debut, 1974), California Split, Nashville, Next Stop Greenwich Village, St. Ives, Special Delivery, The Sentinel, Annie Hall, Between the Lines, Remember My Name, Thank God It's Friday, Invasion of the Body Snatchers, Threshold, The Big Chill, The Right Stuff, The Adventures of Buckaroo Banzai, Into the Night, Silverado, Transylvania 6-5000, The Fly, Beyond Therapy, Vibes, Earth Girls Are Easy, Twisted Obsession, The Tall Guy, Mr. Frost, The Player, Deep Cover, The Favor the Watch and the Very Big Fish, Fathers and Sons, Jurassic Park, Hideaway, Nine Months, Powder, The Great White Hype, Independence Day, Mad Dog Time, The Lost World: Jurassic Park, Welcome to Hollywood, The Prince of Egypt (voice), Holy Man, The Prince of Egypt (voice), Playmate Pajama Party, Chain of Fools, One of the Hollywood Ten, Auggie Rose, Cats & Dogs, Igby Goes Down, Festival in Cannes, Run Ronnie Run, Perfume (exec. prod. & actor), Dumpling Ground, Spinning Boris, Dallas 362.
TELEVISION: *Movies:* The Legend of Sleepy Hollow, Rehearsal for Murder, Ernie Kovacs: Between the Laughter, The Double Helix (BBC), Framed, Lush Life, The Story of Bean. *Series:* Tenspeed and Brownshoe, Future Quest (host), War Stories. *Guest:* The Blue Knight, It's Garry Shandling's Show.

GOLDEN, PAT
Casting Director, Director. b. Pittsburgh, PA, July 21, 1951. e. U. Pittsburgh, Carnegie-Mellon U. Has directed plays for theatre incl. Homeboy at Perry St. Th. in NY. Was in casting dept. of NY Shakespeare Festival Public Th. Served as assoc. prod. on PBS series The Negro Ensemble Company's 20th Anniversary. Assoc. prod.: Hallelujah (PBS); dir.: House Party 2 documentary, My Secret Place (tv pilot).
PICTURES: Ragtime, Beat Street, Krush Groove, The Killing Fields, Blue Velvet, Platoon (Awarded Casting Society of America Award), Dear America, The Handmaid's Tale, House Party 2 (assoc. prod.), New Jack City, True Identity, Fly by Night, Posse, Kalifornia.
TELEVISION: *Movies:* The Josephine Baker Story (casting consultant), Hallelujah. *Series:* Linc's.

GOLDMAN, BO
Writer. b. New York, NY, Sept. 10, 1932. e. Princeton U., B.A., 1953. Wrote lyrics for B'way musical version of Pride and Prejudice entitled First Impressions (1959). Assoc. prod. & script editor for Playhouse 90 1958-60; writer-prod., NET Playhouse 1970-71, Theater in America 1972-74.
PICTURES: One Flew Over the Cuckoo's Nest (co-s.p.; WGA & Academy Awards, 1975), The Rose (co-s.p.), Melvin and Howard (NY Film Critics, WGA & Academy Awards, 1980), Shoot the Moon, Swing Shift (uncredited), Little Nikita (co-s.p.), Dick Tracy (uncredited), Scent of a Woman (Golden Globe Award, Acad. Award nom.), First Knight (co-s.p.), City Hall (co-s.p.), Meet Joe Black, Children of Angels.

GOLDMAN, EDMUND
Executive, Producer. b. Shanghai, China, Nov. 12, 1906. e. Shanghai and San Francisco. Entered ind. as asst. mgr., for Universal in Shanghai, 1935-36; named mgr. Columbia Pictures' Philippine office, 1937. 1951 named Far East. supvr. for Columbia, headquartering in Tokyo. 1953, co-founded Manson Intl. 1953-91 indep. m.p. dist., specializing in foreign mktg. representing indep. prods. and dist. Retired, 1991. PICTURES: Surrender Hell (prod.), The Quick and the Dead (exec. prod.).

GOLDMAN, MICHAEL F.
Executive. b. Manila, Philippines, Sept. 28, 1939. e. UCLA, B.S. in acct., 1962 California C.P.A. certificate issued June, 1972. In 1962 incorporated Manson International, which was sold in 1986. Incorporated Quixote Prods., 1979. Also owner and sole proprietor Taurus Film co. of Hollywood, founded 1964. Co-founder and first chief financial officer of American Film Marketing Association, sponsor of First American Film Market in Los Angeles in 1981; v.p. of AFMA 1982 and 1983, President AFMA 1984 and 1985. Chmn. AFMA, 1992-3. AFMA bd. mbr., 1981-87, 1988-present; Co-founder, Cinema Consultants Group, 1988. Produced feature, Jessi's Girls in 1975. Founded Manson Interactive, 1995. Member A.M.P.A.S. since 1979. Director, Foundation of Motion Picture Pioneers, bd. AFMA.

GOLDMAN, STEVE
Executive. e. Univ. of IL. 1980, joined Paramount as Midwest division mngr., Chicago. Then served in NY as v.p. Eastern regional mngr. 1983, to Hollywood office. 1985, exec. v.p., sls. & mktg. 1989, exec. v.p. 1992, pres. Paramount Domestic Television. 1995, named exec. v.p. of Paramount Television Group. Currently, EVP and Chief Administrative Officer for Paramount TV Group.

GOLDMAN, WILLIAM
Writer. b. Chicago, IL, Aug. 12, 1931. e. Oberlin College, B.A.; Columbia U., M.A.
WRITER: The Temple of Gold, Your Turn to Curtsy—My Turn to Bow, Soldier in the Rain (filmed), Boys and Girls Together, No Way to Treat a Lady (filmed), The Thing of It Is, Father's Day, The Princess Bride (filmed), Marathon Man (filmed), Magic (filmed), Tinsel, Control, Heat (filmed), The Silent Gondoliers, The Color of Light, Brothers, Absolute Power(filmed), Four Screenplays, Five Screenplays, The Ghost & The Darkness (filmed). *Non-fiction:* The Season: A Candid Look at Broadway, Adventures in the Screen Trade, Wait Until Next Year (w/Mike Lupica), Hype and Glory, Which Lie Did I Tell? : More Adventures in the Screen Trade, others.
PICTURES: Harper, Butch Cassidy and the Sundance Kid (Academy Award, 1969), The Hot Rock, The Stepford Wives, The Great Waldo Pepper, All the President's Men (Academy Award, 1976), Marathon Man (based on his novel), A Bridge Too Far, Magic (based on his novel), Mr. Horn, Heat (based on his novel), The Princess Bride (based on his novel), Misery, Memoirs of an Invisible Man (co-s.p.), Year of the Comet, Chaplin (co-s.p.), Last Action Hero (co-s.p.), Maverick, The Chamber, The Ghost and the Darkness (based on his novel), Fierce Creatures (co-s.p.), Absolute Power (based.on his novel), The General's Daughter, Jurassic Park III, Hearts in Atlantis, Dreamcatcher.

GOLDSMITH, JERRY
Composer. b. Los Angeles, CA, Feb. 10, 1929. e. Los Angeles City Coll. Studied piano with Jakob Gimpel and music composition, harmony, theory with Mario Castelnuovo-Tedesco. With CBS radio first with own show (Romance) and then moved on to others (Suspense). Began scoring for TV, including Climax, Playhouse 90, Studio One, Gunsmoke. Emmy Awards for QB VIII, Masada, Babe, The Red Pony, Star Trek Voyager Theme.
PICTURES: Black Patch (debut, 1957), Lonely Are the Brave, Freud (Acad. Award nom.), The Stripper, The Prize, Seven Days in May, Lilies of the Field, In Harm's Way, Von Ryan's Express, Our Man Flint, A Patch of Blue (Acad. Award nom.), The Blue Max, Seconds, Stagecoach, The Sand Pebbles (Acad. Award nom.), In Like Flint, Planet of the Apes (Acad. Award nom.), The Ballad of Cable Hogue, Tora! Tora! Tora!, Patton (Acad. Award nom.), The Wild Rovers, The Other, Papillon (Acad. Award nom.), The Reincarnation of Peter Proud, Chinatown (Acad. Award nom.), Logan's Run, The Wind and the Lion (Acad. Award nom.), The Omen (Academy Award, 1976), Islands in the Stream, MacArthur, Coma, Damien: Omen II, The Boys From Brazil (Acad. Award nom.), The Great Train Robbery, Alien, Star Trek-The Motion Picture (Acad. Award nom.), The Final Conflict, Outland, Raggedy Man, The Secret of NIMH, Poltergeist (Acad. Award nom.), First Blood, Twilight Zone—The Movie, Psycho II, Under Fire (Acad. Award nom.), Gremlins, Legend (European ver.), Explorers, Rambo: First Blood II, Poltergeist II: The Other Side, Hoosiers (Acad. Award nom.), Extreme Prejudice, Innerspace, Lionheart, Rent-a-Cop, Rambo III, Criminal Law, The 'Burbs, Leviathan, Star Trek V: The Final Frontier, Total Recall, Gremlins 2: The New Batch (also cameo), The Russia House, Not Without My Daughter, Sleeping With the Enemy, Medicine Man, Basic Instinct (Acad. Award nom.), Mom and Dad Save the World, Mr. Baseball, Love Field, Forever Young, Matinee, The Vanishing, Dennis the Menace, Malice, Rudy, Six Degrees of Separation, Angie, Bad Girls, The Shadow, The River Wild, I.Q., Congo, First Knight, Powder, City Hall, Executive Decision, Powder, Chain Reaction, The Ghost and the Darkness, Star Trek: First Contact, Fierce Creatures, Air Force One, L.A. Confidential (Acad. Award nom.), Deep Rising, The Edge, U.S. Marshalls, Mulan, Small Soldiers, Star Trek: Insurrection, The Haunting, The Mummy, The 13th Warrior, The Haunting, Hollow Man, Along Came a Spider, The Last Castle, The Sum of All Fears, Star Trek: Nemesis, The Real Nam: Voices From Within, Guts & Glory, Looney Tunes: Back in Action, Picasso at the Lapin Agile, The Game of Their Lives.
TELEVISION: *Specials:* The 75th Annual Acad. Awards (Oscar fanfare). *Series:* Line of Fire (theme).

GOLDSMITH, MARVIN F.
Executive. b. Brooklyn, NY. e. NY Inst. of Tech. Started as page at CBS, eventually becoming film editor. Was tv group supervisor with Batten Barton Durstine & Osborne. 1973, joined ABC as mgr. nighttime sales proposals; 1976-78, account exec. in sports sales, then v.p. prime time sales proposals, then v.p. Eastern Sales. 1986, promoted to sr. v.p., natl. sls. mngr.; 1989, became sr. v.p. gen. sls. mngr. 1992-present, pres., sls. & marketing, ABC Television Network.

GOLDSTEIN, MILTON
Executive. b. New York, NY, Aug. 1, 1926. e. NYU, 1949. In exec. capac., Paramount; foreign sales coord., The Ten Commandments, Psycho; v.p. foreign sales, Samuel Bronston

org.; asst. to Pres., Paramount Int'l, special prods., 1964; Foreign sales mgr., 1966; v.p., world wide sales, 1967, Cinerama; Sr. v.p. Cinema Center Films, 1969; pres., Cinema Center Films, 1971; v.p. Theatrical Mktg. & Sales, Metromedia Producers Corp., 1973; in March, 1974, formed Boasberg-Goldstein, Inc., consultants in prod. and dist. of m.p.; 1975, named exec. vice pres., Avco Embassy Pictures; 1978, named exec. v.p. & chief operating officer, Melvin Simon Prods. 1980, named pres.; 1985, pres. Milt Goldstein Enterprises, Inc.; 1990, chairman and CEO, HKM Films. 1991, pres., Introvision movies. In 2001, teamed with ent. attorneys Leroy Bobbitt and Virgil Roberts to forma StreetSmart Pictures, a dist. co. specializing in the release of African-American films.

GOLDTHWAIT, BOBCAT (BOB)
Comedian, Actor. b. Syracuse, NY, May 1, 1962. Performed with The Generic Comics in early 1980's. Album: Meat Bob.
PICTURES: Police Academy 2: Their First Assignment (debut, 1985), One Crazy Summer, Police Academy 3: Back in Training, Burglar, Police Academy 4: Citizens on Patrol, Hot to Trot, Scrooged, Shakes the Clown (also dir., s.p.), Freaked, Radioland Murders, Destiny Turns on the Radio, Hercules (voice), Rusty: A Dog's Tale (voice), G-Men From Hell, Open Mic, Lion of Oz (voice), Blow, Hansel & Gretel.
TELEVISION: *Movies*: Out There, Encino Woman, Back to Back. *Guest*: Tales From the Crypt, Married... With Children, The Larry Sanders Show, E.R., Beavis and Butthead (voice), Comic Relief, The John Laroquette Show, The Simpsons (voice). *Series*: Capitol Critters (voice), Unhappily Ever After (voice), Bobcat's Big Ass Show, Hercules (voice), Hollywood Squares, Stories From My Childhood, Late Friday, Crank Yankers. *Specials*: Bob Goldthwait: Don't Watch This Show, Share the Warmth, Is He Like That All the Time? (also dir., writer), Bob Saget: In the Dream Suite, Comic Relief, Medusa: Dare to Be Truthful.

GOLDWATER, CHARLES
Executive, Exhibitor. b. New Orleans, LA. e. Boston U., B.S. Broadcasting & Film. Began career with Walter Reade Organization as usher in 1971-74, promoted to manager. Sack Theatres/USA Cinemas 1974-88, began as manager, promoted to s.v.p. & g.m. National Amusements, exec. dir. Project Development, 1988-90. Loews/Sony Theatres, sr. v.p. & general manager, 1990-1995. Pres. & CEO, Cinamerica/Mann Theatres, 1995-1998. March, 1998 became Pres., CEO and Chairman of the Board, Iwerks Entertainment. March '98-Feb. '00. Pres., Clearview Cinemas, July '00-present. In June 2002, named pres./CEO of NDC, NewCo Digital Cinema, the corp. coalition formed by seven major film studios to develop digital cinema technology. NATO bd. of dir. 1987-present. Chmn. CARA/Product Committee, 1991-1996; Exec Comm.,1995-. Gen. chmn. Showeast 1992-1995; chmn of the bd. Showeast, 1995-present. Bd. of directors, Motion Picture Pioneers, Will Rogers. Past pres./chmn. of bd., Theatre Owners of New England. Past bd. of directors, Variety Clubs of New England & New York.

GOLDWYN, JOHN
Executive. Grandson of Samuel Goldwyn. Began career as exec. story editor, The Ladd Co., 1982; later promoted to v.p., creative affairs, served as exec. producer on Police Academy II. Became senior v.p., motion picture production, MGM/UA Entertainment Co., 1985, and was named exec. v.p., motion picture production for MGM in 1988. Joined Paramount Pictures in 1990 as exec. v.p., production and was promoted to president, Motion Picture Grp./production, 1991. 1997, became president, Paramount Pictures. Currently, vice chmn. & co-pres. of Paramount Pictures.

GOLDWYN, SAMUEL, JR.
Producer, Director. b. Los Angeles, CA, Sept. 7, 1926. e. U. of Virginia. Father of actor Tony Goldwyn. U.S. Army, 1944; following war writer, assoc. prod., J. Arthur Rank Org.; prod. Gathering Storm on London stage; returned to U.S., 1948; assoc. prod., Universal; recalled to Army service, 1951; prod., dir., Army documentary films including Alliance for Peace (Edinburgh Film Festival prize); prod. TV shows, Adventure series for CBS, 1952-53; prod. TV series, The Unexpected, 1954; pres., The Samuel Goldwyn Company, 1955-. Also established Samuel Goldwyn Home Entertainment, and Goldwyn Pavilion Cinemas.
PICTURES: *Prod.*: Man With the Gun, The Sharkfighters, The Proud Rebel, The Adventures of Huckleberry Finn, The Young Lovers (also dir.), Cotton Comes to Harlem, Come Back Charleston Blue, The Golden Seal, Mystic Pizza (exec. prod.), Stella, The Preacher's Wife, Tortilla Soup, Master and Commander.
TELEVISION: The Academy Awards, 1987, 1988; April Morning (co-exec. prod.).

GOLDWYN, TONY
Actor. b. Los Angeles, CA, May 20, 1960. e. Brandeis U., London Acad. of Music & Dramatic Art.
THEATRE: Digby, The Foreigner, The Real Thing, Pride and Prejudice, The Sum of Us, Spike Heels, Inherit the Wind.
PICTURES: Friday the 13th Part VI: Jason Live, Gaby-A True Story, Ghost, Kuffs, Traces of Red, The Pelican Brief, Reckless, The Substance of Fire, Nixon, The Substance of Fire, Kiss the Girls, Trouble on the Corner, The Lesser Evil, Tarzan (voice), The

6th Day, Bounce, Someone Like You, An American Rhapsody, Joshua, Abandon, The Last Samurai, Ash Tuesday.
TELEVISION: *Movies*: Favorite Son, Dark Holiday, Iran: Days of Crisis, Taking the Heat, Love Matters, Doomsday Gun, The Last Word, The Boys Next Door, Truman, The Song of the Lark. *Mini-Series*: A Woman of Independent Means. *Special*: The Last Mile. *Guest*: L.A. Law, Tales from the Crypt.

GOLINO, VALERIA
Actress. b. Naples, Italy, Oct. 22, 1966. Raised in Athens, Greece. Was model at age 14 before being discovered by dir. Lina Wertmuller for film debut.
PICTURES: A Joke of Destiny (debut, 1983), Blind Date, My Son Infinitely Beloved, Little Fires, Dumb Dicks, Storia d'Amore (Love Story), Last Summer in Tangiers, The Gold-Rimmed Glasses, Three Sisters, Big Top Pee-wee, Rain Man, Torrents of Spring, The King's Whore, Traces of an Amorous Life, Hot Shots!, The Indian Runner, Hot Shots! Part Deux, Clean Slate, Immortal Beloved, Leaving Las Vegas, Four Rooms, Escape From L.A., The Acrobats, Side Streets, Le Acrobate, The Pear Tree, Harem Square, Spanish Judges, Things You Can Tell Just By Looking at her, Il Fratello minore, Ivansxtc, Against the Wind, Word of Honor, Hotel, L'Inverno, Boccanera, Respiro: Grazia's Island, Frida.

GOMEZ, NICK
Director, Writer. b Sommerville, MA, 1963. Stunts in film Powder. Acted in films Mob War and Blue Vengeance.
PICTURES: Laws of Gravity, New Jersey Drive (also story), Illtown, Drowning Mona.
TELEVISION: Movies: Final Jeopardy, Hunter: Return to Justice. *Series:* Homicide: Life on the Street, Oz, The Sopranos, Mondo Picasso, Night Visions, Crossing Jordan, The Agency, The Shield, Push Nevada, Robbery Homicide Division.

GONZALEZ-GONZALEZ, PEDRO
Actor. r.n. Ramiro Gonzalez-Gonzalez. b. Aguilares, TX, May 24, 1925. Comedian in San Antonio Mexican theatres.
PICTURES: Wings of the Hawk, Ring of Fear, Ricochet Romance, The High and the Mighty, Strange Lady in Town, Bengazi, I Died a Thousand Times, Bottom of the Bottle, The Sheepman, Gun the Man Down, Rio Bravo, The Young Land, The Adventures of Bullwhip Griffin, The Love Bug, The Love God, Hellfighters, Hook Line and Sinker, Chisum, Support Your Local Gunfighter, Zachariah, Six-Pack Annie, Won Ton Ton the Dog Who Saved Hollywood, Dreamer, Lust in the Dust, Uphill All the Way, Down the Drain, Ruby Cairo..
TELEVISION: *Movies*: Donor, Ghost Writer, Bates Motel (pilot), Dazzle. *Guest*: O'Henry Playhouse, Felix the Fourth, Ann Southern Show, No Time for Sergeants, Gunsmoke, Perry Mason, The Monkees, Love American Style, Adam 12, Farmer's Daughter, Danny Kaye Show, National Velvet, Bachelor Father, Bonanza, The Fall Guy, Moonlighting, many others.

GOOD, CHARLES E.
Executive. b. 1922. Joined Buena Vista in 1957 in Chicago office; progressed from salesman to branch mgr. and then district mgr. Later moved to Burbank as domestic sales mgr. in 1975; 1978, named v.p. & general sales mgr.; 1980, appointed pres., BV Distribution Co. Resigned presidency 1984; became BV consultant until retirement, 1987.

GOODALL, CAROLINE
Actress. b. London, England, Nov. 13, 1959. e. Natl Youth Theatre of Great Britain; Bristol Univ. On stage with Royal Court Theatre, Royal Natl. Theatre, Royal Shakespeare Co. Toured Australia in Richard III for RSC, 1986.
PICTURES: Every Time We Say Goodbye (debut, 1986), Hook, The Silver Brumby, The Webbers' 15 Minutes, Cliffhanger, Schindler's List, Disclosure, Hotel Sorrento, White Squall, Casualties, Rhapsody in Bloom, The Secret Laughter of Women, Harrison's Flowers, The Princess Diaries.
TELEVISION: *Movies* (Australia): Cassidy, Ring of Scorpio, The Great Air Race, Diamond Swords (Fr.), The Sculptress, Opera Ball, Sex n' Death, Love and Murder, Me & Mrs. Jones. *Mini-Series*: After the War, A Difficult Woman, The Mists of Avalon. *Guest*: Remington Steele, Tales of the Unexpected, Quantum Leap, The Commish, Rumpole of the Bailey, Poirot: Curse of the Western Star. *Series*: Murder in Mind.

GOODING, CUBA, JR.
Actor. b. Bronx, NY, Sept. 2, 1968. Son of rhythm and blues vocalist Cuba Gooding. Raised in California. Prof. debut as dancer backing up Lionel Richie at 1984 Olympic Games. Recipient of NAACP Image Awards for Boyz in the Hood and tv movie, Murder Without Motive. Voted by NATO/Showest as Newcomer of the Year, 1992.
PICTURES: Coming to America (debut, 1988), Sing, Boyz in the Hood, Hitz, Gladiator, A Few Good Men, Judgment Night, Lightning Jack, Outbreak, Losing Isaiah, Jerry Maguire (Acad. Award, 1996; Chicago Film Critics Award; Screen Actors Guild Award), Do Me a Favor (cameo), As Good As It Gets, What Dreams May Come, Welcome to Hollywood, Chill Factor, A Murder of Crows (also prod.), Instinct, Men of Honor, Pearl Harbor, Rat Race, In the Shadows, Zoolander, Snow Dogs, Boat Trip, Sweating Bullets (voice), The Fighting Temptations, Radio, Home on the Range (voice).
TELEVISION: *Movies*: Murder Without Motive: The Edmund Perry Story, Daybreak, The Tuskegee Airmen. *Specials*: No Means No, America: A Tribute to Heroes.

GOODMAN, DAVID Z.
Writer. e. Queens Coll., Yale School of Drama.
PICTURES: Lovers and Other Strangers, Straw Dogs, Farewell My Lovely, Logan's Run, Eyes of Laura Mars, Fighting Back, Man Woman and Child (co.-s.p.).
TELEVISION: *Movies:* Monte Walsh.

GOODMAN, JOHN
Actor. b. Affton, MO, June 20, 1952. e. Southwest Missouri State U. Moved to NY in 1975 when he appeared on stage (incl. A Midsummer Night's Dream) and in commercials. On Broadway in Loose Ends, Big River. L.A. stage in Antony and Cleopatra.
PICTURES: Eddie Macon's Run (1983, debut), The Survivors, Revenge of the Nerds, C.H.U.D., Maria's Lovers, Sweet Dreams, True Stories, Raising Arizona, Burglar, The Big Easy, The Wrong Guys, Punchline, Everybody's All-American, Sea of Love, Always, Stella, Arachnophobia, King Ralph, Barton Fink, The Babe, Matinee, Born Yesterday, We're Back! A Dinosaur's Story (voice), The Flintstones, The Hudsucker Proxy (cameo), Pie in the Sky, Mother Night, The Borrowers, The Big Lebowski, Fallen, Blues Brothers 2000, Dirty Work (cameo), The Runner, Bringing Out the Dead, Coyote Ugly, What Planet Are You From, O Brother Where Art Thou? Happy Birthday, My First Mister, One Night at McCool's, The Emperor's New Groove (voice), Storytelling, Monsters Inc. (voice), Dirty Deeds, Masked & Anonymous, The Jungle Book 2 (voice), Home of Phobia.
TELEVISION: *Movies:* The Face of Rage, Heart of Steel, The Mystery of Moro Castle, Murder Ordained, Kingfish: A Story of Huey P. Long (also co-prod.), A Streetcar Named Desire, The Jack Bull. *Mini-Series:* Chiefs. *Series:* Roseanne, Normal Ohio. *Guest:* The Equalizer, Moonlighting, The West Wing.

GOODRICH, ROBERT EMMETT
Executive. b. Grand Rapids, MI, June 27, 1940. e. U. of Michigan, B.A., 1962; J.D., 1964; NYU. LL.M, 1966. Pres. & Secty., Goodrich Quality Theaters, Inc. 1967-present, developed circuit from father's one theater to 13 screens plus Wabash Landing at 38 locations in 17 Mich. cities, 4 Indiana cities, 4 Illinois cities, 2 Kansas cities, 4 Missouri cities. Owns and operates 2 AM radio stations in Grand Rapids, MI. NATO; Will Rogers Inst. advisory comm; bd. of dirs., Mich. Millers Mutual Insurance Co.; bd. of dirs., Western Migh. Branch ACLU. State of MI Bar Assn.

GOODWIN, RICHARD B.
Producer. b. Bombay, India, Sept. 13, 1934. e. Rugby. Entered film world by chance: while waiting to go to Cambridge U. took temporary job as tea boy at studio which led to 20-year-long association with producer Lord Brabourne.
PICTURES: *Prod. Mgr.:* The Sheriff of Fractured Jaw, Carve Her Name with Pride, The Grass Is Greener, Sink the Bismarck, HMS Defiant. *Prod.:* The Tales of Beatrix Potter. *Co-Prod.:* Murder on the Orient Express, Death on the Nile, The Mirror Crack'd, Evil Under the Sun, A Passage to India, Little Dorrit, Seven Years In Tibet (exec. prod.).

GOODWIN, RONALD
Composer, Arranger, Conductor. b. Plymouth, Eng., Feb. 17, 1925. e. Pinner County Grammar Sch. Early career: arranger for BBC dance orchestra; mus. dir., Parlophone Records; orchestra leader for radio, TV and records. Fut. m.p. ind., 1958. Many major film scores. Guest cond. R.P.O., B.S.O., Toronto Symph. Orch. New Zealand Symphony Orch., Sydney Symphony Orch. Royal Scottish Natl. Orch., BBC Scottish Symphony Orch., BBC Welsh Symphony Orch., BBC Radio Orch., BBC Concert Orch., London Philharmonic Orch., Gothenberg Symphony Orch., Norwegian Opera Orch. & Chorus, Halle Orchestra, Singapore Symphony Orch., Australian Pops Orch., Detroit Symphony Orchestra, Danish Radio Orchestra, Odense Symphony Orch., Norrkoping Symphony Orch.
PICTURES: Whirlpool, I'm All Right Jack, The Trials of Oscar Wilde, Johnny Nobody, Village of the Damned, Murder She Said, Follow the Boys, Murder at the Gallop, Children of the Damned, 633 Squadron, Murder Most Foul, Murder Ahoy, Operation Crossbow, The ABC Murders, Of Human Bondage, Those Magnificent Men in Their Flying Machines, The Trap, Mrs. Brown, You've Got a Lovely Daughter; Submarine X-1, Decline and Fall, Where Eagles Dare, Monte Carlo or Bust, Battle of Britain, The Executioner, The Selfish Giant, Frenzy, Diamonds on Wheels, The Little Mermaid, The Happy Prince, One of Our Dinosaurs Is Missing, Escape From the Dark, Born to Run, Beauty and the Beast, Candleshoe, Force Ten from Navarone, Spaceman and King Arthur, Clash of Loyalties, Valhalla.
(d. Jan. 8, 2003)

GORDON, ALEX
Producer. b. London, Eng., Sept. 8, 1922. e. Canford Coll., Dorset, 1939. Writer, m.p. fan magazines, 1939-41; British Army, 1942-45; pub. dir. Renown Pictures Corp., 1946-47; PR. and pub. rep. for Gene Autry, 1948-53; v.p. and prod. Golden State Productions, 1954-58; prod. Alex Gordon Prods., 1958-66; producer Twentieth Century-Fox Television, 1967-76; film archivist/preservationist, 1976-84; v.p., Gene Autry's Flying A Pictures, 1985.
PICTURES: Lawless Rider, Bride of the Monster, Apache Woman, Day the World Ended, Oklahoma Woman, Girls in Prison, The She-Creature, Runaway Daughters, Shake Rattle and Rock, Flesh and the Spur, Voodoo Woman, Dragstrip Girl,

Motorcycle Gang, Jet Attack, Submarine Seahawk, Atomic Submarine, The Underwater City, The Bounty Killer, Requiem for a Gunfighter.
TELEVISION: Movie of the Year, Golden Century, Great Moments in Motion Pictures.
(d. June 24, 2003)

GORDON, BERT I.
Producer, Director, Writer. b. Kenosha, WI, Sept. 24, 1932. e. Univ. of WI. Started on tv as commercial prod.
PICTURES: *Dir./Prod.:* Serpent Island (debut, 1954), King Dinosaur, Beginning of the End, Cyclops (also s.p.), The Amazing Colossal Man (also co-s.p.), Attack of the Puppet People (also story), War of the Colossal Beast, The Spider, Tormented, The Boy and the Pirates, The Magic Sword (also story), Village of the Giants (also story), Picture Mommy Dead, How to Succeed With Sex (dir., s.p.), The Big Bet, Necromancy (also s.p.), The Mad Bomber (also s.p.), The Police Connection (also s.p.), The Food of the Gods (also s.p.), Empire of the Ants (also s.p.), Burned at the Stake, The Coming (also s.p.), Let's Do It!, The Big Bet, Satan's Princess, Malediction.

GORDON, BRUCE
Executive. e. B.S. in bus. admin. from Syracuse Univ.; M.B.A. from Hofstra Univ. Career with Price Waterhouse and Company before joining ABC in 1981. 1981-1985 asst. dir./finance for KGO-TV, an ABC-owned tv station in San Francisco. 1985-1997, held sr. mgt. position at KABC-TV, the ABC-owned tv station in Los Angeles. There he led the station's finance, admin. & strategic planning operations. 1997-2001, pres. & gen. mgr. of WTVD-TV, the ABC-owned tv affiliate in Raleigh, NC. Currently, Gordon is SVP & CFO of the Walt Disney Internet Group, headquartered in North Hollywood, CA.

GORDON, CHARLES
Executive, Producer. b. Belzoni, MS. Began career as a talent agent with William Morris Agency. Left to write and develop television programming creating and producing 5 pilots and 3 series. Left TV to enter motion picture production in partnership with brother Lawrence Gordon. President and chief operating officer, The Gordon Company.
PICTURES: *Exec. prod.:* Die Hard, Leviathan. *Co-prod.:* Night of the Creeps, The Wrong Guys, Field of Dreams, K-9, Lock Up, The Rocketeer, The Super, Unlawful Entry, Waterworld, Trojan War (prod.), October Sky, Small World, The Tree, The Girl Next Door.
TELEVISION: *Writer-creator:* When the Whistle Blows. *Exec. prod.:* The Renegades, Just Our Luck (also creator), Our Family Honor (also creator).

GORDON, DON
Actor. r.n. Donald Walter Guadagno. b. Los Angeles, CA, Nov. 13, 1926. Served, U.S. Navy, 1941-45. Studied acting with Michael Chekhov. e. Columbia U. Theatre includes On an Open Roof, Stockade.
PICTURES: Bullitt, The Lollipop Cover (best actor, Chicago Film Fest.), W.U.S.A., The Last Movie, Papillon, The Gambler, Out of the Blue, The Final Conflict, The Beast Within, Lethal Weapon, Skin Deep, The Exorcist III, The Borrower.
TELEVISION: *Series:* The Blue Angels, Lucan, The Contender. *Guest:* The Defenders, Remington Steele, Charlie's Angels, Twilight Zone, Simon & Simon, Outer Limits, MacGyver, etc. *Movies:* Happiness is a Warm Clue, Street Killing, Confessions of a Married Man.

GORDON, JEROME
Executive, Exhibitor. b. Newport News, VA, Mar. 1, 1915. Began movie career at age 10 as usher in father's theatre. At age 18, owned and operated two theatres. Spent one year in theater decorating business in Philadelphia. Worked for Fox West Coast circuit in Los Angeles, 1937-40. Returned to VA and developed small theater circuit with brothers. Served as pres. of Virginia NATO for 4 yrs. 1975-; exec. dir., Virginia NATO; 1976-, exec. dir., Maryland & D.C. NATO. Coordinated Mid-Atlantic NATO convention from 1975 until it merged with ShowEast in 1989. 1978-86, spec. asst. to pres., NATO; coordinated campaigns to pass Anti-Blind Bidding Laws in individual states. Edited Regional Presidents' NATO Handbook. Member, bd. of dirs., NATO; chmn., NATO Membership Development Committee; secretary NATO, 1996-. Currently exec. dir., Mid-Atlantic NATO. Exec. Committee, ShowEast. Recipient of Distinguished Service Award, ShowEast, 1992; B.V. Sturdivant Award, NATO/ShowEast, 1992.

GORDON, KEITH
Actor, Director, Writer. b. Bronx, NY, Feb. 3, 1961.
THEATRE: A Traveling Companion, Richard III, Album, Back to Back The Buddy System, Third Street.
PICTURES: *Actor:* Jaws 2 (debut, 1978), All That Jazz, Home Movies, Dressed to Kill, Christine, The Legend of Billie Jean, Static (also co-s.p., co-prod.), Back to School, I Love Trouble, Delivering Milo. *Director and/or Writer:* The Chocolate War, A Midnight Clear. Mother Night (also prod.), Waking the Dead (also prod.), The Singing Detective.
TELEVISION: *Mini-Series:* Studs Lonigan. *Movies:* Kent State, Single Bars Single Women, Combat High, Shadow Realm. *Special:* My Palikari (Amer. Playhouse). *Series:* Gideon's

Crossing. *Director*: Wild Palms, Homicide (1 episode), Fallen Angels: The Black Bargain.

GORDON, LAWRENCE
Producer, Executive. b. Yazoo City, MS, March 25, 1936. e. Tulane U. (business admin.). Assist. to prod. Aaron Spelling at Four Star Television, 1964. Writer and assoc. prod. on several Spelling shows. 1965, joined ABC-TV as head of west coast talent dev; 1966, TV and motion pictures exec. with Bob Banner Associates; 1968 joined AIP as v.p. in charge of project dev.; 1971 named v.p., Screen Gems (TV div. of Columbia Pictures) where he helped dev. Brian's Song and QB VII. Returned to AIP as v.p. worldwide prod. Formed Lawrence Gordon Prods. at Columbia Pictures; 1984-86, pres. and COO 20th Century Fox. In 1987, he went independent again as head of Largo Productions. Currently indep. prod. with 20th Century Fox. Producer of B'way musical Smile.
PICTURES: Dillinger (1973), Hard Times, Rolling Thunder, The Driver, The End, Hooper, The Warriors, Xanadu, Paternity, Jekyll and Hyde, Together Again, 48 Hours, Streets of Fire, Brewster's Millions, Lucas, Jumpin' Jack Flash, Predator, The Couch Trip, The Wrong Guys, Die Hard, Leviathan (exec. prod.), K-9, Field of Dreams, Lock Up, Family Business, Another 48 HRS, Die Hard 2, Predator 2, The Rocketeer, Used People, The Devil's Own, Boogie Nights, Event Horizon, Tomb Raider, Thieves, Mystery Men, Thieves, Lara Croft: Tombraider, K-PAX, Hellboy, Band Camp.
TELEVISION: Co-creator and co-exec. prod.: Dog and Cat, Matt Houston, Renegades, Just Our Luck, Our Family Honor, Timecop.

GORDON, RICHARD
Producer. b. London, Eng., Dec. 31, 1925. e. U. of London, 1943. Served in Brit. Royal Navy, 1944-46; ed. & writer on fan magazines & repr. independent American cos. 1946, with publicity dept. Assoc. Brit. Pathe 1947; org. export-import business for independent, British and American product; formed Gordon Films, Inc., 1949; formed Amalgamated prod., 1956; formed Grenadier Films Ltd. 1971. 1992, prod. of A Tribute to Orson Welles.
PICTURES: The Counterfeit Plan, The Haunted Strangler, Fiend Without a Face, The Secret Man, First Man into Space, Corridors of Blood, Devil Doll, Curse of Simba, The Projected Man, Naked Evil, Island of Terror, Tales of the Bizarre, Tower of Evil, Horrorplanet, The Cat and the Canary.

GORDON, STUART
Director, Writer. b. Chicago, IL, Aug. 11, 1947. e. Univ. of WI. Worked at commercial art studio prior to founding Broom Street Theater in Madison, WI. Later founder and prod. dir. of Organic Theater Co. in Madison, then Chicago, 1969-85. Was fight choreographer on 1976 film The Last Affair.
PICTURES: *Director*: Re-Animator (also co-s.p.), From Beyond (also co-s.p.), Dolls, Robot Jox (also wrote story), Honey I Shrunk the Kids (co-story only), The Pit and the Pendulum, Honey I Blew Up the Kid (exec. prod., co-story only), Fortress, Body Snatchers (co-s.p. only), Castle Freak (also co-story), Space Truckers (dir., prod., co-story), The Wonderful Ice Cream Suit, Dagon, King of the Ants.
TELEVISION: *Director*: Bleacher Bums (special).

GORDY, BERRY
Executive. b. Detroit, MI, Nov. 28, 1929. Was working on auto assembly line in Detroit when decided to launch record co., Motown. In 1961 wrote song, Shop Around; recording by Smokey Robinson made it his first million dollar record. Expanded into music publishing, personal mgt., recording studios, film and TV, also backing stage shows. Former bd. chmn., Motown Industries. Chmn. The Gordy Co. Received Business Achievement Award, Interracial Council for Business Opportunity, 1967; Whitney M. Young Jr. Award, L.A. Urban League, 1980; Inducted into Rock and Roll Hall of Fame, 1988. Recipient of NARAS Trustee Award, 1991. Author of To Be Loved (1994). Member BMI, NAACP, A.M.P.A.S., DGI, NARAS.
PICTURES: Lady Sings the Blues (prod.), Bingo Long Traveling All-Stars and Motor Kings (exec. prod.), Mahogany (dir.), Almost Summer, The Last Dragon (exec. prod.).

GORE, MICHAEL
Composer, Producer. b. New York City, New York, March 5, 1951. e. Yale University and studied in Paris with composer Max Deustch. Began writing pop songs for his sister singer Lesley Gore; as a staff songwriter for Screen Gems-Columbia; and as a producer of classical recordings for CBS Records. Prod. for Philips Classics recording of The King and I (with Julie Andrews, Ben Kingsley). Wrote Whitney Houston's hit single All the Man That I Need.
PICTURES: Fame (2 Academy Awards for Best Score and Title Song, 1980), Terms of Endearment, Footloose, Pretty in Pink, Broadcast News, Defending Your Life, The Butcher's Wife, Mr. Wonderful, Superstar.
TELEVISION: Generations (theme); Fame (theme) South Pacific (tv movie).

GORSHIN, FRANK
Actor. b. Pittsburgh, PA, Apr. 5, 1933. Also nightclub comic and impressionist. On B'way stage in Jimmy.
PICTURES: Hot Rod Girl, Dragstrip Girl, Invasion of the Saucer Men, Portland Exposse, Warlock, Bells Are Ringing, Studs Lonigan, Where the Boys Are, The Great Impostor, Ring

of Fire, The George Raft Story, Sail a Crooked Ship, That Darn Cat, Ride Beyond Vengeance, Batman, Skidoo, Record City, Underground Aces, The Uppercrust, Hot Resort, Uphill All the Way, Hollywood Vice Squad, Midnight, Beverly Hills Bodysnatchers, Hail Caesar, The Meteor Man, Twelve Monkeys, From Hare to Eternity (voice), Twilight of the Ice Nymphs, Bloodmoon, After the Game, Pullet Surprise (voice), Man of the Century, Final Rinse, Everything's George, All Shook Up, Luck of the Draw, Manna from Heaven, High Times Potluck, Bloodhead.
TELEVISION: *Movies*: Sky Heist, Death on the Freeway, Goliath Awaits, A Masterpiece of Murder. *Guest*: Hennessey, The Detectives, Have Gun Will Travel, The Defenders, Naked City, The Munsters, Batman, Police Woman, SWAT, The Fall Guy, Murder She Wrote. *Series*: ABC Comedy Hour (The Kopycats), The Edge of Night, Black Scorpion, General Hospital, The Bold and the Beautiful.

GORTNER, MARJOE
Actor, Producer. b. Long Beach, CA, Jan. 14, 1944. Was child evangelist, whose career as such was basis for Oscar-winning documentary film, Marjoe. Acted in films and TV; turned producer in 1978 for When You Comin' Back Red Ryder?
PICTURES: Earthquake, Bobbie Joe and the Outlaw, The Food of the Gods, Viva Knievel, Sidewinder One, Acapulco Gold, Starcrash, When You Comin' Back Red Ryder?, Mausoleum, Jungle Warriors, Hellhole, American Ninja III: Blood Hunt, Fire Ice and Dynamite, Wild Bill.
TELEVISION: *Movies*: The Marcus-Nelson Murders, Pray for the Wildcats, The Gun and the Pulpit, Mayday at 40000 Feet. *Guest*: Police Story, Barnaby Jones, The A-Team. *Series*: Falcon Crest.

GOSSETT, LOUIS, JR.
Actor. b. Brooklyn, NY, May 27, 1936. e. NYU, B.S. Also nightclub singer during 1960s.
THEATRE: Take a Giant Step (debut, 1953), The Desk Set, Lost in the Stars, A Raisin in the Sun, Golden Boy, The Blacks, Blood Knot, The Zulu and the Zayda, My Sweet Charlie, Carry Me Back to Morningside Heights, Murderous Angels (L.A. Drama Critics Award).
PICTURES: A Raisin in the Sun (debut, 1961), The Bushbaby, The Landlord, Skin Game, Travels With My Aunt, The Laughing Policeman, The White Dawn, The River Niger, J.D.'s Revenge, The Deep, The Choirboys, An Officer and a Gentleman (Academy Award, best supporting actor, 1982), Jaws 3-D, Finders Keepers, Enemy Mine, Iron Eagle, Firewalker, The Principal, Iron Eagle II, Toy Soldiers, The Punisher, Aces: Iron Eagle III, Diggstown, Monolith, Flashfire, Blue Chips (unbilled), A Good Man in Africa, Iron Eagle IV, Inside, Managua, Bram Stoker's Legend of the Mummy, Y2K, The Highwayman, Delgo (voice).
TELEVISION: *Series*: The Young Rebels, The Lazarus Syndrome, The Powers of Matthew Star, Gideon Oliver, The Great War (voice), Hercules (voice), Walking After Midnight. *Movies*: Companions in Nightmare, It's Good to Be Alive, Sidekicks, Delancey Street, The Crisis Within, Don't Look Back, Little Ladies of the Night, To Kill a Cop, The Critical List, This Man Stands Alone, Sadat, The Guardian, A Gathering of Old Men, The Father Clements Story, Roots: The Gift, El Diablo, Sudie and Simpson, The Josephine Baker Story, Carolina Skeletons, Father & Son: Dangerous Relations (also co-exec. prod.), Ray Alexander: A Taste for Justice, A Father for Charlie (also co-exec. prod.), Curse of the Starving Class, Zooman, Ray Alexander: A Menu for Murder, Captive Heart: The James Mink Story, to Dance with Olivia, The Inspectors, Love Songs, Strange Justice, The Color of Love: Jacey's Story, Dr. Lucille, For Love of Olivia, What About Your Friends: Weekend Getaway, Momentum, Jasper Texas. *Mini-Series*: Roots (Emmy Award, 1977), Backstairs at the White House. *Specials*: Welcome Home, A Triple Play: Sam Found Out, Zora Is My Name, The Century Collection Presents Ben Vereen: His Roots, In His Father's Shoes (Emmy Award, 1998). *Series*: Resurrection Blvd. *Guest*: The Mod Squad, Bill Cosby Show, Partridge Family, The Rookies, Love American Style, Police Story, Rockford Files.

GOTTESMAN, STUART
Executive. b. New York, NY, June 11, 1949. Started career in mailroom of Warner Bros., 1972; later named promo. asst. to southwestern regional fieldman; promoted to that post which held for 10 years. 1987, named WB dir. field activities; 1990, appointed v.p. WB national field operations. 1997, named v.p. regional publicity and promo. for Paramount Pictures' m.p. group.

GOTTLIEB, CARL
Writer, Director, Actor. b. New York, NY, March 18, 1938. e. Syracuse U., B.S., 1960. Directed short film The Absent-Minded Waiter.
PICTURES: *Actor*: Maryjane, M*A*S*H, Up the Sandbox, Cannonball, The Sting II, Johnny Dangerously, The Committee, Into the Night, Clueless. *Director*: Caveman (also co-s.p.), Amazon Women on the Moon (co-dir.). *Co-Writer*: Jaws (also actor), Which Way Is Up?, Jaws II, The Jerk (also actor), Doctor Detroit, Jaws 3-D, The Sting II, Jonny Dangerously, Into the Night, Clueless.
TELEVISION: *Writer*: Smothers Bros. Comedy Hour (Emmy Award, 1969), The Odd Couple, Flip Wilson, Bob Newhart Show,

The Super, Crisis at Sun Valley, The Deadly Triangle. *Director*: Paul Reiser: Out on a Whim, Partners In Life, Campus Cops, Honey I Shrunk the Kids, The Lot (consulting prod.). *Director-Co-creator*: Leo & Liz in Beverly Hills. *Co-creator*: George Burns' Comedy Week.

GOUGH, MICHAEL
Actor. b. Malaya, Nov. 23, 1917. e. Rose Hill Sch., in Kent, England, and at Durham School. Studied at Old Vic School in London; first stage appearance in 1936 at Old Vic Theatre. N.Y. stage debut 1937 in Love of Women. London debut in 1938 in The Zeal of Thy House. Won 1979 Tony Award for Bedroom Farce.
PICTURES: Blanche Fury (debut, 1947), Anna Karenina, Saraband for Dead Lovers, The Small Back Room, The Man in the White Suit, Rob Roy, The Sword and the Rose, Richard III, Reach for the Sky, Horror of Dracula (Dracula), Horrors of the Black Museum, The Horse's Mouth, Konga, Candidate for Murder, I Like Money (Mr. Topaze), The Phantom of the Opera, Black Zoo, Dr. Terror's House of Horrors, The Skull, Berserk, They Came From Beyond Space, A Walk With Love and Death, Women in Love, Trog, Julius Caesar, The Go-Between, Savage Messiah, Legend of Hell House, Horror Hospital (Computer Killers), Galileo, The Boys from Brazil, Venom, The Dresser, Top Secret!, Oxford Blues, Out of Africa, Caravaggio, Memed My Hawk, The Fourth Protocol, The Serpent and the Rainbow, Batman, Strapless, Let Him Have It, Blackeyes, Batman Returns, Little Nemo (voice), The Age of Innocence, Wittgenstein, Uncovered, Batman Forever, Batman & Robin, What Rats Won't Do, The Whisper, St. Ives, Sleepy Hollow, The Cherry Orchard.
TELEVISION: The Search for the Nile, Six Wives of Henry VIII, QB VII, Shoulder to Shoulder, The Citadel, Smiley's People, Brideshead Revisited, Mistral's Daughter, Lace II, Inside the Third Reich, To the Lighthouse, Suez, Vincent the Dutchman, Heart Attack Hotel, After the War, The Shell Seekers, Children of the North, Dr. Who, Sleepers.

GOULD, ELLIOTT
Actor. r.n. Elliott Goldstein. b. Brooklyn, NY, August 29, 1938. e. Professional Children's Sch., NY 1955. Vaudeville: appeared at Palace Theater, 1950. Broadway debut in Rumple (1957). Son is actor Jason Gould.
THEATRE: Say Darling, Irma La Douce, I Can Get It for You Wholesale, On the Town (London), Fantasticks (tour), Drat the Cat, Little Murders, Luv (tour), Hit the Deck (Jones Beach), Rumors, Breakfast With Les & Bess.
PICTURES: Quick Let's Get Married (debut, 1965), The Night They Raided Minsky's, Bob & Carol & Ted & Alice (Acad. Award nom.), M*A*S*H, Getting Straight, Move, I Love My Wife, Little Murders (also prod.), The Touch, The Long Goodbye, Busting, S*P*Y*S!, California Split, Who?, Nashville (cameo), Whiffs, I Will I Will... For Now, Harry and Walter Go to New York, Mean Johnny Barrows, A Bridge Too Far, Capricorn One, Matilda, The Silent Partner, Escape to Athena, The Muppet Movie, The Last Flight of Noah's Ark, The Lady Vanishes, Falling in Love Again, The Devil and Max Devlin, Dirty Tricks, The Naked Face, Over the Brooklyn Bridge, The Muppets Take Manhattan, Inside Out, My First 40 Years, Lethal Obsession, The Telephone, The Big Picture, Dangerous Love, Night Visitor, The Wounded King, The Lemon Sisters, Judgment, Dead Men Don't Die, Bugsy, Strawanser, The Player, Exchange Lifeguards, Wet and Wild Summer, Naked Gun 33 1/3: The Final Insult (cameo), White Man's Burden, The Glass Shield, Kicking and Screaming, A Boy Called Hate, Johns, City of Industry (cameo), Camp Stories, Michael Kael in Katango, The Big Hit, American History X, Picking up the Pieces, Playing Mona Lisa, Boys Life 3, Ocean's Eleven, Puckoon, The Experience Box (also prod.), A Yiddish World Remembered (documentary, narrator).
TELEVISION: *Movies*: The Rules of Marriage, Vanishing Act, Conspiracy: The Trial of the Chicago 8, Stolen: One Husband, Somebody's Daughter, Bloodlines: Murder in the Family, The Shining, Good As Gold, The Kentucky Derby. *Specials*: Once Upon A Mattress, Come Blow Your Horn, Jack and the Beanstalk (Faerie Tale Theater), Paul Reiser: Out on a Whim, Prime Time, Out to Lunch, Casey at the Bat (Tall Tales & Legends), *Guest*: Twilight Zone, Electric Company, Saturday Night Live, George Burns Comedy Week, Ray Bradbury Theatre, The Hitchhiker, Friends, It's Like You Know.... *Series*: ER, Together We Stand, Sessions (HBO), Getting Personal, Baby Bob.

GOULD, HAROLD
Actor. b. Schenectady, NY, Dec. 10, 1923. e. SUNY, Albany, B.A. Cornell U., MA., Ph.D. Instructor of theatre and speech, 1953-56, Randolph Macon's Woman's Col., Lynchburg, VA. Asst. prof. drama and speech, 1956-60, Univ. of Calif., Riverside.Acted with Ashland, OR Shakespeare Fest. in 1958 and Mark Taper Forum (The Miser, Once in a Lifetime). Won Obie Award for Off-B'way debut in The Increased Difficulty of Concentration, 1969. ACE Award for Ray Bradbury Theatre. L.A. Drama Critics Award, 1994.
THEATER: The House of Blue Leaves, Fools, Grown Ups, Artist Descending a Staircase, I Never Sang For My Father, Freud (one man show), Love Letters, Incommunicado, King Lear (Utah Shakespearean Fest.), Mixed Emotions, Old Business, The Tempest (Utah Shakespearean Fest.), Substance of Five (San Diego Olde Globe).
PICTURES: Two for the Seesaw, The Couch, Harper, Inside Daisy Clover, Marnie, An American Dream, The Arrangement, The Lawyer, Mrs. Pollifax: Spy, Where Does It Hurt?, The Sting, The Front Page, Love and Death, The Big Bus, Silent Movie,

The One and Only, Seems Like Old Times, Playing for Keeps, Romero, Flesh Suitcase, Killer, Lover's Knot, My Giant, Beloved, Patch Adams, Brown's Requiem, Stuart Little, Dying on the Edge, The Master of Disguise, Freaky Friday.
TELEVISION: *Movies*: To Catch a Star, Moviola (Emmy nom.), Washington Behind Closed Doors, Aunt Mary, Better Late Than Never, King Crab, Have I Got a Christmas for You, Man in the Santa Claus Suit, I Never Sang For My Father, Get Smart Again!, Mrs. Delafield Wants to Marry (Emmy nom.), Love Bug II, Fox Hope. *Special*: The Sunset Gang. *Series*: Rhoda (Emmy nom.), Park Place, Foot in the Door, Under One Roof, Singer and Sons, Golden Girls, Feather and Father Gang. *Guest*: Police Story (Emmy nom.), Tales from the Hollywood Hills: The Closed Set, Ray Bradbury Theater (Emmy nom.).

GOULET, ROBERT
Singer, Actor. b. Lawrence, MA., Nov. 26, 1933. e. Edmonton; scholarship, Royal Conservatory of Music. Sang in choirs, appeared with numerous orchestras; disk jockey, CKUA, Edmonton; pub. rel., Rogo & Rove,Inc.
THEATRE: *NY*: Camelot (as Lancelot; Theatre World Award), The Happy Time (Tony Award, 1968), Camelot (as King Arthur; 1993 revival).
PICTURES: Gay Purr-ee (voice), Honeymoon Hotel, I'd Rather Be Rich, I Deal in Danger, Atlantic City, Beetlejuice, Scrooged, The Naked Gun 2 1/2: The Smell of Fear, Mr. Wrong, The Line King: Al Hirschfield, Toy Story 2 (voice), The Last Producer, G-Men From Hell, Recess: School's Out (voice), Broadway: The Golden Age by the Legends Who Were There.
TELEVISION: *Movie*: Based on an Untrue Story. *Series*: Robert Goulet Show, Blue Light. *Guest*: The Ed Sullivan Show, Garry Moore, The Enchanted Nutcracker, Omnibus, The Broadway of Lerner and Loewe, Rainbow of Stars, Judy Garland Show, Bob Hope Show, The Bell Telephone Hour, Granada-TV special (U.K.), Jack Benny, Dean Martin, Andy Williams, Jack Paar, Red Skelton, Hollywood Palace, Patty Duke Show, The Big Valley, Mission: Impossible, Police Woman, Cannon, Murder She Wrote, Mr. Belvedere, Fantasy Island, Matt Houston, Glitter, WKRP in Cincinnati, The Simpsons. *Pilot*: Make My Day. *Specials*: Brigadoon, Carousel, Kiss Me Kate.

GOWDY, CURT
Sportscaster. b. Green River, WY, July 31, 1919. Basketball star at U. of Wyoming. All-Conference member; graduated U. of Wyoming. 1942. Officer in U.S. Air Force WWII, then became sportscaster. Voted Sportscaster of the Year, 1967, Nat'l Assn. of Sportswriters Broadcasters. Best Sportscaster, Fame, 1967. Did play-by-play telecasts for 16 World Series, 7 Super Bowls, 12 Rose Bowls, 8 Orange Bowls, 18 NCAA Final 4 college basketball championships. In 1970 was the first individual from the field of sports to receive the George Foster Peabody Award. Hosted the American Sportsman outdoor TV show on ABC for 20 years. (Received 8 Emmy Awards). Inducted into the Sportscasters Hall of Fame in 1981, the Fishing Hall of Fame in 1982, and the Baseball Hall of Fame in 1984, Pro Football Hall of Fame in 1992.
PICTURES: The World of Sport Fishing, Heaven Can Wait, The Naked Gun: From the Files of Police Squad!, BASEketball, Frequency, Summer Catch.

GRADE, MICHAEL, C.B.E.
Executive. b. London, England, March 8, 1943. e. Stowe. Entered industry in 1966 as a theatrical agent with the Grade organisation. Early career as newspaper columnist, became an executive at London Weekend Television then Embassy Television in Hollywood. Joined BBC Television, 1983 as controller of BBC 1 and director of programmes (TV), 1986. Joined Channel 4 as chief executive, 1988-1997. Became chief executive of First Leisure Corporation plc, where he oversaw that company's restructuring in 1999. He then became chmn. of Pinewood-Shepperton Limited, the result of the merger between the two studios. Currently, non-exec. chairman of Hemscott plc, chairman of Octopus Publishing Group Limited and Pinewood Studios Holdings Limited; dir., Camelot Group plc and The New Millennium Experience Company Limited.

GRAFF, RICHARD B.
Executive. b. Milwaukee, WI, Nov. 9, 1924. e. U. of Illinois. Served U.S. Air Force; Universal Pictures 1946 to 1964 in Chicago, Detroit, Chicago and NY home office as asst. to genl. sales mgr.; 1964 joined National General in Los Angeles. 1967 became v.p. and general sales mgr. of National General Pictures, formed and operated company. 1968, exec. v.p. in charge of world-wide sales and marketing. 1968 made v.p. of parent company; v.p. general sales mgr. AIP in 1971; 1975, pres. Cine Artists Pictures; 1977, pres. Richard Graff Company Inc; 1983, pres. of domestic distribution, MGM/UA. 1987, pres., worldwide distribution, Weintraub Entertainment Group. 1990, president, The Richard Graff Company, Inc. Distribution consultant to Danjaq Inc., producers of James Bond films, both theatrically and all television worldwide.

GRAFF, TODD
Actor, Writer. b. New York, NY, Oct. 22, 1959. e. SUNY / Purchase.
THEATRE: *NY*: Baby (Tony nom., Theatre World Award), Birds of Paradise.
PICTURES: *Actor*: Sweet Lorraine (also composed songs), Five Corners, Dominick & Eugene, The Abyss, An Innocent Man, Opportunity Knocks, City of Hope, Death to Smoochy. *Writer*:

Used People, The Vanishing (also co-prod.), Fly by Night (also actor), Angie (also co-prod., cameo), The Beautician and the Beast, Camp (and dir.).

GRAHAM, HEATHER
Actress. b. Milwaukee, WI. Jan. 29, 1970.
PICTURES: License to Drive, Twins, Drugstore Cowboy, I Love You to Death, Shout, Guilty as Charged, Twin Peaks: Fire Walk With Me, Diggstown, Six Degrees of Separation, Even Cowgirls Get the Blues, The Ballad of Little Jo, Mrs. Parker and the Vicious Circle, Don't Do It, Terrified, Desert Winds, Swingers, Entertaining Angels: The Dorothy Day Story, Two Girls and a Guy, Boogie Nights, Nowhere, Scream 2, Committed, Bowfinger, Lost in Space, Austin Powers: The Spy Who Shagged Me, Kiss & Tell, Committed, Sidewalks of New York, When the Cat's Away, Alien Love Triangle, Killing Me Softly, From Hell, .45, Say It Isn't So, The Guru, Austin Powers in Goldmember, Hope Springs.
TELEVISION: Movies: Student Exchange, O Pioneers!. Series: Twin Peaks.

GRAHAM, LAUREN
Actress. b. Honolulu, Hawaii. March. 16, 1967.
PICTURES: Nightwatch, One True Thing, Confessions of a Sexist Pig, Dill Scallion, Lucky 13, Chasing Destiny, Sweet November, Bad Santa, Seeing Other People.
TELEVISION: Series: Good Company, Townies, Conrad Bloom, M.Y.O.B, Gilmore Girls (SAG nom.), Golden Globe nom.). Guest: Caroline in the City, 3rd Rock From the Sun, Law and Order,Seinfeld, News Radio, The Late Late Show with Craig Kilborn.

GRAMMER, KELSEY
Actor. b. St. Thomas, Virgin Islands, Feb. 20, 1955. e. Juilliard. Acting debut on tv in Another World. On B'way in Sunday in the Park With George. Supplied voice for Disney/Mickey Mouse short Runaway Brain.
PICTURES: Down Periscope, Star Trek: First Contact (cameo), Anastasia (voice), The Real Howard Spitz, Standing on Fishes, Toy Story 2 (voice), New Jersey Turnpikes, The Hand Behind the Mouse: The Ub Iwerks Story (narr.), 15 Minutes, Just Visiting, The Big Empty.
TELEVISION: Series: Cheers, Frasier (3 Emmy Awards, Golden Globe Award), Fired Up (exec. prod. only), Gary the Rat (voice, exec. prod.), In-Laws (exec. prod. only), The Simpsons (voice), Just Shoot Me. Movies: Dance 'Til Dawn, Beyond Suspicion, The Innocent, London Suite, The Pentagon Wars, Animal Farm (voice), Mr. St. Nick.

GRANATH, HERBERT A.
Executive. e. Fordham U. Started with ABC TV in sales, marketing and production. 1979, became v.p. of Capital Cities/ABC Video Enterprises Inc.; 1982-93, served as pres. of same; Oct. 1993, named pres. ABC Cable and International Broadcast Group, sr. v.p. Capital Cities/ABC Inc.

GRANET, BERT
Producer, Writer. b. New York, NY, July 10, 1910. e. Yale U. Sch. of Fine Arts (47 workshop). From 1936 author s.p. orig. & adapt. numerous pictures. Exec. prod.: Universal, 1967-69, CBS, Desilu Studios.
PICTURES: Quick Money, The Affairs of Annabel, Mr. Doodle Kicks Off, Laddie, A Girl a Guy and a Gob, My Favorite Wife, Bride by Mistake, Sing Your Way Home, Those Endearing Young Charms, The Locket, Do You Love Me?, The Marrying Kind, Berlin Express, The Torch, Scarface Mob.
TELEVISION: Desilu (1957-61), Twilight Zone (pilot), The Untouchables (pilot), Scarface Mob; Loretta Young Show (1955-56), Walter Winchell File 1956-57, Lucille Ball-Desi Arnaz Show 1957-60, Westinghouse Desilu Playhouse, The Great Adventure.
(d. Nov. 15, 2002)

GRANGER, FARLEY
Actor. b. San Jose, CA, July 1, 1925. e. Hollywood. U.S. Armed Forces 1944-46. Joined Eva Le Gallienne's National Rep. Co. in 1960s (The Sea Gull, The Crucible, Ring Round the Moon).
PICTURES: The North Star (debut, 1943), The Purple Heart, Rope, Enchantment, The Live By Night, Roseanna McCoy, Side Street, Our Very Own, Edge of Doom, Strangers on a Train, Behave Yourself, I Want You, O. Henry's Full House, Hans Christian Andersen, Story of Three Loves, Small Town Girl, Senso, Naked Street, Girl in the Red Velvet Swing, Rogue's Gallery, Something Creeping in the Dark, They Call Me Trinity, Replica of a Crime, Amuk, The Slasher, The Redhead with the Translucent Skin, Kill Me My Love, Planet Venus, Night Flight From Moscow, Man Called Neon, Arnold, Savage Lady, The Co-ed Murders, Deathmask, The Prowler, The Imagemaker, Very Close Quarters, The Whoopee Boys, The Celluloid Closet, The Next Big Thing, Goldwyn (documentary), Broadway: The Golden Age by the Legends Who Were There.
TELEVISION: Movies: The Challengers, The Lives of Jenny Dolan, Widow, Black Beauty, Visconti (documentary). Series: One Life to Live (1976-7), As the World Turns (1986-8). Guest: Playhouse of Stars, U.S. Steel Hour, Producer's Showcase, Climax, Ford Theatre, Playhouse 90, 20th Century Fox Hour, Robert Montgomery Presents, Arthur Murray Dance Party, Wagon Train, Masquerade Party, Kojak, 6 Million Dollar Man, Ellery Queen.

GRANT, DAVID MARSHALL
Actor. b. Westport, CT, June 21, 1955. e. Yale School of Drama.
THEATRE: NY: Sganarelle, Table Settings, The Tempest, Bent, The Survivor, Making Movies, Angels in America: Millenium Approaches/Perestroika, Three Sisters. Regional: Bent (also dir.), Once in a Lifetime, Lake Boat, Free and Clear, True West, The Wager, Rat in the Skull, Snakebit (author), The End of the Day.
PICTURES: French Postcards (debut, 1979), Happy Birthday Gemini, The End of August, American Flyers, The Big Town, Bat 21, Air America, Strictly Business, Forever Young, The Rock, The Chamber, Remembering Sex, People I Know.
TELEVISION: Movies: Kent State, Legs, Sessions, Dallas: The Early Years, What She Doesn't Know, Citizen Cohn, Through the Eyes of a Killer, Noriega: God's Favorite, Jenifer (s.p. only). Special: A Doonesbury Special (voice). Pilot: Graham. Host: The Legend of Billy the Kid, Night Sins. Series: thirtysomething.

GRANT, HUGH
Actor. b. London, England, Sept. 9, 1960. e. New Coll., Oxford U. Acted with OUDS before landing role in Oxford Film Foundation's Privileged. Acted at Nottingham Playhouse and formed revue group, The Jockeys of Norfolk.
PICTURES: Privileged (debut, 1982), Maurice, White Mischief, The Lair of the White Worm, The Dawning, Remando al Viento (Rowing With the Wind), Bengali Night, Impromptu, Crossing the Line, The Remains of the Day, Night Train to Venice, Sirens, Four Weddings and a Funeral (BAFTA & Golden Globe Awards), Bitter Moon, The Englishman Who Went Up a Hill But Came Down a Mountain, Nine Months, An Awfully Big Adventure, Restoration, Sense and Sensibility, Extreme Measures (also prod.), Notting Hill (Golden Globe nom.), Mickey Blue-Eyes, Small Time Crooks, Bridget Jones's Diary, About a Boy, Two Weeks Notice, Love Actually.
TELEVISION: Movies/Specials: The Detective, Handel: Honour, Profit and Pleasure, Jenny's War, The Lady and the Highwayman, Champagne Charlie, 'Til We Meet Again, Our Sons (U.S.), The Changeling. Mini-Series: The Last Place in Earth. Series: The Demon Lover, Ladies in Charge.

GRANT, LEE
Actress. r.n. Lyova Rosenthal. b. New York, NY, Oct. 31, 1931. m. producer Joseph Feury. Daughter is actress Dinah Manoff. At 4 was member of Metropolitan Opera Company; played princess in L'Orocolo. Member of the American Ballet at 11. e. Juilliard Sch. of Music, studied voice, violin and dance. At 18 with road co. Oklahoma as understudy. Acting debut: Joy to the World.
THEATRE: Acted in a series of one-acters at ANTA with Henry Fonda. Detective Story (Critics Circle Award, 1949), Lo and Behold, A Hole in the Head, Wedding Breakfast; road co. Two for the Seesaw, The Captains and the Kings; toured with Electra, Silk Stockings, St. Joan, Arms and the Man, The Maids (Obie Award), Prisoner of Second Avenue.
PICTURES: Detective Story (debut, 1951; Acad. Award nom.), Storm Fear, Middle of the Night, Affair of the Skin, The Balcony, Terror in the City, Divorce American Style, In the Heat of the Night, Valley of the Dolls, Buona Sera Mrs. Campbell, The Big Bounce, Marooned, The Landlord (Acad. Award nom.), There Was a Crooked Man, Plaza Suite, Portnoy's Complaint, The Internecine Project, Shampoo (Academy Award, best supporting actress, 1975), Voyage of the Damned (Acad. Award nom.), Airport '77, Damien: Omen II, The Swarm, The Mafu Cage, When You Comin' Back Red Ryder, Little Miss Marker, Charlie Chan and the Curse of the Dragon Queen, Visiting Hours, Teachers, The Big Town, Defending Your Life, Under Heat, It's My Party, The Substance of Fire, Poor Liza, Dr. T & the Women, Mulholland Dr. Dir.: Tell Me a Riddle, Willmar Eight, Staying Together.
TELEVISION: Movies: Night Slaves, The Love Song of Bernard Kempenski, BBC's The Respectful Prostitute, The Neon Ceiling (Emmy Award, 1971), Ransom for a Dead Man, Lt. Schuster's Wife, Partners in Crime, What Are Best Friends For?, Perilous Voyage, The Spell, Million Dollar Face, For Ladies Only, Thou Shalt Not Kill, Bare Essence, Will There Really Be A Morning?, The Hijacking of the Achille Lauro, She Said No, Something to Live For: The Alison Gertz Story, In My Daughter's Name, Citizen Cohn. Mini-Series: Backstairs at the White House, Mussolini--The Untold Story. Special: Plaza Suite. Series: Search for Tomorrow (1953-4), Peyton Place (Emmy Award, 1965), Fay. Guest: Studio One, The Kraft Theatre, Slattery's People, The Fugitive, Ben Casey, The Nurses, The Defenders, East Side/West Side, One Day at a Time, Bob Hope Show (Emmy nom.). Director: Nobody's Child, Shape of Things, When Women Kill, A Matter of Sex, Down and Out in America, No Place Like Home, Following Her Heart, "Intimate Portrait" series.

GRANT, RICHARD E.
Actor. b. Mbabane, Swaziland, May 5, 1957. e. Cape Town U., South Africa (combined English and drama course). Co-founded multi-racial Troupe Theatre Company with fellow former students and members of Athol Fugard and Yvonne Bryceland's Space Theatre, acting in and directing contemporary and classic plays. Moved to London 1982 where performed in fringe and rep. theater. Nominated most promising newcomer in Plays and Players, 1985, for Tramway Road.

PICTURES: Withnail and I, Hidden City, How to Get Ahead in Advertising, Killing Dad, Mountains of the Moon, Henry and June, Warlock, L.A. Story, Hudson Hawk, The Player, Bram Stoker's Dracula, Franz Kafka's It's A Wonderful Life (short), The Age of Innocence, Ready to Wear (Pret-a-Porter), Jack and Sarah, Twelfth Night, The Portrait of a Lady, Spice World, Keep the Aspidstra Flying, The Serpent's Kiss, St. Ives, Cash in Hand, The Match, The Little Vampire, William Shakespeare, Cocozza's Way, Hildegarde, Gosford Park, Monsieur N. Bright Young Things.
TELEVISION: Series: Sweet Sixteen, Captain Star (voice), Posh Nosh. Movies/Specials: Honest Decent and True, Lizzie's Pictures, Codename Kyril, Thieves in the Night (also released theatrically), Here Is the News, Suddenly Last Summer, Hard Times, Bed, Karaoke, Cold Lazarus, The Scarlet Pimpernel, The Miracle Maker (voice) Moonshot-The Spirit of '69 (voice), Trial & Tribulation III, The Scarlet Pimpernel Meets Madame Guillotine, The Scarlet Pimpernel and the Kidnapped King, A Christmas Carol, Victoria's Secrets, The Miracle Maker, Victoria Wood with All the Trimmings, The Scarlet Pimpernel: A Good Name, We Know Where You Live, Case of Evil, The Hound of the Baskervilles, The 100 Greatest Movie Stars (documentary, narrator).

GRANT, SUSANNAH
Writer b. New York, NY, January 4, 1963.
PICTURES: Pocahontas, Ever After, Erin Brockovich, 28 Days, Unfaithful.
TELEVISION: Series: Party of Five (prod. & dir.).

GRASSHOFF, ALEX
Director. b. Boston, MA, Dec. 10, 1930. e. USC. 3 Acad. Award nominations for feature documentaries; Really Big Family; Journey to the Outer Limits; Young Americans (Acad. Award, 1968).
PICTURES: Billions For Boris, J.D. and the Salt Flat Kid, The Last Dinosaur, The Jailbreakers.
TELEVISION: Movies: The Wave (short), Backwards: The Riddle of Dyslexia, I Want to Go Home. Series: The Rockford Files, Toma, Chips, Night Stalker, Barbary Coast, Movin' On. Specials: The Wave (Emmy Award), Future Shock (1973 Cannes Film Fest. Awards), Frank Sinatra, Family and Friends.

GRASSO, MARY ANN
Executive. b. Rome, NY, Nov. 3, 1952. e. U. of Calif., Riverside, B.A. art history, 1973; U. of Oregon, Eugene, Master of Library Science, 1974. Dir., Warner Research Collection, 1975-85; mgr., CBS-TV, docu-drama, 1985-88; Instructor 1980-88 UCLA Extension, American Film Institute. v.p. & exec. dir. National Association of Theater Owners, 1988-present. Theatre Arts instructor UCLA 1980-85. Amer. Film Inst., LA, 1985-88. Member: Acad. Motion Picture Arts & Sciences, Foundation of the Motion Picture Pioneers, American Society of Association Executives, Phi Beta Kappa. Woman of Achievement, BPOA Awarded 1984, Friend of Tripod 1999. TV credits: The Scarlet O'Hara Wars, This Year's Blonde, The Silent Lovers, A Bunnies Tale, Embassy. Member: NATO (VP); Business and Prof'l. Women's Assoc. ;AMPAS; Foundation Motion Picture Pioneer; Commissioner Burbank Heritage Commission; Board of Directors Burbank Historical Society; Board Center of Film and Television Design.

GRAVES, PETER
Actor. r.n. Peter Aurness. b. Minneapolis, MN, March 18, 1926. e. U. of Minnesota. Brother of actor James Arness. Played with bands, radio announcer, while at school; U.S. Air Force 2 yrs.; summer stock appearances.
PICTURES: Rogue River (debut, 1950), Fort Defiance, Red Planet Mars, Stalag 17, East of Sumatra, Beneath the 12-Mile Reef, Killers From Space, The Raid, Black Tuesday, Wichita, Long Gray Line, Night of the Hunter, Naked Street, Fort Yuma, Court Martial of Billy Mitchell, It Conquered the World, The Beginning of the End, Death in Small Doses, Poor White Trash (Bayou), Wolf Larsen, A Rage to Live, Texas Across the River, Valley of Mystery, The Ballad of Josie, Sergeant Ryker, The Five Man Army, Sidecar Racers, Parts: The Clonus Horror, Survival Run, Airplane!, Savannah Smiles, Airplane II: The Sequel, Number One With a Bullet, Addams Family Values, House on Haunted Hill, Men In Black II.
TELEVISION: Movies: A Call to Danger, The President's Plane is Missing, Scream of the Wolf, The Underground Man, Where Have All the People Gone?, Dead Man on the Run, SST-Death Flight, The Rebels, Death on the Freeway, The Memory of Eva Ryker, 300 Miles for Stephanie, If It's Tuesday It Still Must Be Belgium, These Old Broads. Mini-Series: Winds of War, War and Remembrance. Series: Fury, Whiplash, Court-Martial, Mission Impossible, New Mission: Impossible, With You in Spirit. Host/narrator: Discover! The World of Science, A&E Biography series narrator, Tarzan the Legacy of Edgar Rice Burroughs.

GRAVES, RUPERT
Actor. b. Weston-Super-Mare, England, June 30, 1963. Before film debut worked as a clown with the Delta travelling circus in England.
THEATRE: The Killing of Mr. Toad, 'Tis Pity She's a Whore, St. Ursula's in Danger, Sufficient Carbohydrates, Amadeus, Torch Song Trilogy, Candida, Pitchfork Disney, History of Tom Jones, A Madhouse in Goa, A Midsummer Night's Dream, Design for Living.
PICTURES: A Room with a View, Maurice, A Handful of Dust,

The Children, Where Angels Fear to Tread, Damage, The Madness of King George, The Innocent Sleep, Different for Girls, Mrs. Dalloway, Bent, The Revengers Comedies, Dreaming of Joseph Lees, All My Loved Ones, Room to Rent, Extreme Ops.
TELEVISION: Vice Versa, All for Love, A Life of Puccini, Fortunes of War, The Plot to Kill Hitler, The Sheltering Desert, Union Matters, Starting Out, Royal Celebration, Good and Bad at Games, Inspector Morse, Doomsday Gun, Take a Girl Like You, The Forsyth Saga, Charles II.

GRAY, COLEEN
Actress. r.n. Doris Jensen. b. Staplehurst, NB, Oct. 23, 1922. e. Hamline U., B.A. summa cum laude, 1943, Actor's Lab. m. Fritz Zeiser. Member: Nat'l Collegiate Players, Kappa Phi, a capella choir, little theatres, 1943-44.
PICTURES: State Fair (debut, 1945), Kiss of Death, Nightmare Alley, Fury at Furnace Creek, Red River, Sleeping City, Riding High, Father Is a Bachelor, Apache Drums, Lucky Nick Cain, Models Inc., Kansas City Confidential, Sabre Jet, Arrow in the Dust, The Fake, The Vanquished, Las Vegas Shakedown, Twinkle in God's Eye, Tennessee's Partner, The Killing, Wild Dakotas, Death of a Scoundrel, Frontier Gambler, Black Whip, Star in the Dust, The Vampire, Hell's Five Hours, Copper Sky, Johnny Rocco, The Leech Woman, The Phantom Planet, Town Tamer, P.J., The Late Liz, Cry from the Mountain.
TELEVISION: Movies: Ellery Queen: Don't Look Behind You, The Best Place to Be. Series: Window on Main Street, Days of Our Lives, (1966-67), Bright Promise (1968-72). Guest: Family Affair, Ironside, Bonanza, Judd for the Defense, Name of the Game, The FBI, The Bold Ones, World Premiere, Mannix, Sixth Sense, McCloud, Tales from the Dark Side.

GRAY, DULCIE
C.B.E., F.L.S., F.R.S.A. Actress b. Malaya, Nov. 20, 1919. e. Webber Douglas Sch. Stage debut 1939, Aberdeen, Hay Fever, Author: Love Affair (play), 18 detective novels, book of short stories. 8 radio plays; co-author with husband Michael Denison, The Actor and His World; Butterflies on My Mind, The Glanville Women, Anna Starr; Mirror Image, Looking Forward Looking Back.
THEATRE: Over 50 West End plays including Little Foxes, Brighton Rock, Dear Ruth, Rain on the Just, Candida, An Ideal Husband (1965, 1962, 1996 London & NY), Where Angels Fear to Tread, Heartbreak House, On Approval, Happy Family, No. 10, Out of the Question, Village Wooing, Wild Duck, At The End of the Day, The Pay Off, A Murder Has Been Announced, Bedroom Farce, A Coat of Varnish, School for Scandal, The Living Room, Tartuffe, Cavell, Pygmalion, The School Mistress (Chicester), Two of a Kind.
PICTURES: Two Thousand Women, A Man About the House, Mine Own Executioner, My Brother Jonathan, The Glass Mountain, They Were Sisters Wanted for Murder, The Franchise Affair, Angels One Five, There Was a Young Lady, A Man Could Get Killed, The Trail of the Pink Panther, The Curse of the Pink Panther, The Black Crow.
TELEVISION: Milestones, The Will, Crime Passionel, Art and Opportunity, Fish in the Family, The Governess, What the Public Wants, Lesson in Love, The Happy McBaines, Winter Cruise, The Letter, Tribute to Maugham, Virtue, Beautiful Forever, East Lynne, Unexpectedly Vacant, The Importance of Being Earnest, This Is Your Life (1977; and with Michael Denison, 1995), Crown Court, Making Faces, Read All About It, The Voysey Inheritance, Life After Death, The Pink Pearl, Britain in the Thirties, Rumpole (The Old Boy Net.), Cold Warrior, Hook, Line and Sinker, Howard's Way (series, 6 yrs.), Three Up, Two Down, The Time and the Place.

GRAY, LINDA
Actress. b. Santa Monica, CA, Sept. 12, 1940.
PICTURES: Under the Yum Yum Tree, Palm Springs Weekend, Dogs, Fun With Dick and Jane, Oscar, Star of Jaipur.
TELEVISION: Movies: The Big Ripoff, Murder in Peyton Place, The Grass is Always Greener Over the Septic Tank, Two Worlds of Jennie Logan, Haywire, The Wild and the Fire, Not in Front of the Children, The Entertainers, Highway Heartbreaker, Moment of Truth: Why My Daughter?, Bonanza: The Return, To My Daughter with Love, Accidental Meeting, Moment of Truth: Broken Pledges, When the Cradle Falls, Dallas: War of the Ewings, Doing Dallas, When Shoulderpads Ruled the World, After Dallas, Intimate Portrait: Linda Gray. Series: Dallas, Melrose Place, Models Inc. Guest: Melrose Place, Touched By an Angel.

GRAY, SPALDING
Performance artist, Actor, Writer. b. Barrington, RI, June 5, 1941. Began career as actor in 1965 at Alley Theater, Housten, then off-B'way in Tom Paine at LaMama Co. In 1969 joined the Wooster Group, experimental performance group. Has written and performed autobiographical monologues (Three Places in Rhode Island, Sex and Death to the Age 14, Swimming to Cambodia, Monster in a Box, Gray's Anatomy) throughout U.S, Europe and Australia. Taught theatre workshops for adults and children and is recipient of Guggenheim fellowship. Artist in residence Mark Taper Forum, 1986-87. B'way debut: Our Town (1988).
PICTURES: Actor: Almost You, The Killing Fields, Hard Choices, True Stories, Swimming to Cambodia (also s.p.), Stars and Bars, Clara's Heart, Beaches, Heavy Petting, Straight Talk, Monster in a Box (also s.p.), The Pickle, King of the Hill, Twenty Bucks, The Paper, Bad Company, Beyond Rangoon, Drunks, Diabolique, Gray's Anatomy, Bliss, Coming Soon, Jimmy Zip, Revolution #9, Julie Johnson, How High, Kate & Leopold.

TELEVISION: *Special*: Terrors of Pleasure (HBO). *Movies*: The Image, To Save a Child, Zelda. *Guest*: The Nanny, Missing Links.

GRAY, THOMAS K.
Executive, producer. b. New York City, N. Y., July 1, 1945. e. U. of Arizona, B.A., post grad work at American Graduate School of Int'l Management, Phoenix. Began career as management trainee with United Atists film exchange in Spain, 1970, and year later became managing director, UA, Chile. Also managing director for UA, New Zealand, 1972; Columbia, 1973; South and East Africa, 1974. Joined Cinema Int'l Corp., London, as exec. assist. to co-chairman, 1974, and moved up to managing director of CIC/Warner, South Africa, 1976. Returned to UA as vice pres. Far East, Latin America, Africa and Australia, 1977. Joined Golden Communications Overseas Ltd., London, as vice pres. foreign sales, 1980. With Golden Harvest Films, Inc. since 1984 as sr. vice. pres., production. Executive in charge of prod. for Golden Harvest features: Flying, The Protector, China O'Brien, China O'Brien II, A Show of Force, Teenage Mutant Ninja Turtles, Best of Martial Arts (prod.), Teenage Mutant Ninja Turtles II: Secret of the Ooze (prod.), Teenage Mutant Ninja Turtles III. 1992, pres. and CEO of Rim Film Distribution Inc.

GRAYSON, KATHRYN
Actress, Singer. r.n. Zelma Hedrick. b. Winston-Salem, NC, Feb. 9, 1923. e. St. Louis schools.
THEATRE: Camelot, Rosalinda, Merry Widow, Kiss Me Kate, Showboat.
PICTURES: Andy Hardy's Private Secretary (debut, 1941), The Vanishing Virginian, Rio Rita, Seven Sweethearts, Thousands Cheer; Anchors Aweigh, Ziegfeld Follies, Two Sisters from Boston, Till the Clouds Roll By, It Happened in Brooklyn, The Kissing Bandit, That Midnight Kiss, The Toast of New Orleans, Grounds for Marriage, Show Boat, Lovely to Look At, The Desert Song, So This Is Love, Kiss Me Kate, The Vagabond King, A Century of Cinema, Too Damn Hot (video short).
TELEVISION: *Guest*: GE Theatre (Emmy nom.), Playhouse 90, Lux Playhouse, Murder She Wrote. *Special*: Die Fliedermaus.

GRAZER, BRIAN
Producer. b. Los Angeles, CA, July 12, 1951. e. U. of Southern California. Started as legal intern at Warner Bros.; later script reader (for Brut/Faberge) & talent agent. Joined Edgar J. Scherick-Daniel Blatt Co.; then with Ron Howard as partner in Imagine Films Entertainment. Received NATO/ShoWest Producer of the Year Award, 1992.
PICTURES: Night Shift, Splash (also co-story), Real Genius, Spies Like Us, Armed and Dangerous (also co-story), Like Father Like Son, Vibes, The 'burbs, Parenthood, Cry-Baby (co-exec. prod.), Kindergarten Cop, The Doors (co-exec. prod.), Closet Land (co-exec. prod.), Backdraft (exec. prod.), My Girl, Far and Away, Housesitter, Boomerang, CB4 (co-exec. prod.), Cop and a Half, For Love or Money, My Girl 2, Greedy, The Paper, The Cowboy Way, Apollo 13, Fear, Sgt. Bilko, The Nutty Professor, Ransom, Inventing the Abbotts, Liar Liar, Mercury Rising, Psycho, Life, Into thin Air, How to Eat Fried Worms, Edtv, Bowfinger, Sprockets, The Nutty Professor II, How the Grinch Stole Christmas, A Beautiful Mind (Acad. Award), D-Tox, Undercover Brother, Blue Crush, Stealing Harvard, 8 Mile, Curious George, Intolerable Cruelty, The Incredible Shrinking Man, The Cat in the Hat, The Missing, The Alamo.
TELEVISION: *Movies*: Zuma Beach, Thou Shalt Not Commit Adultery, Splash Too, Student Affairs. *Series* (executive prod.): Shadow Chasers, Take Five, Ohara, Parenthood, Hiller & Diller, Felicity, Sports Night, The PJs, Wonderland, The Beast, 24, BS*. *Special*: Poison (prod.), From Earth to the Moon.

GREATREX, RICHARD
Cinematographer.
PICTURES: Forbidden Sun, For Queen and Country, War Requiem, A Foreign Field, Deadly Advice, Blue Juice, Mrs. Brown, Shakespeare in Love (Acad. Award nom.), Where the Heart Is, A Knight's Tale, Happy Now, I Capture the Castle, Connie and Carla.
TELEVISION: *Movies*: Aderyn Papur...and Pigs Might Fly, Truth or Dare, The Woman in White, Dalziel and Pascoe: Exit Lines, Tess of the D'Urbervilles, Getting Hurt, Warriors, The Last of the Blonde Bombshells, Sons and Lovers.

GREEN, ADOLPH
Writer, Actor. b. New York, NY, Dec. 2, 1915. m. actress-singer Phyllis Newman. Began career in the cabaret act The Revuers with partner Betty Comden and Judy Holliday (1944).
THEATER: Wrote book, sketches and/or lyrics for many Broadway shows including: On the Town (also actor), Billion Dollar Baby, Bonanza Bound! (also actor), Two on the Aisle, Wonderful Town (Tony Award for lyrics, 1953), Peter Pan (Mary Martin), Say Darling, Bells Are Ringing, A Party with Comden and Green (1959 & 1977), Do Re Mi, Subways Are For Sleeping, Fade Out Fade In, Halleuljah Baby (Tony Awards for lyrics & best musical, 1968), Applause (Tony Award for book, 1970), Lorelei: Or Gentlemen Still Prefer Blondes (new lyrics), By Bernstein (book), On the Twentieth Century (Tony Awards for book & lyrics, 1978), A Doll's Life, The Will Rogers Follies (Tony Award for lyrics, 1991).
PICTURES: *Writer* (with Betty Comden): Good News, On the

Town, The Barkleys of Broadway, Take Me Out to the Ball Game (co-lyrics), Singin' in the Rain, The Band Wagon, It's Always Fair Weather, Auntie Mame, What a Way to Go. *Actor*: Greenwich Village, Simon, My Favorite Year, Lily in Love, Garbo Talks, I Want to Go Home, The Substance of Fire.
(d. Oct. 23, 2002)

GREEN, GUY
Director. b. Somerset, Eng. Nov. 5, 1913. Joined Film Advertising Co. as projectionist & camera asst. 1933; camera asst., Elstree Studios (BIP) 1935; started as camera operator on films including One of Our Aircraft Is Missing, In Which We Serve, This Happy Breed. 1944: Director of Photography; Dir of Allied Film Makers Ltd.
PICTURES: *Dir. of Photography*: The Way Ahead, Great Expectations (Acad. Award, 1947), Oliver Twist, Captain Horatio Hornblower, I Am a Camera. *Director*: River Beat (debut, 1954), Portrait of Alison, Tears for Simon, House of Secrets, The Snorkel, Desert Patrol (Sea of Sand), The Angry Silence, The Mark, Light in the Piazza, Diamond Head, A Patch of Blue (also co-exec. prod., s.p.), Pretty Polly (A Matter of Innocence), The Magus, A Walk in the Spring Rain (also co-exec. prod.), Luther, Once Is Not Enough, The Devil's Advocate (1978).
TELEVISION: (U.S.) Incredible Journey of Dr. Meg Laurel; Isabel's Choice; Jennifer: A Woman's Story; Arthur Hailey's Strong Medicine, Jimmy B. and Andre, Inmates.

GREEN, JACK N.
Cinematographer. b. San Francisco, Nov. 18, 1946. Started as camera operator for Bruce Surtees.
PICTURES: *Camera operator*: Fighting Mad, Firefox, Honky Tonk Man, Risky Business, Sudden Impact, Tightrope, Beverly Hills Cop, City Heat, Pale Rider, Ratboy. *Cinematographer*: Heartbreak Ridge, Like Father Like Son, The Dead Pool, Bird, Pink Cadillac, Race for Glory, White Hunter Black Heart, The Rookie, Deceived, Unforgiven, Rookie of the Year, A Perfect World, Bad Company, The Bridges of Madison County, The Net, The Amazing Panda Adventure, Twister, Speed 2: Cruise Control, Midnight in the Garden of Good and Evil, True Crime, Girl Interrupted, Space Cowboys, Pretty When You Cry, Golden Dreams, Wounded, Against the Ropes, Secondhand Lions, Fifty First Kisses.

GREEN, MALCOLM C.
Theatre Executive. b. Boston, MA, Mar. 1, 1925. e. Harvard Coll. Began career as asst. mgr., Translux Theatre, Boston & Revere Theatre, Revere, MA. Treas., Interstate Theatres, 1959-64. Film Buyer, Interstate, 1959-72. Formed Theatre Management Services in 1972 with H. Rifkin and P. Lowe and Cinema Centers Corp. with Rifkin and Lowe families in 1973. Treas., Cinema Center, & pres., Theatre Mgmt. Services. Cinema Center grew to 116 theatres in 6 Northeast states, sold to Hoyts Cinemas Corp., 1986. Sr. v.p., Hoyts Cinemas Corp. 1986-89. Pres., Theatre Owners of New England, 1964-65; chmn bd., 1965-69; treas., 1970-84. Pres., NATO, 1986-88, Chmn Bd, 1988-90. Dir., Natl. Assoc. Theatre Owners. Chmn., NATO of New York State. Director, Vision Foundation. Dir., The Lyric Stage, Boston 1990-94; dir. & v.p., New Hampshire Music Festival, 1988-1996.

GREEN, SETH
Actor. b. Philadelphia, PA, Feb. 8, 1974.
PICTURES: The Hotel New Hampshire, Willy/Milly, Radio Days, Can't Buy Me Love, My Stepmother is an Alien, Big Business, Pump Up the Volume, Ticks, The Double 0 Kid, Airborne, White Man's Burden, To Gillian on Her 37th Birthday, Austin Powers: International Man of Mystery, Enemy of the State, The Attic Expeditions, Can't Hardly Wait, Austin Powers: The Spy Who Shagged Me, Stonebrook, Idle Hands, The Attic Expeditions, The Trumpet of the Swan, Knockaround Guys, Diary of a Mad Freshman, Rat Race, Josie and the Pussycats, America's Sweethearts, Knockaround Guys, Rock Star 101, Rat Race, Austin Powers in Goldmember, Party Monster, The Italian Job, Scooby-Doo 2: Monsters Unleashed.
TELEVISION: *Movies*: Stephen King's It, Our Shining Moment, Arcade, The Day My Parents Ran Away. *Series*: Good & Evil, The Byrds of Paradise, Buffy the Vampire Slayer, Temporarily Yours, Batman Beyond (voice), Family Guy (voice), Greg the Bunny. *Guest*: Amazing Stories, Life Goes On, The Wonder Years, Beverly Hills 90210, The X Files, SeaQuest DSV, Mad About You, The Drew Carey Show, Angel, Greg the Bunny.

GREENAWAY, PETER
Director, Writer. b. Newport, Wales, Apr. 5, 1942. Trained as a painter, first exhibition was at Lord's Gallery in 1964. Started making short films and documentaries in 1966, including: A Walk Through H, The Falls, Act of God, Vertical Features Remake. Directorial feature debut in 1982. Author of numerous books including, 100 Objects to Represent the World, The Physical Self, Les Bruits des Nuages.
PICTURES: The Draughtsman's Contract, A Zed and Two Noughts, The Belly of an Architect, Drowning By Numbers, The Cook The Thief His Wife and Her Lover, Prospero's Books, The Baby of Macon, The Pillow Book (also ed.), The Bridge, Death of a Composer (also act.), 8 1/2 Women, The Death of a Composer: Rosa, a Horse Drama, The Man in the Bath, The

Tulse Luper Suitcases.
TELEVISION: Death in the Seine, series of 9 Cantos from Dante's Inferno in collaboration with painter Tom Phillips, M Is for Man Music Mozart, Darwin.

GREENE, DAVID
Director, Writer. b. Manchester, Eng., Feb. 22, 1921. Early career as actor. To U.S. with Shakespeare company early 1950's; remained to direct TV in Canada, New York and Hollywood.
PICTURES: The Shuttered Room, Sebastian, The Strange Affair, I Start Counting, Godspell, Gray Lady Down, London Conspiracy, Hard Country (prod., dir.).
TELEVISION: The Defenders. *Movies:* The People Next Door, Mdame Sin, Count of Monte Cristo, Friendly Fire, The Trial of Lee Harvey Oswald, A Vacation in Hell, The Choice, World War III, Rehearsal For Murder, Take Your Best Shot, Ghost Dancing, Prototype, Sweet Revenge, The Guardian, Fatal Vision (Emmy nom.), Guilty Conscience, This Child Is Mine, Vanishing Act, Miles to Go, Circle of Violence, The Betty Ford Story, After the Promise; Inherit the Wind, Liberace: Behind the Music, Red Earth, White Earth; The Penthouse (dir., exec. prod.), Small Sacrifices (Peabody Award), Bella Mafia, others.
(d. April 7, 2003)

GREENE, ELLEN
Actress, Singer. b. Brooklyn, NY, Feb. 22, 1950. e. Ryder Coll. After coll. joined musical road show. Appeared in cabaret act at The Brothers & the Sisters Club and Reno Sweeney's, NY. Off-B'way debut, Rachel Lily Rosenbloom. B'way in the The Little Prince and The Aviator. With NY Shakespeare Fest. in In the Boom Boom Room, The Sorrows of Steven, The Threepenny Opera (Tony nom.). Film debut Next Stop, Greenwich Village (1976). Off B'way co-starred in musical Little Shop of Horrors 1982, repeated role in film. Also Off-B'way in Weird Romance. L.A. stage: David's Mother.
PICTURES: Next Stop Greenwich Village (debut, 1976), I'm Dancing as Fast as I Can, Little Shop of Horrors, Me and Him, Talk Radio, Pump Up the Volume, Stepping Out, Rock a Doodle (voice), Fathers and Sons, Naked Gun 33 1/3: The Final Insult, Wagons East!, The Professional, A Journal of Murder, Jaded, One Fine Day, States of Control, Alex in Wonder, The Cooler, Love Object..
TELEVISION: *Special:* Rock Follies. *Movie:* Glory Glory. *Mini-Series:* Seventh Avenue. Pilot: Road Show.

GREENE, GRAHAM
Actor. b. Six Nations Reserve, Ontario, Canada, June 22, 1952. Member of the Oneida tribe. First show business job as audio technician for several rock bands. Began acting in theatre in England.
THEATRE: Diary of a Crazy Boy, Coming Through Slaughter, Crackwalker, Jessica, Dry Lips Oughta Move to Kapuskasing.
PICTURES: Running Brave, Revolution, Powwow Highway, Dances With Wolves (Acad. Award nom.), Thunderheart, Clearcut, Savage Land, Rain Without Thunder, Benefit of the Doubt, Maverick, North, Camilla, Die Hard With a Vengeance, Sabotage, The Pathfinder, Dead Innocent, Song of Hiawatha, Wounded, The Education of the Little Tree, Shattered Image, Bad Money, Grey Owl, The Green Mile, Desire, Christmas in the Clouds, Lost and Delirious, Skins, Snow Dogs, Duct Tape Forever.
TELEVISION: *U.S.: Movies:* Unnatural Causes, The Last of His Tribe, Cooperstown, Huck and the King of Hearts, Rugged Gold, The Pathfinder, Stranger in Town, Wolf Lake, The New Beachcombers, Big Spender. *Series:* Northern Exposure, 500 Nations, Cover Me: Based on the True Life of an FBI Family. *Guest:* Adderly, L.A. Law. *Canada: Series:* 9B, Spirit Bay. *Movies:* Murder Sees the Light, The Great Detective, Street Legal.

GREENHUT, ROBERT
Producer. b. New York, NY. e. Univ. of Miami. Began career as prod. asst. on Arthur Hiller's The Tiger Makes Out, 1967. Worked as prod. manager and asst. director on such films as Pretty Poison, The Night They Raided Minsky's, Where's Poppa?, The Owl and the Pussycat, Husbands, Born to Win, Panic in Needle Park, The Last of the Red Hot Lovers. Received Crystal Apple from city of NY and Eastman Kodak Award for lifetime achievement.
PICTURES: *Prod./assoc. prod./exec. prod.:* Huckleberry Finn, Lenny, Dog Day Afternoon, The Front, Annie Hall, Interiors, Hair, Manhattan, Stardust Memories, Arthur, A Midsummer Night's Sex Comedy, The King of Comedy, Zelig, Broadway Danny Rose, The Purple Rose of Cairo, Hannah and Her Sisters, Heartburn, Radio Days, September, Big, Another Woman, Working Girl, New York Stories, Crimes and Misdemeanors, Quick Change, Postcards From the Edge, Alice, Regarding Henry, Shadows and Fog, A League of Their Own, Husbands and Wives, Manhattan Murder Mystery, Renaissance Man, Wolf, Bullets Over Broadway, Mighty Aphrodite, Everyone Says I Love You, The Preacher's Wife, Mom's On the Roof, With Friends Like These, Siegfried and Roy: The Magic Box, White River Kid, Company Man, Seabiscuit (production exec.), Constellation, The Wedding Contract, Stateside.
TELEVISION: *Movie:* Don't Drink the Water.

GREENSPAN, ALAN
Producer.
PICTURES: *Exec. Prod.:* Photographing Fairies, Donnie Brasco, Best Laid Plans, High Fidelity, My Little Eye, Bookies, Adrenaline (assoc. prod.), Fever Pitch (prod.).

GREENWALD, ROBERT
Director, Producer, Teacher. b. New York, NY, Aug. 28, 1948. e. Antioch Coll., New School for Social Research. Teaches film and theatre at NYU, New Lincoln, New School. Formed Robert Greenwald Prods.
THEATRE: A Sense of Humor, I Have a Dream, Me and Bessie.
PICTURES: *Director:* Xanadu, Sweet Hearts Dance (also exec. prod.), Hear No Evil, Breaking Up (also prod.), Steal This Movie (also prod.), My Dark Places: An L.A. Crime Memoir.
TELEVISION: *Prod.:* The Desperate Miles, 21 Hours at Munich, Delta Country USA, Escape From Bogen County, Getting Married, Portrait of a Stripper, Miracle on Ice, The Texas Rangers, The First Time, The Crooked E: The Unshredded Truth About Enron. *Exec. prod.:* My Brother's Wife, Hiroshima, Zelda, The Portrait, Daddy, Scattered Dreams, Murder in New Hampshire, Death in Small Doses, Blood on Her Hands, The Day Lincoln Was Shot, The Secret Path, Our Guys: Outrage at Glen Ridge, The Audrey Hepburn Story, Deadlocked, Livin' for Love: The Natalie Cole Story, Sharing the Secret, And Never Let Her Go, Blonde, Disappearance, Redeemer, Unprecedented: the 2000 Presidential Election (documentary). *Director:* Sharon: Portrait of a Mistress, In the Custody of Strangers, The Burning Bed, Katie: Portrait of a Centerfold, Flatbed Annie and Sweetpie: Lady Truckers, Shattered Spirits (also exec. prod.), Forgotten Prisoners, A Woman of Independent Means (also co-exec. prod.).

GREENWOOD, BRUCE
Actor. b. Noranda, Quebec, Canada, Aug. 14, 1956. e. Univ. of British Columbia, London Sch. of Speech and Learning, AADA. Worked in Canadian theater and as lead singer/guitarist with blues/rock band in Vancouver before arriving in LA in 1983.
PICTURES: Bear Island (debut, 1980), First Blood, Malibu Bikini Shop, Another Chance, Wild Orchid, Passenger 57, Exotica, Paint Cans, Dream Man, Father's Day, The Sweet Hereafter, Disturbing Behavior, Thick as Thieves, The Lost Son, Double Jeopardy, Here on Earth, Rules of Engagement, Cord, Thirteen Days, Below, Love Sex Drugs & Money, The Core, The Water Giant, Ararat, The Republic of Love, I-Robert.
TELEVISION: *Series:* Legmen, St. Elsewhere, Knots Landing, Hardball, Nowhere Man, Sleepwalkers. *Movies:* Peyton Place: The Next Generation, Destination: America, In the Line of Duty: The FBI Murders, Spy, Summer Dreams: The Story of the Beach Boys, The Great Pretender, Rio Diablo, Adrift, The Heart of a Child, Bitter Vengeance, Treacherous Beauties, The Companion, Servants of Twilight, Little Kindappers, Twist of Fate, Woman on the Run: The Lawrencia Bembenek Story, Dazzle, The Judds: Love Can Build a Bridge, Tell Me No Secrets, The Absolute Truth, The Color of Courage, The Soul Collector, Haven, The Magnificent Amberson, A Girl Thing (mini). *Guest:* Hitchhiker, Jake and the Fatman, Road to Avonlea.

GREGORY, DORIAN
Actor. b. January 26, 1971.
PICTURES: Just Write, Deliver Us From Eva.
TELEVISION:*Movies:* The Barefoot Detective. *Series:* Baywatch Nights, Charmed, The Other Half. *Guest:* Baywatch, Beverly Hills 90210, Too Something, Pacific Blue, Prey.

GREIST, KIM
Actress. b. Stamford, CT, May 12, 1958. e. New School.
THEATRE: Second Prize: Two Months in Leningrad, Twelfth Night (NY Shakespeare Fest.).
PICTURES: C.H.U.D. (debut, 1984), Brazil, Manhunter, Throw Momma from the Train, Punchline, Why Me?, Homeward Bound: The Incredible Journey, Houseguest, Homeward Bound II: Lost in San Francisco, The Rose Sisters, H-E Double Hockeysticks, Rockin' Good Times, A Smaller Place, Zoe.
TELEVISION: *Movies:* Payoff, Duplicates, Roswell. *Guest:* Miami Vice, Tales From the Darkside, Chicago Hope (recurring).

GREY, BRAD
Producer. e. SUNY Buffalo. Managed comedians and signed first client, Bob Saget, while still an undergraduate; mngr., for Garry Shandling, Dana Carvey, Dennis Miller. With manager, Bernie Brillstein, formed the prod. co., Brillstein-Grey; later bought out Brillstein's share, and currently runs the co.
PICTURES: The Burning, Opportunity Knocks, The Celluloid Closet, Cat and Mouse, Happy Gilmore, The Cable Guy, Bulletproof, Dirty Work, What Planet Are You From? Screwed, Scary Movie, City by the Sea, A View from the Top.
TELEVISION: The Larry Sanders Show, Mr. Show, The Naked Truth, The Steve Harvey Show, Just Shoot Me, Alright Already, C-16: FBI, The Sopranos, Sammy, Pasadena, Real Time with Bill Maher (exec. prod.), Married to the Kellys (prod.& exec. prod.).

GREY, JENNIFER
Actress. b. New York, NY, Mar. 26, 1960. Father is actor Joel Grey. Appeared as dancer in Dr. Pepper commercial before making NY stage debut in Off-B'way play Album. B'way in The Twilight of the Golds.
PICTURES: Reckless (debut, 1984), Red Dawn, The Cotton Club, American Flyers, Ferris Bueller's Day Off, Dirty Dancing, Bloodhounds of Broadway, Stroke of Midnight (If the Shoe Fits), Wind, Portraits of a Killer, Lover's Knot, Red Meat, The Secrets of My Heart, Bounce, Ritual.
TELEVISION: Movies: Murder in Mississippi, Criminal Justice, Eyes of a Witness, A Case for Murder, The West Side, Waltz, Outrage, Since You've Been Gone, Tales from the Crypt Presents: Revelation. Series: It's Like You Know....

GREY, JOEL
Actor, Singer, Dancer. r.n. Joel Katz. b. Cleveland, OH, April 11, 1932. Father was performer Mickey Katz; daughter is actress Jennifer Grey. e. Alexander Hamilton H.S., L.A. Acting debut at 9 years in On Borrowed Time at Cleveland Playhouse. Extensive nightclub appearances before returning to theatre and TV. Performed Silverlake in NY.
THEATRE: NY: Come Blow Your Horn, Stop the World—I Want to Get Off, Half a Sixpence, Harry: Noon and Night, Littlest Revue, Cabaret (Tony Award, 1967), George M!, Goodtime Charley, The Grand Tour, Cabaret (1987, B'way revival), Chicago. Regional: Herringbone.
PICTURES: About Face (debut, 1952), Calypso Heat Wave, Come September, Cabaret (Academy Award, best supporting actor, 1972), Man on a Swing, Buffalo Bill and the Indians or Sitting Bull's History Lesson, The Seven Percent Solution, Remo Williams: The Adventure Begins..., Kafka, The Player, The Music of Chance, The Fantasticks, My Friend Joe, The Empty Mirror, Reaching Normal, Dancer in the Dark, The Fantasticks.
TELEVISION: Movies: Man on a String, Queenie, A Christmas Carol, Just Deserts, Further Tales of the City (mini), On the Edge. Specials: Jack and the Beanstalk, George M!, The Wizard of Oz in Concert. Series: Oz. Guest: Maverick, December Bride, Ironside, Night Gallery, The Burt Bacharach Show, The Tom Jones Show, The Carol Burnett Show, The Julie Andrews Hour, Dallas, Brooklyn Bridge, Star Trek Voyager, others.

GREY, VIRGINIA
Actress. b. Los Angeles, CA, March 22, 1917. Screen career started 1927 with Uncle Tom's Cabin.
PICTURES: Misbehaving Ladies, Secrets, Dames, The Firebird, The Great Ziegfeld, Rosalie, Test Pilot, The Hardys Ride High, Hullaballoo, Blonde Inspiration, The Big Store, Grand Central Murder, Idaho, Strangers in the Night, Blonde Ranson, Unconquered, Who Killed Doc Robbin, The Bullfighter and the Lady, Highway 301, Slaughter Trail, Desert Pursuit, Perilous Journey, Forty-Niners, Target Earth, Eternal Sea, Last Command, Rose Tattoo, All That Heaven Allows, Crime of Passion, Jeanne Eagles, The Restless Years, No Name on the Bullet, Portrait in Black, Tammy Tell Me True, Back Street, Bachelor In Paradise, Black Zoo, The Naked Kiss, Love Has Many Faces, Madame X, Rosie, Airport, That's Entertainment.
TELEVISION: Movies: The Lives of Jenny Dolan, Joan Crawford: The Ultimate Movie Star (documentary). Mini-series: Arthur Hailey's The Moneychangers.

GREYSON, JOHN
Director, Writer. b. Canada, 1960.
PICTURES: Kipling Meets the Cowboy (dir. only), The Jungle Boy (dir. only), Moscow Does Not Believe in Queers (dir. only), A Moffie Called Simon (dir. only), Pissoir, Zero Patience, Lilies (dir. only), Uncut (also prod.), The Law of Enclosures.
TELEVISION: Series: The Industry, Queer as Folk.

GRIECO, RICHARD
Actor. b. Watertown, NY, 1966. Started with Elite Modeling Agency. Studied acting at Warren Robertson Theatre Workshop appearing in prods. of Orphans, Golden Boy. As musician released album Waiting for the Sky to Fall.
PICTURES: Born to Ride, If Looks Could Kill, Mobsters, Tomcat: Dangerous Desires, Bolt, The Demolitionist, Mutual Needs, Heaven or Vegas, Against the Law, A Night at the Roxbury, Blackheart, Vital Parts, Point Doom, Final Payback, Raging Silence, Last Cry, Sweet Revenge, Manhattan Midnight, Fish Don't Blink, Death-Deceit-And Destiny Aboard the Orient Express, Samhain, Wounded.
TELEVISION: Movies: Sin and Redemption, A Vow to Kill, It Was Him or Us, When Time Expires, Sinbad: Battle of the Dark Knights Ultimate Deception, Webs. Series: One Life to Live, 21 Jump Street, Booker, Marker.

GRIEM, HELMUT
Actor. b. Hamburg, Germany, April 6, 1932. e. Hamburg U.
PICTURES: The Girl From Hong Kong, The Damned, The Mackenzie Break, Cabaret, Ludwig, Children of Rage, Desert of the Tartars, Voyage of the Damned, Germany in Autumn, The Glass Cell, Sgt. Steiner (Breakthrough), Berlin Alexanderplatz, Malou, La Passante, The Second Victory.
TELEVISION: Mini-Series: Peter the Great. Various European movies and specials.

GRIER, DAVID ALAN
Actor. b. Detroit, MI, June 30, 1955. e. U. of MI, Yale. Acted with Yale Rep.
THEATRE: NY: A Soldier's Play, The First (Theatre World Award), Richard III, Dreamgirls, The Merry Wives of Windsor.
PICTURES: Streamers (debut, 1983), A Soldier's Story, Beer, From the Hip, Amazon Women on the Moon, Off Limits, I'm Gonna Git You Sucka, Me and Him, Loose Cannons, Almost an Angel, The Player, Boomerang, In the Army Now, Blankman, Tales From the Hood, Jumanji, Top of the World, McHale's Navy, Return to Me, The Adventures of Rocky and Bullwinkle, 15 Minutes, I Shaved My Legs for This, The Woodsman, Gettin' the Man's Foot Outta Your Ass and Other Life Lessons.
TELEVISION: Movies: A Saintly Switch, The '60s, King of Texas. Specials: Young Hollywood Awards (host, 2003). Series: All Is Forgiven, In Living Color, The Preston Episodes (also co-exec. prod.), Damon, Random Acts of Comedy, DAG, Premium Blend, Life with Bonnie. Crank Yankers, Jimmy Kimmel Live (guest host), Tough Crowd with Colin Quinn..

GRIER, PAM
Actress. b. Winston-Salem, NC, May 26, 1949.
PICTURES: The Big Doll House, Big Bird Cage, Black Mama White Mama, Cool Breeze, Hit Man, Women in Cages, Coffy, Scream Blacula Scream, Twilight People, The Arena, Foxy Brown, Bucktown, Friday Foster, Sheba Baby, Drum, Greased Lightning, Fort Apache The Bronx, Tough Enough, Something Wicked This Way Comes, The Vindicator, On the Edge, Stand Alone, The Allnighter, Above the Law, The Package, Class of 1999, Bill & Ted's Bogus Journey, Posse, Original Gangstas, Mars Attacks!, Jackie Brown, Jawbreaker, Holy Smoke, Fortress 2, In Too Deep, Holy Smoke, Fortress 2, Snow Day, Wilder, 3 a.m., It Conquered Hollywood! The Story of American International Pictures, Ghosts of Mars, Bones, The Adventures of Pluto Nash, Baby of the Family.
TELEVISION: Mini-Series: Roots: The Next Generations, Feast of All Saints. Movies: A Mother's Right: The Elizabeth Morgan Story, Family Blessings, Hayley Wagner: Star, 1st to Die. Series: The L Word. Guest: Miami Vice, Crime Story, Pacific Station, Frank's Place, The Cosby Show, Night Court, In Living Color, Sinbad Show, Fresh Prince of Bel Air. Series: Linc's.

GRIFFIN, MERV
Executive, Singer, Emcee. b. San Mateo, CA, July 6, 1925. e. U. of San Francisco, Stanford U. Host of The Merv Griffin Show, KFRC-Radio, 1945-48; vocalist, Freddy Martin's orch., 1948-52; recorded hit song I've Got a Lovely Bunch of Coconuts; contract Warner Bros., 1952-54; Prod. Finian's Rainbow, City Center, NY, 1955. In 1962, The Merv Griffin Show first aired after Griffin's successful guest host stints on The Tonight Show. Griffin's talk show style and format remain popular today. In addition to talk show notoriety, he is known for creating the game shows Jeopardy and Wheel of Fortune and still serves as both shows' exec. prod. He sold Merv Griffin Enterprises in 1986, but continues to develop and produce game shows and other forms of tv programming. He is chmn. of Merv Griffin Prods., a premier special events co. which puts on movie premieres, benefits, galas, concerts and other high-profile ent. ind. events, such as the Grammys. Additionally, he owns several world-class hotels which complement Merv Griffin Productions' event planning/hosting. He is the recipient of numerous ent. industry recognitions and awards, including several Emmys.
PICTURES: By the Light of the Silvery Moon, So This Is Love, Boy From Oklahoma, Phantom of the Rue Morgue, Hello Down There, Two Minute Warning, The Seduction of Joe Tynan, The Man With Two Brains, The Lonely Guy, Slapstick of Another Kind, Off the Menu: The Last Days of Chasen's.
TELEVISION: Series: The Freddy Martin Show (vocalist), Summer Holiday, Morning Show, The Robert Q. Lewis Show, Keep Talking (emcee), Play Your Hunch (emcee), Saturday Prom, The Merv Griffin Show (1962-63), Talent Scouts, Word for Word, The Merv Griffin Show (1965-86; Emmy Award for writing, 2 Emmy Awards for hosting), Secrets Women Never Share (exec. prod., host, 1987), Hercules (voice). Creator and Exec. Prod: Jeopardy (Emmy Award, 1998), Wheel of Fortune.

GRIFFITH, ANDY
Actor. b. Mount Airy, NC, June 1, 1926. e. U. of North Carolina. Began career as standup comedian, monologist, recording artist (What It Was Was Football, 1954). TV acting debut in U.S. Steel Hour production of No Time for Sergeants, which he later played on Broadway and film.
THEATRE: B'way: No Time for Sergeants (Theatre World Award), Destry Rides Again.
PICTURES: A Face in the Crowd (debut, 1957), No Time for Sergeants, Onionhead, The Second Time Around, Angel in My Pocket, Hearts of the West, Rustler's Rhapsody, Spy Hard, Daddy and Them.
TELEVISION: Movies: Strangers in 7A, Go Ask Alice, Pray for the Wildcats, Winter Kill, Savages, Street Killing, Girl in the Empty Grave, Deadly Games, Salvage, Murder in Texas, For Lovers Only, Murder in Coweta County, The Demon Murder Case, Fatal Vision, Crime of Innocence, Diary of a Perfect Murder, Return to Mayberry, Under the Influence, Matlock: The Vacation (also co-exec. prod.), The Gift of Love, Gramps,

Scattering Dad, A Holiday Romance. *Mini-Series*: Washington Behind Closed Doors, Centennial, From Here to Eternity, Roots: The Next Generations. *Series*: The Andy Griffith Show, The Headmaster, The New Andy Griffith Show, Salvage One, Matlock.

GRIFFITH, MELANIE
Actress. b. New York, NY, Aug. 9, 1957. m. Anotnio Banderas. Mother is actress Tippi Hedren. Moved to Los Angeles at 4. e. Catholic academies until Hollywood Prof. Sch., 1974. Did some modeling before being cast in Night Moves at 16. Studied acting with Stella Adler, Harry Mastrogeorge and Sandra Seacat.
PICTURES: The Harrad Experiment (debut, 1973), Smile, Night Moves, The Drowning Pool, One on One, Joyride, Underground Aces, Roar, Fear City, Body Double, Something Wild, Cherry 2000, The Milagro Beanfield War, Stormy Monday, Working Girl (Acad. Award nom.), In the Spirit, Pacific Heights, The Bonfire of the Vanities, Paradise, Shining Through, A Stranger Among Us, Born Yesterday, Milk Money, Nobody's Fool, Now and Then, Two Much, Mulholland Falls, Lolita, Celebrity, Another Day in Paradise, Shadow of a Doubt, RKO 281, Crazy in Alabama, Forever Lulu, Life with Big Cats, Tart, Searching for Debra Winger, Stuart Little 2 (voice), Tempo, Shade, The Night We Called It a Day.
TELEVISION: *Movies*: Daddy I Don't Like It Like This, Steel Cowboy, The Star Maker, She's in the Army Now, Golden Gate, Women & Men: Stories of Seduction (Hills Like White Elephants), Buffalo Girls. *Mini-Series*: Once an Eagle. *Series*: Carter Country. *Guest*: Vega$, Miami Vice, Alfred Hitchcock Presents.

GRIFFITHS, RACHEL
Actress. b. Melbourne, Australia, Feb. 20, 1968.
PICTURES: Muriel's Wedding, Jude, Cosi, Children of the Revolution, Welcome to Woop Woop, To Have and to Hold, My Best Friend's Wedding, Hilary and Jackie (Acad. Award nom.), Among Giants, Amy, My Myself I, Blow Dry, Blow, Very Annie Mary, The Rookie, The Hard Word, Ned Kelly.
TELEVISION: *Movies*: Since You've Been Gone, Plainsong *Mini-Series*: After the Deluge. *Series*: Jimeoin, Six Feet Under (Golden Globe Award).

GRIMALDI, ALBERTO
Producer. b. Naples, Italy, Mar. 28, 1925. Studied law, serving as counsel to Italian film companies, before turning to production with Italian westerns starring Clint Eastwood and Lee Van Cleef. Is owner of P.E.A. (Produzioni Europee Associate, s.r.l.).
PICTURES: For a Few Dollars More, The Good the Bad and the Ugly, The Big Gundown, Three Steps in Delirium, A Quiet Place in the Country, The Mercenary, Satyricon, Burn!, The Decameron, Man of the East, The Canterbury Tales, Last Tango in Paris, Bawdy Tales, Arabian Nights, Salo or the 100 Days of Sodom, Burnt Offerings, Fellini's Casanova, 1900, Illustrious Corpses, Lovers and Liars, Hurricane Rosy, Ginger and Fred, The Gangs of New York.

GRIMES, GARY
Actor. b. San Francisco, CA, June 2, 1955. Family moved to L.A. when he was nine. Made film debut at 15 in Summer of '42, 1971. Voted Star of Tomorrow in QP poll, 1971.
PICTURES: Summer of '42, The Culpepper Cattle Company, Cahill: U.S. Marshal, Class of '44, The Spikes Gang, Gus, Concrete Angels.
TELEVISION: *Mini-Series*: Once an Eagle.

GRIMES, TAMMY
Actress. b. Boston, MA, Jan. 30, 1934. Daughter is actress Amanda Plummer. e. Stephens Coll, The Neighborhood Playhouse. Recipient: Woman of Achievement Award (ADL), Mother of the Year Award, Mayor's Outstanding Contribution to the Arts Award (NYC). Member: bd. dirs. & v.p. of the Upper East-Side Historic Preservation District (NYC).
THEATRE: Look After Lulu (Theatre World Award, 1959), Clerambard, The Littlest Revue, Stratford (Ont.) Shakespeare Fest., Bus Stop, The Cradle Will Rock, The Unsinkable Molly Brown (Tony Award, 1961), Rattle of a Simple Man, High Spirits, Private Lives (Tony Award, 1970), Trick, California Suite, 42nd Street, Tartuffe, A Month in the Country, The Guardsman, The Millionairess, Imaginary Invalid, The Importance of Being Earnest, Mademoiselle Columbe, Blythe Spirit, Waltz of the Toreadors, Molly, Taming of the Shrew, Orpheus Descending, Tammy Grimes: A Concert in Words and Music, A Little Night Music, Pygmalion.
PICTURES: Three Bites of the Apple (debut, 1967), Play It as It Lays, Somebody Killed Her Husband, The Runner Stumbles, Can't Stop the Music, The Last Unicorn (voice), The Stuff, No Big Deal, America, Mr. North, Slaves of New York, A Modern Affair, Trouble on the Corner, High Art, Broadway: The Golden Age by the Legends Who Were There.
TELEVISION: *Specials*: Omnibus, Hollywood Sings, Hour of Great Mysteries, Four Poster. *Guest*: St. Elsewhere, The Young Riders. Series: The Tammy Grimes Show, Loving. *Movies*: The Other Man, The Horror at 37,000 Feet, The Borrowers, You Can't Go Home Again, An Invasion of Privacy.

GRIZZARD, GEORGE
Actor. b. Roanoke Rapids, NC, April 1, 1928. e. U. of North Carolina, B.A., 1949. Has been member of Arena Stage, Washington, D.C., APA repertory company and Tyrone Guthrie resident company in Minneapolis.
THEATRE: The Desperate Hours. (B'way debut, 1955), The Happiest Millionaire (Theatre World Award), The Disenchanted, Face of a Hero, Big Fish, Little Fish, Who's Afraid of Virginia Woolf?, The Glass Menagerie, You Know I Can't Hear You When the Water's Running, The Gingham Dog, Inquest, The Country Girl, The Creation of the World and Other Business, Crown Matrimonial, The Royal Family, California Suite, Man and Superman, Another Antiqone, Show Boat, A Delicate Balance (Tony Award, 1996).
PICTURES: From the Terrace, Advise and Consent, Warning Shot, Happy Birthday Wanda June, Comes a Horseman, Firepower, Seems Like Old Times, Wrong Is Right, Bachelor Party, Wonder Boys, Small Time Crooks.
TELEVISION: *Movies*: Travis Logan D.A., Indict & Convict, The Stranger Within, Attack on Terror: The FBI vs. the Ku Klux Klan, The Lives of Jenny Dolan, The Night Rider, Attica, Not In Front of the Children, The Deliberate Stranger, Underseige, That Secret Sunday, International Airport, Embassy, The Shady Hill Kidnapping, Oldest Living Graduate (Emmy Award, 1980), Perry Mason: The Case of the Scandalous Scoundrel, David, Caroline?, Iran: Days of Crisis, Not in My Family, Triumph Over Disaster: The Hurricane Andrew Story, Sisters & Other Strangers. *Specials*: Enemy of the People. *Mini-Series*: The Adams Chronicles, Robert Kennedy and His Times, Queen, Scarlett.

GRODIN, CHARLES
Actor, Director, Writer. b. Pittsburgh, PA, April 21, 1935. e. U. of Miami. After time with Pittsburgh Playhouse studied acting with Uta Hagen and Lee Strasberg; began directing career in New York 1965 as asst. to Gene Saks. Has appeared in some 75 plays all over the country. Has also written scripts, produced plays. *Books*: It Would Be So Nice If You Weren't Here, How I Get Through Life, We're Ready for You Mr. Grodin.
THEATRE: Tchin-Tchin (B'way debut, 1962), Absence of a Cello, Same Time Next Year, It's a Glorious Day... And All That (dir., co-author), Lovers and Other Strangers (dir.), Thieves (prod., dir.), Unexpected Guests (prod., dir.), Price of Fame (also author), One of the All-Time Greats (author).
PICTURES: Sex and the College Girl (debut, 1964), Rosemary's Baby, Catch-22, The Heartbreak Kid, 11 Harrowhouse (also adapt.), King Kong, Thieves, Heaven Can Wait, Real Life, Sunburn, It's My Turn, Seems Like Old Times, The Incredible Shrinking Woman, The Great Muppet Caper, The Lonely Guy, The Woman in Red, Movers and Shakers (also s.p., co-prod.), Last Resort, Ishtar, The Couch Trip, You Can't Hurry Love, Midnight Run, Taking Care of Business, Beethoven, Dave, So I Married an Axe Murderer, Heart and Souls, Beethoven's 2nd, Clifford, It Runs in the Family (My Summer Story).
TELEVISION: *Specials* (writer): Candid Camera (also dir.), The Simon & Garfunkel Special, Paul Simon Special (also dir.; Emmy Award for writing, 1978). *Specials* (dir.): Acts of Love and Other Comedies, Paradise (also prod.). *Actor*: *Guest*: The Defenders, My Mother the Car, The FBI, Guns of Will Sonnett, The Big Valley. *Specials*: Grown Ups, Love Sex and Marriage (also writer), Charley's Aunt. *Movies*: Just Me and You, The Grass Is Always Greener Over the Septic Tank. *Mini-Series*: Fresno. *Series*: Charles Grodin (talk), The Charles Grodin Show, 60 Minutes II.

GROENING, MATT
Animator, Cartoonist. b. Portland, OR, Feb. 14, 1954. Moved to LA in mid 1980s, started drawing comic strip named "Life in Hell". In 1988 created The Simpsons, originally filler in The Tracy Ullman show, later TV series. Author of Kevin Newcombe (bio.).
PICTURES: The Simpsons Movie (exec. prod.).
TELEVISION: *Movies*: Olive the Other Reindeer, My Wasted Life (as himself). Specials: The Simpsons: America's First Family. *Series*: The Simpsons (exec. prod., creator), Futurama (exec. prod., creator).

GROSBARD, ULU
Director. b. Antwerp, Belgium. Jan. 9, 1929. e. U. of Chicago, B.A. 1950, M.A. 1952. Trained at Yale Sch. of Drama 1952-53. Asst. dir. to Eliza Kazan on Splendor in the Grass, 1961; asst. dir.: West Side Story, The Hustler, The Miracle Worker. Unit mgr.: The Pawnbroker.
THEATRE: The Days and Nights of Beebee Fenstermaker, The Subject Was Roses, A View From the Bridge, The Investigation, That Summer—That Fall, The Price, American Buffalo, The Woods, The Wake of Jamie Foster, The Tenth Man.
PICTURES: The Subject Was Roses (debut, 1968), Who Is Harry Kellerman and Why Is He Saying Those Terrible Things About Me? (also co-prod.), Straight Time, True Confessions, Falling in Love, Georgia (also co-prod.), The Deep End of the Ocean, The Hustler: The Inside Story (video documentary short, as himself).

GROSS, KENNETH H.
Executive. b. Columbus, OH, Feb. 12, 1949. e. New School for Social Research, U. of London. Conducted film seminars at New

School and active in several indep. film projects. Published film criticism in various journals and magazines. Joined ABC Ent. 1971. Named supvr. of feature films for ABC-TV. Appt. mgr. of feature films, 1974. Promoted 1975 to program exec., ABC Ent. Prime Time/West Coast. Promoted to exec. prod., movies for TV, ABC Ent. 1976 in L.A.; 1978, with literary agency F.C.A. as partner in L.A.; 1979 prod. for Lorimar; then with Intl. Creative Mgt; 1982, formed own literary talent agency, The Literary Group; 1985, merged agency with Robinson-Weintraub & Assoc. to become Robinson-Weintraub-Gross & Assoc. 1993, founding partner of Paradigm, a talent and literary agency. 1997, formed Ken Gross Management, mgmt. and prod. co.

GROSS, MARY
Actress. b. Chicago, IL, March 25, 1953. Brother is actor Michael Gross. e. Loyola U. Is also student of the harp. In 1980 discovered by John Belushi who saw her perform as resident member of Chicago's Second City comedy troupe, where she won Chicago's Joseph Jefferson Award as best actress for the revue, Well, I'm Off to the Thirty Years War. First came to national attention as regular on Saturday Night Live, 1981-85.
PICTURES: Club Paradise, The Couch Trip, Casual Sex, Baby Boom, Big Business, Feds, Troop Beverly Hills, The Santa Clause, The Evening Star, Mixed Nuts (voice), Practical Magic, The Rugrats Movie (voice), 40 Days and 40 Nights, A Mighty Wind.
TELEVISION: Series: Saturday Night Live, The People Next Door, Billy, Sabrina the Teenage Witch, Animaniacs (voice), Detention (voice). Specials: Comic Relief I, The Second City 25th Anniversary Reunion, Saturday Night Live: TV Tales. Movie: Jailbait.

GROSS, MICHAEL
Actor. b. Chicago, IL, June 21, 1947. m. casting dir. Elza Bergeron. Sister is actress Mary Gross. e. U. Illinois, B.A., Yale School of Drama, M.F.A.
THEATRE: NY Shakespeare Fest. (Sganarelle, An Evening of Moliere Farces, Othello). Off-B'way: Endgame, No End of Blame (Obie Award), Put Them All Together, Geniuses, Territorial Rites. B'way: Bent, The Philadelphia Story. L.A. stage: Hedda Gabler, The Real Thing, Love Letters, Money & Friends.
PICTURES: Just Tell Me What You Want, Big Business, Tremors, Midnight Murders, Cool as Ice, Alan & Naomi, Tremors II: Aftershocks, Ground Control, Tremors III: Back to Perfection, Tremors 4.
TELEVISION: Movies: A Girl Named Sooner, FDR: The Last Year, Dream House, The Neighborhood, Little Gloria Happy at Last, Cook and Peary-The Race to the Pole, Summer Fantasy, Family Ties Vacation, A Letter to Three Wives, Right to Die, In the Line of Duty: The FBI Murders, A Connecticut Yankee in King Arthur's Court, Vestige of Honor, In the Line of Duty: Manhunt in the Dakotas, With a Vengeance, Snowbound: The Jim and Jennifer Stolpa Story, In the Line of Duty: The Price of Vengeance, Avalanche, Awake to Danger, Deceived by Trust, Hijacked: Flight 285, Ed McBain's 87th Precinct tv movies: Ice and Heatwave, Batman Beyond: The Movie (voice). Series: Family Ties, Tremors. Guest: ER.

GROSSBART, JACK
Producer. b. Newark, NJ, Apr. 18, 1948. e. Rutgers Univ. Was agent, 1975-80, then personal manager, Litke-Grossbart Mgmt., 1980-87. Became tv prod., Jack Grossbart Prods., 1987.
TELEVISION: Movies: Exec. prod./prod.: Shattered Vows, The Seduction of Gina, Rockabye, Killer in the Mirror, Something in Common, Dangerous Affection, Echoes in the Darkness, She Was Marked for Murder, The Preppie Murder, Joshua's Heart, Lies Before Kisses, Honor Bright, Last Wish, Something to Live For: The Alison Gertz Story, A Jury of One, Comrades of Summer, The Woman Who Loved Elvis, One of Her Own, Leave of Absence, Between Love & Honor, Rage Against Time: A Search for Sara, Unforgivable, Breaking Through, A Father for Brittany, At the Mercy of a Stranger, Personally Yours, Phantom of the Megaplex. Series: Exec. prod.: Sydney, Cafe Americain.

GRUENBERG, ANDY
Executive. b. Minneapolis, MN, March 10, 1950. e. University of Wisconsin. Held various sales positions with 20th Century Fox and Warner Bros. from 1976 to 1984. Joined Columbia Pictures as asst. general sales mgr. Lorimar Pictures s.v.p. and general sales mgr. 1985-89. Hemdale Prods. pres. of distribution, 1989-91. Joined MGM/UA in 1991, as exec. v.p. of distribution.

GRUSIN, DAVID
Composer, Conductor, Performer. b. Littleton, CO, June 26, 1934. Directed music for the Andy Williams Show on TV for 7 yrs in the 1960s, where he met Norman Lear and Bud Yorkin, producers of the series, who signed him to score their first feature film, Divorce, American Style (1967).
PICTURES: Waterhole No. 3, The Graduate, Candy, The Heart Is a Lonely Hunter, Winning, Where Were You When the Lights Went Out?, Generation, A Man Called Gannon, Tell Them Willie Boy Is Here, Adam at 6 A.M., Halls of Anger, The Gang That Couldn't Shoot Straight, The Pursuit of Happiness, Shoot Out, Fuzz, The Great Northfield Minnesota Raid, The Friends of Eddie Coyle, The Midnight Ride, W.W. and the Dixie

Dance Kings, The Yakuza, Three Days of the Condor, Murder By Death, The Front, Fire Sale, Mr. Billion, Bobby Deerfield, The Goodbye Girl, Heaven Can Wait, And Justice for All, The Champ, The Electric Horseman, My Bodyguard, Absence of Malice, On Golden Pond, Reds, Author! Author!, Tootsie, Scandalous, Racing with the Moon, The Pope of Greenwich Village, The Little Drummer Girl, Falling in Love, Lucas, The Goonies, The Milagro Beanfield War (Acad. Award, 1988), Clara's Heart, Tequila Sunrise, A Dry White Season, Havana, The Bonfire of the Vanities, For the Boys, The Cure, The Firm, Mulholland Falls, Selena, Hope Floats, Random Hearts.
TELEVISION: Movies: Deadly Dream, Prescription: Murder, Scorpio Letters, Eric, The Family Rico, The Death Squad, Dinner with Friends. Series: Maude, Good Times, Baretta, The Name of the Game, It Takes a Thief, The Girl From Uncle, St. Elsewhere, In the Gloaming, Hope.

GUBER, PETER
Producer. b. 1942. e. Syracuse U., B.A.; U. at Florence (Italy), S.S.P.; Sch. of Law, J.D., L.L.M. Recruited by Columbia Pictures as exec. asst. in 1968 while at NYU. Graduate Sch. of Business Adm. With Col. seven yrs. in key prod. exec. capacities, serving last three as studio chief. Formed own company, Peter Guber's Filmworks, which in 1976 was merged with his Casablanca Records to become Casablanca Record and Filmworks where he was co-owner & chmn. bd. 1980 formed Polygram Pictures later bringing in Jon Peters as partner. 1983 sold Polygram and formed Guber-Peters. 1988 merged co. with Burt Sugarman's Barris Industries to form Guber-Peters-Barris Entertainment Co. Co-chmn. & man. dir. 1989 took full control of co. with Sugarman's exit and addition of Australia's Frank Lowy as new partner. 1989 became CEO of Columbia Pictures Ent.; 1992 became chairman and CEO of Sony Pictures Ent. Awards: Producer of Year, NATO, 1979; NYU Albert Gallatin Fellowship; Syracuse U. Ardent Award. Visiting prof., & chmn. producer's dept., UCLA Sch. of Theatre Arts. Member of NY, CA and Wash. DC Bars. Books: Inside the Deep, Above the Title.
PICTURES: The Deep (first under own banner), Midnight Express. Co-Prod. with Jon Peters: An American Werewolf in London, Missing, Flashdance (exec. prod.), D.C. Cab (exec. prod.), Endless Love, Vision Quest (exec. prod.), The Legend of Billie Jean, Head Office, Clan of the Cave Bear, Six Weeks (exec. prod.), The Pursuit of D.B. Cooper (exec. prod.), Clue (exec. prod.), The Color Purple (exec. prod.), The Witches of Eastwick (prod.), Innerspace (exec. prod.), Who's That Girl (exec. prod.), Gorillas in the Mist (exec. prod.), Caddyshack II, Rain Man (exec. prod.), Batman (prod.), Johnny Handsome, Tango and Cash (prod.), Batman Returns, This Boy's Life (exec. prod.), With Honors (exec. prod.), Galapagos: The Enchanted Voyage, Alex & Emma (exec. prod), The Jacket.
TELEVISION: Mysteries of the Sea (doc. Emmy Award). Exec. prod.: Television and the Presidency, Double Platinum, Dreams (series), Rude Awakening (series). Movies: Stand By Your Man, The Toughest Man in the World (exec. prod.), Bay Coven, Oceanquest, Brotherhood of Justice, Nightmare at Bitter Creek, Finish Line.

GUEST, CHRISTOPHER
Actor, Writer, Composer, Director. b. New York, NY, Feb. 5, 1948. m. actress Jamie Lee Curtis. Brother is actor Nicholas Guest. Wrote the musical score and acted in National Lampoon's Lemmings off-B'way. On B'way in Room Service, Moonchildren.
PICTURES: Actor: The Hospital (debut, 1971), The Hot Rock, Death Wish, The Fortune, Girlfriends, The Last Word, The Long Riders, Heartbeeps, This Is Spinal Tap (also co-s.p.), Little Shop of Horrors, Beyond Therapy, The Princess Bride, Sticky Fingers, The Big Picture (also dir. co-s.p., story), A Few Good Men, Waiting for Guffman (also dir.), Edwards and Hunt (also dir.), Small Soldiers (voice), Best in Show, A Mighty Wind (also s.p., dir. & composer/songs).
TELEVISION: Movies: It Happened One Christmas, Haywire, Million Dollar Infield, A Piano for Mrs. Cimino, Attack of the 50 Ft. Woman (dir.). Specials: The TV Show, The Chevy Chase Special (also writer), The Billion Dollar Bubble, Lily Tomlin (also writer, Emmy Award, 1976), A Nice Place to Visit (writer only), Spinal Tap Reunion (also co-writer). Mini-Series: Blind Ambition. Series: Saturday Night Live (1984-5).

GUEST, LANCE
Actor. b. Saratoga, CA, July 21, 1960. e. UCLA.
PICTURES: Halloween II, I Ought To Be in Pictures, The Last Starfighter, Jaws-The Revenge, The Wizard of Loneliness, Plan B, Mach 2.
TELEVISION:Movies: Confessions of a Married Man, Stepsister From Planet Weird, The Jenny Project. Specials: One Too Many, My Father My Rival, The Roommate. Mini-Series: Favorite Son. Series: Lou Grant, Knots Landing, Life Goes On. Guest: St. Elsewhere.

GUEST, VAL
Writer, Director, Producer. b. London, England, Dec. 11, 1911. e. England and America. Journalist with Hollywood Reporter, Zit's Los Angeles Examiner and Walter Winchell. Debuted as dir. & writer of 1942 short film The Nose Has It.

PICTURES: *Director/Writer*: Miss London Ltd. (feature debut, 1943), Murder at the Windmill, Miss Pilgrim's Progress, The Body Said No, Mr. Drake's Duck, Happy Go Lovely, Another Man's Poison, Penny Princess, The Runaway Bus, Life With the Lyons, Dance Little Lady, Men of Sherwood Forest, Lyons in Paris, Break in the Circle, It's A Great Life, The Quatermass Experiment (The Creeping Unknown), They Can't Hang Me, The Weapon, It's a Wonderful World, Quatermass II (Enemy From Space), The Abominable Snowman, Carry on Admiral, The Camp on Blood Island, Up the Creek, Further Up the Creek, Yesterday's Enemy, Expresso Bongo (also prod.), Life Is a Circus, Hell Is a City, Full Treatment (Stop Me Before I Kill; also prod.), The Day the Earth Caught Fire (also prod.), Jigsaw (also prod.), 80,000 Suspects (also prod.), The Beauty Jungle (Contest Girl; also co-prod.), Where the Spies Are (also co-prod.), Casino Royale (co-dir.), Assignment K, When Dinosaurs Ruled the Earth, Tomorrow, The Persuaders, Au Pair Girls, Confessions of a Window Cleaner, Killer Force (Diamond Mercenaries; dir. only), The Boys in Blue.
TELEVISION: Space 1999, The Persuaders, The Adventurer, The Shillingbury Blowers, The Band Played On, Sherlock Holmes & Dr. Watson, Shillingbury Tales, Dangerous Davies, The Last Detective, In Possession, Mark of the Devil, Child's Play, Scent of Fear.

GUILLAUME, ROBERT
Actor. b. St. Louis, MO, Nov. 30, 1937. e. St. Louis U., Washington U. Scholarship for musical fest. in Aspen, CO. Then apprenticed with Karamu Theatre where performed in operas and musicals. B'way plays and musicals include Fly Blackbird, Kwamina, Guys and Dolls, Purlie, Jacques Brel is Alive and Well and Living in Paris, Cyrano. In L.A. in Phantom of the Opera.
PICTURES: Super Fly T.N.T. (debut, 1973), Seems Like Old Times, Prince Jack, They Still Call Me Bruce, Wanted Dead or Alive, Lean On Me, Death Warrant, The Meteor Man, The Lion King I & II (voice), First Kid, Spy Hard, Silicon Towers, The 13th Child Legend of the Jersey Devil, The Land Before Time VIII: The Big Freeze (voice), The Adventures of Tom Thumb & Thumbelina (voice), Unchained Memories: Readings from the Slave Narratives, Big Fish, The Lion King 1 1/2 (voice).
TELEVISION: *Movies*: The Kid From Left Field, The Kid with the Broken Halo, You Must Remember This, The Kid with the 100 I.Q. (also exec. prod.), Perry Mason: The Case of the Scandalous Scoundrel, The Penthouse, Fire and Rain, Greyhounds, Children of the Dust, A Good Day to Die, Panic in the Skies!, Merry Christmas George Bailey, His Bodyguard, The Happy Prince. *Specials*: Purlie, 'S Wonderful 'S Marvellous 'S Gershwin, John Grin's Christmas, Martin Luther King: A Look Back A Look Forward, Living the Dream: A Tribute to Dr. Martin Luther King Jr. (host), The Debbie Allen Special, Carol & Company, Sister Kate, Story of a People (host), Mastergate, Cosmic Slop. *Pilot*: Driving Miss Daisy. *Series*: Soap (Emmy Award, 1979), Benson (Emmy Award, 1985), The Robert Guillaume Show, Saturdays, Pacific Station, Fish Police (voice), Happily Ever After... Fairytales for Every Child, Sports Night. *Guest*: Dinah, Mel and Susan Together, Rich Little's Washington Follies, Jim Nabors, All in the Family, Sanford and Son, The Jeffersons, Marcus Welby, M.D., Carol & Company, Sister Kate, A Different World. *Mini-Series*: North and South, Pandora's Clock.

GUILLERMIN, JOHN
Director, Producer, Writer. b. London, England, Nov. 11, 1925. e. City of London Sch., Cambridge U. RAF pilot prior to entering film industry.
PICTURES: *Director*: Torment (debut, 1949; also co-prod., s.p.), Smart Alec, Two on the Tiles, Four Days, Song of Paris, Miss Robin Hood, Operation Diplomat (also co-s.p.), Adventure in the Hopfields, The Crowded Day, Dust and Gold, Thunderstorm, Town on Trial, The Whole Truth, I Was Monty's Double, Tarzan's Greatest Adventure (also co-s.p.), The Day They Robbed the Bank of England, Never Let Go (also co-story), Waltz of the Toreadors, Tarzan Goes to India (also co-s.p.), Guns at Batasi, Rapture, The Blue Max. P.J. (U.S. debut, 1968), House of Cards, The Bridge of Remagen, El Condor, Skyjacked, Shaft in Africa, The Towering Inferno, King Kong, Death on the Nile, Mr. Patman, Sheena, King Kong Lives, The Favorite.
TELEVISION: *Movie*: The Tracker.

GULAGER, CLU
Actor. b. Holdenville, OK, Nov. 16, 1928. Father, John Gulager, cowboy entertainer. e. Baylor U. Starred at school in original play, A Different Drummer, where spotted by prod. of TV's Omnibus; invited to New York to recreate role on TV.
PICTURES: The Killers, Winning, The Last Picture Show, Company of Killers, McQ, The Other Side of Midnight, A Force of One, Touched by Love, The Initiation, Lies, Into the Night, Prime Risk, The Return of the Living Dead, Hunter's Blood, The Hidden, Tapeheads, Uninvited, I'm Gonna Git You Sucka, Teen Vamp, My Heroes Have Always Been Cowboys, The Killing Device, Eddie Pressley, Puppet Master, Gunfighter, Palmer's Pick Up, Final Act (short).
TELEVISION: *Movies*: San Francisco International, Glass House, Footsteps, Smile Jenny You're Dead, Houston We've Got a Problem, Hit Lady, Killer Who Wouldn't Die, Charlie Cobb:

Nice Night for a Hanging, Ski Lift to Death, Sticking Together, A Question of Love, Willa, This Man Stands Alone, Kenny Rogers as The Gambler, Skyward, Living Proof: The Hank Williams Jr. Story, Bridge Across Time. *Mini-Series*: Once an Eagle, Black Beauty, King, North and South II, Space, Dan Turner Hollywood Detective, In the Line of Duty (Ambush in Waco). *Series*: The Tall Man, The Virginian, The Survivors, San Francisco International Airport, MacKenzies of Paradise Cove.

GUMBEL, BRYANT
Announcer, News Show Host. b. New Orleans, LA, Sept. 29, 1948. e. Bates Coll. Started as writer for Black Sports Magazine, NY, 1971; sportscaster, then sports dir., KNBC, Los Angeles. Sports host NBC Sports NY 1975-82. New York Emmy Awards, 1976, 1977. A Host of the Today Show (1982-1997).
PICTURES: Heaven Can Wait, The Hard Way, Contact.
TELEVISION: Super Bowl games, '88 Olympics, Games People Play, The R.A.C.E, Real Sports with Bryant Gumbel (anchor), Public Eye With Bryant Gumbel, The Early Show (host, 1999-2002), and various tv documentaries and specials.

GUMPERT, JON
Executive. e. Cornell U. Law Sch. Sr. v.p., business affairs, MGM/UA Entertainment; pres., World Film Services, Inc., indep. prod. co. in N.Y. 1985, named v.p., business affairs, Warner Bros; 1986 sr. v.p. Vista Films. Named sr. v.p. legal bus. affairs, Universal Pictures 1990. Named exec. v.p., legal business affairs, Universal Pictures, 1994. Group ex. v.p., Universal Pictures, 1996. Currently head of m.p. operations with IM Internationalmedia AG.

GUNTON, BOB
Actor. b. Santa Monica, CA, Nov. 15, 1945. e. U. of Cal. Served in army during Vietnam War. Prof. acting debut at Cumberland County Playhouse in Tennesse U.S.A.
THEATRE: *Off-B'way*: Who Am I? (debut, 1971), How I Got That Story (Obie Award), Tip Toes, The Death of Von Richtofen. *B'way*: Happy End (debut, 1977), Working, Evita (Drama Desk Award; Tony nom.), Passion, King of Hearts, Big River, Rozsa, Sweeney Todd (Drama Desk Award; Tony nom.).
PICTURES: Rollerover (debut, 1981), Static, Matewan, The Pick-Up Artist, Cookie, Born on the Fourth of July, Glory, JFK, Patriot Games, The Public Eye, Jennifer Eight, Demolition Man, The Shawshank Redemption, Dolores Claiborne, Ace Ventura: When Nature Calls, Broken Arrow, The Glimmer Man, Changing Habits, Midnight in the Garden of Good and Evil, Patch Adams, Bats, The Perfect Storm, Scenes of the Crime, Boat Trip, Dallas 362.
TELEVISION: *Movies*: Lois Gibbs and the Love Canal, A Woman Named Jackie, Finnegan Begin Again, Ned Blessing, Dead Ahead: The Exxon Valdez Disaster, Murder in the Heartland, Sinatra, Ruby Ridge: An American Tragedy, Elvis Meets Nixon, Buffalo Soldiers, Judas & Jesus, The Pact, Peacemakers. *Mini-Series*: Wild Palms. *Series*: Comedy Zone, Hot House, Courthouse, Greg the Bunny.

GURIAN, PAUL R.
Executive, Producer. b. New Haven, CT, Oct.18, 1946. e. Lake Forest Coll., U. of Vienna, NYU. Started producing films in 1971 with Cats and Dogs, a dramatic short which won prizes at Chicago Int. Film Fest and Edinburgh Fest. In 1977 formed Gurian Entertainment Corp., to acquire film properties for production.
PICTURES: Cutter and Bone, Peggy Sue Got Married, The Seventh Sign (exec. prod.), Arizona Dream, The Viking Sagas.
TELEVISION: The Garden Party (PBS program), Profile Ricardo Alegria (short), Bernice Bobs Her Hair (shown at 1977 N.Y. Film Festival)

GUTTENBERG, STEVE
Actor. b. Brooklyn, NY, Aug. 24, 1958. e. Sch. of Performing Arts, N.Y. Off-B'way in The Lion in Winter; studied under John Houseman at Juilliard; classes with Lee Strasberg and Uta Hagen. Moved to West Coast in 1976; landed first TV role in movie, Something for Joey. B'way debut 1991 in Prelude to a Kiss.
PICTURES: Rollercoaster, The Chicken Chronicles, The Boys from Brazil, Players, Can't Stop the Music, Diner, The Man Who Wasn't There, Police Academy, Police Academy 2: Their First Assignment, Cocoon, Bad Medicine, Police Academy 3: Back in Training, Short Circuit, The Bedroom Window, Police Academy 4: Citizens on Patrol (also prod. assoc.), Amazon Women on the Moon, Surrender, Three Men and a Baby, High Spirits, Cocoon: The Return, Don't Tell Her It's Me, Three Men and a Little Lady, The Big Green, Home for the Holidays, It Takes Two, Zeus and Roxanne, Casper, Airborne, Home Team, Love and Fear, Sheer Bliss, P.S. Your Cat Is Dead, Snow Job, Jackson, The Stranger (short).
TELEVISION: *Movies*: Something for Joey, To Race the Wind, Miracle on Ice, The Day After. *Specials*: Gangs (co-prod.), Pecos Bill: King of the Cowboys. *Guest*: Police Story, Doc. *Series*: Billy, No Soap Radio.

GUY, JASMINE
Actress. b. Boston, MA, March 10, 1964. Toured with Grease!, 1996-97.
PICTURES: School Daze, Harlem Nights, Kla$h, America's Dream, Cats Don't Dance (voice), Lillie, Guinevere, Madeline,

Diamond Men, Dying on the Edge, Unchained Memories: Readings from the Slave Narratives (reader). TELEVISION: *Movies*: At Mother's Request, A Killer Among Us, Stomping at the Savoy, Perfect Crime, Carrie. *Series*: A Different World, Dead Like Me. *Mini-series*: Alex Haley's Queen, A Century of Women, Feast of All Saints. *Guest*: Melrose Place, Lois & Clark, Touched by an Angel, The Outer Limits.

GUZMAN, LUIS
Actor. b. Puerto Rico, 1957.
PICTURES: Short Eyes, Variety, Heartbeat, Crocodile Dundee 2, True Believer, Rooftops, Family Business, Black Rain, Q & A, The Hard Way, McBain, Jumpin' at the Boneyard, Empire City, Innocent Blood, Guilty As Sin, Mr. Wonderful, Carlito's Way, The Cowboy Way, Handgun, Stonewall, Lotto Land, The Substitute, The Brave, Boogie Nights, Out of Sight, Snake Eyes, One Tough Cop, The Limey, Mystery Men, The Bone Collector, Magnolia, Luckytown Blues, Traffic, Table One, Sam the Man, Home Invaders, Double Whammy, The Salton Sea, Welcome to Collinwood, The Count of Monte Cristo, Punch Drunk Love, Confidence, Anger Management, Dumb & Dumberer: When Harry Met Loyd, Runaway Jury.
TELEVISION: *Movies*: In The Shadow of a Killer, Double Deception, The Burning Season, Empire City, Quiet Killer, On Seventh Avenue, Pronto, Mind Prey, The Huntress, Thin Air. *Series*: Oz, Luis. *Guest*: NYPD Blue, Miami Vice, The Equilizer, Hunter, Law and Order, Homicide: Life on the Street, Walker, Texas Ranger, New York Undercover, Early Edition, Trinity, The Beat.

GYLLENHAAL, STEPHEN
Director. b. Pennsylvania. e. Trinity Col, CT. Started career in NYC making industrial films. Directed short film Exit 10.m.. writer-producer Naomi Foner.
PICTURES: Waterland, A Dangerous Woman, Losing Isaiah, Piece of My Heart, Homegrown.
TELEVISION: *Movies*: The Abduction of Kari Swenson, Promised a Miracle, Leap of Faith, Family of Spies, A Killing in a Small Town, Paris Trout, Shattered Mind, The Patron Saint of Liars, Resurrection, The Warden, Warden of Red Rock. *Series*: The Shield, Metro, Everwood, Robbery Homicide Division, Lucky. *Mini-Series*: Living with the Dead.

H

HAAS, LUKAS
Actor. b. West Hollywood, CA, Apr. 16, 1976. Kindergarten school principal told casting dir. about him which resulted in film debut in Testament. NY theater debut in Mike Nichols' Lincoln Center production of Waiting for Godot (1988). Appeared in AFI film The Doctor.
PICTURES: Testament (debut, 1983), Witness, Solarbabies, Lady in White, The Wizard of Loneliness, See You in the Morning, Music Box, Rambling Rose, Convicts, Alan and Naomi, Leap of Faith, Warrior Spirit, Boys, Johns, Palookaville, Mars Attacks!, Everyone Says I Love You, Boys, Mars Attacks!, Johns, In the Quiet Night, Breakfast of Champions, Running Free (voice), Kiss and Tell, Zoolander, The Pearl, Long Time Dead, Bookies.
TELEVISION: *Movies*: Love Thy Neighbor, Shattered Spirits, The Ryan White Story, The Perfect Tribute, Kiss and Tell, David and Lisa, The Lathe of Heaven. *Guest*: Amazing Stories (Ghost Train), Twilight Zone, The Young Indiana Jones Chronicles. *Pilot*: Brothers-in-Law. *Specials*: A Place at the Table, My Dissident Mom, Peacemaker (Triple Play II), Child Stars: Their Story. *Series*: Heavy Gear: The Animated Series (voice).

HACK, SHELLEY
Actress. b. Greenwich, CT, July 6, 1952. e. Smith Coll. and U. of Sydney, Australia. Made modeling debut at 14 on cover of Glamour Magazine. Gained fame as Revlon's Charlie Girl on TV commercials.
PICTURES: Annie Hall, If Ever I See You Again, Time After Time, The King of Comedy, Troll, The Stepfather, Blind Fear, Me Myself and I, The Finishing Touch, House Arrest.
TELEVISION:*Movies*: Death on the Freeway, Trackdown: Finding the Goodbar Killer, Found Money, Single Bars Single Women, Bridesmaids, Casualty of War, Taking Back My Life: The Nancy Ziegenmeyer Story, Not in My Family, The Case of the Wicked Wives, SeaQuest DSV, Falling From the Sky: Flight 174, Freefall, Frequent Flyer. *Series*: Charlie's Angels, Cutter to Houston, Jack and Mike.

HACKER, CHARLES R.
Executive. b. Milwaukee, WI, Oct. 8, 1920. e. U. of Wisconsin. Thea. mgr., Fox Wisc. Amuse. Corp., 1940; served in U.S.A.F. 1943-45; rejoined Fox Wisconsin Amusement Corp.; joined Standard Theatres Management Corp. 1947, on special assignments; apptd. district mgr. of Milwaukee & Waukesha theatres 1948; joined Radio City Music Hall Corp. as administrative asst. July, 1948; mgr. of oper., 1952; asst. to the pres., Feb. 1957; v.p.; Radio City Music Hall Corp., 1964; appointed executive vice

president and chief operating officer, February 1, 1973. Pres., Landmark Pictures, May, 1979. Treas. Will Rogers Memorial Fund, 1978-95. Award: Quigley Silver Grand Award for Showmanship, 1947. Member: U.S. Small Business Admin. Region 1, Hartford Advisory Council 1983-93.

HACKETT, BUDDY
Actor. r.n. Leonard Hacker. b. Brooklyn, NY, Aug. 31, 1924. Prof. debut, borscht circuit.
THEATRE: *B'way*: Call Me Mister, Lunatics and Lovers, I Had a Ball.
PICTURES: Walking My Baby Back Home (debut, 1953), Fireman Save My Child, God's Little Acre, Everything's Ducky, All Hands on Deck, The Music Man, The Wonderful World of the Brothers Grimm, It's a Mad Mad Mad Mad World, Muscle Beach Party, The Golden Head, The Good Guys and the Bad Guys (cameo), The Love Bug, Loose Shoes, Hey Babe!, Scrooged, The Little Mermaid (voice), Paulie, Let Me In I Hear Laughter.
TELEVISION: *Movies*: Bud and Lou.*Specials*: Entertainment 55, Variety, The Mama Cass TV Program, Plimpton: Did You Hear the One About...?, Jack Frost (voice), Circus of the Stars, Buddy Hackett—Live and Uncensored. *Series*: School House, Stanley, Jackie Gleason Show, Jack Paar Show, You Bet Your Life (1980), Fish Police (voice), Action, Last Comic Standing (celeb. talent scout, 2003).
(d. June 30, 2003)

HACKFORD, TAYLOR
Director, Producer. b. Santa Barbara, CA, Dec. 31, 1944. e. USC, B.A., int'l. relations. m. actress Helen Mirren. Was Peace Corps volunteer in Bolivia 1968-69. Began career with KCET in Los Angeles 1970-77. As prod-dir. won Oscar for short, Teenage Father, 1978. Theatrical film debut as dir. with The Idolmaker (1980).
PICTURES: *Dir. &/or Prod.*: The Idolmaker, An Officer and a Gentleman, Against All Odds, White Nights, Chuck Berry: Hail! Hail! Rock 'n' Roll, Everyone's All-American, Bound By Honor/Blood In Blood Out, Dolores Claiborne, The Devil's Advocate, Proof of Life (also. prod), Unchain My Heart: The Ray Charles Story. *Prod.*: Rooftops, La Bamba, The Long Walk Home, Sweet Talker, Queens Logic, Defenseless, Mortal Thoughts, When We Were Kings, Greenwich Mean Time.

HACKMAN, GENE
Actor. b. San Bernardino, CA, Jan. 30, 1930. First major broadway role in Any Wednesday. Other stage productions include: Poor Richard, Children from Their Games, A Rainy Day in Newark, The Natural Look, Death and the Maiden. Formed own production co., Chelly Ltd.
PICTURES: Mad Dog Coll (debut, 1961), Lilith, Hawaii, A Covenant With Death, Bonnie and Clyde (Acad. Award nom.), First to Fight, Banning, The Split, Riot, The Gypsy Moths, Downhill Racer, Marooned, I Never Sang for My Father (Acad. Award nom.), Doctors' Wives, The Hunting Party, The French Connection (Acad. Award, 1971), Cisco Pike, Prime Cut, The Poseidon Adventure, Scarecrow, The Conversation, Zandy's Bride, Young Frankenstein, Night Moves, Bite the Bullet, French Connection II, Lucky Lady, The Domino Principle, A Bridge Too Far, March or Die, Superman, All Night Long, Superman II, Reds, Eureka, Under Fire, Uncommon Valor, Misunderstood, Target, Twice in a Lifetime, Power, Hoosiers, Superman IV, No Way Out, Another Woman, Bat-21, Split Decisions, Full Moon in Blue Water, Mississippi Burning (Acad. Award nom.), The Package, Loose Cannons, Postcards From the Edge, Narrow Margin, Class Action, Company Business, Unforgiven (Acad. Award, Natl. Soc. of Film Critics, NY Film Critics, BAFTA, LA Film Critics & Golden Globe Awards, best supporting actor, 1992), The Firm, Geronimo: An American Legend, The Quick and the Dead, Crimson Tide, Get Shorty, Birdcage, Extreme Measures, The Chamber, Absolute Power, Antz (voice), Twilight, Enemy of the State, Under Suspicion, The Replacements, The Heist, Breakers, Behind Enemy Lines, The Royal Tenenbaums, The Runaway Jury, Welcome to Mooseport.
TELEVISION: *Movie*: Shadow on the Land. *Guest*: U.S. Steel Hour, The Defenders, Trials of O'Brien, Hawk, CBS Playhouse's My Father My Mother, The F.B.I., The Invaders, The Iron Horse.

HAGERTY, JULIE
Actress. b. Cincinnati, OH, June 15, 1955. Studied drama for six years before leaving for NY where studied with William Hickey. Made acting debut in her brother Michael's theatre group in Greenwich Village called the Production Company.
THEATRE: The Front Page (Lincoln Center), The House of Blue Leaves (Theatre World Award, 1986), Wild Life, Born Yesterday (Phil. Drama Guild), The Years, Three Men on a Horse, Wifey, A Cheever Evening, Raised in Captivity.
PICTURES: Airplane! (debut, 1980), A Midsummer Night's Sex Comedy, Airplane II: The Sequel, Lost in America, Goodbye New York, Bad Medicine, Beyond Therapy, Aria, Bloodhounds of Broadway, Rude Awakening, Reversal of Fortune, What About Bob?, Noises Off, The Wife, U Turn, Mel, Held Up, The Story of Us, Gut Feeling, Baby Bedlam, Freddy Got Fingered, Sotrytelling, Bridget, A Guy Thing.
TELEVISION: *Movies*: The Day the Women Got Even, Jackie's Back!, London Suite, Tourist Trap, The Badge. *Series*:

Princesses, Women of the House, Reunited. *Specials:* The Visit (Trying Times). House of Blue Leaves, Necessary Parties.

HAGGAR, PAUL JOHN
Executive. b. Brooklyn, NY, Aug. 5, 1928. e. LA h.s. Veteran of over 40 yrs. with Paramount Pictures, working way up from studio mail room to become apprentice editor in 1953; promoted to asst. editor 1955; music editor, 1957. 1968, named head of post-prod. for all films and TV made by Paramount. 1985, named sr. v.p., post-prod. for the Motion Picture Group. Currently exec. v.p., post-prod., Motion Picture Group.

HAGGARD, PIERS
Director. b. London, March 18, 1939. e. U. of Edinburgh. Son of actor Stephen Haggard; great grandnephew of author Rider Haggard. Began career in theatre in 1960 as asst. to artistic dir. at London's Royal Court. Named dir. of Glasgow Citizens' Theatre, 1962. 1963-65 worked with the National Theatre, where co-directed Hobson's Choice and The Dutch Courtesan. Has directed many prize winning TV commercials.
PICTURES: Wedding Night (debut, 1969; also co-s.p.), Blood on Satan's Claw (Satan's Skin), The Fiendish Plot of Dr. Fu Manchu, Venom, A Summer Story, Conquest.
TELEVISION: *Specials/Movies:* A Triple Play: Sam Found Out (Liza Minnelli special), The Fulfillment of Mary Gray, Back Home, Quatermass Conclusion, Chester Cycle of Mystery Plays, Mrs. Reinhardt, Knockback, Visitors, Heartstones, I'll Take Romance, Four Eyes and Six-Guns, Eskimo Day, The Double (s.p.), Lifeforce Experiment, Cold Enough for Snow, The Hunt. *Series:* Pennies from Heaven, Quatermass, Return to Treasure Island, Centrepoint, Space Precinct, Big Bad World.

HAGMAN, LARRY
Actor. b. Fort Worth, TX, Sept. 21, 1931. e. Bard Coll. Son of late actress Mary Martin. First stage experience with Margo Jones Theatre in the Round in Dallas. Appeared in N.Y. in Taming of the Shrew; one year with London production of South Pacific. 1952-56 was in London with U.S. Air Force where produced and directed show for servicemen. Returned to N.Y. for plays on and off B'way: God and Kate Murphy (Theatre World Award), The Nervous Set, The Warm Peninsula, The Beauty Part.
PICTURES: Ensign Pulver, Fail Safe, In Harm's Way, The Group, The Cavern, Up in the Cellar, Son of Blob (aka: Beware! The Blob; also dir.), Harry and Tonto, Stardust, Mother Jugs and Speed, The Big Bus, The Eagle Has Landed, Checkered Flag or Crash, Superman, S.O.B., Nixon, Primary Colors, Toscano.
TELEVISION: *Movies:* Three's a Crowd, Vanished, A Howling in the Woods, Getting Away from It All, No Place to Run, The Alpha Caper, Blood Sport, What Are Best Friends For?, Sidekicks, Hurricane, Sarah T.-Portrait of a Teenage Alcoholic, The Big Rip-Off, Return of the World's Greatest Detective, Intimate Strangers, The President's Mistress, Last of the Good Guys, A Double Life, Deadly Encounter, Dallas: The Early Years, Staying Afloat, In the Heat of the Night: Who Was Geli Bendl? (dir. only), Dallas: War of the Ewings, Dallas: Who Killed J.R.?, Dallas: J.R. Returns, The Third Twin, Dallas: War of the Ewings, Doing Dallas, When Shoulderpads Ruled the World, After Dallas; has appeared in several Intimate Portrait documentaries: Barbara Eden, Victoria Principal & Linda Gray. *Specials:* Applause, Lone Star. *Mini-series:* The Third Twin, The Rhinemann Exchange. *Series:* The Edge of Night, I Dream of Jeannie, The Good Life, Here We Go Again, Orleans, Dallas.

HAHN, HELENE
Executive. b. New York, NY. e. Loyola U. Sch. of Law. Instructor of entertainment law at Loyola. Attorney for ABC before joining Paramount in 1977 in studio legal dept. 1980, v.p.; 1981; sr. v.p., 1983. Left in 1985 to join Walt Disney Pictures as sr. v.p., business & legal affairs for m.p. division. 1987, promoted to exec. v.p., Walt Disney Studios. Currently, co-COO, Dreamworks SKG.

HAID, CHARLES
Actor, Director, Producer. b. San Francisco, CA, June 2, 1943. e. Carnegie Tech. Appeared on NY stage in Elizabeth the First. Co-produced Godspell. Prod. & dir. short film The Last Supper.
PICTURES: *Actor:* The Choirboys, Who'll Stop the Rain, Oliver's Story, House of God, Altered States, Square Dance (co-exec. prod. only), Cop, The Rescue, Nightbreed, Storyville, The Third Miracle. *Director:* Iron Will.
TELEVISION: *Movies:* The Execution of Private Slovik, Remember When, Things in Their Season, Kate McShane (pilot), Foster and Laurie, A Death in Canaan, The Bastard, Death Moon, Twirl, Divorce Wars, Children in the Crossfire (also co-prod.), Code of Vengeance, Six Against the Rock, Weekend War, The Great Escape II: The Untold Story, A Deadly Silence, Fire and Rain, Man Against the Mob: The Chinatown Murders, In the Line of Duty: A Cop for the Killing (also co-prod.), In the Line of Duty: Siege at Marion (dir. only), The Nightman (dir., prod. only), Cooperstown (also dir.), For Their Own Good, The Fire Next Time, Broken Trust, Sally Hemings: An American Scandal (dir. only). *Series:* Kate McShane, Delvecchio, Hill Street Blues, Cop Rock (prod. only). *Dir./series:* NYPD Blue (1993)), Murder One, High Incident, Buddy Faro, Big Apple (also

co-exec. prod., The Guardian, Citizen Baines, The Court, Presidio Med.

HAIM, COREY
Actor. b. Toronto, Canada, Dec. 23, 1972. Performed in TV commercials at 10; regular on children's show, The Edison Twins.
PICTURES: Firstborn (debut, 1984), Secret Admirer, Silver Bullet, Murphy's Romance, Lucas, The Lost Boys, License to Drive, Watchers, Dream a Little Dream, Fast Getaway (also assoc. prod.), Prayer of the Roller Boys, The Dream Machine, Oh What a Night, Blown Away, The Double-O Kid, National Lampoon's Last Resort, Fast Getaway 2, Dream a Little Dream 2, Life 101 (also assoc. prod.), Snowboard Academy, Fever Lake, Demolition High, Busted, Never Too Late, Tales From the Crypt: Bordello of Blood, Demolition University (also exec. prod.), Universal Groove, The Back Lot Murders.
TELEVISION: *Movies:* A Time to Live, Just One of the Girls, Merlin, Without Malice. *Series:* Roomies.

HAINES, RANDA
Director, Producer. b. Los Angeles, CA, Feb. 20, 1945. Raised in NYC. Studied acting with Lee Strasberg. e. School of Visual Arts. 1975 accepted into AFI's Directing Workshop for Women. Dir. & co-wrote short film August/September, which led to work as writer for series Family. Appeared in documentary Calling the Shots.
PICTURES: Children of a Lesser God, The Doctor, Wrestling Ernest Hemingway, A Family Thing (co-prod. only), Dance with Me, Antwone Fisher (prod. only)
TELEVISION: *Movies:* Something About Amelia, The Outsider. *Specials:* Under This Sky, The Jilting of Granny Weatherall, Just Pals. *Series:* Family (writer), Hill Street Blues (dir. of 4 episodes), Alfred Hitchcock Presents (Bang You're Dead).

HALE, BARBARA
Actress. b. DeKalb, IL, Feb. 18, 1922. Was married to late actor Bill Williams. Son is actor William Katt. e. Chicago Acad. of Fine Arts. Beauty contest winner, Little Theatre actress. Screen debut, 1943.
PICTURES: Gildersleeve's Bad Day, The Seventh Victim, Higher and Higher, Belle of the Yukon, The Falcon Out West, Falcon in Hollywood, Heavenly Days, West of the Pecos, First Yank in Tokyo, Lady Luck, A Likely Story, Boy with Green Hair, The Clay Pigeon, Window, Jolson Sings Again, And Baby Makes Three, Emergency Wedding, Jackpot, Lorna Doone, First Time, Last of the Comanches, Seminole, Lone Hand, A Lion Is in the Streets, Unchained, Far Horizons, Houston Story, 7th Cavalry, Oklahoman, Slim Carter, Desert Hell, Buckskin, Airport, Soul Soldier, Giant Spider Invasion, Big Wednesday.
TELEVISION: *Movies:* Flight of the Grey Wolf, Perry Mason Returns (1985) and more than 29 other Perry Mason's incl. The Case of the... Murdered Madam, Avenging Ace, Lady in the Lake, Scandalous Scoundrel, Lethal Lesson, Wicked Wives, Lethal Lifestyle, Grimacing Governor, Jealous Jokester (1995). *Series:* Perry Mason (Emmy Award, 1959).

HALL, ANTHONY MICHAEL
Actor. r.n. Michael Anthony Hall. b. Boston, MA, Apr. 14, 1968.
PICTURES: Six Pack (debut, 1982), National Lampoon's Vacation, Sixteen Candles, The Breakfast Club, Weird Science, Out of Bounds, Johnny Be Good, Edward Scissorhands, A Gnome Named Gnorm, Into the Sun, Hail Caesar (also dir.), Six Degrees of Separation, Me and the Mob, The Grave, Exit in Red, Trojan War, The Killing Grounds, Cold Night Into Dawn, Blunt, Revenge, Dirt Merchant, Happy Accidents, 2 Little 2 Late, The Photographer, The Caveman's Valentine, Freddy Got Fingered, All About the Benjamins, Funny Valentine.
TELEVISION: *Movies:* Rascals and Robbers: The Secret Adventures of Tom Sawyer and Huck Finn, Running Out, A Bucket of Blood, Hijacked: Flight 285, A Touch of Hope, Pirates of Silicon Valley, Hysteria: The Def Leppard Story, Hitched. *Series:* Saturday Night Live (1985-86), Stephen King's Dead Zone. *Mini-Series:* Texas. *Guest:* NYPD Blue, Tales from the Crypt, Boys and Girls.

HALL, ARSENIO
Actor, Comedian. b. Cleveland, OH. Feb. 12, 1959. e. Kent State U. Became interested in magic at 7, which later led to own local TV special, The Magic of Christmas. Switched from advertising career to stand-up comedy, 1979. Discovered at Chicago nightclub by singer Nancy Wilson.
PICTURES: Amazon Women on the Moon (debut, 1987), Coming to America, Harlem Nights, Bopha! (exec. prod. only), Blankman (cameo).
TELEVISION: Movies: Uptown Comedy Express. *Series:* The 1/2 Hour Comedy Hour (1983, co-host), Thicke of the Night, Motown Revue, The Real Ghost Busters (voice), The Late Show (1987, host), The Arsenio Hall Show, The Party Machine With Nia Peeples (prod. only), Arsenio, Martial Law, Arsenio Jams, Star Search (host, 2002-). *Special:*s Happy Birthday Elizabeth: A Celebration of Life, Inside TV Land: African Americans in Television, 16th Annual Soul Train Music Awards, World's Greatest Commercials (co-host), 40 Years of Laughter: At the Improv.

HALL, CONRAD L.
Cinematographer. b. Papeete, Tahiti, June 21, 1926. Worked as camera operator with Robert Surtees, Ted McCord, Ernest Haller; moved to TV as dir. of photography before feature films. PICTURES: Wild Seed, The Saboteur–Code Name: Morituri, Harper, The Professionals, Rogue's Gallery, Incubus, Divorce American Style, In Cold Blood, Cool Hand Luke, Hell in the Pacific, Butch Cassidy and the Sundance Kid (Academy Award, 1969), Tell Them Willie Boy Is Here, The Happy Ending, Fat City, Electra Glide in Blue, The Day of the Locust, Smile, Marathon Man, Black Widow, Tequila Sunrise, Class Action, Jennifer Eight, Searching for Bobby Fischer, Love Affair, A Civil Action (Acad. Award nom.), Without Limits, American Beauty (Acad. Award), The Road to Perdition.
TELEVISION: Movie: It Happened One Christmas, Stoney Burke. Series: Outer Limits.
(d. Jan. 4, 2003)

HALL, KURT C.
Executive. b. Burlington, VT. e. Univ. of VT. Served as dir. of financial reporting, dir. of finance, and v.p. & treas. of UA Entertainment before becoming v.p. & treas. of United States Theatre Circuit, 1990-91. Named exec. v.p. and CFO of United Artists Theatre Circuit, Inc. From 1998-Aug. 2002, pres. & CEO of United Artists Theatre Company. Currently, a director, Co-chmn., and co-CEO of Regal Entertainment Group (REG) and pres., CEO of Regal CineMedia Corp. Hall serves on the exec. committee of NATO's bd. of directors.

HALL, MONTY; O.C.
Actor. b. Winnipeg, Manitoba, Canada, Aug. 25, 1925. e. U. of Manitoba, B.S. Host of Keep Talking, 1958. Host of Let's Make a Deal, 1964-86. International chmn., Variety Clubs International. TELEVISION: Movies: The Courage & The Passion (1978), It's Howdy Doody Time. Series/Host: The Little Revue (1953), Floor Show, Matinee Party, Keep Talking, Video Village, Let's Make A Deal (1963), It's Anybody's Guess, Beat the Clock. Series/Exec. Prod: Split Second (1972 & 1986), Masquerade Party, Let's Make A Deal (2003).

HALL, PHILIP BAKER
Actor. b. Toldeo, Ohio, September 10, 1931. e. Univ. of Toldeo. PICTURES: Cowards, The Man With Bogart's Face, The Last Reunion, Dream On, Secret Honor, Three O'Clock High, Midnight Run, Ghostbusters II, Say Anything, An Innocent Man, How I Got Into College, Blue Desert, Live Wire, Cigarettes and Coffee, Kiss of Death, The Little Death, Eye for an Eye, Hit Me, Hard Eight, The Rock, Buddy, Air Force One, Boogie Nights, Sour Grapes, The Truman Show, Judas Kiss, Rush Hour, Enemy of the State, Psycho, Implicated, Cradle Will Rock, The Insider, Magnolia, The Talented Mr. Ripley, Let the Devil Wear Black, Rules of Engagement, The Contender, Lost Souls, A Gentleman's Game, The Sum of All Fears, Die Die Mommie, Bruce Almighty, Dogville, In Control of All Things.
TELEVISION: Movies: The Last Survivors, Mayday at 40000 Feet, Man from Atlantis, Kill Me If You Can, The Bastard, Terror Out of the Sky, Samurai, The Night the Bridge Fell Down, This House Possessed, Games Mother Never Taught You, Who is Julia?, Goddess of Love, A Cry for Help: The Tracey Thurman Story, Incident at Dark River, Crash Landing: The Rescue of Flight 232, Stormy Weathers, M.A.N.T.I.S, Roswell, Without Warning, Tempting Fate, Witness to the Mob, Path to War. Series: Mariah, Falcon Crest, Pasadena. Guest: Good Times, Emergency!, MASH, The Waltons, Quincy, Cheers, Matlock, T.J. Hooker, Bagdad Cafe, Murder, She Wrote, Seinfeld, Life's Work, Hardball, The Good Life, Chicago Hope, Third Rock from the Sun, The Practice, Millenium. Mini-Series: Jackie Bouvier Kennedy Onassis.

HALLSTROM, LASSE
Director. b. Stockholm, Sweden, June 2, 1946. m. actress Lena Olin. As teenager made 16mm film which was eventually screened on Swedish tv. Began professional career filming and editing inserts for Swedish TV. Directed program Shall We Dance? for Danish TV, followed by TV prod. on The Love Seeker, dir. of program Shall We Go to My or to Your Place or Each Go Home Alone?.
PICTURES: A Love and His Lass (debut, 1974), ABBA: The Movie, Father-to-Be, The Rooster, Happy We, The Children of Bullerbo Village, More About the Children of Bullerby Village, My Life as a Dog (also co-s.p.; Acad. Award noms. for dir. & s.p.), Once Around (U.S. debut, 1991), What's Eating Gilbert Grape (also co-exec. prod.), Lumiere & Company, Something to Talk About, The Cider House Rules (Acad. Award nom.), Chocolat, The Shipping News, An Unfinished Life.

HALMI, ROBERT JR.
Producer. Father is Robert Halmi, Sr. Emmys for Outstanding Children's Special for Run the Wild Fields (2001, shared with Paul Rauch, Paul Kaufman & Rodney P. Vaccaro); and A Storm in Summer (2001, shared with Renee Valente.) Won Emmy-Outstanding Drama/Comedy Special in 1990 for The Incident. PICTURES: Hugo the Hippo, Braxton, Ascent, Just a Dream, Back to the Secret Garden.

TELEVISION: Movies/Exec. Prod.: Nairobi Affair, Pack of Lies, April Morning, Mr. & Mrs. Bridge, Bump In The Night, The Josephine Baker Story, Eyes of a Witness. The Fire Next Time, Blind Spot, The Yearling, Seasons of the Heart, The Ascent, Black Fox, Black Fox: The Price of Peace, Black Fox: Good Men & Bad, September, The Tale of Sweeney Todd, Still Holding On: The Legend of Cadillac Jack, Creature, The Ransom of Red Chief, The Baby Dance, Hard Time, The Premonition, Alice in Wonderland, Cleopatra, Journey to the Center of the Earth, In A Class of His Own, Hostage Hotel, Aftershock: Earthquake in New York, The Wishing Tree, Finding Buck McHenry, Arabian Nights, Jason & the Argonauts, Seventeen Again, Hamlet, David Copperfield, By Dawn's Early Light, The Lost Empire, Walter & Henry, The Infinite Worlds of H.G. Wells, Prince Charming, Snow White: The Fairest of Them All, They Call Me Sirr, Off Season, Roughing It, Just A Dream, Gentle Ben (2002), Night of the Wolf, The Snow Queen, Gentle Ben 2, The Last Cowboy, Straight from the Heart, Love Comes Softly, Audrey's Rain, The King & Queen of Moonlight Bay, Hard Ground, Mystery Woman, Turning Homeward, Monster Makers, Til' the River Runs Dry, Frankenstein, Dinotopia: Curse of the Ruby Sunstone. Mini-series: Lonesome Dove, Return to Lonesome Dove, The Old Curiosity Shop, Streets of Laredo, Dead Man's Walk, The 10th Kingdom, In the Beginning, A Girl Thing, Voyage of the Unicorn, Dinotopia, La Femme Musketeer. Series: Chillers, Lonesome Dove: The Outlaw Years, Farscape, Dinotopia (series, 2002).

HALMI, ROBERT SR.
Producer. b. Budapest, Hungary, Jan 22, 1924. Originally writer-photographer under contract to Life Magazine. CEO, Hallmark Entertainment.
PICTURES: Created documentaries for U.N. Features include: Hugo the Hippo, Visit to a Chief's Son, The One and Only, Brady's Escape, Cheetah, Mr. and Mrs. Bridge.
TELEVISION: Bold Journey (dir.-cin.), American Sportsman, The Oriental Sportsman, The Flying Doctor, The Outdoorsman, Julius Boros Series, Rexford, Who Needs Elephants, Calloway's Climb, Oberndorf Revisited, True Position, Wilson's Reward, Nurse, Buckley Sails, A Private Battle, My Old Man, Mr. Griffin and Me, When the Circus Came to Town, Best of Friends, Bush Doctor, Peking Encounter, Svengali, China Rose, Cook and Peary-The Race to the Pole, Terrible Joe Moran, Nairobi Affair, The Night They Saved Christmas, Spies, Lies and Naked Thighs. Exec. prod.: The Prize Pulitzer, Paradise, Bridesmaids, Face to Face, Margaret Bourke-White, The Incident, Josephine Baker Story, The Secret, An American Story, Call of the Wild, Blind Spot, Incident in a Small Town, Spoils of War, The Yearling, A Promise Kept: The Oksana Baiul Story, A Mother's Gift, Scarlett, Reunion, My Brother's Keeper, White Dwarf, Secrets, Bye Bye Birdie, Kidnapped, Gulliver's Travels (Emmy Award, 1996), Captains Courageous, Dead Man's Walk, The Oddysey, In Cold Blood, Mrs. Santa Claus, Forbidden Territory: Stanley's Search for Livingstone, A Christmas Memory, Mary and Tim, Moby Dick, Merlin, The Long Way Home, Moby Dick, Merlin, Crime and Punishment, Only Love, Rear Window, Alice in Wonderland, Noah's Ark, Cleopatra, Animal Farm, The Magical Legend of the Leprechauns, A Christmas Carol, The 10th Kingdom, Don Quixote, Arabian Nights, The Land of Oz, The Lost Empire, Voyage of the Unicorn, The Infinite Worlds of H.G. Wells, Mike Bassett: England Manager, Prince Charming, Snow White, King of Texas, Dinotopia, The Snow Queen, Teenage Mutant Ninja Turtles, The Lion in Winter, DC 9/11: Time of Crisis.

HAMADY, RON
Producer, Director. b. Flint, MI, June 16, 1947. e. U. of California, B.A. 1971. Co-founder of The Crystal Jukebox, record prod's., music mgmt. and music pub. co. Prod. 12 hit albums for Decca Records of England and London Records, U.S. Entered m.p. industry in 1975, producing Train Ride to Hollywood for Taylor-Laughlin dist. Co.
PICTURES: Fade to Black, Surf II, And God Created Woman (1987), Out Cold, Don't Tell Her It's Me, Pandemonium (video, dir., writer only).

HAMEL, VERONICA
Actress. b. Philadelphia, PA, Nov. 20, 1943. e. Temple U. Moved to NY and began a modelling career with Eileen Ford Agency. Off B'way debut: The Big Knife. Acted in dinner theater prods. Moved to L.A. 1975.
THEATRE: B'way: Rumors. Off B'way: The Big Knife, The Ballad of Boris K.
PICTURES: Cannonball, Beyond the Poseidon Adventure, When Time Ran Out, A New Life, Taking Care of Business, The Last Leprechaun, Determination of Death.
TELEVISION: Movies: The Gathering, Ski Lift to Death, The Gathering II, The Hustler of Muscle Beach, Valley of the Dolls, Sessions, Twist of Fate, She Said No, Stop at Nothing, Deadly Medicine (also co-exec. prod.), Baby Snatcher (also co-exec. prod.), The Disappearance of Nora, The Conviction of Kitty Dodds, Shadow of Obsession, A Child's Cry for Help, Intensive Care, Secrets, Here Come the Munsters, Blink of an Eye, Talk to Me, Stranger in My Home, Home Invasion. Mini-Series: 79 Park Avenue, Kane & Abel. Series: Hill Street Blues, Philly, Third Watch. Guest: Kojak, Rockford Files, Bob Newhart Show.

HAMILL, MARK

Actor. b. Oakland, CA, Sept. 25, 1951. While studying acting at LA City Col. made prof. debut in episode of The Bill Cosby Show, 1970. Featured in CD-ROM interactive game Wing Commander III.
THEATRE: NY: The Elephant Man (B'way debut), Amadeus (also Natl. tour), Harrigan 'n' Hart, Room Service (off-B'way), The Nerd.
PICTURES: Star Wars (debut, 1977), Wizards (voice), Corvette Summer, The Empire Strikes Back, The Big Red One, The Night the Lights Went Out in Georgia, Britannia Hospital, Return of the Jedi, Slipstream, Midnight Ride, Black Magic Woman, Sleepwalkers (cameo), Time Runner, The Guyver, Batman: Mask of the Phantasm (voice), Village of the Damned, Laserhawk, Gen 13 (voice), Hamilton, Wing Commander (cameo, voice), Walking Across Egypt, Sinbad: Beyond the Veil of Mists (voice), Earth Day (voice), Jay and Silent Bob Strike Back, Thank You Good Night, Baxter and Bananas, Reeseville, Comic Book: The Movie (also dir.).
TELEVISION: Movies: Sarah T.-Portrait of a Teenage Alcoholic, Eric, Delancey Street: The Crisis Within, Mallory: Circumstantial Evidence, The City, Earth Angel, Body Bags, Hollyrock-a-Bye Baby (voice), When Time Expires, Sinbad: Beyond the Veil of Mists. Guest: Room 222, The Partridge Family, Headmaster, Medical Center, Owen Marshall, The FBI, Streets of San Francisco, One Day at a Time, Manhunter, Hooperman, Alfred Hitchcock Presents, Amazing Stories, The Flash, seaQuest DSV, The Simpsons (voice), Just Shoot Me. Series: General Hospital, The Texas Wheelers, Batman (voice), The Incredible Hulk (voice), Bruno the Kid (voice), Wing Commander Academy (voice), Cow and Chicken, The Legend of Calamity Jane, Superstructures of the World, The Sci-Fi Files, The Powerpuff Girls, .COM, Justice League, Teamo Supremo (voice), Stripperella. Specials: Get High on Yourself, Night of 100 Stars.

HAMILTON, GEORGE

Actor. b. Memphis, TN, Aug. 12, 1939. e. grammar, Hawthorne, CA; military sch., Gulfport, MS, N.Y. Hackley Prep Sch., FL, Palm Beach H.S. Won best actor award in Florida, high sch. contest.
PICTURES: Crime and Punishment USA (debut, 1959), Home From the Hill, All the Fine Young Cannibals, Where the Boys Are, Angel Baby, By Love Possessed, A Thunder of Drums, Light in the Piazza, Two Weeks in Another Town, Act One, The Victors, Looking for Love, Your Cheatin' Heart, Viva Maria, That Man George, Doctor You've Got to Be Kidding!, Jack of Diamonds, A Time for Killing, The Power, Togetherness, Evel Knievel (also co-p), Medusa (also exec. prod.), The Man Who Loved Cat Dancing, Once Is Not Enough, The Happy Hooker Goes to Washington, Love at First Bite (also co-exec. prod.), Sextette, From Hell to Victory, Zorro the Gay Blade (also co-prod.), The Godfather Part III, Doc Hollywood, Once Upon a Crime, Double Dragon, Amore!, Playback, Meet Wally Sparks, 8 Heads in a Duffel Bag, She's Too Tall, Bulworth (cameo), The Little Unicorn, Pets, Crocodile Dundee in Los Angeles, Off Key, The Trip (exec. prod. only), Hollywood Ending.
TELEVISION: Movies: Two Fathers' Justice, Monte Carlo, Poker Alice, Caution: Murder Can Be Hazardous to Your Health, The House on Sycamore Street, Two Fathers: Justice for the Innocent, Danielle Steel's Vanished, Rough Riders. Mini-Series: Roots, P.T. Barnum. Series: The Survivors, Paris 7000, Dynasty, Spies, The Bold & the Beautiful, The George and Alana Show (also prod.), The Guilt, Jenny, Match Game, The Family (host, 2003). Guest: Rin Tin Tin, The Donna Reed Show, Dream On, The John Laroquette Show, The Bonnie Hunt Show, The Naked Truth. Special: The Veil.

HAMILTON, GUY

Director. b. Paris, France, Sept. 24, 1922. Ent. m.p. industry 1939 as apprentice at Victorine Studio, Nice; Royal Navy, 1940-45, in England asst. dir., Fallen Idol, Third Man, Outcast of the Islands, African Queen.
PICTURES: The Ringer, The Intruder, An Inspector Calls, Dragnet (actor only), Colditz Story, Manuela, The Devil's Disciple, A Touch of Larceny, The Best of Enemies, The Party's Over, Man in the Middle, Goldfinger, Funeral in Berlin, Battle of Britain, Diamonds Are Forever, Live and Let Die, The Man with the Golden Gun, Force Ten from Navarone, The Mirror Crack'd, Evil Under the Sun, Remo Williams, Try This One For Size.

HAMILTON, LINDA

Actress. b. Salisbury, MD, Sept. 26, 1956. Appeared on NY stage in Looice and Richard III.
PICTURES: Tag: The Assassination Game, Children of the Corn, The Stone Boy, The Terminator, Black Moon Rising, King Kong Lives!, Mr. Destiny, Terminator 2: Judgment Day, Silent Fall, The Shadow Conspiracy, Dante's Peak, Unglued The Secret Life of Girls, Skeletons in the Closet, Wholey Moses.
TELEVISION: Movies: Reunion, Rape and Marriage-The Rideout Case, Country Gold, Secrets of a Mother and Daughter, Secret Weapons, Club Med, Go Toward the Light, A Mother's Prayer, Rescuers: Stories of Courage: Two Couples, On the Line, Point Last Seen, The Color of Courage, Batman Beyond: The Movie, Sex & Mrs X, A Girl Thing (mini), Bailey's Mistake, Silent Night. Series: Secrets of Midland Heights, King's Crossing, Beauty and the Beast, Hercules. Guest: Hill Street Blues, Murder She Wrote.

HAMLIN, HARRY

Actor. b. Pasadena, CA, Oct. 30, 1951. e. U. of California, Yale U., 1974 in theatre, psychology. Awarded IT&T Fulbright Grant, 1977. 1974-1976 with the American Conservatory Theatre, San Francisco, then joined McCarter Theatre, Princeton (Hamlet, Faustus in Hell, Equus). B'way debut Awake and Sing! (1984). Also performed in Henry V, Smoke.
PICTURES: Movie Movie (debut, 1978), King of the Mountain, Clash of the Titans, Making Love, Blue Skies Again Maxie, Ebbtide, Save Me, The Celluloid Closet, Badge of Bertrayal, Allie & Me, Frogs for Snakes, Perfume, Roads to Riches, Shoot or Be Shot.
TELEVISION: Movies: Laguna Heat, Deceptions, Deadly Intentions... Again?, Deliver Them From Evil: The Taking of Alta View, Poisoned By Love: The Kern County Murders, In the Best of Families: Marriage Pride & Madness, Tom Clancy's Op Center, Her Deadly Rival, The Hunted, Like Father Like Santa, Silent Predators, Quarantine, Sex Lies and Obsession, Disappearance, L.A. Law: Return to Justice. Mini-series: Studs Lonigan, Master of the Game, Space, Favorite Son, Night Sins. Series: L.A. Law, Ink, Movie Stars.

HAMLISCH, MARVIN

Composer. b. New York, NY, June 2, 1944. e. Juilliard. Accompanist and straight man on tour with Groucho Marx 1974-75; debut as concert pianist 1975 with Minn. Orch. Scores of B'way shows: A Chorus Line (Tony Award & Pulitzer Prize); They're Playing Our Song, Smile, The Goodbye Girl. Composer of popular songs: Sunshine Lollipops and Rainbows, Nobody Does It Better. Winner 4 Grammy awards, 3 Oscars, 2 Emmys, 1 Tony, 3 Golden Globe awards. Autobiography, The Way I Was, 1992. Conductor for the Pittsburgh Symphony Orchestra, 1995; Baltimore Symphony Orchestra, 1996.
PICTURES: The Swimmer, Take the Money and Run, Bananas, Save the Tiger, Kotch, The Way We Were (2 Acad. Awards for orig. score and title song, 1973), The Sting (Acad. Award for music adapt., 1973), The Spy Who Loved Me, Same Time Next Year, Ice Castles, Chapter Two, Seems Like Old Times, Starting Over, Ordinary People, The Fan, Sophie's Choice, I Ought to Be in Pictures, Romantic Comedy, D.A.R.Y.L., Three Men and a Baby, Little Nikita, The January Man, The Experts, Frankie and Johnny, Open Season, The Mirror Has Two Faces, Austin Powers: The Spy Who Shagged Me, Standing Room Only.
TELEVISION: Movies: The Entertainer (also prod.), A Streetcar Named Desire, The Two Mrs. Grenvilles, Women & Men: Stories of Seduction, Switched at Birth, Seasons of the Heart. Series: Good Morning America (theme), Brooklyn Bridge.

HAMMOND, PETER

Actor, Writer, Director. b. London, England,, Nov.15, 1923. e. Harrow Sch. of Art. Stage debut: Landslide, Westminster Theatre. Screen debut: Holiday Camp. Dir./writer, 1959-61, tv plays.
PICTURES: The Huggetts, Helter Skelter, Fools Rush In, The Reluctant Widow, Fly Away Peter, The Adventurers, Operation Disaster, Come Back, Peter, Little Lambs Eat Ivy, Its Never Too Late, The Unknown, Morning Departure, Confession. Dir.: Spring and Port Wine.
TELEVISION: Series: William Tell, Robin Hood, The Buccaneers. Dir.: Avengers, 4 Armchair Theatres, Theatre 625, BBC classic serials Count of Monte Cristo, Three Musketeers, Hereward the Wake, Treasure Island, Lord Raingo, Cold Comfort Farm, The White Rabbit, Out of the Unknown, Follyfoot; Lukes Kingdom, Time to Think, Franklin's Farm, Sea Song, Shades of Greene, Our Mutual Friend, The House that Jack Built, The King of the Castle, The Black Knight, Kilvert's Diary, Turgenev's Liza, Wuthering Heights, Funnyman, Little World of Don Camillo, Rumpole of the Bailey, Bring on the Girls, Hallelujah Mary Plum, Aubrey Beardsley, The Happy Autumn Fields, The Combination, Tales of the Unexpected, The Glory Hole, The Hard Word, Shades of Darkness-The Maze, Uncle Silas, The Master Blackmailer, The Eligible Bachelor, The Memoirs of Sherlock Holmes.

HAMNER, EARL

Producer, Writer. b. Schuyler, VA, July 10, 1923. e. U. of Richmond 1940-43, Northwestern U.; U. of Cincinnati, Coll. Conservatory of Music, B.F.A., 1958. With WLW, Cincinnati, as radio writer-prod.; joined NBC 1949 as writer; (The Georgia Gibbs Show, The Helen O'Connell Show); freelance 1961-71; writer, prod. Lorimar Prods. 1971-86; writer prod. Taft Entertainment 1986-; Pres. Amanda Prods.
PICTURES: Palm Springs Weekend, Spencer's Mountain, The Tamarind Seed, Charlotte's Web (adaptor), Where the Lilies Bloom.
TELEVISION: Movies: The Homecoming: A Christmas Story (writer only), You Can't Get There From Here (writer only), A Wedding on Walton's Mountain, Mother's Day on Walton's Mountain, A Day of Thanks on Walton's Mountain (also actor), The Gift of Love--A Christmas Story (also writer), A Walton Thanksgiving Reunion, A Walton Wedding, A Mother's Gift, A Walton Easter, The Education of Little Tree. Exec. prod.: Series: The Waltons (creator, co-prod., narrator), Apple's Way (creator), The Young Pioneers (creator), Joshua's World, Falcon Crest, Boone (also creator), Morning Star/Evening Star (also narrator) Night Visions (writer).

HAMPSHIRE, SUSAN
O.B.E., 1995. Actress. b. London, England,, May 12, 1941.
THEATRE: Expresso Bongo, Follow That Girl, Fairy Tales of New York, Ginger Man, Past Imperfect, She Stoops to Conquer, On Approval, The Sleeping Prince, A Doll's House, Taming of the Shrew, Peter Pan, Romeo & Jeanette, As You Like It, Miss Julie, The Circle, Arms and the Man, Man and Superman, Tribades, An Audience Called Edward, The Crucifer of Blood, Night and Day, The Revolt, House Guest, Blithe Spirit, Married Love, A Little Night Music, The King and I, Noel & Gertie, Relative Values, Susanna Andler, Black Chiffon.
PICTURES: The Three Lives of Thomasina, Night Must Fall, Wonderful Life, Paris Au Mois d'Aout, The Fighting Prince of Donegal, The Trygon Factor, Monte Carlo or Bust, Rogan, David Copperfield, A Room in Paris, Living Free, Time for Loving, Malpertius, Baffled, Neither the Sea nor the Sand, Roses and Green Peppers, David the King, Bang.
TELEVISION: Andromeda, The Forsyte Saga, Vanity Fair, Katy, The First Churchills; An Ideal Husband, The Lady Is a Liar, The Improbable Mr. Clayville, Dr. Jekyll and Mr. Hyde (musical), The Pallisers, Barchester Chronicles, Leaving, Leaving II, Going to Pot (I, II, and III), Don't Tell Father, The Grand I & II, Coming Home, Nancherrow, Monarch of the Glen.

HAMPTON, JAMES
Actor. b. Oklahoma City, OK, July 9, 1936. e. N. Texas St. Univ.
PICTURES: Fade In, Soldier Blue, The Man Who Loved Cat Dancing, The Longest Yard, W.W. & The Dixie Dancekings, Hustle, Hawmps!, The Cat from Outer Space, Mackintosh & T.J., The China Syndrome, Hangar 18, Condorman, Teen Wolf, Teen Wolf Too, Police Academy 5, Pump Up the Volume, The Giant of Thunder Mountain, Sling Blade, Lost in the Pershing Point Hotel, Danny & Max.
TELEVISION: Movies: Attack on Terror: The FBI Versus the Ku Klux Klan, Force Five, The Amazing Howard Hughes, Three on a Date, Thaddeus Rose and Eddie, Stand By Your Man, Through the Magic Pyramid, World War III, The Burning Bed. Mini-Series: Centennial. Series: F Troop, The Doris Day Show, Love—American Style, Mary, Maggie.

HANCOCK, JOHN
Director. b. Kansas City, MO, Feb. 12, 1939. e. Harvard. Was musician and theatre dir. before turning to films. Dir. play A Man's a Man, NY 1962. Artistic dir. San Francisco Actors Workshop 1965-66, Pittsburgh Playhouse 1966-67. Obie for dir. Midsummer Night's Dream, NY 1968. Nominated for Acad. Award for short, Sticky My Fingers, Fleet My Feet.
PICTURES: Let's Scare Jessica to Death, Bang the Drum Slowly, Baby Blue Marine, California Dreaming, Weeds (also co-s.p.), Prancer, Steal the Sky, A Piece of Eden, Suspended Animation.
TELEVISION: The Twilight Zone (1986), Lady Blue, Hill Street Blues.

HAND, BETHLYN J.
Executive. b. Alton, IL. e. U. of Texas. Entered motion picture industry in 1966 as administrative assistant to president of Motion Picture Association of America, Inc. In 1975 became associate dir. of advertising administration of MPAA. In 1976 became dir. of advertising administration; in 1979 became; v.p.-west coast activities, board of directors, Los Angeles. S.P.C.A. 1981, appointed by Governor to Calif. Motion Picture Council 1983, elected vice chmn., California Motion Picture Council. 1990, named sr. v.p. MPAA. Hand retired full-time duties with MPAA March 28, 2003, but continued consulting for the org. through year-end. She remains a member of the Academy of Motion Picture Arts and Sciences and serves on the exec. committee for public relations and the PR Coordinating Committee, which handles press during the Acad. Awards.

HANDEL, LEO A.
Producer, Director. b. Vienna, Austria, Mar. 7, 1924. e. Univ. of Vienna (Ph.D. economics). Dir. audience research, MGM, 1942-51; organized Meteor Prod., 1951; organized Leo A. Handel Prod., for TV films, 1953; author, Hollywood Looks at Its Audience, also TV plays; press., Handel Film Corp. Exec. prod. & v.p., Four Crown Prods., Inc. Prod.-writer-dir., feature film, The Case of Patty Smith, 1961; book, A Dog Named Duke, 1965.
TELEVISION: prod. TV series including Everyday Adventures, Magic of the Atom. exec. prod., Phantom Planet, Americana Series. Also produced numerous educational specials and videos.

HANEKE, MICHAEL
Director, Writer. b. Munich, Germany, March 23, 1942.
PICTURES: The Seventh Continent, Benny's Video, 71 Fragments of a Chronology of Chance, The Age of the Wolves, Lumiere and Company (dir. only), The Moor's Head (s.p. only), The Castle, Funny Games, Code Unkown: Incomplete Tales of Several Journeys, La Pianiste, Le Temps du loup.
TELEVISION: Movies: After Liverpool, Sperrmull (dir. only), Drei Wege zum See, Variation, Wer war Edgar Allan?, Fraulein, Nachruf fur einen Morder, Die Rebellion.

HANKS, TOM
Actor, Producer. b. Concord, CA, July 9, 1956. m. actress Rita Wilson. Traveled around Northern CA. with family before settling in Oakland, CA. e. Chabot Jr. Col., California State U. Began career with Great Lakes Shakespeare Festival, Cleveland (3 seasons) and NY's Riverside Theater (Taming of the Shrew).
PICTURES: He Knows You're Alone (debut, 1980), Splash, Bachelor Party, The Man With One Red Shoe, Volunteers, The Money Pit, Nothing in Common, Every Time We Say Goodbye, Dragnet, Big (Acad. Award nom.), Punchline, The 'Burbs, Turner and Hooch, Joe Versus the Volcano, The Bonfire of the Vanities, Radio Flyer, A League of Their Own, Sleepless in Seattle, Philadelphia (Academy Award, 1993; Golden Globe Award), Forrest Gump (Academy Award, 1994; Golden Globe Award),The Celluloid Closet, Apollo 13, Toy Story (voice), That Thing You Do! (also dir.), Saving Private Ryan (Acad. Award nom.), You've Got Mail, Toy Story 2 (voice), The Green Mile, Cast Away, The Road to Perdition, Catch Me If You Can, The Polar Express (also prod.), The Terminal, The Ladykillers, Connie & Carla.
TELEVISION: Movies: Rona Jaffe's Mazes and Monsters, Rutles 2: Can't Buy Me Lunch. Episode Dir.: A League of Their Own. Series: Bosom Buddies, My Big Fat Greek Life (exec. prod. only). Guest: The Love Boat, Taxi, Happy Days, Family Ties, Tales From the Crypt (None but the Lonely Heart; also dir.), Fallen Angels (I'll Be Waiting; also dir.), The Naked Truth, From the Earth to the Moon (also dir., co-s.p., co-exec. prod.), Band of Brothers (also dir, writer, prod.).

HANN-BYRD, ADAM
Actor. b. Feb. 23, 1982.
PICTURES: Little Man Tate, Digger, Jumanji, Diabolique, The Ice Storm, Souvenir (voice), Halloween: H20, The Uninvited, Storytelling.
TELEVISION: Guest: NYPD Blue.

HANNAH, DARYL
Actress. b. Chicago, IL, Dec. 3, 1960. Niece of cinematographer Haskell Wexler. e. UCLA. Studied ballet with Maria Tallchief. Studied acting with Stella Adler.
PICTURES: The Fury (debut, 1978), The Final Terror, Hard Country, Blade Runner, Summer Lovers, Reckless, Splash, The Pope of Greenwich Village, Clan of the Cave Bear, Legal Eagles, Roxanne, Wall Street, High Spirits, Crimes and Misdemeanors, Steel Magnolias, Crazy People, At Play in the Fields of the Lord, Memoirs of an Invisible Man, Grumpy Old Men, The Little Rascals, The Tie That Binds, Two Much, Grumpier Old Men, The Real Blonde, The Gingerbread Man, Hi-Life, Wild Flowers, Speedway Junky, Enemy of My Enemy, Diplomatic Siege, My Favorite Martian, Zapatista, Cord, Dancing At the Blue Iguana, Ring of Fire, Jackpot, A Walk to Remember, Run for the Money, Searching for Debra Winger, Bank, Northfolk, Casa des los Babys, Kill Bill, The Job, The Big Empty.
TELEVISION: Movies: Paper Dolls, Attack of the 50 Ft. Woman (also co-prod.), The Last Don, Rear Window, First Target, On the Edge of Blade Runner, Jack and the Beanstalk: The Real Story. Series: Robert Altman's Gun.

HANNAH, JOHN
Actor. b. Kilbride, Scotland, UK, April 23, 1962. Was an apprentice electrician before entering mp industry.
PICTURES: Harbour Beat, Four Weddings and a Funeral, Madagascar Skin, The Innocent Sleep, The Final Cut, The James Gang, Sliding Doors, The Mummy, The Hurricane, The Intruder, Circus, Pandaemonium, The Mummy Returns, Camouflage, I'm With Lucy, Before You Go, I Accuse.
TELEVISION: Movies: Paul Calf's Video Diary, Pauline Calf's Wedding Video, Truth or Dare, Romance and Rejection, Circles of Deceit: Kalon, The Love Bug, Rebus: Black and Blue, Rebus: The Hanging Garden, Rebus: Dead Souls, Rebus: Mortal Causes, Dr. Jekyll & Mr. Hyde. Series: Out of the Blue, McCallum, MDs. Guest: Taggart.

HANNIGAN, ALYSON
Actress. r.n. Allison Lee Hannigan. b. Washington, DC, March 24, 1974.
PICTURES: My Stepmother Is an Alien, Dead Man on Campus, American Pie, Boys and Girls, American Pie 2, Beyond the City Limits, American Pie: The Wedding.
TELEVISION: Movies: Switched at Birth, The Stranger Beside Me, Indecent Seduction. Series: Free Spirit, Buffy the Vampire Slayer, Buffy: The Animated Series (voice). Guest: Roseanne, Almost Home, Touched by an Angel, Picket Fences.

HANSON, CURTIS
Director, Writer. b. Reno, NV, March 24, 1945. Editor of Cinema magazine before becoming screenwriter.
PICTURES: Writer: The Silent Partner, White Dog, Never Cry Wolf. Director: Sweet Kill, Little Dragons, Losin' It, The Bedroom Window (also s.p.), Bad Influence, The Hand That Rocks the Cradle, The River Wild, L.A. Confidential (also co-s.p., prod., Acad. Award, Best Adapted Screenplay, Chicago Film Crits. Award, LA Film Crits. Award, NY Film Crits. Award, Best Director, Best Screenplay, 1997), Wonder Boys (also prod.), 8

Mile (also prod.)Lucky You. *Actor:* The Goonies, Adaptation. TELEVISION: *Movie:* Killing at Hell's Gate, The Children of Times Square. *Series:* Greg the Bunny.

HARBACH, WILLIAM O.
Producer. b. Yonkers, NY, Oct. 12, 1919, e. Brown U. Father was lyricst Otto Harbach. Served with U.S. Coast Guard, 1940-45; actor, MGM, 1945-47; broadcast co-ordinator. NBC, 1947-49; stage mgr., 1949-50; dir., NBC, 1950-53
TELEVISION: *Producer:* Tonight, Steve Allen Show, Bing Crosby shows (also dir.), Milton Berle Special, Hollywood Palace, The Julie Andrews Show (Emmy Award, 1973), Shirley MacLaine's Gypsy in My Soul (Emmy Award, 1976), Bob Hope Specials.

HARBERT, TED
Executive. e. Boston Univ. 1976-77, prod. of new dept. at WHDH radio in Boston. Joined ABC, 1977 as feature film coordinator; 1979, named supervisor, feature film and late-night program planning, then assst. to v.p., program planning & scheduling; 1981, became dir. program planning & scheduling; 1984, promoted to v.p. program planning & scheduling; 1987, named v.p. motion pictures and scheduling, ABC Entertainment; 1988, v.p., prime time, ABC Entertainment; 1989, became exec. v.p., Prime Time, ABC Entertainment; 1993, promoted to pres. of ABC Entertainment. Producer with Dreamworks SKG, 1997. Named pres., NBC Studios, August, 1999. Left NBC June 2003. Member, Dean's Advisory Board of the USC School of Theater, Film and Television; board member, USC School of Cinema-Television's Television Advisory Council; exec. committee, Boston University's School of Communications; bd. of governors, UCLA's Center for Communication Policy; bd. of directors, Friends of the L.A. Free Clinic. He is a past president of the Hollywood Radio & TV Society.

HARDEN, MARCIA GAY
Actress. b. La Jolla, CA, Aug. 14, 1959.
Father was naval captain. Schooled in Athens, Munich, then returned to states attending Univ. of TX, NYU. Stage work in Washington D.C. in Crimes of the Heart, The Miss Firecracker Contest.
THEATRE: *Off-B'way:* The Man Who Shot Lincoln (debut, 1989), Those the River Keeps, The Skin of Our Teeth, The Years, Simpatico. *B'way:* Angels in America: Millenium Approaches/ Perestroika (Theatre World Award; Tony nom.)
PICTURES: Miller's Crossing (debut, 1990), Late for Dinner, Used People, Crush, Safe Passage, The Spitfire Grill, The Daytrippers, The First Wives Club, Spy Hard, Desperate Measures, Flubber, Meet Joe Black, Labor of Love, Curtain Call, Space Cowboys, Pollock (Academy Award), Just Like Mona, Gaudi Afternoon, Mystic River, Casa de los Babys, Mona Lisa Smile.
TELEVISION: *Movies:* Fever, Path to Paradise, Spenser, Small Vices, Thin Air, See You In My Dreams, From Where I Sit, Walking Shadow, King of Texas. *Mini-Series:* Sinatra, Guilty Hearts. *Series:* The Education of Max Bickford.

HARDISON, KADEEM
Actor. b. Brooklyn, NY, July 24, 1966. Studied acting with Earl Hyman and at H.B.Studios.
PICTURES: Beat Street (debut, 1984), Rappin', School Daze, I'm Gonna Git You Sucka, Def by Temptation, White Men Can't Jump, Gunmen, Renaissance Man, Panther, Vampire in Brooklyn, Drive, The Sixth Man, Blind Faith, Dancing in September, Who's Your Daddy, Thank Heaven, Dunsmore, Thirty Years to Life, Showtime, Biker Boyz, Who's Your Daddy?, Face of Terror.
TELEVISION: *Movies:* Dream Date, Fire & Ice. *Specials:* The Color of Friendship, Amazing Grace, Don't Touch, Go Tell It on the Mountain.*Series:* A Different World, Between Brothers. *Guest:* The Cosby Show, Spenser for Hire.

HARE, DAVID
Writer, Director. b. St. Leonards, Sussex, England, June 5, 1947. e. Lancing Coll., Jesus Coll., Cambridge. After leaving univ. in 1968 formed Portable Theatre Company, experimental touring group. Hired by Royal Court Theater as literary manager, 1969. 1970, first full-length play, Slag, prod. at Hampstead Theatre Club. Resident dramatist, Royal Court (1970-71), and Nottingham Playhouse (1973). Assoc. dir., National Theatre. West End debut, Knuckle.
THEATRE: Slag, The Great Exhibition, Brassneck, Knuckle, Fanshen, Teeth 'n' Smiles, Plenty, A Map of the World, Pravda, The Bay at Nice, Secret Rapture, Racing Demon, Murmuring Judges, Rules of the Game (new version of Pirandello Play), Brecht's The Absence of War, Skylight, Galileo, Mother Courage.
PICTURES: *Writer:* Plenty, Wetherby (also dir.), Paris by Night (also dir.), Strapless (also dir.), Damage, The Secret Rapture (also prod.), Via Dolorosa, The Designated Mourner (dir., prod. only), Via Dolorosa, The Papp Project (documentary, himself), The Hours.
TELEVISION: *Writer:* Licking Hitler (also dir.), Dreams of Leaving (also dir.), Saigon: Year of the Cat, Knuckle, Heading Home (also dir.), The Absence of War.

HAREWOOD, DORIAN
Actor. b. Dayton, OH, Aug. 6, 1950. m. actress Ann McCurry. e. U. of Cincinnati.
THEATRE: Jesus Christ Superstar (road co.), Two Gentlemen of Verona, Miss Moffat, Streamers, Over Here, Don't Call Back (Theatre World Award), The Mighty Gents, Kiss of the Spider Woman.
PICTURES: Sparkle (debut, 1976), Gray Lady Down, Looker, Tank, Against All Odds, The Falcon and the Snowman, Full Metal Jacket, Pacific Heights, Solar Crisis, The Pagemaster (voice), Sudden Death, Space Jam (voice), Archibald the Rainbow Painter, Evasive Action, Glitter, Levity, Gothika.
TELEVISION: *Movies:* Foster and Laurie, Panic in Echo Park, Siege, An American Christmas Carol, High Ice, Beulah Land, The Ambush Murders, I Desire, The Jesse Owens Story, Guilty of Innocence, God Bless the Child, Kiss Shot, Polly, Polly-Comin' Home!, Getting Up and Going Home, Bermuda Grace, Shattered Image, When the Cradle Falls, 12 Angry Men, A Change of Heart, Framed, The Christmas Shoes. *Mini-Series:* Roots: The Next Generations, Amerika, Christianity: The First Two Thousand Years.*Pilot:* Half 'n' Half. *Series:* Strike Force, Trauma Center, Glitter, The Trials of Rosie O'Neill, Viper, The Tick (voice), Mortal Kombat: The Animated Series (voice), The Hoop Life.

HARGREAVES, JOHN
Executive. b. Freckleton, Lancashire, England,, July 1921. Joined Gainsborough Pictures 1945. Transferred to Denham Studios 1946 and later Pinewood Studios. Joined Allied Film Makers 1960, then Salamander Film Productions as Bryan Forbes' financial controller and asst. prod. 1965. Joined EMI Film Prods. Ltd. as asst. man. dir. and prod. controller 1969-72. 1983-, U.K. dir. and production executive for Completion Bond Company, Inc. Cal. USA.
PICTURES: Don Quixote (prod.), The Slipper and the Rose (prod. asst.), International Velvet (assoc. prod.), The Awakening (prod. rep.), The Fiendish Plot of Dr. Fu Manchu (post-prod. exec.), Excalibur (prod. rep.), The Year of Living Dangerously, Carrington (financial consultant).

HARK, TSUI
Director, Producer. b. Vietnam, Jan. 2, 1951. e. University of Texas. Started filming 8mm movies at 13. Moved to Hong Kong in 1966, then in 1975 relocated to NY where he became editor for a local Chinese newspaper. Returned to Hong Kong in 1977 and made his directorial debut with The Butterfly Murders. In the 1990's played a major part in reviving "swordsfighting" and "kung-fu" movies.
PICTURES: *Director:* Dangerous Encounter, Hell Has No Door, All the Wrong Clues, Zu: Warriors From the Magic Mountain, Aces go Places III, Shanghai Blues, Working Class, Peking Opera Blues, A Better Tomorrow III, Once Upon A Time in China (also II, III, V), The Master, Green Snake, The Lovers, A Chinese Feast, Love In a Time of Twilight, Tri-Star, Blade, Double Team. *Co-director:* Swordsman, The Banquet, Chess King, Twin Dragons. *Producer:* A Chinese Ghost Story (also II, III) A Better Tomorrow, I Love Maria, Deception, Gunmen, Diary of a Big Man, The Big Heat, The Killer, Spy Games, The Raid, The Wicked City, Swordsman II, Dragon Inn, The East is Red, Once Upon a Time in China (also IV), The Magic Crane, Burning Paradise, Shanghai Grand, Black Mask, Once Upon a Time in China & America, Chinese Ghost Story: The Tsui Hark Animation., Time and Tide, Old Master Q2001, Zu Warrios, Black Mask 2: City of Masks, The Era of the Vampire.

HARKINS, DANIEL E.
Executive, Exhibitor. b. Mesa, AZ, Feb. 6, 1953. e. Arizona State U. Joined Harkins Theatres in 1968. Acquired company in 1975. President and CEO Harkins Amusement Enterprises, Inc. National NATO bd. member. Pres., Arizona Theatre Assoc. V.P., Governor's Film Commission. Recipient of United Motion Picture Assoc. National Showman of the Year award 1976, 1980, 1981. Hollywood Reported Marketing Concept award, 1983. Box Office Showmandizer award, 1976, 1978. Phoenix Artistic Achievement award, 1989. American Institute of Architects award. 1996. Arizona Best awards, 1991-1995.

HARLIN, RENNY
Director.b. Helsinki, Finland, March 15, 1959. e. Univ. of Helsinki film school. r.n. Lauri Mauritz Harjola. Formed prod. co. The Forge with actress Geena Davis.
PICTURES: Born American (debut, 1986), Arctic Heat (also s.p.), Prison, A Nightmare on Elm Street IV: The Dream Master, Die Hard 2, The Adventures of Ford Fairlane, Rambling Rose (prod. only), Cliffhanger, Speechless (co-prod. only), Cutthroat Island (also prod.), Exit Zero, The Long Kiss Goodnight (also prod.), Blast From the Past (prod. only), Deep Blue Sea, Driven, Mindhunters, A Sound of Thunder (prod. only).
TELEVISION: *Movie:* Mistrial, T.R.A.X.

HARMON, MARK
Actor. b. Burbank, CA, Sept. 2, 1951. Son of actress Elyse Knox and football star Tom Harmon. m. actress Pam Dawber. Brother of actresses Kelly and Kristin Harmon. On stage in

Wrestlers, The Wager (both L.A.), Key Exchange (Toronto). PICTURES: Comes a Horseman, Beyond the Poseidon Adventure, Let's Get Harry, Summer School, The Presidio, Stealing Home, Worth Winning, Till There Was You, Cold Heaven, Wyatt Earp, Natural Born Killers (cameo), Magic in the Water, The Last Supper, Casualties, Fear and Loathing in Las Vegas (cameo), I'll Remember April, Local Boys, Freaky Friday. TELEVISION: *Movies*: Eleanor and Franklin: The White House Years, Getting Married, Little Mo, Flamingo Road (pilot), The Dream Merchants, Goliath Awaits, Intimate Agony, The Deliberate Stranger, Prince of Bel Air, Sweet Bird of Youth, Dillinger, Fourth Story, Long Road Home, Shadow of a Doubt, For All Time, The Amati Girls, Crossfire Trail. *Series*: Sam, 240-Robert, Flamingo Road, St. Elsewhere, Reasonable Doubts, Charlie Grace, Chicago Hope, West Wing, NCIS. *Guest*: Adam-12, Laverne & Shirley, Nancy Drew, Police Story, Moonlighting. *Mini-Series*: Centennial, From the Earth to the Moon.

HARNELL, STEWART D.
Executive. b. New York, NY, Aug. 18, 1938. e. U. of Miami, UCLA, New School for Social Research. Entertainer with Youth Parade in Coral Gables, FL,1948-55, performing for handicapped children, Variety Club, etc. as singer, dancer, musician. Had own bands, Teen Aces & Rhythm Rascals, 1950-56; performed on Cactus Jim TV show and Wood & Ivory, 1953-54, WTVJ, Miami. Catskills,1954-55. Joined National Screen Service as exec. trainee in 1960 writing trailer scripts for major studio releases in L.A. Relocated to Chicago as booker & salesman. Transferred to NY home office in 1963 to manage special trailer production. Promoted to asst. General Sales Manager, 1964-66; New Orleans branch mgr., 1966-67; Atlanta division mgr., 1967-70. Formed own distribution co., 1970-76 Harnell Independent Productions. Resumed post as Exec. VP Worldwide General Sales Manager of NSS, New York, 1977-78; In 1978, founded Cinema Concepts Theatre Service Co. serving motion picture, advertising and broadcast industries with high end animation. Chief barker of Variety Club of Atlanta, Tent 21, 1972, 1976,1979, 1988, 1989, 1993, 1994. Presidential Citation 1988. Motion Picture Pioneers Bd. of Directors (1990-2003).

HARPER, JESSICA
Actress. b. Chicago, IL, Oct. 10, 1949. m. prod. exec. Thomas E. Rothman. e. Sarah Lawrence Coll. Understudied on Broadway for Hair for one year. Appeared in summer stock and off-B'way shows (Richard Farina: Long Time Coming Longtime Gone, Doctor Selavy's Magic Theatre.)
PICTURES: Taking Off, Phantom of the Paradise, Love and Death, Inserts, Suspiria, The Evictors, Stardust Memories, Shock Treatment, Pennies from Heaven, My Favorite Year, The Imagemaker, Dario Argento's World of Horror, The Blue Iguana, Big Man on Campus, Mr. Wonderful, Safe, Boys, Minority Report.
TELEVISION: *Series*: Little Women, It's Garry Shandling's Show. *Mini-Series*: Studs Lonigan, Aspen (The Innocent and the Damned), When Dreams Come True. *Special*: The Garden Party. *Guest*: Tales from the Darkside, The Equalizer, Trying Times (Bedtime Story), Wiseguy, Chicago Hope, Moonlighting.

HARPER, TESS
Actress. b. Mammoth Springs, AR, 1952. e. Southwest Missouri State Coll., Springfield. Worked in Houston, then Dallas in children's theater, dinner theater, and commercials.
PICTURES: Tender Mercies (debut, 1983), Amityville 3-D, Silkwood, Flashpoint, Crimes of the Heart (Acad. Award nom.), Ishtar, Far North, Her Alibi, Criminal Law, Daddy's Dyin'... Who's Got the Will?, My Heroes Have Always Been Cowboys, The Man in the Moon, My New Gun, Dirty Laundry, The Jackal, Lonely Place, The In Crowd, Morning, The Rising Place, No Prom for Cindy, Studio City (short), Jesus-Mary-And Joey.
TELEVISION: *Movies*: Kentucky Woman, Starflight: The Plane That Couldn't Land, A Summer to Remember, Promises to Keep, Little Girl Lost, Unconquered, In the Line of Duty: Siege at Marion, Willing to Kill: The Texas Cheerleader Story, Death in Small Doses, Beyond the Prairie: The True Story of Laura Ingalls Wilder. *Mini-Series*: Chiefs, Celebrity.

HARPER, VALERIE
Actress. b. Suffern, NY, Aug. 22, 1940. e. Hunter Coll, New Sch. for Social Research. Started as dancer in stage shows at Radio City Music Hall. First professional acting in summer stock in Conn.; actress with Second City Chicago 1964-69; Appeared on B'way. in Lil' Abner, Take Me Along, Wildcat, Subways Are for Sleeping, Something Different, Story Theatre, Metamorphoses. Won 3 Emmys for best performance in supporting role in comedy for portrayal of Rhoda on The Mary Tyler Moore Show and 1 for best leading actress on Rhoda. Off B'way, Death Defying Acts (1995-96).
PICTURES: Rock Rock Rock, Lil Abner, Freebie and the Bean, Chapter Two, The Last Married Couple in America, Blame It on Rio, Eight Characters In Search of a Sitcom (documentary).
TELEVISION: *Movies*: Thursday's Game, Night Terror, Fun and Games, The Shadow Box, The Day the Loving Stopped, Farrell for the People (pilot), Don't Go to Sleep, An Invasion of Privacy, Execution, Strange Voices, Drop Out Mother, The People Across the Lake, Stolen: One Husband, A Friend To Die For, The Great

Mom Swap, Dog's Best Friend (voice), Mary & Rhoda, The Mary Tyler Moore Reunion, Dancing at the Harvest Moon. *Series*: The Mary Tyler Show, Rhoda, Valerie, City, The Office, Melrose Place.

HARRINGTON, CURTIS
Director, Writer. b. Los Angeles, CA, Sept. 17, 1928. e. U. of Southern California, B.A. Exec. asst. to Jerry Wald, 1955-61 Associate prod. at 20th Cent. Fox.PICTURES: Assoc. Prod.: Mardi Gras (also story), Hound Dog Man, Return to Peyton Place, The Stripper. Director: Night Tide (also s.p.), Queen of Blood (Planet of Blood; also s.p.), Games (also co-story), What's the Matter with Helen?, Who Slew Auntie Roo?, The Killing Kind, Ruby, Mata Hari, The World of Gods and Monsters: A Journey with James Whale (himself), Usher (short).
TELEVISION: *Series episodes*: Hotel, Dynasty, The Colby's, Tales of the Unexpected, Twilight Zone, Baretta, Vega$, Glitter, Logan's Run. *Movies*: How Awful About Allan, The Cat Creature, Killer Bees, The Dead Don't Die, Devil Dog: The Hound of Hell.

HARRINGTON, PAT
Actor. b. New York, NY, Aug. 13, 1929. e. Fordham U. Served USAF as 1st Lt., 1952-54. Time salesman for NBC, 1954-58. Voice in over 40 animation shorts.
PICTURES: The Wheeler Dealers, Move Over Darling, Easy Come Easy Go, The President's Analyst, 2000 Years Later, The Candidate, Every Little Crook and Nanny, The Nine Lives of Fritz the Cat (voice), Round Trip to Heaven, Ablaze.
TELEVISION: *Series*: The Steve Allen Show, The Danny Thomas Show, The Jack Paar Show, Stump the Stars (host), Mr. Deeds Goes to Town, One Day at a Time (Emmy Award, 1984). *Movies*: Savage, The Affair, The Healers, Columbo: An Exercise in Fatality, Let's Switch, Benny and Barney: Las Vegas Undercover, The New Love Boat, The Critical List, The Last Convertible, Between Two Brothers, A Garfield Christmas, I Yabba Dabba Do, Spring Fling, These Old Broads.

HARRIS, BARBARA
Actress. r.n. Sandra Markowitz. b. Evanston, IL, July 25, 1935. e. Wright Junior Coll., Chicago; Goodman Sch. of the Theatre; U. of Chicago. Joined acting troup, The Compass. Founding member, Second City Players, 1960. Came to NY where first role was in Oh Dad Poor Dad Mama's Hung You in the Closet and I'm Feeling So Sad (Theatre World Award), repeating role in film version.
THEATRE: Mother Courage and Her Children, Dynamite Tonight, On a Clear Day You Can See Forever, The Apple Tree (Tony Award, 1967), Mahogany.
PICTURES: A Thousand Clowns (debut, 1965), Oh Dad Poor Dad Mama's Hung You in the Closet and I'm Feeling So Sad, Plaza Suite, Who Is Harry Kellerman and Why Is He Saying Those Terrible Things About Me? (Acad. Award nom.), The War Between Men and Women, The Manchu Eagle Murder Caper Mystery, Mixed Company, Nashville, Family Plot, Freaky Friday, Movie Movie, The North Avenue Irregulars, The Seduction of Joe Tynan, Second Hand Hearts, Peggy Sue Got Married, Nice Girls Don't Explode, Dirty Rotten Scoundrels, The Pamela Principal, Grosse Pointe Blank.
TELEVISION: *Guest*: Alfred Hitchcock Presents, Naked City, The Defenders.

HARRIS, BURTT
Producer, Actor. Began career as actor; later worked with Elia Kazan as prod. asst. and asst. dir. on America America, Splendor in the Grass, and The Arrangement. Worked as second unit dir. and asst. dir. on many films as well as prod. and actor.
PICTURES: *Exec. prod./line prod./assoc. prod.*: The Wiz, Just Tell Me What You Want, Cruising, Prince of the City, The Verdict (also actor), Deathtrap, Garbo Talks, D.A.R.Y.L. (co-prod., actor), The Glass Menagerie, See No Evil Hear No Evil, Q & A (also actor), A Stranger Among Us (also actor), Drunks (also actor), The Last Good Time. *Assoc. prod.*: Little Murders, Gilda Live, Family Business. *Actor*: Splendor in the Grass, Fail Safe, The Taking of Pelham 1-2-3, The Wanderers, Undertow, Hudson Hawk, The Last Good Time. *Asst. dir.*: Illtown, Grace of My Heart, Affliction, The Devil's Advocate.
TELEVISION: *Movies*: Zoya.

HARRIS, ED
Actor. b. Tenafly, NJ, Nov. 28, 1950. m. actress Amy Madigan. Played football 2 years at Columbia U. prior to enrolling in acting classes at OK State U. Summer stock. Grad. CA Institute of the Arts, B.F.A. 1975. Worked in West Coast Theatre.
THEATRE: *NY*: Fool For Love (Off-B'way debut; Obie Award), Precious Sons (B'way debut; Theatre World Award), Simpatico, Taking Sides. *LA*: Scar.
PICTURES: Coma (debut, 1978), Borderline, Knightriders, Dream On, Creepshow, The Right Stuff, Under Fire, Swing Shift, Places in the Heart, Alamo Bay, A Flash of Green, Sweet Dreams, Code Name: Emerald, Walker, To Kill a Priest, Jacknife, The Abyss, State of Grace, Glengarry Glen Ross, The Firm, Needful Things, China Moon, Milk Money, Just Cause, Apollo 13 (Acad. Award nom.), Eye for an Eye, Nixon, The Rock, Absolute Power, The Truman Show (Acad. Award nom.), Stepmom, The Third Miracle, Waking the Dead, The Prime Gig, Pollock (Acad. Award nom.), Enemy at the Gates, Absolute Zero, Buffalo

Soldiers, A Beautiful Mind, The Hours, Just a Dream, Radio, The Human Stain.
TELEVISION: *Movies*: The Amazing Howard Hughes, The Seekers, The Aliens Are Coming (Alien Force), The Last Innocent Man, Paris Trout, Running Mates, Riders of the Purple Sage. *Mini-Series*: The Stand, Baseball (voice).

HARRIS, JAMES B.
Producer, Director, Writer. b. New York, NY, Aug. 3, 1928. e. Juilliard Sch. U.S. film export, 1947; Realart Pictures, 1948; formed Flamingo Films, 1949; formed Harris-Kubrick Productions, 1954. formed James B. Harris Prods., Inc., 1963.
PICTURES: *Producer*: The Killing, Paths of Glory, Lolita, The Bedford Incident (also dir.), Some Call It Loving (also dir., s.p.), Telefon, Fast-Walking (also dir., s.p.), Cop (also dir., s.p.), Boiling Point (dir., s.p.).

HARRIS, JULIE
Designer. b. London, England. e. Chelsea Arts Sch. Entered industry in 1945 designing for Gainsborough Studios. First film, Holiday Camp.
PICTURES: Greengage Summer, Naked Edge, The War Lover, Fast Lady, Chalk Garden, Psyche 59, A Hard Day's Night, Darling, Help!, The Wrong Box, Casino Royale, Deadfall, Prudence and the Pill, Decline and Fall, Goodbye Mr. Chips, Sherlock Holmes, Follow Me!, Live and Let Die, Rollerball, Slipper and The Rose, Dracula, The Great Muppet Caper.
TELEVISION: Laura (with Lee Radziwill), Candleshoe, The Sailor's Return, Lost and Found, The Kingfisher, Arch of Triumph, Sign of Four, Hound of the Baskervilles, A Hazard of Hearts, A Perfect Hero.

HARRIS, JULIE
Actress. b. Grosse Pointe, MI, Dec. 2, 1925. e. Yale Drama Sch.
THEATRE: Sundown Beach, Playboy of the Western World, Macbeth, Young and the Fair, Magnolia Alley, Monserrat, Member of the Wedding, I Am a Camera (Tony Award, 1952), Colombe, The Lark (Tony Award, 1956), A Shot in the Dark, Marathon 33, Ready When You Are, C.B., Break a Leg, Skyscraper, Voices, And Miss Reardon Drinks a Little, 40 Carats (Tony Award, 1969), The Last of Mrs. Lincoln (Tony Award, 1973), In Praise of Love, The Belle of Amherst (Tony Award, 1973), Driving Miss Daisy (Natl. co.), Lucifer's Child, Lettice & Lovage (tour), The Fiery Furnace (Off-B'way debut, 1993), The Glass Menagerie.
PICTURES: The Member of the Wedding (debut, 1952; Acad. Award nom.), East of Eden, I Am a Camera, The Truth About Women, The Poacher's Daughter, Requiem for a Heavyweight, The Haunting, Harper, You're a Big Boy Now, Reflections in a Golden Eye, The Split, The People Next Door, The Hiding Place, Voyage of the Damned, The Bell Jar, Nutcracker: The Motion Picture (voice), Gorillas in the Mist, Housesitter, The Dark Half, Carried Away, Passage to Paradise, Bad Manners, Frank Lloyd Wright, The First of May, Broadway: The Golden Age by the Legends Who Were There.
TELEVISION: *Specials*: Little Moon of Alban (Emmy Award, 1959), Johnny Belinda, A Doll's House, Ethan Frome, The Good Fairy, The Lark, He Who Gets Slapped, The Heiress, Victoria Regina (Emmy Award, 1962), Pygmalion, Anastasia, The Holy Terror, The Power and The Glory, The Woman He Loved. *Movies*: The House on Greenapple Road, How Awful About Alan, Home for the Holidays, The Greatest Gift, The Gift, Too Good To Be True, The Christmas Wife, They've Taken Our Children: The Chowchilla Kidnapping, When Love Kills: The Seduction of John Hearn, One Christmas. *Series*: Thicker Than Water, The Family Holvak, Knots Landing. *Mini-Series*: Backstairs at the White House, Scarlett.

HARRIS, MEL
Executive. b. Arkansas City, Kansas, 1942. e. Ph.D., mass comm., Ohio U. Broadcaster, Kaiser and Metromedia; pres., TV Group, Paramount Pictures, 1978-92, where he co-founded Paramount Home Video and CIC Home Video, engineered the formation of USA Cable Network and the introduction of satellite distribution for first-run programming, launching Entertainment Tonight; president, Sony Pictures Entertainment (SPE) Television Group, 1992-95, Currently president and COO, SPE.

HARRIS, MEL
Actress. r.n. Mary Ellen Harris. b. Bethlehem, PA, July 12, 1957. e. Columbia. Career as model before turning to acting in 1984. NY theatre debut in Empty Hearts, 1992 (Theatre World Award).
PICTURES: Wanted: Dead or Alive, Cameron's Closet, K-9, Raising Cain, Desperate Motive (Distant Cousins), Suture, The Pagemaster, Sonic Impact, Firetrap, Dynamite, The Veritas Project: Hangman's Curse.
TELEVISION: *Movies*: Seduced, Harry's Hong Kong, Cross of Fire, My Brother's Wife, The Burden of Proof, Grass Roots, Child of Rage, With Hostile Intent, Desperate Journey: The Allison Wilcox Story, Ultimate Betrayal, The Spider and the Fly, The Women of Spring Break, Sharon's Secret, The Secretary, A Case for Life, Murder She Wrote: South by Southwest, The Retrievers, Another Pretty Face. *Series*: thirtysomething, Something So Right. *Guest*: M*A*S*H, Alfred Hitchcock Presents, Rags to Riches, Heart of the City, The Wizard.

HARRIS, NEIL PATRICK
Actor. b. Albuquerque, NM, June 15, 1973. While attending week-long theatre camp at New Mexico St. Univ. met writer Mark Medoff who suggested him for co-starring role in Clara's Heart.
THEATRE: Luck Pluck and Virtue (Off-B'way debut, 1995).
PICTURES: Clara's Heart (debut, 1988), Purple People Eater, Hairspray, Starship Troopers, The Proposition, The Next Best Thing, The Mesmerist, Undercover Brother.
TELEVISION: *Movies*: Too Good to Be True, Home Fires Burning, Cold Sassy Tree, Stranger in the Family, A Family Torn Apart, Snowbound: The Jim and Jennifer Stolpa Story, Not Our Son, My Antonia, The Man in the Attic, Legacy of Sin: The William Coit Story, The Christmas Wish, Joan of Arc, The Wedding Dress, Sweeney Todd: The Demon Barber of Fleet Street In Concert. *Series*: Doogie Howser M.D., Capitol Critters (voice), Stark Raving Mad, Spider Man: The Animated Series (voice). *Guest*: B. J. Stryker, Carol & Company, Roseanne, Quantum Leap, Murder She Wrote, The Simpsons (voice).

HARRIS, RICHARD
Actor. b. Limerick, Ireland, Oct. 1, 1930. Attended London Acad. of Music and Dramatic Arts. Prod.-dir. Winter Journey 1956. Prof. acting debut in Joan Littlewood's prod. of The Quare Fellow, Royal Stratford, 1956. Recorded hit song MacArthur's Park, 1968. Author of novel Honor Bound (1982) and poetry compilation: I in the Membership of My Days (1973).
THEATRE: *London*: A View from the Bridge, Man Beast and Virtue, The Ginger Man. *B'way*: Camelot.
PICTURES: Alive and Kicking (debut, 1958), Shake Hands With the Devil, The Wreck of the Mary Deare, A Terrible Beauty (Night Fighters), The Long The Short and The Tall (Jungle Fighters), The Guns of Navarone, Mutiny on the Bounty, This Sporting Life (Acad. Award nom.), Red Desert, Major Dundee, The Heroes of Telemark, The Bible, Hawaii, Caprice, Camelot, The Molly Maguires, A Man Called Horse, Cromwell, The Hero (Bloomfield; also dir., s.p.), Man in the Wilderness, The Deadly Trackers, 99 and 44/100% Dead, Juggernaut, Echoes of a Summer (also co-exec. prod.), Robin and Marian, Return of a Man Called Horse (also co-exec. prod.), The Cassandra Crossing, Gulliver's Travels, Orca, Golden Rendezvous, The Wild Geese, Ravagers, The Last Word, Game for Vultures, Your Ticket Is No Longer Valid, Highpoint, Tarzan the Ape Man, Martin's Day, Triumphs of a Man Called Horse, Mack the Knife, The Field (Acad. Award nom.), Patriot Games, Unforgiven, Wrestling Ernest Hemingway, Silent Tongue, Savage Hearts, Cry the Beloved Country, Trojan Eddie, Smilla's Sense of Snow, The Barber of Siberia, This is the Sea, To Walk with Lions, Harry Potter and the Sorcerer's Stone, The Pearl, My Kingdom, The Count of Monte Cristo, Harry Potter and the Chamber of Secrets, The Apocalypse.
TELEVISION: *Specials*: Ricardo, The Iron Harp, The Snow Goose, Camelot. *Movies*: Maigret, The Return, The Hunchback, The Apocalypse, Julius Caesar (mini).
(d. Oct. 25, 2002)

HARRIS, RICHARD A.
Editor.
PICTURES: The Bamboo Saucer, Downhill Racer, The Christian Licorice Store, Chandler, The Candidate, Catch My Soul, Smile, The Bad News Bears, Semi-Tough, The Bad News Bears Go to Japan, An Almost Perfect Affair, The Island, The Toy, The Survivors, Fletch, The Golden Child, Wildcats, The Couch Trip, Fletch Lives, L.A. Story, Terminator 2: Judgment Day, The Bodyguard, Last Action Hero, True Lies, Titanic (Acad. Award, 1997).
TELEVISION: *Movies*: Dracula, The Kansas City Massacre, Murder at the World Series, The Executioner's Song, Tiger Town, 14 Going on 30, My Boyfriend's Back, A Mother's Courage: The Mary Thomas Story, Indictment: The McMartin Trial, Running Mates.

HARRIS, ROBERT A.
Archivist, Producer. b. New York, NY, Dec. 27, 1945. e. NYU Sch. of Commerce and Sch. of Arts, 1968. Worked as exec. trainee with 7 Arts assoc., NY while in school, 1966-68; worked in corp. communications, Pepsico, 1970-71; formed Center for Instructional Resources, SUNY Purchase, 1971-73; organized Images Film Archive, dist. of classic theatrical and non theat. films, 1974; pres., Images Video and Film Archive, 1985; formed Davnor Prods., pres., 1986; formed The Film Preserve, Ltd. pres. 1989-. 1975-80: restored Abel Gance films Beethoven, J'Accuse, Lucretia Borgia; 1974-79: worked with Kevin Brownlow to complete restoration of Abel Gance's Napoleon. Partnered with Francis Coppola/Zoetrope Studios to present Napoleon at Radio City Music Hall, 1981 and worldwide tour; 1986-89: reconstruction and restoration of David Lean's Lawrence of Arabia for Columbia Pictures, released 1989; The Grifters (prod.); restoration and reconstruction of Stanley Kubrick's Spartacus for Univ. Pictures, 1991; restoration of George Cukor's My Fair Lady for CBS Video, 1994, restoration in SuperVistaVision 70 of Alfred Hitchcock's Vertigo, 1996. Prod.: Alien Space Avenger, The Grifters (1990).

HARRIS, ROSEMARY
Actress. b. Ashby, Suffolk, Sept. 19, 1930. e. India and England. Early career, nursing; studied Royal Acad. of Dramatic Art, 1951-52.
THEATRE: Climate of Eden (NY debut 1952), Seven Year Itch, Confidential Clerk (Paris Festival), and with Bristol Old Vic in The Crucible, Much Ado About Nothing, Merchant of Venice. With Old Vic, 1955-56; U.S. tour, 1956-57; U.S. stage, 1958-63. Chichester Festivals 1962 and 63; Nat'l Theatre 1963-64; You Can't Take It With You, 1965; The Lion in Winter (Tony Award, 1966), 1967, APA Repertory Co., Heartbreak House, The Royal Family, The New York Idea (Obie Award), Pack of Lies, Hay Fever, Lost in Yonkers, An Inspector Calls, A Delicate Balance.
PICTURES: Beau Brummell, The Shiralee, A Flea in Her Ear, The Boys from Brazil, The Ploughman's Lunch, Heartbreak House, Crossing Delancey, The Delinquents, The Bridge, Tom and Viv (Acad. Award nom.), Looking for Richard, Hamlet, World of Moses, My Life So Far, Sunshine, The Gift, Blow Dry, Spider-Man, Broadway: The Golden Age by the Legends Who Were There, Spider-Man II.
TELEVISION: Movie: The Little Riders. Series: The Chisholms. Specials: Cradle of Willow (debut, 1951), Othello, The Prince and the Pauper, Twelfth Night, Wuthering Heights, Blithe Spirit, Profiles in Courage, To the Lighthouse, Strange Interlude, Tales From the Hollywood Hills: The Old Reliable. Mini-Series: Notorious Woman (Emmy Award, 1976), Holocaust (Golden Globe Award), The Chisholms, The Camomille Lawn.

HARRIS, TIMOTHY
Writer, Producer. b. Los Angeles, CA, July 21, 1946. e. Charterhouse, 1963-65; Peterhouse Coll., Cambridge, 1966-69, M.A. Honors Degree, Eng. lit. Author of novels, Knonski/McSmash, Kyd For Hire, Goodnight and Goodbye; author of novelizations, Steelyard Blues, Hit, Heatwave, American Gigolo.
PICTURES: Co-writer with Herschel Weingrod: Cheaper to Keep Her, Trading Places (BAFTA nom., orig. s.p.; NAACP Image Awards, best m.p. 1983), Brewster's Millions, My Stepmother is an Alien, Paint It Black, Twins (People's Choice Award, best comedy, 1988), Kindergarten Cop, Pure Luck. Co-Prod.: Falling Down, Space Jam (s.p. only).
TELEVISION: Street of Dreams (based on his novel Goodnight and Goodbye; also exec. prod.).

HARRISON, GREGORY
Actor, Producer, Director. b. Avalon, CA, May 31, 1950. Started acting in school plays; then joined Army (1969-71). Studied at Estelle Harman Actors Workshop; later with Lee Strasberg and Stella Adler. Formed Catalina Productions with Franklin Levy, 1981.
THEATRE: Child's Play, Carnal Knowledge, Picnic, The Hasty Heart, Love Letters, Festival, Billy Budd, The Subject Was Roses, The Promise, The Music Man, Paper Moon—The Musical.
PICTURES: Jim: the World's Greatest (debut, 1976), Fraternity Row, Razorback, North Shore (also 2nd unit dir.), Voice of a Stranger (also 2nd unit dir.), Cadillac Girls, It's My Party, Hard Evidence, Air Bud 2: Golden Retriever, Canone inverso - making love.
TELEVISION: Movies (actor): The Gathering, Enola Gay, Trilogy in Terror, The Best Place To Be, The Women's Room, For Ladies Only (also co-prod.), The Fighter, Seduced (also exec. prod.), Oceans of Fire, Spot Marks the X (exec. prod. only), Hot Paint, Red River, Dangerous Pursuit, Angel of Death, Bare Essentials, Breaking the Silence, Duplicates, Split Images, Caught in the Act, The Tower (exec. prod. only), A Family Torn Apart, Lies of the Heart: The Story of Laurie Kellogg, Robin Cook's Mortal Fear, A Christmas Romance, A Dangerous Affair, When Secrets Kill, Running Wild, Murder at 75 Birch, First Daughter, Au Pair, First Target, Au Pair II, First Shot. Mini-series: Centennial, Fresno, 500 Nations (narrator), Nothing Lasts Forever. Movies (exec. prod. only): Thursday's Child, Legs, Samson & Delilah. Series: Logan's Run, Trapper John M.D. (also dir. 6 episodes), Falcon Crest, The Family Man, True Detectives, New York News, Safe Harbor, St. Sass. Guest: M*A*S*H, Barnaby Jones, Sisters.

HARROLD, KATHRYN
Actress. b. Tazewell, VA, Aug. 2, 1950. e. Mills Coll. Studied acting at Neighborhood Playhouse in N.Y., also with Uta Hagen. Appeared in Off-Off-B'way. plays for year; then joined experimental theatre group, Section Ten, touring East, performing and teaching at Connecticut Coll. and NYU. Cast in TV daytime serial, The Doctors.
PICTURES: Nightwing (debut, 1979), The Hunter, Modern Romance, The Pursuit of D.B. Cooper, Yes Gorgio, The Sender, Heartbreakers, Into the Night, Raw Deal, Someone to Love, A Woman's A Helluva Thing.
TELEVISION: Movies: Son-Rise: A Miracle of Love, Vampire, The Women's Room, Bogie, An Uncommon Love, Women in White, Man Against the Mob, Dead Solid Perfect, Capital News, Rainbow Drive, Deadly Desire, The Companion, Rockford Files: The Crime & Punishment, Tell Me No Secrets, Outrage, The 70s. Series: The Doctors (1976-78), MacGruder and Loud, Bronx Zoo, I'll Fly Away, The Larry Sanders Show, Chicago Hope.

HARRON, MARY
Director, Writer.
PICTURES: I Shot Andy Warhol, American Psycho, The Weather Underground.
TELEVISION: Movies: A Darkness More Than Night (s.p. only). Hollywood High, (documentary). Series: Homicide: Life on the Street, Oz.

HARRYHAUSEN, RAY
Special Effects Expert, Producer, Writer. b. Los Angeles, CA, June 29, 1920. e. Los Angeles City Coll. While at coll. made 16mm animated film, Evolution, which got him job as model animator for George Pal's Puppetoons in early '40s. Served in U.S. Signal Corps; then made series of filmed fairy tales with animated puppets for schools and churches. In 1946 worked on Mighty Joe Young as ass't. to Willis O'Brien. Designed and created special visual effects for The Beast from 20,000 Fathoms; then began evolving own model animation system called Dynarama. In 1952 joined forces with prod. Charles H. Schneer, using new process for first time in It Came from Beneath the Sea. Subsequently made many films with Schneer in Dynamation. Received Gordon E. Sawyer Award for Acad. of Motion Picture Arts & Sciences, 1992. Appeared in films Spies Like Us, Beverly Hills Cop III, Comic Book: The Movie.
PICTURES: Mighty Joe Young, The Beast From 20000 Fathoms, It Came From Beneath the Sea, Earth Vs. the Flying Saucers, Animal World, Twenty Million Miles to Earth, 7th Voyage of Sinbad, The Three Worlds of Gulliver, Mysterious Island, Jason and the Argonauts, First Men in the Moon, One Million Years B.C., The Valley of Gwangi, The Golden Voyage of Sinbad, Sinbad and the Eye of the Tiger (also co-prod.), Clash of the Titans (also co. prod.).

HART, GARRETT S.
Executive. e. Univ. of MA, Amherst; Queens Col/CUNY. 1979, joined Paramount as mngr. then v.p. of research; 1982, became dir. of comedy develp. Served as sr. v.p., research for Lorimar-Telepictures Corp. before joining Universal 1987; 1990, became sr. v.p., current programs. 1993, named pres. of the network tv division of the Paramount Television Group. Currently, pres. Paramount Television Group.

HART, MELISSA JOAN
Actress. b. Smithtown, NY, April 18, 1976.
PICTURES: Can't Hardly Wait (cameo), The Specials, Drive Me Crazy, The Bachelor and the Bobby-Soxer, Backflash, Rent Control, Jesus-Mary-And Joey.
TELEVISION: Movies: Family Reunion: A Relative Nightmare, Sabrina the Teenage Witch (pilot), Twisted Desire, The Right Connections, Two Came Back, Silencing Mary, Sabrina Goes to Rome (also prod.), Sabrina Down Under. Mini-Series: Kane & Abel. Series: Clarissa Explains It All, Sabrina the Teenage Witch, Witchright Hall, Express Yourself. Guest: The Equalizer, Are You Afraid of the Dark?, Touched by an Angel, Clueless, Boy Meets World, Teen Angel, You Wish.

HARTLEY, HAL
Director, Writer, Composer. b. Long Island, NY, November 3, 1959. e. SUNY/Purchase (film). Following graduation made 3 short movies: Kid, The Cartographer's Girlfriend, Dogs. For PBS made the shorts Theory of Achievement, Ambition, Surviving Desire; also NYC 3/94, Opera No. 1. Music videos: The Only Living Boy in New York (Everything But the Girl), From a Motel 6 (Yo La Tengo), Iris.
PICTURES: Director/Writer: The Unbelievable Truth (debut, 1990), Trust, Simple Men, Amateur, Flirt (also actor, editor), Henry Fool (Cannes Film Festival Award, Best Screenplay, 1998), The Book of Life, Kimono, No Such Thing, The Cloud of Unknowing (prod), Milk and Honey (composer only).

HARTLEY, MARIETTE
Actress. b. New York, NY, June 21, 1940. Student Carnegie Tech. Inst. 1956-57; studied with Eva Le Gallienne. Appeared with Shakespeare Festival, Stratford 1957-60. Co-host Today Show, 1980. Co-host on CBS Morning Show, 1987. Returned to stage in King John (NYSF in Central Park), 1989. Nominated for 6 Emmys for Best Actress. Received 3 Clio Awards, 1979, 1980, and 1981, for acting in commercials. Autobiography: Breaking the Silence.
THEATRE: The Sisters Rosensweig, Deathtrap, Sylvia.
PICTURES: Ride the High Country (debut, 1962), Drums of Africa, Marnie, Marooned, Barquero, The Return of Count Yorga, Skyjacked, The Magnificent Seven Ride!, Improper Channels, O'Hara's Wife, 1969, Encino Man, Snitch, Baggage.
TELEVISION: Movies: Earth II, Sandcastles, Genesis II, Killer Who Wouldn't Die, Last Hurrah, M.A.D.D.: Mothers Against Drunk Drivers, Drop-Out Father, One Terrific Guy, Silence of the Heart. Series: Peyton Place, The Hero, Good Night Beantown, WIOU, To Have and to Hold, One Life to Live, Healthy Solution with Mariette Hartley. Guest: The Rockford Files, The Incredible Hulk (Emmy Award, 1979), Stone, Caroline in the City. My Two Loves, Murder C.O.D., Diagnosis of Murder, The House on Sycamore Street, Child of Rage, Heaven & Hell: North and South Book III, Falling From the Sky!: Flight 174. Mini-Series: Passion and Paradise. Specials: Wild About Animals (host).

HARTMAN BLACK, LISA
Actress. Houston, TX, June 1, 1956. m. musician Clint Black. Attended NYC's H.S. of Performing Arts prior to becoming a nightclub performer.
PICTURES: Deadly Blessing, Where the Boys Are.
TELEVISION: *Series*: Tabitha, Knots Landing, High Performance, 2000 Malibu Road. *Movies*: Murder at the World Series, Valentine Magic on Love Island, Where the Ladies Go, Gridlock, Jacqueline Susann's Valley of the Dolls 1981, Beverly Hills Cowgirl Blues, Full Exposure: The Sex Tapes Scandal, The Operation, The Take, Bare Essentials, Fire: Trapped on the 39th Floor, Not of This World, Red Wind, The Return of Eliot Ness, Without a Kiss Goodbye, Search for Grace, Dazzle, Someone Else's Child, Have You Seen My Son?, Out of Nowhere, Elvis: His Life and Times (host), Still Holding On: The Legend of Cadillac Jack, Intimate Portrait: Lisa Hartman-Black (herself).

HARTNETT, JOSH
Actor. b. San Francisco, CA, July 21, 1978. e. SUNY Purchase. Voted 'Star of Tomorrow' in Quigley's Top Ten MoneyMakers Poll of 2001-2002.
PICTURES: Halloween H20: 20 Years Later, Debutante, The Faculty, The Virgin Suicides, Here on Earth, Member, Blow Dry, Town & Country, Pearl Harbor, O, Black Hawk Down, 40 Days and 40 Nights, Halloween: Resurrection, Hollywood Homicide, The Rum Diary, Obsessed.
TELEVISION: *Series*: Cracker. *Special*: AFI's 100 Years, 100 Thrills: America's Most Heart-Pounding Movies, Young Hollywood Awards, 2003 MTV Movie Awards (himself).

HARVEY, ANTHONY
Director, Editor. b. London, England,, June 3, 1931. Royal Acad. of Dramatic Art. Two yrs. as actor. Ent. m.p. ind. 1949 with Crown Film Unit.
PICTURES: *Editor*: Private's Progress, Brothers-in-Law, Man in a Cocked Hat (Carlton Brown of the F.O.), I'm Alright Jack, The Angry Silence, The Millionairess, Lolita, The L-Shaped Room, Dr. Strangelove, The Spy Who Came In From the Cold, The Whisperers. *Director*: Dutchman (debut, 1966), The Lion in Winter, They Might Be Giants, Eagles' Wing, Players, The Abdication, Richard's Things, Grace Quigley.
TELEVISION: *Movies*: The Disappearance of Aimee, Svengali, The Patricia Neal Story, The Glass Menagerie, This Can't Be Love.

HARWOOD, RONALD
Writer. b. Cape Town, South Africa, November 9, 1934. e. Royal Acad. of Dramatic Art.
THEATRE: The Dresser, Interpreters, J.J. Farr, Another Time, Reflected Glory, Poison Pen, Taking Sides.
PICTURES: Barber of Stamford Hill, Private Potter, High Wind in Jamaica, Arrivederci Baby, Diamonds for Breakfast, Sudden Terror (Eye Witness), One Day in the Life of Ivan Denisovich, Operation Daybreak (Price of Freedom), The Dresser (also prod.), The Doctor and the Devils, Tchin-Tchin, The Browning Version, Cry the Beloved Country, Taking Sides, The Pianist., The Statement, Being Julia.
TELEVISION: The Barber of Stamford Hill, Private Potter, Take a Fellow Like Me, The Lads, Convalescence, Guests of Honor, The Guests. Adapted several of the Tales of the Unexpected, The Deliberate Death of a Polish Priest, Mandela, Breakthrough at Rykjavik, Countdown to War, All the World's a Stage (series), Garderober, Majstor.

HASSANEIN, RICHARD C.
Executive. b. New York, NY, Aug. 13, 1951; e. Staunton Military Acad., 1966-70; American U., 1970-74. Booker/real estate dept. opns., United Artists Theater Circuit, 1974-77; joined United Film Distribution Co., 1977; 1978-88, pres. of UFD. 1988-91 served as pres., prod.s' rep., foreign & U.S. sls., of Myriad Enterprises. Joined Todd-AO Glen Glenn Studios in 1991 as v.p. of new bus. ventures. 1991 appointed exec. v.p. of Todd-AO Studios East, NY. 1993, elected to bd. of dirs. of Todd-AO Corp. 1995, appointed v.p. of Todd-AO Studios West, Los Angeles; 1996, pres. and COO of Todd-AO Studios West. 1999, Executive Vice President of Todd Studios (formerly Todd AO Studios). Joined Advanced Digital Services, Jan. 2002

HASSANEIN, SALAH M.
Executive. b. Suez, Egypt, May 31, 1921. e. British Sch., Alexandria, Egypt. Nat'l Bank of Egypt, Cairo, 1939-42. Asst. division mgr. Middle East, 20th-Fox, Cairo, Egypt, 1942-44: U.S. armed forces, 1945-47; usher, asst. mgr., Rivoli Theatre, N.Y., 1947-48. Film buyer, booker, oper. v.p. U.A. Eastern Theas., 1948-59; pres. 1960; exec. v.p. U.A. Communications, Inc. 1960; v.p. United Artists Cable Corp., 1963. Exec. v.p., Todd-AO Corp., 1980. President, Warner Bros. International Theaters, 1988. President, Todd AO Corp., 1994-2000. Currently, president, SMH Entertainment; bd. chmn., PointSource Technology, bd. directors, SeeBeyond Technology Corp. Chairman, Variety Boys & Girls Club of Queens; past chmn. and pres., Variety Clubs International; hon. chmn., Will Rogers Memorial Fund; past chmn. and pres., Foundation of Motion Picture Pioneers; member, New York State Motion Picture and Television Advisory Board; advisory board member, National Bank of New York City;

past member, Board of Television & Film Committee of the United States Information Agency; trustee, North Shore Hospital, Manhasset, N.Y.; board member, Board of Aging in America, Inc.; chmn., Variety International Lifeline Program.
PICTURES: *Exec. prod.*: Knightriders, Creepshow, Hello Again, Love or Money.

HASSELHOFF, DAVID
Actor. b. Baltimore, MD, July 17, 1952.
PICTURES: Starcrash, Starke Zeiten, Witchery, W.B. Blue and the Bean, The Final Alliance, Ring of the Musketeers, Dear God (cameo), The Big Tease, The Target Shoots First, Layover, The New Guy, Don't Call Me Tonto..
TELEVISION: *Movies*: Griffin and Phoenix, Semi Tough, The Cartier Affair, Bridge Across Time, Perry Mason: The Case of the Lady in the Lake, Baywatch: Panic at Malibu Pier, Fire & Rain, Knight Rider 2000, Avalanche, Baywatch: Forbidden Paradise, Gridlock, Nick Fury, Baywatch: White Thunder at Glacier Bay, One True Love, Shaka Zulu: The Citadel, Baywatch: Hawaiian Wedding. *Series*: The Young and the Restless, Knight Rider, Baywatch, Baywatch Nights.

HASTINGS, DON
Actor. b. Brooklyn, NY, Apr. 1, 1934. e. Professional Children's Sch., Lodge H.S. On B'way in I Remember Mama, Summer and Smoke, etc.; Natl. co. of Life With Father; on various radio shows. Also wrote scripts for tv series The Guiding Light.
TELEVISION: *Series*: Captain Video, The Edge of Night, As the World Turns (1960-present, also writer).

HATFIELD, TED
Executive. b. Wilton Junction, IA. e. Hot Springs, AR. Started in industry ABC Paramount Theatres, advancing from usher to district mgr. 1970-1991, MGM/UA V.P. Field Operations, then V.P. Exhibitor Relations. 1991-1997, Sony Pictures V.P. Exhibitor Relations. 1998, Regal Cinemas Nationwide Promotion Director.

HATOSY, SHAWN
Actor. b. Fredrick, MD, Dec. 29, 1975.
PICTURES: Home for the Holidays, In & Out, No Way Home, Inventing the Abbotts, All Over Me, The Postman, The Faculty, Simpatico, The Joyriders, Anywhere But Here, Outside Providence, Simpatico, Anywhere But Here, Down to You, Borstal Boy, Tangled, John Q., A Guy Thing, The Cooler, Deadrockstar, The Cooler, 11:14, Dallas 362.
TELEVISION: *Guest*: Homicide: Life on the Street, Law & Order.

HAUER, RUTGER
Actor. b. Breukelen, Netherlands, Jan. 23, 1944. Stage actor in Amsterdam for six years.
PICTURES: Repelsteeltje (debut, 1973), Turkish Delight, Pustelblume, The Wilby Conspiracy, Keetje Tippel, Het Jaar van de Kreeft, Max Havelaar, Griechische Feigen, Soldier of Orange, Pastorale 1943, Femme Entre Chien et Loup, Mysteries (also co-prod.), Gripsta en de Gier, Spetters, Nighthawks, Chanel Solitaire, Blade Runner, Eureka, The Osterman Weekend, A Breed Apart, Ladyhawke, Flesh and Blood, The Hitcher, Wanted: Dead or Alive, The Legend of the Holy Drinker, Bloodhounds of Broadway, The Blood of Heroes, Blind Fury, Ocean Point, On a Moonlit Night, Past Midnight, Split Second, Buffy the Vampire Slayer, Arctic Blue, Beyond Forgiveness, Surviving the Game, Nostradamus, The Beans of Egypt Maine, Angel of Death, Hemoglobin, Deathline, Tactical Assault, Bone Daddy, New World Disorder, Partners in Crime, Wilder, Lying in Wait, The Room, Jungle Juice, God's Bankers, Flying Virus, Confessions of a Dangerous Mind, Warrior Angels, Scorcher, In the Shadow of the Cobra, Dracula II: The Ascension, Dracula III: Legacy.
TELEVISION: *Movies*: Escape from Sobibor, Inside The Third Reich, Deadlock, Blind Side, Voyage, Amelia Earhart: The Final Flight, Fatherland, Hostile Waters, Merlin. *Series*: Floris (Netherlands TV). *Mini-Series*: Maketub: The Law of the Desert (Italy), The 10th Kingdom.

HAUSER, WINGS
Actor. b. Hollywood, CA, Dec. 12, 1947. Nickname derived from playing wing back on h.s. football team. Began studying acting in 1975.
PICTURES: First to Fight, Who'll Stop the Rain, Homework, Vice Squad, Deadly Force, Uncommon Valor (assoc. prod., story only), Night Shadows, A Soldier's Story, Jo Jo Dancer Your Life is Calling, 3:15, Tough Guys Don't Dance, Nightmare at Noon, The Wind, Hostage, Dead Man Walking, The Carpenter, The Siege of Firebase Gloria, No Safe Haven (also co-s.p.), Reason to Die, L.A. Bounty, Street Asylum, Pale Blood, Out of Sight Out of Mind, Nightmare at Noon, Living to Die, Exiled in America, Bedroom Eyes II, Wilding, The Killer's Edge, In Between, Frame Up, Cold Fire, Beastmaster 2: Through the Portal of Time, The Art of Dying, Mind Body & Soul, Frame-up III: The Cover Up, Watchers 3, Tales From the Hood, Victim of Desire, Life Among the Cannibals, Original Gangstas, Going Home, The Insider, Clean and Narrow, Savage Season, Irish Eyes..
TELEVISION: *Series*: The Young and the Restless, The Last Precinct, Lightning Force, Command 5, Roseanne, Beverly Hills 90210. *Movies*: Hear No Evil, Ghost Dancing, Sweet Revenge, The Long Hot Summer, Perry Mason: The Case of the

Scandalous Scoundrel, Highway Man, Bump In the Night, Kingpin (mini). *Guest*: Murder She Wrote, China Beach, Hard Ball, The Young Riders, Space Rangers, Walker Texas Ranger, Jag.

HAUSMAN, MICHAEL
Producer. Former stockbroker and still photographer. Entered film industry as assoc. prod. and prod. mgr. on The Heartbreak Kid and Taking Off. Worked as head of prod. for Robert Stigwood on Saturday Night Fever.
PICTURES: I Never Promised You a Rose Garden, Alambrista!, Heartland, Rich Kids, One-Trick Pony, Ragtime (exec. prod., 1st asst. dir.), The Ballad of Gregorio Cortez, Silkwood, Amadeus (exec. prod.), Places in the Heart (exec. prod.), Desert Bloom, Flight of the Spruce Goose, No Mercy, House of Games, Things Change, Valmont, State of Grace, Homicide, Nobody's Fool, A Family Thing, Twilight, Man on the Moon, American Saint, Gangs of New York. Eternal Sunshine of the Spotless Mind (first asst. dir.).
TELEVISION: Lip Service (exec. prod.).

HAVERS, NIGEL
Actor. b. London, England,, Nov. 6, 1949. e. Leicester U., trained for stage at Arts Educational Trust. Father, Sir Michael Havers, was Attorney General of Britain. As child played Billy Owen on British radio series, Mrs. Dale's Diary. Records voice overs and books for the blind.
THEATRE: Conduct Unbecoming, Richard II, Man and , Superman (RSC), Family Voices, Season's Greetings, The Importance of Being Earnest.
PICTURES: Pope Joan (debut, 1972), Full Circle, Who is Killing the Great Chefs of Europe?, Chariots of Fire, A Passage to India, Burke and Wills, The Whistle Blower, Empire of the Sun, Farewell to the King, Clichy Days, Prophecy, Element of Doubt, Paradise Lost.
TELEVISION: *Movies*: The Charmer, Private War of Lucina Smith, Lie Down With Lions, The Burning Season, The Gentleman Thief. *Mini-Series*: The Glittering Prizes, Nicholas Nickleby, Pennies From Heaven, Winston Churchill: The Wilderness Years, Nancy Astor, The Little Princess, Death of the Heart, Naked Under Capricorn, Sleepers, The Afternoon Play. *Series*: A Horseman Riding By, Don't Wait Up, OK! TV, Murder in Mind, Manchild. *Guest*: Thriller, Star Quality: Noel Coward Stories (Bon Voyage), A Question of Guilt, Aspects of Love, Upstairs Downstairs, Edward VII, Liz: The Elizabeth Taylor Story.

HAVOC, JUNE
Actress. r.n. Hovick. b. Seattle, WA, Nov. 8, 1916. Sister was late Gypsy Rose Lee. Made film bow at 2 yrs. old in Hal Roach/Harold Lloyd productions billed as Baby June. Danced with Anna Pavlova troupe, then entered vaudeville in own act. Later, joined Municipal Opera Company, St. Louis, and appeared in Shubert shows. Musical comedy debut: Forbidden Melody (1936). To Hollywood, 1942. Author: Early Havoc (1959), More Havoc (1980).
THEATRE: Pal Joey, Sadie Thompson, Mexican Hayride, Dunnigan's Daughter, Dream Girl, Affairs of State, The Skin of Our Teeth, A Midsummer Night's Dream (Stratford, CT. American Shakespeare Fest., 1958), Tour for U.S. Dept. of St., 1961; wrote Marathon 33, The Ryan Girl, The Infernal Machine, The Beaux Strategem, A Warm Peninsula, Dinner at Eight, Habeas Corpus. An Unexpected Evening with June Havoc (one woman show, London 1985), The Gift (tour), Eleemosynary, The Old Lady's Guide to Survival, Do Not Go Gently.
PICTURES: Four Jacks and a Jill (debut, 1941), Powder Town, My Sister Eileen, Sing Your Worries Away, Hi Diddle Diddle, Hello Frisco Hello, No Time for Love, Casanova Burlesque, Timber Queen, Sweet and Low Down, Brewster's Millions, Intrigue, Gentleman's Agreement, When My Baby Smiles at Me, The Iron Curtain, The Story of Molly X, Red Hot and Blue, Chicago Deadline, Mother Didn't Tell Me, Once a Thief, Follow the Sun, Lady Possessed, Three for Jamie Dawn, The Private Files of J. Edgar Hoover, Can't Stop the Music, Return to Salem's Lot, Broadway: The Golden Age by the Legends Who Were There.
TELEVISION: Anna Christie, The Bear, Cakes and Ale, Daisy Mayme, The Untouchables, Willy, MacMillan & Wife, The Paper Chase, Murder She Wrote, Rodgers & Hart Story: Thou Swell, Thou Witty, Marlene: Inventing Dietrich. *Series*: More Havoc (1964-65), Search for Tomorrow, General Hospital.

HAWKE, ETHAN
Actor. b. Austin, TX, Nov. 6, 1970. Attended NYU. Studied acting at McCarter Theatre in Princeton, NJ, the British Theatre Assn., Carnegie Mellon U. Stage debut in St. Joan. Co-founder of Malaparte Theatre Co. in NYC. Dir. & wrote short film Straight to One. Author of novel The Hottest State, 1996.
THEATRE: *NY*: Casanova (Off-B'way debut, 1991), A Joke, The Seagull (B'way debut, 1992), Sophistry, Hesh, The Great Unwashed.
PICTURES: Explorers (debut, 1985), Dead Poets Society, Dad, White Fang, Mystery Date, A Midnight Clear, Waterland, Alive, Rich in Love, Reality Bites, White Fang 2: Myth of the White Wolf (cameo), Quiz Show (cameo), Floundering, Before Sunrise, Search and Destroy, Gattaca, Snow Falling on Cedars, The Newton Boys, Great Expectations, Hamlet, Joe the King, Waking

Life, Training Day, Tape, The Jimmy Show, Corso: The Last Beat.

HAWN, GOLDIE
Actress, Producer. b. Washington, DC, November 21, 1945. Started as professional dancer (performed in Can-Can at the N.Y. World's Fair, 1964), and made TV debut dancing on an Andy Griffith Special. Daughter is actress Kate Hudson.
PICTURES: The One and Only Genuine Original Family Band (debut, 1968), Cactus Flower (Academy Award, best supporting actress, 1969), There's a Girl in My Soup, $ (Dollars), Butterflies Are Free, The Sugarland Express, The Girl From Petrovka, Shampoo, The Duchess and the Dirtwater Fox, Foul Play, Private Benjamin (Acad. Award nom.; also exec. prod.), Seems Like Old Times, Lovers and Liars (Travels With Anita), Best Friends, Swing Shift, Protocol (also exec. prod.), Wildcats (also exec. prod.), Overboard (also exec. prod.), Bird on a Wire, My Blue Heaven (co-exec. prod. only), Deceived, Crisscross (also co-exec. prod.), Housesitter, Death Becomes Her, Something to Talk About (exec. prod. only), The First Wives Club, Everyone Says I Love You, The Out-of-Towners, Town and Country, The Banger Sisters.
TELEVISION: Movies: Hope (exec. prod., dir.), When Billie Beat Bobby (exec. prod.), The Matthew Shepard Story (exec. prod.) *Series*: Good Morning World, Rowan & Martin's Laugh-In (1968-70). *Specials*: The Goldie Hawn Special, Goldie & Liza Together, Goldie and the Kids: Listen to Us.

HAYEK, SALMA
Actress. b. Coatzacoalcos, Veracruz, Mexico, Sept. 2, 1968. Began her acting career in the 1980's in Mexican TV soap operas. Was first noticed in 1995 for her role in Desperado.
PICTURES: My Crazy Life, Midaq Alley, Desperado, Fair Game, Four Rooms, From Dusk Till Dawn, Fled, Fools Rush In, Breaking Up, The Velocity of Gary, The Faculty, Dogma, 54, Wild Wild West, Forever Hollywood, Timecode, Chain of Fools, Traffic, La Gran Vida, Frida, Hotel, In the Time of the Butterflies, Once Upon a Time in Mexico, The Ground Beneath Her Feet, Searching for Debra Winger.
TELEVISION: *Movies*: Roadracers, The Hunchback, The Maldonado Miracle (sr. exec. prod., dir.) *Series*: Teresa, The Sinbad Show. *Guest*: Dream On, Nurses.

HAYES, ISAAC
Musician, Actor. b. Covington, TN, Aug. 20, 1942. Was session musician with Stax Records in Memphis, eventually working as composer, prod.. Debuted with solo album Presenting Isaac Hayes in 1968.
PICTURES: Music: Shaft (Academy Award for best song: Theme from Shaft, 1971), Shaft's Big Score. Actor: Wattstax, Save the Children, Three Tough Guys (also music), Truck Turner (also music), Escape From New York, I'm Gonna Git You Sucka, Guilty as Charged, Posse, Robin Hood: Men in Tights, It Could Happen to You, Illtown, Once Upon a Time...When We Were Colored, Flipper, Six Ways to Sunday, Blues Brothers 2000, Ninth Street (also comp.), South Park: Bigger, Longer,Uncut (voice), Reindeer Games, Shaft, Dr. Dolittle 2, Chelsea Walls, Only the Strong Survive, 8 Mile (composer-C.R.E.A.M.), A Man Called Rage (acting), Dode City: A Spaghetto Western (acting).
TELEVISION: *Movies*: Book of Days (acting), Soul Comes Home (acting). *Series*: South Park (voice).

HAYES, JOHN EDWARD
Broadcasting Executive. b. Niagara Falls, NY, Sept. 14, 1941. e. U. FL, BS broadcasting, 1963. State capital bur. chief Sta. WTVJ- TV, FL, 1963-67. Exec. asst. FL, Dept. Comsumer Svcs., 1967-71. State capitol bur. chief Sta. WTVT-TV, Tallahassee, 1971-77. Asst. news dir. Sta. WTVT-TV, FL, 1977-79. News dir. Sta. WBRC-TV, AL 1979-82; Sta. KNTV-TV, CA, 1982-83. V.p. gen. mgr. Sta. KLAS-TV, NV, 1983-87. Gen mgr. Sta. WIVB-TV, NY 1987-89. Pres. Jour. Broadcasting of Charlotte Co., 1989-92. V.p. TV Providence Jour. Co., 1992. Recipient of: Nat. Headliners award Headliner Club, 1973; Emmy award TV Acad. Arts & Sci., 1982. Mem.: Nat. Assn. Broadcasters; TV Bur. Advertisers & NBC Affiliates.

HAYES, JOHN MICHAEL
Writer. b. Worcester, MA, May 11, 1919. e. U. of Mass., 1941.
PICTURES: Red Ball Express, Thunder Bay, Torch Song, War Arrow, Rear Window, To Catch a Thief, The Trouble with Harry, It's a Dog's Life, The Man Who Knew Too Much, The Matchmaker, Peyton Place, But Not for Me, Butterfield 8, The Children's Hour, Where Love Has Gone, The Chalk Garden, Judith, Iron Will.
TELEVISION: Movie: Winter Kill, Nevada Smith, Pancho Barnes.

HAYNES, TODD
Director, Writer, Producer, Editor, Actor. b. Jan. 2, 1961.
PICTURES: Superstar: The Karen Carpenter Story, He Was Once, Poison (Sundance Film Fest. Grand Jury Prize, 1991), Swoon, Safe (Seattle Int'l. Film Fest. Amer. Indep. Award, 1995), Velvet Goldmine (Cannes Film Fest., Best Art. Contribution, 1998), Far From Heaven.
TELEVISION: *Movies*: Dottie Gets Spanked.

HAYS, ROBERT
Actor. b. Bethesda, MD, July 24, 1947. e. Grossmont Coll., San Diego State U. Left school to join San Diego's Old Globe Theatre five years, appearing in such plays as The Glass Menagerie, The Man in the Glass Booth, Richard III.
PICTURES: Airplane! (debut, 1980), Take This Job and Shove It!, Utilities, Airplane II: The Sequel, Trenchcoat, Touched, Scandalous, Cat's Eye, Honeymoon Academy, Hot Chocolate, Homeward Bound: The Incredible Journey, Fifty Fifty, Raw Justice, Homeward Bound II: Lost in San Francisco, Dr. T & The Women, Alex in Wonder.
TELEVISION: Movies: Young Pioneers, Young Pioneers' Christmas, Delta County U.S.A., The Initiation of Sarah, The Girl The Gold Watch and Everything, California Gold Rush, The Fall of the House of Usher, The Day the Bubble Burst, Murder by the Book, Running Against Time, No Dessert Dad 'Til You Mow the Lawn, Deadly Invasion: The Killer Bee Nightmare, Danielle Steel's Vanished, Christmas Every Day, Unabomber: The True Story, The Abduction, I'll Be Home for Christmas, Nightworld: 30 Years to Life, Deadly Appearances, The Retrievers, The Santa Trap. Mini-Series: Will Rogers: Champion of the People. Specials: Mr. Roberts, Partners. Guest: Love Boat, Harry O, Laverne and Shirley. Series: Angie, Starman, FM, Cutters, Kelly Kelly, To Tell the Truth, Bette.

HAYSBERT, DENNIS
Actor. b. San Mateo, CA, June 2, 1954.
THEATRE: Wedding Band, Yanks-3 Detroit-0 Top of the Seventh, Diplomacy, Othello, On the Death of, All Over Town, Blood Knot, No Place to Be Somebody, Jimmy Shine, The Time of Your Life, Ten Little Indians.
PICTURES: Major League, Navy SEALS, Mr. Baseball, Love Field, Suture, Major League 2, Amanda, Waiting to Exhale, Absolute Power, Heat, Prairie Fire, Insomnia, Standoff, How to Make the Cruelest Month, Major League 2: Back to the Minors, The Minus Man, The Thirteenth Floor, Random Hearts, What's Cooking, .Love and Basketball, Far From Heaven, The Hire: Ticker (short), Sinbad: Legend of the Seven Seas (voice).
TELEVISION: Movies: A Summer to Remember, Grambling's White Tiger, K-9000. Specials: The Upper Room, Hallelujah. Series: Code Red, Off the Rack, Now and Again, 24, Justice League. Mini-Series: Queen.

HEAD, ANTHONY
Actor. b. Camden, London, England, February 20, 1954.
PICTURES: Lady Chatterly's Lover, A Prayer for the Dying, Woof Again! Why Me?, I'll Be There.
TELEVISION: Movies: Royce, Roger Roger, Best Actress, And Starring Pancho Villa As Himself, Reversals. Mini-Series: Lillie. Guest: The Comic Strip Presents, Spenser for Hire, Boon, Woof!, The Detectives, Highlander, Ghostbusters of East Finchley, NYPD Blue, Jonathan Creek, Bergerace, Two Guys, a Girl, and a Pizza Place. Series: Woof, VR5, Buffy the Vampire Slayer, Jonathan Creek, Manchild, MI-5 Spooks, Ripper.

HEADLY, GLENNE
Actress. b. New London, CT, March 13, 1957. e. High Sch. of Performing Arts. Studied at HB Studios. In Chicago joined St. Nicholas New Works Ensemble. Won 3 Joseph Jefferson awards for work with Steppenwolf Ensemble in Say Goodnight Gracie, Miss Firecracker Contest, Balm in Gilead, Coyote Ugly, Loose Ends. Directed Canadian Gothic.
THEATRE: NY: Balm in Gilead, Arms and the Man, Extremities, The Philanthropist (Theatre World Award).
PICTURES: Four Friends (debut, 1981), Dr. Detroit, Fandango, The Purple Rose of Cairo, Eleni, Making Mr. Right, Nadine, Stars and Bars, Dirty Rotten Scoundrels, Paperhouse, Dick Tracy, Mortal Thoughts, Grand Isle, Ordinary Magic, Gettingeven with Dad, Mr. Holland's Opus, Bastard Out of Carolina, Sgt. Bilko, Days in the Valley, The X Files: Fight the Future, Babe: Pig in the City (voice), Breakfast of Champions, Timecode, Bartleby, What's the Worst That Could Happen, Don't You Cry For Me.
TELEVISION: Movies: Say Goodnight Gracie, Seize the Day, And the Band Played On, Pronto, Winchell, My Own Country, The Darkest Day, The Sandy Bottom Orchestra, On Golden Pond, Oomph!. Mini-series: Lonesome Dove (Emmy nom.), A Girl Thing. Series: David Lynch's Hotel Room, Encore! Encore! Guest: Frasier, ER.

HEALD, ANTHONY
Actor. b. New Rochelle, NY, Aug. 25, 1944. e. Michigan St. Univ.
THEATRE: B'way: The Wake of Jamey Foster, The Marriage of Figaro, Anything Goes, A Small Family Business, Love! Valour! Compassion!, Inherit the Wind. Off-B'way: The Glass Menagerie, The Electra Myth, Inadmissible Evidence, Misalliance (Theatre World Award), The Caretaker, The Fox, The Philanthropist, Henry V, The Foreigner, Digby, Principia Scriptoriae, The Lisbon Traviata, Elliot Loves, Lips Together Teeth Apart, Pygmalion, Later Life, Love! Valour! Compassion! Regional: Quartermaine's Terms, J.B., Look Back in Anger, The Rose Tattoo, Bonjour la Bonjour, The Matchmaker.
PICTURES: Silkwood (debut, 1983), Teachers, Outrageous Fortune, Happy New Year, Orphans, Postcards From the Edge, The Silence of the Lambs, The Super, Whispers in the Dark, Searching for Bobby Fisher, The Ballad of Little Jo, The Pelican Brief, The Client, Kiss of Death, Bushwacked, A Time to Kill, Deep Rising, 8MM, Proof of Life, The Ruby Princess Runs Away, Red Dragon.
TELEVISION: Movies: A Case of Deadly Force, Royce. Mini-Series: Fresno, Boston Public. Pilot: After Midnight. Special: Abby My Love. Guest: Hard Copy, Crime Story, Spenser for Hire, Miami Vice, Tales From the Darkside, Against the Law, Law and Order, Class of '96, Cheers, Murder She Wrote, Under Suspicion.

HEARD, JOHN
Actor. b. Washington, D.C., Mar. 7, 1947. e. Catholic U. Career began at Organic Theatre, starring in Chicago & N.Y. productions of Warp. Other stage roles include Streamers, G.R. Point (Theatre World Award), Othello, Split, The Glass Menagerie, Total Abandon, The Last Yankee.
PICTURES: Between the Lines (debut, 1977), First Love, On the Yard, Head Over Heels (Chilly Scenes of Winter), Heart Beat, Cutter and Bone (Cutter's Way), Cat People, Best Revenge, Violated, Heaven Help Us, Lies, C.H.U.D., Too Scared to Scream, After Hours, The Trip to Bountiful, The Telephone, The Milagro Beanfield War, The Seventh Sign, Big, Betrayed, Beaches, The Package, Home Alone, End of Innocence, Awakenings, Rambling Rose, Deceived, Mindwalk, Radio Flyer, Gladiator, Waterland, Home Alone 2: Lost in New York, In the Line of Fire, Me and Veronica, The Pelican Brief, Before and After, My Fellow Americans, 187, Executive Power, Men, Snake Eyes, Desert Blue, Freak Weather, The Secret Pact, Jazz Night, Fish Out of Water, Animal Factory, The Photographer, Pollock, Above Ground, The Boys of Sunset Ridge, O, Dying on the Edge, Tracks, Researching Raymond Burke.
TELEVISION: Series: John Grisham's The Client. Specials: The Scarlet Letter, Edgar Allan Poe: Terror of the Soul. Mini-Series: Tender Is the Night, Perfect Murder Perfect Town. Movies: Will There Really Be a Morning?, Legs, Out on a Limb, Necessity, Cross of Fire, Dead Ahead: The Exxon Valdez Disaster, There Was a Little Boy, Spoils of War, Because Mommy Works, The Wednesday Woman, The Big Heist, The Pilot's Wife, Monday Night Mayhem.

HECHE, ANNE
Actress. b. Aurora, OH, May 25, 1969.
PICTURES: An Ambush of Ghosts, The Adventures of Huck Finn, A Simple Twist of Fate, Milk Money, I'll Do Anything, The Wild Side, Pie in the Sky, The Juror, Walking and Talking, Donnie Brasco, Volcano, I Know What You Did Last Summer, Six Days Seven Nights, Wag the Dog, Return to Paradise, Psycho, The Third Miracle, Karen Black: Actress At Work, Auggie Rose, Prozac Nation, Timepiece, John Q.
TELEVISION: Series: Another World. Movies: O Pioneers!, Against the Wall, Girls in Prison, Kingfish: A Story of Huey P. Long, If These Walls Could Talk, Subway Stories, One Kill. Guest: Murphy Brown, Ellen, Ally McBeal.

HECHT, ALBIE
Producer, Executive. b. Queens, NY. e. B.A., Columbia U. Exec. producer and founding principal, Chauncey Street Prods. Currently president, Film and TV Entertainment for Nickelodeon. Recipient of three CableACE Awards and an ACT Award for excellence in children's television; also the first recipient of the Children's Museum of Los Angeles Freedom Award.
PICTURES: Exec. prod.: Doom Runners, Snow Day, Rugrats in Paris: The Movie, Jimmy Neutron: Boy Genius, How to Eat Fried Worms, Clockstoppers, Hey Arnold! The Movie, The Wild Thornberrys.
TELEVISION: Exec. prod.: Clarissa Explains It All, Cry Baby Lane, Pop Across America.

HECKERLING, AMY
Director. b. New York, NY, May 7, 1954. e. Art & Design H.S., NYU, (film and TV), American Film Institute. Made shorts (Modern Times, High Finance, Getting It Over With), before turning to features.
PICTURES: Fast Times at Ridgemont High, Johnny Dangerously, Into the Night (actor only), National Lampoon's European Vacation, Look Who's Talking, Look Who's Talking Too, Look Who's Talking 3 (co-exec. prod. only), Clueless (WGA nom.), A Night at the Roxbury (prod.,s.p.), Molly (prod. only), Loser. (also prod.).
TELEVISION: George Burns Comedy Hour, Fast Times, They Came From Queens. Series: Clueless.

HEDAYA, DAN
Actor. b. Brooklyn, NY, July 24, 1940. e. Tufts Univ. Taught junior high school for seven yrs. before turning to acting. Joined NY Shakespeare Fest. in 1973.
THEATRE: NY: Last Days of British Honduras, Golden Boy, Museum, The Basic Training of Pavlo Hummel, Conjuring an Event, Survivors, Henry V.
PICTURES: The Passover Plot (debut, 1976), The Seduction of Joe Tynan, Night of the Juggler, True Confessions, I'm Dancing As Fast As I Can, Endangered Species, The Hunger, The Adventures of Buckaroo Banzai, Blood Simple, Reckless, Tightrope, Commando, Wise Guys, Running Scared, Joe Vs. the Volcano, Pacific Heights, Tune in Tomorrow, The Addams Family,

Boiling Point, Benny & Joon, Rookie of the Year, For Love or Money, Mr. Wonderful, Maverick, Search and Destroy, Clueless, Nixon, The Usual Suspects, To Die For, Marvin's Room, Freeway, Ransom, Daylight, In & Out, Alien: Resurrection, A Life Less Ordinary, A Night at the Roxbury, A Civil Action, Dick, The Hurricane, Shaft, The Crew, Down, Mulholland Dr., Quicksand, The Myersons, Swimfan, New Suit.
TELEVISION: Series: The Tortellis, One of the Boys, ER. Movies: The Prince of Central Park, Death Penalty, The Courage, Slow Burn, A Smoky Mountain Christmas, Betrayal of Trust, Reluctant Agent, The Whereabouts of Jenny, The Garden of Redemption. Guest: Hill Street Blues, Cheers, L.A. Law. Pilots: The Earthlings, The Flamingo Kid, The Rock. Special: Just Like Family, Mama's Boy, Veronica Clare, The Second Civil War.

HEDLUND, DENNIS
Executive. b. Hedley, TX, Sept. 3, 1946. e. U. of Texas, Austin, B.A., business admin., 1968. Captain U.S. Marine Corp, 1966-72. 1970-74, newscaster and disc jockey, KGNC Amarillo, TX; KOMA Oklahoma City, OK; WTIX New Orleans, LA; WFLA Tampa, FL. 1974-77, nat'l sales mgr., Ampex Corp., NY. 1977-80, v.p., Allied Artists Video Corp., NY. 1980-present, founder and pres., Kultur International Films Ltd., distributor of over 800 performing arts programs on home video. 1990, created White Star Ent., prod. of original programs for tv, and marketer of over 400 non-theatrical home video titles. Acquired Duke USA, 1200 motorsports programs for tv and home video.
TELEVISION: Roger Miller: King of the Road, Jackie Mason: An Equal Opportunity Offender, Merle Haggard: A Portrait of a Proud Man, History of Talk Radio, George Jones: Golden Hits, Raised Catholic: Still Catholic After All These Fears.

HEDREN, TIPPI
Actress. r.n. Nathalie Hedren. b. Lafayette, MN, Jan. 18, 1935. Daughter is actress Melanie Griffith. Was hired by Alfred Hitchcock for leading role in The Birds after being spotted on a commercial on the Today Show. Author of The Cats of Shambala. Founder and pres. of The Roar Foundation. Founder of the Shambala preserve. Bd. member, The Wildlife Safari, The Elsa Wild Animal Appeal, The ASPCA, The American Heart Assoc.
THEATRE: Black Comedy, A Hatful of Rain, Love Letters.
PICTURES: The Birds (debut, 1963), Marnie, A Countess From Hong Kong, The Man and the Albatross, Satan's Harvest, Tiger By the Tail, Mr. Kingstreet's War, The Harrad Experiment, Where the Wind Dies, Roar (also prod.), Foxfire Light, Deadly Spygames, Pacific Heights, In the Cold of the Night, Inevitable Grace, Theresa's Tattoo, Mind Lies, The Devil Inside, Citizen Ruth, I Woke Up Early the Day I Died, The Breakup, Internet Love, Expose, The Storytellers, The Hand Behind the Mouse: The Ub Iwerks Story, Mind Rage, Life with Big Cats, Tea with Grandma, Ice Cream Sundae, Mob Dot Com.
TELEVISION: Series: The Bold and the Beautiful, Dream On. Movies: Alfred Hitchcock Presents..., Through the Eyes of a Killer, Shadow of a Doubt, Perry Mason: The Case of the Skin-Deep Scandal, The Birds II: Land's End, Treacherous Beauties, Return to Green Acres, Kraft Suspense Theatre: The Trains of Silence, The Book of Virtues (voice), Freakazoid! (voice), Sixth Sense (short), Mulligans (short), The Darklings, Replacing Dad. Guest: Run for Your Life, The Courtship of Eddie's Father, Alfred Hitchcock Presents (1985), Baby Boom, Hart to Hart, In the Heat of the Night, Hotel, Improv (guest host), Tales From the Darkside, Murder She Wrote, Capitol News, The Guardian, Heroes Die Hard, Our Time. Special: Inside The Birds.

HEFFNER, RICHARD D.
Executive. b. New York, NY, Aug. 5, 1925. e. Columbia U. Instrumental in acquisition of Channel 13 (WNET) as New York's educational tv station; served as its first gen. mngr. Previously had produced and moderated Man of the Year, The Open Mind, etc. for commercial and public TV. Served as dir. of public affairs programs for WNBC-TV in NY. Was also dir. of special projects for CBS TV Network and editorial consultant to CBS, Inc. Editorial Board. Was radio newsman for ABC. Exec. editor of From The Editor's Desk on WPIX-TV in NY. Taught history at U. of California at Berkeley, Sarah Lawrence Coll., Columbia U. and New School for Social Research, NY. Served as American specialist in communications for U.S. Dept. of State in Japan, Soviet Union, Germany, Yugoslavia, Israel, etc. Prof. of Communications and Public Policy at Rutgers U. 1974-94, chmn. of classification and rating admin. rating board. 1994-95, sr. fellow, Freedom Forum Media Studies Center at Columbia Univ.

HEFFRON, RICHARD T.
Director. b. Chicago, Oct. 6, 1930.
PICTURES: Fillmore, Newman's Law, Trackdown, Futureworld, Outlaw Blues, I the Jury, The French Revolution.
TELEVISION: The Morning After, Dick Van Dyke Special, I Will Fight No More Forever, Toma (pilot), Rockford Files (pilot), North and South (mini-series). Movies: The California Kid, Young Joe Kennedy, A Rumor of War, A Whale for the Killing, The Mystic Warrior, V: The Final Battle, Anatomy of an Illness, Convicted: A Mother's Story, Guilty of Innocence, Samaritan, Napoleon and Josephine: A Love Story, Broken Angel, Pancho Barnes, Tagget, Deadly Family Secrets, No Greater Love, Le Braon.

HEIDER, FREDERICK
Producer. b. Milwaukee, WI, Apr. 9, 1917. e. Notre Dame U.Actor in Globe Theatre, Orson Welles' Mercury Theatre.
TELEVISION & RADIO: Chesterfield Supper Club, Sammy Kaye's So You Want to Lead a Band, Frankie Carle Show, Jo Stafford Show, Paul Whiteman Goodyear Revue, Billy Daniels Show, Martha Wright Show, Earl Wrightson Show, Club Seven, Mindy Carson Show; Ted Mack Family Hour, Dr. I.Q., Miss America Pageant, Bishop Sheen's Life Is Worth Living, Voice of Firestone, Music for a Summer Night. Music for a Spring Night, The Bell Telephone Hour. Publisher, Television Quarterly, National Academy of Television Arts and Sciences. Became columnist, The Desert Sun, Palm Springs, CA.

HEILMAN, CLAUDE
Executive. b. Cologne, Germany, June 27, 1927. Early career in Europe in prod. and distribution. In U.S. joined Fox in Hollywood and NY; incl. mgmt of Grauman's Chinese and other Fox theatres.Formed Vintage Prods. Inc., United Film Associates Int'l., Inter Road Shows. President/chief executive GEM Communications and Islandia Enterprises.
PICTURES: This Earth is Mine, Odyssey of Justice Lee, The Adventures of Gulliver, Desamor, Sound General Quarters, Islandia.

HELGELAND, BRIAN
Writer, Director, Producer. b. Providence, RI, 1961.
PICTURES: Writer: A Nightmare on Elm Street 4: The Dream Master, 976-EVIL, Highway to Hell, Assassins, L.A. Confidential (also co-prod., Acad. Award, Best Adapted Screenplay, Chicago Film Crits. Award, LA Film Crits. Award, NY Film Crits. Awards Best Screenplay, 1997), Conspiracy Theory, The Postman, Payback, A Knight's Tale, Bloodwork, The Sin Eater.
TELEVISION: Series: Tales from the Crypt (dir.).

HELGENBERGER, MARG
Actress. b. North Bend, NE, Nov. 16, 1958. e. Northwestern U. Came to NY where she landed first professional job as regular on daytime serial Ryan's Hope.
PICTURES: After Midnight (debut, 1989), Always, Crooked Hearts, Distant Cousins, The Cowboy Way, Bad Boys, Species, My Fellow Americans, Fire Down Below, Species II, Erin Brockovich.
TELEVISION: Series: Ryan's Hope, Shell Game, China Beach (Emmy Award, 1990), Fallen Angels, Partners, CSI. Movies: Blind Vengeance, Death Dreams, The Hidden Room, Deadline (pilot), Through the Eyes of a Killer, The Tommyknockers, When Love Kills: The Seduction of John Hearn, Where Are My Children?, Red Eagle, Partners, Inflammable, Conundrum, Murder Live!, The Last Time I Commited Suicide, Gold Coast, Thanks of a Grateful Nation, Giving Up the Ghost, The Happyface Murders, Lethal Vows. Special: Fallen Angels. Guest: Spenser for Hire, thirtysomething, Tales From the Crypt, The Larry Sanders Show, ER. Mini-series: When Love Kills: The Seduction of John Hearn, Perfect Murder Perfect Town.

HELLER, PAUL M.
Producer. b. New York, NY, Sept. 25, 1927. e. Hunter Coll., Drexel Inst. of Technology. President, Intrepid Productions. Studied engineering until entry into U.S. Army as member of security agency, special branch of signal corps. Worked as set designer (Westport, East Hampton, Palm Beach) and in live TV and then on theatrical films. Produced the NY Experience and South Street Venture. Debut as film prod., David and Lisa, 1963. From 1964 to 1969 was president of MPO Pictures Inc. Joined Warner Bros. as prod. exec., 1970. Founded the Community Film Workshop Council for the American Film Institute. In 1972 founded Sequoia Pictures, Inc. with Fred Weintraub. Pres. of Paul Heller Prods. Inc. formed in 1978. Founded the Audrey Skirball-Kenis Theatre. Bd. of dirs., the British Academy of Film and Television - Los Angeles, The Hearst Monument Foundation, The Geffen Theatre.
PICTURES: David and Lisa, The Eavesdropper, Secret Ceremony, Enter the Dragon, Truck Turner, Golden Needles, Dirty Knight's Work, Outlaw Blues, The Pack, The Promise, First Monday in October, Withnail and I, My Left Foot (exec. prod.), The Lunatic, Fatal Inheritance, The Annihilation of Fish.
TELEVISION: Pygmalion, Falcon's Gold, David & Lisa.

HELLMAN, JEROME
Producer. b. New York, NY, Sept. 4, 1928. e. NYU. Joined ad dept. of New York Times then went to William Morris Agency as apprentice. Made asst. in TV dept. Worked as agent for Jaffe Agency. After hiatus in Europe joined Ashley-Steiner Agency (later IFA) where clients included Franklin Schaffner, Sidney Lumet, George Roy Hill, John Frankenheimer. Functioned as TV prod., inc. Kaiser Aluminum Hour. Left to form own agency, Ziegler, Hellman and Ross. Switched to feature prod. with The World of Henry Orient in 1964.
PICTURES: The World of Henry Orient, A Fine Madness, Midnight Cowboy (Academy Award for Best Picture, 1969), The Day of the Locust, Coming Home, Promises in the Dark (also dir.), The Mosquito Coast.

HELLMAN, MONTE
Director, Editor. b. New York, NY, 1932. e. Stanford Univ., UCLA. Started by working for Roger Corman's company as dir., editor, 2nd Unit dir. Replaced deceased directors on the films The Greatest, Avalanche Express. Dialogue Director: St. Valentine's Day Massacre. Acted in The Christian Licorice Store, Someone to Love.
PICTURES: Director: Beast from Haunted Cave, Back Door to Hell, Flight to Fury (also story) , Ride in the Whirlwind (also edit., prod.), The Shooting (also edit., prod.), Two-Lane Blacktop (also edit.), Cockfighter, China 9 Liberty 37 (also prod.), Iguana (also s.p., edit.), Silent Night Deadly Night 3 (also story). Editor: The Wild Angels, The Long Ride Home, How to Make It, The Killer Elite, Harry and Walter Go to New York, China 9 Liberty 37, The Awakening, Iguana, Silent Night, Deadly Night 3: Better Watch Out!, The Killing Box. Second Unit Director: Last Woman on Earth, Ski Troop Attack, Creature from the Haunted Sea, The Terror. Exec. Prod.: Reservoir Dogs.

HELMOND, KATHERINE
Actress. b. Galveston, TX, July 5, 1934. Initial stage work with Houston Playhouse and Margo Jones Theatre, Dallas. Joined APA Theatre, NY, and Trinity Square Rep. Co., RI, Hartford Stage, CT and Phoenix Rep. NY. In 1950s opened summer stock theatre in the Catskills. Taught acting at American Musical and Dramatic Acad., Brown U. and Carnegie-Mellon U. 1983, accepted into AFI's Directing Workshop for Women. Directed Bankrupt.
THEATER: The Great God Brown, House of Blue Leaves (Clarence Derwent, NY and LA Drama Critics Awards, 1972), Mixed Emotions.
PICTURES: The Hindenberg, Baby Blue Marine, Family Plot, Time Bandits, Brazil, Shadey, Overboard, Lady in White, Inside Monkey Zetterland, Amore!, The Flight of the Dove, Fear & Loathing in Las Vegas, The Perfect Nanny, Living in Fear.
TELEVISION: Series: Soap, Who's The Boss? (also episode dir.), Benson (episode dir. only), Coach. Movies: Dr. Max, Larry, Locusts, The Autobiography of Miss Jane Pittman, The Legend of Lizzie Borden, The Family Nobody Wanted, Cage Without a Key, The First 36 Hours of Dr. Durant, James Dean, Wanted: The Sundance Woman, Little Ladies of the Night, Getting Married, Diary of a Teenage Hitchhiker, Scout's Honor, World War III, For Lovers Only, Rosie: The Rosemary Clooney Story, Meeting of the Minds, Save the Dog, When Will I Be Loved?, The Perfect Tribute, Deception: A Mother's Secret, Grass Roots, Liz: The Elizabeth Taylor Story, Ms. Scrooge, How to Marry a Billionaire: A Christmas Tale. Special: Christmas Snow.

HEMINGWAY, MARIEL
Actress. b. Ketchum, ID, Nov. 22, 1961. Granddaughter of writer Ernest Hemingway. Sister of late actress-model Margaux Hemingway.
PICTURES: Lipstick (debut, 1976), Manhattan (Acad. Award nom.), Personal Best, Star 80, The Mean Season, Creator, Superman IV: The Quest for Peace, Sunset, The Suicide Club (also co-prod.), Delirious, Falling From Grace, Naked Gun 33 1/3: The Final Insult, Deceptions II: Edge of Deception, Bad Moon, Road Ends, Little Men, Deconstructing Harry, Drop-Dead, American Reel, The Contender, Londinium, Perfume.
TELEVISION: Series: Civil Wars, Central Park West. Movies: I Want to Keep My Baby, Steal the Sky, Into the Badlands, Desperate Rescue: The Cathy Mahone Story, September, The Crying Child, First Shot, Warning: Parental Advisory. Mini-Series: Amerika. Guest: Tales From the Crypt, Roseanne.

HEMMINGS, DAVID
Actor, Director. b. Guildford, England, Nov.18, 1941. Early career in opera. Ent. m.p. ind. 1956. Former co-partner in Hemdale Company.
THEATER: Adventures in the Skin Trade, Jeeves.
PICTURES: Five Clues to Fortune, Saint Joan, The Heart Within, In the Wake of a Stranger, No Trees in the Street, Men of Tomorrow, The Wind of Change, The Painted Smile (Murder Can Be Deadly), Some People, Play It Cool, Two Left Feet, West 11, Live It Up (Sing and Swing), The System (The Girl-Getters), Be My Guest, Dateline Diamonds, Eye of the Devil, Blow-Up, Camelot, The Charge of the Light Brigade, Only When I Larf, Barbarella, The Long Day's Dying, The Best House in London, Alfred the Great, The Walking Stick, Fragment of Fear, The Love Machine, Unman Wittering and Zigo, Voices, Juggernaut, Running Scared (dir.only), The 14 (dir. only), Mr. Quilp, Deep Red, Islands in the Stream, The Squeeze, The Disappearance, Blood Relatives, Crossed Swords, Power Play, Murder by Decree, Just a Gigolo (also dir.), Thirst, Beyond Reasonable Doubt, The Survivor (dir. only), Harlequin, Race to the Yankee Zephyr (dir., prod. only), Man Woman and Child, Prisoners (also exec. prod.), Coup D'Grat (also prod.), The Rainbow, Dark Horse (dir. only), Gladiator, Last Orders, Spy Game, Mean Machine, Gangs of New York.
TELEVISION: Auto Stop, The Big Toe, Out of the Unknown, Beverly Hills Cowgirl Blues, Clouds of Glory, Davy Crockett: Rainbow in the Thunder (also dir.). Director only: Hardball, Magnum PI, A-Team, Airwolf, Murder She Wrote, In the Heat of the Night, Quantum Leap, The Turn of the Screw, Tales From the Crypt, Passport to Murder (movie). Guest: Northern Exposure, The Raven, Ned Blessing.

HEMSLEY, SHERMAN
Actor. b. Philadelphia, PA, Feb. 1, 1938. On NY stage in Purlie.
PICTURES: Love at First Bite, Stewardess School, Ghost Fever, Mr. Nanny, Home Angels, Casper: A Spirited Beginning, Sprung, Senseless, Jane Austen's Mafia!, Screwed.
TELEVISION: Series: All in the Family, The Jeffersons, Amen, Dinosaurs (voice), Townsend Television, Goode Behavior. Guest: The Rich Little Show, Love Boat, E/R, 227, Family Matters, Lois & Clark, Fresh Prince of Bel Air, Sister Sister. Movies: Alice in Wonderland, Combat High, Camp Cucamonga, Clip's Place, Up Up and Away.

HENDERSON, FLORENCE
Actress, Singer. b. Dale, IN, Feb. 14, 1934. e. AADA. Made B'way debut while teenager in musical Wish You Were Here.
THEATER: Oklahoma!, The Great Waltz, Fanny, The Sound of Music, The Girl Who Came to Supper, South Pacific. Tour: Annie Get Your Gun.
PICTURES: Song of Norway, Shakes the Clown, Naked Gun 33 1/3: The Final Insult, The Brady Bunch Movie, Holy Man (cameo), Get Bruce (cameo).
TELEVISION: Series: Sing Along, The Jack Paar Show, Oldsmobile Music Theatre, The Brady Bunch, The Brady Bunch Hour, The Brady Brides, Florence Henderson's Home Cooking, The Brady's, Later Today. Movies: The Love Boat (pilot), The Brady Girls Get Married, A Very Brady Christmas, Fudge-A-Mania, Moms on Strike. Guest: Car 54 Where Are You?, Garry Moore Show, Ed Sullivan Show, Medical Center, The Love Boat, Fantasy Island, It's Garry Shandling's Show, Police Squad, many others. Specials: Huck Finn, Little Women, An Evening With Richard Rodgers.

HENDERSON, SKITCH
Music Director. r.n. Lyle Cedric Henderson. b. Birmingham, England, Jan. 27, 1918. e. U. of California. Began as pianist in dance bands, then theatre orchestras, films and radio on West Coast. Accompanist to Judy Garland on tour. Served, USAF, WW II. Music dir. radio, Bing Crosby. Toured with own dance band, 47-49. Music Dir. for NBC Network, Steve Allen Show, Tonight Show, Today Show, Street Scene (NY Opera). Guest conductor, symphony orchestras including NY Philharmonic, London Philharmonic. Founder and Music Dir., NY Pops Orchestra. Music Dir., Florida Orchestra Pops, Virginia Symphony Pops, Louisville Orchestra Pops. Grammy Award for RCA album NY Philharmonic with Leontyne Price and William Warfield, highlights from Porgy and Bess. Instrumental works: Skitch's Blues, Minuet on the Rocks, Skitch in Time, Come Thursday, Curacao. Scores: American Fantasy, Act One (film).

HENNER, MARILU
Actress. b. Chicago, IL, Apr. 6, 1952. e. U. of Chicago. Studied singing and dancing, appearing in musicals in Chicago and on Broadway in Over Here and Pal Joey. Autobiography: By All Means Keep on Moving (1994).
PICTURES: Between the Lines (debut, 1977), Blood Brothers, Hammett, The Man Who Loved Women, Cannonball Run II, Johnny Dangerously, Rustler's Rhapsody, Perfect, L.A. Story, Noises Off, Chasers, Grease, Social Security, Chicago, Man on the Moon, The Titanic Chronicles, Lost in the Pershing Point Hotel, Enemies of Laughter.
TELEVISION: Series: Taxi, Evening Shade, Marilu, Hollywood Squares. Movies: Dream House, Stark, Love with a Perfect Stranger, Ladykillers, Chains of Gold, Abandoned and Deceived (co-exec. prod. only), Fight for Justice, Grand Larceny, My Son Is Innocent, For the Future: The Irvine Fertility Scandal, A Tale of Two Bunnies, Rocket's Red Glare. Mini-series: Titanic.

HENNING, LINDA
Actress, Singer. b. Toluca Lake, CA, Sept. 16, 1944. Daughter of prod. Paul Henning. e. Cal State Northridge, UCLA. Member of California Artists Radio Theatre.
THEATER: Gypsy, Applause, Damn Yankees, I Do, I Do, Pajama Game, Sugar, Wonderful Town, Fiddler on the Roof, Sound of Music, Vanities, Born Yesterday, Mary, Mary, Bus Stop, etc.
PICTURES: Bye Bye Birdie, Mad About You.
TELEVISION: Series: Petticoat Junction, Sliders. Guest: Beverly Hillbillies, Happy Days, Mork & Mindy, Double Trouble, Barnaby Jones, The New Gidget, Hunter. Pilots: Kudzu, The Circle, Family. Movie: The Return of the Beverly Hillbillies.

HENNING, PAUL
Producer, Writer. b. Independence, MO, Sept. 16, 1911. e. Kansas City Sch. of Law, grad. 1932. Radio singer and disc jockey. Also acted, ran sound effects, sang, wrote scripts. To Chicago 1937-38, to write for Fibber McGee and Molly. To Hollywood as writer for Rudy Vallee, 1939. Wrote scripts for Burns and Allen 10 years, including transition radio to TV.
PICTURES: Writer: Lover Come Back, Bedtime Story, Dirty Rotten Scoundrels.
TELEVISION: Series (creator, writer, prod.): The Bob Cummings Show, The Beverly Hillbillies, Petticoat Junction, Green Acres.

HENRIKSEN, LANCE
Actor. b. New York, NY, May 5, 1943. Appeared on B'way in The Basic Training of Pavo Hummel, Richard III.

PICTURES: It Ain't Easy (debut, 1972), Dog Day Afternoon, The Next Man, Mansion of the Doomed, Close Encounters of the Third Kind, Damien: Omen II, The Visitor, The Dark End of the Street, Prince of the City, Piranha II: The Spawning, Nightmares, The Right Stuff, Savage Dawn, The Terminator, Jagged Edge, Choke Canyon, Aliens, Near Dark, Deadly Intent, Pumpkinhead, Hit List, The Horror Show, Johnny Handsome, Survival Quest, The Last Samurai, Stone Cold, Comrades in Arms, Delta Heat, Alien[3], Jennifer Eight, Excessive Force, The Outfit, Super Mario Bros., Hard Target, Man's Best Friend, No Escape, Color of Night, The Quick and the Dead, Powder, The Criminal Mind, Profile for Murder, No Contest II, Tarzan (voice), Scream 3, The Untold, The Lost Voyage, Unspeakable, The Mangler 2, The Invitation, Antibody.
TELEVISION: Series: Millennium. Guest: Scene of the Crime, Paul Reiser: Out on a Whim, Tales From the Crypt. Movies: Return to Earth, Question of Honor, Blood Feud, Reason for Living: The Jill Ireland Story, Wes Craven Presents Mind Ripper, The Day Lincoln Was Shot, Alien Evolution, The Omen Legacy.

HENRY, BUCK
Actor, Writer. r.n. Henry Zuckerman. b. New York, NY, Dec. 9, 1930. e. Dartmouth Coll. Acted in Life with Father, (tour, 1948), Fortress of Glass, Bernardine, B'way; 1952-54, U.S. Army; No Time for Sergeants (Nat'l. Co.), The Premise, improv. theatre, off-B'way.
PICTURES: Actor: The Secret War of Harry Frigg, Taking Off, The Man Who Fell to Earth, Old Boyfriends, Gloria, Eating Raoul, Aria, Dark Before Dawn, Rude Awakening, Tune in Tomorrow, Defending Your Life, The Player, The Linguini Incident, Short Cuts, Even Cowgirls Get the Blues, Grumpy Old Men Shotgun Freeway: Drives Through Lost L.A., The Real Blonde, Later Life, I'm Losing You, 1999, Curtain Call, Breakfast of Champions, Curtain Call, Famous, Serendipity. Actor-Writer: The Troublemaker, The Graduate, Is There Sex After Death?,Catch-22, Heaven Can Wait (also dir.), First Family (also dir.), To Die For, Town and Country. Writer: Candy, The Owl and the Pussycat, What's Up Doc?, The Day of the Dolphin, Protocol.
TELEVISION: Series (writer): Garry Moore Show, Steve Allen Show (also performer), The Bean Show, That Was the Week That Was (also performer), Get Smart (co-creator, story ed.), Captain Nice (also exec. prod.), Alfred Hitchcock Presents (1985, also actor), Quark, The New Show (also performer), Falcon Crest (actor only), Trying Times: Hunger Chic (dir. only), Saturday Night Live. Guest: Murphy Brown. Movies: Keep the Change, Harrison Bergeron. Special: Mastergate.

HENRY, JUSTIN
Actor. b. Rye, NY, May 25, 1971. Debut at age 8 in Kramer vs. Kramer, 1979 for which he received an Academy Award nom.
PICTURES: Kramer vs Kramer, Sixteen Candles, Martin's Day, Sweet Hearts Dance, Groupies, Not Afraid to Say, Chasing Destiny, My Dinner with Jimi, Finding Home.
TELEVISION: Movies: Tiger Town, Andersonville. Guest: ER.

HENSON, LISA
Executive. b. 1960. e. Harvard U. Father was performer-pup-peteer-director Jim Henson. Joined Warner Bros., 1983, as exec. asst. to head of prod. 1985, named dir. of creative affairs. 1985, promoted to v.p., prod. 1992, became exec. v.p., production. 1993, named pres. of worldwide prod. of Columbia Pictures. 1994, named pres. of Columbia Pictures. Resigned in 1996 to form own production company. Currently, prod. & partner, Manifest Film Co.

HEPBURN, KATHARINE
Actress. b. Hartford, CT, May 12, 1907. Author: The Making of the African Queen (1987), Me: Stories of My Life (1991). Received a record 12 Academy Award nominations for acting.
THEATRE: Death Takes a Holiday, The Warrior's Husband, The Lake, The Philadelphia Story, As You Like It, The Millionairess, The Merchant of Venice, The Taming of the Shrew, Measure for Measure, A Matter of Gravity, West Side Waltz.
PICTURES: A Bill of Divorcement (debut, 1932), Christopher Strong, Morning Glory (Academy Award, 1933), Little Women, Spitfire, The Little Minister, Break of Hearts, Alice Adams, Sylvia Scarlett, Mary of Scotland, A Woman Rebels, Quality Street, Stage Door, Bringing Up Baby, Holiday, The Philadelphia Story, Woman of the Year, Keeper of the Flame, Stage Door Canteen, Dragon Seed, Without Love, Undercurrent, The Sea of Grass, Song of Love, State of the Union, Mrs. Parkington, Adam's Rib, The African Queen, Pat and Mike, Summertime, The Iron Petticoat, The Rainmaker, The Desk Set, Suddenly Last Summer, Long Day's Journey Into Night, Guess Who's Coming to Dinner (Academy Award, 1967), The Lion in Winter (Academy Award, 1968), The Madwoman of Chaillot, The Trojan Women, A Delicate Balance, Rooster Cogburn, Olly Olly Oxen Free, On Golden Pond (Academy Award, 1981), Grace Quigley, Love Affair, The Line King: Al Hirschfeld.
TELEVISION: Movies: The Glass Menagerie, Love Among the Ruins (Emmy Award, 1975), The Corn Is Green, Mrs. Delafield Wants To Marry, Laura Lansing Slept Here, The Man Upstairs, This Can't Be Love, One Christmas. Specials: Katharine Hepburn: All About Me (host, co-writer), AFI's 100 Years, 100 Thrills: America's Most Heart-Pounding Movies.
(d. June 29, 2003)

HERALD, PETER
Executive. b. Berlin, Germany, Dec. 20, 1930. e. UCLA, B.A. U.S. Gov't. film officer in Europe 8 years. In charge of continental European prod. operation for Walt Disney Prods., 6 years. Supervisory prod. manager, Columbia Pictures, 3 years. Corporate Prod. mgr. Universal 3 years.
PICTURES: Executive-, Co-, Assoc.-, Line Producer and/or Production Mgr.: Almost Angels, Magnificent Rebel, Miracle of the White Stallions, Emil and the Detectives, There Was a Crooked Man, Outrageous Fortune, National Lampoon's Class Reunion, Doctor Detroit, D. C. Cab; The Great Waltz, Foul Play, Nightwing. W. W. and the Dixie Dancekings, Mandingo, W. C. Fields and Me, Alex and the Gypsy, Silver Streak, Star Wars, Stick, Married to It, others.

HEREK, STEPHEN
Director. b. San Antonio, TX, Nov. 10, 1958.
PICTURES: Critters (also s.p.), Bill & Ted's Excellent Adventure, Don't Tell Mom the Babysitter's Dead, The Mighty Ducks, The Three Musketeers, Mr. Holland's Opus, 101 Dalmatians, Holy Man (also prod.), Rock Star, Life or Something Like It.

HERMAN, NORMAN
Producer, Director. b. Newark, NJ. e. Rutgers U., NYU. Was accountant in California; in 1955 switched to film ind., joining American Int'l Pictures. Headed AIP prod. dept. 4 years, incl. prod., post-prod., labor negotiations, supervising story dept., etc. Pres. of Century Plaza Prods. for 9 yrs. Sr. v.p./staff writer DEG, 1986-9; Pres. No. Carolina Studios, 1989-90.
PICTURES: Prod. except as noted: Sierra Stranger, Hot Rod Girl, Hot Rod Rumble, Crime Beneath Seas, Look in any Window (exec. prod. mgr.), Tokyo After Dark (also dir., s.p.), Everybody Loves It (dir.), Mondy Teeno (dir. co-s.p.), Glory Stompers, Three in the Attic (assoc. prod.), Pretty Boy Floyd, Dunwich Horror, Three in the Cellar, Angel Unchained, Psych-Out, Sadismo (s.p.), Bloody Mama, Bunny O'Hare, Killers Three, Frogs (exec. prod.), Planet of Life (s.p.), Blacula, Dillinger (s.p.), Legend of Hell House, Dirty Mary Crazy Larry, Rolling Thunder, In God We Trust (exec. prod.).
TELEVISION: Writer: Robert Taylor Detective, Iron Horse, Invaders, Adam 12, Lancer. Dir. Prod.: Hannibal Cobb, You Are the Judge.

HEROUX, CLAUDE
Producer. b. Montreal, Canada, Jan. 26, 1942. e. U. of Montreal. 1979, prod. v.p., Film Plan Intl., Montreal.
PICTURES: Valerie, L'Initiation, L'Amour Humain, Je t'aime, Echoes of a Summer, Jacques Brel Is Alive and Well and Living in Paris, Breaking Point,Born for Hell, Hog Wild, City of Fire, Dirty Tricks, Gas, Visiting Hours, Videodrome, The Funny Farm, Going Berserk, Of Unknown Origin, Covergirl, Tous pour un.
TELEVISION: The Park is Mine, Popeye Doyle, Desjardins, others.

HERRMANN, EDWARD
Actor. b. Washington, DC, July 21, 1943. Raised in Grosse Pointe, MI. e. Bucknell U. Postgrad. Fulbright scholar, London Acad. Music and Dramatic Art 1968-69. Acted with Dallas Theater Center for 4 years.
THEATRE: NY: The Basic Training of Pavlo Hummel, Moonchildren, Mrs. Warren's Profession (Tony Award, 1976), Journey's End, The Beach House, The Philadelphia Story, Plenty, Tom and Viv, Julius Caesar, Not About Heroes, Life Sentences. London: A Walk in the Woods.
PICTURES: Lady Liberty, The Paper Chase, The Day of the Dolphin, The Great Gatsby, The Great Waldo Pepper, The Betsy, Brass Target, Take Down, The North Avenue Irregulars, Harry's War, Reds, Death Valley, A Little Sex, Annie, Mrs. Soffel, The Purple Rose of Cairo, The Man With One Red Shoe, Compromising Positions, The Lost Boys, Overboard, Big Business, Hero (unbilled), Born Yesterday, My Boyfriend's Back, Foreign Student, Richie Rich, Critical Care, Frank Lloyd Wright, A Civil Action, Better Living, Walking Across Egypt, Miss Congeniality, Double Take, Down, The Cat's Meow.
TELEVISION: Series: Beacon Hill, Our Century (host), The Practice, Oz, Gilmore Girls. Guest: M*A*S*H, St. Elsewhere, Gilmore Girls. Mini-Series: Freedom Road, The Korean War: Fire & Ice, A Season in Purgatory. Movies: Eleanor and Franklin, Eleanor and Franklin: The White House Years, A Love Affair: The Eleanor and Lou Gehrig Story, Portrait of a Stripper, The Gift of Life, Memorial Day, So Proudly We Hail, Sweet Poison, Fire in the Dark, The Face on the Milk Carton, Hostile Waters, The Soul of the Game, Pandora's Clock, Liberty! The American Revolution. Specials: Sorrows of Gin, The Private History of The Campaign That Failed, Murrow, Dear Liar, Concealed Enemies, The Return of Hickey, The Beginning of the Firm, Last Act is a Solo, The End of a Sentence, A Foreign Field, Don't Drink the Water, The Face on the Milk Carton, Here Come the Munsters, Soul of the Game, What Loves Sees, Pandora's Clock, Atomic Train, Vendetta, James Dean, The Impressionists, Horror in the East.

HERSHEY, BARBARA
Actress. r.n. Barbara Herzstein. b. Los Angeles, CA, Feb. 5, 1948. e. Hollywood H.S. m. painter Stephen Douglas. Briefly, in the mid-1970's, acted under the name Barbara Seagull.
PICTURES: With Six You Get Eggroll (debut, 1968), Heaven With a Gun, Last Summer, The Liberation of L.B. Jones, The Baby Maker, The Pursuit of Happiness, Dealing, Boxcar Bertha, Angela (Love Comes Quietly), The Crazy World of Julius Vrooder, Diamonds, You and Me, The Last Hard Men, Dirty Knights' Work, The Stunt Man, Americana, Take This Job and Shove It, The Entity, The Right Stuff, The Natural, Hannah and Her Sisters, Hoosiers, Tin Men, Shy People (Cannes Film Fest. Award, 1987), A World Apart (Cannes Film Fest. Award, 1988), The Last Temptation of Christ, Beaches, Tune in Tomorrow, Defenseless, The Public Eye, Falling Down, Swing Kids, Splitting Heirs, A Dangerous Woman, Last of the Dogmen, Portrait of a Lady (LA Film Critics Award; Natl Society of Film Critics Award) , The Pallbearer, A Soldier's Daughter Never Cries, Frogs for Snakes, Breakfast of Champions, Passion, Drowning on Dry Land, Lantana. TELEVISION: Series: The Monroes, From Here to Eternity. Guest: Gidget, The Farmer's Daughter, Run for Your Life, The Invaders, Daniel Boone, CBS Playhouse, Chrysler Theatre, Kung Fu, Alfred Hitchcock Presents (1985). Movies: Flood, In the Glitter Palace, Just a Little Inconvenience, Sunshine Christmas, Angel on My Shoulder, My Wicked Wicked Ways... , The Legend of Errol Flynn, Passion Flower, A Killing in a Small Town (Emmy & Golden Globe Awards, 1990), Paris Trout, Stay the Night, Abraham, The Staircase. Mini-Series: A Man Called Intrepid, Return to Lonesome Dove. Special: Working.

HERSKOVITZ, MARSHALL
Producer, Director, Writer. b. Philadelphia, PA, Feb. 23, 1952. e. Brandeis U., BA, 1973; American Film Inst., MFA. 1975. Worked as freelance writer, dir., and prod. on several TV shows. Received Humanitas Award, 1983 and Writers Guild award, 1984.
PICTURE: Jack the Bear (dir.), Legends of the Fall (co-prod.), Dangerous Beauty, Executive Search, Traffic, I Am Sam, Lone Star State of Mind.
TELEVISION: Family (writer, dir.), White Shadow (writer), Special Bulletin (prod., writer, 2 Emmys for writing and dramatic special), thirtysomething (exec. prod., co-writer, dir.; 2 Emmy awards for writing and dramatic series, 1988; Also Humanitas Award and Directors Guild Award, 1988 & 1989, Peabody Award, 1989.), My So-Called Life, Relativity, Once and Again.

HERZFELD, JOHN
Writer, Director, Actor, Producer.
PICTURES: Writer: Voices, Hard Feelings, Two of a Kind (also dir.), The Last Winter, Ha-Kala, 2 Days in the Valley, Turbulence. TELEVISION: Movies: Lieutenant Schuster's Wife (actor only), Cannonball (actor only), Shattered Spirits (actor only), Cobra (actor only), On Fire (also actor), Daddy (also dir.), The Ryan White Story (actor, dir.), The Preppie Murder (also dir.), Casualties of Love: The Long Island Lolita Story (also dir., prod.), Barbara Taylor Bradford's 'Remember,' (also dir.), Don King: Only in America (dir. only, Directors' Guild Award, 1998). Series: Tales from the Crypt (dir.)

HERZOG, WERNER
Director, Producer, Writer. r.n. Werner Stipetic. b. Sachrang, Germany, September 5, 1942. e. U. of Munich, Duquesne U., Pittsburgh. Wrote first s.p. 1957; 1961 worked nights in steel factory to raise money for films; 1966, worked for U.S. National Aeronautics and Space Admin.
PICTURES: Signs of Life (debut, 1968), Precautions Against Fanatics, Even Dwarfs Started Small (also composer), Fata Morgana, The Land of Silence and Darkness, Aguirre—Wrath of God, The Great Ecstasy of Woodcarver Steiner, The Mysery of Kasper Hauser, Nobody Wants to Play With Me, How Much Wood Would a Woodchuck Chuck, Heart of Glass, Stroszek, La Soufriere, Nosferatu: The Vampyre (also cameo), Woyzeck, Garlic Is As Good As Ten Mothers (actor), Werner Herzog Eats His Shoe (actor), Fitzcarraldo, Burden of Dreams (actor), Man of Flowers (actor), Tokyo-Ga (actor), Where the Green Ants Dream, Les Gauloises, Cobra Verde, Scream of Stone, Lessons in Darkness, Bride of the Orient (actor), It Isn't Easy Being God (actor), Echoes of a Somber Empire, Burning Heart (actor), Little Dieter Needs to Fly, Mexico, My Best Friend, Invincible, Pilgrimage, Ten Minutes Older: The Trumpet. TELEVISION: Movies: Huie's Sermon, God's Angry Man, Chambre 666, The Dark Glow of the Mountains, Ballad of the Little Soldier, Herdsmen of the Sun, The Transformation of the World Into Music (actor), Death for Five Voices, and many others.

HESSEMAN, HOWARD
Actor. b. Salem, OR, Feb. 27, 1940. Started with the San Francisco group, The Committee and worked as a disc jockey in San Francisco in the late 1960s.
PICTURES: Petulia, Billy Jack, Steelyard Blues, Shampoo, The Sunshine Boys, Jackson County Jail, The Big Bus, The Other Side of Midnight, Silent Movie, Honky Tonk Freeway, Private Lessons, Loose Shoes, Doctor Detroit, This is Spinal Tap, Police Academy 2: Their First Assignment, Clue, My Chauffeur, Flight of the Navigator, Heat, Amazon Women on the Moon, Rubin and

Ed, Little Miss Millions, Munchie Strikes Back (voice), Out of Sync, Boys Night Out, Gridlock'd, The Sky is Falling, The Mesmerist, Teddy Bears' Picnic, About Schmidt.
TELEVISION: Series: WKRP in Cincinnati, One Day at a Time, Head of the Class. Guest: Mary Hartman Mary Hartman, Fernwood 2night, George Burns Comedy Week. Movies: Hustling, The Blue Knight (pilot), Tail Gunner Joe, The Amazing Howard Hughes, Tarantulas: The Deadly Cargo, The Ghost on Flight 401, The Comedy Company, More Than Friends, Outside Chance, The Great American Traffic Jam, Victims, One Shoe Makes It Murder, Best Kept Secrets, The Diamond Trap, Call Me Anna, Murder in New Hampshire: The Pamela Smart Story, Quiet Killer, Lethal Exposure, High Stakes, On the 2nd Day of Christmas.

HESSLER, GORDON
Producer, Director. b. Berlin, Germany, 1930. e. Reading U., England. Dir., vice pres., Fordel Films, Inc., 1950-58; dir., St. John's Story (Edinborough Film Festival), March of Medicine Series, Dr. Albert Lasker Award; story edit., Alfred Hitchcock Presents 1960-62; assoc. prod., dir., Alfred Hitchcock Hour, 1962; prod., Alfred Hitchcock Hour; prod., dir., Universal TV 1964-66.
PICTURES: The Woman Who Wouldn't Die, The Last Shot You Hear, The Oblong Box, Scream and Scream Again, Cry of the Banshee, Murders of the Rue Morgue, Sinbad's Golden Voyage, Medusa, Embassy, Puzzle, Pray for Death, Rage of Honour, The Misfit Brigade, The Girl in a Swing (also s.p.), Out on Bail, Mayeda, Journey of Honor.
TELEVISION: Series: Alfred Hitchcock Presents (1960-62), Alfred Hitchcock Hour, Run for Your Life, Convoy, Bob Hope Chrysler Show, ABC Suspense Movies of the Week, ABC Movies of the Week, Lucas Tanner, Night Stalker, Amy Prentiss, Switch, Kung Fu, Sara, Hawaii Five-O, Blue Knight, Wonder Woman, Master, CHiPs, Tales of the Unexpected, Equilizer. Pilots: Tender Warriors.

HESTON, CHARLTON
Actor. b. Evanston, IL, Oct. 4, 1924. e. Northwestern U. Sch. of Speech. Radio, stage, TV experience. Following coll. served 3 yrs. 11th Air Force, Aleutians. After war, dir. and co-starred with wife at Thomas Wolfe Memorial Theatre, Asheville, NC in State of the Union, Glass Menagerie; member, Katharine Cornell's Co., during first year on Broadway; Anthony and Cleopatra, other B'way. plays, Leaf and Bough, Cockadoodle Doo; Studio One (TV): Macbeth, Taming of the Shrew, Of Human Bondage, Julius Caesar. Pres. Screen Actors Guild 1966-71; Member, Natl. Council on the Arts, 1967-72; Trustee: Los Angeles Center Theater Group, American Film Inst. 1971, chmn. 1981-; Received Jean Hersholt Humanitarian award, 1978. Pres., Nat'l Rifle Assoc., 1998-2003. Autobiographies: The Actor's Life (1978), In the Arena (1995).
RECENT THEATRE: A Man for All Seasons, The Caine Mutiny (dir., in China).
PICTURES: Dark City (debut, 1950), The Greatest Show on Earth, The Savage, Ruby Gentry, The President's Lady, Pony Express, Arrowhead, Bad for Each Other, The Naked Jungle, The Secret of the Incas, The Far Horizons, Lucy Gallant, The Private War of Major Benson, The Ten Commandments, Three Violent People, Touch of Evil, The Big Country, The Buccaneer, Ben-Hur (Academy Award, 1959), The Wreck of the Mary Deare, El Cid, The Pigeon That Took Rome, 55 Days at Peking, Major Dundee, The Agony and the Ecstasy, The War Lord, The Greatest Story Ever Told, Khartoum, Counterpoint, Planet of the Apes, Will Penny, Number One, Beneath the Planet of the Apes, Julius Caesar, The Hawaiians, The Omega Man, Antony and Cleopatra (also dir.), Skyjacked, Soylent Green, The Three Musketeers, Airport 1975, Earthquake, The Four Musketeers, The Last Hard Men, Midway, Two Minute Warning, Crossed Swords (The Prince and the Pauper), Gray Lady Down, Mountain Men, The Awakening, Mother Lode (also dir.), Almost an Angel (cameo), Solar Crisis, Wayne's World 2 (cameo), Tombstone, True Lies, In the Mouth of Madness, Alaska, Hamlet, Hercules (voice), Alaska: Spirit of the Wild (voice), Illusion Infinity, Gideon's Webb, Armageddon (voice), Any Given Sunday, Toscano, Forever Hollywood, Town & Country, Cats & Dogs (voice), Planet of the Apes, The Order, Papà Rua Alguem 5555. TELEVISION: Series: The Colbys. Mini-Series: Chiefs, Camino de Santiago. Movies: The Nairobi Affair, The Proud Men, A Man For All Seasons (also dir.), Original Sin, Treasure Island, The Little Kidnappers, The Crucifer of Blood, Crash Landing: The Rescue of Flight 232, The Avenging Angel, Texas (narrator), Larry and Vivien: The Oliviers in Love. Specials: Charlton Heston Presents the Bible (also writer), AFI's 100 Years, 100 Thrills: America's Most Heart-Pounding Movies, The Gun Deadlock.

HEWITT, JENNIFER LOVE
Actress. b. Waco, TX, Feb. 21, 1979.
PICTURES: Munchie, Little Miss Millions, Sister Act 2: Back in the Habit, House Arrest, Trojan War, I Know What You Did Last Summer, Telling You, Can't Hardly Wait, I Still Know What You Did Last Summer, The Suburbans, The Adventures of Tom Thumb and Thumbelina (voice), The Hunchback of Notre Dame II, The Tuxedo, Why Can't I Be Audrey Hepburn?, Magic 7, The Devil and Daniel Webster.

TELEVISION: *Movies:* Audrey Hepburn. *Series:* Kids Incorporated, Shaky Ground, The Byrds of Paradise, McKenna, Party of Five, Time of Your Life. *Guest:* Boy Meets World.

HEYER, STEVEN
Executive. b. New York, NY, June 13, 1952. e. Cornell U., BS industrial relations, 1974; Stern Sch. of Business at NYU, MBA, 1976. Various positions with Booz, Allen & Hamilton, finally SVP/managing partner, 1976-92. Pres./COO Young & Rubicam Adv. Worldwide and exec. VP Young & Rubicam, Inc., 1992-94. Pres., Turner Broadcasting Sales Inc., 1994-98. Pres., worldwide sales/mktng./distribution/int'l. networks, Turner Broadcasting System, 1996-98. Pres/COO Turner Broadcasting System Inc., 1998-2000 where he was instrumental in launching 14 new television networks, including Turner South, Boomerang, CNN En Espanol, the Cartoon Network in Japan and Brazil, and a partial-day, German language version of CNN, a European and Asian version of Turner Classic Movies. Led the effort to expand the Company's Internet presence, introducing 19 websites for its CNN, Cartoon Network, and its Turner Classic Movie brands in various languages. Acquired NASCAR rights, the renewal of the NBA contract, and the acquisition of over 200 world broadcast premier movies for TBS and TNT. Departed Time Warner to join Coca-Cola as exec. v.p., pres. and COO, Coca-Cola Ventures, and pres., Latin American Operations

HEYMAN, JOHN
Producer. b. Germany, 1933. e. Oxford U. Started with Independent British Television creating,. writing and producing entertainment and documentary programs. Had 5 top-ten programs 1955-57. Expanded into personal management, forming International Artists, representing Elizabeth Taylor, Richard Burton, Richard Harris, Shirley Bassey, Laurence Harvey, Trevor Howard, among others. In 1963, formed World Film Services Ltd. to produce package and finance films and World Film Sales Ltd., the first major independent film sales co. Co-financed 250 major studio films 1969-91. In 1973, formed Genesis Project. In 1989 co-founded Island World and Islet. Island sold to Polygram, and in 1994, formed World Group of Companies Ltd., parent co. to World Production Ltd.
PICTURES: Privilege, Boom!, Secret Ceremony, Twinky, Bloomfield, The Go-Between (Grand Prix, Cannes 1971), Superstars, Hitler: The Last Ten Days, Black Gunn, Divorce His, Divorce Hers, The Hireling (Grand Prix, Cannes 1973), A Doll's House, Daniel, Beyond the Limit, The Dresser, A Passage to India (co-prod.), Martin's Day, Steaming, D.A.R.Y.L., Saturday Night Fever, Grease, Heaven Can Wait, Home Alone, Reds.

HICKS, CATHERINE
Actress. b. New York NY, Aug. 6, 1951. e. St. Mary's Notre Dame; Cornell U. (2 year classical acting prog.). On B'way. in Tribute, Present Laughter.
PICTURES: Death Valley, Better Late Than Never, Garbo Talks, The Razor's Edge, Fever Pitch, Peggy Sue Got Married, Star Trek IV: The Voyage Home, Like Father Like Son, Child's Play, She's Out of Control, Cognac, Liebestraum, Dillinger and Capone, Eight Days a Week, Turbulence.
TELEVISION: *Series:* Ryan's Hope (1976-8), The Bad News Bears, Tucker's Witch, Winnetka Road, 7th Heaven, Celebrity Dish. *Movies:* Love for Rent, To Race the Wind, Marilyn- the Untold Story, Valley of the Dolls 1981, Happy Endings, Laguna Heat, Spy, Hi Honey I'm Dead, Redwood Curtain, For All Time. *Pilot:* The Circle Game.

HICKS, SCOTT
Director, Writer, Producer. b. Australia, March 4, 1953.
PICTURES: *Director:* Down the Wind (also prodr.), Freedom, Call Me Mr. Brown (also writer), Sebastian and the Sparrow (also writer & prodr.), Shine (also writer; Golden Globe nom.; Acad. Award nom), Snow Falling on Cedars, Arkansas, Hearts in Atlantis (dir. only).

HILL, ARTHUR
Actor. b. Melfort, Saskatchewan, Canada, Aug. 1, 1922. e. U. of British Columbia. Moved to England in 1948, spending ten years in varied stage & screen pursuits
THEATRE: *B'way:* The Matchmaker, Home of the Brave, The Male Animal, Look Homeward Angel, All the Way Home, Who's Afraid of Virginia Woolf? (Tony Award, 1963), More Stately Mansions.
PICTURES: Miss Pilgrim's Progress, Scarlet Thread, Mr. Drake's Duck, A Day to Remember, Life With the Lyons, The Crowded Day, The Deep Blue Sea, Raising a Riot, The Young Doctors, The Ugly American, In the Cool of the Day, Moment to Moment, Harper, Petulia, The Chairman, Rabbit Run, The Pursuit of Happiness, The Andromeda Strain, The Killer Elite, Futureworld, A Bridge Too Far, A Little Romance, Butch and Sundance: The Early Days, The Champ, Dirty Tricks, Making Love, The Amateur, Something Wicked This Way Comes (narrator), One Magic Christmas, A Fine Mess.
TELEVISION: *Series:* Owen Marshall: Counselor-At-Law, Hagen, Glitter. *Movies:* The Other Man, Vanished, Ordeal, Owen Marshall: Counselor at Law (pilot; a.k.a. A Pattern of Morality), Death Be Not Proud, Judge Horton and the Scottsboro Boys, Tell Me My Name, The Ordeal of Dr. Mudd, Revenge of the

Stepford Wives, The Return of Frank Cannon, Angel Dusted, Tomorrow's Child, Intimate Agony, Prototype, Love Leads the Way, Murder in Space, Churchill and the Generals, The Guardian, Perry Mason: The Case of the Notorious Nun, Christmas Eve, Columbo: Agenda for Murder.

HILL, BERNARD
Actor: b. Manchester, England,, Dec. 17, 1944. Joined amateur dramatic society in Manchester then studied drama at Manchester Art Coll. Joined Liverpool Everyman rep. co. West End debut as John Lennon in John, Paul, George, Ringo... and Burt. Also in Normal Service, Shortlist, Twelfth Night, Macbeth, Cherry Orchard, Gasping, A View From the Bridge.
PICTURES: Gandhi, The Bounty, The Chain, Restless Natives, No Surrender, Bellman and True, Drowning by Numbers, Shirley Valentine, Mountains of the Moon, Double X: The Name of the Game, Skallagrigg, Madagascar Skin, The Ghost and the Darkness, The Wind in the Willows, Titanic, The Mill on the Floss, A Midsummer Night's Dream, Blessed Art Thou, True Crime, The Loss of Sexual Innocence, The Red Door, The Titanic Chronicles, Blessed Art Thou, Einstein, Going Off Big Time, The Criminal, The Scorpion King, Lord of the Rings: The Two Towers, Lord of the Rings: The Return of the King.
TELEVISION: I Claudius, Squaring the Circle, John Lennon: A Journey in the Life, New World, St. Luke's Gospel, Boys from the Blackstuff, Burston Rebellion, Great Expectations.

HILL, DEBRA
Producer, Director, Writer. b. Philadelphia, PA. Career on feature films started with work as script supvr., asst. dir. and 2nd unit dir. of 13 pictures. Producer's debut with Halloween, 1980, for which also co-wrote script with dir. John Carpenter.
PICTURES: Halloween (also co-s.p.), The Fog (and co-s.p.), Escape from New York, Halloween II (and co-s.p.), Halloween III: Season of the Witch, The Dead Zone, Clue, Head Office, Adventures in Babysitting, Big Top Pee-wee, Heartbreak Hotel, The Fisher King, Escape From L.A., The Replacement Killers, Crazy in Alabama.
TELEVISION: Adventures in Babysitting (pilot, exec. prod.), Monsters (dir. episodes), Dream On (dir. episodes). *Movies:* El Diablo, Attack of the 50 Ft. Woman. *Rebel Highway Film Series:* Roadracers, Confessions of a Sorority Girl (also co-writer), Dragstrip Girl, Shake Rattle and Roll, The Cool and the Crazy, Runaway Daughters, Motocycle Gang, Drag Strip Girl, Reform School Girl, Jailbreakers (also co-writer), Girls in Prison.

HILL, GEORGE ROY
Director. b. Minneapolis, MN, Dec. 20, 1921. e. Yale U., Trinity Coll., Dublin. Started as actor, Irish theatres and U.S. Margaret Webster's Shakespeare Repertory Co., also off-B'way. Served as Marine pilot in WWII and Korean War. Wrote TV play, My Brother's Keeper, for Kraft Theatre, later rose to dir. with show.
THEATRE: Look Homeward Angel (B'way debut, 1957), The Gang's All Here, Greenwillow, Period of Adjustment, Moon on a Rainbow Shawl (also prod.), Henry Sweet Henry.
PICTURES: Period of Adjustment (debut, 1962), Toys in the Attic, The World of Henry Orient, Hawaii, Thoroughly Modern Millie, Butch Cassidy and the Sundance Kid, Slaughterhouse Five, The Sting (Academy Award, 1973), The Great Waldo Pepper (also prod., story), Slap Shot, A Little Romance (also co-exec. prod.), The World According to Garp (also co-prod., cameo), The Little Drummer Girl, Funny Farm.
TELEVISION: *Writer-Dir.:* A Night to Remember, The Helen Morgan Story, Judgment at Nuremberg, Child of Our Time. (d. Dec. 27, 2002)

HILL, TERENCE
Actor, Director. r.n. Mario Girotti. b. Venice, March 29, 1939. Debuted as actor under his real name. First attracted attention as actor in Visconti's The Leopard, 1963. Gained fame in European-made westerns. Formed Paloma Films.
PICTURES: *as Mario Girotti:* Vacanze col Gangster (debut, 1951), Villa Borghese, Il Viale della speranza, La Vena d'oro, The Wide Blue Road, Mary Magdalene, Anna of Brooklyn, Hannibal, Pecado de amor, Carthage in Flames, Joseph and His Brethren, The Wonders of Aladdin, Seven Seas to Calais, The Leopard, Games of Desire, Last of the Renegades, Arizona Wildcat, Duell vor Sonnenuntergang, Ruf de Walder, Rampage at Apache Wells, Flaming Frontier, Whom the Gods Destroy, Blood River; *as Terence Hill:* The Crazy Kids of the War, Io non protesto io amo, Preparati la bara!, Rita in the West, God Forgives I Don't, Viva Django, Boot Hill, Ace High, Barbagia, Blackie the Pirate, Anger of the Wind, They Call Me Trinity, The True and the False, A Reason to Live a Reason to Die, Trinity Is Still My Name, Man of the East, Baron Blood, All the Way Boys!, My Name Is Nobody, The Two Missionaries, The Genius, Crime Busters, Mr. Billion, March or Die, Odds & Evens, I'm for the Hippopotamus, Super Fuzz, Watch Out We're Mad, Double Trouble, Don Camillo (also dir.), Miami Supercops, Renegade Luke (also exec. prod.), Go for It!, Lucky Luke (also dir.), The F(N)ight Before Christmas (also dir.), Botte di Natale, Troublemakers, Cyberflic.
TELEVISION: *Series:* Don Matteo, Don Matteo II, Don Matteo III.

HILL, WALTER
Director, Writer, Producer. b. Long Beach, CA, Jan. 10, 1942. e. Michigan State U.; Mexico City College; U. of the Americas. PICTURES: *Writer*: Hickey and Boggs, Thief Who Came to Dinner, The Getaway (1972), The Mackintosh Man, The Drowning Pool, Blue City (also prod.), Alien 3 (also prod.), The Getaway (1993; co-s.p.). *Writer/Dir.*: Hard Times, The Driver, The Warriors, Southern Comfort , 48 HRS, Streets of Fire (also exec. prod.), Red Heat (also prod.). *Director*: The Long Riders, Brewster's Millions, Crossroads, Extreme Prejudice, Johnny Handsome, Another 48 HRS, Trespass, Geronimo: An American Legend (also co-prod.), Wild Bill, Last Man Standing, Undisputed, The Prophecy (video, dir.), *Other*: Alien (prod.), Aliens (exec. prod., story), Tales From the Crypt Presents Demon Knight (co-exec. prod.).
TELEVISION: *Series*: Dog and Cat (creator, writer), Deadwood (dir.), Tales From the Crypt (exec. prod.; also dir. & writer of episodes: The Man Who Was Death, Cutting Cards, Deadline (Cable ACE Award, Best Dir.).

HILLER, ARTHUR
Director. b. Edmonton, Alberta, Can., Nov. 22, 1923. e. U. of Alberta, U. of Toronto, U. of British Columbia. Worked for Canadian Broadcasting Corp. as dir. of live tv before moving to L.A. Pres. of DGA. 1993, became pres. of AMPAS where he served until 1997. Appeared in Beverly Hills Cop III. Chartable work includes: Motion Picture and Television Fund, KCET, Amnesty International, Inner City Filmmakers, the Los Angeles Central Library's reading program, the Deaf Arts Council, the Anti-Defamation League, Los Angeles County Museum programs on film and television, Humanitas, the Streisand Centre at UCLA and the Venice Family Clinic
PICTURES: The Careless Years (debut, 1957), Miracle of the White Stallions, The Wheeler Dealers, The Americanization of Emily, Promise Her Anything, Penelope, Tobruk, The Tiger Makes Out, Popi, The Out-of-Towners, Love Story, Plaza Suite, The Hospital, Man of La Mancha, The Crazy World of Julius Vrooder (also co-prod.), The Man in the Glass Booth, W. C. Fields and Me, Silver Streak, Nightwing, The In-Laws (also co-prod.), Making Love, Author Author, Romantic Comedy, The Lonely Guy (also prod.), Teachers, Outrageous Fortune, See No Evil Hear No Evil, Taking Care of Business, The Babe, Married to It, Beverly Hills Cop III (actor only), Wild Bill: A Hollywood Maverick (actor only), Carpool, An Alan Smithee Film: Burn Hollywood Burn, Speakeasy (acting only).
TELEVISION: Matinee Theatre, Playhouse 90, Climax, Alfred Hitchcock Presents, Gunsmoke, Ben Casey, Rte. 66, Naked City, The Dick Powell Show, Roswell (actor only), Frank Capra's American Dream (actor only).

HILLER, DAME WENDY
Actress. D.B.E., 1975, O.B.E., 1971, Hon. LLD, Manchester, 1984. b. Bramhall, Cheshire, Eng., Aug. 15, 1912. e. Winceby House Sch., Bexhill. On stage 1930, Manchester Repertory Theatre, England; then on British tour. London debut 1935 in Love On the Dole; to N.Y., same role 1936. m.p. debut in Lancashire Luck, 1937.
THEATRE: First Gentleman, Cradle Song, Tess of the D'Urbervilles, Heiress (NY & London), Ann Veronica, Waters of the Moon, Night of the Ball, Old Vic Theatre, Wings of the Dove, Sacred Flame, Battle of Shrivings, Crown Matrimonial, John Gabriel Borkman, Waters of the Moon (revival), Aspern Papers (revival), The Importance of Being Earnest, Driving Miss Daisy.
PICTURES: Lancashire Luck (debut, 1937), Pygmalion, Major Barbara, I Know Where I'm Going, Outcast of the Islands, Single Handed (Sailor of the King), Something of Value, How to Murder a Rich Uncle, Separate Tables (Academy Award, best supporting actress, 1958) Sons and Lovers, Toys in the Attic, A Man For All Seasons, Murder on the Orient Express, Voyage of the Damned, The Cat and the Canary, The Elephant Man, Making Love, The Lonely Passion of Judith Hearne, The Countess Alice, A New Window Pane.
TELEVISION: The Curse of King Tut's Tomb, David Copperfield (theatrical in U.K.), Witness for the Prosecution, Anne of Green Gables-The Sequel, Peer Gynt, The Kingfisher, All Passion Spent, A Taste for Death, Ending Up, The Best of Friends, I Know Where I'm Going Revisited.
(d. May 14, 2003)

HILLERMAN, JOHN
Actor. b. Denison, TX, Dec. 20, 1932. e. U. of Texas. While in U.S. Air Force joined community theatre group and went to New York after completing military service. Studied at American Theatre Wing, leading to summer stock and off-B'way.
PICTURES: The Last Picture Show, Lawman, The Carey Treatment, What's Up Doc?, Skyjacked, High Plains Drifter, The Outside Man, The Thief Who Came to Dinner, Paper Moon, Blazing Saddles, Chinatown, At Long Last Love, The Nickel Ride, The Day of the Locust, Lucky Lady, Audrey Rose, Sunburn, History of the World Part I, Up the Creek, A Very Brady Sequel.
TELEVISION: *Movies*: Sweet Sweet Rachel, The Great Man's Whiskers, The Law, Ellery Queen, The Invasion of Johnson County, Relentless, Kill Me If You Can, A Guide for the Married Woman, Betrayal, Marathon, The Murder That Wouldn't Die, Little Gloria... Happy at Last, Assault and Matrimony, Street of

Dreams, Hands of a Murderer, Sink the Bismark. *Mini-Series*: Around the World in 80 Days. *Series*: Ellery Queen, The Betty White Show, Magnum P.I. (Emmy Award, 1987), The Hogan Family, Berlin Break.

HILLMAN, WILLIAM BRYON
Writer, Director, Producer. b. Chicago, IL, Feb. 3, 1951. e. Oklahoma Military Acad., UCLA. Head of production at Intro-Media Prod.; Fairchild Ent.; Spectro Prod.; Double Eagle Ent. Corp; Excellent Films Inc.; Creative consultant for The Hit 'Em Corp. Presently head of SpectroMedia Ent.
AUTHOR: *Novels*: Silent Changes, The Combination, The Liar, Additives The Perfect Crime, Why Me, The Loner.
PICTURES: *Dir.-Writer*: His Name is Joey (also exec. prod.), Tis the Season (also co-prod.), Strangers (also co-prod.), Back on the Street (also co-prod.), Loner (also co-prod.), Fast & Furious, The Master, Lovelines (s.p. only), Double Exposure (also co-prod.), The Passage, Campus, The Photographer (also prod.), The Man From Clover Grove (also co-prod.), Thetus, The Trail Ride (also co-prod.), Betta Betta (also prod.), Ragin' Cajun (also co-prod.), The Adventures of Ragtime, Quigley.
TELEVISION: Working Together (pilot writer), Disco-Theque Pilot (dir., writer), Everything Will Be Alright (writer), Money (dir., writer), RIPA (writer).

HINDERY, LEO JOSEPH , JR.
Media Co. Executive. b. Springfield, Ill, Oct. 31, 1947. e. Seattle U, BA 1969; Stanford U, MBA 1971. With U.S. army, 1968-70. Asst. treas., Utah Internat, 1971-80. Treas. Natomas Co., 1980-82. Exec. v.p. fin. Jefferies & Co., 1982-83. Chief fin. officer A.G. Becker Paribas, 1983-85. Chief officer. planning & fin. Chronicle Pub. Co., 1985-88. Mng. gen. ptnr. Intermedia Ptnrs., 1988. Became pres., Tele-Communications, Inc. and its affiliated companies, March 1997, then pres. CEO, AT&T Broadband (the successor company to TCI. March, 2000, pres. & CEO, Global Crossing Ltd. Currently, pres. and CEO The YES Network, a new regional sports network formed around the broadcast rights to the New York Yankees, the New Jersey Nets, and the New Jersey Devils. Also currently serves on bd. as dir., Akamai Technologies and Knowledge Universe, Inc. and chmn., GT Group Telecom. Received International Cable Executive of the Year award, 1998; .Foundation Award of the International Radio & Television Society, 1998; Executive Achievement Award of the National Association of Minorities in Cable, 1998; named Cable Television Operator of the Year, 1999; National Cable Television Association Distinguished Vanguard Award for Leadership, 1999; named by Business Week as one of its "Top 25 Executives of the Year, 1999. Vice chmn., Museum of Television & Radio; dir., Daniels Fund; member, Stanford Business School Advisory Council.

HINES, GREGORY
Actor, Dancer. b. NY, Feb. 14, 1946. Early career as junior member of family dancing act starting at age 2. Nightclub debut at 5 as Hines Kids with brother Maurice (later renamed Hines Brothers as teenagers) and joined by father as Hines, Hines and Dad. B'way debut at 8 in The Girl in Pink Tights. Continued dancing with brother until 1973. Formed and performed with jazz-rock band, Severance. Solo album, Gregory Hines (1988).
THEATRE: The Last Minstral Show (closed out of town). B'way: Eubie (Theatre World Award), Comin' Uptown (Tony nom.), Sophisticated Ladies (Tony nom.), Twelfth Night, Jelly's Last Jam (Tony Award, 1992).
PICTURES: History of the World Part 1 (debut, 1981), Wolfen, Deal of the Century, The Muppets Take Manhattan, The Cotton Club (also choreog.), White Nights, Running Scared, Off Limits, Tap (also choreog.), Eve of Destruction, A Rage in Harlem, Renaissance Man, Waiting to Exhale, Mad Dog Time, The Preacher's Wife., Good Luck, The Tic Code, Things You Can Tell Just By Looking at Her, Once in the Life.
TELEVISION: *Movies*: White Lie, T Bone N Weasel, Dead Air, A Stranger in Town, The Cherokee Kid, Subway Stories: Tales from the Underground, Color of Justice, Who Killed Atlanta's Children, Bojangles, The Red Sneakers, Santa Baby! (voice). *Guest*: Motown Returns to the Apollo. *Series*: The Gregory Hines Show, Little Bill, Will & Grace (recurring guest role), Lost at Home.
(d. Aug. 9, 2003)

HINGLE, PAT
Actor. b. Miami, FL, July 19, 1924. e. U. of Texas, 1949. Studied at Herbert Berghof Studio, American Theatre Wing, Actor's Studio.
THEATRE: End as a Man (N.Y. debut, 1953), The Rainmaker, Festival, Cat on a Hot Tin Roof, Girls of Summer, Dark at the Top of the Stairs, J.B., The Deadly Game, Macbeth and Troilus and Cresida (with American Shakespeare Festival, Stratford, CT), Strange Interlude, Blues for Mr. Charlie, A Girl Could Get Lucky, The Glass Menagerie, The Odd Couple, Johnny No-Trump, The Price, Child's Play, The Selling of the President, That Championship Season, The Lady from the Sea, A Life, Thomas Edison: Reflections of a Genius (one man show).
RADIO: Voice of America.
PICTURES: On the Waterfront (debut, 1954), The Strange One, No Down Payment, Splendor in the Grass, All the Way Home, The Ugly American, Invitation to a Gunfighter, Nevada Smith, Sol

Madrid, Hang 'em High, Jigsaw, Norwood, Bloody Mama, WUSA, The Carey Treatment, One Little Indian, Running Wild, Nightmare Honeymoon, The Super Cops, The Gauntlet, When You Comin' Back Red Ryder?, Norma Rae, America: Lost and Found (narrator), Sudden Impact, Running Brave, Going Berserk, The Falcon and the Snowman, Brewster's Millions, Maximum Overdrive, Baby Boom, The Land Before Time (voice), Batman, The Grifters, Batman Returns, Lightning Jack, The Quick and the Dead, Batman Forever, Larger Than Life, Batman & Robin, A Thousand Acres, Muppets From Space, The Hunter's Moon, Shaft, Morning, The Angel Doll, Road to Redemption, The Greatest Adventure of My Life.
TELEVISION: Movies: The Ballad of Andy Crocker, A Clear and Present Danger, The City, Sweet Sweet Rachel, If Tomorrow Comes, Trouble Comes to Town, The Last Angry Man, The Secret Life of John Chapman, Escape from Bogen County, Sunshine Christmas, Tarantulas, Elvis, Stone (pilot), Disaster at the Coastliner, Wild Times, Of Mice and Men, Washington Mistress, The Fighter, Stranger on My Land, The Town Bully, Everybody's Baby: The Rescue of Jessica McClure, Not of This World, Gunsmoke: To the Last Man, Citizen Cohn, The Habitation of Dragons, Simple Justice, Against Her Will: The Carrie Buck Story, Truman. Mini-Series: War and Remembrance, The Kennedy's of Massachusetts, The Shining. Series: Stone, The Court. Guest: Gunsmoke, MASH, Blue Skies, Matlock, Twilight Zone, The Untouchables, Trapper John M.D., Murder She Wrote, In the Heat of the Night, Cheers, Wings, American Gothic.

HINKLE, ROBERT
Actor, Producer, Director. b. Brownfield, TX, July 25, 1930. e. Texas Tech. U. Joined Rodeo Cowboys Association, 1950 and rodeoed professionally until 1953 when began acting career in Outlaw Treasure. Pres. Cinema Pictures, Inc.
PICTURES: Actor: Giant, All the Fine Young Cannibals, Hud, The First Texan, Dakota Incident, Gun the Man Down, The Oklahoman, First Traveling Saleslady, No Place to Land, Under Fire, Speed Crazy, The Gunfight at Dodge City, Broken Land, Law in Silver City, Producer-Director: Ole Rex, Born Hunter, Trauma, Something Can Be Done, Mr. Chat, Stuntman, Jumping Frog Jubilee, Mr. Chat-Mexico Safari, Trail Ride, Virginia City Cent., Texas Today, Texas Long Horns, Kentucky Thoroughbred Racing, Country Music, Guns of a Stranger.
TELEVISION: Prod. & Dir.: Test Pilot, Dial 111, Juvenile Squad, X13 Vertijet, Cellist Extraordinary, Sunday Challenge, The Drifter, Country Music Tribute, World of Horses, Country Music Videos.

HIRD, DAME THORA
Actress. b. Morecambe, Lancashire, England,, May 28, 1911. e. The Nelson Sch., Morecambe.
PICTURES: (Screen debut, 1940) The Black Sheep of Whitehall; Street Corner, Turn the Key Softly, Personal Affair, The Great Game, Storks Don't Talk, Shop Soiled, For Better or Worse; Love Match, One Good Turn, Quatermass Experiment, Simon and Laura, Lost, Sailor Beware, Home and Away, Good Companions, The Entertainer, A Kind of Loving, Term of Trial, Bitter Harvest, Rattle of a Simple Man, Some Will Some Won't, The Nightcomers, Consuming Passions, Julie and the Cadillacs.
TELEVISION: The Winslow Boy, The Bachelor, What Happens to Love, The Witching Hour, So Many Children, The Queen Came By, Albert Hope, All Things Bright and Beautiful, Say Nothing, Meet the Wife, Who's a Good Boy Then? I AM! Dixon of Dock Green, Romeo and Juliet, The First Lady, Ours Is a Nice House, The Foxtrot, Seasons, She Stoops to Conquer, Villa Maroc, When We Are Married, In Loving Memory, Flesh and Blood, Your Songs of Praise Choice, Hallelujah, Happiness, That's the Main Thing, Intensive Care, In Loving Memory, Praise Be, Last of the Summer Wine, The Fall, Cream Cracker Under the Settee (Talking Heads), Perfect Scoundrels, Wide Eyed and Legless... It's a Girl, Pat & Margaret, Thora on the Broad 'n' Narrow, South Bank Show, The Queen's Nose, Lost for Word, Talking Heads 2, T, Nearly Complete and Utter History of Everything.
(d. March 15, 2003)

HIRSCH, JUDD
Actor. b. New York, NY, March 15, 1935. e City Coll. of New York. Studied physics but turned to acting; studied at Amer. Acad. of Dramatic Arts., HB Studios. First acting job in 1962 in Crisis in the Old Sawmill in Estes, Colorado; then to Woodstock Playhouse, before returning to N.Y.C.
THEATRE: NY: On the Necessity of Being Polygamous, Barefoot in the Park, Scuba Duba, Mystery Play, HotL Baltimore, King of the United States, Prodigal, Knock Knock, Chapter Two, Talley's Folly (Obie Award), I'm Not Rappaport (Tony Award), Conversations With My Father (Tony Award).
PICTURES: Serpico (debut, 1973), King of the Gypsies, Ordinary People (Acad. Award nom.), Without a Trace, The Goodbye People, Teachers, Running on Empty, Independence Day, Out of the Cold, Man on the Moon, A Beautiful Mind.
TELEVISION: Series: Delvecchio, Taxi (2 Emmy Awards: 1981, 1983), Detective in the House, Dear John, George & Leo, Regular Joe. Movies: The Law, Fear on Trial, Legend of Valentino, The Keegans, Sooner or Later, Marriage is Alive and

Well, Brotherly Love, First Steps, The Great Escape II: The Untold Story, She Said No, Betrayal of Trust, Color of Justice, Rocky Marciano. Special: The Halloween That Almost Wasn't.

HIRSCHFIELD, ALAN J.
Executive. b. Oklahoma City, OK; Oct.10, 1935. e. U. of Oklahoma, B.A.; Harvard Business School, M.B.A. V.P., Allen & Co., 1959-66; Financial v.p. & dir. Warner/7 Arts, 1967-68; v.p. & dir., American Diversified Enterprises, 1969-73; pres. & chief exec. officer, Columbia Pictures Industries, 1973-78; consultant, Warner Communications, 1979, 1980-85, chmn. and chief exec. officer, 20th Century-Fox. 1986-1990, consultant/investor in the entertainment/media industry. 1990-1992, mng. dir., Wertheim Schroder & Co., Inc., investment bankers, and co-CEO, Financial News Network. 1992-2000, co-CEO, Data Broadcasting Corporation, which merged with Financial Times/Pearsons, Inc. Currently, independent investor. Serves as dir. on the boards of: Carmike Cinemas, Chyron Corp., Interactive Data Corp.; vice-chmn., Cantel Medical Corp. and JNet Medical Enterprises, Inc.

HIRSHAN, LEONARD
Theatrical Agent. b. New York, NY, Dec.27, 1927. e. NYU. Joined William Morris Agency as agent trainee, New York, 1951. Agent legit theatre & TV dept. 1952-54. Sr. exec. agent M.P. dept., California office, 1955; sr. v.p., 1983; head of m.p. dept., west coast, 1986; named exec. v.p. and mem. bd. of dir., William Morris Agency, 1989; mem. bd. of dir., Center Theater Group, 1988; bd. governors Cedars-Sinai Hospital in L.A. 1987. Formed own management company, Leonard Hirshan Management, 2001.

HIRSCHHORN, JOEL
Composer. b. Bronx, NY, Dec. 18, 1937. e. HS for the Performing Arts, Hunter Col.
PICTURES: Songs (with collaborator Al Kasha): The Fat Spy, The Cheyenne Social Club, The Poseidon Adventure (Academy Award for best song: The Morning After, 1972), The Towering Inferno (Acad. Award for best song: We May Never Love Like This Again, 1974), Freaky Friday, Pete's Dragon, Hot Lead Cold Feet, The North Avenue Irregulars, All Dogs Go to Heaven, Rescue Me, Hungry For You, Club V.R., Cheyenne.
TELEVISION: Movies: Trapped Beneath the Sea, Someone I Touch, Charles Dickens' David Copperfield. Series: Kids Inc., First and Ten, Getting in Touch, The Challengers. Specials: Kingdom Chums, A Precious Moments Christmas, The Magic Paintbrush, Caddie Woodlawn.

HITZIG, RUPERT
Producer, Director. b. New York, NY, Aug. 15, 1942. e. Harvard. At CBS as doc. writer-prod.-dir.; later moved into dramas and comedy. Alan King's partner in King-Hitzig Prods.
PICTURES: Prod.: Electra Glide in Blue, Happy Birthday Gemini, Cattle Annie and Little Britches, Wolfen (also 2nd unit dir.), Jaws 3-D, The Last Dragon, The Squeeze. Dir.: Night Visitor, Backstreet Dreams, The Legend of O.B. Taggart, Last Lives (dir.), Nowhere Land (dir.), Static (prod.).
TELEVISION: Much Ado About Nothing, The Wonderful World of Jonathan Winters, Playboy After Dark, How to Pick Up Girls, Return to Earth, Saturday Night Live, Birds of Prey, Date My Dad, Save Our Streets, Snakes and Ladders (prod., dir.), annual comedy awards, television series and numerous specials.

HOBERMAN, DAVID
Executive. b. 1953. Started career as prod. exec. with TAT Communications for five years. 1982-85, worked as m.p. agent with Writers and Artists Agency and later at Ziegler Associates and ICM. 1985, named v.p. of prod. for Walt Disney Pictures based at studio. 1987, promoted to sr. v.p.; prod. 1988, named president, production. 1989, pres. Touchstone Pictures. 1994, appointed head of all motion pictures produced by Walt Disney. Resigned from Disney, 1995, to form Mandeville Films, where he is CEO. Recent releases include: Bringing Down the House. Hoberman also serves as creator and exec. prod. of the USA Network orig. series Monk. He is also a professor with UCLA's grad. school in the producers program. Member: bd. of the Starbright Foundation; and, is on the collections & acquisitions committee at L.A.'s Museum of Contemporary Art.

HOCK, MORT
Executive. Blaine-Thompson Agency; A. E. Warner Bros., 1948; David Merrick B'way Prod., 1958; asst. adv. mgr., Paramount Pictures Corp., 1960; adv. mgr., United Artists Corp., 1962; dir. adv., UA Corp., 1964; adv. dir., Paramount, 1965; v.p. adv. & public rltns., Paramount, 1968-71; v.p., marketing, Rastar Prods., 1971; exec. v.p., Charles Schlaifer & Co., 1974; sr. v.p. entertainment div., DDB Needham Worldwide, 1983; exec. v.p. DDB, 1994.

HODGE, PATRICIA
Actress. b. Cleethorpes, Lincolnshire, England, Sept. 29, 1946. Studied at London Acad. of Music and Dramatic Arts.
THEATRE: Popkiss, Two Gentlemen of Verona, Pippin, The Mitford Girls, Benefactors, Noel and Gertie, Separate Tables, The Prime of Miss Jean Brodie.
PICTURES: The Elephant Man, Betrayal, Sunset, Thieves in the

Night, Diamond's Edge, The Leading Man, Lies and Whispers, Jilting Joe, Before You Go.
TELEVISION: The Naked Civil Servant, Rumpole of the Bailey, Edward and Mrs. Simpson, Holding the Fort, Jemima Shore Investigates, Hay Fever, Hotel Du Lac, The Life and Loves of a She-Devil, Exclusive Yarns, Let's Face the Music of..., Inspector Morse, The Shell Seekers, The Secret Life of Ian Fleming, The Heat of the Day, Rich Tea and Sympathy, The Cloning of Joanna May, The Moonstone, The People's Passion, The Falklands Play, RIP 2002 (documentary).

HOFFMAN, DUSTIN
Actor. b. Los Angeles, CA, Aug. 8, 1937. m. Lisa Hoffman. e. Los Angeles Conservatory of Music, Santa Monica Coll., Pasadena Playhouse, 1958. Worked as an attendant at a psychiatric institution, a demonstrator in Macy's toy dept., and a waiter. First stage role 1960 in Yes Is for a Very Young Man at Sarah Lawrence Coll. Acted in summer stock, television and dir. at community theatre. Asst. dir. Off-B'way of A View From the Bridge. Recipient of the Golden Globe Cecil B. DeMille Award, 1997.
THEATRE: B'way and Off B'way: A Cook for Mr. General (bit part, B'way debut), Harry Noon and Night, Journey of the Fifth Horse (Obie Award), Eh? (Vernon Rice & Theatre World Awards), Jimmy Shine, All Over Town (dir. only), Death of a Salesman (Drama Desk Award), The Merchant of Venice (also London).
PICTURES: The Tiger Makes Out (debut, 1967), Madigan's Millions, The Graduate, Midnight Cowboy, John and Mary, Little Big Man, Who Is Harry Kellerman and Why Is He Saying Those Terrible Things About Me?, Straw Dogs, Alfredo Alfredo, Papillon, Lenny, All the President's Men, Marathon Man, Straight Time, Agatha, Kramer vs. Kramer (Academy Award, 1979), Tootsie, Ishtar, Rain Man (Academy Award, 1988), Family Business, Dick Tracy, Billy Bathgate, Hook, Hero, Outbreak, American Buffalo, Sleepers, Mad City, Wag the Dog, Sphere, Being John Malkovich, The Messenger: The Story of Joan of Arc, Shylock, Tuesday, Goldwyn, Moonlight Mile, Confidence, Runaway Jury, J.M. Barrie's Neverland.
TELEVISION: Specials: Journey of the Fifth Horse, The Star Wagons, Free to Be You and Me, Bette Midler: Old Red Hair Is Back, Common Threads: Stories from the Quilt (narrator), The Earth Day Special. Movies: The Point (narrator), Death of a Salesman (Emmy Award, 1985), AFI's 100 Years, 100 Laughs: America's Funniest Movies. Guest: Naked City, The Defenders, The Simpsons (voice).

HOFFMAN, PHILIP SEYMOUR
Actor. b. Fairport, NY, July 23, 1967.
PICTURES: Triple Bogey On A Par Five Hole, My New Gun, Szuler, Scent of a Woman, Leap of Faith, My Boyfriend's Back, Money for Nothing, Joey Breaker The Getaway, The Yearling, Nobody's Fool, When A Man Loves A Woman, The Fifteen Minute Hamlet, Twister, Hard Eight, Boogie Nights (SAG nom.), Montana, Next Stop Wonderland, The Big Lebowski, Happiness, Patch Adams, Culture, Flawless, Magnolia (SAG nom.), The Talented Mr. Ripley, State And Main, Almost Famous (SAG nom.), Last Party 2000, Love Liza, Punch-Drunk Love, The Sweet Spot, Red Dragon, The 25th Hour, Voltage, Owning Mahowny, Captured.

HOGAN, P.J.
Director, Writer. b. Australia, 1962.
PICTURES: Getting Wet, The Humpty Dumpty Man, Sloth, Vicious!, Muriel's Wedding (AFI, BAFTA, WGA noms.), My Best Friend's Wedding, Unconditional Love, Peter Pan.
TELEVISION: Series: The Flying Doctors.

HOGAN, PAUL
Actor, Writer. b. Lightning Ridge, New South Wales, Australia, Oct. 8, 1939. m. actress Linda Kozlowski. Worked as rigger before gaining fame on Australian TV as host of nightly current affairs show (A Current Affair) and The Paul Hogan Show. Shows now syndicated in 26 countries. In U.S. gained attention with commercials for Australian Tourist Commission. 1985, starred in dramatic role on Australian TV in series, Anzacs. Live one-man show, Paul Hogan's America, 1991. PICTURES: Fatty Finn (debut, 1980), Crocodile Dundee (also co-s.p.), Crocodile Dundee II (also exec. prod., co-s.p.), Almost an Angel (also exec. prod., s.p.), Lightning Jack (also s.p., co-prod.), Flipper, Floating Away, Crocodile Dundee in Los Angeles, Pipe Dream (2nd asst. dir. only), Hardcore Action News (1st asst. dir. only).
TELEVISION: Anzacs: The War Down Under.

HOLBROOK, HAL
Actor. r.n. Harold Rowe Holbrook Jr. b. Cleveland, OH, Feb. 17, 1925. m. actress Dixie Carter. e. Denison U., 1948. Summer stock 1947-53. Gained fame and several awards for performance as Mark Twain on stage in Mark Twain Tonight over a period of years throughout the U.S. and abroad.
THEATRE: Mark Twain Tonight (Tony Award, 1966), Do You Know the Milky Way?, Abe Lincoln in Illinois, American Shakespeare Fest., Lincoln Center Repertory (After the Fall), Marco Millions, Incident at Vichy, Tartuffe), The Glass Menagerie, The Apple Tree, I Never Sang For My Father, Man of

La Mancha, Does a Tiger Wear a Necktie?, Lake of the Woods, Buried Inside Extra, The Country Girl, King Lear. Regional: Our Town, The Merchant of Venice, Uncle Vanya, Eye of God.
PICTURES: The Group (debut, 1966), Wild in the Streets, The People Next Door, The Great White Hope, They Only Kill Their Masters, Jonathan Livingston Seagull (voice), Magnum Force, The Girl From Petrovka, All the President's Men, Midway, Julia, Rituals (The Creeper), Capricorn One, Natural Enemies, The Fog, The Kidnapping of the President, Creepshow, The Star Chamber, Girls Night Out (The Scaremaker), Wall Street, The Unholy, Fletch Lives, The Firm, Carried Away, Hercules (voice), Cats Don't Dance, Eye of God, Judas Kiss, Hush, The Florentine, The Bachelor, Walking to the Waterline, Waking the Dead, Men of Honor, The Majestic, Purpose, Shade, Our Country (documentary short, narrator).
TELEVISION: Movies: Coronet Blue, The Whole World is Watching, A Clear and Present Danger, Travis Logan, Suddenly Single, Goodbye Raggedy Ann, That Certain Summer, Murder by Natural Causes, Legend of the Golden Gun, When Hell Was in Session, Off the Minnesota Strip, The Killing of Randy Webster, Under Siege, Behind Enemy Lines, Dress Gray, The Fortunate Pilgrim, Three Wishes for Billy Grier, Emma, Queen of the South Seas, Day One, Sorry Wrong Number, A Killing in a Small Town, Bonds of Love, A Perry Mason Mystery: The Case of the Lethal Lifestyle, A Perry Mason Mystery: The Case of the Grimacing Governor, A Perry Mason Mystery: The Case of the Jealous Jokester, She Stood Alone: The Tailhook Scandal, Beauty. Specials: Mark Twain Tonight, Pueblo (Emmy Award, 1974), Sandburg's Lincoln (Emmy Award, 1976), Our Town, Plaza Suite, The Glass Menagerie, The Awakening Land, The Oath: 33 Hours in the Life of God, Omnibus. Mini-Series: North and South Books I & II, Celebrity, George Washington, Rockport Christmas, Lewis & Clark: The Journey of the Corps of Discovery, The Third Twin, Founding Fathers, Mark Twain. Series: The Bold Ones: The Senator (Emmy Award, 1971), Designing Women, Portrait of America (4 annual ACE Awards, 2 Emmy Awards, 1988, 1989), Evening Shade, Hercules (voice), The Street Lawyer.

HOLDRIDGE, LEE
Composer. b. Port-au-Prince, Haiti, March 3, 1944. e. Manhattan School of Music. Music arranger for Neil Diamond, 1969-73, with whom he collaborated on the score for Jonathan Livingston Seagull. Wrote score for B'way musical Into the Light (1986). With Alan Raph wrote score for the Joffrey Ballet's Trinity. One-act opera for L.A. Opera commission: Journey to Cordoba.
PICTURES: Jeremy, Jonathan Livingston Seagull, Forever Young Forever Free, Mustang Country, The Other Side of the Mountain—Part 2, The Pack, Moment By Moment, Oliver's Story, French Postcards, Tilt, American Pop, The Beastmaster, Mr. Mom, Micki and Maude, Splash, Sylvester, 16 Days of Glory, Transylvania 6-5000, The Men's Club, Big Business, Old Gringo, Pastime, Freefall, The Long Way Home, Family Plan, Puerto Vallarta Squeeze.
TELEVISION: Movies/Mini-Series: East of Eden, Fly Away Home, The Day the Loving Stopped, For Ladies Only, The Sharks, The Story Lady, One Against the Wind, In Love With an Older Woman, Running Out, Thursday's Child, Wizards and Warriors, The Mississippi, Legs, I Want to Live, Letting Go, Fatal Judgment, The Tenth Man, I'll Take Manhattan, Do You Know the Muffin Man?, Incident at Dark River, A Mother's Courage, In the Arms of a Killer, Face of a Stranger, Deadly Matrimony, Killer Rules, One Against the Wind, Call of the Wild, Torch Song, Barcelona '92: 16 Days of Glory, Jack Reed: Badge of Honor, Incident in a Small Town, The Yearling, Heidi, Texas, Buffalo Girls, The Tuskegee Airmen, Nothing Lasts Forever, Twilight of the Golds, Into Thin Air, A Christmas Memory, Two for Texas, Her Own Rules, Replacing Dad, Mutiny, Blue Moon, Love Letters, Atomic Train, Sealed with a Kiss, Anya's Bell, A Gift of Love: The Daniel Huffman Story, Take Me Home: The John Denver Story, Into the Arms of Strangers: Stories of the Kindertransport, The Mists of Avalon, The Pilot's Wife, Almost a Woman, Sounder. Series: One Life to Live, Hec Ramsey, Moonlighting, Beauty and the Beast, Bob, American Family.

HOLLAND, AGNIESZKA
Director, Writer. b. Warsaw, Poland, Nov. 28, 1948. e. FAMU, Prague. m. dir. Laco Adamik. Studied filmmaking in Czechoslovakia. Worked in Poland with dir. Andrzej Wajda. Moved to Paris in 1981.
PICTURES: Dir./s.p.: Screen Tests, Provincial Actors, Bez Znieczulenia (s.p. only), A Woman Alone (co-s.p.), Danton (co-s.p.), Interrogation (actor only), A Love in Germany (co-s.p.), Angry Harvest (co-s.p.), Anna (only s.p., story), Les Possedes (only co-s.p.), La Amiga (only co-s.p.), To Kill a Priest (co-s.p.), Korczak (s.p. only), Europa Europa, Olivier Olivier, Three Colors: Blue (s.p. only)The Secret Garden (dir. only), Total Eclipse (dir. only), Washington Square (dir. only), The Third Miracle (dir. only), Julie Walking Home, Golden Dreams (dir. only).
TELEVISION: Movies: Evening With Abdon, The Children of Sunday, Something for Something, Lorenzaccio, The Trial, Largo Desolato, Shot in the Heart (dir. only). Series: Fallen Angels (dir. only).

HOLLAND, TODD
Director.
PICTURES: The Wizard, Krippendorf's Tribe.
TELEVISION: *Series*: Amazing Stories, Vietman War Story, Max Headroom, Tales from the Crypt, Twin Peaks, Eerie Indiana, Bill & Ted's Excellent Adventures, The Larry Sanders Show (Emmy Award, 1998), My So-Called Life, Friends, Maximum Bob, Felicity, Malcolm in the Middle, D.C., Freaky Links (pilot), Ball & Chain, Wonderfalls (also exec. prod., creator). *Movies*: Kilroy, The Time Tunnel.

HOLLAND, TOM
Director, Writer. b. Highland, NY, July 11, 1945. e. Northwestern U. Started as actor, working at Bucks County Playhouse in PA and HB Studios in NY. Appeared on daytime serials Love of Life, Love is a Many-Splendored Thing. Turned to commercial prod. while attended UCLA law school, then took up screenwriting.
PICTURES: *Writer*: The Beast Within, The Class of 1984, Pyscho II (also actor), Scream for Help, Cloak and Dagger. *Director*: Fright Night (also s.p.), Fatal Beauty, Child's Play (also co-s.p.), The Temp, Stephen King's Thinner (also s.p.).
TELEVISION: *Movies*: The Stranger Within. *Series*: Tales From the Crypt (dir. 3 episodes: Love Come Hack to Me-also co-writer, Four-Sided Triangle-also co-writer, King of the Road). *Mini-Series*: Stephen King's The Langoliers (also writer, actor), The Stand.

HOLLIMAN, EARL
Actor. b. Delhi, LA, Sept. 11, 1928. e. U. of Southern California, Pasadena Playhouse. Pres., Actors and Others for Animals.
THEATRE: Camino Real (Mark Taper Forum), A Streetcar Named Desire (Ahmanson).
PICTURES: Scared Stiff, The Girls of Pleasure Island, Destination Gobi, East of Sumatra, Devil's Canyon, Tennessee Champ, The Bridges at Toko-Ri, Broken Lance, The Big Combo, I Died a Thousand Times, Forbidden Planet, Giant, The Burning Hills, The Rainmaker, Giant, Gunfight at the OK Corral, Trooper Hook, Don't Go Near the Water, Hot Spell, The Trap, Last Train From Gun Hill, Visit to a Small Planet, Armored Command, Summer and Smoke, The Sons of Katie Elder, A Covenant With Death, The Power, Anzio, The Biscuit Eater, Good Luck Miss Wyckoff, Sharky's Machine, Bad City Blues, The Perfect Tenant.
TELEVISION: *Movies*: Tribes, Alias Smith and Jones, Cannon, The Desperate Mission, Trapped, Cry Panic, I Love You... Goodbye, Alexander: The Other Side of Down, The Solitary Man, Where the Ladies Go, Country Gold, Gunsmoke: Return to Dodge, American Harvest, P.S. I Luv You (pilot). *Mini-Series*: The Thorn Birds. *Series*: Hotel de Paree, Wide Country, Police Woman, P.S. I Luv You, Delta, Night Man. *Pilot*: Twilight Zone. *Specials*: The Dark Side of the Earth, The Return of Ansel Gibbs, Intimate Portrait: Lisa Hartman Black (himself).

HOLLOWOOD, ANN
Costume Designer.
PICTURES: Nightbreed, The Second Jungle Book: Mowgli & Baloo, Mother Teresa: In the Name of God's Poor.
TELEVISION: *Movies*: Tears in the Rain, The Old Man and the Sea. *Mini-series*: The Storyteller, The Storyteller: Greek Myths, Merlin (Emmy Award, 1998), The Magical Legend of the Leprechauns, Jack and the Beanstalk: The Real Story.

HOLLY, LAUREN
Actress. b. Bristol, PA, October 28, 1963.
PICTURES: Seven Minutes in Heaven, Band of the Hand, The Adventures of Ford Fairlane, Dragon: The Bruce Lee Story, Dumb & Dumber, Sabrina, Beautiful Girls, Down Periscope, Turbulence, A Smile Like Yours, No Looking Back, Entropy, Any Given Sunday, The Last Producer, What Women Want, Colored Eggs, Don't Cry For Me, Changing Hearts, Pavement, Counting Sheep, In Enemy Hands.
TELEVISION: *Movies*: Archie: To Riverdale and Back Again, Fugitive Among Us, Dangerous Heart, Vig, King of Texas, Santa Jr., Just Desserts. *Mini-Series*: Jackie, Ethel, Joan: The Women of Camelot. *Series*: All My Children, The Antagonists, Picket Fences.

HOLM, CELESTE
Actress. b. New York, NY, Apr. 29, 1919. e. Univ. Sch. for Girls, Chicago, Francis W. Parker, Chicago, Lyceae Victor Durui (Paris), U. of Chicago, UCLA. p. Theodor Holm and Jean Parke Holm. m. actor Wesley Addy.
THEATRE: *B'way*: Gloriana, The Time of Your Life, 8 O'Clock Tuesday, Another Sun, Return of the Vagabond, My Fair Ladies, Papa Is All, All the Comforts of Home, The Damask Cheek, Oklahoma!, Bloomer Girl, She Stoops to Conquer, Affairs of State, Anna Christie, The King and I, Interlock, Third Best Sport, Invitation to a March, Mame, Candida, Habeas Corpus, The Utter Glory of Morrissey Hall, I Hate Hamlet. *Off-B'way*: A Month in the Country. Theatre-in-Concert for the U.S. State Department in 8 countries May-July 1966. *Regional*: Janet Flanner's Paris Was Yesterday. *Natl. Tour*: Mame (Sarah Siddons Award), Hay Fever, Road to Mecca, Cocktail Hour.
PICTURES: Three Little Girls in Blue (debut, 1946), Carnival in Costa Rica, Gentleman's Agreement (Academy Award, best supporting actress, 1947), Road House, The Snake Pit, Chicken Every Sunday, Come to the Stable (Acad. Award nom.), A Letter to Three Wives (voice), Everybody Does It, Champagne for Caesar, All About Eve (Acad. Award nom.), The Tender Trap, High Society, Bachelor Flat, Doctor You've Got To Be Kidding, Tom Sawyer, Bittersweet Love, The Private Files of J. Edgar Hoover, Three Men and a Baby, Once You Meet a Stranger, Still Breathing, Broadway: The Golden Age by the Legends Who Were There.
TELEVISION: *Specials*: A Clearing in the Wood, Play of the Week, Cinderella, Nora's Christmas Gift. *Mini-Series*: Backstairs at the White House (Emmy nom.). *Movies*: Underground Man, Death Cruise, Love Boat II, Midnight Lace, The Shady Hill Kidnapping, This Girl for Hire, Murder by the Book, Polly, Polly-Comin' Home!, Home of the Brave. *Pilot*: Road Show. *Series*: Honestly Celeste, Who Pays, Nancy, Jessie, Falcon Crest, Christine Cromwell, Loving, Promised Land, The Beat. *Guest*: Love Boat, Trapper John M.D., Magnum P.I.

HOLM, IAN
C.B.E. Actor. r.n. Ian Holm Cuthbert. b. Ilford, Essex, England, Sept. 12, 1931. e. RADA. On British stage in Love Affair, Titus Andronicus, Henry IV, Ondine, Becket, The Homecoming (B'way: Tony Award, 1967), Henry V, Richard III, Romeo and Juliet, The Sea. Knighted, 1998.
PICTURES: The Bofors Gun (debut, 1968), A Midsummer Night's Dream, The Fixer, Oh! What a Lovely War, A Severed Head, Nicholas and Alexandra, Mary Queen of Scots, Young Winston, The Homecoming, Juggernaut, Robin and Marian, Shout at the Devil, March or Die, Alien, Chariots of Fire (Acad. Award nom.), Time Bandits, Return of the Soldier, Greystoke: The Legend of Tarzan Lord of the Apes, Dance With a Stranger, Wetherby, Dreamchild, Brazil, Laughterhouse, Another Woman, Henry V, Hamlet, Kafka, Naked Lunch, The Advocate, Mary Shelley's Frankenstein, The Madness of King George, Big Night, Night Falls On Manhattan, The Fifth Element, The Sweet Hereafter, A Life Less Ordinary, Joe Gould's Secret, eXistenZ, The Match, Wisconsin Death Trip, Shergar, Joe Gould's Secret, Esther Kahn, Beautiful Joe, Bless the Child, From Hell, The Emperor's New Clothes, The Lord of the Rings: The Fellowship of the Ring, The Lord of the Rings: The Return of the King.
TELEVISION: *Mini-Series/Movies*: Les Miserables, S.O.S. Titanic, Napoleon, We the Accused, All Quiet on the Western Front, Holocaust, Man in the Iron Mask, Jesus of Nazareth, Thief of Bagdad, Game Set and Match, A Season of Giants, The Borrowers, The Miracle Maker (voice), Alice Through the Looking Glass, Animal Farm (voice), The Last of the Blonde Bombshells. *Specials*: The Browning Version, Murder By the Book, Uncle Vanya, Tailor of Gloucester, The Lost Boys, The Last Romantics.

HOLMES, KATIE
Actress. r.n. Kate Noelle Holmes. b. Toledo, OH, Dec. 18, 1978.
PICTURES: The Ice Storm, Disturbing Behavior, Go, Muppets From Space, Teaching Mrs. Tingle, The Gift, The Wonder Boys, Abandon, Phone Booth, The Singing Detective, Pieces of April.
TELEVISION: *Movies*: Christmas in Washington. *Series*: Dawson's Creek, Disney's Hercules (voice) *Guest*: Fanatic.

HOMEIER, SKIP
Actor. r.n. George Vincent Homeier. b. Chicago, IL, Oct. 5, 1930. e. UCLA. Started in radio, 1936-43; on B'way stage, Tomorrow the World, 1943-44 which led to film debut in adaptation of same (billed as Skippy Homeier).
PICTURES: Tomorrow the World (debut, 1944), Boys' Ranch, Mickey, Arthur Takes Over, The Big Cat, The Gunfighter, Halls of Montezuma, Fixed Bayonets, Sealed Cargo, Sailor Beware, Has Anybody Seem My Gal?, The Last Posse, The Lone Gun, Beachhead, Black Widow, Dawn at Socorro, Ten Wanted Men, The Road to Denver, At Gunpoint, Cry Vengeance, The Burning Hills, Between Heaven and Hell, Dakota Incident, No Road Back, Stranger at My Door, Thunder Over Arizona, The Tall T, Lure of the Swamp, Decision at Durango, Day of the Badman, Journey Into Darkness, The Punderers of Painted Flats, Commanche Station, Showdown, Bullet for a Badman, Stark Fear, The Ghost and Mr. Chicken, Dead Heat on a Merry-Go-Round, Tiger By the Tail, The Greatest.
TELEVISION: *Movies*: The Challenge, Two for the Money, Voyage of the Yes, Helter Skelter, Overboard, The Wild Wild West Revisited. Washington: Behind Closed Doors. *Series*: Dan Raven, The Interns. *Guest*: Playhouse 90, Alcoa Hour, Kraft Theatre, Studio 1, Armstrong Circle Theatre, Alfred Hitchcock.

HOOKS, KEVIN
Actor, Director. b. Philadelphia, PA, Sept. 19, 1958. Son of actor-dir. Robert Hooks.
PICTURES: Sounder, Aaron Loves Angela, A Hero Ain't Nothin' But a Sandwich, Take Down, Innerspace, Strictly Business (also dir.), Passenger 57 (dir. only), Fled, Glory & Honor (also dir.), Black Dog (dir. only), Lie Detector.
TELEVISION: *Movies*: Just an Old Sweet Song, The Greatest Thing That Almost Happened, Friendly Fire, Can You Hear the Laughter?-The Story of Freddie Prinze, Roots: The Gift (dir.), Murder Without Motive: The Edmund Perry Story (dir.), Glory and Honor, Mutiny (dir.), The Color of Friendship (dir.), Sounder (dir., prod.). *Mini-Series*: Backstairs at the White House. *Special*:

Home Sweet Homeless (dir.). *Series*: The White Shadow, He's the Mayor, The Hoop Life (dir.), City of Angels (dir.), Soul Food (dir.), Philly (dir.), Without A Trace (dir. only), Dragnet (dir., co-exec. prod.).

HOOKS, ROBERT
Actor, Director, Producer. b. Washington, D.C., April 18, 1937. Father of actor-dir. Kevin Hooks. Co-founder and exec. dir. Negro Ensemble Co. NY 1967-present. Founder DC Black Repertory Company, 1970-77. Co-star of TV series NYPD, 1967-69.
THEATRE: *B'way*: A Raisin In the Sun (B'way debut, 1960), A Taste of Honey, Tiger Tiger Burning Bright, Arturo Ui, The Milktrain Doesn't Stop Here Anymore, Where's Daddy? (Theatre World Award for last two), Hallelujah, Baby?. *Off B'way.*: The Blacks, Dutchman, Happy Ending, Day of Absence, Henry V, Ballad for Bimshire, Kongi's Harvest. A Soldier's Play (Mark Taper Forum, LA). *Co-prod.* (with Gerald S. Krone): Song of the Lusitanian Bogey, Daddy Goodness, Ceremonies in Dark Old Men, Day of Absence, The Sty of the Blind Pig, The River Niger, The First Breeze of Summer.
PICTURES: Sweet Love Bitter, Hurry Sundown, The Last of the Mobile Hot-Shots, Trouble Man, Aaron Loves Angela, Airport '77, Fast-Walking, Star Trek III: The Search For Spock, Passenger 57, Posse, Fled, Glory and Honor, Free of Eden, Seventeen Again.
TELEVISION: *Movies*: Carter's Army, Vanished, The Cable Car Murder, Crosscurrent, Trapped, Ceremonies in Dark Old Men, Just an Old Sweet Song, The Killer Who Wouldn't Die, The Courage and the Passion, To Kill a Cop, A Woman Called Moses, Hollow Image, Madame X, The Oklahoma City Dolls, The Sophisticated Gents, Cassie and Co., Starflight-The Plane that Couldn't Land, Feel the Heat, Sister Sister, The Execution. *Series*: N.Y.P.D., Supercarrier, Seinfeld, Parenthood, Family Matters, Different World, Murder She Wrote, The Hoop Life. *Pilots*: The Cliff Dweller, Two for the Money, Down Home.

HOOL, LANCE
Producer, Director. b. Mexico City, Mex., May 11, 1948. e. Univ. of the Americas.
PICTURES: *Producer*: Cabo Blanco, Ten to Midnight, The Evil That Men Do, Missing in Action (also s.p.), Missing in Action 2 (dir.), Steel Dawn (also dir.), Options, Damned River, Pure Luck, The Air Up There, Gunmen, Road Flower, Flipper, McHale's Navy, One Man's Hero, Crocodile Dundee in Los Angeles. *Exec. prod.*: Broken Lizard's Club Dread, Man on Fire.
TELEVISION: The Tracker, Born To Run, Cover Girl Murders, Flashfire.

HOOPER, TOBE
Director. b. Austin, Texas, Jan. 25, 1943. e. Univ. of TX. Began film career making documentary and industrial films and commercials in Texas. Was asst. dir. of U. of Texas film program, continuing filmmaking while working with students. First feature film: documentary Peter Paul & Mary, followed by Eggshells. Directed Billy Idol video Dancing With Myself.
PICTURES: The Texas Chainsaw Massacre (also prod., co-s.p.), Eaten Alive (Death Trap), The Funhouse, Poltergeist, Lifeforce, Invaders from Mars, The Texas Chainsaw Massacre Part 2 (also co-prod., co- music), Spontaneous Combustion, Sleepwalkers (actor only), Night Terrors, The Mangler (also co-s.p.), Crocodile, The Toolbox Murders.
TELEVISION: *Movie*: I'm Dangerous Tonight. *Mini-Series*: Salem's Lot, Taken. *Series episodes*: Amazing Stories, Freddy's Nightmares (No More Mr. Nice Guy-1st episode), Equalizer (No Place Like Home), Tales from the Crypt (Dead Wait), Nowhere Man, Dark Skies, Perversions of Science, The Others, Night Visions. *Pilots*: Haunted Lives, Body Bags.

HOPE, BOB
Actor. r.n. Leslie Townes Hope. b. Eltham, England, May 29, 1903. To U.S. at age 4; raised in Cleveland, OH. Became American citizen in 1920. Was amateur boxer before appearing in vaudeville as comedian/song and dance man. Debuted on B'way 1933 in Roberta, followed by stage work in Ziegfeld Follies, Red Hot & Blue. Began film career 1934, appearing in 8 short films made in NY, before going to Hollywood for feature debut, 1938, signing contract with Paramount. Starred on radio, 1938-56; made countless trips overseas to entertain U.S. troops during wartime; lent name to Bob Hope Desert Classic golf tournament. Voted one of top ten Money-Making Stars in M.P. Herald-Fame Poll: 1941-47, 1949-53. Recipient: 5 special Academy Awards (1940, 1944, 1952, 1959, 1965); special Emmy Awards: Trustees Award (1959), Governors Award (1984); Kennedy Center Honors (1985); Presidential Medal of Freedom, and many other awards. Author (or-co-author): They Got Me Covered, I Never Left Home, So This Is Peace, Have Tux Will Travel, I Owe Russia $1,200, Five Women I Love, Hope's Vietnam Story, The Last Christmas Show, The Road to Hollywood: My 40-Year Love Affair With the Movies, Confessions of a Hooker: My Lifelong Love Affair With Golf, Don't Shoot It's Only Me.
PICTURES: The Big Broadcast of 1938 (feature debut, 1938), College Swing, Give Me a Sailor, Thanks for the Memory, Never Say Die, Some Like It Hot, The Cat and the Canary, Road to Singapore, The Ghost Breakers, Road to Zanzibar, Caught in the Draft, Louisiana Purchase, My Favorite Blonde, Road to Morocco, Nothing But the Truth, They Got Me Covered, Star Spangled Rhythm, Let's Face It, Road to Utopia, The Princess and the Pirate, Monsieur Beaucaire, My Favorite Brunette, Where There's Life, Road to Rio, The Paleface, Sorrowful Jones, The Great Lover, Fancy Pants, The Lemon Drop Kid, My Favorite Spy, Son of Paleface, Road to Bali, Off Limits, Scared Stiff (cameo), Here Come the Girls, Casanova's Big Night, The Seven Little Foys, That Certain Feeling, The Iron Petticoat, Beau James, Paris Holiday (also prod., story), Alias Jesse James (also prod.), The Five Pennies (cameo), The Facts of Life, Bachelor in Paradise, The Road to Hong Kong, Call Me Bwana, A Global Affair, I'll Take Sweden, The Oscar (cameo), Boy Did I Get a Wrong Number!, Not With My Wife You Don't (cameo), Eight on the Lam, The Private Navy of Sgt. O'Farrell, How to Commit Marriage, Cancel My Reservation (also exec. prod.), The Muppet Movie (cameo), Spies Like Us (cameo).
TELEVISION: *Movies*: A Masterpiece of Murder. Many specials incl. prod. of Roberta, annual variety shows; also was frequent host of annual Academy Award telecast. *Series*: Chesterfield Sound Off Time, Colgate Comedy Hour (rotating host), Bob Hope Presents the Chrysler Theatre (Emmy Award as exec. prod. and host, 1966).
(d. July 27, 2003)

HOPE, TED
Producer. b. 1962.
PICTURES: Tiger Warsaw (assoc.), The Unbelievable Truth, (1st asst. dir.), Theory of Achievement, Surviving Desire, Ambition, Pushing Hands (Tui Shou), I Was on Mars (also actor), Simple Men, The Wedding Banquet, Roy Cohn/Jack Smith, Eat Drink Man Woman, (assoc.), Amateur, Safe (exec.), The Brothers McMullen (exec.), Flirt, Walking and Talking, She's the One, Little Cobras, Arresting Gena, The Myth of Fingerprints (exec. prod.), The Ice Storm, Office Killer, Love God, No Looking Back, The Lifestyle (exec.), Ride with the Devil, The Tao of Steve, In the Bedroom, Storytelling, Human Nature, Lovely & Amazing, The Laramie Project, American Splendor (also exec. prod.), 21 Grams, Door in the Floor, Thumbsucker (exec. prod.).
TELEVISION: Punch and Judy Get Divorced.

HOPKINS, SIR ANTHONY
C.B.E.: Actor. r.n. Philip Anthony Hopkins. b. Port Talbot, South Wales, Dec. 31, 1937. Trained at Royal Acad. of Dramatic Art; Welsh Coll. of Music & Drama. Joined National Theatre, gaining fame on stage in England, then TV and films. Appeared in short The White Bus. Recordings: Under Milk Wood (1988), Shostakovich Symphony No. 13 Babi Yar (reciting Yevtushenko's poem, 1994). Dir. An Evening With Dylan Thomas, 1993. Received special award at Montreal Film Festival for Career Excellence, 1992; Evening Standard Film Awards Special Award for Body of Work, 1994; BAFTA Britannia Award for Outstanding Contribution to the International Film and TV Industry, 1995.
THEATRE: Julius Caesar (debut, 1964), Juno and the Paycock, A Flea in Her Ear, The Three Sisters, Dance of Death, As You Like It, The Architect and the Emperor of Assyria, A Woman Killed With Kindness, Coriolanus, The Taming of the Shrew, Macbeth, Equus (NY, 1974-75; Outer Critics Circle, NY Drama Desk, U.S. Authors & Celebrities Forum Awards), Equus (LA 1977, also dir.; LA Drama Critics Award), The Tempest, Old Times, The Lonely Road, Pravda (Variety Club Stage Actor Award, 1985; British Theatre Association Best Actor, Laurence Olivier & Observer Awards), King Lear, Antony and Cleopatra, M. Butterfly, August (also dir.).
PICTURES: The Lion in Winter (debut, 1967), The Looking Glass War, Hamlet, When Eight Bells Toll, Young Winston, A Doll's House, The Girl from Petrovka, Juggernaut, Audrey Rose, A Bridge Too Far, International Velvet, Magic, The Elephant Man, A Change of Seasons, The Bounty (Variety Club UK Film Actor Award, 1983), 84 Charing Cross Road (Moscow Film Fest. Award, 1987), The Good Father, The Dawning, A Chorus of Disapproval, Desperate Hours, The Silence of the Lambs (Academy Award, Natl. Board of Review, NY Film Critics, Boston Film Critics & BAFTA Awards, 1991), Freejack, One Man's War, Howards End, The Efficiency Expert (Spotswood), Bram Stoker's Dracula, Chaplin, The Remains of the Day (BAFTA, Variety Club UK Film Actor, LA Film Critics, Japan Critics Awards, 1993), The Trial, Shadowlands (Natl. Board of Review & LA Film Critics Award, 1993, BAFTA, Best Actor-Leading, 1994), The Road to Wellville, Legends of The Fall, The Innocent, August (also dir.), Nixon, Surviving Picasso, The Edge, Amistad, Meet Joe Black, The Mask of Zorro, Instinct, Titus, How the Grinch Stole Christmas (voice), Mission Impossible 2, The Making of Titus, Hannibal, Hearts in Atlantis, The Devil and Daniel Webster, Red Dragon, Bad Company, The Human Stain.
TELEVISION: A Heritage and Its History, Vanya, Hearts and Flowers, Decision to Burn, War & Peace, Cuculus Canorus, Lloyd George, QB VII, Find Me, A Childhood Friend, Possessions, All Creatures Great and Small, The Arcata Promise, Dark Victory, The Lindbergh Kidnapping Case (Emmy Award, 1976), Victory at Entebbe, Kean, Mayflower: The Pilgrim's Adventure, The Bunker (Emmy Award, 1981), Peter and Paul, Othello, Little Eyolf, The Hunchback of Notre Dame, A Married Man, Corridors of Power, Strangers and Brothers, Arch of Triumph, Mussolini and I / Mussolini: The Rise and Fall of Il Duce (ACE Award), Guilty

Conscience, The Dawning, Across the Lake, Heartland, The Tenth Man, Great Expectations, One Man's War, To Be the Best, A Few Selected Exits, Big Cats.

HOPKINS, BO
Actor. b. Greenwood, SC, Feb. 2, 1942. Studied with Uta Hagen in N.Y. then with Desilu Playhouse training school in Hollywood. Parts in several prods. for that group won him an agent, an audition with dir. Sam Peckinpah and his first role in latter's The Wild Bunch.
PICTURES: The Wild Bunch (debut, 1969), Monte Walsh, The Moonshine War, The Culpepper Cattle Co., The Getaway, White Lightning, The Man Who Loved Cat Dancing, American Graffiti, The Nickel Ride, The Day of the Locust, Posse, The Killer Elite, A Small Town in Texas, Tentacles, Midnight Express, More American Graffiti, The Fifth Floor, Sweet Sixteen, Night Shadows, Trapper Country, What Comes Around, War, The Bounty Hunter, The Stalker, Nightmare at Noon, The Tenth Man, Big Bad John, Center of the Web, Inside Monkey Zetterland, The Ballad of Little Jo, Cheyenne Warrior, Radioland Murders, Riders in the Storm, The Feminine Touch, Ben Johnson: Third Cowboy on the Right, Painted Hero, Fever Lake, U Turn, Uncle Sam, Lunker Lake, Phantoms, The Newton Boys, Getting to Know You, Time Served, South of Heaven West of Hell, Big Brother Trouble, Vice, The Thundering 8th, Ring of Fire, A Crack in the Door, Land of Canaan, Choosing Matthias, Don't Let Go, Mending Fences (also prod.), The Road Home, Shade (also exec. prod.).
TELEVISION: *Series*: Doc Elliott, The Rockford Files, Dynasty. *Movies*: The Runaway Barge, Kansas City Massacre, Charlie's Angels (pilot), The Invasion of Johnson County, Dawn: Portrait of a Teenage Runaway, Thaddeus Rose and Eddie, Crisis in Sun Valley, Plutonium Incident, A Smoky Mountain Christmas, Beggerman Thief, Down the Long Hills, Last Ride of the Dalton Gang, Casino, Rodeo Girl, Ghost Dancing, Blood Ties, Movie Lover's Road Trip (himself, 2003). *Special*: Wyatt Earp: Return to Tombstone.

HOPPER, DENNIS
Actor, Director. b. Dodge City, KS, May 17, 1936. e. San Diego, CA, public schools. *Author*: Out of the Sixties (1988; book of his photographs).
PICTURES: Rebel Without a Cause, I Died a Thousand Times, Giant, The Steel Jungle, The Story of Mankind, Gunfight at the OK Corral, From Hell to Texas, The Young Land, Key Witness, Night Tide, Tarzan and Jane Regained Sort Of, The Sons of Katie Elder, Queen of Blood, Cool Hand Luke, Glory Stompers, The Trip, Panic in the City, Hang 'Em High, True Grit, Easy Rider (also dir., co-s.p.), The Last Movie (also dir., s.p.), Kid Blue, James Dean-The First American Teenager, Bloodbath (The Sky Is Falling), Mad Dog Morgan, Tracks, The American Friend, Douleur Chair, The Sorcerer's Appentices, L'Ordre et la Securite du Monde, Resurrection, Apocalypse Now, Out of the Blue (also dir.), King of the Mountain, Renacida, White Star, Human Highway, Rumble Fish, The Osterman Weekend, My Science Project, The Texas Chainsaw Massacre Part 2, Hoosiers (Acad. Award nom.), Blue Velvet, Black Widow, River's Edge, Straight to Hell, The Pick Up Artist, O.C. and Stiggs, Riders of the Storm, Blood Red, Colors (dir. only), Flashback, Chattachoochee, The Hot Spot (dir. only), Superstar: The Life and Times of Andy Warhol, The Indian Runner, Hearts of Darkness: A Filmmaker's Apocalypse, Midnight Heat, Eye of the Storm, Boiling Point, Super Mario Bros., True Romance, Red Rock West, Chasers (also dir.), Speed, Search and Destroy, Waterworld, Acts of Love, Basquiat, Carried Away, Star Truckers, The Blackout, Tycus, Meet the Deedles, The Source, The Prophet's Game, Lured Innocence, Jesus' Son, Bad City Blues, EDtv, Straight Shooter, Luck of the Draw, Listen With Your Eyes, Choke, Ticker, Knockaround Guys, Unspeakable, My Little Hollywood, LAPD: To Protect and to Serve, I Don't Know Jack, Firecracker, One Giant Leap, The Piano Player, Knockaround Guys, Leopold Bloom, Dumping Ground, Out of Season, The Keeper, The Crow: Wicked Prayer, Americano (2004).
TELEVISION: *Movies*: Wild Times, Stark, Paris Trout, Doublecrossed, Backtrack (also dir.), Nails, The Heart of Justice, Witch Hunt, Suspense. *Guest*: Pursuit, Espionage, Medic, Loretta Young Show, King of the Hill (voice), The Art of Dennis Hopper. *Series*: Flatland, 24.

HORN, ALAN
Executive. b. 1944. e. M.B.A., Harvard Bus. Sch. Began career in brand management with Proctor & Gamble, then five years in the U.S. Air Force, rank of Captain. Entered entertainment as an executive for Tandem Prods., T.A.T. Communications, and as CEO for Embassy Communications (with Norman Lear and Jerry Perenchio), 1973-86. In 1986, he served as pres. & COO of 20th Century Fox Film Corp. Left 20th Century in 1987 to form Castle Rock Ent. as a co-founder, chair & CEO (1987-99). Named to current position of pres. & COO, Warner Bros. Entertainment, Inc., 1999. Serves on the board of Univision Communications, The Natural Resources Defense Council (NRDC) as vice chmn., The Board of Trustees for the Autry Museum of Western Heritage in Los Angeles, The Buffalo Bill Historical Center in Cody, Wyoming, The Board of Directors of KCET-TV, the Los Angeles PBS affiliate, and the John Thomas Dye School in Los Angeles. Founding bd. member, Environmental Media

Association. He is also a member of the Acad. of Television Arts & Sciences , Acad. of Motion Picture Arts & Sciences, AFI, the Hollywood Radio and Television Society & the Museum of Broadcasting.

HORNE, LENA
Singer, Actress. b. Brooklyn, NY, June 30, 1917. Radio with Noble Sissle, Charlie Barnet, other bands. Floor shows at Cotton Club, Cafe Society, Little Troc. Started screen career 1942. Appeared in short subjects Harlem Hotshots, Boogie Woogie Dream. Autobiographies: In Person (1950), Lena (1965) Recipient Kennedy Center Honors for Lifetime contribution to the Arts, 1984. Spingarn Award, NAACP, 1983; Paul Robeson Award, Actors Equity Assn., 1985.
THEATRE: Blackbirds, Dance With Your Gods, Jamaica, Pal Joey (L.A. Music Center), Lena Horne: The Lady and Her Music (Tony Award).
PICTURES: The Duke Is Tops (debut, 1938), Panama Hattie, Cabin in the Sky, Stormy Weather, I Dood It, Thousands Cheer, Broadway Rhythm, Swing Fever, Two Girls and a Sailor, Ziegfeld Follies, Till the Clouds Roll By, Words and Music, Duchess of Idaho, Meet Me in Las Vegas, Death of a Gunfighter, The Wiz, That's Entertainment III.
TELEVISION: *Guest*: Music '55, Perry Como Show, Here's to the Ladies, The Flip Wilson Show, Dean Martin Show, Sesame Street, Ed Sullivan Show, Sanford & Sons, Laugh-In, Hollywood Palace, The Cosby Show. *Specials*: The Lena Horne Show (1959), The Frank Sinatra Timex Show, Lena in Concert, Harry and Lena, The Tony & Lena Show, Lena Horne: The Lady and Her Music, Small Steps-Big Strides: The Black Experience in Hollywood (tv documentary).

HORNER, JAMES
Composer. b. Los Angeles, CA, Aug. 14, 1953. e. Royal Col. of Music: London, USC, UCLA. Received Grammy Awards for the song Somewhere Out There (from the film An American Tail), and for instrumental composition from Glory. Has won more than 10 ASCAP awards for his film compositioins.
PICTURES: The Lady in Red, Battle Beyond the Stars, Humanoids From the Deep, Deadly Blessing, The Hand, Wolfen, The Pursuit of D.B. Cooper, 48 HRS, Star Trek II: The Wrath of Khan, Something Wicked This Way Comes, Krull, Brainstorm, Testament, Gorky Park, The Dresser, Uncommon Valor, The Stone Boy, Star Trek III: The Search for Spock, Heaven Help Us, Cocoon, Volunteers, Journey of Natty Gann, Commando, Aliens, Where the River Runs Black, The Name of the Rose, An American Tail, PK. and the Kid, Project X, Batteries Not Included, Willow, Red Heat, Vibes, Cocoon: The Return, The Land Before Time, Field of Dreams, Honey I Shrunk the Kids, Dad, Glory, I Love You to Death, Another 48 HRS., Once Around, My Heroes Have Always Been Cowboys, Class Action, The Rocketeer, An American Tail: Fievel Goes West, Thunderheart, Patriot Games, Unlawful Entry, Sneakers, Swing Kids, A Far Off Place, Jack the Bear, Once Upon a Forest, Searching for Bobby Fischer, The Man Without a Face, Bopha!, The Pelican Brief, Clear and Present Danger, Legends of the Fall, Braveheart, Casper, Apollo 13 (Acad. Award nom.), Jumanji, Courage Under Fire, Ransom, To Gillian on Her 37th Birthday, Titanic (Acad. Award, Best Dramatic Score, Best Orig. Score, Best Orig. Song, Golden Globe Award, Best Orig. Score, Best Orig. Song, Chicago Film Crits. Award, Best Musical Score, 1997), The Devil's Own, Deep Impact, The Mask of Zorro, Mighty Joe Young, Bicentennial Man, The Perfect Storm, How the Grinch Stole Christmas, Enemy at the Gates, A Beautiful Mind (Acad. Award nom.), Iris, Windtalkers, Four Feathers, The Land Before Time: Journey to Big Water (video), Soul Calibur, Beyond Borders, Radio, The Missing, House of Sand and Fog, The Passion.

HORSLEY, LEE
Actor. b. Muleshoe, TX, May 15, 1955. e. U. of No. Colorado. On stage in Mack and Mabel, West Side Story, Sound of Music, Oklahoma!, Forty Carats, 1776, Damn Yankees.
PICTURE: The Sword and the Sorcerer, Unlawful Passage, Nightmare Man, Dismembered.
TELEVISION: *Movies*: The Wild Women of Chastity Gulch, Infidelity, When Dreams Come True, Thirteen at Dinner, Single Women Married Men, The Face of Fear, Danielle Steel's Palomino, French Silk, The Corpse Had a Familiar Face, Home Song, The Care and Handling of Roses, Nightmare Man. *Miniseries*: Crossings, North and South Book II. *Documentary*: Western Ranching Culture In Crisis, The Forest Wars. *Series*: Nero Wolfe, Matt Houston, Guns of Paradise, Bodies of Evidence, Hawkeye, Wind on Water.

HORTON, PETER
Actor. b. Bellevue, DC, Aug. 20, 1953. e. Univ. of CA, Santa Barbara. Stage work includes appearances with Lobero Rep. Co. Theatre in Santa Barbara, Butterflies Are Free in L.A.
PICTURES: Serial, Fade to Black, Split Image, Children of the Corn, Where the River Runs Black, Amazon Women on the Moon (also co-dir.), Sideout, Singles, The Cure (dir. only), The Baby-sitters Club, 2 Days in the Valley, Death Benefit, T-Rex: Back to the Cretaceous, The Dust Factory.
TELEVISION: *Series*: Seven Brides for Seven Brothers, thirtysomething (also dir.), The Wonder Years (dir. only), Class of '96

dir., actor), Brimstone(also prod.), The Geena Davis Show, Karen Sisco. *Pilot:* Sawyer and Finn. *Movies:* She's Dressed to Kill, Miracle on Ice, Freedom, Choices of the Heart, Children of the Dark, Crazy Horse, One Too Many (dir. only), Murder Live!, Into Thin Air: Death on Everest, From the Earth to the Moon.

HORTON, ROBERT
Actor. b. Los Angeles, CA, July 29, 1924. e. U. of Miami. UCLA, B.A. Cum Laude, 1949. Yale Grad School, 1949-50. With U.S.Coast Guard; many legit. plays; many radio & TV appearances. Star of Broadway musical 110 in the Shade.
PICTURES: A Walk in the Sun, The Tanks Are Coming, Return of the Texan, Pony Soldier, Apache War Smoke, Bright Road, The Story of Three Loves, Code Two, Arena, Prisoner of War, Men of the Fighting Lady, The Green Slime, The Dangerous Days of Kiowa Jones, The Spy Killer, Foreign Exchange.
TELEVISION: *Series:* Kings Row, Wagon Train, A Man Called Shenandoah, As the World Turns. *Movies:* The Spy Killer, Red River. *Guest:* Alfred Hitchcock Presents, Suspense, Houston Knights, Murder She Wrote.

HOSKINS, BOB
Actor. b. Bury St. Edmunds, Suffolk, England, Oct. 26, 1942. Porter and steeplejack before becoming actor at 25. Veteran of Royal Shakespeare Co. Appeared with Britain's National Theatre (Man Is Man, King Lear, Guys and Dolls.)
PICTURES: The National Health (debut, 1973), Royal Flash, Inserts, Zulu Dawn, The Long Good Friday, Pink Floyd: The Wall, Beyond the Limit, Lassiter, The Cotton Club, Brazil, Sweet Liberty, Mona Lisa (Acad. Award nom.), A Prayer for the Dying, The Lonely Passion of Judith Hearne, Who Framed Roger Rabbit, The Raggedy Rawney (also dir., co-s.p.), Heart Condition, Mermaids, Shattered, The Inner Circle, The Favor the Watch and the Very Big Fish, Hook, Passed Away, Super Mario Bros., The Rainbow, The Secret Agent, Nixon, Balto (voice), Joseph Conrad's The Secret Agent, Michael, Spice World (cameo), Twenty Four Seven, Parting Shots, Captain Jack, Cousin Bette, The White River Kid, A Room for Romeo Bass, American Virgin, Felicia's Journey, Enemy at the Gates, Last Orders, The Sleeping Dictionary, Where Eskimos Live, Maid in Manhattan, Tortoise vs. Hare, Den of Lions, Danny the Dog.
TELEVISION: Villains on the High Road (debut, 1972), New Scotland Yard, On the Move, Rock Follies, In the Looking Glass, Napoleon, Flickers, Pennies from Heaven, Othello, Mussolini, The Dunera Boys, World War II: When Lions Roar, The Changeling, The Forgotten Toys, David Copperfield, Don Quixote, Noriega: God's Favorite, The Lost World, The Good Pope: Pope John XXIII (tv documentary).

HOU, HSIAO-HSIEN
Director. b. Meixian, China, April 8, 1947.
PICTURES: Cute Girl, Cheerful Wind, Six is Company (s.p. only), Growing Up (s.p., prod. only), The Green Green Grass of Home, All the Youthful Days, The Sandwich Man, A Summer at Grandpa's, The Time to Live and the Time to Die (also s.p.), Dust in the Wind, Daughter of the Nile, City of Sadness, Raise the Red Lantern (exec. prod. only), Dust of Angels (exec. prod. only), The Puppetmaster, A Borrowed Life (exec. prod. only), Good Men Good Women, Heartbreak Island (s.p., exec. prod. only), Goodbye South Goodbye, Flowers of Shanghai, Borderline (prod. only)., Mirror Image (co-exec. prod.), Millenium Mambo

HOUGH, JOHN
Director. b. London, England,, Nov. 21, 1941. Worked in British film prod. in various capacities; impressed execs. at EMI-MGM Studios, Elstree, London, so was given chance to direct The Avengers series for TV. Began theatrical films with Sudden Terror for prod. Irving Allen, 1971.
PICTURES: Sudden Terror, The Practice, Twins of Evil, Treasure Island, The Legend of Hell House, Twins of Evil, Treasure Larry, Escape to Witch Mountain, Return From Witch Mountain, Brass Target, The Watcher in the Woods, The Incubus, Triumphs of a Man Called Horse, Biggles: Adventures in Time, American Gothic, Howling IV—The Original Nightmare, The Backyard (documentary, exec. prod.), Something to Believe In (also prod., writer), Bad Karma.
TELEVISION: A Hazard of Hearts (also co-prod.), The Lady and the Highwayman (also prod.), A Ghost in Monte Carlo (also prod.), Duel of Hearts (also prod.), Distant Scream, Black Carrion, Check-Mate.

HOUNSOU, DJIMON
Actor. b. Benin, West Africa, April 24, 1964. Was model before he began acting.
PICTURES: Without You I'm Nothing, Unlawful Entry, Stargate, Amistad, Ill Gotten Gains, Deep Rising, Gladiator, The Middle Passage, Dead Weight, Four Feathers, In America, Heroes (short), Biker Boyz, Lara Croft Tomb Raider: The Cradle of Life, Blueberry.
TELEVISION: *Guest:* ER, Soul Food. *Series:* Beverly Hills 90210.

HOWARD, ARLISS
Actor. b. Independence, MO, 1955. e. Columbia Col., MO. m. actress Debra Winger.

THEATRE: American Buffalo, Lie of the Mind.
PICTURES: The Prodigal, Sylvester, Door to Door, The Ladies Club, The Lightship, Full Metal Jacket, Plain Clothes, Tequila Sunrise, Men Don't Leave, For the Boys, Ruby, Crisscross, The Sandlot, Wilder Napalm, Natural Born Killers, Wet, To Wong Foo—Thanks for Everything—Julie Newmar, Johns, Beyond the Call, The Lost World: Jurassic Park, Amistad, The Lesser Evil, A Map of the World, Big Bad Love, Dandelion, Birth.
TELEVISION: *Movies:* Hands of a Stranger, I Know My First Name is Steven, Somebody Has to Shoot the Picture, Iran: Days of Crisis, Till Death Us Do Part, Those Secrets, The Infiltrator, The Man Who Captured Eichmann, Old Man, You Know My Name, The Song of the Lark, Word of Honor.

HOWARD, CLINT
Actor. b. Burbank, CA, Apr. 20, 1959. Brother is dir. Ron Howard; father is actor Rance Howard.
PICTURES: An Eye for an Eye, Gentle Giant, The Jungle Book (voice), Winnie the Pooh and the Blustery Day (voice), The Wild Country, The Grand Auto Theft, The Many Adventures of Winnie the Pooh (voice), Harper Valley P.T.A., Rock 'n' Roll High School, Evil Speak, Night Shift, Flip Out, Splash, Cocoon, Gung Ho, The Wraith, End of the Line, Freeway, B.O.R.N.,An Innocent Man, Parenthood, Tango and Cash, Silent Night Deadly Night 4: Inititation, Disturbed, Backdraft, The Rocketeer, Silent Night Deadly Night 5: The Toy Maker, Voice of a Stranger, Far and Away, Ticks, Forced to Kill, Carnosaur, Leprechaun 2, The Paper, Bigfoot: The Unforgettable Encounter, Not Like Us, The Ice Cream Man, Fist of the North Star, Dillinger and Capone, Digital Man, Baby Face Nelson, Forget Paris, Apollo 13, Twisted Love, That Thing You Do!, Rattled, Barb Wire, Unhook the Stars, Santa with Muscles, The Protector, Austin Powers: International Man of Mystery, Telling You, Twilight, The Dentist II, The Waterboy, Sparkle and Charm, My Dog Skip, Fortune Hunters, Austin Powers: The Spy Who Shagged Me, Arthur's Quest, Edtv, The Million Dollar Kid, My Dog Skip, Little Nicky, How the Grinch Stole Christmas, Sparkle and Charm, Ping!, Blackwoods, Austin Powers in Goldmember, You'll Never Wiez in This Town Again, The Sure Hand of God, Home Room, The House of the Dead, Searching for Haizmann, You'll Never Wiez in This Town Again (documentary), The Great Commission, Big Paw: Beethoven 5 (video), The Missing.
TELEVISION: *Series:* The Andy Griffith Show, The Baileys of Balboa, Gentle Ben, Salty, The Cowboys, Gung Ho, Space Rangers. *Movies:* The Red Pony, Huckleberry Finn, The Death of Richie, Cotton Candy (also writer), Skyward, Little White Lies, Cheyenne Warrior, Sawbones, Humanoids from the Deep. *Guest:* The Streets of San Francisco, Happy Days, Star Trek, Night Gallery, Seinfeld, Star Trek: Deep Space Nine, Silk Stalkings, The Outer Limits, Gun.

HOWARD, JAMES NEWTON
Composer. Started as keyboard player for Elton John, before composing and producing for such artists as Cher, Diana Ross, Barbra Streisand, Chaka Khan, Randy Newman.
PICTURES: Tough Guys, Nobody's Fool, Head Office, Wildcats, 8 Million Ways to Die, Five Corners, Campus Man, Promised Land, Off Limits, Tap, Some Girls, Everybody's All-American, Major League, The Package, Marked for Death, Pretty Woman, Coupe de Ville, Flatliners, Three Men and a Little Lady, Dying Young, The Man in the Moon, My Girl, The Prince of Tides (Acad. Award nom.), Grand Canyon, Guilty by Suspicion, King Ralph, Dying Young, The Man in the Moon, Glengarry Glen Ross, Night and the City, American Heart, Diggstown, Alive, Falling Down, Dave, The Fugitive (Acad. Award nom.), The Saint of Fort Washington, Intersection, Wyatt Earp, Junior (Acad. Award nom; Golden Globe nom.), Restoration, Just Cause, Outbreak, Eye for an Eye, The Juror, Primal Fear, The Trigger Effect, The Rich Man's Wife, Space Jam, One Fine Day (Acad. Award nom.), Dante's Peak, Liar Liar, Fathers' Day, My Best Friend's Wedding (Acad. Award nom.), The Devil's Advocate, The Postman, Snow Falling on Cedars, A Perfect Murder, Runaway Bride, Stir of Echoes, The Sixth Sense, Mumford, Snow Falling on Cedars, Wayward Son, Dinosaur, Unbreakable, Vertical Limit, Atlantis: The Lost Empire, America's Sweethearts, Big Trouble, Signs, Treasure Planet, Unconditional Love, The Palace Thief, Dreamcatcher, Peter Pan (2003), Hidalgo.
TELEVISION: *Movies:* The Image, Revealing Evidence: Stalking the Honolulu Strangler, Somebody Has to Shoot the Picture, Descending Angel, A Private Matter. *Series:* ER (Emmy nom.), Gideon's Crossing (Emmy award), The Fugitive.

HOWARD, KEN
Actor. b. El Centro, CA, March 28, 1944. e. Yale Drama Sch. Left studies to do walk-on in B'way. musical, Promises Promises.
THEATRE: Promises Promises, 1776 (Theatre World Award), Child's Play (Tony Award, 1970), Equus, Rumors, Camping With Henry and Tom.
PICTURES: Tell Me That You Love Me Junie Moon (debut, 1970), Such Good Friends, The Strange Vengeance of Rosalie, 1776, Second Thoughts, Oscar, Clear and Present Danger, The Net, Tactical Assault, At First Sight, Mark Twain's Greatest Adventure: 'It's a Matter of Time'.
TELEVISION: *Movies:* Manhunter, Superdome, Critical List, A Real American Hero, Damien: The Leper Priest, Victims, Rage of

Angels, The Trial of George Armstrong Custer, He's Not Your Son, Rage of Angels: The Story Continues, Murder in New Hampshire: The Pamela Smart Story, Memories of Midnight, Hart to Hart Returns, Moment of Truth: To Walk Again, Tom Clancy's Op Center, Her Hidden Truth, Something Borrowed Something Blue, A Vow to Cherish, Chasing the Sun, Chasing the Sun (documentary, narrator). *Specials*: Strange Interlude, The Man in the Brown Suit, Mastergate. *Mini-Series*: The Thorn Birds, Perfect Murder Perfect Town. *Series*: Adam's Rib, The Manhunter, The White Shadow, It's Not Easy, The Colbys, Dynasty, Dream Girl U.S.A., What Happened? (host), Crossing Jordan.

HOWARD, RON
Actor, Director, Producer. b. Duncan, OK, March 1, 1954. e. Univ. of So. Calif. Los Angeles Valley Col. Acting debut as Ronny Howard at age of 2 with parents, Rance and Jean Howard, in The Seven Year Itch at Baltimore's Hilltop Theatre. Two years later traveled to Vienna to appear in first film, The Journey. Brother is actor Clint Howard, also former child actor. Co-Chairman of Imagine Films Entertainment.
PICTURES: *Actor*: The Journey (debut, 1959), Door-to-Door Maniac, The Music Man, The Courtship of Eddie's Father, Village of the Giants, The Wild Country, American Graffiti, Happy Mother's Day... Love George, The Spikes Gang, Eat My Dust!, I'm a Fool, The Shootist, The First Nudie Musical (cameo), More American Graffiti, The Magical World of Chuck Jones, Osmosis Jones (voice). *Director*: Grand Theft Auto (dir. debut, 1977; also actor, co-s.p.),Night Shift, Splash, Cocoon, Gung Ho (also exec. prod.), Willow, Parenthood (also co-story), Backdraft, Far and Away (also co-prod., co-story), The Paper, Apollo 13, Ransom, Edtv (also prod.), How the Grinch Stole Christman, A Beautiful Mind (Acad. Award, AFI nom., BAFTA nom., DGA Award, Golden Globe nom.), The Missing. *Exec. prod/prod.*: Leo & Loree, No Man's Land, Vibes, Clean and Sober, Closet Land, Far and Away, The Chamber, Inventing the Abbotts, Edtv, Beyond the Mat, How the Grinch Stole Christmas, A Beautiful Mind (Acad. Award), The Alamo (prod.).
TELEVISION: *Movies*: The Migrants, Locusts, Huckleberry Finn, Cotton Candy (dir., co-writer), Act of Love, Bitter Harvest, Fire on the Mountain, When Your Lover Leaves (also co.exec. prod.), Through the Magic Pyramid (exec. prod., dir.), Splash Too, Skyward (co-exec. prod., dir.), Into Thin Air (exec. prod.), Return to Mayberry, Frank Capra's American Dream, Boarding School (exec. prod). *Mini-series*: From the Earth to the Moon. *Series*: The Andy Griffith Show, The Smith Family, Happy Days, Fonz and the Happy Days Gang (voice), Parenthood, Hiller & Diller (exec. prod), Felicity (prod.), The PJs (exec. prod.), Wonderland (exec. prod.), The Beast (exec. prod.), 24 (exec. prod.), Arrested Development (exec. prod.). *Guest*: Red Skelton Hour, Playhouse 90, Dennis the Menace, Many Loves of Dobie Gillis, Five Fingers, Twilight Zone, Dinah Shore Show, The Fugitive, Dr. Kildare, The Big Valley, I Spy, Danny Kaye Show, Gomer Pyle USMC, The Monroes, Love American Style, Gentle Ben, Gunsmoke; Disney TV films (incl. A Boy Called Nuthin', Smoke), The Simpsons (voice).

HOWARD, SANDY
Producer. b. Aug. 1, 1927. e. Florida So. Coll. Ent. m.p. ind. 1946.
PICTURES: Tarzan and the Trappers (dir. only), Perils of the Deep, Diary of a Bachelor (dir. only), Gamera the Invincible (dir. only), One Step to Hell (also dir. & s.p.), Jack of Diamonds (s.p. only), A Man Called Horse, Man in the Wilderness, Together Brothers, Neptune Factor, The Devil's Rain (exec. prod.), Sky Riders, The Last Castle, Embryo, Magna I-Beyond the Barrier Reef, The Battle, Island of Dr. Moreau, City on Fire, Death Ship (exec. prod.), Avenging Angel, Vice Squad (s.p. only), Kidnapped, The Boys Next Door, Nightstick, Dark Tower (exec. prod.), Blue Monkey (exec. prod.), Street Justice (exec. prod.).

HOWELL, C. THOMAS
Actor. r.n. Christopher Thomas Howell. b. Los Angeles, CA, Dec. 7, 1966. Former junior rodeo circuit champion.
PICTURES: E.T.: The Extra Terrestrial (debut, 1982), The Outsiders, Tank, Grandview U.S.A., Red Dawn, Secret Admirer, The Hitcher, Soul Man, A Tiger's Tale, Young Toscanini, Side Out, Far Out Man, The Return of the Musketeers, Kid, Nickel and Dime, Breaking the Rules, First Force, That Night, Tattle Tale, Streetwise, To Protect and Serve, Gettysburg, Jail Bate, Teresa's Tattoo, Power Play, Treacherous, Payback, Dangerous Indiscretion, Hourglass (also dir.), Baby Face Nelson, Mad Dogs and Englishmen, Pure Danger (also dir.), The Big Fall (also dir.), Sleeping Dogs, Last Lives, Dilemma, The Prince and the Surfer, The Glass Jar, Felons, Fortune Hunters, Shepherd, Red Team, The Million Dollar Kid, Hot Boyz, Enemy Action, WillFull, XCU: Extreme Closeup, Separate Ways, Asylum Days, Nursie, Net Games, Gods and Generals, The Hitcher II: I've Been Waiting (video), The Keeper: The Legend of Omar Khayyam, Fighting Words.
TELEVISION: *Movies*: It Happened One Christmas, Into the Homeland, Curiosity Kills, Acting on Impulse, Dark Reflection, Suspect Device, Dead. Fire, Night of the Wolf, Killer Bees!, Hope Ranch (s.p., prod.) *Series*: Little People (only 4 yrs. old), Two Marriages, Kindred: The Embraced, Ollie. *Guest*: Nightmare Classics (Eye of the Panther).

HOWELLS, URSULA
Actress. b. Sept. 17, 1922. e. St. Paul's Sch., London. Stage debut, 1939, at Dundee Repertory with Bird in Hand followed by several plays inc. Springtime for Henry in N.Y., 1951; m.p. debut in Flesh and Blood, 1950; TV debut in Case of the Frightened Lady for BBC, 1948.
PICTURES: Lolly Madonna XXX, Catch My Soul, Hardcore, Escape from New York, Vice Squad, Total Exposure, Twist of Fate, I Believe in You, The Weak and the Wicked, The Horse's Mouth, Track the Man Down, Handcuffs London, The Constant Husband, The Third Key, Keep It Clean, Account Rendered, The Sicilians, The Blood Suckers, Torture Garden, Assignment K, Girly, Crossplot, Time After Time, The Tichborne Claimant.
TELEVISION: *Movies*: King Lear, The Small Back Room, For Services Rendered, The Cocktail Party, Father Dear Father, A Murder is Announced, The Cold Room, Jewels, A Pinch of Snuff, A Rather English Marriage. *Series*: The Forsyte Saga, The Many Wives of Patrick, The Cazalets.

HUBBARD, STANLEY
Satellite Broadcast Executive. b. St. Paul, MN, May 28, 1933. B.A. Univ. MN 1955. With Hubbard Broadcasting from 1950, named president 1967, chmn. & CEO 1983. Chairman & CEO U.S. Satellite Broadcasting Corp. Currently, chmn. & CEO, Hubbard Broadcasting. Broadcasting & Cable Hall of Fame 1991, Dist. Service Award, NAB 1995.

HUBLEY, SEASON
Actress. b. New York, NY, Mar. 14, 1951. Studied acting with Herbert Berghoff.
THEATRE: *LA*: Heat, Triplet Collection, Rhythm of Torn Stars.
PICTURES: The Oracle (Horse's Mouth), Track the Man Down, They Can't Hang Me, Keep It Clean, Long Arm (Third Key), Death and The Sky Above, Mumsy Nanny Sonny and Girly, Vice Squad, Caddie Woodlawn, Total Exposure, Crossplot, Children of the Corn V: Fields of Terror (video), Kiss the Sky.
TELEVISION: *Movies/Specials*: She Lives, The Healers, SST—Death Flight, Loose Change, Elvis, Mrs. R's Daughter, Three Wishes of Billy Grier, Under the Influence, Christmas Eve, Shakedown on Sunset Strip, Unspeakable Acts, Child of the Night, Steel Justice, Key to Rebecca, All I Could See From Where I Stood, Stepfather III, Caribbean Mystery, Black Carrion, Vestige of Honor, Humanoids From the Deep. *Series*: Kung Fu, Family, All My Children, *Pilots*: Lond and Davis in New York, Blues Skies, The City. *Guest*: The Partridge Family, The Rookies, Kojak, Twilight Zone, Alfred Hitchcock Presents, Twilight Zone, Hitchhiker.

HUDDLESTON, DAVID
Actor, Producer. b. Vinton, VA, Sept. 17, 1930. e. American Acad. of Dramatic Arts. Son is actor Michael Huddleston.
THEATER: A Man for All Seasons, Front Page, Everybody Loves Opal, Ten Little Indians, Silk Stockings, Fanny, Guys and Dolls, The Music Man, Desert Song, Mame. Broadway: The First, Death of a Salesman.
PICTURES: All the Way Home, A Lovely Way to Die, Slaves, Norwood, Rio Lobo, Fools, Parade, Bad Company, Blazing Saddles, McQ, The World's Greatest Lover, Capricorn One, Gorp, Smokey and the Bandit II, The Act, Santa Claus, Frantic, Life With Mikey, Cultivating Charlie. Something to Talk About (unbilled), Joe's Apartment, The Man Next Door, The Big Lebowski, G-Men From Hell.
TELEVISION: *Movies*: Sarge, The Badge or the Cross, The Priest Killer, Suddenly Single, The Homecoming, Brian's Song, Tenafly (pilot), Brock's Last Case, Hawkins on Murder, Heatwave, The Gun and the Pulpit, The Oregon Trail, Shark Kill, Sherlock Holmes in New York, Kate Bliss and the Ticker Tape Kid, Oklahoma City Dolls, Family Reunion, Computerside, M.A.D.D.: Mothers Against Drunk Drivers, Finnegan Begin Again, Family Reunion, Spot Marks the X, The Tracker, Margaret Bourke-White, In a Child's Name. *Mini-Series*: Once an Eagle. *Series*: Tenafly, Petrocelli, The Kallikaks, Hizzoner.

HUDSON, ERNIE
Actor. b. Benton Harbor, MI, Dec. 17, 1945. e. Wayne St. Univ., Yale Sch. of Drama. Former Actors Ensemble Theater while in Detroit. Stage debut in L.A. production of Daddy Goodness.
PICTURES: Leadbelly (debut, 1976), The Main Event, The Jazz Singer, Penitentiary II, Spacehunter: Adventures in the Forbidden Zone, Going Berserk, Ghostbusters, The Joy of Sex, Weeds, Leviathan, Ghostbusters II, The Hand That Rocks the Cradle, Sugar Hill, No Escape, The Crow, The Cowboy Way, Airheads, Speechless, The Basketball Diaries, Congo, The Substitute, Operation Delta Force, Levitation, Fakin' Da Funk, Mr Magoo, Stranger in the Kingdom, Butter, Lillie, Shark Attack, Paper Bullets, Interceptors, Hijack, Everything's Jake, Red Letters, The Watcher, Miss Congeniality, Anne B. Real, Halfway Decent.
TELEVISION: *Movies*: White Mama, Dirty Dozen: The Fatal Mission, Love on the Run, Clover, Tornado!, The Cherokee Kid, Miracle on the 17th Green, Nowhere to Land, Walking Shadow, A Town Without Christmas. *Guest*: Fantasy Island, Little House on the Praire, One Day at a Time, Diff'rent Strokes, St. Elsewhere. *Mini-Series*: Roots: The Next Generations, Wild Palms. *Series*: Highcliffe Manor, The Last Precinct, Broken Badges, Oz, H.R.T., 10-8.

HUDSON, HUGH
Producer, Director. b. England. e. Eton. Began career as head of casting dept. with ad agency in London; left for Paris to work as editor for small film co. Returned to London to form Cammell-Hudson-Brownjohn Film Co., production house., turning out award-winning documentaries (Tortoise and Hare, A is for Apple). 1970, joined Ridley Scott to make TV commercials. 1975, formed Hudson Films to produce.
PICTURES: Director: Chariots of Fire, Greystoke: The Legend of Tarzan Lord of the Apes (also prod.), Revolution, Lost Angels, Lumiere and Company, My Life So Far, I Dreamed of Africa.

HUEY, WARD L. JR.,
Media Executive. b. Dallas, TX, Apr. 26, 1938. e. So. Meth. U, BA, 1960. With dept. prodn., sales svc. mgr., regional sales mgr., gen sales mgr. Sta. WFAA-TV, TX 1960-67; sta. mgr., 1972-75. V.p. gen. mgr. Belo Broadcasting Corp., 1975; vice chmn. bd. dirs., pres. broadcast div, Belo Corp., 1987-July 2000. Chmn. affiliate bd. govs. ABC-TV, 1981-82. Chmn. bd. TV Operators Caucus, 1989. Mem.: exec. com., So. Meth. U. Meadows Sch. Arts, 1986-; So. Meth. U. Bd. of Trustees; a Trustee of the Belo Foundation. Goodwill Industries Dallas, 1978-79; State Fair Tex., 1992. Bd. Dirs.: Children's Med. Found., 1985-94; Dallas Found. 1993-. Mem.: Maximum Svc TV Assn. (vice chmn., 1988-94); TV Bur. ADvt. (bd. dirs., exec. com., 1984-88); Assn. Broadast Execs. Tex. (bd. dirs., 1977-78); Dallas Advt. league (bd. dirs 1975-76); Salesman Club Dallas (pres. 1992-93); Dallas Country Club.

HUGH-KELLY, DANIEL
Actor. b. Hoboken, NJ, Aug. 10, 1949. Began acting with the National Players touring U.S. in such plays as Henry IV Part 1, Charlie's Aunt, School for Wives.
THEATRE: Arena Stage (DC): An Enemy of the People, Once in a Lifetime, Long Day's Journey Into Night. Actors Theatre (Louisville): Much Ado About Nothing, The Best Man, The Taming of the Shrew, The Rainmaker. Off-B'way: Hunchback of Notre Dame, Miss Margarita's way, Juno's Swans, Fishing, Short-Changed Revue. B'way: Born Yesterday, Cat on a Hot Tin Roof.
PICTURES: Cujo, Nowhere to Hide, Someone to Watch Over Me, The Good Son, Bad Company, Star Trek: Insurrection, Chill Factor, The In Crowd, Guardian.
TELEVISION: Movies: Nutcracker, Thin Ice, Murder Ink, Night of Courage, Citizen Cohn, Moment of Truth: A Mother's Deception, A Child's Cry for Help, The Tuskegee Airmen, Never Say Never: The Deidre Hall Story, No Greater Love, Stranger in My Home, Five Desperate Hours, Bad As I Wanna Be: The Dennis Rodman Story, Labor of Love, Atomic Dog, Passing Glory, Growing Up Brady, Joe and Max. Mini-Series: From the Earth to the Moon, Jackie Ethel Joan: The Women of Camelot. Series: Chicago Story, Hardcastle and McCormick, Second Noah, Ponderosa (2001).

HUGHES, BARNARD
Actor. b. Bedford Hills, NY, July 16, 1915. Winner of Emmy for role as Judge in Lou Grant series (1978) and Tony Award for Da (1978). Inducted into Theatre Hall of Fame (1993).
PICTURES: Midnight Cowboy, Where's Poppa?, Cold Turkey, The Pursuit of Happiness, The Hospital, Rage, Sisters, Deadhead Miles, Oh God!, First Monday in October, Tron, Best Friends, Maxie, Where Are the Children?, The Lost Boys, Da, Doc Hollywood, Sister Act 2: Back in the Habit, The Odd Couple II, Cradle Will Rock, The Fantasticks.
TELEVISION: Movies: Guilty or Innocent, The Sam Sheppard Murder Case, See How She Runs, The Caryl Chessman Story, Tell Me My Name, Look Homeward, Angel, Father Brown: Detective, Nova, Homeward Bound, The Sky's No Limit, A Caribbean Mystery, Night of Courage, A Hobo's Christmas, Day One, Home Fires Burning, Guts and Glory: The Rise and Fall of Oliver North, The Incident, Miracle Child, Trick of the Eye, Past the Bleachers. Series: Doc, Mr. Merlin, The Cavanaughs, Blossom. Guest: Homicide, The Marshal.

HUGHES, JOHN
Writer, Director, Producer. b. Detroit, MI, Feb. 18, 1950. e. Univ. of AZ. Editor of National Lampoon before writing film script of National Lampoon's Class Reunion (1982). Made directorial debut with Sixteen Candles in 1984 which also wrote. In 1985 entered into deal with Paramount Pictures to write, direct and produce films with his own production unit, The John Hughes Co.
PICTURES: Writer: National Lampoon's Class Reunion, National Lampoon's Vacation, Mr. Mom, Nate and Hayes, Sixteen Candles (also dir.), The Breakfast Club (also dir., co-prod.), National Lampoon's European Vacation, Weird Science (also dir.), Pretty in Pink (also co-exec. prod.), Beethoven's 4th (video, writer, as Edmond Dantes), Big Paw: Beethoven 5 (video), Maid in Manhattan (as Edmond Dantes). Writer/Prod.: Ferris Bueller's Day Off (also dir.), Some Kind of Wonderful, Planes Trains & Automobiles (also dir.), She's Having a Baby (also dir.), The Great Outdoors (exec. prod., s.p.), Uncle Buck (also dir.), National Lampoon's Christmas Vacation, Home Alone, Career Opportunities (exec. prod., co-s.p.), Only the Lonely (co-prod. only), Dutch, Curly Sue (also dir.), Home Alone 2: Lost in New York, Dennis the Menace, Baby's Day Out, Miracle on 34th Street, 101 Dalmations, Reach the Rock, Flubber, Home Alone 3, Reach the Rock, Just Visiting, Uptown Girl, New Port South (prod. only).

HUGHES, KATHLEEN
Actress. r.n. Betty von Gerkan; b. Hollywood, CA, Nov. 14, 1928. e. Los Angeles City Coll., UCLA. m. Stanley Rubin, prod., mother of 4, Michael played Baby Matthew on Peyton Place. Studied drama; under contract, 20th-Fox, 1948-51; starred in Seven Year Itch 1954, La Jolla Playhouse; signed by UI, 1952. Theatre includes You Can't Take It With You, An Evening With Tennessee Williams, The Bar Off Melrose.
PICTURES: Road House, Mother is a Freshman, Mr. Belvedere Goes to College, Take Care of My Little Girl, It Happens Every Spring, When Willie Comes Marching Home, My Blue Heaven, Mister 880, No Way Out, I'll See You in My Dreams, Thy Neighbor's Wife, For Men Only (The Tall Lie), Sally and Saint Anne, Golden Blade, It Came From Outer Space, Dawn at Socorro, Glass Web, Cult of the Cobra, Three Bad Sisters, Promise Her Anything, The President's Analyst, The Take, Pete and Tillie, Ironweed, The Couch Trip, Revenge, Welcome to Hollywood.
TELEVISION: Movies: Babe, Forbidden Love, The Spell, Portrait of an Escort, Capitol, Mirror, Mirror, And Your Name is Jonah. Guest: Bob Cummings Show, Hitchcock, 77 Sunset Strip, G.E. Theatre, Bachelor Father, Frank Sinatra Show, Ed Wynn Show, Alan Young Show, The Tall Man, Dante, Tightrope, Markham, I Dream of Jeannie, Peyton Place, Gomer Pyle, Kismet, Ghost and Mrs. Muir, Bracken's World, The Survivors, Julia, Here's Lucy, To Rome with Love, The Interns, The Man and the City, Mission Impossible, The Bold Ones, Lucas Tanner, Marcus Welby, Barnaby Jones, Medical Center, M.A.S.H., General Hospital, Quincy, Finder of Lost Loves, The Young and the Restless.

HUGHES, WENDY
Actress. b. Melbourne, Australia, July 29, 1952. Studied acting at National Institute of Dramatic Art, Sydney.
PICTURES: Petersen, Sidecar Racers, High Rolling, Newsfront, My Brilliant Career, Kostas, Lucinda Brayford, Touch and Go, Hoodwink, A Dangerous Summer, Partners, Duet for Four, Lonely Hearts, Careful He Might Hear You, My First Wife, Remember Me, An Indecent Obsession, Happy New Year, Echoes of Paradise, Warm Nights on a Slow Moving Train, Boundaries of the Heart, Luigi's Ladies (also co-s.p.), Wild Orchid II, Princess Caraboo, Lust & Revenge, Paradise Road, The Man Who Sued God.
TELEVISION: Movies: Coralie Landsdowne Says No, Puzzle, Promises to Keep, Can't Get Started, The Heist, Donor. Mini-series: Power Without Glory, Return to Eden, Amerika, A Woman Named Jackie, Series: Rush, Snowy River: The McGregor Saga, State Coroner. Guest: Star Trek: The Next Generation, Homicide: Life on the Street.

HUIZENGA, HARRY WAYNE
Entrepreneur, Entertainment Executive. b. Evergreen Park, IL, Dec 29, 1939. e. Calvin College, 1957-58. m. Martha Jean Pike, Apr. 17, 1972. Vice chmn., pres., chief operating officer Waste Mgmt. Inc., Oak Brook, IL, 1968-84; prin. Huizenga Holdings, Inc., Ft. Lauderdale, FL, 1984-; chmn., chief exec. officer Blockbuster Entertainment Corp., Ft. Lauderdale, 1987-1995, at which time sold to Viacom; Various ownership in sport enterprises: owns Miami Dolphins, Joe Robbie Stadium, Pro Player Stadium in South Florida. Part-owner NHL's Panthers; former owner of Florida Marlins.
MEMBERSHIPS/RECOGNITIONS: Florida Victory Com., 1988-89, Team Repub. Nat. com., Washington, 1988-90. Recipient Entrepeneur of Yr. award Wharton Sch. U. Pa., 1989, Excalibur award Bus. Leader of Yr. News/Sun Sentinel, 1990, Silver Medallion Brotherhood award Broward Region Nat. Conf. Christians and Jews, 1990, Laureates award Jr. Achievement Broward and Palm Beach Counties, 1990, Jim Murphy Humanitarian Award The Emerald Soc., 1990, Entrepreneur of Yr. award Disting. Panel Judges Fla., 1990, Man of Yr. Billboard/Time Mag., 1990, Man of Yr. Juvenile Diabetes Found., 1990, Florida Free Enterpriser of Yr. award Fla. Coun. on Econ. Edn., 1990, commendation for youth restricted video State of Fla. Office of Gov., 1989, Hon. Mem. Appreciation award Bond Club Ft. Lauderdale, 1989, honored with endowed teaching chair Broward Community Coll., 1990. Mem. Lauderdale Yacht Club, Tournament Players Club, Coral Ridge Country Club, Fisher Island Club, Ocean Reef Club, Cat Cay Yacht Club, Linville Ridge Country Club.
PROFESSIONAL AFFILIATIONS: Director for: AutoNation, Inc.; ANC Rental Corporation; NationsRent, Inc.; Republic Services, Inc. Chairman of: Boca Resorts, Inc.; Extended Stay America, Inc.; Miami Dolphins Ltd., Inc. and owner). Former chmn. of AutoNation, Inc.; Huizenga Holdings, Inc; & former vice chmn. of Zix Corporation. Still active in various global entreprunial business ventures.

HULCE, TOM
Actor. b. White Water, WI, Dec. 6, 1953. e. NC School of the Arts. Understudied and then co-starred in Equus on Broadway. Directorial stage debut Sleep Around Town. Appeared in IMAX

film Wings of Courage. Recipient of Emmy Award, 1996.
THEATRE: A Memory of Two Mondays, Julius Caesar, Candida, The Sea Gull, The Rise and Rise of Daniel Rocket, Eastern Standard, A Few Good Men (Tony nom.), Hamlet.
PICTURES: September 30, 1955 (debut, 1978), National Lampoon's Animal House, Those Lips Those Eyes, Amadeus (Acad. Award nom.), Echo Park, Slamdance, Dominick and Eugene, Parenthood, Shadowman, The Inner Circle, Fearless, Mary Shelley's Frankenstein, Wings of Courage, The Hunchback of Notre Dame (voice), Paul Monette: The Brink of Summer's End, Hunchback of Notre Dame II (voice), A Home at the End of the World (prod. only).
TELEVISION: Movies: Murder in Mississippi, Black Rainbow, The Heidi Chronicles. Mini-Series: The Adams Chronicles. Specials: Emily Emily, The Rise and Rise of Daniel Rocket, Song of Myself, Forget-Me-Not Lane, Tall Tales and Legends (John Henry).

HUNDT, REED
Executive. b. Ann Arbor, MI, March 3, 1948. B.A. Yale 1969, J.D. 1974. Served on various U.S. circuit courts 1975-80. Associate Latham & Watkins 1975, partner 1982. Named to FCC in 1994 as Chairman. Resigned 1997. Serves as chmn., The Forum on Communications and Society at The Aspen Institute; is a senior advisor on information industries to McKinsey & Company, and as a special advisor to Blackstone Group. Also currently a venture partner at Benchmark Capital, a principal of Charles Ross Partners, LLC; member of the board of directors, Intel Corp. Also a director for: Allegiance Telecom, Inc. & Expedia, Inc.

HUNNICUT, GAYLE
Actress. b. Fort Worth, TX, February 6, 1943. e. UCLA, B.A., with honors, theater arts & English major. Early career, community theatres in Los Angeles.
THEATRE: The Ride Across Lake Constance, Twelfth Night, The Tempest, Dog Days, The Admirable Crichton, A Woman of No Importance, Hedda Gabler, Peter Pan, Macbeth, Uncle Vanya, The Philadelphia Story, Miss Firecracker Contest, Exit The King, The Doctor's Dilemma, So Long on Lonely Street, The Big Knife, Edith Wharton at Home, The Little Foxes, Dangerous Corner.
PICTURES: The Wild Angels (debut, 1966), P.J., Eye of the Cat, Marlowe, Fragment of Fear, The Freelance, Voices, Running Scared, Legend of Hell House, Scorpio, L'Homme Sans Visage, The Spiral Staircase, The Sell Out, Strange Shadows in an Empty Room, Once in Paris, One Take Two, Fantomas, Privilege, Sherlock Holmes, Target, Dream Lover, Turnaround, Silence Like Glass.
TELEVISION: Movies: The Smugglers, The Million Dollar Face, The Return of the Man From U.N.C.L.E., The First Olympics: Athens 1896, Voices in the Garden. Series: Dallas (1989-91). Specials: Man and Boy, The Golden Bowl, The Ambassadors, The Ripening Seed, Fall of Eagles, The Switch, Humboldt's Gift, The Life and Death of Dylan Thomas, Return of the Saint, The Lady Killers, Savage in the Orient, Strong Medicine. Mini-Series: A Man Called Intrepid, The Martian Chronicles, Dream West. Guest: Taxi.

HUNT, HELEN
Actress. b. Los Angeles, CA, June 15, 1963. Daughter of dir. Gordon Hunt.
THEATRE: Been Taken, Our Town, The Taming of the Shrew, Methusalem.
PICTURES: Rollercoaster, Girls Just Want to Have Fun, Peggy Sue Got Married, Project X, Miles From Home, Trancers, Stealing Home, Next of Kin, The Waterdance, Only You, Bob Roberts, Mr. Saturday Night, Kiss of Death, Twister, As Good as It Gets (Acad. Award, Golden Globe Award, Best Actress, 1997), Twister: Ride it Out, Dr. T and the Women, Pay it Forward, Cast Away, What Women Want, The Curse of the Jade Scorpion, Pulse Pounders, Timepiece (co-prod. only).
TELEVISION: Movies: Pioneer Woman, All Together Now, Death Scream, The Spell, Transplant, Angel Dusted, Child Bride of Short Creek, The Miracle of Kathy Miller, Quarterback Princess, Bill: On His Own, Sweet Revenge, Incident at Dark River, Into the Badlands, Murder in New Hampshire: The Pamela Smart Story, In the Company of Darkness. Specials: Weekend, Land of Little Rain, Twelfth Night. Special: Sexual Healing. Series: Swiss Family Robinson, Amy Prentiss, The Fitzpatricks, It Takes Two, Mad About You (Emmy Award, 1996, 1997, 1999; Golden Globe Award, 1997). Guest: St. Elsewhere, Family, Mary Tyler Moore Show, The Hitchhiker, The Simpsons (voice).

HUNT, LINDA
Actress. b. Morristown, NJ, Apr. 2, 1945. e. Interlochen Arts Acad., MI, and Chicago's Goodman Theatre & Sch. of Drama. Narrated documentary Ecological Design: Inventing the Future.
THEATRE: Long Wharf (New Haven):Hamlet, The Rose Tattoo, Ah Wilderness. NY: Mother Courage, End of the World (Tony nom.), A Metamorphosis in Miniature (Obie Award), Top Girls (Obie Award), Aunt Dan and Lemon, The Cherry Orchard. Regional: The Three Sisters.
PICTURES: Popeye (debut, 1980) The Year of Living Dangerously (Academy Award, best supporting actress, 1983), The Bostonians, Dune, Silverado, Eleni, Waiting for the Moon, She-Devil, Kindergarten Cop, If Looks Could Kill, Rain Without Thunder, Twenty Bucks, Younger and Younger, Ready to Wear (Pret-a-Porter), Pocahontas (voice), The Relic, Eat Your Heart Out, Amazon, Paul Monette: The Brink of Summer's End, Amazon, Out of the Past, Pocahontas II: Journey to a New World (voice), Island of the Sharks, Dragonfly, Shadow Play: Indonesia's Year of Living Dangerously (documentary, narrator).
TELEVISION: Movies: The Room Upstairs. Specials: Ah Wilderness, The Room. Guest: Fame. Mini-Series: The Century. Series: Space Rangers, The Practice, Before We Ruled the Earth (host, voice).

HUNT, MARSHA
Actress. b. Chicago, IL, Oct. 17, 1917.
THEATRE: B'way: Joy to the World, Devils Disciple, Legend of Sarah, Borned in Texas, Tunnel of Love, The Paisley Convertible.
PICTURES: The Virginia Judge (debut, 1935), College Holiday, Easy to Take, Blossoms in the Dust, Panama Hattie, Joe Smith American, These Glamour Girls, Winter Carnival, Irene, Pride and Prejudice, Flight Command, The Affairs of Martha, Kid Glove Killer, Seven Sweethearts, Cheers for Miss Bishop, Trial of Mary Dugan, Lost Angel, Cry Havoc, Bride by Mistake, Music for Millions, Valley of Decision, A Letter for Evie, Smash-Up, Carnegie Hall, The Inside Story, Raw Deal, Take One False Step, Actors and Sin, Happy Time, No Place to Hide, Back from the Dead, Bombers B-52, Blue Denim, The Plunderers, Johnny Got His Gun.
TELEVISION: Movies: Fear No Evil, Jigsaw, Terror Among Us. Series: Peck's Bad Girl. Guest: Philco, Studio One, Ford Theatre, Show of Shows, G.E. Theatre, Climax, Hitchcock, The Defenders, Twilight Zone, Cains Hundred, Gunsmoke, The Breaking Point, Outer Limits, Profiles in Courage, Ben Casey, Accidental Family, Run For Your Life, My Three Sons, The Outsiders, Name of the Game, Univ.'s 120, Ironside, Marcus Welby, M.D., Police Story, The Young Lawyers, Harry-O, The Mississippi, Hot Pursuit, Shadow Chaser, Matlock, Murder She Wrote, Star Trek: The Next Generation.

HUNT, PETER R.
Director, Editor. b. London, England,, March 11, 1928. e. Romford, England and Rome, Italy, London Sch. of Music. Actor English Rep. Entered film as camera asst. documentary, later asst film editor documentary, then asst editor features, London Films.
PICTURES: Editor: Stranger from Venus (Immediate Decision), Doublecross, A Hill in Korea, Secret Tent, Admirable Crichton, A Cry From the Streets, Next to No Time, Ferry to Hong Kong, Sink the Bismark!, There was a Crooked Man, The Greengage Summer (Loss of Innocence), On the Fiddle (Operation Snafu) H.M.S. Defiant (Damn the Defiant). Supervising editor/2nd Unit Director: Dr. No, Call Me Bwana, From Russia With Love,Goldfinger, The Ipcress File, Thunderball, You Only Live Twice. Assoc. Prod.: Chitty Chitty Bang Bang. Director: On Her Majesty's Secret Service, Gullivers Travels, Gold, Shout at the Devil, Death Hunt, Wild Geese II, Hyper Sapien, Assassination.
TELEVISION: Director: Series: The Persuaders, Shirley's World, The Pencil, Smart Alec Kill (Philip Marlowe). Movies: The Beasts Are in the Streets, Eyes of a Witness. Mini-Series: Last Days of Pompeii.
(d. Aug. 14, 2002)

HUNT, PETER H.
Director. b. Pasadena, CA, Dec. 16, 1938. e. Hotchkiss, Yale U., Yale Drama Sch. m. actress Barbette Tweed. Dir. for Williamston Theatre since 1957. Lighting designer on B'way. (1963-69) Awards: Tony, Ace, Peabody (twice), N.Y. Drama Critics, London Drama Critics, Edgar Allan Poe, Christopher.
THEATRE: 1776 (London & B'way.), Georgy (B'way.), Scratch (B'way.), Goodtime Charley (B'way.), Give 'Em Hell Harry, Magnificent Yankee (Kennedy Center). Tours: Bully, Three Penny Opera, Sherlock Holmes, Bus Stop.
PICTURES: 1776, Give 'Em Hell Harry.
TELEVISION: Specials: Adventures of Huckleberry Finn, Life on the Mississippi, A Private History of a Campaign That Failed, A New Start, Mysterious Stranger, Sherlock Holmes (cable), Bus Stop (cable). Movies: Flying High, Rendezvous Motel, When She Was Bad, Skeezer, The Parade, Sins of the Past, It Came Upon the Midnight Clear, Charley Hannah, Danielle Steel's Secrets, Sworn to Vengeance, four Hart to Hart movies. Pilots: Adam's Rib, Hello Mother Goodbye, Ivan the Terrible, Quark, Mixed Nuts, Wilder and Wilder, The Main Event, Nuts and Bolts, The Good Witch of Laurel Canyon, Masquerade, Stir Crazy, The Wizard of Elm Street, Travelling Man, My Africa., Dead Man's Island. Series: One West Waikiki, Touched by an Angel, Bay Watch Nights, Promised Land.

HUNT, WILLIE
Executive Producer. b. Van Nuys, CA, Oct. 1, 1941. e. Utah State U., B.A., 1963. m. writer Tim Considine. Started in industry as secretary at Warner Bros., 1965; named exec. secty. to Ted Ashley, WB, 1969; story analyst, WB, 1974; story editor, WB, 1975; named West Coast story editor for WB, 1978; joined MGM in 1979 as v.p., motion picture development. Moved to U,A, as v.p.-prod., 1982. 1983 sr. v.p. of prod. at Rastar Prods.; 1984, indep. prod., Tri-Star; 1986, sr. v.p., Freddie Fields Prods. 1988: Loverboy (co-prod.) 1989, sr. v.p. Considine Prods. 1993, partner, Creative Entertainment Group.

HUNTER, HOLLY
Actress. b. Conyers, GA. March 20, 1958. e. studied acting, Carnegie-Mellon Univ. Appeared Off-B'way in Battery (1981) and Weekend Near Madison. Appeared in 5 Beth Henley plays: The Miss Firecracker Contest (Off-B'way), as a replacement in Crimes of the Heart (B'way) The Wake of Jamey Foster (B'way), Lucky Spot (Williamstown Theater Festival), and Control Freaks (L.A.; also co-prod.). Also: A Lie of the Mind (L.A.).
PICTURES: The Burning (debut, 1981), Swing Shift, Raising Arizona, Broadcast News (NY Film Critics, LA Film Critics and Natl. Board of Review Awards, Acad. Award nom., 1987), End of the Line, Miss Firecracker, Animal Behavior, Always, Once Around, The Firm (Acad. Award nom.), The Piano (Academy Award, Cannes Film Fest., LA Film Critics, NY Film Critics, Natl. Board of Review, Natl. Society of Film Critics & Golden Globe Awards, 1993), Home for the Holidays, Copycat, Crash, A Life Less Ordinary, Living Out Loud, Woman Wanted, Jesus' Son, Things You Can Tell Just By Looking At Her, Timecode, O Brother Where Art Thou?, Down From the Mountain, Festival in Cannes, Searching for Debra Winger, Moonlight Mile, Levity, Thirteen (also exec. prod).
TELEVISION: Movies: Svengali, An Uncommon Love, With Intent to Kill, A Gathering of Old Men, Roe vs. Wade (Emmy Award, 1989), Crazy in Love, The Positively True Adventures of the Alleged Texas Cheerleader-Murdering Mom (Emmy Award, 1993), When Billy Beat Bobby, Harlan County War. Guest: Fame (pilot).

HUNTER, KIM
Actress. r.n. Janet Cole. b. Detroit, MI, Nov. 12, 1922. e. public schools. d. Donald and Grace Mabel (Lind) Cole. Studied acting with Charmine Lantaff Camine, 1938-40, Actors Studio; First stage appearance, 1939; played in stock, 1940-42; Broadway debut in A Streetcar Named Desire, 1947; frequent appearances in summer stock and repertory theater, 1940-; appeared Am. Shakespeare Festival, Stratford, CT, 1961. Autobiography-cookbook: Loose in the Kitchen (1975).
THEATRE: Over 50 NY and Regional productions.
PICTURES: The Seventh Victim (debut, 1943), Tender Comrade, When Strangers Marry (Betrayed), You Came Along, Stairway to Heaven (A Matter of Life and Death), A Canterbury Tale, A Streetcar Named Desire (Academy Award, best supporting actress, 1951), Anything Can Happen, Deadline: U.S.A., The Young Stranger, Bermuda Affair, Storm Center, Money Women and Guns, Lilith, Planet of the Apes, The Swimmer, Beneath the Planet of the Apes, Escape from the Planet of the Apes, Dark August, The Kindred, Two Evil Eyes, Midnight in the Garden of Good and Evil, A Price Above Rubies, A Smaller Place, Abilene, Out of the Cold, Here's to Life!, Broadway: The Golden Age by the Legends Who Were There.
TELEVISION: Made TV debut on Actors Studio Program, 1948. Series: The Edge of Night (1979-80). Specials: Requiem for a Heavyweight, The Comedian (both on Playhouse 90); Give Us Barabbas, Stubby Pringle's Christmas, Project: U.F.O., Three Sovereigns for Sarah, Vivien Leigh: Scarlett and Beyond, Martin Luther King: The Dream and the Drum, AFI's 100 Years, 100 Thrills: America's Most Heart-Pounding Movies. Guest: Love American Style, Columbo, Cannon, Night Gallery, Mission Impossible, Marcus Welby, Hec Ramsey, Griff, Police Story, Ironside, Medical Center, Baretta, Gibbsville, The Oregon Trail, Scene of the Crime, Hunter, Murder She Wrote, Class of '96, Mad About You, L.A. Law, All My Children, As the World Turns. Movies: Dial Hot Line, In Search of America, The Magician (pilot), Unwed Father, Born Innocent, Bad Ronald, Ellery Queen (Too Many Suspects), The Dark Side of Innocence, The Golden Gate Murders, F.D.R.: The Last Year, Skokie, Private Sessions, Drop-Out Mother, Cross of Fire, Bloodlines: Murder in the Family, Hurricane Andrew, Larry and Vivien: The Oliviers in Love, Blue Moon. Mini-Series: Once an Eagle, Backstairs at the White House.
(d. Sept. 11, 2002)

HUNTER, TAB
Actor. r.n. Arthur Gelien. b. New York, NY, July 11, 1931. Served with U.S. Coast Guard. Entered industry in 1948.
PICTURES: The Lawless (debut, 1950), Island of Desire, Gun Belt, Steel Lady, Return to Treasure Island, Track of the Cat, Battle Cry, Sea Chase, The Burning Hills, The Girl He Left Behind, Lafayette Escadrille, Gunman's Walk, Damn Yankees, That Kind of Woman, They Came to Cordura, The Pleasure of His Company, Operation Bikini, The Golden Arrow, Ride the Wild Surf, The Loved One, War Gods of the Deep, Birds Do It, Fickle Finger of Fate, Hostile Guns, The Arousers (Sweet Kill), Life and Times of Judge Roy Bean, Timber Tramp, Won Ton Ton the Dog Who Saved Hollywood, Polyester, Pandemonium, Grease 2, Lust in the Dust (also co-prod.), Cameron's Closet, Grotesque, Out of the Dark, Dark Horse (also story), Wild Bill: Hollywood Maverick.
TELEVISION: Movies: San Francisco International, Katie: Portrait of a Centerfold. Series: The Tab Hunter Show, Mary Hartman Mary Hartman.

HUNTER, TIM
Director. e. Harvard, AFI.
PICTURES: Over the Edge (co-s.p.). Dir.: Tex (also s.p.), Sylvester, River's Edge, Paint It Black, The Saint of Fort Washington, The Maker, Reflections of Eden, The Failures.
TELEVISION: Movies: Lies of the Twins, People Next Door, Rescuers: Stories of Courage, Anatomy of a Hate Crime. Mini-

series: Out of Order. Series: Homicide: Life on the Street, Chicago Hope, Nowhere Man, Sins of the City, Soul Food, Carnivale.

HUPPERT, ISABELLE
Actress. b. Paris, France, March 16, 1955. e. Conservatoire National d'Art Dramatique.
PICTURES: Faustine and the Beautiful Summer (Growing Up; debut, 1971), Cesar and Rosalie, Going Places, Rosebud, The Rape of Innocence, The Judge and the Assassin, The Lacemaker, Violette (Cannes Fest. Award, 1977), The Bronte Sisters, Loulou, Heaven's Gate, Coup de Torchon, Every Man for Himself, The True Story of Camille, Wings of the Dove, Deep Water, Entre Nous, The Trout, Cactus, Signed Charlotte, The Bedroom Window, The Possessed, Story of Women (Venice Fest Award, 1988), Milan Noir, Madame Bovary, Revenge of a Woman, Malina, Apres l'Amour (After Love), Amateur, The Separation, A Judgment in Stone, Love's Debris, The Elective Affinities, Les Palmes de M. Schultz, Rien ne va Plus, Keep it Quiet, Modern Life, False Servant, The King's Daughters, Les Destinees Sentimentales, Comedy of Innocence, Nightcap, Clara, La Pianiste, 8 femmes, La Vie Promise, Deux, Ghost River, Le Temps du loup.
TELEVISION: Movies: Médée. Gulliver's Travels (voice). Mini-series: Seobe.

HURD, GALE ANNE
Producer. b. Los Angeles, CA, Oct. 25, 1955. e. Stanford U., Phi Beta Kappa, 1977. Joined New World Pictures in 1977 as exec. asst. to pres. Roger Corman, then named dir. of advertising and pub. and moved into prod. management capacities on several New World films. Left in 1982 to form own co., Pacific Western Productions. Honored by NATO with special merit award for Aliens. Served as juror, U.S. Film Fest., Utah, 1988 and for 1989 Focus Student Film Awards. Member, Hollywood Women's Political Committee. Board of Trustees, AFI. The Amer. Film Inst. created Gale Anne Hurd production grants for Institute's Directing Workshop for Women. Bd. of dir. The Independent Feature Project/West.
PICTURES: Smokey Bites the Dust (co-prod. with Roger Corman, 1981), The Terminator (Grand Prix, Avoriaz Film Fest.,France), Aliens (Hugo Award) Alien Nation (Saturn nom.), The Abyss, Downtown (exec. prod.), Tremors (exec. prod.), Terminator 2 (exec. prod.), The Waterdance, Raising Cain, No Escape, Safe Passage, The Relic, The Ghost and The Darkness, Dante's Peak, Switchback, Snake Eyes, Armageddon, Dead Man on Campus, Virus, Dick, Clockstoppers, The Hulk, Terminator 3: Rise of the Machines (exec. prod., writer), The Punisher..
TELEVISION: Movies: Cast a Deadly Spell, Witch Hunt, Sugartime. Series: Adenture Inc. (exec. prod.)

HURLEY, ELIZABETH
Actress, Producer. b. Hampshire, England, June 10, 1965. Also model.
PICTURE: Rowing In the Wind, Aria, Kill Cruise, The Long Winter of '39, Passenger 57, Beyond Bedlam, Mad Dogs and Englishmen, Extreme Measures (prod. only), Dangerous Ground, Austin Powers: International Man of Mystery, Permanent Midnight, Austin Powers: The Spy Who Shagged Me, My Favorite Martian, Edtv, Mickey Blue Eyes (prod. only), The Weight of Water, Bedazzled, Double Whammy, Serving Sarah, Bad Boy, Psyclops (video, exec. prod.), Method (exec. prod.)
TELEVISION: Movies/Specials: Christabel, Act of Will, Death Has a Bad Reputation, Orchid House, Sharpe's Enemy, The World of 007 (host), Samson and Delilah, The Human Face. Guest: The Young Indiana Jones Chronicles.

HURT, JOHN
Actor. b. Shirebrook, Derbyshire, Jan. 22, 1940. e. St. Martin's Sch. for Art, London, RADA.
THEATRE: The Dwarfs, Little Malcolm and His Struggle Against the Eunichs, Man and Superman, Belcher's Luck, Ride a Cock Horse, The Caretaker, Romeo and Juliet, Ruffian on the Streets, The Dumb Waiter, Travesties, The Arrest, The Seagull, The London Vertigo, A Month in the Country.
PICTURES: The Wild and the Willing (debut, 1962), This is My Street, A Man for All Seasons, The Sailor from Gibraltar, Before Winter Comes, Sinful Davey, In Search of Gregory, 10 Rillington Place, Mr. Forbush and the Penguins, The Pied Piper, Little Malcolm, The Naked Civil Servant, La Linea del Fiume, The Ghoul, East of Elephant Rock, The Disappearance, Midnight Express (Acad. Award nom.), Watership Down (voice), The Lord of the Rings (voice), The Shout, Alien, The Elephant Man (Acad. Award nom.), Heaven's Gate, History of the World Part I, Night Crossing, Partners, The Plague Dogs (voice), The Osterman Weekend, Champions, The Hit, Success Is the Best Revenge, 1984, After Darkness, The Black Cauldron (voice), Jake Speed, From the Hip, Spaceballs, Aria, Vincent (voice), White Mischief, Little Sweetheart, Poison Candy, Bengali Night, Scandal, Frankenstein Unbound, The Field, King Ralph, Romeo-Juliet, Resident Alien, Windprints, I Dreamt I Woke Up, Lapse of Memory, Dark at Noon or Eyes and Lies, Monolith, Hans Christian Andersen's Thumbelina (voice), Even Cowgirls Get the Blues, Crime and Punishment, Great Moments in Aviation, Second Best, Betrayal (voice), Rob Roy, Wild Bill, Two Nudes Bathing, Saigon Baby, Dead Man, Love & Death on Long Island, Contact, The Climb, Bandyta, If... Dog... Rabbit, Desert Blue, The Commissioner, All the Little Animals, The Tigger Movie, Lost Souls, Crime and Punishment, Captain Corelli's Mandolin,

Harry Potter and the Sorcerer's Stone, Tabloid, Miranda, Owning Mahowny, Dogville (narrator), Hellboy.
TELEVISION: Playboy of the Western World, A Tragedy of Two Ambitions, Green Julia, Nijinsky, Ten from the Twenties, The Peddler, The Naked Civil Servant, Spectre, Deadline, The Jim Henson Hour, King Lear, The Investigation: Inside a Terrorist Bombing, Six Characters in Search of an Author, Shades of Fear, Prisoners in Time, Bait. *Mini-series*: Crime and Punishment, I Claudius, The Storyteller, Red Fox.

HURT, MARY BETH
Actress. r.n. Mary Beth Supinger. b. Marshalltown, IA, Sept. 26, 1946. m. writer-dir. Paul Schrader. e. U. of Iowa, NYU Sch. of Arts. Stage debut in 1973 with N.Y. Shakespeare Fest. (More Than You Deserve, Pericles, The Cherry Orchard).
THEATRE: As You Like It (Central Park), 2 seasons with Phoenix Theater, Love For Love, Tralawny of the Wells, Secret Service, Boy Meets Girl, Father's Day, Crimes of the Heart, The Misanthrope, Benefactors, The Nest of the Wood Grouse, The Day Room, Othello, A Delicate Balance.
PICTURES: Interiors (debut, 1978), Head Over Heels (Chilly Scenes of Winter), A Change of Seasons, The World According to Garp, D.A.R.Y.L., Compromising Positions, Parents, Slaves of New York, Defenseless, Light Sleeper, My Boyfriend's Back, The Age of Innocence, Six Degrees of Separation, From the Journals of Jean Seberg, Alkali Iowa, Affliction, Boy's Life 2, Bringing Out the Dead, Autumn in New York, The Family Man, Red Dragon.
TELEVISION: *Series*: Nick and Hillary, Working It Out. *Movies*: Baby Girl Scott, Shimmer, After Amy. *Specials*: The Five-Forty-Eight, Secret Service (NET Theatre). *Guest*: Kojak, Law and Order.

HURT, WILLIAM
Actor. b. Washington, DC, Mar. 20, 1950. Lived as child in South Pacific when father was dir. of Trust Territories for U.S. State Dept. e. Tufts as theology major, switched to drama in jr. year, Juilliard. Acted with Oregon Shakespearean Fest. Leading actor with New York's Circle Repertory Company (Theatre World Award), since 1976.
THEATRE: *NY*: The Fifth of July, My Life (Obie Award), Ulysses in Traction, The Runner Stumbles, Hamlet, Childe Byron, Beside Herself. *NY Shakespeare Festival*: Henry V, A Midsummer's Night's Dream, Hurlyburly (off-B'way and B'way). *Regional*: Good (S.F.), Ivanov (Yale).
PICTURES: Altered States (debut, 1980), Eyewitness, Body Heat, The Big Chill, Gorky Park, Kiss of the Spider Woman (Academy Award, 1985), Children of a Lesser God, Broadcast News, A Time of Destiny, The Accidental Tourist, I Love You to Death, Alice, The Doctor, Until the End of the World, Mr. Wonderful, The Plague, Trial by Jury, Second Best, Smoke, Jane Eyre, A Couch in New York, Michael, Loved, Dark City, The Proposition, Lost in Space, One True Thing, The Taste of Sunshine, The Big Brass Ring, The 4th Floor, The Simian Line, The Contaminated Man, Artificial Intelligence: AI, Rare Birds, Changing Lanes, Tuck Everlasting, Au plus pres du paradis, The Blue Butterfly.
TELEVISION: *Specials*: Verna: USO Girl, Best of Families, All the Way Home, The Odyssey of John Dos Passos (voice). *Movies*: The Miracle Maker, The Flamingo Rising, Varian's War., Frankenstein (2004). *Mini-Series*: Dune.

HUSSEY, OLIVIA
Actress. b. Buenos Aires, Apr. 17, 1951. Attended Italia Conti Stage School, London. Began acting at age 8.
PICTURES: The Battle of the Villa Fiorita (debut, 1965), Cup Fever, All the Right Noises, Romeo and Juliet, Summertime Killer, Lost Horizon, Black Christmas, Death on the Nile, The Cat and the Canary, Virus, The Man With Bogart's Face, Escape 2000, Distortions, The Jeweler's Shop, The Undeclared War, Save Me, Ice Cream Man, Bad English I: Tales of a Son of a Brit, Saving Grace, Shame Shame Shame, Tortilla Heaven, El Grito, Island Prey.
TELEVISION: *Movies/Mini-Series*: Jesus of Nazareth, The Pirate, The Bastard, Ivanhoe, Last Days of Pompeii, The Corsican Brothers, Psycho IV: The Beginning, Stephen King's IT, Save Me, Quest of the Delta Knights, H-Bomb, Dead Man's Island, Lonesome Dove, Shame, The Gardener. *Guest*: Murder She Wrote, Boy Meets World.

HUSTON, ANJELICA
Actress. b. Santa Monica, CA, July 8, 1951. Father is late writer-dir.-actor, John Huston. Brother is dir. Danny Huston. Raised in St. Clerans, Ireland. Studied acting at the Loft Studio and with Peggy Furey, Martin Landau. Appeared in 3-D Disney short Captain Eo.
PICTURES: A Walk With Love and Death (debut, 1969), Sinful Davey, Swashbuckler, The Last Tycoon, The Postman Always Rings Twice, Frances, The Ice Pirates, This is Spinal Tap, Prizzi's Honor (Academy Award, best supporting actress, 1985), Good to Go (Short Fuse), Gardens of Stone, The Dead, A Handful of Dust, Mr. North, Crimes and Misdemeanors, Enemies a Love Story (Acad. Award nom.), The Witches, The Grifters (Acad. Award nom.), The Addams Family, The Player (cameo), Manhattan Murder Mystery, Addams Family Values,

The Perez Family, The Crossing Guard, Bastard Out of Carolina (dir.), Buffalo '66, Phoenix, Ever After: A Cinderella Story, Agnes Browne (also dir., prod.), The Golden Bowl, Time of Our Lives, The Man from Elysian Fields, The Royal Tenenbaums, Searching for Debra Winger, Blood Work, Barbie as Rapunzel (video, voice), Daddy Day Care, Kaena: The Prophecy (voice).
TELEVISION: *Movies*: The Cowboy and the Ballerina, Family Pictures, And the Band Played On, Iron Jawed Angels. *Specials*: Faerie Tale Theatre, A Rose for Miss Emily. *Mini-Series*: Lonesome Dove, Buffalo Girls, The Mists of Avalon.

HUSTON, DANNY
Director. b. Rome, Italy, May 14, 1962. Youngest son of dir.-actor John Huston and actress Zoe Sallis. Brother of actress Anjelica and screenwriter Tony Huston. e. Overseas School, Rome; Intl branch of Milfield School in Exeter, London Film School. A constant visitor to his father's sets throughout the world, he began working on his father's films, beginning in Cuernavaca, Mexico as second-unit dir. on Under the Volcano. Directed TV doc. on Peru and on making of Santa Claus: The Movie; and TV features Bigfoot and Mr. Corbett's Ghost.
PICTURES: Mr. North (debut, 1988), Becoming Colette, The Maddening, Amparo. *Actor*: Leaving Las Vegas, Ana Karenina, Susan's Plan, Spanish Fly, Rockin' Good Times, Timecode, Ivansxtc, Eden, Hotel, The Bacchae, 21 Grams, Birth.
TELEVISION: *Movie*: Ice Princess.

HUTTON, BETTY
Actress. r.n. Betty June Thornburg. b. Battle Creek, MI, Feb. 26, 1921. Sister was singer-actress Marion Hutton. Was vocalist for Vincent Lopez orchestra earning nickname the Blonde Bombshell. Debuted on B'way 1940 in Two for the Show, followed by Panama Hattie. Signed by Paramount in 1941. Returned to stage in Fade Out Fade In, Annie.
PICTURES: The Fleet's In (debut, 1942), Star Spangled Rhythm, Happy Go Lucky, Let's Face It, The Miracle of Morgan's Creek, And the Angels Sing, Here Come the Waves, Incendiary Blonde, Duffy's Tavern, The Stork Club, Cross My Heart, The Perils of Pauline, Dream Girl, Red Hot and Blue, Annie Get Your Gun, Let's Dance, Sailor Beware (cameo), The Greatest Show on Earth, Somebody Loves Me, Spring Reunion.
TELEVISION: *Series*: The Betty Hutton Show (1959-60). *Special*: Satins and Spurs. *Guest*: Dinah Shore Chevy Show, Greatest Show on Earth, Burke's Law, Gunsmoke.

HUTTON, BRIAN, G.
Director. b. New York, NY, 1935. Started as bit player in films (incl. Fear Strikes Out, Gunfight at the O.K. Corral) before dir. for tv, then features.
PICTURES: The Wild Seed (debut, 1965), The Pad and How to Use It, Sol Madrid, Where Eagles Dare, Kelly's Heroes, X Y and Zee (Zee & Company), Night Watch, The First Deadly Sin, High Road to China, Hostile Takeover.
TELEVISION: Institute For Revenge.

HUTTON, LAUREN
Actress. r.n. Mary Laurence Hutton. b. Charleston, SC, Nov. 17, 1943. e. U. of South Florida, Sophie Newcombe Coll. As model featured on more covers than any other American. Stage debut at LA Public Theatre in Extremities.
PICTURES: Paper Lion (debut, 1968), Pieces of Dreams, Little Fauss and Big Halsy, Rocco Papaleo, The Gambler, Gator, Welcome to L.A., Viva Knievel!, A Wedding, American Gigolo, Paternity, Zorro the Gay Blade, Tout Feu tout Flamme (Hecate), Lassiter, Once Bitten, Flagrant Desire, Malone, Blue Blood, Bulldance (Forbidden Sun), Run For Your Life, Billions, Guilty as Charged, Missing Pieces, My Father the Hero, A Rat's Tale, 54, Loser Love, Just a Little Harmless Sex, The Venice Project.
TELEVISION: *Movies*: Someone Is Watching Me, Institute for Revenge, Starflight, The Cradle Will Fall, Scandal Sheet, The Return of Mike Hammer, Time Stalker, Monte Carlo, Perfect People, Fear, We the Jury, Caracara, The Last Witness, The Bunny Years. *Mini-Series*: The Rhinemann Exchange, Sins. *Series*: Paper Dolls, Falcon Crest, Lauren Hutton and... (talk show), Central Park West.

HUTTON, TIMOTHY
Actor, Director. b. Malibu, CA, Aug. 16, 1960. Father was late actor Jim Hutton. Debut in bit part in father's film Never Too Late. Acted in high school plays; toured with father in Harvey during vacation. Directed Cars video Drive (1984).
PICTURES: Never Too Late (debut, 1965), Ordinary People (Academy Award, best supporting actor, 1980; also Golden Globe & LA Film Critics Awards), Taps, Daniel, Iceman, The Falcon and The Snowman, Turk 182, Made in Heaven, A Time of Destiny, Betrayed (cameo), Everybody's All American, Torrents of Spring, Q&A, Strangers, The Temp, The Dark Half, French Kiss, Beautiful Girls, The Substance of Fire, City of Industry, City of Industry, Playing God, Deterrence, The General's Daughter, Deterrence, Just One Night, The Lucky Strike, Sunshine State.
TELEVISION: *Movies*: Zuma Beach, Friendly Fire, The Best Place to Be, And Baby Makes Six, Young Love First Love, Father Figure, A Long Way Home, Zelda, The Last Word, Mr. & Mrs. Loving, Dead by Midnight, Vig, Aldrich Ames: Traitor Within, Deliberate Intent, WWIII. *Director*: Amazing Stories (Grandpa's Ghost). *Series*: A Nero Wolfe Mystery.

HUVANE, KEVIN
Executive. b. New York, NY. e. Fordham U. Began career in mailroom of William Morris Agency in New York. Promoted to agent in motion picture talent department. 1988, joined Creative Artists Agency where he is currently a partner and managing dir. Helped to create the CAA Foundation which encourages philanthropy in the entertainment community and develops public/private partnerships to support educational programs and charities. Recipient of David Niven Award for his contribution to Project ALS (Lou Gehrig's Disease).

HUYCK, WILLARD
Writer, Director. e. USC. Worked as reader for Larry Gordon, executive at American-International Pictures; named Gordon's asst., working on scene rewrites for AIP films. First screen credit on The Devil's Eight as co-writer with John Milius.
PICTURES: Writer: American Graffiti , Dead People (also dir., prod.), Lucky Lady, More American Graffiti, French Postcards (also dir., prod.), Indiana Jones and the Temple of Doom, Best Defense (also dir.), Howard the Duck (also dir.), Radioland Murders.
TELEVISION: A Father's Homecoming (co-exec. prod., co-s.p.), American River (co-exec. prod., co-s.p.), Mothers-Daughters & Lovers (also exec. prod.).

HYAMS, JOSEPH
Advertising & Publicity Executive. b. New York, NY, Sept. 21, 1926. e. NYU Ent. industry, 1947. Various publicity posts, 20th Century-Fox, Columbia Pictures, 1947-55; eastern pub. mgr., Figaro Prods., 1955-56; West Coast pub. mgr., Hecht-Hill-Lancaster, 1955-58; pub. adv. dir., Batjac Prods. 1959-60 national adv. & pub. dir., Warner Bros.-7 Arts, 1960. v.p., worldwide pub., Warner Bros., Inc., 1970-87; sr. v.p., special projects, 1987.

HYAMS, PETER
Director, Writer, Cinematographer. b. New York, NY, July 26, 1943. e. Hunter Coll., Syracuse U. Joined CBS news staff N.Y. and made anchor man. Filmed documentary on Vietnam in 1966. Left CBS in 1970 and joined Paramount in Hollywood as writer. Hired by ABC to direct TV features.
PICTURES: Writer: T.R. Baskin (also prod.), Telefon, The Hunter. Exec. Prod.: The Monster Squad. Director: Busting (dir. debut 1974; also s.p.), Our Time (also s.p.), Peeper, Capricorn One (also s.p.), Hanover Street (also s.p.), Outland (also s.p.), The Star Chamber (also s.p.), 2010 (also prod., s.p., photog.), Running Scared (also exec. prod., photog.), The Presidio (also photog.), Narrow Margin (also s.p., photog.), Stay Tuned (also photog.), Timecop (also photog.), Sudden Death (also photog.), The Relic (also photog.), End of Days, The Musketeer (also photog.), Sound of Thunder.
TELEVISION: Movies (dir., writer): The Rolling Man, Goodnight My Love.

HYER, MARTHA
Actress. b. Fort Worth, TX, Aug. 10, 1924. e. Northwestern U., Pasadena Playhouse.
PICTURES: The Locket (debut, 1946), Thunder Mountain, Born to Kill, Woman on the Beach, The Velvet Touch, Gun Smugglers, The Judge Steps Out, Clay Pigeon, Roughshod, The Rustlers, The Lawless, Outcast of Black Mesa, Salt Lake Raiders, Frisco Tornado, Geisha Girl, The Kangaroo Kid, The Invisible Mr. Unmei, Wild Stallion, Yukon Gold, Abbott and Costello Go to Mars, So Big, Riders to the Stars, Scarlet Spear, Battle of Rogue River, Lucky Me, Down Three Dark Streets, Sabrina, Cry Vengeance, Wyoming Renegades, Kiss of Fire, Paris Follies of 1956, Francis in the Navy, Red Sundown, Showdown at Abilene, Battle Hymn, Kelly and Me, Mister Cory, The Delicate Delinquent, My Man Godfrey, Paris Holiday, Once Upon a Horse, Houseboat, Some Came Running (Acad. Award nom.), The Big Fisherman, The Best of Everything, Ice Palace, Desire in the Dust, Mistress of the World, The Right Approach, The Last Time I Saw Archie, Girl Named Tamiko, The Man from the Diner's Club, Wives and Lovers, Pyro, The Carpetbaggers, First Men in the Moon, Blood on the Arrow, Bikini Beach, The Sons of Katie Elder, The Chase, Night of the Grizzly, Picture Mommy Dead, War Italian Style, The Happening, Some May Live, Lo Scatenato (Catch as Catch Can), House of 1000 Dolls, Once You Kiss a Stranger, Crossplot, Day of the Wolves.
TELEVISION: Guest: Adventures of Wild Bill Hickock, Zane Gray Theatre, The Virginian, The Alfred Hitchcock Hour, Bewitched, The Young Lawyers.

HYMAN, DICK
Composer. b. New York, NY, March 8, 1927.
PICTURES: Erased Off, French Quarter, Stardust Memories, Zelig, Broadway Danny Rose (also mus. supv.), The Purple Rose of Cairo, Moonstruck, Thelonious Monk: Straight—No Chaser, Radio Days (mus. supv.), The Lemon Sisters, Alan & Naomi, Mighty Aphrodite, Everyone Says I Love You, Sweet & Lowdown, The Curse of the Jade Scorpion (band leader).
TELEVISION: Bernice Bobs Her Hair, The Last Tenant, Natica Jackson, Ask Me Again.

I

IANNUCCI, SALVATORE J.
Executive. b. Brooklyn, NY, Sept. 24, 1927. e. NYU, B.A., 1949; Harvard Law School, J.D., 1952. 2 yrs. legal departments RCA and American Broadcasting Companies, Inc.; 14 yrs. with CBS Television Network: asst. dir. of bus. affairs, dir. of bus. affairs, v.p. of bus. affairs; 2 yrs. v.p. admin. National General Corp.; 2-1/2 yrs. pres. of Capital Records; 4-1/2 yrs. Corp. v.p. and dir. of Entertainment Div. of Playboy Enterprises, Inc.; 4 yrs. partner with Jones, Day Reavis & Pogue in Los Angeles office, handling entertainment legal work; Pres., Filmways Entertainment, and sr. v.p., Filmways, Inc.; exec. v.p., Embassy Communications; COO, Aaron Spelling Prods.; sr. partner Bushkin, Gaims, Gaines, & Jonas; pres. and chief operating officer, Brad Marks International; prod. of features, tv movies and infomercials. Retired.

ICE CUBE
Actor, Singer. r.n. O'Shea Jackson. b. Los Angeles, CA, June 15, 1969. e. Phoenix Inst. of Tech. Debuted as rap performer with group N.W.A. Solo debut 1990 with album Amerikkka's Most Wanted.
PICTURES: Boyz N the Hood (debut, 1991), Trespass, CB4 (cameo), Higher Learning, Friday (also co-s.p., co-exec. prod.), The Glass Shield, Anaconda, Dangerous Ground (also exec. prod.), The Players' Club (also co-s.p., co-exec. prod., dir.), I Got the Hook-up, Three Kings, Next Friday (also co-s.p., co-exec. prod.), Ghosts of Mars, All About the Benjamins, Friday After Next, Torque, The Extractors, Barbershop.

ICE-T
Actor, Singer. r.n. Tracy Marrow. b. Newark, NJ, February 16, 1958. Raised in Los Angeles. Served 4 yrs. as ranger in U.S. Army. Made debut as rap performer with 1982 single The Coldest Rap. Received Grammy Award 1990 for Back on the Block.
PICTURES: Breakin' (debut, 1984), Breakin' 2: Electric Boogaloo, New Jack City, Ricochet, Trespass, Who's the Man?, Surviving the Game, Tank Girl, Johnny Mnemonic, Below Utopia, Rhyme & Reason (cameo), The Deli, Crazy Six, Jacob Two Two Meets the Hooded Fang, Final Voyage, Corrupt, The Wrecking Crew, Sonic Impact, Point Doom, The Heist, The Alternate, Leprechaun in the Hood, The Luck of the Draw, Los Angeles, Ablaze, 3000 Miles to Graceland, Deadly Rhapsody, R-Xmas, Ticker, Crime Partners 2000, Out Kold, Ablaze, Space Station, Playback, Air Rage, Stranded, Tracks, Pimpin' 101 (video, host, composer, 2002), Pimpin' 101 (video, host, 2003).
TELEVISION: Movies: Exiled. Series: Players, Law & Order: Special Victims Unit. Guest: New York Undercover.

IDLE, ERIC
Actor, Writer. b. South Shields, England, March 29, 1943. e. Pembroke Coll., Cambridge, 1962-65. Pres. Cambridge's Footlights appearing at Edinburgh Fest. 1963-64. Member Monty Python's Flying Circus appearing on BBC, 1969-74.
THEATRE: Oh What a Lovely War, Monty Python Live at the Hollywood Bowl, Monty Python Live, The Mikado (English Natl. Opera, 1986).
BOOKS: Hello Sailor, The Rutland Dirty Weekend Book, Pass the Butler; as well as co-author of Monty Python books: Monty Python's Big Red Book, The Brand New Monty Python Book, Monty Python and the Holy Grail, The Complete Works of Shakespeare and Monty Python.
PICTURES: And Now for Something Completely Different (also co-s.p.), Monty Python and the Holy Grail (also co-s.p.), Monty Python's Life of Brian (also co-s.p.), Monty Python Live at the Hollywood Bowl (also co-s.p.), Monty Python's The Meaning of Life (also co-s.p.), Yellowbeard, National Lampoon's European Vacation, Transformers (voice), The Adventures of Baron Munchausen, Nuns on the Run, Too Much Sun, Missing Pieces, Mom & Dad Save the World, Splitting Heirs (also s.p., exec. prod.), Casper, The Wind and the Willows, An Alan Smithee Film: Burn Hollywood Burn, Quest for Camelot, Dudley Do-Right, South Park: Bigger Longer and Uncut (voice), 102 Dalmations, Dudley Do-Right, Pirates: 3D Show (writer), Journey Into Your Imagination, It's Only Rock 'n' Roll (video documentary), Brightness (short), Pinocchio (voice, U.S. version), Hollywood Homicide, Ella Enchanted (narrator), Delgo (voice). TELEVISION: Isadora (debut, 1965), The Frost Report (writer), Do Not Adjust Your Set, Monty Python's Flying Circus, Rutland Weekend Television (series), All You Need is Cash (The Rutles), Faerie Tale Theater (The Frog Prince; dir., writer ACE Award, 1982; The Pied Piper), Saturday Night Live, The Mikado, Around the World in 80 Days, Nearly Departed (series), House of Mouse, The Scream Team, The Soul Patrol, Rutles 2: Can't Buy Me Lunch.

IDZIAK, SLAVOMIR
Cinematogrpaher.
PICTURES: A Woman's Decision, The Scar, Partita for a Wooden Instrument, The Conductor, Constancy, The Contract, Imperative, The Year of the Quiet Sun, Power of Evil, Harmagedon, A Short Film About Killing, Yasemin, Wherever You Are, Inventory, The Double Life of Veronique, Blue,

Weltmesiter, The Journey of August King, Lilian's Story, Mannerpension, Tears of Stone, Men With Guns, Gattaca, Commandments, I Want You, Love and Rage, The Last September, Paranoid, LiebesLuder, Proof of Life, Black Hawk Down.
TELEVISION: *Movies:* Podrozni jak inni, Gory o zmierzchu, Pizama, The Underground Passage, From A Far Country: Pope John Paul, The Unapproachable, The Decalogue, Long Conversation with a Bird.

IGER, ROBERT
Executive. b. New York, NY, 1951. e. Ithaca Col. Joined ABC in 1974 as studio supervisor. 1976 moved to ABC Sports. 1985, named v.p. in charge of program plan. & dev. as well as scheduling and rights acquisitions for all ABC Sports properties. 1987, named v.p. program. for ABC Sports and mgr. & dir. for ABC's Wide World of Sports; 1988, appt. exec. v.p., ABC Network Group. 1989 named pres., ABC Entertainment. 1992 became pres. of ABC TV Network Group.; 1993, sr. v.p. CC/ABC Inc., exec. v.p. of Capital Cities/ABC Inc. Sept., 1994, elected pres. & COO. Feb. 1999 named chair of ABC Group & pres., Walt Disney International. Jan. 2000 named pres. & COO of The Walt Disney Co. Currently pres., COO., and director, The Walt Disney Company.

IMAMURA, SHOHEI
Director, Producer, Writer. b. Tokyo, Japan, Sept. 15, 1926. e. Waseda U. Joined Shochiku Ofuna Studio 1951 asst. dir., transferred Nikkatsu in 1954 as asst. dir., director Stolen Desire 1958 then 4 more films before refusing to work on any film distasteful to him; and wrote play later made into film directed by him in 1968; later turned to documentaries and from 1976 onward as independent; Ballad of Narayama awarded Golden Palm Prize, Cannes Festival, 1983.
PICTURES: *Director*: Bakumatsu Taiyoden (writer, asst. dir. only), Stolen Desire, Lights of Night, Endless Desire, Nianchan, Big Brother, Pigs and Battleships, Insect Woman, Intentions of Murder, The Pornographers, A Man Vanishes, The Profound Desire of the Gods, Human Evaporation, History of Postwar Japan, Karayuki-san—the Making of a Prostitue, Vengeance Is Mine, Why Not?, The Ballad of Narayama (also writer), Zegen, Black Rain (also writer), Unagi (The Eel, also writer; Palme d'Or), Dr. Akagi, Warm Water Under a Red Bridge, September 11 (dir., documentary, 2001).

IMI, TONY
Cinematographer. b. London, March 27, 1937. Ent. ind. 1959.
PICTURES: The Raging Moon, Dulcima, The Slipper and the Rose, International Velvet, Brass Target, Ffolkes, The Sea Wolves, Night Crossing, Not Quite Jerusalem, Enemy Mine, Empire State, American Roulette, Options, Wired, Fire Birds, Pretty Hattie's Baby, Shopping, Downtime, Aimee and Jaguar, Dead of Night, Rancid Aluminium, The Testimony of Taliesin Jones, Goodbye Charlie Bright, Silent Cry, A Flight of Fancy, Lighthouse Hill, Chaos and Cadavers, School for Seduction.
TELEVISION: Queenie, The Return of Sherlock Holmes, Oceans of Fire, The Last Days of Frank and Jesse James, Reunion at Fairborough, A Christmas Carol, Sakharov, Princess Daisy, John Paul II, Little Gloria–Happy at Last, Inside the Third Reich, Dreams Don't Die, For Ladies Only, Nicholas Nickleby, A Tale of Two Cities, Babycakes, Old Man and the Sea, Fourth Story, The Last to Go, Our Sons, Carolina Skeletons, Child of Rage, Queen, Cobb's Law, For the Love of My Child: The Anissa Ayala Story, Blind Angel, Scarlett, The Sunshine Boys, The Turn of the Screw, Dalva, The Abduction, Desperate Justice, Victoria & Albert, Blackwater Lightship.

IMMERMAN, WILLIAM J.
Producer, Attorney, Executive. b. New York, NY, Dec. 29, 1937. e. Univ. Wisconsin, BS, 1959; Stanford Law, J.D., 1963. 1963-65, served as deputy district attorney, LA County. 1965-72, assoc. counsel, v.p.-bus. affairs, American Intl. Pictures. 1972-77, v.p., business affairs, sr. v.p. feature film division 20th Century-Fox. He represented Fox on the bd. of dir. of M.P.A.A. & the Assoc. of Motion Picture and Television Producers. 1977-1979, producer at Warner Bros. 1979-82, founder and chmn. of bd. of Cinema Group Inc., spec. vice chmn. Cannon Pictures, consultant to office of pres., Pathe Communications. 1989-90, 1986-90, dir. Heritage Ent., Inc. 1991, v.p. The Crime Channel 1983-93. Has also practiced law as sr. entertainment atty. with the law firms of Barash & Hill, Kenoff & Machtinger, and, most recently, The Law Offices of William J. Immerman. Member of the Academy of Motion Picture Arts and Sciences and serves as an arbitrator for the American Film Marketing Association.
Stage Productions: Berlin to Broadway (LA), The Knife Thrower's Assistant (LA, tour), The Wiz (B'way).
PICTURES: *Exec. prod.:* Highpoint, Southern Comfort, Hysterical, Mind Games, Take this Job and Shove It, Where the Red Ferns Grows Part II, The St. Tammany Miracle, The Lost Treasure of Sawtooth Island, Bring Him Home, Swimming Upstream, Danny Deckchair, The Game of Their Lives, Unchain My Heart: The Ray Charles Story. *Prod.:* Primal Rage, Nightmare Beach (Welcome to Spring Break), Children on Their Birthdays.

INGALLS, DON
Producer, Writer. b. Humboldt, NE, July 29, 1928. e. George Washington U., 1948. Columnist, Washington Post; producer-writer, ATV England and Australia; writer-prod., Have Gun Will Travel, also prod. for TV: The Travels of Jamie McPheeters, The Virginian, Honey West, Serpico, Kingston: Confidential. Exec. story consultant The Sixth Sense; prod.: Fantasy Island, T.J. Hooker, Duel at Shiloh, Smile of the Dragon, In Preparation: Watchers on the Mountain, Hearts & Diamonds, Motherwit, Funny Man, Beaumaris.
PICTURES: Airport—1975, Who's Got the Body?
TELEVISION: *Writer*: Gunsmoke, Have Gun Will Travel, The Bold Ones, Marcus Welby M.D., Mod Squad, Star Trek, Honey West, Bonanza, The Sixth Sense, Then Came Bronson, Police Story, World Premier Movie, Shamus, Flood, Capt. America, The Initiation of Sarah, Blood Sport, Fantasy Island, T.J. Hooker.

INGELS, MARTY
Actor, Former Comedian, Executive. b. Brooklyn, NY, Mar. 9, 1936. m actress-singer Shirley Jones. U.S. Infantry 1954-58. Ent. show business representing Army, Name That Tune. Stage: Sketchbook revue, Las Vegas. Pres., Celebrity Brokerage, packaging celebrity events and endorsements. Active in community affairs and charity funding.
PICTURES: The Ladies Man, Armored Command, The Horizontal Lieutenant, The Busy Body, Wild and Wonderful, A Guide for the Married Man, If It's Tuesday It Must be Belgium, For Singles Only, Instant Karma, Round Numbers, The Opposite Sex, How to Live with Them, Cops n Roberts, Kartenspieler, Luxury of Love.
TELEVISION: *Series*: I'm Dickens... He's Fenster, The Phyllis Diller Show.

INMAN, ROBERT
Writer.
TELEVISION: *Movies*: Home Fires Burning, My Son Is Innocent, The Summer of Ben Tyler (also prod., Writers' Guild Award, 1998), Family Blessings.

INSDORF, ANNETTE
Film Professor, Critic, Translator, TV Host. b. Paris, France. e. 1963-68 studied voice, Juilliard Sch. of Music and performed as singer; Queens Coll. (summa cum laude), B.A. 1972; Yale U., M.A., 1973; Yale U., Ph.D., 1975. 1973: soloist in Leonard Bernstein's Mass (European premiere in Vienna and BBC/WNET TV). 1975-87: professor of film, Yale U. Author of Francois Truffaut (1979; updated 1989), Indelible Shadows: Film and the Holocaust (1983, updated 1989). Since 1979: frequent contributor to NY Times (Arts and Leisure), Los Angeles Times, San Francisco Chronicle, Film Comment, and Premiere. Named Chevalier dans l'ordre des arts et lettres by French Ministry of Culture, 1986. Since 1987, dir. of Undergrad. Film Studies, Columbia U., and prof. Graduate Film Div. 1990 named chmn. of Film Div. 1987: exec.-prod. Shoeshine (short film nom. for Oscar). 1989: exec. prod., Tom Abrams' Performance Pieces (named best fiction short, Cannes Fest). 2002-2003, Host of Bravo Cable Network's Weekend at Cannes: Closing Ceremonies.

IRELAND, SIMONE
Casting Director.
PICTURES: Circle of Friends, Madagascar Skin, Jude, Hamlet, Welcome to Sarajevo, Under the Skin, Spice World, My Son the Fanatic, Resurrection Man, I Want You, What Rat's Won't Do, Appetite, Elizabeth, Hilary and Jackie, Alegria, The Lost Son, Heart, Go Now, Jakob the Liar, The Innocent Sleep, Stella Does Tricks.

IRONS, JEREMY
Actor. b. Isle of Wight, UK, Sept. 19, 1948. m. actress Sinead Cusack. e. Sherborne Sch., Dorset. Stage career began at Marlowe Theatre, Canterbury, where he was student asst. stage manager. Accepted at Bristol Old Vic Theatre Sch. for two-yr. course; then joined Bristol Old Vic Co. In London played in Godspell, Much Ado About Nothing, The Caretaker, Taming of the Shrew, Wild Oats, Rear Column, An Audience Called Edouard, etc. N.Y. stage debut, The Real Thing (Tony Award, 1984).
PICTURES: Nijinsky (debut, 1980), The French Lieutenant's Woman, Moonlighting, Betrayal, The Wild Duck, Swann in Love, The Mission, Dead Ringers, A Chorus of Disapproval, Danny the Champion of the World (tv in U.S.), Australia, Reversal of Fortune (Academy Award, 1990), Kafka, Waterland, Damage, M. Butterfly, The House of the Spirits, The Lion King (voice), Die Hard With a Vengeance,Stealing Beauty, Lolita, The Man in the Iron Mask, Chinese Box, Longitude, Dungeons & Dragons, The Fourth Angel, The Night of the Iguana, Callas Forever, The Time Machine, And Now Ladies and Gentleman, Mathilde, Broadway: The Golden Age by the Legends Who Were There.
TELEVISION: The Palliers, Notorious Woman, Love for Lydia, Langrishe Go Down, Brideshead Revisited, The Captain's Doll, Autogeddon, Tales From Hollywood, The Dream of a Ridiculous Man, The Great War (voice), Ohio Impromptu, Last Call.

IRONSIDE, MICHAEL
Actor. b. Toronto, Ontario, Canada, Feb. 12, 1950. e. Ontario Col. of Art.
PICTURES: Scanners, Visiting Hours, Spacehunter: Adventures in the Forbidden Zone, The Falcon and the Snowman, Jo Jo Dancer Your Life Is Calling, Top Gun, Extreme Prejudice, Nowhere to Hide, Hello Mary Lou: Prom Night II, Watchers, Total Recall, McBain, Highlander II: The Quickening, The Vagrant, Fortunes of War, The Killing Man, Free Willy, The Next Karate Kid, Major Payne, The Glass Shield, Starship Troopers, Desert Blue, Chicago Cab, Captive, Black Light, Going to Kansas City, One of Our Own, Ivory Tower, The Omega Code, Southern Cross, Ivory Tower, Crime and Punishment in Suburbia, Heavy Metal, The Perfect Storm, Cause of Death, Borderline Normal, Mindstorm, Down, Soulkeeper, Dead Awake, Extreme Honor, Fallen Angels, Fairtales & Pornography, Maximum Velocity, The Failures.
TELEVISION: *Movies*: Probable Cause (also co-exec. prod.), The Arrow, Voyage of Terror, Nuremberg, Jett Jackson: The Movie, The Red Phone, The Last Chapter, The Last Chapter: The War Continues.. *Series*: V, ER, SeaQuest DSV.

IRVIN, JOHN
Director. b. Cheshire, England, May 7, 1940. In cutting rooms at Rank Organisation before making first film documentary, Gala Day, on grant from British Film Inst.; made other award-winning documentaries before turning to features.
PICTURES: The Dogs of War (debut, 1981), Ghost Story, Champions, Turtle Diary, Raw Deal, Hamburger Hill, Next of Kin, Eminent Domain, Widow's Peak, A Month by the Lake, City of Industry, Wisegirls, Shiner, The Fourth Angel, The Great Ceili War.
TELEVISION: The Nearly Man, Hard Times, Tinker Tailor Soldier Spy, Robin Hood (foreign theatrical), Crazy Horse, When Trumphets Fade, Noah's Ark.

IRVING, AMY
Actress. b. Palo Alto, CA, Sept. 10, 1953. e. American Conservatory Theatre, London Acad. of Dramatic Art. Daughter of late theatre dir. Jules Irving and actress Priscilla Pointer. m. dir. Bruno Barreto.
THEATRE: *NY*: Amadeus, Heartbreak House, Road to Mecca, Broken Glass. *LA*: The Heidi Chronicles.
PICTURES: Carrie (debut, 1976), The Fury, Voices, Honeysuckle Rose, The Competition, Yentl (Acad. Award nom.), Micki and Maude, Rumpelstiltskin, Who Framed Roger Rabbit (voice), Crossing Delancey, A Show of Force, An American Tail: Fievel Goes West (voice), Benefit of the Doubt, Kleptomania, Acts of Love (also co- exec. prod.), I'm Not Rappaport, Carried Away, Deconstructing Harry, One Tough Cop, Blue Ridge Fall, The Confession, The Rage: Carrie 2, Blue Ridge Fall, Bossa Nova, Traffic, 13 Conversations About One Thing, Tuck Everlasting.
TELEVISION: *Movies*: James Dean, James A. Michener's Dynasty, Panache, Anastasia: The Mystery of Anna. Mini-*Series*: Once an Eagle, The Far Pavilions, The Impressionists. *Specials*: I'm a Fool, Turn of the Screw, Heartbreak House, Twilight Zone: Rod Serling's Lost Classics: The Theater. *Series*: Alias. *Guest*: The Rookies, Police Woman.

IRWIN, BILL
Actor. b. Santa Monica, CA, April 11, 1950.
THEATRE: *B'way*: Accidental Death of an Anarchist, 5-6-7-8 Dance, Largely New York, Fool Moon. *Off-B'way*: The Regard of Flight, The Courtroom, Not Quite New York, Waiting for Godot. Regional: Scapin (also dir., adaptation).
PICTURES: Popeye (debut, 1980), A New Life, Eight Men Out, My Blue Heaven, Scenes From a Mall, Hot Shots!, Stepping Out, Silent Tongue, Manhattan by Numbers, Water Ride, Illuminata, Just the Ticket, A Midsummer Night's Dream, Stanley's Gig, How the Grinch Stole Christmas, The Laramie Project, Igby Goes Down, The Truth About Miranda.
TELEVISION: *Movies*: Subway Stories: Tales from the Underground. *Specials*: The Regard of Flight, Bette Midler—Mondo Beyondo, The Paul Daniels Magic Show (BBC), The Last Mile. *Guest*: Cosby Show, Northern Exposure. *Series*: Sesame Street.

ISAACS, CHERYL BOONE
Executive. b. Springfield, MA. Entered m.p. industry 1977 as staff publicist for Columbia Pictures. Worked five years after that for Melvin Simon Prods., named v.p. Left to become dir. of adv./pub. for The Ladd Co. 1984, named dir., pub. & promo., West Coast, for Paramount Pictures. Promoted to vice pres., Worldwide Publicity, Paramount, 1986; sr. v.p., Worldwide Publicity, Paramount, 1991; exec. v.p., Worldwide Publicity, Paramount, 1994. Pres., theatrical marketing, New Line until 1999. Currently, marketing consultant for New Line. Member A.M.P.A.S. Board of Governors since 1988 and v.p. 2003-2004. Also a vice chmn. for A.M.P.A.S. 2003 Governors Ball.

ISAACS, PHIL
Executive. b. New York, NY, May 20, 1922. e. City Coll. of New York. In U.S. Navy, 1943-46. Joined Paramount Pictures in 1946 as bookers asst., N.Y. exch. Branch mgr. in Washington; then mgr. Rocky Mt. div. In 1966 was Eastern-Southern sls. mgr.;

1967 joined Cinema Center Films as v.p. domestic dist. In 1972 named v.p., marketing, for Tomorrow Entertainment; Joined Avco-Embassy 1975 as v.p., gen. sls. mgr., named exec. v.p., 1977. 1978 joined General Cinema Corp. as v.p. 1980 v.p., gen. sls. mgr., Orion Pictures. 1983, formed Phil Isaacs Co; 1988, v.p., general sales mgr., TWE Theatrical; 1989, appointed pres. Became pres. South Gate Entertainment 1989. Retired.

ISRAEL, NEAL
Writer, Director, Producer.
PICTURES: Cracking Up (s.p., actor), Americathon (dir., s.p.), Police Academy (s.p.), Bachelor Party (dir., s.p.), Johnny Dangerously (actor), Moving Violations (dir., s.p.), Real Genius (s.p.), It's Alive III (s.p.), Buy and Cell (co-s.p.), Look Who's Talking Too (co-prod., actor), Spurting Blood (exec. prod., s.p.), All I Want for Christmas (co-s.p.), Breaking the Rules (dir.), Surf Ninjas (dir., actor), Tunnelvision (co-dir.),Three O'clock High (co-prod.), Police Academy: Mission to Moscow (s.p.), The Adventures of Mary-Kate & Ashley: The Case of the Sea World Adventure & The Case of the Mystery Cruise (video, dir.), Chocolate for Breakfast (exec. prod.), The Runner (exec. prod.).
TELEVISION: *Movies*: The Cover Girl and the Cop (dir.), Woman With a Past (co-exec. prod.), Combat High (dir.), Taking the Heat (co-prod.), Dream Date (prod.), Bonnie and Clyde: The True Story (co-prod.), A Quiet Little Neighborhood (co-prod.), Foster's Field Trip (dir., writer), Family Reunion: A Relative Nightmare (dir., co-writer, co-prod.), National Lampoon's Dad's Week Off (dir., writer), The Patty Duke Show: Still Rockin' in Brooklyn Heights (s.p.), Hounded, The Poof Point, The Brady Bunch in the White House, Thanksgiving Family Reunion (dir.). *Specials*: Lola Falana Special (writer), Mac Davis Show, Ringo, Marie (prod.), Twilight Theatre (writer, prod.), Man of the People (co-prod.), *Series*: The Wonder Years (dir.), Harts of the West (dir.). Nash Bridges (dir.) Clueless (dir.), Love Boat: The Next Wave, Lizzie McGuire, Shasta McNasty, Even Stevens (dir.), The Mind of the Married Man (dir.), Family Affair (dir., 2002), Do Over, Miracles (co-prod.), Phil of the Future (dir.).

IVANEK, ZELJKO
Actor. b. Ljubljana, Yugoslavia, Aug. 15, 1957. Came to U.S. with family in 1960 and returned to homeland before settling in Palo Alto, CA, in 1967. Studied at Yale, majoring in theatre studies: graduated in 1978. Also graduate of London Acad. of Music and Dramatic Arts. Was member of Williamstown Theatre Festival, appearing in Hay Fever, Charley's Aunt, Front Page. B'way debut in The Survivor.
THEATRE: *B'way*: The Survivor, Brighton Beach Memoirs, Loot, Two Shakespearean Actors, The Glass Menagerie. Regional: Master Harold... and the Boys (Yale Rep. premiere prod.), Hamlet (Guthrie), Ivanov (Yale Rep.). *Off B'way*: Cloud 9, A Map of the World, The Cherry Orchard.
PICTURES: Tex, The Sender, The Soldier, Mass Appeal, Rachel River, School Ties, White Squall, Courage Under Fire, Infinity, The Associate, Donnie Brasco, Julian Po, Nowhere to Go, A Civil Action, Snow Falling on Cedars, Dancer in the Dark, Hannibal, Black Hawk Down, Unfaithful, Dogville.
TELEVISION: *Movies*: The Sun Also Rises, Echoes in the Darkness, Aftermath: A Test of Love, Our Sons, My Brother's Keeper, Truman, After Jimmy, Ellen Foster, The Rat Pack, Dash and Lilly, Sally Hemmings: An American Scandal. *Special*: All My Sons. *Series*: Homicide: Life on the Street, 24. *Mini-Series*: From the Earth to the Moon.

IVANY, PETER
Executive. b. Melbourne, Australia, Aug. 23, 1954. e. Monash U. Melbourne, B.A. Victoria Health Commission as strategic planning analyst, 1978-80. Kodak Australia, estimating and planning analyst, 1980-81. Joined Hoyts Corporation Pty Ltd. in 1982 as cinema mgr., then general mgr., Hoyts Video; general mgr., corporate development, 1988. CEO, Hoyts Corp. Resigned 1999 after selling out his share to Kerry Packer who bought Hoyts. Formed Ivany Investment Group, taking over IMAX operations in Australia.

IVEY, JUDITH
Actress. b. El Paso, TX, Sept. 4, 1951. m. ind. prod., Tim Braine. e. Illinois State U. Stage debut in The Sea in Chicago, 1974.
THEATRE: Bedroom Farce, The Goodbye People, Oh Coward!, Design for Living, Piaf, Romeo and Juliet, Pastorale, Two Small Bodies, Steaming (Tony & Drama Desk Awards), Second Lady (off-B'way work she helped develop), Hurlyburly (Tony & Drama Desk Awards), Precious Sons (Drama Desk nom.), Blithe Spirit, Mrs. Dally Has a Lover, Park Your Car in Harvard Yard (Tony nom.), The Moonshot Tape (Obie Award), A Fair Country, A Madhouse in Goa.
PICTURES: Harry and Son (debut, 1984), The Lonely Guy, The Woman in Red, Compromising Positions, Brighton Beach Memoirs, Hello Again, Sister Sister, Miles from Home, In Country, Everybody Wins, Alice, Love Hurts, There Goes the Neighborhood, Washington Square, The Devil's Advocate, Without Limits, Mystery Alaska, The Stand-In, What Alice Found.
TELEVISION:*Movies*: The Shady Hill Kidnapping, Dixie: Changing Habits, We Are the Children, The Long Hot Summer,

Jesse and the Bandit Queen, Decoration Day, Her Final Fury: Betty Broderick—The Last Chapter, On Promised Land, Almost Golden: The Jessica Savitch Story, What the Deaf Man Heard, Texarkana, Life's Little Struggles. *Special:* Other Mothers (Afterschool Special). *Mini-Series:* Rose Red. *Series:* Down Home, Designing Women, The Critic (voice), The Five Mrs. Buchanans, Buddies.

IVORY, JAMES
Director. b. Berkeley, CA, June 7, 1928. e. U. of Oregon, B.F.A., 1951; U. of Southern California, M.A. (cinema) 1956. First film Venice: Theme and Variations (doc. made as M.A. thesis, 1957). Early work: The Sword and the Flute, The Delhi Way. Formed Merchant Ivory Productions with prod. Ismail Merchant and script writer Ruth Prawer Jhabvala. Received D.W. Griffith Lifetime Achievement Award from DGA, 1995, Commandeur Des Arts et Des Lettres, France 1996.
PICTURES: The Householder, Shakespeare Wallah (also co-s.p.), The Guru (also co-s.p.), Bombay Talkie (also co-s.p.), Savages, The Wild Party, Roseland, The Europeans (also cameo), Quartet, Heat and Dust, The Bostonians, A Room With a View, Maurice (also co-s.p.), Slaves of New York, Mr. and Mrs. Bridge, Howards End, The Remains of the Day, Jefferson in Paris, Surviving Picasso, A Soldier's Daughter Never Cries (also s.p.), The Golden Bowl, Le Divorce (also s.p).
TELEVISION: Noon Wine (exec. prod.). Dir: Adventures of a Brown Man in Search of Civilization, Autobiography of a Princess (also released theatrically), Hullabaloo Over George and Bonnie's Pictures, Jane Austen in Manhattan (also released theatrically), The Five Forty Eight.

J

JACKSON, ANNE
Actress. b. Allegheny, PA, Sept. 3, 1926. e. Neighborhood Playhouse, Actors Studio. m. to actor Eli Wallach. Stage debut in The Cherry Orchard, 1944. Autobiography: Early Stages.
THEATRE: Major Barbara, Middle of the Night, The Typist and the Tiger, Luv, Waltz of the Toreadors, Twice Around the Park, Summer and Smoke, Nest of the Woodgrouse, Marco Polo Sings a Solo, The Mad Woman of Chaillot, Cafe Crown, Lost in Yonkers, In Persons, The Flowering Peach, Love Letters.
PICTURES: So Young So Bad (debut, 1950), The Journey, Tall Story, The Tiger Makes Out, How to Save a Marriage and Ruin Your Life, The Secret Life of an American Wife, The Angel Levine, Zig Zag, Lovers and Other Strangers, Dirty Dingus Magee, Nasty Habits, The Bell Jar, The Shining, Sam's Son, Funny About Love, Folks!, Man of the Century, Something Sweet, Broadway: The Golden Age by the Legends Who Were There.
TELEVISION: *Movies:* The Family Man, A Woman Called Golda, Private Battle, Blinded By the Light, Leave 'em Laughing, Baby M, Rescuers: Stories of Courage: Two Women. *Series:* Everything's Relative. *Special:* 84 Charing Cross Road.

JACKSON, BRIAN
Actor, Film & Theatre Producer. b. Bolton, England, 1931. Early career in photography then numerous stage performances incl. Old Vic, Royal Shakespeare. Ent. film/TV industry 1958. Formed Quintus Plays, 1965; formed Brian Jackson Productions 1966; formed Hampden Gurney Studios Ltd. 1970. Co-produced The Others 1967; presented The Button, 1969; co-produced the documentary film Village in Mayfair, 1970; 1971: Formed Brian Jackson Film Ltd.; produced Yesterday, The Red Deer, The Story of Tutankhamen.
THEATRE: Mame, Drury Lane, Fallen Angels, In Praise of Love.
PICTURES: Incident in Karandi, Carry On Sergeant, Gorgo, Jack the Ripper, Taste of Fear, Heroes of Telemark, Only the Lonely, The Deadly Females, The Revenge of the Pink Panther, Deceptions, Shadow Chasers.
TELEVISION: Moon Fleet, Private Investigator, Life of Lord Lister, Z Cars, Vendetta, Sherlock Holmes, Mr. Rose, Hardy Heating International, Nearest & Dearest, The Persuaders, The Paradise Makers, The New Avengers, Smugglers Bay, The Tomorrow People, Secret Army, Last Visitor for Hugh Peters, Six Men of Dorset, Commercials: featured as the man from Delmonte for 5 years.

JACKSON, GLENDA
Actress. b. Birkenhead, England, May 9, 1936. Stage debut: Separate Tales (Worthing, England, 1957). 1964 joined Peter Brooks' Theatre of Cruelty which led to film debut. Became Member of Parliament, 1992.
THEATRE: (Eng.): All Kinds of Men, Hammersmith, The Idiot, Alfie. Joined Royal Shakespeare Co in experimental Theatre of Cruelty season. Marat Sade (London, N.Y.), Three Sisters, The Maids, Hedda Gabler, The White Devil, Rose, Strange Interlude (N.Y.), Macbeth (N.Y.), Who's Afraid of Virginia Wolf? (L.A.).
PICTURES: The Persecution and Assassination of Jean-Paul Marat as Performed by the Inmates of the Asylum at Charenton Under the Direction of the Marquis de Sade (debut, 1967), Tell Me Lies, Negatives, Women in Love (Academy Award, 1970),

The Music Lovers, Sunday Bloody Sunday, Mary Queen of Scots, The Boy Friend, Triple Echo, The Nelson Affair, A Touch of Class (Academy Award, 1973), The Maids, The Temptress, The Romantic Englishwoman, The Devil is a Woman, Hedda, The Incredible Sarah, Nasty Habits, House Calls, Stevie, The Class of Miss McMichael, Lost and Found, Health, Hopscotch, Giro City, The Return of the Soldier, Turtle Diary, Beyond Therapy, Business as Usual, Salome's Last Dance, The Rainbow, The Visit, King of the Wind, Doombeach, William Shakespeare.
TELEVISION: *Movies:* The Patricia Neal Story, Sakharov, Strange Interlude, Jerry Springer on Sunday. *Mini-Series:* Elizabeth R (2 Emmy Awards, 1972). *Special:* Strange Interlude, A Murder of Quality, The House of Bernarda Alba, Secret Life of Sir Arnold Bax, I Love a 1970s Christmas.

JACKSON, JOSHUA
Actor. b. Vancouver, Canada, June 11, 1978.
PICTURES: Crooked Hearts, The Mighty Ducks, Digger, Andre, D2: The Mighty Ducks, Magic in the Water, Robin of Locksley, D3: The Mighty Ducks, Scream 2, Apt Pupil, Urban Legend, Cruel Intentions, Muppets From Space, The Skulls, Gossip, The Safety of Objects, Ocean's Eleven, The Laramie Project, Road To Hell (2002), I Love Your Work.
TELEVISION: *Movies:* Ronnie & Julie, The Laramie Project. *Series:* Dawson's Creek. *Guest:* The Outer Limits.

JACKSON, KATE
Actress. b. Birmingham, AL, Oct. 29, 1949. e. U. of Miss., Birmingham Southern U. Did stock before going to N.Y. to enter American Acad. of Dramatic Arts, appearing in Night Must Fall, The Constant Wife, Little Moon of Alban. Worked as model and became tour guide at NBC. First role on TV in Dark Shadows (series).
PICTURES: Night of Dark Shadows, Limbo, Thunder and Lightning, Dirty Tricks, Making Love, Loverboy, Error in Judgment, Larceny.
TELEVISION: *Movies:* Satan's School for Girls, Killer Bees, Death Cruise, Death Scream, Charlie's Angels (pilot), Death at Love House, James at 15 (pilot), Topper, Inmates: A Love Story, Thin Ice, Listen to Your Heart, The Stranger Within, Quiet Killer, Homewrecker (voice), Adrift, Empty Cradle, Armed and Innocent, Justice in a Small Town, The Silence of Adultery, Murder on the Iditarod Trail, A Kidnapping in the Family, Panic in the Skies, What Happened to Bobby Earl, Satan's School for Girls, A Mother's Testimony, Charlie's Angels: TV Tales (documentary), Miracle Dogs. *Series:* Dark Shadows, The Rookies, Charlie's Angels, Scarecrow and Mrs. King, Baby Boom. *Guest:* The Jimmy Stewart Show.

JACKSON, MICHAEL
Singer, Composer. b. Gary, IN, Aug. 29, 1958. Musical recording artist with family group known as Jackson 5: all brothers, Jackie, Jermaine, Tito, Marlon, and Michael. Sister is singer Janet Jackson.
PICTURES: Save the Children, The Wiz, Moonwalker (also exec. prod., story), Get on the Bus (singer, "Put Your Heart on the Line"), Ghosts (short, acting, composer), Men in Black II (as himself), They Cage the Animals at Night (dir. only). *Composer:* Ben (and singer, title song), We Are the World (video documentary short), Captain Eo (also acting, s.p.), Lola,Superman (song "Beat It"), Back to the Future Part II (song "Beat It"), Black or White, Free Willy (song, "Will You Be There"), Free Willy II (song, "Childhood"), Rush Hour, Center State, Charlie's Angels (2000), Rush Hour II, Zoolander, Undercover Brother.
TELEVISION: *Series:* The Jacksons (1976-77), The Simpsons (composer songs). *Specials:* Free to Be You and Me, Sandy in Disneyland, Motown on Showtime: Michael Jackson.

JACKSON, MICK
Director. b. Grays, England. e. Bristol Univ. Joined BBC as film editor, following post-grad work in film & tv. Produced and directed many documentaries for the BBC.
PICTURES: Chattahoochee, L.A. Story, The Bodyguard, Clean Slate, Volcano, Josiah's Canon, The First $20 Million is Always the Hardest.
TELEVISION: *Movies/Specials:* Threads, The Race for the Double Helix, Yuri Nosenko KGB (HBO), Live from Baghdad, Street Boss *Mini-Series:* A Very British Coup. *Series:* That's Life, The Handler.

JACKSON, PETER
Director, Writer, Producer. b. New Zealand, Oct. 31, 1961.
PICTURES: Bad Taste, Meet the Feebles, Dead Alive, Heavenly Creatures (Academy Award nom.), Forgotten Silver, The Frighteners, Contact (special effects only), The Lord of the Rings: The Fellowship of the Ring (Acad. Award nom., AFI Award), The Lord of the Rings: The Two Towers, The Lord of the Rings: The Return of the King .

JACKSON, SAMUEL L.
Actor. b. Washington, D.C., Dec. 21, 1948. e. Morehouse Col. m. actress LaTanya Richardson. Co-founder, member of the Just Us Theatre Co. in Atlanta.
THEATRE: *Negro Ensemble Company:* Home, A Soldier's Story,

Sally/Prince, Colored People's Time. *NY Shakespeare Fest*: Mother Courage, Spell No. 7, The Mighty Gents. *Yale Rep*: The Piano Lesson, Two Trains Running. *Seattle Rep*: Fences.
PICTURES: Ragtime (debut, 1981), Eddie Murphy Raw, School Daze, Coming to America, Do the Right Thing, Sea of Love, A Shock to the System, Def by Temptation, Betsy's Wedding, Mo' Better Blues, The Exorcist III, GoodFellas, Mob Justice, Jungle Fever (Cannes Film Fest. & NY Film Critics Awards, 1991), Strictly Business, Juice, White Sands, Patriot Games, Johnny Suede, Jumpin at the Boneyard, Fathers and Sons, National Lampoon's Loaded Weapon 1, Amos & Andrew, Menace II Society, Jurassic Park, True Romance, Hail Caesar, Fresh, The New Age, Pulp Fiction (Acad. Award nom.), Losing Isaiah, Kiss of Death, Die Hard With a Vengeance, Fluke (voice), The Great White Hype, A Time to Kill, The Long Kiss Goodnight, 187, Eve's Bayou (also prod.), Jackie Brown, The Red Violin, Sphere, Out of Sight (cameo), The Negotiator, Rules of Engagement, Deep Blue Sea, Star Wars: Episode I-The Phantom Menace, Forever Hollywood, Rules of Engagement, Shaft, Unbreakable, The Caveman's Valentine, Changing Lanes, 51st State, Mefisto in Onyx, Stars Wars: Episode 2: Attack of the Clones, XXX, No Good Deed, S.W.A.T., Basic, Kill Bill: Volume 1, Country of My Skull, The Blackout Murders.
TELEVISION: *Movies*: Assault at West Point: The Court-Martial of Johnson Whittaker, Against the Wall, 2004: A Light Knight's Odyssey.

JACOBI, DEREK
O.B.E. **Actor**. b. London, England, Oct. 22, 1938. e. Cambridge. On stage in Pericles, The Hollow Crown, Hobson's Choice, The Suicide, Breaking the Code (London, NY).
PICTURES: Othello (debut, 1965), Interlude, The Three Sisters, The Day of the Jackal, Blue Blood, The Odessa File, The Medusa Touch, The Human Factor, Enigma, The Secret of NIMH (voice), Little Dorrit, Henry V, Dead Again, Hamlet, Basil, Up at the Villa, Love Is the Devil, Molokai: The Story of Father Damian, Gladiator, Up at the Villa, The Body, Joan of Arc: Virgin Warrior, Revelation, Gosford Park, Fairy Feller, The Diaries of Vaslav Nijinsky, Two Men Went to War, A Revenger's Tragedy, Broadway: The Golden Age by the Legends Who Were There.
TELEVISION: *Movies/Mini-Series*: She Stoops to Conquer, Man of Straw, The Pallisers; I, Claudius; Philby, Burgess and MacLean, Hamlet. Movies: Othello, Three Sisters, Interlude, Charlotte, The Man Who Went Up in Smoke, The Hunchback of Notre Dame, Inside the Third Reich, The Secret Garden, The Tenth Man (Emmy Award), The Civil War, Storyteller: The Greek Myths, Circle of Deceit, Baseball, The Secret Garden, Witness Against Hitler, Breaking the Code, Animated Epics: Beowulf, The Wyvern Mystery, Jason and the Argonauts, Victoria Wood and All the Trimmings, Larry and Viven: The Oliviers in Love, The Gathering Storm, Manor House, Dinosaur Hunters (narrator), Mr. Ambassador. *Series*: Minder, Tales of the Unexpected, Mr. Pye, The Leper of St. Giles, Cadfael, Flora Britannica.

JACOBS, MICHAEL
Producer, Writer. b. New Brunswick, NJ. Studied at Neighborhood Playhouse in NY. Had first play, Cheaters, prod. on B'way when he was only 22 yrs. old.
PICTURE: 3:15 (writer only), Halloween 5 (writer only) Quiz Show, Treehouse Hostage, Trapped: Beneath the Snow, Peace Virus, Fangs.
TELEVISION: *Movies*: Wild Grizzly.*Series*: *Creator/prod.*: Charles in Charge, No Soap Radio, Together We Stand, Singer and Songs, My Two Dads (also dir.), Dinosaurs, The Torkelsons (Almost Home), Boy Meets World, Where I Live, You Wish, Misery Loves Company, The Brainiacs.com.

JACOBSEN, JOHN M.
Producer, Executive. b. Oslo, Norway, Dec. 27, 1944. Produced number of feature films incl. Pathfinder (Acad. Award nom.), Shipwrecked, Head Above Water. Pres., Norwegian Film and HTV Producers Assn.; Pres. AB Svensk Filmindustri Norwegian Operation.
PICTURES: Prima Veras saga om Olav den hellige, Hard asfalt, Pathfinder, Showbiz - eller hvordan bli kjendis på en-to-tre!, Shipwrecked, Giftige logner, De Bla ulvene, Head Above Water (1993), Chasing the Kidneystone, Head Above Water (1996), Gurin with the Foxtail, Only Clouds Move the Stars, Sleepwalker.
TELEVISION: Sofies verdin (mini).

JACOBY, FRANK DAVID
Director, Producer. b. New York, NY, July 15, 1925. e. Hunter Coll., Brooklyn Coll. m. Doris Storm, producer/director educational films, actress. 1949-52, NBC network tv dir.; 1952-56, B.B.D.O., Biow Co., tv prod./dir.; 1956-58 Metropolitan Educational TV Assn., dir. of prod.; 1958-65, United Nation, film-prod./dir.; 1965 to present, pres., Jacoby/Storm Prods., Inc., Westport, CT—documentary, industrial, educational films and filmstrips. Clients include Xerox Corp., Random House, Publ., Lippincott Co., IBM, Heublein, G.E., and Pitney Bowes. Winner, Sherwood Award, Peabody Award. Member, Director's Guild of America; winner, Int'l TV & Film Festival, National Educational Film Festival, American Film Festival. Retired.

JACOBY, JOSEPH
Producer, Director, Writer. b. Brooklyn, NY, Sept. 22, 1942. e. NYU. Sch. of Arts and Sciences, majoring in m.p. As undergraduate worked part-time as prod. asst. on daytime network TV shows and as puppeteer for Bunin Puppets. 1964 joined Bil Baird Marionettes as full-time puppeteer, working also on Baird film commercials. Made feature m.p. debut as prod.-dir of Shame Shame Everybody Knows Her Name, 1968. Contributing essayist, NY Woman Magazine. Founder/Dir.-Prod., Children's Video Theatre starring The Bil Baird Marionettes. Adjunct professor, New School for Social Reserach, NY.
PICTURES: *Dir./Prod./Writer*: Hurry Up or I'll Be 30, The Great Bank Hoax, Shenanigans, Davy Jones' Locker.

JACOBY, SCOTT
Actor, Director. b. Chicago, IL, Nov. 26, 1956.
PICTURES: The Little Girl Who Lives Down the Lane, Love and the Midnight Auto Supply, Our Winning Season, Return to Horror High, To Die For, To Die For II. *Dir.*: To Kill a Mockingbird, Rage: 20 Years of Punk Rock West Coast Style.
TELEVISION: *Movies*: No Place to Run, That Certain Summer (Emmy Award, 1973), The Man Who Could Talk to Kids, Bad Ronald, Smash-Up on I 5, No Other Love, The Diary of Anne Frank. *Mini-Series*: 79 Park Avenue. *Series*: One Life to Live (73-74). *Guest*: Medical Center, Marcus Welby M.D., The Golden Girls.

JAFFE, STANLEY R.
Producer. b. New York, NY, July, 31, 1940. Graduate of U. of Pennsylvania Wharton Sch. of Finance. Joined Seven Arts Associates, 1962; named exec. ass't to pres., 1964; later, head of East Coast TV programming. Produced Goodbye, Columbus, in 1968 for Paramount; joined that company as exec. v.p., 1969. Named pres. of Paramount in 1970; resigned 1971 to form own prod. unit. Joined Columbia as exec. v.p. of global prod. in 1976, but resigned to be independent prod. Named pres. & COO of Paramount Communications in 1991-1994. Owner of Jaffilms LLC, 1994-.
PICTURES: Goodbye Columbus, A New Leaf, Bad Company, Man on a Swing, The Bad News Bears, Kramer vs. Kramer (Academy Award for Best Picture, 1979), Taps, Without a Trace (also dir.), Madeline (exec.). *Co-prod.*(with Sherry Lansing): Racing with the Moon, Firstborn, Fatal Attraction, The Accused, Black Rain, School Ties, I Dreamed of Africa, Four Feathers.

JAFFE, STEVEN-CHARLES
Producer. b. Brooklyn, NY, 1954. e. U. of Southern California, cinema. First professional job as documentary prod. on John Huston's Fat City. Served as prod. asst. on The Wind and the Lion in Spain. Assoc. prod. on Demon Seed (written by brother Robert); served as location mgr. on Who'll Stop the Rain; assoc. prod. on Time After Time. On tv worked as 2nd unit dir. on The Day After.
PICTURES: Those Lips Those Eyes, Motel Hell (also co-s.p.), Scarab (dir.), Flesh + Blood (2nd unit. dir.), Near Dark, Plain Clothes (exec. prod.), The Fly II, Ghost (exec. prod., 2nd unit dir.), Company Business, Star Trek VI: The Undiscovered Country, Strange Days, The Informant, The Weight of Water, K-19: The Widowmaker.

JAGGER, MICK
Singer, Composer, Actor. b. Dartford, Kent, England, July 26, 1943. Lead singer with the Rolling Stones.
PICTURES: The Rolling Stones Rock and Roll Circus, Performance, Ned Kelly, Popcorn, Gimme Shelter, Sympathy for the Devil, Ladies and Gentlemen: The Rolling Stones, The London Rock 'n' Roll Show, Let's Spend the Night Together, At the Max, Freejack, Bent, My Best Friend, The Man From Elysian Fields, Enigma, The Mayor of Sunset Strip. Composer: (Songs appeared in the following:) Made in U.S.A, Zabriskie Point, Mean Streets, Coming Home, FM, Divine Madness!, Night Shift, The Big Chill, Jumpin' Jack Flash, Full Metal Jacket, Adventures in Babysitting, Flashback, Goodfellas, Interview with the Vampire, Nine Months, Assassins, Casino, Bottle Rocket, The Fan, The Devil's Advocate, Fallen, Hope Floats, Rushmore, The Other Sister, The Replacements, The Way of the Gun, The Family Man, Blow, The Royal Tenenbaums, Life or Something Like It, Moonlight Mile, Adaptation, Bruce Almighty.
TELEVISION: *Special*:s The Nightingale (Faerie Tale Theatre), History of Rock 'N' Roll Pt. 3, 5 and 6, The Concert for New York City, America: A Tribute to Heroes, Being Mick.

JAGGS, STEVE
Executive. b. London, England, June 29, 1946. Ent. motion picture industry, 1964. Gained experience in the film production and laboratory areas with Colour Film Service and Universal Laboratories. Joined Agfa-Gevaert Ltd., Motion Picture Division, 1976. Appt. sales manager, 1979; divisional manager, 1984. Joined Rank Organisation, 1992. 1993-present (2003), mng. dir. of Pinewood Studios, Buckinghamshire, United Kingdom.

JAGLOM, HENRY
Director, Writer, Editor, Actor. b. London, Eng., Jan. 26, 1943. Studied acting, writing and directing with Lee Strasberg and at Actors Studio. Did off-B'way. shows; went to West Coast where

guest-starred in TV series (Gidget, The Flying Nun, etc.). Shot documentary film in Israel during Six Day War. Hired as edit consultant for Easy Rider by producer Bert Schneider. Acted in Psych Out, Drive He Said, The Last Movie, Thousand Plane Raid, Lili Aime Moi, The Other Side of the Wind (Orson Welles' unreleased last film). Wrote and dir. first feature, A Safe Place, in 1971. Created The Women's Film Co. (to prod. and distrib. motion pictures by women filmmakers), and Jagfilms Inc., Rainbow Film Company, and Rainbow Releasing. Presented Academy Award winning documentary Hearts and Minds, 1974.
PICTURES: Dir.-Writer-Prod.-Editor: A Safe Place, Tracks, Sitting Ducks (also actor), National Lampoon Goes to the Movies (co-dir. only), Can She Bake A Cherry Pie?, Always (also actor), Someone To Love (also actor), New Year's Day (also actor), Eating, Venice Venice (also actor), Babyfever, Last Summer in the Hamptons (dir., co-s.p., edit., actor), Deja Vu (dir., s.p., edit.), Shopping, Festival in Cannes.

JALBERT, JOE JAY
Executive. e. U. of Washington. Was ski captain in school and began film career as technical director on Downhill Racer, 1969, also cinematographer and double for Robert Redford. 1970, produced Impressions of Utah, documentary, with Redford. Won Emmy for cinematography on TV's Peggy Fleming Special. In 1970 formed Jalbert Productions, Inc., to make feature films, TV sports, specials, commercials, etc. Co. has prod. Winter Sportscast and 9 official films at Innsbruck Winter Olympics (1976), Lake Placid (1980), Sarajevo (1984). Albertville Winter Olympic Games official film, One Light One World, 1992. For more than 10 years the co. has been the official film prod. for the U.S. ski team.

JAMES, CLIFTON
Actor. b. Portland, OR, May 29, 1925. e. U. of Oregon. Studied at Actors Studio. Made numerous appearances on stage and TV, as well as theatrical films.
THEATRE: NY: B'way: J.B., All the Way Home, The Shadow Box, American Buffalo. Off-B'way: All the King's Men.
PICTURES: On The Waterfront, The Strange One, The Last Mile, Something Wild, Experiment in Terror, David and Lisa, Black Like Me, The Chase, The Happening, Cool Hand Luke, Will Penny, The Reivers, ...tick...tick...tick..., WUSA, The Biscuit Eater, The New Centurions, Kid Blue, Live and Let Die, The Iceman Cometh, Werewolf of Washington, The Last Detail, Bank Shot, Juggernaut, The Man with the Golden Gun, Rancho DeLuxe, Silver Streak, The Bad News Bears in Breaking Training, Superman II, Where Are the Children?, Whoops Apocalypse, Eight Men Out, The Bonfire of the Vanities, Lone Star, Interstate 84, Sunshine State, Counting Sheep.
TELEVISION: Series: City of Angels, Lewis and Clark. Movies: Runaway Barge, Friendly Persuasion, The Deadly Tower, Hart to Hart (pilot), Undercover With the KKK, Guyana Tragedy: The Story of Jim Jones, Carolina Skeletons, The John Vernon Story, The Summer of Ben Tyler. Mini-Series: Captains and the Kings.

JAMES, FRANCESCA.
Actress, Director.
TELEVISION: Series: One Life to Live, All My Children (also dir. Emmy Awards, 1980, 1998), Loving (dir.only), Santa Barbara (prod. only), Port Charles (dir. only).

JAMESON, JERRY
Director. b. Hollywood, CA. Started as editorial asst.; then editor and supv. editor for Danny Thomas Prods. Turned to directing.
PICTURES: Dirt Gang, The Bat People, Brute Core, Airport '77, Raise the Titanic, Land of the Free, Running Red (exec. prod.), Last Flight Out.
TELEVISION: Movies: Heatwave!, The Elevator, Hurricane, Terror on the 40th Floor, The Secret Night Caller, The Deadly Tower, The Lives of Jenny Dolan, The Call of the Wild, The Invasion of Johnson County, Superdome, A Fire in the Sky, High Noon--Part II, The Return of Will Kane, Stand By Your Man, Killing at Hell's Gate, Hotline, Starflight: The Plane That Couldn't Land, Cowboy, This Girl for Hire, Last of the Great Survivors, The Cowboy and the Ballerina, Stormin' Home, One Police Plaza, The Red Spider, Terror on Highway 91, Fire and Rain, Gunsmoke: The Long Ride, Bonanza: The Return, Gunsmoke: One Man's Justice, Gone in a Heartbeat, The Red Phone. Series: The Six Million Dollar Man, Murder She Wrote, B.L. Stryker, Dr. Quinn: Medicine Woman, Walker Texas Ranger, Models Inc., Touched by an Angel, JAG, The Lazarus Man, The Magnificent Seven.

JANKOWSKI, GENE F.
Executive. b. Buffalo, NY, May 21, 1934. e. Canisius Coll., B.S., Michigan State U., M.A. in radio, TV and film. Joined CBS radio network sls, 1961 as acct. exec.; eastern sls. mgr., 1966; moved to CBS-TV as acct. exec. 1969; gen. sls. mgr. WCBS-TV, 1970; dir. sls, 1971; v.p. sls., CBS-TV Stations Divisions, 1973; v.p., finance & planning, 1974; v.p., controller, CBS Inc. 1976; v.p. adm., 1977; exec. v.p. CBS/Broadcast Group, 1977; pres., CBS/Broadcast Group, 1977; chmn. CBS/Broadcast Group, 1988-89; chmn. Jankowski Communications Systems, Inc. 1989-. Member: pres., Intl. Council of National Acad. of Television Arts & Sciences; chmn. & trustee Amer. Film Institute; trustee,

Catholic U. of Amer.; director, Georgetown U.; bd. of gov. American Red Cross; vice chmn., business comm. Metropolitan Museum of Art. Member, Library of Congress Film Preservation Board; adjunct prof. telecommunications, Michigan St.U. Chmn. of Trans-Lux Corporation; an advisor-managing director of Veronis Suhler & Associates, Inc.; and dir. of TV Azteca. Also Co-chmn. of St. Vincent's College and a trustee of St. Vincent's Medical Center. AWARDS: Received Distinguished Communications Medal from South Baptist Radio & Television Commission; honorary Doctorate of Humanities, Michigan State U.; Humanitarian Award, National Conference of Christians and Jews.

JANNEY, ALLISON
Actress. b. Dayton, Ohio, November 19, 1960.
PICTURES: Who Shot Patakango?, Dead Funny, The Cowboy Way, Miracle on 34th Street, Wolf, Heading Home, Big Night, Faithful, Walking and Talking, The Associate, Flux, Private Parts, The Ice Storm, Julian Po, Anita Liberty, Primary Colors, The Object of My Affection, Six Days Seven Nights, Celebrity, The Impostors, 10 Things I Hate About You, Drop Dead Gorgeous, American Beauty, Nurse Betty, Leaving Drew, The Hours, Finding Nemo (voice), How to Deal.
TELEVISION: -Movies: Blind Spot, First Do No Harm, David and Lisa, Path to Paradise: The Untold Story of the World Trade Center Bombing. Mini-Series: A Girl Thing. Series: The Guiding Light, The West Wing (Emmy Awards, 2000 and 2001). Guest: Law and Order, New York Undercover, Aliens in the Family, Cosby, Late Line.

JARMAN, CLAUDE, JR.
Actor. b. Nashville, TN, Sept. 27, 1934. e. MGM Sch. Received special Oscar for The Yearling. Exec. prod. of concert film Fillmore.
PICTURES: The Yearling (debut, 1946), High Barbaree, The Sun Comes Up, Intruder in the Dust, Roughshod, The Outriders, Inside Straight, Rio Grande, Hangman's Knot, Fair Wind to Java, The Great Locomotive Chase.
TELEVISION: Mini-Series: Centennial, The Story of Lassie.

JARMUSCH, JIM
Director, Writer, Composer, Actor. b. Akron, OH, 1953. e. attended Columbia U., went to Paris in senior year. NYU Film Sch., studied with Nicholas Ray and became his teaching asst. Appeared as an actor in Red Italy and Fraulein Berlin. Composed scores for The State of Things and Reverse Angle. Wrote and directed The New World using 30 minutes of leftover, unused film from another director. (Won International Critics Prize, Rotterdam Film Festival). Expanded it into Stranger Than Paradise.
PICTURES: Director-Writer: Permanent Vacation (dir. debut, 1980; also prod., music, edit.), Stranger Than Paradise (also edit., Golden Leopard, Locarno Film Festival; Camera d'Or best new director, Cannes), Down by Law, Mystery Train (also actor) Night on Earth (also prod.), Whips Fly (prod. only), Coffee and Cigarettes (also II & III), Dead Man, Year of the Horse, Ghost Dog: The Way of the Samurai (also prod.), Ten Minutes Older: The Trumpet. Actor: American Autobahn, Straight to Hell, Running Out of Luck, Helsinki Napoli All Night Long, Candy Mountain, Leningrad Cowboys Go America, The Golden Boat, Iron Horsemen, In the Soup, Tigrero: A Film That Was Never Made, Blue in the Face, The Typewriter the Rifle & the Movie Camera, Cannes Man, Sling Blade, Divine Trash, Year of the Horse, RIP: Rest in Pieces, Screamin' Jay Hawkins: I Put a Spell On Me. Ten Minutes Older: The Trumpet.

JARRE, MAURICE
Composer. b. Lyons, France, Sept. 13, 1924. Studied at Paris Cons. Was orchestra conductor for Jean Louis Barrault's theatre company four years. 1951 joined Jean Vilar's nat'l theatre co., composing for plays. Musical dir., French National Theatre for 12 years before scoring films. Also has written ballets (Masques de Femmes, Facheuse Rencontre, The Murdered Poet, Maldroros, The Hunchback of Notre Dame) and served as cond. with Royal Phil. Orch., London, Japan Phil. Orch., Osaka Symph. Orch., Quebec Symp. Orch, Central Orchestra of People's Republic of China.
PICTURES: La Tete contre les Murs (The Keepers; feature debut, 1959), Eyes Without a Face, Crack in the Mirror, The Big Gamble, Sundays and Cybele, The Longest Day, Lawrence of Arabia (Academy Award, 1962), To Die in Madrid, Behold a Pale Horse, The Train, The Collector, Is Paris Burning?, Weekend at Dunkirk, Doctor Zhivago (Academy Award, 1965), The Professionals, Grand Prix, Gambit, The Night of the Generals, Villa Rides!, Five Card Stud, Barbarella, Isadora, The Extraordinary Seaman, The Damned, Topaz, The Only Game in Town, El Condor, Ryan's Daughter, Plaza Suite, Red Sun, Pope Joan, The Life and Times of Judge Roy Bean, The Effect of Gamma Rays on Man-in-the-Moon Marigolds, The Mackintosh Man, Ash Wednesday, Island at the Top of the World, Mandingo, Posse, The Man Who Would Be King, Shout at the Devil, The Last Tycoon, Crossed Swords, Winter Kills, The Magician of Lublin, Resurrection, The American Success Company, The Black Marble, Taps, Firefox, Young Doctors in Love, Don't Cry It's Only Thunder, The Year of Living Dangerously, Dreamscape, A Passage to India (Academy Award, 1984), Top Secret!, Witness

(BAFTA Award, 1985), Mad Max Beyond Thunderdome, Solarbabies, The Mosquito Coast, Tai-Pan, No Way Out, Fatal Attraction, Gaby--A True Story, Julia and Julia, Moon Over Parador, Gorillas in the Mist, Wildfire, Distant Thunder, Chances Are, Dead Poets Society (BAFTA Award, 1989), Prancer, Enemies a Love Story, Ghost, After Dark My Sweet, Jacob's Ladder, Almost an Angel, Only the Lonely, Fires Within, School Ties, Shadow of the Wolf, Mr. Jones, Fearless, A Walk in the Clouds (Golden Globe, 1996), The Mirror Has Two Faces, The Sunchaser, Day and Night, Sunshine, I Dreamed of Africa.
TELEVISION: several productions, 1960s to present.

JARROTT, CHARLES
Director. b. London, England, June 16, 1927. Joined British Navy; wartime service in Far East. After military service turned to theatre as asst. stage mgr. with Arts Council touring co. 1949 joined Nottingham Repertory Theatre as stage dir. and juvenile acting lead. 1953 joined new co. formed to tour Canada; was leading man and became resident leading actor for Ottawa Theatre. 1955 moved to Toronto and made TV acting debut opposite Katharine Blake whom he later wed. 1957 dir. debut in TV for Canadian Bdcstg. Co. Became CBC resident dir. Moved to London to direct for Armchair Theatre for ABC-TV. Then became freelance dir., doing stage work, films, TV. Received BAFTA Best Director Award, 1962. Golden Globe Awards, 1969, 1987.
THEATRE: The Duel, Galileo, The Basement, Tea Party, The Dutchman, etc.
PICTURES: Time to Remember (debut, 1962), Anne of the Thousand Days, Mary Queen of Scots, Lost Horizon, The Dove, The Littlest Horse Thieves, The Other Side of Midnight, The Last Flight of Noah's Ark, Condorman, The Amateur, The Boy in Blue, Morning Glory (co-s.p. only), Byron (s.p., dir.), The Secret Life of Algernon (also s.p.), Turn of Faith.
TELEVISION: The Hot Picture Boys, Roll On, Bloomin' Death, Girl in a Birdcage, The Picture of Dorian Gray, Rain, The Rose Affair, Roman Gesture, Silent Song, The Male of the Species, The Young Elizabeth, A Case of Libel, Dr. Jekyll and Mr. Hyde.
U.S. Movies/Mini-Series: A Married Man, Poor Little Rich Girl: The Barbara Hutton Story, The Woman He Loved, Till We Meet Again (mini-series), Night of the Fox (mini-series), Lucy & Desi: Before the Laughter, Changes, Yes Virginia There is a Santa Claus, Stranger in the Mirror, Jackie Collins' Lady Boss, Treacherous Beauties, Trade Winds, A Promise Kept: The Oksana Baiul Story (Emmy Award for dir.), At The Midnight Hour, The Christmas List.

JAYSTON, MICHAEL
Actor. b. Nottingham, England, Oct. 28, 1935. Member of Old Vic theatre Co. & Bristol Old Vic.
PICTURES: A Midsummer Night's Dream, Cromwell, Nicholas and Alexandra, The Public Eye, Alice's Adventures in Wonderland, The Nelson Affair, Tales That Witness Madness, The Homecoming, Craze, The Internecine Project, Dominique, Zulu Dawn, From a Far Country, MacBeth, Element of Doubt.
TELEVISION: Movies/Mini-Series: She Fell Among Thieves, Tinker Tailor Soldier Spy, Dust to Dust, Still Crazy Like a Fox, Shake Hands Forever, A Guilty Thing Surprised, Somewhere to Run, A Bit of a Do, 20,000 Leagues Under the Sea, A Dinner of Herbs. Series: Haggard, The Casebook of Sherlock Holmes, Outside Edge, Fun at the Funeral Parlour.

JEFFREYS, ANNE
Actress. b. Goldsboro, NC, Jan. 26, 1923. m. actor Robert Sterling. Named by Theatre Arts Magazine as one of the 10 outstanding beauties of the stage. Trained for operatic career. Sang with NY's Municipal Opera Co. while supplementing income as a Powers model. Appeared as Tess Trueheart in Dick Tracy features.
THEATRE: B'way: in Street Scene, Kiss Me Kate, Romance, Three Wishes for Jamie, Kismet. Stock: Camelot, King & I, Kismet, Song of Norway, Bells Are Ringing, Marriage Go Round, No Sex Please, We're British, Take Me Along, Carousel, Anniversary Waltz, Do I Hear a Waltz, Ninotchka, Pal Joey, Name of the Game, Destry Rides Again, The Merry Widow, Bitter Sweet, Desert Song, High Button Shoes, Sound of Music.
PICTURES: I Married an Angel, Billy the Kid, Trapped, Joan of Ozark, The Old Homestead, Tarzan's New York Adventure, X Marks the Spot, Yokel Boy, Catterbox, Man from Thunder River, Nevada, Step Lively, Dillinger, Sing Your Way Home, Those Endearing Young Charms, Zombies on Broadway, Dick Tracy Vs. Cueball, Genius at Work, Step By Step, Vacation in Reno, Trail Street, Riffraff, Return of the Bad Men, Boys' Night Out, Panic in the City, Southern Double Cross, Clifford.
TELEVISION: Movies: Beggarman Thief, A Message From Holly, American Movie Classics (host). Series: Topper, Love That Jill, Bright Promise, Delphi Bureau, General Hospital, Finder of Lost Loves, Port Charles. Guest: Falcon Crest, Hotel, Murder She Wrote, L.A. Law, Baywatch.

JEFFRIES, LIONEL
Actor, Director. b. Forest Hill, London, England, June 10, 1926. e. Queens Elizabeth's Grammar Sch, Wimbone Dorset. Ent. m.p. ind. 1952.
THEATRE: Hello, Dolly!, See How They Run, Two Into One, Pygmalion (U.S.), The Wild Duck.

PICTURES: The Black Rider, The Colditz Story, No Smoking, Will Any Gentleman?, Windfall, All for Mary, Bhowani Junction, Eyewitness, Jumping for Joy, Lust for Life, Creeping Unknown (Quatermass Experiment), Baby and the Battleship, Decision Against Time, Doctor at Large, High Terrace, Hour of Decision, Up in the World, Behind the Mask, Blue Murder at St. Trinian's, Dunkirk, Girls at Sea, Law and Disorder, Orders to Kill, Revenge of Frankenstein, Up the Creek, Bobbikins, The Vicious Circle, Idol on Parade, Nowhere to Go, The Nun's Story, Jazzboat, Let's Get Married, Trials of Oscar Wilde, Please Turn Over, Tarzan the Magnificent, Two-Way Stretch, Fanny, The Hellions, Life is a Circus, Kill or Cure, Mrs. Gibbons' Boys, Operation Snatch, The Notorious Landlady, The Wrong Arm of the Law, Call Me Bwana, The Crimson Blade, First Men in the Moon, The Long Ships, Murder Ahoy, The Secret of My Success, The Truth About Spring, You Must Be Joking!, Arrivederci Baby!, The Spy With a Cold Nose, Oh Dad Poor Dad, Blast Off!, Camelot, Chitty Chitty Bang Bang, Sudden Terror, The Railway Children (dir., s.p. only), Lola, Who Slew Auntie Roo?, The Amazing Mr. Blunden (dir., s.p. only), Baxter (dir. only), Royal Flash, Wombling Free (voice, also dir., s.p.), The Water Babies (dir. only), The Prisoner of Zenda, Better Late Than Never, A Chorus of Disapproval.
TELEVISION: Father Charlie, Tom Dick and Harriet, Cream in My Coffee, Minder, Danny: the Champion of the World, Jekyll and Hyde, Boon Morse, Ending Up, Look at It This Way, Bed, Woof!, Heaven on Earth, I Love 1970s, I Love a 1970s Christmas.

JENKINS, GEORGE
Art Director. b. Baltimore, MD, Nov. 19, 1908. e. U. of Pennsylvania. Hollywood-New York art dir. since 1946; TV pictures for Four Star Playhouse and Revue productions; NBC-TV opera, Carmen; color dir., CBS-TV, 1954; NBC color spec. Annie Get Your Gun, 1957; TV music with Mary Martin, 1959. Professor, Motion Picture Design, UCLA, 1985-88.
THEATRE: Mexican Hayride, I Remember Mama, Dark of the Moon, Lost in the Stars, Bell Book and Candle, The Bad Seed, The Happiest Millionaire, Two for the Seesaw, Ice Capades, Song of Norway, Paradise Island, Around the World in 80 Days, Mardi Gras, The Miracle Worker, Critic's Choice, A Thousand Clowns, Jennie, Generation, Wait Until Dark, Only Game in Town, Night Watch, Sly Fox.
PICTURES: The Best Years of Our Lives, The Secret Life of Walter Mitty, A Song Is Born, Rosanna McCoy, The Miracle Worker, Mickey One, Up the Down Staircase, Wait Until Dark, The Subject Was Roses, Klute, 1776, The Paper Chase, The Parallax View, Night Moves, Funny Lady, All the President's Men (Academy Award, 1976), Comes a Horseman, The China Syndrome (Acad. Award nom.), Starting Over, The Postman Always Rings Twice, Rollover, Sophie's Choice, Orphans, See You in the Morning, Presumed Innocent.
TELEVISION: Movie: The Dollmaker.

JENNINGS, PETER
TV News Anchor. b. Toronto, Canada, July 29, 1938. Son of Canadian b'caster Charles Jennings. e. Carleton U.; Rider Coll. Worked as a bank teller and late night radio host in Canada. Started career as host of Club 13, a Canadian American Bandstand-like dance prog., then as a newsman on CFJR (radio), Ottawa; then with CJOH-TV and CBC. Joined ABC in 1964 as NY corr.; 1965, anchor, Peter Jennings with the News; 1969, overseas assignments for ABC news; 1975, Washington corr. and anchor for AM America; 1977, chief foreign corr.; 1978, foreign desk anchor, World News Tonight; 1983-, anchor, sr. editor, World News Tonight. Has appeared/reported numerous documentaries.

JENS, SALOME
Actress. b. Milwaukee, WI, May 8, 1935. e. Northwestern U. Member Actors Studio.
THEATRE: The Disenchanted, Far Country, Night Life, Winter's Tale, Mary Stuart, Antony and Cleopatra, After the Fall, Moon For the Misbegotten, The Balcony.
PICTURES: Angel Baby (debut, 1961), The Fool Killer, Seconds, Me Natalie, Cloud Dancer, Harry's War, Just Between Friends, Coming Out Under Fire (narrator), I'm Losing You, Cats and Dogs (voice), Room 101.
TELEVISION: Movies: In the Glitter Palace, Sharon: Portrait of a Mistress, The Golden Moment: An Olympic Love Story, A Killer in the Family, Playing with Fire, Uncommon Valor. Guest: Mary Hartman, Mary Hartman. Series: Falcon Crest. Mini-Series: From Here to Eternity, The Great War.

JERGENS, ADELE
Actress. b. Brooklyn, NY, Nov. 26, 1917. Began career in musical shows during summer vacation at 15; won contest, New York's World Fair, as model; appeared on New York stage; night clubs, U.S. and abroad.
PICTURES: A Thousand and One Nights, She Wouldn't Say Yes, The Corpse Came C.O.D., Dwon to Earth, Woman From Tangier, The Fuller Brush Man, The Dark Past, Treasure of Monte Cristo, SLightly French, Edge of Doom, Side Street, Abbott and Costello Meet the Invisible Man, Sugarfoot, Try and Get Me, Show Boat, Somebody Loves Me, Aaron Slick from Punkin' Crick, Overland Pacific, Miami Story, Fireman Save My Child, Big Chase, Strange

Lady in Town, The Cobweb, Girls in Prison, The Lonesome Trail, Treasure of Monte Cristo, Runaway Daughters, Fighting Trouble, The Day the World Ended.
(d. Nov. 22, 2002)

JETER, MICHAEL
Actor. b. Lawrenceberg, TN, Aug. 20, 1952.e. Memphis St. U.
THEATRE: Alice, G.R. Point (Theatre World Award), Cloud 9, Greater Tuna, Once in a Lifetime, Zoo Story, Waiting for Godot, Only Kidding, The Boys Next Door, Grand Hotel (Tony Award, 1990).
PICTURES: Hair, Ragtime, Soup for One, Zelig, The Money Pit, Dead-Bang, Tango & Cash, Just Like in the Movies, Miller's Crossing, The Fisher King, Bank Robber, Sister Act 2: Back in the Habit, Drop Zone, Waterworld, Air Bud, Mouse Hunt, Race for Atlantis, Fear and Loathing in Las Vegas, Thursday, Zack and Reba, Patch Adams, The Naked Man, True Crime, Jakob the Liar, The Green Mile, South of Heaven West of Hell, The Gift, Kid Quick, Jurassic Park III, Welcome to Collinwood.
TELEVISION: Series: One Life to Live, Hothouse, Evening Shade (Emmy Award, 1992), Sesame Street. Movies: My Old Man, Sentimental Journey, When Love Kills: The Seduction of John Hearn, Gypsy, The Ransom of Red Chief. Mini-Series: From Here to Eternity. Guest: Lou Grant, Designing Women.
(d. March 30, 2003)

JEWISON, NORMAN
Producer, Director. b. Toronto, Canada, July 21, 1926. e. Malvern Collegiate Inst., Toronto, 1940-44; Victoria Coll., U. of Toronto, 1946-50, B.A. Stage and TV actor 1950-52. Director, Canadian Broadcasting Corp 1953-58. Awarded 1988 Acad. of Canadian Cinema and Television Special Achievement Award. Made Companion Order of Canada, 1992. Thalberg Award, 1998.
PICTURES: Director: 40 Pounds of Trouble (debut, 1962), The Thrill of It All, Send Me No Flowers, The Art of Love, The Cincinnati Kid. Director-Producer: The Russians Are Coming! The Russians Are Coming! (Acad. Award nom. for picture), In the Heat of the Night (dir. only; Acad. Award nom.), The Thomas Crown Affair, Gaily Gaily, Fiddler on the Roof (Acad. Award nom. for dir. & picture), Jesus Christ Superstar (also co-s.p.), Rollerball, F.I.S.T., ... And Justice for All, Best Friends, A Soldier's Story (Acad. Award nom. for picture), Agnes of God, Moonstruck (Acad. Award noms. for dir. & picture), In Country, Other People's Money, Only You, Bogus, The Hurricane, The Statement. Producer: The Landlord, Billy Two Hats, The Dogs of War (exec.), Iceman, The January Man, Dance Me Outside (exec.), A Brother's Kiss (exec.).
TELEVISION: Exec. prod. of 8 episodes of The Judy Garland Show, Walter and Henry. Prod.-Dir.: Judy Garland specials, The Andy Williams Show, Dinner with Friends. Dir. of Specials: Tonight with Harry Belafonte, The Broadway of Lerner and Loewe.

JEUNET, JEAN-PIERRE
Director, Writer. b. Roanne, Loire, France, Sept. 3, 1953.
PICTURES: The Escape, Le Manege, The Bunker of the Last Gunshots, Pas du repos pour Billy Brakko, Things I Like, Things I Don't Like, Delicatessen (also s.p.), The City of Lost Children (also s.p.), Alien: Resurrection, Amélie (dir., s.p., Acad. Award nom., BAFTA Award), A Very Long Engagement.

JHABVALA, RUTH PRAWER
Writer. b. Cologne, Germany, May 7, 1927. Emigrated with her family to England, 1939. e. Hendon County Sch., Queen Mary Coll., London U. (degree in English). m. architect C.S.H. Jhabvala, 1951 and moved to Delhi. Has written most of the screenplays for the films of Ismail Merchant and James Ivory.
AUTHOR: To Whom She Will, Esmond in India, The Nature of Passion, The Householder, Get Ready for Battle, Heat and Dust, In Search of Love and Beauty, Three Continents, Poet and Dancer, Shards of Memory.
PICTURES: The Householder (debut, 1963; based on her novel), Shakespeare Wallah (with Ivory), The Guru (with Ivory), Bombay Talkie (with Ivory), Roseland, The Europeans, Quartet, Heat and Dust (based on her own novel; BAFTA Award), The Bostonians, A Room with a View (Academy Award, 1986), Madame Sousatzka (co.-s.p. with John Schlesinger), Mr. and Mrs. Bridge (NY Film Critics Award), Howards End (Academy Award, 1992), The Remains of the Day, Jefferson in Paris, Surviving Picasso, A Soldier's Daughter Never Cries, The Golden Bowl, Le Divorce.
TELEVISION: Hullabaloo Over Georgie and Bonnie's Pictures, Autobiography of a Princess, Jane Austen in Manhattan.

JILLIAN, ANN
Actress. b. Cambridge, MA, Jan. 29, 1951. Began career at age 10 in Disney's Babes in Toyland; in film version of Gypsy at age 12. Broadway debut in musical, Sugar Babies, 1979. Formed own company: 9-J Productions, developing TV movies and series.
PICTURES: Babes in Toyland, Gypsy, Mr. Mom, Sammy the Way Out Seal.
TELEVISION: Movies: Mae West (Emmy & Golden Globe nom.), Death Ride to Osaka, Killer in the Mirror, Convicted: A Mother's

Story, Perry Mason: The Case of the Murdered Madam, The Ann Jillian Story (Golden Globe Award; Emmy nom.), Original Sin, This Wife for Hire, Little White Lies, Mario and the Mob, Labor of Love: The Arlette Schweitzer Story, Heart of a Child, The Disappearance of Vonnie, Fast Company, It's Him Or Us, My Son The Match Maker, The Care and Handling of Roses, I'll Be Home for Christmas. Series: Hazel, It's a Living, Jennifer Slept Here, Ann Jillian. Guest: Love Boat, Fantasy Island, Twilight Zone, Ben Casey, etc. Mini-Series: Ellis Island (Emmy & Golden Globe nom.), Alice in Wonderland, Malibu.

JOANOU, PHIL
Director. b. La Canada, CA, Nov. 20, 1961. e. UCLA, USC. Student film The Last Chance Dance won him first professional job directing 2 episodes of tv's Amazing Stories.
PICTURES: Three O'Clock High (debut, 1987), U2: Rattle and Hum (also edit., camera operator), State of Grace, Final Analysis, Heaven's Prisoners, Entropy, 14 Up in America, U2: The Best of 1980-1990 (music video documentary), Entropy (also s.p. and prod.), The Regulators.
TELEVISION: Mini-Series: Wild Palms (co-dir.). Series: Fallen Angels (Dead-End for Delia).

JOFFE, CHARLES H.
Executive. b. Brooklyn, NY, July 16, 1929. e. Syracuse U. Joined with Jack Rollins to set up management-production org., clients including Woody Allen, Ted Bessell, Billy Crystal, David Letterman, Tom Poston, Robin Williams.
PICTURES: Producer: Don't Drink the Water, Take the Money and Run, Everything You Always Wanted to Know About Sex but Were Afraid To Ask, Love and Death, Annie Hall (Academy Award for Best Picture, 1977), House of God. Exec./Co-Exec. prod.: Play It Again Sam, Bananas, Sleeper, Manhattan, Interiors, Stardust Memories, Arthur, A Midsummer Nights' Sex Comedy, Zelig, Broadway Danny Rose, The Purple Rose of Cairo, Hannah and Her Sisters, Radio Days, September, Another Woman, New York Stories (Oedipus Wrecks), Crimes and Misdemeanors, Alice, Shadows and Fog, Husbands and Wives, Manhattan Murder Mystery, Bullets Over Broadway, Everyone Says I Love You (co-exec. prod.), Deconstructing Harry, Celebrity, Sweet and Lowdown, Small Time Crooks, The Curse of the Jade Scorpion, Hollywood Ending, Anything Else.
TELEVISION: Woody Allen specials. Star of the Family, Good Time Harry, Triplecross.

JOFFE, EDWARD
Producer, Director, Writer, Production Consultant. Worked in m.p., theatre, commercial radio and as journalist before ent. TV ind. in Britain as writer/prod with ATV. 1959-61 staff prod. Granada TV. 1962, dir., Traitor's Gate & Traveling Light for Robt Stigwood; prod. dir. numerous series for Grampian TV; 1967, dir. film The Price of a Record—Emmy finalist; 1967-68 films, Columba's Folk & So Many Partings ITV entries in Golden Harp Fest.; 1968, prod., dir. Tony Hancock Down Under in Australia, prod. dir. Up At The Cross; prod. dir. ind. film, Will Ye No' Come Back Again; dir., This Is... Tom Jones; prod. dir., The Golden Shot; 1971, senior production lecturer, Thomson TV College; dir., films for U.S. for London Television Service; Evening Standard Commercials for Thames TV. Co. prod. dir.,ind. film Sound Scene, 1972-8, Contract prod. dir. Thames TV various series: Magpie, Today, Opportunity Knocks, The David Nixon Show, Seven Ages of Man, Problems, Finding Out; 1980 production consultant, CBC-TV; 1978-82, prod. dir. series Writers' Workshop, About Books; 1978, film, Places & Things (British Academy Award nom.) film, Who Do You Think You Are? (British Academy Award nom.), ITV's Japan Prize entry, Special Jury Award San Francisco Intl. Film Fest), 1981, Film Images, (British Academy Award nom.; Gold Plaque Chicago Intl. Film Fest.); The Protectors (medal winner Intl. Film & TV Festival, N.Y.). 1982-86: film Rainbow Coloured Disco Dancer. Various Series: Taste of China, Jobs Ltd., Spin-Offs, The Buzz. Doc.: War Games in Italy. 1989-95, devised, prod., dir. Video View for ITV Network; Co-prod. & dir. 2 series Sprockets; dir. Challenge. Dir. Screen Scene Prods, String of Pearls, PLC, String of Pearls 2 PLC. Companies produced mopics Double X, Little Devils - The Birth, To Catch a Yeti, Big Game, Shepherd on the Rock.

JOFFE, ROLAND
Director, Producer. b. London, England, Nov. 17, 1945. e. Lycee Francaise, Carmel Col. Manchester U., England. Worked in British theatre with the Young Vic, the National Theatre and the Old Vic. 1973 became youngest director at National Theatre. 1978, moved into directing TV for Granada TV, then Thames and B.B.C. before feature debut in 1984 with The Killing Fields.
PICTURES: Director: The Killing Fields (debut, 1984), The Mission, Fat Man and Little Boy (also co-s.p.), City of Joy (also co-prod.), The Scarlet Letter (also prod.). Producer: Made in Bangkok, Super Mario Bros, Goodbye Lover, Waterproof, Vatel, Shabana!-Actor-Activist-Woman (short, as himself)
TELEVISION: Documentaries: Rope, Ann, No Mama No. Plays: The Spongers, Tis Pity She's a Whore, The Legion Hall Bombing, United Kingdom (also co-wrote). Series: Coronation Street, Bill Brand, The Stars Look Down.

JOHNS, GLYNIS
Actress. b. Durban, South Africa, Oct. 5, 1923. e. in England. Daughter of Mervyn Johns, actor, and Alys Steele, pianist. On London stage from 1935 (Buckie's Bears, The Children's Hour, A Kiss for Cinderella, Quiet Week-End; Gertie, N.Y. stage, 1952; Major Barbara, N.Y., 1956-57.) Voted one of top ten British Money-making stars in Motion Picture Herald-Pathe poll, 1951-54.
THEATRE: Too Good to Be True (NY), The King's Mare, Come as You Are, The Marquise (tour), A Little Night Music (NY; Tony Award), Cause Celebre, Harold and Maude (Canada, Hay Fever (U.K. tour), The Boy Friend (Toronto), The Circle (NY).
PICTURES: South Riding (debut, 1938), Murder in the Family, Prison Without Bars, On the Night of the Fire, Mr. Brigg's Family, Under Your Hat, The Prime Minister, 49th Parallel, Adventures of Tartu, Half-Way House, Perfect Strangers, This Man Is Mine, Frieda, An Ideal Husband, Miranda, Third Time Lucky, Dear Mr. Prohack, State Secret, Flesh and Blood, No Highway in the Sky, Appointment With Venus (Island Rescue), Encore, The Magic Box, The Card (The Promoter), The Sword and the Rose, Rob Roy the Highland Rogue, Personal Affair, The Weak and the Wicked, The Seekers (Land of Fury), The Beachcomber, Mad About Men, Court Jester, Josephine and Men, Loser Takes All, All Mine to Give, Around the World in 80 Days, Another Time Another Place, Shake Hands with the Devil, The Sundowners, The Spider's Web, The Cabinet of Caligari, The Chapman Report, Papa's Delicate Condition, Mary Poppins, Dear Brigette, Don't Just Stand There, Lock Up Your Daughters, Under Milk Wood, Vault of Horror, Zelly and Me, Nukie, The Ref, While You Were Sleeping, Superstar.
TELEVISION: Series: Glynis, Coming of Age. Guest: Dr. Kildare, Roaring Twenties, Naked City, The Defenders, Danny Kaye Show. Also: Noel Coward's Star Quality, Mrs. Amworth, All You Need Is Love, Across a Crowded Room, Little Gloria... Happy at Last, Skagg.

JOHNSON, ARTE
Actor. b. Chicago, IL, Jan. 20, 1934. e. Univ. of IL: To NY in 1950's where he landed role on B'way in Gentlemen Prefer Blondes. Also worked in nightclubs, summer stock, tv commercials. Gained fame on Rowan and Martin's Laugh-In in late 1960's. Much voice work on tv cartoons.
PICTURES: Miracle in the Rain, The Subterraneans, The Third Day, The President's Analyst, Love at First Bite, A Night at the Magic Castle, What Comes Around, Tax Season, Evil Spirits, Munchie, Second Chance, Captiva Island, The Modern Adventures of Tom Sawyer, The Stan Freberg Commercials (video).
TELEVISION: Series: It's Always Jan, Sally, Hennesey, Don't Call Me Charlie, Rowan & Martin's Laugh-In (Emmy Award, 1969), Ben Vereen... Comin' at Ya!, The Gong Show (panelist), Games People Play, Glitter, General Hospital. Movies: Twice in a Lifetime, Bud and Lou, If Things Were Different, Detour to Terror, The Love Tapes, Condominium, Making of a Male Model, Alice in Wonderland, Dan Turner—Hollywood Detective.

JOHNSON, DON
Actor. b. Flatt Creek, MO, Dec. 15, 1949. Worked at ACT (Amer. Conservatory Th.), San Francisco. On stage in Your Own Thing. In L.A. in Fortune and Men's Eyes. Recording: Heartbeat (1986).
PICTURES: The Magic Garden of Stanley Sweetheart (debut, 1970), Zachariah, The Harrad Experiment, A Boy and His Dog, Return to Macon County, Soggy Bottom USA, Cease Fire, Sweet Hearts Dance, Dead-Bang, The Hot Spot, Harley Davidson and the Marlboro Man, Paradise, Born Yesterday, Guilty as Sin, Tin Cup, Goodbye Lover.
TELEVISION: Movies: First You Cry, Ski Lift to Death, Katie: Portrait of a Centerfold, Revenge of the Stepford Wives, Amateur Night at the Dixie Bar and Grill, Elvis and the Beauty Queen, The Two Lives of Carol Letner, In Pursuit of Honor, Word of Honor. Special: Don Johnson's Heartbeat (music video, also exec. prod.). Mini-Series: The Rebels, Beulah Land, The Long Hot Summer. Series: From Here to Eternity, Miami Vice, Nash Bridges (also prod.).

JOHNSON, J. BOND
Producer, Executive. b. Fort Worth, TX, June 18, 1926. e. Texas Wesleyan Univ., B.S., 1947; Texas Christian U., M.Ed., 1948; Southern Methodist U., B.D., 1952; USC, Ph.D., 1967. Army Air Forces, WWII; public info. officer, captain, U.S. Marine Corps, Korean War. Formerly member Marine Corps Reserve, Motion Picture Prod. Unit, Hollywood. Was Col. U.S. Army; now retired. Newspaper reporter, Fort Worth Star-Telegram, 1942-48; pres., West Coast News Service, 1960; pres., exec. prod., Bonjo Prods., Inc., 1960, President, CEO, Cine-Media International, 1975 managing partner, Capra-Johnson Productions, Ltd., 1978.
PICTURES: Sands of Iwo Jima, Retreat Hell, Flying Leathernecks; photographed aerial portions, Jamboree 53, Norfleet, Devil at My Heels, Kingdom of the Spiders, Ordeal at Donner Pass, Place of the Dawn, Lies I Told Myself, Backstretch, Airs Above The Ground, The Jerusalem Concert, The Berkshire Terror, The Seventh Gate.
TELEVISION: Series: Creator, story consultant, tech. advisor, Whirlpool. Exec. producer, creator: On The Go (TV News-Sports), Coasties, Desert Rangers. Producer: Fandango.

JOHNSON, LAMONT
Director, Producer. b. Stockton, CA, Sept. 30, 1922. e. UCLA. 4 time winner of Director's Guild Award for TV work. Directed plays The Egg, Yes Is For a Very Young Man. Dir. two operas, L.A. Philharmonic, 1964; founder, dir., UCLA Professional Theatre Group.
PICTURES: A Covenant With Death (debut, 1967), Kona Coast, The McKenzie Break, A Gunfight, The Groundstar Conspiracy, You'll Like My Mother, The Last American Hero, Visit to a Chief's Son, Lipstick, One on One (also actor), Somebody Killed Her Husband, Cattle Annie and Little Britches, Spacehunter: Adventures in the Forbidden Zone.
TELEVISION: Movies/Mini-Series: Deadlock, My Sweet Charlie, That Certain Summer, The Execution of Pvt. Slovik, Fear on Trial, Off the Minnesota Strip, Crisis at Central High, Escape from Iran, Dangerous Company, Life of the Party: The Story of Beatrice, Ernie Kovacs: Between the Laughter, Wallenberg: A Hero's Story (also co-prod.; Emmy Award, 1985), Unnatural Causes, Gore Vidal's Lincoln (Emmy Award, 1988), The Kennedys of Massachusetts, Voices Within: The Lives of Truddi Chase, Crash Landing: The Rescue of Flight 232, The Broken Chain (also prod.), The Man Next Door, All the Winters That Have Been. Series: The Defenders, Profiles in Courage, Twilight Zone, Felicity.

JOHNSON, MARK
Producer. b. Washington, DC, Dec. 27, 1945. Moved to Spain at age 7, lived there for eleven years before returning to America. e. Univ. of VA, Univ. of IA. Joined Directors Guild training program receiving first credit on Next Stop Greenwich Village. Worked as prod. asst., then asst. dir. on High Anxiety, Movie Movie, The Brink's Job, and Escape From Alcatraz. Starting with Diner in 1982 served as executive prod. or prod. on all Barry Levinson films. With Levinson formed Baltimore Pictures in 1989.
PICTURES: Diner (exec. prod.), Kafka (co-exec. prod.), The Astronaut's Wife (exec. prod.), My Dog Skip (exec. prod.), Mouse Hunt (exec. prod.), What Lies Beneath (exec. prod.). Producer: The Natural, Young Sherlock Holmes, Tin Men, Good Morning Vietnam, Rain Man (Academy Award for Best Picture of 1988), Avalon, Bugsy (L.A. Film Critics & Golden Globe Awards for Best Picture of 1991), Toys, Sniper, Wilder Napalm, A Perfect World, A Little Princess, Donnie Brasco, Home Fries, An Everlasting Piece, Dragonfly, The Rookie, Moonlight Mile, The Banger Sisters, The Alamo, The Notebook, The Lion, the Witch and the Wardrobe.
TELEVISION: Series: The Guardian (exec. prod.), HRT (exec. prod.), Hack (exec. in charge of production).

JOHNSON, RICHARD
Actor. b. Upminster, Essex, England, July 30, 1927. Studied at Royal Acad. of Dramatic Art. First stage appearance Opera House, Manchester, then with John Gielgud's repertory season, 1944. Served in Royal Navy 1945-48. Subsequent stage appearances incl. The Madwoman of Chaillot, The Lark. Visited Moscow with Peter Brook's production of Hamlet. Royal Shakespeare Thea.: Stratford, London, 1957-62. Royal Shakespeare Co. 1972-73. National Theatre, 1976-77. Founded United British Artists, 1983.
PICTURES: Captain Horatio Hornblower (debut, 1951), Calling Bulldog Drummond, Scotland Yard Inspector (Lady in the Fog), Saadia, Never So Few, Cairo, The Haunting, 80,000 Suspects, The Pumpkin Eater, The Amorous Adventures of Moll Flanders, Operation Crossbow, Khartoum, The Witch in Love, Deadlier Than the Male, The Rover, Danger Route, A Twist of Sand, Oedipus the King, Lady Hamilton, Some Girls Do, Julius Caesar, The Tyrant, The Beloved, Behind the Door, Hennessy, Night Child, The Cursed Medallion, Aces High, The Last Day of Spring, The Comeback, Zombie, The Monster Club, Screamers, What Waits Below, Lady Jane, Turtle Diary, Foreign Student, Diving In, Milk, Lara Croft: Tombraider, The Dark (video short, voice).
TELEVISION: The Flame is Love, Haywire, The Four Feathers, Portrait of a Rebel: Margaret Sanger, A Man For All Seasons, Voice of the Heart, The Crucifer of Blood, Duel of Hearts. Guest: Wagon Train, Lou Grant, Ironside, Knots Landing, That Girl, MacGyver, Police Story, Route 66, many others. Live TV incl. Lux Video Theatre, Front Row Center, Hallmark Hall of Fame.

JOHNSON, RUSSELL
Actor. b. Ashley, PA, Nov. 10, 1924. e. Girard Coll, Actors Laboratory, L.A. W.W.II, Army Air Corps. Author: Here on Gilligan's Isle (1993).
PICTURES: A Town of the 80's, Stand at Apache Landing, A Distant Trumpet, Ma & Pa Kettle at Waikiki, Rogue Cop, Loan Shark, Seminole, Tumbleweed, Blue Movies, It Came From Outer Space, Many Rivers to Cross, Law and Order, Black Tuesday, This Island Earth, Rock All Night, Attack of the Crab Monsters, The Space Children, For Men Only, The Greatest Story Ever Told, MacArthur, Hitchhike to Hell, Off the Wall, Robotech II: The Sentinels, Blue Movies, Christian Scare Films Vol. 4. (video).
TELEVISION: Movies: The Movie Murderer, Vanished, Horror at 37,000 Feet, Beg-Borrow or Steal, Aloha Means Goodbye,

Adventures of the Queen, Collision Course: Truman vs. MacArthur, Nowhere to Hide, Hewitt's Just Different, The Ghost of Flight 401, The Bastard, Rescue from Gilligan's Island, The Castaways on Gilligan's Island, The Harlem Globetrotters on Gilligan's Island, With a Vengeance. Series: Black Saddle, Gilligan's Island. Guest: Studio One, Front Row Center, Playhouse 90, Lux Video Theatre, Mobile One, The Great Adventure Jane Powell Show, Climax, You Are There, Rawhide, Twilight Zone, Gunsmoke, Outer Limits, Cannon, Marcus Welby, That Girl, The FBI, Dallas, Fame, Dynasty, My Two Dads, Bosom Buddies, Buffalo Bill, Vanished, Harry Truman Biography, Truman vs. MacArthur, Knots Landing, Santa Barbara, Roseanne.

JOHNSON, TOM
Sound.
PICTURES: Star Wars: Return of the Jedi, Indiana Jones and the Temple of Doom, Seize the Day, Howard the Duck, Dirty Rotten Scoundrels, Colors, The Couch Trip, Tucker: The Man and His Dream, The Karate Kid III, To Cross the Rubicon, The Five Heartbeats, Terminator II: Judgment Day, F/X2, Single White Female, Quiz Show, Forrest Gump, Nine Months, Strange Days, Stealing Beauty, Jack, One Fine Day, Titanic (Acad. Award, Best Sound, 1997), Beverly Hills Ninja, Contact, Wag the Dog, Sphere, The Horse Whisperer, A Midsummer Night's Dream, Star Wars: Episode 1 - The Phantom Menace, Liberty Heights, Galaxy Quest, The Yards, Requiem for a Dream, When the Sky Falls, Cirque du Soleil: Journey of Man, What Lies Beneath, Cast Away, An Everlasting Piece, The Tailor of Panama, Atlantis: The Lost Empire, Bandits. Blood Work, LThe Good Thief, The Ring, Maid in Manhattan.
TELEVISION: Movies: The Dreamer of Oz.

JOHNSON, VAN
Actor. b. Newport, RI, Aug. 25, 1916. Began in vaudeville; then on N.Y. stage New Faces of 1937, Eight Men of Manhattan, Too Many Girls, Pal Joey. Voted one of the top ten Money Making Stars in Motion Picture Herald-Fame Poll 1945-46. Stage includes The Music Man (London), La Cage aux Folles (NY) and numerous tours.
PICTURES: Too Many Girls (debut, 1940), Murder in the Big House, Somewhere I'll Find You, War Against Mrs. Hadley, Dr. Gillespie's New Assistant, The Human Comedy, Pilot No. 5, Dr. Gillespies's Criminal Case, Guy Named Joe, White Cliffs of Dover, Three Men in White, Two Girls and a Sailor, Thirty Seconds Over Tokyo, Between Two Women, Thrill of Romance, Weekend at the Waldorf, Easy to Wed, No Leave No Love, Till the Clouds Roll By, High Barbaree, Romance of Rosy Ridge, Bride Goes Wild, State of the Union, Command Decision, Mother is a Freshman, In the Good Old Summertime, Scene of the Crime, Battleground, Big Hangover, Duchess of Idaho, Three Guys Named Mike, Grounds for Marriage, Go For Broke, Too Young to Kiss, It's a Big Country, Invitation, When in Rome, Washington Story, Plymouth Adventure, Confidentially Connie, Remains to Be Seen, Easy to Love, Caine Mutiny, Siege at Red River, Men of the Fighting Lady, Brigadoon, Last Time I Saw Paris, End of the Affair, Bottom of the Bottle, Miracle in the Rain, 23 Paces to Baker Street, Slander, Kelly and Me, Action of the Tiger, The Last Blitzkreig, Subway in the Sky, Beyond This Place, Enemy General, Wives and Lovers, Divorce American Style, Yours Mine and Ours, Where Angels Go... Trouble Follows, Company of Killers, Eagles Over London, The Kidnapping of the President, The Purple Rose of Cairo, Down There in the Jungle, Escape From Paradise, Three Days to a Kill, Clowning Around, Junket Whore.
TELEVISION: Special: Pied Piper of Hamelin. Mini-Series: Rich Man Poor Man, Black Beauty. Movies: Doomsday Flight, San Francisco International, Call Her Mom, The Girl on the Late Late Show, Superdome. Guest: I Love Lucy, G.E. Theatre, Batman, Love American Style, The Love Boat, Murder She Wrote.

JOHNSTON, JOANNA
Costume Designer.
PICTURES: Hellraiser, Who Framed Roger Rabbit, Indiana Jones and the Last Crusade, Back to the Future Part II, Back to the Future Part III, Far and Away, Death Becomes, Forrest Gump, French Kiss, Contact, Saving Private Ryan, The Sixth Sense, Unbreakable, Cast Away, About a Boy, Love Actually.

JOHNSTON, MARGARET
Actress. b. Sydney, Australia, Aug. 10, 1918. e. Sydney U., Australia; RADA. London stage debut: Murder Without Crime.
THEATRE: Ring of Truth, The Masterpiece, Lady Macbeth, Merchant of Venice, Measure for Measure, Othello.
PICTURES: The Prime Minister, The Rake's Progress (The Notorious Gentleman), A Man About the House, Portrait of Clare, The Magic Box, Knave of Hearts, Touch and Go, Burn With Burn (Night of the Eagle), The Nose on My Face, Girl in the Headlines (The Model Murder Case), Life at the Top, The Psychopath, Schizo, Sebastian.
TELEVISION: Always Juliet, Taming of the Shrew, Man with a Load of Mischief, Light of Heart, Autumn Crocus, Androcles and the Lion, Sulky Five, Windmill Near a Frontier, The Shrike, The Out of Towners, Looking for Garrow, The Typewriter, The Glass

Menagerie, That's Where the Town's Going, The Vortex. (d. June 29, 2002)

JOLIE, ANGELINA
Actress. b. Los Angeles, CA, June 4, 1975. Father is actor Jon Voight.
PICTURES: Lookin' to Get Out, Cyborg 2: Glass Shadow, Angela & Viril (short), Hackers, Without Evidence, Mojave Moon, Foxfire, Love Is All There Is, Playing God, Pushing Tin, Hell's Kitchen, Dancing About Architecture, Girl Interrupted (Academy Award, best actress in a supporting role), The Bone Collector, Gone in Sixty Seconds, Original Sin, Tomb Raider, Beyond Borders, Life or Something Like It, Trading Women (documentary, narrator), Tomb Raider: The Cradle of Life, Beyond Borders, Lovesick (prod. only), The World of Tomorrow, Sharkslayer (voice).
TELEVISION: Movies: True Women, George Wallace (Golden Globe Award, 1998), Gia. Mini-series: True Women.

JOLLEY, STAN
Producer, Director, Production Designer, Art Director. b. New York, NY, May 17, 1926. e. U. of Southern California, col. of architecture. Son of actor I. Stanford Jolley. In Navy in W.W.II. Has acted in capacities listed for many feature films and TV series. One of orig. designers of Disneyland.
PICTURES: Prod./Prod. Designer: Knife for the Ladies. Assoc. Prod./ Prod. Designer: The Good Guys and the Bad Guys. 2nd Unit Dir.: Superman. Prod. Designer: Dutch, The Good Mother, Witness (Acad. Award nom.), Taps, Caddyshack, Cattle Annie and Little Britches, Americathon (also second unit director), The Swarm, Drum, Framed, Dion Brothers, Mixed Company, Walking Tall, Terror in the Wax Museum, Night of the Lepus (also second unit director), War Between Men and Women, Law Man, The Phynx. Art Director: Young Billy Young, Ride Beyond Vengeance, Broken Saber, The Restless Ones, Mail Order Bride, Toby Tyler, The Grass Harp, Mr. Ed. Assoc. Prod./Prod. designer & 2nd unit dir.: Happily Ever After.
TELEVISION: Movies: 2nd Unit Dir./Prod. Designer: Swiss Family Robinson, Adventures of the Queen, Woman Hunter, Abduction of Carrie Swenson, Eagle One, No Man's Land, Last of the Great Survivors, Like Normal People, Rescue From Gilligan's Island, Flood, Voyage of the Yes, The Stranger, Punch & Jody, City Beneath the Sea, Women of San Quentin. Mini-series: Howards, The Amazing Mr. Hughes. Series: Dir./Prod. Designer: MacGyver, Today's FBI. Assoc. Prod./Prod. Designer: Jessie. Prod. Designer: Walking Tall, For Love and Honor. Art Dir.: Walt Disney Presents, Pete and Gladys, Gunsmoke, Mr. Ed, Branded, Voyage to the Bottom of the Sea, Land of the Giants, O'Hara Shane, Acapulco, The Racers, Docu-drama: Under Fire. Pilots: Get Smart, Some Like It Hot. Cartoon: Donald in Mathmagic Land. Documentary: Crisis in the Wetlands (prod./dir.). Writer: Novel: "Dichotomy-Amish Justice", Chake (s.p.).

JONES, AMY HOLDEN
Director, Writer. b. Philadelphia, PA, Sept. 17, 1953. m. cinematographer, Michael Chapman. e. Wellesley Coll., B.A., 1974; film and photography courses, Massachusetts Inst. of Technology. Winner, first place, Washington National Student Film Festival, 1973.
PICTURES: Editor: Hollywood Boulevard (debut, 1976), American Boy, Corvette Summer, Second Hand Hearts. Director: Slumber Party Massacre, Love Letters (also s.p.), Mystic Pizza (s.p. only), Maid to Order (also co-s.p.), Rich Man's Wife (also s.p.). Writer: Beethoven (1, 2, 3, 4 & 5), Indecent Proposal, The Getaway, It Had to Be Steve (co-s.p.), The Relic (co-s.p.).
TELEVISION: Pilot (writer): Jack's Place.

JONES, DAVID HUGH
Director, Producer. b. Poole, Eng., Feb. 19, 1934. e. Christ's Coll., Cambridge U., B.A., 1954, M.A., 1957. Immigrated to U.S. in 1979. Artistic controller, then assoc. dir., Royal Shakespeare Co., 1964-75; artistic dir, RSC at Aldwych Theatre 1975-78; artistic dir, Brooklyn Acad. of Music Theatre Co., NY 1979-81; prof. Yale Sch. of Drama, 1981.
THEATRE: Sweeney Agonistes (debut, 1961); U.S.: Summerfolk, Loves Labour's Lost, Winter's Tale, Barbarians, Jungle of Cities.
PICTURES: Look Back in Anger, Betrayal, 84 Charing Cross Road, Jacknife, The Trial, Time to Say Goodbye?,
TELEVISION: Prod.: Monitor 1958-64 (BBC series), Play of the Month. Movies/Dir: Barbara of the House of Grebe, The Merry Wives of Windsor, Pericles-Prince of Tyre, The Christmas Wife, Sensibility & Sense, Fire in the Dark, And then there was One, Is There Life Out There?, Requiem Apache, Sophie and the Moonhanger, An Unexpected Life, A Christmas Carol, Custody of the Heart. Series/Dir.: Shakespeare series, BBC 1982-83; The Education of Max Bickford.

JONES, DEAN
Actor. b. Decatur, AL, Jan. 25, 1931. e. Asbury Coll., Wilmore, KY. Prof. debut as blues singer, New Orleans; U.S. Navy, 1950-54. Author: Under Running Laughter.
THEATRE: There Was a Little Girl, Under the Yum-Yum Tree, Company, Into the Light, Show Boat.
PICTURES: Tea and Sympathy (debut, 1956), The Rack, The

Opposite Sex, These Wilder Years, The Great American Pastime, Designing Woman, Ten Thousand Bedrooms, Jailhouse Rock, Until They Sail, Imitation General, Torpedo Run, Handle with Care, Night of the Quarter Moon, Never So Few, Under the Yum-Yum Tree, The New Interns, That Darn Cat, Two on a Guillotine, Any Wednesday, The Ugly Dachshund, Monkeys Go Home, Blackbeard's Ghost, The Horse in the Grey Flannel Suit, The Love Bug, $1,000,000 Duck, Snowball Express, Mr. Super Invisible, The Shaggy D.A., Herbie Goes to Monte Carlo, Born Again, Other People's Money, Beethoven, Clear and Present Danger, That Darn Cat II, Subzero (dubb).
TELEVISION: Movies: Guess Who's Sleeping in My Bed?, When Every Day Was the 4th of July, Long Days of Summer, Fire and Rain, The Great Man's Whiskers, Saved By the Bell: Hawaiian Style, The Computer Wore Tennis Shoes, The Love Bug Reunion, Who Is This Jesus? Scrooge and Marley. Series: Ensign O'Toole, The Chicago Teddy Bears, What's It All About World?, Herbie the Love Bug, Beethoven (animated; voice). Specials: Journey to Mars, Out of Jerusalem.

JONES, GEMMA
Actress. b. London, Eng., Dec. 4, 1942. e. Royal Acad. of Dramatic Art.
THEATRE: Baal, Alfie, The Cavern, The Marriage of Figaro, And A Nightingale Sang, reaking the Silence, Howards End, A Midsummer Night's Dream, The Homecoming, Mount Morgan, The Winter's Tale.
PICTURES: The Devils, The Paper House, On the Black Hill, The Devils Feast of July, Sense and Sensibility, Wilde, The Winslow Boy, O.K. Garage, The Theory of Flight, Captain Jack, Cotton Mary, Bridget Jones's Diary, Don't Tempt Me, Harry Potter and the Chamber of Secrets, Shanghai Knights.
TELEVISION: The Lie, The Way of the World, The Merchant of Venice, The Duchess of Duke Street (series), The Jim Henson Hour, Forget Me Not Lane,Call My Bluff, Dial M For Murder, The Way of the World, Churchill's People, The Cherry Orchard, The Lie, Man In A Sidecar, Shadows of Fear, Crimes of Passion, The Spoils of Poynton, The Duchess of Duke Street, The Importance of Being Earnest, Chelworth, After The Dance, Inspector Morse, The Storyteller, Sevises and Desires, Some Lie Some Die, Wycliffe, The Borrowers, Faith, Wilderness, Jane Eyre, The Phoenix and the Carpet, An Unsuitable Job for a Woman, Longitude, An Evil Streak, Bootleg.

JONES, GLENN R.
Executive. Began career in law, representing cable TV cos. in acquisition efforts. Purchased his first cable TV system in 1967 which became part of Jones Intercable, Inc., founded 1970. Pres. and CEO of the corp. since its inception. Co. changed name to Jones Media Networks, Ltd. Currently, chmn. Served as a member of the Board of Directors and the Executive Committee for the National Cable Television Association (NCTA) and as a member of the Board of Governors for the American Society for Training and Development (ASTD). Currently on the Board and Education Council of the National Alliance of Business (NAB). Founding member of the James Madison National Council. Recipient of numerous honors including: named Man of the Year by the Denver chapter of the Achievement Rewards for College Scientists (ARCS) and inducted into Broadcasting and Cable's Hall of Fame.

JONES, GRACE
Singer, Actress. r.n. Grace Mendoza. b. Spanishtown, Jamaica, May 19, 1948. e. Syracuse U. Modelled and appeared in several Italian pictures before career as singer.
PICTURES: Conan the Destroyer, A View to a Kill, Vamp, Straight to Hell, Siesta, Boomerang, Cyber Bandits, McCinsey's Island, Palmer's Pick Up.
TELEVISION: Wolf Girl, Shaka Zulu: The Citadel.

JONES, JAMES EARL
Actor. r.n. Todd Jones. b. Arkabutla, MS, Jan. 17, 1931. e. U. of Michigan. Son of actor Robert Earl Jones. Awarded Hon. Doctor of Fine Arts (Yale, Princeton); Medal for Spoken Language (Amer. Acad. and Inst. of Arts and Letter; Hon. Doctor of Humane Letters (Columbia Coll. & U. of Mich.).
THEATRE: Moon on a Rainbow Shawl (Theatre World Award), The Cool World, Othello, Paul Robeson, Les Blancs, The Great White Hope (Tony Award, 1969), The Iceman Cometh, Of Mice and Men, A Lesson from Aloes, Master Harold ... and the Boys, Fences (Tony Award, 1986).
PICTURES: Dr. Strangelove, or: How I Learned to Stop Worrying and Love the Bomb (debut, 1964), The Comedians, King: A Filmed Record ... Montgomery to Memphis, End of the Road, The Great White Hope (Acad. Award nom.), Malcolm X (narrator), The Man, Claudine, Deadly Hero, Swashbuckler, The Bingo Long Travelling All-Stars and Motor Kings, The River Niger, The Greatest, Star Wars (voice), Exorcist II: The Heretic, The Last Remake of Beau Geste, A Piece of the Action, The Bushido Blade, The Empire Strikes Back (voice), Conan the Barbarian, Blood Tide (The Red Tide), Return of the Jedi (voice), City Limits, My Little Girl, Soul Man, Allan Quartermain and the Lost City of Gold, Gardens of Stone, Matewan, Pinocchio and the Emperor of the Night (voice), Coming to America, Three Fugitives, Field of Dreams, Best of the Best, The Hunt for Red

October, Grim Prairie Tales, The Ambulance, True Identity, Convicts, Patriot Games, Sneakers, Sommersby, The Sandlot, The Meteor Man, Naked Gun 33 1/3: The Final Insult, Clean Slate, The Lion King (voice), Clear and Present Danger, Jefferson in Paris, Judge Dredd (voice), Cry the Beloved Country, Lone Star, A Family Thing, Good Luck (cameo), Gang Related, Summer's End, The Lion King II: Simba's Pride (voice), The Annihilation of Fish, Fantasia/2000, Undercover Angel, Quest for Atlantis, Antietam: A Documentary Drama, Finder's Fee, The Papp Project, Disney's American Legends (documentary, narrator).
TELEVISION:Movies: The UFO Incident, Jesus of Nazareth, The Greatest Thing That Almost Happened, Guyana Tragedy—The Story of Jim Jones, Golden Moment: An Olympic Love Story, Philby, Burgess and MacLean, The Atlanta Child Murders, The Vegas Strip War, By Dawn's Early Light, Heat Wave (Emmy Award, 1991), Last Flight Out, The Last Elephant, Percy & Thunder, The Vernon Johns Story, Confessions: Two Faces of Evil, Alone, The Second Civil War, What the Deaf Man Heard, Merlin, Summer's End, Santa and Pete, In Search of Liberty Bell 7, 2004: A Light Knight's Odyssey, The Magic 7. Mini-Series: Roots: The Next Generations, Feast of All Saints. Specials: King Lear, Soldier Boy, Mathnet, Bailey's Bridge, Third and Oak: The Pool Hall, Teach 109, Hallelujah. Host: Black Omnibus, Vegetable Soup, Summer Show, Long Ago and Far Away. Series: As the World Turns, The Guiding Light, Paris, Me and Mom, Gabriel's Fire (Emmy Award, 1991), Pros & Cons, Under One Roof.

JONES, JEFFREY
Actor. b. Buffalo, NY, Sept. 28, 1947. e. Lawrence U., Wisconsin. While pre-med student, performed in 1967 prod. of Hobson's Choice and was invited by Sir Tyrone Guthrie to join Guthrie Theatre in Minneapolis. After short time in South America, studied at London Acad. of Music and Dramatic Arts before joining Stratford Theater in Ontario. 1973-74 worked with Vancouver touring children's theater co. Playhouse Holiday. Moved to N.Y. where performed on stage.
THEATRE: The Elephant Man (B'way debut), Trelawney of the Wells, Secret Service, Boy Meets Girl, Cloud Nine, Comedy of Errors, The Tempest, The Death of Von Richtoven, London Suite.
PICTURES: The Revolutionary, The Soldier, Easy Money, Amadeus, Transylvania 6-5000, Ferris Bueller's Day Off, Howard the Duck, The Hanoi Hilton, Beetlejuice, Without a Clue, Who Is Harry Crumb?, Valmont, The Hunt for Red October, Over Her Dead Body, Mom and Dad Save the World, Stay Tuned, Out on a Limb, Heaven and Earth (cameo), Ed Wood, Houseguest, The Pest, The Crucible, Sante Fe, Flypaper, The Pest, The Devil's Advocate, There Is No Fish Food in Heaven, Ravenous, Sleepy Hollow, Stuart Little, Robots of Mars, Company Man, Heartbreakers, Dr. Dolittle 2, How High, Per 6.
TELEVISION: Mini-Series: George Washington: The Forging of a Nation, Fresno. Movies: Kenny Rogers as The Gambler III—The Legend Continues, The Avenging Angel, Till Dad Do Us Part. Guest: Amazing Stories, Twilight Zone, Remington Steele. Series: The People Next Door, Deadwood.

JONES, JENNIFER
Actress. r.n. Phyllis Isley. b. Tulsa, OK, Mar. 2, 1919. e. Northwestern U., American Acad. of Dramatic Arts. Daughter of Phil R., Flora Mae (Suber) Isley, exhib. m. industrialist Norton Simon. Son is actor Robert Walker Jr. Toured with parents stock company as child; in summer stock in East; little theat. East & West. Began screen career as Phyllis Isley. Pres., Norton Simon Museum.
PICTURES: Dick Tracy's G-Men (debut, 1939), The New Frontier, The Song of Bernadette (Academy Award, 1943; first film billed as Jennifer Jones), Since You Went Away, Love Letters, Cluny Brown, Duel in the Sun, Portrait of Jennie, We Were Strangers, Madame Bovary, Carrie, Wild Heart (Gone to Earth), Ruby Gentry, Indiscretion of an American Wife (Terminal Station), Beat the Devil, Love Is a Many-Splendored Thing, Good Morning Miss Dove, The Man in the Gray Flannel Suit, The Barretts of Wimpole Street, A Farewell to Arms, Tender Is the Night, The Idol, Angel Angel Down We Go (Cult of the Damned), The Towering Inferno.
TELEVISION: Numerous appearances on various specials: AFI Salutes and Academy Award specials.

JONES, KATHY
Executive. b. Aug. 27, 1949. Began career as acct. exec. for m.p. clients, Stan Levinson assoc., Dallas. Joined Paramount Pictures in 1977 as sr. publicist in field marketing then exec. dir., field mktg. Left to join Time-Life Films as v.p., domestic mktg. for m.p. div. Returned to Paramount 1981 as v.p., domestic pub. & promo. 1984, appt. sr. v.p., domestic pub. & promo. for Motion Picture Group, Paramount. Formed m.p. consultancy with Buffy Shutt, 1987. 1989, appt. exec. v.p., marketing, Columbia Pictures. 1991, appt. exec. v.p. marketing, TriStar Pictures. Currently partnered with Buffy Shutt in feature & tv production co., Shutt-Jones Productions, based at Universal Studios in Universal City.

JONES, QUINCY
Producer, Composer, Arranger, Recording Artist. b. Chicago, IL, March 14, 1933. e. Seattle U., Berklee Sch. Music, Boston Conservatory, Trumpeter and arranger for Lionel Hampton's orch. 1950-53, played with Dizzy Gillespie, Count Basie and arranged for orchs., singers-Frank Sinatra, Sarah Vaughn, Peggy Lee, Dinah Washington and led own orch. for European tours, and recordings. Prod. recordings for Michael Jackson, Tevin Campbell, Barbra Streisand, Donna Summer. Music dir. and v.p., Mercury Records 1961-64 before scoring films. Prod. & arranged We Are the World recording. Owns Qwest Records record company. Received Jean Hersholt Humanitarian Award, 1995. Wrote autobiography in 2001, Q: The Autobiography of Quincy Jones.
PICTURES: The Pawnbroker, Mirage, The Slender Thread, Made in Paris, Walk Don't Run, Banning, The Deadly Affair, In the Heat of the Night, In Cold Blood (Acad. Award nom.), Enter Laughing, A Dandy in Aspic, For Love of Ivy, The Hell With Heroes, The Split, Up Your Teddy Bear, Jocelyn, McKenna's Gold, The Italian Job, Bob & Carol & Ted & Alice, The Lost Man, Cactus Flower, John and Mary, The Last of the Mobile Hotshots, The Out-of-Towners, They Call Me Mister Tibbs, Brother John, $ (Dollars), The Anderson Tapes, Yao of the Jungle, The Hot Rock, The New Centurions, Come Back Charleston Blue, The Getaway, The Wiz (also cameo), The Color Purple (also co-prod.; Acad. Award nom.), Listen Up: The Lives of Quincy Jones, Steel, Austin Powers: International Man of Mystery, Austin Powers: The Spy Who Shagged Me, The Smokers (exec. prod. only), Vaccuums (exec. prod. only), Thug Angel (exec. prod. only), Austin Powers in Goldmember (also actor), Vaccuums (exec. prod., prod), Keeping Time: The Life-Music & Photography of Milt Hinton (as himself).
TELEVISION: Movies: The Palladium: Where Mambo Was King. Mini-Series: Roots (Emmy, 1977). Special: An American Reunion (exec. prod.). Series: Fresh Prince of Bel Air, In the House (prod.).

JONES, SAM J.
Actor. b. Chicago, IL, Aug. 12, 1954.
PICTURES: "10," Davinci's War, One Man Force, Night Rhythms, South Beach, Iron Fist, Where the Truth Lies, Evasive Action, Flash Gordon, Lady Dragon II, Last Breath, My Chauffeur, Under the Gun, Silent Assassins, Jane & the Lost City, White Fire, Trigon Factor, Driving Force, In Gold We Trust, Human Shields, Fists of Honor, Ballistic, American Strays, Texas Payback, Hard Vice, R.I.O.T., American Tigers, Baja Run, Earth Minus Zero, Baja Run, American Tigers, T.N.T., Evasive Action, The Killer Inside, Gangland, Down n' Dirty, Dead Sexy (video), Van Hook, Psychotic, Redemption.
TELEVISION: Series: Training Camp, Code Red, The Highwayman, Hollywood Safari. Movies: This Wife for Hire, Ray Alexander. Pilot: Hat Squad, Cobra, Thunder in Paradise,Stunts Unlimited, No Man's Land, The Spirit. Guest: Co-ed Fever, A-Team, Riptide, Hunter, Baywatch, Diagnosis Murder, Pacific Blue.

JONES, SHIRLEY
Actress. b. Smithton, PA, March 31, 1934. m. agent-prod. Marty Ingels. Mother of actors Shaun and Patrick Cassidy. Former Miss Pittsburgh. Natl. chair, Leukemia Foundation. Book: Shirley & Marty: An Unlikely Love Story (Wm. Morrow, 1990). Received hon. Doctor of Humane Letters degree from Point Park Col. 1991.
THEATRE: Appeared with Pittsburgh Civic Light Opera in Lady in the Dark, Call Me Madam. B'way: South Pacific, Me and Juliet, Maggie Flynn.
PICTURES: Oklahoma! (debut, 1955), Carousel, April Love, Never Steal Anything Small, Bobbikins, Elmer Gantry (Academy Award, best supporting actress, 1960), Pepe, Two Rode Together, The Music Man, The Courtship of Eddie's Father, A Ticklish Affair, Dark Purpose, Bedtime Story, Fluffy, The Secret of My Success, The Happy Ending, El Golfo, Oddly Coupled, The Cheyenne Social Club, Beyond the Poseidon Adventure, Tank, There Were Times Dear, Jack L. Warner: The Last Mogul, Cops n' Roberts, Gideon, Shriek If You Know What I Did Last Friday the Thirteenth (video), Ping!, The Adventures of Cinderella's Daughter, Manna From Heaven, Bloodhead.
TELEVISION: Movies: Silent Night Lonely Night, But I Don't Want to Get Married, The Girls of Huntington House, The Family Nobody Wanted, Winner Take All, The Lives of Jenny Dolan, Yesterday's Child, Evening in Byzantium, Who'll Save Our Children? A Last Cry For Help, Children of An Lac, Intimates: A Love Story, Widow, Charlie, Dog's Best Friend, Intimate Portrait: Shirley Jones (as herself), We Are Family (documentary, as herself). Series: The Partridge Family, Shirley, The Slap Maxwell Story. Guest: McMillan and Wife, The Love Boat, Hotel, Murder She Wrote, Empty Nest.

JONES, TERRY
Writer, Actor, Director. b. Colwyn Bay, North Wales, Feb. 1, 1942. Worked with various rep. groups before joining BBC script dept. Was member of Monty Python's Flying Circus.
PICTURES: Actor: And Now for Something Completely Different (also co-s.p.), Monty Python and the Holy Grail (also co-dir., co-s.p.), Monty Python's Life of Brian (also dir., co-s.p.), Monty Python's The Meaning of Life (also co-s.p., dir., music), Labyrinth (s.p. only), Personal Services (dir. only), Erik the Viking (also dir., s.p.), LA Story, The Wind in the Willows, Magdalen, The Creator, Help I'm a Fish, Bitter Jester (documentary), Green Card Fever.
TELEVISION: Late Night Lineup, The Late Show, A Series of Birds, Do Not Adjust Your Set, The Complete and Utter History of Britain, Monty Python's Flying Circus, Secrets, The Crusades (also dir., writer), So This Is Progress, It's the Monty Python Story, Crusades, Monty Python's Flying Circus: Live at Aspen, 30 Years of Monty Python: A Revelation, The Boy in Darkness, Top Ten Comedy Records, The Sketch Show Story, Dinotopia.

JONES, TOMMY LEE
Actor. b. San Saba, TX, Sept. 15, 1946. Worked in oil fields; graduated Harvard, where earned a degree, cum laude, in English. Broadway debut in A Patriot for Me; appeared on stage in Four in a Garden, Ulysses in Nighttown, Fortune and Men's Eyes.
PICTURES: Love Story (debut, 1970), Eliza's Horoscope, Jackson County Jail, Rolling Thunder, The Betsy, Eyes of Laura Mars, Coal Miner's Daughter, Back Roads, Nate and Hayes, The River Rat, Black Moon Rising, The Big Town, Stormy Monday, The Package, Firebirds, JFK (Acad. Award nom.), Under Siege, House of Cards, The Fugitive (Acad. Award, best supporting actor, 1993; LA Film Critics & Golden Globe Awards), Heaven and Earth, Blown Away, The Client, Natural Born Killers, Blue Sky, Cobb, Batman Forever, Men in Black, Volcano, U.S. Marshalls, Small Soldiers (voice), Rules of Engagement, Double Jeopardy, Space Cowboys, Men in Black 2, The Hunted, The Missing.
TELEVISION: Movies: Charlie's Angels (pilot), Smash-Up on Interstate 5, The Amazing Howard Hughes, The Executioner's Song (Emmy Award, 1983), Broken Vows, The Park is Mine, Yuri Nosenko: KGB, Gotham, Stranger on My Land, April Morning, The Good Old Boys (also dir., co-writer). Mini-Series: Lonesome Dove. Specials: The Rainmaker, Cat on a Hot Tin Roof.

JONES, TREVOR
Composer, conductor. b. Cape Town, S. Africa, March 23, 1949.
PICTURES: The Dollar Bottom, Brothers and Sisters, The Beneficiary, The Appointment, Excalibur, The Sender, The Dark Crystal, Nate and Hayes, Runaway Train, From an Immigrant's Diary, Labyrinth, Angel Heart, Sweet Lies, A Private Life, Mississippi Burning, Just Ask For Diamond, Dominick and Eugene, Sea of Love, Bad Influence, Arachnophobia, Ture Colors, CrissCross, Blame It on the Bellboy, Freejack, The Last of the Mohicans (Golden Globe nom.), In the Name of the Father, Cliffhanger, De Baby huilt, LochNess, Hideaway, Kiss of Death, Richard III, Brassed Off, Lawn Dogs, Roseanna's Grave, Talk of Angels, Desperate Measures, G.I. Jane, Titanic Town, Plunkett & MacLeane, Analyse This, Dark City, The Mighty, Notting Hill, Molly, Frederic Wilde, From Hell, Crossroads, I'll Be There, The League of Extraordinary Gentlemen.
TELEVISION: Movies: Those Glory Glory Days, One of Ourselves, Aderyn Papur.. and Pigs Might Fly, Dr. Fischer of Geneva, A Private Life, Murder by Moonlight, By Dawn's Early Light, Chains of Gold, Guns... A Day In the Death of America, Death Train, Mini-series: Joni Jones, The Last Days of Pompeii, Jim Henson Presents the World of International Puppeteering, The Last Place on Earth, Gulliver's Travels, Merlin, Cleopatra, Dinotopia.

JONZE, SPIKE
Actor, Director. b. Rockville, Maryland, 1969. r.n. Adam Speigel. Has directed many television commercials and music videos for artists. Is heir to the Spiegel mail order catalog.
PICTURES: Mi Vida Loca (actor), The Game (actor only), Being John Malkovich, Three Kings (actor only), Hannibal (actor only), Adaptation, Keep Your Eyes Open (actor only), Jackass (documentary, writer, prod.), Adaptation (actor, dir.), Yeah Right! (video, dir. exec. prod.).

JORDAN, GLENN
Director, Producer. b. San Antonio, TX, April 5, 1936. e. Harvard, B.A.; Yale Drama Sch. Directed plays off-B'way and on tour.
PICTURES: Director: Only When I Laugh, The Buddy System, Mass Appeal.
TELEVISION: Movies: Director: Frankenstein, The Picture of Dorian Gray, Shell Game, One of My Wives is Missing, The Displaced Person, Delta County U.S.A., In the Matter of Karen Ann Quinlan, Sunshine Christmas, Les Miserables, One Sunrise: A Miracle of Love, The Family Man, The , The Princess and the Cabbie, Lois Gibbs and the Love Canal, Heartsounds, Dress Gray (also prod.), Promise (also prod., 2 Emmy Awards), Something in Common (also prod.), Echoes in the Darkness (also prod.), Jesse, Home Fires Burning (also prod.), Challenger, Sarah Plain & Tall (also prod.), Aftermath: A Test of Love, The Boys (also prod.), O Pioneers (also prod.), Barbarians at the Gate (Emmy Award; co-exec. prod.), To Dance with the White Dog (also prod.), Jane's House (also prod.), My Brother's Keeper, A Streetcar Named Desire (1995), Jake's Women (also prod.), After Jimmy, Mary & Tim, A Christmas Memory, The Long Way Home, Legalese, Night Ride Home, Sarah Plain & Tall:

Winter's End, Midwives, Lucy. *Specials*: Hogan's Goat, Paradise Lost, Benjamin Franklin (prod.; Emmy Award), Eccentricities of a Nightingale, The Oath, The Court Martial of Gen. George Armstrong Custer. *Series*: Family.

JORDAN, NEIL
Director, Writer. b. Sligo, Ireland, Feb. 25, 1950. e. University Coll, B.A., 1972. Novels: The Past, Night in Tunisia, Dream of a Beast.
PICTURES: Traveller (s.p.), The Courier (co-exec. prod.). *Dir.-Writer*: Angel, The Company of Wolves, Mona Lisa (LA Film Critics Award for s.p., 1986), High Spirits, We're No Angels (dir. only), The Miracle, The Crying Game (Academy Award, WGA & NY Film Critics Awards for s.p., 1992), Interview With the Vampire, Michael Collins, The Butcher Boy, In Dreams, The End of the Affair, Not I (dir. only), The Good Thief, Borgia, The Actors (story only), Intermission (prod. only).
TELEVISION: Mr. Solomon Wept (BBC), RTE (Ireland), Seduction, Tree, Miracles and Miss Langan.

JOSEPHSON, ERLAND
Actor, Director, Writer. b. Stockholm, Sweden, June 15, 1923. Acted in over 100 plays in Sweden. Joined Sweden's Royal Dramatic Theatre in 1956 replacing Ingmar Bergman as head of the theater, 1966-76. Closely associated with Bergman, with whom he staged plays in his late teens. Co-authored s.p. The Pleasure Garden and Now About These Women. Also has pub. poetry, six novels, and scripts for stage, screen and radio. American stage debut: The Cherry Orchard, 1988. In numerous movies on Swedish television.
PICTURES: It Rains on Our Love, To Joy (uncredited), Sceningang, Som man baddar, Brink of Life, The Magician, Hour of the Wolf, The Girls, Eva: Diary of Half Virgin, The Passion of Anna, Cries and Whispers, Scenes from a Marriage, Monismanien, Face to Face, A Look at Liv, Io ho paura, Beyond Good and Evil, Games of Love and Loneliness, I'm Afraid, Autumn Sonata, Die Erste Polka, To Forget Venice, One and One (also dir.), The Marmalade Revolution (also dir., s.p.), Karleken, Victor Sjostrom (voice), You Love Only Once, Montenegro, Sezona Mira u Parizu, Fanny and Alexander, Bella Donna, Nostalgia, House of the Yellow Carpet, After the Rehearsal, Angela's War, Bakom jalusin, Behind the Shutters, A Case of Irresponsibility, Dirty Story, Amorosa, The Flying Devils, Garibaldi, The General, The Last Mazurka, The Sacrifice, The Malady of Love, Saving Grace, Le Testament d'un poete juif assassine, Unbearable Lightness of Being, Directed by Andrei Tarkovsky, Hanussen, Good Evening Mr. Wallenberg, The Wicked, Meeting Venus, Prospero's Books, The Ox, The Accidental Golfer, Sofie, Holozan, The Dancer, Dreamplay, Ulysses' Gaze, Vendetta, Waiting for Sunset, Kristin Lavransdatter, I Am Curious Film, Al la recherche de Erland Josephson, Magnetist's Fifth Winter, Light Keeps Me Company, Faithless, Hr. Boe & Co's Anxiety, Scener ur ett aktenskap II, The Good Pope: Pope John XXIII, Nu..

JOSEPHSON, MARVIN
Executive. b. Atlantic City, NJ, March 6, 1927. e. Cornell U., B.A., 1949; L.L.B. NYU, 1952. Lawyer at CBS Television 1952-55; founded company which today is ICM Holdings Inc. in 1955. ICM Holdings Inc. is the parent company of Intl. Creative Management Inc. and ICM Artists Ltd.

JOST, JON
Director, Writer, Cinematographer, Editor. b. May 16, 1943. PICTURES: Speaking Directly, Angel City, Last Chants for a Slow Dance, Chameleon (also prod.), Stagefright, Psalm, Slow Moves, Bell Diamond, Rembrandt Laughing, Plain Talk & Common Sense, Blood Orgy of the Leather Girls (assoc. prod. only), All the Vermeers in New York, The Living End (exec. prod. only), Sure Fire, Frame Up, The Bed You Sleep In, One for You One for Me and One for Raphael, Albrecht's Wings, Frame Up, London Brief, Roman Walls.

JOURDAN, LOUIS
Actor, r.n. Louis Gendre. b. Marseille, France, June 19, 1921. Stage actor prior to m.p.
PICTURES: Le Corsaire (debut, 1940), Her First Affair, La Boheme, L'Arlesienne, La Belle, Adventure, Felicie Nanteuil, The Paradine Case, Letter from an Unknown Woman, No Minor Vices, Madame Bovary, Bird of Paradise, Anne of the Indies, The Happy Time, Decameron Nights, Three Coins in the Fountain, The Swan, Julie, The Bride is Much Too Beautiful, Dangerous Exile, Gigi, The Best of Everything, Can-Can, Leviathan, Streets of Montmartre, Story of the Count of Monte Cristo, Mathias Sandorf, The VIPs, Made in Paris, To Commit a Murder, A Flea in Her Ear, Young Rebel (Cervantes), The Silver Bears, Double Deal, Swamp Thing, Octopussy, The Return of Swamp Thing, Counterforce, Year of the Comet.
TELEVISION: *Movies*: Run a Crooked Mile, Fear No Evil, Ritual of Evil, The Great American Beauty Contest, The Count of Monte Cristo, The Man in the Iron Mask, The First Olympics-Athens, Beverly Hills Madam. *Series*: Paris Precinct, Romance Theatre (host). *Mini-Series*: The French Atlantic Affair, Dracula.

JOY, ROBERT
Actor. b. Montreal, Canada, Aug. 17, 1951. e. Memorial Univ. of Newfoundland; Rhodes Scholar. Acted in regional and off-Broadway theatre. Off-B'way debut The Diary of Anne Frank (1978). Has composed music for stage, radio and film.
THEATRE: NY Shakespeare Fest. (Found a Peanut, Lenny and the Heartbreakers, The Death of von Richtofen), Life and Limb, Fables for Friends, Welcome to the Moon, What I Did Last Summer, Lydie Breeze, Romeo and Juliet (La Jolla Playhouse; Drama-Logue Award), Hay Fever (B'way debut), Big River (premiere), The Nerd, Hyde in Hollywood, The Taming of the Shrew, Shimada, Goodnight Desdemona (Good Morning Juliet), Abe Lincoln in Illinois, No One Will Be Immune, June Moon.
PICTURES: Atlantic City, Ragtime, Ticket to Heaven, Threshold, Terminal Choice, Amityville 3-D, Desperately Seeking Susan, Joshua Then and Now, Adventure of Faustus Bidgood (also co-prod. music), Radio Days, Big Shots, The Suicide Club, She's Back!, Millenium, Longtime Companion, Shadows and Fog, The Dark Half, Death Wish 5: The Face of Death, I'll Do Anything, Henry & Verlin, Waterworld, A Modern Affair, Pharoah's Army, Dangerous Offender, Harriet the Spy, The Divine Ryans, Fallen, Resurrection, The Divine Ryans, Advice From a Caterpillar, Bonhoeefer: Agent of Grace, Perfume, Sweet November, The Shipping News, Joe Somebody.
TELEVISION: *Movies*: Escape from Iran: The Canadian Caper, Gregory K, Woman on the Run: The Lawrencia Bembenek Story, The High Life, Moonlight Becomes You, The Bookfair Murders, Cheaters, Haven, 61*, Series: One Life to Live, The High Life, MDs. *Guest*: The Equalizer, Moonlighting, Law and Order, The Marshal, New York Undercover, Wings. *Specials*: The Prodigious Hickey, The Return of Hickey, The Beginning of the Firm, Hyde in Hollywood.

JUDD, ASHLEY
Actress. b. Los Angeles, CA, April 19, 1968. Mother and sister are country singers, Naomi and Wynona Judd.
PICTURES: Kuffs, Ruby in Paradise, The Passion of Darkly Noon, Smoke, Heat, A Time to Kill, Normal Life, The Locusts, Kiss the Girls, Simon Birch, Eye of the Beholder, Double Jeopardy, Where the Heart Is, Killing Priscilla (video documentary), Someone Like You, High Crimes, Frida, Divine Secrets of the Ya Ya Sisterhood, Star Trek: Nemesis, The Blackout Murders, De-Lovely.
TELEVISION: *Series*: Sisters. *Movies*: Till Death Us Do Part, Norma Jean and Marilyn, The Ryan Interview. *Special*: Naomi & Wynona: Love Can Build a Bridge. *Guest*: Star Trek: The Next Generation.

JUDGE, MIKE
Animator, actor, director, producer. b. Guayaquil, Ecuador, Oct. 17, 1962. e. UC San Diego. *Shorts*: Frog Baseball (also voices, dir. prod., s.p.), Inbred Jed (also voices, dir., prod., s.p.), Office Space (voice, composer, dir.)
PICTURES: Airheads (voice), Beavis & Butt-head Do America (also dir., prod., composer, voices), Mene Tekel (voices), Office Space (dir., s.p., act.), South Park: Bigger Longer and Uncut (voice), Spy Kids, Spy Kids 2: The Island of Lost Dreams, The Animation Show (co-prod. only), Spy Kids 3-D: Game Over (acting)..
TELEVISION: *Series*: Beavis and Butt-head, (also dir., prod., composer, voices), King of the Hill (also prod., voices), Monsignor Martinez (dir., s.p.,). *Guest*: The Simpsons (voice).

JURADO, KATY
Actress. r.n. Maria Christina Jurado Garcia. b. Guadalajara, Mexico, Jan. 16, 1927. Appeared in numerous Mexican films beginning in 1943. Also m.p. columnist for Mexican publications.
PICTURES: No Maturas (debut, 1943), El Museo del Crimen, Rosa del Caribe, The Bullfighter and the Lady (U.S. debut, 1951), High Noon, San Antone, Arrowhead, Broken Lance (Acad. Award nom.), The Sword of Granada, The Racers, Trial, Trapeze, Man from Del Rio, Dragoon Wells Massacre, Badlanders, One Eyed Jacks, Barabbas, Seduction of the South, Target for Killing, Smoky, A Covenant With Death, Stay Away Joe, Bridge in the Jungle, Pat Garrett and Billy the Kid, Once Upon a Scoundrel, The Children of Sanchez, Reasons of State, Under the Volcano, Divine, The Hi-Lo Country A Beautiful Secret (2002).
TELEVISION: *Movies*: Any Second Now, A Little Game, Evita Peron, Lady Blue. *Series*: A.K.A. Pablo, To sigo amando.
(d. July 5, 2002)

K

KAGAN, JEREMY
Director, Writer. b. Mt. Vernon, NY, Dec. 14, 1945. e. Harvard; NYU, MFA; student Amer. Film Inst. 1971. Film animator, 1968; multi-media show designer White House Conf. on Youth and Ed. Previously credited as Jeremy Paul Kagan.
PICTURES: Scott Joplin, Heroes, The Big Fix, The Chosen (Montreal World Film Fest. Prize, 1981), The Sting II, The Journey of Natty Gann (Gold Prize, Moscow Film Fest., 1987), Big Man on Campus, By the Sword, Incoming.
TELEVISION: *Movies*: Unwed Father, Judge Dee and the

Monastery Murders, Katherine (also writer), Courage, Roswell (also co-prod., co-story), My Dad Lives in a Downtown Hotel, Conspiracy: The Trial of the Chicago 8 (also writer; ACE Award, 1988), Descending Angel, The Hired Heart, The Ballad of Lucie Whipple, Bobbie's Girl, Taken (mini).
Series: Columbo, The Bold Ones, Chicago Hope (Emmy Award, 1996), Ally McBeal, Family Law, The West Wing, Resurrection Blvd., Boomtown, Karen Sisco.

KAHN, MILTON
Publicist. b. Brooklyn, NY, May 3, 1934. e. Syracuse U., Ohio U., B.S.J. 1957. Formed Milton Kahn Associates, Inc. in 1958. Represented: Gregory Peck, Joan Crawford, Steve Allen, Glenn Ford, Lee Grant, Herb Alpert, Roger Corman, Robert Aldrich, Arthur Hiller, Chuck Norris, Bob Cousy, Gordie Howe, Michael Landon, Dean Hargrove, Bill Conti, etc. and New World Pictures (1970-83), Avco-Embassy, Vista Films, Roger Corman's Concorde (1983-), Electric Shadow Prods. Named Publicist of the Year by Book Pub. of So. CA, 1996.

KAHN, RICHARD
Executive. b. New Rochelle, NY, Aug. 19, 1929. e. Wharton Sch. of Finance and Commerce, U. of Pennsylvania, B.S., 1951; U.S. Navy, 3 yrs.; joined Buchanan & Co., 1954; ent. m.p. ind. as pressbook writer, Columbia Pictures, 1955; exploitation mgr., 1958; natl. coord. adv. and pub., 1963; natl. dir. of adv., pub. and exploitation, 1968; v.p., 1969; 1974 v.p. in chg. of special marketing projects; 1975; moved to MGM as v.p. in chg. of worldwide advertising, publicity and exploitation; 1978, named sr. v.p. in chg. worldwide mktg. & pres., MGM Intl. 1980, elected bd. of govrs., Academy of M.P. Arts & Sciences. 1982, named exec. v.p. of adv., pub., promo. for MGM/UA; 1983, formed the Richard Kahn Co., dist. & mktg. consultancy. 1984-88. Faculty mem. Peter Stark m.p. producing prog., USC Sch. of Cinema & TV. Exec. chmn., Film Inf. Council. 1982-95 elected secretary Acad. of Motion Picture Arts & Sciences; elected v.p. 1983-87; elected pres. 1988.

KALB, MARVIN
TV news reporter. e. City Coll. of NY; Harvard, M.A., 1953, Russian Language Sch., Middlebury Coll. Worked for U.S. State Dept., American Embassy, Moscow; CBS News, 1957; writer, reporter-researcher Where We Stand; reporter-assignment editor; Moscow Bureau Chief, 1960-63; first diplomatic corresp., Washington Bureau, 1963. Chief diplomatic corresp. CBS News and NBC News, moderator Meet the Press; Teacher and lecturer; first dir. Joan Shorenstein Barone Center on the Press, Politics and Public Policy at J.F.K. Sch. of Govt. of Harvard U., since 1987. Host of PBS series, Candidates '88. Author: Eastern Exposure, Kissinger, Dragon in the Kremlin, Roots of Involvement, The U.S. in Asia 1784-1971, Candidates '88 (with Hendrik Hertzberg). Retired.

KALISH, EDDIE
Executive. b. New York, NY, April 27, 1939. Reporter/reviewer, Variety, 1959-64; sr. publicist, Paramount, 1964-65; adv./pub./promo dir., Ken Greengras Personal Management, 1965-66; pub. dir., Harold Rand & Co., 1966-67; indept. publicist overseas, 1967-75; rejoined Paramount in 1975 as dir. of intl. mktg.; later named v.p.; 1978, v.p., worldwide pub. & promo. 1979 appt. sr. v.p., worldwide mktg. 1980 joined UA as v.p. domestic mktg.; sr. v.p., adv., pub., promo. for MGM/UA 1981-82; became sr. v.p., worldwide mkt., PSO, 1982-1986. Now pres., Kalish/Davidson Marketing, Inc.

KAMEN, MICHAEL
Composer, conductor, arranger. b. New York, NY, April 15, 1948. Began career composing music for the Joffrey Ballet and the La Scala Opera Co. Wrote his first film score in 1970 for The Next Man. Has also written for David Bowie, Eric Clapton and the Eurythmics.
PICTURES: *Scores*: The Next Man (debut), Stunts, Between the Lines, Polyester, Venom, Pink Floyd—The Wall, Angelo My Love, The Dead Zone, Brazil, Lifeforce, Shoot for the Sun, Rita—Sue and Bob Too, Highlander, Mona Lisa, Shanghai Surprise, Suspect, Someone to Watch Over Me, Adventures in Babysitting, Lethal Weapon, The Raggedy Rawney, Crusoe, Action Jackson, Homeboy, Die Hard, Rooftops, For Queen and Country, The Adventures of Baron Munchausen, Road House, License to Kill, Dead-Bang, Lethal Weapon, Renegades, The Krays, Cold Dog Soup, Die Hard 2, Nothing But Trouble, Let Him Have It, Company Business, Robin Hood: Prince of Thieves (Acad. award nom.), Golden Globe nom.), Hudson Hawk, The Last Boy Scout, Blue Ice, Shining Through, Lethal Weapon 3, Wilder Napalm, Splitting Hairs, Last Action Hero, The Three Musketeers, Stonewall, Mr Holland's Opus, Circle of Friends, Don Juan DeMarco, Die Hard: With a Vengeance, Jack, 101 Dalmations, Remember Me?, Inventing the Abbotts, Event Horizon, The Winter Guest, Lethal Weapon 4, The Avengers, What Dreams May Come, The Iron Giant, Frequency, X-Men, XII, Open Range, Against the Ropes.
TELEVISION: *Scores*: Liza's Pioneer Diary, S*H*E, Amazing Stories, Edge of Darkness, Tales from the Crypt, The Heart Surgeon, Band of Brothers, Mr. Dreyfuss Goes to Washington.

KAMINSKI, JANUSZ
Cinematographer. b. Ziembice, Poland, June 27, 1959. Second unit work on films: Watchers II, To Die Standing, One False Move.
PICTURES: The Terror Within II (debut, 1990), Grim Prairie Tales, The Rain Killer, Pyrates, Cool as Ice, Trouble Bound, Mad Dog Coll, The Adventures of Huck Finn, Schindler's List, Little Giants, Tall Tale, How to Make an American Quilt, Jerry Maguire, Amistad, The Lost World: Jurassic Park, Armageddon (addt'l), Saving Private Ryan (Acad. Award), A.I., Minority Report, Collateral, Catch Me If You Can, Jumbo Girl (short). *Dir*: Lost Souls.
TELEVISION: *Movies*: Wildflower, Class of '61.

KANAKAREDES, MELINA
Actress. b. Akron, OH, April 23, 1967.
PICTURES: White Man's Burden, The Long Kiss Goodnight, Rounders, Dangerous Beauty, 15 Minutes.
TELEVISION: *Movies*: Saint Maybe. *Series*: The Guiding Light, NYPD Blue, New York News, Leaving L.A., Providence. *Guest*: Due South, The Practice, Oz.

KANE, CAROL
Actress. b. Cleveland, OH, June 18, 1952. e. Professional Children's Sch., NY. Began professional acting career at age 14, touring, then on B'way in The Prime of Miss Jean Brodie.
THEATRE: The Tempest, The Effect of Gamma Rays on Man-in-the-Moon Marigolds, Are You Now or Have You Ever Been? Arturo Ui, The Enchanted, The Tempest, Macbeth, Tales of the Vienna Woods, Frankie and Johnny in the Claire de Lune, Control Freaks.
PICTURES: Carnal Knowledge (debut, 1971), Desperate Characters, Wedding in White, The Last Detail, Dog Day Afternoon, Hester Street, Harry and Walter Go to New York, Annie Hall, Valentino, The World's Greatest Lover, The Mafu Cage, The Muppet Movie, When a Stranger Calls, Pandemonium, Norman Loves Rose, Over the Brooklyn Bridge, Racing With the Moon, The Secret Diary of Sigmund Freud, Transylvania 6-5000, Jumpin' Jack Flash, Ishtar, The Princess Bride, Sticky Fingers, License to Drive, Scrooged, Flashback, Joe Vs. the Volcano, My Blue Heaven, The Lemon Sisters, Ted and Venus, In the Soup, Addams Family Values, Even Cowgirls Get the Blues, Big Bully, The Pallbearer, Sunset Park, The Pallbearer, American Strays, Office Killer, Gone Fishin', The Tic Code, Jawbreaker, Man on the Moon, Tomorrow by Midnight, The Shrink Is In, The Office Party, My First Mister, D.C. Smalls, Love in the Time of Money.
TELEVISION: *Movies*: An Invasion of Privacy, Burning Rage, Drop Out Mother, Dad the Angel and the Freaky Friday, Merry Christmas George Bailey, Audrey's Rain, Cosmopolitan. *Specials*: Faerie Tale Theatre, Paul Reiser: Out on a Whim, Tales From the Crypt (Judy, You're Not Yourself Today), Noah's Ark. *Series*: Taxi (2 Emmy Awards: 1982, 1983), All Is Forgiven, American Dreamer, Pearl, Beggars and Choosers.

KANEW, JEFF
Director. b. Dec. 16, 1944
PICTURES: Black Rodeo (also prod., edit.), Natural Enemies (also s.p., edit.), Eddie Macon's Run (also s.p., edit.), Revenge of the Nerds, Gotcha!, Tough Guys, Troop Beverly Hills, V. I. Warshawski, Babij Jar (documentary, dir., editor)
TELEVISION: Alfred Hitchcock Presents (1985), Touched by an Angel.

KANFER, MICHAEL
Special Effects.
PICTURES: Apollo 13, Titanic (Acad. Award, Best Visual Effects, 1997), Edtv, Fight Club, Rules of Engagement, O Brother Where Art Thou, Stormrider, Harry Potter & the Sorcerer's Stone, We Were Soldiers (digital mastering supervisor).

KANIN, FAY
Writer. b. New York, NY, May 9. 1917. e. Elmira Coll., U. of Southern California, 1937. m. Michael Kanin, writer. Contrib. fiction to mags., Writers Guild of Amer. pres. screen branch, 1971-73; Acad. Motion Picture Arts & Sciences 1983-88. also bd. mem. of latter. Co-chair, National Center for Film and Video Preservation; Bd. of trustees, Amer. Film Institute; Chair, Natl. Film Preservation Board.
THEATRE: Goodbye My Fancy, His and Hers, Rashomon, The High Life, Grind (1985).
PICTURES: My Pal Gus, Rhapsody, The Opposite Sex, Teacher's Pet, Swordsman of Siena, The Right Approach, The Outrage, Rich & Famous (acting only), Mary Pickford: A Life on Film (writer, prod.),
TELEVISION: Heat of Anger, Tell Me Where It Hurts (Emmy Award, 1974), Hustling (also co-prod.), Friendly Fire (also co-prod., Emmy Award, San Francisco Film Fest. Award, Peabody Award), Heartsounds (Peabody Award; also co-prod.), American Masters: On Cukor (documentary, as herself), Without Lying Down: Frances Marion and the Power of Women in Hollywood (documentary, as herself).

KANTER, HAL
Writer, Director, Producer. b. Savannah, GA, Dec. 18, 1918. On B'way contributor to Hellzapoppin. Then began writing radio dramas before mil. service, WW II. Served as combat corresp. Armed Forces Radio; writer, Paramount, 1951-54; dir., RKO, 1956; writer, prod. for Lucille Ball Prods., 1979-80. Savannah Prods., 1982-86. Received Writers Guild Paddy Chayefsky Laurel Award, 1989. Writer (radio): Danny Kaye Show, Amos 'n Andy, Bing Crosby Show, Jack Paar, Beulah. Winner 3 Emmy Awards for writing, 1954, 1991, 1992; W.G.A.W. Valentine Davies award. Was member: bd. of dir., WGAW; bd. of govs. AMPAS; v.p. Writers Guild Foundation.
PICTURES: Writer: My Favorite Spy, Off Limits, Road to Bali, Casanova's Big Night, About Mrs. Leslie, Money from Home, Artists and Models, The Rose Tattoo, I Married a Woman (dir. only), Loving You (also dir.), Mardi Gras, Once Upon a Horse (also dir., prod.), Blue Hawaii, Pocketful of Miracles, Bachelor in Paradise, Move Over Darling, Dear Brigitte.
TELEVISION: Writer: Ed Wynn Show, George Gobel Show (also creator, prod.), Kraft Music Hall (also dir., prod.; 1958-59), Chrysler Theatre (also prod., dir.; 1966-67), Julia (also dir., prod., creator), Jimmy Stewart Show (also prod., dir., creator), All In The Family (exec. prod.: 1975-76), Chico & The Man (spv. prod., 1976-77), You Can't Take It With You. Specials (writer): AFI Life Achievement Awards for Henry Fonda & Alfred Hitchcock, 1991-1998 Academy Awards and many others.

KANTER, JAY
Executive. b. Chicago, IL, Dec. 12, 1926. Entered industry with MCA, Inc., where was v.p. Left after more than 20 yrs. to become indep. prod., then pres. of First Artists Production Co., Ltd. 1975 joined 20th-Fox as v.p. prod.; 1976, named sr. v.p., worldwide prod. Named v.p., The Ladd Co., 1979. Joined MGM/UA Entertainment Co. as pres., worldwide prod., Motion Picture Division, 1984. 1985, named pres., worldwide prod., UA Corp.; then pres., production MGM Pictures Inc.; 1989, named chmn. of prod. of Pathe Entertainment Co. 1991, became COO & chmn. of prod., MGM-Pathe Commun. Co. (MGM Communi-cations, 1992). 1994-95, MGM consultant. March, 1995, independent prod.

KANTOR, IGO
Producer, Film Editor. b. Vienna, Austria, Aug. 18, 1930. e. UCLA, A.A. 1950; B.S., 1952; M.S., 1954. Foreign corres., Portugal magazine, FLAMA, 1949-57, music supvr., Screen Gems, Columbia 1954-63; post-prod. supvr., film ed., features, TV; assoc. prod., 1963-64; prod., exec., International Entertainment Corp., 1965; pres., Synchrofilm, Inc., post-production co. and Duque Films Inc., production co. 1968-74. 1975-present, produced and edited films. 1982, pres., Laurelwood Prods; 1988, pres. Major Arts Corp.
PICTURES: Assoc. Producer: Bye Bye Birdie, Under the Yum Yum Tree, Gidget Goes to Rome, A House Is Not a Home, Pattern for Murder, Willy. Producer: Assault on Agathon (also edit.), FTA, Dixie Dynamite (assoc. prod., edit.), Kingdom of the Spiders (also edit., music spvr.), The Dark (assoc. prod.), Good Luck Miss Wyckoff (prod. spvr.), Hardly Working, Kill and Kill Again, Shaker Run, Act of Piracy, Legends of the West (exec. prod.).
TELEVISION: From Hawaii with Love (1984), The Grand Tour, It's a Wonderful World (prod.-dir.), Nosotros Golden Eagle Awards (prod.), United We Stand (pre-Olympic special), Legends of the West With Jack Palance, Mom U.S.A., A Desperate Affair, Holiday Classics Cartoons (special).

KAPLAN, GABRIEL
Actor, Comedian. b. Brooklyn, NY, March 31, 1945. After high school worked as bellboy at Lakewood, NJ hotel, spending free time studying comedians doing routines. Put together a comedy act, landing engagements in small clubs and coffee houses all over U.S. Made several appearances on Tonight Show, Merv Griffin Show, Mike Douglas Show, etc. Has played Las Vegas clubs.
PICTURES: Fast Break, Tulips, Nobody's Perfekt, Groucho.
TELEVISION: Series: Welcome Back Kotter, Gabriel Kaplan Presents Future Stars, Lewis and Clark. Movie: Love Boat (pilot). Specials: Welcome Back Kotter: The E! True Hollywood Story, Just For Laughs: Montreal Comedy Festival.

KAPLAN, JONATHAN
Director, Writer. b. Paris, France, Nov. 25, 1947. Son of composer Sol Kaplan. e. U. of Chicago, B.A.; NYU, M.F.A. Made short film Stanley Stanley. Member of tech. staff Fillmore East, NY 1969-71. New World Pictures' Roger Corman post-grad. sch. of filmmaking, Hollywood, 1971-73. As actor on B'way in Dark at the Top of the Stairs. Appeared in films: Cannonball, Hollywood Boulevard.
PICTURES: Director: Night Call Nurses, Student Teachers, The Slams, Truck Turner, White Line Fever (also co-s.p.), Mr. Billion, Over the Edge, Heart Like a Wheel, Project X, The Accused, Immediate Family, Unlawful Entry, Love Field, Bad Girls, Brokedown Palace.
TELEVISION: Movies: The 11th Victim, The Hustler of Muscle Beach, The Gentleman Bandit, Girls of the White Orchid, Reform School Girl, In Cold Blood. Series: Fallen Angels, JAG, ER, The Court.

KAPOOR, SHASHI
Actor. b. Calcutta, India, March 18, 1938. Son of late Prithviraj Kapoor, Indian film and stage actor. As child worked in Prithvi Theatre and in brother, Raj's films. Toured with father's co. at 18 and joined the Kendals' Shakespeareana Co. in India. Starred in over 200 Indian films as well as several Merchant-Ivory Prods.
PICTURES: Aag, Awara, Prem Patra, The Householder, Waqt, Shakespeare Wallah, A Matter of Innocence, Pretty Polly, Bombay Talkie, Sharmilee, Siddhartha, Roti Kapda Aur Makaan, Deewar, Kabhie Kabhie, Imaan Dharam, Trishul; Satyam, Shivam, Sundaram; Junoon (also prod.), Suhaag, Kaala Pathar, Shaan, Kalyug (also prod.), Do Aur do Paanch, 36 Chowringhee Lane (prod. only), Silsila, Bezubaan, Namak Halal, Heat and Dust, Door-desh, Utsav (also prod.), New Delhi Times, Abodh, Sammy and Rosie Get Laid, Ijaazat, The Deceivers, Nomads, Akayla, Ajooba (dir. only), In Custody, Side Streets, Jinnah.
TELEVISION: Movie: Gulliver's Travels.

KAPUR, SHEKHAR
Director. b. Lahore, Pakistan, 1945.
PICTURES: Masoom, Joshilar, Mr. India, Time Machine, Bandit Queen, From the Heart (exec. prod. only), Dushmani, Dil Se (exec. prod. only), Elizabeth, Four Feathers, Phantom of the Opera, The Guru (exec. prod. only) Paani (also writer), Long Walk to Freedom.
TELEVISION: Tahqiqat, 100 Greatest Movie Stars (documentary, as himself).

KARANOVIC, SRDJAN
Director. b. Belgrade, Yugoslavia, November 17, 1945. 1994-1996, Guest Instructor, Boston University.
PICTURES: Stvar Srca, Pani Vratna, Neblbni, Drustvena Igra, If It Kills Me (s.p. only), Miris Poljskog Cveca, Bravo Maestro (s.p. only), Nesto Izmedju (also s.p.), Jagode U Grlu, A Film with No Name, Virdzina (also writer), Pavle Vuisic 1926-1988 (video documentary), Zoran Radmilovic 1933-1985 (video documentary).
TELEVISION: Movies: Apotekarica, Dom, Pogledaj Me Nevernice. Series: Grlom U Jagode, Petria's Wreath (also s.p.).

KARDISH, LAURENCE
Curator, Dept. of Film, Museum of Modern Art. b. Ottawa, Ontario, Canada, Jan. 5, 1945. e. Carlton U. Ottawa, Canada, 1966, Honors B.A. in philosophy; Columbia U., Sch. of the Arts, 1968, M.F.A. in film, radio, and television. 1965-66: Canadian Film Inst., programmer for National Film Theatre, Ottawa; researched a history of Canadian filmmaking. 1965: founded first film society in Canada to exhibit Amer. avant-garde films (Carleton U. Cine Club); directed summer seminar on film, Carleton U., 1966. 1966-68: New American Cinema Group, Inc., NY, worked for the Film-Makers' Distribution Center. 1968: joined Dept. of Film, MOMA; made curator 1984. Since 1968 involved with Cineprobe prog. Since 1972 participated in selection of films for New Directors/New Films series; dir. exhibitions of surveys of national cinemas (Senegal, Scandinavia, French-speaking Canada) and retrospectives of indel. Amer. filmmakers (includ. Rudolph Burkhardt, Stan Brakhage, Shirley Clarke), The Lubitsch Touch, Columbia Pictures, Warner Bros., MGM, Universal, RKO, and directors. 1980: toured Europe with prog. of indep. Amer. films. Author: Reel Plastic Magic (1972); also essays and monographs. Dir.feature Slow Run (1968). On jury for Channel 13's Indep. Focus series and on Board of Advisors, Collective for Living Cinema, NY. 1982-82: bd. of dirs. of National Alliance of Media Arts Centers; 1987-89: on Jerome Foundation panel. 1986 on Camera d'Or jury, Cannes Film Fest. Received France's medal of the Order of Arts and Letters, June 2003. AUTHOR: Michael Balcon: The Puirsuit of British Cinema, Rainer Werner Fassbinder, Reel Plastic Magic: A History of Films and Filmmaking in America.

KARLIN, FRED
Composer, Conductor. b. Chicago, IL, June 16, 1936. e. Amherst Coll., B.A. Composer and arranger for Benny Goodman. Won Academy Award for Best Song for For All We Know (from Lovers and Other Strangers) and Emmy for original music in The Autobiography of Miss Jane Pittman. 4 Acad. Award noms., 11 Emmy Award noms.; Image Award for score to Minstrel Man. Author: On the Track: A Guide to Contemporary Film Scoring (with Rayburn Wright), Listening to Movies. Creator and instructor of the ASCAP/Fred Karlin Film Scoring Workshop, since 1988.
PICTURES: Up the Down Staircase, Yours Mine and Ours, The Sterile Cuckoo (including music for song, Come Saturday Morning, Acad. Award nom.), The Stalking Moon, Westworld, Futureworld, Lovers and Other Strangers (Acad. Award, Best Music, Song: "For All We Know", 1971), Leadbelly, Loving Couples.
TELEVISION: The Autobiography of Miss Jane Pittman, The Awakening Land, The Plutonium Incident, Minstrel Man, Sophia Loren—Her Own Story, Green Eyes, Strangers: The Story of a Mother and Daughter, Calamity Jane, Ike: the War Years, Inside the Third Reich, Hollywood—The Gift of Laughter, Homeward Bound, Dream West, Hostage Flight, A Place to Call Home, Robert Kennedy and His Times, Dadah is Death, Bridge to Silence, The Secret, Film Music Masters: Jerry Goldsmith

(prod.and dir.), Film Music Masters: Elmer Bernstein (prod. and dir.), Lost Treasure of Dos Santos (1997); many others.

KARLIN, MYRON D.
Executive. b. Revere, MA, Sept. 21, 1918. e. UCLA. Joined m.p. business in 1946 as gen. mgr. for MGM in Ecuador. Two yrs. later assigned same spot for MGM in Venezuela. 1952-53 was gen. sales mgr. for MGM in Germany, after which managing dir. in Argentina, returning to Germany as mgr. dir. in 1956. Named mgr. dir. for United Artists in Italy. 1960-68 was pres. of Brunswick Int'l., while also serving as advisor to World Health Organization and UNESCO. 1969 was European mgr. for MGM and mgn. dir. in Italy. Joined Warner Bros. Int'l. in 1970 as v.p. of European dist. 1972 appt. v.p. in chg. of int'l. operations for WB; 1977, appt. pres., WB Intl. & exec. v.p., Warner Bros., Inc; 1985, named exec. v.p., intl. affairs, WB, Inc. Pres. & COO, Motion Picture Export Assn. July, 1994, sr. consultant, Motion Picture Assoc. Decorations: Commander of the Italian Republic; Office of Order of Arts and Letters (France); Commander of Order of King Leopold (Belgium).

KARMAZIN, MELVIN ALLEN
Executive. b. 1944, New York. e. Pace University, BA in business administration, 1965. Station Mgr., CBS Radio, NY, 1960-70. VP and Gen'l Mgr. Metromedia Inc., 1970-81. Pres. Infinity Broadcast Corp., 1981-96. CEO Infinity Broadcast Corp., 1988-96. Chairman, CEO CBS Station Group, 1996-1998. 1999, Chairman & CEO, CBS, Inc. At CBS, Karmazin amassed over 160 major-market radio stations, along with the nation's premier outdoor advertising companies. He also orchestrated the spin-off of Infinity Broadcasting in the largest IPO in media history at the time. Additionally, he invested in Internet properties such as CBS MarketWatch, CBS SportsLine, and iWon.com. The CBS Television Network also experienced a dramatic turnaround under Karmazin's leadership. Upon merger of CBS and Viacom, became pres. & COO, Viacom, May 2000. In March 2003, signed a three-year contract to remain in current position through May 2006. Serves on Viacom bd. of dirs., as well as Westwood One and the NY Stock Exchange. Vice-chmn., Museum of Television and Radio. Inductee, Broadcasting Hall of Fame. Recipient, NAB National Radio Award and the IRTS Gold Medal Award. Creator of the Prism Fund to encourage minority ownership of media outlets.

KARP, ALLEN
Executive. b. Toronto, Ontario, Canada, Sept. 18, 1940. e. Univ. of Toronto, law degree, 1964; called to Ontario bar in 1966; masters of business law degree 1975, from Osgoode Hall Law School, York Univ. Upon graduation joined the firm of Goodman & Carr, became a partner in 1970. Served as business lawyer and sr. legal advisor, becoming dir. of Odeon Theatre Film circuit, 1977. 1986, named sr. exec. v.p. of Cineplex Odeon Corp; 1988, became pres. North American Theatres Division; 1989, pres. & COO; 1990, elected pres. & CEO Cineplex Odeon Canada (Loews Cineplex Ent. Corp.). Chmn. since 1998. A director of Alliance Atlantis Communications Co. Member of the Canadian Civil Liberties Assn., New York City Partnership of CEO's.

KARRAS, ALEX
Actor. b. Gary, IN, July 15, 1935. e. Univ. of Iowa. As football player with Iowa State U., picked for All Amer. team. Received Outland Trophy, 1957. Former professional football player with Detroit Lions, 1958-62, and 1964-71. Sportswriter, Detroit Free Press, 1972-73. Also worked as prof. wrestler, salesman, steel worker and lecturer. m. actress Susan Clark. With her formed Georgian Bay Prods., 1979. Books: Even Big Guys Cry (with Herb Gluck, 1977), Alex Karras: My Life in Football Television and Movies (1979), Tuesday Night Football (1991).
PICTURES: Paper Lion (as himself; debut, 1968), Blazing Saddles, FM, Win Place or Steal, Jacob Two-Two Meets the Hooded Fang, When Time Ran Out, Nobody's Perfekt, Porky's, Victor/Victoria, Against All Odds, The Street Corner Kids, The Street Corner Kids: The Sequel, Buffalo '66.
TELEVISION: Commentator and host: Monday Night Football (1974-76). Mini-Series: Centennial. Movies: Hardcase, The 500-Pound Jerk, Babe, Mulligan's Stew, Mad Bull, Jimmy B. & Andre (also exec. prod.), Alcatraz: The Whole Shocking Story, Word of Honor (also exec. prod.), Maid in America (also exec. prod.), Fudge-a-Mania, Tracy Takes On... Series: Webster (also co-prod.), The Tom Show.

KARTOZIAN, WILLIAM F.
Executive. b. San Francisco, CA, July 27, 1938. e. Stanford U., 1960; Harvard Law Sch., 1963. Deputy Attorney General State of CA, 1963-64; assoc. in law firm of Lillick, McHose Wheat Adams & Charles, San Francisco, 1964-65; corp. counsel and dir., Natl. Convenience Stores, Houston, 1965-67; v.p. and corp. counsel, UA Theatres, 1967-75; owner, Festival Enterprises, Inc., 1970-86; chmn. San Francisco Theatre Employers Assoc., 1973-76; Theatre Assoc. of CA, Inc., dir. 1972-86, v.p. 1974-75, pres. 1975-79, chmn. of bd. 1979-81; member, State of CA Industrial Welfare Comm. Amusement and Recreation Industries Wage Board, 1975-76; Natl Assoc. of Theatre Owners: dir. 1976-86, v.p. 1980-86, president 1988-2000. Owner, Regency Enterprises, Inc., 1986-present; chmn. of bd., Lakeside Inn & Casino,

Stateline, NV 1985-present. former member: Calif. Film Commission.

KAR-WAI, WONG
Director. b. Shanghai, 1959. e. B.A. in graphic design, Hong Kong, 1980.
PICTURES: Dir.: As Tears Go By (also s.p.), The True Story of Ah Fei (also s.p.), Let's Go Slam Dunk, Fallen Angels (also prod., s.p.), Ashes of Time (also s.p.), Chunking Express (also s.p.), Fallen Angels, Happy Together (also prod., s.p., Cannes 2000, Best Dir.), In the Mood For Love (also prod., s.p.), The Hire: Follow, 2046, Six Days (video) Writer: Intellectual Trio, The Final Test, The Final Victory, The Haunted Copshop, Dragon and Tiger Fight, The Haunted Copshop II, Saviour of Souls, Beijing Summer. Prod.: The Eagle Shooting Heroes, First Love: A Litter on the Breeze, Chinese Odyssey 2002.

KARYO, TCHEKY
Actor. b. Istanbul, Turkey, Oct. 4, 1953. Studied drama at the Cyrano Theatre and became a member of the Daniel Sorano Company, National Theatre of Strasbourg. Received the Jean Gabin Prize, 1986.
PICTURES: Vincent and Me, La Balance, The Return of Martin Guerre, All Night Long, La Java des ombres, The Outsider, Full Moon in Paris, Amour braque, L' Actor, États d'âme, Bleu comme l'enfer, L' Unique, Spirale, Sorceress, The Bear, Australia, La Fille des Collines, La Femme Nikita, Corps Perdus, Exposure, Isabelle Eberhardt, 1492: Conquest of Paradise, Sketch Artist, On Guard, Husbands and Lovers, And the Band Played On, The Black Angel, Nostradamus, Fear City: A Family-Style Comedy, Zadoc et le bonheur, GoldenEye, Operation Dumbo Drop, Bad Boys, Colpo di luna, Crying Freeman, Foreign Land, Albergo Roma, Gentle Into the Night, To Have and to Hold, Follow Your Heart, Les Mille merveilles de l'univers, Dobermann, Addicted to Love, Habitat, Que la lumière soit, World of Moss, Wing Commander, Babel, Comme un poisson hors de l'eau, My Life So Far, The Messenger: The Story of Joan of Arc, Saving Grace, The Patriot, The King is Dancing, Kiss of the Dragon, The Core, The Good Thief, Cinemagique, Utopia, Blueberry.

KASDAN, LAWRENCE
Writer, Director, Producer. b. West Virginia, Jan. 14, 1949. e. U. of Michigan. Clio award-winning adv. copywriter, Detroit and LA before becoming screen writer. Became dir. with Body Heat (1981).
PICTURES: Dir./s.p./co-s.p.: The Empire Strikes Back, Raiders of the Lost Ark, Continental Divide, Body Heat, Return of the Jedi, The Big Chill (also co-exec. prod.), Into the Night (actor), Silverado (also prod), Cross My Heart (prod.), The Accidental Tourist (also co-prod.), Immediate Family (exec. prod.), I Love You to Death (also actor), Grand Canyon (also co-prod., actor), Jumpin at the Boneyard (exec. prod.), The Bodyguard (also co-prod.), Wyatt Earp (also co-prod.), French Kiss, Home Fires (prod.), Mumford, Dreamcatcher.

KASLOFF, STEVE
Writer. b. New York, NY, Nov. 13, 1952. e. Pratt Institute, 1974, cum laude. Writer/supvr., Young & Rubicam, 1974-76; writer/sprv., Ally & Gargano, 1976; writer/supvr., Marsteller Inc., 1976-79; writer/creative supvr., Scali, McCabe, Sloves, 1979-82. hired as youngest v.p., Columbia Pictures, 1982; promoted to sr. v.p., creative dir., Columbia, 1983. Sr. v.p. creative dir., 20th Century Fox, 1992. Member, WGA. Winner of numerous Clio and Key Arts Awards and over 200 others for creative work (trailers, TV commercials, posters, etc.) on such films as Tootsie, Ghostbusters, Total Recall, Home Alone, Dances With Wolves, Terminator 2, Home Alone 2, Last Action Hero, Jurassic Park, Schindler's List, Dumb and Dumber, etc. Has directed stage productions, commercials & special teaser trailers. Screen-writing/Production deal with Columbia Pictures, 1988; 20th Century Fox Films, 1993-present.

KASSAR, MARIO
Executive, Producer. b. Lebanon, Oct. 10, 1951. At age of 18 formed own foreign distribution co. Kassar Films International, specializing in sale, dist. and exhibition of films in Asia and Europe. In 1976 became partners with Andrew Vajna who had own dist. co., forming Carolco. First prod. First Blood, followed by Rambo: First Blood Part II. Became sole chmn. of Carolco in 1989. Formed own production co. in 1996.
PICTURES: Exec. Prod.: Angel Heart, Extreme Prejudice, Rambo III, Red Heat, Iron Eagle II, Deep Star Six, Johnny Handsome, Mountains of the Moon, Total Recall, Air America, Jacob's Ladder, L.A. Story, The Doors, Terminator 2: Judgment Day, Rambling Rose, Basic Instinct, Universal Soldier, Light Sleeper, Chaplin, Cliffhanger, Heaven & Earth, Stargate, Last of the Dogmen, Showgirls, Cutthroat Island, Lolita (prod.), Icarus (prod.), I Spy, Terminator 3: Rise of the Machines.

KASTNER, ELLIOTT
Producer. b. New York, NY, Jan. 7, 1933. e. U. of Miami, Columbia U. Was agent then v.p. with MCA, before becoming indep. prod., financing and personally producing 65 feature films in 25 yrs. Based in London, NY & LA.
PICTURES: Bus Riley's Back in Town, Harper, Kaleidoscope,

The Bobo, Sweet November (1968), Sol Madrid, Michael Kohlaas, Laughter in the Dark, Night of the Following Day, Where Eagles Dare, A Severed Head, Tam Lin, The Walking Stick, X Y and Zee (Zee & Company), The Nightcomers, Big Truck and Poor Clare, Face to the Wind, Fear Is the Key, The Long Goodbye, Cops and Robbers, Jeremy, 11 Harrowhouse, Spot, Rancho Deluxe, 92 in the Shade, Farewell My Lovely, Russian Roulette, Breakheart Pass, The Missouri Breaks, Swashbuckler, Equus, A Little Night Music, The Medusa Touch, The Big Sleep, Absolution, Goldengirl, Yesterday's Hero, Ffolkes, The First Deadly Sin, Death Valley, Man Woman and Child, Garbo Talks, Oxford Blues, Nomads, Heat, Angel Heart, Black Joy, Spy Trap, Jack's Back, The Blob, White of the Eye, Zombie High, Never on Tuesday, Homeboy, A Chorus of Disapproval, The Last Party, Love is All There Is, Franke and Jesse, Sweet November (2001).

KATLEMAN, HARRIS L.
Executive. b. Omaha, NB, Aug. 19, 1928. e. UCLA. Joined MCA in 1949; 1952 transferred to NY as head of TV Packaging Dept. Left to join Goodson-Todman Prods. in 1955, where named v.p., 1956; exec. v.p., 1958; sr. exec. v.p., 1968. Was directly responsible for all programs prod. in L.A., including The Rebel, Branded, The Richard Boone Show, and Don Rickles Show, on which was exec. prod. Joined M-G-M in 1972 as v.p. of MGM-TV; promoted following year to pres., MGM-TV and sr. v.p. of MGM, Inc. Resigned as pres., MGM-TV, 1977. Formed Bennett/Katleman Productions under contract to Columbia Pictures. Exec. prod.: From Here to Eternity, Salvage 1; 1980, named bd. chmn. 20th-Fox Television. Appointed pres. & CEO, Twentieth TV, 1982. Oversaw prod. of final years of M*A*S*H, as well as Mr. Belvedere, The Fall Guy, Trapper John M.D., L.A. Law, Hooperman, Anything But Love, Tracey Ullman Show, Alien Nation, The Simpsons, In Living Color. Resigned, 1992. Formed Shadow Hill Prods. under contract to Twentieth TV. Joined Mark Goodson Prods., 1993, as COO. Retired.

KATSELAS, MILTON GEORGE
Director, Writer, Teacher, Painter. b. Pittsburgh, PA, Feb. 22, 1933. e. drama dept., Carnegie Inst. of Technology (now Carnegie-Mellon U.). Acting teacher-owner, Beverly Hills Playhouse. Has exhibited paintings in several major solo exhibitions. Awards: 3 time recipient of the L.A. Drama Critics Circle Award, Drama Logue Best Director Award, NAACP and Tony Nominations for Best Director.
THEATRE: B'way: The Rose Tattoo, Butterflies are Free, Camino Real. Off-B'way: Call Me By My Rightful Name, The Zoo Story.
PICTURES: Butterflies Are Free, 40 Carats, Report to the Commissioner, When You Comin' Back Red Ryder?
TELEVISION: Movies: The Rules of Marriage, Strangers—The Story of a Mother and Daughter.

KATT, WILLIAM
Actor. b. Los Angeles, CA, Feb. 16, 1955. Son of actors Barbara Hale and Bill Williams. e. Orange Coast Coll. Majored in music, playing piano and guitar. Acted with South Coast Repertory Theatre, later working in productions at the Ahmanson and Mark Taper Theatres in L.A. Phoenix Rep (N.Y.): Bonjour La Bonjour. Regional: Sarah and Abraham, Days of Wine and Roses.
PICTURES: Carrie (debut, 1976), First Love, Big Wednesday, Butch and Sundance: The Early Days, Baby, Rising Storm, House, White Ghost, Wedding Band, Naked Obsession, Double X: The Name of the Game, House IV: Home Deadly Home, Desperate Motive (Distant Cousins), Tollbooth, The Paperboy, Stranger by Night, Cyborg 3: The Recycler, Rattled, Devil's Food, Daddy's Girl, Whacked, U'bejani, Mother Teresa: In the Name of God's Poor, Hyacinth, Jawbreaker, The Rage: Carrie 2, Twin Falls Idaho, Clean and Narrow, Learning to Surf, Circuit, Determination of Death, Treading Water, Descendent-Descendent, Nexus.
TELEVISION: Movies: Night Chase, The Daughters of Joshua Cabe, Can Ellen Be Saved?, Perry Mason Returns and several Perry Mason follow-ups (Case of the...Murdered Madam, Avenging Ace, Scandalous Scoundrel, Lady in the Lake, Notorious Nun, Shooting Star, Lost Love, Sinister Spirit), Swim Suit, Americanski Blues, Problem Child 3: Junior in Love, Piranha, Rough Riders, Hide and Seek, Gentle Ben. Specials: Pippin, The Rainmaker. Series: The Greatest American Hero, Top of the Hill, Good Sports, Models Inc.

KATZ, GLORIA
Producer, Writer. e. UCLA. Film Sch. Joined Universal Pictures as editor, cutting educational films. Later joined forces with Willard Huyck, whom she had met at U.C.L.A. Pair signed by Francis Ford Coppola to write and direct for his newly created company, American Zoetrope.
PICTURES: Writer: American Graffiti, Lucky Lady, French Postcards (also prod.), Indiana Jones and the Temple of Doom, Best Defense (also prod.), Howard the Duck (also prod.), Radioland Murders.
TELEVISION: Co-Producer, Co-Writer: A Father's Homecoming, Mothers Daughters and Lovers.

KATZ, JAMES C.
Producer, Executive. b. New York, NY, March 17, 1939. e. Ohio St. U. Started in publicity dept. of United Artists, 1963,

eventually serving as v.p. of publicity for UA, 1966-68. Publicity co-ord. on film Khartoum, 1964. To London, 1968 as unit publicist for The Charge of the Light Brigade, Joanna. Prod. & dir. for C.I.C. special shorts and documentaries. 1973-78, prod./dir. commercials for own company in London. 1980, pres. Universal Classics Dept.; 1984, v.p. prod, Universal Pictures. With Robert A. Harris worked on restoration of Spartacus, My Fair Lady and Alfred Hitchcock's Vertigo.
PICTURES: Three Sisters (co-prod.), Lust in the Dust (exec. prod.), Nobody's Fool (prod.), Scenes From the Class Struggle in Beverly Hills (prod.).

KATZ, MARTY
Producer. b. Landsburg, West Germany, Sept. 2, 1947. e. UCLA, U. of Maryland. Served in Vietnam War as U.S. Army first lieut.; awarded Bronze Star as combat pictorial unit director. 1971, dir. of film prod., ABC Circle Films; 1976, exec. v.p., prod., Quinn Martin Prods'; 1978-80, producer and consultant, Paramount Pictures' 1981-85, independent producer (Lost in America, Heart Like a Wheel). 1985, joined Walt Disney Prods. as sr. v.p., motion picture & TV prod. Named exec. v.p. motion picture and TV production, 1988-92. 1992-present, prod. Marty Katz Prods./Buena Vista.
PICTURES: Heart Like a Wheel, Lost in America, Man of the House, Mr. Wrong, Reindeer Games, Imposter, Below, Four Feathers.
TELEVISION: 11th Victim, The Day the Bubble Burst, Triplecross.

KATZ, NORMAN B.
Executive. b. Scranton, PA, Aug. 23, 1919. e. Columbia U. In U.S. Army 1941-46 as intelligence officer, airborne forces. Entered m.p. industry in 1947 with Discina Films, Paris, France, as prod. asst. Named exec. asst. to head of prod. in 1948. 1950 named v.p. Discina Int'l. Films and in 1952 exec. v.p. 1954 joined Associated Artists Prods. as foreign mgr.; named dir. of foreign operation in 1958. 1959 became dir. of foreign operations for United Artists Associated. 1961 joined 7 Arts Associated Corp. as v.p. in chg. of foreign optns.; 1964, named exec. v.p., 7 Arts Prods. Int'l.; 1967, exec. v.p. Warner Bros.-7 Arts Int'l. 1969 appt. exec. v.p. & CEO WB Int'l. & bd. mem. of WB Inc. 1974 named sr. v.p. int'l. div. of American Film Theatre. Pres. of Cinema Arts Assoc. Corp. 1979, exec. v.p. and bd. member, American Communications Industries and pres., CEO of ACI subsidiary, American Cinema; 1983, pres., The Norkat Co., Also, bd. chmn., CEO, American Film Mktg. Assoc.; 1985-87; chmn. Amer. Film Export Assn. 1988-92.

KATZENBERG, JEFFREY
Executive, Executive Producer. b. 1950. Entered motion picture industry in 1975 as asst. to Paramount Pictures chmn. and CEO Barry Diller in NY. In 1977, became exec. dir. of mktg.; later same year moved to west coast as v.p. of programming for Paramount TV. Promoted to v.p., feature production for Paramount Pictures 1978; 2 years later assumed role of sr. v.p. prod. of m.p. div; 1982, pres. of prod., m.p. and TV, Paramount Pictures. Left to join The Walt Disney Company, 1984; chairman of The Walt Disney Studios, 1984-94. With Steven Spielberg and David Geffen formed DreamWorks SKG entertainment company, 1995.
PICTURES: Exec. Prod: The Prince of Egypt, Road to El Dorado, Chicken Run, Shrek, Spirit: Stallion of the Cimarron, Wallace and Gromit: The Great Vegetable Plot, Shrek 2.

KAUFFMAN, MARTA
Producer. b. 1956. Partner in Kauffman-Crane Prods.
TELEVISION: Series: Dream On (co-creator), Friends (exec., co-creator), Veronica's Closet (exec., co-creator), Jesse (exec.).

KAUFMAN, AVY
Casting Director.
PICTURES: Little Man Tate, The Super, The Basketball Diaries, Home for the Holidays, Across thr Sea of Time, Lone Star, Gotti, Boys Life 2, The Ice Storm, The Real Blonde, Critical Care, Snitch, Wide Awake, Rounders, Claire Dolan, A Civil Action, The Sixth Sense, Music of the Heart, Ride With the Devil, A Map of the World, The Hurricane, O, Keeping the Faith, Dancer in the Dark, Blow, Save the Last Dance, The Heist, Don't Say a Word, Divine Secrets of the Ya Ya Sisterhood, Moonlight Mile, Smack in the Kisser, Dogville, The Hulk, The Human Stain, Against the Ropes.
TELEVISION: On Seventh Avenue, Dinner With Friends, The Job.

KAUFMAN, CHARLIE
Producer, Writer.
PICTURES: Being John Malkovich (Acad. Award nom., Golden Globe nom., BAFTA Award), Human Nature, Adaptation, Confessions of a Dangerous Mind.
TELEVISION: Series: Get A Life, Ned and Stacey, The Dana Carvey Show.

KAUFMAN, HAL
Creative Director, TV Writer, Producer. b. New York, NY, Dec. 16, 1924. e. U. of TX, 1943-44; U. of MI, 1944-47. Started career as petroleum geologist, Western Geophysical Co., 1947-48; TV writer-prod-dir., KDYL-TV, Salt Lake City, 1948-49; prog. dir., LAV-TV, Grand Rapids, 1949-51; prod. mgr., WOOD-TV, Grand Rapids, 1951-54; TV writer-prod., Leo Burnett Co., Chicago, 1954-56; TV writer-prod., Gordon Best Company, Chicago, 1957-58; with Needham Louis & Brorby Inc.; 1959, sr. writer, TV/Radio creative dept.; 1962, v.p., asst. copy dir.; 1963, dir., tv, radio prod.; 1964, dir. b'cast design, production; assoc. creat. dir., asst. exec. v.p., Needham, Harper & Steers, Inc., 1965; creat. dir. L.A., 1966; sr. v.p. and mem. bd. of dir., 1966. 1969, creative & mktg consultant in Beverly Hills. 1970, exec. v.p., principle, Kaufman, Lansky Inc., Beverly Hills and San Diego; 1974 editor and publisher Z Magazine; prog. dir., Z Channel, Theta Cable TV. 1979, sr. v.p./adv. & p.r & asst. to pres. & bd. chmn., World Airways, Inc. 1982, v.p., creative dir., Admarketing, Inc., Los Angeles. 1985, mktg. & adv. consultant copy dir., Teleflora, Inc.; pres. Hal Kaufman Inc., mktg. & adv. consultant; pres. Brochures on Video, library division, creators and prods. of promotional videos, distribs. religious videos to libraries; pres. Pious Publications, prods. and distribs. of religious videos. Member, DGA, SAG, AFTRA. 1974.

KAUFMAN, LEONARD B.
Producer, Writer, Director. b. Newark, NJ, Aug. 31, 1927. e. NYU. In W.W.II served with Army Special Services writing and directing camp shows. Nat'l magazine writer, 1945-48; radio writer, including Errol Flynn Show, 1948-50; radio and TV writer, 1950-52. Headed own public relations firm: Kaufman, Schwartz, and Associates, 1952-64.
PICTURES: Clarence the Cross-eyed Lion, Birds Do It (story).
TELEVISION: Daktari, Ivan Tors' Jambo, O'Hara U.S. Treasury (pilot feature and series). Producer: Hawaii-Five O, The New Sea Hunt, Scruples (mini-series), The Hawaiian (pilot), Writer: Knightrider, Dukes of Hazzard, Hawaii-Five O, Wet Heat (pilot), Hawaiian Heat, Island Sons (movie).

KAUFMAN, LLOYD
Executive. e. Yale Univ., 1969. From 1974-present, pres. of Troma, Inc. Co-writer of book, All I Need To Know About Filmmaking I Learned from the Toxic Avenger.
PICTURES: The Girl Who Returned (prod., dir., s.p.), Cry Uncle (prod. mgr.), Joe (prod. asst.), Sugar Cookie (exec. prod., s.p.), Silent Night Bloody Night (assoc. prod.), Battle of Love's Return (dir., prod., s.p., actor), Big Gus What's the Fuss (dir., prod.), Sweet Savior (prod. mgr.), Mother's Day (assoc. prod.), Rocky (pre-prod. spvr.), Slow Dancing in the Big City (prod. spvr.), The Final Countdown (assoc. prod.), Squeeze Play (dir., prod.), Waitress (Co-dir., prod.), Stuck on You (co-dir., co-prod., co-s.p.), The First Turn-On (co-dir., co-prod.), Screamplay (exec. prod.), When Nature Calls (assoc. prod.), The Toxic Avenger (co-dir., co-prod., co-s.p., story), Blood Hook (exec. prod.), Girl School Screams (exec. prod.), Class of Nuke 'Em High (co-dir., co-prod.), Lust for Freedom (exec. prod.), Monster in the Closet (exec. prod.), Troma's War (Co-dir., co-prod., co-s.p., story), Toxic Avenger Part II (co-dir., co-prod., co-s.p., story), Fortress of Amerikkka (prod.), Toxic Avenger III: The Last Temptation of Toxie (co-dir., co-s.p., co-prod.), Class of Nuke 'Em High Part II: Subhumanoid Meltdown (co-s.p., co-prod., story), Sgt. Kabukiman N.Y.P.D. (co-dir., co-prod., co-s.p.), The Good the Bad and the Subhumanoid (co-s.p., co-prod., co-story), Tromeo and Juliet (dir., co-s.p., co-prod.), Rowdy Girls (prod.), Terror Firmer (co-s.p., prod., dir.), Alien Blood, Sidney Pink on 'Pyro'.

KAUFMAN, PHILIP
Writer, Director, Producer. b. Chicago, IL, Oct. 23, 1936. e. U. of Chicago, Harvard Law Sch. Was teacher in Italy and Greece before turning to film medium.
PICTURES: Co-Writer: The Outlaw Josey Wales, Raiders of the Lost Ark. Director: Goldstein (co-dir., co-s.p., co-prod.), Fearless Frank (also s.p., prod.), The Great Northfield Minnesota Raid (also s.p., prod.), The White Dawn, Invasion of the Body Snatchers, The Wanderers (also co-s.p.), The Right Stuff (also s.p.), The Unbearable Lightness of Being (also co-s.p.), Henry & June (also co-s.p.), Rising Sun (also co-s.p.), Quills, Blackout.

KAUFMAN, VICTOR
Executive. b. New York, NY, June 21, 1943. e. Queens Coll.; NYU Sch. of Law, J.D., 1967. Taught criminal law at UCLA before joining Wall St. law firm, Simpson Thacher & Bartlett. Joined Columbia Pictures as asst. general counsel, 1974. Named chief counsel, 1975; then made vice chmn. Columbia Pictures. Later exec. v.p. Columbia Pictures Industries and vice chmn. Columbia Pictures motion picture div. when conceived a new studio as a joint venture between Coca-Cola, Time Inc.'s Home Box Office and CBS, Inc. forming Tri-Star Pictures. Named chmn. and CEO Tri-Star, 1983. When Columbia Pictures and Tri-Star merged in late 1987, became pres. and CEO of new entity, Columbia Pictures Entertainment. In June 1988, dropped title of chmn. of Tri-Star. 1993 became head of Savoy Pictures. CFO, USA Networks, Nov., 1997. Currently, vice-chmn., USA Interactive overseeing all strategic planning, financial and legal matters for USAi. Also on boards of Ticketmaster, Hotels.com and Expedia.

KAUFMANN, CHRISTINE
Actress. b. Lansdorf, Graz, Austria, Jan. 11, 1945. e. school in Munich, Germany. Film debut as a dancer. Salto Mortale at age 7.
PICTURES: The White Horse Inn, Salto Mortale, Der Klosterjager, Staatsanwaltin Corda, Rosenrosli (Little Rosie), Schweigende Engel (Silent Angel), Wenn die Alpenrosen Bluh'n, Ein Herz Schlagt fur Erika, Stimme der Sehnsucht, Witwer mit 5 Tochtern, Die Winzerin von Langenlois, Sag ja Mutti!, First Love, Madchen in Uniform, Embezzled Heaven, Winter Vacation, Madchen von denen man spricht, Everybody Loves Peter, Toto Fabrizio e i Giovani D'oggi, Der Letzte Fubganger, The Last Days of Pompeii, Red Lips, Un Trono Para Cristy, A Man Named Rocca, Town Without Pity, Via Mala, The Phony American, Swordsman of Siena, Taras Bulba (U.S debut), Escape from East Berlin, Constantine the Great, Neunzig Minuten nach Mitternacht, Wild & Wonderful, Love Birds, The Death of Maria Malibran, Murder in the Rue Morgue, Willow Springs, Goodbye with Mums, Auf Biegen oder Brechen, Goldflocken, Rich and Respectable, Orgie des Todes, It Can only Get Worse, Day of the Idiots, Egon Schiele - Exzesse, Lili Marleen, Lola, Ziemlich weit Weg, The Wild Fifties, The Excluded, Peppermint Peace, The Swing, Bagdad Cafe, Hard to Be a God, Der Geschichtenerzahler, The Talking Grave, War of Neighbours, The Sleeper, Blutiger Ernst.
TELEVISION: Movies: World on a Wire, Immobilien, Inflation im Paradies, Birkenhof & Kirchenau, Weihnachten mit Willy Wuff II - Eine Mama fur Lieschen, Ein Flotter Dreier. Mini-series: Wie ein Blitz, Lockruf des Goldes, Monaco Franze - Der Ewige Stenz.

KAURISMAKI, AKI
Director, Writer. b. Finland, April 4, 1957. Brother is filmmaker Mika Kaurismaki. First film credit was acting and writing his brother's The Liar in 1980. Directed short subjects: Rocky VI, Thru the Wire, Those Were the Days, These Boots. Served as writer on brother's features: Jackpot 2, The Worthless (also actor), The Clan: The Tale of the Frogs, Rosso.
PICTURES: Director: The Saimaa Gesture (co-dir., with Mika), Crime and Punishment, Calamari Union, Shadows in Paradise, Hamlet Goes Business, Ariel, Leningrad Cowboys Go America, The Match Factory Girl, I Hired a Contract Killer, La Vie de Boheme (The Bohemian Life), Leningrad Cowboys Meet Moses (also s.p., prod., edit.), Total Balalaika Show (also s.p.), Take Care of Your Scarf Tatiana (also s.p., prod., edit.), Drifting Clouds (also s.p.), Quiet Village, Juha, Kovat miehet, The Man Without a Past (Cannes Grand Jury Prize), Ten Minutes Older: The Trumpet.

KAVNER, JULIE
Actress. b. Los Angeles, CA, Sept. 7, 1951. e. San Diego State U. Professional debut as Brenda Morgenstern on TV's Rhoda, 1974.
THEATRE: Particular Friendships (Off-B'way), Two for the Seesaw (Jupiter, FLA), It Had to Be You (Canada).
PICTURES: National Lampoon Goes to the Movies, Bad Medicine, Hannah and Her Sisters, Radio Days, Surrender, New York Stories (Oedipus Wrecks), Awakenings, Alice, This Is My Life, Shadows and Fog, I'll Do Anything, Forget Paris, Deconstructin Harry, Doctor Dolittle (voice), A Walk on the Moon, Judy Berlin, Cyberworld (voice), Someone Like You... (voice).
TELEVISION: Series: Rhoda (Emmy Award, 1978), The Tracey Ullman Show, The Simpsons (voice), Tracey Takes On.... Special: The Girl Who Couldn't Lose (Afternoon Playbreak). Movies: Katherine, No Other Love, The Revenge of the Stepford Wives, Don't Drink the Water, The Simpsons: America's First Family. Pilot: A Fine Romance. Guest: Lou Grant, Petrocelli, Taxi.

KAYLOR, ROBERT
Director. b. Plains, MT, Aug. 1, 1934. e. Art Center Sch. of Design. Received awards at Cannes, San Francisco and Dallas Film Festivals, Guggenheim Fellow, Amer. Film Inst.
PICTURES: Derby, Carny, Nobody's Perfect.

KAZAN, ELIA
Director. b. Constantinople, Turkey, Sept. 7, 1909. e. Williams Coll., Yale Dramatic Sch. With Group Theatre as apprentice & stage mgr.; on stage, 1934-41; plays include: Waiting for Lefty, Golden Boy, Gentle People, Five-Alarm, Lilliom. Author (novels): The Arrangement, The Assassins, The Understudy, Acts of Love, The Anatolian, A Life (autobiography, 1988), Beyond the Aegean (1994).Honorary Oscar Award, 1998.
THEATRE: Director: Skin of Our Teeth, All My Sons, Streetcar Named Desire, Death of a Salesman, Cat on a Hot Tin Roof (co-dir.), One Touch of Venus, Harriet, Jocobowsky and the Colonel, Tea and Sympathy, Dark at the Top of the Stairs, J.B., Sweet Bird of Youth, Lincoln Center Repertory Theatre (co-dir., prod.), After The Fall, But For Whom Charlie.
PICTURES: Actor: City for Conquest, Blues in the Night. Director: A Tree Grows in Brooklyn (debut, 1945), Boomerang!, The Sea of Grass, Gentleman's Agreement (Acad. Award, 1947), Pinky, Panic in the Streets, A Streetcar Named Desire, Viva Zapata!, Man on a Tightrope, On the Waterfront (Academy Award, 1954). Prod./Director: East of Eden, Baby Doll, A Face in the Crowd, Wild River, Splendor in the Grass, America America (also s.p.), The Arrangement (also s.p.), The Visitors, The Last Tycoon.
(d. Sept. 28, 2003)

KAZAN, LAINIE

Singer, Actress. b. New York, NY, May 15, 1942. e. Hofstra U.
PICTURES: Dayton's Devils, Lady in Cement, Romance of a Horse Thief, One from the Heart, My Favorite Year, Lust in the Dust, The Delta Force, The Journey of Natty Gann, Harry and the Hendersons, Beaches, Eternity, 29th Street, I Don't Buy Kisses Anymore, The Cemetery Club, Love Is All There Is, The Associate, Movies Money Murder, The Unknown Cyclist, Allie & Me, The Big Hit, Permanent Midnight, Kimberly, What's Cooking?, If You Only Knew, Bruno, The Crew, My Big Fat Greek Wedding.
TELEVISION: Series: The Dean Martin Summer Show, Tough Cookies, Karen's Song. Pilot: Family Business, The Lainie Kazan Show. Movies: A Love Affair: The Eleanor and Lou Gehrig Story, A Cry for Love, Sunset Limousine, The Jerk Too, Obsessive Love, Prince for a Day, Safety Patrol. Guest: Too Close for Comfort, Dick Van Dyke Show, Beverly Hills 90210, Tales From the Crypt, Faerie Tale Theatre (Pinocchio), Hotel, Johnny Carson Show, Dean Martin, Merv Griffin, Joan Rivers, Amazing Stories, Pat Sajak Show, The Famous Teddy Z, Murder She Wrote.

KAZANJIAN, HOWARD G.

Producer. b. Pasadena, CA, July 26, 1943. e. U. of Southern California Film Sch.; DGA Training Program.
PICTURES: Asst. dir.: Cool Hand Luke, Camelot, Finian's Rainbow, The Wild Bunch, The Great Bank Robbery, I Love You Alice B. Toklas, Christine, The Arrangement, The Girl From Petrovka, The Front Page, The Hindenberg, Family Plot. Producer: Rollercoaster (assoc. prod.) More American Graffiti, Raiders of the Lost Ark, Return of the Jedi, The Rookie, Demolition Man, One Dozen, Rattled, Carlo's Wake, The Sky Is Falling, Extreme Days, The Homecoming of Jimmy Whitecloud.
TELEVISION: The Making of More American Graffiti, The Making of Raiders of the Lost Ark (Emmy award), The Making of Return of the Jedi, JAG, Amati Girls.

KAZURINSKY, TIM

Actor, Writer. b. Johnstown, PA, March 3, 1950. Raised in Australia. Worked as copywriter for Chicago ad agency. Took acting class at Second City and quit job to become actor and head writer for Second City Comedy Troupe. Co-starred with John Candy in CTV/NBC's series Big City Comedy, 1980. Joined cast of Saturday Night Live as writer-actor 1981-84.
PICTURES: Actor: My Bodyguard, Somewhere in Time, Continental Divide, Neighbors, Police Academy II: Their First Assignment, Police Academy III: Back in Training, About Last Night (also co-s.p.), Police Academy IV: Citizens on Patrol, For Keeps (s.p. only), Road to Ruin (also s.p.), Hot to Trot, Wedding Band, A Billion for Boris, Shakes the Clown, Plump Fiction, Poor White Trash, Betaville.
TELEVISION: Movies: This Wife for Hire, Dinner at Eight, The Cherokee Kid (also s.p.), My Beautiful Son.

KEACH, STACY

Actor, Director, Producer. b. Savannah, GA, June 2, 1942. Brother is actor James Keach. Began professional acting career in Joseph Papp's 1964 Central Park prod. of Hamlet.
THEATRE: Long Day's Journey into Night (Obie Award), Macbird (Drama Desk & Obie Awards), Indians (Drama Desk Award & Tony nom.), Hamlet, Deathtrap, Hughie, Barnum, Cyrano de Bergerac, Peer Gynt, Henry IV Parts I & II, Idiot's Delight, Solitary Confinement, Richard III, The Kentucky Cycle (Helen Hayes Award), Steiglitz Loves O'Keefe.
PICTURES: The Heart Is a Lonely Hunter (debut, 1968), End of the Road, The Traveling Executioner, Brewster McCloud, Doc, The New Centurions, Fat City, Watched!, The Life and Times of Judge Roy Bean, Luther, The Gravy Train, The Killer Inside Me, Conduct Unbecoming, Street People, The Squeeze, The Duellists (narrator), Slave of the Cannibal God, The Great Battle, Gray Lady Down, Up in Smoke, The Ninth Configuration (Twinkle Twinkle Killer Kane), The Long Riders (also exec. prod., co-s.p.), Nice Dreams, Road Games, Butterfly, That Championship Season, Class of 1999, False Identity, Milena, Raw Justice, Batman: Mask of the Phantasm (voice), New Crime City, Escape from L.A., Prey of the Jaguar, Sea Wolf, Future Fear, American History X, Birds of Passage, Olympic Glory, Icebreaker, Militia, Mercy Streets, Unshackled, Lightning: Fire From the Sky, Sunstorm., El Padrino, Jesus-Mary-And Joey, The Hollow, Keep Your Distance.
TELEVISION: Series: Caribe, Mickey Spillane's Mike Hammer, Case Closed (host), Mike Hammer Private Eye, World's Most Amazing Videos, Stupid Behavior: Caught on Tape, Rods!, Titus. Movies: All the Kind Strangers, Caribe, The Blue and the Gray, Princess Daisy, Murder Me Murder You, More Than Murder, Wait Until Dark, Mistral's Daughter, Hemingway, Mickey Spillane's Mike Hammer: Murder Takes All, The Forgotten, Mission of the Shark, Revenge on the Highway, Rio Diablo, Body Bags, Against Their Will: Women in Prison, Texas, Amanda & the Alien, Young Ivanhoe, Plague Fighters, The Pathfinder, Legend of the Lost Tomb, Savage Seas, Murder in My Mind, The Courage to Love, Warship, The Santa Trap, Frozen Impact.. Director: Incident at Vichy, Six Characters in Search of an Author.

KEACH, SR., STACY

Executive. b. Chicago, IL, May 29, 1914. Father of actors, Stacy and James. e. Northwestern U., B.S. & M.A. Was instructor in theatre arts at Northwestern and Armstrong Coll. and dir. at Pasadena Playhouse before entering industry. For 4-1/2 yrs. was under contract at Universal Pictures; 3 yrs. at RKO; had own prod. on NBC, CBS. In 1946 began producing and directing industrial stage presentations for Union Oil Co. and from then on became full-time prod. of m.p. and stage industrial shows. In 1946 formed Stacy Keach Productions. In addition to directing, producing and writing occasionally appears as actor in films. Created radio show, Tales of the Texas Rangers, 1950-53. Played Clarence Birds Eye on TV commercials as well as other commercials. Voiceovers/ spokesman for many major American Cos. Autobiography: Stacy Keach, Go Home! (1996). Received Man of the Year Award from Pasadena Playhouse Alumni in 1995. Recipient of the Diamond Circle Award from the Pacific Pioneers Broadcasters Assoc., 1996.
(d. Feb. 13, 2003)

KEATON, DIANE

Actress, Director. r.n. Diane Hall. b. Santa Ana, CA, Jan. 5, 1946. e. Santa Ana Coll. Appeared in summer stock and studied at Neighborhood Playhouse in N.Y. Made prof. debut in B'way prod. of Hair (1968); then co-starred with Woody Allen in Play It Again Sam, repeating role for film version. Off-B'way: The Primary English Class. Author: photography books: Reservations (co-ed.), Still Life. Directed 1982 short What Does Dorrie Want?
PICTURES: Lovers and Other Strangers (debut, 1970), The Godfather, Play It Again Sam, Sleeper, The Godfather Part II, Love and Death, I Will I Will... for Now, Harry and Walter Go to New York, Annie Hall (Acad. Award, 1977), Looking for Mr. Goodbar, Interiors, Manhattan, Reds, Shoot the Moon, The Little Drummer Girl, Mrs. Soffel, Crimes of the Heart, Radio Days, Heaven (dir. only), Baby Boom, The Good Mother, The Lemon Sisters (also prod.), The Godfather Part III, Father of the Bride, Manhattan Murder Mystery, Look Who's Talking Now (voice), Unstrung Heroes (dir. only), Father of the Bride 2, Marvin's Room, The First Wives Club, The Only Thrill, Northern Lights, Town and Country, The Other Sister, Hanging Up, Plan B, Elephant (exec. prod. only), Something's Gotta Give.
TELEVISION: Movies: Running Mates, Amelia Earhart: The Final Flight, Northern Lights, Sister Mary Explains It All, Crossed Over, On Thin Ice. Guest: Love American Style, The FBI, Mannix. Director: The Girl With the Crazy Brother, Twin Peaks, Wildflower (movie).

KEATON, MICHAEL

Actor. r.n. Michael Douglas. b. Coraopolis, PA, Sept. 5, 1951. Speech major, Kent State U, 2 years. Drove cab and ice-cream truck, worked for PBS station in Pittsburgh and appeared in regional theatre prods. while performing in local coffeehouses. Became memb. of improvisational troupe Jerry Vale. Moved to L.A. where honed craft at Comedy Store and Second City Improv. Workshops as stand-up comic.
PICTURES: Night Shift (debut, 1982), Mr. Mom, Johnny Dangerously, Gung Ho, Touch and Go, The Squeeze, Beetlejuice, Clean and Sober, The Dream Team, Batman, Pacific Heights, One Good Cop, Batman Returns, Much Ado About Nothing, My Life, The Paper, Speechless, Multiplicity, Inventing the Abbotts (narrator), Jackie Brown, Desperate Measures, Out of Sight (cameo), Jack Frost, A Shot At Glory, Quicksand.
TELEVISION: Series: All's Fair, Mary, The Mary Tyler Moore Hour, Working Stiffs, Report to Murphy. Movies: Roosevelt and Truman, Live From Baghdad. Special: Frank Capra's American Dream.

KEENER, CATHERINE

Actress. b. Miami, FL 1961. m. actor Dermot Mulroney
PICTURES: About Last Night, The Education of Allison Tate, Survival Quest, Catchfire, Switch, Johnny Suede, The Gun in Betty Lou's Handbag, Living in Oblivion, Boys, Walking and Talking, Box of Moonlight, The Destiny of Marty Fine, The Real Blonde, Out of Sight, Your Friends & Neighbors, 8MM, Being John Malkovich, Simpatico, Simone, How to Survive a Hotel Room Fire, Death to Smoochy, Full Frontal, Simone, Adaptation.
TELEVISION: Series: Seinfeld, L.A. Law, Ohara.

KEEL, HOWARD

Actor. r.n. Harold Keel. b. Gillespie, IL, April 13, 1919. e. high school, Fallbrook, CA. Began career following George Walker scholarship award for singing, L.A.; appeared in plays, Pasadena Auditorium, concerts; won awards, Mississippi Valley and Chicago Musical Fest.. Stage debut: Carousel, 1945; followed by London prod. of Oklahoma! which led to contract with MGM.
THEATRE: Carousel, Oklahoma!, Saratoga, No Strings, The Ambassador, Man of La Mancha.
PICTURES: The Small Voice (debut, 1948), Annie Get Your Gun, Pagan Love Song, Three Guys Named Mike, Show Boat, Texas Carnival, Callaway Went Thataway, Lovely to Look At, Desperate Search, I Love Melvin (cameo), Ride Vaquero!, Fast Company, Kiss Me Kate, Calamity Jane, Rose Marie, Seven Brides for Seven Brothers, Deep in My Heart, Jupiter's Darling, Kismet, Floods of Fear, The Big Fisherman, Armored Command, The Day of the Triffids, The Man From Button Willow (voice), Waco, Red Tomahawk, The War Wagon, Arizona Bushwhackers, That's

Entertainment III, Too Darn Hot (video).
TELEVISION: *Series*: Dallas. *Movie*: Hart to Hart: Home Is Where the Hart Is. *Guest*: Zane Grey Theatre, Bell Telephone Hour, Tales of Wells Fargo, Death Valley Days, Here's Lucy, Sonny and Cher, The Love Boat, etc. *Specials*: A Toast to Jerome Kern, Roberta, Music of Richard Rodgers, The Making of 'Seven Brides for Seven Brothers'.

KEESHAN, BOB
Performer. b. Lynbrook, NY, June 27, 1927. e. Fordham U. As network page boy became assistant to Howdy Doody's Bob Smith and originated role of Clarabelle the Clown; created children's programs Time for Fun, Tinker's Workshop, Mister Mayor, Captain Kangaroo (1955-85).

KEITEL, HARVEY
Actor. b. Brooklyn, NY, May 13, 1939. Served in U.S. Marine Corps. Studied with Frank Corsaro, Lee Strasberg, Stella Adler. Member of the Actors' Studio. Debuted in Martin Scorsese's student film Who's That Knocking at My Door?
THEATRE: *NY*: Up to Thursday, Death of a Salesman, Hurlyburly, A Lie of the Mind.
PICTURES: Who's That Knocking at My Door? (debut, 1968), Mean Streets, Alice Doesn't Live Here Anymore, That's the Way of the World, Taxi Driver, Mother Jugs and Speed, Buffalo Bill and the Indians or: Sitting Bull's History Lesson, Welcome to L.A., The Duellists, Fingers, Blue Collar, Eagle's Wing, Deathwatch, Saturn 3, Bad Timing, The Border, Exposed, La Nuit de Varennes, Corrupt, Falling in Love, Knight of the Dragon (Star Knight), Camorra, Off Beat, Wise Guys, The Investigation (The Inquiry), The Pick-Up Artist, The Last Temptation of Christ, The January Man, The Two Jakes, Mortal Thoughts, Thelma & Louise, Two Evil Eyes, Bugsy (Acad. Award nom.), Sister Act, Reservoir Dogs (also co-prod.), Bad Lieutenant, Point of No Return, Rising Sun, The Piano, Dangerous Game, The Young Americans, Monkey Trouble, Pulp Fiction, Imaginary Crimes, Somebody to Love, Smoke, Clockers, Blue in the Face, Ulysses' Gaze, From Dusk Till Dawn, Head Above Water, Somebody to Love, City of Industry, Cop Land, Shadrach, Finding Graceland, Lulu on the Bridge, My West, Three Seasons, Prince of Central Park, Holy Smoke, U-571, Little Nicky, Taking Sides, La Soutane Tourquoise, Nailed, Je Viens Apres La Pluie, Jack Shepard and Jonathan Wild, Taking Sides, The Grey Zone, Viper, Je viens apres la pluie, Dreaming of Julia, Beeper, Nowhere, Red Dragon, Crime Spree, Who Killed the Idea?, The Galindez File, National Treasure, The Bridge of San Luis Rey.
TELEVISION: *Movie*: The Virginia Hill Story. *Special*: This Ain't Bebop (Amer. Playhouse).

KEITH, DAVID
Actor, **Director**. b. Knoxville, TN, May 8, 1954. e. U. of Tennessee, B.A., speech and theater. Appearance at Goodspeed Opera House in musical led to role in CBS sitcom pilot, Co-Ed Fever.
PICTURES: The Rose (debut, 1979), The Great Santini, Brubaker, Back Roads, Take This Job and Shove It, An Officer and a Gentleman, Independence Day, The Lords of Discipline, Firestarter, The Curse (dir. only), White of the Eye, The Further Adventures of Tennessee Buck (also dir.), Heartbreak Hotel, The Two Jakes, Off and Running, Desperate Motive, Caged Fear, Raw Justice, Temptation, Major League II, Liar's Edge, Till the End of the Night, Born Wild, Gold Diggers: The Secret of Bear Mountain, Deadly Sins, The Indian in the Cupboard, A Family Thing, Invasion of Privacy, Secret of the Andes, Ambushed, Judge & Jury, Red Blooded American Girl II, If... Dog... Rabbit, U-571, Men of Honor, Cahoots, Epoch, World Traveler, Anthrax, License to Steal, Clover Bend, Sabretooth, Behind Enemy Lines, The Stick Up, Deep Shock, Daredevil, The Veritas Project: Hangman's Curse.
TELEVISION: *Series*: Co-ed Fever, Flesh 'N' Blood, Strangers, High Incident, Local Heroes. *Movies*: Are You in the House Alone?, Friendly Fire, Gulag, Whose Child Is This?: The War for Baby Jessica, XXX's & OOO's (pilot), James Michener's Texas, If Looks Could Kill: From the Files of America's Most Wanted, Poodle Springs. *Mini-Series*: If Tomorrow Comes, Golden Moment: An Olympic Love Story, Guts and Glory: The Rise and Fall of Oliver North, The Great War (voice). *Guest*: Happy Days, Runaways.

KEITH, PENELOPE
O.B.E. Actress. b. Sutton, Surrey, Eng., 1939. London stage debut, The Wars of the Roses (RSC, 1964). Theater work including The Norman Conquests, Donkey's Years, The Apple Cart, Hobson's Choice, Captain Brassbound's Conversion, Hay Fever.
PICTURES: Think Dirty (Every Home Should Have One), Take a Girl Like You, Penny Gold, Priest of Love.
TELEVISION: *Series*: Kate, The Good Life, To the Manor Born, Executive Stress, No Job for a Lady, Law and Disorder, Next of Kin. *Movies-Specials*: Private Lives, The Norman Conquests, Donkey's Years, Laughter in the House: The Story of the British Sitcom.

KELLER, MARTHE
Actress. b. Basel, Switzerland, 1945. e. Stanislavsky Sch., Munich. Joined a Heidelberg repertory group and Schiller Rep. in

Berlin. Started acting in France and attracted attention of U.S. directors after appearing in Claude Lelouch's And Now My Love. Has acted in over 50 plays in French, German, Eng. & Italian.
PICTURES: Funeral in Berlin (debut, 1967), The Devil by the Tail, ive Her the Moon, La Vieille Fille, The Loser, Elle Court (Love in the Suburbs), And Now My Love, Down the Ancient Staircase, Le Guepier, Marathon Man, Black Sunday, Bobby Deerfield, Fedora, The Formula, Les Uns et les Autres, The Amateur, Wagner, Femmes de Personne, Joan Lui, I Come on Monday, Dark Eyes, Rouge Basier, The Artisan, Una Vittoria, Lapse of Memory, Mon Amie Max, According to Pereira, Nuits Blanches, K, Elles, The School of Flesh, From Behind, Time of the Wolf.
TELEVISION: Liberez mon Fils, Mein oder Dein, The Chartreuse of Parma, Wagner, Die Frau des Reporters, La Ruelle de Clair de Lune, The Nightmare Years, Young Catherine, Turbulences, Im Kreis der Iris.

KELLERMAN, SALLY
Actress. b. Long Beach, CA, June 2, 1936. e. Hollywood H.S. Studied acting in N.Y. at the Actors Studio and in Hollywood with Jeff Corey. Recorded album Roll With the Feeling. Has done voice-overs for many commercials. m. Jonathan Krane.
THEATRE: Women Behind Bars, Holiday.
PICTURES: Reform School Girl (debut, 1959), Hands of a Stranger, The Third Day, The Boston Strangler, The April Fools, M*A*S*H (Acad. Award nom.), Brewster McCloud, Last of the Red Hot Lovers, Lost Horizon, Slither, Reflection of Fear, Rafferty and the Gold Dust Twins, The Big Bus, Welcome to L.A., The Mouse and His Child (voice), Magee and the Lady, A Little Romance, Serial, Head On (Fatal Attraction), Foxes, Loving Couples, Moving Violations, Lethal (KGB: The Secret War), Back to School, That's Life!, Meatballs III, Three For the Road, Someone to Love, You Can't Hurry Love, Paramedics (voice), All's Fair, Limit Up, The Secret of the Ice Cave, The Player, Doppelganger, Happily Ever After (voice), Younger and Younger, Ready to Wear (Pret-a-Porter), Mirror Mirror 2: Raven Dance, It's My Party, The Maze, The Lay of the Land (also prod.), Live Virgin, Ugly, Open House, Delgo (voice).
TELEVISION: *Mini-Series*: Centennial. *Movies*: For Lovers Only, Dempsey, Secret Weapons, September Gun, Drop Dead Gorgeous, Boris and Natasha (also assoc. prod.), Columbo: Ashes to Ashes, Bar Hopping, Verdict in Blood. *Specials*: Big Blonde, Verna: USO Girl, Elena, Faerie Tale Theatre, Dr. Paradise. *Guest*: Mannix, It Takes a Thief, Chrysler Theatre, Robert Altman's Gun.

KELLEY, DAVID E.
Producer, Writer. b. Waterville, ME, April 4, 1956. e. Princeton U., Boston U. Law. m. actress Michelle Pfeiffer. Formerly a lawyer at Fine & Ambrogne when in 1983 he wrote a film script based on some of his legal experiences. The script was optioned and later becamse the film "From the Hip." Was invited to L.A. by Steven Bochco and Terry Louise Fisher to become story editor for "L.A. Law." In 1987, became exec. story editor, then exec. prod. and writer after Bochco left. Now CEO, writer and exec. prod. at David E. Kelley Prods. in L.A.
PICTURES: *Writer*: From the Hip, To Gillian on Her 37th Birthday (also prod.), Lake Placid, Mystery Alaska (also prod.).
TELEVISION: *Movies*: Annie O (cam.). *Series exec. prod.*: L.A Law (Emmy Award, 1989, 1990, 1991), Doogie Howser M.D., Picket Fences (Emmy Award, 1993 and 1994) Chicago Hope, The Practice (Emmy Award, 1999), Ally McBeal (Emmy Award, 1999), Boston Public, Girls Club.

KELLEY, SHEILA
Actress. b. Philadelphia, PA, Sept. 9, 1963.
PICTURES: Wish You Were Here, Hostile Witness, Staying Together, Some Girls, Breaking In, Mortal Passions, Where the Heart Is, Wild Blade, Soapdish, Pure Luck, Singles, Passion Fish, Passion to Kill, Mona Must Die, One Fine Day, Sante Fe, Nurse Betty, Dancing at the Blue Iguana.
TELEVISION: *Series*: L.A. Law, Sisters, Moving Story. *Movie*: Tonight's the Night, The Betty Ford Story, Terrorist on Trial: The United States vs. Salim Ajami, Fulfillment, The Chase, Deconstructing Sarah, The Secretary, Mind Prey, The Jennie Project. *Guest*: Wings.

KELLY, FRANK
Executive. Was assoc. prod. of AM Los Angeles, then exec. prod./program dir. for KABC-TV prior to joining Paramount. 1983, named v.p. programming for Paramount domestic tv division; 1985, promoted to sr. v.p. 1989, became exec. v.p. programming. 1995, named pres. of creative affairs for domestic tv division of Paramount Television Group.

KELLY, MOIRA
Actress. b. Queens, NY, March 6, 1968. e. Marymount Col. In addition to acting also trained as violinist, operatic soprano.
PICTURES: The Boy Who Cried Bitch (debut, 1991), Billy Bathgate, The Cutting Edge, Twin Peaks: Fire Walk With Me, Chaplin, With Honors, The Lion King (voice), Little Odessa, The Tie That Binds, Enterlang Angels: The Dorothy Day Story, Unhook the Stars, Henry Hill, Drive She Said, Changing Habits, The Lion King II: Simba's Pride, Love Walked In, Dangerous

Beauty, Hi-Life, Henry Hill, The Safety of Objects.
TELEVISION: *Movies:* Love Lies and Murder, Daybreak, Monday After the Miracle. *Series:* To Have & To Hold, The West Wing.

KELSEY, LINDA
Actress. b. Minneapolis, MN, July 28, 1946. e. U. of Minn. B.A.
TELEVISION: *Series:* Lou Grant, Day by Day, Sessions. *Movies:* The Picture of Dorian Gray, Something for Joey; Eleanor and Franklin: The White House Years, The Last of Mrs. Lincoln, A Perfect Match, Attack on Fear, His Mistress, Nutcracker, Baby Girl Scott, A Place to Be Loved, A Family Torn Apart, If Someone Had Known, The Babysitter's Seduction. *Special:* Home Sweet Homeless. *Mini-Series:* Captains and the Kings.

KEMENY, JOHN
Producer. b. Budapest, Hungary. Producer for National Film Board of Canada, 1957-69. Formed International Cinemedia Center, Ltd. in 1969 in Montreal, as partner.
PICTURES: Ladies and Gentlemen... Mr. Leonard Cohen, Don't Let the Angels Fall, Seven Times a Day, The Apprenticeship of Duddy Kravitz, White Line Fever, Shadow of the Hawk, Ice Castles, The Plouffe Family (exec. prod.), Quest for Fire (co-prod.), The Bad Boy, Murder in the Family (exec. prod.), The Wraith, The Boy in Blue, The Gate, Iron Eagle II, Gate II.
TELEVISION: Louisiana, The Blood of Others, Sword of Gideon (exec. prod.), The Park is Mine, Murderers Among Us: The Simon Wiesenthal Story (co-prod.), Red King White King, The Josephine Baker Story, The Teamster Boss: The Jackie Presser Story, Dead Silence.

KEMP, JEREMY
Actor. b. Chesterfield, England, Feb. 3, 1935. e. Abbottsholme Sch., Central Sch. of Speech and Drama. Service with Gordon Highlanders. Early career on stage incl. Old Vic Theatre Company, 1959-61. Recent theatre: Celebration, Incident at Vichy, Spoiled, The Caretaker. National Theatre, 1979-80.
PICTURES: Cleopatra (debut, 1963), Dr. Terror's House of Horrors, Face of a Stanger, Operation Crossbow (The Great Spy Mission), Cast a Giant Shadow, The Blue Max, Assignment K, Twist of Sand, The Strange Affair, Darling Lili, The Games, Sudden Terror (Eye Witness), Pope Joan, The Bellstone Fox, The Blockhouse, The Seven Percent Solution, East of Elephant Rock, Queen of Diamonds, A Bridge Too Far, The Thoroughbreds (Treasure Seekers), Leopard in the Snow, Caravans, The Prisoner of Zenda, The Return of the Soldier, Top Secret!, When the Whales Came, Angels and Insects, Four Weddings and a Funeral.
TELEVISION: Z Cars, The Lovers of Florence, The Last Reunion, Colditz, Brassneck, Rhinemann Exchange, Lisa, Goodbye, Henry VIII, St. Joan, The Winter's Tale, Unity, The Contract, Sadat, King Lear, Sherlock Holmes, George Washington, Peter the Great, The Winds of War, War and Remembrance, Slip-Up (The Great Paper Chase), Cop-out, Summers Lease, Prisoner of Honor, Duel of Hearts, The Magician, Conan: The Adventurer. *Series:* Star Trek: The Next Generation (guest), Conan.

KEMPER, VICTOR J.
Cinematographer. b. Newark, NJ, April 14, 1927. e. Seton Hall, B.S./Engineer. Channel 13, Newark 1949-54; Tech. supervisor EUE Screen Gems NY 1954-56; v.p. engineering General TV Network. Pres. VJK Prods.
PICTURES: Husbands, The Magic Garden of Stanley Sweetheart, They Might Be Giants, Who is Harry Kellerman?, The Hospital, The Candidate, Last of the Red Hot Lovers, Shamus, The Friends of Eddie Coyle, Gordon's War, The Hideaways, The Gambler, The Reincarnation of Peter Proud, Dog Day Afternoon, Stay Hungry, The Last Tycoon, Mikey and Nicky, Slapshot, Audrey Rose, Oh God!, The One and Only, Coma, Eyes of Laura Mars, Magic, Night of the Juggler, And Justice for All, The Jerk, The Final Countdown, Xanadu, The Four Seasons, Chu Chu and the Philly Flash, Partner, Author! Author!, National Lampoon's Vacation, Mr. Mom, The Lonely Guy, Cloak and Dagger, Secret Admirer, Pee-wee's Big Adventure, Clue, Bobo, Hot to Trot, Cohen and Tate, See No Evil, Hear No Evil, Crazy People, FX2, Another You, Married to It, Beethoven, Tommy Boy, Eddie, Jingle All the Way
TELEVISION: Too Rich: The Secret Life of Doris Duke, On Golden Pond..

KENNEDY, GEORGE
Actor. b. New York, NY, Feb. 18, 1925. At 2 acted in touring co. of Bringing Up Father. At 7, disc jockey with his own radio show for children. Served in Army during WWII, earning two Bronze Stars and combat and service ribbons. In Army 16 years, became Capt. and Armed Forces Radio and TV officer. 1957, opened first Army Information Office, N.Y. Served as technical advisor to Phil Silvers's Sergeant Bilko TV series. Began acting in 1959 when discharged from Army.
PICTURES: The Little Shepard of Kingdom Come (debut, 1961), Lonely Are the Brave, The Man From the Diner's Club, Charade, Strait- Jacket, Island of the Blue Dolphins, McHale's Navy, Hush... Hush... Sweet Charlotte, Mirage, In Harm's Way, The Sons of Katie Elder, The Flight of the Phoenix, Shenandoah, Hurry Sundown, The Dirty Dozen, Cool Hand Luke (Acad.

Award, best supporting actor, 1967), The Ballad of Josie, The Pink Jungle, Bandolero!, The Boston Strangler, The Legend of Lylah Claire, Guns of the Magnificent Seven, Gaily Gaily, The Good Guys and the Bad Guys, Airport, ... tick ... tick ... tick ..., Zigzag, Dirty Dingus Magee, Fool's Parade, Lost Horizon, Cahill: U.S. Marshal, Thunderbolt and Lightfoot, Airport 1975, Earthquake, The Human Factor, The Eiger Sanction, Airport '77, Ningen no Shomei (Proof of the Man), Mean Dog Blues, Death on the Nile, Brass Target, The Concorde—Airport '79, Death Ship, The Double McGuffin, Steel, Virus, Just Before Dawn, Modern Romance, A Rare Breed, Search and Destroy, Wacko, The Jupiter Menace, Bolero, Chattanooga Choo Choo, Hit and Run, Savage Dawn, The Delta Force, Radioactive Dreams, Creepshow 2, Born to Race, Demonwarp, Counterforce, Nightmare at Noon, Private Roads, Uninvited, The Terror Within, The Naked Gun: From the Files of Police Squad, Esmeralda Bay, Ministry of Vengeance, Brain Dead, Hangfire, The Naked Gun 2 1/2: The Smell of Fear, Driving Me Crazy, Distant Justice, Naked Gun 33 1/3: The Final Insult, Cats Don't Dance (voice), Dennis the Menace 2, Bayou Ghost, Small Soldiers (voice) .
TELEVISION: *Series:* The Blue Knight, Sarge, Counterattack: Crime in America, Dallas, Santo Bugito (voice). *Guest:* Sugarfoot, Cheyenne. *Movies:* See How They Run, Sarge: The Badge or the Cross, Priest Killer, A Great American Tragedy, Deliver Us From Evil, A Cry in the Wilderness, The Blue Knight, The Archer: Fugitive from the Empire, Jesse Owens Story, Liberty, International Airport, Kenny Rogers as the Gambler III, The Gunfighters, What Price Victory, Good Cops Bad Cops, Final Shot: The Hank Gathers Story, Dallas: J.R. Returns, Dallas: War of the Ewings, Men in White, Holy War, Un-Holy Victory. *Mini-Series:* Backstairs at the White House.

KENNEDY, JAMES C.
Publishing & Media Executive. b. 1947. e. U. Denver, BBA, 1970. Prodn. asst. with Atlanta Newspapers, 1972-76, then exec. v.p. gen. mgr. 1976-79. Pres. Grand Junction newpapers, 1979-80. Pub. Grand Junction Daily Sentinel, 1980-83. V.p. Cox newspapers div. Cox Enterprises, Inc., 1985-86; exec. v.p. 1986-87; pres., COO, Exec. v.p., 1986-87; chmn., 1987-; chmn., CEO, Cox Enterprises, Inc., 1988-present. Currently serves on the boards of Flagler System, Inc., Ducks Unlimited, the PATH Foundation (People of Atlanta for Trails Here) and the Women's United Soccer Association (WUSA). Advisory dir. of J. P. Morgan – Chase & Company (Texas Region) and pres. of Wetlands America Trust, Inc.

KENNEDY, KATHLEEN
Producer. b. 1954. Raised in Weaverville and Redding in No. Calif. e. San Diego State U. Early TV experience on KCST, San Diego, working as camera operator, video editor, floor director and news production coordinator. Produced talk show, You're On. Left to enter m.p. industry as prod. asst. on Steven Spielberg's 1941. Founding member and pres. of Amblin Entertainment. 1992, with husband and partner Frank Marshall formed the Kennedy/Marshall Company.
PICTURES: Raiders of the Lost Ark (prod. assoc.), Poltergeist (assoc. prod.), E.T.: The Extra-Terrestrial (prod.), Twilight Zone: The Movie (co-assoc. prod.), Indiana Jones and the Temple of Doom (assoc. prod.). *Exec. prod.* (with Frank Marshall): Gremlins, The Goonies, Back to the Future, The Color Purple (prod.), Young Sherlock Holmes (co-prod.), An American Tail, Innerspace, Empire of the Sun, Batteries Not Included, Who Framed Roger Rabbit, The Land Before Time, Indiana Jones and the Last Crusade, (prod. exec.), Dad, Always (prod.), Joe Versus the Volcano, Gremlins II, Hook (co-prod.), Noises Off, Alive, A Far Off Place, Jurassic Park, Milk Money, The Bridges of Madison County, Congo, The Indian in the Cupboard, Twister, The Thief of Always, The Sixth Sense, Snow Falling on Cedars., A Map of trhe World, Artificial Intelligence: AI, Jurassic Park III, The Young Black Stallion. *Exec. Prod:* Schindler's List, A Dangerous Woman, The Flintstones, The Lost World: Jurassic Park, Olympic Glory, Signs.
TELEVISION: Amazing Stories (spv. prod.), You're On (prod.), Roger Rabbit & the Secrets of Toontown (exec. prod.), The Sports Pages (exec. prod.).

KENNEY, H. WESLEY
Producer, Director. b. Dayton, OH, Jan. 3, 1926. e. Carnegie Inst. of Tech. Guest Instructor, UCLA; guest lecturer, Televisia: Mexico City.
THEATRE: *Dir:* Ten Little Indians (Advent Th., L.A.), The Best Christmas Pageant Ever, Love Letters (WV State Theatre), Shadowlands (Tracey Roberts Theatre).
TELEVISION: *Series:* All in the Family (dir.), The Jefferson (pilot dir.), Days of Our Lives (exec. prod. 1979-81), Ladies Man (dir.), Filthy Rich (dir.), Flo (dir.), The Young and the Restless (exec. prod. 1981-86), General Hospital (exec. prod. 1986-89). *Dir.* Sopa Break. Infomercials (dir.): Elements of Beauty, Merle Norman Experience,

KENSIT, PATSY
Actress. b. London, England, March 4, 1968. Made film debut at the age of 4 in The Great Gatsby. Later appeared in commercials directed by Tony Scott and Adrian Lyne.
PICTURES: The Great Gatsby (debut, 1974), Alfie Darling, The

Blue Bird, Hanover Street, Absolute Beginners, Lethal Weapon 2, A Chorus of Disapproval, Chicago Joe and the Showgirl, Timebomb, Twenty-One, Blue Tornado, Blame It on the Bellboy, Beltenebros, Kleptomania, The Turn of the Screw, Bitter Harvest, Angels and Insects, Grace of My Heart, Speedway Junky, Best, Janice Beard: 45 Words Per Minute, The Pavilion, Best, Things Behind the Sun, The One and Only, Bad Karma, Darkness Falling.
TELEVISION: BBC: Great Expectations, Silas Marner, Tycoon: The Story of a Woman, Adam Bede, French & Saunders. U.S.: The Corsican Brothers, Fall from Grace, Love and Betrayal: The Mia Farrow Story, Human Bomb, The Last Don, The Last Don II, Murder in Mind, Love Music Loves to Dance.

KENT, JEAN
Actress. r.n. Joan Summerfield. b. London, England, June 29, 1921. e. Marist Coll., Peekham, London. First stage appearance at 3; at age 10 played in parents' act; chorus girl at Windmill Theatre, London, 1935; 2 yrs. repertory before debuting on screen under real name.
PICTURES: The Rocks of Valpre (High Treason; debut, 1934), It's That Man Again (first film as Jean Kent, 1943), Fanny by Gaslight (Man of Evil), Champagne Charlie, 2000 Women, Madonna of the Seven Moons, The Wicked Lady, The Rake's Progress (The Notorious Gentleman), Caravan, The Magic Bow, The Man Within (The Smugglers), Good Time Girl, Bond Street, Sleeping Car to Trieste, Trottie True (Gay Lady), Her Favorite Husband, The Woman in Question, The Browning Version, The Big Frame (The Lost Hours), Before I Wake (Shadow of Fear), The Prince and the Showgirl, Bonjour Tristesse, Grip of the Strangler (The Haunted Strangler), Beyond This Place (Web of Evidence), Please Turn Over, Bluebeard's Ten Honeymoons, Shout at the Devil, The Saving of Aunt Esther.
TELEVISION: A Call on the Widow, The Lovebird, The Morning Star, November Voyage, Love Her to Death, The Lion and the Mouse, The Web, Sir Francis Drake series, Yvette, Emergency Ward 10, County Policy, Coach 7, Smile on the Face of the Tiger, No Hiding Place, Kipling, This Man Craig, The Killers, Vanity Fair, A Night with Mrs. Da Tanka, United serial. The Family of Fred, After Dark, Thicker than Water series, The Young Doctors, Brother and Sister, Up Pompei, Steptoe and Son, Doctor at Large, Family at War, K is for Killing, Night School, Tycoon series, Crossroads (series), Lyttons Diary, Lovejoy (series), Missing Persons, After Henry (series), Shrinks (series).

KENT, JOHN B.
Theatre executive, Attorney. b. Jacksonville, FL, Sept. 5, 1939. e. Yale U., U. of FL, Law Sch., NYU grad. sch. of law (L.L.M. in taxation, 1964). Partner in Kent Ridge & Crawford, P.A.; pres. & dir, Kent Investments, Inc. 1977-; dir. & v.p. & gen. counsel, Kent Theatres, Inc. 1970-; dir. & v.p., Kent Enterprises, Inc. 1961-; dir. & v.p. Kent Cinemas Inc. 1993-. Was pres. of Kent Theatres Inc. 1967-70; resigned to devote full time to law practice. NATO dir. 1972 and Presidents' Advisory Cabinet, 1979-; v.p./dir. NATO of FL, 1968-. Member of Rotary Club ofJacksonville, Fla. Bar Ass'n., American Bar Ass'n.

KENYON, CURTIS
Writer. b. New York, NY, March 12, 1914.
PICTURES: Woman Who Dared, Lloyds of London, Wake Up and Live, Love and Hisses, She Knew All the Answers, Twin Beds, Seven Days' Leave, Thanks for Everything, Bathing Beauty, Fabulous Dorseys, Tulsa, Two Flags West, Mr. Ricco.
TELEVISION: Cavalcade of America, Fireside Theatre, Schlitz Playhouse, U.S. Steel Hour, 20th Century-Fox Hour. Series: Hawaii 5-O.

KERKORIAN, KIRK
Executive. b. Fresno, CA, June 6, 1917. e. Los Angeles public schools. Served as capt., transport command, RAF, 1942-44. Commercial air line pilot from 1940; founder Los Angeles Air Service (later Trans Intl. Airlines Corp.), 1948; Intl. Leisure Corp., 1968; controlling stockholder, Western Airlines, 1970; chief exec. officer, MGM, Inc., 1973-74; chmn. exec. com., vice-chmn. bd., 1974-1978. Stepped down from exec. positions while retaining financial interest in MGM/UA. Repurchased MGM in the summer of 1996. Currently, director of MGM and MGM Mirage and co-chmn., pres., & CEO of Tracinda Corp.

KERNER, JORDAN
Producer. e. Stanford U, A.B. Political Science & Comm.; U.C. Berkely, J.D.-M.B.A.. Bgean career in entertainment working for CBS affiliate KPIX-TV. Joined law firm of Ball, Hunt, Brown & Baerwitz. Talent & Program Negotiator for CBS. Worked for Universal Pictures & QM Prods., 1978-81. Joined ABC Entertainment as dir., Dramatic Series Develop-ment. Promoted to v.p., 1983. While at ABC, placed Moonlight-ing, MacGyver, Dynasty, Spencer for Hire, Call To Glory. Founded the Avnet/Kerner Co. in 1986 with Avent. Currently dir., Allied Communications, Inc. Member, bd. of dirs., The Starbright Foundation, The Chrysalis Foundation. Member, President's Advisory Council for the City of Hope, Sen. Dianne Feinstein's California Cabinet, Planned Parenthood, Earth Communications Office, A.M.P.A.S., A.F.I. Former gov., Academy of Television Arts & Sciences. Founder and former co-chmn., Committee for the

Arts of the Beverly Hills Bar Asoc. Founder, COMM/ENT, the Journal of Communications & Entertainment Law.
PICTURES: Less Than Zero, Funny About Love, The Mighty Ducks, Fried Green Tomatoes, The War, The Three Musketeers, When A Man Loves A Woman, D2: The Mighty Ducks, Miami Rhapsody (exec. prod.), Up Close and Personal, Swiss Family Robinson, Dinner For Two at the El Cortez, To Live For, Friday Night Lights, Blaze of Glory, D3: The Mighty Ducks, Red Corner, George of the Jungle, Thirty Wishes, Inspector Gadget, Snow Dogs.
TELEVISION: Breaking Point, Do You Know the Muffin Man?, Heat Wave, Backfield in Motion, The Watchman, The Switch, For Their Own Good, The War, Love Can Build a Bridge, Poodle Springs, Mama Flora's Family, My Last Love, A House Divided, Uprising, A Wrinkle in Time.

KERNS, JOANNA
Actress. r.n. Joanna de Varona. b. San Francisco, CA, Feb. 12, 1953. Former gymnast, became dancer, appeared on tv com-mercials. Sister is Olympic swimmer and tv commentator Donna de Varona. NY stage: Ulysses in Nighttown.
PICTURES: Coma, Cross My Heart, Street Justice, An American Summer, No Dessert Dad Til You Mow the Lawn, No One Could Protect Her, Girl Interrupted, All Over the Guy.
TELEVISION: Series: The Four Seasons, Growing Pains (also wrote one episode). Guest: Three's Company, Magnum P.I., Hill Street Blues, Hunter, etc. Movies: The Million Dollar Rip-Off, Marriage Is Alive and Well, Mother's Day on Walton's Mountain, A Wedding on Walton's Mountain, A Day of Thanks on Walton's Mountain, The Return of Marcus Welby M.D., A Bunny's Tale, The Rape of Richard Beck, Stormin' Home, Mistress, Those She Left Behind, Like Mother Like Daughter, The Preppie Murder, Blind Faith, Captive, The Nightman, Not in My Family, The Man With 3 Wives, Shameful Secrets, No Dessert Dad 'Til You Mow the Lawn, Robin Cook's Mortal Fear, See Jane Run, Whose Daughter Is She?, Sisters and Other Strangers, Mother Knows Best, Morning Glory, Terror In the Family, Emma's Wish, At the Mercy of a Stranger, The Growing Pains Movie, Someone to Love.

KERR, DEBORAH
Actress. b. Helensburgh, Scotland, Sept. 30, 1921; e. Phyllis Smale Ballet Sch. On stage 1939 in repertory before Brit. screen career began the following year. Voted Star of Tomorrow by Motion Picture Herald-Fame Poll, 1942. Voted one of top ten British money-making stars in Motion Picture Herald-Fame Poll, 1947. B'way debut in Tea and Sympathy, 1953. Received special Academy Award, 1994.
PICTURES: Major Barbara (debut, 1940), Love on the Dole, Penn of Pennsylvania, Hatter's Castle, The Day Will Dawn (The Avengers), The Life and Death of Colonel Blimp, Perfect Strangers (Vacation From Marriage), I See a Dark Stranger (The Adventuress), Black Narcissus (Acad. Award nom.), The Hucksters (U.S. debut), If Winter Comes, Edward My Son, Please Believe Me, King Solomon's Mines, Quo Vadis, The Prisoner of Zenda, Thunder in the East, Dream Wife, Julius Caesar, Young Bess, From Here to Eternity (Acad. Award nom.), End of the Affair, The King and I (Acad. Award nom.), The Proud and the Profane, Tea and Sympathy, Heaven Knows Mr. Allison (Acad. Award nom.), An Affair to Remember, Bonjour Tristesse, Separate Tables (Acad. Award nom.), The Journey, Count Your Blessings, Beloved Infidel, The Sundowners (Acad. Award nom.), The Grass Is Greener, The Innocents, The Naked Edge, The Chalk Garden, The Night of the Iguana, Marriage On the Rocks, Casino Royale, Eye of the Devil, Prudence and the Pill, The Gypsy Moths, The Arrangement, The Assam Garden, L.A. Confidential, Off the Menu: The Last Days of Chasen's.
TELEVISION: Movies: A Woman of Substance, Reunion at Fairborough, Hold the Dream, Witness for the Prosecution.

KERSHNER, IRVIN
Director. b. Philadelphia, PA, April 29, 1923. e. Tyler Sch. of Fine Arts of Temple U., 1946; Art Center Sch., U. of Southern California. Designer, photography, adv., documentary, architec-tural; doc. filmmaker, U.S.I.S., Middle East, 1950-52; dir., cam-eraman, TV doc., Confidential File, 1953-55; dir.-prod.-writer, Ophite Prod. Appeared as actor in film The Last Temptation of Christ.
PICTURES: Stakeout on Dope Street (debut, 1958; also co-s.p.), The Young Captives, The Hoodlum Priest, A Face in the Rain, The Luck of Ginger Coffey, A Fine Madness, The Flim-Flam Man, Loving, Up the Sandbox, S*P*Y*S, The Return of a Man Called Horse, Eyes of Laura Mars, The Empire Strikes Back, Never Say Never Again, Robocop 2, American Perkect (prod.).
TELEVISION: Series: The Rebel, Naked City, numerous pilots and other nat'l. shows. Movies: Raid on Entebbe (theatrical in Europe), The Traveling Man. Pilot: seaQuest dsv.

KERWIN, BRIAN
Actor. b. Chicago, IL, Oct. 25, 1949. e. USC.
THEATRE: NY: Emily (Theatre World Award), Lips Together Teeth Apart, Raised in Captivity. LA: Strange Snow (LA Drama Critics Award), Who's Afraid of Virginia Woolf?, A Loss of Roses, Torch Song Trilogy.
PICTURES: Hometown USA (debut, 1979), Nickel Mountain,

Murphy's Romance, King Kong Lives, Torch Song Trilogy, S.P.O.O.K.S., Hard Promises, Love Field, Gold Diggers: The Secret of Bear Mountain, Getting Away With Murder, Jack, The Myth of Fingerprints, Mr. Jealousy.
TELEVISION: *Series*: The Young and the Restless (1976-77), The Misadventures of Sheriff Lobo, Angel Falls, Beggars and Choosers. *Mini-Series*: The Chisholms, The Blue and the Gray, Bluegrass, A Girl Thing. *Movies*: A Real American Hero, Power, Miss All-American Beauty, Intimate Agony, Wet Gold, The Greatest Thing That Almost Happened, Challenger, Switched at Birth, Against Her Will: An Incident in Baltimore, Abandoned and Deceived, It Came From Outer Space, Sins of Silence, Critical Choices, Volcano: Fire on the Mountain, Flash, The Hunt for the Unicorn Killer, Common Ground. *Special*: Natica Jackson. *Guest*: St. Elsewhere, The Love Boat, B.J. and the Bear, Roseanne, Murder She Wrote, Simon & Simon, Highway to Heaven.

KEYES, EVELYN
Actress. b. Port Arthur, TX, Nov. 20, 1919. e. high school. Began career as a dancer in night clubs.
AUTHOR: *Novel*: I Am a Billboard (1971). *Autobiographies*: Scarlett O'Hara's Younger Sister (1977), I'll Think About That Tomorrow (1991).
PICTURES: Artists and Models (debut, 1937), The Buccaneer, Men With Wings, Artists and Models Abroad, Sons of the Legion, Dangerous to Know, Paris Honeymoon, Union Pacific, Sudden Money, Gone with the Wind, Slightly Honorable, Before I Hang, Beyond Sacramento, The Lady in Question, The Face Behind the Mask, Here Comes Mr. Jordan, Ladies in Retirement, The Adventures of Martin Eden, Flight Lieutenant, There's Something About a Soldier, Dangerous Blondes, The Desperadoes, Nine Girls, Strange Affair, A Thousand and One Nights, The Jolson Story, Renegades, The Thrill of Brazil, The Mating of Millie, Johnny O'Clock, Enchantment, Mrs. Mike, Mr. Soft Touch, The Killer That Stalked New York, Smuggler's Island, The Iron Man, The Prowler, One Big Affair, Shoot First, 99 River Street, Hell's Half Acre, It Happend in Paris, Top of the World, The Seven Year Itch, Around the World in 80 Days, Across 110th Street, Return to Salem's Lot, Wicked Stepmother.
TELEVISION: *Guest*: Murder She Wrote. *Specials*: Glorious Technicolor, Larry and Vivien: The Oliviers in Love.

KHONDJI, DARIUS
Cinematographer. b. Tehran, Iran, Oct. 21, 1955.e. NYU, Film.
PICTURES: Rive droite, rive gauche (first assistant cameraman), Le Tresor des chiennes, Delicatessen, Prague, Shadow of a Doubt, Before the Rain, Marie-Lousie ou la permission, City of Lost Children, Seven, Stealing Beauty, Evita (Academy Award nom.), Alien: Resurrection, In Dreams, The Ninth Gate, The Beach., The Panic Room.

KIAROSTAMI, ABBAS
Director, Producer, Writer, Editor. b. Teheran, Iran, June 22, 1940. Recipient of the 1997 UNESCO Fellini-Medal in Gold for achievement in film, freedom, peace & tolerance.
PICTURES: The Window, The Bread & Alley, The Breaktime, The Experience, The Traveller, So I Can, Two Solutions for One Problem, The Colours, Suit for Wedding, The Report (Gozaresh), Tribute to the Teachers, How to Make Use of Our Leisure Time?, Solution No. 1, First Case—Second Case, Dental Hygiene, Orderly or Unorderly, The Chorus, Fellow Citizen, Toothache, First Graders, Where is the Friend's Home, The Key, Homework, Close Up, And Life Goes on..., Journey to the Land of the Traveller, Under the Olive Trees, The Journey, Lumiere & Company, The White Balloon, The Taste of Cherry (Cannes Film Festival Palme d'Or, 1997), The Wind Will Carry Us, Volte sempre Abbas!, Willow and Wind, Ten.

KIDD, MICHAEL
Choreographer, Dancer, Actor. r.n. Milton Greenwald. b. Brooklyn, NY, Aug. 12, 1919. e. CCNY. Studied dance at School of the American Ballet. Was dancer with Lincoln Kirstein's Ballet Caravan, Eugene Loring's Dance Players, Ballet Theatre. Became stage choreographer starting in 1945. Recipient of the Academy Award for Career Achievement, 1997.
THEATRE: *B'way (choreographer):* Finian's Rainbow (Tony Award, 1947), Love Life, Arms and the Girl, Guys and Dolls (Tony Award, 1951), Can-Can (Tony Award, 1954), Li'l Abner (Tony Award, 1957; also dir., prod.), Destry Rides Again (Tony Award, 1960; also dir.), Wildcat (also dir., co-prod.), Subways Are for Sleeping (also dir.), Here's Love, Ben Franklin in Paris, Skyscraper, The Rothschilds (also dir.). *B'way (dir.):* Cyrano, Good News, Pal Joey, The Music Man, The Goodbye Girl.
PICTURES: *Choreographer:* Where's Charley?, The Band Wagon, Knock on Wood, Seven Brides for Seven Brothers, Guys and Dolls, Merry Andrew (also dir.), Li'l Abner, Star!, Hello Dolly!, Movie Movie (also actor). *Actor*: It's Always Fair Weather, Smile, Skin Deep.
TELEVISION: *Specials (choreographer):* Baryshnikov in Hollywood, Academy Awards. *Movie (actor):* For the Love of It.

KIDDER, MARGOT
Actress. r.n. Margaret Kidder. b. Yellowknife, Ca., Oct. 17, 1948.
PICTURES: The Best Damned Fiddler From Calabogie to Kaladar (debut, 1968), Gaily Gaily, Quackser Fortune Has a

Cousin in the Bronx, Sisters, A Quiet Day in Belfast, The Gravy Train, Black Christmas, The Great Waldo Pepper, 92 in the Shade, The Reincarnation of Peter Proud, Superman, Mr. Mike's Mondo Video, The Amityville Horror, Willie and Phil, Superman II, Heartaches, Shoot the Sun Down, Some Kind of Hero, Trenchcoat, Superman III, Little Treasure, GoBots (voice), Superman IV: The Quest for Peace, Miss Right, Mob Story, White Room, Crime and Punishment, Maverick, Henry & Verlin, Beanstalk, The Pornographer, La Florida, Aaron Sent Me, Windrunner, Never Met Picasso, The Planet of Junior Brown, Silent Cradle, Shadow Zone: My Teacher Ate My Homework, The Clown at Midnight, The Annihilation of Fish, Tail Lights Fade, Nightmare Man, The Hi-Line, Tribulation, Crime and Punishment, Angel Blade.
TELEVISION: *Series*: Nichols, Shell Game. *Movies*: Suddenly Single, The Bounty Man, Honky Tonk, Louisiana, The Glitter Dome, Picking Up the Pieces, Vanishing Act, Body of Evidence, To Catch a Killer, One Woman's Courage, Bloodknot, Phantom 2040: The Ghost Who Walks, Young Ivanhoe, Crime in Connecticut: The Story of Alex Kelly, Common Ground, Someone Is Watching, Society's Child. *Specials*: Bus Stop, Pygmalion. *Guest*: Murder She Wrote, Bostom Common. *Director*: White People, Love 40.

KIDMAN, NICOLE
Actress. b. Hawaii, June 20, 1967. Raised in Australia. Made acting debut at 14 in Australian film Bush Christmas. On Australian stage in Steel Magnolias (Sydney Theatre Critics Award for Best Newcomer).
PICTURES: Bush Christmas (debut, 1982), BMZ Bandits, Windrider, Dead Calm, Emerald City, Days of Thunder, Billy Bathgate, Far and Away, Flirting, Malice, My Life, Batman Forever, To Die For (Golden Globe, 1996), Portrait of a Lady, The Peacemaker, Practical Magic, Eyes Wide Shut, Birthday Girl, Moulin Rouge (Acad. Award nom.), The Panic Room (voice), The Others (BAFTA nom.), The Hours (Acad. Award- best actress, BAFTA-best actress, 2003), Dogville, Cold Mountain, The Human Stain, Birth, In the Cut (prod. only).
TELEVISION: *Mini-Series* (Australia): Five-Mile Creek, Vietnam, Bangkok Hilton.

KIDRON, BEEBAN
Director. b. London, England. e. National Film School. Made co-dir. debut (with Amanda Richardson) with documentary Carry Greenham Home (Chicago Film Fest. Hugo Award, 1983).
PICTURES: Antonia and Jane, Used People, Great Moments in Aviation, To Wong Foo—Thanks for Everything—Julie Newmar, Swept from the Sea (prod. only).
TELEVISION: The Global Gamble, Vroom, Oranges Are Not the Only Fruit, Great Moments in Aviation, Texarkana, Cinderella, Murder.

KIEL, RICHARD
Actor. b. Detroit, MI, Sept. 13, 1939. Former nightclub bouncer.
PICTURES: The Phantom Planet (debut, 1961), Eegah!, House of the Damned, The Magic Sword, Roustabout, The Human Duplicators, Las Vegas Hillbillies, A Man Called Dagger, Skidoo, The Longest Yard, Flash and the Firecat, Silver Streak, The Spy Who Loved Me, Force 10 from Navarone, Moonraker, The Humanoid, So Fine, Hysterical, Cannonball Run II, Pale Rider, Think Big, The Giant of Thunder Mountain (also co-s.p., co-exec. prod.), Happy Gilmore, Inspector Gadget (cameo).
TELEVISION: *Series*: The Barbary Coast, Van Dyke & Company. *Movies*: Now You See It Now You Don't, The Barbary Coast (pilot).

KIER, UDO
Actor. b. Cologne, Germany, October 14, 1944.
PICTURES: Road to St. Tropez, Season of the Senses, Schamlos, La Horse, Satan, Provocation, Erotomaneis, The Salzburg Connection, Sexual Eroticism, Pan, Olifant, Andy Warhol's Frankenstein, Andy Warhol's Dracula, The Last Word, The Story of O, Trauma, Goldflocken, Spermula, Suspiria, Bolweiser, Belcanto oder Darf eine Nutte schluchzen?, Counterfeit Commandos, Das Funfte Gebot, Kretakor, The Third Generation, Hungarian Rhapsody, Lulu, Psyche, Deutschland privat, Lili Marleen, Lola, The Blood of Dr. Jekyll, Escape from Blood Plantation, The Wild Fifties, Pankow '95, Hur und Heilig, Seduction: The Cruel Woman, Der Unbesiegbare, Die Einsteiger, Egomania - Insel ohne Hoffmung, Die Schlacht der Idioten, Am nachsten Morgen kehrte der Minister nicht an seinen Arbeitsplatz zuruck, Mutters Mask, Epidemic, 100 Jahre Adolf Hitler- Die letzte Stunde im Fuhrerbunker, Blackest Heart, Europa, My Own Private Idaho, Der Unbekannte Deserteur, Terror 2000 - Intesivstation Deutschland, Even Cowgirls Get The Blues, Three Shake-A-Leg Steps to Heaven, Plotzlich und unerwarten, Josn and S.A.M, Ace Ventura: Pet Detective, For Love or Money, The Kingdom, Rotwang Must Go, Johnny Mnemonic, Over My Dead Body, Unter Druck, Paradise Framed, A Trick of the Light, Duke of Groove, Dog Daze, Ausgerstoben, United Trash, Barb Wire, Breaking the Waves, Pinocchio, Lea, The End of Violence, Prince Valiant, The Kingdom 2, Betty, Die 120 Tage von Bottrop, Armageddon, Blade, Modern Vampires, Ice, Simon Says, Guilty, Killer Deal, Besat, Spy Games, History is Made at

Night, The Debtors, Under the Palms, The New Adventures of Pinocchio, End of Days, The Last Call, Doomsdayer, Shadow of the Vamprie, Dancer in the Dark, Just One Night, Red Letters, There's No Fish Food in Heaven, Invincible, Black Widow, Final Payback, Broken Cookies, Critical Mass, Citizens of Perpetual Indulgence, Cadillac Tramps, The Bloodcountess, All the Queen's Men, The 8th Day, The Last Minute, Revelation, Double Deception, Yuri's Revenge, Herz und Nieren, FearDotCom, Dogville, Broken Cookies.

KIERZEK, TERRY
Executive. b. Chicago, IL, Feb. 15, 1951. e. U. of Il. Joined Paramount Pictures Domestic Distrib., as booker in Chicago, 1974. Promoted to Sales in 1976, Dallas, TX. Named branch mgr., Dallas/OK City, 1978. V.P., Eastern Division in Washington, D.C., 1982-84. V.P., Southern Division, Dallas, TX., 1984-86. V.P., Western Division, Los Angeles, 1986-89. Orion Pictures v.p., Western Division, 1990-92. Joined National Film Service in 1993 as v.p., sales & mktg. Named exec. v.p., 1995. Appointed pres., National Film Service in 1996.

KILMER, VAL
Actor. b. Los Angeles, CA, Dec. 31, 1959. e. Hollywood Professional Sch., Juilliard, NY. Appeared in IMAX film Wings of Courage.
THEATRE: NY: Electra and Orestes, How It All Began (also co-writer), Henry IV Part One, Slab Boys (B'way debut), 'Tis Pity She's a Whore. Also: As You Like It (Gutherie MN), Hamlet (Colorado Shakespeare Fest.).
PICTURES: Top Secret! (debut, 1984), Real Genius, Top Gun, Willow, Kill Me Again, The Doors, Thunderheart, True Romance, The Real McCoy, Tombstone, Batman Forever, Heat, The Island of Dr. Moreau, The Ghost and the Darkness, The Saint, The Prince of Egypt (voice), Joe the King, At First Sight, Pollock, Red Planet, The Salton Sea, Run For the Money, Mindhunters, The Missing, Prophet: The Story of Joseph Smith, Spartan, Delgo (voice).
TELEVISION: Movies: Murders in the Rue Morgue, The Man Who Broke 1000 Chains, Gore Vidal's Billy the Kid.

KIMBLEY, DENNIS
Executive. Early career in Kodak Testing Dept. responsible for quality control motion picture films. Joined Marketing Division 1966. Chairman BKSTS FILM 75 and FILM 79 Conference Committee. President BKSTS 1976-78. Governor, London International Film School, 1983. Bd. member, British Board of Film Classification; dir. of Children's Film Unit.

KIMBROUGH, CHARLES
Actor. b. St. Paul, MN, May 23, 1936. e. Indiana U., Yale U.
THEATRE: NY: All in Love (debut, 1961), Cop-Out (B'way debut, 1969), Company (Tony nom.), Candide, Love for Love, The Rules of the Game, Secret Service, Mr. Happiness, Same Time Next Year, Drinks Before Dinner, The Dining Room, Sunday in the Park With George, Hay Fever. Several prods. with Milwaukee Rep. Theatre (1966-73).
PICTURES: The Front (debut, 1976), The Seduction of Joe Tynan, Starting Over, It's My Turn, Switching Channels, The Good Mother, The Hunchback of Notre Dame (voice), The Wedding Planner, Recess: School's Out (voice), Marci X.
TELEVISION: Series: Murphy Brown (Emmy nom.). Movies: For Ladies Only, A Doctor's Story, Weekend War, Cast the First Stone. Pilot: The Recovery Room. Special: Sunday in the Park With George.

KIMMELMAN, KEN
Producer, Director, Animator. b. New York, NY. Aug. 6, 1940. e. School of Visual Arts. Has produced tv programs, political films, theatricals, TV commercials, and many films for Sesame Street. Consultant on the faculty of the Aesthetic Realism Roundation. Pres. of Imagery Film Ltd; prod. films for UN. Recipient of: National Emmy Award 1995 (The Heart Knows Better), Newark Black Film Festival's Paul Robeson Award; Atlanta Film Festival's Dir's. Choice Award; Cindy Award; ASIFA East's Best Children's Film Award. Taught and lectured at NYU, presently at School of Visual Arts, NY. Published numerous articles & letters.
TELEVISION: Director/Producer: People Are Trying to Put Opposites Together (documentary). Series: Doug (Emmy nom., 1992, 93), The Head, Daria, Mr. Hiccup.

KING, ALAN
Actor, Producer. r.n. Irwin Alan Kingberg. b. Brooklyn, NY, Dec. 26, 1927. Started as musician, stand-up comedian in Catskills, then nightclubs. Author: Anybody Who Owns His Own Home Deserves It, Help I'm a Prisoner in a Chinese Bakery.
THEATRE: Actor: The Impossible Years, The Investigation, Dinner at Eight, The Lion in Winter, Something Different.
PICTURES: Actor: Hit the Deck (debut, 1955), Miracle in the Rain, The Girl He Left Behind, The Helen Morgan Story, On the Fiddle (Operation Snafu), Bye Bye Braverman, The Anderson Tapes, Just Tell Me What You Want, Prince of the City (cameo), Author! Author!, I the Jury, Lovesick, Cat's Eye, You Talkin' to Me?, Memories of Me (also co-prod.), Enemies a Love Story,

The Bonfire of the Vanities, Night and the City, Casino, Under the Gun, Let Me In I Hear Laughter, Saltwater, Rush Hour 2, Sunshine State. Producer: Happy Birthday Gemini, Cattle Annie and Little Britches (co-prod.), Wolfen (exec. prod.).
TELEVISION: Guest/Host: The Tonight Show, Kraft Music Hall. Prod-star NBC-TV specials: Comedy is King, On Location: An Evening With Alan King at Carnegie Hall, The College of Comedy, etc. Mini-Series: Seventh Avenue. Movies: Return to Earth (co-exec. prod. only), How to Pick Up Girls (also exec. prod.), Pleasure Palace, Dad the Angel and Me, The Infiltrator. Host: Alan King: Inside the Comic Mind (Comedy Central).

KING, ANDREA
Actress. r.n. Georgette Barry. b. Paris, France, Feb. 1, 1919. e. Edgewood H.S., Greenwich, CT. m. N.H. Willis, attorney. Started career on NY stage, following high school; in Growing Pains & Fly Away Home, Boy Meets Girl, Angel Street (Boston); Life with Father (Chicago); signed by Warner, 1943. Screen debut as Georgette McKee in The Ramparts We Watch, 1940.
PICTURES: Hotel Berlin, God is My Co-Pilot, The Very Thought of You, The Man I Love, The Beast With Five Fingers, Shadow of a Woman, Roughly Speaking, My Wild Irish Rose, Ride the Pink Horse, Mr. Peabody and the Mermaid, Song of Surrender, Southside 1-10001, I Was a Shoplifter, Dial 1119, The Lemon Drop Kid, Mark of the Renegade, World in His Arms, Red Planet Mars, Darby's Rangers, Band of Angels, Daddy's Gone A-Hunting, The Linguini Incident, The Color of Evening.
TELEVISION: Movie: Prescription Murder. Specials: Dream Girl, Officer and the Lady, Witness for the Prosecution. Guest: Fireside Theatre, Maya.

KING, LARRY
Talk Show Host, Writer. b. Brooklyn, NY, Nov. 19, 1933. Started as disc jockey on various Miami radio stations from 1958-64. Became host of radio talk show, broadcast from Miami before moving to Arlington, VA, in 1978. Host of CNN tv talk show since 1985, Larry King Live. Starred in tv special Larry King Extra. Columnist for Miami Beach Sun-Reporter, Sporting News, USA Today.
AUTHOR: Larry King by Larry King, Tell It to the King, When You're Having a Heart Attack, Tell Me More, How to Talk to Anyone Anytime Anywhere: The Secrets of Good Conversation.
PICTURES: Ghostbusters, Lost in America, Eddie and the Cruisers II: Eddie Lives, The Exorcist III, Dave, Open Season, Courage Under Fire, The Long Kiss Goodnight, Contact, An Alan Smithee Film: Burn Hollywood Burn, Mad City, The Jackal, Primary Colors, Bulworth, Enemy of the State, The Kid, The Contender, America's Sweethearts, John Q., Shrek 2 (voice), Catching Kringle (voice).
TELEVISION: Larry King Live, Sam Kinison: Why Did We Laugh?, I Love Lucy's 50th Anniversary Special, Roots: Celebrating 25 Years.

KING, PERRY
Actor. b. Alliance, OH, April 30, 1948. e. Yale. Studied with John Houseman at Juilliard. B'way debut 1990 in A Few Good Men.
PICTURES: Slaughterhouse-Five (debut, 1972), The Possession of Joel Delaney, The Lords of Flatbush, Mandingo, The Wild Party, Lipstick, Andy Warhol's Bad, The Choirboys, A Different Story, Search and Destroy (Striking Back), Class of 1984, Killing Hour (The Clairvoyant), Switch, A Cry in the Night.
TELEVISION: Series: The Quest, Riptide, Almost Home, The Trouble with Larry. Guest: Medical Center, Hawaii Five-O, Apple's Way, Cannon. Mini-Series: Aspen, The Last Convertible, Captain and the Kings. Movies: Foster and Laurie, The Cracker Factory, Love's Savage Fury, City in Fear, Inmates: A Love Story, Golden Gate, Helen Keller: The Miracle Continues, Stranded, Perfect People, Shakedown on Sunset Strip, The Man Who Lived at the Ritz, Disaster at Silo 7, The Prize Pulitzer, Danielle Steel's Kaleidoscope, Only One Survived, Something to Live For, Sidney Sheldon's A Stranger in the Mirror, Jericho Fever, Good King Wenceslas, She Led Two Lives. Pilot: Half 'n' Half.

KING, PETER
Executive, Barrister-at-law. b. London, England, March 22, 1928. e. Marlborough, Oxford U. (MA, honors). Bd., Shipman & King Cinemas Ltd., 1956; borough councillor, 1959-61; chmn., London & Home counties branch, CEA, 1962-63; pres., CEA, 1964; mang. dir. Shipman & King Cinemas Ltd., 1959-68; chmn. & mang. dir. Paramount Pictures (U.K.) Ltd. Britain, 1968-70; mang. dir., EMI Cinemas and Leisure Ltd., 1970-74; chmn. & mang. dir. King Publications/pub. Screen Intl., 1974-89; pres., Screen Intl., 1989-90; chmn. & mang. dir., Rex Publications Ltd., 1990-; pub. Majesty, 1990-; pub. Preview.

KING, STEPHEN
Writer. b. Portland, ME, Sept. 21, 1947. e. Univ. of Maine at Orono (B.S.). Best-selling novelist specializing in thrillers many of which have been adapted to film by others. Movie adaptations: Carrie, The Shining, The Dead Zone, Christine, Cujo, Children of the Corn, Firestarter, Cat's Eye, Stand By Me (The Body), The Running Man, Pet Sematary, Misery, Apt Pupil, The Lawnmower Man, The Dark Half, Needful Things, The Shawshank Redemption, The Mangler, Dolores Claiborne, Thinner, Night Flier, Apt Pupil, The Green Mile, Stud City (The Body),

Desperation, Secret Window. *TV adaptations:* Salem's Lot, It, The Stand, Trucks, The Tommyknockers, The Langoliers, The Shining, Rose Madder, The Diary of .Ellen Rimbauer.
PICTURES: Knightriders (actor), Creepshow (s.p., actor), Children of the Corn (s.p.), Silver Bullet (s.p.), Maximum Overdrive (dir., s.p., actor), Creepshow II (actor), Pet Sematary (s.p., actor), Sleepwalkers (s.p., actor).
TELEVISION: *Series:* Golden Years (creator, writer). *Movies/Mini-Series:* Sometimes They Come Back (s.p.), The Stand (actor), The Langoliers (actor), Sometimes They Come Back...Again (s.p.),Quicksilver Highway, Sometimes They Come Back..For More (s.p.), Storm of the Century (also prod.), Rose Red.

KING, ZALMAN
Actor, Director, Writer. r.n. Zalman King Lefkowitz. b. Trenton, NJ, 1941. m. writer Patricia Knop.
PICTURES: *Actor*: The Ski Bum, You've Got to Walk It Like You Talk It or You'll Lose the Beat, Neither by Day Nor Night, Some Call It Loving, Trip with the Teacher, Sammy Somebody, The Passover Plot, Blue Sunshine, Tell a Me a Riddle, Galaxy of Terror. *Exec. Prod.*: Roadie (also co-story), Endangered Species, Siesta, Female Perversions, Boca, Business for Pleasure, In God's Hands, A Place Called Truth, Black Sea 213. *Prod./Writer:* 9 1/2 Weeks. *Director-Writer:* Wildfire, Two Moon Junction, Wild Orchid, Wild Orchid II: Two Shades of Blue, Delta of Venus.
TELEVISION: *Series:* The Young Lawyers, Red Shoe Diaries (exec. prod., creator, dir. episodes), Wind on Water. *Guest:* Alfred Hitchcock Presents, Land of the Giants, Gunsmoke, Adam 12, Charlie's Angels, etc. *Movies:* The Dangerous Days of Kiowa Jones, Stranger on the Run, The Young Lawyers (pilot), The Intruders, Smile Jenny You're Dead, Like Normal People, Lake Consequence (co-prod., co-writer), ChromiumBlue.com.

KINGMAN, DONG
Fine Artist. b. Oakland, CA, March 31, 1911. e. Hong Kong 1916-1920. 1928, mem. motion picture co., Hong Kong branch; 1935; began to exhibit as fine artist in San Francisco; promotional, advertising or main title artwork for following films: World of Suzie Wong, Flower Drum Song, 55 Days of Peking, Circus World, King Rat, The Desperados, The Sand Pebbles, Lost Horizon. 1966-67, created 12 paintings for Universal Studio Tour for posters and promotion; 1968, cover painting for souvenir program for Ringling Bros.,Barnum and Bailey Circus; treasurer for Living Master Artist Production since 1954; Exec. V.P. 22nd-Century Films, Inc. since 1968, Prod. & dir. short, Hongkong Dong. Also short subject film Dong Kingman, filmed and directed by James Wong Howe. 1993 Chinese-American Arts Council exhibition of all motion picture work. 1996, created official poster for Olympic Games.

KINGSLEY, BEN
Actor. r.n. Krishna Banji. b. Snaiton, Yorkshire, England, Dec. 31, 1943. Started career with Salford Players, amateur co. in Manchester. Turned pro in 1966 and appeared on London stage at a Chichester Festival Theatre. 1967, joined Royal Shakespeare Co., appearing in A Midsummer Night's Dream, Tempest, Measure for Measure, Merry Wives of Windsor, Volpone, Cherry Orchard, Hamlet, Othello, Judgement. On NY stage in Kean. Played Squeers in Nicholas Nickleby in 1980 in London.
PICTURES: Fear Is the Key (debut, 1972), Gandhi (Acad. Award, 1982), Betrayal, Turtle Diary, Harem, Maurice, Testimony, Pascali's Island, Without a Clue, Bugsy (Acad. Award nom.), Sneakers, Dave, Searching for Bobby Fisher (Innocent Moves), Schindler's List, Death and the Maiden, Species, Twelfth Night, The Assignment, Photographing Fairies, Parting Shots, Spooky House, Sexy Beast (Acad. Award nom.), Rules of Engagement, The Confession, A.I. Artificial Intelligence (voice), The Triumph of Love, Tuck Everlasting, All for Nothin', A Sound of Thunder, The House of Sand and Fog.
TELEVISION: *Movies/Specials:* Silas Marner, Kean, Oxbridge Blues, Camille, Murderers Among Us: The Simon Wiesenthal Story, Joseph, Moses, The Tale of Sweeney Todd, Crime and Punishment, Alice in Wonderland, Anne Frank (Emmy nom., Golden Globe nom.).

KINOY, ERNEST
Writer. Started career in radio writing sci. fic. programs (X Minus One, Dimension X). Wrote for nearly all early dramatic shows, including Studio One, Philco Playhouse, Playhouse 90.
PICTURES: Brother John, Buck and the Preacher, Leadbelly, White Water Summer (co-s.p.).
TELEVISION: The Defenders (Emmy Award, 1964), Naked City, Dr. Kildare, Jacob and Joseph, David the King, Roots I & II, Victory at Entebbe, Skokie, Murrow, The President's Plane is Missing, Stones for Ibarra, Gore Vidal's Lincoln, The Fatal Shore, White Water Summer, Tad, Diagnosis Murder, Rescuers: Stories of Courage: Two Women.

KINSKI, NASTASSJA
Actress. r.n. Nastassja Nakszynski. b. Berlin, Germany, Jan. 24, 1960. Daughter of late actor Klaus Kinski.
PICTURES: Falsche Bewegung (The Wrong Move; debut, 1975), To the Devil a Daughter, Passion Flower Hotel, Stay as You Are,

Tess, One From the Heart, Cat People, For Your Love Only, Exposed, The Moon in the Gutter, Unfaithfully Yours, The Hotel New Hampshire, Maria's Lovers, Paris Texas, Revolution, Symphony of Love, Harem, Malady of Love, Silent Night, Torrents of Spring, On a Moonlit Night, Magdalene, The Secret, Night Sun, Faraway So Close!, Crackerjack, Terminal Velocity, The Blonde, The Ring, One Night Stand, Little Boy Blue, Your Friends and Neighbors, Fathers' Day, The Magic of Marciano, Timeshare, Town and Country, The Claim, Off the Menu: The Last Days of Chasen's, Beyond City Limits, American Rhapsody, Say Nothing, .com for Murder, Diary of a Sex Addict, Paradise Found, Beyond the City Limits, All Around the Town, A ton image.
TELEVISION: For Your Love Only, The Ring, Bella Mafia, Quarantine, A Storm in Summer, Blind Terror, The Day the World Ended, Les Liasons Dangereuses.

KIRBY, BRUNO
Actor. b. New York, NY, April 28, 1949. Also acted as B. Kirby Jr., and Bruce Kirby Jr. Father is actor Bruce Kirby. On B'way 1991 in Lost in Yonkers.
PICTURES: The Harrad Experiment (debut, 1973), Cinderella Liberty, Superdad, The Godfather Part 2, Baby Blue Marine, Between the Lines, Almost Summer, Where the Buffalo Roam, Borderline, Modern Romance, This Is Spinal Tap, Birdy, Flesh + Blood, Tin Men, Good Morning Vietnam, Bert Rigby You're a Fool, When Harry Met Sally ..., We're No Angels, The Freshman, City Slickers, Hoffa (cameo), Golden Gate, The Basketball Diaries, Donnie Brasco, A Slipping Down Life, Stuart Little (voice), One Eyed King, Waiting for Ronald.
TELEVISION: *Series:* The Super. *Movies:* All My Darling Daughters, A Summer Without Boys, Some Kind of Miracle, Million Dollar Infield, American Tragedy. *Specials:* Run Don't Walk, The Trap, Mastergate. *Guest:* Room 222, Columbo, Kojak, Emergency, It's Garry Shandling's Show, Tales From the Crypt, The Larry Sanders Show, Fallen Angels.

KIRK (BUSH), PHYLLIS
Actress. r.n. Phyllis Kirkegaard. b. Syracuse, NY, Sept. 18, 1926. Perfume repr. model, Conover Agcy.; B'way debut in My Name Is Aquilon followed by Point of No Return. Worked as interviewer-host on all three major networks Executive with ICPR and Stone Associates. Joined CBS News in Los Angeles, 1978; 1988 named v.p. media relations Stone/Hallinan Associates.
PICTURES: Our Very Own (debut, 1950), A Life of Her Own, Two Weeks with Love, Mrs. O'Malley and Mr. Malone, Three Guys Named Mike, About Face, The Iron Mistress, Thunder Over the Plains, House of Wax, Crime Wave, River Beat, Canyon Crossroads, Johnny Concho, Back From Eternity, City After Midnight, The Sad Sack.
TELEVISION: *Series:* The Red Buttons Show, The Thin Man.

KIRKLAND, SALLY
Actress. b. NY, NY, Oct. 31, 1944. e. Actors Studio, studied acting with Uta Hagen and Lee Strasberg. Achieved notoriety in the 1960s for on-stage nudity (Sweet Eros, Futz), for work in experimental off-off B'way theater and as part of Andy Warhol's inner circle. Appeared as featured actress in over 25 films and countless avant-garde shows, before winning acclaim (and Acad. Award nom.) as the star of Anna (1987). 1983 founded Sally Kirkland Acting Workshop, a traveling transcendental meditation, yoga and theatrical seminar. Formed Artists Alliance Prods. with Mark and David Buntzman, 1988.
THEATRE: The Love Nest, Futz, Tom Paine, Sweet Eros, Witness, One Night Stand of a Noisy Passenger, The Justice Box, Where Has Tommy Flowers Gone?, In the Boom Boom Room (L.A., Drama-Logue's best actress award, 1981), Largo Desolato.
PICTURES: The Thirteen Most Beautiful Woman (1964), Blue, Futz!, Coming Apart, Going Home, The Young Nurses, The Way We Were, Cinderella Liberty, The Sting, Candy Stripe Nurses, Big Bad Mama, Bite the Bullet, Crazy Mama, Breakheart Pass, A Star is Born, Pipe Dreams, Hometown U.S.A., Private Benjamin, The Incredible Shrinking Woman, Human Highway, Love Letters, Fatal Games, Talking Walls, Anna (Golden Globe Award), Melanie Rose (High Stakes), Crack in the Mirror (White Hot), Paint It Black, Cold Feet, Best of the Best, Revenge, Bullseye, Two Evil Eyes, JFK, In the Heat of Passion, The Player, Blast 'Em, Primary Motive, Double Threat, Forever, Paper Hearts (also co-exec. prod.), Eye of the Stranger, Gunmen, Little Ghost, Amnesia, Excess Baggage, Wilbur Falls, Paranoia, It's All About You (cameo), The Island, Edtv, Starry Night, Men Named Milo Women Named Greta, Wish You Were Dead, The Boys Behind the Desk, The Audit, Out of the Black, Thank You Goodnight, The Rose Technique, A Month of Sunday, Mango Me, The Chocolate Fairy, Bruce Almighty, Neo Ned.
TELEVISION: *Movies:* Kansas City Massacre, Death Scream, Stonestreet: Who Killed the Centerfold Model?, Georgia Peaches, Heat Wave, The Haunted. Double Jeopardy, The Woman Who Loved Elvis, Double Deception, Another Woman's Husband, Night of the Wolf. *Specials:* Willow B—Women in Prison, Summer, Largo Desolato, The Westing Game, Brave New World. *Series:* Falcon Crest, Valley of the Dolls, Days of Our Lives. *Guest:* Roseanne.

KIRKWOOD, GENE
Producer. The Kirkwood Company.
PICTURES: Rocky, New York New York (assoc. prod.), Comes a Horseman, Uncle Joe Shannon, The Idolmaker, Gorky Park, The Keep, The Pope of Greenwich Village, What Makes Sammy Run, Gia a Thing of Beauty, The Duke of Deception.

KIRKWOOD, PAT
Actress, Singer. r.n. Patricia Kirkwood. b. Pendleton, Manchester, England, Feb. 24, 1921. British stage debut 1936. U.S. cabaret debut 1954. Autobiography The Time of My Life (1999). Recorded CD Miss Show Business (1999).
THEATRE: LONDON: Cinderella, Black Velvet, Top of the World, Lady Behave, Let's Face It, Happidrome, Starlight Roof, Roundabout, Ace of Clubs, Fancy Free, Peter Pan, Wonderful Town, Chrysanthemum, Pools Paradise, Villa Sleeps Four, Lock Up Your Daughters, The Constant Wife, The Rumpus, Hay Fever, Lady Frederick, A Chorus of Murder, Move Over Mrs. Markham, Pal Joey, The Cabinet Minister, An Evening with Pat Kirkwood, A Talent to Amuse, A Glamorous Night with Evelyn Laye and Friends, Glamorous Nights of Music, Noel/Cole-Let's Do It.
PICTURES: Save A Little Sunshine, Me and My Pal, Band Waggon, Come On George, Flight from Folly, No Leave No Love, Once A Sinner, Stars in Your Eyes, After the Ball, To See Such Fun.
TELEVISION: Starlight, Two of Everything, What's My Line?, The Pat Kirkwood Show, Our Marie, Pygmalion, The Great Little Tilley, From Me To You, Pat, Looks Familiar, Pebble Mill, Paul Merton's Palladium Story, This Is Your Life (subject).

KITANO, TAKESHI
Director, Writer. b. Tokyo, Japan, Jan. 18, 1948. Also actor in numerous Japanese films.
PICTURES: Merry Christmas Mr. Lawrence (actor only), Yasha (actor only), Comic Magazine (actor only), Violent Cop (also actor), Boiling Point (also actor), A Scene at the Sea (also ed.), Sonatine (also ed., actor), Many Happy Returns (actor, novel only), Getting Any? (also actor, ed.), Johnny Mnemonic (actor only), The Five (actor only), Kids Return (also ed.), Fireworks (also actor, ed.), Tokyo Eyes (actor only), Kikujiro no natsu, Brother.

KITT, EARTHA
Actress, Singer. b. Columbia, SC, Jan. 26, 1928. Professional career started as dancer in Katherine Dunham group; toured U.S., Mexico & Europe with group, then opened night club in Paris; in Orson Welles stage prod. of Faust (European tour); N.Y. night clubs before B'way debut in New Faces of 1952. Author: Thursday's Child, A Tart Is Not a Sweet, Alone with Me, Confessions of a Sex Kitten.
THEATRE: NY: New Faces of 1952, Shinbone Alley, Mrs. Patterson, The Skin of Our Teeth, The Owl and the Pussycat, Timbuktu.
PICTURES: New Faces (debut, 1954), The Mark of the Hawk (Accused), St. Louis Blues, Anna Lucasta, Saint of Devil's Island, Synanon, Uncle Tom's Cabin, Up the Chastity Belt, Friday Foster, The Last Resort, The Serpent Warriors, The Pink Chiquitas (voice), Master of Dragonard Hill, Erik the Viking, Ernest Scared Stupid, Boomerang, Fatal Instinct, Unzipped, Harriet the Spy, Ill Gotten Gains, I Woke Up Early the Day I Died, Kingdom of the Sun, The Emperor's New Groove (voice).
TELEVISION: Movies: Lt. Schuster's Wife, To Kill a Cop. Guest: Batman (as Catwoman), I Spy, Miami Vice. Mini-Series: The Feast of All Saints. Series: The Wild Thornberrys (voice).

KLEIN, ALLEN
Producer. b. New Jersey, Dec. 18, 1931. e. Upsala. Pres. ABKCO Films, a division of ABKCO Music & Records, Inc.
PICTURES: Force of Impulse, Pity Me Not, Charlie is My Darling, Stranger in Town, Sympathy for the Devil, Mrs. Brown You've Got a Lovely Daughter, The Stranger Returns, The Silent Stranger, Come Together, Pearl & The Pole, Let It Be, Gimme Shelter, El Topo, Blind Man, The Concert for Bangladesh, The Holy Mountain, The Greek Tycoon, Personal Best, It Had to Be You, The Rolling Stones Rock and Roll Circus.

KLEIN, MALCOLM C.
Executive. b. Los Angeles, CA, Nov. 22, 1927. e. UCLA, grad., 1948; U. of Denver. Prod. dir. management, KLAC-TV (KCOP), L.A., 1948-52; acct. exec., KABC-TV, 1952-56; asst. gen. sales mgr., KABC-TV, 1956-59; exec. v.p. gen. mgr., NTA Broadcasting, N.Y., 1959; v.p.; gen. mgr., RKO-General-KHJ-TV, 1960. Joined National General Corp. 1968, v.p. creative services and marketing; pres. Nat. Gen. TV Prods. Inc.; pres. NGC Broadcasting Corp. 1971, pres. Filmways TV Presentations. 1972, pres. Malcolm C. Klein & Assoc. mgmt. & mktg. consultants. 1973, gen'l. exec. Sterling Recreation Org. & Gen'l Mgr. B'cast Division. 1976, pres., American Song Festival. Member of faculty, UCLA, USC. Exec. v.p.; Telease Inc. & American Subscription Television. 1981, sr. v.p., mng. dir., STAR-TV (subscription TV). 1982, sr. v.p., InterAmerican Satellite TV Network. 1983, pres. Malcolm C. Klein & Assoc., management consultant. Exec. dir. prog., Interactive Network Inc; v.p.; bus. development, Interactive Network Inc. 1995, exec. v.p., Vivid Travel Network. Consultant, Central European Media. Member of bd., Media Shower Inc.

KLEIN, ROBERT
Actor, Comedian. b. New York, NY, Feb. 8, 1942. e. Alfred U, Yale Drama School. Was member of Chicago's Second City comedy group. Comedy albums: Child of the '50s (Grammy nom.), Mind Over Matter, New Teeth, Let's Not Make Love.
THEATRE: NY: The Apple Tree, Morning Noon and Night, New Faces of 1968, They're Playing Our Song (Tony Award nom.), The Sisters Rosensweig.
PICTURES: The Landlord, The Owl and the Pussycat, Rivals, The Bell Jar, Hooper, Nobody's Perfekt, The Last Unicorn (voice), Tales from the Darkside—The Movie, Radioland Murders, Mixed Nuts, Jeffrey, One Fine Day, Next Stop Wonderland, Primary Colors, Suits, Labor Pains, The Safety of Objects, Pinero, People I know, Two Weeks Notice.
TELEVISION: Series: Comedy Tonight, Robert Klein Time, TV's Bloopers and Practical Jokes, Sisters, Bob Patterson. Movies: Your Place or Mine, Poison Ivy, This Wife for Hire. Guest: The Tonight Show, ABC Comedy Special, George Burns Comedy Week, Twilight Zone, Late Night With David Letterman. Also appeared in HBO comedy specials, including recent From Where I Sit and Child in His 50's.

KLEINER, HARRY
Writer, Producer. b. Philadelphia, PA, Sept. 10, 1916. e. Temple U., B.S.; Yale U., M.F.A.
PICTURES: Fallen Angel, The Street With No Name, Red Skies of Mountain, Kangaroo, Miss Sadie Thompson, Salome, Carmen Jones, The Violent Men, The Garment Jungle (also prod.), Cry Tough (also prod.), The Rabbit Trap (prod. only), Ice Palace, Fever in the Blood, Fantastic Voyage, Bullitt, Le Mans, Extreme Prejudice, Red Heat.
TELEVISION: Writer: Rosenberg Trial.

KLEISER, RANDAL
Director, Producer. b. Lebanon, PA, July 20, 1946. e. U. of Southern California. For Disney Theme Parks dir. 70mm 3-D film Honey I Shrunk the Audience.
PICTURES: Street People (s.p.). Director: Grease, The Blue Lagoon, Summer Lovers (also s.p.), Grandview U.S.A., Flight of the Navigator, North Shore (exec. prod., co-story only), Big Top Pee-Wee, Getting It Right (also co-prod.), White Fang, Return to the Blue Lagoon (exec. prod. only), Honey I Blew Up the Kid, It's My Party, Shadow of Doubt, Vanilla Gorilla.
TELEVISION: Movies: All Together Now, Dawn: Portrait of a Teenage Runaway, The Boy in the Plastic Bubble, The Gathering, Royal Standard, The O.Z. Series: Marcus Welby, M.D., The Rookies, Starsky and Hutch, Family.

KLINE, KEVIN
Actor. b. St. Louis, MO, Oct. 24, 1947. e. Indiana U, School of Music. Studied at Juilliard Drama Center (1970-72), and became founding member of John Houseman's The Acting Company, touring in classics, incl. The School for Scandal, She Stoops to Conquer, The Lower Depths, The Way of the World. Associate prod., NY Shakespeare Festival, 1993-1997.
THEATRE: Understudied Raul Julia in Lincoln Center's The Threepenny Opera; The Three Sisters (B'way debut, 1973), On the Twentieth Century (Tony Award, 1978), Loose Ends, The Pirates of Penzance (Tony Award, 1981), Richard III, Henry V (Central Park), Arms and the Man, Hamlet, Much Ado About Nothing, Hamlet (1990, also dir.), Measure for Measure.
PICTURES: Sophie's Choice (debut, 1982), The Pirates of Penzance, The Big Chill, Silverado, Violets Are Blue, Cry Freedom, A Fish Called Wanda (Acad. Award for Best Supporting Actor, 1988), The January Man, I Love You to Death, Soapdish, Grand Canyon, Consenting Adults, Chaplin, Dave, George Balanchine's The Nutcracker (narrator), Princess Caraboo, French Kiss, Fierce Creatures, The Hunchback of Notre Dame (voice), The Ice Storm, In & Out, Looking for Richard, Wild Wild West, A Midsummer Night's Dream, The Road to El Dorado, The Hunchback of Notre Dame II (voice), The Anniversary Party, Life As A House, The Palace Thief, Orange County, The Hunchback of Notre Dame II (voice), Picasso at The Lapin Agile, She's De Lovely.
TELEVISION: Series: Search For Tomorrow (1976-77). Specials: The Time of Your Life, Hamlet (also co-dir.).

KLUGMAN, JACK
Actor. b. Philadelphia, PA, April 27, 1922. e. Carnegie Tech. Much tv work in 1950's incl. Captain Video, Tom Corbett— Space Cadet, U.S. Steel Hour, Kraft Television Theatre, Playhouse 90.
THEATRE: B'way: Saint Joan, Stevedore, Mister Roberts, Gypsy, I'm Not Rappaport, Three Men on a Horse. Tour/Stock: The Odd Couple.
PICTURES: Timetable (debut, 1956), Twelve Angry Men, Cry Terror, The Scarface Mob, Days of Wine and Roses, I Could Go on Singing, The Yellow Canary, Act One, Hail Mafia, The Detective, The Split, Goodbye Columbus, Who Says I Can't Ride a Rainbow?, Two Minute Warning, Dear God, Scene Smoking: Cigarettes, Cinema & the Myth of Cool.
TELEVISION: Series: The Greatest Gift (daytime serial; 1954-55), Harris Against the World, The Odd Couple (2 Emmy Awards: 1971, 1973), Quincy M.E., You Again? Guest: The Defenders (Emmy Award, 1964), The Twilight Zone, The FBI, Ben Casey, 90 Bristol Court. Movies: Fame Is the Name of the Game, Poor

Devil, The Underground Man, One of My Wives Is Missing, The Odd Couple: Together Again, Parallel Lives, The Twilight of the Golds. *Mini-Series*: Around the World in 80 Days.

KNIGHT, SHIRLEY
Actress. b. Goessell, KS, July 5, 1936. e. Lake Forest Coll., D.F.A., 1978. Won 1976 Tony Award for Kennedy's Children; Joseph Jefferson Award for Landscape of the Body, 1977; New Jersey Drama Critics Awards for A Streetcar Named Desire, 1979.
PICTURES: Five Gates to Hell (debut, 1959), Ice Palace, The Dark at the Top of the Stairs (Acad. Award nom.) The Couch, Sweet Bird of Youth (Acad. Award nom.), House of Women, Flight from Ashiya, The Group, Dutchman (Venice Film Fest. Award), Petulia, The Counterfeit Killer, The Rain People, Juggernaut, Secrets, Beyond the Poseidon Adventure, Endless Love, The Sender, Prisoners, Color of Night, Stuart Saves His Family, Diabolique, Somebody Is Waiting, The Man Who Counted, As Good as It Gets, Little Boy Blue, 75 Degrees in July, The Center of the World, Angel Eyes, The Salton Sea, Divine Secrets of the Ya-Ya Sisterhood.
TELEVISION: *Movies*: The Outsider, Shadow Over Elveron, Friendly Persuasion, Medical Story, Return to Earth, 21 Hours at Munich, The Defection of Simas Kudirka, Champions: A Love Story, Playing for Time (Emmy nom.), Billionaire Boys Club, Bump in the Night, Shadow of a Doubt, To Save a Child, When Love Kills: The Seduction of John Hearn, A Mother's Revenge, Baby Brokers, The Yarn Princess, A Part of the Family, Children of the Dust, Indictment: The McMartin Trial (Emmy Award, 1995; Golden Globe Award, 1996), Stolen Memories: Secrets from the Rose Garden, Fudge-A-Mania, Dad the Angel and Me, A Promise to Carolyn, If These Walls Could Talk, The Uninvited, Mary & Tim, Convictions, Dying to Be Perfect: The Ellen Hart Pena Story, The Wedding (mini), A Father for Brittany, A Marriage of Convenience, My Louisiana Sky. *Specials:* The Country Girl, The Lie. *Guest:* The Equalizer (Emmy nom.), thirtysomething (Emmy Award), Law and Order (Emmy nom.), NYPD Blue (Emmy Award, 1995), Cybill, Outer Limits Tribute. *Series:* Maggie Winters.

KNOTTS, DON
Actor. b. Morgantown, WV, July 21, 1924. e. WV U., U. of AZ. Drafted into U.S. Army where became part of show called Stars and Gripes, teamed with comedian Mickey Shaughnessy. After schooling resumed was offered teaching fellowship but went to New York to try acting instead. Started out in radio show Bobby Benson and the B Bar B's. Appeared on TV, leading to role in No Time for Sergeants on B'way; appeared in film version.
PICTURES: No Time for Sergeants (debut, 1958), Wake Me When It's Over, The Last Time I Saw Archie, It's a Mad Mad Mad Mad World, Move Over Darling, The Incredible Mr. Limpet, The Ghost and Mr. Chicken, The Reluctant Astronaut, The Shakiest Gun in the West, The Love God?, How to Frame a Figg (also co-story), The Apple Dumpling Gang, No Deposit No Return, Gus, Herbie Goes to Monte Carlo, Hot Lead and Cold Feet, The Apple Dumpling Gang Rides Again, The Prize Fighter, Their Private Eyes, Cannonball Run II, Big Bully, Cats Don't Dance (voice), Pleasantville, Heart of Love.
TELEVISION: *Series*: Search for Tomorrow (1953-55), The Steve Allen Show, The Andy Griffith Show (5 Emmy Awards: 1961, 1962, 1963, 1966, 1967), The Don Knotts Show, Three's Company, What a Country, Matlock. *Movies*: I Love a Mystery, Return to Mayberry, Quints.

KOCH, HOWARD W., JR.
Producer. b. Los Angeles, CA, Dec. 14, 1945. Was asst. dir. and in other industry posts before turning to production. Pres. & chief exec. off., Rastar (Peggy Sue Got Married, The Secret of My Success, Nothing in Common, Violets Are Blue, Amazing Chuck and Grace prod. under presidency); 1987, set up own prod. co. at De Laurentiis Entertainment Group. Oct. 1987: named president of the De Laurentiis Entertainment Group, Resigned April 1988 to produce independently.
PICTURES: Heaven Can Wait, The Other Side of Midnight, The Frisco Kid (exec.). *Co-prod./prod.*: The Idolmaker, Gorky Park, Honky Tonk Freeway, The Keep, A Night in Heaven, The Pope of Greenwich Village, Rooftops, The Long Walk Home, Necessary Roughness, Wayne's World, The Temp, Sliver, Wayne's World 2, Losing Isaiah, Virtuosity, Primal Fear (exec.), The Beautician and the Beast, Keeping the Faith, Frequency, Collateral Damage.
TELEVISION: The Riverman.

KOCH, JOANNE
Executive Director. The Film Society of Lincoln Center. b. NY, NY, Oct. 7, 1929. e. Goddard College, B.A. political science, 1950. Dept. of Film, Museum of Modern Art, as circulation asst., film researcher, motion picture stills archivist, 1950. Early 1960s, technical dir., film dept. MOMA, supervised the implementation of MOMA's film preservation program. 1967, asst. to publisher of Grove Press, active in preparation of Grove's case in I Am Curious Yellow censorship trial. Joined film div., Grove, first in distribution then as tech. dir. and prod. coord. 1971 joined Film Society of Lincoln Center as prog. dir. of Movies-in-the-Parks. 1971 made admin. dir. Exec. dir. of N.Y. Film Festival, Film Comment magazine, Film-in-Education, New Directors/New Films, annual Film Society Tribute and Walter Reade Theater at Lincoln Center.

KOEPP, DAVID
Writer,
PICTURES: Apartment Zero (also prod.), Bad Influence, Toy Soldiers, Death Becomes Her, Jurassic Park, Carlito's Way, The Paper (also prod.) The Shadow, Mission Impossible, Suspicious (dir. only), The Trigger Effect (also dir.), The Lost World: Jurassic Park (also actor), Snake Eyes, Stir of Echoes (also dir.), The Panic Room (also prod.), Spider-Man, Big Trouble (actor only).
TELEVISION: Hack.

KOENEKAMP, FRED J.
Cinematographer. b. Los Angeles, CA, Nov. 11, 1922. Father was special effects cinematographer Hans F. Koenekamp. Member of American Society of Cinematographers.
PICTURES: Doctor You've Got to Be Kidding, Sol Madrid, Stay Away Joe, Live a Little Love a Little, Heaven With a Gun, The Great Bank Robbery, Patton (Acad. Award nom.), Beyond the Valley of the Dolls, Flap, Skin Game, Billy Jack, Happy Birthday Wanda June, Stand Up and Be Counted, Kansas City Bomber, The Magnificent Seven Ride, Rage, Harry in Your Pocket, Papillon, Uptown Saturday Night, The Towering Inferno (Acad. Award, 1974), The Wild McCullochs, Doc Savage, Posse, Embryo, Fun With Dick and Jane, The Other Side of Midnight, Islands in the Streams (Acad. Award nom.), The Bad News Bears in Breaking Training, The Dominic Principle, White Line Fever, The Swarm, The Champ, The Amityville Horror, Love and Bullets, When Time Ran Out, The Hunter, First Family, First Monday in October, Carbon Copy, Yes Giorgio, It Came From Hollywood, Two of a Kind, The Adventures of Buckaroo Banzai: Across the 8th Dimension, Stewardess School, Listen to Me, Welcome Home, Flight of the Intruder.
TELEVISION: *Movies*: Disaster on the Coastline, Tales of the Gold Monkey, Money on the Side, Return of the Man from U.N.C.L.E., Summer Fantasies, Whiz Kids, Flight 90—Disaster on the Potomac, Obsessive Love, City Killer, Las Vegas Strip War, A Touch of Scandal, Not My Kid, Hard Time on Planet Earth (pilot), Return of the Shaggy Dog, Foreign Exchange, Splash Too, Hard Times. *Series*: The Man From U.N.C.L.E. (Emmy nom.)

KOENIG, WALTER
Actor, Writer. b. Chicago, IL, Sept. 14, 1936. e. Grinnell Coll. (IA), U. of California. Performed in summer stock; after college enrolled at Neighborhood Playhouse, N.Y.; first acting job in TV's Day in Court. *Books:* Chekov's Enterprise, Buck Alice and the Actor Robot. Creator and writer of comic book series Raver.
PICTURES: Strange Lovers, The Deadly Honeymoon, Star Trek—The Motion Picture, Star Trek II: The Wrath of Khan, Star Trek III: The Search for Spock, Star Trek IV: The Voyage Home, Star Trek V: the Final Frontier, Moontrap, Star Trek VI: The Undiscovered Country, Star Trek: Generations, Drawing Down the Moon, Trekkies.
TELEVISION: *Series*: Star Trek. *Guest*: Colombo, Medical Center, Ironside, Mannix, Alfred Hitchcock Presents, Mr. Novak, Ben Casey, The Untouchables, Combat, Babylon 5. *Movies*: The Questor Tapes, Goodbye Raggedy Ann, The Privateers. *Writer*: Family, The Class of '65, The Powers of Matthew Starr.

KOHNER, PANCHO
Producer. b. Los Angeles, CA, Jan. 7, 1939. e. U. of Southern California, U. of Mexico, Sorbonne.
PICTURES: The Bridge in the Jungle (also dir., s.p.), The Lie, Victoria (also s.p.), Mr. Sycamore (also dir., s.p.), St. Ives, The White Buffalo, Love and Bullets, Why Would I Lie?, 10 to Midnight, The Evil That Men Do, Murphy's Law, Assassination, Death Wish IV, Messenger of Death, Kinjite, Madeline.

KOHNER, SUSAN
Actress. b. Los Angeles, CA. Nov. 11, 1936. m. designer & author John Weitz. Sons Paul and Christopher Weitz are screenwriters. Mother, Lupita Tovar, was one of Mexico's leading film actresses. Father was talent rep. Paul Kohner. e. U. of California, 1954-55. Received Golden Globe Awards, 1959 and 1960. Retired from acting in 1964. Co-chair, Juilliard Council, Juilliard Sch. NY.
THEATER: Love Me Little, He Who Gets Slapped, A Quiet Place, Rose Tatoo, Bus Stop, St. Joan, Sunday in New York, Take Her She's Mine, Pullman Car, Hiawatha, as well as summer stock.
PICTURES: To Hell and Back (debut, 1955), The Last Wagon, Trooper Hook, Dino, Imitation of Life (Acad. Award nom.), The Big Fisherman, The Gene Krupa Story, All the Fine Young Cannibals, By Love Possessed, Freud.
TELEVISION: Alcoa Hour, Schlitz Playhouse, Four Star Theatre, Matinee Theatre, Climax, Suspicion, Playhouse 90, Route 66, Dick Powell Theatre.

KONCHALOVSKY, ANDREI
Director, Writer. a.k.a. Mikhalkov Konchalovski. b. Moscow, Soviet Union, Aug. 20, 1937. Great grandfather: painter Sourikov; grandfather: painter Konchalovski; father is a writer; mother poet Natalia Konchalovskaia; brother is director Nikita Mikhalkov. e. as pianist Moscow Conservatoire, 1947-57; State

Film Sch. (VGIK) under Mikhail Romm (1964). Dir. debut with 1961 short film The Boy and the Pigeon. Worked as scriptwriter during 1960s especially with Andrei Tarkovsky. 1962: asst. to Tarkovsky on Ivan's Childhood. In 1980, moved to U.S. In 1991, moved back to Russia.

THEATRE/OPERA: The Seagull (Theatre de L'Odeon, Paris), Eugene Onegin (La Scala, Milan), La Pique Dame (La Scala, Milan & Bastille Opera, Pairs).

PICTURES: Writer: The Steamroller and the Violin, Andrey Rublev, Tashkent City of Bread, The Song of Manshuk, The End of Chieftain. Director: The First Teacher (feature debut, 1965), Asya's Happiness, A Nest of Gentlefolk, Uncle Vanya, Romance for Lovers, Siberiade (Cannes Film Fest. Award, 1979), Maria's Lovers, Runaway Train, Duet for One, Shy People (also co-s.p.), Tango and Cash, Homer and Eddie, Ryaba, My Chicken (writer, dir.), The Inner Circle (also co-s.p.), Assia and the Hen with the Golden Eyes, The Royal Way.

TELEVISION: Split Cherry Terry (short). Mini-series: The Odyssey (Part I & II, Emmy Award, 1996).

KONIGSBERG, FRANK

Executive. b. Kew Gardens, NY, March 10, 1933. e. Yale, Yale Law Sch. Worked as lawyer at CBS for six years; moved to NBC 1960-65 in legal dept. as dir. prog. and talent administration. Left to package TV special for Artists Agency Rep. (later AFA) in Los Angeles; sr. v.p. of West Coast office seven years. Executive producer of many TV series, pilots, variety specials and made-for-TV movies. Formed own Konigsberg Company.

PICTURES: The Joy of Sex, Nine 1/2 Weeks.

TELEVISION: Movies (all exec. prod.): Pearl, Ellis Island, Bing Crosby: His Life and Legend, Dummy, Before and After, Guyana Tragedy, A Christmas Without Snow, The Pride of Jesse Hallam, Hard Case, Divorce Wars, Coming Out of the Ice, The Glitter Done, Wet Gold, Surviving, Act of Vengeance, As Summers Die, Strong Medicine, Onassis: The Richest Man in the World, Dance til Dawn, Fourth Story, Paris Trout, To Save a Child, In Sickness and in Health, Double Edge, Charles and Diana: Unhappily Ever After, Love Can Be Murder, The Tommyknockers, The Yarn Princess, Oldest Living Confederate Widow Tells All, A Good Day to Die, A Face to Die for, Titanic, Sweet Temptation, A Loss of Innocence, Deadly Pursuits, The Price of Heaven, Bella Mafia, Jesus, Like Mother Like Son: The Strange Story of Sante and Kenny Kimes, Living in Fear.Series (exec. prod.): It's Not Easy, Breaking Away, Dorothy, Rituals, Angel Falls. Mini-Series: Pearl, Ellis Island, The Last Don, The Last Don II.

KOPELSON, ANNE

Producer. m. Producer, Arnold Kopelson.

PICTURES: Exec. prod.: Outbreak, Seven, Eraser, Murder at 1600, Mad City, Devil's Advocate, A Perfect Murder, U.S. Marshals, Don't Say a Word, Joe Somebody, Blackout.

TELEVISION: Movies: Past Tense. Series: The Fugitive, Thieves.

KOPELSON, ARNOLD

Producer, Financier, Intl. Distributor. b. New York, NY, Feb. 14, 1935. e. New York Law Sch., J.D., 1959; NYU, B.S. 1956. Has executive-produced, produced, packaged, developed or distributed with wife, Anne Kopelson over 100 films. Chmn. Arnold Kopelson Prods., Co-chmn. Inter-Ocean Film Sales, Ltd. Named NATO/ShoWest Producer of the Year, 1994.

PICTURES: Exec. Prod.: The Legacy, Lost and Found, Night of the Juggler, Dirty Tricks, Final Assignment, Gimme an "F", Fire Birds, Warlock. Producer: Foolin' Around, Platoon (Acad. Award for Best Picture, 1986), Triumph of the Spirit, Out for Justice, Falling Down, The Fugitive (Acad. Award nom.), Outbreak, Seven, Eraser, Murder at 1600, Mad City, The Devil's Advocate, A Perfect Murder, U.S. Marshals, Don't Say a Word, Joe Somebody, Blackout.

TELEVISION: Movie: Past Tense. Series: The Fugitive, Thieves.

KOPLOVITZ, KAY

Executive. b. Milwaukee, WI, April 11, 1945. e. U. Wis., 1967, BA, Mich. State U., MA, Communications, 1968. Radio/TV prod., WTMJ-TV, Milwaukee 1967. Ed. Comm. Satellite Corp. 1968-72. Dir. Communications Svcs. UA Columbia Cablevision 1973-75. VP, Exec. dir. UA Columbia Satellite Services, Inc. 1977-80. Founder, pres., CEO USA Network and Sci-Fi Channel 1980-1998. June-June 2001, CEO Working Women Network. Currently a principal of Koplovitz & Co., a media investment firm. Also, chmn., Broadway Television Network, serves on the board of Liz Claiborne and Instinet. Member Nat'l Cable TV Assn. 1984-. Nat'l Acad. TV Arts and Scis. 1984-95. Women in Cable 1979-83. Non-profit bds. include New York City Partnership, the Central Park Conservancy, the Museum of Television and Radio and the Tennis Hall of Fame.

KOPPEL, TED

TV News Correspondent, Anchor, Host. b. Lancashire, England, Feb. 8, 1940. To U.S. in 1953; became citizen, 1963. e. Syracuse U, Stanford U. Started as writer and news correspondent for WMCA radio in NYC. Joined ABC News in New York, 1963, serving as correspondent in Vietnam, 1967, 1969-71; Miami Bureau chief, 1968; Hong Kong Bureau chief, 1969-71; diplomatic correspondent, 1971-76, 1977-79. Anchor of NBC Saturday Night News, 1976-77. Host of Nightline, beginning in 1980. Author: The Wit and Wisdom of Adlai Stevenson, In the National Interest.

TELEVISION: Series: ABC News (1971-80), ABC Saturday Night News (1975-77); Nightline (1980-), 20/20 (1986). Host/anchor/writer of many ABC news specials.

KOPPLE, BARBARA

Director, Producer.

PICTURES: Dir.: Harlan County USA (also prod., Acad. Award, Best Doc., LA Film Crits. Special Award, 1976), American Dream (Acad. Award, Best Doc., 1990, Directors' Guild Award, 1992, Cannes Film Festival Grand Jury Prize, 1991), Beyond JFK: The Question of Conspiracy, Woodstock '94 (also prod.), Wild Man Blues, A Conversation with Gregory Peck, My Generation (also s.p.). Prod.: Fallen Champ: The Mike Tyson Story (Directors' Guild Award, 1994).

TELEVISION: Movies, dir.: Keeping On, The Hamptons Project. Series, dir.: Homicide: Life in the Street (Directors' Guild Award, 1998). Mini-series, dir.: A Century of Women.

KORMAN, HARVEY

Actor, Director. b. Chicago, IL, Feb. 15, 1927. e. Wright Junior Coll. Began dramatic studies at Chicago's Goodman Sch. of Drama at the Arts Inst. Acted in small roles in Broadway plays and did TV commercials until break came as comedian for Danny Kaye Show on TV. Staged comedy sketches for Steve Allen variety series in 1967. Became Carol Burnett's leading man on her show 1967-77. Directed two episodes of The New Dick Van Dyke Show.

PICTURES: Living Venus (debut, 1961), Gypsy, Lord Love a Duck, The Last of the Secret Agents?, The Man Called Flintstone (voice), Three Bites of the Apple, Don't Just Stand There, The April Fools, Blazing Saddles, Huckleberry Finn, High Anxiety, Americathon, Herbie Goes Bananas, First Family, History of the World Part I, Trail of the Pink Panther, Curse of the Pink Panther, The Longshot, Munchie, The Flintstones (voice), Radioland Murders, Dracula: Dead and Loving It, Jingle All the Way, Gideon's Webb, The Flintstones in Viva Rock Vegas, The Ruby Princess Runs Away (voice).

TELEVISION: Series: The Danny Kaye Show, The Carol Burnett Show (4 Emmy Awards: 1969, 1971, 1972, 1974), The Tim Conway Show, Mama's Family, Leo and Liz in Beverly Hills, The Nutt House. Movies: Three's a Crowd, Suddenly Single, The Love Boat (pilot), Bud and Lou, The Invisible Woman, Carpool, Crash Course, Based on an Untrue Story. Special: The Carol Burnett Show: A Reunion (also co-exec. prod.).

KORMAN, LEWIS J.

Executive. b. 1945. Partner, Kaye, Scholer, Fierman, Hays & Handler 1978; founding partner, Gelberg & Abrams where pioneered dev. of public limited partnerships, Delphi Partners, to help finance Columbia Pictures' and Tri-Star Pictures' films. 1986, became consultant to Tri-Star involved in negotiations that led to acquisition of Loews Theatre Corp. that year. Joined Tri-Star, 1987, as sr. exec. v.p. 1988 appt. to additional post of COO and named dir. of Columbia Pictures Entertainment Inc.; 1989 also became chmn, Motion Picture Group. 1990, resigned his positions after Columbia sale to Sony. Co-founder, pres. & COO of Savoy Pictures Ent., Inc., 1992. Currently, vice-chmn., R.A.B. Holdings, Inc. and dir., The B. Manischewitz Company, LLC.

KORTY, JOHN

Director, Producer, Writer, Animator. b. Lafayette, IN, June 22, 1936. e. Antioch Coll, B.A. 1959. President, Korty Films. Documentary: Who Are the DeBolts? And Where Did They Get Nineteen Kids? (Acad. Award: 1977; Emmy & DGA Awards: 1978-79). Short Films: The Language of Faces (AFSC, 1961), Imogen Cunningham: Photographer (AFI grant, 1970), The Music School. Animation: Breaking the Habit (Oscar nom.), Twice Upon a Time.

PICTURES: Crazy Quilt (1966), Funnyman, Riverrun, Alex and the Gypsy, Oliver's Story, Twice Upon a Time.

TELEVISION: Movies: The People, Go Ask Alice, Class of '63, The Autobiography of Miss Jane Pittman (Emmy & DGA Awards, 1974), Farewell to Manzanar (Humanitas, Christopher Awards), Forever, A Christmas Without Snow (also writer, prod.), The Haunting Passion, Second Sight: A Love Story, The Ewok Adventure, Resting Place, Baby Girl Scott, Eye on the Sparrow, Winnie, Cast the First Stone, A Son's Promise, Line of Fire: The Morris Dees Story, Long Road Home, Deadly Matrimony, They, Getting Out, Redwood Curtain, Scrooge, Oklahoma City: A Survivor's Story, Gift of Love: The Daniel Huffman Story.

KOTCHEFF, TED

Director. r.n. William Theodore Kotcheff. b. Toronto, Canada, April 7, 1931. Ent. TV ind. 1952. After five years with Canadian Broadcasting Corp. joined ABC-TV in London, 1957.

THEATRE: London: Progress the Park, Play with a Tiger, Luv, Maggie May, The Au Pair Man, Have You Any Dirty Washing, Mother Dear?

PICTURES: Tiara Tahiti (debut, 1963), Life at the Top, Two Gentlemen Sharing, Wake in Fright, Outback, Billy Two Hats, The Apprenticeship of Duddy Kravitz, Fun with Dick and Jane, Who Is Killing the Great Chefs of Europe?, North Dallas Forty (also co-s.p.), First Blood, Split Image (also prod.), Uncommon Valor

(also exec. prod.), Joshua Then and Now, The Check is in the Mail (prod. only), Switching Channels, Winter People, Weekend at Bernie's (also actor), Folks!, The Shooter, The Populist.
TELEVISION: *Movies:* A Family of Cops, A Husband a Wife and a Lover, Borrowed Hearts, The Return of Alex Kelly. *Specials:* Of Mice and Men, Desperate Hours, The Human Voice. *Series:* Buddy Faro, Law and Order: SVU.

KOTEAS, ELIAS
Actor. b. Montreal, Quebec, Canada, 1961. e. AADA.
PICTURES: One Magic Christmas, Some Kind of Wonderful, Gardens of Stone, Tucker: The Man and His Dream, Full Moon in Blue Water, Malarek, Blood Red, Friends Lovers and Lunatics, Teenage Mutant Ninja Turtles, Backstreet Dreams, Desperate Hours, Look Who's Talking Too, Almost an Angel, Teenage Mutant Ninja Turtles III, Chain of Desire, Camilla, Exotica, The Prophecy, Hit Me, Crash, Gattaca, The Thin Red Line, Fallen, Apt Pupil, Divorce: A Contemporary Western, Dancing at the Blue Iguana, Harrison's Flowers, Lost Souls, Novocaine, Collateral Damage, Ararat.
TELEVISION: Private Sessions, Onassis: The Richest Man in the World, The Habitation of Dragons, Sugartime, Shot in the Heart.

KOTTO, YAPHET
Actor. b. New York, NY, Nov. 15, 1937. Has many stage credits, including starring roles on Broadway in The Great White Hope, The Zulu and the Zayda. Off-B'way: Blood Knot, Black Monday, In White America, A Good Place To Raise a Boy.
PICTURES: The Limit (also prod.), 4 for Texas, Nothing But a Man, 5 Card Stud, Thomas Crown Affair, The Liberation of L. B. Jones, Man and Boy, Across 110th Street, Bone, Live and Let Die, Truck Turner, Report to the Commissioner, Sharks' Treasure, Friday Foster, Drum, Monkey Hustle, Blue Collar, Alien, Brubaker, Fighting Back, Star Chamber, Eye of the Tiger, Warning Sign, Prettykill, The Running Man, Midnight Run, Nightmare of the Devil (also prod., dir.), Terminal Entry, Jigsaw, A Whisper to a Scream, Tripwire, Ministry of Vengeance, Hangfire, Freddy's Dead, Almost Blue, Intent to Kill, The Puppet Masters, Two If By Sea.
TELEVISION: *Series:* Homicide. *Movies:* Night Chase, Raid on Entebbe, Rage, Playing With Fire, The Park Is Mine, Women of San Quentin, Badge of the Assassin, Harem, Desperado, Perry Mason: The Case of the Scandalous Scoundrel, Prime Target, After the Shock, Chrome Soldiers, It's Nothing Personal, Extreme Justice, The American Clock, The Corpse Had a Familiar Face, Deadline for Murder: From the Files of Edna Buchanan, Defenders: The Payback, Homicide: The Movie, The Ride, Stiletto Dance. *Guest:* Alfred Hitchcock Presents.

KOVACS, LASZLO
Cinematographer. b. Hungary, May 14, 1933. Came to U.S. 1957; naturalized 1963. e. Acad. Drama and M.P. Arts, Budapest, MA 1956.
PICTURES: Hell's Angels on Wheels, Hell's Bloody Devils, Psych Out, The Savage Seven, Targets, A Man Called Dagger, Single Room Furnished, Easy Rider, That Cold Day in the Park, Getting Straight, Alex in Wonderland, Five Easy Pieces, The Last Movie, Marriage of a Young Stockbroker, The King of Marvin Gardens, Pocket Money, What's Up Doc?, Steelyard Blues, Paper Moon, Slither, A Reflection of Fear, Huckleberry Finn, For Pete's Sake, Freebie and the Bean, Shampoo, At Long Last Love, Baby Blue Marine, Nickelodeon, Close Encounters of the Third Kind (addl. photog. only), Harry and Walter Go to New York, New York New York, F.I.S.T., The Last Waltz, Paradise Alley, Butch and Sundance: The Early Days, The Runner Stumbles, Heart Beat, Inside Moves, The Legend of the Lone Ranger, Frances, The Toy, Crackers, Ghostbusters, Mask, Legal Eagles, Little Nikita, Say Anything..., Shattered, Radio Flyer, Life With Mikey, Deception, The Next Karate Kid, The Scout, Free Willy 2: The Adventure Home, Copycat, Multiplicity, My Best Friend's Wedding, Jack Frost, Return to Me, Miss Congeniality, Two Weeks Notice.

KOZAK, HARLEY JANE
Actress. b. Wilkes-Barre, PA, Jan. 28, 1957. e. NYU's School of the Arts. Member of Nebraska Repertory Theatre.
PICTURES: House on Sorority Row, Clean and Sober, When Harry Met Sally..., Parenthood, Sideout, Arachnophobia, Necessary Roughness, The Taking of Beverly Hills, All I Want for Christmas, The Favor, Magic in the Water, Dark Planet.
TELEVISION: *Series:* The Guiding Light, Santa Barbara, Texas, Harts of the West, Bringing Up Jack, You Wish. *Guest:* L.A. Law, Highway to Heaven. *Movies:* So Proudly We Hail, The Amy Fisher Story, The Android Affair, Unforgivable, A Friend's Betrayal, The Love Master, Emma's Wish. *Mini-series:* Titanic.

KOZLOWSKI, LINDA
Actress. b. 1956. m. actor Paul Hogan. Began professional acting career soon after graduating from Juilliard Sch., N.Y., 1981. Stage debut in How It All Began at the Public Theatre. In regional theatre appeared in Requiem, Translations, Make and Break, as well as on Broadway and on tour with Dustin Hoffman in Death of a Salesman and the TV adaptation.
PICTURES: Crocodile Dundee, Crocodile Dundee II, Pass the

Ammo, Helena, Almost an Angel, The Neighbor, Backstreet Justice, Zorn, Village of the Damned, Crocodile Dundee in Los Angeles.
TELEVISION: *Movies:* Favorite Son, Shaughnessy.

KRABBE, JEROEN
Actor. b. Amsterdam, The Netherlands, Dec. 5, 1944. Trained for stage at De Toneelschool, Acad. of Dramatic Art, Amsterdam, 1965. Also studied at painting at Acad. of Fine Arts, grad. 1981. Founded touring theater co. in the Netherlands and translated plays into Dutch. Also costume designer. As a painter, work has been widely exhibited (one-man show at Francis Kyle Galleries, London). Author: The Economy Cookbook. Theatre dir. debut, new stage adaptation of The Diary of Anne Frank, 1985 in Amsterdam.
PICTURES: Soldier of Orange, A Flight of Rainbirds, Spetters, The Fourth Man, Turtle Diary, Jumpin' Jack Flash, No Mercy, The Living Daylights, Shadow of Victory, A World Apart, Crossing Delancey, Shadowman, Scandal, The Punisher, Melancholia, Till There Was You, Kafka, The Prince of Tides, For a Lost Soldier, The Fugitive, King of the Hill, Immortal Beloved, Farinelli, Blood of a Poet, Business for Pleasure, Lorca, Dangerous Beauty, Left Luggage (dir. debut), Dangerous Beauty, Ever After, An Ideal Husband, Ausverkauft, The Sky Will Fall, The Discovery of Heaven.
TELEVISION: Danton's Death (debut, 1966), William of Orange, World War III. *Movies:* One for the Dancer, Family of Spies, After the War, Secret Weapon, Robin Hood (theatrical in Europe), Murder East Murder West, Dynasty: The Reunion, Stalin, Only Love, Jesus. *Mini-series:* The Odyssey, The Great War.

KRAMER, LARRY
Writer, Producer. b. Bridgeport, CT, June 25, 1935. e. Yale U., B.A. 1957. Ent. m.p. ind. 1958. Story edit. Columbia Pictures, N.Y. London 1960-65. Asst. to David Picker and Herb Jaffe, UA, 1965. Assoc. prod. and additional dialogue Here We Go Round the Mulberry Bush, 1968. Writ. prod. Women in Love (Acad. Award nom. for s.p., 1970). Lost Horizon, 1973 (s.p.). Novel: Faggots (1978). Theater: The Normal Heart (NY Shakespeare Festival and throughout the world), Just Say No, The Destiny of Me. Cofounder: Gay Men's Health Crisis, Inc. (community AIDS org.). Founder: ACT UP: AIDS Coalition to Unleash Power (AIDS activist andprotest org.). Book of Essays: Reports from the Holocaust: The Story of an AIDS Activist (St. Martin's Press, 1995).

KRANE, JONATHAN
Executive. b. 1952. m. actress Sally Kellerman. e. St. Johns Coll. grad. with honors, 1972; Yale Law Sch., 1976. Joined Blake Edwards Entertainment in 1981, becoming pres. Formed talent management co. Management Company Entertainment Group representing clients such as John Travolta, Sally Kellerman, Kathryn Harrold, Sandra Bernhard, Howie Mandel, Drew Barrymore, others. Began producing vehicles for clients and transformed co. into production, distribution, management and finance co. Chairman and chief exec. officer, Management Company Entertainment Group (MCEG).
PICTURES: *Exec. prod./prod.:* Boardwalk, Honeymoon, Fly Away Home, The Man Who Loved Women, Micki & Maude, A Fine Mess, That's Life, The Chocolate War, The Experts, Fatal Charm, Boris and Natasha, Look Who's Talking, Chud II: Bud the Chud, Without You I'm Nothing (prod.), Look Who's Talking Too, Convicts, Cold Heaven, Breaking the Rules, Look Who's Talking Now, Face/Off, Lay of the Land, Primary Colors, Mad City, The General's Daughter, Battlefield Earth, Lucky Numbers, Bar Hopping, Starfish, Domestic Disturbance, Standing Room Only.
TELEVISION: *Prod.:* Howie Mandel Life at Carnegie Hall, Howie Mandel: The North American Watusi Tour.

KRANTZ, STEVE
Executive. b. New York, NY, May 20, 1923. m. novelist Judith Krantz. e. Columbia U., B.A. Dir. progs., NBC, New York, 1953; dir. prog. dev., Screen Gems, N.Y., 1955; v.p.; gen. mgr. Screen Gems, Canada, 1958; dir. int. sls.; 1960; formed Steve Krantz Productions, Inc. 1964.
PICTURES: *Producer:* Fritz the Cat, Heavy Traffic, The Nine Lives of Fritz the Cat, Cooley High, Ruby, Which Way Is Up?, Jennifer. Swap Meet (also writer).
TELEVISION: *Series:* Steve Allen Show, Kate Smith Show, Hazel, Dennis the Menace, Winston Churchill—The Valiant Years, Marvel Super Heroes, Rocket Robin Hood. *Mini-series:* Princess Daisy, Sins, Mistral's Daughter, I'll Take Manhattan. *Movies:* Dadah is Death (exec. prod.), Till We Meet Again, Deadly Medicine, Deadly Matrimony, Torch Song, Jack Reed: Badge of Honor, House of Secrets, Children of the Dark, Dazzle, Jack Reed: One of Our Own, Jack Reed: Death and Vengeance.

KRAUSE, BRIAN
Actor. b. El Toro, California, February 1, 1969.
PICTURES: Return to the Blue Lagoon, December, An American Summer, Sleepwalkers, The Liars Club, Naked Souls, Breaking Free, Within the Rock, Mind Games, Get a Job, Trash, Dreamers.
TELEVISION: *Movies:* Earth Angel, Teen Vid 2, American Eyes, Bandit: Bandit Goes Country, Bandit: Bandit Bandit, Bandit:

Beauty and the Bandit, Bandit: Bandit's Silver Angel, Family Album, Extreme Blue, 919 Fifth Avenue, The Women of Charmed, Return to Cabin by the Lake. *Series:* Another World, Charmed. *Guest:* Highway to Heaven, Tales from the Crypt, Walker,Texas Ranger, High Tide.

KREUGER, KURT
Actor. b. St. Moritz, Switzerland, July 23, 1917. e. U. of Lausanne, Polytechnic. London. Came to U.S. 1937, partner in travel bureau: acted in Wharf Theat. group. Cape Cod, 1939; Broadway debut in Candle in the Wind with Helen Hayes, 1941.
PICTURES: The Moon Is Down, Edge of Darkness, The Strange Death of Adolph Hitler, Sahara, Mademoiselle Fifi, None Shall Escape, Escape in the Desert, Hotel Berlin, Paris Underground, The Spider, Dark Corner, Unfaithfully Yours, Spy Hunt, Fear, The Enemy Below, Legion of the Doomed, What Did You Do in the War Daddy?, The St. Valentine's Day Massacre.

KRIGE, ALICE
Actress. b. Upington, South Africa. Moved to London at 21 and studied at Central School of Speech and Drama. Professional debut on British TV: The Happy Autumn Fields. In London prod. of Forever Yours, Maylou. West End debut, Arms and the Man, 1981. Two seasons with Royal Shakespeare Co. at Stratford and London (The Tempest, King Lear, The Taming of the Shrew, Cyrano de Bergerac, Bond's Lear.), Venice Preserved at the Almeida, 1995.
PICTURES: Chariots of Fire (debut, 1981), Ghost Story, King David, Barfly, Haunted Summer, See You in the Morning, S.P.O.O.K.S., Sleepwalkers, Habitat, Institute Benjamenta, Amanda, Star Trek: First Contact, Twilight of the Icenymphs, The Commissioner, The Little Vampire, Molokai: The Story of Father Damien, The Calling, Superstition, Falling, Reign of Fire.
TELEVISION: *Movies:* Wallenberg: A Hero's Story, Dream West, A Tale of Two Cities, Second Serve, Baja Oklahoma, Max and Helen, Iran: Days of Crisis, Ladykiller, Judgment Day: The John List Story, Double Deception, Jack Reed: Badge of Honor, Scarlet & Black, Sharpes Honour, Summer, Devil's Advocate, Donor Unknown, Joseph, Hidden in America, Like Father Like Son, Indefensible: The Truth About Edward Brannigan, Deep in My Heart. *Mini-Series:* Ellis Island, Close Relations, Atilla, Dinotopia, Children of Dune.

KRISTOFFERSON, KRIS
Actor, Singer. b. Brownsville, TX, June 22, 1936. e. Pomona Coll., Oxford U. (Rhodes Scholar). Joined U.S. Army briefly and taught English literature at West Point. Started writing songs (country music), hits have included Me and Bobby McGee, Why Me, Lord, Sunday Mornin' Comin' Down.
PICTURES: The Last Movie, Cisco Pike, Pat Garrett and Billy the Kid, Blume in Love, Bring Me the Head of Alfredo Garcia, Alice Doesn't Live Here Anymore, Vigilante Force, The Sailor Who Fell from Grace with the Sea, A Star Is Born, Semi-Tough, Convoy, Heaven's Gate, Rollover, Flashpoint, Songwriter, Trouble in Mind, Big Top Pee-wee, Millennium, Welcome Home, Original Intent, Night of the Cyclone, Sandino, No Place to Hide, Cheatin' Hearts, Lone Star, Fire Down Below, A Soldier's Daughter Never Cries, Girls' Night, Blade, Dance with Me, Limbo, The Joyriders, Payback, Molokai: The Story of Father Damien, Detox, Comanche, The Ballad of Ramblin' Jack, Planet of the Apes, Wooly Boys, Chelsea Walls, Eye See You, Disappearances, D-Tox, Blade 2.
TELEVISION: *Movies/Mini-Series:* Freedom Road, The Lost Honor of Kathryn Beck, The Last Days of Frank and Jesse James, Blood and Orchids, Stagecoach, The Tracker, Dead or Alive, Pair of Aces, Another Pair of Aces, Miracle in the Wilderness, Christmas in Connecticut, Troubleshooters: Trapped Beneath the Earth, Big Dreams & Broken Hearts: The Dottie West Story, Tad, Outlaw Justice, Two for Texas. *Mini-Series:* Amerika, Netforce, Perfect Murder Perfect Town.

KRONICK, WILLIAM
Writer, Director. b. Amsterdam, NY. e. Columbia Coll., A.B. U.S. Navy photography; wrote, dir. featurette, A Bowl of Cherries.
PICTURES: Nights in White Satin (s.p.), Horowitz in Dublin (dir., s.p.), Flash Gordon and King Kong (2nd unit dir.).
TELEVISION: *Documentaries: Wrote, dir., prod.:* The Ultimate Stuntman: a Tribute to Dar Robinson, To the Ends of the Earth, Mysteries of the Great Pyramid; George Plimpton Specials; National Geographic, Ripley's Believe It or Not, The World's Greatest Stunts. *Prod.:* In Search of... Series. *Dir.:* (movie) The 500 Pound Jerk.

KRUEGER, RONALD P.
Executive. b. St. Louis, MO, Oct. 19, 1940. e. Westminister Coll., 1961. Began working in theatres as a teenager. Assumed presidency Wehrenberg Theatres, 1963. Member: NATO, bd. member; American Film Inst.; Motion Picture Pioneers; Demolay Legion of Honor; Mercantile Bank, bd. member; Big Game Hunters; World Presidents Org. Bd. trustees, Westminster Col. at Fulton, MO. Divan member. Moolah Temple Shrine. Past Master Tuscan Lodge 360 AF & AM. Scottish Rite 32 KCCH. Advisory bd. chmn., Salvation Army. Recipient of the NATO B.V. Sturdivant award for Community Svc. Member & past pres. of Safari Club Intl.

KRUGER, HARDY
Actor, Writer. b. Berlin, Germany, April 12, 1928. Ent. m.p. ind. 1943; on stage since 1945. Starred in approx. 25 German films). Has published 11 books, novels, travelogues.
PICTURES: The One That Got Away, Bachelor of Hearts, The Rest Is Silence (German film of Hamlet), Blind Date, Taxi Pour Tobrouk, Sundays and Cybele, Hatari! (U.S. debut, 1963), Le Gros Coup, Les Pianos Mecaniques (The Uninhibited), Le Chant du Monde, Flight of the Phoenix, The Defector, La Grande Sauterelle, Le Franciscain de Bourges, The Nun of Monza, The Secret of Santa Vittoria, The Battle of Neretva, The Red Tent, Night Hair Child, Death of a Stranger, Barry Lyndon, Paper Tiger, Un Solitaire, Potato Fritz, A Bridge Too Far, L'Autopsie d'un Monstre, The Wild Geese, Society Limited, Wrong Is Right, The Inside Man.
TELEVISION: *Mini-Series:* War and Remembrance. *Series:* The Globe Trotter Parts 1 & 2 (writer, prod; 1986). *Special:* Schlussklappe '45 - Szenen aus dem deutschen Film.

KUDROW, LISA
Actress. e. Vassar College, NY, B.S., in biology. Member of The Groundlings improvisational theatre group, 1989-.
PICTURES: L.A. on $5 a Day, The Unborn, Dance with Death, In the Heat of Passion, Unfaithful, Behind Closed Doors, The Crazysitter, Mother, Hacks, Romy and Michele's High School Reunion, Clockwatchers, The Opposite of Sex, I Dream of Jeannie, Analyze This, All Over the Guy, I've Got 2 Babe, Analyze That, Bark, Marci X., Wonderland.
TELEVISION: *Series:* Bob, Mad About You, Friends (Emmy Award, 1998; Emmy noms. 1995, 1997-2001), Hercules (voice). *Guest:* Cheers, Newhart, Life Goes On, Coach, Flying Blind, Hope & Gloria, The Simpsons (voice).

KUHN, THOMAS G.
Executive/Executive Producer. e. Northwestern U., B.A.; USC, M.B.A. KNBC-TV sales; NBC business affairs; dir. live night time progs. Warner Bros. TV, v.p. prod. TV *Exec. prod.:* Alice, The Awakening Land, Torn Between Two Lovers, The Jayne Mansfield Story, Long Way Home. Pres., RCA Video Prods. Pres., Lightyear Ent., 1987. *Exec. prod.:* Aria, The Return of Swamp Thing, Heaven, The Lemon Sisters, Stories to Remember. With partner Fred Weintraub: The JFK Assassination: The Jim Garrison Tapes, Trouble Bound, Gypsy Eyes, Backstreet Justice, Guinevere, Triplecross, Young Ivanhoe, Young Connecticut Yankee, Undertow, Playboy's Really Naked Truth, Iron Fist, Bruce Lee: Curse of the Dragon, Triplecross, The New Adventures of Robin Hood.

KUREISHI, HANIF
Writer. b. South London, Eng., Dec. 5, 1956. e. King's Coll. (philosophy). At 18, first play presented at Royal Court Theatre where he ushered before becoming writer in residence. Early in career, wrote pornography as Antonia French. Stage and TV plays include: The Mother Country, Outskirts, Borderline and adaptations (Mother Courage). The Rainbow Sign, With Your Tongue Down My Throat (novella) and short stories have been pub. Anglo-Pakistani writer's first s.p. My Beautiful Laundrette earned Acad. Award nom., 1986 and began creative relationship with dir. Stephen Frears.
PICTURES: My Beautiful Laundrette, Sammy and Rosie Get Laid, London Kills Me (also dir.), My Son the Fanatic, Mauvaise passe, Intimacy.
TELEVISION: The Buddha of Suburbia.

KURI, JOHN A.
Producer, Writer. b. Los Angeles, CA, Feb. 16, 1945. Son of set decorator and Disneyland co-designer, Emile Kuri. Began 13 yr. employment with Disney at age 16 in construction and maintenance at Disneyland. Progressed through mgmt. in Park Operations. 1969 transferred to Disney Studios in set decorating. 1973 became art director. 1975 at 20th Century Fox as exec. asst. to prod. Irwin Allen. 1976, formed own co., wrote and prod. both television and motion picture projects. 1979 thru 1982 developed and prod. television in partnership with Ron Howard. 1988 thru 1990 as pres. of Sheffield Ent. developed master broadcasting plan for KCMY TV, Sacramento, CA. Published works: Determined to Live: An American Epic, Remember Wes.
PICTURES: Captive Hearts (prod., co-s.p. 2nd unit dir., co-lyrics.) *Set decorator:* Apple Dumpling Gang, Leadbelly, Report to the Commissioner, Castaway Cowboy, Superdad.
TELEVISION: One More Mountain (prod., writer, 2nd unit dir.; Christopher Award, 1994), Conagher (prod.; Western Heritage Award from Cowboy Hall of Fame), O'Hara (co-creator of series), Airwolf (2nd unit prod., dir.), Skyward (prod., 2nd unit dir.), Golden Halo Award), Skyward Christmas (prod., 2nd unit dir.), Through the Magic Pyramid (assoc. prod., art dir.). Art dir.: The Plutonium Incident, Scared Straight Another Story, Young Love First Love, Marriage is Alive and Well, Little Shots, The Red Pony (and set decorator, Emmy nom., 1973). Set decorator: Michael O'Hara IV, The Mouse Factory (22 episodes).

KURTZ, GARY
Producer, Director. b. Los Angeles, CA, July 27, 1940. e. USC Cinema Sch. Began prof. career during college. Has worked as cameraman, soundman, editor, prod. supervisor and asst. dir. on

documentaries and features. Worked on many low budget features for Roger Corman including: The Terror, Beach Ball, Track of the Vampire, Planet of Blood, The Shooting, Ride in the Whirlwind. Drafted into Marines. Spent 2 yrs. in photo field as cameraman, editor and still photo.
PICTURES: The Hostage (prod. spvr., ed.), Two-Lane Blacktop (line prod.), Chandler (line prod.), American Graffiti (co.-prod.); Star Wars (prod.), The Empire Strikes Back (prod.), The Dark Crystal (prod., 2nd unit dir.), Return to Oz (exec. prod.), Slipstream (prod.) The Steal (prod.), 5-25-77 (prod.).

KURTZ, SWOOSIE
Actress. b. Omaha, NE, September 6, 1944. e. Studied at U. Southern Calif., London Acad. of Music and Dramatic Art.
THEATRE: A History of the American Film (Drama Desk Award), Ah Wilderness (Tony nom.), Who's Afraid of Virginia Woolf? (with Mike Nichols and Elaine May), The Effect of Gamma Rays on Man-in-the Moon Marigolds, Fifth of July (Tony, Outer Critics Circle & Drama Desk Awards), House of Blue Leaves (Tony and Obie Awards), Uncommon Women and Others (Obie & Drama Desk Awards), Hunting Cockroaches (Drama League nom.), Six Degrees of Separation, Lips Together Teeth Apart.
PICTURES: Slap Shot, First Love, Oliver's Story, The World According to Garp, Against All Odds, Wildcats, True Stories, Vice Versa, Bright Lights Big City, Dangerous Liaisons, Stanley and Iris, A Shock to the System, Reality Bites, Storybook, Citizen Ruth, Liar Liar, Outside Ozona, The White River Kid, Cruel Intentions, Sleep Easy, Hutch Rimes, Get Over It, Bubble Boy, The Wild Girls, The Rules of Attraction, Duplex.
TELEVISION: Series: As the World Turns (1971), Mary, Love Sidney (Emmy noms.), Sisters (Emmy & SAG noms.), Suddenly Susan. Movies: Walking Through the Fire, Marriage Is Alive and Well, Mating Season, A Caribbean Mystery, Guilty Conscience, A Time to Live, Baja Oklahoma (Golden Globe nom.), The Image (Emmy & Cable ACE noms.), Terror on Track 9, The Positively True Adventures of the Alleged Texas Cheerleader-Murdering Mom, And the Band Played On (Emmy & Cable Ace noms.), One Christmas, Betrayed: A Story of Three Women, A Promise to Carolyn, Little Girls in Pretty Boxes, My Own Country, More Tales of the City. Specials: Uncommon Women, Fifth of July, House of Blue Leaves, The Visit (Trying Times). Guest: Kojak, Carol & Company (Emmy Award, 1990).

KURYS, DIANE
Director, Writer. b. Lyons, France, Dec. 3, 1948. In 1970 joined Jean-Louis Barrault's theatre group, acted for 8 years on stage, television and film. Adapted and translated staged plays. 1977, wrote screenplay for Dibolo Menthe (Peppermint Soda) which she also directed and co-prod. Film won Prix Louis Deluc, Best Picture. Co-prod. Alexandre Arcady's Coup de Sirocco and Le Grand Pardon.
PICTURES: Dir./Writer: Peppermint Soda (also co-prod.), Cocktail Molotov, Entre Nous, A Man in Love, C'est la vie, Apres L'amour, Six Days Six Nights, Children of the Century.

KUSHNER, DONALD
Producer, Executive. Exec. producer, all programming produced by Kushner Locke; producer, Tron, 1982. Currently co-chairman, co-CEO, & secretary, Kushner-Locke, 1983.
PICTURES: Animalympics, Tron, Nutcracker: The Motion Picture, The Brave Little Toaster, Lady In Waiting, Andre, Dangerous Intentions, Last Gasp, The Adventures of Pinocchio, The Whole Wide World, Shadow of the Night, The Grave, The Last Time I Committed Suicide, Little Ghost, The Incredible Genie, The Secret Kingdom, Girl, Basil, Possums, The Shrunken City, Small Time, Susan's Plan, Ringmaster, Denial, Bone Daddy, Murdercycle, Beowulf, Blooddolls, Freeway II: Confessions of a Trickbaby, But I'm a Cheerleader, The Boy with the X-Ray Eyes, Piking Up the Pieces, The Last Producer, Harvard Man.
TELEVISION: Series: 1st and Ten, Jem. Movies: Your Mother Wears Combat Boots, Sweet Bird of Youth, Carolina Skeletons, Fire in the Dark, Father & Son: Dangerous Relations, Getting Gotti, A Strange Affair, Unlikely Angel, others.

KUSTURICA, EMIR
Director. b. Sarajevo, Yugoslavia, 1955. e. FAMU.
PICTURES: Do You Remember Dolly Bell? (debut, 1981), When Father Was Away on Business (Golden Palme at Cannes Film Fest., 1985), Time of the Gypsies (also co-s.p.), Arizona Dream, Underground (Golden Palme at Cannes Film Fest., 1995), White Cat Black Cat, Super 8 Stories, The Nose.

KWAN, NANCY
Actress. b. Hong Kong, May 19, 1939. Trained as dancer at British Royal Ballet.
PICTURES: The World of Suzie Wong (debut, 1960), Flower Drum Song, The Main Attraction, Tamahine, Fate Is the Hunter, The Wild Affair, Honeymoon Hotel, Arrivederci Baby, Lt. Robin Crusoe USN, The Corrupt Ones, Nobody's Perfect, The Wrecking Crew, The Girl Who Knew Too Much, The McMasters, Girl From Peking, Supercock, The Pacific Connection, Project: Kill, Night Creature, Streets of Hong Kong, Angkor, Walking the Edge, Night Children, Cold Dog Soup, Dragon: The Bruce Lee Story, Mr. P's Dancing Sushi Bar. TELEVISION: Movies: The Last Ninja, Blade in Hong Kong, Miracle Landing.

KWIETNIOWSKI, RICHARD
Director. b. London, England, March 17, 1957.
PICTURES: Alfalfa, Ballad of Reading Gaol, Flames of Passion, Proust's Favorite Fantasy, Cost of Love, Actions Speak Louder Than Words, I Was a Jewish Sex Worker (D.P. only), Love and Death on Long Island (also s.p.), Owning Mahowny.

KWIT, NATHANIEL TROY, JR.
Executive. b. New York, NY, May 29, 1941. e. Cornell U., B.A.; NYU, M.B.A. 1964-68, American Broadcasting Co., Inc., exec. asst. to pres. of ABC Films. 1968-71, National Screen Service Corp., New York branch mgr., asst. genl. sls. mgr. 1971, founder, CEO Audience Marketing, Inc., later acquired by Viacom International as operating subsidiary. 1974 named v.p. marketing services, Warner Bros., Inc. 1979, named v.p. in charge video and special markets division, United Artists Corp.; 1981, named sr. v.p. in chg. UA television, video, special market div. Following acquisition of UA Corp. by MGM in 1981 promoted to pres., dist. & mktg. for MGM/UA Entertainment Co. 1983, pres. & CEO, United Satellite Communications, direct broadcast TV co. 1986, founder, pres. Palladium Entertainment, Inc.

L

LaBUTE, NEIL
Director, Writer. b. Detroit, MI, March 19, 1963. Graduate of Brigham Young University Theatre and Film program.
PICTURES: In the Company of Men, Your Friends & Neighbors, Nurse Betty (dir. only), Possession, The Shape of Things.
TELEVISION: Bash: Latter Day Plays.

LACHMAN, ED
Cinematographer. b. 1948. Son of a Morristown, NJ movie theater owner. e. Ohio U., BFA. Filmed documentaries Ornette: Made in America, Strippers, Huie's Sermon. Assisted Sven Nykvist on King of the Gypsies, Hurricane; Vittorio Storaro on Luna; Robby Muller on The American Friend and They All Laughed. Co-director of photography on Werner Herzog's La Soufriere and Stroszek and Wim Wenders' Lightning Over Water and A Tokyo Story.
PICTURES: Scalpel, Union City, Say Amen Somebody, Little Wars, Split Cherry Tree, Strippers, The Little Sister, Insignificance, Desperately Seeking Susan, True Stories, Making Mr. Right, Chuck Berry: Hail Hail Rock 'n' Roll, Less Than Zero, El Dia Que Me Quieras, Mississippi Masala, Light Sleeper, London Kills Me, My New Gun, My Family/Mi Familia, Selena, Why Do Fools Fall In Love, The Virgin Suicides, The Limey, Erin Brockovich, Sweet November, Simone, Far From Heaven, Bad Santa, Moonlight Mile (photographer).
TELEVISION: Get Your Kicks on Route 66 (dir., cinematography, American Playhouse.), A Gathering of Old Men, Backtrack.

LACK, ANDREW
Executive. b. New York, NY, May 16, 1947. e. Sorbonne, Boston Univ. School of Fine Arts (BFA). Starting in 1976, worked at CBS as prod. for Who's Who, 60 Minutes, CBS Reports. 1981, named sr. prod. of CBS Reports and CBS News correspondent, 1983 became exec. prod. Exec. prod. and creator of Face to Face with Connie Chung, West 57th, Crossroads, Our Times With Bill Moyers. Exec. prod. of Street Stories, specials The 20th Anniversary of Watergate, Malcolm X. 1993, appointed pres. of NBC News. Appointed pres. and CEO of NBC on June 4, 2001. Currently, chairman and CEO of Sony Music Entertainment, Inc. (2003).

LADD, JR., ALAN
Executive. b. Los Angeles, CA, Oct. 22, 1937. Son of late actor Alan Ladd. M. P. agent, Creative Mgmt. Associates, 1963-69.; m.p. prod., 1969-73. Joined 20th Century-Fox in 1973 in chg. of creative affairs in feature div.; promoted to v.p., prod., 1974; 1975, named sr. v.p. for worldwide prod.; 1976, promoted to pres. of 20th Century-Fox Pictures. Resigned & formed The Ladd Co., 1979. 1985, appt. pres. & COO, MGM/UA Ent. Film Corp; appt. chmn. of bd., CEO, MGM Pictures Inc., 1986; resigned 1988. 1989, named co-chmn. Pathe Communications Corp. and chmn., CEO, Pathe Ent.; chmn., & CEO, MGM-Pathe Ent., 1990; chmn. & CEO MGM-Pathe Comm. Co., 1991-92; co-chmn. & co-CEO, MGM, 1992-93. Founded Ladd Pictures.
PICTURES: Prod.: Walking Stick, A Severed Head, Tam Lin, Villian, Zee and Co., Fear Is the Key, Braveheart (Acad. Award), The Phantom, A Very Brady Sequel, The Man in the Iron Mask. Exec. prod.: Nightcomers, Vice Versa, The Brady Bunch Movie.

LADD, CHERYL
Actress. r.n. Cheryl Stoppelmoor. b. Huron, S.D., July 12, 1951. Joined professional Music Shop Band while in high school; after graduation toured with group ending up in Los Angeles. Cast as voice of Melody character in animated Josie and the Pussycats. Studied acting with Milton Katselas. Did TV commercials, small parts in TV. Film debut 1972 in Jamaica Reef (unreleased).
PICTURES: Purple Hearts, Now and Forever, Millennium, Lisa, Poison Ivy, Permanent Midnight, Perfect Little Angels, A Dog of

Flanders.
TELEVISION: *Series*: The Ken Berry "Wow" Show, Charlie's Angels, One West Waikiki. *Specials*: Ben Vereen... His Roots, General Electric's All-Star Anniversary, John Denver and the Ladies; The Cheryl Ladd Special, Looking Back: Souvenirs, Scenes From a Special. *Guest*: Police Woman, Happy Days, Switch. *Movies*: Satan's School for Girls, When She Was Bad, Grace Kelly Story, Romance on the Orient Express, A Death in California, Crossings, Deadly Care, Bluegrass, Kentucky Woman, Jekyll & Hyde, The Fulfillment of Mary Gray, The Girl Who Came Between Them, Crash: The Mystery of Flight 1501, Danielle Steel's Changes, Locked Up: A Mother's Rage, Dead Before Dawn, Broken Promises: Taking Emily Back, Dancing With Danger, The Haunting of Lisa, Kiss & Tell, Tangled Web, Kiss and Tell, Every Mother's Worst Fear, Michael Landon: The Father I Knew, Her Best Friend's Husband.

LADD, DAVID ALAN
Actor, Producer, Motion Picture Executive. b. Los Angeles, CA, Feb. 5, 1947. e. USC. Son of late actor Alan Ladd. Exec. v.p. motion picture prod. at Pathe Entertainment and MGM.
PICTURES: *Actor*: The Big Land, The Proud Rebel (Golden Globe Award), The Sad Horse, A Dog of Flanders, Raymie, Misty, R.P.M., Catlow, Deathline (Raw Meat), The Klansman, The Day of the Locust, Wild Geese. *Producer*: The Serpent and the Rainbow, The Mod Squad, Hart's War, A Guy Thing, Godspeed Lawrence Mann.
TELEVISION: *Guest*: Zane Gray Theatre, Wagon Train, Pursuit, Ben Casey, Gunsmoke, Love American Style (pilot), Kojak, Emergency, Tom Sawyer, Bonanza, Quest, Police Story, Medical Story, etc. *Producer*: When She Was Bad, ABC Variety specials.

LADD, DIANE
Actress. r.n. Diane Rose Lanier. b. Meridian, MS. Daughter is actress Laura Dern. e. St. Aloysius Acad.; trained for stage with Curt Conway and Frank Corsaro. Member of Actors Studio. Worked as model, singer and as Copacabana nightclub dancer. At 17 in touring co. of Hatful of Rain. NY debut: Orpheus Descending.
THEATRE: Carry Me Back to Morningside Heights, One Night Stands of a Noisy Passenger. The Wall, The Goddess, The Fantastiks, Women Speak, Texas Trilogy; Lu Ann Hampton Laverty, Love Letters.
PICTURES: Wild Angels (debut, 1966), Rebel Rousers, The Reivers, Macho Calahan, WUSA, White Lightning, Chinatown, Alice Doesn't Live Here Anymore (Acad. Award nom.), Embryo, All Night Long, Sweetwater, The Reivers, Something Wicked This Way Comes, Black Widow, Plain Clothes, National Lampoon's Christmas Vacation, Wild at Heart (Acad. Award nom.), A Kiss Before Dying, Rambling Rose (Acad. Award nom.), The Cemetery Club, Forever, Carnosaur, Hold Me Thrill Me Kiss Me, Father Hood, Ghost of Mississippi, Primary Colors, Can't Be Heaven, 28 Days, The Law of Enclosures, Redemption of the Ghost, More Than Puppy Love, Daddy and Them, The Virgin, Rain.
TELEVISION: *Movies*: The Devil's Daughter, Black Beauty, Thaddeus Rose and Eddie, Willa, Guyana Tragedy, Desperate Lives, Grace Kelly, Crime of Innocence, Bluegrass, Rock Hudson, The Lookalike, Shadow of a Doubt, Hush Little Baby, Mrs. Munck (also dir., writer), The Staircase, Late Last Night, Best Actress, Sharing the Secret, Christy: The Movie, Aftermath, Damaged Care. *Mini-Series*: Christy, Choices of the Heart, Part II: A New Beginning, Living With the Dead. *Guest*: Hazel, Gunsmoke, City of Angels, The Love Boat, Dr. Quinn Medicine Woman (pilot), Grace Under Fire, Touched By An Angel. *Series*: The Secret Storm, Alice (Golden Globe Award). *Special*: The Gift.

LAFFERTY, PERRY
Executive. b. Davenport, IA, Oct. 3, 1920. e. Yale U. With CBS-TV as v.p., programs, Hollywood, 1965-76. Sr. v.p., programs and talent, west coast, for NBC Entertainment, 1979-85.
TELEVISION: Maybe Baby (exec. prod.), Murder C.O.D.

LaGRAVENESE, RICHARD
Writer. b. Brooklyn, NY, Oct.30, 1959.
PICTURES: Rude Awakening, The Fisher King (also actor, Acad. Award nom.), The Ref (also prod.), A Little Princess, The Bridges of Madison County, Unstrung Heroes, The Mirror has Two Faces, The Kiss (also dir.), The Horse Whisperer, Living Out Loud, Beloved, Blow (actor only).

LAHTI, CHRISTINE
Actress. b. Birmingham, MI, April 4, 1950. m. dir. Thomas Schlamme. e. U. of Michigan. Trained for stage at Herbert Berghof Studios with Uta Hagen. TV commercials. As a mime, performed with Edinburgh Scotland's Travis Theatre. N.Y. stage debut in The Woods, 1978.
THEATRE: The Zinger, Hooter (Playwrights Horizon), Loose Ends, Division St., The Woods (Theatre World Award), Scenes and Revelations, Present Laughter, The Lucky Spot, Summer and Smoke (LA), The Heidi Chronicles, Three Hotels.
PICTURES: ...And Justice For All (debut, 1979), Whose Life Is It Anyway?, Ladies and Gentlemen the Fabulous Stains, Swing Shift (Acad. Award nom.), Just Between Friends, Housekeeping,

Stacking, Running on Empty, Miss Firecracker (cameo), Gross Anatomy, Funny About Love, The Doctor, Leaving Normal, Hideaway, Pie in the Sky, Judgment Day: The Ellie Nesler Story. *Director*: Lieberman In Love (short; Academy Award).
TELEVISION: *Movies*: Dr. Scorpion, The Last Tenant, The Henderson Monster, The Executioner's Song, Love Lives On, Single Bars Single Women, No Place Like Home, Crazy From the Heart, The Fear Inside, The Good Fight, The Four Diamonds, A Weekend in the Country, Subway Stories: Tales from the Underground, Hope, An American Daughter, The Pilot's Wife, Oooph!, Gisella Perl. *Mini-Series*: Amerika.*Series*: Chicago Hope (Golden Globe Award, Emmy Award, 1998).

LAI, FRANCIS
Composer. b. France, April 26, 1932.
PICTURES: A Man and a Woman, I'll Never Forget What's 'is Name, The Bobo, Three Into Two Won't Go, Hello Goodbye, Hannibal Brooks, The Games, Mayerling, House of Cards, Rider on the Rain, Love Story (Academy Award, 1970), Le Petit Matin, Another Man, Another Chance, Wanted: Babysitter, Bilitis, The Good and the Bad, Widow's Nest, Cat and Mouse, The Body of My Enemy, Emmanuelle 2; The Forbidden Room, International Velvet, Oliver's Story, Passion Flower Hotel, Robert and Robert, The Small Timers, By the Blood Brothers, Beyond the Reef, Bolero, A Second Chance, Edith and Marcel, My New Partner, Marie, A Man and a Woman: 20 Years Later, Bernadette, Itinerary of a Spoiled Child., Der Aten (The Spirit), La Belle Histoire, Le Provincial, Keys to Paradise, Il y a des jours... et des lunes, Stranger in the House, I'll Be Going Now, All That...For This?, The Thief and the Liar, Les Miserables, Men Women: A User's Manual, My Best Friend's Wedding, One 4 All.

LAKE, RICKI
Actress. b. New York, NY, Sept. 21, 1968. e. Manhattan's Professional Children's School. Won role in Hairspray while attending Ithaca Col. Theatre in LA: A Girl's Guide to Chaos.
PICTURES: Hairspray (debut, 1988), Working Girl, Starlight: A Musical Movie, Cookie, Cry-Baby, Last Exit to Brooklyn, Where the Day Takes You, Inside Monkey Zetterland, Cabin Boy, Serial Mom, Skinner, Mrs. Winterbourne, Cecil B. Demented, In Bad Taste.
TELEVISION: *Series*: China Beach, Ricki Lake (synd. talk show), The King of Queens. *Movies*: Babycakes, The Chase, Based on an Untrue Story, Jackie's Back!, Murder She Purred: A Mrs. Murphy Mystery, Jackie's Back!

LAM, RINGO
Director. e. York University, Toronto. Started training as an actor in 1973 but switched to production as asst. until 1976, then as TV dir. until 1978. In 1981 he returned to Hong Kong and two years later made his dir. debut with Esprit D'Amour.
PICTURES: The Other Side of a Gentleman, Cupid One, Aces Go Places IV: Mad Mission, City on Fire, Prison on Fire, School on Fire, Wild Search, Undeclared War, Touch and Go, Prison on Fire II, Full Contact, Twin Dragons, Burning Paradise (Rape of the Red Temple), The Adventurers, The Exchange, Full Alert, The Suspect, Victim, Replicant, The Monk, Finding Mr. Perfect.

LAMAS, LORENZO
Actor. b. Los Angeles, CA, Jan. 20, 1958. e. Santa Monica City Coll. Son of the late actor Fernando Lamas and actress Arlene Dahl. Studied at Tony Barr's Film Actors Workshop (Burbank Studios). Appeared on commercials for Diet Coke, BVD, Coors.
PICTURES: Grease, Tilt, Take Down, Body Rock, Snakeater, Night of the Warrior, Snakeater II, Final Impact, Snakeater III: His Law, Killing Streets, The Swordsman, Bounty Tracker, Final Round, Bad Blood, Midnight Man, Gladiator Cop, CIA II Target: Alexa, Terminal Justice, Mask of Death, Black Dawn, The Rage, Undercurrent, Back to Even, The Muse.
TELEVISION: *Series*: California Fever, Secrets of Midland Heights, Falcon Crest, Dancin' to the Hits (host), Renegade, Air American, The Immortal. *Guest*: The Love Boat, Switch, Sword of Justice, The Hitchhiker, Dear John. *Movies*: Detour to Terror, Snakeeater, La Carne e il diavolo

LAMBERT, CHRISTOPHER (also CHRISTOPHE)
Actor, Producer. b. New York , NY, Mar. 29, 1957; reared in Geneva; parents French. Studied at Paris Conservatoire Drama Academy.
PICTURES: La Bar du Telephone (debut, 1981), Putain d'Historie d'Amour, Legitime Violence, Greystoke: The Legend of Tarzan Lord of the Apes, Love Songs, Subway (Cesar Award), Highlander, I Love You, The Sicilian, Love Dream, To Kill a Priest, Un Plan d'Enfer, Why Me?, Highlander 2: The Quickening, Priceless Beauty, Knight Moves, Fortress, Gunmen, Road Flower, Highlander III: The Sorcerer, The Hunted, Nine Months (exec. prod. only), Mortal Kombat, North Star (also exec. prod.), When Saturday Comes (exec. prod. only), Adrenalin, Hercule et Sherlock, Nirvana, Arlette, Mean Guns, Operation Splitsville (also prod.), Beowulf, Resurrection (also prod., story), Gideon (also prod.), Fortress 2, Highlander: Endgame, Druids, The Point Men, The Piano Player, Absolon.

LAMBERT, MARY
Director. b. Arkansas. e. attended U. of Denver, Rhode Island Sch. of Design where began making short films. Worked in variety of prod. jobs before moving to L.A. and directing TV commercials and music videos (includ. Madonna's Material Girl, Like a Virgin, Like a Prayer, others for Sting, Janet Jackson and Mick Jagger).
PICTURES: Siesta, Pet Sematary, Pet Sematary 2, Clubland, The In Crowd, In Between.
TELEVISION: *Movie*: Dragstrip Girl, Face of Evil, My Stepson My Lover, Strange Frequency.

LAMBERT, VERITY
Producer. b. London, England, Nov. 27. Ent. TV 1961; prod. Dr. Who, Adam Adamant Lives, Detective, Somerset Maugham (all BBC series). Since 1971: (series), Budgie, Between The Wars. 1974: Appt. controller of Drama, Thames Television. 1979: Chief exec. Euston Films. 1983: Director of Production Thorn EMI Films Ltd. Relinquished her position as controller of Drama Thames Television and retained position as chief exec., Euston Films. Became indep. prod. developing projects for film and TV incl. BBC. Founded own company, Cinema Verity Ltd., 1985.
PICTURES: Link, Morons from Outer Space, Restless Natives, Dreamchild, Not for Publication, Clockwise, A Cry in the Dark.
TELEVISION: May to December, The Boys from the Bush, Sleepers, So Haunt Me, Comics, Coasting, Sam Saturday, Running Late, Class Act, She's Out, Heavy Weather. *Series*: Doctor Who, Budgie, Rock Follies, Quatermass, Minder, Widows 2, GBH, El Dorado, She's Out, Jonathan Creek, The Cazalets.

LAMONT, PETER
Production designer.
PICTURES: Watch Your Stern, Night of the Eagle, This Sporting Life, On Her Majesty's Secret Service, Daimonds Are Forever, Sleuth, Live and Let Die, The Dove, The Main with the Golden Gun, Inside Out, Seven-Per-Cent Solution, The Spy Who Loved Me, The Boys from Brazil, Moonraker, For Your Eyes Only, Octopussy, Top Secret!, A View to a Kill, Aliens, The Living Daylights, Consuming Passions, Licence to Kill, Eve of Destruction, The Taking of Beverly Hills, True Lies, GoldenEye, Titanic (Acad. Award, Best Art Dir., LA Film Crits. Award, Best Prod. Design, 1997), Wing Commander, The World is Not Enough, Die Another Day.

LANDAU, JON
Producer. b. New York, NY.
PICTURES: *Prod.*: Campus Man (also unit prod. mgr.), Honey I Shrunk the Kids, Dick Tracy (also unit prod. mgr.), Titanic (Acad. Award, Best Pic., 1997), Mr. Hughes, Solaris. *Unit prod. mgr.*: Manhunter, F/X, Making Mr. Right.
TELEVISION: Winter Break.

LANDAU, JULIET
Actress. Father is actor Martin Landau.
PICTURES: The Grifters, Pump Up the Volume, Neon City, Direct Hit, Ed Wood, Theodore Rex, Ravager, Citizens of Perpetual Indulgence, Carlo's Wake,Citizens of Perpetual Indulgence, Freedom Park, Repossessed.
TELEVISION: *Series*: Buffy the Vampire Slayer, Angel. *Guest*: Parker Lewis Can't Lose, Millennium, La Femme Nikita.

LANDAU, MARTIN
Actor. b. Brooklyn, NY, June 20, 1930. e. Pratt Inst., Art Students League, Was cartoon and staff artist on NY Daily News; studied at Actors Studio. Daughter is actress Juliet Landau. Recipient: Lifetime Achievement Awards from Houston Film Fest. and Charleston Film Fest. Spoken word recording, Harry Truman: The journey to Independence, 1997 (Grammy nom.).
THEATER: Middle of the Night, Uncle Vanya, Stalag 17, Wedding Breakfast, First Love, The Goat Song.
PICTURES: Pork Chop Hill (debut, 1959), North by Northwest, The Gazebo, Stagecoach to Dancer's Rock, Cleopatra, The Hallelujah Trail, The Greatest Story Ever Told, Decision at Midnight, Alien Attack, Nevada Smith, They Call Me Mister Tibbs, Situation Normal But All Fouled Up, A Town Called Hell, Black Gunn, Strange Shadows in an Empty Room, Meteor, Destination Moonbase Alpha, Without Warning, Trial By Terror, Cosmic Princess, Journey Through the Black Sun, The Last Word, The Return, Alone in the Dark, The Being, Access Code, Treasure Island, Run ... If You Can, Death Blow, W.A.R.: Women Against Rape, Sweet Revenge, Cyclone, Real Bullets, Empire State, Delta Fever, Tucker: The Man and His Dream (Acad. Award nom.), Crimes and Misdemeanors (Golden Globe Award, Acad. Award nom.), Paint It Black, Firehead, Tipperary, The Color of Evening, Mistress, Eye of the Stranger, Sliver, Intersection, Time Is Money, Ed Wood (Academy Award, best supporting actor, 1994; also Golden Globe, SAG, American Comedy, NY Film Critics, LA Film Critics, Natl. Society of Film Critics, Boston Film Critics, Chicago Film Critics & Texas Film Critics Awards), City Hall, Pinocchio, B.A.P.S., The Elevator, The X Files: Fight the Future, Rounders, The Joy Riders, Edtv, The New Adventures of Pinocchio, Sleepy Hollow, Carlo's Wake, Ready to Rumble, Very Mean Men, Shiner, The Majestic, An Existential Affair.
TELEVISION: *Series*: Mission Impossible (1966-69; 3 Emmy noms., Golden Globe Award), Space 1999, In The Beginning, Haven, Rosebud. *Movies*: Welcome Home Johnny Bristol, Savage, The Death of Ocean View Park, Harlem Globetrotters on Gilligan's Island, Fall of the House of Usher, Max and Helen

(ACE Award nom.), The Neon Empire, By Dawn's Early Light (ACE Award nom.), Something to Live For: The Alison Gertz Story, Legacy of Lies (ACE Award), 12:01, Bonanno: A Godfather's Story. Numerous guest appearances.

LANDES, MICHAEL
Executive, Producer.. b. Bronx, NY, Feb. 4, 1939. e. Fairleigh Dickinson, B.A., 1961; Rutgers, J.D., 1964; NYU, L.L.M., 1965. Bars passed: NJ 1965, NY 1966, U.S. Supreme Ct. 1969. 17 years of corporate law and financing experience as sr. partner in law firm of Hahn and Hessen. Co-chmn of The ALMI Group formed, 1978. Co-chmn. & CEO of Almi Pictures Inc. formed, 1982. 1986, Almi sold its 97-screen RKO Century Warner Theatre chain to Cineplex Odeon. 1986, purchased Video Shack Inc. assets and formed RKO Warner Video, Inc.; Chmn since inception. 1988, became chmn, Damon Creations, Inc. which merged with Enro Holding Corp. and Enro Shirt Co. into Damon Creations. Sold Damon, 1988. Chmn./CEO, RKO Warner Intl. Ltd. a video franchisor and chmn./CEO of The Lexington Group Ltd., org. 1990. Member: World Presidents Organization (WPO). Chief Executives Organization (CEO); Association for a Better New York; bd. of dirs. Motion Picture Pioneers; Academy of Motion Picture Arts and Sciences; bd. of dirs. Periwinkle Theatre Productions.
PICTURES: Spaceship, The Big Score, I Am the Cheese, Rosebud Beach Hotel, Night Stalker, B.C. Roch, The Bostonians.

LANDIS, JOHN
Director, Producer, Writer, Actor. b. Chicago, IL, Aug. 3, 1950. Raised in Los Angeles. Started in mailroom at 20th Century-Fox, then worked in Europe as prod. asst. and stuntman before making first low-budget film, Schlock.
PICTURES: *Director &/or Actor*: Schlock (also writer), The Kentucky Fried Movie, National Lampoon's Animal House, The Blues Brothers (also co-s.p.), An American Werewolf in London (also s.p.), Trading Places, Twilight Zone—The Movie (sequence dir., also s.p., co-prod.), Into the Night, Spies Like Us, Clue (co-exec. prod., co-story only), Three Amigos!, Amazon Women on the Moon (sequence dir.; also co-exec. prod.), Coming to America, Oscar, Innocent Blood, Beverly Hills Cop III, The Stupids, Battle for the Planet of the Apes, Death Race 2000, 1941, The Muppets Take Manhattan, Spontaneous Combustion, Darkman, Diva Las Vegas, Voice of a Stranger, Sleepwalkers, Venice/Venice, The Silence of the Hams., Vampirella, Mad City, Susan's Plan, Blues Brothers 2000.
TELEVISION: *Series*: *Exec. prod.*: Dream On (also. dir., actor). Topper (also dir.), Weird Science, Sliders, Campus Cops. *Movie*: Psycho IV (actor), Quicksilver Highway, Slasher (documentary). *Mini-series*: The Stand. *Specials*: B.B. King Into the Night, Disneyland's 35th Anniversary Celebration. *Videos*: Thriller, Black or White (both for Michael Jackson).

LANDSBURG, ALAN
Executive, Producer, Writer. b. New York, NY, May 10, 1933. e. NYU. Producer for NBC News Dept., 1951-59; producer-writer, CBS, 1959-60; exec. prod., Wolper Productions/ Metromedia Producers Corp., 1961-70; chairman, The Alan Landsburg Company, 1970-present.
PICTURES: *Co-exec. prod.*: Jaws 3-D, Porky's II: The Next Day.
TELEVISION: *Exec. prod.*: Biography, National Geographic Specials (1965-70): The Undersea World of Jacques Cousteau; In Search of..., That's Incredible. *Movies*: Adam, Fear on Trial, Parent Trap II, Adam: His Song Continues, The George McKenna Story, Long Gone, Strange Voices, Bluegrass, A Place at the Table, Too Young the Hero, A Stoning in Fulham County, High Risk, Destined to Live, Quiet Victory: The Charlie Wedemeyer Story, The Ryan White Story, Unspeakable Acts (co-exec. prod., writer), A Mother's Right: The Elizabeth Morgan Story (writer), The Hunter (writer), The Lottery, Country Justice.

LANE, DIANE
Actress. b. New York, NY, Jan. 2, 1965. Acted in stage classics (Medea, Electra, As You Like It) at La Mama Experimental Theatre Club, NY. Addtl. stage: The Cherry Orchard, Agamemnon, Runaways, Twelfth Night.
PICTURES: A Little Romance (debut, 1979), Touched by Love, National Lampoon Goes to the Movies, Cattle Annie and Little Britches, Six Pack, Ladies and Gentlemen the Fabulous Stains, The Outsiders, Rumble Fish, Streets of Fire, The Cotton Club, The Big Town, Lady Beware, Priceless Beauty, Vital Signs, My New Gun, Chaplin, Knight Moves, Indian Summer, Judge Dredd, Wild Bill, Mad Dog Time, Jack, Murder at 1600, The Only Thrill, A Walk on the Moon, The Virginian, My Dog Skip, The Perfect Storm, Hardball, The Glass House, Just Like Mona, Unfaithful, Searching for Debra Winger, Under the Tuscan Sun.
TELEVISION: *Movies*: Child Bride of Short Creek, Miss All-American Beauty, Descending Angel, Oldest Living Confederate Widow Tells All, Grace and Glorie. *Special*: Edith Wharton's Summer. *Guest*: Fallen Angels. *Mini-Series*: Lonesome Dove.

LANE, NATHAN
Actor. r.n. Joseph Lane. b. Jersey City, NJ, Feb. 3, 1956. Received 1992 Obie Award for Sustained Excellence in Off-B'way Theatre.
THEATRE: *B'way*: Present Laughter (Drama Desk nom.), Merlin, The Wind in the Willows, Some Americans Abroad, On Borrowed Time, Guys & Dolls (Drama Desk & Outer Critics Circle Awards; Tony nom.), Laughter on the 23rd Floor, Love! Valour! Compassion! (Drama Desk, Outer Critics Circle and

Obie Awards; also Off-B'way), A Funny Thing Happened On The Way To The Forum (Tony Award), The Producers. *Off-B'way*: A Midsummer Night's Dream, Measure for Measure, The Merry Wives of Windsor, She Stoops to Conquer, Claptrap, The Common Pursuit (Dramalogue Award), In a Pig's Valise, The Film Society, Uncounted Blessings, Hidden in This Picture, Love, The Lisbon Traviata (also L.A.; Drama Desk, Lucille Lortel, LA Drama Critics Circle & Dramalogue Awards), Bad Habits, Lips Together Teeth Apart (also L.A.).
PICTURES: Ironweed (debut, 1987), Joe Vs. the Volcano, The Lemon Sisters, He Said She Said, Frankie and Johnny, Life With Mikey, Addams Family Values, The Lion King (voice), Jeffrey (American Comedy Award nom.), The Birdcage (Golden Globe nom., American Comedy Award, SAG award), Mouse Hunt, Trixie, The Lion King II: Simba's Pride, Love's Labour's Lost, Isn't She Great, Get Bruce (cameo), At First Sight, Titan A.E. (voice), Trixie, Stuart Little 2 (voice), Nicholas Nickleby.
TELEVISION: *Movies*: Hallmark Hall of Fame's The Boys Next Door, Timon and Pumba (Emmy Award), Merry Christmas George Bailey, The Man Who Came to Dinner, Laughter on the 23rd Floor. *Specials*: Alice in Wonderland, The Last Mile, Co-host 1995 Tony Awards, 1995 Kennedy Center Honors, Host 1996 Tony Awards (American Comedy Award nom.). *Series*: One of the Boys, Encore! Encore! *Guest*: The Days and Nights of Molly Dodd, Miami Vice, Frasier (Emmy nom., American Comedy Award nom.), Sex and the City.

LANG, OTTO
Producer, Director. b. Tesanj, Austria (now Yugoslavia), Jan. 21, 1908. e. Salzburg, Austria. Four Academy Award nominations for Cinemascope Specials, Twentieth Century-Fox Film Corp.
PICTURES: *Dir.*: Search for Paradise. *Prod.*: Call Northside 777, Five Fingers, White Witch Doctor. *Assoc. prod*: Tora! Tora! Tora! TELEVISION: Man from U.N.C.L.E., Daktari, Iron Horse, Cheyenne, Dick Powell Show, Zane Gray Theatre, Ann Sothern Show, Rifleman, Bat Masterson, Seahunt, The Deputy, Surfside 6, Hawaiian Eye. Prod. Twentieth Century Fox Hour. *Dir.*: Man and the Challenge, Aquanauts, World of Giants, The Legend of Cortez, Beethoven: Ordeal and Triumph, Saga of Western Man.

LANG, STEPHEN
Actor. b. Queens, NY, July 11, 1952. e. Swarthmore Col. Professional debut 1974 at Washington D.C.'s Folger Theatre.
THEATRE: *NY*: Rosencrantz and Guildenstern Are Dead, Henry V, Bloomsday on Broadway, The Shadow of a Gun, Saint Joan, Hamlet, Johnny on the Spot, Death of a Salesman, Barbarians, The Winter's Tale, A Few Good Men, The Speed of Darkness.
PICTURES: Twice in a Lifetime (debut, 1985), Band of the Hand, Manhunter, Project X, Last Exit to Brooklyn, The Hard Way, Another You, Guilty As Sin, Gettysburg, Tombstone, Tall Tale, The Amazing Panda Adventure, The Shadow Conspiracy, An Occasional Hell, Fire Down Below, Story of a Bad Boy, Trixie, The Proposal, After the Storm, D-Tox, Gods and Generals.
TELEVISION: *Series*: Crime Story, The Fugitive. *Movies*: King of America, Death of a Salesman, Stone Pillow, Babe Ruth, Taking Back My Life: The Nancy Ziegenmeyer Story, Darkness Before Dawn, Murder Between Friends, A Season of Hope, The Possession of Michael D., The Phantoms, Strangers, Escape: Human Cargo, A Town Has Turned to Dust, At the Mercy of a Stranger. *Specials*: Anyone for Tennyson?, The Mother.

LANGE, HOPE
Actress. b. Redding Ridge, CT, Nov. 28, 1936. e. Reed Coll., Portland, OR; Barmore Jr. Coll., N.Y. Parents: John Lange, musician and Minnette Buddecke Lange, actress. Prof. stage debut in The Patriots on Broadway
THEATRE: The Hot Corner, Same Time Next Year, The Supporting Cast.
PICTURES: Bus Stop (debut, 1956), The True Story of Jesse James, Peyton Place (Acad. Award nom.), The Young Lions, In Love and War, The Best of Everything, Wild in the Country, Pocketful of Miracles, Love Is a Ball, Jigsaw, Death Wish, I Am the Cheese, The Prodigal, A Nightmare on Elm Street Part 2, Blue Velvet, Tune in Tomorrow, Clear and Present Danger, Just Cause.
TELEVISION: *Series*: The Ghost and Mrs. Muir (2 Emmy Awards: 1969, 1970), The New Dick Van Dyke Show, Knight and Dave. *Movies*: Crowhaven Farm, That Certain Summer (Emmy nom.), The 500 Pound Jerk, I Love You— Goodbye, Fer-de-Lance, The Secret Night Caller, Love Boat II, Like Normal People, The Day Christ Died, Beulah Land, Pleasure Palace, Private Sessions, Dead Before Dawn, Cooperstown. Special: A Family Tree (Trying Times), Before He Wakes, AMC Backstory: Bus Stop. *Mini-Series*: The Henry Ford Story: Man and the Machine, Message from Nam. Guest: Murder She Wrote.

LANGE, JESSICA
Actress. b. Cloquet, MN, Apr. 20, 1949. e. U. of Minnesota. Left to study mime 2 years under Etienne Decroux in Paris. Dancer, Opera Comique, Paris; model with Wilhelmina, N.Y. Worked in experimental theatre in New York. Broadway debut 1992 in A Streetcar Named Desire (Theatre World Award).
PICTURES: King Kong (debut, 1976), All That Jazz, How to Beat the High Cost of Living, The Postman Always Rings Twice,

Frances, Tootsie (Academy Award, best supporting actress, 1982), Country (also co-prod.), Sweet Dreams, Crimes of the Heart, Far North, Everybody's All-American, Music Box, Men Don't Leave, Cape Fear, Night and the City, Blue Sky (Acad. Award, 1994), Losing Isaiah, Rob Roy, A Thousand Acres, Hush, Cousin Bette, Titus, Prozac Nation, Normal, Masked & Anonymous, Big Fish..
TELEVISION: *Special*: Cat on a Hot Tin Roof. *Movies*: O Pioneers!, A Streetcar Named Desire (Golden Globe, 1996).

LANGELLA, FRANK
Actor. b. Bayonne, NJ, Jan. 1, 1938. Studied acting at Syracuse U.; later in regional repertory, summer stock, and On- and Off-B'way. Joined Lincoln Ctr. Rep. Co., 1963.
THEATRE: *NY*: The Immoralist (Off-B'way debut, 1963), Benito Cereno, The Old Glory (Obie Award), Good Day (Obie Award), The White Devil (Obie Award), Long Day's Journey Into Night, Yerma, Seascape (B'way debut, 1975; Tony Award), Dracula, A Cry of Players, Cyrano de Bergerac, The Tooth of the Crime, Ring Around the Moon, Amadeus, Passion, Design for Living, Sherlock's Last Case, The Tempest, Booth. *L.A.*: The Devils, Les Liaisons Dangereuses, My Fair Lady, Scenes From an Execution.
PICTURES: Diary of a Mad Housewife (debut, 1970), The Twelve Chairs, The Deadly Trap, The Wrath of God, Dracula, Those Lips Those Eyes, Sphinx, The Men's Club, Masters of the Universe, And God Created Woman, True Identity, 1492: Conquest of Paradise, Body of Evidence, Dave, Brainscan, Junior, Bad Company, Cutthroat Island, Eddie, Lolita, I'm Losing You, Small Soldiers, The Ninth Gate, Stardom, Sweet November.
TELEVISION: *Specials*: Benito Cereno, The Good Day, The Ambassador, The Sea Gull, The American Woman: Portrait in Courage, Eccentricities of a Nightingale, Sherlock Holmes, Fortitude (Kurt Vonnegut's Monkey House). *Movies*: The Mark of Zorro, Liberty, Doomsday Gun, Cry Baby Lane. *Series*: The Beast.

LANGFORD, FRANCES
Singer, Actress. b. Lakeland, FL, April 4, 1913. e. Southern Coll. Stage experience in vaudeville, nightclubs, national radio programs.
PICTURES: Every Night at Eight, Collegiate, Broadway Melody of 1936, Palm Springs, Born to Dance, The Hit Parade, Hollywood Hotel, Dreaming Out Loud, Too Many Girls, The Hit Parade of 1941, All-American Coed, Mississippi Gambler, Yankee Doodle Dandy, Cowboy in Manhattan, This Is the Army, Never a Dull Moment, Career Girl, The Girl Rush, Dixie Jamboree, Radio Stars on Parade, Bamboo Blonde, Make Mine Laughs, People Are Funny, Deputy Marshall, Purple Heart Diary, The Glenn Miller Story.

LANGNER, PHILIP
Producer. b. New York, NY, Aug. 24, 1926. e. Yale U. President of The Theatre Guild and Theatre Guild Films, Inc. Producer the Westport Country Playhouse 1947-53. Joined The Theatre Guild 1954.
THEATRE: The Matchmaker, Bells Are Ringing, The Tunnel of Love, Sunrise at Campobello, A Majority of One, The Unsinkable Molly Brown, A Passage to India, Seidman and Son, The Royal Hunt of the Sun, The Homecoming, Absurd Person Singular, Golda.
PICTURES: *Producer*: The Pawnbroker, Slaves, Born to Win. Associate Prod.: Judgment at Nuremberg, A Child Is Waiting.

LANSBURY, ANGELA
Actress. b. London, England, Oct. 16, 1925. Brothers are producers Bruce and Edgar Lansbury. e. South Hampstead Sch. for Girls, England; Acad. of Music, London; Feagin Dramatic Sch., N.Y. Mother was actress Moyna Macgill. To NY 1940 to study drama. Signed to contract by MGM, 1944. Exercise and lifestyle video: Positive Moves, 1988. *Book*: Positive Moves, 1990.
THEATRE: *B'way*: Hotel Paradiso (NY debut, 1957), A Taste of Honey, Anyone Can Whistle, Mame (Tony Award, 1966), Dear World (Tony Award, 1969), Prettybelle (closed out of town), All Over, Gypsy (Tony Award, 1975), Hamlet, The King and I, Sweeney Todd: The Demon Barber of Fleet Street (Tony Award, 1979), A Little Family Business, Mame (1983 revival).
PICTURES: Gaslight (debut, 1944; Acad. Award nom.), National Velvet, The Picture of Dorian Gray (Acad. Award nom.), The Harvey Girls, The Hoodlum Saint, The Private Affairs of Bel Ami, Till the Clouds Roll By, If Winter Comes, Tenth Avenue Angel, State of the Union, The Three Musketeers, The Red Danube, Samson and Delilah, Kind Lady, Mutiny, Remains to Be Seen, The Purple Mask, A Lawless Street, The Court Jester, Please Murder Me, The Key Man (A Life at Stake), The Long Hot Summer, The Reluctant Debutante, The Summer of the 17th Doll (Season of Passion), The Dark at the Top of the Stairs, A Breath of Scandal, Blue Hawaii, All Fall Down, The Manchurian Candidate (Acad. Award nom.), In the Cool of the Day, The World of Henry Orient, Dear Heart, The Greatest Story Ever Told, Harlow, The Amorous Adventures of Moll Flanders, Mister Buddwing, Something for Everyone, Bedknobs and Broomsticks, Death on the Nile, The Lady Vanishes, The Mirror Crack'd, The Last Unicorn (voice), The Pirates of Penzance, The Company of Wolves, Beauty and the Beast (voice), Beauty and the Beast:

The Enchanted Christmas (voice), Anastasia (voice), Fantasia 2000, Forever Hollywood, Broadway: The Golden Age by the Legends Who Were There, The Last Unicorn.
TELEVISION: *Specials*: Sweeney Todd, Elizabeth Taylor: England's Other Elizabeth. *Movies*: Little Gloria... Happy at Last, The Gift of Love: A Christmas Story, The First Olympics: Athens 1896, A Talent for Murder, Lace, Rage of Angels: The Story Continues, Shootdown, The Shell Seekers, The Love She Sought, Mrs. Harris Goes to Paris, Mrs. Santa Claus, Murder She Wrote: South by Southwest, The Unexpected Mrs. Pollifax, Murder She Wrote: A Story to Die For, Murder She Wrote: The Last Free Man, AMC Backstory: The Long Hot Summer. *Series*: Pantomime Quiz, Murder She Wrote (also exec. prod.). *Guest*: Robert Montgomery Presents, Four Star Playhouse, Studio 57, Playhouse 90, GE Theatre, Fireside Theatre, Lux Video Theatre, Revlon Mirror Theatre, Ford Theatre, Schlitz Playhouse of the Stars, Stage 7, Front Row Center, Screen Directors Playhouse, Eleventh Hour, The Man from U.N.C.L.E., Climax, The Perry Como Show, The Julie Andrews Hour.

LANSBURY, BRUCE
Executive. b. London, England, Jan. 12, 1930. Brother of Angela and twin Edgar. e. UCLA. Mother was actress Moyna Macgill. Writer, prod. KABC-TV, Los Angeles, 1957-59; joined CBS-TV, 1959, was ass't. dir., program dev., Hollywood, director for daytime and nighttime programs, and v.p., programs, New York; 1964-66, indep. prod.; Broadway stage; 1966-69 producer, Wild Wild West, CBS series; 1969-72, prod. Mission: Impossible, Paramount Movies of Week; then v.p., creative affairs, Paramount TV. Retired.
TELEVISION: Great Adventure (series; prod.), Wings of the Water (exec. prod.), Murder She Wrote.

LANSBURY, EDGAR
Producer, Director, Designer. b. London, England, Jan. 12, 1930. e. UCLA. Brother of Angela and Bruce Lansbury. Started career as scenic designer and art dir. 1955-60, art dir., CBS; 1962-63, exec. art dir. prod. for WNDT-TV, educational station.
THEATRE: *Producer–B'way*: The Subject Was Roses, That Summer That Fall, Promenade, Waiting for Godot, Long Day's Journey into Night, Godspell, Gypsy, The Night That Made America Famous, American Buffalo, Amphigorey: The Musical, Any Given Day, In Circles, As Bees in Honey Drown, June Moon, etc. *Director*: Without Apologies, Advice From a Caterpillar, The Country Club.
PICTURES: *Producer*: The Subject Was Roses, Godspell, The Wild Party, Squirm, Blue Sunshine, He Knows You're Alone, The Clairvoyant, Advice from a Caterpillar.
TELEVISION: The Defenders (art. dir.), Summer Girl (exec. prod.), Wings of the Water (exec. prod.), A Stranger Waits.

LANSING, SHERRY
Executive. b. Chicago, IL, July 31, 1944. e. B.S., science, Northwestern Univ., 1966 (cum laude). m. director William Friedkin. Taught math and English in Los Angeles city schools, 1966-69. Acted in films (Loving, Rio Lobo) and numerous TV shows. Exec. story editor, movies, Wagner Intl. Prod. Co. 1970-74; v.p., production, Heyday Prods., 1973-75; director, West Coast Develop., 1974-75; story editor, mgr., 1975-77, v.p., creative affairs, 1977, senior v.p., production, 1977-80, Columbia Pictures. Became president of production, 20th Century Fox, 1980-83, being the first woman to hold this position in the motion picture industry. Founded Jaffe-Lansing Prods. with Stanley Jaffe, 1983; indpt. producer, Jaffe-Lansing Prods., 1983-91. Named chairman, Paramount Motion Pictures Grp. in 1992, a position she holds today. (Paramount Pictures Corporation is now a unit of Viacom Entertainment Grp.). Recipient of a star on Hollywood Walk of Fame, 1996. Member, board of directors: Music Center of Los Angeles, American Film Institute, Teach for America, American Found. for AIDS Research (AMFAR), Cedars Sinai Hospital, Stop Cancer, Big Sisters of Los Angeles Endowment Fund (co-founder); member, board of governors, National Conference of Christians and Jews, member, advisory board, Revlon/UCLA Women's Health Research Prog.; member, board of trustees, American Museum of the Moving Image, Regents of the U. of Calif.
PICTURES: *Co-prod*: Racing with the Moon, Firstborn, Fatal Attraction, The Accused, Black Rain, School Ties, Indecent Proposal.
TELEVISION: *Exec. producer*: When the Time Comes, Mistress.

LaPAGLIA, ANTHONY
Actor. b. Adelaide, Australia, 1959. Former teacher, moved to U.S. in 1984. Made Off-B'way debut in Bouncers, followed by On the Open Road. B'way: The Rose Tattoo (Theatre World Award).
PICTURES: Slaves of New York (debut, 1989), Dangerous Obsession (Mortal Sins), Betsy's Wedding, He Said/She Said, One Good Cop, 29th Street, Whispers in the Dark, Innocent Blood, So I Married an Axe Murderer, The Client, The Custodian, Mixed Nuts, Bulletproof Heart, Lucky Break, Empire Records, The Funeral, Brilliant Lies, The Garden of Redemption, Phoenix, Summer of Sam, The House of Mirth, Sweet and Lowdown, Black and Blue, Company Man, Looking for Alibrandi, Autumn in New York, The Bank, The Salton Sea, I Fought the Law, Happy Hour, I'm With Lucy .

TELEVISION: *Movies*: Criminal Justice, Keeper of the City, Black Magic, Past Tense, Nitti: The Enforcer, Lansky, The Other Side. *Series*: Murder One, Normal Ohio, Frasier.

LARKIN, JAMES J.
Executive. b. Brooklyn, NY, Nov. 2, 1925. e. Columbia U., 1947-52. U.S. Air Force, 1943-46; BOAC rep. to entertainment ind., 1948-60; pres., Transportation Counselors Inc., 1960-62; pres., Larkin Associates, Inc., 1962-65; exec. Radio N.Y. Worldwide, 1965-68; v.p. Grolier Educational Corp., 1968-69; v.p. Visual Informational Systems, 1969-73; pres., Business TV Services, Inc., 1973-; exec. prod., Madhouse Brigade, 1977-79; prod.-writer, All Those Beautiful Girls, 1979-80.

LARROQUETTE, JOHN
Actor. b. New Orleans, LA., Nov. 25, 1947. Disc jockey on FM radio during 1960s and early 70s. Acted on L.A. stage from 1973 (The Crucible, Enter Laughing, Endgame). Prof. debut, TV series Doctor's Hospital, 1976-78. Was narrator for film Texas Chainsaw Massacre.
PICTURES: Altered States, Heart Beat, Green Ice, Stripes, Cat People, Hysterical, Twilight Zone—The Movie, Choose Me, Meatballs Part II, Star Trek III: The Search for Spock, Summer Rental, Blind Date, Second Sight, Madhouse, Tune in Tomorrow, Richie Rich, Tales from the Crypt Presents: Demon Knight (cameo), Isn't She Great, The Texas Chainsaw Massacre (2003, narrator).
TELEVISION: *Series*: Doctor's Hospital, Baa Baa Black Sheep, Night Court (4 Emmy Awards, 1985-88), The John Larroquette Show, Payne, Rosebud, Corsairs, Happy Family. *Movies*: Bare Essence, The Last Ninja, Hot Paint, Convicted, One Special Victory (also co-exec. prod.), The Defenders: Payback, The Tenth Kingdom, Walter and Henry, Till Dad Do Us Part, The Heart Department. *Guest*: Kojak, Dallas, Remington Steele, Mork and Mindy, Three's Company, The Practice (Emmy Award, 1997), The West Wing.

LASSALLY, WALTER
Cinematographer. b. Berlin, Germany, Dec. 18, 1926. Entered indust. as clapper-boy at Riverside Studios. During 1950s allied himself with Britain's Free Cinema filmmakers working for Lindsay Anderson, Gavin Lambert, Tony Richardson and Karel Reisz.
PICTURES: A Girl in Black (feature debut, 1956), Beat Girl, A Taste of Honey, Electra, The Loneliness of the Long Distance Runner, Tom Jones, Zorba the Greek (Academy Award, 1964), The Day the Fish Came Out, Joanna, Oedipus the King, The Adding Machine, Three Into Two Won't Go, Something for Everyone, Twinky (Lola), Savages, Happy Mother's Day... Love George, To Kill a Clown, The Wild Party, Pleasantville, The Great Bank Hoax, The Woman Across the Way, Hullabaloo Over George and Bonnie's Pictures, Something Short of Paradise, The Blood of Hussain, Angel of Iron, Memoirs of a Survivor, Too Far to Go, Heat and Dust, Private School, The Bostonians, The Deceivers, Fragments of Isabella, The Perfect Murder, Ballad of the Sad Cafe, The Little Dolphins, Ta Delfinakia tou Amvrakikou, Silent Film, Aci gonul.
TELEVISION: Mrs. Delafield Wants to Marry, The Man Upstairs.

LASSER, LOUISE
Actress. b. New York, NY, April 11, 1939. e. Brandeis U., New School for Social Research. Appeared on stage before theatrical film debut in 1965 with What's New Pussycat? Won first Clio Award for best actress in a commercial.
THEATRE: I Can Get it For You Wholesale, The Third Ear, Henry Sweet Henry, Lime Green/Khaki Blue, The Chinese, Marie & Bruce, A Coupla White Chicks Sitting Around Talking.
PICTURES: What's Up Tiger Lily? (voice), Take the Money and Run, Bananas, Such Good Friends, Everything You Always Wanted to Know About Sex, Slither, Simon, In God We Trust, Stardust Memories, Crimewave, Nightmare at Shadow Woods (Blood Rage), Surrender, Sing, Rude Awakening, Modern Love, Frankenhooker, The Night We Never Met, Layin' Low, Sudden Manhattan, Happiness, Mystery Men, Requiem for a Dream, Fast Food, Fast Women, Queenie in Love.
TELEVISION: *Series*: Mary Hartman Mary Hartman, It's a Living. *Movies*: Coffee Tea or Me?, Isn't It Shocking?, Just Me and You (also writer), For Ladies Only, Clubland. *Guest*: Bob Newhart Show, Mary Tyler Moor Show, Taxi, St. Elsewhere, Empty Nest, many others.

LASZLO, ANDREW
Cinematographer. b. Papa, Hungary, Jan. 12, 1926. To U.S. in 1947, working as cameraman on tv before turning to feature films.
PICTURES: One Potato Two Potato, You're a Big Boy Now, The Night They Raided Minskys, Popi, The Out of Towners, Lovers and Other Strangers, The Owl and the Pussycat, Jennifer on My Mind, To Find a Man, The Effect of Gamma Rays on Man-in-the-Moon Marigolds, Class of '44, Countdown at Kusini, Thieves, Somebody Killed Her Husband, The Warriors, The Funhouse, Southern Comfort, I the Jury, First Blood, Streets of Fire, Thief of Hearts, Remo Williams: The Adventure Begins, Poltergeist II, Innerspace, Star Trek V: The Final Frontier, Ghost Dad, Newsies.
TELEVISION: *Documentaries*: High Adventure with Lowell

Thomas, The Twentieth Century. *Series:* The Phil Silvers Show, Joe and Mabel, Mama, Brenner, Naked City, The Nurses, Doctors and Nurses, Coronet Blue. Specials: New York New York, The Beatles at Shea Stadium, Ed Sullivan *Specials. Movies and feature pilots:* The Happeners, The Cliffdwellers, Daphne, Teacher Teacher, Blue Water Gold, The Man Without a Country, The Unwanted, Spanner's Key, Thin Ice, Love is Forever. *Mini-series:* Washington Behind Closed Doors, The Dain Curse, Top of the Hill, Shogun, and numerous commericals.

LATSIS, PETER C.
Publicist. b. Chicago, IL, Mar. 9, 1919. e. Wright Jr. Coll., Chicago. Newspaper reporter, Chicago Herald-American, 1942-45; Army, 1943; joined Fox West Coast Theatres, Los Angeles, in theatre operations 1945; adv.-pub. dept. 1946; asst. dir. adv.-pub. 1955; press rep. National Theatres, 1958; press relations dir., National General Corp., 1963; home office special field pub. repr., American International Pictures, 1973; Filmways Pictures, 1980-82; Recipient of Publicists Guild's Robert Yeager Award, 1983. Member, Motion Picture Pioneers. Unit rep., Executive Bd. of Publicists Guild of America, 1993-95.

LATTANZI, MATT
Actor. m. actress-singer Olivia Newton-John.
PICTURES: Xanadu (1980), Rich and Famous, Grease 2, My Tutor, That's Life!, Roxanne, Blueberry Hill, Catch Me If You Can, Diving In.
TELEVISION: *Series:* Paradise Beach.

LATTUADA, ALBERTO
Director. b. Milan, Italy, 1914. Son of Felice Lattuada, musician, opera composer, and writer of scores of many of son's films, Studied architecture; founded the periodical Cominare. Later founded Italian Film Library of which he still pres. Also, pres., Cinema D'Essay, First screen work as scriptwriter and asst. dir. of two films, 1940.
PICTURES: Mill on the Po, Anna, The Overcoat, La Lupa, Love in the City, White Sister, Flesh Will Surrender, Without Pity, The She Wolf, Tempest, The Unexpected, Mafioso, The Mandrake, Matchless, The Betrayal, The Steppe, Oh Serafina, Stay as You Are, The Cricket, Portrait of a Nude Woman, Una Spina nel cuore, 12 registi per 12 città.

LAUGHLIN, TOM
Actor, Producer, Director, Writer. b. Minneapolis, MN, 1938. e. U. of Indiana, U. of Minnesota where had athletic scholarships. m. actress Delores Taylor. Travelled around world, studying in Italy with Dr. Maria Montessori. Established, ran a Montessori school in Santa Monica for several yrs. Worked his way to Hollywood, where acted in bit parts until stardom came in Born Losers in 1967. Produced and starred in Billy Jack and The Trial of Billy Jack, also writing s.p. with wife under pseudonym Frank Christina. Heads own prod. co., Billy Jack Enterprises.
PICTURES: *Actor:* Tea and Sympathy, The Delinquents, South Pacific, Senior Prom, Lafayette Escadrille, Gidget, Battle of the Coral Sea, Tall Story, Born Losers, Callan, Brannigan, Voyage of the Damned, The Littlest Horse Thieves, The Big Sleep, The Legend of the Lone Ranger, Murder Elite, No Escape, Wild Bill: A Hollywood Maverick. *Actor-Dir.-Prod.-Writer:* The Proper Time, The Young Sinner, Born Losers, Billy Jack, The Trial of Billy Jack, The Master Gunfighter, Billy Jack Goes to Washington.
TELEVISION: *Movies:* The War That Never Ends, Zoya.

LAUNER, DALE
Writer. b. Cleveland, OH. E. Cal State Northridge.
PICTURES: Ruthless People, Blind Date, Dirty Rotten Scoundrels, My Cousin Vinny, Love Potion #9 (also dir.).

LAURENTS, ARTHUR
Writer, Director. b. New York, NY, July 14, 1917. e. Cornell U., B.A., 1937. First Professional writing as radio script writer in 1939. In Army 1941-45. Member of the Council of the Dramatists Guild; Theatre Hall of Fame.
THEATRE: *Author:* Home of the Brave (Sidney Howard Award), Heartsong, The Bird Cage, The Time of the Cuckoo, A Clearing in the Woods, Invitation to a March, West Side Story, Gypsy, Hallelujah, Baby! (Tony Award), Scream, The Enclave, Running Time, Jolson Sings Again, The Radical Mystique. Director: Invitation to a March, I Can Get It for You Wholesale, La Cage aux Folles (Tony Award), Birds of Paradise. *Author-Director:* Anyone Can Whistle, Do I Hear a Waltz?, The Madwoman of Central Park West, Gypsy (revival), Nick and Nora.
PICTURES: *Writer:* The Snake Pit, Rope, Caught, Anna Lucasta, Anastasia, Bonjour Tristesse, The Way We Were (from his own novel), The Turning Point (also co-prod.; Golden Globe, WGA Award). *Actor:* The Celluloid Closet, Leonard Bernstein Reaching for the Note, Broadway: The Golden Age by the Legends Who Were There

LAURIA, DAN
Actor. b. Brooklyn, NY, April 12, 1947. e. So Conn. St. Col., Univ. of Conn. Served in U.S. Marine Corps., 1970-73.
PICTURES: Without a Trace, Stakeout, Another Stakeout, Excessive Force II: Force on Force, Dog Watch, Independence Day, Ricochet River, Justice, Rhapsody in Bloom, True Friends,

Wide Awake, A Wake in Providence, Stranger in My House, Fear Runs Silent, Full Circle, High Times Potluck, The Empath, Contagion.
TELEVISION: *Series:* Love of Life, One Life to Live, Hooperman, The Wonder Years, Amazing Grace, Party of Five, The Hoop Life, Costello, N.Y.U.K. *Movies:* Johnny Brass, Johnny Bull, Doing Life, At Mother's Request, Angel in Green, David, Howard Beach: Making the Case for Murder, The Big One: The Great Los Angeles Earthquake, Overexposed, Dead and Alive, From the Files of Joseph Wambaugh: A Jury of One, In the Line of Duty: Ambush in Waco, In the Line of Duty: Hunt for Justice, Between Mother and Daughter, Terror in the Family The Bachelor's Baby, Prison of Secrets, Merry Christmas George Bailey, Mr. Murder, From the Earth to the Moon, Justice, Common Ground, Never Say Day. *Guest:* Growing Pains, Mike Hammer, Moonlighting, Hill Street Blues, NYPD Blue, Chicago Hope. *Special:* Between Mother and Daughter.

LAURIE, PIPER
Actress. r.n. Rosetta Jacobs. b. Detroit, MI, Jan. 22, 1932. e. Los Angeles H.S. Acted in school plays, signed by U.I. in 1949.
THEATRE: The Glass Menagerie (revival), Marco Polo Sings a Solo, The Innocents, Biography, Rosemary, The Alligators, The Last Flapper (tour), The Destiny of Me.
PICTURES: Louisa (debut, 1950), The Milkman, Francis Goes to the Races, The Prince Who was a Thief, Son of Ali Baba, Has Anybody Seen My Gal, No Room for the Groom, Mississippi Gambler, Golden Blade, Dangerous Mission, Johnny Dark, Dawn at Socorro, Smoke Signal, Ain't Misbehavin', Kelly and Me, Until They Sail, The Hustler (Acad. Award nom.), Carrie (Acad. Award nom.), Ruby, The Boss's Son, Tim, Return to Oz, Children of a Lesser God (Acad. Award nom.), Distortions, Appointment with Death, Tiger Warsaw, Dream a Little Dream, Mother Mother, Other People's Money, Storyville, Rich in Love, Trauma, Wrestling Ernest Hemingway, The Crossing Guard, The Grass Harp, The Faculty, Palmer's Pick Up, The Rage: Carrie 2 (voice), The Mao Game, Acting "Carrie".
TELEVISION: *Specials:* Days of Wine and Roses (Emmy nom.), The Road That Led Afar (Emmy nom.), The Deaf Heart (Emmy nom.), The Secret Life of Margaret Sanger. *Movies:* In the Matter of Karen Ann Quinlan, Rainbow, Skag, The Bunker (Emmy nom.), Mae West, Love Mary, Toughlove, Promise (Emmy Award, 1987), Go To the Light, Rising Son, Poisoned By Love: The Kern County Murders, Lies and Lullabies, Shadows of Desire, Fighting for My Daughter, In the Blink of an Eye, Road to Galveston, Alone, Inherit the Wind, Possessed, Dario Argento: An Eye for Horror, The Last Brickmaker in America. *Series:* Skag, Twin Peaks (Golden Globe Award, Emmy nom.), Partners. *Mini-Series:* The Thorn Birds (Emmy nom.), Tender is the Night, Intensity. *Guest:* St. Elsewhere (Emmy nom.)

LAUTER, ED
Actor. b. Long Beach, NY, Oct. 30, 1940.
PICTURES: The New Centurions, Hickey & Boggs, The Last American Hero, Executive Action, Lolly Madonna XXX, The Longest Yard, French Connection II, Breakheart Pass, Family Plot, King Kong, The Chicken Chronicles, Magic, The Amateur, Death Hunt, Timerider, The Big Score, Eureka, Lassiter, Cujo, Finders Keepers, Death Wish 3, Girls Just Want to Have Fun, Youngblood, 3:15, Raw Deal, Chief Zabu, Revenge of the Nerds II, Gleaming the Cube, Fat Man and Little Boy, Tennessee Waltz, School Ties, Wagons East!, Trial by Jury, Girl in the Cadillac, Digital Man, Crash, Rattled, Coyote Summer, Mulholland Falls, Top of the World, Allie & Me, Out in Fifty, Farewell My Love, Civility, Python, Thirteen Days, Gentleman B., Blast, Not Another Teen Sex Movie, Go For Broke.
TELEVISION: *Series:* B.J. and the Bear. *Movies:* Class of '63, The Migrants, The Godchild, Satan's Triangle, A Shadow in the Streets, Last Hours Before Morning, The Clone Master, The Jericho Mile, Love's Savage Fury, Undercover with the KKK, The Boy Who Drank Too Much, Guyana Tragedy—The Story of Jim Jones, AlcatrazThe Whole Shocking Story, In the Custody of Strangers, Rooster, The Seduction of Gina, Three Wishes of Billy Grier, The Last Days of Patton, The Thanksgiving Promise, Calendar Girl Cop Killer?: The Bambi Bembenek Story, Extreme Justice, The Return of Ironside, Secret Sins of the Father, Tuskegee Airmen, Ravenhawk, Under Wraps, Mercenary, A Bright Shining Lie.

LAVEN, ARNOLD
Director, Producer. b. Chicago, IL, Feb. 23, 1922.
PICTURES: Without Warning (debut, 1952), Vice Squad, Down Three Dark Streets, The Rack, The Monster That Challenged the World, Slaughter on Tenth Ave., Anna Lucasta, Geronimo (also prod.), The Glory Guys (also co-prod.), Clambake (co-prod. only), Rough Night in Jericho, Sam Whiskey (also co-prod.).
TELEVISION: Part creator and director TV pilots: The Rifleman, Robert Taylor's Detectives, The Plainsmen. *Dir.:* over 20 series including Planet of the Apes, Eight is Enough, CHiPs, Hill Street Blues, etc.

LAVIN, LINDA
Actress. b. Portland, ME, Oct. 15, 1937. e. Coll. of William & Mary. First professional job in chorus of Camden County (N.J.) Music Circus. Worked in plays both off and on Broadway before

turning to TV, where guest-starred on such series as Family, Rhoda, Phyllis and Harry O.
THEATRE: Oh Kay! (Off-B'way debut, 1960), A Family Affair (B'way debut), Revues: Wet Paint (Theatre World Award), The Game Is Up, The Mad Show, member acting co.: Eugene O'Neil Playwright's Unit, 1968; It's a Bird It's a Plane... It's Superman, Something Different, Little Murders (Outer Critics Circle & Sat. Review Awards), Cop Out, The Last of the Red Hot Lovers (Tony nom.), Story Theatre, Dynamite Tonight, Broadway Bound (Tony, Drama Desk, Outer Critics Circle & Helen Hayes Awards), Gypsy, The Sisters Rosensweig, Death Defying Acts.
PICTURES: The Muppets Take Manhattan, See You in the Morning, I Want to Go Home, Whitewash.
TELEVISION: Series: Barney Miller, Alice (2 Golden Globe Awards; 2 Emmy noms.), Room for Two (also co-exec. prod.), COnrad Bloom. Movies: The Morning After, Like Mom and Me, The $5.20 an Hour Dream, A Matter of Life and Death (also exec. prod. & developed), Another Woman's Child, A Place to Call Home (also exec. prod. & developed), Lena: My Hundred Children, Room for Two, Stolen Moments, Secrets from the Rose Garden, A Dream Is a Wish Your Heart Makes, The Annette Funicello Story, The Ring, For the Children: The Irvine Fertility Scandal, Best Friends for Life, Collected Stories.

LAW, JOHN PHILLIP
Actor. b. Hollywood, CA, Sept. 7, 1937. e. Neighborhood Playhouse. B'way debut in Coming on Strong. Appeared at Lincoln Center in After the Fall, Marco Millions, The Changeling, and Tartuffe. Has made more than 50 films in more than 20 countries world wide.
PICTURES: High Infidelity, Three Nights of Love, The Russians Are Coming The Russians Are Coming the Russians Are Coming (U.S. debut), Hurry Sundown, Barbarella, Danger Diabolik, The Sergeant, Death Rides a Horse, Skidoo, Diary of a Telephone Operator, Von Richtofen and Brown, The Hawaiians, Michael Strogoff, The Love Machine, The Last Movie, The Golden Voyage of Sinbad, Stardust, Open Season, Your God My Hell, The Spiral Staircase, Dr. Justice, African Rage, Whisper in the Dark, Portrait of an Assassin, The Crystal Man, Death in November, Ring of Darkness, The Cassandra Crossing, Der Schimmelreiter, Attack Force Z, Tarzan the Ape Man, Night Train to Terror, The Tin Man, Rainy Day Friends (L.A. Bad), No Time to Die, American Commandos (Mr. Salvage), Johann Strauss, The Moon Under the Trees, Moon in Scorpio, Striker, The Overthrow, Mutiny in Space, Thunder Warrior III, A Case of Honor, Blood Delirium, Alienator, L.A. Heat, Gorilla, The Guest, Alaska Stories, Angel Eyes, Shining Blood, Marilyn Behind Bars, Day of the Pig, The Mountain of the Lord, Europa Mission, Angel Eyes, Burning Heart, Hindsight, Ghost Dog, Wanted, Vic, Citizens of Perpetual Indulgence, CQ.
TELEVISION: Series: The Young and the Restless (1989). Movie: The Best Place to Be, A Great Love Story (It.), Experiences (It.), The Fourth Man (Austrian), Little Women of Today (It.). Guest: The Love Boat, Murder She Wrote.

LAW, JUDE
Actor. b. London, England, Dec. 29, 1972.
PICTURES: Shopping, I Love You I Love You Not, Wilde, Gattaca, Bent, Midnight in the Garden of Good and Evil, Final Cut, Music From Another Room, The Wisdom of Crocodiles, The Talented Mr. Ripley (Acad. Award nom., BAFTA Award), eXistenZ, Love, Honour and Obey, A.I., Enemy at the Gates, The Road to Perdition, Marlowe, The Diary of a Young London Physician, Cold Mountain, The World of Tomorrow.
TELEVISION: Movies: The Marshal. Series: The Casebook of Sherlock Holmes, Families.

LAW, LINDSAY
Producer. e. NYU School of the Arts. Producer of specials for Warner Bros. Television, head of drama for WNET/New York and prod. for Theatre in America before becoming exec. prod. of American Playhouse. Advisory Board of Independent Feature Project/West, Sundance Film Festival.
PICTURES: Exec. prod.: On Valentine's Day, Smooth Talk, Native Son, In a Shallow Grave, Stand and Deliver, The Thin Blue Line, El Norte, The Wizard of Loneliness, Signs of Life, Bloodhounds of Broadway, Big Time, Eat a Bowl of Tea, Longtime Companion, Thousand Pieces of Gold, Straight Out of Brooklyn, Daughters of the Dust, Thank You and Goodnight, All the Vermeers in New York, Brother's Keeper, Ethan Frome, The Music of Chance, Golden Gate, I Shot Andy Warhol, Fast Cheap and Out of Control.
TELEVISION: Prod.: The Girls in Their Summer Dresses, The Time of Your Life, You Can't Take It With You, The Good Doctor, The Most Happy Fella, The Eccentricities of a Nightingale, Cyrano de Bergerac (assoc. prod.). Prod. for American Playhouse: Working, for Colored Girls Who Have Considered Suicide/When the Rainbow Is Enuf, Private Contentment, Exec. prod.: Concealed Enemies (Emmy Award, 1984), Land of Little Rain, Ask Me Again, The Diaries of Adam and Eve, A Walk in the Woods, Fires in the Mirror.

LAWRENCE, BARBARA
Actress. b. Carnegie, OK, Feb. 24, 1930. e. UCLA. Mother Berenice Lawrence. Child model; successful screen try-out,

1944; screen debut in Billy Rose Diamond Horse Shoe (1945).
PICTURES: Margie, Captain from Castile, You Were Meant for Me, Give My Regards to Broadway, Street with No Name, Unfaithfully Yours, Letter to Three Wives, Mother Is a Freshman, Thieves Highway, Two Tickets to Broadway, Here Come the Nelsons, The Star, Arena, Paris Model, Her 12 Men, Oklahoma, Man with the Gun, Joe Dakota, Kronos.

LAWRENCE, JOEY
Actor. b. Montgomery, PA, Apr. 20, 1976. e. USC.
PICTURES: Summer Rental, Oliver and Company (voice), Pulse, Radioland Murders, Tequila Body Shots, Urban Legends: Final Cut, Do You Wanna Know a Secret?, A Christmas Adventure from a Book Called Wisely's Tales (voice), Pandora's Box, R3.
TELEVISION: Series: Gimme a Break, Blossom, Brotherly Love, Express Yourself, American Dreams, Run of the House. Pilots: Scamps, Little Shots. Specials: Andy Williams and the NBC Kids, Don't Touch, Alvin Goes Back to School, Umbrella Jack, Adventures in Babysitting, Disney's Countdown to Kids' Day, All That, Blossom in Paris, Kids' Choice Awards (host). Movies: Chains of Gold, Prince for a Day, Brothers of the Frontier, Jumping Ship, Romantic Comedy 101.

LAWRENCE, MARC
Actor. r.n. Max Goldsmith. b. New York, NY, Feb. 17, 1914. e. City Coll. of New York. On stage in the Tree (Eva La Gallience Rep. Theatre.), Sour Mountain, Waiting for Lefty, Golden Boy, View From the Bridge.
PICTURES: White Woman, Little Big Shot, Dr. Socrates, Road Gang, San Quentin, The Ox Bow Incident, I Am the Law, While New York Sleeps, Dillinger, Flame of Barbary Coast, Club Havana, Don't Fence Me In, The Virginian, Life with Blondie, Yankee Fakir, Captain from Castile, I Walk Alone, Calamity Jane and Sam Bass, The Asphalt Jungle, Hurricane Island, My Favorite Spy, Girls Marked Danger, Helen of Troy, Johnny Cool, Nightmare in the Sun, Savage Pampas, Johnny Tiger, Custer of the West, Nightmare in the Sun (dir. co- prod., co-story only), Krakatoa East of Java, The Kremlin Letter, Fraser: The Sensuous Lion, The Man With the Golden Gun, Marathon Man, A Piece of the Action, Foul Play, Goin' Cocoanuts, Hot Stuff, Night Train to Terror, The Big Easy, Ruby, Newsies, Marilyn I Love You, Four Rooms, From Dusk Till Dawn, End of Days, The Shipping News.

LAWRENCE, MARTIN
Actor, Comedian. b. Frankfurt, Germany, 1965. Started as stand-up comic in Washington D.C.
PICTURES: Do the Right Thing (debut, 1989), House Party, Talkin' Dirty After Dark, House Party 2, Boomerang, You So Crazy (also exec. prod.), Bad Boys, Nothing to Lose, A Thin Line Between Love and Hate (also, exec. prod., dir., s.p.), Life, Blue Streak, Big Momma's House, What's the Worst that Could Happen?, Black Knight, National Security, Bad Boys 2.
TELEVISION: Series: What's Happening Now?, Kid 'n' Play (voice), Russell Simmons' Def Comedy Jam (host, prod. consultant), Martin (also creator, co-exec. prod.). Pilots: Hammer Slammer & Slade, A Little Bit Strange. Guest: Stand Up Spotlight, Yo! MTV Laffs, An Evening at the Improv.

LAWRENCE, STEVE
Actor. r.n. Sydney Leibowitz. b. Brooklyn, NY, July 8, 1935. m. singer Eydie Gorme. Singer in nightclubs and on TV.
THEATRE: What Makes Sammy Run?, Golden Rainbow.
PICTURES: Stand Up and Be Counted, The Blues Brothers, The Lonely Guy, Blues Brothers 2000, Play It to the Bone, The Contract, The Yards, Ocean's Eleven.
TELEVISION: Specials: Steve and Eydie Celebrate Irving Berlin (also co-exec. prod.; Emmy Award, 1979), many specials. Series: Tonight, The Steve Lawrence-Eydie Gorme Show (1958), The Steve Lawrence Show (1965), Foul-Ups Bleeps and Blunders (host). Guest: Police Story, Murder, She Wrote. Movie: Alice in Wonderland.

LAWRENCE, VICKI
Actress. b. Inglewood, CA, March 26, 1949. Singer and recording artist appearing with Young Americans (1965-67). Gained fame on The Carol Burnett Show as comedienne (1967-78), winning Emmy Award in 1976. Gold record for The Night the Lights Went Out in Georgia (1972). Author: Vicki!: The True Life Adventures of Miss Fireball (Simon & Schuster, 1995).
TELEVISION: Movies: Having Babies, Hart to Hart: Old Friends Never Die. Series: Carol Burnett Show, Jimmie Rodgers Show, Mama's Family. Host: Win Lose or Draw (1987-88), Vicki!, Fox After Breakfast (synd. talk shows).

LAWSON, SARAH
Actress. b. London, Eng., Aug. 6, 1928. e. Heron's Ghyll Sch., Sussex. Stage debut in Everyman (Edinburgh Festival) 1947.
PICTURES: The Browning Version (debut, 1951), The Night Won't Talk, Street Corner, Street Corner (Both Sides of the Law), Three Steps in the Dark, Meet Mr. Malcolm, You Know What Sailors Are, Blue Peter (Navy Heroes), It's Never Too Late, Links of Justice, Three Crooked Men, The Solitary Child, Night Without Pity, On the Run, The World Ten Times Over, Island of the Burning Doomed, The Devil's Bride (The Devil Rides Out), Battle

of Britain, The Stud, The Dawning (prod.).
TELEVISION: Face to Face, River Line, Whole Truth, Lady From the Sea, Mrs. Moonlight, Silver Card, An Ideal Husband, Love and Money, Rendezvous, Invisible Man, Saber Buccaneers, White Hunter, Flying Doctor, On the Night of the Murder, Haven in Sunset, The Odd Man, Zero 1 (series), The Innocent Ceremony, Department S, The Marrying Kind, The Expert, The Persuaders, Trial, Starcast, The Midsummer of Colonel Blossum, Callen, Crime of Passion, Full House, Father Brown, Within These Walls These Walls Series, The Standard, The Purple Twilight, The Professionals, Bergerac, Cuffy, Lovejoy.

LAYBOURNE, GERALDINE
Executive. e. Vassar College, B.A.; U. Penn, M.S. Joined Nickelodeon in 1980. Was vice chmn., MTV Networks; pres., Nickelodeon/Nick at Nite. Bd. member Viacom exec. committee. Left Nickelodeon to join ABC as pres., Disney/ABC Cable Networks. Inducted into Broadcast and Cable Hall of Fame, 1996. Resigned ABC/Cable post in 1998 and started own network/cable/internet production company, Oxygen Media of which she is chmn. and CEO.

LAZARUS, PAUL N. III
Executive. b. New York, NY, May 25, 1938. e. Williams Coll., BA.; Yale Law Sch., L.L.B. Third generation film exec. Began career with Palomar Pictures Int'l. as exec. v.p.; joined ABC Pictures Corp. as v.p. in chg. of creative affairs. Mng. dir., CRM Productions, maker of educational films; v.p. for motion pictures. Marble Arch Productions; 1983, v.p. in chg. of prod., Home Box Office. 1985, Film Commissioner, New Mexico; 1987, Dir. of Film Program, U. of Miami.
PICTURES: *Prod.:* Extreme Close-Up, Westworld, Futureworld, Capricorn One, Hanover Street, Barbarosa, Doubles.

LAZENBY, GEORGE
Actor. b. Gouburn, Australia, Sept. 5, 1939. Appeared in Australian and British tv commericals before being chosen to star as James Bond.
PICTURES: On Her Majesty's Secret Service (debut, 1969), Universal Soldier, Who Saw Her Die?, The Dragon Flies, Stoner, The Man From Hong Kong, The Kentucky Fried Movie, Death Dimension, The Falcon's Ultimatum, Saint Jack, L'ultimo Harem, Never Too Young to Die, Hell Hunters, Gettysburg, Eyes of the Beholder, Emmanuelle's Revenge, Emmanuelle's Love, Emmanuelle Forever, Death By Misadventure, .Twin Sitters, Gut Feeling, Four Dogs Playing Poker, Bruce Lee: A Warrior's Journey, Bruce Lee in G.O.D, Sheer Bliss.
TELEVISION: *Series:* General Hospital, Rituals. *Movies:* Is Anybody There?, Cover Girls, The Newman Shame, Evening in Byzantium, The Return of the Man From U.N.C.L.E., Batman Beyond: The Movie *Guest:* Hawaii Five-O, Bring "Em Back Alive, The Master, Freddy's Nightmares, Aldred Hitchcock Presents, Superboy, Kung Fu: The Legend Continues, Diagnosis Murder, Batham Beyond, Baywatch, The Pretender.

LEACHMAN, CLORIS
Actress. b. Des Moines, IA, April 30, 1926. e. Northwestern U. Broadway stage, television, motion pictures.
PICTURES: Kiss Me Deadly (debut, 1955), The Rack, The Chapman Report, Butch Cassidy and the Sundance Kid, Lovers and Other Strangers, The People Next Door, W.U.S.A., The Steagle, The Last Picture Show (Acad. Award, best supporting actress, 1971), Dillinger, Charlie and the Angel, Happy Mother's Day... Love George, Daisy Miller, Young Frankenstein, Crazy Mama, High Anxiety, The Mouse and His Child (voice), North Avenue Irregulars, The Muppet Movie, Scavenger Hunt, Foolin' Around, Yesterday, Herbie Goes Bananas, History of the World—Part I, My Little Pony (voice), Shadow Play, Walk Like a Man, Hansel and Gretel, Prancer, Texasville, Love Hurts, My Boyfriend's Back, The Beverly Hillbillies, A Troll in Central park (voice), Now and Then, Beavis and Butt-Head Do America (voice), Never Too Late, Gen 13, The Iron Giant, Music of the Heart, Hanging Up, The Amati Girls, Animal, Manna From Heaven. .
TELEVISION: *Series:* Hold It Please, Charlie Wild: Private Detective, Bob and Ray, Lassie, Mary Tyler Moore Show (Emmy Awards 1974, 1975), Phyllis (Golden Globe Award), The Facts of Life, The Nutt House, Walter & Emily, The Ellen Show. *Movies:* Silent Night Lonely Night, Suddenly Single, Haunts of the Very Rich, A Brand New Life (Emmy Award, 1973), Crime Club, Dying Room Only, The Migrants, Hitchhike!, Thursday's Game, Death Sentence, Someone I Touched, A Girl Named Sooner, Death Scream, The New Original Wonder Woman, The Love Boat (pilot), It Happened One Christmas, Long Journey Back, Willa, Mrs. R's Daughter, S.O.S. Titanic, The Acorn People, Advice to the Lovelorn, Miss All-American Beauty, Dixie: Changing Habits, Demon Murder Case, Ernie Kovacs: Between the Laughter, Deadly Intentions, Love Is Never Silent, Wedding Bell Blues, Danielle Steel's Fine Things, In Broad Daylight, A Little Piece of Heaven, Fade to Black, Without a Kiss Goodbye, Miracle Child, Double Double Toil and Trouble, Between Love and Honor, Annabella Wish. *Specials:* Oldest Living Graduate, Of Thee I Sing, Breakfast With Les and Bess, Screen Actors Guild 50th Anniversary Celebration (Emmy Award, 1984). *Guest:* Twilight Zone, Untouchables, Big Valley, That Girl, Marcus Welby, Night

Gallery, Cher (Emmy Award, 1975), Love Boat, Promised Land (Emmy Award, 1997), The Simpsons, The Nanny, Touched By An Angel, The Norm Show, many others.

LEAR, NORMAN
Producer, Director, Writer. b. New Haven, CT, July 27, 1922. e. Emerson Coll. In public relations 1945-49. Began in TV as co-writer of weekly one-hour variety show, The Ford Star Revue in 1950. Followed as writer for Dean Martin and Jerry Lewis on the Colgate Comedy Hour and for the Martha Raye and George Gobel TV shows. With partner, Bud Yorkin, created and produced such specials as Another Evening with Fred Astaire, Henry Fonda and the Family, An Evening with Carol Channing, and The Many Sides of Don Rickles. In 1965 their company, Tandem Productions, also produced the original Andy Williams Show. Moved into motion pictures in 1963, writing and producing Come Blow Your Horn. Formed Act III Communications, 1987.
PICTURES: Come Blow Your Horn (co-prod., s.p.), Never Too Late (prod.), Divorce-American Style (prod., s.p.), The Night They Raided Minsky's (co.-prod., co-s.p.), Start the Revolution Without Me (exec. prod.), Cold Turkey (dir, s.p., prod.), The Princess Bride (exec. prod.), Fried Green Tomatoes (co-exec. prod.), Way Past Cool (exec. prod.).
TELEVISION: *Creator-dir.:* TV Guide Award Show (1962), Henry Fonda and the Family (1963), Andy Williams Specials, Robert Young and the Family. Exec. prod. and creator or developer: All in the Family (3 Emmy Awards), Maude, Good Times, Sanford and Son, The Jeffersons, Mary Hartman Mary Hartman, One Day at a Time, All's Fair, A Year at the Top, All that Glitters, Fernwood 2 Night, The Baxters, Palmerstown, I Love Liberty, Heartsounds, Sunday Dinner, The Powers That Be, 704 Hauser.

LEARNED, MICHAEL
Actress. b. Washington, DC, Apr. 9, 1939. Studied ballet and dramatics in school. Many stage credits include Under Milkwood, The Three Sisters, A God Slept Here, The Sisters Rosensweig, etc.; resident performances with Shakespeare festivals in Canada, Stratford, CT, and San Diego, CA. Gained fame on hit TV series, The Waltons, as the mother, Olivia.
PICTURES: Touched by Love, Shanghai Shadows (narrator), Power, Dragon: The Bruce Lee Story, Life During Wartime, For the Love of May, Shallow End.
TELEVISION: *Series:* The Waltons (3 Emmy Awards: 1973, 1974, 1976), Nurse (Emmy Award, 1982), Hothouse, Living Dolls. *Guest:* Gunsmoke, Police Story, St. Elsewhere, Murder She Wrote, Who's the Boss?. *Movies:* Hurricane, It Couldn't Happen to a Nicer Guy, Widow, Little Mo, Nurse (pilot), Off the Minnesota Strip, A Christmas Without Snow, Mother's Day on Walton Mountain, The Parade, A Deadly Business, Mercy or Murder?, Roots: The Gift, Gunsmoke: The Last Apache, Aftermath: A Test of Love, Keeping Secrets, A Walton Thanksgiving Reunion, A Walton Wedding, A Father for Brittany. *Specials:* All My Sons, Picnic.

LEARY, DENIS
Actor. b. Boston, MA, Aug. 18, 1957. e. Emerson Coll. Performed with the New Voices Theater Company, Charlestown Working Theater. Debuted one-man stand-up show No Cure for Cancer at Edinburgh Intl. Arts Fest., then later in London, Off-B'way, and cable tv. Appeared in and dir. short film for Showtime, Thy Neighbor's Wife.
PICTURES: Strictly Business (debut), National Lampoon's Loaded Weapon 1, The Sandlot, Who's the Man?, Gunmen, Demolition Man, Judgment Night, The Ref, Operation Dumbo Drop, The Neon Bible, Two If by Sea (also co-s.p.), Suicide Kings, The Real Blonde, Underworld, The MatchMaker, Wag the Dog, Snitch, A Bug's Life (voice), Love Walked In, Wide Awake, Small Soldiers, The Thomas Crown Affair, Sand, Jesus' Son, True Crime, Company Man, Lakeboat, Double Whammy, Final, Dawg, The Ice Age, The Secret Lives of Dentists.
TELEVISION: *Movies:* The Second Civil War, Subway Stories: Tales from the Underground. *Series:* The Job.

LEAUD, JEAN-PIERRE
Actor. b. Paris, France, May 5, 1944. Parents were screenwriter Pierre Leaud and actress Jacqueline Pierreux. At 14 chosen to play Antoine Doinel in Truffaut's The 400 Blows and subsequent autobiographical films Love at 20, Stolen Kisses, Bed and Board, Love on the Run. Closely identified with major films by Jean-Luc Godard.
PICTURES: The 400 Blows, Boulevard, The Testament of Orpheus, Love at Twenty, Masculine-Feminine, Made in USA, Le Depart, La Chinoise, Weekend, Stolen Kisses, Le Gai Savoir, Pigsty, The Oldest Profession, Bed and Board, Two English Girls, Last Tango in Paris, Day for Night, Lola's Lolos, Love on the Run, Rebelote, Detective, Just a Movie, Seen by... 20 Years After, Treasure Island, The Grandeur and Decadence of a Small-Time Filmmaker, With All Hands, Time to Aim, Jane B, par Agnes V.; 36 Fillete, La Femme de Paille (The Straw Woman), The Color of the Wind, Bunker Palace Hotel, Treasure Island, I Hired a Contract Killer, Paris at Dawn, The Birth of Love, Nobody Loves Me, The Seducer's Diary, A Hundred & One Nights, Irma Vep, Mon Homme, Pour Rire!, Elizabeth, Innocent, A Question of Taste, The Marcorelle Affair, What Time Is It There?, Barra 68 - Sem Perder a Ternura, The Pornographer, La Guerre a Paris.

LeBLANC, MATT
Actor. b. Newton, MA, July 25, 1967.
PICTURES: The Killing Box, Lookin' Italian, Ed, Lost in Space, Charlie's Angels, All the Queen's Men, Broad Daylight, Charlie's Angels: Full Throttle.
TELEVISION: Movies: Anything to Survive, Reform School Girl. Series: TV 101, Top of the Heap, Vinnie & Bobby, Friends, Friends: The Stuff You've Never Seen. Guest: Just the Ten of Us, Married...with Children, Red Shoe Diaries.

LEDER, HERBERT JAY
Writer, Director, Producer. b. New York, NY, Aug. 15, 1922. e. B.A., Ph.D. Play Doctor on Broadway; Director TV dept., Benton and Bowles Adv. chg. all T.V. & Film production, 13 yrs. Sponsored Films: Child Molester, Bank Robber, Shoplifter, Untouchables.
PICTURES: Writer: Fiend Without a Face, Pretty Boy Floyd (also dir., co-prod.), Nine Miles to Noon (also dir., co-prod.), Aquarius Mission, Love Keeps No Score of Wrongs, The Frozen Dead (also dir., prod.), It (also dir., prod.), Candyman (also dir.), The Winners, The Way It Is, The Cool Crazies.

LEDER, MIMI
Director, Script Supervisor. b. 1952. Daughter of late Producer.Director Paul Leder.
PICTURES: The Peacemaker, Deep Impact, Sentimental Journey, Pay It Forward, Smoke & Mirrors.
TELEVISION: Script Supervisor: Dummy, The Boy Who Drank too Much, A Long Way Home, A time to Live, L.A. Law. Director: L.A. Law, China Beach, Nightingales, Midnight Caller, A Little Piece of Heaven, A Woman with a Past, Marked for Muder, There Was a Little Boy, Rio Shannon, Baby Broker, ER, The Innocent. Series Dir.: The Beast.

LEDERER, RICHARD
Executive. b. New York, NY, Sept. 22, 1916. e. U. of Virginia, B.S., 1938. Freelance writer, 1939-41; U.S. Army. Cryptanalyst, Signal Intell. Serv 1941-45; Adv. copywriter, Columbia Pictures, 1946-50; Adv. copywriter, Warner Bros., 1950-53; copy chief, Warner Bros., 1950-53; copy chief, Warner Bros., 1953-57; Asst. Nat'l Adv. mgr., Warner Bros. studios, 1957-59; Prod., theatrical, TV. Warner Bros. studios, 1959-60; Dir. of adv., publicity, Warner Bros. Pictures, 1960; v.p. Warner Bros. Pictures, 1963. V.P. production, Warner Bros. Studio, 1969-70; indep. prod. to 1971, when returned to WB as adv.-pub., v.p. Independent producer. 1980: Hollywood Knights. Joined Orion Pictures as v.p., adv. Resigned, 1984.

LEDGER, HEATH
Actor. r.n. Heathcliff Andrew Ledger. b. Perth, Australia, April 4, 1979.
PICTURES: Blackrock, Paws, Two Hands, 10 Things I Hate About You, Patriot, A Knight's Tale, Four Feathers, Monster's Ball, The Sin Eater, Ned Kelly, The Order.
TELEVISION: Series: Sweat, Roar, Bush Patrol.

LEE, ANG
Director, Producer, Writer. b. Pingtung, Taiwan, Oct. 23, 1954.
PICTURES: Joe's Bed-Stuy Barbershop: We Cut Heads, Pushing Hands, The Wedding Banquet, Eat Drink Man Woman, Siao Yu, Sense and Sensibility (BAFTA Award), The Ice Storm, Ride with the Devil, Crouching Tiger Hidden Dragon (Acad. Award nom., BAFTA Award, DGA Award), Chosen, The Incredible Hulk.

LEE, ANNA
Actress. M.B.E. r.n. Joan Boniface Winnifrith. b. Kent, England, Jan. 2, 1913. e. Central School of Speech Training and Dramatic Art, Royal Albert Hall. With London Repertory Theatre; toured in the Constant Nymph and Jane Eyre. In 1930s known as Britain's Glamour Girl. 1939 came to U.S. to star in My Life With Caroline. Entertained troops with U.S.O. during WWII. 1950 moved to N.Y. to appear in live TV.
PICTURES: Ebb Tide (debut, 1932), Yes Mr. Brown, Say It With Music, Mayfair Girl, King's Cup, Chelsea Life, Mannequin, Faces, The Bermondsey Kid, Lucky Loser, The Camels Are Coming, Rolling in Money, Heat Wave, Passing of the Third Floor Back, First a Girl, The Man Who Changed His Mind, O.H.M.S., King Solomon's Mines, Non-Stop New York, The Four Just Men, Return to Yesterday, Young Man's Fancy, Seven Sinners, My Life With Caroline, How Green Was My Valley, Flying Tigers, The Commandos Strike at Dawn, Hangmen Also Die, Flesh and Fantasy, Forever and a Day, Summer Storm, Abroad With Two Yanks, Bedlam, G.I. War Brides, High Conquest, The Ghost and Mrs. Muir, Best Man Wins, Fort Apache, Prison Warden, Wyoming Mail, Boots Malone, Daniel Boone—Trail Blazer, Gideon of Scotland Yard, The Last Hurrah, The Horse Soldiers, Jet Over the Atlantic, This Eath Is Mine, The Big Night, The Crimson Kimono, Jack the Giant Killer, Two Rode Together, The Man Who Shot Liberty Valance, What Ever Happend to Baby Jane?, The Prize, The Unsinkable Molly Brown, For Those Who Think Young, The Sound of Music, Torn Curtain, Seven Women, Picture Mommy Dead, In Like Flint, Star!, Clash, The Right Hand Man, Listen to Me, Beyond the Next Mountain, Beverly Hills Brats, What Can I Do?

TELEVISION: Guest on many major television shows from 1950-77. Series: General Hospital (1978-present). Movies: Eleanor and Franklin, The Night Rider, The Beasts are Loose, Scruples.

LEE, CHRISTOPHER
Actor. b. London, England, May 27, 1922. e. Wellington Coll. Served RAF 1940-46. Ent. m.p. ind. 1947. Autobiography: Tall, Dark and Gruesome (1977).
PICTURES: include: Corridor of Mirrors (debut, 1947), One Night With You, A Song for Tomorrow, Scott of the Antarctic, Hamlet, The Gay Lady, Capt. Horatio Hornblower, Valley of the Eagles, The Crimson Pirate, Babes in Bagdad, Moulin Rouge, Innocents of Paris, That Lady, The Warriors, Cockleshell Heroes, Storm Over the Nile, Port Afrique, Private's Progress, Beyond Mombasa, Battle of the River Plate, Night Ambush, She Played With Fire, The Traitors, Curse of Frankenstein, Bitter Victory, Truth About Women, Tale of Two Cities, Dracula, Man Who Could Cheat Death, The Mummy, Too Hot to Handle, Beat Girl, City of the Dead (Horror Hotel), Two Faces of Dr. Jekyll, The Terror of the Tongs, The Hands of Orlac, Taste of Fear, The Devil's Daffodil, Pirates of Blood River, Devil's Agent, Red Orchid, Valley of Fear, Katharsis, Faust '63, The Virgin of Nuremberg, The Whip and the Body, Carmilla, The Devil Ship Pirates, The Gorgon, The Sign of Satan, The House of Blood, Dr. Terror's House of Horrors, She, The Skull, The Mask of Fu Manchu, Dracula, Prince of Darkness, Rasputin, Theatre of Death, Circus of Fear, The Brides of Fu Manchu, Five Golden Dragons, Vengeance of Fu Manchu, Night of the Big Heat, The Pendulum, The Face of Eve, The Devil Rides Out, The Blood of Fu Manchu, The Crimson Altar, Dracula Has Risen from the Grave, The Oblong Box, De Sade 70, Scream and Scream Again, The Magic Christian, Julius Caesar, One More Time, Count Dracula, Bloody Judge, Taste the Blood of Dracula, The Private Life of Sherlock Holmes, El Umbragolo, Scars ofDracula, The House That Dripped Blood, I Monster, Hannie Caulder, Dracula A.D. 1972, Horror Express, Death Line (Raw Meat), Nothing But the Night (also co-exec. prod.), The Creeping Flesh, The Wicker Man, Poor Devil, Dark Places, Satanic Rites of Dracula, Eulalie Quitte les Champs, The Three Musketeers, Earthbound, The Man with the Golden Gun, The Four Musketeers, Killer Force, Diagnosis—Murder, Whispering Death, The Keeper, To the Devil a Daughter, Dracula and Son, Airport '77, Starship Invasions, The End of the World, Return from Witch Mountain, Caravans, The Passage, Arabian Adventure, Jaguar Lives, Circle of Iron, 1941, Bear Island, Serial, The Salamander, An Eye for an Eye, Safari 3000, House of Long Shadows, The Return of Captain Invincible, The Rosebud Beach Hotel, Roadtrip, Dark Mission, The Howling II: Your Sister is a Werewolf, Olympus Force, Jocks, Murder Story, Mio In the Land of Faraway, The Girl, The Return of the Musketeers, Honeymoon Academy, The French Revolution, Gremlins 2: The New Batch, Curse III: Blood Sacrifice, The Rainbow Thief, L'Avaro, Jackpot, Double Vision, Shogun Mayeda, Special Class, Journey of Honor, Cybereden, Funny Man, Police Academy: Mission to Moscow, A Feast at Midnight, The Stupids, Sorellina, Jinnah, Russell Mulcahy's Tale of the Mummy, Sleepy Hollow, The Lord of the Rings: The Fellowship of the Ring, The Rocky Horror Interactive Show, Cries in the Night: Orloff, The Lord of the Rings: The Two Towers, Star Wars: Episode 2: Attack of the Clones, The Last Unicorn: The Movie, The Lord of the Rings: The Return on the King
TELEVISION: The Disputation, Metier du Seigneur, Movies: Poor Devil, Harold Robbins' The Pirate, Captain America II, Once a Spy, Charles and Diana: A Royal Love Story, Far Pavilions, Shaka Zulu, Goliath Awaits, Massarati and the Brain, Around the World in 80 Days, Treasure Island, Young Indiana Jones, The Care of Time, Sherlock Holmes & the Leading Lady, Sherlock Holmes and the Incident at Victoria Falls, Death Train, The Tomorrow People, Tales of Mystery & Imagination, Moses, Ivanhoe, Gormenghast, In the Beginning, Ghost Stories for Christmas, Les Redoutables.

LEE, JASON SCOTT
Actor. b. Los Angeles, CA, 1966. Raised in Hawaii. e. Fullerton Col., Orange County, CA.
PICTURES: Born in East L.A. (debut, 1987), Back to the Future II, Map of the Human Heart, Dragon: The Bruce Lee Story, Rapa Nui, Rudyard Kipling's The Jungle Book, Tale of the Mummy, Soldier, Arabian Nights (voice), Lilo & Stitch (voice), Dracula II: Ascencion.
TELEVISION: Movie: Vestige of Honor. Special: American Eyes. Guest: Showtime's Hunger Series.

LEE, JOIE
Actress. b. 1968. e. Sarah Lawrence Col. Brother is director-writer Spike Lee. On NY stage in Mulebone. Appeared in short film Coffee and Cigarettes Part Two. Has also been billed as Joy Lee, Joie Susannah Lee.
PICTURES: She's Gotta Have It (debut, 1986), School Daze, Do the Right Thing, Bail Jumper, Mo' Better Blues, A Kiss Before Dying, Fathers and Sons, Crooklyn (also story, co-s.p., assoc. prod.), Losing Isaiah, Girl 6, Get on the Bus, Summer of Sam, Snapped (prod. only).

LEE, MICHELE
Actress. b. Los Angeles, CA, June 24, 1942. On Broadway in How to Succeed in Business Without Really Trying, Seesaw.
PICTURES: How to Succeed in Business Without Really Trying, The Love Bug, The Comic, Nutcracker Fantasy.
TELEVISION: Movies: Dark Victory, Bud and Lou, Letter to Three Wives, Single Women Married Men (also exec. prod.), The Fatal Image, My Son Johnny, Broadway Bound, When No One Would Listen (also exec. prod.), Big Dreams & Broken Hearts: The Dottie West Story (also exec. prod.), Color Me Perfect (also dir., prod., co-s.p.), Scandalous Me: The Jacqueline Susann Story, A Murder on Shadow Mountain, AMC Backstory: Valley of the Dolls. Mini-Series: Knots Landing: Back to the Cul de Sac. Series: Knots Landing (also dir. several episodes).

LEE, SHERYL
Actress. b. Augsburg, Germany, April 22, 1967.
PICTURES: Wild at Heart, I Love You to Death, Twin Peaks: Fire Walk With Me, Jersey Girl, Backbeat, Don't Do It, Fall Times, Notes From Underground, Homage, Mother Night, Bliss, This World, Then the Fireworks, The Blood Oranges, Vampires, Kiss the Sky, Dante's View, Angel's Dance.
TELEVISION: Movies: Love, Lies, and Murder, Guinevere, Follow the River, David, Hitched. Series: Twin Peaks, L.A. Doctors. Guest: Red Shoe Diaries, Dr. Quinn, Medicine Woman.

LEE, SPIKE
Director, Producer, Writer, Actor. r.n. Shelton Jackson Lee. b. Atlanta, GA, Mar. 20, 1957. Son of jazz bass musician, composer Bill Lee. Sister is actress Joie Lee. e. Morehouse Coll B.A., Mass Comm., MFA NYU Film Sch. Completed 2 student features and hour-long thesis: Joe's Bed-Stuy Barbershop: We Cut Heads which won student Acad. Award from Acad. M.P. Arts & Sciences. Wrote, prod., dir., co-starred in indep. feature, She's Gotta Have It, budgeted at $175,000. Appeared in films Lonely in America, Hoop Dreams. Author of five books on his films. Director of numerous tv commercials for Nike, Levi's, ESPN and others. Director of over 35 music videos for Michael Jackson, Stevie Wonder, Miles Davis, and others.
PICTURES: Joe's Bed-Stuy Barbershop: We Cut Heads (co-prod., dir., s.p., editor). Dir.-Prod.-Writer-Actor: She's Gotta Have It (LA Film Critics Award for best new director, 1986), School Daze, Do the Right Thing (LA Film Critics Awards for best picture & dir., 1989), Mo' Better Blues, Jungle Fever, Malcolm X, Crooklyn, Clockers, Girl 6, Get On the Bus, 4 Little Girls, He Got Game, Summer of Sam, Michael Jordan to the Max (actor only), Famous (actor), The Original Kings of Comedy, Bamboozled, Rent . Executive Producer: Drop Squad (also actor), New Jersey Drive, Tales From the Hood, Subway Stories: Tales from the Underground, 3 AM.
TELEVISION: Guest: The Debbie Allen's Special, Spike & Co. Do It A Capella. Movies: A Huey P. Newton Story, Good Fences (exec. prod.) Mini-Series: The Blues

LEEDS, MARTIN N.
Film-TV Executive. b. New York, NY, Apr. 6, 1916. e. NYU, B.S., 1936; J.D., 1938. Admitted NY Bar, 1938, CA Bar, 1948; dir. ind. rltns. Wabash Appliance Corp., 1943-44; ind. bus. rltns. cons. Davis & Gilbert, 1944-45; dir. ind. rltns. Flying Tiger Lines, 1947; dir. bus. affairs CBS TV div., 1947-53; exec. v.p. Desilu Productions, Inc., 1953-60; v.p. Motion Picture Center Studios, Inc.: memb. Industry comm. War Manpower Comm., 1943; chmn. Comm. to form Television Code of Ethics: U.S. Army 1941. Exec. v.p. in chg. of West Coast oper. & member of bd. of dir. Talent Associates—Paramount Ltd., Hollywood, 1962; TV production consultant; exec. v.p., Electronovision Prods. Inc., 1964; TV prod. & MP prod. consultant, 1965; pres., CEO, memb. of bd., Beverly Hills Studios, Inc., 1969; sr. v.p., American Film Theatre, 1973; 1975, motion picture and TV attorney & consultant. Retired.

LEEWOOD, JACK
Producer. b. New York, NY. May 20, 1913. e. Upsala Coll., Newark U., NYU. 1926-31 with Gottesman-Stern circuit as usher, asst. and relief mgr.; 1931-43 Stanley-Warner, mgr. of Ritz, Capitol and Hollywood theatres 1943-47. Joined Warner Bros. field forces in Denver-Salt Lake; Seattle-Portland, 1947-48. Dir. pub. & adv. Screen Guild Prod.; 1948-52, Lippert Productions; prod. exec., 1953-56, Allied Artists; 1957-62 prod. 20th Cent. Fox; 1965-68, prod., Universal; 1976-78. Affiliated Theatre S.F. & HTN.; 1978-83. Hamner Prod.
PICTURES: Holiday Rhythm, Gunfire, Hi-Jacked, Roaring City, Danger Zone, Lost Continent, F.B.I. Girl, Pier 23, Train to Tombstone, I Shot Billy the Kid, Bandit Queen, Motor Patrol, Savage Drums, Three Desperate Men, Border Rangers, Western Pacific Agent, Thundering Jets, Lone Texan, Little Savage, Alligator People, 13 Fighting Men, Young Jesse James, Swingin' Along, We'll Bury You, 20,000 Eyes, Thunder Island, The Plainsman.
TELEVISION: Longest 100 Miles, Escape to Mindanao, Dallas Cowboys Cheerleaders, When Hell Was in Session, Fugitive Family, Dallas Cowboys Cheerleaders II, Million Dollar Face, Portrait of a Showgirl, Margin For Murder, Anatomy of an Illness, Malibu.

LEFFERTS, GEORGE
Producer, Writer, Director. b. Paterson, NJ. e. Univ. of MI. Dir., numerous award-winning TV series, films. Exec. prod.-Time-Life films prod./writer, Movie of the Week (NBC) Biog: Who's Who in America, Who's Who in the World. Exec. prod., Bing Crosby Productions, prod., NBC 10 yrs, Independent. Exec. prod. David Wolper prods. 4 Emmy Awards, 2 Golden Globe Awards, 2 New England Journalism Awards, 1 Cine Golden Eagle Award.
PICTURES: The Stake, Mean Dog Blues, The Living End, The Boat, The Teenager.
TELEVISION: Specials: Teacher Teacher (Emmy Award, 1969), Benjamin Franklin (Emmy Award, 1975), Purex Specials for Women (Emmy Award, Producer's Guild Award; writer, prod. dir.), Our Group (writer), Jean Seberg Story. Series: Breaking Point (exec. prod.), The Bill Cosby Show, Studio One, Kraft Theatre, Chrysler Theatre, Sinatra Show, Lights Out, Alcoa, The Bold Ones, One Life to Live (WGA Award), Ryan's Hope (prod.). Movies: The Harness, She's Dressed to Kill, The Night They Took Miss Beautiful, Smithsonian Institution Specials (exec. prod.).

LEGATO, ROBERT
Special Effects, Director.
PICTURES: Interview with the Vampire, Apollo 13, Titanic (Acad. Award, Best Visual Effects, 1997), Armageddon, What Lies Beneath, Harry Potter and the Sorcerer's Stone (AFI nom., BAFTA nom.).
TELEVISION: Series: Star Trek: The Next Generation (also dir.), Star Trek: Deep Space 9 (also dir.) Movies: Star Trek: Deep Space Nine-Emissary.

LEGRAND, MICHEL JEAN
Composer, Conductor. b. France, Feb. 24, 1932. Son of well-known arranger, composer and pianist, Raymond Legrand. At 11 Michel, a child prodigy, entered Paris Cons. and graduated nine years later with top honors in composition and as solo pianist. In late fifties turned to composing for films and has composed, orchestrated and conducted scores of more than 140 films.
PICTURES: Lola, Eva, Vivre Sa Vie, La Baie des Anges, The Umbrellas of Cherbourg, Banda a Part, Un Femme Mariee, Une Femme est une Femme, The Young Girls of Rochefort, Ice Station Zebra, The Thomas Crown Affair (Academy Award for best song: The Windmills of Your Mind, 1968), Pieces of Dreams, The Happy Ending, Picasso Summer, Wuthering Heights, The Go-Between, Summer of '42 (Academy Award, 1971), Lady Sings the Blues, The Nelson Affair, Breezy, The Three Musketeers, Sheila Levine, Gable and Lombard, Ode to Billy Joe, The Savage, The Other Side of Midnight, The Fabulous Adventures of the Legendary Baron Munchausen, The Roads of the South, The Hunter, The Mountain Men, Atlantic City, Falling in Love Again, Best Friends, A Love in Germany, Never Say Never Again, Yentl (Academy Award, 1983), Hell Train, Micki and Maude, Secret Places, Spirale, Parking, Switching Channels, Three Seats for the 26th Cinq jours en juin (dir. debut, s.p., music), Dingo, The Pickle, Ready to Wear (Pret-a-Porter), Les Miserables, The Children of Lumiere, Aaron's Magic Village, Madeline, Doggy Bag, Season's Beatings, And Now...Ladies and Gentlemen.
TELEVISION: Movies: Brian's Song, The Jesse Owens Story, A Woman Called Golda, As Summers Die, Crossings, Sins, Promises to Keep, Not a Penny More Not a Penny Less, The Burning Shore, The Ring. Mini-Series: La Bicyclette bleu.

LE GROS, JAMES
Actor. b. Minneapolis, MN, Apr. 27, 1962.
THEATRE: The Cherry Orchard, Galileo, Ceremony of Innocence, Table Settings, Curse of the Starving Class, American Buffalo, Bits and Bytes, Becoming Memories, Slab Boys.
PICTURES: Solarbabies, Near Dark, Fatal Beauty, Phantasm II, Drugstore Cowboy, Point Break, Blood & Concrete, Gun Crazy, The Rapture, Where the Day Takes You, Singles, My New Gun, Bad Girls, Floundering, Mrs. Parker and the Vicious Circle, Destiny Turns on the Radio, Panther, Safe, Living in Oblivion, Infinity, The Low Life, Boys, The Destiny of Marty Fine, Countdown, The Myth of Fingerprints, Wishful Thinking, The Pass, L.A. Without a Map, Thursday, Enemy of the State, Psycho, Jump, Drop Back Ten, If You Only Knew, There's No Fish Food in Heaven, Scotland,PA, Lovely and Amazing, World Traveler
TELEVISION: Movie: The Ratings Game, Pronto, Border Line, Common Ground, Big Shot: Confessions of a Campus Bookie, Damaged Care. Series: Ally McBeal.

LEGUIZAMO, JOHN
Actor. b. Bogota, Colombia, July 22, 1964. Moved to Queens, NY at age 5. e. NYU. Appeared in award-winning student film Five Out of Six, while in school. Studied acting with Lee Strasberg and Wynn Handman. Made professional debut on Miami Vice on tv.
THEATRE: A Midsummer Night's Dream, La Puta Vida, Parting Gestures, Mambo Mouth (also writer; Obie & Outer Critics Circle Awards), Spic-O-Rama (also writer; Drama Desk & Theatre World Awards).
PICTURES: Casualties of War, Revenge, Die Hard 2, Gentile

Alouette, Street Hunter, Out for Justice, Hangin' With the Homeboys, Regarding Henry, Whispers in the Dark, Super Mario Bros., Night Owl, Carlito's Way, A Pyromaniac's Love Story, To Wong Foo—Thanks for Everything—Julie Newmar, Executive Decision, Romeo and Juliet, The Pest, A Brother's Kiss, Spawn, Frogs for Snakes, Doctor Dolittle (voice), The Split, Summer of Sam, Joe the King (also exec. prod.), Moulin Rouge, Titan A.E. (voice), King of the Jungle, What's The Worst That Could Happen?, Collateral Damage, Empire, Spun, ZigZag, Ice Age (voice).
TELEVISION: Series: House of Buggin', The Brothers Garcia (voice). Specials: Talent Pool Comedy Special (ACE Award), Mambo Mouth (also writer), Spic-O-Rama (also writer; 3 Cable ACE Awards), Sexaholix: A Love Story.

LEHMAN, ERNEST
Writer, Producer, Director. b. New York, NY, 1923. e. City Coll. of New York. Began career as free-lance journalist and magazine fiction writer. First pub. books, The Comedian, The Sweet Smell of Success. First hardcover novel, The French Atlantic Affair followed by Farewell Performance, and first non-fiction book, Screening Sickness. Pres., WGAW, 1983-85.1987, 1988, 1990: Acad. Awards show (co-writer). The Ernest Lehman Collection is archived at the Humanities Research Center, Univ. of TX at Austin, and in part at USC Film Library and Margaret Herrick Library. Co-prod. of musical stage adaptation of Sweet Smell of Success. Laurel Award for Screen Achievement, WGAW, 1973. Five Best Screenplay Awards, WGAW.
PICTURES: Writer: Executive Suite, Sabrina (co-s.p.; Acad. Award nom.), The King and I, Somebody Up There Likes Me, Sweet Smell of Success (co-s.p.; based on his own novelette), North By Northwest (Acad. Award nom.), From the Terrace, West Side Story (Acad. Award nom.), The Prize, The Sound of Music, Who's Afraid of Virginia Woolf? (also prod.; 2 Acad. Award noms. for picture & s.p.), Hello Dolly! (also prod.; Acad. Award nom. for picture), Portnoy's Complaint (also dir., prod.), Family Plot, Black Sunday (co-s.p.), Sabrina.
TELEVISION: The French Atlantic Affair.

LEHMANN, MICHAEL
Director. b. San Francisco, CA, March 30, 1957. e. U. Cal, Berkeley, Columbia U. Started in industry supervising video systems used in the Francis Ford Coppola films One From the Heart, Rumble Fish, The Outsiders. Dir. short films for Saturday Night Live incl. Ed's Secret Life. Served as exec. prod. on Ed Wood.
PICTURES: Heathers (debut, 1989), Meet the Applegates, Hudson Hawk, Airheads, Ed Wood (exec. prod. only), The Truth About Cats and Dogs, My Giant, Killing Mrs. Duke, 40 Days and 40 Nights.
TELEVISION: Series: The Larry Sanders Show, Homicide: Life on the Street, The West Wing, Watching Ellie.

LEHRER, JIM
News Anchor. b. Wichita, KS, 1934. e. Victoria Col., Univ. of MO. Served in U.S. Marine Corps. 1959-66, reporter for Dallas Morning News, Dallas Times-Herald; 1968 became Times-Herald's city editor before moving into tv as exec. dir. of public affairs, host and editor of news program on KERA-TV in Dallas. To Washington where he became public affairs coord. for PBS, then corresp. for the Natl. Public Affairs Center for Television. 1973 first teamed with Robert MacNeil to cover Senate Watergate hearings. 1975, served as D.C. corresp. for the Robert MacNeil Report on PBS (showed was re-named The MacNeil/Lehrer Report in 1976). 1983, started The MacNeil/Lehrer NewsHour. 1995, became exec. editor and anchor of new version of series The NewsHour With Jim Lehrer. Host of series: Character Above All (1996).

LEIBMAN, RON
Actor. b. New York, NY, Oct. 11, 1937. m. actress Jessica Walter. e. Ohio Wesleyan U. Joined Actor's Studio in N.Y.; first professional appearance in summer theatre production of A View from the Bridge.
THEATRE: The Premise, Dear Me, The Sky Is Falling, We Bombed in New Haven (Theatre World Award), Cop Out, Room Service, I Oughta Be in Pictures, The Deputy, Bicycle Ride to Nevada, Doubles, Rumors, Angels in America: Millenium Approaches (Tony & Drama Desk Awards).
PICTURES: Where's Poppa (debut, 1970), The Hot Rock, Slaughterhouse Five, Your Three Minutes Are Up, Super Cops, Won Ton Ton the Dog Who Saved Hollywood, Norma Rae, Up the Academy, Zorro the Gay Blade, Romantic Comedy, Phar Lap, Rhinestone, Door to Door, Seven Hours to Judgement, Night Falls on Manhattan, Just the Ticket, Shylock, Dummy, Personal Velocity: Three Portraits.
TELEVISION: Series: Kaz (Emmy Award, 1979), Pacific Station, Central Park West. Movies: The Art of Crime, A Question of Guilt, Rivkin: Bounty Hunter, Many Happy Returns, Christmas Eve, Terrorist on Trial: The United States vs. Salim Ajami, Don King: Only in America.

LEIDER, GERALD J.
Producer, Executive. b. Camden, NJ, May 28, 1931. e. Syracuse U., 1953; Bristol U., Eng., 1954, Fulbright Fellow-ship in drama. m. Susan Trustman. 1955 joined MCA, Inc., N.Y.; 1956-59 theatre producer in NY, London: Shinbone Alley, Garden District, and Sir John Gielgud's Ages of Man. 1960-61; director of special programs, CBS/TV; 1961-62, dir. of program sales, CBS-TV; 1962-69, v.p., tv optns., Ashley Famous Agency, Inc.; 1969-74, pres. Warner Bros. TV, Burbank; 1975-76, exec. v.p. for-eign prod. Warner Bros. Pictures, Rome; 1977-82, indept. prod. under Jerry Leider Prods.; 1982-87, pres., ITC Prods., Inc; named pres. and CEO, ITC Entertain-ment Group, 1987-91.
PICTURES: Wild Horse Hank, The Jazz Singer, Trenchcoat, Dr. Jekyll and Ms. Hyde, My Favorite Martian.
TELEVISION: Movies: And I Alone Survived, Willa, The Hostage Tower, The Scarlet and the Black, Secrets of a Married Man, The Haunting Passion, Letting Go, A Time to Live, The Girl Who Spelled Freedom, Unnatural Causes, Poor Little Rich Girl, Sydney Sheldon's The Sands of Time, Morning Glory, Home Song, Family Blessings, Trucks, Cadet Kelly, Fall From the Sky. Series: Major Payne.

LEIGH, JANET
Actress. r.n. Jeanette Helen Morrison. b. Merced, CA, July 6, 1927. Mother of actresses Jamie Lee Curtis and Kelly Curtis. e. Coll. of Pacific, music. Author: There Really Was a Hollywood (autobiography, 1984), Behind the Scenes of Psycho (1995), House of Destiny (novel; 1995).
THEATRE: includes: Murder Among Friends, Love Letters (with Van Johnson).
PICTURES: The Romance of Rosy Ridge (debut, 1947), If Winter Comes, Hills of Home, Words and Music, Act of Violence, Little Women, That Forsyte Woman, Red Danube, Doctor and the Girl, Holiday Affair, Two Tickets to Broadway, Strictly Dishonorable, Angels in the Outfield, It's a Big Country, Just This Once, Scaramouche, Fearless Fagan, Naked Spur, Confidentially Connie, Houdini, Walking My Baby Back Home, Prince Valiant, Living It Up, Black Shield of Falworth, Rogue Cop, My Sister Eileen, Pete Kelly's Blues, Safari, Jet Pilot, Touch of Evil, The Vikings, The Perfect Furlough, Who Was That Lady?, Psycho (Acad. Award nom.), Pepe, The Manchurian Candidate, Bye Bye Birdie, Wives and Lovers, Three on a Couch, Harper, An American Dream, Kid Rodelo, Grand Slam, Hello Down There, One Is a Lonely Number, Night of the Lepus, Boardwalk, The Fog, Other Realms, Halloween H20: Twenty Years Later, Mary Pickford: A Life on Film, A Fate Totally Worse Than Death.
TELEVISION: Movies: Honeymoon With a Stranger, House on Green Apple Road, The Monk, Deadly Dream, Mirror Mirror, Telethon, Murder at the World Series, Carriage from Britain, Murder in the First, Dear Deductible, Catch Me If You Can, One for My Baby, My Wives, Jane, The Chairman, Death's Head, This Is Maggie Mulligan, Tales of the Unexpected, On the Road, In My Sister's Shadow, Hitchcock: Shadow of a Genius, Howard Hughes: His Women and His Movies. Guest: Matt Houston, Starman, Murder She Wrote.

LEIGH, JENNIFER JASON
Actress. r.n. Jennifer Leigh Morrow. b. Los Angeles, CA, Feb. 5, 1962. Daughter of late actor Vic Morrow and TV writer Barbara Turner. At age 14 debuted in Disney tv movie The Young Runaway. Won L.A. Valley Coll. best actress award for stage prod. The Shadow Box (1979).
PICTURES: Eyes of a Stranger (debut, 1981), Wrong Is Right, Fast Times at Ridgemont High, Easy Money, Grandview U.S.A., The Hitcher, Flesh + Blood, The Men's Club, Undercover, Sister Sister, Heart of Midnight, The Big Picture, Miami Blues (NY Film Critics Award, 1990), Last Exit to Brooklyn (NY Film Critics Award, 1990), Backdraft, Crooked Hearts, Rush, Single White Female, Short Cuts, The Hudsucker Proxy, Mrs. Parker and the Vicious Circle (Natl. Society of Film Critics & Chicago Film Critics Awards, 1994), Dolores Claiborne, Georgia (also co-prod.), Kansas City, A Thousand Acres, Washington Square, eXistenZ, The King is Alive, Skipped Parts, Beautiful View, The Quickie, The Anniversary Party (also dir.), The Road to Perdition, Hey Arnold: The Movie (voice).
TELEVISION: Movies: The Young Runaway, Angel City, The Killing of Randy Webster, The Best Little Girl in the World, The First Time, Girls of the White Orchid, Buried Alive, The Love Letter, Thanks of a Grateful Nation, Crossed Over.

LEIGH, MIKE
Director, Writer. b. Salford, England, Feb. 20, 1943. e. RADA, Camberwell Art Sch., Central Sch. of Arts & Crafts, London Film Sch. m. actress Alison Steadman. Began career in experimental theatre. Plays include Waste Paper Guards, The Box Play, Neena, Individual Fruit Pies, Down Here and Up There, Big Basil, Epilogue, Bleak Moments, A Rancid Pong, Wholesome Glory, The Jaws of Death, Dick Whittington and His Cat, Babies Grow Old, The Silent Majority, Abigail's Party, Ecstacy, Goose-Pimples, Smelling the Rat, Greek Tragedy, It's a Great Big Shame. Directed 1977 TV drama Abigail's Party. 1987 short: The Short and Curlies. Recipient of 1995 BAFTA Award for Outstanding British Contribution to Cinema.
PICTURES: Bleak Moments, Hard Labour, Nuts in May, The Kiss of Death, Who's Who, Grown-Ups, Home Sweet Home,

Meantime, Four Days in July, High Hopes, Life Is Sweet, Naked, Secrets & Lies (Palme d'Or, Cannes 1996; LA Film Critics Award; BAFTA for Best Original S.P.), Career Girls, Topsy-Turvy, All or Nothing.
TELEVISION: A Mug's Game, Plays for Britain.

LEIGH, SUZANNA
Actress. b. Reading, England, 1945. Studied at the Arts Educational Sch. and Webber Douglas Sch. 1965-66, under contract to Hal Wallis and Paramount.
PICTURES: Oscar Wilde, Bomb in High Street, Boeing Boeing, Paradise Hawaiian Style, The Deadly Bees, Deadlier Than the Male, The Lost Continent, Subterfuge, Lust for a Vampire (To Love a Vampire), Beware My Brethren, Son of Dracula.
TELEVISION: Series: Three Stars (France), One on an Island (West Indies). Special: The Plastic People. Guest: The Persuaders.

LEITCH, DONOVAN
Actor. Son of folksinger Donovan. Brother of actress Ione Skye. Acted in jr. high sch. musical then had bit part in PBS. show K.I.D.S.
PICTURES: And God Created Women (1988), The Blob, The In Crowd, Cutting Class, Glory, Gas Food Lodging, Dark Horse, I Shot Andy Warhol, One Night Stand, Love Kills, Cherry, Big City Blues, Men Make Women Crazy Theoryq.
TELEVISION: Movie: For the Very First Time, The '60s. Guest: Life Goes On, 21 Jump Street, Friends, Sex and the City.

LELAND, DAVID
Director, Writer, Actor. b. Cambridge, Eng., April 20, 1947. Began as actor at Nottingham Playhouse. Then joined newly formed company at Royal Court Theatre, London. Also appeared in films Time Bandits, The Missionary, and his own Personal Services (Peter Sellers Award for Comedy) and on TV in The Jewel in the Crown. As stage director specialized in complete seasons of new works at the Crucible in Sheffield and London venues. Wrote play Psy-Warriors.
PICTURES: Mona Lisa (co-s.p.), Personal Services (s.p.), Wish You Were Here (dir., s.p.; BAFTA Award for s.p.), Checking Out (dir.), The Big Man (dir.; a.k.a. Crossing the Line), Land Girls (co-s.p., dir.), The White River Kid (also s.p.), Running Wild.
TELEVISION: Wrote Birth of a Nation, Flying Into the Wind, Rhino, Made in Britain, Beloved Enemy, Ligmalion, Psy-Warriors, Band of Brothers.

LELOUCH, CLAUDE
Director, Writer, Producer, Cinematographer, Editor. b. Paris, France, Oct. 30, 1937. Began m.p. career with short subjects, 1956; French military service, motion picture department, 1957-60; formed Films 13, 1960; publicity Films and Scopitones, 1961-62.
PICTURES: Le Propre de l'Homme (The Right of Man; debut, 1960; also s.p., prod., actor), L'amour avec des Si (Love With Ifs; aalso prod., s.p.), La Femme Spectacle (Night Women; also prod., photog.), Une Fille et des Fusils (To Be a Crook; also co-s.p., prod., edit.), Les Grands Moments (also co-prod.), A Man and A Woman (also co-s.p., story, prod., photog., edit.; Academy Awards for Best Foreign Language Film & Original Screenplay, 1966; also Acad. Award nom. for dir.), Live for Life (also co-s.p., co-photog. , edit.), Farm From Vietnam (segment), 13 Jours in France (Grenoble; co-dir., co-s.p.), Life Love Death (also co-s.p.), Love Is a Funny Thing (also photog., co-s.p.), The Crook (also co- photog., co-s.p.), Smic Smac Smoc (also prod., s.p., photog., actor), Money Money Money (also s.p., prod., photog.), La Bonne Annee (Happy New Year; also prod., s.p., co-photog.), Visions of Eight (segment: The Losers), And Now My Love (also s.p., prod.), Marriage (also co-s.p.), Cat and Mouse (also s.p.), The Good and Bad (also s.p., photog.), Second Chance (also s.p., prod.), Another Man Another Chance (also s.p.), Robert and Robert (also s.p.), Adventure for Two, Bolero (also s.p., prod.), Edith and Marcel (also prod., s.p.), Vive la Vie (also prod., s.p., photog.), Partier Revenir (also prod., co-s.p.), A Man and a Woman: 20 Years Later (also prod., co-s.p.), Bandits (also prod., s.p.), Itinerary of a Spoiled Child (also co-prod., s.p.), There Were Days and Moons (also prod., co-s.p.), Les Miserables, Lumiere and Company, Men Women: A User's Manual, Chance or Coincidence, All 4 One, And Now...Ladies and Gentlemen.
TELEVISION: Moliere (prod. only).

LE MAT, PAUL
Actor. b. Rahway, NJ, Sept. 22, 1945. Studied with Milton Katselas, Herbert Berghof Studio, A.C.T., San Francisco, Mitchel Ryan-Actor's Studio.
PICTURES: American Graffiti (debut, 1973), Aloha—Bobby and Rose, Citizens Band (Handle With Care), More American Graffiti, Melvin and Howard, Death Valley, Jimmy the Kid, Strange Invaders, PK. and the Kid, Rock & Rule (voice), The Hanoi Hilton, Private Investigations, Puppet Master, Easy Wheels, Deuce Coupe, Grave Secrets, Veiled Threat, Wishman, Caroline at Midnight, Sensation, Deep Down, The Outfitters, Big Bad Love.
TELEVISION: Movies: Firehouse, The Gift of Life, The Night They Saved Christmas, The Burning Bed, Long Time Gone, Secret Witness, On Wings of Eagles, Into the Homeland, Blind Witness, In the Line of Duty: Siege at Marion, Woman With a Past. Series: Lonesome Dove.

LEMBERGER, KEN
Executive. e. B.A., Queen's College, CUNY and J.D., NYU School of Law. Began tenure with Sony Pictures Entertainment (SPE) in the legal dept., 1979-81; senior v.p., Studio Legal Affairs, 1981-83; senior v.p. & gen. counsel, SPE, 1983; vice chairman, TriStar Pictures, 1992-94; corporate exec. v.p., SPE, 1994-97. 1997, pres., Columbia TriStar Motion Picture Group. Currently, co-pres., Sony Pictures Entertainment.

LENFEST, H. F. "GERRY"
Executive. b. Jacksonville, FL. e. Mercersburg Academy, Washington and Lee U. and Columbia Law School. Served in U.S. Navy, retired Captain. Practiced law in NYC before joining Triangle Publications., Inc. in Philadelphia as assoc. counsel in 1965. Became head of Triangle's Communications Div., 1970. Formed new co. in 1974 and bought two cable cos. from Triangle. Owns with his children Lenfest Communications, Inc. Subsidiaries incl. Suburban Cable, StarNet and Micronet.

LENO, JAY
Comedian, Actor. r.n. James Leno. b. New Rochelle, NY, April 28, 1950. e. Emerson College, B.A. speech therapy, 1973. Raised in Andover, MA. Worked as Rolls Royce auto mechanic and deliveryman while seeking work as stand-up comedian. Performed in comedy clubs throughout the U.S. and as opening act for Perry Como, Johnny Mathis, John Denver and Tom Jones. Guest on numerous talk shows and specials.
PICTURES: Fun With Dick and Jane, The Silver Bears, American Hot Wax, Americathon, Collision Course, What's Up Hideous Sun Demon? (voice), Dave, We're Back! (voice), Wayne's World 2, Major League 2, The Flintstones, The Birdcage (cameo), Meet Wally Sparks, In & Out, Contact, Wag the Dog, EDtv, Space Cowboys, John Q., Stuck on You, Calendar Girls.
TELEVISION: Series: The Marilyn McCoo & Billy Davis Jr. Show, The Tonight Show (guest host: 1987-92; host: 1992-; Emmy Award, 1995). Specials: Jay Leno and the American Dream (also prod.), The Jay Leno Show, Our Planet Tonight, Jay Leno's Family Comedy Hour, Comedy Store: The E! True Hollywood Story. Guest: The Simpsons (voice).

LENZ, KAY
Actress. b. Los Angeles, CA, March 4, 1953.
PICTURES: Breezy (debut, 1973), White Line Fever, The Great Scout and Cathouse Thursday, Moving Violation, Mean Dog Blues, The Passage, Fast-Walking, House, Stripped to Kill, Death Wish IV: The Crackdown, Headhunter, Physical Evidence, Fear, Streets, Falling From Grace, Trapped in Space, Gunfighter's Moon, A Gun A Car A Blonde, The Adventures of Ragtime, Southside.
TELEVISION: Series: Reasonable Doubts, The Tick (voice), Cover Me: Based on the True Life of an FBI Family. Movies: The Weekend Nun, Lisa, Bright and Dark, A Summer Without Boys, Unwed Father, The Underground Man, The FBI Story: The FBI Versus Alvin Karpis, Journey from Darkness, Rich Man, Poor Man, The Initiation of Sarah, The Seeding of Sarah Burns, Sanctuary of Fear, The Hustler of Muscle Beach, Murder by Night, Heart in Hiding, How the West Was Won, Traveling Man, Escape, Hitler's Daughter, Against Their Will: Women in Prison, Trapped in Space, Shame II: The Secret, Journey of the Heart. Guest: Midnight Caller (Emmy Award, 1989), Moonlighting, Hill St. Blues, Hotel, Cannon, McGyver, Cagney & Lacey, McCloud, Riptide, Law & Order: SVU. Mini-Series: Rich Man Poor Man—Book II.

LEONARD, ROBERT SEAN
Actor. b. Westwood, NJ, Feb. 28, 1969. Raised in Ridgewood, NJ. Started acting at age 12 in local summer stock. Joined NY Shakespeare Festival at 15.
THEATRE: Off-B'way: Coming of Age in Soho, Sally's Gone—She Left Her Name, The Beach House, When She Danced, Romeo and Juliet, Good Evening, The Great Unwashed. B'way: Brighton Beach Memoirs, Breaking the Code, The Speed of Darkness, Candida (Tony nom.), Philadelphia Here I Come!, Arcadia. Regional: Biloxi Blues (tour), Rocky and Diego, Long Day's Journey Into Night, King Lear, The Double Inconstancy.
PICTURES: The Manhattan Project (debut, 1986), My Best Friend Is a Vampire, Dead Poets Society, Mr. & Mrs. Bridge, Swing Kids, Married to It, Much Ado About Nothing, The Age of Innocence, Safe Passage, Killer: A Journal of Murder, I Love You—I Love You Not, Ground Control, Stand Off, The Last Days of Disco, Tape, Driven, Chelsea Walls.
TELEVISION: Movies: My Two Loves, Bluffing It, In the Gloaming, A Glimpse of Hell. Pilot: The Robert Klein Show. Series: Rosebud.

LEONI, TEA
Actress. b. New York, NY Feb. 25, 1966. m. actor David Duchovny
PICTURES: Switch, A League of Their Own, Wyatt Earp, Bad Boys, Flirting with Disaster, Deep Impact, There's No Fish Food In Heaven (also exec. prod.), The Family Man, Jurassic Park III, Hollywood Ending, People I Know.

TELEVISION: *Movies:* The Counterfeit Contessa. *Series:* Santa Barbara, Flying Blind, The Naked Truth. *Guest:* Frasier.

LERNER, JOSEPH
Producer, Director, Writer. m. Geraldine Lerner. Actor on Broadway; radio actor & dir.; with RKO, Columbia and Republic as dir., dial. dir., writer, 2nd unit dir., test dir.; dir.-writer & head of special productions U.S. Army Signal Corps Photographic Center; writer of commercial and educational films 1946-47; v.p. in chg. of prod. Visual Arts Productions 1947; v.p. in chg. prod. Laurel Films 1949; Girl on the Run, comm. ind. films; dir., prod., writer, many TV commercials, documentaries 1967-73; pres., The Place for Film Making, Inc.; pres., Astracor Associates Ltd.; writer & line prod. for Gold Shield Prods; also lecturer and instructor at NYU, Wm. Patterson Coll., Broward Community Coll. (FL), College at Boca Raton. Member: Eastern Council of the Directors Guild of America. Trip the Light Fantastic, musical play in collaboration with song writer Dan Costello
TELEVISION: *Dir./Prod.:* Gangbusters, Grand Tour, Three Musketeers, United Nations Case Book. *Dir./Prod./Writer:* C-Man, Guilty Bystander, Mr. Universe, Dark of the Day, The Fight Never Ends, etc. *Prod./Writer:* Olympic Cavalcade, King of The Olympics, and many other documentaries.

LERNER, MICHAEL
Actor. b. Brooklyn, NY, June 22, 1941. e. Brooklyn Col., Univ. of CA, Berkeley. Prior to acting was professor of dramatic literature at San Francisco St. Col., 1968-69. Studied acting in London on Fullbright Scholarship. Was member of San Francisco's American Conservatory Theatre. On NY stage in Twelfth Night; L.A. stage in The Women of Trachis, Hurlyburly.
PICTURES: Alex in Wonderland (debut, 1970), The Candidate, Busting, Newman's Law, Hangup (Superdude), St. Ives, The Other Side of Midnight, Outlaw Blues, Goldengirl, Borderline, Coast to Coast, The Baltimore Bullet, The Postman Always Rings Twice, National Lampoon's Class Reunion, Threshold, Strange Invaders, Movers and Shakers, Anguish, Vibes, Eight Men Out, Harlem Nights, Any Man's Death, The Closer, Barton Fink (Acad. Award nom.), Newsies, Amos & Andrew, Blank Check, No Escape, Radioland Murders, The Road to Wellville, Girl in the Cadillac, A Pyromaniac's Love Story, The Beautician and the Beast, for Richer or Poorer, Russell Mulcahy's Tale of the Mummy, Godzilla, Celebrity, Safe Men, The Mod Squad, My Favorite Martian, Attention Shoppers, The Mockingbird Don't Sing, Larceny, 29 Palms.
TELEVISION: *Movies:* Thief, Marriage Year One, What's a Nice Girl Like You...?, Magic Carpet, Firehouse (pilot), Reflections of Murder, The Rockford Files (pilot), The Death of Sammy, A Cry for Help, Starsky and Hutch (pilot), Sarah T: Portrait of a Teenage Alcoholic, Dark Victory, F. Scott Fitzgerald in Hollywood, Scott Free, Killer on Board, A Love Affair: The Eleanor and Lou Gehrig Story, Vega$ (pilot), Ruby & Oswald, Hart to Hart (pilot), Moviola: This Year's Blonde, Gridlock, Blood Feud, Rita Hayworth: Love Goddess, The Execution, This Child is Mine, Betrayal of Trust, Hands of a Stranger, King of Love, Framed, Omen IV: The Awakening, The Comrades of Summer, Murder at the Cannes Film Festival, The Omen Legacy. *Series:* Courthouse. *Special:* The Missiles of October. *Guest:* Amazing Stories, Macgyver. *Pilots:* Grandpa Max, The Boys, I Gave at the Office.

LESLIE, ALEEN
Writer. b. Pittsburgh, PA, Feb. 5, 1908. e. Ohio State U. Contributor to magazines; columnist Pittsburgh Press; orig. & wrote radio series A Date with Judy 1941-50. B'way play Slightly Married, 1943; wrote, prod. Date with Judy, TV series; author, The Scent of the Roses, The Windfall.
PICTURES: Doctor Takes a Wife, Affectionately Yours, Henry Aldrich Plays Cupid, Stork Pays Off, Henry Aldrich Gets Glamour, It Comes Up Love, Rosie the Riveter, A Date With Judy, Father Was a Fullback, Father Is a Bachelor.

LESLIE, JOAN
Actress. r.n. Joan Brodell. b. Detroit, MI, January 26, 1925. e. St. Benedicts, Detroit; Our Lady of Lourdes, Toronto; St. Mary's Montreal; Immaculate Heart. H.S., L.A. Child performer on stage as part of The Three Brodels. Became model before going to Hollywood in 1936. Voted Star of Tomorrow, 1946. Now on bd. of dir., St. Anne's Maternity Home, Damon Runyon Foundation.
PICTURES: *(as Joan Brodel):* Camille (debut, 1937), Men with Wings, Nancy Drew—Reporter, Love Affair, Winter Carnival, Two Thoroughbreds, High School, Young as You Feel, Star Dust, Susan and God, Military Academy, Foreign Correspondent, Laddie. *(as Joan Leslie):* Thieves Fall Out, The Wagons Roll at Night, High Sierra, The Great Mr. Nobody, Sergeant York, The Hard Way, The Male Animal, Yankee Doodle Dandy, The Sky's the Limit, This Is the Army, Thank Your Lucky Stars, Hollywood Canteen, Rhapsody in Blue, Where Do We Go From Here?, Too Young to Know, Janie Gets Married, Cinderella Jones, Two Guys From Milwaukee, Repeat Performance, Northwest Stampede, Born To Be Bad, The Skipper Surprised His Wife, Man in the Saddle, Hellgate, Toughest Man in Arizona, The Woman They Almost Lynched, Flight Nurse, Hell's Outpost, Jubilee Trail, The Revolt of Mamie Stover.
TELEVISION: *Guest:* Ford Theatre, G.E. Theatre, Queen for a Day, Simon and Simon, Murder, She Wrote. *Movies:* Charley Hannah, The Keegans, Turn Back the Clock. Various commercials.

LESTER, MARK
Actor. b. Oxford, England, July 11, 1958. Ent. m.p. ind. 1963.
THEATER: The Murder Game, The Prince and the Pauper 1976.
PICTURES: *Director and/or Producer:* The Counterfeit Constable; debut, 1963), Spaceflight IC-1, Fahrenheit 451, Arrividerci Baby!, Our Mother's House, Oliver!, Run Wild Run Free, Sudden Terror (Eye Witness), Melody, Black Beauty, Who Slew Auntie Roo?, Redneck, Scalawag, Jungle Boy, Crossed Swords (The Prince and the Pauper).
TELEVISION: The Boy Who Stole the Elephants, Graduation Trip, Danza Alla Porto Gli Olmi (Italian Entry Berlin '75), Seen Dimly Before Dawn.

LESTER, MARK LESLIE
Director. b. Cleveland, OH, Nov. 26, 1949. e. Cal. State Univ. Northridge, B.A.
PICTURES: *Director and/or Producer:* Steel Arena (debut, 1973; also co-prod., s.p.), Truck Stop Women (also co-s.p.), Bobbie Jo and the Outlaw, Stunts, Roller Boogie, The Funhouse (co-exec. prod. only), The Class of 1984 (also co-exec. prod., co-s.p.), Firestarter, Commando, Armed and Dangerous, Class of 1999 (also story), Showdown in Little Tokyo, Extreme Justice, Night of the Running Man, The Ex, Public Enemy #1, Double Take, Misbegotten, The Ex, Hitman's Run, Blowback, Betrayal.
TELEVISION: Gold of the Amazon Women, Sacrifice, Guilty As Charged.

LESTER, RICHARD
Director. b. Philadelphia, PA, Jan. 19, 1932. e. Univ. of PA. Started as stagehand at tv studio before becoming dir. and music. dir. CBS-TV in Philadelphia, then CBC-TV, Toronto. To England in 1956 where he resumed work as tv dir. TV dir. The Goon Shows. Composed (with Reg. Owen) Sea War Series. Short Film: composer and dir., The Running Jumping and Standing Still Film. Directed sequences for Mondo Teeno/Teenage Rebellion, Superman.
PICTURES: It's Trad Dad (debut, 1962; aka Ring-a-Ding Rhythm; also prod.), The Mouse on the Moon, A Hard Day's Night, The Knack... and How to Get It, Help!, A Funny Thing Happened on the Way to the Forum, How I Won the War (also prod.), Petulia, The Bed-Sitting Room (also co-prod.), The Three Musketeers, Juggernaut, The Four Musketeers, Royal Flash, Robin & Marian (also co-prod.), The Ritz, Butch and Sundance: The Early Days, Cuba, Superman II, Superman III, Finders Keepers (also exec. prod.), The Return of the Musketeers (tv in U.S.), Get Back.

LETTERMAN, DAVID
Performer, Writer. b. Indianapolis, IN, Apr. 12, 1947. e. Ball State U. Began career as weatherman and talk show host on Indianapolis TV before going to Hollywood. Cameo appearances in films Cabin Boy, Beavis and Butt-head Do America (voice), Private Parts, Man on the Moon, Meeting People Is Easy.
TELEVISION: *Series Writer:* Good Times, Paul Lynde Comedy Hour. *Writer* (specials): John Denver Special, Bob Hope Special. *Series Performer:* The Starland Vocal Band (also writer), Mary (1978), Tonight Show (guest host 1978-82), The David Letterman Show (Daytime Emmy Award for writing, 1981), Late Night with David Letterman (1982-93, on NBC; 4 Emmy Awards for Writing), Late Show With David Letterman (1993-, on CBS, 1994 Emmy Award, Emmy nom., 1995-2001). *Exec. Prod:* Ed. *Guest:* An NBC Family Christmas, The Larry Sanders Show.

LEVIN, GERALD M.
Executive. b. Philadelphia, PA, May 6, 1939. e. Haverford Col., Univ. of PA Law Sch. Attorney, 1963-67. Gen. mgr. & COO of Development Sources Corp., 1969. IBEC rep. in Tehran, Iran, 1971. Joined HBO in 1972 as v.p. of programming, then pres. & CEO, 1973-76; promoted to chmn, 1976. Became v.p. Time Inc., 1975; group v.p., video, 1979; exec. v.p. in 1984; on bd. of dirs., 1983-87. Named vice-chmn, Time Warner, 1989; COO, 1991; pres. & co-CEO of Time Warner, Inc., 1992; chmn. & CEO of Time Warner Inc., 1993. Became CEO and dir., AOL Time Warner, Inc. after the merger and CEO, Time Warner Entertainment Group LP. Bd. of directors, Federal Reserve Bank of NY, dir., The New York Stock Exchange. He is also a member of the board and treasurer of the New York Philharmonic, bd. member, National Cable Television Center and Museum, The Aspen Institute and the Museum of Jewish Heritage – A Living Memorial to the Holocaust, and is a member of the Council on Foreign Relations. Retired from Time Warner, 2002.

LEVIN, JULIAN
Executive. b. South Africa. Held various positions at Morgan Creek International, Vestron Motion Pictures and other independent production and distribution companies. Joined Fox in 1991, holding several exec. position in intl. sales and distrib. 1995, promoted to exec. v.p., sales and distrib., Twentieth Century Fox Intl. Played an integral role in the distribution of such films as Mrs. Doubtfire, Independence Day, Braveheart, Titanic, and Moulin Rouge. Feb. 2002, appointed to newly creative position of exec. v.p., digital exhibition and special projects, Twentieth Century Fox. Responsible for development of corporate strategies for digital exhibition and analysis of key initiatives in new theatrical technologies. Levin is also the key exec. representing Twentieth Century Fox in NEWCO, the entity formed by the seven major studioes to develop technical standards for digital cinema technology.

LEVIN, MARC
Director, Writer, Actor, Producer.
PICTURES: The Last Party, CIA: America's Secret Warriors, Slam (Cannes Film Fest. Awards, Camera d'Or, Grand Jury Prize, 1998) ,Whiteboys, Soldiers in the Army of God, Speak Truth to Power (dir. only), Brooklyn Babylon, Street Time (dir. only).
TELEVISION: Series: Cleghorne! (cinematographer).   Mini-Series: The Blues (dir. only).

LEVIN, ROBERT B.
Executive. b. Chicago, IL, May 31, 1943. e. U. of Illinois, BS Journalism, 1965. Copywriter Sears Roebuck & Co. 1965-66, PR Natural Gas Pipeline Co. of Amer. 1966-69. Acct. Exec. Hurvis Binzer & Churchill 1969-70. McCann-Erickson 1975-82 Acct. Super. 1975-79, Mgmt. Super. Needham Harper Worldwide 1982-85. Pres. Mktg. WD Co. 1985-94, Chief Corp. Mktg. & Comm. 1994-95. Pres. Worldwide Mktg. Savoy Pictures 1995-96, Sony Pictures Entertainment, 1996. Currently, pres,. Worldwide Theatrical Mktg. & Distrib., MGM.

LEVINSON, BARRY
Director, Producer, Writer, Actor. b. Baltimore, MD, Apr. 6, 1942. e. American Univ. Wrote and acted in L.A. comedy show leading to work on network tv incl. writing and performing on The Carol Burnett Show. Co-wrote film scripts with Mel Brooks, and then-wife Valerie Curtin. Apppeared as actor in History of the World Part I, Quiz Show.
PICTURES: Writer: Silent Movie (also actor), High Anxiety (also actor), ... And Justice for All (Acad. Award nom.), Inside Moves, Best Friends, Unfaithfully Yours. Director/Producer: Diner (also s.p.; Acad. Award nom. for s.p.), The Natural, Young Sherlock Holmes, Tin Men (also s.p.), Good Morning Vietnam, Rain Man (also actor; Acad. Award for Best Director, 1988), Avalon (also s.p.; WGA Award, Acad. Award nom. for s.p.), Bugsy (Acad. Award nom.), Toys (also co-s.p.), Jimmy Hollywood (also s.p., co-prod.), Disclosure (also co-prod.), Sleepers (also s.p., co-prod.), Donnie Brasco (prod. only), Wag the Dog (also co-prod.), Sphere (also co-prod.), Liberty Heights (also prod.), The Perfect Storm (exec. prod.), An Everlasting Piece, Bandits (dir. only), Possession (prod. only), Analyze That.
TELEVISION: Series: The Tim Conway Comedy Hour (writer), The Marty Feldman Comedy Machine (writer), The Carol Burnett Show (writer; Emmy Awards: 1974, 1975), Harry (exec. prod.), Homicide: Life on the Streets (dir., co-exec. prod.; Emmy Award for directing, 1993), The Beat, Falcone, Baseball Wives. Pilot: Diner (exec. prod., dir.), Oz (exec. prod.). Specials: Stopwatch 30 Minutes of Investigative Ticking (exec. prod.). Movies: The Second Civil War, Homicide: The Movie, American Tragedy, Shot in the Heart.

LEVINSON, NORM
Executive. b. New Haven, CT, Mar. 17, 1925. Started theatre business as usher for Loew's Theatres, 1940. U.S. Army, 1943-46. Returned Loew's Theatres managerial positions New Haven and Hartford, CT. MGM press representative, Minneapolis, Jacksonville, Atlanta, Dallas. General Manager, Trans-Texas Theatres, Dallas. President, Academy Theatres, Inc., Dallas. Promoted World Championship Boxing, Dallas and Johannesburg, South Africa. Executive Vice President, Cobb Theatres, Birmingham, Alabama; v.p., world-wide mktg., Artists Releasing Corp., Encino, CA.; head film buyer, Chakeres Theatres, Ohio & Kentucky. Retired.

LEVITAN, STEVEN
Producer.
TELEVISION: Series: Frasier (consult. and writer), The Larry Sanders Show (writer only), Just Shoot Me (also dir., creator), Yes, Dear (dir. only), Men Behaving Badly (writer only), Stark Raving Mad (exec. prod.), Greg the Bunny (exec. prod.), With You in Spirit (writer, exec. prod.), Oliver Beene

LEVY, BERNARD
Executive. b. Boca Raton, FL. e. Brooklyn Law Sch., L.L.B. Legal staff of Superintendent of Insurance of the state of New York in the rehabilitation and liquidation of guaranteed title and mortgage companies, 1934-36; private practice of law, 1936-46; legal staff, Paramount Pictures, Inc., 1946-50; legal staff, United Paramount Theatres, 1950-51; exec. asst. to Edward L. Hyman, v.p., ABC, Inc., in chg. of theatre administration, north, 1951-62; apptd. exec. liaison officer for southern motion picture theatres, ABC, Inc., 1962-64; exec. liaison officer, m.p. theas., ABC, Inc., 1965-72; v.p., ABC Theatre Division, 1973. Retired, 1976.

LEVY, BUD
Executive. b. Jackson Heights, NY, April 3, 1928. e. NYU. Member: Variety Clubs Int'l., M.P. Pioneers, President's Advisory Board-NATO. Director: NATO, TOP, CATO. Elected pres., Trans-Lux Corp., 1980; pres. Trans Lux Theatres, (a subsidiary of Paramount Pictures), 1986-1991. Will Rogers Memorial Fund; chmn., Cara Committee for NATO; chmn. ShowEast; v.p. NATO; dir. Motion Picture Pioneers. Retired.

LEVY, EUGENE
Actor, Writer, Director. b. Hamilton, Canada, Dec. 17, 1946. e. McMaster U. Acted with coll. ensemble theater. Film debut in Ivan Reitman's Cannibal Girls, 1970
PICTURES: Cannibal Girls, Running, Nothing Personal, double Negative, Heavy Metal (voice), National Lampoon's Vacation, Vacation, Strange Brew, Going Berserk, Splash, Tears Are Not Enough, Armed and Dangerous, Club Paradise, Speed Zone, Father of the Bride, Once Upon a Crime (also dir.), Stay Tuned, I Love Trouble, Father of the Bride 2, Multiplicity, Waiting for Guffman (also s.p.), Dogmatic, Almost Heroes, Holy Man, Akbar's Adventure Tours, The Secret Life of Girls, Unglued, America Pie, Best In Show (also s.p.), The Ladies Man, Silver Man, Down to Earth, Josie and the Pussycats, American Pie 2, Serendipity, Repli-Kate, Like Mike, A Mighty Wind, In the Houze.
TELEVISION: Series: Stay Tuned, Second City TV (also writer), The Sunshine Hour, SCTV Network 90, SCTV Network (Emmy Award as writer, 1983), Hiller & Diller, Hercules (voice), Greg the Bunny. Movies: Partners 'n Love, Sodbusters (dir., co-writer, co-exec. prod.), Harrison Bergeron, D.O.A., Committed, Club Land, The Kid. Specials: The Canadian Conspiracy, Bully Crystal: Don't Get Me Started, Biographies: The Enigma of Bobbie Bittman.

LEVY, JULES
Producer. b. Los Angeles, CA, Feb. 12, 1923. e. USC. Started in property dept. of WB, 1941; first m.p. unit Army Air Force.
PICTURES: The Vampire, Return of Dracula, Vice Squad, Without Warning, Down Three Dark Streets, Geronimo, The Glory Guys, Clambake, The Scalphunters, Sam Whiskey, The McKenzie Break, The Hunting Party, Kansas City Bomber, The Honkers, McQ, Branningan, White Lightning, Gator, Safari 3000.
TELEVISION: Series: The Rifleman, Robert Taylor in The Detectives, Law of the Plainsman, The Big Valley.

LEVY, MICHAEL
Executive. b. Brooklyn, NY. e. Brown U. Started in industry in editorial dept. of trade-paper Variety; held posts in New York with ABC Motion Pictures and with Diener/Hauser/Bates Advertising. Worked for Lawrence Gordon Productions as exec. asst. to Gordon and as story editor. Joined 20th Century Fox in January, 1985, as dir. of creative affairs for studio. 1986, named v.p., production, m.p. div., Fox; appointed sr. v.p. production, 20th Century Fox, 1988; named pres., Silver Pictures, 1989. Currently with Lawrence Gordon Prods.
PICTURES: Exec. Prod/Prod.: Die Hard 2, Predator 2, Ricochet, The Last Boy Scout, Demolition Man, Lara Croft: Tombraider, K-PAX, Band Camp.

LEVY, NORMAN
Executive. b. Bronx, NY, Jan. 3, 1935. e. City Coll. of New York. 1957 joined Universal Pictures, holding various sales positions; 1967, went to National General Pictures, ultimately being named v.p. and exec. asst. to pres.; 1974, Columbia Pictures, v.p., gen. sls. mgr. 1975 named Columbia exec. v.p. in chg. of domestic sls.; 1977, exec. v.p., mktg; 1978. pres., Columbia Pictures Domestic Distribution. 1980 joined 20th-Fox as pres. of Entertainment Group; 1981, vice-chmn., 20th Century-Fox Film Corp. Resigned 1985 to become chmn, ceo, New Century/Vista Film Co. 1991, chmn. and CEO, Creative Film Enterprises.

LEWELLEN, A. WAYNE
Executive. b. Dallas, TX, Feb. 16, 1944. e. U. of Texas. Joined Paramount Pictures 1973 as brch. mgr., Dallas-Oklahoma City territory; 1978, v.p. Southern div.; 1984, exec. v.p., gen. sls. mngr.; 1986, pres. domestic distrib.; 1993-present, pres. M.P. distrib. chairman, Will Rogers Memorial Fund Board, dir. for the Found. of the Motion Picture Pioneers.

LEWINE, JEFFREY G.
Executive. b. New York, NY, 1955. e. Syracuse U. Entered the industry while young, working as an usher, a ticker-take, a janitor, and eventually as a theatre manager while in high school and during summers in college. 1977, named general sl's. mng'r., of Cinema 5, responsible for marketing and distribution of notable Cinema 5 films such as Pumping Iron, Endless Summer, Swept Away and Monty Python and The Holy Grail; 1980, named v.p., managing company's theatre and distibution activities. 1981, became managing dir., Cinema Int'l. Corp.,
in Sydney, Australia; created a new division to manage merchandising and ancillary film sales which expanded to the Far

East. 1987, returned to the U.S., and with his partners, the Edgar Bronfman family, acquired Cinemette, movie theatre circuit based in Pittsburgh; became pres. and CEO, of the renamed Cinema World; 1994, sold Cinema World to Carmike Cinemas, Inc. 1995-96, consultant for Coca-Cola USA in several divisions. 1997, founded JJL Consultants, Inc., agc'y. dealing with theatre and real estate negotiations. Nov. 1997, together with Warburg Pinctus Ventures, formed WestStar Cinemas to acquire Cinamerica Theatres which operates as Mann Theatres, and was named pres. and CEO of WestStar Cinemas. Resigned, 1999. Partner, KLM Theatre Partners, 1999-present. On Bd. of Dir's.: NATO, Will Rogers Memorial Foundation.

LEWIS, ARTHUR
Producer, Director, Writer. b. New York, NY, Sept. 15, 1918. e. USC, Yale U. Began career as writer and assoc. prod. on the Jones Family TV series. Five years in U.S. Army; returned to screenwriting before producing Three Wishes for Jamie on Broadway and producing and directing Guys and Dolls in London's West End. In mid-60s and 70s produced over 25 plays with Bernard Delfont in the West End of London.
PICTURES: *Producer*: Loot, Baxter, The Killer Elite, Brass Target.
TELEVISION: Brenner, The Asphalt Jungle, The Nurses. *Movies*: The Diary of Anne Frank, Splendor in the Grass.

LEWIS, EDWARD
Producer. b. Camden, NJ, Dec. 16, 1922. e. Bucknell U. Began entertainment career as script writer, then co-produced The Admiral Was a Lady and teamed with Marion Parsonnet to bring the Faye Emerson Show to TV. Subsequently prod. first Schlitz Playhouse and China Smith series. Was v.p. of Kirk Douglas' indep. prod. co., where was assoc. prod. and writer-prod. Collaborated with John Frankenheimer on 8 films.
PICTURES: Lizzie (assoc. prod.), The Careless Years (prod., s.p.), Spartacus, The Last Sunset, Lonely Are the Brave, The List of Adrian Messenger, Seconds, Grand Prix, The Fixer (exec. prod.), The Gypsy Moths (exec.), I Walk the Line (exec.), The Horsemen, The Iceman Cometh (exec.), Executive Action, Rhinoceros, Lost in the Stars, Missing (co-prod.), Crackers, The River, Brothers (prod., s.p.).
TELEVISION: Ishi: The Last of His Tribe (exec. prod.), The Thorn Birds (exec. prod.).

LEWIS, GEOFFREY
Actor. b. San Diego, CA, 1935. Father of actress Juliette Lewis, actors Lightfield & Peter Lewis.
PICTURES: Welcome Home Soldier Boys, The Culpepper Cattle Company, Bad Company, High Plains Drifter, Dillinger, Thunderbolt and Lightfoot, Macon County Line, The Great Waldo Pepper, Smile, The Wind and the Lion, Lucky Lady, The Return of a Man Called Horse, Every Which Way But Loose, Tilt, Human Experiments, Tom Horn, Broncho Billy, Heaven's Gate, Any Which Way You Can, Shoot the Sun Down, I the Jury, Ten to Midnight, Night of the Comet, Lust in the Dust, Stitches, Fletch Lives, Out of the Dark, Pink Cadillac, Catch Me If You Can, Disturbed, Double Impact, The Lawnmower Man, Point of No Return, Wishman, The Man Without a Face, Only the Strong, Army of One, Maverick, White Fang II: Myth of the White Wolf, Last Resort, The Dragon Gate, An Occassional Hell, American Perfekt, Midnight in the Garden of Good and Evil, Five Aces, The Prophet's Game, The Way of the Gun, Highway 395, A Light in the Darkness, The New Guy, Something Borrowed.
TELEVISION: *Series*: Flo, Gun Shy, Land's End. *Movies*: Moon of the Wolf, Honky Tonk, The Great Ice Rip-Off, Attack on Terror: The FBI Versus the Ku Klux Klan, The New Daughters of Joshua Cabe, The Great Houndinis, The Deadly Triangle, The Hunted Lady, When Every Day Was the Fourth of July, The Jericho Mile, Samurai, Salem's Lot, Belle Starr, The Shadow Riders, Life of the Party: The Story of Beatrice, The Return of the Man From U.N.C.L.E., Travis McGee, September Gun, Stormin' Home, Dallas: The Early Years, Day of Reckoning, Gambler V: Playing for Keeps, When the Dark Man Calls, Kansas, Trilogy of Terror II, Rough Riders. *Guest*: Mannix, Barnaby Jones, Starsky and Hutch, Streets of San Francisco, Police Woman, Little House on the Prairie, Laverne & Shirley, Lou Grant, Magnum P.I., Amazing Stories, Murder She Wrote, Paradise.

LEWIS, HAROLD G.
Executive. b. New York, NY, Sept. 18, 1938. e. Union Coll., 1960, electrical engineer. Joined ATA Trading Corp. in 1960 and has been pres. since 1977. Producer of feature animation. Importer and exporter for theatrical and TV features, documentaries, series, classics. Pres., ATA Trading Corp., and Favorite TV, Inc.

LEWIS, JERRY
Actor, Director, Writer, Producer. r.n. Joseph Levitch. b. Newark, NJ, Mar. 16, 1926. e. Irvington H.S. Parents Danny and Rae Lewis, prof. entertainers. Debut at 5 at a NY Borscht Circuit hotel singing Brother Can You Spare a Dime? 1946 formed comedy-team with Dean Martin at 500 Club, Atlantic City, NJ; then appeared on NBC tv, performed many theatres before being signed by Hal Wallis for m.p. debut. Voted Most Promising Male Star in Television in m.p. Daily's 2nd annual TV poll, 1950. Voted (as team) one of top ten money making stars in m.p. Herald-

Fame poll: 1951-56 (including no. 1 position in 1952), voted as solo performer: 1957-59, 1961-64; named best comedy team in m.p. Daily's 16th annual radio poll, 1951-53. 1956 formed Jerry Lewis Prods. Inc., functioning as prod., dir., writer & star. National Chairman & bd. member, Muscular Dystrophy Association. Full professor USC; taught grad. film dir. Book: The Total Filmmaker (1971) based on classroom lectures. *Autobiography*: Jerry Lewis In Person (1982).
THEATRE: Hellzapoppin (regional), Damn Yankees (B'way debut, 1995).
PICTURES: My Friend Irma (debut, 1949), My Friend Irma Goes West, At War With the Army, That's My Boy, Sailor Beware, Jumping Jacks, Scared Stiff, The Stooge, Road to Bali (cameo), The Caddy, Money From Home, Living It Up, Three Ring Circus, You're Never Too Young, Artists and Models, Pardners, Hollywood or Bust, The Delicate Delinquent (also prod.), The Sad Sack, Rock-a-Bye Baby, The Geisha Boy (also prod.), Don't Give Up the Ship, Li'l Abner (cameo), Visit to a Small Planet, Cinderfella (also prod.), The Bellboy (also dir., prod., s.p.), The Ladies Man (also dir., prod., co-s.p.), The Errand Boy (also dir., co-s.p.), It's Only Money, The Nutty Professor (also dir., co-s.p.), Who's Minding the Store?, It's a Mad Mad Mad Mad World (cameo), The Patsy (also dir., co-s.p.), The Disorderly Orderly, Boeing-Boeing, The Family Jewels (also dir., prod., co-s.p.), Three on a Couch (also dir., prod.), Way... Way Out, The Big Mouth (also dir., prod., co-s.p.), Don't Raise the Bridge Lower the River, Hook Line and Sinker (also prod.), Which Way to the Front? (also dir., prod.), One More Time (dir. only), The Day the Clown Cried (also dir., co-s.p.), Hardly Working (also dir., co-s.p.), The King of Comedy, Smorgasbord (Cracking Up; also dir., co-s.p.), Slapstick of Another Kind, Cookie, Mr. Saturday Night (cameo), Arizona Dream, Funny Bones, Off the Menu: The Last Days of Chasen's, Encounter in the Third Dimension.
TELEVISION: *Movie*: Fight for Life. *Series*: Colgate Comedy Hour, The Jerry Lewis Show (1963), The Jerry Lewis Show (1967-69). *Guest*: Wiseguy (5 episodes).

LEWIS, JULIETTE
Actress. b. California, June 21, 1973. Father is actor Geoffrey Lewis.
PICTURES: My Stepmother Is an Alien (debut, 1988), Meet the Hollowheads, National Lampoon's Christmas Vacation, Crooked Hearts, Cape Fear (Acad. Award nom.), Husbands and Wives, That Night, Kalifornia, What's Eating Gilbert Grape, Romeo Is Bleeding, Natural Born Killers, Mixed Nuts, The Basketball Diaries, Strange Days, From Dusk Till Dawn, The Evening Star, The Audition, Full Tilt Boogie, The Other Sister, The 4th Floor, The Way of the Gun, Room to Rent, Picture Claire, Gaudi Afternoon, Armitage: Dual Matrix, Hysterical Blindness, Enough, Old School, Cold Creek Manor, Blueberry, Starsky & Hutch (2004).
TELEVISION: *Series*: Homefires, I Married Dora, A Family for Joe. *Movie*: Too Young to Die?

LEWIS, MICHAEL J.
Composer. b. Wales, 1939. First film score 1969, The Mad Woman of Chaillot, won Ivor Novello Award for best film score. 1973: first Broadway musical, Cyrano, Grammy nomination '74, Caesar and Cleopatra (T.V. '76), The Lion the Witch and the Wardrobe (Emmy, 1979).
PICTURES: The Man Who Haunted Himself, Julius Caesar. Upon This Rock, Unman Wittering and Zigo, Running Scared, Baxter, Theatre of Blood, 11 Harrowhouse, 92 in the Shade, Russian Roulette, The Stick-Up, The Medusa Touch, The Legacy, The Passage, The Unseen, Sphinx, Yes Giorgio, The Hound of the Baskervilles, On the Third Day, The Naked Face.

LEWIS, RICHARD
Comedian, Actor. b. Brooklyn, NY, June 29, 1949. e. Ohio St. Univ. (marketing degree). Was copywriter for adv. agency before becoming stand-up comic performing in nightclubs in NYC, Las Vegas, 1971.
PICTURES: The Wrong Guys (debut, 1988), That's Adequate, Once Upon a Crime, Robin Hood: Men in Tights, Wagons East!, Leaving Las Vegas, Drunks, Game Day.
TELEVISION: *Series*: Harry, Anything But Love, Hiller & Diller, Curb Your Enthusiasm. *Specials*: Richard Lewis: I'm in Pain, Richard Lewis: I'm Exhausted, Richard Lewis: I'm Doomed, Living Against the Odds (also writer). *Pilot*: King of the Building.

LI, GONG
Actress. b. Shenyang, Liaoning Province, China, Dec. 31, 1965.
PICTURES: Red Field, Red Sorghum, The Terracotta Warrior, Ju Dou, God of Gamblers III: Back to Shanghai, Raise the Red Lantern, The Story of Qiu Ju, Mary from Beijing, Farewell—My Concubine, Flirting Scholar, La Peintre, Semi-Gods and Semi-Devils, The Great Conqueror's Concubine, To Live, Shanghai Triad, Temptress Moon, Chinese Box, Breaking the Silence, The Assassin.

LIBERMAN, FRANK P.
Publicist. b. New York, NY, May 29, 1917. e. Cheshire Acad., CT, 1934; Lafayette Coll., Easton, PA, B.A. 1938. m. Patricia Harris, casting dir. Worked as copy boy, N.Y. Daily News, 1938-39. Began career as publicist at Warner Bros., home office as

messenger, 1939, promoted to pressbooks dept., transferred to Warner's Chicago office as field exploitation man. U.S. Signal Corps, 1941, public relations officer, Army Pictorial Service, on temporary duty with War Dept., Bureau of Public Relations in Pentagon. Discharged as Capt., 1946. Rejoined Warner Bros. on coast 2 years, 1947, est. own public relations office, 1947. Owner, Frank Liberman and Associates, Inc. Retired.

LIBERTINI, RICHARD
Actor. b. Cambridge, MA, May 21. Original member of Second City troupe in Chicago. With MacIntyre Dixon appeared as the Stewed Prunes in cabaret performances.
THEATRE: Three by Three (1961), Plays for Bleecker Street, The Cat's Pajamas, The Mad Show, . Bad Habits. Solo: The White House Murder Case, Don't Drink the Water, Paul Sill's Story Theatre, Ovid's Metamorphoses, The Primary English Class, Neopolitan Ghosts, Love's Labour's Lost, As You Like It.
PICTURES: The Night They Raided Minsky's, Don't Drink the Water, Catch-22, The Out-of-Towners, Lovers and Other Strangers, Lady Liberty, Fire Sale, Days of Heaven, The In-Laws, Popeye, Sharky's Machine, Soup for One, Best Friends, Deal of the Century, Going Berserk, Unfaithfully Yours, All of Me, Fletch, Big Trouble, Betrayed, Fletch Lives, Animal Behavior. Duck Tales: The Movie (voice), Lemon Sisters, Awakenings, The Bonfire of the Vanities, Cultivating Charlie, Nell, Lethal Weapon 4, Telling You.
TELEVISION: Series: Story Theatre, The Melba Moore-Clifton Davis Show, Soap, Family Man, The Fanelli Boys, Pacific Station, Pinky and the Brain. Guest: George Burns Comedy Week, Barney Miller, Bob Newhart. Pilots: Calling Dr. Storm, M.D., Fair Game. Movies: Three on a Date, Extreme Close-Up, House of Frankenstein, Cutty Whitman, Columbo: Ashes to Ashes. Specials: Let's Celebrate, The Fourth Wise Man, Fame (Hallmark Hall of Fame), The Trial of Bernhard Goetz.**LIEBER-FARB, WARREN N.**
Executive. e. Wharton Sch. of Commerce and Finance, U. of PA, B.S., economics; U. of Michigan. Started career in industry at Paramount Pictures as dir. of mktg. and exec. asst. to Stanley Jaffe, then pres. Later joined 20th-Fox as v.p., special market dist. (cable, pay-TV, non-theatrical). Joined Warner Bros. as v.p., exec. asst. to Ted Ashley, bd. chmn.; later named v.p., intl. adv.-pub. In 1979 joined Lorimar as v.p., of Lorimar Productions, Inc., the parent company, based in New York, Promoted to sr. v.p. 1982, named v.p. mktg., Warner Home Video; named pres. 1984. In 1999, the Acad. of Television Arts & Sciences awarded him an Emmy for the development of DVD technology. Serves on the Bd. of Trustees of AFI; on bd. of directors for Digital Theater Systems, Inc.; SIRIUS bd. (satellite radio); Bd. of Trustees of Univ. of PA and its Wharton Undergraduate exec. bd. Member of Academy of Motion Picture Arts & Sciences.

LIEBERMAN, ROBERT
Director, Producer. b. Buffalo, NY, July 16, 1947. e. Univ. of Buffalo. m. actress Marilu Henner. Moved to LA, became editor for Desort-Fisher commercial production house, which led to dir. tv ad spots. Formed own commercial company, Harmony Pictures.
PICTURES: Table for Five, All I Want for Christmas, Fire in the Sky, D3: The Mighty Ducks, Rag and Bone.
TELEVISION: Movies: Fighting Back: The Story of Rocky Blier, Will: G. Gordon Liddy, To Save a Child (also exec. prod.), Titanic, Second String. Series: thirtysomething, Dream Street (pilot), The Young Riders (pilot), Gabriel's Fire (also exec. prod.), Pros and Cons (exec. consultant), Under Suspicion (also exec. prod.), Medicine Ball (also exec. prod.), Moloney, NetForce (mini), Once and Again, Strong Medicine, The Dead Zone.

LIEBERSON, SANFORD
Producer. b. Los Angeles, CA, 1936. Early career with William Morris Agency. 1961-62, agent in Rome for Grade Org. Returned to LA as Founding Member CMA agency then exec. in charge of European operations. 1979, named pres. of 20th-Fox Productions, which company he joined in 1977 as v.p. European production. Previously an independent producer forming Good Times. With David Putnam formed Visual Programming Systems to produce, acquire and consult in the Home Video area for CBS, Phillips, Time/Life, etc. As v.p. intl. prod. at Fox, spv. intl. release of such films as Star Wars, 1900, Alien, Chariots of Fire, Nine to Five, Quest for Fire. V.P. Intl. prod. for The Ladd Company. Outland, Body Heat, Blade Runner, The Right Stuff, Police Academy, etc. Chief of prod. at Goldcrest Harvest: Dance With a Stranger, Room With a View, Absolute Beginners, etc. Pres. intl. prod. MGM spv. Russia House, Thelma & Louise, Liebestraum, Not Without My Daughter, Criss Cross, etc. Currently head of prod. at the Natl. Film and Television School of Great Britain.
PICTURES: Producer: Melody, Pied Piper, Radio Wonderful, James Dean: First American Teenager, Bugsy Malone, Slade in Flame, Final Programme, Stardust, That'll Be the Day, Brother Can You Spare a Dime, Swastika, Double Headed Eagle, All This and World War II, Mahler, Lisztomania, Jabberwocky, Rita Sue and Bob Too, Stars and Bars, The Mighty Quinn, Performance.
TELEVISION: Movie: Frank & Jessie (exec. prod.).

LIGHT, JUDITH
Actress. b. Trenton, NJ, Feb. 9. e. Carnegie-Mellon Univ. (BFA). Toured with USO in prod. of Guys and Dolls during college. Acted with Milwaukee and Seattle rep. companies. Made B'way debut in 1975 prod. of A Doll's House with Liv Ullmann. Other stage work: A Streetcar Named Desire, As You Like It, Richard III. Landed role of Karen Wolek on daytime serial One Life to Live in 1977.
PICTURES: Paul Monette: The Brink of Summer's End.
TELEVISION: Series: One Life to Live (2 Emmy Awards), Who's the Boss?, Phenom, The Simple Life, Law & Order: SVU. Movies: Intimate Agony, Dangerous Affection, The Ryan White Story, My Boyfriend's Back, In Defense of a Married Man, Wife Mother Murderer, Men Don't Tell, Betrayal of Trust, Against Their Will: Women in Prison, Lady Killer, A Husband, A Wife and A Lover, Murder at My Door, A Step Toward Tomorrow, Too Close to Home, Carriers.

LIGHTMAN, M. A.
Exhibitor. b. Nashville, TN, Apr. 21, 1915. e. Southwestern U., Vanderbilt U., 1936, B.A. Bd. chmn. Malco Theatres, Inc., Memphis, Tenn.

LILLARD, MATTHEW
Actor. b. Lansing, MI, Jan. 24, 1970.
PICTURES: Ghoulies 3: Ghoulies Go to College, Serial Mom, Ride for Your Life, Mad Love, Hackers, Tarantella, Scream, Telling You, Dish Dogs, The Curve, Senseless, Without Limits, S.L.C. Punk!, Love's Labour's Lost, She's All That, Wing Commander, Spanish Judges, Finder's Fee, Triangle Square, Summer Catch, Thirteen Ghosts, Scooby-Doo.
TELEVISION: Movies: Vanishing Son IV, If These Walls Could Talk, The Devil's Child. Guest: Nash Bridges.

LIMAN, DOUG
Director. e. Brown University, USC Film.
PICTURES: Getting In, Swingers (also photog.), Go (also photog.), See Jane Run (prod. only), Kissing Jessica Stein (prod. only), The Bourne Identity.

LINDBLOM, GUNNEL
Actress, Director. b. Gothenburg, Sweden, 1931. Discovered by Ingmar Bergman while studying at drama school of Gothenburg Municipal Theatre, 1950-53; she moved to Malmo, where he was director of the local Municipal Theatre. Under Bergman's direction she played in Easter, Peer Gynt, Faust, etc. between 1954-59. Later appeared in many Bergman films. Since 1968 has been on staff of Stockholm's Royal Dramatic Theatre, assisting Bergman and then beginning to direct on her own. Made film debut as director with Summer Paradise in 1977.
PICTURES: Actress: Love, Girl in the Rain, Song of the Scarlet Flower, The Seventh Seal, Wild Strawberries, The Virgin Spring, Winter Light, The Silence, My Love Is a Rose, Rapture, Loving Couples, Hunger, Woman of Darkness, The Girls, The Father, Brother Carl, Scenes From a Marriage, Misfire, Bakom Jalusin, Capitan Escalaborns, Betraktelse (also dir., s.p.), Nadja, Lines From the Heart, Expectations, Passing Darkness, Light Keeps Me Company. Director: Summer Paradise (also co-s.p.), Sally and Freedom, Summer Nights on Planet Earth (also s.p.).

LINDEN, HAL
Actor. b. Bronx, NY, March 20, 1931. e. City Coll. of New York. Began career as saxophone player and singer, playing with bands of Sammy Kaye, Bobby Sherwood, etc. Drafted and performed in revues for Special Services. After discharge enrolled at N.Y.'s American Theatre Wing; appeared on B'way in Bells Are Ringing, replacing Sydney Chaplin.
THEATRE: Wildcat, Something More, Subways Are for Sleeping, Ilya Darling, The Apple Tree, The Education of H*Y*M*A*N K*A*P*L*A*N, On a Clear Day You Can See Forever, Three Men on a Horse, The Pajama Game, The Rothschilds (Tony Award, 1971), I'm Not Rappaport, Unfinished Stories, The Sisters Rosensweig.
PICTURES: Bells Are Ringing, When You Comin' Back Red Ryder?, A New Life, Out to Sea, The Others, Just Friends, Jump, Dumb Luck, Time Changer, Broadway: The Golden Age by the Legends Who Were There.
TELEVISION: Series: Animals Animals Animals (host), Barney Miller, Blacke's Magic, F.Y.I. (Emmy Awards, 1983, 1984), Jack's Place, The Boys Are Back. Specials: I Do! I Do!, The Best of Everything. Movies: Mr. Inside/Mr. Outside, The Love Boat (pilot), How to Break Up a Happy Divorce, Father Figure, Starflight: The Plane That Couldn't Land, The Other Woman, My Wicked Wicked Ways: The Legend of Errol Flynn, The O'Connors, Dream Breakers, The Colony, Killers in the House, Rockford Files: If It Bleeds It Leads, The Glow.

LINDHEIM, RICHARD D.
Executive. b. New York, NY, May 28, 1939. e. Univ. of Redlands, USC. Admin. Asst. Story Dept., CBS, 1962-64. Project Dir. Entertainment Testing ASI Mkt. Research, 1964-69. VP Prog. Research NBC 1969-78, VP Dramatic Prog. 1978-79, Prod. Universal TV 1979-81, VP Current Prog. 1981-85, SVP Series Prog. 1986-87. Exec. VP Creative Affairs 1987-91, Exec. VP

Prog. Strategy MCA TV Group 1991-92. Exec. VP Paramount TV 1992. Asst. Prof. CSU. Sr. Lecturer, USC, UCLA. Author: Primetime Network TV Programming (w/ Richard Blum) 1987, Inside TV Producing 1991.

LINDO, DELROY
Actor. b. London, England, Nov. 18, 1952. Received NAACP Image Awards for film Malcolm X and play A Raisin in the Sun.
THEATRE: B'way: Joe Turner's Come and Gone (Tony nom.), Master Harold and the Boys. Off-B'way: District Line, As You Like It, Romeo and Juliet, Spell #7, The Heliotrope Bouquet. Regional: Othello, Mrs. Ever's Boys, Cobb, A Raisin in the Sun, My Mark My Name, Union Boys, Macbeth, Black Branch, Home.
PICTURES: The Blood of Heroes (Salute to the Jugger; debut, 1990), Mountains of the Moon, Perfect Witness, The Hard Way, Bright Angel, Malcolm X, Bound by Honor, Mr. Jones, Benhanzin, Crooklyn, Congo, Clockers, Get Shorty, Feeling Minnesota, Broken Arrow, Ransom, The Devil's Advocate, A Life Less Ordinary, Glory & Honor, Romeo Must Die, The Cider House Rules, The Book of Stars, Romeo Must Die, Gone In Sixty Seconds, Heist, The Last Castle, The One, The Core.
TELEVISION: Movies: First-Time Felon, Strange Justice. Guest: Going to Extremes, Against the Law, Hawk, Beauty and the Beast. Mini-series: Jazz.

LINDSAY, ROBERT
Actor. b. Ilkeston, Derbyshire, Eng., Dec. 13, 1949. e. GLadstone Boys School, Ilkeston, Royal Acad. of Dramatic Art. With Manchester's Royal Exchange Theatre Co. (Hamlet, The Cherry Orchard, The Lower Depths). Also in Godspell, The Three Musketeers, Me and My Girl, (London—Olivier Award, NY—Tony, Theatre World & Drama Desk Awards, 1987), Becket (Olivier & Variety Club Awards), Cyrano de Bergerac.
PICTURES: That'll Be the Day, Bert Rigby You're a Fool, Strike It Rich, Fierce Creatures, Remember Me, Divorcing Jack.
TELEVISION: Series: Citizen Smith, Give Us A Break, GBH, In Your Dreams, My Family, The Heat Is On, Don't Eat the Neighbours. Mini-series: The Wimbledon Poisoner, Jake's Progress, Oliver Twist, Hawk. Specials: Victoria Wood with All the Trimmings. Movies: Twelfth Night, All's Well That Ends Well, A Midsummer Night's Dream, Cymbeline, Much Ado About Nothing, King Lear, Confessional, Genghis Cohn, The Office, Brazen Hussies, Hornblower: The Even Chance, Hornblower: The Duchess and the Devil, Hornblower: The Frogs and the Lobsters, Jack the Ripper: On Going Mystery, Hornblower: Mutiny, Hornblower: Retribution.

LINDSAY-HOGG, MICHAEL
Director. b. England, 1940. Mother is actress Geraldine Fitzgerald.
PICTURES: Let It Be, Nasty Habits, The Object of Beauty (also s.p.), Frankie Starlight, Celebration: The Music of Pete Townshend and The Who, Rolling Stones Rock and Roll Circus, Guy, Waiting for Godot.
TELEVISION: Brideshead Revisted (co-dir.), Master Harold and the Boys, As Is, Nazi Hunter: The Beate Klarsfeld Story, The Little Match Girl, Murder by Moonlight, The Strange Case of Dr. Jekyll and Mr. Hyde, Nightmare Classics, The Habitation of Dragons, Running Mates, Marsalis on Music, Alone, Two of Us.

LINK, WILLIAM
Writer, Producer. b. Philadelphia, PA, Dec. 15, 1933. e. U. of Pennsylvania, B.S., 1956. With partner, late Richard Levinson, wrote and created numerous TV series and movies, specializing in detective-mystery genre. Books: Fineman, Stay Tuned: An Inside Look at the Making of Prime-Time Television, Off Camera. Stage incl.: Prescription Murder, Guilty Conscience, Merlin.
PICTURES: The Hindenberg, Rollercoaster.
TELEVISION: Series writer-creator: Mannix, Ellery Queen, Tenafly, Columbo (Emmy Award as writer, 1972), Murder She Wrote. Movies writer-prod.: That Certain Summer, My Sweet Charlie (Emmy Award as writer, 1970), The Judge and Jake Wyler, Savage (exec. prod., writer), The Execution of Private Slovik, The Gun, A Cry for Help (prod. only), The Storyteller, Murder by Natural Causes, Stone, Crisis at Central High, Rehearsal For Murder (also exec. prod.), Take Your Best Shot, Prototype (also exec. prod.), The Guardian (also exec. prod.), Guilty Conscience (also exec. prod.), Vanishing Act (also exec. prod.), The United States Vs. Salim Ajami, The Boys, Over My Dead Body, The Cosby Mysteries.

LINKLATER, RICHARD
Director, Writer, Producer. b. Houston, TX, 1961. Founded Austin Film Society, serving as artistic director. Filmed several super 8 films incl. feature It's Impossible to Learn to Plow by Reading Books.
PICTURES: Director/Writer: Slacker (also actor & prod.), Dazed and Confused (also co-prod.), The Underneath (actor only), Beavis & Butt-Head Do America (voice), Before Sunrise, Suburbia (dir. only), The Newton Boys, Waking Life, Tape (dir. only).

LINKLETTER, ART
Emcee, Producer, Author. b. Moose Jaw, Saskatchewan, Canada, July 17, 1912. Raised in San Diego. e. San Diego State

Coll. Radio prg. mgr., San Diego Exposition, 1935; radio pgm. mgr. S.F. World's Fair, 1937-39; freelance radio announcer and m.c. 1939-42; m.c. series People Are Funny starting in 1942. Author: The Secret World of Kids, 1959; Kids Say the Darndest Things, 1957; Linkletter Down Under, 1969; Yes You Can, 1979; Old Age Is Not For Sissies, 1988; Cavalcade of the Golden West; Cavalcade of America. Recorded albums: Howls, Boners & Shockers and We Love You, Call Collect (Grammy Award winner, 1966). Bd. of dir., MGM, 1979-88.
PICTURES: People Are Funny, Champagne for Caesar, The Snow Queen, Matinee, Off the Menu: The Last Days of Chasen's, Let Me In I Hear Laughter.
TELEVISION: Series: Art Linkletter's House Party, Life With Linkletter, People Are Funny (emcee), The Art Linkletter Show (emcee), Hollywood Talent Scouts, Kids Say the Darndest Things. Specials: Inside Salute to Baseball (exec. prod., host), Art Linkletter's Secret World of Kids (host), Ford Startime, Young Man With A Band, Linkletters Spend Christmas in the Holy Land, Kid's Eye View of Washington, Walt: The Man Behind the Myth. Movies: Zane Grey Theatre, G.E. Theatre, Wagon Train: Kid at the Stick.

LINN-BAKER, MARK
Actor, Director. b. St. Louis, MO, June 17, 1954. e. Yale Univ., Yale Sch. of Drama (M.F.A., 1979). Founding memb. American Repertory Th. in Cambridge, MA; founding prod./dir. NY Stage & Film Co. in NYC & Poughkeepsie. Co-founder of True Pictures, 1990.
THEATRE: B'way: Doonesbury, Laughter on the 23rd Floor, A Funny Thing Happened On The Way To The Forum.
PICTURES: Manhattan (bit), The End of August, My Favorite Year, Me and Him (voice only), Noises Off, Me and Veronica (co-prod. only).
TELEVISION: Series: Comedy Zone, Perfect Strangers, Hangin' With Mr. Cooper (dir. only). Movies: Wedding Bell Blues, Bare Essentials. Specials: Doonesbury (voice of Kirby), The Ghost Writer (Amer. Playhouse), The Whole Shebang, Laughter on the 23rd Floor. Director: episodes of Family Matters, Family Man, Going Places.

LINSON, ART
Producer, Director. b. Chicago, IL, 1942. e. UCLA; LLD. UCLA, 1967. Was rock music manager with record prod. Lou Adler and ran own record co., Spin Dizzy records before turning to film production. Debuted as director with Where the Buffalo Roam.
PICTURES: Prod. &/or dir.: Rafferty and the Gold Dust Twins (co.-prod.), Car Wash, American Hot Wax (also co-s.p.), Where the Buffalo Roam, Melvin and Howard, Fast Times at Ridgemont High (co-prod.), The Wild Life, The Untouchables, Scrooged (co-prod.), Casualties of War, We're No Angels, Dick Tracy (exec. prod.), Singles, Point of No Return, This Boy's Life, Heat, The Edge, Pushing Tin, Great Expectations, Fight Club, Sunset Strip, Heist.

LIOTTA, RAY
Actor. b. Newark, NJ, Dec. 18, 1955. e. Univ. of Miami. First prof. job on tv commercial, followed by continuing role on daytime serial, Another World.
PICTURES: Something Wild (debut, 1983), The Lonely Lady, Dominick and Eugene, Field of Dreams, GoodFellas, Article 99, Unlawful Entry, No Escape, Corrina Corrina, Operation Dumbo Drop, Unforgettable, Turbulence, Cop Land, Phoenix, A Rumor of Angels, Forever Mine, Muppets from Space, Pilgrim, Blow, Hannibal, John Q, Heartbreakers, Point of Origin, Narc, Identity, Slow Burn (also co-exec. prod.), Control.
TELEVISION: Series: Another World, Casablanca, Our Family Honor. Movies: Hardhat and Legs, Crazy Times, Women and Men 2: In Love There Are No Rules, The Rat Pack.

LIPPERT, ROBERT L., JR.
Producer, Exhibitor. b. Alameda, CA, Feb. 28, 1928. e. St Mary's Coll., 1946; all conference football 1947. Career began in theatre exhibition. Entered m.p. production in 1951. Film editor of 45 "b" features. Produced 9 pictures for Lippert Features and 20th Century Fox Films. Returned in 1966 to theatre exhibition. Became pres. of Affiliated, Lippert, Transcontinental theatres (180 theatres nation-wide). Retired.

LIPSTONE, HOWARD H.
Executive, Producer. b. Chicago, IL, Apr. 28, 1928. e. UCLA, USC. Ass't to gen. mgr. at KLTA, 1950-55; program dir. at KABC-TV, 1955-65; exec. ass't to pres. at Selmur Prods., ABC subsidiary, 1965-69. Ivan Tors Films & Studios as exec. v.p., 1969-70; pres., Alan Landsburg Prods., 1970-1985; The Landsburg Co., 1985-. Co-exec. prod.: The Outer Space Connection, The Bermuda Triangle, Mysteries, The White Lions, Jaws 3-D.
TELEVISION: Exec. in charge of prod.: The Savage Bees, Ruby and Oswald, The Triangle Factory Fire Scandal, Strange Voices, A Place at the Table, Kate & Allie, Gimme a Break, A Stoning in Fulham County, The Ryan White Story, Quiet Victory, Unspeakable Acts, In Defense of a Married Man, Triumph of the Heart, Nightmare in Columbia County, A Mother's Right, The Elizabeth Morgan Story, The Diamond Fleece, Terror in the Night, If Someone Had Known, The Lottery, Country Justice.

LIPTON, PEGGY
Actress. b. New York, NY, Aug. 30, 1947. Former model. Co-wrote song L.A. is My Lady (recorded by Frank Sinatra). Recorded album Peggy Lipton.
PICTURES: The Purple People Eater, Kinjite (Forbidden Subjects), Twin Peaks: Fire Walk With Me, The Postman, The Intern, Skipped Parts, Jackpot.
TELEVISION: Series: The John Forsythe Show, The Mod Squad (Golden Globe Award, 1971), Twin Peaks, Angel Falls. Movies: The Return of the Mod Squad, Addicted to His Love, Fatal Charm, The Spider and the Fly, Deadly Vows, Justice for Annie: A Moment of Truth Movie, The 70s (mini).

LISI, VIRNA
Actress. r.n. Virna Pieralisi. b. Ancona, Italy, Nov. 8, 1936.
PICTURES: Desiderio e Sole, Violenza sul Lago, The Doll That Took the Town, Luna Nova, Vendicatta, La Rossa, Caterina Sforza, Il Mondo dei Miracoli, Duel of the Titans, Eva, Don't Tempt the Devil, The Black Tulip, The Shortest Day, How To Murder Your Wife, Casanova 70, The Possessed, A Virgin for a Prince, Kiss the Other Sheik, The Birds the Bees and the Italians, Made in Italy, La Bamboie (The Dolls), Not With My Wife You Don't, Assault on a Queen, The 25th Hour, Anyone Can Play, The Girl and the General, Arabella, Better a Widow, The Girl Who Couldn't Say No, The Christmas Tree, The Secret of Santa Vittoria, If It's Tuesday This Must Be Belgium, Roma Bene, The Statue, Bluebeard, The Serpent, Ernesto, I Love N.Y., I Ragazzi di Via Panisperna, Beyond Good and Evil, Merry Christmas Happy New Year, Miss Right, Queen Margot (Cannes Film Fest. Award, 1994), A Hundred and One Nights, Follow Your Heart, The Best Day of My Life.
TELEVISION: U.S.: Christopher Columbus. Several European movies and mini-series.

LITHGOW, JOHN
Actor. b. Rochester, NY, Oct. 19, 1945. Father was prod. of Shakespeare Fests. in midwest. e. Harvard. Fulbright fellowship to study at London Acad. of Music and Dramatic Art. Interned in London with Royal Shakespeare Co. and Royal Court Theatre.
THEATRE: NY: The Changing Room (Tony & Drama Desk Awards, 1973), My Fat Friend, Trelawney of the Wells, Comedians, Anna Christie, A Memory of Two Mondays, Once in a Lifetime, Spokesong, Bedroom Farce, Salt Lake City Skyline, Division Street (also LA), Kaufman at Large (also dir., writer), Beyond Therapy, Requiem for a Heavyweight (Drama Desk Award), The Front Page, M Butterfly. Regional: The Beggar's Opera, Pygmalion, Of Mice and Men, Troilus and Cressida, The Roar of the Greasepaint, What Price Glory?, The Lady's Not for Burning, Who's Afraid of Virginia Woolf? (LA Drama Critics Circle Award).
PICTURES: Dealing or The Berkeley-to-Boston Forty-Brick Lost-Bag Blues (debut, 1972), Obsession, The Big Fix, Rich Kids, All That Jazz, Blow Out, I'm Dancing as Fast as I Can, The World According to Garp (Acad. Award nom.), Twilight Zone—The Movie, Terms of Endearment (Acad. Award nom.), Footloose, The Adventures of Buckaroo Banzai: Across the Eighth Dimension, 2010, Santa Claus, The Manhattan Project, Mesmerized, Harry and the Hendersons, Distant Thunder, Out Cold, Memphis Belle, Ricochet, At Play in the Fields of the Lord, Raising Cain, Cliffhanger, The Pelican Brief, A Good Man in Africa, Princess Caraboo, Silent Fall, Hollow Point, Officer Buckle and Gloria, Johnny Skidmarks, A Civil Action, Homegrown, Rugrats in Paris: The Movie, C-Scam, Shrek, Orange County, Portofino, Shrek 2, Kinsey.
TELEVISION: Series: Third Rock From the Sun (Emmy Award, 1996, 1997, 1999; Golden Globe Award, 1997). Guest: Amazing Stories (Emmy Award, 1987). Movies: Mom The Wolfman and Me, Not in Front of the Children, The Day After, The Glitter Dome, Resting Place, Baby Girl Scott, The Traveling Man, The Last Elephant (Ivory Hunters), The Boys, The Wrong Man, Love Cheat and Steal, World War II: When Lions Roared, Redwood Curtain, The Tuskegee Airmen, Don Quixote, The Lifeand Death of Peter Sellers. Specials: The Country Girl (TV debut, 1973), Secret Service, Big Blonde, The Oldest Living Graduate, Goldilocks and the Three Bears (Faerie Tale Theatre), Creating a Fairy Tale World: The Making of 'Shrek'.

LITTLE, RICH
Actor. b. Ottawa, Canada, Nov. 26, 1938. Started as radio disc jockey, talk show host in Canada.
PICTURES: Dirty Tricks, Happy Hour, Bebe's Kids (voice), The Brainiacs.com.
TELEVISION: Series: Love on a Rooftop, The John Davidson Show, ABC Comedy Hour (The Kopycats), The Julie Andrews Hour, The Rich Little Show, The New You Asked For It (host), Hollywood Squares. Specials: The Rich Little Show, Rich Little's Christmas Carol (also writer), Rich Little's Washington Follies, The Rich Little Specials (HBO), Rich Little's Robin Hood, others.

LITTLEFIELD, WARREN
Executive. b. Montclair, NJ. e. American Univ. in DC, School of Government and Public Admin.; Hobart Col. (psych. degree). 1975-79, Westfall Prods., developing prime-time specials and movies before being promoted to v.p., develop. & prod. 1979, served as WB TV dir., comedy develop. Joined NBC 1979, as mngr. comedy develop. 1981, v.p. current comedy programs at NBC. 1985, sr. v.p. series specials & variety progs., NBC Entertainment; 1987, exec. v.p., Prime-Time progs. NBC Entertainment. 1990, named pres. NBC Entertainment. Resigned, 1998. Formed the Littlefield Co. first producing programming with NBC and now with Paramount.

LITTMAN, LYNNE
Director, Producer. b. New York, NY, June 26. e. Sarah Lawrence. B.A., 1962; Student the Sorbonne 1960-61. Researcher for CBS News 1965; assoc. prod. Natl. Educational TV 1964-68; dir. NIMH film series on drug abuse UCLA Media Center 1970; prod., dir. documentary films, news and pub. affairs series KCET Community TV, So. Calif. 1971-77; dir. WNET non-fiction film, Once a Daughter 1979; exec. v.p., movies-for-TV ABC, 1980-81; Received Ford Fdn. Grant 1978 and numerous awards. Acad. Award film tribute to women, 1993.
PICTURES: In the Matter of Kenneth (doc.), Wanted-Operadoras (doc.), Till Death Do Us Part (doc.), Number Our Days (doc. short; Acad. Award 1977), Testament (co-prod., dir.), In Her Own Time (doc.), Freak City.
TELEVISION: Movies: Cagney & Lacey, Rescuers: Stories of Courage, Having Our Say: The Delany Sisters' First 100 Years.

LITTO, GEORGE
Producer. b. Philadelphia, PA. e. Temple U. Joined William Morris Agency in New York and then became indep. literary agent. Opened own office in Hollywood, 1965. Packaged film and TV productions, including M*A*S*H, Hang 'Em High, Hawaii Five-O for TV prior to entering indep. prod.; 1981-82, chmn. bd. & CEO, Filmways; 1983-85 indep. prod. 20th Century Fox.
PICTURES: Thieves Like Us (exec. prod.), Drive-In (exec. prod.), Obsession (prod.), Over the Edge (prod.), Dressed To Kill (prod.). Blow Out (prod.), Kansas (prod.), Night Game (prod.), The Crew, Sentimental Journey.

LITVINOFF, SI
Producer, Executive. b. New York, NY, April 5. e. Adelphi Coll., A.B.; NYU Sch. of Law, LL.B. Theatrical lawyer, personal and business manager in New York until 1967 when left firm of Barovick, Konecky & Litvinoff to produce plays and films. June, 1987: sr. v.p. for production and dev., Hawkeye Entertainment, Inc.
THEATRE: Leonard Bernstein's Theatre Songs, Cry of the Raindrop, Girl of the Golden West, Little Malcolm and His Struggle Against the Eunuchs, I and Albert (London).
PICTURES: The Queen, All the Right Noises, Walkabout, A Clockwork Orange (exec. prod.), Glastonbury Fayre (exec. in chg. prod.), The Man Who Fell to Earth (exec. prod.)
TELEVISION: Exec. prod.: 15th Annual Saturn Awards, Doobie Brothers Retrospective, Listen to the Music 1989.

LIU, LUCY ALEXIS
Actress. b. Jackson Heights, NY, 1967.
PICTURES: The Big Bang Theory, Guy, Jerry Maguire, Flypaper, Gridlock'd, City of Industry, Payback, Love Kills, True Crime, The Mating Habits of the Earthbound Human, Play it To the Bone, Molly, Shanghai Noon, Charlie's Angels, Hotel, Ecks vs. Sever, Company Man, Chicago: The Musical, Charlie's Angels 2, Kill Bill.
TELEVISION: Movies: Riot. Series: Pearl, Ally McBeal. Guest: Beverly Hills 90210, L.A. Law, Coach, Home Improvement, Hercules: The Legendary Journeys, ER, The X Files.

LLOYD, CHRISTOPHER
Actor. b. Stamford, CT, Oct. 22, 1938. Studied at Neighborhood Playhouse, NY.
THEATRE: NY: Kaspar (Drama Desk & Obie Awards, 1973), Happy End, Red White and Maddox. Regional: The Father, Hot L Baltimore, The Possessed, A Midsummer Night's Dream.
PICTURES: One Flew Over the Cuckoo's Nest (debut, 1975), Goin' South, Butch and Sundance: The Early Days, The Onion Field, The Lady in Red, Schizoid, The Black Marble, The Postman Always Rings Twice, The Legend of the Lone Ranger, National Lampoon Goes to the Movies, Mr. Mom, To Be or Not to Be, Star Trek III: The Search for Spock, The Adventures of Buckaroo Banzai Across the Eighth Dimension, Joy of Sex, Back to the Future, Clue, Legend of the White Horse, Miracles, Walk Like a Man, Who Framed Roger Rabbit, Track 29, Eight Men Out, The Dream Team, Back to the Future Part II, Why Me?, Back to the Future Part III, Duck Tales: The Movie (voice), White Dragon, Suburban Commando, The Addams Family, Dennis the Menace, Twenty Bucks, Addams Family Values, Angels in the Outfield, Camp Nowhere, Radioland Murders, The Pagemaster, Things to Do in Denver When You're Dead, Cadillac Ranch, Changing Habits, Anastasia, Tom Sawyer, It Came from the Sky, Dinner at Fred's, Convegence, Baby Geniuses, My Favorite Martian, Man on the Moon, Dinner At Fred's, Wish You Were Dead, Happy Birthday, A Fate Totally Worse Than Death, Chasing Destiny, Kids World, Interstate 60, Hey Arnold! The Movie, Haunted Lighthouse.
TELEVISION: Series: Taxi (Emmy Awards: 1982, 1983), Back to the Future (voice for animated series), Deadly Games, Cyberchase. Specials: Pilgrim Farewell, The Penny Elf, Tales From Hollywood Hills: Pat Hobby—Teamed With Genius, In

Search of Dr. Seuss. *Movies*: Lacy and the Mississippi Queen, The Word, Stunt Seven, Money on the Side, September Gun, The Cowboy and the Ballerina, T Bone N Weasel, Dead Ahead: The Exxon Valdez Disaster, It Came from the Sky, Wit. *Guest*: Barney Miller, Best of the West, Cheers, Amazing Stories, Avonlea (Emmy Award, 1992), Angels in the End Zone.

LLOYD, EMILY
Actress. r.n. Emily Lloyd Pack. b. North London, Eng., Sept. 29, 1970. Father is stage actor Roger Lloyd Pack, mother worked as Harold Pinter's secretary. Father's agent recommended that she audition for screenwriter David Leland's directorial debut Wish You Were Here when she was 15.
PICTURES: Wish You Were Here (Natl. Society of Film Critics & London Evening Standard Awards, 1987; BAFTA nom.), Cookie, In Country, Chicago Joe and the Showgirl, Scorchers, A River Runs Through It, Under the Hula Moon, When Saturday Comes, Dead Girl, Welcome to Sarajevo, Livers Ain't Cheap, Boogie Boy, Woundings, The Honey Trap.
TELEVISION: Override, Riverworld.

LLOYD, EUAN
Producer. b. Rugby, Warwick, England, Dec. 6, 1923. e. Rugby. Entered m.p. ind. in 1939 as theatre manager, then pub. dir.; dir. of Publ. Rank, 1946; joined Associated British-Pathe, Ltd. in same capacity; 1952 asst. to prod., Warwick Film Prod. Ltd. v.p. Highroad Productions, 1962-64. Rep. Europe Goldwyn's Porgy & Bess 1959.
PICTURES: April in Portugal, Heart of Variety, Invitation to Monte Carlo, The Secret Ways, Genghis Khan, Poppy Is Also a Flower, Murderer's Row, Shalako, Catlow, The Man Called Noon, Paper Tiger, The Wild Geese, The Sea Wolves, Who Dares Wins, Wild Geese II, The Final Option.

LLOYD, NORMAN
Actor, Producer, Director. b. Jersey City, NJ, Nov. 8, 1914. e. NYU, 1932. Acted on B'way in: Noah, Liberty Jones, Everywhere I Roam, 1935-44; in various stock companies. Joined Orson Welles and John Houseman in the original company of Mercury Theatre, NY, 1937-38. Prod. asst. on films Arch of Triumph, The Red Pony. Produced film Up Above the World.
THEATRE: *With the Civic Repertory Theatre, 1932-33 and The Living Newspapers of The Federal Theatre, 1936*: Triple a Plowed Under, Injunction Granted. *Regional*: Power, Medicine Show, Ask My Friend, Sandy, Volpone. *American Shakespeare Festival*: Measure for Measure, Taming of the Shrew (also dir.). *With La Jolla Playhouse, 1948-1955*: Village Green, King Lear, The Cocktail Party, The Lady's Not for Burning, Madame Will You Walk, The Golden Apple, Major Barbara, The Will & Bart Show, Quiet City
PICTURES: *Actor*: Saboteur, Spellbound, The Southerner, A Walk in the Sun, A Letter for Evie, The Unseen, Green Years, The Beginning or The End, Limelight, Young Widow, No Minor Vices, The Black Book, Scene of the Crime, Calamity Jane and Sam Bass, Buccaneer's Girl, The Flame and the Arrow, He Ran All the Way, The Light Touch, Audrey Rose, FM, The Nude Bomb, Jaws of Satan, Dead Poets Society, Journey of Honor (Shogun Mayeda), The Age of Innocence, Jean Renoir, The Adventures of Rocky and Bullwinkle.
TELEVISION: *Assoc. prod./exec. prod.*: The Alfred Hitchcock Show. *Prod.-Dir.*: The Alfred Hitchcock Hour, The Name of the Game, Hollywood Television Theater, Tales of the Unexpected, Omnibus (dir. of The Lincoln Films, 1952), Journey to the Unknown (series). *Actor*: St. Elsewhere (series), Harvest Home. *Movies* (prod.-dir.): The Smugglers, Companions in Nightmare, What's a Nice Girl Like You (prod.), The Bravos (prod.), Amityville: The Evil Escapes, The Battle Over Citizen Kane, Seven Days, Hitchcock: Shadow of a Genius, Fail Safe, The Song of the Lark.

LOACH, KEN
Director, Writer. b. Nuneaton, England, June 17, 1936. e. Oxford (studied law). Served in Royal Air Force; then became actor. Began dir. career on British tv in early 1960's.
PICTURES: Poor Cow (debut, 1968; also co-s.p.), Kes (also co-s.p.), Family Life, Black Jack (also co-s.p.), Looks and Smiles (also co- s.p.), Fatherland (Singing the Blues in Red), Hidden Agenda, Riff-Raff, Raining Stones, Land and Freedom, Ladybird Ladybird, Carla's Song, The Flickering Flame, My Name is Joe, Bread and Roses, The Navigators, Sweet Sixteen.
TELEVISION: Diary of a Young Man, 3 Clear Sundays, The End of Arthur's Marriage, Up the Junction, Coming Out Party, Cathy Come Home, In Two Minds, The Golden Vision, The Big Flame, In Black and White, After a Lifetime, The Rank and the File, Days of Hope, The Price of Coal, Auditions: The Gamekeeper, A Question of Leadership, Which Side Are You On.

LOBELL, MICHAEL
Producer. b. Brooklyn, NY, May 7, 1941. e. Michigan State U. on athletic baseball scholarship. Worked briefly in garment indust. Entered film industry in 1974 by buying Danish distribution rights to The Apprenticeship of Duddy Kravitz. Formed Lobell/ Bergman Prods. with Andrew Bergman.
PICTURES: Dreamer, Windows, So Fine, The Journey of Natty Gann, Chances Are, The Freshman, White Fang, Honeymoon in

Vegas, Undercover Blues, Little Big League, It Could Happen to You, Striptease, Isn't She Great, This Man This Woman, Hostile Rescue.

Lo BIANCO, TONY
Actor. b. New York, NY. Oct. 19, 1936. Performed on N.Y. stage as well as in films and TV. Former artistic dir. Triangle Theatre, NY.
THEATRE: Yanks 3—Detroit 0—Top of the Seventh (Obie Award), The Office, The Rose Tattoo, A View From the Bridge (Outer Critics Circle Award), The Royal Hunt of the Sun, Hizzoner, Other People's Money (tour).
PICTURES: The Honeymoon Killers (debut, 1970), The French Connection, The Seven Ups, Demon (God Told Me To), F.I.S.T., Bloodbrothers, Separate Ways, City Heat, Too Scared to Scream (dir. only), Mean Frankie and Crazy Tony, La Romana, City of Hope, The Spiders Web, Boiling Point, The Ascent, The Last Home Run (dir. only), The Juror, Sworn to Justics, Cold Night Into Dawn, Jane Austen's Mafia, The Pawn, The Day the Ponies Come Back, Friends and Family, Down n' Dirty, The Last Request, Endagered Species.
TELEVISION: *Series*: Love of Life, Jessie, Palace Guard. *Guest*: Police Story. *Movies/Mini-Series*: Mr. Inside Mr. Outside, The Story of Joseph and Jacob, Magee and the Lady (She'll Be Sweet), Jesus of Nazareth, Hidden Faces, Legend of the Black Hand, Lady Blue, Marco Polo, Welcome Home Bobby, Blood Ties, A Last Cry for Help, Marciano, Another Woman's Child, The Last Tenant, Goldenrod, Shadow in the Streets, Eugene O'Neill's A Glory of Ghosts, Police Story: The Freeway Killings, The Ann Jillian Story, Body of Evidence, Off Duty, True Blue, Perry Mason: The Case of the Poisoned Pen, Malcolm Takes a Shot, In the Shadow of a Killer, Stormy Weathers, Teamster Boss: The Jackie Presser Story, The First Circle, The Maharajah's Daughter, Tyson, Rocky Marciano, Bella Mafia, Lucky Day. *Specials*: Hizzoner (Emmy Award), A Glory of Ghosts. *Director*: Police Story, Kaz, Cliffhangers, When the Whistle Blows, The Duke.

LOCKE, PETER
Producer, Executive. Exec. producer, all programming produced by Kushner Locke. Producer, Stockard Channing Show, The Star Maker, The Hills Have Eyes, Parts I & II. Co-founder and currently co-chairman & co-CEO, Kushner-Locke, 1983.
PICTURES: *Producer*: The Hills Have Eyes, Nutcracker: The Motion Picture, Dorothy Meets Ozma of Oz, The Brave Little Toaster. *Exec. Producer*: Lady In Waiting, Adnre, Dangerous Intentions, Last Gasp, The Adventures of Pinocchio, The Whole Wide World, Shadow of the World, The Grave, The Last Time I Committed Suicide, Little Ghost, The Incredible Geneie, The Brave Little Toaster Goes to Mars, Possums, Basil, The Shrunken City, Small Time, Susan's Plan, Ringmaster, Teen Knight, Denial, Clockmaker, Bone Daddy, Phantom Town, Mudercycle, Beowulf, Girl, The Brave Little Toaster to the Rescue, Blooddolls, Freeway II: Confessions of a Trickbaby, But I'm a Cheerleader, The Boy with the X-Ray Eyes, Picking Up the Pieces, The Last Producer, Harvard Man.
TELEVISION: *Exec. Producer*: Sweet Bird of Youth, Your Mother Wears Combat Boots, Carolina Skeletons, Fire in the Dar, Father & Son: Dangerous Relations, A Strange Affair, Jack Reed: Death and Vengeance, Unlikely Angel, Every Woman's Dream, Gun (series), Echo, Dragonworld: The Legend Continues, The Search for the Jewel of Polaris: Mysterious Museum, They Nest, Dark Prince: The True Story of Dracula, Thrills (series), Wolf Girl.

LOCKE, SONDRA
Actress, Director. b. Shelbyville, TN, May 28, 1947. Autobiography: The Good the Bad and the Very Ugly, 1997.
PICTURES: The Heart Is a Lonely Hunter (debut, 1968; Acad. Award nom.), Cover Me Babe, Willard, A Reflection of Fear, The Second Coming of Suzanne, Death Game (The Seducers), The Outlaw Josey Wales, The Gauntlet, Every Which Way But Loose, Bronco Billy, Any Which Way You Can, Sudden Impact, Ratboy (also dir.), Impulse (dir. only), Do Me a Favor (dir.), The Prophet's Game, Clean and Narrow.
TELEVISION: *Movies*: Friendships, Secrets and Lies, Rosie: The Rosemary Clooney Story. *Guest*: Amazing Stories. *Director*: Death in Small Doses (movie).

LOCKHART, JUNE
Actress. b. New York, NY, June 25, 1925. p. actors, Gene and Kathleen Lockhart. B'way debut For Love or Money, 1947.
PICTURES: A Christmas Carol (debut, 1938), All This and Heaven Too, Adam Had Four Sons, Sergeant York, Miss Annie Rooney, Forever and a Day, White Cliffs of Dover, Meet Me in St. Louis, Son of Lassie, Keep Your Powder Dry, Easy to Wed, She-Wolf of London, Bury Me Dead, The Yearling, T-Men, It's a Joke Son, Time Limit, Butterfly, Deadly Games, Strange Invaders, Troll, Rented Lips, The Big Picture, Dead Women in Lingerie, Tis the Season, Sleep With Me, Lost in Space, Deterrence, The Thundering 8th.
TELEVISION: *Series*: Who Said That? (panelist), Lassie, Lost in Space, Petticoat Junction, General Hospital, Roseanne, Step By Step, Fired Up. *Movies*: But I Don't Want to Get Married, The Bait, Who is the Black Dahlia?, Curse of the Black Widow, The Gift of Love, Walking Through the Fire, The Night They Saved

Christmas, Perfect People, A Whisper Kills, Danger Island, The Au Pair II. *Mini-Series*: Loose Change.

LOCKLEAR, HEATHER
Actress. b. Los Angeles, CA, Sept. 25, 1961. e. UCLA. Appeared in commercials while in college.
PICTURES: Firestarter (debut, 1984), The Return of Swamp Thing, The Big Slice, Illusions, Wayne's World 2, The First Wives Club, Money Talks, Double Tap, Uptown Girls, Looney Tunes: Back in Action..
TELEVISION: *Movies*: Return of the Beverly Hillbillies, Twirl, City Killer, Blood Sport, Rich Men Single Women, Jury Duty: The Comedy, Her Wicked Ways, Dynasty: The Reunion, Body Language, Highway Heartbreaker, Fade to Black, Texas Justice, Too Many Lovers, Once Around the Park. Specials: Battle of the Network Stars, Hollywood Starr, TV Guide 40th Anniversary Special (host). *Series*: Dynasty, T.J. Hooker, Fright Night Videos (host), Going Places, Melrose Place, Hercules (voice), Spin City. *Guest*: Fantasy Island, The Fall Guy, Matt Houston, Hotel, The Love Boat.

LOCKWOOD, GARY
Actor. r.n. John Gary Yusolfsky. b. Van Nuys, CA, Feb. 21, 1937. Began in Hollywood as stuntman.
PICTURES: Tall Story, Splendor in the Grass, Wild in the Country, The Magic Sword, It Happened at the World's Fair, Firecreek, 2001: A Space Odyssey, They Came to Rob Las Vegas, Model Shop, The Body, R.P.M., Stand Up and Be Counted, The Wild Pair, Night of the Scarecrow, Trekkies, A Bedfull of Foreigners.
TELEVISION: *Series:* Follow the Sun, The Lieutenant. *Movies*: Earth II, Manhunter,

LOCKWOOD, ROGER
Executive. b. Middletown, CT, June 7, 1936. e. Ohio Wesleyan U. Sports writer for Akron Beacon Journal, 1960-62. On executive staff of Lockwood & Gordon Theatres; exec. v.p. SBC Theatres, 1969-73. 1974 asst. to exec. v.p., General Cinema Corp. 1975 formed Lockwood/Friedman Theatres, buying-booking and exhibition organization. Pres., Theatre Owners of New England, 1971-72; pres., Young NATO 1965-67; bd. of dir. NATO, 1962-1968. Board of dir. Tone, 1968-present; pres., Jimmy Fund, present; 1979-80, Variety Club of New England, pres. Director, Dana-Farber Cancer Institute, 1983-present. 1988, formed Lockwood/McKinnon Company Inc. operating theatres and Taco Bell Restaurants.

LOEKS, BARRIE LAWSON
Executive. b. Pittsburgh, PA. e. Univ. of MI, Univ. of MI Law Sch., 1979. Began career as associate in Grand Rapids, MI, law firm of Warner Norcross & Judd before serving for 7 yrs. as v.p. and gen. counsel of Jack Loeks Theatres; promoted to pres. of Loeks Michigan Theatres and Loeks-Star joint venture, 1988; Nov. 1992 named co-chmn., with husband Jim Loeks, of Sony/Loews Theatres, a Sony Retail Entertainment Co. April 1998 resigned from Loews Cineplex Entertainment; president and co-owner of Loeks-Star Theatres; named president of Loeks and Loeks Entertainment, Inc. Loeks-Star Theatres was bought by Onex (Loews Cineplex) in April 2002. Lawson Loeks remained in management until June, 2002 after acquisition. Recipient of Entrepreneur Award for the State of Michigan, 1998. November 1998, named Chairman National Association of Theatre Owners. Member: Board of Directors of Meijer, Inc. and Carlow College; Visitor's Committee of the University of Michigan.

LOEKS, JIM
Executive. b. Grand Rapids, MI. e. Univ. of MI. Started as gen. mgr. of John Ball Concessions Inc, becoming chmn. of bd. and owner, 1976-91. 1978, elected v.p. of Jack Loeks Theatres Inc.; named pres. of chain in 1983. 1988, became chmn. & co-owner of Loeks Michigan Theatres Inc., also gen. partner & operating agent of Loeks-Star joint venture with Sony Pictures Entertainment. Nov., 1992 named co-chmn., with wife Barrie Lawson Loeks, of Sony/Loews Theatres. April 1998, resigned from Loews Cineplex Entertainment; chairman and co-owner of Loeks-Star Theatres; named chairman of Loeks and Loeks Entertainment, Inc. Loeks-Star Theatres was bought by Onex (Loews Cineplex) in April 2002. Loeks remained in management until June, 2002 after acquisition. Recipient of Entrepreneur Award for State of Michican, 1998.

LOEKS, JOHN D. Jr.
Executive. b. Grand Rapids, MI, Feb 24, 1945. e. Wheaton Coll., B.A. 1967; Wayne State U., J.D. 1970. Began own law practice in 1970 until 1990. President, Showspan Inc., Jack Loeks Theatres Inc. Bd. member, Ausable Institute, Grand Rapids Symphony Orchestra, InterVarsity Christian Fellowship.

LOEWY, VICTOR
Executive. e. B.A., economics and German, McGill U., 1970. Co-founded Vivafilm, 1972; after Vivafilm became Alliance Communications Corp. in 1985, led that company to a dominant position in Canada's independent film distribution industry. Currently board member, Canadian Film Centre, Toronto

International Film Festival; chairman, National Assn. of Canadian Film Distributors; chairman, Alliance Atlantis Motion Picture Grp.; board member and member of Executive Committee, Alliance Atlantis Communications, Inc.

LOGAN, JEFF
Exhibitor. b. Mitchell, SD, Dec. 29, 1950. e. Dakota Wesleyan U. & U. of SD. Started working in family's Roxy Theatre at 9 yrs. old. Worked as announcer on KORN radio, 1969-70. Announcer, reporter & photgrapher KUSD-TV, 1970-71. Relief anchor KXON-TV, 1972-78. Took over management of family theatre. Built co. into present circuit, Logan Luxury Theatres. Member Bd. of trustess Dakota Wesleyan U., 1990-present. Bd. of trustees Queen of Peace Hospital, 1991-1997. V.P. Variety Club of SD, 1994-96. Dir. NATO/North Central, 1980-90. V.P. VSDA of SD, 1989-1994. Dir., NATO, 1997-present. Chairman NATO Theatre Operations Committee, 1999.

LOGGIA, ROBERT
Actor. b. New York, NY, Jan. 3, 1930. e. U. of Missouri, B.A. journalism, 1951. Studied with Stella Adler and at The Actors Studio. Broadway debut, The Man with the Golden Arm, 1955. THEATRE: Toys in the Attic, The Three Sisters, In the Boom Boom Room, Wedding Band.
PICTURES: Somebody Up There Likes Me (debut, 1956), The Garment Jungle, Cop Hater, The Lost Missile, Cattle King, The Greatest Story Ever Told, Che, First Love, Speed Trap, Revenge of the Pink Panther, The Ninth Configuration (Twinkle Twinkle Killer Kane), S.O.B., An Officer and a Gentleman, Trail of the Pink Panther, Psycho II, Curse of the Pink Panther, Scarface, Prizzi's Honor, Jagged Edge (Acad. Award nom.), Armed and Dangerous, That's Life, Over the Top, Hot Pursuit, The Believers, Gaby: A True Story, Big, Oliver & Company (voice), Relentless, S.P.O.O.K.S. (Code Name: Chaos), Triumph of the Spirit, Opportunity Knocks, The Marrying Man, Necessary Roughness, Gladiator, Innocent Blood, The Last Tattoo, Bad Girls, I Love Trouble, Man With a Gun, Independence Day, Lost Highway, Smilla's Sense of Snow, Wide Awake, The Proposition, Holy Man, American Virgin, The Suburbans, Return to Me, All Over Again, The Shipment, A Galaxy Far Far Away .
TELEVISION: *Specials:* Miss Julie, The Nine Lives of Elfego Baca, Conspiracy: The Trial of the Chicago 8, Merry Christmas Baby. *Movies:* Mallory: Circumstantial Evidence, Street Killing, Scott Free, Raid on Entebbe, No Other Love, Casino, A Woman Called Golda, A Touch of Scandal, Streets of Justice, Intrigue, Dream Breakers, Afterburn, Lifepod, Nurses on the Line: The Crash of Flight 7, White Mile, Jake Lassiter: Justice on the Bayou, Between Love and Honor, Mercy Mission: The Rescue of Flight 771, Right to Remain Silent, Joe Torre: Curveballs Along the Way, Hard Time: The Premonition, Dodson's Journey, Queen's Supreme. *Mini-Series*: Arthur Hailey's The Moneychangers, Echoes in the Darkness, Favorite Son, Wild Palms, Joan of Arc. *Series*: T.H.E. Cat, Emerald Point N.A.S., Mancuso FBI, Sunday Dinner, Queens Supreme.

LOLLOBRIGIDA, GINA
Actress. b. Subiaco, Italy, July 4, 1927. e. Acad. of Fine Arts, Rome. Film debut (Italy) L'aguila nera, 1946. Published several volumes of her photography incl. Italia Mia, The Wonder of Innocence.
PICTURES: Pagliacci, The City Defends Itself, The White Line, Fanfan the Tulip, Times Gone By, Beat the Devil, Crossed Swords, The Great Game, Beauties of the Night, Wayward Wife, Bread Love and Dreams, Bread Love and Jealousy, Young Caruso, World's Most Beautiful Woman, Trapeze, Hunchback of Notre Dame, Solomon and Sheba, Never So Few, The Unfaithfuls, Fast and Sexy, Where the Hot Wind Blows, Go Naked in the World, Come September, Imperial Venus, Woman of Straw, That Splendid November, Hotel Paradiso, Buona Sera Mrs. Campbell, Plucked, The Private Navy of Sgt. O'Farrell, Bad Man's River, King Queen Knave, The Lonely Woman, Bambole, Wandering Stars, A Hundred and One Nights, XXL.
TELEVISION: *Movie*: Deceptions, Cheer for Charlie. *Series*: Falcon Crest.

LOMIS, ERIK
Executive. b. Philadelphia, PA, November 21, 1958. e. B.S. Philadelphia Textile. Began career in 1979 at Sameric Theatres, where he held numerous positions including head film buyer. 1988-1993 United Artists Theatre Circuit, Sr. V.P. National Film Dept. 1993 joined MGM Distribution Co. as Sr. V.P. and G.S.M. Currently, pres. distribution at MGM. President, Will Rogers Foundation; Board Member, Variety Club and Foundation of Motion Picture Pioneers.

LOMITA, SOLOMON
Executive. b. New York, NY, April 23, 1937. Started industry career with United Artists Corp. as follows: adm., intl. dept., 1962; asst., intl. sales, same year. 1963, asst. intl. print mgr.; 1965, intl., print mgr. 1973 appt. dir. of film services. 1981, v.p., film services. 1985 named v.p., post-prod., Orion Pictures; 1989-92; then sr. v.p. post-prod. Retired.

LONDON, BARRY
Executive. Joined Paramount Pictures 1971 in L.A. branch office as booker; later salesman. 1973, sls. mgr., Kansas City-St. Louis; 1974, branch mgr. Transferred to San Francisco, first as branch mgr.; later as district mgr. 1977, eastern div. mgr. in Washington, DC, 1978-81, western div. mgr. 1981, named v.p., gen. sls. mgr. 1983, advanced to sr. v.p., domestic distrib.1984, named pres., domestic div., for Motion Picture Group of Paramount; 1985, named pres., marketing and domestic distrib.; 1988, named pres. worldwide distrib., Motion Picture Group. Producer, Barry London Co. Member: Variety Club NYC (VP, 1984-), Will Rogers Hospital Dist. Chmn., 1985-.

LONDON, JASON
Actor. b. San Diego, CA, Nov. 7, 1972. Twin brother of actor Jeremy London. Raised in Oklahoma and Texas. Appeared in Aerosmith video Amazing.
PICTURES: The Man in the Moon (debut, 1991), December, Dazed and Confused, Safe Passage, To Wong Foo—Thanks for Everything—Julie Newmar, My Generation, Learning Curves, The Barefoot Executive, Fall Time, Countdown, Mixed Signals, Frontline, Broken Vessels, The Rage: Carrie 2, Goodbye Sunrise, Poor White Trash, $pent, Out Cold, Dracula II: Ascension.
TELEVISION: Movie: A Matter of Justice, Alien Cargo, The Hound of the Baskervilles. Guest: I'll Fly Away, Tales From the Crypt, Friends Til the End.

LONDON, JEREMY
Actor. b. San Diego, CA, Nov. 7, 1972. Twin brother of actor Jason London. Raised in OK and TX.
PICTURES: Breaking Free, The Babysitter, Mallrats, Levitation, Happenstance, Get a Job, Scene Smoking: Cigarettes, Cinema & the Myth of Cool, Gods and Generals.
TELEVISION: Movies: In Broad Daylight, A Seduction in Travis County, A Season of Hope, A Mother's Gift, Bad to the Bone, The Defenders: Taking the First, Journey to the Center of the Earth. Series: I'll Fly Away, Angel Falls, Party of Five, Hollywood Squares. Guest: Perversions of Science.

LONDON, JERRY
Director. b. Los Angeles, CA, Jan 21, 1937. Apprentice film editor, Desilu Prods., 1955; film ed., Daniel Boone, 1962; staged plays in local theater workshops; editor, assoc. prod., then dir. Hogan's Heroes. Formed Jerry London Prods., 1984.
PICTURE: Rent-a-Cop (feature debut, 1988).
TELEVISION: Series: Mary Tyler Moore Show, Love American Style, The Bob Newhart Show, Marcus Welby, M.D., Kojak, The Six Million Dollar Man, Police Story, Rockford Files, Police Woman, Switch, Joe Forrester, The Bionic Woman, Delvecchio, The Feather and Father Gang, Dream On, Diagnosis Murder, The Cosby Mysteries, JAG, 100 Centre Street. Mini-series: Wheels, Shogun (DGA, best dir., special award), Chiefs (also sprv. prod.), Ellis Island (also sprv. prod.), If Tomorrow Comes, A Long Way From Home. Movies: Killdozer, McNaughton's Daughter, Cover Girls, Evening in Byzantium, Women in White, Father Figure, The Chicago Story, The Ordeal of Bill Carney (also prod.), The Gift of Life (also prod.), The Scarlet and the Black, Arthur Hailey's Hotel (also prod.), With Intent to Kill (exec. prod. only), Dark Mansions, Manhunt For Claude Dallas, Harry's Hong Kong, Family Sins (exec. prod. only), Macgruder and Loud (also prod.), Dadah Is Death (also prod.), Kiss Shot (also exec. prod.), The Haunting of Sarah Hardy (also exec. prod.), Vestige of Honor, A Season of Giants, Victim of Love, Grass Roots, Calendar Girl Cop Killer?: The Bambi Bembenek Story (also prod.), A Twist of the Knife, Labor of Love: The Arlette Schweitzer Story, A Mother's Gift, A Promise to Carolyn, A Holiday For Love, Get to the Heart: The Barbara Mandrell Story, I'll Be Home for Christmas, Stolen Women Captured Hearts, Beauty, As Time Runs Out, Take Me Home: The John Denver Story, Dr. Quinn Medicine Woman: The Heart Within, Attack on the Queen.

LONDON, MILTON H.
Executive. b. Detroit, MI, Jan. 12, 1916. e. U. of Michigan, B.A., 1937. Wayne U. Law Sch., 1938. U.S. Army 1943-46. Invented Ticograph system of positive admissions control for theatres, 1950; pres. Theatre Control Corp., 1950-62; secy-treas. Co-op. Theas. of Michigan Inc., 1956-63; exec. comm., Council of M.P. Organizations, 1957-66; dir. M.P. Investors, 1960-67; exec. dir. Allied States Assoc. of M.P. Exhib., 1961-66; exec. dir. National Assoc. of Theatre Owners, 1966-69; pres., NATO of Michigan, 1954-74; Chief Barker, Variety Club of Detroit, Tent No. 5. 1975-76; Life Patron and Lifeliner, Variety Clubs International; trustee, Variety Club Charity for Children; chmn., Variety Club Myoelectric Center; dir., Motion Picture Pioneers; dir., Will Rogers Inst.; trustee, Detroit Inst. for Children; pres., Metropolitan Adv. Co.; Intl. ambassador, Variety Clubs Int'l; Detroit News 1991 Michiganian of the Year. Retired.

LONE, JOHN
Actor. b. Hong Kong. Studied at Chin Ciu Academy of the Peking Opera in Hong Kong, Moved to LA where he studied acting at Pasadena's American Acad. of Dramatic Art, becoming member of the East-West Players.
THEATRE: NY: F.O.B., The Dance and the Railroad (Obie Awards for both plays), Paper Angels (dir.), Sound and Beauty (also dir.).
PICTURES: Iceman (debut, 1984), Year of the Dragon, The Last Emperor, The Moderns, Echoes of Paradise, Shadow of China, Shanghai 1920, M. Butterfly, The Shadow, The Hunted, Task Force, Rush Hour 2.
TELEVISION: The Dance and the Railroad, Paper Angels (dir.).

LONG, SHELLEY
Actress. b. Ft. Wayne, IN, Aug. 23, 1949. e. Northwestern U. Was co-host, assoc. prod. of local tv show Sorting It Out.
PICTURES: A Small Circle of Friends (debut, 1980), Caveman, Night Shift, Losin' It, Irreconcilable Differences, The Money Pit, Outrageous Fortune, Hello Again, Troop Beverly Hills, Don't Tell Her It's Me, Frozen Assets, The Brady Bunch Movie, A Very Brady Sequel, The Adventures of Ragtime, Dr. T. & the Women.
TELEVISION: Series: Cheers (Emmy Award, 1983), Good Advice, Kelly Kelly. Movies: The Cracker Factory, Princess and the Cabbie, Promise of Love, Voices Within: The Lives of Truddi Chase, Fatal Memories, A Message From Holly, The Women of Spring Break, Freaky Friday, Susie Q, A Different Kind of Christmas, Brady Bunch in the Whitehouse. Special: Basic Values: Sex Shock & Censorship in the '90's.

LONSDALE, PAMELA
Producer and Executive Producer for Children's drama, Thames TV for 15 years. Prod. short feature film plays, Exploits at West Poley (for CFTF), Prod.:News at Twelve (Central TV comedy series). Exec. prod. for E.B.U.'s world drama exchange for 2 years. Winner British Acad. Award for Rainbow, 1975.
TELEVISION: Exploits at West Poley (prod.), Ace of Wands (series, dir., prod.).

LOPEZ, JENNIFER
Actress. b. Bronx, NY, July 24, 1970.
PICTURES: My Little Girl, My Family—Mi Familia, Money Train, Jack, Blood and Wine, Selena, Anaconda, U-Turn, Out of Sight, Antz (voice), Thieves, The Cell, The Wedding Planner, Angel Eyes, Enough, Uptown Girl, Gigli, Jersey Girl, Shall We Dance?, An Unfinished Life.
TELEVISION: Movies: Nurses on the Line: The Crash of Flight 7. Series: Second Chances, Hotel Malibu, In Living Color.

LORD, PETER
Director, Producer. b. England, 1953.
PICTURES: Director: On Probation, Late Edition, Early Bird, Babylon, My Baby Just Carres For Me, Going Equipped, War Story, Adam, Wat's Pig, Chicken Run. Producer: On Probation, Adam (exec.), Not Without My Handbag (exec.), Wallace & Gromit: The Wrong Trousers (exec.), Wat's Pig (exec.), Stage Fight (exec.), Chicken Run, Wee Wee (exec.), Superhero (exec.), Horror (exec.), Hardface (exec.), Chips (exec.), Buzz Off (exec.), Bone (exec.), Wallace and Gromit: The Great Vegetable Plot.

LOREN, SOPHIA
Actress. b. Rome, Italy, Sept. 20, 1934. e. Naples. m. producer Carlo Ponti. Autobiography: Sophia: Living and Loving (with A.E. Hotchner, 1979).
PICTURES: Africa Beneath the Seas, Village of the Bells, Good People's Sunday, Neapolitan Carousel, Day in the District Court, Pilgrim of Love, Aida, Two Nights with Cleopatra, Our Times, Attila, Scourge of God, Gold of Naples, Too Bad She's Bad, Scandal in Sorrento, Miller's Beautiful Wife, Lucky to Be a Woman, Boy on a Dolphin (U.S. debut, 1957), The Pride and the Passion, Legend of the Lost, Desire Under the Elms, The Key, Houseboat, The Black Orchid, That Kind of Woman, Heller in Pink Tights, It Started in Naples, A Breath of Scandal, The Millionairess, Two Women (Academy Award, 1961), El Cid, Boccaccio 70, Madame Sans-Gene, Five Miles to Midnight, The Condemned of Altona, Yesterday Today and Tomorrow, The Fall of the Roman Empire, Marriage Italian Style, Operation Crossbow, Lady I, Judith, Arabesque, A Countess from Hong Kong, More than a Miracle, Ghosts—Italian Style, Sunflower, The Priest's Wife, Lady Liberty, White Sister, Man of La Mancha, The Voyage, The Verdict, The Cassandra Crossing, A Special Day, Angela, Brass Target, Firepower, Blood Feud, Ready to Wear (Pret-a-Porter), Grumpier Old Men, Messages, Soleil, Destinazione Verna, Francesca e Nunziata, Between Strangers.
TELEVISION: Movies/Specials: Brief Encounter, Sophia Loren—Her Own Story, Softly Softly, Rivals of Sherlock Holmes, Fantasy Island, Aurora, Courage, Mario Puzo's The Fortunate Pilgrim.

LOUDON, DOROTHY
Actress. b. Boston, MA, Sept. 17, 1933.
THEATRE: B'way: Nowhere to Go But Up (Theatre World Award), The Fig Leaves Are Falling, Sweet Potato, Three Men on a Horse, The Women, Annie (Tony Award, 1977), Ballroom, Sweeney Todd, West Side Waltz, Noises Off, Jerry's Girls, Comedy Tonight. Off-B'way: The Matchmaker. Regional: Driving Miss Daisy, Love Letters.
PICTURE: Garbo Talks, Midnight in the Garden of Good and Evil.

TELEVISION: *Series:* It's a Business?, Laugh Line, The Garry Moore Show, Dorothy, The Thorns (sang opening song). *Specials:* Many appearances on the Tony Awards; also Carnegie Hall Salutes Stephen Sondheim.

LOUGHLIN, LORI
Actress. b. Long Island, NY, July 28, 1964. Started modeling at age 7 for catalogues, then tv commercials. First professional acting job at 18 as regular on daytime serial The Edge of Night.
PICTURES: Amityville 3-D, The New Kids, Secret Admirer, Back to the Beach, The Night Before, Suckers, Critical Mass.
TELEVISION: *Series:* The Edge of Night, Full House, Hudson Street. *Movies:* North Beach and Rawhide, Brotherhood of Justice, A Place to Call Home, Doing Time on Maple Drive, A Stranger in the Mirror, Empty Cradle, One of Her Own, Abandoned and Deceived, In the Line of Duty: Blaze of Glory, Tell Me No Secrets, The Price of Heaven, Medusa's Child (mini).

LOUIS-DREYFUS, JULIA
Actress. b. New York, NY, Jan. 13, 1961. e. Northwestern Univ. Member of Second City comedy troupe which resulted in casting on Saturday Night Live.
PICTURES: Troll (debut, 1986), Hannah and Her Sisters, Soul Man, National Lampoon's Christmas Vacation, Jack the Bear, North, Deconstructing Harry, Father's Day, A Bug's Life (voice), Gilligan's Island, Speak Truth to Power, The Queen of the Whole Wide World.
TELEVISION: *Series:* Saturday Night Live (1982-85), Day by Day, Seinfeld (Golden Globe, 1994; Emmy Award, 1996), Watching Ellie. *Specials:* The Art of Being Nick, Spy Magazine's Hit List (host), Sesame Street's All-Star 25th Birthday. *Movies:* London Suite, Animal Farm (voice), Geppetto. *Guest:* Dinosaurs (voice), Dr Katz Professional Therapist.

LOUISE, TINA
Actress. r.n. Tina Blacker. b. New York, NY, Feb. 11. e. Miami U., N.Y. Neighborhood Playhouse, Actors Studio. Author, Sunday, 1997.
PICTURES: God's Little Acre (debut), The Trap, The Hangman, Day of the Outlaw, The Warrior Empress, Siege of Syracuse, Armored Command, For Those Who Think Young, The Wrecking Crew, The Good Guys and the Bad Guys, How to Commit Marriage, The Happy Ending, The Stepford Wives, Mean Dog Blues, Dogsday, Hellriders, Evils of the Night, O.C. and Stiggs, Dixie Lanes, The Pool, Johnny Suede, Little Pieces, Going Down in Brooklyn.
TELEVISION: *Series:* Jan Murray Time, Gilligan's Island, Dallas, Rituals. *Guest:* Mannix, Ironside, Kung Fu, Police Story, Kojak, Roseanne. *Movies:* But I Don't Want to Get Married, A Call to Danger, Death Scream, Look What's Happened to Rosemary's Baby, Nightmare in Badham Country, SST—Death Flight, Friendships Secrets and Lies, The Day the Women Got Even, Advice to the Lovelorn. *Special:* Surviving Gilligan's Island: The Incredibly True Story of the Longest Three Hour Tour in History.

LOURD, BRYAN
Executive. b. New Iberia, LA. e. Cambridge U., George Washington U., U.S.C. Began as a page at CBS Studios. Joined William Morris Agency in the mailroom, 1983. Promoted to agent in motion picture dept. 1988, joined Creative Artists Agency where he currently a partner and managing dir. In April 2000, he received the David Niven Award for his contribution to Project ALS (Lou Gehrig's disease).

LOVE, COURTNEY
Actress, Musician. r.n. Love Michelle Harrison. b. San Francisco, CA, July 9, 1965. Late husband was musician Kurt Cobain. Fronts music group Hole. Began career as punk rock extra in films, television before acting debut in Sid and Nancy, 1986.
PICTURES: Sid and Nancy, Straight to Hell, Tapeheads, Tank Girl (exec. music co-ord. only), Basquiat, Feeling Minnesota, Not Bad for a Girl (also co-prod.), The People vs. Larry Flint, 200 Cigarettes, Man on the Moon, Clara Bow: Discovering the It Girl (voice), Bounce: Behind the Velvet Rope, Julie Johnson, Trapped, Last Party 2000, Mayor of Sunset Strip.

LOVETT, RICHARD
Executive. e. U. of Wisconsin, Madison. Began career in mailroom at Creative Artists Agency. Promoted from agent trainee to agent in motion picture department. Appointed pres., CAA, October 1995. He and his partners created the CAA Foundation which works to involve the entertainment community in philanthropy and encourages organizations to lend their support to educational programs. Named one of the most influential people in entertainment by numerous media outlets. Serves on the boards of Communities & Schools, the National Urban League, and the Artists Rights Foundation. Recipient of City of Angels Helen Bernstein Award and David Niven Award for his contribution to Project ALS.

LOVITZ, JON
Actor, Comedian. b. Tarzana, CA, July 21, 1957. e. U. of California at Irvine. Studied acting at Film Actors Workshop. Took classes at the Groundlings, 1982. Performed with Groundling's

Sunday Company, before joining main company in Chick Hazzard: Olympic Trials. Developed comedy character of pathological liar which he later performed when he became regular member of Saturday Night Live in 1985.
PICTURES: The Last Resort, Ratboy, Jumpin' Jack Flash, Three Amigos, Big, My Stepmother Is an Alien, The Brave Little Toaster (voice), Mr. Destiny, An American Tail: Fievel Goes West (voice), A League of Their Own, Mom and Dad Save the World, National Lampoon's Loaded Weapon 1, Coneheads, City Slickers II: The Legend of Curly's Gold, North, Trapped in Paradise, The Great White Hype, High School High, Happiness, The Wedding Singer, Happiness, Lost and Found, Small Time Crooks, Little Nicky, Sand In the Boom Boom Room, 2000 Miles to Graceland, Cats and Dogs (voice), Rat Race, Good Advice, 8 Crazy Nights.
TELEVISION: *Series:* Foley Square, Saturday Night Live (1985-90), The Critic (voice), NewsRadio. *Specials:* The Please Watch the Jon Lovitz Special, One Night With Robbie Williams. *Guest:* The Paper Chase, The Simpsons (voice).

LOWE, CHAD
Actor. b. Dayton, OH, Jan. 15, 1968. Brother is actor Rob Lowe. m. actress Hilary Swank. Stage debut in L.A. production of Blue Denim. On NY stage in Grotesque Love Songs.
PICTURES: Oxford Blues (debut, 1984), Apprentice to Murder, True Blood, Nobody's Perfect, Highway to Hell, Driven, Floating, Do Me a Favor, The Way We Are, Suicide: The Comedy, The Audition, Take Me Home, Red Betsy, Unfaithful.
TELEVISION: *Movies:* Silence of the Heart, There Must Be a Pony, April Morning, So Proudly We Hail, An Inconvenient Woman, Captive, Candles in the Dark, Fighting for My Daughter, In the Presence of Mine Enemies, Target Earth, Take Me Home: The John Denver Story, The Apartment Complex, Acceptable Risk. *Series:* Spencer, Life Goes On (Emmy Award, 1993), Melrose Place, Now and Again, Popular. *Special:* No Means No (Emmy nom.).

LOWE, PHILIP L.
Executive. b. Brookline, MA, Apr. 17, 1917. e. Harvard. Army 1943-46. Checker, Loew's 1937-39; treasurer, Theatre Candy Co., 1941-58; Pres., ITT Sheraton Corp., 1969-70; Principal, Philip L. Lowe and Assoc. Retired.

LOWE, PHILIP M.
Executive. b. New Rochelle, NY, May 9, 1944. e. Deerfield Acad., Harvard Coll., cum laude in psychology, 1966; Columbia Business Sch., 1968. Work experience includes major marketing positions at General Foods, Gillette, Gray Advertising, and Estee Lauder Cosmetics before co-founding Cinema Centers Corp. and Theatre Management Services in Boston. Pres. of Lowe Group of Companies (cable television, broadcasting, hotels, real estate and management consulting). Past pres. and chmn. of the bd; National Association of Concessionaires (NAC); past director, National Association of Theater Owners (NATO). Professor of Marketing, Bentley Coll., Waltham, MA.; Contributing Editor; The Movie Business Book, Prentice-Hall, Inc. 1983.

LOWE, ROB
Actor. r.n. Robert Helper Lowe. b. Charlottesville, VA, Mar. 17, 1964. Brother is Chad Lowe. Raised in Dayton, OH. Started acting as child appearing in commercials, local tv spots, summer stock. Family moved to California when he was 13 yrs. old.
PICTURES: The Outsiders (debut, 1983), Class, The Hotel New Hampshire, Oxford Blues, St. Elmo's Fire, Youngblood, About Last Night..., Square Dance, Home Is Where the Heart Is, Masquerade, Illegally Yours, Mulholland Falls, Bad Influence, Stroke of Midnight (if the Shoe Fits), Desert Shield, The Dark Backward, The Finest Hour, Wayne's World, Tommy Boy, For Hire, Contact, Hostile Intent, Crazy Six, The Specials, Austin Powers: The Spy Who Shagged Me, Statistics, Dead Silent, The Specials, Under Pressure, Proximity, A View From the Top.
TELEVISION: *Movies:* Thursday's Child, Frank and Jesse (also co-prod.), First Degree, Desert's Edge (s.p. dir.), Outrage, Atomic Train, Jane Doe, Framed. *Series:* A New Kind of Family, The West Wing, The Lyon's Den *Mini-Series:* Stephen King's The Stand. *Specials:* A Matter of Time, Schoolboy Father, Suddenly Last Summer, On Dangerous Ground, Midnight Man.

LOWRY, DICK
Director. b. Oklahoma City, OK. e. U. of Oklahoma. Commercial photographer before being accepted by AFI. Dir. short film The Drought.
PICTURE: Smokey and the Bandit Part 3.
TELEVISION: *Mini-Series:* Dream West, Texas Justice, Dean Koontz's Mr. Murder. *Movies:* OHMS, Kenny Rogers as the Gambler, The Jayne Mansfield Story, Angel Dusted, Coward of the County, A Few Days in Weasel Creek, Rascals and Robbers: The Secret Adventures of Tom Sawyer and Huck Finn, Missing Children—A Mother's Story, Living Proof: The Hank Williams Jr. Story, Kenny Rogers as the Gambler—The Adventure Continues (also prod.), Off Sides (Pigs Vs. Freaks), Wet Gold, The Toughest Man in the World, Murder with Mirrors, American Harvest, Kenny Rogers as The Gambler III (also co-exec. prod.), Case Closed, In the Line of Duty: The FBI Murders, Unconquered (also prod.), Howard Beach: Making the Case For Murder, Miracle Landing (also prod.), Archie: To Riverdale and

Back, In the Line of Duty: A Cop for the Killing (also prod.), In the Line of Duty: Manhunt in the Dakotas (also prod.), A Woman Scorned: The Betty Broderick Story (also co-prod.), In the Line of Duty: Ambush in Waco (also prod.), In the Line of Duty: The Price of Vengeance, One More Mountain, A Horse for Danny, In The Line of Duty: Hunt for Justice (also prod.), Forgotten Sins, Project Alf, In The Line of Duty: Smoke Jumpers (also prod.), Last Stand at Saber River, Blaze of Glory (also prod.), Mr. Murder, Atomic Train, A Murder on Shadow Mountain, Y2K, Atilla, Follow the Stars Home, The Diamon of Jeru, Little John. *Series*: Crossing Jordan.

LOWRY, HUNT
Producer. b. Oklahoma City, OK, Aug. 21, 1954. e. Rollins Coll., & Wake Forest. Abandoned plans to study medicine to enter film-making industry; first job for New World Pictures where he met Jon Davison, with whom was later to co-produce. Next made TV commercials as prod. asst. and then producer. Left to go free-lance as commercials producer. 1980, appt. assoc. prod. to Davison on Airplane!
PICTURES: Humanoids from the Deep, Get Crazy, Top Secret!, Revenge, Career Opportunities, Only the Lonely, Last of the Mohicans, Striking Distance, My Life, First Knight, A Time to Kill, Instinct, The Kid, Donnie Darko, A Walk to Remember, Welcome to Collinwood, Divine Secrets of the Ya-Ya Sisterhood, White Oleander, The Heart of Me, Company Man.
TELEVISION: *Movies* (exec. prod.): Rascals and Robbers: The Secret Adventures of Tom Sawyer and Huckleberry Finn, Baja Oklahoma. *Movies* (prod.): His Mistress, Surviving, Wild Horses. *Mini-Series*: Dream West (prod.).

LUCAS, GEORGE
Producer, Director, Writer. b. Modesto, CA, May 14, 1944. e. USC, cinema. Made short film called THX-1138 and won National Student Film Festival Grand Prize, 1967. Signed contract with WB. Ass't. to Francis Ford Coppola on The Rain People, during which Lucas made 2-hr. documentary on filming of that feature entitled Filmmaker. Appeared as actor in film Beverly Hills Cop III. *Novel*: Shadow Moon (1995). Pres., Lucas Films, Industrial Light & Magic.
PICTURES: *Director/Writer*: THX-1138, American Graffiti, Star Wars: Episode IV-A New Hope, Star Wars: Episode I-The Phantom Menace (also exec. prod.), Star Wars: Episode II-Attack of the Clones (also prod.), Star Wars: Episode III (also prod.). *Executive Producer*: More American Graffiti, Star Wars: Episode V-The Empire Strikes Back (also story), Raiders of the Lost Ark (also co-story), Star Wars: Episode VI-Return of the Jedi (also co-s.p., story), Twice Upon a Time, Indiana Jones and the Temple of Doom (also story), Mishima, Labyrinth, Howard the Duck, Willow (also story), Tucker: The Man and His Dream, The Land Before Time, Indiana Jones and the Last Crusade (also co-story), Radioland Murders (also story), Indiana Jones and the Lost Continent.
TELEVISION: *Exec. Prod.*: The Ewok Adventure (movie), Ewoks: The Battle for Endor (movie); The Young Indiana Jones Chronicles (series).

LUCCHESI, GARY
Executive. b. San Francisco, CA, 1955. e. UCLA. Entered industry as a trainee with the William Morris Agency, 1977. Joined Tri-Star, 1983, as vice pres. of production, became sr. vice pres., 1985. Joined Paramount Pictures as exec. vice pres., April 1987; pres. of motion picture production division, 1987-92. Pres. of the Really Useful Film Company, Inc., 1994-1998. President LakeShore Entertainment, Oct. 1998.
PICTURES: *Producer/Executive Producer*: Jennifer Eight, Three Wishes, Virtuosity, Primal Fear, Gotti, Runaway Bride, Passion of Mind, The Next Best Thing, Autumn in New York, The Gift, The Mothman Prophecies, The Human Stain.
TELEVISION: Breast Men, Gotti, Vendetta, Wild Iris.

LUCCI, SUSAN
Actress. b. Scarsdale, NY, Feb. 23, 1948. e. Marymount Col. Was semifinalist in NY State Miss Universe Pageant. First professional job as "color girl" for CBS, sitting for cameras as new lighting system for color tv was developed. Had bit parts in films Me Natalie and Goodbye Columbus. Performed on 1983 album Love in the Afternoon.
PICTURES: Daddy You Kill Me, Young Doctors in Love (cameo).
TELEVISION: *Series*: All My Children (1970-; Daytime Emmy 1999). *Movies*: Invitation to Hell, Mafia Princess, Anastasia: The Story of Anna, Haunted By Her Past, Lady Mobster, The Bride in Black, The Woman Who Sinned, Double Edge, Between Love and Hate, French Silk, Seduced and Betrayed, Ebbie, Blood on Her Hands.

LUCKINBILL, LAURENCE
Actor. b. Fort Smith, AR, Nov. 21, 1934. m. actress Lucie PICTURES: The Boys in the Band, Such Good Friends, The Promise, Not for Publication, Cocktail, Messenger of Death, Star Trek V: The Final Frontier.
TELEVISION: *Series*: The Secret Storm, Where the Heart Is, The Delphi Bureau. *Movies*: The Delphi Bureau (pilot), Death Sentence, Panic on the 5:22, Winner Take All, The Lindbergh Kidnapping Case, The Mating Season, To Heal a Nation, Lincoln,

Dash & Lilly. *Mini-Series*: Ike. *Specials*: Lyndon Johnson (one-man show), Voices and Visions (narrator), The 5:48, Lucy & Desi: A Home Movie (co-exec. prod., co-dir., writer).

LUDDY, TOM
Producer. e. U. of California at Berkeley where he operated student film societies and rep. cinemas. Entered industry via Brandon Films. 1972, prog. dir. and curator of Pacific Film Archives. 1979, joined Zoetrope Studios as dir. of special projects where dev. and supervised revival of Gance's Napoleon and Our Hitler—A Film From Germany. Coordinated Koyaanisqatsi, Every Man For Himself, Passion. A founder, Telluride Film Fest.
PICTURES: Mishima (co-prod.), Tough Guys Don't Dance (co-exec. prod.), Barfly, King Lear (assoc. prod.), Manifesto (exec. prod.), Powwaqatsi (assoc. prod.), Wait Until Spring Bandini, Wind, The Secret Garden (co-prod.), Mi Familia (exec. prod.).

LUDWIG, IRVING H.
Executive. b. Nov. 3. Rivoli Theatre, N.Y., mgr., theatre oper., Rugoff and Becker, 1938-39; opened first modern art type theatre, Greenwich Village, 1940. With Walt Disney Prod. in charge of theatre oper. on Fantasia, 1940-41; buyer-booker, Rugoff and Becker, 1942-45; film sales admin., Walt Disney Prod. home office, 1945-53; v.p. and domestic sales mgr., Buena Vista Dist. Co., 1953; pres. sales & mktg., 1959-80. Member of bd. of dirs., Will Rogers Memorial Fund, Foundation of M.P. Pioneers; Motion Picture Club; Academy of M.P. Arts & Sciences.

LUEDTKE, KURT
Writer. b. Grand Rapids, MI, Sept. 29, 1938. e. Brown U., B.A., 1961. Reporter Grand Rapids Press 1961-62. Miami Herald, 1963-65; Detroit Free Press (reporter, asst. photography dir., asst. mgr. ed., asst. exec. ed., exec. ed. 1965-78.).
PICTURES: Absence of Malice, Out of Africa (Academy Award, 1985), Random Hearts.

LUFT, LORNA
Actress, Singer. b. Hollywood, CA, Nov. 21, 1952. Daughter of actress-singer Judy Garland and producer Sid Luft. Has sung in nightclubs. Appeared on 1990 recording of Girl Crazy.
THEATRE: *NY*: Judy Garland at Home at the Palace, Promises Promises, Snoopy, Extremities. PICTURES: I Could Go on Singing (cameo), Grease 2, Where the Boys Are, 54.
TELEVISION: *Series*: Trapper John. *Movies*: Fear Stalk, Life with Judy Garland: Me and My Shadows. *Guest*: Twilight Zone, Hooperman, Murder She Wrote, Tales from the Dark Side, The Cosby Show.

LUHRMANN, BAZ
Director. r.n.Bazmark Luhrmann.
PICTURES: *Dir./Writer.*: Strictly Ballroom, Romeo + Juliet (also prod., BAFTA Award, Best Direction, Best Adapted Screenplay, 1997), Moulin Rouge (Acad. Award nom., BAFTA nom., AFI nom.), Rent. *Actor*: Winter of Our Dreams, The Dark Room.

LUKE, PETER
Writer, Director. b. England, Aug. 12, 1919. *Autobiography*: Sisyphus & Reilly.
TELEVISION: *Writer*: Small Fish Are Sweet, Pigs Ear with Flowers, Roll on Bloomin' Death, A Man on Her Back (with William Sansom), Devil a Monk Won't Be, Anach 'Cuan (also dir.), Black Sound—Deep Song (also dir.), several others.

LUMET, SIDNEY
Director. b. Philadelphia, PA, June 25, 1924. e. Professional Children's Sch.; Columbia U. Child actor in plays: Dead End, George Washington Slept Here, My Heart's in the Highlands, and films: The 400 Million, One Third of a Nation. U.S. Armed Forces, WWII, 1942-46; dir. summer stock, 1947-49; taught acting, H.S. of Prof. Arts. Assoc. dir. CBS, 1950, dir. 1951. Appeared in documentary List Up: The Lives of Quincy Jones. Author: Making Movies (Alfred A. Knopf, 1995).
PICTURES: 12 Angry Men (debut, 1957), Stage Struck, That Kind of Woman, The Fugitive Kind, A View from the Bridge, Long Day's Journey Into Night, Fail-Safe, The Pawnbroker, The Hill, The Group, The Deadly Affair (also prod.), Bye Bye Braverman (also prod.), The Sea Gull (also prod.), The Appointment, The Last of the Mobile Hotshots (also prod.), King: A Filmed Record... Montgomery to Memphis (co-dir., prod.), The Anderson Tapes, Child's Play, The Offence, Serpico, Lovin' Molly, Murder on the Orient Express, Dog Day Afternoon, Network, Equus, The Wiz, Just Tell Me What You Want (also co-prod.), Prince of the City (also co-s.p.), Deathtrap, The Verdict, Daniel (also co-exec. prod.), Garbo Talks, Power, The Morning After, Running on Empty, Family Business, Q & A (also s.p.), A Stranger Among Us, Guilty As Sin, Night Falls On Manhattan (also s.p.), Critical Care, The Beautiful Mrs. Seidelmann, Gloria, Whistle.
TELEVISION: *Series episodes*: Mama, Danger, You Are There, Omnibus, Best of Broadway, Alcoa, Goodyear Playhouse, Kraft Television Theatre (Mooney's Kid Don't Cry, The Last of My Gold Watches, This Property is Condemned), Playhouse 90, Play of the Week (The Dybbuk, Rashomon, The Iceman Cometh—Emmy Award), 100 Centre Street. *Specials*: The Sacco and

Vanzetti Story, John Brown's Raid, Cry Vengeance.

LUNDGREN, DOLPH
Actor. r.n. Hans Lundren. b. Stockholm, Sweden, Nov. 3, 1959. e. Washington State U., won Fulbright to Massachusetts Inst. of Technology, Royal Inst. of Technology, Stockholm, M.S.C. Was doorman at Limelight disco in NY while studying acting. Full Contact Karate champion. Made workout video, Maximum Potential. On stage in Another Octopus.
PICTURES: A View to a Kill, Rocky IV, Masters of the Universe, Red Scorpion, The Punisher, I Come in Peace, Cover-Up, Showdown in Little Tokyo, Universal Soldier, Army of One, Pentathlon, Men of War, Johnny Mnemonic, The Shooter, The Algonquin Goodbye, The Peacekeeper, The Minion, Sweepers, Storm Catcher, Bridge of Dragons, Storm Catcher, Jill Rips, The Last Patrol, Captured, Hideen Agenda, Straight Blast, Alien Agent.
TELEVISION: Movie: John Woo's Blackjack.

LUPONE, PATTI
Actress. b. Northport, NY, Apr. 21, 1949. e. Juilliard.
THEATRE: School for Scandal, Three Sisters, The Beggars Opera, The Robber Bridegroom, Meaure for Measure, Edward II, The Water Engine, Working, Evita (Tony Award, 1980), Oliver!, Anything Goes, Les Miserables (London), Sunset Boulevard (London), Master Class, The Old Neighborhood.
PICTURES: 1941, Fighting Back, Witness, Wise Guys, Driving Miss Daisy, Family Prayers, Summer of Sam, State and Main, 24 Hour Woman, Bad Faith, Heist, The Victim, City by the Sea.
TELEVISION: Series: Life Goes On, Falcone. Movies: LBJ: The Early Years, The Water Engine, The Song Spinner, Her Last Chance, Bonanno: A Godfather's Story, Monday Night Mayhem. Special: Sweeney Todd: The Demon Barber of Fleet Street In Concert. Guest: Law & Order.

LURIE, JOHN
Composer, Actor
PICTURES: Composer: The Offenders, The Loveless, Permanent Vacation, Stranger than Paradise, Variety, City Limits, Down By Law, Mystery Train, On the Beautiful Blue Danube, Blue in the Face, Get Shorty, Manny & Lo, Excess Baggage, Lulu on the Bridge, Clay Pigeons, The Animal Factory, Atlantic City Serenade. Actor: The Offenders, Subway Rider, Permanent Vacation, Paris, Texas, Stranger than Paradise, Desperately Seeking Susan, Down by Law, The Last Temptation of Christ, The Little Devil, Wild at Heart, John Lurie and the Lounge Lizard Live in Berlin, Smoke, Blue in the Face, Just Your Luck, New Rose Hotel, Sleepwalk.

LYDON, JAMES
Actor. b. Harrington Park, NJ, May 30, 1923; e. St. Johns Mil. Sch. On N.Y. stage in Prologue to Glory, Sing Out the News. For 20th Century Fox tv was assoc. prod. of series Anna and the King, Roll Out. Prod./Writer/Dir. of special The Incredible 20th Century. Dir. for Universal TV: 6 Million Dollar Man, Simon & Simon, Beggarman Thief.
PICTURES: Actor: Back Door to Heaven (debut, 1939), Two Thoroughbreds, Racing Luck, Tom Brown's Schooldays, Little Men, Naval Academy, Bowery Boy, Henry Aldrich for President, Cadets on Parade, The Mad Martindales, Star Spangled Rhythm, Henry Aldrich— Editor, Henry Aldrich Gets Glamour, Henry Aldrich Swings It, Henry Aldrich Haunts a House, Henry Aldrich Plays Cupid, Aerial Gunner, Henry Aldrich—Boy Scout, My Best Gal, The Town Went Wild, Henry Aldrich's Little Secret, When the Lights Go on Again, Out of the Night, Twice Blessed, The Affairs of Geraldine, Life With Father, Cynthia, Sweet Genevieve, The Time of Your Life, Out of the Storm, Joan of Arc, An Old-Fashioned Girl, Bad Boy, Miss Mink of 1949, Tucson, Gasoline Alley, Tarnished, When Willie Comes Marching Home, Destination Big House, Hot Rod, September Affair, The Magnificent Yankee, Island in the Sky, The Desperado, Battle Stations, Chain of Evidence, The Hypnotic Eye, I Passed for White, The Last Time I Saw Archie, Brainstorm, Death of a Gunfighter, Scandalous John, Bonnie's Kids, Vigilante Force. Assoc. Prod.: My Blood Runs Cold, An American Dream, A Covenant With Death, First to Fight, The Cool Ones, Chubasco, Countdown, Assignment to Kill, The Learning Tree.
TELEVISION: Guest: Frontier Circus (also assoc. prod.). Co-ordin. Prod.: Wagon Train, Alfred Hitchcock Hour. Assoc. Prod.: McHale's Navy, 77 Sunset Strip, Mr. Roberts. Series (actor): So This Is Hollywood, The First Hundred Years, Love That Jill. Movies: Ellery Queen, The New Daughters of Joshua Cabe, Peter Lundy and the Medicine Hat Stallion.

LYLES, A. C.
Producer. b. Jacksonville, FL. May 17, 1918. e. Andrew Jackson H.S. Paramount Publix's Florida Theatre, 1928; interviewed Hollywood celebrities, Jacksonville Journal, 1932; mail boy, Paramount Studios, Hollywood, 1937; publicity dept., 1938; hd. of adv., publ. dept., Pine-Thomas unit at Paramount, 1940; assoc. prod., The Mountain. President, A. C. Lyles Productions, Inc. (Paramount Pictures). Retired.
PICTURES: Short Cut to Hell, Raymie, The Young and the Brave, Law of the Lawless, Stage to Thunder Rock, Young Fury,

Black Spurs, Hostile Guns, Arizona Bushwackers, Town Tamer, Apache Uprising, Johnny Reno, Waco, Red Tomahawk, Fort Utah, Buckskin, Rogue's Gallery, Night of the Lepus, The Last Day, Flight to Holocaust.
TELEVISION: Rawhide (series; assoc. prod.), A Christmas for Boomer, Here's Boomer (series), Dear Mr. President, Conversations With the Presidents.

LYNCH, DAVID
Director, Writer. b. Missoula, MT, Jan. 20, 1946. e. Pennsylvania Acad. of Fine Arts, where received an independent filmmaker grant from America Film Institute. Made 16mm film, The Grandmother. Accepted by Center for Advanced Film Studies in Los Angeles, 1970. Wrote and directed Eraserhead (with partial AFI financing). Acted in films Zelly & Me, Nadja (also exec. prod.). Daughter is director Jennifer Lynch.
PICTURES: Director-Writer: Eraserhead (also prod., edit., prod.-design, f/x), The Elephant Man, Dune, Blue Velvet, Wild at Heart, Twin Peaks: Fire Walk With Me (also co-exec. prod., actor), Lost Highway, The Straight Story (also s.p.), Mulholland Drive, Darkened Room (also exec. prod.), Cabin Fever (exec. prod. only).
TELEVISION: Series: Twin Peaks (dir., exec. prod., writer), On the Air (exec. prod., dir., writer), Mulholland Drive (also exec prod.). Special: Hotel Room (co-dir., co-exec. prod.).

LYNCH, KELLY
Actress. b. Minneapolis, MN, 1959. Former model.
PICTURES: Osa, Bright Lights Big City, Cocktail, Road House, Warm Summer Rain, Drugstore Cowboy, Desperate Hours, Curly Sue, For Better and For Worse, Three of Hearts, Imaginary Crimes, The Beans of Egypt Maine, Virtuosity, White Man's Burden, Heaven's Prisoners, Persons Unknown, Cold Around the Heart, Mr. Magoo, Homegrown, Charlie's Angels, Joe Somebody, The Slaughter Rule, Searching for Debra Winger, Dallas and Rusty.
TELEVISION: Guest: Miami Vice, The Equalizer, Spenser for Hire, The Hitcher, The Edge (Black Pudding). Movie: Something in Common. Pilot: San Berdoo.

LYNCH, PAUL M.
Director.
PICTURES: Hard Part Begins, Blood and Guts, Prom Night, Cross Country, Flying, Blindside, Bullies, Mania, Flying, Blindside, No Contest, No Contest II, More to Love, Frozen With Fear.
TELEVISION: Series: Voyagers, Blacke's Magic, Murder She Wrote, In the Heat of the Night, Tour of Duty, Beauty and the Beast, Twilight Zone (1987), Moonlighting, Star Trek: The Next Generation, Dark Shadows, Tour of Duty, Top Cops, Mike Hammer, Hooperman, Bronx Zoo, various other series episodes. Movies: Cameo By Night, Going to the Chapel, She Knows Too Much, Murder by Night, Drop Dead Gorgeous.

LYNCH, RICHARD
Actor. b. Brooklyn, NY. Trained with Lee Strasberg at Carnegie Hall. In 1970 became life time member of the Actors Studio, NY.
THEATRE: NY: The Devils (On and Off-B'way debut), The Basic Training of Pavlo Hummel, Lion in Winter, The Orphan, Arturo-U, The Lady From the Sea, One Night Stands of a Noisy Passenger, Action, Richard III, Live Like Pigs, The Man with the Flower in His Mouth, A View from the Bridge.
PICTURES: Scarecrow (debut, 1973), The Seven Ups, The Delta Fox, The Premonition, Steel, Open Season, The Formula, The Sword and the Sorcerer, Little Nikita, Savage Dawn, Invasion U.S.A., Cut and Run, Night Force, The Barbarians, Bad Dreams, The Ninth Configuration, Melanie Rose (High Stakes), Spirit, Aftershock, Return to Justice, One Man Force, The Forbidden Dance, October 32nd, Alligator II: The Mutation, Double Threat, H.P. Lovecraft's Necromonicon, Scanner Cop, Crime & Punishment, Takedown, Dragon Fury, Destination Vegas, Werewolf, Terrified, Loving Deadly, Deathmatch, Midnight Confessions, Warrior of Justice, Diamond Run, Under Oath, Total Force, Ground Rules, Divine Lovers, Armstrong, Love and War II, Lone Tiger, Breaking the Silence, Strike Zone, Enemy Action, Eastside, Battlestar Galactica: The Second Coming, First Watch, Ancient Warriors, Outta Time.
TELEVISION: Series: Battlestar Gallactica, The Phoenix. Movies: Starsky and Hutch (pilot), Roger & Harry: The Mitera Target, Good Against Evil, Dog and Cat, Vampire, Alcatraz—The Whole Shocking Story, Sizzle, White Water Rebels, The Last Ninja.

LYNDON, VICTOR
Producer, Writer. b. London. e. St. Paul's. Ent. m.p. ind. 1942 as asst. dir., Gainsborough Pictures. Novel: Bermuda Blue (1984).
PICTURES: Prod. mgr.: The African Queen. Assoc. Prod.: Dr. Strangelove, Darling, 2001: A Space Odyssey. Prod.: Spare the Rod, Station Six—Sahara, The Optimists.

LYNE, ADRIAN
Director. b. Peterborough, England, March 4, 1941. Started as director of commercials.
PICTURES: Foxes, Flashdance, Nine 1/2 Weeks, Fatal Attraction, Jacob's Ladder, Indecent Proposal, Lolita, Unfaithful (also prod.).

LYNLEY, CAROL
Actress. b. New York, NY, Feb. 13, 1942. Was model as teenager.
PICTURES: The Light in the Forest (debut, 1958), Holiday for Lovers, Blue Denim, Hound-Dog Man, Return to Peyton Place, The Last Sunset, The Stripper, Under the Yum-Yum Tree, The Cardinal, The Pleasure Seekers, Shock Treatment, Harlow, Bunny Lake Is Missing, The Shuttered Room, Danger Route, Once You Kiss a Stranger, The Maltese Bippy, Norwood, Beware the Blob!, The Poseidon Adventure, Cotter, The Four Deuces, The Washington Affair, The Cat and the Canary, The Shape of Things to Come, Vigilante, Dark Tower, Blackout, Howling VI: The Freaks, Neon Signs, Off the Menu: The Last Days of Chasen's, Vic, Drowning on Dry Land, A Light in the Forest.
TELEVISION: Series: The Immortal. Movies: Shadow on the Land, The Smugglers, The Immortal (pilot), Weekend of Terror, The Cable Car Murder, The Night Stalker, The Elevator, Death Stalk, Willow B, Women in Prison, Flood, Fantasy Island, Having Babies II, Cops and Robin, The Beasts Are on the Streets.

LYNN, ANN
Actress. b. London, England, 1934. Ent. films and TV, 1958.
PICTURES: Johnny You're Wanted (debut, 1955), Moment of Indiscretion, Naked Fury, Piccadilly Third Stop, The Wind of Change, Strip Tease Murder, Strongroom, Flame in the Streets, HMS Defiant (Damn the Defiant), The Party's Over, Doctor in Distress, The Black Torment, The System (The Girl Getters), A Shot in the Dark, The Uncle, Four in the Morning, Separation, I'll Never Forget What's 'is Name, Baby Love, Hitler—The Last Ten Days, Screamtime.
TELEVISION: Specials/Movies: After The Show, All Summer Long, Trump Card, Man at the Top, The Expert, Hine, The Intruders, Too Far, King Lear, The Zoo Gang, Morning Tide, Estuary, Who Pays the Ferryman, The Professionals, Zeticula, Westway, The Perfect House, Minder, To the Sound of Guns, Crown Court, Just Good Friends, Starting Out, Paradise Park. Series: The Cheaters, The Other Side of the Underneath.

LYNN, JONATHAN
Director, Writer, Actor. b. Bath, England, Apr. 3, 1943. Was artistic dir. of Cambridge Theatre Company, 1976-81; Company Director of Natl. Theatre, 1987. Playwright: Pig of the Month. Books: A Proper Man, The Complete Yes Prime Minister, Mayday. Appeared as actor in Into the Night, Three Men and a Little Lady.
PICTURES: The Internecine Project (s.p.). Director: Clue (also s.p.), Nuns on the Run (also s.p.), My Cousin Vinny, The Distinguished Gentleman, Greedy (also actor), Sgt. Bilko, Trial and Error (also prod.).
TELEVISION: Doctor on the Go, My Name is Harry Worth, My Brother's Keeper, Yes Minister, Yes Prime Minister.

LYONNE, NATASHA
Actress. r.n. Natasha Braunstein. b. NY, April 4, 1979.
PICTURES: Heartburn (debut, 1986), Dennis the Menace, Everyone Says I Love You, Slums of Beverly Hills, Krippendorf's Tribe, Modern Vampyres, Freeway II: Confessions of a Trickbaby, Detroit Rock City, But I'm a Cheerleader, American Pie, The Auteur Theory, When Autumn Leaves, Rat Girl, Plan B, Scary Movie 2, American Pie 2, The Grey Zone, Kate & Leopold, Zigzag, Night at the Golden Eagle, Fast Sofa, Comic Book Villains.
TELEVISION: Movies/Specials: If These Walls Could Talk 2. Series: Pee-Wee's Playhouse.

LYONS, S. DANIEL
Executive. b. Toronto, Canada, Sept., 9, 1955. e. Brandeis Univ., B.A. magna cum laude 1977. Univ. of Toronto, LL.B. 1981. 1985, joined Astral Films as a lawyer. Promoted to dir. of bus. affairs, then v.p., Dist. for the Astral Entertainment Group. 1997, became v.p., Dist & Mktg., Coscient/Astral Dist. Author of: Public Strategy and Motion Pictures, and Showman (play, Cubiculo Theatre, NY).

LYON, SUE
Actress. b. Davenport, IA, July 10, 1946. e. Hollywood Prof. Sch.
PICTURES: Lolita (debut, 1962), The Night of the Iguana, Seven Women, Tony Rome, The Flim Flam Man, Evel Knievel, Crash, End of the World, Alligator, Invisible Strangler.
TELEVISION: Movies: But I Don't Want to Get Married!, Smash-Up on Interstate 5, Don't Push—I'll Charge When I'm Ready.

M

MacARTHUR, JAMES
Actor. b. Los Angeles, CA, Dec. 8, 1937. e. Harvard. p. actress Helen Hayes, writer Charles MacArthur. Stage debut, summer stock; The Corn Is Green, Life with Father.
PICTURES: The Young Stranger (debut, 1957), The Light in the Forest, Third Man on the Mountain, Kidnapped, Swiss Family Robinson, The Interns, Spencer's Mountain, Cry of Battle, The Truth About Spring, The Battle of the Bulge, The Bedford Incident, Ride Beyond Vengeance, The Love-Ins, Hang 'em

High, The Angry Breed, JFK.
TELEVISION: Series: Hawaii Five-0. Movies: Alcatraz—The Whole Shocking Story, The Night the Bridge Fell Down, Storm Chasers: Revenge of the Twister. Special: Willie and the Yank (Mosby's Marauders).

MACCHIO, RALPH
Actor. b. Long Island, NY, Nov. 4, 1962. Started in TV commercials at age 16 before winning role in series Eight Is Enough. Broadway debut in Cuba and His Teddy Bear, 1986; Off-B'way in Only Kidding.
PICTURES: Up the Academy (debut, 1980), The Outsiders, The Karate Kid, Teachers, Crossroads, The Karate Kid Part II, Distant Thunder, The Karate Kid Part III, Too Much Sun, My Cousin Vinny, Naked in New York, Dizzyland, Can't be Heaven, Popcorn Shrimp, The Office Party, A Cold Day in August.
TELEVISION: Series: Eight Is Enough. Movies: Journey to Survival, Dangerous Company, The Three Wishes of Billy Grier, The Last P.O.W.?: The Bobby Garwood Story.

MacCORKINDALE, SIMON
Actor, Producer, Director, Writer. b. Isle-of-Ely, England, Feb. 2, 1952. m. actress Susan George. On stage in Dark Lady of the Sonnets, Pygmalion, French Without Tears, etc.
PICTURES: Actor: Death on the Nile, Quatermass Conclusion, Caboblanco, Robbers of the Sacred Mountain, The Sword and the Sorcerer, Jaws 3-D, The Riddle of the Sands, Sincerely Violet. Producer: Stealing Heaven, That Summer of White Roses (also co-s.p.), The House That Mary Bought (also dir., co-s.p.), Such a Long Journey.
TELEVISION: Specials: I Claudius, Romeo and Juliet, Quatermass. Movies: The Manions of America, Falcon's Gold, Jesus of Nazareth, Twist of Fate, Obsessive Love, No Greater Love, At The Midnight Hour, A Family of Cops, While My Pretty One Sleeps, The Sands of Eden. Mini-Series: Pursuit, The Way to Dusty Death. Series: Manimal, Falcon Crest, Counterstrike. Series Prod.: The Relic Hunter, Queen of Swords.

MacCURDY, JEAN
Executive. Began career in the Children's Prog. dept., NBC TV network. Joined Warner Bros. Cartoons in 1979, as dir. of Animation and Prog.; named v.p. & gen. mngr, WB Cartoons & served as prodn. exec., 1982. Named v.p., Children's Prog., 1983. Returned to WB Animation as v.p. & gen. mngr., 1988; named sr. v.p. & gen. mngr. 1991; became first pres., WB TV Animation, 1992.

MacDOWELL, ANDIE
Actress. r.n. Rose Anderson MacDowell. b. Gaffney, SC, April 21, 1958. Started as model for Elite Agency in NY appearing for L'Ordeal Cosmetics, The Gap, Calvin Klein.
PICTURES: Greystoke: The Legend of Tarzan Lord of the Apes (debut, 1984), St. Elmo's Fire, Sex Lies and Videotape (L.A. Film Critics Award, 1989), Green Card, The Object of Beauty, Hudson Hawk, The Player, Groundhog Day, Short Cuts, Deception, Four Weddings and a Funeral, Bad Girls, Unstrung Heroes, Michael, Multiplicity, The End of Violence, Shadrach, Just the Ticket (also exec. prod.), Muppets from Space, The Muse, Reaching Normal, Harrison's Flowers, Ginostra, Town & Country, Crush.
TELEVISION: Movies: Women and Men 2: In Love There Are No Rules (Domestic Dilemma), Dinner with Friends. Mini-Series (Italy): Sahara's Secret.

MACGILLIVRAY, GREG
Executive. President & co-founder, MacGillivray Freeman Films, which specializes in large format documentary films, 1965-present. Director/producer, To Fly!, 1976 (the highest grossing documentary film of all time, selected by the Library of Congress for inclusion in the National Film Registry), To the Limit, Everst, The Living Sea, Dolphins, Adventures in Wild California, Living Caves.

MacGRAW, ALI
Actress. b. Pound Ridge, NY, April 1, 1939. e. Wellesley Coll. Son is actor Josh Evans. Editorial asst. Harper's Bazaar Mag.; asst. to photographer Melvin Sokolsky. Was top fashion model. Author: Moving Pictures (autobiography, 1991), Yoga Mind & Body (1995).
PICTURES: A Lovely Way to Die (debut, 1968), Goodbye Columbus, Love Story (Acad. Award nom.), The Getaway, Convoy, Players, Just Tell Me What You Want, Natural Causes, Glam.
TELEVISION: Mini-Series: The Winds of War. Movies: China Rose, Survive the Savage Sea, Gunsmoke: The Long Ride, The Hollywood Fashion Machine. Series: Dynasty.

MacLACHLAN, KYLE
Actor. b. Yakima, WA, Feb. 22, 1959. e. Univ. of WA. Acted in high school and college, then in summer stock. Joined Oregon Shakespeare Festival (Romeo and Juliet, Julius Caesar, Henry V). Cast as lead in Dune by dir. David Lynch in a nationwide search.
THEATRE: NY: Palace of Amateurs (Off-B'way).
PICTURES: Dune (debut, 1984), Blue Velvet, The Hidden, Don't Tell Her It's Me, The Doors, Twin Peaks: Fire Walk With Me, Where the Day Takes You, Rich in Love, The Trial, The Flintstones, Showgirls, Trigger Effect, Mad Dog Time, One Night

Stand, Hamlet, Timecode, XChange, Perfume, Me Without You, Miranda.
TELEVISION: *Series*: Twin Peaks, Sex and the City. *Guest*: Tales From the Crypt (Carrion Death). *Movies*: Dream Breakers, Against the Wall, Roswell, Windsor Protocol, Route 9, The Spring.

MacLAINE, SHIRLEY
Actress. r.n. Shirley MacLean Beaty. b. Richmond, VA, April 24, 1934. Brother is actor-prod. Warren Beatty. e. Washington and Lee H.S., Arlington, VA. Started as dancer; on B'way as understudy for Carol Haney in The Pajama Game, which resulted in contract with film prod. Hal Wallis. Prod., writer and co- dir. of Oscar-nominated film documentary: The Other Half of The Sky: A China Memoir. Returned to stage in Gypsy in My Soul, Shirley MacLaine on Broadway. Videos: Shirley MacLaine's Inner Workout, Relaxing Within.
AUTHOR: Don't Fall off the Mountain, You Can Get There from Here, Out on a Limb, Dancing in the Light, It's All In the Playing, Going Within, Dance While You Can, My Lucky Stars. *Editor*: McGovern: The Man and His Beliefs (1972).
PICTURES: The Trouble With Harry (debut, 1955), Artists and Models, Around the World in 80 Days, Hot Spell, The Matchmaker, The Sheepman, Some Came Running (Acad. Award nom.), Ask Any Girl, Career, Can-Can, The Apartment (Acad. Award nom.), Ocean's Eleven (cameo), All in a Night's Work, Two Loves, My Geisha, The Children's Hour, Two for the Seesaw, Irma La Douce (Acad. Award nom.), What a Way to Go!, John Goldfarb Please Come Home, The Yellow Rolls Royce, Gambit, Woman Times Seven, The Bliss of Mrs. Blossom, Sweet Charity, Two Mules for Sister Sara, Desperate Characters, The Possession of Joel Delaney, The Turning Point (Acad. Award nom.), Being There, Loving Couples, A Change of Seasons, Terms of Endearment (Acad. Award, 1983), Cannonball Run II, Madame Sousatzka, Steel Magnolias, Postcards From the Edge, Waiting for the Light, Defending Your Life (cameo), Used People, Wrestling Ernest Hemingway, Guarding Tess, Mrs. Winterbourne, The Celluloid Closet, Evening Star, A Smile Like Yours (cameo), Looking for Lulu, Bet Bruce, Bruno (also dir.), Salem Witch Trials, Carolina, Broadway: The Golden Age by the Legends Who Were There.
TELEVISION: *Series*: Shirley's World. Variety *Specials*: The Other Half of the Sky: A China Memoir (also prod., co-writer), If They Could See Me Now, Where Do We Go From Here?, Shirley MacLaine at the Lido, Every Little Movement (Emmy Award for co-writing, 1980), Illusions, The Shirley MacLaine Show. *Movies*: Out on a Limb (also co-writer), The West Side Waltz, Joan of Arc, These Old Broads.

MacLEOD, GAVIN
Actor. b. Mt. Kisco, NY, Feb. 28, 1930. e. Ithaca Coll.
PICTURES: I Want to Live, Compulsion, Operation Petticoat, McHale's Navy, McHale's Navy Joins the Air Force, The Sand Pebbles, Deathwatch, The Party, Kelly's Heroes, Time Changer.
TELEVISION: *Series*: McHale's Navy, The Mary Tyler Moore Show, The Love Boat, The King of Queens, Oz. *Movies*: The Intruders, Only with Married Men, Ransom for Alice, Murder Can Hurt You, Student Exchange, The Love Boat: The Valentine Voyage. *Mini-Series*: Scruples. *Specials*: Last Act Is a Solo, If I Die Before I Wake.

MACMILLAN, MICHAEL
Executive. b. Scarborough, Ontario, Canada, 1956. e. Queen's U., Ontario. Co-founded and served as first cinematographer for Atlantis Films Ltd.,1978; chairman and CEO, Alliance Atlantis Communications, Inc. Producer/exec. producer, Boys and Girls, The Painted Door, Curse of the Viking Crane, Lost in the Barrens. Currently on the board of directors, Canadian Stage Co., Toronto East General Hospital Foundation, and The Canadian Film and Television Production Assn. Also vice-chair Canadian Film Centre.

MacNAUGHTON, ROBERT
Actor. b. New York, NY, Dec. 19, 1966. Entered entertainment industry in 1979. Member Circle Rep. Co., N.Y.
THEATRE: Critic's Choice, A Thousand Clowns, Camelot, The Diviners, The Adventures of Huckleberry Finn, Henry V, Tobacco Road, Master Harold... and the Boys, Tomorrow's Monday, Talley and Son.
PICTURES: E.T.: The Extra-Terrestrial, I Am the Cheese.
TELEVISION: *Movies*: Angel City, A Place to Call Home. *Specials*: Big Bend Country, The Electric Grandmother, Hear My Cry, Visitors.

MacNICOL, PETER
Actor. b. Dallas, TX, April 10, 1954. e. U. of Minnesota.
THEATRE: Manhattan Theatre Club: Crimes of the Heart. NY Shakespeare Fest: Found a Peanut, Rum and Coke, Twelfth Night, Richard II, Romeo & Juliet. Regional theatre includes Guthrie, Alaska Rep., Long Wharf, Dallas Theatre Center, Trinity Rep. B'way: Crimes of the Heart (Theatre World Award), The Nerd, Black Comedy/White Liars.
PICTURES: Dragonslayer (debut, 1981), Sophie's Choice, Heat, Ghostbusters II, American Blue Note, Hard Promises, Housesitter, Addams Family Values, Radioland Murders,

Dracula: Dead and Loving It, Mojave Moon, Bean, Baby Geniuses, Recess: School's Out.
TELEVISION: *Movies*: Johnny Bull, By Dawn's Early Light, Roswel, Olive the Other Reindeer (voice), Silencing Mary, The Ponder Heart. *Guest*: Faerie Tale Theatre, Days and Nights of Molly Dodd, Cheers. *Series*: Powers That Be, Chicago Hope, Abducted: A Father's Love, Silencing Mary, Ally McBeal, Ally.

MACY, WILLIAM H.
Actor. b. Miami, FL, March 13, 1950. e. Goddard Col.
THEATRE: *NY*: The Man in 605 (debut, 1980), Twelfth Night, Beaurecrat, A Call From the East, The Dining Room, Speakeasy, Wild Life, Flirtations, Baby With the Bathwater, The Nice and the Nasty, Bodies Rest and Motion, Oh Hell!, Life During Wartime, Mr. Gogol and Mr. Preen, Oleanna, Our Town (B'way).
PICTURES: Without a Trace, The Last Dragon, Radio Days, House of Games, Things Change, Homicide, Shadows and Fog, Benny and Joon, Searching for Bobby Fischer, The Client, Oleanna, Murder in the First, Mr. Holland's Opus, Down Periscope, Fargo (Acad. Award nom.), Ghosts of Mississippi, Boogie Nights, Air Force One, Wag the Dog, Pleasantville, Jerry & Tom, A Civil Action, Psycho, Mystery Men, Happy Texas, Magnolia, State and Maine, Panic, Jurassic Park III, Focus, Welcome to Collinwood, The Cooler, Voltage, Stealing Sinatra, Seabiscuit, Minnesota Nice (video short), Spartan, In Enemy Hands.
TELEVISION: *Movies*: The Murder of Mary Phagan, Texan, A Murderous Affair, The Water Engine, Heart of Justice, A Private Matter, The Con, A Slight Case of Murder, Night of the Headless Horseman (voice), Door to Door. *Guest*: ER, Law and Order, Chicago Hope, King of the Hill (voice).

MADDEN, BILL
Executive. b. New York, NY, March 1, 1915. e. Boston U. Joined Metro-Goldwyn-Mayer as office boy, 1930; student salesman, 1938; asst. Eastern div. sales mgr., 1939; U.S. Navy, 1942-46; Boston sales rep., MGM, 1947-53; Philadelphia branch mgr., 1954-59; Midwest div. sales mgr., 1960-68; roadshow sales mgr., 1969; v.p., gen. sales mgr., 1969-74, MGM; corp., v.p. & gen. sls. mgr., MGM, 1974; retired from MGM, 1975; 1976-present, exec. consultant to motion picture industry; lecturer and instructor at UCLA. Member: AMPAS, Motion Picture Associates, American Film Institute. Motion Picture Pioneers.

MADDEN, DAVID
Executive, Producer, Director. b. Chicago, IL, July 25, 1955. e. Harvard U., 1976; UCLA, M.A., 1978. Joined 20th Century-Fox in 1978 as story analyst. Named story editor, 1980; exec. story editor, 1982. Appt. v.p., creative affairs for 20th-Fox Prods., 1983; v.p., prod., 20th Century-Fox Prods; 1984, v.p., prod., Paramount Pictures. 1987, joined Interscope Commun. as prod. 1996, Formed Cort Madden Co. at Paramount with Robert Cort.
PICTURES: *Producer*: Renegades, Blind Fury (exec. prod.), The First Power, Eve of Destruction, Jersey Girls, The Hand That Rocks the Cradle, Holy Matrimony, Operation Dumbo Drop, The Tie That Binds, Separate Lives (dir only.), The Associate, Odd Couple II, The Out of Towners, Runaway Bride, Save the Last Dance, The Colony, Against the Ropes.
TELEVISION: *Movies*: A Part of the Family (dir., writer), Body Language (co-exec. prod.), In the Company of Spies, Harlan County War, L.A. Law: The Movie.

MADDEN, JOHN
Director. b. Portsmouth, NH, April 8, 1949.
PICTURES: Ethan Frome, Golden Gate, Mrs. Brown, Shakespeare in Love (Acad. Award nom.), Captain Corelli's Mandolin.
TELEVISION: *Movies*: Grown-ups, A Wreath of Roses, The Widowmaker, The Storyteller: Greek Myths, Meat, Prime Suspect 4: The Lost Child, Truth or Dare. *Series*: The Return of Sherlock Holmes, Inspector Morse, The Casebook of Sherlock Holmes.

MADDIN, GUY
Director, Writer. b. Winnipeg, Canada, Feb. 28, 1956.
PICTURES: The Dead Father, Tales from the Gimli Hospital (also ed., d.p.), Indigo High-Hatters, Tyro, BBB, Mauve Decade, The Pomps of Satan, Archangel (also ed., d.p.), Careful (also ed., d.p.), Sea Begger, Odilon Redon or The Eye Like a Strange Balloon Mounts Toward Infinity, The Hands of Ida, Imperial Orgies, Twilight of the Ice Nymphs (dir. only), Maldoror: Tygers, The Hoyden, The Cock Crew, Hospital Fragment, The Heart of the World, Fleshpots of Antiquity, Dracula: Pages From a Virgin's Diary (dir. only).

MADIGAN, AMY
Actress. b. Chicago, IL, Sept. 11, 1951. m. actor Ed Harris. For 10 years traveled country performing in bars and clubs with band. Then studied at Lee Strasberg Inst., L.A. NY Stage: The Lucky Spot (Theatre World Award), A Streetcar Named Desire.
PICTURES: Love Child (debut, 1982), Love Letters, Streets of Fire, Places in the Heart, Alamo Bay, Twice in a Lifetime (Acad. Award nom.), Nowhere To Hide, The Prince of Pennsylvania, Field of Dreams, Uncle Buck, The Dark Half, Female Perversions, Loved, With Friends Like These, Pollock, A Time for Dancing, The Sleepy Time Gal, Just a Dream, The Laramie

Project.
TELEVISION: *Special*: The Laundromat. *Movies*: Crazy Times, The Ambush Murders, Victims, Travis McGee, The Day After, Roe vs. Wade, Lucky Day, And Then There Was One, Riders of the Purple Sage, Big Guns Talk: The Story of the Western, A Bright Shining Lie, Having Our Say: The Delany Sisters' First 100 Years, In the Name of the People, Shot in the Heart. *Mini-Series*: Not for Ourselves Alone: The Story of Elizabeth Cady Stanton & Susan B. Anthony, Jazz, Mark Twain.

MADONNA
Singer, Actress. r.n. Madonna Louise Veronica Ciccone. b. Pontiac, MI, Aug. 16, 1958. e. U. of Michigan. m. director Guy Ritchie. Gained fame as rock & recording star before professional acting debut in Desperately Seeking Susan, 1985. NY stage debut: Speed-the-Plow, 1988. Author: Sex (1992).
PICTURES: A Certain Sacrifice (debut, 1983), Vision Quest, Desperately Seeking Susan, Shanghai Surprise, Who's That Girl?, Bloodhounds of Broadway, Dick Tracy, Truth or Dare (also exec. prod.), Shadows and Fog, A League of Their Own, Body of Evidence, Dangerous Game, Blue in the Face, Four Rooms, Girl 6, Evita (Golden Globe Award for Actress, 1997), Junket Whore, The Next Best Thing, Star, Swept Away.
TELEVISION: Various specials and performances.

MADSEN, MICHAEL
Actor. b. Chicago, IL, Sept. 25, 1958. Sister is actress Virginia Madsen. Started acting with Chicago's Steppenwolf Theatre appearing in such plays as Of Mice and Men, A Streetcar Named Desire. On B'way in A Streetcar Named Desire (1992).
PICTURES: WarGames (debut, 1983), Racing With the Moon, The Natural, The Killing Time, Shadows in the Storm, Blood Red, Kill Me Again, The End of Innocence, The Doors, Thelma & Louise, Straight Talk, Inside Edge, Reservoir Dogs, Trouble Bound, House in the Hills, Free Willy, Money for Nothing, Fixing the Shadow, The Getaway, Beyond the Law, Dead Connection, Wyatt Earp, Man With a Gun, Species, Free Willy 2: The Adventure Home, Mulholland Falls, Donnie Brasco, The Maker, The Thief & The Stripper, Detour, Species II, The Replacement, The Florentine, Luck of the Draw, The Price of Air, Love.com, Ides of March, The Ghost, Fall, Choke, Bad Guys, Pressure Point, Outlaw, Microwave Park, LAPD: To Protect and Serve, Extreme Honor, The Real Deal, Where's Angelo?, Die Another Day, The Confidence Game, A Christmas Cop, Blueberry, Kill Bill.
TELEVISION: *Movies:* Our Family Honor, Montana, Baby Snatcher, Supreme Sanction. *Specials:* Steve McQueen: The King of Cool. *Pilot:* Diner. *Series:* Vengeance Unlimited.

MADSEN, VIRGINIA
Actress. b. Chicago, IL, Sept. 11, 1963. Mother is Emmy-winning Chicago filmmaker; brother is actor Michael Madsen. Studied with Chicago acting coach Ted Liss. Prof. debut, PBS, A Matter of Principle. Received Avoriaz & Saturn Awards for Best Actress for Candyman.
PICTURES: Class (debut, 1983), Electric Dreams, Dune, Creator, Fire With Fire, Modern Girls, Zombie High, Slam Dance, Mr. North, Hot to Trot, Heart of Dixie, The Hot Spot, Highlander 2: The Quickening, Candyman, Becoming Colette, Caroline at Midnight, Blue Tiger, The Prophecy, Ghosts of Mississippi, Suicide Kings, The Rainmaker, McClintocks Peach, The Florentine, Ballad of the Nightingale, Ambushed, The Haunting, All the Fine Lines, After Sex, Lying in Wait, American Gun, Almost Salinas.
TELEVISION: *Movies*: Mussolini: The Untold Story, The Hearst and Davies Affair, Long Gone, Gotham, Third Degree Burn, Ironclads, Victim of Love, Love Kills, Linda, A Murderous Affair: The Carolyn Warmus Story, Bitter Revenge, Robert Ludlum's The Apocalypse Watch, Children of Fortune, The Inspector General, Crossfire Trail, Just Ask My Children. *Guest:* The Hitchhiker, Frasier.

MAGNOLI, ALBERT
Director, Writer, Editor.
PICTURES: Jazz (dir., editor, s.p.), Reckless (edit.), Purple Rain (dir., edit., s.p.), American Anthem (dir. only), Sign 'o' the Times, Tango and Cash, Street Knight, Dark Planet.
TELEVISION: *Movie*: Born to Run. *Series*: Nash Bridges.

MAGNUSON, ANN
Actress, Writer, Performance Artist. b. Charleston, WV, Jan. 4, 1956. e. Denison U. Intern at Ensemble Studio Theatre when she came to NY in 1978. Ran Club 57, an East Village club, 1979. Has performed Off-B'way, in East Village clubs, downtown art spaces, on college campuses since 1980, and at Whitney Museum, Soguestu Hall (Tokyo), Walker Art Ctr. (Minn.), Lincoln Center, Serious Fun Festival, Joseph Papp's Public Theatre. Also performed with band Bongwater. Debut as solo recording artist on Geffen Records with The Luv Show, 1995.
PICTURES: Vortex, The Hunger, Perfect Strangers, Desperately Seeking Susan, Making Mr. Right, A Night in the Life of Jimmy Reardon, Sleepwalk, Mondo New York, Tequila Sunrise, Checking Out, Heavy Petting, Love at Large, Cabin Boy, Clear and Present Danger, Tank Girl, Before and After, Hugo Pool, Still Breathing, Levitation, Small Soldiers, I Woke Up Early The Day I Died, Still Breathing, Love & Sex, Friends & Lovers,

Housebound, The Caveman's Valentine, Glitter, Ghost Light, Panic Room, Night at the Golden Eagle, The United States of Leland.
TELEVISION: *Movies/Specials:* Night Flight, Made for TV, Alive from Off Center (co-host), Vandemonium, Table at Ciro's (Tales From the Hollywood Hills), The Hidden Room, The Adventures of Pete and Pete, From the Earth to the Moon. *Guest:* The John Laroquette Show, Caroline in the City, The Drew Carey Show. *Series:* Anything But Love.

MAGUIRE, TOBEY
Actor. b. Santa Monica, CA, June 27, 1975.
PICTURES: This Boy's Life, S.F.W., Plane Fear, Duke of Groove, Joyride, The Ice Storm, Deconstructing Harry, Pleasantville, Fear and Loathing in Las Vegas, Wonder Boys, The Cider House Rules, Ride with the Devil, Cats & Dogs, Don's Plum, Spider-Man, The 25th Hour, Seabiscuit (also exec. prod.), Spider-Man 2.
TELEVISION: *Movie*: Spoils of War. *Series*: Great Scott!. *Guest*: Roseanne, Walker Texas Ranger, Blossom.

MAHARIS, GEORGE
Actor. b. Astoria, NY, Sept. 1, 1928. Studied at The Actors Studio.
PICTURES: Exodus (debut, 1960), Quick Before It Melts, Sylvia, The Satan Bug, A Covenant With Death, The Happening, The Desperadoes, Last Day of the War, The Land Raiders, The Sword and the Sorcerer, Doppelganger.
TELEVISION: *Series*: Search for Tomorrow, Route 66, Most Deadly Game. *Guest*: Naked City. *Movies*: Escape to Mindanao, The Monk, The Victim, Murder on Flight 502, Look What's Happened to Rosemary's Baby, SST—Death Flight, Return to Fantasy Island, Crash, A Small Rebellion, Rock of Ages (exec. prod. only). *Mini-Series*: Rich Man Poor Man. *Special*: A Death of Princes.

MAHONEY, JOHN
Actor. b. Manchester, England, June 20, 1940. Mem. of Stratford Children's Theatre from age 10-13. Moved to U.S. at 19, taught Eng. at Western Illinois U. Then freelance ed. of medical manuscripts; assoc. ed., Quality Review Bulletin. At 35 quit medical book editing to become an actor. Studied acting, Chicago's St. Nicholas Theatre. Prof. debut, The Water Engine, 1977. Joined Steppenwolf Theatre Co., 1979.
THEATRE: Orphans (Theatre World Award), The House of Blue Leaves (Tony & Clarence Derwent Awards), The Subject Was Roses.
PICTURES: Mission Hill, Code of Silence, The Manhattan Project, Streets of Gold, Tin Men, Suspect, Moonstruck, Frantic, Betrayed, Eight Men Out, Say Anything..., Love Hurts, The Russia House, Barton Fink, Article 99, In the Line of Fire, Striking Distance, Reality Bites, The Hudsucker Proxy, The American President, Primal Fear, She's the One, Antz (voice), The Iron Giant (voice), The Broken Hearts Club, Atlantis: The Lost Empire (voice), Almost Salinas.
TELEVISION: *Movies*: The Killing Floor, Chicago Story, First Steps, Listen to Your Heart, Dance of the Phoenix, First Steps, Trapped in Silence, Favorite Son, The Image, Dinner at Eight, The 10 Million Dollar Getaway, The Secret Passion of Robert Clayton, Unnatural Pursuits. *Special*: The House of Blue Leaves. *Series*: Lady Blue, H.E.L.P., The Human Factor, Frasier.

MAJORS, LEE
Actor. r.n. Lee Yeary. b. Wyandotte, MI, April 23, 1939. Star athlete in high school; turned down offer from St. Louis Cardinals in final year at Eastern Kentucky State Coll. to pursue acting career. In L.A. got job as playground supervisor for park dept. while studying acting at MGM Studio. Debuted in films 1964 under his real name.
PICTURES: Strait-Jacket (debut, 1964), Will Penny, The Liberation of L. B. Jones, The Norsemen, Killer Fish, Steel, Agency, The Last Chase, Scrooged, Keaton's Cop, Trojan War, Musketeers Forever, Chapter Zero, The Protector, New Jersey Turnpikes, Primary Suspect, Here, Out Cold, Big Fat Liar, Waitin' to Live.
TELEVISION: *Series*: The Big Valley, The Men From Shiloh, Owen Marshall-Counselor at Law, The Six Million Dollar Man, The Fall Guy, Tour of Duty, Raven, Too Much Sun. *Movies*: The Ballad of Andy Crocker, Weekend of Terror, The Gary Francis Powers Story, The Cowboy and the Ballerina, A Rocky Mountain Christmas, The Return of the Six Million Dollar Man and the Bionic Woman, Danger Down Under (exec. prod., actor), The Bionic Showdown: the Six Million Dollar Man and the Bionic Woman, Fire!, Trapped on the 37th Floor, The Cover Girl Murders, Bionic Ever After?, Lost Treasures of Dos Santos.

MAKAVEJEV, DUSAN
Director. b. Belgrade, Yugoslavia, Oct. 13, 1932.
PICTURES: Jatagan Mala, Pecat, Antonijevo Razbijeno Ogledalo, Spomenicima ne Treba Verovati, Slikovnica Pcelara, Prokleti Praznik, Boje Sanjaju, Sto je Radnicki Savjet?, Pedagoska Bajka, Osmjeh 61, Eci Pec Pec, Parada, Ljepotica 62, Film o Knjizi ABC, Dole Plotovi, Nova Igracka, Nova Domaca Zivotinja, Man is Not a Bird, An Affair of the Heart, Innocence Unprotected, Mystery of Body (also s.p.), I Miss Sonia Henie, Wet Dreams, Sweet Movie (also s.p.), Montenegro (also s.p.),

The Coca-Cola Kid, Manifesto (also s.p.), Gorilla Bathes at Noon (also s.p.), A Hole in the Soul, Danish Girls Show Everything.

MAKEPEACE, CHRIS
Actor. b. Montreal, Canada, April 22, 1964. e. Jarvis Collegiate Institute. Trained for stage at Second City Workshop.
PICTURES: Meatballs (debut, 1979), My Bodyguard, The Last Chase, The Oasis, The Falcon and the Snowman, Vamp, Captive Hearts, Aloha Summer, Memory Run, Short for Nothing.
TELEVISION: *Movies*: The Terry Fox Story, The Mysterious Stranger, Mazes and Monsters, The Undergrads, Christmas in My Hometown. *Series*: Going Great (host, 1982-84), Why On Earth?

MAKO
Actor. r.n. Makoto Iwamatsu. b. Kobe, Japan, Dec. 10, 1933. e. Pratt Inst.
THEATRE: *NY*: Pacific Overtures (Tony nom.), Shimada. *Regional*: Rashomon.
PICTURES: The Ugly Dachshund, The Sand Pebbles (Acad. Award nom.), The Private Navy of Sgt. O'Farrell, The Great Bank Robbery, The Hawaiians, The Island at the Top of the World, Prisoners, The Killer Elite, The Big Brawl, The Bushido Blade, Under the Rainbow, An Eye for an Eye, Conan the Barbarian, The House Where Evil Dwells, Testament, Conan the Destroyer, Armed Response, P.O.W. The Escape, Silent Assassins, The Wash, Tucker: The Man and His Dream, An Unremarkable Life, Taking Care of Business, Pacific Heights, The Perfect Weapon, Sidekicks, Robocop 3, Rising Sun, Cultivating Charlie, A Dangerous Place, Highlander III: The Sorcerer, Midnight Man, Crying Freeman, Sworn to Justice, Balance of Power, Seven Years in Tibet, The Bird People in China, Alegria, Talk to Taka, Rugrats in Paris: The Movie (voice), Pearl Harbor, She Said I Love You, Straight Blast, Bulletproof Monk.
TELEVISION: *Series*: Hawaiian Heat, Dexter's Laboratory. *Movies*: The Challenge, If Tomorrow Comes, The Streets of San Francisco (pilot), Judge Dee and the Monastery Murders, Farewell to Manzanar, When Hell Was in Session, The Last Ninja, Girls of the White Orchid, Kung Fu: The Movie, Hiroshima: Out of the Ashes, Riot. *Guest*: McHale's Navy, Ensign O'Toole, 77 Sunset Strip, I Spy, F Troop, Hawaii Five-O.

MALDEN, KARL
Actor. r.n. Mladen Sekulovich. b. Gary, IN, March 22, 1914. e. Art Inst. of Chicago 1933-36; Goodman Theatre Sch. Elected pres., Acad. of Motion Picture Arts & Sciences, 1989.
THEATRE: *B'way*: Golden Boy, Key Largo, Flight to West, Missouri Legend, Uncle Harry, Counterattack, Truckline Cafe, All My Sons, Streetcar Named Desire, Desperate Hours, Desire Under the Elms, The Egghead.
PICTURES: They Knew What They Wanted (debut, 1940), Winged Victory, 13 Rue Madeleine, Boomerang!, Kiss of Death, The Gunfighter, Where the Sidewalk Ends, Halls of Montezuma, A Streetcar Named Desire (Acad. Award, best supporting actor, 1951), The Sellout, Diplomatic Courier, Operation Secret, Ruby Gentry, I Confess, Take the High Ground, Phantom of the Rue Morgue, On the Waterfront (Acad. Award nom.), Baby Doll, Bombers B-52, Time Limit (dir. only), Fear Strikes Out, The Hanging Tree, One Eyed Jacks, Pollyanna, The Great Impostor, Parrish, All Fall Down, Birdman of Alcatraz, Gypsy, How the West Was Won, Come Fly With Me, Cheyenne Autumn, Dead Ringer, The Cincinnati Kid, Nevada Smith, Murderer's Row, Hotel, Blue, The Adventures of Bullwhip Griffin, Billion Dollar Brain, Hot Millions, Patton, Cat O'Nine Tails, Wild Rovers, Summertime Killer, Beyond the Poseidon Adventure, Meteor, The Sting II, Twilight Time, Billy Galvin, Nuts.
TELEVISION: *Series*: Streets of San Francisco, Skag. *Movies*: Captains Courageous, Word of Honor, With Intent to Kill, Alice in Wonderland, Fatal Vision (Emmy Award, 1985), My Father My Son, The Hijacking of the Achille Lauro, Call Me Anna, Absolute Strangers, Back to the Streets of San Francisco, They've Taken Our Children: The Chowchilla Kidnapping.

MALICK, TERRENCE
Wrtier, Director. b. Bartlesville, OK, November 30, 1943. e. Harvard University. Former Rhodes Scholar.
PICTURES: *Writer*: Deadhead Miles, Pocket Money, The Gravy Train, Bear's Kiss, The Beautiful Country (also prod.). *Writer, Director*: Days of Heaven, Badlands (also prod.), The Thin Red Line (Acad. Award nom for dir., s.p. adapt.). *Producer*: Endurance, Endurance: Shackleton's Legendary Antarctic Expedition.
TELEVISION: *Actor*: Golden Fiddles, The Beast.

MALIN, AMIR JACOB
Producer, Executive. b. Tel-Aviv, Israel, March 22, 1954. e. Brandeis U., 1972-76, Boston U. School of Law, 1976-79. Staff atty., WGBH-TV, Boston, 1979-81; president and co-CEO, Cinecom Entertainment Grp., Inc., 1982-88; co-president, October Films, Inc., where he oversaw some of the industry's most important films and championed its most important film-makers; 1989-97; president & CEO, Millennium Pictures, a joint venture with Nu-Image, Inc., Phoenician Films, and October Films; CEO, Artisan Entertainment, 1997-present.
PICTURES: *Executive producer*: Swimming to Cambodia,

Matewan, Miles From Home, Scenes from the Class Struggle in Beverly Hills, The Handmaid's Tale, Tune in Tomorrow.

MALKOVICH, JOHN
Actor. b. Christopher, IL, Dec. 9, 1953. e. Illinois State U. Founding member Steppenwolf Ensemble in Chicago with group of college friends, 1976. Starred in Say Goodnight Gracie and True West (Obie Award).Stage work includes Death of Salesman, Burn This, States of Shock. *Dir.*: Balm in Gilead, Arms and the Man, The Caretaker, Libra (also writer).
PICTURES: Places in the Heart (Acad. Award nom.), The Killing Fields, Eleni, Making Mr. Right, The Glass Menagerie, Empire of the Sun, Miles From Home, Dangerous Liaisons, The Accidental Tourist (co-exec. prod. only), The Sheltering Sky, Queens Logic, The Object of Beauty, Shadows and Fog, Of Mice and Men, Jennifer Eight, Alive, In the Line of Fire (Acad. Award nom.), The Convent, Beyond the Clouds, Mary Reilly, Mulholland Falls, Portrait of a Lady, Con Air, Rounders, The Man in the Iron Mask, Time Regained, Ladies Room, Being John Malkovich, The Messenger: The Story of Joan of Arc, Burned to Light, Shadow of the Vampire, Speak Truth to Power, Savage Souls, Hotel, Knockaround Guys, Ripley's Game, I'm Going Home, Johnny English, A Talking Picture, Kill the Poor (prod. only), Art School Confidential (also prod.).
TELEVISION: *Special*: Rocket to the Moon. *Movies*: True West, Word of Honor, American Dream, Death of a Salesman (Emmy Award, 1986), Heart of Darkness, RKO 281 (Emmy nom.). *Mini-series*: Les Miserables, Napoleon.

MALMUTH, BRUCE
Director, Actor. b. Brooklyn, NY, Feb. 4, 1937. e. City Coll. of New York, Brooklyn Coll. Grad. studies in film, Columbia U. and U. of Southern California. Acted in and dir. college productions. Moved to California and obtained job as page at NBC. In Army assigned to special services as dir.; reassigned to New York. Upon release began 10-year Clio-winning career as dir. of TV commercials. Debut as dir. of features with Nighthawks, 1981. Founder, Los Angeles Aspiring Actors and Directors Workshop.
PICTURES: *Director*: Nighthawks, The Man Who Wasn't There, Where Are the Children? (also actor), Hard to Kill, Pentathalon (also actor). *Actor*: The Karate Kid (also part II), For Keeps?, Happy New Year, Lean on Me, Pentathlon.
TELEVISION: *Baseballs or Switchblades?* (prod., writer, dir., Emmy Award), A Boy's Dream, Twilight Zone, Beauty and the Beast, Heartbreak Winner.

MALONE, DOROTHY
Actress. b. Chicago, IL, Jan. 30, 1925. e. Southern Methodist U., USC, AADA. Started as RKO starlet, 1943. Stage work incl. Little Me, Practice to Deceive.
PICTURES: The Big Sleep, Night and Day, One Sunday Afternoon, Two Guys From Texas, The Nevadan, The Bushwackers, Jack Slade, The Killer That Stalked New York, Scared Stiff, Torpedo Alley, The Lone Gun, Pushover, Security Risk, Private Hell 36, The Fast and the Furious, Young at Heart, Battle Cry, Sincerely Yours, Artists and Models, At Gunpoint, Five Guns West, Tall Man Riding, Pillars of the Sky, Tension at Table Rock, Written on the Wind (Acad. Award, best supporting actress, 1956), Man of a Thousand Faces, Quantez, The Tarnished Angels, Tip on a Dead Jockey, Too Much Toon Soon, Warlock, The Last Voyage, The Last Sunset, Beach Party, Fate is the Hunter (unbilled), Abduction, Golden Rendezvous, Good Luck Miss Wyckoff, Winter Kills, The Day Time Ended, The Being, Basic Instinct, Beverly Hills.
TELEVISION: *Series*: Peyton Place. *Guest*: Dick Powell Theatre, Loretta Young Show (twice hosted), others. *Movies*: The Pigeon, Little Ladies of the Night, Murder in Peyton Place, Katie: Portrait of a Centerfold, Condominium, Peyton Place: The Next Generation. *Mini-Series*: Rich Man Poor Man. *Specials*: Gertrude Stein Story, The Family That Prays Together.

MALONE, JOHN C.
Executive. b. Milford, CT, Mar. 7, 1941. e. Yale U, B.S; Johns Hopkins, M.S.; Johns Hopkins, Ph.D., 1967. Began career in 1963 with Bell Telephone Labs/AT&T. Joined McKinsey & Co., 1968. 1970, became Group v.p. at General Instrument Corp. Later named pres., Jerrold Electronics, a GI subsidiary. Joined Tele-Communications, Inc. in 1973. Pres. & CEO, TCI, 1973-1996. 1996-1999, chmn. & CEO, TCI until merger with AT&T. Chmn., Liberty Media Corp., 1990-present. Dir., AT&T Corp.; bd. of dirs., Bank of New York, the CATO Institute, Discovery Communications, Inc., BET Holdings II, Inc., At Home Corp., USANi, UnitedGlobalCom, Inc. and Cendant Corp. Dir., National Cable Television Assoc., 1974-1977 and 1980-1993. Recipient of NCTA Vanguard Award; TVC Magazine Man of the Year Award 1981; Wall Street Trascript's Gold Award for the cable industry's best CEO, 1982, 1985, 1986 and 1987; Women in Cable's Betsy Magness Fellowship Honoree; U. Penn Wharton School Sol C. Snider Entrepreneurial Center Award of Merit; American Jewish Committee Sherrill C. Corwin Human Relations Award; Denver U. Honorary Degree, 1992, etc.

MAMET, DAVID
Writer, Director. b. Chicago, IL, Nov. 30, 1947. m. actress Rebecca Pidgeon. e. Goddard Coll. Artist-in-residence, Goddard

Coll. 1971-73. Artistic dir. St. Nicholas Theatre Co., Chicago, 1973-75. Co-founder Dinglefest Theatre; assoc. artistic dir.,Goodman Theatre, Chicago. Appeared as actor in film Black Widow. *Novel*: The Village (1994).
THEATRE: Lakefront, The Woods, American Buffalo, Sexual Perversity in Chicago, Duck Variations, Edmond, A Life in the Theatre, The Water Engine, Prairie du Chien, Glengarry Glen Ross (Pulitzer Prize, Tony Award, 1984), Speed-the-Plow, Sketches of War (benefit for homeless Vietnam Veterans), Oleanna, An Interview (Death Defying Acts), The Cryptogram.
PICTURES: *Writer*: The Postman Always Rings Twice, The Verdict, The Untouchables, House of Games (also dir.), Things Change (also dir.), We're No Angels, Homicide (also dir.), Hoffa, Vanya on 42nd Street (adaptation), Oleanna (also dir.), The Spanish Prisoner (also dir.), The Edge, Wag the Dog, Ronin, The Winslow Boy (also dir.), State and Maine, Lakeboat, Hannibal, Heist, The Diary of a Young London Physician, Whistle.
TELEVISION: Lip Service (exec. prod.), Hill Street Blues, A Life in the Theatre, Texan, Lansky (also exec. prod.), Catastrophe.

MANASSE, GEORGE
Producer. b. Florence, Italy, Jan. 1, 1938. e. U. of North Carolina.
PICTURES: *Prod.*: Who Killed Mary What's 'er Name?, Squirm, Blue Sunshine, He Knows You're Alone. Prod. Mgr.: Greetings, Joe, Fury on Wheels, Slow Dancing in the Big City, Tribute, Porky's II: The Next Day, Neighbors, Death Wish III, Torch Song Trilogy, Indecent Proposal, Coneheads, Lassie, Die Hard With a Vengeance, Eraser, others.
TELEVISION: *Line Prod.*: Series: American Playwright's Theatre (Arts & Ent.) The Saint in Manhattan (pilot), Movie: The Killing Floor, Vengeance: The Story of Tony Cimo. *Prod. Mgr.*: Series: St. Elsewhere, Annie McGuire. *Movies*: Sanctuary of Fear, Mr. Griffith and Me, Peking Encounter, When the Circus Came to Town, Murder, Inc. Muggable Mary, Running Out, Dropout Father, He's Hired, She's Fired, Intimate Strangers, Drop Out Mother, Vengeance: The Story of Tony Cimo, The Saint in Manhattan, The Diamond Trap, The Prize Pulitzer (also suprv. prod.), Orpheus Descending (also suprv. prod.), John and Yoko, Marilyn and Me, The Woman Who Sinned, The Hunley.

MANCIA, ADRIENNE
Curator, Dept. of Film, Museum of Modern Art. b. New York, NY. e. U. of Wisconsin. B.A.; Columbia U., M.A. Worked in film distribution industry in New York prior to joining Dept. of Film & Video, Museum of Modern Art, 1964; responsible for film exhibition since 1965. 1977, appointed curator. Restructured Museums' Auditorium Exhibition Prog., creating a balance between classic cinema and contemporary work. Initiated innovative programs such as Cineprobe and New Documentaries (formerly What's Happening?) Served on numerous int'l film juries. Co-founder New Directors/New Films. Chevalier de l'Ordre des Arts et des Lettres (France, 1985). Ufficiale dell Ordine al Merito della Repubblica Italiana, 1988.

MANCUSO, FRANK G.
Executive. b. Buffalo, NY, July 25, 1933. e. State U. of New York. Film buyer and operations supvr. for Basil Enterprises, theatre circuit, 1958-62. Joined Paramount as booker in Buffalo branch, 1962. Named sls. repr. for branch in 1964 and branch mgr. in 1967. 1970 appt. v.p./gen. sls. mgr., Paramount Pictures Canada, Ltd., becoming pres. in 1972. 1976 relocated with Paramount in U.S. as western div. mgr. in LA. 1977, appt. gen. sls. mgr. of NY, office; two months later promoted to v.p. domestic distribution; 1979, named exec. v.p., distrib. & mktg. 1983 made pres. of entire Paramount Motion Picture Group. 1984, appointed chmn. and CEO, Paramount Pictures; resigned 1991. Appointed chmn. and CEO, MGM. Resigned from post, April 1999 but remains on MGM's board to present. Named Motion Picture Pioneers Man of the Year, 1987. Member of Board: AMPAS, M.P. Assoc. of America, Will Rogers Memorial Fund, Variety Clubs Intl., Sundance Institute, Amer. Film Institute, Museum of Broadcasting, Motion Picture Pioneers. Appointed Chmn. & CEO of MGM, 1993. 1998 Women in film Mentor Award. 1998 Ellis Island Medal of Honor Award.

MANCUSO, JR., FRANK
Producer. b. Buffalo, NY, Oct. 9, 1958. Son of Frank G. Mancuso. e. Upsala Coll. Began with industry at age 14, booking short subjects in Canadian theatres. Worked in gross receipts dept. in Paramount corporate offices in New York and later with paralegal div. Initial prod. work as location asst. for Urban Cowboy in Houston, TX. Served as assoc. prod. of Friday the 13th Part II and prod. of Friday the 13th Part III in 3-D.
PICTURES: Off the Wall, The Man Who Wasn't There, April Fool's Day, Friday the 13th, Part IV: The Final Chapter; Friday the 13th—A New Beginning (exec. prod.), Friday the 13th, Part VII (exec. prod.); Back to the Beach; Permanent Record, Internal Affairs, He Said/She Said, Species, Fled, Hoodlum, Toby's Story, Species II, Ronin, Stigmata, New Best Friend.
TELEVISION: Friday the 13th: The Series, The Escape.

MANDEL, BABALOO
Writer. r.n. Marc Mandel. b. 1949. Started as comedy writer for Joan Rivers, among others. First teamed with Lowell Ganz on

script for 1982 film Night Shift.
PICTURES: Night Shift, Splash (Acad. Award nom.; also actor), Spies Like Us, Gung Ho, Vibes, Parenthood, City Slickers, A League of Their Own, Mr. Saturday Night, Greedy, City Slickers II: The Legend of Curly's Gold, Forget Paris, Multiplicity, Father's Day, The Secret LIfe of Walter Mitty, Edtv, Where the Heart Is, Down and Under.
TELEVISION: *Series co-writer*: Laverne and Shirley, Busting Loose, Take Five (also co-creator). *Series co-exec. prod.*: Gung Ho, Knight and Daye, Parenthood.

MANDEL, LORING
Writer. b. Chicago, IL, May 5, 1928. e. U. of Wisconsin, B.S. 1949. Long career writing scripts for TV, dating back to 1955 when penned Shakedown Cruise. Governor, Natl. Acad. of TV Arts & Sciences 1964-68; Pres. Writers Guild of America East 1975-77; Natl. Chmn. 1977-79.
PICTURES: Countdown, Promises in the Dark, Little Drummer Girl.
TELEVISION: Do Not Go Gentle Into That Good Night (Emmy, 1967), Breaking Up, Project Immortality (Sylvania Award, 1959), A House His Own, Trial of Chaplain Jensen, The Raider, Conspiracy.

MANDEL, ROBERT
Director. e. Columbia Univ.
PICTURES: Night at O'Rears (also prod.), Independence Day, F/X, Touch and Go, Big Shots, School Ties, The Substitute.
TELEVISION: *Movies*: Hard Time on Planet Earth, The X Files (pilot), Kansas, Special Report: Journey to Mars, Thin Air, WWIII, A Season on the Brink. *Series*: Nash Bridges, The Practice, The District.

MANDELL, ABE
Executive. b. Oct. 4, 1922. e. U. of Cincinnati. Entered broadcasting as actor on Cincinnati radio station prior to W.W.II. Served U.S. Army in Southwest Pacific, 1942-45. Formed indep. motion picture distribution co. in the Far East. Company, also operated and owned motion picture theaters throughout the Phillipines and Indonesia, 1946-56; network-regional sales exec., Ziv Television, 1956-58; dir. foreign operations, Independent Television Corporation, 1959; v.p.-foreign oper., 1960; v.p.-sales and adm., 1961; exec. v.p., 1962; pres. 1965. 1976 corporate name changed to ITC Entertainment, Inc. President to 1983 of ITC Ent.; with Robert Mandell headed New Frontier Prods. Retired.

MANDOKI, LUIS
Director. b. Mexico City, Mexico. e. San Francisco Art Institute, London Intl. Film School, London College's School of Film. Dir. short film Silent Music which won Intl. Amateur Film Fest. Award at 1976 Cannes Film Fest. Back in Mexico dir. shorts and documentaries for the Instituto Nacional Indignista Concaine, Centro de Produccionde Cortometraje. Won Ariel Award.
PICTURES: Motel (debut, 1982), Gaby--A True Story, White Palace, Born Yesterday, When a Man Loves a Woman, Message in a Bottle, Amazing Grace, Angel Eyes, Trapped, The Untold Love Story: Marie-Antoinette and Count Fersen.

MANES, FRITZ
Producer. b. Oakland, CA, April 22, 1936. e. U.C., Berkeley, B.A. UCLA, 1956. Armed Service: 1951-54. U.S. Marines, Korea, Purple Heart. TV ad. exec. and stuntman before becoming exec. prod. on films for Clint Eastwood. Has formed own production co., Sundancer Prods. Membership, DGA, SAG.
PICTURES: *in various capacities*: The Outlaw Josey Wales, The Enforcer. *Assoc. prod.*: The Gauntlet, Every Which Way But Loose, Escape From Alcatraz, Bronco Billy. *Prod.*: Any Which Way You Can (Acad. of Country Music Tex Ritter award), Firefox (exec. prod.), Honky Tonk Man (exec. prod.), Tightrope (prod.), Sudden Impact (exec. prod.), City Heat (prod.), Pale Rider (exec. prod.), Ratboy (exec. prod.), Heartbreak Ridge, James Dean.

MANHEIM, CAMRYN
Actress. b. Peoria, IL, March 8, 1961.
PICTURES: The Bonfire of the Vanities, The Road to Wellville, David Searching, Jeffrey, Eraser, Romy and Michele's High School Reunion, The Tic Code, Mercury Rising, Fool's Gold, Happiness, Wide Awake, David Searching, Your Are Here, Joe the King, What Planet Are You From?, Just Like Mona, The Laramie Project.
TELEVISION: *Movies*: Deadley Whispers, Jackie's Back, The Loretta Claiborne Story, Kiss My Act. *Mini-Series*: The 10th Kingdom, A Girl Thing. *Series*: The Practice (Emmy Award, 1998).

MANKIEWICZ, DON M.
Writer. b. Berlin, Germany, Jan. 20, 1922. p. Herman J. Mankiewicz. e. Columbia, B.A., 1942; Columbia Law Sch. Served in U.S. Army, 1942-46; reporter, New Yorker magazine, 1946-48; author of novels See How They Run, Trial, It Only Hurts a Minute; magazine articles, short stories. President, Producers Guild of America, 1987; on bd. of dirs., Writers Guild of America, 1992.
PICTURES: Trial, I Want to Live, (Acad. Award nom.), The

Chapman Report, The Black Bird.
TELEVISION: Studio One, On Trial, One Step Beyond, Playhouse 90, Profiles in Courage. Exec. story consultant: Hart to Hart, Simon & Simon, Crazy Like a Fox, Adderly. Pilots: Ironside, Marcus Welby M.D., Sarge, Lanigan's Rabbi (collab.), Rosetti and Ryan (collab.)

MANKIEWICZ, TOM
Writer, Director. b. Los Angeles, CA, June 1, 1942. e. Yale U.
PICTURES: *Writer*: The Sweet Ride (debut), Diamonds Are Forever, Live and Let Die, The Man with the Golden Gun, Mother Jugs and Speed (also prod.), The Cassandra Crossing, The Eagle Has Landed, Ladyhawke. *Exec. Prod.*: Hot Pursuit. *Creative consultant*: Superman, Superman II. *Director*: Dragnet (also s.p.), Delirious.
TELEVISION: *Pilot*: Hart to Hart (writer, dir.). *Movie*: Taking the Heat (dir.), `Till Death Do Us Hart. *Episode*: Tales of the Crypt (dir.)

MANN, ABBY
Writer. b. Philadelphia, PA, 1927. e. NYU. First gained fame on TV writing for Robert Montgomery Theatre, Playhouse 90, Studio One, Alcoa, Goodyear Theatre. Acad. Award for film adaptation of own teleplay Judgment at Nuremberg into theatrical film.
PICTURES: Judgment at Nuremberg, A Child Is Waiting, The Condemned of Altona, Ship of Fools (Acad. Award nom.), The Detective, Report to the Commissioner.
TELEVISION: *Series*: Kojak (creator), Skag, Medical Story. *Movies*: The Marcus-Nelson Murders (Emmy Award, 1973; also exec. prod.), Medical Story (also exec. prod.), The Atlanta Child Murders, King (Emmy nom.), Murderers Among Us: The Simon Wiesenthal Story (Emmy Award, 1989; co-writer, co-exec. prod.), Teamster Boss: The Jackie Presser Story (also co-exec. prod.), Indictment: The McMartin Trial (also co-exec. prod.; Emmy Award, 1995, Golden Globe Award), Whitewash: The Clarence Brandley Story.

MANN, DELBERT
Director, Producer. b. Lawrence, KS, Jan. 30, 1920. e. Vanderbilt U., Yale U. U.S. Air Force, 1942-45. Stage mgr., summer stock, dir. Columbia, S.C. Town Theatre, 1947-49. Asst. dir., NBC-TV, 1949; dir., NBC-TV, 1949-55. Past pres., Directors Guild of America.
PICTURES: Marty (Acad. Award, 1955), The Bachelor Party, Desire Under the Elms, Separate Tables, Middle of the Night, The Dark at the Top of the Stairs, The Outsider, Lover Come Back, That Touch of Mink, A Gathering of Eagles, Dear Heart, Quick Before It Melts (also prod.), Mister Buddwing (also prod.), Fitzwilly, The Pink Jungle, Kidnapped, Birch Interval, Night Crossing.
TELEVISION: Philco-Goodyear TV Playhouse, Producer's Showcase, Omnibus, Playwrights '56, Playhouse 90, Ford Star Jubilee, Lights Out, Mary Kay and Johnny, The Little Show, Masterpiece Theatre, Ford Startime. *Movies/Specials*: Heidi, David Copperfield, No Place to Run, She Waits (also prod.), Jane Eyre, The Man Without a Country, A Girl Named Sooner, Francis Gary Powers: The True Story of the U-2 Spy Incident, Tell Me My Name, Breaking Up, Home to Stay, Love's Dark Ride, Thou Shalt Not Commit Adultery, All Quiet on the Western Front, Torn Between Two Lovers, To Find My Son, All the Way Home, The Member of the Wedding, The Gift of Love, Bronte, Love Leads the Way, A Death in California, The Last Days of Patton, The Ted Kennedy, Jr. Story, April Morning (also co-prod.), Ironclads, Against Her Will: An Incident in Baltimore (also prod.), Incident in a Small Town (also prod.), Lily in Winter.

MANN, MICHAEL
Director, Writer, Producer. b. Chicago, IL, Feb. 5, 1943. e. U. of Wisconsin, London Film Sch. Directed shorts, commercials and documentaries in England. Returned to U.S. in 1972. Wrote for prime-time TV.
PICTURES: *Exec. Prod.*: Band of the Hand. *Director-Writer*: Thief (also exec. prod.), The Keep, Manhunter, The Last of the Mohicans (also co-prod.), Heat, The Insider (also prod.), Ali (s.p.).
TELEVISION: The Jericho Mile (writer, dir.; DGA Award for dir., Emmy Award for writing, 1980), Miami Vice (exec. prod.), Crime Story (exec. prod.), L.A. Takedown (dir., writer, exec. prod.), Metro. *Mini-Series*: Drug Wars: The Camarena Story (exec. prod.; Emmy Award, 1990), Drug Wars: The Cocaine Cartel (exec. prod.).

MANNE, S. ANTHONY
Executive. b. New York, NY, July 19, 1940. e. Wharton School, Univ. of Pennsylvania, B.S. economics. Joined Columbia Pictures, 1963; intl. dept., 1964; asst. mgr., Brazil, 1968; mgr., Brazil, 1969-72. Joined JAD Films, 1976. V.p. United Artists, Latin American supervisor, 1980. V.p. Columbia Pictures Intl., continental mgr., 1981; sr. v.p., sales manager, 1984; exec. v.p., Tri-Star Intl, 1987; exec. v.p., Columbia Tri-Star Film Dist. Intl., 1988.Cine Asia Distributor of the Year, 1997. Intl. Consultant, Sony Pictures, 2002. Founder and President, Bristol Media Intl., Inc. 2002.

MANNING, MICHELLE
Executive. Began production career at Zoetrope Studios as prod. supervisor, then VP Production, Orion Pictures. Sr. VP Production, Viacom, Inc., 1991; promoted to Exec. VP, 1993. Pres. production, Paramount Motion Pictures, 1997.
PICTURES: Blue City (dir.), Another 48 Hours.

MANOFF, DINAH
Actress. b. New York, NY, Jan. 25, 1958. e. CalArts. Daughter of actress-dir. Lee Grant and late writer Arnold Manoff. Prof. debut in PBS prod., The Great Cherub Knitwear Strike. Guest starred on Welcome Back Kotter.
THEATRE: I Ought to Be in Pictures (Tony & Theatre World Awards, 1980), others.
PICTURES: Grease (debut, 1978), Ordinary People, I Ought to Be in Pictures, Child's Play, Staying Together, Bloodhounds of Broadway, Welcome Home Roxy Carmichael, Zigs.
TELEVISION: *Series*: Soap, Empty Nest, State of Grace. *Movies*: Raid on Entebbe, Night Terror, The Possessed, For Ladies Only, A Matter of Sex, The Seduction of Gina, Flight No. 90: Disaster on the Potomac, Classified Love, Crossing the Mob, Backfire, Babies, Maid for Each Other (also co-exec. prod., co-story), The Amati Girls. *Mini-Series*: Celebrity.

MANSON, ARTHUR
Executive. b. Brooklyn, NY, Feb. 21, 1928. e. City Coll. of New York, grad. Inst. Film Technique, 1945. Editor, American Traveler, U.S. Army, 1946. Advance agent, co. mgr., Henry V, U.S., 1948-50; producer's publ. rep., Stanley Kramer Distributing Corp., Samuel Goldwyn Productions, 1951-52, dir. of adv. and publ., MGM Pictures of Canada, Ltd., 1952-53; publ. and adv. rep., Cinerama widescreen process, 1953-58; dir. worldwide ad-pub Cinerama 1958-60; adv. mgr., Columbia Pictures, 1961-62; nat'l dir. of adv., publ., Dino De Laurentiis, 1962-64; exec. asst. to v.p. adv. & pub., 20th Century-Fox, 1964-67; v.p., adv. & pub. Cinerama. Inc., and Cinerama Releasing Corp.; 1967-74; exec. v.p., sales & marketing, BCP, service of Cox Broadcasting Corp., 1974-75; v.p. worldwide marketing Warner Bros., 1976. 1977 formed own company, CineManson Mkt. & Dist. Corp. and is pres. Chmn. and founder NY events committee, AMPAS.

MANTEGNA, JOE
Actor. b. Chicago, IL, Nov. 13, 1947. e. Morton Jr. Coll., Goodman Sch. of Drama, 1967-69. Member: The Organic Theatre Company, Chicago (The Wonderful Ice Cream Suit, Cops, and 2 European tours with ensemble). Later member of Goodman Theater where he began long creative assoc. with playwright-dir. David Mamet (A Life in the Theatre, The Disappearance of the Jews). In national co. of Hair, Godspell, Lenny. B'way debut: Working. Narrated documentaries Crack U.S.A. and Death on the Job.
THEATRE: Bleacher Bums (also conceived and co-author), Leonardo (L.A., co-author), Glengarry Glen Ross (Tony Award).
PICTURES: Who Stole My Wheels? (Towing), Second Thoughts, Compromising Positions, The Money Pit, Off Beat, Three Amigos, Critical Condition, House of Games, Weeds, Suspect, Things Change (Venice Film Fest. Award, 1988), Wait Until Spring Bandini, Alice, The Godfather Part III, Queens Logic, Homicide, Bugsy, Body of Evidence, Family Prayers, Searching for Bobby Fisher, Baby's Day Out, Airheads, For Better or Worse, Forget Paris, Up Close and Personal, Eye for an Eye, Thinner, Albino Alligator, Personal Unknowns, For Hire, Underworld, The Wonderful Ice Cream Suit, Jerry & Tom, Conundrum, Celebrity, Body And Soul, Airspeed, The Runner, More Dogs Than Bones, The Last Producer, Lakeboat, Fall, The Trumpet of the Swan (voice), Mother Ghost, , Uncle Nino, Pontormo.
TELEVISION: *Series*: Comedy Zone, First Monday, Joan of Arcadia. *Guest*: Soap, Bosom Buddies, Archie Bunker's Place, Magnum P.I., Open All Night, Fallen Angels, The Simpsons (voice). *Special*: Bleacher Bums (Emmy Award). *Movies*: Elvis, Comrades of Summer, The Water Engine, State of Emergency, Above Suspicion, A Call to Remember, Face Down, Merry Christmas George Bailey, The Rat Pack, Spenser: Small Vices, My Little Assassin, Thin Air, Walking Shadow, Oomph!., And Thou Shalt Honor (narrator). *Mini-series*: The Last Don, The Last Don II.

MANULIS, MARTIN
Producer, Director. b. New York, NY, May 30, 1915. e. Columbia Col., B.A. 1935. Lt. USN, 1941-45. Head of prod. John C. Wilson, 1941-49; mgr. dir., Westport Country Playhouse, 1945-50; dir. B'way plays; staff prod. & dir. CBS-TV, 1951-58; head prod. 20th-Fox Television. Now pres., Martin Manulis Prods. Ltd. 1987, artistic dir., Ahmanson Theatre, L.A.
THEATRE: B'way/and on tour: Private Lives, Made in Heaven, The Philadelphia Story, Pride's Crossing, Laura, The Men We Marry, The Hasty Heart, The Show Off.
PICTURES: *Producer*: Days of Wine and Roses, Dear Heart, Luv, Duffy, The Out-of-Towners.
TELEVISION: *Producer*: Suspense, Studio One, Climax, Best of Broadway, Playhouse 90. *Mini-Series*: Chiefs, Space, The Day Christ Died, Grass Roots.

MARA, ADELE
Actress. r.n. Adelaida Delgado; b. Dearborn, MI, April 28, 1923. m. writer-prod. Roy Huggins. Singer, dancer with Xavier Cugat.
PICTURES: Navy Blues (feature debut, 1941), Shut My Big Mouth, Blondie Goes to College, Alias Boston Blackie, You Were Never Lovelier, Lucky Legs, Vengeance of the West, Reveille With Beverly, Riders of the Northwest Mounted, The Magnificent Rogue, Passkey to Danger, Traffic in Crime, Exposed, The Trespasser, Blackmail, Campus Honeymoon, Twilight on the Rio Grande, Robin Hood of Texas, Nighttime in Nevada, The Gallant Legion, Sands of Iwo Jima, Wake of the Red Witch, Rock Island Trail, California Passage, The Avengers, The Sea Hornet, Count The Hours, The Black Whip, Back from Eternity, Curse of the Faceless Man, The Big Circus.
TELEVISION: Series: Cool Million. Mini-Series: Wheels.

MARBUT, ROBERT GORDON
Broadcast Executive. b. Athens, GA, April 11, 1935. Bachelor Industrial Engineering, Georgia Tech, 1957. M.B.A., Harvard, 1963. Copley Newspapers, 1963-91, named pres. & CEO 1971. Founder, chmn. & CEO Argyle communications, 1991.

MARCOVICCI, ANDREA
Actress, Singer. b. New York, NY, Nov. 18, 1948. e. Bennett Col. Studied acting with Herbert Berghof. Acted on NY stage in The Wedding of Iphigenia, The Ambassadors, Nefertiti, Hamlet, Any Given Day. Frequent performer in night clubs.
PICTURES: The Front (debut, 1976), The Concorde: Airport 1979, The Hand, Spacehunter: Adventures in the Forbidden Zone, Kings and Desperate Men, The Stuff, Someone to Love, White Dragon, Jack the Bear, The Beatnicks, Who Is Henry Jaglom?
TELEVISION: Series: Love Is a Many-Splendored Thing, Berrenger's, Trapper John M.D. Movies: Cry Rape!, Smile Jenny You're Dead, Some Kind of Miracle, A Vacation in Hell, Packin' It In, Spraggue, Velvet, The Canterville Ghost, The Water Engine.

MARCUS, JEFFREY A.
Executive. Began cable TV career selling cable door-to-door in college. Founded Marcus Communiations, Inc., in 1982 which merged in 1988 with Western Tele-Communications, Inc. to form WestMarc Communications, Inc. at which he served as Chairman and CEO. Created Marcus Cable Co. in 1990 by merging cable systems in Wisconsin, Texas, Delaware and Maryland. Pres. & CEO, AMFM, Inc. (formerly Chancellor Media), 1998-1999. Partner, Marcus & Partners, a private equity investment firm, 1999-2000. Chmn. & CEO, Novo Networks, Inc., 2000-2001. Currently, private investor and dir., Brinker International, Inc.

MARCUS, MICHAEL E.
Executive. b. Pittsburgh, PA, June 5, 1945. e. Penn State, 1963-67. Moved to LA where he started in industry in mailroom of General Artists Corp. Promoted to agent when co. merged with Creative Management Assocs. 1972 joined Bart/Levy Agency; 1980, became full partner and co-owner of Kohner/Levy/Marcus Agency. 1981, became sr. agent at Creative Artists Agency. 1993, named pres. & COO of MGM Pictures.

MARENSTEIN, HAROLD
Executive b. New York, NY, Nov. 30, 1916. e. City Coll. of New York, 1937. Shipping, picture checking service, Warner Bros., 1935-45; booking, Loew's Inc., 1945-48; booking, contracts, Selznick Rel. Org., 1948-51; contracts, Paramount, 1951-52; asst. sls. gr., International Rel. Org., 1952; asst. sls. mgr., Janus Films, 1961-64; sls. exec., Rizzoli Films, 1965; 1967, nat'l. sales dir., Continental Dist.; gen. sales mgr., Cinemation Industries, 1968; v.p.-sales, dir., Cinemation Industries, 1971; 1976, gen. sls. mgr., General National Films; 1980, gen. sls. mgr., Lima Productions. Now retired.

MARGOLIN, STUART
Actor, Director, Writer. b. Davenport, IA, Jan. 31, 1940. Wrote play Sad Choices which was produced Off-B'way when he was only 20.
PICTURES: The Gamblers, Kelly's Heroes, Limbo, Death Wish, The Big Bus, Futureworld, Days of Heaven, S.O.B., Class, Running Hot, A Fine Mess, Paramedics (dir. only), Iron Eagle II, Bye Bye Blues, Guilty By Suspicion, The Lay of the Land, The Hi-Line.
TELEVISION: Series: Occasional Wife, Love American Style, Nichols, The Rockford Files (Emmy Awards, 1979, 1980), Bret Maverick, Mr. Smith, These Arms of Mine, Tom Stone. Guest: Hey Landlord, He & She, The Monkees, M*A*S*H, others.Movies: The Intruders, The Ballad of Andy Crocker (writer, associate prod. only), A Summer Without Boys (voice), The Rockford Files (pilot), The California Kid, This is the West That Was, Lanigan's Rabbi, Perilous Voyage, A Killer in the Family, Three of a Kind, To Grandmother's House We Go, How the West Was Fun (dir. only), The Rockford Files: I Still Love L.A, The Rockford Files: A Blessing in Disguise. Director: Suddenly Love, A Shining Season, The Long Summer of George Adams, Double Double Toil and Trouble, Salt Water Moose (Dir.'s. Guild of America Award, 1997).

MARGULIES, JULIANNA
Actor. b. Spring Valley, NY, June 8, 1966. e. Sarah Lawrence College, BA.
PICTURES: Out of Justice, Paradise Road, Traveller, A Price Below Rubies, The Newton Boys, Dinosaur, The Man From Elysian Fields, Searching for Debra Winger, Ghost Ship, Evelyn.
TELEVISION: Movies: Hitler: The Rise of Evil. Series: ER (Emmy Award, 1995). Guest: The Larry Sanders Show, Homicide: Life on the Street, Murder She Wrote, Law & Order. Mini-series: The Mists of Avalon.

MARILL, ALVIN H.
Writer. b. Brockton, MA, Jan. 10, 1934. e. Boston U., 1955. Dir. music programming, writer/prod., WNAC, Boston 1961-65; dir. music prog., WRFM, NY 1966-67; publicity writer, RCA Records 1967-72; sr. writer/editor, RCA Direct Marketing 1972-80; partner, TLK Direct Marketing 1977-80; mgr., A & R Administration, RCA Direct Marketing 1980-83; exec. editor, CBS TV (1984-88); editor, Carol Publ. Group (1988-94); v.p., Sandal Enterprises (1994-pre sent). Television editor, Films in Review 1973-84. Writer/researcher: The Great Singers (record/tape collections). Jury member: 1983 Locarno Film Fest. Television Movie Hall of Fame.
AUTHOR: Samuel Goldwyn Presents, Robert Mitchum on the Screen, The Films of Anthony Quinn, The Films of Sidney Poitier, Katharine Hepburn: A Pictorial Study, Boris Karloff—A Pictorial Biography, Errol Flynn—A Pictorial Biography, The Complete Films of Edward G. Robinson, More Theatre: Stage to Screen to Television, Movies Made for Television 1964-96, The Films of Tyrone Power; Editor: Moe Howard & The 3 Stooges, The Films of Tommy Lee Jones, The Ultimate John Wayne Trivia Book. Assoc. editor: Leonard Maltin's Movie & Video Guide.

MARIN, CHEECH (RICHARD)
Actor, Writer. b. Los Angeles, CA, July 13, 1946. e. California State U, B.S. Teamed with Tommy Chong in improvisational group, City Works (Vancouver). Comedy recordings include Sleeping Beauty, Cheech and Chong Big Bama, Los Cochinos, The Wedding Album (Grammy Award), Get Out of My Room.
PICTURES: Up in Smoke (also co-s.p.), Cheech and Chong's Next Movie (also co-s.p.), Cheech and Chong's Nice Dreams (also co-s.p.), Things Are Tough All Over (also co-s.p.), It Came from Hollywood, Still Smokin' (also co-s.p.), Yellowbeard, Cheech and Chong's The Corsican Brothers (also s.p., dir.), After Hours, Echo Park, Born in East L.A. (also s.p., dir.), Fatal Beauty, Oliver & Company (voice), Troop Beverly Hills (cameo), Ghostbusters II (cameo), Rude Awakening, Far Out Man, The Shrimp on the Barbie, FernGully... The Last Rainforest (voice), A Million to Juan, The Lion King (voice), Desperado, From Dusk Till Dawn, The Great White Hype, Tin Cup, Paulie, Picking Up the Pieces, Luminarias, It's Tough to Be a Bug, Spy Kids, Spy Kids 2: The Island of Lost Dreams, Once Upon a Time in Mexico.
TELEVISION: Series: The Golden Palace, Nash Bridges, Resurrection Blvd. Movie: The Cisco Kid. Specials: Get Out of My Room (also dir., songs), Charlie Barnett—Terms of Enrollment.

MARK, LAURENCE M.
Producer, Executive. b. New York, NY. e. Wesleyan U., B.A.; NYU, M.A. Started career as trainee and publicist for United Artists; also asst. to prod. on Lenny, Smile. Joined Paramount Pictures as mktg./prod. liaison dir. and then exec. dir., pub. for m.p. division in NY. Named v.p., prod./mktg. at Paramount Studio; 1980, v.p., west coast mktg.; 1982 promoted to post as v.p., prod. 1984 (projects incl. Trading Places, Terms of Endearment, Falling in Love, Lady Jane); joined 20th Century-Fox as exec. v.p., prod. (projects incl. The Fly, Broadcast News); 1986, established Laurence Mark Productions at Fox; 1989 moved headquarters to Walt Disney Studios. 1998 moved headquarters to Columbia Pictures at Sony Studios.
THEATRE: Brooklyn Laundry (L.A.), Big (N.Y.).
PICTURES: Producer/Exec. prod.: Black Widow, Working Girl, My Stepmother is an Alien, Cookie, Mr. Destiny, True Colors, One Good Cop, The Adventures of Huck Finn, Gunmen, Sister Act 2: Back in the Habit, Cutthroat Island, Tom & Huck, Jerry Maguire, Romy & Michele's High School Reunion, Deep Rising, As Good As It Gets, The Object of My Affection, Simon Birch, Anywhere But Here, Bicentennial Man, Hanging Up, Center Stage, Finding Forrester, Glitter, Riding In Cars With Boys.
TELEVISION: Exec. prod.: Sweet Bird of Youth, Oliver Twist, These Old Broads, Kiss My Act. The Last Laugh.

MARKHAM, MONTE
Actor. b. Manatee, FL, June 21, 1938. e. U. of Georgia. Military service in Coast Guard after which joined resident theatre co. at Stephens College, MO, where he also taught acting. Joined Actor's Workshop Theatre, San Francisco, for three years. Made TV debut in Mission: Impossible episode. June, 1992 formed Perpetual Motion Films with Adam Friedman.
THEATRE: B'way: Irene (Theatre World Award), Same Time Next Year.
PICTURES: Hour of the Gun, Guns of the Magnificent Seven, One Is a Lonely Number, Midway, Airport '77, Ginger in the Morning, Off the Wall, Jake Speed, Hot Pursuit, Defense Play (also dir.), Neon City (also dir.), At First Sight.
TELEVISION: Series: The Second Hundred Years, Mr. Deeds

Goes to Town, The New Perry Mason, Dallas, Rituals, Baywatch (also dir. episodes), Melrose Place, Campus Cops. *Movies*: Death Takes a Holiday, The Astronaut, Visions, Hustling, Ellery Queen, Relentless, Drop-Out Father, Hotline, Baywatch: Panic at Malibu Pier. *Host-narrator-prod.-dir.*: Air Combat, Combat at Sea, Master of War, Epic Biographies, The Great Ships.

MARKLE, PETER
Director. b. Danville, PA, Sept. 24, 1946.
PICTURES: The Personals (also s.p., photog.), Hot Dog ... The Movie, Youngblood (also co-story, s.p.), Bat-21, Wagons East!, The Last Days of Frankie the Fly, Virginia's Run.
TELEVISION: *Movies*: Desperate, Nightbreaker, Breaking Point, El Diablo, Through the Eyes of a Killer, Jake Lassiter: Justice on the Bayou, White Dwarf, Mob Justice, Target Earth, Strange World. *Series*: Millenium, EZ Streets, The Magnificent Seven, L.A. Doctors, Strange World, CSI, The District.

MARKOWITZ, ROBERT
Director. b. Irvington, NJ, Feb. 7, 1935. e. Boston Univ. Mostly on TV before theatrical debut with Voices, 1979.
TELEVISION: *Movies*: Children of the Night, Phantom of the Opera, The Deadliest Season, The Storyteller, Kojak: The Belarus File, My Mother's Secret Life, Pray TV, A Long Way Home, Alex: The Life of a Child, Adam: His Song Continues, The Wall, A Cry for Help: The Tracey Thurman Story, Too Young to Die, A Dangerous Life, Decoration Day, Love Lies and Murder, Afterburn, Overexposed, Murder in the Heartland, Because Mommy Works, The Tuskegee Airmen, Into Thin Air: Death on Everest, David, Nicholas' Gift, Spenser: Small Vices, The Great Gatsby, The Big Heist, The Pilot's Wife. *Special*: Twilight Zone: Rod Serling's Lost Classics.

MARKS, ARTHUR
Producer, Director, Writer, Film Executive. b. Los Angeles, CA, Aug. 2, 1927. At 19 began work at MGM Studios as production messenger. Became asst. dir. in 1950, youngest dir. member of Directors Guild of Amer., 1957. President and board member of Arthur Prod., Inc.
PICTURES: Togetherness (prod., dir., s.p.), Class of '74 (prod., s.p.), Bonnie's Kids (dir., s.p.), Roommates (dir., s.p.), Detroit 9000 (prod., dir.), The Centerfold Girls (prod., dir.), A Woman For All Men (dir.), Wonder Woman (exec. prod.), The Candy Snatchers (exec. prod.), Bucktown (dir.), Friday Foster (prod., dir.), J.D.'s Revenge (prod., dir.), Monkey Hustle (prod., dir.).
Writer: Empress of the China Seas, Gold Stars, Mean Intentions, Hot Times, Starfire, There's A Killer in Philly.
TELEVISION: *Series*: Perry Mason series (1961-66; prod., also dir. of over 100 episodes); writer-dir. of numerous TV shows including: I Spy, Mannix, Starsky & Hutch, Dukes of Hazzard, Young Daniel Boone, My Friend Tony.

MARKS, RICHARD E.
Executive. e. UCLA; UCLA Sch. of Law. 1978-82, v.p., legal & business affairs for Ziegler/Diskant Literary Agency. Joined Paramount Pictures 1984 as sr. atty. for Network TV Div., as project atty. for Family Ties, Cheers, etc. 1985, named sr. atty. for M.P. Group for The Golden Child, Beverly Hills Cop II, etc.; 1987 joined Weintraub Ent. Group as v.p. business affairs; m.p. div. 1990; counsel for Disney projects such as The Rocketeer, Beauty and the Beast. 1991, joined Media Home Entertainment as sr. v.p. in charge of all business and legal affairs. 1994, joined the Kushner-Locke Company as sr. v.p., business affairs for feature division; currently exec. v.p., gen. counselor.

MARS, KENNETH
Actor. b. Chicago, IL, 1936.
PICTURES: The Producers, Butch Cassidy and the Sundance Kid, Desperate Characters, What's Up Doc?, The Parallax View, Young Frankenstein, Night Moves, The Apple Dumpling Gang Rides Again, Full Moon High, Yellowbeard, Protocol, Prince Jack, Beer, Fletch, Radio Days, For Keeps?, Illegally Yours, Rented Lips, Police Academy 6: City Under Siege, The Little Mermaid (voice), Shadows and Fog, We're Back (voice), The Land Before Time II: The Great Valley Adventure (voice), Thumbelina (voice), Land Before Time III, Rough Magic, Citizen Ruth, Teddy Bears' Picnic.
TELEVISION: *Series*: He & She, The Don Knotts Show, Sha Na Na, The Carol Burnett Show (1979), Bruno the Kid. *Guest*: Facts of Life, Murder She Wrote, The Twilight Zone, Garfield & Friends, Civil Wars, Tom, Star Trek Deep Space Nine, The Drew Carrey Show and many others. *Movies*: Second Chance, Guess Who's Sleeping in My Bed?, Someone I Touched, The New Original Wonder Woman, Before and After, The Rules of Marriage, Get Smart Again, Runaway Virus, How to Marry a Billionaire: A Christmas Tale.

MARSH, JEAN
Actress, Writer. b. London, England, July 1, 1934. NY stage debut in Much Ado About Nothing, 1959. As a child appeared in films: Tales of Hoffman; as principal dancer in Where's Charley. Co-creator, co-author and starred as Rose, in Upstairs, Downstairs.
THEATRE: *B'way*: Travesties, The Importance of Being Earnest, Too True to Be Good, My Fat Friend, Whose Life Is It Anyway?,

Blithe Spirit.
PICTURES: Cleopatra, Unearthly Stranger, The Limbo Line, Frenzy, Dark Places, The Eagle Has Landed, The Changeling, Return to Oz, Willow, Monarch.
TELEVISION: Upstairs Downstairs (Emmy Award, 1975), Nine to Five, The Grover Monster, A State Dinner with Queen Elizabeth II, Mad About the Boy: Noel Coward—A Celebration, Habeas Corpus, Uncle Vanya, Twelfth Night, Pygmalion, On the Rocks Theatre, The Corsican Brothers, Master of the Game, Danny, the Champion of the World, Act of Will, A Connecticut Yankee in King Arthur's Court, Act of Will, No Strings, Backstage at Masterpiece Theatre, Adam Bede, The Tomorrow People, The All New Alexei Sayle Show, Fatherland, The Ring, The Pale Horse, The Ghosthunter.

MARSHALL, ALAN
Producer. b. London, England, Aug. 12, 1938. Co-founder Alan Parker Film Company, 1970. Formerly film editor. Received Michael Balcon Award, British Acad., Outstanding Contribution to Cinema, 1985.
PICTURES: Bugsy Malone, Midnight Express, Fame, Shoot the Moon, Pink Floyd: The Wall, Another Country (Cannes Film Fest. Award, 1984), Birdy (Special Jury Award, Cannes Film Fest., 1985), Angel Heart, Homeboy, Jacob's Ladder, Basic Instinct, Cliffhanger, Showgirls, Starship Troopers, The Hollow Man.
TELEVISION: No Hard Feelings, Our Cissy, Footsteps.

MARSHALL, FRANK
Producer, Director. b. 1954. Raised in Newport Beach, CA. Worked on first feature film in 1967 while still a student at UCLA. Protege of Peter Bogdanovich, working on his production crew and as asst. on Targets, location manager on The Last Picture Show, What's Up Doc?, assoc. prod. on Paper Moon, Daisy Miller, Nickelodeon, etc. Line prod. on Orson Welles' The Other Side of the Wind (unreleased) and Martin Scorsese's The Last Waltz. Worked with Walter Hill on The Driver (assoc. prod.) and The Warriors (exec. prod.). Began collaboration with Steven Spielberg as prod. for Raiders of the Lost Ark. 1992, with wife and partner Kathleen Kennedy formed The Kennedy/Marshall Company.
PICTURES: Raiders of the Lost Ark (prod.), Poltergeist (prod.), E.T.: The Extra-Terrestrial (prod. supvr.). *Exec. Producer*: Twilight Zone—The Movie, Indiana Jones and the Temple of Doom, Fandango, Gremlins, The Goonies, Back to the Future (also 2nd unit dir.), The Color Purple (prod.), Young Sherlock Holmes, An American Tail, Innerspace, The Money Pit (prod.), Empire of the Sun (prod.), Who Framed Roger Rabbit (prod., 2nd unit dir.), The Land Before Time, Indiana Jones and the Last Crusade, Dad, Back to the Future Part II, Always (prod.), Joe Versus the Volcano, Back to the Future Part III, Gremlins II, Arachnophobia (also dir.), Cape Fear, An American Tail: Fievel Goes West, Hook (co-prod.), Noises Off (prod.), Alive (also dir.), Swing Kids, A Far Off Place, We're Back, Milk Money, Congo (also dir.), The Indian in the Cupboard, The Thief of Always, Snow Falling on Cedars, A Map of the World, The Bourne Identity, Signs, The Young Black Stallion.
TELEVISION: Amazing Stories (series exec. prod.), Roger Rabbit and the Secrets of Toontown (exec. prod.), Alive: The Miracle of the Andes (exec. prod.), A Wish for Wings That Work, The Sports Pages.

MARSHALL, GARRY
Producer, Director, Writer, Actor. r.n. Garry Marscharelli. b. New York, NY, Nov. 13, 1934. Sister is dir.-actress Penny Marshall. e. Northwestern U. Copy boy and reporter for NY Daily News while writing comedy material for Phil Foster, Joey Bishop. Was drummer in his own jazz band and successful stand-up comedian and playwright. Turned Neil Simon's play The Odd Couple into long running TV series (1970). Partner with Jerry Belson many years. *Playwright*: The Roast (with Belson, 1980), Wrong Turn at Lungfish (with Lowell Ganz, 1992; also dir., actor). *Autobiography*: Wake Me When It's Funny (1995).
PICTURES: *Writer-Producer*: How Sweet It Is, The Grasshopper. *Director*: Young Doctors in Love (also exec. prod.), The Flamingo Kid (also co-s.p.), Nothing in Common, Overboard, Beaches, Pretty Woman, Frankie and Johnny (also co-prod.), Exit to Eden, Dear God (also cameo), Runaway Bride (also cameo), The Other Sister (also story), The Princess Diaries, Raising Helen (dir. only). *Actor*: Psych-Out, Mary Jane, The Escape Artist, Lost in America, Jumpin' Jack Flash, Soapdish, A League of Their Own, Hocus Pocus, With Friends Like These, This Space Between Us, Can't Be Heaven, Never Been Kissed., Runaway Bride, Can't Be Heaven, This Space Between Us, It's A Shame About Ray, The Hollywood Sign, The Long Ride Home, Mother Ghost, Orange County, They Call Him Sasquatch, Devil's Knight.
TELEVISION: *Series Writer*: Jack Paar Show, Joey Bishop Show, Bill Dana Show, Danny Thomas Show, Lucy Show, Dick Van Dyke Show, I Spy, Sheriff Who??, Love, American Style. *Series creator/exec. prod./writer*: Hey Landlord! (also dir.), The Odd Couple, Barefoot in the Park, Me and the Chimp, The Little People, Happy Days, Laverne & Shirley, Angie. *Series exec. prod./writer*: Blansky's Beauties (also dir.), Who's Watching the Kids?, Mork and Mindy (also dir.), Joanie Loves Chachi. *Series exec. prod.*: The New Odd Couple, Nothing in Common. *Actor*: *Series* A League of Their Own, Murphy Brown. *Movie*: Evil Roy

Slade (also co-prod., co-writer), The Twilight of the Golds, CHiPs '99. *Special*: The Last Shot.

MARSHALL, PENNY
Actress, Director. b. New York, NY, Oct. 15, 1942. Father: industrial filmmaker and Laverne and Shirley prod., Tony Marscharelli. Brother is prod.-dir. Garry Marshall. Daughter is actress Tracy Reiner. Acted in summer stock and competed on The Original Amateur Hour before going to Hollywood to make TV debut in The Danny Thomas Hour (1967-68).
PICTURES: *Actress*: How Sweet It Is, The Savage Seven, The Grasshopper, 1941, Movers and Shakers, The Hard Way, Hocus Pocus, Odd Couple: Together Again, Get Shorty, One Vision, Special Delivery, Stateside. *Director*: Jumpin' Jack Flash (debut, 1986), Big, Awakenings, A League of Their Own (also exec. prod.), Renaissance Man (also exec. prod.), The Preacher's Wife, Riding in Cars With Boys. *Prod.*: Calendar Girl (exec.), Getting Away with Murder, With Friends Like These, Saving Grace, Risk.
TELEVISION: *Actress*: *Series*: The Bob Newhart Show, The Odd Couple, Friends and Lovers, Laverne and Shirley. *Guest*: Danny Thomas Hour, The Super, Happy Days, Comedy Zone, Chico and the Man. *Movies*: The Feminist and the Fuzz, Evil Roy Slade, The Couple Takes a Wife, The Crooked Hearts, Love Thy Neighbor, Let's Switch, More Than Friends, Challenge of a Lifetime, The Odd Couple: Together Again. *Specials*: Lily for President, The Laverne and Shirley Reunion. *Series Director*: Laverne and Shirley, Working Stiffs, Tracey Ullman Show, A League of Their Own (also prod.).

MARSHALL, PETER
Actor, TV Show Host. r.n. Pierre La Cock. b. Clarksburg, WV, March 30. Sister is actress Joanne Dru. Began career as NBC page in N.Y. Teamed with the late Tommy Noonan in comedy act for nightclubs, guesting on Ed Sullivan Show and other variety shows. In 1950, made Las Vegas stage debut and since has been headliner there and in Reno and Lake Tahoe. New York stage, in B'way musical Skyscraper. On London stage in H.M.S. Pinafore, Bye Bye Birdie. In La Cage aux Folles (national company and B'way), 42nd St. (Atlantic City), Rumors (natl. co.).
PICTURES: Holiday Rhythm, FBI Girl, Starlift, The Rookie, Swingin' Along (Double Trouble), I Love You Love, Ensign Pulver, The Cavern, Mary Jane, Americathon, Annie, HMS Pinafore, The Fortress, The Last Dance, Teddy Bears' Picnic.
TELEVISION: *Host*: The Hollywood Squares, NBC Action Playhouse, The Peter Marshall Variety Show, Mrs. America Pageant, Mrs. World.

MARSHALL, MERYL
Executive. b. Los Angeles, CA, Oct. 16, 1949. e. UCLA, BA sociology, 1971. JD Loyola Marymount U., 1974. Deputy pub. defender, LA County, 1975-77. Partner, Markman & Markman, 1978-79. NBC: Sr. Atty., 1979-80. Dir. programs/contracts/bus. affairs, 1980; asst. gen'l counsel, 1980-82; VP, compliance/practices, 1982-87. VP prog. affairs, Group W Prods., 1987-92. Founder, Two Oceans Ent. Grp., 1992. Chmn. & CEO, Acad. of TV Arts and Sciences, 1997..

MARTEL, GENE
Producer, Director. b. New York, NY, June 19, 1906. e. City Coll. of New York , U. of Alabama, Sorbonne, Paris. Newspaperman, New York and Birmingham, AL; dancer, actor, choreographer, dir. Broadway; prod. dir., many documentaries; films for State Dept., others; dir. for Paramount Pictures. Joined Princess Pictures 1952 to make films in Europe; formed own co., Martel Productions Inc., 1956.
PICTURES: Check-mate, Double-Barrelled Miracle, The Lie, Double Profile, Sergeant and the Spy, Black Forest, Eight Witnesses, Fire One, Phantom Caravan, Doorway to Suspicion, Diplomatic Passport, Immediate Disaster.

MARTIN, ANDREA
Actress. b. Portland, ME, Jan. 15, 1947.
THEATRE: *NY*: My Favorite Year (Tony Award & Theatre World Award), The Merry Wives of Windsor.
PICTURES: Cannibal Girls, Soup for One, Club Paradise, Rude Awakening, Worth Winning, Too Much Sun, Stepping Out, All I Want for Christmas, Ted and Venus,. Bogus, Anastasia, Wag the Dog, The Rugrats Movie (voice), Believe, Hedwig and the Angry Inch, Recess: School's Out (voice), All Over the Guy, Jimmy Neutron: Boy Genius, My Big Fat Greek Wedding.
TELEVISION: *Series*: Second City TV, SCTV Network 90 (2 Emmy Awards for writing), The Martin Short Show, Life and Stuff, Damon, Hercules (voice), George and Martha, Committed. *Special*: In Search of Dr. Seuss. *Movies*: Harrison Bergeron, Frosty Returns, Prince Charming, The Kid.

MARTIN, DEWEY
Actor. b. Katy, TX, Dec. 8, 1923. e. U. of Georgia. U.S. Navy, WWII. In stock before film debut in 1949.
PICTURES: Knock on Any Door, Kansas Raiders, The Thing, The Big Sky, Tennessee Champ, Prisoner of War, Men of the Fighting Lady, Land of the Pharaohs, Desperate Hours, The Proud and Profane, 10,000 Bedrooms, Battle Ground, The Longest Day, Savage Sam, Seven Alone.

TELEVISION: G.E. Theatre, U.S. Steel, Playhouse 90, Playwrights 56, Daniel Boone, Doc Holliday, Wheeler and Murdoch, Outer Limits, Twilight Zone.

MARTIN, EDWIN DENNIS
Executive. b. Columbus, GA, Jan. 30, 1920. e. U. of Georgia, B.S., 1940. Past pres., Martin Theatre Cos.; past pres., TOA, International, past pres., Variety. Retired.

MARTIN, GARY
Executive. b. Santa Monica, CA, Aug, 14, 1944. e. CSU Northridge, 1962-65. V.P. of production, Columbia Pictures, 1984-86; exec. v.p., production, 1986-88. Pres. of production admin., Columbia Pictures and TriStar Pictures 1988-95, Columbia TriStar Motion Pictures, 1995-. Member, AMPAS., D.G.A.

MARTIN, JUDSON W.
Executive. Began career with Pricewaterhouse Coopers in Calgary, Alberta, Canada, 1979. Twenty years in various mgmt roles with affiliates of EdperBrascan Corp., including president & CEO, Trilon Securities Corp., v.p., corporate finance & treasurer, Trizec Hahn; senior exec. v.p., CEO, and director, MDC Corp. Currently director and non-exec. chairman, Board of Intl. Properties Group, Ltd.; director, TGS Properties, Ltd.. exec. v.p & CFO, Alliance Atlantis Communications, Inc.-present.

MARTIN, MILLICENT
Actress, Singer. b. Romford, England, June 8, 1934. Toured U.S. in The Boy Friend, 1954-57.
THEATRE: Expresso Bongo, The Crooked Mile, Our Man Crichton, Tonight at 8:30, The Beggar's Opera, Puss 'n Boots, Aladdin, Peter Pan, The Card, Absurd Person Singular, Aladdin, Side by Side by Sondheim, King of Hearts, Move Over Mrs. Markham, Noises Off, One Into Two, 42nd Street (N.Y. & L.A.), The Cemetery Club, Shirley Valentine, The Boyfriend, Noel, Follies, The Rivals, The Rise and Fall of Little Voice.
TELEVISION: *Series*: The Picadilly Palace, From a Bird's Eye View, Mainly Millicent, Millie, Dowtown. Also: Harry Moorings, Kiss Me Kate, London Palladium Color Show, Tom Jones, Englebert Humperdinck show, That Was the Week That Was, LA Law, Max Headroom, Newhart, Murphy Brown, Coach.
PICTURES: Libel, The Horsemasters (tv in U.S.), The Girl on the Boat, Nothing But the Best, Those Magnificent Men in Their Flying Machines, Alfie, Stop the World I Want To Get Off, Invasion Quartet, Moon and Son, Days of Our Lives.

MARTIN, PAMELA SUE
Actress. b. Westport, CT, Jan. 15, 1953. Did modelling and TV commercials before entering films.
PICTURES: To Find a Man, The Poseidon Adventure, Buster and Billie, Our Time, The Lady in Red, Torchlight (also assoc. prod. & s.p.), Flicks, A Cry in the Wild.
TELEVISION: *Series*: Nancy Drew Mysteries, Hardy Boys Mysteries, Dynasty, The Star Games (host). *Movies*: The Girls of Huntington House, The Gun and the Pulpit, Human Feelings, Bay Coven, Sky Trackers.

MARTIN, STEVE
Actor, Writer. b. Waco, TX, Aug. 14, 1945. e. Long Beach Col., UCLA. Raised in Southern California. Worked at Disneyland, teaching himself juggling, magic and the banjo. Became writer for various TV comedy shows, incl. Smothers Brothers Comedy Hour (Emmy Award for writing, 1968-69), Glen Campbell Show, Sonny & Cher. Co-writer for special Van Dyke and Company. Wrote and starred in Acad. Award nominated short The Absent-Minded Waiter. *Author*: Cruel Shoes (1980). *Albums*: Let's Get Small (Grammy Award, 1977), A Wild and Crazy Guy (Grammy Award, 1978), Comedy Is Not Pretty, The Steve Martin Brothers. Gold Record for single King Tut.
THEATRE: *Actor*: Waiting for Godot (Off-B'way debut, 1988). *Author*: Picasso at the Lapin Agile (regional, 1993), WASP (Off-B'way).
PICTURES: Sgt. Pepper's Lonely Hearts Club Band (debut, 1978), The Kids Are Alright, The Muppet Movie, The Jerk (also co-s.p.), Pennies From Heaven, Dead Men Don't Wear Plaid (also co-s.p.), The Man With Two Brains (also co-s.p.), The Lonely Guy, All of Me (NY Film Critics & Natl. Board of Review Awards, 1984), Movers and Shakers, Three Amigos! (also co-s.p., exec. prod.), Little Shop of Horrors, Roxanne (also s.p., exec. prod.; Natl. Society of Film Critics & L.A. Film Critics Awards for actor, WGA Award for adapt. s.p., 1987), Planes Trains & Automobiles, Dirty Rotten Scoundrels, Parenthood, My Blue Heaven, L.A. Story (also s.p., co-exec. prod.), Father of the Bride, Grand Canyon, Housesitter, Leap of Faith, A Simple Twist of Fate (also s.p., exec. prod.), Mixed Nuts, Father of the Bride 2, Sgt. Bilko, The Spanish Prisoner, The Prince of Egypt (voice), Joe Gould's Secret, The Out-of-Towners, Bowfinger (also s.p.), The Venice Project, Fantasia/2000, Joe Gould's Secret, Thin Ice, Novocaine, Brining Down the House, Looney Tunes: Back in Action, Cheaper By the Dozen, Picasso at the Lapini Agile (s.p. only).
TELEVISION: *Series*: Andy Williams Presents Ray Stevens, The Ken Berry "WOW" Show, Half the George Kirby Comedy Hour, The Sonny and Cher Comedy Hour, The Smothers Brothers

Show (1975), The Johnny Cash Show. *Guest*: The Tonight Show, Cher, The Carol Burnett Show, The Simpsons (voice), The Muppet Show, Steve Allen Comedy Hour. *Specials*: HBO On Location: Steve Martin, Steve Martin—A Wild and Crazy Guy, Comedy Is Not Pretty, All Commercials: A Steve Martin Special, Steve Martin's Best Show Ever, The Winds of Whoopie, Texas 150--A Celebration, The Smothers Brothers Comedy Hour 20th Reunion, Learned Pigs and Fireproof Women, Saturday Night Live 25th Anniversary. *Producer*: Domestic Life (series). *Pilot*: Leo & Liz in Beverly Hills (writer, creator, co-prod., dir.). *Movies*: The Jerk Too (exec. prod. only), And the Band Played On, The Rutles 2: Can't Buy Me Lunch.

MARTIN, TONY
Singer, Musician, Actor. r.n. Alvin Morris. b. Oakland, CA, Dec. 25, 1913. e. Oakland H.S., St. Mary's Coll. m. actress-dancer Cyd Charisse. Sang, played saxophone & clarinet in high school band, engaged by nearby theatres for vaudeville; with Five Red Peppers, jazz group at 14 yrs.; two yrs. later with band, Palace Hotel, San Francisco; radio debut Walter Winchell program, 1932; joined Tom Gerund's band, World's Fair Chicago, 1933; played night clubs. First starring radio show, Tune Up Time (singer & emcee); on Burns and Allen program; own show for Texaco, Carnation Contented Hour. *Recordings*: Begin the Beguine,Intermezzo, The Last Time I Saw Paris, I'll See You in My Dreams, Domino, September Song, For Every Man There's a Woman.
PICTURES: Pigskin Parade (debut, 1936), Banjo on My Knee, Sing Baby Sing, Follow the Fleet, Back to Nature, The Holy Terror, Sing and Be Happy, You Can't Have Everything, Life Begins in College, Ali Baba Goes to Town, Sally Irene and Mary, Kentucky Moonshine, Thanks for Everything, Up the River, Winner Take All, Music in My Heart, Ziegfeld Girl, The Big Store, Till the Clouds Roll By, Casbah, Two Tickets to Broadway, Here Come the Girls, Easy to Love, Deep in My Heart, Hit the Deck, Quincannon—Frontier Scout, Let's Be Happy, Dear Mr. Wonderful.

MASLANSKY, PAUL
Producer. b. New York, NY, Nov. 23, 1933. e. Washington and Lee U., 1954. Moved to Europe performing as jazz musician in Paris, 1959-60. Entered film business with documentary, Letter from Paris. Asst. to prods. Charles Shneer and Irving Allen in England, Italy and Yugoslavia, 1961-62. In charge of physical prod. in Europe for UA, 1965-67.
PICTURES: Castle of the Living Dead, Revenge of the Blood Beast, Sudden Terror (Eye Witness), Raw Meat, Deathline, Sister of Satan, Big Truck, Poor Claire, Deathline, Sugar Hill (also dir.), Race With the Devil, Hard Times, The Blue Bird, Circle of Iron, Damnation Alley (co-prod.), When You Comin' Back Red Ryder (co-prod.), Hot Stuff, The Villain, Scavenger Hunt, The Salamander, Ruckus, Love Child, Police Academy, Police Academy 2: Their First Assignment, Return to Oz, Police Academy 3: Back in Training, Police Academy 4: Citizens on Patrol, Police Academy 5: Assignment Miami Beach, For Better or Worse (exec. prod.), Police Academy 6: City Under Siege, Ski Patrol (exec. prod.), Honeymoon Academy (exec. prod.), The Russia House, Cop and a Half, Police Academy: Mission to Moscow, Fluke.
TELEVISION: *Movie*: The Gun and the Pulpit. *Mini-Series*: King. *Series*: Police Academy: The Series.

MASON, JACKIE
Comedian, Actor. b. Sheboygan, WI June 9, 1934. e. City College. Was a rabbi before becoming stand-up comedian. Records include The World According to Me! Has lectureship in his name at Oxford Univ. in England.
THEATRE: Enter Solly Gold (1965), A Teaspoon Every Four Hours (Amer. National Theatre & Academy Theatre), Sex-a-Poppin (revue, prod. only), The World According to Me! (one-man show, special Tony Award, 1987), Jackie Mason: Brand New, Politically Incorrect.
PICTURES: Operation Delilah (debut, 1966), The Stoolie (also prod.), The Jerk, History of the World Part I, Caddyshack II.
TELEVISION: *Guest*: Steve Allen, Ed Sullivan, Jack Paar, Garry Moore, Perry Como and Merv Griffin Shows. Johnny Carson, Arsenio Hall, Evening at the Improv, Late Night with David Letterman. *Series*: Chicken Soup, Jackie Mason (synd.). *Specials*: Jack Paar is Alive and Well!, The World According to Me! (ACE Award), Jackie Mason on Broadway (Emmy Award for Writing), But...Seriously, The Royal Variety Performance 2001.

MASON, JOHN DUDLEY
Executive. b. Ashland, KY, Oct 29, 1949. e. Amherst Coll., B.A., cum laude, 1971; Claremont Graduate Sch. and University Center, M.A., 1973; Amos Tuck Sch. of Business Administration, Dartmouth Coll., M.B.A., 1978. Program officer, National Endowment for the Humanities, 1972-76; analyst (1978-79), asst. mgr. (1979-80), mgr. (1980) strategic planning, Consolidated Rail Corp.; Consultant, Frito-Lay, Division, PepsiCo (1980-82); mgr, corporate planning, Dun & Bradstreet Corp. (1982-86); finance dir., anti-piracy (1986-90), v.p. finance, anti-piracy (1990-92), Motion Picture Association of America, Inc. Chmn., New Century Artists' Mgmt., 1990-98. Chmn., Finance Comm. and mem., bd. of dir. Association de Gestion Int'l.

Collective des Oeuvres Audiovisuelles (AGICOA) 1987-88. Dir., Instituto Venezolano de Representacion Cinematografica (INVERECI), Caracas, Venezuela (1988-92). Dir.: Foundation for the Protection of Film & Video Works (FVWP), Taipei, Taiwan (1987-92). Dir. sec. Korean Federation Against Copyright Theft, 1990-92; Dir., Japan & Intl. M.P.Copyright Assn., Tokyo, 1990-92; Trustee and Treasurer, Design Industries Foundation for AIDS, 1990-94. Mng. dir., B.L. Nickerson & Associates, 1997-present.

MASON, MARSHA
Actress b. St. Louis. April 3, 1942. e. Webster Coll. Came to N.Y. to continue dramatic studies and embark on theatre career. Member of American Conservatory Theatre, San Francisco.
THEATRE: The Deer Park, Cactus Flower, The Indian Wants the Bronx, Happy Birthday Wanda June, King Richard III, Cactus Flower, Private Lives, You Can't Take It With You, Cyrano de Bergerac, A Doll's House, The Merchant of Venice, The Crucible, Twelfth Night, The Good Doctor, Old Times, The Big Love, Lake No Bottom. Escape from Happiness, Amazing Grace, Night of the Iguana. *Director*: Juno's Swans.
PICTURES: Hot Rod Hullabaloo (debut, 1966), Blume in Love, Cinderella Liberty (Acad. Award nom.), Audrey Rose, The Goodbye Girl (Acad. Award nom.), The Cheap Detective, Promises in the Dark, Murder by Death, Max Dugan Returns, Chapter Two (Acad. Award nom.), Only When I Laugh (Acad. Award nom.), Max Dugan Returns, Heartbreak Ridge, Stella, Drop Dead Fred, I Love Trouble, Nick of Time, 2 Days in the Valley.
TELEVISION: *Specials/Movies*: Brewsie and Willie, The Good Doctor, Cyrano de Bergerac. *Movies*: Lois Gibbs and the Love Canal, Surviving, Trapped in Silence, The Image, Dinner at Eight, Broken Trust, Dead Aviators, Life With Judy Garland: Me and My Shadows. *Dir.*: Little Miss Perfect. *Series*: Love of Life, Sibs, Frazier.

MASSEN, OSA
Actress. b. Denmark, Copenhagen. Jan. 13, 1916.
PICTURES: Honeymoon in Bali, Honeymoon for Three, A Woman's Face, Accent on Love, You'll Never Get Rich, The Devil Pays Off, Iceland, Jack London, Cry of the Werewolf, Tokyo Rose, Strange Journey, Night Unto Night, Deadline at Dawn, Gentleman Misbehaves, Rocketship XM, Outcasts of the City.

MASSEY, ANNA
Actress. b. Sussex, England, Aug. 11, 1937. Daughter of late actor Raymond Massey. Brother is actor Daniel Massey. On London stage in The Reluctant Debutante (debut, 1958), The Prime of Jean Brodie, Slag, The Importance of Being Earnest, Spoiled, Doctor's Delimma, School for Scandal, With National Theatre, 1989.
PICTURES: Gideon of Scotland Yard, Peeping Tom, Bunny Lake Is Missing, DeSade, The Looking Glass War, David Copperfield (TV in U.S.), Frenzy, A Doll's House, Vault of Horror, A Little Romance, Sweet William, Another Country, The Chain, Five Days One Summer, Foreign Body, Mountains of the Moon, La Couleur du Vent, The Tall Guy, Killing Dad, Impromptu, Emily's Ghost, The Grotesque, Angels & Insects, Haunted, Sweet Angel Mine, Driftwood, The Slab Boys, Deja Vu, Captain Jack, Mad Cows, Room to Rent, Dark Blue World, The Importance of Being Earnest, Possession.
TELEVISION: Remember the Germans, Wicked Woman, The Corn Is Green, Sakharov, Hotel Du Lac (BAFTA Award), A Hazard of Hearts, Around the World in 80 Days, Tears in the Rain, The Man from the PRU, A Tale of Two Cities, The Return of the Psammead, A Very British Psycho, A Respectable Trade, The Sleeper.

MASTERS, BEN
Actor. b. Corvallis, OR, May 6, 1947. e. Univ. of Oregon.
THEATRE: The Cherry Orchard, Waltz of the Toreadors, Plenty, Captain Brassbound's Conversion, The Boys in the Band, Eden Court, What the Butler Saw, The White Whore and the Bit Player, Key Exchange.
PICTURES: Mandingo, All That Jazz, Key Exchange, Dream Lover, Making Mr. Right.
TELEVISION: *Series*: Another World, Heartbeat, Passions. *Guest*: Barnaby Jones, Kojack. *Movies*: One of Our Own, The Shadow Box, The Neighborhood, Illusions, The Deliberate Stranger, Street of Dreams, Cruel Doubt, Running Mates, A Twist of the Knife, A Time to Heal, Lady Killer, The Second Civil War. *Mini-Series*: Loose Change, Celebrity, Noble House.

MASTERSON, MARY STUART
Actress. b. Los Angeles, CA, June 28, 1966. Daughter of writer-dir.-actor Peter Masterson and actress Carlin Glynn. e. Goddard Col. Made film debut at age 8 in The Stepford Wives (1975), which featured her father. Spent summer at Stage Door Manor in Catskills; two summers at Sundance Inst. Studied acting with Gary Swanson. Member of the Actor's Studio. Off-off B'way debut in Been Taken. Off-B'way debut in Lily Dale followed by The Lucky Spot (Manhattan Theatre Club). Regional: Moonlight and Valentines, Three Sisters.
PICTURES: The Stepford Wives (debut, 1975), Heaven Help Us, At Close Range, My Little Girl, Some Kind of Wonderful, Gardens of Stone, Mr. North, Chances Are, Immediate Family

(Natl. Board of Review Award, 1989), Funny About Love, Fried Green Tomatoes, Mad at the Moon, Married to It, Benny & Joon, Bad Girls, Radioland Murders, Heaven's Prisoners, Bed of Roses, Dogtown, On the Second Day of Christmas, The Postman, The Florentine, Digging to China, The Book of Stars, West of Here, Leopold Bloom.
TELEVISION: *Movies:* Love Lives On, Lily Dale, On the 2nd Day of Christmas, Black and Blue, Three Blind Mice. *Guest:* Amazing Stories (Go to the Head of the Class). *Series:* Kate Brasher, R.U.S./H.

MASTERSON, PETER
Actor, Writer, Director. r.n. Carlos Bee Masterson, Jr. b. Houston, TX, June 1, 1934. m. actress Carlin Glynn. Daughter is actress Mary Stuart Masterson. e. Rice U., Houston, BA. 1957. NY stage debut, Call Me By My Rightful Name, 1961.
THEATRE: Marathon '33, Blues for Mr. Charlie, The Trial of Lee Harvey Oswald, The Great White Hope, That Championship Season, The Poison Tree, The Best Little Whorehouse in Texas (co-author, dir.), The Last of the Knucklemen (dir.).
PICTURES: *Actor:* Ambush Bay (debut, 1965), Counterpoint, In the Heat of the Night, Tomorrow, The Exorcist, Man on a Swing, The Stepford Wives, Gardens of Stone. *Writer:* The Best Little Whore House in Texas. *Director:* The Trip to Bountiful, Full Moon in Blue Water, Blood Red, Night Game, Convicts, The Only Thrill, Lost Junction.
TELEVISION: Camera Three, Pueblo; The Quinns; A Question of Guilt, Mermaid (dir.).

MASTORAKIS, NICO
Writer, Director, Producer. b. Athens, Greece, 1941. Writer of novels and screenplays, including Fire Below Zero, and Keepers of the Secret (co-author). Pres. Omega Entertainment Ltd. since 1978.
PICTURES: *Writer/dir./prod.:* The Time Traveller, Blind Date, Sky High, The Zero Boys, The Wind, Terminal Exposure, Nightmare at Noon, Glitch, Ninja Academy, Hired to Kill, In the Cool of the Night, At Random. *Prod.:* The Greek Tycoon, Red Tide, Grandmother's House, Darkroom, Bloodstone (prod., co-s.p.)., Nightmare at Noon, The Naked Truth, .com for Murder.

MASTRANTONIO, MARY ELIZABETH
Actress. b. Oak Park, IL, Nov. 17, 1958. e. U. of Illinois 1976-78 where she trained for opera. m. dir. Pat O'Connor. Worked as singer & dancer for summer at Opryland Theme Park in Nashville. Came to NY as understudy and vacation replacement as Maria in West Side Story revival.
THEATRE: *NY:* Copperfield (1981), Oh Brother, Amadeus, Sunday in the Park With George (Playwright's Horizons), The Human Comedy, Henry V, The Marriage of Figaro, Measure for Measure, The Knife, Twelfth Night.
PICTURES: Scarface (debut, 1983), The Color of Money (Acad. Award nom.), Slamdance, The January Man, The Abyss, Fools of Fortune, Class Action, Robin Hood: Prince of Thieves, White Sands, Consenting Adults, A Day to Remember, Three Wishes, Two Bits, My Life So Far, Limbo, The Perfect Storm, Tabloid, Standing Room Only.
TELEVISION: *Mini-Series:* Mussolini: The Untold Story, Witness Protection. *Special:* Uncle Vanya (BBC).

MASUR, RICHARD
Actor. b. New York, NY, Nov. 20, 1948. Directed Oscar-nominated short, Love Struck, 1987. Pres., Screen Actors Guild, 1995.
THEATRE: *B'way:* The Changing Room.
PICTURES: Whiffs (debut, 1975), Bittersweet Love, Semi-Tough, Who'll Stop the Rain, Hanover Street, Scavenger Hunt, Heaven's Gate, I'm Dancing as Fast as I Can, The Thing, Timerider, Risky Business, Under Fire, Nightmares, The Mean Season, My Science Project, Head Office, Heartburn, The Believers, Walker, Rent-a-Cop, Shoot to Kill, License to Drive, Far from Home, Flashback, Going Under, My Girl, Encino Man, The Man Without a Face, Six Degrees of Separation, My Girl 2, Forget Paris, Multiplicity, Fire Down Below, Play It To the Bone.
TELEVISION: *Series:* Hot L Baltimore, One Day at a Time, Empire. *Mini-Series:* East of Eden. *Movies:* Having Babies, Betrayal, Mr. Horn, Walking Through the Fire, Fallen Angel, Money on the Side, An Invasion of Privacy, The Demon Murder Case, Adam, John Steinbeck's The Winter of Our Discontent, Flight #90: Disaster on the Potomac, The Burning Bed, Obsessed With a Married Woman, Wild Horses, Embassy, Adam: His Song Continues, Roses Are for the Rich, Cast the First Stone, When the Bough Breaks, Settle the Score, Always Remember I Love You, Stephen King's IT, The Story Lady, And the Band Played On, Search for Grace, My Brother's Keeper, The Face on the Milk Carton, Hiroshima, It Was Him or Us, Undue Influence, Noriega: God's Favorite, 61*. *Director:* Torn Between Two Fathers (After School Special, DGA nom.).

MATARAZZO, HEATHER
Actress. b. Long Island, NY, Nov. 10, 1982.
PICTURES: Welcome to the Dollhouse, Arresting Gena, The Devil's Advocate, The Deli, Hurricane Streets, 54, The Hairy Bird, Getting to Know You, Cherry, Blue Moon, Scream 3, Company Man, The Princess Diaries, Sorority Boys, The Pink House, 10029.

TELEVISION: *Movies:* Our Guys: Outrage at Glen Ridge. *Series:* The Adventures of Pete & Pete, Roseanne, Now & Again. *Guest:* Townies, Roseanne, ER.

MATHESON, TIM
Actor. b. Los Angeles, CA, Dec. 31, 1947. e. California State U. Debut on TV at age 12 in Window on Main Street. At 19, contract player for Universal. 1985, turned to direction: St. Elsewhere episode and music videos. Set up production co. at Burbank Studios 1985; acted off-B'way in True West. With partner Daniel Grodnick bought National Lampoon from founder Matty Simons, becoming exec. officer and chmn. 1989; resigned in 1991.
PICTURES: Divorce American Style (debut, 1967), Yours Mine and Ours, How to Commit Marriage, Magnum Force, Almost Summer, National Lampoon's Animal House, Dreamer, The Apple Dumpling Gang Rides Again, 1941, House of God, A Little Sex, To Be or Not To Be, Up the Creek, Impulse, Fletch, Speed Zone, Drop Dead Fred, Solar Crisis, Black Sheep, A Very Brady Sequel, A Very Unlucky Leprechaun, She's All That, The Story of Us, Chump Change, Van Wilder.
TELEVISION: *Movies:* Owen Marshall: Counselor-at-Law, Lock Stock and Barrel, Hitched, Remember When, The Last Day, The Runaway Barge, The Quest, Mary White, Listen to Your Heart, Obsessed with a Married Woman, Blind Justice, Warm Hearts Cold Feet, Bay Coven, The Littlest Victims, Little White Lies, Buried Alive, Joshua's Heart, Stephen King's Sometimes They Come Back, The Woman Who Sinned, Quicksand: No Escape, Relentless: Mind of a Killer, Trial & Error, Dying to Love You, A Kiss to Die For, Robin Cook's Harmful Intent, Target of Suspicion, Breach of Conduct (dir., co-exec. prod. only), While Justice Sleeps, Fast Company, An Unfinished Affair, Buried Alive 2 (also dir.), Sleeping with the Devil, Forever Love, Catch Me If You Can, In the Company of Spies (also dir.), Fishing with John, At the Mercy of a Stranger, Navigating the Heart, Hell Swarm (also dir.), Sharing the Secret, Second Honeymoon, Wolf Lake, Judas & Jesus, Moms on Strike. *Series:* Window on Main Street, Jonny Quest (voice), The Virginian, Bonanza, The Quest, Tucker's Witch, Just in Time (also co-exec. prod.), Charlie Hoover, The Legend of Calamity Jane (voice), The West Wing, Wolf Lake, Breaking News. *Pilot:* Nikki & Alexander. *Special:* Bus Stop. *Mini-Series:* How the West Was Won, Jackie Bouvier Kennedy Onassis.

MATHIS, SAMANTHA
Actress. b. New York, NY, 1971. Mother is actress Bibi Besch; grandmother was actress Gusti Huber. Began acting as teen landing role in tv pilot Aaron's Way at age 16.
PICTURES: The Bulldance (debut, 1988 in Yugoslav film), Pump Up the Volume, This Is My Life, FernGully ... The Last Rainforest (voice), Super Mario Bros., The Music of Chance, The Thing Called Love, Little Women, Jack and Sarah, How to Make an American Quilt, The American President, Broken Arrow, Waiting for Woody, Sweet Jane, Freak City, American Psycho, Attraction, Searching for Debra Winger.
TELEVISION: *Series:* Knightwatch, Harsh Realm, First Years. *Movies:* Cold Sassy Tree, To My Daughter, 83 Hours 'Til Dawn, Collected Stories. *Mini-series:* The Mists of Avalon.

MATLIN, MARLEE
Actress. b. Morton Grove, IL, Aug. 24, 1965. e. John Hersey H.S., Chicago, public school with special education program for deaf; William Rainey Harper Coll.Performed at Children's Theatre of the Deaf in Des Plaines at age 8, playing many leading roles. Theatrical film debut in Children of a Lesser God. Production company, Solo One Productions.
PICTURES: Children of a Lesser God (debut, 1986; Acad. Award, Golden Globe), Walker, The Player, The Linguini Incident, Hear No Evil, It's My Party, Snitch, Two Shades of Blue.
TELEVISION: *Series:* Reasonable Doubts, The Outer Limits, Picket Fences, The West Wing, Ollie. *Movies:* Bridge to Silence, Against Her Will: The Carrie Buck Story, Dead Silence, Kiss My Act *Specials:* Face the Hate, Meaning of Life, Free to Laugh, Creative Spirit, The Big Help, People In Motion (host). *Guest:* Sesame Street, Adventures in Wonderland, Picket Fences (Emmy Award nom.), Seinfeld (Emmy Award nom.).

MATTHAU, CHARLES
Director. b. New York, NY, Dec. 10, 1964. Son of actor Walter Matthau. e. U. of Southern California Film School. While at USC wrote and dir. The Duck Film, a silent comedy short (Golden Seal Award, London Amateur Film Fest. and C.I.N.E. Eagle Award.) Also dir. short, I Was a Teenage Fundraiser. President, The Matthau Company, organized 1990.
PICTURES: Doin' Time on Planet Earth. (nom. Saturn Award, best dir., Acad. of Science Fiction.), The Grass Harp (dir., prod.; Acad. of Family Films award, best dir., 1996), Hanging Up (actor only), An Ordinary Killer (actor only).
TELEVISION: *Movies:* Mrs. Lambert Remembers Love (dir., prod.; Golden Eagle, Golden Medal & Houston Fest. Grand & Angel Awards, 1993), The Marriage Fool (actor, dir., writer).

MAURA, CARMEN
Actress. b. Madrid, Spain, Sept. 15, 1945. e. Madrid's Catholic Inst. Daughter of ophthalmologist; faced family disapproval and custody battle when she became an actress. Met aspiring dir.

Pedro Almodovar when they were cast in stage prod. of Sartre's Dirty Hands and starred in several of his films. Hosted weekly Spanish tv talk show Esta Noche.
PICTURES: El Hombre Oculto (debut, 1970), El Love Feroz, The Petition, Paper Tigers, Que Hace una Chica Como tu en un Sitio Como Este?, Pepi Luci Bom ... And Other Girls on the Heap (1980), El Cid Cabreador, Dark Habits, What Have I Done to Deserve This?, Extramuros, Se Infiel y No Mires Con Quien, Matador, Law of Desire, Women on the Verge of a Nervous Breakdown, Baton Rouge, How to Be a Woman and Not Die Trying, Ay Carmela!, Chatarra, Between Heaven and Earth, The Anonymous Queen, Shadows in a Conflict, Louis the Child King, How to Be Miserable and Enjoy It, The Flowers of My Secret, Una Pareja de Tres, El Palomo cojo, Happiness Is in the Field, Tortilla y cinema, Alliance cherche doigt, Elles, Vivir despeus, Alice and Martin, Enthusiasm, Superlove, The Comet, Lisbon, Harem of Madame Osmane, Common Wealth, To the End of the Road, Hold Up, Arregui la noticia del dia, Cara y Elena, Shutdown, Valentin, Le Ventre de Juliette, 800 balas.

MAUREY, NICOLE
Actress. b. France, Dec. 20, 1926. Studied dancing; French films include Blondine, Pamela, Le Cavalier Noir, Journal D'Un Cure De Campagne, Les Compagnes de la Nuit; many television and stage appearances in France; U.S. film debut in Little Boy Lost (1953).
PICTURES: Little Boy Lost, The Secret of the Incas, The Bold and the Brave, The Weapon, The Constant Husband, The Scapegoat, Me and the Colonel, The Jayhawkers, House of the Seven Hawks, High Time, Day of the Triffids, Why Bother to Knock?, The Very Edge.
TELEVISION: U.S. and U.K.: Tomorrow We Will Love, Casablanca, The Billion Franc Mystery, Champion House, I Thought They Died Years Ago.

MAXWELL, LOIS
Actress. r.n. Lois Hooker. b. Canada, 1927. Started in U.S. films in late 1940's before working in Italy then Britain. Has done numerous Canadian films for tv.
PICTURES: That Hagen Girl, The Decision of Christopher Blake, The Big Punch, The Dark Past, Kazan, Domani e troppa Tardi (Tomorrow Is Too Late), La Grande Speranza (The Great Hope), Aida, Passport to Treason, Satellite in the Sky, Time Without Pity, Lolita, Dr. No, Come Fly With Me, The Haunting, From Russia With Love, Goldfinger, Thunderball, Operation Kid Brother, You Only Live Twice, On Her Majesty's Secret Service, Adventure in Rainbow Country, The Adventurers, Diamonds Are Forever, Live and Let Die, The Man With the Golden Gun, The Spy Who Loved Me, Moonraker, Mr. Patman, For Your Eyes Only, Octopussy, A View to a Kill, Martha Ruth and Eddie, The Fourth Angel.
TELEVISION: Adventures in Rainbow Country, Peep, The Blue Man, Rescue Me, Lady in the Corner, Hard to Forget.

MAXWELL, RONALD F.
Director, Writer, Producer. b. Jan. 5, 1947. e. NYU Coll. of Arts & Sciences; NYU Sch. of the Arts, Inst. of Film & Television Graduate Sch., M.F.A., 1970. Prod., dir,. for PBS Theater-in-America (1974-78).
PICTURES: Director: The Guest, Little Darlings, The Night the Lights Went Out in Georgia, Kidco, Gettysburg (also co-s.p.), Joan of Arc: The Virgin Warrior (also s.p.), Gods and Generals (also s.p.).
TELEVISION: Director: Sea Marks (also prod.), Verna: USO Girl (also prod.), Parent Trap II.

MAY, ELAINE
Actress, Director, Writer. b. Philadelphia, PA, April 21, 1932. Daughter is actress Jeannie Berlin. Father was prod.-dir. Jack Berlin whose travelling theater she acted with from age 6 to 10. Repertory theatre in Chicago, 1954; comedy team with Mike Nichols starting in 1955. Appeared with improvisational theater group, The Compass, Chicago. Co-starred in An Evening with Mike Nichols and Elaine May.
THEATRE: Playwright: A Matter of Position, Not Enough Rope, Hot Line, Better Point of Valour, Mr. Gogol & Mr. Preen, Hotline (Death Defying Acts).
PICTURES: Luv (actress), Enter Laughing (actress), A New Leaf (actress, dir., s.p.), Such Good Friends (s.p. as Esther Dale), The Heartbreak Kid (dir.), Mikey and Nicky (dir., s.p.), Heaven Can Wait (co-s.p.), California Suite (actress), Ishtar (dir., s.p.), In the Spirit (actress), The Birdcage (s.p.), Primary Colors (Acad, Award nom. for s.p. adapt.), Small Time Crooks, Down to Earth (s.p.).
TELEVISION: Series regular: Keep Talking (1958-59). Guest: Jack Paar, Omnibus, Dinah Shore Show, Perry Como, Laugh Lines.

MAY, JODHI
Actress. b. London, England, 1975.
PICTURES: A World Apart, Isabelle Eberhardt, Eminent Domain, The Last of the Mohicans, Sister My Sister, Second Best, The Scarlet Letter (voice), The Woodlanders, The Gambler, The House of Mirth, The Escapist, The Dish.
TELEVISION: Movies: For the Greater Good, Max and Helen, Signs and Wonders, Warriors, The Turn of the Screw, The Mayor

of Casterbridge. Mini-series: Aristocrats.

MAYER, MICHAEL F.
Attorney, Executive. b. White Plains, NY, Sept. 8, 1917. e. Harvard Coll., B.S., 1939; Yale Law Sch., L.L.B., 1942. Armed Forces 1942-46, Air Medal (1945). V.P., Kingsley International Pictures Corp., 1954-62. Exec. dir. and gen. counsel, Independent Film Importers and Distributors of America Inc. (IFIDA), 1959-67. Special Counsel, French Society of Authors, Composers and Publishers, 1961-72; British Performing Rights Society, 1962-67. Author: Foreign Films on American Screens (1966), Divorce and Annulment (1967), What You Should Know About Libel and Slander (1968), Rights of Privacy (1972), The Film Industries (1973, revised ed. pub. in 1978). Teacher of courses on Business Problems in Film, New School (1971-82). Secty. of Film Society of Lincoln Center, Inc. (1972-88). Retired.

MAYER, ROGER LAURANCE
Executive. b. New York, NY, April 21, 1926. e. Yale U., B.A. 1948; Yale Law Sch., L.L.B. and J.D. 1951. In 1952 was practicing attorney; joined Columbia Pictures that year as atty. and named general studio exec., 1957. Left in 1961 to join MGM Studio as asst. gen. mgr. With MGM as follows: v.p., operations, 1964; v.p., administration, 1975-84. Also exec. v.p., MGM Laboratories, 1974-83. Named pres., MGM Laboratories and sr. v.p., studio admin.; MGM Entertainment Co. 1983-86; joined Turner Entertainment Co. as pres. and COO, 1986. Member of Los Angeles County Bar Assn., Calif. Bar Assn., Los Angeles Copyright Society, bd of govs., Acad. of Motion Picture Arts & Sciences. Trustee, chmn. Motion Picture & TV Fund. Chmn National Film Preservation Foundation.

MAYO, VIRGINIA
Actress. r.n. Virginia Jones. b. St. Louis, MO, Nov. 30, 1920. e. St. Louis dramatic school. With Billy Rose's Diamond Horseshoe; then N.Y. stage, Banjo Eyes.
PICTURES: Jack London (debut, 1943), Up in Arms, The Princess and the Pirate, Wonder Man, The Kid from Brooklyn, The Best Years of Our Lives, The Secret Life of Walter Mitty, Out of the Blue, A Song Is Born, Smart Girls Don't Talk, The Girl from Jones Beach, Flaxy Martin, Colorado Territory, Always Leave Them Laughing, White Heat, Red Light, Backfire, The Flame and the Arrow, West Point Story, Along the Great Divide, Captain Horatio Hornblower, Painting the Clouds with Sunshine, Starlift, She's Working Her Way Through College, Iron Mistress, She's Back on Broadway, South Sea Woman, Devil's Canyon, King Richard and the Crusaders, The Silver Chalice, Pearl of the South Pacific, Great Day in the Morning, The Proud Ones, Congo Crossing, The Big Land, The Story of Mankind, The Tall Stranger, Fort Dobbs, Westbound, Jet Over the Atlantic, Young Fury, Fort Utah, Castle of Evil, Won Ton Ton the Dog Who Saved Hollywood, French Quarter, Evil Spirits, Seven Days Ashore, The Man Next Door.

MAYRON, MELANIE
Actress, Director. b. Philadelphia, PA, Oct. 20, 1952. e. American Academy of Dramatic Arts, 1972. Debut Godspell (tour), NY stage debut: The Goodbye People, 1979.
PICTURES: Actress: Harry and Tonto (debut, 1974), Gable and Lombard, Car Wash, The Great Smokey Roadblock, You Light Up My Life, Girl Friends (Locarno Film Fest. Award) Heartbeeps, Missing, The Boss' Wife, Sticky Fingers (also co-s.p., co-prod.), Checking Out, My Blue Heaven, Drop Zone, East of A, Clockstoppers. Dir.: The Babysitters Club, Slap Her She's French.
TELEVISION: Series: thirtysomething (Emmy Award, 1989). Movies: Playing For Time, Will There Really Be a Morning?, Hustling, The Best Little Girl in the World, Wallenberg: A Hero's Story, Ordeal in the Arctic, Other Women's Children. Guest: Rhoda. Specials: Lily Tomlin: Sold Out, Cinder Ella: A Modern Fairy Tale, Wanted: The Perfect Guy, Mad About You, Toothless, Something So Right, Range of Motion. Dir.: Tribeca: Stepping Back (also writer), thirtysomething, Sirens, Moon Over Miami, Winnetka Road, Freaky Friday, Nash Bridges, New York Undercover, Arliss, The Larry Sanders Show, Freaky Friday, Toothless, Dawson's Creek, Providence, Wasteland, Ed, State of Grace.

MAYSLES, ALBERT
Director, Cinematographer. b. Boston, MA, Nov. 1926. e. Syracuse (B.A.), Boston U, M.A. Taught psychology there for 3 years. With late brother David (1932-87) pioneer in direct cinema documentary filmmaking. Entered filmmaking photographing Primary with D.A. Pennebaker, Richard Leacock and Robert Drew, 1960. Formed Maysles Films, Inc. 1962, making non-fiction feature films, commercials and corp. films.
PICTURES: Showman (1962), Salesman, What's Happening! The Beatles in the U.S.A., Meet Marlon Brando, Gimme Shelter, Christo's Valley Curtain, Grey Gardens, Running Fence, Vladimir Horowitz: The Last Romantic, Ozawa, Islands, Horowitz Plays Mozart, Fellow Passengers, Christo in Paris, Soldiers of Music: Rostropovitch Returns to Russia, Baroque Duet, Umbrellas, Letting Go: A Hospice Journey, Concert of Wills: Making the Getty Center, LaLee's Kin: The Legacy of Cotton.
TELEVISION: Vladimir Horowitz: The Last Romantic (Emmy

Award, 1987), Soldiers of Music: Rostopovich Returns to Russia (Emmy Award, 1991), Sports Illustrated: The Making of the Swimsuit Issue (co-dir.), Abortion: Desperate Choices (Emmy Award, 1992, Cable Ace Award), Letting Go: A Hospice Journey (Emmy Award, 1996).

MAZURSKY, PAUL

Producer, Director, Writer, Actor. b. Brooklyn, NY, April 25, 1930. e. Brooklyn Coll. Started acting in 1951 Off-B'way (Hello Out There, The Seagull, Major Barbara, Death of a Salesman, He Who Gets Slapped), TV and films. Was nightclub comic 1954-1960 and directed plays. Began association with Larry Tucker by producing, directing, writing and performing in Second City, semi-improvisational revue. For four years they wrote the Danny Kaye TV show and created the Monkees series. First theatrical film I Love You Alice B. Toklas, 1968, which he wrote and exec. produced with Tucker. Exec. prod. of film Taking Care of Business.
PICTURES: *Dir.-Writer*: Bob and Carol and Ted and Alice, *Dir.-Prod.-Writer-Actor*: Alex in Wonderland, Blume in Love, Harry and Tonto, Next Stop Greenwich Village (dir., prod., s.p. only), An Unmarried Woman, Willie and Phil, Tempest, Moscow on the Hudson, Down and Out in Beverly Hills, Moon Over Parador, Enemies: a Love Story, Scenes From a Mall, The Pickle, Faithful. *Actor*: Fear and Desire, Blackboard Jungle, Deathwatch, A Star Is Born, A Man a Woman and a Bank, History of the World Part 1, Into the Night, Punchline, Scenes From the Class Struggle in Beverly Hills, Man Trouble, Carlito's Way, Love Affair, Miami Rhapsody, Faithful, 2 Days in the Valley, Touch, Bulworth, Why Do Fools Fall in Love, Antz (voice), Crazy in Alabama, Stanley Kubrick: A Life in Pictures, Big Shot's Funeral, The Majestic, Do It For Uncle Manny.
TELEVISION: *Movies*: Weapons of Mass Distruction, A Slight Case of Murder.

MAZZELLO, JOSEPH

Actor. b. Rhineback, NY, Sept. 21, 1983. Made acting debut at age 5 in tv movie Unspeakable Acts.
PICTURES: Presumed Innocent (debut, 1990), Radio Flyer, Jurassic Park, Shadowlands, The River Wild, The Cure, Three Wishes, The Lost World: Jurassic Park, Star Kid, Simon Birch, Wooly Boys.
TELEVISION: *Movies*: Unspeakable Acts, Desperate Choices: To Save My Child, A Father for Charlie.

McBRIDE, JIM

Director, Writer. b. New York, NY, Sept. 16, 1941. e. NYU. m. costume designer Tracy Tynan. Began in underground film scene in New York. First film: David Holzman's Diary, 1967, which won grand prize at Mannheim and Pesaro Film Festivals, and was named to the Library of Congress' list of important American films designated for preservation in 1991. Appeared as actor in film Last Embrace.
PICTURES: *Director*: David Holzman's Diary (also prod.), My Girlfriend's Wedding (also actor, s.p.), Glen and Randa (also s.p.), Hot Times (also s.p., actor), Breathless (also co-s.p.), The Big Easy, Great Balls of Fire, Uncovered (also co-s.p.).
TELEVISION: *Series*: The Wonder Years (3 episodes), Twilight Zone (The Once and Future King, 1986), Six Feet Under. *Movies*: Blood Ties, The Wrong Man, The Informant, Pronto, Dead by Midnight. *Special*: Fallen Angels (Fearless), Dead Before Midnight, Meatloaf: To Hell and Back.

McCALL, JOAN

Writer, Actress. b. Grahn, KY. e. Berea Coll. Staff writer for Days of Our Lives, Another World, As the World Turns, under the pen name Joan Pommer; also Search for Tomorrow, Capitol, Santa Barbara, Divorce Court. Starred on B'way in Barefoot in the Park, The Star Spangled Girl, A Race of Hairy Men, and road companies of Barefoot in the Park, Any Wednesday, Star Spangled Girl, and Don't Drink the Water
PICTURES: Grizzly, Act of Vengeance, The Devil Times Five. Screenwriter: Predator, Between Two Worlds, Timelapse, Heart Like a Wheel.

McCALLUM, DAVID

Actor. b. Glasgow, Scotland, Sept. 19, 1933. Early career in rep. theatres and dir. plays for Army. Entered industry in 1953.
PICTURES: The Secret Place (debut, 1957), Hell Drivers, Robbery Under Arms, Violent Playground, A Night to Remember, The Long and the Short and the Tall, Carolina, Jungle Street, Billy Budd, Freud, The Great Escape, The Greatest Story Ever Told, To Trap a Spy, The Spy With My Face, Around the World Under the Sea, One Spy Too Many, Three Bites of the Apple, Sol Madrid, Mosquito Squadron, The Kingfisher Caper, Dogs, King Solomon's Treasure, The Watcher in the Woods, Terminal Choice, The Wind, The Haunting of Morella, Hear My Song, Dirty Weekend, Healer.
TELEVISION: *Series*: The Man From U.N.C.L.E., Colditz (BBC, 1972-74), The Invisible Man, Sapphire and Steel (BBC), Trainer (BBC), VR. 5, The Education of Max Bickford. *Guest*: Hitchcock, Murder She Wrote. *Movies*: Teacher Teacher, Hauser's Memory, Frankenstein: The True Story, Behind Enemy Lines, Freedom Fighters, She Waits, The Man Who Lived at the Ritz, The Return

of Sam McCloud, Mother Love (BBC), Shattered Image, Death Game, Coming Home, Beyond Titanic.

McCAMBRIDGE, MERCEDES

Actress. b. Joliet, IL, March 17, 1918. e. Mundelein Coll., Chicago, B.A. Did some radio work while in college; opposite Orson Welles two seasons, on Ford Theatre, other air shows; New York stage in: Hope for the Best, (1945); Place of Our Own, Twilight Bar, Woman Bites Dog, The Young and Fair, Lost in Yonkers. Starred on own radio show, 1952. Autobiography: The Two of Us.
PICTURES: All the King's Men (debut, 1949; Acad. Award, best supporting actress), Lightning Strikes Twice, Inside Straight, The Scarf, Johnny Guitar, Giant, A Farewell to Arms, Touch of Evil (cameo), Suddenly Last Summer, Cimarron, Angel Baby, 99 Women, Like a Crow on a June Bug, The Exorcist (voice), Thieves, The Concorde—Airport '79, Echoes.
TELEVISION: *Series*: One Man's Family, Wire Service; also numerous guest appearances. *Movies*: Killer By Night, Two For the Money, The Girls of Huntington House, The President's Plane Is Missing, Who Is the Black Dahlia?, The Sacketts.

McCARTHY, ANDREW

Actor. b. Westfield, NJ, Nov. 29, 1962. Raised in Bernardsville, NJ. e. NYU. While at college won role in film Class. Studied acting at Circle-in-the-Square.
THEATRE: *B'way*: The Boys of Winter. *Off B'way*: Bodies Rest and Motion, Life Under Water, Neptune's Hips, Mariens Kammer.
PICTURES: Class (debut, 1983), Heaven Help Us, St. Elmo's Fire, Pretty in Pink, Mannequin, Waiting for the Moon, Less Than Zero, Kansas, Fresh Horses, Weekend at Bernie's, Quiet Days in Clichy, Dr. M, Year of the Gun, Only You, Weekend at Bernie's 2, The Joy Luck Club, Getting In, Night of the Running Man, Mrs. Parker & the Vicious Circle, Dream Man, Dead Funny, Mulholland Falls, Things I Never Told You, Stag, I Woke Up Early the Day I Died, Bela Donna A Breed Apart, New World Disorder, Jump, A Twist of Faith, Standard Time, Diggity: Home at Last.
TELEVISION: *Movies*: The Courtyard, The Christmas Tree, Hostile Force, A Father For Brittany, Perfect Assassins, A Storm in Summer, The Sight. *Specials*: Dear Lola, Common Pursuit. *Guest*: Amazing Stories (Grandpa's Ghost), Tales From the Crypt (Loved to Death). *Mini-Series*: Jackie Bouvier Kennedy Onassis.

McCARTHY, KEVIN

Actor. b. Seattle, WA, Feb. 15, 1914. Sister was late author Mary McCarthy. e. U. of Minnesota. Acted in sch. plays, stock; B'way debut in Abe Lincoln in Illinois. Served in U.S. Army.
THEATRE: *B'way*: Flight to West, Winged Victory, Truckline Cafe, Joan of Lorraine, The Survivors, Death of a Salesman (London), Anna Christie, The Deep Blue Sea, others.
PICTURES: Death of a Salesman (debut, 1951; Acad. Award nom.), Drive a Crooked Road, The Gambler From Natchez, Stranger on Horseback, Annapolis Story, Nightmare, Invasion of the Body Snatchers, The Misfits, 40 Pounds of Trouble, A Gathering of Eagles, The Prize, The Best Man, An Affair of the Skin, Mirage, A Big Hand for the Little Lady, Three Sisters, Hotel, The Hell With Heroes, If He Hollers Let Him Go, Revenge in El Paso, Ace High, Kansas City Bomber, Alien Thunder, Order to Kill, Buffalo Bill and the Indians, Piranha, Invasion of the Body Snatchers (1978, cameo), Hero at Large, Those Lips Those Eyes, The Howling, My Tutor, Twilight Zone—The Movie, Hostage, Innerspace, UHF, Fast Food, Dark Tower, Love or Money, The Sleeping Car, Eve of Destruction, Final Approach, The Distinguished Gentleman, Matinee, Greedy, Just Cause, Steal Big Steal Little, Mommy, Razorback.
TELEVISION: Active on TV since 1949. *Movies*: U.M.C., A Great American Tragedy, Exo-Man, Mary Jane Harper Cried Last Night, Flamingo Road, Portrait of an Escort, Rosie: The Story of Rosemary Clooney, Making of a Male Model, Invitation to Hell, Deadly Intentions, The Midnight Hour, A Masterpiece of Murder, Poor Little Rich Girl: The Barbara Hutton Story, The Long Journey Home, Once Upon a Texas Train, In the Heat of the Night, Channel 99, The Rose and the Jackal, Dead on the Money, Duplicates, The Sister-in-Law, Liz: The Elizabeth Taylor Story, Marlon Brando: The Wild One, The Second World War, Elvis Meets Nixon. *Mini-series*: Passion and Paradise. *Series*: The Colbys, The Survivors, Flamingo Road, Amanda's, Second Start. *Guest*: Dynasty. *Pilot*: Second Stage.

McCARTNEY PAUL

Singer, Musician. r.n. James Paul McCartney. b. Liverpool, England, June 18, 1942. Formerly with The Beatles, Wings.
PICTURES: *Performer*: A Hard Day's Night, (debut, 1964; also songs) Help! (also songs), Yellow Submarine (cameo; also songs), Let It Be (also songs; Acad. Award for best original song score, 1970), Rockshow (concert film), Give My Regards to Broad Street (also s.p., songs), Eat the Rich (cameo), Get Back (concert film) *Songs for films*: Live and Let Die (title song; Acad. Award nom.), Oh Heavenly Dog, Spies Like Us, many others. *Scores*: The Family Way, Beyond the Limit.
TELEVISION: *Specials*: James Paul McCartney, Sgt. Pepper: It

Was 20 Years Ago Today, Put It There, Paul McCartney Live in the New World, The Beatles Anthology, The Concert for New York City, many others.

McCLANAHAN, RUE
Actress. b. Healdton, OK, Feb. 21. e. U. of Tulsa (B.A. cum laude). Member: Actors Studio, NYC.
THEATRE: On B'way in Sticks and Bones, Jimmy Shine, California Suite. Off-B'way: Who's Happy Now? (Obie Award, 1970), After Play. Vienna: Lettice and Lovage. London: Harvey.
PICTURES: Five Minutes to Love, Hollywood After Dark, How to Succeed With Girls, They Might Be Giants, The People Next Door, The Pursuit of Happiness, Modern Love, This World Then The Fireworks, Dear God, Starship Troopers, Out to Sea, This Rusty: A Dog's Tale, Lugosi: Hollywood's Dracula, Border to Border.
TELEVISION: Series: Maude, Mama's Family, The Golden Girls (Emmy Award, 1987), The Golden Palace, Apple Pie, Balckbird Hall, Safe Harbor. Movies: Having Babies III, Sgt. Matlovich Vs. the U.S. Air Force, Rainbow, Topper, The Great American Traffic Jam, Word of Honor, The Day the Bubble Burst, The Little Match Girl, Liberace, Take My Daughters Please, Let Me Hear You Whisper, To the Heroes, After the Shock, Children of the Bride, To My Daughter, The Dreamer of Oz, Baby of the Bride, Mother of the Bride (also co-exec. prod.), A Burning Passion: The Margaret Mitchell Story, Innocent Victims, A Christmas Love, Columbo: Ashes to Ashes, A Saintly Switch, The Moving of Sophia Myles. Specials: The Wickedest Witch, The Man in the Brown Suit, Nunsense 2: The Sequel. Mini-Series: Message From Nam.

McCLORY, SEÁN
Actor. b. Dublin, Ireland, March 8, 1924. e. Jesuit Coll., Nat'l U. at Galway (medical sch.). With Gaelic Theatre, Galway; Abbey Theatre, Dublin. Brought to U.S. in 1946 under contract to RKO Pictures, then Warners, then Batjac (John Wayne's co.). Prod. and dir. numerous plays, member of the Directors Guild of America and author of drama, Moment of Truth; Pax: The Benedictions in China. Editor: The Jester: The Masques Club 50th Anniv. Mng. Editor: A.N.T.A. News (2 yrs). For past 4 years starred in 40 ninety-minute radio dramas for California Artists Radio Theatre and written some 90 min. shows for National Public Radio. Recipient, Irish American Partnership Special CA Achievement Award, 1998.
THEATRE: Shining Hour, Juno and the Paycock, Anna Christie, Shadow of a Gunman (Dramalogue Award), many others.
PICTURES: Roughshod, Beyond Glory, The Daughter of Rosie O'Grady, Anne of the Indies, Storm Warning, Lorna Doone, What Price Glory?, The Quiet Man, Rogue's March, Plunder of the Sun, Island in the Sky, Them, Ring of Fear, Man in the Attic, The Long Grey Lane, Diane, I Cover the Underworld, The King's Thief, Moonfleet, Guns of Fort Petticoat, Valley of the Dragons, Cheyenne Autumn, Follow Me Boys, The Gnome-Mobile, Bandolero, Day of the Wolves, Roller Boogie, In Search of Historic Jesus, My Chauffeur, The Dead, John Huston and the Dubliners.
TELEVISION: Series: The Californians (also dir. episodes), Kate McShane, Bring 'Em Back Alive, General Hospital. Mini-Series: The Captains and the Kings, Once an Eagle. Movies: Kate McShane (pilot), The New Daughters of Joshua Cabe, Young Harry Houdini. Guest: Matinee Theatre, Climax, Lost in Space, My Three Sons, many others.

McCLUGGAGE, KERRY
Executive. b. 1955. e. USC, Harvard U. 1978, programming asst. at Universal; 1979, dir. of current srs. programming; 1980, became v.p., Universal TV. 1982, sr. v.p. creative affairs. Served as v.p. of production, Universal Pictures and supv. prod. on series Miami Vice. 1987-991, pres. of Universal Television. 1991, joined Paramount as pres. of the Television Group. 1992, named chmn. of the Television Group of Paramount Pictures. Resigned Dec. 2001. Will remain with Paramount as independent producer of programming.

McCLURE, MARC
Actor. b. San Mateo, CA, March 31, 1957.
PICTURES: Freaky Friday, Coming Home, I Wanna Hold Your Hand, Superman, Superman II, Superman III, Supergirl, Back to the Future, Superman IV: The Quest for Peace, Amazon Women on the Moon, Perfect Match, Chances Are, After Midnight, Back to the Future Part III, Grim Prairie Tales, The Vagrant, Apollo 13, Sleepstalker.
TELEVISION: Series: California Fever. Movies: James at 15, Little White Lies. Guest: The Commish.

McCLURG, EDIE
Actress. b. Kansas City, MO, July 23, 1951. e. Syracuse Univ. Newswriter and documentary prod. for National Public Radio affiliate, KCUR-FM. Became member of the Groundlings Improv Comedy Revue.
PICTURES: Carrie (debut, 1976), Cheech and Chong's Next Movie, Oh God Book II, Secret of NIMH (voice), Pandemonium, Cracking Up, Eating Raoul, Mr. Mom, The Corsican Brothers, Ferris Bueller's Day Off, Back to School, The Longshot, Planes Trains and Automobiles, She's Having a Baby, Elvira: Mistress of the Dark, The Little Mermaid (voice), Curly Sue, A River Runs Through It, Stepmonster, Airborne, Natural Born Killers, Under the Hula Moon, Carpool, Circuit Breaker, Casper: A Spirited Beginning, Flubber, Meeting Daddy, A Bug's Life (voice), Holy Man, The Rugrats Movie (voice), Can't Stop Dancing, The Manor, Hanging Up, Van Wilder, Colored Eggs, The Master of Disguise, Now You Know.
TELEVISION: Series: Tony Orlando and Dawn, The Kallikaks, The Big Show, Harper Valley PTA, No Soap Radio, Madame's Place, Small Wonder, Toegther We Stand, Valerie (The Hogan Family), Drexell's Class, Life with Louie, Martin Mull's White Politics in America, Rocket Power, The Kids From Room 402. Specials: Cinderella (Faerie Tale Theatre), The Pee-wee Herman Show, Martin Mull's History of White People in America, Once Upon a Brothers Grimm, The Chevy Chase Show, A Home Run for Love. Guest: WKRP in Cincinnati, The Richard Pryor Show, The Jeffersons, Trapper John M.D., Alice, Diff'rent Strokes, The Incredible Hulk, Madame's Place, Picket Fences. Movies: Bill on His Own, Crash Course, Dance 'til Dawn, Menu for Murder, Columbo: Ashes to Ashes, Murder She Purred. Voice Characterizations: The Snorks, The 13 Ghosts of Scooby Doo, The New Jetsons, Casper, Problem Child, Bobby's World of Monsters.

McCONAUGHEY, MATTHEW
Actor. b. Uvalde, Texas, November 4, 1969
PICTURES: Dazed and Confused, My Boyfriend's Back, Angels in the Outfield, The Return of the Texas Chainsaw Massacre, Boys on the Side, Scorpion Spring, Submission, Glory Daze, Larger Than Life, A Time to Kill, Lone Star, Amistad, Contact, Making Sandwiches, The Newton Boys, South Beach, Last Flight of the Raven (prod. only), Johnny Diamond, Edtv, U-571, Last Flight of the Raven, The Wedding Planner, Reign of Fire, Dexterity, 13 Conversations About One Thing, Frailty, Tiptoes, How to Lose a Guy in 10 Days.

McCORMICK, PAT
Writer, Actor. b. July 17, 1934. Served as comedy writer for such performers as Jonathan Winters, Phyllis Diller.
PICTURES: Actor: Buffalo Bill and the Indians, Smokey and the Bandit, A Wedding, Hot Stuff, Scavenger Hunt, Smokey and the Bandit 2, History of the World Part 1, Under the Rainbow (also co-s.p.), Smokey and the Bandit 3, Bombs Away, Rented Lips, Scrooged, Beverly Hills Vamp, Nerds of a Feather, Chinatown Connection, Ted and Venus.
TELEVISION: Series (as writer): Jack Paar Show, Tonight Show, etc. Series (as actor): The Don Rickles Show, The New Bill Cosby Show, Gun Shy. Movies (as actor): Mr. Horn, Rooster, The Jerk Too.

McCOWEN, ALEC
Actor. b. Tunbridge Wells, England, May 26, 1925. e. Royal Acad. of Dramatic Art. On stage in London in Hadrian the Seventh, among others. On B'way in Antony and Cleopatra, After the Rain, The Philanthropist, The Misanthrope, Equus, Someone Who'll Watch Over Me, etc.
PICTURES: The Cruel Sea, The Divided Heart, The Deep Blue Sea, The Good Companions, The Third Key (The Long Arm), Time Without Pity, Town on Trial, The Doctor's Dilemma, A Night to Remember, The One That Got Away, Silent Enemy, The Loneliness of the Long Distance Runner, In the Cool of the Day, The Devil's Own, The Hawaiians, Frenzy, Travels with My Aunt, Stevie, Hanover Street, Never Say Never Again, The Assam Garden, Personal Services, Cry Freedom, Henry V, The Age of Innocence, Maria's Child, The American.
TELEVISION: numerous productions in the U.K.

McCRANE, PAUL
Actor. b. Philadelphia, PA, Jan. 19, 1961. Stage debut at age 16 in NY Shakespeare Fest. prod. of Landscape of the Body.
THEATRE: NY: Dispatches, Runaway, Split, The House of Blue Leaves, The Palace of Amateurs, Hooters, The Hostage, Curse of an Aching Heart
PICTURES: Rocky II (debut, 1979), Fame (also songwriter), The Hotel New Hampshire, Purple Hearts, Robocop, The Blob, The Shawshank Redemption, The Last Producer, Last Mistake, New Suit.
TELEVISION: Series: Cop Rock, Under Suspicion, ER, Champs. Movies: Baby Comes Home, We're Fighting Back, Money— Power— Murder, With Murder in Mind, The Portrait, Strapped, Zelda. Mini-series: North & South II, Heaven and Hell: North and South Book III, From the Earth to the Moon.

McDERMOTT, DYLAN
Actor. b. Connecticut, Oct. 26, 1961. Raised in New York City. e. Fordham U., studied acting at Neighborhood Playhouse with Sanford Meisner.
THEATRE: The Seagull, Golden Boy, The Glass Menagerie, Biloxi Blues (B'way), Floating Rhoda and the Glue Man.
PICTURES: Hamburger Hill, The Blue Iguana, Twister, Steel Magnolias, Where Sleeping Dogs Lie, Hardware, In the Line of Fire, The Cowboy Way, Miracle on 34th Street, Destiny Turns on the Radio, Home for the Holidays, `Til There Was You, Three to Tango, Texas Rangers.
TELEVISION: Movies: The Neon Empire, Into the Badlands, The Fear Inside. Series: The Practice.

McDONNELL, MARY
Actress. b. Wilkes Bare, PA.
THEATRE: *NY:* Buried Child, Savage in Limbo, All Night Long, Black Angel, A Weekend Near Madison, Three Ways Home, Still Life, The Heidi Chronicles, Summer and Smoke. *Regional:* National Athems, A Doll's House, A Midsummer Night's Dream, The Three Sisters.
PICTURES: Matewan, Tiger Warsaw, Dances With Wolves (Acad. Award nom.), Golden Globe Award), Grand Canyon, Sneakers, Passion Fish (Acad. Award nom.), Blue Chips, Mariette in Ecstasy, Independence Day, You Can Thank Me Later, Spanish Fly (voice), Mumford, Fly Girls, Amargosa, Donnie Darko, Nola, Crazy Like a Fox.
TELEVISION: *Series:* ER, High Society, Ryan Caulfield. *Movies:* Money on the Side, Courage, Evidence of Blood, Behind the Mask, A Father's Choice, For All Time, Chestnut Hill.

McDORMAND, FRANCES
Actress. b. Illinois, 1958. m. dir. Joel Coen. Daughter of a Disciples of Christ preacher, traveled Bible Belt with family settling in PA at 8. e. Yale Drama School. Regional theater includes Twelfth Night, Awake and Sing, The Three Sisters, All My Sons. Two seasons with O'Neill Playwrights Conference.
THEATRE: Awake and Sing, Painting Churches, On the Verge, A Streetcar Named Desire (Tony nom.), The Sisters Rosensweig, The Swan.
PICTURES: Blood Simple, Raising Arizona, Mississippi Burning (Acad. Award nom.), Chattahoochee, Dark Man, Miller's Crossing (unbilled), Hidden Agenda, The Butcher's Wife, Passed Away, Short Cuts, Beyond Rangoon, Fargo (Acad. Award, 1996; Chicago Film Critics Award; Screen Actors Guild Award; Ind't Spirit Award), Lone Star, Primal Fear, Palookaville, Paradise Road, Johnny Skidmarks, Madeline, Talk of Angels, Wonder Boys, Almost Famous, Scottsboro: An American Tragedy, The Man Who Wasn't There, Searching for Debra Winger, City By the Sea, Laurel Canyon.
TELEVISION: *Series:* Leg Work, State of Grace (voice). *Guest:* Twilight Zone, Spenser: For Hire, Hill St. Blues. *Movies:* Crazy in Love, The Good Old Boys.

McDOWELL, MALCOLM
Actor. b. Leeds, England, June 13, 1943. Was spearholder for the Royal Shakespeare Co. in season of 1965-66 when turned to TV and then to films. *NY stage:* Look Back in Anger (also on video), In Celebration, Another Time. *LA stage:* Hunting Cockroaches.
PICTURES: Poor Cow (debut, 1967), If..., Figures in a Landscape, The Raging Moon (Long Ago Tomorrow), A Clockwork Orange, O Lucky Man!, Royal Flash, Voyage of the Damned, Aces High, The Passage, Time After Time, Caligula, Cat People, Britannia Hospital, Blue Thunder, Cross Creek, Get Crazy, Sunset, Buy and Cell, The Caller, Class of 1999, Disturbed, In the Eye of the Snake, Moon 44, The Maestro, Schweitzer, Assassin of the Tsar, The Player, Happily Ever After (voice), Chain of Desire, East Wind, Night Train to Venice, Bopha!, Milk Money, Star Trek: Generations, Tank Girl, Kids of the Round Table, Where Truth Lies, Hugo Pool, Mr. Magoo, The Gardener, The First 9 1/2 Weeks, Beings, Y2K, Southern Cross, My Life So Far, Stanley and Us, Gangster No. 1, Island of the Dead, Stanley Kubrick: A Life in Pictures, Just Visiting, The Void, Dorian, The Chemical Wedding, The Barber, Between Strangers, I Spy, Tempo, I'll Sleep When I'm Dead.
TELEVISION: *Series:* Pearl, Fantasy Island, Captain Simian and the Space Monkeys, Pearl, Wing Commander Academy. *Guest:* Faerie Tale Theatre (Little Red Riding Hood), Tales from the Crypt (Reluctant Vampire). *Movies:* Arthur the King, Gulag, Monte Carlo, Seasons of the Heart, The Man Who Wouldn't Die, The Little Rider, Superman: The Last Son of Krypton, Can of Worms, The David Cassidy Story, St. Patrick: The Irish Legend, Faces of Evil, Princess of Thieves, Firestarter II: Rekindled. *Mini-Series:* Our Friends in the North, The Great War, Lexx: The Dark Zone.

McELWAINE, GUY
Executive. b. Culver City, CA, June 29, 1936. Started career in pub. dept. of MGM, 1955; 1959, joined m.p. div. of Rogers and Cowen; 1964, formed own public relations firm; then joined CMA. Left to become sr. exec. v.p. in chg. worldwide m.p. production, Warner Bros., 1975. 1977 became sr. exec. v.p. in chg. worldwide m.p. activities and pres. of intl. film mktg. at Intl. Creative Management (formerly CMA. 1981, named pres. and CEO Rastar Films. Left in 1982 to become pres., Columbia Pictures; given additional title of CEO, 1983. 1985 named chmn. and on board of Columbia Pictures Industries. Resigned, 1986. Joined Weintraub Entertainment Group as exec. v.p. and chmn., m.p. div. 1987-89; returned to ICM, 1989 as vice chmn. Currently, pres., Morgan Creek Productions.

McEVEETY, BERNARD
Director. Father was pioneer as unit mgr. at New York's Edison Studios; Brothers dir. Vincent and writer Joseph. Began career in 1953 at Paramount where he was asst. dir. for 6 yrs. Dir. debut on TV series, The Rebel.
PICTURES: Ride Beyond Vengeance, Brotherhood of Satan, Napoleon and Samantha, One Little Indian, The Bears and I.

TELEVISION: Numerous episodes of Bonanza, Gunsmoke, Combat and Cimarron Strip (also prod.), Centennial, Roughnecks, The Machans.

McEVEETY, VINCENT
Director. Brother is dir. Bernard McEveety. Joined Hal Roach Studios in 1954 as second asst. dir. Then to Republic for The Last Command. First Disney assignments: Davy Crockett shows and Mickey Mouse Club. Moved to Desilu as first asst. dir. on The Untouchables; made assoc. prod. with option to direct. Did segments of many series, including 34 Gunsmoke episodes.
PICTURES: Firecreek (debut, 1968), $1,000,000 Duck, The Biscuit Eater, Charley and the Angel, Superdad, The Strongest Man in the World, Gus, Treasure of Matecumbe, Herbie Goes to Monte Carlo, The Apple Dumpling Gang Rides Again, Herbie Goes Bananas, Amy.
TELEVISION: Blood Sport, Wonder Woman, High Flying Spy, Ask Max, Gunsmoke: Return to Dodge, Murder She Wrote, Simon and Simon (26 episodes), Columbo: Rest in Peace Mrs. Columbo, may other movies and series episodes.

McGAVIN, DARREN
Actor. b. Spokane, WA, May 7, 1922. e. Coll. of the Pacific. Studied acting at Neighborhood Playhouse, Actors Studio. Landed bit roles in films starting in 1945.
THEATRE: Death of a Salesman, My Three Angels, The Rainmaker, The Lovers, The King and I, Dinner at Eight (revival), Captain Brassbound's Conversion (LA), The Night Hank Williams Died, Greetings.
PICTURES: A Song to Remember (debut, 1945), Kiss and Tell, Counter-Attack, She Wouldn't Say Yes, Fear, Queen for a Day, Summertime, The Man With the Golden Arm, The Court Martial of Billy Mitchell, Beau James, The Delicate Delinquent, The Case Against Brooklyn, Bullet for a Badman, The Great Sioux Massacre, Ride the High Wind, Mission Mars, Mrs. Polifax—Spy, Happy Mother's Day... Love George (dir. only), No Deposit No Return, Airport '77, Hot Lead and Cold Feet, Zero to Sixty, Hangar 18, Firebird 2015 A.D., A Christmas Story, The Natural, Turk 182, Raw Deal, From the Hip, Dead Heat, Blood and Concrete: A Love Story, Billy Madison, Still Waters Burn, Small Time, Pros and Cons.
TELEVISION: *Series:* Crime Photographer, Mike Hammer, Riverboat, The Outsider, Kolchak: The Night Stalker, Small & Frye. *Movies:* The Outsider (pilot), The Challenge, The Challengers, Berlin Affair, Tribes, Banyon, The Death of Me Yet, Night Stalker, Something Evil, The Rookies, Say Goodbye Maggie Cole, The Night Strangler, The Six Million Dollar Man (pilot), Brink's: The Great Robbery, Law and Order, The Users, Love for Rent, Waikiki, Return of Marcus Welby M.D., My Wicked Wicked Ways, Inherit the Wind, The Diamond Trap, By Dawn's Early Light, The American Clock, Danielle Steel's A Perfect Stranger, Derby. *Specials:* Unclaimed Fortunes (host), Clara (ACE Award), Mastergate, Miracles and Ohter Wonders (host), The Secret Discovery of Noah's Ark (host). *Mini-Series:* Ike, The Martian Chronicles, Around the World in 80 Days. *Guest:* Goodyear TV Playhouse, Alfred Hitchcock Presents, Route 66, U.S. Steel Hour, The Defenders, Love American Style, The Name of the Game, Owen Marshall, Police Story, The Love Boat, Murphy Brown (Emmy Award, 1990), The X Files.

McGILLIS, KELLY
Actress. b. Newport Beach, CA, July 9, 1957. Studied acting at Pacific Conservatory of Performing Arts in Santa Maria, CA; Juilliard. While at latter, won role in film Reuben Reuben.
THEATRE: *D.C. Stage:* The Merchant of Venice, Twelfth Night, Measure for Measure, Much Ado About Nothing. *NY Stage:* Hedda Gabler.
PICTURES: Reuben Reuben (debut, 1983), Witness, Top Gun, Once We Were Dreamers, Made in Heaven, The House on Carroll Street, The Accused, Winter People, Cat Chaser, Before and After Death, The Babe, North, Painted Angels, Morgan's Ferry, At First Sight, The Settlement, The Monkey's Mask, No On Can Hear You.
TELEVISION: *Movies:* Sweet Revenge, Private Sessions, Grand Isle (also prod.), Bonds of Love, In the Best of Families: Marriage Pride & Madness, We the Jury, The Third Twin, Perfect Prey, Storm Chasers: Revenge of the Twister. *Special:* Out of Ireland (narrator).

McGINLEY, JOHN C.
Actor. b. New York, NY, Aug. 3, 1959. e. NYU (M.F.A.), 1984.
THEATRE: *NY:* Danny and the Deep Blue Sea, The Ballad of Soapy Smith, Jesse and the Games, Requiem for a Heavyweight, Love as We Know It, Talk Radio, Florida Crackers, Breast Men.
PICTURES: Sweet Liberty, Platoon, Wall Street, Shakedown, Talk Radio, Lost Angels, Fat Man and Little Boy, Born on the Fourth of July, Point Break, Highlander 2: The Quickening, Article 99, Little Noises, A Midnight Clear, Fathers and Sons, Hear No Evil, Watch It (also co-prod.), Car 54 Where Are You?, On Deadly Ground, Surviving the Game, Suffrin' Bastards (also co-s.p.), Wagons East!, Born to Be Wild, Captive (co-prod. only), Seven, Nixon, Johns, The Rock, Nothing to Lose, A.W.O.L, Three to Tango, Any Given Sunday, Get Carter, The Animal, Summer Catch, Highway, Crazy As Hell, Stealing Harvard, I.D.

TELEVISION: *Movies*: Clinton & Nadine, Cruel Doubt, The Last Outlaw, The Return of Hunter, Intensity, The Pentagon Wars, Target Earth, The Jack Bull. *Guest*: Frasier. *Series*: Scrubs.

McGOOHAN, PATRICK
Actor, Director. b. New York, March 19, 1928. Early career in repertory in Britain. London stage 1954 in Serious Charge; 1955, Orson Welles' Moby Dick. On B'way in Pack of Lies (1987).
PICTURES: The Dam Busters (debut, 1954), I Am a Camera, The Dark Avenger, Passage Home, Zarak, High Tide at Noon, Hell Drivers, The Gypsy and the Gentleman, Nor the Moon by Night, Two Living One Dead, All Night Long, Life for Ruth (Walk in the Shadow), The Quare Fellow, The Three Lives of Thomasina, Dr. Syn: Alias the Scarecrow (U.S. tv as: The Scarecrow of Romney Marsh), Ice Station Zebra, The Moonshine War, Mary—Queen of Scots, Catch My Soul (dir. only), Un Genio due Campari e un Pollo, Porgi d'altra Guancia, Silver Streak, Brass Target, Escape From Alcatraz, Scanners, Kings and Desperate Men, Finding Katie, Baby: Secret of the Lost Legend, Braveheart, The Phantom, A Time to Kill, Hysteria.
TELEVISION: *Series*: Danger Man (also dir. episodes), Secret Agent, The Prisoner (also creator, prod.), Rafferty. *Movies/Specials*: The Hard Way, Jamaica Inn, Of Pure Blood, The Man in the Iron Mask, Three Sovereigns for Sarah. *Guest*: Columbo (Emmy Awards: 1975, 1990; also dir. several Columbo movies).

McGOVERN, ELIZABETH
Actress. b. Evanston, IL, July 18, 1961. Family moved to Southern California when she was 10. Acted in high school in North Hollywood; performance in prod. of The Skin of Our Teeth won her agency represenation. Studied at American Conservatory Theatre, San Francisco and Juilliard Sch. of Dramatic Art. Open audition for Ordinary People resulted in her film debut. Appeared in IMAX film Wings of Courage.
THEATRE: *NY*: To Be Young Gifted and Black (1981, debut), My Sister in This House (Theatre World, Obie Awards), Painting Churches, The Hitch-Hiker, A Map of the World, Aunt Dan and Lemon (L.A.), Two Gentlemen of Verona, A Midsummer Night's Dream (NY Shakespeare Fest.), Love Letters, Twelfth Night (Boston), Major Barbara (Alaska), King Aroung the Moon (D.C.), Maids of Honor, The Three Sisters, As You Like It.
PICTURES: Ordinary People (debut, 1980), Ragtime (Acad. Award nom.), Lovesick, Racing with the Moon, Once Upon a Time in America, Native Son, The Bedroom Window, She's Having a Baby, Johnny Handsome, The Handmaid's Tale, A Shock to the System, Tune in Tomorrow, King of the Hill, Me and Veronica, The Favor, Wings of Courage, The Wings of the Dove, The Man With Rain in His Shoes, The Misadventures of Margaret, Manila, The House of Mirth, Buffalo Soldiers.
TELEVISION: *Series*: If Not for You, Table 12. *Movies*: Women and Men: Stories of Seduction (The Man in the Brooks Brothers Shirt), Broken Trust, The Summer of Ben Tyler, Broken Glass, Clover, The Scarlet Pimpernel Meets Madame Guillotine, The Scarlet Pimpernel and the Kidnapped King, Thursday the 12th, The Flamingo Rising. *Specials*: Ashenden, Tales From Hollywood, The Changeling (BBC). *Mini-Series*: The Scarlet Pimpernel, Hawk.

McGRATH, JUDY
Executive. e. Cedar Crest Coll. President, MTV Music Networks Group. Began at MTV as on-air promotions writer. Created Unplugged, MTV Books, MTV Online, Video Music Awards, MTV Movie Awards, Total Request Live, The Real World, The Osbournes, etc.

McGRATH, THOMAS J.
Producer, Attorney, Writer, Lecturer. b. New York, NY, Oct. 8, 1932. e. Washington Square Coll. of NYU, B.A., 1956; NYU Sch. of Law, LL.B., 1960. Served in Korea with U.S. Army, 1953-54. Has practiced law in N.Y. from 1960 to date. Became indep. prod. with Deadly Hero in 1976; Author, Carryover Basis Under The 1976 Tax Reform Act, published in 1977. Cobntributing author, Estate and Gift Tax After ERTA, 1982. Lecturer and writer: American Law Institute 1976-81; Practicing Law Institute, 1976-97. Dir., New York Philharmonic; Oloffson Corp.; Fast Food Development Corp. Pres.: American Austrian Foundation; Tanzania Wildlife Fund.

McGREGOR, EWAN
Actor. b. Crieff, Scotland, March 31, 1971. Formed Natural Nylon, prodn. co., with Johnny Lee Miller & Jude Law.
PICTURES: Being Human, Shallow Grave, Blue Juice, The Pillow Book, Trainspotting, Emma, Brassed Off, The Serpent's Kiss, Nightwatch, A Life Less Ordinary, Velvet Goldmine, Little Voice, Desserts, Nightwatch, Rogue Trader, Nora, Star Wars: Episode I-The Phantom Menace, Eye of the Beholder, Moulin Rouge, Nora, Killing Priscilla, Anno Domini, Black Hawk Down, Star Wars: Episode II-Attack of the Clones, Young Adam, Down With Love, Borgia.
TELEVISION: *Movies*: Lipstick on Your Collar. *Mini-series*: Scarlet & Black, Karaoke. *Guest*: Tales from the Crypt, ER.

McHATTIE, STEPHEN
Actor. b. Antigonish, Nova Scotia, Canada, Feb. 3, e. Acadia U. Trained for stage at American Acad. of Dramatic Arts.

PICTURES: Von Richthofen and Brown (debut, 1970), The People Next Door, The Ultimate Warrior, Moving Violation, Tomorrow Never Comes, Death Valley, Best Revenge, Belizaire the Cajun, Salvation!, Call Me, Sticky Fingers, Caribe, Bloodhounds on Broadway, Erik, The Dark, Geronimo: An American Legend, Beverly Hills Cop III, Art Deco Detective, Pterodactyl Woman From Beverly Hills, Nonnie & Alex, Theodore Rex, My Friend Joe, The Climb, BASEketball, The Highwayman, Secretary.
TELEVISION: *Series*: Highcliffe Manor, Mariah, Scene of the Crime, Emily of the New Moon, Cold Squad. *Mini-series*: Centennial. *Movies*: Search for the Gods, James Dean, Look What's Happened to Rosemary's Baby, Mary and Joseph: A Story of Faith, Roughnecks, Terror on Track 9, Jonathan Stone: Threat of Innocence, Deadlocked: Escape From Zone 14, Convict Cowboy, Visitors of the Night, Deadly Love, Midnight Flight, American Whiskey Bar, A Sordid Affair.

McKEAN, MICHAEL
Actor, Writer. b. NYC, Oct. 17, 1947. e. NYU. Featured on L.A. radio show, The Credibility Gap.
THEATRE: Accomplice (Theatre World Award).
PICTURES: 1941, Used Cars, Young Doctors in Love, This is Spinal Tap (also co-s.p., co-wrote songs), D.A.R.Y.L., Clue, Jumpin' Jack Flash, Light of Day, Planes Trains and Automobiles, Short Circuit 2, Earth Girls Are Easy, The Big Picture (also co-s.p.), Hider in the House, Flashback, Book of Love, True Identity, Memoirs of an Invisible Man, Man Trouble, Coneheads, Airheads, Radioland Murders, Across the Moon, The Brady Bunch Movie, Edie and Pen, Jack, No Strings Attached, That Darn Cat, Nothing to Lose, With Friends Like These, Still Breathing, The Pass, Archibald the Rainbow Painter, Final Justice, Small Soldiers (voice), Teaching Mrs. Tingle, Kill the Man, True Crime, Mystery Alaska, Sugar: The Fall of the West, Best in Show, Beautiful, Little Nicky, My First Mister, Never Again, Dr. Dolittle 2 (voice), Teddy Bears' Picnic, The Guru, A Mighty Wind, Haunted Lighthouse, 100 Mile Rule.
TELEVISION: *Series*: Laverne & Shirley, Grand, Sessions, Saturday Night Live, Dream On, Road Rovers, Secret Service Guy, The X Files, Totally Ridiculous (host), Clerks, Primetime Glick, Harvey Birdman: Attorney At Law. *Movies*: More Than Friends, Classified Love, Murder in High Places, MacSharpe: The Final Roll of the Dice, The Sunshine Boys. *Specials*: Spinal Tap Reunion, The Laverne and Shirley Reunion. *Guest*: The X Files, The Simpsons (voice).

McKEE, GINA
Actress. b. 1964.
PICTURES: The Lair of the White Worm, The Rachel Papers, The Misadventures of Mr. Wilt, Naked, Element of Doubt, Croupier, Wonderland, Notting Hill, The Loss of Sexual Innocence, Women Talking Dirty, Messenger: The Story of Joan of Arc, There's Only One Jimmy Gimble, The Zookeeper, The Reckoning, Divine Secrets of the Ya Ya Sisterhood.
TELEVISION: *Movies*: Treasure Seekers, Mothertime, Beyond Fear, Our Friends in the North, The Passion, The Real Yoko Ono. *Series*: An Actor's Life for Me, The Lenny Henry Show, Brass Eye. *Guest*: Drop the Dead Donkey. *Mini-Series*: Our Friends in the North, Dice, The Forsyte Saga.

McKELLEN, SIR IAN
Actor. b. Burnley, England, May 25, 1939. e. Cambridge. C.B.E. 1979, Knighted 1991.
THEATRE: *London*: A Scent of Flowers (debut, 1964), Trelawny of the Wells, A Lily in Little India, The Man of Destiny, Black Comedy, Dr. Faustus, Henceforward, Bent, Uncle Vanya, Hamlet, Macbeth, Romeo & Juliet, Richard III. B'way: The Promise, Amadeus (Tony Award, 1981), Ian McKellen Acting Shakespeare, Wild Honey (also London), Richard III (Brooklyn), A Knight Out. Assoc. Dir. Nat'l Theatre. Prof. of Contemporary Theatre, Oxford Univ., 1991.
PICTURES: Alfred the Great, Thank You All Very Much, A Touch of Love, Priest of Love, The Keep, Plenty, Zina, Scandal, Last Action Hero, The Ballad of Little Jo, Six Degrees of Separation, The Shadow, Jack & Sarah, Restoration, Thin Ice, Richard III (also co-s.p.), Apt Pupil, Gods and Monsters (Acad. Award nom.), X-Men, The Lord of the Rings: The Fellowship of the Ring, Cirque du Soleil: Journey of Man (voice), The Lord of the Rings: The Two Towers, X2, The Lord of the Rings: The Return of the King, Asylum.
TELEVISION: *Movies*: Hamlet, David Copperfield, The Scarlet Pimpernel, Hedda Gabler, Ian McKellen Acting Shakespeare, Every Good Boy Deserves Favor, Loving Walter, Windmills of the Gods, Macbeth, Othello, Countdown to War, And the Band Played On, Mister Shaw's Missing Millions, Tales of the City, Cold Comfort Farm, Rasputin (Golden Globe Award, 1997), Great Composers (voice).

McKEON, DOUG
Actor. b. Pompton Plains, NJ, June 10, 1966.
THEATRE: Dandelion Wine, Truckload, Brighton Beach Memoirs, Death of a Buick, The Big Day.
PICTURES: Uncle Joe Shannon, On Golden Pond, Night Crossing, Mischief, Turnaround, Where the Red Fern Grows Part 2, The Empty Mirror, Courting Courtney, Sub Down, Critical

Mass.
TELEVISION: *Series*: Edge of Night, Big Shamus Little Shamus, Little Niagra. *Mini-Series*: Centennial, At Mother's Request, From the Earth to the Moon. *Movies*: Tell Me My Name, Daddy I Don't Like It Like This, The Comeback Kid, An Innocent Love, Desperate Lives, Silent Eye, Heart of a Champion: The Ray Mancini Story, Breaking Home Ties, Without Consent, Rocket's Red Glare.

McKEON, NANCY
Actress. b. Westbury, NY, April 4, 1966.
PICTURE: Where the Day Takes You, Teresa's Tattoo, Just Write.
TELEVISION: *Series:* Stone, The Facts of Life, Can't Hurry Love, Style and Substance, The Division. *Movies:* A Question of Love, The Facts of Life Goes to Paris, High School U.S.A., This Child Is Mine, Poison Ivy, Firefighter (also co-exec. prod.), The Facts of Life Down Under, Strange Voices (also co-exec. prod.), A Cry for Help: The Tracey Thurman Story, A Mother's Gift, Style and Substance, Just Right. *Specials:* Schoolboy Father, Scruffy (voice), Please Don't Hit Me Mom, Candid Kids (co-host).

McKERN, LEO
Actor. r.n. Reginald McKern. b. Sydney, New South Wales, Australia, March 16, 1920.
THEATRE: She Stoops to Conquer, Hamlet, Merry Wives of Windsor, Cat on a Hot Tin Roof, A Man for All Seasons, Boswell for the Defence, Hobson's Choice.
PICTURES: Murder in the Cathedral, All For Mary, X the Unknown, Time Without Pity, A Tale of Two Cities, The Mouse That Roared, Yesterday's Enemy, Scent of Mystery, Jazz Boat, Mr. Topaze, The Day the Earth Caught Fire, Lisa, Doctor in Distress, A Jolly Bad Fellow, King and Country, Agent 8 3/4, Help!, The Amorous Adventures of Moll Flanders, A Man for All Seasons, Assignment K, Decline and Fall of a Bird Watcher, The Shoes of the Fisherman, Ryan's Daughter, Massacre in Rome, The Adventure of Sherlock Holmes' Smarter Brother, The Omen, Candleshoe, Damien: Omen II, The Last Tasmanian, The Blue Lagoon, The French Lieutenant's Woman, Ladyhawke, The Chain, Traveling North (Australian Film Award), Dave and Dad on Our Selection, Molokai: The Story of Father Damien.
TELEVISION: King Lear, Murder with Mirrors, House on Garibaldi Street, Reilly: Ace of Spies, Rumpole of the Bailey, The Master Builder, The Last Romantics, A Foreign Field, Good King Wenceslas.

McLAGLEN, ANDREW V.
Director. b. London, England, July 28, 1920. Son of late actor Victor McLaglen. e. U. of Virginia, 1939-40. Asst. m.p. dir., 1944-54.
PICTURES: Gun the Man Down (debut, 1956), Man in the Vault, The Abductors, Freckles, The Little Shepherd of Kingdom Come, McLintock!, Shenandoah, The Rare Breed, The Way West, Monkeys Go Home!, The Ballad of Josie. The Devil's Brigade, Bandolero, Hellfighters, The Undefeated, Chisum, Fool's Parade (also prod.), Something Big (also prod.), One More Train to Rob, Cahill: U.S. Marshal, Mitchell, The Last Hard Men, The Wild Geese, Breakthrough (Sergeant Steiner), ffolkes (North Sea Hijack), The Sea Wolves, Sahara, Return to the River Kwai, Eye of the Widow.
TELEVISION: *Series:* Gunsmoke, Have Gun—Will Travel, Perry Mason, Rawhide, The Lineup, The Lieutenant. *Movies:* Log of the Black Pearl, Stowaway to the Moon, Banjo Hackett: Roamin' Free, Murder at the World Series, Louis L'Amour's The Shadow Riders, Travis McGee, The Dirty Dozen: The Next Mission. *Mini-Series:* The Blue and the Gray, On Wings of Eagles.

McLEAN, SEATON
Executive. b. Florida, raised in Montreal, Quebec, Canada. Founding partner, Atlantis Films, Ltd., 1978. Writer and editor of several award-winning films. producer/co-producer, Boys and Girls, Lost in the Barrens, Ray Bradbury Theater, Traders. Co-exec. producer, Marlowe, Petticoat Wars. Formerly in charge of Television Production for Alliance Atlantis. Currently president motion picture production, Alliance Atlantis Motion Picture Production.

McLERIE, ALLYN ANN
Actress. b. Grand Mere, Quebec, Canada, Dec. 1, 1926. e. Prof. childrens school. m. actor-singer George Gaynes. e. high school, N.Y. Dancer since 15 in many B'way shows.
THEATRE: One Touch of Venus, On the Town, Finian's Rainbow, Where's Charley?, Miss Liberty, Time Limit, South Pacific, Night of the Iguana, Julius Caesar, West Side Story, My Fair Lady, The Beast in Me, To Dorothy a Son.
PICTURES: Words and Music (debut 1948), Where's Charley?, Desert Song, Calamity Jane, Phantom of the Rue Morgue, Battle Cry, They Shoot Horses Don't They?, Monte Walsh, The Cowboys, Jeremiah Johnson, The Magnificent Seven Ride, The Way We Were, Cinderella Liberty, All the President's Men.
TELEVISION: *Series:* Tony Randall Show, Punky Brewster, Days and Nights of Molly Dodd. *Mini-Series:* The Thorn Birds, Beulah Land. *Specials:* Oldest Living Graduate, The Entertainer, Return Engagement, Shadow of a Gunman. *Guest:* WKRP in Cincinnati, Barney Miller, St. Elsewhere, Hart to Hart, Love Boat, Dynasty.

McMAHON, ED
Performer. b. Detroit, MI, March 6, 1923. e. Boston Coll.; Catholic U. of America, B.A., 1949. U.S. Marines, 1942-53. First

job on TV was as the clown on Big Top, 1950-51. First joined Johnny Carson as his sidekick on daytime quiz show Who Do You Trust? in 1958.
THEATRE: stock; *B'way*: Impossible Years.
PICTURES: The Incident, Slaughter's Big Rip-Off, Fun with Dick and Jane, The Last Remake of Beau Geste (cameo), Butterfly, Full Moon High, Love Affair, For Which He Stands, Just Write, Off the Menu: The Last Days of Chasen's, Mixed Blessings, The Pitch People, The Vegas Connection, Let Me In I Hear Laughter.
TELEVISION: *Series:* Big Top, Who Do You Trust?, The Tonight Show (1962-92), Missing Links (emcee), Snap Judgment (emcee), The Kraft Music Hall (host, 1968), Concentration (emcee), NBC Adventure Theatre (host), Whodunnit? (emcee), Star Search (host), TV's Bloopers and Practical Jokes (host). Movies: Star Marker, The Great American Traffic Jam (Gridlock), The Kid From Left Field, Star Seach, Bruno the Kid, The Tom Show. *Specials:* Macy's Thanksgiving Day Parade (host), Jerry Lewis Labor Day Telethon (co-host).

McMAHON, JOHN J.
Executive. b. Chicago, IL, 1932. e. Northwestern U. Served with U.S. Army in Korea, beginning career on WGN-TV, Chicago; associated with ZIV-United Artists TV Productions during 1950s; joined ABC in 1958: v.p. & gen. mgr., WXYTZ-TV, Detroit, then KABC-TV, Los Angeles, 1968; v.p., ABC, 1968-72; joined NBC in 1972 as v.p., programs; west coast, NBC-TV; president, Hollywood Radio & Television Society; board member, Permanent Charities Committee. 1980, named pres. of Carson Prods. (Johnny Carson's prod. co.).
TELEVISION: John & Yoko: A Love Story, If It's Tuesday It Still Must Be Belgium (exec. prod.), My Father My Son (exec. prod.), Passions, Brother of the Wind, Warning: Parental Advisory.

McMARTIN, JOHN
Actor. Warsaw, IN, e. Columbia U. Off-B'way debut: Little Mary Sunshine (1959: Theatre World Award).
THEATRE: The Conquering Hero, Blood Sweat and Stanley Poole, Children from Their Games, A Rainy Day in Newark, Pleasures and Palaces (Detroit), Sweet Charity (Tony nom.), Follies, The Great God Brown (Drama Desk Award), Sondheim: A Musical Tribute, Forget-Me-Not-Lane (Mark Taper Forum), The Visit, Chemin de Fer, The Rules of the Game, A Little Family Business, Passion (Mark Taper), Solomon's Child, Julius Caesar, A Little Night Music (Ahmanson), Love for Love, Happy New Year, Don Juan (Drama Desk Award, Tony nom.), Artist Descending a Staircase, Henry IV (Kennedy Ctr.), Custer (Kennedy Ctr.), Money & Friends (L.A.), Show Boat (Tony nom.), High Society.
PICTURES: A Thousand Clowns, What's So Bad About Feeling Good?, Sweet Charity, All The President's Men, Thieves, Brubaker, Blow Out, Pennies From Heaven, Dream Lover, Legal Eagles, Native Son, Who's That Girl, A Shock to the System, Three Businessmen, The Dish.
TELEVISION: *Series:* Falcon Crest, Beauty and the Beast. *Guest:* Cheers, Mary Tyler Moore Show, Murder She Wrote, Magnum P.I., The Golden Girls, Empty Nest, Law and Order, others. American Playhouse *Specials:* Edith Wharton Story, Rules of the Game, The Greatest Man in the World, Private Contentment, The Fatal Weakness, Concealed Enemies. *Movies:* Ritual of Evil, Fear on Trial, The Defection of Simas Kudirka, The Last Ninja, Murrow, Day One, Roots: The Gift, Citizen Cohn, H.U.D.

McNAMARA, WILLIAM
Actor. b. Dallas, TX, March 31, 1965. e. Columbia U. Joined Act I theatre group at Williamstown Theatre Festival, 1986; studied acting at Lee Strasberg Institute.
PICTURES: The Beat (debut, 1988), Stealing Home, Dream a Little Dream, Stella, Texasville, Terror at the Opera, Aspen Extreme, Surviving the Game, Chasers, Storybook, Dead in the Cadillac, Copycat, Dead Girl, The Brylcreem Boys, Sweet Jane, Something to Believe In, Stag, The Deli, Knockout, Implicated, Glam, Ringmaster, Paper Bullets, Just Sue Me, The Calling.
TELEVISION: *Series:* Island Son, Beggars and Choosers. *Specials:* Soldier Boys (Afterschool Special), Secret of the Sahara, The Edge (Indian Poker), It's Only Rock 'n' Roll (Afterschool Special). *Movies:* Wildflower (ACE Award nom.), Doing Time on Maple Drive, Honor Thy Mother, Sworn to Vengeance, Radio Inside, Liz: The Elizabeth Taylor Story, Natural Enemy, Trapped. *Pilot:* The Wyatts.

McNAUGHTON, JOHN
Director. b. Chicago, IL, Jan. 13, 1950.
PICTURES: Henry: Portrait of a Serial Killer, The Borrower, Sex Drugs Rock & Roll, Mad Dog and Glory, Girls in Prison, Normal Life, Veeck as a Wreck, Condo Painting, Wild Things, Speaking of Sex.
TELEVISION: *Movies:* Lansky. *Series:* Push Nevada.

McNEELY, JOEL
Composer.
PICTURES: The Pick-Up Artist (add'l. music score), Iron Will (orchestration), You Talkin' to Me?, Samantha, Police Story III: Supercop, Squanto: A Warrior's Tale, Iron Will, Terminal Velocity, Radioland Murders, Gold Diggers: The Secret of Bear Mountain, Flipper, Virus, Vegas Vacation, Wild America, Air Force One (add'l.), The Avengers, Zack and Reba, Soldier, Virus, All Forgotten, Return to Never Land, The Jungle Book II.
TELEVISION: *Movies:* Parent Trap III, Parent Trap Hawaiian Honemoon, Frankenstein: The College Years, Buffalo Soldiers, Road Rage, Sally Hemmings: An American Scandal, Santa

Who?. *Series*: Tiny Toon Adventures, The Young Indiana Jones Chronicles, Buddy Faro, Dark Angel.

McNICHOL, KRISTY
Actress. b. Los Angeles, CA, Sept. 11, 1962. Brother is actor Jimmy McNichol. Made debut at age of 7 performing in commercials. Given regular role in Apple's Way; began appearing on such series as Love American Style and The Bionic Woman. Attracted attention of Spelling-Goldberg Productions, who cast her as Buddy Lawrence in Family series, 1976-80.
PICTURES: The End (debut, 1978), Little Darlings, The Night the Lights Went Out in Georgia, Only When I Laugh, White Dog, The Pirate Movie, Just the Way You Are, Dream Lover, You Can't Hurry Love, Two Moon Junction, The Forgotten One.
TELEVISION: *Series*: Apple's Way, Family (2 Emmy Awards: 1977, 1979), Empty Nest. *Movies*: The Love Boat II, Like Mom Like Me, Summer of My German Soldier, My Old Man, Blinded by the Light, Love Mary, Women of Valor, Children of the Bride, Baby of the Bride, Mother of the Bride (also co-exec. prod.).

McRANEY, GERALD
Actor. b. Collins, MS, Aug. 19, 1948. m. actress Delta Burke. e. U. of Mississippi. Left school to become surveyor in oil fields after which joined acting company in New Orleans. Studied acting with Jeff Corey; landed guest role on TV series, Night Gallery.
PICTURES: Night of Bloody Horror, Keep Off My Grass, The Neverending Story, American Justice, Blind Vengeance, Hansel & Gretel.
TELEVISION: *Series*: Simon & Simon, Major Dad (also exec. prod.), Home of the Brave, Promised Land, The Protector. *Guest*: The Incredible Hulk, The Rockford Files, The Dukes of Hazzard, Eight Is Enough, How the West Was Won, Hawaii Five-O, Barnaby Jones, Gunsmoke, Designing Women, The West Wing. *Movies*: Roots II, The Jordan Chance, Women in White, Trial of Chaplain Jenson, The Law, The Haunting Passion, A Hobo's Christmas, Where the Hell's That Gold?!!?, The People Across the Lake, Dark of the Moon, Murder By Moonlight, Blind Vengeance, Vestige of Honor, Love and Curses... And All That Jazz (also dir., co-exec. prod.), Fatal Friendship, Scattered Dreams: The Kathryn Messenger Story, Armed and Innocent, Motorcycle Gang, Deadly Vows, Someone She Knows, Not Our Son, Simon & Simon: In Trouble Again, The Stranger Beside Me, Nothing Lasts Forever, Home of the Brave, A Nightmare Come True, A Thousand Men and a Baby, A Holiday Romance, Take Me Home: The John Denver Story, Danger Beneath the Sea. *Special*: Fast Forward.

McSHANE, IAN
Actor. b. Blackburn, England, Sept. 29, 1942. e. RADA.
THEATRE: *England*: The House of Fred Ginger, The Easter Man, The Glass Menagerie, Rashomon, Next Time I'll Sing to You, Loot, The Big Knife, The Admirable Crichton. *NY*: The Promise. *LA*: Inadmissible Evidence, Betrayal, As You Like It.
PICTURES: The Wild and the Willing (debut, 1962), The Pleasure Girls, Gypsy Girl (Sky West and Crooked), If It's Tuesday This Must Be Belgium, The Battle of Britain, Freelance, Pussycat Pussycat I Love You, The Devil's Widow (Tam-Lin), Villain, Sitting Target, The Left Hand of Gemini, The Last of Sheila, Ransom, Journey Into Fear, The Fifth Musketeer, Yesterday's Hero, Cheaper to Keep Her, Exposed, Torchlight, Ordeal By Innocence, Too Scared to Scream, Grand Larceny, Con Man, Sexy Beast.
TELEVISION: Wuthering Heights, The Pirate, Disraeli, The Letter, Marco Polo, Bare Essence, Grace Kelly, Evergreen, A.D., The Murders in the Rue Morgue, Grand Larceny, War and Remembrance, Chain Letter (pilot), The Great Escape II: the Untold Story, The Young Charlie Chaplin, Lovejoy, Sauce For Goose, Dick Francis Mysteries (Blood Sport), Perry Mason: The Case of the Desperate Deception, Columbo: Rest in Peace Mrs. Columbo, White Goods, Soul Survivors (prod.), Madson (prod.), Lovejoy (prod., dir.), Man and Boy.

McTEER, JANET
Actress. b. New Castle, England, May 8, 1961. Tony Award Winner in 1991 as Best Actress in a revival of Ibsen's "A Doll's House."
PICTURES: Half Moon Street, Hawks, I Dreamt I Woke Up, Prince, Wuthering Heights, Carrington, Saint-Ex, Velvet Goldmine (voice), Tumbleweeds (Academy Award nom.), Waking the Dead, Songcatcher, The King is Alive.
TELEVISION: *Movies*: Precious Bane, Portrait of a Marriage, Yellowbacks, A Masculine Ending, Don't Leave Me This Way, The Black Velvet Gown. *Series*: The Governor.

McTIERNAN, JOHN
Director. b. Albany, NY, Jan. 8, 1951. e. Juilliard (acting), SUNY/Old Westbury (filmmaking). m. prod. Donna Dubrow. First effort was film The Demon's Daughter, unreleased to date. Appeared in film Death of a Soldier.
PICTURES: Nomads (also s.p.), Predator, Die Hard, The Hunt for Red October, Medicine Man, Last Action Hero (also co-prod.), Die Hard With a Vengeance, The Thomas Crown Affair, The 13th Warrior, Rollerball, Basic.

MEADOWS, JAYNE
Actress. b. Wu Chang, China, Sept. 27, 1924. m. performer Steve Allen. Sister of deceased actress Audrey Meadows. Parents were Episcopal missionaries. Came to U.S. in 1931. Studied acting with Stella Adler, Lee Strasberg, David Craig. Made B'way debut in 1941 in Spring Again.
THEATRE: *NY*: Once in a Lifetime (revival), The Gazebo, Spring Again, Another Love Story, Kiss Them for Me, Many Happy Returns, Odds on Mrs. Oakley. *Regional*: Lost in Yonkers, Love Letters, Cinderella, The Fourposter, Tonight at 8:30, Powerful Women in History (1 woman show).
PICTURES: Undercurrent (debut, 1946), Dark Delusion, Lady in the Lake, Luck of the Irish, Song of the Thin Man, David and Bathsheba, Enchantment, Norman Is That You?, The Fat Man, College Confidential, Da Capo (Finland), City Slickers (voice), City Slickers II: The Legend of Curly's Gold (voice), The Player, Casino, The Story of Us.
TELEVISION: *Series*: Meeting of Minds, St. Elsewhere, Medical Center, I've Got a Secret, High Society, It's Not Easy, The Steve Allen Show, Art Linkletter Show, Steve Allen Comedy Hour, Steve Allen's Laugh Back. *Movies*: Alice in Wonderland, Alice Through the Looking Glass, Ten Speed and Brownshoe, Masterpiece of Murder, The Ratings Game, Miss All-American Beauty, The James Dean Story, Sex and the Married Woman, The Gossip Columnist, Parent Trap Hawaiian Honeymoon, Now You See It Now You Don't. *Guest*: Your Show of Shows, The Hollywood Palace, The Red Skelton Show, The Love Boat, Fantasy Island, The Paper Chase, Here's Lucy, Uncle Buck, Sisters, The Nanny, Murder She Wrote.

MEANEY, COLM
Actor. b. Ireland. Started acting as a teen, appearing at Gate Theatre in Dublin in play, The Hostage. Studied at Abbey Theatre then joined London's 7-84 Theatre Co., Half Moon Theatre Co., Belt and Braces touring co. On NY stage in Breaking the Code.
PICTURES: The Dead, Dick Tracy, Die Hard 2, Come See the Paradise, The Commitments, The Last of the Mohicans, Under Siege, Far and Away, Into the West, The Snapper (Golden Globe nom.), The Road to Wellville, The Englishman Who Went Up a Hill But Came Down a Mountain, The Van, The Last of the High Kings, Con Air, This is My Father, Snitch, October 22, Claire Dolan, Four Days, Chapter Zero, Mystery Alaska, Star Trek 3D, Most Important, How Harry Became a Tree, Backflash, Blueberry.
TELEVISION: *Series*: Star Trek: The Next Generation, Deep Space Nine, R.U.S./H. *Movies/Mini-Series*: Scarlett, Vig, Leprechauns, Random Passage, King of Texas.

MEANEY, DONALD V.
Executive. b. Newark, NJ. e. Rutgers U. Sch. of Journalism. Worked as reporter for Plainfield (NJ) Courier-News, Newark Evening News. Became news dir. of radio station WCTC in New Brunswick, NJ; later for WNJR, Newark. Joined NBC in 1952 as news writer; two years later became nat'l TV news editor. Promoted to mgr., national news, 1960 and mrg., special news programs, 1961. Appt. dir. of news programs 1962 and gen. mgr., NBC News, 1965; v.p., news programming, NBC, 1967; v.p. news, Washington, 1974; mng. dir., affiliate & intl. liaison, 1979; sr. mng. editor, intl. liaison, 1984; retired from NBC, 1985. Now on faculty of American U. Sch. of Communications.

MEARA, ANNE
Actress, Writer. b. Brooklyn, NY Sept. 20, 1929. m. actor-writer Jerry Stiller. Son is actor-dir. Ben Stiller; daughter is actress Amy Stiller. e. Herbert Berghof Studio, 1953-54. Apprenticed in summer stock on Long Island and Woodstock NY, 1950-53. Acted with NY Shakespeare Fest. 1957 and 1988 (Romeo and Juliet). With husband joined St. Louis improv. theater The Compass, 1959 and Chicago's Medium Fare. They formed comedy act in 1962 appearing (34 times) on The Ed Sullivan Show and making the nightclub and comedy club circuit incl. The Village Gate, The Blue Angel, The Establishment. Formed own prod. company, writing, prod. and recording award-winning radio and TV commercials. With husband co-hosted video, So You Want to Be an Actor?
THEATRE: A Month in the Country, Maedchen in Uniform, Ulysses in Nightown, The House of Blue Leaves, Spookhouse, Bosoms and Neglect, Eastern Standard, Anna Christie (Tony nom.), After-Play (also author, Outer Critics Circle Award, 1996).
PICTURES: The Out-of-Towners, Lovers and Other Strangers, Nasty Habits, The Boys From Brazil, Fame, The Perils of P.K., The Longshot, My Little Girl, Awakenings, Highway to Hell, Reality Bites, Heavyweights, Kiss of Death, An Open Window, The Daytrippers, Brass Ring, Fish in the Bathtub, Brooklyn Thrill Killers, The Indepedent, Chump Change, Amy Stiller's Breast, Zoolander, Get Well Soon, Crooked Lines, Like Mike, The Yard Sale.
TELEVISION: Guest on numerous TV game and talk shows and variety shows. *Series*: The Greatest Gift (1954 soap opera), The Paul Lynde Show, The Corner Bar, Take Five with Stiller and Meara (1977-78; synd.), Kate McShane, Rhoda, Archie Bunker's Place, ALF, All My Children. *Movies*: Kate McShane (pilot), The Other Woman (co-writer), Jitters, What Makes a Family. *Specials*: The Sunset Gang, Avenue Z Afternoon.

MECHANIC, WILLIAM M.
Executive. V.p. & Head of Programming, Select TV Programming, Inc., 1978-82. v.p., pay TV & post-theatrical markets, Paramount; senior creative exec., Paramount Pictures; senior v.p. & v.p., pay TV sales, Walt Disney Co., 1984; president, Intl. Distribution & Worldwide Video, Walt Disney Studios, where he set up Buena Vista Intl;. president & COO, Twentieth Century Fox, 1993; president & COO, Fox Filmed Entertainment, 1994-96. Chairman & CEO, Fox Filmed Entertainment, where he oversees all operations including worldwide feature film production, marketing, and distribution, and all worldwide operations for Fox Video, Fox Interactive, Licensing & Merchandising, and Fox Music. Resigned June, 2000. Set up own production co., Pandemonium Films which has a five year deal, 2002-2007, with Disney.

MEDAK, PETER
Director. b. Budapest, Hungary, Dec. 23, 1940. Appeared in film Beverly Hills Cop III.
THEATRE: Miss Julie. Operas: Salome, La Voix Humaine, Rigoletto.
PICTURES: Negatives, A Day in the Death of Joe Egg, The Ruling Class, Ghost in the Noonday Sun, The Odd Job, The Changeling, Zorro the Gay Blade, The Men's Club, The Krays, Let Him Have It, Romeo Is Bleeding, Pontiac Moon, Species 2, Understanding Virginia.
TELEVISION: Third Girl from the Left, The Babysitter, The Dark Secret of Black Bayou, Mistress of Paradise, Cry for the Stranger, Faerie Tale Theatre, Twilight Zone, Nabokov, Crime Story, Mount Royal, La Voix Humaine, Tales From the Crypt, Homicide, Homicide, The Hunchback of Notre Dame, Law and Order: SVU, David Copperfield, Feast of All Saints.

MEDAVOY, MIKE
Executive. b. Shanghai, China, Jan. 21, 1941. e. UCLA, grad. 1963 with honors in history. Lived in China until 1947 when family moved to Chile. Came to U.S. in 1957. Started working in mail room at Universal Studios and became a casting dir., then went to work for Bill Robinson as an agent trainee. Two years later joined GAC and CMA where he was a v.p. in the m. p. dept. 1971 joined IFA as v.p. in charge of m. p. dept. Represented American and foreign creative talents, incl. Jane Fonda, Donald Sutherland, Michelangelo Antonioni, Jean-Louis Trintignant, Karel Reisz, Steven Spielberg, Robert Aldrich, George Cukor, John Milius, Terry Malick, Raquel Welch, Gene Wilder and Jeanne Moreau. While at IFA was involved in packaging The Sting, Young Frankenstein, Jaws and others, before joining United Artists Corp. in 1974, as sr. v.p. in chg. of West Coast prod. While at UA, was responsible for One Flew Over the Cuckoo's Nest, Annie Hall and Rocky among others. 1978 named exec. v.p., Orion Pictures Co. where he was responsible for Platoon, Amadeus, Dances With Wolves and Silence of the Lambs. (In 1982 Orion team took over Filmways, Inc.). 1990, apptd. chmn. Tri-Star Pictures, & mem. Columbia Pictures Bd. of Dir. Resigned in 1994. Became chmn. and CEO of Phoenix Pictures in 1995. Co-chmn., St. Petersburg Film Festival, 1994. Chmn. of the Jury, Tokyo Film Festival, 1994. Member of Filmex d.; bd. of trustees, UCLA Foundation; chmn. advisory bd., College for Intl. Strategic Affairs at UCLA; steering comm. of Royce 270, UCLA; visiting comm., Boston Museum of Fine Arts; advisory bd., Tel Aviv U.; bd., Museum of Science & Industry; Co-Chmn.: Olympic Sports Federation, Music Center Unified Fund Campaign; founding bd. of governors, Sundance Inst. Recipient: Motion Picture Pioneer Award, 1993; Cannes Film Festival Award, 1998; UCLA Alumni Award for Excellence.

MEDOFF, MARK
Writer. e. U. of Miami, Stanford U. Honorary doctor of humane letters, Gallaudet Univ. Prof. & dramatist in residence, New Mexico St. Univ. Novel: Dreams of Long Ladies.
THEATRE: When You Comin' Back Red Ryder? (Obie Award), Children of a Lesser God (Tony Award), The Wager, Kringle's Window.
PICTURES: Good Guys Wear Black, Children of a Lesser God (Acad. Award nom.), Clara's Heart, City of Joy, Homage (also prod.), Santa Fe, Mighty Joe Young.
TELEVISION: Movie: Apology, The Twilight of the Golds..

MEDWIN, MICHAEL
Actor, Writer, Producer. b. London, England, 1923. e. Institut Fischer, Switzerland. Stage debut 1940; m.p. acting debut in Root of All Evil, 1946. Acted with National Theatre 1977-78.
THEATRE: Spring and Port Wine, Joe Egg, Forget-me-not Lane, Chez Nous, Alpha Beta, Another Country, Crystal Clear, Interpreters, Orpheus, Noises Off.
PICTURES: Actor: My Sister and I, Mrs. Christopher, Gay One, Children of Chance, Operation Diamond, Black Memory, Just William's Luck, Ideal Husband, Picadilly Incident, Night Beat, Courtney's of Curzon Street, Call of the Blood, Anna Karenina, William Comes to Town, Woman Hater, Look Before You Love, Forbidden, For Them That Trespass, Queen of Spades, Trottie True, Boys in Brown, Trio, Long Dark Hall, Curtain Up, Street Corner, I Only Asked, Carry on Nurse, Wind Cannot Read, Heart of a Man, Crooks Anonymous, It's All Happening, Night Must Fall, I've Gotta Horse, 24 Hours To Kill, Scrooge, The Jigsaw

Man, Fanny and Elvis. Prod.: Charlie Bubbles, If..., Spring and Port Wine, O Lucky Man! Gumshoe, Law and Disorder, Memoirs of a Survivor, Diamond's Edge.
TELEVISION: Granada's Army Game, Shoestring, The Love of Mike, Three Live Wires.

MEIER, JIM
Executive. b. Newport Beach, CA, Aug. 9, 1971. Pres., Meier Entertainment Group, Vancouver, BC, 1994-98. Dir., British Columbia Motion Picture Assoc., 1996-98. Member, Academy of Canadian Cinema and Television. Pres., CEO and Chairman, Meier Worldwide Intermedia, Inc., 1996-.

MELCHIOR, IB
Director, Writer. b. Copenhagen, Denmark, Sept. 17, 1917. Son of late singer Lauritz Melchior. e. Coll., Stenhus, Denmark, 1936; U. of Copenhagen, 1937. Actor. stage mgr., English Players, 1937-38; co-dir. 1938; actor in 21 stage prod. in Europe and U.S. on radio; set designer; stage man. dept., Radio City Music Hall, 1941-42; U.S. Military Intelligence, 1942-45; writer, dir., m.p. shorts for TV, 1947-48; TV actor, 1949-50; assoc. dir., CBS-TV, 1950; assoc. prod., G-L Enterprises, 1952-53; dir., Perry Como Show, 1951-54; dir. March of Medicine, 1955-56. Documentary writ. & dir., received Top Award by Nat'l. Comm. for Films for Safety, 1960. Golden Scroll Award, Acad. of Science Fiction, Best Writing, 1976; Hamlet Award, Shakespeare Society of America, excellence in playwriting, Hour of Vengeance, 1982.
AUTHOR: Order of Battle, Sleeper Agent, The Haigerloch Project, The Watchdogs of Abaddon, The Marcus Device, The Tombstone Cipher, Eva, V-3, Code Name: Grand Guignol, Steps & Stairways, Quest, Order of Battle: Hitler's Werewolves, Case by Case.
PICTURES: Writer: When Hell Broke Loose, Live Fast—Die Young, The Angry Red Planet (also dir.), The Case of Patty Smith (assoc. prod.), Reptilicus, Journey to the Seventh Planet, Robinson Crusoe on Mars, The Time Travellers (also dir.), Ambush Bay, Planet of the Vampires, Death Race 2000.

MELNICK, DANIEL
Executive. b. New York, NY, April 21, 1934. e. NYU. 1952-54, prod. The Children's Theatre at Circle in the Sq., NY. In 1954 was (youngest) staff prod. for CBS-TV; then exec. prod., East Side West Side and N.Y.P.D. Joined ABC-TV as v.p. in chg. of programming. Partner in Talent Associates. Joined MGM as v.p. in chg. of prod.; in 1974 named sr. v.p. & worldwide head of prod.; 1977 in charge of worldwide production, Columbia Pictures; named pres., 1978. Resigned to form independent production co., IndieProd. Company.
PICTURES: Prod.: Straw Dogs, That's Entertainment (exec. prod.), That's Entertainment Part 2, All That Jazz (exec. prod.), Altered States (exec. prod.), First Family, Making Love, Unfaithfully Yours (exec. prod.), Footloose (exec. prod.), Quicksilver, Roxanne, Punchline, Mountains of the Moon, Total Recall, Air America, L.A. Story, Universal Soldier: The Return, Blue Streak.
TELEVISION: Specials: Death of a Salesman (prod.; Emmy Award, 1967), The Ages of Man (prod.; Emmy Award, 1966). Exec. prod.: East Side/West Side, N.Y.P.D., Get Smart, Chain Letter (pilot, exec. prod.). Movie: Get Smart Again!

MELNIKER, BENJAMIN
Producer, Attorney. b. Bayonne, NJ. e. Brooklyn Coll., LL.B., Fordham Law Sch. Loew's Theatres usher; private law practice. Employed by Legal Department MGM; v.p. & gen. counsel, 1954-69; exec. v.p., 1968-70; resigned from MGM, 1971; also member MGM bd. of dirs. and mem. MGM exec. com. Pres., & CEO of Jerry Lewis Cinemas, 1972. Prod. & exec. prod. motion pictures and television movies and series, 1974 to present. Adjunct assoc. prof., NY Law Sch., 1976-77. Former m.p. chmn. Anti-Defamation League, B'nai Brith. Mem. Amer., NY State bar assns., Bar Assn. of City NY, AMPAS.
PICTURES: Winter Kills. Exec. prod.: Mitchell, Shoot, Batman, Batman Returns, Batman Forever, Batman & Robin, Batman: Year One. Producer: Swamp Thing. The Return of the Swamp Thing, Batman: Mask of the Phantasm.
TELEVISION: Exec. prod.:Three Sovereigns for Sarah, Television's Greatest Hits, Where On Earth Is Carmen Sandiego (Emmy Award), Little Orphan Annie's Very Animated Christmas, Swamp Thing, Harmful Intent, Fish Police, Dinosaucers, Doomsday.

MELVIN, MURRAY
Actor. b. London, England, 1932. On stage with Theatre Workshop.
PICTURES: The Criminal (debut, 1960), A Taste of Honey, HMS Defiant (Damn the Defiant), Sparrows Can't Sing, The Ceremony, Alfie, Kaleidoscope, Smashing Time, The Fixer, Start the Revolution Without Me, A Day in the Death of Joe Egg, The Devils, The Boy Friend, Ghost in the Noonday Sun, Barry Lyndon, The Bawdy Adventures of Tom Jones, Joseph Andrews, Comrades, Testimony, Little Dorrit, The Krays, Let Him Have It, Princess Caraboo, England My England, The Emperor's New Clothes.
TELEVISION: Little World of Don Camillo, The Soldiers Tale, A Christmas Carol, This Office Life, Bulman, William Tell, Stuff of

Madness, Sunday Pursuit, The Memorandum, The Stone of Montezuma, Surprises, England My England, The Village, Prisoner of Honor, Doomsday Gun, Alice in Wonderland, David Copperfield.

MENDES, SAM
Director. England, UK, August 1, 1965. Runs the Donmar Warehouse in London.
PICTURES: American Beauty (Academy Award), Road to Perdition.

MENGES, CHRIS
Cinematographer, Director. b. Kington, England, Sept. 15, 1940.
PICTURES: *Cinematographer*: Kes, Gumshoe, The Empire Strikes Back (second unit), Local Hero, Comfort and Joy, The Killing Fields (Acad. Award, 1984), Marie, The Mission (Acad. Award, 1986), Singing the Blues in Red, Shy People, High Season, Michael Collins (LA Film Critics Award, 1997), The Boxer, The Pledge, The Honest Thief, Dirty Pretty Things. *Director*: A World Apart, Crisscross, Second Best, The Lost Son.
TELEVISION: World in Action, Opium Warlords, Opium Trail, East 103rd Street.

MENKEN, ALAN
Composer. b. New York, NY, July 22, 1949. Raised in New Rochelle, NY. e. NYU. Began composing and performing at Lehman Engel Musical Theatre Workshop at BMI, where he met future partner, lyricist Howard Ashman. With Ashman made Off-B'way debut in 1979 with score of God Bless You Mr. Rosewater. Wrote music for workshop Battle of the Giants, and music and lyrics for Manhattan Theatre Club Prod. of Real Life Funnies. With Ashman wrote 1982 Off-B'way hit Little Shop of Horrors. Other theatre credits include: The Apprenticeship of Duddy Kravitz, Diamonds, Personals, Let Freedom Sing, Weird Romance, Beauty and the Beast, A Christmas Carol. Grammy Awards: The Little Mermaid (2), Beauty and the Beast (3), Aladdin (4), Pocahontas (1).
PICTURES: Little Shop of Horrors (Acad. Award nom. for song Mean Green Mother From Outer Space), The Little Mermaid (2 Acad. Awards: best song, Under the Sea, and music score, 1989), Rocky V (song), Beauty and the Beast (2 Acad. Awards: best song, title song, and music score, 1991), Newsies, Aladdin (2 Acad. Awards: for song, A Whole New World, and music score, 1992), Home Alone 2: Lost in New York (song), Life With Mikey, Pocahontas (Acad. Awards for Best Score & Best Original Song), The Hunchback of Notre Dame, Hercules, Little Mermaid II: Return to the Sea.
TELEVISION: *Special*: Lincoln. *Movie*: Polly (song). *Series*: Hercules.

MENZEL, JIRI
Actor, Director. b. Prague, Czechoslovakia, Feb. 23, 1938.
PICTURES: *Actor*: Defendant, Kdyby tisic klarinetu, Everday Courage, Closely Watched Trains, Return of the Prodigal Son, Soukroma vichrie, Hotel pro ciznice, Dita Saxova, Capricious Summer, The Cremator, Sechse kommen durch die ganze Welt, 30 panen a Pythagoras, The Apple Game, The Blue Planet, Magicians of the Silverscreen, Miniden szerdain, Koportos, Upir z Feratu, Szivzur, Buldoci a tresme, Srdecny pozdrav ze zemek-oule, Fandy, O Fandy, Albert, Utekajme, uzide, Hard Bodies, Tender Barbarians, Larks on a String, The Elementary School, Long Conversation with a Bird, Everything I Like, The Little Apocalypse, Joint Venture, Vengeance is Mine, Jak si zaslouziat princeznu, Truck Stop, Every Sunday, Hannah's Ragtime, Velvet Hangover. *Director;* Domy z panleu, Umrel nam pan Forester, Crime at the Girls School, Pearls of the Deep, Koncert 65, Closely Watched Trains, Capricious Summer, Zlocin v santanu, Promeny krajiny, Who Looks for Gold?, Seclusion Near A Forest, Magicians of the Silverscreen, Short Cut, Krasosmutneni, The Snowdrop Festival, My Sweet Little Village, Die Schokladenschnuffler, Prague, The End of Old Times, Larks on a String, The Beggar's Opera, Life and Extraordinary Adventures of Private Ivan Chonkin, Ten Minutes Older: The Cello.

MERCHANT, ISMAIL
Producer, Director. b. Bombay, India, Dec. 25, 1936. e. St. Xavier's Coll., Bombay; NYU, M.A. business admin. Formed Merchant Ivory Prods., 1961 with James Ivory. First film, The Creation of Women (theatrical short, 1961, nom. for Acad. Award). Published 3 cookbooks. Other books: Hullabaloo in Old Jeypore: The Making of The Deceivers (1989), The Proprietor: The Screenplay and Story Behind the Film.
PICTURES: *Producer*: The Householder, Shakespeare Wallah, The Guru, Bombay Talkie, Savages, Autobiography of a Princess, The Wild Party, Roseland, Hullabaloo Over Georgie and Bonnie's Pictures, The Europeans, Jane Austen in Manhattan, Quartet, Heat and Dust, The Bostonians, A Room With a View, Maurice, My Little Girl (exec. prod.), The Deceivers, Slaves of New York, The Perfect Murder (exec. prod.), Mr. and Mrs. Bridge, Ballad of the Sad Cafe, Howards End (BAFTA Award), The Remains of the Day, In Custody (dir. debut), Jefferson in Paris (also cameo), Feast of July (exec. prod.), The

Proprietor (dir.), Surviving Picasso, Side Streets, Gaach, A Soldier's Daughter Never Cries, The Mystic Masseur (dir. only), Cotton Mary, The Golden Bowl, Le Divorce.
TELEVISION: *Director*: Mahatma and the Mad Boy, Courtesans of Bombay.

MEREDITH, ANNE
Writer, Producer.
PICTURES: Losing Chase, Bastard Out of Carolina (writer only, Writers' Guild Award, 1998), Rated X.
TELEVISION: Gisella Perl.

MERHIGE, E. ELIAS
Director. b. Brooklyn, NY, 1964. r.n. Edmund Elias Merhige.
PICTURES: Implosion, Spring Rain, A Taste of Youth, Begotten (also prod.,s.p.,photog.), Shadow of the Vampire (numerous film festival awards).

MERRILL, DINA
Actress. r.n. Nedenia Hutton. b. New York, NY, Dec. 29, 1928. Fashion model, 1944-46. A co-owner and vice-chmn., RKO Pictures, m.p. and TV prod. co.
THEATER: *B'way*: Angel Street, Are You Now or Have You Ever Been?, On Your Toes.
PICTURES: The Desk Set (debut, 1957), A Nice Little Bank That Should Be Robbed, Don't Give Up the Ship, Operation Petticoat, The Sundowners, Butterfield 8, Twenty Plus Two, The Young Savages, The Courtship of Eddie's Father, I'll Take Sweden, Running Wild, The Meal, The Greatest, A Wedding, Just Tell Me What You Want, Twisted, Caddyshack II, True Colors, The Player, Open Season, The Point of Betrayal, Milk & Money, Mighty Joe Young.
TELEVISION: *Debut:* Kate Smith Show 1956. *Guest*: Four Star Theatre, Playwrights '56, Climax!, Playhouse 90, Westing-house Presents, The Investigators, Checkmate, The Rogues, Bob Hope Presents, To Tell the Truth, The Doctors, The Name of the Game, Hotel, Hawaii Five-O, Murder She Wrote, Something Wilder, The Nanny, Rosanne. *Series*: Hot Pursuit. *Mini-Series*: Roots: The Next Generations. *Movies*: The Sunshine Patriot, Seven in Darkness, The Lonely Profession, Mr. & Mrs. Bo Jo Jones, Family Flight, The Letters, Kingston: The Power Play, The Tenth Month, Repeat Performance, Turn Back the Clock, Fear, Brass Ring, Anne to the Infinite, Not in My Family, Something Borrowed Something Blue, A Chance of Snow, The Glow, The Magnificent Ambersons.

MERSON, MARC
Producer. b. New York, NY, Sept. 9, 1931. e. Swarthmore Coll. Entered Navy in 1953; assigned as publicist to Admiral's Staff of Sixth Fleet Command in the Mediterranean. Upon discharge joined trade paper Show Business as feature editor. Joined CBS-TV as asst. to casting dir.. Left after 3 yrs. to work for Ely Landau as casting dir., packager and sometime prod. of The Play of the Week on TV. Returned to CBS for 3-yr. stint doing specials and live programs. Left to organize Brownstone Productions as indep. prod. Partner with Alan Alda in Helix Productions to package and produce TV shows. PICTURES: The Heart Is a Lonely Hunter, People Soup (short), Leadbelly, Doc Hollywood (exec. prod.).
TELEVISION: *Series*: Kaz, We'll Get By, Off the Rack, Jessica Novak, Waverly Wonders, Stage 67, Androcles and the Lion, Dummler and Son (pilot), The David Frost Revue (synd. series), We'll Get By. *Movie*: Rules of Marriage (spr. prod.).

MESSIER, JEAN MARIE
Executive. b. Grenoble, France, Dec. 13, 1956. e. Ecole Polytechnique, Ecole Nationale d'Adiministration. Began career as Inspecteur des Finances for the French Ministry of Economy and Finance (1982-1986). Then head of the cabinet of Camille Cabana, Deputy Minister in charge of the Privatization pro-gram.1986 to 1988, served as Advisor to Edouard Balladur, Minster of Economy, Finance and Privatization at the time. 1989, General Partner of the investment bank Lazard Frères et Cie. Joined Compagnie Générale des Eaux (renamed Vivendi in 1998) in Nov. 1994, as CEO and chmn. Chmn. & CEO, Vivendi, 1996-2000; then Vivendi Universal, 2001-2002. Stepped down, July, 2002. Member of the Board of Directors of Alcatel, BNP-Paribas, Cegetel, Compagnie de Saint-Gobain, LVMH-Moët Hennessy Louis Vuitton, the New York Stock Exchange, UGC, USA Networks, the Whitney Museum (New York) and is Chairman of the Supervisory Board of Canal +. Chevalier de la Légion d'Honneur.

MESTRES, RICARDO A. III
Executive. b. New York, NY, Jan. 23, 1958. e. Harvard U., A.B. 1980. Gained filmmaking experience during summers as prod. asst. on TV features. Joined Paramount Pictures as creative exec. 1981. Promoted to exec. dir. of production in 1982 and to v.p., prod. in 1984. Named v.p. of prod., Walt Disney Pictures, 1985. Promoted to sr. v.p., prod.,1986-88. Named pres. production, Touchstone Pictures, 1988-89. In 1989, became pres., Hollywood Pictures. Resigned, 1994. Co-founder Great Oaks Entertainment with John Hughes, 1995-1997. Principal Ricardo Mestres Productions associated with Disney, 1997-present. Member, AMPAS.

PICTURES: *Prod.*: Jack, 101 Dalmatians, Flubber, Home Alone III, Reach the Rock, The Visitors, The Hunted.

METCALF, LAURIE
Actress. b. Edwardsville, IL, June 16, 1955. e. Illinois St. Univ. One of the original members of the Steppenwolf Theatre Company. On B'way in My Thing of Love.
PICTURES: Desperately Seeking Susan (debut, 1985), Making Mr. Right, Candy Mountain, Stars and Bars, Miles From Home, Uncle Buck, Internal Affairs, Pacific Heights, JFK, Mistress, A Dangerous Woman, Blink, Leaving Las Vegas, Dear God, U Turn, Scream 2, Chicago Cab, Bulworth, Runaway Bride, Toy Story 2 (voice), Timecode.
TELEVISION: *Series*: Roseanne (3 Emmy Awards: 1992-4), Norm, God the Devil and Bob. *Movies*: The Execution of Raymond Graham, Balloon Farm, Always Outnumbered, The Long Island Incident.

METZLER, JIM
Actor. b. Oneonta, NY, June 23, 1951. e. Dartmouth Coll.
PICTURES: Four Friends, Tex, River's Edge, Hot to Trot, Sundown: The Vampire in Retreat, 976-EVIL, Old Gringo, Circuitry Man, Delusion, One False Move, Waxwork II: Lost in Time, A Weekend with Barbara und Ingrid, Gypsy Eyes, C.I.A. Trackdown, Plughead Rewired: Circuitry Man II, Children of the Corn III: Urban Harvest, Cadillac Ranch, A Gun A Car A Blonde, L.A. Confidential, St Patrick's Day, Under the Influence, Phantom Town, Warm Texas Rain, A Gun A Car A Blonde, Big Brass Ring, Bad City Blues, The Doe Boy, Megiddo: The Omega Code 2, What Matters Most, Under the Influence.
TELEVISION: *Series*: Cutter to Houston, The Best Times. *Mini-Series*: North and South, North and South Book II, On Wings of Eagles. *Movies*: Do You Remember Love, Princess Daisy, Christmas Star, The Alamo: 13 Days to Glory, The Little Match Girl, Murder By Night, Crash: The Mystery of Flight 1501, Love Kills, French Silk, Don't Look Back, Apollo 11, Little Girls in Pretty Boxes, A Wing and a Prayer, Hefner: Unauthorized, Witness Protection.

MEYER, BARRY M.
Executive. b. New York, NY, Nov. 28, 1943. e. B.A., U. of Rochester, J.D., Case Western Reserve U. School of Law. Began in legal & business affairs, ABC Television Network, 1968; director, Business Affairs, 1971; v.p., Business Affairs, 1972, Warner Bros. Television; exec. v.p., Television Division, Warner Bros., 1978; exec. v.p., Warner Bros., Inc., 1984, in charge of all television operations. Became CEO, Warner Bros., Inc., 1994. Named chairman & CEO, Warner Bros., 1999. Currently member and former Governor, Academy of Television Arts & Sciences; member and past board member, Hollywood Radio & Television Society; member, Academy of Motion Picture Arts & Sciences; member, Board of Councilors, USC School of Cinema-Television; member of the board, Museum of Radio & Television; member, Board of Directors, City National Corp. and City National Bank; involved in various charitable and community service activities.

MEYER, BRECKIN
Actor. b. Minneapolis, MN, May 7, 1974.
PICTURES: Freddy's Dead: The Final Nightmare, Payback, Clueless, The Craft, Escape from L.A., Prefontaine, Touch, Dancer Texas Pop. 81, Can't Hardly Wait, 54, Go, The Insider, Tail Lights Fade, Road Trip, Josie and the Pussycats, Rat Race, Kate & Leopold, Old School.
TELEVISION: *Movies*: Camp Cucamonga, Betrayed: A Story of Three Women. *Series*: The Jackie Thomas Show, The Home Court, King of the Hill, Rocky Times, The Near Future, Inside Schwartz. *Guest*: The Wonder Years, Clueless, Party of Five.

MEYER, NICHOLAS
Director, Writer. b. New York, NY, Dec. 24, 1945. e. U. of Iowa. Was unit publicist for Love Story, 1969. Story ed. Warner Bros. 1970-71.
AUTHOR: The Love Story Story, The Seven Percent Solution, Target Practice, The West End Horror, Black Orchid, Confession of a Homing Pigeon, The Canary Trainer.
PICTURES: The Seven Percent Solution (s.p.), Time After Time (s.p., dir.), Star Trek II: The Wrath of Khan (dir.), Volunteers (dir.), The Deceivers (dir.), Company Business (dir., s.p.) Star Trek VI: The Undiscovered Country (dir., co-s.p.), Sommersby (co-s.p.), Voices, The Informant, The Prince of Egypt, The Human Stain, Collateral Damage (exec. prod. only).
TELEVISION: *Movies*: Judge Dee (writer), The Night That Panicked America (writer), The Day After (dir.), Fall From the Sky.

MEYER, RON
Executive. b. 1945. Served in U.S. Marine Corps. Agent with William Morris. 1975, co-founded with Mike Ovitz, Creative Artists talent agency, eventually serving as pres. 1995, appointed pres. & COO of Universal Studios, now Vivendi Universal Entertainment..

MEYER, RUSS
Producer, Director. b. Oakland, CA, March 21, 1922. In 1942 joined Army Signal Corps, learned m.p. photography and shot combat newsreels. Worked as photographer for Playboy Magazine. Pres., RM Films Intl. Inc. 3 vol. autobiography: A Clean Breast: The Life and Loves of Russ Meyer.
PICTURES: The Immoral Mr. Teas, Eve and the Handyman, Erotica, Wild Gals of the Naked West, Heavenly Bodies, Lorna, Motor Psycho, Fanny Hill, Mudhoney, Mondo Topless, Faster Pussycat Kill Kill, Finders Keepers Lovers Weepers, Goodmorning and Goodbye, Common Law Cabin, Vixen, Cherry Harry & Raquel, Beyond the Valley of the Dolls, The Seven Minutes, Black Snake, Supervixens, Up, Beneath the Valley of the Ultra Vixens, Amazon Women on the Moon (actor), Pandora Peaks, Europe In the Raw!, Melissa Mounds, others.

MEYERS, NANCY
Writer, Producer. b. Philadelphia, PA. e. American U., D.C. Began as story editor for Ray Stark. First teamed with Charles Shyer to write screenplay for Private Benjamin.
PICTURES: *Writer/Producer*: Private Benjamin (Acad. Award nom., Writers Guild Annual Award), Irreconcilable Differences, Baby Boom, Father of the Bride, I Love Trouble, Father of Bride II, The Parent Trap, What Women Want, The Affair of the Necklace (exec. prod. only). *Director*: The Parent Trap, What Women Want.

MEYERS, ROBERT
Executive. b. Mount Vernon, NY, Oct. 3, 1934. e. NYU. Entered m.p. industry as exec. trainee in domestic div. of Columbia Pictures, 1956; sales and adv. 1956-60; transferred to sales dept. Columbia Pictures Int'l, NY: posts there included supervisor of int'l roadshows and exec. assistant. to continental mgr. Joined National General Pictures as v.p.-foreign sales, 1969. Created JAD Films International Inc. in Feb. 1974 for independent selling and packaging of films around the world. September, 1977, joined Lorimar Productions Inc. as sr. v.p. of Lorimar Distribution Intl. Became pres. in 1978. Joined Filmways Pictures in 1980, named pres. & COO. Pres. of American Film Mktg. Assn.; 1982, formed new co., R.M. Films International. Rejoined Lorimar 1985. as pres., Lorimar Motion Pictures, int'l distribution. 1988-92, pres., Orion Pictures Int'l. 1993-94, pres., Odyssey Entertainment. In 1995, joined Village Roadshow International as pres.

MICHAELS, JOEL B.
Producer. b. Buffalo, NY, Oct. 24, 1938. Studied acting with Stella Adler. Many co-prods. with Garth Drabinsky, Cineplex Corp. Pres. of Cineplex Odeon, 1986-90.
PICTURES: The Peace Killers, Your Three Minutes Are Up (prod. spvr.), Student Teachers (prod. spvr.), The Prisoners (assoc. prod.), Lepke (assoc. prod.), The Four Deuces (assoc. prod.), Bittersweet Love, The Silent Partner, The Changeling, Tribute, The Amateur, Losin' It (exec. prod.), The Philadelphia Experiment, Black Moon Rising, Universal Soldier, Three of Hearts (exec. prod.), Stargate, Cutthroat Island (co-prod.), Last of the Dogmen, Lolita, Terminator 3: Rise of the Machines.

MICHAELS, LORNE
Writer, Producer. b. Toronto, Canada, Nov. 17, 1944. e. U. of Toronto, 1966. CEO, Broadway Video, since 1979. Named B'caster of the Year by the International Radio and TV Society, 1992.
THEATRE: Gilda Radner Live From New York (prod., dir.).
PICTURES: *Producer*: Gilda Live (also co-s.p.), Nothing Lasts Forever, Three Amigos (also co-s.p.), Wayne's World, Coneheads, Wayne's World 2, Lassie, Tommy Boy, Stuart Saves His Family, Black Sheep, Kids In the Hall: Brain Candy, A Night at the Roxbury, The Ladies Man, Enigma.
TELEVISION: *Series*: Rowan and Martin's Laugh-In (writer, 1968-69), Saturday Night Live (creator, prod., writer: 1975-80, 4 Emmy Awards; 1985-), The New Show (prod.), The Kids in the Hall (series co-prod.), Late Night With Conan O'Brien (exec. prod.), The Colin Quinn Show. *Specials*: Lily Tomlin Specials (writer, prod.: 1972-75, 2 Emmy Awards), Perry Como (writer, prod., 1974), Flip Wilson (writer, prod.), Beach Boys (writer, prod., 1978), The Rutles: All You Need Is Cash (writer, prod.), Steve Martin's Best Show Ever (prod.), Simon and Garfunkel: The Concert in the Park (exec. prod.), The Coneheads (exec. prod.), 1988 Emmy Awards (prod.), Coca-Cola Presents Live: The Hard Rock, On Location: Kids in the Hall (exec. prod.), The Rolling Stones: Steel Wheels Concert (exec. prod.), Paul Simon: Born at the Right Time in Central Park (exec. prod.), various Saturday Night Live specials. *Movie*: The Rutles 2: Can't Buy Me Lunch.

MICHAELS, RICHARD
Director. b. Brooklyn, NY, Feb. 15, 1936. e. Cornell U. Script supervisor 1955-64 and associate prod. before starting directing career in 1968 with Bewitched (54 episodes; also assoc. prod.).
PICTURES: How Come Nobody's On Our Side?, Blue Skies Again.
TELEVISION: *Series*: Love American Style, The Odd Couple, Delvecchio, Ellery Queen, Room 222. *Movies*: Once an Eagle (mini-series), Charlie Cobb, Having Babies II, Leave Yesterday Behind, My Husband Is Missing, ... And Your Name Is Jonah (winner, Christopher Award), Once Upon a Family, The Plutonium Incident, Scared Straight, Another Story (Scott Newman Drug Abuse Prevention Award), Homeward Bound

(Banff Intl. TV Fest. Special Jury Award & Christopher Award), Berlin Tunnel 21, The Children Nobody Wanted, One Cooks, The Other Doesn't, Jessie (pilot), Silence of the Heart, Heart of a Champion: The Ray Mancini Story, Rockabye, Kay O'Brien (pilot), Leg Work (pilot), Red River (movie), Indiscreet, Love and Betrayal, Her Wicked Ways, Leona Helmsley: The Queen of Mean, Triumph of the Heart: The Ricky Bell Story, Backfield in Motion, Miss America: Behind the Crown, Father and Scout. *Mini-series*: Sadat, I'll Take Manhattan.

MICHEL, WERNER
Executive. e. U. of Berlin, U. of Paris, Ph.D., Sorbonne, 1931. Radio writer, dir., co-author two Broadway revues, 1938, 1940. Broadcast dir., Voice of America, 1942-46. Prod. & dir., CBS, 1946-48; asst. prog. dir., CBS, 1948-50. Prod. Ford TV Theatre, 1950-52 Prod. DuMont TV network, 1952-55. Dir. Electronicam TV-Film Prod., 1955-56. Prod. of Edge of Night, Procter and Gamble, 1956-57. V.P. & dir., TV-radio dept., Reach, McClinton Advertising, Inc., 1957-62. Consultant, TV Programming & Comm'l-Prod., N.W. Ayer & Son Inc. V.P. & dir., TV dept., SSCB Advertising, 1963. Program exec. at ABC-TV Hollywood, 1975. Sr. v.p. of creative affairs, MGM-TV, 1977. Exec. v.p., Wrather Entertainment Intl., 1979. Returned to MGM-TV as sr. v.p., creative affairs, 1980-82. COO, Guber-Peters TV, 1982-84. Sr. v.p., corporate TV dept., Kenyon & Eckhart, & NY, 1984-86. Currently sr. v.p., sr. partner of TV dept., Bozell, Inc. NY.

MICHELL, KEITH
Actor. b. Adelaide, Australia, Dec. 1, 1926. Early career as art teacher, radio actor; toured Australia with Stratford Shakespearean Co. 1952-53; Stratford Memorial Theatre 1954-55, Old Vic Theatre 1956-57. Served as artistic dir., Chichester Festival Theatre, touring Australia.
PICTURES: True as a Turtle, Dangerous Exile, Gypsy and the Gentleman, The Hellfire Club, All Night Long, Seven Seas to Calais, Prudence and the Pill, House of Cards, Henry VIII and his Six Wives, Moments, The Deceivers, The Tales of Helpmann.
TELEVISION: *U.K.*: Pygmalion, Act of Violence, Mayerling Affair, Wuthering Heights, The Bergonzi Hand, Ring Round The Moon, Spread of the Eagle, The Shifting Heart, Loyalties, Julius Caesar, Antony and Cleopatra, Kain, The Ideal Husband, The Six Wives of Henry VIII (series), Dear Love, Captain Beaky & His Band, Captain Beaky, Volume 2, The Gondoliers, The Pirates of Penzance, Ruddigore. *U.S.*: Story of the Marlboroughs, Jacob and Joseph, Story of David, The Tenth Month, The Day Christ Died, The Miracle, Murder She Wrote. *Australia: Series*: My Brother Tom, Captain James Cook.

MIDLER, BETTE
Actress, Singer. b. Honolulu, HI, Dec. 1, 1945. e. U. of Hawaii. Studied acting at Berghof Studios. Appeared on B'way in Fiddler on the Roof, Salvation; also in Tommy with Seattle Opera Co., 1971. Gained fame as singer-comic in nightclubs and cabarets. Has toured extensively with own stage shows: The Divine Miss M, Clams on the Half-Shell, Divine Madness, Art of Bust, Experience the Divine. Grammy Awards: The Divine Miss M, The Rose, Blueberry Pie (from In Harmony), Wind Beneath My Wings. *Author*: A View From a Broad, The Saga of Baby Divine. Special Tony Award, 1973.
PICTURES: Hawaii (debut, 1966), The Rose (Acad. Award nom.; 2 Golden Globe Awards), Divine Madness, Jinxed, Down and Out in Beverly Hills, Ruthless People, Outrageous Fortune, Big Business, Oliver & Company (voice), Beaches (also co-prod.), Stella, Scenes from a Mall, For the Boys (Acad. Award nom., Golden Globe Award; also co-prod.), Hocus Pocus, Get Shorty, First Wives Club, Divine Secrets of the Ya Ya Sisterhood (exec. prod. only), That Old Feeling, Isn't She Great, Get Bruce, Drowning Mona, What Women Want.
TELEVISION: *Series*: Bette. *Specials*: The Fabulous Bette Midler Show, Ol' Red Hair is Back (Emmy Award, 1978; also co-writer), Art or Bust (also prod., co-writer), Bette Midler's Mondo Beyondo (also creator, co-writer), Mud Will Be Flung Tonight, Bette Midler in Concert: Diva Las Vegas. *Movies*: Gypsy, Jackie's Back!, Crossover. *Guest*: Cher, The Tonight Show (Emmy Award, 1992).
RECORDINGS: The Divine Miss M, Bette Midler, Songs for the New Depression, Live at Last, The Rose, Thighs and Whispers, Divine Madness, No Frills, Mud Will Be Flung Tonight, Beaches, Some People's Lives, For the Boys, Experience the Divine, Bette of Roses, others.

MIGDEN, CHESTER L.
Executive. b. New York, NY, May 21, 1921; e. City Coll. of New York, B.A., 1941, Columbia U., J.D., 1947. Member New York Bar. Attorney for National Labor Relations Board 1947-51. Exec of Screen Actors Guild 1952-81. Nat'l exec. dir., 1973-81. Exec. dir., Assn. of Talent Agents, 1982-94. Arbitrator, consultant 1994.

MIKELL, GEORGE
Actor. b. Lithuania. In Australia 1950-56 acting with Old Vic Co. Ent. films 1955. TV 1957. To England 1957.
PICTURES: The Guns of Navarone, The Password Is Courage, The Great Escape, Deadline for Diamonds, Where The Spies Are, The Spy Who Came in From the Cold, I Predoni Del Sahara (Italy), Sabina (Israel), The Double Man, Attack on the Iron Coast, Zeppelin, Young Winston, Scorpio, The Tamarind Seed,

Sweeney Two, The Sea Wolves, Victory, Emerald, Kommissar Zufall.
TELEVISION: Counsel at Law, Six Eyes on a Stranger, The Mask of a Clown, Green Grows the Grass, Opportunity Taken, OSS Series, Espinage, The Danger Man, Strange Report, The Survivors, The Adventurer, Colditz, The Hanged Man, Quiller, Martin Hartwell, Flambards, Sweeney, The Secret Army, Sherlock Holmes, When the Boat Comes In, Brack Report, many others.

MILCH, DAVID
Producer, Consultant.
TELEVISION: *Movies*: Capital News. *Mini-series*: Murder One: Diary of a Serial Killer. *Series*: Capital News, NYPD Blue (Emmy Award, 1997), Murder One, Total Security, Brooklyn South, Big Apple.

MILCHAN, ARNON
Producer. b. Israel, Dec. 6, 1944. Began producing and financing films in Israel.
PICTURES: Black Joy, The Medusa Touch, Dizengoff 99, The King of Comedy, Once Upon a Time in America (also actor), Brazil, Stripper (exec. prod.), Legend, Man on Fire, Who's Harry Crumb?, The War of the Roses, Big Man on Campus, Pretty Woman, Q & A, Guilty by Suspicion, JFK (exec. prod.), The Mambo Kings, Memoirs of an Invisible Man (exec. prod.), The Power of One, Under Siege, Sommersby, Falling Down (exec. prod.), Made in America, Free Willy (exec. prod.), That Night, Striking Distance, George Balanchine's The Nutcracker (exec. prod.), Six Degrees of Separation, Heaven and Earth, The Client, The New Age, Second Best, Boys on the Side, Copycat (co-prod.), Under Siege 2: Dark Territory, Free Willy 2: The Adventure Home, Heat, Bogus, Tin Cup (exec. prod.), A Time to Kill, The Mirror Has Two Faces, Murder at 1600, L.A. Confidential, Fight Club, Up at the Villa, Big Momma's House, Tigerland, Freddy Got Fingered, Joy Ride, Don't Say A Word, High Crimes, Dare Devil, Black Knight, Joe Somebody, Life Or Something Like It, Unfaithful, Daredevil, The Runaway Jury.
TELEVISION: *Mini-Series:* Masada. *Series:* John Grisham's The Client (exec. prod.), Michael Hayes. *Movie:* Noriega: God's Favorite.

MILES, CHRISTOPHER
Director. b. London, England, April 19, 1939. e. I.D.H.E.C., 1962. Sister is actress Sarah Miles. Studied film in Paris at the Institut des Hautes Etudes Cinematographiques.
PICTURES: The Six-Sided Triangle, Up Jumped a Swagman, The Virgin and the Gypsy, Time for Loving, The Maids (also co-s.p.), That Lucky Touch, Alternative 3 (also co-s.p.), Priest of Love (also prod.), The Marathon (also co-s.p.), Aphrodisias (also co-s.p.), Some Stones of No Value (also co-s.p.), Love In The Ancient World (also s.p.), The Clandestine Marriage.

MILES, SARAH
Actress. b. Ingatestone, England, Dec. 31, 1941. e. RADA. Was married to late writer Robert Bolt. Brother is actor Christopher Miles. Appeared in short film Six-Sided Triangle.
PICTURES: Term of Trial (debut, 1962), The Servant, The Ceremony, Those Magnificent Men in Their Flying Machines, I Was Happy Here, Blow-Up, Ryan's Daughter (Acad. Award nom.), Lady Caroline Lamb, The Man Who Loved Cat Dancing, The Hireling, Bride to Be, The Sailor Who Fell From Grace With the Sea, The Big Sleep, Priest of Love, Venom, Ordeal by Innocence, Steaming, Hope and Glory, White Mischief, The Silent Touch, Accidental Detective, Days of Grace.
TELEVISION: Loving Walter (Walter and June), James Michener's Dynasty, Great Expectations, Harem, Queenie, A Ghost in Monte Carlo, Dandelion Dead, Ring Round the Moon, The Rehearsal.

MILES, SYLVIA
Actress. b. New York, NY, Sept. 9, 1934. Attended Pratt Inst., NYC. e. Washington Irving H.S., Actors Studio, Dramatic Workshop of the New School.
THEATRE: Rosebloom, The Iceman Cometh, The Balcony, The Riot Act, Vieux Carre, Before Breakfast, others.
PICTURES: Murder Inc. (debut, 1960), Parrish, Pie in the Sky, Violent Midnight, Terror in the City, Midnight Cowboy (Acad. Award nom.), The Last Movie, Who Killed Mary Whats'ername?, Heat, 92 in the Shade, Farewell My Lovely (Acad. Award nom.), The Great Scout and Cathouse Thursday, The Sentinel, Shalimar, Zero to Sixty, The Funhouse, Evil Under the Sun, No Big Deal, Critical Condition, Sleeping Beauty, Wall Street, Crossing Delancey, Spike of Bensonhurst, She-Devil, Denise Calls Up, Superstar: The Life and Times of Andy Warhol, Rose's, The Boys Behind the Desk, High Times Potluck.
TELEVISION: *Series*: All My Children. *Guest*: Miami Vice, The Equalizer, Tonight Show, etc.

MILES, VERA
Actress. r.n. Vera Ralston. b. Boise City, OK, Aug. 23, 1929. e. public schools, Pratt and Wichita, KS.
PICTURES: Two Tickets to Broadway (debut, 1951), For Men Only, Rose Bowl Story, Charge at Feather River, So Big, Pride of the Blue Grass, Tarzan's Hidden Jungle, Wichita, The

Searchers, 23 Paces to Baker Street, Autumn Leaves, Wrong Man, Beau James, Web of Evidence, FBI Story, Touch of Larceny, Five Branded Women, Psycho, Back Street, The Man Who Shot Liberty Valance, A Tiger Walks, Those Calloways, Follow Me Boys!, The Spirit Is Willing, Gentle Giant, Sergeant Ryker, Kona Coast, It Takes All Kinds, Hellfighters, Mission Batangas, The Wild Country, Molly and Lawless John, One Little Indian, The Castaway Cowboy, Twilight's Last Gleaming, Thoroughbred, Run for the Roses, Brainwaves, Psycho II, The Initiation, Into the Night, Separate Lives.
TELEVISION: *Movies*: The Hanged Man, In Search of America, Cannon (pilot), Owen Marshall: Counselor at Law (pilot), A Howling in the Woods, Jigsaw, A Great American Tragedy, Baffled!, Runaway!, Live Again Die Again, Underground Man, The Strange and Deadly Occurence, NcNaughton's Daughter, Judge Horton and the Scottsboro Boys, Smash-up on Interstate 5, Fire!, And I Alone Survived, Roughnecks, Our Family Business, Rona Jaffe's Mazes and Monsters, Travis McGee, Helen Keller: The Miracle Continues, The Hijacking of the Achille Lauro. *Guest*: Climax, Pepsi Cola Playhouse, Schlitz Playhouse, Ford Theatre.

MILGRAM, HANK
Theatre Executive. b. Philadelphia, PA, April 20, 1926. e. U. of PA, Wharton Sch. Exec. v.p., Milgram Theatres. Variety Club Board member, past president and chairman of the board of Variety Club of Philadelphia; past Variety Club Intl. v.p.; President's council. Served for 12 yrs. as bd. member, Hahneman Univ. until 1993.

MILIUS, JOHN
Writer, Director. b. St. Louis, MO. April 11, 1944. e. Los Angeles City Coll., U. of Southern California (cinema course). While at latter, won National Student Film Festival Award. Started career as ass't. to Lawrence Gordon at AIP. Began writing screenplays, then became dir. with Dillinger (1973). Appeared in documentary Hearts of Darkness.
PICTURES: The Devil's Eight (co-s.p.), Evel Knievel (co-s.p.), The Life and Times of Judge Roy Bean (s.p.), Jeremiah Johnson (co-s.p.), Deadhead Miles (actor), Dillinger (dir. debut, 1973; also s.p.), Magnum Force (co-s.p.), The Wind and the Lion (dir., s.p.), Big Wednesday (dir., co-s.p., actor), Hardcore (exec. prod.), Apocalypse Now (dir.), 1941 (exec. prod., co-story), Used Cars (co-exec. prod.), Conan the Barbarian (dir., co-s.p.), Uncommon Valor (co-prod.), Red Dawn (dir. co-s.p.), Extreme Prejudice (story), Farewell to the King (dir., s.p.), Flight of the Intruder (dir., co-s.p), Geronimo: An American Legend (co-s.p., story), Clear and Present Danger (co-s.p.), The Son Tay Raid (s.p.,dir)
TELEVISION: Movies: Motorcycle Gang (dir.), Rough Riders, (writer, dir.) Series: Miami Vice (writer).

MILLAR, STUART
Producer, Director. b. New York, NY, 1929. e. Stanford U.; Sorbonne, Paris. Ent. industry working for Motion Picture Branch, State Dept., Germany. documentaries, Army Signal Corps, Long Island, Germany; journalist, International News Service, San Francisco; assoc. prod.-dir., The Desperate Hours; assoc. prod.-dir., Friendly Persuasion.
PICTURES: *Producer*: The Young Stranger, Stage Struck, Birdman of Alcatraz, I Could Go On Singing, The Young Doctors, Stolen Hours, The Best Man, Paper Lion, Little Big Man, When The Legends Die (also dir.), Rooster Cogburn (dir. only), Shoot the Moon (co-exec. prod.).
TELEVISION: *Producer*: Isabel's Choice, Vital Signs (also dir.), Killer Instinct, Dream Breaker (also dir.), Lady in a Corner.

MILLER, ANN
Actress. r.n. Lucille Ann Collier. b. Houston, TX, April 12, 1923. e. Albert Sidney Johnson H.S., Houston; Lawler Prof. Sch., Hollywood. Studied dance as child; played West Coast vaudeville theatres. Autobiography: Miller's High Life (1974), Tapping Into the Force.
THEATRE: George White's Scandals, Mame, Sugar Babies.
PICTURES: Anne of Green Gables (debut, 1934), The Good Fairy, Devil on Horseback, New Faces of 1937, Life of the Party, Stage Door, Radio City Revels, Having Wonderful Time, Room Service, You Can't Take It with You, Tarnished Angel, Too Many Girls, Hit Parade of 1941, Melody Ranch, Time Out for Rhythm, Go West Young Lady, True to the Army, Priorities on Parade, Reveille with Beverly, What's Buzzin' Cousin?, Jam Session, Hey Rookie, Carolina Blues, Eadie Was a Lady, Eve Knew Her Apples, Thrill of Brazil, Easter Parade, The Kissing Bandit, On the Town, Watch the Birdie, Texas Carnival, Two Tickets to Broadway, Lovely To Look At, Small Town Girl, Kiss Me Kate, Deep in My Heart, Hit the Deck, The Opposite Sex, The Great American Pastime, Won Ton Ton the Dog Who Saved Hollywood, That's Entertainment III, Mulholland Dr., Marlene Dietrich: Her Own Song, Broadway: The Golden Age by the Legends Who Were There.TELEVISION: *Specials*: Dames at Sea, Disney-MGM Special. *Guest*: Love American Style, The Love Boat.

MILLER, ARTHUR
Writer. b. New York, NY, Oct. 17, 1915. e. U. of Michigan. Plays include All My Sons, Death of a Salesman (Pulitzer Prize, 1949),

The Crucible (Tony Award), A View from the Bridge, After the Fall, Incident at Vichy, The Price, Up From Paradise, Situation Normal, The American Clock, I Can't Remember Anything, Some Kind of Love Story, Clara, Broken Glass. Novel: Focus. Novella: Homely Girl. *Autobiography*: Time-bends (1987).
PICTURES: Film versions of plays: All My Sons, Death of a Salesman, The Crucible, A View From the Bridge. Original s.p.: The Misfits, Everybody Wins, The Crucible, Broken Glass, Den sista Yankeen, Eden, Focus.
TELEVISION: Death of a Salesman (Emmy Award, 1967), Fame, After The Fall, Playing for Time (Emmy Award, 1981).

MILLER, BARRY
Actor. b. Los Angeles, CA, Feb. 6, 1958. New York stage debut, My Mother My Father and Me, 1980.
THEATRE: Forty Deuce, The Tempest, Biloxi Blues (Tony, Theatre World, Outer Critics Circle and Drama Desk Awards, 1985), Crazy He Calls Me.
PICTURES: Lepke (debut, 1975), Saturday Night Fever, Voices, Fame, The Chosen, The Journey of Natty Gann, Peggy Sue Got Married, The Sicilian, The Last Temptation of Christ, Love at Large, The Pickle, Love Affair, Flawless, The Devil and Daniel Webster.
TELEVISION: *Specials*: The Roommate, Conspiracy: The Trial of the Chicago Eight. *Series*: Joe and Sons, Szysznyk, Equal Justice, The Practice (3 episodes). *Guest*: The Bill Cosby Show. *Movies*: Brock's Last Case, Having Babies, The Death of Richie.

MILLER, CHERYL
Actress. b. Sherman Oaks, CA, Feb. 4, 1942. e. UCLA, Los Angeles Conservatory of Music.
PICTURES: Casanova Brown, Marriage is a Private Affair, Unconquered, Cheaper by the Dozen, Fourteen Hours, Mr. 880, Executive Suite, The Next Voice You Hear, The Matchmaker, Blue Denim, North by Northwest, The Parent Trap, The Monkey's Uncle, Clarence the Cross-Eyed Lion, The Initiation, Doctor Death, Mr. Too Little.
TELEVISION: *Series*: Daktari, Bright Promise. *Guest*: Perry Mason, Bachelor Father, Flipper, Donna Reed, Leave It to Beaver, Farmer's Daughter, Wonderful World of Color, Moutain Man, Dobie Gillis, Bright Promise, Love American Style, Emergency, Cade's County. *Movie*: Gemini Man.

MILLER, DENNIS
Comedian, Actor. b. Pittsburgh, PA, Nov. 3, 1953. e. Point Park Coll., (journalism degree). Began as stand-up comic in local clubs, then moved to NY appearing at Catch a Rising Star and the Comic Strip. Back in Pittsburgh wrote essays for PM Magazine and hosted Saturday-morning series for teens, Punchline. Recording: The Off-White Album.
PICTURES: Madhouse, Disclosure, The Net, Tales From the Crypt: Bordello of Blood, Murder at 1600, Joe Dirt.
TELEVISION: *Series*: Saturday Night Live (1985-91), The Dennis Miller Show (talk), Dennis Miller Live (also writer; Emmy Award for writing, 1996), Monday Night Football. *Specials* (also exec. prod./writer): Mr. Miller Goes to Washington, Dennis Miller: Black and White, They Shoot HBO Specials Don't They?, MTV Video Awards (host, 1996), Dennis Miller: Citizen Arcane (also exec. prod./writer; Emmy Award, 1996, Writers' Guild Award, 1998), Real Time with Bill Mayer.

MILLER, DICK (RICHARD)
Actor, Writer. b. New York, NY, Dec. 25, 1928. e. City Coll. of New York, Columbia U. Grad. NYU. Theater Sch. of Dramatic Arts. Commercial artist, psychologist (Bellevue Mental Hygiene Clinic, Queens General Hosp. Psychiatric dept.) Served in U.S. Navy, WWII. Boxing champ, U.S. Navy. Semi-pro football. Broadway stage, radio disc jockey, The Dick Miller Show, WMCA, WOR-TV. Over 500 live shows. Did first live night talk show with Bobby Sherwood, Midnight Snack, CBS, 1950. Wrote, produced and directed radio and TV shows in NY in early 1950s. Wrote screenplays; T.N.T. Jackson, Which Way to the Front, Four Rode Out and others. Has appeared on many major TV series and was a regular on Fame (3 years) and The Flash.
PICTURES: Has appeared in over 150 features, including: Apache Woman, Oklahoma Woman, It Conquered the World, The Undead, Not of This Earth, The Gunslinger, War of the Satellites, Naked Paradise, Rock All Night, Sorority Girl, Carnival Rock, A Bucket of Blood, Little Shop of Horrors, Atlas, Capture That Capsule, Premature Burial, X—The Man With the X Ray Eyes, The Terror, Beach Ball, Ski Party, Wild Wild Winter, Wild Angels, Hell's Angels on Wheels, The Trip, St. Valentine's Day Masacre, A Time for Killing, The Dirty Dozen, Targets, The Legend of Lilah Clare, Wild Racers, Target Harry, Which Way to the Front (also co-s.p.), Night Call Nurses, The Grissom Gang, Ulzana's Raid, Executive Action, The Slams, Student Nurses, Big Bad Mama, Truck Turner, Capone, T.N.T. Jackson, The Fortune, White Line Fever, Crazy Mama, Moving Violation, Hustle, Cannonball, Vigilante Force, New York New York, Mr. Billion, Hollywood Boulevard, Grand Theft Auto, I Wanna Hold Your Hand, Piranha, Corvette Summer, Rock 'n' Roll High School, Lady in Red, Dr.

Heckle and Mr. Hype, The Happy Hooker Goes Hollywood, Used Cars, The Howling, Heartbeeps, White Dog, Get Crazy, Lies, Heart Like a Wheel, All the Right Moves, Twilight Zone: The Movie, National Lampoon Goes to the Movies, Space Raiders, Swing Shift, Gremlins, The Terminator, Explorers, After Hours, Night of the Creeps, Project X, Armed Response, Chopping Mall, Amazon Women on the Moon, Innerspace, Angel III, The 'Burbs, Under the Boardwalk, Far From Home, Mob Boss, Gremlins 2: The New Batch, Unlawful Entry, Amityville 1992: It's About Time, Motorama, Matinee, Batman: Mask of the Phantasm (voice), Mona Must Die, Number One Fan, Tales From the Crypt Presents Demon Knight, Second Civil War, Small Soldiers, Route 666, It Conquered Hollywood! The Story of American International Pictures, Looney Tunes: Back in Action.

MILLER, (DR.) GEORGE
Director, Producer. b. Chinchilla, Queensland, Australia, 1945. Practiced medicine in Sydney; quit to work on films with Byron Kennedy, who became longtime partner until his death in 1983. Early work: Violence in the Cinema Part One (short: dir., s.p.), Frieze—An Underground Film (doc.: editor only), Devil in Evening Dress (doc.: dir., s.p.). First worldwide success with Mad Max.
PICTURES: Mad Max (dir., s.p.), Chain Reaction (assoc. prod.), The Road Warrior (dir., co-s.p.), Twilight Zone—The Movie (dir. segment), Mad Max Beyond Thunderdome (co-dir., prod., co-s.p.), The Witches of Eastwick (dir.), The Year My Voice Broke (exec. prod.), Dead Calm (exec. prod.), Flirting (exec. prod.), Lorenzo's Oil (dir., co-s.p., co-prod.), Babe (co-s.p.), 40000 Years of Dreaming (also s.p.), Babe: Pig in the City (also s.p.).
TELEVISION: The Dismissal (mini-series; exec. prod., co-writer & dir. of first episode). Prod.: Bodyline, The Cowra Breakout. Exec. Prod.: Vietnam (mini-series), Dirtwater Dynasty, Sports Crazy.

MILLER, GEORGE
Director. b. Scotland, 1945.
PICTURES: In Search of Anna (asst. dir.), The Man from Snowy River, The Aviator, The Never Ending Story II, Over the Hill, Frozen Assets, Gross Misconduct, Andre, Zeus and Roxanne, Cybermutt.
TELEVISION: Cash and Company, Against the Wind, The Last Outlaw, All the Rivers Run.

MILLER, MAX B.
Executive. b. Los Angeles, Feb. 23, 1937. Father, Max Otto Miller, prod. silent features and shorts. Great grandfather was Brigham Young. e. Los Angeles Valley Coll., UCLA, Sherwood Oaks Coll. Writer of articles on cinema for American Cinematographer and other publications. Owns and manages Fotos Intl., entertainment photo agency with offices in 46 countries. Recipient of Golden Globe Award in 1976 for Youthquake, documentary feature. Also dir. of Films International (prod., Shoot Los Angeles) and pres. of MBM Prod., Inc. Active member of Hollywood Foreign Press Assn. (from 1974-82 bd member; twice chmn.), Independent Feature Project, Acad. of TV Arts & Sciences, L.A. Int'l, Film Exhibition, Soc. of M.P. & TV Engineers, Film Forum, Amer. Cinemateque.

MILLER, PENELOPE ANN
Actress. b. Los Angeles, CA, Jan. 13, 1964. Daughter of actor-filmmaker Mark Miller and journalist-yoga instructor Bea Ammidown. e. studied acting with Herbert Berghof.
THEATRE: NY: The People From Work (1984), Biloxi Blues (B'way and LA), Moonchildren, Our Town (Tony nom.), On the Waterfront.
PICTURES: Adventures in Babysitting (1987, debut), Biloxi Blues, Big Top Pee-Wee, Miles From Home, Dead-Bang, Downtown, The Freshman, Awakenings, Kindergarten Cop, Other People's Money, Year of the Comet, The Gun in Betty Lou's Handbag, Chaplin, Carlito's Way, The Shadow, The Relic, Rhapsody in Bloom, Little City, The Break Up, Outside Ozona, Killing Moon, Chapter Zero, All the Fine Lines, Famous, Forever Lulu, A Woman's a Helluva Thing, Along Came a Spider, Full Disclosure, Carry Me Home.
TELEVISION: Series: The Guiding Light, As the World Turns, The Popcorn Kid, The Closer, A Minute with Stan Hooper. Movies: Rudy: The Rudy Guiliani Story. Guest: Tales From the Darkside, Miami Vice, St. Elsewhere, Family Ties, The Facts of Life. Specials: Tales From the Hollywood Hills: The Closed Set, Our Town. Movies: Witchhunt, The Last Don, The Hired Heart, Merry Christmas George Bailey, Ruby Bridges, Rocky Marciano, Killing Moon, Dodson's Journey, Dead in a Heartbeat, Scared Silent.

MILLER, ROBERT ELLIS
Director. b. New York, NY, July 18, 1932. e. Harvard U. Worked on Broadway and TV before feature film debut with Any Wednesday (1966).
PICTURES: Any Wednesday (debut, 1966), Sweet November, The Heart Is a Lonely Hunter, The Buttercup Chain, The Big Truck, The Girl from Petrovka, The Baltimore Bullet, Reuben Reuben, Brenda Starr, Hawks, Bed and Breakfast, Angel of Pennsylvania Ave.

TELEVISION: The Voice of Charlie Pont, The Other Lover, Madame X, Just an Old Sweet Song, Her Life as a Man, Ishi: Last of His Tribe, Intimate Strangers, Killer Rules, Point Man (pilot), A Walton Wedding.

MILLS, DONNA
Actress. b. Chicago, IL, Dec. 11, 1945. e. U. of Illinois. Left school to pursue career in theatre, beginning as dancer with stage companies around Chicago and touring. In NY became regular on soap opera, The Secret Storm. On B'way in Don't Drink the Water.
PICTURES: The Incident (debut, 1968), Play Misty for Me, Murph the Surf, Cursed Part III.
TELEVISION: Series: Love Is a Many Splendored Thing, The Good Life, Knots Landing. Guest: Lancer, Dan August. Movies/Mini-Series: Haunts of the Very Rich, Rolling Man, Night of Terror, The Bait, Live Again Die Again, Who is the Black Dahlia?, Beyond the Bermuda Triangle, Look What's Happened to Rosemary's Baby, Smash-Up on Interstate 5, Fire!, Curse of the Black Widow, The Hunted Lady, Superdome, Doctors' Private Lives, Hanging by a Thread, Waikiki, Bare Essence, He's Not Your Son, Woman on the Run, Outback Bound, The Lady Forgets, Intimate Encounters (also exec. prod.), The World's Oldest Living Bridesmaid (also exec. prod.), Runaway Father (also co-exec. prod.), False Arrest, In My Daughter's Name (also co-exec. prod.), The President's Child, Barbara Taylor Bradford's Remember, My Name Is Kate (also exec. prod.), Dangerous Intentions, Element of Truth (exec. prod.), Stepford Husbands, Knots Landing: Back to the Cul-de-Sac, Moonlight Becomes You.

MILLS, HAYLEY
Actress. b. London, England, April 18, 1946. Father is actor John Mills. Sister is actress Juliet Mills. e. Elmhurst Boarding Sch., Surrey, and Institute Alpine Vidamanette, Switz. Made m.p. debut in Tiger Bay 1959 with father; then signed Disney contract 1960. Received special Academy Award for her role in Pollyanna.
THEATRE: The Wild Duck, Peter Pan, Trelawney of the Wells, The Three Sisters, A Touch of Spring, The Importance of Being Earnest, Rebecca, The Summer Party, Hush & Hide, My Fat Friend, Tally's Folly, Dial M for Murder, The Secretary Bird, Toys in the Attic, The Kidnap Game, The King and I (Australian tour), Fallen Angels (U.K., Australia, New Zealand), Dead and Guilty.
PICTURES: Tiger Bay (debut, 1959), Pollyanna, The Parent Trap, Whistle Down the Wind, In Search of the Castaways, Summer Magic, The Chalk Garden, The Moonspinners, That Darn Cat, The Truth About Spring, Sky West and Crooked (Gypsy Girl), The Trouble With Angels, The Family Way, A Matter of Innocence (Pretty Polly), Twisted Nerve, Take a Girl Like You, Mr. Forbush and the Penguins (Cry of the Penguins), Endless Night, Deadly Strangers, Silhouettes, What Changed Charley Farthing, The Kingfisher Caper, Appointment with Death, After Midnight, A Troll in Central Park (voice).
TELEVISION: The Flame Trees of Thika (mini-series), Parent Trap (Parts II, III, IV, V), Amazing Stories, Illusion of Life, Good Morning Miss Bliss (series), Murder She Wrote, Back Home (series), Tales of the Unexpected, Deadly Strangers, Only a Scream Away, Walk of Life, Child Stars: Their Story.

MILLS, SIR JOHN
Actor, Producer. b. Suffolk, England, February 22, 1908. m. Mary Hayley Bell. Father of actresses Hayley and Juliet Mills. Worked as clerk before becoming actor. One of top ten money-making Brit. stars in Motion Picture Herald-Fame Poll, 1945, 1947, 1949-50, 1954, 1956-58. Knighted, 1977. Recipient special award 1988, British Academy of Film and Television Arts. Autobiography: Up in the Clouds Gentlemen Please (1981).
THEATRE: London: Good Companions, Great Expectations, Separate Tables, Goodbye Mr. Chips, Little Lies (also Toronto), The Petition, Pygmalion (NY), An Evening With John Mills.
PICTURES: The Midshipmaid (debut, 1932), Britannia of Billingsgate, The Ghost Camera, The River Wolves, A Political Party, The Lash, Those Were the Days, Blind Justice, Doctor's Orders, Regal Cavalcade, Born for Glory, Car of Dreams, Charing Cross Road, First Offence, Nine Days a Queen, OHMS, The Green Cockatoo, Goodbye Mr. Chips, Old Bill and Son, Cottage to Let, The Black Sheep of Whitehall, The Big Blockade, The Young Mr. Pitt, In Which We Serve, We Dive at Dawn, This Happy Breed, Waterloo Road, The Way to the Stars, Great Expectations, So Well Remembered, The October Man, Scott of the Antarctic, The History of Mr. Polly, The Rocking Horse Winner (also prod.), Morning Departure, Mr. Denning Drives North, The Gentle Gunman, The Long Memory, Hobson's Choice, The End of the Affair, The Colditz Story, Above Us the Waves, Escapade, It's Great to Be Young, War and Peace, Around the World in 80 Days, Baby and the Battleship, Town on Trial, Vicious Circle, I Was Monty's Double, Dunkirk, Ice Cold in Alex, Summer of the 17th Doll, Tiger Bay, Tunes of Glory, The Singer Not the Song, Swiss Family Robinson, Flame in the Streets, Tiara Tahiti, The Valiant, The Chalk Garden, The Truth About Spring, Operation Crossbow, King Rat, The Wrong Box, Sky West and Crooked (dir., prod. only), The Family Way, Africa—Texas Style, Chuka, Emma Hamilton, La Morte non ha Sesso, Oh! What a Lovely War, Run Wild Run Free, Ryan's Daughter (Acad. Award, best supporting actor, 1970), A Black Veil for Lisa, Adam's Woman, Dulcima, Oklahoma Crude, Young Winston, Lady Caroline Lamb,

The Human Factor, Trial By Combat, The Devil's Advocate, The Big Sleep, Zulu Dawn, The 39 Steps, Gandhi, Sahara, Who's That Girl, When the Wind Blows (voice), Deadly Advice, The Big Freeze, The Grotesque, Hamlet, Bean. TELEVISION: Masks of Death, Murder with Mirrors, Woman of Substance, Hold the Dream, Edge of the Wind, When the Wind Blows, Around the World in 80 Days, The Lady and the Highwayman, The True Story of Spit MacPhee, A Tale of Two Cities, Ending Up, Frankenstein, Martin Chuzzlewit, Forty years on Coronation Street, The Gentleman Thief.

MILLS, JULIET
Actress. b. London, England, Nov. 21, 1941. m. actor Maxwell Caulfield. Father is actor John Mills. Mother is writer Mary Hayley Bell. Sister is actress Hayley Mills. Made stage debut at 14 in Alice Through the Looking Glass. Also toured with Fallen Angels with sister; 1995, The Cherry Orchard, in Canada. Also in 1995, The Molière Comedies and Time of My Life; in 1996, It Could Be Any One of Us..
PICTURES: So Well Remembered, The History of Mr. Polly, No My Darling Daughter, Twice Round the Daffodils, Nurse on Wheels, Carry on Jack, The Rare Breed, Oh! What a Lovely War, Avanti!, Beyond the Door, The Man With the Green Cross, Primevals, The Other Sister.
TELEVISION: Series: Nanny and the Professor, Passions, Harmony's Passions. Movies: Wings of Fire, The Challengers, Letters from Three Lovers, Alexander: The Other Side of Dawn, The Cracker Factory, Barnaby and Me (Australia), Columbo: No Time to Die, A Stranger in the Mirror. Mini-Series: QB VII (Emmy Award, 1975), Once an Eagle. Guest: Hotel, Dynasty, The Love Boat. Special: She Stoops to Conquer.

MILNER, MARTIN
Actor. b. Detroit, MI, Dec. 28, 1927. e. USC. Army 1952-54, directed 20 training films.
PICTURES: Life With Father (debut, 1947), Sands of Iwo Jima, The Halls of Montezuma, Our Very Own, Operation Pacific, I Want You, The Captive City, Battle Zone, Mr. Roberts, Pete Kelly's Blues, On the Threshold of Space, Gunfight at the O.K. Corral, Sweet Smell of Success, Marjorie Morningstar, Too Much Too Soon, Compulsion, 13 Ghosts, Valley of the Dolls.
TELEVISION: Series: The Stu Erwin Show, The Life of Riley, Route 66, Adam-12, Swiss Family Robinson. Movies: Emergency!, Runaway!, Hurricane, Swiss Family Robinson (pilot), Flood, SST—Death Flight, Black Beauty, Little Mo, Crisis in Mid-Air, The Seekers, The Ordeal of Bill Carney, Nashville Beat. Mini-Series: The Last Convertible.

MIMIEUX, YVETTE
Actress. b. Los Angeles, CA, Jan. 8, 1942. e. Vine Street Sch., Le Conte Jr. H.S., Los Angeles, Los Ninos Heroes de Chapultepec, Mexico City, Hollywood H.S., CA. Appeared with a theatrical group, Theatre Events; Concerts: Persephone, Oakland Orchestra, 1965, N.Y. Philharmonic, Lincoln Center, L.A. Philharmonic, Hollywood Bowl.
THEATRE: I Am a Camera (1963), The Owl and the Pussycat.
PICTURES: Platinum High School (debut, 1960), The Time Machine, Where the Boys Are, The Four Horsemen of the Apocalypse, Light in the Piazza, The Wonderful World of the Brothers Grimm, Diamond Head, Toys in the Attic, Joy in the Morning, The Reward, Monkeys Go Home, The Caper of the Golden Bulls, Dark of the Sun, The Picasso Summer, Three in the Attic, The Delta Factor, Skyjacked, The Neptune Factor, Journey Into Fear, Jackson County Jail, The Black Hole, Mystique, Lady Boss.
TELEVISION: Series: The Most Deadly Game, Berrenger's. Movies: Death Takes A Holiday, Black Noon, Hit Lady (also writer), The Legend of Valentino, Snowbeast, Ransom for Alice, Devil Dog: The Hound of Hell, Outside Chance, Disaster on the Coastliner, Forbidden Love, Night Partners, Obsessive Love (also co-prod., co-writer), Perry Mason: The Case of the Desperate Deception.

MINER, STEVE
Director. b. Chicago, IL, June 18, 1951. e. Dean Junior Col. Began career as prod. asst. on Last House on the Left (1970). Launched a NY-based editorial service, and dir., prod., edited sport, educational and indust. films.
PICTURES: Here Come the Tigers! (co-prod.), Manny's Orphans (co-prod., s.p.), Friday the 13th (assoc. prod.). Director: Friday the 13th Part 2 (also prod.), Friday the 13th Part 3, Soul Man, House, Warlock (also prod.), Wild Hearts Can't Be Broken, Forever Young, My Father the Hero, Big Bully, Halloween H20: Twenty Years Later, Lake Placid, Texas Rangers.
TELEVISION: Series: The Wonder Years (sprv. prod., dir., DGA Award for pilot), Chicago Hope, The Practice, Dawson's Creek (also prod.), The Third Degree, Wasteland, Kate Brasher, Felicity, Home of the Brave. Pilots: B-Men, Elvis, Laurie Hill, Against the Grain.

MINGHELLA, ANTHONY
Director, Writer. b. Ryde, Isle of Wight, UK, Jan. 6, 1954.
PICTURES: Truly Madly Deeply, Mr Wonderful (writer only), The English Patient (Acad. award., Golden Globe nom.), The Talented Mr. Ripley (Acad. Award nom.), Play (dir. only), Cold Mountain, The Assumption (s.p. & prod. only), The Quiet American (exec. prod.)
TELEVISION: Writer: Grange Hill, Jim Henson's The Storyteller, Living With Dinosaurs, Boon, Inspector Morse..

MINNELLI, LIZA
Actress, Singer. b. Los Angeles, CA, March 12, 1946. p. actress-singer Judy Garland & dir. Vincente Minnelli. e. attended sch. in CA, Switzerland, and the Sorbonne. Left to tour as lead in The Diary of Anne Frank, The Fantastiks, Carnival and The Pajama Game. In concert with mother, London Palladium 1964. In concert Carnegie Hall, 1979, 1987, 1993. Film debut as child in mother's film In the Good Old Summertime (1949). Recordings incl. Liza with a Z, The Singer, Live at the Winter Garden, Tropical Nights, Live at Carnegie Hall, Liza Minnelli at Carnegie Hall, Results, Live at Radio City Music Hall, The Day After That.
THEATRE: Best Foot Forward (off-B'way debut, 1963, Theatre World Award), Flora The Red Menace (Tony Award, 1965), Liza at the Winter Garden (special Tony Award, 1974), Chicago, The Act (Tony Award, 1978), Are You Now or Have You Ever Been?, The Rink (Tony nom.).
PICTURES: In the Good Old Summertime, Journey Back to Oz (voice; 1964, released in U.S. in 1974), Charlie Bubbles, The Sterile Cuckoo (Acad. Award nom.), Tell Me That You Love Me Junie Moon, Cabaret (Acad. Award; also British Acad. & Golden Globe Awards, 1972), That's Entertainment!, Lucky Lady, Silent Movie, A Matter of Time, New York New York, Arthur, The Muppets Take Manhattan, That's Dancing!, Rent-a-Cop, Arthur 2 on the Rocks, Stepping Out, A Century of Cinema.
TELEVISION: Specials: Judy and Liza at the London Palladium, The Dangerous Christmas of Red Riding Hood, Liza, Liza with a Z (Emmy Award, 1972). Goldie and Liza Together, Baryshnikov on Broadway, Liza in London, Faerie Tale Theater (Princess and the Pea), A Triple Play: Sam Found Out, Frank Sammy and Liza: The Ultimate Event, Liza Minnelli Live From Radio City Music Hall, Jackie's Back, My Favorite Broadway: The Leading Ladies, AFI's 100 Years...100 Stars, New York at the Movies. Movies: A Time to Live (Golden Globe Award), Parallel Lives, The West Side Waltz.

MIOU-MIOU
Actress r.n. Sylvette Herry. b. Paris, France, Feb. 22, 1950. First job as apprentice in upholstery workshop. In 1968, helped to create Montparnasse cafe-theatre, Cafe de la Gare, with comedian Coluche. Returned to stage in Marguerite Duras' La Musica, 1985.
PICTURES: La Cavale (debut, 1971), Themroc, Quelques Messieurs Trop Tranquilles, Elle Court, Elle Court La Banlieue, Les Granges Brulees, The Mad Adventures of Rabbi Jacob, Going Places, Un Genie Deux Associes une Cloche, D'Amour et D'Eau Fraiche, Victory March, F... comme Fairbanks, On Aura Tout Vu, Jonah Who Will Be 25 in the Year 2000, Dites-lui Que Je l'aime, Les Routes du Sud, Le Grand Embouteillage, Memoirs of a French Whore, Au Revoir...a Lundi, La Femme Flic (Lady Cop), Est-ce Bien Raisonnable?, La Geule du Loup, Josepha, Guy De Maupassant, Coup de Foudre, Canicule, Le Vol du Sphinx, Blanche et Marie, Menage, The Revolving Doors, La Lectrice, Milou in May, La Totale, Le Bal des Casse-Pieds, Tango, Montparnasse-Pondichery, Germinal., An Indian in Paris, My Woman Is Leaving Me, The Eighth Day, Dry Cleaning, Elles, Foul Play, Everything's Fine We're Leaving.
TELEVISION: Various French productions.

MIRISCH, DAVID
Executive. b. Gettysburg, PA, July 24, 1935. e. Ripon Coll. United Artists Corp., 1960-63. Former exec. with Braverman-Mirisch, adv. public rel. firm. Pres. of David Mirisch Ent., intl prom. firm. Also member of Mirisch Film Co, which has produced Hawaii, West Side Story, Fiddler on the Roof, The Great Escape, The Pink Panther, Some Like It Hot, In the Heat of the Night and The Magnificent Seven.

MIRISCH, MARVIN E.
Executive. b. New York, NY, March 19, 1918. e. CCNY, B.A., 1940. Print dept., contract dept., asst. booker, NY exch.; head booker, Grand National Pictures, Inc., 1936-40; officer, gen. mgr. vending concession operation 800 theatres, Midwest, Theatres Candy Co., Inc., Milwaukee, Wisc., 1941-52; exec., corporate officer in chg., indep. prod. negotiations, other mgmt. functions, Allied Artists Pictures, Inc., 1953-57; chmn. of bd., CEO in chg. of all business affairs, admin. & financing, distr. liaison, The Mirisch Company, Inc., 1957 to present. Member of Board of Governors and former v.p., AMPAS. Member Motion Pictures Pioneers.
PICTURES: Exec. prod.: Dracula, Romantic Comedy.

MIRISCH, WALTER
Producer. b. New York, NY, Nov. 8, 1921. e. U. of Wisconsin, B.A., 1942; Harvard Grad. Sch. of Business Admin., 1943. In m.p. indust. with Skouras Theatres Corp., 1938-40; Oriental Theatre Corp., 1940-42. 1945 with Monogram/Allied Artists; apptd. exec. prod. Allied Artists, 1951 (spv. such films as The Big Combo, The Phoenix City Story, Invasion of the Body Snatchers, Friendly Persuasion, Love in the Afternoon);established The Mirisch Company, supervising such films as Some Like It Hot,

The Horse Soldiers, The Apartment, West Side Story, Irma La Douce, The Great Escape, The Pink Panther, A Shot in the Dark, The Fortune Cookie, The Russians Are Coming the Russians Are Coming, Fiddler on the Roof; 1960-61 Pres. of Screen Prod. Guild; 1962, mem. bd. dir., MPAA; bd. Gvnrs., AMPAS, 1964, 1972; 1967, pres., Center Thea. Group of L.A.; named pres. and exec. head of prod., The Mirisch Corporation, 1969; pres., Permanent Charities Committee 1962-63; pres., AMPAS, 1973-77. Recipient: Irving Thalberg Award 1978, Jean Hersholt Humanitarian Award 1984, Honorary Doctor of Humanities, Univ. of WI 1989, UCLA Medal 1989.
PICTURES: *Producer or Exec. Producer*: Fall Guy, I Wouldn't Be in Your Shoes, Bomba on Panther Island, Bomba the Jungle Boy, Bomba and the Hidden City, County Fair, The Lost Volcano, Cavalry Scout, Elephant Stampede, Flight to Mars, The Lion Hunters, Rodeo, African Treasure, Wild Stallion, The Rose Bowl Story, Flat Top, Bomba and the Jungle Girl, Hiawatha, Safari Drums, The Maze, The Golden Idol, Killer Leopard, The Warriors, Annapolis Story, Lord of the Jungle, Wichita, The First Texan, The Oklahoman, The Tall Stranger, Fort Massacre, Man of the West, Cast a Long Shadow, Gunfight at Dodge City, The Man in the Net, The Magnificent Seven, By Love Possessed, Two for the Seesaw, Toys in the Attic, In the Heat of the Night (Acad. Award for Best Picture, 1967), Sinful Davey, Some Kind of a Nut, Halls of Anger, The Hawaiians, They Call Me Mister Tibbs, The Organization, Scorpio, Mr. Majestyk, Midway, Gray Lady Down, Same Time Next Year, The Prisoner of Zenda, Dracula, Romantic Comedy.
TELEVISION: *Movies* (exec. prod.): Desperado, Return of Desperado, Desperado: Avalanche at Devil's Ridge, Desperado: The Outlaw Wars, Desperado: Badlands Justice, Troubleshooters: Trapped Beneath the Earth, Lily In Winter, A Case for Life. *Series*: The Magnificent Seven.

MIRREN, HELEN
Actress. b. London, England, July 26, 1946.
THEATRE: Troilus and Cressida, 2 Gentlemen of Verona, Hamlet, Miss Julie, Macbeth, Teeth 'n' Smiles, The Seagull, Bed Before Yesterday, Henry VI, Measure for Measure, The Duchess of Malfi, Faith Healer, Antony and Cleopatra, Roaring Girl, Extremities, Madame Bovary, Two Way Mirror, Sex Please We're Italian!, Woman in Mind (LA), A Month in the Country (also B'way).
PICTURES: A Midsummer's Night Dream (debut, 1968), Age of Consent, Savage Messiah, O Lucky Man!, Hamlet, Caligula, Hussy, The Fiendish Plot of Dr. Fu Manchu, Excalibur, The Long Good Friday, Cal, 2010, White Nights, Heavenly Pursuits, The Mosquito Coast, Pascali's Island, When the Whales Came, The Cook The Thief His Wife and Her Lover, The Comfort of Strangers, Where Angels Fear to Tread, Dr. Bethune, The Gift, The Hawk, Prince of Jutland, The Madness of King George (Acad. Award nom.; Cannes Film Fest. Award), Losing Chase, (Golden Globe Award, 1997), Some Mother's Son, Critical Care, The Prince of Egypt (voice), Teaching Mrs. Tingle, The Passion of Ayn Rand, Green Fingers, Happy Birthday, The Pledge, Last Orders, Gosford Park, No Such Thing.
TELEVISION: Miss Julie, The Applecart, The Little Minister, The Changeling, Blue Remembered Hills, As You Like It, A Midsummer Night's Dream, Mrs. Reinhart, After the Party, Cymbeline, Coming Through, Cause Celebre, Red King White Knight, Prime Suspect (BAFTA Award), Prime Suspect 2, Prime Suspect 3 (Emmy Award, 1996), Prime Suspect 4, Prime Suspect 5: Errors of Judgment, Painted Lady, French and Saunders Spring Special, Door to Door, The Roman Spring of Mrs. Stone.

MISCHER, DON
Producer, Director. b. San Antonio, TX, March 5, 1941. e. U. of TX, B.A. 1963, M.A. 1965. Pres., Don Mischer Productions. Founded Don Mischer Productions, 1978. Recipient of 12 Emmy Awards, 9 Directors Guild Awards, 3 NAACP Image Awards, Peabody Award.
TELEVISION: *Producer*: Opening and closing ceremonies of the 1996 Centennial Olympics Games (Emmy Award, 1997), Michael Jackson's Super Bowl XXVII Halftime Show, The Kennedy Center Honors (Emmy Awards, 1981, 1987, 1994, 1996), Tony Awards (3 yrs; Emmy Awards, 1987, 1989), Carnegie Hall 100th Anniversary, Gregory Hines Tap Dance in America, Opening of EuroDisney, The Muppets Celebrate Jim Henson, AFI Salutes to Billy Wilder and Gene Kelly, Irving Berlin's 100th Birthday (Emmy Award, 1988), Baryshnikov by Tharp, Motown 25: Yesterday Today Forever (Emmy Award, 1983), Motown Returns to the Apollo (Emmy Award, 1985), Grand Reopening of Carnegie Hall, specials with Goldie Hawn, Liza Minnelli, Bob Hope, Robin Williams, Pointer Sisters. Also: The Great American Dream Machine, Donohue and Kids: Project Peacock (Emmy Award, 1981), The Presidential Inaugural, 6 Barbara Walters Specials, Ain't Misbehavin', It's Garry Shandling's Show, The Wayne Brady Show, other specials, award programs, etc.

MOCIUK, YAR W.
Executive. b. Ukraine, Jan. 26, 1927. e. CCNY; World U.; Peoples U. of Americas, Puerto Rico. Expert in field of m.p. care and repair; holds U.S. patent for method and apparatus for treating m.p. film. Has also been film prod. and dir.. Founder and pres.

of CM Films Service, Inc. until 1973. Now chmn. of bd. and pres. of Filmtreat International Corp. Member: M.P. & TV Engineers; Univ. Film Assn. Pres., Ukrainian Cinema Assn. of America.

MODINE, MATTHEW
Actor. b. Loma Linda, CA, March 22, 1959. Raised in Utah. Studied acting with Stella Adler. Stage work incl. Our Town, Tea and Sympathy, The Brick and the Rose.
PICTURES: Baby It's You (debut, 1983), Private School, Streamers, The Hotel New Hampshire, Mrs. Soffel, Birdy, Vision Quest, Full Metal Jacket, Orphans, Married to the Mob, La Partita, Gross Anatomy, Pacific Heights, Memphis Belle, Wind, Equinox, Short Cuts, The Browning Version, Bye Bye Love, Fluke, Cutthroat Island., The Real Blonde, The Blackout, The Maker, If...Dog...Rabbit, Notting Hill (cameo), Any Given Sunday, Very Mean Men, Bamboozled, In the Shadows, Stanley Kubrick: A Life in Pictures, The Shipment, Nobody's Baby, Le Divorce, Hollywood North, Hairy Tale.
TELEVISION: *Movies*: And the Band Played On, Jacob, What the Deaf Man Heard, Flowers for Algernon, Redeemer, Hitler: The Rise of Evil. *Specials*: Amy and the Angel, Eugene O'Neill: Journey Into Greatness. *Series*: Texas (daytime serial) *Mini-Series*: Jack and the Beanstalk.

MOFFAT, DONALD
Actor. b. Plymouth, England, Dec. 26, 1930. Studied acting Royal Academy of Dramatic Art, 1952-54. London stage debut Macbeth, 1954. With Old Vic before Broadway debut in Under Milkwood, 1957. Worked with APA-Phoenix Theatre Co. and as actor and dir. of numerous B'way and regional productions.
THEATRE: The Bald Soprano, Jack, Ivanov, Much Ado About Nothing, The Tumbler, Duel of Angels, A Passage to India, The Affair, The Taming of the Shrew, The Caretaker, Man and Superman, War and Peace, You Can't Take It With You, Right You Are... If You Think You Are, School for Scandal, The Wild Duck, The Cherry Orchard, Cock-a-Doodle Dandy, Hamlet, Chemin de Fer, Father's Day, Forget-Me-Not-Lane, Terra Nova, The Kitchen, Waiting for Godot, Painting Churches, Play Memory, Passion Play, The Iceman Cometh, Uncommon Ground, Love Letters, As You Like It, The Heiress.
PICTURES: Pursuit of the Graf Spee (The Battle of the River Plate; debut, 1957), Rachel Rachel, The Trial of the Catonsville Nine, R.P.M., The Great Northfield Minnesota Raid, Showdown, The Terminal Man, Earthquake, Land of No Return, Promises in the Dark, Health, On the Nickel, Popeye, The Thing, The Right Stuff, Alamo Bay, The Best of Times, Monster in the Closet, The Unbearable Lightness of Being, Far North, Music Box, The Bonfire of the Vanities, Class Action, Regarding Henry, Housesitter, Clear and Present Danger, Trapped in Paradise, The Evening Star, Just In Time, A Smile Like Yours, Cookie's Fortune, The Sleep Room.
TELEVISION: *Series*: The New Land, Logan's Run. *Guest*: Camera Three (1958), You Can't Have Everything (U.S. Steel Hour), Murder, She Wrote, Dallas, Bull. *Specials*: Forget-Me-Not Lane, Tartuffe, Waiting for Godot. *Movies*: Devil and Miss Sarah, Call of the Wild, Eleanor and Franklin: The White House Years, Exo-Man, Mary White, Sergeant Matlovich vs. the U.S. Air Force, The Word, The Gift of Love, Strangers: The Story of a Mother and Daughter, Ebony Ivory and Jade, Mrs. R's Daughter, The Long Days of Summer, Jacqueline Bouvier Kennedy, Who Will Love My Children?, Through Naked Eyes, License to Kill, Cross of Fire, A Son's Promise, Kaleidoscope, The Great Pretender, Babe Ruth, Columbo: No Time to Die, Teamster Boss: The Jackie Presser Story, Majority Rule, Love Cheat and Steal, Is There Life Out There?, 61*. *Mini-Series*: Tales of the City.

MOGER, STANLEY H.
Executive. b. Boston, MA, Nov. 13, 1936. e. Colby Coll., Waterville, ME, B.A., 1958. Announcer/TV personality/WVDA and WORL (Boston) 1953-54; WGHM (Skowhegan) 1955-56; WTWO-TV (Bangor) 1955; WMHB (Waterville) 1956-57; WTVL (Waterville) 1957-58; unit pub. dir., Jaguar Prods., 1958-59; U.S. Army reserve, 1958-64, with calls to active duty in 1958-59, 1961-62. Account exec., NBC Films/California National Productions, Chicago 1959-60; asst. sales mgr., Midwest, RCA/NBC Medical Radio System, 1960; acct. exec. Hollingbery Co., Chicago, 1960-63; and NY 1963-66; acct. exec., Storer TV Sales, 1966-69; co-founded SFM, 1969. 1978, named pres., SFM Entertainment which was responsible for the revival of Walt Disney's Mickey Mouse Club, The Adventures of Rin-Tin-Tin; Mobil Showcase Network, SFM Holiday Network. Pres.: SFM Entertainment, Inc. Exec. prod.: Television-Annual, 1978-79: Your New Day with Vidal Sassoon, The Origins Game, Believe You Can and You Can, Walt Disney Presents Sport Goofy (series), The World of Tomorrow, March of Time ... on the March (England), Sports Pros and Cons, Unclaimed Fortunes, Sea World Summer Night Magic, America's Dance Honors, Allen & Rossi's 25th Anniversary Special, Paris '89 Celebration, U.S. Sports Academy Awards, K-Nite Color Radio, Into the Night With Brad Garrett (ABC-TV), Family Film Awards (CBS), Sea World/Busch Gardens Annual Specials (CBS and Nickelodeon), Everybody Rides the Carousel (Lifetime), Gift of the Magi (Lifetime), Zoobilee Zoo (PBS), Pillar of Fire (History Channel), AFI Life Achievement Awards (CBS, ABC, NBC, Fox), AFI's 100 Years...100 Movies (CBS & TNT), The Journey Inside (Sci-Fi),

Open Book (A&E), Indomitable Teddy Roosevelt (ABC), Ray Harryhausen Chronicles (AMC), Crusade in Europe (History/A&E), Visions of Light (PBS/Encore), Alice Through the Looking Glass (Disney), Witness to the Execution (HBO/Cinemax.)

MOKAE, ZAKES
Actor. b. Johanesburg, South Africa, Aug. 5, 1935. e. RADA. Came to U.S. in 1969. Has appeared in many plays written by Athol Fugard incl. Master Harold...and the Boys, Blood Knot.PIC-TURES: The Comedians, The Island, Roar, Cry Freedom, The Serpent and the Rainbow, A Dry White Season, Gross Anatomy, Dad, A Rage in Harlem, The Doctor, Body Parts, Dust Devil, Outbreak, Waterworld, Vampire in Brooklyn, Krippendorf's Tribe. TELEVISION: *Special*: Master Harold... and the Boys. *Movies*: One in a Million: The Ron LeFlore Story, Parker Kane, Percy & Thunder, Slaughter of the Innocents, Rise & Walk: The Dennis Byrd Story. *Series*: Oz.

MOL, GRETCHEN
Actress. b. Deep River, CT, November 8, 1973. e. William Esper Studio.
PICTURES: The Funeral, Girl 6, Donnie Brasco, The Last Time I Committed Suicide, The Deli, Rounders, The 13th Floor, Music From Another Room, Bleach, Too Tired to Die, Celebrity, Sweet and Lowdown, Forever Mine, Just Looking, Attraction, Get Carter, The Shape of Things.
TELEVISION: *Movie*: Calm at Sunset Calm at Dawn, Subway Stories, Tales from the Underground, Picnic. *Mini-series*: Dead Man's Walk, The Magnificent Ambersons. *Guest*: Spin City. *Series*: Girls' Club.

MOLEN, GERALD R.
Producer. b. Jan. 6, 1935. Unit prod. mngr. on The Postman Always Rings Twice, Tootsie, Let's Spend the Night Together, A Soldier's Story, The Color Purple. Assoc. prod. on Batteries Not Included. Co-prod. on Rain Man. Joined Amblin Entertainment to oversee prod. of feature film projects.
PICTURES: *Exec. Producer*: Bright Lights Big City, Days of Thunder, A Far Off Place, The Flintstones, The Little Rascals, Little Giants, Casper, Twister, The Trigger Effect. *Producer*: Hook, Jurassic Park, Schindler's List (Acad. Award for Best Picture, 1993), The Lost World: Jurassic Park, View From the Swing, The Other Side of Heaven, Minority Report, The Legend of Johnny Lingo, Catch Me If You Can (actor).

MOLINA, ALFRED
Actor. b. London, England, May 24, 1953. e. Guildhall Sch. of Music and Drama. Began acting with the National Youth Theatre. Worked as stand-up comic for street theatre group. Joined Royal Shakespeare Co., 1977.
THEATRE: Frozen Assets, The Steve Biko Inquest, Dingo, Bandits, Taming of the Shrew, Happy End, Serious Money, Speed-the-Plow, Accidental Death of an Anarchist (Plays and Players' Most Promising New Actor Award), The Night of the Iguana, Molly Sweeney (off-B'way).
PICTURES: Raiders of the Lost Ark (debut, 1981), Meantime, Number One, Ladyhawke, Eleni, Water, Letter to Brezhnev, Prick Up Your Ears, Manifesto, Not Without My Daughter, Enchanted April, American Friends, The Trial, When Pigs Fly, Cabin Boy, White Fang 2: Myth of the White Wolf, Maverick, Hideaway, The Perez Family, The Steal, Species, Before and After, Dead Man, Scorpion Spring, Anna Karenina, Boogie Nights, The Man Who Knew Too Little, The Treat, The Imposters, The Odd Couple II, Dudley Do-Right, Texas Rangers, Magnolia, Chocolat, Texas Rangers, Frida, Plots With a View, My Life Without Me, Luther, Identity.
TELEVISION: The Losers, Anyone for Dennis, Joni Jones, Cats' Eyes, Blat, Casualty, Virtuoso, Apocolyptic Butterflies, The Accountant, Drowning in the Shallow End, El C.I.D., Ashenden, Hancock, A Polish Practice, Year in Provence, Requiem Apache, Nervous Energy, Ladies Man (series), Murder on the Orient Express, The Miracel Maker (voice). *Series*: Bram and Alice.

MOLL, RICHARD
Actor. b. Pasadena, CA, Jan. 13, 1943.
PICTURES: Caveman, The Sword and the Sorcerer, Metal-storm: The Destruction of Jared-Syn, The Dungeonmaster, House, Wicked Stepmother, Think Big, Driving Me Crazy, National Lampoon's Loaded Weapon 1, Sidekicks, The Flintstones, Storybook, Galaxis, The Glass Cage, The Secret Agent Club, The Perils of Being Walter Wood, Jingle All the Way, The Elevator, Living in Peril, Me and the Gods, Little Cobras: Operation Dalmation, The Survivor, Snide and Prejudice, Route 66, Monkey Business, Dish Dogs, The Defectors, Big Monster on Campus, Foreign Correspondents, But I'm a Cheerleader, Shadow Hours, That Summer in L.A., Flamingo Dreams, Spiders II, Evolution, Scary Movie 2, No Place Like Home, Dumb Luck, Angel Blade, Pulse Pounders, The Biggest Fan, Uh Oh!, Cats and Mice.
TELEVISION: *Series*: Night Court, Mighty Max (voice), Batman: The Animated Series (voice), Spider-Man (voice), Batman: Gotham Knights, 100 Deeds for Eddie McDowd. *Movies*: The Jericho Mile, The Archer: Fugitive from the Empire, Combat High, Dream Date, Class Cruise, Summertime Switch, The

Ransom of Red Chief, Casper Meets Wendy, Call Me Claus. *Specials*: Reach for the Sun, The Last Halloween, Words Up! *Guest*: Remington Steele, Facts of Life, Sledge Hammer, My Two Dads, Highlander, Weird Science, Married...With Children.

MONASH, PAUL
Producer, Writer. b. New York, NY, June 14, 1917. e. U. of WI, Columbia U. Was in U.S. Army Signal Corps and Merchant Marine; newspaper reporter, high school teacher, and civilian employee of U.S. gov't. in Europe. Wrote two novels: How Brave We Live, The Ambassadors. Entered industry writing TV scripts for Playhouse 90, Studio One, Theatre Guild of the Air, Climax, etc. Authored two-part teleplay which launched The Untouchables. 1958 won Emmy award for The Lonely Wizard (Schlitz Playhouse of Stars), dramatization of life of German-born electrical inventor Charles Steinmetz. Made m.p. debut as exec. prod. of Butch Cassidy and the Sundance Kid, 1969.
PICTURES: *Exec. Prod.*: Butch Cassidy and the Sundance Kid. *Producer*: Slaughterhouse-Five, The Friends of Eddie Coyle (also s.p.), The Front Page, Carrie, The Rage: Carrie 2, Big Trouble in Little China.
TELEVISION: *Series*: Peyton Place (exec. prod.). *Movies* (exec. prod.): The Trial of Chaplain Jensen, The Day the Loving Stopped, Child Bride of Short Creek, Killer Rules (writer), Stalin (writer), Kingfish: A Story of Huey P. Long (writer), George Wallace, Rescuers: Stories of Courage: Two Couples, The Golden Spiders: A Nero Wolfe Mystery.

MONICELLI, MARIO
Director. b. Rome, Italy, May 15, 1915. Ent. m.p. industry in pro-duction; later co-authored, collab., comedies.
PICTURES: The Tailor's Maid (also s.p.), Big Deal on Madonna Street (also s.p.), The Great War, The Passionate Thief, Boccaccio '70 (dir. segment; cut for U.S. release), The Organizer (also s.p.), Casanova '70 (also s.p.), Girl With a Pistol, The Queens, Lady Liberty (Mortadella), Romanzo Popolare (also s.p.), My Friends, Caro Michele, Signore e Signori Buonanotte (also s.p.), The New Monsters, Hurricane Rosy, Sono Fotogencio, Lovers and Liars (also s.p.), Il Marchese del Grillo (also s.p.), Amici Miei Atto (All My Friends 2; also s.p.), Bertoldo Bertoldino e Cacasenna (also s.p.), The Two Lives of Mattia Pascal (also s.p.), Let's Hope It's a Girl (also s.p.), The Rogues (also co-s.p.), The Obscure Illness (also s.p.), Looking for Paradise, various other Italian films.

MONKHOUSE, BOB
Comedian, Writer. b. Beckenham, Kent, England, June 1, 1928. e. Dulwich Coll. Debut 1948 while serving in RAF, own radio com-edy series 1949-83 (winters), own TV series, BBC 1952-56, ITV 1956-83, BBC 1983-90, ITV 1990-. Major cabaret attraction. Voted Comedian of the Year, 1987. After-Dinner Speaker of the Year, 1989.
THEATRE: The Boys from Syracuse, Come Blow Your Horn; The Gulls, several West End revues.
PICTURES: Carry On Sergeant, Weekend with Lulu, Dentist in the Chair, She'll Have to Go, The Bliss of Mrs. Blossom
TELEVISION: *Series*: What's My Line?; Who Do You Trust?, Mad Movies, Quick on the Draw, Bob Monkhouse Comedy Hour, The Golden Shot, Celebrity Squares, I'm Bob He's Dickie!, Family Fortunes, Bob Monkhouse Tonight (1983-86), Bob's Full House (1984-90), Bob Says Opportunity Knocks (1987-89), $64,000 Question (1990-ongoing), others. *Movies*: A Perfect Two Ronnies Show, Aaagh!, It's The Mr. Hell Show!, Wipeout.

MONTAGNE, EDWARD J.
Producer, Director. b. Brooklyn, NY, May 20, 1912. e. Loyola U., Univ. of Notre Dame. RKO Pathe, 1942; U.S. Army, 1942-46; prod. many cos. after army. Exec. prod. of film-CBS-N.Y. Prod. & head of programming, Wm. Esty Adv. Co., 1950; Program con-sultant, William Esty Co.; v.p. Universal TV prod. & dir.
PICTURES: Tattooed Stranger, The Man with My Face, McHale's Navy, McHale's Navy Joins the Air Force, P.J., The Reluctant Astronaut, Angel in My Pocket.
TELEVISION: Man Against Crime, Cavalier Theatre, The Vaughn Monroe Show, The Hunter, I Spy, McHale's Navy, Phil Silvers Show. TV *Movies*: Ellery Queen: A Very Missing Person, Short Walk to Daylight, Hurricane, Terror on the 40th Floor, Francis Gary Powers, Million Dollar Ripoff, Crash of Flight 401, High Noon—Part 2.

MONTALBAN, RICARDO
Actor. b. Mexico City, Mex., Nov. 25, 1920. Appeared in Mexican pictures 1941-45. On B'way in Her Cardboard Lover with Tallulah Bankhead. Later in Jamaica, The King and I, Don Juan in Hell. Autobiography: Reflections: A Life in Two Worlds (1980).
PICTURES: Fiesta (U.S. debut, 1947), On an Island With You, The Kissing Bandit, Neptune's Daughter, Battleground, Border Incident, Mystery Street, Right Cross, Two Weeks with Love, Across the Wide Missouri, Mark of the Renegade, My Man and I, Sombrero, Latin Lovers, The Saracen Blade, The Courtesans of Babylon (Queen of Babylon), Sombra Verde, A Life in the Balance, Untouched, The Son of the Sheik, Three for Jamie Dawn, Sayonara, Let No Man Write My Epitaph, The Black Buccaneer, Hemingway's Adventures of a Young Man, The Reluctant Saint, Love Is a Ball, Cheyenne Autumn, The Money

Trap, Madame X, The Singing Nun, Sol Madrid, Blue, Sweet Charity, The Deserter, Escape From the Planet of the Apes, Conquest of the Planet of the Apes, The Train Robbers, Joe Panther, Won Ton Ton the Dog Who Saved Hollywood, Star Trek II: The Wrath of Khan, Cannonball Run II, The Naked Gun: From the Files of Police Squad, Spy Kids 2: The Island of Lost Dreams, Spy Kids 3-D: Game Over.
TELEVISION: Series: Fantasy Island, The Colbys, Heaven Help Us, Freakazoid, Kim Possible. Guest: How the West Was Won Part II (Emmy Award, 1978). Movies: The Longest Hundred Miles, The Pigeon, Black Water Gold, The Aquarians, Sarge: The Badge or the Cross, Face of Fear, Desperate Mission, Fireball Foreward, Wonder Woman, The Mark of Zorro, McNaughton's Daughter, Fantasy Island (pilot).

MONTENEGRO, FERNANDA
Actress. r.n. Arlette Pinheiro Monteiro Torres. b. Rio de Janeiro, Brazil, Oct. 16,1929.
PICTURES: Tudo Bem, A Hora da Estrela, O Que E Isso, Companheiro, Central Station (Acad. Award nom.), Treason, Gemeas, O Auto da Compadecida, O Rendentor.
TELEVISION: Movies: O Auto da Compadecida. Series: Baila Comigo, Brilhante, Guerra dos Sexos, Cambalacho, O Dono do Mundo, Renascer, Zaza, A Incrivel Batalha das Filhas da Mãe no Jardim do Éden. Mini-series: O Auto da Compadecida.

MOODY, RON
Actor. r.n. Ronald Moodnick. b. London, England, Jan. 8, 1924. e. London Sch. of Economics. Novels: The Devil You Don't, Very Very Slightly Imperfect, Off The Cuff, The Amazon Box.
THEATRE: London: Intimacy at Eight (debut, 1952), For Adults Only, Candide, Oliver! (also NY revival: Theatre World Award), Joey Joey (Bristol; also writer, composer, lyricist), Peter Pan, Hamlet, The Clandestine Marriage, The Showman (also writer), Sherlock Holmes—The Musical. Author: Saturnalia, Move Along Sideways.
PICTURES: Davy (debut, 1958), Follow a Star, Make Mine Mink, Five Golden Hours, The Mouse on the Moon, A Pair of Briefs, Summer Holiday, Ladies Who Do, Murder Most Foul, San Ferry Ann, The Sandwich Man, Oliver! (Acad. Award nom.), The Twelve Chairs, Flight of the Doves, Dogpound Shuffle, Dominique, Unidentified Flying Oddball, Wrong Is Right, Where Is Parsifal?, A Kid in King Arthur's Court, Quality Time, The Paradise Grove, The Three Kings, Revelation.
TELEVISION: Series: Nobody's Perfect, Tales of the Gold Monkey. Mini-Series: The Word. Movies: David Copperfield (theatrical in U.K.), Dial M for Murder (U.S.), The Caucasian Chalk Circle, Hideaway, The Curse of the Golden Monkey, A Ghost in Monte Carlo, The People's Passion. Specials: Portrait of Petulia, Bing Crosby's Merrie Olde Christmas, Winter's Tale, Othello, Other Side of London, Baden Powell, Lights Camera Action, Last of the Summer Wine.

MOONJEAN, HANK
Producer, Director. Began as asst. dir. at MGM. Later producer.
PICTURES: Assoc. Prod.: The Great Gatsby, WUSA, The Secret Life of An American Wife, Child's Play, Welcome to Hard Times, The Singing Nun. Exec. Prod.: The Fortune, The End. Producer: Hooper, Smokey and the Bandit II, The Incredible Shrinking Woman, Paternity, Sharky's Machine, Stroker Ace, Stealing Home, Dangerous Liaisons.

MOORE, CONSTANCE
Actress. b. Sioux City, IA, Jan. 18, 1922. Sang on radio: Lockheed program, Jurgen's Show. Screen debut 1938. TV shows, nightclubs. N.Y. Stage: The Boys from Syracuse, By Jupiter, Annie Get Your Gun, Bells Are Ringing, Affairs of State.
PICTURES: Prison Break, A Letter of Introduction, You Can't Cheat an Honest Man, I Wanted Wings, Take a Letter Darling, Show Business, Atlantic City, Delightfully Dangerous, Earl Carroll Vanities, In Old Sacramento, Hit Parade of 1947, Spree.
TELEVISION: Captured on Film: The True Story of Marion Davies.

MOORE, DAN
Costumer Designer.
PICTURES: Southern Comfort, Rocky III, Brewster's Millions, Blue City, Crossroads, Punchline, Red Heat, She's Out of Control, Johnny Handsome, Another 48 Hrs., Necessary Roughness, Trespass, Geronimo: An American Legend, Wild Bill, This World Then the Fireworks, Last Man Standing, Broken Arrow, Agua Dulce, Hart's War, Charlie's Angels: Full Throttle, Slugger, (prod.), Austin Powers in Goldmember, (prod.).
TELEVISION: Movies: Twisted Desire, The Cherokee Kid, The Second Civil War, 12 Angry Men. Series: The Magnificent Seven (Emmy Award, 1998), Two For Texas, Houdini, 61*.

MOORE, DEMI
Actress. r.n. Demetria Guynes. b. Roswell, NM, Nov. 11, 1962. Began modeling at age 16. Off-B'way debut: The Early Girl, 1987 (Theatre World Award).
PICTURES: Choices (debut, 1981), Parasite, Young Doctors in Love, Blame It on Rio, No Small Affair, St. Elmo's Fire, About Last Night, One Crazy Summer, Wisdom, The Seventh Sign, We're No Angels, Ghost, Nothing But Trouble, Mortal Thoughts (also

co-prod.), The Butcher's Wife, A Few Good Men, Indecent Proposal, A Century of Cinema, Disclosure, The Scarlett Letter, Now and Then (also co-prod.), The Juror, The Hunchback of Notre Dame (voice), Striptease, Destination Anywhere, G.I. Jane (also prod.), Austin Powers: International Man of Mystery (prod. only), Deconstructing Harry, Passion of Mind, The Hunchback of Notre Dame 2 (voice), Charlie's Angels: Full Throttle, The Magic 7 (voice).
TELEVISION: Series: General Hospital. Guest: Kaz, Vega$, Moonlighting, Tales from the Crypt (Dead Right). Specials: Bedrooms, The New Homeowner's Guide to Happiness. Movies: If These Walls Could Talk.

MOORE, DICKIE
Actor. b. Los Angeles, CA, Sept. 12, 1925. m. actress Jane Powell. Began picture career when only 11 months old, playing John Barrymore as a baby in The Beloved Rogue. Appeared in numerous radio, television and stage prods. in NY and L.A. and over 100 films; appeared in several Our Gang shorts. Co-author and star, RKO short subject, The Boy and the Eagle (Acad. Award nom.). Author: Opportunities in Acting, Twinkle Twinkle Little Star (But Don't Have Sex or Take the Car), 1984. Now public relations executive.
PICTURES: Passion Flower, The Squaw Man, Manhattan Parade, Million Dollar Legs, Blonde Venus, So Big, Gabriel Over the White House, Oliver Twist, Cradle Song, This Side of Heaven, Upper World, Little Men, Peter Ibbetson, So Red the Rose, The Story of Louis Pasteur, The Life of Emile Zola, The Arkansas Traveler, The Under-Pup, The Blue Bird, A Dispatch From Reuters, Sergeant York, Adventures of Martin Eden, Miss Annie Rooney, Heaven Can Wait, The Happy Land, The Eve of St. Mark, Youth Runs Wild, Out of the Past, Killer Shark, 16 Fathoms Deep, Eight Iron Men, The Member of the Wedding.

MOORE, ELLIS
Consultant. b. New York, NY, May 12, 1924. e. Washington and Lee U., 1941-43. Newspaperman in AK, TN, 1946-52. Joined NBC 1952; mgr. of bus. pub., 1953; dir., press dept., 1954; dir., press & publicity, 1959; vice-pres., 1961; pub. rel. dept., Standard Oil Co. (N.J.), 1963-66; v.p. press relations, ABC-TV Network, 1966-68; v.p. public relations ABC-TV Network, 1968-70; v.p. public relations, ABC, 1970, v.p. public relations ABC, Inc., 1972; v.p. corporate relations, ABC, Inc., 1979; v.p., public affairs, ABC, Inc., 1982-85. P.R. consultant, 1985. Retired, 1992.

MOORE, JULIANNE
Actress. b. Fayetteville, North Carolina, December 3,1961. e. Boston Univ. Sch. for the Arts.
THEATRE: Off-B'way: Serious Money, Ice Cream/Hot Fudge, The Road to Nirvana, Hamlet, The Father.
PICTURES: Tales From the Darkside (debut, 1990), The Hand That Rocks the Cradle, Body of Evidence, Benny & Joon, The Fugitive, Short Cuts, Vanya on 42nd Street, Roommates, Safe, Nine Months, Assassins, Surviving Picasso, The Lost World: Jurassic Park, The Myth of Fingerprints, Boogie Nights (LA Film Crits. Award, Best Supporting Actress, 1997), The Big Lebowski, Psycho, A Map of the World, Cookie's Fortune, An Ideal Husband, The End of the Affair, Magnolia, The Ladies Man, Hannibal, Evolution, World Traveler, Not I, The Shipping News, The Hours, Far From Heaven, Laws of Attraction.
TELEVISION: Series: As the World Turns (Emmy Award). Movies: I'll Take Manhattan, Money Power Murder, The Last to Go, Cast a Deadly Spell.

MOORE, MARY TYLER
Actress. b. Brooklyn, NY, Dec. 29, 1936. Began as professional dancer and got first break as teenager in commercials (notably the elf in Hotpoint appliance ads); then small roles in series Bachelor Father, Steve Canyon, and finally as the switchboard oper. in series Richard Diamond Private Detective (though only her legs were seen). Chairman of Bd., MTM Enterprises, Inc, which she founded with then-husband Grant Tinker.
THEATRE: B'way: Breakfast at Tiffany's (debut), Whose Life Is It Anyway? (special Tony Award, 1980), Sweet Sue.
PICTURES: X-15, Thoroughly Modern Millie, Don't Just Stand There, What's So Bad About Feeling Good?, Change of Habit, Ordinary People (Acad. Award nom.), Six Weeks, Just Between Friends, Flirting With Disaster, Reno Finds Her Mom, Keys to Tulsa, Labor Pains, Cheaters, The Gin Game, (also co. exec. prod.)
TELEVISION: Series: Richard Diamond—Private Detective, The Dick Van Dyke Show (2 Emmy Awards: 1964, 1966), The Mary Tyler Moore Show (1970-77; 4 Emmy Awards: 1973, 1974 (2), 1976), Mary (1978), The Mary Tyler Moore Hour (1979), Mary (1985-86), Annie McGuire, New York News, Mary & Rhoda. Guest: Bachelor Father, Steve Canyon, 77 Sunset Strip, Hawaiian Eye, Love American Style, Rhoda. Movies: Run a Crooked Mile, First You Cry, Heartsounds, Finnegan Begin Again, Gore Vidal's Lincoln, The Last Best Year, Thanksgiving Day, Stolen Babies (Emmy Award, 1993), Forbidden Memories, Payback, Mary and Rhoda, Like Mother Like Son: The Strange Story of Sante and Kenny Kimes, Miss Lettie and Me. Specials: Dick Van Dyke and the Other Woman, How to Survive the 70's, How to Raise a Drugfree Child, Three Cats from Miami and Other Pet Practictioners (host).

MOORE, MICHAEL
Director, Writer. b. Davison, MI, April 23, 1954. e. Univ. of MI. Was editor of The Michigan Voice and Mother Jones magazine, commentator on radio show All Things Considered, before gaining fame with first film Roger & Me. Established Center for Alternative Media to support indept. filmmakers.
PICTURES: Dir./Prod./Writer/Actor: Roger & Me (debut, 1989), Canadian Bacon, The Big One, Trade Off, Lucky Numbers, Fever Pitch (actor only), Bowling for Columbine (55th Anniversary Prize, Cannes Film Fest.).
TELEVISION: Series: Dir., Exec. Prod., Writer, Host: TV Nation, The Awful Truth. Special: Pets and Meat: The Return to Flint. Mini Series: A Brief History of the United States of America, (writer).

MOORE, ROGER
Actor. b. London, England, Oct. 14, 1927. e. art school, London; Royal Acad. of Dramatic Art. Had bit parts in British films Vacation From Marriage, Caesar and Cleopatra, Piccadilly Incident, Gay Lady. Appointed Special Ambassador for UNICEF, 1991.
THEATRE: Mr. Roberts, I Capture the Castle, Little Hut, others. B'way: A Pin to See the Peepshow.
PICTURES: The Last Time I Saw Paris, Interrupted Melody, The King's Thief, Diane, The Miracle, Gold of the Seven Saints, The Sins of Rachel Cade, Rape of the Sabines, Crossplot, The Man Who Haunted Himself, Live and Let Die, Gold, The Man With the Golden Gun, That Lucky Touch, Street People, Shout at the Devil, The Spy Who Loved Me, The Wild Geese, Escape To Athena, Moonraker, ffolkes, The Sea Wolves, Sunday Lovers, For Your Eyes Only, The Cannonball Run, Octopussy, The Curse of the Pink Panther, The Naked Face, A View to a Kill, The Magic Snowman (voice), Fire Ice and Dynamite, Bed and Breakfast, Bullseye!, The Quest, The Saint, Spice World, The Enemy, Boat Trip.
TELEVISION: Series: The Alaskans, Maverick, The Saint, The Persuaders. Movies: Sherlock Holmes in New York, The Man Who Wouldn't Die (also co-exec. prod.). Various specials.

MOORE, TERRY
Actress. r.n. Helen Koford. b. Los Angeles, CA, Jan. 7, 1929. Mother was Luella Bickmore, actress. Photographer's model as a child; acted on radio; with Pasadena Playhouse 1940. Voted Star of Tomorrow: 1958. Author: The Beauty and the Billionaire (1984). Formed Moore/Rivers Productions, 1988 with partner-manager Jerry Rivers. Has also acted as Helen Koford, Judy Ford, and Jan Ford.
PICTURES: Maryland (debut as Helen Koford, 1940), The Howards of Virginia, On the Sunny Side (billed as Judy Ford), A-Haunting We Will Go, My Gal Sal, True to Life, Date With Destiny, Gaslight, Since You Went Away, Son of Lassie, Sweet and Low Down, Shadowed, Summer Holiday, Devil on Wheels, The Return of October (1st billing as Terry Moore), Mighty Joe Young, The Great Ruppert, He's a Cockeyed Wonder, Gambling House, The Barefoot Mailman, Two of a Kind, Sunny Side of the Street, Come Back Little Sheba (Acad. Award nom.), Man on a Tightrope, Beneath the 12-Mile Reef, King of the Khyber Rifles, Daddy Long Legs, Shack Out on 101, Postmark for Danger (Portrait of Alison), Between Heaven and Hell, Peyton Place, Bernardine, A Private's Affair, Cast a Long Shadow, Why Must I Die?, Platinum High School, City of Fear, Black Spurs, Town Tamer, Waco, A Man Called Dagger, Daredevil, Death Dimension, Double Exposure, Hellhole, W.A.R., Beverly Hills Brats (also co-prod., co-story), Mighty Joe Young, Second Chances, Stageghost, Sweet Deadly Dreams.
TELEVISION: Series: Empire. Movies: Quarantined, Smash-Up on Interstate 5, Jake Spanner: Private Eye, Marilyn and Me.

MOORE, THOMAS W.
Executive. e. U. of Missouri. Naval aviator, USNR, 1940-45. Adv. dept., The Star, Meridian, MS; v.p., adv. mgr., Forest Lawn Memorial Park; account exec., CBS-TV Film Sales, Los Angeles; gen. sales mgr., CBS-TV Film Sales, 1956; v.p. in chg. programming & talent, 1958; pres., ABC-TV Network, 1962; chmn. bd., Ticketron, 1968; pres., Tomorrow Entertainment, Inc. 1971; chmn., 1981.

MORALES, ESAI
Actor. b. Brooklyn, NY, October 1, 1963. e. NY's High School for the Performing Arts. NY stage debut at age 17 in NY Shakespeare Fest. prod. of The Tempest, 1981.
THEATRE: Short Eyes, Tamer of Horses, El Mermano, Salome.
PICTURES: Forty Deuce (debut, 1982), Bad Boys, L.A. Bad, Rainy Day Friends, La Bamba, The Principal, Bloodhounds of Broadway, Naked Tango, Amazon, Freejack, In the Army Now, Rapa Nui, My Family/Mi Familia, Scorpion Spring, The Disappearance of Garcia Lorca, Livers Ain't Cheap, The Wonderful Ice Cream Suit, Southern Cross, Doomsday Man, American Virgin, How to Go Out on a Date in Queens, Spin Cycle, Paid In Full.
TELEVISION: Mini-Series: On Wings of Eagles. Movies: The Burning Season, Deadlocked: Escape From Zone 14, Atomic Train, The Elian Gonzalez Story. Special: The Great Love Experiment. Guest: The Equalizer, Miami Vice. Series: NYPD Blue, American Family.

MORANIS, RICK
Actor, Writer. b. Toronto, Canada, April 18, 1954. Began career as part-time radio engineer while still in high school. Hosted own comedy show on radio then performed in Toronto cabarets and nightclubs and on TV. Joined satirical TV series SCTV during its 3rd season on CBC, for which he won Emmy for writing when broadcast in U.S. Created characters of the McKenzie Brothers with Dave Thomas and won Grammy nom. for McKenzie Brothers album. With Thomas co-wrote, co-directed and starred in film debut Strange Brew, 1983. Supplied voice for cartoon series Rick Moranis in Gravedale High.
PICTURES: Strange Brew (debut, 1983; also co-dir., co-s.p.), Streets of Fire, Ghostbusters, The Wild Life, Brewster's Millions, Head Office, Club Paradise, Little Shop of Horrors, Spaceballs, Ghostbusters II, Honey I Shrunk the Kids, Parenthood, My Blue Heaven, L.A. Story, Honey I Blew Up the Kid, Splitting Heirs, The Flintstones, Little Giants, Big Bully, Honey We Shrunk Ourselves, Rudolph the Red-Nosed Reindeer and the Island of Misfit Toys (voice), Brother Bear, The Animated Adventures of Bob and Doug McKenzie, (voice).

MOREAU, JEANNE
Actress. b. Paris, France, Jan. 23, 1928. e. Nat'l Conservatory of Dramatic Art. Stage debut with Comedie Francaise, acting there until 1952 when she joined the Theatre Nationale Populaire. Directorial debut: La Lumiere (film), 1976. Recipient of 1995 BAFTA Film Craft Fellowship Award.
THEATRE: A Month in the Country, La Machine Infernale, Pygmalion, Cat on a Hot Tin Roof.
PICTURES: The She-Wolves, Elevator to the Scaffold, The Lovers, Le Dialogue Des Carmelites, Les Liaisons Dangereuses, Moderato Cantabile, La Notte, Jules and Jim, A Woman Is a Woman, Eva, The Trial, Bay of Angels, The Victors, Le Feu Follet, Diary of a Chambermaid, The Yellow Rolls-Royce, The Train, Mata Hari, Viva Maria, Mademoiselle, Chimes at Midnight, Sailor From Gibraltar, The Bride Wore Black, The Immortal Story, Great Catherine, Monte Walsh, Alex in Wonderland, The Little Theatre of Jean Renoir, Louise, The Last Tycoon, French Provincial, La Lumiere (also dir., s.p.), Mr. Klein, The Adolescent (dir., s.p. only), Plein Sud, Querelle, The Trout, Le Miracule, La Femme Nikita, The Suspended Step of the Stork, La Femme Farde, Until the End of the World, Alberto Express, The Lover (voice), Map of the Human Heart, Anna Karamazova, The Summer House, See You Tomorrow, My Name Is Victor, The Old Lady Who Walks in the Sea, Beyond the Clouds, I Love You I Love You Not, The Proprietor, Orson Welles: The One-Man Band, Amour et confusions, Un amour de sorciere, Ever After, The Prince's Manuscript, Fassbinder's Women, Lisa, Cet amour-la, The Will to Resist, The Birch Tree Meadow, (writer).
TELEVISION: A Foreign Field (BBC), The Summer House, Catherine the Great, Balzac, Les Miserables, Zaide un petit air de vengeance, Movies: Les Parents Terribles, Attila.

MORENO, RITA
Actress. r.n. Rosa Dolores Alvario. b. Humacao, Puerto Rico, Dec. 11, 1931. Spanish dancer since childhood; night club entertainer. Has won all 4 major show business awards: Oscar, Tony, 2 Emmys and Grammy (for Best Recording for Children: The Electric Company, 1972).
THEATRE: Skydrift (debut, 1945), The Sign in Sidney Brustein's Window, Gantry, Last of the Red Hot Lovers, The National Health (Long Wharf, CT), The Ritz (Tony Award, 1975), Wally's Cafe, The Odd Couple (female version), Sunset Boulevard (London).
PICTURES: So Young So Bad (debut, 1950, as Rosita Moreno), Pagan Love Song, The Toast of New Orleans, Singin' in the Rain, The Ring, Cattle Town, Ma and Pa Kettle on Vacation, Latin Lovers, Fort Vengeance, Jivaro, El Alamein, Yellow Tomahawk, Garden of Evil, Untamed, Seven Cities of Gold, Lieutenant Wore Skirts, The King and I, The Vagabond King, The Deerslayer, This Rebel Breed, Summer and Smoke, West Side Story (Acad. Award, best supporting actress, 1961), Cry of Battle, The Night of the Following Day, Marlowe, Popi, Carnal Knowledge, The Ritz, The Boss' Son, Happy Birthday Gemini, The Four Seasons, Life in the Food Chain, The Italian Movie, Blackout, I Like It Like That, Angus, Slums of Beverly Hills, Carlo's Wake, Blue Moon, Speak Truth to Power, Pinero, Casa de los Babys, The Pursuit of Happiness.
TELEVISION: Series: The Electric Company, Nine to Five, B.L. Styker, Top of the Heap, The Cosby Mysteries, Oz, The Remarkable Journey, American Family. Movies: Evita Peron, Anatomy of a Seduction, Portrait of a Showgirl, The Spree, Resurrection, The Rockford Files: It It Bleeds...It Leads. Guest: The Muppet Show (Emmy Award, 1977), The Rockford Files (Emmy Award, 1978). Special: Tales From the Hollywood Hills: The Golden Land, When It Was a Game III, Bourne to Dance, Open House.

MORGAN, ANDRE
Producer. b. Morocco, 1952. e. U. of Kansas. Golden Harvest Films prod., 1972-84. Exec. v.p., Golden Communications 1976-84. Formed Ruddy-Morgan Organization with Albert S. Ruddy, 1984. Exec. prod. with Golden Harvest.
PICTURES: Enter the Dragon, The Amsterdam Kill, The Boys in Company C, Cannonball Run II, High Road to China, Lassiter, Farewell to the King, Speed Zone, Impulse, Ladybugs, Bad Girls,

The Scout, Heaven's Prisoners, Mr. Magoo, Solo, China Strike Force.
TELEVISION: *Series:* Walker Texas Ranger, Martial Law. *Movies:* Miracle in the Wilderness, Staying Afloat.

MORGAN, DEBBI
Actress. b. Dunn, NC, Sept. 20, 1956.
PICTURES: Cry Uncle! (debut, 1971), Mandingo, Monkey Hustle, Dirty Mary, Eve's Bayou (Chicago Crits. Award, Best Supporting Actress, 1997), Asunder, She's All That, The Hurricane, Love & Basketball, Once in a Wife Time.
TELEVISION: *Movies:* Love's Savage Fury, The Jesse Owens Story, Guilty of Innocence: The Lenell Geter Story, Perry Mason: The Case of the Fatal Framing. *Mini-series:* Roots: The Next Generations. *Series:* General Hospital, Behind the Screen, All My Children, Generations, Loving, The City, Port Charles, Spawn, Soul Food, Charmed, For the People.

MORGAN, HARRY
Actor. r.n. Harry Bratsburg. b. Detroit, MI, April 10, 1915. e. U. of Chicago. Previously acted as Henry Morgan.
THEATRE: Gentle People, My Heart's in the Highlands, Thunder Rock, Night Music, Night Before Christmas.
PICTURES: To the Shores of Tripoli (debut, 1942), The Loves of Edgar Allen Poe, Crash Dive, Orchestra Wives, The Ox-Bow Incident, Happy Land, Wing and a Prayer, A Bell for Adano, Dragonwyck, From This Day Forward, The Gangster, All My Sons, The Big Clock, Moonrise, Yellow Sky, Madame Bovary, The Saxon Charm, Dark City, Appointment with Danger, The Highwayman, When I Grow Up, The Well, The Blue Veil, Bend of the River, Scandal Sheet, My Six Convicts, Boots Malone, High Noon, What Price Glory, Stop You're Killing Me, Arena, Torch Song, Thunder Bay, The Glenn Miller Story, About Mrs. Leslie, Forty-Niners, The Far Country, Not as a Stranger, Backlash, Strategic Air Command, The Teahouse of the August Moon, Inherit the Wind, The Mountain Road, How the West Was Won, John Goldfarb Please Come Home, What Did You Do in the War Daddy?, Frankie and Johnny, The Flim Flam Man, Support Your Local Sheriff, Viva Max!, The Barefoot Executive, Support Your Local Gunfighter, Scandalous John, Snowball Express, Charlie and the Angel, The Apple Dumpling Gang, The Greatest, The Shootist, The Cat From Outer Space, The Apple Dumpling Gang Rides Again, Dragnet, Wild Bill: Hollywood Maverick, Family Plan, Crosswalk.
TELEVISION: *Series:* December Bride, Pete and Gladys, The Richard Boone Show, Kentucky Jones, Dragnet, The D.A., Hec Ramsey, M*A*S*H (Emmy Award, 1980), After M*A*S*H, Blacke's Magic, You Can't Take It With You, 3rd Rock From the Sun. *Movies:* Dragnet (pilot), But I Don't Want to Get Married!, The Feminist and the Fuzz, Ellery Queen: Don't Look Behind You, Hec Ramsey (pilot), Sidekicks, The Last Day (narrator), Exo-Man, The Magnificent Magnet of Santa Mesa, Maneaters Are Loose!, Murder at the Mardi Gras, The Bastard, Kate Bliss and the Ticker Tape Kid, The Wild Wild West Revisited, Better Late Than Never, Roughnecks, Scout's Honor, More Wild Wild West, Rivkin: Bounty Hunter, Agatha Christie's Sparkling Cyanide, The Incident, Against Her Will: An Incident in Baltimore, Incident in a Small Town. *Mini-series:* Backstairs at the White House, Roots: The Next Generations.

MORGAN, MICHELE
Actress. r.n. Simone Roussel. b. Paris, France, Feb. 29, 1920. e. Dieppe, dramatic school, Paris. Won starring role at 17 opposite Charles Boyer in Gribouille (The Lady in Question). Made several pictures abroad; to U.S. 1941. Recent theatre includes Les Monstres Sacres. *Autobiography:* With Those Eyes (1977).
PICTURES: Gribouille, Port of Sahadows, Joan of Paris (U.S. debut, 1942), The Heart of a Nation, Two Tickets to London, Higher and Higher, Passage to Marseilles, The Chase, La Symphonie Pastorale, The Fallen Idol, Fabiola, Souvenir, The Naked Heart (Maria Chapdelaine), The Moment of Truth, Daughters of Destiny, The Proud and the Beautiful, Napoleon, Grand Maneuver, Marguerite de la Nuit, Marie Antoinette, There's Always a Price Tag, The Mirror Has Two Faces, Maxime, Love on the Riviera, Three Faces of Sin, Crime Does Not Pay, Landru (Bluebeard), Web of Fear, Lost Command, Benjamin, Cat and Mouse, Robert et Robert, A Man and a Woman: 20 Years Later, Everybody's Fine.

MORIARTY, CATHY
Actress. b. Bronx, NY, Nov. 29, 1960. Raised in Yonkers, NY.
PICTURES: Raging Bull (debut, 1980; Acad. Award nom.), Neighbors, White of the Eye, Burndown, Kindergarten Cop, Soapdish, The Mambo Kings, The Gun in Betty Lou's Handbag, Matinee, Another Stakeout, Me and the Kid, Pontiac Moon, Forget Paris, Casper, Foxfire, Opposite Corners, Cop Land, Hugo Pool, P.U.N.K.S., Digging to China, New Waterford Girl, But I'm A Cheerleader, Gloria, Crazy in Alabama, Red Team, Prince of Central Park, Little Pieces, Lady and the Tramp 2: Scamp's Adventure, Next Stop Eternity, Analyze That.
TELEVISION: *Series:* Bless This House. *Movie:* Another Midnight Run. *Guest:* Tales from the Crypt (ACE Award).

MORIARTY, MICHAEL
Actor. b. Detroit, MI, April 5, 1941. e. Dartmouth. Studied at London Acad. of Music and Dramatic Arts. Appeared with New

York Shakespeare Festival, Charles Street Playhouse (Boston), Alley Theatre (Houston) and Tyrone Guthrie Theatre (Minneapolis). B'way debut in The Trial of the Catonsville Nine.
THEATRE: Find Your Way Home (Tony & Theatre World Awards, 1974), Richard III, Long Day's Journey Into Night, Henry V, GR Point, Whose Life Is It Anyway (Kennedy Center), The Ballad of Dexter Creed, Uncle Vanya, The Caine Mutiny Court-Martial, My Fair Lady.
PICTURES: Glory Boy (debut, 1971), Hickey and Boggs, Bang the Drum Slowly, The Last Detail, Shoot It Black Shoot It Blue Report to the Commissioner, Who'll Stop the Rain, Q, Blood Link, Odd Birds, Pale Rider, The Stuff, Troll, The Hanoi Hilton, It's Alive III: Island of the Alive, Return to Salem's Lot, Dark Tower, Full Fathom Five, The Secret of the Ice Cave, Courage Under Fire, Managua, Shiloh, The Life and Times of Hank Greenberh, Shiloh 2: Shiloh Season, Woman Wanted, The Art of Murder, House of Luk, Hitler Meets Christ, Bad Faith, Out of Line, Mindstorm, Along Came a Spider, Swimming Upstream.
TELEVISION: *Series:* Law and Order, The Dead Zone..*Movies:* A Summer Without Boys, The Glass Menagerie (Emmy Award, 1974), The Deadliest Season, The Winds of Kitty Hawk, Too Far to Go (also distributed theatrically), Windmills of the Gods, Frank Nitti: The Enforcer, Tailspin: Behind the Korean Airline Tragedy, Born Too Soon, Children of the Dust, Children of My Heart, Children of Fortune, Galileo: On the Shoulders of Giants, Earthquake in New York, Calm at Sunset, Crome of the Century. *Mini-Series:* Holocaust (Emmy Award, 1978), Taken, Living With the Dead. *Guest:* The Equalizer.

MORITA, NORIYUKI "PAT"
Actor. b. Isleton, CA, June 28, 1932. Began show business career as comedian in nightclubs for such stars as Ella Fitzgerald, Johnny Mathis, Diana Ross and the Supremes, Glen Campbell, etc. Worked in saloons, coffee houses, and dinner theatres before becoming headliner in Las Vegas showrooms, Playboy Clubs, Carnegie Hall, etc. Guest on most TV talk, variety shows and series: M*A*S*H, Love Boat, Magnum, PI. etc.
PICTURES: Thoroughly Modern Millie, Every Little Crook and Nanny, Cancel My Reservation, Where Does It Hurt?, Midway, When Time Ran Out, Full Moon High, Savannah Smiles, Jimmy the Kid, The Karate Kid (Acad. Award nom.), Night Patrol, Slapstick of Another Kind, The Karate Kid Part II, Captive Hearts, Collision Course, The Karate Kid Part III, Do Or Die, Lena's Holiday, Honeymoon in Vegas, Miracle Beach, Even Cowgirls Get the Blues, The Next Karate Kid, American Ninja 5, Singapore Sling: Road to Mandalay, The Misery Brothers, Captured Alive, Timemaster, Reggie's Prayer, Earth Minus Zero, Bloodsport 3, Bloodsport 2, Spy Hard, Beyond Barbed Wire, Seth, Mulan (voice), I'll Remember April, King Cobra, Los Gringos, Talk to Taka, House of Luk, Hammerlock, The Boys of Sunset Ridge, The Center of the World, Shadow Fury, Unleashed, The Stone Man, Bombshell, The Biggest Fan, Cats and Mice, The Karate Dog, Stuey.
TELEVISION: *Series:* The Queen and I, Sanford and Son, Happy Days, Mr. T and Tina, Blansky's Beauties, Ohara, The Karate Kid (voice for animated series), The Mystery Files of Shelby Woo, Adventures with Kanga Roddy. *Movies:* Evil Roy Slade, A Very Missing Person, Brock's Last Case, Punch and Jody, Farewell to Manzanar, Human Feelings, For the Love of It, The Vegas Strip Wars, Amos, Babes in Toyland, Hiroshima: Out of the Ashes, Greyhounds, Hart to Hart: Secrets of the Hart, Gone to Maui.

MORITZ, MILTON I
Executive. b. Pittsburgh, PA, April 27, 1933. e. Woodbury Coll., grad. 1955. Owned, operated theatres in L.A., 1953-55; U.S. Navy 1955-57; American International Pictures asst. gen. sls. mgr., 1957; nat'l. dir. of adv. and publ. 1958; v.p. and bd. mem. of American International Pictures, 1967; pres. of Variety Club of So. Cal, Tent 25, 1975-76; 1975, named sr. v.p.; in 1980, formed own co., The Milton I. Moritz Co., Inc., Inc., mktg. & dist. consultant. 1987-94, joined Pacific Theatres as v.p. in chg. of adv., p.r. & promotions. 1995, reactivated the Milton I. Moritz Co., Inc.

MORRICONE, ENNIO
Composer, Arranger. b. Rome, Italy, Nov. 10, 1928. Studied with Goffredo Petrassi at the Acad. of Santa Cecilia in Rome. Began career composing chamber music and symphonies as well as music for radio, TV and theater. Wrote for popular performers including Gianni Morandi. Early film scores for light comedies. Gained recognition for assoc. with Italian westerns of Sergio Leone (under name of Dan Davio).
PICTURES: Il Federal (1961, debut), A Fistful of Dollars, The Good the Bad and the Ugly, El Greco, Fists in the Pocket, Battle of Algiers, Matchless, Theorem, Once Upon a Time in the West, Investigation of a Citizen, Fraulein Doktor, Burn, The Bird with the Crystal Plumage, Cat O'Nine Tails, The Red Tent, Four Flies in Grey Velvet, The Decameron, The Black Belly of the Tarantula, Bluebeard, The Serpent, Blood in the Streets, Eye of the Cat, The Human Factor, Murder on the Bridge, Sunday Woman, The Inheritance, Partner, Orca, Exorcist II: The Heretic, 1900, Days of Heaven, La Cage aux Folles, Bloodline, Stay as You Are, The Humanoid, The Meadow, A Time to Die, Travels With Anita (Lovers and Liars), When You Comin' Back Red Ryder?, Almost Human, La Cage aux Folles II, The Island, Tragedy of a Ridiculous Man, Windows, Butterfly, So Fine, White Dog,

Copkiller, Nana, The Thing, Treasure of the Four Crowns, Sahara, Once Upon a Time in America, Thieves After Dark, The Cage, La Cage aux Folles III, The Forester's Sons, The Red Sonja, Repentier, The Mission, The Venetian Woman, The Untouchables, Quartiere, Rampage, Frantic, A Time of Destiny, Casualties of War, Cinema Paradiso, State of Grace, Hamlet, Bugsy, City of Joy, The Bachelor, In the Line of Fire, Wolf, Love Affair, Disclosure, Lolita, U Turn, Phantom of the Opera, Bulworth, The Legend of 1900, Canone Inverso, Missions to Mars, Vatel, Before Night Falls, Malena, Say It Isn't So, The Sleeping Wife, Another World Is Possible, Aida of the Trees, Senso '45, Ripley's Game, Kill Bill: Volume One, Marvelous Light.
TELEVISION: U.S.: Marco Polo, Moses—The Lawgiver, Scarlet and the Black, C.A.T. Squad, The Endless Game, Octopus 4, Abraham, Musashi, Maria Goretti.

MORRIS, ERROL
Director, Writer. b. Hewlett, NY, Feb. 5, 1948. e. Univ. of WI, Univ. of CA/Berkeley.
PICTURES: Gates of Heaven, Vernon Florida, The Thin Blue Line, The Dark Wind, A Brief History of Time, Fast Cheap & Out Of Control, Stairway to Heaven, Mr. Death: The Rise and Fall of Fred A Leuchter Jr.
TELEVISION: Series: First Person.

MORRIS, GARRETT
Actor. b. New Orleans, LA, Feb. 1, 1937. e. Dillard Univ., Juilliard Sch. of Music, Manhattan Sch. of Music. Was singer and arranger for Harry Belafonte Folk Singers and B'way actor before achieving fame as original cast member of Saturday Night Live.
THEATRE: Porgy and Bess, I'm Solomon, Show Boat, Hallelujah Baby!, The Basic Training of Pavlo Hummel, Finian's Rainbow, The Great White Hope, Ain't Supposed to Die a Natural Death, The Unvarnished Truth.
PICTURES: Where's Poppa? (debut, 1970), The Anderson Tapes, Cooley High, Car Wash, How to Beat the High Cost of Living, The Census Taker, The Stuff, Critical Condition, The Underachievers, Dance to Win, Motorama, Children of the Night, Almost Blue, Coneheads, Black Rose of Harlem, Black Scorpion II: Aftershock, Santa with Muscles, Black Rose of Harlem, Palmer's Pick Up, Twin Falls Idaho, Graham's Diner, Jackpot, How High, Connecting Dots.
TELEVISION: Series: Roll Out, Saturday Night Live (1975-80), It's Your Move, Hunter, Martin, Cleghorne!, The Jamie Foxx Show, Justice League. Movies: The Invisible Woman, Earth Angel, Maid for Each Other, Black Scorpion, Maniac Magee. Guest: Scarecrow and Mrs. King, Love Boat, Married With Children, Murder She Wrote, The Jeffersons.

MORRIS, HOWARD
Actor, Director, Writer. b. New York, NY, Sept. 4, 1919. e. NYU. U.S. Army, 4 yrs.
THEATRE: Hamlet, Call Me Mister, John Loves Mary, Gentlemen Prefer Blondes, Finian's Rainbow.
PICTURES: Director: Who's Minding the Mint?, With Six You Get Egg Roll, Don't Drink the Water, Goin' Cocoanuts. Actor: Boys' Night Out, 40 Pounds of Trouble, The Nutty Professor, Fluffy, Way... Way Out, High Anxiety, History of the World Part 1, Splash, Transylvania Twist, Life Stinks, Tom and Jerry: The Movie, Lasting Silents, The Wonderful Ice Cream Suit, Hail Sid Caeser: The Golden Age of Comedy.
TELEVISION: Series: Your Show of Shows (also writer), Caesar's Hour, The Nudnik Show, Cow and Chicken. Movies: The Munster's Revenge, Portrait of a Showgirl, Return to Mayberry. Voices: Jetsons, Flintstones, Mr. Magoo. Producer: The Corner Bar. Director: Dick Van Dyke Show, Get Smart, Andy Griffith Show (also frequent guest); also many commericals.

MORRIS, JOHN
Composer, Conductor, Arranger. b. Elizabeth, NJ. e. Juilliard Sch. Music 1946-48, U. of Washington. 1947, New Sch. Social Research 1946-49. Member: ASCAP, Acad. of M.P. Arts & Sciences, American Federation of Musicians.
THEATRE: Composer: B'way: My Mother My Father and Me, A Doll's House, Camino Real, A Time For Singing (musical), Take One Step, Young Andy Jackson, 15 Shakespeare plays for NY Shakespeare Fest. & Amer. Shakespeare Fest, Stratford CT. Musical supervisor, conductor, dance music arranger: Mack and Mabel, Much Ado About Nothing, Bells Are Ringing, Bye Bye Birdie and 23 other B'way musicals. Off-B'way: Hair.
PICTURES: The Producers, The Twelve Chairs, Blazing Saddles (Acad. Award nom.), Bank Shot, Young Frankenstein, The Adventure of Sherlock Holmes' Smarter Brother, Silent Movie, The Last Remake of Beau Geste, The World's Greatest Lover, High Anxiety, The In-Laws, In God We Trust, The Elephant Man (Acad. Award nom.), History of the World Part 1, Table for Five, Yellowbeard, To Be or Not to Be, The Woman in Red, Johnny Dangerously, The Doctor and the Devils, Clue, Haunted Honeymoon, Dirty Dancing, Spaceballs, Ironweed, The Wash, Second Sight, Stella, Life Stinks.
TELEVISION: Composer: Fresno, Katherine Anne Porter, Ghost Dancing, The Firm, The Mating Season, Splendor in the Grass, The Electric Grandmother, The Scarlet Letter, Georgia O'Keeffe, The Adams Chronicles, The Franken Project, The Tap Dance Kid (Emmy Award, 1986), Make Believe Marriage, The Desperate

Hours, The Skirts of Happy Chance, Infancy and Childhood, The Fig Tree, The Little Match Girl, Favorite Son, The Last Best Year, The Last to Go, The Sunset Gang, Our Sons, When Lions Roared, Scarlett, Carolina Skeletons, The Fig Tree, Scarlett, Ellen Foster, Only Love, Murder in a Small Town, The Lady in Question. Themes: ABC After School Special, Making Things Grow, The French Chef, Coach. Musical sprv., conductor, arranger Specials: Anne Bancroft Special (Emmy Award), S'Wonderful S'Marvelous S'Gershwin (Emmy Award), Hallmark Christmas specials.
RECORDINGS: Wildcat, All-American, Bells Are Ringing, First Impressions, Bye Bye Birdie, Kwamina, Baker Street, Rodgers and Hart, George Gershwin Vols. 1 & 2, Jerome Kern, Lyrics of Ira Gershwin, Cole Porter, others.

MORRIS, OSWALD
Cinematographer. b. London, England, Nov. 22, 1915. Left school at 16 to work for two years as camera dept. helper at studios. Was lensman for cameraman Ronald Neame who gave Morris first job as cameraman; in 1949, when Neame directed The Golden Salamander, he made Morris dir. of photography.
PICTURES: The Golden Salamander, The Card, The Man Who Never Was, Moulin Rouge, Beat the Devil, Moby Dick, Heaven Knows Mr. Allison, A Farewell to Arms, The Roots of Heaven, The Key, The Guns of Navarone, Lolita, Term of Trial, Of Human Bondage, The Pumpkin Eater (BFA Award, 1964), Mister Moses, The Hill (BFA Award, 1965), The Spy Who Came in from the Cold, Life at the Top, Stop the World- -I Want to Get Off, The Taming of the Shrew, Reflections in a Golden Eye, Oliver!, Gooodbye Mr. Chips, Scrooge, Fiddler on the Roof (Acad. Award, 1971), Sleuth, Lady Caroline Lamb, The Mackintosh Man, The Odessa File, The Man Who Would Be King, The Seven Per Cent Solution, Equus, The Wiz, Just Tell Me What You Want, The Great Muppet Caper, The Dark Crystal.
TELEVISION: Dracula (1974).

MORRISSEY, PAUL
Writer, Director, Photographer. b. New York, NY, 1938. e. Fordham U. 2nd lt. in Army. A writer, cameraman and dir. in indt. film prod. prior to becoming Andy Warhol's mgr. in all areas except painting. Discovered and managed The Velvet Underground and Nico. Founded Interview magazine. Story, casting, dir. & photog. for Warhol Productions' Chelsea Girls, Four Stars, Bike Boy, I A Man, Lonesome Cowboys, Blue Movie, and San Diego Surf.
PICTURES: writer/photog./edit./dir.: Flesh, Trash, Heat, L'Amour, Women in Revolt. writer/dir.: Flesh For Frankenstein, Blood for Dracula, The Hound of the Baskervilles, Madame Wang's, Forty Deuce, Mixed Blood, Beethoven's Nephew, Spike of Bensonhurst.

MORROW, ROB
Actor. b. New Rochelle, NY, Sept. 21, 1962.
THEATRE: NY: The Substance of Fire, Aven'U Boys, The Chosen, Scandal (workshop), Soulful Scream of a Chosen Son, The Boys of Winter, Slam, Third Secret.
PICTURES: Private Resort, Quiz Show, The Last Dance, Mother, Magic, Labor Pains, Shopping, Fairy Teller, The Guru, The Emperor's Club, Night's Noontime, Shopping.
TELEVISION: Movies: The Day Lincoln Was Shot, Only Love, The Thin Blue Lie, The Jennifer Estes Story. Series: Tattinger's, Northern Exposure, Nearly Yours, Street Time. Guest: Spenser: For Hire, Everything's Relative, Fame.

MORSE, DAVID
Actor. b. Beverly, MA, Oct. 11, 1953.
THEATRE: B'way: On the Waterfront.
PICTURES: Inside Moves, Desperate Hours, The Indian Runner, The Good Son, The Getaway, The Crossing Guard, Twelve Monkeys, The Rock, Contact, The Legend of Pig Eye, A.W.O.L., The Negotiator, The Green Mile, Dancer in the Dark, Bait, Von Trier's 100 Eyes, Proof of Life, Diary of a City Priest, Hearts in Atlantis, The Slaughter Rule, Double Vision.
TELEVISION: Series: St. Elsewhere, Big Wave Dave's, Friday the 13th (dir. only). Movies: Shattered Vows, When Dreams Come True, Prototype, Downpayment on Murder, Six Against the Rock, Winnie, Brotherhood of the Rose, Cross of Fire, A Cry in the Wild: The Taking of Peggy Ann, Dead Ahead: The Exxon Valdez Disaster, Miracle on Interstate 880, Tecumseh: The Last Warrior, Murder Live, Hack. Mini-Series: Stephen King's The Langoliers, Abraham and Mary Lincoln: A House Divided. Guest: Nurse. Special: A Place at the Table.

MORSE, ROBERT
Actor. b. Newton, MA, May 18, 1931. Served U.S. Navy. Studied with American Theatre Wing, New York. Following radio work, appeared on B'way stage in The Matchmaker, 1956.
THEATRE: The Matchmaker, Say Darling (Theatre World Award), Take Me Along, How to Succeed in Business Without Really Trying (Tony Award, 1962), Sugar, So Long 174th Street, Tru (Tony Award, 1990).
PICTURES: The Proud and the Profane (debut, 1956), The Matchmaker, The Cardinal, Honeymoon Hotel, Quick Before It Melts, The Loved One, Oh Dad Poor Dad Mama's Hung You in the Closet and I'm Feeling So Sad, How to Succeed in Business

Without Really Trying, A Guide for the Married Man, Where Were You When the Lights Went Out?, The Boatniks, Hunk, The Emperor's New Clothes, Broadway: The Golden Age by the Legends Who Were There.
TELEVISION: *Series*: The Secret Storm (1954), That's Life, All My Children, Pound Puppies (voice). *Specials*: The Stingiest Man in Town (voice), Kennedy Center Tonight—Broadway to Washington, Tru (Emmy Award, 1993), City of Angels. *Movie*: The Calendar Girl Murders, Here Come the Munsters. *Mini-Series*: Wild Palms. *Guest*: Masquerade, Alfred Hitchcock Presents, Naked City, Love American Style, Twilight Zone, Murder She Wrote.

MORTENSEN, VIGGO
Actor. b. New York, NY, Oct. 20, 1958.
PICTURES: Witness, Salvation!, Prison, Fresh Horses, Tripwire, Leatherface: Texas Chainsaw Massacre III, Young Guns II, The Reflecting Skin, The Indian Runner, The Young Americans, Ruby Cairo, Ewangelia wedlug Harry'ego, Carlito's Way, Boiling Point, Floundering, Desert Lunch, The Crew, American Yakuza, The Passion of Darkly Noon, Gimlet, Crimson Tide, The Prophecy, Albino Alligator, The Portrait of a Lady, Daylight, La Pistola de mi hermano, G. I. Jane, Blouse Man, A Perfect Murder, Psycho, A Walk on the Moon, 28 Days, Lord of the Rings: The Fellowship of the Ring, Lord of the Rings: The Two Towers, Hidalgo, Lord of the Rings: The Return of the King.
TELEVISION: *Movie*: Vanishing Point. *Mini-series*: George Washington.

MORTON, JOE
Actor. b. New York, NY, Oct. 18, 1947. e. Hofstra U.
THEATRE: *NY*: Hair, Raisin (Theatre World Award), Oh Brother, Honky Tonk Nights, A Midsummer Night's Dream, King John, Cheapside, Electra, A Winter's Tale, Oedipus Rex, Julius Caesar, The Tempest. Dir.: Heliotrope Bouquet.
PICTURES: ...And Justice for All, The Brother From Another Planet, Trouble in Mind, Zelly and Me, The Good Mother, Tap, Terminator 2: Judgment Day, City of Hope, Of Mice and Men, Forever Young, The Inkwell, Speed, The Walking Dead, Lone Star, Executive Decision, Lone Star, The Pest, Speed 2: Cruise Control, Trouble on the Corner, Blues Brothers 2000, Apt Pupil, When It Clicks, The Astronaut's Wife, What Lies Beneath, Bounce, Ali, Dragonfly.
TELEVISION: *Series*: Grady, Equal Justice, Tribeca (also dir.), Under One Roof, New York News, Prince Street, Mercy Point, Smallville, The Fritz Pollard Story, All My Children. *Movies*: The Challenger, Terrorist on Trial: The United States vs. Salim Ajami, Howard Beach: Making a Case for Murder, Death Penalty, Legacy of Lies, In the Shadow of Evil, Y2K, Mutiny, Ali: An American Hero, Jasper Texas. *Special*: The File of Jill Hatch. *Guest*: A Different World, Hawk, Homicide: Life on the Street.

MOSK, RICHARD M.
Executive. b. Los Angeles, CA, May 18, 1939. e. Stanford U, Harvard Law School. Admitted to California Bar, 1964. Principal in firm of Sanders Barnet Goldman Simons & Mosk, a prof. corp. Named chmn. of the movie industry's voluntary rating system, the Classification & Rating Administration, June 1994; co-chmn. 1997-. Judge, Iran-U.S. Claims Tribunal.

MOSLEY, ROGER E.
Actor. b. Los Angeles, CA. Dec. 18, 1938. Planned career in broadcasting but turned to acting, first appearing in small roles on TV in: Night Gallery, Baretta, Kojak, Cannon, Switch.
PICTURES: The New Centurions (debut, 1972), Hit Man, Terminal Island, Stay Hungry, Leadbelly, The Greatest, Semi-Tough, Steel, Heart Condition, Unlawful Entry, Pentathlon, A Thin Line Between Love and Hate, Letters From a Killer.
TELEVISION: *Series*: Magnum P.I., You Take the Kids, Hangin' With Mr. Cooper, You Take the Kids. *Guest*: Cannon, Switch. *Movies*: Cruise Into Terror, I Know Why the Caged Bird Sings, The Jericho Mile, Attica. *Mini-Series*: Roots, The Next Generations.

MOSS, CARRIE-ANNE
Actress. b. Vancouver, Canada, Aug. 21, 1970.
PICTURES: Flashfire, The Soft Kill, Terrified, Sabotage, Secret Life of Algernon, Lethal Tender, New Blood, The Matrix, Memento, Red Planet, Chocolat, The Matrix Revisited, The Matrix Reloaded, The Matrix 3. Suspect Zero.
TELEVISION: *Series*: Dark Justice, Matrix, Models Inc., F/X: The Series. *Guest*: Street Justice, Nightmare Cafe, Forever Knight, Silk Stalkings, Baywatch, Nowhere Man, Due South, Viper, Spider-Man, L.A. Law.

MOSS, IRWIN
Executive. e. Syracuse U., Harvard Law Sch. Member NY State Bar. Began industry career as dir. of package negotiations for CBS-TV; 1970-80, exec. v.p. & natl. head of business affairs for I.C.M.; 1978-80, sr. v.p., NBC Entertainment; 1980, pres., Marble Arch TV. 1982, joined Paramount Pictures as sr. v.p. for motion picture div. 1984, exec. v.p., D.L. Taffner Ltd.

MOSTEL, JOSH
Actor, Director. b. New York, NY, Dec. 21, 1946. Father was late actor Zero Mostel. m. prod. Peggy Rajski. e. Brandeis U., B.A. 1970. Part of The Proposition, a Boston improvisational comedy group. Stage debut, The Homecoming (Provincetown Playhouse, MA).
THEATRE: *Actor*: Unlikely Heroes, The Proposition, An American Millionaire, A Texas Trilogy, Gemini, Men in the Kitchen, The Dog Play, The Boys Next Door, A Perfect Diamond, Threepenny Opera, My Favorite Year, The Flowering Peach. *Director*: Ferocious Kisses, Love As We Know It, Misconceptions, Red Diaper Baby.
PICTURES: Going Home (debut, 1971), The King of Marvin Gardens, Jesus Christ Superstar, Harry and Tonto, Deadly Hero, Fighting Back, Sophie's Choice, Star 80, Almost You, The Brother from Another Planet, Windy City, Compromising Positions, The Money Pit, Stoogemania, Radio Days, Matewan, Wall Street, Heavy Petting, Animal Behavior, City Slickers, Naked Tango, Little Man Tate, City of Hope, Searching for Bobby Fischer, The Chase, City Slickers II: The Legend of Curly's Gold, Billy Madison, The Basketball Diaries, The Maddening, Big Daddy, Rounders, The Out of Towners, Knockaround Guys.
TELEVISION: *Series*: Delta House, At Ease, Murphy's Law. *Mini-Series*: Seventh Avenue. *Special*: The Boy Who Loved Trolls (PBS). *Co-writer*: Media Probes: The Language Show. *Movies*: Thicker than Blood.

MOUND, FRED
Executive. b. St. Louis, MO, April 10, 1932. e. St. Louis U., Quincy Coll. 1946-52, assoc. with father, Charles Mound, at Park Theatre in Valley Park, Mo.; 1952-53, Universal Pictures (St. Louis); 1953, booker, UA, St. Louis; 1955 promoted to salesman in Kansas City; 1957, salesman, St. Louis; 1962, Indianapolis branch mgr. 1967 named UA regional mgr., Dallas and in 1970 became S.W. div. mgr; 1976-77, asst. gen. sls. mgr. for Southern, N.W. and S.W. div. operating out of Dallas. 1977 appt. v.p., asst. gen. sls. mgr. of UA; 1978, appt. v.p. gen sls. mgr. for AFD Pictures in Los Angeles; 1981, v.p. asst. gen. sls. mgr. for Universal; 1984, sr. v.p., gen. sls. mgr., Universal Pictures Distribution; named exec. v.p. 1988. Foundation of Motion Picture Pioneers v.p., 1989. Appointed pres. Universal distrib., 1990. Currently, v.p., creative svcs., Carsey-Werner.

MOUNT, THOM
Executive. b. Durham, NC, May 26, 1948. e. Bard Coll.; CA Institute of the Arts, MFA. Started career with Roger Corman and as asst. to prod., Danny Selznick at MGM. Moved to Universal under prod. exec. Ned Tanen. At 26, named pres. and head of prod. at Universal. During 8-year tenure, was responsible for dev. and prod. of more than 140 films (including Smokey and the Bandit, Animal House, others).
THEATRE: Open Admissions (co-prod.), Death and the Maiden.
PICTURES: Pirates (exec. prod.), My Man Adam, Can't Buy Me Love, Frantic, Bull Durham (co-prod.), Stealing Home, Tequila Sunrise, Roger Corman's Frankenstein Unbound, The Indian Runner (exec. prod.), Death and the Maiden, Natural Born Killers, Night Falls on Manhattan (prod.).
TELEVISION: Son of the Morning Star, Open Admissions.

MOYERS, BILL
TV Correspondent. b. Hugo, OK, June 5, 1934. e. U. of Texas; Southwestern Baptist Theological Sem. Aide to Lyndon B. Johnson; assoc. dir., Peace Corps, 1961-62, and deputy dir., 1963. Spec. asst. to Pres. Johnson, 1963-65 and press secty., 1965-67. Editor and chief corr., CBS Reports. Bill Moyers Journal on PBS. Established Public Affairs TV, Inc., 1986.

MUDD, ROGER
Newscaster. b. Washington, DC, Feb. 9, 1928. e. Washington & Lee U., U. of North Carolina. Reporter for Richmond News-Leader, 1953; news. dir., WRNL, 1954; WTOP, Washington, 1956; joined CBS News 1961 as Congressional correspondent (2 Emmy Awards). 1977, Natl. Aff. corr.; 1978, corr., CBS Reports; 1980-87: NBC News as chief Washington corr., chief political corr., co-anchor; 1987 joined The MacNeil/Lehrer News Hour as special correspondent; essayist, and chief congressional correspondent. 1992 became contributing correspondent. Host of numerous specials and history series.

MUELLER-STAHL, ARMIN
Actor. b. Tilsit, East Prussia, Dec. 17, 1930. Moved to West Germany in 1980. e. Berlin Conservatory. Studied violin before turning to acting. Author: Verordneter Sonntag (Lost Sunday), Drehtage, Nuterwegs Nach Hause (On the Way Home).
PICTURES: Naked Among the Wolves, The Third, Jacob the Liar, The Flight, Lite Trap, Lola, Wings of Night, Veronika Voss, A Cop's Sunday, A Love in Germany, Thousand Eyes, Trauma, Colonel Redl, L'Homme blesse, God Doesn't Believe in Us Anymore, Angry Harvest, The Blind Director, Following the Fuhrer, Momo, The Jungle Mission, Lethal Obsession, Midnight Cop, Music Box, Das Spinnenetz, Just for Kicks, Avalon, Bronstein's Children, Kafka, The Power of One, Night on Earth, Utz, The House of the Spirits, Holy Matrimony, The Last Good Time, A Pyromaniac's Love Story, Taxandria, Shine, Theodore Rex, The Peacemaker, The Game, The Commissioner, The X

Files: Fight the Future, Jakob the Liar, The Thirteenth Floor, The Third Miracle, Pilgrim, Mission to Mars, The Long Run, .
TELEVISION: *Mini-Series: Amerika, Jesus, Crociati.* Several German movies and specials.

MUIR, E. ROGER
Producer. b. Canada, Dec. 16, 1918. e. U. of Minnesota. Partner Minn. Advertising Services Co.; Photographer, Great Northern Railway; motion picture prod. Army Signal corps; NBC TV prod., Howdy Doody; exec. prod., Concentration. Now pres. Nicholson-Muir Prods, TV program packager, U.S. Spin-Off, Pay Cards, Canada Pay Cards, Headline Hunters, Definition, Celebrity Dominoes; co-creator Newlywed Game, exec. prod. I Am Joe's Heart, I Am Joe's Lung, I Am Joe's Spine, I Am Joe's Stomach, The New Howdy Doody Show, Supermates, Second Honeymoon, Groaner, Generation Jury, Shopping Game, Guess What, I Am Joe's Kidney, I Am Joe's Liver, It's Howdy Doody Time: A 40 Year Celebration. Retired 1993.

MULDAUR, DIANA
Actress. b. New York, NY, Aug. 19, 1943. e. Sweet Briar Coll. Began on New York stage then turned to films and TV, appearing on numerous major network shows.
PICTURES: The Swimmer (debut, 1968), Number One, The Lawyer, One More Train to Rob, The Other, McQ, Chosen Survivors, Beyond Reason.
TELEVISION: *Series:* The Secret Storm, The Survivors, McCloud, Born Free, The Tony Randall Show, Hizzoner, Fitz and Bones, A Year in the Life, L.A. Law, Star Trek: The Next Generation, Hearts Are Wild, Batman: The Animated Series. *Movies:* McCloud: Who Killed Miss U.S.A.?, Call to Danger, Ordeal, Planet Earth, Charlie's Angels (pilot), Pine Canyon is Burning, Deadly Triangle, Black Beauty, To Kill a Cop, Maneaters Are Loose!, The Word, The Miracle Worker, The Return of Frank Cannon, Terror at Alcatraz, The Return of Sam McCloud.

MULGREW, KATE
Actress. b. Dubuque, IA, April 29, 1955. e. NYU. Stage work includes stints with American Shakespeare Festival, NY Shakespeare Festival, Seattle Rep. Theatre, Mark Taper Forum (LA). B'way: Black Comedy.
PICTURES: Lovespell, A Stranger Is Watching, Remo Williams: The Adventure Begins, Throw Momma from the Train, Camp Nowhere, Round Numbers, Camp Nowhere, Captain Nuke and the Bomber Boys, Trekkies, Star Trek: Nemesis.
TELEVISION: *Series:* Ryan's Hope (1975-77), Kate Columbo (Kate Loves a Mystery), Heartbeat, Man of the People, Star Trek: Voyager, Gargoyles (voice). *Movies:* The Word, Jennifer: A Woman's Story, A Time for Miracles, The Manions of America, Roses Are for the Rich, Roots: The Gift, Danielle Steel's Daddy, Fatal Friendship, For Love and Glory, Nightworld: Riddler's Moon.

MULHERN, MATT
Actor. b. Philadelphia, PA, July 21, 1960. e. Rutgers Univ.
THEATRE: *NY:* Biloxi Blues, Wasted, The Night Hank Williams Died.
PICTURES: One Crazy Summer, Extreme Prejudice, Biloxi Blues, Junior, Infinity, The Sunchaser, Walking the Waterline.
TELEVISION: *Series:* Major Dad. *Movie:* Gunsmoke: To the Last Man, Terror in the Night, A Burning Passion: The Margaret Mitchell Story.

MULHOLLAND, ROBERT E.
Executive. b. 1933. e. Northwestern U. Joined NBC News as newswriter in Chicago in 1962. 1964 made midwestern field prod. for Huntley-Brinkley Report. 1964 moved to London as European prod. for NBC News; 1965, named Washington prod. of Huntley-Brinkley Report. Transferred to L.A. in 1967 to be dir. of news, west coast. Named exec. prod. of NBC Nightly News. 1973 appt. v.p., NBC news.; 1974 exec. v.p. of NBC News. 1977 appt. pres. of NBC Television Network; also elected to board of directors; 1981, pres. & CEO. Resigned, 1984. Dir. Television Info. Office, NYC 1985-87. Prof. Northwestern U. 1988-.

MULL, MARTIN
Actor. b. Chicago, IL, Aug. 18, 1943. e. Rhode Island Sch. of Design. Started as humorist, making recordings for Warner Bros., Capricorn, ABC Records.
PICTURES: FM (debut, 1978), My Bodyguard, Serial, Take This Job and Shove It, Flicks, Mr. Mom, Bad Manners, Clue, O.C. and Stiggs, Home Is Where the Hart Is, Rented Lips (also s.p., exec. prod.), Cutting Class, Ski Patrol, Far Out Man, Think Big, Ted and Venus, The Player, Miracle Beach, Mrs. Doubtfire, Mr. Write, Edie and Pen, Jingle All the Way, Movies Money Murder, Zack and Reba, Attention Shoppers, The Year That Trembled.
TELEVISION: *Series:* Mary Hartman Mary Hartman, Fernwood 2-Night, America 2-Night, Domestic Life, His and Hers, Roseanne, The Jackie Thomas Show, Family Dog (voice), Sabrina The Teenage Witch, Hollywood Squares, The Ellen Show, Teamo Supremo. *Specials:* The History of White People in America (also prod.), Candid Camera Christmas Special (1987), Portrait of a White Marriage, The Whole Shebang. *Movies:* Sunset Limousine, California Girls, The Day My Parents Ran Away, How the West Was Fun, Sister Mary Explains It All.

MULLAN, PETER
Actor. b. Glasgow, Scotland. 1954.
PICTURES: *Actor:* The Big Man, Shallow Grave, Ruffian Hearts, Good Day for the Bad Guys, Braveheart, Trainspotting, Fairy Tale: A True Story, My Name Is Joe (Cannes Film Fest. Award, Best Actor, 1998), Miss Julie, Mauvaise passe, Ordinary Decent Criminal, The Claim, Session 9, Young Adam, Kiss of Life. *Director:* Good Day for the Bad Guys, Fridge, Orphans, Magdalena Sisters.
TELEVISION: *Movies:* Bogwoman, Nightlife.

MULLER, ROBBY
Cinematographer. b. Netherlands, April 4, 1940. e. Dutch Film Acad. Asst. cameraman in Holland before moving to Germany where he shot 9 films for Wim Wenders.
PICTURES: Alabama: 2000 Light Years, Summer in the City, Jonathan, Carlos, The Goalkeeper's Fear of the Penalty Kick, The Scarlet Letter, Die Reise Nach Wien, Kings of the Road, Alice in the Cities, Perahim Die Zweite Chance, Wrong Move, The American Friend, Mysteries, The Glass Cell, Opname, Saint Jack, Honeysuckle Rose, A Cop's Sunday, They All Laughed, Body Rock, Repo Man, Paris Texas, To Live and Die in L.A., The Longshot, Down By Law, Tricheurs, The Believers, Barfly, Il Piccolo Diavolo (The Little Devil), Mystery Train, Korczak, Until the End of the World, When Pigs Fly, The Ditvoorst Domains (actor only), Mad Dog and Glory, Breaking the Waves (NY Society of Film Critics Award and Natl Society of Film Critics Awards, 1997), Dead Man (NY Society of Film Critics Awards, 1997), Last Call, Beyond the Clouds, The Tango Lesson, Shattered Image, Ghost Dog: The Way of the Samurai, Buena Vista Social Club, Dancer in the Dark, My Brother Tom, 24 Hour Party People.

MULLIGAN, ROBERT
Director. b. Bronx, NY. Aug. 23, 1925. e. Fordham U. Served in Navy during WWII. After working as copyboy for NY Times joined CBS in mailroom. Eventually became TV dir. before moving into features.
PICTURES: Fear Strikes Out (debut, 1957), The Rat Race, The Great Imposter, Come September, The Spiral Road, To Kill a Mockingbird, Love With the Proper Stranger, Baby the Rain Must Fall, Inside Daisy Clover, Up the Down Staircase, The Stalking Moon, The Pursuit of Happiness, Summer of '42, The Other, The Nickel Ride, Bloodbrothers, Same Time Next Year, Kiss Me Goodbye, Clara's Heart, The Man in the Moon.
TELEVISION: The Moon and the Sixpence (Emmy Award, 1960), Billy Budd, Ah Wilderness, A Tale of Two Cities, The Bridge of San Luis Rey, Playhouse 90, Philco-Goodyear, Suspense, Studio One, Hallmark Hall of Fame.

MULRONEY, DERMOT
Actor. b. Alexandria, VA, Oct. 31, 1963. e. Northwestern Univ.
PICTURES: Sunset, Young Guns, Survival Quest, Staying Together, Longtime Companion, Career Opportunities, Bright Angel, Where the Day Takes You, Samantha, Point of No Return, The Thing Called Love, Silent Tongue, Bad Girls, Angels in the Outfield, There Goes My Baby, Living in Oblivion, Copycat, How to Make an American Quilt, Kansas City, Trigger Effect, My Best Friend's Wedding, Where the Money Is, Trixie, Goodbye Lover, Where the Money Is, The Safety of Objects, Lovely & Amazing, Investigating Sex, About Schmidt.
TELEVISION: *Movies:* Sin of Innocence, Daddy, Unconquered, Long Gone, The Heart of Justice, Family Pictures, The Last Outlaw. *Special:* Toma: The Drug Knot.

MUMY, BILL
Actor. r.n. Charles William Mumy Jr. b. El Centro, CA, Feb. 1, 1954. Began acting as Billy Mumy at age 6. Played with band America in 1970's, also with bands Bill Mumy & The Igloos, and The Jenerators. Has made 8 albums with Barnes & Barnes. With actor Miguel Ferrer, wrote comic books Comet Man and Trip to the Acid Dog. Has also written stories for Star Trek, The Hulk, and Spiderman comic books, and Lost in Space comic published by Innovation. Wrote music for Disney's Adventures in Wonderland series (Emmy nom.)
PICTURES: Tammy Tell Me True, Palm Springs Weekend, A Ticklish Affair, A Child is Waiting, Dear Brigitte, Rascal, Bless the Beasts and Children, Papillon, Twilight Zone—The Movie, Hard to Hold, Captain America, Double Trouble, Three Wishes, The Fantasy Worlds of Irwin Allen.
TELEVISION: *Series:* Lost in Space, Sunshine. *Movies:* Sunshine, The Rockford Files (pilot), Sunshine Christmas. *Guest:* The Twilight Zone, Alfred Hitchcock Presents, Bewitched, The Virginian, I Dream of Jeannie, The Adventures of Ozzie and Harriet, Ben Casey, The Red Skelton Show, Lancer, Here Come the Brides, Riverboat, Have Gun Will Travel, Matlock, Me and Mom, The Flash, Superboy, Babylon 5. *Pilots:* The Two of Us, Archie, Space Family Robinson.

MURDOCH, K. RUPERT
Executive. b. Australia, March 11, 1931. Son of Sir Keith Murdoch, head of The Melbourne Herald and leading figure in Australian journalism. e. Oxford U., England. Spent two years on Fleet St. before returning home to take over family paper, The Adelaide News. Acquired more Australian papers and in

1969, expanded to Britain, buying The News of the World. Moved to U.S. in 1973, buying San Antonio Express and News. Conglomerate in 1985 included New York Post, New York Magazine, The Star, The Times of London, The Boston Herald, The Chicago Sun-Times along with TV stations, book publishing companies, airline, oil and gas companies, etc. 1985, made deal to buy 20th Century-Fox Film Corp. from owner Martin Davis. Sold the NY Post, 1988 to conform with FCC regulations. Purchased Triangle Publications 1988 (including TV Guide). Currently, chmn, Sky Global Networks; chmn & CEO, News Corp. and Fox Entertainment; CEO, Fox Broadcasting; chmn., British Sky Broadcasting Group; director, Gemstar-TV Guide International, Inc.; director, Knowledge Universe.

MUREN, DENNIS E.
Visual Effects Creator and Director. b. Glendale, CA, Nov. 1, 1946. AA Pasadena CC, 1966. Studied at UCLA. Freelance special effects 1968-75. Cameraman Cascade 1975-76. Dir. of photography, visual effects Industrial Light Magic 1976-80. AMPAS Scientific/Technical Award, 1981. Member ASC, AMPAS.
PICTURES: Star Wars, Close Encounters of the Third Kind, The Empire Strikes Back (Acad. Award), Dragonslayer, E.T.: the Extraterrestrial (Acad. Award), Return of the Jedi (Acad. Award, BAFTA Award), Indiana Jones and the Temple of Doom (Acad. Award, BAFTA award), Young Sherlock Holmes, Captain Eo (short feature), Innerspace (Acad. Award), Empire of the Sun, Willow, Ghostbusters II, The Abyss (Acad. Award), Terminator 2 (Acad. Award, BAFTA award), Jurassic Park (Acad. Award, BAFTA award), Casper, Star Wars: Episode I - The Phantom Menace (Acad. Award nom.), Artifical Intelligence: AI (Acad. Award nom.), Star Wars: Episode II - Attack of the Clones, The Hulk.
TELEVISION: Battlestar Galactica, Caravan of Courage (Emmy).

MURPHY, BEN
Actor. b. Jonesboro, AR, March 6, 1942. e. U. of Illinois. Degree in drama from Pasadena Playhouse. Acted in campus productions and toured in summer stock. Film debut with small role in The Graduate, 1967.
PICTURES: Yours Mine and Ours, The Thousand Plane Raid, Sidecar Racers, Time Walker, To Protect and Serve.
TELEVISION: Movies: The Letters, Wild Bill Hickock, Bridger, Heat Wave, Runaway, This Is the West That Was, Gemini Man, Hospital Fire, The Cradle Will Fall, Stark: Mirror Image. Series: The Name of the Game, Alias Smith and Jones, Griff, Gemini Man, The Chisholms, Lottery!, Berrenger's, The Dirty Dozen. Mini-Series: The Winds of War.

MURPHY, BRITTANY
Actress. b. Nov. 10, 1977.
PICTURES: Family Prayers, Clueless, Drive, Freeway, The Prophecy II, Phoenix, Falling Sky, Bongwater, Trixie, Piece of My Heart, Drop Dead Gorgeous, Cherry Falls, Girl Interrupted, The Audition, Sidewalks of New York, Summer Catch, Trixie, Don't Say a Word, Riding in Cars with Boys, 8 Mile, Spun, Just Married, Molly Gunn, Uptown Girls.
TELEVISION: Movies: David and Lisa, Devil's Arithmetic. Series: Drexell's Class, Almost Home, Sister Sister, King of the Hill (voice). Guest: Murphy Brown, Blossom, Frasier, Party of Five, SeaQuest DSV, Boy Meet World, Clueless, Nash Bridges.

MURPHY, EDDIE
Actor. b. Brooklyn, NY, April 3, 1961. e. Roosevelt High Sch. Wrote and performed own comedy routines at youth centers and local bars at age 15. Worked on comedy club circuit; at 19 joined TV's Saturday Night Live as writer and performer. Recordings: Eddie Murphy, Eddie Murphy: Comedian, How Could It Be?, Love's Alright. Voted Top-Money Making Star of 1988 on Quigley Poll, NATO/ShoWest Star of the Decade, for 1980's.
PICTURES: 48 HRS. (debut, 1982), Trading Places, Best Defense, Beverly Hills Cop, The Golden Child, Beverly Hills Cop II, Eddie Murphy Raw (also s.p., exec. prod.), Coming to America (also story), Harlem Nights (also dir., s.p, exec. prod.), Another 48 HRS., Boomerang (also story), The Distinguished Gentleman, Beverly Hills Cop III, Vampire in Brooklyn (also co-prod.), The Nutty Professor (also co-exec. prod.; Nat'l Society of Film Critics Award, 1997), Metro, Mulan (voice), Doctor Dolittle, Holy Man, Life, Bowfinger, The Nutty Professor II, Shrek, Dr. Dolittle 2, Showtime, The Adventures of Pluto Nash, I Spy, The Incredible Shrinking Man, Daddy Day Care, Shrek 2.
TELEVISION: Series: Saturday Night Live (1981-84), The PJs. Pilots (exec. prod.): What's Alan Watching? (also cameo), Coming to America. Movie (exec. prod.): The Kid Who Loved Christmas.

MURPHY, MICHAEL
Actor. b. Los Angeles, CA, May 5, 1938. e. U. of Arizona. m. actress Wendy Crewson. Taught English and Drama in L.A. city school system, 1962-64. N.Y. stage debut as dir. of Rat's Nest, 1978.
PICTURES: Double Trouble (debut, 1967), Countdown, The Legend of Lylah Clare, The Arrangement, That Cold Day in the Park, M*A*S*H, Count Yorga: Vampire, Brewster McCloud, McCabe and Mrs. Miller, What's Up Doc?, The Thief Who Came

o Dinner, Phase IV, Nashville, The Front, An Unmarried Woman, The Great Bank Hoax, The Class of Miss MacMichael, Manhattan, The Year of Living Dangerously, Strange Behavior, Cloak and Dagger, Salvador, Mesmerized, Shocker, Folks!, Batman Returns, Clean Slate, Bad Company, Kansas City, Private Parts, The Island, Magnolia, Tricks.
TELEVISION: Series: Two Marriages, Hard Copy. Guest: Saints and Sinners, Ben Casey, Dr. Kildare, Bonanza, Combat. Movies: The Autobiography of Miss Jane Pittman, The Caine Mutiny Court-Martial, Tailspin: Behind the Korean Airlines Tragedy, Special Report: Journey to Mars, Breaking the Surface: The Greg Louganis Story, Indiscretion of An American Wife, The Day Reagan Was Shot. Specials: John Cheever's Oh Youth and Beauty, Tanner '88.

MURPHY, THOMAS S.
Executive. e. Cornell Univ (B.S.M.E.), Harvard U. Grad. Sch. of Bus. Admin. (M.B.A.). Joined Capital Cities at its inception in 1954. Named a dir. in 1957, then pres. in 1964. Chmn. & CEO of Capital Cities, 1966-90. Company named Capital Cities/ABC Inc. in 1986 after acquistion of American Broadcasting Companies Inc. 1990-94, chmn. of bd. Resumed position of chmn. & CEO in Feb., 1994. Retired, 1996. Currently serves on boards of Walt Disney, DoubleClick, Inc., and New York University.

MURRAY, BARBARA
Actress. b. London, England, Sept. 27, 1929. Stage debut in Variety, 1946.
PICTURES: Badger's Green (debut, 1948), Passport to Pimlico, Don't Ever Leave Me, Boys in Brown, Poets Pub, Tony Draws a Horse, Dark Man, Frightened Man, Mystery Junction, Another Man's Poison, Hot Ice, Street Corner (Both Sides of the Law), Meet Mr. Lucifer, Doctor at Large, Campbell's Kingdom, A Cry from the Streets, Girls in Arms, A Dandy in Aspic, Tales From the Crypt.
TELEVISION: Series: The Power Game, The Bretts.

MURRAY, BILL
Actor. b. Wilmette, IL, Sept. 21, 1950. e. attended Regis Coll. Was pre-med student; left to join brother, Brian Doyle-Murray, in Second City the Chicago improvisational troupe. Appeared with brother on radio in National Lampoon Radio Hour, and in off-B'way revue, National Lampoon Show. Also on radio provided voice of Johnny Storm the Human Torch on Marvel Comics' Fantastic Four. Hired by ABC for Saturday Night Live with Howard Cosell; then by NBC for Saturday Night Live, 1977.
PICTURES: Jungle Burger (debut, 1975), Meatballs, Mr. Mike's Mondo Video, Where the Buffalo Roam, Loose Shoes, Caddyshack, Stripes, Tootsie, Ghostbusters, The Razor's Edge (also co-s.p.), Nothing Lasts Forever, Little Shop of Horrors, Scrooged, Ghostbusters II, Quick Change (also co-dir., co-prod.), What About Bob?, Groundhog Day, Mad Dog and Glory, Ed Wood, Space Jam, Larger Than Life, Kingpin, The Man Who Knew Too Little, With Friends Like These, Veeck As in Wreck, Rushmore, Wild Things, The Cradle Will Rock, Hamlet, Scout's Honor, Company Man, Charlie's Angels, Osmosis Jones, The Royal Tenenbaums, Speaking of Sex, The Wedding Contract.
TELEVISION: Series: Saturday Night Live (1977-80; also writer; Emmy Award for writing 1977), The Sweet Spot. Pilot: The TV TV Show. Movie: All You Need Is Cash. Specials: It's Not Easy Being Me—The Rodney Dangerfield Show, Steve Martin's Best Show Ever, Second City—25 Years in Revue.

MURRAY, DON
Actor, Director, Writer. b. Hollywood, CA, July 31, 1929. e. AADA. Mother was a Ziegfeld Girl, father was dance dir. for Fox Studio.
THEATRE: B'way: Insect Comedy, The Rose Tattoo, The Skin of Our Teeth, The Hot Corner, Smith (musical), The Norman Conquests, Same Time Next Year. National tours: California Suite, Chicago.
PICTURES: Bus Stop (debut, 1956; Acad. Award nom.), The Bachelor Party, A Hatful of Rain, From Hell to Texas, These Thousand Hills, Shake Hands With the Devil, One Foot in Hell, The Hoodlum Priest (also co-prod., co-s.p. as Don Deer), Advise and Consent, Escape From East Berlin, One Man's Way, Baby the Rain Must Fall, Kid Rodelo, The Plainsman, Sweet Love Bitter, The Viking Queen, Childish Things (Confession of Tom Harris; also prod., co-s.p.), The Cross and the Switchblade (dir., co-s.p. only), Happy Birthday Wanda June, Conquest of the Planet of the Apes, Cotter, Call Me by My Rightful Name (also prod., co-s.p.), Deadly Hero, Damien (dir., s.p. only), Endless Love, I Am the Cheese, Radioactive Dreams, Peggy Sue Got Married, Scorpion, Made in Heaven, Ghosts Can't Do It, Island Prety, Elvis Is Alive.
TELEVISION: Series: Made in America (panelist), The Outcasts, Knots Landing, Brand New Life, Sons and Daughters. Movies: The Borgia Stick, Daughter of the Mind, The Intruders, The Girl on the Late Late Show, The Sex Symbol, A Girl Named Sooner, Rainbow, Crisis in Mid-Air, If Things Were Different, The Boy Who Drank to Much, Fugitive Family, Return of the Rebels, Thursday's Child, Quarterback Princess, License to Kill, A Touch of Scandal, Something in Common, Stillwatch, The Stepford Children, Mistress, Brand New Life. Specials: For I Have Loved Strangers (also writer), Hasty Heart, Billy Budd, Winterset, Alas

Babylon, Justin Morgan Had a Horse, My Dad Isn't Crazy Is He?, Montana Crossroads (Emmy nom.)

MURRAY, JAN
Comedian, Actor. b. Bronx, NY, Oct. 4, 1917. Started as comedian, nightclub performer, continuing on radio, tv.
THEATRE: A Funny Thing Happened on the Way to the Forum, Guys and Dolls, Silk Stockings, Bye Bye Birdie, A Thousand Clowns, Come Blow Your Horn, The Odd Couple, Make a Million, Don't Drink the Water, Critic's Choice, You Know I Can't Hear You When the Water Is Running.
PICTURES: Who Killed Teddy Bear? (debut, 1965), Tarzan and the Great River, The Busy Body, A Man Called Dagger, Which Way to the Front?, History of the World Part I, Fear City.
TELEVISION: Series: (emcee/host): Songs for Sale, Go Lucky, Sing It Again, Blind Date, Dollar a Second (also creator, prod.), Jan Murray Time, Treasure Hunt (also creator, prod.), Charge Account (also creator, prod.), Chain Letter. Guest: Zane Grey Theatre, Dr., Kildare, Burke's Law, The Lucy Show, Love American Style, Mannix, Ellery Queen, Hardcastle and McCormick. Movies: Roll Freddy Roll, Banjo Hackett: Roamin' Free, The Dream Merchants.

MUSANTE, TONY
Actor. b. Bridgeport, CT, June 30, 1936. e. Oberlin Coll. B.A. Directed local theatre, then appeared off-Broadway, in regional theater, and on Dupont Show of the Month (Ride With Terror).
THEATRE: B'way: The Lady From Dubuque, P.S. Your Cat Is Dead, 27 Wagons Full of Cotton, Memory of Two Mondays. Off-B'way: Grand Magic, Cassatt, A Gun Play, Benito Cereno, L'Histoire du Soldat, Match-Play, The Zoo Story, The Pinter Plays (The Collection), Kiss Mama, The Balcony, Snow Orchid, The Flip Side, Frankie and Johnny in the Claire de Lune. Regional: The Big Knife, A Streetcar Named Desire, The Taming of the Shrew, Widows, The Archbishop's Ceiling, Dancing in the Endzone, Two Brothers, Souvenir, APA Shakespeare Rep., Wait Until Dark, Anthony Rose, Mount Allegro, Double Play, Falling Man, Breaking Legs, Love Letters, The Sisters, Italian Funerals and Other Festive Occasions.
PICTURES: Once a Thief, The Incident, The Detective, The Mercenary, The Bird with the Crystal Plumage, The Grissom Gang, The Last Run, Anonymous Venetian, Collector's Item, The Repenter, The Pisciotta Case, Goodbye and Amen, Break Up, Nocturne, The Pope of Greenwich Village, One Night at Dinner, Appointment in Trieste, Devil's Hill, The Deep End of the Ocean, The Seventh Scroll, The Yards.
TELEVISION: Series: Toma, Oz. Guest: Chrysler Theatre, Alfred Hitchcock Hour, N.Y.P.D., The Fugitive, Trials of O'Brien, Police Story, Medical Story, Thomas Gottschallk's Late Night TV, Loving, Acapulco H.E.A.T., Nothing Sacred, As the World Turns. Movies: Rearview Mirror, The Court Martial of Lt. William Calley, Desperate Miles, The Quality of Mercy, Nowhere to Hide, My Husband is Missing, The Story of Esther, High Ice, Last Waltz on a Tightrope, Weekend (Amer. Playhouse), Nutcracker: Money Madness & Murder, Breaking Up Is Hard To Do, The Baron, The Seventh Scroll, Deep Family Secrets.

MYERS, JULIAN F.
Public Relations Executive. b. Detroit, MI, Feb. 22, 1918. e. Wayne U., 1935-37, USC, 1937-39. Distribution, Loew's Detroit, 1941-42; asst. story editor, idea man, Columbia, 1942-46; publicist, 20th Century-Fox, 1948-62; public relations, Julian F. Myers, Inc., 1962; pres., Myers Studios, Inc., 1966; pres., New Horizons Broadcasting Corp., 1968-69; sr. publicist American Intl. Pictures, 1970-80. Pres., Hollywood Press Club; former member Variety Club; Academy of Motion Pictures Arts & Sciences; Board of Governors Film Industry Workshops, Inc. 1977, 1979, western v.p.; Publicists Guild; Recipient of Publicists Guild's Robert Yeager Award. First male member Hollywood Women's Press Club. Co-founder HANDS (Hollywood Answering Needs of Disaster Survivors). Member, M.P. Pioneers. Winner, 1980 Publicists Guild Les Mason Award. Instructor in publicity, UCLA, 1979-present, and at Loyola Marymount U, 1991-present. Filmways Pictures, pub. dept., 1980-81. Exec. v.p., worldwide m.p. and TV pub./mktg., Hanson & Schwam Public Relations 1981-91. Author of Myersystem and Myerscope guides. Member: USC Cinema & TV Alumni Assn., West Coast P.R. Will Rogers Inst., Acad. TV Arts Sciences; p.r. coord. comm., Academy of Motion Picture Arts & Sciences. Bd. of dirs., Show Biz Expo. Publicist, Prods. Guild of America. Pres. Julian Myers Public Relations, nominated MoPic Showmanship of the Year, Publicists Guild of America, 1993. Columnist, Drama-Logue Magazine. Special Award of Merit, Publicists Guild of America, 1998. Member, Women in Film.

MYERS, MIKE
Actor. b. Scarborough, Ontario, Canada, May 25, 1963.
PICTURES: Elvis Stories, Wayne's World (also s.p.), So I Married an Axe Murderer(also s.p.), Wayne's World 2 (also s.p.), Austin Powers: International Man of Mystery (also s.p., prod.), 54, Austin Powers: The Spy Who Shagged Me (also s.p., prod.), Mystery Alaska, Shrek (voice), A View from the Top, Austin Powers in Goldmember (also s.p. & prod.), The Cat in the Hat, Shrek 2.
TELEVISION: Series: Mullarky & Myers, Saturday Night Live.

Guest: King of Kensington, The Littlest Hobo.

MYERSON, BERNARD
Executive. b. New York, NY, March 25, 1918. Entered m.p. ind. with Fabian Theatres, 1938-63; last position as exec. v.p.; joined Loew's Theatres as v.p., 1963; exec. v.p. and board member, Loew's Corp.; pres. Loew's Theatres, 1971. Chmn. & pres., Loews Theatre Management Corp., 1985, presently retired. Member of Executive Committee Greater N.Y. Chapter, National Foundation of March of Dimes; Honorary chmn., bd. mem., & former pres., Will Rogers Memorial Fund; exec. comm., bd., National Assn. Theatre Owners; bd. member & former pres., Motion Picture Pioneers; treas. Variety Intl.; member bd. of dirs., Burke Rehabilitation Center; member, N.Y.S. Governor's Council on M.P. & T.V. Development; vice-chmn., adv. bd. of Tisch Sch. of Arts, NYU.

N

NABORS, JIM
Actor. b. Sylacauga, AL, June 12, 1932. Discovered performing in an L.A. nightclub in early 1960's by Andy Griffith, who asked him to appear on his series. Developed a second career as a singer. Between 1966-72 had 12 albums on best selling charts.
PICTURES: The Best Little Whorehouse in Texas, Stroker Ace, Cannonball Run II.
TELEVISION: Series: The Andy Griffith Show, Gomer Pyle USMC, The Jim Nabors Hour, The Lost Saucer, The Jim Nabors Show (synd. talk show). Movie: Return to Mayberry.

NAIFY, ROBERT
Executive. b. Sacramento, CA. e. Attended Stanford U. Worked for United California Theatres starting in 1946 in various capacities including: theatre manager, purchasing agent, film buyer, general manager and president. 1963 became exec. v.p. United Artists Communications; 1971 became pres. & CEO until 1987. Then president, Todd-AO Corporation.

NAIR, MIRA
Director, Producer. b. Bhubaneshwar, India, October 15, 1957. e. Irish Catholic Missionary School in India, Delhi U., Harvard U. A course in documentary filmmaking at Harvard led to directing 4 non-fiction films including India Cabaret (1985) and Children of Desired Sex.
PICTURES: Director-Producer: Salaam Bombay! (Cannes Film Fest. Camera d'Or/Prix du Publique; Acad. Award nom.), Mississippi Masala (also s.p.), The Perez Family, Kama Sutra: A Tale of Love, Monsoon Wedding (also prod.), Hysterical Blindness.

NAMATH, JOE
Actor. b. Beaver Falls, PA, May 31, 1943. e. U. of Alabama. Former professional football star.
PICTURES: Norwood (debut, 1970), C.C. & Company, The Last Rebel, Avalanche Express, Chattanooga Choo Choo, Going Under.
TELEVISION: Series: The Waverly Wonders, Figure It Out. Host: Monday Night Football (1985). Movies: Marriage Is Alive and Well, The Bear: The Legend of Coach Paul Bryant. Guest: Here's Lucy, The Brady Bunch, The Love Boat, Kate and Allie.

NARIZZANO, SILVIO
Producer, Director. b. Montreal, Canada, Feb. 8, 1927. e. U. of Bishop's, Lennoxville, Quebec, B.A. Was active as actor-director in Canadian theatre before going to England for drama and theatrical film work.
PICTURES: Director: Under Ten Flags (co-dir.), Die! Die! My Darling!, Georgy Girl, Blue, Loot, Redneck (also prod.), The Sky Is Falling, Why Shoot the Teacher?, The Class of Miss MacMichael, Choices, Double Play. Producer: Negatives, Fade-In.
TELEVISION: The Babysitter, Poet Game, The Little Farm, Come Back Little Sheba, Staying On, Young Shoulders, The Body in the Library. Series: Miss Marple.

NATHANSON, MICHAEL
Executive. Began his career at NBC Sports, NY. In 1977 moved to LA and worked as prod. asst. on The Deep, Sinbad the Eye of the Tiger. 1980-85, v.p., prod., MGM, United Artists, Warner Bros. 1987, exec. v.p., prod., Columbia Pictures; 1989-94, pres. of Worldwide Prod. at Columbia Pictures; projects included: Awakenings, The Prince of Tides, Boyz N the Hood, A River Runs Through It, A League of Their Own, In the Line of Fire, Groundhog Day, Bram Stoker's Dracula, and others. 1994-97, chmn. & CEO, Regency Productions; produced: A Time to Kill, Tin Cup, Natural Born Killers, Heat, Copy Cat. 1997-, pres. & CEO, MGM Pictures; produced: Species 2, Dirty Work.

NAUGHTON, DAVID
Actor, Singer. b. Hartford, CT, Feb. 13, 1951. Brother is actor James Naughton. e. U. of Pennsylvania, B.A. Studied at London Acad. of Music and Dramatic Arts. Numerous TV commercials,

including music for Dr. Pepper. On B'way in Hamlet, Da, Poor Little Lambs.
PICTURES: Midnight Madness (debut, 1980), An American Werewolf in London, Separate Ways, Hot Dog... The Movie, Not for Publication, The Boy in Blue, Separate Vacations, Kidnapped, Quite By Chance, Beanstalk, The Sleeping Car, Overexposed, Wild Cactus, Desert Steel, Amityville: A New Generation, Beanstalk, Ice Cream Man, Urban Safari, Little Insects, A Crack in the Floor, Flying Virus.
TELEVISION: Series: Makin' It, At Ease, My Sister Sam, Temporary Insanity, The Belles of Bleeker St., Those Two. Movies: I Desire, Getting Physical, Goddess of Love. Guest: Twilight Zone, Murder She Wrote, Touched By An Angel, Seinfeld, Cybil, Melrose Place.

NAUGHTON, JAMES
Actor. b. Middletown, CT, Dec. 6, 1945. Father of actors Greg Naughton and Keira Naughton. e. Brown U., A.B., 1967; Yale U., M.F.A., drama, 1970.
THEATRE: NY: I Love My Wife (B'way debut, 1977), Long Day's Journey Into Night (Theatre World, Drama Desk and New York Critics Circle Awards, 1971), Whose Life Is It Anyway?, Losing Time, Drinks Before Dinner, City of Angels (Tony & Drama Desk Awards, 1990), Four Baboons Adoring the Sun. Regional: Who's Afraid of Virginia Woolf? (Long Wharf), The Glass Menagerie (Long Wharf), Hamlet (Long Wharf), Julius Caesar (Amer. Shakespeare Festival), 8 seasons at Williamstown Theatre Festival, Chicago (B'way, 1996-97).
PICTURES: The Paper Chase (debut, 1973), Second Wind, A Stranger is Watching, Cat's Eye, The Glass Menagerie, The Good Mother, First Kid, Broadway: The Golden Age by the Legends Who Were There, Fascination.
TELEVISION: Special: Look Homeward Angel (1972). Series: Faraday and Company, Planet of the Apes, Making the Grade, Trauma Center, Raising Miranda, The Cosby Mysteries. Movies: F. Scott Fitzgerald and the Last of the Belles, The Last 36 Hours of Dr. Durant, The Bunker, My Body My Child, Parole, The Last of the Great Survivors, Between Darkness and the Dawn, Sin of Innocence, Traveling Man, Antigone, The Cosby Mysteries (pilot), The Birds II: Land's End, Cagney & Lacey: The Return, Cagney & Lacey: Together Again, Raising Caines, Crime Stories: The Capture and Trial of Adolf Eichmann, The Truth About Jane, Our Town.

NEAL, PATRICIA
Actress. b. Packard, KY, Jan. 20, 1926. e. Northwestern U. Worker as doctor's asst., cashier, hostess, model, jewelry store clerk prior to prof. career as actress. In summer stock before B'way debut in The Voice of the Turtle, 1946. Autobiography: As I Am (with Richard DeNeut, 1988).
THEATRE: NY: The Voice of the Turtle, Another Part of the Forest (Tony, Donaldson & Drama Critic Awards), The Children's Hour, Roomful of Roses, The Miracle Worker. England: Suddenly Last Summer.
PICTURES: John Loves Mary (debut 1949), The Fountainhead, It's a Great Feeling, The Hasty Heart, Bright Leaf, Three Secrets, The Breaking Point, Raton Pass, Operation Pacific, The Day the Earth Stood Still, Weekend With Father, Diplomatic Courier, Washington Story, Something for the Birds, Stranger From Venus (Immediate Disaster), Your Woman, A Face in the Crowd, Breakfast at Tiffany's, Hud (Academy Award, BFA Award, 1963), Psyche '59, In Harm's Way (BFA Award, 1965), The Subject Was Roses (Acad. Award nom.), The Night Digger, Baxter, Happy Mother's Day Love George, "B" Must Die, The Passage, Ghost Story, An Unremarkable Life, Theremin: An Electronic Odyssey, From Russia to Hollywood: The 100-Year Odyssey of Chekhov and Shdanoff, Cookie's Fortune, For the Love of May, Broadway: The Golden Age by the Legends Who Were There.
TELEVISION: Movies: The Homecoming, Things in Their Season, Eric, Tail Gunner Joe, A Love Affair: The Eleanor and Lou Gehrig Story, The Bastard, All Quiet on the Western Front, Shattered Vows, Love Leads the Way, Caroline?, A Mother's Right: The Elizabeth Morgan Story, Heidi. Guest: Little House on the Prairie, Murder She Wrote. BBC: Days & Nights of Beebee Finstermaker, The Country Girl, Clash By Night, The Royal Family.

NEAME, RONALD
C.B.E. Cinematographer, Producer, Director. b. Hendon, Eng. April 23, 1911. e. U. Coll. Sch., London. p. Elwin Neame, London photog., & Ivy Close, m.p. actress. Entered m.p. ind. 1928; asst. cameraman on first full-length Brit. sound film, Blackmail, dir. by Alfred Hitchcock, 1929; became chief cameraman & lighting expert, 1934; in 1945 joint assoc. prod., Noel Coward Prods.
PICTURES: Cinematographer: Girls Will Be Boys (co-cine.), Happy (co-cine.), Elizabeth of England, Honours Easy (co-cine.), Joy Ride, Music Hath Charms, The Crimes of Stephen Hawke, The Improper Dutchess, A Star Fell From Heaven, Against the Tide, Brief Ecstasy, Feather Your Nest, Keep Fit, Weekend Millionaire, Gaunt Stranger, The Phantom Strikes, The Crime of Peter Frame, Dangerous Secrets, Penny Paradise, Who Goes Next? Cheers Boys Cheer, Sweeney Todd: The Demon Barber of Fleet Street, Let's Be Famous, Trouble Brewing, The Ware Case, Let George Do It, Return to Yesterday, Saloon Bar, Four Just Men, Major Barbara, A Yank in the R.A.F. (Brit. flying sequence),

In Which We Serve, This Happy Breed, Blithe Spirit, Brief Encounter, Great Expectations (also co-s.p.), Oliver Twist (also co-s.p.), A Young Man's Fancy, Passionate Friends. Director: Take My Life, Golden Salamander (also co-s.p.), The Card (The Promoter; also prod.), Man With a Million (The Million Pound Note), The Man Who Never Was, The Seventh Sin, Windom's Way, The Horse's Mouth, Tunes of Glory, I Could Go on Singing, The Chalk Garden, Mister Moses, Gambit, A Man Could Get Killed (co-dir.), Prudence and the Pill (co-dir.), The Prime of Miss Jean Brodie, Scrooge, The Poseidon Adventure, The Odessa File, Meteor, Hopscotch, First Monday in October, Foreign Body, The Magic Balloon.

NEEDHAM, HAL
Director, Writer. b. Memphis, TN, March 6, 1931. e. Student public schools. Served with Paratroopers, U.S. Army 1951-54. Founder Stunts Unlimited, Los Angeles, 1970; stuntman Stunts Unlimited, 1956-65; dir. and stunt coordinator second unit, 1965-75. Chmn. of bd., Camera Platforms International, Inc. 1985. Owner Budweiser Rocket Car (fastest car in the world). Member Screen Actors Guild, AFTRA, Writers Guild of America, Directors Guild of America.
PICTURES: Dir.: Smokey and the Bandit (debut, 1977; also co-story), Hooper, The Villain, Smokey and the Bandit II, The Cannonball Run, Megaforce (also co-s.p.), Stroker Ace (also co-s.p.), Cannonball Run II (also co-s.p.), RAD, Body Slam.
TELEVISION: Series: Hal Needham's Wild World of Stunts (synd. series; also writer, star). Movie: Death Car on the Freeway, Hostage Hotel, The Sunchaser, (stunts). Pilot: Stunts Unlimited (pilot). Episode: B.L. Stryker.

NEESON, LIAM
Actor. b. Ballymena, Northern Ireland, June 7, 1952. m. actress Natasha Richardson. Former amateur boxer. Was driving a fork lift truck for a brewery when he joined the Lyric Player's Theatre in Belfast. Made prof. debut in The Risen (1976) and stayed with rep. co. 2 years. Moved to Dublin as freelance actor before joining the Abbey Theatre.
THEATRE: The Informer (Dublin Theatre Fest.), Translations (National Theatre, London). NY theatre debut 1992 in Anna Christie (Theatre World Award).
PICTURES: Excalibur (debut, 1981), Krull, The Bounty, Lamb, The Innocent, The Mission, Duet For One, A Prayer for the Dying, Suspect, Satisfaction, The Dead Pool, The Good Mother, High Spirits, Next of Kin, Dark Man, Crossing the Line (The Big Man), Shining Through, Under Suspicion, Husbands and Wives, Leap of Faith, Ethan Frome, Deception, Schindler's List (Acad. Award nom.), Nell, Rob Roy, Before and After, Michael Collins, A Leap of Faith (voice), Alaska: Spirit of the Wild (voice), Ambrose Chapel, Everest (narrator), Les Miserables, The Haunting, Star Wars: Episode I-The Phantom Menace, Omagh the Legacy: Clarie and Stephen's Story (voice), Gun Shy, Endurance: Shackleton's Legendary Antarctic Expedition (voice), Journey into Amazing Caves (voice), Gangs of New York, Star Wars: Episode 2 - Attack of the Clones (voice), K-19: The Widowmaker, Exorcist 4:1.
TELEVISION: Merlin and the Sword, Across the Water (BBC), Ellis Island, A Woman of Substance, Sweet As You Are, The Great War, The Greeks: Crucible of Civilization, The Man Who Came to Dinner, Inside the Space Station (voice), Revenge of the Whale, Nobel Prize Peace Concert, Who Is Alan Smithee?. Mini-Series: The Greeks.

NEILL, SAM
Actor. r.n. Nigel Neill. b. Northern Ireland, Sept. 14, 1947. Raised in New Zealand. e. U. of Canterbury. In repertory before joining N.Z. National Film Unit, acting and directing documentaries and shorts. 1992, awarded the O.B.E. for his services to acting. Co-directed, co-wrote and appeared in New Zealand documentary Cinema of Unease: A Personal Journey by Sam Neill.
PICTURES: Sleeping Dogs (debut, 1977), The Journalist, My Brilliant Career, Just Out of Reach, Attack Force Z, The Final Conflict, Possession, Enigma, Le Sang des Autres, Robbery Under Arms, Plenty, For Love Alone, The Good Wife, A Cry in the Dark (Australian Film Inst. Award), Dead Calm, The French Revolution, The Hunt for Red October, Until the End of the World, Hostage, Memoirs of an Invisible Man, Death in Brunswick, Jurassic Park, The Piano, Sirens, Rudyard Kipling's The Jungle Book, In the Mouth of Madness, Country Life, Restoration, Victory, Event Horizon, The Revengers' Comedies, The Horse Whisperer, My Mother Frank, Molokai: The Story of Father Damien, Bicentennial Man, The Magic Pudding (voice), Numero Bruno, Jurassic Park 3, The Zookeeper, Dirty Deeds, Spider-Man 2.
TELEVISION: The Sullivans, Young Ramsay, Lucinda Brayford, The Country Girls. Mini-Series: Kane and Abel, Reilly Ace of Spies, Amerika, Merlin, Doctor Zhivago. Movies: From a Far Country: Pope John Paul II, Ivanhoe, The Blood of Others, Arthur Hailey's Strong Medicine, Leap of Faith, Fever, One Against the Wind, The Sinking of the Rainbow Warrior, Family Pictures, Sally Hemmings: An American Scandal, Submerged, Space, Framed, SuperCroc. Guest: The Simpsons (voice).

NELLIGAN, KATE
Actress. r.n. Patricia Colleen Nelligan. b. London, Ontario, Canada, March 16, 1951.
THEATRE: Barefoot in the Park, A Streetcar Named Desire, Playboy of the Western World, Private Lives, Plenty, Serious Money, Spoils of War, Bad Habits.
PICTURES: The Romantic Englishwoman, Dracula, Mr. Patman, Eye of the Needle, Without a Trace, The Mystery of Henry Moore, Eleni, Frankie and Johnny (BAFTA Award), The Prince of Tides (Acad. Award nom.), Shadows and Fog, Fatal Instinct, Wolf, Margaret's Museum, How to Make an American Quilt, Up Close and Personal, U.S. Marshals, Stolen Moments, Rape: A Crime of War, Boy Meets Girl, The Cider House Rules.
TELEVISION: Movies/Specials: The Onedin Line, The Lady of the Camelias, Therese Raquin, Count of Monte Cristo, Victims, Kojak: The Price of Justice, Love and Hate: The Story of Colin and Joann Thatcher, Three Hotels, Terror Strikes the Class Reunion, Diamond Fleece, Liar Liar, Shattered Trust: The Shari Karney Story, Spoils of War, Million Dollar Babies, Captive Heart: The James Mink Story, Calm At Susnet, Love Is Strange, Swing Vote, Walter and Henry, A Wrinkle in Time, Blessed Stranger: After Flight 111.

NELSON, BARRY
Actor. r.n. Robert Neilson. b. Oakland, CA, Apr. 16, 1920. e. U. of California. London stage in No Time for Sergeants, 1957.
THEATRE: B'way: Light Up the Sky, The Rat Race, The Moon Is Blue, Mary Mary, Cactus Flower, Everything in the Garden, Seascape, The Norman Conquests, The Act, 42nd Street.
PICTURES: Shadow of the Thin Man, Johnny Eager, Dr. Kildare's Victory, Rio Rita, Eyes in the Night, Bataan, The Human Comedy, A Guy Named Joe, Winged Victory, The Beginning or the End, Undercover Maisie, The Man With My Face, The First Traveling Saleslady, Mary Mary, Airport, Pete 'n' Tillie, The Shining, Island Claws.
TELEVISION: Series: The Hunter, My Favorite Husband. Mini-Series: Washington: Behind Closed Doors. Movies: The Borgia Stick, Seven in Darkness, Climb an Angry Mountain. Guest: Suspense, Alfred Hitchcock Presents, Longstreet, Taxi, Magnum P.I., Murder She Wrote.

NELSON, CRAIG T.
Actor. b. Spokane, WA, April 4, 1946. Began career as writer/performer on Lohman and Barkley Show in Los Angeles. Teamed with Barry Levinson as a comedy writer. Wrote for Tim Conway Show, Alan King TV special; guest appearances on talk shows and Mary Tyler Moore Show. Produced series of 52 half-hour films on American artists, American Still. Returned to L.A. in 1978 and acting career.
PICTURES: And Justice for All (debut, 1979), Where the Buffalo Roam, Private Benjamin, Stir Crazy, The Formula, Poltergeist, Man Woman and Child, All the Right Moves, The Osterman Weekend, Silkwood, The Killing Fields, Poltergeist II, Red Riding Hood, Action Jackson, Rachel River, Me and Him, Troop Beverly Hills, Turner & Hooch, I'm Not Rappaport, Ghosts of Mississippi, The Devil's Advocate, Wag the Dog, Top of the World, The Skulls, All Over Again.
TELEVISION: Series: Call to Glory, Coach (Emmy Award, 1992), The District.Guest: Wonder Woman, Charlie's Angels, How the West Was Won. Movies: Diary of a Teenage Hitchhiker, Rage, Promise of Love, Inmates: A Love Story, Chicago Story, Paper Dolls, Alex: The Life of a Child, The Ted Kennedy Jr. Story, Murderers Among Us: The Simon Wiesenthal Story, Extreme Close-Up, The Josephine Baker Story, The Switch, The Fire Next Time, Ride With the Wind (also co-writer), Probable Cause, Take Me Home Again, If These Walls Could Talk, The Huntress, Dirty Pictures Mini-Series: Drug Wars: The Camarena Story, To Serve and Protect, The Fifty, Creature.

NELSON, DAVID
Actor. b. New York, NY, Oct. 24, 1936. e. Hollywood H.S., U. of Southern California. Son of Ozzie Nelson and Harriet Hilliard Nelson; brother of late Rick Nelson.
PICTURES: Here Comes the Nelsons, Peyton Place, The Remarkable Mr. Pennypacker, Day of the Outlaw, The Big Circus, "30," The Big Show, No Drums No Bugles, Up In Smoke, Cry-Baby, Ozzie and Harriet: The Adventures of America's Favorite Family. Director: A Rare Breed, The Last Plane Out, Death Screams, Cry-Baby.
TELEVISION: Series: The Adventures of Ozzie and Harriet (also dir. episodes). Movies: Smash-Up on Interstate 5, High School U.S.A. Guest: Hondo, The Love Boat. Dir.: Easy To Be Free (special), OK Crackerby (series).

NELSON, JUDD
Actor. b. Portland, ME, Nov. 28, 1959. e. Haverford/Bryn Mawr Coll. Studied acting at Stella Adler Conservatory. NY theatre includes Carnal Knowledge.
PICTURES: Making the Grade (debut, 1984), Fandango, The Breakfast Club, St. Elmo's Fire, Blue City, Transformers (voice), From the Hip, Relentless, Far Out Man, New Jack City, The Dark Backward, Primary Motive, Entangled, Conflict of Interest, Caroline at Midnight, Hail Caesar, Every Breath (also s.p.), Flinch, Circumstances Unknown, Blackwater Trail, Steel, Endsville, Light It Up, The Big Beat Heat, Falcon Down, The Cure

for Boredom, Jay and Silent Bob Strike Back, Dark Asylum, The Last Voyage, Deceived, Cybermutt.
TELEVISION: Series: Suddenly Susan. Guest: Moonlighting. Movies: Billionaire Boys Club, Hiroshima: Out of the Ashes, Conflict of Interest, Blindfold: Acts of Obsession, Cabin by the Lake, Mr. Rock 'n' Roll, The Spiral Staircase, The New Adventures of Spin and Marty: Suspect Behavior, Return to Cabin by the Lake, Strange Frequency, Cybermutt.

NELSON, LORI
Actress. r.n. Dixie Kay Nelson. b. Santa Fe, NM, Aug. 15, 1933. e. Canoga Park H.S. Started as child actress, photographer's model before film debut in 1952.
THEATRE: The Pleasure of His Company, Who Was That Lady I Saw You With, Affairs of Mildred Wilde, Sweet Bird of Youth, Picnic, 'Night Mother.
PICTURES: Ma and Pa Kettle at the Fair (debut, 1952), Bend of the River, Francis Goes to West Point, All I Desire, All-American, Walking My Baby Back Home, Tumbleweed, Underwater, Destry, Revenge of the Creature, I Died a Thousand Times, Sincerely Yours, Mohawk, Day the World Ended, Pardners, Hot Rod Girl, Ma and Pa Kettle at Waikiki, Gambling Man, Untamed Youth, Outlaw's Son, Mom Can I Keep Her?, Back to the Black Lagoon.
TELEVISION: Series: How to Marry a Millionaire. Guest: Wagon Train, Laramie, Family Affair, The Texan, Wanted Dead or Alive, Sam Spade, G.E. Theatre, Riverboat, Sugarfoot, The Young and the Restless, Climax, The Millionaire, Wells Fargo, etc. Special: The Pied Piper of Hamelin.

NELSON, TRACY
Actress, Singer, Dancer. b. Santa Monica, CA, Oct. 25, 1963. e. Bard Coll. Daughter of late singer-actor Rick Nelson. Sister of singers Matthew & Gunnar Nelson. Studied acting in England.
THEATRE: Grease (Nat'l touring co. & B'way).
PICTURES: Yours Mine and Ours (debut, 1968), Maria's Lovers, Down and Out in Beverly Hills, Chapters, The Night Caller, The Bus Stop, The Perfect Tenant, The Perfect Nanny, Home the Horror Story, Fangs, Dumb Luck.
TELEVISION: Series: Square Pegs, Glitter, Father Dowling Mysteries, A League of Their Own, Melrose Place, The Man from Snowy River. Movies: Katie's Secret, Tonight's the Night, If It's Tuesday It Still Must Be Belgium, Fatal Confessions, For Hope, In the Shadow of Evil, Pleasures, Highway Heartbreaker, Ray Alexander: Murder in Mind, Ray Alexander: A Taste for Justice, No Child of Mine. Guest: The Adventures of Ozzie and Harriet, Hotel, Family Ties, The Love Boat.

NELSON, WILLIE
Composer, Singer, Actor. b. Abbott, TX, April 30, 1933. Worked as salesman, announcer, host of country music shows on local Texas stations; bass player with Ray Price's band. Started writing songs in the 60's; performing in the 70's.
PICTURES: The Electric Horseman (debut, 1979), Honeysuckle Rose, Thief, Barbarosa, Hell's Angels Forever, Songwriter, Red-Headed Stranger (also prod.), Walking After Midnight, Gone Fishin', Anthem, Wag the Dog, Half Baked, Dill Scallion (cameo), Austin Powers: The Spy Who Shagged Me (cameo), Stardust, The Journeyman, Freedom Highway, The Country Bears.
TELEVISION: Movies: The Last Days of Frank and Jesse James, Stagecoach, Coming Out of the Ice, Baja Oklahoma, Once Upon a Texas Train, Where the Hell's That Gold?!!?, Pair of Aces, Another Pair of Aces, Wild Texas Wind, Big Dreams & Broken Hearts: The Dottie West Story, Outlaw Justice. Specials: Willie Nelson—Texas Style (also prod.), America: A Tribute to Heroes, Korean War Stories.

NEMEC, CORIN
Actor. r.n. Joseph Charles Nemec IV. b. Little Rock, AR, Nov. 5, 1971. Began acting in commercials at age 13.
PICTURES: Tucker: The Man and His Dream, Solar Crisis, Drop Zone, Operation Dumbo Drop, The War at Home, Mojave Moon, Quality Time, The First to Go, Goodbye America, Legacy, Foreign Correspondents, Shadow Hours, Quality Time, Killer Bud, Free.
TELEVISION: Series: Parker Lewis Can't Lose, Stargate-SG1. Movies: I Know My First Name is Steven (Emmy nom.), For the Very First Time, My Son Johnny, The Lifeforce Experiment, Summer of Fear, Blade Squad, Silencing Mary, My Brother's Keeper. Mini-Series: The Stand. Pilot: What's Alan Watching? Guest: Webster, Sidekicks.

NERO, FRANCO
Actor. r.n. Franceso Spartanero. b. Parma, Italy, Nov. 23, 1942. e. Univ. La Bocconi, Milan. m. Vanessa Redgrave.
PICTURES: Celestina (Made at Your Service; debut, 1964), The Deadly Diaphanoids, I Knew Her Well, Wild Wild Planet, The Third Eyes, The Bible, The Tramplers, Django, The Avenger, Hired Killer, The Brute and the Beast, Mafia, Camelot, L'uomo l'Orgoglio la Vendetta, Island of Crime, The Mercenary, The Day of the Owl, A Quiet Place in the Country, The Battle of Neretva, Detective Belli, Sardinia: Ramsom, Companeros, Tristana, The Virgin and the Gypsy, Drop Out!, Confessions of a Police Commissioner, Killer From Yuma, Redneck, The Monk, The Vacation, Pope Joan, Deaf Smith and Johnny Ears, The Fifth Day of Peace, The Aquarian, High Crime, Blood Brothers, Cry Onion, The Anonymous Avenger, Challenge to White Fang,

Death Drive, Violent Breed, Submission, The Last Days of Mussolini, Force Ten From Navarone, The Man With Bogart's Face, The Visitor, Shark Hunter, Blue-Eyed Bandit, Danzig Roses, Day of the Cobra, The Falcon, The Salamander, Sahara Cross, Enter the Ninja, Mexico in Flames, Querelle, Wagner, Sweet Country, The Girl, Garibaldi the General, Race to Danger, Marathon, Django Strikes Again, Top Line, Silent Night, Young Toscanini, The Betrothed, The Magistrate, Heart of Victory, The Repenter, The Forester's Sons, Die Hard 2, Brothers and Sisters, Crimson Down, Oro, Deep Blue, The Lucona Affair, Babylon Complot, A Breath of Life, Jonathan of the Bears, Conflict of Interest, The Dragon's Ring, Talk of Angels, The Innocent Sleep, The King and Me, various others in Europe and USA.
TELEVISION: *Mini-series*: The Last Days of Pompeii, Desideria, The Return of Sandokan, Bella Mafia, Painted Lady, Crociati. *Movies*: The Legend of Valentino, 21 Hours at Munich, The Pirate, Young Catherine, David, The Versace Murder, Das Babylon Komplott, Il Deserto di fuoco.

NESMITH, MICHAEL
Musician, Producer. r.n. Robert Michael Nesmith. b. Houston, TX, Dec. 30, 1942. Original member of The Monkees, later became producer of videos and films. Chmn. & CEO Pacific Arts Publishing video company. Won Grammy award for music video Elephant Parts. Exec. prod. & performer in video Dr. Duck's Super Secret All-Purpose Sauce.
PICTURES: *Actor*: Head, Burglar (cameo), Heart and Soul. *Exec. Prod.*: Timerider (also co-s.p.), Repo Man, Square Dance, Tapeheads.
TELEVISION: *Series*: The Monkees, Michael Nesmith in Television Parts (also prod.). *Special*: 33-1/3 Revolutions Per Monkee, Hey Hey It's the Monkees (also exec. prod.).

NETTER, DOUGLAS
Executive, Producer. b. Seattle, WA. 1955-57, gen. mgr. Todd A.O.; 1958-60, Sam Goldwyn Productions; 1961-67, formed own co. representing producers; 1968-69, Jalem Productions; 1969-75, exec. v.p. MGM. Films: Mr. Ricco (prod.), The Wild Geese (co-prod.).
TELEVISION: Louis L'Amour's The Sacketts (prod.), The Buffalo Soldiers (exec. prod.), Wild Times (prod.), Roughnecks (exec. prod.), Cherokee Trail (exec. prod.), Five Mile Creek (exec. prod.; Australian based TV series for Disney Channel), Captain Power and the Soldiers of the Future (exec. prod.), Stealth F22 (exec. prod.), Babylon 5 (exec. prod.), Crusade, Babylon 5: The Legend of the Rangers: To Live and Die in Starlight, Babylon 5: In the Beginning, Babylon 5: Thirdspace, Babylon 5: The River of Souls, Babylon 5: A Call to Arms.

NETTLETON, LOIS
Actress. b. Oak Park, IL, August 16, 1931. e. Studied at Goodman Theatre, Chicago and Actors Studio. Replaced Kim Hunter in Darkness at Noon on B'way. Emmy Award: Performer Best Daytime Drama Spec., The American Woman: Portraits in Courage (1977). Also Emmy: Religious Program, Insight (1983).
THEATER: Cat on a Hot Tin Roof, Silent Night, Lonely Night, God and Kate Murphy, The Wayward Stork, The Rainmaker, A Streetcar Named Desire.
PICTURES: A Face in the Crowd (debut, 1957), Period of Adjustment, Come Fly with Me, Mail Order Bride, Valley of Mystery, Bamboo Saucer, The Good Guys and the Bad Guys, Dirty Dingus Magee, The Sidelong Glances of a Pigeon Kicker, The Honkers, The Man in the Glass Booth, Echoes of a Summer, Deadly Blessing, Butterfly, Soggy Bottom U.S.A., The Best Little Whorehouse in Texas.
TELEVISION: *Series*: Accidental Family, You Can't Take It With You, In the Heat of the Night, Spider-Man (voice), General Hospital, House of Mouse. *Guest*: Medical Center, Barnaby Jones, Alfred Hitchcock, All That Glitters, In the Heat of the Night. *Movies*: Any Second Now, Weekend of Terror, The Forgotten Man, Terror in the Sky, Women in Chains, Fear on Trial, Tourist, Brass, Manhunt for Claude Dallas, The Good Doctor: The Paul Fleiss Story, Traveler's Rest, The Making of a Hollywood Madam. *Mini-Series*: Washington: Behind Closed Doors, Centennial. *Specials*: Rendezvous, Meet Me in St. Louis, Traveler's Rest.

NEUFELD, MACE
Producer. b. New York, NY, July 13, 1928. e. Yale Col. Started as professional photographer, before becoming prod. asst. at Dumont Television Network. Wrote musical material for performers incl. Sammy Davis Jr., Dorothy Loudon, Ritz Brothers, etc., and theme for Heckle and Jeckle animated series. In 1951, formed independent TV prod. and personal mgmt. co. For TV produced programs for Dick Van Dyke, Elaine May and Mike Nichols. Formed independent production co. with Nichols and Buck Henry. In 1980, created Neufeld-Davis Prods. with Marvin Davis. Formed Neufeld/Rehme Prods. with Robert G. Rehme in 1989; Mace Neufeld Prods., 1997. On B'way, prod. Flying Karamazov Brothers show. Voted Producer of the Year by NATO/ShoWest, 1992.
PICTURES: The Omen, Damien: Omen II, The Frisco Kid, The Funhouse, The Aviator, Transylvania 6-5000, No Way Out, The Hunt for Red October, Flight of the Intruder, Necessary Roughness, Patriot Games, Gettysburg, Beverly Hills Cop III,

Clear and Present Danger, The Saint, The General's Daughter, Lost in Space, Black Dog, Bless the Child, The Sum of All Fears, Gods and Generals, (exec. prod.).
TELEVISION: *Movies/Miniseries*: East of Eden, Angel on My Shoulder, American Dream, Cagney and Lacey (pilot), A Death in California, White Hot, Woman Undone, Escape: Human Cargo, Love and Treason. *Specials*: The Magic Planet, The Flying Karamazov Brothers, Blind Faith.

NEUWIRTH, BEBE
Actress. b. Newark, NJ, Dec. 31, 1958. e. Juilliard. Started as chorus dancer.
THEATRE: *NY*: Little Me, Dancin', Upstairs at O'Neal, The Road to Hollywood, Sweet Charity (Tony Award, 1986), Showing Off, Damn Yankees. *Tour*: A Chorus Line. Regional: Just So, Kicks (also choreog.), Chicago. *London*: Kiss of the Spider Woman.
PICTURES: Say Anything... (debut, 1989), Green Card, Bugsy, Paint Job, Malice, Jumanji, All Dogs Go to Heaven (voice), The Associate, The Faculty, Celebrity, An All Dogs Christmas Carol (voice), Summer of Sam, Dash and Lilly, Getting to Know You, Liberty Heights, An Extremely Goofy Movie (voice), The Adventures of Tom Thumb and Tumbelina, Tadpole, Le Divorce, How To Lose a Guy in 10 Days.
TELEVISION: *Series*: Cheers (2 Emmy Awards), All Dogs Go to Heaven: The Series (voice), Deadline. *Movies*: Without Her Consent, Unspeakable Acts, Dash and Lilly, Cupid and Cate, My Favorite Broadway: The LoveSongs. *Mini-Series*: Wild Palms. *Guest*: Frasier.

NEWELL, MIKE
Director. b. St. Albans, England, March 28, 1942. e. Cambridge U. Took directorial training course at Granada Television.
PICTURES: The Awakening (debut, 1980), Bad Blood, Dance With a Stranger, The Good Father, Amazing Grace and Chuck, Common Ground, Enchanted April, Into the West, Four Weddings and a Funeral, An Awfully Big Adventure, Donnie Brasco, Pushing Tin, Mona Lisa Smile. *Exec. Prod.*: Photographing Fairies, 200 Cigarettes, Best Laid Plans, High Fidelity, Traffic, Ripleys' Game, I Capture the Castle.
TELEVISION: Baa Baa Black Sheep, Silver Wedding, Jill and Jack, Ready When You Are Mr. McGill, Lost Your Tongue, Mr. & Mrs. Bureaucrat, Just Your Luck, The Man in the Iron Mask, The Gift of Friendship, Destiny, Tales Out of School, Birth of a Nation, Blood Feud, The Young Indiana Jones Chronicles.

NEWHART, BOB
Actor, Comedian. b. Chicago, IL, Sept. 5, 1929. e. Loyola U. In Army 2 yrs., then law school; left to become copywriter and accountant. Acted with theatrical stock co. in Oak Park; hired for TV man-in-street show in Chicago. Recorded hit comedy album for Warner Bros., The Button-Down Mind of Bob Newhart (Grammy Award, 1960), followed by two more successful albums. Did series of nightclub engagements and then acquired own TV variety series in 1961. Grand Marshall: Tournament of Roses Parde, 1991. Inducted into TV Hall of Fame, 1993.
PICTURES: Hell Is for Heroes (debut, 1962), Hot Millions, Catch-22, On a Clear Day You Can See Forever, Cold Turkey, The Rescuers (voice), Little Miss Marker, First Family, The Rescuers Down Under (voice), In & Out, Legally Blonde 2: Red, White and Blonde, Elf.
TELEVISION: *Series*: The Bob Newhart Show (1961-62, variety), The Entertainers, The Bob Newhart Show (1972-78, sitcom), Newhart, Bob, George & Leo. *Movies*: Thursday's Game, Marathon, The Entertainers, The Sports Pages.

NEWMAN, ALFRED S.
Executive. b. Brooklyn, NY, Nov. 16. e. NYU. Public relations work for Equitable Life Insurance, Trans World Airlines prior to joining Columbia Pictures in 1968 as writer in publicity dept.; named New York publicity mgr., 1970; national publicity mgr., 1972; joined MGM as East adv.-pub. dir., 1972; named director of adv., pub. and promotion, 1974; named v.p., worldwide adv., pub., promo., 1978; v.p., pub.-promo., MGM/UA, 1981. With 20th Century-Fox as v.p. adv.-pub.-promo. for TV & corporate, 1984-85; joined Rogers & Cowan as sr. v.p. & head of film and corporate entertainment dept., 1985; named exec. v.p., 1987; Oct. 1988 named pres. and CEO. Sterling Entertainment Co. and exec. v.p. worldwide marketing of parent co. MCEG; formed Newman & Associates, 1989; joined Hill and Knowl Entertainment as founding mng. dir., 1990. Re-opened Newman and Assocs., 1991. Joined Imax Corp. as Sr V.P. & Head of Worldwide Communications, 1996. Formed Newman & Company, 1998.

NEWMAN, BARRY
Actor. b. Boston, MA, Nov. 7, 1938. e. Brandeis U.
PICTURES: Pretty Boy Floyd (debut, 1960), The Moving Finger, The Lawyer, Vanishing Point, The Salzburg Connection, Fear is the Key, City on Fire, Amy, Daylight, Brown's Requiem, Goodbye Lover, The Limey, Bowfinger, G-Men From Hell, Jack the Dog, Good Advice, True Blue, 40 Days and 40 Nights.
TELEVISION: *Series*: Petrocelli, Nightingales. *Movies*: Night Games, Sex and the Married Woman, King Crab, Fantasies, Having It All, Second Sight: A Love Story, Fatal Vision, My Two Loves, The Mirror Crack'd (BBC).

NEWMAN, DAVID
Composer. b. Los Angeles, CA, Mar. 11, 1954. e. USC (masters degree). Son of late composer Alfred Newman. Cousin of composer Randy Newman. Music director at Robert Redford's Sundance Institute.
PICTURES: Critters, Vendetta, The Kindred, My Demon Lover, Malone, Dragnet, Throw Momma from the Train, Pass the Ammo, Bill & Ted's Excellent Adventure, Disorganized Crime, The Brave Little Toaster, Heathers, Little Monsters, Gross Anatomy, The War of the Roses, Madhouse, Fire Birds, The Freshman, DuckTales: The Movie, Mr. Destiny, Meet the Applegates, The Marrying Man, Talent for the Game, Don't Tell Mom the Babysitter's Dead, Bill & Ted's Bogus Journey, Rover Dangerfield, Paradise, Other People's Money, The Runestone, The Mighty Ducks, Hoffa, The Sandlot, Coneheads, The Air Up There, My Father the Hero, The Flintstones, The Cowboy Way, Tommy Boy, Operation Dumbo Drop, The Phantom, Mathilda, The Nutty Professor, Out to Sea, Anastasia, 1001 Nights, Never Been Kissed, Brokedown Palace, Bowfinger, Galaxy Quest, The Flintstones in Viva Rock Vegas, Nutty Professor II: The Klumps, Duets, Bedazzled, 102 Dalmatians, Dr. Dolittle 2, The Affair of the Necklace, Death to Smoochy, Ice Age, Life or Something Like It, Scooby Doo, How To Lose a Guy in 10 Days, Daddy Day Care.

NEWMAN, DAVID
Writer. b. New York, NY, Feb. 4, 1937. e. U. of Michigan, M.S., 1959. Was writer-editor at Esquire Magazine where he met Robert Benton, an art director, and formed writing partnership. All early credits co-written with Benton; later ones with Leslie Newman and others.
THEATRE: It's a Bird... It's a Plane... It's Superman (libretto), Oh! Calcutta (one sketch).
PICTURES: Bonnie and Clyde, There Was a Crooked Man, What's Up Doc?, Bad Company, Superman, Superman II, Jinxed, Still of the Night (co-story), Superman III, Sheena, Santa Claus, Moonwalker, Takedown, Brasil 1500, La Trampa de Fu Manchu.

NEWMAN, EDWIN
News Correspondent. b. New York, NY, Jan. 25, 1919. Joined NBC News in 1952, based in N.Y. since 1961. Reports news on NBC-TV and often assigned to anchor instant specials. Has been substitute host on Today, appeared on Meet the Press and has reported NBC News documentaries. Series host: Edwin Newman Reporting, The Nation's Future, What's Happening to America, Comment, Speaking Freely, Television (PBS series).

NEWMAN, JOSEPH M.
Producer, Director, Writer. b. Logan, UT, Aug. 7, 1909. Started as office boy MGM, 1925; jobs in production dept. to 1931; asst. to George Hill; Ernst Lubitsch, etc., 1936-37; asstd. in organization of MGM British studios 1937; dir. short subjects 1938; dir. Crime Does Not Pay series 1938-42; Major in U.S. Army Signal Corps 1942-46; dir. 32 Army Pictorial Service Pictures. TV work includes Alfred Hitchcock Presents, Twilight Zone. Member of AMPAS, SDG Masons.
PICTURES: Northwest Rangers, Abandoned, Jungle Patrol, Great Dan Pitch, 711 Ocean Drive, Lucky Nick Cain, The Guy Who Came Back, Love Nest, Red Skies of Montana, Outcasts of Poker Flat, Pony Soldier, Dangerous Crossing, Human Jungle, Kiss of Fire, This Island Earth, Flight to Hong Kong, Fort Massacre, The Big Circus, Tarzan the Ape Man, King of the Roaring Twenties, Twenty Plus Two, The George Raft Story, Thunder of Drums.

NEWMAN, LARAINE
Actress. b. Los Angeles, CA, Mar. 2, 1952. Founding member of comedy troupe the Groundlings.
THEATRE: B'way: Fifth of July.
PICTURES: Tunnelvision (debut, 1976), American Hot Wax, Wholly Moses!, Stardust Memories (cameo), Perfect, Sesame Street Presents Follow That Bird (voice), Invaders from Mars, Problem Child 2, Witchboard II, Coneheads, The Flintstones, Jingle All the Way, Chow Bella, Alone in the Woods, Rusty: A Dog's Tale, Naked in the Cold Sun, Demolition University, Fear and Loathing in Las Vegas, I'm Losing You, The Modern Adventures of Tom Sawyer, Just Add Water, The Flunky, Endsville, Monsters, Inc., Jimmy Neutron Boy Genius, The Wild Thornberrys Movie, Finding Nemo, (voices).
TELEVISION: Series: Manhattan Transfer, Saturday Night Live, Bone Chillers, Histeria, As Told By Ginger, Grim & Evil. Guest: George Burns Comedy Week, St. Elsewhere, Laverne & Shirley, Alfred Hitchcock Presents, Amazing Stories, Faerie Tale Theatre (The Little Mermaid), Twilight Zone, Dream On, Likely Suspects, Friends, Chicago Hope, Third Rock From the Sun. Specials: Steve Martin's Best Show Ever, The Lily Tomlin Special, Bob Ray Jane Laraine & Gilda, Saturday Night Live: 25th Anniversary. Movies: Her Life as a Man, This Wife for Hire, The Rugrats: All Growed Up. Voice: Pinky and the Brain, Sylvester & Tweetie, The Tick, Rapunzel, Superman, Wonder Woman.

NEWMAN, NANETTE
Actress, Writer. b. Northampton, Eng., May 29, 1934. m. prod.-dir.-writer Bryan Forbes. Ent. films in 1946 and TV in 1951.

AUTHOR: God Bless Love, That Dog, Reflections, The Root Children, Amy Rainbow, Pigalev, Archie, Christmas Cookbook, Summer Cookbook, Small Beginnings, Bad Baby, Entertaining with Nanette Newman and Her Daughters, Charlie the Noisy Caterpillar, Sharing, The Pig Who Never Was, ABC, 123, Cooking for Friends, Spider the Horrible Cat, There's a Bear in the Bath, Karmic Mothers, There's a Bear in the Classroom, The Importance of Being Ernest, The Earwig, Take 3 Cooks.
PICTURES: The Personal Affair, The League of Gentlemen, The Rebel, Twice Around the Daffodils, The L-Shaped Room, The Wrong Arm of the Law, Of Human Bondage, Seance on a Wet Afternoon, The Wrong Box, The Whisperers, Deadfall, The Madwoman of Chaillot, Captain Nemo and the Underwater City, The Raging Moon, The Stepford Wives, It's a 2'2" Above the Ground World, Man at the Top, International Velvet, Restless Natives, The Mystery of Edwin Drood.
TELEVISION: The Glorious Days, The Wedding Veil, Broken Honeymoon, At Home, Trial by Candlelight, Diary of Samuel Pepys, Faces in the Dark, Balzac (BBC), Fun Food Factory, TV series, Stay with Me Till Morning, Let There Be Love (series), West Country Tales, Jessie, Late Expectations (series), Ideal Cooks (presenter), The Endless Game.

NEWMAN, PAUL
Actor, Director, Producer. b. Cleveland, OH, Jan. 26, 1925. m. actress Joanne Woodward. e. Kenyon Coll., Yale Sch. of Drama, The Actors Studio. Formed First Artists Prod. Co., Ltd. 1969 with Sidney Poitier, Steve McQueen and Barbra Streisand. Appeared in documentaries: King: A Filmed Record... Memphis to Montgomery, Hello Actors Studio. Recipient of special Academy Award, 1986; Jean Hersholt Humanitarian Award, 1994.
THEATRE: B'way: Picnic, The Desperate Hours, Sweet Bird of Youth, Baby Want a Kiss.
PICTURES: The Silver Chalice (debut, 1954), The Rack, Somebody Up There Likes Me, The Helen Morgan Story, Until They Sail, The Long Hot Summer, The Left-Handed Gun, Cat on a Hot Tin Roof, Rally 'Round the Flag Boys!, The Young Philadelphians, From the Terrace, Exodus, The Hustler, Paris Blues, Sweet Bird of Youth, Hemingway's Adventures of a Young Man, Hud, A New Kind of Love, The Prize, What a Way to Go!, The Outrage, Harper, Lady L, Torn Curtain, Hombre, Cool Hand Luke, The Secret War of Harry Frigg, Rachel Rachel (dir. prod. only), Winning, Butch Cassidy and the Sundance Kid, WUSA (also prod.), Sometimes a Great Notion (also dir.), Pocket Money, The Life and Times of Judge Roy Bean, The Effect of Gamma Rays on Man-in-the-Moon Marigolds (dir., prod. only), The Mackintosh Man, The Sting, The Towering Inferno, The Drowning Pool, Buffalo Bill and the Indians or Sitting Bull's History Lesson, Silent Movie, Slap Shot, Quintet, When Time Ran Out..., Fort Apache the Bronx, Absence of Malice, The Verdict, Harry and Son (also dir., co-s.p., co-prod.), The Color of Money (Academy Award, 1986), The Glass Menagerie (dir. only), Fat Man & Little Boy, Blaze, Mr. and Mrs. Bridge, The Hudsucker Proxy, Nobody's Fool, Twilight, Where the Money Is, Message in a Bottle, The Road to Perdition, The Life Between.
TELEVISION: Guest (on 1950's anthology series): The Web (Bell of Damon, One for the Road), Goodyear TV Playhouse (Guilty is the Stranger), Danger (Knife in the Dark), Appointment With Adventure (Five in Judgment), Philco TV Playhouse (Death of Billy the Kid), Producers Showcase (Our Town), Kaiser Aluminum Hour (The Army Game, Rag Jungle), U.S. Steel Hour (Bang the Drum Slowly), Playhouse 90 (The 80-Yard Run). Movie (dir. only): The Shadow Box.

NEWMAN, RANDY
Composer, Singer. b. Los Angeles, CA, Nov. 28, 1943. Nephew of musicians Lionel and Alfred Newman. Studied music at UCLA. Debut album: Randy Newman Creates Something New Under the Sun. Songs include Short People, I Think It's Gonna Rain Today, I Love L.A. Was music director on film Performance. Began writing songs and scores for films in 1971 with The Pursuit of Happiness. Composed opera, Faust.
PICTURES: Pursuit of Happiness, Cold Turkey, Ragtime, The Natural, Three Amigos (also co-wrote s.p.), Parenthood, Avalon, Awakenings, The Paper, Maverick, James and the Giant Peach, The Quest, Michael, Cat's Don't Dance, Pleasantville (Acad. Award nom.), A Bug's Life (Acad. Award nom.), Toy Story 2, Meet the Parents (Acad. Award nom.), Monsters, Inc. (Acad. Award), Meet the Fockers, Seabiscuit, (composer).

NEWMAR, JULIE
Actress. r.n. Julie Newmeyer. b. Hollywood, CA, Aug. 16, 1933. e. UCLA. Studied acting with Lee Strasberg at the Actor's Studio. Holds patent for special panty hose design. Appeared in George Michael video Too Funky.
THEATRE: NY: Silk Stockings, Li'l Abner, The Marriage-Go-Round (Tony Award, 1959). Other: In the Boom Boom Room (L.A.), Damn Yankees, Irma La Douce, Guys and Dolls, Dames at Sea, Stop the World, The Women.
PICTURES: Just for You (debut, 1952), Seven Brides for Seven Brothers, The Rookie, Li'l Abner, The Marriage-Go-Round, For Love or Money, McKenna's Gold, The Maltese Bippy, Hysterical, Streetwalkin', Body Beat, Nudity Required, Ghosts Can't Do It, Oblivion, To Wong Foo—Thanks for Everything—Julie Newmar, Oblivion 2: Backlash, If...Dog...Rabbit.

TELEVISION: *Series*: My Living Doll, Batman (frequent guest; as Catwoman). *Movies*: McCloud: Who Killed Miss U.S.A.?, The Feminist and the Fuzz, A Very Missing Person, Terraces. *Guest*: Omnibus, Route 66, Jonathan Winters Show, Beverly Hillbillies, The Monkees, Love American Style, Love Boat, Half Nelson, Fantasy Island, Hart to Hart, Buck Rogers.

NEWTON-JOHN, OLIVIA
Actress, Singer. b. Cambridge, Eng. Sept. 26, 1948. m. actor Matt Lattanzi. Brought up in Melbourne, Australia, where won first talent contest at 15, winning trip to England. Stayed there 2 yrs. performing as part of duo with Australian girl singer Pat Carroll (Farrar) in cabarets and on TV. Started recording; several hit records. Became a regular guest on TV series, It's Cliff Richard. Gained world-wide prominence as singer, winning several Grammys and other music awards. 1983 opened Koala Blue, U.S. Clothing Stores featuring Australian style clothes and goods.
PICTURES: Tomorrow (debut, 1970), Grease, Xanadu, Two of a Kind, The Golbal Forum, Madonna: Truth or Dare, It's My Party, Sordid Lives, Not Under My Roof, The Wilde Girls.
TELEVISION: *Specials*: Olivia Newton-John: Let's Get Physical, Standing Room Only: Olivia Newton-John, Olivia Newton-John in Australia, Christmas in Washington. *Movies*: A Mom for Christmas, A Christmas Romance, Snowden on Ice (voice), Mariah Carey: Around the World, The Main Event.

NEY, RICHARD
Actor, Writer, Producer, Financier. b. New York, NY, Nov. 12, 1917. e. Columbia U., B.A., 1940. Acted in RCA TV demonstration, New York World's Fair; on stage in Life with Father. Was Naval Officer in WWII. Financial advisor consultant, Richard Ney and Associates; financial advisor, lecturer; author, The Wall Street Jungle, The Wall Street Gang, Making it in the Market.
PICTURES: Mrs. Miniver, The War Against Mrs. Hadley, The Late George Apley, Ivy, Joan of Arc, The Fan, Secret of St. Ives, Lovable Cheat, Babes in Bagdad, Miss Italia, Sergeant and The Spy, Midnight Lace, The Premature Burial.

NICHOLAS, DENISE
Actress, Writer. b. Detroit, MI, July 12, 1946. e. USC.
THEATRE: Performances with the Free Southern Theatre, The Negro Ensemble Company, Crossroads Theatre Co., New Federal Theatre, Los Angeles Theatre Company, Media Forum.
PICTURES: Ghost Dad, Capricorn One, A Piece of the Action, Let's Do It Again, Blacula, The Soul of Nigger Charley, Marvin and Tige, Ghost Dad, Ritual.
TELEVISION: *Series*: Room 222, Baby I'm Back, In the Heat of the Night (also wrote 6 episodes). *Movies*: incl. The Sophisticated Gents, On Thin Ice, Mother's Day, Ring of Passion, In the Heat of the Night, others. *Guest*: The Cosby Show, A Different World, Benson, Magnum P.I., The Paper Chase, Police Story, Living Single, many others.
AUTHOR: Buses (one act play), Augustine, Myrtle, Marty and Me (short story, Essence Magazine), various published articles and poetry.

NICHOLS, MIKE
Director, Producer, Performer. r.n. Michael Igor Peschkowsky. b. Berlin, Germany, Nov. 6, 1931. m. news correspondent Diane Sawyer. e. U. of Chicago. Member of Compass Players; later teamed with Elaine May in night clubs.
THEATRE: *Director*: Barefoot in the Park (Tony Award), The Knack, Luv (Tony Award), The Odd Couple, The Apple Tree, The Little Foxes, Plaza Suite (Tony Award), Uncle Vanya, The Prisoner of 2nd Avenue (Tony Award), Streamers, Comedians, The Gin Game, Drinks Before Dinner, Annie (prod. only; Tony Award), The Real Thing (2 Tony Awards), Hurlyburly, Social Security, Waiting for Godot, Elliot Loves, Death and the Maiden.
PICTURES: *Director*: Who's Afraid of Virginia Woolf? (debut, 1966), The Graduate (Academy Award, 1967), Catch-22, Carnal Knowledge, The Day of the Dolphin, The Fortune, Gilda Live, Silkwood (also co-prod.), The Longshot (exec. prod. only), Heartburn, Biloxi Blues, Working Girl, Postcards From the Edge, Regarding Henry, The Remains of the Day (co-prod. only), Wolf, The Birdcage, Primary Colors, What Planet Are You From? (also prod.), Wit (also exec. prod), Angels in America.
TELEVISION: *Specials*: B'way, An Evening with Mike Nichols and Elaine May. *Exec. prod.*: Family, The Thorns. *Series*: Dismissed (exec. prod.).

NICHOLS, NICHELLE
Actress. b. Robbins, IL, Dec. 28, 1936. Started singing and dancing with Duke Ellington and his band at age 16. Was appointee to the bd. of dirs. of the National Space Institute in the 1970's; recruited women and minority astronauts for Space Shuttle Program. Received NASA's distinguished Public Service Award. Member of the bd. of govs. of the National Space Society. One of the original founders of KWANZA Foundation. Awarded star on Hollywood Walk of Fame (1992). *Autobiography*: Beyond (1994). Novels: Saturn's Child (1995), Saturna's Quest (1996).
THEATRE: Horowitz and Mrs. Washington, Reflections (one woman show). Nominated for Sarah Siddons Award for performances in Kicks and Company, The Blacks.
PICTURES: Porgy and Bess, Mr. Buddwing, Made in Paris, Truck

Turner, Star Trek: The Motion Picture, Star Trek II: The Wrath of Khan, Star Trek III: The Search for Spock, Star Trek IV: The Voyage Home, The Supernaturals, Star Trek V: The Final Frontier, Star Trek VI: The Undiscovered Country, Trekkies, Snow Dogs.
TELEVISION: *Series*: Star Trek. *Guest*: The Lieutenant, Tarzan. *Specials*: Antony and Cleopatra, Moonshot: The Spirit of '69, Inside TV Land: African Americans in Television. *Movies*: various Star Trek movies.

NICHOLSON, JACK
Actor, Producer, Director, Writer. b. Neptune, NJ, April 22, 1937. Began career in cartoon department of MGM. Made acting debut in Hollywood stage production of Tea and Sympathy. Made directing debut with Drive, He Said (1971). Twelve Academy Award nominations and three wins. Recipient of American Film Institute's Life Achievement Award, 1994.
PICTURES: Cry Baby Killer (debut, 1958), Too Soon to Love, Little Shop of Horrors, Studs Lonigan, The Wild Ride, The Broken Land, The Raven, The Terror, Thunder Island (co-s.p. only), Back Door to Hell, Flight to Fury (also s.p.), Ensign Pulver, Ride in the Whirlwind (also co-prod., s.p.), The Shooting (also co-prod.), The St. Valentine's Day Massacre, Rebel Rousers, Hell's Angels on Wheels, The Trip (s.p. only), Head (also co-prod., co-s.p.), Psych-Out, Easy Rider, On a Clear Day You Can See Forever, Five Easy Pieces, Carnal Knowledge, Drive He Said (dir., co-prod., co-s.p. only), A Safe Place, The King of Marvin Gardens, The Last Detail, Chinatown, Tommy, The Passenger, The Fortune, One Flew Over the Cuckoo's Nest (Academy Award, 1975), The Missouri Breaks, The Last Tycoon, Goin' South (also dir.), The Shining, The Postman Always Rings Twice, Reds, The Border, Terms of Endearment (Academy Award, best supporting actor, 1983), Prizzi's Honor, Heartburn, The Witches of Eastwick, Broadcast News, Ironweed, Batman, The Two Jakes (also dir.), Man Trouble, A Few Good Men, Hoffa, Wolf, The Crossing Guard, Mars Attacks!, The Evening Star, As Good As It Gets (Acad. Award, Golden Globe Award, Best Actor, 1997), The Pledge, Stanley Kubrick: A Life in Pictures, Velocity, About Schmidt, Anger Management, Stuck on You, Something's Gotta Give.
TELEVISION: *Guest*: Tales of Wells Fargo, Cheyenne, Hawaiian Eye, Dr. Kildare, Andy Griffith Show, Guns of Will Sonnett.

NICHOLSON, WILLIAM
Writer. b. England, 1948. e. Cambridge U. Was graduate trainee at BBC, becoming prod./dir./writer of over 40 documentaries.
THEATRE: Shadowlands, Map of the Heart.
PICTURES: Sarafina!, Shadowlands (Acad. Award nom.), Nell, First Knight, Firelight (also dir.), Gray Owl, Gladiator.
TELEVISION: *Exec. Prod.*: Everyman, Global Report, Lovelaw. *Writer*: Martin Luther, New World, Life Story, The Vision, Shadowlands, Sweet as You Are, The Race for the Double Helix, The March, A Private Matter, Crime of the Century.

NICITA, RICK
Executive. e. Wesleyan U. m. agent/producer, Paula Wagner. Began career at William Morris Agency, 1968 where he worked in the Motion Picture Dept. until 1980. Joined Creative Artists Agency, 1980. Co-head, Motion Picture Dept., then Head of the Talent Dept. Currently, co-chmn., CAA. Listed as one of the most influential people in Hollywood by several magazines. Helped pioneer strategy of actor-based properties and prod. companies.

NICKSAY, DAVID
Executive, Producer. e. Mass., Hampshire Coll. Entered industry through Directors Guild of America's training program, apprenticing on Rich Man Poor Man and rising to second asst. dir. on Oh, God. Producer of many TV projects and theatrical films with Edgar Scherick prod. co. In 1986, joined Paramount Pictures as v.p., prod., for M.P. Group. Assoc. prod., prod. mgr.: I'm Dancing as Fast as I Can. Became sr. v.p., prod. Paramount, M.P. Group, 1987; resigned 1989 to become pres. and head of prod. at Morgan Creek Prods. Mem. of bd.
PICTURES: The One & Only, When I am King, Mrs. Soffel, Lucas, Young Guns II, Pacific Heights, Robin Hood:Prince of Thieves, Freejak, White Sands, Big Top Pee-Wee, Summer School, Coming to America, The Untouchables, Scrooged, Star Trek V: The Final Frontier, Major League, We're No Angels, Harlem Nights, The Two Jakes, Stay Tuned, Addams Family Values, Up Close and Personal, Flubber, The Negotiator, The Adventures of Rocky & Bullwinkle, AntiTrust, What's the Worst That Could Happen?, Legally Blonde, A Guy Thing, Agent Cody Banks, Legally Blonde 2: Red, White & Blonde.
TELEVISION: Call to Glory (pilot), Little Gloria Happy at Last.

NIELSEN, LESLIE
Actor. b. Regina, Sask., Canada, Feb. 11, 1926. e. Victoria H.S., Edmonton. Disc jockey, announcer for Canadian radio station; studied at Lorne Greene's Acad. of Radio Arts, Toronto and at Neighborhood Playhouse; N.Y. radio actor summer stock. Toured country in one-man show, Darrow, 1979. *Author*: The Naked Truth (1993), Leslie Nielsen's Stupid Little Golf Book (1995).
PICTURES: Ransom (debut, 1956), Forbidden Planet, The Vagabond King, The Opposite Sex, Hot Summer Night, Tammy and the Bachelor, The Sheepman, Night Train To Paris, Harlow, Dark Intruder, Beau Geste, The Plainsman, Gunfight in Abilene,

The Reluctant Astronaut, Rosie!, Counterpoint, Dayton's Devils, How to Commit Marriage, Change of Mind, Four Rode Out, The Resurrection of Zachary Wheeler, The Poseidon Adventure, And Millions Will Die, Day of the Animals, Viva Knievel!, The Amsterdam Kill, City on Fire, Airplane!, Prom Night, The Creature Wasn't Nice, Wrong Is Right, Creepshow, The Patriot, Soul Man, Nightstick, Nuts, Home Is Where the Hart Is, The Naked Gun: From the Files of Police Squad!, Dangerous Curves, Repossessed, The Naked Gun 2 1/2: The Smell of Fear, All I Want for Christmas, Surf Ninjas, Naked Gun 33 1/3: The Final Insult, Dracula: Dead and Loving It, Spy Hard (also co-exec. prod.), Family Plan, Mr. Magoo, Wrongfully Accused, Camouflage, 2001: A Space Travesty, The Best of So Graham Norton, Men With Brooms, Kevin of the North.
TELEVISION: Series: The New Breed, Peyton Place, The Protectors, Bracken's World, The Explorers (host), Police Squad, Shaping Up, Liography, N.Y.U.K. Guest: Studio One, Kraft, Philco Playhouse, Robert Montgomery Presents, Pulitzer Prize Playhouse, Suspense, Danger, Justice, Man Behind the Badge, Ben Casey, Walt Disney (Swamp Fox), Wild Wild West, The Virginian, The Loner. Special: Death of a Salesman. Movies: See How They Run, Shadow Over Elveron, Hawaii Five-O (pilot), Companions in Nightmare, Trial Run, Deadlock, Night Slaves, The Aquarians, Hauser's Memory, Incident in San Francisco, They Call It Murder, Snatched, The Letters, The Return of Charlie Chan, Can Ellen Be Saved?, Brink's: The Great Robbery, Little Mo, Institute for Revenge, OHMS, The Night the Bridge Fell Down, Cave-In!, Reckless Disregard, Blade in Hong Kong, Fatal Confession: A Father Dowling Mystery, Chance of a Lifetime, Safety Patrol. Mini-Series: Backstairs at the White House.

NIMOY, LEONARD
Actor, Director. b. Boston, MA, Mar. 26, 1931. e. Boston Col. Joined Pasadena Playhouse. Along with active career in films, TV and stage, has been writer and photographer. Author of three books on photography and poetry, as well as autobiography, I Am Not Spock. Has also been speaker on college lecture circuit. Created comic book Primortals.
THEATRE: Full Circle, Equus, Sherlock Holmes, Vincent (also dir., writer; one-man show), Love Letters.
PICTURES: Queen for a Day, Rhubarb, Francis Goes to West Point, Them!, Satan's Satellite's (edited from serial Zombies of the Stratosphere), The Brain Eaters, The Balcony, Catlow, Invasion of the Body Snatchers, Star Trek—The Motion Picture, Star Trek II: The Wrath of Khan, Star Trek III: The Search for Spock (also dir.), Transformers: The Movie (voice), Star Trek IV: The Voyage Home (also. dir., co-story), Three Men and a Baby (dir. only), The Good Mother (dir. only), Star Trek V: The Final Frontier, Funny About Love (dir. only), Star Trek VI: The Undiscovered Country (also exec. prod., co-story), Holy Matrimony (dir. only), The Pagemaster (voice), Jellies & Other Ocean Drifters (voice), Carpati: 50 Miles, 50 Years (voice), A Life Apart: Hasidism in America (voice), Sinbad: Beyond the Veil of Mists, Trekkies, Armageddon: Target Earth, Rashi: A Light After the Dark Ages, Minyan in Kaifeng (voice), Atlantis: The Lost Empire.
TELEVISION: Series: Star Trek, Mission: Impossible, In Search Of... (host), Outer Limits. Movies: Assault on the Wayne, Baffled, The Alpha Caper, The Missing Are Deadly, The Sun Also Rises, A Woman Called Golda, Never Forget (also co-prod.), Bonanza: Under Attack, David, Alien Voices, Brave New World. Mini-Series: Marco Polo. Guest: Bonanza, Twilight Zone, Perry Mason, Laramie, Wagon Train, Man From U.N.C.L.E., The Virginian, Get Smart, Night Gallery, Columbo, T.J. Hooker, Star Trek: The Next Generation, The Simpsons (voice). Special: Seapower: A Global Journey (narrator). Episode Dir.: Deadly Games.

NIVEN, DAVID, JR.
Executive. b. London, England, Dec. 15, 1942. e. Univ. of Grenoble; London Sch. of Economics. Joined William Morris Agency in Beverly Hills in 1963. Transferred same yr. to New York; over next five yrs. worked for agency's European offices in Rome, Madrid and London. 1968-72, Columbia Pictures' U.K. office as v.p. of production; 1972-76, mng. dir. and v.p. of Paramount Pictures in U.K. 1976 became indep. prod. West Coast corresp. & interviewer for Inside Edition. Appeared as actor in films Lisa, Cool Surface, and on tv series, America's Most Wanted. 1993, became chmn. of R.A.D.D. (Recording-Artists Against Drunk Driving)
PICTURES: Producer: The Eagle Has Landed, Escape to Athena, Monsignor, Better Late Than Never, Kidco, That's Dancing!, Pyscho Cop II, Girl With the Hungry Eyes, Cool Surface (also actor), Blue Flame.
TELEVISION: The Night They Saved Christmas (exec. prod., s.p.), Cary Grant: A Celebration, Minnelli on Minnelli, The Wonderful Wizard of Oz. Panelist: To Tell the Truth (1991-92).

NIX, WILLIAM PATTERSON
Executive. b. Philadelphia, PA, April 10, 1948. e. Georgetown U., A.B., 1970; Antioch, M.A., 1971; Hofstra U. Sch. of Law, J.D., 1976; NYU Sch. of Law, LL.M., 1979. Member, Baker & Botts, LLP New York, NY. Formerly, V.P. Bus. Affairs, NBA Properties Inc., NY, ent. & media firm. Prior to that, was sr. v.p. of both the MPAA and Motion Picture Export Assoc. of America. Chmn. of

MPAA committee on copyright and literary property matters, and COO of film industry's intellectual property protection division (1976-91). Lifetime voting member, AMPAS.

NIXON, AGNES
Writer, Producer. b. Nashville, TN, Dec. 10, 1927. e. Northwestern Sch. of Speech, Catholic U. Landed 1st job writing radio serial dialogue (Woman in White, 1948-51), three days after graduating from college. Became a freelance writer for TV dramatic series. Guest writer, New York Times 1968-72, and TV Guide. Trustee, Television Conference Inst., 1979-82. Received National Acad. of Television Arts & Sciences' Trustee Award, 1981; Junior Diabetic Assn. Super Achiever Award, 1982; Communicator Award for American Women in Radio and Television, 1984. Gold Plate Award, American Acad. Achievement, 1993; inducted into TV Hall of Fame, 1993. Popular Culture Lifetime Achievement Award, 1995; Public Service Award, Johns Hopkins Hospital, 1995. Humanitarian Award, National Osteoporosis Foundation, 1996. Member, Int'l Radio & TV Society; Nat'l Acad. of TV Arts & Sciences; bd. of Harvard Foundation; The Friars Club.
TELEVISION: Series writer: Studio One, Philco Playhouse, Robert Montgomery Presents, Somerset Maugham Theatre, Armstrong Circle Theatre, Hallmark Hall of Fame, My True Story, Cameo Theatre, Search For Tomorrow, As The World Turns, Guiding Light, Another World. Series creator-producer: One Life to Live, All My Children, Loving. Mini-Series: The Manions of America.

NIXON, CYNTHIA
Actress. b. New York, NY, April 9, 1966. e. Barnard Coll. Started stage career at age 14.
THEATRE: B'way: The Philadelphia Story (Theatre World Award), Hurlyburly, The Real Thing, The Heidi Chronicles, Angels in America: Millenium Aproaches/Perestroika, Indiscretions. Off-B'way: Moonchildren, Romeo and Juliet, The Balcony Scene, Servy N Bernice 4-Ever, On the Bum, The Illusion, The Scarlet Letter.
PICTURES: Little Darlings (debut, 1980), Tattoo, Prince of the City, I Am the Cheese, Amadeus, The Manhattan Project, Let It Ride, Addams Family Values, The Pelican Brief, Baby's Day Out, Marvin's Room, The Out-of-Towners, Advice from a Caterpillar, Igby Goes Down.
TELEVISION: Movies: The Murder of Mary Phagan, The Love She Sought, Love Lies and Murder, Face of a Stranger, Papa's Angels, Sex and the Matrix, Mark Twain (voice), Stage On Screen: The Women. Specials: The Fifth of July, Kiss Kiss Dahlings, Tanner '88. Series: Sex and the City. Guest: The Equalizer, Gideon Oliver, Murder She Wrote.

NOIRET, PHILIPPE
Actor. b. Lille, France, Oct. 1, 1930. e. Centre Dramatique de l'Ouest. Company member of Theatre National Populaire 1951-63; nightclub entertainer before film debut in Agnes Varda's short, La Pointe Court. B'way debut Lorenzaccio (1958).
PICTURES: Gigi (debut, 1948), Olivia, Agence Matrimoniale, La Pointe Courte, Ravissante, Zazie dans le Metro, The Billionaire, Crime Does Not Pay, Therese Desqueyroux, Cyrano and D'Artagnan, None But the Lonely Spy, Death Where Is Thy Victory?, Monsieur, Les Copains, Lady L, La Vie de Chateau, Tender Scoundrel, The Night of the Generals, Woman Times Seven, The Assassination Bureau, Mr. Freedom, Justine, Topaz, Clerambard, Give Her the Moon, A Room in Paris, Murphy's War, A Time for Loving, Five-Leaf Clover, The Assassination, Sweet Deception, Poil de Carotte, The French Conspiracy, The Serpent, The Day of the Jackal, La Grande Bouffe, Let Joy Reign Supreme, The Old Gun, The Judge and the Assassin, A Woman at Her Window, Purple Taxi, Dear Inspector, Due Pezzi di Pane, Who Is Killing the Great Chefs of Europe?, Heads or Tails, Three Brothers, Kill Birgitt Haas, Coup de Torchon, L'Etoile du Nord, Amici, Miei, tito 2, L'Africain, A Friend of Vincents, Le Grand Carnival, Fort Saganne, Les Ripoux, Souvenirs, Next Summer, The Gold-Rimmed Glasses, No Downing Allowed, My New Partner, 'Round Midnight, Let's Hope It's a Girl, The 4th Power, The Thrill of Genius, The Secret Wife, Twist Again in Moscow, Masks, The Family Chouans!, IL Frullo del Passero, Young Toscanini, The Return of the Musketeers, Moments of Love, Cinema Paradiso, Life and Nothing But, Palermo Connection, My New Partner 2, Uranus, I Don't Kiss, The Two of Us, Especially on Sunday, The Postman, Grosse Fatigue, D'Artagnan's Daughter, The King of Paris, Marianna Ucria, Le Grand ducs, Fantome avec Chauffeur, Soleil, Les Palmes de M. Schutz, On Guard, Lulu Kreutz's Picnic, Un honnette commercant, Les Cotelettes.

NOLTE, NICK
Actor. b. Omaha, NB, Feb. 8, 1941. Attended 5 colleges in 4 yrs. on football scholarships, including Pasadena City Coll. and Phoenix City Coll. Joined Actors Inner Circle at Phoenix and appeared in Orpheus Descending, After the Fall, Requiem For a Nun. Did stock in Colorado. In 1968, joined Old Log Theatre in MN and after 3 yrs. left for New York, appearing at Cafe La Mama. Went to L.A. and did plays The Last Pad and Picnic, as well as several guest spots on TV series before big break in mini-series, Rich Man Poor Man as Tom Jordache.

PICTURES: Return to Macon County (debut, 1975), The Deep, Who'll Stop the Rain, North Dallas Forty, Heart Beat, Cannery Row, 48 HRS., Under Fire, Teachers, Grace Quigley, Down and Out in Beverly Hills, Extreme Prejudice, Weeds, Three Fugitives, New York Stories (Life Lessons), Farewell to the King, Everybody Wins, Q&A, Another 48 HRS, Cape Fear, The Prince of Tides (Golden Globe Award, Acad. Award nom.), The Player, Lorenzo's Oil, I'll Do Anything, Blue Chips, I Love Trouble, Jefferson in Paris, Mulholland Falls, Nightwatch, Mother Night, Afterglow, Affliction (Acad. Award nom.), U-Turn, Thin Red Line, Breakfast of Champions, Simpatico, The Best of Enemies, The Golden Bowl, Trixie, Investigating Sex, Double Down, The Honest Thief, Hulk, Beautiful Country.
TELEVISION: Mini-Series: Rich Man Poor Man. Movies: Winter Kill (pilot), The California Kid, Death Sentence, The Runaway Barge. Guest: Medical Center, Streets of San Francisco, The Rookies.

NOONAN, TOM
Actor, Writer. b. Greenwich, CT, Apr. 12, 1951. e. Yale.
THEATRE: Buried Child (Off-B'way debut, 1978), Invitational Farmyard, The Breakers, Five of Us, Spookhouse, What Happened Was (also writer), Wifey (also writer).
PICTURES: Heaven's Gate, Wolfen, Eddie Macon's Run, Easy Money, The Man With One Red Shoe, F/X, Manhunter, The Monster Squad, Mystery Train, Robocop 2, Last Action Hero, What Happened Was (also dir., s.p.), The Wife (also composer, s.p., & dir.), Heat, Phoenix, The Astronaut's Wife, Wang Dang, The Photographer, The Opportunists, The Pledge, Knockaround Guys.
TELEVISION: Mini-series: Monsters, North & South II. Movies: Rage, Red Wind (s.p.), The 10 Million Dollar Getaway, Heaven & Hell: North & South Book III. Guest: X-Files.

NORMAN, BARRY
Writer/presenter. b. London. Early career as show business editor London Daily Mail; humorous columnist for The Guardian. Entered TV as writer, presenter FILM 1972-81 and 1983-93. 1982, presenter Omnibus. Writer/host: The Hollywood Greats and Talking Pictures. Radio work incl.: Going Places, The News Quiz, Breakaway, The Chip Shop.
AUTHOR: The Hollywood Greats, Movie Greats, Film Greats, Talking Pictures, 100 Best Films of the Century. Novels: A Series of Defeats, Have a Nice Day, Sticky Wicket, The Bird Dog Tapes.
PICTURES: Blues for the Avatar (dir.).

NORRIS, CHUCK
Actor. r.n. Carlos Ray Norris. b. Ryan, OK, Mar. 10, 1940. World middle weight karate champion 1968-74. Owner of LA karate schools which led to film career.
PICTURES: The Wrecking Crew (debut, 1969), Slaughter in San Francisco, Return of the Dragon, The Student Teachers, Breaker! Breaker!, Good Guys Wear Black, Game of Death, A Force of One, The Octagon, An Eye for an Eye, Silent Rage, Forced Vengeance, Lone Wolf McQuade, Missing in Action, Missing in Action 2, Code of Silence, Invasion U.S.A. (also co-s.p.), Delta Force, Firewalker, Braddock: Missing in Action III (also co-s.p.), Hero and the Terror, Delta Force II, The Hitman, Sidekicks (also co-exec. prod.), Hellbound, Top Dog, Forest Warrior, The Bells of Innocence.
TELEVISION: Series: Chuck Norris's Karate Kommandos (animated series, voice), Walker: Texas Ranger (also co-exec. prod.). Movies: Logan's War: Bound by Honor, The President's Man, The President's Man: A Line in the Sand. Special: The Ultimate Stuntman: A Tribute to Dar Robinson (host), Wind in the Wire.

NORTH, SHEREE
Actress. r.n. Dawn Bethel. b. Los Angeles, CA, Jan. 17, 1933. e. Hollywood H.S. Amateur dancer with USO at 11; prof. debut at 13; many TV appearances
THEATRE: B'way: Hazel Flagg (Drama Desk Award, Critics' Award), I Can Get It For You Wholesale. Bye Bye Birdie, Your Own Thing, Can-Can, Two for the Seesaw, Breaking Up the Act, etc. Also directed and produced several productions.
PICTURES: Excuse My Dust, Here Come the Girls, Living It Up, How to Be Very Very Popular, The Lieutenant Wore Skirts, The Best Things in Life Are Free, Way to the Gold, No Down Payment, In Love and War, Mardi Gras, Destination Inner Space, Madigan, The Gypsy Moths, The Trouble With Girls, Lawman, The Organization, Charley Varick, The Outfit, Breakout, The Shootist, Telefon, Rabbit Test, Telefon, Cold Dog Soup, Defenseless, Susan's Plan.
TELEVISION: Series: Big Eddie, I'm a Big Girl Now, Bay City Blues. Movies: Then Came Bronson (pilot), Vanished, Rolling Man, Trouble Comes to Town, Snatched, Maneater, Key West, Winter Kill, A Shadow in the Streets, Most Wanted, The Night They Took Miss Beautiful, A Real American Hero, Amateur Night at the Dixie Bar and Grill, Women in White, Portrait of a Stripper, Marilyn: The Untold Story, Legs, Scorned and Swindled, Jake Spanner—Private Eye, Dead on the Money.

NORTON, EDWARD
Actor. b. Boston, MA, Aug. 18, 1969. e. Yale University. Board member of Edward Albee's Signature Company. Works as a board member of the Enterprise Foundation in New York.

PICTURES: Primal Fear, The People vs. Larry Flynt, Everyone Says I Love You, Rounders, Out of the Past (voice), American History X (Acad. Award nom), Fight Club, Keeping the Faith (also dir. and prod.), Forever Hollywood, The Score, Death to Smoochy, Frida (also s.p.), Red Dragon, The 25th Hour, The Italian Job.
TELEVISION:Specials: A Salute to Dustin Hoffman, AFI's 100 Years...100 Stars. Guest: The Simpsons (voice).

NOSSECK, NOEL
Director, Producer. b. Los Angeles, CA, Dec. 10, 1943. Began as editor with David Wolper Prods; made documentaries; turned to features.
PICTURES: Director: Best Friends (also prod.), Youngblood, Dreamer, King of the Mountain.
TELEVISION: Movies: Return of the Rebels, The First Time, Night Partners, Summer Fantasies, Different Affair, Stark, A Mirror Image, Roman Holiday, Full Exposure: The Sex Tapes Scandal, Follow Your Heart, Opposites Attract, A Mother's Justice, Without a Kiss Goodbye, Born Too Soon, French Silk, Sister in Law, Down Out and Dangerous, Justice For Annie: A Moment of Truth Movie, No One Would Tell, Tornado!, What Kind of Mother Are You?, The Secret, Nightscream, The Fury Within, Silent Predators, Another Woman's Husband. Pilots: Aaron's Way, Half 'n Half, Fair Game, Heaven Help Us. Series: Charmed.

NOURI, MICHAEL
Actor. b. Washington, DC, Dec. 9, 1945. e. Avon Old Farms, Rollins Coll., Emerson Coll. Studied for theatre with Larry Moss and Lee Strasberg. New York stage debut in Forty Carats, 1969.
THEATRE: Forty Carats, Victor/Victoria.
PICTURES: Goodbye Columbus (debut, 1969), Flashdance, Gobots (voice), The Imagemaker, The Hidden, Chameleon, Fatal Sky, Total Exposure, Black Ice, Fortunes of War, To the Limit, Hologram Man, Overkill, Picture This, Finding Forrester, Carman: The Champion, Lovely & Amazing, Peace Virus.
TELEVISION: Series: Beacon Hill, Search for Tomorrow, The Curse of Dracula, The Gangster Chronicles, Bay City Blues, Downtown, Love and War. Movies: Contract on Cherry Street, Fun and Games, Secrets of a Mother and Daughter, Sprague, Between Two Women, Rage of Angels: The Story Continues, Quiet Victory: the Charlie Wedemeyer Story, Shattered Dreams, Danielle Steel's Changes, In the Arms of a Killer, Psychic, Exclusive, The Sands of Time, The Hidden 2, Eyes of Terror, Between Love and Honor, This Matter of Marriage, Second Honeymoon, 61*. Mini-Series: The Last Convertible, Too Rich: The Secret Life of Doris Duke.

NOVAK, KIM
Actress. r.n. Marilyn Novak. b. Chicago, IL, Feb, 13, 1933. e. Wright Junior Coll., Los Angeles City Coll. Started as model, named World's Favorite Actress, Brussels World's Fair.
PICTURES: The French Line (debut, 1954), Pushover, Phffft!, Five Against the House, Son of Sinbad, Picnic, The Man with the Golden Arm, The Eddy Duchin Story, Jeanne Eagles, Pal Joey, Vertigo, Bell Book and Candle, Middle of the Night, Pepe, Strangers When We Meet, The Notorious Landlady, Boys' Night Out, Of Human Bondage, Kiss Me Stupid, The Amorous Adventures of Moll Flanders, The Legend of Lylah Clare, The Great Bank Robbery, Tales That Witness Madness, The White Buffalo, The Mirror Crack'd, Just a Gigolo, The Children, Liebestraum.
TELEVISION: Series: Falcon Crest. Guest: Alfred Hitchcock Presents (1985). Movies: Third Girl From the Left, Satan's Triangle, Malibu. Special: Obsessed With Vertigo.

NOVELLO, DON
Writer, Comedian, Actor. b. Ashtabula, OH, Jan. 1, 1943. e. U. of Dayton, B.A., 1964. Best known as Father Guido Sarducci on Saturday Night Live. Was advertising copy writer before writing and performing on The Smothers Brothers Comedy Hour (1975). Writer for Van Dyke and Company, and writer-performer on Saturday Night Live 1978-80. Producer: SCTV Comedy Network (1982) and performer-writer on B'way in Gilda Radner—Live From New York (1979), as well as filmed version (Gilda Live!). Recordings: Live at St. Douglas Convent, Breakfast in Heaven. Author: The Lazlo Letters: The Amazing Real-Life Actual Correspondence of Lazlo Toth, American!, The Blade, Citizen Lazlo.
PICTURES: Gilda Live!, Head Office, Tucker: The Man and His Dream, New York Stories (Life Without Zoe), The Godfather Part III, Casper (cameo), One Night Stand, Jack, Touch, Nothing Sacred, Just the Ticket, The Adventures of Rocky & Bullwinkle, Just One Night, Atlantis: The Lost Empire (voice), Rent Control.
TELEVISION: Cable specials: Fr. Guido Sarducci Goes to College, The Vatican Inquirer—The Pope Tour.

NOYCE, PHILLIP
Director. b. Griffith, New South Wales, Australia, April 29, 1950. Began making films at school and university. Made first short film at age 15, Better to Reign in Hell. In 1980, became part-time mgr., Sydney Filmmaker's Co-operative and in 1973 was selected for Australian Nat'l Film School in Sydney, for year-long training prog. which resulted in shorts, Good Afternoon, Caravan Park, Castor and Pollux, God Knows Why But It Works, and 60-

minute film Backroads.
PICTURES: Backroads (also prod., s.p.), Newsfront (also s.p.; Australian Acad. Awards for best dir. & s.p., 1978), Heatwave (also co-s.p.), Echoes of Paradise, Dead Calm, Blind Fury, Patriot Games, Sliver (also cameo), Clear and Present Danger, The Saint, The Bone Collector, Blast Off (also s.p.), The Repair Shop, Rabbit Proof Fence, The Quiet American.
TELEVISION: *Mini-Series*: Dismissal, Cowra Breakout. *Episodes*: The Hitchhiker, Nightmare Cafe.

NOZOE, YUKI
Executive. Began career with Sony Pictures Entertainment (SPE) in 1972. Director, senior v.p. & gen. mgr. , Sony Electronics Consumer Video Co., 1986; exec. v.p. & senior v.p. of mktg., Consumer Products Group, Sony Electronics, Inc., 1993-96, where he was instrumental in developing and standardizing DVD format; co-president, SPE, 1999.

NUNN, BILL
Actor. b. Pittsburgh, PA. Teamed with friend Al Cooper as member of comedy team Nunn and Cooper in nightclubs, 1980-83. On stage with various theatrical companies including the Alliance, the Academy, Theatrical Oufit, Just Us Theatre.
THEATRE: T-Bone and Weasel, Split Second, Home, A Lesson From Aloes, A Soldier's Play, Macbeth, The River Niger, Fences.
PICTURES: School Daze, Do the Right Thing, Def by Temptation, Cadillac Man, Mo' Better Blues, New Jack City, Regarding Henry, Sister Act, National Lampoon's Loaded Weapon 1, The Last Seduction, Canadian Bacon, Things to Do in Denver When You're Dead, Candyman 2, Money Train, Mr. & Mrs. Loving, BulletProof, Extreme Measures, Kiss the Girls, Mad City, He Got Game, Ambushed, The Legend of 1900, The Tic Code, Foolish, The Hungry Bachelors Club, Lockdown, Spider-Man, People I Know.
TELEVISION: *Movies*: The Littlest Victims, The Affair, Carriers, Quicksilver Highway, Ellen Foster, Always Outnumbered, Stolen From the Heart, The Price of a Broken Heart. *Specials*: Native Strangers, Dangerous Heart, War Stories, A Yankee in King Arthur's Court. *Guest*: Fallen Angels. *Series*: The Job.

NYKVIST, SVEN
Cinematographer. b. Moheda, Sweden, Dec. 3, 1922. e. Stockholm Photog. Sch. Asst. cameraman 1941-44. Became internationally known by photographing most of Ingmar Bergman's pictures. Recipient of American Society of Cinematographers Life Achievement Award, 1996.
PICTURES: Sawdust and Tinsel, The Virgin Spring, Winter Light, Karin Mansdotter, The Silence, Loving Couples, Persona, Hour of the Wolf, Cries and Whispers (Academy Award, 1973), The Dove, Black Moon, Scenes from a Marriage, The Magic Flute, Face to Face, One Day in the Life of Ivan Denisovich, The Tenant, The Serpents' Egg, Pretty Baby, Autumn Sonata, King of the Gypsies, Hurricane, Starting Over, Willie and Phil, From the Life of the Marionettes, The Postman Always Rings Twice, Cannery Row, Fanny and Alexander (Academy Award, 1983), Swann in Love, The Tragedy of Carmen, After the Rehearsal, Agnes of God, Dream Lover, The Sacrifice, The Unbearable Lightness of Being, Katinka, Another Woman, New York Stories (Oedipus Wrecks), Crimes and Misdemeanors, The Ox (dir., co-s.p. only), Chaplin, Sleepless in Seattle, What's Eating Gilbert Grape, With Honors, Kirsten Lavrandatter, Only You, Mixed Nuts, Something to Talk About, Celebrity, Curtain Call.
TELEVISION: Movie: Nobody's Child, Private Confessions.

O

O'BRIAN, HUGH
Actor. r.n. Hugh C. Krampe. b. Rochester, NY, Apr. 19, 1925. Raised in Chicago. e. Kemper Military Sch., U. of Cincinnati, UCLA. U.S. Marine Corps, where at age 18 he served as youngest drill instructor in Marine Corps history. Actor in stock cos. before film career. Founder, chmn. development: Hugh O'Brian Youth Foundation, 1958; Nat'l Chmn., Cystic Fibrosis Research Foundation 1969-74; Co-founder and pres. Thalians 1955-58; Founder Hugh O'Brian Annual Acting Awards at UCLA, 1962.
THEATRE: B'way: Destry Rides Again, First Love, Guys and Dolls, Cactus Flower, The Decision. Regional: The Music Man, Rainmaker, Plaza Suite, On 20th Century, Stalag 17, Thousand Clowns, etc.
PICTURES: Young Lovers (debut, 1949), Never Fear, Rocketship X-M, The Return of Jesse James, Vengeance Valley, Fighting Coast Guard, Little Big Horn, On the Loose, The Cimarron Kid, Red Ball Express, The Battle at Apache Pass, Sally and Saint Anne, Son of Ali Baba, The Raiders, The Lawless Breed, Meet Me at the Fair, Seminole, Man from the Alamo, Back to God's Country, The Stand at Apache River, Saskatchewan, Fireman Save My Child, Drums Across the River, Broken Lance, There's No Business Like Show Business, White Feather, The Twinkle in

God's Eye, Brass Legend, The Fiend Who Walked the West, Alias Jesse James, Come Fly with Me, Love Has Many Faces, In Harm's Way, Ten Little Indians, Ambush Bay, Africa--Texas Style!, Killer Force, The Shootist, Game of Death, Doin' Time on Planet Earth, Twins, Wyatt Earp: Return to Tombstone.
TELEVISION: *Series*: The Life and Legend of Wyatt Earp, Search. *Specials*: Dial M for Murder, A Punt a Pass and a Prayer, Going Home, Engagement Ring, Invitation to a Gunfighter, Reunion, Chain of Command, It's a Man's World, Wyatt Earp: Return to Tombstone. *Movies*: Wild Women, Harpy, Probe (Search), Murder on Flight 502, Benny & Barney: Las Vegas Undercover, Fantasy Island, Murder at the World Series, Cruise Into Terror, The Seekers, Gunsmoke: The Last Apache, The Gambler Returns: Luck of the Draw. *Mini-Series*: Y2K: A World in Crisis.

O'BRIEN, CONAN
Performer, Writer. b. Brookline, MA, Apr. 18, 1963. e. Harvard. Served two years as pres. of Harvard Lampoon before landing work as tv writer for The Simpsons, Saturday Night Live (Emmy Award, 1989), Winner WGA Award 1996-2003. Prod. of pilot Lookwell.
TELEVISION: *Series*: Not Necessarily the News, NBC's Late Night With Conan O'Brien (Emmy nom., 1996). *Host*: Emmy Awards, 2002.

O'BRIEN, MARGARET
Actress. r.n. Angela Maxine O'Brien. Los Angeles, CA, Jan. 15, 1938. Screen debut at 3 in Babes on Broadway (1941). Awarded special Academy Award as best child actress, 1944. Voted one of ten best money-making stars in Motion Picture Herald-Fame Poll 1945-46.
PICTURES: Babes on Broadway (debut, 1941), Journey for Margaret, Dr. Gillespie's Criminal Case, Lost Angel, Thousands Cheer, Madame Curie, Jane Eyre, The Canterville Ghost, Meet Me in St. Louis, Music for Millions, Our Vines Have Tender Grapes, Bad Bascomb, Three Wise Fools, Unfinished Dance, Tenth Avenue Angel, The Big City, The Secret Garden, Little Women, Her First Romance, Two Persons Eyes (Jap.), Agente S3S Operazione Uranio (It.), Glory, Heller in Pink Tights, Anabelle Lee, Diabolic Wedding, Amy, Sunset After Dark, Hollywood Mortuary, Off the Menu: The Last Days of Chasen's.
TELEVISION: *Movies*: Death in Space, Split Second to an Epitaph, Testimony of Two Men. *Guest*: Robert Montgomery Presents, Lux Video Theatre, Playhouse 90, Wagon Train, Studio One, U.S. Steel Hour, Dr. Kildare, Love American Style, Marcus Welby M.D.

OBST, LYNDA
Producer. b. New York, NY, Apr. 14, 1950. e. Pomona Col., Columbia Univ. Former editor for New York Times Magazine, 1976-79; then exec. at Polygram Pictures, 1979-81; Geffen Films, 1981-83, co-prod. at Paramount, 1983-85; prod. for Walt Disney, 1986, before moving over to Columbia. Co-Author: Dirty Dreams (with Carol Wolper).
PICTURES: Flashdance (assoc. prod.). *Producer*: Adventures in Babysitting, Heartbreak Hotel, The Fisher King, This Is My Life, Bad Girls, One Fine Day, Hope Floats, The Siege, The Wishbones, Abandon, How to Lose a Guy in 10 Days. *Exec. Prod.*: Sleepless in Seattle, Someone Like You...
TELEVISION: The '60s (exec. prod.), Hello, He Lied & Other Truths From the Hollywood Trenches (exec. prod.).
AUTHOR: Hello, He Lied and Other Truths From the Hollywood Trenches.

OCHS, MILLARD L.
Executive. e. U. of Akron. Beginning in July 1946, worked as an usher, projectionist and concession manager and later as cinema manager for his father Lee A. Ochs, while in college. After graduation, became city mng'r. for RKO Stanley Warner Theatre, Cincinnati, OH; followed by district mng'r. for AMC, covering SW territoris of AR and S. CA. 1985, while with AMC, transferred to England and began developing the multiplex concept at Milton Keynes; over next three years, AMC opened eight locations in England, then sold their interest to Univ./Paramount Studio Joint Venture of United Cinema Int'l.; stayed on with UCI until June 1993. Joined WB Int'l. Theatres as exec. v.p.; July 1994, promoted to pres. and began working with Ira Stiegler, v.p., architecture & planning, to introduce the Looney Tune Themed lobby. Awards: Exhibitor of the Year, Cinema Expo in Amsterdam, June 1996; co-recipient, Exhibitor of the Year, ShoWest, March 1998.

O'CONNELL, JACK
Producer, Director, Writer. b. Boston, MA. e. Princeton U., Harvard Business Sch. After being a creative group head in all media and doing 500 tv commercials entered feature films working with Fellini on La Dolce Vita, then asst. dir. to Antonioni on L'Avventura.
PICTURES: *Writer/Prod./Dir.*: Greenwich Village Story, Revolution, Christa (aka Swedish Flygirls), Up the Girls Means Three Cheers for Them All, The Hippie Revolution.

O'CONNOR, DAVID
Executive. e. Dartmouth College. Joined Creative Artists Agency 1983 as agent trainee and was soon promotion to motion picture literary agent. In 1996, created the CAA Foundation to involve the entertainment community in philanthropy, developing public/private partnerships at local and national levels. Currently, partner and managing dir., CAA. Serves on bd. of overseers, Dartmouth College and National Council for the Environmental Defense Fund. In April 2000, he received the David Niven Award for his contribution to Project ALS (Lou Gehrig's disease).

O'CONNOR, DONALD
Actor. b. Chicago, IL, Aug. 28, 1925. In vaudeville with family and Sons o' Fun (Syracuse, N.Y.) before screen debut 1938 in Sing You Sinners; return to vaudeville 1940-41, then resumed screen career with What's Cookin'?, 1942. Entered armed services, 1943. Voted Star of Tomorrow, 1943; best TV performer by M.P. Daily poll, 1953.
PICTURES: Sing You Sinners (debut, 1938), Sons of the Legion, Men With Wings, Tom Sawyer—Private Detective, Unmarried, Death of a Champion, Million Dollar Legs, Night Work, On Your Toes, Beau Geste, Private Buckaroo, Give Out Sisters, Get Hep to Love, When Johnny Comes Marching Home, Strictly in the Groove, It Comes Up Love, Mr. Big, Top Man, Chip Off the Old Block, Patrick the Great, Follow the Boys, The Merry Monahans, Bowery to Broadway, This Is the Life, Something in the Wind, Are You With It?, Feudin' Fussin' and a-Fightin', Yes Sir That's My Baby, Francis, Curtain Call at Cactus Creek, The Milkman, Double Crossbones, Francis Goes to the Races, Singin' in the Rain, Francis Goes to West Point, I Love Melvin, Call Me Madam, Francis Covers the Big Town, Walking My Baby Back Home, Francis Joins the WACS, There's No Business Like Show Business, Francis in the Navy, Anything Goes, The Buster Keaton Story, Cry for Happy, The Wonders of Aladdin, That Funny Feeling, That's Entertainment, Ragtime, Pandemonium, A Time to Remember, Toys, Father Frost, Out to Sea.
TELEVISION: Series: The Colgate Comedy Hour (host: 1951-54; Emmy Award, 1954), The Donald O'Connor Texaco Show (1954-55), The Donald O'Connor (synd., 1968). Movies: Alice in Wonderland, Bandit and the Silver Angel. Guest: Dinah Shore, Hollywood Palace, Carol Burnett, Julie Andrews, Ellery Queen, The Love Boat, Highway to Heaven, Tales From the Crypt. Specials: The Red Mill, Hollywood Melody, Olympus 7-0000. (d. Sept. 27, 2003).

O'CONNOR, GLYNNIS
Actress. b. New York, NY, Nov. 19, 1955. Daughter of ABC News prod. Daniel O'Connor and actress Lenka Peterson. e. State U., NY at Purchase. Stage includes Domestic Issues (Circle Rep., NY, 1983), The Taming of the Shrew (Great Lakes Shakespeare Fest.), The Seagull (Mirror Rep.).
PICTURES: Jeremy (debut, 1973), Baby Blue Marine, Ode to Billy Joe, Kid Vengeance, California Dreaming, Those Lips Those Eyes, Night Crossing, Melanie, Johnny Dangerously, New Best Friend.
TELEVISION: Series: Sons and Daughters. Mini-series: Black Beauty. Movies: The Chisholms, Someone I Touched, All Together Now, The Boy in the Plastic Bubble, Little Mo, My Kidnapper, My Love, The Fighter, Love Leads the Way, Why Me?, Sins of the Father, The Deliberate Stranger, To Heal a Nation, Death in Small Doses, Past the Bleachers, Summer of Fear, Saint Maybe, Ellen Foster.

O'CONNOR, KEVIN J.
Actor. b. Nov. 15, 1964. e. DePaul Univ.'s Goodman Sch. of Drama. On stage in Colorado Catechism (NY), El Salvador (Chicago).
PICTURES: One More Saturday Night, Peggy Sue Got Married, Candy Mountain, The Moderns, Signs of Life, Steel Magnolias, Love at Large, F/X 2, Hero, Equinox, No Escape, Color of Night, Virtuosity, Lord of Illusions, Canadian Bacon, Hit Me, Amistad, Gods & Monsters, Chicago Cab, Deep Rising, If...Dog...Rabbit, Chill Factor, The Mummy, Van Helsing.
TELEVISION: Movie: The Caine Mutiny Court Martial, The Love Bug, Black Cat Run. Special: Tanner 88. Guest: Birdland. Guest: Law & Order, Birdland. Series: The Others, Gideon's Crossing.

O'CONNOR, PAT
Director. b. Ardmore, Ireland, 1943. After working in London at odd jobs (putting corks in wine bottles, paving roads), came to U.S. e. UCLA, B.A. Studied film and TV at Ryerson Institute in Toronto. 1970, trainee prod., dir. with Radio Telefis Eireann. 1970-78 prod. and dir. over 45 TV features and current affairs documentaries. (The Four Roads, The Shankhill, Kiltyclogher, One of Ourselves, Night in Ginitia). A Ballroom of Romance won BAFTA Award (1981).
PICTURES: Cal (debut, 1984), A Month in the Country, Stars and Bars, The January Man, Fools of Fortune, Circle of Friends, Sacred Hearts, Inventing the Abbotts, Dancing at Lughnasa, Sweet November.
TELEVISION: Movie: Zelda.

O'DONNELL, CHRIS
Actor. b. Winetka, IL, June 26, 1970. e. Boston College.
PICTURES: Men Don't Leave (debut, 1990), Fried Green Tomatoes, School Ties, Scent of a Woman, The Three Musketeers, Blue Sky, Circle of Friends, Mad Love, Batman Forever, The Chamber, In Love and War, Batman & Robin, Cookie's Fortune, The Bachelor (also exec. prod.), Vertical Limit, 29 Palms.
TELEVISION: Movies: Miracle on the 17th Green (exec. prod.), The Triangle (exec. prod.). Guest: Rove Live.

O'DONNELL, ROSIE
Actress. b. Commack, NY, March 21, 1962. e. Dickinson Col., Boston Univ. Stand-up comic first gaining attention on series Star Search.
THEATRE: Grease! (B'way debut, 1994).
PICTURES: A League of Their Own, Sleepless in Seattle, Another Stakeout, Car 54 Where Are You?, I'll Do Anything, The Flintstones, Exit to Eden, Now and Then, Beautiful Girls, Harriet the Spy, A Very Brady Sequel (cameo), Wide Awake, Tarzan (voice), Get Bruce, The Flintstones in Viva Rock Vegas (voice), Hedwig and the Angry Inch, Secrets Through the Smoke, Artists and Orphans: A True Drama.
TELEVISION: Series: Gimme a Break, Stand-Up Spotlight (host, exec. prod.), Stand by Your Man, The Rosie O'Donnell Show (host; Emmy, 1997-98). Movies/Specials: Elmopalooza!, The Twilight of the Golds, Jackie's Back!, Elmopalooza, My Favorite Broadway: Leading Ladies, The Gun Deadlock, The 42nd Annual Academy Awards, Rugrats: Still Babies After All These Years.

O'HARA, CATHERINE
Actress, Writer, Director. b. Toronto, Canada, Mar. 4, 1954. Professional debut in 1974 with Toronto's Second City. Co-founder of SCTV in 1976 (Emmy and Canadian Nellie Awards for writing).
PICTURES: Nothing Personal, Rock & Rule (voice), After Hours, Heartburn, Beetlejuice, Dick Tracy, Betsy's Wedding, Home Alone, Little Vegas, There Goes the Neighborhood, Home Alone 2: Lost in New York, The Nightmare Before Christmas (voice), The Paper, Wyatt Earp, A Simple Twist of Fate, Tall Tale, Last of the High Kings, Pippi Longstocking, Home Fries, The Life Before This, Best in Show, Edward Fudwupper Fibbed Big, Bartok the Magnificent (voice), Speaking of Sex, Orange County, Searching for Debra Winger, A Mighty Wind, (also comp.).
TELEVISION: Series: SCTV, Steve Allen Comedy Hour, SCTV Network 90. Movie: Hope, Late Last Night, Committed. Guest: Trying Times, Dream On (also dir.), The Simpsons (voice).

O'HARA, GERRY
Director, Writer. b. Boston, Lincolnshire, England 1924. e. St. Mary's Catholic Sch., Boston. Junior Reporter Boston Guardian. Entered industry in 1942 with documentaries and propaganda subjects.
PICTURES: Director: That Kind of Girl (debut, 1963), Game for Three Lovers, Pleasure Girls (also s.p.), Maroc 7, Love in Amsterdam, All the Right Noises (also s.p.), Leopard in the Snow, The Bitch, Fanny Hill, The Mummy Lives (also co-s.p.). Writer: Ten Little Indians, Havoc in Chase County, Phantom of the Opera, De Sade's Nightmare, Sherlock Holmes and the Affair in Transylvania, Catherine the Great.
TELEVISION: The Avengers, Man in a Suitcase, Journey into the Unknown, The Professionals (story editor, writer), Special Squad (story consultant), Cats Eyes (exec. story editor), Operation Julie (writer; mini-series), Sherlock Holmes & The Leading Lady, Sherlock Holmes & The Incident at Victoria Falls (co-writer).

O'HARA, MAUREEN
Actress. r.n. Maureen FitzSimons. b. Dublin, Ireland. Aug. 17, 1921. Abbey Sch. of Acting. Won numerous prizes for elocution. Under contract to Erich Pommer-Charles Laughton. Co-starred, Abbey & Repertory Theatre.
PICTURES: Kicking the Moon Around (debut, 1938), My Irish Molly, Jamaica Inn, The Hunchback of Notre Dame, A Bill of Divorcement, Dance Girl Dance, They Met in Argentina, How Green Was My Valley, To the Shores of Tripoli, Ten Gentlemen From West Point, The Black Swan, The Immortal Sergeant, This Land Is Mine, The Fallen Sparrow, Buffalo Bill, The Spanish Main, Sentimental Journey, Do You Love Me?, Miracle on 34th Street, Sinbad the Sailor, The Homestretch, The Foxes of Harrow, Sitting Pretty, Woman's Secret, Forbidden Street, Father Was a Fullback, Bagdad, Comanche Territory, Tripoli, Rio Grande, At Sword's Point, Flame of Araby, The Quiet Man, Kangaroo, Against All Flags, The Redhead From Wyoming, War Arrow, Fire Over Africa, The Magnificent Matador, Lady Godiva, Long Gray Line, Lisbon, Everything But the Truth, Wings of Eagles, Our Man in Havana, The Parent Trap, The Deadly Companions, Mr. Hobbs Takes a Vacation, McLintock!, Spencer's Mountain, The Battle of the Villa Fiorita, The Rare Breed, How Do I Love Thee?, Big Jake, Only the Lonely, A Century of Cinema.
TELEVISION: Movie: The Red Pony, The Christmas Box, Cab to Canada, The Last Dance. Specials: Mrs. Miniver, Scarlet Pimpernel, Spellbound, High Button Shoes, Who's Afraid of Mother Goose.

O'HERLIHY, DAN
Actor. b. Wexford, Ireland, May 1, 1919. e. National U. of Ireland (Bachelor of Architecture). Actor with Abbey Theatre, Dublin Gate, Longford Prod.; announcer on Radio Eireann; on

Broadway in The Ivy Green.
PICTURES: Odd Man Out (debut, 1946), Kidnapped, Larceny, Macbeth, Iroquois Trail, The Blue Veil, The Desert Fox, The Highwayman, Soldiers Three, At Swords Point, Invasion U.S.A., Operation Secret, Actors and Sin, Sword of Venus, The Adventures of Robinson Crusoe (Acad. Award nom.), The Black Shield of Falworth, Bengal Brigade, The Purple Mask, The Virgin Queen, City After Midnight, Home Before Dark, Imitation of Life, The Young Land, Night Fighters, One Foot in Hell, The Cabinet of Caligari, Fail-Safe, The Big Cube, 100 Rifles, Waterloo, The Carey Treatment, The Tamarind Seed, MacArthur, Halloween III: The Season of the Witch, The Last Starfighter, The Whoopee Boys, Robocop, The Dead, Robocop 2.
TELEVISION: Series: The Travels of Jamie McPheeters, The Long Hot Summer, Hunter's Moon, Whiz Kids, Man Called Sloane, Twin Peaks. Mini-series: QB VII, Jennie: Lady Randolph Churchill, Nancy Astor. Movies: The People, Deadly Game, Woman on the Run, Good Against Evil, Love Cheat and Steal. Guest: The Equalizer, L.A. Law, Murder She Wrote, Ray Bradbury Theatre, Father Dowling. BBC: Colditz, The Secret Servant, Artemis, The Last Day, Jennie, Nancy Astor, The Rat Pack.

OHLMEYER, DONALD W., JR.
Executive, Producer, Director. b. New Orleans, LA, Feb. 3, 1945. e. U. of Notre Dame, B.A. (Communications), 1967. Producer and director at both ABC and NBC. Formed Ohlmeyer Communications Company, 1982 (diversified prod. and dist. of entertainment and sports prog.). Assoc. dir., ABC Sports, NY 1967-70; director, ABC Sports, 1971-72 (dir. 1972 Olympic Games); prod.: ABC Sports, NY 1972-77 (prod. and dir. 1976 Winter and Summer Olympics; prod. ABC's Monday Night Football, 1972-76); exec. prod.: NBC Sports, NY 1977-82 (exec. prod., 1980 Olympics, The World Series, The Super Bowl). Special Bulletin (exec. prod.), John Denver's Christmas in Aspen (exec. prod.). Chmn. and CEO, Ohlmeyer Communications Co., LA, 1982-present. 1993, named pres. NBC West Coast. Resigned from post 1999. Recipient of 14 Emmy Awards, Humanitas Prize, Award for Excellence, National Film Board. Member, Directors Guild of America.
TELEVISION: Specials: Heroes of Desert Storm (dir.), Disney's Christmas on Ice (dir.), Crimes of the Century (prod.). Series: Lifestories (dir./exec. prod.), Fast Copy (prod.). Movies: Cold Sassy Tree (exec. prod.), Crazy in Love (exec. prod.), Right to Die.

OKAWARA, TAKAO
Director.
PICTURES: Psychic Girl Reiko, Godzilla and Mothra: The Battle for Earth, Godzilla vs. Mechagodzilla II, Orochi the Eight-Headed Dragon, Godzilla vs. Destroyah, Abduction, Godzilla 2000.

O'KEEFE, MICHAEL
Actor. b. Larchmont, NY, April 24, 1955. e. NYU, AADA. m. singer Bonnie Raitt. Co-founder, Colonnades Theatre Lab, NY.
THEATRE: B'way: Mass Appeal (Theatre World Award), Fifth of July. Off-B'way: Killdere (NYSF), Moliere in Spite of Himself, Christmas on Mars, Short Eyes. Regional: Streamers, A Few Good Men (tour).
PICTURES: Gray Lady Down (debut, 1978), The Great Santini (Acad. Award nom.), Caddyshack, Split Image, Nate and Hayes, Finders Keepers, The Slugger's Wife, Ironweed, Out of the Rain, Me and Veronica, Nina Takes a Lover, Three Lovers, Edie and Pen, Ghosts of Mississippi, Herman U.S.A., Just One Night, The Pledge, The Glass House, Prancer Returns, Taking A Chance on Love, The Hot Chick.
TELEVISION: Series: Against the Law, Roseanne. Movies: The Lindbergh Kidnapping Case, Friendly Persuasion, Panache, The Dark Secret of Harvest Home, A Rumor of War, Unholy Matrimony, Bridge to Silence, Disaster at Silo 7, Too Young to Die?, In the Best Interest of the Child, Fear, Incident at Deception Ridge, The People Next Door, Swing Vote.

OLDMAN, GARY
Actor. r.n. Leonard Gary Oldman. b. New Cross, South London, England, March 21, 1958. Won scholarship to Rose Bruford Drama College (B.A. Theatre Arts) after studying with Greenwich Young People's Theatre. Acted with Theatre Royal, York and joined touring theatre co. Then in 1980 appeared with Glasgow Citizens Theatre in Massacre at Paris, Chinchilla, Desperado Corner, A Waste of Time (also touring Europe and South America). Received Evening Standard Film Award for Best Newcomer for Sid and Nancy, 1986.
THEATRE: London: Minnesota Moon, Summit Conference, Rat in the Skull, Women Beware Women, The War Plays, Real Dreams, The Desert Air, Serious Money (Royal Shakespeare Co.), The Pope's Wedding (Time Out's Fringe Award, best newcomer 1985-86; British Theatre Assc. Drama Mag. Award, Best Actor 1985).
PICTURES: Sid and Nancy (debut, 1986), Prick Up Your Ears, Track 29, We Think the World of You, Criminal Law, Chattahoochee, State of Grace, Rosencrantz and Guildenstern Are Dead, Exile, Before and After Death, JFK, Bram Stoker's Dracula, True Romance, Romeo Is Bleeding, The Professional, Immortal Beloved, Murder in the First, Dead Presidents, The

Scarlet Letter, Basquiat, Air Force One, Nil by Mouth (s.p., dir., prod. only, BAFTA Award, Outstanding Brit. Film, Best Orig. Screenplay, 1997), Lost in Space, Quest for Camelot (voice), The Contender, Anasazi Moon, Hannibal, Interstate 60, Nobody's Baby, Sin, Tiptoes.
TELEVISION: Remembrance, Meantime, Honest Decent and True, Rat in the Skull, The Firm, Heading Home, Fallen Angels, Jesus (mini-series), Friends, Alias, (dir.).

OLIN, KEN
Actor, Director. b. Chicago, IL, July 30, 1954. e. Univ. of PA. m. actress Patricia Wettig. Studied acting with Warren Robertson and Stella Adler. Made Off-B'way deput in Taxi Tales, 1978.
PICTURES: Ghost Story, Queen's Logic, White Fang 2: Myth of the White Wolf (dir.), 'Til There Was You.
TELEVISION: Series: The Bay City Blues, Hill Street Blues, Falcon Crest, thirtysomething (also dir.), EZ Streets (also dir.), L.A. Doctors (also dir.). Series: (director only): Felicity, Judging Amy, The West Wing, Freaks and Geeks, Alias. Movies (actor): Women at West Point, Flight 90: Disaster on the Potomac, There Must Be a Pony, Tonight's the Night, Cop Killer, A Stoning in Fulham County, Goodnight Sweet Wife: A Murder in Boston, Telling Secrets, Nothing But the Truth, The Advocate's Devil, Evolution's Child, Y2K. Movies (director): The Broken Cord, Doing Time on Maple Drive, In Pursuit of Honor. Guest: Murder She Wrote, Hotel, The Hitchhiker.

OLIN, LENA
Actress. b. Stockholm, Sweden, March 22, 1955. Member of the Royal Dramatic Theatre in Stockholm. Daughter of actor-director Stig Olin. m. director Lasse Hallstrom.
THEATRE: NY: Miss Julie.
PICTURES: The Adventures of Picasso, Karleken, Fanny and Alexander, Grasanklingar, After the Rehearsal, A Matter of Life and Death, Friends, The Unbearable Lightness of Being, S/Y Joy (Gladjen), Enemies a Love Story (Acad. Award nom.), Havana, Mr. Jones, Romeo Is Bleeding, The Night and the Moment, Night Falls on Manhattan, Polish Wedding, Hamilton, Mystery Men, The Ninth Gate, Chocolat, Ignition, Darkness, Queen of the Damned, The United States of Leland, Darkness, Hollywood Homicide.
TELEVISION: Movies: Friaren som inte ville gifta sig, Wallenberg: A Hero's Story, Glasmastarna, Hebriana, Hamilton.

OLMI, ERMANNO
Director, Writer, Producer, Editor. b. Bergamo, Italy, July 24, 1931. e. Accademia d'Arte Drammatica, Milan. Worked as a clerk for an electric company Edisonvolta 1949-52 until 1952 when he began directing theatrical and cinematic activities sponsored by co. 1952-61, directed or supervised over 40 short 16mm and 35mm documentary films. 1959 first feature film, semi-doc. Time Stood Still. With other friends and Tullio Kezich formed prod. co., 22 December S.P.A., 1961. 1982, Helped found Hypothesis Cinema, a sch. for aspiring dirs.
PICTURES: Director/Writer: Time Stood Still (debut, 1959), The Sound of Trumpets, The Fiances (also prod.), And There Came a Man (A Man Named John), One Fine Day (also edit.), The Tree of the Wood Clogs (Cannes Film Fest. Award, 1978; also photog., edit.), Camminacammina (also photog., edit., design), Milano '83 (also photog., edit.), Long Live the Lady (also co-photog., edit.), Legend of the Holy Drinker (also edit.), Il Segreto Del Bosco Vecchio. Documenatries: Artigiani Veneti, Lungo Il Fiume, The Secret of the Old Woods, Genesis: The Creation and the Flood, 12 registi per 12 città, Il Denaro non esiste, Professions of Arms.
TELEVISION: The Scavengers (also photog.), During the Summer (also photog., edit.), The Circumstance (also photog., edit.), Genesis: The Creation & the Flood.

OLMOS, EDWARD JAMES
Actor. b. East Los Angeles, CA, February 24, 1947. e. East Los Angeles City Coll., CA State U. m. actress Lorraine Bracco. Started as rock singer with group Eddie James and the Pacific Ocean. By the early 1970s acted in small roles on Kojak and Hawaii Five-O. 1978 starred in Luis Valdez's musical drama Zoot Suit at Mark Taper Forum (L.A. Drama Critics Circle Award, 1978), later on B'way (Theatre World Award, Tony nom.), and in film version. Formed YOY Productions with director Robert Young. Numerous awards for humanitarian work.
PICTURES: Aloha Bobby and Rose (debut, 1975), Alambrista!, Virus, Wolfen, Zoot Suit, Blade Runner, The Ballad of Gregorio Cortez (also assoc. prod., composer and musical adaptor), Saving Grace, Stand and Deliver (Acad. Award nom.; also co-prod.), Triumph of the Spirit, Talent for the Game, American Me (also dir., co-prod.), A Million to Juan, Mirage, My Family/Mi Familia, Roosters, Caught, Selena, The Wonderful Ice Cream Suit, The Wall, Zaoatista (narrator), The Road to El Dorado (voice), Gossip, In the Time of the Butterflies.
TELEVISION: Movies: Evening in Byzantium, 300 Miles for Stephanie, Menendez: A Killing in Beverly Hills, The Burning Season, The Taking of Pelham One Two Three, Bonanno: A Godfather's Story, The Princess and the Barrio Boy, The Judge. Specials: Sequin, Y.E.S. Inc, The Story of Fathers & Sons. Series: Miami Vice (Golden Globe & Emmy Awards, 1985; also dir. episodes), American Family.

O'LOUGHLIN, GERALD STUART
Actor. b. New York, NY, Dec. 23, 1921. e. Lafayette Col., U. of Rochester, Neighborhood Playhouse. U.S. Marine, WWII.
THEATRE: B'way: Streetcar (ANTA series), Shadow of a Gunman, Dark at the Top of the Stairs, A Touch of the Poet, Cook for Mr. General, One Flew Over the Cuckoo's Nest, Calculated Risk, Lovers and Other Strangers. Off-B'way: Who'll Save the Plowboy (Obie Award), Harry Noon and Night, Machinal.
PICTURES: Lovers and Lollipops, Cop Hater, A Hatful of Rain, Ensign Pulver, A Fine Madness, In Cold Blood, Ice Station Zebra, Desperate Characters, The Organization, The Valachi Papers, Twilight's Last Gleaming, Frances, Crimes of Passion, City Heat, Quicksilver, The Secret Kingdom, 3 Strikes. Audio narration, The Secret Kingdom.
TELEVISION: Movies: The D.A.: Murder One, Murder at the World Series, Something for Joey, A Love Affair: The Eleanor and Lou Gehrig Story, Crash of Flight 401, Detour to Terror, Pleasure Palace, A Matter of Life and Death, Under Siege, Perry Mason: The Case of the Notorious Nun, Child's Cry, In the Arms of a Killer, The Crime of the Century. Mini-Series: Wheels, Roots: The Next Generations, Blind Ambition, Women in White, The Blue and the Gray. Series: The Storefront Lawyers (Men at Law), The Rookies, Automan, Our House. Guest: Alcoa Premiere, Philco-Goodyear, Suspense, The Defenders, Ben Casey, Dr. Kildare, 12 O'Clock High, Going My Way, Naked City, Gunsmoke, Green Hornet, Mission Impossible, Mannix, Judd For The Defense, Hawaii 5-0, Cannon, Room 222, Charlie's Angels, M*A*S*H, Trapper John M.D., Fame, T.J. Hooker, Murder She Wrote, Highway to Heaven, Dirty Dancing, Equal Justice, ER.

OLSON, DALE C.
Executive. b. Fargo, ND, Feb. 20, 1934. e. Portland State Coll., OR. Owner, Dale C. Olson & Associates; formerly sn. v.p. & pres., m.p. div., Rogers & Cowan public relations. Journalist on Oregonian newspaper, West Coast editor, Boxoffice Magazine, 1958-60; critic and reporter, Daily Variety, 1960-66; dir. of publ., Mirisch Corp., 1966-68; Rogers & Cowan, 1968-85. Past pres., Hollywood Press Club, awarded Bob Yaeger and Les Mason award by Publicists Guild; v.p. Diamond Circle, City of Hope; delegate for U.S. to Manila International Film Festival. Chmn. public rltns. coordin. committee & member nat'l bd. of trustees, A.M.P.A.S., 1989-91. Chmn. Western Council, Actors Fund of America, 1991. On Nat'l Bd. of Trustees, 1992-present.

OLSON, JAMES
Actor. b. Evanston, IL, Oct. 8, 1930. e. Northwestern U.
THEATRE: NY: The Young and the Beautiful, Romulus, The Chinese Prime Minister, J.B., Slapstick Tragedy, Three Sisters, Sin of Pat Muldoon, Winter's Tale, Of Love Remembered, Twelve Dreams.
PICTURES: The Sharkfighters, The Strange One, Rachel Rachel, Moon Zero Two, The Andromeda Strain, The Groundstar Conspiracy, The Mafu Cage, Ragtime, Amityville II: The Possession, Commando, Rachel River.
TELEVISION: Movies: Paper Man, Incident on a Dark Street, Manhunter, A Tree Grows in Brooklyn, The Sex Symbol, The Family Nobody Wanted, Someone I Touched, Man on the Outside, Strange New World, Law and Order, The Spell, Moviola: The Silent Years, Cave-In!, The Parade. Specials: Missiles of October, Vince Lombardi Story, Court-Martial of Geoge Armstrong Custer.

OLSON, NANCY
Actress. b. Milwaukee, WI, July 14, 1929. e. U. of Wisconsin, UCLA. No prof. experience prior to films.
PICTURES: Canadian Pacific (debut, 1949), Sunset Boulevard (Acad. Award nom.), Union Station, Mr. Music, Submarine Command, Force of Arms, Big Jim McLain, So Big, The Boy From Oklahoma, Battle Cry, Pollyanna, The Absent-Minded Professor, Son of Flubber, Smith!, Snowball Express, Airport 1975, Making Love.
TELEVISION: Series: Kingston: Confidential, Paper Dolls. Special: High Tor.

OLYPHANT, TIMOTHY
Actor. b. Hawaii, May 20, 1968.
PICTURES: The First Wives Club, A Life Less Ordinary, Scream 2, 1999, No Vacancy, Go, Advice From a Caterpillar, The Broken Hearts Club: A Romantic Comedy, Gone in Sixty Seconds, Auggie Rose, Head Over Heels, The Safety of Objects, Rockstar, Coastlines, El Diablo, Dreamcatcher, A Man Apart.
TELEVISION: Movies: When Trumphets Fade, Shadow Realm. Guest: High Incident, Mr. & Mrs. Smith, Sex and the City.

O'NEAL, RON
Actor. b. Utica, NY, Sept. 1, 1937. e. Ohio State U. Spent 9 yrs. at Karamu House in Cleveland (inter-racial theatre) from 1957 to 1966, acting in 40 plays. 1967-68 spent in N.Y. teaching acting in Harlem. Appeared in all-black revue 1968, The Best of Broadway, then in summer stock. Off-B'way in American Pastorale and The Mummer's Play. 1970 joined the Public Theatre. Break came with No Place To Be Somebody, which won him the Obie, Clarence Derwent, Drama Desk and Theatre World Awards.

THEATRE: Tiny Alice, The Dream of Monkey Mountain.
PICTURES: Move (debut, 1970), The Organization, Super Fly, Super Fly TNT (also dir., co-story), The Master Gunfighter, Brothers, A Force of One, When a Stranger Calls, The Final Countdown, St. Helens, Red Dawn, Mercenary Fighters, Hero and the Terror, Up Against the Wall (also dir.), Death House, Original Gangstas.
TELEVISION: Series: Bring 'em Back Alive, The Equalizer. Mini-Series: North and South. Movies: Freedom Road, Brave New World, Guyana Tragedy: The Story of Jim Jones, Sophisticated Gents, Playing with Fire, North Beach and Rawhide, As Summers Die.

O'NEAL, RYAN
Actor. r.n. Patrick Ryan O'Neal. b. Los Angeles, CA, April 20, 1941. Parents, screenwriter-novelist, Charles O'Neal, and actress Patricia Callaghan. Daughter is actress Tatum O'Neal; son is actor Griffin O'Neal. Boxer, L.A. Golden Gloves, 1956-57. Began career as stand-in, stunt man, then actor in Tales of the Vikings series, in Germany, 1959; freelanced in Hollywood.
PICTURES: The Big Bounce (debut, 1969), The Games, Love Story (Acad. Award nom.), Wild Rovers, What's Up Doc?, Paper Moon, The Thief Who Came to Dinner, Barry Lyndon, Nickelodeon, A Bridge Too Far, The Driver, Oliver's Story, The Main Event, So Fine, Green Ice, Partners, Irreconcilable Differences, Fever Pitch, Tough Guys Don't Dance, Chances Are, Faithful, Hacks, An Alan Smithee Film: Burn Hollywood Burn, Zero Effect, Coming Soon, The List, Gentleman B., Epoch, People I Know, Malibu's Most Wanted.
TELEVISION: Movies: Love Hate Love, Small Sacrifices, The Man Upstairs. Special: Liza Minnelli: A Triple Play. Guest: Dobie Gillis, Bachelor Father, Leave It to Beaver, My Three Sons, Perry Mason, The Larry Sanders Show, Bull. Pilot: 1775.Series: Empire, Peyton Place, Good Sports, Miss Match.

O'NEAL, TATUM
Actress. b. Los Angeles, CA, Nov. 5, 1963. p. actors Ryan O'Neal and Joanna Moore. NY stage debut 1992 in A Terrible Beauty, followed by Adroscoggin Fugue.
PICTURES: Paper Moon (debut, 1973; Academy Award, best supporting actress), The Bad News Bears, Nickelodeon, International Velvet, Little Darlings, Circle of Two, Certain Fury, Little Noises, Basquiat, The Scoundrel's Wife.
TELEVISION: Movie: Woman on the Run: The Lawrencia Bembenek Story. Special: 15 and Getting Straight. Guest: Cher, Faerie Tale Theatre (Goldilocks and the Three Bears).

O'NEILL, ED
Actor. b. Youngstown, OH, Apr. 12, 1946. e. Ohio Univ., Youngstown State. Taught social studies in Youngstown prior to becoming an actor. Made NY stage debut Off-Off-B'way in Requiem for a Heavyweight at SoHo Rep. Theatre. B'way debut in Knockout.
PICTURES: Deliverance, Cruising, The Dogs of War, Disorganized Crime, K-9, The Adventures of Ford Fairlane, Sibling Rivalry, Dutch, Wayne's World, Wayne's World 2, Blue Chips, Little Giants, Prefontaine, The Spanish Prisoner, The Bone Collector, Lucky Numbers, Nobody's Baby.
TELEVISION: Series: Married... With Children, Big Apple. Pilot: Farrell for the People. Movies: When Your Lover Leaves, The Day the Women Got Even, Popeye Doyle, A Winner Never Quits, Right to Die, Police School, The Whereabouts of Jenny, W.E.I.R.D. World, The Tenth Kingdom.

O'NEILL, JENNIFER
Actress. b. Rio de Janeiro, Brazil, Feb. 20, 1949. e. Dalton Sch. Model before entering films. Spokeswoman: CoverGirl cosmetics. Pres., Point of View Productions and Management.
PICTURES: Rio Lobo, Summer of '42, Such Good Friends, The Carey Treatment, Glass Houses, Lady Ice, The Reincarnation of Peter Proud, Whiffs, Caravans, The Psychic, The Innocent, A Force of One, Cloud Dancer, Steel, Scanners, Committed, I Love N.Y., Love is Like That, Invasion of Privacy, The Gentle People, Discretion Assured, The Corporate Ladder, The Ride, Time Changer.
TELEVISION: Series: Bare Essence, Cover Up. Movies: Love's Savage Fury, The Other Victim, An Invasion of Privacy, Chase, Perry Mason: The Case of the Shooting Star, The Red Spider, Glory Days, Full Exposure: The Sex Tapes Scandal, Passions, Perfect Family, The Cover Girl Murders, Frame-up, Jonathan Stone: Threat of Innocence, Silver Strand. Mini-Series: A.D.

ONTKEAN, MICHAEL
Actor. b. Vancouver, British Columbia, Canada, Jan. 24, 1946. e. U. of New Hampshire. Son of Leonard and Muriel Cooper Ontkean, actors. Acting debut at 4 with father's rep. theater. Child actor with Stratford Shakespeare Fest., CBC and Natl Film Bd. Attended coll. 4 years on hockey scholarship. Has performed with Public Theatre, NY, Willamstown Theatre Fest., Mark Taper Lab, The Kitchen, Soho.
PICTURES: The Peace Killers (debut, 1971), Pick Up on 101, Necromancy, Hot Summer Week, Slap Shot, Voices, Willie and Phil, Making Love, Just the Way You Are, The Allnighter, Maid to Order, Clara's Heart, Street Justice, Cold Front, Bye Bye Blues, Postcards From the Edge, Bayou Boy, The Toy Factory, Summer,

Access All Areas, Le Sang des Autres, Cutting Loose, Square Deal, Rapture, Just A Little Harmless Sex.
TELEVISION: *Series:* The Rookies, Twin Peaks. *Movies:* The Rookies (pilot), The Blood of Others, Kids Don't Tell, The Right of the People, Twin Peaks (pilot), Defense of a Married Man, In a Child's Name, Legacy of Lies, Whose Child Is This? The War for Baby Jessica, Vendetta 2: The New Mafia, Danielle Steel's Family Album, The Man Next Door, Man From the South.

OPHULS, MARCEL
Director, Writer. r.n. Hans Marcel Oppenheimer. b. Frankfurt-am-Main, Germany, Nov. 1, 1927. Son of German director Max Ophuls. e. Occidental Coll., U. of California, Berkeley, Sorbonne (philosophy). Family moved to France, 1932, then to Hollywood, 1941. Military service with Occupation forces in Japan, 1946; performed with theater unit, Tokyo. 1951 began working in French film industry as asst. dir., using name Marcel Wall. Asst. dir. on Moulin Rouge, Act of Love, Marianne de ma Jeunesse, Lola Montes. 1956-59, radio and TV story ed., West Germany. Later worked for French TV as reporter and dir. news mag. features. Dir. & wrote short film Henri Matisse. 1968 doc. dir. for German TV. 1975-78 staff prod. CBS News, then ABC News. MacArthur Fellowship 1991. Member of AMPAS.
PICTURES: *Director/Writer:* Love at 20 (dir. segment), Banana Peel, Fire at Will, Munich or Peace in Our Time, The Sorrow and the Pity (also prod.; Natl. Soc. of Film Critics, NY Film Critics & Prix de Dinard Awards, 1970), The Harvest at Mai Lai, A Sense of Loss, The Memory of Justice, Hotel Terminus--The Life and Times of Klaus Barbie (also prod.; Academy Award, Berlin Peace Prize, Cannes Jury Prize, 1988), The Troubles We've Seen (also prod., Intl. Film Critics Prize, 1994).
TELEVISION: America Revisited, Two Whole Days, November Days.

OPOTOWSKY, STAN
Executive. b. New Orleans, LA, Apr. 13, 1923. e. Tulane U. Served in U.S. Marine Corps as combat corr. and later joined United Press, working in New Orleans, Denver, and New York. Published own weekly newspaper in Mississippi before returning to N.Y. to join New York Post as mgr. editor and traveling natl. corr. Is also cinematographer and film editor. Joined ABC News as TV assignment editor; named asst. assignment mgr. 1974 named dir. of operations for ABC News TV Documentaries. 1975 named dir. of TV News Coverage, ABC News.
TELEVISION: *Author:* The Big Picture, The Longs of Louisiana, The Kennedy Government, Men Behind Bars.

O'QUINN, TERRY
Actor. b. Michigan, July 15, 1952.
THEATRE: *B'way:* Foxfire, Curse of an Aching Heart. *Off-B'way:* Richard III, Groves of Academy, Total Abandon. *Regional:* Streamers, Measure for Measure, The Front Page.
PICTURES: Heaven's Gate, Without a Trace, All the Right Moves, Places in the Heart, Mrs. Soffel, Mischief, Silver Bullet, SpaceCamp, The Stepfather, Black Widow, Young Guns, Pin, Stepfather 2, Blind Fury, The Rocketeer, Prisoners of the Sun, Company Business, The Cutting Edge, Amityville: A New Generation, Tombstone, Lipstick Camera, American Outlaws, Old School, Primal Fear, Ghosts of Mississippi, Shadow Conspiracy, The X Files.
TELEVISION: *Movies:* FDR: The Final Year, Prisoner Without a Name Cell Without a Number, Right to Kill, Unfinished Business, An Early Frost, Stranger on My Land, Women of Valor, When the Time Comes, Perry Mason: The Case of the Desperate Deception, Son of the Morning Star, The Last to Go, Deliver Them From Evil: The Taking of Alta View, Trial: The Price of Passion, Sexual Advances, Wild Card, The Good Fight, Born Too Soon, Visions of Murder, Heart of a Child, Don't Talk To Strangers, Justice in a Small Town, A Friend to Die For, Ray Alexander: A Menu for Murder. *Television: Series:* Alias, Jag, Harsh Realm, Millennium.

ORBACH, JERRY
Actor. b. Bronx, NY, Oct. 20, 1935. e. U. of Illinois, Northwestern U. Trained for stage with Herbert Berghof and Lee Strasberg. N.Y. stage debut in Threepenny Opera, 1955.
THEATRE: The Fantasticks (original cast, 1960), Carnival, The Cradle Will Rock, Guys and Dolls, Scuba Duba, Promises Promises (Tony Award, 1969), 6 Rms Riv Vu, Chicago, 42nd Street.
PICTURES: Cop Hater, Mad Dog Coll, John Goldfarb Please Come Home, The Gang That Couldn't Shoot Straight, A Fan's Notes, Foreplay (The President's Woman), The Sentinel, Underground Aces, Prince of the City, Brewster's Millions, F/X, The Imagemaker, Dirty Dancing, Someone to Watch Over Me, Crimes and Misdemeanors, Last Exit to Brooklyn, I Love N.Y., A Gnome Named Norm, California Casanova, Dead Women in Lingerie, Out for Justice, Toy Soldiers (cameo), Delusion, Delirious, Beauty and the Beast (voice), Straight Talk, Universal Soldier, Mr. Saturday Night, The Cemetery Club, Disney Sing-Along-Songs: Be Our Guest (voice), Aladdin and the King of Thieves (voice), Beauty and the Beast: The Enchanted Christmas (voice), Belle's Magical World (voice), Chinese Coffee, Prince of Central Park, The Acting Class.
TELEVISION: *Series:* The Law and Harry McGraw, Law and

Order, House of Mouse (voice), Encounters with the Unexplained. *Guest:* Shari Lewis Show, Jack Paar, Bob Hope Presents, Love American Style, Murder She Wrote, Kojak, Golden Girls, Hunter, Who's the Boss?, Homicide: Life on the Street, Law & Order: Special Victims Unit. *Movies:* An Invasion of Privacy, Out on a Limb, Love Among Thieves, In Defense of a Married Man, Broadway Bound, Quiet Killer, Mastergate, Exiled. *Mini-Series:* Dream West.

ORMOND, JULIA
Actress. b. England, Jan. 4, 1965. Studied acting at Webber Douglas Acad., London.
THEATRE: The Rehearsal, Wuthering Heights, Arms and the Man, The Crucible, Faith Hope and Charity (London Drama Critics Award, 1989).
PICTURES: The Baby of Macon, Nostradamus, Legends of the Fall, First Knight, Captives, Sabrina, Smilla's Sense of Snow, The Barber of Siberia, The Prime Gig.
TELEVISION: *Mini-Series:* Traffik. *Movies:* Young Catherine, Stalin, Animal Farm (voice), Varian's War.

ORTEGA, KENNY
Director, Choreographer. b. Palo Alto, CA. e. American Conserv. Theatre, Canada Coll. Started acting at age 13. Earned several scholarships to dance academies in San Francisco Bay area. Regional theatre roles in Oliver, Hair, The Last Sweet Days of Isaac, before staging shows for rock band The Tubes. First major tv job choreographing Cher special. Directed/choreographed concerts and/or music videos for such performers as Michael Jackson, Kiss, Elton John, Cher, Rod Stewart, Diana Ross, Madonna, Billy Joel, Oingo Boingo, Miami Sound Machine, Pointer Sisters, Toto. Artistic dir. and choreographer, 1996 Centennial Olympic Games opening and closing ceremonies.
PICTURES: *Director/Choreographer:* Newsies, Hocus Pocus. *Choreographer:* Quest for Camelot, Ferris Bueller's Day Off, To Wong Foo—Thanks for Everything–Julie Newmar, Dirty Dancing, Road House, Shag, The Great Outdoors, Lost Boys, Pretty in Pink, Salsa, God Created Woman, One from the Heart, St. Elmo's Fire, Xanadu, The Rose.
TELEVISION: *Series Director:* Dirty Dancing (also choreog.), Hull Street High, Chicago Hope (also choreog.), Fame L.A., McKenna, Second Noah. *Choreographer:* American Music Awards, Academy Awards, NAACP Awards, 1996 Olympics, Mickey's 60th Birthday, Totally Mine, America Picks the #1 Hit, Nosotros Awards, Good Time Rock 'n' Roll, Jump, Grounded For Life, (dir.), Ally McBeal, (dir.), Gilmore Girls, Wasteland. *Movies:* The Way She Moves. *Specials Choreographer:* Olivia Newton-John, Cher, The Pointer Sisters, Neil Diamond, Smokey Robinson, Cheryl Ladd.

O'SHEA, MILO
Actor. b. Dublin, Ireland, June 2, 1926. Member of Dublin Gate Theatre Co., 1944, before screen career.
THEATRE: *NY:* Staircase, Dear World, The Comedians, A Touch of the Poet, Waiting For Godot (Brooklyn Acad. of Music), Mass Appeal, My Fair Lady, Corpse!, Meet Me in St. Louis, Remembrance (Off-B'way), Philadelphia Here I Come!, Alive Alive Oh! (alo co-writer), Mrs. Warren's Profession. *London:* Treasure Hunt, Glory Be, Hans Andersen, Corpse, Can-Can.
PICTURES: Carry on Cabby, Never Put It in Writing, Ulysses, Romeo and Juliet, Barbarella, The Adding Machine, The Angel Levine, Paddy, Sacco and Vanzetti, Loot, Theatre of Blood, Digby: The Biggest Dog in the World, It's Not the Size That Counts, Arabian Adventure, The Pilot, The Verdict, The Purple Rose of Cairo, The Dream Team, Opportunity Knocks, Only the Lonely, The Playboys, Rooney, Never Put It In Writing, The Butcher Boy, The Match Maker.
TELEVISION: *Series:* Once a Hero, Frasier, Oz. *Mini-Series:* QB VII, Ellis Island, The Best of Families. *Movies/Specials:* Two Forsythe, Peter Lundy and the Medicine Hat Stallion, Portrait of a Rebel: Margaret Sanger, And No One Could Save Her, A Times for Miracles, Broken Vows, Angel in Green, Murder in the Heartland, Swing Vote. *Guest:* The Golden Girls, Cheers, Who's the Boss, Beauty and the Beast, St. Elsewhere.

OSHIMA, NAGISA
Director, Writer. b. Kyoto, Japan, March 31, 1932. e. U. of Kyoto (law), 1954. Joined Shochiku Ofuna Studios in 1954 as asst. dir.; 1956 wrote film criticism and became editor-in-chief of film revue Eiga hihyo; 1959 promoted to director. 1962-65 worked exclusively in TV; 1962-64 made documentaries in Korea and Vietnam; 1975 formed Oshima Prods. 1976, his book of Realm of the Senses seized by police. With editor, prosecuted for obscenity, acquitted. Pres. of Directors Guild of Japan, 1980-present.
PICTURES: *Dir./Writer:* A Town of Love and Hope (debut, 1959), Cruel Story of Youth, The Sun's Burial, Night and Fog in Japan, The Catch (dir. only), The Christian Rebel, A Child's First Adventure, I'm Here Bellett, The Pleasures of the Flesh, Violence at Noon (dir. only), Band of Ninja (also co-prod.), Sing a Song of Sex (also co- prod.), Japanese Summer: Double Suicide (also co-prod.), Death By Hanging, Three Resurrected Drunkards, Diary of a Shinjuku Thief, Boy (dir. only), He Died After the War, The Ceremony, Dear Summer Sister, In the Realm of the Senses, Phantom Love, Empire of Passion (also co-prod.), Merry Christmas Mr. Lawrence, Max My Love, Taboo.

OSMENT, HALEY JOEL
Actor. b. Los Angeles, CA, April 10, 1988.
PICTURES: Forrest Gump, Mixed Nuts, Bogus, For Better or Worse, The Sixth Sense, I'll Remember April, Discover Spot (voice), Pay It Forward, Edwurd Fudwupper Fibbed Big (voice), A.I., The Hunchback of Notre Dame II (voice), Edges of the Lord, Edwurd Fudwupper Fibbed Big (voice), The Jungle Book 2 (voice), The Country Bears (voice).
TELEVISION: *Series:* Thunder Alley, The Jeff Foxworthy Show, Murphy Brown. *Movies:* Lies of the Heart: The Story of Laurie Kellog, Beauty and the Beast: The Enchanted Christmas (voice), The Ransom of Red Chief, Cab to Canada. *Guest:* The Larry Sanders Show, Touched By An Angel, The Pretender, Alley McBeal, Walker, Texas Ranger, Chicago Hope, Buzz Lightyear of Star Command, Rove Live.

OSMOND, DONNY
Singer, TV Host. b. Ogden, UT, Dec. 9, 1957. Seventh of 9 children, he was fifth member of family to become professional singer. (Four brothers: Alan, Wayne, Merrill and Jay, were original members of Osmond Bros., who originally sang barbershop quartet.) Made debut at 4 on Andy Williams Show. Has had 12 gold albums. Was co-host with sister of Donny & Marie on TV.
THEATRE: Little Johnny Jones, Joseph and the Amazing Technicolor Dreamcoat.
PICTURE: Goin' Coconuts, Mulan (voice).
TELEVISION: *Series:* The Andy Williams Show, Donny and Marie, Pyramid, (host). *Movie:* The Wild Women of Chastity Gulch, Inside The Osmonds. *Guest:* The Jerry Lewis Show, Here's Lucy, The Love Boat.

OSMOND, MARIE
Singer, TV Host. b. Ogden, UT, Oct. 13, 1959. Began career at age of 3 on Andy Williams Show. Her first album, Paper Roses went gold. Appeared with brother Donny in feature film Goin' Coconuts.
TELEVISION: *Series:* Donny and Marie, Marie, Ripley's Believe It or Not (co-host), Maybe This Time. *Movies:* Gift of Love, I Married Wyatt Earp, Side By Side, Inside The Osmonds.

O'SULLIVAN, KEVIN P.
Executive. b. New York, NY, April 13, 1928. e. Queens Coll., Flushing, NY. Associated with television 40 yrs., initially as a talent; later as businessman. Won first prize in Arthur Godfrey Talent Scouts competition in 1948. 1950-55 professional singer, actor on TV, in theatre, night clubs. 1955-57 on radio-TV promotion staff, Ronson Corp. 1958-61, salesman, Television Programs of America. 1961-67 dir. of program services, Harrington, Righter and Parsons. 1967 joined ABC Films, domestic sales div. as v.p. & gen. sales mgr. 1969 named v.p., gen. mgr. then pres., ABC Films, Inc.; 1970 made pres., ABC Int'l. TV, while retaining position as pres., ABC Films. 1973 became pres., COO, Worldvision Enterprises, Inc., co. formed to succeed ABC Films when FCC stopped networks from TV program dist. Elected chmn. & CEO, Worldvision, 1982. Named pres., Great American Broadcasting Group, 1987. Resigned, 1988. Named pres., Kenmare Prods. Inc., 1988.

O'TOOLE, ANNETTE
Actress. b. Houston, TX, April 1, 1953. e. UCLA.
PICTURES: Smile (debut, 1975), One on One, King of the Gypsies, Foolin' Around, Cat People, 48 HRS, Superman III, Cross My Heart, Love at Large, Andre (voice), Imaginary Crimes, A Mighty Wind, (composer).
TELEVISION: *Movies:* The Girl Most Likely To..., The Entertainer, The War Between the Tates, Love For Rent, Stand By Your Man, Copacabana, Arthur Hailey's Strong Medicine, Broken Vows, Stephen King's It, The Dreamer of Oz, White Lies, Kiss of a Killer, Love Matters, A Mother's Revenge, My Brother's Keeper, The Christmas Box, The Man Next Door, Keeping The Promise, Final Descent, Final Justice, The Huntress. *Mini-Series:* The Kennedys of Massachusetts. *Specials:* Vanities, Best Legs in the Eighth Grade, Secret World of the Very Young, Unpublished Letters, On Hope, Smallville.

O'TOOLE, PETER
Actor. b. Connemara, Ireland, Aug. 2, 1932. Studied at Royal Acad. of Dramatic Art. Early career with Bristol Old Vic. Partner with Jules Buck, Keep Films, Ltd. Autobiography: Loitering With Intent (1993).
THEATRE: *London:* Major Barbara, Oh My Papa, The Long the Short and the Tall, Baal, Hamlet, Ride a Cock Horse, Macbeth, Man and Superman, Jeffrey Bernard is Unwell, Our Song. 1960, with the Stratford-on-Avon Company (The Taming of the Shrew, Merchant of Venice, etc). *Dublin:* Arms and the Man, Waiting for Godot. *Toronto:* Present Laughter, Uncle Vanya. B'way debut 1987: Pygmalion.
PICTURES: Kidnapped (debut, 1959), The Savage Innocents, The Day They Robbed the Bank of England, Lawrence of Arabia, Becket, Lord Jim, What's New Pussycat?, The Bible, How to Steal a Million, The Night of the Generals, Casino Royale (cameo), Great Catherine, The Lion in Winter, Goodbye Mr. Chips, Brotherly Love (Country Dance), Murphy's War, Under Milk Wood, The Ruling Class, Man of La Mancha, Rosebud, Man

Friday, Foxtrot, Caligula, Power Play, Zulu Dawn, The Stunt Man, My Favorite Year, Supergirl, Creator, Club Paradise, The Last Emperor, High Spirits, On a Moonlit Night, Helena, Wings of Fame, The Nutcracker Prince (voice), The Rainbow Thief, Isabelle Eberhardt, King Ralph, Rebecca's Daughters, The Seventh Coin, FairyTale: A True Story, Phantoms, The Manor, Molokai: The Story of Father Damien, Coming Home, The Sinister Saga of Making "The Stunt Man," The Final Curtain, Global Heresy.
TELEVISION: *Movies:* Rogue Male (BBC), Svengali, Kim, Crossing to Freedom, Civvies, Gulliver's Travels, Jeffrey Bernard is Unwell, Hitler: The Rise of Evil. *Specials:* Present Laughter, Pygmalion, The Dark Angel. *Series:* Strumpet City (BBC), Heavy Weather. *Mini-Series:* Masada, Heaven & Hell: North and South Book III, Joan of Arc.

OTWELL, RONNIE RAY
Theatre Executive. b. Carrollton, GA, Aug. 13, 1929. e. Georgia Inst. of Technology. Entered industry as mgr., Bremen Theatre, GA, 1950: dir. pub., adv., Martin Theatres, Columbus, GA, 1950-63; v.p., dir. Martin Theatres of Ga., Inc., 1963, Martin Theatres of Ala., Inc., 1963; dir. Martin Theatres of Columbus, 1963; sr. v.p., Martin Theatres Companies, 1971.

OVERALL, PARK
Actress. b. Nashville, TN, March 15, 1957. Attended British boarding school, earned teaching degree, before turning to acting.
THEATRE: *NY:* Biloxi Blues, Wild Blue, Only You, Loose Ends, Something About Baseball, Marathon '88.
PICTURES: Body Passion, Biloxi Blues, Mississippi Burning, Talk Radio (voice), Lost Angels, Kindergarten Cop, The Vanishing, House of Cards, Undercover Blues, Sparkler.
TELEVISION: *Series:* Empty Nest. *Movies:* Luck of the Draw: The Gambler Returns, Overkill: The Aileen Wuornos Story, Precious Victims, The Good Old Boys, Inflammable, Fifteen and Pregnant, The Price of a Broken Heart, When Andrew Came Home. *Pilot:* The Line.

OVITZ, MICHAEL
Talent Agent, Executive. b. Chicago, IL, Dec. 14, 1946. e. UCLA, 1968. Began ent. career as a tour guide at Universal Studios. Started as a trainee at William Morris Agency before becoming agent, 1969-75. Co-founder of Creative Artists Agency, 1975; became chmn. and chief stock holder. 1995 named pres. The Walt Disney Company; resigned from The Walt Disney Company, Jan. 1997. Co-founder of Artists Management Group, 1999.
Member: Bd. of Dir. Gulfstream Aerospace Corp., Bd. of Dir. J. Crew Inc., Bd. of Dir. Livent Inc., Bd. of Dir. of D.A.R.E. America, National Bd. of Advisors for the Children's Scholarship Fund, Bd. of Advisors at the UCLA School of Theater Film and Television. Also serves on the Exec. Advisory Bd. of the Pediatric Aids Foundations.

OWENSBY, EARL
Producer, Actor. b. North Carolina, 1935. Set up his own studio in Shelby, NC. Built new studio in Gaffney, SC, 1985.
PICTURES: Challenge, Dark Sunday, Buckstone County Prison, Frank Challenge—Manhunter, Death Driver, Wolfman, Seabo, Day of Judgment, Living Legend, Lady Grey, Rottweiler, Last Game, Hyperspace, Hit the Road Running, Rutherford County Line.

OXENBERG, CATHERINE
Actress. b. NY, NY, Sept. 21, 1961. Daughter of the exiled Princess Elizabeth of Yugoslavia, raised among intl. jet set with Richard Burton acting as her tutor. Modeled before making TV debut in The Royal Romance of Charles and Diana (1982).
PICTURES: The Lair of the White Worm, The Return of the Musketeers, The Omega Code.
TELEVISION: *Series:* Dynasty, Acapulco H.E.A.T. *Movies:* The Royal Romance of Charles and Diana, Roman Holiday, Swimsuit, Trenchcoat in Paradise, Ring of Scorpio, K-9000, Charles & Diana: Unhappily Ever After, Rubdown, Treacherous Beauties, Hide and Seek, Thrill Seekers, The Miracle of the Cards.

OZ, FRANK
Puppeteer, Director, Performer. r.n. Frank Oznowicz. b. Hereford, England, May 25, 1944. Gained fame as creator and performer of various characters on Sesame Street and the Muppet Show (Fozzie Bear, Miss Piggy, Animal, Cookie Monster, Grover and Bert). V.P., Jim Henson Prods.
PICTURES: *Performer:* The Muppet Movie, The Blues Brothers, Star Wars: Episode V-The Empire Strikes Back, The Great Muppet Caper (also prod.), An American Werewolf in London, The Dark Crystal (also co-dir.), Star Wars: Episode VI-Return of the Jedi, Trading Places, The Muppets Take Manhattan (also dir., co-s.p.), Spies Like Us, Labyrinth, Innocent Blood, The Muppet Christmas Carol (also exec. prod.), Muppet Treasure Island (voice), Blues Brothers 2000, Star Wars: Episode I-The Phantom Menace (voice), Muppets from Space (voice), The Adventures of Elmo in Grouchland (voice), Muppet Race Mania, Star Wars 2: Attack of the Clones. *Director only:* Little Shop of Horrors, Dirty

Rotten Scoundrels, What About Bob?, Housesitter, The Indian in the Cupboard, In & Out, Bowfinger, Ump, The Score, Ump, Monsters Inc. (voices), S1mOne.
TELEVISION: *Series:* Sesame Street (3 Emmy Awards), The Muppet Show (Emmy Award, 1978), Saturday Night Live.

P

PAAR, JACK
Actor. b. Canton, OH, May 1, 1918. Radio announcer in Cleveland, Buffalo; served in U.S. Armed Forces, WWII; entertained in Pacific zone with 28th Special Service Div. On radio with own show, then quiz show Take It or Leave It. First host of The Tonight Show; various specials.
AUTHOR: I Kid You Not, My Sabre Is Bent, Three on a Toothbrush, P.S. Jack Paar.
PICTURES: Variety Time (debut, 1948), Easy Living, Walk Softly Stranger, Footlight Varieties, Love Nest, Down Among the Sheltering Palms.
TELEVISION: Series: Up to Paar (emcee, 1952), Bank on the Stars (emcee, 1953), The Jack Paar Show (1954), The Morning Show (1954), The Tonight Show (retitled The Jack Paar Show: 1957-62), The Jack Paar Program (1962-65), ABC Late Night (1973). Specials: Jack Paar Diary, Jack Paar Remembers, Jack Paar Is Alive and Well (also prod.), He Kids You Not, Jack Paar "As I Was Saying..."

PACINO, AL
Actor. b. New York, NY, April 25, 1940. e. High Sch. for the Performing Arts, NY; Actors Studio, 1966; HB Studios, NY. Gained attention as stage actor initially at Charles Playhouse, Boston (Why Is a Crooked Letter, The Peace Creeps, Arturo Ui). Served as artistic dir. (with Ellen Burstyn), Actors Studio (1982-84).
THEATRE: NY: The Indian Wants the Bronx (Obie Award), Does a Tiger Wear a Necktie? (Tony & Theatre World Awards, 1969), The Local Stigmatic, Camino Real, The Connection, Hello Out There, Tiger at the Gates, The Basic Training of Pavlo Hummel (Tony Award, 1977), Richard III, American Buffalo, Julius Caesar, Chinese Coffee, Salome, Hughie (also dir.).
PICTURES: Me Natalie (debut, 1969), The Panic in Needle Park, The Godfather, Scarecrow, Serpico, The Godfather Part II, Dog Day Afternoon, Bobby Deerfield, ... And Justice for All, Cruising, Author! Author!, Scarface, Revolution, Sea of Love, Dick Tracy, The Godfather Part III, Frankie and Johnny, Glengarry Glen Ross, Scent of a Woman (Acad. Award, 1992), Carlito's Way, A Day to Remember, City Hall, Heat, Two Bits, Looking for Richard (also dir.), Donnie Brasco, The Devil's Advocate, Chinese Coffee (also dir.), The Insider, Any Given Sunday, Chinese Coffee (also dir.), Simone, People I Know, Insomnia, The Recruit, Gigli, Angels in America.
TELEVISION: America: A Tribute to Heroes.

PACULA, JOANNA
Actress. b. Tomszowau, Poland, Jan. 2, 1957. Member of Polish National Theatre School. Model in Poland, France, then U.S. where she moved in early 1980's.
PICTURES: Gorky Park, Not Quite Paradise, Death Before Dishonor, The Kiss, Sweet Lies, Options, Marked for Death, Husbands and Lovers, Tombstone, Warlock: The Armageddon, Private Lessons 2, Every Breath, The Silence of the Hams, Kim Novak is on the Phone, Deep Red, Timemaster, Not Like Us, Last Gasp, Captain Nuke and the Bomber Boys, In Praise of Older Women, Business for Pleasure, Heaven Before I Die, Haunted Sea, My Giant, The White Raven, Error in Judgement, Virus, Crash and Byrnes, The Art of Murder, No Place Like Home, The Hit, Warrior Angels, Cupid's Prey, Virus.
TELEVISION: Series: E.A.R.T.H. Force, Brutally Normal. Movies: Escape From Sobibor, Breaking Point, Condition Critical, Under Investigation, Sweet Deception.

PAGE, ANTHONY
Director. b. Bangalore, India, Sept. 21, 1935. e. Oxford. Stage work includes Inadmissible Evidence, Waiting for Godot, A Patriot for Me, Look Back in Anger, Uncle Vanya, Mrs. Warren's Profession, Alpha Beta, Heartbreak House, Absolute Hell.
PICTURES: Inadmissible Evidence (debut, 1968), Alpha Beta, I Never Promised You a Rose Garden, Absolution, The Lady Vanishes, Forbidden, Silent Cries.
TELEVISION: Movies: The Parachute, Pueblo, The Missiles of October, F. Scott Fitzgerald in Hollywood, Collision Course, F.D.R.: The Last Year, The Patricia Neal Story, Bill, Johnny Belinda, Grace Kelly, Bill: On His Own, Murder: By Reason of Insanity, Second Serve, Monte Carlo, Heartbreak House, Pack of Lies, Scandal in a Small Town, Chernobyl: The Final Warning, Absolute Hell, Human Bomb. Mini-Series: The Nightmare Year, Middlemarch.

PAGE, PATTI
Performer, Recording Artist. r.n. Clara Ann Fowler. b. Claremore, OK, Nov. 8, 1927. e. U. of Tulsa. Staff performer, radio stat. KTUL, Tulsa; Top recording star of the 1950's and 60's (The Tennessee Waltz, Cross Over the Bridge, How Much is That

Doggie in the Window?, etc.). Appeared on CBS radio show. Author of Once Upon a Dream, Åke Hasselgård story.
PICTURES: Elmer Gantry (debut, 1960), Dondi, Boys' Night Out.
TELEVISION: Series host: Music Hall, Scott Music Hall, The Patti Page Show, The Big Record, The Patti Page Olds Show. Guest: U.S. Steel Hour, Bachelor Father.

PAGET, DEBRA
Actress. r.n. Debrahlee Griffin. b. Denver, CO, Aug. 19, 1933. e. Hollywood Prof. Sch. , also studied drama & dancing privately. Stage debut in Merry Wives of Windsor, 1946; in Jeanne D'Arc little theatre prod.
PICTURES: Cry of the City (debut, 1948), It Happens Every Spring, House of Strangers, Broken Arrow, Fourteen Hours, Bird of Paradise, Anne of the Indies, Belles on Their Toes, Les Miserables, Stars & Stripes Forever, Prince Valiant, Demetrius & the Gladiators, Princess of the Nile, Gambler from Natchez, White Feather, Seven Angry Men, Last Hunt, The Ten Commandments, Love Me Tender, The River's Edge, Omar Khayyam, From the Earth to the Moon, Why Must I Die?, Cleopatra's Daughter, Journey to the Lost City, The Most Dangerous Man Alive, Tales of Terror, The Haunted Palace.
TELEVISION: Guest: Steve Allen, Colgate Comedy Hour, Climax, Wagon Train, Rawhide, Burke's Law.

PAGETT, NICOLA
Actress. r.n. Nicola Scott. b. Cairo, Egypt, June 15, 1945. e. Royal Acad. of Dramatic Art. Appeared with Citizen's Rep. Theatre, Glasgow.
THEATRE: Cornelia (debut, 1964, Worthing, U.K.), A Boston Story (London debut, 1968), A Midsummer Night's Dream, Widowers' Houses, The Misanthrope, A Voyage 'Round My Father, The Ride Across Lake Constance, Ghosts, The Seagull, Hamlet, The Marriage of Figaro, A Family and a Fortune, Gaslight, Yahoo, Old Times (L.A.).
PICTURES: Anne of the Thousand Days, There's a Girl in My Soup, Operation Daybreak, Oliver's Story, Privates on Parade, An Awfully Big Adventure.
TELEVISION: Series: Upstairs Downstairs. A Bit of a Do, Ain't Misbehavin'. Movies: Franken-stein: The True Story, The Sweeney, Aren't We All. Mini-Series: A Woman of Substance, Anna Karenina, Up Rising.

PAIGE, JANIS
Actress r.n. Donna Mae Jaden. b. Tacoma, WA, Sept. 16, 1923. Sang with Tacoma Opera Co. Star of Tomorrow, 1947. Album: Let's Fall in Love. Owns and operates Ipanema, Janeiro, Rio-Cali, and Dindi Music Cos.
THEATRE: Pajama Game, Remains to Be Seen, Here's Love, Mame, Alone Together.
PICTURES: Hollywood Canteen (debut, 1944), Of Human Bondage, Two Gals and a Guy, The Time the Place and the Girl, Two Guys from Milwaukee, Her Kind of Man, Cheyenne, Love and Learn, Always Together, Wallflower, Winter Meeting, One Sunday Afternoon, Romance on the High Seas, House Across the Street, The Younger Brothers, Mr. Universe, Fugitive Lady, Two Guys and a Gal, Silk Stockings, Please Don't Eat the Daisies, Bachelor in Paradise, The Caretakers, Welcome to Hard Times, Love at the Top, The Dark Road (It.), Follow the Boys (Fr.), Natural Causes, Broadway: The Golden Age by the Legends Who Were There.
TELEVISION: Movies: The Turning Point of Jim Malloy, Return of Joe Forrester, Lanigan's Rabbi (pilot), Valentine Magic on Love Island, Angel on My Shoulder, The Other Woman, No Man's Land. Special: Roberta (1958 and 1969). Series: It's Always Jan, Lanigan's Rabbi, Gun Shy, Baby Makes Five, Trapper John M.D., Capitol, General Hospital, Santa Barbara. Guest: Plymouth Playhouse, Alcoa Premiere, Columbo, Banacek, Flamingo Road, St. Elsewhere.

PAINE, CHARLES F.
Executive. b. Cushing, TX, Dec. 23, 1920. e. Stephen F. Austin U. Pres. Tercar Theatre Company; pres., NATO of Texas, 1972-73. NATO board member, 1973 to present; Motion Picture Pioneers member; Variety Club of Texas member.

PALANCE, JACK
Actor. r.n. Vladimir Palanuik. b. Lattimer, PA, Feb. 18, 1920. e. U. of North Carolina. Professional fighter; U.S. Air Corps.
THEATRE: The Big Two, Temporary Island, The Vigil, A Streetcar Named Desire, Darkness at Head.
PICTURES: Panic in the Streets (debut, 1950), Halls of Montezuma, Sudden Fear (Acad. Award nom.), Shane (Acad. Award nom.), Flight to Tangier, Arrowhead, Second Chance, Man in the Attic, Sign of the Pagan, Silver Chalice, Kiss of Fire, Big Knife, I Died a Thousand Times, Attack!, Lonely Man, House of Numbers, The Man Inside, Ten Seconds to Hell, Battle of Austerliz, Sword of the Conqueror, The Mongols, Barabbas, Warriors Five, Contempt, Once a Thief, The Professionals, Torture Garden, Kill a Dragon, The Mercenary, Deadly Sanctuary, They Came to Rob Las Vegas, The Desperados, Che, Legion of the Damned, A Bullet for Rommel, The McMasters, Monte Walsh, Companeros, The Horsemen, Chato's Land, Oklahoma Crude, Craze, The Four Deuces, The Great Adventure, The Sensuous Nurse, Portrait of a Hitman, One Man

Jury, Angel's Brigade, The Shape of Things to Come, Cocaine Cowboys, Hawk the Slayer, Without Warning, Alone in the Dark, Gor, Bagdad Cafe, Young Guns, Outlaw of Gor, Batman, Tango and Cash, City Slickers (Acad. Award, best supporting actor, 1991), Solar Crisis, Cops and Robbersons, City Slickers II: The Legend of Curly's Gold, The Swan Princess (voice), War Games, The Incredible Adventures of Marco Polo, Treasure Island, Cast and Crew, Prancer Returns.
TELEVISION: *Specials:* Requiem for a Heavyweight (Emmy Award, 1957), Dr. Jekyll and Mr. Hyde, Twilight Zone: Rod Serling's Lost Classics: Where the Dead Are. *Movies:* Dracula, The Godchild, The Hatfields and the McCoys, Bronk (pilot), Last Ride of the Dalton Gang, The Ivory Ape, Golden Moment: An Olympic Love Story, Keep the Change, Buffalo Girls, Ebenezer, I'll Be Home for Christmas, Sarah Plain: Winter's End, The Omen Legacy, Living With the Dead (mini). *Series:* The Greatest Show on Earth, Bronk, Ripley's Believe It or Not (host). *Guest:* Studio One, Your Show of Shows, Motorola TV Theatre, the Web, Suspense, The Tonight Show, Playhouse 90, Zane Grey Theatre, Convoy, Man from U.N.C.L.E., The Carol Burnett Show, Buck Rodgers in the 25th Century, Dame Edna's Hollywood, Night Visions.

PALCY, EUZHAN
Director, Writer. b. Martinique, Jan. 13, 1957. e. Earned a degree in French lit., Sorbonne and a film degree from Vaugirard School in Paris. Began career working as TV writer and dir. in Martinique. Also made 2 children's records. In Paris worked as film editor, screenwriter and dir. of shorts. She received grant from French gov. to make 1st feature Sugar Cane Alley which cost $800,000 and won Silver Lion Prize at Venice Film Fest., 1983.
PICTURES: Sugar Cane Alley (also writer), A Dry White Season (also co-s.p.), Simeon (also writer), Aime Cesaire: A Voice for History, Wings Against the Wind (also story).
TELEVISION: Ruby Bridges, The Killing Yard.

PALIN, MICHAEL
Actor, Writer. b. Sheffield, Yorkshire, England, May 5, 1943. e. Oxford. Performed there in Pinter's The Birthday Party and in revue Hang Your Head Down and Die (also in West End prod., 1964). At Oxford met Terry Jones, began writing comedy together, incl. TV series The Frost Report. Became member of Monty Python's Flying Circus. On stage with troupe both in London and on B'way.
PICTURES: And Now for Something Completely Different (also co-s.p.), Monty Python and the Holy Grail (also co-s.p.), Jabberwocky, Life of Brian (also co-s.p.), Time Bandits, The Secret Policeman's Other Ball, Monty Python Live at the Hollywood Bowl (also co-s.p.), The Missionary (also co-prod., s.p.), A Private Function, Brazil, A Fish Called Wanda, American Friends (also co-s.p.), Fierce Creatures, The Wind In The Willows (voice).
TELEVISION: Do Not Adjust Your Set, The Frost Report, Monty Python's Flying Circus, Marty Feldman Comedy Machine, How To Irritate People, Pythons in Deutschland, Secrets, Ripping Yarns, Around the World in 80 Days, GBH, Pole to Pole, The Willows in Winter, Ex-S, Live from the Lighthouse, Comic Relief: The Record Breaker, Hemmingway Adventure, Monty Python Night, It's the Monty Python Story, 2000 Today, The Human Face (mini-series), Full Circle with Michael Palin, Monty Python's Flying Circus: Live at Aspen, Pythonland, The Unknown Peter Sellers, The Sketch Show Story.

PALMER, BETSY
Actress. b. East Chicago, IN, Nov. 1, 1929. e. DePaul U. Studied at Neighborhood Playhouse, HB Studio with Uta Hagen. On Broadway in The Grand Prize, South Pacific, Affair of Honor, Cactus Flower, Roar Like a Dove, Eccentricities of a Nightingale, Same Time Next Year and many regional prods.
PICTURES: Mister Roberts, The Long Gray Line, Queen Bee, The Tin Star, The Last Angry Man, Friday the 13th, Friday the 13th Part 2, Unveiled, The Fear: Resurrection.
TELEVISION: All major live shows such as Studio One, U.S. Steel Hour, Kraft Theatre. *Series:* Masquerade Party (panelist), What's It For? (panelist), I've Got a Secret (panelist, 11 years), No. 96 (series), Candid Camera (host), The Today Show (host), Wifeline (host). *Guest:* As the World Turns, Murder She Wrote, Out of This World, Charles in Charge, Knots Landing, Newhart, Love Boat. *Movies:* Isabel's Choice, Windmills of the Gods, Goddess of Love, Still Not Quite Human, Columbo: Death Hits the Jackpot, Not Quite Human III.

PALMER, GREGG
Actor. r.n. Palmer Lee. b. San Francisco, CA, Jan. 25, 1927. e. U. of Utah. U.S. Air Force, 1945-46; radio announcer, disc jockey; then to Hollywood.
PICTURES: Cimarron Kid, Battle at Apache Pass, Son of Ali Baba, Red Ball Express, Francis Goes to West Point, Sally and St. Anne, The Raiders, Back at the Front, The Redhead From Wyoming, Column South, Veils of Bagdad, Golden Blade, The All American, Taza Son of Cochise, Magnificent Obsession, Playgirl, To Hell and Back, Creature Walks Among Us, Hilda Crane, Zombies of Mora Tau, Revolt of Fort Laramie, Rebel Set,

Commancheros, Quick Gun, Prize, It Happened Every Thursday, Female Animal, Thundering Jets, Forty Pounds of Trouble, Night Hunt, The Undefeated, Chisum, Rio Lobo, Big Jake, Providenza (It.), Ci Risiamo Vero Providenza (It-Sp), Cat Man, The Sad Horse, Most Dangerous Man Alive, Cutter's Trail, The Shootist, The Man With Bogart's Face, Scream.
TELEVISION (has appeared in over 400 TV programs): *Series:* Run Buddy Run. *Guest:* Wagon Train, Loretta Young, Wyatt Earp, Have Gun Will Travel, Sea Hunt, Roaring 20's, Mannix, The High Chaparral, Cannon, Baretta, Gunsmoke, etc. *Movies:* Mongo's Back in Town, Go West Young Girl, Hostage Heart, How the West Was Won, True Grit, Beggarman Thief, The Blue and the Gray (mini-series).

PALMER, PATRICK J.
Producer. b. Los Angeles, CA, Dec. 28, 1936. Began career with 10-year apprenticeship at Mirisch Company, involved in making of West Side Story, Seven Days in May, The Fortune Cookie, etc. 1966, began association with Norman Jewison, serving as assoc. prod. on The Landlord, Fiddler on the Roof, Jesus Christ Superstar, Rollerball. 1972, prod., with Jewison, Billy Two Hats; exec. prod. on The Dogs of War.
PICTURES: *Co-prod.:* And Justice for All, Best Friends, Iceman, A Soldier's Story, Agnes of God, Children of a Lesser God, Moonstruck, Stanley & Iris, Mermaids, Paradise (also writer), Made in America, Don Juan Demarco. *Exec. prod:* Milk Money, Iron Will, Mrs. Winterbourne, The Rage: Carrie 2. *Prod:* Blade II, Hellboy, The Shrink Is In (also unit prod. mngr.).

PALMINTERI, CHAZZ
Actor, Writer. r.n. Calogero Lorenzo Palminteri. b. Bronx, NY, May 15, 1951. e. Bronx Comm. Coll. NY stage in The Guys in the Truck (B'way), The King's Men, 22 Years, The Flatbush Faithful, A Bronx Tale (which he also wrote).
PICTURES: The Last Dragon (debut, 1985), Oscar, Innocent Blood, There Goes the Neighborhood, A Bronx Tale (also s.p.), Bullets Over Broadway (Acad. Award nom.), The Perez Family, The Usual Suspects, Faithful (also s.p.), Dante and the Debutante (s.p. and prod.), Jade, Mulholland Falls, Diabolique, Scar City, A Night at the Roxbury (cameo), Hurlyburly, Excellent Cadavers, Analyze This, Stuart Little (voice), Company Man, Down to Earth, One Eyed King, Lady and the Tramp II, Scamp's Adventure (voice), Just Like Mona, Poolhall Junkies.
TELEVISION: *Movie:* The Last Word, Ooooph! (dir.), Women vs. Men (dir.). *Guest:* Dallas, Matlock, Valerie, Wiseguy, Dilbert, Oz (dir.).

PALTROW, GWYNETH
Actress. b. Los Angeles, CA, Sept. 28, 1973. p. actress Blythe Danner, and the late-prod. Bruce Paltrow. Moved to NY when she was 11. In 1999, won best actress Academy Award for Shakespeare in Love.
THEATRE: *Williamstown:* Picnic, The Adventures of Huck Finn, Sweet Bye and Bye, The Seagull.
PICTURES: Shout (debut, 1991), Hook, Malice, Flesh and Bone, Mrs. Parker and the Vicious Circle, Jefferson in Paris, Moonlight and Valentino, Seven, The Pallbearer, Sydney, Emma, Hush, Out of the Past, Sliding Doors, Great Expectations, A Perfect Murder, Duets, Shakespeare in Love (Acad. Award for best actress), The Talented Mr. Ripley, The Intern, Duets, Bounce, Shallow Hal, The Anniversary Party, Pootie Tang, The Royal Tenenbaums, Searching for Debra Winger, Austin Powers in Goldmember, Possession, A View From the Top.
TELEVISION: *Movie:* Cruel Doubt.

PANAMA, CHARLES A. (CHUCK)
Publicist, b. Chicago, IL, Feb. 2, 1925. e. Northwestern U., Beloit Coll., UCLA. Publicist, Los Angeles Jr. Chamber of Commerce; So. Calif. sports ed., Los Angeles bureau, INS; publicist, 20th Century-Fox Studios; adv.-pub. dir., Arcola Pics.; opened L.A. office, John Springer Associates; v.p. Jerry Pam & Assoc.; account exec., Rogers, Cowan & Brenner, Inc.; dir. m.p. div., Jim Mahoney & Assoc.; v.p. Guttman & Pam, Ltd.; asst. pub. dir., Twentieth TV. Owner, pres. Chuck Panama P.R.; winner 1990 Les Mason Award and 1993 Robert Yeager Award, Publicists Guild of America. Docent, Santa Monica (CA) Museum of Flying.

PANAMA, NORMAN
Writer, Producer, Director. b. Chicago, IL, April 21, 1914. Co-authored The Glass Bed (novel), and plays: A Talent for Murder, The Bats of Portobello.
PICTURES: *Co-Writer:* My Favorite Blonde, Happy Go Lucky, Star-Spangled Rhythm, Thank Your Lucky Stars, And the Angels Sing, Duffy's Tavern, Road to Utopia (Acad. Award nom.), Our Hearts Were Growing Up, Monsieur Beaucaire, It Had to Be You, Mr. Blandings Builds His Dream House, Return of October, White Christmas, Li'l Abner, The Facts of Life. *Co-Dir./Co-Writer* (with Melvin Frank): The Reformer and the Redhead, Strictly Dishonorable, Callaway Went Thataway, Above and Beyond, Knock on Wood (Acad. Award nom. for s.p.), The Court Jester. *Dir./Writer:* The Road to Hong Kong, Not With My Wife You Don't, How to Commit Marriage, I Will I Will... for Now.
TELEVISION: *Dir.:* Barnaby and Me, The Stewardesses, Li'l Abner, Mrs. Katz and Katz (pilot), How Come You Never See Dr. Jekyll and Mr. Hyde Together?, Coffee Tea or Me.
(d. Jan. 13, 2003)

PANKIN, STUART
Actor. b. Philadelphia, PA, April 8, 1946. e. Dickinson Coll., Columbia U. Stage debut 1968 in The War of the Roses.
THEATRE: NY: Timon of Athens, Tale of Cymbeline, Mary Stuart, The Crucible, Twelfth Night, Glorious Age, Wings, Gorky, Joseph and the Amazing Technicolor Dreamcoat, Three Sisters, The Inspector General.
PICTURES: Scavenger Hunt, Hangar 18, The Hollywood Knights, An Eye for an Eye, Earthbound, Irreconcilable Differences, The Dirt Bike Kid, Fatal Attraction, Love at Stake, Second Sight, That's Adequate, Arachnophobia, Mannequin 2 on the Move, The Vagrant, I Love Trouble, The Silence of the Hams, Squanto: A Warrior's Tale, Congo, Striptease, Honey We Shrunk Ourselves, Encounter in the Third Dimension, The Settlement, Chasing Destiny, Now You Know.
TELEVISION: Series: The San Pedro Beach Bums, No Soap Radio, Not Necessarily the News (ACE Award), Nearly Departed, Dinosaurs (voice). Movies: Valentine Magic on Love Island, Father & Scout, Down Out and Dangerous, Babylon 5: The River of Souls, Like Father Like Santa, Zenon: Girl of the 21st Century, Batman Beyond: The Movie, Uncle Gus in: For the Love of Monkeys, Zenon: The Sequel, The Settlement. Pilots: Car Wash, Wonderful World of Philip Malley. Guest: Night Court, Crazy Like a Fox, Golden Girls, Stingray, Family Ties, It's Garry Shandling's Show, Hooperman, Barney Miller. Special: Stuart Pankin (also co-exec. prod., co-writer).

PANTOLIANO, JOE
Actor. b. Jersey City, NJ, Sept. 12, 1954.
THEATRE: NY: The Kitchen, The Off Season, The Death Star, Visions of Kerouac. Regional: One Flew Over the Cuckoo's Nest, Skaters, Brothers, Italian American Reconciliation (Dramalogue Award), Orphans (Dramalogue Award, Drama Critic Circle nomination), Pvt. Wars.
PICTURES: The Idolmaker, Monsignor, Risky Business, Eddie and the Cruisers, The Mean Season, The Goonies, Running Scared, La Bamba, The Squeeze, Amazon Women on the Moon, Empire of the Sun, The In Crowd, Midnight Run, Downtown, The Last of the Finest, Short Time, Zandalee, Used People, Three of Hearts, Goin' to Mexico, The Fugitive, Calendar Girl, Me and the Kid, Teresa's Tattoo, Baby's Day Out, Bad Boys, Congo (cameo), Steal Big Steal Little, Bound, The Immortals, Top of the World, Tinseltown, U.S. Marshals, The Taxman, New Blood, The Life Before This, Black and White, The Matrix, Ready to Rumble, Memento, Silver Man, Pray for the Cardinal, A Better Way to Die, Cats and Dogs (voice), The Adventures of Pluto Nash, A Piece of My Heart, Daredevil, Bad Boys II, Second Best (also prod.), Just Like Mona (s.p., dir. only), 5-25-77.
TELEVISION: Series: Free Country, The Fanelli Boys, EZ Streets, Godzilla (voice), Sugar Hill, The Sopranos, The Handler. Mini-Series: Robert F. Kennedy: His Life and Times, From Here to Eternity. Guest: Tales from the Crypt (ACE Award nomination), Amazing Stories, L.A. Law, The Hitchhiker. Movies: More Than Friends, Alcatraz: The Whole Shocking Story, Nightbreaker, Destination America, El Diablo, One Special Victory, Through the Eyes of a Killer, The Last (also co-assoc. prod.), EZ Streets (pilot), Ed McBain's 87th Precinct: Ice, Natural Enemy.

PAPAS, IRENE
Actress. b. Chiliomodion, Greece, Sept. 3, 1926. Entered dramatic school at 12. At 16 sang and danced in variety shows before debuting in Greek films, 1950. 1958 appeared with Greek Popular Theatre in Athens. Received Salonika Film Fest. Awards for the films Antigone, Electra.
THEATRE: The Idiot, Journey's End, The Merchant of Venice, Inherit the Wind, That Summer, That Fall, Iphigenia in Aulis.
PICTURES: Lost Angels (debut, 1950), Dead City, The Unfaithful, Atilla the Hun, Theodora the Slave Empress, Whirlpool, Tribute to a Bad Man, Antigone, The Guns of Navarone, Electra, The Moon-Spinners, Zorba the Greek, We Still Kill the Old Way, The Desperate Ones, The Brotherhood, Anne of the Thousand Days, Z, A Dream of Kings, The Trojan Women, Roma Bene, Bambina, Mohammed: Messenger of God, Iphigenia, Bloodline, Eboli, Lion of the Desert, Erendira, Into the Night, The Assisi Underground, Sweet Country, High Season, Chronicle of a Death Foretold, Island, Drums of Fire, Banquet, Zoe, Up Down and Sideways, Party, Anxiety, The Wog Boy, Captain Corelli's Mandolin, Returning in Autumn.
TELEVISION: Movies: Moses the Lawgiver, Jacob, The Odyssey.

PAQUIN, ANNA
Actress. b. Winnipeg, Manitoba, Canada, July 24, 1982.
PICTURES: The Piano (Acad. Award, 1994; Golden Globe nom.), Fly Away Home, Jane Eyre, Amistad, Hurlyburly, Begin the Beguine, A Walk on the Moon, Sleepless Beauty, Castle in the Sky (voice), All the Rage, She's All That, X-Men, Almost Famous, Finding Forrester, Buffalo Soldiers, Darkness, The 25th Hour, X2.
TELEVISION: Movie: The Member of the Wedding. Guest: The Practice.

PARE, MICHAEL
Actor. b. Brooklyn, NY, Oct. 9, 1959. e. Culinary Inst. of America, Hyde Park, NY. Worked as chef and model before being discovered by ABC talent agent.

PICTURES: Eddie and the Cruisers (debut, 1983), Streets of Fire, The Philadelphia Experiment, Under Cover (Aust.), Space Rage, Instant Justice, The Women's Club, World Gone Wild, Eddie and the Cruisers II: Eddie Lives, Moon 44, Dragon Fight, Concrete War, The Closer, Into the Sun, Midnight Heat, First Light, Point of Impact, Village of the Damned, Bad Moon, Coyote Run, Strip Search, Merchant of Death, Falling Fire, 2103: The Deadly Wake, Hope Floats, October 22, Back to Even, The Virgin Suicides, Men of Means, Space Fury, Sanctimony, Peril, A Month of Sundays, Blackwoods, Two Faced, Red Serpent, Heart of America.
TELEVISION: Series: The Greatest American Hero, Houston Knights, Starhunter. Movie: Crazy Times, The Colony, Carver's Gate, The Malibu Branch, Falling Fire.

PARISH, JAMES ROBERT
Film Historian, Biographer. b. Cambridge, MA, April 21, 1944. e. U. of PA (BA, Phi Beta Kappa); U. of PA Law School (LLB). Member of NY Bar. Founder Entertainment Copyright Research Co., Inc. 1968-69, film reporter, Motion Picture Daily, Weekly Variety. 1969-70, entertainment publicist, Harold Rand & Co. (NY). Currently author, contributor to arts sections of major national newspapers and entertainment trade papers, on-air interviewee for cable/TV documentaries, and series editor of show business book series.
AUTHOR: Hollywood's Great Musicals, Prostitution in Hollywood Films, Ghosts & Angels in Hollywood Films, Hollywood Songsters, Prison Pictures From Hollywood, Hollywood Baby Boomers, The Great Detective Pictures, The Great Cop Pictures, The Great Science Fiction Pictures II, Complete Actors TV Credits (1948-88), The Great Combat Pictures, Black Action Pictures From Hollywood, The Great Detective Pictures, The Great Western Pictures II: The Great Gangster Pictures II: The Great Spy Pictures II, Actors TV Credits, The Best of MGM, The Forties Gals, The Great American Movies Book, Hollywood Happiness, The Funsters, Hollywood on Hollywood, The Hollywood Beauties, Elvis!, The Great Science Fiction Pictures, The Child Stars, The Jeannette MacDonald Story, Great Movie Heroes, Liza!, The RKO Gals, Vincent Price Unmasked, The George Raft File, The Emmy Awards, Hollywood Death Book, Gays & Lesbians in Mainstream Cinema, Hollywood Celebrity Death Book (updated), Let's Talk! America's Favorite TV Talk Show Hosts, Today's Black Hollywood, Pirates and Seafaring Swashbucklers, Rosie: Rosie O'Donnell's Story, The Unofficial 'Murder She Wrote' Casebook, Whoopi Goldberg: Her Journey From Poverty to Mega-Stardom.

PARK, NICK
Director, Writer, Animator. b. Preston, Lancashire, England, December 6, 1958. e. Sheffield Hallam Univeristy. Awarded honorary doctor of arts degree by Bath University, UK.
PICTURES: War Story (anim. only), Creature Comforts, Wallace & Gromit: A Grand Day Out, Wallace & Gromit: The Wrong Trousers, Wallace & Gromit: A Close Shave, Wallace & Gromit: The Best of Aardman Animation, Wallace & Gromit: The Aardman Collection 2, Chicken Run (also prod.), Wallace & Gromit: The Great Vegetable Plot.

PARKER, ALAN
Director, Writer. b. Islington, London, England, Feb. 14, 1944. Worked way up in advertising industry from mail room to top writer and dir. of nearly 500 TV commercials between 1969-78. Appointed chmn. of British Film Institute, 1997.
PICTURES: Melody (s.p., 1968). Director/Writer: No Hard Feelings, Our Cissy, Footsteps, Bugsy Malone (Brit. Acad. Award for best s.p.), Midnight Express (Brit. Acad. Award), Fame, Shoot the Moon, Pink Floyd—The Wall, Birdy, Angel Heart, Mississippi Burning, Come and See the Paradise, The Commitments (also cameo; BAFTA Award for best dir., 1991), The Road to Wellville (also co-prod.), Evita (also prod), Angela's Ashes (also prod.), The Life of David Gale (also prod.).
TELEVISION: The Evacuees (Brit. Acad. Award), Bomber (composer).

PARKER, COREY
Actor. b. New York, NY, July 8, 1965. e. NYU.
THEATRE: NY: Meeting the Winter Bike Rider (Off-B'way debut, 1984), Been Taken, The Bloodletters, The Semi-Formal.
PICTURES: Scream for Help (debut, 1984), Friday the 13th Part V: A New Beginning, Something Special, Nine 1/2 Weeks, Biloxi Blues, How I Got Into College, Big Man on Campus, White Palace, Flesh Suitcase, Mr. & Mrs. Loving, Fool's Paradise, My Angel Is a Centerfold.
TELEVISION: Series: Eddie Dodd, Flying Blind, Blue Skies, The Love Boat: The Next Wave. Movies: Courage, At Mother's Request, Liz: The Elizabeth Taylor Story, A Mother's Prayer, Encino Woman. Specials: Don't Touch, Teen Father, The Lost Language of Cranes. Pilot: Sons of Gunz. Guest: The Bronx Zoo, thirtysomething.

PARKER, ELEANOR
Actress. b. Cedarville, OH, June 26, 1922. In Cleveland play group; in summer stock Martha's Vineyard; at Pasadena Community Playhouse.

PICTURES: They Died With Their Boots On (debut, 1941), Buses Roar, Mysterious Doctor, Mission to Moscow, Between Two Worlds, The Very Thought of You, Crime By Night, Hollywood Canteen, Last Ride, Pride of the Marines, Never Say Goodbye, Of Human Bondage, Escape Me Never, Woman in White, Voice of the Turtle, It's a Great Feeling, Chain Lightning, Caged (Acad. Award nom.), Three Secrets, Valentino, Millionaire for Christy, Detective Story (Acad. Award nom.), Scaramouche, Above and Beyond, Escape from Fort Bravo, Naked Jungle, Valley of the Kings, Many Rivers to Cross, Interrupted Melody (Acad. Award nom.), Man with the Golden Arm, King and Four Queens, Lizzie, Seventh Sin, A Hole in the Head, Home from the Hill, Return to Peyton Place, Madison Avenue, Panic Button, The Sound of Music, The Oscar, An American Dream, Warning Shot, Tiger and the Pussycat, Eye of the Cat, Sunburn.
TELEVISION: Series: Bracken's World. Movies: Maybe I'll Come Home in the Spring, Vanished, Home for the Holidays, The Great American Beauty Contest, Fantasy Island (pilot), The Bastard, She's Dressed to Kill, Once Upon a Spy, Madame X, Dead on the Money. Pilot: Guess Who's Coming to Dinner. Special: Hans Brinker. Guest: Buick Electra Playhouse, Kraft Suspense Theatre, The Man from U.N.C.L.E., Vega$, Hawaii 5-0, The Love Boat, Hotel, Murder She Wrote.

PARKER, FESS
Actor. b. Fort Worth, TX, Aug. 16, 1924. e. USC. U.S. Navy, 1943-46; national co., Mr. Roberts, 1951.
PICTURES: Untamed Frontier (debut, 1952), No Room for the Groom, Springfield Rifle, Thunder Over the Plains, Island in the Sky, The Kid From Left Field, Take Me to Town, Them!, Battle Cry, Davy Crockett—King of the Wild Frontier (from Disney TV show), Davy Crockett and the River Pirates (from TV show), The Great Locomotive Chase, Westward Ho! the Wagons, Old Yeller, The Light in the Forest, The Hangman, Alias Jesse James (cameo), The Jayhawkers, Hell Is for Heroes, Smoky.
TELEVISION: Series: Mr. Smith Goes to Washington, Daniel Boone. Guest: Jonathan Winters, Walt Disney presents (Davy Crockett), Playhouse 90 (Turn Left at Mount Everest), Ed Sullivan, Danny Kaye Show, Phyllis Diller, Joey Bishop, Dean Martin, Red Skelton, Glen Campbell, Andy Williams, Vicki Lawrence. Movie: Climb an Angry Mountain. Special: Walt: The Man Behind the Myth.

PARKER, JAMESON
Actor. b. Baltimore, MD, Nov. 18, 1947. e. Beloit Coll. Professional stage debut in Washington Theatre Club production, Caligula. Acted with Arena Stage in DC; worked in dinner theatres and summer stock. Moved to N.Y., working in TV commercials and acted in play, Equus (Coconut Grove Playhouse).
PICTURES: The Bell Jar (debut, 1979), A Small Circle of Friends, White Dog, American Justice (also prod.), Jackals, Prince of Darkness, Curse of the Crystal Eye.
TELEVISION: Series: Somerset, One Life to Live, Simon and Simon. Movies: Women at West Point, Anatomy of a Seduction, The Gathering Part II, The Promise of Love, Callie and Son, A Caribbean Mystery, Who Is Julia?, Spy, She Says She's Innocent, Dead Before Dawn, Simon & Simon: In Trouble Again, Have You Seen My Son?, Dead Man's Island; Something Borrowed Something Blue.

PARKER, MARY-LOUISE
Actress. b. Ft. Jackson, SC, Aug. 2, 1964. e. Bard Coll. 1990, received Clarence Derwent Award for her work in the theatre.
THEATRE: B'way: Prelude to a Kiss (Theatre World Award). Off-B'way: Hayfever, The Girl in Pink, Babylon Gardens, Throwing Your Voice, Four Dogs and a Bone, Communicating Doors. Regional: The Importance of Being Earnest, Up in Saratoga, The Miser, Hay Fever, The Night of the Iguana, The Age of Pie.
PICTURES: Signs of Life (debut, 1989), Longtime Companion, Grand Canyon, Fried Green Tomatoes, Mr. Wonderful, Naked in New York, The Client, Bullets Over Broadway, Boys on the Side, Reckless, The Portrait of a Lady, Murder in Mind, The Maker, Let the Devil Wear Black, Goodbye Lover, The Five Senses, Pipe Dream, Red Dragon.
TELEVISION: Movies: Too Young the Hero, A Place for Annie, The Simple Life of Noah Dearborn, Cupid & Cate. Series: The West Wing, Angels in America.

PARKER, SARAH JESSICA
Actress. b. Nelsonville, OH, March 25, 1965. Was dancer with Cincinnati Ballet and American Ballet Theatre. Professional debut at age 8 in TV special The Little Match Girl.
THEATRE: NY: The Innocents, By Strouse, Annie (title role for 2 yrs.), To Gillian on Her 37th Birthday, The Heidi Chronicles, The Substance of Fire, Sylvia, How To Succeed In Business Without Really Trying, Once Upon A Mattress, others.
PICTURES: Rich Kids (debut, 1979), Somewhere Tomorrow, Footloose, Firstborn, Girls Just Want to Have Fun, Flight of the Navigator, L.A. Story, Honeymoon in Vegas, Hocus Pocus, Striking Distance, Ed Wood, Miami Rhapsody, If Lucy Fell, The Substance of Fire, First Wives Club, Extreme Measures, Mars Attacks!, 'Til There Was You, Isn't She Great, Dudley Do-Right, State and Main, Life Without Dick, Sweating Bullets (voice).
TELEVISION: Series: Square Pegs, A Year in the Life, Equal Justice, Stories From My Childhood, Sex and the City (Emmy

Award, 2001, Emmy Noms., 1999 & 2000; Golden Globe Awards, 2000, 2001 & 2002). Specials: The Almost Royal Family, Life Under Water, America: A Tribute to Heroes. Movies: My Body My Child, Going for the Gold: The Bill Johnson Story, A Year in the Life (pilot), The Room Upstairs, Dadah Is Death, Twist of Fate, The Ryan White Story, In the Best Interest of the Children, The Sunshine Boys, Sex and the Matrix, The Big Show.

PARKER, SUZY
Actress. r.n. Cecelia Parker. b. San Antonio, TX, Oct. 28, 1933. m. actor Bradford Dillman. Began career at 17 as fashion model; becoming the highest paid fashion model and cover girl in U.S.; went to Paris under contract to fashion magazine; film debut as model in Funny Face (1957); signed by 20th-Fox prod. chief Buddy Adler for part opposite Cary Grant in Kiss Them for Me.
PICTURES: Funny Face, Kiss Them For Me, Ten North Frederick, The Best of Everything, Circle of Deception, The Interns, Flight From Ashiya, Chamber of Horrors.
TELEVISION: Special: Cleopatra: The Film That Changed Hollywood.
(d. May 3, 2003)

PARKES, WALTER F.
Producer, Writer. b. Bakersfield, CA. e. Yale, Stanford Univ. 1978 prod. & dir. documentary The California Reich which was nominated for Acad. Award.
PICTURES: WarGames (s.p.; Acad. Award nom.). Prod./Exec. Prod.: Volunteers, Project X, True Believer, Awakenings (Acad. Award nom.), Sneakers (also co-s.p.), Little Giants; To Wong Foo,-Thanks for Everything-Julie Newmar; How to Make an American Quilt, Twister, The Trigger Effect, Amistad, Men In Black, The Peacemaker, Deep Impact, Small Soldiers, The Mask of Zorro, Gladiator, Artificial Intelligence: AI, The Time Machine, Minority Report, Men in Black II, Road to Perdition, The Tuxedo, Ring, Catch Me If You Can.
TELEVISION: Series: Eddie Dodd (prod., writer). Pilot: Birdland (prod., writer).

PARKINS, BARBARA
Actress. b. Vancouver, British Columbia, Canada, May 22, 1942.
PICTURES: Valley of the Dolls, The Kremlin Letter, The Mephisto Waltz, Puppet on a Chain, Asylum, Shout at the Devil, Bear Island, Breakfast in Paris, Vengeance.
TELEVISION: Series: Peyton Place, Scene of the Crime. Mini-Series: Captains and the Kings, Jennie: Lady Randolph Churchill, Testimony of Two Men, The Manions of America. Movies: A Taste of Evil, Snatched, Law of the Land, Testimony of Two Men, Young Joe: The Forgotten Kennedy, Ziegfield: The Man and His Women, The Critical List, The Manions of America, Uncommon Valor, To Catch a King, Calendar Girl Murders, Peyton Place: The Next Generation, Perry Mason: The Case of the Notorious Nun, Scandalous Me: The Jacqueline Susann Story. Guest: G.E. Theatre, My Three Sons, Dr. Kildare, Gibbsville, Hotel, The Love Boat, Murder She Wrote. Specials: Jennie.

PARKS, GORDON
Director, Writer, Photographer, Composer, Photojournalist. b. Fort Scott, KS, Nov. 30, 1912. From the age of 15 worked as piano player, bus boy, dining car waiter and prof. basketball player in MN before taking up photography in late 1930's. Awarded 1st Julius Rosenwald Fellowship in photog., 1942. Worked with Roy Stryker at Farm Security Admin., WWII Office of War Info. correspondent. Photo-journalist, Life Mag., 1949-68, editorial dir. (and founder): Essence Magazine 1970-73. Film debut 1961 with doc. Flavio (dir. and writer), followed by Diary of a Harlem Family (doc.; Emmy Award). Winner of numerous awards including NAACP's Spingarn Medal and Kansas Governor's Medal of Honor, Nat'l Medal of Arts, 1988. Recipient of 23 honorary degrees in lit., fine arts, humane letters. Member of NAACP, AMPAS, PEN American Center, AFI, etc.
AUTHOR: The Learning Tree, A Choice of Weapons, A Poet and His Camera, Whispers of Intimate Things, In Love, Born Black, Moments Without Proper Names, Flavio, To Smile in Autumn, Shannon, Voices in the Mirror, Irias In Silence, Glimpses Toward Infinity.
PICTURES: The Learning Tree (Library of Congress Nat'l Film Registry Classics honor, 1989), Shaft, Shaft's Big Score, Super Cops, Leadbelly.
TELEVISION: The Odyssey of Solomon Northup, Moments Without Proper Names, Martin, Malcolm X: Make It Plain, Half Past Autumn: The Life and Works of Gordon Parks.

PARKS, MICHAEL
Actor. b. Corona, CA, April 4, 1938.
PICTURES: Wild Seed (debut, 1964), Bus Riley's Back in Town, The Bible, The Idol, The Happening, The Last Hard Men, Sidewinder One, ffolkes, Hard Country, Savannah Smiles, Spiker, Club Life, The Return of Josey Wales (also dir.), Spiker, Arizona Heat, Nightmare Beach, Prime Suspect, The Hitman, Storyville, Death Wish 5: The Face of Death, Stranger by Night, Sorceress, Niagara Niagara, Deceiver, Julian Po, Full Tilt Boogie, Wicked, Bullfighter, Big Bad Love, A Chance of Life.
TELEVISION: Series: Then Came Bronson, The Colbys, Twin Peaks. Movies: Can Ellen Be Saved?, Savage Bees, Chase,

Dangerous Affection, Gore Vidal's Billy the Kid, The China Lake Murders, Hart to Hart: Secrets of the Hart.

PARKS, VAN DYKE
Composer, actor. b. Jan. 3, 1941. Albums include: Song Cycle, Discover America, Clang of the Yankee Reaper, Jump!, Tokyo Rose, Orange Crate Art (with Brian Wilson).
PICTURES: The Swan, A Gift for Heidi (actor only), Goin' South, Popeye (actor only), Loose Shoes (actor only), Sesame Street Presents Follow That Bird, Club Paradies, The Brave Little Toaster (songs), Vibes (actor only), Casual Sex?, The Two Jakes (actor only), He Said She Said (actor only), Out on a Limb, Wild Bill, Bastard Out of Carolina, Private Parts, Shadrach.
TELEVISION: *Movies:* Mother Goose Rock 'n' Rhyme (actor only), One Christmas, Next Door, The Summer of Ben Tyler, Oliver Twist, A Chance of Snow, Borderline, Harlan County War, The Ponder Heart, Call Me Claus, Charms for the Easy Life, Monday Night Mayhem, Whitewash: The Clarence Bradley Story. *Series:* Bonino (actor only), Harold and the Purple Crayon.

PARRETTI, GIANCARLO
Executive. b. Orvieto, Italy, Oct. 23, 1941. Hotelier in Sicily in the late 1970's. Managing dir. of Naples newspaper Diario, until 1981. 1987, purchased Cannon Group, renaming it Pathe Comm. 1990, company acquired MGM/UA, Communications. Resigned 1991.

PARSONS, ESTELLE
Actress. b. Marblehead, MA, Nov. 20, 1927. e. Connecticut Coll. for Women, Bachelor's degree in political science. Attended Boston U. Law Sch. Helped harvest crops in England with the Women's Land Army. Was active in politics; worked for the Committee for the Nation's Health in Wash. and the Republican Finance Committee in Boston. Was elected to public office in Marblehead, Mass. Joined NBC-TV's Today Show as prod. asst.; then writer, feature prod. and commentator. Appeared in two Julius Monk revues, Jerry Herman's Nightcap.
THEATRE: Happy Hunting, Whoop Up, Beg Borrow or Steal, Mrs. Dally Has a Lover (Theater World Award), Next Time I'll Sing to You (Obie Award), In the Summer House (Obie Award), Ready When You Are C.B., Malcolm, The Seven Descents of Myrtle, ...And Miss Reardon Drinks a Little, The Norman Conquests, Ladies of the Alamo, Miss Margarida's Way, Pirates of Penzance, The Unguided Missile, Threepenny Opera, Lincoln Center Repertory Theatre, Mahagonny, Forgiving Typhoid Mary, Shimada, The Shadow Box, Twice Removed, Grace & Glorie.
PICTURES: Ladybug Ladybug (debut, 1963), Bonnie and Clyde (Acad. Award, best supporting actress, 1967), Rachel Rachel (Acad. Award nom.), Don't Drink the Water, Watermelon Man, I Walk the Line, I Never Sang for My Father, Two People, For Pete's Sake, Foreplay, Dick Tracy, The Lemon Sisters, Boys on the Side, That Darn Cat, Looking for Richard, Freak City.
TELEVISION: *Mini-Series:* Backstairs at the White House. *Special:* The Front Page. *Movies:* Terror on the Beach, The Gun and the Pulpit, The UFO Incident, The Gentleman Bandit, Open Admissions, A Private Matter, The American Clock, The Love Letter. *Series:* Roseanne. *Guest:* All in the Family.

PARTON, DOLLY
Singer, Composer, Actress. b. Sevierville, TN, Jan. 19, 1946. Gained fame as country music singer, composer and radio and TV personality. Co-partner with Sandy Gallin, Sandollar Prods. *Author:* My Life and Other Unfinished Business (autobiography), Coat of Many Colors.
PICTURES: Nine to Five (debut, 1980; also wrote & sang title song), The Best Little Whorehouse in Texas (also wrote addtl. songs), Rhinestone (also songs), Steel Magnolias, Straight Talk (also songs), The Beverly Hillbillies, Heartsong, Frank McKlusky C.I, Moulin Rouge ! (comp.), Songcatcher (comp.), Women Talking Dirty (comp./singer).
TELEVISION: *Series:* Dolly (1976), Dolly (1987-88), Mindin' My Own Business. *Guest:* Porter Wagoner Show, Cass Walker Program, Bill Anderson Show, Wilbur Bros. Show. *Specials:* Kenny Dolly & Willie: Something Inside So Strong, A Tennessee Mountain Thanksgiving, Dolly Parton: Treasures. *Movies:* A Smoky Mountain Christmas (also songs), Wild Texas Wind (also co-writer, co-prod.), Big Dreams & Broken Hearts: The Dottie West Story, Naomi & Wynonna: Love Can Build a Bridge, Unlikely Angel, Blue Valley Songbird, Graham Goes to Dollywood.

PASDAR, ADRIAN
Actor. b. Pittsfield, MA, April 30, 1965. e. Univ. of Central FL. Studied acting with People's Light and Theatre Co., Lee Strasberg Institute.
THEATRE: *Regional:* The Glass Menagerie, Shadow Box, Hotters, Sorry Wrong Number, Cold Foot, Monkey's Paw.
PICTURES: Top Gun (debut, 1986), Streets of Gold, Solarbabies, Near Dark, Made in USA, Cookie, Vital Signs, Torn Apart, Just Like a Woman, The Pompatus of Love, Ties to Rachel, Wounded, A Brother's Kiss, Desert Son, The Big Day.
TELEVISION: *Series:* Profit, Feds, Mysterious Ways. *Movies:* The Lost Capone, A Mother's Gift, Touched by Evil, Love in Another Town, The Perfect Getaway, Mutiny, Crossing the Line. *Mini-Series:* House of Frankenstein. *Special:* Big Time.

PASETTA, MARTY
Producer-Director. b. June 16, 1932. e. U. Santa Clara.
TELEVISION: AFI Salutes to Fred Astaire, John Huston, Lillian Gish, Alfred Hitchcock and Jimmy Stewart, Gene Kelly Special, Elvis Aloha From Hawaii, Oscar (17), Emmy (2) and Grammy (8) Award Shows, A Country Christmas (1978-81), The Monte Carlo Show, Texaco Star Theatre-Opening Night, Burnett Discovers Domingo, Disneyland's 30th Anniversary Celebration, 15 Years of Cerebral Palsy Telethons, A Night at the Moulin Rouge, Soap Opera Awards, An All-Star Celebration Honoring Martin Luther King, Disneyland's Summer Vacation Party, Disney's Captain EO Grand Opening, 15th Anniversary of Disney World; Beach Boys... 25 Years Together, Super Night at the Superbowl, 20th Anniversary of Caesars Palace, Paris by Night with George Burns, I Call You Friend Papal Spacebridge '87, Walt Disney World's Celebrity Circus, Las Vegas: An All-Star 75th Anniversary, Julio Iglesias—Sold Out, The Ice Capades with Kirk Cameron, American All-Star Tribute Honoring Elizabeth Taylor.

PASOLINI, UBERTO
Producer.
PICTURES: The Killing Fields, The Frog Prince, The Mission, Meeting Venus, Palookaville, The Full Monty (BAFTA Award, Outstanding Brit. Film, 1997), The Closer You Get, The Emperor's New Clothes.
TELEVISION: *Movies:* A Dangerous Man: Lawrence After Arabia.

PASSER, IVAN
Director, Writer. b. Prague, Czechoslovakia, July 10, 1933. e. Film Faculty of Acad. of Musical Arts, Prague. 1961, asst. dir. to Milos Forman on Audition which led to scripting for Forman. 1969, moved to U.S., worked in NY as longshoreman while studying Eng. U.S. dir. debut: Born to Win, 1971.
PICTURES: *Writer:* Loves of a Blonde, A Boring Afternoon, Fireman's Ball. *Director:* Intimate Lighting (also s.p.), Born to Win, Law and Disorder, Crime and Passion, The Silver Bears, Cutter and Bone, Creator, Haunted Summer, Pretty Hattie's Baby, The Wishing Tree.
TELEVISION: *U.S.:* Faerie Tale Theatre. *Movies:* Fourth Story, Stalin, While Justice Sleeps, Kidnapped, Picnic.

PASTER, GARY M.
Executive. b. St. Louis, MO, July 4, 1943. e. U. of MO, B.A.; UCLA, USC Graduate Sch. of Business. 1970, joined Burbank Studios as asst. to pres., treas.; 1976 v.p., admin. and chmn. of the exec. comm.; 1977 pres. Member: AMPAS, LA Film Dev. Council, Hollywood Radio & T.V. Society, Acad. of Television Arts and Sciences. Advisory bd., Kaufman Astoria Studios, N.Y.

PASTORELLI, ROBERT
Actor. b. New Brunswick, NJ, June 21, 1954.
PICTURES: Outrageous Fortune, Memories of Me, Beverly Hills Cop II, Dances With Wolves, Folks!, The Paint Job, Ferngully: The Last Rainforest (voice), Sister Act 2: Back in the Habit, Striking Distance, Eraser, Michael, A Simple Wish, Heist, Scotch and Milk, Modern Vampires, Bait.
TELEVISION: I Married a Centerfold, California Girls, Hands of a Stranger, Lady Mobster, Dances with Wolves, Painted Heart, F, Robin Cook's Harmful Intent, The Yam Princess, The West Side Waltz, The Ballad of Lucy Whipple, South Pacific, Oooph!, Women vs. Men. *Series:* Murphy Brown, Double Rush, Cracker. *Guest:* Tucker's Witch, Hill Street Blues, MacGyver, Batman.

PATINKIN, MANDY
Actor. r.n. Mandel Patinkin. b. Chicago, IL, Nov. 30, 1952. e. U. of Kansas, Juilliard Sch. (Drama Div.; 1972-74). m. actress Kathryn Grody. In regional theatre before coming to New York where played with Shakespeare Festival Public Theater (Trelawny of the Wells, Hamlet, Rebel Women). Recordings: Mandy Patinkin, Dress Casual, Experiment.
THEATRE: Savages, The Shadow Box (B'way debut), Evita (Tony Award, 1980), Henry IV, Part I (Central Park), Sunday in the Park With George (Tony nom.), The Knife, Follies in Concert, A Winter's Tale, Mandy Patinkin: Dress Casual (solo concert), The Secret Garden, Falsettos, others.
PICTURES: The Big Fix (debut, 1978), Last Embrace, French Postcards, Night of the Juggler, Ragtime, Daniel, Yentl, Maxie, The Princess Bride, The House on Carroll Street, Alien Nation, Dick Tracy, True Colors, Impromptu, The Doctor, The Music of Chance, Life With Mikey (cameo), Squanto: A Warrior's Tale, Men with Guns, Lulu on the Bridge, The Adventures of Elmo in Grouchland, Pinero, The Papp Project.
TELEVISION: *Series:* Chicago Hope (Emmy Award, 1995). *Guest:* That Thing on ABC, That 2nd Thing on ABC, Taxi, Sparrow, Streets of Gold, Midnight Special. *Movie:* Charleston, Broken Glass, The Hunchback, Strange Justice, Everything That Rises.

PATRIC, JASON
Actor. Jason Patric Miller Jr .b. Queens, NY, June 17, 1966. Son of playwright-actor Jason Miller. Grandson of performer Jackie Gleason. Began professional career with Vermont's Champlain Shakespeare Festival.
THEATRE: *NY:* Beirut. *LA:* Out of Gas on Lovers' Leap.

PICTURES: Solarbabies (debut, 1986), The Lost Boys, The Beast, Denial, After Dark My Sweet, Roger Corman's Frankenstein Unbound, Rush, Geronimo: An American Legend, The Journey of August King, Sleepers, Speed 2: Cruise Control, Incognito, Your Friends & Neighbors (also prod.), 3 Days of Rain, Narc, Scene Smoking: Cigarettes, Cinema & the Myth of Cool, The Alamo.
TELEVISION: Movie: Tough Love. Special: Teach 109.

PATRICK, Sr., C.L.
Theatre Executive. b. Honaker, VA, Dec. 6, 1918. Former pres. of Fuqua Industries which owned Martin Theatres and Gulf States Theatres. Prior to this was pres. and chairman of Martin Theatres. Presently chairman of board Carmike Cinemas, Inc.; v.p. Variety International; dir., Will Rogers Institute; Motion Picture Pioneer of 1976; Recipient of: Sherrill Corwin Award, 1984; Salah Hassanein Humanitarian Award, ShowEast '88; Show South's Exhibitor of the Decade Award, 1990.

PATRICK, MICHAEL W.
Executive. b. Columbus, GA, May 17, 1950. e. Columbus Coll., B.S., 1972. Pres., CEO, Carmike Cinemas. 1989-present. *Board of dir.:* Columbus Bank and Trust Co. *Member:* exec. comm., Will Rogers Institute; Variety Int'l; Motion Picture Pioneers. *Bd. of Trustees:* Columbus State University Foundation Inc.

PATRICK, ROBERT
Actor. b. Marietta, GA. November 5, 1959.
PICTURES: Eye of the Eagle, Equalizer 2000, Killer Instinct, Hollywood Boulevard II, Future Hunters, Die Hard 2, Terminator 2: Judgment Day, Double Dragon, Body Shot, Fire in the Sky, Zero Tolerance, Hong Kong 97, The Cool Surface, Last Gasp, Decoy, Asylum, Striptease, The Only Thrill, Hacks, Rosewood, Cop Land, Ravager (prod. only), Very Bad Things, Winter, Counter Force, A Breed Apart, From Dusk Till Dawn 2: Texas Blood Money, The Faculty, Ambushed, Texas Funeral, Shogun Cop, All the Pretty Horses, Mexico City, Angels Don't Sleep Here, Spy Kids, Texas Rangers, Eye See You, Blackflash, D-Tox, Charlie's Angels: Full Throttle, Ladder 49.
TELEVISION: Movies: Resident Alien, Body Language. Series: Real Adventures of Jonny Quest. Guest: The Outer Limits. The X- Files.

PATTON, WILL
Actor. b. Charleston, SC, June 14, 1954. e. NC School of the Arts, 1975.
THEATRE: NY: Tourists and Refugees #2 (La Mama E.T.C., Obie Award), Fool For Love (Obie Award), Goose and Tomtom (Public Theatre), A Lie of the Mind.
PICTURES: King Blank, Silkwood, Variety, Desperately Seeking Susan, After Hours, Chinese Boxes, Belizaire the Cajun, No Way Out, Stars and Bars, Wildfire, Signs of Life, Everybody Wins, A Shock to the System, The Rapture, Cold Heaven, In the Soup, The Paint Job, Romeo Is Bleeding, Natural Causes, Midnight Edition, Tollbooth, The Client, The Puppet Masters, Copycat, Johns, The Spitfire Grill, Inventing the Abbotts, The Postman, O.K. Garage, I Woke Up Early the Day I Died, Breakfast of Champions, Armageddon, I Woke Up Early the Day I Died, Breakfast of Champions, Entrapment, Jesus' Son, Gone In Sixty Seconds, Trixie, Remember the Titans, The Mothman Prophecies, The Rough South of Larry Brown.
TELEVISION: Movies: Kent State, Dillinger, A Gathering of Old Men, The Deadly Desire, In the Deep Woods, A Child Lost Forever, Taking the Heat, Judicial Consent. Series: Ryan's Hope, Search For Tomorrow, The Protector, The Agency.

PAULEY, JANE
TV Host, Journalist. b. Indianapolis, IN, Oct. 31, 1950. m. Doonesbury creator Garry Trudeau. e. Indiana U. Involved in Indiana state politics before joining WISH-TV, Indianapolis, as reporter. Co-anchored midday news reports and anchored weekend news reports. Co-anchor of nightly news at WMAQ-TV, NBC station in Chicago. Joined Today Show in October, 1976, as featured regular, prior to which had made guest appearances on that program; co-host until 1990. Began own series Real Life With Jane Pauley in 1991. Dateline NBC, 1992-present.

PAVAN, MARISA
Actress. r.n. Marisa Pierangeli. b. Cagliari, Sardinia, Italy, June 19, 1932. e. Torquato Tasso Coll. Twin sister of late actress Pier Angeli. Came to U.S. 1950.
PICTURES: What Price Glory? (debut, 1952), Down Three Dark Streets, Drum Beat, The Rose Tattoo (Acad. Award nom.), Diane, The Man in the Gray Flannel Suit, The Midnight Story, John Paul Jones, Solomon and Sheba, A Slightly Pregnant Man, Antoine and Sebastien, Wandering Stars, Adieu marin.
TELEVISION: Movies/Mini-Series: The Diary of Anne Frank, Arthur Hailey's The Moneychangers, The Trial of Lee Harvey Oswald, Johnny Monroe, Jean-Pierre Aumont charme et fou-ri. Series: Ryan's Hope.

PAVLIK, JOHN M.
Executive. b. Melrose, IA, Dec. 3, 1939. e. U. of Minnesota, B.A., 1963. Reporter, Racine (WI) Journal-Times, San Bernardino (CA) Sun-Telegram, 1963-66; writer, News Bureau, Pacific

Telephone, Los Angeles, 1966-68; asst. dir. of publ. rltns., Association of Motion Picture and Television Producers, 1968-72; dir. of PR, 1972-78; v.p., 1978-79; special consultant, California Motion Picture Council, 1974-79; member, exec. council, Los Angeles Film Dev. Committee, v.p., 1977-78; exec. admin., Academy of Motion Picture Arts and Sciences, 1979-82; member, bd. of dir., Permanent Charities Comm. of the Entertainment Industries, 1979-84; member, bd. of dir., Hollywood Chamber of Commerce, 1979-85; exec. dir., M.P. & TV Fund, 1982-88; consultant, 1988-89; member, advisory board, Assn. of Film Commissioners Int'l, 1988-91; dir. of endowment dev., Academy Foundation, 1989-92; dir. of communications, AAMPA, 1992-present.

PAXSON, LOWELL W.
Executive. b. Rochester, NY. e. Syracuse U. As teenager worked in Rochester radio and became announcer while in college. Purchased first broadcast entity, WACK radio in Newark NY, 1954. Began selling merchandise on a Florida AM station in 1977. Conceived and founded Home Shopping Network, 1982. Est. Silver King Communications, 1986. Sold interest in HSN and Silver King in 1990 and bought WCRJ radio in Florida, start of Paxson Communications Corp. Sold radio interests in 1997 and acquired The Travel Channel, which has since been sold to Discovery Communications, Inc. Launched PAX TV, the seventh U.S. TV network, in 1998. Currently, chmn., Paxson Communications Corp.

PAXTON, BILL
Actor. b. Fort Worth, TX, May 17, 1955. e. NYU. First professional job as set dresser for film Big Bad Mamma. Studied acting with Stella Adler. Dir. short films Fish Heads, Scoop (also s.p.)
PICTURES: Stripes, The Lords of Discipline, Mortuary, Streets of Fire, Impulse, The Terminator, Weird Science, Commando, Aliens, Near Dark, Pass the Ammo, Slipstream, Next of Kin, Back to Back, Brain Dead, The Last of the Finest, Navy SEALS, Predator 2, The Dark Backward, One False Move, The Vagrant, Trespass, Indian Summer, Boxing Helena, Future Shock, Monolith, Tombstone, True Lies, Apollo 13, The Last Supper, Twister, The Evening Star, Titanic, Traveller, A Simple Plan, Mighty Joe Young, U-571, Vertical Limit, Frailty (also dir.), Spy Kids 2: The Island of Lost Dreams, Resistance, Spy Kids 3D: Game Over.
TELEVISION: Mini-Series: Fresno. Movies: Deadly Lessons, The Atlanta Child Murders, An Early Frost, Frank and Jesse, A Bright Shining Lie, War Letters. Guest: Miami Vice.

PAYMER, DAVID
Actor. b. Long Island, NY, Aug. 30, 1954. e. Univ. of Mich. First professional job with natl. company of Grease, which he later appeared in on B'way. Has also taught acting at UCLA and the Film Actor's Workshop, performed stand-up comedy and served as staff writer on The New Leave It to Beaver Show.
PICTURES: The In-Laws (debut, 1979), Airplane II: The Sequel, Best Defense, Irreconcilable Differences, Perfect, Howard the Duck, No Way Out, Crazy People, City Slickers, Mr. Saturday Night (Acad. Award nom.), Searching for Bobby Fischer, Heart and Souls, City Slickers II: The Legend of Curly's Gold, Quiz Show, City Hall, The American President, Unforgettable, Nixon, Get Shorty, The Sixth Man, Amistad, The Long Way Home (voice), Gang Related, Mighty Joe Young, Chill Factor, The Hurricane, Mumford, Payback, Outside Ozona, State and Main, Bait, Enemies of Laughter, Bounce, Partners, Bartleby, Focus, The Burial Society, Alex and Emma.
TELEVISION: Series: The Commish. Guest: Cagney & Lacy, The Paper Chase, Taxi, Cheers, L.A. Law, Hill Street Blues, Moonlighting, Murphy Brown, Channel Umptee-3, Justice League. Movies: Grace Kelly, Pleasure, Cagney & Lacey: The Return, Cagney & Lacey: Together Again, Crime of the Century, Dash & Lilly, For Love or Country: The Arturo Sandoval Story, From Where I Sit, Joe and Max, RFK. Special: In Search of Dr. Seuss.

PAYNE, ALEXANDER
Director, Writer. b. Omaha, Nebraska, Feb. 10, 1961.
PICTURES: The Passion of Martin (dir. only), Inside Out, Citizen Ruth, Election, Jurassic Park III (s.p. only), Sideways (dir. only), About Schmidt, A Decade Under the Influence (doc. Winner Golden Globe Award, best s.p. 2003).

PAYNTER, ROBERT
Cinematographer. b. London, England, March 12, 1928. e. Mercer Sch. First job in industry at 15 years as camera trainee with Government Film Dept.
PICTURES: Hannibal Brooks (debut, 1969), The Games, Lawman, The Nightcomers, Chato's Land, The Mechanic, Scorpio, The Big Sleep, Superman, Firepower, The Final Conflict, Superman II, An American Werewolf in London, Superman III, Trading Places, The Muppets Take Manhattan, Into the Night, National Lampoon's European Vacation, Spies Like Us, Little Shop of Horrors, When the Whales Came, Strike It Rich, Get Back.

PAYS, AMANDA
Actress. b. Berkshire, England, June 6, 1959. m. actor Corbin Bernsen. Began as a model. Studied French, art and pottery at Hammersmith Polytechnic. Acting debut: Cold Room (HBO).
PICTURES: Oxford Blues, The Kindred, Off Limits, Leviathan, Exposure, Solitaire for Two, Subterfuge, Spacejacked, Ablaze.
TELEVISION: Series: Max Headroom, The Flash, Thief Takers. Mini-Series: A.D. Movies: 13 at Dinner, The Pretenders, Parker Kane, Dead on the Money, The Thorn Birds: The Lost Years, Hollywood Confidential, The Santa Trap.

PAYSON, MARTIN D.
Executive. b. Brooklyn, NY, Jan. 4, 1936. e. Cornell U., NYU Sch. of Law, LLB, 1961. Practiced law privately before joining Warner Communications, Inc. as v.p. 1970. Later named exec. v.p., gen. counsel. 1987, appt. to 3-member office of pres., WCI. Was vice chmn. Time Warner Inc., until Dec. 1992. Retired.

PEAKER, E. J.
Actress, Singer, Dancer. r.n. Edra Jeanne Peaker. b. Tulsa, OK, Feb. 22, 1944. e. U. of New Mexico, U. of Vienna, Austria. Stage debut Bye, Bye Birdie
PICTURES: Hello Dolly! (debut, 1969), All American Boy, Private Roads, The Four Deuces, Graduation Day, Fire in the Night, I Can't Lose, Out of This World, The Banker, Dreamrider, The Last Producer.
TELEVISION: Series: That's Life. Guest: The Flying Nun, That Girl, Love American Style, Odd Couple, Police Woman, Rockford Files, Get Christie Love, Houston Knights, Hunter, Quincy, Charlie's Angels, Six Million Dollar Man. Movies: Three's a Crowd, Getting Away From It All, Broken Promises (assoc. prod., writer), Surviving Gilligan's Island: The Incredibly True Story of the Longest Three Hour Tour in History.

PEARCE, CHRISTOPHER
Producer. b. Dursley, Eng, Nov. 19, 1943. Entered industry as gen. mgr. American Zoetrope. From 1982 to 1985 served as exec. in chg. of prod. for Cannon Films Inc. overseeing prod. on 150 films incl. That Championship Season, Runaway Train, Fool For Love and Barfly. 1987 became sr. v.p. and COO Cannon Group. Has since become pres. & CEO Cannon Pictures. Producer of numerous pictures and tv movies.

PEARCE, CRAIG
Actor, Writer.
PICTURES: I Can't Get Started, Vicious!, Mad Bomber in Love, The Seventh Floor. Writer: Strictly Ballroom, Romeo + Juliet (BAFTA Award, Best Adapted Screenplay, 1997), Moulin Rouge (BAFTA nom., WGA nom.), The Season, Rent.

PEARCE, RICHARD
Director, Cinematographer. b. San Diego, CA, Jan. 25, 1943. e. Yale U., B.A. degree in Eng. lit., 1965. New School for Social Research, M.A., degree in political economics. Worked with Don Pennebaker and Richard Leacock on documentaries. Photographed Emile de Antonio's America Is Hard to See. In 1970 went to Chile where he dir., photographed and edited Campamento, an award-winning documentary.
PICTURES: As photographer (Acad. Award winning documentaries): Woodstock, Marjoe, Interviews With My Lai Veterans, Hearts and Minds. Director: Heartland (debut, 1979), Threshold, Country, No Mercy, The Long Walk Home, Leap of Faith, A Family Thing.
TELEVISION: Series Dir.: Alfred Hitchcock Presents, Homicide: Life on the Streets, Party of Five, Nothing Sacred. Movies Dir.: Siege, No Other Love, Sessions, Dead Man Out, The Final Days, Thicker Than Blood, Witness Protection, South Pacific.

PECK, GREGORY
Actor, Producer. r.n. Eldred Gregory Peck. b. La Jolla, CA, April 5, 1916. e. U. of California; Neighborhood Playhouse Sch. of Dramatics. Father of actors Tony and Cecilia Peck. On dramatic stage (The Doctor's Dilemma, The Male Animal, Once in a Lifetime, The Play's the Thing, You Can't Take It With You, The Morning Star, The Willow and I, Sons and Soldiers, etc.). Voted one of ten best Money-Making Stars Motion Picture Herald-Fame Poll, 1947, 1952. Co-prod. and starred in Big Country, for his company, Anthony Productions; prod. the Trial of the Catonsville Nine, The Dove (St. George Productions). Pres., Acad. M.P. Arts and Sciences, 1967-70. Founding mem., bd. mem. and chmn. American Film Inst. Recipient, Jean Hersholt Humanitarian Award, 1986. AFI Life Achievement Award, 1989. Voice of Florenz Ziegfeld in 1991 B'way musical The Will Rogers Follies.
PICTURES: Days of Glory (debut, 1944), The Keys of the Kingdom, The Valley of Decision, Spellbound, The Yearling, Duel in the Sun, The Macomber Affair, Gentleman's Agreement, The Paradine Case, Yellow Sky, The Great Sinner, Twelve O'Clock High, The Gunfighter, Only the Valiant, David and Bathsheba, Captain Horatio Hornblower, The World in His Arms, The Snows of Kilimanjaro, Roman Holiday, Night People, Man With a Million, The Purple Plain, The Man in the Gray Flannel Suit, Moby Dick, Designing Woman, The Bravados, The Big Country (also co-prod.), Pork Chop Hill (also prod.), Beloved Infidel, On the Beach, Guns of Navarone, To Kill a Mockingbird (Acad. Award, 1962),

Cape Fear (also prod.), How the West Was Won, Captain Newman M.D., Behold a Pale Horse (also prod.), John F. Kennedy: Years of Lightning—Day of Drums (narrator), Mirage, Arabesque, MacKenna's Gold, Stalking Moon, The Chairman, Marooned, I Walk the Line, Shootout, Billy Two Hats, The Omen, MacArthur (also prod.), The Boys from Brazil (also prod.), The Sea Wolves (also prod.), Amazing Grace and Chuck, Old Gringo, Other People's Money, Cape Fear (1991), Theremin: An Electronic Odyssey, Passage a l'acte, L'Hidato Shel Adolf Eichmann, Wild Bill: Hollywood Maverick, From Russia to Hollywood: The 100-Year Odyssey of Chekhov and Shdanoff, A Conversation with Gregory Peck, The Art of Norton Simon, American Prophet: The Story of Joseph Smith.
TELEVISION: Mini-series: The Blue and the Gray. Movies: The Scarlet and the Black (also prod.),The Portrait. Specials: We the People 200: The Constitutional Gala, The First 50 Years.
(d. June 12, 2003)

PEDAS, JIM
Executive. b. Youngstown, OH. e. Thiel College. Opened Circle Theatre in Washington, D.C. in 1957 with brother Ted. 1984 formed Circle Releasing, serving as Secretary/ Treasurer; Circle Films, serving as v.p. See Ted Pedas entry for releases.

PEDAS, TED
Executive. b. Farrell, PA, May 6, 1931. e. B.S.B.A, Youngstown St. Univ. M.B.A., Wharton Sch. of Business at Univ. of PA. J.D., Geo. Washington Univ. 1957, with brother Jim, opened Circle Theatre in Washington D.C. one of the first repertory houses. Circle/Showcase group of m.p. theatres expanded to over 80 quality screens before being sold in 1988. 1973-78, served on board of Cinema 5 in NY. 1984. Pres. NATO D.C.; National Film Preservation Board, Joseph Wharton Award 1988. Circle Releasing formed to distribute films with Ted serving as president. Releases include Blood Simple, The Navigator and the Killer. Circle Films has produced: Raising Arizona, Miller's Crossing, Barton Fink, Caught, Whatever.

PEERCE, LARRY
Director. b. Bronx, NY. April 19, 1930. Father was late singer Jan Peerce.
PICTURES: One Potato Two Potato, The Big T.N.T. Show, The Incident, Goodbye Columbus, The Sporting Club, A Separate Peace, Ash Wednesday, The Other Side of the Mountain, Two Minute Warning, The Other Side of the Mountain—Part II, The Bell Jar (also exec. prod.), Why Would I Lie?, Love Child, Hard to Hold, Wired.
TELEVISION: Movies: A Stranger Who Looks Like Me, Love Lives On, I Take These Men, The Fifth Missile, Prison for Children, Queenie, Elvis and Me, The Neon Empire, The Court-Martial of Jackie Robinson, Child of Rage, Poisoned by Love: The Kern County Murders, Heaven & Hell: North and South Book III, A Burning Passion: The Margaret Mitchell Story, In Pursuit of Honor (co-exec. prod. only), An Element of Truth, The Abduction, Love-Struck, Christmas Every Day, Holy Joe, A Test of Love, A Secret Life, Second Honeymoon.

PEÑA, ELIZABETH
Actress. b. N.J., Sept. 23, 1961 of Cuban parents. Moved to New York in 1969 where she attended NY High School for Performing Arts. Off-B'way in Blood Wedding, Antigone, Romeo & Juliet, Act One & Only, Italian American Reconciliation, and many others.
PICTURES: El Super, Times Square, They All Laughed, Fat Chance, Crossover Dreams, Down and Out in Beverly Hills, La Bamba, Batteries Not Included, Vibes, Blue Steel, Jacob's Ladder, The Waterdance, Across the Moon, Free Willy 2: The Adventure Home, Dead Funny, Lone Star (Ind't Spirit Award, 1997), Strangeland, The Pass, Rush Hour, Strangeland, Seven Girlfriends, On the Borderline, Things Behind the Sun, Tortilla Soup, Ten Tiny Love Stories, Imposter, Zigzag.
TELEVISION: Series: Tough Cookies, I Married Dora, Shannon's Deal, Resurrection Blvd. Movies: Fugitive Among Us, Roommates, It Came From Outer Space, Contagious, The Second Civil War, Border Line. Miniseries: Drug War, The Camarena Story, The Invaders, Aldrich Ames: America Betrayed.

PENDLETON, AUSTIN
Actor. b. Warren, OH, March 27, 1940. e. Yale Univ. Started acting with Williamstown Theatre Festival. Teaches acting at the Herbert Berghof Studio. Named artistic dir. of NY's Circle Rep. Theatre, 1995.
THEATRE: Actor: Oh Dad Poor Dad Mama's Hung You in the Closet and I'm Feeling So Sad, Fiddler on the Roof, The Little Foxes, The Last Sweet Days of Isaac (NY Drama Critics & Outer Critics Circle Awards), Educating Rita, Doubles, The Sorrows of Frederick, Grand Hotel, Hamlet, Sophistry. Director: The Runner Stumbles, Say Goodnight Gracie, John Gabriel Borkman, The Little Foxes. Author: Booth, Uncle Bob.
PICTURES: Skidoo (debut, 1968), Catch-22, What's Up Doc?, Every Little Crook and Nanny, The Thief Who Came to Dinner, The Front Page, The Great Smokey Roadblock (The Last of the Cowboys), The Muppet Movie, Starting Over, Simon, First Family, My Man Adam, Off Beat, Short Circuit, Hello Again, Mr. & Mrs. Bridge, The Ballad of the Sad Cafe, True Identity, My Cousin

Vinny, Charlie's Ear, Rain Without Thunder, My Boyfriend's Back, Searching for Bobby Fischer, Mr. Nanny, Greedy, Guarding Tess, Dangerous Minds, Two Much, Home for the Holidays, Sgt. Bilko, Trial and Error, 2 Days in the Valley, The Proprietor, The Associate, The Mirror Has Two Faces, Sue, Amistad, A River Made to Drown In, Charlie Hoboken, Joe the King, Men of Means, Brokendown Love Story, The 4th Floor, Broke Even, Fast Food Fast Women, Erotic Tales IV, Clowns, Angela, The Acting Class, Queenie in Love, Manna From Heaven, A Beautiful Mind, Sex & Violence, Don't You Cry For Me, Finding Nemo (voice).
TELEVISION: *Movie*: Don't Drink the Water. *Guest*: Miami Vice, The Equalizer.

PENN, ARTHUR
Director. b. Philadelphia, PA, Sept. 27, 1922. e. Black Mountain Coll., Asheville, NC; U. of Perugia, U. of Florence in Italy. Began as TV dir. in 1953, twice winner of Sylvania Award. Appeared in 1994 film Naked in New York.
THEATRE: Two for the Seesaw, Miracle Worker (Tony Award, 1960), Toys in the Attic, All the Way Home, Golden Boy, Wait Until Dark, Sly Fox, Monday After the Miracle, Hunting Cockroaches.
PICTURES: The Left-Handed Gun (debut, 1958), The Miracle Worker (Acad. Award nom.), Mickey One (also prod.), The Chase, Bonnie and Clyde (Acad. Award nom.), Alice's Restaurant (Acad. Award nom.; also co-s.p.), Little Big Man, Visions of Eight (dir. segment: The Highest), Night Moves, The Missouri Breaks, Four Friends (also co-prod.), Target, Dead of Winter, Penn and Teller Get Killed (also prod.), Lumiere and Company.
TELEVISION: *Movies*: Flesh and Blood, The Portrait, Inside. *Series*: American Playhouse, 100 Centre Street.

PENN, CHRISTOPHER
Actor. b. Malibu, CA. Son of dir. Leo Penn and actress Eileen Ryan. Brother of actor Sean Penn and musician Michael Penn. Studied acting with Peggy Feury.
PICTURES: Rumble Fish (debut, 1983), All the Right Moves, Footloose, The Wild Life, Pale Rider, At Close Range, Made in USA, Return From the River Kwai, Best of the Best, Mobsters, Leather Jackets, Reservoir Dogs, Best of the Best 2, The Pickle, The Music of Chance, True Romance, Short Cuts, Josh and S.A.M., Beethoven's 2nd, Imaginary Crimes, Fist of the Northstar, Under the Hula Moon, To Wong Foo–Thanks for Everything–Julie Newmar, Sacred Cargo, Mulholland Falls, The Boys Club, The Funeral, Papertrail, Deceiver, One Tough Cop, Rush Hour, The Florentine, Cement, Bread and Roses, Kiss Kiss (Bang Bang), Redemption, Corky Romano, Microwave Park, Murder By Numbers, Stealing Harvard, Redemption, Shelter Island.
TELEVISION: *Guest*: Magnum P.I., The Young Riders, North Beach, Rawhide, Chicago Hope. *Series*: A.F.P.: American Fighter Pilot (voice).

PENN, ROBIN WRIGHT
Actress. b. Dallas, TX, April 8, 1966. m. actor Sean Penn. Was model at age 14 before making acting debut on tv series The Yellow Rose.
PICTURES: Hollywood Vice Squad (debut, 1986), The Princess Bride, Denial, State of Grace, The Playboys, Toys, Forrest Gump, The Crossing Guard, Moll Flanders, Loved, She's So Lovely, Message In a Bottle, Hurlyburly, How to Kill Your Neighbor's Dog, Unbreakable, The Pledge, The Last Castle, White Oleander, Searching for Debra Winger, The Singing Detective.
TELEVISION: *Series*: Santa Barbara. *Pilot*: Home.

PENN, SEAN
Actor, Director, Writer. b. Burbank, CA, Aug. 17, 1960. Son of actor-dir. Leo Penn and actress Eileen Ryan. Brother of actor Christopher Penn and musician Michael Penn. m. actress Robin Wright. e. Santa Monica H.S. Served as apprentice for two years at Group Repertory Theatre, L.A. Acted in: Terrible Jim Fitch, Earthworms, The Girl on the Via Flaminia. First prof. appearance as guest star on TV's Barnaby Jones. On B'way in Heartland, Slab Boys. Also in Hurlyburly (Westwood Playhouse, LA), Goose & Tom Tom (Lincoln Center Theater). Directed, The Kindness of Women (Santa Monica Pink Theater); exec. prod., Remembrance (Santa Monica Playhouse).
PICTURES: *Actor*: Taps (debut, 1981), Fast Times at Ridgemont High, Bad Boys, Crackers, Racing with the Moon, Falcon and the Snowman, At Close Range, Shanghai Surprise, Colors, Judgment in Berlin, Casualties of War, We're No Angels, State of Grace, Carlito's Way, Dead Man Walking (Acad. Award nom.), She's So Lovely (also exec. prod.; Cannes Film Festival Award, 1997), Loved (also prod.), U-Turn (also prod.), The Game, Hurlyburly, The Thin Red Line, Sweet and Lowdown (Acad. Award nom.), Being John Malkovich (cameo), Up at the Villa, Before Night Falls, The Weight of Water, Beaver Trilogy, I Am Sam (Acad. Award nom.), You'll Never Wiez in this Town Again, Scene Smoking: Cigarettes, Cinema & the Myth of Cool, The Art of Dennis Hopper, Mystic River, The Assassination of Richard Nixon. *Dir./Writer*: The Indian Runner, The Crossing Guard (also co-prod.), The Pledge.
TELEVISION: *Movie*: The Killing of Randy Webster. *Guest*: Barnaby Jones, Friends. *Special*: Dear America (reader).

PENNEBAKER, D.A.
Director, Cinematographer. r.n. Donn Alan Pennebaker. b. Evanston, IL, July 15, 1925. e. Yale U. Studied engineering, set up own electronics firm. Worked in advertising, before writing and directing documentaries, as well as experimental films. 1958 joined Richard Leacock, Willard Van Dyke and Shirley Clarke in equipment-sharing film co-op, Filmakers. 1960 joined Robert Drew operating out of Time Life with Leacock, Albert Maysles and others. Set up Leacock Pennebaker with Leacock and made several films that were blown up from 16mm to 35mm and released in theatres. Currently works with co-dir. and wife Chris Hegedus and son Frazer Pennebaker, continuing to film unscripted dramas of real events in cinema verite style. Dir. music videos for Suzanne Vega, Victoria Williams, Branford Marsalis, Randy Newman.
PICTURES: Daybreak Express (1956), Opening in Moscow, Primary, David, Jane, Crisis, The Chair, On the Pole, Mr. Pearson, Don't Look Back, Monterey Pop, Beyond the Law, One P.M., Sweet Toronto, Maidstone, Ziggy Stardust and the Spiders from Mars, On the Pole, Town Bloody Hall, The Energy War, Dance Black America, Rockaby, Depeche Mode: 101, The Music Tells You, The War Room, Keine Zeit, Moon Over Broadway, Woodstock Diary (also ed.), Down From the Mountain, Only the Strong Survive.

PEPLOE, MARK
Writer. b. Kenya. Sister is writer Clare Peploe. Raised in England and Italy. e. Magdalen Col., Oxford. Became researcher for documentary dept. of the BBC; then worked as research, writer and dir. for series Creative Persons.
PICTURES: The Pied Piper, The Passenger, The Babysitter, High Season, The Last Emperor (Acad. Award, 1987), The Sheltering Sky, Afraid of the Dark (also dir.), Little Buddha, Victory.

PERAKOS, SPERIE P.
Executive. b. New Britain, CT, Nov. 12, 1920. e. Cheshire Acad., Yale U., Harvard Law Sch. Student mgr., Stanley-Warner Theatres, 1939-40; Perakos Theatres 1940 to present; Capt., U.S.A. Intelligence with 35 inf. division. Fellow, Pierson Coll., Yale, 1946-present; Yale Alumni Bd., 1949 to present; Yale Alumni Film Bd. 1952 to 1980; member Alumni Council for Yale Drama Sch.; Past pres. Yale Club of New Britain, Conn.; dir. of Films & Filmings Seminars, Pierson Coll., Yale; prod. Antigone, 1964; pres. Norma Film Prod., Inc., 1962 to present. Past pres. and chmn. Yale's Peabody Museum Associates. Pres., Perakos Theatres, Conn. Theatre Associates, Inc. Past Pres., Connecticut Association of Theatre Owners, Secretary, ShowEast. *Member*: Exec. Board of Natl' Assn. of Theatre Owners, C.A.R.A.

PERENCHIO, ANDREW J.
Executive. b. Fresno, CA, Dec. 20, 1930. e. U. of California. Vice pres., Music Corp. of America, 1958-62; General Artists Corp., 1962-64; pres., owner, Chartwell Artists, Ltd., theatrical agency, Los Angeles, 1964; pres. & CEO, Tandem Productions, Inc., and TAT Communications Co., 1973-83, then became principal with Norman Lear in Embassy Communications. Held post of pres. & CEO of Embassy Pictures.

PERENCHIO, A. JERROLD
Executive. Owned and been active in Chartwell Partners LLC, a media and communications investment co., since it was formed in 1983. Chairman of the Board and CEO of Univision since Dec., 1992. From Dec. 1992 through Jan. 1997, he was also the Company's President.

PEREIRA, VANESSA
Casting Director.
PICTURES: Jude, Hamlet, Welcome to Sarajevo, Under the Skin, Spice World, My Son the Fanatic, Resurrection Man, I Want You, Dark City, What Rats Won't Do, Appetite, Elizabeth, Hilary and Jackie, Alegria, The Lost Son, Heart,Jakob the Liar.
TELEVISION: Flowers of the Forest, The Hunger.

PEREZ, ROSIE
Actress. b. Brooklyn, NY Sept.6,1964. Attended sch. in L.A. where she became a dancer on Soul Train; then choreographer for music videos and stage shows for such performers as Bobby Brown, The Boys, Diana Ross, LL Cool J, etc. Acting debut in Do the Right Thing.
PICTURES: Do the Right Thing (also choreog.; debut, 1989), White Men Can't Jump, Night on Earth, Untamed Heart, Fearless (Acad. Award nom.), It Could Happen to You, Somebody to Love, A Brother's Kiss, Perdita Durango, The 24 Hour Woman (also co-prod.), The Road to El Dorado (voice), King of the Jungle, Human Nature, Riding in Cars with Boys,King of the Jungle.
TELEVISION: *Movies*: Criminal Justice, Subway Stories: Tales from the Underground (also exec. prod.). *Series*: In Living Color (choreographer). *Specials*: Rosie Perez Presents Society's Ride (exec. prod.), In a New Light: Sex Unplugged (co-host).

PERKINS, ELIZABETH
Actress. b. Forest Hills, Queens, NY, Nov. 18, 1960. Grew up in Vermont. After high school moved to Chicago to study at Goodman School of Drama. Two months after moving to NY in 1984, landed a role in the national touring co. of Brighton Beach Memoirs, later performing part on Broadway. Acted with Playwright's Horizon, NY Ensemble Theater, Shakespeare in the Park and Steppenwolf Theatre Co. Appeared in short film Teach 109.
PICTURES: About Last Night..., From the Hip, Big, Sweet Hearts Dance, Love at Large, Avalon, Enid Is Sleeping, He Said She Said, The Doctor, Indian Summer, The Flintstones, Miracle on 34th Street, Moonlight and Valentino, Lesser Prophets, I'm Losing You, Crazy in Alabama, 28 Days, Cats & Dogs, Finding Nemo (voice).
TELEVISION: Movies: For Their Own Good, If These Walls Could Talk 2, What Girls Learn, My Sister's Keeper. Mini-series: The Rescuers: Two Women, From the Earth to the Moon.

PERKINS, MILLIE
Actress. b. Passaic, NJ, May 12, 1938. Was model when chosen by dir. George Stevens for starring role in The Diary of Anne Frank.
PICTURES: The Diary of Anne Frank (debut, 1959), Wild in the Country, Dulcinea, Ensign Pulver, Ride in the Whirlwind, The Shooting, Wild in the Streets, Cockfighter, Lady Cocoa, The Witch Who Came From the Sea, Table for Five, At Close Range, Jake Speed, Slam Dance, Wall Street, Necronomicon, Two Moon Junction, The Pistol, Bodily Harm, The Chamber, Harvest of Fire, A Woman's a Helluva Thing.
TELEVISION: Series: Knots Landing, Elvis, Any Day Now. Guest: U.S. Steel Hour, Breaking Point, Murder She Wrote, Our House, Jessie, Hart to Hart, Glitter, Wagon Train, thirtysomething, Touched By An Angel. Movies: A.D., The Thanksgiving Promise, Penalty Phase, Anatomy of an Illness, Shattered Vows, License to Kill, Strange Voices, Broken Angel, Best Intentions, The Other Love, Haunting Passion, A Gun in the House, Model Mother, Macbeth (cable tv), Call Me Anna, 72 Hours, Murder of Innocence, The Writing on the Wall, God, The Universe and Hot Fudge Sundaes, The Bounty Hunter: Miles To Go Before I Sleep, The Summer of Ben Tyler.

PERKINS, ROWLAND
Executive. Vice-President, Creative Services, William Morris Agency, 1952–75. Founding President, Creative Artists Agency, 1975–95. Established The Rowland Perkins Company (a.k.a. Double Eagle Entertainment) in 1994 to develop and produce feature, network and cable films; television series and specials; Broadway shows. Subsequently founded Talentclick.com, Maliboo Magic, and Imagine Nation.

PERLMAN, RHEA
Actress. b. Brooklyn, NY, March 31, 1948. e. Hunter Coll. m. actor-dir. Danny DeVito. Co-founder Colonnades Theatre Lab., NY and New Street prod. co with Danny DeVito.
PICTURES: Love Child, My Little Pony (voice), Enid is Sleeping (Over Her Dead Body), Ted & Venus, Class Act, There Goes the Neighborhood, Canadian Bacon, Sunset Park, Matilda, H-E Double Hockey Sticks.
TELEVISION: Series: Cheers (4 Emmy Awards: 1984, 1985, 1986, 1989), Pearl (co-exec. prod.), Kate Brasher. Movies: I Want to Keep My Baby!, Stalk the Wild Child, Having Babies II, Intimate Strangers, Mary Jane Harper Cried Last Night, Like Normal People, Drop-out Father, The Ratings Game, Dangerous Affection, A Family Again, To Grandmother's House We Go, A Place to Be Loved, Spoils of War, In the Doghouse, Houdini, The Frasier Story, A Tail of Two Bunnies, Secret Cutting, How to Marry a Billionaire: A Christmas Tale. Specials: Funny You Don't Look 200, Two Daddies (voice), The Last Halloween.

PERLMAN, RON
Actor. b. New York, NY, April 13, 1950. While in high school, part of comedy team that played clubs. e. City U. of NY, U. of Minnesota, M.F.A. Joined Classic Stage Company, NY, for 2 years.
THEATRE: NY: The Architect and the Emperor of Assyria (also toured Europe), American Heroes, The Resistible Rise of Arturo Ui, Tiebele and Her Demon, La Tragedie de Carmen, A Few Good Men.
PICTURES: Quest for Fire, The Ice Pirates, The Name of the Rose, Sleepwalkers, The Adventures of Huck Finn, Double Exposure, Romeo Is Bleeding, Crime and Punishment, Cronos, Fluke, The City of Lost Children, The Last Summer, The Island of Dr. Moreau, Prince Valiant, Alien Resurrection, Tinsletown, The Protector, Betty, Frogs for Snakes, I Woke Up Early the Day I Died, Happy,Texas, Price of Glory, Bread and Roses, Titan A.E. (voice), The King's Guard, The Trial of Old Drum, Crime and Punishment, Enemy at the Gates, Down, Quiet Kill, Rtas, Night Class, How to Go Out on a Date in Queens, Boys on the Run, Blade 2, G-S.P.O.T., Star Trek: Nemesis, Two Soldiers, Shakedown, Hoodlum & Son, Absolon, Hellboy.
TELEVISION: Series: Beauty and the Beast. Movies: A Stoning in Fulham County, Blind Man's Bluff, Original Sins, Mr.Stitch, The Adventures of Captain Zoom in Outer Space, The Second Civil War, A Town Has Turned to Dust, Houdini, Supreme Sanction, Primal Force, Operation Sandman.

PERLMUTTER, DAVID M.
Producer. b. Toronto, Canada, 1934. e. U. of Toronto. Pres., Quadrant Films Ltd.
PICTURES: The Neptune Factor, Vengeance In Sime, It Seemed Like a Good Idea at the Time, Find the Lady, Fast Company, Nothing Personal, Soft Deceit, Bloodknot, Undertow, Hostile Intent, Ms. Bear, Teenage Space Vampires, Teen Knight, The Excalibur Kid, Bone Daddy, Falling Through, Bear with Me, Zebra Lounge, Time of the Wold, Touching Wild Horses, Tempo.
TELEVISION: Model by Day, Nightworld: 30 Years to Life, Nightworld: Lost Souls, Valentine's Day, Survivor, The Cyberstalking, Stiletto Dance, Murder Amoung Friends, Recipe for Murder, Drive Time Murders, Cybermutt.

PERMUT, DAVID A.
Producer. b. New York, NY, March 23, 1954. In 1974, became pres., Diversified Artists Intl.; 1975, pres., Theatre Television Corp.; 1979, formed Permut Presentations, Inc., of which is pres. Production deals with Columbia Pictures (1979), Lorimar Productions (1981), Universal (1985), United Artists (1986), and New Line Cinema (1991).
PICTURES: Give 'Em Hell Harry, Fighting Back (exec. prod.), Blind Date, Richard Pryor—Live in Concert (exec. prod.), Dragnet, The Marrying Man, 29th Street, Captain Ron, Consenting Adults, The Temp, Three of Hearts, Surviving the Game, Trapped in Paradise, Eddie, Face/Off, Woodstuck, Double Take, Uncoupled, Route 52, Kings for a Day, DysFunktional Family.
TELEVISION: Mistress (sprv. prod.), Love Leads the Way (exec. prod.), Triumph of the Heart: The Ricky Bell Story (prod.), Breaking the Silence (prod.).

PERREAU, GIGI
Actress. r.n. Ghislaine Perreau. b. Los Angeles, CA, Feb. 6, 1941. e. Immaculate Heart H.S. & College. Many stage and TV guest appearances. Now teaching and directing. Among first 50 stars to be honored with star on Hollywood Walk of Fame.
PICTURES: Madame Currie (debut, 1943), Abigail, Dear Heart, Dark Waters, San Diego I Love You, Two Girls and a Sailor, The Master Race, The Seventh Cross, Mr. Skeffington, Yoland and the Thief, Voice of the Whistler, God Is My Co-Pilot, To Each His Own, Alias Mr. Twilight, High Barbaree, Song of Love, Green Dolphin Street, Family Honeymoon, Enchantment, Sainted Sisters, Roseanna McCoy, Song of Surrender, My Foolish Heart, Shadow on the Wall, For Heaven's Sake, Never a Dull Moment, Reunion in Reno, The Lady Pays Off, Weekend with Father, Has Anybody Seen My Gal, Bonzo Goes to College, There's Always Tomorrow, The Man in the Gray Flannel Suit, Dance With Me Henry, Wild Heritage, The Cool and the Crazy, Girls' Town, Tammy Tell Me True, Look in Any Window, Journey to the Center of Time, Hell on Wheels, The Sleepless.
TELEVISION: Series: The Betty Hutton Show, Follow the Sun. Guest: Alfred Hitchcock Presents, Perry Mason, The Rifleman, The Brady Bunch.

PERRINE, VALERIE
Actress. b. Galveston, TX, Sept. 3 1943. e. U. of Arizona. Was showgirl in Las Vegas before discovered by agent Robert Walker who got her contract with Universal Pictures.
PICTURES: Slaughterhouse 5 (debut, 1972), The Last American Hero, Lenny (NY Film Critics & Cannes Film Fest. Awards; Acad. Award nom.), W. C. Fields & Me, Mr. Billion, Superman, The Magician of Lublin, The Electric Horseman, Can't Stop the Music, Superman II, Agency, The Border, Water, Maid to Order, Reflections in a Dark Sky, Bright Angel, Boiling Point, Girl in the Cadillac, The Break, My Girlfriend's Boyfriend, Curtain Call, 54, Shame Shame Shame, A Place Called Truth, Brown's Requiem, Picture This, My Girlfriend's Boyfriend, What Women Want, Directing Eddie, My Angel Is a Centerfold.
TELEVISION: Movies: The Couple Takes a Wife, Ziegfeld: The Man and His Women, Marian Rose White, Malibu, When Your Lover Leaves, Sweet Bird of Youth, Un Casa a Roma, The Burning Shore. Series: Leo and Liz in Beverly Hills. Special: Steambath.

PERRY, LUKE
Actor. r.n. Coy Luther Perry III. b. Mansfield, OH, Oct. 11, 1966. To LA from NY as teen to become actor, landing role on daytime serial Loving.
PICTURES: Terminal Bliss (debut, 1992), Scorchers, Buffy the Vampire Slayer, At Home With the Webbers (cameo), 8 Seconds, From the Edge, Christmas Vacation, Normal Life, American Strays, Lifebreath, The Fifth Element, Last Breath, Indiscreet, The Florentine, The Heist, Attention Shoppers, The Enemy, Dirt, Luxury of Love, Fogbound.
TELEVISION: Movies: Riot, Storm, Indiscreet, The Last Buckaroo, The Night of the Headless Horseman, The Triangle. Series: Loving, Another World, Beverly Hills 90210, Jeremiah, Oz. Mini-Series: Johnson County War. Guest: The Simpsons (voice), Spin City, Night Visions, Johnny Bravo.

PERRY, MATTHEW
Actor. b. Williamstown, MA, Aug. 19, 1969.
PICTURES: A Night in the Life of Jimmy Reardon, She's Out of Control, Getting In, Fools Rush In, Almost Heroes, Three to Tango, Imagining Emily (s.p. only), The Whole Nine Yards, The Kid, Serving Sarah.
TELEVISION: *Movies:* Dance 'til Dawn, Call Me Anna, Deadly Relations, Parallel Lives. *Series:* Second Chance, Sydney, Home Free, Friends. *Guest:* Silver Spoons, The Tracey Ullman Show, Just the Ten of Us, Highway to Heaven, Growing Pains, Empty Nest, Who's the Boss, Beverly Hills 90210, Dream On, Caroline in the City, The West Wing (in recurring role). *Special:* Friends: The Stuff You've Never Seen.

PERRY, SIMON
Producer, Writer. b. Farnham, England, Aug. 5, 1943. e. Cambridge Univ., 1965. Ent. ind. 1974. Early career in stage and television production. Prod. mini-budget feature Knots; prod. dir. Eclipse. Served on bureau staff of Variety. Ran the National Film Development Fund for two years. 1982 set up Umbrella Films to produce Another Time Another Place, Loose Connections, Nineteen Eighty Four, Hotel Du Paradis, Nanou, White Mischief, The Playboys, Innocent Lies. Chief exec. of British Screen Finance since 1991.

PERSKY, LESTER
Executive. b. New York, NY, July 6, 1927. e. Brooklyn Coll. Officer in U.S. Merchant Marine, 1946-48. Founder and pres. of own adv. agency, 1951-1964. Theatrical stage prod., 1966-69. 1973, creative dir. and co-owner Persky Bright Org. (owner-financier of numerous motion pictures for private investment group). Films: Last Detail, Golden Voyage of Sinbad, For Pete's Sake, California Split, The Man Who Would Be King, The Front, Shampoo, Hard Times, Taxi Driver, Missouri Breaks, Funny Lady, Gator, Bound for Glory, Sinbad and the Eye of the Tiger. Lester Persky Productions, Inc.
PICTURES: *Producer:* Fortune and Men's Eyes, Equus, Hair, Yanks.
TELEVISION: *Mini-Series:* Poor Little Rich Girl (Golden Globe Award, 1987), A Woman Named Jackie (Emmy Award, 1992), Liz: The Elizabeth Taylor Story.
(d. Dec. 16, 2001)

PERSOFF, NEHEMIAH
Actor. b. Jerusalem, Israel, Aug. 2, 1919. e. Hebrew Technical Inst., 1934-37. Electrician, 1937-39; signal maint., N.Y. subway, 1939-41. Studied acting with Stella Adler and the Actors Studio. L.A. Critics Award 1971 for Sholem-Sholem Alecheim, and The Dybbuk. Has had exhibitions of his watercolor paintings in California, Florida; on permanent exhibit in Cambria, Ca.
THEATRE: Sundown Beach, Galileo, Richard III, King Lear, Peter Pan, Peer Gynt, Tiger At the Gates, Colombe, Flahooly, Montserrat, Only in America. Tour: Fiddler on the Roof, Man of La Mancha, Oliver, Death of a Salesman (Stratford, Ont.), Peter Pan, I'm Not Rappaport, Sholem Aleichem (Drama Log & Bay Area Critics Circle Awards).
PICTURES: On the Waterfront, The Wild Party, The Harder They Fall, The Wrong Man, Men in War, This Angry Age, The Badlanders, Never Steal Anything Small, Al Capone, Some Like It Hot, Green Mansions, The Big Show, The Comancheros, The Hook, A Global Affair, Fate Is the Hunter, The Greatest Story Ever Told, The Power, The Money Jungle, Panic in the City, Mafia, The People Next Door, Mrs. Pollifax—Spy, Red Sky at Morning, Psychic Killer, Voyage of the Damned, In Search of Historic Jesus, Yentl, An American Tail (voice), The Last Temptation of Christ, Twins, Day of the Outlaw, The Dispossessed, An American Tail: Fievel Goes West (voice), An American Tail III (voice).
TELEVISION: *Guest:* Playhouse 90, Philco-Goodyear Show, Kraft, For Whom the Bells Tolls (Sylvania Award, 1958), Producers Showcase, Danger, You Are There, Untouchables, Route 66, Naked City, Wagon Train, Rawhide, Gunsmoke, Thriller, Hitchcock, Bus Stop, Mission Impossible, Henderson Monster, Rebels, Twilight Zone, Five Fingers, Mr. Lucky, The Wild Wild West, I Spy, Hawaii 5-0, Columbo, Barney Miller, L.A. Law, Star Trek, Law and Order, Reasonable Doubts. *Movies:* Sadat, Adderly, The French Atlantic Affair, Sex Symbol, Stranger Within.

PESCI, JOE
Actor. b. Newark, NJ, Feb. 9, 1943. Raised in Belleville, NJ. First show business job as child on TV's Star Time Kids. Worked as mason's laborer, restaurant owner, prior to becoming actor.
PICTURES: Death Collector, Raging Bull, I'm Dancing as Fast as I Can, Dear Mr. Wonderful (Ruby's Dream), Easy Money, Eureka, Once Upon a Time in America, Man on Fire, Moonwalker, Lethal Weapon 2, Betsy's Wedding, Goodfellas (Acad. Award, best supporting actor, 1990), Home Alone, The Super, JFK, My Cousin Vinny, Lethal Weapon 3, The Public Eye, Home Alone 2: Lost in New York, A Bronx Tale, Jimmy Hollywood, With Honors, Casino, 8 Heads in a Duffel Bag, Gone Fishing, Lethal Weapon 4, A Galaxy Far Far Away.
TELEVISION: *Series:* Half Nelson. *Movies:* Half Nelson (pilot), Backtrack. *Guest:* Tales From the Crypt (Split Personality).

PETERS, BERNADETTE
Actress. r.n. Bernadette Lazzara. b. New York, NY, Feb. 28, 1948. e. Quintano Sch. for Young Professionals, NY. Professional debut at age 5 on TV's Horn & Hardart Children's Hour, followed by Juvenile Jury and Name That Tune. Stage debut with N.Y. City Center production of The Most Happy Fella (1959).
THEATRE: Gypsy (1961), This is Goggle, Riverwind, The Penny Friend, Curley McDimple, Johnny No-Trump, George M! (Theatre World Award), Dames at Sea (Drama Desk Award), La Strada, W.C. & Me, On the Town (1971 revival), Tartuffe, Mack and Mabel, Sally and Marsha, Sunday in the Park With George, Song and Dance (Tony, Drama Desk & Drama League Awards), Into the Woods, The Goodbye Girl.
PICTURES: Ace Eli and Rodger of the Skies (debut, 1973), The Longest Yard, W.C. Fields & Me, Vigilante Force, Silent Movie, The Jerk, Tulips, Pennies from Heaven, Heartbeeps, Annie, Slaves of New York, Pink Cadillac, Alice, Impromptu, Anastasia (voice), Hey Mr. Producer, Snow Days, Wako's Wish, A Few Good Years, It Runs in the Family.
TELEVISION: *Series:* All's Fair, The Closer. *Mini-Series:* The Martian Chronicles. *Specials:* George M, They Said It with Music, Party at Annapolis, Rich Thin and Beautiful (host), Faerie Tale Theatre, The Last Mile. *Pilot:* The Owl and the Pussycat. *Movies:* The Islander, David, Fall from Grace, The Last Best Year, Into the Woods, The Odyssey, Cinderella, What the Deaf Man Heard, Holiday in Your Heart, Prince Charming, Bobbie's Girl. *Guest:* The Larry Sanders Show, Frasier, Ally McBeal, others.

PETERS, BROCK
Actor. r.n. Brock Fisher. b. Harlem, NY, July 2, 1927. e. CCNY, U. of Chicago. Had numerous featured roles on and off B'way. in road and stock cos., nightclubs, TV. Toured with DePaur Infantry Chorus as bass soloist, 1947-50.
THEATRE: Porgy and Bess (debut, 1943), Anna Lucasta, My Darlin' Aida, Mister Johnson, King of the Dark Chamber, Othello, Kwamina, The Great White Hope (tour), Lost in the Stars, Driving Miss Daisy (Natl. Co.).
PICTURES: Carmen Jones (debut, 1954), Porgy and Bess, To Kill a Mockingbird, Heavens Above, The L-Shaped Room, The Pawnbroker, Major Dundee, The Incident, P.J., The Daring Game, Ace High, The MacMasters, Black Girl, Soylent Green, Slaughter's Big Rip-off, Lost in the Stars, Million Dollar Dixie Deliverance, Framed, Two-Minute Warning, Star Trek IV: The Voyage Home, Star Trek VI: The Undiscovered Country, Alligator II: The Mutation, The Importance of Being Earnest, Ghosts of Mississippi, Two Weeks From Sunday, Park Day, The Last Place on Earth, No Prom For Cindy, The Wild Thornberrys Movie.
TELEVISION: Arthur Godfrey's Talent Scouts (debut, 1953). *Series:* The Young and the Restless. *Guest:* Eleventh Hour, It Takes a Thief, Mannix, Mod Squad, Swat Kats: The Radical Squadron (voice). *Mini-series:* Seventh Avenue, Black Beauty, Roots: The Next Generations, Le Baron. *Movies:* Welcome Home Johnny Bristol, SST: Death Flight, The Incredible Journey of Doctor Meg Laurel, The Adventures of Huckleberry Finn, Agatha Christie's Caribbean Mystery, To Heal a Nation, Broken Angel, The Big One: The Great Los Angeles Earthquake, Highway Heartbreakers, The Secret, You Must Remember This, Cosmic Slop, An Element of Truth, 10,000 Black Men Named George, The Locket. *Specials:* Challenge of the Go Bots (voice), Living the Dream: A Tribute to Dr. Martin Luther King. *Co-prod.:* This Far By Faith.

PETERS, JANICE C.
Executive. e. Wayne State U., BS, and Stanford U., masters in mgmt. Began in local/long distance telecom. field. Became pres., CEO, U S WEST NewVector Group, a cellular comm. co., and pres. of wireless ops., U S WEST MediaOne before becoming managing dir. of One 2 One, a cellular comm. co. in the UK in 1996. Currently pres. and CEO of MediaOne, broadband svcs. under MediaOne Group.

PETERS, JON
Producer. b. Van Nuys, CA, 1947. Started hair-styling business; built it into multimillion-dollar firm before turning film producer. Formed Jon Peters Organization. 1980, joined with Peter Guber and Neil Bogart to form The Boardwalk Co. (dissolved 1981). Later Guber-Peters-Barris Company. 1989, became co-chairman of Columbia Pictures. Resigned, 1991.
PICTURES: A Star Is Born, Eyes of Laura Mars, The Main Event, Die Laughing, Caddyshack. *Co-Prod./Co-Exec. Prod. with Peter Guber:* An American Werewolf in London, Missing, Six Weeks, Flashdance, D.C. Cab, Vision Quest, Legend of Billie Jean, Clue, The Color Purple, Head Office, The Clan of the Cave Bear, Youngblood, The Witches of Eastwick, Innerspace, Who's That Girl, Gorillas in the Mist, Caddyshack II, Rain Man, Batman, Tango and Cash, The Bonfire of the Vanities, Batman Returns, This Boy's Life, With Honors, Money Train. *Also: Prod.:* My Fellow Americans (prod.), Rosewood, Wild Wild West, Ali.
TELEVISION: *Movies:* Bay Coven (co-exec. prod.), Nightmare at Bitter Creek (exec. prod.).

PETERSEN, PAUL
Actor. b. Glendale, CA, Sept. 23, 1945. e. Valley Coll. Original Disney Mouseketeer (TV). Recorded hit songs She Can't Find Her Keys, and My Dad in 1962. In the late 1960's turned to writing beginning with a Marcus Welby script followed by paperback novels in 1970's. Author of book about Disney empire, Walt Mickey and Me (1977), and co-author of It's a Wonderful Life Trivia Book (1992). President and founder of A Minor Consideration, a support foundation for former kid actors with a current membership of 150 movie, tv and sports stars spanning the past 70 years.
PICTURES: Houseboat, This Could Be the Night, The Happiest Millionaire, Journey to Shiloh, A Time for Killing.
TELEVISION: Series: The Donna Reed Show. Guest: Playhouse 90, Lux Video Theatre, GE Theatre, The Virginian, Ford Theatre, Valentine's Day, Shindig. Movies: Something for a Lonely Man, Gidget Grows Up, Scout's Honor. Special: Child Stars: Their Story.

PETERSEN, WILLIAM
Actor. b. Chicago, IL, Feb. 21, 1953. e. Idaho State U. Active in Chicago theatre; helped to found Ix, an ensemble acting group now called the Remains Theatre. Acted in Moby Dick, In the Belly of the Beast, A Streetcar Named Desire, etc. 1986, formed company with prod. Cynthia Chvatal called High Horse Prods.
THEATRE: NY: Night of the Iguana.
PICTURES: To Live and Die in L.A., Manhunter, Amazing Grace and Chuck, Cousins, Young Guns II, Hard Promises (also co-prod.), In the Kingdom of the Blind the Man with One Eye Is King, Passed Away, Fear, Mulholland Falls, The Beast, Gunshy, Kiss the Sky, The Skulls, The Contender.
TELEVISION: Movies: Long Gone (HBO), Keep the Change (also co-prod.), Curacao, Present Tense Past Perfect, 12 Angry Men, The Staircase, The Rat Pack, Haven. Mini-Series: The Kennedys of Massachusetts, Return to Lonesome Dove, The Beast. Series: C.S.I.: Crime Scene Investigation.

PETERSEN, WOLFGANG
Director, Writer. b. Emden, Germany, March 14, 1941. Career as asst. stage dir. at Ernst Deutsch Theatre in Hamburg before entering 4 year program at the German Film & TV Academy wher he directed for television and later theatrical films.
PICTURES: One of Us Two, Black and White Like Day and Night (also s.p.), The Consequence (also s.p.), Das Boot (The Boat; also s.p.; Acad. Award nom. for dir.), The Neverending Story (also s.p.), Enemy Mine, Shattered (also s.p., co-prod.), In the Line of Fire (also co-exec.prod.), Outbreak (also co-prod.), Air Force One (also prod.), The Perfect Storm (also prod.).
TELEVISION: I Will Kill You Wolf (dir. debut 1970), Tatort (series), Smog (Prix Futura Award, 1975), For Your Love Only (also released theatrically), Scene of the Crime (series), The Agency (prod. only).

PETERSON, S. DEAN
Executive. b. Toronto, Canada, December 18, 1923. e. Victoria Coll., U. of Toronto. WWII service RCNVR; 1946 TV newsreel cameraman NBC; founded own prod. co. in 1947; incorporated Dordean Realty Limited to acquire new studios 1959; formed Peterson Productions Limited in 1957 to make TV commercials and sponsored theatrical shorts; formed Studio City Limited in 1965 to produce TV series and features acquiring an additional studio complex and backlot in Kleinberg, Ontario; 1972 formed SDP Communications Ltd. to package M.P. and TV; 1970 incorporated Intermedia Financial Services Limited to provide specialized financing and consultation to companies in M.P. and TV industries. Past-President Canadian Film and Television Production Assn., mbr. Variety Club, Tent 28; Canadian Society of Cinematographers; Directors Guild of America, Directors Guild of Canada, SMPTE.

PETERSON, RICHARD W.
Executive. b. Denver, CO, June 15, 1949. e. Col. Sch. of Broadcasting, Harper Coll. Joined Kennedy Theatres, Chicago, 1966. 1968 went with Great States Theatres (now Cineplex Odeon), Chicago. Was city mgr. of Crocker and Grove Theatres, Elgin, IL. 1973 joined American Automated Theatres, Oklahoma City, as dir. of adv., pub. Promoted to dir. of U.S. theatre operations. Worked for American International Pictures, Dallas, TX. Then moved to Dal Art Film Exchange and B & B Theatres as general mgr.; 1987 took over 7 screens from McLendon and formed own co., Peterson Theatres, Inc.

PETIT, HENRI-DOMINIQUE
Executive. b. Baden-Baden, Germany. e. Ecole Superieure de Physique et Chimie de Paris, Univ. of Paris. Joined Kodak 1975 as asst. mgr. of the Purchasing Division, Kodak Pathe, France. 1980, asst., then mgr. of Kodak Pathe Photofinishing Lab (1981). 1984, became bus. mgr. Business Information Systems and Corporate Accounts, Kodak Pathe. 1987, named bus. mgr. of Photofinishing Systems Division. 1989, appointed gen. mgr. and v.p. Motion Picture and Television Imaging, Europe/ Africa/Middle East Region. Dec., 1992, named v.p. and gen. mgr. Motion Picture and Television Imaging.

PETRIE, DANIEL
Director. b. Glace Bay, Nova Scotia, Nov. 26, 1920. e. St. Francis Xavier U., Nova Scotia; Columbia U., MA, 1945; postgrad. Northwestern U. Broadway actor 1945-46. TV dir. from 1950. Son Daniel Petrie Jr. is a screenwriter; son Donald Petrie is a dir.
THEATRE: Shadow of My Enemy, Who'll Save the Plowboy?, Mornin' Sun, Monopoly, The Cherry Orchard, Volpone, A Lesson from Aloes.
PICTURES: The Bramble Bush (debut, 1960), A Raisin in the Sun, The Main Attraction, Stolen Hours, The Idol, The Spy With a Cold Nose, The Neptune Factor, Buster and Billie, Lifeguard, The Betsy, Resurrection, Fort Apache The Bronx, Six Pack, The Bay Boy (also s.p.; Genie Award), Square Dance (also prod.), Rocket Gibraltar, Cocoon: The Return, Lassie, The Associate.
TELEVISION: Movies: Silent Night Lonely Night, A Howling in the Woods, A Stranger in Town, Moon of the Wolf, Trouble Comes to Town, Mousey, Returning Home, Eleanor and Franklin (Emmy Award, 1976), Sybil, Eleanor and Franklin: The White House Years (Emmy Award, 1977), Harry Truman, Plain Speaking (Emmy nom.), The Dollmaker (Emmy nom.), The Execution of Raymond Graham (Emmy nom.), Half a Lifetime, My Name is Bill W. (also prod.; Emmy nom.), Mark Twain and Me (also prod., Emmy Award), A Town Torn Apart (also prod., Emmy nom.), Kissinger and Nixon, Calm at Sunset, Monday After the Miracle, Inherit the Wind (DGA nom.), Walter and Henry (DGA nom.), Wild Iris, DC 9/11: Time of Crisis. Mini-Series: Seasons of Love.

PETRIE, DONALD
Director. b. New York, NY. Son of dir. Daniel Petrie. Moved to LA as teenager, becoming tv actor. Attended American Film Inst. dir. program, where he made short film The Expert. Was then hired to dir. Mister Magic esisode of Amazing Stories.
PICTURES: Mystic Pizza (debut, 1988), Opportunity Knocks, Grumpy Old Men, The Favor, Richie Rich, The Associate, My Favorite Martian, Miss Congeniality, How to Lose a Guy in 10 Days.
TELEVISION: DC 9/11: Time of Crisis. Series episodes: MacGyver, The Equalizer, L.A. Law, Players, Opposite Sex. Special: Have You Tried Talking to Patty?

PETROU, DAVID MICHAEL
Writer, Producer, Public Relations Executive. b. Washington, DC, Nov. 3, 1949. e. U. of Maryland, B.A.; Georgetown U., M.A. Publicity assoc., Psychiatric Institutes of America, Washington, DC, 1971; assoc. dir. of publicity & film liaison, Random House, 1974; guest lecturer, screen writing & film production, The American University Consortium, Washington, DC, spring, 1980; Woodrow Wilson Fellowship, 1971. Entered industry in 1975. Joined Salkind Organization in chg. of literary projects. Worked in numerous production capacities on Crossed Swords, Superman, Superman II. 1977, exec. in chg. of literary development, Salkind. Wrote Crossed Swords (1978) and The Making of Superman. Co-authored screenplay, Shoot to Kill. 1978-79, promotional dev. on Time after Time for Warner Bros.; 1980-83, dir., special projects Joseph Kennedy Foundation. 1983-84, sr. edit. for entertainment, Regardie's Magazine; 1984-86, sr. exec., p.r. div., Abramson Associates; 1986-88, sr. v.p., Eisner, Held & Petrou, Inc., p.r. agency; 1988-present, pres. & COO, Eisner Petrou & Associates Inc. Baltimore-Wash., marketing communications agency. 1992, named chmn. of American Film Institute's Second Decade Council. Bd. Member: Choral Arts Society of Washington, University of Maryland Center for the Performing Arts, Foundation for Contemporary Mental Health, Washington Men's Camerata.

PETTET, JOANNA
Actress. b. London, England, Nov. 16, 1944. Raised in Canada. Studied acting at Neighborhood Playhouse in NY.
PICTURES: The Group (debut, 1966), The Night of the Generals, Casino Royale, Robbery, Blue, The Best House in London, Welcome to Arrow Beach, The Evil, An Eye for an Eye, Double Exposure, Sweet Country, Terror in Paradise.
TELEVISION: Series: Knots Landing. Mini-Series: Captains and the Kings. Movies: Footsteps, The Delphi Bureau, The Weekend Nun, Pioneer Woman, A Cry in the Wilderness, The Desperate Miles, The Hancocks, The Dark Side of Innocence, Sex and the Married Woman, Cry of the Innocent, The Return of Frank Cannon.

PETTY, LORI
Actress. b. Chattanooga, TN, March 23, 1964. Worked as graphic artist before turning to acting.
PICTURES: Cadillac Man, Point Break, A League of Their Own, Free Willy, Poetic Justice, In the Army Now,The Johnny Johnson Trial, Tank Girl, The Glass Shield, Relax...It's Just Sex, Clubland, MacArthur Park, Horrible Accident, Firetrap, Route 666.
TELEVISION: Series: The Thorns, Booker, Lush Life, Brimstone. Guest: The Equalizer, The Twilight Zone, Stingray, Miami Vice, Freddy's Nightmares, Booker, Alien Nation, The New Batman/ Superman Adventures (voice), Profiler, Superman (voice), Batman: Gotham Knights (voice), Star Trek: Voyager, The Beast.

PFEIFFER, MICHELLE
Actress. b. Santa Ana, CA, April 29, 1957. Sister of actress Deedee Pfeiffer. m. David E. Kelley. While attending jr. coll. and working as supermarket checkout clerk, won Miss Orange County beauty contest. Began taking acting classes in L.A. Stage debut in L.A. prod. of A Playground in the Fall. NY Theatre debut 1989 in Twelfth Night (Central Park).
PICTURES: The Hollywood Nights (debut, 1980), Falling in Love Again, Charlie Chan and the Curse of the Dragon Queen, Grease 2, Scarface, Into the Night, Ladyhawke, Sweet Liberty, The Witches of Eastwick, Amazon Women on the Moon, Married to the Mob, Tequila Sunrise, Dangerous Liaisons (Acad. Award nom.), The Fabulous Baker Boys (NY, LA & & Natl. Society of Film Critics Awards; Acad. Award nom.), The Russia House, Frankie and Johnny, Batman Returns, Love Field (Acad. Award nom.), The Age of Innocence, Wolf, Dangerous Minds, Up Close and Personal, To Gillian On Her 37th Birthday, One Fine Day (also exec. prod.), A Thousand Acres, A Midsummer Night's Dream, The Deep End of the Ocean (also prod.), Prince of Egypt (voice), The Story of Us, What Lies Beneath, I Am Sam, White Oleander, Sinbad: Legend of the Seven Seas (voice).
TELEVISION: Series: Delta House, B.A.D. Cats. Movies: The Solitary Man, Callie and Son, Splendor in the Grass, The Children Nobody Wanted. Specials: One Too Many, Tales from the Hollywood Hills (Natica Jackson). Guest: Fantasy Island, The Simpsons (voice).

PHILLIPPE, RYAN
Actor. r.n. Matthew Ryan Phillippe. b. New Castle, DE, Sept. 10, 1974. m. actress Reese Witherspoon.
PICTURES: Crimson Tide, Invader, White Squall, Nowhere, I Know What You Did Last Summer, Playing by Heart, Homegrown, Little Boy Blue, 54, Cruel Intentions, The Way of the Gun, Anti-Trust, Company Man, Gosford Park, Igby Goes Down, Light in the Sky, The Honest Thief.
TELEVISION: Movies/Specials: The Secrets of Lake Success, Deadly Invasion: The Killer Bee Nightmare. Series: One Life to Live. Guest: Matlock, Due South, Chicago Hope, The Outer Limits, King of the Hill (voice).

PHILLIPS, LESLIE
Actor, Producer. b. London, England, April 20, 1924. Early career as child actor. Ent. m.p. ind. 1935.
PICTURES: A Lassie From Lancashire (debut, 1935), The Citadel, Rhythm Serenade, Train of Events, The Woman With No Name, Pool of London, The Galloping Major, Breaking the Sound Barrier, The Fake, The Limping Man, Time Bomb, The Price of Greed, Value for Money, The Gamma People, As Long as They're Happy, The Big Money, Brothers in Law, The Barretts of Wimpole Street, Just My Luck, Les Girls, The Smallest Show on Earth, High Flight, I Was Monte's Double, The Man Who Liked Funerals, The Angry Hills, Carry on Nurse, Ferdinand of Naples, This Other Eden, Carry on Teacher, Please Turn Over, The Navy Lark, Doctor in Love, Watch Your Stern, No Kidding, Carry on Constable, Inn for Trouble, Raising the Wind, In the Doghouse, Very Important Persons, Crooks Anonymous, The Longest Day, The Fast Lady, Father Came Too, Doctor in Clover, You Must Be Joking, Maroc 7, Some Will Some Won't, Doctor in Trouble, The Magnificent 7 Deadly Sins, Not Now Darling, Don't Just Lie There Say Something!, Spanish Fly, Not Now Comrade, Out of Africa, Empire of the Sun, Scandal, Mountains of the Moon, King Ralph, Carry on Columbus, August, Caught In The Act, The Jackal, Saving Grace, Lara Croft: Tomb Raider, Harry Potter and the Sorcerer's Stone (voice),Harry Potter and the Chamber of Secrets (voice), Thunderpants.
TELEVISION: Our Man at St. Marks, Impasse, The Gong Game, Time and Motion Man, Reluctant Debutante, A Very Fine Line, The Suit, The Culture Vultures (series), Edward Woodward Show, Casanova 74 (series), Redundant—or the Wife's Revenge, You'll Never See Me Again, Mr. Palfrey of Westminister, Monte Carlo, Rumpole, Summers Lease, Chancer, Comic Strip, Who Bombed Birmingham, Life After Life, Thacker, Chancer II, The Oz Trial, Lovejoy, Boon, The Changeling, Bermuda Grace, Royal Celebration, Honey for Tea, House of Windsor, Two Golden Balls, Love on a Branch Line, Vanity Dies Hard, Edgar Wallace (Germany), Canterville Ghost, Woof, The Bill, The Pale Horse, Cinderella, Dalziel and Pascoe: Recalled to Life, Take a Girl Like You, Sword of Honour, Outside the Rules.

PHILLIPS, LOU DIAMOND
Actor. r.n. Lou Upchurch. b. Philippines, Feb. 17, 1962. Raised in Corpus Christi, TX. e. U. of Texas, Arlington (BFA. drama). Studied film technique with Adam Roarke, becoming asst. dir./instructor with the Film Actor's Lab, 1983-86. Regional theater includes: A Hatful of Rain, Whose Life Is It Anyway?, P.S. Your Cat Is Dead, The Lady's Not for Burning, Doctor Faustus, Hamlet.
THEATRE: NY: The King and I (Bdwy. debut, Tony nom.)
PICTURES: Angel Alley, Interface, Trespasses (also co-s.p.), Harley, La Bamba, Stand and Deliver, Young Guns, Dakota (also assoc. prod.), Disorganized Crime, Renegades, The First Power, A Show of Force, Young Guns II, Ambition (also s.p.), The Dark Wind, Shadow of the Wolf, Dangerous Touch (also dir.), Teresa's Tattoo, Sioux City (also dir.), Undertow, Boulevard, Courage Under Fire, Another Day in Paradise (cameo), The Big Hit,

Picking Up the Pieces, Brokedown Palace, Bats, Supernova, Picking Up the Pieces, A Better Wya to Die, Route 666, Knight Club, Lone Hero, Stark Raving Mad, Naked Movie, Malevolent, Hollywood Homicide.
TELEVISION: Movies: Time Bomb, The Three Kings, Extreme Justice, The Wharf Rat, In a Class of His Own, Hangman. Specials: Avenue Z Afternoon, Wind in the Wire. Guest: Dallas, Miami Vice. Series: Wolf Lake, 24.

PHILLIPS, MICHAEL
Producer. b. Brooklyn, NY, June 29, 1943. e. Dartmouth Coll., B.A., 1965. NYU, Law Sch. J.D., 1968. Indep. m.p. prod. 1971.
PICTURES: Steelyard Blues, The Sting (Acad. Award for Best Picture, 1973), Taxi Driver (Golden Palm Award at Cannes), The Big Bus, Close Encounters of the Third Kind, Heartbeeps, Cannery Row, The Flamingo Kid, Don't Tell Mom the Babysitter's Dead, Mom and Dad Save the World, Eyes of an Angel, The Companion, Mimic (exec.), Imposter (exec.).
TELEVISION: Movie: Jane's House, The Companion.

PHILLIPS, MICHELLE
Actress. r.n. Holly Michelle Gilliam. b. Long Beach, CA, June 4, 1944. Daughter is actress-singer Chynna Phillips. Former member of The Mamas and the Papas. Co-wrote hit single California Dreamin'. Author: California Dreamin': The Story of The Mamas and The Papas (1986).
PICTURES: Monterey Pop, The Last Movie, Dillinger, Valentino, Sidney Sheldon's Bloodline, The Man With Bogart's Face, Savage Harvest, American Anthem, Let It Ride, Scissors, Army of One, Keep on Running, Lost in the Pershing Point Hotel, Price of Air, Jane White is Sick and Twisted, March.
TELEVISION: Series: Hotel, Knots Landing, Second Chances. Mini-Series: Aspen, The French Atlantic Affair. Movies: The Death Squad, The California Kid, The Users, Moonlight, Mickey Spillane's Mike Hammer: Murder Me Murder You, Secrets of a Married Man, Stark: Mirror Image, Assault and Matrimony, Trenchcoat in Paradise, Rubdown, Paint Me a Murder, Covenant, 919 Fifth Avenue, No One Would Tell, Pretty Poison, Sweetwater. Guest: Owen Marshall, Matt Houston, The Fall Guy, Murder She Wrote, T.J. Hooker, Hotel, Fantasy Island, Love Boat, Burke's Law, Robin's Hood, Lois & Clark, Herman's Head.

PHILLIPS, SIAN
Actress. b. Bettws, Wales, May 14,1934. e. Univ. of Wales. Studied acting at RADA. London stage debut 1957 in title role in Hedda. Has made numerous recordings including Pal Joey, Gigi, A Little Night Music, Remember Mama.
THEATRE: Saint Joan, The Three Sisters, Taming of the Shrew, Duchess of Malfi, Lizard on the Rock, Gentle Jack, The Night of the Iguana, Ride a Cock Horse, Man and Superman, The Burglar, The Cardinal of Spain, Alpha Beta, Spinechiller, A Woman of No Importance, You Never Can Tell, Dear Liar, Pal Joey (SWET nom.), Major Barbara, Gigi, Paris Match, Painting Churches, Vanilla, Ghosts (Artist of the Year nom.), Marlene, A Little Night Music (Olivier nom.), Snow Spider, many others. B'way debut 1994 in An Inspector Calls.
PICTURES: Becket, Young Cassidy, Laughter in the Dark, Goodbye Mr. Chips (NY Film Critics & Critics Circle Awards, 1969), Murphy's War, Under Milk Wood, Clash of the Titans, Dune, The Doctor and the Devils, Valmont, The Age of Innocence, A Painful Case, House of America.
TELEVISION: Mini-Series: Shoulder to Shoulder, How Green Was My Valley (BAFTA Award), I Claudius (BAFTA & Royal TV Society Awards), Crime and Punishment, Tinker Tailor Soldier Spy, Vanity Fair, Red Empire, Aristocrats, Ivanhoe, Attila. Movies: Ewoks: The Battle for Endor–Dark River, The Two Mrs. Grenvilles, Out of Time, Dark River, The Black Candle, Heidi, The Borrowers, The Return of the Borrowers, The Vacillations of Poppy Carew, The Scold's Bridle, Alice Through the Looking Glass, The Magician's House, Cinderella, The Magician's House II, Come and Go. Specials: Off to Philadelphia in the Morning, Sean O'Casey, How Many Miles to Babylon?, Lady Windermere's Fan, Language and Landscape, Heartbreak House, Don Juan in Hell, Summer Silence, Shadow of the Noose, Snow Spider, The Quiet Man, The Sex Game, A Mind To Kill, Ivanhoe, Chestnut Soldier (BAFTA nom.).

PHOENIX, JOAQUIN
Actor. b.San Juan, Puerto Rico, Oct. 28, 1974. Brother of late River Phoenix.
PICTURES: SpaceCamp, Russkies, Parenthood, To Die For, Inventing the Abbotts, U Turn, Clay Pigeons, 8 MM, The Yards, Gladiator (Acad. Award nom.), Quills, Buffalo Soldiers, Signs, It's All About Love, Ladder 49, Brother Bear (voice), Voltage, Aurora Island.
TELEVISION: Movie: Secret Witness. Series: Morningstar/Eveningstar. Guest: Seven Brides for Seven Brothers, The Fall Guy, Murder She Wrote, Superboy.

PIALAT, MAURICE
Director, Writer. b. Cunlhat, Puy de Dome, France, Aug. 21, 1925. Worked as a painter and sometime actor before turning to film in 1952. Made a number of short films including L'Amour Existe (award winner Venice Film Fest., 1960). Worked in television before feature debut in 1967.

PICTURES: *Dir./Writer*: L'Enfance Nue (Naked Childhood; Prix Jean Vigo Award), We Will Not Grow Old Together, La Gueule Ouverte (also prod.), Passe ton Bac d'Abord (Graduate First), Loulou, A Nos Amours (also actor; Prix Louis Delluc Award), Police, Under Satan's Sun (also actor; Golden Palm Award, Cannes Festival), Van Gogh, Le Garcu, Bastard Brood (actor only), Les Auto-Stoppeuses.
TELEVISION: Janine, Maitre Galip, La Maison des Bois.
(d. Jan. 11, 2003)

PICARDO, ROBERT
Actor. b. Philadelphia, PA, Oct. 27, 1953. e. Yale. Studied acting at Circle in the Square Theater School.
THEATRE: *NY*: Sexual Perversity in Chicago, Gemini, Tribute.
PICTURES: The Howling, Star 80, Oh God You Devil, Explorers, Legend, Back to School, Munchies, Innerspace, Amazon Women on the Moon, Jack's Back, Dead Heat, The 'burbs, 976-EVIL, Loverboy, Total Recall, Gremlins II, Samantha, Motorama, Matinee, Wagons East!, The Pagemaster (voice), Menno's Mind, Star Trek: First Contact, Small Soldiers, Archibald the Rainbow Painter, Until Morning, Looney Tunes: Back in Action.
TELEVISION: *Series*: China Beach, The Wonder Years, Star Trek: Voyager. *Movies*: The Dream Merchants, The Violation of Sarah McDavid, Lois Gibbs and the Love Canal, Dixie: Habits, The Other Woman, Runaway Daughters, White Mile, Out There, Out There, The Second Civil War, Pfish and Chip, The Amati Girls.

PICCOLI, MICHEL
Actor. r.n. Jacques Piccoli. b. Paris, France, Dec. 27, 1925. Since his film debut in The Sorcerer in 1945 has had impressive career on the French stage and in films working for major French dirs. Renoir, Bunuel, Melville, Resnais, Clouzot, Godard as well as Hitchcock. Until 1957 was mgr. of Theatre Babylone in Paris. Formed prod. co. Films 66. Produced: Themroc (1972); La Faille; Les Enfants Gates.
PICTURES: The Sorcerer, Le Point du Jour, French Can Can, The Witches of Salem, Le Bal des Espiona, Gina, Le Doulos, Contempt, Diary of a Chambermaid, Lady L, La Guerre Est Finie, The Young Girls of Rochefort, Un Homme de Trop, Belle de Jour, La Chamade, Dillinger Is Dead, L'Invasion, The Milky Way, Topaz, The Things of Life, Ten Days' Wonder, The Discreet Charm of the Bourgeoisie, Themroc, Wedding in Blood, La Grande Bouffe, The Last Woman, Leonor, 7 Deaths by Prescription, The Weak Spot, F For Fairbanks, Mado, Todo Modo, Rene the Cane, Spoiled Children, Strauberg Is Here, The Fire's Share, Little Girl in Blue Velvet, The Savage State, The Sugar, The Bit Between the Teeth, La Divorcement, Leap into the Void, The Price for Survival, Atlantic City, The Prodigal Daughter, Beyond the Door, The Eyes The Mouth, Passion, A Room in Town, Will the High Salaried Workers Please Raise Their Hands!!!, The General of the Dead Army, La Passante, The Prize of Peril, Adieu Bonaparte, Dangerous Moves, Danger in the House, Long Live Life!, Success Is the Best Revenge, The Sailor 512, Departure, Return, Mon Beau-Frere a Tue Ma Soeur, The Nonentity, The Prude, Bad Blood, Undiscovered Country, Blanc de Chine, Le Peuple Singe (narrator), The French Revolution, May Fools, La Belle Noiseuse, The Children Thief, Archipelago, Punctured Life, Martha and I, others.

PICERNI, PAUL
Actor. b. New York, NY, Dec. 1, 1922. e. Loyola U., Los Angeles. U.S. Air Force 1943-46; head of drama dept. Mt. St. Mary's Coll., 1949-50.
PICTURES: Saddle Tramp, Breakthrough, Operation Pacific, The Tanks Are Coming, Force of Arms, I Was a Communist for the FBI, Mara Maru, Operation Secret, The Desert Song, She's Back on Broadway, House of Wax, The System, Shanghai Story, To Hell and Back, Bobby Ware Is Missing, Miracle in the Rain, Omar Khayyam, The Brothers Rico, Marjorie Morningstar, The Young Philadelphians, Strangers When We Meet, The Young Marrieds, The Scarface Mob, The Scalphunters, Che!, Airport, Kotch, Beyond the Poseidon Adventure, Capricorn One.
TELEVISION: *Series*: The Untouchables. *Movies*: The Old Man Who Cried Wolf, Something for Joey,The Last Hurrah, Alcatraz: The Whole Shocking Story. *Guest*: Philco Playhouse, Climax, Lux, Loretta Young Show, Desilu, Kojak, Mannix, Police Story, Lucy Special, Quincy, Alice, Trapper John M.D., Vegas, Fall Guy, Capitol, Hardcastle and McCormick, Matt Houston, Simon and Simon.

PICKER, DAVID V.
Executive. b. New York, NY, May 14, 1931. e. Dartmouth Coll., B.A., 1953. Father Eugene Picker, exec. Loew's Theatres. Ent. industry in 1956 as adv. pub. & exploitation liaison with sls. dept., United Artists Corp.; exec. v.p. U.A. Records; asst. to Max Youngstein, v.p.; v.p. U.A.; first v.p. UA; pres. 1969. Resigned 1973 to form own production co. 1976 joined Paramount Pictures as pres. of m.p. div.; v.p., Lorimar Productions; independent; 1987, pres. & COO, Columbia Pictures. Resigned.
PICTURES: Juggernaut, Lenny, Smile, Royal Flash, Won Ton Ton the Dog Who Saved Hollywood, The One and Only, Oliver's Story, Bloodline (prod.), The Jerk (prod.), Dead Men Don't Wear Plaid (prod.), The Man with Two Brains, Beat Street (prod.), The Appointments of Dennis Jennings (short, prod.), Stella (exec

prod.), Traces of Red, Leap of Faith, Matinee, The Saint of Fort Washington, The Crucible, Back to the Secret Garden.
TELEVISION: *Mini-Series*: The Temptations, P.T. Barnum, In the Beginning, Fidel. *Movies*: Rear Window, Journey to the Center of the Earth, Aftershock: Earthquake in New York, David Copperfield, Hans Christian Andersen.

PICKMAN, JEROME
Executive. b. New York, NY, Aug. 24, 1916. e. St. John's U.; Brooklyn Law Sch. of St. Lawrence U., LL.B. Reporter N.Y. newspapers; U.S. Army World War II; Ad-pub exec. 20th-Fox, 1945-46; v.p., dir., adv. & pub., later v.p. domestic gen. sls. mgr., Paramount Pictures; sr. sls. exec. Columbia Pictures; pres. Motion Picture Div. of Walter Reade Org.; pres., Levitt-Pickman Film Corp.; sr. v.p., domestic distribution, Lorimar Productions; pres., Pickman Film Corp., Cineworld Enterprises Corp.; pres. Scotti Bros. Pictures Distribution, 1986. Consultant, various entertainment entities, legal and financial individuals and organizations.

PIDGEON, REBECCA
Actress. b. Cambridge, MA, October 10, 1963. m. wr.-dir. David Mamet.
PICTURES: The Dawning, She's Been Away, Oleanna (comp. only), The Spanish Prisoner, The Winslow Boy, State and Main, Catastrophe, Heist, The Diary of a Young London Physician, Before the Devil Knows You're Dead, Advice and Dissent.
TELEVISION: *Movies*: Uncle Vanya, Homicide (pilot), The Water Engine, Catastrophe.

PIERCE, DAVID HYDE
Actor. b. Saratoga Sprins, NY, April 3, 1959. e. Yale U.
THEATRE: *Off-B'way*: Summer, That's It Folks, Donuts, Hamlet, The Moderati, The Cherry Orchard, Zero Positive, Much About Nothing, Elliot Loves. *B'way*: Beyond Therapy, The Heidi Chronicles. *Regional*: work with Long Wharf, Guthrie, Goodman, Doolittle Theatres.
PICTURES: Bright Lights Big City, Crossing Delancey, Rocket Gibraltar, The Fisher King, Little Man Tate, Sleepless in Seattle, Addams Family Values, Wolf, Nixon, The Mating Habits of the Earthbound Human, A Bug's Life (voice), Isn't She Great, Chain of Fools, The Tangerine BEar, Happy Birthday, Osmosis Jones (voice), Wet Hot American Summer, Treasure Planet (voice), Full Frontal, Down With Love.
TELEVISION: *Movies*: Jackie's Back!, On the Edge, War Letters. *Series*: The Powers That Be, Frasier (Emmy Award, 1995, 1997, 1999; Emmy nom., 1996, 2000, 2001, 2003), Hercules (voice), The 100 Greatest TV Characters. *Guest*: Dream On, Crime Story, Spenser: For Hire, The Outer Limits, The Simpsons (voice), Caroline in the City, Titus.

PIERCE, FREDERICK S.
Executive. b. New York, NY, April 8, 1933. e. Bernard Baruch Sch. of B.A., City Coll. of New York. Served with U.S. Combat Engineers in Korean War. Associated with Benj. Harrow & Son, CAP, before joining ABC in 1956. Served as analyst in TV research dep.; prom. to supvr. of audience measurements, 1961; named mgr. next year. 1961 made dir. of research; 1962 dir. of research, sales dev. Named dir. of sales planning, sales devel. 1962; elec. v.p., 1964 and made nat. dir. of sales for TV. 1968 named v.p., planning; 1970 named asst. to pres.; 1972, named v.p, in chg. ABC TV planning and devel. and asst. to pres. ABC TV, 1973. Named sr. v.p., ABC TV, 1974. Elected pres., ABC Television Division, 1974. Pres. & COO, ABC, Inc., 1983. Formed Frederick Pierce Co. and also Pierce/Silverman co. with Fred Silverman, 1989. Retired.

PIERSON, FRANK
Producer, Director, Writer. b. Chappaqua, NY, May 12, 1925. e. Harvard U. Was correspondent for Time magazine before entering show business as story editor of TV series, Have Gun, Will Travel. Later served as both prod. and dir. for show. Developed a number of properties for Screen Gems before writing theatrical screenplays.
PICTURES: *Writer*: Cat Ballou, The Happening, Cool Hand Luke, The Anderson Tapes, Dog Day Afternoon (Acad. Award, 1975), In Country, Presumed Innocent. *Director-Writer*: The Looking Glass War, A Star Is Born, King of the Gypsies.
TELEVISION: *Series*: Nichols (prod.), Alfred Hitchcock Presents (1985; dir.). *Movies*: The Neon Ceiling (dir.), Haywire (co-writer), Somebody Has to Shoot the Picture (dir.), ACE Award, 1990), Citizen Cohn (dir.), Lakota Woman: Siege at Wounded Knee (dir.), Truman, Dirty Pictures, Conspiracy, A Soldier's Girl.

PIGOTT-SMITH, TIM
Actor. b. Rugby, England, May 13, 1946. e. U. of Bristol, B.A., Bristol Old Vic Theatre Sch., 1969. Acted with Bristol Old Vic, Royal Shakespeare Co. Artistic Director of Compass Theatre, 1989-93.
THEATRE: *Actor*: As You Like It, Major Barbara, Hamlet, School for Scandal, Sherlock Holmes (B'way debut), Hedda and Gabbles, Entertaining Strangers, The Winter's Tale, Antony and Cleopatra, Cymbeline, The Tempest, Jane Eyre, The Picture of Dorian Gray, Retreat. *Director*: Company, Royal Hunt of the Sun, Playing the Wife, Hamlet, The Letter, Retreat, Mary Stuart.
PICTURES: Aces High (debut, 1975), Man in a Fog, Sweet

William, Richard's Things, Joseph Andrews, Clash of the Titans, Lucky Village, Victory, State of Emergency, The Remains of the Day, Laissez-passez, Bloody Sunday, Four Feathers, Johnny English, Gangs of New York.
TELEVISION: *Series*: Dr. Who, Nightmares of Nature (voice). *Mini-series*: Winston Churchill: The Wilderness Years, The Jewel in the Crown, The Challenge, The Great War, The Vice. *Movies*: Eustace and Hilda, The Lost Boys, I Remember Nelson, Measure for Measure, Henry IV, Day Christ Died, The Hunchback of Notre Dame, Fame Is the Spur, Glittering Prizes, Dead Man's Folly, The Case of Sherlock Holmes (host), Life Story, Hannah, The True Adventures of Christopher Columbus, The Chief, Bullion Boys, The Shadowy Third, Calcutta Chronicles, The Inspector Lynley Mysteries: For the Sake of Elena.

PIKE, CORNELIA M.
Executive. b. Holyoke, MA, 1933. e. Boston U. Sch. of Comm., BS Magna Cum Laude. Asst. promotion & publicity dir. WNAC/WNAC-TV 1954-56, Boston, MA. Women's dir./on-air personality: WKNE, Keene, NH, 1957-60; WSMN, Nashua, NH, 1963-67; WHOB, Nashua, NH, 1967-68. Mngr., Trade Winds Interior Design, Boston, MA, 1979-81; Sales Mngr./V.P. Pike Productions, Inc.,1981-present. Company produces and markets trailers to exhibitors in U.S., UK, Germany, Australia and New Zealand. Bd. Dirs., Variety Club of New England. Life Patron, Variety Clubs International.

PINCHOT, BRONSON
Actor. b. New York, NY, May 20, 1959. e. Yale U. Grew up in Pasadena. Studied acting at Yale. On NY stage in Poor Little Lambs, Zoya's Apartment.
PICTURES: Risky Business (debut, 1983), Beverly Hills Cop, The Flamingo Kid, Hot Resort, After Hours, Second Sight, Blame It on the Bellboy, True Romance, Beverly Hills Cop III, It's My Party, Courage Under Fire, The First Wives Club, Babes in Toyland, Slappy and the Stinkers, Quest for Camelot, Beach Movie, The All New Adventures of Laurel & Hardy: For Love or Mummy, Out of the Cold.
TELEVISION: *Series*: Sara, Perfect Strangers, Eek the Cat, The Trouble With Larry, Dumb and Dumber, Bruno the Kid, Meego. *Movies*: Jury Duty—The Comedy, Merry Christmas George Bailey, Putting It Together. *Mini-Series*: Stephen King's The Langoliers.

PINKETT-SMITH, JADA
Actress. b. Baltimore, MD, Sept. 18, 1971. m. actor Will Smith.
PICTURES: Menace II Society, A Low Down Dirty Shame, Jason's Lyric, The Inkwell, Tales from the Crypt Presents: Demon Knight, The Nutty Professor, Set It Off, Scream 2, Love For Hire (writer only), Return to Paradise, Woo, Welcome to Hollywood, Bamboozled, Kingdom Come, Ali, The Matrix Reloaded, The Matrix Revolutions.
TELEVISION: *Series*: A Different World. *Movie*: If These Walls Could Talk. *Guest*: 21 Jump Street.

PINSKER, ALLEN
Executive. b. New York, NY, Jan. 23, 1930. e. NYU. Mgr., Hempstead Theatre, 1950. 1954 joined Island Theatre Circuit as booker-buyer; named head buyer 1958. 1968 joined United Artists Eastern Theatres as film buyer; head buyer, 1969, v.p., 1970. Named v.p. United Artists Theatre Circuit, 1972. 1973. named UAET exec. v.p., member bd., 1974. Appt. pres. & COO, UA Communications, Inc., theatre division, 1987. 1987, named pres. and CEO United Artists Theatre Circuit, Inc. and exec. v.p., United Artists Communications, Inc.; 1988, became member, bd. dir. United Artists Comm. Inc. Retired.

PINTER, HAROLD
Writer, Director, Actor. b. London, England, Oct. 10, 1930. Began career as actor then turned to writing and direction.
THEATRE: The Dumb Waiter, Slight Ache, The Room, The Birthday Party, The Caretaker, The Homecoming, The Collection, Landscape, Silence, Old Times, No Man's Land, The Hothouse, Betrayal, One for the Road, Mountain Language, Party Time, Moonlight.
PICTURES: *Writer*: The Caretaker (The Guest), The Servant (also actor), The Pumpkin Eater, The Quiller Memorandum, Accident (also actor), The Birthday Party, The Go-Between, The Homecoming, Butley (dir. only), The Last Tycoon, The French Lieutenant's Woman, Betrayal, Turtle Diary (also actor), The Handmaid's Tale, Reunion, The Comfort of Strangers, The Trial. *Actor*: The Rise and Rise of Michael Rimmer, Mojo, Mansfield Park, Catastrophe, The Tailor of Panama.
TELEVISION: *Writer*: A Night Out, Night School, The Lover, Tea Party, The Basement, Langrishe Go Down (also actor), Heat of the Day, Party Time, Old times, Bez pogovra. *Actor*: Rogue Male, The Birthday Party, Breaking the Code, Changing Stages, Wit.

PISANO, A. ROBERT
Executive. e. San Jose St. Univ., Boalt Hall School of Law at Univ. of CA, Berkeley. Was partner at law firm of O'Melveny & Myers prior to entering m.p. industry. 1985-91, exec. v.p. of Paramount Pictures serving as gen. counsel, member of office of chmn.; 1993, named exec. v.p. of MGM responsible for all

business and legal affairs, home video and pay tv. In 1997, became Vice Chairman, with overall responsibility for business operations of MGM. Resigned, 1999. Currently on board of Netflix, Inc. and CEO and exec. dir., Screen Actors Guild.

PISCOPO, JOE
Actor, Comedian. b. Passaic, NJ, June 17, 1951. Stage appearances in regional and dinner theaters in South and Northeast. Worked as stand-up comic at the Improvisation and the Comic Strip clubs, NY 1976-80. Author: The Piscopo Tapes. Television debut as regular on Saturday Night Live, 1980.
PICTURES: American Tickler or the Winner of 10 Academy Awards (1976), King Kong, Johnny Dangerously, Wise Guys, Dead Heat, Sidekicks, Huck and the King of Hearts, Two Bits & Pepper, Captain Nuke and the Bomber Boys, Open Season, Baby Bedlam, Bartleby, The Last Request. (also exec. prod.)
TELEVISION: *Series*: Saturday Night Live (1980-84). *Guest*: Comic Relief. *Special*: The Joe Piscopo Special (HBO). *Movie*: Huck and the King of Hearts.

PISIER, MARIE-FRANCE
Actress. b. Dalat, Indochina, May 10, 1944. Began appearing in French films at age 17. Returned to school at Univ. of Paris for degrees in law and political science; continued to work in films.
PICTURES: Qui sec nous Accuser? (debut, 1961), Love at Twenty (Truffaut episode), La Mort d'un Tueur, Les Yeux cernes, Trans-Europe Express, Stolen Kisses, Celine and Julie Go Boating, French Provincial, Cousin Cousine, Serail, Barocco, The Other Side of Midnight, Love on the Run, Les Apprentis Sourciers, The Bronte Sisters, French Postcards, La Banquiere, Chanel Solitaire, Der Zauberberg (The Magic Mountain), Miss Right, Hot Touch, The Prize of Peril, The Silent Ocean, L'Ami de Vincent, Les Nanas, Parking, Blue Note, Why is My Mother in My Bed?, Seven Sundays, Son of Gascogne, La Gazelle, Marion, Why Not Me?, The Ice Rink, Time Regained, Highway Melody, Love Torn in Dream, Inch'Allah Sunday, Like an Airplane.
TELEVISION: *U.S.*: French Atlantic Affair, Scruples.

PITT, BRAD
Actor. r.n. William Bradley Pitt. b. Shawnee, OK, Dec. 18, 1963. m. actress Jennifer Aniston. Raised in Springfield, MO. Studied journalism at Univ. of MO at Columbia. Moved to L.A. to attend art school, instead studied acting with Roy London. Appeared in short film Contact.
PICTURES: Cutting Class (debut, 1989), Happy Together, Across the Tracks, Thelma & Louise, Cool World, Johnny Suede, A River Runs Through It, Kalifornia, True Romance, The Favor, Interview With the Vampire. Legends of the Fall, Se7en, Twelve Monkeys (Golden Globe, 1996), Sleepers, The Devil's Own, Seven Years In Tibet, Meet Joe Black, Fight Club, Being John Malkovich (cameo), Snatch, The Mexican, Ocean's Eleven, Spy Game, Full Frontal, Confessions of a Dangerous Mind, Sinbad: Legend of the Seven Seas (voice), Troy.
TELEVISION: *Series*: Another World, Glory Days. *Movies*: A Stoning in Fulham County, Too Young to Die, The Image. *Guest*: Dallas, Growing Pains, Head of the Class, Jackass.

PIVEN, JEREMY
Actor. b. New York, NY. July 26, 1965. Raised in Chicago where parents ran Piven Theater Workshop. e. Drake Univ. Studied acting at Eugene O'Neill Theater Center, Natl. Theater of Great Britain, NYU. Eventually joined Chicago's Second City comedy troupe. Co-founded Chicago's New Criminals Theatre Company, 1988.
THEATRE: Fear & Loathing in Las Vegas, Peacekeeper, Methusalen, Knuckle, Macbeth.
PICTURES: Lucas, One Crazy Summer, Say Anything..., White Palace, The Grifters, Pay Dirt, The Player, Bob Roberts, Singles, Judgment Night, Twenty Bucks, Car 54 Where Are You?, Twogether, PCU, Miami Rhapsody, Dr. Jekyll and Ms. Hyde, Heat, Grosse Pointe Blank, Very Bad Things, Music From Another Room, Phoenix, The Crew, Red Letters, The Family Man, Serendipity, Highway, Black Hawk Down, Rush Hour 2, Highway, Old School, Scary Movie 3, Runaway Jury.
TELEVISION: *Series*: Carol and Company, The Larry Sanders Show, Pride and Joy, Ellen, Cupid, The Twilight Zone. *Pilots*: Heads Will Roll, Ready or Not. *Movie*: Don King: Only in America. *Guest*: The Drew Carey Show, Chicago Hope, Seinfeld, Coach, Grace Under Fire, Duckman (voice), Will and Grace, Buzz Lightyear of Star Command (voice).

PLACE, MARY KAY
Actress, Writer. b. Tulsa, OK, Sept. 23, 1947. e. U. of Tulsa. Worked in production jobs and as Tim Conway's asst. for his TV show also as sect. for Norman Lear on Maude before starting to write for TV series (Mary Tyler Moore Show, Phyllis, Maude, M*A*S*H, etc.).
PICTURES: Bound For Glory (debut, 1976), New York New York, More American Graffiti, Starting Over, Private Benjamin, Modern Problems, Waltz Across Texas, The Big Chill, Smooth Talk, A New Life, Bright Angel, Captain Ron, Samantha, Teresa's Tattoo, Manny and Lo, Precious, Citizen Ruth, Eye of God, The Rainmaker, How to Make the Cruelest Month, Pecker, Nobody Knows Anything, Naturally Native, Judgment Day: The Ellie Nesler Story, Being John Malkovich, Girl Interrupted, Committed,

A Woman's a Helluva Thing, My First Mister, Nailed, The Safety of Objects, Human Nature, Junk, Sweet Home Alabama.
TELEVISION: *Series:* Mary Hartman Mary Hartman (Emmy Award, 1977). *Guest:* All in the Family, Mary Tyler Moore Show, Fernwood 2-Night, Tonight Show, Saturday Night Live (host), thirtysomething. *Movies:* The Girl Who Spelled Freedom, Act of Love, For Love or Money, Out on the Edge, Just My Imagination, Telling Secrets, In the Line of Duty: The Pride of Vengeance. *Specials:* John Denver Special, Martin Mull's History of White People in America I & II, Portrait of a White Marriage, The Gift, Tales of the City, Leslie's Folly, My Very Best Friend, For My Daughter's Honor, Love in Another Town, Point Last Seen, Further Tales of the City.

PLATT, OLIVER
Actor. b. Windsor, Ontario, Canada, January 12, 1962. Raised in Asia, Africa and Washington DC. e. Tufts Univ.
THEATRE: *Off-B'way:* The Tempest, Moon Over Miami, Sparks in the Park, Urban Blight, Ubu, Elliot Loves.
PICTURES: Married to the Mob (debut, 1988), Working Girl, Crusoe, Flatliners, Postcards From the Edge, Beethoven, Diggstown, The Temp, Indecent Proposal, Benny & Joon, The Three Musketeers, Tall Tale, Funny Bones, Executive Decision, A Time to Kill, Dangerous Beauty, Bulworth, Simon Birch, Lake Placid, Three to Tango, Bicentennial Man, Gun Shy, Ready to Rumble, Don't Say a Word, Zigzag, Liberty Stands Still, Ash Wednesday, Hope Springs, Pieces of April.
TELEVISION: *Movies:* The Infiltrator, Cinderelmo, Queens Supreme. *Series:* Deadline. *Guest:* The Equalizer, Miami Vice, Wiseguy, The West Wing.

PLESHETTE, SUZANNE
Actress. b. New York, NY. Jan. 31, 1937. e. H.S. for the Performing Arts, Finch Coll., Syracuse U. Broadway debut, Compulsion.
THEATRE: The Cold Wind and the Warm, The Golden Fleecing, The Miracle Worker, Compulsion, Two for the Seesaw, Special Occasions.
PICTURES: The Geisha Boy (debut, 1958), Rome Adventure, 40 Pounds of Trouble, The Birds, Wall of Noise, A Distant Trumpet, Fate Is the Hunter, Youngblood Hawke, A Rage to Live, The Ugly Dachshund, Nevada Smith, Mister Buddwing, The Adventures of Bullwhip Griffin, Blackbeard's Ghost, The Power, If It's Tuesday This Must Be Belgium, Suppose They Gave a War and Nobody Came, Target Harry, Support Your Local Gunfighter, The Shaggy D.A., Hot Stuff, Oh God! Book II, Lion King II, Off the Menu: The Last Days of Chasen's.
TELEVISION: *Series:* The Bob Newhart Show, Suzanne Pleshette Is Maggie Briggs, Bridges to Cross, Nightingales, The Boys Are Back, The Single Guy, Good Morning Miami. *Movies:* Wings of Fire, Along Came a Spider, Hunters Are for Killing, River of Gold, In Broad Daylight, Law and Order, Richie Brockelman: Missing 24 Hours, Kate Bliss and the Ticker Tape Kid, Flesh and Blood, For Love or Money, Fantasies, If Things Were Different, Help Wanted—Male, Starmaker, One Cooks, The Other Doesn't, Legend of Valentino, Kojak The Belarus File, A Stranger Waits, Alone in the Neon Jungle, Leona Helmsley: The Queen of Mean, Battling for Baby, A Twist of the Knife.

PLESKOW, ERIC
Executive. b., Vienna, Austria, April 24, 1924. Served as film offcer, U.S. War dept., 1946-48; entered industry in 1948 as asst. gen. mgr., Motion Picture Export Association, Germany; 1950-51, continental rep. for Sol Lesser Prods.; joined United Artists in 1951 as Far East Sales Mgr.; named mgr., S. Africa, 1952; mgr., Germany, 1953-58; exec. asst. to continental mgr., 1958-59; asst. continental mgr., 1959-60; continental mgr., 1960-62; v.p. in charge of foreign distrib., 1962; exec. v.p. & CEO, Jan., 1973; pres. & CEO, Oct. , 1973. Resigned in 1978 to become pres. and CEO of Orion Pictures Co.; 1982, became pres. & CEO, Orion Pictures Corp; appointed chmn. of bd. 1991. Resigned 1992. Partner, Pleskow/Spikings Partnership, Beverly Hills, 1992-present. Prod., Beyond Rangoon.

PLIMPTON, MARTHA
Actress. b. New York, NY, Nov. 16, 1970. Daughter of actors Shelley Plimpton and Keith Carradine. Acting debut in film workshop of Elizabeth Swados' musical Runaways.
At 11 gained recognition as model in Richard Avedon's commercials for Calvin Klein jeans. Also on stage in The Hagadah, Pericles, The Heidi Chronicles, Robbers, subUrbia, The Great Unwashed.
PICTURES: Rollover (debut 1981, in bit role), The River Rat, The Goonies, The Mosquito Coast, Shy People, Stars and Bars, Running on Empty, Another Woman, Parenthood, Stanley and Iris, Silence Like Glass, Samantha, Inside Monkey Zetterland, Josh and S.A.M., My Life's in Turnaround, Mrs. Parker and the Vicious Circle, The Beans of Egypt Maine, Last Summer in the Hamptons, Beautiful Girls, I Shot Andy Warhol, I'm Not Rappaport, Eye of God, Pecker, Music From Another Room, 200 Cigarettes, The Sleepy Time Gal, Searching for Debra Winger.
TELEVISION: *Movies:* Daybreak, Chantilly Lace, The Defenders: Choice of Evils, The Defenders: Taking the First. *Guest:* Family Ties, Law and Order: SVU.

PLOWRIGHT, JOAN
C.B.E. Actress. b. Scunthrope, Brigg, Lincolnshire, England, Oct. 28, 1929. m. late actor, Lord Laurence Olivier. Trained for stage at Laban Art of Movement Studio, 1949-50; Old Vic Theatre Sch. 1950-52; with Michel St. Denis, Glen Byam Shaw and George Devine. London stage debut The Duenna, 1954. Broadway debut The Entertainer, 1958. Won Tony Award in 1961 for A Taste of Honey. With Bristol Old Vic Rep., Royal Court, National Theatre in numerous classics and contemporary plays.
RECENT THEATER: Saturday Sunday Monday, The Seagull, The Bed Before Yesterday, Filumena, Enjoy, Who's Afraid of Virginia Woolf?, Cavell, The Cherry Orchard, The Way of the World, Mrs. Warren's Profession, Time and the Conways, If We Are Women.
PICTURES: Moby Dick (debut, 1956), Time Without Pity, The Entertainer, Uncle Vanya, Three Sisters, Equus, Brimstone and Treacle, Britannia Hospital, Wagner (tv in U.S.), Revolution, The Dressmaker, Drowning By Numbers, I Love You to Death, Avalon, Enchanted April (Acad. Award nom.), Last Action Hero, Dennis the Menace, A Pin for the Butterfly, The Summer House, Widow's Peak, A Pyromaniac's Love Story, Hotel Sorrento, The Scarlett Letter, Jane Eyre, Mr. Wrong, Surviving Picasso, 101 Dalmatians, The Assistant, Dance with Me, Tom's Midnight Garden, Tea with Mussolini, Dinosaur (voice), Back to the Secret Garden, Global Heresy, Callas Forever, George and the Dragon, I am David, Bringing Down the House.
TELEVISION: Odd Man In, Secret Agent, School for Scandal, The Diary of Anne Frank, Twelfth Night, Merchant of Venice, Daphne Laureola, The Divider, Conquest of the South Pole, A Nightingale Sang, House of Bernarda Alba, Stalin, On Promised Land, A Place for Annie, The Return of the Native, This Could Be the Last Time, Encore! Encore!, others. *Pilot:* Driving Miss Daisy (U.S.).

PLUMMER, AMANDA
Actress. b. New York, NY, March 23, 1957. e. Middlebury Coll. Daughter of actors Christopher Plummer and Tammy Grimes.
THEATRE: Artichokes, A Month in the Country, A Taste of Honey (Theatre World Award), Agnes of God (Tony Award, 1982), The Glass Menagerie, A Lie of the Mind, Life Under Water, You Never Can Tell, Pygmalion, The Milk Train Doesn't Stop Here Anymore.
PICTURES: Cattle Annie and Little Britches (debut, 1981), The World According to Garp, Daniel, The Hotel New Hampshire, Static, The Courtship, Made in Heaven, Prisoners of Inertia, Joe Versus the Volcano, California Casanova, The Fisher King, Freejack, So I Married an Axe Murderer, Needful Things, Nostradamus, Pulp Fiction, Pax, Butterfly Kiss, The Propechy, Drunks, Freeway, A Simple Wish, American Perfekt, You Can Thank Me Later, L.A. Without a Map, Elizabeth Jane, 8 1/2 Women, The Million Dollar Hotel, Seven Days to Live, Triggerman, Ken Park, Darkness, My Life Wihout Me, The Last Angel, Broadway: The Golden Age by the Legends Who Were There.
TELEVISION: *Movies:* The Dollmaker, The Unforgivable Secret, Riders to the Sea, Miss Rose White (Emmy Award, 1992), The Sands of Time, Last Light, Whose Child Is This? The War for Baby Jessica, The Apartment Complex, Get a Clue. *Guest:* Outer Limits (Emmy Award, 1996). *Series:* Stories from my Childhood. *Specials:* Gryphon, The Courtship. *Pilot:* True Blue.

PLUMMER, CHRISTOPHER
Actor. b. Toronto, Canada, Dec. 13, 1927. Daughter is actress Amanda Plummer. Stage & radio career began in Canada (French & English).
THEATRE: toured U.S. in The Constant Wife; B'way debut in The Starcross Story, 1953. *B'way:* The Dark is Light Enough, Home Is the Hero, J.B., The Lark, The Good Doctor, Cyrano (Tony Award, 1974), Othello (Tony nom.), Macbeth, No Man's Land. *London:* leading actor, Royal Shakespeare Theatre, 1961-62, Becket (Evening Standard Award), Natl. Theatre, 1969-70. *Canada:* leading actor, Stratford Festival (6 yrs.).
PICTURES: Stage Struck (debut, 1958), Wind Across the Everglades, The Fall of the Roman Empire, The Sound of Music, Inside Daisy Clover, The Night of the Generals, Triple Cross, Oedipus the King, The High Commissioner (Nobody Runs Forever), The Battle of Britain, The Royal Hunt of the Sun, Lock Up Your Daughters, Waterloo, The Pyx, The Return of the Pink Panther, Conduct Unbecoming, The Man Who Would Be King, The Spiral Staircase, Aces High, Assassination at Sarajevo (The Day That Shook the World), The Assignment, The Disappearance, International Velvet, Murder by Decree, The Silent Partner, Hanover Street, Starcrash, RIEL, Highpoint, Somewhere in Time, Eyewitness, Being Different (narrator), The Amateur, Dreamscape, Ordeal by Innocence, Lily in Love, The Boy in Blue, The Boss' Wife, An American Tail (voice), Dragnet, Souvenir, Light Years (voice), Nosferatu in Venice, I Love N.Y., Shadow Dancing, Mindfield, Kingsgate, Red-Blooded American Girl, Where the Heart Is, Don't Tell Mom the Babysitter's Dead, Star Trek VI: The Undiscovered Country, Firehead, Rock-a-Doodle (voice), Money, Liar's Edge, Impolite, Malcolm X, Wolf, Dolores Claiborne, Twelve Monkeys, Skeletons, Babes in Toyland, Hidden Agenda, The Clown at Midnight, Blackheart, All the Fine Lines, The Insider, The Dinosaur Hunter, Dracula 2000, Star Trek: Klingon Academy, Lucky Break, Full Disclosure, A Beautiful Mind, Ararat, Ted Allan: Minstrel Boy of the Twentieth

Century, Nicholas Nickleby, Blizzard.
TELEVISION: *Series*: Counterstrike. *Movies/Specials*: Hamlet at Elsinore (Emmy nom.), Don Juan in Hell (BBC), Little Moon of Alban, Prince and the Pauper, Jesus of Nazareth, Steiglitz and O'Keefe, Oedipus Rex, Omnibus, After the Fall, The Moneychangers (Emmy Award, 1977), Desperate Voyage, The Shadow Box, When the Circus Came to Town, Dial M for Murder, Little Gloria—Happy at Last, The Scarlet and the Black, The Thorn Birds, The Velveteen Rabbit, Crossings, A Hazard of Hearts, A Ghost in Monte Carlo, Young Catherine, Danielle Steel's Secrets, Stranger in the Mirror, Liar's Edge, Madeline (narrator; Emmy Award, 1994), Harrison Bergeron, We the Jury, The Conspiracy of Fear, The Arrow, Winchell, Celebrate the Century (narrator), Nuremberg, Possessed, American Tragedy, Leo's Journey, On Golden Pond, Night Flight, Agent of Influence.

PODELL, ALBERT N.
Attorney. b. New York, NY, Feb. 25, 1937. e. Cornell U., U. of Chicago, NYU Sch. of Law. Non-fiction ed., Playboy magazine, 1959-60; dir. of photog. and m.p. reviewer Argosy magazine, 1961-64; Author: Who Needs a Road? (Bobbs-Merrill, 1967; re-published, Wolfenden, 1999), mng. ed., The Players Magazine, 1965-66; acct. exec. on 20th Century-Fox at Diener, Hauser, Greenthal, 1966-68; natl. advt. mgr., Cinema Center Films, 1969; acct. supervisor and creative dir. on Columbia Pictures at Charles Schlaifer, 1969-72; creator & dir. of Annual Motion Picture Advertising Awards sponsored by Cinema Lodge, B'nai B'rith. Attorney specializing in litigation, matrimonial law, rep. of performers and producers (1976-present). Pres., 1990-95 Jean Cocteau Rep. Th. Chmn. of Trustees; 1980-90, Assn. for Development of Dramatic Arts. Pres., Far Above Films. *Dir. & Writer*: A Class Above, The Class on the Cutting Edge, Lift the Chorus, This Is Christmas.

PODHORZER, MUNIO
Executive. b. Berlin, Germany, Sept. 18, 1911. e. Jahn-Realgymnasium, U. of Berlin Medical Sch. U.S. Army, 1943-47; pres. United Film Enterprises, Inc.; formerly secy.-treas. 86th St. Casino Theatre, N.Y.; former v.p. Atlantic Pictures Corp.; former pres. Casino Films, Inc.; former pres. Film Development Corp.; former rep. Export-Union of the German Film Ind.; former U.S. rep. Franco-London Film, Paris; former pres., Venus Productions Corp.; former U.S. rep. Atlas Int'l Film GmbH, Munich; former U.S. rep. Bavaria Atelier Gesellschaft U.S.; past rep. Israfilm Ltd., Tel-Aviv; past rep. Tigon British Film Prod., London; past rep. Elias Querejeta, P.C., Madrid; past rep. Equiluz Films, Madrid; past rep. Airport Cine, Haiti; Les Films Du Capricorne, Paris; Schongerfilm, German; Profilmes, Spain; Ligno, Spain; Films D'Alma, France; Intra Films, Italy. Member: Variety Club, Cinema Lodge, B'nai B'rith, Past Board of Governors IFIDA; past pres. CID Agents Assoc. Former gen. foreign sales mgr.; theatrical division of National Telefilm Associates; past rep. Barcino Films, S.A. Spain; Eagle Films Ltd., UK; Les Films Jacques Leitienne, France; Nero Film Classics, USA; Schongerfilm, Germany; Profilmes, S.A. Spain; VIP Ltd., Israel. Presently representing Atlas Film & AV, Germany; KFM Films, Inc. U.S.A.; Compagnie France Film, Canada; Cia. Iberoamerican de TV, S.A. Spain; Israel. Co-chmn., entertainment div., United Jewish Appeal, Federation of Jewish Philanthropies, 1981-83

PODHORZER, NATHAN
Executive. b. Brody, Poland, Nov. 27, 1919. e. City Coll. of New York, Rutgers U., U. of Southern California. U.S. Army, 1942-46; documentary film prod., Israel, 1946-57; CEO, United Film Enterprises, Inc. U.S. purchasing agent: Atlas Air, Atlas Film & Medien (Germany), Co. France Film (Canada).

POITIER, SIDNEY
Actor, Director. b. Miami, FL, Feb. 20, 1927. Raised in the Bahamas. m. actress Joanna Shimkus. e. Miami, FL. On stage with Amer. Negro Theatre in Days of Our Youth. Appeared in Army Signal Corps documentary From Whence Cometh My Help. Formed First Artists Prod. Co. Ltd., 1969, with Paul Newman and Barbra Streisand. *Autobiography*: This Life (1980). Recipient 1992 AFI Life Achievement Award. Won honorary Acad. Award in 2002.
THEATRE: Strivers Road, You Can't Take It With You, Anna Lucasta (B'way debut, 1948), Lysistrata, Freight, A Raisin in the Sun.
PICTURES: No Way Out (debut 1950), Cry the Beloved Country, Red Ball Express, Go Man Go, Blackboard Jungle, Goodbye My Lady, Edge of the City, Something of Value, Band of Angels, Mark of the Hawk, The Defiant Ones, Virgin Island, Porgy and Bess, All the Young Men, A Raisin in the Sun, Paris Blues, Pressure Point, Lilies of the Field (Acad. Award, 1963), The Long Ships, The Greatest Story Ever Told, The Bedford Incident, The Slender Thread, A Patch of Blue, Duel at Diablo, To Sir With Love, In the Heat of the Night, Guess Who's Coming to Dinner, For Love of Ivy, The Lost Man, They Call Me Mister Tibbs, Brother John, The Organization, Buck and the Preacher (also dir.), A Warm December (also dir.), Uptown Saturday Night (also dir.), The Wilby Conspiracy, Let's Do It Again (also dir.), A Piece of the Action (also dir.), Stir Crazy (dir. only), Hanky Panky (dir. only), Fast Forward (dir. only), Shoot To Kill, Little Nikita, Ghost Dad (dir. only), Sneakers, The Jackal, Scandalize My Name:

Stories from the Blacklist, Ralph Bunche: An American Odyssey.
TELEVISION: *Movies*: Separate But Equal, Children of the Dust, To Sir With Love II, Mandela and de Klerk, Free of Eden, The Simple Life of Noah Dearborn, The Last Bricklayer in America. *Guest*: Philco TV Playhouse, ABC Stage '67.

POLANSKI, ROMAN
Director, Writer. b. Paris, France, Aug. 18, 1933. m. actress Emmanuelle Seigner. Lived in Poland from age of three. Early career, art school in Cracow; Polish Natl. Film Acad., Lodz 1954-59. Radio Actor 1945-47; on stage 1947-53; asst. dir., Kamera film prod. group 1959-61. Co-founder Cadre Films, 1964. Wrote, dir. and acted in short films: Two Men and a Wardrobe, When Angels Fall, The Fat and the Lean, Mammals. On stage as actor in Amadeus (and dir., Warsaw & Paris), Metamorphosis (Paris, 1988). *Autobiography*: Roman (1984).
PICTURES: *Dir./Writer*: Knife in the Water (feature debut, 1962), Repulsion, Cul-de-Sac, The Fearless Vampire Killers or: Pardon Me But Your Teeth Are in My Neck (also actor), Rosemary's Baby, A Day at the Beach (s.p. only), Weekend of a Champion (prod. only), Macbeth (also prod.), What? (a.k.a. Che?; also actor), Chinatown (dir. & actor only), The Tenant (also actor), Tess, Pirates, Frantic, Bitter Moon, Death and the Maiden, The Ninth Gate, The Pianist (acad. award, dir., (dir. only; Golden Palm Award). *Actor only*: The Generation, The Magic Christian, Andy Warhol's Dracula, Back in the U.S.S.R., A Pure Formality, Grosse Fatigue, the Story of X, Light Keeps Me Company, Tribute to Alfred Lepetit, Zemsta.

POLEDOURIS, BASIL
Composer. b. Kansas City, MO, Aug. 21, 1945. e. Long Beach St. Univ., USC. While at USC composed music for short films by John Milius and Randal Kleiser. Became first American Film Institute intern.
PICTURES: Big Wednesday, Tintorera, Dolphin, The Blue Lagoon, Conan the Barbarian, Summer Lovers, House of God, Conan the Destroyer, Making the Grade, Red Dawn, Protocol, Flesh and Blood, Iron Eagle, Robocop, No Man's Land, Cherry 2000, Spellbinder, Split Decisions, Farewell to the King, Wired, The Hunt for Red October, Quigley Down Under, Flight of the Intruder, White Fang, Return to the Blue Lagoon, Harley Davidson & the Marlboro Man, Wind, Hot Shots Part Deux, Free Willy, Robocop 3, On Deadly Ground, Serial Mom, Lassie, The Jungle Book, Under Siege 2: Dark Territory, Free Willy 2: The Adventure Home, It's My Party, Celtic Pride, Breakdown, Starship Troopers, Les Miserables, Mickey Blue Eyes, Kimberly, For Love of the Game, Cecil B. DeMented, Crocodile Dundee in Los Angeles, The Touch.
TELEVISION: *Mini-Series*: Amerika, Lonesome Dove (Emmy Award, 1989). *Movies*: Congratulations It's a Boy, A Whale for the Killing, Fire on the Mountain, Amazons, Single Women Single Bars, Prison for Children, Misfits of Science, Island Sons, Intrigue, L.A. Takedown, Nasty Boys, Ned Blessing, Lone Justice, Danielle Steel's Zoya, If These Walls Could Talk 2, Love and Treason.

POLL, MARTIN H.
Producer. b. New York, NY, Nov. 24, 1926. e. Wharton Sch., U. of Pennsylvania. Pres. Gold Medal Studios (1956-61).
PICTURES: A Face in the Crowd, Middle of the Night, The Goddess, Butterfield 8, Love Is a Ball, Sylvia, The Lion in Winter, The Appointment, The Magic Garden of Stanley Sweetheart, The Man Who Loved Cat Dancing, Night Watch, Love and Death (exec. prod.); The Man Who Would Be King, The Sailor Who Fell From Grace with the Sea, Somebody Killed Her Husband, Nighthawks, Gimme an F, Haunted Summer, My Heroes Have Always Been Cowboys, Lion's Share.
TELEVISION: *Series*: Car 54 Where Are You? *Movies*: Arthur the King, Stunt Seven, The Lion in Winter. *Mini-Series*: A Town Called Alice, The Dain Curse, Diana: Her True Story.

POLLACK, SYDNEY
Director, Producer. b. South Bend, IN, July 1, 1934. m. Claire Griswold. e. Neighborhood Playhouse. Assistant to Sanford Meisner at Neighborhood Playhouse. Appeared as actor on B'way in A Stone for Danny Fisher, The Dark is Light Enough. Dir. debut in 1960. Dir. play at UCLA, P.S. 193. Prepared the American version of The Leopard.
PICTURES: *Director*: The Slender Thread (debut, 1965), This Property Is Condemned, The Scalphunters, Castle Keep, They Shoot Horses Don't They? (also prod.), Jeremiah Johnson, The Way We Were (also prod.), The Yakuza (also prod.), Three Days of the Condor, Bobby Deerfield (also prod.), The Electric Horseman, Asence of Malice (also prod.), Tootsie (also prod., actor), Out of Africa (also prod.; Acad. Awards for Best Picture & dir., 1985), Havana (also prod.), The Firm, Sabrina (also prod.), Random Hearts. *Producer*: Songwriter, Bright Lights Big City, The Fabulous Baker Boys, Presumed Innocent, Random Hearts (also prod.), 20 Billion. *Exec. Producer*: Honeysuckle Rose, White Palace, King Ralph, Dead Again, Leaving Normal, Searching for Bobby Fischer, Flesh and Bone, Sense and Sensibility, The Talented Mr. Ripley, Up at the Villa, Blow Dry, Heaven, The Quiet American, The Assumption (also dir.), Iris, 20 Billion, Cold Mountain, Birthday Girl. *Actor*: War Hunt, The Player, Death Becomes Her, Husbands and Wives, A Civil Action,

Eyes Wide Shut, Random Hearts, Lost Angeles, Stanley Kubrick: A Life in Pictures, The Majestic, Changing Lanes.
TELEVISION: *As actor:* Playhouse 90 (several segments), Shotgun Slade. *Dir.:* Ben Casey (15 episodes), The Game (Bob Hope-Chrysler Theatre; Emmy Award), Two is the Number. *Co-prod.* (movie): A Private Matter. *Exec. prod.* (series): Fallen Angels.

POLLAK, KEVIN
Actor. b. San Francisco, CA, Oct. 30, 1958. Started doing stand-up comedy in the San Francisco Bay area, then continued in L.A. clubs.
PICTURES: Million Dollar Mystery (debut, 1987), Willow, Avalon, L.A. Story, Another You, Ricochet, A Few Good Men, The Opposite Sex and How to Live With Them, Indian Summer, Wayne's World 2, Grumpy Old Men, Reality Bites, Clean Slate, Miami Rhapsody, The Usual Suspects, Canadian Bacon, Casino, Nowhere Man, Chameleon, House Arrest, Grumpier Old Men, That Thing You Do!, National Lampoon's The Don's Analyst, Truth or Consequences N.M., Buffalo 66, Outside Ozona, Steal This Movie, The Sex Monster, She's All That, Deterrence, The Whole Nine Yards, Deal of a Lifetime, The Wedding Planner, 3000 Miles to Graceland, Dr. Dolittle 2, Juwanna Mann, Frank McKlusky C.I., The Santa Clause 2, Stolen Summer, Rolling Kansas, Mob Dot Com, Blizzard.
TELEVISION: *Series:* Coming of Age, Morton and Hayes, Work with Me, Project Greenlight. *Specials:* One Night Stand (also prod., writer), Stop With the Kicking (also prod., writer), The Seven Deadly Sins (also writer, dir.). *Movie:* Ruby Bridges. *Mini-series:* From the Earth to the Moon.

POLLAN, TRACY
Actress. b. New York, NY, June 22, 1960. m. actor Michael J. Fox.
THEATRE: *B'way:* Jake's Women.
PICTURES: Promised Land, Bright Lights Big City, A Stranger Among Us.
TELEVISION: *Series:* Family Ties, Anna Says (also exec. prod.). *Movies:* For Lovers Only, Sessions, Trackdown: Finding the Goodbar Killer, A Good Sport, Fine Things, Dying to Love You, Children of the Dark, 1st to Die. *Guest:* Law and Order.

POLLARD, MICHAEL J.
Actor. r.n. Michael J. Pollack. b. Passaic, NJ, May 30, 1939. e. Montclair Academy, Actors Studio.
THEATRE: Comes a Day, Loss of Roses, Enter Laughing, Bye Bye Birdie, Leda Had a Little Swan, Our Town.
PICTURES: Adventures of a Young Man (debut, 1962), The Stripper, Summer Magic, The Russians Are Coming The Russians Are Coming, The Wild Angels, Caprice, Enter Laughing, Bonnie and Clyde (Acad. Award nom.), Jigsaw, Hannibal Brooks, Little Fauss and Big Halsy, The Legend of Frenchie King, Dirty Little Billy, Between the Lines, Melvin and Howard, Heated Vengeance, America, The Patriot, The American Way, Roxanne, Scrooged, Fast Food, Season of Fear, Next of Kin, Tango and Cash, Night Vision, Sleepaway Camp 3, Why Me?, Dick Tracy, I Come in Peace, Joey Takes a Cab, The Art of Dying, Another You, Enid Is Sleeping (Over Her Dead Body), Split Second, The Arrival, Heartstopper, Arizona Dream, Motorama, Skeeter, Heartstopper, Mad Dog Time, The Unknown Cyclist, Stir, Merchants of Venus, Tumbleweeds, The Debtors, Forever Lulu, Danny and Max, Out of the Black, House of 1000 Corpses.
TELEVISION: *Series:* Leo and Liz in Beverly Hills. *Guest:* Alfred Hitchcock Presents (Anniversary Gift), Going My Way, Route 66, Here's Lucy, Mr. Novak, Honey West, I Spy, Lost in Space, Dobie Gillis, Get Christie Love, Star Trek, Simon & Simon, The Fall Guy, Gunsmoke, Guns of Paradise, The Young Riders, Nasty Boys. *Movies:* The Smugglers, Stuck With Each Other, Working Trash, The Odyssey.

POLLEXFEN, JACK
Producer, Director, Writer. b. San Diego, CA, June 10, 1918. e. Los Angeles City Coll. Newspaperman, magazine writer, playwright; prod. for RKO, United Artists, Columbia, Allied Artists.
PICTURES: Son of Sinbad, At Swords Point, Secret of Convict Lake, Desert Hawk, Lady in the Iron Mask, Dragon's Gold, Problem Girls, Captive Women, Captain Kidd and the Slave Girl, Neanderthal Man, Captain John Smith and Pocahontas, Return to Treasure Island, Sword of Venus, Daughter of Dr. Jekyll, Monstrosity, Son of Dr. Jekyll, Mr. Big, Man from Planet X, Indestructible Man, Port Sinister, Treasure of Monte Cristo, Bulldog Drummond, Grey City.

POLLEY, SARAH
Actress. b. Canada, Jan. 8, 1979. Daughter of late actress and casting director Diane Polley.
PICTURES: One Magic Christmas, The Big Town, The Adventures of Baron Munchausen, Babar: The Movie (voice), Exotica, Joe's So Mean to Josephine, The Sweet Hereafter, The Planet of Junior Brown, The Hanging Garden, Last Night, Guinevere, Go, eXistenZ, The Life Before This, The Weight of Water, Love Come Down, The Law of Enclosures, The Claim, This Might Be Good, No Such Thing, My Life Without Me, The Event.
TELEVISION: *Movies:* Lantern Hill, Johann's Gift to Christmas, White Lies. *Series:* Ramona, Road to Avonlea. *Guest:* Friday the 13th.

POLLOCK, DALE
Producer. b. Cleveland, OH, May 18, 1950. e. Brandeis U., B.A. anthropology, San Jose State, M.S., mass communication. Began journalistic career in Santa Cruz in early '70s, serving as reporter and film critic for Daily Variety, 1977-80. Joined Los Angeles Times as film writer, winning paper's Award for Sustained Excellence in 1984. 1985 left to take post with The Geffen Film Co. as executive in chg. creative development. Joined A&M Films as v.p. in chg. prod., 1986. Became pres., 1989. Author: Skywalking (about George Lucas).
PICTURES: The Beast (exec. prod.), The Mighty Quinn (exec. prod.). Producer: House of Cards, Worth Winning, Blaze, Crooked Hearts, A Midnight Clear, A Home of Our Own, S.F.W., Mrs. Winterbourne, Set It Off, Meet the Deedles (also s.p.), Bats.

POLLOCK, THOMAS
Executive. b. 1943. In 1971, after 3 years as business mgr. for American Film Institute's film marketing wing, formed law firm Pollock Bloom, and Dekom with young filmmakers such as George Lucas and Matthew Robbins as clients. Served as chmn. Filmex, 1973-81. 1986, named chmn. MCA's Universal motion picture group., then vice chmn., MCA, Inc. Currently, partner in the Montecito Film Co.

PONTECORVO, GILLO
Director. b. Pisa, Italy, Nov. 19, 1919. Younger brother of Prof. Bruno Pontecorvo, Harwell scientist who defected in 1950. Former photo-journalist. Worked as asst. dir., directed documentary shorts before feature debut in 1957.
PICTURES: Die Windrose (Giovanna episode), La Grande Strada Azzurra (The Long Blue Road; also co-s.p.), Kapo (also co-s.p.), The Battle of Algiers (also story; Acad. Award noms. as dir. & writer), Queimada! (also co-story), Ogro (also co-s.p.), L'Addio a Enrico Berlinguer, Nostalgia di protezione (also s.p.), I Corti italiani (also s.p.), 12 registi per 12 città, Another World Is Possible.

PONTI, CARLO
Producer. b. Milan, Italy, Dec. 11, 1913. m. actress Sophia Loren. e. U. of Milan. 1934. Prod. first picture in Milan, Little Old World; prod. Lux Film Rome; prod. first of a series of famous Toto pictures, Toto Househunting.
PICTURES: A Dog's Life, The Knight Has Arrived, Musolino, The Outlaw, Romanticism, Sensuality, The White Slave, Europe 1951, Toto in Color, The Three Corsairs, The Gold of Naples, Ulysses, The Woman of the River, An American of Rome, Attila, La Strada, War and Peace, The Last Lover, The Black Orchid, That Kind of Woman, A Breath of Scandal, Heller in Pink Tights, Two Women, Boccaccio '70, Bluebeard, The Condemned of Altona, Marriage Italian Style, Casanova '70, Operation Crossbow, Doctor Zhivago, Lady L, Blow Up, More Than a Miracle, The Girl and the General, Sunflower, The Best House in London, Zabriskie Point, The Priest's Wife, Lady Liberty, White Sister, What?, Andy Warhol's Frankenstein, The Passenger, The Cassandra Crossing, A Special Day, Saturday Sunday Monday, Twilight of Love, The Squeeze, Claretta and Ben, Liv.
TELEVISION: Mario Puzo's The Fortunate Pilgrim (exec. prod.), Running Away (prod.)

POP, IGGY
Musician, Actor. r.n. James Osterberg. b. MI, April 21, 1947. Has recorded 16 albums with band the Stooges and solo.
PICTURES: *Actor:* Cry Baby, Hardware (voice only), Dead Man, The Crow: City of Angels, Private Parts (cameo), The Rugrats Movie (voice), Snow Day. *Songs:* Rock 'N' Rule. *Score:* The Brave, Repo Man, The Wedding Singer (comp.), Almost Famous (comp.), Freddy Got Fingered (singer)
TELEVISION: *Mini-Series:* Rock and Roll. *Special:* 25 Years of Punk.

POPE, DICK
Cinematographer.
PICTURES: The Girl in the Picture, Coming Up Roses, The Fruit Machine, The Reflecting Skin, Life is Sweet, Dark City, Naked, The Air Up There, An Awfully Big Adventure, Nothing Personal, Secrets and Lies, Career Girls, Swept from the Sea, The Debt Collector, Topsy-Turvy, The Way of the Gun, 13 Conversations About One Thing, All or Nothing, Nicholas Nickleby.
TELEVISION: Series: Porterhouse Blue, Forever Green. Movies: A Sense of History, Fool's Gold: The Story of the Brink's-Mat Robbery, The Blackheath Poisonings, Pleasure, The Great Kandinsky.

PORTMAN, NATALIE
Actress. b. Jerusalem, Israel, June 9, 1981. e. Stagedoor Manor Performing Arts, Harvard. B'way debut in The Diary of Anne Frank, 1997.
PICTURES: The Professional, Heat, Everyone Says I Love You, Beautiful Girls, Mars Attacks!, South Beach, Prince of Egypt (voice), The Little Black Book, Anywhere But Here, Star Wars: Episode I-The Phantom Menace, Where the Heart Is, Zoolander, Star Wars: Episode II: Attack of the Clones, Cold Mountain, Star Wars: Episode III.
TELEVISION: *Series:* Hercules (voice).

PORTMAN, RACHEL
Composer. b. Haslemere, England, Dec. 11, 1960.
PICTURES: Privileged, First Love, Last Day of Summer, Sharma and Beyond, 90 Degrees South, High Hopes, Oranges Are Not the Only Fruit, Life Is Sweet, Antonia and Jane, Where Angels Fear to Tread, Used People, Rebecca's Daughters, The Joy Luck Club, Great Moments in Aviation, Friends, Ethan Frome, Benny & Joon, War of the Buttons, Only You, Sirens, The Road to Wellville, To Wong Foo—Thanks for Everything! Julie Newmar, A Pyromaniac's Love Story, Smoke, The Adventures of Pinocchio, Emma (Acad. Award, 1996), Palookaville, Marvin's Room, Home Fries, Beauty and the Beast: The Enchanted Christmas, Addicted to Love, Mulan, Beloved, The Other Sister, Ratcatcher, Cider House Rules (Acad. Award nom.), The Legend of Bagger Vance, Chocolat (Acad. Award nom.), The Emperor's New Clothes, Hart's War, The Truth About Charlie, Nicholas Nickleby.
TELEVISION: Movies: Reflections, Four Days in July, Good as Gold, The Short and Curlies, 1914 All Out, Sometime in August, Loving Hazel, Young Charlie Chaplin, The Woman in Black, Precious Bane, Monster Maker, Living with Dinosaurs, The Widowmaker, Shoot to Kill, Flea Bites, The Cloning of Joanna , Great Moments in Aviation, May. Mini-series: A Little Princess, Jim Henson's The Storyteller, Jim Henson's The Storyteller: Greek Myths.

POSEY, PARKER
Actress. b. Laurel, MS, Nov. 8, 1968. e. NC School of the Arts; SUNY Purchase.
PICTURES: Joey Breaker, Dazed and Confused, Coneheads, Mixed Nuts, Dead Connection, Amateur, Sleep with Me, Frisk, Drunks, Party Girl, Kicking and Screaming, The Doom Generation, Flirt, Waiting for Guffman, The Daytrippers, Basquiat, Henry Fool, Dinner at Fred's, SubUrbia, Clockwatchers, The House of Yes, The Misadventures of Margaret, Cross Country, You've Got Mail, Dinner at Fred's, Scream 3, Best in Show, Josie and the Pussycats, The Anniversary Party, The Sweetest Thing, Personal Velocity: Three Portraits, The Event, A Mighty Wind.
TELEVISION: Series: As The World Turns. Mini-series: Tales of the City, More Tales of the City, Further Tales of the City.

POST, TED
Producer, Director. b. Brooklyn, NY, March 31, 1918. Dir. many stage plays; dir. CBS-TV Repertoire Thea.; Prod.-dir., NBC-TV Coney Island of the Mind. Directed Everyone Can Make Music.
PICTURES: The Peacemaker (debut, 1956), The Legend of Tom Dooley, Hang 'em High, Beneath The Planet of the Apes, The Baby, The Harrad Experiment, Magnum Force, Whiffs, Good Guys Wear Black, Go Tell the Spartans, Nightkill, The Human Shield, 4 Faces, Old Pals.
TELEVISION: Series: Studio One, Ford Theatre, Playhouse of Stars, Alcoa Theatre, Gunsmoke, Rawhide, Twilight Zone, Wagon Train, Combat, Peyton Place, Alcoa, Defenders, Route 66, Baretta, Columbo. Movies: Night Slaves, Dr. Cook's Garden, Yuma, Five Desperate Women, Do Not Fold Spindle or Mutilate, The Bravos, Sandcastles, Girls in the Office, Diary of a Hitchhiker, Stagecoach. Pilots: Cagney & Lacey, Beyond Westworld, Steve Canyon, Perry Mason. Mini-series: Rich Man, Poor Man II (episode 3).

POSTER, STEVEN
Cinematographer. A.S.C. b. Chicago, IL, March 1, 1944. e. L.A. Art Center Coll. Started as commercial cinematographer before moving into feature films. 2nd unit work includes: Close Encounters of the Third Kind, Blade Runner. 2nd v.p., American Society of Cinematographers.
PICTURES: Blood Beach, Dead and Buried, Spring Break, Strange Brew, Testament, The New Kids, The Heavenly Kid, Blue City, The Boy Who Could Fly, Aloha Summer, Someone to Watch Over Me, Big Top Pee-wee, Next of Kin, Opportunity Knocks, Rocky V, Life Stinks, The Cemetery Club, Once You Meet a Stranger, A Midwife's Tale, Boy's Life 2, Rocket Man, Half a Chance, Donnie Darko, Stuart Little 2, Daddy Day Care
TELEVISION: Movies: The Grass is Always Greener, The Night Rider, The Beggarman Thief, Coward of the County, Mysterious Two, The Cradle Will Fall, I'll Take Manhattan, Class of '65, Courage, Shanghai La Plaza, Roswell, The Color of Justice.

POSTLETHWAITE, PETE
Actor. b. Lancashire, England. Feb. 16, 1946.
THEATRE: RSC: Every Man and His Humour, A Midsummer Night's Dream, MacBeth, King Lear, The Taming of the Shrew.
PICTURES: The Duellists, A Private Function, Distant Voices Still Lives, The Dressmaker, To Kill a Priest, Hamlet, Alien^3, The Last of the Mohicans, Waterland, In the Name of the Father (Acad. Award nom.), Anchoress, The Usual Suspects, James and the Giant Peach (voice), Dragonheart, When Saturday Comes, William Shakespeare's Romeo + Juliet, Brassed Off, Bandyta, Amistad, The Serpent's Kiss, The Lost World: Jurrasic Park, Among Giants, The Divine Ryans, When the Sky Falls, Rat, The Shipping News, Triggermen, Between Strangers, Ring of Fire.
TELEVISION: The Muscle Market, A Child From the South, Treasure Island (theatrical in U.K.), Martin Chuzzlewit, Lost for Words, Alic in Wonderland, Butterfly Collectors (mini-series),

Animal Farm (voice) The Sins (mini-series), Victoria Wood with all the Trimmings.

POSTON, TOM
Actor. b. Columbus, OH, Oct. 17, 1927. Made B'way debut 1947 in Cyrano de Bergerac.
PICTURES: City That Never Sleeps (debut, 1953), Zotz!, The Old Dark House, Soldier in the Rain, Cold Turkey, The Happy Hooker, Rabbit Test, Up the Academy, Carbon Copy, Krippendorf's Tribe, The Story of Us.
TELEVISION: Movies: The Girl The Gold Watch and Everything, Save the Dog!, A Quiet Little Neighborhood A Perfect Little Murder. Series: The Steve Allen Show (Emmy Award, 1959), Pantomime Quiz, To Tell the Truth, On the Rocks, We've Got Each Other, Mork and Mindy, Newhart, Grace Under Fire, Apple Valley Knights. Guest: Goodyear Playhouse, Phil Silvers Show, Password, The Defenders, Fame, The Love Boat, Dream On, The Simpsons (voice).

POTTS, ANNIE
Actress. b. Nashville, TN, Oct. 28, 1952. e. Stephens Coll., MO, BFA. Amateur stage debut at 12 in Heidi. Then in summer stock; on road in Charley's Aunt, 1976. Serves on auxilliary bd. of MADD (Mothers Against Drunk Driving). Ambassador for Women for the Amer. Arthritis Fdn.
PICTURES: Corvette Summer (debut, 1978), King of the Gypsies, Heartaches, Ghostbusters, Crimes of Passion, Pretty in Pink, Jumpin' Jack Flash, Pass the Ammo, Who's Harry Crumb?, Ghostbusters II, Texasville, Breaking the Rules, Toy Story (voice), Toy Story 2 (voice).
TELEVISION: Movies: Black Market Baby, Flatbed Annie and Sweetie Pie, Cowboy, It Came Upon the Midnight Clear, Why Me?, Her Deadly Rival. Series: Goodtime Girls, Designing Women, Love & War, Dangerous Minds, Over the Top, Any Day Now, Hercules (voice). Guest: Remington Steele, Magnum P.I., Twilight Zone.

POUND, LESLIE
Executive. b. London, England, Nov. 3, 1926. Entered industry in 1943 as reporter on British trade paper, The Cinema. Now, Screen International. Following military service in India and Singapore returned to work for that publication until 1952 when joined Paramount pub. office in London on the The Greatest Show on Earth. Named dir. of adv/pub. in U.K. for Paramount. 1958, retained Paramount position when Cinema Int'l Corp. was formed. 1977, joined Lew Grade in ITC Entertainment as worldwide dir. of pub./adv. 1977, int'l pub. chief for Embassy Pictures in Los Angeles. 1982, named Paramount Pictures v.p., int'l mktg. for motion picture div., N.Y. 1983. Relocated to L.A. with mktg. div. as sr. v.p. Returned to London, 1993 as sr. v.p. International markets for Paramount Pictures. Retired.

POWELL, JANE
Actress, Singer. r.n. Suzanne Burce. b. Portland, OR, April 1, 1929. m. pub. relations exec. Dick Moore. Had own radio program over KOIN, Portland; singer on nat'l networks; Star of Tomorrow, 1948. Autobiography: The Girl Next Door ... and How She Grew (1998). Video: Jane Powell's Fight Back With Fitness.
THEATRE: Irene (B'way, 1974). After-Play (off-B'way, 1996). Toured nationally with South Pacific, Peter Pan, My Fair Lady, The Unsinkable Molly Brown, I Do I Do, Same Time Next Year, PICTURES: Song of the Open Road (debut, 1944), Delightfully Dangerous, Holiday in Mexico, Three Daring Daughters, A Date With Judy, Luxury Liner, Nancy Goes to Rio, Two Weeks With Love, Royal Wedding, Rich Young and Pretty, Small Town Girl, Three Sailors and a Girl, Seven Brides for Seven Brothers, Athena, Deep in My Heart, Hit the Deck, The Girl Most Likely, The Female Animal, Enchanted Island, That's Entertainment, Tubby the Tuba, That's Dancing, Marie, Picture This, Broadway: The Golden Age by the Legends Who Were There.
TELEVISION: Specials: Ruggles of Red Gap, Give My Regards to Broadway, Meet Me in St. Louis, Jane Powell Show. Series: Alcoa Theatre, Loving, As the World Turns, Growing Pains. Guest: The Love Boat, Growing Pains, Murder She Wrote, others. Movies: The Letters, Mayday at 40,000 Feet, The Making of Seven Brides for Seven Brothers, The Sandy Bottom Orchestra. Host: The Movie Musicals. Mini-Series: Perfect Murder Perfect Town.

POWELL, MICHAEL
Executive. b. Birmingham, AL, March 23, 1963. e. College of William and Mary, AB, government, 1985. Georgetown U. Law Center, JD, 1993. U.S. Army officer, 1985-88. Policy adviser to Sec'y of Defense, Defense Dept., 1988-90. Law clerk for Harry Edwards, chief judge, U.S. Court of Appeals, 1993-94. Associate, O'Melveny & Myers, 1994-96. Chief of staff, Justice Dept. antitrust div., 1996-97. Commissioner of the FCC, 1997.

POWELL, ROBERT
Actor. b. Salford, England, June 1, 1944. e. Manchester U. Stage work includes Tovarich.
PICTURES: Robbery (debut, 1967), Far From the Madding Crowd, Joanna, The Italian Job, Walk a Crooked Path, Secrets, Running Scared, Asylum, The Asphyx, Mahler, Tommy, Oltre il Bene e il Male, Cocktails for Three, The Thirty-Nine Steps, The Dilessi Affair, Harlequin, Jane Austin in Manhattan, The Survivor,

Imperative (Venice Film Fest. Award), The Jigsaw Man, What Waits Below, D'Annunio and I Down There in the Jungle, Romeo-Juliet (voice), The Sign of Command, Chunuk Bair, The Mystery of Edwin Drood.
TELEVISION: *Series*: Doomwatch, Hannay, Canned Carrott, The Detectives, Escape. *Mini-Series*: Jesus of Nazareth, The Century of Welfare. *Movies/Specials*: Shelley, Jude the Obscure, Mrs. Warren's Profession, Mr. Rolls & Mr. Royce, Looking for Clancy, The Four Feathers, The Hunchback of Notre Dame, Pygmalion, Frankenstein, Shaka Zulu, Merlin of the Crystal Cave, The Golden Years, The First Circle, Pride of Africa.

POWERS, MALA
Actress. r.n. Mary Ellen Powers. b. San Francisco, CA, Dec. 20, 1931. p. George and Dell Powers, latter, dramatic coach. e. Studied acting with Michael Chekhov. e. UCLA. Pasadena Playhouse in For Keeps, 1946, followed by Distant Isle; Actor's Lab, Hollywood; did considerable radio, theatre and tv work.
Writer, narrator Children's Story, and Dial A Story (1979). *Author*: Follow the Star (1980), Follow the Year (1984). Teaches Michael Chekhov technique of acting.
PICTURES: Tough as They Come (debut, 1942), Outrage, Edge of Doom, Cyrano de Bergerac, Rose of Cimarron, City Beneath the Sea, City That Never Sleeps, Geraldine, The Yellow Mountain, Rage at Dawn, Bengazi, Tammy and the Bachelor, The Storm Rider, Death in Small Doses, The Colossus of New York, Sierra Baron, The Unknown Terror, Man on the Prowl, Flight of the Lost Balloon, Rogue's Gallery, Doomsday, Daddy's Gone-A-Hunting, Six Tickets to Hell, Where the Wind Dies, From Russia to Hollywood: The 100-Year Odyssey of Chekhov and Shdanoff.
TELEVISION: *Series*: Hazel, The Man and the City. *Guest*: Daniel Boone.

POWERS, C. F. (MIKE) JR.
Executive. b. San Francisco, CA, March 6, 1923. e. Park Coll., MO, Columbia U., N.Y., graduated U. of Oregon. Entered film business with P.R.C. in Portland, OR, 1947. Became Eagle Lion branch mgr. in Portland, 1950, and then United Artists. Moved to Seattle, WA as branch mgr. of 20th Century Fox, 1960. Was then western division mgr. for 20th Century Fox until 1967, then western division mgr. for Cinerama until 1973. Became exec. v.p., head film buyer for Robert L. Lippert Theatres, Transcontinental Theatres and Affiliated Theatres until 1978. Western div. mgr. Orion Pictures, 1982-4. Mike Powers Ent. (a buying and booking combine and indept. film distrib.). 1984-86 Western district mgr. Embassy Pictures. Became western division mgr. for Filmways Pictures. Past president of Catholic Entertainment Guild of Northern Calif.; past pres. of Variety Club Tent 32, San Francisco. Consultant to U.S. Federal Govt. Retired.

POWERS, STEFANIE
Actress. r.n. Stefania Federkiewicz. b. Hollywood, CA, Nov. 2, 1942. After graduation from Hollywood High signed by Columbia Studios.
PICTURES: Tammy Tell Me True (debut, 1962), Experiment in Terror, The Young Sinner, The Interns, If a Man Answers, McClintock!, Palm Springs Weekend, The New Interns, Love Has Many Faces, Die Die My Darling, Stagecoach, Warning Shot, The Boatniks, Crescendo, The Magnificent 7 Ride, Herbie Rides Again, Gone With the West, It Seemed Like a Good Idea at the Time, Escape to Athena, Invisible Stranger.
TELEVISION: *Series*: The Girl From U.N.C.L.E., Feather and Father Gang, Hart to Hart, Doctors, Dale's All Stars. *Mini-series*: Washington: Behind Closed Doors, Hollywood Wives. *Movies*: Five Desperate Women, Paper Man, Sweet Sweet Rachel, Hardcase, No Place to Run, Shootout in a One-Dog Town, Skyway to Death, Sky Heist, Return to Earth, Family Secrets (also prod.), A Death in Canaan, Nowhere to Run, Mistral's Daughter, Deceptions, At Mother's Request, Beryl Markham: A Shadow on the Sun (also co-prod.), She Was Marked for Murder, Love and Betrayal, When Will I Be Loved?, The Burden of Proof, Survive the Night, Hart to Hart Returns (also co-prod.), Hart to Hart: Home is Where the Hart Is, Hart to Hart: Crimes of the Hart (also co-prod.), Hart to Hart: Old Friends Never Die, The Good Ride, Good King Wenceslas, Hart to Hart: Secrets of the Hart, Hart to Hart: Til Death Do Us Hart, Someone Is Watching.

PREISNER, ZBIGNIEW
Composer. b. Bielsko-Biala, Poland, May 20, 1955.
PICTURES: The Weather Forecast, No End, By Touch, Ucieczka, The Lullabye, Kocham Kino, To Kill a Priest, A Short Film About Killing, A Short Film About Love, The Last Schoolbell, Europa, Europa, The Double Life of Veronique, Eminent Domain, At Play in the Fields of the Lord, Dismissed from Life, Olivier, Olivier, Damage, The Secret Garden, Blue, White, Red, The Line of the Horizon, To Have and to Hold, Desire in Motion, Elisa, Feast of July, Krysztof Kieslowski: I'm So-So, De Aegypto, Bridges, Fairy Tale: A True Story, The Island on Bird Street, Foolish Heart, Liv, The Last September, Dreaming of Joseph Lees, Aberdeen, Weiser.
TELEVISION: Mini-series: The Decalogue, Radetzky March.

PRENTISS, PAULA
Actress. r.n. Paula Ragusa. b. San Antonio, TX, March 4, 1939. m. actor-dir. Richard Benjamin. e. Northwestern U., Bachelor degree in drama, 1959. On stage in As You Like It, Arf!, The Norman Conquests, Love Letters, Secrets, Demons (Amer. Rep. Theatre, Cambridge, MA), Angel's Share (Tiffany Theater, L.A.).
PICTURES: Where the Boys Are (debut, 1960), The Honeymoon Machine, Bachelor in Paradise, The Horizontal Lieutenant, Follow the Boys, Man's Favorite Sport?, The World of Henry Orient, Looking for Love, In Harm's Way, What's New Pussycat?, Catch-22, Move, Born to Win, Last of the Red Hot Lovers, Crazy Joe, The Parallax View, The Stepford Wives, The Black Marble, Saturday the 14th, Buddy Buddy, Mrs. Winterbourne.
TELEVISION: *Series*: He & She, Burke's Law. *Movies*: The Couple Takes a Wife, Having Babies II, No Room to Run (Australian), Friendships Secrets and Lies, Top of the Hill, Packin' It In, M.A.D.D.: Mothers Against Drunk Drivers.

PRESLE, MICHELINE
Actress. r.n. Micheline Chassagne. b. Paris, France, Aug. 22, 1922. e. Raymond Rouleau Dram. Sch. m.p. debut in Je Chante; on stage in Colinette. Am. Stram Gram, Spectacle des Allies; to U.S., 1945; Flea in Her Ear, Magic Circus, Who's Afraid of Virginia Woolf? (tour), Gigi, Nuit de Valognes, Boomerang, Adriana Mont, etc.
PICTURES: Jeunes Filles en Detresse, L'Histoire de Rire, La Nuit Fantastique, Felicie Nanteuil, Seul Amour, Faibalas, Boule de Suif, Jeux Sont Faix, Diable au Corps, Under My Skin, Some Kind of News, An American Guerilla in the Philippines, Adventures of Captain Fabian, Sins of Pompeii, House of Ricordi, Archipelago of Love, Thieves After Dark, Le Chien, At the Top of the Stairs, Le Jour de Rois. Fine Weather, But Storms Due Towards Evening, Confidences, Alouette je te plumerai, I Want to Go Home, others.
TELEVISION: The Blood of Others, several European productions.

PRESLEY, PRISCILLA
Actress. b. Brooklyn, NY, May 24, 1945. Raised in Connecticut. e. Wiesbaden, West Germany where met and married Elvis Presley (1967-73). Studied acting with Milton Katselas, dance at Steven Peck Theatre Art School and karate at Chuck Norris Karate School. Formed a business, Bis and Beau, marketing exclusive dress designs. Became TV spokesperson for beauty products.
PICTURES: The Naked Gun: From the Files of Police Squad! (debut, 1988), The Adventures of Ford Fairlane, The Naked Gun 2 1/2: The Smell of Fear, Naked Gun 33 1/3: The Final Insult. *Exec. Prod.*: Finding Graceland.
TELEVISION: *Series*: Those Amazing Animals (host, 1980-81), Dallas. *Movies*: Love is Forever, Elvis and Me (prod. only), Breakfast with Einstein, Haley Wagner Star.

PRESSMAN, EDWARD R.
Producer. b. New York, N.Y. 1943. e. Fieldston Sch.; grad., Stanford U.; studied at London Sch. of Economics. Began career with film short, Girl, in collaboration with dir. Paul Williams in London. They formed Pressman-Williams Enterprises.
PICTURES: *Prod. or Exec. prod.*: Out of It, The Revolutionary, Dealing: or the Berkeley to Boston Forty Brick, Lost Bag Blues, Sisters, Badlands, Phantom of the Paradise, Despair, Paradise Alley, Old Boyfriends, Heartbeat, The Hand, Conan the Barbarian, Das Boot, The Pirates of Penzance, Crimewave, Plenty, Half Moon Street, True Stories, Good Morning Babylon, Masters of the Universe, Walker, Wall Street, Cherry 2000, Paris By Night, Talk Radio, Martians Go Home, Blue Steel, Reversal of Fortune, To Sleep with Anger, Waiting for the Light, Homicide, Year of the Gun, Iron Maze (co-exec. prod.), Storyville, Bad Lieutenant, Hoffa, Dream Lover, The Crow, Street Fighter, Judge Dredd, City Hall, The Island of Dr. Moreau, The Crow: City of Angels, The Winter Guest, Two Girls and a Guy, The Blackout, The Crow: World of Gods and Monsters, American Psycho, The Crow: Salvation, Endurance: Shackleton's Legendary Antarctic Expedition, Harvard Man, The Cooler, The Beautiful Country, The Guys, The Hebrew Hammer, Owning Mahowny, 10th Victim.

PRESSMAN, LAWRENCE
Actor. b. Cynthiana, KY, July 10, 1939. e. Kentucky Northwestern U. On B'way in Man in the Glass Booth, Play It Again, Sam.
PICTURES: The Man in the Glass Booth, The Crazy World of Julius Vrooder, Hellstrom Chronicle, Shaft, Making It, Walk Proud, Nine to Five, Some Kind of Hero, The Hanoi Hilton, The Waterdance, The Maker, Trial & Error, Mighty Joe Young, My Giant, Very Bad Things, American Pie, Alex in Wonder, American Pie: The Wedding, Dr. Dolittle 2.
TELEVISION: *Series*: Mulligan's Stew, Doogie Howser M.D., Law and Order, N.Y.P.D. Blue, The Late Shift, Dark Angel. *Movies*: Cannon, The Snoop Sisters, The Marcus-Nelson Murder, Winter Kill, The First 36 Hours of Dr. Durant, Rich Man, Poor Man, Man from Atlantis, The Trial of Lee Harvey Oswald, The Gathering, Like Mom, Like Me, Blind Ambition, Little Girl Lost, She Knows Too Much, Breaking Point, Fire and Rain, White Hot: The Mysterious Murder of Thelma Todd, To My Daughter with Love, The Enemy Within, The Rockford Files: I Still Love L.A.

PRESSMAN, MICHAEL
Director, Producer. b. New York, NY, July 1, 1950. e. California Inst. of Arts. From show business family; was actor in college.
PICTURES: *Director*: The Great Texas Dynamite Chase, The Bad News Bears Breaking Training, Boulevard Nights, Those Lips Those Eyes (also prod.), Some Kind of Hero, Doctor Detroit, Teenage Mutant Ninja Turtles II: The Secret of the Ooze, To Gillian On Her 37th Birthday, Lake Placid.
TELEVISION: *Movies*: Like Mom, Like Me, The Imposter, The Christmas Gift, Final Jeopardy, Private Sessions, Haunted by Her Past, To Heal a Nation, Shootdown, The Revenge of Al Capone, Incident at Dark River, Man Against the Mob (also co-prod.), Joshua's Heart, Quicksand: No Escape, Saint Maybe, A Season for Miracles. *Series*: The Practice, Boston Public, The Guardian.

PRESTON, KELLY
Actress. b. Honolulu, HI, Oct. 13, 1962. e. UCLA, USC. m. actor John Travolta.
PICTURES: Metalstorm: The Destruction of Jared-Syn (debut, 1983), Christine, Mischief, Secret Admirer, SpaceCamp, 52 Pick-Up, Amazon Women on the Moon, A Tiger's Tale, Love at Stake, Spellbinder, Twins, The Experts, Run, Only You, Love Is a Gun, Cheyenne Warrior, Waiting to Exhale, From Dusk Till Dawn, Citizen Ruth, Addicted to Love, Jerry Maguire, Nothing to Lose, Jack Frost, Holy Man, For Love of the Game, Bar Hopping, Battlefield Earth, Daddy and Them, Not Under My Roof, A View from the Top, What a Girl Wants.
TELEVISION: *Series*: For Love and Honor, Capitol. *Movies*: The Perfect Bride, The American Clock, Mrs. Munck, Bar Hopping. *Guest*: Quincy, Blue Thunder, Riptide.

PREVIN, ANDRE
Composer, Conductor. b. Berlin, Germany, April 6, 1929. Composed and conducted over 50 m.p. scores. Music dir., Pittsburgh Symphony Orchestra, & conductor emeritus of London Symphony Orchestra. Music dir., Royal Philharmonic Orch., 1985-89. Guest conductor of most major symphony orchestras in U.S. and Europe. Music dir., Pittsburgh Symphony 1972-81. Conductor, London Symphony, 1968-78. Conductor Emeritus London Symphony, 1992-present. Received Knighthood of British Empire in 1996.
PICTURES: Three Little Words, Cause for Alarm, It's Always Fair Weather, Bad Day at Black Rock, Invitation to the Dance, Catered Affair, Designing Woman, Silk Stockings, Gigi (Acad. Award, 1958), Porgy and Bess (Acad. Award, 1959), The Subterraneans, Bells Are Ringing, Pepe, Elmer Gantry, The Four Horsemen of the Apocalypse, One Two Three, Two for the Seesaw, Long Day's Journey Into Night, Irma LaDouce (Acad. Award, 1963), My Fair Lady (Acad. Award, 1964), Goodbye Charlie, Inside Daisy Clover, The Fortune Cookie, Thoroughly Modern Millie, Valley of the Dolls, Paint Your Wagon, The Music Lovers, Jesus Christ Superstar, Rollerball, One Trick Pony, The Music Lovers, Mrs. Pollifax—Spy, Bang Bang.
TELEVISION: Jennie: Lady Randolph Churchill, A Streetcar Named Desire.

PRICE, FRANK
Executive, Producer. b. Decatur, IL, May 17, 1930. e. Michigan State U. following naval service. Joined CBS in N.Y. in 1951 as story editor and writer. Moved to Hollywood in 1953, serving as story editor first at Columbia and then NBC (Matinee Theatre). In 1958 joined Universal as an assoc. prod. and writer. In 1961 named exec. prod. of The Virginian TV series. Appt. exec. prod. of Ironside; later did It Takes a Thief and several World Premiere movies. 1964 named v.p. of Universal TV; 1971, sr. v.p.; 1974, pres. Also v.p., MCA, Inc. 1978 left to join Columbia as pres. of new company unit, Columbia Pictures Productions. In 1979 named chmn. & CEO of Columbia Pictures. In 1983 joined Universal: named chmn., motion picture group, pres. of UniversalPictures, and v.p. of MCA. In 1987 formed Price Entertainment Inc. as chmn. & CEO to produce movies and create TV shows for dist. through Columbia Pictures Entertainment. 1990, integrated Price Entertainment Inc., into Columbia and was named chairman. Resigned, 1991.
PICTURES: Gladiator, The Walking Dead, Circle of Friends, Getting Away with Murder, Zeus and Roxanne, Texas Rangers.
TELEVISION: *Series*: Matinee Theatre, The Virginian, Ironside, It Takes a Thief, Rich Man, Poor Man. *Movies*: Sullivan's Empire, Split Second to an Epitaph, Alias Smith and Jones, The City, I Love a Mystery, The Tuskegee Airmen.

PRICE, RICHARD
Writer. b. Bronx, NY, Oct. 12, 1949. e. Cornell U., Columbia U.
AUTHOR: The Wanderers, Bloodbrothers, Ladies' Man, The Breaks, Clockers.
PICTURES: *Cameos*: The Wanderers, The Paper. *Writer*: The Color of Money (Acad. Award nom.; also cameo), Streets of Gold, New York Stories (Life Lessons; also cameo), Sea of Love, Night and the City (also cameo), Mad Dog and Glory (also exec. prod., cameo), Ethan Frome (exec. prod. only), Kiss of Death (also co-prod., cameo), Clockers (also co-prod.), Ransom (also cameo), Money Train, Shaft.

PRIESTLEY, JASON
Actor. b. Vancouver, Canada, Aug. 28, 1969. First screen appearance was as baby in 1969 film That Cold Day in the Park, in which his mother had bit part. Child actor in many Canadian TV commercials. First major U.S. acting job in 1986 TV movie Nobody's Child. Moved to L.A. in 1987. Theatre includes The Addict, The Breakfast Club.
PICTURES: The Boy Who Could Fly, Nowhere to Run, Watchers, Calendar Girl, Tombstone, Coldblooded, Love and Death on Long Island, Hacks, Standing on Fishes, Dill Scallion, Barenaked in America (also dir., prod.), Eye of the Beholder, The Highwayman (also exec. prod.), Choose Life, Zigs, Lion of Oz (voice), The Fourth Angel, Civer Story, Darkness Falling, Time of the Wolf, Call Me Irresponsible, Cherish.
TELEVISION: *Series*: Sister Kate, Beverly Hills 90210 (also co-prod., dir.). *Movies*: Stacie (Canada), Nobody's Child, Teen Angel & Teen Angel Returns (Disney TV), Vanishing Point, Kiss Tomorrow Goodbye. *Guest*: Danger Bay (Canada), MacGyver, 21 Jump Street, Adventures of Beans Baxter, Quantum Leap, Parker Lewis Can't Lose.

PRIMUS, BARRY
Actor. b. New York, NY, Feb. 16, 1938. e. Bennington Coll., City Coll. of NY.
THEATRE: The King and the Duke, The Nervous Set, Henry IV, Parts I and II, Creating the World, Teibele and the Demon, Lincoln Center Rep. (The Changling, After the Fall).
PICTURES: The Brotherhood, Puzzle of a Downfall Child, Been Down So Long It Looks Like Up to Me, Von Richtofen and Brown, Boxcar Bertha, The Gravy Train, New York New York, Avalanche, Autopsy, The Rose, Heartland, Night Games, Absence of Malice, The River, Down and Out in Beverly Hills, Jake Speed, Space Camp, Talking Walls, The Stranger, Big Business, Cannibal Women in the Avocado Jungle of Death, Torn Apart, Guilty by Suspicion, Mistress (dir., s.p. only), Night and the City, Flipping, Black & White, 15 Minutes, Life as a House, Jackson, Break a Leg.
TELEVISION: *Series*: Cagney and Lacey. *Mini-Series*: Washington Behind Closed Doors. *Movies*: Big Rose, Roger & Harry: The Mitera Target, Portrait of a Showgirl, Paper Dolls, I Want to Live, Heart of Steel, Brotherly Love, The Women of Spring Break, Trade Off, Crime of the Century, Gold Coast, James Dean. *Guest*: Law and Order.

PRINCE
Singer, Actor. r.n. Prince Rogers Nelson. b. Minneapolis, MN, June 7, 1958. Rock star and recording artist.
PICTURES: Purple Rain (also wrote songs; Acad. Award for best orig. song score, 1984), Under the Cherry Moon (also dir., s.p., songs), Sign O' the Times (also dir., songs), Graffiti Bridge (also dir., s.p., songs). *Songs only*: Still Smokin', Bright Lights Big City, Batman, Show Girls, Girl 6, Striptease, Bamboozled, Scream 2.

PRINCE, HAROLD
Director. b. New York, NY, Jan. 30, 1928. e. U. of Pennsylvania. Worked as stage mgr. for George Abbott on three shows, later co-produced, produced and/or directed the following: The Pajama Game (Tony Award), Damn Yankees (Tony Award), New Girl In Town, West Side Story, A Swim in the Sea, Fiorello! (Tony Award, Pulitzer Prize), Tenderloin, A Call on Kurpin, Take Her She's Mine, A Funny Thing Happened on the Way to the Forum (Tony Award), She Loves Me, The Matchmaker (revival), Fiddler on the Roof, Poor Bitos, Baker Street, Flora, The Red Menace, Superman, Cabaret (Tony Award), Zorba, Company, Follies, The Great God Brown, The Visit, Love for Love (the last three all revivals), A Little Night Music (Tony Award), Candide (Tony Award), Pacific Overtures, Side by Side by Sondheim, Some of My Best Friends, On the Twentieth Century, Evita (also London), Sweeney Todd (Tony Award 1979; also London), Merrily We Roll Along, A Doll's Life, Play Memory, End of the World, Diamonds, Grind, Roza, Cabaret (revival), Phantom of the Opera (Tony Award, 1988; also London), Grandchild of Kings (dir. & adapt.), Kiss of the Spider Woman (Tony Award, 1993), Show Boat (Tony Award, 1995); and also directed the operas Ashmadei, Silverlake, Sweeney Todd, Candide and Don Giovanni for N.Y. City Opera, Girl of Golden West for Chicago Lyric Opera Co. and San Francisco Opera; Willie Stark for Houston Grand Opera; Madama Butterfly for Chicago Lyric Opera and Turandot for Vienna State Opera and Faust for Metropolitan Opera.
AUTHOR: Contradictions: Notes on Twenty-Six Years in the Theatre (1974).
PICTURES: *Co-producer*: The Pajama Game, Damn Yankees. *Director*: Something for Everyone, A Little Night Music.
TELEVISION: Sweeney Todd, Candide.

PRINCIPAL, VICTORIA
Actress. b. Fukuoka, Japan, Jan 3, 1946. Father was in U.S. air force. Went to New York to become model; studied acting privately with Jean Scott at Royal Acad. of Dramatic Art in London before moving to Hollywood. Worked as talent agent in the mid-1970's.
PICTURES: The Life and Times of Judge Roy Bean (debut, 1972), The Naked Ape, Earthquake, I Will I Will... for Now, Vigilante Force, Michael Kael contre la World News Company.
TELEVISION: *Series*: Dallas, Titans. *Guest*: Fantasy Island

(pilot), Love Story, Love American Style, Greatest Heroes of the Bible. *Movies:* The Night They Stole Miss Beautiful, The Pleasure Palace, Last Hours Before Morning, Not Just Another Affair, Mistress, Naked Lie (also exec. prod.), Blind Witness (also exec. prod.), Sparks: The Price of Passion (also exec. prod.), Don't Touch My Daughter (also exec. prod.), The Burden of Proof, Seduction: Three Tales From the Inner Sanctum (also co-exec. prod.), Midnight's Child (exec. prod. only), Beyond Obsession, River of Rage: The Taking of Maggie Keene, Dancing in the Dark, The Abduction, Love in Another Town, Titans, Doing Dallas.

PRINE, ANDREW
Actor. b. Jennings, FL, Feb. 14, 1936. e. U. of Miami. m. actress Heather Lowe. Mem. Actors Studio. On stage in Look Homeward, Angel, A Distant Bell, Mrs. Patterson, Borak. Ahmanson Theatre, LA: Long Day's Journey into Night, The Caine Mutiny. South Coast Rep.: Goodbye Freddy.
PICTURES: The Miracle Worker, Advance to the Rear, Texas Across the River, Bandolero!, The Devil's Brigade, This Savage Land, Generation, Chisum, Riding Tall, Simon: King of the Witches, Barn of the Naked Dead (Terror Circus), One Little Indian, The Centerfold Girls, Grizzly, The Town That Dreaded Sundown, Winds of Autumn, High Flying Love, The Evil, Amityville II: The Possession, Playing with Fire, Eliminators, Chill Factor, The Big One, Life on the Edge, Double Exposure, Gettysburg, Inferno, Dark Dancer, Gathering Evidence, Without Evidence, Serial Killer, The Shadow Men, Possums, The Boy with X-Ray Eyes, Critical Mass, Scooby-Doo, Sweet Home Alabama, Gods and Generals, Collector of Souls.
TELEVISION: *Series:* The Wide Country, The Road West, W.E.B., Dallas, Room for Two, Weird Science. *Movies:* And the Children Shall Lead, Roughing It, Callie & Son, The Deputies, Another Part of the Forest, Night Slaves, Split Second to an Epitaph, Along Came a Spider, Night Slaves, Wonder Woman, Law of the Land, Tail Gunner Joe, Last of the Mohicans, A Small Killing, Mind over Murder, M-Station Hawaii, Christmas Miracle in Caulfield, Young Abe Lincoln, U.S.A., Donner Pass: The Road to Survival, Mission of the Shark, Scattered Dreams: The Kathryn Messenger Story, The Avenging Angel, The Mircale Worker, James Dean. *Mini-Series:* V: The Final Battle.

PRINZE, JR., FREDDIE
Actor. b. Los Angeles, CA, March 8, 1976. Son of late actor Freddie Prinze.
PICTURES: To Gillian on Her 37th Birthday, The House of Yes, I Know What You Did Last Summer, Sparkler, I Still Know What You Did Last Summer, Down to You, She's All That, Wing Commander, Head Over Heels, Boys and Girls, Summer Catch, Scooby-Doo, Happily N'Ever After, Scooby-Doo 2: Monsters Unleashed.
TELEVISION: *Movies:* Detention: The Siege at Johnson High, Vig. *Guest:* Family Matters, Friends.

PROCHNOW, JURGEN
Actor. b. Berlin, Germany, June 10, 1941. Studied acting at the Folkwang-Schule. In provincial theatre before making tv debut on the series Harbour at the Rhine River, 1970.
PICTURES: Zoff (debut, 1971), Zartlichkeit der Wolfe, The Lost Honor of Katharina Blum, The Consequence, Einer von uns bei-den, Das Boot (The Boat; Berlin Film Fest. Award), The Keep, Dune, Der Bulle und das Madchen, Killing Cars, Terminus, Beverly Hills Cop II, Devil's Paradise, The Seventh Sign, A Dry White Season, The Fourth War, The Man Inside, Twin Peaks: Fire Walk With Me, Body of Evidence, In the Mouth of Madness, Judge Dredd, The Replacement Killers, The Fall, Chinadream, The Last Stop, Wing Commander, Jack the Dog, Gunblast Vodka, Elite, Last Run, Ripper: Letter From Hell, Dark Asylum, Heart of America, The House of the Dead, Baltic Storm.
TELEVISION: Forbidden, Murder by Reason of Insanity, Danielle Steel's Jewels, The Lucona Affair, Love Is Forever, Robin Hood, The Fire Next Time, Esther, Heaven's Fire, Final Ascent, Poison, Padre Pio.

PROSKY, ROBERT
Actor. b. Philadelphia, PA, Dec. 13, 1930. Won TV amateur talent search contest, leading to scholarship with American Theatre Wing. 23-year veteran with Washington's Arena stage. Taught acting and appeared in over 150 plays
THEATRE: Death of a Salesman, Galileo, The Caucasian Chalk Circle, You Can't Take it With You, Our Town, The Price (Helen Hayes Award). *B'way:* Moonchildren, A View from the Bridge, Pale Horse Pale Rider, Arms and the Man, Glengarry Glen Ross (Tony nom.), A Walk in the Woods (Tony nom.).
PICTURES: Thief, Hanky Panky, Monsignor, The Lords of Discipline, Christine, The Keep, The Natural, Outrageous Fortune, Big Shots, Broadcast News, The Great Outdoors, Things Change, Loose Cannons, Gremlins II: The New Batch, Funny About Love, Green Card, Life in the Food Chain (Age Isn't Everything), Far and Away, Hoffa, Last Action Hero, Rudy, Mrs. Doubtfire, Miracle on 34th Street, The Scarlet Letter, Dead Man Walking, Mad City, Dudley Do-Right, Grandfather's Birthday, D-Tox, Death to Smoochy.
TELEVISION: *Series:* Hill Street Blues, Lifestories (host), Veronica's Closet, Danny. *Movies:* World War III, The Ordeal of

Bill Carny, Lou Grant, The Adams Chronicles, Old Dogs, Into Thin Air, The Murder of Mary Phagan, Home Fires Burning, From the Dead of Night, Heist, Dangerous Pursuit, Johnny Ryan, Against the Mob, A Green Journey, The Love She Sought, Double Edge, Life on the High Wire, Teamster Boss: The Jackie Presser Story, Brother's Destiny, The Lake, Swing Vote. *Guest:* Coach, Frasier, The Practice.

PROVINE, DOROTHY
Actress. b. Deadwood, SD, Jan. 20, 1937. e. U. of Washington. Retired from films in 1969.
PICTURES: The Bonnie Parker Story (debut, 1958), Live Fast Die Young, Riot in Juvenile Prison, The 30 Foot Bride of Candy Rock, Wall of Noise, It's a Mad Mad Mad Mad World, Good Neighbor Sam, The Great Race, That Darn Cat, One Spy Too Many, Kiss the Girls and Make Them Die, Who's Minding the Mint?, Never a Dull Moment.
TELEVISION: *Series:* The Alaskans, The Roaring 20's. *Movie:* The Sound of Anger.

PRYCE, JONATHAN
Actor. b. North Wales, June 1, 1947. e. Royal Acad. of Dramatic Art. Actor and artistic dir. of Liverpool Everyman Theatre Co.
THEATRE: *London:* Comedians, Taming of the Shrew, Antony and Cleopatra, Tally's Folly, Hamlet (Olivier Award), The Caretaker, Macbeth, The Seagull, Uncle Vanya, Miss Saigon (Olivier & Variety Club Awards), Oliver! *NY:* Comedians (Tony & Theatre World Awards, 1977), Accidental Death of an Anarchist, Miss Saigon (Tony & Drama Desk Awards, 1991).
PICTURES: Voyage of the Damned (debut, 1976), Breaking Glass, Loophole, The Ploughman's Lunch, Something Wicked This Way Comes, The Doctor and the Devils, Brazil, Haunted Honeymoon, Jumpin' Jack Flash, Man on Fire, Consuming Passions, The Adventures of Baron Munchausen, The Rachel Papers, Freddie as F.R.O. 7 (voice), Glengarry Glen Ross, The Age of Innocence, A Business Affair, Great Moments in Aviation, A Troll in Central Park (voice), Deadly Advice, Shopping, Carrington (Cannes Film Fest. Award, 1995), Evita, Tomorrow Never Dies, Ronin, Stigmata, The Testimony of Taliesin Jones, Very Annie Mary, The Suicide Club, Il Gioco, Bride of the Wind, The Affair of the Necklace, Who Shot Victor Fox, What a Girl Wants, Pirates of the Caribbean: The Curse of the Black Pearl.
TELEVISION: Comedians, Playthings, Partisans, For Tea on Sunday, Timon of Athens, Praying Mantis, Murder Is Easy, Daft as a Brush, Martin Luther Heretic, The Caretaker, Glad Day, The Man From the Pru, Roger Doesn't Live Here Anymore, Selling Hitler, Whose Line is It Anyway?, Mr. Wroes Virgins, Barbarians at the Gate, Thicker Than Water, David, The Union Game: A Rugby History, Confessions of an Ugly Stepsister, Victoria and Albert (mini-series).

PRYOR, RICHARD
Actor. b. Peoria, IL, Dec. 1, 1940. At age 7 played drums with professionals. Made NY debut as standup comic in 1963, leading to appearances on TV (Johnny Carson, Merv Griffin, Ed Sullivan). Co-wrote TV scripts for Lily Tomlin (Emmy Award, 1974) and Flip Wilson. Won Grammy Awards for albums That Nigger's Crazy, Is It Something I Said?, Bicentennial Nigger. *Autobiography:* Pryor Convictions and Other Life Sentences (1995).
PICTURES: The Busy Body (debut, 1967), The Green Berets, Wild in the Streets, The Phynx, You've Got to Walk It Like You Talk It Or You'll Lose That Beat, Dynamite Chicken, Lady Sings the Blues, Hit!, Wattstax, The Mack, Some Call It Loving, Blazing Saddles (co-s.p. only), Uptown Saturday Night, Adios Amigo, The Bingo Long Traveling All-Stars and Motor Kings, Car Wash, Silver Streak, Greased Lightning, Which Way Is Up?, Blue Collar, The Wiz, California Suite, Richard Pryor—Live in Concert (also prod., s.p.), The Muppet Movie, Richard Pryor Is Back Live in Concert (also s.p.), Wholly Moses, In God We Trust, Stir Crazy, Bustin' Loose (also co-prod., co-s.p.), Richard Pryor Live on the Sunset Strip (also prod., s.p.), Some Kind of Hero, The Toy, Superman III, Richard Pryor Here and Now (also dir., s.p.), Brewster's Millions, Jo Jo Dancer Your Life Is Calling (also dir., prod., s.p.), Critical Condition, Moving, See No Evil Hear No Evil, Harlem Nights, Another You, A Century of Cinema, Mad Dog Time, Lost Highway, Me Myself and Irene.
TELEVISION: *Series:* The Richard Pryor Show (1977), Pryor's Place. *Guest:* Wild Wild West, The Partridge Family, The Mod Squad, Chicago Hope. *Movies:* The Young Lawyers, Carter's Army.

PTAK, JOHN
Agent. b. San Diego, CA. Graduated UCLA film department, 1968. Theatre mgr. and booker for Walter Reade Organization and Laemmle Theatres, 1966-1969. Admin. exec. at American Film Institute's Center for Advanced Studies, 1969-1971. International Famous Agency (ICM), 1971-1975, William Morris Agency, 1976-91, Creative Artists Agency, 1991-. Represents motion picture and television talent. Co-chmn., Center for Film & Video Preservation at AFI. Member, National film Preservation Board. Bd. of dir., National Film Preservation Foundation, Motion Picture & Television Fund Foundation.

PULLMAN, BILL
Actor. b. Hornell, NY, Dec. 17, 1953. e. SUNY at Oneonta, Univ. of Mass. at Amherst. Worked with various theater companies, most notably the Folger Theater Groupe and the Los Angeles Theater Center.
THEATRE: *NY*: Dramathon '84, Curse of the Starving Class. *LA*: All My Sons, Barabbas, Nanawatai, Demon Wine, Control Freaks.
PICTURES: Ruthless People (debut, 1986), Spaceballs, The Serpent and the Rainbow, Rocket Gibraltar, The Accidental Tourist, Cold Feet, Brain Dead, Sibling Rivalry, Bright Angel, Going Under, Newsies, A League of Their Own, Singles, Nervous Ticks, Sommersby, Sleepless in Seattle, Malice, Mr. Jones, The Favor, Wyatt Earp, While You Were Sleeping, Casper, Mr. Wrong, Independence Day, The End of Violence, Lost Highway, Zero Effect, The Virginian (also dir.), A Man is Mostly Water, The Guilty, Lake Placid, Brokedown Palace, Titan A.E. (voice), Lucky Numbers, Ignition, Igby Goes Down, 29 Palms.
TELEVISION: *Movies*: Home Fires Burning, Crazy in Love, The Last Seduction (also released theatrically), Merry Christmas George Bailey. *Special*: Opening the Tombs of the Golden Mummies: Live.

PURCELL, PATRICK B.
Executive. b. Dublin, Ireland, March 16, 1943. e. Fordham U., M.B.A., 1973. In pub. & acct., England, 1969-69; acct., Associated Hosp. Service, N.Y., 1968-70; joined Paramount Pictures, 1970; v.p., fin., 1980-83; exec. v.p. chief fin. & admin. officer 1983-1998.

PURI, OM
Actor. b. Ambala, India, October 18, 1950.
PICTURES: Ghashiram Kotwal, The Strange Fate of Arvind Desai, Sparsh, A Folk Tale, Cry of the Wounded, Gandhi, The Ascent, Market Place, Who Pays the Piper, Half Truth, The Wave, Party, The Crossing, The Festival of Fire, Spices, New Delhi Times, Genesis, Sam & Me, Narasimha, The Inner Voice, City of Dreams, City of Joy, In Custody, The Burning Season, Ankuram, The Kite, Wold, Target, Kartavya, Brothers in Trouble, The Ghost and the Darkness, Maachis, Ghatak, Droh Kaal, Mrityu Dand, Gupt, My Son the Fanatic, Such a Long Journey, China Gate, Chachi 420, East is East, Hey Ram, Zandagi Zindabad, Kunuwara, The Zookeeper, The Parole Officer, Happy Now, Mystic Masseur Indian, Deewaanapan, The Zookeeper, Bollywood Calling, Pitaah, Ansh, Awara Paagal Deewana.
TELEVISION: Deliverance, The Jewel in the Crown. *Mini-Series*: White Teeth.

PURL, LINDA
Actress. b. Greenwich, CT, Sept. 2, 1955. Moved to Japan at age 2. Appeared in Japanese theatre, TV. e. Toho Geino Academy. Back to U.S. in 1971.
THEATRE: The Baby Dance (New Haven, NYC), Hedda Gabler, The Real Thing (Mark Taper), The Merchant of Venice (Old Globe Theatre), Romeo & Juliet, Doll's House, Hallelujah Hallelujah (NYC), Three Penny Opera, Nora, All the Way Home, The Road to Mecca, Long Wharf, Beyond Therapy.
PICTURES: Jory, Crazy Mama, W.C. Fields & Me, Leo and Loree, The High Country, Visiting Hours, Viper, Natural Causes, Mighty Joe Young, Sunday, The Perfect Tennant, Fear of the Dark.
TELEVISION: *Series*: The Secret Storm, Beacon Hill, Happy Days, Matlock, Under Cover, Young Pioneers, Robin's Hoods, Port Charles, First Monday. *Movies*: Eleanor and Franklin, Little Ladies of the Night, Testimony of Two Men, A Last Cry for Help, Women at West Point, Like Normal People, The Flame is Love, The Night the City Screamed, The Adventures of Nellie Bly, The Last Days of Pompeii, The Manions of America, Addicted to His Love, Spies Lies and Naked Thighs, Before the Storm, Spy Games, Danielle Steel's Secrets, Body Language, Accidental Meeting, Incident at Deception Ridge, Born Free: A New Adventure, Absolute Truth, Holy Joe, The Griffin and the Minor Canon, Frozen Impact.

PUTTNAM, LORD DAVID
CBE: Hon. LL.D Bristol 1983; Hon. D. Litt, Leicester 1986. Hon. Litt. D., Leeds 1992. Knighted, 1995. Producer. b. London, England, Feb. 25, 1941. e. Michenden Sch. In advertising before joining VPS/Goodtimes Prod. Co. Dir. of Britain's National Film Finance Corp. (1980-85); Also served on Cinema Films Council and governing council of the British Acad. of Film & Television Arts. Officier dans L'Ordre des Arts et des Lettres, 1986. Chmn. National Film and Television Sch., 1988. Past Pres., Council for the Protection of Rural England; Fellow, Royal Soc. of Arts; Fellow, Royal Geographical Soc., Hon. Fellow, The Chartered Society of Designers. appt. Chmn. & CEO, Columbia Pictures. Resigned 1987. Received Eastman 2nd Century Award, 1988. 1988 formed a joint venture for his Enigma Productions Ltd. with Warner Bros., Fujisankei Comm. Gp. of Japan, British Satellite Broadcasting & Country Nat West to prod. 4 films. Appt. chmn. ITEL intl. TV dist. agency, 1989. Dir., Anglia Television Group and Survival Anglia. V.P., BAFTA. Founding pres., Atelier du Cinema Europeen. Member, European Commission's 'Think Tank' for audio-visual policy.
PICTURES: Melody, The Pied Piper, That'll Be The Day, Stardust, Mahler, Bugsy Malone, The Duellists, Midnight Express, Foxes, Chariots of Fire (Acad. Award for Best Picture, 1981), Local Hero, Cal, The Killing Fields, The Mission, Defence of the Realm, Memphis Belle, Meeting Venus, Being Human, War of the Buttons, Le Confessional, My Life So Far. Co-produced documentaries: Swastika, James Dean—The First American Teenager, Double-Headed Eagle, Brother Can You Spare a Dime?
TELEVISION: P'Tang Yang Kipperbang, Experience Preferred, Secrets, Those Glory Glory Days, Sharma and Beyond, Winter Flight, Josephine Baker, Without Warning: The James Brady Story, A Dangerous Man: Lawrence After Arabia, The Burning Season.

Q

QUAID, DENNIS
Actor. b. Houston, TX Apr. 9, 1954. Brother is actor Randy Quaid. e. U. of Houston. Appeared in Houston stage productions before leaving for Hollywood. On N.Y. stage with his brother in True West, 1984. Performer with rock band The Electrics; wrote songs for films The Night the Lights Went Out in Georgia, Tough Enough, The Big Easy. Formed Summers/Quaid Productions with producer Cathleen Summers, 1989.
PICTURES: Crazy Mama (debut, 1975), I Never Promised You a Rose Garden, September 30, 1955, Our Winning Season, Seniors, G.O.R.P., Breaking Away, The Long Riders, All Night Long, Caveman, The Night the Lights Went Out in Georgia, Tough Enough, Jaws 3-D, The Right Stuff, Dreamscape, Enemy Mine, The Big Easy, Innerspace, Suspect, D.O.A., Everybody's All-American, Great Balls of Fire, Postcards From the Edge, Come See the Paradise, Wilder Napalm, Undercover Blues, Flesh & Bone, Wyatt Earp, Hideaway (co-prod. only), Something to Talk About, Dragonheart, Gang Related, Switchback, Playing by Heart, The Parent Trap, Savior, Any Given Sunday, Frequency, Traffic, Stranger than the Wheel, The Rookie, Far From Heaven, The Alamo, The Day After Tomorrow, Cold Creek Manor.
TELEVISION: *Movies*: Are You in the House Alone?, Amateur Night at the Dixie Bar and Grill, Bill, Johnny Belinda, Bill: On His Own, Everything That Rises (also dir., exec. prod.), Dinner with Friends.

QUAID, RANDY
Actor. b. Houston, TX, Oct. 1, 1950. Brother is actor Dennis Quaid. Discovered by Peter Bogdanovich while still jr. at Drama Dept. at U. of Houston and cast in his Targets and The Last Picture Show, 1971. Off-B'way debut: True West (1983).
PICTURES: Targets (debut, 1968), The Last Picture Show, What's Up Doc?, Paper Moon, Lolly-Madonna XXX, The Last Detail (Acad. Award nom.), The Apprenticeship of Duddy Kravitz, Breakout, The Missouri Breaks, Bound for Glory, The Choirboys, Midnight Express, Three Warriors, Foxes, The Long Riders, Heartbeeps, National Lampoon's Vacation, The Wild Life, The Slugger's Wife, Fool for Love, The Wraith, Sweet Country, No Man's Land, Moving, Caddyshack II, Parents, Bloodhounds of Broadway, Out Cold, National Lampoon's Christmas Vacation, Martians Go Home!, Days of Thunder, Quick Change, Cold Dog Soup, Texasville, Freaked, The Paper, Major League 2, Bye Bye Love, The Last Dance, Independence Day, Kingpin, Vegas Vacation, P.U.N.K.S., Bug Buster, Hard Rain, The Adventures of Rocky and Bullwinkle, George Wallace: Settin' the Woods on Fire (narrator), Not Another Teen Movie, Under the Mimosa, Milwaukee, Minnesota, The Adventures of Pluto Nash, Frank McKlusky C.I., Carolina, Kart Racer, Black Cadillac, Back By Midnight, Milwaukee / Minnesota, Carolina, Grind, Kart Racer, Home on the Range (voice).
TELEVISION: *Movies*: Getting Away From It All, The Great Niagara, The Last Ride of the Dalton Gang, To Race the Wind, Guyana Tragedy: The Story of Jim Jones, Of Mice and Men, Inside the Third Reich, Cowboy, A Streetcar Named Desire, LBJ: The Early Years, Dead Solid Perfect, Evil in Clear River, Frankenstein, Roommates, Next Door, Ed McBain's 87th Precinct, Purgatory West of the Pecos, Mail to the Chief, Leprechauns, The Day the World Ended, The Thin Blue Lie, Christmas Vacation 2: Cousin Eddie's Island Adventure. *Series*: Saturday Night Live (1985-86), Davis Rules, Gun, The Grubbs, The Brotherhood of Poland-NH, *Special*: Dear America (reader).

QUIGLEY, MARTIN, JR.
Educator, Writer. b. Chicago, IL, Nov. 24, 1917. e. A.B. Georgetown U.; M.A., Ed. D., Columbia U. M.P. Herald, Oct. 1939; spcl. ed. rep., M.P. Herald & M.P. Daily, May, 1941. U.S. Office of Coordination of Info., 1942; U.S. Office of Strategic Svc's., Special Intelligence Div., Eire & Italy, 1943-45. Assoc. ed., Quigley Pub., Oct. 1945; ed. M.P. Herald, July, 1949; also edit. dir. of all Quigley Pub., 1956; pres. Quigley Pub. Co., 1964-2001. Editor: New Screen Techniques, 1953; m.p. tech. section, Encyclopaedia Brit., 1956. Co-author: Catholic Action in Practice, 1963; Films in America, 1929-69, 1970. Pres., QWS, Inc., ed. cons., 1975-81. Adjunct prof. of higher ed., Baruch College Univ. City of N.Y. 1977-89; Teachers College, Columbia Univ., 1990. Village of Larchmont, N.Y., trustee, 1977-79; mayor, 1980-84. Bd. of trustees, American Bible Society, 1984-; Religious Ed. Ass'n., treasurer, 1975-80 & chairperson, 1981-84; Laymen's Nat'l. Bible Ass'n., chmn. ed. com., 1983-93; Will Rogers Institute, chmn. Health ed. com., 1980-97; dir, William J. Donovan Memorial Foundation, 1995-2002. Publisher of The International Motion Picture Almanac and International Television & Video Almanac. AUTHOR: Great Gaels, 1944; Roman Notes, 1946; Magic Shadows—The Story of the Origin of Motion Pictures, 1948; Gov't. Relations of Five Universities, 1975; Peace Without Hiroshima, 1991; First Century of Film, 1995; A U.S. Spy In Ireland, 1999; Amercian edition 2002; Community College Movement In Perspective, 2003.

QUIGLEY, WILLIAM J.
Executive. b. New York, NY, July 6, 1951. e. Wesleyan U., B.A., 1973; Columbia U., M.S., 1983. From 1973 to 1974 was advt. circulation mgr. for Quigley Publishing Co. Taught school in Kenya in 1974; returned to U.S. to join Grey Advt. as media planner. 1975 joined Walter Reade Organization as asst. film buyer; promoted to head film buyer in 1977. Named v.p., 1982. In 1986 joined Vestron, Inc. as sr. v.p. to establish Vestron Pictures. Named pres., Vestron Pictures, 1987-89. In 1990 joined Fair Lanes Entertainment, Inc. as v.p. mktg. 1993, joined United Artists Theatre as sr. v.p., marketing & new business. 1997, pres. Entertainment Express; partner, Spellbound Pictures. Exec. V.P. Mann Theatres, 1998-99. Founder and pres., QP Media 1999-present. President, Quigley Publishing Company, Inc., 2001-present.
PICTURES: Exec. prod.: Steel Dawn, The Dead, Salome's Last Dance, The Unholy, Waxwork, Burning Secret, The Lair of the White Worm, Paint It Black, The Rainbow, Twister.

QUINLAN, KATHLEEN
Actress. b. Pasadena, CA, Nov. 19, 1954. Played small role in film, One Is a Lonely Number, while in high school.
THEATRE: Taken in Marriage (NY Public Theatre; Theatre World Award), Uncommon Women and Others, Accent on Youth (Long Wharf, CT), Les Liaisons Dangereuses.
PICTURES: One Is a Lonely Number (debut, 1972), American Graffiti, Lifeguard, Airport '77, I Never Promised You a Rose Garden, The Promise, The Runner Stumbles, Sunday Lovers, Hanky Panky, Independence Day, Twilight Zone—The Movie, The Last Winter, Warning Sign, Wild Thing, Man Outside, Sunset, Clara's Heart, The Doors, Trial by Jury, Apollo 13, Zeus and Roxanne, Breakdown, Event Horizon, Lawn Dogs, A Civil Action, My Giant.
TELEVISION: Movies: Can Ellen Be Saved?, Lucas Tanner (pilot), Where Have All the People Gone?, The Missing Are Deadly, The Abduction of St. Anne, Turning Point of Jim Malloy, Little Ladies of the Night, She's in the Army Now, When She Says No, Blackout, Children of the Night, Dreams Lost Dreams Found, Trapped, The Operation, Strays, An American Story, Stolen Babies, Last Light, Perfect Alibi, Too Rich: The Secret Life of Doris Duke. Series: Hollywood Squares, Family Law.

QUINN, AIDAN
Actor. b. Chicago, IL, March 8, 1959. Raised in Rockwell, IL, also spent time in Ireland as a boy and following high sch. graduation. Returned to Chicago at 19, worked as tar roofer before debuting on Chicago stage in The Man in 605, followed by Scheherazade, The Irish Hebrew Lesson, Hamlet.
THEATRE: Fool for Love (off-B'way debut), A Lie of the Mind, A Streetcar Named Desire (Theatre World Award).
PICTURES: Reckless (debut, 1984), Desperately Seeking Susan, The Mission, Stakeout, Crusoe, The Handmaid's Tale, The Lemon Sisters, Avalon, At Play in the Fields of the Lord, The Playboys, Benny & Joon, Blink, Mary Shelley's Frankenstein, Legends of the Fall, The Stars Fell on Henrietta, Haunted, Looking for Richard, Michael Collins, Commandments, The Assignment, This is My Father (also exec. prod.), Practical Magic, Songcatcher, Music of the Heart, In Dreams, Songcatcher, The Messiah XXI, Stolen Summer, Evelyn.
TELEVISION: Special: All My Sons. Movies: An Early Frost, Perfect Witness, Lies of the Twins, A Private Matter, Forbidden Territory: Stanley's Search for Livingstone, Two of Us, The Passenger List, The Prince and the Pauper, Benedict Arnold: A Question of Honor, Plainsong. Series: Prokect Greenlight.

R

RABE, DAVID WILLIAM
Writer. b. Dubuque, IA, March 10, 1940. m. actress Jill Clayburgh. e. Loras Coll.
THEATRE: The Basic Training of Pavlo Hummel (Obie Award, 1971), Sticks and Bones (Tony Award, 1971), The Orphan, In the Boom Boom Room, Streamers, Hurlyburly, Those the River Keeps.
PICTURES: I'm Dancing As Fast As I Can (also exec. prod.), Streamers, Casualties of War, State of Grace, The Firm, Hurlyburly.
TELEVISION: Special: Sticks and Bones.

RABINOVITZ, JASON
Executive. b. Boston, MA, e. Harvard Coll., B.A. where elected to Phi Beta Kappa. Following WWII service as military intelligence captain with paratroops, took M.B.A. at Harvard Business Sch., 1948. Started in industry in 1949 as asst. to secty.-treas., United Paramount Theatres. Asst. controller, ABC, 1953; adm v.p., ABC-TV, 1956; joined MGM as asst. treas., 1957; named MGM-TV gen. mgr., dir. of business & financial affairs, 1958; treas. & CFO, MGM, Inc., 1963; financial v.p. & CFO, 1967. 1971, named exec. v.p. & dir. Encyclopedia Britannica Education Corp.; sr. v.p., American Film Theatre, 1974-75. Rejoined MGM as v.p./exec. asst. to the pres., 1976. Elected v.p. finance, 1979; promoted to sr. v.p., finance & corporate admin., MGM Film Co. & UA Communications, Inc. Resigned, 1984. Now film & TV consultant and indep. prod. Dir., Pacific Rim Entertainment, 1993-95. Retired.

RADFORD, MICHAEL
Director, Writer. b. New Dehli, India, Feb. 24, 1946. e. Oxford U. Worked briefly as a teacher before beginning work as documentary filmmaker.
PICTURES: Director & Writer: Another TIme Another Place, Nineteen Eight-Four (1984), White Mischief, Il Postino (Academy Award nom., Directors Guild Award nom.), The Swedish Cavalier, The Postman, B. Monkey, Dancing at the Blue Iguana. Director: Delta of Venus, The Elixir, Tania, Ten Minutes Older: The Cello, The Letters.
TELEVISION: Series: Homicide: Life on the Street.

RADNITZ, ROBERT B.
Producer. b. Great Neck, NY, Aug. 9, 1924. e. U. of VA. Taught 2 years at U. of VA, then became reader for Harold Clurman; wrote several RKO This Is America scripts, then to Broadway where co-prod. The Frogs of Spring; prod. The Young and the Beautiful; to Hollywood working at United Artists, then as story consultant to Buddy Adler, head of prod., 20th Century-Fox, 1957-58. V.P., Producer Guild of America, 1982, 1984, 1985; bd. member, Producers Branch, AMPAS, last 4 yrs. First producer with retrospective at Museum of Modern Art, and first producer honored by joint resolution of both houses of Congress for his work, 1973. Pres. Robert B. Radnitz Productions, Ltd.
PICTURES: Producer: A Dog of Flanders (debut, 1960; first U.S. film to win Golden Lion Award at Venice Film Fest.), Misty, Island of the Blue Dolphins, And Now Miguel, My Side of the Mountain, The Little Ark, Sounder (Acad. Award nom.), Where the Lilies Bloom, Birch Interval, Sounder 2, A Hero Ain't Nothin' But a Sandwich, Cross Creek.
TELEVISION: Mary White (Emmy & Christopher Awards), Never Forget (ACE Award nom.).

RAFELSON, BOB
Producer, Director, Writer. b. New York, NY, Feb. 21, 1933. e. Dartmouth, B.A. (philosophy). Left NY in teens to ride in rodeos in AZ. Worked on cruise ship, then played drums and bass with jazz combos in Acapulco. 1953 won Frost Natl. Playwriting competition. Dir. his award-winning play at Hanover Experimental Theatre, N.H. After Army Service did program promotion for a radio station, was advisor for Shochiku Films, Japan, then hired by David Susskind to read scripts for Talent Assocs. Writer-assoc. prod., DuPont Show of the Month and Play of the Week (also script sprv.). Joined Screen Gems in California, developing program ideas for Jackie Cooper, then head of TV prod. arm of Columbia. Later formed BBS Productions with Burt Schneider and Steve Blauner. Appeared as actor in 1985 film Always.
PICTURES: Co-Prod. only: Easy Rider, The Last Picture Show, Drive He Said. Director: Head (debut, 1968; also co-prod., co-s.p.), Five Easy Pieces (also co-prod., co-story; Acad. Award noms. for picture & writing), The King of Marvin Gardens (also prod., co-s.p.), Stay Hungry (also co-prod., co-s.p.), The Postman Always Rings Twice (also co-prod.), Black Widow, Mountains of the Moon (also co-s.p.), Man Trouble, Blood and Wine, Wet (also s.p.), Tales of Erotica, Always (actor only), Leaving Las Vegas (actor only), Who is Henry Jaglon (actor only), No Good Deed..
TELEVISION: Movies: Poodle Springs. Series: The Monkees (1966-68, creator, writer, dir.; Emmy Award, 1967), Adapted 34 prods., Play of the Week. Dir. music video: All Night Long, with Lionel Ritchie.

RAFFERTY, FRANCES
Actress. b. Sioux City, IA, June 26, 1922. e. U. of California, premed student UCLA. TV series, December Bride, Pete and Gladys.
PICTURES: Seven Sweethearts, Private Miss Jones, Girl Crazy, War Against Mrs. Hadley, Thousands Cheer, Dragon Seed, Barbary Coast Gent, Hidden Eye, Abbott and Costello in Hollywood, Adventures of Don Coyote, Lady at Midnight, Old Fashioned Girl, Rodeo, Shanghai Story, Wings of Chance.

RAFFIN, DEBORAH
Actress. b. Los Angeles, CA, March 13, 1953. m. producer Michael Viner. Mother is actress Trudy Marshall. e. Valley Coll. Was active fashion model before turning to acting when discovered by Ted Witzer. Author: Sharing Christmas (Vols. I & II). Debut in 40 Carats (1973). Publisher Dove Books On Tape. Head of Dove Films, prod. co.
PICTURES: 40 Carats (debut, 1973), The Dove, Once Is Not Enough, God Told Me To, Assault on Paradise, The Sentinel, Touched by Love, Dance of the Dwarfs, Death Wish 3, Claudia, Scanners II, Wilde, Family Blessings.
TELEVISION: Series: Foul Play. Movies: A Nightmare in Badham County, Ski Lift to Death, How to Pick Up Girls, Willa, Mind Over Murder, Haywire, For the Love of It, Killing at Hell's Gate, For Lovers Only, Running Out, Sparkling Cyanide, Threesome, The Sands of Time, Morning Glory (also co-s.p.), A Perry Mason Mystery: The Case of the Grimacing Governor, Home Song, Unwed Father, Book of Days, Futuresport (exec. prod.) Mini-Series: The Last Convertible, James Clavell's Noble House, Windmills of the Gods (also co-prod.). Guest: B.L. Stryker.

RAGLAND, ROBERT O.
Composer. b. Chicago, IL, July 3, 1931. e. Northwestern U., American Conservatory of Music, Vienna Acad. of Music. Professional pianist at Chicago nightclubs. In U.S. Navy; on discharge joined Dorsey Bros. Orchestra as arranger. On sls. staff at NBC-TV, Chicago. 1970, moved to Hollywood to become composer for movies; has scored 67 feature films plus many TV movies and series segments. Has also written some 45 original songs.
PICTURES: The Touch of Melissa, The Yin and Yang of Mr. Go, The Thing with Two Heads, Project: Kill, Abby, Seven Alone, The Eyes of Dr. Chaney, Return to Macon County, The Daring Dobermans, Shark's Treasure, Grizzly, Pony Express Rider, Mansion of the Doomed, Mountain Family Robinson, Only Once in a Lifetime, Jaguar Lives, The Glove, Lovely But Deadly, "Q", The Day of the Assassin, A Time To Die, The Winged Serpent, Trial by Terror, The Guardian, Ten to Midnight, Dirty Rebel, Hysterical, Brainwaves, Where's Willie?, The Supernaturals, Nightstick, Pretty Kill, Deep Space, Messenger of Death, The Fifth Monkey, No Place to Hide, The Buffalo Soldiers, The Raffle, Morty, Crime and Punishment, The Fear, Evil Obsession, Warhead, Top of the World, Plato's Run, Motel Blue.
TELEVISION: Photoplay's Stars of Tomorrow, Wonder Woman, Barnaby Jones, Streets of San Francisco, High Ice, The Girl on the Edge of Town, The Guardian, Conspiracy of Silence, Nightstick.

RAILSBACK, STEVE
Actor. b. Dallas, TX, Nov. 16,1948. Studied with Lee Strasberg. On stage in Orpheus Descending, This Property Is Condemned, Cherry Orchard, Skin of Our Teeth, etc.
PICTURES: The Visitors, Cockfighter, Angela, The Stunt Man, Deadly Games, Turkey Shoot, The Golden Seal, Torchlight, Lifeforce, Armed and Dangerous, Blue Monkey, The Wind, Distortions, Deadly Intent, Alligator II: The Mutation, After-Shock, Private Wars, Forever, Calendar Girl, Nukie, Save Me, Barb Wire, Disturbing Behavior, Storytelling.
TELEVISION: Movies: Helter Skelter, Good Cops Bad Cops, The Forgotten, Spearfield's Daughter, Sunstroke, Bonds of Love, Separated by Murder, Vanishing Point. Mini-Series: From Here to Eternity.

RAIMI, SAM
Director, Writer, Producer, Actor. b. Royal Oak, MI, Oct. 23, 1959. e. Michigan St. Univ. Formed Renaissance Pictures, Inc.
PICTURES: Dir./Writer: The Evil Dead, Crimewave, Evil Dead II, Darkman, Army of Darkness, The Quick and the Dead (dir. only), A Simple Plan, For Love of the Game, The Gift, Spider Man, Spider-Man II. Co-Producer: Hard Target, Timecop, Darkman III (exec. prod.) Actor: Spies Like Us, Thou Shalt Not Kill... Except, Maniac Cop, Miller's Crossing, Innocent Blood, Indian Summer, Intruder, The Hudsucker Proxy (also co-writer), The Flintstones, Galaxis.
TELEVISION: Movies: Journey to the Center of the Earth (actor), Mantis (prod., writer), Body Bags (actor), The Stand (actor). Series: American Gothic (exec. prod.), Xena: Warrior Princess (exec. prod.), Hercules: The Legendary Journeys (exec. prod.), Spy Game (exec. prod.), Hercules and Xena-The Animated Movie:The Battle for Mount Olympus, Young Hercules, Jack of All Trades, Cleopatra 2525. Mini-Series: The Shining (actor).

RAJSKI, PEGGY
Producer. b. Stevens Point, WI. e. Univ. of Wisconsin. m. actor Josh Mostel. Began film career as prod. manager on John Sayles film Lianna, before becoming producer. Prod. of Bruce

Springsteen music videos, incld. Glory Days which won American Video Award. Received 1994 Academy Award for short film Trevor.
PICTURES: The Brother From Another Planet, Matewan, Eight Men Out, The Grifters, Little Man Tate, Used People, Home for the Holidays, Boy's Life 2.

RAKSIN, DAVID
Composer. b. Philadelphia, PA, Aug. 4, 1912. e. U. of Pennsylvania, studied music with Isadore Freed and Arnold Schoenberg. Composer for films, ballet, dramatic and musical comedy, stage, radio and TV, symphony orchestra and chamber ensembles. Arranger of music of Chaplin film, Modern Times; pres. Composers and Lyricists Guild of America, 1962-70; animated films include Madeline and The Unicorn in the Garden (UPA). Professor of Music and Urban Semester, U. of Southern California. Coolidge Commission from the Library of Congress: Oedipus Memneitai (Oedipus Remembers) for bass/baritone, part chorus and chamber orchestra premiered there under dir. of composer, Oct. 1986. Pres., Society for the Preservation of Film Music, 1992. Recipient of ASCAP Golden Score Award for Career Achievement, 1992. Elected to ASCAP bd. of dirs., 1995.
PICTURES: Laura, Secret Life of Walter Mitty, Smoky, Force of Evil, Across the Wide Missouri, Carrie, Bad and the Beautiful, Apache, Suddenly, Big Combo, Jubal, Hilda Crane, Separate Tables, Al Capone, Night Tide, Too-Late Blues, Best of the Bolshoi (music for visual interludes), Two Weeks in Another Town, The Redeemer, Invitation to a Gunfighter, Sylvia, A Big Hand for the Little Lady, Will Penny, Glass Houses, What's the Matter With Helen?
TELEVISION: Series: Five Fingers, Life With Father, Father of the Bride, Ben Casey, Breaking Point. Movies: The Ghost of Flight 401. Specials: Journey, Tender is the Night, Prayer of the Ages, Report from America, The Olympics (CBC), The Day After, Lady in a Corner.

RALPH, SHERYL LEE
Actress. b. Waterbury, CT, Dec. 30, 1956. e. Rutgers U. Studied with Negro Ensemble Company in NYC.
THEATRE: NY: Reggae, Dreamgirls. LA: Identical Twins From Baltimore.
PICTURES: A Piece of the Action (debut, 1977), Oliver and Company (voice), The Mighty Quinn, Skin Deep, To Sleep With Anger, Mistress, The Distinguished Gentleman, Sister Act 2: Back in the Habit, The Flintstones, White Man's Burden, Bogus, Deterrence, Unconditional Love, Lost in the Pershing Point Hotel, Baby of the Family.
TELEVISION: Series: Code Name: Foxfire, Search for Tomorrow, It's a Living, Designing Women, George. Movies: The Neighborhood, Sister Margaret and the Saturday Night Ladies, Luck of the Draw: The Gambler Returns, No Child of Mine, Acapulco Black Film Festival, The Jennie Project. Specials: Happy Birthday Hollywood, Voices That Care, Story of a People: The Black Road to Hollywood (host).

RAMIS, HAROLD
Writer, Director, Actor, Producer. b. Chicago, IL, Nov. 21, 1944. e. Washington U., St. Louis. Assoc. ed. Playboy Mag. 1968-70; writer, actor, Second City, Chicago 1970-73; National Lampoon Radio Show, 1974-75. Recipient of Chicago Film Critics "Commitment to Chicago" Award, 1997.
PICTURES: National Lampoon's Animal House (co-s.p.), Meatballs (co-s.p.), Caddyshack (co-s.p., dir.), Stripes (co-s.p., actor), Heavy Metal (voice), National Lampoon's Vacation (dir.), Ghostbusters (co-s.p., actor), Back to School (co-s.p., exec. prod.), Club Paradise (co-s.p., dir.), Armed and Dangerous (exec. prod., co-s.p.), Baby Boom (actor), Caddyshack II (co-s.p.), Stealing Home (actor), Ghostbusters II (co-s.p., actor), Rover Dangerfield (co-story), Groundhog Day (dir., co-s.p., co-prod., actor), Airheads (actor), Love Affair (actor), Stuart Saves His Family (dir.), Multiplicity (dir., co-prod.), As Good As It Gets (actor), Run for Your Wife (dir.), Analyze This (dir.), High Fidelity (actor), American Storytellers (actor), Bedazzled (dir), Analyze That, Orange County (actor), The First $20 Million Is Always the Hardest (exec prod.), I'm With Lucy (actor).
TELEVISION: Series: SCTV (head writer, performer, 1976-78), Rodney Dangerfield Show (head writer, prod.). Special: Will Rogers—Look Back and Laugh (exec. prod.).

RAMPLING, CHARLOTTE
Actress. b. Sturmer, England, Feb. 5, 1946. e. Jeanne D'Arc Academie pour Jeune Filles, Versailles; St. Hilda's, Bushey, England.
PICTURES: The Knack... and How to Get It (debut, 1965), Rotten to the Core, Georgy Girl, The Long Duel, Sequestro di Persona, The Damned, Target: Harry, Three, The Ski Bum, Corky, Addio Fratello Crrudele, Asylum, The Night Porter, Giordano Bruno, Zardoz, Caravan to Vaccares, La Chair de L'orchidee, Farewell My Lovely, Foxtrot, Yuppi-Du, Orca, Purple Taxi, Stardust Memories, The Verdict, Viva La Vie, Tristesse et Beaute, On ne Meurt que deux Fois, Angel Heart, Mascara, D.O.A., Max My Love, Rebus, Paris By Night, Helmut Newton: Frames from the Edge (doc.), Hammers Over the Anvil, Time is Money, Invasion of Privacy, Asphalt Tango, Wings of the Dove, Varya, Signs and Wonders, Tribute to Alfred Lepetit, Aberdeen,

Under the Sand, Clouds: Letters to My Son, The Fourth Angel, Supersitition, Voyez comme on danse, Spy Game, Swimming Pool.
TELEVISION: *BBC Series*: The Six Wives of Henry VIII, The Superlative Seven, The Avengers. *Movies*: Sherlock Holmes in New York, Mystery of Cader Iscom, The Fantasists, What's in it for Henry, Zinotchka, Infidelities, La Femme Abandonnee, Radetzky March, Murder In Mind, Samson Le Maqnifique, La Dernière Fête.

RANDALL, TONY
Actor. r.n. Leonard Rosenberg. b. Tulsa, OK, Feb. 26, 1920. e. Northwestern U. Prof. N.Y. debut as actor in Circle of Chalk; U.S. Army 1942-46; radio actor on many shows. Founder/Artistic Director of National Actors Theatre in NYC, 1991.
THEATRE: Candida, The Corn is Green, Antony & Cleopatra, Caesar & Cleopatra, Inherit the Wind, Oh Men! Oh Women!, Oh Captain, The Sea Gull, The Master Builder, M. Butterfly, A Little Hotel on the Side, Three Men on a Horse, The Government Inspector, The Odd Couple (tour).
PICTURES: Oh Men! Oh Women! (debut, 1957), Will Success Spoil Rock Hunter?, No Down Payment, The Mating Game, Pillow Talk, The Adventures of Huckleberry Finn, Let's Make Love, Lover Come Back, Boys' Night Out, Island of Love, The Brass Bottle, 7 Faces of Dr. Lao, Send Me No Flowers, Fluffy, The Alphabet Murders, Bang Bang You're Dead, Hello Down There, Everything You Always Wanted to Know About Sex* But Were Afraid to Ask, Scavenger Hunt, Foolin' Around, The King of Comedy, My Little Pony (voice), It Had to Be You, That's Adequate, Gremlins 2: The New Batch (voice), Fatal Instinct.; Pixielon's iBash; Down With Love;
TELEVISION: *Series*: One Man's Family, Mr. Peepers, The Odd Couple (Emmy Award, 1975), The Tony Randall Show, Love Sidney. *Guest*: TV Playhouse, Max Liebman Spectaculars, Sid Caesar, Dinah Shore, Playhouse 90, Walt Disney World Celebrity Circus;The Majic School Busl Brother's Keeper. *Movies*: Kate Bliss and the Ticker Tape Kid, Sidney Shorr: A Girl's Best Friend, Off Sides, Hitler's SS: Portrait in Evil, Sunday Drive, Save the Dog!, The Odd Couple: Together Again; Howard Cosell, Telling It Like It Is; Playboy: The Party Continues

RANSOHOFF, MARTIN
Executive. b. New Orleans, LA, 1927. e. Colgate U., 1949. Adv., Young & Rubicam, 1948-49; slsmn, writer, dir., Caravel Films, 1951; formed own co., Filmways, 1952; industrial films, commercials; formed Filmways TV Prods., Filmways, Inc., Filmways of Calif.; bd. chmn. Filmways, Inc. Resigned from Filmways in 1972 and formed Martin Ransohoff Prods., Inc, independent m. p. and tv prod. co.
PICTURES: Boys' Night Out, The Wheeler Dealers, The Americanization of Emily, The Loved One, The Sandpiper, The Cincinnati Kid, The Fearless Vampire Killers, Don't Make Waves, Ice Station Zebra, Castle Keep, Hamlet (exec. prod.), Catch-22, The Moonshine War, King Lear, See No Evil, 10 Rillington Place, Fuzz, Save The Tiger, The White Dawn, Silver Streak (exec. prod.), Nightwing, The Wanderers, The Mountain Men, A Change of Seasons, American Pop, Hanky Panky, Class, Jagged Edge, The Big Town, Switching Channels, Physical Evidence, Welcome Home, Guilty as Sin, Turbulence (prod.).
TELEVISION: *Series*: Mister Ed, The Beverly Hillbillies, Petticoat Junction, Green Acres, The Addams Family.

RAPAPORT, MICHAEL
Actor. b. New York, NY, March 20, 1970. Started as stand-up comic appearing at Improv in LA before becoming actor.
PICTURES: Zebrahead, Point of No Return, Poetic Justice, Money for Nothing, True Romance, The Scout, Higher Learning, The Basketball Diaries, Kiss of Death, Mighty Aphrodite, The Pallbearer, A Brother's Kiss, Metro, Cop Land, Men, Palmetto, Kiss Toledo Goodbye, Deep Blue Sea, Kiss Toledo Goodbye, Next Friday, Small Time Crooks, Lucky Numbers, Men of Honor, Chain of Fools, Bamboozled, The 6th Day, Tell Me, King of the Jungle, Dr. Doolittle 2, Triggermen, A Cold Day in August, 29 Palms, Comic Book Villains; Triggermen; Paper Soldiers; A Cold Day in August, 29 Palms (also exec. prod.)
TELEVISION: *Series*: Subway Stories: Tales from the Underground, Boston Public. *Guest*: Friends, ER, NYPD Blue.; Night Visions, Celebrity Adventures.

RAPHAEL, FREDERIC
Writer. b. Chicago, IL, Aug. 14, 1931. e. Charterhouse, St. John's Coll., Cambridge.
AUTHOR: The Earlsdon Way, The Limits of Love, A Wild Surmise, The Graduate Wife, The Trouble With England, Lindmann, Orchestra and Beginners, Like Men Betrayed, Who Were You With Last Night?, April June and November, Richard's Things, California Time, The Glittering Prizes, Sleeps Six & Other Stories, Oxbridge Blues & Other Stories, Heaven & Earth, Think of England and other stories, After the War, A Double Life, The Latin over and other stories, Old Scores. Biographies: Somerset Maugham and His World, Byron. Translations: (with Kenneth McLeish), Poems of Catullus The Oresteia. Essays: Cracks in the Ice, Of Gods and Men.

THEATRE: From the Greek (1979), An Early Life.
PICTURES: Nothing But the Best, Darling (Academy Award, 1965), Two for the Road, Far from the Madding Crowd, A Severed Head, Daisy Miller, Richard's Things, La Putain du roi, Eyes Wide Shut, This Man,This Woman, Hiding Room.
TELEVISION: The Glittering Prizes (Royal TV Society Writer Award 1976), Rogue Male, School Play, Something's Wrong, Best of Friends, Richard's Things, Oxbridge Blues (ACE Award, best writer), After the War, Byrow, The Man in the Brooks Brothers Shirt (also dir.; ACE Award best picture), Women and Men: Stories of Seduction, Women & Men 2: In Love There Are No Rules.

RAPPOPORT, GERALD J.
Executive, Film Producer. b. New York, NY, Aug. 25, 1925. e. NYU. U.S. Marine Corps. Pres., Major Artists Representatives Corp., 1954-58; dir. of Coast Sound Services, Hollywood; 1959-61, pres., International Film Exchange Ltd.; 1960-91, CEO of IFEX Int'l; 1991-94, pres. CIFEX Corporation, 1995-present.

RASHAD, PHYLICIA
Actress-singer. b. Houston, TX, June 19, 1948. m. sportscaster Ahmad Rashad. Sister of Debbie Allen. e. Howard U., B.F.A., magna cum laude, 1970. NY School of Ballet. Acted under maiden name of Phylicia Ayers-Allen. Recording, Josephine Superstar (1979). Conceived (with Michael Peters) and appeared in revue Phylicia Rashad & Co. in 1989 in Las Vegas.
THEATRE: Ain't Supposed to Die a Natural Death, The Duplex, The Cherry Orchard, The Wiz, Weep Not For Me, Zooman and the Sign, In an Upstate Motel, Zora, Dreamgirls, Sons and Fathers of Sons, Puppetplay, A Raisin in the Sun, Into the Woods, Jelly's Last Jam.
PICTURE: Once Upon A Time...When We Were Colored; The Visit
TELEVISION: *Series*: One Life to Live, The Cosby Show (People's Choice Award, NAACP Image Award, Emmy nom.), Cosby;.*Movies*: Uncle Tom's Cabin, False Witness, Polly, Polly—Comin' Home!, Jailbirds, David's Mother, The Possession of Michael D;.Madelain Kahn; The Old Settler(also exec.prod.) , The Babysitter's Seduction. *Specials*: Nell Carter—Never Too Old to Dream, Superstars and Their Moms, Our Kids and the Best of Everything, The Debbie Allen Special, Hallelujah.; Intimate Portrait: ; Murder She Wrote: The Last Free Man; The Cosby Show: A Look Back

RATHER, DAN
News Correspondent, Anchor. b. Wharton, TX, Oct. 31, 1931. e. Sam Houston State Teachers Coll., BA journalism, 1953. Instructor there for 1 year. Graduate e.: U. of Houston Law School, S. Texas School of Law. Worked for UPI and Houston Chronicle. Radio: KSAM, Huntsville, KTRH, Houston. Joined CBS News in 1962 as chief of southwest bureau in Dallas. Transferred to overseas burs. (including chief of London Bureau 1965-66), then Vietnam before returning as White House corr. 1966. White House Correspondent, 1964-74. Covered top news events, from Democratic and Republican national conventions to President Nixon's trip to Europe (1970) and to Peking and Moscow (1972). Anchored CBS Reports, 1974-75. Presently co-editor of 60 minutes (since 1975) and anchors Dan Rather Reporting on CBS Radio Network (since 1977). Anchor for 48 Hours, 1988. Winner of numerous awards, including 5 Emmys. Anchorman on CBS-TV Evening News, 1981-;The Cold War; 60 Minutes II; Breaking The News . Books: The Palace Guard (1974); The Camera Never Blinks (1977); I Remember (1991); The Camera Never Blinks Twice (1994); Mark Sullivan's Our Times (editor, 1995).

RAUCHER, HERMAN
Writer. b. Apr. 13, 1928. e. NYU. Author of novels Watermelon Man, Summer of '42 and Ode to Billy Joe, adapted to films by him. Other novels inc. A Glimpse of Tiger, There Should Have Been Castles, Maynard's House.
PICTURES: Sweet November, Can Hieronymous Merkin Ever Forget Mercy Humppe and Find True Happiness?, Watermelon Man, Summer of '42, Class of '44, Ode to Billy Joe, The Other Side of Midnight.
TELEVISION: Studio One, Alcoa Hour, Goodyear Playhouse, Matinee Theatre, Remember When? (movie).

RAVETCH, IRVING
Writer, Producer. b. Newark, NJ, Nov. 14, 1920. e. UCLA. m. Harriet Frank, with whom he often collaborated.
PICTURES: *Writer*: Living in a Big Way, The Outriders, Vengeance Valley, Ten Wanted Men, The Long Hot Summer, The Sound and the Fury, Home from the Hill, The Dark at the Top of the Stairs, Hud (also co-prod.), Hombre (also co-prod.), The Reivers (also prod.), House of Cards (as James P. Bonner), The Cowboys, Conrack, Norma Rae, Murphy's Romance, Stanley and Iris.

RAYMOND, PAULA
Actress. r.n. Paula Ramona Wright, b. San Francisco, CA., Nov. 23, 1925. e. San Francisco Jr. Coll. 1942. Started career in little theatre groups, concerts, recitals, San Francisco; leading stage roles in Ah! Wilderness, Peter Pan, etc.; also sang lead coloratura rules in Madame Butterfly, Aidia, Rigoletto, Faust, etc.;

ballerina with S.F. Opera Ballet; classical pianist; model, Meade-Maddick Photographers.
PICTURES: Racing Luck, Rusty Leads the Way, Blondie's Secret, East Side West Side, Challenge of the Range, Adam's Rib, Devil's Doorway, Sons of New Mexico, Duchess of Idaho, Crisis, Grounds For Marriage, Inside Straight, The Tall Target, Texas Carnival, The Sellout, Bandits of Corsica, City That Never Sleeps, The Beast from 20,000 Fathoms, The Human Jungle, King Richard & the Crusaders, The Gun That Won the West, Hand of Death, The Flight That Disappeared, The Spy With My Face, Blood of Dracula's Castle, Five Bloody Graves, Mind Twister.
TELEVISION: Guest: Perry Mason, 77 Sunset Strip, Wyatt Earp, Man from U.N.C.L.E., Maverick, The Untouchables, Bachelor Father, Bat Masterson, Temple Houston, Peter Gunn.

RAYNOR, LYNN S.
Producer, Production Executive. b. Chicago, IL, Feb. 11, 1940. Produced West Coast premiere of The Balcony by Genet, The Crawling Arnold Review by Feiffer. Joined Television Enterprises, 1965; Commonwealth United, 1968 as business affairs exec. later prod. spvr. 1972 opened London branch of the Vidtronics Co. 1974, formed Paragon Entertainment & RAH Records. 1980-95, prod. of TV Movies and Mini-Series. Prod. & editor of 12 minute tv vignettes, A Hall of Fame Story.
PICTURE: Freejack.
TELEVISION: Special: Waiting for Godot. Movies: Marilyn: The Untold Story, The Execution, A Winner Never Quits, On Wings of Eagles, Stranger in My Bed, Hands of a Stranger, The High Price of Passion, The Kennedys of Massachusetts, Common Ground, Face of Love, The Rape of Doctor Willis, Quiet Killer, Love Honor & Obey: The Last Mafia Marriage, Tony & Nancy: The Inside Story, Tecumseh: The Last Warrior, It Was Him Or Us, The Lover Letter, Glory & Honor, The Wall, Double Platinum, The Virginian, American Tragedy, A Town Without Christmas, Two Against Time, Erotomania, Obsessed. Series: Camp Wilderness, Falcone. Mini-Series: True Women. Pilot: Murphy's Law.

REA, STEPHEN
Actor. b. Belfast, Northern Ireland, Oct. 31, 1948. e. Queens Univ. (BA in English Lit.). Started acting at Abbey Theatre in Dublin. Formed the Field Day Theatre Co. in 1980 in Londonderry, acting in or directing most of their productions. Also acted with Royal Natl. Theatre.
THEATRE: Playboy of the Western World, Comedians, High Society, Endgame, Freedom of the City, Someone Who'll Watch Over Me (also B'way; Theatre World Award, Tony nom.).
PICTURES: Danny Boy (Angel), Loose Connections, The Company of Wolves, The Doctor and the Devils, The House, Life Is Sweet, The Crying Game (Acad. Award nom.), Bad Behavior, Angie, Princess Caraboo, Ready to Wear (Pret-a-Porter), Between the Devil and the Deep Blue Sea, Interview With A Vampire, All Men Are Mortal, Trojan Eddie, Michael Collins, A Further Gesture, Last of the High Kings, Hacks, Fever Pitch, Double Top, This Is My Father, Still Crazy, The Butcher Boy, Blue Vision, The Life Before This, Guinevere, In Dreams, The End of the Affair, On the Edge, Snow in August, The Musketeer, Ulysses, FearDotCom, Evelyn.
TELEVISION: Shadow of a Gunman, Fugitive, I Didn't Know You Cared, Professional Foul, The Seagull, Out of Town Boys, Calbe Williams, Joyce in June, The House, Four Days in July, Shergar, Scout, Lost Belongings, The Big Gamble, Not With a Bang, Saint Oscar, Hedda Gabler, Citizen X, Crime of the Century, Armadillo.

REAGAN, RONALD
Actor, Politician. b. Tampico, IL, Feb. 6, 1911. e. high school, Eureka Coll. m. former actress Nancy Davis. Wrote weekly sports column for a Des Moines, IA newspaper; broadcast sporting events. Signed as actor by Warner Bros. in 1937. In WWII 1942-45, capt., USAAF. Actor until 1966. Served as Governor, California, 1967-74. Businessman and rancher. Elected President of the United States, 1980. Re-elected, 1984. Autobiography: Where's the Rest of Me? (1965).
PICTURES: Love Is On the Air (debut, 1937), Hollywood Hotel, Sergeant Murphy, Swing Your Lady, Brother Rat, Going Places, Accidents Will Happen, Cowboy from Brooklyn, Boy Meets Girl, Girls on Probation, Dark Victory, Naughty but Nice, Hell's Kitchen, Code of the Secret Service, Smashing the Money Ring, Angels Wash Their Faces, Brother Rat and a Baby, Murder in the Air, Tugboat Annie Sails Again, Knute Rockne—All American, Santa Fe Trail, Angel From Texas, Nine Lives Are Not Enough, The Bad Man, International Squadron, Million Dollar Baby, Kings Row, Juke Girl, Desperate Journey, This Is the Army, Stallion Road, That Hagen Girl, The Voice of the Turtle, Night Unto Night, John Loves Mary, The Girl From Jones Beach, It's a Great Feeling (cameo), The Hasty Heart, Louisa, Storm Warning, The Last Outpost, Bedtime for Bonzo, Hong Kong, She's Working Her Way Through College, The Winning Team, Tropic Zone, Law & Order, Prisoner of War, Cattle Queen of Montana, Tennessee's Partner, Hellcats of the Navy, The Young Doctors (narrator), The Killers, Guts & Glory, Afghanistan: Land in Crisis.
TELEVISION: Series: The Orchid Award (emcee), General Electric Theater (host, frequent star), Death Valley Days (host), Cold War. Guest: Ford Theratre, Schlitz Playhouse of Stars, Lux

Video Theatre, Startime,Walt: The Man Behind the Myth, Air Force One.

REARDON, BARRY
Executive. b. Hartford, CT, Mar. 8, 1931. e. Holy Cross Col., Trinity Col. Began industry career with Paramount Pictures; named v.p.; left to join General Cinema Theatres Corp. as sr. v.p., Warner Bros. pres. of domestic distribution co., retired 1999. Now serves on the Board of various companies.

REASON, REX
Actor. b. Berlin, Germany, Nov. 30, 1928. e. Hoover H.S., Glendale, CA. Worked at various jobs; studied dramatics at Pasadena Playhouse.
PICTURES: Storm Over Tibet, Salome, Mission Over Korea, Taza Son of Cochise, This Island Earth, Smoke Signal, Lady Godiva, Kiss of Fire, Creature Walks Among Us, Raw Edge, The Rawhide Trail, Under Fire, Thundering Jets, The Sad Horse, Yankee Pasha, Band of Angels, Miracle of the Hills.
TELEVISION: Series: Man Without a Gun, Roaring Twenties.

REDDY, HELEN
Singer. b. Melbourne, Australia, Oct. 25, 1942. Parents were producer-writer-actor Max Reddy and actress Stella Lamond. e. in Australia. Began career at age four as singer and appeared in hundreds of stage and radio roles with parents by age of 15. Came to New York in 1966, played nightclubs, appeared on TV. First single hit record: I Don't Know How To Love Him (Capitol). Grammy Award, 1973, as best female singer of year for I Am Woman. Most Played Artist by the music operators of America: American Music Award 1974; Los Angeles Times Woman of the Year (1975); No. 1 Female Vocalist in 1975 and 1976; Record World, Cash Box and Billboard. Heads prod. co. Helen Reddy, Inc.
THEATRE: B'way: Blood Brothers.
PICTURES: Airport 1975 (debut), Pete's Dragon, Sgt. Pepper's Lonely Hearts Club Band, Disorderlies.
TELEVISION: Series: The Helen Reddy Show (Summer, 1973), Permanent host of Midnight Special. Appearances: David Frost Show, Flip Wilson Show, Mike Douglas Show, Tonight Show, Mac Davis Show, Merv Griffin Show (guest host), Sesame Street, Live in Australia (host, 1988); Muppet Show, Home for Easter.

REDFORD, ROBERT
Actor, Director, Producer. r.n. Charles Robert Redford Jr.. b. Santa Monica, CA, Aug. 18, 1937. Attended U. of Colorado; left to travel in Europe, 1957. Attended Pratt Inst. and American Acad. of Dramatic Arts. Founded Sundance Film Institute, Park City, Utah, workshop for young filmmakers.
THEATRE: B'way: Tall Story (walk on), The Highest Tree, Sunday in New York (Theatre World Award), Barefoot in the Park.
PICTURES: Actor: War Hunt (debut, 1962), Situation Hopeless But Not Serious, Inside Daisy Clover, The Chase, This Property Is Condemned, Barefoot in the Park, Downhill Racer (also exec. prod.), Butch Cassidy and the Sundance Kid, Tell Them Willie Boy is Here, Little Fauss and Big Halsy, The Hot Rock, The Candidate (also co-exec. prod.), Jeremiah Johnson, The Way We Were, The Sting (Acad. Award nom.), The Great Gatsby, The Great Waldo Pepper, Three Days of the Condor, All The President's Men (also exec. prod.), A Bridge Too Far, The Electric Horseman, Brubaker, The Natural, Out of Africa, Legal Eagles, Havana, Sneakers, Indecent Proposal, Up Close and Personal, Anthem, Forever Hollywood, New York in the 50's, The Last Castle, Spy Game. Exec. Producer: Promised Land, Some Girls, Yosemite: The Fate of Heaven (also narrator), The Dark Wind, Incident at Oglala (also narrator), Strawberry & Chocolate (presenter), She's the One, Slums of Beverly Hills, A Civil Action, No Looking Back, People I Know, The Motorcycle Diaries. Director: Ordinary People (Acad. Award, 1980), The Milagro Beanfield War (also co-prod.), A River Runs Through It (also prod., narrator), Quiz Show (also prod.; NY Film Critics Award for Best Picture; Acad. Award noms. for picture & dir.), The Horse Whisperer (also actor, prod.), The Legend of Bagger Vance (also prod.), Enredando Sombras, Forever Hollywood, In the Shadow of Hollywood, New York in the 50;s, The Last Castle, Spy Game, The Motorcycle Diaries (exec. prod.).
TELEVISION: Actor: Guest: Maverick, Playhouse 90, Play of the Week (The Iceman Cometh), Alfred Hitchcock Presents, Route 66, Twilight Zone, Dr. Kildare, The Untouchables, The Virginian, The Defenders. Exec. Prod.: Grand Avenue. Skinwalkers, The Mystery of Chaco Canyon.

REDGRAVE, CORIN
Actor. b. London, England, July 16, 1939. e. Cambridge. p. late Sir Michael Redgrave and Rachel Kempson. Brother of Vanessa and Lynn Redgrave.
THEATRE: On stage with England Stage Co.: A Midsummer Night's Dream, Chips with Everything. RSC: Lady Windermere's

Fan, Julius Caesar, Comedy of Errors, Antony and Cleopatra. Young Vic: Rosmersholm.
PICTURES: A Man for All Seasons, The Deadly Affair, Charge of the Light Brigade, The Magus, Oh What a Lovely War, When Eight Bells Toll, Serail, Excalibur, Eureka, Between Wars, The Fool, In the Name of the Father, Four Weddings and a Funeral, Persuasion, England, My England, Honest, Die Erika und Klaus Mann Story, Enigma, Doctor Sleep, Cromwell and Fairfax.
TELEVISION: I Berlioz, Measure for Measure, Persuasion, Henry IV, Circle of Deceit, Trial and Retribution, Shackleton, Bertie and Elizabeth, The Forsythe Saga, Sunday.

REDGRAVE, LYNN

Actress. b. London, England, Mar. 8, 1943. Sister of Vanessa and Corin Redgrave. p. late Sir Michael Redgrave and Rachel Kempson. m. dir.-actor-manager John Clark. Ent. m.p. and TV industries, 1962.
THEATRE: NY: Black Comedy (B'way debut), My Fat Friend (1974), Mrs. Warren's Profession, Knock Knock, Misalliance, St. Joan, Twelfth Night (Amer. Shakespeare Fest), Sister Mary Ignatius Explains It All For You, Aren't We All?, Sweet Sue, A Little Hotel on the Side, The Master Builder, Shakespeare for My Father (also writer). LA: Les Liaisons Dangereuses.
PICTURES: Tom Jones (debut, 1963), Girl With Green Eyes, Georgy Girl (Acad. Award nom.), The Deadly Affair, Smashing Time, The Virgin Soldiers, Last of the Mobile Hot-Shots, Los Guerilleros, Viva la Muerta—Tua!, Every Little Crook and Nanny, Everything You Always Wanted to Know About Sex* But Were Afraid to Ask, The National Health, The Happy Hooker, The Big Bus, Sunday Lovers, Morgan Stewart's Coming Home, Midnight, Getting It Right, Shine, Strike, Gods and Monsters (Acad. Award nom.), Touched, The Annihilation of Fish, The Simian Line, The Next Best Thing, Deeply, How to Kill Your Neighbor's Dog, Venus and Mars, My Kingdom, Spider, Anita and Me, Who Shot Victor Fox, Hansel and Gretel.
TELEVISION: BBC: Pretty Polly, Ain't Afraid to Dance, The End of the Tunnel, I Am Osango, What's Wrong with Humpty Dumpty, Egg On the Face of the Tiger, Blank Pages, A Midsummer Night's Dream, Pygmalion, William, Vienna 1900, Daft as a Brush, Not For Women Only, Calling the Shots. United States: Co-host: A.M. America. Movies: Turn of the Screw, Sooner or Later, Beggarman Thief, Gauguin the Savage, Seduction of Miss Leona, Rehearsal for Murder, The Bad Seed, My Two Loves, Jury Duty: The Comedy, What Ever Happened to Baby Jane?, Toothless, Indefensible: The Truth About Edward Brannigan, White Lies, Different, A Season For Miracles, Varian's War, My Sister's Keeper,. Mini-Series: Centennial. Series: House Calls, Teachers Only, Chicken Soup, Rude Awakening. Guest: The Muppet Show, Walking on Air, Candid Camera Christmas Special, Woman Alone, Tales From the Hollywood Hills: The Old Reliable, Death of a Son.

REDGRAVE, VANESSA

O.B.E. Actress. b. London, England, Jan. 30, 1937. p. Sir Michael Redgrave and Rachel Kempson. Sister of Lynn and Corin Redgrave. Mother of actresses Joely and Natasha Richardson. Early career with Royal Shakespeare Company. Appeared in documentary Tonight Let's All Make Love in London. Autobiography, 1994.
THEATRE: Daniel Deronda, Cato Street, The Threepenny Opera, Twelfth Night, As You Like It, The Taming of the Shrew, Cymbeline, The Sea Gull, The Prime of Miss Jean Brodie, Antony & Cleopatra, Design for Living, Macbeth, Lady from the Sea, The Aspern Papers, Ghosts, Anthony and Cleopatra, Tomorrow Was War, A Touch of the Poet, Orpheus Descending, Madhouse in Goa, The Three Sisters, When She Danced, Maybe, Heartbreak House, Vita & Virginia.
PICTURES: Behind the Mask (debut, 1958), Morgan!: A Suitable Case for Treatment (Acad. Award nom.), A Man for All Seasons, Blow-Up, The Sailor From Gibraltar, Red and Blue, Camelot, The Charge of the Light Brigade, Isadora (Acad. Award nom.), Oh! What a Lovely War, The Sea Gull, A Quiet Place in the Country, Drop Out, The Trojan Women, La Vacanza, The Devils, Mary—Queen of Scots (Acad. Award nom.), Murder on the Orient Express, Out of Season, The Seven Percent Solution, Julia (Acad. Award, best supporting actress, 1977), Agatha, Yanks, Bear Island, The Bostonians (Acad. Award nom.), Steaming, Wetherby, Prick Up Your Ears, Consuming Passions, Comrades, The Ballad of the Sad Cafe, Romeo-Juliet (voice), Howards End (Acad. Award nom.), Breath of Life, Sparrow, The House of the Spirits, Crime and Punishment, Mother's Boys, Great Moments in Aviation, Little Odessa, A Month by the Lake, Mrs. Dalloway, Deep Impact, Lulu on the Bridge, A Rumor of Angels, Mirka, Girl Interrupted, The Cradle Will Rock, The 3 Kings, The Pledge, Searching for Debra Winger, The Riding of the Laddie, The Assumption.
TELEVISION: Movies/Specials: A Farewell to Arms, Katherine Mansfield, Playing for Time (Emmy Award, 1981), My Body My Child, Wagner (theatrical in Europe), Three Sovereigns for Sarah, Peter the Great, Second Serve, A Man For All Seasons, Orpheus Descending, Young Catherine, What Ever Happened to Baby Jane?, They, Down Came a Blackbird, Bella Mafia, If These Walls Could Talk 2., The Gathering Storm, The Locket .Guest: Faerie Tale Theatre (Snow White and the 7 Dwarfs).

REDSTONE, SUMNER M.

Executive, Attorney; b. Boston, MA, May 27, 1923. e. Harvard, B.A., 1944, LLB., 1947. Served to 1st Lt. AUS, 1943-45. Admitted to MA Bar 1947; U.S. Ct. Appeals 1st Circuit 1948, 8th Circuit 1950, 9th Circuit 1948; D.C. 1951; U.S. Supreme Ct. 1952; law sec. U.S. Ct. Appeals for 9th Circuit 1947-48; instr. U. San Francisco Law Sch. and Labor Management Sch., 1947; special asst. to U.S. Atty. General, 1948-51; partner firm Ford Bergson Adams Borkland & Redstone, Washington, D.C. 1951-54; exec. v.p. Northeast Drive-In Theatre Corp., 1954-68; pres. Northeast Theatre Corp.; chmn. bd., pres. & CEO, National Amusements, Inc.; chmn. bd., Viacom Int'l, Inc., 1987; asst. pres. Theatre Owners of America, 1960-63; pres. 1964-65; bd. chmn, National Assoc. of Theatre Owners, 1965-66. Member: Presidential Advisory Committee John F. Kennedy Center for the Performing Arts; chmn. Jimmy Fund, Boston 1960; chmn., met. div. Combined Jewish Philanthropies 1963; sponsor Boston Museum of Science; Trustee Children's Cancer Research Foundation; Art Lending Library; bd. of dirs. of TV Acad. of Arts and Sciences Fund; bd. dirs. Boston Arts Festival; v.p.; exec. committee Will Rogers Memorial Fund; bd. overseers Dana Farber Cancer Institute; corp. New England Medical Center; Motion Picture Pioneers; bd. mem. John F. Kennedy Library Foundation; 1984-85; 1985-86 State Crusade Chairman American Cancer Society; Board of Overseers Boston Museum of Fine Arts; Professor, Boston U. Law Sch. 1982-83, 1985-86; Boston Latin School's Graduate of the Year, 1989; Acquired Viacom in 1987 which purchased Paramount Communications in 1993. Member of exec. committe of the National Assoc. of Theatre Owners. Member, exec. bd., Combined Jewish Philanthropies. Judge on Kennedy Library Foundation. Founding trustee, American Cancer Society. Visiting professor, Brandeis University; lecturer, Harvard Law School. AWARDS: (Entertainment related) include: Communicator of the Year B'nai B'rith Communications, Cinema Lodge 1980; Man of the Year, Entertainment Industries div.; UJA-Federation, NY, 1988; Variety of New England Humanitarian Award, 1989; Motion Picture Pioneers Pioneer of the Year, 1991; Golden Plate Award American Acad. Achievement 32nd Annual Salute to Excellence Program; 1994, Man of the Year Award from MIPCOM, the Int'l Film and Programme Market for TV Video Cable and Satellite; 1995, Variety Club International Humanitarian Award; Hall of Fame Award, Broadcast & Cable Magazine, 1995; Honoree 7th Annual Fundraiser, Montefiore Medical Center; Expeditioner's Award, New York City Outward Bound Center, 1996; Patron of the Arts Award, Songwriter's Hall of Fame, 1996; Vision 21 Award and Doctor of Humane Letter, New York Institute of Technology, 1996; Trustees Award, The National Academy of Television Arts and Sciences, 1997; Gold Medal Award, International Radio and Television Society, 1998.

Redstone, Shari E.

Executive. b. 1954, Washington, D.C. Daughter of Sumner Redstone. e. Tufts University, B.A., 1976; Boston University, law degree, 1978; Boston University, master's degree in law, 1980. Practiced law from 1978-1993. E.V.P. of National Amusements, 1994-Dec. 1999. Jan. 2000, named president, National Amusements. Member, bd. of directors and exec. comm. for National Assn. of Theatre Owners, co-chmn. and co-CEO of MovieTickets.com, Inc.; chmn. and CEO of CineBridge Ventures, Inc.; chmn. and CEO of Rising Star Media; a member of bd. of trustees at Dana Farber Cancer Institute; bd. member at Combined Jewish Philanthropies; on bd. of directors of the John F. Kennedy Library Foundation and member of Bd. of Overseers at Brandeis Univ. A director of Viacom, Inc., since 1994.

REED, PAMELA

Actress. b. Tacoma, WA, Apr. 2, 1953. Ran day-care center and worked with Head Start children before studying drama at U. of Washington. Worked on Trans-Alaska pipeline. Off-Broadway showcases.
THEATRE: Curse of the Starving Class (Off-B'way debut, 1978), All's Well That Ends Well (Central Park), Getting Out (Drama Desk Award), Aunt Dan and Lemon, Fools, The November People (Broadway debut), Sorrows of Stephen, Mrs. Warren's Profession, Getting Through the Night, Best Little Whorehouse in Texas, Fen, Standing on My Knees, Elektra.
PICTURES: The Long Riders (debut, 1980), Melvin and Howard, Eyewitness, Young Doctors in Love, The Right Stuff, The Goodbye People, The Best of Times, Clan of the Cave Bear, Rachel River, Chattahoochee, Cadillac Man, Kindergarten Cop, Passed Away, Bob Roberts, Junior, Santa Fe, Bean, Santa Fe, Why Do Fools Fall in Love, Standing on Fishes, Proof of Life.
TELEVISION: Series: The Andros Targets (TV debut, 1977), Grand, Family Album, The Home Court. Movies: Inmates—A Love Story, I Want To Live, Heart of Steel, Scandal Sheet, Caroline?, Woman With a Past, Born Too Soon, Deadly Whispers, The Man Next Door, Critical Choices, Carriers, Book of Days. Special: Tanner '88. Mini-Series: Hemingway. Guest: L.A. Law, The Simpsons (voice).

REES, ROGER

Actor. b. Aberystwyth, Wales, May 5, 1944. e. Camberwell Sch. of Art, Slade Sch. of Fine Art. Stage debut Hindle Wakes (Wimbledon, U.K., 1964). With Royal Shakespeare Co. from 1967. Starred in the title role The Adventures of Nicholas

Nickleby (London and NY, Tony Award), also on stage in Hapgood (London, L.A.), Indiscretions (NY). Off-B'way in The End of the Day. Assoc. dir. Bristol Old Vic Theatre Co., 1986-present. Playwright with Eric Elice of Double Double and Elephant Manse.
PICTURES: Star 80 (debut, 1983), Keine Storung Bitte, Mountains of the Moon, If Looks Could Kill, Stop! Or My Mom Will Shoot, Robin Hood: Men in Tights, Sudden Manhattan, Trouble on the Corner, Next Stop Wonderland, A Midsummer Night's Dream, Jump, The Bumblebee Flies Away, Blackmale, 3 A.M., Loop Dreams- The Making of a Low Budget Movie, Return to Neverland, The Scorpion King, The Palace Thief, Frida, Crazy Like a Fox, The Emperor's Club.
TELEVISION: Movies: A Christmas Carol (released theatrically in Europe), Place of Peace, Under Western Eyes, Bouquet of Barbed Wire, Saigon: The Year of the Cat, Imaginary Friends, The Adventures of Nicolas Nickleby, The Comedy of Errors, Macbeth, The Voysey Inheritance, The Ebony Tower, The Finding, The Return of Sam McCloud, Charles & Diana: Unhappily Ever After, The Tower, The Possession of Michael D., Titanic, Double Platinum, The Crossing Series: Cheers, Singles, M.A.N.T.I.S., Liberty! The American Revolution, Damian Cromwell's Postcards from America.

REESE, DELLA
Actress, Singer. r.n. Deloreese Patricia Early. b. Detroit, MI, July 6, 1932. e. Wayne St. Univ. As teen toured with Mahalia Jackson. Began recording in 1950's. Hit songs include Don't You Know.
PICTURES: Let's Rock!, Psychic Killer, Harlem Nights, The Distinguished Gentleman, A Thin Line Between Love and Hate, Dinosaur, (voice).
TELEVISION: Series: The Della Reese Show, Chico and the Man, It Takes Two, Charlie & Company, The Royal Family, Touched by an Angel. Guest: The Ed Sullivan Show, Sanford and Son, The Rookies, McCloud, Welcome Back Kotter, The Love Boat, Night Court, The A-Team. Movies: The Voyage of the Yes, Twice in a Lifetime, The Return of Joe Forrester, Nightmare in Badham County, The Secret Path, Mama Flora's Family, Anya's Bell, The Moving of Sophie Miles Mini-Series: Roots: The Next Generations.

REEVE, CHRISTOPHER
Actor. b. New York, NY, Sept. 25, 1952. e. Cornell U., B.A.; graduate work at Juilliard. Stage debut at McCarter Theatre in Princeton at age 9. B'way debut with Katharine Hepburn in A Matter of Gravity.
THEATRE: NY: A Matter of Gravity, My Life, Fifth of July, The Marriage of Figaro, A Winter's Tale, Love Letters. LA: Summer and Smoke. Williamstown: The Front Page, Mesmer, Richard Corey, Royal Family, The Seagull, The Greeks, Holiday, Camino Real, John Brown's Body, Death Takes a Holiday, The Guardsman. Regional: The Irregular Verb to Love, Beggar's Opera, Troilus and Cressida, The Love Cure. London debut: The Aspern Papers.
PICTURES: Gray Lady Down (debut, 1978), Superman, Somewhere in Time, Superman II, Deathtrap, Monsignor, Superman III, The Bostonians, The Aviator, Street Smart, Superman IV: The Quest for Peace (also co-story), Switching Channels, Noises Off, Morning Glory, The Remains of the Day, Above Suspicion, Speechless, Village of the Damned, A Step Toward Tomorrow.
TELEVISION: Series: Love of Life. Mini-Series: Kidnapped. Movies: Anna Karenina, The Great Escape II: The Untold Story, The Rose and the Jackal, Bump in the Night, Death Dreams, Mortal Sins, Nightmare in the Daylight, The Sea Wolf, Black Fox, Black Fox: The Price of Peace, Black Fox: Good Men and Bad, Rear Window (also exec. prod.). Toughest Break: The Martin's Story, Intimate Portrait: Margot Kidder Specials: Faerie Tale Theatre (Sleeping Beauty), The Last Ferry Home, Earth and the American Dream, Without Pity: A Film About Abilities, BBC and The BAFTA: A Tribute to Michael Kaine Guest: Tales From the Crypt, Frasier.

REEVES, KEANU
Actor. b. Beirut, Lebanon, Sept. 2, 1964. Lived in Australia and NY before family settled in Toronto. e. Toronto's High School for the Performing Arts, then continued training at Second City Workshop. Made Coca-Cola commercial at 16. At 18 studied at Hedgerow Theatre in PA for summer. Professional debut on Hanging In, CBC local Toronto TV show. Toronto stage debut in Wolf Boy; later on stage in Romeo and Juliet, Hamlet.
PICTURES: Youngblood (debut, 1986), River's Edge, The Night Before, Permanent Record, The Prince of Pennsylvania, Dangerous Liaisons, Bill and Ted's Excellent Adventure, Parenthood, I Love You to Death, Tune in Tomorrow, Point Break, Bill and Ted's Bogus Journey, My Own Private Idaho, Bram Stoker's Dracula, Much Ado About Nothing, Freaked (cameo), Even Cowgirls Get the Blues, Little Buddha, Speed, Johnny Mnemonic, A Walk in the Clouds, Chain Reaction, Feeling Minnesota, The Last Time I Committed Suicide, The Devil's Advocate, Me and Will (cameo), The Matrix, The Replacements, The Watcher, The Gift, Sweet November, Hardball, The Matrix Reloaded, The Matrix Revisited, Mayor of Sunset Strip, The Matrix 3, The Matrix Revolutions.
TELEVISION: Movies: Act of Vengeance, Under the Influence,

Brotherhood of Justice, Babes In Toyland. Specials: I Wish I Were Eighteen Again, Life Under Water. Guest: The Tracey Ullman Show, Action.

REGNIER, NATACHA
Actress. b. Belgium, April 11. 1974.
PICTURES: The Motorcycle Girl, Le nid tombe de l'oiseau, Dismoi oiu..., Cecile mon enfant, Encore, La Mouette, The Dreamlife of Angels (Cannes Film Fest. Award, Best Actress, 1998), Harlem, Calino Maneige, Tempo dell ámore, Les amants criminels, Tout va bien- on s'en va, La fille de son pere, Comment j'ai tue mon pere, How I Killed My Father.

REHME, ROBERT G.
Executive. b. Cincinnati, OH, May 5, 1935. e. U. of Cincinnati. 1953, mgr., RKO Theatres, Inc., Cincinnati; 1961, adv. mgr., Cincinnati Theatre Co.; 1966, dir. of field adv., United Artists Pictures; 1969, named dir. of pub. and field adv./promotion, Paramount Pictures; 1972, pres., BR Theatres and v.p., April Fools Films, gen. mgr. Tri-State Theatre Service; 1976, v.p. & gen. sls. mgr., New World Pictures; 1978, joined Avco Embassy Pictures as sr. v.p. & COO, then named exec. v.p.; 1979, named pres., Avco Embassy Pictures, Inc.; 1981, joined Universal Pictures as pres. of distrib. & marketing; 1982, named pres. of Universal Pictures; 1983, joined New World Pictures as co-chmn. & CEO; elected pres., Academy Foundation, 1988; pres. Foundation of Motion Picture Pioneers, 1989; 1st v.p., AMPAS; 1989, partner, Neufeld/Rehme prods. at Paramount; 1992, pres. of Academy of Motion Picture Arts & Sciences.
PICTURES: Flight of the Intruder, Necessary Roughness, Patriot Games, Gettysburg, Beverly Hills Cop III, Clear and Present Danger, Woman Undone, Blind Faith, Lost in Space, Black Dog, Joan of Arc: The Virgin Warrior, Love and Treason, The General's Daughter, Gods and Generals, Conviction.
TELEVISION: Movies: Gridock, For the Children: The Irvine Fertility Scandal, Escape, Human Cargo. Series: Lightning Force.

REID, TIM
Actor. b. Norfolk, VA, Dec. 19, 1944. m. actress Daphne Maxwell. Started as half of comedy team of Tim and Tom in 1969, before becoming solo stand-up comedian. Published photo/poetry collection As I Feel It, 1982.
PICTURES: Dead Bang, The Fourth War, Out of Sync (also prod.). Prod/dir: Once Upon A Time...When We Were Colored, For Real.
TELEVISION: Series: Easy Does It... Starring Frankie Avalon, The Marilyn McCoo and Billy Davis Jr. Show, The Richard Pryor Show, WKRP in Cincinnati, Teachers Only, Simon and Simon, Frank's Place (also co-exec. prod.), Snoops (also co-exec. prod.), Sister Sister, Save Our Streets, Lincs (also exec. prod.), Alley Cats Strike. Guest: That's My Mama, Rhoda, What's Happening, Matlock. Movies: Perry Mason: The Case of the Silenced Singer, Stephen King's It, Race to Freedom: The Underground Railroad (also co-exec. prod.), Simon & Simon: In Trouble Again, You Wish!, For Real, (also writer,dir.), Las Vegas Warrior, Blue Moon, (exec.prod.) Special: Mastergate.

REID, TRAVIS
Executive.
V.p. with General Cinema Corporation's Midwest, Southwest and Western regions before joining Loews theatres in 1991 as v.p. of film. Promoted to sr. v.p. in 1993; by 1995, promoted to executive v.p., with expanded responsibilities for strategic planning, corporate development, and theatre circuit expansion. Named president of Loews Theatres, 1996. Company merged with Cineplex Odeon Corporation in 1998 and formed Loews Cineplex Entertainment (LCE). Reid then assumed current position as president, Loews Cineplex United States, a division of LCE.

REILLY, CHARLES NELSON
Actor, Director. b. New York, NY, Jan. 13. 1931. e. U. of CT. On Broadway mostly in comedy roles before turning to TV and films. Recently directed stage plays.
THEATRE: As actor: Bye Bye Birdie (debut), How to Succeed in Business Without Really Trying (Tony Award, 1962), Hello Dolly!, Skyscraper, God's Favorite. Acted in 22 off-B'way plays. Founded musical comedy dept. HB Studios. Conceived and dir.: The Belle of Amherst, Paul Robeson, The Nerd (dir.). Resident dir.: Burt Reynolds' Jupiter Theatre.
PICTURES: A Face in the Crowd, Two Tickets to Paris, The Tiger Makes Out, Cannonball Run II, Body Slam, All Dogs Go to Heaven (voice), Rock-a-Doodle (voice), A Troll in Central Park (voice), Bows will be Boys, Babes in Toyland, An All Dogs Christmas Carol, The First of May, Broadway- The Golden Age.
TELEVISION: Series: The Steve Lawrence Show, The Ghost and Mrs. Muir, Dean Martin Presents The Golddiggers, Liddsville, Arnie, It Pays to Be Ignorant (1973-74), Match Game P.M., Sweethearts (game show host), Hercules. Guest: Tonight Show (guest host), Dean Martin Show. Movies: Call Her Mom, The Three Kings, Bandit, Bandit Goes Country. Special: Wind in the Wire.

REINER, CARL
Actor, Director, Writer, Producer. b. New York, NY, March 20, 1922. Son is actor-director-writer Rob Reiner. Comedian on B'way: Call Me Mr., Inside U.S.A., Alive and Kicking. *Author* (novels): Enter Laughing, All Kinds of Love, Continue Laughing. *Playwright*: Something Different.
PICTURES: *Actor only*: Happy Anniversary, Gidget Goes Hawaiian, It's a Mad Mad Mad Mad World, The Russians Are Coming! The Russians Are Coming!, Don't Worry We'll Think of a Title, A Guide for the Married Man, Generation, The End, The Spirit of '76, Ocean's Eleven. *Writer-Actor*: The Gazebo, The Thrill of It All (also co-prod.), The Art of Love. *Director*: Enter Laughing (also co-s.p.), The Comic (also s.p., actor), Where's Poppa?, Oh God! (also actor), The One and Only, The Jerk (also actor), Dead Men Don't Wear Plaid (also co-s.p., actor), The Man With Two Brains (also co-s.p.), All of Me, Summer Rental, Summer School (also actor), Bert Rigby You're a Fool (also s.p.), Sibling Rivalry, Fatal Instinct (also actor), That Old Feeling, The Slums of Beverly Hills (actor only), Ocean's Eleven, Hail Syd Caesar! The Golden Age of Comedy, The Majestic, (voice), The Adventures of Rocky & Bullwinkle.
TELEVISION: *Series*: The Fashion Story, The Fifty-Fourth Street Revue, Eddie Condon's Floor Show, Your Show of Shows (also writer), Droodles (panelist), Caesar's Hour (also writer; 2 Emmy Awards for supporting actor, 1956, 1957), Sid Caesar Invites You, Keep Talking, Dinah Shore Chevy Show (writer), Take a Good Look (panelist), The Dick Van Dyke Show (also creator-prod.-dir-writer; 5 Emmy Awards: writing 1962, 1963, 1964, producing: 1965, 1966), Art Linkletter Show, The Celebrity Game (host), The New Dick Van Dyke Show (creator-prod.-writer), Good Heavens (also exec. prod.), Sunday Best (host), Hercules (voice). *Movies*: Medical Story, Skokie. *Guest*: Comedy Spot, Judy Garland Show, Burke's Law, That Girl, Night Gallery, Faerie Tale Theatre (Pinocchio), It's Garry Shandling's Show, Mad About You (Emmy Award, 1995). *Special*: The Sid Caesar-Imogene Coca-Carl Reiner-Howard Morris Special (Emmy Award for writing, 1967).
RECORDINGS: Carl Reiner and Mel Brooks, The 2000 Year Old Man, The 2001 Year Old Man, The 2013 Year Old Man, Continue Laughing, A Connecticut Yankee in King Arthur's Court, Miracle on 34th Street, Jack and the Beanstalk, Aesop's Fables, The Prince and the Pauper.

REINER, ROB
Actor, Director, Writer. b. New York, NY, March 6, 1947. Father is actor-writer-director-producer Carl Reiner. Worked as actor with regional theatres and improvisational comedy troupes. Wrote for the Smothers Brothers Comedy Hour. Breakthrough as actor came in 1971 when signed by Norman Lear for All in the Family. Directorial debut with This Is Spinal Tap, 1984. Co-founder of Castle Rock Entertainment.
PICTURES: *Actor*: Enter Laughing, Halls of Anger, Where's Poppa?, Summertree, Fire Sale, Throw Momma From the Train, Postcards From the Edge, The Spirit of '76, Sleepless in Seattle, Bullets Over Broadway, Mixed Nuts, Bye Bye Love, Mad Dog Time, For Better or Worse, The First Wives Club, Primary Colors, Edtv, The Muse (cameo). *Director/Prod.*: This is Spinal Tap (also actor, co-s.p., co-prod.), The Sure Thing (dir. only), Stand by Me (dir. only), The Princess Bride (dir. only), When Harry Met Sally..., Misery, A Few Good Men (Acad. Award nom. for best picture; DGA nom.), North, The American President, Ghosts of Mississippi, The Story of Us (also actor), Forever Hollywood, Hail Syd Caesar! The Golden Age of Comedy, The Majestic, Alex and Emma, (also prod./dir.).
TELEVISION: *Series*: All in the Family (2 Emmy Awards: 1974, 1978), Free Country (also co-writer), Morton & Hayes (also co-creator, co-exec. prod.). *Movies*: Thursday's Game, More Than Friends (also co-writer, co-exec. prod.), Million Dollar Infield (also co-prod., co-writer). *Guest*: Gomer Pyle, Batman, Beverly Hillbillies, Room 222, Partridge Family, Odd Couple, It's Garry Shandling's Show. *Special*: But... Seriously (exec. prod.).

REINHOLD, JUDGE
Actor. r.n. Edward Ernest Reinhold Jr. b. Wilmington, DE, May 21, 1957. e. Mary Washington Coll., North Carolina Sch. of Arts. Acted in regional theatres including Burt Reynolds dinner theater in FL before signed to TV contract at Paramount.
PICTURES: Running Scared (debut, 1979), Stripes, Pandemonium, Fast Times at Ridgemont High, Lords of Discipline, Roadhouse 66, Gremlins, Beverly Hills Cop, Head Office, Off Beat, Ruthless People, Beverly Hills Cop II, Vice Versa, Rosalie Goes Shopping, Daddy's Dyin', Enid is Sleeping, Zandalee, Near Misses, Baby on Board, Bank Robber, Beverly Hills Cop III, The Santa Clause, Crackerjack 2, Last Lives, Family Plan, Homegrown, Redemption High, My Brother the Pig, Beethoven's 3rd, Enemies of Laughter, Ping, Newsbreak, Mindstorm, Camp Ninja, Beethoven's 4th, No Plave Like Home, The Meeksville Ghost, Hollywood Palms, Betaville, Dead in a Heartbeat, The Santa Clause 2, Whacked!
TELEVISION: *Series*: Secret Service Guy. *Movies*: Survival of Dana, A Matter of Sex, Promised a Miracle, Black Magic, Four Eyes and Six-Guns, Dad the Angel and Me, As Good as Dead, The Wharf Rat, The Right to Remain Silent, Runaway Car, Netforce, The O'Keefes. *Guest*: Seinfeld. *Specials*: A Step Too Slow, The Willmar Eight, The Parallax Garden.

REISENBACH, SANFORD E.
Executive. e. NYU. Associated with Grey Advertising for 20 years; exec. v.p. and pres./founder of Grey's Leisure & Entertainment division in N.Y. In August, 1979, joined Warner Bros. as exec. v.p. of worldwide adv. & pub.; named pres. worldwide adv. & pub., 1985. Appt. corporate exec. of marketing and planning, Warner Bros., 1989.

REISER, PAUL
Actor. b. New York, NY, Mar. 30, 1957. e. SUNY/Binghamton. Started performing as a stand-up comic in such clubs as Catch a Rising Star, the Improv, and the Comic Strip. Author: Couplehood (1994).
PICTURES: Diner (debut, 1982), Beverly Hills Cop, Aliens, Beverly Hills Cop II, Cross My Heart, Crazy People, The Marrying Man, Mr. Write, Bye Bye Love, Get Bruce (cameo), the Story of Us, One Night at McCool's, Purpose.
TELEVISION: *Series*: My Two Dads, Mad About You (Emmy Award). *Special*: Paul Reiser—Out on a Whim. *Movies*: Sunset Limousine, The Tower, Oooph!, Women Vs. Men. *Pilots*: Diner, Just Married.

REISNER, ALLEN
Director. b. New York, NY.
PICTURES: The Day They Gave the Babies Away, St. Louis Blues, All Mine to Give.
TELEVISION: *Movies/Specials*: Captain and the Kings, Mary Jane Harper Cried Last Night, Your Money or Your Wife, To Die in Paris, The Clift, Skag, They're Playing Our Song, The Gentleman From Seventh Avenue, Escape of Pierre Mendes-France, Deliverance of Sister Cecelia, The Sound of Silence. *Series*: Murder She Wrote, Twilight Zone, Hardcastle & McCormick, Airwolf, The Mississippi, Hawaii Five-O, Blacke's Magic, Law and Harry McGraw, Playhouse 90, Studio One, Climax, United States Steel Hour, Suspense, Danger.

REISS, JEFFREY C.
Executive. b. Brooklyn, NY, April 14, 1942. e. Washington U., St. Louis, B.A., 1963. Consultant at NYU and Manhattanville Coll. and instructor at Brooklyn Coll. before entering industry. Agent in literary dept. for General Artists Corp., 1966. Supervised development in NY of Tandem Prods. for Norman Lear, 1968. Produced off-B'way plays 1968-70. Dir. of program acquistion devel. for Cartridge TV, Inc. (mfg. of first home video cassette players-recorders), 1970-73. Joined ABC Entertainment as director of network feature films, 1973-75. Founder and pres., Showtime Pay TV Network, 1976-80. Co-founder, pres. & CEO, Cable Health Network, 1981-83. 1983, named vice chmn. & CEO, Lifetime Cable Network following Cable Health Network merger with Daytime. Chmn. of the board, pres. & CEO, Reiss Media Enterprises, Inc. 1984. Founder & chmn. of board, Request Television (pay-per-view svc.), 1985.

REISS, STUART A.
Set Decorator. b. Chicago, IL, July 15, 1921. e. L.A. High Sch., 1939. Property man, 20th-Fox, 1939-42; U.S. Army Air Corps, 1942-45; joined 20th-Fox as set decorator in 1945. Worked on over 30 tv shows and over 100 motion pictures, receiving 6 Academy Award noms. and 2 Oscars.
PICTURES: Titanic, How to Marry a Millionaire, Hell and High Water, There's No Business Like Show Business, Soldier of Fortune, The Seven Year Itch, Man in the Grey Flannel Suit, Teen Age Rebel, The Diary of Anne Frank (Academy Award, 1959), What a Way to Go, Fantastic Voyage (Academy Award, 1966), Doctor Doolittle, Che!, Beyond the Valley of the Dolls, Escape from the Planet of the Apes, Oh God!, The Swarm, Beyond the Poseidon Adventure, Carbon Copy, When Time Ran Out... , All the Marbles, The Man Who Loved Women, Micki and Maude, A Fine Mess,

REITMAN, IVAN
Director, Producer. b. Komarno, Czechoslovakia, Oct. 26, 1946. Moved to Canada at age 4. e. McMaster U. Attended National Film Board's Summer Institute directing three short films including Orientation (1968) which received theatrical distribution. Produced Canadian TV show in 1970s.
THEATRE: *Prod.*: The National Lampoon Show, The Magic Show, Merlin (also dir.).
PICTURES: *Dir./Prod.*: Foxy Lady (debut, 1971; also edit., music), Cannibal Girls, Meatballs (dir. only), Stripes, Ghostbusters, Legal Eagles (also co-story), Twins, Ghostbusters II, Kindergarten Cop, Dave, Junior, Father's Day, Six Days Seven Nights, Evolution. *Prod. only*: Columbus of Sex, They Came From Within (Shivers), Death Weekend, Rabid (co-exec. prod.), Blackout, National Lampoon's Animal House, Heavy Metal, Spacehunter: Adventures in the Forbidden Zone (exec. prod.), Big Shots (exec. prod.), Casual Sex? (exec. prod.), Feds (exec. prod.), Stop! Or My Mom Will Shoot, Beethoven (exec. prod.), Beethoven's 2nd (exec. prod.), Space Jam, Commandments (exec. prod.), Private Parts, Road Trip (exec.), Killing Me Softly, Evolution, Old School (exec. prod.).
TELEVISION: *Series*: Delta House.

RELPH, MICHAEL
Producer, Director, Writer, Designer. b. 1915. Became art dir. Ealing Studios then assoc. prod. to Michael Balcon on The Captive Heart, Frieda, Kind Hearts and Coronets, Saraband (also designed: Oscar nom.). 1948 appt. producer and formed prod./dir. partnership Basil Dearden (until 1972). 1971-76, Governor, Brit. Film Institute. Chairman BFI Prod. Board. Chairman Film Prod. Assoc. of G.B.; member Films Council.
PICTURES: For Ealing: The Blue Lamp (BFA Award, 1950), I Believe in You, The Gentle Gunman, The Square Ring, The Rainbow Jacket, Out of the Clouds, The Ship That Died of Shame, Davy, The Smallest Show on Earth (for Brit. Lion), Violent Playground (for Rank), Rockets Galore (Island Fling), Sapphire (BFA Award, 1959). 1960 Founder Dir. Allied Film Makers: Prod. The League of Gentlemen, Man in the Moon (co-s.p.), Victim, Life For Ruth (Walk in the Shadow). Also produced: Secret Partner, All Night Long, The Mind Benders, A Place To Go (s.p.), Woman of Straw (co-s.p.), Masquerade (co-s.p.), The Assassination Bureau (prod., s.p., designer), The Man Who Haunted Himself (prod., co-s.p.). 1978, exec. in chg. prod., Kendon Films, Ltd. Exec. prod., Scum, 1982. Co-prod., An Unsuitable Job for a Woman. 1984, exec. prod.: Treasure Houses of Britain; TV series, prod., Heavenly Pursuits, 1985-86; Gospel According to Vic (U.S.). Prod. Consultant: Torrents of Spring.

RELPH, SIMON
Producer. b. London, Eng., April 13, 1940. Entered industry 1961.
PICTURES: Reds (exec. prod.), The Return of the Soldier, Privates on Parade, The Ploughman's Lunch, Secret Places, Laughterhouse (exec. prod.), Wetherby, Comrades, Enchanted April (exec. prod.), Damage (coprod.), The Secret Rapture, Camilla, Look Me In The Eye, Blue Juice, The Slab Boys, The Land Girls, Hideous Kinky, (Exec.Prod.)

RELYEA, ROBERT E.
Producer, Executive. b. Santa Monica, CA, May 3, 1930. e. UCLA, B.S., 1952. In Army 1953-55. Entered industry in 1955; asst. dir. on The Magnificent Seven and West Side Story; assoc. prod. and 2nd unit dir. on The Great Escape; partnered with Steve McQueen as exec. prod. on Bullitt and The Reivers. 1979-82, exec. v.p. with Melvin Simon Prods. Served as exec. v.p. in chg. world wide prod., Keith Barish Prods. 1983-85. Served as sr. v.p. prod., Lorimar Prods. 1985-90. Named sr. v.p. features prod. management, Paramount Pictures Motion Picture Gp., 1989.
PICTURES: Exec. Prod.: Bullitt, The Reivers, Day of the Dolphin. Prod.: Love at First Bite, My Bodyguard, Porky's, Blame It On Rio (assoc. prod.), Last Action Hero (co-prod.). Actor: Seven.

REMAR, JAMES
Actor. b. Boston, MA, Dec. 31, 1953. Studied acting at NY's Neighborhood Playhouse and with Stella Adler. Appeared on NY stage in Yo-Yo, Early Dark, Bent, California Dog Fight.
PICTURES: On the Yard (debut, 1979), The Warriors, Cruising, The Long Riders, Windwalker, Partners, 48 HRS, The Cotton Club, The Clan of the Cave Bear, Band of the Hand, Quiet Cool, Rent-a-Cop, The Dream Team, Drugstore Cowboy, Tales from the Darkside, Silence Like Glass, White Fang, Fatal Instinct, Blink, Renaissance Man, Miracle on 34th Street, Boys on the Side, Session Man (Academy Award, Best Action Short, 1991), Across the Moon, Judge Dredd (cameo), The Quest, The Phantom, Robo-Warriors, Tale From The Darkside: The Movie, Wild Bill, Exquisite Tenderness, The Phantom, Born Bad, Mortal Kombat: Annihilation, Psycho, Rites of Passage, Blowback, What Lies beneath, Inferno Hellraiser, Guardian, Dying on the Edge, Betrayal, Fear the X, Duplex, Down with the Joneses, 2 Fast 2 Furious.
TELEVISION: Movies: The Mystic Warrior, Desperado, Deadlock, Brotherhood of the Gun, Fatal Charm, Indecency, Night Vision, Inferno. Guest: Hill Street Blues, Miami Vice, The Equalizer, The Hitchhiker, Tales From The Crypt, Total Security, Cutty Whitman, Inferno, DREAM Team, The Huntress, Guilty as Charged.

REMBUSCH, MICHAEL J.
Executive. b. Indianapolis, IN, April 8, 1950. e. Ball State U. Son of Trueman T. Rembusch. Began working for father's circuit, Syndicate Theatres, Inc., in 1967. From 1970-80, managed various theatres in circuit. 1980-85, v.p., operations. 1985-90, acquired Heaston circuit (Indianapolis). Became pres., Syndicate Theatres, Inc. 1987-90, chmn, Indiana Film Commission. 1992 to present, pres., Theatre Owners of Indiana.

RENO, JEAN
Actor. r.n. Juan Moreno b. Casablanca, Morocco July 30, 1948. To France in early 1970's to serve in French military. Began acting in Paris with theatre workshop, then established his own travelling acting company.
PICTURES: Claire de Femme, Le Dernier Combat, Subway, Signes Exterieurs de Richesse, Notre Histoire, I Love You, The Big Blue, La Femme Nikita, L'homme au Masque d'Or, L'Operation Corned Beef, Loulou Graffiti, The Professional (Leon), French Kiss, The Visitors (also s.p.), Beyond the Clouds, Mission Impossible, Le Jaguar, Witch Way Love, Roseanna's

Grave, Ronin, Le Couloirs du Temps, Godzilla, Tripwire, Les Rivieres pourpres, Just Visitors, Wasabi, Rollerball, Décalage horaire, Ruby & Quentin, Borgia, Crimson Rivers 2: Angels of the Apocalypse.

RESNAIS, ALAIN
Director. b. Cannes, France, June 3, 1922. Began career as asst. dir. to Nicole Vedres on compilation of film for Paris 1900. During '50s worked as asst. editor and editor; experimented with making his own 16mm films. Directed or co-dir. several short films: Van Gogh, Gauguin, Guernica, The Statues Also Die, Night and Fog.
PICTURES: Hiroshima Mon Amour (feature debut, 1959), Last Year at Marienbad, Muriel, La Guerre Est Finie (The War Is Over), Je t'Aime Je t'Aime (also co-s.p.), Stavisky, Providence, Life Is a Bed of Roses, L'Amour a Mort (Love Unto Death), Melo, I Want to Go Home, Smoking/No Smoking, Same Old Song, On connaît la chanson .

RESNICK, JOEL H.
Executive. b. New York, NY, April 28, 1936. e. U. of PA, B.A., 1958; NY Law Sch. 1961, admitted to NY State Bar. 1962 received Masters of Law degree in taxation; 1961-66 served as associate with NY law firm, Phillips Nizer Benjamin Krim & Ballon; Was in-house counsel to United Artists Corp. 1967, joined UA as spec. asst. to the sr. v.p. & gen. mgr.; 1970, moved to American Multi-Cinema, Inc., Kansas City, as asst. to pres.; 1972, named v.p. in chg. dev.; 1976, promoted to v.p. in chg. film development; 1977, named exec. v.p.; 1983, elected exec. v.p. & dir., AMC Entertainment; 1984, appt. to office of pres. as chmn. & CEO, film mktg.; 1986, resigned to join Orion Pictures Distribution Corp. as pres.; has served as co-chmn. NATO trade practices comm. since 1979. 1982 elected pres., NATO; 1984, became chmn. NATO bd.; 1989, v.p. Foundation of Motion Picture Pioneers; 1990, resigned from Orion; pres., GKC Theatres, Springfield, IL, 1991-92; Cinemark Theatres, Intl. Dev., 1994-.

REUBENS, PAUL
Actor, Writer. r.n. Paul Rubenfeld. b. Peekskill, NY, Aug. 27, 1952. Raised in Sarasota, FL. e. Boston U., California Inst. of the Arts (1976). Also acted as Pee-Wee Herman. Pee-wee character made debut, 1978 at Groundlings, improvisational theater, Los Angeles followed by The Pee-wee Herman Show, a live show which gave 5 months of sold-out performances at the L.A. rock club, Roxy, and was later taped for HBO special. Guest appearances on Late Night With David Letterman, The Gong Show, 227, Tonight Show, Mork & Mindy, Joan Rivers' The Late Show, and The Dating Game.
PICTURES: Midnight Madness, The Blues Brothers, Cheech & Chong's Next Movie, Cheech and Chong's Nice Dreams, Pandemonium, Meatballs Part II, Pee-wee's Big Adventure (also co-s.p.), Flight of the Navigator (voice), Back to the Beach, Big Top Pee-wee (also co-s.p., co-prod.), Batman Returns, Buffy the Vampire Slayer, Tim Burton's The Nightmare Before Christmas (voice), Dunston Checks In, Matilda, Buddy, Doctor Doolittle (voice), Mystery Men, Blow, South of Heaven,West of Hell, Mayor of Sunset Strip.
TELEVISION: Series: Pee-wee's Playhouse (also creator, co-dir., co-writer, exec. prod.; 12 Emmy Awards), Hercules (voice), You Don't Know Jack. Specials: Pinocchio (Faerie Tale Theatre), Pee-wee Herman Show, Pee-wee's Playhouse Christmas Special (also exec. prod., co-dir. co-writer). Guest: Murphy Brown.

REVELL, GRAEME
Composer.
b. New Zealand, Oct. 23, 1955.
PICTURES: Spontaneous Combustion, Dead Calm, Till There Was You, Child's Play 2, Love Crimes, Until the End of the Crime, Traces of Red, Deadly, The People Under the Stairs, The Hand That Rocks the Cradle, Hear No Evil, Ghost, in the Machine, The Crush, Body of Evidence, Boxing Helena, Hard Target, Street Fighter, S.F.W., No Escape, The Crow, Killer: A Journal of Murder, The Basketball Diaries, Tank Girl, Mighty Morphin Power Rangers: The Movie, The Tie That Binds, Strange Days, From Dusk Till Dawn, Race the Sun, The Craft, Fled, The Crow: City of Angels, Chinese Box, The Saint, Spawn, Suicide Kings, Lulu on the Bridge, The Big Hit, The Negotiator, Phoenix, Strike, Bride of Chucky, The Siege, Idle Hands, Three to Tango, Gossip, Bats, Red Planet, Doubletake, Blow, Human Nature, Anne Frank, Lara Croft: Tomb Raider, Don't Say a Word, Collateral Damage, High Crimes, Below, Daredevil, Freddy Vs. Jason.

REVILL, CLIVE
Actor. r.n. Clive Selsby. b. Wellington, New Zealand, Apr. 18, 1930. e. Rongotal Coll., Victoria U.
THEATRE: Irma La Douce, The Mikado, Oliver, Marat/Sade, Jew of Malta, Sherry, Chichester Season, The Incomparable Max, Sherlock Holmes, Lolita, Pirates of Penzance, Mystery of Edwin Drood, My Fair Lady, Bandido.
PICTURES: Reach for the Sky, The Headless Ghost, Bunny Lake Is Missing, Once Upon a Tractor, Modesty Blaise, A Fine Madness, Kaleidoscope, The Double Man, Fathom, Italian

Secret Service, Nobody Runs Forever, Shoes of the Fisherman, Assassination Bureau, The Private Life of Sherlock Holmes, The Buttercup Chain, A Severed Head, Boulevard de Rhum, Avanti!, Escape to the Sun, Ghost in the Noonday Sun, The Legend of Hell House, The Little Prince, The Black Windmill, One of Our Dinosaurs Is Missing, Galileo, Matilda, Zorro the Gay Blade, Transformers (voice), Rumpelstiltskin, The Emperor's New Clothes, Mack the Knife, CHUD II: Bud the Chud, Frog Prince, Let Him Have It, Robin Hood: Men in Tights, Crime and Punishment, Arabian Knight (voice), The Wacky Adventures of Dr. Boris and Nurse Shirley, Dracula—Dead and Loving It!, Possums, Intrepid, Crime & Punishment, Return to Neverland (voice).
TELEVISION: Chicken Soup with Barley, Volpone, Bam Pow Zapp, Candida, Platonov, A Bit of Vision, Mill Hill, The Piano Player, Hopcroft in Europe, A Sprig of Broome, Ben Franklin in Paris, Pinocchio, The Great Houdini, Show Business Hall of Fame, Feather and Father, Winner Take All, The New Avengers, Licking Hitler, Columbo, Centennial, A Man Called Sloane, Nobody's Perfect, Marya, Moviola, Diary of Anne Frank, Mikado, The Sorcerer, Wizards & Warriors, George Washington, Murder She Wrote, Faerie Tale Theatre, Twilight Zone, Newhart, Hunter, Star Trek, The Sea Wolf, Babylon 5, Fortune Hunter, The Preston Episodes (series), Murphy Brown., Feast of All Saints, Return to Never Land (voice).

REYNOLDS, BURT
Actor, Director. b. Waycross, GA, Feb. 11, 1936. Former Florida State U. football star; TV and film stunt performer. Won fame as actor on TV in series Riverboat. Founded the Burt Reynolds Dinner Theater in Jupiter, FL, 1979. *Autobiography*: My Life (1994).
THEATRE: Mister Roberts (NY City Center), Look We've Come Through (B'way debut, 1956), The Rainmaker.
PICTURES: Angel Baby (debut, 1961), Armored Command, Operation CIA, Navajo Joe, Fade In, Impasse, Shark, Sam Whiskey, 100 Rifles, Skullduggery, Fuzz, Deliverance, Everything You Always Wanted To Know About Sex, Shamus, White Lightning, The Man Who Loved Cat Dancing, The Longest Yard, W.W. & The Dixie Dancekings, At Long Last Love, Hustle, Lucky Lady, Gator (also dir.), Silent Movie, Nickelodeon, Smokey and the Bandit, Semi-Tough, The End (also dir.), Hooper, Starting Over, Rough Cut, Smokey and the Bandit II, Cannonball Run, Paternity, Sharky's Machine (also dir.), The Best Little Whorehouse in Texas, Best Friends, Stroker Ace, Smokey and the Bandit III (cameo), The Man Who Loved Women, Cannonball Run II, City Heat, Stick (also dir.), Uphill All the Way (cameo), Heat, Malone, Rent-a-Cop, Switching Channels, Physical Evidence, Breaking In, All Dogs Go to Heaven (voice), Modern Love, The Player (cameo), Cop and a Half, The Maddening, Devil Inside, Meet Wally Sparks, Striptease, Mad Dog Time, Citizen Ruth, Boogie Nights (Golden Globe Award, Chicago Film Crits. Award, LA Film Crits. Award, NY Film Circle Crits. Award, Best Supporting Actor, 1997), Raven, Bean, Crazy Six, Pups, The Last Producer (also dir.), The Hunter's Moon, Mystery Alaska, The Crew, The Last Producer, The Hollywood Sign, Driven, Big City Blues, Tempted, The Librarians, Hotel, A Woman in Love, The Hermit of Amsterdam, Time of the Wolf.
TELEVISION: *Movies*: Hunters Are for Killing, Run Simon Run, The Man Upstairs (co-exec. prod. only), The Man From Left Field (also dir.), Universal Soldier II: Brothers in Arms, Universal Soldier III: Unfinished Business, Hard Time (also dir.), Hard Time: Hostage Hotel, Hard Time: Hide and Seek, Hard Time: The Premonition., Miss Lettie and Me. *Host*: The Story of Hollywood. *Special*: Wind in the Wire. *Dir.*: Alfred Hitchcock Presents (1985), Johnson County War. *Series*: Riverboat, Gunsmoke, Hawk, Dan August, Out of This World (voice), B.L. Stryker (also co-exec. prod.), Evening Shade (Emmy Award, 1991), Founding Fathers, Johnson County War.

REYNOLDS, DEBBIE
Actress. r.n. Mary Frances Reynolds. b. El Paso, TX, April 1, 1932. Daughter is actress Carrie Fisher. e. Burbank & John Burroughs H.S., Burbank, CA. With Burbank Youth Symphony during h.s.; beauty contest winner (Miss Burbank) 1948; signed by Warner Bros.; on stage in Personal Appearances, Blis-Hayden Theater. Voted Star of Tomorrow, 1952. *Autobiography*: Debbie: My Life (1988).
THEATRE: B'way: Irene, Woman of the Year.
PICTURES: June Bride (debut, 1948), The Daughter of Rosie O'Grady, Three Little Words, Two Weeks With Love, Mr. Imperium, Singin' in the Rain, Skirts Ahoy, I Love Melvin, Give a Girl a Break, The Affairs of Dobie Gillis, Susan Slept Here, Athena, Hit the Deck, The Tender Trap, The Catered Affair, Bundle of Joy, Tammy and the Bachelor, This Happy Feeling, The Mating Game, Say One for Me, It Started with a Kiss, The Gazebo, The Rat Race, Pepe (cameo), The Pleasure of His Company, The Second Time Around, How the West Was Won, My Six Loves, Mary Mary, Goodbye Charlie, The Unsinkable Molly Brown (Acad. Award nom.), The Singing Nun, Divorce American Style, How Sweet It Is, What's the Matter with Helen?, Charlotte's Web (voice), That's Entertainment!, The Bodyguard (cameo), Heaven and Earth, That's Entertainment III, Mother, In & Out, Wedding Bell Blues, Fear and Loathing in Las Vegas (voice), Keepers of the Frame, Rugrats in Paris- The

Movie(voice), Cinerama Adventure.
TELEVISION: *Series*: The Debbie Reynolds Show, Aloha Paradise. *Movies*: Sadie and Son, Perry Mason: The Case of the Musical Murders, Battling for Baby, Halloweentown, The Christmas Wish, Virtual Mom, These Old Broads, Halloween Town II, Gene Kelly- Anatomy of a Dancer *Special*: Jack Paar Is Alive and Well.

REYNOLDS, GENE
Actor, Executive, Producer. b. Cleveland, OH, April 4, 1925. Acted from 1936-55. Currently pres. Director's Guild of America, Inc.
PICTURES: *Actor*: Thank You, Jeeves, The San, Thunder Trail, In Old Chicago, The Californian, Of Human Hearts, Love Finds Andy Hardy, The Crowd Roars, Boys Town, The Spirit of Culver, The Flying Irishman, Bad Little Angel, They Shall Have Music, Santa Fe Trail, The Mortal Storm, Gallant Sons, The Blue Bird, Edison, the man; Andy Hardy's Private Secretary, Adventure in Washington, The Penalty, The Tuttles of Tahiti, Junior G-men of the Air, Eagle Squadron, Jungle Patrol, The Big Cat, Slattery's Hurricane, 99 River Street, The Country Girl, The Bridges at Toko-Ri, Down Three Dark Streets.
TELEVISION: *Director: Series:* Wanted: Dead or Alive, My Three Sons, Hogan's Heroes, F Troop, The Ghost and Mrs. Muir, M*A*S*H (also exec. prod.), Lou Grant (also exec. prod), Christy, Touched by and Angel. *Movies:* In Defense of Kids, Doing Life (also exec. prod.), The Whereabouts of Jenny (also prod.).

REYNOLDS, KEVIN
Director, Writer. b. Jan. 17, 1950. e. Texas Marine Acad., Trinity Univ., Baylor Univ. (law degree), USC film school. Student film Proof led to offer to do expanded feature version subsequently retitled Fandango.
PICTURES: Red Dawn (co-s.p.). *Director:* Fandango (dir. debut, 1985; also s.p.), The Beast, Robin Hood: Prince of Thieves, Rapa Nui (also s.p.), Waterworld, 187, The Count of Monte Christo.

REYNOLDS, NORMAN
Production Designer, Art Director.
PICTURES: *Production Designer:* The Empire Strikes Back, Raiders of the Lost Ark, Return of the Jedi, Return to Oz, Young Sherlock Holmes, Empire of the Sun, Mountains of the Moon, Avalon, Alien 3, Alive, Clean Slate, Mission: Impossible, Sphere, Bicentennial Man. *Art Director:* The Old Curiosity Shop, Lucky Lady, The Incredible Sarah, Star Wars, Superman, Star Wars: Episode V - The Empire Strikes Back, The Exorcist III.

REYNOLDS, SHELDON
Writer, Producer, Director. b. Philadelphia, PA, 1923. e. NYU. Radio-TV writer; programs include My Silent Partner, Robert Q. Lewis Show, We the People, Danger, Adventures of Sherlock Holmes (prod., dir., writer), Dick and the Duchess (prod., dir., writer), Foreign Intrigue (dir., prod., writer). TV Special: Sophia Loren's Rome (dir., writer). Movies: Foreign Intrigue (dir., prod., s.p.), Assignment to Kill (dir., s.p.).
(d. Jan. 25, 2003).

REZNOR, TRENT
Composer. r.n. Michael Trent Reznor. b. Mercer, PA, May 17, 1965. Head of Nothing Records, a division of Interscope Records. Fronts industrial-rock band Nine Inch Nails. Composed music and sounds for id Software's computergame QUAKE.
PICTURES: Light of Day (actor), Seven, Natural Born Killers, Lost Highway, Closure, Lara Croft: Tomb Raider, Nine Inch Nails Live: And All That Could Have Been, World Traveler, (musician).

RHAMES, VING
Actor. b. May 12, 1959. e. Juilliard Sch. of Drama.
THEATRE: B'way: The Boys of Winter. Off-B'way: Map of the World, Short Eyes, Richard III, Ascension Day. Europe: Ajax.
PICTURES: Native Son, Patty Hearst, Casualties of War, Jacob's Ladder, The Long Walk Home, Flight of the Intruder, Homicide, The People Under the Stairs, Stop! Or My Mom Will Shoot, Bound by Honor, Dave, The Saint of Fort Washington, Pulp Fiction, Drop Squad, Kiss of Death, Mission: Impossible, Striptease, Rosewood, Con Air, Dangerous Ground, The Split, Out of Sight, Mission: Impossible 2, Duets, Bringing Out the Dead, Entrapment, Final Fantasy (voice), Undisputed, Lilo and Stitch (voice), The Plague Seasons, Dark Blue, RFK, Sin, Mission Impossible 3.
TELEVISION: *Movies*: Go Tell It on the Mountain, Rising Son, When You Remember Me, Iran: Days of Crisis, Terror on Track 9, Ed McBain's 87th Precinct: Lightning, Deadly Whispers, Don King: Only in America (Golden Globe Award, 1998), Holiday Heart, American Tragedy, Sins of the Father. *Series*: Another World, Men, UC: Undercover. *Guest:* Miami Vice, Spenser: For Hire, Tour of Duty, Crime Story.

RHODES, CYNTHIA
Actress, Dancer. b. Nashville, TN, Nov. 21, 1956. m. singer Richard Marx. Appeared on many TV specials, inc. Opryland USA, Music Hall America.
PICTURES: Xanadu, One From the Heart, Flashdance, Staying Alive, Runaway, Dirty Dancing, Curse of the Crystal Eye.

RHYS-DAVIES, JOHN
Actor. b. Salisbury, England, May 5, 1944. Grew up in Wales and East Africa. Began acting at Truro School in Cornwall at 15. e. U. of East Angelia where he founded school's dramatic society. Worked as teacher before studying at Royal Academy of Dramatic Art, 1969. Appeared in 23 Shakespearean plays.
PICTURES: The Black Windmill, Sphinx, Raiders of the Lost Ark, Victor/Victoria, Sahara, Sword of the Valiant, Best Revenge, King Solomon's Mines, In the Shadow of Kilimanjaro, Firewalker, The Living Daylights, Waxwork, Rising Storm, Indiana Jones and the Last Crusade, Young Toscanini, Journey of Honor, Unnameable II, The Seventh Coin, The Great White Hype, Glory Days, Marquis de Sade, Cas Don't Dance (voice), Bloodsport 3, Aladdin and the King of Thieves, The Protector, Secret of the Andes, Sinbad: Beyond the Veil of Mists, The Gold Cross, The Lord of the Rings: The Fellowship of the Ring, The Lord of the Rings: The Two Towers, Sabretooth, Highbinders, The Lord of the Rings: The Return of the King, The Medallion.
TELEVISION: Mini-series: Shogun, James Clavell's Noble House, Riley, Ace of Spies, I, Claudius, War and Remembrance. Movies: The Little Match Girl, Sadat, Kim, The Naked Civil Servant, The Trial of the Incredible Hulk, Goddess of Love, The Gifted One, Great Expectations, Desperado, Secret Weapon, Before the Storm, Spy Games, Perry Mason: The Case of the Fatal Framing. Series: Under Cover, The Untouchables, Archaeology, Sliders.

RIBISI, GIOVANNI
Actor. b. Los Angeles, CA, March 31, 1976.
PICTURES: The Outpost, That Thing You Do!, The Grave, First Love Last Rites, Lost Highway, SubUrbia, The Postman, Scotch and Milk, Phoenix, Men, Saving Private Ryan, The Virgin Suicides (voice), The Mod Squad, The Other Sister, The Boiler Room, Gone in 60 Seconds, The Gift, According to Spencer, Heaven, Cold Mountain, Masked & Anonymous, Love's Brother, Basic.
TELEVISION: Movies: Promised a Mircle, Blossom, The Positively True Adventures of the Alleged Texas Cheerleader-Murdering Mom, Alptraum im Airport, Shot in the Heart. Series: My Two Dads, The Wonder Years, Davis Rules, Family Album. Guest: Highway to Heaven, Married...with Children, The Commish, Walker Texas Ranger, Ellen, NYPD Blue, Marker, The X Files, Chicago Hope, Friends, The Hunger, Black of Life.

RICCI, CHRISTINA
Actress. b. Santa Monica, CA, February 12, 1980. Raised in Long Island, NY, and Montclair, NJ. Started acting career in commercials.
PICTURES: Mermaids (debut, 1990), The Hard Way, The Addams Family, The Cemetery Club, Addams Family Values, Casper, Gold Diggers: The Secret of Bear Mountain, Now and Then, Last of the High Kings, The Ice Storm, That Darn Cat, Souvenir, I Woke Up Early the Day I Died, Buffalo 66, 200 Cigarettes, The Opposite of Sex, Fear and Loathing in Las Vegas, Pecker, Desert Blue, Small Soldiers (voice), No Vacancy, Sleepy Hollow, Bless the Child, The Man Who Cried, Prozac Nation (also prod.), All Over the Guy, Adrenalynn (also prod.), Pumpkin (also prod.), Miranda, The Gathering, The Speed Queen, Borgia, Anything Else, I Love Your Work, Monster.
TELEVISION: Movie: The Laramie Project. Guest: The Simpsons (voice), The Late Late Show with Craig Kilborn.

RICH, JOHN
Producer, Director. b. Rockaway Beach, NY, e. U. of Michigan, B.A., Phi Beta Kappa, 1948; M.A. 1949; Sesquicentennial Award, 1967; bd. of dir., Screen Dir. Guild of America, 1954-1960; v.p. 1958-1960, Founder-Trustee, Producers-Directors Pension Plan, chmn. of bd. 1965, 1968, 1970; treasurer, Directors Guild of America, 1966-67; v.p. 1967-72. Awards: Directors Guild Award, Most Outstanding Directorial Achievement, 1971. Christopher award: Henry Fonda as Clarence Darrow, 1975. NAACP Image Award, 1974; 2 Golden Globe Awards: All in the Family, 1972-73. DGA Robert B. Aldrich Award for 1992.
PICTURES: Director: Wives and Lovers, The New Interns, Roustabout, Boeing-Boeing, Easy Come Easy Go.
TELEVISION: Director: Academy Awards, The Dick Van Dyke Show, All in the Family (also prod.), Mr. Sunshine, Dear John, MacGyver, The Good Life.

RICH, LEE
Producer, Executive. b. Cleveland, OH, Dec. 10, 1926. e. Ohio U. Adv. exec.; resigned as sr. v.p., Benton & Bowles, to become producer for Mirisch-Rich TV, 1965 (Rat Patrol, Hey Landlord). Resigned 1967 to join Leo Burnett Agency. Left to form Lorimar Productions in 1969 and served as pres. until 1986 when left to join MGM/UA Communications as chmn. & CEO. Resigned 1988; signed 3-year deal with Warner Bros. setting up Lee Rich Prods. there. Twice named Television Showman of the Year by Publishers' Guild of America.
PICTURES: Producer: The Sporting Club, Just Cause, The Amazing Panda Adventure, Big Bully. Executive Producer: The Man, The Choirboys, Who Is Killing the Great Chefs of Europe?, The Big Red One, Hard to Kill, Innocent Blood, Passenger 57, Just Cause, The Amazine Panda Adventure, Big Bully, Desperate Measures, Gloria, The Score.

RICHARD, SIR CLIFF
O.B.E. Singer, Actor. r.n. Harry Webb. b. India, Oct. 14, 1940. Ent. show business 1958 in TV series Oh Boy. Other TV includes Sunday Night at the London Palladium, several Cliff Richard Shows; top British Singer, 1960-71. Voted top box-office star of Great Britain, 1962-63, 1963-64. Twice rep. U.K. in Eurovision Song Contest. Innumerable platinum, gold and silver discs. 1989 became first UK artist to release 100 singles; voted top male vocalist of the 80's by UK Indept. TV viewers. Has made numerous videos. Knighted, 1995.
THEATRE: Aladdin, Five Finger Exercise, The Potting Shed, Time.
PICTURES: Serious Charge (debut, 1959), Expresso Bongo, The Young Ones, Summer Holiday, Wonderful Life, Finder's Keepers, Two a Penny, Take Me High, Xanadu.
TELEVISION: Getaway with Cliff, The Case, It's Cliff and Friends (series), Comic Relief, The Grand Knockout Tournament, The Girl with the Giggle in Her Voice, Stars 2001: Die- Aids-Gala, Party at the Palace.

RICHARDS, DENISE
Actress. b. Downers Grove, IL, Feb. 17, 1972.
PICTURES: Loaded Weapon I, Tammy and the T-Rex, Lookin' Italian, Nowhere, Starship Troopers, Wild Things, Drop Dead Gorgeous, The World is Not Enough, Valentine, The Third Wheel, Good Advice, You Stupid Man, Empire, Undercover Brother.
TELEVISION: Movies: 919 Fifth Avenue, In the Blink of an Eye. Series: Melrose Place. Guest: Life Goes On, Saved by the Bell, Married...with Children, Beverly Hills 90210, Seinfeld, Bodies of Evidence, Lois & Clark: The New Adventures of Superman.

RICHARDS, DICK
Director, Producer, Writer. b. New York, NY, July 9, 1934. In U.S. Army as photo-journalist; work appeared in Life, Look, Time, Esquire, etc. Won over 100 int'l. awards for commercials and photographic art work.
PICTURES: Director: The Culpepper Cattle Co. (also story), Rafferty and the Gold Dust Twins, Farewell My Lovely, March or Die (also co- prod., co-story), Death Valley, Tootsie (co-prod. only), Man Woman and Child, Heat.

RICHARDS, MICHAEL
Actor. b. Culver City, July 14, 1950. e. California Inst. of Arts. Work as stand-up comedian led to appearances on tv including regular stint on series Fridays. Acted on stage with San Diego Rep. Co.
THEATRE: LA: The American Clock, Wild Oats.
PICTURES: Young Doctors in Love, Transylvania 6-5000, Whoops Apocalypse, UHF, Problem Child, Coneheads, So I Married an Axe Murderer, Airheads, Unstrung Heroes, Trial and Error, Redux Riding Hood (voice).
TELEVISION: Series: Fridays, Marblehead Manor, Seinfeld (3 Emmy Awards: 1993, 1994, 1997), The Michael Richards Show. Movie: David Copperfield.

RICHARDSON, JOELY
Actress. b. London, Eng., January 9, 1965. Daughter of actress Vanessa Redgrave and director Tony Richardson, sister of actress Natasha Richardson. e. Lycee, St. Paul's Girl's School, London; Pinellas Park H.S. (Florida), The Thacher Sch. (Ojai, CA), Royal Acad. of Dramatic Art. London stage: Steel Magnolias, Beauty and the Beast (Old Vic); also at Liverpool Playhouse, RSC.
PICTURES: Wetherby (debut, 1985 with mother), Drowning By Numbers, About That Strange Girl, King Ralph, Shining Through, Rebecca's Daughters, I'll Do Anything, Sister My Sister, Hollow Reed, Lochness, 101 Dalmations, Event Horizon, Wrestling with Alligators, Under Heaven, Maybe Baby, Return to Me, The Patriot, The Affair of the Necklace, The Family Business.
TELEVISION: Body Contact, Behaving Badly, Available Light, Heading Home, Lady Chatterly, The Tribe, Echo.

RICHARDSON, MIRANDA
Actress. b. Southport, England, 1958. Studied acting at the drama program at Bristol's Old Vic Theatre School. Began acting on stage, 1979. Appeared in Moving, at the Queen's Theatre and

TELEVISION: Exec. Prod.: Series: The Waltons (Emmy Award, 1973), Dallas, Knots Landing, Against the Grain. Mini-series: The Blue Knight, Helter Skelter, Studs Lonigan. Movies: Do Not Fold Spindle or Mutilate, The Homecoming: A Christmas Story, The Crooked Hearts, Pursuit, The Girls of Huntington House, Dying Room Only, Don't Be Afraid of the Dark, A Dream for Christmas, The Stranger Within, Bad Ronald, The Runaway Barge, Runaways, Returning Home, Eric, Conspiracy of Terror, Widow, Green Eyes, Killer on Board, Desperate Women, Long Journey Back, Mary and Joseph: A Story of Faith, Mr. Horn, Some Kind of Miracle, Young Love, First Love, A Man Called Intrepid, Flamingo Road, Marriage Is Alive and Well, A Perfect Match, Reward, Skag, Killjoy, A Matter of Life and Death, Our Family Business, Mother's Day on Walton's Mountain, This is Kate Bennett, Two of a Kind, A Wedding on Walton's Mountain, A Day of Thanks on Walton's Mountain, Secret of Midland Heights, Face of Fear, Killer Rules, A Walton Thanksgiving Reunion.

continued in All My Sons, Who's Afraid of Virginia Woolf?, The Life of Einstein in provincial theatres. Also A Lie of the Mind (London), The Changeling, Mountain Language.
PICTURES: Dance With a Stranger (debut, 1985), The Innocent, Empire of the Sun, Eat the Rich, Twisted Obsession, The Bachelor, Enchanted April, The Crying Game, Damage (BAFTA Award; Acad. Award nom.), Tom and Viv, Century, The Night and the Moment, Kansas City, The Evening Star, The Apostle, The Designated Mourner, St. Ives, Jacob Two Two Meets the Hooded Fang, The Big Brass Ring, The King and I (voice), Sleepy Hollow, Chicken Run (voice), Get Carter, Constance & Carlotta, The Hours, Spider, Nicholas Nickleby, The Rage in Placid Lake, The Actors.
TELEVISION: The Hard Word, Sorrel and Son, A Woman of Substance, After Pilkington, Underworld, Death of the Heart, The Black Adder (series), Die Kinder (mini-series), Sweet as You Are (Royal TV Society Award), Fatherland (Golden Globe Award), A Dance to the Music of Time (mini-series), The Scold's Bridle, Merlin, Ted & Ralph, The Miracle Maker (voice), Alice in Wonderland, Absolutely Fabulous, Snow White, The Lost Prince.

RICHARDSON, NATASHA
Actress. b. London, England, May 11, 1963. m. actor Liam Neeson. Daughter of actress Vanessa Redgrave and director Tony Richardson; sister is actress Joely Richardson. e. Central Sch. of Speech and Drama. Appeared at the Leeds Playhouse in On the Razzle, Top Girls, Charley's Aunt. Performed A Midsummer Night's Dream and Hamlet with the Young Vic. 1985 starred with mother in The Seagull (London), also starred in the musical High Society. Won London Theatre Critics Most Promising Newcomer award, 1986. NY stage debut 1992 in Anna Christie.
PICTURES: Every Picture Tells a Story (debut, 1984). Gothic, A Month in the Country, Patty Hearst, Fat Man and Little Boy, The Handmaid's Tale, The Comfort of Strangers, The Favor the Watch and the Very Big Fish, Widow's Peak, Nell, The Parent Trap, Blow Dry, Waking Up in Reno, Chelsea Walls, Uptown Girl, Maid in Manhattan.
TELEVISION: Ellis Island (mini-series), In a Secret State, The Copper Beeches (epis. of Sherlock Holmes), Ghosts, Past Midnight, Suddenly Last Summer, Hostages, Zelda, Tales From the Crypt (guest), The Man Who Came to Dinner, Haven.

RICHARDSON, PATRICIA
Actress. b. Bethesda, MD, Feb. 23, 1951. e. Southern Methodist Univ.
THEATRE: NY: Gypsy, Loose Ends, The Wake of Jamie Foster, The Collected Works of Billy the Kid, The Frequency, Vanities, The Miss Firecracker Contest, The Coroner's Plot, Fables for Friends. Regional: The Killing of Sister George, King Lear, The Philadelphia Story, Fifth of July, About Face.
PICTURES: Gas, C.H.U.D., You Better Watch Out, Lost Angels, In Country, Ulee's Gold, Viva Las Nowhere.
TELEVISION: Series: Double Trouble, Eisenhower and Lutz, FM, Home Improvement, Storytime (PBS), Strong Medicine. Mini-Series: Blonde. Movies: Hands of a Stranger, Parent Trap III, Sophie and the Moonhanger, Undue Influence, Blonde. Guest: Love Sidney, Kate and Allie, The Cosby Show, Quantum Leap.

RICHMAN, PETER MARK
Actor. b. Philadelphia, PA, April 16, 1927. e. Philadelphia Coll. of Pharmacy & Science with Bachelor of Science Degree in Pharmacy. Previously acted as Mark Richman. Member of Actors Studio since 1954.
THEATRE: B'way: End as a Man, Masquerade, A Hatful of Rain. Off B'way: The Dybbuk, The Zoo Story, 4 Faces (also author). Regional: Blithe Spirit, The Night of the Iguana, 12 Angry Men, Babes in Toyland, Funny Girl, The Best Man, Equus, The Rainmaker, 4 Faces.
PICTURES: Friendly Persuasion, The Strange One, The Black Orchid, Dark Intruder, Agent for H.A.R.M., For Singles Only, Friday 13th Part VIII—Jason Takes Manahattan, The Naked Gun 2 1/2: The Smell of Fear, Judgment Day (Manila), Poolhall Junkies.
TELEVISION: Series: Longstreet, Dynasty, Cain's Hundred, My Secret Summer (Berlin). Movies: House on Greenapple Road, Yuma, Mallory: Circumstantial Evidence, The Islander, The Psi Factor, Dempsey, Blind Ambition, City Killer, Bonanza: The Next Generation. Guest: Three's Company, Murder She Wrote, Star Trek: The Next Generation, Matlock, Beverly Hills 90210, Nothing Sacred and over 500 guest roles.

RICHMOND, TED
Producer. b. Norfolk, VA, June 10, 1912. e. MIT. Entered m.p. ind. as publicity dir.; RKO Theatres; later mgr. Albany dist.; publ. dir. Fabian circuit, NY; Paramount upper NY state theats.; Grand Nat'l Pictures. Author Grand Nat'l series Trigger Pal, Six Gun Rhythm. Formed T. H. Richmond Prods., Inc., 1941. Formed Copa Prod. with Tyrone Power, 1954. Formed Ted Richmond Prod. Inc. for MGM release, 1959. Reactivated Copa Prod. Ltd., England, 1960.
PICTURES: Hit the Hay, The Milkman, Kansas Raiders, Shakedown, Smuggler's Island, Strange Door, Cimarron Kid, Bronco Buster, Has Anybody Seen My Gal, No Room for the Groom, Weekend with Father, The Mississippi Gambler, Desert Legion, Column South, Bonzo Goes to College, Forbidden, Walking My Baby Back Home, Francis Joins the Wacs, Bengal Brigade, Count Three and Pray, Nightfall, Abandon Ship, Solomon and Sheba, Charlemagne, Bachelor in Paradise, Advance to the Rear, Pancho Villa, Return of the 7, Red Sun, Papillon (exec. prod.), The Fifth Musketeer.

RICHTER, W. D.
Writer, Director. b. New Britain, CT, Dec. 7, 1945. e. Dartmouth Coll, B.A.; U. of Southern California Film Sch., grad. study.
PICTURES: Writer: Slither, Peeper, Nickelodeon, Invasion of the Body Snatchers, Dracula, Brubaker, All Night Long, Big Trouble in Little China, Needful Things, Home for the Holidays. Prod.-Dir.: Adventures of Buckaroo Banzai Across the Eighth Dimension, Late for Dinner.

RICKERT, JOHN F.
Executive. b. Kansas City, MO, Oct. 29, 1924. e. USC. Joined Universal Pictures in 1951; left in 1957 to start independent productions. 1960-68 handled indep. roadshow distribution (4-walling). 1969 formed Cineworld Corporation, natl. dist. co., of which he is pres. 1975-76 did tax shelter financing for 13 films. Currently involved in distribution, production packaging and intl. co-production as pres. of Coproducers Corp.

RICKLES, DON
Actor, Comedian. b. New York, NY, May 8, 1926. e. AADA.
PICTURES: Run Silent Run Deep, Rabbit Trap, The Rat Race, X: The Man With the X-Ray Eyes, Muscle Beach Party, Bikini Beach, Beach Blanket Bingo, Enter Laughing, The Money Jungle, Where It's At, Kelly's Heroes, Keaton's Cop, Innocent Blood, Casino, Toy Story (voice), Little Redux Riding Hood (voice), Dennis the Menace 2, Quest for Camelot (voice), Dirty Work, Toy Story 2 (voice),.
TELEVISION: Series: The Don Rickles Show (1968), The Don Rickles Show (1972), C.P.O. Sharkey, Foul-Ups Bleeps and Blunders, Daddy Dearest. Movie: For the Love of It. Guest: The Big Show, F Troop, Laugh-In, Kraft Music Hall, Dean Martin's Celebrity Roasts, Tales From the Crypt.

RICKMAN, ALAN
Actor. b. London, England, Feb. 21, 1946. Began as graphic designer before studying acting at RADA. Joined the Royal Shakespeare Co. where he starred in Les Liaisons Dangereuses; received Tony Award nomination for 1987 NY production.
THEATRE: Commitments, The Last Elephant, The Grass Widow, Lucky Chance, The Seagull, As You Like It, Troilus and Cressida, Tango At the End of Winter, Hamlet.
PICTURES: Die Hard (debut, 1988), The January Man, Quigley Down Under, Closet Land, Truly Madly Deeply, Robin Hood: Prince of Thieves (BAFTA Award, 1991), Close My Eyes, Bob Roberts, Mesmer, An Awfully Big Adventure, Sense and Sensibility, Michael Collins, The Winter Guest (also dir.), Judas Kiss, Dogma, Dark Harbor, Galaxy Quest, Play, Blow Dry, Harry Potter and the Sorcerer's Stone, The Search for John Gissing, Harry Potter and the Chamber of Secrets, Standing Room Only, Harry Potter and the Prisoner of Azkaban.
TELEVISION: Series: The Barchester Chronicles (BBC). Specials: Romeo and Juliet. Guest: Fallen Angels (Murder Obliquely). Movie: Rasputin (Emmy, 1996, 1997; Golden Globe, Screen Actors Guild Awards 1996), Revolutionary Witness, Spirit of Man, Victoria Wood with all the Trimmings, Nikki, We Know Where You Live.

RIEGERT, PETER
Actor. b. New York, NY, Apr. 11, 1947. e. U. of Buffalo, B.A. Brief stints as 8th grade English teacher, social worker, and aide de camp to politician Bella Abzug 1970, before turned actor, off-off B'way. Appeared with improvisational comedy group War Babies. Film debut in short, A Director Talks About His Film.
THEATRE: Dance with Me (B'way debut), Minnie's Boys (as Chico Marx), Sexual Perversity in Chicago, Isn't it Romantic?, La Brea Tarpits, A Rosen By Any Other Name, The Nerd, Mountain Language/The Birthday Party, The Road to Nirvana.
PICTURES: National Lampoon's Animal House, Americathon, Head Over Heels, National Lampoon Goes to the Movies, Local Hero, City Girl, A Man in Love, Le Grand Carnaval, The Stranger, Crossing Delancey, That's Adequate, The Passport, A Shock to the System, The Object of Beauty, Beyond the Ocean, Oscar, The Runestone, Passed Away, Utz, The Mask, White Man's Burden, Coldblooded, Pie in the Sky, Infinity, Jerry and Tom, Hi Life, Passion of Mind, In the Weeds, How to Kill your Neighbor's Dog, Traffic, C-Scam.
TELEVISION: Specials: Concealed Enemies, The Hit List, W. Eugene Smith: Photography Made Difficult. Mini-Series: Ellis Island. Movies: News at Eleven, Barbarians at the Gate, Gypsy, The Infiltrator, Element of Truth, North Shore Fish, Face Down, The Baby Dance, Bojangles, The Bleacher Bums. Series: The Middle Ages.

RIFKIN, MONROE M.
Executive. e. New York U., BA Finance. Began career with Amer. TV and Communications Corp. as CEO, 1968-82, and Chairman, 1974-82. Bd. member, Nat'l. Cable TV Assoc., 1968-84, and as Chairman, 1983-84. Founder, dir. and Chairman of Rifkin & Associates.

RIFKIN, RON
Actor. b. New York, NY, Oct. 31, 1939. e. NYU.
THEATRE: B'way: Come Blow Your Horn, The Goodbye People, The Tenth Man. Off-B'way: Rosebloom, The Art of Dining, Temple, The Substance of Fire.
PICTURES: The Devil's 8 (debut, 1969), Flareup, Silent Running, The Sunshine Boys, The Big Fix, The Sting II, Husbands and Wives, Manhattan Murder Mystery, Wolf, Last Summer in the Hamptons, The Substance of Fire, I'm Not Rappaport, L.A. Confidential, The Negotiator, Drop Back Ten, Keeping the Faith, Sam the Man, The Majestic, Tadpole, Dragonfly, Sum of All Fears, Just a Kiss.
TELEVISION: Series: Adam's Rib, When Things Were Rotten, Husbands Wives & Lovers, One Day at a Time, Falcon Crest, Leaving L.A., Alias Mini-Series: The Winds of War. Movie: Norma Jean & Marilyn, Flowers for Algernon, Deliberate Intent, The Warden, Prisoner's Base: A Nero Wolfe Mystery.

RIGG, DIANA
C.B.E. (1987). Actress. b. Doncaster, England, July 20, 1938. With the Royal Shakespeare Co. at Aldwych Theatre, 1962-64. Recent London stage: Follies, Medea (also B'way).
PICTURES: A Midsummer's Night Dream (debut, 1968), The Assassination Bureau, On Her Majesty's Secret Service, Julius Caesar, The Hospital, Theatre of Blood, A Little Night Music, The Great Muppet Caper, Evil Under the Sun, Snow White, A Good Man in Africa, Parting Shots, The American, Cannon Movie Tales: Cinderella.
TELEVISION: Series: The Avengers, Diana, Mystery (host). Movies: In This House of Brede, Witness for the Prosecution, A Hazard of Hearts, Mother Love, Mrs. 'arris Goes to Paris, Running Delilah, Genghis Cohn, Danielle Steel's Zoya, The Haunting of Helen Walker, Fortunes and Misfortunes of Moll Flanders, Samson and Delilah, Rebecca, Mrs. Bradley Mysteries, Victoria and Albert. Specials: King Lear, Bleak House, Rebecca (Emmy, 1997).

RINGWALD, MOLLY
Actress. b. Sacramento, CA, Feb. 16, 1968. Daughter of jazz musician Bob Ringwald; began performing at age 4 with his Great Pacific Jazz Band and at 6 recorded album, Molly Sings. Professional debut at 5 in stage play, The Glass Harp. Appeared in bit on TV's New Mickey Mouse Club, a West Coast stage production of Annie and in TV series, The Facts of Life, Off-B'way debut: Lily Dale (Theatre World Award, 1986).
PICTURES: Tempest (debut, 1982), P.K. and the Kid, Spacehunter: Adventures in the Forbidden Zone, Sixteen Candles, The Breakfast Club, Pretty in Pink, The Pick-Up Artist, For Keeps?, King Lear, Fresh Horses, Strike It Rich, Betsy's Wedding, Face the Music, Seven Sundays, Malicious, Baja, Bastard Brood, Office Killer, Requiem for Murder, Teaching Mrs. Tingle, Kimberly, Cut, The Giving Tree, In the Weeds, The Translator, Ring of Fire, Not Another Teen Movie, Jupiter City, The Tulse Luper Suitcases.
TELEVISION: Series: The Facts of Life, Townies. Movies: Packin' It In, Surviving, Women and Men: Stories of Seduction (Dust Before Fireworks), Something to Live For: The Alison Gertz Story, Since You've Been Gone, Twice Upon a Time. Mini-Series: The Stand.

RISHER, SARA
Executive. Chair of production, New Line Productions, Inc.
PICTURES: Co-prod./assoc. prod.: Polyester, A Nightmare on Elm Street, Quiet Cool, Critters. A Nightmare on Elm Street 3: Dream Warriors, My Demon Lover. Exec. prod.: A Nightmare on Elm Street 4: The Dream Master, A Nightmare on Elm Street 5: The Dream Child, Book of Love, Pump Up the Volume, Wide Sargasso Sea, Surf Ninjas, Blink, A Nightmare on Elm Street 7 (also actress), In Love & War, Last Man Standing, The Deep Blue.

RISSIEN, EDWARD L.
Executive. b. Des Moines, IA. e. Grinnell Coll., Stanford U., B.A., 1949. Army Air Force, WWII. B'way stage, mgr., 1950-53; v.p., Mark Stevens. Prods., 1954-56; prod., v.p., Four Star, 1958-60; prog. execs., ABC-TV, 1960-62; v.p., Bing Crosby Prods., 1963-66; v.p., Filmways TV Prods.; assoc. prod., Columbia, 1968-69; indept. prod., 1970; prod., WB, 1971; exec. v.p., Playboy Prods., 1972-80; consultant & indept. prod., 1981-82; sr. consultant, cable, Playboy Prods., 1982-85; pres., Playboy Programs, 1985-88; bd. of dirs.: Heritage Entertainment, Inc. 1985-88; indept. prod., 1989-present. Theatre producer in London: The School of Night.
PICTURES: Snow Job (prod.), Castle Keep (prod. exec.), The Crazy World of Julius Vrooder (prod.), Saint Jack (exec. prod.).
TELEVISION: Movies: Minstrel Man, A Whale for the Killing, The Death of Ocean View Park, Big Bob Johnson, The Great Niagara, Third Girl from the Left, A Summer Without Boys.

RISSNER, DANTON
Executive. b. Brooklyn, NY, March 27, 1940. e. Florida So. Col. Began as agent with Ashley Famous (later Intl. Famous), 1967-69. 1969 joined Warner Bros. as v.p., chg. European prod.; 1970, moved to United Artists as v.p., chg. European prod.; 1973, named v.p. in chg. East Coast & European prod. for UA; 1975-78, v.p. in chg. of world-wide prod.; 1981, exec. v.p., 20th Century-Fox.; 1984, joined UA as sr. v.p., motion pictures.
PICTURES: Prod.: Up the Academy, A Summer Story.
TELEVISION: Backfire (prod.).

RITCHIE, GUY
Writer, Director. b. Hatfield, Hertfordshire, England, September 10, 1968. m. singer/actress Madonna.
PICTURES: The Hard Case, Lock Stock and Two Smoking Barrels (also cast. dir.), Snatch (also actor), What It Feels Like For a Girl (dir. only), Star, Swept Away, Mean Machine (supervising. prod.).
TELEVISION: Series: Lock, Stock...(exec. prod.). Guest: Independent Focus.

RITTER, JOHN
Actor. b. Burbank, CA, Sept. 17, 1948. Father was late Tex Ritter, country-western star. Attended Hollywood H.S. Began acting at USC in 1968. Appeared with college cast at Edinburgh Festival; later with Eva Marie Saint in Desire Under the Elms.
PICTURES: The Barefoot Executive (debut, 1971), Scandalous John, The Other, The Stone Killer, Nickelodeon, Americathon, Hero at Large, Wholly Moses, They All Laughed, Real Men, Skin Deep, Problem Child, Problem Child II, Noises Off, Stay Tuned, North, Slingblade. Montana, I Woke Up Early the Day I Died, A Gun A Car A Blonde, Bride of Chucky, Shadow of Doubt, TripFall, Lost in the Pershing Point Hotel, Terror Tract, Your Aura is Throbbing, Nuncrackers (narrator), Tadpole, Man of the Year, Manhood, Bad Santa.
TELEVISION: Movies: The Night That Panicked America, Leave Yesterday Behind, The Comeback Kid, Pray TV, In Love With an Older Woman, Sunset Limousine, Love Thy Neighbor, Letting Go, Unnatural Causes, A Smoky Mountain Christmas, The Last Fling, Prison for Children, Tricks of the Trade, My Brother's Wife, Stephen King's It, The Dreamer of Oz, The Summer My Father Grew Up, Danielle Steel's Heartbeat, The Only Way Out, Gramps, The Colony, Unforgivable, Chance of a Lifetime, Dead Husbands, Holy Joe, It Came From the Sky. Series: The Waltons, Three's Company (Emmy Award, 1984), Three's a Crowd, Hooper-man, Have Faith (exec. prod.), Anything But Love (exec. prod., also guest), Fish Police (voice), Hearts Afire, Buffy the Vampire (guest), 8 Simple Rules for Dating My Teenage Daughter. (d. Sept. 11, 2003).

RIVERA, CHITA
Actress, Dancer. r.n. Concita del Rivero. b. Washington, DC, Jan. 23, 1933. Trained for stage at American School of Ballet.
THEATRE: Call Me Madam (1952), Guys and Dolls, Can-Can, Shoestring Revue, Seventh Heaven, Mr. Wonderful, Shinbone Alley, West Side Story, Bye Bye Birdie, Bajour, Sondheim: A Musical Tribute, Chicago, Hey Look Me Over, Merlin, The Rink (Tony Award, 1984), Jerry's Girls, Kiss of the Spider Woman (Tony Award, 1993), Broadway- The Golden Age.
PICTURES: Sweet Charity (1969), Chicago- The Musical.
TELEVISION: Series: The New Dick Van Dyke Show. Specials: Kennedy Center Tonight—Broadway to Washington!, Pippin, Toller Cranston's Strawberry Ice, TV Academy Hall of Fame, 1985. Movies: The Marcus-Nelson Murders, Mayflower Madam.

RIVERA, GERALDO
Journalist. b. New York, NY, July 4, 1943. e. U. of Arizona, Brooklyn Law Sch., 1969, Columbia Sch. of Journalism. Started legal career 1st as lawyer with Harlem Assertion of Rights Community Action for Legal Services 1968-70. Switched to journalism, joined WABC-TV, New York, 1970. Made several TV documentaries on such subjects as institutions for retarded, drug addiction, migrant workers, etc. Chmn.: One-to-One Foundation, Maravilla Foundation. Winner 3 national and 4 local Emmys, George Peabody Award, 2 Robert F. Kennedy Awards. Appeared in film The Bonfire of the Vanities.
PICTURES: Meet Wally Sparks, Contact, Copland, Primary Colors.
TELEVISION: Series: Good Morning America (contributor), Good Night America, 20/20, The Geraldo Rivera Show, Now It Can Be Told, Rivera Live. Specials: The Mystery of Al Capone's Vault, American Vice: The Doping of a Nation, Innocence Lost: The Erosion of American Childhood, Sons of Scarface: The New Mafia, Murder: Live From Death Row, Devil Worship: Exposing Satan's Underground. Movie: Perry Mason: The Case of the Reckless Romeo, Back to Bedlam.

RIVERS, JOAN
Actress, Writer, Director. r.n. Joan Molinsky. b. New York, NY, June 8, 1933. e. Barnard Coll. (Phi Beta Kappa). Formerly fashion coordinator for Bond clothing stores. Performed comedy act in nightclubs, then with Second City 1961-62; TV debut: Johnny Carson Show, 1965; nat'l syndicated columnist, Chicago Tribune 1973-76; Hadassah Woman of the Year, 1983; Jimmy Award for Best Comedian 1981; Chair., National Cystic Fibrosis

Foundation. 1978 created TV series Husbands Wives and Lovers.
AUTHOR: Having a Baby Can Be a Scream (1974), Can We Talk? (1983), The Life and Hard Times of Heidi Abramowitz (1984), Enter Talking (1986), Still Talking (1990).
THEATER: B'way: City (also co-writer), Broadway Bound, Sally Marr... and Her Escorts (also co-writer).
PICTURES: The Swimmer, Rabbit Test (also dir., s.p.), The Muppets Take Manhattan, Spaceballs (voice), Serial Mom, Goosed, The Intern, Hip Edgy Quirky!,
TELEVISION: Series: Fun City (regular substitute guest host: 1983-86), The Late Show (host), The New Hollywood Squares, The Joan Rivers Show (morning talk show). Movies: How to Murder a Millionaire, Tears and Laughter: The Joan and Melissa Rivers Story.

ROBARDS, SAM
Actor. b. New York, NY, December 16, 1961. m. actress Suzy Amis. Son of actors Jason Robards and Lauren Bacall. e. National Theater Institute and studied with Uta Hagen at H.B. Studios.
THEATRE: Off-B'way: Album, Flux, Taking Steps, Moonchildren. Kennedy Center: Idiot's Delight and regional theatre.
PICTURES: Tempest, Not Quite Paradise, Fandango, Bright Lights Big City, Bird, Casualties of War, The Ballad of Little Jo, Mrs. Parker and the Vicious Circle, Donor Unknown, Beautiful Girls, Dinner and Driving, American Beauty, Bounce, Artificial Intelligence: AI, Life as a House.
TELEVISION: Series: Movin' Right Along (PBS), TV 101, Get a Life!, Maximum Bob. Movies: Jacobo Timerman: Prisoner Without a Name Cell Without a Number, Into Thin Air, Pancho Barnes, The Man Who Captured Eichmann, Black and Blue, Hamlet, The Warden, On Golden Pond, Obsessed.

ROBBINS, MATTHEW
Writer, Director. e. U.S.C. Sch. of Cinema. Wrote early scripts in collaboration with Hal Barwood, Robbins branching out into directing with Corvette Summer in 1978.
PICTURES: Writer: The Sugarland Express, The Bingo Long Traveling All-Stars and Motor Kings, Corvette Summer (also dir.), Dragonslayer (also dir.), Warning Sign, Batteries Not Included (also dir.), Bingo (dir. only), Mimic (also story).

ROBBINS, RICHARD
Composer. b. Boston, MA, Dec. 4, 1940. Bachelor of Music and Graduate Studies at New England Conservatory of Music. Received Frank Huntington Beebe Fellowship to Austria where he studied musicology, chamber music. Later became dir. of Mannes College of Music Preparatory School, N.Y. Has worked closely with James Ivory and Ismail Merchant. Also dir. doc. films Sweet Sounds, Street Musicians of Bombay. Awards: Best Score, Venice Film Festival for Maurice; Best Score, BFI Anthony Asquith Award for A Room With a View. Acad. Award nom. for Howards End and The Remains of the Day.
PICTURES: The Europeans (supr. score), Jane Austen in Manhattan, Quartet, Heat and Dust, The Bostonians, A Room with a View, Maurice, Sweet Lorraine, My Little Girl, Slaves of New York, Mr. & Mrs. Bridge, The Ballad of the Sad Cafe, Howards End, The Remains of the Day, Jefferson in Paris, Surviving Picasso, The Proprietor, The Hidden Dimension, A Soldier's Daughter Never Cries, Place Vendome, Cotton Mary, The Girl, The Golden Bowl, The Mystic Masseur, Le Divorce.
TELEVISION: Love and Other Sorrows, In The Gloaming.

ROBBINS, TIM
Actor, Director. b. West Covina, CA, Oct. 16, 1958. Son of Greenwich Village folksinger, worked as actor while in high school. e. NYU. Transferred to UCLA theatre program appearing in guest roles on tv. 1981, co-founder and artistic dir., The Actors Gang, in L.A.; dir. them in and co-authored Alagazam: After the Dog Wars, Violence: The Misadventures of Spike Spangle—Farmer, Carnage: A Comedy (also prod. in NY).
PICTURES: Toy Soldiers (debut, 1984), No Small Affair, Fraternity Vacation, The Sure Thing, Top Gun, Howard the Duck, Five Corners, Bull Durham, Tapeheads, Miss Firecracker, Twister (cameo), Erik the Viking, Cadillac Man, Jacob's Ladder, Jungle Fever, The Player (Cannes Film Fest. Award, 1992), Bob Roberts (also dir., s.p., co-wrote songs), Short Cuts, The Hudsucker Proxy, The Shawshank Redemption, Ready to Wear (Pret-a-Porter), I.Q., Dead Man Walking (dir.), Nothing to Lose, Arlington Road, The Cradle Will Rock (dir and prod.), The Spectre of Hope (prod. only), Mission to Mars, High Fidelity, Anti-Trust, Human Nature, The Truth About Charlie, Mystic River, Code 46.
TELEVISION: Movies: Quarterback Princess, Malice in Wonderland, Queens Supreme, (alos dir. pilot). Guest: Hardcastle and McCormick, St. Elsewhere, Hill Street Blues.

ROBERTS, BRIAN L.
Executive. b. Philadelphia, PA. e. Wharton School at U. of Penn. Joined Comcast Corp. a major cable TV and cell. tele. network operating co., in 1982. Several mgt. positions, incl. exec. VP of ops., before becoming president in 1990. CEO and Director of Comcast since 1999.

ROBERTS, CURTIS
Producer. b. Dover, England. e. Cambridge U., Yale U., Oxford U. Child actor. England, Germany; numerous pictures for Rank Org.; prod. England, on Broadway in Gertie, Island Visit; co-prod. on Broadway, Horses in Midstream, Golden Apple, Tonight or Never; tour and NY The Journey. Recipient: Lawrence J. Quirk Photoplay Award 1990. Now pres., CGC Films, Munich.
AUTHOR: The History of Summer Theatre, The History of Vaudeville, Other Side of the Coin, History of Music (Popular) 1900-70, The History of English Music Halls, Latta, Then There Were Some, I Live to Love, Gabor the Merrier, I Live to Love II.
THEATRE: Tours: Blithe Spirit, Showboat, Kiss Me Kate, Generation, The Camel Bell, Farewell Party, Twentieth Century, Great Sebastians, Goodbye Charlie, Time of the Cuckoo, Under Papa's Picture, Everybody's Gal, Divorce Me Darling, Gingerbread Lady, September Song, Same Time Next Year, Funny Girl, Pal Joey, South Pacific, It Girl, Fanny, Breaking Up the Act, Good, Good Friends, Together, I Remember Mama, Applause Too.
PICTURES: An Actress in Love, La Die, Hypocrite, Jet Over the Atlantic, The Vixen, Farewell Party, Polly's Return, Rain Before Seven, Halloween, Malaga, My Dear Children, Norma, The Lion's Consort, Whispers, Golden Idol, London Belongs To Me, The Ann Moriss Story, My Brother's Keeper, Highland Fling.
TELEVISION: Rendezvous, Deadly Species, Top Secret, The Ilona Massey Show, When In Rome, Ethan Frome, Black Chiffon, Illusion in Java (mini-series), Diamonds Don't Burn (mini-series), Mama. BBC Specials: My Family Right Or Wrong, The Psychopathic Dog.

ROBERTS, ERIC
Actor. b. Biloxi, MS, April 18, 1956. Father founded Actors and Writers Workshop in Atlanta, 1963. Sister is actress Julia Roberts. Began appearing in stage prods. at age 5. Studied at American Acad. of Dramatic Arts. Stage debut in Rebel Women.
THEATRE: Mass Appeal, The Glass Menagerie (Hartford Stage Co.), A Streetcar Named Desire (Princeton's McCarter Theater), Alms for the Middle Class (Long Wharf), Burn This (B'way debut; Theatre World Award).
PICTURES: King of the Gypsies (debut, 1978), Raggedy Man, Star 80, The Pope of Greenwich Village, The Coca Cola Kid, Runaway Train (Acad. Award nom., Golden Globe nom.), Nobody's Fool, Rude Awakening, Blood Red, Best of the Best, The Ambulance, Lonely Hearts, Final Analysis, Best of the Best 2, By the Sword, Freefall, Babyfever, Love Is a Gun, The Specialist, Nature of the Beast, The Grave, Heaven's Prisoners, It's My Party, From the Edge, The Immortals, Power 98, The Cable Guy, American Strays, TNT, The Shadow Men, Making Sandwiches, Most Wanted, Two Shades of Blue, The Prophecy II, La Cucaracha, Dead End, Bittersweet, Spawn 3: Ultimate Battle, Hitman's Run, Facade, The Alternate, No Alibi, Luck of the Draw, Cecil B. Demented. Tripfall, The King's Guard, Mercy Streets, Sanctimony, The Flying Dutchman, The Beat Nicks, Mindstorm, Raptor, Con Games, Wrong Number, The Week-End, Sol Goode, Rough Air: Danger on Flight 534, National Security, Murder by Numbers, The Long Ride Home, Fast Sofa, Spun, Sex and Violence, Fool Proof, , Endangered Species, Brotherhood 3, National Security, Break A Leg.
TELEVISION: Movies: Pauls' Case, Slow Burn, To Heal a Nation, The Lost Capone, Descending Angel, Vendetta: Secrets of a Mafia Bride, Fugitive Among Us, Love Honor & Obey: The Last Mafia Marriage, Voyage, Love Cheat and Steal, Saved by the Light, The Odyssey, Dr. Who, Dark Angel, In Cold Blood, Purgatory West of the Pecos, Christmas Rush, Less than Perfect. Series: Another World, C-16: FBI, Less Than Perfect. Specials: Miss Lonelyhearts, Dear America: Letters Home from Vietnam (reader).

ROBERTS, JULIA
Actress. b. Smyrna, GA, Oct. 28, 1967. Brother is actor Eric Roberts. Parents ran theatre workshop in Atlanta. Moved to NY to study acting; modeled for the Click Agency before making prof. debut in brother's film Blood Red. Voted Hasty Pudding Woman of the Year, 1997. People's Choice Award, 1991, 1992, 1994, 1998, 2000 and ShoWest Awards, 1991 and 1998. Number one on Quigley's Top Ten MoneyMaking Stars of 1999.
PICTURES: Blood Red (debut, 1986), Firehouse, Satisfaction, Mystic Pizza, Steel Magnolias (Acad. Award nom., Golden Globe award), Pretty Woman (Acad. Award nom., BAFTA nom., Golden Globe award), Flatliners, Sleeping With the Enemy, Dying Young, Hook, The Player, The Pelican Brief, I Love Trouble, Ready to Wear (Pret-a-Porter), Something to Talk About, Mary Reilly, Michael Collins, Everyone Says I Love You, My Best Friend's Wedding (Golden Globe nom.), Conspiracy Theory, Notting Hill (Golden Globe nom.), Runaway Bride, Stepmom (also exec. prod.), Erin Brockovich, The Mexican, America's Sweethearts, Ocean's Eleven, How to Survive a Hotel Room Fire, Full Frontal, Confessions of a Dangerous Mind, Mona Lisa Smile.
TELEVISION: Movie: Baja Oklahoma. Guest: Crime Story, Miami Vice, Inside the Actors Átudio, Friends, Murphy Brown, Sesame Street, Law & Order (Emmy nom.). Specials: In the Wild, AFI's 100 Years...100 Stars, America: A Tribute to Heroes.

ROBERTS, PERNELL
Actor. b. Waycross, GA, May 18, 1928. e. U. of Maryland. Left college to begin working with summer stock companies, joining Arena Stage in Washington, DC in 1950. 1952 began appearing off-B'way (where he won a Drama Desk Award for Macbeth, 1957); made B'way debut in 1958 in Tonight in Samarkand.
PICTURES: Desire Under the Elms (debut, 1958), The Sheepman, Ride Lonesome, The Errand Boy (cameo), Four Rode Out, The Magic of Lassie, Checkered Flag.
TELEVISION: *Movies:* The Silent Gun, San Francisco International, The Bravos, Adventures of Nick Carter, Assignment: Munich, Dead Man on the Run, The Deadly Tower, The Lives of Jenny Dolan, Charlie Cobb: Nice Night for a Hanging, The Immigrants, The Night Rider, Hot Rod, High Noon Part II: The Return of Will Kane, Incident at Crestridge, Desperado, Perry Mason: The Case of the Sudden Death Payoff, Perry Mason: The Case of the All-Star Assassin, Donor. *Mini-Series:* Captains and the Kings, Centennial, Around the World in 80 Days, FBI: The Untold Stories. *Series:* Bonanza, Trapper John M.D., FBI: The Untold Stories (host).

ROBERTS, RALPH J.
Executive. b. Philadelphia, PA. Father of Brian L. Roberts. e. Wharton School at U. of Penn. Served 4-year tour of duty in U.S. Navy. Began career in 1950's as acct. exec., Aitken Kynett Advertising Agency. VP, Muzak Corp. Exec. VP, dir. of advertising and later pres. and CEO of Pioneer Industries, a men's accessory co. Pres. and Chairman, Comcast Corp., a cable TV and cell. tel. network operating co. Chairman only since 1989.

ROBERTS, TONY
Actor. b. New York, NY, Oct. 22, 1939. e. Northwestern U.
THEATRE: B'way: How Now Dow Jones, Don't Drink the Water, Play It Again Sam, Promises Promises, Barefoot in the Park, Absurd Person Singular, Sugar, Murder at the Howard Johnson's, They're Playing Our Song, Doubles, Arsenic and Old Lace, Jerome Robbins' Broadway, The Seagull, The Sisters Rosensweig, Victor/Victoria. *Off-B'way:* The Cradle Will Rock, The Good Parts, Four Dogs and a Bone. NY City Opera: Brigadoon, South Pacific. *Dir:* One of the All-Time Greats (Off-B'way).
PICTURES: Million Dollar Duck, Star Spangled Girl, Play It Again Sam, Serpico, The Taking of Pelham One Two Three, Lovers Like Us, Annie Hall, Just Tell Me What You Want, Stardust Memories, A Midsummer Night's Sex Comedy, Amityville 3-D, Key Exchange, Hannah and Her Sisters, Radio Days, 18 Again, Popcorn, Switch, Dead Broke, Grownups.
TELEVISION: *Series:* Rosetti and Ryan, The Four Seasons, The Lucie Arnaz Show, The Thorns. *Movies:* The Lindbergh Kidnapping Case, Girls in the Office, If Things Were Different, Seize the Day, Messiah on Mott Street, A Question of Honor, A Different Affair, Our Sons, Not in My Family, The American Clock, A Perry Mason Mystery: The Case of the Jealous Jokester, Victor/Victoria, My Favorite Broadway: The Leading Ladies, Sounds From a Town I Love. *Guest:* The Defenders, Phyllis, Storefront Lawyers, MacMillan, Trapper John M.D., Love American Style, Love Boat, Hotel.

ROBERTSON, CLIFF
Actor, Writer, Director. b. La Jolla, CA, Sept. 9, 1925.
THEATRE: Mr. Roberts, Late Love, The Lady and the Tiger, Ghosts of 87 (one-man show). B'way: The Wisteria Tree, Orpheus Descending (Theatre World Award), Love Letters.
PICTURES: *Actor:* Picnic (debut, 1955), Autumn Leaves, The Girl Most Likely, The Naked and the Dead, Gidget, Battle of the Coral Sea, As the Sea Rages, All in a Night's Work, Underworld USA, The Big Show, The Interns, My Six Loves, PT 109, Sunday in New York, The Best Man, 633 Squadron, Love Has Many Faces, Masquerade, Up From the Beach, The Honey Pot, The Devil's Brigade (also s.p.), Charly (Academy Award, 1968), Too Late the Hero, J.W. Coop (also dir., s.p.), The Great Northfield Minnesota Raid, Ace Eli and Rodger of the Skies, Man on a Swing, Out of Season, Three Days of the Condor, Shoot, Obsession, Dominique, Fraternity Row (narrator), Class, Brainstorm, Star 80, Shaker Run, Malone, Wild Hearts Can't Be Broken, Wind, Renaissance Man, Dazzle, The Sunset Boys, Escape From L.A., Melting Pot, Family Tree, Paranoid III, March 2, Falcon Down, The 13th Child, Spider-Man.
TELEVISION: *Series:* Falcon Crest. *Guest:* Philco-Goodyear, Studio One, Robert Montgomery Presents, The Game (Emmy Award, 1966), Batman. *Movies:* Man Without a Country, My Father's House, Washington: Behind Closed Doors, Dreams of Gold, Key to Rebecca, Henry Ford—The Man and the Machine, Dead Reckoning, Dazzle, The Last Best Days, Assignment Berlin. *Special:* Days of Wine and Roses (Playhouse 90). Also spokesman for AT&T.

ROBERTSON, DALE
Actor, Producer. r.n. Dayle Robertson. b. Harrah, OK, July 14, 1923. e. Oklahoma Military Coll. Prof. prizefighter; U.S. Army, 1942-45. Film debut as bit player. Voted Star of Tomorrow, M.P. Herald Fame Poll, 1951.
PICTURES: The Boy With Green Hair (debut, 1948), Flamingo Road, Fighting Man of the Plains, Caribou Trail, Two Flags West, Call Me Mister, Take Care of My Little Girl, Golden Girl, Lydia Bailey, Return of the Texan, The Outcasts of Poker Flat, O. Henry's Full House, The Farmer Takes a Wife, Devil's Canyon, The Silver Whip, City of Bad Men, The Gambler from Natchez, Sitting Bull, Son of Sinbad, Day of Fury, Dakota Incident, Hell Canyon Outlaws, Fast and Sexy, Law of the Lawless, Blood on the Arrow, Coast of Skeletons, The One-Eyed Soldier.
TELEVISION: *Series:* Tales of Wells Fargo, The Iron Horse, Death Valley Days, Dynasty, Dallas, J.J. Starbuck. *Movies:* Scalplock, Melvin Purvis: G-Man, Kansas City Massacre, Last Ride of the Dalton Gang. *Guest:* The Love Boat, Matt Houston,

ROBERTSON, KATHLEEN
Actress. b. Hamilton, Canada, July 8, 1973.
PICTURES: Blown Away, Lapse of Memory, Nowhere, Dog Park, Splendor, Runaway Bride (cameo), Psycho Beach Party, Scary Movie 2, Beautiful, I am Sam, Speaking of Sex, XX/XY, Torso: The Evelyn Dick Story, Girls Club.
TELEVISION: *Movies:* Liar's Edge, Quiet Killer, Survive the Night. *Series:* Maniac Mansion, Beverly Hills 90210. *Guest:* My Secret Identity, ENG, Burke's Law.

ROBERTSON, TIMOTHY B.
Executive. e. Univ of VA, Gordon-Conwell Thelogical Seminary, Columbia Univ. Manager of WXNE-TV in Boston, 1980-82; supervisor of Christian Broadcasting Network's tv facility; 1982-90, in charge of Middle East Television after purchase by CBN. Became President & CEO of International Family Entertainment Inc., holdings include The Family Channel, Fit TV, United Family Communications.

ROBINSON, BRUCE
Actor, Director, Writer. b. Kent, England, May 1, 1946. e. Central School of Speech and Drama. As actor appeared in 12 films but began writing novels and screenplays long before he gave up acting in 1975.
PICTURES: *Actor:* Romeo and Juliet (debut), The Story of Adele H., Paid in Full. *Writer:* The Killing Fields (Acad. Award nom.), Fat Man and Little Boy. *Director-Writer:* Withnail and I, How to Get Ahead in Advertising, Jennifer Eight, Return to Paradise, In Dreams, Harry's War, Still Crazy, Jennifer Eight,

ROBINSON, JAMES G.
Executive, Producer. e. Univ. of Maryland. Was prof. photographer and business entreprenur prior to entering m.p. industry as co-prod. of The Stone Boy, and exec. prod. of Where the River Runs Black, Streets of Gold. Founded Morgan Creek Prods. in 1988, Morgan Creek Intl. in 1989, Morgan Creek Music Group in 1990, Morgan Creek Theatres and Morgan Creek International Theatres in 1992. Chairman and CEO of Morgan Creek.
PICTURES: *Exec. Prod. for Morgan Creek:* Young Guns, Skin Deep, Renegades, Enemies a Love Story, Nightbreed, Coupe de Ville, Young Guns II, The Exorcist III, Pacific Heights, Robin Hood: Prince of Thieves, Freejack, White Sands, The Last of the Mohicans, True Romance. *Prod. for Morgan Creek:* Stay Tuned, The Crush, Ace Ventura: Pet Detective, Major League II, Chasers, Trial by Jury, Silent Fall, Imaginary Crimes, A Walk in the Clouds, Big Bully, Ace Ventura: When Nature Calls, Two If By Sea, Diabolique, Bad Moon, Wild America, Incognito, Major League: Back to the Minors, Wrongfully Accused, Soldier, The King and I, Chill Factor, The In Crowd, American Outlaws, Juwanna Mann.

ROBINSON, PHIL ALDEN
Director, Writer. b. Long Beach, NY, Mar. 1, 1950. e. Union Coll., Schenectady. Write and directed training films for Air Force, before writing two episodes for series Trapper John M.D.
PICTURES: Rhinestone (co-s.p.), All of Me (s.p., assoc. prod.). *Dir./Writer:* In the Mood, Field of Dreams, Sneakers. All the Queen's Men (exec. prod.), The Sum of All Fears.
TELEVISION: *Series:* Trapper John M.D. (writer), The George Burns Comedy Week (dir.), Freedom Song(writer). *Mini-Series:* Band of Brothers.

ROCCO, ALEX
Actor. b. Cambridge, MA, Feb. 29, 1936.
PICTURES: Motor Psycho, St. Valentine's Day Massacre, Blood Mania, The Godfather, Slither, Detroit 9000, Friends of Eddie Coyle, The Outside Man, Stanley, Freebie and the Bean, Three the Hard Way, Rafferty and the Gold Dust Twins, Hearts of the West, Fire Sale, House Calls, Rabbit Test, Voices, Herbie Goes Bananas, The Stunt Man, Nobody's Perfekt, The Entity, Cannonball Run II, Stick, Gotcha!, P.K. and the Kid, Return to Horror High, Dream a Little Dream, Wired, The Pope Must Die, That Thing You Do!, Just-Write, Dead of Night, A Bug's Life (voice), Dudley Do-Right, Goodbye Lover, The Last Producer, The Wedding Planner, Face to Face, The Country Bears.
TELEVISION: Over 400 television shows incl: *Series:* Three for the Road, The Famous Teddy Z (Emmy Award, 1990), Sibs, The George Carlin Show. *Movies:* Hustling, The Blue Knight, A Question of Guilt, The Grass is Always Greener Over the Septic Tank, Badge of the Assassin, Rock 'n' Roll Mom, The First Time, A Quiet Little Neighborhood A Perfect Little Murder, An Inconvenient Woman, Boris & Natasha, Love Honor & Obey: The Last Mafia Marriage, Robin Cook's Harmful Intent, Big Shot: Confessions of a Campus Bookie. *Mini-Series:* 79 Park Avenue,

Heart of the City. *Guest:* The Simpsons (voice).

ROCK, CHRIS
Actor, Comedian. b. Brooklyn, NY, Feb. 7, 1966.
PICTURES: Beverly Hills Cop II, I'm Gonna Git You Sucka, New Jack City, Boomerang, CB4 (also writer, co-prod.), The Immortals, Panther, Sgt. Bilko, Beverly Hills Ninja, Doctor Dolittle (voice), Lethal Weapon 4, Dogma, Nurse Betty, Spin Doctor, Bamboozled, Osmosis Jones, Down to Earth (also s.p. & exec. prod.), A.I. Artificial Intelligence (voice), Pootie Tang (also prod.), Jay and Silent Bob Strike Back, You'll Never Wiez in this Town Again, Bad Company, Head of State.
TELEVISION: *Specials:* Chris Rock: Bigger & Blacker (also exec. prod.), Jackie's Back!, Whatever Happened to Michael Ray?. *Series:* Saturday Night Live, In Living Color, The Chris Rock Show. *Guest:* Miami Vice, The Fresh Prince of Bel-Air, Homicide: Life on the Street, King of the Hill (voice), DAG, Rove Live, The Big Schmooze.

RODAT, ROBERT
Writer. b. 1953.
PICTURES: Tall Tale: The Unbelievable Adventures of Pecos Bill, Fly Away Home, Saving Private Ryan (Acad. Award nom.), The Patriot.
TELEVISION: Comrades of Summer, The Ripper, 36 Hours to Die.

RODDAM, FRANC
Director. b. Stockton, England, Apr. 29, 1946. Studied at London Film Sch. Spent two years as adv. copywriter/prod. with Ogilvy, Benson, Mather before joining BBC as documentary filmmaker. Founder of Union Pictures 1991.
PICTURES: Quadrophenia (also co-s.p.), The Lords of Discipline, Rain Forest (s.p. only), The Bride, Aria (sequence), War Party (also co-exec. prod.), K2.
TELEVISION: *Director:* The Family, Mini, Dummy, Moby Dick, Cleopatra. *Creator:* Aufwiedersehen Pet, Making Out, Masterchief, Harry.

RODRIGUEZ, ROBERT
Director, Writer, Producer, Editor. b. June 20,1968. e. Univ. of TX. While in college created comic strip Los Hooligans. Made many short films including Bedhead which won several festival awards.
PICTURES: *Director/Writer:* El Mariachi (feature debut, 1993; also co-prod., story, photog., editor, sound), Desperado (also prod., editor), Four Rooms (segment), From Dusk Till Dawn (dir.), The Facult, Spy Kids, Once Upon a Time in Mexico, Spy Kids 2: Island of Lost Dreams, Spy Kids 3-D: Game Over.
TELEVISION: *Movie (dir./writer):* Roadracers.

ROEG, NICOLAS
Director, Cameraman. b. London, England. Aug. 15, 1928. m. actress Theresa Russell. Entered film industry through cutting rooms of MGM's British Studios, dubbing French films into English. Moved into prod. as clapper boy and part of photographer Freddie Young's crew at Marylebone Studios London, 1947. Next became camera operator (Trials of Oscar Wilde, The Sundowners). Had first experience as cameraman on TV series (Police Dog and Ghost Squad). Debut as director on Performance, co-directed with Donald Cammell. First solo dir. film, Walkabout.
PICTURES: *Cameraman:* The Miniver Story, The Trial of Oscar Wilde, The Sundowners, Lawrence of Arabia, Jazz Boat, Information Received, The Great Van Robbery. *Dir. of Photography:* The Caretaker, Dr. Crippen, Nothing But the Best, Masque of the Red Death, A Funny Thing Happened on the Way to the Forum, Fahrenheit 451, Far from the Madding Crowd, The Girl-Getters, Petulia. *Director-Cameraman:* Performance (co.-dir.), Walkabout. *Director:* Don't Look Now, The Man Who Fell To Earth, Bad Timing, Eureka, Insignificance, Castaway, Aria (sequence, also co-s.p.), Track 29, The Witches, Without You I'm Nothing (exec. prod. only), Cold Heaven.
TELEVISION: *Movies:* Sweet Bird of Youth, Heart of Darkness.

ROËVES, MAURICE
Actor, Director, Writer. b. Sunderland, England, Mar. 19, 1937. Ent. industry, 1964. Played Macduff to Alec Guinness's Macbeth, London stage. Early films: Ulysses, Oh! What a Lovely War, Young Winston, The Eagle Has Landed, Who Dares Wins. Dir. many stage plays.
THEATER: The Killing of Michael Malloy.
PICTURES: Hidden Agenda, Last of the Mohicans, Judge Dredd, The Acid House, Beautiful Creatures.
TELEVISION: In *USA* and *UK* incl.: Scobie (series), The Gambler, Allergy, Magnum P.I., Remington Steele, Escape to Victoria, Inside the Third Reich, Journal of Bridgitte Hitler, Tutti Frutti, Unreported Incident, Bookie, North & South Part II, 919 Fifth Ave., Moses (mini-series), Hillborough, David, The Sight, Grafters, Vanity Fair, Forgive and Forget, Reach for the Moon.

ROGERS, FRED
Television Host, Producer. b. Latrobe, PA, March 20, 1928. e. Rollins Coll., B.A., music composition, 1951; Pittsburgh Theol. Seminary, M. Div. 1962. 1951 served as asst. prod. of NBC-TV's The Voice of Firestone and NBC-TV Opera Theatre. Later promoted to network floor dir., supervising Your Lucky Strike Hit Parade, Kate Smith Hour, etc. 1953, joined WQED-TV in Pittsburgh, educational TV station, to handle programming. 1954 started Children's Corner series, writing, producing and performing; it ran 7 years. 1963 was ordained minister of Presbyterian Church, dedicated to working with children and families through media. Same year introduced Mister Rogers on Canadian Broadcasting Corp. of 15-min. daily program. Ran for one year—was similar in content to present half-hour program, Mister Rogers' Neighborhood. 1964 programs were incorporated into larger, half-hour format on ABC affiliate in Pittsburgh. 1966, 100 programs acquired by Eastern Educational Network, broadcast in Pittsburgh, and seen for first time in other cities (and on some cable services) with underwriting by Sears & Roebuck Foundation. Mister Rogers' Neighborhood in its present format began on Feb. 19, 1968 on NET (now PBS). Program now carried over 300 PBS stations. Author of numerous fiction books for children and non-fiction books for adults; and albums and videos released by Family Communication. Also prod. 20-part PBS series Old Friends New Friends, interview/documentary format for adults, 1978-9. Produced Fred Rogers' Heroes (adult special for PBS). Recipient of 2 Emmy Awards, 2 Peabody Awards and over 25 honorary degrees from colleges and universities.
(d. Feb. 27, 2003)

ROGERS, IVAN
Actor. b. Indianapolis, IN, Sept. 20, 1954. e. Ball State Univ. on a music scholarship.
PICTURES: Tigershark (co-s.p. only), One Way Out (also prod., s.p.), Two Wrongs Make a Right (also s.p., prod.), Slow Burn, Ballbuster (also co-prod.), The Runner, Karate Commando: Jungle Wolf 3, Striking Point, Caged Women II (also co-prod., s.p., dir.), Laserhawk, Forgive Me Father (also prod., s.p., dir.), Down N Dirty.

ROGERS, KENNY
Singer, Actor, Songwriter. b. Crockett, TX, Aug. 21, 1938. Country and western singer. Member Bobby Doyle Trio, Christy Minstrels, 1966-67; The First Edition 1967-76. On screen in Six Pack (1982).
TELEVISION: *Series:* McShane (NBC Friday Night Mystery). *Movies:* The Dream Makers, Kenny Rogers as The Gambler, Coward of the County, Wild Horses; Kenny Rogers as The Gambler Part III: The Legend Continues, Christmas in America, The Gambler Returns: Luck of the Draw, Real West, Rio Diablo, MacShayne: The Final Roll of the Dice, Gambler IV: Playing for Keeps, Big Dreams & Broken Hearts: The Dottie West Story., Jack of All Trades (pilot). *Specials:* Kenny, Dolly & Willie: Something Inside So Strong, and numerous others. *Guest:* Dr. Quinn, Medicine Woman.

ROGERS, MIMI
Actress. b. Coral Gables, FL, Jan. 27, 1959.
PICTURES: Blue Skies Again (debut, 1983), Gung Ho, Street Smart, Someone to Watch Over Me, The Mighty Quinn, Hider in the House, Desperate Hours, The Doors, The Rapture, The Palermo Connection, The Player, White Sands, Dark Horse, Monkey Trouble, Far From Home: The Adventures of Yellow Dog, Bulletproof Heart, Reflections in the Dark, The Mirror Has Two Faces, Lost In Space, Austin Powers International Man of Mystery, Seven Girlfriends, Ginger Snaps, The Upgrade, Dumb and Dumberer: When Harry Met Lloyd.
TELEVISION: *Series:* The Rousters, Paper Dolls. *Episodes:* Magnum, P.I., Hart to Hart, Quincy, M.E., Hill Street Blues, Tales From the Crypt, The X Files. *Movies:* Divorce Wars, Hear No Evil, You Ruined My Life, Fourth Story, Deadlock, Ladykiller, Bloodlines: Murder in the Family, A Kiss to Die For, Weapons of Mass Distraction, Full Body Massage, Tricks, The Devil's Arithmetic, Common Ground, Cruel Intentions 2, My Horrible Year!, Charms for the Easy Life.

ROGERS, THOMAS C.
Executive. e. Columbia Law School, Wesleyan Univ. 1981-86, sr. counsel, U.S. House of Representatives Subcommittee on Telecommunications, Consumer Protection and Finance; Joined NBC in 1987 as v.p., policy and planning and business development. 1988 became pres. of NBC Cable and Business Development. 1992, also named exec. v.p. of NBC.

ROGERS, WAYNE
Actor. b. Birmingham, AL, April 7, 1933. e. Princeton U. After graduation entered the army for three yrs.; studied at Sanford's Meisner's Neighborhood Playhouse and with Martha Graham. Currently gen. partner of Balanced Value Fund, an investment firm; founder, mem on advisory bd., of Plaza Bank of Commerce. Chmn., Easter Seals. Member: Executive Committee of the Arthritis Foundation; Juvenile Diabetes Foundation; Trustees of the Webb School; Kenan Institute of Private Enterprise. Affiliate, School of Business Adm. of the U. of NC. Spokeperson, J.B. Oxford & Co.
PICTURES: Odds Against Tomorrow (debut, 1959), The Glory Guys, Chamber of Horrors, Cool Hand Luke, WUSA, Pocket Money, Once in Paris, The Gig, The Killing Time, Ghosts of

Mississippi, Nobody Knows Anything, Love Lies Bleeding, Frozen With Fear, 3 Days of Rain.
TELEVISION: *Movies*: Lamp Unto My Feet, Attack on Terror: The FBI Versus the Ku Klux Klan, Making Babies II, It Happened One Christmas, The Top of the Hill, Chiefs, He's Fired She's Hired, The Lady from Yesterday, American Harvest, Drop-Out Mother, One Terrific Guy, Bluegrass, Passion and Paradise, Miracle Landing, The Goodbye Bird. *Series*: Edge of Night, Stagecoach West, M*A*S*H, City of the Angels, House Calls, High Risk (host). *Mini-Series*: Chiefs. *Exec. prod.*: Perfect Witness, Age-Old Friends, The Charlie Rose Special, AMC Hollywood Report (also host), Money Plays.

ROHRBECK, JOHN H.
Executive. e. Univ. of WA. 1967, account exec. for NBC Spot Sales in San Francisco, then NY. 1969-78, with KNBC-TV in mgmt. and sales, became station manager in 1976. 1978-84, v.p. & gen. mngr. WRC-TV in Washington DC. Became pres. & gen. mngr. of KNBC-TV in 1984. Named pres. of NBC Television Stations, 1991. Also in charge of network's daytime programming 1992-95.

ROHMER, ERIC
Director. Writer. r.n. Jean Maurice Scherer. b. Nancy, France, April 4, 1920. Professor of literature. Film critic for La Gazette du Cinema and its successor Cahiers du Cinema which he edited, 1957-63. With Claude Chabrol wrote book on Alfred Hitchcock as a Catholic moralist, 1957. 1959 directorial debut, Le Signe du Lion. 1962 began a series of 6 Moral Tales; from 1980 with The Aviator's Wife began another series of 7 films called Comedies and Proverbs. Staged Catherine de Heilbronn in Nanterre, 1979.
PICTURES: *Short films*: Presentation ou Charlotte et Son Steack (1961), La Boulangere de Monceau, Veronique et Son Cancre, Nadja a Paris, Place de L'etoile, Une Etudiante d'aujourd'hui, Fermiere a Montfaucon. *Feature films* (dir. & s.p.): Le Signe du Lion (The Sign of Leo; debut, 1959), La Carriere de Suzanne, Six in Paris (episode), La Collectionneuse, My Night at Maude's, Claire's Knee, Chloe in the Afternoon, The Marquise of O, Perceval, The Aviator's Wife, Le Beau Mariage, Pauline at the Beach, Full Moon in Paris, Summer, Boyfriends and Girlfriends, Four Adventures of Reinette and Mirabelle (also prod.), A Tale of Springtime, A Tale of Winter, The Tree, The Mayor and the Mediatheque, Citizen Langlois (actor), Rendezvous in Paris, A Summer's Tale; An Autumn Tale, The Lady and the Duke.
TELEVISION: Carl Dreyer, Le Celluloid et le Marbre, Ville Nouvelle, Catherine de Heilbronn. Between 1964-69 directed series of documentaries for French TV: Les Cabinets et Physique du XVIII siecle, Les Metamorphoses du Paysage Industriel, Don Quichotte, Edgar Poe, Pascal, Louis Lumiere.

ROIZMAN, OWEN
Cinematographer. b. Brooklyn, NY, Sept. 22, 1936. e. Gettysburg Col.
PICTURES: The French Connection, The Gang That Couldn't Shoot Straight, Play It Again Sam, The Heartbreak Kid, The Exorcist, The Taking of Pelham 1-2-3, The Stepford Wives, Independence, Three Days of the Condor, The Return of the Man Called Horse, Network, Straight Time, Sgt. Pepper's Lonely Hearts Club Band, The Electric Horseman, The Black Marble, True Confessions, Absence of Malice, Taps, Tootsie, Vision Quest, I Love You to Death, Havana, The Addams Family, Grand Canyon, Wyatt Earp, French Kiss.

ROLLINS, JACK
Producer. b. 1914. Co-founder of talent management firm Rollins, Joffe, Mora and Brezner Inc. handling careers of Woody Allen, Nichols and May, Robin Williams, Robert Klein, David Letterman, Dick Cavett, Billy Crystal.
PICTURES: *Co-prod./exec. prod.* with Charles Joffe: Take the Money and Run, Bananas, Everything You Always Wanted to Know About Sex, Sleeper, Love and Death, The Front, Annie Hall (Acad. Award for Best Picture, 1977), Interiors, Manhattan, Stardust Memories, Zelig, Broadway Danny Rose (also actor), The Purple Rose of Cairo, Hannah and Her Sisters, Radio Days, September, Another Woman, New York Stories (Oedipus Wrecks), Crimes and Misdemeanors, Alice, Shadows and Fog, Husbands and Wives, Manhattan Murder Mystery, Bullets Over Broadway, Mighty Aphrodite, Everyone Says I Love You, Deconstructing Harry, Celebrity, Sweet and Lowdown, Small Time Crooks, The Curse of the Jade Scorpion, Hollywood Ending.
TELEVISION: *Prod./exec. prod.*: The Dick Cavett Show, Late Night With David Letterman.

ROMAN, LAWRENCE
Writer. b. Jersey City, NJ, May 30, 1921. e. UCLA, 1943.
THEATRE: *Author*: Under the Yum Yum Tree, P.S. I Love You, Alone Together, Buying Out, Crystal, Crystal Chandelier (prod. in Stockbridge, Mass), Coulda Woulda Shoulda (premiered in Berlin, Germany), Moving Mountains (premiered in Berlin as Grapes and Raisins).
PICTURES: Drums Across the River, Vice Squad, Naked Alibi, One Desire, Man from Bitter Ridge, Kiss Before Dying, Slaughter on Tenth Avenue, Under the Yum Yum Tree, The Swinger, Paper

Lion, Red Sun, A Warm December, McQ.
TELEVISION: *Movies*: Anatomy of an Illness, Badge of the Assassin, Three Wishes for Jamie, Final Verdict, The Ernest Green Story (Peabody Award).

ROMERO, GEORGE A.
Director, Writer, Editor. b. New York, NY, Feb. 4, 1940. e. Carnegie-Mellon Univ.
PICTURES: *Dir./Writer/Cameraman*: Night of the Living Dead (debut, 1968), There's Always Vanilla, The Crazies, Jack's Wife (also edit.). *Director-Writer*: Martin (also edit., actor), Dawn of the Dead (dir. only), Knightriders, Creepshow (dir., co-edit. only), Day of the Dead, Monkey Shines, Night of the Living Dead (s.p., co-exec. prod. only), Two Evil Eyes, The Dark Half (also exec. prod.), Bruiser, The III (s.p.), The Girl Who Loved Tom Gordon.TELEVISION: Tales from the Dark Side (exec. prod., writer).

RONA, JEFF
Composer. b. March 3, 1957.
PICTURES: *Composer*: Lipstick Camera, White Squall, Do Me a Favor, Net Force, Mind Prey, The In Croud, Exit Wounds, The Follow, Black Hawk Down, The Mothman Prophecies. *Additional Music*: Toys, The Net, Assassins, The Fan, Black Cat Run, Shelter Island.
TELEVISION: *Movies*: Toys, Death in Small Doses. *Series*: Homicide: Life on the Street, Chicago Hope, Profiler, High Incident, Gun, Teen Angel, Sleepwalkers, The Dead Zone.

ROOKER, MICHAEL
Actor. b. Jasper, AL, April 6, 1955. e. Goodman School of Drama. Studied Japanese martial art of Aikido prior to establishing himself in Chicago theatre, where he appeared in Union Boys, The Crack Walker and Moon Children.
PICTURES: Streets of Fire (debut, 1984), Light of Day, Rent-a-Cop, Eight Men Out, Mississippi Burning, Sea of Love, Music Box, Henry: Portrait of a Serial Killer, Days of Thunder, JFK, The Dark Half, Cliffhanger, Tombstone, The Hard Truth, Mallrats, The Trigger Effect, Rosewood, Liar, The Replacement Killers, Renegade Force, Brown's Requiem, The Bone Collector, A Table for One, Here on Earth, The 6th Day, Newsbreak, Replicant, Undisputed.
TELEVISION: *Movies*: Afterburn, Johnny & Clyde, HRT.

ROONEY, ANDREW A
Writer, Producer. b. Albany, NY, Jan. 14, 1919. e. Colgate U. Started career as writer at MGM 1946-7, then for Arthur Godfrey, Garry Moore; wrote and produced documentaries, including Black History: Lost Stolen or Strayed (Emmy Award, 1969), An Essay on War, An Essay on Bridges, In Praise of New York City, Mr. Rooney Goes to Washington, etc. Commentator, 60 Minutes (CBS), 1978-present. Newspaper columnist for Tribune Syndicate, 1979-present.
AUTHOR: Air Gunner, The Story of the Stars and Stripes, Conqueror's Peace, A Few Minutes With Andy Rooney, And More Any Rooney, Pieces of My Mind, Sweet and Sour, The Fortunes of War, Not That You Asked, Word for Word, My War.

ROONEY, MICKEY
Actor. r.n. Joe Yule, Jr. b. Brooklyn, NY, Sept. 23, 1920. Son of Joe Yule & Nell Carter, vaudeville performers. U.S. Army, WWII. In vaudeville as child with parents and others before m.p. debut and after; from age of 5 to 12 (1926-33) created screen version of Fontaine Fox newspaper comic character Mickey McGuire in series of short subjects (also billed as Mickey McGuire). Adopted name of Mickey Rooney, returned to vaudeville, then resumed screen career in features. Special Academy Award 1940 for Andy Hardy characterization; voted among first ten Money-Making Stars in M.P. Herald-Fame Poll: 1938-43. Autobiographies: i.e. (1965), Life is Too Short (1991). Novel: The Search for Sonny Skies (1994). Received honorary Academy Award, 1983.
THEATRE: *B'way*: Sugar Babies, The Will Rogers Follies. *Regional*: W.C., Lend Me a Tenor.
PICTURES: Orchids and Ermine (feature debut, 1927), Emma, The Beast of the City, Sin's Pay Day, High Speed, Officer Thirteen, Fast Companions, My Pal the King, The Big Cage, The Life of Jimmy Dolan, The Big Chance, Broadway to Hollywood, The World Changes, The Chief, Beloved, I Like It That Way, Love Birds, Half a Sinner, The Lost Jungle, Manhattan Melodrama, Upperworld, Hide-Out, Chained, Blind Date, Death on the Diamond, The County Chairman, Reckless, The Healer, A Midsummer Night's Dream, Ah Wilderness, Riff-Raff, Little Lord Fauntleroy, The Devil is a Sissy, Down the Stretch, Captains Courageous, Slave Ship, A Family Affair, Hoosier Schoolboy, Live Love and Learn, Thoroughbreds Don't Cry, You're Only Young Once, Love is a Headache, Judge Hardy's Children, Hold That Kiss, Lord Jeff, Love Finds Andy Hardy, Boys Town, Stablemates, Out West With the Hardys, The Adventures of Huckleberry Finn, The Hardys Ride High, Andy Hardy Gets Spring Fever, Babes in Arms (Acad. Award nom.), Judge Hardy and Son, Young Tom Edison, Andy Hardy Meets Debutante, Strike Up the Band, Andy Hardy's Private Secretary, Men of Boy's Town, Life Begins for Andy Hardy, Babes on Broadway, The Courtship of Andy Hardy, A Yank at Eton, Andy Hardy's Double Life, The Human Comedy (Acad. Award nom.), Girl Crazy, Thousands Cheer, Andy Hardy's

Blonde Trouble, National Velvet, Love Laughs at Andy Hardy, Killer McCoy, Summer Holiday, Words and Music, The Big Wheel, Quicksand, He's a Cockeyed Wonder, The Fireball, My Outlaw Brother, The Strip, Sound Off, All Ashore, Off Limits, A Slight Case of Larceny, Drive a Crooked Road, The Atomic Kid (also prod.), The Bridges at Toko-Ri, The Twinkle in God's Eye, Francis in the Haunted House, The Bold and the Brave (Acad. Award nom.), Magnificent Roughnecks, Operation Mad Ball, Baby Face Nelson, Andy Hardy Comes Home, A Nice Little Bank That Should Be Robbed, The Last Mile, The Big Operator, Platinum High School, The Private Lives of Adam and Eve (also co-dir.), Breakfast at Tiffany's, King of the Roaring Twenties, Requiem for a Heavyweight, Everything's Ducky, It's a Mad Mad Mad Mad World, Secret Invasion, 24 Hours to Kill, The Devil in Love, Ambush Bay, How to Stuff a Wild Bikini, The Extraordinary Seaman, Skidoo, The Comic, 80 Steps to Jonah, The Cockeyed Cowboys of Calico County, Hollywood Blue, B.J. Lang Presents (The Manipulator), Richard, Pulp, The Godmothers (also s.p., music), Ace of Hearts, Thunder County, That's Entertainment, Journey Back to Oz (voice), From Hong Kong With Love, Rachel's Man, Find the Lady, The Domino Principle, Pete's Dragon, The Magic of Lassie, The Black Stallion (Acad. Award nom.), Arabian Adventure, The Fox and the Hound (voice), The Emperor of Peru, The Black Stallion Returns, The Care Bears Movie (voice), Lightning the White Stallion, Erik the Viking, My Heroes Have Always Been Cowboys, Sweet Justice, The Legend of Wolf Mountain, Little Nemo (voice), Silent Night Deadly Night 5: The Toymaker, The Milky Life, Revenge of the Red Baron, That's Entertainment III, Animals, Internet Love, Topa Topa Bluffs.
TELEVISION: Series: Hey Mickey, One of the Boys, The Black Stallion. Many specials including: Playhouse 90, Pinocchio, Eddie, Somebody's Waiting, The Dick Powell Theater. Movies: Evil Roy Slade, My Kidnapper My Love, Leave 'Em Laughing, Bill (Emmy Award, 1982), Senior Trip, Bill: On His Own, It Came Upon the Midnight Clear, Bluegrass, Home for Christmas, The Gambler Returns: Luck of the Draw. Many guest appearances including: The Golden Girls, The Judy Garland Show, Naked City, Wagon Train, Twilight Zone, The Lucy Show, Hollywood Squares, Night Gallery, The Love Boat.

ROONEY, PAT E.
Producer. e. Santa Monica College, Marquette U., Denver U., UCLA. Was Captain in U.S. Army. Entertainer Far East Command Forces, Korean War. In 1960, joined CBS Films, producing TV series and pilot films. 1962 formed Pat Rooney Prods. with Del E. Webb and Jerry Buss. Has worked as independent producer for MGM, Paramount, Universal, 20th Century Fox, Warber Bros, Goldwyn. 1993 partnered with John Veitch (former pres. of Columbia Pictures).
PICTURES: Dime With A Halo, Danger Pass, Caged, Law of the Lawless, Requiem for a Gunfighter, Bounty Killer, Young Once, Hell's Angels, Fools, Christmas Couple, Black Eye, Deadman's Curve, Deadly Attack, Secret Ceremony, Kings Row, Devil Planes, Gentlemen of the Night, Kapo Women, Lillies of the Field, Light Fingers, Poison Ivy, Nylon Noose, A Love Story, Gattling Gun.

ROOS, FRED
Producer. b. Santa Monica, CA, May 22, 1934. e. UCLA, B.A. Directed documentary films for Armed Forces Radio and Television Network. Worked briefly as agent for MCA and story editor for Robert Lippert Productions. Worked as casting dir. in 1960s and served as casting dir. on The Godfather, beginning longtime association with filmmakers Francis Coppola and George Lucas.
PICTURES: The Conversation, The Godfather Part II, Apocalypse Now, The Black Stallion, The Escape Artist (exec. prod.), The Black Stallion Returns, Hammett, One From the Heart, The Outsiders, Rumble Fish, The Cotton Club, One Magic Christmas, Seven Minutes in Heaven, Peggy Sue Got Married (special consultant), Barfly, Gardens of Stone (co-exec. prod.), Tucker: The Man and His Dream, New York Stories (Life Without Zoe), Wait Until Spring Bandini, The Godfather Part III, Hearts of Darkness: A Filmmaker's Apocalypse (exec. prod.), The Secret Garden, Radioland Murders, Jack (spec. consultant), The Rainmaker (exec. consultant), The Virgin Suicides, Town & Country.
TELEVISION: Series: The Outsiders (exec. prod.). Movie: Montana.

ROSE, ALEX
Producer. r.n. Alexandra Rose. b. Jan. 20, 1946. e. U. of WI, BS. Started in m.p. distribution with Medford Films. Later became asst. sls. mgr. for New World Pictures.
PICTURES: Co-prod.: Drive-In, I Wanna Hold Your Hand, Big Wednesday, Norma Rae, Nothing in Common (solo prod.), Overboard (co-prod.), Quigley Down Under, Frankie and Johnny, Exit to Eden, The Other Sister (prod./writer).
TELEVISION: Nothing in Common (co-exec. prod. with Garry Marshall), Pilots: Norma Rae, Just Us Kids.

ROSE, CHARLIE
Talk Show Host. b. Henderson, NC, Jan. 5, 1942. e. Duke Univ. (history, law). Was exec. prod. for Bill Moyers' Journal, 1975.
TELEVISION: Series (host/anchor): A.M. Chicago, The Charlie Rose Show (NBC, 1979, 1981), CBS News Nightwatch, E.D.J. Entertainment Daily Journal (Personalities), Charlie Rose (synd; also exec. prod., editor). Specials: Public Debate With Charlie Rose, In Concert at the United Nations (host).

ROSE, STEPHEN
Executive. Entered m.p. industry in 1964 with Columbia Pictures; named adv. dir. 1970 joined Cinema V Distributing, Inc. as dir. of adv.; left in 1971 to take post at Cinemation Industries, where was named v.p. and bd. member. 1975 joined Paramount Pictures as dir. of adv.; promoted to v.p./adv. 1979 formed Barrich Prods. with Gordon Weaver. 1982, rejoined Paramount as v.p., mktg.; 1983, named v.p. of mktg. for Paramount; sr. v.p., mktg., 1983. Resigned in 1984 to form Barrich Marketing with Gordon Weaver.

ROSEANNE
Actress. r.n. Roseanne Cherrie Barr. b. Salt Lake City, UT, Nov. 3, 1952. Started performing in bars; prod. showcase for women performers, Take Back the Mike at U. of Boulder. 1983 won Denver Laff-Off. Moved to Los Angeles where performed at The Comedy Store, and showcased on TV special Funny and The Tonight Show. Has previously performed under the names Roseanne Barr, Roseanne Arnold. Autobiographies: My Life as a Woman (1989), My Lives (1994).
PICTURES: She-Devil (debut, 1989), Look Who's Talking Too (voice), Freddy's Dead, Even Cowgirls Get the Blues, Blue in the Face, Meet Wally Sparks, Get Bruce, The Eyes of Tammy Faye, Cecil B. Demented, 15 Minutes, Sweating Bullets.
TELEVISION: Series: Roseanne (also co-exec. prod.; Peabody & Golden Globe Awards for Best Series; Emmy Award for Best Actress, 1993), The Jackie Thomas Show (co-exec. prod, guest), Tom (co-exec. prod.), The Roseanne Show (also exec. prod.). The Real Roseanne Show. Specials: Fast Copy, Rodney Dangerfield—It's Not Easy Bein' Me, Live From Minneapolis: Roseanne, Roseanne Arnold: Live From Trump Castle. Movies: Backfield in Motion, The Woman Who Loved Elvis (also co-exec. prod.), I Am Your Child.

ROSEN, ROBERT L.
Producer. b. Palm Springs, CA, Jan. 7, 1937. e. U. of Southern Calif.
PICTURES: Exec. prod.: French Connection II, Black Sunday, Prophecy, Going Ape, The Challenge, Courage (also dir.), Porky's Revenge, World Gone Wild, Dead-Bang (exec. prod.), Year of the Gun, Spy Hard, Mr. Magoo, Wrongfully Accused, Sniper. Exec. in chg. of prod.: Little Big Man, Le Mans, The Reivers, Rio Lobo, Big Jake, Scrooge, Fourth War (Line Producer).
TELEVISION: Gilligan's Island, Hawaii Five-O, Have Gun Will Travel.

ROSENBERG, GRANT E.
Executive. b. San Francisco, CA, 1952. e. Univ. of Cal. at Davis. Started career in research dept., NBC; 1977, joined Paramount in research and later in development; 1984, v.p., dramatic dev.; then sr. v.p., dev., for TV group, Paramount. 1985, named sr. v.p., network TV for Walt Disney Pictures; 1988, named pres., Lee Rich Productions, TV div., and exec. prod. of Molloy TV series. 1990, writer, prod., Paramount TV. Series: MacGyver (writer), Star Trek: The Next Generation (writer), Time Trax (exec. prod., creator), Lois & Clark (writer, prod.). Writer, prod. for Warner Bros. TV.

ROSENBERG, RICHARD K.
Executive, Attorney. b. Paterson, NJ, Apr. 4, 1942. e. Indiana Univ. Corporation & intl. entertainment attorney for major corps. and celebrities. Formed RKR Entertainment Group in 1977 with subsidiaries RKR Releasing, RKR Artists and RKR Productions. Subsequently consolidated into RKR Pictures Inc. Author: Negotiating Motion Picture Contracts. Films include Alice Sweet Alice (Holy Terror), Hell's Angels Forever, Mother Lode, Best Revenge, The Wild Duck, Primary Motive, Fatal Past, Dutchman's Creek. V.p., Cinetel Films, 1991-93. Exec. v.p. and bd. mem., Jones Entertainment Group Ltd., 1995.

ROSENBERG, RICK
Producer. b. Los Angeles, CA. e. Los Angeles City Coll., UCLA. Started career in mail room of Columbia Pictures, then asst. to prod. Jerry Bresler on Major Dundee and Love Has Many Faces. Asst. to Col. v.p., Arthur Kramer. Was assoc. prod. on The Reivers and in 1970 prod. first feature, Adam at Six A.M., with Bob Christiansen, with whom co-prod. all credits listed below.
PICTURES: Adam at Six A.M., Hide in Plain Sight, Down in the Delta.
TELEVISION: Suddenly Single, The Glass House, A Brand New Life, The Man Who Could Talk to Kids, The Autobiography of Miss Jane Pittman, I Love You... Goodbye, Queen of the Stardust Ballroom, Born Innocent, A Death in Canaan, Strangers, Robert Kennedy and His Times, Kids Don't Tell, As Summers Die, Gore Vidal's Lincoln, Red Earth White Earth, Heist, A House

of Secrets and Lies, The Last Hit, Heart of Darkness, Tad, Kingfish: A Story of Huey P. Long, Redwood Curtain, Death Benefit, Beyond the Call, Sudden Terror: The Hijacking of School Bus #17, Home Invasion, Lost Treasure of Dos Santos, The Long Island Incident, Southern Man, The Crossing.

ROSENBERG, STUART
Director, Producer. b. New York, NY, Aug. 11, 1927. e. NYU.
PICTURES: Murder, Inc. (co-dir.; debut, 1960), Question 7, Cool Hand Luke, The April Fools, Move (also co-exec. prod.), WUSA (also co-exec. prod.), Pocket Money, The Laughing Policeman (also prod.), The Drowning Pool, Voyage of the Damned, The Amityville Horror, Love and Bullets, Brubaker, The Pope of Greenwich Village, Let's Get Harry (under pseudonym Allan Smithee), My Heroes Have Always Been Cowboys.
TELEVISION: Numerous episodes of such series as The Untouchables, Naked City, The Defenders (Emmy Award, 1963), Espionage, Chrysler Theatre, Twilight Zone, Alfred Hitchcock Theater.

ROSENFELT, FRANK E.
Executive. b. Peabody, MA, Nov. 15, 1921. e. Cornell U., B.S.; Cornell Law Sch., L.L.B. Served as atty. for RKO Radio Pictures, before joining MGM in 1955 as member of legal dept. Appt. secty. in 1966. Named v.p., gen. counsel in 1969 and pres. in 1973. 1974-81, CEO, bd. chmn. & CEO, MGM; Later became vice chmn., MGM/UA Communications Co. Member: Bd. of Governors, Academy of M.P. Arts & Sciences for 9 years. Retired from MGM/UA in Aug. 1990, now consultant to MGM-Pathe Commun. Co.

ROSENFELT, SCOTT
Producer, Director. b. Easton, PA, Dec. 20, 1955. e. NYU.
PICTURES: Producer: Teen Wolf, Extremities, Russkies, Mystic Pizza, Big Man on Campus (co-prod.), Home Alone, Family Prayers (dir.), Smoke Signals, Getting to Know You (exec.), The Book of Stars, The Business of Fancydancing.
TELEVISION: Movie: T-Bone N Weasel.

ROSENMAN, HOWARD
Producer. b. Brooklyn, NY, Feb. 1, 1945. e. Brooklyn Col. Asst. to Sir Michael Benthall on B'way show; prod., Benton & Bowles Agency; ABC-TV; RSO Prods. Co-pres., Sandollar Prods.; currently pres. Brillstein-Grey Motion Pictures.
PICTURES: Sparkle, The Main Event, Resurrection, Lost Angels, Gross Anatomy, True Identity, Father of the Bride, Shining Through, Straight Talk, A Stranger Among Us, Buffy the Vampire Slayer, The Celluloid Closet, The Family Man, My First Mister, Girl on Fire: The Edie Sedgwick Story.
TELEVISION: Movies: Isn't It Shocking? Altogether Now, Death Scream, Virginia Hill, Killer Bees. Specials: Common Threads: Stories from the Quilt (co-exec. prod.), Tidy Endings.

ROSENMAN, LEONARD
Composer. b. New York, NY, Sept. 7, 1924.
PICTURES: East of Eden, Cobweb, Rebel Without a Cause, Edge of the City, The Savage Eye, The Chapman Report, Fantastic Voyage, Hellfighters, Beneath the Planet of the Apes, Barry Lyndon (Academy Award, 1975), Birch Interval, Race With the Devil, Bound For Glory (Academy Award, 1976), A Man Called Horse, The Car, September 30, 1955, The Enemy of the People, The Lord of the Rings, Promises in the Dark, Prophecy, Hide in Plain Sight, The Jazz Singer, Making Love, Miss Lonely Hearts, Cross Creek, Heart of the Stag, Star Trek IV: The Voyage Home, Robocop 2, Ambition, The Color of Evening, Mrs. Munck, Levitation.
TELEVISION: Movies/Mini-Series: Sybil (Emmy Award), Friendly Fire (Emmy Award), City in Fear, Murder in Texas, Vanished, The Wall, Miss Lonelyhearts, Celebrity, The Return of Marcus Welby MD, Heartsounds, First Steps, Promised a Miracle, Keeper of the City, The Face on the Milk Carton.

ROSENSTEIN, GERTRUDE
Director. b. New York, NY. e. Barnard Coll., B.A., Neighborhood Playhouse. Exec. asst. to George Balanchine & Lincoln Kirstein, N.Y.C. Ballet. Assoc. with Gian Carlo Menotti, Festival of Two Worlds, Spoleto, Italy. Assoc. dir., NBC Opera Theatre, Emmy Awards, Kennedy Memorial Mass. TV staff dir., NBC. Now freelance director, news programs, election coverages, music and dance programs, commercials. Governor, NY Television Academy. Member, Emmy Awards Committee.

ROSENTHAL, BUD
Executive. b. Brooklyn, NY, Mar. 21, 1934. e. Brooklyn Coll., B.A., 1954, NYU. U.S. Army, 1954-56; college correspondent, NY Times. Entered m.p. ind. as assoc. editor, Independent Film Journal, 1957-59. Publicist, Columbia Pictures, 1959-61.Natl. publ mgr.,
Columbia Pictures, 1962-67. Publ. dir. for Anderson Tapes, Such Good Friends, The Blue Bird; Story edit. and casting dir., Otto Preminger's Sigma Productions, 1972-75. Assoc. prod., Broadway play, Full Circle. Warner Bros. worldwide mtg. coordinator, Superman, Superman II, Superman III, Batman, Space Jam. Project coordinator, Time Warner Earth Day Special, Warner Bros. Studio Rededication, Celebration of Tradition.

International mktg. consultant, 1976-present.
PICTURES: Something for Everyone (asst. prod.), Rosebud (assoc. prod.). Int'l mktg. co-ord. on films: Ghostbusters, Labyrinth, Tune in Tomorrow, Boyz 'N the Hood, Addams Family, Bugsy, Batman Returns, A Few Good Men, Last Action Hero, Jumanji, Star Trek: Insurrection, The Rugrats Movie.

ROSENTHAL, JANE
Executive. b. Denver, CO. e. NYU. 1976-84, dir. of film for TV at CBS; 1984-87, v.p. prod. Disney; 1987-88, v.p. of TV & Mini-Series, Warners TV; 1988-93, co-founder, Tribeca Prods., Tribeca Film Center; 1993-present, pres. of Tribeca Prods.; 1992-93, exec. prod. of series Tribeca. Producer of films Thunderheart, Faithful, Night and the City, Bronx Tale, Marvin's Room, Wag the Dog, Analyze This, Entropy, Flawless, Rocky and Bullwinkle, Meet the Parents, About a Boy, Showtime, Scared Guys., Holiday Heart, Analyze That, Rent.

ROSENTHAL, RICK
Director. b. New York, NY, June 15, 1949. e. Harvard, B.A. cum laude, 1971. Launched career as filmmaker-in-residence with New Hampshire TV Network. Moved to Los Angeles to study at American Film Institute where filmed Moonface, 1973.
PICTURES: Halloween II (debut, 1981), Bad Boys, American Dreamer, Russkies, Distant Thunder, Halloween: Resurrection, Just a Little Harmless Sex.
TELEVISION: Movies: Fire on the Mountain, Code of Vengeance, Secrets of Midland Heights, Nasty Boys, Devlin, Birds II, The Land's End. Series: Life Goes On, Witches of Eastwick, The Practice, Feds, Early Edition, Dellaventura, Roar, LA Doctors, Providence, D.C., Falcone, The District, Witchblade, Crossing Jordan, Smallville, Law & Order: Special Victims Unit.

ROSENZWEIG, BARNEY
Producer. b. Los Angeles, CA, Dec. 23, 1937. e. USC, 1959. m. actress Sharon Gless.
PICTURES: Morituri (assoc. prod.), Do Not Disturb (assoc. prod.), Caprice (assoc. prod.), Who Fears the Devil (prod.).
TELEVISION: Prod.: Daniel Boone (series), Men of the Dragon, One of My Wives Is Missing, Charlie's Angels (series), Angel on My Shoulder, American Dream (pilot), John Steinbeck's East of Eden (mini-series; Golden Globe Award). Exec. prod.: Modesty Blasie (pilot), This Girl for Hire (movie), Cagney and Lacey (series; 2 Emmy Awards: 1985, 1986), The Trials of Rosie O'Neill (series), Christy (movie, series), Cagney & Lacey: The Return (movie), Cagney & Lacey: Together Again (movie), Cagney & Lacey: The View Through the Glass Ceiling (movie), Cagney & Lacey: True Convictions (movie).

ROSS, DIANA
Singer, Actress. b. Detroit, MI, Mar. 26, 1944. Formed musical group at age 14 with two friends, Mary Wilson and Florence Ballard. In 1960 they auditioned for Berry Gordy, head of Motown Record Corp. After completing high school, the trio was named the Supremes and went on tour with Motor Town Revue. Over period of 10 yrs. Supremes had 15 consecutive hit records and once had five consecutive records in the number one spot on charts. In 1969 Diana Ross went on her own, appearing on TV and in nightclubs. Memoirs: Secrets of a Sparrow (1993).
PICTURES: Lady Sings the Blues (debut as actress, 1972; Acad. Award nom.), Mahogany, The Wiz.
TELEVISION: Movie: Out of Darkness (also co-exec. prod.). Specials: Diana! (also exec. prod. & writer), Motown 25: Yesterday Today Forever, Motown Returns to the Apollo, Diana's World Tour.

ROSS, KATHARINE
Actress. b. Los Angeles, CA, Jan. 29, 1943. m. actor Sam Elliott. e. Santa Rosa Coll. Joined the San Francisco Workshop, appeared in The Devil's Disciple, The Balcony. TV debut, 1962 in Sam Benedict segment.
PICTURES: Shenandoah (debut, 1965), Mister Buddwing, The Singing Nun, Games, The Graduate (Golden Globe Award, Acad. Award nom.), Hellfighters, Butch Cassidy and the Sundance Kid, Tell Them Willie Boy is Here, Fools, Get to Know Your Rabbit, They Only Kill Their Masters, The Stepford Wives, Voyage of the Damned, The Betsy, The Swarm, The Legacy, The Final Countdown, Wrong Is Right, Daddy's Deadly Darling, The Red-Headed Stranger, A Climate for Killing, Home Before Dark, Donnie Darko, Don't Let Go.
TELEVISION: Movies: The Longest Hundred Miles, Wanted: The Sundance Woman, Murder by Natural Causes, Rodeo Girl, Murder in Texas, Marian Rose White, Shadow Riders, Travis McGee, Secrets of a Mother and Daughter, Conagher (also co-script), Houston: The Legend of Texas, Tattle, Conagher, Snow in August. Guest: Ben Casey, The Bob Hope-Chrysler Theatre, The Virginian, Wagon Train, Kraft Mystery Theatre, The Lieutenant, The Road West. Series: The Colbys.

ROSS, KENNETH
Writer. b. London, Sept. 16, 1941. Entered m.p. industry 1970.
THEATRE: The Raft, Under The Skin, Mr. Kilt & The Great I Am.
PICTURES: Brother Sun Sister Moon, Slag, The Reckless Years (also orig. story), Abelard & Heloise, The Day of the Jackal (So.

Cal. M.P. Council Award; nom. for Writers' Guild, SFTA, and Golden Globes), The Devil's Lieutenant, The Odessa File (nom. for Writers' Guild Award), Quest (also orig. story), Black Sunday (Edgar Allen Poe Award, Mystery Writers of America, 1977), The Fourth War, Epiphany (also orig. story), The Jackal.
TELEVISION: The Roundelay, The Messenger.

ROSSELLINI, ISABELLA
Actress. b. Rome, Italy, June 18, 1952. Daughter of actress Ingrid Bergman and director Roberto Rossellini. Came to America in 1972. Worked as translator for Italian News Bureau. Taught Italian at New Sch. for Social Research. Worked 3 years on second unit assignments for journalist Gianni Mina and as NY corresp. for Ital. TV series, The Other Sunday. Model for Vogue, Harper's Bazaar, Italian Elle, Lancome Cosmetics.
PICTURES: A Matter of Time (debut 1976; with her mother), The Meadow, Il Pap'Occhio, White Nights, Blue Velvet, Tough Guys Don't Dance, Siesta, Red Riding Hood, Zelly and Me, Cousins, Les Dames Galantes, The Siege of Venice, Wild at Heart, Death Becomes Her, The Pickle, Fearless, Wyatt Earp, Immortal Beloved, The Innocent, Big Night, Left Luggage, The Imposters, The Sky Will Fall, Empire, The Wedding Contract, The Tulse Luper Suitcases, Roger Dodger.
TELEVISION: Movies: The Last Elephant, Lies of the Twins, The Crime of the Century, The Odyssey, Merlin, Don Quixote, Monte Walsh. Guest: The Tracey Ullman Show, Tales From the Crypt (You Murderer), Friends, The Simpsons (voice). Specials: The Gift, Fallen Angels (The Frightening Frammis). Mini-Series: Napoleon.

ROSSOVICH, RICK
Actor. b. Palo Alto, CA, August 28, 1957. e. Calif. St. Univ. Sacramento (art history). Studied acting with coach Vincent Chase.
PICTURES: The Lords of Discipline (debut, 1983), Losin' It, Streets of Fire, The Terminator, Fast Forward, Warning Sign, Top Gun, Let's Get Harry, The Morning After, Roxanne, Paint It Black, The Witching Hour, Spellbinder, Navy SEALS, Cognac, Tropical Heat, New Crime City, Cover Me, Black Scorpion II, Truth or Consequences N.M., Telling You, Cross Country.
TELEVISION: Series: MacGruder and Loud, Sons and Daughters, ER. Guest: Tales from the Crypt (The Switch), Pacific Blue. Special: 14 Going On 30. Movies: Deadly Lessons, The Gambler Returns: Luck of the Draw, Black Scorpion, Fatally Yours, Legend of the Lost Tomb, Killer Deal, Miracle in Lane 2.

ROTH, BOBBY
Director, Writer, Producer.
b. 1950.
PICTURES: The Boss' Son, Circle of Power, Independence Day, Heartbreakers, The Man Inside, Amanda, Jack the Dog, Dancing at the Harvest Moon, Manhood.
TELEVISION: Episodes: Miami Vice, The Insiders, Crime Story. Movies: Tonight's the Night, The Man Who Fell to Earth, Dead Solid Perfect (dir., co-s.p.), Baja Oklahoma (dir., co-s.p.), The Man Inside, Rainbow Drive, Keeper of the City, The Switch, Judgement Day: The John List Story, Ride With the Wind, Nowhere to Hide, Love Can Build a Bridge, In the Line of Duty: Kidnapped, Tell Me No Secrets, Inheritance, The Devil's Child, Vengeance Unlimited, Her Own Rules, A Secret Affair, A Holiday Romance, Crossed Over, Unfinished Business, A Date with Darkness: The Trial and Capture of Andrew Luster, Dancing at the Harvest Moon.

ROTH, JOE
Executive, Producer, Director. b. New York, NY, June 13, 1948. Began career working as prod. assistant on commercials and feature films in San Francisco. Also ran the rights for improv group Pitchel Players. Moved with them to Los Angeles, and prod. their shows incl. the $250,000 film Tunnelvision. 1987, co-founder of independent film prod. co. Morgan Creek Productions. 1989, left to become chmn. of newly-formed Fox Film Corp., the theatrical film unit of 20th Century Fox Film Corp. Also named head of News Corp. unit. Resigned from Fox, 1993. Pres. & founder, Caravan Pictures, 1993. 1994, became chmn. Walt Disney Motion Pictures Group. In 2000, left Disney to start own company, Revolution Studios.
PICTURES: Producer: Tunnelvision, Cracking Up, Americathon, Our Winning Season, The Final Terror, The Stone Boy, Where the River Runs Black, Bachelor Party, Off Beat, Streets of Gold (also dir. debut), Tall Tale, Angels in the Outfield. Exec. prod.: Revenge of the Nerds II: Nerds in Paradise (also dir.), Young Guns, Dead Ringers, Skin Deep, Major League, Renegades, Enemies a Love Story, Pacific Heights, The Three Musketeers, Angie, I Love Trouble, Angels in the Outfield, A Low Down Dirty Shame, Houseguest, Tall Tale, While You Were Sleeping, Before and After, Tears of the Sun, Daddy Day Care, Hollywood Homicide, Mona Lisa Smile. Dir.: Coupe de Ville, Tomcats, Butterfly, Hostile Rescue, America's Sweethearts.

ROTH, PETER
Executive. b. Larchmont, NY. e. U. of Pennsylvania, graduated cum laude, Tufts U., 1972. Began career in television at ABC Television Network as manager, then director, Children's Programs, 1976; moving to director, Current Programs, 1979;

became v.p., Current Primetime Series, 1981-86; president, Stephen J. Cannell Prods., 1986-92, president of production, Twentieth Network Television (currently 20th Century Fox Television), 1992; president, Twentieth Network Television, 1993; president, 20th Century Fox Television, 1994. Currently president, Warner Bros. Television.

ROTH, RICHARD A.
Producer. b. Beverly Hills, CA, 1943. e. Stanford U. Law Sch. Worked for L.A. law firm before beginning film career as lawyer and literary agent for Ziegler-Ross Agency. In 1970 left to develop s.p. Summer of '42 with Herman Raucher.
PICTURES: Summer of '42, Our Time, The Adventures of Sherlock Holmes' Smarter Brother, Julia, Outland, In Country, Blue Velvet, Manhunter.

ROTH, TIM
Actor. b. London, England, May 14,1961. Started acting with various fringe theatre groups such as Glasgow Citizen's Theatre, The Oval House, and the Royal Court. Also on London stage in Metamorphosis.
PICTURES: The Hit, A World Apart, The Cook the Thief His Wife and Her Lover, Vincent & Theo, Rosencrantz and Guildenstern Are Dead, Jumpin at the Boneyard, Reservoir Dogs, Backsliding, Bodies Rest and Motion, Pulp Fiction, Rob Roy (BAFTA Award, 1995), Little Odessa, Captives, Hoodlum, Four Rooms, Everyone Say I Love You, Liar, Animals, No Way Home, Gridlock'd, The Legend of 1900, The Million Dollar Hotel, Vatel, Lucky Numbers, Invincible, Planet of the Apes, The Musketeer, Inside Job, Emmett's Mark, Cromwell & Fairfax.
TELEVISION: Specials/Movies (BBC): Meantime, Made in Britain, Metamorphosis, Knuckle, Yellow Backs, King of the Ghetto, The Common Pursuit, Murder in the Heartland (U.S.), Heart of Darkness.

ROTHMAN, THOMAS E.
Executive. b. Baltimore, MD, Nov. 21, 1954. m. actress Jessica Harper. e. Brown U., B.A. 1976; Columbia Law Sch., J.D. 1980. Worked as law clerk with Second Circuit Court of Appeals 1981-82 before becoming partner at entertainment law firm, Frankfurt Garbus Klein & Selz 1982-87; exec. v.p. of production, Columbia Pictures; president of worldwide production, Samuel Goldwyn Co.; founder and president, Fox Searchlight Pictures; president of production, Twentieth Century Fox, 1995. Currently president, Twentieth Century Fox Film Group; member, Board of Directors, Sundance Institute; recipient, Arthur B. Krim Award, Columbia U.
PICTURES: Co-prod.: Down By Law, Candy Mountain. Exec. Prod.: The Program.

ROTUNNO, GIUSEPPE
Cinematographer. b. Rome, Italy, March 19, 1923. Gained fame as leading cinematographer of Italian films working with Federico Fellini. Later worked in Hollywood.
PICTURES: Tosca, Monte Carlo Story, White Nights, The Naked Maja, On the Beach, Fast and Sexy, The Angel Wore Red, Five Branded Women, Rocco and His Brothers, Boccaccio '70, The Leopard, The Organizer, Juliet of the Spirits, The Bible, Anizo, Candy, Spirits of the Dead, Fellini Satyricon, The Secret of Santa Vittoria, Carnal Knowledge, Fellini's Roma, Man of La Mancha, Amarcord, Love and Anarchy, Fellini's Casanova, All Screwed Up, End of the World in Our Usual Bed in a Night Full of Rain, Orchestra Rehearsal, All That Jazz, City of Women, Popeye, Rollover, Five Days One Summer, And the Ship Sails On, American Dreamer, Desire, Nothing Left to Do But Cry, The Red Sonja, Hotel Colonial, Julia and Julia, Rent-a-Cop, Rebus, Haunted Summer, The Adventures of Baron Munchausen, Regarding Henry, Once Upon a Crime, Wolf, The Night the Moment, Sabrina, La Sindrome di Stendhal, Marcello Mastroianni: I Remember.
TELEVISION: The Scarlet and the Black.

ROUNDTREE, RICHARD
Actor. b. New Rochelle, NY, July 9, 1942. e. Southern Illinos U. Former model, Ebony Magazine Fashion Fair; joined workshop of Negro Ensemble Company, appeared in Kongi's Harvest, Man Better Man, Mau Mau Room; played lead role in Philadelphia road company of The Great White Hope before film debut.
PICTURES: What Do You Say to a Naked Lady? (debut, 1970), Shaft, Embassy, Charley One-Eye, Shaft's Big Score, Embassy, Shaft in Africa, Earthquake, Diamonds, Man Friday, Portrait of a Hitman, Escape to Athena, Game for Vultures, An Eye for an Eye, Inchon, Q, One Down Two to Go, The Big Score, Young Warriors, Killpoint, City Heat, Opposing Force, Jocks, Maniac Cop, Homer and Eddie, Angel III: The Final Chapter, The Party Line, Getting Even, American Cops, The Banker, Night Visitor, Crack House, Bad Jim, Lost Memories, Body of Influence, Deadly Rivals, Amityville: A New Generation, Gypsy Angels, Mind Twister, Seven, Once Upon A Time...When We Were Colored, Theodore Rex, Original Gangstas, George of the Jungle, Steel, Shaft, Hawaiian Gardens, Antitrust, Shoot!, Corkey Romano, Al's Lads, Boat Trip.
TELEVISION: Series: Shaft, Outlaws, Cop Files (host), 413 Hope St. Movies: Firehouse, The Fifth Missile, Christmas in Connecticut, Bonanza: The Return, Shadows of Desire, Bonanza: Under Attack, Buddies, 413 Hope St., Any Place but

Home, Rescue 77, Y2K: A World in Crisis, Joe and Max, As the World Turns. *Mini-Series*: Roots, A.D.

ROURKE, MICKEY
Actor. b. Schenectady, NY, Sept. 16, 1956. Moved to Miami as a boy. Fought as an amateur boxer 4 years in Miami. Studied acting with Sandra Seacat while working as a nightclub bouncer, a sidewalk pretzel vendor and other odd jobs. Moved to LA, 1978. Debut: TV movie City in Fear (1978).
PICTURES: 1941 (debut, 1979), Fade to Black, Heaven's Gate, Body Heat, Diner (Natl. Society of Film Critics Award, 1982), Rumblefish, Eureka, The Pope of Greenwich Village, Year of the Dragon, 9-1/2 Weeks, Angel Heart, A Prayer for the Dying, Barfly, Homeboy (also wrote orig. story), Francesco, Johnny Handsome, Wild Orchid, Desperate Hours, Harley Davidson and the Marlboro Man, White Sands, F.T.W., Fall Time, Double Team, Another 9-1/2 Weeks, The Rainmaker, Buffalo 66, Thursday, Shades, Out in Fifty, Animal Factory, Get Carter, The Pledge, The Follow, Picture Claire, Spun, Once Upon a Time in Mexico, Masked & Anonymous.
TELEVISION: *Movies*: City in Fear, Rape and Marriage: The Rideout Case, Act of Love, The Last Outlaw, Thicker than Blood.

ROUSSELOT, PHILIPPE
Cinematographer. b. Meurthe-et-Moselle, France, 1945. e. Vaugirard Film Sch., Paris. Worked as camera assistant to Nestor Almendros on My Night at Maud's, Claire's Knee, Love in the Afternoon.
PICTURES: The Guinea Pig Couple, Adom ou le sang d'Abel, Paradiso, Pauline et l'ordinateur, Peppermint Soda, For Clemence, Cocktail Molotov, La Provinciale, A Girl From Lorraine, Diva (Cesar, Natl. Society of Film Critics, and Moscow Awards), The Jaws of the Wolf, The Moon in the Gutter, Thieves After Dark, The Emerald Forest, Therese (Cesar Award), Hope and Glory, Dangerous Liaisons, The Bear, We're No Angels, Too Beautiful for You, Henry and June, A River Runs Through It (Academy Award, 1992), Sommersby, Interview With the Vampire, Queen Margot, Mary Reilly, The People vs. Larry Flynt, Instinct, Random Hearts, Remember the Titans, The Tailor of Panama, Planet of the Apes, Antwone Fisher, Big Fish.

ROWLANDS, GENA
Actress. r.n. Virginia Cathryn Rowlands. b. Cambria, WI, June 19, 1934. e. U. of Wisconsin. Son is actor Nicholas Cassavetes. Came to New York to attend American Acad. of Dramatic Arts, where she met and married John Cassavetes. Made B'way debut as understudy and then succeeded to role of The Girl in The Seven Year Itch. Launched as star with part in The Middle of the Night, which she played 18 mos.
PICTURES: The High Cost of Loving (debut, 1958), Lonely Are the Brave, The Spiral Road, A Child Is Waiting, Tony Rome, Faces, Machine Gun McCain, Minnie and Moskowitz, A Woman Under the Influence (Acad. Award nom.), Two Minute Warning, The Brink's Job, Opening Night, Gloria (Acad. Award nom.), Tempest, Love Streams, Light of Day, Another Woman, Once Around, Ted and Venus, Night on Earth, The Neon Bible, Something to Talk About, Unhook The Stars, She's So Lovely, Playing by Heart, The Mighty, Paulie, Hope Floats, The Weekend, The Incredible Mrs. Ritchie.
TELEVISION: *Movies*: A Question of Love, Strangers: The Story of a Mother & Daughter, Thursday's Child, An Early Frost, The Betty Ford Story (Emmy Award, 1987), Montana, Face of a Stranger (Emmy Award, 1992), Crazy in Love, Silent Cries, Parallel Lives, Best Friends for Life, Grace and Glorie, Charms for the Easy Life, Hysterical Blindness. *Guest*: The Philco TV Playhouse, Studio One, Alfred Hitchcock Presents, Dr. Kildare, Bonanza, The Kraft Mystery Theatre, Columbo. *Series*: Top Secret USA, 87th Precinct, Peyton Place.

ROWLEY, JOHN H.
Executive. b. San Angelo, TX, Oct. 6, 1917. e. U. of TX, 1935-39. Past pres., NATO of Texas; past Int'l Chief barker, Variety Clubs Int'l; past pres., TOA. Currently exec. dir. NATO of TX.

ROY, DEEP
Actor, Stunts.
PICTURES: Greystoke: The Legend of Tarzan, Lord of the Apes, Poltergeist II: The Other Side, Hook, Leprechaun, The Little Rascals, New Nightmare, The War, Sudden Death, Matilda, BASEketball, How the Grinch Stole Christmas, Planet of the Apes, A Man Apart.
TELEVISION: Desperado: The Outlaw Wars (actor), Evil Has a Face.

RUBEN, JOSEPH
Director. b. Briarcliff, NY, 1951. e. U. of Michigan, majoring in theater and film; Brandeis U., B.A. Interest in film began in high sch. Bought a Super-8 camera and filmed his first movie, a teenage love story. First feature, The Sister-in-Law, a low budget feature which he wrote and dir. in 1975.
PICTURES: *Dir./Writer*: The Sister-in-Law (also prod.), The Pom-Pom Girls (also prod.), Joy Ride, Our Winning Season. *Dir.*: G.O.R.P., Dreamscape (also co-s.p.), The Stepfather, True Believer, Sleeping With the Enemy, The Good Son, Money Train, Return to Paradise.
TELEVISION: Breaking Away (pilot), Eddie Dodd.

RUBIN, STANLEY
Producer, Writer. b. New York, NY, Oct. 8, 1917; ed. UCLA, 1933-37. Phi Beta Kappa. Writer for radio, magazines, pictures, 1937-41; U.S. Army Air Force, 1942-45; writer, prod., owner, Your Show Time, Story Theatre TV series; winner of 1st Emmy awarded to filmed series: The Necklace, 1949. Producer, RKO, 20th-Fox, U.I., MGM, Paramount, Rastar.
PICTURES: The Narrow Margin, My Pal Gus, Destination Gobi, River of No Return, Destry, Francis in the Navy, Behind the High Wall, Rawhide Years, The Girl Most Likely, Promise Her Anything, The President's Analyst, Revenge, Black Heart.
TELEVISION: G.E. Theatre, Ghost and Mrs. Muir, Bracken's World, The Man and the City, Executive Suite. *Movies*: Babe (co-prod.; Golden Globe Award) and Your Name is Jonah, Don't Look Back: The Story of Satchel Page (Image Award), Escape From Iran: The Canadian Caper (exec. prod.).

RUBINEK, SAUL
Actor. b. Fohrenwold, Germany, July 2, 1948. Family moved to Canada when he was a baby. Acting debut at age 8 with local theatre groups. Founding member of the Toronto Free Stage Theatre.
PICTURES: Nothing Personal, Highpoint, Agency, Death Ship, Ticket to Heaven, Soup for One, Young Doctors in Love, By Design, Against All Odds, Martin's Day, Sweet Liberty, Taking Care, Wall Street, Obsessed, The Outside Chance of Maximillian Glick, The Bonfire of the Vanities, Man Trouble, Unforgiven, The Quarrel, True Romance, Undercover Blues, Death Wish V, Getting Even With Dad, I Love Trouble, Open Season, Nixon, Past Perfect, Bad Manners, Dick, The Contender, The Family Man, Lakeboat, Rush Hour 2, Fairy Fellar, Triggermen.
TELEVISION: Concealed Enemies, The Terry Fox Story, Clown White, Interrogation in Budapest, Woman on the Run, And the Band Played On, The Android Affair, Color of Justice, John Woo's Blackjack, 36 Hours to Die, Golden Spiders, The Bookfair Mystery, Laughter on the 23rd Floor, A Nero Wolfe Mystery, Gleason, The Brady Bunch in the White House, Coast to Coast.

RUBINSTEIN, JOHN
Actor, Composer, Director. b. Los Angeles, CA, December 8, 1946. Son of concert pianist Arthur Rubinstein and dancer-writer Aniela Rubinstein. e. UCLA.
THEATRE: Pippin (NY debut, 1972; Theatre World Award), Picture (Mark Taper, LA), Children of a Lesser God (Tony Award, Drama Desk, L.A. Drama Critics Awards, 1980), Fools, The Caine Mutiny Court-Martial, M. Butterfly, Kiss of the Spider Woman, Love Letters, Hurlyburly, Getting Away With Murder, Camelot, Ragtime, On A Clear Day You Can See Forever, Counsellor-at-Law (also dir; Drama-Logue, Ovation, L.A. Drama Critics Awards, 1995), Into the Woods (also dir.), Merrily We Roll Along, Streamers, The Tempest, Candida, Arms and the Man, Three Hotels, Broken Glass, Sight Unseen. *Director*: The Rover, Les Liaisons Dangereuses, Phantasie, Nightingale, The Old Boy, She Loves Me.
PICTURES: Journey to Shiloh (debut, 1968), The Trouble With Girls, Getting Straight, The Wild Pack, Zachariah, The Car, The Boys From Brazil, In Search of Historic Jesus, Daniel, Someone to Watch Over Me, Another Stakeout, Mercy, Kid Cop, Red Dragon.
TELEVISION: *Series*: Family, Crazy Like a Fox. *Guest*: The Virginian, Ironside, Dragnet, Room 222, The Psychiatrist, The Mary Tyler Moore Show, Cannon, The Mod Squad, Nichols, Hawaii Five-O, Barnaby Jones, Policewoman, Barbary Coast, The Rookies, The Streets of San Francisco, Harry O, Vegas, The Class of '65, Movin' On, Stop the Presses, Wonder Woman, Lou Grant, Fantasy Island, The Quest, Quincy, Trapper John M.D., The Love Boat, Father Dowling, The Paper Chase, Murder She Wrote, Against the Grain, Frasier, Jake and the Fatman, Hotel, Matlock, Highway to Heaven, NYPD Blue, Lois and Clark, Party of Five, Diagnosis Murder, Star Trek: Voyager, Early Edition, E.R., Robocop. *Special*: Triple Play—Sam Found Out. *Movies*: The Marriage Proposal, God Bless the Children, A Howling in the Woods, Something Evil, All Together Now, The Gift of the Magi, Roots: The Next Generations, Just Make Me an Offer, The French Atlantic Affair, Corey: For the People, Happily Ever After, Moviola, Skokie, The Mr. and Ms. Mysteries, Killjoy, Freedom to Speak, Someone's Killing the High Fashion Models; I Take These Men, M.A.D.D.: Mothers Against Drunk Driving, Liberace, Voices Within: The Lives of Truddi Chase, In My Daughter's Name, The American Clock, Perry Mason, Norma and Marilyn, The Sleepwalker Killing, Perfect Murder, Perfect Town: JonBenét and the City of Boulder. *Director*: A Matter of Conscience, Summer Stories: The Mall, High Tide.
SCORES: *Films*: Paddy, Jeremiah Johnson, The Candidate, Kid Blue, The Killer Inside Me. *Television*: All Together Now, Emily, Emily, Stalk the Wild Child, Champions: A Love Story, To Race the Wind, The Ordeal of Patty Hearst, Amber Waves, Johnny Belinda, Secrets of a Mother and Daughter, Choices of the Heart, The Dollmaker, Family (Emmy nom.), The Fitzpatricks, The Mackenzies of Paradise Cove, The New Land, For Heaven's Sake, The Lazarus Syndrome, The City Killer, China Beach, A Walton Wedding.

RUBINSTEIN, RICHARD P.
Producer, Executive. b. New York, NY, June 15, 1947. e. American U. B.S. 1969, Columbia U. MBA 1971. Pres. & CEO, New Amsterdam Entertainment, Inc.
PICTURES: Martin, Dawn Of The Dead, Knightriders, Creepshow, Day Of The Dead, Creepshow 2, Pet Sematary, Tales From the Darkside: The Movie, Stephen King's The Night Flier.
TELEVISION: *Exec. Prod.: Series*: Tales From the Darkside, Monsters, Stephen King's Golden Years. *Mini-Series*: Stephen King's The Stand. *Movies*: The Vernon Johns Story, Precious Victims., Dune, Children of Dune.

RUDDY, ALBERT S.
Producer. b. Montreal, Canada, March 28, 1934. e. U. of Southern California, B.S. in design, Sch. of Architecture, 1956. Exec. prod. of 1991 TV movie Miracle in the Wilderness.
PICTURES: The Wild Seed, Little Fauss & Big Halsey, Making It, The Godfather, The Longest Yard, Coonskin, Matilda, The Cannonball Run, Megaforce, Lassiter, Cannonball Run II, Farewell to the King, Paramedics, Speed Zone, Impulse, Ladybugs, Bad Girls, The Scout, Heaven's Prisoners, Mean Machine.
TELEVISION: *Series*: Walker—Texas Ranger. *Movies*: Miracle in the Wilderness, Staying Afloat, Married to a Stranger, Running Mates, Atlas Shrugged.

RUDIE, EVELYN
Actress, Singer, Songwriter. r.n. Evelyn Rudie Bernauer, b. Hollywood, Calif. March 28. e. Hollywood H.S., UCLA. At 19, after childstar career in TV and films, stage debut at Gallery Theatre in Hollywood as songwriter, musical dir., choreographer and star performer: Ostrogoths and King of the Schnorrers. Currently producer, artistic dir., Santa Monica Playhouse; founder of own repertoire co. Received Emmy Nomination for first TV leading role, Eloise, Playhouse 90, 1956. Filmdom's Famous Fives critics award, 1958. Star on Hollywood's Walk of Fame.
PICTURES: Daddy Long Legs (debut, 1955). The Wings of Eagles, Gift of Love, Bye Bye Birdie.
TELEVISION: Hostess with the Mostess, Playhouse 90, Dinah Shore, Red Skelton Show, George Gobel Show, Omnibus, Matinee Theatre, Hitchcock Presents, Gale Storm Show, Jack Paar, Wagon Train, G.E. Theatre, 77 Sunset Strip.

RUDIN, SCOTT
Executive. b. New York, NY, July 14, 1958. Began career as prod. asst. on B'way for producers Kermit Bloomgarden, Robert Whitehead; then casting director. 1984, became producer for 20th Century Fox; named exec. v.p. prod.; 1986, appt. pres. prod., 20th-Fox. Resigned 1987 becoming independent producer.
PICTURES: *Prod.*: I'm Dancing as Fast as I Can, Reckless, Mrs. Soffel, Flatliners (exec. prod.), Pacific Heights, Regarding Henry, Little Man Tate, The Addams Family, White Sands, Sister Act, Jennifer Eight, Life With Mikey, The Firm, Searching for Bobby Fisher, Addams Family Values, Sister Act 2: Back in the Habit, Nobody's Fool, I.Q., Clueless, Sabrina, Up Close and Personal, Marvin's Room, In & Out, The Truman Show, Civil Action, Southpark:Bigger, Longer and Uncut,Bringing Out the Dead, Angela's Ashes, Wonder Boys, Rules of Engagement, Shaft, Brokeback Mountain, Zoolander, The Royal Tennenbaums, Iris, Orange County, Changing Lanes, Marci X, The Hours.
TELEVISION: Little Gloria... Happy at Last (exec. prod.).

RUDNER, RITA
Actress, Writer. b. Miami, FL, Sept. 17, 1956. m. producer Martin Bergman. Was stage dancer then stand-up comic. Author: Naked Beneath My Clothes, Rita Rudner's Guide to Men.
THEATRE: Annie (B'way), Promises Promises, Follies, Mack and Mabel.
PICTURES: The Wrong Guys (debut, 1988), Gleaming the Cube, That's Adequate, Peter's Friends (also co-s.p.), A Weekend in the Country (also s.p.).
TELEVISION: *Series*: George Schlatter's Funny People (co-host). *Specials*: Women of the Night, One Night Stand: Rita Rudner, Rita Rudner: Born to Be Mild, The Rita Rudner Comedy Specials (also writer), Comic Relief, Rita Rudner: Married Without Children.

RUDOLPH, ALAN
Director, Writer. b. Los Angeles, CA, Dec. 18, 1943. Son of Oscar Rudolph, TV director of '50s and '60s. Made his screen debut in his father's The Rocket Man (1954). Began in industry doing odd jobs in Hollywood studios. 1969 accepted for Directors Guild assistant director's training program. Worked with Robert Altman as asst. dir. on California Split, The Long Goodbye and Nashville and co-writer on Buffalo Bill and the Indians.
PICTURES: *Director*: Welcome to L.A. (debut, 1977; also s.p.), Remember My Name (also s.p.), Roadie (also story), Endangered Species (also co-s.p.), Return Engagement, Songwriter, Choose Me (also s.p.), Trouble in Mind (also s.p.), Made in Heaven, The Moderns (also co-s.p.), Love at Large (also s.p.), Mortal Thoughts, The Player (actor only), Equinox (also s.p.), Mrs. Parker and the Vicious Circle (also co-s.p.), Afterglow, Trixie (also s.p.), Breakfast of Champions (also s.p.), Investigating Sex, The Secret Lives of Dentists.

RUEHL, MERCEDES
Actress. b. Queens, NY, Feb.28, 1950. Raised in Silver Spring, MD. e. College of New Rochelle, B.A. English lit. Worked for years in regional theater, mostly in classics.
THEATRE: *B'way*: I'm Not Rappaport, Lost in Yonkers (Tony Award, 1991), The Shadow Box, The Rose Tattoo. *Off-B'way*: American Notes, The Marriage of Bette and Boo (Obie Award), Coming of Age in Soho, Other People's Money.
PICTURES: The Warriors (debut, 1979), Four Friends, Heartburn, Radio Days, 84 Charing Cross Road, The Secret of My Success, Leader of the Band, Big, Married to the Mob, Slaves of New York, Crazy People, Another You, The Fisher King (Acad. Award, best supporting actress, 1991), Lost in Yonkers, Last Action Hero, Roseanna's Grave, Spooky House, Out of the Cold, The Minus Man, The Amati Girls, What's Cooking?.
TELEVISION: *Movie*: Indictment: The McMartin Trial, Gia, Subway Stories: Tales from the Underground, Widows, Guilt By Association, The Lost Child, The Mary Kay Letourneau Story: All-American Girl, North Shore Fish. *Pilot*: Late Bloomer. *Guest*: Our Family Honor, Frasier. *Special*: On Hope.

RUGOLO, PETE
Composer, Arranger. b. Sicily, Italy, Dec. 25, 1915. To U.S., 1919. e. San Francisco State Coll., Mills Coll., Oakland. Armed Forces, 1942-46; pianist, arr. for many orch. including Stan Kenton. Conductor and arrang. for Nat King Cole, Peggy Lee, Harry Belafonte, many others. Received 3 Emmy Awards.
PICTURES: The Strip, Skirts Ahoy, Glory Alley, Latin Lovers, Easy to Love, Jack the Ripper, Foxtrot, Buddy Buddy, Chu Chu and the Philly Flash.
TELEVISION: Richard Diamond, The Thin Man, Thriller, The Fugitive, Run for Your Life, The Bold Ones, Leave It to Beaver, more than 25 movies.

RUIZ-ANCHIA, JUAN
Cinematographer. b. Bilbao, Spain, 1949. e. Escuela Official de Cinematografica, 1972. Worked on such Spanish prods. as 19/19, Cornica del Alba, Odd and Even, Soldier of Metal. Moved to L.A. Granted 2 yr. fellowship at American Film Inst. from which he graduated in 1981. First U.S. prod. was Reborn, 1982.
PICTURES: The Stone Boy, That Was Then This Is Now, Maria's Lovers, At Close Range, Where the River Runs Black, House of Games, Surrender, The Seventh Sign, Things Change, Lost Angels, The Last of the Finest, Dying Young, Naked Tango, Liebstraum, Glengarry Glen Ross, A Far Off Place, Mr. Jones, The Jungle Book, Two Bits, The Adventures of Pinocchio, Lorca, Mararia, The Corrupter, The Crew, New Port South, Focus, No Good Deed, Confidence, Spartan.

RULE, JANICE
Actress. b. Cincinnati, OH, Aug. 15, 1931. e. Wheaton & Glenbard H.S., Glen Ellyn, IL. Received Phd in Clinical & Research Psychoanalysis, 1983. Dancer 4 yrs. in Chicago & New York nightclubs; stage experience in It's Great To Be Alive, as understudy of Bambi Lynn.
THEATRE: Miss Liberty, Picnic (B'way debut, 1953), The Happiest Girl in the World.
PICTURES: Goodbye My Fancy (debut, 1951), Starlift, Holiday for Sinners, Rogue's March, A Woman's Devotion, Gun for a Coward, Bell Book and Candle, The Subterraneans, Invitation to a Gunfighter, The Chase, Alvarez Kelly, Welcome to Hard Times, The Swimmer, The Ambushers, Doctors' Wives, Gumshoe, Kid Blue, 3 Women, Missing, Rainy Day Friends, American Flyers.
TELEVISION: *Movies*: Shadow on the Land, Trial Run, The Devil and Miss Sarah, The Word.

RUSH, BARBARA
Actress. b. Denver, CO, Jan. 4, 1927. e. U. of CA. First stage appearance at age of ten, Loberto Theatre, Santa Barbara, CA, in fantasy, Golden Ball; won acting award in college for characterization of Birdie (The Little Foxes); scholarship, Pasadena Playhouse Theatre Arts Coll.
THEATRE: A Woman of Independent Means, 40 Carats, Same Time Next Year, Steel Magnolias, The Golden Age.
PICTURES: Molly (debut, 1950), The First Legion, Quebec, When Worlds Collide, Flaming Feather, Prince of Pirates, It Came From Outer Space, Taza—Son of Cochise, The Magnificent Obsession, The Black Shield of Falworth, Captain Lightfoot, Kiss of Fire, World in My Corner, Bigger Than Life, Flight to Hong Kong, Oh Men! Oh Women!, No Down Payment, The Young Lions, Harry Black and the Tiger, The Young Philadelphians, The Bramble Bush, Strangers When We Meet, Come Blow Your Horn, Robin and the 7 Hoods, Hombre, The Man, Superdad, Can't Stop the Music, Summer Lovers, Gatta alla pari.
TELEVISION: *Series*: Saints and Sinners, Peyton Place, The New Dick Van Dyke Show, Flamingo Road, 7th Heaven. *Movies*: Suddenly Single, Cutter, Eyes of Charles Sand, Moon of the Wolf, Crime Club, The Last Day, Death on the Freeway, The Seekers, Flamingo Road (pilot), The Night the Bridge Fell Down, The Widow's Kiss, Web of Deceit.

RUSH, GEOFFREY
Actor. b. Toowomba, Queensland, Australia, July 6,1951. 1996 Acad. Award winner for performance in Shine.
PICTURES: Hoodwink, Starstruck, Twelfth Night, Dad and Dave: On Our Selection, Call Me Sal, Shine (Acad. Award, 1996; Golden Globe), Children of the Revolution, Les Miserables, A Little Bit of Soul, Oscar and Lucinda, Shakespeare in Love (Acad. Award nom.), Elizabeth, Mystery Men, The House on Haunted Hill, Quills, The Magic Pudding (voice), The Tailor of Panama, Lantana, Frida, The Banger Sisters, The Assumption of the Virgin, Swimming Upstream, Finding Nemo, Ned Kelly, Intolerable Cruelty, The Assumption, Pirates of the Caribbean: The Curse of the Black Pearl.

RUSH, HERMAN
Executive. b. Philadelphia, PA, June 20, 1929. e. Temple U., Sales mgr., Official Films Inc., 1952-57. Headed Flamingo Telefilms, Inc. 1957-60; 1960-71, pres., tv div. of Creative Mgt. Assoc.; pres., Herman Rush Assoc. Inc., 1971-77; 1977-78 chmn. bd., Rush-Flaherty Agency, Inc.; 1970 headed Marble Arch TV; 1980 named pres., Columbia TV; 1984, pres. of newly formed Columbia Pictures TV Group; 1986, chmn. of newly formed Coca-Cola Telecommunications, Inc.; 1988, chmn., Rush Entertainment Group; 1989, became creative consultant for CBN Producers Group; 1992, Katz/Rush Ent., partner; co-founder, dir. of Transactional Media, Informercial and Transactional Program Production Co.; 1993-94 exec. prod., Willard Scott's New Original Amateur Hour; 1994-95, exec. prod. Susan Powter Show; exec. prod. of The Montel Williams Show.

RUSH, RICHARD
Director, Producer, Writer. b. New York, NY, 1930.
PICTURES: Director: Too Soon To Love (also prod., s.p.), Of Love and Desire (also prod., s.p.), A Man Called Dagger, Fickle Finger of Fate, Thunder Alley, Hell's Angels on Wheels, Psych-Out (also s.p.), Savage Seven, Getting Straight (also prod.), Freebie and the Bean (also prod.), The Stunt Man (also prod., s.p.; Acad. Award nom. for best dir., s.p.), Air America (co-s.p.), Color of Night.

RUSSELL, CHUCK
Director. Asst. dir., and line prod. on many low-budget films for Roger Corman and Sunn Classics, including Death Race 2000.
PICTURES: Dreamscape (co-s.p., line prod.), Back to School (prod.), Nightmare on Elm Street III (dir., co-s.p.), The Blob (dir., co-s.p.), The Mask, Eraser,Bless the Child, The Scorpion King.
TELEVISION: Black Cat Run.

RUSSELL, DAVID O.
Director, Writer. b. New York, NY, August 20, 1958
PICTURES: Spanking the Monkey (also exec. prod.), Flirting with Disaster, Three Kings, The Slaughter Rule (prod. only), Adaptation (actor only).

RUSSELL, JANE
Actress. r.n. Ernestine Jane Russell. b. Bemidji, MN, June 21, 1921. e. Max Reinhardt's Theatrical Workshop & Mme. Ouspenskaya. Photographer's model.
PICTURES: The Outlaw (debut, 1943), Young Widow, The Paleface, His Kind of Woman, Double Dynamite, Macao, Son of Paleface, Montana Belle, Las Vegas Story, Road to Bali (cameo), Gentlemen Prefer Blondes, The French Line, Underwater, Gentlemen Marry Brunettes, Foxfire, Tall Men, Hot Blood, The Revolt of Mamie Stover, The Fuzzy Pink Nightgown, Fate Is the Hunter, Waco, Johnny Reno, Born Losers, Darker Than Amber, L.A. Confidential.
TELEVISION: Series: Yellow Rose.

RUSSELL, KEN
Director, Producer, Writer. b. Southampton, England, July 3, 1927. e. Walthamstow Art Sch. Early career as dancer, actor, stills photographer, TV documentarian. Ent. TV ind. 1959. Made 33 documentaries for BBC-TV. Also made numerous pop videos.
PICTURES: French Dressing, Billion Dollar Brain, Women in Love, The Music Lovers (also prod.), The Devils (also prod., s.p.), The Boy Friend (also prod., s.p.), Savage Messiah (also prod.), Mahler (also s.p.), Tommy (also prod., s.p.), Lisztomania (also s.p.), Valentino, Altered States, Crimes of Passion, Gothic, Aria (sequence), Salome's Last Dance (also s.p., actor), The Lair of the White Worm (also prod., s.p.), The Rainbow (also prod., co-s.p.), The Russia House (actor only), Whore (also s.p.), Mindbender, Lion's Mouth, The Fall of the House of Usher, Pretty Boy Floyd, Charged: The Life of Nikola Tesla.
TELEVISION: The Secret Life of Sir Arnold Box, Lady Chatterly's Lover, Portrait of a Soviet Composer, Elgar, A House in Bayswater, Always on Sunday, The Debussy Film, Isadora Duncan, Dantes Inferno, Song of Summer—Delius, Dance of the Seven Veils. HBO: Dust Before Fireworks, Prisoner of Honor, Dogboys.

RUSSELL, KERI
Actress. b. Fountain Valley, CA, March 23, 1976.
PICTURES: Honey I Blew Up the Kid, Eight Days a Week, The Curve, Mad About Mambo, We Were Soldiers.
TELEVISION: Movies: The Babysitter's Seduction, The Lottery,

When Innocence Is Lost. Series: The Mickey Mouse Club, Emerald Cove, Daddy's Girls, Malibu Shores, Roar, Felicity. Guest: Boy Meets World, Married...with Children, 7th Heaven, Cinderelmo.

RUSSELL, KURT
Actor. b. Springfield, MA, March 17, 1951. Son of former base-ball player-turned-actor Bing Russell (deputy sheriff on Bonanza). At 12 got lead in tv series The Travels of Jamie McPheeters (1963-64). Starred as child in many Disney shows and films. Professional baseball player 1971-73. Host, Kurt Russell Celebrity Shoot Out, 4-day hunting tournament.
PICTURES: It Happened at the World's Fair (debut, 1963), Follow Me Boys, The One and Only Genuine Original Family Band, The Horse in the Grey Flannel Suit, The Computer Wore Tennis Shoes, The Barefoot Executive, Fools' Parade, Now You See Him Now You Don't, Charley and the Angel, Superdad, The Strongest Man in the World, Used Cars, Escape from New York, The Fox and The Hound (voice), The Thing, Silkwood, Swing Shift, The Mean Season, The Best of Times, Big Trouble in Little China, Overboard, Tequila Sunrise, Winter People, Tango and Cash, Backdraft, Unlawful Entry, Captain Ron, Tombstone, StarGate, Executive Decision, Escape From L.A., Breakdown, Soldier, 3000 Miles to Graceland, Vanilla Sky, The Plague Season, Interstate 60, Dark Blue.
TELEVISION: Series: The Travels of Jamie McPheeters, The New Land, The Quest. Movies: Search for the Gods, The Deadly Tower, The Quest (pilot), Christmas Miracle in Caulfield U.S.A., Elvis, Amber Waves. Guest: The Fugitive, Daniel Boone, Gilligan's Island, Lost in Space, The F.B.I., Love American Style, Gunsmoke, Hawaii Five-O.

RUSSELL, THERESA
Actress. r.n. Theresa Paup. b. San Diego, CA, Mar. 20, 1957. m. dir.-cinematographer Nicolas Roeg. e. Burbank H.S. Began mod-eling career at 12. Studied at Actors' Studio in Hollywood.
PICTURES: The Last Tycoon (debut, 1976), Straight Time, Bad Timing/A Sensual Obsession, Eureka, The Razor's Edge, Insignificance, Black Widow, Aria, Track 29, Physical Evidence, Impulse, Whore, Kafka, Cold Heaven, The Grotesque, Trade Off,The Spy Within, EroticTales II, Wild Things, Running Woman, Luckytown Blues, The Believer, Passionada, Now and Forever, The House Next Door, Project V.I.P.E.R., Searching for Debra Winger, Passionada, Now and Forever, Destiny.
TELEVISION: Mini-Series: Blind Ambition. Movie: Thicker Than Water, Flight of the Dove, The Trade Off, The Proposition, Woman's Guide to Adultery, Hotel Paradise, When You Meet a Stranger, Public Enemy, Earth vs. the Spider, Love Comes Softly. Series: Glory Days.

RUSSO, JAMES
Actor. b. New York, NY, Apr. 23, 1953. e. NYU, where he wrote and starred in prize-winning short film Candy Store.
THEATRE: NY: Welcome to Andromeda, Deathwatch, Marat/Sade, Extremities (Theatre World Award).
PICTURES: A Strange Is Watching (debut, 1982), Fast Times at Ridgemont High, Vortex, Exposed, Once Upon a Time in America, Beverly Hills Cop, The Cotton Club, Extremities, China Girl, The Blue Iguana, Freeway, We're No Angels, State of Grace, A Kiss Before Dying, My Own Private Idaho, Cold Heaven, Dangerous Game, Bad Girls, Donnie Brasco, The Postman, Felons, Detour, Sonic Impact, Jimmy Zip, The Ninth Gate, Diamonds, The Unscarred, Sonic Impact, Paper Bullets, Deep Core, Pendulum, Shattered Lies, Microwave Park, The House Next Door, Double Deception, Stealing Sinatra, Redemption, Paris, My Daughter's Tears, Cold Day in August, Open Range, Firecracker.
TELEVISION: Movie: The Secretary, The Hidden War.

RUSSO, RENE
Actress. b. California, Feb. 17, 1955. Raised in Burbank. Worked as top fashion model for Eileen Ford Agency prior to acting.
PICTURES: Major League (debut, 1989), Mr. Destiny, One Good Cop, Freejack, Lethal Weapon 3, In the Line of Fire, Outbreak, Get Shorty, Tin Cup, Ransom, Buddy, Lethal Weapon 4, The Thomas Crown Affair, The Adventures of Rocky and Bullwinkle, Big Trouble, Showtime.
TELEVISION: Series: Sable.

RUTHERFORD, ANN
Actress. b. Toronto, Canada, Nov. 2, 1920. Trained by mother (cousin of Richard Mansfield); with parents in stock as child; later on Los Angeles radio programs. Screen debut, 1935.
PICTURES: Waterfront Lady (debut, 1935), Judge Hardy's Children, Of Human Hearts, A Christmas Carol, You're Only Young Once, Dramatic School, Love Finds Andy Hardy, Out West With the Hardys, The Hardys Ride High, Four Girls in White, Dancing Co-Ed, Andy Hardy Gets Spring Fever, Gone With the Wind, These Glamour Girls, Judge Hardy and Son, Wyoming, Pride and Prejudice, The Ghost Comes Home, Andy Hardy Meets Debutante, Washington Melodrama, Life Begins for Andy Hardy, Badlands of Dakota, Andy Hardy's Private Secretary, Whistling in the Dark, Orchestra Wives, The Courtship of Andy Hardy, Whistling in Dixie, Andy Hardy's Double Life, This Time for Keeps, Happy Land, Whistling in Brooklyn, Bermuda Mystery,

Two O'Clock Courage, Bedside Manner, The Madonna's Secret, Murder in the Music Hall, Inside Job, The Secret Life of Walter Mitty, Operation Haylift, Adventures of Don Juan, They Only Kill Their Masters, Won Ton Ton the Dog Who Saved Hollywood.

RYAN, ARTHUR N.
Executive. Joined Paramount in N.Y. in 1967 as asst. treas; later made dir. of admin. and business affairs, exec. asst. to Robert Evans and asst. scty. 1970 appt. v.p.-prod. adm. 1975 named sr. v.p. handling all prod. operations for Paramount's m.p. and TV divisions; 1976, asst. to the chmn. & CEO; chmn. & pres. Magicam, Inc.; chmn. Fortune General Corp.; chmn. Paramount Communications; co-chmn. of scholarship comm. of AMPAS; trustee of Univ. Film Study Center in Boston; joined Technicolor in 1976 as pres., COO & dir.; vice chmn., 1983-85; chmn. & CEO, 1985-; chmn. Technicolor Audio-Visual Systems International, Inc.; dir. Technicolor S.P.A.; dir. Technicolor, Film Intl.; and chmn. of exec. committee, Technicolor Graphics Services, Inc.; dir., Technicolor, Inc.; chmn., Technicolor Fotografica, S.A.; chmn. Technicolor Film Intl. Service Company, Inc.; dir. & deputy chmn. Technicolor Ltd.; chmn. & dir., The Vidtronics Company, Inc.; chmn. & CEO, Compact Video, Inc., 1984-; dir, Four Star Int'l., 1983-; dir., MacAndrews & Forbes, Inc. 1985-; Permanent charities committee of the Ent. Industry; Hollywood Canteen Foundations. Vice-chmn. & dir., Calif. Inst. of Arts. Trustee: Motion Picture & Television Fund. 1985 named chmn., Technicolor.

RYAN, JOHN
Actor. b. New York, NY, July 30, 1936. e. City Coll. of NY.
THEATRE: *NY:* Duet for Three, Sgt. Musgrave's Dance, Yerma, Nobody Hears a Broken Drum, The Love Suicide at Schofield Barracks, The Silent Partner, Twelve Angry Men, Medea.
PICTURES: The Tiger Makes Out (debut, 1967), A Lovely Way to Die, What's So Bad About Feeling Good?, Five Easy Pieces, The King of Marvin Gardens, The Legend of Nigger Charley, Cops and Robbers, Dillinger, Shamus, It's Alive, The Missouri Breaks, Futureworld, It Lives Again, The Last Flight of Noah's Ark, On the Nickel, The Postman Always Rings Twice, The Escape Artist, Breathless, The Right Stuff, The Cotton Club, Runaway Train, Avenging Force, Death Wish 4: The Crackdown, Delta Force II, Fatal Beauty, Three O'Clock High, Rent-a-Cop, Paramedics, City of Shadows, Best of the Best, White Sands, Hoffa, Star Time, Young Goodman Brown, Batman: Mask of the Phantasm (voice), Tall Tale, Bound.
TELEVISION: *Series:* Archer. *Guest:* M*A*S*H, Kojak, Starsky & Hutch, Matt Helm, Hart to Hart, Houston, Miami Vice. *Movies:* Target Risk, Death Scream, Kill Me If You Can, A Killing Affair, Houston: The Legend of Texas, Blood River, Shooting Stars.

RYAN, MEG
Actress. r.n. Margaret Mary Emily Anne Hyra. b. Bethel, CT, Nov. 19, 1961. e. NYU. While studying journalism at NYU, supported herself by making commercials. Auditioned for and won first prof. role as Candice Bergen's daughter in film Rich and Famous.
PICTURES: Rich and Famous (debut, 1981), Amityville 3-D, Top Gun, Armed and Dangerous, Innerspace, Promised Land, D.O.A., The Presidio, When Harry Met Sally, Joe Versus the Volcano, The Doors, Prelude to a Kiss, Sleepless in Seattle, Flesh & Bone, When a Man Loves a Woman, I.Q., French Kiss, Restoration, Courage Under Fire, Addicted to Love, Anastasia (voice), Hurlyburly, City of Angels, You've Got Mail, Hanging Up, Proof of Life, Kate and Leopold, Searching for Debra Winger, In the Cut, Against the Ropes.
TELEVISION: *Series:* One of the Boys, As the World Turns (1982-84), Wild Side (Disney TV).

RYAN, MITCHELL
Actor. b. Louisville, KY, Jan. 11, 1928. Entered acting following service in Navy during Korean War. Was New York stage actor working off-B'way for Ted Mann and Joseph Papp; on B'way in Wait Until Dark. Member of Arena Stage group in Washington.
PICTURES: Monte Walsh, The Hunting Party, My Old Man's Place, High Plains Drifter, The Friends of Eddie Coyle, ElectraGlide in Blue, Magnum Force, Labyrinth, Winter People.
TELEVISION: *Series:* Chase, Executive Suite, Having Babies, The Chisholms, Dark Shadows, High Performance, King Crossings. *Movies:* Angel City, The Five of Me, Death of a Centerfold—The Dorothy Stratten Story, Uncommon Valor, Medea, Kenny Rogers as the Gambler—The Adventure Continues, Robert Kennedy & His Times, Fatal Vision, Favorite Son, The Ryan White Story, Margaret Bourke-White.

RYDELL, MARK
Director, Producer, Actor. b. New York, NY March 23, 1934. e. Juilliard Sch. of Music. Studied acting with Sanford Meisner of NY Neighborhood Playhouse. Became member of Actors Studio. Was leading actor for six years on daytime CBS serial, As The World Turns. Made Broadway debut in Seagulls over Sorrento and film debut in Crime in the Streets. Went to Hollywood as TV director (Ben Casey, I Spy, Gunsmoke, etc.). Partner with Sydney Pollack in Sanford Prods., film, TV prod. co. Formed own production co., Concourse Productions.
PICTURES: *Director:* The Fox (debut, 1968), The Reivers, The Cowboys (also prod.), Cinderella Liberty (also prod.), Harry and Walter Go To New York, The Rose, On Golden Pond, The River, Man in the Moon (prod. only), For the Boys (also exec. prod.), Intersection (also co-prod.), Crime of the Century. *Actor:* Crime in the Streets, The Long Goodbye, Punchline, Havana, Hollywood Ending.

RYDER, WINONA
Actress. r.n. Winona Horowitz. b. Winona, MN, Oct. 29, 1971. Grew up in San Francisco. At 7, moved with family to Northern CA commune. At 13 discovered by talent scout during a performance at San Francisco's American Conservatory theatre, where she was studying, and given screen test.
PICTURES: Lucas (debut, 1986), Square Dance, Beetlejuice, 1969, Heathers, Great Balls of Fire, Welcome Home Roxy Carmichael, Edward Scissorhands, Mermaids, Night on Earth, Bram Stoker's Dracula, The Age of Innocence (Golden Globe Award; Acad. Award nom.), Reality Bites, The House of the Spirits, Little Women (Acad. Award nom.), How to Make an American Quilt, Boys, Looking for Richard, The Crucible, Alien: Resurrection, Just to Be Together, Celebrity, Lost Souls, Girl Interrupted (also exec. prod.), Autumn in New York, Mr. Deeds, Zoolander, Lily and the Secret Planting, Killing Mrs. Duke (exec.prod. only), S1m0ne.
TELEVISION: *Guest:* The Simpsons (voice), Dr. Katz, Professional Therapist, The Larry Sanders Show, Strangers with Candy, Friends, Saturday Night Live.

RYDSTROM, GARY
Sound.
PICTURES: Indiana Jones and the Temple of Doom, Cocoon, Luxo Jr., Red's Dream, Spaceballs, Tin Toy, Cocoon: The Return, Willow, Colors, Knickknack, Ghostbusters II, Always, Romero, The Hot Spot, Rush, Luxo Jr. in 'Surprise' and 'Light & Heavy,' Backdraft, Terminator 2: Judgment Day, F/X2, A River Runs Through It, Single White Female, Mrs. Doubtfire, Meteor Man, Jurassic Park, Quiz Show, Baby's Day Out, Casper, Strange Days, Toy Story, Jumanji, James and the Giant Peach, Mission: Impossible, Sleepers, Titanic (Acad. Award, Best Sound, 1997), Hercules, The Lost World: Jurassic Park, A Bug's Life, The Horse Whisperer, Saving Private Ryan, Reach the Rock, Rules of Engagement, The Haunting, Star Wars: Episode I-The Phantom Menace, Toy Story 2, It's Tough to be a Bug, The Yards, X-Men, The Legend of Bagger Vance, 102 Dalmatians, The Mexican, Atlantis: The Lost Empire, Artificial Intelligence, Monsters Inc., Star Wars Episode II: Attack of the Clones, Punch Drunk Love, Minority Report, Amandla: A Revolution in Four Part Harmony, Finding Nemo (voice), Hulk.

S

SACKHEIM, WILLIAM B.
Producer, Writer. b. Gloversville, NY, Oct. 31, 1921. e. UCLA.
PICTURES: The Art of Love, The In-Laws (co-prod.), The Competition, First Blood (co-s.p.), The Survivors (prod.), No Small Affair (prod.), The Hard Way (prod.), Pacific Heights (prod.), White Sands (prod.).
TELEVISION: The Law (Emmy Award, Peabody Award, 1975), Gideon Oliver (series, exec. prod.), Almost Grown (exec. prod.), The Antagonists (exec. prod.), The Human Factor (exec. prod.), The Harness (prod.), The Neon Ceiling (prod.), The Senator.

SACKS, SAMUEL
Attorney, Agent. b. New York, NY, March 29, 1908. e. CCNY, St. John's Law Sch., LL.B., 1930. Admitted Calif. Bar, 1943; priv. law practice, NY 1931-42; attorney, William Morris Agency, Inc., 1942; head of west coast TV business affairs, 1948-75; bd. of dir., Alliance of Television Film Producers, 1956-60; LA Copyright Society Treasurer, Beverly Hills Bar Assn., LA Bar Assn., American Bar Assn.; Academy of TV Arts & Sciences; Hollywood Radio & TV Society; counsel, entertainment field; Simon & Sheridan, 1975-89, Los Angeles Citizens' Olympic Committee; arbitrator for Screen Actors Guild, Assn. of Talent Agents and American Arbitration Assn.; bd. of dirs., Friars Club, 1991-95; Counsel for the Caucus for Producers, Writers & Directors, 1975-95.

SADLER, WILLIAM
Actor. b. Buffalo, NY, April 13, 1950. e. SUNY, Cornell U. Made stage debut in title role in Hamlet for Colorado Shakespeare Fest. Also acted with La Jolla Playhouse, Yale Rep.
THEATRE: *NY:* Ivanov (Off-B'way debut, 1975), Limbo Tales (Obie Award), Chinese Viewing Pavilion, Lennon, Necessary Ends, Hannah, Biloxi Blues (B'way debut, 1985; Clarence Derwent & Dramalogue Awards). *Regional:* Journey's End, A Mad World My Masters, Romeo and Juliet, Night Must Fall, etc.
PICTURES: Hanky Panky, Off Beat, Project X, K-9, Hard to Kill, Die Hard 2, The Hot Spot, Bill & Ted's Bogus Journey, Rush, Trespass, Freaked, The Shawshank Redemption, Tales From the Crypt Presents Demon Knight, Solo, Skippy, Rocket Man, Ambushed, Disturbing Behavior, Reach the Rock, The Green Mile, Stealth Fighter, Another Life, Cold Water, The Battle of Shaker Heights

TELEVISION: *Series:* Private Eye, Roswell. *Movies:* The Great Walendas, Charlie and the Great Balloon Race, Face of Fear, The Last to Go, Bermuda Grace, Witness Protection, Shawshank: The Redeeming Feature. *Guest:* Hooperman, Roseanne, Dear John, Gideon Oliver, The Equalizer, In the Heat of the Night, Tales From the Crypt, Murphy Brown.

SAFER, MORLEY
News Correspondent. b. Toronto, Ont., Nov. 8, 1931. e. U. of Western Ontario. Started as corresp. and prod. with Canadian Broadcasting Corp. Joined CBS News London Bureau 1964, chief of Saigon Bureau, 1965. Chief of CBS London bureau 1967-70. Joined 60 Minutes as co-editor in Dec., 1970.

SAFFLE, M. W. "BUD"
Executive. b. Spokane, WA, June 29, 1923. e. U. of Washington. In service 1943-46. Started in m.p. business as booker, 1948. Entire career with Saffle Theatre Service as buyer-booker; named pres. in 1970. Also pres. of Grays Harbor Theatres, Inc., operating theatres in Aberdeen, WA. Also operates drive-in in Centralia, WA. On bd. of NATO of WA for 15 yrs; pres. of same for 2 terms and secty.-treas. 6 yrs. Elected to National NATO bd. in 1972. Founder of Variety Tent 46, serving as chief barker three times.

SAGAL, KATEY
Actress. b. Los Angeles, CA, Nov. 18, 1953.
PICTURES: Maid to Order, The Good Mother, Dropping Out, Recess: Schools Out (voice).
TELEVISION: *Movies:* The Failing of Raymond, Mother Goose Rock 'n' Rhyme, She Says She's Innocent, Trail of Tears, Mr. Headmistress, Chance of a Lifetime, God's New Plan. *Series:* Mary, Married...with Children, Futurama (voice), Tucker, The Hank Azaria Show, Imagine That, 8 Simple Rules for Dating My Teenage Daughter. *Guest:* Tales from the Crypt, Duckman (voice), That '70s Show (voice).

SAGANSKY, JEFF
Executive. b. 1953. Joined CBS 1976 in bdcst. finance; 1977, NBC, assoc. in pgm. development.; 1977, mgr. film pgms.; 1978, dir. dramatic dev.; 1978, v.p., dev. David Gerber Co.; 1981, returned to NBC as series dev. v.p.; 1983, sr. v.p. series programming; 1985, joined Tri-Star Pictures as pres. of production; 1989 promoted to president of Tri-Star, later that year joined CBS as entertainment division president. Resigned, 1994.

SAGEBRECHT, MARIANNE
Actress. b. Starnberg, Germany, Aug. 27, 1945. In 1977 conceived revue Opera Curiosa.
PICTURES: Die Schaukel (debut, 1983), Sugarbaby, Crazy Boys, Bagdad Cafe, Moon Over Parador, The War of the Roses, Rosalie Goes Shopping, Martha and I, The Milky Life, Dust Devil, Mr. Bluesman, Il Piccolo lord, Erotique, Mona Must Die, All Men Are Mortal, Lorenz Im Land Der Lugner, The Ogre, Soleil, Johnny, Left Luggage, Asterix et Obelix.
TELEVISION: *Movies:* Herr Kischott, Eine Mutter Kampft un Ihren Sohn, My Lord, Und Plotzlich War Alles Anders, Frau Nach Mab Eine, Private Lies, Without Family.

SAGET, BOB
Actor. b. Philadelphia, PA, May 17, 1956. Started as stand-up comedian.
PICTURE: Through Adam's Eyes (dir. only), Spaced Out (voice), Full Moon High, Moving (also dir.), Devics, Critical Condition, For Goodness Sake, Dirty Work (dir. only), Meet Wally Sparks, Half Baked, Dumb and Dumberer: When Harry Met Lloyd.
TELEVISION: *Series:* Full House, America's Funniest Home Videos (host), Raising Dad. *Movie:* Father and Scout (also co-exec. prod.), Jitters (dir.), For Hope (dir. and exec.prod.), A Comedy Salute to Andy Kaufman, Becoming Dick (also dir.).

SAINT, EVA MARIE
Actress. b. Newark, NJ, July 4, 1924. e. Bowling Green State U., Ohio, Actors Studio. Radio, tv actress; on Broadway in Trip to Bountiful before film debut.
THEATRE: Trip to Bountiful, The Rainmaker, Desire Under the Elms, The Lincoln Mask, Summer and Smoke, Candida, Winesburg Ohio, First Monday in October, Duet for One, The Country Girl, Death of a Salesman, Love Letters, The Fatal Weakness, On The Divide.
PICTURES: On the Waterfront (debut, 1954; Acad. Award, best supporting actress), That Certain Feeling, Raintree County, Hatful of Rain, North by Northwest, Exodus, All Fall Down, 36 Hours, The Sandpiper, The Russians Are Coming! The Russians Are Coming!, Grand Prix, The Stalking Moon, Loving, Cancel My Reservation, Nothing in Common, Mariette in Ecstasy, I Dreamed of Africa.
TELEVISION: *Movies:* Carol for Another Christmas, The Macahans, A Christmas to Remember, When Hell Was in Session, Fatal Weakness, Curse of King Tut's Tomb, Best Little Girl in the World, Splendor in the Grass, Malibu, Jane Doe, Love Leads the Way, Fatal Vision, The Last Days of Patton, A Year in the Life, Norman Rockwell's Breaking Ties, I'll Be Home for Christmas, Voyage of Terror: The Achille Lauro Affair, People Like Us (Emmy Award, 1991), Danielle Steel's Palomino, Kiss of

a Killer, My Antonia, After Jimmy, Titanic, Jackie's Back!, Papa's Angels. *Series:* Campus Hoopla, One Man's Family, Moonlighting. *Special:* Our Town, First Woman President, Primary Colors: The Story of Corita.

SAINT JAMES, SUSAN
Actress. r.n. Susan Miller. b. Los Angeles, CA, Aug. 14, 1946. e. Connecticut Coll. for Women. Was model for 2 years; then signed to contract by Universal Pictures.
PICTURES: P.J., Where Angels Go... Trouble Follows, What's So Bad About Feeling Good?, Jigsaw, Outlaw Blues, Love at First Bite, How to Beat the High Cost of Living, Carbon Copy, Don't Cry It's Only Thunder.
TELEVISION: *Series:* The Name of the Game (Emmy Award, 1969), McMillan & Wife, Kate and Allie. *Movies:* Fame Is the Name of the Game, Alias Smith and Jones, Once Upon a Dead Man, Magic Carpet, Scott Free, Night Cries, Desperate Women, The Girls in the Office, Sex and the Single Parent, S.O.S. Titanic, The Kid from Nowhere, I Take These Men. *Special:* A Very Special Christmas Party.

SAJAK, PAT
TV Host. b. Chicago, IL, Oct. 26, 1946. e. Columbia Coll., Chicago. Broadcasting career began as newscaster for Chicago radio station. 1968 drafted into Army, where served 4 years as disc jockey for Armed Forces Radio in Saigon, Vietnam. Moved to Nashville, where continued radio career while also working as weatherman and host of public affairs prog. for local TV station. 1977 moved to LA to become nightly weatherman on KNBC. Took over as host of daytime edition of Wheel of Fortune and later the syndicated nighttime edition (4 Emmy nom.; Emmy, 1997). 1989, The Pat Sajak Show.
PICTURE: Airplane II: The Sequel.
TELEVISION: *Host:* The Thanksgiving Day Parade, The Rose Parade.

SAKS, GENE
Director, Actor. b. New York, NY, Nov. 8, 1921. e. Cornell U. Attended dramatic workshop, New School for Social Research. Active in off-Broadway in 1948-49, forming cooperative theatre group at Cherry Lane Theatre. Joined Actor's Studio, followed by touring and stock. Also appeared in live TV dramas (Philco Playhouse, Producer's Showcase). Directed many Broadway plays before turning to film direction with Barefoot in the Park (1967) President of SSDC.
THEATRE: *B'way: Director:* Enter Laughing, Nobody Loves an Albatross, Generation, Half a Sixpence, Mame, A Mother's Kisses, Sheep on the Runway, How the Other Half Loves, Same Time Next Year, California Suite, I Love My Wife (Tony Award), Brighton Beach Memoirs (Tony Award), Biloxi Blues (Tony Award), The Odd Couple (1985), Broadway Bound, Rumors, Lost in Yonkers, Jake's Women. *Actor:* Middle of the Night, Howie, The Tenth Man, A Shot in the Dark, A Thousand Clowns.
PICTURES: *Director:* Barefoot in the Park, The Odd Couple, Cactus Flower, Last of the Red Hot Lovers, Mame, Brighton Beach Memoirs, Tchin-Tchin, A Fine Romance. *Actor:* A Thousand Clowns, Prisoner of Second Avenue, The One and Only, Lovesick, The Goodbye People, Nobody's Fool, I.Q., Deconstructing Harry.
TELEVISION: *Movie:* Bye Bye Birdie, On Seventh Avenue. *Guest:* Law & Order.

SALANT, RICHARD S.
Executive. b. New York, NY, April 14, 1914. e. Harvard Coll. A.B., 1931-35; Harvard Law Sch., 1935-38. Atty. Gen.'s Com. on Admin. Procedure, 1939-41; Office of Solicitor Gen., U.S. Dept. of Justice, 1941-43; U.S. Naval Res., 1943-46; assoc., Roseman, Goldmark, Colin & Kave, 1946-48; then partner, 1948-51; pres. CBS news div., 1961-64; v.p. special asst. to pres. CBS, Inc., 1951-61, 1964-66; pres., CBS news div., 1966; mem. bd. of dir., CBS, Inc. 1964-69; vice chmn., NBC bd., 1979-81; sr. adviser, 1981-83; pres. CEO, National News Council, 1983-84. Retired.

SALDANA, THERESA
Actress. b. Brooklyn, NY, Aug. 20, 1954. Following attack by stalker founded advocacy group Victims for Victims. *Author:* Beyond Survival, 1986.
PICTURES: Nunzio, I Wanna Hold Your Hand, Defiance, Raging Bull, Double Revenge, Angel Town, Carlo's Wake.
TELEVISION: *Series:* The Commish, All My Children. *Movies:* Sophia Loren: Her Own Story, Victims for Victims: The Theresa Saldana Story, Confessions of a Crime, The Highwayman, Shameful Secrets, She Woke Up Pregnant, The Time Shifters, Ready to Run.

SALEM, KARIO
Actor, Writer.
PICTURES: Underground Aces, Triumph of the Spirit, 1492: Conquest of Paradise, Killing Zoe, Savage, The Score (s.p.).
TELEVISION: *Movies:* Under the Influence, The Red Spider, Shooter, Liberace, Kojak: Ariana, Jericho Fever, Without Warning, Mr. Stitch, Divas (writer), Don King: Only in America (writer, Emmy Award, 1998), The Rat Pack (writer). *Mini-series:* Centennial. *Series:* Heart of the City, The Beast (s.p. and prod.).

SALES, SOUPY
Comedian. r.n. Milton Hines. b. Franklinton, NC, Jan. 8, 1926. Was radio DJ before debuting with his own children show in Detroit, 1953. Program was picked up by ABC in 1955. Continued to perform on radio over the years.
PICTURES: Birds Do It, And God Spoke, A Little Bit of Lipstick, Behind the Seams, Everything's George, Palmer's Pick Up, Conundrum, Holy Man, Black Scorpion Returns, This Train.
TELEVISION: Series: Soupy Sales (1955), Lunch With Soupy Sales, The Soupy Sales Show (1962), The Soupy Sales Show (1965-67), What's My Line (panelist), The Soupy Sales Show (1978-79), Sha Na Na. Guest: The Rebel, The Real McCoys, Route 66, The Beverly Hillbillies, Love American Style, The Love Boat, Wings.

SALHANY, LUCIE
Executive. e. Kent State U., Kent, OH. Began career 1967 WKBF-TV, Cleveland, OH. Prog. mgr., WLVI-TV, Boston, 1975. VP, TV and cable prog., Taft Broadcasting Co., 1979-85. Pres. & CEO, Paramount Domestic TV, 1985. Chairman, 20th TV, 1991. Chairman, Fox Broadcasting Co., 1993. Pres., UPN, 1995.

SALKIND, ILYA
Producer. b. Mexico City, July 27, 1947. e. U. of London. Father is producer, Alexander Salkind. First film job as production runner on The Life of Cervantes for father.
PICTURES: The Three Musketeers, The Four Musketeers, Superman, Superman II (exec. prod.), Supergirl (exec. prod.), Superman III (exec. prod.), Santa Claus, Christopher Columbus: The Discovery, Brasil (1500).
TELEVISION: Superboy (exec. prod.).

SALOMON, MIKAEL
Cinematographer, Director. b. Copenhagen, Feb. 24, 1945.
PICTURES: Europe: The Dreamers, Z.P.G., Three From Haparanda, The Five, Me and My Kid Brothers, The Owlfarm Brothers, Five on the Run, Magic in Town, 24 Hours With Ilse, Why?, Bedside Freeway, My Sister's Children Goes Astray, Around the World, Tumult, Welcome to the Club, Violets Are Blue, Tintomare, Tell It Like It Is Boys, Cop, Elvis Elvis, Hearts Are Trump, The Marksman, The Flying Devils, Peter von Scholten, The Baron, Once a Cop..., Early Spring, The Wolf at the Door, U.S.: Zelly and Me, Torch Song Trilogy, Stealing Heaven, The Abyss (Acad. Award nom.), Always, Arachnophobia, Backdraft, Far and Away, A Far Off Place (dir. only), Congo (2nd unit dir.), Judge Dredd (trailer dir.), Hard Rain (dir. only).
TELEVISION: Movie: The Man Who Broke 1,000 Chains (ACE Award), Salem's Lot, Benedict Arnold: A Question of Honor. Series: Space Rangers (dir.), The Agency, Band of Brothers. Also commercials for Mitsubishi, Nescafe, Converse, Mazda, etc.

SALZBURG, JOSEPH S.
Producer, Editor. b. New York, NY, July 27, 1917. Film librarian, then rose to v.p. in chg. of prod., Pictorial Films, 1935-42; civilian chief film ed. U.S. Army Signal Corps Photo Center, 1942-44; U.S. Army Air Forces, 1944-46; prod. mgr., Pictorial Films, 1946-50; prod. mgr. Associated Artists Prod., then M.P. for TV, 1950-51; org. m.p. prod. & edit. service for theatrical, non-theatrical & TV films 1951-56; prod. mgr., dir. of films oper., official Films. 1956-59; prod. sup. tech. dir. Lynn Romero Prod. features and TV; assoc. prod. Lynn Romero Prod. TV series, Counterthrust 1959-60; v.p., sec'y, B.L. Coleman Assoc., Inc. & Newspix, Inc. 1961; pres. National Production Assoc., Inc. 1960-1962, chief of production, UPI Newsfilm, 1963-66. Prod./account exec. Fred A. Niles Comm. Center, 1966. Appt. v.p., F.A. Niles Communications Centers Inc., N.Y., 1969. 1979 appointed in addition exec. producer & gen. mgr., F. A. Niles Comm., N.Y. studio. 1989, elected mem. bd. dir., Florida Motion Pictures & Television Assn., Palm Beach area chap.; 1989 professor m.p. & TV prod. course at Palm Beach Comm. Coll.: Breaking into TV and Movie Making in South Florida.

SAMMS, EMMA
Actress. b. London, England, Aug. 28, 1960. Former fashion model. Has worked as commercial photographer for such magazines as Ritz, Metro, and Architectural Digest. Co-founder of charitable org. the Starlight Foundation.
PICTURES: Arabian Adventure (debut, 1979), The Shrimp on the Barbie, Delirious, Fatal Inheritance, Terminal Voyage, The Little Unicorn, Pets, The Adventures of Tom Thumb and Thumbelina (voice).
TELEVISION: Series: General Hospital, Dynasty, The Colbys. Movies: Goliath Awaits, Agatha Christie's Murder in Three Acts, The Lady and the Highwayman, A Connecticut Yankee in King Arthur's Court, Bejeweled, Shadow of a Stranger, Robin Cook's Harmful Intent, Treacherous Beauties, Humanoids from the Deep, Pretend You Don't See Her. Guest: Hotel, The New Mike Hammer, Murder She Wrote, Newhart, My Two Dads.

SAMUELSON, DAVID W.
F.R.P.S., F.B.K.S., B.S.C.: Executive. b. London, England, July 6, 1924. Son of early producer G.B. Samuelson. Joined ind. 1941 with British Movietone News. Later film cameraman, 1947. Left Movietone 1960 to join family company, Samuelson Film Service Ltd. Dir., Samuelson Group Plc, 1958-84. Past president

British Kinematograph Sound & TV Soc., Past Chmn, British Board of Film Classification, London Intl. Film Sch. Author: Hands On Manual for Cinematographer, Motion Picture Camera and Lighting Equipment, Motion Picture Camera Techniques, Motion Picture Camera Data, Samuelson Manual of Cinematography, Panaflex User's Manual and Cinematographers Computer Program. Currently consultant on technology film making, author, lecturer. Won Acad. Award for Engineering, 1980 and Acad. Award for Tech. Achievement, 1987.

SAMUELSON, PETER GEORGE WYLIE
Producer. b. London, England, October 16, 1951. e. Cambridge U., M.A., English literature. Early career as interpreter, production assistant, then prod. mgr. 1975, Return of the Pink Panther. 1979-85, exec. v.p., Interscope Comm., Inc. 1982-present, Intl. Pres., Starlight Foundation. 1986-present, pres., Film Associates, Inc. 1985-90 chmn., Samuelson Group, Inc. 1990-present, partner, Samuelson Prods. of L.A. and London.
PICTURES: Speed Merchants, High Velocity, One by One, Return of the Pink Panther, Santa Fe, A Man a Woman and a Bank, Revenge of the Nerds, Turk 182, Tom and Viv, Playmaker, Wilde, The Commissioner, This is the Sea, Arlington Road, Guest House Paradiso, Gabriel and Me, The Gathering, The Blind Bastards Club, Tales not Told, Good Omens.
TELEVISION: Movies: Dog's Best Friend, The Pact.

SAMUELSON, SIR SYDNEY
C.B.E., B.S.C., Hon. F.B.K.S., Executive. b. London, England, Dec. 7, 1925. e. Irene Avenue Council Sch., Lancing, Sussex. Early career as cinema projectionist, 1939-42; Gaumont British News, 1942-43; Royal Air Force, 1943-47; asst. cameraman, cameraman, director/cameraman until 1960; founded Samuelson Film Service, 1954; Trustee and chmn. board of management, British Acad. of Film and Television Arts (chmn. of Council 1973-76). Member (Pres. 1983-86; Trustee: 1982-89) Cinema and Television Benevolent Fund. Member of Executive, Cinema & Television Veterans (pres. 1980-81); assoc. member, American Society of Cinematographers. Hon. Tech. Adviser, Royal Naval Film Corp. Hon. member, Guild of British Camera Technicians, 1986 (now BECTU); Member, British Society of Cinematographers (governor, 1969-79; 1st vice pres., 1976-77), Hon. Mem. for Life, Assn. of Cinema & Television Technicians, 1990. Appointed first British Film Commissioner by U.K. government, 1991. Recipient of two British Academy Awards: Michael Balcon (1985), Fellowship (1993). Received knighthood for services to British Film Industry, 1995. Lifetime Honorary Fellowship, British Kinematograph, Sound & Television Society, 1995.

SANDA, DOMINIQUE
Actress. r.n. Dominique Varaigne. b. Paris, France, March 11, 1951. e. Saint Vincent de Paul, Paris. Was a popular model for women's magazines when cast by Robert Bresson as the tragic heroine in his Dostoyevsky adaptation Un Femme Douce (1968).
THEATRE: Madame Klein, Les Liaisons Dangereuses, Un Mari Ideal, Carte Blanche de Dominique Sanda.
PICTURES: Un Femme Douce, First Love, The Conformist, The Garden of the Finzi-Continis, La Notte Dei Fiori, Sans Mobile Apparent, Impossible Object, Steppenwolf, Conversation Piece, 1900, L'Heritage, Le Berceau de Cristal, Damnation Alley, Au Dela du Bien et du Mal, Beyond Good and Evil, The Song of Roland, Utopia, The Navire Night, Travels on the Sly, Caboblanco, A Room in Town, Dust of the Empire, The Way to Bresson, The Sailor 512, Corps et Biens, Les Mendiants, On a Moonlit Night, Warrior and Prisoners, Je Ne Vous Derangerai Plus, Moi La Pire De Toutes, Le Voyage, Emile Rosen, Henri Le Vert, Albert Salvarus, The Universe of Jacques Demy, Garage Olimpo, The Island of the Mapmaker's Wife.
TELEVISION: The Sealed Train, La Naissance Du Jour, Il Decimo Clandestino, Voglia Di Vivere, Achille Lauro, Warburg, Comme Par Hazard, Non Siamo Soli, Albert Savarus, Der Lange Weg des Lukas B, The Lucona Affair, Nobody's Children, Brennendes Herz, Joseph.

SANDERS, JAY O.
Actor. b. Austin, TX, April 16, 1953. e. SUNY/Purchase. First professional theatre experience with NY Shakespeare-in-the Park prods. of Henry V and Measure for Measure. Appeared in Abel's Sister for England's Royal Court Theatre.
THEATRE: NY: Loose Ends, The Caine Mutiny Court-Martial, Buried Child, In Trousers, Geniuses, The Incredibly Famous Willy Powers, Heaven on Earth, Girls Girls Girls, King John, Saint Joan, Three Birds Alighting on a Field.
PICTURES: Starting Over (debut, 1979), Hanky Panky, Eddie Macon's Run, Cross Creek, Tucker: The Man and His Dream, The Prince of Pennsylvania, Glory, Just Like in the Movies, Mr. Destiny, V.I. Warshawski, Defenseless, Meeting Venus, JFK, Angels in the Outfield, Kiss of Death, Down Came a Blackbird, The Big Green, Three Wishes, Kiss the Girls, Daylight, The Matchmaker, For Richer or Poorer, Wrestling With Alligators, The Odd Couple II, Tumbleweeds, Music of the Heart, Endsville, The Confession, Dead Dog, Along Came a Spider, Rumor Has It, The Day After Tomorrow.
TELEVISION: Series: Aftermash, Crime Story, Lonesome Dove. Movies: The Day Christ Died, Living Proof: The Hank Williams Jr.

Story, A Doctor's Story, Cold Sassy Tree, Hostages, State of Emergency, Nobody's Children, Rio Shannon, The Prosecutors, Earthly Possessions, The Jack Bull, A.T.F., Boss of Bosses, Picnic, The Familiar Stranger, The Last Brickmaker in America. *Mini-Series:* Salem Witch Trials, Widows. *Special:* The Revolt of Mother. *Guest:* Roseanne, The Young Riders, Spenser: For Hire, A Man Called Hawk, Kate and Allie, Miami Vice, Northern Exposure, NY Undercover, The Outer Limits, Nothing Sacred, Widows.

SANDERS, TERRY BARRETT
Producer, Director, Writer. b. New York, NY, Dec. 20, 1931. e. UCLA, 1951; Co-prod., photographed, A Time Out of War, 1954. Academy Award best two-reel subject, and won first prize Venice Film Festival, etc.; co-wrote The Day Lincoln Was Shot, CBS-TV; s.p. The Naked and the Dead; prod. Crime and Punishment—USA., prod., co-dir. War Hunt; prod. and dir. Portrait of Zubin Mehta for U.S.I.A. Assoc. dean, Film Sch., California Inst. of the Arts. Prod.-Dir.: Four Stones for Kanemitsu (Acad. Award nom.). Prod.-Dir.-Writer: Rose Kennedy: A Life to Remember (Acad. Award nom.) Professor, UCLA. Pres., American Film Foundation. PICTURES: Maya Lin: A Strong Clear Vision (prod., Acad. Award), Never Give Up: The 20th Century Odyssey of Herbert Zipper (prod., dir., Acad. Award nom.).
TELEVISION: *Prod./dir.:* Hollywood and the Stars, The Legend of Marilyn Monroe, National Geographic Society specials, The Kids from Fame, Film Bios Kennedy Center Honors, Slow Fires, Lillian Gish: The Actor's Life for Me (Emmy Award).

SANDLER, ADAM
Actor, Writer, Comedian. b. Brooklyn, NY, Sept. 9, 1966. PICTURES: Going Overboard, Shakes the Clown, Coneheads, Mixed Nuts, Airheads, Billy Madison (also s.p.), Happy Gilmore (also s.p.), Bulletproof, The Wedding Singer (also comp. 2 songs), Dirty Work, The Waterboy (also s.p., exec. prod.), Big Daddy (also s.p., exec. prod.), Little Nicky (also s.p.), Joe Dirt (exec. prod.), The Animal (exec. prod.), Master of Disguise (exec. prod.), Mr. Deeds, 8 Crazy Nights (voice & exec.prod. and s.p.), The Hot Chick, Anger Management, Dickie Roberts: Former Child Star, (exec. prod.), Fifty First Kisses.
TELEVISION: *Series:* Remote Control, Saturday Night Live. *Guest:* The Cosby Show, The Marshall Chronicles, The Larry Sanders Show, Today, Clive Anderson All Talk, WWF Smackdown

SANDRICH, JAY
Director. b. Los Angeles, CA, Feb. 24, 1932. e. UCLA. PICTURES: Seems Like Old Times, Neil Simon's London Suite. TELEVISION: *Special:* The Lily Tomlin Show (DGA Award, 1975). *Movies:* The Crooked Hearts, What Are Best Friends For?, For Richer For Poorer, The Man Who Came to Dinner. *Series:* The Mary Tyler Moore Show (Emmy Awards: 1971, 1973), Soap, Phyllis (pilot), Tony Randall Show (pilot), Bob Newhart Show (pilot), Benson (pilot), Golden Girls (pilot; DGA Award, 1985), Empty Nest (pilot), The Cosby Show (Emmy Awards: 1985, 1986; DGA Award 1985), The Secret Lives of Men, Thanks, My Family, The Three Sisters,

SANDS, JULIAN
Actor. b. Yorkshire, England, Jan. 4,1958. e. Central School of Speech and Drama, London 1979. Formed small theater co. that played in schools and youth clubs. Professional debut in Derek Jarman's short, Broken English and one-line part in Privates on Parade. Then opposite Anthony Hopkins in British TV series A Married Man (1981).
PICTURES: Privates on Parade (debut, 1982), Oxford Blues, The Killing Fields, After Darkness, The Doctor and the Devils, A Room with a View, Gothic, Siesta, Vibes, Wherever You Are, Manika: The Girl Who Lived Twice, Arachnophobia, Warlock, Night Sun, Impromptu, Naked Lunch, Wicked, Husbands and Lovers, Tale of a Vampire, Boxing Helena, Warlock: The Armageddon, Black Water, The Browning Version, Leaving Las Vegas, Never Ever, One Night Stand, Long Time Since, Phantom of the Opera, The Loss of Sexual Innocence, Autumn Heart, The Million Dollar Hotel, Mercy, Love Me, Timecode, Vatel, Pokemon: The Movie 2000, Hotel, The Scoundrel's Wife, The Visitors, Highbinders, The Medallion.
TELEVISION: *Series:* A Married Man, Jackie Chan Adventures (voice). *Mini-Series:* Rose Red. *Movies:* Romance on the Orient Express, Harem, The Room, Murder By Moonlight, Grand Isle, Crazy in Love, Witch Hunt, The Great Elephant Escape, The Tomorrow Man, End of Summer, Napoléon, Rose Red.

SANDS, RICK
Executive. Began career as v.p. of distribution, Columbia Pictures, 1978; exec. v.p. & CFO, Miramax Films, 1990; exec. v.p. & CFO, Hallmark/RHI Entertainment, 1993; president, Miramax Intl., 1995. Currently chairman, Worldwide Distribution, Miramax, (since1997), where he is responsible for worldwide theatrical, home video, television, co-productions and acquisitions; member, Board of Directors, AFMA, AMPAS, BAFTA, and IFP; awarded Distributor of the Year, Cinema Expo Intl., 2000.

SANDS, TOMMY
Singer. b. Chicago, IL, Aug. 27, 1937. e. Schools there and Houston, TX, Greenwood, LA. Father, Benny Sands, concert pianist. Started career as guitar player, singer when 5, at KWKH station, Shreveport. One of pioneers of rock music. First manager was Col. Tom Parker. Acting debut: Kraft TV show The Singin' Idol; recording contract won him million record sales of Teen Age Crush.
PICTURES: Sing Boy Sing, Mardi Gras, Love in a Goldfish Bowl, Babes in Toyland, The Longest Day, Ensign Pulver, None But the Brave, The Violent Ones.

SANFORD, ISABEL
Actress. b. New York, NY, Aug. 29, 1929. e. Textile H.S., Evander Childs H.S. Began acting in elementary school and continued through high school. Joined American Negro Theatre in the 1930's (then The Star Players) which disbanded in W.W.II. Later associated with YWCA project and off-B'way plays. B'way debut in The Amen Corner.
PICTURES: Guess Who's Coming to Dinner, The Young Runaways, Pendulum, The Comic, Stand Up and Be Counted, The New Centurions, Love at First Bite, South Beach, Original Gangstas, Sprung, Jane Austen's Mafia!, Click Three Times.
TELEVISION: *Series:* All in the Family, The Jeffersons (Emmy Award, 1981). *Movie:* The Great Man's Whiskers, Jackie's Back: Portrait of a Diva. *Guest:* Fresh Prince of Bel Air, Roseanne, Hangin' With Mr. Cooper, Living Single, In the House, Fresh Prince of Bel Air, Lois & Clark, Cybill.

SAN GIACOMO, LAURA
Actress. b. New Jersey, Nov. 14, 1962. e. Carnegie Melon Univ. m. actor Cameron Dye. Appeared Off-B'way in North Shore Fish, Beirut, The Love Talker, Italian American Reconciliation, Wrong Turn at Lungfish, Three Sisters.
PICTURES: Sex Lies and Videotape (debut, 1989), Pretty Woman, Vital Signs, Quigley Down Under, Once Around, Under Suspicion, Where the Day Takes You, Nina Takes a Lover, Stuart Saves His Family, Suicide Kings, Eat Your Heart Out, The Apocalypse, With Friends Like These.
TELEVISION: *Series:* Just Shoot Me, Stories From My Childhood. *Movie:* For Their Own Good, The Right to Remain Silent, Sister Mary Explains It All, The Jennifer Estess Story. *Mini-Series:* Stephen King's The Stand. *Guest:* The Equalizer, Crime Story, Hollywood Sqaures.

SANSOM, LESTER A.
Producer. b. Salt Lake City, UT, April 24, 1910. e. U. of Utah. Radio singer under name of Jack Allen, 1930; ent. m.p. ind. in editorial dept., Fox Film Corp., 1931; served in U.S. Navy as head of film library, Washington, DC, 1942-45; head of edit. dept. & post-prod., Allied Artists, from 1953; assoc. prod. Skabenga; prod., co-writer, Battle Flame; assoc. prod. Hell to Eternity, exec. prod. The Thin Red Line, prod. Crack in the World; prod. Bikini Paradise, Battle of the Bulge, Custer of the West, Co-prod., Krakatoa—East of Java; exec. prod. 12+1.

SAPERSTEIN, DAVID
Writer, Director. b. Brooklyn, NY. e. Bronx H.S. of Science, CCNY, Film Institute, Chemical Engineering. 1960-80 wrote, prod. and dir. documentary films, TV commercials. Also wrote lyrics and managed rhythm and blues and rock 'n roll groups. Assoc. Professor NYU Graduate Film & TV, Manhattan Marymount College. Has directed various music videos.Wrote libretto and lyrics for Blue Planet Blue, Clowns and Cocoon: The Musical.
AUTHOR: Cocoon, Metamorphosis, Red Devil, Funerama, Fatal Reunion, Dark Again.
PICTURES: Cocoon (story), Killing Affair (dir., s.p.), Personal Choice (dir., s.p.), Cocoon: The Return. Fatal Reunion (s.p.), Queen of America (s.p.), Torch, Sara Deri, Hearts & Diamonds, Vets, Do Not Disturb, Point of Honor, Snatched, Jack in the Box, Schoolhouse, Roberto: The Roberto Clemente Story, Roamers, Joshua's Golden Band, Beyond the Stars (dir., s.p.), Bab's Labs (s.p.), Fighting Back (s.p.), Silyan (s.p.).
TELEVISION: The Vintage Years (pilot), Dance of the Athletes (dir., writer), Rodeo—A Matter of Style (dir., writer), Mama Sings, The Corky Project, OB/GYN (pilot), Reppies (prod.). *Movies:* A Christmas Visitor.

SARA, MIA
Actress. b. Brooklyn, NY, June 19, 1968. Started doing TV commercials; landed role in soap opera, All My Children.
PICTURES: Legend (debut, 1986), Ferris Bueller's Day Off, The Long Lost Friend, Apprentice to Murder, A Row of Crows, Imagination, Any Man's Death, Shadows in the Storm, A Stranger Among Us, By the Sword, Timecop, The Pompatus of Love, The Maddening, Undertow, Bullet to Beijing, Black Day Blue Night, Dazzle, Little Insects, The Impossible Elephant, Turn of Faith, Hoodlum & Son.
TELEVISION: *Movies:* Queenie, Till We Meet Again, Daughter of Darkness, Blindsided, Call of the Wild, The Set Up, Hard Time *Special:* Big Time. *Guest:* Alfred Hitchcock Presents. *Mini-series:* 20,000 Leagues Under the Sea, Jack and the Beanstalk- The Real Story. *Series:* Lost in Oz

SARAFIAN, RICHARD C.
Director. b. New York, NY. April 28, 1935. Studied medicine and law before entering film industry with director Robert Altman making industrial documentaries.
PICTURES: Andy (debut, 1965), Run Wild Run Free, Ballad of a Badman, Fragment of Fear, Man in the Wilderness, Vanishing Point, Lolly Madonna XXX, The Man Who Loved Cat Dancing, The Next Man (also prod.), Sunburn, The Bear, Songwriter (actor only), Street Justice (also actor), Crisis 2050, Truk Lagoon, *As Actor*: Bugsy, Ruby, Gunmen, Don Juan DeMarco, The Crossing Guard, Bound, Bulworth, Blue Streak, Dr. Dolittle 2, (voice), Masked and Anonymous.
TELEVISION: Gunsmoke, Bonanza, Guns of Will Sonnet, I Spy Wild, Wild West; Maverick, Twilight Zone, Gangster Chronicles. *Movies*: Shadow on the Land, Disaster on the Coastline, Splendor in the Grass, A Killing Affair, Liberty, Golden Moment—An Olympic Love Story. *As Actor*: Foley Square, Long Time Gone, Miami Hustle, Gotti, Miami Hustle.

SARANDON, CHRIS
Actor. b. Beckley, WV, July 24, 1942. e. U. of West Virginia. Mem. Catholic U.'s National Players touring U.S. in Shakespeare and Moliere. Acted with Washington, D.C. improvisational theater co. and Long Wharf. B'way debut, The Rothschilds.
THEATRE: Two Gentlemen of Verona, Censored Scenes from King Kong, Marco Polo Sings a Solo, The Devil's Disciple, The Soldier's Tale, The Woods, Nick & Nora.
PICTURES: Dog Day Afternoon (debut, 1975; Acad. Award nom.), Lipstick, The Sentinel, Cuba, The Osterman Weekend, Protocol, Fright Night, Collision Course, The Princess Bride, Child's Play, Slaves of New York, Forced March, Whispers, The Resurrected, Dark Tide, The Nightmare Before Christmas (voice), Just Cause, Tales From the Crypt: Bordello of Blood, Edie and Pen, Road Ends, Little Men, Reaper, Let the Devil Wear Black, Perfume, Rescued From the Closet, As You Wish: The Story of the Princess Bride.
TELEVISION: *Series*: The Guiding Light, Felicity, The Court. *Movies*: Thursday's Game, You Can't Go Home Again, The Day Christ Died, A Tale of Two Cities, This Child Is Mine, Broken Promises, Liberty, Mayflower Madam, Tailspin: Behind the Korean Airliner Tragedy, The Stranger Within, A Murderous Affair: The Carolyn Warmus Story, David's Mother, When the Dark Man Calls, No Greater Love, Race Against Time.

SARANDON, SUSAN
Actress. r.n. Susan Abigail Tomaling. b. New York, NY, Oct. 4, 1946. e. Catholic U. Raised in Metuchen, New Jersey. Returned to New York to pursue acting, first signing with Ford Model Agency.
THEATRE: *NY*: An Evening with Richard Nixon and..., A Coupla White Chicks Sitting Around Talking, Extremities.
PICTURES: Joe (debut, 1970), Lady Liberty, Lovin' Molly, The Front Page, The Great Waldo Pepper, The Rocky Horror Picture Show, Dragonfly (One Summer Love), Checkered Flag or Crash, The Last of the Cowboys (The Great Smokey Roadblock; also co-prod.), The Other Side of Midnight, Pretty Baby, King of the Gypsies, Something Short of Paradise, Loving Couples, Atlantic City (Acad. Award nom.), Tempest, The Hunger, The Buddy System, Compromising Positions, The Witches of Eastwick, Bull Durham, Sweet Hearts Dance, The January Man, A Dry White Season, Through the Wire (narrator), White Palace, Thelma & Louise (Acad. Award nom.), The Player, Light Sleeper, Bob Roberts, Lorenzo's Oil (Acad. Award nom.), The Client (Acad. Award nom.), Little Women, Safe Passage, The Celluloid Closet, Dead Man Walking (Acad. Award), James and the Giant Peach (voice), 187, Illuminata, Twilight, Stepmom (also exec. prod.), Joe Gould's Secret, The Cradle Will Rock, Anywhere But Here, Our Friend, Martin (voice), Rugrats in Paris: The Movie (voice), Cats & Dogs, Baby's in Black, The Banger Sisters, This Child of Mine, Igby Goes Down, Uphill All the Way (voice), Rudyland (narrator), Moonlight Mile.
TELEVISION: *Series*: Search For Tomorrow. *Guest*: Calucci's Dept, Owen Marshall: Counsellor at Law, The Simpsons (voice). *Specials*: Rimers of Eldritch, June Moon, Who Am I This Time?, One Woman One Vote (narrator). *Mini-Series*: A.D. *Movies*: F. Scott Fitzgerald & the Last of the Belles, Mussolini: Decline and Fall of Il Duce, Women of Valor, Father Roy: Inside the School of Assassins, Earthly Possessions, Children of Dune, Ice Bound.

SARDI, JAN
Writer.
PICTURES: Moving Out, Street Hero, Ground Zero, Breakaway, Secrets, Shine, Love's Brother.
TELEVISION: Mission Impossible, Phoenix, The Feds, The Man From Snowy River, Halifax f.p: Lies of the Mind.

SARGENT ALVIN
Writer. b. Philadelphia, PA, April 12, 1927. Began career as writer for TV, then turned to theatrical films.
PICTURES: Gambit (co-s.p.), The Stalking Moon, The Sterile Cuckoo, I Walk the Line, The Effect of Gamma Rays on Man-in-the-Moon Marigolds, Paper Moon (Acad. Award nom.), Love and Pain (and the Whole Damn Thing), Julia (Acad. Award, 1977), Bobby Deerfield, Straight Time (co-s.p.), Ordinary People (Acad. Award, 1980), Nuts (co-s.p.), Dominick and Eugene (co-s.p.),

White Palace (co-s.p.), What About Bob? (co-story), Other People's Money, Hero (co-story), Bogus, Anywhere But Here, Unfaithful (s.p.), Spider-Man II.
TELEVISION: *Movies*: Footsteps, The Impatient Heart. *Series*: The Naked City, Route 66, Ben Casey, Alfred Hitchcock Presents, The Nurses, Mr. Novak, Empire.

SARGENT, HERB
Executive. Pres., Writer Guild of America East, Inc. Prod. radio program, NPR's Backfire; s.p., Bye Bye Branerman; writer, prod. for many comedy shows.

SARGENT, JOSEPH
Director. r.n. Giuseppe Danielle Sargente. b. Jersey City, NJ, July 25, 1925. e. studied theatre, New Sch. for Social Research 1946-49.
PICTURES: One Spy Too Many, The Hell With Heroes, Colossus: The Forbin Project, White Lightning, The Taking of Pelham One Two Three, MacArthur, Goldengirl, Coast to Coast, Nightmares, Jaws—The Revenge (also prod.).
TELEVISION: *Special*: The Spy in the Green Hat. *Mini-series*: The Manions of America, James Mitchener's Space. *Movies*: The Sunshine Patriot, The Immortal (pilot), The Man, Tribes, The Marcus-Nelson Murders (Emmy Award, 1973), Maybe I'll Come Home in the Spring (also prod.), The Man Who Died Twice, The Night That Panicked America, Sunshine (also prod.), Friendly Persuasion, Amber Waves, Hustling, Freedom, Tomorrow's Child, Memorial Day, Terrible Joe Moran, Choices of the Heart (also prod.), Space, Love Is Never Silent (Emmy Award, 1986), Passion Flower, Of Pure Blood, There Must Be a Pony, The Karen Carpenter Story, Day One, The Incident, Caroline? (Emmy Award, 1990), The Last Elephant, Never Forget, Miss Rose White (Emmy Award, 1992), Somebody's Daughter (also prod.), Skylark (also prod.), Abraham, World War II: When Lions Roared, My Antonia, Mandela and de Klerk, Miss Evers' Boys, The Long Island Incident, The Wall, Crime and Punishment, A Lesson Before Dying, Bojangles, Gisella Perl, The Arturo Sandoval Story, Vola Sciusciù, Salem Witch Trials, Out of the Ashes.

SARLUI, ED
Executive. b. Amsterdam, The Netherlands, Nov. 10, 1925. Owner, Peruvian Films, S.A.; pres., Radio Films of Peru, S.A.; pres. Bryant Films Educatoriana, S.A.; partner, United Producers de Colombia Ltd.; pres. Royal Film N.V.; pres., United Producers de Centroamerica, S.A.; pres. United Producers de Mexico, S.A.; pres., United Producers Int'l, Inc., Continental Motion Pictures, Inc. 1988, formed Cinema Corp. of America with Moshe Diamant and Elliott Kastner. Co-chmn. Epic Prods. Inc.
PICTURES: *Exec. prod.*: Full Moon in Blue Water, High Spirits, Teen Witch, Courage Mountain, Night Game.

SARNOFF, THOMAS W.
Executive. b. New York, NY, Feb. 23, 1927. e. Phillips Acad., Andover, MA, 1939-43; Princeton U., 1943-45; Stanford U. grad. 1948, B.S. in E.E.; Grad Sch. of Bus. Admin. 1948-49. Sgt., U.S. Army Signal Corps, 1945-46; prod. & sales, ABC-TV, Hollywood 1949-50; prod. dept. MGM, 1951-52; asst. to dir. of finance and oper., NBC, 1952-54; dir. of prod. and bus. affairs, 1954-57; v.p.; prod. and bus. affairs, 1957-60; v.p. adm. west coast, 1960-62; v.p. west coast, 1962; exec. v.p. 1965-77; bd. of dir., NBC prods 1961-77; bd of dir. Hope Enterprises 1960-75; dir. NABCAT, Inc. 1967-75; dir. Valley County Cable TV, Inc. 1969-75; Pres. NBC Entertainment Corp. 1972-77; pres. Sarnoff International Enterprises, Inc. 1977-81; pres., Sarnoff Entertainment Corp., 1981-; pres., Venturetainment Corp. 1986-93; past pres. Research Foundation at St. Joseph Hospital of Burbank; past pres. Permanent Charities of the Entertainment Ind.; past ch. bd. of trustees, National Acad. of TV Arts and Sciences. Pres. Acad. of TV Arts & Sciences Foundation 1990-99. Chairman and C.E.O. Acad. of TV Arts & Sciences Foundation, 1999-. Bd. of Dir. Multimedia Games Inc., 1998-

SARRAZIN, MICHAEL
Actor. r.n. Jacques Michel Andre Sarrazin. b. Quebec, Canada, May 22, 1940. Began acting at 17 on CBC TV; signed by Universal, 1965.
PICTURES: Gunfight in Abilene (debut, 1967), The Flim-Flam Man, The Sweet Ride, Journey to Shiloh, A Man Called Gannon, Eye of the Cat, In Search of Gregory, They Shoot Horses Don't They?, The Pursuit of Happiness, Sometimes a Great Notion, Believe in Me, The Groundstar Conspiracy, Harry in Your Pocket, For Pete's Sake, The Reincarnation of Peter Proud, The Loves and Times of Scaramouche, The Gumball Rally, Caravans, Double Negative, The Seduction, Fighting Back, Joshua Then and Now, Captive Hearts, Mascara, Keeping Track, Malarek, Lena's Holiday, Bullet to Beijing, Crackerjack II, The Peacekeeper, The Second Arrival, FearDotCom.
TELEVISION: *Movies*: The Doomsday Flight, Frankenstein: The True Story, Beulah Land, Passion and Paradise, Earthquake in New York, The Phone Call, Bullet to Beijing, Midnight Man, *Guest*: Chrysler Theatre, The Virginian, *Series:* The City.

SAUNDERS, DAVID
Executive. Pres., Triumph Films, Inc.
PICTURES: *Exec. prod.*: Hellraiser, High Spirits, Bat *21 (co-prod.), Wild Orchid, Wild Orchid II: Two Shades of Blue, The Assignment, Masterminds, In God's Hands, Baby Geniuses.
TELEVISION: *Series*: Red Shoe Diaries. *Movies*: Red Shoe Diaries, Red Shoes Diaries 3: Another Woman's Lipstick.

SAUNDERS, WILLIAM
Executive. b. London, England, Jan. 4, 1923. e. left Upton House Central Sch. at 16. Served in British Eighth Army, 1941-47. Entered industry in 1947 as salesman with 20th Century Fox Film Co. in London; sales mgr., Anglo-Amalgamated Film Co., London, 1951-61; with Motion Picture Producers Assoc. of Amer. as sales dir. in Lagos, Nigeria, dist. Amer. feature films to West African countries, 1962-64; joined 20th Century Fox TV Intl., Paris as v.p. European TV sales, 1964-83; 20th Century TV Intl., Los Angeles as sr. v.p.; 1983; named exec. v.p. 1987 and pres., 1988. Retired.

SAURA, CARLOS
Director. b. Huesca, Spain, January 4, 1932. e. educated as engineer. Worked as professional photographer from 1949. Studied at Instituto de Investigaciones y Experiencias Cinematograficos, Madrid, 1952-57 where he then taught from 1957-64 until being dismissed for political reasons. 1957-58 dir. shorts La tarde del domingo and Cuenca.
PICTURES: *Director &/or Writer*: Los Golfos (The Urchins), Lament for a Bandit, La Caza (The Hunt), Peppermint Frappe, Stress es Tres Tres, La Madriguera (The Honeycomb), The Garden of Delights, Anna and the Wolves, Cousin Angelica (Cannes Fest. jury prize, 1974), Cria! (Cannes Fest. jury prize, 1976), Elisa Vide Mia, Los ojos Vendados (Blindfold), Mama Turns 100, Hurry Hurry (Golden Bear, Berlin Fest., 1981), Blood Wedding, Dulces Horas (Sweet Hours), Antonieta, Carmen, Los Zancos (The Stilts), El Amor Brujo (Love the Magician), El Dorado, The Dark Night, Ay Carmela!, Sevillanas, Outrage, Flamenco, Taxi, Tango, Pajarico, Esa luz!, Goya, Bunuel y la mesa del rey Salomon.

SAVAGE, FRED
Actor. b. Highland Park, IL, July 9, 1976. e. Stanford Univ. While in kindergarten auditioned for commercial at local community center. Didn't get the job but called back by same dir. for two more tests. Chosen for Pac-Man vitamin ad which led to 27 on-camera TV commercials and 36 voice-over radio spots.
PICTURES: The Boy Who Could Fly, The Princess Bride, Vice Versa, Little Monsters, The Wizard, Guy Walks into a Bar, As You Wish: The Story of the Princess Bride, The Jungle Book: Mowgli's Story (voice), Austin Powers in Goldmember, The Rules of Attraction.
TELEVISION: *Series*: Morningstar/Eveningstar, The Wonder Years, Working, Oswald (voice). *Movies*: Convicted: A Mother's Story, Run Till You Fall, When You Remember Me, Christmas on Division Street, No One Would Tell, Area 52. *Special*: Runaway Ralph. *Guest*: The Twilight Zone, Seinfeld, The Outer Limits.

SAVAGE, JOHN
Actor. r.n. John Youngs. b. Old Bethpage, Long Island, NY, Aug. 25, 1949. Studied at American Acad. of Dramatic Arts. In Manhattan organized Children's Theatre Group which performed in public housing. Won Drama Desk Award for performance in One Flew Over the Cuckoo's Nest (Chicago & LA).
THEATRE: Fiddler on the Roof, Ari, Siamese Connections, The Hostage, American Buffalo, Of Mice and Men.
PICTURES: Bad Company (debut, 1972), Steelyard Blues, The Killing Kind, The Sister in Law (also composed score), The Deer Hunter, Hair, The Onion Field, Inside Moves, Cattle Annie and Little Britches, The Amateur, Brady's Escape, Maria's Lovers, Salvador, Beauty and the Beast, Hotel Colonial, Soldier's Revenge, The Beat, Caribe, Do the Right Thing, Point of View, Any Man's Death, The Godfather Part III, Hunting, Primary Motive, My Forgotten Man, C.I.A. II: Target Alexa, Red Scorpion 2, Killing Obsession, Carnosaur 2, From the Edge, The Dangerous, Centurion Force, The Crossing Guard, White Squall, Where Truth Lies, American Strays, Little Boy Blue, The Mouse, Burning Down the House, Amnesia, Hostile Intent, Summer of Sam, Frontline, Message in a Bottle, Something Between Us, Christina's House, Redemption of the Ghost, Dead Man's Run, The Anarchists' Cookbook, Downtown: A Street Tale, Wounded.
TELEVISION: *Series*: Gibbsville. *Movies*: All the Kind Strangers, Eric (also wrote and performed songs), The Turning Point of Jim Malloy, Coming Out of the Ice, The Tender Age (The Little Sister), Silent Witness, The Nairobi Affair, Desperate, The Burning Shore, Daybreak, Shattered Image, Tom Clancy's Op Center, Before Women Had Wings, The Jack Bull, Dark Angel, The Virginian, Nightworld: Lost Souls, They Nest. *Special*: Date Rape (Afterschool Special). *Guest*: Tales From the Crypt, Birdland, X Files, Walker Texas Ranger, The Outer Limits.

SAVOCA, NANCY
Director. b. July 23, 1959. e. NYU film sch. m. prod.-writer Richard Guay. While in school directed and wrote short films Renata and Bad Timing. Received Haig P. Manoogian Award for filmmaking at 1984 NYU Student Film Festival. Made feature debut with True Love which won Grand Jury Prize at 1989 United States Film Festival.
PICTURES: True Love (also co-s.p.), Dogfight, Household Saints (also co-s.p.), 24-Hour Woman.

SAWYER, DIANE
News Correspondent, Anchor. b. Glasgow, KY, Dec. 22, 1945. m. director Mike Nichols. e. Wellesley Coll. Studied law before deciding on career in TV. Former Junior Miss winner and weather reporter on a Louisville TV station before arriving in Washington, 1970. Worked for Nixon Administration in press office from 1970-74; assisted Nixon in writing memoirs, 1975-78. Joined CBS News as reporter in Washington bureau in 1978; named correspondent in 1980. Served as CBS State Dept. correspondent 1980-81. Joined Charles Kuralt as co-anchor of the weekday editions of CBS Morning News in 1981; 1984-89 correspondent on 60 Minutes; 1989, signed by ABC News as co-anchor of Primetime Live news prog. with Sam Donaldson. 1994, co-anchor of Turning Point, Good Morning America, (co-host).

SAXON, JOHN
Actor. r.n. Carmine Orrico. b. Brooklyn, NY, Aug. 5, 1936.
PICTURES: Running Wild (debut, 1955), The Unguarded Moment, Rock Pretty Baby, Summer Love, The Reluctant Debutante, This Happy Feeling, The Restless Years, The Big Fisherman, Cry Tough, Portrait in Black, The Unforgiven, The Plunderers, Posse from Hell, Mr. Hobbs Takes a Vacation, War Hunt, Evil Eye, The Cardinal, The Ravagers, The Cavern, The Appaloosa, Queen of Blood, Night Caller From Outer Space, For Singles Only, Death of a Gunfighter, Company of Killers, Joe Kidd, Enter The Dragon, Black Christmas, Mitchell, The Swiss Conspiracy, Strange Shadows in an Empty Room, Moonshine County Express, Shalimar, The Bees, The Glove, The Electric Horseman, Battle Beyond the Stars, Beyond Evil, Blood Beach, Cannibal in the Streets, Wrong Is Right, The Big Score, Nightmare on Elm Street, Prisioners of the Lost Universe, Fever Pitch, Nightmare on Elm Street 3: Dream Warriors, Criminal Act, Death House (also dir.), My Mom's a Werewolf, Aftershock, Blood Salvage, Hellmaster, Crossing the Line, Maximum Force, No Escape No Return, Jonathan of the Bears, Killing Obsession, Beverly Hills Cop III, Wes Craven's New Nightmare, Nonstop Pyramid Action, The Killers Within, From Dusk till Dawn, Lancelot: Guardian of Time, The Path of the Dragon, Joseph's Gift, Criminal Mind, The Party Crashers, Final Payback, Living in Fear, Night Class, Outta Time.
TELEVISION: *Series*: The Bold Ones (The New Doctors), Falcon Crest, Unseen Hollywood. *Movies*: The Doomsday Flight, Winchester 73, Istanbul Express, The Intruders, Snatched, Linda, Can Ellen Be Saved?, Planet Earth, Crossfire, Strange New World, Raid on Entebbe, The Immigrants, Golden Gate, Rooster, Prisoners of the Lost Universe, Payoff, Blackmail, Genghis Khan, Liz: The Elizabeth Taylor Story.

SAYLES, JOHN
Writer, Director, Editor, Actor. b. Schnectady, NY, Sept. 28, 1950. e. Williams Coll., B.S. psychology, 1972. Wrote two novels: Pride of the Bimbos, 1975 and Union Dues, 1978; also The Anarchist's Convention, collection of short stories and, Thinking in Pictures: The Making of the Movie Matewan (1987). Wrote and directed plays off-B'way (New Hope for the Dead, Turnbuckle). Directed Bruce Springsteen music videos (Born in the U.S.A., I'm on Fire, Glory Days). Recipient of MacArthur Foundation Grant for genius.
PICTURES: Piranha (s.p., co-story, actor), Lady in Red (s.p.), Battle Beyond the Stars (story, s.p.), Return of the Secaucus Seven, Alligator (s.p., story), The Howling (co-s.p., actor), The Challenge (co-s.p.), Lianna, Baby It's You (dir., s.p.), The Brother from Another Planet, Enormous Changes at the Last Minute (co-s.p.), The Clan of the Cave Bear (s.p.), Hard Choices (actor), Something Wild (actor), Wild Thing (s.p.), Matewan (dir., s.p., actor), Eight Men Out (dir., s.p., actor), Breaking In (s.p.), Little Vegas (actor), City of Hope, Straight Talk (actor), Malcolm X (actor), Passion Fish (dir., s.p., edit.), Matinee (actor), My Life's in Turnaround (actor), The Secret of Roan Inish (dir., s.p., edit.), Lone Star (dir., s.p.), Men With Guns (dir., s.p., edit.), Limbo (dir., s.p., ed.), Sunshine State, Casa de los Babys, The Alamo (s.p.)
TELEVISION: *Movies*: A Perfect Match, Unnatural Causes (actor, writer), Shannon's Deal (writer, creative consult.). *Special*: Mountain View (Alive From Off Center).

SCACCHI, GRETA
Actress. b. Milan, Italy, Feb. 18, 1960. e. England and Australia. Acted in Bristol Old Vic Theatre in England.
PICTURES: Das Zweiter Gesicht, Heat and Dust, The Coca Cola Kid, Burke & Wills, Defence of the Realm, A Man in Love, Good Morning Babylon, White Mischief, Paura e Amore (Fear and Love), Woman in the Moon, Presumed Innocent, Fires Within, Shattered, The Player, Turtle Beach, Desire, The Browning Version, Jefferson in Paris, Country Life, Cosi (cameo), Emma, The Serpent's Kiss, The Red Violin, Love and Rage, Tom's Midnight Garden, Ladies Room, Cotton Mary, The Manor, Looking for Alibrandi, One of the Hollywood Ten, Festival in Cannes, Baltic Storm.
TELEVISION: *Mini-Series*: Waterfront (Australia), The Odyssey, The Farm. *Movies*: Ebony Tower, Dr. Fischer of Geneva, Camille,

Rasputin (Emmy Award, 1996), Macbeth, Christmas Glory 2000, Jeffrey Archer: The Truth.

SCARWID, DIANA
Actress. b. Savannah, GA. August 27, 1955. e. St. Vincent's Acad., American Acad. of Dramatic Arts, Pace U., 1975. Member of National Shakespeare Conservatory (Woodstock, NY) and worked in regional theatres before moving to Hollywood 1976.
PICTURES: Pretty Baby (debut, 1978), Honeysuckle Rose, Inside Moves (Acad. Award nom.), Mommie Dearest, Rumble Fish, Strange Invaders, Silkwood, The Ladies Club, Psycho III, Extremities, Heat, Brenda Starr, Gold Diggers: The Secret of Bear Mountain, The Cure, The Neon Bible, Bastard Out of Carolina, Angel of Pennsylvania Avenue, What Lies Beneath, The Angel Doll, A Guy Thing, Party Monster.
TELEVISION: Mini-Series: Studs Lonigan, From the Earth to the Moon, A Will of their Own. Movies: In the Glitter Palace, The Possessed, Forever, Battered, Guyana Tragedy: The Story of Jim Jones, Desperate Lives, Thou Shalt Not Kill, A Bunny's Tale, After the Promise, Night of the Hunter, Simple Justice, Labor of Love: The Arlette Schweitzer Story, JFK: Reckless Youth, Truman, If These Walls Could Talk, Critical Choice, Ruby Bridges, Before He Wakes, Down Will Come Baby, Dirty Pictures, Path to War. Mini Series: A Will of Their Own. Series: The Outer Limits.

SCHAEFER, CARL
Media Consultant, Publicist, b. Cleveland, OH, Sept. 2, 1908. e. UCLA. Contr. to mag., including Vanity Fair, Hollywood Citizen-News, 1931-35; Warner Bros., 1935.; Huespéd de Honor, Mexico, 1943; OSS WWII, 1944-45; Int'l Comt. AMPS, chmn. 1966-67; Italian Order of Merit, 1957; Chevalier de l'ordre de la Couronne, Belgium, 1963. Pres., Foreign Trade Assn. of Southern Calif., 1954; chmn. of bd., 1955; British-American C. of C., Dir., 1962; Chevalier French Legion d'Honneur, 1955; Comm. Hollywood Museum; dir., intl. relations, Warner Bros. Seven Arts Int'l Corp., 1960; formed own firm, Carl Schaefer Enterprises, 1971. Dir. pub. rel., British-American Chamber of Commerce, 1971; dir. pub. rel. for Iota Intl. Pictures, 1971; dir. pub. rel. Lyric Films Intl., 1971; bureau chief (Hollywood) Movie/TV Marketing, 1971; man. dir., Intl. Festival Advisory Council, 1971; dir. pub. rel. & adv. Francis Lederer Enterprises Inc. (American National Acad. of Performing Arts, and Canoga Mission Gallery) 1974; West Coast rep. Angelika Films of N.Y. 1974, Hwd. rep Korwitz/Geiger Products. 1975-; Hwd. corresp. Movie News, S'pore, & Femina, Hong Kong, 1974-; member Westn. Publications Assn. 1975-; field rep. Birch Records 1975; Hollywood rep Antena Magazine, Buenos Aires; dir. pub. rel., Style Magazine. Coordinator Hollywood Reporter Annual Key Art Awards; coordinator Hollywood Reporter Annual Marketing Concept Awards; exec. comm. & historian ShoWest; Mem: National Panel of Consumer Arbitrators, 1985; Hollywood Corr., Gold Coast Times of Australia, 1986-87. Winner 1990 Key Art Award. Member: AMPAS, awarded certif. of Appreciation, 1962; charter member, Publicists Guild of America; pres. Pacific Intercollegiate Press Assn., while UCLA Daily Bruin Editor, 1930-31. Poetry anthologies, 1995-96, National Library of Poetry.

SCHAFFEL, ROBERT
Producer. b. Washington, DC, March 2, 1944. Partner with Jon Voight in Voight-Schaffel Prods. Now heads Robert Schaffel Prods.
PICTURES: Gordon's War, Sunnyside, Lookin' to Get Out, Table for Five, American Anthem, Distant Thunder, Jacknife, Diggstown, Pontiac Moon.

SCHAPIRO, KEN
Executive. e. B.A., UC Berkeley, graduate, Harvard Law School. Joined Morgan Creek films, 1990, where he was responsible for business & legal affairs on the production of all films; executive v.p., Morgan Creek Prods. & Morgan Creek Intl.; executive v.p., Artisan Entertainment, 1998. Currently COO, Artisan.

SCHATZBERG, JERRY
Director. b. New York, NY, June 26, 1927. e. U. of Miami, 1947-48. Early career in photography as asst. to Bill Helburn 1954-56. Freelance still photographer and TV commercials dir. 1956-69. Contrib. photographs to several mags. incl. Life.
PICTURES: Puzzle of a Downfall Child (debut, 1970), The Panic in Needle Park, Scarecrow, Sweet Revenge (also prod.), The Seduction of Joe Tynan, Honeysuckle Rose, Misunderstood, No Small Affair, Street Smart, Reunion, The Day the Ponies Came Back, A Decade Under the Influence.
TELEVISION: Movie: Clinton and Nadine.

SCHEIDER, ROY
Actor. b. Orange, NJ, Nov. 10, 1932. e. Franklin and Marshall Coll. where he twice won the Theresa Helburn Acting Award. First professional acting in 1961 NY Shakespeare Festival prod. of Romeo and Juliet. Became member of Lincoln Center Repertory Co. and acted with Boston Arts Festival, American Shakespeare Festival, Arena Stage (Wash., DC) and American Repertory Co. Appeared in documentary In Our Hands.
THEATRE: Richard III, Stephen D, Sergeant Musgrave's Dance, The Alchemist, Betrayal.

PICTURES: Curse of the Living Corpse (debut, 1964), Paper Lion, Star!, Stiletto, Loving, Puzzle of a Downfall Child, Klute, The French Connection (Acad. Award nom.), The Outside Man, The French Conspiracy, The Seven Ups, Sheila Levine is Dead and Living in New York, Jaws, Marathon Man, Sorcerer, Jaws 2, Last Embrace, All That Jazz (Acad. Award nom.), Still of the Night, Blue Thunder, 2010, Mishima (narrator), The Men's Club, 52 Pickup, Cohen and Tate, Listen to Me, Night Game, The Fourth War, The Russia House, Naked Lunch, Romeo Is Bleeding, The Rage, Plato's Run, The Peacekeeper, The Myth of Fingerprints, Executive Target, The Definite Maybe, The Rainmaker, The White Raven, Better Living, Silver Wolf, Falling Through, The Doorway, Daybreak, The Best of So Graham Norton, Angel's Don't Sleep Here, Texas 46, Joplin: The Movie, Red Serpent, Love thy Neighbor, Dracula II: The Ascencion.
TELEVISION: Movies: Assignment Munich, Jacobo Timerman: Prisoner Without a Name Cell Without a Number, Tiger Town, Somebody Has to Shoot the Picture, Wild Justice, Money Plays, RKO 281, King of Texas. Series: seaQuest DSV. Guest: Hallmark Hall of Fame, Studio One, N.Y.P.D., Diamond Hunters. Special: Portrait of the Soviet Union (host).

SCHEINMAN, ANDREW
Producer. b. 1948. e. Univ. of VA, law degree. Professional tennis player before entering film business as producer of three Charlton Heston films. Became one of 5 founding partners of Castle Rock Entertainment.
PICTURES: Prod/Exec. Prod.: The Mountain Man, The Awakening, Modern Romance, Mother Lode, The Sure Thing, Stand By Me, The Princess Bride, When Harry Met Sally..., Misery, A Few Good Men, North (also co-s.p.), Ghosts of Mississippi, Extreme Measures. Director: Little Big League, Bait, (writer).
TELEVISION: Series: Seinfeld (exec. prod.)

SCHELL, MARIA
Actress. b. Vienna, Austria, Jan. 5, 1926. Brother is actor Maximilian Schell. Made debut as teenager in Swiss film, Steinbruch (Quarry). Subsequently appeared in many British and American films.
PICTURES: Quarry (debut, 1941), Angel with the Trumpet, The Affairs of Dr. Holl, The Magic Box, Angelika, So Little Time, The Heart of the Matter, Der Traumende Mund (Dreaming Lips), The Last Bridge (Cannes Film Fest. Award, 1954), Angelika, The Rats, Napoleon, Gervaise (Venice Film Fest. Award, 1956), Liebe (Love), Rose Bernd, Le Notti Bianche (White Nights), Une Vie (End of Desire), The Brothers Karamazov, The Hanging Tree, Der Schinderhannes (Duel in the Forest), As the Sea Rages, Cimarron, The Mark, Only a Woman, La Assassin connait la Musique, Rendezvous in Trieste, Who Has Seen the Wind?, 99 Women, Devil By the Tail, Night of the Blood Monster, Lust in the Sun, The Odessa File, Voyage of the Damned, Folies Bourgeoises (The Twist), Superman, Just a Gigolo, 1919, Meine Schwester Maria.
TELEVISION: U.S.: Heidi, Christmas Lilies of the Field, Inside the Third Reich, Martian Chronicles, Samson and Delilah, Tatort-Heileg Blut, Le Dernier mot.

SCHELL, MAXIMILIAN
Actor, Director. b. Vienna, Dec. 8, 1930. Sister is actress Maria Schell. e. Switzerland. Stage debut 1952. B'way debut in Interlock.
PICTURES: Children Mother and the General (debut, 1955), The Young Lions (U.S. debut, 1958), Judgment at Nuremberg (Acad. Award, 1961), Five Finger Exercise, The Reluctant Saint, The Condemned of Altona, Topkapi, Return from the Ashes, The Deadly Affair, Counterpoint, The Desperate Ones, The Castle (also dir.), Krakatoa—East of Java, Simon Bolivar, First Love (also dir., co-s.p., co-prod.), Trotta (co-s.p.), Pope Joan, Paulina 1880, The Pedestrian (also dir., prod., s.p.), The Odessa File, The Man in the Glass Booth, End of the Game (also dir., co-prod., co-s.p.), St. Ives, The Day That Shook the World, A Bridge Too Far, Cross of Iron, Julia, Players, Avalanche Express, Together?, The Black Hole, Tales From the Vienna Woods (also dir., s.p.), The Chosen, Les Iles, Morgen in Alabama, Marlene (dir., s.p., interviewer), The Rose Garden, The Freshman, Labyrinth, A Far Off Place, Little Odessa, The Vampyre Wars, Telling Lies in America, Zwischen Rosen, The Fifteenth Angel, Left Luggage, Vampires, Deep Impact, On the Wings of Love, I Love You Baby, Fisimatenten, Hamlet in Hollywood, Festival in Cannes, Meine Schwester Maria, Light in the Sky.
TELEVISION: Judgment at Nuremberg (Playhouse 90), The Fifth Column, The Diary of Anne Frank, Turn The Key Deftly, Phantom of the Opera, Heidi, The Assisi Underground, Peter the Great (mini-series), Young Catherine, Stalin, Miss Rose White, Candles in the Dark (also dir.), Abraham, Thorn Birds: The Missing Years, Joan of Arc, The Song of the Lark, Coast to Coast.

SCHEPISI, FRED
Producer, Director, Writer. b. Melbourne, Australia, Dec. 26, 1939. e. Assumption Col., Marist Bros. Juniorate, Marcellin Col. Assessed student films at Melbourne's Swinburne Inst. of Tech.; worked on gov. sponsored experimental Film Fund; made TV commercials. Founded The Film House prod. co. Dir. short film The Party.

PICTURES: *Director*: Libido (co-dir.), Barbarosa, Iceman, Plenty, Roxanne, A Cry in the Dark (also co-s.p.; Australian Film Inst. Award for best dir. & s.p.), Fierce Creatures. *Dir./Prod.*: The Devil's Playground (also s.p.), The Chant of Jimmie Blacksmith (also s.p.), The Russia House, Mr. Baseball, Six Degrees of Separation, I.Q., Fierce Creatures, Picasso at the Lapin Agile, It Runs in the Family. *Producer*: That Eye the Sky (exec.), Levity, (exec. prod.).

SCHIAVELLI, VINCENT
Actor. b. Brooklyn, NY, November 10, 1948. e. NYU. On Stage in Hunting Cockroaches, Alphabetical Order, Angel City.
AUTHOR: Papa Andrea's Sicilian Table, Bruculinu America.
PICTURES: Taking Off, The Great Gatsby, For Pete's Sake, One Flew Over the Cuckoo' Nest, The Happy Hooker, Next Stop Greenwich Village, An Unmarried Woman, The Frisco Kid, Butch and Sundance: The Early Days, Seed of Innocence, The Return, American Pop (voice), Chu Chu and the Philly Flash, Night Shift, Fast Times at Ridgemont High, Kidco, The Adventures of Buckaroo Banzai Across the 8th Dimension, Amadeus, Better Off Dead, Valmont, Homer and Eddie, Cold Feet, Ghost, Waiting for the Light, Playroom, Penny Ante, Mister Frost, Ted and Venus, Another You, Miracle Beach, Batman Returns, Lurking Fear, Cultivating Charlie, Lod of Illusions, A Little Princess, Ninjas Knuckle Up, Two Much, The People vs. Larry Flynt, Back to Back, The Beautician and the Beast, Tomorrow Never Dies, Milo, The Prince and the Surfer, Coyote Moon, Man on the Moon, Treehouse Hostage, Baggage, American Virgin, 3 Strikes, American Saint, Death to Smoochy, Solino, Hey Arnold! (movie).
TELEVISION: *Series*: The Corner Bar, Taxi, Fast Times, The Eddie Files. *Movies*: Rescue from Gilligan's Island, White Mama, Escape, The Ratings Game, Bride of Boogedy, Escape to Witch Mountain, The Whipping Boy, Snow White: The Fairest of Them All, Heat Vision and Jack, The Pooch and the Pauper, Casper Meets Wendy, Back to Back, Brothers' Destiny, The Courtyard, Escape to Witch Mountain. *Guest*: Moonlighting, Shell Game, Star Trek: The Next Generation, Batman: The Animated Series (voice), Knots Landing, Eerie Indiana, The X Files, Buffy the Vampire Slayer.

SCHIFRIN, LALO
Composer, b. Buenos Aires, Argentina, June 21, 1932. Father was conductor of Teatro Colon in B.A. for 30 years. Schifrin studied with Juan Carlos Paz in Arg. and later Paris Cons. Returned to homeland and wrote for stage, modern dance, TV. Became interested in jazz and joined Dizzie Gillespie's band in 1962 as pianist and composer. Settled in L.A. Pres. Young Musicians Fed. Music; dir. and conductor, Paris Philharmonic 1987.
PICTURES: El Jefe, Rhino!, Joy House/Les Felins, Once A Thief, Gone With the Wave, Dark Intruder, The Cincinnati Kid, Way...Way Out!, The Liquidator, I Deal in Danger, Blindfold, Who's Minding the Mint?, The Venetian Affair, Sullivan's Empire, The President's Analyst, Murderer's Row, Cool Hand Luke (Acad. Award nom.), Sol Madrid, Hell in the Pacific, The Fox (Acad. Award nom.), Coogan's Bluff, Bullitt, The Bortherhood/The Heroin Gang, The Eye of the Cat, Che!, W.U.S.A., Pussycat Pussycat I love You, Kelly's Heroes, Imago, I Love My Wife, THX-1138, Pretty Maids All in a Row, Mrs. Pollifax–Spy, The Hellstrom Chronicle, Dirty Harry, The Christian Licorice Store, The Beguiled, The Wrath of God, Rage, Prime Cut, Joe Kidd, The Neptune Factor, Magnum Force, Hit!, Harry in Your Pocket, Enter the Dragon, Charlie Varrick, Man On a Swing, Golden Needles, The Master Gunfighter, The Four Musketeers, Voyage of the Damned (Acad. Award nom.), St. Ives, Special Delivery, The Sky Riders, Return From Witch Mountain, Telefon, Rollercoaster, The Eagle Has Landed, The Day of the Animals, Nunzio, The Manitou, The Cat From Outer Space, Love and Bullets, Escape to Athena, Boulevard Nights, The Concorde: Airport '79, The Amityville Horror, When Time Ran Out, Serial, The Nude Bomb, The Competition (Acad. Award nom.), Brubaker, The Big Brawl, The Seduction, La Pelle, Loophole, Caveman, Buddy Buddy, Las Viernes de la Etertnidad, Fast-Walking, The Class of 1984, A Stranger Is Watching, Amytiville II–The Possession, Airplane II–The Sequel, Sudden Impact, The Sting II, The Osterman Weekend, Dr. Detroit, Tank, The New Kids, The Mean Season, The Ladies Club, Black Moon Rising, The Fourth Protocol, The Silence at Bethany, Little Sweetheart, The Dead Pool, Berlin Blues, Return to the River Kwai, Fridays to Eternity, Naked Tango, FX 2, The Beverly Hillbillies, Rice Beans & Ketchuo, Scoprion Spring, Mission: Impossible, Tango, Something to Believe In, Money Talks, Rush Hour, Rush Hour 2, Longshot, Mission Impossible 2, Rush Hour 3, Mission Impossible 3.
TELEVISION: *Theme, Episode, Movie & Miniseries scores*: Mission Impossible, Mannix, Medical Center, Starsky and Hutch, Bronk, Braddock, The Blue Light, Dr. Kildare, 90 Bristol Court, The Young Lawyers, The Black Cloak, The Cliff Dwellers, Ben Casey, I.F.M., Johnny Comes Home, Delancy Street, Foster and Laurie, Egan, How I Spent My Summer Vacation, The World of Jacques Cousteau, Three for Danger, Brenda Starr, Good Against Evil, The Chicago Story, The Victims, Starflight One, Princess Diasy, Sprague, House Detective, Command 5, Glitter, A.D., Hollywood Wives, Terror at London Bridge, Private Sessions, The Equalizer, Beverly Hills Madam, Out on a Limb, Hunter, The Doomsday Flight, Jericho, The Highest Fall of All, Maryk, The Nativity,

Quest, Petrocelli, The President's Mistress, Pay the Piper, The Rise and Fall of the Third Reich, The Hidden World of Insects, The Way-Out Men, Sullivan Country, The Aquarians, Shipwreck, Sam Sheppard, Sixth Sense, Memo From Purgatory, Kraft Suspense Theatre, The Virginians, Wagon Train, Private Eye, Shakedown on the Sunset Strip, Earthstar Voyager, Noon Empire, Little White Lies, Face to Face, Original Sins, Berlin Blues, El Quixote, A Woman Named Jackie, Danger Theater.

SCHILLER, FRED
Playwright, Screen & TV Writer. b. Vienna, Austria, Jan. 6, 1924. e. Columbia Univ. (B.A.). Awarded: New York Literary Prize for McCall magazine story Ten Men and a Prayer. Member of Dramatists' Guild and Writer's Guild of America. Formerly chief corresp. European Newspaper Feature Services. Honored by the U. of Wyoming and the American Heritage Center for literary achievements with a special Fred Schiller Collection for their library. Awarded the Honor Silver Cross by Austrian Govt., for literary achievements and for advancing cultural relations between Austria and U.S. Screen plays for pictures by MGM, Columbia, and others.
THEATRE: Come On Up (U.S. key citiies , London), Anything Can Happen (London), Demandez Vicky (Paris), Finder Please Return (L.A., San Francisco, Madrid, Vienna), Finder Bitte Melden (Berlin, Baden-Baden, Vienna), The Love Trap.
TELEVISION: Wrote some 53 TV plays incl. The Inca of Jerusalem, Demandez Vicky! for Paris and Finder Bitte Melden! for Austria, She- Me and Her.
(d. Feb. 8, 2003).

SCHILLER, LAWRENCE J.
Producer, Director. b. New York, NY, Dec. 28, 1936. Photojournalist with Life Magazine & Saturday Evening Post, 1958-70; collaborated on numerous books including three by Norman Mailer: The Executioner's Song, Marilyn, and The Faith of Graffiti; also Muhammad Ali (with Wilfrid Sheed), Minamata (with Eugene Smith).
PICTURES: The Man Who Skied Down Everest (editorial concept & direction), Butch Cassidy & the Sundance Kid (conceived and executed special still montages & titles); The American Dreamer (prod., dir.).
TELEVISION: *Prod.*: Hey I'm Alive (also dir.), The Trial of Lee Harvey Oswald, The Winds of Kitty Hawk, Marilyn, The Untold Story, An Act of Love, The Executioner's Song (also dir.), Peter the Great, Margaret Bourke-White (also dir.), The Patricia Neal Story, The Executioner's Song, Murder: By Reason of Insanity, The Plot to Kill Hitler, Master Spy: The Robert Hanssen Story, American Tragedy, Perfect Murder, Perfect Town: JonBenét and the City of Boulder, Double Jeopardy.

SCHLATTER, GEORGE
Producer, Director, Writer. b. Birmingham, AL, Dec. 31, 1932. m. former actress Jolene Brand. e. Pepperdine U. on football scholarship. First industry job was MCA agent in band and act dept. Then gen. mgr. and show producer Ciro's nightclub (where he met Dick Martin and Dan Rowan). Produced shows at Frontier Hotel and Silver Slipper, Las Vegas. Sang 2 seasons St. Louis Municipal Opera Co.
TELEVISION: *Created*: Laugh-In, Real People (3 Emmys, 27 nominations). *Specials with*: Goldie Hawn, Robin Williams, Shirley MacLaine, Doris Day, John Denver, Frank Sinatra, Jackie Gleason, Danny Thomas, Bob Hope, Milton Berle, Danny Kaye, George Burns, Dinah Shore, Lucille Ball, Goldie & Liza Together, Salute to Lady Liberty, Las Vegas 75th Anniversary, Speak Up America, Real Kids, Best of Times, Look At Us, Shape of Things, Magic or Miracle, Grammy Awards (first 5 years: also writer), series with Dinah Shore, Judy Garland, Bill Cosby, Steve Lawrence; also ABC American Comedy Awards (3 years), George Schlatter's Comedy Club, George Schlatter's Funny People, Beverly Hills 75th Anniversary, Humor and the Presidency, Frank Liza & Sammy... The Ultimate Event, Comedy Hall of Fame, She TV (series), Sinatra's 75th Birthday, The Best Is Yet to Come, Muhammad Ali's 50th Birthday, Welcome Home America, Laugh-In 25th Anniversary Reunion. *Movies*: Tracey Ullman in the Trailer Tales.

SCHLESINGER, JOHN
Director, Producer. b. London, England, Feb. 16, 1926. e. Oxford U., BBC dir. 1958-60: Wrote and dir. Terminus for British Transport Films (Golden Lion, best doc., Venice); The Class. Some episodes The Valiant Years series. Appeared as actor in films: Sailor of the King (1953), Pursuit of the Graf Spee, Brothers in Law, The Divided Heart, The Last Man to Hang, Fifty Years of action (DGA doc.). Assoc. dir., National Theatre, London 1973-89. Recipient of 1995 BAFTA Fellowship.
THEATRE: Heartbreak House (NT), Julius Caesar (NT), True West (NT).
PICTURES: A Kind of Loving (Berlin Golden Bear Award, 1961), Billy Liar, Darling (NY Film Critics Award), Far From the Madding Crowd, Midnight Cowboy (Acad. Award, 1969), Sunday Bloody Sunday, Visions of Eight (sequence), The Day of the Locust, Marathon Man, Yanks, Honky Tonk Freeway, The Falcon and the Snowman (also co-prod.), The Believers (also co-prod.), Madame Sousatzka (also co-s.p.), Pacific Heights (also cameo), The Innocent, Eye for an Eye, Cold Comfort Farm, The Next Best Thing.

TELEVISION: Separate Tables, An Englishman Abroad (BAFTA Award), The Lost Language of Cranes (actor only), A Question of Attribution (BAFTA Award), The Tale of Sweeney Todd.
OPERA: Les Contes d'Hoffmann (Royal Opera House 1981; SWET award), Der Rosenkavalier.
(d. Feb. 16, 2003).

SCHLONDORFF, VOLKER

Director. b. Wiesbaden, Germany, March 31, 1939. m. dir.-actress Margarethe von Trotta. Studied in France, acquiring degree in political science in Paris. Studied at French Intl. Film Sch. (IDHEC) before becoming asst. to Jean-Pierre Melville, Alain Resnais, and Louis Malle.
PICTURES: Young Torless (debut, 1966; also s.p.), A Degree of Murder (also s.p.), Michael Kohlhass, Baal, The Sudden Fortune of the Poor People of Kombach, Die Moral der Ruth Halbfass, A Free Woman, The Lost Honor of Katharina Blum (also s.p.), Coup de Grace, The Tin Drum (also s.p.), Valeska Gert (also s.p.), Circle of Deceit, Swann in Love (also s.p.), The Handmaid's Tale, Voyager (also co-s.p.), The Ogre, Palmetto, Legend of Rita.
TELEVISION: Movies: Death of a Salesman, A Gathering of Old Men. Series: Billy How Did You Do It?

SCHLOSSBERG, JULIAN

Producer, Distributor, Director, Radio TV Host. b. New York, NY, Jan. 26, 1942. e. N.Y. Joined ABC-TV network 1964 as asst. acct. rep.; named act. rep. 1965; 1966, joined Walter Reade Organization as asst. v.p. chg. of TV; 1969, moved to WRO Theatre Div.; 1970, joined faculty of School of Visual Arts; 1971 named v.p. of WRO Theatres; 1976, joined Paramount Pictures as v.p. in charge of feature film acquisition. Since 1978 pres. & owner of Castle Hill Productions; 1974, prod. & moderated An Evening with Joseph E. Levine at Town Hall, N.Y.; 1974-1980, host of radio show Movie Talk on WMCA (N.Y.), WMEX (Boston), WICE (Providence); 1982-83 host of syndicated TV show, Julian Schlossbergs' Movie Talk; producers' rep. for Dustin Hoffman, Elaine May and the late John Cassavetes and Elia Kazan,. Responsible for restored version of Orson Welles' Othello, re-released in 1992.
THEATRE: Unexpected Man, Madame Melville, Vita & Virginia, Death Defying Acts, Moscow Stations, Below the Belt, Cakewalk, Beauty Queen of Leenane, Power Plays, Tennessee Williiams Remembered, If Love Were All, Street of Dreams, Taller Than A Dwarf, It Had To Be You, Adult Entertainment, Tommy Tune: White Tie & Tails and Fortune's Fool.
PICTURES: Going Hollywood: The War Years, Hollywood Uncensored, Hollywood Ghost Stories, No Nukes, Going Hollywood: The 30's, 10 From Your Show of Shows, In the Spirit, Bad Girls, Widow's Peak.
TELEVISION: Steve Allen's Golden Age of Comedy; All the Best, Steve Allen, Sex & Justice: The Anita Hill/Clarence Thomas Hearings, Slapstick Too, Elia Kazan: A Director's Journey (Emmy nom.), Nichols & May: Take Two, Claire Bloom's Shakespeare's Women, The Lives of Lillian Hellman.

SCHLOSSER, HERBERT S.

Executive. b. Atlantic City, NJ, April 21, 1926. e. Princeton U., Yale Law Sch. Joined law firm of Phillips, Nizer, Benjamin, Krim & Ballon, 1954; attorney, California National Productions subsidiary of National Broadcasting Company) 1957; v.p. & gen. mgr., 1960; joined NBC-TV as director, talent & program admin., 1961; v.p., talent & program admin., 1962; v.p. programs, west coast, 1966-72; exec. v.p., NBC-TV, 1972; pres., 1973; pres. & COO, 1974-76; pres. & CEO, 1977-78; exec. v.p. RCA, 1978-85; sr. advisor, broadcasting & entertainment, Schroder Wertheim & Co., 1986.

SCHMIDT, WOLF

Producer, Distributor. b. Freiburg/Br., Germany, June 30, 1937. Came to U.S. 1962 as freelance journalist. Started producing in 1969, distributing independently since 1972. Now pres. Big Bearing Licensing Corp.
PICTURES: Prod./Exec. Prod.: Ski Fever, Stamping Ground, Young Hannah, Things Fall Apart, The Passover Plot, Run for the Roses, Ghost Fever, Defense Play, Riding the Edge, The Fourth War, Neon City, Extreme Justice, Silent Hunter.

SCHMOELLER, DAVID

Writer, Director. b. Louisville, KY, Dec. 8, 1947. e. Universidad de Las Americas, 1967-69, studied film and theater under Luis Bunuel and Alejandro Jodorowsky; U. of TX, B.A., M.A., 1969-74. Wrote and directed 7 short films while studying at college; won 27 intl. awards. In Hollywood spent 6 months working as intern to Peter Hyams on film, Capricorn One. Now heads own co., The Schmoeller Corp.
AUTHOR: The Seduction.
PICTURES: Tourist Trap (debut as dir.), The Seduction (dir., s.p.), Crawlspace (dir., s.p.). Writer: The Day Time Ended, The Peeper, Last Chance Romance, Thrill Palace, Warriors of the Wind (Eng. adaptation), Ghost Town (story). Director: Catacombs, Curse of the Puppet Master, The Arrival, Netherworld, Catch the Wind (also s.p.), The Secret Kingdom, Please kill Mr. Kinski.
TELEVISION: James at 15 (writer), Kid Flicks (cable; writer, prod.), Silk Stalkings (dir.), Renegades (dir.), Search for the Jewel of Polaris: Mysterious Museum.

SCHNEER, CHARLES H.

Producer, b. Norfolk, VA, May 5, 1920. e. Columbia Coll. pres., Morningside Prods. Inc. & Pictures Corp.; 1956. Founded Andor Films 1974. Chmn, Acad. of MP Arts & Sciences, London Screening Committee.
PICTURES: Prod.: The 3 Worlds of Gulliver, The 7th Voyage of Sinbad, I Aim at the Stars, Face of a Fugitive, Good Day for a Hanging, Battle of the Coral Sea, Tarawa Beachhead, Mysterious Island, Jason and the Argonauts, First Men In The Moon, Half A Sixpence, Land Raiders, Valley of Gwangi, The Executioner, The Golden Voyage of Sinbad, Sinbad & The Eye of the Tiger, Clash of the Titans.

SCHNEIDER, DICK

Producer, Director. b. Cazadero, CA, March 7. e. Univ. of the Pacific, Stockton, CA. U.S. Navy, WWII. Has received 9 Emmy Awards.
TELEVISION: Dough Re Mi, Wide Wide World, Colgate Comedy Hour, Beatrice Lillie, Jackie Gleason, Henry Morgan Show, Kate Smith Show, Big Story, Treasury Men in Action, Doorway to Danger, Today Show, Home, Tonight Show, General Mills Circus, Princess Margaret's Wedding, Paris Summit Conference, Eleanor Roosevelt Specials, Something Special 61, At This Very Moment, Inauguration, Gemini, Papal Mass for all networks at Yankee Stadium, Orange Bowl, Jr. Miss Pageant, College Queen (Emmy Award), New Communication, Big Sur, Dream House, Who What or Where, Stars and Stripes, Post Parade, Salute to Sir Lew, NBC Star Salute, Rose Parade, UCP Telethons, Macy's Parade, People's Choice, Jeopardy, Photo Finish.

SCHNEIDER, JOHN

Actor. b. Mount Kisco, NY, April 8, 1954. Active in drama club in high school in Atlanta. Worked as fashion model and played guitar singing own compositions in various Atlanta clubs. Active in local community theatre. Summer stock in New Hampshire. B'way debut 1991 in Grand Hotel.
PICTURES: Smokey and the Bandit, Million Dollar Dixie Deliverance, Eddie Macon's Run, The Curse, Cocaine Wars, Speed Zone, Ministry of Vengeance, Snow Day.
TELEVISION: Movies: Dream House, Happy Endings, Stagecoach, Christmas Comes to Willow Creek, Outback Bound, Gus Brown and Midnight Brewster, Highway Heartbreaker, Desperate Journey: The Allison Wilcox Story, Texas, Bandit: Bandit Bandit, Night of the Twisters , The Legend of the Ruby Silver, The Dukes of Hazzard: Reunion!, True Women, Michael Landon, the Father I Knew, Sam Churchill: Search for a Homeless Man, The Dukes of Hazzard: Hazzard In Hollywood, Lightning: Fire From the Sky, Christy: The Movie, Many Christmas. Mini- Series: Christy, Choices of the Heart, Part I: A Change of Seasons. Series: Dukes of Hazzard, Grand Slam, Second Chances, Heaven Help Us. Specials: John Schneider—Back Home, Wild Jack.

SCHNEIDER, PETER

Executive. e. B.A., theatre, Purdue U., 1971. Theatrical director, The WPA, Playwrights Horizon, and Circle Repetory Theater, New York; producer & managing director, Chicago's St. Nicholas Theater; general mgr., Apollo Theater Productions; director, 1984 Olympic Arts Festival; president (1985) and supervisor of the development and production of all Disney animated motion pictures; president, Walt Disney Studios; supervised the release of Disney's most successful release to date, the Lion King. Chairman of The Walt Disney Studios through June 2001. Resigned to form independent theatrical co. in New York.

SCHNEIER, FREDERICK

Executive. b. New York, NY, May 31, 1927; e. NYU, 1951, bus. admin.; NYU Grad. Sch., M.B.A., 1953. Dir. sls. planning, Mutual Broadcasting System, 1947-53; media research dir., RKO Teleradio, 1953-55; RKO Teleradio Advisory Comm., 1955-56; exec. staff RKO Teleradio & dir., marketing services, 1956-58; exec. vice-pres., Showcorporation, 1958-71; v.p. TV programming, RKO General, 1972-1973; v.p., Hemdale Leisure Corp., 1973-79; Viacom Enterprises v.p., feature films, 1979; sr. v.p., program acquisitions & motion pictures, 1980-83; sr. v.p., acquisitions, Showtime/The Movie Channel, 1983-85; sr. v.p. program acquisitions, program enterprises, 1985-87; exec. v.p., programming; 1987-89; pres. & CEO, Viacom Pictures Inc., 1989-92; pres. & CEO, FSA Film Enterprises.

SCHOEFFLING, MICHAEL

Actor. b. Philadelphia, PA. 1960. e. Temple Univ.
PICTURES: Sixteen Candles (debut, 1984), Vision Quest, Sylvester, Bellizaire the Cajun, Let's Get Harry, Slaves of New York, Longtime Companion, Mermaids, Wild Hearts Can't Be Broken.

SCHOONMAKER, THELMA

Editor. b. January 3, 1940.
PICTURES: Finnegan's Wake, Who's That Knocking at My Door?, Woodstock, Street Scenes, Taxi Driver, Rock Show, Raging Bull, The King of Comedy, After Hours, The Color of Money, Bad, The Last Temptation of Christ, New York Stories, Made in Milan, Goodfellas, Cape Fear, The Age of Innocence, Casino, Grace of My Heart, Kundun, Bringing out the Dead, The Gangs of New York.

SCHORR, DANIEL

Radio, Television News Correspondent. b. New York, NY, Aug. 31, 1916. e. City Coll. of New York. Started with various news services and newspapers. Joined CBS in 1953 as Washington correspondent; 1955, reopened CBS bureau in Moscow; 1958-60, roving assignment; 1960-1966, chief German Bureau; 1966-76, Washington Bureau; 1979, Public Radio and TV; 1980, sr. Washington correspondent for Cable News Network; 1985, sr. news analyst, National Public Radio.

SCHRADER, PAUL

Writer, Director. b. Grand Rapids, MI, July 22, 1946. m. actress Mary Beth Hurt. e. Calvin Coll. (theology & philosophy); Columbia U., UCLA, M.A., cinema. Served as film critic for L.A. Free Press and Cinema 1970-72. Former professor at Columbia U.
PICTURES: *Writer &/or Director*: The Yakuza (co-s.p.), Taxi Driver, Rolling Thunder, Obsession, Blue Collar (co-s.p., dir). Hardcore, Old Boyfriends (co-s.p., exec. prod.), American Gigolo, Raging Bull (co-s.p.), Cat People, Mishima (co-s.p.), The Mosquito Coast, Light of Day, The Last Temptation of Christ, Patty Hearst, The Comfort of Strangers, Light Sleeper, City Hall (co-s.p.), Touch, Affliction, Bringing out the Dead (s.p.), Auto Focus, Forever Mine (dir., s.p.), Dino (s.p.), Exorcist IV: The Beginning.
TELEVISION: *Movie*: Witch Hunt (dir.), The Hollywood Fashion Machine (act. only).

SCHREIBER, LIEV

Actor. b. San Francisco, CA, October 4, 1967. e. Yale School of Drama. Attended London's Royal Academy of Art and Hampshire College, Amherst, Mass.
PICTURES: Mixed Nuts, Denise Calls Up, Mad Love, Party Girl, Big Night, Walking and Talking, Ransom, Scream, The Daytrippers, Baggage, Scream 2, His and Hers, Phantoms, Sphere, Twilight, Desert Blue (voice), A Walk on the Moon, Jakob the Liar, The Hurricane, Spring Forward, Hamlet, Scream 3, Dial 9 For Love, The Sum of All Fears, Kate and Leopold.
TELEVISION: *Movies*: Janek: The Silent Betrayal, Buffalo Girls, The Sunshine Boys, Since You've Been Gone, Babe Ruth (voice), RKO 281, Bill Russell: My Life,My Way (voice), When It Was a Game 3, Ali-Frazier 1: One Nation...Divisible (narrator), Playing the Field: Sports and Sex in America (narrator), Do You Believe in Miracles? The Story of the 1980 U.S. Hockey Team (narrator), Shot Heard 'Round the World (narrator), A Brilliant Madness, :03 From Gold, Hitler: The Rise of Evil. *Guest*: Nova (narrator).

SCHRODER, RICK

Actor. b. Staten Island, NY, April 13, 1970. Started modelling while only four months; did many TV commercials before theatrical film debut in The Champ, at age eight.
PICTURES: The Champ, The Last Flight of Noah's Ark, The Earthling, Apt Pupil, Across the Tracks, There Goes My Baby, Crimson Tide, Poolhall Junkies, I woke Up Early the Day I Died.
TELEVISION: *Movies*: Little Lord Fauntleroy, Something So Right, Two Kinds of Love, A Reason to Live, Too Young the Hero, Terror on Highway 91, Out on the Edge, A Son's Promise, The Stranger Within, Blood River, My Son Johnny, Miles From Nowhere, Call of the Wild, To My Daughter with Love, Texas, Heart Full of Rain, Ebenezer, Too Close To Home, Detention: The Siege at Johnson High, What we did that Night, Murder at Devil's Glenn, The Lost Batallion. *Mini-Series*: Lonesome Dove, Return to Lonesome Dove. *Series*: Silver Spoons, NYPD Blue.

SCHROEDER, BARBET

Producer, Director. b. Teheran, Iran, Aug. 26, 1941. Critic for Cahiers du Cinema and L'Air de Paris, 1958-63. 1963: asst. to Jean-Luc Godard on Les Carabiniers. 1964: formed own prod. co. Les Films du Losange. As actor only: Paris vu par, La Boulangere de Monceau Roberte, Celline and Julie Go Boating, Beverly Hills Cop III, La Reine Margot, Mars Attacks!
PICTURES: *Producer*: La Boulangere de Monceau (26 mins.), La Carriere de Suzanne (52 mins.), Mediterrannee, Paris Vu Par, La Collectionneuse, Tu Imagines Robinson, My Night at Maud's, Claire's Knee, Chloe in the Afternoon, Out One (co-prod.), The Mother and the Whore (co-prod.), Celine and Julie Go Boating, Flocons D'Or, The Marquise of O, Roulette Chinoise (co-prod.), The American Friend (co-prod.), Le Passe-Montagne, The Rites of Death, Perceval Le Gallois, Le Navire Night, Le Pont du Nord, Mauvaise Conduite, Une Sale Historie. *Director & Producer*: More (1969), Sing-Sing (doc.), La Vallee, General Idi Amin Dada (doc.), Maitresse, Koko a Talking Gorilla (doc.), Charles Bukowski Tapes (doc.), Tricheurs, Barfly, Reversal of Fortune, Single White Female, Kiss of Death, Before and After, Desperate Measures, Shattered Image(prod.), Our Lady of the Assassins, Murder by Numbers,(prod.).

SCHUCK, JOHN

Actor. b. Boston, MA, Feb. 4, 1940. e. Denison (BA). Cabaret act: An Evening With John Schuck.
THEATRE: *B'way*: Annie. *Off-B'way*: The Streets of NY, The Shrike. London: The Caine Mutiny. Regional incl. Long Day's Journey Into Night, As You Like It.
PICTURES: M*A*S*H, The Moonshine War, Brewster McCloud, McCabe and Mrs. Miller, Hammersmith Is Out, Blade, Thieves

Like Us, Butch and Sundance: The Early Days, Just You and Me Kid, Earthbound, Finders Keepers, Star Trek VI: The Voyage Home, Outrageous Fortune, The New Adventures of Pippi Longstocking, My Mom's a Werewolf, Second Sight, Dick Tracy, Star Trek IV: The Undiscovered Country, Holy Matrimony, Pontiac Moon, Tales From the Crypt Presents Demon Knight, The Trial of Old Drum, The Curse of the Jade Scorpion.
TELEVISION: *Series*: McMillan and Wife, Holmes and Yoyo, Turnabout, The New Odd Couple, The Munsters Today. *Mini-Series*: Roots. *Movies*: Once Upon a Dead Man, Hunter, Till Death Us Do Part, Project ALF, Run for the Dream: The Gail Devers Story. *Guest*: Murder She Wrote, Time Trax, Deep Space Nine.

SCHULBERG, BUDD WILSON

Writer. b. New York, NY, March 27, 1914. Son of B. P. Schulberg, prod. e. Dartmouth Coll. Publicist, Paramount Pictures, 1931; writer for screen from 1932. Armed services WWII. Syndicated newspaper columnist: The Schulberg Report.
AUTHOR: *Novels*: What Makes Sammy Run?, The Disenchanted, The Harder They Fall, On the Waterfront, Some Faces in the Crowd, Everything That Moves, Sanctuary V, Love Action Laughter and Other Sad Tales. *Non-fiction books*: Writers in America, Moving Pictures: Memories of a Hollywood Prince, Swan Watch, Loser and Still Champion: Muhammad Ali, Sparring With Hemingway and Other Legends of the Fight Game. *Short stories*: Some Faces In the Crowd, Love, Action, Laughter and Other Sad Tales.
THEATRE: The Disenchanted (with Harvey Breit, 1958), What Makes Sammy Run? (book for musical), On the Waterfront (with Stan Silverman).
PICTURES: A Star is Born (additional dial.), Nothing Sacred (add. dial.), Little Orphan Annie (co-s.p.), Winter Carnival (co-s.p with F. Scott Fitzgerald), Weekend for Three (orig. and co-s.p.), City Without Men (co-story), Government Girl (adapt.). Original s.p.: On the Waterfront (Acad. Award, & Writers Guild Award, 1954), A Face in the Crowd, Wind Across the Everglades, Joe Louis: For All Time (doc., Cine Golden Eagle Award, 1985).
TELEVISION: *Teleplays*: What Makes Sammy Run?, Paso Doble, The Pharmacist's Mate, Memory In White, The Legend That Walks Like A Man, A Question of Honor, A Table at Ciro's.

SCHULMAN, JOHN A.

Executive. b. Washington, D.C., June 13, 1946. e. Yale U., 1968; law degree from Boalt Hall, U. of California, Berkeley, 1972. Founding partner in Beverly Hills law firm, Weissmann, Wolff, Bergman, Coleman & Schulman in 1981 after nine years with firm of Kaplan, Livingston, Goodwin, Berkowitz & Selvin. Joined Warner Bros. 1984 as v.p. & gen. counsel; 1989 sr. v.p. and gen. counsel; 1991, exec. v.p. and gen. counsel.

SCHULMAN, TOM

Writer. e. Vanderbilt U, BA.
PICTURES: Dead Poets Society (Acad. Award, 1989), What About Bob?, Honey I Shrunk the Kids, Second Sight, Medicine Man, Indecent Proposal (exec. prod.), 8 Heads in a Duffel Bag (also dir.), Holy Man, Me, Myself and Irene (exec. prod.)
TELEVISION: *Movies:* The Gladiator, (exec. prod.), Das Rattennest.

SCHULTZ, DWIGHT

Actor. b. Baltimore, MD, Nov. 24, 1947. e. Townson St. Univ. Acted with Williamstown Theatre Fest. prior to NY stage work, incl. The Crucifer of Blood, The Water Engine, Night and Day.
PICTURES: The Fan, Alone in the Dark, Fat Man and Little Boy, The Long Walk Home, The Temp., Star Trek: First Contact, The First Men on the Moon, Sacrifice,Baldur's Gate II, Technu 2, Blood Wake, Spiderman: The Game.
TELEVISION: *Series*: The A-Team, Star Trek: The Next Generation. *Movies*: Child of Rage, When Your Lover Leaves, Perry Mason: The Case of the Sinister Spirit, Perry Mason: The Case of the Musical Murder, A Woman With a Past, The Last Wish, A Killer Among Us, Victim of Love: The Shannon Mohr Story, Menendez: A Killing in Beverly Hills, Star Trek Voyager (series), Spawn, Cat Dog, The Barbara Mandrell Story, The Chimp Channel.

SCHULTZ, MICHAEL

Director, Producer. b. Milwaukee, WI, Nov. 10, 1938. e. U. of Wisconsin, Marquette U.
THEATRE: The Song of the Lusitainian Bogey, Kongi's Harvest, Does a Tiger Wear a Necktie?, Operation Sidewinder, What the Winesellers Buy, The Cherry Orchard, Mulebone, Dream on Monkey Mountain.
PICTURES: *Director*: Together for Days, Honeybaby Honeybaby, Cooley High, Car Wash, Greased Lightning, Which Way Is Up?, Sgt. Pepper's Lonely Hearts Club Band, Scavenger Hunt, Carbon Copy, The Last Dragon, Krush Groove (also prod.), Disorderlies (also co-prod.), Livin' Large, Phat Beach
TELEVISION: *Specials*: To Be Young Gifted and Black, Ceremonies in Dark Old Men, For Us the Living, Fade Out: The Erosion of Black Images in the Media (documentary), Hollywood Follies, Travels With Father. *Series*: The Young Indiana Jones Chronicles, Picket Fences, Chicago Hope, Sisters City of Angels, Boston Public, Ally, Family Law, Charmed, Ally McBeal,

Promised Land, JAG.. *Pilot*: Shock Treatment. *Movies*: Benny's Place, The Jerk Too, Timestalkers, Rock 'n' Roll Mom, Tarzan in Manhattan, Jury Duty, Dayo, Shock Treatment, Young Indiana Jones and the Hollywood Follies,Young Indiana Jones: Travels with Father, L.A. Law: The Movie.

SCHUMACHER, JOEL
Director, Writer. b. New York, NY, Aug. 29, 1939. Worked as design and display artist for Henri Bendel dept. store NY while attending Parson's Sch. of Design. As fashion designer opened own boutique, Paraphernalia. Joined Revlon as designer of clothing and packaging before entering m.p. indus. as costume designer on Play It As It Lays, Sleeper, The Last of Sheila, Blume in Love, Prisoner of 2nd Avenue, Interiors.
PICTURES: *Writer*: Car Wash, Sparkle, The Wiz. *Director*: The Incredible Shrinking Woman (debut, 1981), D.C. Cab (also s.p.), St. Elmo's Fire (also s.p.), The Lost Boys, Cousins, Flatliners, Dying Young, Falling Down, The Client, Batman Forever, A Time to Kill, Batman & Robin, Tigerland, 8mm (also prod.), Flawless (also s.p., prod.), Gossip (exec. prod.), Tigerland, Phone Booth, Bad Company, Veronica Guerin, The Phantom of the Opera.
TELEVISION: *Director*: *Movies*: The Virginia Hill Story (also writer), Amateur Night at the Dixie Bar & Grill (also writer). *Music video*: Devil Inside for rock group INXS (dir.). *Series*: 2000 Malibu Drive. *Exec. Prod.*: Slow Burn.

SCHUMACHER, MARTHA
Producer. a.k.a Martha De Laurentiis. m. Dino De Laurentiis, producer.
PICTURES: Firestarter (assoc. prod.), Silver Bullet, Cat's Eye, King Kong Lives, Raw Deal, Maximum Overdrive, The Bedroom Window, Desperate Hours (exec. prod.). *As Martha De Laurentiis*: Once Upon a Crime (exec. prod.), Temptation (exec. prod.), Slave of Dreams, Unforgettable, Breakdown, U-571, Hannibal, Red Dragon.

SCHUMACHER, THOMAS
Producer, Executive. e. UCLA. Began as production asst., Taper Mainstage, Taper Too, and the literary cabaret, Mark Taper Forum. Producer, three original productions for the Improvisational Theater Project. Olympic Arts Festival staff, 1984; asst. gen. mgr., Los Angeles Ballet; co-founder and assoc. dir., 1987 Los Angeles Festival of Arts. Responsible for the American premiere of Canada's Cirque du Soleil. Producer: The Rescuers Down Under (1990), Walt Disney Feature Animation, 1988; exec. producer, The Lion King, 1994; exec. v.p., Disney Feature Animation and Theatrical Productions, 1994-98. Currently president of Walt Disney Feature Animation, Walt Disney Television Animation, and Buena Vista Theatrical Group. Serves on the Education Council, the Presentations Committee of the Performing Arts Center of Los Angeles County, and the board of directors of the Rachel Rosenthal Co.
PICTURES: The Rescuers Down Under, The Lion King, (exec. prod.).

SCHWAB, SHELLY
Executive. Station mgr., WAGA-TV, Atlanta; various sls. & mgr. posts with CBS. Joined MCA, 1978, becoming exec. v.p., MCA-TV. 1986, appt. pres., MCA TV Enterprises, 1989 appt. pres. MCA TV.

SCHWARTZ, BERNARD
Producer. Brought to Hollywood by the late Howard Hughes to watch his film interests; Schwartz teamed with atty. Greg Bautzer to package movie deals for clients. Re-cut number of Buster Keaton's silent movies into documentary anthologies (The Golden Age of Comedy, When Comedy Was King.). Subsequently made TV series, One Step Beyond, followed by The Wackiest Ship in the Army, Miss Teen International specials, etc. Named pres. Joseph M. Schenck Enterprises, for which he made Journey to the Center of the Earth, Eye of the Cat, A Cold Wind in August, I Passed for White, The Shattered Room, Trackdown. Presently partnered with Alan Silverman.
PICTURES: Coal Miner's Daughter (prod.), Road Games (exec. prod.) Psycho II (exec. prod.), St. Elmo's Fire (co-exec. prod.).
TELEVISION: Elvis and Me (co-exec. prod.).

SCHWARTZ, SHERWOOD
Producer. b. Nov. 14, 1916. Also composed themes for television shows Gilligan's Island and The Brady Bunch.
PICTURES: The Brady Bunch Movie, A Very Brady Sequel.
TELEVISION: *Movies*: Rescue from Gilligan's Island (exec., s.p.), The Invisible Woman (exec., s.p.), The Harlem Globetrotters on Gilligan's Island (s.p. only), The Brady Girls Get Married (s.p. only), The Brady Bunch in the White House. *Series*: Gilligan's Island (also creator), It's About Time, The Brady Bunch (exec.), The brady Kids (exec. consult. only), Dusty's Trail, Big John Little John (exec., also creator), The Brady Bunch Hour, Harper Valley P.T.A., The Bradys (creator only).

SCHWARY, RONALD L.
Producer. b. Oregon, May 23, 1944. e. U. of Southern California. Started as movie extra before becoming asst. dir.; served as assoc. prod. on The Electric Horseman.
PICTURES: Ordinary People (Acad. Award for Best Picture,

1980), Absence of Malice, Tootsie, A Soldier's Story, Batteries Not Included, Havana, Scent of a Woman, Cops and Robbersons, Sabrina, The Mirror Has Two Faces (co-exec. prod.), Meet Joe Black (exec. prod.) , Random Hearts (exec. prod.).
TELEVISION: Tour of Duty, Now and Again.

SCHWARZENEGGER, ARNOLD
Actor. b. Graz, Austria, July 30, 1947. m. NBC reporter Maria Shriver. e. U. Wisconsin, B.A. Bodybuilding Titles: Junior Mr. Europe (at age 18), Mr. Universe (3 time winner), Mr. Olympia (7 times), Mr. Europe, Mr. World. Special Olympics weightlifting Coach (1989), Prison Weightlifting Rehabilitation Prog. Awards: Sportsman of the Year (1977, Assn. Physical Fitness Ctrs.), Golden Globe (best newcomer, 1977), ShoWest '85 Intl. Star, ShoWest Career Achievement Award, NATO Male Star of Yr. (1987). Elected governor of California during 2003 gov. recall election. AUTHOR: Arnold: The Education of a Bodybuilder, Arnold's Bodyshaping for Women, Arnold's Bodybuilding for Men, The Encyclopedia of Modern Bodybuilding, Arnold's Fitness for Kids (3 Vols.).
PICTURES: Hercules in New York (debut, 1970; billed as Arnold Strong), The Long Goodbye, Stay Hungry, Pumping Iron, The Villain, Scavenger Hunt, Conan the Barbarian, Conan the Destroyer, The Terminator, Red Sonja, Commando, Raw Deal, Predator, The Running Man, Red Heat, Twins, Total Recall, Kindergarten Cop, Terminator 2: Judgment Day, Beretta's Island (cameo), Dave (cameo), Last Action Hero (also exec. prod.), True Lies, Junior, Eraser, Jingle All the.Way, Batman and Robin, End of Days, The 6th Day, Collateral Damage, Terminator 3: Rise of the Machines, Around the World in 80 Days.
TELEVISION: *Movie*: The Jayne Mansfield Story. *Special*: A Very Special Christmas Party (host). *Guest*: Streets of San Francisco. *Director*: Tales from the Crypt (The Switch), Christmas in Connecticut (movie).

SCHWIMMER, DAVID
Actor. b. Queens, NY, Nov. 12, 1966.
PICTURES: Flight of the Intruder, Crossing the Bridge, Twenty Bucks, Wolf, The Pallbearer, Apt Pupil, Kissing a Fool (also exec. prod.), Six Days Seven Nights, Love & Sex, Picking up the Pieces, Hotel.
TELEVISION: *Movies*: Breast Men, Since You've Been Gone (also dir.), Uprising. *Series*: The Wonder Years, Monty, Friends, Band of Brothers. *Guest*: L.A. Law, NYPD Blue, Blossom, The Single Guy, ER, The Big Breakfast.

SCHYGULLA, HANNA
Actress. b. Kattowitz, Germany, Dec. 25, 1943. Worked with Rainer Werner Fassbinder in Munich's Action Theater; a founder of the ``anti-theatre'' group. Made film debut in 1968 short Der Brautigam die Komodiantin und der Zuhalter (The Bridegroom, the Comedienne and the Pimp).
PICTURES: Love Is Colder Than Death, Gods of the Plague, Beware of a Holy Whore, The Merchant of Four Seasons, The Bitter Tears of Petra Von Kant, House by the Sea, Jail Bait, Effi Briest, The Marriage of Maria Braun, Berlin Alexanderplatz, Lili Marleen, The Night of Varennes, Passion, A Labor of Love, A Love in Germany, The Delta Force, The Future Is a Woman, Forever Lulu, Miss Arizona, The Summer of Ms. Forbes, Dead Again, Warszawa, Golem: The Ghost of Exile, Mavi Surgun, Life's Little Treasures, Hey Stranger, A Hundred and One Nights, Pakten, Night of the Filmmakers, Milim, Lea, Girl of Your Dreams, Life- Love & Celluloid, Blackout, Hanna Sings, Werckmeister Harmonies, Fassbinder in Hollywood.
TELEVISION: *U.S.*: Rio das Mortes, Peter the Great, Barnum, Casanova, Angelo Nero.

SCIORRA, ANNABELLA
Actress. b. New York, NY, March 24, 1964. As teen studied acting at HB Studio; then AADA. Founded The Brass Ring Theatre Co. Won role of Sophia Loren's daughter in mini-series Fortunate Pilgrim.
THEATRE: Orpheus Descending, Bus Stop, Three Sisters, Snow Angel, Cries and Shouts, Trip Back Down, Love and Junk, Stay With Me, Those the River Keeps.
PICTURES: True Love (debut, 1989), Internal Affairs, Cadillac Man, Reversal of Fortune, The Hard Way, Jungle Fever, The Hand That Rocks the Cradle, Whispers in the Dark, The Night We Never Met, Mr. Wonderful, Romeo is Bleeding, The Cure, The Addiction, The Innocent Sleep, The Funeral, Cop Land, What Dreams May Come, New Rose Hotel, Little City, Above Suspicion, Once in the LIfe, Sam the Man, King of the Jungle, Domenica, American Crime.
TELEVISION: *Mini-Series*: The Fortunate Pilgrim. *Movie*: Prison Stories: Women on the Inside, Jenifer, Queens Supreme. *Series*: The Sopranos.

SCOFIELD, PAUL
Actor. b. Hurstpierpoint, England, Jan. 21, 1922.
THEATRE: Adventure Story, Ring Round the Moon, Richard II, The Way of the World, Venice Preserved, Time Remembered, Hamlet, Power and the Glory, Family Reunion, Espresso Bongo, A Man For All Seasons (also B'way: Tony Award, 1962), Coriolanus, Don Armando, King Lear, Timon, Troilus, Pericles,

Henry V, MacBeth, Staircase, Hotel In Amsterdam, Uncle Vanya, The Captain of Kopernik, Rules of the Game, Savages, The Tempest, Volpone, Madras House, The Family, Amadeus, Othello, Don Quixote, A Midsummer Night's Dream, I'm Not Rappaport, Heartbreak Housem, John Gabriel Borkman.
PICTURES: That Lady (debut, 1955), Carve Her Name With Pride, The Train, A Man for All Seasons (Acad. Award, 1966), Tell Me Lies, King Lear, Bartleby, Scorpio, A Delicate Balance, 1919, When the Whales Came, Henry V, Hamlet, Utz, Quiz Show, London (narrator), The Crucible (BAFTA Award, 1997), Robinson in Space (narrator), Kurosawa.
TELEVISION: Movies: Anna Karenina, The Attic: The Hiding of Anne Frank, The Disabled Century, Animal Farm (voice). Specials: The Male of the Species (Emmy Award, 1969), The Ambassadors, The Potting Shed, Martin Chuzzlewit, Little Riders.

SCOGGINS, TRACY
Actress. b. Galveston, TX, Nov. 13, 1959. Studied acting at H.B. Studies, Wynn Handman Studios. Appeared on stage in L.A. in The Sicilian Bachelor.
PICTURES: Some Kind of Hero, Toy Soldier, In Dangerous Company, The Gumshoe Kid, Watchers II, Time Bomb, Silhouette, Ultimate Desires, Alien Intruder, Demonic Toys, Dead On, A Crack in the Floor.
TELEVISION: Series: Renegades, Hawaiian Heat, The Colbys, Lois & Clark: The New Adventures of Superman. Movies: Twirl, Jury Duty, Dan Turner: Hollywood Detective, Jake Lassiter: Justice on the Bayou, Dallas: J.R. Returns, Dallas: War of the Ewings, Babylon 5: The River of Souls, Babylon 5: A Call to Arms. Pilots: The Naturals, High Life, Unauthorized Biographies. Guest: Hotel, Crazy Like a Fox, Dallas, Magnum P.I., The Fall Guy, Mike Hammer, The Heights.

SCOLA, ETTORE
Director, Writer. b. Trevico, Italy, May 10, 1931. e. U. of Rome. Began career in 1947 as journalist; 1950, wrote for radio shows. Then made first film as script writer 1954; debut as director-writer, 1964. Has written 50 other scripts for other directors.
PICTURES: Dir/Writer: Let's Talk about Women (debut, 1964), La Congiuntura, Thrilling (segment: Il Vittimista), The Devil in Love, Will Your Heroes Find Their Friends Who Disappeared so Mysteriously in Africa?, Inspector Pepe, The Pizza Triangle, Rocco Papaleo, The Greatest Evening of My Life, We All Loved Each Other So Much, Down and Dirty, Signore e Signori Buonanotte (segment), A Special Day, Viva Italia! (segment), The Terrace, Passion d'Amore, La Nuit de Varennes, Le Bal, Macaroni, The Family, Splendor, What Time is It?, Le Capitain Fracassa, Mario Maria and Mario, Romanzo di un Giovane Povero, Corti italiani, 1943-1997, La Cena, Concorrenza Sleale.

SCOLARI, PETER
Actor. b. New Rochelle, NY, Sept. 12, 1954.
PICTURES: The Rosebud Beach Hotel, Corporate Affairs, Ticks, Camp Nowhere, That Thing You Do!, Buckle Up, Sorority Boys, The Polar Express.
TELEVISION: Series: Goodtime Girls, Bosom Buddies, Baby Makes Five, Newhart, Family Album, Dweebs, Honey I Shrunk the Kids: The TV Show., From the Earth to the Moon. Movies: Carpool, Amazon, Fatal Confession, The Ryan White Story, Stop the World I Want to Get Off, The Ultimate Christmas Present, For Hope. Mini-Series: From the Earth to the Moon. Guest: Remington Steele, The Love Boat, Family Ties, The New Mike Hammer, Trying Times, Fallen Angels.

SCORSESE, MARTIN
Writer, Director, Editor, Actor. b. New York, NY, Nov. 17, 1942. Began career while film arts student at NYU, doing shorts What's A Nice Girl Like You Doing in a Place Like This? (dir., s.p.), It's Not Just You Murray and The Big Shave. Other short films: Street Scenes, Italianamerican, American Boy, Mirror Mirror, Somewhere Down the Crazy River. Dir. 2 commercials for Armani. Currently campaigning for the preservation and restoration of historic films. Recipient of the American Film Institute Life Achievement Award, ,1997.
THEATRE: The Act.
PICTURES: Editor: Woodstock, Medicine Ball Caravan, Unholy Rollers, Elvis on Tour. Producer: The Grifters, Mad Dog and Glory, Naked in New York (exec. prod.), Clockers. Actor: Cannonball, 'Round Midnight, Akira Kurosawa's Dreams, Guilty by Suspicion, Quiz Show, Search and Destroy (also co-exec. prod.). Director: Who's That Knocking at My Door? (also s.p., assoc. prod., actor), Boxcar Bertha (also actor), Mean Streets (also co-s.p., actor), Alice Doesn't Live Here Anymore, Taxi Driver (also actor), New York New York, The Last Waltz (also cameo), Raging Bull, The King of Comedy (also actor), After Hours (also cameo), The Color of Money, The Last Temptation of Christ, New York Stories (Life Lessons; also cameo), GoodFellas (also co-s.p.), Cape Fear, The Age of Innocence (also co-s.p., cameo), Casino (also co-s.p.), Kundun, Bringing Out the Dead, The Gangs of New York, Dino, Revisiting the Last Waltz, Sharkslayer.
TELEVISION: Series episode: Amazing Stories (dir.). Specials: A Personal Journey With Martin Scorsese Through American Movies (dir. writer), Il Dolce Cinema, New York at the Movies.

SCOTT, CAMPBELL
Actor. b. New York, NY, July 19, 1962. e. Lawrence Univ. Son of George C. Scott and Colleen Dewhurst. Studied with Geraldine Page and Stella Adler.
THEATRE: NY: The Last Outpost, The Real Thing, Copper-head, The Queen and the Rebels, Hay Fever, A Man For All Seasons, Long Day's Journey Into Night, Measure for Measure, Pericles, On the Bum. Regional: Romeo and Juliet, Our Town, Gilette, School for Wives, Hamlet.
PICTURES: Five Corners (debut, 1988), From Hollywood to Deadwood, Longtime Companion, The Sheltering Sky, Dying Young, Dead Again, Singles, Mrs. Parker and the Vicious Circle, The Innocent, The Daytrippers, Big Night (also co-dir., prod.), The Spanish Prisoner, The Imposters, Hi-Life, Top of the Food Chain, Lush, Other Voices, Delivering Milo, Final, Rodger Dodger, The Secret Lives of Dentists.
TELEVISION: Mini-Series: The Kennedys of Massachusetts, LIBERTY! The American Revolution. Guest: Family Ties, L.A. Law. Movie: The Perfect Tribute, The Love Letter, The Tale of Sweeney Todd, Follow the Stars Home, Hamlet (also prod.), The Pilot's Wife.

SCOTT, DEBORAH LYNN
Costume Designer. b. 1954.
PICTURES: The Private Eyes, Don't Answer the Phone!, E.T. the Extra-Terrestrial, Never Cty Wolf, Back to the Future, Armed and Dangerous, Blue City, About Last Night..., Who's That Girl?, Life Is Sweet, Coupe de Ville, Hear My Song, Defending Your Life, Eve of Destruction, Blame It on the Bellboy, Hoffa, Jack the Bear, Sliver, Legends of the Fall, Sister My Sister, Persuasion, Funny Bones, Jack and Sarah, The Indian in the Cupboard, Wild Heat, Looking for Richard, To Gillian on Her 37th Birthday, Titanic (Acad. Award, 1997), Wild Wild West, The Patriot, Minority Report, Bad Boys II.
TELEVISION: Movies: Dancing Queen.

SCOTT, MARTHA
Actress. b. Jamesport, MO, September 22, 1914. e. U. of Michigan. In little theatres over U.S.; summer stock NY; on radio with Orson Welles; Broadway debut Our Town (1938), film debut in film adaptation of same. Became theater producer in 1968 with Henry Fonda and Alfred De Liagre at Kennedy Center and on B'way (Time of Your Life, First Monday in October).
THEATRE: Our Town, Soldier's Wife, The Voice of the Turtle, The Number, The Male Animal, The Remarkable Mr. Pennypacker, Forty-Second Cousin, The Crucible.
PICTURES: Our Town (Acad. Award nom.), The Howards of Virginia, Cheers for Miss Bishop, They Dare Not Love, One Foot in Heaven, In Old Oklahoma (The War of the Wildcats), Hi Diddle Diddle, So Well Remembered, Strange Bargain, When I Grow Up, The Desperate Hours, The Ten Commandments, Eighteen and Anxious, Sayonara, Ben-Hur, Charlotte's Web (voice), Airport 1975, The Turning Point, Doin' Time on Planet Earth.
TELEVISION: Movies: The Devil's Daughter, Thursday's Game, The Abduction of Saint Anne, Medical Story, Charleston, Father Figure, Summer Girl, Adam, Adam: His Song Continues, Love and Betrayal, Daughter of the Streets. Mini-Series: The Word, Beulah Land. Guest: Murder She Wrote, Hotel, A Girl's Life (pilot). (d. May 28, 2003).

SCOTT, RIDLEY
Director, Producer. b. South Shields, Northumberland, England, Nov. 30, 1937. Brother is director Tony Scott. e. Royal College of Art, London. Joined newly formed Film Sch. First film: Boy on Bicycle (short). Won design scholarship in NY. Returned to London and joined BBC as set designer (Z-Cars, The Informer series). Directed almost 3,000 commercials in 18 years. Formed Percy Main Prods. Also mng. dir. of Ridley Scott Assocs.Exec.
PICTURES: Director: The Duellists (debut, 1978), Alien, Blade Runner, Legend, Someone to Watch Over Me (also exec. prod.), Black Rain, Thelma & Louise (also prod.), 1492: Conquest of Paradise (also prod.), White Squall (also exec. prod.), G.I. Jane (also prod.), G.I. Jane, Gladiator, Hannibal, Black Hawk Down (also prod.), Matchstick Men. Prod: Monkey Trouble, The Browning Version, Clay Pigeons, Six Bullets from Now.

SCOTT, TONY
Director. b. Newcastle, England, July 21, 1944. Began career in TV commercials, being partnered with his brother Ridley in prod. co. Winner of numerous Clios, Gold & Silver Lions, and other awards. Entered m.p. industry 1972, directing half-hr. film, One of the Missing, for British Film Inst. and Loving Memory, 1-hr. feature for Albert Finney.
PICTURES: Loving Memory, One of the Missing, The Hunger, Top Gun, Beverly Hills Cop II, Revenge, Days of Thunder, The Last Boy Scout, True Romance, Crimson Tide, The Fan, Clay Pigeons (exec. prod. only), Enemy of the State, Spy Game, Six Bullets from Now (exec. prod.), Tick Tock.
TELEVISION: Series Dir.: The Hunger. Movies: RKO 281, The Last Debate, The Gathering Storm.

SCOTT-THOMAS, KRISTIN
Actress. b. Redruth, Cornwall, England, May 24, 1960. Lived in France since 18. e. Central School of Speech and Drama, London; Ecole Nationale des Arts et Technique de Theatre,

Paris. Stage debut in La Lune Declinante Sur 4 Ou 5 Personnes Qui Danse. Other theatre work in Paris.
PICTURES: Djomel et Juliette, L'Agent Troube, La Meridienne, Under the Cherry Moon, A Handful of Dust, Force Majeure, Bille en tete, Autobus/In the Eyes of the World, The Governor's Party, The Bachelor, Bitter Moon, Somebody to Love, Four Weddings and a Funeral, An Unforgettable Summer, Mayday, The Confessional, Angels and Insects, Les Milles, Richard III, The Pompatus of Love, Portraits Chinois, Mission: Impossible, Microcosmos: Le Peuple de L'Herbe, The English Patient, Amour et Confusions, The Revengers' Comedies, The Horse Whisperer, Up at the Villa, Random Hearts, Play, Life as a House, Gosford Park, Petites Coupures.
TELEVISION: L'Ami D'Enfance de Maigret, Blockhaus, Chameleon/La Tricheuse (Aust.), Sentimental Journey (Germany), The Tenth Man, The Endless Game, Framed, The Secret Life of Ian Fleming, Titmuss Regained, Look at it This Way, Weep No More My Lady, Body & Soul, La Belle Epoque, Gulliver's Travels.

SCULLY, JOE
Talent Executive, Casting Director, Producer, Writer. b. Kearny, NJ, March 1, 1926. e. Goodman Memorial Theatre of the Art Inst. of Chicago, 1946. m. Penelope Gillette. Acted until 1951. CBS-TV, N.Y. Casting Dir., Danger, You Are There, Omnibus, The Web, 1951-56. Wrote The Little Woman for CBS Danger Anthology Series, 1954. 1956-60, CBS-TV, Associate Prod., Studio One, Dupont Show of the Month, Playhouse 90; 1962-64, Writer for CBS Repertoire Workshop anthology series; 1963-64, CBS Stations div. KNXT, prod., Repertoire Workshop; 1965-70 casting dir., 20th Century-Fox Films; 1970-74, indept. casting dir.; 1974-75 Universal TV, casting dir. Member, AMPAS since 1975; NBC-TV Manager, Casting & Talent; 1978, re-established Joe Scully Casting, indept. service to the industry. Founding member, CSA, 1982; 1983, casting dir., Walt Disney Pictures. 1991 published story in Emmy Magazine: Have You Ever... You Know? Conducted AMPAS Seminar, 'The Casting Process in Motion Pictures.'
PICTURES: Hello Dolly, In Like Flint, Valley of the Dolls, Planet of the Apes, The Flim-Flam Man, Sounder, Lady Sings the Blues, Play It as It Lays, The Stone Killer, Parallax View, Lifeguard, Man in the Glass Booth, Middle Age Crazy, Death Wish II, Frankenweenie (short), North of Chiang Mai, Chained in Paradiso (video).
TELEVISION: Series: Peyton Place, Bonanza, Room 222, Nichols, Snoop Sisters, Columbo, Switch, McMillan & Wife, Tales of the Unexpected, Gone Are the Days (Disney Channel). Pilots: Julia, The Ghost and Mrs. Muir, The Bill Cosby Show. Movies: Thief, Missiles of October, Gone Are the Days, Earth II. Australian: Flair (mini-series), Ebb Tide (movie).

SEAGAL, STEVEN
Actor, Director, Producer, Writer. b. Lansing, MI, April 10, 1952. Became skilled at martial arts at an early age, studying Aikido. Lived in Japan for 15 yrs. where he opened a martial arts academy. Opened similar academy upon his return to U.S. in Los Angeles. Was martial arts choreographer/coordinator on film The Challenge.
PICTURES: Above the Law (debut, 1988; also co-prod., co-story), Hard to Kill, Marked for Death (also co-prod.), Out for Justice (also co-prod.), Under Siege (also co-prod.), On Deadly Ground (also dir., co-prod.). Under Siege 2: Dark Territory (also co-prod.), Executive Decision, The Glimmer Man, Fire Down Below (also prod.), My Giant (cameo), The Patriot (also prod.), Get Bruce, Exit Wounds, Ticker, The Path Beyond Thought, Half Past Dead, The Foreigner, Out for a Kill.

SEAGROVE, JENNY
Actress. b. Kuala Lumpur, Malaysia, July 4, 1957. e. Bristol Old Vic. Theatre Sch. Stage debut 1979. Early TV: The Brack Report, The Woman in White, Diana. Recent stage: Jane Eyre, King Lear, Present Laughter, The Miracle Worker, Dead Guilty.
PICTURES: Moonlighting, Local Hero, Nate and Hayes, Appointment With Death, A Chorus of Disapproval, The Guardian, Bullseye!, Miss Beatty's Children, New Order Story, Don't Go Breaking My Heart, Zoe, Boogeymen:The Killer Compilation.
TELEVISION: A Woman of Substance, Hold The Dream, In Like Flynn, Killer, Lucy Walker, Magic Moments, Some Other Spring, The Betrothed, Deadly Game, The Sign of Four, The Incident at Victoria Falls, A Shocking Accident, Mark of the Devil, Judge John Deed.

SEALE, JOHN
Cinematographer. b. Warwick, Australia, 1943. Camera operator on several films before becoming director of photography.
PICTURES: Deathcheaters, Fatty Finn, The Survivor, Doctors & Nurses, Fighting Back, Ginger Meggs, Goodbye Paradise, Careful He Might Hear You, BMX Bandits, Silver City, Witness, The Empty Beach, The Mosquito Coast, The Hitcher, Children of a Lesser God, Stakeout, Gorillas in the Mist, Rain Man, Dead Poets Society, Till There Was You (dir. only), The Doctor, Lorenzo's Oil, The Firm, The Paper, Beyond Rangoon, The American President, Ghosts of Mississippi, The English Patient, City of Angels, The Talented Mr. Ripley, Cold Mountain, At First

Sight, The Perfect Storm, Harry Potter and the Sorcerer's Stone, Dreamcatcher, Cold Mountain.
TELEVISION: Movies: Top Kid.

SEDGWICK, KYRA
Actress. b. New York, NY, Aug. 19, 1965. e. USC. m. actor Kevin Bacon.
THEATRE: NY: Time Was, Dakota's Belly Wyoming, Ah Wilderness (Theatre World Award), Maids of Honor. LA: Oleanna.
PICTURES: War and Love, Tai-Pan, Kansas, Born on the Fourth of July, Mr. & Mrs. Bridge, Pyrates, Singles, Heart & Souls, Murder in the First, Something to Talk About, The Low Life, Losing Chase, Phenomenon, Montana (also assoc. prod.), Critical Care, Labor Pains, What's Cooking, Just A Kiss, Rumor Has It, Behind the Red Door.
TELEVISION: Movies: The Man Who Broke 1000 Chains, Women & Men II (In Love There Are No Rules), Miss Rose White, Family Pictures, The Wide Net, Twelfth Night, Lemon Sky, Enter Fleeing, Door to Door, Queens Supreme. Series: Another World. Guest: Amazing Stories. Specials: Cinder Ella: A Modern Fairy Tale.

SEGAL, GEORGE
Actor. b. New York, NY, Feb. 13, 1934. e. Columbia U., B.A., 1955. Worked as janitor, ticket-taker, soft-drink salesman, usher and under-study at NY's Circle in the Square theatre. Acting debut: Downtown Theatre's revival of Don Juan. Formed a night-club singing act with Patricia Scott. Record album of ragtime songs and banjo music: The Yama Yama Man. Dir. debut: Bucks County Playhouse prod. Scuba Duba.
THEATRE: The Iceman Cometh (1956 revival), Antony and Cleopatra N.Y. Shakespeare Festival, Leave It to Jane, The Premise (satiric improv revue), Gideon, Rattle of a Simple Man, The Knack, Requiem for a Heavyweight, The Fourth Wall.
PICTURES: The Young Doctors (debut, 1961), The Longest Day, Act One, The New Interns, Invitation to a Gunfighter, Ship of Fools, King Rat, Lost Command, Who's Afraid of Virginia Woolf? (Acad. Award nom.), The Quiller Memorandum, The St. Valentine's Day Massacre, Bye Bye Braverman, No Way to Treat a Lady, The Southern Star, The Bridge at Remagen, The Girl Who Couldn't Say No, Loving, The Owl and the Pussycat, Where's Poppa?, Born to Win, The Hot Rock, A Touch of Class, Blume in Love, The Terminal Man, California Split, Russian Roulette, The Black Bird, The Duchess and the Dirtwater Fox, Fun with Dick and Jane, Rollercoaster, Who Is Killing the Great Chefs of Europe?, Lost and Found, The Last Married Couple in America, Carbon Copy, Killing 'em Softly, Stick, All's Fair, Look Who's Talking, The Clearing, For the Boys, Look Who's Talking Now, Army of One, Direct Hit, Deep Down, Flirting With Disaster, The Cable Guy, The Feminine Touch, The Mirror Has Two Faces.
TELEVISION: Movies: Trackdown: Finding the Goodbar Killer, The Cold Room, The Zany Adventures of Robin Hood, Not My Kid, Many Happy Returns, Endless Game, Taking the Heat, Following Her Heart, Houdini, The Linda McCartney Story, The Making of a Hollywood Madam. Series: Take Five, Murphy's Law, High Tide, Just Shoot Me. Specials: Death of a Salesman, Of Mice and Men, The Desperate Hours. Guest: The Nurses, Naked City, Alfred Hitchcock Presents.

SEIDELMAN, ARTHUR ALLAN
Director, Producer, Writer. b. New York, NY, October 11. e. Whittier Coll., B.A.; UCLA, M.A. Former staff member, Repertory Theatre of Lincoln Center and Phoenix Theatre, NY.
THEATRE: Dir.: LA: The Sisters, Gypsy Princess, The Beautiful People, Five Finger Exercise, The Purification, etc. Dir.: NY: Awakening of Spring, Hamp, Ceremony of Innocence, The Justice Box, Billy, Vieux Carre, The World of My America, Awake and Sing, The Four Seasons, Inherit the Wind, The Most Happy Fella, as well as numerous regional prods. and national tours.
PICTURES: Hercules in New York, Children of Rage (dir., s.p.), Echoes, The Caller, Rescue Me, Walking Across Egypt.
TELEVISION: Director: Family, Magnum, P.I., Murder She Wrote, Hill Street Blues, Trapper John M.D., Paper Chase, Knots Landing, Bay City Blues, Capitol News, WIOU, L.A. Law, FBI: The Untold Stories, Sweet Justice, Heaven Help Us, Amazing Grace. Movies: Which Mother is Mine? A Special Gift, Schoolboy Father, A Matter of Time, I Think I'm Having a Baby, Sin of Innocence, Kate's Secret, Ceremony of Innocence, Poker Alice, The People Across the Lake, Addicted to His Love, Kate's Secret, A Friendship in Vienna, A Place at the Table, An Enemy Among Us, Glory Years, Strange Voices, A Taste of Honey, Look Away, False Witness, The Kid Who Loved Christmas, Body Language, Trapped in Space, Dying to Remember, Wing and a Prayer, Harvest of Fire, I Love Liberty, The Summer of Ben Tyler, Deep Family Secrets, Miracle in the Woods, Grace and Glorie, Sex and Mrs. X, The Runaway, By Dawn's Early Light, Like Mother- Like Son.

SEIDELMAN, SUSAN
Director. b. near Philadelphia, PA, Dec.11, 1952. e. Drexel Univ. B.A. Worked at a UHF television station in Phila., NYU film school M.F.A. Debut: 28-min. student film And You Act Like One Too. Then dir. Deficit (short, funded by AFI), and Yours Truly, Andrea G. Stern.
PICTURES: Smithereens (dir., prod., co-s.p.); 1st Amer. indep.

feature accepted into competition at Cannes Film Fest., 1982), Desperately Seeking Susan, Making Mr. Right, Cookie (also exec. prod.), She-Devil, The Dutch Master (short, Acad. Award nom.), Tales of Erotica, Gaudi Afternoon.
TELEVISION: Sex and the City, Confessions of a Suburban Girl (BBC; also writer, actress), The Barefoot Executive, A Cooler Climate, Beauty and Power.

SEINFELD, JERRY
Comedian, Actor. b. Brooklyn, NY, April 29, 1954. e. Queens Col. Stand-up comic; guested on such shows as The Tonight Show, Late Night With David Letterman. Received American Comedy Award for funniest male comedy stand-up, 1988. Author: Seinlanguage (1993).
TELEVISION: Series: Benson, Seinfeld (also co-creator, writer). Pilot: The Seinfeld Chronicles. Specials: Jerry Seinfeld—Stand-Up Confidental (also writer), Abbott and Costello Meet Jerry Seinfeld (host). Guest: The Cosby Sow, The New WKRP in Cincinatti, The Larry Sanders Show, NewsRadio, Mad About You, Dilbert (voice), Primetime Glick. Numerous appearances on Awards shows and network specials.

SELBY, DAVID
Actor. b. Morganstown, WV. Feb. 5, 1941. e. West Virginia U. Acted in outdoor dramas in home state and did regional theatre elsewhere. Was asst. instructor in lit. at Southern Illinois U.
PICTURES: Night of Dark Shadows, Up the Sandbox, Super Cops, Rich Kids, Raise the Titanic, Rich and Famous, Dying Young, Intersection, Headless Body in Topless Bar, White Squall, D3: The Mighty Ducks.
TELEVISION: Series: Dark Shadows, Flamingo Road, Falcon Crest. Mini-Series: Washington: Behind Closed Doors. Movies: Telethon, The Night Rider, Love for Rent, Doctor Franken, King of the Olympics: The Lives and Loves of Avery Brundage, Grave Secrets: The Legacy of Hilltop Drive, Lady Boss, Alone, Soldier of Fortune. Guest: Kojak, Doogie Howser M.D.

SELF, WILLIAM
Producer. b. Dayton, OH, June 21, 1921. e. U. of Chicago, 1943. Prod.-dir., Schlitz Playhouse of Stars, 1952-56; prod., The Frank Sinatra Show, 1957; exec. prod., CBS-TV, The Twilight Zone, Hotel De Paree; 1960-61 exec. prod., 20th Century-Fox TV: Hong Kong, Adventures in Paradise, Bus Stop, Follow The Sun, Margie; v.p. in chg. of prod., 20th Century-Fox TV, 1962; exec. v.p.; 1964; pres., Fox TV 1969; v.p. 20th Century Fox Film Corp., 1969; pres. of William Self Productions, Inc., partner, Frankovich/Self Productions; 1975; v.p., programs, Hollywood CBS TV Network, 1976; 1977, v.p., tv movies and miniseries, CBS TV; 1982, pres., CBS Theatrical Films; 1985, pres., William Self Prods. in association with CBS Prods; 1990, pres. Self Productions, Inc.
PICTURES: Red River, Sands of Iwo Jima, The Shootist.
TELEVISION: Movies (exec. prod.): The Tenth Man (also prod.), Sarah Plain & Tall: Winter's End, Skylark.

SELIG, ROBERT WILLIAM
Exhibitor. b. Cripple Creek, CO, Feb., 1910. e. U. of Denver, 1932, B.A.; doctorate, 1959. 1932 joined advertising sales div., 20th Century Fox, Denver. Founding mem. Theatre Owners of Amer. and NATO. Consultant, Pacific Theatres. Lifetime Trustee, U. of Denver. Member Kappa Sigma, Omicron Delta Kappa, Beta Gamma Sigma; Nat'l Methodist Church Foundation; Past Pres., Theatre Association of California and CEO NATO of CA; board of directors L.A. Chamber of Commerce; founder NATO/ShoWest Conventions. Received NATO Sherrill C. Corwin Award, 1989.

SELLECCA, CONNIE
Actress. b. Bronx, NY, May 25, 1955. m. John Tesh.
PICTURES: I Saw Mommy Kissing Santa Claus.
TELEVISION: Series: Flying High, Beyond Westworld, The Greatest American Hero, Hotel, P.S. I Luv U, Second Chances. Movies: The Bermuda Depths (debut, 1978), Flying High (pilot), Captain America II, She's Dressed to Kill, The Last Fling, International Airport, Downpayment on Murder, Brotherhood of the Rose, Turn Back the Clock, Miracle Landing, People Like Us, P.S.I. Luv U, A House of Secrets and Lies (also co-exec. prod.), Passport to Murder, She Led Two Lives, A Dangerous Affair, The Surrogate, A Holiday to Remember, Something Borrowed, Something Blue, Doomsday Rock, While My Pretty One Sleeps, Dangers Waters, Imminent Danger, I Saw Mommy Kissing Santa Claus, Anna's Dream. Specials: The Celebrity Football Classic, Celebrity Challenge of the Sexes, Circus of the Stars.

SELLECK, TOM
Actor. b. Detroit, MI, Jan. 29, 1945. e. U. of Southern California. Grew up in Southern California, appearing in several commercials before being signed to 20th Century Fox. First acting job was on tv series Lancer.
PICTURES: Myra Breckenridge (debut, 1970), Midway, The Washington Affair, Coma, High Road to China, Lassiter, Runaway, Three Men and a Baby, Her Alibi, An Innocent Man, Quigley Down Under, Three Men and a Little Lady, Folks!, Christopher Columbus: The Discovery, Mr. Baseball, In & Out, The Love Letter, Running Mates.

TELEVISION: Series: Magnum P.I. (Emmy Award, 1984; also Golden Globe & People's Choice Awards), The Closer. Movies: Most Wanted, Superdome, Returning Home, The Sacketts, The Concrete Cowboys, Divorce Wars, Louis L'Amour's The Shadow Riders, Broken Trust, Ruby Jean and Joe, Last Stand at Saber River, Memoir of the 1997 Cowboy, Hall of Fame Heritage Award, Crossfire Trail, Monte Walsh, 12 Mile Road. Guest: The Young and the Restless, The Rockford Files, Friends.

SELTZER, DAVID
Writer, Director. b. Highland Park, IL, 1940. m. flutist Eugenia Zukerman. e. Northwestern U. School for Film and Television. Moved to NY where worked on TV game show I've Got a Secret. Made short My Trip to New York. 1966 moved to LA to write for David Wolper's Incredible World of Animals. Then dir. and prod. Wolper documentaries. Worked as ghostwriter on film Willy Wonka and the Chocolate Factory.
PICTURES: Writer: The Hellstrom Chronicle, One Is a Lonely Number, The Omen, Damien: The Omen Part II, The Other Side of the Mountain, Six Weeks, Table for Five, Lucas (also dir.), Punchline (also dir.), Bird on a Wire, Shining Through (also dir., co-exec. prod.), The Eighteenth Angel, My Giant, Nobody's Baby (also dir.), Dragonfly.
TELEVISION: National Geographic Specials (prod., dir., writer), William Holden in Unconquered Worlds (prod., dir., writer), The Underworld World of Jacques Cousteau. Movies (writer): The Story of Eric, Green Eyes, My Father's House, Larry, Omen IV: The Awakening.

SELTZER, WALTER
Executive. b. Philadelphia, PA, Nov. 7, 1914. e. U. of PA. Publicity Asst. for Warner Bros. Theatres, Philadelphia; Fox West Coast Theatres; with MGM 1936-39; Warner Bros., 1939-40; Columbia, 1940-41. Enlisted U.S. Marine Corp., 1941-44. Publ. dir., Hal Wallis, 1945-54; v.p. in chg. adv & pub., Hecht-Lancaster Orgn., 1954-56; assoc. prod., The Boss; partner, Glass-Seltzer, pub. rel. firm; v.p. & exec. prod, Pennebaker Production; 1982, v.p., M.P. & TV Fund; Pres., WSP Inc. Bd. of trustees of Motion Picture and TV Fund.
PICTURES: One-Eyed Jacks, Shake Hands With the Devil, Paris Blues, The Naked Edge, Man in the Middle, Wild Seed, War Lord, Beau Geste, Will Penny, Number One, Darker Than Amber, The Omega Man, Skyjacked, Soylent Green, The Cay, The Last Hard Men.

SEMEL, TERRY
Executive. b. New York, NY, Feb. 24, 1943. e. Long Island Univ., B.S. Accounting 1964. Warner Bros. sales trainee 1966. Branch mgr., Cleveland, Los Angeles. V.P. Domestic sls. mgr. for CBS, 1971-73. Buena Vista as v.p., gen. sls. mgr., 1973-5. 1975 went to Warner Bros. as pres. domestic sls. 1978 named exec. v.p. and COO WB Inc. Named pres., Warner Bros. & COO, 1980. Named Pioneer of the Year by Foundation of Motion Picture Pioneers, 1990. Named to his current position of Chairman and CEO of Yahoo! Inc. in 2001.

SEMLER, DEAN
Cinematographer. b. Australia, 1943. Served as 2nd unit dir. and cameraman on the mini-series Lonesome Dove, Son of the Morningstar.
PICTURES: The Earthling, The Coca Cola Kid, The Road Warrior, Hoodwink, Kitty and the Bagman, Razorback, Mad Max Beyond Thunderdome, The Coca-Cola Kid, Going Sane, The Lighthorsemen, Cocktail, Young Guns, Farewell to the King, K-9, Dead Calm, Impulse, Young Guns II, Dances With Wolves (Acad. Award, 1990), City Slickers, The Power of One, Super Mario Bros., Last Action Hero, The Three Musketeers, The Cowboy Way, Waterworld, Gone Fishin', Firestorm, The Bone Collector, The Nutty Professor II, The Patriot (dir.), D-Tox, Dragonfly, We Were Soldiers, XXX, The Adventures of Pluto Nash, Bruce Almighty, The Alamo.

SEMPLE, LORENZO, JR.
Writer.
THEATRE: The Golden Fleecing.
PICTURES: Fathom, Pretty Poison, Daddy's Gone A-Hunting (co-s.p.), The Sporting Club, The Marriage of a Young Stockbroker, Papillon (co-s.p.), Super Cops, The Parallax View (co-s.p.), The Drowning Pool (co-s.p.), Three Days of the Condor (co-s.p.), King Kong, Hurricane (and exec. prod.), Flash Gordon, Never Say Never Again, Sheena (co-s.p.), Never Too Young to Die.
TELEVISION: Series: Batman (1966). Movie: Rearview Mirror, Rapture, Pretty Poison.

SENA, DOMINIC
Director. b. Niles, Ohio, April 26, 1949.
PICTURES: Rhythm Nation 1814, Kalifornia, Gone in Sixty Seconds, Swordfish, A Normal Life.

SENDREY, ALBERT
Music Composer, Arranger, Conductor. b. Chicago, IL, Dec. 26, 1921. e. Trinity Coll. Music, London, USC, Paris, & Leipzig Conservatories. Composer, arr., orch. for many plays, films and TV. On stage was pianist/conductor for Kathryn Grayson, Ray

Bolger, Danny Kaye, Tony Martin, Buddy Ebsen. Numerous B'way productions, including Mary Martin's Peter Pan, Ginger Rogers' Pink Jungle and Yul Brynner's Penelope.
PICTURES: *Orchestrations*: The Yearling, Three Musketeers, Father's Little Dividend, Duchess of Idaho, Royal Wedding, Easy to Love, Great Caruso, An American in Paris, Brigadoon, Guys and Dolls, Meet Me in Las Vegas, High Society, Raintree County, Ride the High Country, Hallelujah Trail, The Hook, The Comancheros, Nevada Smith, The Oscar, Thoroughly Modern Millie, Hello Down There, Private Navy of Sgt. O'Farrell.
TELEVISION: *Comp. music*: Laramie, Wagon Train, Ben Casey, Wolper Documentaries, Americans Abroad, J. F. Kennedy Anthology, Young Man from Boston, High Chaparral, The Monroes, Ken Murray's Hollywood.
(d. May 18, 2003).

SERNA, ASSUMPTA
Actress. b. Barcelona, Spain, Sept. 16, 1957. Abandoned plans to be a lawyer, making stage debut 1978 with anti- Franco theatre company.
PICTURES: Sweet Hours (debut, 1980), The Hunting Ground, Crime of Cuenca, Revolt of the Birds, Circle of Passions, Tin Soldier, Secret Garden, Extramuros, The Old Music, Lola, Matador, Ballad of Dogs, Lucky Ravi, La Brute, La Nuite de L'Ocean, What Belongs to Caesar, Neon Man, Wild Orchid, I the Worst of All, Rossini Rossini, Adelaide, Chain of Desire, Cracked Nut, Fencing Master, Green Henry, Nostradamus, Shortcut to Paradise, Belle al Bar, The Shooter, Como un Relampago, The Craft, Stolen Moments, Managua, Como un relampago, Why Not Me?, Nana, The Journeyman, Bullfighter, Single Again.
TELEVISION: Valentina, First Parade, Falcon Crest, Fur Elise, Drug Wars, Revolver, Sharpe, Day of Reckoning, Les Derniers Jours de la Victime, Caligula, Germanes de sang.

SEWELL, RUFUS
Actor. b. Twickenham, England, Oct. 29, 1967. e. London's Central School of Speech and Drama.
THEATRE: *London*: (stage debut) Making It Better, Arcadia. *B'way*: (debut) Translations.
PICTURES: Twenty-One, Dirty Weekend, A Man of No Importance, Victory, Cold Comfort Farm, Carrington, Hamlet, The Woodlanders, Illuminata, Dark City, Dangerous Beauty, Martha Meet Frank Daniel and Laurence, In a Savage Land, Bless the Child, A Knight's Tale, The Extremists, Light in the Sky.
TELEVISION: *Movie*: The Last Romantics, Arabian Nights, She Creature. *Mini-series*: Middlemarch, Helen of Troy.

SEYMOUR, JANE
Actress. r.n. Joyce Frankenberg. b. Hillingdon, England, Feb. 15, 1951. Dancer with London Festival Ballet at 13. On B'way in Amadeus (1980). British Repetory including Canterbury, Harrogate, Sussex, Windsor.
PICTURES: Oh! What a Lovely, The Only Way, Young Winston, Live and Let Die, Sinbad and the Eye of the Tiger, Battlestar Galactica, Oh Heavenly Dog, Somewhere in Time, Lassiter, Head Office, The Tunnel, The French Revolution, Keys to Freedom, Touching Wild Horses.
TELEVISION: *Series*: The Onedine Line, Dr. Quinn: Medicine Woman (Golden Globe, 1996). *Movies/Mini-Series*: Here Come the Double Deckers, Frankenstein: The True Story, Captains and the Kings, Benny and Barney: Las Vegas Undercover, Seventh Avenue, Killer on Board, Our Mutual Friend, The Four Feathers, The Awakening Land, Love's Dark Ride, The Hanged Man, Dallas Cowboys Cheerleaders, The Story of David, McCloud, East of Eden, The Scarlet Pimpernal, Phantom of the Opera, The Haunting Passion, Dark Mirror, The Sun Also Rises, Obsessed with a Married Woman, Jamaica Inn, Crossings, War and Remembrance, The Woman He Loved, Onassis: The Richest Man in the World (Emmy Award, 1988), Jack the Ripper, Angel of Death, I Remember You, Memories of Midnight, Are You Lonesome Tonight?, Matters of the Heart, Sunstroke (also exec. prod.), Heidi, Praying Mantis (also co-exec. prod.), A Passion for Justice: The Hazel Brannon Smith Story (also co-exec. prod.), The Absolute Truth, A Marriage of Convenience, A Memory in My Heart, Murder in the Mirror, Yesterday's Children, Blackout, Dr. Quinn, Medicine Woman: The Heart Within, (also exec. prod.), Heart of a Stranger. *Host*: The Heart of Healing.

SHAFER, MARTIN
Producer, Executive. b. 1954. e. UCLA, 1975. J.D., Southwestern U. Law School, 1978.president of production, Embassy Pictures, 1985; exec. v.p., Twentieth Century Fox Film Corp. Motion Picture Division, 1986; co-founder, Castle Rock Entertainment, 1987. Currently president, Castle Rock Pictures, where his is responsible for the development, production, and distribution of all movies.
PICTURES: The Awakening, Mother Lode, Modern Romance; co-producer, The Mountain Men (Columbia Pictures)

SHAGAN, STEVE
Writer. b. New York, NY. Oct. 25, 1927. Apprenticed in little theatres, film lab chores, stagehand jobs. Wrote, produced and directed film short, One Every Second; moved to Hollywood in 1959. Was IATSE technician, working as grip, stagehand, electrician to support film writing. Also did freelance advertising and publicity; produced Tarzan TV show. In 1968 began writing and producing two-hour films for TV.
AUTHOR: Save the Tiger, City of Angels, The Formula, The Circle, The Discovery, Vendetta, Pillars of Fire, A Cast of Thousands.
PICTURES: *Writer*: Save the Tiger (also prod.; Acad. Award nom., WGA Award, 1973), W.W. and the Dixie Dancekings (exec. prod.), Hustle, Voyage of the Damned (co.-s.p.; Acad. Award nom.), Nightwing (co-s.p.), The Formula (also prod.), The Sicilian, Primal Fear (co-s.p.).
TELEVISION: *Writer-producer*: River of Mystery, Spanish Portrait, Sole Survivor, A Step Out of Line, House on Garibaldi Street (exec. prod.), John Gotti.

SHAIMAN, MARC
Composer, Arranger. b. Newark, NJ, Oct. 22, 1959. Began career at 16 as vocal arranger for Bette Midler; became her Musical Director and Co-producer as well as writing special material for The Divine Miss M! Wrote music for Saturday Night Live; co-wrote musical material for Billy Crystal for the Academy Awards (Emmy Award for "Oscar Medleys"). Prod. and arranger for several Harry Connick, Jr. albums. Received Grammy noms. for "When Harry Met Sally" and "We Are In Love". Appeared on stage in Harlem Nocturne.
PICTURES: Divine Madness (music dir., arranger), The Cotton Club (music sprv., arranger), Broadcast News (cameo), Big Business (music sprv., arranger), Beaches (arranger), When Harry Met Sally... (music spvr.), Misery (music), Scenes From a Mall (music, adapt., cameo), City Slickers (music), Hot Shots (cameo), For the Boys (music sprv., arranger, co-composer), The Addams Family (music, cameo, co-wrote song "Mamuschka"), Sister Act (music, adapt.), Mr. Saturday Night (music, cameo), A Few Good Men (music), Life With Mikey (music spvr.), Sleepless in Seattle (musical spvr., co-wrote song "With a Wink and a Smile"; Acad. Award nom.), Hocus Pocus (music prod.), Heart and Souls (music, cameo), For Love or Money (co-composer), Addams Family Values (music), Sister Act 2: Back in the Habit (music, adaptations), That's Entertainment III (music spvr.), City Slickers II: The Legend of Curly's Gold (music), North (music, cameo), The American President (Acad. Award nom.), Speechless, Stuart Saves His Family, Forget Paris, The First Wives Club (Acad. Award nom.), Ghosts of Mississippi, Mother, George of the Jungle, In & Out, Patch Adams, My Giant, Simon Birch, The Out-of-Towners, South Park: Bigger Longer and Uncut, The Story of Us, The Kid, How Harry Met Sally, Get Over It, One Night at McCool's, What's the Worst that Could Happen, Down with Love, Alex and Emma, Marci X, The Cat in the Hat.
TELEVISION: From the Earth to the Moon (part eleven), Jackie's Back!, Greg the Bunny(series). *Movies*: 61.

SHALIT, GENE
Critic. b. New York, NY, March 25, 1932. e. U. of Illinois. Started as freelance writer; joined NBC Radio Network, working on Monitor, 1968. Has been book and film critic, sports and general columnist. Since 1973 has been featured regularly on NBC Today Show. Edits newsletter Shalit's Sampler.

SHANDLING, GARRY
Actor, Comedian, Writer, Producer. b. Chicago, IL, Nov. 29, 1949. e. Univ. of AZ. Moved to LA where he became writer for such sitcoms as Sandford & Son, Welcome Back Kotter, Three's Company. Became stand-up comedian in nightclubs which led to appearances on The Tonight Show.
PICTURES: The Night We Never Met (debut, 1993), Love Affair, Mixed Nuts, Hurlyburly, Doctor Dolittle (voice), What Planet Are You From? (also s.p. & prod.), Town and Country, Zoolander, Run,Ronnie,Run, Tusker.
TELEVISION: *Series*: It's Garry Shandling's Show (also exec. prod., writer; ACE Awards for Best Series & Actor), The Larry Sanders Show (also co-exec. prod., co-creator, co-writer, Emmy Award, 1998). *Specials*: Garry Shandling—Alone in Las Vegas (also writer, prod.), It's Garry Shandling's Show—25th Anniversary Special (also exec. prod., writer), Grammy Awards (host) Garry Shandling: Stand-Up (also writer), Rutles 2: Can't Buy Me Lunch. Guest: Tonight Show (also frequent guest host), Dr Katz: Professional Therapist (voice).

SHANLEY, JOHN PATRICK
Writer, Director. b. New York, NY, 1950. e. NYU. Cameo role in 1988 film Crossing Delancey. Dir. and s.p. for short I am Angry.
THEATRE: *Writer*: Rockaway, Welcome to the Moon, Danny and the Deep Blue Sea, Savage in Limbo, Dreamer Examines His Pillow. *Writer-Dir.*: Italian-American Reconciliation, Beggars in the House of Plenty, Four Dogs and a Bone
PICTURES: *Writer*: Moonstruck (Acad. Award & Writers Guild Award, 1987), Five Corners (also assoc. prod.), The January Man, Joe Versus the Volcano (also dir.), Alive, We're Back!, Congo, Papillionns de nuit.
TELEVISION: *Movies*: Live From Baghdad.

SHAPIRO, ROBERT W.
Producer. b. Brooklyn, NY, March 1, 1938. e. USC. Joined William Morris Agency, Inc., 1958; dir. and head of motion picture dept., William Morris Agency (UK) Ltd., 1969; mng. dir., 1970; 1974 v.p., head int'l. m.p. dept.; 1977 joined Warner Bros. as

exec. v.p. in chg. of worldwide production; 1981, named WB pres., theatrical production div. Resigned 1983 to produce films.
PICTURES: Pee-Wee's Big Adventure, Empire of the Sun (exec. prod.), Arthur 2 On the Rocks, There Goes My Baby, Black Beauty, The Last Days of Paradise, Dr. Jekyll and Ms. Hyde, An Alan Smithee Film: Burn Hollywood Burn (actor only), My Favorite Martian, Baby Geniuses, Somewhere in the City (actor only), Princess of Paradise Park.
TELEVISION: Movie: The Summer My Father Grew Up, Do You Know the Muffin Man, Cadet Kelly.

SHARIF, OMAR
Actor. r.n. Michel Shahoub. b. Alexandria, Egypt, April 10, 1932. e. Victoria Coll., Cairo.; pres. of College Dramatic Society.Starred in 21 Egyptian (billed as Omar el Cherif or Omar Cherif) and two French films prior to English-language debut in Lawrence of Arabia. Left Egypt 1964. Champion contract bridge player. 1983 made rare stage appearance in The Sleeping Prince (Chichester, then West End).
PICTURES: The Blazing Sun (debut, 1954), Our Happy Days, La Chatelane du Liban, Goha, The Mameluks, Lawrence of Arabia (Acad. Award nom.), The Fall of the Roman Empire, Behold a Pale Horse, Marco the Magnificent, Genghis Khan, The Yellow Rolls-Royce, Doctor Zhivago, The Poppy Is Also a Flower, The Night of the Generals, More Than a Miracle, Funny Girl, Mackenna's Gold, The Appointment, Mayerling, Che!, The Last Valley, The Horsemen, The Burglars, The Right to Love (Brainwashed), The Tamarind Seed, The Mysterious Island of Captain Nemo, Juggernaut, Funny Lady, Crime and Passion, The Pink Panther Strikes Again (cameo), Ashanti, Bloodline, The Baltimore Bullet, Oh Heavenly Dog, Green Ice, Chanel Solitaire, Top Secret!, The Possessed, Paradise Calling, The Blue Pyramids, Keys to Freedom, Novice, Mountains of the Moon, Michelangelo and Me, Drums of Fire, Le Guignol, The Puppet, The Rainbow Thief, Journey of Love, Mother, 588 Rue Paradis, Bridge Deluxe with Omar Sharif, Umm Kulthum, Lebanon: Imprisoned Splendour, Heaven Before I Die, Mysteries of Egypt, The 13th Warrior, The Parole Officer, Return of the Thief of Baghdad.
TELEVISION: S*H*E, Pleasure Palace, The Far Pavilions, Peter the Great, Harem, Anastasia, Grand Larceny, Omar Sharif Returns to Egypt, The Mysteries of the Pyramids Live (host), Memories of Midnight, Mrs. 'arris Goes to Paris, Lie Down with Lions, Gulliver's Travels, Katharina die Grosse, Shaka Zulu: The Citadel.

SHARP, ALAN
Writer. b. Glasgow, Scotland.
PICTURES: The Hired Hand, Ulzana's Raid, Billy Two Hats, Night Moves, The Osterman Weekend, Little Treasure (also dir.), Freeway, Cat Chaser (co-s.p.), Rob Roy.
TELEVISION: The Snoop Sisters, Coming Out of the Ice, Love and Lies, Descending Angel, Mission of the Shark: The Saga of the U.S.S. Indianapolis, The Last Hit, Betrayed by Love, The Poet, Lathe of Heaven.

SHATNER, WILLIAM
Actor. b. Montreal, Quebec, March 22, 1931. e. McGill U. Toured Canada in various stock, repertory companies before U.S. tv debut in 1956. Author: TekWar, TekLords, TekLab, Tek Vengeance, TekSecret, Believe, Star Trek Memories (co-author with Chris Kreski), Star Trek Movie Memories (co-author with Kreski), The Return, Man O'War.
THEATRE: NY: Tamburlaine the Great, The World of Susie Wong (Theatre World Award), A Shot in the Dark, L'Idiote.
PICTURES: The Brothers Karamazov (debut, 1958), Judgment at Nuremberg, The Explosive Generation, The Intruder, The Outrage, Incubus, White Comanche, Impulse, Big Bad Mama, The Devil's Rain, Kingdom of the Spiders, Land of No Return, Star Trek—The Motion Picture, The Kidnapping of the President, Visiting Hours, Star Trek II: The Wrath of Khan, Airplane II: The Sequel, Star Trek III: The Search for Spock, Star Trek IV: The Voyage Home, Star Trek V: The Final Frontier (also dir., orig. story), Bill & Ted's Bogus Journey (cameo), Star Trek VI: The Undiscovered Country, National Lampoon's Loaded Weapon 1, Star Trek: Generations, Trekkies, Land of the Free, Trinity and Beyond, Jefftowne, Free Enterprise, Nukes in Space, The First Men on the Moon, Miss Congeniality, Falcon Down, Osmosis Jones, Festival in Cannes, Shoot or be Shot, Showtime, American Psycho II, Groom Lake, Dumb Fellas, Lil'Pimp.
TELEVISION: Series: For the People, Star Trek, Barbary Coast, T.J. Hooker, Rescue 911 (host), TekWar: The Series (also dir., co-exec. prod.), Hercules (voice). Movies: Sole Survivor, Vanished, Owen Marshall: Counselor at Law (pilot), The People, The Hound of the Baskervilles, Incident on a Dark Street, Go Ask Alice, The Horror at 37000 Feet, Pioneer Woman, Indict and Convict, Pray for the Wildcats, Barbary Coast (pilot), Perilous Voyage, The Bastard, Little Women, Crash, Disaster on the Coastliner, The Baby Sitter, Secrets of a Married Man, North Beach and Rawhide, Broken Angel, Family of Strangers, Columbo: Butterfly in Shades of Grey, TekWar (also dir., co-exec. prod.), TekLab, TekWar: TekJustice, Janek: The Silent Betrayal, Prisoner of Zenda Inc., Dead Man's Island. Special: The Andersonville Trial, TekPower, TekMoney, Ashes of Money, Trinity and Beyond. Mini-Series: Testimony of Two Men, A Twist in the Tale, Iron Chef(series).

SHAVELSON, MELVILLE
Writer, Director. b. Brooklyn, NY, April 1, 1917. e. Cornell U., 1937, A.B. Radio writer: We The People, Bicycle Party, 1937, Bob Hope Show, 1938-43, then screen writer; apptd. prod., Warner Bros. 1951. Conceived for TV: Make Room for Daddy, My World and Welcome To It. Author: book, How To Make a Jewish Movie, Lualda, The Great Houdinis, The Eleventh Commandment, Ike, Don't Shoot It's Only Me. Pres., Writers Guild of America, West, 1969-71, 1979-81, 1985-87; Pres., Writers Guild Foundation 1978-96.
PICTURES: Writer: The Princess and the Pirate, Wonder Man, The Kid From Brooklyn, Sorrowful Jones, It's a Great Feeling, The Daughter of Rosie O'Grady, Always Leave Them Laughing, Where There's Life, On Moonlight Bay, Double Dynamite, I'll See You in My Dreams, Room for One More, April in Paris, Trouble Along the Way, Living It Up. Director-Writer: The Seven Little Foys (dir. debut, 1955), Beau James, Houseboat, It Started in Naples, The Five Pennies, On the Double, The Pigeon That Took Rome (also prod.), A New Kind of Love (also prod.), Cast a Giant Shadow (also prod.), Yours Mine and Ours, The War Between Men and Women, Mixed Company.
TELEVISION: Movies: The Legend of Valentino, The Great Houdinis, Ike, The Other Woman, Deceptions. Specials: Academy Awards, 1988, 1990 (writer).

SHAVER, HELEN
Actress. b. St. Thomas, Ontario, Canada, Feb. 24, 1951. e. Banff Sch. of Fine Arts, Alberta. Worked on stage and screen in Canada before coming to Los Angeles 1978.
THEATRE: Tamara, Are You Lookin'? Ghost on Fire, A Doll's House, The Master Builder, The Hostage, Jake's Women (B'way debut; Theatre World Award).
PICTURES: Christina, Shoot, Starship Invasions, Outrageous!, High-Ballin', The Amityville Horror, In Praise of Older Women, Who Has Seen the Wind, Gas, Harry Tracy, The Osterman Weekend, Best Defense, Desert Hearts, The Color of Money, The Believers, The Land Before Time (voice), Walking After Midnight, Innocent Victim (Tree of Hands), Zebrahead, That Night, Dr. Bethune, Morning Glory, Change of Heart, Open Season, Born to Be Wild, The Craft, Rowing Through, Egg Salad, The Wishing Tree, We All Fall Down, Bear With Me.
TELEVISION: Series: United States, Jessica Novak, WIOU, The Education of Max Bickford. Movies: Lovey: Circle of Children II, Between Two Brothers, Many Happy Returns, The Park is Mine, Countdown To Looking Glass, No Blame, B.L. Stryker: The Dancer's Touch, Pair of Aces, Columbo: Rest in Peace Mrs. Columbo, Survive the Night, Poisoned By Love: The Kern County Murders, Trial & Error, The Forget-Me-Not Murders, Ride With the Wind, Without Consent, Janek: A Silent Betrayal, Falling for You, Trial & Error, The Sweetest Gift, Summer's End, Common Ground, Due East, The Risen. Guest: Ray Bradbury Theatre, Amazing Stories.

SHAW, MICHAEL M. (JOHN)
Executive. b. Ashland, KY, Jan. 10, 1945. e. Eastern KY Univ., Univ. of KY, Univ of MS. 1968-69, asst. booker, 20th Century Fox, Denver; 1969, head booker, Fox; 1970, salesman, Paramount Pictures, S.F.; 1970-71, head booker, sales Paramount L.A.; 1971-73, booker, Commonwealth Theatres; 1973, booker, McLendon theatres, Dallas; 1973-78, div. mngr. Mulberry Square Prods., Dallas; 1978-79, branch mngr. Filmways Pictures, Dallas; 1980-82, owner, Sequoyah Cinema Svc., Denver; 1983-87, head film buyer, Presidio Theatres, Austin; 1987-88, head film buyer, Santikos Theatres, San Antonio; 1988-present, pres./CEO, Film Booking Office Corp., Movieline Int'l, Dallas. Member: Motion Picture Pioneers, Variety Club.

SHAW, STAN
Actor. b. Chicago, IL, July 14, 1952. On stage received NAACP Image Award for West Coast premiere of Home, 1982.
PICTURES: The Bingo Long Travelling All-Stars and Motor Kings, Rocky, The Boys in Company C, The Great Santini, Tough Enough, Runaway, The Monster Squad, Harlem Nights, Fried Green Tomatoes, Body of Evidence, Rising Sun, Houseguest, Cutthroat Island, Daylight, Snake Eyes.
TELEVISION: Series: The Mississippi. Mini-Series: Roots: The Next Generations, Heaven & Hell: North & South, Book III. When Love Kills: The Seduction of John Hearn. Movies: Call to Glory, Maximum Security, The Gladiator, The Billionaire Boys Club, The Three Kings, The Court-Martial of Jackie Robinson, Lifepod, Freedom Song, Rag and Bone. Guest: Starsky and Hutch, Wiseguy, Murder She Wrote, Hill Street Blues, Matlock.

SHAWN, WALLACE
Playwright, Actor. b. New York, NY, Nov. 12, 1943. Son of former New Yorker editor William Shawn. e. Harvard; Oxford U. Taught English in India on a Fulbright scholarship 1965-66. English, Latin and drama teacher, NY 1968-70.
THEATRE: Writer: Our Late Night (1975, Obie Award), The Mandrake (translation, also actor), A Thought in Three Parts, Marie and Bruce, The Hotel Play, Aunt Dan and Lemon (also actor), The Fever (Obie Award, 1991; also actor). Opera: The Music Teacher (with Allen Shawn). Actor: The Master and Margarita, Chinchilla, Wifey.
PICTURES: Manhattan (debut, 1979), Starting Over, All That

Jazz, Strong Medicine, Simon, Atlantic City, My Dinner With Andre (also co-s.p.), A Little Sex, Lovesick, The First Time, Deal of the Century, Strange Invaders, Saigon—Year of the Cat, Crackers, The Hotel New Hampshire, The Bostonians, Micki and Maude, Heaven Help Us, Head Office, The Bedroom Window, Radio Days, Prick Up Your Ears, Nice Girls Don't Explode, The Princess Bride, The Moderns, She's Out of Control, Scenes From the Class Struggle in Beverly Hills, We're No Angels, Shadows and Fog, Mom and Dad Save the World, Nickel and Dime, The Cemetery Club, Un-Becoming Age, The Meteor Man, Vanya on 42nd Street, Mrs. Parker and the Vicious Circle, A Goofy Movie (voice), Clueless, Canadian Bacon, Toy Story (voice), The Wife, House Arrest, All Dogs Go to Heaven II (voice), Just Write, National Lampoon's Vegas Vacation, Critical Care, My Favorite Martian, Toy Story 2 (voice), The Hurdy Gurdy Man, Buzz Lightyear of the Star Command: The Adventure Begins (voice), The Prime Gig, The Curse of the Jade Scorpion, Monsters Inc. As You Wish: The Story of the Princess Bride, Personal Velocity, Love Thy Neighbor.
TELEVISION: *Series:* Clueless, The Lionhearts, Teacher's Pet (voice), Blonde (mini-series), Star Trek: Deep Space Nine . *Movies:* How to Be a Perfect Person In Just Three Days, Just Like Dad, Noah, Blind Men, Mr. St. Nick, Monte Walsh. *Guest:* Crossing Jordan.

SHAYE, ROBERT
Executive. b. Detroit, MI, March 4, 1939. e. U. of Michigan, B.B.A.; Columbia U. Law. At 15 wrote, prod. dir. training film for father's supermarket staff. Later won first prize in Society of Cinematologists' Rosenthal Competition (best m.p. by American dir. under 25). Wrote, prod., dir., edited short films, trailers and TV commercials, including award-winning shorts, Image and On Fighting Witches (prod., dir.). Founded New Line Cinema 1967. Chmn. & CEO, New Line Cinema.
PICTURES: *Prod./exec. prod.:* Stunts, XTRO, Alone in the Dark, The First Time, Polyester, Critters, Quiet Cool, My Demon Lover, A Nightmare on Elm Street (also parts 2,3,4,5,6), The Hidden, Stranded, Critters 2, Hairspray, Heart Condition, Book of Love (dir.), Wes Craven's New Nightmare (also actor).
TELEVISION: Freddy's Nightmare: the Series (exec. prod.).

SHEA, JOHN
Actor. b. Conway, NH, April 14, 1949. Raised in MA. e. Bates Coll., ME, B.A. 1970; Yale Drama School, M.F.A. 1973. Worked as asst. dir. Chelsea Theater; taught part-time at Pratt Inst.
THEATRE: Yentl (debut 1975, Off-B'way and B'way; Theatre World Award), Sorrows of Stephen, Long Day's Journey Into Night (Joseph Jefferson Award nom.), The Master and Margarita, Romeo and Juliet (Circle in the Sq.), American Days (Drama Desk Award), The Dining Room, End of the World (B'way), The Normal Heart (London, 1987), Animal Kingdom, Rosmersholm (La Mama), Impossible Spy (China's Golden Panda Award).
PICTURES: Hussy, Missing, Windy City (Best Actor Montreal Film Festival), A New Life, Unsettled Land, Honeymoon, Stealing Home, Freejack, Honey I Blew Up the Kid, A Weekend in the Country, Brass Ring (also dir., co-writer), Nowhere to Go, Southie, The Adventures of Sebastian Cole, Lost & Found, Getting Personal, Catalina Trust, Heartbreak Hospital.
TELEVISION: *Series:* WIOU, Lois and Clark. *Movies:* The Nativity, Family Reunion, Coast to Coast (BBC), Hitler's S.S.: Portrait in Evil, A Case of Deadly Force, The Impossible Spy, Magic Moments, Baby M (Emmy Award), Do You Know the Muffin Man, Small Sacrifices, Notorious, Ladykiller, Justice in a Small Town, See Jane Run, Forgotten Sins, A Weekend in the Country, The Dining Room. *Mini-Series:* The Last Convertible, Kennedy, The Apocalypse Watch, A Will of Their Own. *Special:* Leslie's Folly.

SHEARER, HARRY
Writer, Actor. b. Los Angeles, CA, Dec. 23, 1943. e. UCLA (pol. science); grad. work in urban gov., Harvard. At 7 appeared on The Jack Benny Show. Worked as freelance journalist for Newsweek, L.A. Times and publ. articles in New West, L.A. Magazine and Film Comment. Also taught h.s. Eng. and social studies and worked in CA State Legislature in Sacramento. Founding mem. The Credibility Gap, co-wrote, co-prod. and performed on comedy group's albums (A Great Gift Idea, The Bronze Age of Radio). Co-wrote, co-prod. Albert Brooks' album A Star is Bought. Performed with group Spinal Tap. Host of Le Show, L.A. radio prog. Writer-cast mem. Saturday Night Live (1979-80 & 1984-85).
THEATRE: Accomplice (Pasadena Playhouse).
PICTURES: *Actor:* Abbott and Costello Go to Mars (debut, as child, 1953), Cracking Up, Real Life (also co-s.p.), Animalympics (voice), The Fish That Saved Pittsburgh, Serial, One-Trick Pony, The Right Stuff, This is Spinal Tap (also co-s.p.), Plain Clothes, My Stepmother is an Alien (voice), Oscar, Pure Luck, Blood & Concrete, The Fisher King, A League of Their Own, Wayne's World 2, I'll Do Anything, Speechless, My Best Friend's Wedding, Godzilla, Encounters in the Third Dimension (voice), Almost Heroes, The Truman Show, Small Soldiers (voice), Dick, Edtv, Ghost Dog: The Way of the Samurai (voice), Cyber World (voice), Edwurd Fudwupper Fibbed Big (voice), Haiku Tunnel, Haunted Castle (voice), Teddy Bears' Picnic, A Mighty Wind.
TELEVISION: *Series:* Fernwood 2-Night (creative consultant),

The Simpsons (voice), Harry Shearer's News Quiz. *Specials:* Likely Stories, It's Just TV, Paul Shaffer: Viva Shaf Vegas, Comedy Hour, Portrait of a White Marriage (also dir.), The Magic of Live, Spinal Tap Reunion (also co-writer).

SHEEDY, ALLY
Actress. r.n. Alexandra Sheedy. b. New York, NY, June 13, 1962. e. USC. m. actor David Lansbury. Daughter of literary agent Charlotte Sheedy. As child performed with American Ballet Theatre. At age 12 wrote children's book, She Was Nice to Mice; later wrote pieces for NY Times, Village Voice, Ms. Published book of poetry: Yesterday I Saw the Sun. Began acting in TV commercials at 15. Chicago Theatre in Wrong Turn at Lungfish; NY stage debut in Advice from a Caterpillar.
PICTURES: Bad Boys (debut, 1983), WarGames, Oxford Blues, The Breakfast Club, St. Elmo's Fire, Twice in a Lifetime, Blue City, Short Circuit, Maid to Order, Heart of Dixie, Betsy's Wedding, Only the Lonely, Home Alone 2: Lost in New York (cameo), Tattletale, The Pickle, Man's Best Friend, One Night Stand, High Art, Sugar Town, Autmn Heart, I'll Take You There, Advice from a Caterpillar, Happy Here and Now, A Cold Day in August, Searching for Debra Winger, Shelter Island.
TELEVISION: *Movies:* The Best Little Girl in the World, The Violation of Sarah McDavid, The Day the Loving Stopped, Splendor in the Grass, Deadly Lessons, We Are the Children, Fear, The Lost Capone, Lethal Exposure, Chantilly Lace, Ultimate Betrayal, Parallel Lives, The Haunting of Seacliff Inn, The Tin Soldier, The Fury Within, Our Guys: Outrage at Glen Ridge, Walking After Midnight, The Warden, The Interrogation of Michael Crowe. *Series:* Walking After Midnight. *Guest:* Hill Street Blues, St. Elsewhere.

SHEEN, CHARLIE
Actor. r.n. Carlos Irwin Estevez. b. Los Angeles, Sept. 3, 1965. Father is actor Martin Sheen. Brother of actors Emilio, Ramon and Renee Estevez. m. actress Denise Richards. Made debut as extra in TV movie, The Execution of Private Slovik (starring father) and as extra in Apocalypse Now (also starring father).
PICTURES: Grizzly II—The Predator, Red Dawn, The Boys Next Door, Lucas, Ferris Bueller's Day Off, The Wraith, Platoon, Wisdom, Three for the Road, No Man's Land, Wall Street, Never on Tuesday, Young Guns, Eight Men Out, Major League, Beverly Hills Brats, Courage Mountain, Navy Seals, Men at Work, The Rookie, Cadence, Hot Shots!, National Lampoon's Loaded Weapon 1 (cameo), Hot Shots Part Deux!, DeadFall, The Three Musketeers, The Chase (also co-exec. prod.), Major League 2, Beyond the Law, Terminal Velocity, The Shadow Conspiracy, All Dogs Go to Heaven II (voice), The Arrival, Money Talks, Postmortem, No Code of Conduct, Free Money, Being John Malkovich (cameo), Five Aces, Rated X, Famous, Good Advice, Scary Movie 3, Deeper than Deep, The Big Bounce.
TELEVISION: *Movies:* Silence of the Heart, Backtrack. *Series:* Sugar Hill, Spin City, Two and a Half Men.

SHEEN, MARTIN
Actor. r.n. Ramon Estevez. b. Dayton, OH, Aug. 3, 1940. Father of actors Emilio Estevez, Charlie Sheen, Ramon Estevez and Renee Estevez. Wrote play (as Ramon G. Estevez) Down the Morning Line (prod. Public Theatre, 1969). Emmy Award as dir., exec. prod. Babies Having Babies (1986).
THEATRE: The Connection (debut, 1959 with the Living Theater), Women of Trachis, Many Loves, In the Jungle of Cities, Never Live Over a Pretzel Factory, The Subject Was Roses, The Wicked Crooks, Hamlet, Romeo and Juliet, Hello Goodbye, The Happiness Cage, Death of a Salesman (with George C. Scott), Julius Caesar, The Crucible.
PICTURES: The Incident (debut, 1967), The Subject Was Roses, Catch-22, No Drums No Bugles, Rage, Pickup on 101, Badlands, The Legend of Earl Durrand, The Cassandra Crossing, The Little Girl Who Lives Down the Lane, Apocalypse Now, Eagle's Wing, The Final Countdown, Loophole, Gandhi, That Championship Season, Enigma, Man Woman and Child, The Dead Zone, Firestarter, The Believers, Siesta, Wall Street, Walking After Midnight, Da (also co-exec. prod.), Judgment in Berlin (also exec. prod.), Beverly Hills Brats, Cold Front, Beyond the Stars, The Maid, Cadence (also dir.), JFK (narrator), Hear No Evil, Hot Shots Part Deux (cameo), Gettysburg, Trigger Fast, Hits!, Fortunes of War, Sacred Cargo, The Break, Dillinger & Capone, Captain Nuke and the Bomber Boys, Ghost Brigade, The Cradle Will Rock, Dead Presidents, Dorothy Day, Gospa, The American President, The War At Home, Spawn, Taylor's Campaign, Stranger in the Kingdom, Snitch, Shadrach (voice), No Code of Conduct, Gunfighter, Free Money, Texas Funeral, Ninth Street, Lucky Town, O, The Papp Project, The Confidence Game.
TELEVISION: *Series:* As the World Turns, The West Wing (Emmy noms., 2000-2002). *Movies:* Then Came Bronson, Mongo's Back in Town, Welcome Home Johnny Bristol, That Certain Summer, Letters for Three Lovers, Pursuit, Catholics, Message to My Daughter, The Execution of Private Slovik, The California Kid, The Missiles of October, The Story of Pretty Boy Floyd, Sweet Hostage, The Guardian, The Last Survivors, Blind Ambition, The Long Road Home (Emmy Award, 1981), In the Custody of Strangers, Choices of the Heart, The Atlanta Child Murders, Consenting Adult, Shattered Spirits, News at Eleven,

Out of the Darkness, Samaritan, Conspiracy: The Trial of the Chicago 8, No Means No (exec. prod. only), Nightbreaker (also exec. prod.), Guilty Until Proven Innocent, The Water Engine (voice), The Last P.O.W.?: The Bobby Garwood Story, A Matter of Justice, One of Her Own, Roswell, Voyage of Terror, Babylon 5: The River of Souls, The Darklings, Storm, The Time Shifters, D.R.E.A.M. Team, Forget Me Never, Thrill Seekers. *Mini-Series*: Kennedy, Queen, Medusa's Child. *Guest*: Tales From the Crypt, Murphy Brown (Emmy Award, 1994), The Simpsons (voice). *Narrator*: Eyewitness (PBS).

SHEFFER, CRAIG
Actor. b. York, PA, 1960. e. East Stroudsberg Univ., PA. Started career in tv commercials; in soap opera, One Life to Live. On NY stage in Fresh Horses, G.R. Point, Torch Song Trilogy (B'way & Off-B'way). Starred in IMAX film Wings of Courage.
PICTURES: That Was Then This Is Now (debut, 1985), Fire with Fire, Some Kind of Wonderful, Voyage of the Rock Aliens, Split Decisions, Nightbreed, Instant Karma (also exec. prod.), Blue Desert, Eye of the Storm, A River Runs Through It, Fire in the Sky, The Program, Sleep With Me, Roadflower, The Grave, Head Above Water, Flypaper, Double Take, Bliss, Executive Power, The Fall, Rhapsody in Bloom, Shadow of Doubt, Net Worth, Quest for Atlantis, Inc, Million, Deep Core, Fear of Flying, Ritual, Flying Virus, Deadly Little Secrets, Berserker, Final Breakdown, Mob Dot Com, Dracula II: Ascension.
TELEVISION: *Series*: The Hamptons. *Movies*: Babycakes, In Pursuit of Honor, The Desperate Trail, Miss Evers' Boys, Merry Christmas George Bailey, Without Malice, Cabin Pressure.

SHEFFIELD, JOHN
Actor. b. Pasadena, CA, April 11, 1931. e. UCLA. Stage debut at 7 in On Borrowed Time. Created screen role of Tarzan's son in Tarzan Finds a Son, followed by 7 other entries in Tarzan series, and role of Bomba in Bomba series.
PICTURES: Babes in Arms, Tarzan Finds a Son, Lucky Cisco Kid, Little Orvie, Knute Rockne—All-American, Million Dollar Baby, Tarzan's Secret Treasure, Tarzan's New York Adventure, Tarzan Triumphs, Tarzan's Desert Mystery, Tarzan and the Amazons, Tarzan and the Leopard Woman, Tarzan and the Huntress, Roughly Speaking, Bomba the Jungle Boy, Bomba on Panther Island, Lost Volcano, Bomba and the Hidden City, The Lion Huntress, Bomba and the Elephant Stampede, African Treasure, Bomba and the Jungle Girl, Safari Drums, The Golden Idol, Killer Leopard, Lord of the Jungle.
TELEVISION: *Series*: Bantu the Zebra Boy.

SHEINBERG, SIDNEY JAY
Executive. b. Corpus Christi, TX, Jan. 14, 1935. e. Columbia Coll., A.B. 1955; LL.B., 1958. Admitted to Calif. bar, 1958; assoc. in law U. of California Sch. of Law, Los Angeles, 1958-59; joined MCA, Inc, 1959; pres., TV div., 1971-74; exec. v.p., parent co., 1969-73. Named MCA pres. & chief oper. off., 1973. Resigned from position 1995 to form company The Bubble Factory to produce films for MCA. 1997, prod. films: The Pest, A Simple Wish.

SHELDON, DAVID
Producer, Director, Writer. b. New York, NY. e. Yale U. Sch. of Drama, M.F.A.; Principia Coll., B.A.; Actors Studio, directors unit. 1972-74 was exec. at American Int'l Pictures supervising development and production of 18 films include: Futureworld, Walking Tall, Dillinger, Sisters, Macon County Line, Reincarnation of Peter Proud, Slaughter, Dr. Phibes. *Prod./Dir.*, The Gateway Playhouse in NY where dir. over 50 plays and musicals. Started the Sheldon/Post Company in 1991 with Ira Post. *Exec. prod./writer* of Secret of a Small Town.
PICTURES: *Prod./Dir.*: Grizzly Adams and The Legend of Dark Mountain. *Producer*: Just Before Dawn, Abby, Day of the Animals, The Manitou. *Director*: Lovely But Deadly. *Writer*: The Predator. *Prod./Writer*: Grizzly, Sheba Baby, The Evil, Project: Kill.

SHELDON, JAMES
Director. r.n. James Schleifer. b. New York, NY. Nov. 12. e. U. of NC. Page boy, NBC; announcer-writer-dir., NBC Internat'l Div.; staff dir., ABC radio; staff prod. dir., Young & Rubicam; free lance prod. dir. of many programs live tape and film, N.Y. and Hollywood.
TELEVISION: *Series* (prod./ dir.): Mr. Peepers, Armstrong Circle Theatre, Robert Montgomery Presents, Schlitz Playhouse, West Point, Zane Grey Theatre, The Millionaire, Desilu Playhouse, Perry Mason, Twilight Zone, Route 66, Naked City, The Virginian, Alfred Hitchcock Presents, Fugitive, Espionage, Defenders, Nurses, Bing Crosby Show, Family Affair, Wonderful World of Disney, Man From UNCLE, Felony Squad, That Girl, Ironside, My World and Welcome To It, To Rome With Love, Owen Marshall, Room 222, Apple's Way, Love American Style, McMillan and Wife, Sanford and Son, Ellery Queen, Rich Man, Poor Man II, Family, MASH, Switch, Loveboat, Sheriff Lobo, Knots Landing, The Waltons, 240-Robert, Nurse, Dukes of Hazard, Todays F.B.I., McLain's Law, 7 Brides for 7 Brothers, Lottery, Partners in Crime, Jessie, Santa Barbara, Half Nelson, Stir Crazy, The Equalizer, Sledge Hammer, Cagney & Lacey. *Movies*: Gidget Grows Up, With This Ring, The Gossip Columnist.

SHELDON, SIDNEY
Writer, Director, Producer, Novelist. b. Chicago, IL, Feb. 11, 1917. e. Northwestern U.
AUTHOR: The Naked Face, The Other Side of Midnight, A Stranger in the Mirror, Bloodline, Rage of Angels, Master of the Game, If Tomorrow Comes, Windmills of the Gods, The Sands of Time, Memories of Midnight, The Doomsday Conspiracy, The Stars Shine Down, Nothing Lasts Forever, Morning Noon & Night, The Best Laid Plans, Tell Me Your Dreams.
THEATRE: Redhead (Tony Award, 1959). Alice in Arms, Jackpot, Dream With Music, Merry Widow (revision), Roman Candle.
PICTURES: *Writer*: The Bachelor and the Bobbysoxer (Acad. Award, 1947), Easter Parade, Annie Get Your Gun, Three Guys Named Mike, Dream Wife (also dir.), Remains to Be Seen, You're Never Too Young, Pardners, The Buster Keaton Story (also prod., dir.), The Birds and the Bees, Gambling Daughters, Dangerous Lady, Bill Rose's Jumbo. *Novels made into films:* The Naked Face, The Other Side of Midnight, Bloodline.
TELEVISION: *Series*: Patty Duke Show (creator), I Dream of Jeannie (creator, prod.), Nancy (creator, prod.), Hart to Hart (creator). *Novels made into Mini-Series/Movies*: Rage of Angels, Master of the Game, Windmills of the Gods, If Tomorrow Comes, Memories of Midnight, The Sands of Time, Stranger in the Mirror, Nothing Lasts Forever.

SHELLEY, CAROLE
Actress. b. London, England, Aug. 16, 1939. e. Arts Educational Sch., RADA.
THEATRE: *NY*: The Odd Couple (debut, 1965), The Astrakhan Coat, Loot, Sweet Potato, Little Murders, Hay Fever, Absurd Person Singular (Tony nom.), The Norman Conquests, The Elephant Man (Tony Award, 1979), Twelve Dreams (Obie Award), The Misanthrope, Noises Off, Stepping Out (Tony nom.), What the Butler Saw, The Miser, Maggie and Misha, The Destiny of Me, Later Life, London Suite, Show Boat. *London*: Simon and Laura (debut, 1955), New Cranks, Boeing-Boeing, Mary Mary, Lettice and Lovage. Also appearances with Shaw Festival, Stratford Fest., Amer. Shakespeare Fest., etc.
PICTURES: Give Us this Day (debut, 1949), Cure for Love, It's Great to Be Young, Carry on Regardless, Carry on Cabby, The Odd Couple, The Boston Strangler, The Aristocats (voice), Robin Hood (voice), The Super, Little Noises, Quiz Show, The Road to Wellville, Hercules (voice), Jungle2Jungle.
TELEVISION: *Series*: The Odd Couple. *Specials*: Coconut Downs, Gabby, A Salute to Noel Coward. *Movie*: Devlin. *Guest*: Brian Rix, Dickie Henderson Show, The Avengers.

SHELTON, RON
Writer, Director, Producer. b. Whittier, CA, Sept. 15, 1945. e. Westmont Coll., Santa Barbara, CA, 1967; U. of Arizona, Tucson, AZ, 1974. For 5 years played second base for Baltimore Orioles farm team. Cleaned bars and dressed mannequins to support his art: painting and sculpture. A script he wrote, A Player to Be Named Later (which he later himself made as Bull Durham), attracted attention of dir. Roger Spottiswoode who directed his first two scripts.
PICTURES: The Pursuit of D. B. Cooper (assoc. prod.), Open Season (exec. prod.). Writer: Under Fire (also 2nd unit dir.), The Best of Times (also 2nd unit dir.), Bull Durham (also dir.), Blaze (also dir.), White Men Can't Jump (also dir.), Blue Chips (also co-exec. prod.), Cobb (also dir.), The Great White Hype (co-s.p.), Tin Cup (also prod., s.p.), Play it to the Bone, Dark Blue, Hollywood Homicide, Bad Boys II.

SHEPARD, SAM
Writer, Actor. r.n. Samuel Shepard Rogers. b. Fort Sheridan, IL, Nov. 5, 1943. Raised in California, Montana and South Dakota. Worked as stable hand, sheep shearer, orange picker in CA, a car wrecker in MA and musician with rock group Holy Modal Rounders. Lived near San Francisco, where, in addition to writing, ran a drama workshop at the U. of California at Davis. Recipient of Brandeis U. Creative Arts Citation, 1976, and American Acad. of Arts and Letters Award, 1975.
THEATRE: *Playwright*: Icarus' Mother, Red Cross (triple bill—Obie Award, 1966), La Turista (Obie Award, 1967), Forensic and the Navigators, Melodrama Play, Tooth of Crime (Obie Award, 1973), Back Dog Beast Bait, Operation Sidewinder, 4-H Club, The Unseen Hand, Mad Dog Blues, Shaved Splits, Rock Garden, Curse of the Starving Class (Obie Award, 1978), Buried Child (Obie Award & Pulitzer Prize, 1979), True West, Fool For Love, A Lie of the Mind, Simpatico.
PICTURES: *Actor*: Renaldo and Clara (debut, 1978), Days of Heaven, Resurrection, Raggedy Man, Frances, The Right Stuff (Acad. Award nom.), Country, Fool for Love, Crimes of the Heart, Baby Boom, Steel Magnolias, Bright Angel, Defenseless, Voyager, Thunderheart, The Pelican Brief, Safe Passage, The Only Thrill, Snow Falling on Cedars, Hamlet, Curtain Call, All the Pretty Horses, The Pledge, Swordfish, Black Hawk Down. *Writer*: Me and My Brother (co-s.p.), Zabriskie Point (co-s.p.), Oh Calcutta! (contributor), Renaldo and Clara (co-s.p.), Paris Texas, Fool for Love, Far North (also dir.), Silent Tongue (also dir.), In America, Curtain Call, Snow Falling on Cedars, Hamlet, All the Pretty Horses, The Pledge, Swordfish, Kurosawa, Blackhawk Down, Leopold Bloom, The Notebook.
TELEVISION: *Special*: Fourteen Hundred Thousand Blue Bitch

(BBC). *Movie*: The Good Old Boys, Purgatory, Dash and Lilly, One Kill, After the Harvest, Shot in the Heart, True West, (writer, play).

SHEPHERD, CYBILL
Actress, Singer. b. Memphis, TN, Feb. 18, 1950. e. Hunter Coll., NYU, USC. Was fashion model (won Model of the Year title, 1968) before acting debut in 1971. Debut record album, Cybill Does It... To Cole Porter, 1974, followed by Stan Getz: Mad About the Boy, Vanilla, Somewhere Down the Road.
PICTURES: The Last Picture Show (debut, 1971), The Heartbreak Kid, Daisy Miller, At Long Last Love, Taxi Driver, Special Delivery, Silver Bears, The Lady Vanishes, The Return, Chances Are, Texasville, Alice, Once Upon a Crime, Married to It, The Muse (cameo), The Last Picture Show: A Look Back, Marine Life, Falling off the Verge.
TELEVISION: *Series*: The Yellow Rose, Moonlighting, Cybill (also co-exec. prod.; Golden Globe, 1996). *Movies*: A Guide for the Married Woman, Secrets of a Married Man, Seduced, The Long Hot Summer, Which Way Home, Memphis (also co-writer, co-exec. prod.), Stormy Weathers, Telling Secrets, There Was a Little Boy, Baby Brokers, For the Love of My Daughter, While Justice Sleeps, The Last Word, Journey of the Heart, Due East, Martha, Inc.: The Story of Martha Stewart.

SHEPHERD, RICHARD
Producer. b. Kansas City, MO, June 4, 1927. e. Stanford U. In U.S. Naval Reserve, 1944-45. Entered entertainment field as exec. with MCA, 1948, functioning in radio, TV, and m.p. fields until 1956, with time out for U.S. Army, 1950-52. 1956 became head of talent for Columbia Pictures. 1962 joined CMA talent agency on its founding, becoming exec. v.p. in chg. of m.p. div.; 1972-74, exec. v.p. for prod. Warner Bros.; 1974 became indept. prod.; 1976 named MGM sr. vp. & worldwide head of theatrical prod. 1985 to present, partner in The Artists Agency.
PICTURES: Twelve Angry Men, The Hanging Tree, The Fugitive Kind, Breakfast at Tiffany's, Alex and the Gypsy, Robin and Marian, Volunteers, The Hunger, The Man in the Iron Mask,(prod. assist.).

SHERAK, THOMAS
Executive. e. B.A., marketing, New York City Community College. Began film career in distribution, Paramount Pictures, 1970; v.p. & head film buyer, General Cinema; president, domestic dist. & mktg, Twentieth Century Fox, 1983-84 & 1986-90; senior exec. v.p., Twentieth Century Fox. Currently chairman, 20th Domestic Film Group (since 1997); senior exec. v.p., Fox Filmed Entertainment, 1994-2000. Board member, National Multiple Sclerosis Society, the Weizmann Institute, Fulfillment Fund of Southern Calif., and Southern Calif. Variety; member, Endowment Campaign Committee for the Academy Found.; chairman, Found. for Motion Picture Pioneers. Partner, Revolution Studios.

SHERIDAN, JAMEY
Actor. b. Pasadena, CA, July 12, 1951. e. UC Santa Barbara.
THEATRE: *Off-B'way*: Just a Little Bit Less Than Normal, The Arbor, One Wedding Two Rooms Three Friends. *B'way*: The Man Who Came to Dinner, Hamlet, Biloxi Blues, All My Sons, Long Day's Journey Into Night, Ah Wilderness, The Shadow Box. *Regional*: Major Barbara, Loose Ends, Deathtrap, Homesteaders.
PICTURES: Jumpin' Jack Flash (debut, 1986), The House on Carroll Street, Distant Thunder, Stanley & Iris, Quick Change, Talent for the Game, All I Want for Christmas, A Stranger Among Us, Whispers in the Dark, White Squall, Sherwood's Travels, The Ice Storm, Wild America, Luminous Motion, Cradle Will Rock, The Amati Girls, Let the Devil Wear Black, The Simian Line, Life as a House, Desert Saints, Rain.
TELEVISION: *Series*: Shannon's Deal, Chicago Hope, Law & Order:Criminal Intent. *Movies*: One Police Plaza, Shannon's Deal (pilot), A Mother's Courage: The Mary Thomas Story, Murder in High Places, My Breast, Spring Awakening, Killer Rules, All Lies End in Murder, The Echo of Thunder, Beauty, The Lost Child, Hamlet, *Mini-Series*: The Stand. *Guest*: The Doctors, St. Elsewhere, Spenser: For Hire, Picket Fences, The Equalizer.

SHERIDAN, JIM
Director, Writer. b. Dublin, Ireland, 1949. e. Univ Col. in Dublin, NYU Inst. of Films & TV. Started as director-writer at Lyric Theatre in Belfast and Abbey Theatre in Dublin; also at Project Arts Theatre (1976-80), NY Irish Arts Center (1982-87) as artistic director. Founded Children's Theatre Company in Dublin.
PICTURES: *Dir.-Writer*: My Left Foot, The Field, In the West (s.p. only), In the Name of the Father, Some Mother's Son (also prod.), The Boxer (also prod.), East of Harlem, The General, Agnes Browne, Borstal Boy, On the Edge, Bloody Sunday.
THEATRE: *Writer*: Mobile Homes, Spike in the First World War (Edinburgh Festival Fringe Award for best play, 1983).

SHERIDAN, NICOLLETTE
Actress. b. Worthing, Sussex, England, Nov. 21, 1963. Moved to LA in 1973. Became model in NYC before turning to acting.
PICTURES: The Sure Thing (debut, 1985), Noises Off, Spy Hard, Beverly Hills Ninja, Raw Nerve, .com for Murder, Tarzan &Jane.

TELEVISION: *Series*: Paper Dolls, Knots Landing. *Movies*: Dark Mansions, Agatha Christie's Dead Man's Folly, Jackie Collins' Lucky/Chances, Deceptions, A Time to Heal, Shadows of Desire, Robin Cook's Virus, Murder in My Mind, Knots Landing: Back to the Cul-de-Sac, Dead Husbands, The Spiral Staircase, Haven't We Met Before, Deadly Betrayal.

SHERMAN, RICHARD M.
Composer, Lyricist, Screenwriter. b. New York, NY, June 12, 1928. e. Bard Coll., B.A., 1949. Info. & Educ. Br., U.S. Army, 1953-55. Songwriter, composer, Walt Disney Prods 1960-71, then freelance. With partner-brother Robert has won, 9 Acad. Award nom., 2 Grammys, 17 gold and platinum albums, 1st Prize, Moscow Film Fest. (for Tom Sawyer) and a star on Hollywood Walk of Fame. Have written over 500 pub. and recorded songs. Also wrote score for B'way musical Over Here (1974) and songs for Disney Theme Parks.
SONGS: Things I Might Have Been, Tall Paul, Christmas in New Orleans, Mad Passionate Love, Midnight Oil, The Ugly Bug Ball, You're Sixteen, That Darn Cat, The Wonderful Thing About Tiggers, It's a Small World, A Spoonful of Sugar, Supercalifragilistic, Feed the Birds, Let's Go Fly a Kite, Age of Not Believing, When You're Loved, Pineapple Princess, Let's Get Together, Maggie's Theme, Chim Chim Cheree (Acad. Award, 1964), Chitty Chitty Bang Bang, Hushabye Mountain, Winnie the Pooh, Fortuosity, Slipper and the Rose Waltz, many others. Comedy Album: Smash Flops.
PICTURES: Nightmare, The Cruel Tower, The Absent Minded Professor, The Parent Trap, Big Red, In Search of the Castaways, Moon Pilot, Bon Voyage, Legend of Lobo, Summer Magic, Miracle of the White Stallions, The Sword in the Stone, The Misadventures of Merlin Jones, Mary Poppins (2 Acad. Awards for song & score, 1964), Those Calloways, The Monkey's Uncle, That Darn Cat, Follow Me Boys!, Winnie the Pooh, Monkeys Go Home!, Chitty Chitty Bang Bang, The Gnome-Mobile, The Jungle Book, The Happiest Millionaire, The One and Only Genuine Original Family Band, The Aristocats, Bedknobs & Broomsticks, Snoopy Come Home, Charlotte's Web, Beverly Hills Cop III, The Mighty Kong. Songs & S.P.: Tom Sawyer, The Slipper and the Rose, The Magic of Lassie, Huckleberry Finn, Little Nemo: Adventures in Slumberland, The Tigger Movie.
TELEVISION: Wonderful World of Color, Bell Telephone Hour, Welcome to Pooh Corner, The Enchanted Musical Playhouse, The Timberwood Tales, Goldilocks, Harry Anderson's Sideshow.

SHERMAN, ROBERT B.
Composer, Lyricist, Screenwriter. b. New York, NY, Dec. 19, 1925. e. Bard Coll., B.A., 1949. U.S. Army, WWII, 1943-45 (purple heart). Songwriter, 1952-60; pres., Music World Corp., 1958; songwriter, composer, Walt Disney, 1971, then freelance. Hon. Phd., Lincoln Col, 1990. With partner-brother Richard Sherman, has won, 9 Acad. Award nom., 2 Grammys, 17 gold and platinum albums, 1st Prize, Moscow Film Fest. (for Tom Sawyer) and a star on Hollywood Walk of Fame. Have written over 500 pub. and recorded songs. Also wrote score for B'way musical Over Here (1974) and songs for Disney Theme Parks. (see Richard M. Sherman for co-writing credits.)

SHERMAN, SAMUEL M.
Producer, Director, Writer. b. New York, NY. April 23, 1940. e. CCNY, B.A. Entered m.p. ind. as writer, cameraman, film ed., rep. & sound cutter; nat'l mag. ed., Westerns Magazine 1959; pres., Signature Films; prod., dir., TV pilot, The Three Mesquiteers, 1960; prod., Pulse Pounding Perils, 1961; helped create, ed., dir., Screen Thrills Illustrated; exec. prod., Screen Thrills; v.p., Golden Age Films, 1962; prod., Joe Franklin's Silent Screen, 1963; NY rep., Victor Adamson Prods.; NY rep., Tal prods., Hlywd.; adv. & pub. Hemisphere Pictures; prod., writer, Chaplin's Art of Comedy, The Strongman; prod., Hollywood's Greatest Stuntman; story adapt., Fiend With the Electronic Brain; tech. consul., Hal Roach Studios, Music from the Land; 1968, NY rep. East West Pict. of Hollywood. 1968, N.Y. rep., Al Adamson Prods. of Hollywood; Ed.-in-chief, bk., The Strongman; pres., Independent-International Pictures Corp. (and tv div.); pres., Producers Commercial Productions, Inc. Chmn. of Creditors' Committee, Allied Artists Television Corp.; pres., Technovision Inc.; pres., Super Video, Inc.
PICTURES: *Assoc. prod.*: Horror of the Blood Monsters, Blood of Ghastly Horror. *Prod., s.p.*: Brain of Blood. *Prod. supervisor*: Dracula vs. Frankenstein. *Exec. prod.*: Angels, Wild Women, The Naughty Stewardesses (prod., s.p.), Girls For Rent, The Dynamite Brothers, Blazing Stewardesses (prod., s.p.), Cinderella 2000, Team-Mates (also story), Raiders of the Living Dead (dir., s.p.).

SHERMAN, VINCENT
Director. b. Vienna, GA, July 16, 1906. e. Oglethorpe U. B.A. Writer, actor, dialogue dir., then prod. dir.
PICTURES: The Return of Doctor X (debut, 1939), Saturday's Children, The Man Who Talked Too Much, Underground, Flight from Destiny, The Hard Way, All Through the Night, Old Acquaintance, In Our Time, Mr. Skeffington, Pillow to Post, Janie Gets Married, Nora Prentiss, The Unfaithful, Adventures of Don Juan, The Hasty Heart, The Damned Don't Cry, Harriet Craig, Goodbye My Fancy, Lone Star, Affair in Trinidad, Difendo il mio

Amore, The Garment Jungle, The Naked Earth, The Young Philadelphians, Ice Palace, A Fever in the Blood, The Second Time Around, Cervantes.
TELEVISION: 35 episodes of Medical Center, Westside Medical, Baretta, Waltons, Doctors Hospital, Trapper John, Movies: Women at West Point, Bogey, The Dream Merchants, Trouble in High Timber Country, High Hopes—The Capra Years.

SHERRIN, NED
Producer, Director, Writer. b. Low Ham, Somerset, England, Feb. 18, 1931. Early career writing plays and musical plays. Prod., dir., ATV Birmingham, 1955-57; prod., Midlands Affairs, Paper Talk, etc. Joined BBC-TV 1957 and produced many TV talk programs. Novels: (with Caryl Brahms) Cindy-Ella or I Gotta Shoe (also prod. as stage play), Rappell 1910, Benbow Was His Name.
AUTHOR: *Autobiography*: A Small Thing Like a Earthquake. *Anthology*: Cutting Edge Theatrical Anecdotes. 1995, edit. of Oxford Dictionary of Humorous Quotations. *Novel*: Scratch an Actor. *Diaries*: Serrin's Year: 1995.
PICTURES: *Prod.*: The Virgin Soldiers (with Leslie Gilliat), Every Home Should Have One, Up Pompeii, Girl Stroke Boy (co-author with Caryl Brahms), Up the Chastity Belt, Rentadick, The Garnet Saga, Up the Front, The National Health, The Cobblers of Umbridge (dir. with Ian Wilson). *Actor*: Orlando.
TELEVISION: *England: Prod.*: Ask Me Another, Henry Hall Show, Laugh Line, Parasol. *Assoc. prod.*: Tonight series, Little Beggars. *Prod., creator*: That Was The Week That Was. *Prod., dir.*: Benbow Was His Name (co-author), Take a Sapphire (co-author), The Long Garden Party, The Long Cocktail Party. ABC of Britain revue, Not So Much a Programme—More a Way of Life. Appearances inc.: Your Witness, Quiz of The Week, Terra Firma, Who Said That, The Rather Reassuring Programme, Song by Song, Loose Ends Radio 4.

SHERWOOD, MADELEINE
Actress. b. Montreal, Canada, Nov. 13, 1922. e. Yale Drama Sch. Trained with Montreal Rep. and Actors Studio. Has dir. prods. at Actors Studio and regional theaters, as well as 2 AFI films Goodnight Sweet Prince and Sunday.
THEATRE: The Crucible, Sweet Bird of Youth, Cat on a Hot Tin Roof, Invitation to a March, The Garden of Sweets, Camelot, Hey You, Light Man!, Brecht on Brecht, Night of the Iguana, Arturo Ui, Do I Hear a Waltz?, Inadmissible Evidence, All Over, Older People, Getting Out, The Suicide, Eclipse, Miss Edwina.
PICTURES: Baby Doll, Cat on a Hot Tin Roof, Parrish, Sweet Bird of Youth, The 91st Day, Hurry Sundown, Pendulum, Wicked Wicked, The Changeling, Resurrection, Teachers, An Unremarkable Life, Silence Like Glass, Zwei Frauen.
TELEVISION: *Series*: The Flying Nun. *Mini-Series*: Rich Man Poor Man. *Movies*: The Manhunter, Nobody's Child, Palace Guard; many guest appearances.

SHIELDS, BROOKE
Actress. r.n. Christa Brooke Camille Shields. b. New York, NY, May 31, 1965. e. Princeton U. Honors in French Lit. Discovered at age 11 months by photographer Francesco Scavullo to pose in Ivory Soap ads.
THEATRE: *Off-B'way*: The Eden Cinema; B'way debut 1994 in Grease! (Theatre World Award).
PICTURES: Alice Sweet Alice (debut 1977), Pretty Baby, King of the Gypsies, Tilt, Wanda Nevada, Just You and Me Kid, The Blue Lagoon, Endless Love, Sahara, The Muppets Take Manhattan (cameo), Speed Zone (cameo), Back Street Dreams, Brenda Starr, An American Love (It.), The Seventh Floor, Freeway, The Misadventures of Margaret, Black and White, The Weekend, The Bachelor, After Sex, Massholes.
TELEVISION: *Movies*: The Prince of Central Park, Wet Gold, The Diamond Trap, I Can Make You Love Me: The Stalking of Laura Black; Nothing Lasts Forever; Almost Perfect Bank Robbery, What Makes a Family. *Guest*: Friends, The Simpsons (voice). *Series*: Suddenly Susan, Widows (mini-series).

SHIELDS, WILLIAM A.
Executive. b. New York, NY, 1946. e. El Camino Coll., California State Coll. at LA. Entered the motion picture industry in 1966 with Pacific Theatres, then MGM sales dept., L.A. and Denver, 1970; New World Pictures, 1972; 20th Century-Fox, Washington, 1973; NY district manager, 20th Century-Fox, 1973-75; joined Mann Theatres Corp. of California as head booker in 1975; gen. sls. mgr., Far West Films, 1977-79; joined Avco Embassy as Western div. mgr., promoted to asst. gen. sls. mgr., 1980; promoted to v.p.-gen. sls. mgr., 1981; 1983 joined New World Pictures as exec. v.p., worldwide mktg. & acquisitions; promoted to pres., worldwide sls. & mktg., 1985; 1987, pres. CEO, New World Intl.; 1989, joined Trans Atlantic Pictures as pres., CEO when company purchased assets of New World's feature film division. Sold ownership in Trans Atlantic and formed G.E.L. Prod. & Distrib., 1992. Exec. prod. Au Pair (1991); exec. in charge of prod. Death Ring (1992). Exec. prod. of Uninvited. Past chmn, American Film Mktg. Assn. (1987-91). Presently chmn. American Film Export Assn.

SHIRE, DAVID
Composer. b. Buffalo, NY, July 3, 1937. m. actress Didi Conn. e. Yale U., 1959, B.A. Composer of theater scores: The Sap of Life, Urban Blight, Starting Here Starting Now, Baby, Closer Than Ever, Big. Emmy noms. Raid on Entebbe, The Defection of Simas Kudirka, Do You Remember Love? and The Kennedys of Massachusetts. Grammy Awards for Saturday Night Fever.
PICTURES: One More Train to Rob, Summertree, Drive, He Said; Skin Game, To Find a Man, Showdown, Two People, Steelyard Blues (adapt.), Class of '44, The Conversation, The Taking of Pelham 1-2-3, The Fortune, Farewell My Lovely, The Hindenberg, All the President's Men, The Big Bus, Harry and Walter Go to New York, Saturday Night Fever (adapt. & add. music), Straight Time, The Promise (Acad. Award nom.), Old Boyfriends, Norma Rae (Acad. Award for best song, It Goes Like It Goes, 1979), Only When I Laugh, The Night the Lights Went Out in Georgia, Paternity, The World According to Garp, Max Dugan Returns, Oh God You Devil, 2010, Fast Break, Return to Oz, Short Circuit, 'night mother, Vice Versa, Monkey Shines, Bed and Breakfast, One Night Stand, Ash Wednesday.
TELEVISION: *Series themes*: Sarge, McCloud, The Practice, Sirota's Court, Joe & Sons, Lucas Tanner, Alice, Tales of the Unexpected, Brewster Place, Room for Two. *Movies*: Priest Killer, McCloud, Harpy, Three Faces of Love, Killer Bees, Tell Me Where It Hurts, The Defection of Simus Kudirka, Three for the Road, Amelia Earhart, Something for Joey, Raid on Entebbe, The Storyteller, Promise, Mayflower Madam, Echoes in the Darkness, Jesse, God Bless the Child, Common Ground, The Clinic, Convicted, The Women of Brewster Place, I Know My First Name is Steven, The Kennedys of Massachusetts (mini-series), The Great Los Angeles Earthquake, The Boys, Sarah: Plain and Tall, Always Remember I Love You, Paris Trout, Four Eyes, Broadway Bound, Bed of Lies, Last Wish, Alison, Habitation of Dragons, Lily in Winter, Reunion, Serving in Silence, My Brother's Keeper, My Antonia, The Heidi Chronicles, The Man Who Wouldn't Die, Tecumseh: The Last Warrior, Almost Golden: The Jessica Savitch Story, many others.

SHIRE, TALIA
Actress. r.n. Talia Coppola. b. New York, NY, April 25, 1946. Raised on road by her father, arranger-conductor Carmine Coppola, who toured with Broadway musicals. After 2 yrs. at Yale Sch. of Drama she moved to L.A. where appeared in many theatrical productions. Brother is dir. Francis Ford Coppola. Started in films as Talia Coppola.
PICTURES: The Wild Racers, The Dunwich Horror, Gas-s-s-s, The Christian Licorice Store, The Outside Man, The Godfather, The Godfather Part II (Acad. Award nom.), Rocky (Acad. Award nom.), Old Boyfriends, Prophecy, Rocky II, Windows, Rocky III, Rocky IV, RAD, Lionheart (co-prod.), New York Stories (Life Without Zoe), Rocky V, The Godfather III, Bed and Breakfast, Cold Heaven, DeadFall, One Night Stand (dir. only), Lured Innocence, A River Made to Drown In, The Landlady, Divorce: A Contemporary Western, Can I Play?, Palmer's Pick Up, Caminho dos Sonhos, The Visit, Your Aura is Throbbing, The Whole Shebang, Pomegranate, Dunsmore, Kiss the Bride.
TELEVISION: *Mini-Series*: Rich Man Poor Man. *Movies*: Foster and Laurie, Kill Me If You Can, Daddy I Don't Like It Like This, For Richer For Poorer, Chantilly Lace, Born Into Exile. *Special*: Please God I'm Only 17.

SHIVAS, MARK
Producer. e. Oxford.
PICTURES: *Producer*: Richard's Things, Moonlighting, A Private Function, The Witches. *Exec. Prod.*: Bad Blood, Truly Madly Deeply, Enchanted April, The Grass Arena, Memento Mori, The Snapper, Priest, An Awfully Big Adventure, Jude, The Van, Small Faces, Designated Mourner, Regeneration, I Went Down, Painted Angels, Hideous Kinky, The Revengers' Comedies, The Claim, I Capture the Castle.
TELEVISION: Presenter of Cinema. *Producer*: The Six Wives of Henry VIII, Casanova, The Edwardians, The Evacuees, The Glittering Prizes, Abide With Me, Rogue Male, 84 Charing Cross Road, The Three Hostages, She Fell Among Thieves, Professional Foul, Telford's Change, On Giant's Shoulders, The Price, What If it's Raining?, The Storytellers. *Exec. prod.*: Regeneration, Talking Heads 2. *Mini-Series*: Cambridge Spies.

SHORE, HOWARD
Composer, Musician. b. Oct., 18, 1946, Toronto, Ontario, Canada. Began as musical director for Saturday Night Live, 1975.
PICTURES: I Miss You Hugs and Kisses, The Brood, Scanners, Gilda Live (actor), Videodrome, The Fly, Nothing Lasts Forever, After Hours, Fire with Fire, The Fly, Heaven, Belizaire the Cajun, Nadine, Moving, Big, Dead Ringers, Signs of Life, She-Devil, The Local Stigmatic, An Innocent Man, The Lemon Sisters, Made in Milan, Postcards From the Edge (musical numbers sprv.), The Silence of the Lambs, A Kiss Before Dying, Naked Lunch, Prelude to a Kiss, Single White Female, Sliver, Guilty as Sin, M. Butterfly, Mrs. Doubtfire, Philadelphia, Ed Wood, The Truth About Cats & Dogs, Striptease, Looking for Richard, Crash, That Thing You Do!, The Game, Cop Land, eXistenZ, Chinese Coffee, Dogma, Gloria, Analyze This, High Fidelity, The Yards, Esther Kahn, the Cell, Camera, The Score, The Lord of the Rings: The Fellowship of the Ring, The Lord of the Rings: The

Two Towers, Gangs of New York, The Panic Room, Spider, The Lord of the Rings: The Return of the King.
TELEVISION: Saturday Night Live, Coca-Cola Presents Live: The Hard Rock, Late Night with Conan O'Brien.

SHORE, PAULY
Actor. b. Los Angeles, CA, Feb. 1, 1968. Son of comedian Sammy Shore and nightclub owner Mitzi Shore. Worked as stand-up comedian at mother's club, The Comedy Store.
PICTURES: For Keeps? (debut, 1988), 18 Again!, Lost Angels, Phantom of the Mall, Wedding Band, Encino Man, Class Act, Son-in-Law, In the Army Now, Jury Duty, Bio-Dome, The Curse of Inferno, Junket Whore, Love and Fear, An Extremely Goofy Movie, Red Letters, The Wash, You'll Never Wiez in this Town Again.
TELEVISION: Series: Totally Pauly, Totally Different Pauly, Paul. Special: Pauly Does Dallas. Movie: Home By Midnight, The Curse of Inferno, Casper Meets Wendy, The Bogus Witch Project, The Princess and the Barrio Boy.. Guest: 21 Jump Street, Married... with Children, King of the Hill (voice). Mini-Series: I Love the '70s.

SHORT, MARTIN
Actor, Comedian, Writer. b. Toronto, Can., March 26, 1950. e. McMaster U. Trained as social worker but instead performed on stage in Godspell as well as in revues and cabarets in Toronto, 1973-78, including a stint as a member of the Toronto unit of the Second City comedy troupe, 1977-78. Created such characters as Ed Grimley, Jackie Rogers Jr. B'way debut 1993 in The Goodbye Girl (Theatre World Award; Tony nom.).
PICTURES: Lost and Found, The Outsider, Three Amigos!, Innerspace, Cross My Heart, Three Fugitives, The Big Picture, Pure Luck, Father of the Bride, Captain Ron, Clifford, The Pebble and the Penguin (voice), Father of the Bride Part 2, An Indian in the City, Mars Attacks!, Jungle 2 Jungle, A Simple Wish, Mumford, Akbar's Adventure Tours, Prince of Egypt (voice), Get Over It, Jimmy Neutron: Boy Genius, Treasure Planet, Cinemagimique, 101 Dalmatians 2: Patch's London Adventure.
TELEVISION: Series: The Associates, I'm a Big Girl Now, SCTV Network (Emmy Award for writing, 1983), Saturday Night Live (1985- 86), The Completely Mental Misadventures of Ed Grimley (cartoon series), The Martin Short Show (also exec. prod., writer), Primetime Glick. Specials: All's Well That Ends Well, Really Weird Tales, Martin Short's Concert for the North Americas (SHO), Martin Short Goes Hollywood (HBO), The Show Formerly Known as the Martin Short Show (also exec. prod., co-writer). Movies: The Family Man, Sunset Limousine, Money for Nothing (BBC), Alice in Wonderland, Prince Charming.

SHORT, THOMAS C.
Executive. International Pres., International Alliance of Theatrical Stage Employees, Moving Picture Technicians, Artists and Allied Crafts of the United States and Canada AFL-CIO, CLC.

SHUE, ELISABETH
Actress. b. South Orange, NJ, Oct. 6, 1963. e. Harvard. Brother is actor Andrew Shue.
PICTURES: The Karate Kid (debut, 1984), Adventures in Babysitting, Link, Cocktail, Back to the Future Part II, Back to the Future Part III, The Marrying Man, Soapdish, Twenty Bucks, The Underneath, Leaving Las Vegas (Chicago Film Critics Award; Nat'l Film Critics Award; LA Film Critics Award), Trigger Effect, The Saint, Radio Inside, Palmetto, Deconstructing Harry, Cousine Bette (LA Film Critics Award), Molly, Hollow Man, Leopold Bloom, Tuck Everlasting, (narrator voice).
TELEVISION: Series: Call to Glory. Movies: Charles and Diana, Double Switch, Hale the Hero, Blind Justice, Amy and Isabelle, The First Year.

SHUGRUE, J. EDWARD
Executive. Began career in theater management with General Cinema Corp, 1970-71. Joined Columbia Pictures as sales manager, 1971; became branch manager, 1976. Eastern Div. Mgr., 20th Century Fox, 1981-1983. 1983-1987, exec. v.p., North American Distribution, TriStar Pictures. Pres., Columbia TriStar Film Distributors International, 1987-1996. Exec. v.p., Sony Pictures Entertainment and exec. v.p. Sony Retail Entertainment, 1996-1998. Became pres., Loews Cineplex International 1998. Also serves as director, Yelmo Cineplex (Spain), DeLaurentiis Cineplex (Italy), and Megabox Cineplex (Korea).

SHULER-DONNER, LAUREN
Producer. b. Cleveland, OH. June 23, 1949. B.S. in film & bdc-stg., Boston U. m. dir.-prod. Richard Donner. Began filmmaking career as ed. of educational films then camera-woman in TV prod., assoc. prod., story editor, creative affairs exec.; TV movie: Amateur Night at the Dixie Bar and Grill (prod.). Assoc. prod. on film Thank God It's Friday. Cameo in film Maverick.
PICTURES: Mr. Mom, Ladyhawke, St. Elmo's Fire, Pretty in Pink, Three Fugitives, The Favor, Radio Flyer, Dave, Free Willy, Free Willy 2: The Adventure Home, Assassins, Volcano, Free Willy 3, Bulworth, You've Got Mail, Any Given Sunday, X-Men, Out Cold, X-Men 2, Just Married, X2, Timeline.

SHUTT, BUFFY
Executive. e. Sarah Lawrence Col. Joined Paramount 1973 as sect. with N.Y. pub. staff; 1975, natl. mag. contact. 1978, named dir. of pub.; later exec. dir. of pub. Promoted 1980 to v.p., pub. & promo. Resigned to join Time-Life Films as v.p. east coast prod; returned to Paramount in 1981 as sr. v.p. & asst. to pres. of Motion Picture Group. 1983, appointed pres. of mktg. 1986, resigned. Formed Shutt-Jones Communications, 1987, marketing consultancy with Kathy Jones. 1989, pres. of marketing, Columbia Pictures & TriStar Pictures. 1991, pres. of marketing, TriStar Pictures. 1994, pres. of marketing, Universal Pictures.

SHYER, CHARLES
Director, Writer. b. Los Angeles, CA. Oct. 11, 1941. e. UCLA. Was asst. dir. and prod. mgr. before becoming head writer for tv series The Odd Couple. First teamed with Nancy Meyers on Private Benjamin.
PICTURES: Writer: Smokey and the Bandit, House Calls, Goin' South, Private Benjamin (Acad. Award nom.; also prod.), The Parent Trap (also prod.). Director-Writer: Irreconcilable Differences, Baby Boom, Father of the Bride, I Love Trouble, Father of the Bride Part II, The Affair of the Necklace.

SHYAMALAN, M. NIGHT
Writer, Director. b. Pondicherry, Tamil-Nadu province, India, August 6, 1970.
PICTURES: Praying With Anger (also prod.), Wide Awake, The Sixth Sense, Stuart Little (s.p. only), Unbreakable (also prod.), Signs, (also prod.).

SIDARIS, ANDY
Producer, Director, Writer. b. Chicago, IL, Feb. 20, 1932. e. Southern Methodist U., B.A., radio-TV. Began television career in 1950 in Dallas, TX as a director at station WFAA-TV; now pres., The Sidaris Company. Won 8 Emmy Awards.
PICTURES: Dir.: Stacey, The Racing Scene, M*A*S*H (football sequences), Seven (also prod.). Dir.-Writer: Malibu Express (also prod.), Hard Ticket to Hawaii, Picasso Trigger, Savage Beach, Guns, Do or Die, Hard Hunted, Fit to Kill, Day of the Warrior, Return to Savage Beach. Exec. Prod.: Enemy Gold, The Dallas Connection.
TELEVISION: Dir.: The Racers/Mario Andretti/Joe Leonard/Al Unser, ABC's Championship Auto Racing, ABC's NCAA Game of the Week, 1968 Summer Olympics: 1968 (Mexico City), 1972 (Munich), 1976 (Montreal), 1984 (L.A.), Winter Olympics: 1964 (Innsbruck), 1968 (Grenoble), 1976 (Innsbruck), 1980 (Lake Placid), 1988 (Calgary), Wide World of Sports, The Racers/Craig and Lee Breedlove, The Burt Reynolds Late Show, Kojak episode, Nancy Drew episodes.

SIEMASZKO, CASEY
Actor. r.n. Kazimierz Siemaszko. b. Chicago, IL, March 17, 1961. e. Goodman Theatre School of Drama, Chicago.
PICTURES: Class (debut, 1983), Secret Admirer, Back to the Future, Stand By Me, Gardens of Stone, Three O'Clock High, Biloxi Blues, Young Guns, Breaking In, Back to the Future Part II, Of Mice and Men, Teresa's Tattoo, My Life's in Turnaround, Milk Money, The Phantom, Bliss, The Taxman, Limbo, The Crew.
TELEVISION: Movie: Miracle of the Heart: A Boys Town Story, The Chase, Children Remember the Holocaust, Black Scorpion, Rose Hill, Mistrial, Chameleon II: Death Match. Mini-series: Storm of the Century.

SIGHVATSSON, SIGURJON (JONI)
Producer. b. Reykjavik, Iceland, June 15, 1952. e. Iceland Community Col, Univ. of Iceland. Came to U.S. in 1978. Also attended USC. Was film and music video dir. for Blue-Ice Prods. Founder and chairperson with Steve Golin of Propaganda Films.
PICTURE: Assoc. Prod: Hard Rock Zombies, American Drive-In. Producer: Private Investigations, The Blue Iguana, Kill Me Again, Fear Anxiety and Depression, Daddy's Dyin'... Who's Got the Will?, Wild at Heart, Truth or Dare, Ruby, A Stranger Among Us, Candyman, Kalifornia, Red Rock West, S.F.W., Lord of Illusions, Canadian Bacon, The Kids in the Hall: Brain Candy, Basquiat, A Thousand Acres. Exec. Prod.: 'Til There Was You , The Real Blonde, Polish Wedding, Phoenix, Homegrown, 200 Cigarettes, Arlington Road, Passion of Mind, The Weight of Water, K-19 The Widowmaker.
TELEVISION: Movie: Memphis. Specials: Rock the Vote, Education First, Tales of the City. Series: Twin Peaks.

SIKKING, JAMES B.
Actor. b. Los Angeles, CA, March 5, 1934. e. UCLA, B.A. Theatre includes Waltz of the Toreadors, Plaza Suite, Damn Yankees, The Big Knife.
PICTURES: The Magnificent Seven, Von Ryan's Express, Chandler, The New Centurions, The Electric Horseman, Capricorn One, Ordinary People, Outland, The Star Chamber, Up the Creek, Star Trek III—The Search for Spock, Morons from Outer Space, Soul Man, Narrow Margin, Final Approach, The Pelican Brief.
TELEVISION: Series: General Hospital, Turnabout, Hill Street Blues. Doogie Howser, M.D., Brooklyn South. Movies: The Jesse Owens Story, First Steps, Bay Coven, Brotherhood of the Rose,

Too Good to be True, Desperado: Badlands Justice, Doing Time on Maple Drive, The Final Days, Jake Lassiter: Justice on the Bayou, In Pursuit of Honor, Seduced by Evil, Tyson, Dare to Love, Dead Badge, The Ring, Mutiny, Nowhere to Land, Submerged. Mini-Series: Around the World in 80 Days. Specials: Tales from the Hollywood Hills (Golden Land), Ollie Hopnoodle's Haven of Bliss.

SILVA, HENRY
Actor. b. Brooklyn, NY, Sept. 15, 1928. Studied acting with Group Theatre, Actors Studio.
PICTURES: Viva Zapata!, Crowded Paradise, A Hatful of Rain, The Law and Jake Wade, The Bravados, Green Mansions, Cinderfella, Ocean's Eleven, Sergeants 3, The Manchurian Candidate, A Gathering of Eagles, Johnny Cool, The Secret Invasion, Hail Mafia, The Return of Mr. Moto, The Reward, The Hills Ran Red, The Plainsman, Matchless, Never a Dull Moment, The Animals, Man and Boy, The Italian Connection,
The Kidnap of Mary Lou, Shoot, Thirst, Buck Rogers in the 25th Century, Love and Bullets, Virus, Alligator, Sharky's Machine, Wrong Is Right, Megaforce, Cannonball Run II, Lust in the Dust, Code of Silence, Alan Quartermain and the Lost City of Gold, Amazon Women on the Moon, Above the Law, Bulletproof, Dick Tracy, Fists of Steel, Trained to Kill, Possessed by the Night, The Silence of the Hams, The Prince, Mad Dog Time, The End of Violence, Unconditional Love, Ghost Dog: The Way of the Samurai, Ocean's Eleven.
TELEVISION: Movies: Black Noon, Drive Hard Drive Fast, Contract on Cherry Street, Happy, Justice, Seduced by Evil, Backlash. Series: Buck Rogers in the 25th Century.

SILVER, CASEY
Executive. Chmn., Universal Pictures, Inc. Began career in motion picture industry as a screenwriter. Was asst. to dir. Adrian Lyne on Flashdance. Became dir. of devt. and prod. for Simpson-Bruckheimer Prods. V.P., prod., TriStar Pictures. Sr. v.p., prod., TriStar. Joined Universal Pictures as exec. v.p., prod., 1987. Became pres. of prod. in January, 1989; pres., Universal Pictures, June, 1994. Appointed chmn., Universal Pictures, November, 1995. In October 1999, Silver formed Casey Silver Productions, a motion picture company.

SILVER, JOAN MICKLIN
Writer, Director. b. Omaha, NB, May 24, 1935. m. producer Raphael Silver. Daughter is dir. Marisa Silver. e. Sarah Lawrence Coll. Began career as writer for educational films. Original s.p., Limbo, purchased by Universal Pictures. In 1972 Learning Corp. of Am. commissioned her to write and direct a 30-min. film, The Immigrant Experience. Also wrote and directed two children's films for same co; dir. & wrote short film Bernice Bobs Her Hair. First feature was Hester Street, which she wrote and directed.
THEATRE: Director: Album, Maybe I'm Doing It Wrong, A ... My Name is Alice, A ... My Name is Still Alice (co-conceived & co-dir. with Julianne Boyd).
PICTURES: Director: Hester Street (also s.p.), Between the Lines, On the Yard (prod.), Head Over Heels (also s.p.; retitled Chilly Scenes of Winter), Crossing Delancey, Loverboy, Big Girls Don't Cry... They Get Even, A Fish In the Bathtub.
TELEVISION: Bernice Bobs Her Hair, How to Be a Perfect Person In Just Three Days, Finnegan Begin Again (dir.), The Nightingale: Faerie Tale Theatre (writer), Parole Board (Prison Stories: Women on the Inside), A Private Matter (dir.), Miss Sherri, In the Presence of Mine Enemies, Invisible Child, Charms for the Easy Life, Hunger Point.

SILVER, JOEL
Producer. b. South Orange, NJ, July 14, 1952. e. NYU. Made first film, a short called Ten Pin Alley; moved to Los Angeles with job as asst. to Lawrence Gordon. Named pres., Lawrence Gordon Prods.; developed with Gordon and produced and marketed Hooper, The End, The Driver, The Warriors (also assoc. prod.). At Universal Pictures as prod. v.p.; supervising Smokey and the Bandit II. Honored 1990 as NATO/Showest's Producer of the Year. Appeared in 1988 film Who Framed Roger Rabbit.
PICTURES: Xanadu (co-prod.), Jekyll & Hyde ... Together Again (exec. prod.), 48 HRS., Streets of Fire, Brewster's Millions, Weird Science, Commando, Jumpin' Jack Flash, Lethal Weapon, Predator, Action Jackson, Die Hard, Road House, Lethal Weapon 2, The Adventures of Ford Fairlane, Die Hard 2, Predator 2, Hudson Hawk, Ricochet, The Last Boy Scout, Lethal Weapon 3, Demoliton Man, The Hudsucker Proxy, Richie Rich, Tales From the Crypt Presents Demon Knight (co-exec. prod.), Fair Game, Assassins, Executive Decision, Conspiracy Theory, Father's Day, Conspiracy Theory, The Matrix, Lethal Weapon 4, Romeo Must Die, The House on Haunted Hill, Made Men, Dungeon & Dragons, Exit Wounds, Chimera, Proximity, Swordfish, 13 Ghosts, Ritual, Adrenalynn, Macabre, The Matrix Reloaded, The Matrix 3, Cradle 2: The Grave, Adrenalynn, The Matrix Revolutions.
TELEVISION: Tales from the Crypt (exec. prod. & prod.; also dir. episode), Two Fisted Tales, Parker Can, W.E.I.R.D. World (co-exec. prod.), The Strip (exec. prod), Action (exec. prod.), Jane Doe.

SILVER, MARISA
Director. b. New York, NY, April 23, 1960. Daughter of director Joan Micklin Silver and prod.-dir. Raphael Silver. e. Harvard U. where she directed short Dexter T. and edited doc. Light Coming Through: a Portrait of Maud Morgan.
PICTURES: Old Enough, Permanent Record, Vital Signs, He Said/She Said (co-dir.).
TELEVISION: Series: L.A. Law. Co-dir.: A Community of Praise (an episode of PBS series Middletown, 1982). Movies: Indecency.

SILVER, RAPHAEL D.
Producer. b. Cleveland, OH, 1930. e. Harvard Coll. and Harvard Graduate Sch. of Business Adm. Is pres. of Middex Devel. Corp. 1973 formed Midwest Film Productions to produce Hester Street, written and directed by Joan Micklin Silver. Also distributed film independently. Also produced Between the Lines. Exec. prod. of Crossing Delancey. Directed On the Yard, A Walk on the Moon; writer/prod. A Fish in the Bathtub. Currently pres. Silverfilm Prods. Inc.

SILVER, RON
Actor, Director. b. New York, NY, July 2, 1946. e. U. of Buffalo, St. John's U., Taiwan, M.A. Trained for stage at Herbert Berghof Studios and Actors Studio. N.Y. stage debut in Kasper and Public Insult, 1971. Elected pres. of Actors Equity Assn., 1991.
THEATRE: El Grande de Coca Cola, Lotta, More Than You Deserve, Angel City (Mark Taper, LA), Hurlyburly, Social Security, Hunting Cockroaches, Speed-the-Plow (Tony & Drama Desk Award), Gorilla (Chicago, Jefferson Award nom.; N.YU. & L.A., Dramalogue Award), Friends, And, Broken Glass.
PICTURES: Tunnelvision, Welcome to L.A., Semi-Tough, Silent Rage, Best Friends, The Entity, Lovesick, Silkwood, Garbo Talks, Oh God! You Devil, Goodbye People, Eat and Run, Enemies A Love Story, Blue Steel, Reversal of Fortune, Mr. Saturday Night, Married to It, Timecop, Danger Zone, Deadly Takeover, Girl 6, The Arrival, Rhapsody in Bloom, Black & White, The White Raven, Exposure, Cutaway, Ali, Festival in Cannes.
TELEVISION: Series: Mac Davis Show, Rhoda, Dear Detective, The Stockard Channing Show, Baker's Dozen, Chicago Hope, The West Wing. Movies: The Return of the World's Greatest Detective, Murder at the Mardi Gras, Betrayal, Word of Honor, Billionaire Boys Club, Fellow Traveler, Forgotten Prisoners: The Amnesty Files, Live Wire, Blindside, Lifepod (also dir.), Almost Golden: The Jessica Savitch Story, Billionaire Boys Club (Emmy nom.), Shadow Zone: The Undead, Express, The Beneficiary, In the Company of Spies, Love Is Strange, Master Spy: The Robert Hanssen Story, Two Babies: Switched at Birth, Ratz, American Tragedy, When Billie Beat Bobby. Mini-Series: A Zoman of Independent Means. Guest: Trying Times, Hill Street Blues. Special: Loyalty and Betrayal: The Story of the American Mob (narrator).

SILVERMAN, FRED
Producer. b. New York, NY, Sept., 1937. e. Syracuse U., Ohio State U., master's in TV and theatre arts. Joined WGN-TV, indep. sta. in Chicago. Came to NY for exec. post at WPIX-TV, where stayed only six weeks. CBS-TV hired him as dir. of daytime programs. Named v.p., programs 1970. 1975 left CBS to become pres., ABC Entertainment. 1978, named pres. and CEO of NBC.In 1981 NBC to make programs via The Fred Silverman Company, where he is currently president.
TELEVISION: Prod./exec. prod.: Series: Perry Mason Movies, Matlock, In the Heat of the Night, Jake and the Fatman, Father Dowling Mysteries, Diagnosis Murder, Bonechillers, Bedtime Stories, Twenty One, Movies: Gramps, My Very Best Friend, Journey to Mars, Murder Among Friends, Recipe for Murder, Drive Time Murders, A Town Without Pity, Without Warning.

SILVERMAN, JONATHAN
Actor. b. Los Angeles, CA, Aug. 5, 1966. e. USC, NYU.
THEATRE: NY: Brighton Beach Memoirs, Biloxi Blues, Broadway Bound. LA: The Illusion (Dramalogue Award), Pay or Play (Dramalogue Award), Sticks and Stones (Dramalogue Award).
PICTURES: Brighton Beach Memoirs (debut, 1986), Caddyshack II, Stealing Home, Weekend at Bernie's, Class Action, Breaking the Rules, Life in the Food Chain, Little Sister, Weekend at Bernie's II, Little Big League, Teresa's Tattoo, French Exit, At First Sight, Denial, 12 Bucks, The Odd Couple II, Just a Little Harmless Sex, Freak City, Men Named Milo,Women Named Greta, Dick and Betty, Made, Lip Service, The Medicine Show, It Is What it Is.
TELEVISION: Series: Gimme a Break, The Single Guy. Movies: Challenge of a Lifetime, Traveling Man, For Richer For Poorer, Broadway Bound, 12:01, Sketch Artist II: Hands That See, London Suite, The Inspectors, These Old Broads, Inspectors 2: A Shred of Evidence, Bobbie's Girl, Deacons for Defense.

SILVERSTEIN, ELLIOT
Director. b. Boston, MA, Aug. 3, 1937. e. Boston Coll., Yale U. Started career in television.
PICTURES: Cat Ballou, The Happening, A Man Called Horse, Deadly Honeymoon, The Car (also co-prod.), Flashfire.
TELEVISION: Pilot: Belle Sommers (debut, 1962). Movies: Betrayed by Innocence, Night of Courage, Fight for Life, Rich Men Single Women. Series: Tales From the Crypt.

SILVERSTONE, ALICIA
Actress. b. San Francisco, California, October 4, 1976. Made stage debut at Met Theater in Los Angeles in Carol's Eve. Starred in three Aerosmith videos including Cryin'. Formed own production co., First Kiss Prods.
PICTURES: The Crush (debut, 1993), The Babysitter, True Crime, Le Nouveau Monde, Hideaway, Clueless, Excess Baggage (also prod.), Batman & Robin, Love's Labour's Lost, Blast from the Past, Global Heresy, Scorched, Scooby-Doo 2: Monsters Unleashed.
TELEVISION: *Movies:* Torch Song, Shattered Dreams, The Cool and the Crazy. *Series:* Braceface (voice), Miss Match. *Guest:* The Wonder Years.

SILVESTRI, ALAN
Composer. b. March 26, 1950.
PICTURES: The Doberman Gang, The Amazing Dobermans, The Fifth Floor, Romancing the Stone, Summer Rental, Fandango, Cat's Eye, Back to the Future, No Mercy, Flight of the Navigator, American Anthem, The Delta Force, The Clan of the Cave Bear, Overboard, Critical Condition, Predator, Outrageous Fortune, My Stepmother Is an Alien, Mac and Me, Who Framed Roger Rabbit, She's Out of Control, The Abyss, Back to the Future Part II, Downtown, Back to the Future Part III, Young Guns II, Predator 2, Father of the Bride, Dutch, Back to the Future... The Ride, Soapdish, Shattered (also orchestration), Ricochet, FernGully: The Last Rainforest, Stop! Or My Mom Will Shoot, The Bodyguard, Sidekicks, Death Becomes Her, Judgment Night, In Search of the Obelisk, Grumpy Old Men, Super Mario Bros., Cop & 1/2, Richie Rich, Clean Slate, Forrest Gump (Acad. Award nom., Golden Globe nom.), Blown Away, The Quick and the Dead, The Perez Family, Judge Dredd, Father of the Bride Part II, Grumpier Old Men, Sgt. Bilko, Eraser, The Long Kiss Goodnight, Fools Rush In, Volcano, Contact, Mouse Hunt, The Odd Couple II, Holy Man, Practical Magic, Stuart Little, Reindeer Games, What Lies Beneath, Cast Away, What Women Want, The Mexican, The Mummy Returns, Serendipity, Lilo and Stitch, Stuart Little 2, Macabre, Uptown Girl, Showtime, Maid in Manhattan, Identity, Lara Croft Tomb Raider: The Cradle of Life, Something's Gotta Give, Van Helsing, The Polar Express.
TELEVISION: Starsky and Hutch, CHiPs, Airwolf, Tales From the Crypt.

SIMMONS, ANTHONY
Director, Writer. b. London, England. 1924. e. Grad. from the LSE with LL.B. Practiced briefly as a barrister before entering the industry as writer/director of documentaries, then commercials and feature films. Awards: Grand Prix (shorts), Venice, Grand Prix, Locarno; 2 Int. Emmys, Intl. Awards for commercials. Publications: The Optimists of Nine Elms, A Little Space for Issie Brown.
PICTURES: Sunday By the Sea, Bow Bells, Time Without Pity (co- prod.), Four in the Morning, The Optimists, Black Joy, Little Sweetheart, Poison Candy.
TELEVISION: On Giant's Shoulders, Supergran and the Magic Ray, Harry Carpenter Never Said It Was Like This, Life After Death, Day After the Fair, Inspector Morse, Van de Valk, Inspector Frost, The Good Guys, 99-1.

SIMMONS, JEAN
Actress. b. London, England, Jan. 31, 1929. e. Aida Foster Sch., London. Screen debut 1944 at age 14. Voted one of top ten British money-making stars in M.P. Herald-Fame Poll, 1950-51. London stage: A Little Night Music. Awards: Cannes Film Festival Homage 1988, Italian Outstanding Film Achievement Award 1989, French Govt. Commandeur de L'Ordre des Arts des Lettres. 1990.
PICTURES: Give Us the Moon (debut, 1944), Mr. Emmanuel, Meet Sexton Blake, Kiss the Bride Goodbye, Sports Day, Caesar and Cleopatra, Way to the Stars, Great Expectations, Hungry Hill, Black Narcissus, Uncle Silas, The Women In the Hall, Hamlet (Acad. Award nom.), Blue Lagoon, Adam and Evelyne, Trio, So Long at the Fair, Cage of Gold, The Clouded Yellow, Androcles and the Lion (U.S. film debut, 1953), Angel Face, Young Bess, Affair with a Stranger, The Actress, The Robe, She Couldn't Say No, A Bullet Is Waiting, The Egyptian, Desiree, Footsteps in the Fog, Guys and Dolls, Hilda Crane, This Could Be the Night, Until They Sail, The Big Country, Home Before Dark, This Earth Is Mine, Elmer Gantry, Spartacus, The Grass Is Greener, All the Way Home, Life at the Top, Mister Buddwing, Rough Night in Jericho, Divorce American Style, The Happy Ending (Acad. Award nom.), Say Hello to Yesterday, Mr. Sycamore, Dominique, Going Undercover, The Dawning, How to Make an American Quilt, Final Fantasy: The Spirits Within.
TELEVISION: *Movies & Specials:* Heidi, Beggarman Thief, The Easter Promise, The Home Front, Golden Gate, Jacqueline Susann's Valley of the Dolls 1981, A Small Killing, Inherit the Wind, Great Expectations, Sensibility and Sense, The Laker Girls, Perry Mason: The Case of Lost Love, People Like Us, December Flower, One More Mountain, Daisies in December, Her Own Rules, On Cukor, The Oliviers in Love.. *Mini-Series:* The Dain Curse, The Thorn Birds (Emmy Award, 1983), North and South Book II, Great Expectations *Series:* Dark Shadows (1991), Mysteries of the Bible.

SIMMONS, MATTY
Producer. b. Oct. 3. As bd. chmn., National Lampoon, Inc. pro- duced National Lampoon Radio Hour, National Lampoon Lemmings, National Lampoon Show. Resigned from National Lampoon Inc. 1989. Now heads Matty Simmons Productions.
PICTURES: National Lampoon's Animal House, National Lampoon's Vacation, National Lampoon Goes to the Movies, National Lampoon's Class Reunion, National Lampoon's European Vacation, National Lampoon's Christmas Vacation (exec. prod.), National Lampoon's Vegas Vacation (exec. prod.).
TELEVISION: National Lampoon's Disco Beavers, National Lampoon's Class of '86 (exec. prod.), Delta House.

SIMON, MELVIN
Executive. b. New York, NY, Oct. 21, 1926. e. City Coll.of New York, B.B.A., 1949; graduate work at Indiana U. Law Sch. Owner and operator, in partnership with two brothers, of over 110 shop- ping centers in U.S. 1978 formed Melvin Simon Productions, pri- vately owned corp., to finance films. Dissolved Co. in 1983.
PICTURES: *Exec. Prod.:* Dominique, Love at First Bite, When a Stranger Calls, The Runner Stumbles, Scavenger Hunt, Cloud Dancer, The Stunt Man, My Bodyguard, Zorro the Gay Blade, Chu Chu and the Philly Flash, Porky's, Porky's II—The Next Day, Uforia, Wolf Lake, Porky's Revenge.

SIMON, NEIL
Playwright, Screenwriter, Producer. r.n. Marvin Neil Simon. b. Bronx, NY, July 4, 1927. e. NYU. U.S. Army Air Force, 1945-46. Wrote comedy for radio with brother, Danny, (Robert Q. Lewis Show and for Goodman Ace), also TV scripts for Sid Caesar, Red Buttons, Jackie Gleason, Phil Silvers, Garry Moore, Tallulah Bankhead Show. With Danny contributed to B'way revues Catch a Star (1955), and New Faces of 1956.
THEATRE: *Playwright:* Come Blow Your Horn, Little Me, Barefoot in the Park, The Odd Couple (Tony Award, 1965), Sweet Charity, The Star Spangled Girl, Plaza Suite, Promises Promises, Last of the Red Hot Lovers, The Gingerbread Lady, The Prisoner of Second Avenue, The Sunshine Boys, The Good Doctor, God's Favorite, California Suite, Chapter Two, They're Playing Our Song, I Ought to Be in Pictures, Fools, Little Me (revised version), Brighton Beach Memoirs, Biloxi Blues (Tony Award, 1985), The Odd Couple (female version), Broadway Bound, Rumors, Lost in Yonkers (Pulitzer Prize, Tony Award, 1991), Jake's Women, The Goodbye Girl (musical), Laughter on the 23rd Floor, London Suite (Off-B'way), The Out-of-Towners, The Odd Couple II.
PICTURES: After the Fox, Barefoot in the Park (also assoc. prod.), The Odd Couple, The Out-of-Towners, Plaza Suite, Last of the Red Hot Lovers, The Heartbreak Kid, The Prisoner of Second Avenue, The Sunshine Boys, Murder by Death, The Goodbye Girl, The Cheap Detective, California Suite, Chapter Two, Seems Like Old Times, Only When I Laugh (also co-prod.), I Ought to Be in Pictures (also co-prod.), Max Dugan Returns (also co-prod.), The Lonely Guy (adaptation), The Slugger's Wife, Brighton Beach Memoirs, Biloxi Blues (also co-prod.), The Marrying Man, Lost in Yonkers, The Odd Couple II, The Out-of-Towners (1999).
TELEVISION: *Specials:* The Trouble With People, Plaza Suite. *Movie:* Broadway Bound, Jake's Women, London Suite, Sonny Boys, Laughter on the 23rd Floor.

SIMON, PAUL
Singer, Composer, Actor. b. Newark, NJ, Oct. 13, 1941. e. Queens Coll., BA; postgrad. Brooklyn Law Sch. Teamed with Art Garfunkel in 1964, writing and performing own songs; they part- ed in 1970. Reunited for concert in New York, 1982, which was televised on HBO. Songs: With Garfunkel incl.: Mrs. Robinson (Grammy Award), The Boxer, Bridge Over Troubled Water (Grammy Award).
ALBUMS: with Garfunkel: Wednesday Morning 3 a.m., Sounds of Silence, Parsley, Sage, Rosemary and Thyme, The Graduate (Grammy Award), Bookends, Bridge Over Troubled Water (Grammy Award), Simon & Garfunkel's Greatest Hits, Concert in the Park. *Solo:* Paul Simon, There Goes Rhymin' Simon, Live Rhymin', Still Crazy After All These Years (Grammy Award), Greatest Hits, One Trick Pony, Hearts and Bones, Graceland (Grammy Award), Negotiations and Love Songs, The Rhythm of the Saints, Paul Simon's Concert in the Park.
PICTURES: The Graduate (songs), Annie Hall (actor), One Trick Pony (s.p., actor, composer), Graceland, On Tiptoe: Gentle Steps to Freedom, Old School, The Wild Thornberrys Movie, 40 Days and 40 Nights, American Pie 2, Almost Famous, Forrest Gump, Baby, It's You.
TELEVISION: *Specials:* The Fred Astaire Show, The Paul Simon Special (Emmy Award), Home Box Office Presents Paul Simon, Graceland: The African Concert, Mother Goose Rock 'n' Rhyme, Paul Simon's Concert in the Park. *Guest:* Sesame Street, America: A Tribute to Heroes.

SIMON, SIMONE
Actress. b. April 23, 1911, Marseilles, France. Played in many films in Europe, among them Les Beaux Jours, La Bete Humaine, and Lac aux Dames. On stage in Toi C'est Moi, and others.
PICTURES: Girl's Dormitory (U.S. debut, 1936), Ladies in Love, Seventh Heaven, All That Money Can Buy, Cat People, Tahiti

Honey, Johnny Doesn't Live Here Any More, The Curse of the Cat People, Mademoiselle Fifi, Petrus, Temptation Harbor, La Ronde, Olivia (Pit of Loneliness), Le Plaisir (House of Pleasure), Double Destin, The Extra Day, La Femme en Bleu, On connaît la chanson.

SIMPSON, GARRY
Producer, Director, Executive. b. Camden, MI, Feb. 16, 1914. e. Stanford U. Major shows with NBC-TV: Jimmy Durante Show, Armstrong Circle Theatre, Campbell Soundstage, Comedy Hour, Ford Festival, Chevrolet Tele-Theater, Ed Wynn Show, The World of Mr. Sweeney, Philco TV Playhouse, Wide Wide World, Ballet Theatre. Dir. of programming, Vermont State PBS Network and writer-prod. of documentary films. Awards: Peabody, NY Film & TV Fest., Chicago Film Fest., & 3 Emmys.

SIMPSON, O.J.
Actor. r.n. Orenthal James Simpson. b. San Francisco, CA, July 9, 1947. e. U. of Southern California. Was star collegiate and professional football player and winner of Heisman Trophy. Began sportscasting in 1969.
PICTURES: The Klansman (debut, 1974), The Towering Inferno, Killer Force, The Cassandra Crossing, Capricorn One, Firepower, Hambone & Hillie, The Naked Gun: From the Files of Police Squad, The Naked Gun 2 1/2: The Smell of Fear, Naked Gun 33 1/3: The Final Insult, Bamboozled.
TELEVISION: Mini-Series: Roots. Movies: A Killing Affair, Goldie and the Boxer (also exec. prod.), Detour to Terror (also exec. prod.), Goldie and the Boxer Go to Hollywood (also exec. prod.), Cocaine and Blue Eyes (also exec. prod.), Student Exchange. Prod.: High Five (pilot), Frogmen, Superbowl Saturday Night (host & co-prod.). Series: First and Ten (HBO), NFL Live (co-host).

SINBAD
Actor. r.n. David Adkins. b. Benton Harbor, MI, Nov. 10, 1956. e. Univ. of Denver. Served in Air Force before becoming stand-up comic. Career was subsquently launched by appearances on tv series Star Search.
PICTURES: Necessary Roughness (debut, 1991), Coneheads, The Meteor Man, Houseguest, First Kid (also co-exec. prod.), Jingle All the Way, Homeward Bound II: Lost in San Francisco, First Kid, Jingle All the Way, Good Burger, Crazy as Hell, Treading Water, Hansel & Gretel.
TELEVISION: Movies: Club Med, Sinbad: Brain Damaged, Circus of the Stars and Sideshow, Aliens for Breakfast, The Cherokee Kid, (also exec. prod.), Ready to Run, Inside TV Land: African Americans in Television, (documentary). Series: The Redd Foxx Show, A Different World, It's Showtime at the Apollo (host), The Sinbad Show (also exec. prod.), Vibe. Specials: Afros and Bellbottoms, Take No Prisoners, Sinbad and Friends All the Way Live... Almost (also writer). Guest: The Cosby Show, Miss Universe Pageant.

SINDEN, DONALD
Actor. b. Plymouth, England, Oct. 9, 1923. Stage debut 1942 in fit-up shows; London stage includes There's a Girl in My Soup, The Relapse, Not Now Darling, King Lear, Othello, Present Laughter, Uncle Vanya, The School for Scandal, Two Into One, The Scarlet Pimpernel, Oscar Wilde, Major Barbara, Out of Order, Venus Observed, She Stoops to Conquer, Hamlet, That Good Night. B'way: London Assurance, Habeas Corpus. TV debut 1948.
PICTURES: Portrait From Life (The Girl in the Painting; debut, 1948), The Cruel Sea, Mogambo, A Day to Remember, You Know What Sailors Are, Doctor in the House, The Beachcomber, Mad About Men, An Alligator Named Daisy, Black Tent, Eyewitness, Tiger in the Smoke, Doctor at Large, Rockets Galore (Mad Little Island), The Captain's Table, Operation Bullshine, Your Money or Your Wife, The Siege of Sydney Street, Twice Around the Daffodils, Mix Me a Person, Decline and Fall, Villain, Rentadick, The Island at the Top of the World, That Lucky Touch, The Children, The Canterville Ghost, Hey Mr. Producer, Accidental Detective.
TELEVISION: Bullet in the Ballet, Road to Rome, Dinner With the Family, Odd Man In, Love from Italy, The Frog, The Glove, The Mystery of Edwin Drood, The Happy Ones, The Comedy of Errors, The Wars of the Roses, The Red House, Blackmail, A Bachelor Gray, Our Man at St. Marks (3 series), The Wind in the Tall Paper Chimney, A Woman Above Reproach, Call My Bluff, Relatively Speaking, Father Dear Father, The 19th Hole, Seven Days in the Life of Andrew Pelham (serial), The Assyrian Rejuvenator, The Organization (serial), The Confederacy of Wives, Tell It to the Chancellor, The Rivals, Two's Company (4 series), All's Well That Ends Well, Never the Twain (11 series), Cuts.
Alice in Wonderland, Nancherrow, Judge John Deed.

SINGER, LORI
Actress. b. Corpus Christi, TX, Nov. 6, 1962. Brother is actor Marc Singer; father was symphony conductor Jacques Singer. Concert cellist while in teens. Won starring role in TV series Fame (1981).
PICTURES: Footloose (debut, 1984), The Falcon and The Snowman, The Man with One Red Shoe, Trouble in Mind,

Summer Heat, Made in U.S.A., Warlock, Equinox, Sunset Grill, Short Cuts (Golden Globe Award), F.T.W., Luck, Trust and Ketchup: Robert Altman in Carver County, Bach Cello Suite #4: Sarabande, Marcus Timberwolf.
TELEVISION: Series: Fame, VR5. Movies: Born Beautiful, Storm and Sorrow, Inspired by Bach. Special: Sensibility and Sense.

SINGER, MARC
Actor. b. Vancouver, B.C., Canada, Jan. 29. Brother of actress Lori Singer. Son of symphony conductor Jacques Singer. Trained in summer stock and regional theatre.
PICTURES: Go Tell the Spartans, If You Could See What I Hear, The Beastmaster, Born to Race, A Man Called Sarge, Watchers II, Body Chemistry, Dead Space, In the Cold of the Night, Beastmaster 2, Sweet Justice, The Berlin Conspiracy, Alien Intruder, Beastmaster 3, Streetcorner 3, Lancelot: Guardian of Time, Determination to Death, Angel Blade.
TELEVISION: Series: The Contender, V, Dallas, The Young and The Restless, Beastmaster. Mini-Series: 79 Park Avenue, Roots: The Next Generation. Movies: Things in Their Season, Journey from Darkness, Something for Joey, Never Con a Killer, Sergeant Matlovich vs. the U.S. Air Force, The Two Worlds of Jennie Logan, For Ladies Only, Paper Dolls, V, Her Life as a Man, V—The Final Battle, Deadly Game, The Sea Wolf, Beastmaster III.

SINGLETON, JOHN
Director, Writer. b. Los Angeles, CA, Jan. 6, 1968. Entered USC's Filmic Writing Program, where he received a Robert Riskin Writing Award and two Jack Nicholson Writing Awards. With debut feature Boyz N the Hood (1991) he became the first African-American and youngest person ever to be nominated for an Academy Award for Best Director. Appeared in film Beverly Hills Cop III.
PICTURES: Director-Writer: Boyz N the Hood (Acad. Award noms. for dir. & s.p.), Poetic Justice (also co-prod.), Beverly Hills Cop III, Higher Learning (also co-prod.), Rosewood, Woo , (also exec. prod.), Shaft (also prod. & s.p.), Baby Boy (also prod. and s.p.), 2 Fast 2 Furious.

SINGLETON, PENNY
Actress. r.n. Dorothy McNulty. b. Philadelphia, PA, September 15, 1908. e. Columbia U. First Broadway success came as top comedienne in Good News., exec. pres. AGVA.
PICTURES: Outside of Paradise, Swing Your Lady, Men Are Such Fools, Boy Meets Girl, Mr. Chump, Mad Miss Manton, Garden of the Moon, Secrets of an Actress, Hard to Get, 28 films in Blondie series (from Blondie, 1938, to Blondie's Hero, 1950), Rocket Busters, Go West Young Lady, Footlight Glamor, Young Widow, The Best Man, Jetsons: The Movie (voice).
TELEVISION: Series: The Jetsons (voice).

SINISE, GARY
Actor, Director. b. Blue Island, Illinois, March 17, 1955. Co-founder and artistic dir. of Chicago's Steppenwolf Theatre Company, 1974.
THEATRE: NY: Balm in Gilead, True West, The Caretaker, The Grapes of Wrath. Chicago: Of Mice and Men, Getting Out. Director: True West (Obie Award), Orphans, Buried Child.
PICTURES: Miles From Home (dir. only), A Midnight Clear, Of Mice and Men (also dir., co-prod.), Jack the Bear, Forrest Gump (Acad. Award nom.), The Quick and the Dead, Apollo 13, Albino Alligator, Ransom., Snake Eyes, Bruno, All the Rage, The Green Mile, Reindeer Games, Mission to Mars, Imposter, A Gentleman's Game, Made Up, The Human Stain.
TELEVISION: Mini-Series: The Stand. Movies: Family Secrets, My Name is Bill W, The Final Days, Truman (Golden Globe Award), George Wallace (Emmy Award, 1998), That Championship Season, Path to War. Director: Crime Story, thirtysomething, China Beach.

SIZEMORE, TOM
Actor. b. Detroit, MI.September 29, 1964. e. Wayne St. Univ., Temple Univ.Stage incl. The Land of the Astronauts in NYC and Washington, D.C.
PICTURES: Lock Up, Rude Awakening, Penn and Teller Get Killed, Born on the Fourth of July, Blue Steel, Flight of the Intruder, Guilty by Suspicion, Harley Davidson and the Marlboro Man, A Matter of Degrees, Passenger 57, Watch It, Heart and Souls, True Romance, Striking Distance, Wyatt Earp, Natural Born Killers, Devil in a Blue Dress, Strange Days, Heat, The Relic, Enemy of the State (cameo), Saving Private Ryan, The Florentine, The Match, Bringing Out the Dead, Play It To The Bone, Red Planet, Pearl Harbor, Ticker, Big Trouble, Black Hawk Down, You'll Never Wiez in this Town Again, $windle, Dreamcatcher.
TELEVISION: Movies: An American Story, Witness to the Mob, Witness Protection, Sins of the Father, R.H.D./L.A. (series.)

SKARSGARD, STELLAN
Actor. b. Gothenburg, Vastergotland, Sweden, June 13, 1951.
PICTURES: Raid in the Summer, The Office Party, Brollopet, Anita, Taboo, Homeward in the Night, The Simple-Minded Murder, P & B, Ake and His World, False as Water, Peter-No-Tail in Americat, The Serpents Way, Jim and the Pirates, Hipp hipp hurra!, Time of the Wolf, Friends, The Unbearable Lightness of

Being, S/Y Joy, Code Name Coq Rouge, The Women on the Roof, The Hunt for Red October, The Perfect Murder, The Ox, The Democratic Terrorist, Wind, The Slingshot, The Last Dance, Jonssonligans storsta kupp, Zero Kelvin, Hundarna i Riga, Harry och Sonja, Breaking the Waves, Insomnia, The Volcano Man, The Kingdom 2, Amistad, Good Will Hunting, Tranceformer - A Portait of Lars von Trier, My Son the Fanatic, The Glass-Blower's Children, Savior, Ronin, Deep Blue Sea, Passion of Mind, Light Keeps Me Company, Signs & Wonders, Timecode, Dancer in the Dark, Aberdeen, Kiss Kiss Bang Bang, Taking Sides, The Glass House, Powder Keg, Beneath the Banyan Trees, No Good Deed, Dogville, City of Ghosts, Exorcist IV: The Beginning.
TELEVISION: Noon Wine, The Wild Duck, Parker Kane, D-dag - Lise, D-dag, Harlan County War. *Mini-Series:* Helen of Troy.

SKASE, CHRISTOPHER
Executive. b. Australia, 1946. Began career as reporter for Fairfax publication, Australian Financial Review. In 1970s set up investment company with about $20,000. Revived Australian TV Seven network in Melbourne and in U.S. bought Hal Roach Studios and NY based prod.-dist. Robert Halmi which he merged into Qintex Entertainment. Qintex Entertainment produced TV mini-series Lonesome Dove.

SKERRITT, TOM
Actor. b. Detroit, MI, Aug. 25, 1933. e. Wayne State U., UCLA. Model for Guess? jeans ads.
PICTURES: War Hunt (debut, 1962), One Man's Way, Those Calloways, M*A*S*H, Wild Rovers, Fuzz, Harold and Maude, Run Joe Run, Big Bad Mama, Thieves Like Us, The Devil's Rain, La Madonna, The Turning Point, Up in Smoke, Ice Castles, Alien, Savage Harvest, The Silence of the North, A Dangerous Summer (The Burning Man), Fighting Back, The Dead Zone, Top Gun, Opposing Force (Hell Camp), SpaceCamp, Wisdom, Maid to Order, The Big Town, Poltergeist III, Steel Magnolias, Big Man on Campus, Honor Bound, The Rookie, Wild Orchid II: Two Shades of Blue, Poison Ivy, Singles, A River Runs Through It, Knight Moves, Contact, Not Like You, Smoke Signals, The Other Sister, Texas Rangers, Greenmail, Colored Eggs, Tears of the Sun.
TELEVISION: *Series:* Ryan's Four, Cheers, Picket Fences (Emmy Award, 1993). *Movies:* The Bird Men, The Last Day, Maneaters Are Loose!, The Calendar Girl Murders, Miles to Go, Parent Trap II, A Touch of Scandal, Poker Alice, Moving Target, Nightmare at Bitter Creek, The Heist, Red King White Knight, The China Lake Murders, Child of the Night, In Sickness and in Health, Getting Up and Going Home, What the Deaf Man Heard, Two for Texas, The Hunt for the Unicorn Killer, Aftershock, An American Daughter, High Noon, Voyage to Atlantis, Alien Evolution, Chestnut Hill, Path to War, Homeland Security. *Director:* A Question of Sex (Afterschool Special), Picket Fences (3 episodes), Divided by Hate.

SKLAR, MARTIN A.
Executive. e. UCLA, 1956. editor, the Daily Bruin, 1955. Began as asst. news editor, MAC (Media Agency Clients) Publications, 1956. Worked in publicity & mktg., Disneyland, 1956-61; writer, advertising and publicity, WED Enterprises (now Walt Disney Imagineering - WDI) where he served on a team assigned by Walt Disney to develop special projects for industry. Wrote personal materials for Showman of the World and other publications, television and special films aimed at communicating Walt Disney's visionary concepts. Primary strategist, Imagineering, 1960s-90s; v.p.; concepts/planning, 1974; v.p., creative development, 1979; exec. v.p., 1982; president, 1987-96, Walt Disney Imagineering, responsible for the creation and expansion of Disney's theme parks and other creative initiatives. Currently vice chairman and principal creative executive, Walt Disney Imagineering (WDI), which is responsible for all aspects of every theme park project; featured speaker at numerous art design and recreation-related conferences. Elected member & president, Board of Education, Anaheim City School District, 1969 & 1973; former president, Orange City. School Board Assoc.; former City Commissioner, Anaheim; founding chairman, Michael L. Roston Creative Writing Awards; recipient, Community Service Award for Anaheim, 1977; Disney Legend Award, 1995; recipient, Lifetime Achievement Award, Themed Entertainment Assoc., 1995; member, Board of the Manned Space Flight Education Found.; president, Ryman-Carroll Found., which fosters the teaching of art and cultural diversity in public education.

SKOLIMOWSKI, JERZY
Director, Writer. b. Lodz, Poland, May 5, 1938. e. Warsaw U., State Superior Film Sch., Lodz, Poland. Scriptwriter for Wajda's Innocent Sorcerers (also actor), Polanski's Knife in the Water and Lomnicki's Poslizg. Author: Somewhere Close to Oneself, Somebody Got Drowned.
PICTURES: *Director-Writer:* Identification Marks—None (also actor, edit., art dir.), Walkover (also actor, edit.), Barrier, The Departure, Hands Up (also actor), Dialogue, The Adventures of Gerard, Deep End, King Queen Knave (dir. only), The Shout, Circle of Deceit (actor only), Moonlighting (also prod., actor), Success Is the Best Revenge, The Lightship, White Nights

(actor), Big Shots (actor), Torrents of Spring (also actor), 30 Door Key (also co-s.p., prod.), The Hollow Men (prod.), Mars Attacks! (actor), Before Night Falls, (actor).

SKYE, IONE
Actress. r.n. Ione Skye Leitch. b. London, England, Sept. 4, 1971. Daughter of folksinger Donovan (Leitch) and sister of actor Donovan Leitch. Raised in San Francisco, Connecticut, Los Angeles. Magazine photo led to audition for film River's Edge.
PICTURES: River's Edge (debut, 1987 as Ione Skye Leitch), Stranded, A Night in the Life of Jimmy Reardon, Say Anything..., The Rachel Papers, Mindwalk, Samantha, Guncrazy, Carmilla, Wayne's World, The Color of Evening, Gas Food Lodging, Four Rooms, Wayne's World, Guncrazy, The Size of Watermelons, One Night Stand, Dream for an Insomniac, Went to Coney Island on a Mission from God...Be Back by Five, Jump, The Good Doctor, Mascara, Men Make Women Crazy Theory, Southlander, Free, Chicken Night, Babylon Revisited, Angryman.
TELEVISION: *Series:* Covington Cross. *Movies:* Napoleon and Josephine, Girls in Prison, The Perfect Mother, The Sands of Time. *Specials:* It's Called the Sugar Plum, Nightmare Classics (Carmilla).

SLATER, CHRISTIAN
Actor. r.n. Christian Michael Leonard Hawkins. b. New York, NY, Aug. 18, 1969. Mother is NY casting dir. Mary Jo Slater; father Los Angeles stage actor Michael Hawkins. Made prof. debut at 9 in The Music Man starring Dick Van Dyke, natl. tour, then on B'way Also on B'way in Macbeth, A Christmas Carol, David Copperfield and Merlin. Off-B'way in Landscape of the Body, Between Daylight and Boonville, Somewhere's Better. Also summer theatre. Directed 1992 L.A. prod. of The Laughter Epidemic.
PICTURES: The Legend of Billie Jean (debut, 1985), Twisted, The Name of the Rose, Tucker: The Man and His Dream, Gleaming the Cube, Heathers, The Wizard, Tales from the Dark Side: The Movie, Beyond the Stars (Personal Choice), Young Guns II, Pump Up the Volume, Robin Hood: Prince of Thieves, Mobsters, Star Trek VI: The Undiscovered Country (cameo), Kuffs, FernGully... The Last Rainforest (voice), Where the Day Takes You, Untamed Heart, True Romance, Jimmy Hollywood, Interview With the Vampire, Murder in the First, Broken Arrow, Austin Powers: International Man of Mystery (cameo), Bed of Roses, Julian Po, Very Bad Things, Hard Rain, Basil, Love Stinks (cameo), The Contender, 3000 Miles to Graceland, Windtalkers, Who is Cletis Tout? Zoolander, In God We Trust, Naked Movie, Mindhunters, Masked & Anonymous, Churchill: The Hollywood Years, Alone in the Dark.
TELEVISION: *Series:* One Life to Live, Ryan's Hope. *Specials:* Sherlock Holmes, Pardon Me for Living, The Haunted Mansion Mystery, Cry Wolf, The Edge (Professional Man). *Movies:* Living Proof: The Hank Williams Jr. Story, Desperate For Love, Merry Christmas George Bailey, A Light Knight's Odyssey.

SLATER, HELEN
Actress. b. New York, NY, Dec. 19, 1963. *Off-B'way:* Responsible Parties, Almost Romance.
PICTURES: Supergirl (debut, 1984), The Legend of Billie Jean, Ruthless People, The Secret of My Succe$s, Sticky Fingers, Happy Together, City Slickers, A House in the Hills, Betrayal of the Dove, Lassie, The Steal, The Long Way Home (voice), Nowhere in Sight, Carlo's Wake,
TELEVISION: *Series:* Capital News. *Movies:* The Great Air Race, 12:01, Chantilly Lace, Parallel Lives, Toothless, Best Friend for Life, American Adventure.

SLATZER, ROBERT FRANKLIN
Writer, Director, Producer. b. Marion, OH, April 4, 1927. e. Ohio State U., UCLA, 1947. Radio news commentator sportscaster; wrote radio serials; adv. dir., Brush-Moore Newspapers; feature writer, Scripps-Howard Newspapers; adv. exec., The Columbus Dispatch; syn. columnist, NY Journal-American; wrote guest columns for Dorothy Kilgallen; author of western short stories and novels; wrote, dir., prod. industrial films, docs., sports specials and commercials; 1949-51, writer for Grand National Studios Prods, Monogram Pictures, Republic Studios, Eagle-Lion Films; 1951, publicist, Hope Enterprises; pub. dir., Paramount Pictures; 1952, personal mgr. to Marilyn Monroe, Ken Maynard, James Craig, Gail Russell and other stars; 1953, story editor and assoc. prod., Joe Palooka Productions; 1953-54, staff writer Universal Studios, RKO Radio Pictures, MGM, Columbia and Paramount; 1958, formed Robert F. Slatzer Productions; 1960, exec. in chg. of prod., Jaguar Pictures Corp.; 1963-65, pres., Slatzer Oil & Gas Co.; 1966-67, bd. dir., United Mining & Milling Corp.; 1970-74, exec., Columbia Pictures Corp.; 1974, resumed producing and financing features and television films; 1976, honored as Fellow, Mark Twain Inst.
AUTHOR: *Novels:* Desert Empire, Rose of the Range, Rio, Rawhide Range, The Cowboy and the Heiress, Daphne, Campaign Girl, Scarlet, The Dance Studio Hucksters, Born to Be Wild, Single Room Furnished, The West is Still Wild, Gusher, The Young Wildcats. *Biographies:* The Life and Curious Death of Marilyn Monroe, The Life and Legend of Ken Maynard, Who Killed Thelma Todd?, The Duke of Thieves, Bing Crosby—The Hollow Man, Duke: The Life and Times of John Wayne, The Marilyn Files.

PICTURES: White Gold, The Obsessed, Mike and the Heiress, Under Texas Skies, They Came To Kill, Trail of the Mounties, Jungle Goddess, Montana Desperado, Pride of the Blue, Green Grass of Wyoming, The Naked Jungle, Warpaint, Broken Lance, Elephant Walk, South of Death Valley, The Big Gusher, Arctic Flight, The Hellcats, Bigfoot, John Wayne's No Substitute for Victory', Joniko-Eskimo Boy, Operation North Slope, Claws, Don't Go West, Mulefeathers, The Unfinished, Single Room Furnished, Viva Zapata, Inchon.
TELEVISION: The Great Outdoors, Adventures of White Arrow, Let's Go Boating, The Joe Palooka Story, Amos & Andy, I Am the Law, Files of Jeffrey Jones, Fireside Theatre, The Unser Story, Year of Opportunity, The Big Ones, Ken Maynard's West, Where are They Now?, The Groovy Seven, The Untouchables, The Detectives, Wild Wild West, Wagon Train, Playhouse 90, Highway Patrol, David Frost Special, Today Show, ABC News, 20/20, Inside Edition, The Reporters, Current Affair, The Geraldo Show, Hard Copy, Larry King Show, Marilyn and Me, The Marilyn Files.

SLOAN, JOHN R.
Producer. e. Merchiston Castle Sch., Edinburgh, 1932-39; asst. dir. and prod. man. Warners, London, Hollywood; 1939-46, Army.
PICTURES: Sea Devils, The End of the Affair, Port Afrique, Abandon Ship, The Safecracker, Beyond this Place, The Killers of Kilimanjaro, Johnny Nobody, The Reluctant Saint, The Running Man, The Last Command, To Sir With Love, Fragment of Fear, Dad's Army, Lord Jim, No Sex Please, We're British, The Odessa File, High-Ballin', Force 10 From Navarone, The Children's Story.

SLOCOMBE, DOUGLAS
Cinematographer. b. England, Feb. 10, 1913. Former journalist. Filmed the invasion of Poland and Holland. Under contract to Ealing Studios 17 years.
PICTURES: Dead of Night, The Captive Heart, Hue and Cry, The Loves of Joanna Godden, It Always Rains on Sunday, Saraband for Dead Lovers, Kind Hearts and Coronets, Cage of Gold, The Lavender Hill Mob, Mandy, The Man in the White Suit, The Titfield Thunderbolt, Man in the Sky, Ludwig II, Lease on Life, The Smallest Show on Earth, Tread Softly, Stranger, Circus of Horrors, The Young Ones, The Mark, The L-Shaped Room, Freud, The Servant (BAFTA Award), Guns at Batashi, A High Wind in Jamaica, The Blue Max, Promise Her Anything, The Vampire Killers, Fathom, Robbery, Boom, The Lion in Winter, The Italian Job, The Music Lovers, Murphy's War, The Buttercup Chain, Travels With My Aunt (Acad. Award nom.), Jesus Christ Superstar, The Great Gatsby, Rollerball, Hedda, The Sailor Who Fell From Grace With the Sea, Nasty Habits, Julia (Acad. Award nom.), Close Encounters of the Third Kind (co-photog.), Caravans, Lost and Found, The Lady Vanishes, Nijinsky, Raiders of the Lost Ark (Acad. Award nom.), The Pirates of Penzance, Never Say Never Again, Indiana Jones and the Temple of Doom, Water, Lady Jane, Indiana Jones and the Last Crusade.
TELEVISION: Movie: Love Among the Ruins.

SLUIZER, GEORGE
Director. b. Paris, France, June 25, 1932.
PICTURES: De lage landen, Jolio en het mes, Twice a Woman, Red Desert Penetentiary, Spoorloos, Utz, The Vanishing, Dying to Go Home, Crimetime, The Commissioner, The Stone Raft.

SMART, JEAN
Actress. b. Seattle, WA, Sept. 13, 1951. e. Univ. of WA. Member of Oregon Shakespeare Fest, 1975-77; also with Hartford Stage Co., Pittsburgh Public Theatre Co., Intiman Theatre Co.
THEATRE: Regional: Equus, Much Ado About Nothing, A Moon for the Misbegotten, Terra Nova, Cat's Play, Saint Joan, A History of the American Film, Last Summer at Bluefish Cove (LA Drama Critics Circle, Dramalogue & LA Drama Desk Awards), Mrs. California, Strange Snow. NY: Last Summer at Bluefish Cove, Piaf (B'way debut, 1981).
PICTURES: Flashpoint (debut, 1984), Protocol, Fire With Fire, Project X, Mistress, Homeward Bound: The Incredible Journey, The Brady Bunch Movie, Edie & Pen, The Odd Couple II, Guinevere, Snow Day, The Kid, Forever Fabulous, Sweet Home Alabama, Bringing Down the House.
TELEVISION: Series: Reggie, Teachers Only, Designing Women, High Society, Hey Arnold, Style and Substance, The District, The Oblongs, Im Possible, In Laws. Movies: Single Bars Single Women, A Fight for Jenny, A Seduction in Travis County, A Stranger in Town (also co-prod.), The Yarn Princess, The Yearling, A Stranger in Town, Undue Influence, The Man Who Came to Dinner, Audrey's Rain. Specials: Piaf, Maximum Security, Royal Match, A Place at the Table.

SMITH, CHARLES MARTIN
Actor, Director. b. Los Angeles, CA, Oct. 30, 1953. e. California State U. Father is animation artist Frank Smith.
PICTURES: The Culpepper Cattle Company (debut, 1972), Fuzz, The Spikes Gang, American Graffiti, Pat Garrett and Billy the Kid, Rafferty and the Gold Dust Twins, No Deposit No Return, The Hazing, The Buddy Holly Story, More American Graffiti, Herbie Goes Bananas, Never Cry Wolf (also co-wrote

narration), Starman, Trick or Treat (also dir.), The Untouchables, The Experts, The Hot Spot, Deep Cover, Fifty-Fifty (also dir.), I Love Trouble, Perfect Alibi, Speechless, He Ain't Heavy, The Final Cut, Wedding Bell Blues, Deep Impact, Hoods, Here's to Life!, Air Bud, (dir.).
TELEVISION: Series: Buffy the Vampire Slayer, (dir.), Speed Buggy (voice), The Apartment Complex Guest: The Brady Bunch, Monte Nash, Baretta, Streets of San Francisco, Petrocelli, The Rookies, Grizzly Adams, Twilight Zone, Ray Bradbury Theatre, Outer Limits, L.A. Law, Picket Fences, Northern Exposure, Tales From the Crypt. Movies: Go Ask Alice, The Deputies, Law of the Land, Cotton Candy, Boris and Natasha (also dir.), And the Band Played On, Roswell, Brother's Destiny, Dead Silence, Blackout Effect, The Apartment Complex, Roughing It. Special: Partners. Mini-Series: Streets of Laredo, The Beast, P.T. Barnum.

SMITH, DAVID R.
Archivist. b. Pasadena, CA, Oct. 13, 1940. e. Pasadena City Coll., A.A., 1960; U. of California, Berkeley, B.A. 1962, MLS 1963. Writer of numerous historical articles. Worked as librarian at Library of Congress, 1963-65 and as reference librarian, UCLA 1965-70 before becoming archivist for The Walt Disney Co. 1970-present. Exec. dir., The Manuscript Society, 1980-; member, Society of CA Archivists, Fellow of the Manuscript Society, 1993. Received service award, ASIFA, and award of distinction, Manuscript Soc, 1983. Co-Author: The Ultimate Disney Trivia Book (1992, 1994, 1997), Disney: The First 100 Years (1999). Author: Disney A to Z: The Official Encyclopedia (1996, 1998).

SMITH, HY
Executive. b. New York, NY, June 3, 1934. e. Baruch Sch., CCNY, B.B.A. Joined Paramount Pictures 1967, foreign ad.-pub coordinator; 1969, joined United Artists as foreign ad.-pub mgr.; named intl. ad.-pub dir., 1970; named v.p., intl. adv.-pub 1976; v.p. worldwide adv., publ. & promo.; 1978; 1981, named first v.p., adv./pub./promo; 1982, joined Rastar Films as v.p., intl. project director for Annie; 1983, joined United Intl. Pictures as sr. v.p., adv/pub, based in London. 1984, named sr. v.p., mktg. 1995, promoted to exec. v.p., mktg.

SMITH, JACLYN
Actress. b. Houston, TX, Oct. 26, 1947. Started acting while in high school and studied drama and psychology at Trinity U. in San Antonio. Appeared in many commercials as model.
PICTURES: The Adventurers, Bootleggers, Nightkill, Deja Vu, Charlie's Angels 2, Charlie's Angels: Full Throttle.
TELEVISION: Series: Charlie's Angels, Christine Cromwell. Guest: McCloud, Get Christy Love, The Rookies. Movies: Probe (Switch), Charlie's Angels (pilot), Escape From Bogen County, The Users, Jacqueline Bouvier Kennedy, Rage of Angels, The Night They Saved Christmas, Sentimental Journey, Florence Nightingale, Rage of Angels: The Story Continues, Windmills of the Gods, The Bourne Identity, Settle the Score, Danielle Steel's Kaleidoscope, Lies Before Kisses, The Rape of Dr. Willis, In the Arms of a Killer, Nightmare in the Daylight, Love Can Be Murder, Cries Unheard: The Donna Yalich Story, Danielle Steel's Family Album, My Very Best Friend, Married to a Stranger, Before He Wakes, Freefall, Three Secrets, Navigating the Heart.

SMITH, JOSEPH P.
Executive. b. Brooklyn, NY, March 28, 1921. e. Columbia U. Started career Wall Street; joined RKO Radio Pictures, served in sales and managerial posts; exec. v.p., Lippert Productions, Hollywood; v.p., Telepictures, Inc.; formed and pres., Cinema-Vue Corp.; pres., Pathe Pictures, Inc.; Pathe News, Inc.

SMITH, KEVIN
Director, Writer, Editor. b. Red Bank, NJ, Aug. 2, 1970. Also co-authored comic book series featuring Jay and Silent Bob characters.
PICTURES: Clerks (debut, 1994. also actor, editor, prod.), Mallrats (also actor), Drawing Flies (prod. only), Chasing Amy (also actor, editor), Good Will Hunting (co-exec. prod. only), Vulgar (exec. prod., actor only), Dogma (also actor, editor), Coyote Ugly (s.p. only), The Blair Crown Project (actor only), Big Helium Dog (actor only), Chasing Kevin (actor only), Starwoids (actor only),Jay and Silent Bob Strike Back (also actor), Now You Know (actor only), Clerks: Sell Out (voice), Jersey Girl, Fletch Won, Daredevil.

SMITH, KURTWOOD
Actor. b. New Lisbon, WI, July 3, 1943. e. B.A. San Jose (1966), M.F.A. Stanford (1969). Starred in Oscar-nom short 12:01 P.M.
THEATRE: Plymouth Rock, The Price, Faces by Chekhov, Familiar Faces, Enemy of the People, The Debutante Ball (all in Calif.), The Lucky Spot (Williamston), Signature, Hamlet, Taming of the Shrew, and over 20 other Shakespeare productions in CA.
PICTURES: Roadie (debut, 1980), Zoot Suit, Going Berserk, Staying Alive, Flashpoint, Robocop, Rambo III, True Believer, Dead Poets Society, Heart of Dixie, Quick Change, Oscar, Company Business, Star Trek VI: The Undiscovered Country, Shadows and Fog, The Crush, Heart and Souls, Fortress, Boxing Helena, Under Siege 2: Dark Territory, Last of the Dogmen, To

Die For, Broken Arrow, A Time to Kill, Citizen Ruth, Precious, Shelter, Prefontaine, Deep Impact, Girl Interrupted, Freespace 2, Fallout Tactics, Teddy Bears' Picnic.
TELEVISION: *Series:* The Renegades, The New Adventures of Beans Baxter, Big Wave Dave's, That '70s Show. *Movies:* Murder in Texas, Missing Pieces, The Midnight Hour, International Airport, Deadly Messages, The Christmas Gift, Doorways, While Justice Sleeps, A Bright Shining Lie, Black Jaq. *Mini-Series:* North and South Book II, The Nightmare Years (Ace Award nom.), Robocop: Prime Detectives, Gary & Mike, The Zeta Project. *Guest:* Stir Crazy, Stingray, Newhart, 21 Jump Street, It's Garry Shandling's Show, The Famous Teddy Z, Picket Fences.

SMITH, LANE
Actor. b. Memphis, TN, April 29, 1936.
THEATRE: *NY:* Visions of Kerouac, Brechtesgarten, Glengarry Glen Ross (Drama Desk Award).
PICTURES: Network, Honeysuckle Rose, Prince of the City, Frances, Purple Hearts, Red Dawn, Places in the Heart, Weeds, Prison, Race for Glory, Air America, My Cousin Vinny, The Mighty Ducks, The Distinguished Gentleman, Son-in-Law, The Scout, Lost & Found, The Flight of the Dove, The War at Home, Why Do Fools Fall in Love?, The Hi-Lo Country, Getting Personal, The Legend of Bagger Vance, The Caprice.
TELEVISION: *Series:* V, Kay O'Brien, Good Sports, Good and Evil. *Mini-Series:* Chiefs, From the Earth to the Moon. *Movies:* A Death in Canaan, Crash, The Solitary Man, Disaster on the Coastliner, City in Fear, Gideon's Trumpet, A Rumor of War, The Georgia Peaches, Mark I Love You, Dark Night of the Scarecrow, Prime Suspect, Thou Shalt Not Kill, Special Bulletin, Something About Amelia, Dress Gray, The Final Days, False Arrest, Duplicates, Alien Nation: The Udara Legacy, Alien Nation, Inherit the Wind, WWIII. *Specials:* Displaced Person, Member of the Wedding.

SMITH, DAME MAGGIE
D.B.E. C.B.E. Actress. b. Ilford, England, Dec. 28, 1934. Early career Oxford Playhouse. With the Old Vic 1959-60. Also with Stratford Ontario Shakespeare Fest. 1975-78, & 1980. Received C.B.E. 1970; D.B.E., 1990.
THEATRE: Twelfth Night (debut, 1952), Cakes and Ale, New Faces of 1956 (NY debut, as comedienne), Share My Lettuce, The Stepmother, What Every Woman Knows, Rhinoceros, The Rehearsal, The Private Ear, The Public Eye, Mary Mary, The Recruiting Officer, Othello, The Master Builder, Hay Fever, Much Ado About Nothing, Black Comedy, Miss Julie, Trelawney of the Wells, The Beaux Stratagem, The Three Sisters, Hedda Gabler, Design for Living (L.A.), Private Lives (London & NY), Slap, Peter Pan, As You Like It, Macbeth, Night and Day (London & NY), Virginia, Way of the World, Lettice and Lovage (London & NY, Tony Award), The Importance of Being Earnest, Three Tall Women.
PICTURES: Nowhere to Go (debut, 1958), Go to Blazes, The V.I.Ps, The Pumpkin Eater, Young Cassidy, Othello, The Honey Pot, Hot Millions, The Prime of Miss Jean Brodie (Acad. Award, BAFTA Award, 1969), Oh! What a Lovely War, Travels With My Aunt, Love and Pain and the Whole Damn Thing, Murder by Death, Death on the Nile, California Suite (Acad. Award, best supporting actress, 1978), Clash of the Titans, Quartet, Evil Under the Sun, The Missionary, Better Late Than Never, A Private Function (BAFTA Award, 1985), Lily in Love, A Room with a View, The Lonely Passion of Judith Hearne, Romeo-Juliet (voice), Hook, Sister Act, The Secret Garden, Sister Act 2: Back in the Habit, Richard III, Washington Square, Tea With Mussolini, Curtain Call, Harry Potter and the Sorcerer's Stone, Gosford Park, The Divine Secrets of the Ya Ya Sisterhood, Harry Potter and the Chamber of Secrets, Harry Potter and the Prisoner of Azkaban.
TELEVISION: Much Ado About Nothing, Man and Superman, On Approval, Home and Beauty, Mrs. Silly, Bed Among the Lentils, Memento Mori, Suddenly Last Summer, All the King's Men, David Copperfield, My House in Umbria.

SMITH, ROGER
Actor, Producer. b. South Gate, CA, Dec. 18, 1932. m. actress-performer Ann Margret. e. U. of Arizona. Started career at age 7, one of the Meglin Kiddies, appearing at the Mayan Theater, Wilshire, Ebell. Sings, composes, American folk songs. Producer: Ann-Margret cabaret and theater shows.
PICTURES: No Time to Be Young, Crash Landing, Operation Madball, Man of a Thousand Faces, Never Steal Anything Small, Auntie Mame, Rogues Gallery.
TELEVISION: The Horace Heidt Show, Ted Mack Original Amateur Hour, 77 Sunset Strip (series), writer, ABC-TV. Co-prod.: Homestead.

SMITH, WILL
Actor, Singer. b. Philadelphia, PA, Sept. 25, 1968. Teamed with musician Jeff Townes as rap duo D.J. Jazzy Jeff & the Fresh Prince. Albums: Rock the House, He's the DJ I'm the Rapper, And in This Corner, Homebase. Recipient of 2 Grammy Awards.
PICTURES: Where the Day Takes You (debut, 1992), Made in America, Six Degress of Separation, Bad Boys, Independence Day, Men in Black, Enemy of the State, Wild Wild West, The Legend of Bagger Vance, Men in Black II, Ali, Bad Boys II, Sharkslayer.

TELEVISION: *Series:* Fresh Prince of Bel Air (also co-exec. prod. , comp. and singer of theme). *Movies:* The Perfect Date, Voices That Care, (lead vocals as Fresh Prince).

SMITH, WILLIAM
Actor. b. Columbia, MO, March 24, 1934. e. Syracuse, U., BA; UCLA, MA.
PICTURES: Darker Than Amber, C.C. and Company, The Losers, Run, Angel, Run, Blood and Guts, Seven, Fast Company, No Knife, Twilight's Last Gleaming, The Frisco Kid, Any Which Way You Can, Rumble Fish, Red Dawn, Eye of the Tiger, Commando Squad, Moon in Scorpio, Hell Comes to Frogtown, Maniac Cop, Red Nights, Nam, B.O.R.N., Action U.S.A., Deadly Breed, Evil Altar, Jungle Assault, L.A. Vice, Slow Burn, Terror in Beverly Hills, Hell on the Battleground, Forgotten Heroes, Instant Karma, Empire of Ash, Emperor of the Bronx, Rock n' Roll Cops, Broken Vessels, Merchants of Evil, The Last Riders, Last of the Warriors, Kiss and Be Killed, The Final Sanction, Cybernator, American Me, Third Trail, Shadow of the Dragon, Legend of Skull Canyon, The Feast, Dark Secrets, Road to Revenge, Hard Time Romance, Maverick, Manosaurus, Taken Alive, Raw Energy, Judee Strange, Big Sister 2000, Rasputin, Neon Signs, Deadly Currency, Uncle Sam, The Shooter, Interview with a Zombie, Hollywood Cops, Ground Zero, Broken Vessels, No Rest for the Wicked, Dogs of Damnation, Blood of His Own, Inspector Gadget, Wasteland Justice, Vice, Plastic Boy and His Jokers, Never Look Back, Elite, Dangerous Highway, Never Look Back, The Vampire Hunters Club, Scarlet Countess, Deadman's Bluff, The Killing Point, Zombiegeddon, Y.M.I., Jumper, The Body Shop.
TELEVISION: *Mini-Series:* Rich Man Poor Man. *Series:* Laredo, Rich Man Poor Man: Book II. *Series:* Laredo, Rich Man Poor Man: Book II, Hawaii 5-0, Wildside. *Movies:* The Over-the-Hill Gang, Crowhaven Farm, The Rockford Files (pilot), The Sex Symbol, Death Among Friends, Manhunter, The Rebels, Wild Times, The Jerk Too.

SMITROVICH, BILL
Actor. b. Bridgeport, CT, May 16, 1947. e. Univ. of Bridgeport, Smith Col. Studied acting at Actors and Directors Lab.
THEATER: *B'way:* The American Clock. *Off-B'way:* Never Say Die, Frankie and Johnny in the Claire de Lune, Seks. Regional: Requeim for a Heavyweight, Food from Trash, Of Mice and Men, The Love Suicide at Schofield Barracks.
PICTURES: A Little Sex, Without a Trace, Splash, Maria's Lovers, Key Exchange, Silver Bullet, Band of the Hand, Manhunter, A Killing Affair, Her Alibi, Renegades, Crazy People, Bodily Harm, The Phantom, The Trigger Effect, Independence Day, Air Force One, Around the Fire, Kiss Toledo Goodbye, Thirteen Days Which Shocked the World.
TELEVISION: *Series:* Crime Story, Life Goes On, Millennium. *Guest:* Miami Vice, L.A. Medical, A Nero Wolfe Mystery. *Movies:* Born Beautiful, Miami Vice: Brother's Keeper, Overdrawn at the Memory Bank, Crime Story, Muggable Mary, Gregory K: A Place to Be, Labor of Love: The Arlette Schweitzer Story, Children of the Dark, Texas Justice, Mr. Murder, Futuresport, The '60s, Batman Beyond: The Movie, The Golden Spiders: A Nero Wolfe Mystery, Fail Safe, Far East.

SMITS, JIMMY
Actor. b. New York, NY, July 9, 1955. e. Brooklyn Coll., B.A.; Cornell U., M.F.A. Worked as community organizer before acting with NY Shakespeare Fest. Public Theater.
THEATRE: Hamlet (NY Shakespeare Fest., 1983), Little Victories, Buck, The Ballad of Soapy Smith, Death and the Maiden.
PICTURES: Running Scared (debut, 1986), The Believers, Old Gringo, Vital Signs, Fires Within, Switch, Gross Misconduct, My Family/Mi Familia, Marshal Law, Murder in Mind, Lesser Prophets, The Million Dollar Hotel, Bless the Child, Price of Glory, Star Wars: Episode II - Attack of the Clones, Angel, Star Wars: Episode III.
TELEVISION: *Series:* L.A. Law (Emmy Award, 1990), NYPD Blue (Golden Globe, 1996). *Pilot:* Miami Vice. *Movies:* Rockabye, The Highwayman, Dangerous Affection, Glitz, The Broken Cord, The Tommyknockers, The Cisco Kid, Solomon and Sheba, The Last Word. *Specials:* The Other Side of the Border (narrator), Happily Ever After Fairy Tales: Cinderella, Hispanic Americans: The New Frontier (host), The Story of the Western.

SMOTHERS BROTHERS
Comedians, Singers.
SMOTHERS, DICK: b. New York, NY, Nov. 20, 1939. e. San Jose State College. Films: The Silver Bears (debut, 1978).
PICTURES: Casino.
TELEVISION: *Movies:* Alice Through the Looking Glass.

SMOTHERS, TOM: b. New York, NY, Feb. 2, 1937. e. San Jose State College. In films Get to Know Your Rabbit, The Silver Bears, There Goes the Bride, Serial, Pandemonium.
Began career as coffeehouse folk singers with a bit of comic banter mixed in. After success at some of hipper West Coast clubs, appeared on Jack Paar's Tonight Show, The Jack Benny Show and as regulars on Steve Allen's show, 1961. 1962-65 had a series of popular albums. After starring in a situation comedy show, they hosted their own variety program. On B'way in

musical I Love My Wife. Both appeared in film Speed Zone.
TELEVISION: *Series*: The Steve Allen Show (1961), The Smothers Brothers Show (1965-66), The Smothers Brothers Comedy Hour (1967-69), The Smothers Brothers Show (1970), The Smothers Brothers Show (1975), Fitz and Bones, The Smothers Brothers Comedy Hour, The Vegas Connection., The '70s: The Decade That Changed Television, TV's Most Censored Moments, Smothered: The Censorship Struggles of the Smothers Brothers Comedy Hour. *Specials*: The Smothers Brothers Reunion.

SNELL, PETER R. E.
Producer. b. Nov. 17, 1941. Entered industry 1967. Appt. head of prod. and man. dir. British Lion 1973. Joined Robert Stigwood group 1975. Returned to indep. prod., 1978; Hennessy. Appt. chief exec., Britannic Film & Television Ltd. 1985, purchased British Lion Film Prods., Ltd. from Thorn/EMI 1986-87. 1988: chmn. and chief executive British Lion.
PICTURES: *Prod.*: Winters Tale, Some May Live, A Month in the Country, Carnaby 68, Subterfuge, Julius Caesar, Goodbye Gemini, Antony and Cleopatra, The Wicker Man, Hennessy, Bear Island, Mother Lode, Lady Jane, Turtle Diary, A Prayer for the Dying, Letters from a Killer, Riding of the Laddie.
TELEVISION: *Exec. Prod.*: A Man For All Seasons, Tears in the Rain, Treasure Island, The Crucifer of Blood. *Prod.*: Death Train, Nightwatch.

SNIPES, WESLEY
Actor. b. Bronx, NY, July 31, 1962. e. SUNY/Purchase. Performed with puppet theatre group called Struttin Street Stuff before landing NY stage work. Appeared in Michael Jackson video Bad.
THEATRE: *B'way*: The Boys of Winter, Death and the King's Horsemen, Execution of Justice.
PICTURES: Wildcats (debut, 1986), Streets of Gold, Critical Condition, Major League, Mo' Better Blues, King of New York, New Jack City, Jungle Fever, White Men Can't Jump, The Waterdance, Passenger 57, Boiling Point, Rising Sun, Demolition Man, Sugar Hill, Drop Zone, To Wong Foo—Thanks for Everything—Julie Newmar, Money Train, Waiting to Exhale, The Fan, Murder at 1600, Down in the Delta, Blade (also prod.), U.S. Marshals, One Night Stand, The Art of War, Blade 2, Undisputed, (also exec. prod.), Zigzag, Liberty Stands Still, Nine Lives, Blade: Trinity, (also prod.).
TELEVISION: *Series*: H.E.L.P. *Special*: Vietnam War Stories (ACE Award, 1989). *Guest*: Miami Vice. *Movies*: Futuresport.

SNODGRESS, CARRIE
Actress. b. Chicago, IL, Oct 27, 1945. e. Northern Illinois U. and M.A. degree from the Goodman Theatre. Plays include All Way Home, Oh What a Lovely War, Caesar and Cleopatra and Tartuffe (Sarah Siddons Award, 1966), The Price, Vanities, The Curse of the Starving Class.
PICTURES: Rabbit Run (debut, 1970), Diary of a Mad Housewife (Acad. Award nom.), The Fury, The Attic, Homework, Trick or Treats, A Night in Heaven, Pale Rider, Rainy Day Friends, Murphy's Law, Blueberry Hill, The Chill Factor, Nowhere to Run, Across the Tracks, The Ballad of Little Jo, 8 Seconds, Blue Sky, White Man's Burden, Wild Things, Strangers in the Kingdom, In the Light of the Moon, Bartleby, The Forsaken.
TELEVISION: *Movies*: The Whole World Is Watching, Silent Night Lonely Night, The Impatient Heart, Love's Dark Ride, Fast Friends, The Solitary Man, Nadia, The Rose and the Jackal, Woman With a Past, Rise & Walk: The Dennis Byrd Story, All She Ever Wanted, Death Benefit. *Guest*: The Outsider, The Virginian, Judd for the Defense, Medical Center, Marcus Welby, M.D.

SNOW, MARK
Composer. b. Brooklyn, NY, Aug. 26, 1946. e. Juilliard School of Music, 1968. As co-founder and member of New York Rock 'n' Roll Ensemble, appeared with the Boston Pops, at Carnegie Hall concerts and on the college circuit in the 1960s and 1970s.
PICTURES: Skateboard, Something Short of Paradise, High Risk, Jake Speed, Born to Be Wild, The X-Files: Fight the Future, Disturbing Behavior, Crazy in Alabama, The Dancing Crow, Stranger in My House, Code Name Phoenix, Pearl Harbor II-Pearlmageddon.
TELEVISION: *Series*: The Rookies, Starsky and Hutch, The Gemini Man, Family, The San Pedro Beach Bums, The Love Boat, The Next Step Beyond, Vega$, Hart to Hart, When the Whistle Blows, Dynasty, Falcon Crest, Strike Force, Cagney and Lacey, T.J. Hooker, The Family Tree, Lottery!, Double Trouble, Crazy Like a Fox, Hometown, The X-Files, Millenium, La Femme Nikita, Harsh Realm, Bull, Sole Survival, Dark Realm, Lone Gunmen, Special Unit 2, The Guardian, Pasadena, Smallville. *Mini-series*: Blood and Orchids, Night Sins. *Movies*: The Boy in the Plastic Bubble, Overboard, The Return of the Mod Squad, Angel City, Games Mother Never Taught You, John Steinbeck's Winter of Our Discontent, Packin' It In, I Married a Centerfold, Something About Amelia, Challenge of a Lifetime, California Girls, I Dream of Jeannie: Fifteen Years Later, Not My Kid, The Lady From Yesterday, Beverly Hills Cowgirl Blues, Acceptable Risks, News at Eleven, The Girl Who Spelled Freedom (Emmy nom.), Murder By the Book, A Hobo's Christmas, The Father Clements Story, Still Crazy Like a Fox, Cracked Up, Roman

Holiday, Pals, Murder Ordained, Louis L'Amour's Down the Long Hills, The Saint, The Return of Ben Casey, Bluegrass, Alone in the Neon Jungle, Those She Left Behind, Stuck With Each Other, Settle the Score, Archie: To Riverdale and Back Again, Child of the Night, Dead Reckoning, Follow Your Heart, The Girl Who Came Between Them, The Little Kidnappers, Miracle Landing, When He's Not a Stranger, Opposites Attract, Crash: The Mystery of Flight 1501, In the Line of Duty, The Marla Hanson Story, A Woman Scorned: The Betty Broderick Story, Highway Heartbreaker, Deliver Them From Evil: The Taking of Alta View, An American Story, Telling Secrets, The Man With 3 Wives, Born Too Soon, In the Line of Duty: Ambush in Waco, Precious Victims, Scattered Dreams: The Kathryn Messenger Story, In the Line of Duty: The Price of Heaven, Murder Between Friends, Moment of Truth: Cradle of Conspiracy, Substitute Wife, Down Out and Dangerous, Cloned, The Day Lincoln Was Shot, Le Dernier Combat, Mr. Murder, A Memory in My Heart, A Touch of Hope, In the Name of the People, Another Woman's Husband, Dirty Pictures, For Love of Olivia, Wolf Lake, Ground Zero. *Specials*: Day-to-Day Affairs, Vietnam War Story.

SNYDER, BRUCE M.
Executive. b. New York, NY, July 1, 1946. e. Queens Coll. Began entertainment career with Paramount Pictures as a booker in San Francisco, 1968-69. Paramount sales, NY 1969-76. Became eastern div. mgr., 20th century Fox, 1976-80. New York sales mgr., American Cinema Releasing, 1980-82. Eastern div. mgr., Embassy Pictures, 1982-83. Eastern div. mgr., TriStar Pictures, 1984-85. General sales mgr., 20th Century Fox, 1985-89. Pres., domestic distribution, 20th Century Fox, 1989-present.

SNYDER, TOM
Newscaster, Host. b. Milwaukee, WI, May 12, 1936. e. Marquette U. First job in news dept. of WRIT, Milwaukee. Subsequently with WSAV-TV, Savannah; WAII-TV, Atlanta; KTLA-TV, Los Angeles; and KYW-TV, Philadelphia, before moving to KNBC in L.A. in 1970 as anchorman for weeknight newscast. Named host of NBC-TV's Tomorrow program in 1973 (Emmy Award), moved to NY in 1974, as anchorman of one-hour segment of NewsCenter 4. 1975, inaugurated the NBC News Update, one-minute weeknight prime time news spot. Host for Tomorrow talk show (Tom Snyder Show (ABC Radio), The Late Late Show With Tom Snyder.
TELEVISION: *Movies*: Fire and Rain, (narrator). *Documentaries*: Off the Menu: The Last Days of Chasen's, Ayn Rand: A Sense of Life, Plaster Caster.

SOADY, WILLIAM C.
Executive. b. Toronto, Canada, Oct. 7, 1943. Career with Universal Pictures started in 1970 when named Toronto branch mgr.; promoted to v.p. & gen. sls. mgr. of Universal Film (Canada) in 1971. Promoted to v.p. & gen. sls. mgr., Universal Pictures, 1981, in NY relocating to L.A. later that year. 1983 named pres. of Universal Pictures Distribution, new domestic dist. div. of Universal; resigned, 1988. Named exec. v.p. distrib., Tri-Star Pictures, 1988; pres. of distrib., 1992. Named pres. & CEO of Showscan Entertainment Inc. in 1994. Became pres. of distrib. for Polygram Films in 1997.

SOAMES, RICHARD
Executive. b. London, England, June 6, 1936. Joined Film Finances Ltd. 1972; Appt. director Film Finances Ltd., 1977: Appt. man. dir. 1979. Appt. pres. Film Finances Canada Ltd. 1982: Appt. pres., Film Finances Inc. Also formed Doric Prods, Inc.
PICTURES: The Boss's Wife, The Principal, Honey I Shrunk the Kids, Tap.

SOBIESKI, LEELEE
Actress. r.n. Liliane Rudabet Gloria Elsveta Sobieski. b. New York, NY, June 10, 1982.
PICTURES: Jungle 2 Jungle, A Soldier's Daughter Never Cries, Deep Impact, Never Been Kissed, Eyes Wide Shut, Here on Earth, Squelch, My First Mister, The Glass House, Joy Ride, Hoffman, Uprising, Max, Nailed Right In, Les liasiones dangereuses, L'Idole.
TELEVISION: *Movies*: Reunion, A Horse for Danny, Joan of Arc, Uprising. *Series*: Charlie Grace. *Guest*: F/X: The Series, NewsRadio.

SODERBERGH, STEVEN
Director, Writer, Editor. b. Atlanta, GA, Jan. 14, 1963. First major professional job was directing concert film for rock group Yes for Grammy-nominated video, 1986.
PICTURES: *Director-Editor*: Sex Lies and Videotape (debut, 1989; also s.p.; Cannes Fest. Palme d'Or Award; Acad. Award nom. for s.p.), Kafka, King of the Hill (also s.p.), The Underneath (also s.p.), Schizopolis (also actor), Gray's Anatomy, Out of Sight, The Limey, Erin Brockovich, Traffic, Ocean's Eleven, How to Survive a Hotel Room Fire, Eros. *Producer*: Suture (exec. prod.), The Day Trippers, Pleasantville, Welcome to Collinwood, Insomnia (exec. prod.), Confessions of a Dangerous Mind (exec. prod.), Full Frontal, Solaris, The Informant, Eros, Ocean's Twelve, (exec. prod., dir.).
TELEVISION: *Series*: Fallen Angels (The Quiet Room).

SOKOLOW, DIANE
Executive. b. New York, NY. e. Temple U. m. Mel Sokolow. 1975, v.p., East Coast operations, for Lorimar; with Warner Bros. 1977-81; served as v.p. of East Coast production. Left to form The Sokolow Co. with husband, Mel, to produce films. 1982, returned to WB as v.p., East Coast prod. 1984, joined Motown Prods. as exec. v.p.; producer, MGM-UA 1986-87. Currently S.V.P., East Coast Production, Phoenix Pictures.
PICTURE: My Son's Brother (co-prod.).
TELEVISION: *Exec. Prod.*: Miles from Nowhere, Trial: The Price of Passion, Lady Against the Odds, Fallen Champ, Silent Cries.

SOLO, ROBERT H.
Producer. b. Waterbury, CT, Dec. 4, 1932. e. U. of Connecticut, BA. Early career as agent with Ashley-Famous; later production as exec. asst. to Jack Warner and Walter MacEwen at Warner Bros. 1971, named WB v.p., foreign production 1974, named exec. v.p., prod. at Burbank Studio. Now indep. prod.
PICTURES: Scrooge, The Devils (co-prod.), Invasion of the Body Snatchers, The Awakening, I the Jury, Bad Boys, Colors, Above the Law (exec. prod.), Winter People, Blue Sky, Car 54 Where Are You?, Body Snatchers.

SOLONDZ, TODD
Director, Producer, Writer. b. Newark, NJ, October 15, 1959. e. NYU Film Sch. After first feature film release, left filmmaking to teach English as a Second Language. Returned with Welcome to the Dollhouse.
PICTURES: Feelings (NYU short), Babysitter (NYU short), Schatt's Last Shot (NYU short), Fear Anxiety and Depression, Married to the Mob (actor only), Welcome to the Dollhouse (Jury Prize, Sundance Film Fest.), Happiness, Storytelling. *Actor*: As Good as It Gets.
TELEVISION: How I Became a Leading Artistic Figure in New York City's East Village Cultural Landscape (short for Saturday Night Live).

SOLT, ANDREW W.
Producer, Writer, Director. b. London, England, December 13, 1947. e. UCLA.
PICTURES: Imagine: John Lennon, This is Elvis, It Came From Hollywood.
TELEVISION: Honeymooners' Reunion, The Muppets... A Celebration of 30 Years, Cousteau's Mississippi, Happy Birthday Donald Duck, America Censored, Remembering Marilyn, Great Moments in Disney Animation, ET & Friends, Disney's DTV, Heroes of Rock 'n Roll, Bob Hope's Christmas Tours, Disney Goes To The Oscars, Cousteau: Oasis In Space (series), Cousteau: Odyssey, Best of the Ed Sullivan Show (4 specials), The History of Rock 'n' Roll, (vol. 1-10), Sesame Street's 25th Birthday Special, Grammy's Greatest Moments, TV Guide's 40th Anniversary Special, 25x5: The Continuing Adventures of the Rolling Stones, Andy Griffith Show Reunion, Cousteau: Search for Atlantis I&II, All My Children 25th Anniversary Special, Hunt for Amazing Treasure, Great Moments in Disney Animation, Gimme Some Truth, 50 Years of NBC Late Night, NBC 75th Anniversary Celebration.

SOMERS, SUZANNE
Actress. r.n. Suzanne Mahoney. b. San Bruno, CA, Oct. 16, 1946. e. Lone Mountain Sch., San Francisco Coll. for Women. Pursued modeling career; worked as regular on Mantrap, syndicated talk show. Did summer stock and theatrical films. *Author*: Touch Me Again, Keeping Secrets, Some People Live More Than Others, Wednesday's Children: Adult Survivors of Abuse Speak Out.
PICTURES: Bullitt (debut, 1968), Daddy's Gone A-Hunting, Fools, American Graffiti, Magnum Force, Yesterday's Hero, Nothing Personal, Serial Mom, Rusty: A Dog's Tale, Say It Isn't So.
TELEVISION: *Series*: Three's Company, She's the Sheriff, Step by Step, The Suzanne Somers Show (talk). *Guest*: One Day at a Time, Lotsa Luck, The Rockford Files, Starsky & Hutch, The Rich Little Show, Battle of the Network Stars, Love Boat. *Movies*: Sky Heist, It Happened at Lakewood Manor (Ants), Happily Ever After, Zuma Beach, Rich Men Single Women, Keeping Secrets (also exec. prod.), Exclusive (also co-exec. prod), Seduced by Evil, Devil's Food, No Laughing Matter, The Darklings, The 70's:The Decade that Changed Television, The Truth About Blondes. *Mini-Series*: Hollywood Wives. *Specials*: Us Against the World, Suzanne, Suzanne Somers Presents: Showtime's Triple Crown of Comedy, Disney's Totally Minnie.

SOMMER, ELKE
Actress. r.n. Elke Schletz. b. Berlin, Germany, Nov. 5, 1940. Entered films in Germany, 1958.
PICTURES: Das Totenschiff (debut, 1958), Lampenfieber, The Day It Rained, Heaven and Cupid, Love the Italian Way, Why Bother to Knock? (English-language debut, 1961), Daniela by Night, Violent Ecstasy, Auf Wiedersehen, Cafe Oriental, Bahia de Palma, The Victors, Island of Desire, The Prize, Frontier Hellcat, Le Bambole (The Dolls), A Shot in the Dark, The Art of Love, The Money Trap, The Corrupt Ones, The Oscar, Boy Did I Get a Wrong Number, The Venetian Affair, Deadlier Than the Male, The Wicked Dreams of Paula Schultz, The Invincible Six, They Came to Rob Las Vegas, The Wrecking Crew, Baron Blood, Zeppelin, Percy, It's Not the Size That Counts (Percy's Progress),

Ten Little Indians, The Swiss Conspiracy, Carry on Behind, House of Exorcism (Lisa and the Devil), Das Netz, The Astral Factor (Invisible Strangler), Thoroughbreds, I Miss You—Hugs and Kisses, The Prisoner of Zenda, A Nightingale Sang in Berkeley Square, The Double McGuffin, Exit Sunset Blvd., The Man in Pyjamas, Lily in Love, Death Stone, Himmelshorn, Neat and Tidy, Severed Ties, Alles nur Tarnung, Dangerous Cargo, Flashback -Morderische Ferien.
TELEVISION: *Movies*: Probe, Stunt Seven, The Top of the Hill, Inside the Third Reich, Jenny's War, Anastasia: The Mystery of Anna, Adventures Beyond Belief, Nicht mit uns. *Mini-Series*: Peter the Great.

SOMMER, JOSEF
Actor. b. Greifswald, Germany, June 26, 1934. Raised in North Carolina. e. Carnegie-Mellon U. Studied at American Shakespeare Festival in Stratford, CT, 1962-64. U.S Army, 1958-60. NY stage debut in Othello, 1970.
PICTURES: Dirty Harry (debut, 1971), Man on a Swing, The Front, Close Encounters of the Third Kind, Oliver's Story, Hide in Plain Sight, Absence of Malice, Reds, Rollover, Hanky Panky, Still of the Night, Sophie's Choice (narrator), Independence Day, Silkwood, Iceman, Witness, D.A.R.Y.L., Target, The Rosary Murders, Chances Are, Dracula's Widow, Forced March, Bloodhounds of Broadway, Shadows and Fog, The Mighty Ducks, Malice, Cultivating Charlie, Nobody's Fool, Strange Days, Moonlight & Valentino, The Chamber, The Proposition, Bulworth, Patch Adams, The Next Best Thing, Shaft, The Family Man, Searching for Paradise, The Sum of All Fears.
TELEVISION: *Series*: Hothouse, Under Cover. *Specials*: Morning Becomes Electra, The Scarlet Letter, Saigon. *Movies*: Too Far to Go, Doctor Franken, The Henderson Monster, Sparkling Cyanide, The Betty Ford Story, A Special Friendship, Bridge to Silence, The Bionic Showdown: The Six Million Dollar Man and the Bionic Woman, Money Power Murder, Spy Games, An American Story, Citizen Cohn, Hostages, The Enemy Within, Don't Drink the Water, The Minutes, Kansas, Letter to My Killer, Hidden in America, Mistrial, The Widenet, The Hunt for the Unicorn Killer, The Impressionists. *Mini-Series*: The Kennedys of Massachusetts, A Woman Named Jackie.

SONDHEIM, STEPHEN
Composer, Lyricist. b. New York, NY, March 22, 1930. e. Williams Coll. Writer for Topper TV series, 1953. Wrote incidental music for The Girls of Summer (1956), Invitation to a March (1961), Twigs (1971). Winner of 6 Grammy Awards: Cast Albums 1970, 1973, 1979, 1984, 1988 and song of the year 1975. Named Visiting Prof. of Contemporary Theater, Oxford U. 1990.
THEATRE: *Lyrics only*: West Side Story, Gypsy, Do I Hear a Waltz? *Music and lyrics*: A Funny Thing Happened on the Way to the Forum, Anyone Can Whistle, Company (Tony Award, 1971), Follies (Tony Award, 1972), A Little Night Music (Tony Award, 1973), The Frogs, Candide (new lyrics for revival), Pacific Overtures, Sweeney Todd, (Tony Award, 1979), Merrily We Roll Along, Sunday in the Park with George (Pulitzer Prize, 1985), Into the Woods (Tony Award, 1988), Assassins, Passion (Tony Award, 1994). Theater anthologies of his songs: Side By Side By Sondheim; Marry Me a Little, You're Gonna Love Tomorrow, Putting It Together.*Play*: Getting Away With Murder.
PICTURES: West Side Story (lyrics), Gypsy (lyrics), A Funny Thing Happened on the Way to the Forum (music, lyrics), The Last of Sheila (s.p.), Stavisky (score), A Little Night Music (music, lyrics), Reds (score), Dick Tracy (music, lyrics; Acad. Award for best song: Sooner or Later, 1990), Postcards from the Edge, The Birdcage, Camp.
TELEVISION: *Movies*: Evening Primrose, June Moon, (actor), Sweeney Todd, Sunday in the Park with George, A Little Night Music, Into the Woods, Gypsy, The Sunshine Boys, Passion, Company, Putting It Together, Sweeney Todd: The Demon Barber of Fleet Street In Concert. *Special*: Evening Primrose (music, lyrics; ABC Stage '67), Into the Woods.

SONNENFELD, BARRY
Director, Cinematographer. b. New York, NY April 1, 1953. Received Emmy Award for photography on series Out of Step.
PICTURES: *Cinematographer*: Blood Simple (debut, 1984), Compromising Positions, Raising Arizona, Three O'Clock High, Throw Momma From the Train, Big, When Harry Met Sally..., Miller's Crossing, Misery. *Director*: The Addams Family (debut, 1991), For Love or Money (also co-prod.), Addams Family Values (also cameo), Get Shorty (also prod.), Men in Black., Wild Wild West, Big Trouble, Men in Black 2.
TELEVISION: *Movies*: Doubletake, Welcome Home Bobby, Classified Love. *Series*: Maximum Bob, The Tick.

SORVINO, MIRA
Actress. b. Tenafly, NJ,September 28, 1967. Father is actor Paul Sorvino. e. Harvard U., A.B., 1990.
PICTURES: Amongst Friends (also assoc. prod.), Quiz Show, Parallel Lives, Barcelona, Tarantella, Sweet Nothing, Mighty Aphrodite (Acad. Award, Golden Globe), The Dutch Master (short), The Second Greatest Story Ever Told (short), Blue in the Face, Tales of Erotica, New York Cop, Beautiful Girls, Romy and Michele's High School Reunion, Mimic, The Replacement Killers, Too Tired to Die, Lulu on the Bridge, Free Money, At First Sight,

Summer of Sam, Joan of Arc: The Virgin Warrior, The Triumph of Love, The Grey Zone, Semana Santa, Wise Girls, Gods and Generals, Between Strangers.
TELEVISION: *Movies*: Parallel Lives, Jake's Women, Norma Jean and Marilyn, The Great Gatsby. *Series*: The Guiding Light, Swans Crossing. *Mini-series*: The Buccaneers.

SORVINO, PAUL
Actor. b. New York, NY, 1939. Daughter is actress Mira Sorvino.
THEATRE: Bajour, An American Millionaire, The Mating Dance, King Lear, That Championship Season, Marlon Brando Sat Right Here.
PICTURES: Where's Poppa? (debut, 1970), The Panic in Needle Park, Made for Each Other, A Touch of Class, The Day of the Dolphin, The Gambler, Shoot It Black Shoot It Blue, I Will I Will... For Now, Oh God, Bloodbrothers, Slow Dancing in the Big City, The Brink's Job, Lost and Found, Cruising, Reds, I The Jury, That Championship Season, Off the Wall, Very Close Quarters, Turk 182, The Stuff, A Fine Mess, Vasectomy, Dick Tracy, GoodFellas, The Rocketeer, Life in the Food Chain (Age Isn't Everything), The Firm, Nixon, Romeo + Juliet, Money Talks, American Perfekt, Most Wanted, Bulworth, Knock Off, Harlem Aria, Goodnight Joseph Parker, Dead Broke, Longshot, Ciao America, Perfume, See Spot Run, Plan B, Last Call, Rhode Island Blue, Irishman: The Legend of Danny Greene, The Cooler, Hey Arnold! The Movie.
TELEVISION: *Series*: We'll Get By, Bert D'Angelo: Superstar, The Oldest Rookie, Law and Order, That's Life. *Mini-Series*: Seventh Avenue, Chiefs. *Movies*: Tell Me Where It Hurts, It Couldn't Happen to a Nicer Guy, Dummy, A Question of Honor, My Mother's Secret Life, With Intent to Kill, Surviving, Don't Touch My Daughter, The Case of the Wicked Wives, Parallel Lives, Without Consent, Joe Torre: Curveballs Along the Way, Houdini, That Championship Season, Chearers, Thin Blue Lie, The Amati Girls, Mafia Doctor. *Guest*: Moonlighting, Murder She Wrote. *Special*: The Last Mile.

SOUL, DAVID
Actor. r.n. David Solberg. b. Chicago, IL, Aug. 28, 1943.
PICTURES: Johnny Got His Gun, Magnum Force, Dog Pound Shuffle, The Hanoi Hilton, Appointment with Death, Pentathalon, Tabloid.
TELEVISION: *Series*: Here Come the Brides, Owen Marshall-Counselor at Law, Starsky and Hutch, Casablanca, Yellow Rose, Unsub. *Movies*: The Disappearance of Flight 412, Starsky and Hutch (pilot), Little Ladies of the Night, Salem's Lot, Swan Song (also co-prod.), Rage, Homeward Bound, The Manions of America, World War III, Through Naked Eyes, The Fifth Missile, Harry's Hong Kong, In the Line of Duty: The FBI Murders, Prime Target, So Proudly We Hail, Bride in Black, A Cry in the Wild, The Taking of Peggy Ann, Perry Mason: The Case of the Fatal Framing, Grave Secrets: The Legacy of Hilltop Drive, Vents Contraires, Terror in the Mall.

SPACEK, SISSY
Actress. r.n. Mary Elizabeth Spacek. b. Quitman, TX, Dec. 25, 1949. m. director Jack Fisk. Cousin of actor Rip Torn. Attended acting classes in New York under Lee Strasberg. Had bit role in Andy Warhol's Trash. Worked as set decorator on films Death Game, Phantom of the Paradise.
PICTURES: Prime Cut (debut, 1972), Ginger in the Morning, Badlands, Carrie, Welcome to L.A., 3 Women, Heart Beat, Coal Miner's Daughter (Acad. Award, 1980), Raggedy Man, Missing, The Man With Two Brains (voice), The River, Marie, Violets Are Blue, 'night Mother, Crimes of the Heart, The Long Walk Home, JFK, Hard Promises, Trading Mom, The Grass Harp, Affliction, Blast from the Past, Rage: Carrie 2, The Straight Story, In The Bedroom, Acting Carrie, Tuck Everlasting, A Decade Under the Influence.
TELEVISION: *Movies*: The Girls of Huntington House, The Migrants, Katherine, A Private Matter, The Good Old Boys, If These Walls Could Talk, Songs in Ordinary Times, Midwives, Last Call, Fitzgerald. *Special*: Verna: USO Girl. *Guest*: The Rookies, The Waltons.

SPACEY, KEVIN
Actor. r.n. Kevin Spacey Fowler. b. South Orange, NJ, July 26, 1959. Raised in southern CA. e. L.A. Valley Coll., appearing in stage productions as well as stand-up comedy clubs, before attending Juilliard Sch. of Drama. Has appeared in numerous regional and repertory productions including Kennedy Center (The Seagull), Williamstown Theatre Fest. and Seattle Rep. Theatre, and with New York Shakespeare Fest. Recipient of numerous industry awards, including two Acad. Awards.
THEATRE: Henry IV Part I, The Robbers, Barbarians, Ghosts, Hurlyburly, Long Day's Journey into Night, National Anthems, Lost in Yonkers (Tony Award, 1991), Playland.
PICTURES: Heartburn (debut, 1986), Rocket Gibraltar, Working Girl, See No Evil Hear No Evil, Dad, A Show of Force, Henry and June, Glengarry Glen Ross, Consenting Adults, Iron Will, The Ref, Outbreak, Swimming With Sharks (also co-prod.), The Usual Suspects (Acad. Award, Chicago Film Critics Award, 1996), Seven, Albino Alligator (dir.), A Time to Kill, Looking for Richard, L.A. Confidential, Midnight in the Garden of Good and Evil, Hurly-burly, The Negotiator, A Bug's Life (voice), The Negotiator, Ordinary Decent Criminal, American Beauty (Acad.

Award, best actor, 2000), Pay It Forward, The Shipping News, President Clinton: Final Days, Shackleton's Antarctic Adventure (narrator), K-Pax, The Life of David Gale, The United States of Leland.
TELEVISION: *Specials*: Long Day's Journey into Night, Darrow, Steve McQueen: The King of Cool, Hitchcock: Shadow of a Genius. *Movies*: The Murder of Mary Phagan, Fall from Grace, When You Remember Me, Doomsday Gun. *Series*: Wiseguy, Tribeca. *Guest*: L.A. Law.

SPADE, DAVID
Actor. b. Birmingham, M, Juy 22, 1964. Raised in Scottsdale, AZ. Performed stand-up comedy in clubs and colleges which led to debut on Saturday Night Live in 1990.
PICTURES: Light Sleeper (debut, 1982), Coneheads, Reality Bites, P.C.U., Tommy Boy, Black Sheep, 8 Heads in a Duffel Bag, Senseless, The Rugrats Movie (voice), Lost & Found (also s.p.), Loser, Little Nicky, The Emperor's New Groove (voicd), Joe Dirt, Dickie Roberts: Former Child Star.
TELEVISION: *Series*: Saturday Night Live, Just Shoot Me.

SPADER, JAMES
Actor. b. Boston, MA, Feb. 7, 1960. e. Phillips Academy. Studied acting at Michael Chekhov Studio.
PICTURES: Endless Love (debut, 1981), The New Kids, Tuff Turf, Pretty in Pink, Mannequin, Baby Boom, Less Than Zero, Wall Street, Jack's Back, The Rachel Papers, Sex Lies and Videotape (Cannes Fest. Award, 1989), Bad Influence, White Palace, True Colors, Storyville, Bob Roberts, The Music of Chance, Dream Lover, Wolf, Stargate, 2 Days in the Valley, Crash, Critical Care, Curtain Call, Supernova, The Watcher, Slow Burn, Speaking of Sex, Secretary.
TELEVISION: *Series*: The Family Tree, The Practice. *Movies*: Cocaine: One Man's Seduction, A Killer in the Family, Starcrossed, Family Secrets, Keys to Tulsa, The Pentagon Papers.

SPANO, VINCENT
Actor. b. New York, NY, Oct. 18, 1962. While attending Stuyvesant H.S. made stage debut at 14 in The Shadow Box (Long Wharf and B'way).
THEATRE: The Shadow Box, Balm in Gilead.
PICTURES: Over the Edge (debut, 1979), The Double McGuffin, The Black Stallion Returns, Baby It's You, Rumblefish, Alphabet City, Maria's Lovers, Creator, Good Morning Babylon, And God Created Woman, 1753: Venetian Red, High Frequency (Aquarium), Oscar, City of Hope, Alive, Indian Summer, The Ascent, The Tie That Binds, A Brooklyn State of Mind, The Unknown Cyclist, No Strings Attached, The Christmas Path, Goosed, Prophecy 3, The Deadly Look of Love, The Colony, Texas Rangers, Silence.
TELEVISION: *Series*: Search for Tomorrow. *Movies*: The Gentleman Bandit, Senior Trip, Blood Ties, Afterburn, Downdraft, Medusa's Child, The Deadly Look of Love, Jenifer, The Rats, Deathlands.

SPEARS, JR., HAROLD T.
Executive. b. Atlanta, GA, June 21, 1929. e. U. of Georgia, 1951. With Floyd Theatres, Lakeland, FL, since 1953; now Pres., Sun South Theatres, Inc., 1996.

SPECKTOR, FREDERICK
Executive. b. Los Angeles, CA, April 24, 1933. e. USC, UCLA. M.P. agent, Ashley Famous Agency, 1962-64; Artists Agency Corp., 1964-68; exec. M.P. dept., William Morris Agency, 1968-78; exec. Creative Artists Agency, 1978-present. Trustees Council, Education First, bd. of dirs., Amer. Jewish Committee. Bd. of dirs. for the ACLU and Center for Gun-Violence Prevention.

SPEEDMAN, SCOTT
Actor. b. London, England, Sept. 1, 1975.
PICTURES: Ursa Major, Kitchen Party, Duets, Dark Blue, My Life Without Me, The 24th Day, Underworld.
TELEVISION: *Series*: Felicity. *Movies*: Net Worth, A Brother's Promise: The Dan Jansen Story, Giant Mine, Rescuers Stories of Courage: Two Couples, Dead Silence, What Happened to Bobby Earl?, Every 9 Seconds. *Series*: Nancy Drew, Felicity. *Guest*: Kung Fu: The Legend Continues, Goosebumps.

SPELLING, AARON
Executive, Producer. b. Dallas, TX, April 22, 1923. e. SMU. Daughter is actress Tori Spelling. Was actor/writer before becoming producer at Four Star in 1957. Won Harvard Award for Best Original One-act Play. Producer of series and tv movies: 1967, formed Thomas/Spelling Productions; 1969, formed his own co., Aaron Spelling Productions; 1972, partnered with Leonard Goldberg. Chairman/CEO Spelling TV, Inc. Produced more than 111 movies for television to date. Winston Churchill Medal of Wisdom, 1988. Special People's Choice Award, 1992.
PICTURES: Exec Prod.: Mr. Mom, Surrender, Three O'Clock High, Cross My Heart, Satisfaction (co-prod.), Loose Cannons, Soapdish, The Mod Squad, Charlie's Angels.
TELEVISION: *Exec. Prod./Prod.*: *Series*: The Mod Squad, The Rookies, Charlie's Angels, Fantasy Island, Starsky and Hutch,

Hart to Hart, T.J. Hooker, Family, The Love Boat, Vega$, Dynasty, Matt Houston, Hotel, The Colbys, Life with Lucy, Nightingales, HeartBeat, Beverly Hills 90210, The Heights, Melrose Place, The Round Table, Winnetka Road, 7th Heaven, Sunset Beach, Pacific Palisades, The Love Boat: The Next Wave, Buddy Faro, Charmed, Safe Harbor. *Mini-Series:* Kingpin. *Movies:* The Over-the-Hill Gang, Wake When the War Is Over, The Monk, The Pigeon, The Ballad of Andy Crocker, Say Goodbye Maggie Cole, Rolling Man, Shooting Stars, Dark Mirror, Making of a Male Model, The Three Kings, Nightingales, Day One (Emmy Award, 1989), Rich Men Single Women, The Love Boat: The Valentine Voyage, Jailbirds, Back to the Streets of San Francisco, Grass Roots, Terror on Track 9, A Stranger in the Mirror, And the Band Played On (Emmy Award, 1994), Jane's House, Green Dolphin Beat, Satan's School for Girls, Titans, All Souls, Stop at Nothing, The Deep, Summerland, Hotel.

SPELLING, TORI
Actress. r.n. Victoria Davey Spelling. b. Los Angeles, CA, May 16, 1973. Father is prod. Aaron Spelling.
PICTURES: Troop Beverly Hills, The House of Yes, Scream 2, Perpetrators of the Crime, Trick, Playmate Pajama Party, Scary Movie 2, Sol Goode, Naked Movie.
TELEVISION: *Movies:* Shooting Stars, Beverly Hills 90210 (pilot), A Friend to Die For, Awake to Murder, Mother May I Sleep with Danger, Deadly Pursuits, Co-ed Call Girl, The Alibi . *Series:* Saved by the Bell, Beverly Hills 90210. *Guest:* Vega$, Fantasy Island, The Love Boat, T.J. Hooker, Hotel, Blossom, Parker Lewis Can't Lose, Burke's Law, Melrose Place, Malibu Shores.

SPENGLER, PIERRE
Producer. b. Paris, France, 1947. Went on stage at 15; returned to language studies at Alliance Franccaise. Entered film industry as production runner and office boy. Teamed for first time with friend Ilya Salkind on The Light at the Edge of the World, produced by Alexander Salkind.
PICTURES: Bluebeard, The Three Musketeers, The Four Musketeers, Crossed Swords, Superman, Superman II, Superman III, Santa Claus: The Movie, The Return of the Musketeers (tv in U.S.), Underground(exec. prod.), Joan of Arc(exec. prod.), The Hermit of Amsterdam(prod.), Danny the Dog.

SPHEERIS, PENELOPE
Director. b. New Orleans, LA, 1945. e. UCLA. Film Sch., MFA.
PICTURES: Real Life (prod. only). *Director:* The Decline of Western Civilization (also prod., s.p.), Suburbia (also s.p.), The Boys Next Door, Summer Camp Nightmare (s.p. only), Hollywood Vice Squad, Dudes, The Decline of Western Civilization-Part II: The Metal Years, Wedding Band (actress only), Wayne's World, The Beverly Hillbillies, The Little Rascals, Black Sheep, The Decline of Western Civilization Part III: Gutterpunks, Senseless, The Thing in Bob's Garage, We Sould Our Souls for Rock N' Roll, We Posers, Closers.
TELEVISION: Saturday Night Live (prod. only), Danger Theatre (co-creator, p., co-writer). *Movie:* Prison Stories: Women on the Inside (New Chicks), Applewood 911 (dir.), Dear Doughboy, The Crooked E: The Unshredded Truth About Enron.

SPIEGEL, LARRY
Producer, Writer, Director. b. Brooklyn, NY. e. Ohio U. With CBS-TV; Benton & Bowles; Wells, Rich, Green; BBDO. Now heads Appledown Films, Inc.
PICTURES: Hail (s.p.), Book of Numbers (s.p.), Death Game (prod.), Stunts (prod.), Spree (dir., s.p.), Phobia (prod.), Remo Williams: The Adventure Begins (prod.), Dove Against Death (prod.), The Sunchaser (prod.).
TELEVISION: *ABC Afterschool Specials,* Bear That Slept Through Christmas (writer), Never Fool With A Gypsy Ikon (writer), Planet of The Apes (animated; writer), Jan Stephenson Golf Video (prod.), Remo Williams (pilot ABC; prod.).

SPIELBERG, STEVEN
Director, Producer. b. Cincinnati, OH, Dec. 18, 1947. e. California State Coll. m. actress Kate Capshaw. Made home movies as child; completed first film with story and actors at 12 yrs. old in Phoenix. At 13 won film contest for 40-min. war movie, Escape to Nowhere. At 16 made 140-min. film, Firelight. At California State Coll. made five films. First professional work, Amblin', 20 min. short which led to signing contract with Universal Pictures at age 20. Formed own co. Amblin Entertainment, headquartered at Universal Studios. Received Irving G. Thalberg Memorial Award, 1987; American Film Institute Life Achievement Award, 1995. Partnered with David Geffen and Jeffrey Katzenberg formed film company DreamWorks, 1995.
PICTURES: *Director:* The Sugarland Express (debut, 1974; also story), Jaws, Close Encounters of The Third Kind (also s.p.; Acad. Award nom. for dir.), 1941, Raiders of the Lost Ark (Acad. Award nom.), E.T. The Extra-Terrestrial (also co-prod.; Acad. Award noms. for dir. & picture), Twilight Zone—The Movie (sequence dir.; also exec. prod.), Indiana Jones and the Temple of Doom, The Color Purple (also co-prod.; Acad. Award nom. for picture), Empire of the Sun (also co-prod.), Indiana Jones and the Last Crusade, Always (also co-prod.), Hook, Jurassic Park,

Schindler's List (also co-prod.; Acad. Awards for Best Director & Picture, 1993; DGA, Golden Globe & Natl. Society of Film Critics Awards for director; NY Film Critics, LA Film Critics, Natl. Board of Review. Natl. Society of Film Critics & Golden Globe Awards for picture), The Lost World: Jurassic Park, Amistad (also prod.), Saving Private Ryan (also prod.; Acad. Award for Best Director), The Unfinished Journey, A.I., Minority Report, Catch Me If You Can, Memoirs of a Geisha. Taken. *Co-exec. prod.:* I Wanna Hold Your Hand, Used Cars, Continental Divide (exec. prod.), Poltergeist (co-prod., co-s.p.), Gremlins (also cameo), The Goonies (also story), Back to the Future, Young Sherlock Holmes, The Money Pit, An American Tail, Innerspace, Batteries Not Included, Who Framed Roger Rabbit, The Land Before Time, Dad, Back to the Future Part II, Joe Versus the Volcano, Back to the Future Part III, Gremlins 2: The New Batch, Arachnophobia, Cape Fear, An American Tail: Fievel Goes West (co-prod.), We're Back!: A Dinosaur's Story, The Flintstones, The Little Rascals, Casper (co-prod.), The Bridges of Madison County (co-prod.), Men in Black, Deep Impact (also cameo), The Last Days, The Mask of Zorro, Gladiator, Shrek, Evolution, Jurassic Park 3, Men in Black II, Terminal, Indiana Jones 4. *Actor only:* The Blues Brothers, Listen Up: The Lives of Quincy Jones.
TELEVISION: *Series episodes* (dir.): Columbo, Owen Marshall: Counsellor-at-Law, The Pyschiatrist, Toonsylvania. *Movies* (dir.): Night Gallery (episode dir.), Duel, Something Evil, Savage. *Exec. prod.:* Amazing Stories (series; also dir. of 2 episodes), Tiny Toon Adventures (series; Emmy Award, 1991), Class of '61 (movie), Family Dog (series), seaQuest DSV (series), Pinky and the Brain (series), Band of Brothers (mini-series, Emmy Award), Taken, (mini-series).

SPIKINGS, BARRY
Executive. b. Boston, England, Nov. 23, 1939. Ent. m.p. ind. 1973. Joint man. dir. British Lion Films Ltd., 1975. Appt. jnt. man. dir. EMI Films Ltd., 1977. 1979, appt. chmn. & chief exec., EMI Film & Theatre Corp.; chmn. & chief exec, EMI Films, Ltd., chmn. EMI Cinemas, Ltd.; chmn., Elstree Studios, Ltd.; chmn. EMI-TV Programs, Inc., 1980; appt. chmn. chief exec., EMI Films Group, 1982; 1985 Barry Spikings Productions Inc. (U.S.A.); 1985 became director Galactic Films Inc. (with Lord Anthony Rufus Issacs); 1986, acquired Embassy Home Entertainment from Coca Cola Co., renamed Nelson Entertainment Inc., appointed pres. and COO. 1992, Pleskow/Spikings Partnership, film prod. and distrib. partnership with Eric Pleskow.
PICTURES: *Prod.:* Conduct Unbecoming, The Man Who Fell to Earth, The Deer Hunter, Texasville, Beyond Rangoon. *Exec. prod.:* Convoy.

SPINELLA, STEPHEN
Actor.
THEATRE: Angels in America: Millenium Approaches (Tony award), Angels in America: Perestroika (Tony award).
PICTURES: Tarantella, Virtuosity, Faithful, The Unknown Cyclist, Love! Valour! Compassion!, The Jackal, Ravenous, Out of the Past (voice), Great Expectations, David Searching, Ravenous, Cradle Will Rock, Bubble Boy.
TELEVISION: *Movies:* And the Band Played On, What the Deaf Man Heard, Our Town.

SPINER, BRENT
Actor. b. Houston, TX, Feb. 2, 1949. Recorded album Ol' Yellow Eyes Is Back.
THEATRE: *NY:* The Seagull, The Three Musketeers, Sunday in the Park With George, Big River.
PICTURES: Stardust Memories, The Miss Firecracker Contest, Corrina Corrina, Star Trek: Generations, Independence Day, Phenomenon, Star Trek: First Contact, Out to Sea, Trekkies, Star Trek: Insurrection, South Park: Bigger Longer and Uncut (voice), Geppetto, Dude- Where's My Car?, I am Sam, Star Trek: Bridge Commander, Dating Service, Master of Disguise, Star Trek: Nemesis.TELEVISION: *Series:* Star Trek: The Next Generation. Movie: Introducing Dorothy Dandridge, As Me No Questions, The Ponder Heart, An Unexpected Love.

SPINETTI, VICTOR
Actor. b. South Wales, Sept. 2, 1933. e. Monmouth School. Entered industry in 1955. Appeared on Broadway in Oh! What a Lovely War winning 1965 Tony and Theatre World Awards.
THEATRE: *London:* Expresso Bongo, Candide, Make Me an Offer, Oh What a Lovely War (also B'way), The Odd Couple, Cat Among the Pigeons.
PICTURES: A Hard Day's Night, The Wild Affair, Help!, The Taming of the Shrew, The Biggest Bundle of Them All, Can Hieronymous Merkin Ever Forget Mercy Humppe and Find True Happiness?, Under Milk Wood, The Little Prince, The Return of the Pink Panther, Under the Cherry Moon, The Krays, The Princess and the Goblin (voice), Julie and the Cadillacs.
TELEVISION: The Magical Mystery Tour, Vincent Van Gogh, Paradise Club, The Attic, The Secret Garden, Young Indiana Jones and the Attack of the Hawkmen, In the Beginning (mini-series).

SPINOTTI, DANTE
Cinematographer. b. Tolmezzo, Italy, Aug. 22, 1943.
PICTURES: La Disubbidienza, Cinderella '80, Hearts and Armour, Sogno di una notte di meza estate, Softly Softly, Cosi parlo Bellavista, The Berlin Affair, The Dark Side of Love, Manhunter, Crimes of the Heart, Choke Canyon, From the Hip, The Legend of the Holy Drinker (actor), Illegally Yours, Fair Game, Beaches, Torrents of Spring, A Violent Life, The Comfort of Strangers, True Colors, Hudson Hawk, Frankie and Johnny, The Last of the Mohicans, The Secret of the Old Woods, The End Is Known, Blink, Nell, The Quick and the Dead, The Star Maker, Heat, The Mirror Has Two Faces, L.A. Confidential (LA Film Crits. Award, Best Cinematography, 1997), Goodbye Lover, Other Sister, Man of the People, The Insider, Wonder Boys, The Family Man, Bandits, Red Dragon, Pinocchio.
TELEVISION: Basileus Quartet.

SPIRA, STEVEN S.
Executive. b. New York, NY, March 25, 1955. e. City Coll. of New York; Benjamin Cardozo Sch. of Law. Associated 10 years with N.Y. law firm, Monasch Chazen & Stream. 1984, joined 20th Century Fox as sr. counsel; 1985, to Warner Bros. Now exec. v.p., theatrical business affairs, Warner Bros.

SPODICK, ROBERT C.
Exhibitor. b. New York, NY, Dec. 3, 1919. e. CCNY, 1940; ent. NYC m.p. ind. as errand boy Skouras Park Plaza, Bronx 1932-33; reel boy, asst. mgr., Loew's Theatres; mgr., Little Carnegie and other art theatres; exploitation man, United Artists.
Acquired Lincoln, New Haven art house in 1945 in partnership with cousin Leonard E. Sampson; developed Nutmeg Theatre circuit, which was sold in 1968 to Robert Smerling. Beginning in 1970, built Groton, CT., Cinemas I and II; Norwich Cinemas I and II, Mystic Village Cinemas I, II and III, and Westerley Triple Cinemas in RI as Gemini Cinema Circuit in partnership with Sampson and William Rosen. Gemini sold to Interstate Theatres, 1986. With Sampson presently operates York Square I & II and The New Lincoln in New Haven. Pres., Allied of CT, 1962-64; Pres. NATO of Conn. 1968-73. Past Chmn. Exec. Comm., CT Ass'n of Theatre Owners, and still active member of Board of Directors in 1997.

SPOTTISWOODE, ROGER
Director. b. England, Jan. 5, 1945. Film editor of TV commercials and documentaries before turning to direction.
PICTURES: Editor: Straw Dogs, The Getaway, Pat Garrett and Billy the Kid, Hard Times, The Gambler; Who'll Stop the Rain? (assoc. prod.), Baby: Secret of the Lost Legend (exec. prod.). Director: Terror Train (debut, 1980), The Pursuit of D.B. Cooper, Under Fire, The Best of Times, Shoot to Kill, Turner & Hooch, Air America, Stop Or My Mom Will Shoot, Mesmer, Tomorrow Never Dies, The 6th Day.
TELEVISION: Movies: The Renegades, The Last Innocent Man, Third Degree Burn, And the Band Played On, Hiroshima, Murder Live!, Noriega, The Matthew Shepherd Story, The Yeltsin Project, Ice Bound. Special: Time Flies When You're Alive.

SPRADLIN, G.D.
Actor. b. Daylight Township, Garvin County, OK, Aug. 31, 1920. e. Univ. of Oklahoma-doctor of Juris Prudence (1948). Started career as lawyer, became Independent Oil Producer. Active in local politics before turning to acting. Joined Oklahoma Repertory Theatre in 1964.
PICTURES: Will Penny (debut, 1968), Number One, Zabriskie Point, Monte Walsh, Tora! Tora! Tora!, The Hunting Party, The Godfather Part II, MacArthur, One on One, North Dallas Forty, Apocalypse Now, The Formula, Wrong Is Right, The Lords of Discipline, Tank, The War of the Roses, Clifford, Ed Wood, Canadian Bacon, Nick of Time, The Long Kiss Goodnight, Dick.
TELEVISION: Series: Rich Man Poor Man Book II. Mini-Series: Space, Dream West, Nutcracker: Money Madness and Murder, Robert Kennedy and His Times, War and Remembrance Movies: Dial Hot Line, Sam Hill: Who Killed the Mysterious Mr. Foster?, Oregon Trail, Maneaters Are Loose!, And I Alone Survived, Jayne Mansfield Story, Resting Place, Shoot First: A Cop's Vengeance, Telling Secrets, Riders of the Purple Sage.

SPRINGER, PAUL D.
Executive. e. Brooklyn Law Sch. Served as assoc. for NY law firm, Johnson & Tannebaum. Later with legal dept. of Columbia Pics. 1970, joined Paramount Pictures N.Y. legal dept. 1970; promoted to v.p. Theatrical Distrib. Counsel, 1979; promoted to sr. v.p., chief resident counsel, 1987; promoted to sr. v.p., asst. general counsel responsible for all legal functions for Paramount's distribution and marketing depts. Mem., NY and California Bars.

SPRINGFIELD, RICK
Actor, Singer, Songwriter. b. Sydney, Australia, Aug. 23, 1949.
PICTURES: Battlestar Galactica, Hard to Hold (act., addl. music), Keeping the Faith, (comp. song "Jessie's Girl").
TELEVISION: Series: General Hospital, Human Target, High Tide, A Change of Place, High Tide, Robin's Hoods. Specials: An Evening at the Improv, Countdown '81. Movies: Nick Knight, Dead Reckoning, In the Shadows Someone's Watching, Dying to Dance, Legion.

SQUIRES, BUDDY
Cinematographer.
PICTURES: Brooklyn Bridge (also prod.), Huey Long, The Statue of Liberty (Acad. Award nom.), The Donner Party, High Lonesome: The Story of Bluegrass Music, Out of the Past, Frank Lloyd Wright, Ram Dass- Fierce Grace.
TELEVISION: Mini-series: The Civil War, Baseball, The West, Lewis & Clark, The Irish in America: Long Journey Home, Fatal Twisters: A Season of Fury, Not for Ourselves Alone, American High, Hate.Com: Extremists on the Internet, Not for Ourselves Alone: The Story of Elizabeth Cady Stanton & Susan B. Anthony, New York: A Documentary Film, Jazz, Beyond Tara, Inside Sex: Taboos, The Merchants of Cool, Beyond Tara: The Extraordinary Life of Hattie McDaniel, Mark Twain, Miss America, Law & Order: Crime & Punishment.

STACK, ROBERT
Actor. b. Los Angeles, CA, Jan. 13, 1919. e. U. of Southern California. In U.S. Armed Forces (Navy), W.W.II. Studied acting at Henry Duffy School of Theatre 6 mo. then signed a contract with Universal. National skeet champion at age 16. Autobiography: Straight Shooting (1980).
PICTURES: First Love (debut, 1939), When the Daltons Rode, The Mortal Storm, A Little Bit of Heaven, Nice Girl?, Badlands of Dakota, To Be or Not To Be, Eagle Squadron, Men of Texas, Fighter Squadron, A Date With Judy, Miss Tatlock's Millions, Mr. Music, The Bullfighter and the Lady, My Outlaw Brother, Bwana Devil, War Paint, Conquest of Cochise, Sabre Jet, The Iron Glove, The High and the Mighty, House of Bamboo, Good Morning Miss Dove, Great Day in the Morning, Written on the Wind (Acad. Award nom.), The Gift of Love, The Tarnished Angels, John Paul Jones, The Last Voyage, The Caretakers, Is Paris Burning?, The Corrupt Ones, Action Man, Story of a Woman, A Second Wind, 1941, Airplane!, Uncommon Valor, Big Trouble, Transformers (voice), Plain Clothes, Caddyshack II, Dangerous Curves, Joe Versus the Volcano, Beavis and Butt-Head Do America (voice), BASEketball (cameo), Totally Irresponsible, Top Speed (cameo), Mumford (cameo), Recess:School's Out, Killer Bud.
TELEVISION: Series: The Untouchables (Emmy Award, 1960), The Name of the Game, Most Wanted, Strike Force, Unsolved Mysteries (host), Final Appeal (host), Hercules (voice). Guest: Playhouse 90 (Panic Button). Movies: The Strange and Deadly Occurance, Adventures of the Queen, Murder on Flight 502, Most Wanted (pilot), Undercover With the KKK (narrator), Midas Valley, Perry Mason: The Case of the Sinister Spirit, The Return of Eliot Ness, Sealed With a Kiss, H.U.D. 2000, Walt: The Man Behind the Myth. Mini-Series: George Washington, Hollywood Wives, Butt Ugly Martians.
(d. May 14, 2003).

STAHL, AL
Executive. b. July 3, 1916. Syndicated newspaper cartoonist; asst. animator, Max Fleischer, gag ed. Terrytoons; U.S. Signal Corps; opened own studios, 1946; prod. first animated TV cartoon show; pres., Animated Prod., prod. live and animated commercials; member of bd. NTFC. Developed and built first animation camera and stand, 1950. Designed and produced opening animation for The Honeymooners, The Electric Company, Saturday Night Live. Produced over 5,000 tv spots. Prod. 50 min. documentary War and Pieces for U.S. Army Commander of War in the Gulf, 1991.

STAHL, NICK
Actor. b. Dallas, TX, De. 5, 1980. Started acting at age 4.
PICTURES: The Man Without a Face, Safe Passage, Tall Tale, Eye of God, The Thin Red Line, Disturbing Behavior, Soundman, Sunset Strip, All Forgotten, In the Bedroom, The Sleepy Time Gal, Bully, Taboo, Bookies, Terminator 3: Rise of the Machines, Carnivale.
TELEVISION: Movies: Stranger at My Door, Woman With a Past, Incident in a Small Town, Blue River, My Son Is Innocent, Seasons of Love, Wasted.

STALLONE, SYLVESTER
Actor, Writer, Director. b. New York, NY, July 6, 1946. After high school taught at American Coll. of Switzerland instructing children of career diplomats, young royalty, etc. Returned to U.S. in 1967 and studied drama at U. of Miami, 1969. Came to New York to seek acting career, taking part-time jobs, including usher for Walter Reade Theatres. Then turned to writing, selling several TV scripts.
PICTURES: Actor: Party at Kitty and Studs (debut, 1970), Bananas, Rebel (A Man Called Rainbo), The Lords of Flatbush (also co-s.p.), The Prisoner of 2nd Avenue, Capone, Death Race 2000, Farewell My Lovely, Cannonball, Rocky (also s.p.; Acad. Award noms. for actor & s.p.), F.I.S.T. (also co-s.p.), Paradise Alley (also s.p., dir.), Rocky II (also s.p., dir.), Nighthawks, Victory, Rocky III (also s.p., dir.), First Blood (also co-s.p.), Staying Alive (cameo; also dir., prod., co-s.p.), Rhinestone (also co-s.p.), Rambo: First Blood Part II (also co-s.p.), Rocky IV (also dir., s.p.), Cobra (also s.p.), Over the Top (also co-s.p.), Rambo III (also co-s.p.), Lock Up, Tango and Cash, Rocky V (also s.p.), Oscar, Stop Or My Mom Will Shoot, Cliffhanger (also s.p.), Demolition Man, The Specialist, Judge Dredd, Assassins, Daylight, Cop

Land, Antz (voice), Get Carter, Eye See You, Driven (also s.p.), My Little Hollywood, Eye See You, Avenging Angelo, Dolan's Cadillac, Shade, Spy Kids 3-D: Game Over.
TELEVISION: *Guest:* Kojak, Police Story, Dream On.

STAMOS, JOHN
Actor. b. Cypress, CA, Aug. 19, 1963. m. model Rebecca Romijn Stamos. Landed role of Blackie Parrish on daytime serial General Hospital in 1982. Has toured with his own band John Stamos and the Bad Boyz.
THEATRE: *B'way:* How to Succeed in Business Without Really Trying.
PICTURES: Never Too Young to Die, Born to Ride, Private Parts, Dropping Out, Grownups, Femme Fatale, The Making of Bret Michaels, Party Monster.
TELEVISION: *Series:* General Hospital, Dreams, You Again?, Full House, Celebrity Profile, The List, Thieves. *Movies:* Daughter of the Streets, Captive, The Disappearance of Christina, Fatal Vows: The Alexandra O'Hara Story, Private Parts, A Match Made in Heaven, The Marriage Fool, Sealed with a Kiss, The Beach Boys: An American Family, (exec. prod.), How to Marry a Billionaire: A Christmas Tale, United We Stand, (host), Martin and Lewis, (co-exec. prod.).

STAMP, TERENCE
Actor. b. London, England, July 23, 1938. Stage experience including Alfie on Broadway. Recent stage: Dracula, The Lady from the Sea, Airborne Symphony. *Autobiography:* Coming Attractions (1988).
PICTURES: Billy Budd (debut 1962; Acad. Award nom.), Term of Trial, The Collector (Cannes Film Fest. Award, 1965), Modesty Blaise, Far from the Madding Crowd, Poor Cow, Blue, Teorema, Spirits of the Dead, The Mind of Mr. Soames, A Season in Hell, Hu-Man, The Divine Nymph, Strip-Tease, Superman, Meetings with Remarkable Men, Together?, Superman II, Monster Island, Death in the Vatican, The Hit, The Company of Wolves, Link, Legal Eagles, The Sicilian, Wall Street, Young Guns, Alien Nation, Stranger in the House (also dir., co-s.p.), Genuine Risk, Beltenebros, The Real McCoy, The Adventures of Priscilla-- Queen of the Desert, Mindbender, Limited Edition, Bliss, Kiss the Sky, Love Walked In, The Limey, Bowfinger, Star Wars: Episode I-The Phantom Menace, Red Planet, Ma femme est une actrice, Revelation, Fellini: Je suis un gran menteur, Full Frontal, My Boss's Daughter, The Haunted Mansion.
TELEVISION: *Movie:* The Thief of Bagdad, The Alamut Ambush

STANFILL, DENNIS C.
Executive. b. Centerville, TN, April 1, 1927. e. Lawrenceburg H.S.; U.S. Naval Acad., B.S., 1949; Oxford U. (Rhodes Scholar), M.A., 1953; U. of S. Carolina, L.H.D. (hon.). Corp. finance specialist, Lehman Bros 1959-65; v.p. finance, Times Mirror Company, Los Angeles, 1965-69; exec. v.p. finance, 20th C.-Fox Film Corp., 1969-71, pres., 1971, chmn. bd./CEO, 1971-81; pres., Stanfill, Bowen & Co., venture capital firm, 1981-90; chmn. bd./CEO, AME, Inc., 1990-92; co-chmn. bd./co-CEO, MGM, 1992-93. Sr. advisor to Credit Lyonnais, 1993-95. Private Investments, 1995-.

STANG, ARNOLD
Performer. b. Chelsea, MA, Sept. 28, 1927. Radio, 1935-50; on B'way, in five plays and in m.p. and short subjects; guest appearances on TV shows. Much voice-over cartoon work. Starred in 36 shorts.
TELEVISION: *Series:* School House, Henry Morgan Show, Doc Corkle, Top Cat (voice), Broadside. *Guest:* Captain Video, Milton Berle, Danny Thomas, Perry Como, Ed Sullivan, Red Skelton, Frank Sinatra, Wagon Train, Jack Benny, Johnny Carson, December Bride, Playhouse 90, Batman, Bonanza, Bob Hope, Danny Kaye, Jackie Gleason, Emergency, Feeling Good, Chico & the Man, Super Jaws & Catfish, Busting Loose, Flying High, Robert Klein Specials, Tales from the Dark Side, True Blue, Cosby Show.
PICTURES: Seven Days Leave, My Sister Eileen, Let's Go Steady, They Got Me Covered, So This is New York, Double for Della, Return of Marco Polo, Spirit of '76, The Man with the Golden Arm, Dondi, The Wonderful World of the Brothers Grimm, It's a Mad Mad Mad Mad World, Pinocchio in Outer Space (voice), Alakazam the Great (voice), Hello Down There, Skidoo, The Aristocats (voice), Raggedy Ann & Andy (voice), Gang That Couldn't Shoot Straight, That's Life, Hercules in New York, Ghost Dad, Dennis the Menace, At The Cottonwood.

STANTON, HARRY DEAN
Actor. b. West Irvine, KY, July 14, 1926. Acting debut at Pasadena Playhouse. Billed in early film appearances as Dean Stanton.
PICTURES: Revolt at Fort Laramie (debut, 1957), Tomahawk Trail, The Proud Rebel, Pork Chop Hill, The Adventures of Huckleberry Finn, A Dog's Best Friend, Hero's Island, The Man

From the Diner's Club, Ride in the Whirlwind, The Hostage, A Time for Killing, Rebel Rousers, Cool Hand Luke, Day of the Evil Gun, The Miniskirt Mob, Kelly's Heroes, Cisco Pike, Two-Lane Blacktop, Face to the Wind (Cry for Me Billy), Pat Garrett and Billy the Kid, Dillinger, Where the Lilies Bloom, Cockfighter, Zandy's Bride, The Godfather Part II, Rafferty and the Gold Dust Twins, Rancho Deluxe, Farewell My Lovely, 92 in the Shade, Win Place or Steal, The Missouri Breaks, Straight Time, Renaldo and Clara, Alien, The Rose, Wise Blood, Death Watch, The Black Marble, Private Benjamin, Escape From New York, One From the Heart, Young Doctors in Love, Christine, Repo Man, Red Dawn, The Bear, Paris Texas, The Care Bears Movie (voice), One Magic Christmas, Fool for Love, UFOria, Pretty in Pink, Slamdance, Stars and Bars, Mr. North, The Last Temptation of Christ, Dream a Little Dream, Twister, The Fourth War, Stranger in the House, Wild at Heart, Man Trouble, Twin Peaks: Fire Walk With Me, Blue Tiger, Never Talk to Strangers, Down Periscope, She's So Lovely, Fire Down Below, The Mighty, Fear and Loathing in Las Vegas, The Straight Story, The Green Mile, The Man Who Cried, Sand, Ginostra, Cadillac Tramps, The Pledge, Alien Evolution, Anger Management, Sonny.
TELEVISION: *Movies:* Flatbed Annie & Sweetpie: Lady Truckers, I Want to Live, Payoff, Hostages, Against the Wall. *Special:* Hotel Room (Tricks).

STAPLETON, JEAN
Actress. r.n. Jeanne Murray. b. New York, NY, Jan. 19, 1923. e. Wadleigh H.S. Summer stock in NH, ME, MA, and PA. Broadway debut in In the Summer House (1954). Chair, Advisory bd., Women's Research and Education Inst. (Wash., D.C.); bd.: Eleanor Roosevelt Val-kill, Hyde Park; trustee: Actors Fund of America.
THEATRE: Harvey, Damn Yankees, Bells Are Ringing, Juno, Rhinoceros, Funny Girl, Arsenic and Old Lace (B'way and tour), Mountain Language/The Birthday Party (Obie Award), The Learned Ladies, Bon Appetit, The Roads to Home, Night Seasons, Morning's at Seven, You Can't Take It With You, The Show-Off, The Mystery of Edwin Drood (natl. tour). and extensive regional work at the Totem Pole Playhouse, Fayetteville, PA, Pocono Playhouse, Mountain Home Pa; Peterborough Playhouse, N.H. and others. Operatic debut with Baltimore Opera Co. in Candide, then The Italian Lesson and Bon Appetit. Cinderella, NY City Opera. Starred in San Jose Civic Light Opera Co.'s Sweeney Todd. Off B'way in The Entertainer. The Matchmaker, A.C.T. San Francisco.
PICTURES: Damn Yankees (debut, 1958), Bells Are Ringing, Something Wild, Up the Down Staircase, Cold Turkey, Klute, The Buddy System, Michael, You've Got Mail, This Is My Father, Pursuit of Happiness.
TELEVISION: *Series:* All in the Family (3 Emmy Awards: 1971, 1972, 1978), Bagdad Cafe, Mrs. Piggle-Wiggle. *Movies:* Tail Gunner Joe, Aunt Mary, Angel Dusted, Isabel's Choice, Eleanor: First Lady of the World (Emmy nom.), A Matter of Sex, Dead Man's Folly, Fire in the Dark, The Habitation of Dragons, Ghost Mom, Lily Dale, Chance of a Lifetime, Like Mother Like Son: The Strange Story of Sante and Kenny Kimes. *Specials:* You Can't Take It With You, Grown-Ups (ACE nom.), Jack and the Beanstalk and Cinderella (Faerie Tale Theatre), Something's Afoot, Let Me Hear You Whisper, Mother Goose Rock 'n' Rhyme, Parallax Garden. *Mini-series:* The Great War.

STAPLETON, MAUREEN
Actress. b. Troy, NY, June 21, 1925. e. Siena Col. Worked as a model and waitress while studying acting with Herbert Berghof in NY. Became member of Actors Studio. Broadway debut, 1946, in The Playboy of the Western World. *Autobiography:* A Hell of a Life (1995).
THEATRE: *NY:* Antony and Cleopatra, Detective Story, The Bird Cage, The Rose Tattoo (Tony Award, 1951), The Emperor's Clothes, The Crucible, Richard III, The Seagull, 27 Wagons Full of Cotton, Orpheus Descending, The Cold Wind and the Warm, Toys in the Attic, The Glass Menagerie (1965 & 1975), Plaza Suite, Norman Is That You?, The Gingerbread Lady (Tony Award, 1971), The Country Girl, The Secret Affairs of Mildred Wild, The Gin Game, The Little Foxes. *LA:* Juno and the Paycock.
PICTURES: Lonelyhearts (debut, 1958; Acad. Award nom.), The Fugitive Kind, A View From the Bridge, Bye Bye Birdie, Airport (Acad. Award nom.), Plaza Suite, Interiors (Acad. Award nom.), Lost and Found, The Runner Stumbles, The Fan, On the Right Track, Reds (Acad. Award, best supporting actress, 1981), Johnny Dangerously, The Cosmic Eye (voice), Cocoon, The Money Pit, Heartburn, Sweet Lorraine, Made in Heaven, Nuts, Doin' Time on Planet Earth (cameo), Cocoon: The Return, Passed Away, Trading Mom, The Last Good Time, Addicted to Love, Wilbur Falls.
TELEVISION: *Series:* What Happened? (panelist, 1952), The Thorns. *Specials:* For Whom the Bell Tolls, Among the Paths to Eden (Emmy Award, 1968).*Movies:* Tell Me Where It Hurts, Queen of the Stardust Ballroom, Cat on a Hot Tin Roof, The Gathering, Letters From Frank, The Gathering Part II, The Electric Grandmother, Little Gloria--Happy at Last, Family Secrets, Sentimental Journey, Private Sessions, Liberace: Behind the Music, Last Wish, Miss Rose White.

STARGER, MARTIN
Producer, Executive. b. New York, NY, May 8, 1932. e. CCNY. Served in U.S. Army Signal Corp., where prod. training films. Joined BBDO, starting in TV prod. dept.; later made v.p. & assoc. dir. of TV. Joined ABC in 1966, as v.p. of programs, ABC-TV, East Coast. 1968, promoted to v.p. and natl prog. dir; 1969 named v.p. in chg. progr.; named pres., ABC Entertainment, 1972; 1975 formed & became pres. of Marstar Productions Inc., M.P. & TV prod. co.; 1978 formed Marble Arch Productions, of which he was pres. Formed Rule/Starger Co. with Elton Rule, 1988.
PICTURES: *Exec. prod./Producer*: Nashville, The Domino Principle, Movie/Movie, The Muppet Movie, Raise the Titanic, Saturn 3, The Great Muppet Caper, Hard Country, The Legend of the Lone Ranger, On Golden Pond, Sophie's Choice, Barbarosa, Mask.
TELEVISION: Friendly Fire (Emmy Award, 1979), Escape from Sobibor, Consenting Adult, Earth Star Voyager, Marcus Welby M.D., A Holiday Affair, The Return of Marcus Welby M.D., The Elephant Man, All Quiet on the Western Front, Love Letters, Escape from Sobibor.

STARK, RAY
Producer. b. Oct. 3, 1914. e. Rutgers U. Began career after WWII as agent handling Red Ryder radio scripts, and later literary works for such writers as Costain, Marquand and Hecht. Publicity writer, Warner Bros. Joined Famous Artists Agency, where he represented such personalities as Marilyn Monroe, Kirk Douglas and Richard Burton; in 1957, resigned exec. position to form Seven Arts Prods. with Eliot Hyman, serving as exec. v.p. and head of production until 1966, when he left to take on personal production projects. Founded Rastar Prods. and Ray Stark Prods. Received Irving Thalberg Award from Acad. of M.P. Arts and Sciences 1980. TV production: Barbarians at the Gate (Emmy Award).
PICTURES: The World of Susie Wong, The Night of the Iguana, This Property Is Condemned, Oh Dad Poor Dad Mama's Hung You in the Closet and I'm Feeling So Sad, Reflections in a Golden Eye, Funny Girl, The Owl and the Pussycat, Fat City, The Way We Were, Summer Wishes Winter Dreams, For Pete's Sake, Funny Lady, The Sunshine Boys, Robin and Marian, Murder by Death, The Goodbye Girl, Casey's Shadow, The Cheap Detective, California Suite, The Electric Horseman, Chapter Two, Seems Like Old Times, Annie, The Slugger's Wife, Nothing in Common, Brighton Beach Memoirs, Biloxi Blues, Steel Magnolias, Revenge, Lost in Yonkers, Harriet the Spy, To Gillian on Her 37th Birthday, Random Hearts, The Night of the Iguana.

STARR, MIKE
Actor. b. Queens, N.Y, July 29, 1950. e. Hofstra Univ. Theatre debut with Manhattan Punchline.
THEATRE: NY: Requiem for a Heavyweight, The Guys in the Truck, Map of the World, Vesper's Ever.
PICTURES: Bushido Blade, Cruising, The Natural, The Last Dragon, Cat's Eye, The Money Pit, Violets Are Blue, Off-Beat, Collision Course, Five Corners, Funny Farm, Lean on Me, Blue Steel, Uncle Buck, Last Exit to Brooklyn, Miller's Crossing, GoodFellas, Billy Bathgate, Freejack, The Bodyguard, Mac, Mad Dog and Glory, Son of the Pink Panther, Cabin Boy, On Deadly Ground, The Hudsucker Proxy, Blown Away, Baby's Day Out, Trial by Jury, Ed Wood, Radioland Murders, Dumb & Dumber, A Pyromaniac's Love Story, Clockers, Two If By Sea, James & the Giant Peach, Blood & Wine, Hoodlum, The Deli, Frogs for Snakes, The Adventures of Ragtime, Summer of Sam, Gloria, The taxman, New Jersey Turnpikes, The Cactus, 3 A.M., Tempted, The Next Big Thing, Backflash, Anne B. Real, Jersey Girl.
TELEVISION: *Series*: Hardball. *Mini-series*: The Last Don, Ed. *Movies*: The Frank Nitti Story, Hot Paint, Stone Pillow, Path to Paradise, Murder in a Small Town, The lady in Question. *Guest*: Kojak, Hawk, The Equalizer, Crime Story, Spenser: For Hire.

STARR, RINGO
O.B.E. Singer, Musician, Songwriter, Actor. r.n. Richard Starkey. b. Liverpool, England, July 7, 1940. m. actress Barbara Bach. Former member of The Beatles.
PICTURES: A Hard Day's Night (debut, 1964), Help!, Yellow Submarine (cameo), Candy, The Magic Christian, Let It Be, 200 Motels, Blindman, The Concert for Bangladesh, Lisztomania, The Last Waltz, Sextette, The Kids Are Alright, Caveman, Give My Regards to Broad Street, Water (cameo), Walking After Midnight, Imagine: John Lennon, Secrets, Standing in the Shadows of Motown.
TELEVISION: *Movies*: Princess Daisy, Alice in Wonderland. *Series*: Shining Time Station, Jazz (mini-series).

STEADMAN, ALISON
Actress. b. Liverpool, England, Aug. 26, 1946. m. director Mike Leigh. Studied acting with Good 15 Acting School.
THEATRE: The Prime of Miss Jean Brodie, Hamlet, Wholesome Glory, The Pope's Wedding, The Anchor, The King, Abigail's Party, Joking Apart, Unlce Vanya, The Rise and Fall of Little Voice, Othello, Plotters of Cabbage Patch Corner.
PICTURES: Kipperbang (debut, 1982), Champions, Number One, A Private Function, Clockwise, Stormy Monday, The Misadventures of Mr. Wilt, Shirley Valentine, Life Is Sweet, Blame It on the Bellboy, Secrets & Lies, Topsy Turvy, Happy Now, Bob the Builder: A Christmas to Remember.
TELEVISION: Virtuoso, The Singing Detective, The Finding, Hard Labour, Nuts in May, Throught the Night, Pasmore, Pride & Prejudice, Crapston Villas(series), Karaoke(series), No Bananas(series), The Missing Postman(series), Stressed Eric, Let Them Eat Cake, Fat Friends, Adrian Mole: The Cappuccino Years, Hans Christian Andersen: My Life as a Fairy Tale.

STEELE, BARBARA
Actress. b. Trenton Wirrall, England, Dec. 29, 1937. Studied to be painter prior to joining rep. cos. in 1957.
PICTURES: Bachelor of Hearts (debut, 1958), Sapphire, Your Money or Your Wife, Black Sunday, The Pit and the Pendulum, Revenge of the Mercenaries, The Horrible Dr. Hitchcock, 8 1/2, Danse Macabre (Castle of Blood), The Ghost, The Hours of Love, White Voices, Nightmare Castle, The Maniacs, Terror Creatures From the Grave, The She Beast, Young Torless, Crimson Cult, They Came From Within, Caged Heat, I Never Promised You a Rose Garden, Piranha, Pretty Baby, The Silent Scream, Key is in the Door, Adam Hart I Sahara, Deep Above, Hollywood Rated R, The Prophet.
TELEVISION: *Series*: Dark Shadows, Queer Eye for the Straight Guy, (assoc. prod.). *Mini-Series*: The Winds of War, War and Remembrance, (Singapore Christmans Party, prod.) *Movies*: Honeymoon with a Stranger, Dark Shadows.

STEELE, TOMMY
Performer. r.n. Tommy Hicks. b. London, Dec. 17, 1936. Early career Merchant Navy. 1956 first gained fame as successful pop singer. First TV and film appearances, 1957. Composed and sang title song for The Shiralee.
THEATRE: Half a Sixpence, Hans Andersen, Singin' in the Rain, Some Like It Hot.
PICTURES: Kill Me Tomorrow (debut, 1957), The Tommy Steele Story (Rock Around the World), The Duke Wore Jeans, Tommy the Toreador, Light Up the Sky, It's All Happening (The Dream Maker), The Happiest Millionaire, Half a Sixpence, Finian's Rainbow, Where's Jack?
TELEVISION: Tommy Steele Spectaculars, Richard Whittington Esquire (Rediffusion), Ed Sullivan Show, Gene Kelly in NY NY, Perry Como Show, Twelfth Night, The Tommy Steele Hour, Tommy Steele in Search of Charlie Chaplin, Tommy Steele and a Show, Quincy's Quest.

STEENBURGEN, MARY
Actress. b. Newport, AR, Feb. 8, 1953. m. actor Ted Danson. Graduated from Neighborhood Playhouse. Received honorary doctorate degrees from Univ. of Ark. at Little Rock and Hendrix Col. in Conway, AR. On B'way stage 1993 in Candida.
PICTURES: Goin' South (debut, 1978), Time After Time, Melvin and Howard (Acad. Award, best supporting actress, 1980), Ragtime, A Midsummer Night's Sex Comedy, Cross Creek, Romantic Comedy, One Magic Christmas, Dead of Winter, End of the Line (also exec. prod.), The Whales of August, Miss Firecracker, Parenthood, Back to the Future Part III, The Long Walk Home (narrator), The Butcher's Wife, What's Eating Gilbert Grape, Philadelphia, Clifford, It Runs in the Family (My Summer Story), Pontiac Moon, My Family/Mi Familia, Powder, The Grass Harp, Nixon, Wish You Were Dead, Nobody's Baby, The Trumpet of the Swan, Life as a House, I am Sam, Sunshine State, Hope Springs, Casa de los Babys.
TELEVISION: *Series*: Ink (also co-exec. prod.), Back to the Future (voice). *Mini-Series*: Tender Is the Night. *Specials*: Faerie Tale Theatre (Little Red Riding Hood), The Gift. *Movie*: The Attic: The Hiding of Anne Frank, Gulliver's Travels, About Sarah. Noah's Ark, Picnic, Living With the Dead, Surviving Love.

STEINBERG, DAVID
Actor, Writer, Director. b. Winnipeg, Canada, Aug. 9, 1942. e. U. of Chicago; Hebrew Theological Coll. Member Second City troupe; comedian at comedy clubs: Mr. Kelly's Hungry i, Bitter End. Starred in London and B'way stage prods. B'way includes Little Murders, Carry Me Back to Morningside Heights.
PICTURES: *Actor*: The Lost Man, The End, Something Short of Paradise, The Best of the Big Laff Off, The Tommy Chong Roast. *Director*: Paternity, Going Berserk (also co.-s.p.), Cats Don't Dance (exec. prod. only), The Wrong Guy, Kids in the Hall: Brain Candy (exec. prod. only), All Dogs Go to Heaven, (writer, story), My Giant.
TELEVISION: *Series*: Music Scene (writer, co-host), Tonight Show (guest host), David Steinberg Show, Curb Your Enthusiasm, Even Stevens, The Parent 'Hood. *Director*: Newhart, The Popcorn Kid, Golden Girls, It's Garry Shandling's Show, One Big Family, Faerie Tale Theatre, Richard Belzer Special, Baby on Board, Annie McGuire, Seinfeld, Evening Shade, Get a Life, Mad About You, Evening Shade, Designing Women, Friends, Good Grief, and many commercials. *Movies*: Women of the Night 3, (exec. prod.), Switching Goals, (dir.), Robin Williams: Live on Broadway, (dir.).

STEINMAN, MONTE
Executive. b. New York, NY, May 18, 1955. e. Wharton Sch. of Univ. of PA. Joined Paramount Pictures 1980 as sr. financial analyst. Series of promotions followed, culminating in appt. as

dir. of financial planning of Gulf & Western's Entertainment and Communications Group. 1984. 1985, named exec. dir., financial planning. 1990, joined Viacom Intl., as mgr. financial planning. 1993, dir. financial planning, MTV Networks. 1994, v.p. finance at MTV Networks.

STEMBLER, JOHN H.
Executive. b. Miami, FL, Feb. 18, 1913. e. U. of FL Law Sch., 1937. Asst. U.S. att., South. dist. of FL, 1941; U.S. Air Force, 1941-45; pres. Georgia Theatre Co., 1957; named chmn., 1983; NATO member exec. comm. and past pres.; Major Gen. USAF (Ret); past bd. chmn., National Bank of Georgia.

STEMBLER, WILLIAM J.
Executive. b. Atlanta, GA, Nov. 29, 1946. e. Westminster Sch., 1964; U. of FL, 1968; U. of GA Law Sch., 1971. 1st. lt. U.S. Army, 1971; capt., U.S. Army Reserve; resigned 1976. Enforcement atty., SEC, Atlanta office, 1972-73; joined Georgia Theatre Co., 1973; pres. 1983-86; joined United Artists Communications, Inc., 1986, as v.p.; Incorporated Value Cinemas 1988 and Georgia Theatre Co. II in 1991 as its chmn. & pres. Bd. of dir., & vice chmn., NATO; member, NATO OF GA & past-pres., 1983-85; Rotary Club of Atlanta, pres. 1991-92.

STERLING, JAN
Actress. r.n. Jane Sterling Adriance. b. New Yor, NY, April 3, 1923. e. private tutors; Fay Compton Sch. of Dramatic Art, London. N.Y. stage debut: Bachelor Born.
THEATRE: Panama Hattie, Present Laughter, John Loves Mary, Two Blind Mice, Front Page, Over 21, Born Yesterday, The November People.
PICTURES: Johnny Belinda (debut, 1948), Appointment with Danger, Mystery Street, Caged, Union Station, The Skipper Surprised His Wife, The Big Carnival (Ace in the Hole), The Mating Season, Rhubarb, Flesh and Fury, Sky Full of Moon, Pony Express, The Vanquished, Split Second, Alaska Seas, The High and the Mighty (Acad. Award nom.), Return From the Sea, Human Jungle, Women's Prison, Female on the Beach, Man with the Gun, 1984, The Harder They Fall, Slaughter on Tenth Avenue, Kathy O', The Female Animal, High School Confidential, Love in a Goldfish Bowl, The Incident, The Angry Breed, The Minx, First Monday in October.
TELEVISION: Series: You're in the Picture (panelist, 1961), Made in America, The Guiding Light (1969-70). Mini-Series: Backstairs at the White House. Movies: Having Babies, Dangerous Company, My Kidnapper My Love.

STERLING, ROBERT
Actor. r.n. William Sterling Hart. b. Newcastle, PA, Nov. 13, 1917. e. U. of Pittsburgh. m. Anne Jeffreys, actress. Daughter is actress Tisha Sterling. Fountain pen salesman, day laborer, clerk, industrial branch credit mgr., clothing salesman on West Coast; served as pilot-instructor U.S. Army Corps. 3 yrs.
PICTURES: The Amazing Mr. Williams (debut, 1939), Blondie Brings Up Baby, Blondie Meets the Boss, Only Angels Have Wings, Manhattan Heartbeat, Yesterday's Heroes, Gay Caballero, Penalty, I'll Wait for You, Get-Away, Ringside Maisie, Two-Faced Woman, Dr. Kildare's Victory, Johnny Eager, This Time for Keeps, Somewhere I'll Find You, Secret Heart, Roughshod, Bunco Squad, Sundowners, Show Boat, Column South, Voyage to the Bottom of the Sea, Return to Peyton Place, A Global Affair.
TELEVISION: Series: Topper, Love That Jill, Ichabod and Me. Movies: Letters from Three Lovers, Beggarman, Thief.

STERN, DANIEL
Actor, Director. b. Bethesda, MD, Aug. 28, 1957. e. H.B. Studios. Appeared in 1984 short film Frankenweenie.
PICTURES: Breaking Away (debut, 1979), Starting Over, A Small Circle of Friends, Stardust Memories, It's My Turn, One- Trick Pony, Honky Tonk Freeway, I'm Dancing As Fast As I Can, Diner, Blue Thunder, Get Crazy, C.H.U.D., Key Exchange, The Boss' Wife, Hannah and Her Sisters, Born in East L.A., D.O.A., The Milagro Beanfield War, Leviathan, Little Monsters, Friends Lovers and Lunatics, Coupe de Ville, My Blue Heaven, Home Alone, City Slickers, Home Alone 2: Lost in New York, Rookie of the Year (also dir.), City Slickers II: The Legend of Curly's Gold, Bushwhacked (also exec. prod.), Celtic Pride, Very Bad Things, Viva Las Nowhere.
TELEVISION: Movies: Samson and Delilah, Weekend War, The Court-Martial of Jackie Robinson, Big Guns Talk: The Story of the Western. Series: Hometown, The Wonder Years (narrator; also episode dir.), Dilbert (voice), Danny. Guest: The Simpsons (voice).

STERN, EDDIE
Film buyer.
b. New York, NY, Jan. 13, 1917. e. Columbia Sch. of Journalism. Head film buyer and booker, specializing in art theatres, for Rugoff and Becker, NY; Captain, USAF; joined Wometco Ent. in 1952 as asst. to film buyer; v.p. motion picture theatre film buying and booking, Wometco Enterprises, Inc. Retired from Wometco 1985. 1985-96, film buying and booking, Theatres of Nassau, Ltd. Retired in 1996.

STERN, STEWART
Writer. b. New York, NY, March 22, 1922. e. Ethical Culture Sch., 1927-40; U. of Iowa, 1940-43. Rifle Squad Leader, S/Sgt. 106th Inf. Div., 1943-45; actor, asst. stage mgr., The French Touch, B'way, 1945-46; dialogue dir. Eagle-Lion Studios, 1946-48. 1948 to date: screenwriter.
TELEVISION: Crip, And Crown Thy Good, Thunder of Silence, Heart of Darkness, A Christmas to Remember, Sybil (Emmy Award, 1977), Rita Hayworth: The Love Goddess.
PICTURES: Teresa, Rebel Without a Cause, The Rack, The James Dean Story, The Outsider, The Ugly American, Rachel Rachel, The Last Movie, Summer Wishes Winter Dreams, The Celluloid Closet.

STERNHAGEN, FRANCES
Actress. b. Washington, DC, Jan. 13, 1930. e. Vassar Coll., drama dept.; Perry-Mansfield School of Theatre. Studied with Sanford Meisner at Neighborhood Playhouse, NY. Was teacher at Milton Acad. in MA. Acted with Arena Stage, Washington, DC, 1953-54.
THEATRE: Thieves Carnival (off-B'way debut, 1955), The Skin of Our Teeth, The Carefree Tree, The Admirable Bashville, Ulysses in Night Town, Viva Madison Avenue!, Red Eye of Love, Misalliance, Great Day in the Morning, The Right Honorable Gentleman, The Displaced Person, The Cocktail Party, Cock-a-Doodle Dandy, Playboy of the Western World, The Sign in Sidney Brustein's Window, Enemies, The Good Doctor (Tony Award, 1974), Equus, Angel, On Golden Pond, The Father, Grownups, Summer, You Can't Take It With You, Home Front, Driving Miss Daisy, Remembrance, A Perfect Ganesh, The Heiress (Tony Award, 1995), Long Day's Journey Into Night.
PICTURES: Up the Down Staircase (debut, 1967), The Tiger Makes Out, The Hospital, Two People, Fedora, Starting Over, Outland, Independence Day, Romantic Comedy, Bright Lights Big City, See You in the Morning, Communion, Sibling Rivalry, Misery, Doc Hollywood, Raising Cain, Curtain Call, Landfall, The Laramie Project.
TELEVISION: Series: Love of Life, Doctors, Golden Years, Under One Roof, The Road Home, Sex and the City. Movies: Who'll Save Our Children?, Mother and Daughter: The Loving War, Prototype, Follow Your Heart, She Woke Up, Labor of Love: The Arlette Schweitzer Story, Reunion. Guest: Cheers, Tales From the Crypt, Outer Limits, The Con, To Live Again.

STEUER, ROBERT B.
Executive. b. New Orleans, LA, Nov. 18, 1937. e. U. of Illinois, & 1955-57; Tulane U., 1957-59, B.B.A. Booker-Southern D.I. circuit, New Orleans, 1959; assoc., prod., Poor White Trash; 1960; v.p. Cinema Dist. America, 1961; co-prod., Flesh Eaters, Common Law Wife, Flack Black Pussy Cat; partner, gen. mgr., radio station WTVF, Mobile, 1963; dir. special projects, American Intl. Pictures, 1967; so. div. sls. mgr., AIP, 1971; v.p. asst. gen. sls. mgr., AIP, 1974; partner, United Producers Organization, producing Screamers, 1977; v.p., sls., Ely Landau Org., 1979; v.p., gen. sls. mgr., Film Ventures Intl., 1981; exec. v.p. world-wide mktg., 1983; pres., FVI, 1986-89. 1987, exec. v.p. world-wide mktg. Film Ventures Intl; 1987-88 exec. prod. Operation: Take No Prisoners, Most Dangerous Women Alive, Tunnels, Criminal Act, Au Pair; 1989 sales consultant, 20th Century Fox. 1990-93 Prod. rep: When the Whales Came, China Cry, Twogether, Sweet and Short, Taxi to Soweto, Bound and Gagged: A Love Story, Skin Art, Yankee Zulu. 1994-97 formed Robert B. Steuer and Assoc. distribution and sales consult. to ent. industry. U.S. Rep 1997-98 Marche International du Film (Cannes Film Market). 1998-present, partner in Encore Int'l. Group LTD, a comp. of diversified experienced marketing and public relations specialists.

STEVENS, ANDREW
Actor, Director, Writer, Producer. b. Memphis, TN, June 10, 1955. Mother is actress Stella Stevens. e. Antioch U., L.A., B.A. (psychology). L.A. stage includes Journey's End, Mass Appeal, Leader of the Pack, Billy Budd (also prod.), P.S. Your Cat is Dead, Bouncers (L.A. Drama Circle Critics Award). Pres., CEO Royal Oaks Entertainment Intl. Film Distributors.
PICTURES: Actor: Shampoo, Day of the Animals, Massacre at Central High, Las Vegas Lady, Vigilante Force, The Boys in Company C, The Fury, Death Hunt, The Seduction, Ten to Midnight, Scared Stiff, Tusks, Fine Gold, Deadly Innocents, Down the Drain, Eyewitness to Murder, The Ranch, The Terror Within, Blood Chase, Counterforce, The Terror Within II (also dir., s.p.), Red Blooded American Girl, Night Eyes (also s.p., prod.), Munchie, Double Threat, Night Eyes II (also s.p., prod.), Deadly Rivals, Night Eyes III (also s.p., dir.), Body Chemistry III (also prod.), Scorned (also dir.), Illicit Dreams (also dir.), Victim of Desire (prod. only), The Skateboard Kid 2 (also dir.), Body Chemistry 4 (prod. only), Hard Bounty (prod. only), Grid Runners (dir. only), Munchie Strikes Back. Producers: Victim of Desire, Body Chemistry 4, Starhunter, Cyber Zone, Masseuse, Virtual Desire, Alone in the Woods, Invisible Mom, Innocence Betrayed, Illicit Dreams 2, Over the Wire, Terminal Rush, Flash Frame (also dir.), Hijack, Things you can Tell By Just Looking at Her, Animal Factory, The Whole Nine Yards, Mercy, Get Carter, Submerged, Viva Las Nowhere, Thy Neighbor's Wife, Auggie Rose, Ablaze, The Pledge, Green Dragon, The Caveman's Valentine, 3000 Miles to Graceland, Driven, Angel Eyes, Heist, Six, ZigZag, City

By the Sea, Ballistic, Half Past Dead, Final Exam, The Foreigner, The In-Laws.
TELEVISION: *Series*: Oregon Trail, Code Red, Emerald Point N.A.S., Dallas. *Mini-Series*: Hollywood Wives, Once an Eagle. *Movies*: Beggarman Thief, The Rebels, The Bastard, The Last Survivors, The Oregon Trail, Secrets, Topper (also prod.), Women at Westpoint, Code Red, Miracle on Ice, Journey's End, Forbidden Love, Murder in Malibu (Columbo). *Special*: Werewolf of Woodstock. *Guest*: Adam-12, Apple's Way, The Quest, Police Story, Shazam, Hotel, Westside Medical, Murder She Wrote, Love Boat. *Director*: Swamp Thing (3 episodes), Silk Stalkings (2 episodes), General Hospital (3 eps), Walker—Texas Ranger, Marker.

STEVENS, CONNIE
Actress. r.n. Concetta Ann Ingolia. b. Brooklyn, NY, August 8, 1938. e. Sacred Heart Acad., Hollywood Professional Sch. Began career as winner of several talent contests in Hollywood; prof. debut, Hollywood Repertory Theatre's prod. Finian's Rainbow; B'way in Star Spangled Girl (Theatre World Award); recordings include: Kookie Kookie Lend Me Your Comb, 16 Reasons, What Did You Wanna Make Me Cry For, From Me to You, They're Jealous of Me, A Girl Never Knows.
PICTURES: Eighteen and Anxious (debut, 1957), Young and Dangerous, Dragstrip Riot, Rock-a-Bye Baby, The Party Crashers, Parrish, Susan Slade, Palm Springs Weekend, Two on a Guillotine, Never Too Late, Way ... Way Out, The Grissom Gang, The Last Generation, Scorchy, Sgt. Pepper's Lonely Hearts Club Band (cameo), Grease 2, Back to the Beach, Tapeheads, Love Is All There Is, James Dean: Race With Destiny, Returning Mickey Stern. .
TELEVISION: *Movies*: Mister Jerico, Call Her Mom, Playmates, Every Man Needs One, The Sex Symbol, Love's Savage Fury, Scruples, Bring Me the Head of Dobie Gillis, Race with Destiny: The James Dean Story, Becoming Dick. *Series*: Hawaiian Eye, Wendy and Me, Kraft Music Halls Presents The Des O'Connor Show, Starting from Scratch, Titus.

STEVENS, FISHER
Actor. b. Chicago, IL, Nov. 27, 1963. e. NYU. Artistic Director of Naked Angels Theatre Co. in NYC.
THEATRE: *NY*: Torch Song Trilogy (Off-B'way & B'way), Brighton Beach Memoirs, A Perfect Ganesh, Carousel.
PICTURES: The Burning, Baby It's You, The Brother From Another Planet, The Flamingo Kid, My Science Project, Short Circuit, The Boss's Wife, Short Circuit 2, Point of View, Reversal of Fortune, The Marrying Man, Mystery Date, Bob Roberts, Hero, When the Party's Over, Super Mario Bros., Nina Takes a Lover, Only You, Hackers, Cold Fever, Four Days in September, The Pompatus of Love, The Tic Code, The Taxman, Famous, Sam the Man, Prison Song, 3 A.M., Pinero, Undisputed, Just a Kiss, (dir.), Swimf@n, (exec. prod.), Uptown Girls, (prod.)
TELEVISION: *Series*: Key West, Early Edition. *Guest*: Columbo. *Special*: It's Called the Sugar Plum, The Right to Remain Silent, Jenifer, Is it College Yet?. *Movies*: Columbo: Murder, Smoke & Shadows, Jenifer.

STEVENS, GAIL
Casting Director.
PICTURES: High Season, The Lair of the White Worm, The Rachel Papers, Antonia and Jane, Captives, Paprazzo, Trainspotting, Beautiful Thing, The Slab Boys, Swept From the Sea, The Woodlanders, Still Crazy, Bedrooms & Hallways, Mansfield Park, Hold Back the Night, Saving Grace, The Beach, 15 Minutes, (UK), Late Night Shopping, Blow Dry, The Affair of the Necklace, The One and Only, 28 Days Later..., Peter Pan, (UK).
TELEVISION: Living with Dinosaurs, A Woman at War, A Murder of Quality, The Affair, (UK), Oliver's Travels, Deadly Voyage, Truth or Dare, Painted Lady, Touching Evil, Butterfly Collectors, Great Expectations, All the Kings Men, Ella and the Mothers, White Teeth, Best of Both Worlds, Spooks, Goodbye, Mr. Chips, Dinosaur Hunters, Crime and Punishment,

STEVENS, JR., GEORGE
Director, Writer, Producer. b. Los Angeles, CA, April 3, 1932. Son of late director George Stevens. e. Occidental Coll., 1949-53, B.A. 1st Lieut. U.S. Air Force; TV dir., Alfred Hitchcock Presents, Peter Gunn, 1957-61; prod. asst. Giant Productions, 1953-54; prod. asst. Mark VII, Ltd., 1956-57; dir. M.P. Service, U.S. Information Agency 1962-67; chmn., U.S. deleg. to Film Festivals at Cannes (1962, 1964), Venice (1962, 1963), Moscow (1963); Founding director, American Film Institute, 1967-79; co-chmn., American Film Institute, 1979 to present.
PICTURES: The Diary of Anne Frank (assoc. prod.), The Greatest Story Ever Told (assoc. prod.), John F. Kennedy: Years of Lightning Day of Drums (prod.), America at the Movies (prod.), George Stevens: A Filmmaker's Journey (dir., s.p., prod.; 1988 WGA Award for TV broadcast), The Thin Red Line,(exec. prod.)
TELEVISION: *Specials*: American Film Institute's Salutes (exec. prod./writer, 1973-; received 1975 Emmy Award as exec. prod. of The American Film Institue Salute to James Cagney), The Stars Salute America's Greatest Movies (exec. prod.), The Kennedy Center Honors (prod./writer, 1978-; Emmy Awards: 1984, 1986, 1989, 1996), America Entertains Vice Premier Deng (prod./writer), Christmas in Washington, (exec. prod./writer, 1982-), Star Trek: 30 Years and Beyond , *Movies:* The Murder of Mary Phagan (co-writer, prod.; 1988; Emmy Award for prod.; also Christopher & Peabody Awards), Separate But Equal (dir., writer, co-exec. prod.; Emmy Award for exec. prod.; also Christopher Award, Ohio State Award, Paul Selvin Award by the Writers Guild of America), George Stevens: D-Day to Berlin, The Kennedy Center Honors (co. prod., co-writer; Emmy Award, 1996).

STEVENS, STELLA
Actress, Director. r.n. Estelle Eggleston. b. Yazoo City, MS, Oct. 1, 1938. Mother of actor Andrew Stevens. e. Attended Memphis State U. Modeled in Memphis when she was discovered by talent scouts. Was briefly a term contract actress at 20th Century-Fox, later under exclusive contract to Paramount, then Columbia. *Director*: The American Heroine (feature length doc.), The Ranch (feature comedy). Creator/owner of Sexy Fragrances.
PICTURES: Say One For Me (debut, 1959), The Blue Angel, Li'l Abner, Man Trap, Girls! Girls! Girls!, Too Late Blues, The Nutty Professor, The Courtship of Eddie's Father, Advance to the Rear, Synanon, The Secret of My Success, The Silencers, Rage, Where Angels Go Trouble Follows, How to Save a Marriage and Ruin Your Life, Sol Madrid, The Mad Room, The Ballad of Cable Hogue, A Town Called Hell, Slaughter, Stand Up & Be Counted, The Poseidon Adventure, Arnold, Cleopatra Jones and the Casino of Gold, Las Vegas Lady, Nickelodeon, The Manitou, Wacko, Chained Heat, The Longshot, Monster in the Closet, Down the Drain, Last Call, The Terror Within II, Eye of the Stranger, The Guest, Exiled in America, The Nutty Nut, Hard Drive, Molly & Gina, Body Chemistry 3: Point of Seduction, Illicit Dreams, The Granny, Virtual Combat, Bikini Hotel, Size Em Up, The Long Ride Home, Jim Brown- All American.
TELEVISION: *Series*: Ben Casey, Flamingo Road, Santa Barbara, General Hospital. *Guest*: Bob Hope Bing Crosby Special, Frontier Circus, Johnny Ringo, Alfred Hitchcock, Love Boat, Highway to Heaven, Murder She Wrote, Martin Mull's White America, A Table at Ciros, In the Heat of the Night, Hotel, Night Court, Newhart, Dangerous Curves, The Commish, Burke's Law. *Movies*: In Broad Daylight, In Cold Blood, Climb an Angry Mountain, Linda, The Day The Earth Moved, Honky Tonk, New Original Wonder Woman (pilot), Kiss Me Kill Me, Wanted: The Sundance Woman, Charlie Cobb (pilot), The Night They Took Miss Beautiful, Murder in Peyton Place, The Jordan Chance, Cruise into Terror, New Love Boat (pilot), Friendship Secrets and Lies, Hart to Hart (pilot), The French Atlantic Affair, The Pendragon Affair (Eddie Capra Mystery pilot), Make Me an Offer, Children of Divorce, Twirl, Amazons, Women of San Quentin, No Man's Land, A Masterpiece of Murder, Fatal Confessions (Father Dowling pilot), Power, Passion and Murder, Adventures Beyond Belief, Man Against The Mob, In Cold Blood, Jake Spanner: Private Eye, Attack of the 5 Ft. 2 Women. *Special*: Attack of the 5'2" Woman, The Christmas List, Reunion in Hazzard, In Cold Blood, Subliminal Seduction, By Dawn's Early Light.

STEVENSON, CYNTHIA
Actress. b. Oakland, CA, Aug. 2, 1962. Raised in Washington, Vancouver.
THEATRE: Ladies Room.
PICTURES: The Player, The Gun in Betty Lou's Handbag, Watch It, Forget Paris, Home for the Holidays, Live Nude Girls, Happiness, Air Bud: Golden Receiver, Air Bud: Seventh Inning Sretch, Agent Cody Banks, Agent Cody Banks 2.
TELEVISION: *Series*: My Talk Show, Bob, Hope and Gloria, Oh Baby. *Movie*: Double Your Pleasure, From the Earth to the Moon. *Guest*: Empty Nest, Cheers, Dream On.

STEVENSON, JULIET
Actress. b. England, Oct. 30, 1956. e. RADA.
THEATRE: Other Worlds, Measure for Measure, Breaking the Silence, Troilus and Cressida, As You Like It, Les Liaisons Dangereuses, Yerma, Hedda Gabler, On the Verge, Burn This, Death and the Maiden, Scenes From an Execution (LA), The Duchess of Malfi.
PICTURES: Drowning by Numbers (debut, 1988), Ladder of Swords, Truly Madly Deeply, The Trial, The Secret Rapture, Emma, Play, The Search for John Gissing, Food of Love, Bend it Like Beckham, The One and Only, Nicholas Nickleby, Mona Lisa Smile
TELEVISION: The Mallens (TV debut), *Movies*: Pericles, Prince of Tyre, Maybury, Bazaar and Rummage, Life Story, Stanley, Out of Love, Antigone, Oedipus at Colonus, Amy, The March, A Doll's House, The Politician's Wife, Stone Scissors Paper, Cider with Rosie, Trial by Fire, The Road from Coorain, The Pact, Hear the Silence.

STEVENSON, PARKER
Actor. b. Philadelphia, PA, June 4, 1952. e. Princeton U. m. actress Kirstie Alley. Began professional acting career by starring in film, A Separate Peace, while high school senior, having attracted attention through work on TV commercials.
PICTURES: A Separate Peace (debut, 1972), Our Time, Lifeguard, Stroker Ace, Stitches, Official Denial, Rough Ridin Justice, Probe, Not of this Earth.
TELEVISION: Series: Hardy Boys Mysteries, Falcon Crest, Probe, Baywatch, Melrose Place. Guest: The Streets of San Francisco, Gunsmoke. Mini-Series: North & South Book II, All the Rivers Run. Movies: This House Possessed, Shooting Stars, That Secret Sunday, Baywatch: Panic at Malibu Pier, The Cover Girl and the Cop, Are You Lonesome Tonight?, Nighttide, Shadow of a Stranger, Official Denial, Avalon: Beyond the Abyss, Trapped, Legion, Terror Peak.

STEWART, DOUGLAS DAY
Writer, Director.
PICTURES: Writer: The Blue Lagoon, An Officer and a Gentleman, The Scarlet Letter. Director-Writer: Thief of Hearts, Listen to Me, The Visionary (dir. only).
TELEVISION: Writer: Boy in the Plastic Bubble, The Man Who Could Talk to Kids, Murder or Mercy, Silver Strand.

STEWART, JAMES L.
Executive. e. U. of Southern California, B.A. in cinema-TV and M.B.A. in finance. Worked for two years in sales for CBS Radio Network-West Coast. Spent four years with MGM in promotion and marketing. With Walt Disney Prods. for 12 years, functioning in marketing, management and administrative activities; named v.p.-corp. relations & admin. asst. to pres. 1978 joined in formation of Aurora Pictures, as exec. v.p., secty., & COO.
PICTURES: Exec. prod.: Why Would I Lie?, The Secret of NIMH, Eddie and the Cruisers, Heart Like a Wheel, East of the Sun, West of the Moon, Maxie.

STEWART, MARILYN
Marketing & Public Relations Executive. b. New York, NY. e. Hunter Coll. Entered ind. as scty. then asst. to MGM dir. of adv. Left to become prom.-pub. dir. for Verve/Folkways Records; duties also included ar and talent scouting. In 1966 joined 20th-Fox as radio/tv pub. coordinator. In 1969 went to Para. Pictures as mag. pub. coordinator; 1970 named worldwide dir. of pub. for Para., including creation of overall mkt. concepts, becoming 1st woman to be appt. to that position at major co. Campaigns included Love Story and The Godfather. 1972 opened own consulting office specializing in m.p. marketing and p.r. Headquarters in NY; repr. in L.A. Has represented The Lords of Flatbush, Bang the Drum Slowly, The Kids Are Alright, Autumn Sonata, The Tin Drum, A Cry in the Dark, The Russia House, Filmex, Michael Moriarty, Arthur Hiller, John Shea, Fred Schepisi, Volker Schlondorff, Hemdale Pictures, Lucasfilm.

STEWART, PATRICK
Actor. b. Mirfield, England, July 13, 1940. Trained at Bristol Old Vic Theatre School. Made professional stage debut 1959 in Treasure Island with Lincoln Rep. Co. at the Theatre Royal in Lincoln.
THEATRE: NY: A Midsummer Night's Dream, A Christmas Carol, The Tempest. Numerous London theatre credits incl.: The Investigation, Henry V, The Caretaker, Body and Soul, Who's Afraid of Virginia Woolf?, Yonadab. Associate artist with Royal Shakespeare Co. since 1967; many appearances with them incl. Antony and Cleopatra for which he received the Olivier Award for Best Supporting Actor in 1979.
PICTURES: Hennessey, Hedda, Excalibur, The Plague Dogs (voice), Races, Dune, Lifeforce, Code Name: Emerald, Wild Geese II, The Doctor and the Devils, Lady Jane, L.A. Story, Robin Hood: Men in Tights, Gunmen, Star Trek: Generations, The Pagemaster (voice), Liberation (narrator), Jeffrey, Star Trek: First Contact, Conspiracy Theory, Masterminds, The Prince of Egypt (voice), Dad Savage, Star Trek: Insurrection, Safe House, X-Men, Jimmy Neutron: Boy Genius, X-Men 2, Star Trek X, X2, The Water Warriors.
TELEVISION: Series: Eleventh Hour (BBC), Maybury (BBC), Star Trek: The Next Generation (U.S.). Mini-Series: I Claudius, Smiley's People. Movies: Little Lord Fauntleroy, Pope John Paul II, Death Train, Moby Dick, Animal Farm (voice), King of Texas, The Lion in Winter. Special: In Search of Dr. Seuss. BBC Specials: Oedipus Rex, Miss Julie, Hamlet, The Devil's Disciple, Fall of Eagles, The Artist's Story, Love Girl and the Innocent, Conrad, A Walk With Destiny, Alfred the Great, The Madness, When the Actors Come, Tolstoy: A Question of Faith, The Anatomist, The Mozart Inquest. Guest: The Simpsons (voice).

STIERS, DAVID OGDEN
Actor. b. Peoria, IL, Oct. 31, 1942. Guest conductor: 50 American orchestras incl. Chicago, San Diego, Dallas, Utah, and Chamber Orchestra of Baltimore. Resident conductor of Yaquina Chamber Orchestra in Oregon.
THEATRE: NY: The Magic Show, Ulysses in Nighttown, The Three Sisters, Beggar's Opera, Measure for Measure.
PICTURES: Drive He Said, THX 1138, Oh God!, The Cheap Detective, Magic, Harry's War, The Man With One Red Shoe,

Better Off Dead, Creator, Another Woman, The Accidental Tourist, Doc Hollywood, Beauty and the Beast (voice), Shadows and Fog, Iron Will, Bad Company, Pocahontas (voice), Steal Big Steal Little, Mighty Aphrodite, Meet Wally Sparks, The Hunchback of Notre Dame (voice), Jungle 2 Jungle, Everyone Says I Love You, Krippendorf's Tribe, Toy Story 2 (voice), The Stand In, Tomcats, Atlantis: The Lost Empire (voice), The Curse of the Jade Scorpion, The Majestic, The Assistant, Lilo and Stitch (voice).
TELEVISION: Series: Doc, M*A*S*H, Two Guys and a Girl, Love and Money, Teacher's PetHouse of Mouse (voice). Movies: Charlie's Angels (pilot), A Circle of Children, A Love Affair: The Eleanor and Lou Gehrig Story, Sgt. Matlovich Vs. the U.S. Air Force, Breaking Up is Hard to Do, Damien: The Leper Priest, The Day the Bubble Burst, Anatomy of an Illness, The First Olympics: Athens 1896, The Bad Seed, 5 Perry Mason Movies (Shooting Star, Lost Love, Sinister Spirit, Avenging Ace, Lady in the Lake), Mrs. Delafield Wants to Marry, The Alamo: 13 Days to Glory, The Kissing Place, Final Notice, The Final Days, How to Murder a Millionaire, Wife Mother Murderer, The Last of His Tribe, Without a Kiss Goodbye, To Face Her Past, Murder She Wrote: The Last Free Man. Specials: The Oldest Living Graduate, The Innocents Abroad, Mastergate, Odyssey of Life (voice), The Race For the Superbomb (voice). Mini-Series: North and South (also Book II), MacArthur, Reagan, MacArthur, New York: A Documentary Film (voice), Jazz (voice), The Black River.

STILES, JULIA
Actress. b. New York, NY, March 28, 1981.
PICTURES: I Love You I Love You Not, The Devil's Own, Wicked, Wide Awake, Hamlet, State and Main, Save the Last Dance, 10 Things I Hate About You, Down to You, O, The Bourne Identity, A Guy Thing, Carolina, Mona Lisa Smile.
TELEVISION: Movies: Before Women Had Wings, The '60s. Guest: Ghostwriter, Promised Land, Chicago Hope.

STILES, RYAN
Actor. b. April 22, 1959.
PICTURES: Hot Shots!, Hot Shots! Part Deux, Courting Courtney.
TELEVISION: Series: Whose Line Is It Anyway?, The Drew Carey Show, Whose Line Is It Anyway? (USA, also exec. prod.). Guest: Parker Lewis Can't Lose, The John Larroquette Show, Mad About You, Weird Science, Murphy Brown, Improv All Stars, Rock and Roll Back to School Special.

STILLER, BEN
Actor, Director. b. New York, NY, November 30, 1966. Son of performers Jerry Stiller and Anne Meara. e. UCLA. Made short film parody of The Color of Money, called The Hustler of Money which landed him work on Saturday Night Live. Acting debut in 1985 B'way revival of The House of Blue Leaves.
PICTURES: Hot Pursuit, Empire of the Sun, Fresh Horses, Next of Kin, That's Adequate, Stella, Highway to Hell, Reality Bites (also dir.), Heavyweights, Get Shorty, Flirting With Disaster, The Cable Guy (also dir.), If Lucy Fell, Permanent Midnight, Zero Effect, There's Something About Mary, Your Friends & Neighbors, Mystery Men, Black and White, The Suburbans (also prod.), Meet the Parents, Zoolander (also dir.), The Royal Tenenbaums, You'll Never Wiez in this Town Again, Run Ronnie Run, Duplex, Envy, Starsky & Hutch.
TELEVISION: Series: Saturday Night Live (also writer), The Ben Stiller Show (also creator, dir., writer; Emmy Award as writer). Specials: House of Blue Leaves, Colin Quinn Back in Brooklyn (dir., writer). Movie: Working Trash, Mission Improbable. Guest: Frasier, Friends, Duckman, NewsRadio, The Larry Sanders Show, Mr. Show.

STILLER, JERRY
Actor. b. New York, NY, June 8, 1929. m. actress Anne Meara. Son is actor Ben Stiller, daughter is actress Amy Stiller. With partner Meara gained recognition as comedy team in nightclubs, theatres and on tv, most notably The Ed Sullivan Show. Video with Meara, So You Want to Be An Actor?
THEATRE: B'way: The Ritz, Passione, Hurlyburly, Three Men on a Horse, What's Wrong With This Picture?, The Three Sisters.
PICTURES: The Taking of Pelham One Two Three, Airport 1975, The Ritz, Nasty Habits, Those Lips Those Eyes, Hot Pursuit, Nadine, Hairspray, That's Adequate, Little Vegas, Highway to Hell, The Pickle, Heavyweights, Stag, The Deli, The Suburbans, A Fish in the Bathtub, The Independent, My 5 Wives, Chump Change, Bombshell, Zoolander, On the Line, Serving Sara.
TELEVISION: Movies: Madame X, The Other Woman, Seize the Day, Subway Stories: Tales from the Underground. Series: The Paul Lynde Show, Joe and Sons, Take Five With Stiller and Meara (synd), Tattingers, Seinfeld, The King of Queens. Guest: L.A. Law, In the Heat of the Night, Homicide, Murder She Wrote, Touched By an Angel, The Larry Sanders Show, Hercules (voice), The Eddie Files.

STING
Musician, Actor. r.n. Gordon Matthew Sumner. b. Newcastle-Upon-Tyne, England, Oct. 2, 1951. e. Warwick U. A schoolteacher before helping form rock group, The Police. B'way debut, Threepenny Opera, 1989.
PICTURES: Quadrophenia, Radio On, The Great Rock 'n' Roll Swindle, The Secret Policeman's Other Ball, Brimstone and Treacle, Urgh! A Music War, Dune, The Bride, Plenty, Bring on the Night, Julia and Julia, Stormy Monday, The Adventures of Baron Munchausen, Resident Alien, The Music Tells You, The Grotesque, Lock Stock and Two Smoking Barrels, The Filth and the Fury. Composer: 48 Hrs, Stars and Bars,Four Weddings and a Funeral, The Professional, Leaving Las Vegas, Sabrina, White Squall, The Truth About Cats & Dogs, The Wedding Singer, The Mighty, The X Files, Red Planet, The Emperor's New Groove, Moulin Rouge!, Rush Hour 2, Kate & Leopold.

ST. JOHN, JILL
Actress. r.n. Jill Oppenheim. b. Los Angeles, CA, Aug. 19, 1940. m. actor Robert Wagner. On radio series One Man's family. Television debut, A Christmas Carol, 1948.
PICTURES: Summer Love, The Remarkable Mr. Pennypacker, Holiday for Lovers, The Lost World, The Roman Spring of Mrs. Stone, Tender Is the Night, Come Blow Your Horn, Who's Minding the Store?, Who's Been Sleeping in My Bed?, Honeymoon Hotel, The Liquidator, The Oscar, Banning, Tony Rome, Eight on the Lam, The King's Pirate, Diamonds Are Forever, Sitting Target, The Concrete Jungle, The Act, The Player, Something to Belive In, The Calling, The Trip.
TELEVISION: Series: Emerald Point. Movies: Fame Is the Name of the Game, How I Spent My Summer Vacation, The Spy Killer, Foreign Exchange, Brenda Starr, Telethon, Hart to Hart (pilot), Rooster. Guest: Dupont Theatre, Fireside Theatre, Batman, The Love Boat. Mini-Series: Around the World in 80 Days, Out There.

STOCKWELL, DEAN
Actor. r.n. Robert Dean Stockwell. b. Hollywood, CA, March 5, 1935. p. Harry and Betty Veronica Stockwell. Brother is actor Guy Stockwell. e. Long Island public schools and Martin Milmore, Boston. On stage in Theatre Guild prod. Innocent Voyage. Appeared on radio in Death Valley Days and Dr. Christian. Named in 1949 M.P. Herald-Fame Stars of Tomorrow poll; 1976 retired to Santa Monica as a licensed real estate broker but soon returned to acting.
PICTURES: Anchors Aweigh (debut, 1945), The Valley of Decision, Abbott and Costello in Hollywood, The Green Years, Home Sweet Homicide, The Mighty McGurk, The Arnelo Affair, The Romance of Rosy Ridge, Song of the Thin Man, Gentleman's Agreement, Deep Waters, The Boy With Green Hair, Down to the Sea in Ships, The Secret Garden, The Happy Years, Kim, Stars in My Crown, Kim, Cattle Drive, Gun for a Coward, The Careless Years, Compulsion, Sons and Lovers, Long Day's Journey Into Night, Rapture, Psych-Out, The Dunwich Horror, The Last Movie, The Loners, The Werewolf of Washington, Win Place or Steal (The Big Payoff), Won Ton Ton The Dog Who Saved Hollywood, Stick Fighter (South Pacific Connection), Tracks, She Came to the Valley, Alsino and the Condor, Sandino, Human Highway (also co-dir, s.p.), Wrong Is Right, To Kill a Stranger, Paris Texas, Dune, The Legend of Billie Jean, To Live and Die in L.A., Blue Velvet, Gardens of Stone, Beverly Hills Cop II, Banzai Runner, The Blue Iguana, Tucker: The Man and His Dream, Married to the Mob (Acad. Award nom.), Palais Royale, Limit Up, Buying Time, Time Guardian, The Player, Chasers, Mr. Wrong, Air Force One, McHale's Navy, The Rainmaker, Water Damage, Rites of Passage, Batman Beyond: Return of the Joker, In Pursuit, The Flunky, C.Q., The Quickie, Buffalo Soliders, Inferno, Face to Face.
TELEVISION: Series: Quantum Leap, It's True, The Tony Danza Show, JAG. Guest: Miami Vice, Hart to Hart, Simon and Simon, The A-Team, Wagon Train, Twilight Zone, Playhouse 90, Bonanza, Hallmark Hall of Fame, Hunter, Police Story, Greatest Show on Earth. Movies: Paper Man, The Failing of Raymond, The Adventures of Nick Carter, The Return of Joe Forrester, Three for the Road, A Killing Affair, Born to Be Sold, Sweet Smell of Death (U.K.), The Gambler III: The Legend Continues, Son of the Morning Star, Backtrack, Shame, Fatal Memories, Bonanza: The Return, In the Line of Duty: The Price of Vengeance, Justice in a Small Town, The Innocent, Madonna: Innocence Lost, Deadline for Murder: From the Files of Edna Buchanan, Stephen King's The Langoliers. Pilot: Caught in the Act.

STODDARD, BRANDON
Executive. b. Brideport, CT, March 31, 1937. e. Yale U., BS Amer. Studies, 1958. Columbia Law Sch. Was program ass't. at Batton, Barton, Durstine and Osborn before joining Grey Advertising, 1962, where was successively prog. ops. supvr., dir. daytime prog., VP TV/radio prog. Joined ABC in 1970; named v.p. daytime programs for ABC Entertainment, 1972; v.p. children's programs, 1973. Named v.p., motion pictures for TV, 1974; 1976 named v.p., dramatic progs. and m.p. for TV; 1979, named pres., ABC Motion Pictures; 1985 appt. pres., ABC Entertainment. Resigned 1989 to head ABC Prods. unit to create and prod. series and movies for ABC and other networks. Resigned that position, 1995.

STOLNITZ, ART
Executive. b. Rochester, NY, March 13, 1928. e. U. of Tennessee, LL.B., 1952. U.S. Navy Air Force. Legal dept., William Morris Agency, 1953, dir. business affairs, ZIV, 1959; dir. new program development, ZIV-United Artists, 1960; literary agent, MCA, 1961; dir. business affairs, Selmur Productions, Selmur Pictures, 1963; v.p. ABC Pictures, 1969; v.p. Metromedia Producers Corporation, 1970, executive v.p. Metromedia Producers Corporation; 1975 exec. v.p. and prod. Charles Fries Prods. 1976, prod. Edgar J. Scherick Productions; 1976-77 prod., Grizzly Adams (TV); 1977; v.p. business affairs, Warner Bros.-TV; 1980, sr. v.p., business affairs; 1990, exec. v.p. business & financial affairs, Lorimar; 1993, exec. v.p. business and financial affairs, Warner Bros. TV.

STOLOFF, VICTOR
Producer, Writer, Director, Editor. b. March 17, 1913. e. French Law U. Ac. Fines Arts. Prod. dir. writer of award winning documentaries (Warner Bros. release); Prod. dir. writer first U.S. film made in Italy, When in Rome; contract writer, dir. to Sidney Buchman, Columbia.
PICTURES: Writer: Volcano, The Sinner, Shark Reef, Journey Around the World. Of Love and Desire (also prod.), Intimacy (also prod., dir.), The Washington Affair (prod., dir.), The 300 Year Weekend (also dir.).
TELEVISION: Ford Theatre, Lloyd Bridges series, National Velvet, High Adventure with Lowell Thomas, Prod.: Hawaii Five-O. Created Woman of Russia (dir., writer), Audience (exec. prod., dir.).

STOLTZ, ERIC
Actor. b. Los Angeles, CA, Sept. 30, 1961. Moved to American Samoa at age 3; family returned to California when he was 8. Spent 2 years at U. of Southern California in theatre arts; left to study with Stella Adler and later William Traylor and Peggy Feury.
THEATRE: Off-B'way: The Widow Claire, The American Plan, Down the Road, The Importance of Being Earnest. B'way: Our Town (B'way debut; Theatre World Award, Tony nom. & Drama Desk nom., 1988), Two Shakespearean Actors, Three Sisters. Regional: Tobacco Road, You're a Good Man Charlie Brown, Working (all with an American Rep. Co. in Scotland), Arms and the Man, Glass Menagerie (Williamstown Theater Festival).
PICTURES: Fast Times at Ridgemont High (debut, 1982), Surf II, Running Hot, The Wild Life, The New Kids, Mask, Code Name: Emerald, Some Kind of Wonderful, Lionheart, Sister Sister, Haunted Summer, Manifesto, The Fly II, Say Anything... (cameo), Memphis Belle, The Waterdance, Singles (cameo), Bodies Rest & Motion (also co-prod.), Naked in New York, Killing Zoe, Sleep With Me (also prod.), Pulp Fiction, Little Women, Rob Roy, Fluke, The Prophecy, Kicking and Screaming, Grace of My Heart, 2 Days in the Valley, Inside, Anaconda, Mr. Jealousy (also prod.), The Passion of Ayn Rand, Hi-Life, A Murder of Crows, The House of Mirth, Jesus & Hutch, It's A Shame About Ray, Things Behind the Sun, Harvard Man, Happy Hour, The Rules of Attraction, The Butterfly Effect.
TELEVISION: Movies: The Grass Is Always Greener Over the Septic Tank, The Seekers, The Violation of Sarah McDavid, Paper Dolls, Thursday's Child, A Killer in the Family, Money, The Heart of Justice, Foreign Affairs, Roommates, Keys to Tulsa, Our Guys: Outrage at Glen Ridge, The Lot, Annus Horribilis, War Letters. Specials: Things Are Looking Up, Sensibility and Sense, Our Town. Guest: Mad About You, Homicide. Series: Chicago Hope. Mini-Series: Out of Order.

STONE, AUBREY
Executive. b. Charlotte, NC, Jan. 14, 1964. e. U. of NC-Chapel Hill. Joined Consolidated Theatres Inc. in 1987. Helped to found a new motion picture exhibition company, Consolidated Theatres/The Stone Group, 1990. V.P., Consolidated Theatres/The Stone Group, 1990-95. Assumed role of v.p./general mgr. in 1996. Bd. of dir., NATO of NC & SC, 1991-present; pres., NATO of NC & SC, 1995-96. Bd of dir., National NATO, 1995-present; chmn., Programs & Services Committee, National NATO, present.

STONE, BURTON
Executive. b. Feb. 16, 1928; e. Florida Southern Coll. Was film ed., Hollywood Film Co. 1953-61; serv. mgr., sales mgr. and gen. mgr., Consolidated Film Inds., 1953-61; nat'l sales mgr., Movielab, 1961-63; pres., Allservice Film Laboratories, 1963-64; v.p. Technicolor, Inc., 1964-70. Pres., Precision Film Labs., 1965-76. Pres., Deluxe Laboratories, Inc., a wholly-owned subsidiary of 20th Century Fox, 1976-91. 1991, pres. Deluxe color, a sub of the Rank Org. Member: Board of directors, Will Rogers Foundation and Motion Picture Pioneers; member Acad. of Motion Picture Arts & Sciences, American Society of Cinematographers; awarded fellowship in Society of Motion Picture & Television Engineers; past pres., Association of Cinema & Video Laboratories; awarded fellowship in British Kinematograph, Sound & Television Society.

STONE, DEE WALLACE
Actress. r.n. Deanna Bowers. b. Kansas City, MO, Dec. 14, 1948. m. actor Christopher Stone. e. U. of Kansas, theater and education. Taught high school English. Came to NY to audition for Hal

Prince and spent 2 years working in commercials and industrial shows. First break in Police Story episode.
PICTURES: The Stepford Wives (debut, 1975), The Hills Have Eyes, 10, The Howling, E.T.:. The Extra-Terrestrial, Jimmy the Kid, Cujo, Critters, Secret Admirer, Club Life, Shadow Play, The White Dragon, Alligator II: The Mutation, Popcorn, Rescue Me, The Frighteners, Skeletons, Nevada, Mutual Needs, Black Circle Boys, The Christmas Path, Pirates of the Plain, Deadly Delusions, Killer Instinct, Flamingo Dreams, Artie, Out of the Black, Adjustments, She's No Angel, Land of Canaan, Fish Don't Blink, 18, Virgil, A Month of Sundays.
TELEVISION: Series: Together We Stand, Lassie, High Sierra Search and Rescue, Felicity. Movies: The Sky's No Limit, Young Love First Love, The Secret War of Jackie's Girls, Child Bride of Short Creek, The Five of Me, A Whale for the Killing, Skeezer, Wait Til Your Mother Gets Home, Happy, I Take These Men, Hostage Flight, Sin of Innocence, Addicted to His Love, Stranger on My Land, Terror in the Sky, The Christmas Visitor, I'm Dangerous Tonight, Prophet of Evil: The Ervil LeBaron Story, Witness to the Execution, Search and Rescue, Moment of Truth: Cradle of Conspiracy, Huck and the King of Hearts, Subliminal Seduction, The Perfect Mother, To Love Honor and Betray, Sudden Fear, Paradise, The Magic 7. Guest: CHiPs.

STONE, MARIANNE
Actress. b. London, England, August 23, 1924. Studied Royal Acad. of Dramatic Art, West End debut in The Kingmaker, 1946.
PICTURES: Brighton Rock, Seven Days to Noon, The Clouded Yellow, Wrong Arm of the Law, Heavens Above, Stolen Hours, Nothing But the Best, Curse of the Mummy's Tomb, Hysteria, The Beauty Jungle, A Hard Day's Night, Rattle of a Simple Man, Echo of Diana, Act of Murder, Catch Us If You Can, You Must Be Joking, The Countess from Hong Kong, The Wrong Box, To Sir With Love, The Bliss of Mrs. Blossom, Here We Go Round the Mulberry Bush, Carry on Doctor, The Twisted Nerve, The Best House in London, Oh! What a Lovely War; The Raging Moon, There's a Girl in My Soup, All the Right Noises, Assault, Carry On at Your Convenience, All Coppers Are..., Carry on Girls, Penny Gold, The Vault of Horror, Percy's Progress, Confessions of a Window Cleaner, Carry on Dick, That Lucky Touch, Sarah, Carry on Behind, Confessions from a Holiday Camp, The Chiffy Kids, What's Up Superdoc?; The Class of Miss McMichael, The Human Factor, Dangerous Davies, Funny Money, Terry on the Fence, Carry on Laughing, The Wicked Lady, Deja Vu.
TELEVISION: Maigret, Bootsie and Snudge, Jimmy Edwards Show, Wayne and Schuster Show, Roy Hudd Show, Harry Worth Show, Steptoe and Son, Informer, Love Story, Father Dear Father, Bless This House, The Man Outside, Crown Court, Public Eye, Miss Nightingale, She, Little Lord Fauntleroy, The Secret Army (2 series), Shillingbury Tale, The Bright Side (series), Tickets for the Titanic (series), The Balance of Nature, Always, Hammer House of Mystery & Suspense, The Nineteenth Hole, In Possession.

STONE, OLIVER
Director, Writer. b. New York, NY, Sept. 15, 1946. e. Yale U., NYU, B.F.A., 1971. Teacher in Cholon, Vietnam 1965-66. U.S. Infantry specialist 4th Class. 1967-68 in Vietnam (Purple Heart, Bronze Star with Oak Leaf Cluster honors).
PICTURES: Sugar Cookies (assoc. prod.), Seizure (dir., s.p., co-editor, 1974), Midnight Express (s.p.; Acad. Award, 1978), The Hand (dir., s.p., cameo), Conan the Barbarian (co-s.p.), Scarface (s.p.), Year of the Dragon (co-s.p.), Salvador (dir., co-s.p., co-prod.), 8 Million Ways to Die (co-s.p.), Platoon (dir., s.p., cameo; Acad. Award & DGA Award for Best Director, 1986), Wall Street (dir., co-s.p., cameo), Talk Radio (dir., co-s.p.), Born on the Fourth of July (dir., co-s.p., cameo; Acad. Award & DGA Award for Best Director, 1989), Blue Steel (co-prod.), Reversal of Fortune (co-prod.), The Doors (dir., co-s.p., cameo), Iron Maze (co-exec. prod.), JFK (dir., co-prod., co-s.p.), South Central (co-exec. prod.), Zebrahead (co-exec. prod.), Dave (actor), The Joy Luck Club (co-exec. prod.), Heaven and Earth (dir., co-prod., s.p.), Natural Born Killers (dir., co-prod., co-s.p.), The New Age (exec. prod.), Nixon (dir., co-s.p., co-prod.; Chicago Film Critics Award), Killer: A Journal of Murder (co-exec. prod.), The People vs. Larry Flynt (prod.), Evita, U-Turn, Savior (prod.), Scud: The Disposable Assassin (prod.), Any Given Sunday (dir., prod.), Chains (exec. prod.), The Art of War (prod.), The Corrupter (prod.), Beyond Borders (s.p. only), Alexander (prod.)
TELEVISION: Mini-Series: Wild Palms (co-exec. prod.). Movie: Indictment: The McMartin Trial (co-exec. prod.), Frank Capra's American Dream, The Day Reagan Was Shot.

STONE, PETER
Writer. b. Los Angeles, CA, Feb. 27, 1930. Son of film prod. John Stone and screenwriter Hilda Hess Stone. e. Bard Col., B.A. 1951; Yale U, M.F.A., 1953. Won Mystery Writers of America Award for Charade, Christopher Award for 1776.
THEATRE: Kean, Skyscraper, 1776 (Tony and NY Drama Critics Circle Awards, 1969), Two By Two, Sugar, Full Circle, Woman of the Year (Tony Award, 1981), My One and Only, Will Rogers Follies (Tony, Grammy and NY Drama Critics Circle Awards, 1991), Titanic.
PICTURES: Charade, Father Goose (Acad. Award, 1964), Mirage, Arabesque, The Secret War of Harry Frigg, Jigsaw,

Sweet Charity, Skin Game, The Taking of Pelham One Two Three, 1776, The Silver Bears, Who Is Killing the Great Chefs of Europe?, Why Would I Lie?, Grand Larceny, Just Cause, The Truth About Charlie.
TELEVISION: Movies: Studio One, Brenner, Witness, Asphalt Jungle, The Defenders (Emmy Award, 1962). Androcles and the Lion, Baby on Board, The Taking of Pelham One Two Three. Series: Adam's Rib, Ivan the Terrible.
(d. April 26, 2003).

STONE, SHARON
Actress. b. Meadville, PA, March 10, 1958. e. Edinboro St. Univ. Started as model, appearing in several TV commercials.
PICTURES: Stardust Memories (debut, 1980), Deadly Blessing, Bolero, Irreconcilable Differences, King Soloman's Mines, Allan Quartermain and the Lost City of Gold, Cold Steel, Police Academy 4: Citizens on Patrol, Action Jackson, Above the Law, Blood and Sand, Beyond the Stars (Personal Choice), Total Recall, He Said/She Said, Scissors, Year of the Gun, Basic Instinct, Diary of a Hit Man, Where Sleeping Dogs Lie, Sliver, Last Action Hero (cameo), Intersection, The Specialist, The Quick and the Dead (also co- prod.), Casino (Golden Globe Award), The Last Dance, Diabolique, The Mighty, Sphere, Gloria, Antz (voice), Simpatico, Picking up the Pieces, Gloria, The Muse, Forever Hollywood, Beautiful Joe, CyberWorld, In the Shadow of Hollywood, Searching for Debra Winger, Cold Creek Manor, Catwoman, A Different Loyalty.
TELEVISION: Series: Bay City Blues. Mini-Series: War and Remembrance, Harold and the Purple Crayon (voice). Movies: Not Just Another Affair, The Calendar Girl Murders, The Vegas Strip Wars, Tears in the Rain, If These Walls Could Talk 2, Beyond the Simmit, Who is Alan Smithee. Pilots: Mr. & Mrs. Ryan, Badlands 2005. Guest: T.J. Hooker, Magnum P.I., Roseanne, Big Guns Talk: The Story of the Western.

STOPPARD, TOM
Writer, Director. r.n. Tomas Straussler. b. Zlin, Czechoslovakia, July 3, 1937. Playwright whose works include Rosencrantz and Guildenstern Are Dead, Jumpers, Travesties, The Real Thing, Hapgood, Arcadia.
PICTURES: Writer: The Romantic Englishwoman, Despair, The Human Factor, Squaring the Circle, Brazil, Empire of the Sun, The Russia House, Rosencrantz and Guildenstern Are Dead (also dir.), Billy Bathgate, Fifteen Minute Hamlet, Shakespeare in Love (Acad. Award for orig. s.p.), Enigma, Vatel.
TELEVISION: Movies: Three Men in a Boat, The Dog It Was That Died, Poodle Springs.

STORARO, VITTORIO
Cinematographer. b. Rome, Italy, June 24, 1940. Trained at Rome's Centro Sperimentale Cinematografia and began filming short films. His work as Bernardo Bertolucci's regular cine-matographer won him an international reputation and award-winning work in Europe and America, including 3 Academy Awards.
PICTURES: Giovinezza Giovinezza (Youthful Youthful), The Gallery Murders, The Conformist, The Spider's Stratagem, The Fifth Cord, Malice, 'Tis Pity She's a Whore, Last Tango in Paris, Giordano Bruno, Footprints, The Driver's Seat, 1900, Submission, Agatha, Apocalypse Now (Acad. Award, 1979), La Luna, Reds (Acad. Award, 1981), One From the Heart, Wagner, Ladyhawke, Captain Eo, Ishtar, The Last Emperor (Acad. Award, 1987), Tucker: The Man and His Dream, New York Stories (Life Without Zoe), Dick Tracy, The Sheltering Sky, Tosca, Little Buddha, Roma! Imago Urbis, Flamenco, Taxi, Tango (Canne Film Fest. Award, Tech. Prize, 1998), Bulworth, Goya, Mirka, Picking Up the Pieces. Zapata, Exorcist IV: The Beginning.
TELEVISION: Mini- Series: Dune. Movies: La Traviata à Paris.

STORM, GALE
Actress. r.n. Josephine Cottle. b. Bloomington, TX, April 5, 1922. Won Gateway to Hollywood talent contest while still in high school, in 1939. Also launched successful recording career. Autobiography: I Ain't Down Yet (1981).
PICTURES: Tom Brown's Schooldays (debut, 1939), Smart Alecks, Foreign Agent, Nearly Eighteen, Where Are Your Children?, Revenge of the Zombies, The Right to Live, Sunbonnet Sue, Swing Parade of 1946, It Happened on Fifth Avenue, The Dude Goes West, Stampede, The Kid From Texas, Abandoned, Between Midnight and Dawn, Underworld Story, Curtain Call at Cactus Creek, Al Jennings of Oklahoma, Texas Rangers, Woman of the North Country.
TELEVISION: Series: My Little Margie, The Gale Storm Show.

STOSSEL, JOHN
News Correspondent. b. 1947. e. Princeton U. Started as pro-ducer-reporter with KGW-TV in Portland, OR. Joined WCBS-TV in New York as investigative reporter and consumer editor, winning 15 local Emmy Awards. 1981 joined ABC-TV, appearing on Good Morning America and 20/20 as Correspondent; co-anchor (2003-). Also provides twice-weekly consumer reports on ABC Radio Information Network. Sex, Drugs, and Freedom of Choice (doc.). Author: Shopping Smart (1982).

STOWE, MADELEINE
Actress. b. Los Angeles, CA, Aug. 18, 1958. e. USC. m. actor Brian Benben. Began acting at the Solari Theatre in Beverly Hills where she appeared in The Tenth Man.
PICTURES: Stakeout (debut, 1987), Tropical Snow, Worth Winning, Revenge, The Two Jakes, Closet Land, China Moon, Unlawful Entry, The Last of the Mohicans, Another Stakeout, Short Cuts, Blink, Bad Girls, Twelve Monkeys, The Proposition, Imposter, The General's Daughter, Avenging Angels, We Were Soldiers, Octane.
TELEVISION: Series: The Gangster Chronicles. Movies: The Nativity, The Deerslayer, Amazons, Blood and Orchids. Mini-Series: Beulah Land, The Magnificent Ambersons.

STRATHAIRN, DAVID
Actor. b. San Francisco, CA, Jan. 26, 1949. e. Williams Col.
THEATRE: Einstein and the Polar Bear, Blue Plate Special, Fen, I'm Not Rappaport, Salonika, A Lie of the Mind, The Birthday Party, Danton's Death, Mountain Language, L'Atelier, A Moon for the Misbegotten, Temptation.
PICTURES: Return of the Secaucus 7, Lovesick, Silkwood, Iceman, The Brother from Another Planet, When Nature Calls, Enormous Changes at the Last Minute, At Close Range, Matewan, Stars and Bars, Dominick and Eugene, Call Me, Eight Men Out, The Feud, Memphis Belle, City of Hope, Big Girls Don't Cry... They Get Even, A League of Their Own, Bob Roberts, Sneakers, Passion Fish, Lost in Yonkers, The Firm, A Dangerous Woman, The River Wild, Losing Isaiah, Dolores Claiborne, Mother Night, Home for the Holidays, Song of Hiawatha, L.A. Confidential, The Climb, With Friends Like These, Meschugge, A Good Baby, Simon Birch, Bad Manners, A Midsummer Night's Dream, A Map of the World, Limbo, The Victim, Blue Car, Ball in the house, Speak Easy, Rumor Has It. TELEVISION: Series: The Days and Nights of Molly Dodd, Big Apple. Movies: Day One, Son of the Morning Star, Heat Wave, Judgment, Without Warning: The James Brady Story, O Pioneers!, The American Clock, Beyond the Call, In the Gloaming, Evidence of Blood, Freedom Song, The Miracle Worker, Lathe of Heaven, Master Spy: The Robert Hanssen Story. Guest: Miami Vice, The Equalizer, The Lathe of Heaven.

STRAUSS, PETER
Actor. b. Croton-on-Hudson, NY., Feb. 20, 1947. e. Northwestern U. Spotted at N.U. by talent agent and sent to Hollywood. On stage at Mark Taper Theatre in Dance Next Door, The Dirty Man.
PICTURES: Hail Hero! (debut, 1969), Soldier Blue, The Trial of the Catonsville Nine, The Last Tycoon, Spacehunter: Adventures in the Forbidden Zone, Nick of Time.
TELEVISION: Series: Moloney. Movies: The Man Without a Country, Attack on Terror: The FBI Versus the Ku Klux Klan, Young Joe: The Forgotten Kennedy, The Jericho Mile (Emmy Award, 1979), Angel on My Shoulder, Heart of Steel, Under Siege, A Whale for the Killing, Penalty Phase, Proud Men, Brotherhood of the Rose, Peter Gunn, 83 Hours Till Dawn, Flight of Black Angel, Fugitive Among Us, Trial: The Price of Passion, Men Don't Tell, Thicker Than Blood: The Larry McLinden Story, The Yearling, Reunion, Texas Justice, In the Lake of the Woods, Death in the Shadows, Joan of Arc, A Father's Choice, Murder on the Orient Express. Mini-Series: Rich Man Poor Man, Masada, Kane & Abel, Tender Is The Night, Seasons of Love (also exec. prod.).

STRAUSS, PETER E.
Executive. b. Oct. 7, 1940. e. Oberlin Coll., London Sch. of Economics, Columbia U. Sch. of Law, L.L.B., 1965. Vice pres., University Dormitory Dev. Co., 1965-68; v.p., Allart Cinema 16, 1968-69; v.p. prod., Allied Artists Pictures Corp., 1970; 1978-80, exec. v.p. Rastar Films; left to become independent as pres., Panache Prods., 1980-86. 1987, pres. & CEO of The Movie Group.
PICTURE: Producer: Best of the Best, Cadence, By the Sword, Best of the Best II, Best of the Best III.

STREEP, MERYL
Actress. r.n. Mary Louise Streep. b. Summit, NJ, June 22, 1949. e. Vassar. Acted for a season with traveling theater co. in VT. Awarded scholarship to Yale Drama School, 1972. NY stage debut: Trelawny of the Wells (1975) with New York Shakespeare Fest. Appeared in 1984 documentary In Our Hands.
THEATRE: Off-B'way: 27 Wagons Full of Cotton (Theatre World Award), A Memory of Two Mondays, Secret Service, Henry V. (NY Shakespeare Fest.), Measure for Measure (NYSF), The Cherry Orchard, Happy End (B'way debut, 1977), The Taming of the Shrew (NYSF), Taken in Marriage, Alice in Concert, Isn't It Romantic?
PICTURES: Julia (debut, 1977), The Deer Hunter, Manhattan, The Seduction of Joe Tynan, Kramer vs. Kramer (Acad. Award,

best supporting actress, 1979), The French Lieutenant's Woman, Still of the Night, Sophie's Choice (Acad. Award, 1982), Silkwood, Falling in Love, Plenty, Out of Africa, Heartburn, Ironweed, A Cry in the Dark, She-Devil, Postcards From the Edge, Defending Your Life, Death Becomes Her, The House of the Spirits, The River Wild, The Bridges of Madison County, Before and After, Marvin's Room, One True Thing (Acad. Award nom.), Antz (voice), Dancing at Lughnasa, Music of the Heart, Artificial Intelligence: AI (voice), Clint Eastwood: Out of the Shadows, The Papp Project, The Hours, Adaptation.
TELEVISION: Mini-Series: Holocaust (Emmy Award, 1978). Angels in America. Movies: The Deadliest Season. Specials (PBS): Secret Service, Uncommon Women and Others, Age 7 in America (host), First Do No Harm. Guest: The Simpsons (voice).

STREISAND, BARBRA
Singer, Actress, Director, Producer. b. New York, NY, April 24, 1942. e. Erasmus H.S., Brooklyn. Son is actor Jason Gould. Appeared as singer in NY night clubs. NY stage debut: Another Evening with Harry Stoones (1961), followed by Pins and Needles. On Broadway in I Can Get It For You Wholesale, Funny Girl. Performed song Prisoner for 1978 film Eyes of Laura Mars. Appeared in 1990 documentary Listen Up.
PICTURES: Funny Girl (debut; Acad. Award, 1968), Hello Dolly!, On a Clear Day You Can See Forever, The Owl and the Pussycat, What's Up Doc?, Up the Sandbox, The Way We Were (Acad. Award nom.), For Pete's Sake, Funny Lady, A Star Is Born (also co-composer, exec. prod.; Acad. Award for best song: Evergreen, 1976), The Main Event (also co-prod.), All Night Long, Yentl (also dir., prod., co- s.p.), Nuts (also prod.), co-composer), The Prince of Tides (also dir., co-prod.; Acad. Award nom. for picture), The Mirror Has Two Faces (also dir.).
TELEVISION: Specials: My Name Is Barbra (Emmy Award, 1965), Color Me Barbra, The Belle of 14th Street, A Happening in Central Park, Barbra Streisand... And Other Musical Instruments, Putting It Together, One Voice, Barbra Streisand: The Concert (also co-prod.; 2 Emmy Awards, 1995). Movie: Serving in Silence: The Margarethe Cammermeyer Story (co-exec. prod. only), Rescuers: Stories of Courage: Two Women (exec. prod.), The Long Island Incident (exec. prod.), Rescuers: Stories of Courage: Two Families (exec. prod.), Frankie & Hazel (exec. prod.), What Makes a Family (exec. prod.), Varian's War (exec. prod.), Mame (exec. prod.). Guest: Ed Sullivan, Merv Griffin, Judy Garland Show.

STRICK, WESLEY
Writer. b. New York, NY, Feb. 11, 1954. e. UC at Berkeley, 1975. Was rock critic for magazines Rolling Stone, Cream, Circus.
PICTURES: True Believer, Arachnophobia, Cape Fear, Final Analysis, Batman Returns, Wolf, The Tie That Binds (dir.), The Saint, Return to Paradise, The Glass House, Love is the Drug.
TELEVISION: Series: Eddie Dodd (pilot), Hitched (movie).

STRICKLAND, GAIL
Actress. b. Birmingham, AL, May 18, 1947. e. Florida St. Univ. NY Theatre includes Status Quo Vadis, I Won't Dance.
PICTURES: The Drowning Pool, Bittersweet Love, Bound for Glory, One on One, Who'll Stop the Rain, Norma Rae, Lies, Oxford Blues, Protocol, The Man in the Moon, Three of Hearts, When a Man Loves a Woman, How to Make an American Quilt, The American President, Quality Time.
TELEVISION: Series: The Insiders, What a Country, Heartbeat, First Monday. Movies: Ellery Queen, My Father's House, The Dark Side of Innocence, The Gathering, A Love Affair: The Eleanor and Lou Gehrig Story, The President's Mistress, Ski Lift to Death, Letters from Frank, King Crab, Rape and Marriage: The Rideout Case, A Matter of Life and Death, My Body My Child, Eleanor: First Lady of the World, Life of the Party: The Story of Beatrice, Starlight: The Plane That Couldn't Land, The Burden of Proof, Silent Cries, Spies, Barbara Taylor Bradford's Remember, A Mother's Prayer.

STRINGER, HOWARD
Executive. b. Cardiff, Wales. Feb. 19, 1942. e. Oxford U., B.A., M.A., modern history/international relations. Received Army Commendation Medal for meritorious achievement for service in Vietnam (1965-67). Joined CBS, 1965, at WCBS-TV, NY, rising from assoc. prod., prod. to exec. prod. of documentary broadcasts. Served as prod., dir. and writer of CBS Reports: The Palestinians (Overseas Press Club of America, Writers Guild Awards, 1974); The Rockefellers (Emmy Award, 1973). Won 9 Emmy Awards as exec. prod., prod., writer or dir: CBS Reports: The Boston Goes to China; CBS Reports: The Defense of the United States; CBS Evening News with Dan Rather: The Beirut Bombing; The Countdown Against Cancer; The Black Family. Exec. prod., CBS Reports; exec. prod., CBS Evening News with Dan Rather, 1981-84. Appointed exec. vice pres., CBS News Division, 1984; pres., CBS News, 1986; pres., CBS/Broadcast Group, 1988. Chmn. & CEO, Tele-TV 1995. Pres., Sony Corporation of America. Chmn. & CEO, Sony Corp. of America, appointed vice Chmn., Sony Corporation 2003.

STRITCH, ELAINE
Actress. b. Detroit, MI, Feb. 2, 1926. e. studied acting with Erwin Piscator at the New Sch. for Social Research. Major career on stage. B'way debut 1946 in Loco.
THEATRE: *NY:* Made in Heaven, Angel in the Wings, Call Me Madam, Pal Joey, On Your Toes, Sail Away, Who's Afraid of Virginia Woolf?, Show Boat, A Delicate Balance (Tony Award nom.). *London:* Gingerbread Lady, Small Craft Warnings, Company.
PICTURES: The Scarlet Hour (debut, 1955), Three Violent People, A Farewell to Arms, The Perfect Furlough, Who Killed Teddy Bear?, Sidelong Glances of a Pigeon Kicker, The Spiral Staircase, Providence, September, Cocoon: The Return, Cadillac Man, Out to Sea, Krippendorf's Tribe, Screwed, Small Time Crooks, Autumn in New York.
TELEVISION: *Series:* Growing Paynes (1948), Pantomine Quiz (regular, 1953-55, 1958), My Sister Eileen, The Trials of O'Brien, Two's Company (London), Nobody's Perfect (London; also adapt.) The Ellen Burstyn Show, Egg: The Arts Show. *Specials:* Company: the Making of the Album, Kennedy Center Tonight, Follies in Concert, Sensibility and Sense. Movies: The Secret Life of Archie's Wife, An Inconvenient Woman, Chance of a Lifetime. *Guest:* Law & Order (Emmy Award, 1993).

STROCK, HERBERT L.
Producer, Writer, Director, Film editor. b. Boston, MA, Jan. 13, 1918. e. USC, A.B., M.A. in cinema. Prof. of cinema, USC, 1941. Started career, publicity leg man, Jimmy Fidler, Hollywood columnist; editorial dept., MGM, 1941-47; pres., IMPPRO, Inc., 1955-59; assoc. prod.-supv. film ed., U.A.; director: AIP, Warner Bros. independent, Phoenix Films. Pres., Herbert L. Strock Prods. Lecturer at American Film Institute.
PICTURES: Storm Over Tibet, Magnetic Monster, Riders to the Stars, The Glass Wall. *Director:* Gog, Battle Taxi, Donovan's Brain, Rider on a Dead Horse, Devil's Messenger, Brother on the Run, One Hour of Hell, Witches Brew, Blood of Dracula, I Was a Teenage Frankenstein, The Crawling Hand; Soul Brothers Die Hard, Monstroids. *Writer-film editor*, Hurray for Betty Boop (cartoon). *Sound Effects editor* on Katy Caterpillar (cartoon feature). Editor: Night Screams, Detour. *Post-prod. spvr.:* King Kung Fu, Sidewalk Motel. *Co-director:* Deadly Presence. *Editor:* Snooze You Lose, Gramma's Gold, Distance, Fish Outta Water. *Prod/edit.:* The Visitors, Statistically Speaking.
TELEVISION: Highway Patrol, Harbor Command, Men of Annapolis, I Led Three Lives, The Veil, Dragnet, 77 Sunset Strip, Maverick, Cheyenne, Bronco, Sugarfoot, Colt 45, Science Fiction Thea., Seahunt, Corliss Archer, Bonanza, Hallmark Hall of Fame, The Small Miracle, Hans Brinker, The Inventing of America (specials); What Will We Say to a Hungry World (telethon), They Search for Survival (special), Flipper (series). *Documentaries:* Atlantis, Legends, UFO Journals, UFO Syndrome, Legend of the Lochness Monster, China-Mao to Now, El-Papa—Journey to Tibet. *Editor:* Peace Corps' Partnership in Health. *L.A. Dept. of Water & Power:* Water You Can Trust. Olympic Comm. Your Olympic Legacy—AAF.

STROLLER, LOUIS A.
Producer. b. Brooklyn, NY, April 3, 1942. e. Nicholas Coll. of Business Admin., BBA, 1963. Entered film business in 1963 doing a variety of jobs in local NY studios, and TV commercials. Unit manager on The Producers. Moved to L.A. in 1970s. First asst. dir. Charley, Take the Money and Run, Lovers and Other Strangers, They Might Be Giants, Man on a Swing, 92 in the Shade. Prod. mgr.: Mortadella, Sisters, Sweet Revenge, The Eyes of Laura Mars, Telefon. *Assoc. prod.:* Badlands, Carrie, The Seduction of Joe Tynan.
PICTURES: *Exec. prod. or prod.:* Simon, The Four Seasons, Venom, Eddie Macon's Run, Scarface, Sweet Liberty, Real Men, A New Life, Sea of Love, Betsy's Wedding, Back in the U.S.S.R., The Real McCoy, Carlito's Way, The Shadow, The Rock, Nothing to Lose, Snake Eyes, The Bone Collector, The Adventures of Pluto Nash, Carolina.Lara Croft Tomb Raider: The Cradle of Life.
TELEVISION: Half a Lifetime (exec. prod.; nom. 4 ACE Awards), Blue Ice.

STRONG, JOHN
Producer, Director, Writer, Actor. b. New York, NY, Dec. 3. e. U. of Miami, Cornell U., B.S., architectural engineering. On B'way in Annie Get Your Gun and understudy for James Dean in Immoralist. Appeared in many radio and TV serials, regular on Captain Video and the Video Ranger, later under contract as actor to Universal and Warner Bros. Member, Writers Guild America West, Directors Guild of America, Producers Guild of America, Dramatists Guild. Pres., Cinevent Corp.
PICTURES: Perilous Journey (exec. prod., s.p.), Eddie & the Cruisers (sprv. prod.), Heart Like a Wheel (sprv. prod.), For Your Eyes Only (s.p.), The Earthling (prod.), The Mountain Men (actor, prod.), Savage Streets (prod.), Steel Justice (prod.), Knights of the City (prod.), Garbage Pail Kids (sprv. prod.), Cop (sprv. prod.), Wild Thing (sprv. prod.), Summer Heat (sprv. prod.), Teen Wolf II (sprv. prod.), Atlantic Entertainment (sprv. prod.), Show of Force (prod., s.p.), Prime Directive (prod., s.p.), Sinapore Sling (prod., s.p.), Willie Sutton Story (prod.), Bandit Queen (prod.), Fatal Charm (exec. prod.), Colors of Love (prod.), Black Ice (dir., s.p.).

TELEVISION
TELEVISION: The John Strong Show (host, exec. prod.), The Nurse (special, writer), McCloud (prod., writer), The Thrill of the Fall (prod.), Search (prod., writer, 2nd unit dir.), Outer Limits (exec. chg. prod.), Name of the Game (exec. chg. prod.), I Spy (writer), Love American Style (writer), All in the Family (writer), Changes (prod., dir., writer), Charlie's Angels (writer), Hawaii Five O' (writer).

STROUD, DON
Actor. b. Honolulu, Hawaii, Sept. 1, 1943. e. Kaimuki h.s. Was surfing champion, ranked 4th in the world.
PICTURES: Games, Madigan, Journey to Shiloh, What's So Bad About Feeling Good?, Coogan's Bluff, Bloody Mama, Explosion, Angel Unchained, Tick Tick Tick, Von Richtofen and Brown, Joe Kidd, Slaughter's Big Rip-Off, Scalawag, Murph the Surf, The Killer Inside Me, The House by the Lake, The Choirboys, The Buddy Holly Story, The Amityville Horror, The Night the Lights Went Out in Georgia, Search and Destroy, Sweet Sixteen, Armed and Dangerous, Licence to Kill, Down the Drain, The Divine Enforcer, King of the Kickboxers, Cartel, Mob Boss, Street Wars, Frogtown, Deady Avenger, Danger Sign, Carnosaur II, Of Unknown Origin, Sudden Death, Dillinger and Capone, Twisted Justice, Two to Tango, Ghost Ship, Precious Find, Wild America, Perdita Durango, Little Bigfoot, HauntedSea, Detonator.
TELEVISION: *Series:* Kate Loves a Mystery, Mike Hammer, The New Gidget, Dragnet. *Pilot:* Barefoot in Paradise. *Movies:* Split Second to an Epitaph, Something for a Lonely Man, DA: Conspiracy to Kill, Deadly Dream, Daughters of Joshua Cabe, Rolling Man, The Elevator, Return of Joe Forrester, High Risk, Katie: Portrait of a Centerfold, Out on a Limb, I Want to Live, Manhunters, Murder Me Murder You, The Alien Within, Sawbones, Barefoot in Paradise, Men in White.. *Special:* Hatful of Rain. *Guest:* Murder She Wrote, Quantum Leap, The FBI, Gunsmoke, Baywatch, Starsky and Hutch, The Mod Squad, Marcus Welby, Babylon 5, Walker: Texas Ranger, Nash-Bridges.

STRUTHERS, SALLY
Actress. b. Portland, OR, July 28, 1948. First tv appearance was as dancer on a Herb Alpert special. Appeared on Broadway stage in Wally's Cafe.
PICTURES: The Phynx, Five Easy Pieces, The Getaway, The Others, Out of the Black, A Month of Sundays.
TELEVISION: *Series:* The Summer Smothers (1970), The Tim Conway Comedy Hour, All in the Family (Emmy Awards: 1972, 1979), Pebbles and Bamm-Bamm (voice), Flintstones Comedy Hour (voice), Gloria, 9 to 5, Dinosaurs (voice).. Gilmore Girls, Gneral Hospital. *Movies:* The Great Houdinis, Aloha Means Goodbye, Hey I'm Alive, Intimate Strangers, My Husband is Missing, And Your Name is Jonah, A Gun in the House, A Deadly Silence, In the Best Interest of the Children, New Adventures of Mother Goose.

STUBBS, IMOGEN
Actress. b. Newcastle-upon-Tyne, England, Feb. 2, 1961. Brought up in West London on sailing barge on the Thames. Grandmother was playright Esther McCracken. e. Exeter Coll. First class degree at Oxford U. in English. Joined Oxford U. Dramatic Society appearing in revues and at Edinburgh Festival in play called Poison. Trained for stage at Royal Acad. of Dramatic Art. Prof. stage debut in Cabaret and The Boyfriend, in Ipswich. Acted with Royal Shakespeare Co. in The Two Noble Kinsmen, The Rover (promising newcomer critics award), Richard II, Othello, Heartbreak House, St. Joan, Uncle Vanya.
PICTURES: Privileged, A Summer Story, Nanou, Erik the Viking, True Colors, A Pin for the Butterfly, Sandra C'est la Vie, Jack & Sarah, Sense and Sensibility, Twelfth Night.
TELEVISION: The Browning Version, Deadline, The Rainbow, Fellow Traveller, After the Dance, Relatively Speaking, Othello, Anna Lee, Mother Time, Blind Ambition. Big Kids (series).

STULBERG, GORDON
Executive. b. Toronto, Canada, Dec. 17, 1927. e. U. of Toronto, B.A., Cornell Law Sch., LL.B. Was assoc. & member, Pacht, Ross, Warne & Bernhard; ent. m.p. ind. as exec. asst. to v.p., Columbia Pictures Corp., 1956-60; v.p. & chief studio admin. off., 1960-67; pres. of Cinema Center Films, a division of CBS 1967-71; pres. 20th Century-Fox, 1971-75; 1980, named president & COO, PolyGram Pictures. Member of NY, Calif. bars, Chairman, American Interactive Media (Polygram subsidiary).

SUGAR, LARRY
Executive. b. Phoenix, AZ, May 26, 1945. m. Bonnie Sugar. e. Cheshire Acad., 1962; CSUN, B.A., 1967; U. of Southern Calif., J.D., 1971. Writer and co-author, Calif. Primary Reading Program, 1967-68. Joined Warner Bros. as dir., legal and corp. affairs, 1971-74; 20th Century Fox legal staff, 1974-77; co-owner with Bonnie Sugar, Serendipity Prods., 1977-81; named president, international., Lorimar Prods. 1981-84; executive v.p., distribution, CBS 1984-85; exec. v.p. worldwide distribution, Weintraub Entertainment Group 1987-89; formed Sugar Entertainment, chairman., 1989-1991; president, international, Republic, Pictures, Inc. 1991-93; pres. Larry Sugar Entertainment, 1993-.
PICTURES: *Exec. prod.:* Slapstick, Steel Dawn, Options, Damned River, Fatal Sky, Graveyard Shift, Shattered, Dark

Horse, Family Prayers, The Plague, Boxing Helena. *Prod.*: With Deadly Intent, Annie O, Robin of Locksley, Ronnie & ulie.
TELEVISION: *Movies*: The Prisoner of Zenda Inc., The Halfback of Notre Dame, Dead Man's Gun.

SUGARMAN, BURT
Producer. b. Beverly Hills, CA, Jan. 4. e. U. of Southern California. Chmn. & CEO, GIANT GROUP, LTD., diversified co. traded on NYSE.
PICTURES: Kiss Me Goodbye, Extremities, Children of a Lesser God, Crimes of the Heart.
TELEVISION: Midnight Special, Switched on Symphony, The Mancini Generation, Johnny Mann's Stand Up and Cheer.

SULLIVAN, REV. PATRICK J.
S.J., S.T.D.: Provost, Graduate Center at Tarrytown, Fordham U. b. New York, NY, March 25, 1920. e. Regis H.S.: Georgetown U., A.B., 1943; Woodstock Coll., M.A., 1944; Fordham U., 1945-47; S.T.L. Weston Coll., 1947-51; S.T.D. Gregorian U. (Rome), 1952-54. Prof. of Theology, Woodstock Coll., 1954-57; Consultor, Pontifical Commission for Social Communications, 1968-82; Exec. Dir., U.S. Catholic Conference, Film & Broadcasting Office, 1965-80; Fordham Univ. Graduate School of Business, Assoc. Dean 1982-83, Dean 1983-85.

SUMMERS, GARY
Sound.
PICTURES: Star Wars: Episode IV-A New Hope, Star Wars: Episode V-The Empire Strikes Back, Raiders of the Lost Ark, Star Wars: Episode VI-Return of the Jedi, Indiana Jones and the Temple of Doom, Cocoon, Captain Eo, Howard the Duck, Spaceballs, Always, Indiana Jones and the Last Crusade, Defenseless, The Cross the Rubicon, Rush, The Five Heartbeats, Terminator 2: Judgment Day, F/X2, The Addams Family, House of Cards, Jurassic Park, Miracle on 34th Street, Casper, Toy Story, Special Effects: Anything Can Happen, Titanic (Acad. Award, Best Sound, 1997), The Lost World: Jurassic Park, Stepmom, A Bug's Life, Saving Private Ryan, Stepmom, Lake Placid, The Haunting, Komodo, Toy Story 2, Bicentennial Man, Titus, Frequency, Cirque du Soleil, Legend of Bagger Vance, 102 Dalmatians, The Mexican, Artificial Intelligence, Jurassic Park 3, Monsters Inc., Hart's War, K-19: The Widowmaker, The Lord of the Rings: The Two Towers, Ghosts of the Abyss, Finding Nemo, Lara Croft Tomb Raider: The Cradle of Life.
TELEVISION: *Series*: Fame L.A.

SUNSHINE, ROBERT HOWARD
Publisher. b. Brooklyn, NY, Jan. 17, 1946. e. U. of RI; Brooklyn Law Sch., 1971. Admitted to NY State Bar, 1971. President of Pubsun Corp., owner of Film Journal International (formerly Film Journal). Publisher of Film Journal International. Exec. dir., International Theatre Equipment Association, 1979-present; sec. and exec. dir. Foundation of the Motion Picture Pioneers, 1975-present; exec. dir., Natl. Assoc. of Theatre Owners of NY State, 1985-present; Producer of Variety Telethon, 1985-present; coordinator and producer, Show East Convention; coordinator and prod., Cinema Expo Intl., Amsterdam, Holland; coordinator and producer, CineAsia, Singapore.

SURTEES, BRUCE
Cinematographer. b. Carmel, CA, Aug. 3, 1944. Son of cinematographer Robert L. Surtees.
PICTURES: The Beguiled, Play Misty for Me, Dirty Harry, The Great Northfield Minnesota Raid, Conquest of the Planet of the Apes, Joe Kidd, The Outfit, High Plains Drifter, Blume in Love, Lenny (Acad. Award nom.), Night Moves, Leadbelly, The Outlaw Josey Wales, The Shootist, Three Warriors, Sparkle, Big Wednesday, Movie Movie (segment: Baxter's Beauties of 1933), Dreamer, Escape from Alcatraz, Ladies and Gentlemen the Fabulous Stains, White Dog, Firefox, Inchon, Honkytonk Man, Bad Boys, Risky Business, Sudden Impact, Tightrope, Beverly Hills Cop, Pale Rider, Psycho III, Out of Bounds, Ratboy, Back to the Beach, License to Drive, Men Don't Leave, Run, The Super, The Crush, That Night. Corrina Corrina, The Stars Fell on Henrietta, The Substitute, Isn't It Romantic, Just A Little Harmless Sex Joshua.
TELEVISION: Murder in a Small Town, That Championship Season, Dash and Lilly, That Championship Season, Lethal Vows, The Lady in Question, Thin Air, American Tragedy, Never Let Her Go.

SUSCHITZKY, PETER
Cinematographer. b. Poland, July 25, 1941. Spent long time in Latin America as documentatory cinematographer. Later made commercials in France, England and U.S. First feature was It Happened Here, 1962.
PICTURES: Over 30 features including: A Midsummer Night's Dream, Charlie Bubbles, Leo the Last, Privilege, That'll Be the Day, Lisztomania, The Rocky Horror Picture Show, All Creatures Great and Small (TV in U.S.), Valentino, The Empire Strikes Back, Krull, Falling in Love, In Extremis, Dead Ringers, Where the Heart Is, Naked Lunch, The Public Eye, The Vanishing, M. Butterfly, Immortal Beloved, Crash, Mars Attacks, The Man in the Iron Mask, eXistenZ, Red Planet, Spider.

SUTHERLAND, DONALD
Actor. b. St. John, New Brunswick, Canada, July 17, 1935. Son is actor Kiefer Sutherland. e. U. of Toronto, B.A., 1956. At 14 became a radio announcer and disc jockey. Worked in a mine in Finland. Theatre includes: The Male Animal (debut), The Tempest (Hart House Theatre, U. of Toronto), Two years at London Acad. of Music and Dramatic Art. Spent a year and a half with the Perth Repertory Theatre in Scotland, then repertory at Nottingham, Chesterfield, Bromley and Sheffield.
THEATRE: August for the People (London debut), On a Clear Day You Can See Canterbury, The Shewing Up of Blanco Posnet, The Spoon River Anthology, Lolita (B'way debut, 1981).
PICTURES: Castle of the Living Dead (debut, 1964), The World Ten Times Over, Dr. Terror's House of Horrors, Die Die My Darling (Fanatic), The Bedford Incident, Promise Her Anything, The Dirty Dozen, Billion Dollar Brain, Sebastian, Oedipus the King, Interlude, Joanna, The Split, M*A*S*H, Start the Revolution Without Me, Act of the Heart, Kelly's Heroes, Alex in Wonderland, Little Murders, Klute, Johnny Got His Gun, F.T.A. (also co-prod., co-dir., co-s.p.), Steelyard Blues (also exec. prod.), Lady Ice, Alien Thunder (Dan Candy's Law), Don't Look Now, S*P*Y*S, The Day of the Locust, End of the Game (cameo), Fellini's Casanova, The Eagle Has Landed, 1900, The Disappearance, The Kentucky Fried Movie, National Lampoon's Animal House, Invasion of the Body Snatchers, The Great Train Robbery, Murder by Decree, Bear Island, A Man a Woman and a Bank, Nothing Personal, Ordinary People, Blood Relatives, Gas, Eye of the Needle, Threshold, Max Dugan Returns, Crackers, Ordeal by Innocence, Heaven Help Us, Revolution, Wolf at the Door, The Rosary Murders, The Trouble With Spies, Apprentice to Murder, Lost Angels, Lock Up, A Dry White Season, Eminent Domain, Backdraft, Buster's Bedroom, JFK, Scream of Stone, Buffy the Vampire Slayer, Shadow of the Wolf, Benefit of the Doubt, Dr. Bethune (Bethune: The Making of a Hero), Younger and Younger, Six Degrees of Separation, Robert A. Heinlein's The Puppet Masters, Disclosure, Outbreak, Hollow Point, The Shadow Conspiracy, A Time to Kill, The Assignment, Free Money, Fallen, Without Limits, Virus, Toscano, Instinct, The Setting Sun, The Art of War, Clint Eastwood: Out of the Shadows, .Threads of Hope (narrator), Final Fantasy: The Spirits Within (voice), Big Shot's Funeral, Fellini: Je suis un gran menteur, Baltic Storm, Cold Mountain, The Italian Job.
TELEVISION: *Specials*: (British) Marching to the Sea, The Death of Bessie Smith, Hamlet at Elsinore, Gideon's Way, The Champions, Bethune (Canada), Give Me Your Answer True, The Prize (narrator), People of the Forest: The Chimps of Gombe (narrator). *Guest*: The Saint, The Avengers. *Movies*: The Sunshine Patriot, The Winter of Our Discontent, Quicksand: No Escape, The Railway Station Man, The Lifeforce Experiment, Oldest Living Confederate Widow Tells All, Citizen X (Emmy Award, 1995; Golden Globe Award 1995), Natural Enemy, The Hunley, The Big Heist, Uprising, Salem's Lot, Frankenstein. *Series*: Great Books (narrator). *Mini-Series:* Queen Victoria's Empire (voice), Path to War.

SUTHERLAND, KIEFER
Actor. r.n. William Frederick Dempsey George Sutherland. b. London, England, Dec. 18, 1966. Son of actor Donald Sutherland and actress Shirley Douglas. Moved to Los Angeles at age 4, then to Toronto at 8. Debut with L.A. Odyssey Theater at age 9 in Throne of Straw. Worked in local Toronto theater workshops before landing starring role in The Bay Boy (1984) for which he won Canadian Genie Award.
PICTURES: Max Dugan Returns (debut, 1983), The Bay Boy, At Close Range, Stand By Me, Crazy Moon, The Lost Boys, The Killing Time, Promised Land, Bright Lights Big City, Young Guns, 1969, Renegades, Flashback, Chicago Joe and the Showgirl, Flatliners, Young Guns II, The Nutcracker Prince (voice), Article 99, Twin Peaks: Fire Walk With Me, A Few Good Men, The Vanishing, The Three Musketeers, The Cowboy Way, Teresa's Tattoo, Eye for an Eye, Freeway, A Time To Kill, Truth or Consequences—N.M. (also dir.), Dark City, The Break Up, Woman Wanted, Picking up the Pieces, The Royal Way, Beat, Ring of Fire, The Right Temptation, To End All Wars, The Red Door, Paradise Found, I Fought the Law, Desert Saints, Dead Heat, Behind the Red Door, Phone Booth (caller voice).
TELEVISION: *Movies*: Trapped in Silence, Brotherhood of Justice, Last Light (also dir.), Dark Reflection (co-exec. prod. only). *Series*: 24. *Guest*: Amazing Stories (The Mission).

SUTTON, JAMES T.
Executive. b. California, Sept. 13. e. Columbia U. Film inspector, U.S. government; overseas m.p. service, WW II; co-owner, gen. mgr., Hal Davis Studios; hd. TV commercial div., Allan Sandler Films; Academy Art Pictures; pres., chmn. of bd., exec. prod., Royal Russian Studios, Inc., western hemisphere div.; pres. exec. prod. Gold Lion Prods., Inc.; pres. exec. prod. James T. Sutton-John L. Carpenter Prods.; pres., exec. dir., Airax Corp.; pres. of Skyax (div. of Airax).

SUVARI, MENA
Actress. b. Newport, RI, February 9, 1979. e. Providence High School, Burbank. m. cinematographer Robert Brinkmann.
PICTURES: Nowhere, Kiss the Girls, Slums of Beverly Hills, Snide and Prejudice, The Rage: Carrie 2, American Pie, American Beauty, American Virgin, Loser, Sugar & Spice, American Pie 2, The Musketeer, Spun, Sonny, Light in the Sky, Trauma.
TELEVISION: Movies: Atomic Train. Guest: Boy Meets World, High Incident, Minor Adjustments, ER, Chicago Hope, 413 Hope St, The Late Late Show with Craig Kilborn, Just Shoot Me.

SUZMAN, JANET
Actress. b. Johannesburg, South Africa, Feb. 9, 1939. e. Kingsmead Coll., U. of Witwatersrand. Trained at L.A.M.D.A. London stage debut in The Comedy of Errors. Recent theater: Another Time, Hippolytos, The Sisters Rosensweig. Director: Othello for Market Theatre and Channel 4 (TV), Death of a Salesman, A Dream of People, The Deep Blue Sea.
PICTURES: Nicholas and Alexandra (Acad. Award nom.), A Day in the Death of Joe Egg, The Black Windmill, Nijinsky, Priest of Love, The Draughtsman's Contract, And the Ship Sails On, A Dry White Season, Nuns on the Run, Leon the Pig Farmer, Max.
TELEVISION: Specials/Movies: The Three Sisters, Hedda Gabler, The House on Garibaldi Street, The Zany Adventures of Robin Hood, Miss Nightingale, Macbeth, The Miser, Revolutionary Witness, Saint Joan, Twelfth Night, Master Class on Shakespearean Comedy, Inspector Morse, The Ruth Rendell Mysteries. Series: Mountbatten—Last Viceroy of India, The Singing Detective, Clayhanger.

SVENSON, BO
Actor. b. Goteborg, Sweden, Feb. 13, 1941. e. UCLA, 1970-74. U.S. Marine Corps 1959-65.
PICTURES: Maurie (debut, 1973), The Great Waldo Pepper, Part 2: Walking Tall, Breaking Point, Special Delivery, Portrait of a Hitman, Final Chapter: Walking Tall, Our Man in Mecca, The Inglorious Bastard, North Dallas Forty, Virus, Night Warning, Thunder Warrior, Deadly Impact, Wizards of the Lost Kingdom, The Manhunt, The Delta Force, Choke Canyon, Heartbreak Ridge, War Bus 2, Silent Hero, Thunder Warrior II, White Phantom, Deep Space, Justice Done, The Train, Soda Cracker, Curse II: The Bite, Captain Henkel, Running Combat, Steel Frontier, Private Obsession, Speed 2: Cruise Control, Solitude Point, Crackerjack 3, Outlaw.
TELEVISION: Series: Here Come the Brides, Walking Tall. Movies: The Bravos, Frankenstein, You'll Never See Me Again, Hitched, Target Risk, Snowbeast, Gold of the Amazon Women, Jealousy, Dirty Dozen: The Deadly Mission, 3 Days to Kill, Heartless.

SWAIM, BOB
Director, Writer. b. Evanston, IL, Nov. 2, 1943. e. Calif. State U, B.A.; L'Ecole Nationale de la Cinematographie, Paris, BTS 1969. American director who has often worked in France. Began career making shorts: Le Journal de M Bonnafous, Self Portrait of a Pornographer, Vive les Jacques. Received Cesar award French Acad. M.P., 1982; Chevalier des Arts et des Lettres 1985.
PICTURES: La Nuit de Saint-Germain-des-Pres (1977), La Balance, Spies Like Us, (actor), Half Moon Street, Masquerade, Atlantide, Da Costa, Parfum de Meurte, Femme de Passions, The Climb, A Soldier's Daughter Never Cries.
TELEVISION: Series: Rainbow Drive (actor), Frauen in Angst (s.p.), Target of Suspicion (actor, dir., cam.).

SWANK, HILARY
Actress. Bellingham, Washington, July 30, 1974. m. actor Chad Lowe.
PICTURES: Buffy the Vampire Slayer, The Next Karate Kid, Sometimes They Come Back...Again, Kounterfeit, Quiet Days in Hollywood, Heartwood, Boys Don't Cry (Acad. Award, best actress, 2000), The Gift, The Affair of the Necklace, Insomnia, The Core.
TELEVISION: Series: Camp Wilder, Beverly Hills 90210, Leaving L.A. Movies: Cries Unheard: The Donna Yaklich Story, Terror in the Family, Dying to Belong, The Sleepwalker Killing. Guest: Growing Pains.

SWANSON, DENNIS
Executive. e. Univ. of IL. B.A. in journalism, 1961, M.S. in communications/political science, 1966. 1966-67, news prod. & assignment mngr. for WGN radio & tv in Chicago; 1968-70, assign. edit. & field prod. for NBC news at WMAQ TV in Chicago; 1971-74, sportscaster and prod. WMAQ; worked for TVN in Chicago and served as company's NY dir. of news division; 1976, became exec. prod. of KABC-TV in LA; 1981, appointed station mngr. KABC-TV; 1983, v.p. & gen. mngr. WLS-TV, Chicago; 1985, named pres. of ABC Owned TV Stations; 1986, became pres. of ABC Sports; 1990, pres., ABC Daytime and ABC Children's Programming.

SWANSON, KRISTY
Actress. b. Mission Viejo, CA, Dec. 12, 1969. Signed with modeling agency at age 9, appearing in over 30 commercials. Acting debut at 13 on Disney series Dreamfinders.
PICTURES: Pretty in Pink, Ferris Bueller's Day Off, Deadly Friend, Flowers in the Attic, Diving In, Mannequin Two on the Move, Hot Shots, Highway to Hell, Buffy the Vampire Slayer, The Program, The Chase, Getting In (Student Body), Higher Learning, The Phantom, Marshal Law, Lover Girl, 8 Heads in a Duffel Bag, Tinseltown, Supreme Sanction, Past Imperfect, Meeting Daddy, Big Daddy, Dude, Where's My Car?, Zebra Lounge, Soul Assassin, Silence.
TELEVISION: Series: Dreamfinders, Knots Landing, Nightingales, Early Edition,Grapevine. Movies: Miracle of the Heart: A Boys Town Story, Not Quite Human, Bad to the Bone, Supreme Sanction, Zebra Lounge, Red Water.

SWAYZE, PATRICK
Actor, Dancer. b. Houston, TX. Aug. 18, 1952. e. San Jacinto Col. m. actress-dancer Lisa Niemi. Son of choreographer Patsy Swayze (Urban Cowboy). Brother is actor Don Swayze. Began as dancer appearing in Disney on Parade on tour as Prince Charming. Songwriter and singer with 6 bands. Studied dance at Harkness and Joffrey Ballet Schs. On B'way as dancer in Goodtime Charley, Grease. Co-author of play Without a Word.
PICTURES: Skatetown USA (debut, 1979), The Outsiders, Uncommon Valor, Red Dawn, Grandview USA (also choreographer), Youngblood, Dirty Dancing (also co-wrote and sang She's Like the Wind), Steel Dawn, Tiger Warsaw, Road House, Next of Kin, Ghost, Point Break, City of Joy, Father Hood, Tall Tale, To Wong Foo—Thanks for Everything—Julie Newmar, Three Wishes, Black Dog, Letters from a Killer, Get Bruce, Forever Lulu, Green Dragon, Donnie Darko, Waking Up in Reno, Without a Word, 11:14, George and the Dragon, Dirty Dancing: Havana Nights.
TELEVISION: Mini-Series: North and South: Books I and II. Movies: The Comeback Kid, Return of the Rebels, The Renegades (pilot), Off Sides. Series: Renegades. Guest: M*A*S*H, Amazing Stories.

SWEENEY, ANNE
Executive. e. B.A., College of New Rochelle, and Ed. M., Harvard U. President, Disney Channel and exec. v.p., Disney/ABC Cable Networks, 1996-98. Under her leadership, Disney channel has more than quadrupled its subscriber base to over 62 million homes. Oversaw the launch of Toon Disney, the all-animation cable channel and SoapNet, the 24-hr. soap opera network. Currently president of Disney/ABC Cable Networks, where she is responsible for nonsports cable programming for The Walt Disney Co. and its ABC subsidiary. Oversees the operation of Disney Channel, Toon Disney, and SoapNet, as well as ABC's interests in Lifetime, A&E Television Network, The History Channel, and E! Entertainment Television. Also oversees the creation and management of ABC's Saturday morning children's programming schedule and is in charge of developing future television programming for cable and other platforms. Currently a board member of the National Assoc. of Television Program Executives (NATPE) and the Walter Kaitz Foundation, and honorary chair of Cable Positive. Founding member, Women in Cable, who awarded her Executive of the Year in 1994, Woman of the Year in 1997, and the 1998 Advocate Leader Award from the So. Calif. chapter. Received prestigious STAR Award from American Women in Radio and Television in 1995 and was inducted into the American Adverstising Federation's Advertising Hall of Achievement in 1996. Named to the board of directors, Special Olympics, 2000.

SWEENEY, D. B.
Actor. r.n. Daniel Bernard Sweeney. b. Shoreham, NY, Nov. 14, 1961. e. NYU, 1984 B.F.A.
THEATRE: NY: The Caine Mutiny Court-Martial (B'way), The Seagull: The Hamptons: 1990, Distant Fires (L.A.), among others.
PICTURES: Power (debut, 1986), Fire With Fire, Gardens of Stone, No Man's Land, Eight Men Out, Memphis Belle, Blue Desert, Sons, Leather Jackets, Heaven Is a Playground, The Cutting Edge, A Day in October, Hear No Evil, Fire in the Sky, Roommates, Three Wishes (cameo), Spawn, Goosed, The Book of Stars, The Weekend, Dinosaur, X-Men, After Sex, Warriors of Might and Magic, Hardball, Greenmail, Brother Bear (voice).
TELEVISION: Series: Strange Luck, C-16: FBI, Harsh Realm. Mini-Series: Lonesome Dove. Movies: Out of the Darkness, Miss Rose White, Introducing Dorothy Dandridge, Superfire.

SWERLING, JO, JR.
Executive, Producer. b. Los Angeles, CA, June 18, 1931. e. UCLA, 1948-51; California Maritime Acad., 1951-54. Son of writer Jo Swerling. Active duty U.S. Navy 1954-56. Joined Revue Prods./Universal Television, 1957-81, as prod. coordinator, assoc. prod., prod., assoc. exec. prod., exec. prod., writer, director, actor; currently sr. v.p. and supervising prod., The Cannell Studios.
TELEVISION: Series: Kraft Suspense Theater (prod.), Run for Your Life (prod., writer, Emmy, nom.), The Rockford Files (prod., writer), Cool Million (prod.), Alias Smith & Jones (assoc. exec.

prod.), Baretta (prod., Emmy nom.), City of Angels (exec. prod.), Toma (exec. prod.), Jigsaw (prod.), The Bold Ones (prod., writer), Lawyers (prod., writer). Mini-series: Captains and the Kings (prod., Emmy nom.), Aspen (prod.), The Last Convertible (exec. prod., dir.). Movies (prod.): This Is the West That Was, The Whole World Is Watching, The Invasion of Johnson County, The Outsider, Do You Take This Stranger, Burn the Town Down, The Three-Thousand Mile Chase, How to Steal an Airplane. Supervising prod., Stephen J. Cannell Productions: The Greatest American Hero, Quest, The A-Team, Hardcastle & McCormick, Riptide, The Last Precinct, Hunter, Stingray, Wiseguy, 21 Jump Street, J.J. Starbuck, Sonny Spoon, The Rousters, Unsub, Booker, Top of the Hill, Broken Badges, Dead End Brattigan, The Hat Squad, Traps, Profit.

SWIFT, LELA
Director.
TELEVISION: Studio One, Suspense, The Web, Justice, DuPont Show of the Week, Purex Specials For Women (Emmy Award) Dark Shadows, Norman Corwin Presents, ABC Late Night 90 min. Specials, ABC Daytime 90 min. Play Break, Ryan's Hope (Emmy Awards: 1977, 1979, 1980; Montior Awards: 1985, 1989), The Rope (A & E).

SWIT, LORETTA
Actress. b. Passaic, NJ, Nov. 4, 1939. Stage debut in Any Wednesday. Toured in Mame for year. Arrived in Hollywood in 1971 and began TV career.
THEATRE: Same Time Next Year, The Mystery of Edwin Drood (B'way), Shirley Valentine (Sarah Siddons Award).
PICTURES: Stand Up and Be Counted (debut, 1972), Freebie and the Bean, Race with the Devil, S.O.B., Beer, Whoops Apocalypse, Lords of Tanglewood, Beach Movie, Forest Warrior.
TELEVISION: Series: M*A*S*H (Emmy Awards, 1980, 1982; also Genii, Silver Satellite & People's Choice Awards), Those Incredible Animals (host). Guest: Perry Como Show, Mac Davis, Dolly Parton, Bobby Vinton. Movies: Hostage Heart, Shirts/Skins, The Last Day, Coffeeville, Valentine, Mirror Mirror, Friendships Secrets and Lies, Cagney & Lacey, Games Mother Never Taught You, Friendships Secrets & Lies, First Affair, The Execution, Dreams of Gold: The Mel Fisher Story, Hell Hath No Fury, A Killer Among Friends. Specials: 14 Going on 30, Best Christmas Pageant Ever, Texaco Salute to Broadway, It's a Bird It's a Plane It's Superman, Miracle at Moreauxs, My Dad Can't Be Crazy Can He?, A Matter of Principal, Hell Hath no Fury, A Killer Among Friends,

SWOPE, HERBERT BAYARD, JR.
Director, Producer, Commentator. b. New York, NY, 1920. e. Horace Mann Sch., Princeton U. U.S. Navy, 1941-46; joined CBS-TV as remote unit dir., 1946 directing many firsts in sportscasting; winner, Variety Show Management Award for sports coverage & citation by Amer. TV Society, 1948; joined NBC as dir., 1949; prod. dir., 1951; winner, 1952 Sylvania TV Award Outstanding Achievement in Dir. Technique; became exec. prod., NBC-TV in charge of Wide Wide World; film prod., 20th Century-Fox; 1960-62, exec. prod. 20th-Fox TV; 1970-72 exec. at N.Y. Off-Track Betting Corp. 1973-74; v.p., Walter Reade Organization, Inc.; 1975-76 producer-host, This Was TV, Growth of a Giant; 1976 to present commentator-interviewer, Swope's Scope, (radio—WSBR-AM); Critic's Views (TV: WTVJ, Ch. 5); Column: Now and Then (Palm Beach Pictorial).
THEATRE: Dir./Co-Prod.: Step on a Crack, Fragile Fox, Fair Game for Lovers.
PICTURES: Producer: Hilda Crane, Three Brave Men, True Story of Jesse James, The Bravados, The Fiend Who Walked the West.
TELEVISION: Prod/Dir.: Lights Out, The Clock, The Black Robe, Robert Montgomery Presents, Arsenic and Old Lace, Climax, Many Loves of Dobie Gillis, Five Fingers.

SYKES, ERIC
O.B.E.: Writer, Comedian, Actor. b. Oldham, England, May 4, 1923. Early career as actor; 1948 wrote first three series, BBC's Educating Archie TV comedy series for Frankie Howerd, Max Bygraves, Harry Secombe. BBC panel show member. Sykes Versus TV, The Frankie Howerd Series. Longterm contract with ATV 1956. Own BBC series 1958-78, Sykes and A... Specials: Silent Movies for TV, The Plank (also dir. & s.p.), If You Go Down Into the Woods Today, Rhubarb, It's Your Move, Mr. H Is Late, 19th Hole, The Big Freeze.
THEATRE: Big Bad Mouse (tour: 1966-9 in America, Rhodesia, Australia, Canada), One Man Show (1982), Time and Time Again, Run for Your Wife, Two Into One, The 19th Hole.
PICTURES: Watch Your Stern, Very Important Person, Invasion Quartet, Village of Daughters, Kill or Cure, Heavens Above, The Bargee, One Way Pendulum, Those Magnificent Men in Their Flying Machines, Rotten to the Core, The Liquidator, The Spy

With The Cold Nose, Shalako, Monte Carlo or Bust, Theatre of Blood, Boys in Blue, Gabrielle and the Doodleman, Absolute Beginners, Splitting Heirs, The Big Freeze, The Others.

SYLBERT, ANTHEA
Executive. b. New York, NY, Oct. 6, 1939. e. Barnard Coll., B.A.; Parsons Sch. of Design, M.A. Early career in costume design with range of B'way (The Real Thing), off-B'way and m.p. credits (Rosemary's Baby, John & Mary, Carnal Knowledge, A New Leaf, The Heartbreak Kid, The Cowboys, Bad Company, Shampoo, The Fortune, The Last Tycoon, F.I.S.T.). Two Acad. award. nominations for costume designs for Julia and Chinatown. Joined Warner Bros. in 1977, as v.p., special projects, acting as liaison between creative execs., prod. dept., and creative talent producing films for company. 1978, named v.p., prod. (projects included One Trick Pony, Personal Best.). 1980 appointed v.p. prod., for United Artists, working on Jinxed, Still of the Night, Yentl, etc. 1982 became indept. prod. in partnership with Goldie Hawn (Hawn/Sylbert Movie Co.) producing Swing Shift, Protocol, Wildcats, Overboard, My Blue Heaven, Deceived, Crisscross, Something to Talk About. TV Movie: Truman, Hope.

SYMES, JOHN
Executive. e. Univ. of CA at Berkeley. Started at Paramount in tech. opts. dept. of Paramount's domestic tv distrib. div., then became mngr. of videotape opts., dir. of opts. Became sr. v.p. current programs for Paramount Network tv, then exec. v.p. creative affairs for same. Jan. 1994, became pres. of MGM Worldwide TV.

SYMS, SYLVIA
Actress. b. London, June 1, 1934. e. Convent and Grammar Sch.
PICTURES: My Teenage Daughter (debut, 1956), No Time For Tears, The Birthday Present, Woman in a Dressing Gown, Ice Cold in Alex (Desert Attack), The Moonraker, Bachelor of Hearts, No Trees in the Street, Ferry to Hong Kong, Expresso Bongo, Conspiracy of Hearts, The Virgins of Rome, The World of Suzie Wong, Flame in the Streets, Victim, The Quare Fellow, The Punch and Judy Man, The World Ten Times Over, East of Sudan, Operation Crossbow, The Big Job, Hostile Witness, Danger Route, Run Wild Run Free, The Desperados, Asylum, The Tamarind Seed, Give Us Tomorrow, There Goes the Bride, Absolute Beginners, A Chorus of Disapproval, Shirley Valentine, Shining Through, Dirty Weekend, Staggered, The House of Angelo, Food of Love, What a Girl Wants, I'll Sleep When I'm Dead.
TELEVISION: Something to Declare, Bat Out of Hell, Department in Terror, Friends and Romans, Strange Report, Half-hour Story, The Root of All Evil, The Bridesmaid, Clutterbuck, Movie Quiz, My Good Woman, Looks Familiar, Love and Marriage, The Truth About Verity, I'm Bob, He's Dickie, Blankety Blank, The Story of Nancy Astor, Give Us a Clue, Sykes, Crown Court, A Murder Is Announced, Murder at Lynch Cross, Rockcliffes Follies, Dr. Who, Countdown, Ruth Rendell Mystery, May to December, Intimate Contact, Thatcher: The Final Days, Natural Lies, Mulberry, Peak Practice, Half the Picture, Master of the Moor, Original Sin, Neville's Island. Series: The Human Jungle, The Saint, The Baron, At Home with the Braithwaites. Mini-series: The Glass Virgin, The Jury.

SZABO, ISTVAN
Director. b. Budapest, Hungary, Feb. 18, 1938. e. Academy of Theatre and Film Art, Budapest, 1961. Debut Koncert (short, diploma film) 1961. Short films: Variations on a Theme, You, Piety, Why I Love It, City Map. Appeared in film Stand Off.
PICTURES: Age of Illusions (feature debut, 1964), Father, A Film About Love, 25 Fireman's Street, Premiere, Tales of Budapest, The Hungarians, Confidence (Silver Bear Award, Berlin Fest.), The Green Bird, Mephisto (Hungarian Film Critics Award; Acad. Award, Best Foreign Film, 1982), Bali, Colonel Redl, Hanussen (also co-s.p.), Opera Europa, Meeting Venus, Dear Emma—Sweet Bobe, Offenbach Titkai, Place Vendôme, Sunshine (also s.p.), Taking Sides.

SZWARC, JEANNOT
Director. b. Paris, France, Nov. 21, 1939.
PICTURES: Extreme Close-Up, Bug, Jaws II, Somewhere in Time, Enigma, Supergirl, Santa Claus, Honor Bound, Hercule et Sherlock.
TELEVISION: Series: Ironside, To Catch a Thief, Kojak, Columbo, Night Gallery, Crime Club, True Life Stories, Twilight Zone, JAG, The Practice, Ally McBeal, Seven Days, Providence, Boston Public, C.S.I.: Miami. Movies: Night of Terror, The Weekend Nun, The Devil's Daughter, You'll Never See Me Again, The Small Miracle, Lisa: Bright and Dark, A Summer Without Boys, Crime Club, Code Name: Diamond Head, Murders in the Rue Morgue, The Rockford Files: A Blessing in Disguise, Laura, Shrecklicher Verdacht, The Rockford Files: If the Frame Fits.

T

MR. T
Actor. r.n. Lawrence Tero. b. Chicago, IL, May 21, 1953. Professional bodyguard when hired by Stallone in 1980 for Rocky.
PICTURES: Penitentiary II, Rocky III, D.C. Cab, Freaked, Spy Hard, The Magic of the Golden Bear: Goldy III, Inspector Gadget, Not Another Teen Movie, Judgment, Undercover Brother.
TELEVISION: *Series*: The A Team, T & T. *Movie*: The Toughest Man in the World. *Guest*: Silver Spoons.

TAFFNER DONALD L.
Executive. b. New York, NY. e. St. Johns U. William Morris Agency, 1950-59; Paramount Pictures. 1959-63; D. L. Taffner Ltd., 1963-present.
TELEVISION: *Prod.*: Three's Company, Too Close For Comfort.

TAGAWA, CARY-HIROYUKI
Actor. b. Tokyo, Japan, Sept. 30, 1950.
PICTURES: Armed Response, The Last Emperor, Spellbinder, Twins, The Last Warrior, License to Kill, Showdown in Little Tokyo, The Perfect Weapon, Kickboxer 2: The Road Back, Raven: Return of the Black Dragons, American Me, Nemesis, Rising Sun, Natural Causes, The Dangerous, Soldier Boyz, Picture Pride, Mortal Kombat, White Tiger, Provocateur, Danger Zone, The Phantom, Top of the World, American Dragons, Vampires, Bridge of Dragons, Snow Falling on Cedars, Fixations, The Art of War, The Ghost, Camp Ninja, Pearl Harbor, Planet of the Apes, Speedball: The Movie.
TELEVISION: *Movies*: Star Trek: The Next Generation - Encounter at Farpoint, L.A. Takedown, Murder in Paradise, Vestige of Honor, Not of This World, Mission of the Shark: The Saga of the U.S.S Indianapolis, Raven: Return of the Black Dragons, Day of Reckoning, NetForce, Johnny Tsunami. *Series*: Nash Bridges.

TAKEI, GEORGE
Actor. b. Los Angeles, CA, April 20, 1937. e. UCLA. Professional debut in Playhouse 90 production while training at Desilu Workshop in Hollywood. Gained fame as Sulu in Star Trek TV series. *Author*: Mirror Friend Mirror Foe (novel), To the Stars (autobiography; 1994).
PICTURES: Ice Palace, A Majority of One, Hell to Eternity, PT 109, Red Line 7000, An American Dream, Walk Don't Run, The Green Berets, Star Trek: The Motion Picture, Star Trek II: The Wrath of Khan, Star Trek III: The Search for Spock, Star Trek IV: The Voyage Home, Star Trek V: The Final Frontier, Return From the River Kwai, Prisoners of the Sun, Star Trek VI: The Undiscovered Country, Live by the Fist, Oblivion, Chongbal, Oblivion 2: Backlash, Star Trek: Starfleet Academy, Mulan (voice), Bug Buster, Trekkies, The Magic Pearl, Who Gets the House?, Noon Blue Apples.
TELEVISION: *Series*: General Hospital, Star Trek, Hercules (voice). *Movies*: Kissinger and Nixon, Space Cases, Star Trek Voyager, Batman Beyond: The Movie, OB-1, DC 9/11: Time of Crisis. *Guest*: Perry Mason, Alcoa Premiere, Mr. Novak, The Wackiest Ship in the Army, I Spy, Magnum PI, Trapper John M.D., Miami Vice, Murder She Wrote, McGyver, Hawaiian Eye, Californian, Hawaii Five-O, My Three Sons, John Forsythe Show, Death Valley Days, Theatre in America, Game Night, Kung Fu: The Legend Continues, The Simpsons (voice).

TAMBLYN, RUSS
Actor. b. Los Angeles, CA, Dec. 30, 1934. e. No. Hollywood H.S. West Coast radio shows; on stage with little theater group; song-and-dance act in Los Angeles clubs, veterans hospitals.
PICTURES: The Boy with Green Hair, Reign of Terror, Samson and Delilah, Gun Crazy, Kid from Cleveland, The Vicious Years, Captain Carey U.S.A., Father of the Bride, As Young As You Feel, Father's Little Dividend, Cave of Outlaws, Winning Team, Retreat Hell, Take the High Ground, Seven Brides for Seven Brothers, Deep in My Heart, Many Rivers to Cross, Hit the Deck, Last Hunt, Fastest Gun Alive, The Young Guns, Don't Go Near the Water, Peyton Place (Acad. Award nom.), High School Confidential, Tom Thumb, Cimarron, West Side Story, Wonderful World of the Brothers Grimm, How the West Was Won, Follow the Boys, The Haunting, Long Ships, Son of a Gunfighter, War of the Gargantuas, Scream Free, Dracula Vs. Frankenstein, Satan's Sadists, The Female Bunch, The Last Movie, Win Place or Steal, Murder Gang, Human Highway, Aftershock, Commando Squad, Cyclone, Necromancer, B.O.R.N., Phantom Empire, Bloodscream, Wizards of the Demon Sword, Desert Steel, Cabin Boy, Attack of the 60 Ft. Centerfold, Johnny Mysto: The Boy Wizard, Little Miss Magic, Invisible Dad, Ghost Dog, Inviati Speciali, Cinerama Adventure.
TELEVISION: *Series*: Days of Our Lives, Twin Peaks. *Movies*: Twin Peaks, Running Mates, Inherit the Wind. *Guest*: The Walter Winchell Show, ABC's Wide World of Entertainment, The Ed Sullivan Show, Gunsmoke, Name of the Game, Tarzan, Rags to Riches, Channing, Iron Horse, Perry Como Show, Love American Style, Grizzly Adams, Fame, Running Mates, Greatest Show on Earth, Burke's Law, Cade's County, The Quest, Quantum Leap, Babylon 5, Invisible Mom, Nash Bridges.

TAMBOR, JEFFREY
Actor. b. San Francisco, CA, July 8, 1944. e. San Francisco St. (BA), Wayne St. (MA). Acted with Seattle Rep., Actors Theatre of Louisville, Loeb Drama Ctr. (Harvard), Milwaukee Rep. Theatre, Acad. Festival Theatre (Chicago), Old Globe Theatre in San Diego, South Coast Rep. Theatre. B'way in Measure for Measure, Sly Fox.
PICTURES: And Justice for All, Saturday the 14th, Mr. Mom, The Man Who Wasn't There, No Small Affair, Three O'Clock High, Lisa, City Slickers, Life Stinks, Pastime, Article 99, Brenda Starr, Crossing the Bridge, At Home with the Webbers, Face Dancer, Under Pressure, A House in the Hills, Radioland Murders, Heavyweights, Big Bully, Learning Curves, Bad with Numbers, Big Bully, Meet Joe Black, Teaching Mrs. Tingle, Doctor Dolittle, There's Something About Mary, Girl Interrupted, The Freshman, Muppets From Space, Pollock, How the Grinch Stole Christmas, Never Again, Get Well Soon, Scorched, Malibu's Most Wanted, My Boss's Daughter, Hellboy.
TELEVISION: *Series*: The Ropers, Hill Street Blues, 9 to 5, Mr. Sunshine, Max Headroom, Studio 5-B, American Dreamer, The Larry Sanders Show, Me and George, The Lionhearts, Everything's Relative, Sammy (voice), That Was Then. *Movies*: Alcatraz: The Whole Shocking Story, A Gun in the House, The Star Maker, Take Your Best Shot, Cocaine: One Man's Seduction, Sadat, The Awakening of Candra, The Three Wishes of Billy Grier, The Burden of Proof, Honey Let's Kill the Neighbors, Another Midnight Run, The Man Who Captured Eichmann, Weapons of Mass Destruction, The Lot. *Mini-Series*: Robert Kennedy & His Times, The Lot, Eloise at the Plaza, Eloise at Christmastime. *Guest*: Three's Company, M*A*S*H, Barney Miller, Tales From the Crypt, The Golden Globe, Empty Nest, Doogie Howser M.D., Equal Justice, Murder She Wrote.

TANEN, NED
Executive. b. Los Angeles, CA, 1931. e. UCLA, law degree. Joined MCA, Inc. 1954; appt. v.p. in 1968. Brought Uni Records, since absorbed by MCA Records, to best-seller status with such artists as Neil Diamond, Elton John, Olivia Newton-John. First became active in theatrical prod. in 1972. 1975 began over-seeing feature prod. for Universal. 1976 named pres. of Universal Theatrical Motion Pictures, established as div. of Universal City Studios. Left in 1982 to become independent pro-ducer. 1985, joined Paramount Pictures as pres. of Motion Picture Group. Resigned 1988 to continue as sr. advisor at Paramount. Emerged from retired in 1992 to link his company Channel Productions to Paramount. Producer: Guarding Tess, Cops and Robbersons, Mary Reilly.

TAPLIN, JONATHAN
Producer. b. Cleveland, OH, July 18, 1947. e. Princeton U.
PICTURES: Mean Streets, The Last Waltz, Carny (exec. prod.), Grandview U.S.A. (co-exec. prod.), Under Fire, Baby, My Science Project, Until the End of the World, K2, To Die For (exec. prod.), Rough Magic (exec. prod.).
TELEVISION: Shelly Duvall's Faerie Tale Theatre (6 episodes), 1968: The 25th Anniversary, The Native Americans, The Prize, *Mini-series*: Cadillac Desert (exec. prod.).

TARADASH, DANIEL
Writer, Director. b. Louisville, KY, Jan. 29, 1913. e. Harvard Coll., B.A., 1933; Harvard Law Sch., LL.B., 1936. Passed NY Bar, 1937; won nationwide playwriting contest, 1938; U.S. Army WWII. Pres. Screen Writers Branch, WGA, 1955-56; v.p.; Writers Guild of America, West 1956-59; mem. Writers Guild Council, 1954-65; mem., bd. of govnrs. Motion Picture Acad. Arts & Sciences, 1964-74, 1990-93; v.p. 1968-70 and pres. 1970-73. Trustee, Producers-Writers Guild Pension plan 1960-73. chmn., 1965. Mem. Bd. of Trustees of American Film Institute 1967-69. WGA's Valentine Davies Award, 1971. Pres., Academy M.P. Arts & Sciences, 1970-73, mem. bd. trustees, Entertainment Hall of Fame Foundation. Mem., Public Media General Programs panel for the National Foundation for the Arts, 1975-85, 1992; Pres. Writers Guild of America, West, 1977-79. Natl. chmn., Writers Guild of America, 1979-81. WGA's Morgan Cox Award, 1988. WGA's Edmund H. North Founders Award 1991. Festival to pres-ent Taradash Screenwriting Award 1992-; USC retrospective and tribute, 1992. Writer of TV special Bogie. Recipient of the Writers Guild of America West Laurel Award, 1996.
PICTURES: Golden Boy, A Little Bit of Heaven, Knock on Any Door, Rancho Notorious, Don't Bother to Knock, From Here to Eternity (Academy Award 1953), Desiree, Storm Center (also dir., co-story), Picnic, Bell Book and Candle, The Saboteur Code Name—Morituri, Hawaii, Castle Keep, Doctors' Wives, The Other Side of Midnight.
(d. Feb. 22, 2003).

TARANTINO, QUENTIN
Writer, Director, Actor, Producer. b. Knoxville, TN, March 27, 1963. Graduate of Sundance Institute Director's Workshop and Lab. With producer Lawrence Bender, formed production co. A Band Apart.
PICTURES: Past Midnight (assoc. prod., co-s.p.), Reservoir Dogs (dir., s.p., actor), True Romance (s.p.), Killing Zoe (co-exec. prod.), Natural Born Killers (story), Sleep With Me (actor), Pulp Fiction (dir., s.p., co-story, actor; Cannes Film Fest. Award for

Best Film; LA Film Critics, NY Film Critics, Natl. Soc. of Film Critics, Chicago Film Critics & Independent Spirit Awards for dir. & s.p.; Academy Award & Golden Globe for s.p.; Natl. Bd. of Review Award for dir., 1994), Destiny Turns on the Radio (actor), Somebody to Love (actor), Desperado (actor), Four Rooms (co-s.p., co-exec. prod., actor), From Dusk Till Dawn (s.p., actor, co-exec. prod.), Girl 6 (actor), Curdled (exec. prod.), God Said, Ha (actor); Full Tilt Boogie (actor), Jackie Brown, Forever Hollywood (actor), Little Nicky (actor), From Dusk Till Dawn 2: Texas Blood Money (exec. prod), From Dusk Till Dawn 3: The Hangman's Daughter (exec. prod.), Kill Bill (prod., s.p., dir.), All the Love You Cannes (actor), Planet of the Pitts (actor).
TELEVISION: *Guest:* The Golden Girls, All-American Girl. *Dir:* ER (1 episode).

TARNOFF, JOHN B.
Producer. b. New York, NY, Mar. 3, 1952. e. UCLA, motion pictures & TV, 1973-74; Amherst Coll., B.A., 1969-73. Named field exec. with Taylor-Laughlin Distribution (company arm of Billy Jack Enterprises) 1974; left in 1975 to be literary agent with Bart/Levy, Inc.; later with Michael Levy & Associates, Paul Kohner/Michael Levy Agency; Headed TV dept., Kohner/Levy, 1979. Joined MGM as production exec., 1979; v.p., development, 1979-80; sr. v.p. production & devel., 1981-82; exec. v.p., Kings Road Prods., 1983-84; v.p., prod., Orion Pictures Corp., 1985; exec. prod., Out of Bounds, Columbia Pictures, 1986; v.p., prod., De Laurentiis Entertainment Group, 1987. Head of production, DeLaurentiis Entertainment, Australia, 1987-88. Exec. v.p. production, Village Roadshow Pictures, 1988-. Exec. prod.: The Delinquents, Blood Oath. 1990-93, personal mngr., Addis-Wechsler & Assoc. 1994, New Line Cinema/Overseas Film Group; prod., Nature of the Beast. 1995, founder, Newspeak Media Inc. 1996, founder, Personality Factory, Inc. 1998, exec. prod. Big Brother, cd-rom adventure based on Orwell's 1984; writer/designer, WarGames, cd-rom.

TARSES, JAMIE
Executive. b. Pittsburgh, PA. e. Williams Coll. Prior to joining NBC, worked as a casting director for Lorimar Productions. Joined NBC in Sept. 1987 as Mgr., Creative Affairs for NBC Productions. In Dec. 1987, named Mgr., Current Comedy Programs, NBC Entertainment and was NBC's Program Exec. for such series as Cheers, Amen, 227 and A Different World. In 1988, named Mgr., Comedy Development. In Feb. 1989, promoted to Director, Comedy Development, NBC Entertainment. Was directly involved in the development of Friends, NewsRadio, Caroline in the City, Mad About You, Frasier and several other NBC programs. In Aug. 1994, was named to supervise one of NBC's two programming teams before being promoted in 1995 to S.V.P., Primetime Series. In June of 1996, joined ABC Entertainment as President. Resigned, July 1999. Joined 3 Sisters Ent. in 2001.

TARSES, JAY
Producer, Writer, Actor. b. Baltimore, MD, July 3, 1939. e. Williams Coll., Ithaca Coll., BFA theatre. Daughter is executive Jamie Tarses. Wrote and acted with little-theater co. in Pittsburgh, drove a truck in NY for Allen Funt's Candid Camera and worked in advertising and promotion for Armstrong Cork Co. in Lancaster, PA where he met Tom Patchett. Formed Patchett and Tarses, stand-up comedy team played coffeehouse circuit in the late 1960s. Later twosome became TV writing team and joined writing staff of Carol Burnett Show winning Emmy in 1972.
PICTURES: *Co-s.p. with Patchett:* Up the Academy, The Great Muppet Caper, The Muppets Take Manhattan, Teen Wolf.
TELEVISION: *Series: Actor:* Make Your Own Kind of Music, Open All Night, The Duck Factory, The Days and Nights of Molly Dodd. *Specials: With Tom Patchett:* The Bob Newhart Show (exec. prod., writer), The Tony Randall Show (creator, exec. prod., writer), We've Got Each Other (creator, exec. prod., writer), Mary (prod.), Open All Night (creator, prod., writer), Buffalo Bill (creator, exec. prod., writer). *Solo:* The Days and Nights of Molly Dodd (creator, prod., writer), The "Slap" Maxwell Story (creator, prod., writer), Smoldering Lust (creator, prod., writer), Public Morals (co-creator, exec. prod., writer). *Pilots:* The Chopped Liver Brothers (exec. prod., writer), The Faculty (exec. prod., dir., writer), Baltimore (creator, prod., writer), Harvey Berger: Salesman (co-creator, prod., writer), Jackass Junior High (creator, prod., writer).

TAVERNIER, BERTRAND
Director, Writer. b. Lyon, France, April 25, 1941. After 2 yrs. of law study, quit to become film critic for Cahiers du Cinema and Cinema 60. Asst. to dir. Jean-Pierre Melville on Leon Morin Priest (1961), also worked as film publicist. Wrote film scripts and a book on the Western and a history of American cinema. Partner for 6 yrs. with Pierre Rissient in film promotion company, during which time he studied all aspects of film-making. 1963: Director episode of Les Baisers. Pres., Lumiere Inst., Lyon. Book: 50 Years of American Cinema, Qu'est ce Qu'on Attend?, Amis Americains.
PICTURES: *Director-Co-writer:* The Clockmaker (L'Horloger de Saint-Paul), Let Joy Reign Supreme (Que La Fête Commence), The Judge and the Assassin (Le Judge et l'Assassin), Spoiled

Children (also co-prod.), Deathwatch. *Dir./Co-Writer/Prod.:* A Week's Vacation, Clean Slate (Coup de Torchon; 11 César nom., Oscar nom.), Mississippi Blues (co-dir. with Robert Parrish), A Sunday in the Country (Un Dimanche a la Campagne; Best Direction Cannes, New York Critics Prize), 'Round Midnight, Beatrice (dir. co-prod. only) Life and Nothing But, Daddy Nostalgia, The Undeclared War (co-dir. with Patrick Rutman), L627, La Fille de D'Artagnan, L'Appat, Capitaine Conan, Ca Commence Aujourd'hui, Histoires de vies brisées: les 'double peine' de Lyon, Laissez passer, Safe Conduct, Joan of Arc: The Virgin Warrior.
TELEVISION: Phillippe Soupault, October Country (co-dir. with Robert Parrish), Lyon, le regard interieur, La Lettre, The Other Side of the Tracks, Les Enfants de Thies.

TAVIANI, PAOLO and VITTORIO
Directors, Writers. b. San Miniato, Pisa, Italy, (Paolo: Nov. 8, 1931; Vittorio: Sept. 20, 1929); e. Univ. of Pisa (Paolo: liberal arts; Vittorio: law). The two brothers always work in collaboration from script preparation through shooting and editing. 1950: With Valentino Orsini ran cine-club at Pisa. 1954: In collab. with Caesare Zavattini directed short about Nazi massacre at San Miniato. 1954-59: With Orsini made series of short documentaries (Curatorne e Montanara; Carlo Pisacane; Ville della Brianza; Lavatori della pietra; Pitori in cita; I Pazzi della domenica; Moravia, Cabunara). Worked as assistant to Rosellini, Luciano Emmer and Raymond Pellegrini. 1960: collaborated on an episode of Italy Is Not a Poor Country.
PICTURES (all by both): A Man for Burning (debut, 1962; co-dir. with Valentino Orsini), Matrimonial Outlaws (co-dir. with Orsini), The Subversives, Under the Sign of Scorpio, Saint Michael Had a Rooster, Allonsanfan, Padre Padrone (Cannes Film Fest.: Grand Prix & Critics International Prize, 1977), The Meadow, The Night of the Shooting Stars (1981, Best Director Award, Natl. Society of Film Critics; Special Jury Prize, Cannes), Kaos, Good Morning Babylon, The Sun Also Shines at Night, Fiorile, The Elective Affinities (Le Affinata elettive), You Laugh (Tu ridi), Un Altro mondo e possibile.
TELEVISION: Resurrezione (mini), Luisa Sanfelice.

TAVOULARIS, DEAN
Production Designer. b. Lowell, MA, 1932.
PICTURES: Candy, Zabriskie Point, Little Big Man, The Godfather, The Godfather: Part II, The Conversation, Farewell, My Lovely, The Brink's Job, Apocalypse Now, One From the Heart, The Escape Artist, Hammett, The Outsiders, Rumble Fish, Peggy Sue Got Married, Gardens of Stone, Tucker: The Man and His Dream, New York Stories, The Godfather: Part III, Final Analysis, Rising Sun, I Love Trouble, Jack, Bulworth, The Parent Trap, The Ninth Gate, Angel Eyes, C.Q., Megalopolis.

TAYLOR, DELORES
Actress, Writer, Producer. b. Winner, SD, Sept. 27, 1939. e. U. of South Dakota, studying commercial art. m. Tom Laughlin. First TV experience was heading art dept. at RCA wholesale center in Milwaukee. Established first Montessori School in U.S. in Santa Monica for several yrs., with husband. Made feature film debut as actress in Billy Jack in 1971. Wrote s.p. with husband for that and sequels, The Trial of Billy Jack, Billy Jack Goes to Washington, under pseudonym Teresa Christina.
PICTURES: *Exec. Prod., Writer:* Proper Time, Young Sinners, Born Losers, The Master Gunfighter. *Exec. Prod., Writer, Actress:* Billy Jack, Trial of Billy Jack, Billy Jack Goes to Washington, Return of Billy Jack.

TAYLOR, ELIZABETH
Actress. b. London, Eng., Feb. 27, 1932. e. Bryon House, London. When 3 years old danced before Princess Elizabeth, Margaret Rose. Came to U.S. at outbreak of WWII. *Author:* World Enough and Time (with Richard Burton; 1964), Elizabeth Taylor (1965), Elizabeth Takes Off (1988). Initiated Ben Gurion U.—Elizabeth Taylor Fund for Children of the Negev, 1982. Co-founded American Foundation for AIDS Research, 1985. Named Comdr. Arts & Letters (France) 1985, Legion of Honor, 1987. Established the Elizabeth Taylor AIDS Foundation in 1991. Developed various perfume products: Elizabeth Taylor's Passion, Passion Body Riches, Passion for Men, White Diamonds, Diamonds and Emeralds, Diamonds and Sapphires, Diamond and Rubies; 1993 launched Elizabeth Taylor Fashion Jewelry Collection. Recipient of AFI Life Achievement Award (1993), Jean Hersholt Humanitarian Award (1993).
THEATRE: *B'way:* The Little Foxes (also London), Private Lives.
PICTURES: There's One Born Every Minute (debut, 1942), Lassie Come Home, Jane Eyre, White Cliffs of Dover, National Velvet, Courage of Lassie, Life with Father, Cynthia, A Date With Judy, Julia Misbehaves, Little Women, Conspirator, The Big Hangover, Father of the Bride, Father's Little Dividend, A Place in the Sun, Callaway Went Thataway (cameo), Love Is Better Than Ever, Ivanhoe, The Girl Who Had Everything, Rhapsody, Elephant Walk, Beau Brummel, The Last Time I Saw Paris, Giant, Raintree County, Cat on a Hot Tin Roof, Suddenly Last Summer, Scent of Mystery (cameo), Butterfield 8 (Academy Award, 1960), Cleopatra, The V.I.Ps, The Sandpiper, Who's Afraid of Virginia Woolf? (Academy Award, 1966), The Taming of

the Shrew, Doctor Faustus, Reflections in a Golden Eye, The Comedians, Boom!, Secret Ceremony, The Only Game in Town, X Y and Zee (Zee and Company), Under Milk Wood, Hammersmith Is Out, Night Watch, Ash Wednesday, That's Entertainment!, The Driver's Seat, The Blue Bird, A Little Night Music, Winter Kills (cameo), The Mirror Crack'd, Genocide (narrator), Young Toscanini, The Flintstones, The Visit, Get Bruce, Chop Suey.
TELEVISION: Movies: Divorce His/Divorce Hers, Victory at Entebbe, Return Engagement, Between Friends, Malice in Wonderland, There Must Be a Pony, Poker Alice, Sweet Bird of Youth, These Old Broads. Mini-Series: North and South. Guest: Here's Lucy (1970 with Richard Burton), General Hospital (1981), All My Children (1983), Hotel, The Simpsons (voice). Specials: Elizabeth Taylor in London, America's All-Star Salute to Elizabeth Taylor, numerous appearances in specials and tributes.

TAYLOR, JOHN RUSSELL
Writer, Critic. b. Dover, England, June 19, 1935. e. Cambridge U., B.A., 1956. Editor: Times Educational Supplement, London, 1959-60; film critic, The Times, London, 1962-73; art critic, 1978-; editor, Films and Filming, 1983-; prof., division of Cinema, USC, 1972-78. Member: London Film and TV Press Guild, London Critics Circle, NY Society of Cinematologists.
BOOKS: Joseph L. Mankiewicz: An Index, The Angry Theatre, Anatomy of a Television Play, Cinema Eye Cinema Ear, Shakespeare: A Celebration (cont.), New English Dramatists 8 (ed. & intr.), The Hollywood Musical, The Second Wave: Hollywood Dramatists for the 70s, Masterworks of the British Cinema, Directors and Directions: Peter Shaffer, Hitch, Cukor's Hollywood, Impressionism, Strangers in Paradise, Ingrid Bergman, Alec Guinness: A Celebration, Vivien Leigh, Hollywood 1940s, Portraits of the British Cinema, others.

TAYLOR, JULIET
Casting Director. e. Smith College, Massachussetts.
PICTURES: The Exorcist, The Stepford Wives, Love and Death, Taxi Driver, Next Stop, Greenwich Village, Network, The Front, Close Encounters of the Third Kind, Annie Hall, Julia, Between the Lines, Cindy, Pretty Baby, An Unmarried Woman, Manhattan, Stardust Memories, Willie and Phil, Arthur, Shoot the Moon, A Midsummer Night's Sex Comedy, Tempest, Still of the Night, Zelig, Terms of Endearment, Broadway Danny Rose, The Killing Fields, Falling in Love, Birdy, The Purple Rose of Cairo, Alamo Bay, The Mission, Heartburn, Hannah and Her Sisters, September, Radio Days, Big, Another Woman, Working Girl, Mississippi Burning, Dangerous Liasons, New York Stories, Crimes and Misdemeanors, The Grifters, The Sheltering Sky, Postcards from The Edge, Alice, Harley Davidson and the Marlboro Man, Regarding Henry, Shadows and Fog, This is My Life, Husbands and Wives, Hero, Sleepless in Seattle, Schindler's List, Bullets Over Broadway, Mixed Nuts, Wolf, The Road To Welville, Angie, Mighty Aphrodite, Mary Reilly, The Birdcage, Everyone Says I Love You, Deconstructing Harry, Primary Colors, Celebrity, Meet Joe Black, Sweet and Lowdown, Angela's Ashes, Small Time Crooks, The Curse of the Jade Scorpion, Hollywood Ending, People I Know, The Life of David Gale, The Blind Assassin, Anything Else.
TELEVISION: Wit.

TAYLOR, LILI
Actress. b. Chicago, Feb. 20, 1967.
THEATRE: NY: What Did He See, Aven U Boys. Regional: Mud, The Love Talker, Fun. Director: Collateral Damage.
PICTURES: Mystic Pizza (debut, 1988), Say Anything, Born on the Fourth of July, Bright Angel, Dogfight, Watch It, Household Saints, Short Cuts, Rudy, Arizona Dream, Mrs. Parker and the Vicious Circle, Ready to Wear (Pret-a-Porter), The Addiction, Cold Fever, Four Rooms, Things I Never Told You, I Shot Andy Warhol, Girl's Town, Ransom, Pecker, Kicked in the Head, O.K. Garage, The Imposters, A Slipping Down Forward, Janis, The Haunting, High Fidelity, Julie Johnson, Gaudi Afternoon, Casa de los Babys.
TELEVISION: Movies: Subway Stories: Tales from the Underground, Anne Frank, Live From Baghdad. Guest: Mad About You, The X Files. Series: Deadline, Six Feet Under.

TAYLOR, MESHACH
Actor. b. Boston, MA, Apr. 11, 1947. e. Florida A & M Univ. Hosted Chicago TV show Black Life.
THEATER: Streamers, Sizwe Banzi is Dead, The Island, Native Son, Wonderful Ice Cream Suit, Bloody Bess, Sirens of Titan, Night Feast, Huckleberry Finn, Cops.
PICTURES: Damien: Omen II, The Howling, The Beast Within, Explorers, Warning Sign, One More Saturday Night, From the Hip, Mannequin, The Allnighter, House of Games, Welcome to Oblivion, Mannequin 2: On the Move, Class Act, Jacks or Better, Friends and Family.
TELEVISION: Series: Buffalo Bill, Designing Women, Dave's World, To Tell the Truth. Guest: Lou Grant, Barney Miller, Melba, Golden Girls, M*A*S*H, The White Shadow, What's Happening Now, ALF. Movies: An Innocent Man, How to Murder a Millionaire, Double Double Toil and Trouble, Virtual Seduction, The Right Connections. Specials: Huckleberry Finn, The Rec Room. Mini-Series: Nothing Lasts Forever.

TAYLOR, RENEE
Actress, Writer. b. New York, NY, March 19, 1935. Wife of actor Joseph Bologna, with whom she collaborates in writing. Their B'way plays include Lovers and Other Strangers, It Had to Be You. Stage actress: One of the All-Time Greats.
PICTURES: Actress: The Errand Boy, The Detective, The Producers, A New Leaf, Lovers and Other Strangers (also s.p.), Made for Each Other (also s.p.), Last of the Red Hot Lovers, Lovesick, It Had to Be You (also co-dir., co-s.p.), That's Adequate, White Palace, End of Innocence, Delirious, All I Want for Christmas, Forever, Love Is All There Is, Dr. Dolittle 2 (voice), Dying On the Edge, Returning Mickey Stern.
TELEVISION: Writer: Acts of Love... and Other Comedies (Emmy Award, 1973), Paradise, Calucci's Department, The American Dream Machine, Bedrooms (Writers Guild Award, 1984), etc. Actress: Series regular: The Jack Paar Show, Mary Hartman Mary Hartman, Daddy Dearest, The Nanny. Movies: Woman of the Year (also co-writer), 61, A Match Made in Heaven.

TAYLOR, ROD
Actor. b. Sydney, Australia, Jan. 11, 1930. e. East Sydney Fine Arts Coll. Started out as artist then turned to acting on stage. Formed own company, Rodler, Inc., for TV-film production.
PICTURES: The Sturt Expedition (debut, 1951), King of the Coral Sea, Long John Silver, Top Gun, The Virgin Queen, Hell on Frisco Bay, World Without End, The Rack, Giant, The Catered Affair, Raintree County, Step Down to Terror, Separate Tables, Ask Any Girl, The Time Machine, Seven Seas to Calais, 101 Dalmatians (voice), The Birds, A Gathering of Eagles, The V.I.P.s, Sunday in New York, Fate is the Hunter, 36 Hours, Young Cassidy, Do Not Disturb, The Glass Bottom Boat, The Liquidator, Hotel, Chuka (also prod.), Dark of the Sun, High Commissioner (Nobody Runs Forever), The Hell with Heroes, Zabriskie Point, Darker Than Amber, The Man Who Had Power Over Women, The Heroes, The Train Robbers, Trader Horn, The Deadly Trackers, Hell River, Blondy, Picture Show Man, A Time To Die, On the Run, Close Enemy, Open Season, Point of Betrayal, Welcome to Woop-Woop.
TELEVISION: Movies: Powerkeg, Family Flight, The Oregon Trail, Cry of the Innocent, Jacqueline Bouvier Kennedy, Charles and Diana: A Royal Love Story, Outlaws, Danielle Steel's Palomino, Grass Roots, The Warlord: Battle for the Galaxy. Series: Hong Kong, Bearcats, Masquerade, The Oregon Trail, Outlaws, Falcon Crest.

TAYLOR, RONNIE
Cinematographer. b. London, England, 1924. Ent. m.p. ind. 1941 at Gainsborough Studios
PICTURES: Tommy, The Silent Flute, Circle of Iron, Savage Harvest, Gandhi, High Road to China, The Champions, A Chorus Line, Foreign Body, Cry Freedom, Opera (Italy), The Experts, Sea of Love, Popcorn, The Rainbow Thief, Jewels, Age of Treason, The Steal.
Television: Series: The Avengers. Mini-Series: Master of the Game (UK shoot). Movies: The Hound of the Baskervilles, Nairobi Affair, Shadow of Obsession, Good King Wenceslas, Redwood Curtain.

TAYLOR-YOUNG, LEIGH
Actress. b. Washington, DC, Jan. 25, 1945. e. Northwestern U. B'way debut 1966 in Three Bags Full. Additional stage: The Beckett Plays (Off-B'way, LA), Knives, Sleeping Dogs.
PICTURES: I Love You Alice B. Toklas (debut, 1968), The Games, The Big Bounce, The Adventurers, The Buttercup Chain, The Horsemen, The Gang That Couldn't Shoot Straight, Soylent Green, Can't Stop the Music, Looker, Secret Admirer, Jagged Edge, Honeymoon Academy, Accidents, Dreamrider, Bliss, Slackers.
TELEVISION: Series: Peyton Place, The Devlin Connection, The Hamptons, Dallas, Picket Fences (Emmy Award, 1994), Sunset Beach. Movies: Marathon, Napoleon and Josephine: A Love Story, Perry Mason: The Case of the Sinister Spirit, Who Gets the Friends, Bonnie and McCloud, Moment of Truth: Murder or Memory?, An Unfinished Affair, Stranger in My Home. Guest: Civil Wars, The Young Riders, Alfred Hitchcock Presents, Spenser for Hire, Evening Shade. Pilots: Ghostwriter, Houston Knights.

TEAGUE, LEWIS
Director. b. 1941. e. NYU. Editor and/or 2nd unit dir. on such films as Cockfighter, Crazy Mama, Death Race 2000, Avalanche, Fast Charlie: The Moonbeam Rider, The Big Red One.
PICTURES: Dirty O'Neil (co-dir.), Lady in Red (also editor), Alligator, Fighting Back, Cujo, Cat's Eye, The Jewel of the Nile, Collision Course, Navy SEALS, Fortune Hunter.
TELEVISION: Series episodes: Alfred Hitchcock Presents, Daredevils, Shannon's Deal. Movies: T Bone N Weasel, Tom Clancy's Op Center, Time Traxx, Saved by the Light, Profiler, Justice League of America, The Reunion: Dukes of Hazzard, Love and Treason, The Triangle.

TECHINE, ANDRE
Director, Writer. b. Valence d'Agen, Tarn-et- Garonne, France, March 13, 1943.
PICTURES: Paulina s'en va (dir. only), French Provincial, Barocco, The Bronte Sisters, Hotel des Ameriques, La Matiouette, Rendez-vous, Scene of the Crime, The Innocents, Mauvaise Fille (s.p. only), I Don't Kiss, My Favorite Season, The Wild Reeds (won Cesar, NY Film Critics Circle Award), The Child of the Night, Transatlantique (s.p. only), Alice and Martin, Terminus des anges, Loin, Cafe de la plage (s.p. only), Le Garcon aux yeux gris (dir. only).

TELLER, IRA
Executive. b. New York, NY, July 3, 1940. e. City Coll. of New York, & 1957-61; NYU Graduate Sch. of Arts, 1961-62. Publicist, Pressbook Dept., 20th Century Fox., 1961-62; asst. to adv. mgr., Embassy Pictures Corp., 1962-63; asst. adv. mgr., Columbia Pictures Corp., 1963; adv. mgr., Columbia Pictures Corp., 1964, 1964-65; asst. to chmn. of bd., Diener, Hauser, Greenthal Agy., 1966; adv. mgr., 20th Century-Fox, 1966-67; 1967, adv. dir. 20th Cent.-Fox.; dir. of adv., Nat'l General Pictures Corp., 1969; eastern dir., adv.-pub., 1972; national dir., adv-pub., 1973; Bryanston Distributors, Inc. v.p. adv.-pub., 1974; Cine Artists Pictures Corp. v.p. adv-pub., 1975; Lorimar Productions, v.p., adv.-marketing, 1976-77; 1977-present, pres. Ira Teller and Company, Inc.; This Is It Productions, prod. Instructor, UCLA Extension.

TEMPLE, JULIEN
Director. b. London, England, Nov. 26, 1953. e. Cambridge, London's National Film School. Dir. many rock videos.
PICTURES: The Great Rock 'n' Roll Swindle (debut, 1979), The Secret Policeman's Other Ball, Undercover (also s.p.), Running Out of Luck (also s.p.), Absolute Beginners, Aria (segment: Rigoletto), Earth Girls Are Easy, Rolling Stones: At the Max (creative consultant), Bullet, Catching Fire, Vigo, The Filth and the Fury, Pandaemonium.

TEMPLE (BLACK), SHIRLEY
Actress, Diplomat. b. Santa Monica, CA, April 23, 1928. In 1932 screen debut, Red Haired Alibi. In 1933 To the Last Man; then leading figure in series of Educational shorts called Baby Burlesque and Frolics of Youth, until breakthrough role in Stand Up and Cheer, 1934, which resulted in career as child and teen star. Voted one of ten best Money-Making Stars in Motion Picture Herald-Fame Poll, 1934-39. As an adult, turned her attention to government and international issues. Republican candidate for U.S. House of Representatives, 1967. Rep. to 24th General Assembly of U.N. (1969-70). Special asst. to chmn., President's Council on the Environment (1970-72). U.S. Ambassador to Ghana (1974-76). Chief of Protocol, White House (1976-77); member of U.S. delegation on African Refugee problems, Geneva, 1981; 1987 made 1st honorary U.S. Foreign Service Rep. for State Dept.; 1989, appt. Ambassador to Czechoslovakia. Autobiography: Child Star (1988).
PICTURES: The Red-Haired Alibi (feature debut, 1932), To the Last Man, Out All Night, Mandalay, Carolina, Stand Up and Cheer, Baby Take a Bow, Now and Forever, Bright Eyes, Now I'll Tell, Change of Heart, Little Miss Marker, The Little Colonel, Our Little Girl, Curly Top, The Littlest Rebel, Captain January, Poor Little Rich Girl, Dimples, Stowaway, Wee Willie Winkle, Heidi, Rebecca of Sunnybrook Farm, Little Miss Broadway, Just Around the Corner, Little Princess, Susannah of the Mounties, The Blue Bird, Young People, Kathleen, Miss Annie Rooney. Since You Went Away, I'll Be Seeing You, Kiss and Tell, That Hagen Girl, Honeymoon, Bachelor and the Bobby-Soxer, Fort Apache, Mr. Belvedere Goes to College, Adventure in Baltimore, Story of Seabiscuit, Kiss for Corliss.
TELEVISION: Series: Shirley Temple's Storybook (host, performer). Various tributes and specials.

TENNANT, VICTORIA
Actress. b. London, England, Sept. 30, 1953. e. Central Sch. of Speech & Drama. Daughter of ballerina Irina Baronova and talent agent Cecil Tennant.
THEATRE: Love Letters (Steppenwolf), Getting Married (NY), Taming of the Shrew (NY).
PICTURES: The Ragman's Daughter, Strangers Kiss, All of Me, The Holocraft Covenant, Best Seller, Flowers in the Attic, Fool's Mate, The Handmaid's Tale, L.A. Story, Whispers, The Plague, Edie & Pen, The Legend of the Mummy, We Married Margo.
TELEVISION: Mini-Series: Voice of the Heart, Winds of War, Chiefs, War and Remembrance, Act of Will, The Man from Snowy River. Movies: Maigret, Dempsey, Under Siege, Sister Mary Explains It All (also exec. prod.).

TEWKESBURY, JOAN
Writer, Director. b. Redlands, CA, April 8, 1936. e. USC. Student American Sch. Dance 1947-54. Was ostrich and understudy in Mary Martin's Peter Pan. Directed and choreographed Theatre prods. in L.A., London, Edinburgh Festival, Scotland. Taught dance and theory, American Sch. of Dance 1959-64; taught in theatre arts depts. of two universities: USC, Immaculate Heart. Became script supvr. for Robert Altman on McCabe & Mrs. Miller. Off-B'way: Cowboy Jack Street (writer,

dir.). Teacher in film dept. UCLA. Sundance advisor, 1992-93: directors lab-writers lab. American Musical Theatre Festival in Philadelphia. Chippy (dir.), Jammed (Edinburgh Festival; writer, dir.). Dance Card (Oregon Ballter Theatre; writer, dir., co-choreo.)
PICTURES: Thieves Like Us (co.-s.p.), Nashville, (s.p.), Old Boyfriends (dir.), Hampstead Center (doc. of Anna Freud, writer, dir.), A Night in Heaven (s.p.), The Player (actress).
TELEVISION: Series: Director: Alfred Hitchcock Presents (also writer), Elysian Fields (pilot; also writer, exec. prod.), Almost Grown, Shannon's Deal (also writer), Nothing Sacred, Felicity, The Guardian. Movies: Director/Writer: The Acorn People, The Tenth Month, Cold Sassy Tree, Sudie and Simpson, Wild Texas Wind, The Stranger, On Promised Land, Scattering Dad.

THAXTER, PHYLLIS
Actress. b. Portland, ME, Nov. 20, 1919. e. St. Genevieve Sch., Montreal. Daughter is actress Skye Aubrey.
PICTURES: Thirty Seconds Over Tokyo (debut, 1944), Bewitched, Weekend at the Waldorf, Sea of Grass, Living in a Big Way, Tenth Avenue Angel, Sign of the Ram, Blood on the Moon, Act of Violence, No Man of Her Own, The Breaking Point, Fort Worth, Jim Thorpe_All American, Come Fill the Cup, She's Working Her Way Through College, Springfield Rifle, Operation Secret, Women's Prison, Man Afraid, The World of Henry Orient, Superman.
TELEVISION: Movies: Incident in San Francisco, The Longest Night, Three Sovereigns for Sarah. Mini-Series: Once an Eagle. Guest: Wagon Train, Alfred Hitchcock, Twilight Zone, Purex Specials For Women, Playhouse 90, The Fugitive, The Defenders, Murder She Wrote.

THEODORAKIS, MIKIS
Composer. b. Chios, Greece, 1925.
PICTURES: Eva, Night Ambush, Shadow of the Cat, Phaedra, Five Miles to Midnight, Zorba the Greek, The Day the Fish Came Out, The Trojan Women, State of Siege, Serpico, Iphigenia, Easy Road, Costas, The Man With the Carnation, Les Clowns de Dieu, Le Brouillard, Barluschke, Beware of Greeks Bearing Guns.
TELEVISION: Peri anemon kai ydaton (series).

THERON, CHARLIZE
Actress. b. Benoni, South Africa, August 7, 1975. Trained as a dancer. Worked for Joffrey Ballet in New York prior to an injury that ended her ballet career.
PICTURES: Children of the Corn II, Two Days in the Valley, That Thing You Do!, Trial and Error, The Devil's Advocate, Celebrity, Mighty Joe Young, The Astronaut's Wife, The Cider House Rules, Reindeer Games, The Yards, Men of Honor, The Legend of Bagger Vance, Sweet November, 15 Minutes, The Curse of the Jade Scorpion, Waking Up in Reno, Trapped, The Italian Job, The Husband I Bought. Producer: Sweet Home Alabama.
TELEVISION: Movies: Hollywood Confidential, The Life and Death of Peter Sellers.

THEWLIS, DAVID
Actor. b. Blackpool, England, March 20, 1962. e. Guildhall School of Music and Drama, The Barbicon, London. First prof. job in breakfast food commercial.
PICTURES: Little Dorrit, Resurrected, Life Is Sweet, Afraid of the Dark, Damage, The Trial, Naked (Cannes Film Fest., NY Film Critics & Natl. Soc. of Film Critics Awards, 1993), Black Beauty, Restoration,Total Eclipse, Dragonheart, James and the Giant Peach (voice), The Island of Dr. Moreau, Seven Years in Tibet, American Perfekt, Divorcing Jack, The Big Lebowski, Besieged, Whatever Happened to Harold Smith?, Gangster No. 1, Great Sex, Goodbye Charlie Bright, Timeline, Cheeky, Harry Potter and the Prisoner of Azkaban.
TELEVISION: Movies: Only Fools and Horses, The Singing Detective, Filipino Dreamgirls, Prime Suspect, Dandelion Dead, Love Story, The Miracle Maker (voice), Endgame, Discovering Hamilton Mattress. Mini-series: Dinotopia.

THIGPEN, LYNNE
Actress, Singer. b. Joliet, IL, Dec. 22, 1948.
THEATRE: NY: Godspell, The Magic Show, But Never Jam Today, Tintypes, And I Ain't Finished Yet, Full Hookup, Balm in Gilead, A Month of Sundays, Fences, Boesman & Lena, An American Daughter (B'way).
PICTURES: Godspell (debut, 1973), The Warriors, Tootsie, Streets of Fire, Sweet Liberty, Hello Again, Running on Empty, Lean on Me, Impulse, Article 99, Bob Roberts, The Paper, Naked in New York, Blankman, Just Cause, Random Hearts, The Insider, Bicentennial Man, Shaft, Novocaine, Anger Management.
TELEVISION: Series: Love Sidney, The News is the News, FM, All My Children, Where in the World is Carmen Sandiego?, Where in Time is Carmen Sandiego?, Bear in the Big Blue House (voice), The District. Pilot: Pottsville. Guest: The Equalizer, Gimme a Break, L.A. Law, Days and Nights of Molly Dodd, Roseanne, Frank's Place, The Cosby Show, Dear John, thirtysomething, Preston Episodes, Law & Order, King of the Hill (voice). Movies: Fear Stalk, Separate But Equal, A Mother's Instinct, Boys Next Door, Cagney & Lacey: The View Through the Glass Ceiling, An American Daughter. Pilot: For the People, Those Two, A Mother Instinct, The Boys Next Door, Chance of a Lifetime. (d. March 12, 2003)

THINNES, ROY
Actor. b. Chicago, IL, April 6, 1938. Made tv debut as teen on DuPont Theatre, 1957.
PICTURES: Journey to the Far Side of the Sun, Charlie One-Eye, Airport 75, The Hindenburg, Rush Week, Bar Hopping, A Beautiful Mind.
TELEVISION: Series: General Hospital (1963-65), The Long Hot Summer, The Invaders, The Psychiatrist, From Here to Eternity, One Life to Live, Falcon Crest, Dark Shadows, The X Files. Movies: The Other Man, The Psychiatrist: God Bless the Children, Black Noon, The Horror at 37000 Feet, The Norliss Tales, Satan's School for Girls, Death Race, The Manhunter, Secrets, Code Name: Diamond Head, Sizzle, The Return of the Mod Squad, Freedom, Dark Holiday, Blue Bayou, The Hand in the Glove, An Inconvenient Woman, Lady Against the Odds, Stormy Weathers, The Indians, Terminal, Bar Hopping. Mini-Series: From Here to Eternity, Scruples, The Invaders.

THOMAS, BETTY
Director, Actress. b. St. Louis, MO, July 27, 1949. e. Ohio U, Chicago Art Inst., Roosevelt U. Former member of Chicago's Second City improv group.
PICTURES: Actress: Tunnelvision, Chesty Anderson—U.S. Navy, Loose Shoes, Used Cars, Homework, Troop Beverly Hills, Jackson County Jail. Director: Only You, The Brady Bunch Movie, Private Parts, Doctor Dolittle, 28 Days, Surviving Christmas, The Dreyfus Affair: A Love Story, I Spy, R3. Prod.: Can't Hardly Wait, Charlie's Angels, I Spy, Charlie's Angels: Full Throttle, Surviving Christmas.
TELEVISION: Series: Hill Street Blues (Emmy Award, 1985). Movies: Outside Chance, Nashville Grab, When Your Lover Leaves, Prison for Children. Director (series): Doogie Howser M.D., Dream On (Emmy Award, 1993), Hooperman, Mancusco FBI, Arresting Behavior, Couples. Movie: My Breast. Specials: The Late Shift (Dir's Guild of America Award, 1997).

THOMAS, DAVE
Actor, Writer, Director. b. St. Catherines, Ontario, Canada, May 20, 1949. e. McMaster Univ.
PICTURES: Stripes (debut, 1981), Strange Brew (also co-dir., co-s.p.), My Man Adam, Sesame Street Presents Follow That Bird, Love at Stake, Nightflyers, Moving, The Experts (dir. only), Cold Sweat, Coneheads, Public Enemy #2, MVP: Most Valuable Primate, Rat Race, Fancy Dancing, Trial and Error: The Making of Sequestered, Brother Bear (voice).
TELEVISION: Series (actor/writer): Second City TV, SCTV Network The New Show, The Dave Thomas Comedy Show (also exec. prod., dir.), Maniac Mansion, Grace Under Fire (actor only). Movies: Home to Stay, Just Me and You, The Canadian Conspiracy, Boris and Natasha, Ghost Mom (writer). Pilot: From Cleveland, Picture Perfect, Kidz in the Wood, The New Beachcombers. Specials: Twilight Theatre, Martin Short Concert for the North, Dave Thomas: The Incredible Time Travels of Henry Osgood (also dir., exec. prod., writer), Andrea Martin: Together Again, Inside America's Totally Unsolved Lifestyles (also exec. prod., writer).

THOMAS, HENRY
Actor. b. San Antonio, TX, Sept. 8, 1971. Made film debut at the age of 9 in Raggedy Man, 1981. On stage in Artichoke, The Guardsman.
PICTURES: Raggedy Man (debut, 1981), E.T.: The Extra-Terrestrial, Misunderstood, Cloak and Dagger, The Quest, Murder One, Valmont, Fire in the Sky, Legends of the Fall, Bombshell, Suicide Kings, Niagara Niagara, Hijacking Hollywood, A Good Baby, Fever, All the Pretty Horses, I'm With Lucy, Dead in the Water, Gangs of New York, I Capture the Castle, Briar Patch, Honey Baby, 11:14.
TELEVISION: Movies: Psycho IV: The Beginning, A Taste for Killing, Curse of the Starving Class, Indictment: The McMartin Trial, Riders of the Purple Sage, Moby Dick, Happy Face Murders. Special: The Steeler and the Pittsburgh Kid.

THOMAS, JAY
Actor. b. New Orleans, LA, July 12, 1948. Started as stand-up comedian before pursuing acting career in NY. Appeared on NY stage with Playwrights Horizons and Off-B'way in Isn't It Romantic? Also morning DJ on L.A. radio station KPWR-FM.
PICTURES: C.H.U.D., The Gig, Straight Talk, Mr. Holland's Opus, A Smile Like Yours, Dirty Laundry, A Smile Like Yours, The Adventures of Ragtime, Last Chance, The Big Tease, Stranger in My House, Surfacing, Dragonfly, The Santa Clause 2: The Mrs. Clause.
TELEVISION: Movies: Miracle Landing, A Husband A Wife A Lover, Deserts Edge, Killing Mr. Griffin, My Date with the President's Daughter, Monday Night Mayhem. Series: Mork & Mindy, Cheers, Married People, Love & War, Katie Joplin. Guest: Murphy Brown (Emmy Award, 1991).

THOMAS, JEREMY
Producer. b. London, Eng., July 26, 1949. e. Millfield School. Son of dir. Ralph Thomas (Doctor comedies) and nephew of dir. Gerald Thomas (Carry On... comedies). Entered industry 1969. Worked as film edit. on Brother Can You Spare a Dime, 1974. Received Evening Standard Special Award for Outstanding

Contribution to Cinema in 1990, BAFTA's Michael Balcon Award in 1991. Appointed chmn. of British Film Institute, 1992.
PICTURES: Mad Dog Morgan, The Shout, The Great Rock 'n' Roll Swindle, Bad Timing: A Sensual Obsession, Eureka, Merry Christmas Mr. Lawrence, The Hit, Insignificance, The Last Emperor (Academy Award, 1987), Everybody Wins, The Sheltering Sky, Let Him Have It (exec. prod.), Naked Lunch, Little Buddha, Stealing Beauty, Blood and Wine, The Brave, All the Little Animals (dir.), Phorpa, Gohatto, Brother, Sexy Beast, The Triumph of Love, Heaven and Hell, Rabbit-Proof Fence, Young Adam, The Dreamers.

THOMAS, LEO J.
Executive. b. Grand Rapids, MN. e. Univ. of MI, Univ. of IL. Started as research chemist in 1961 at Color Photog. Division of the Kodak Research Labs. 1967-70, head of Color Physics and Engineering Lab; 1970-72, asst. head of Color Photog. Division; 1972-74, tech. asst. to dir. of the Research Labs; 1974, appointed sec. of Technical Affairs Committee. 1977, named dir. of Research Laboratories; later that year became v.p. of the company; 1978 elected sr. v.p. 1984, appointed gen. mgr. Life Sciences. 1988, v.p. Sterling Drug; 1989, gen. mgr. of Health Group; 1989, v.p. of Health Group; 1991, pres. of Imaging Group; 1994, exec. v.p. Eastman Kodak Company.

THOMAS, MARLO
Actress. b. Detroit, MI, Nov. 21, 1938. Daughter of late Danny Thomas. m. Phil Donahue. Brother is TV producer Tony Thomas. e. U. of Southern California. Started career with small TV roles, summer stock. Appeared in London stage prod. of Barefoot in the Park. Most Promising Newcomer Awards from both Fame and Photoplay for series That Girl. Conceived book, record and TV special Free to Be You and Me (Emmy Award, 1974).
THEATRE: NY: Thieves, Social Security, The Shadow Box. Regional: Six Degrees of Separation.
PICTURES: Jenny, Thieves, In the Spirit, The Real Blonde, Starstruck, Deuce Bigalow: Male Gigalo, Playing Mona Lisa.
TELEVISION: Series: The Joey Bishop Show, That Girl. Specials: Acts of Love and Other Comedies, Free To Be You and Me (also prod.; Emmy Award, 1974), The Body Human: Facts for Girls (Emmy Award, 1981), Love Sex... and Marriage (also exec. prod.), Free to Be a Family (host, exec. prod.; Emmy Award, 1989), Funny Women of Television, Kids Are Punny, Intimate Portrait: Gloria Steinem. Movies: It Happened One Christmas (also co-prod.), The Lost Honor of Kathryn Beck (also exec. prod.), Consenting Adult, Nobody's Child (Emmy Award, 1986), Leap of Faith (co-exec. prod. only), Held Hostage: The Sis and Jerry Levin Story, Ultimate Betrayal, Reunion (also co-exec. prod.), Two Against Time. Guest: Dobie Gillis, Zane Grey Theatre, Thriller, Ally McBeal, Friends.

THOMAS, PHILIP MICHAEL
Actor. b. Columbus, OH, May 26, 1949. e. Oakwood Coll.
PICTURES: Black Fist, Sparkle, Death Drug, The Wizard of Speed and Time, Miami Shakedown, Vampirates.
TELEVISION: Series: Miami Vice. Movies: Toma, The Beasts Are on the Streets, Lawman Without a Gun, Miami Vice: Brother's Keeper, This Man Stands Alone, Valentine, A Fight for Jenny, False Witness, A Little Piece of Sunshine, Extralarge: Moving Target, Perry Mason: The Case of the Ruthless Reporter, Extralarge: Miami Killer, Extralarge: Magic Power , Extralarge: Jo-Jo, Extralarge: Cannonball, Extralarge: Black Magic, Extralarge: Black and White. Special: Disney's Totally Minnie, The Debbie Allen Special.

THOMAS, RICHARD
Actor. b. New York, NY, June 13, 1951. e. Columbia U. Made TV debut at age 7 on Hallmark Hall of Fame The Christmas Tree. That same year appeared on Broadway in Sunrise at Campobello.
THEATRE: Sunrise at Campobello, Everything in the Garden, Fifth of July, The Front Page, Love Letters, Square One, The Lisbon Traviata, Danton's Death, Richard II, Richard III.
PICTURES: Winning (debut, 1969), Last Summer, Red Sky at Morning, The Todd Killings, You'll Like My Mother, September 30, 1955, Battle Beyond the Stars, Andy Colby's Incredible Adventure, Riding the Rails, The Million Dollar Kid, Wonder Boys.
TELEVISION: Series: One Two Three Go, As the World Turns, The Waltons (Emmy Award, 1973). Guest: Great Ghost Tales, Bonanza, Love American Style, Medical Center, Marcus Welby M.D., The F.B.I., Tales From the Crypt (Mute Witness to Murder), The Outer Limits, The Promised Land, The Adventures of Swiss Family Robinson, It's a Miracle, Just Cause. Movies: Homecoming, The Red Badge of Courage, The Silence, Getting Married, No Other Love, All Quiet on the Western Front, To Find My Son, Berlin Tunnel 21, Johnny Belinda, Living Proof: The Hank Williams Jr. Story, Hobson's Choice, The Master of Ballantrae, Final Jeopardy, Glory Glory, Go To the Light, Common Ground, Stephen King's IT, Mission of the Shark, Yes Virginia There Is a Santa Claus, Crash Landing: The Rescue of Flight 232, I Can Make You Love Me: The Stalking of Laura Black, Precious Victims, Linda, A Walton Thanksgiving Reunion, Death in Small Doses, A Walton Wedding, Down Out and Dangerous, The Christmas Box, What Love Sees, Time Piece, A Walton Easter, A Thousand Men and a Baby, Flood: A River's

Rampage, Big and Hairy, Beyond the Prairie: The True Story of Laura Ingalls Wilder, In the Name of the People, The Christmas Secret, The Miracle of the Cards, Beyond the Prairie 2: The True Story of Laura Ingalls Wilder, Anna's Dream. *Specials:* A Doll's House, Give Us Barabbas, HMS Pinafore, Barefoot in the Park, Fifth of July, Andre's Mother.

THOMAS, ROBERT G.
Producer, Director. b. Glen Ridge, NJ, July 21, 1943. e. U. of Bridgeport, Fairleigh Dickinson U. Prod. educational radio programs, 1962, WPKN-FM. Asst. stage mgr. Meadowbrook Dinner Theatre, 1963; 1964, began career as TV cameraman for NY stations. Worked both full-time and freelance for major TV and video tape studios. 1968, started Bob Thomas Productions, producing business/sales films and TV commercials. Has 8 awards from natl. film festivals; nominated for 5 Emmys for TV series called The Jersey Side he produced for WOR-TV. Inventor of Futurevision 2000 multi-imaging video system for conventions and exhibits and museums (American Museum of Natural History: Hall of Human Biology to be shown over 15 years). Inventor and pres. of Video Mail Marketing Inc., low cost, light weight paper board video cassettes for the direct mail video marketing industry. *Shorts:* Valley Forge with Bob Hope, New Jersey—200 Years, Road-Eo '77.
TELEVISION: The Jersey Side (talk/entertainment), Jersey People (weekly talk/entertainment prog.), Movies '89 (synd. film preview series).

THOMOPOULOS, ANTHONY D.
Executive. b. Mt. Vernon, NY, Feb. 7, 1938. e. Georgetown U. Began career in broadcasting at NBC, 1959, starting as mailroom clerk and moving to radio division in prod. & admin. Shortly named to post in int'l division sales, involved with programming for stations and in dev. TV systems for other nations. Joined Four Star Entertainment Corp. as dir. of foreign sales, 1964; named v.p., 1965; exec. v.p., 1969; 1970 joined RCA SelectaVision Div. as dir. of programming; 1971 joined Tomorrow Entertainment as v.p.; 1973 joined ABC as v.p., prime-time programs in N.Y.; 1974, named v.p., prime-time TV creative operations, ABC Entertainment; 1975 named v.p. of special programs, ABC Entertainment; 1976 made v.p., ABC-TV, assisting pres. Frederick S. Pierce in supervising all activities of the division; 1978 named pres. of ABC Entertainment; 1983 promoted to pres., ABC Broadcast Group in chg. all TV & radio operations; 1986-88, pres. & COO, United Artists Corp.; independent prod. with Columbia, 1989. Formed Thomopoulos Productions in 1989. Pres., Amblin Television, 1991-95. Responsible for the original placement of ER in addition to several other series on network television.

THOMPSON, CAROLINE
Writer. b. Washington, DC, Apr. 23, 1956. e. Amherst Col., Harvard. Started as free-lance journalist. Wrote novel First Born, which led to screenwriting.
PICTURES: Edward Scissorhands (also assoc. prod.), The Addams Family, Homeward Bound: The Incredible Journey, The Secret Garden (also assoc. prod.), The Nightmare Before Christmas, Black Beauty (also dir.), Buddy (also dir.).
TELEVISION: Snow White: The Fairest of Them All (also dir.).

THOMPSON, EMMA
Actress. b. London, England, Apr. 15, 1959. e. Cambridge Univ. Daughter of actors Eric Thompson and Phyllida Law. Acted with the Footlights at the Edinburgh Fringe. At Cambridge co-wrote, co-produced, co-directed and co-starred in school's first all-female revue Woman's Hour, as well as solo show Short Vehicle.
THEATRE: *London*: Me and My Girl, Look Back in Anger. Renaissance Theatre Company (World Tour): A Midsummer Night's Dream, King Lear.
PICTURES: Henry V, The Tall Guy, Impromptu, Dead Again, Howards End (Academy Award, BAFTA, NY Film Critics, LA Film Critics, Golden Globe, Nat'l Society of Film Critics & Nat'l Board of Review Awards for Best Actress of 1992), Peter's Friends, Much Ado About Nothing, The Remains of the Day (Acad. Award nom.), In the Name of the Father (Academy Award nom.), My Father the Hero, Junior, Carrington, Sense and Sensibility (also s.p.; BAFTA Award, 1995; Academy Award for s.p.,1996; Writers Guild Award, 1996; Golden Globe Award, 1996), The Winter Guest, Judas Kiss, Primary Colors, Maybe Baby, Treasure Planet, Imagining Argentina.
TELEVISION: *Series*: Thompson (also writer). *Mini-Series*: Tutti Frutti, Fortunes of War (BAFTA Best Actress award), Angels in America. *Specials*: The Emma Thompson Special, The Winslow Boy, Look Back in Anger, Knuckle, The Blue Boy, Hospital. *Guest*: Cheers, Ellen.*Movies*: Wit (Emmy nom.), We Know Where You Live.

THOMPSON, FRED (DALTON)
Actor. b. Sheffield, AL, Aug. 19, 1942. Raised in TN. e. Memphis St. U, Vanderbilt U, studying law. Was Federal prosecutor before going to DC to serve as minority counsel on the Senate Select Committe on Presidential Campaign Activities, which involved investigation of the Watergate scandal. Hired to serve as consultant on film Marie, then was asked to play himself in the movie, resulting in acting career. Elected 1994 to U.S. senate as

Republican representative from Tennessee. *Author*: At That Point in Time (1975).
PICTURES: Marie (debut, 1985), No Way Out, Feds, Fat Man and Little Boy, The Hunt for Red October, Days of Thunder, Die Hard 2, Flight of the Intruder, Class Action, Necessary Roughness, Curly Sue, Cape Fear, Thunderheart, White Sands, Aces: Iron Eagle III, Born Yesterday, In the Line of Fire, Baby's Day Out.
TELEVISION: *Movies*: Bed of Lies, Keep the Change, Stay the Night, Day-O, Barbarians at the Gate. *Series*: Law & Order.

THOMPSON, JACK
Actor. r.n. John Payne. b. Sydney, Australia, Aug. 31, 1940. e. Queensland U. Joined drama workshop at school; first part was in TV soap opera as continuing character. 1988, appt. to bd. of Australian Film Finance Corp. Formed Pan Film Enterprises.
PICTURES: The Savage Wild, Outback (Wake in Fright), Libido, Petersen, A Sunday Too Far Away, Caddie, Scobie Malone, Mad Dog Morgan, The Chant of Jimmie Blacksmith, The Journalist, Breaker Morant, The Earthling, The Club, The Man From Snowy River, Bad Blood, Merry Christmas Mr. Lawrence, Flesh + Blood, Burke & Willis, Ground Zero, Waterfront, Turtle Beach, Wind, A Far Off Place, Deception, The Sum of Us, The Last Dance, Excess Baggage, Midnight in the Garden of Good and Evil, Feeling Sexy, The Magic Pudding, The Yolngu Boy, Original Sin, Star Wars: Episode II-Attack of the Clones, The Assassination of Richard Nixon.
TELEVISION: The Last Frontier, A Woman Called Golda, The Letter, Waterfront, The Letter, Kojak: The Price of Justice, The Riddle of the Stinson, Trouble in Paradise, After the Shock, Beryl Markham: A Shadow on the Sun, Paradise, Last Frontier, Wreck of the Stinson, Thornbirds: The Missing Years, McLeod's Daughters, South Pacific. *Mini-Series*: A Woman of Independent Means, My Brother Jack.

THOMPSON, LEA
Actress. b. Rochester, MN, May 31, 1961. m. director Howard Deutch. Danced professionally since age of 14; won scholarship to Pennsylvania Ballet Co., American Ballet Theatre, San Francisco Ballet. Gave up that career for acting, appearing in several commercials for Burger King. *L.A. stage*: Bus Stop, The Illusion.
PICTURES: Jaws 3-D (debut, 1983), All the Right Moves, Red Dawn, The Wild Life, Back to the Future, SpaceCamp, Howard the Duck, Some Kind of Wonderful, Casual Sex?, Going Undercover, The Wizard of Loneliness, Back to the Future Part II, Back to the Future Part III, Article 99, Dennis the Menace, The Beverly Hillbillies, The Little Rascals, The Unknown Cyclist, Fish Don't Blink, Electric, Haunted Lighthouse.
TELEVISION: *Series*: Caroline in the City, For the People. *Movies*: Nightbreaker, Montana, Stolen Babies, The Substitute Wife, The Unspoken Truth, Right to Remain Silent. *Mini-Series*: A Will of Their Own. *Guest*: Tales From the Crypt.

THOMPSON, SADA
Actress. b. Des Moines, IA, Sept. 27, 1929. e. Carnegie Inst. of Technology, Pittsburgh. First N.Y. stage appearance in Under Milk Wood. B'way incl. The Effect of Gamma Rays (Obie, Drama Desk, Variety Poll), Twigs (Tony Award, 1972), Saturday, Sunday, Monday. Recent theater: Real Estate, Any Given Day.
PICTURES: Pursuit of Happiness, Desperate Characters, This Is My Father, Pollock.
TELEVISION: *Specials*: Sandburg's Lincoln, Our Town, The Skin of Our Teeth, Andre's Mother, Painting Churches. *Movies*: The Entertainer, Princess Daisy, My Two Loves, Fatal Confession: A Father Dowling Mystery, Home Fires Burning, Fear Stalk, Indictment: The McMartin Trial, Any Mother's Son , The Patron Saint of Liars *Series*: Family (Emmy Award, 1978). *Mini-Series*: Queen.

THORNTON, BILLY BOB
Actor, Director, Writer. b. Hot Springs, AR, Aug. 5, 1955.
PICTURES: *Actor*: Hubter's Blood, South of Reno, Babes Ahoy, One False Move (also s.p.), For the Boys, Trouble Bound, Chopper Chicks in Zombietown, Tombstone, Some Call It a Sling Blade (also s.p., dir.), Bound by Honor, On Deadly Ground, Floundering, Stars Fell on Henrietta, Dead Man, The Winner, Sling Blade (also dir. s.p.; Acad. Award, for best adapt. s.p., 1996; Chicago Film Critics Award for best actor; Ind't Spirit Awards), U-Turn, A Thousand Miles, Primary Colors, Homegrown, The Apostle, A Gun A Car A Blonde, Armageddon, A Simple Plan (Acad. Award nom.), Pushing Tin, South of Heaven, West of Hell, All the Pretty Horses (dir., prod.), The Man Who Wasn't There, Franky Goes to Hollywood, The Last Real Cowboys, Wakin' Up in Reno, Daddy and Them (also s.p.), The Barber Project, Bandits, Monster's Ball, Waking Up in Reno, Intolerable, Levity, Bad Santa, Intolerable Cruelty, The Alamo . *Writer*: A Family Thing, Camouflage, The Gift.
TELEVISION: *Movies*: The 1,000 Chains (actor), Don't Look Back (actor, writer). *Series*: The Outsiders (actor), Hearts Afire (actor). *Guest*: Matlock, Ellen.

THULIN, INGRID
Actress, Director. b. Solleftea, Sweden, Jan. 27, 1929. m. Harry Schein. Made acting debut at 18 at the Municipal Theatre in Norrkoping. Studied at Stockholm's Royal Dramatic Theatre. Worked with Malmo and Stockholm repertory. Appeared on Swedish stage in nearly 50 plays including Gigi, Peer Gynt, Two for the Seesaw, Twelfth Night, Miss Julie. Has directed plays and films in Stockholm. N.Y. stage debut, 1967: Of Love Remembered. Author: Somebody I Knew (1993).
PICTURES: Where the Wind Blows, Love Will Conqueror, Jack of Hearts, Foreign Intrigue, Wild Strawberries, Brink of Life (Cannes Film Fest. Award), The Magician, The Judge, The Four Horsemen of the Apocalypse, Winter Light, The Silence, Games of Desire, Return From the Ashes, La Guerre est Finie, Night Games, Adelaide, Hour of the Wolf, I a Virgin, The Ritual, The Damned, Cries and Whispers, A Handful of Love, La Cage, Moses, Madame Kitty, The Cassandra Crossing, Broken Sky, At the Rehearsal, Control, House of Smiles, Rabbit Face, others.

THURMAN, UMA
Actress. b. Boston, MA, Apr. 29, 1970. m. actor Ethan Hawke. Named after a Hindu deity. Raised in Woodstock, NY and Amherst, MA where father taught Asian studies. Father's work took family to India where they lived three years. e. Professional Children's School, NY. Worked as model while still in high school.
PICTURES: Kiss Daddy Good Night (debut, 1988), Johnny Be Good, Dangerous Liaisons, The Adventures of Baron Munchausen, Where the Heart Is, Henry and June, Final Analysis, Jennifer Eight, Mad Dog and Glory, Even Cowgirls Get the Blues, Pulp Fiction (Acad. Award nom.), A Month by the Lake, The Truth About Cats and Dogs, Beautiful Girls, Batman and Robin, Gattaca, Les Miserables, The Avengers, Sweet and Lowdown, Vatel, The Golden Bowl, Tape, Chelsea Walls, Kill Bill: Volume 1, Paycheck.
TELEVISION: *Movies:* Robin Hood, Hysterical Blindness. *Specials:* Without Lying Down: Frances Marion and the Power of Women in Hollywood.

THURSTON, BARRY
Executive. b. Hackensack, NJ. e. B.S., economics, Lehigh U. Began career as broadcaster, director and producer for network telecasts, Sports Network; program mgr., Kaiser Broadcasting, and station mgr., WKBD, 1965-1970; dir. of programming, v.p., programming, Field Communications (formerly Kaiser Broadcasting); v.p., domestic synd., Embassy Communications, 1983-85; senior v.p., domestic synd., and president, Embassy Comm., 1985-86; president of syndication, Columbia/Embassy Television, 1986-87; president of syndication, Columbia Pictures Entertainment and Columbia Pictures Television, 1987-92; president, Columbia Pictures Television Distribution (now Columbia TriStar Television Distribution - CTTD), 1992-present. Responsible for ushering CTTD into new areas of first-run syndication and first-run production for cable, and formed Columbia TriStar Advertiser Sales, 1993. Served on the board for NATPE and Combined Broadcasting and was a member of INTV's planning committee. Currently on the board of directors, TVB.

THURSTON, DONALD A.
Executive. b. Gloucester, MA, April 2, 1930. Began career in broadcasting in 1949. Former Chmn., National Assoc. of Broadcasters. Past Pres., Massachusetts Broadcasters Assoc. Former Commissioner of Massachusetts Cable TV Commission. Former Chmn. of Broadcast Capital Fund, Inc. a venture capital co. that assists minorities in the acquisition of broadcast properties. Pres. Berkshire Broadcasting Co. Inc. Director and Former Chmn., Broadcast Music, Inc. Received Honorary Doctor of Humanities from North Adams State College (1977), Doctor of Humane Letters, Emerson college (1995). Recipient of the Distinguished Service Award of the National Association of Broadcasters.

TICOTIN, RACHEL
Actress. b. Bronx, NY, Nov. 1, 1958. Began career as dancer with the Ballet Hispanico of New York, before becoming a production assist. on such films as The Wanderers, Dressed to Kill and Raging Bull.
PICTURES: King of the Gypsies, Fort Apache: The Bronx, Critical Condition, Total Recall, One Good Cop, FX2, Falling Down, Natural Born Killers, Don Juan DeMarco, Steal Big Steal Little, Turbulence, Con-Air, The Day October Died, Can't Be Heaven, Civility, Desert Saints.
TELEVISION: *Series:* For Love and Honor, Ohara, Crime and Punishment, American Family, Skin. *Movies:* Love Mary, Rockabye, When the Bough Breaks, Spies Lies and Naked Thighs, Prison Stories: Women on the Inside, Keep the Change, From the Files of Joseph Wambaugh: A Jury of One, Thicker Than Blood: The Larry McLinden Story, Deconstructing Sarah, The Wharf Rat, First Time Felon, Aftershock: Earthquake in New York, Warden of Red Rock.

TIERNEY, MAURA
Actress. b. Boston, MA, Feb. 3, 1965.
PICTURES: Dead Women in Lingerie, The Linguini Incident, White Sands, The Temp, Fly by Night, Primal Fear, Mercy, Liar Liar, Primary Colors, Oxygen (also exec. prod.), Forces of

Nature, Instinct, Mexico City, Scotland PA, Insomnia, The Nazi, Phyro-Giants.
TELEVISION: *Movies:* Student Exchange, Crossing the Mob, Flying Blind, Out of Darkness. *Series:* The Van Dyke Show, 704 Hauser, NewsRadio, ER, The Andy Dick Show. *Guest:* Booker, Law & Order.

TIFFIN, PAMELA
Actress. r.n. Pamela Wonso. b. Oklahoma City, OK, Oct. 13, 1942. e. Hunter Coll., Columbia U., Loyola U, Rome Center. Studied acting with Stella Adler and Harold Clurman. Started modeling as a teenager.
THEATRE: Dinner at Eight (Theatre World Award), Uncle Vanya.
PICTURES: Summer and Smoke (debut, 1961), One Two Three, State Fair, Come Fly with Me, For Those Who Think Young, The Lively Set, The Pleasure Seekers, Kiss the Other Sheik, The Hallelujah Trail, Harper, Paranoia, Viva Max!, The Godson, Giornata Nera per l'Ariete, Deaf Smith and Johnny Ears, Puntto e a Capo, Evil Fingers.

TIGHE, KEVIN
Actor. b. Los Angeles, CA, Aug. 13, 1944. e. Cal. State, B.A. in psychology; USC M.F.A. in performing arts. Served in U.S. Army, 1967-69. Received N.E.A. Director's Fellowship, Seattle Rep. Theatre, 1988-89.
PICTURES: The Graduate (debut, 1967), Matewan, Eight Men Out, K-9, Lost Angels, Road House, Another 48 HRS, Bright Angel, City of Hope, Newsies, School Ties, A Man in Uniform (Genie Award), Geronimo: An American Legend, What's Eating Gilbert Grape, Scorpion Spring, Jade, Race the Sun, The Wentonkawa Flash, Mumford, The Big Day.
TELEVISION: *Series:* Emergency, Murder One. *Guest:* Tales From the Crypt (Cutting Cards). *Movies:* Better Off Dead, Betrayal of Trust, The Avenging Angel, Winchell, The Darwin Conspiracy, The Sight, Nancy Drew. *Mini-Series:* Rose Red.

TILLY, JENNIFER
Actress. b. Harbour City, CA, Sept. 16, 1962. Sister is actress Meg Tilly.
THEATRE: One Shoe Off (Off-B'way debut, 1993; Theatre World Award).
PICTURES: No Small Affair, Moving Violations, Inside Out, He's My Girl, Johnny Be Good, Rented Lips, High Spirits, Far From Home, Let It Ride, The Fabulous Baker Boys, Made in America, The Getaway, Bullets Over Broadway (Acad. Award nom.), Man With a Gun, Embrace of the Vampire, House Arrest, The Pompatus of Love, Bound, Bird of Prey, Edie and Pen, American Strays, Liar Liar, Bride of Chucky, Relax...It's Just Sex, The Wrong Guy, Hoods, Music From Another Room, Goosed, The Muse (cameo), Do Not Disturb, Stuart Little, Play It to the Bone, Bruno, Cord, The Crew, Dancing at the Blue Iguana, Dirt, Fast Sofa, The Cat's Meow, Monsters Inc., Sultans of Africa, Joplin: The Movie, Ball in the House, Babylon Revisited, Sex & Violence, A Piece of My Heart, Lil' Pimp, Second Best, El Padrino, Nowhere to Go But Up, Home on the Range (voice), The Haunted Mansion.
TELEVISION: *Series:* Shaping Up, Family Guy. *Movie:* Heads, Bella Mafia, The Kid, Sister Mary Explains It All, The Magnificent Ambersons, Stage on Screen: The Women. *Guest:* Hill Street Blues.

TILLY, MEG
Actress. b. Long Beach, CA, Feb. 14, 1960. m. Producer John Calley. Sister is actress Jennifer Tilly. Began acting and dancing in community theatrical prods. while in high school. To New York at 16; appeared on TV in Hill Street Blues. *Author:* Singing Songs (1994).
PICTURES: Fame (debut, 1980), Tex, Psycho II, One Dark Night, The Big Chill, Impulse, Agnes of God (Acad. Award nom.), Off Beat, Masquerade, The Girl in a Swing, Valmont, The Two Jakes, Leaving Normal, Body Snatchers, Sleep with Me.
TELEVISION: *Series:* Winnetka Road. *Specials:* The Trouble With Grandpa, Camilla (Nightmare Classics). *Movies:* In the Best Interest of the Child, Trick of the Eye, Journey. *Guest:* Fallen Angels (Dead-End for Delia).

TINKER, GRANT A.
Executive. b. Stamford, CT., Jan. 11, 1926. e. Dartmouth Coll., 1947. Joined NBC radio prog. dept. 1949. In 1954 with McCann-Erickson ad agency, TV dept. In 1958, Benton & Bowles Ad Agency, TV dept.; 1961-66 with NBC, v.p., programs, West Coast; v.p. in chg. of programming, NY, 1966-67; joined Universal Television as v.p., 1968-69; 20th-Fox, v.p., 1969-70. Became pres. MTM Enterprises, Inc. 1970. Named NBC bd. chmn. & CEO, 1981-86. Received ATAS Governor's Award in 1987. Formed indep. prod. co. GTG. Entertainment, 1988. The GTG partnership was dissolved in 1990. Retired.

TINKER, MARK
Director, Producer. b. Stamford, CT, Jan. 16, 1951. Brother of John Tinker.
TELEVISION: *Movies:* Private Eye, Capital News, N.Y.P.D. Mounted, Babe Ruth, Bonanza: Under Attack. *Series:* L.A. Law, NYPD Blue, Chicago Hope, ER, Brooklyn South (prod., Emmy Award, 1998).

TINKER, JOHN
Writer, Producer. Brother of Mark Tinker.
TELEVISION: *Writer*: St. Elsewhere, L.A. Law, Tattingers, Home Fires, Chicago Hope, The Practice, Judging Amy. *Exec. Producer*: L.A. Law, Home Fires, The Road Home, Chicago Hope, The Practice, Snoops, HRT.

TISCH, LAURENCE A.
Executive. b. Brooklyn, NY, March 5, 1923. e. NYU, 1941; U. of Pennsylvania Wharton Sch., 1942; Harvard Law Sch., 1946. Pres. Tisch Hotels, Inc., 1950-59; pres. Americana Hotel, Inc., Miami Beach, 1956-59; Chmn. of bd. and co-chief executive officer of Loews Corp since 1960. Also chmn. of bd. of CNA Financial Corp since 1947. President, chief executive officer, CBS Inc., New York City, from 1987, chair, president, chief executive officer, board of directors, from 1990.Chair and member of board of directors, CNA Finance Corporation, Chicago. Board of directors: Bulove Corporation, New York City; ADP Corporation; Petrie Stores Corporation; R. H. Macy & Company board of directors, United Jewish Appeal-Federation; chair, board of trustees, New York University. Trustee: Metropolitan Museum of Art, New York City; New York Public Library; Carnegie Corporation.

TISCH, PRESTON ROBERT
Executive. b. Brooklyn, NY, April 29, 1926. e. Bucknell U., Lewisberg, PA, 1943-44; U. of Michigan, B.A., 1948. Pres. Loew's Corporation. Postmaster General of the U.S. 1986-1988. March, 1988 returned to Loews Corp. as president and co-chief executive. Elected member of bd. CBS Inc. 1988, 1994, position changed to co-chmn. & co-CEO of Loews Corp. , a position he holds today (2003).

TISCH, STEVE
Producer. b. Lakewood, NJ, 1949. e. Tufts U. Son of Preston Tisch. Worked during school breaks for John Avildsen and Fred Weintraub. Signed upon graduation as exec. asst. to Peter Guber, then prod. head at Columbia Pics. Entered producer ranks with Outlaw Blues, 1977, collaborating with Jon Avnet with whom formed Tisch/Avnet Prods. Alliance with Phoenix Entertainment 1988.
PICTURES: Outlaw Blues, Almost Summer, Coast to Coast, Risky Business, Deal of the Century, Soul Man, Big Business, Hot to Trot, Heart of Dixie, Heart Condition, Bad Influence, Forrest Gump (Academy Award for Best Picture, 1994), Corrina Corrina. *Exec. Prod.:* The Long Kiss Goodnight, Dear God, Wild America, American History X, The Postman, Nico the Unicorn, Lock Stock and Two Smoking Barrels, Wayward Son, Looking for an Echo, Snatch: Pigs and Diamonds, Alex and Emma.
TELEVISION: Homeward Bound, No Other Love, Prime Suspect, Something So Right, Calendar Girl Murders, The Burning Bed (exec. prod.), Call to Glory (series), Triple Cross, Silence of the Heart, In Love and War (sole prod.), Evil in Clear River, Dirty Dancing (series), Out on the Edge (exec. prod.), Judgment (exec. prod.), Lies of the Heart, The Vidiots (pilot), Victim of Love, Keep the Change, Afterburn (exec. prod.), Freshman Dorm (pilot & series), The People Next Door, Mission Extreme (series).

TOBACK, JAMES
Writer, Producer, Director. b. New York, NY, Nov. 23, 1944. e. Harvard U. Taught literature at City Coll. of New York; contributed articles and criticism to Harper's, Esquire, Commentary, etc. Wrote book Jim, on actor-athlete Jim Brown (1971). First screenplay, The Gambler, filmed in 1974.
PICTURES: *Writer*: The Gambler, Fingers (also dir.), Love and Money (also dir., prod.), Exposed (also dir., prod.), The Pick-Up Artist (also dir.), The Big Bang (also dir., actor), Alice (actor), Bugsy (also actor), Two Girls and a Guy (also dir.), Black and White (also dir.), Love in Paris (also dir.), Harvard Man (also dir.).

TOBOLOWSKY, STEPHEN
Actor. b. Dallas, TX, May 30, 1951. e. Southern Methodist Univ.
THEATER: *Actor*: Whose Life Is It Anyway?, Crimes of the Heart, Godspell, Three Sisters, The Glass Menagerie, Barabass, The Wake of Jamey Foster, The Wild Duck, No Scratch, The Miss Firecracker Contest, The Importance of Being Earnest, Purlie, Whispers in the Wind. *Director*: The Miss Firecracker Contest, The Lucky Spot, The Bridgehead (Dramalogue Award), The Secret Rapture (Dramalogue Award), Our Town, The Debutante Ball.
PICTURES: Swing Shift, True Stories (co-s.p.), Nobody's Fool, Spaceballs, Mississippi Burning, Checking Out, Two Idiots in Hollywood (dir. & s.p.), Great Balls of Fire!, In Country, Breaking In, Bird on a Wire, Funny About Love, Welcome Home Roxy Carmichael, The Grifters, Thelma & Louise, Memoirs of an Invisible Man, Basic Instinct, Roadside Prophets, Single White Female, Where the Day Takes You, Sneakers, Hero, Groundhog Day, The Pickle, Calendar Girl, Josh and S.A.M., My Father the Hero, Radioland Murders, Murder in the First, Dr. Jekyll and Ms. Hyde, Power 98, The Glimmer Man, The Curse of the Inferno, The Curse of Inferno, The Brave Little Toaster Goes to Mars, Boys Life II, Mr. Magoo, An Alan Smithee Film: Burn Hollywood Burn, The Operator, Black Dog, One Man's Hero, The Insider, Bossa Nova, Alien Fury: Countdown to Invasion, The Prime Gig, Memento, Urban Chaos Theory, Sleep Easy Hutch Rimes, Freddy Got Fingered, Par 6, It Is What It Is, Country Bears, Love

Liza, Adaptation, A View From the Top.
TELEVISION: *Movies*: Last Flight Out, Marla Hanson Story, Perry Mason: The Case of the Maligned Mobster, Tagget, Deadlock, Deadly Medicine, When Love Kills: The Seduction of John Hearn, Night Visitors, Black River, The Day the World Ended. *Series*: Against the Grain, Blue Skies, A Whole New Ballgame, Dweebs. *Guest*: Crazy Like a Fox, Designing Women, L.A. Law, Days and Nights of Molly Dodd, Seinfeld, Picket Fences, Chicago Hope, Hearts of the West, Baby Talk, Knots Landing, Falcon Crest.

TODD, BEVERLY
Actress, Director, Producer. b. Chicago, IL, July 11.
THEATRE: *NY*: Carry Me Back to Morningside Heights, Black Visions. *Producer*: A Tribute to Ella Fitzgerald. *Director*: I Need a Man, Sneaky.
PICTURES: The Lost Man, They Call Me Mister Tibbs!, Brother John, Vice Squad, Homework, The Ladies Club, Happy Hour, Baby Boom, Moving, Clara's Heart, Lean on Me, The Surgeon.
TELEVISION: *Series*: Love of Life, Having Babies, The Redd Foxx Show. *Mini-Series*: Roots. *Movies*: Deadlock, The Ghost of Flight 401, Having Babies II, The Jericho Mile, Don't Look Back, A Touch of Scandal, A Different Affair. *Guest*: Magnum P.I., The Robert Guillaume Show, Falcon Crest, Quincy M.E., Hill Street Blues, Family, Benson, Lou Grant, A Different World, Good News, Sparks. *Special*: A Laugh a Tear: The Story of Black Humor in America (prod.), Don't Hit Me Mom (Afterschool Special), The Class of '61.

TODD, RICHARD
O.B.E. Actor. b. Dublin, Ireland, June 11, 1919. e. Shrewsbury. In repertory, 1937; founder-member, Dundee Repertory Theatre, 1939; distinguished war service, 1939-46; Dundee Repertory, 1946-48; screen debut, 1948; For Them That Trespass, 1948. 1970 Founder-Director Triumph Theatre Productions. Published autobiography, 1986, Volume II, 1989. Awarded O.B.E., 1993.
THEATRE: An Ideal Husband, Dear Octopus. Co-founder, Triumph Theatre Prods., Ltd. plays since 1970: Roar Like a Dove, Grass Is Greener, The Marquise (U.S.), Sleuth (England and Australia). Murder by Numbers, The Hollow Crown (with RSC), Equus. On Approval, Quadrille, This Happy Breed, The Business of Murder (London), Intent to Kill, The Woman in Black, Beyond Reasonable Doubt, Sweet Revenge, Brideshead Revisited.
PICTURES: For Them That Trespass (debut, 1948), The Hasty Heart, Interrupted Journey, Stage Fright, Portrait of Clare, Lightning Strikes Twice (U.S.), Flesh and Blood, Story of Robin Hood, 24 Hours of a Woman's Life, The Venetian Bird, Sword and the Rose, Rob Roy, Les Secrets d'Alcove (Fr.), A Man Called Peter (U.S.), The Virgin Queen (U.S.), Dam Busters, D-Day the Sixth of June (U.S.), Marie Antoinette (Fr.), Yangtse Incident, Saint Joan, Chase a Crooked Shadow, The Naked Earth, Intent to Kill, Danger Within, Never Let Go, The Long the Short and the Tall, Don't Bother to Knock (also exec. prod.), The Hellions, The Longest Day, Crime Does Not Pay (Fr.), The Boys, The Very Edge, Death Drums Along the River, Battle of the Villa Fiorita, Operation Crossbow, Coast of Skeletons, The Love-Ins, Subterfuge, Dorian Gray, Asylum, The Sky is Falling, Number One of the Secret Service, The Big Sleep, House of the Long Shadows, Incident at Victoria Fall.s .
TELEVISION: Wuthering Heights, Carrington V.C., The Brighton Mesmerists, Beautiful Lies, The Boy Dominic, Murder She Wrote, Virtual Murder., Murder One, Marlene Dietrich: Shadow and Light.

TOKOFSKY, JERRY H.
Executive. b. New York, NY, Apr. 14, 1936. e. NYU, B.S., journalism, 1956; New York Law, 1959. Entered William Morris Agency while at NYU 1953, working in night club dept. to live TV. Moved to Beverly Hills office, 1959. Entered m.p. div. WMA, 1960. Joined Columbia Pictures, as Prod. V.P., 1963-70. Joined Paramount Pictures 1970 as prod. v.p. To MGM as prod. v.p., 1971. Producer & Exec. V.P., Zupnik Enterprises, Inc. until 1992.
PICTURES: *Producer*: Where's Poppa, Born to Win, Paternity, Dreamscape, Fear City, Wildfire, Glengarry Glen Ross, The Grass Harp, Constellation.

TOLAN, PETER
Producer, Writer.
PICTURES: Alice (actor). *Writer*: My Fellow Americans, Analyze This, What Planet Are You From?, Bedazzled, America's Sweethearts, Stealing Harvard, Analyze That, The Wedding Party.
TELEVISION: *Series*: Murphy Brown (Emmy Award, 1992), The Larry Sanders Show (Emmy Award, 1998), Style and Substance, The Job, Wednesday 9:30 (8:30 Central).

TOLKAN, JAMES
Actor. b. Calumet, MI, June 20, 1931. e. Univ. of Iowa.
THEATRE: *NY*: Abe Lincoln in Illinois, Once in a Lifetime, Three Sisters, The Cannibals, Mary Stuart, The Silent Partner, 42 Seconds from Broadway, Full Circle, Macbeth, Dream of a Blacklisted Actor, Jungle of Cities, Wings.
PICTURES: Stiletto, They Might Be Giants, The Friends of Eddie Coyle, Serpico, Love and Death, The Amityville Horror, Wolfen, Prince of the City, Author! Author!, Hanky Panky, Nightmares

(voice), WarGames, Iceman, The River, Turk 182!, Flanagan, Back to the Future, Off Beat, Top Gun, Armed and Dangerous, Masters of the Universe, Made in Heaven, Viper, Split Decisions, True Blood, Second Sight, Back to the Future Part II, Family Business, Opportunity Knocks, Back to the Future Part III, Dick Tracy, Hangfire, Problem Child 2, Driving Me Crazy, Boiling Point, Love in Ambush, Robo Warriors, Wings.
TELEVISION: *Series*: Mary, The Hat Squad, Cobra. *Movies*: Little Spies, Leap of Faith, Weekend War, The Case of the Hillside Stranglers, Sketch Artist, Beyond Betrayal, Sketch Artist II: Hands That See. *Guest*: Remington Steele, Miami Vice, The Equalizer, Tales From the Crypt.

TOLKIN, MICHAEL
Writer, Director, Producer. b. New York, NY, Oct. 17, 1950. e. Middlebury Col, VT. Started as writer for LA Times, Village Voice, before becoming story editor on tv series Delta House. Novels: The Player (1988), Among the Dead (1992).
PICTURES: *Writer*: Gleaming the Cube, The Rapture (also dir.), The Player (also co-prod., actor; WGA Award, Acad. Award nom.), Deep Cover (also dir.), The New Age (also dir.), Deep Impact, Changing Lanes, Dawn of the Dead, The Punisher.
TELEVISION: *Movie*: The Burning Season (co-writer).

TOLL, JOHN
Cinematographer.
PICTURES: *Cam. Op.*: Tom Horn, Norma Rae, Zorro: The Gay Blade, Scarface, The Falcon and the Snowman, Peggy Sue Got Married, Black Widow, Tequila Sunrise, The Milagro Beanfield War, Blaze, Always. *Cinematographer*: Wind, Legends of the Fall (Academy Award), Braveheart (Academy Award), Jack, The Rainmaker, The Thin Red Line (Acad. Award nom.), Simpatico, Almost Famous, Captain Corelli's Mandolin, Vanilla Sky, Orange County, The Last Samurai.
TELEVISION: The Boy Who Drank Too Much (cam. op.), The Kid, The Young Riders, Good Night Sweet Wife: A Murder in Boston.

TOMEI, MARISA
Actress. b. Brooklyn, NY, Dec. 4, 1964. e. Boston U.
THEATRE: Beirut (L.A.). *NY*: Daughters (Theatre World Award), The Comedy of Errors, What the Butler Saw, Slavs!
PICTURES: The Flamingo Kid (debut, 1984), Playing for Keeps, Oscar, Zandalee, My Cousin Vinny (Academy Award, best supporting actress, 1992), Chaplin, Untamed Heart, Equinox, The Paper, Only You, The Perez Family, Four Rooms, A Brother's Kiss, Unhook the Stars, Welcome to Sarajevo, The Women, The Slums of Beverly Hills, Only Love, Happy Accidents, The Watcher, What Women Want, King of the Jungle, Dirk and Betty, In the Bedroom, Someone Like You, Just A Kiss, The Guru, The Wild Thornberrys (voice), Anger Management.
TELEVISION: *Series*: As the World Turns, A Different World. *Guest*: Seinfeld. *Movie*: Parker Kane, Since You've Been Gone, Only Love, My Own Country, Jenifer.

TOMLIN, LILY
Actress. r.n. Mary Jean Tomlin. b. Detroit, MI, Sept. 1, 1939. e. Wayne State U. (studied pre-med). Studied mime with Paul Curtis. Started inventing characters for comedy sketches in college, used them in cafe and night club dates in Detroit. 1965 went to NY performing skits on coffee-house circuit, landed job on The Garry Moore Show. Moved to L.A. where she appeared on The Music Scene. 1969, first appeared on Laugh-In TV series, gaining national attention with such characters as telephone operator Ernestine and child Edith Ann.
RECORDS: This Is a Recording (Grammy Award, 1971), Modern Scream, And That's the Truth, Lily Tomlin On Stage.
THEATRE: Appearing Nitely (special Tony Award, 1977), The Search for Signs of Intelligent Life in the Universe (1985, on B'way and on tour; Tony Award).
PICTURES: Nashville (debut, 1975; NY Film Critics Award; Acad Award nom.), The Late Show, Moment by Moment, Nine to Five, The Incredible Shrinking Woman, All of Me, Big Business, The Search for Signs of Intelligent Life in the Universe, Shadows and Fog, The Player, Short Cuts, The Beverly Hillbillies, Blue in the Face, Getting Away With Murder, The Celluloid Closet (narrator), Flirting With Disaster, Krippendorf's Tribe, Get Bruce (cameo), Tea with Mussolini, Picking Up the Pieces, The Kid, Orange County, I Heart Huckabee's.
TELEVISION: *Series*: The Music Scene (host, 1969), Rowan and Martin's Laugh-In (1969-73), Magic School Bus (voice for animated series; Emmy Award), Murphy Brown, The West Wing. *Specials*: Lily (Emmy Award as writer, 1974), Lily Tomlin (Emmy Award as writer, 1976), The Paul Simon Special (Emmy Award as writer, 1978), Lily: Sold Out! (also exec. prod.; Emmy Award as exec. prod., 1981), The Muppets Go to the Movies, Lily for President?, Live—and in Person, Funny You Don't Look 200, Free to Be... a Family, Edith Ann: A Few Pieces of the Puzzle (voice, exec. prod.), Edith Ann: Homeless Go Home (voice, exec. prod.), Edith Ann's Christmas: Just Say Noel (voice, exec. prod; Peabody Award), various others. *Movie*: And the Band Played On. *Guest*: The X Files, Frasier.

TOPOL
Actor. r.n. Chaim Topol. b. Tel-Aviv, Israel, Sept. 9, 1935.
THEATRE: Fiddler on the Roof (London, 1967, 1994-95 also U.K. tour; NY 1989: Tony nom.; Canada & Japan tour) Chicester Fest. Theatre: Caucasian Chalk Circle, Romanov and Juliet, Othello, View From the Bridge.
PICTURES: Sallah, Cast a Giant Shadow, Before Winter Comes, A Talent for Loving, Fiddler on the Roof (Acad. Award nom.), Follow Me, Galileo, Flash Gordon, For Your Eyes Only, Ervinka, A Dime Novel, Left Luggage, Time Elevator.
TELEVISION: *Movies*: House on Garibaldi Street, Queenie. *Mini-Series*: The Winds of War, War and Remembrance. *Series* (BBC): It's Topol, Topol's Israel.

TORN, RIP
Actor. r.n. Elmore Torn, Jr. b. Temple, TX, Feb. 6, 1931. e. Texas A & M U., U. of TX. Served in army. Signed as understudy for lead in Cat on a Hot Tin Roof on Broadway.
THEATRE: Orpheus Descending, Sweet Bird of Youth (Theatre World Award), Daughter of Silence, Macbeth, Desire Under the Elms, Strange Interlude, Blues For Mr. Charlie, The Kitchen, The Deer Park (Obie Award), The Beard, The Cuban Thing, Dream of a Blacklisted Actor, The Dance of Death, Anna Christie.
PICTURES: Baby Doll (debut, 1956), A Face in the Crowd, Time Limit, Pork Chop Hill, King of Kings, Hero's Island, Sweet Bird of Youth, Critic's Choice, The Cincinnati Kid, One Spy Too Many, You're a Big Boy Now, Beach Red, Sol Madrid, Beyond the Law, Coming Apart, Tropic of Cancer, Maidstone, Slaughter, Payday, Crazy Joe, Birch Interval, The Man Who Fell to Earth, Nasty Habits, The Private Files of J. Edgar Hoover, Coma, The Seduction of Joe Tynan, Heartland, One Trick Pony, First Family, A Stranger is Watching, The Beastmaster, Jinxed, Airplane II: The Sequel, Cross Creek (Acad. Award nom.), Misunderstood, Songwriter, Flashpoint, City Heat, Summer Rental, Beer, Extreme Prejudice, Nadine, The Telephone (also dir.), Cold Feet, Hit List, Blind Curve, The Hunt for Red October, Defending Your Life, Silence Like Glass, Beautiful Dreamers, Hard Promises, Robocop 3, Dolly Dearest, Where the Rivers Flow North, Canadian Bacon, How to Make an American Quilt, Down Periscope, Hercules (voice), Trial and Error, Men in Black, The Mouse, Senseless, Wonder Boys, Men in Black Alien Attack, Freddy Got Fingered, Men in Black II, Rolling Kansas, Love Object, Welcome to Mooseport, Eulogy.
TELEVISION: *Series*: The Larry Sanders Show (Emmy Awatd, 1996), Hercules (voice), Ghost Stories (voice). *Movies*: The President's Plane Is Missing, Attack on Terror: The FBI vs. the Ku Klux Klan, Betrayal, Steel Cowboy, A Shining Season, Sophia Loren—Her Own Story, Rape and Marriage—The Rideout Case, Laguna Heat, When She Says No, The Execution, The Atlanta Child Murders, Manhunt for Claude Dallas, J. Edgar Hoover, The King of Love, April Morning, Sweet Bird of Youth, Pair of Aces, By Dawn's Early Light, Another Pair of Aces, My Son Johnny, Death Hits the Jackpot, T Bone N Weasel, A Mother's Right: The Elizabeth Morgan Story, Dead Ahead: The Exxon Valdez Disaster, She Stood Alone: The Tailhook Scandal, Letter to My Killer, Balloon Farm, Seasons of Love, Maniac Magee, The Lyon's Den. *Mini-Series*: Blind Ambition, The Blue and the Gray, Heaven & Hell: North and South Book III, Heart of a Child. *Guest*: Will & Grace.

TORNATORE, GIUSEPPE
Director. b. Bagheria, Sicily, Italy, 1956. Made directorial debut at age 16 with short film Il Carretto. 1978- 85, served as pres. of the CLTC filmmaking cooperative.
PICTURES: The Professor (debut, 1986), Cinema Paradiso, Everybody's Fine, The Blue Dog (segment), Especially on Sunday (segment), A Pure Formality, The Star Maker (L'uomo delle stelle), The Legend of 1900 (La Leggenda del pianista sull'oceano), Malena.
TELEVISION: Portrait of a Thief, Metting With Francesco Rosi, Sicilian Writers and Films, Il Diario di Guttuso, Ethnic Minorities in Sicily (Salerno Film Fest. Prize), A Hundred Days in Palermo (also writer, 2nd unit dir.).

TOTTER, AUDREY
Actress. b. Joliet, IL, Dec. 20, 1918. In many stage plays. On radio 1939-44.
THEATRE: Copperhead, Stage Door, Late Christopher Bean, My Sister Eileen.
PICTURES: Main Street After Dark (debut, 1944), Her Highness and the Bellboy, Dangerous Partners, The Sailor Takes a Wife, Adventure, The Hidden Eye, The Secret Heart, The Postman Always Rings Twice, Cockeyed Miracle, Lady in the Lake, Beginning or the End, Unsuspected, High Wall, The Saxon Charm, Alias Nick Beal, Any Number Can Play, Tension, The Set-Up, Under the Gun, The Blue Veil, Sellout, F.B.I. Girl, Assignment-Paris, My Pal Gus, Woman They Almost Lynched, Cruisin' Down the River, Man in the Dark, Mission Over Korea, Champ for a Day, Massacre Canyon, Women's Prison, A Bullet for Joey, Vanishing American, Ghost Diver, Jet Attack, Man or Gun, The Carpetbaggers, Harlow, Chubasco, The Apple Dumpling Gang Rides Again, Lugosi: Hollywood's Dracula.
TELEVISION: *Series*: Cimarron City, Our Man Higgins, Medical Center (1972-76). *Movies*: The Outsider, U.M.C., The Nativity, The Great Cash Giveaway, City Killer. Guest: Murder, She Wrote.

TOWERS, CONSTANCE
Actress. b. Whitefish, MT, May 20, 1934. m. John Gavin, actor and former U.S. Ambassador to Mexico. e. Juilliard Sch. of Music. Stage work on Broadway and tour. In Concert with John Raitt, 1998.
THEATRE: *B'way*: Ari, Anya, Engagement Baby, The King and I (1977-79 opp. Yul Brynner), Showboat. *Regional*: Steel Magnolias, Follies, Sound of Music, I Do I Do, Mame, 110 In the Shade, Carousel, Oklahoma, Dumas & Son, Guys & Dolls, Oh Coward.
PICTURES: Bring Your Smile Along, Horse Soldiers, Sergeant Rutledge, Fate Is the Hunter, Shock Corridor, Naked Kiss, Sylvester, Fast Forward, Nutty Nut, The Next Karate Kid, The Relic, A Perfect Murder.
TELEVISION: *Series*: Love Is a Many Splendored Thing, VTV, Capitol, 2000 Malibu Road, General Hospital. *Mini-Series*: On Wings of Eagles, Sands of Time. *Guest*: Home Show, The Loner, Murder, She Wrote, Hour Mag, MacGyver, Designing Women, Midnight Caller, Matlock, Baywatch, Prince of Bel Air, Thunder in Paradise, L.A. Law, Civil Wars, Frasier, Robin's Nest, Caroline in the City, The Young & the Restless.

TOWERS, HARRY ALAN
Executive, Producer. b. London, England, 1920.
PICTURES: Sanders of the River (also s.p.), Code Seven Victim Five (also s.p.), City of Fear, Mozambique, Coast of Skeletons, Sandy the Seal, 24 Hours to Kill, The Face of Fu Manchu, Ten Little Indians, Marrakesh, Circus of Fear, The Brides of Fu Manchu, Sumuru, Five Golden Dragons, The Vengeance of Fu Manchu, Jules Verne's Rocket to the Moon, House of a Thousand Dolls, The Face of Eve, Blood of Fu Manchu, 99 Women, Girl From Rio, Marquis de Sade's Justine, Castle of Fu Manchu, Venus in Furs, Philosophy in the Boudoir, Eugenie, Dorian Gray, Count Dracula, The Bloody Judge, Black Beauty, Night Hair Child, The Call of the Wild, Treasure Island, White Fang, Death in Persepolis, Ten Little Indians, End of Innocence, Black Cobra, Black Velvet—White Silk, Night of The High Tide, King Solomon's Treasure, Shape of Things to Come, Klondike Fever, Fanny Hill, Frank and I, Black Venus, Christmas, Black Arrow, Pompeii, Love Circles, Lightning—The White Stallion, Gor, Outlaw of Gor, Dragonard, Skeleton Coast, Master of Dragonard Hill, Nam, Fire With Fire, Jekyll and Hyde, River of Death, Cobra Strike, The Howling IV: The Original Nightmare, Skeleton Coast, Edge of Sanity, Ten Little Indians, Platoon Leader, Captive Rage, American Ninja III: Blood Hunt, The Fall of the House of Usher, Edgar Allan Poe's Buried Alive, Phantom of the Opera, Oddball Hall, Terror of Manhattan, The Lost World, Return to the Lost World, Black Museum, Golden Years of Sherlock Holmes, The Mangler, Midnight in St. Petersburg, Bullet to Beijing (The Return of Harry Palmer), Cry the Beloved Country, China Bill, She, Stanley & Livingstone, The Zodiac Conspiracy, The House of Usher, Edge of Sanity, Ten Little Indians, River of Death, Outlaw of Gor, American Ninja 3: Blood Hunt, Masque of Red Death, Buried Alive, Incident at Victoria Falls, The Hitman, Delta Force 3: The Killing Game, Tobe Hooper's Night Terrors, The Mummy Lives, The Mangler, Cry the Beloved Country, Midnight in St. Petersburg, Bullet to Beijing, Treasure Island, City of Fear, Queen's Messenger, High Explosive, numerous others.

TOWNE, ROBERT
Writer, Director, Producer. b. Los Angeles, CA, Nov. 23, 1936. Raised in San Pedro. Was member of Warren Beatty's production staff on Bonnie and Clyde and contributed to that screenplay. Also uncredited, wrote Pacino-Brando garden scene in The Godfather; script doctor on Marathon Man, The Missouri Breaks and others.
PICTURES: *Writer*: The Last Woman on Earth (as Edward Wain), The Tomb of Ligeia, Villa Rides, The Last Detail, Chinatown (Academy Award, 1974), Shampoo (co-s.p.), The Yakuza (co-s.p.), Personal Best (also dir., prod.), Greystoke: The Legend of Tarzan (s.p., uncredited), Tequila Sunrise (also dir.), Days of Thunder, The Two Jakes, The Firm (co-s.p.), Love Affair (co-s.p.), Mission: Impossible (co-s.p.), Without Limits, Mission: Impossible II, A Decade Under the Influence.
TELEVISION: *Writer*: In the Company of Spies. *Series*: The Outer Limits, Breaking Point, The Man from U.N.C.L.E. *Mini-Series*: Cadillac Desert.

TOWNSEND, ROBERT
Actor, Producer, Director, Writer. b. Chicago, IL, Feb. 6, 1957. e.Illinois State U., Hunter Coll. Veteran of Experimental Black Actors Guild and Second City. TV commercials; stand-up comedy at NY Improvisation; taped Evening at the Improv.
PICTURES: *Actor*: Cooley High (debut, 1974), Willie and Phil, Streets of Fire, A Soldier's Story, American Flyers, Odd Jobs, Ratboy, Hollywood Shuffle (also prod., dir., co-s.p.), Eddie Murphy Raw (dir. only), The Mighty Quinn, That's Adequate, The Five Heartbeats (also dir., exec. prod., co-s.p.), The Meteor Man (also dir., s.p., co-prod.), B.A.P.S. (dir. only), Joseph's Gift, The Taxman, Casting for Glinda, The Book of Love, The Script, Undercover Brother.
TELEVISION: *Series*: Another Page (PBS series), Townsend Television, The Parent 'Hood (also co-creator, exec. prod.). *Specials*: Robert Townsend and His Partners in Crime, Take No Prisoners: Robert Townsend and His Partners in Crime II (HBO).

Movies: Women at West Point, Senior Trip!, In Love With an Older Woman, Love Songs, Jackie's Back, Up Up and Away, I Was a Teenage Faust, 10,000 Black Men Named George. *Mini-Series*: Bliss, Great Drives.

TRAMBUKIS, WILLIAM J.
Executive. b. Providence, R.I., July 26, 1926. e. Mt. Pleasant Bus. Col. Began career as usher with Loew's in Providence, RI, 1941. Served 1943-46 with Navy Seabees. Recipient of Quigley Awards. Managed/supervised Loew's Theatres in several New England cities, Harrisburg, PA, Syracuse, Rochester, Buffalo, NY, Washington, DC, Richmond, Norfolk, VA, Toronto, Canada, Atlanta, GA. Appt. Loew's NorthEastern Division mgr. 1964, Loew's gen. mgr. 1975: v.p. in 1976; sr. v.p., 1985. Retired, 1987.

TRAVANTI, DANIEL J.
Actor. b. Kenosha, WI, March 7, 1940. e. U. of Wisconsin (B.A.), Loyola Marymount Univ. (M.A.), Yale Sch. of Drama. Woodrow Wilson fellow, 1961. Formerly acted as Dan Travanty. On stage in Twigs, Othello, I Never Sang for My Father, Only Kidding, The Taming of the Shrew, Les Liaisons Dangereuses, A Touch of the Poet, Antony & Cleopatra, A Touch of the Poet.
PICTURES: St. Ives, Midnight Crossing, Millenium, Megaville, Weep No More My Lady, Just Cause, Siao Yu, Who Killed Teddy Bear, Something Sweet, Design.
TELEVISION: *Series*: General Hospital, Hill Street Blues (Emmy Awards, 1981, 1982; Golden Globe Award, 1981), Missing Persons, Poltergeist: The Legacy. *Movies*: The Love War, Adam, Aurora, Murrow, Adam: His Song Continues, I Never Sang for My Father, Fellow Traveler, Howard Beach: Making the Case for Murder, Tagget, Eyes of a Witness, The Christmas Stallion, In the Shadows Someone's Watching, My Name is Kate, Wasp Woman, A Case of Libel, To Sir With Love II.

TRAVIS, NANCY
Actress. b. New York, NY, Sept. 21, 1961. Raised in Baltimore, MD, and Farmingham, MA. e. NYU. Attended Circle-in-the-Square Theatre school. Acted with NY Amer. Jewish Theatre before landing role in touring prod. of Brighton Beach Memoirs.3
THEATRE: *NY*: It's Hard to Be a Jew, The Signal Season of Dummy Hoy, I'm Not Rappaport (B'way). Tour: Brighton Beach Memoirs. *La Jolla Playhouse*: My Children My Africa, Three Sisters.
PICTURES: Three Men and a Baby (debut, 1987), Married to the Mob, Eight Men Out, Internal Affairs, Loose Cannons, Air America, Three Men and a Little Lady, Passed Away, Chaplin, The Vanishing, So I Married an Axe Murderer, Greedy, Destiny Turns on the Radio, Fluke, Bogus, Auggie Rose.
TELEVISION: *Series*: Almost Perfect, Work with Me, Becker. *Movies*: Malice in Wonderland, Harem, I'll Be Home for Christmas, Body Language, My Last Love (prod.), Running Mates. *Special*: High School Narc (ABC Afterschool Special). *Mini-Series*: Rose Red.

TRAVOLTA, JOHN
Actor. b. Englewood, NJ, Feb. 18, 1954. m. actress Kelly Preston. First stage role in Who Will Save the Plowboy? Did off-B'way prod. of Rain; then on Broadway in Grease (also on tour for 10 months), Over Here (with the Andrew Sisters). Author of Staying Fit, 1984.
PICTURES: The Devil's Rain (debut, 1975), Carrie, Saturday Night Fever (Acad. Award nom.), Grease, Moment by Moment, Urban Cowboy, Blow Out, Staying Alive, Two of a Kind, Perfect, The Experts, Look Who's Talking, Look Who's Talking Too, Shout, Eyes of an Angel, Look Who's Talking Now, Pulp Fiction (Acad. Award nom.), White Man's Burden, Get Shorty (Golden Globe winner), Broken Arrow, Phenomenon, Michael, Face/Off, She's So Lovely (also exec. prod.), Mad City, The Thin Red Line, A Civil Action, Primary Colors, The General's Daughter, Our Friend, Martin (voice), Forever Hollywood, Battlefield Earth (also prod.), Lucky Numbers, Swordfish, Domestic Disturbance, Basic, Austin Powers in Goldmember, The Punisher.
TELEVISION: *Series*: Welcome Back Kotter. *Movies*: The Boy in the Plastic Bubble, Chains of Gold, Boris & Natasha (cameo). *Special*: The Dumb Waiter. *Guest*: Emergency, Owen Marshall--Counselor at Law, The Rookies, Medical Center.

TREMAYNE, LES
Actor. b. London, England, Apr. 16, 1913. e. Northwestern U., Chicago Art Inst., Columbia U., UCLA. First professional appearance in British mp., 1916, with mother; stock, little theatres, vaudeville, 1925-40; entered radio field, 1930. Blue ribbon award for best perf. of the month for A Man Called Peter; dir. Hollywood Rep. Theatre, 1957; pres. Hollywood Actors' Council, 1951-58; chmn. Actors Div. workshop com. Acad. TV Arts & Sciences; Mem.: The Workshop Comm. of the Hollywood M.P. & TV Museum Comm. One of 17 founding members, Pacific Pioneer Broadcasters; Life member, Actor's Fund; charter/founding mem. AFTRA, Chicago local. (delegate to most conventions since 1938). mem. Local, L.A. and Natl. AFTRA bds.
THEATRE: Woman in My House, Errand of Mercy, You Are There, One Man's Family, Heartbeat Theatre, The First Nighter (lead 7 yrs.); on Broadway in Heads or Tails, Detective Story.
PICTURES: The Racket, Blue Veil, Francis Goes to West Point,

It Grows on Trees, I Love Melvin, Under the Red Sea, Dream Wife, War of the Worlds, Susan Slept Here, Lieutenant Wore Skirts, Unguarded Moment, Everything But the Truth, Monolith Monsters, Perfect Furlough, North by Northwest, Say One for Me, The Gallant Hours, The Angry Red Planet, The Story of Ruth, The Fortune Cookie, Daffy Duck's Movie: Fantastic Island (voice), Starchaser (voice), Rainbow Brite and the Star Stealer.
TELEVISION: Lux Video Theatre, 20th Century-Fox Hour, Navy Log, One Man's Family, Meet Mille, The Millionaire, The Whistler, Truth or Consequences, NBC Matinee, The Girl, O'Henry series, Rin Tin Tin, Bachelor Father, The Texan, Adventures of Ellery Queen, Court of Last Resort, Rifleman, State Trooper, Rescue 8, June Allyson-Dupont Show, Wagon Train, M Squad, Hitchcock Presents, Mr. Ed., Perry Mason, One Life to Live. *Series:* (voice), Challenge of the GoBots, The 13 Ghosts of Scooby-Doo, Jonny Quest, Dark Water.

TREUT, MONIKA
Director, **Writer**, **Editor**. b. West Germany, April 6, 1954.
PICTURES: Seduction: The Cruel Woman, Virgin Machine, My Father is Coming, Female Misbehavior, Erotique ("Taboo Parlor" segment), Danish Girls Show Everything (dir. only), Didn't Do It for Love, Gendernauts (dir. only), Warrior of Light.

TRIKONIS, GUS
Director. b. New York, NY, 1938. Started career in chorus of West Side Story on B'way. Turned to directing, making low-budget weekenders (films shot in 12 days only on weekends).
PICTURES: *Actor:* West Side Story, Pajama Party, The Unsinkable Molly Brown, The Sand Pebbles, The Hell Cats, St. Valentine's Day Massacre, *Director:* Five the Hard Way, The Swinging Mermaids, Supercock (also actor), The Student Body, Nashville Girl, Moonshine County Express, The Evil, Touched by Love, Take This Job and Shove It.
TELEVISION: *Movies:* The Darker Side of Terror, She's Dressed To Kill, Flamingo Road (pilot), Elvis and the Beauty Queen, Twirl, Miss All-American Beauty, Dempsey, First Affair, Dempsey, Dance of the Dwarfs, Midas Valley, Malice in Wonderland, Love on the Run, Christmas Snow, Open Admissions, Unknown Subject, The Great Pretender, Insel der Furcht. *Mini-Series:* The Last Convertible (co-dir.). *Episode:* Twilight Zone (1985). *Series:* Burke's Law, Hercules: The Legendary Journeys, Baywatch Nights, Viper, The Sentinel, Hunter, The Twilight Zone, Beauty and the Beast, Wiseguy, Quantum Leap, Baywatch, The Flash, The Commish, SeaQuest DSV, Thunder in Paradise.

TRINTIGNANT, JEAN-LOUIS
Actor. b. Piolenc, France, Dec. 11, 1930. m. Nadine Marquand, director. Theatre debut: 1951, To Each According to His Hunger. Then Mary Stuart, Macbeth (at the Comedie de Saint-Etienne). 1955 screen debut.
PICTURES: Si Tous Les Gars du Monde, La Loi des Rues, And God Created Woman, Club de Femmes, Les Liaisons Dangereuses, L'Estate Violente, Austerlitz, La Millieme Fenetre, Pleins Feux sur L'Assasin, Coeur Battant, L'Atlantide, The Game of Truth, Horace 62, Les Sept Peches Capitaux (7 Capital Sins), Le Combat dans L'Ile, The Easy Life, Il Successo, Nutty Naughty Chateau, Les Pas Perdus, La Bonne Occase, Mata-Hari, Meurtre a L'Italienne, La Longue Marche, Un Jour a Paris, Is Paris Burning?, The Sleeping Car Murders, A Man and a Woman, Enigma, Safari Diamants, Trans-Europ-Express, Mon Amour, Mon Amour, Un Homme a Abattre, La Morte Ha Fatto L'Uovo, Les Biches, Grand Silence, Z, Ma Nuit Chez Maud (My Night at Maud's), The Conformist, The Crook, Without Apparent Motive, The Outside Man, The French Conspiracy, Simon the Swiss, Agression, Les Violons du Bal, The Sunday Woman, Under Fire, La Nuit de Varennes, Long Live Life!, Next Summer, Departure, Return, The Man With the Silver Eyes, Femme Je Personne, Confidentially Yours, A Man and a Woman: 20 Years Later, La Vallee Fantome; Rendezvous, Bunker Palace Hotel, Three Colors: Red, The City of Lost Children, Fiesta, Un homme est tombe dans la rue, L'Insoumise, Les Bidochon, C'est jamais loin, Self-Made Hero, Tykho Moon, Those Who Love Me Can Take the Train.

TRIPP, STEVEN L.
Executive. b. Worthington, MN, Sept. 29, 1958. e. St. Cloud State U. Managed local hometown theatres from 1978-82, then promoted to operation mgr., Tentelino Enterprises Circuit. Became general mgr. after Tentelino was purchased by Lakes & Rivers Cinemas in 1989. 1994-present, general mgr. and film buyer. Formed Midwest Theatres Corp. dba Cinemagic Theatres in 1996. Currently serving as Pres. & COO.

TRIPPLEHORN, JEANNE
Actress. b. Tulsa, OK, 1964. e. Julliard Sch. of Drama. On stage at NY's Public Theatre in The Big Funk, 'Tis Pity She's a Whore.
PICTURES: Basic Instinct (debut, 1992), The Night We Never Met, The Firm, Waterworld, Reality Bites (cameo), Office Killer, 'Til There Was You, Very Bad Things, Snitch, Sliding Doors, Steal This Movie, Mickey Blue Eyes, Timecode, Paranoid, Relative Values, Dial 9 For Love, Swept Away.
TELEVISION: *Movies:* The Perfect Tribute, Old Man, Breeders, My Brother's Keeper, Word of Honor. *Guest:* The Ben Stiller Show.

TRUMBULL, DOUGLAS
Director, **Cinematographer**. b. Los Angeles, CA, Apr. 8, 1942. Inventor Showscan Film process. Produced and directed Universal Studios attraction Back to the Future: The Ride; Luxor Las Vegas attractions. Director: Showscan short films New Magic, Let's Go, Big Ball, Leonardo's Dream, Night of the Dreams, Chevy Collector. Former Vice Chmn., The Imax Corp. Currently Pres. & CEO, Entertainment Design Workshop.
PICTURES: *Cinematographer:* 2001: A Space Odyssey, Silent Running (also dir.), The Andromeda Strain, Close Encounters of the Third Kind, Star Trek: The Motion Picture, Blade Runner, Brainstorm (also dir., prod.).

TSAI, MING-LIANG
Director, **Writer**. b. Kuching, Malaysia, Oct. 27, 1957.
PICTURES: Rebels of the Neon God, Vive L'Amour (Golden Horse Award, 1994), The River, Last Dance (dir. only), Dong, Fish Underground, Ni neibian jidian, What Time Is It Over There?, The Skywalk Is Gone.

TUBB, BARRY
Actor. b. Snyder, TX, 1963. Former rodeo star. Studied acting at Amer. Conservatory Theatre in SF.
THEATRE: Sweet Sue (B'way), The Authentic Life of Billy the Kid.
PICTURES: Mask, The Legend of Billie Jean, Top Gun, Valentino Returns, Warm Summer Rain, Guilty By Suspicion, The Big Day, American Outlaws, Grand Champion (dir. only).
TELEVISION: *Series:* Bay City Blues. *Guest:* Hill Street Blues. *Movies:* Consenting Adult, The Billionaire Boys Club, Without Her Consent. *Mini-Series:* Lonesome Dove, Return to Lonesome Dove.

TUCCI, STANLEY
Actor. b. Peekskill, NY, Jan. 11, 1960. e. SUNY.
THEATRE: *B'way:* The Misanthrope, Brighton Beach Memoirs, The Iceman Cometh. Moon Over Miami, Scapin, Dalliance, Balm in Gilead.
PICTURES: Who's That Girl, Monkey Shines, Slaves of New York, Fear Anxiety and Depression, The Feud, Quick Change, Men of Respect, Billy Bathgate, Beethoven, Prelude to a Kiss, The Public Eye, In the Soup, Undercover Blues, The Pelican Brief, It Should Happen to You, Mrs. Parker and the Vicious Circle, Kiss of Death, A Modern Affair, The Daytrippers, Big Night (also co-dir; Ind't Spirit Awards, 1997.), Life During Wartime, The Eighteenth Angel, Deconstructing Harry, A Life Less Ordinary, Montana, The Imposters (also prod., dir., s.p.), A Midsummer Night's Dream, Joe Gould's Secret (also prod., dir.), In Too Deep, Sidewalks of New York, The Whole Shebang, America's Sweethearts, The Road to Perdition, Big Trouble, Maid in Manhattan, The Core, Terminal, Spin, Shall We Dance?.
TELEVISION: *Series:* The Street, Wiseguy, Murder One. *Guest:* Miami Vice, The Equalizer, thirtysomething, Equal Justice. *Movies:* Winchell, Conspiracy, The Life and Death of Peter Sellers.

TUCKER, MICHAEL
Actor. b. Baltimore, MD, Feb. 6, 1944. m. actress Jill Eikenberry. e. Carnegie Tech. Drama Sch. Worked in regional theater (Long Wharf, Washington's Arena Stage, Milwaukee Rep.) and with the NY Shakespeare Festival in Trelawney of the Wells, Comedy of Errors, Measure for Measure, The Merry Wives of Windsor. Also prod. revival of El Grande de Coca Cola (1986).
THEATRE: Moonchildren, Modigliani, The Goodbye People, The Rivals, Mother Courage, Waiting for Godot, Oh What a Lovely War, I'm Not Rappaport (American Place Theatre).
PICTURES: A Night Full of Rain (debut, 1977), An Unmarried Woman, Eyes of Laura Mars, Diner, The Goodbye People, The Purple Rose of Cairo, Radio Days, Tin Men, Checking Out, For Love or Money, D2: The Mighty Ducks, 'Til There Was You.
TELEVISION: *Series:* L.A. Law. *Movies:* Concealed Enemies, Vampire, Assault and Matrimony, Day One, Spy, Too Young to Die?, Casey's Gift: For Love of a Child, The Secret Life of Archie's Wife, In the Nick of Time, A Town Torn Apart, Growing Up Brady, L.A. Law: The Movie, The Alibi. *Specials:* Love Sex... and Marriage, A Family Again, On Hope. *Guest:* Hill Street Blues.

TUCKERMAN, DAVID R.
Executive. b. Perth Amboy, NJ, Nov. 9, 1949. e. Monmouth Coll., F.L.U. 1967-70; B.S.B.A. Entered industry with A.I.T. Theatres, 1967; gen. mgr., Music Makers Theatres, 1973; v.p., Leigh Group, MMT, head film buyer, 1976; sr. v.p., MMT, 1980; Loews Film Buyer, 1986; Loews (now Sony) v.p. film, 1993. U.A., Head Film Buyer, Southeat region, 1998. New Line Cinema, Exec. V.P. and Gen. Sales Mgr., 1999. President, New Line Cinema, 2000-present. *Member:* SMPTE, Variety Int., MPBC, AFI, Motion Picture Pioneers.

TUGGLE, RICHARD
Director, **Writer**. b. Coral Gables, FL, Aug. 8, 1948. e. U. Virginia, B.A. 1970. Wrote screenplays before directorial debut with Tightrope, 1984.
PICTURES: Escape from Alcatraz (s.p.), Tightrope (dir., s.p.), Out of Bounds (dir.).

419

TUNE, TOMMY
Actor, Director, Choreographer, Dancer. b. Wichita Falls, TX, Feb. 28, 1939. e. Univ of Texas at Austin. Began professional career dancing in chorus of B'way shows (Baker Street, A Joyful Noise, How Now Dow Jones, etc.). Recipient of 9 Tony Awards.
THEATRE: *Performer:* Seesaw, My One and Only, Bye Bye Birdie (tour), Tommy Tune Tonite! (B'way & tour). *Director and/or choreographer:* The Club, Cloud 9, The Best Little Whorehouse in Texas, Nine, A Day in Hollywood/A Night in the Ukraine, Stepping Out, My One and Only, Grand Hotel, The Will Rogers Follies, Broadway: The Golden Age By the Legends Who Were There.
PICTURES: Hello Dolly!, The Boy Friend.
TELEVISION: *Series:* Dean Martin Presents the Goldiggers, The Bold and the Beautiful, also numerous specials, Tony Award Shows.

TURMAN, LAWRENCE
Producer. b. Los Angeles, CA, Nov. 28, 1926. e. UCLA. In textile business 5 years, then joined Kurt Frings Agency; left in 1960 to form Millar-Turman Prods.
PICTURES: *Prod.:* The Young Doctors, I Could Go on Singing, The Best Man. Formed own prod. co., Lawrence Turman, Inc., to make The Flim-Flam Man, The Graduate, Pretty Poison (exec. prod.), The Great White Hope, The Marriage of a Young Stockbroker (also dir.), The Nickel Ride (exec. prod.), The Drowning Pool, First Love, Heroes, Walk Proud, Tribute, Caveman, The Thing, Second Thoughts (also dir.), Mass Appeal, The Mean Season, Short Circuit, Running Scared, Short Circuit 2, Full Moon in Blue Water, Gleaming the Cube, The Getaway, The River Wild, The Getaway, Booty Call (exec. prod.), American History X (exec. prod.), Kingdom Come, What's the Worst That Could Happen?.
TELEVISION: *Co-prod. with David Foster:* The Gift of Love, News at Eleven, Between Two Brothers. *Prod.:* The Morning After, She Lives, Unwed Father. *Co-exec. prod.:* Jesse. *Exec. prod.:* Miracle on the Mountain: The Kincaid Family Story.

TURNER, JANINE
Actress. r.n. Janine Gauntt. b. Lincoln, NE, Dec. 6, 1962. Raised in Texas. Studied dance, joined Forth Worth Ballet. Started modeling at age 15 in NYC, enrolled in Professional Children's School. First major acting job was on series Dallas. On stage in Full Moon and High Tide in the Ladies Room.
PICTURES: Young Doctors in Love, Knights of the City, Tai-Pan, Monkey Shines, Steel Magnolias, The Ambulance, Cliffhanger, The Curse of the Inferno, Leave It to Beaver, Dr. T and the Women, Birdie and Bogey.
TELEVISION: *Movies:* Stolen Women Captured Hearts, Circle of Deceit, Beauty, Fatal Error, A Secret Affair. *Series:* Behind the Screen, General Hospital (1982-83), Another World (1986-87), Santa Barbara (1984), Northern Exposure, Strong Medicine. *Guest:* The Love Boat, The A-Team, Mike Hammer.

TURNER, KATHLEEN
Actress. b. Springfield, MO, June 19, 1954. e. U. of Maryland, SMSU.
THEATRE: *B'way:* Gemini, Cat on a Hot Tin Roof (Theatre World Award), Indiscretions. *Regional:* Camille (Long Wharf), A Midsummer Night's Dream (DC), Toyer (DC).
PICTURES: Body Heat (debut, 1981), The Man With Two Brains, Romancing the Stone, Crimes of Passion, A Breed Apart, Prizzi's Honor, The Jewel of the Nile, Peggy Sue Got Married (Acad. Award nom.), Julia and Julia, Switching Channels, Who Framed Roger Rabbit (voice), The Accidental Tourist, The War of the Roses, V.I. Warshawski, House of Cards, Undercover Blues, Serial Mom, Naked in New York, Moonlight & Valentino, A Simple Wish, Legalese, Baby Geniuses, The Virgin Suicides, Beautiful, Prince of Central Park, In Bad Taste, Delilah.
TELEVISION: *Series:* The Doctors. *Movies:* Friends at Last, Love in the Ancient World, Cinderella. *Special:* Dear America: Letters Home From Vietnam (reader). *Director:* Leslie's Folly.

TURNER, TED
Executive. r.n. Robert Edward Turner. b. Cincinnati, OH., Nov. 19, 1938. e. Brown U. m. actress Jane Fonda. Began career in Savannah in family's outdoor adv. business, selling space on billboards. Inherited co. in 1963 and in 1970 entered broadcasting with purchase of a failing TV station in Atlanta which he turned into WTBS, a "superstation" which in 1994 reached 95% of U.S. homes equipped with cable. 1980, established CNN a 24-hr. cable news service. Purchased MGM film library. Co-owner of two professional sports teams in Atlanta: Braves (baseball) and Hawks (basketball). Started Headline News, 1982; CNN International 1985; Turner Network Television 1988; Sportsouth, 1990; Cartoon Network in 1992; acquired Castle Rock Entertainment, 1993; merger with New Line Cinema, 1994; started Turner Classic Movies, 1994; CNNfn Financial Network, 1995. Became Vice Chairman of Time Warner in October 1996, with the merger of Time Warner Inc. and Turner Broadcasting System, Inc., Vice Chairman and Senior Advisor of AOL Time Warner, Chairman, Ted's Montana Grill, Inc., 2002-present.

TURNER, TINA
Singer, Actress. r.n. Annie Mae Bullock. b. Nutbush, TN, Nov. 26, 1939. Previously married to Ike Turner and appeared with him on road in Ike and Tina Turner Revue. Many hit records. *Autobiography:* I Tina.
PICTURES: Gimme Shelter, Taking Off, Soul to Soul, Tommy, Sound of the City, Mad Max Beyond Thunderdome, What's Love Got to Do With It (vocals), Last Action Hero, GoldenEye (singer "GoldenEye").
TELEVISION: *Special:* Tina—Live From Rio, Live in Amsterdam, VH1 Divas Live 2, One Last Time Live in Concert.

TURTURRO, JOHN
Actor. b. Brooklyn, NY, Feb. 28, 1957. e. SUNY/New Paltz; Yale Drama School, 1983. m. actress Katherine Borowitz. Worked in regional theater and off-B'way.
THEATRE: Danny and the Deep Blue Sea (Obie & Theatre World Awards, 1985), Men Without Dates, Tooth of the Crime, La Puta Viva, Chaos and Hard Times, The Bald Soprano, Of Mice and Men, The Resistible Rise of Arturo Ui, Death of a Salesman (B'way debut, 1984).
PICTURES: Raging Bull (debut, 1980), Exterminator II, The Flamingo Kid, Desperately Seeking Susan, To Live and Die in L.A., Hannah and Her Sisters, Gung Ho, Off Beat, The Color of Money, The Sicilian, Five Corners, Do the Right Thing, Mo' Better Blues, State of Grace, Miller's Crossing, Men of Respect, Jungle Fever, Barton Fink (Cannes Film Fest. Award), Brain Donors, Mac (also dir., co-s.p.), Fearless, Being Human, Quiz Show, Search and Destroy, Clockers, Unstrung Heroes, Grace of My Hear, Box of Moonlight, Girl 6, The Search for One-eye Johnny, Lesser Prophets, Animals, O.K. Garage, Illuminata, The Big Lebowski, He Got Game, Rounders, The Cradle Will Rock, Summer of Sam, Company Man, O Brother, Where Art Thou?, Two Thousand and None, The Man Who Cried, The Luzhin Defence, Monkeybone, Thirteen Conversations About One Thing, Collateral Damage, Mr. Deeds, Rosy-Fingered Dawn: A Film on Terrence Malick, Fear the X, Secret Passage, Anger Management, 2 B Perfectly Honest.
TELEVISION: *Mini-Series:* The Fortunate Pilgrim. *Movies:* Backtrack, Monday Night Mayhem.

TUSHINGHAM, RITA
Actress. b. Liverpool, England, March 14, 1942. Student at Liverpool Playhouse.
THEATRE: The Giveaway, Lorna and Ted, Mistress of Novices, The Undiscovered Country, Mysteries.
PICTURES: A Taste of Honey (debut, 1961; BFA Award), The Leather Boys, A Place to Go, Girl With Green Eyes, The Knack... and How to Get It, Doctor Zhivago, The Trap, Smashing Time, Diamonds for Breakfast, The Guru, The Bed Sitting Room, Straight on Till Morning, The Case of Laura C., Where Do You Go From Here?, Situation, Instant Coffee, The Human Factor, Rachel's Man, The Slum Boy, The Black Journal, Bread Butter and Jam, Mysteries, Felix Krull, Spaghetti Thing, Dream to Believe, Flying, Seeing Red, The Housekeeper, Resurrected, Dante and Beatrice in Liverpool, Hard Days Night Nights, Paper Marriage, Desert Lunch, An Awfully Big Adventure, The Boy From Mercury, Under the Skin, Swing, Out of Depth.
TELEVISION: *U.S.:* Green Eyes, Bread, Sunday Pursuit, Gutt Ein Journalist, Hamburg Poison.

TWAINE, MICHAEL
Actor, Director. b. New York, NY, Nov. 1, 1939. e. Ohio State U. Served U.S. Army. While studying with Lee Strasberg, worked as private detective, school teacher. Made stage debut City Center, 1956, in Mr. Roberts. Became village coffee house and club comedian 1968 to 1972.
PICTURES: Marriage Italian Style (voice), American Soap, Blood Bath, F.I.S.T., Cheap Shots, Platoon (voice), Billy Bathgate (voice).
TELEVISION: The Silent Drum, Starsky & Hutch, Wonder Woman, Streets of San Francisco, Soap, Lou Grant, Diff'rent Strokes, Nurse, Stalk the Wild Child, The Courage and the Passion, Eischied, America's Most Wanted, Beyond the Universe.

TWIGGY
Actress. r.n. Leslie Hornby. b. London, England, Sept. 19, 1949. m. actor Leigh Lawson. At 17 regarded as world's leading high fashion model. Made m.p. debut in The Boy Friend, 1971. Starred in many London West End Shows, including Cinderella and Captain Beaky Presents. 1983: on Broadway in musical, My One and Only.
PICTURES: The Boyfriend (debut, 1971), W, There Goes the Bride, The Blues Brothers, The Doctor and the Devils, Club Paradise, Madame Sousatzka, Istanbul, Edge of Seventeen.
TELEVISION: *Series:* Twiggy, Twiggy and Friends, Juke Box (U.S.), Princesses (U.S.). *Specials:* Pygmalion, Sun Child, Young Charlie Chaplin. *Movies:* The Diamond Trap, Body Bags.

TYKWER, TOM
Director, Writer, Composer. b. Wuppertal, Germany, May 23, 1965.
PICTURES: Deadly Maria (also prod.), Winter Sleeper, Life Is All You Get (s.p. only), Winter Sleepers, Run Lola Run, Any Given Sunday, Der Krieger und die Kaiserin (The Princess and the Warrior), Head Over Heels, Heaven.

TYLER, LIV
Actress. b. July, 1, 1977. Daughter of fashion model Bebe Buell and musician Steven Tyler. Began as a model at age 14.
PICTURES: Silent Fall (debut), Empire Records, Heavy, Stealing Beauty, That Thing You Do!, Inventing the Abbotts, U-Turn, Plunkett & MacLeane, Eugene Onegin, Armageddon, The Little Black Book, Cookie's Fortune, Franky Goes to Hollywood, Dr.T and the Women, One Night at McCool's, The Lord of the Rings: The Fellowship of the Ring, The Lord of the Rings: The Two Towers, The Lord of the Rings: The Return of the Kings, Jersey Girl.
TELEVISION: Movie: Quest For the Ring.

TYRRELL, SUSAN
Actress. b. San Francisco, CA, March 18, 1946. Made first prof. appearance with Art Carney in summer theatre tour prod. of Time Out for Ginger. Worked in off-B'way prods. and as waitress in coffee house before attracting attention in Lincoln Center Repertory Co. prods. of A Cry of Players, The Time of Your Life, Camino Real.
THEATRE: The Knack, Futz, Father's Day, A Coupla White Chicks Sitting Around Talking, The Rotten Life.
PICTURES: Shoot Out (debut, 1971), The Steagle, Been Down So Long It Looks Like Up to Me, Shoot Out, Fat City (Acad. Award nom.), Catch My Soul, Zandy's Bride, The Killer Inside Me, Islands in the Stream, Andy Warhol's Bad, I Never Promised You a Rose Garden, Another Man Another Chance, September 30, 1955, Racquet, Loose Shoes, Forbidden Zone, Subway Riders, Night Warning, Fast-Walking, Liar's Moon, Tales of Ordinary Madness, Fire and Ice (voice), Angel, The Killers, Avenging Angel, Flesh and Blood, The Chipmunk Adventure (voice), The Offspring, Big Top Pee-Wee, Tapeheads, The Underachievers, Far From Home, Cry-Baby, Motorama, Powder, Digital Man, Poison Ivy: The Last Seduction, Pink As the Day She Was Born, Relax...It's Just Sex, Buddy Boy, Masked and Anonymous .
TELEVISION: Series: Open All Night. Movies: Lady of the House, Midnight Lace, Jealousy, Thompson's Last Run, Poker Alice, The Christmas Star, Windmills of the Gods. Mini-Series: If Tomorrow Comes.

TYSON, CICELY
Actress. b. New York, NY, Dec. 19, 1933. e. NYU. Studied at Actor's Studio. Former secretary and model. Co-founder, Dance Theatre of Harlem.
THEATRE: The Blacks, Moon on a Rainbow Shawl, Tiger Tiger Burning Bright, The Corn Is Green.
PICTURES: A Man Called Adam (debut, 1966), The Comedians, The Heart Is a Lonely Hunter, Sounder (Acad. Award nom.), The Blue Bird, The River Niger, A Hero Ain't Nothin' But a Sandwich, The Concorde—Airport '79, Bustin' Loose, Fried Green Tomatoes, The Grass Harp, Hoodlum, The Double Dutch Divas!.
TELEVISION: Series: East Side West Side, The Guiding Light, Sweet Justice. Movies: Marriage: Year One, The Autobiography of Miss Jane Pittman (Emmy Award, 1974), Just An Old Sweet Song, Wilma, A Woman Called Moses, The Marva Collins Story, Benny's Place, Playing with Fire, Acceptable Risks, Samaritan: The Mitch Snyder Story, The Women of Brewster Place, Heat Wave, The Kid Who Loved Christmas, Duplicates, When No One Would Listen, House of Secrets, Oldest Living Confederate Widow Tells All (Emmy Award, 1994), Mama Flora's Family, Road to Galveston, Bridge of Time, Riot, The Price of Heaven, Ms. Scrooge, Always Outnumbered, A Lesson Before Dying, Aftershock: Earthquake in New York, Jewel, The Rosa Parks Story. Guest: B.L. Stryker. Special: Without Borders (host). Mini-Series: Roots, Aftershock. Pilot: Clippers.

U

UGGAMS, LESLIE
Singer. b. New York, NY, May 25, 1943. e. Professional Children's Sch., grad., 1960. Juilliard Sch. of Music. Beg. singing career age 5. TV debut as Ethel Waters' niece on Beulah. Also on Johnny Olsen's TV kids at age 7, Your Show of Shows as singer, 1953; Recording artist for Columbia Records, Atlantic, Motown Wrote The Leslie Uggams Beauty Book (1962).
THEATRE: Hallelujah Baby (Tony & Theatre World Awards, 1968), Her First Roman, Blues in the Night, Jerry's Girls, Anything Goes (natl. co. & Bdwy), Stringbean (Dallas), Into the Woods (Long Beach, CA).
PICTURES: Two Weeks in Another Town, Poor Pretty Eddie, Black Girl, Heartbreak Motel, Skyjacked, Sugar Hill, Broadway: The Golden Age by the Legends Who Were There.
TELEVISION: Series: Sing Along With Mitch, The Leslie Uggams Show (1969), Fantasy (Emmy Award, 1984), All My Children, Guest: Beulah (1949), Kids and Company, Milton Berle Show, Name That Tune, Jack Paar Show, Garry Moore. Mini-Series: Roots, Backstairs at the White House. Movie: Sizzle. Specials: The Book of Lists (co-host), Fantasy (Emmy Award, 1983, host), I Love Men, 'S Wonderful, 'S Marvelous, 'S Gershwin, Sinatra and Friends, Placido Domingo Steppin' Out With the Ladies, Jerry Herman Tribute, Rooms for Improvement.

RADIO: Peter Lind Hayes-Mary Healy Show, Milton Berle, Arthur Godfrey, Star Time.

ULANO, MARK
Sound.
PICTURES: Think Me Nothing, Hospital Massacre, Time Walker, Cujo, Lovelines, Once Bitten, Sweet Hearts Dance, Desperado, Rough Magic, The Winner, From Dusk Till Dawn, Titanic (Acad. Award, Best Sound Mixing, 1997), The Pest, Austin Powers: International Man of Mystery, Jackie Brown, The Patriot, Molly, Making Sandwiches, 68, Stuart Little, Molly, Spy Kids, The Majestic, Blue Crush, The Hot Chick, Two Paths, Kill Bill: Volume 1, Kill Bill: Volume 2, A Cinderella Story.
TELEVISION: Movies: High School U.S.A., The Parade, The Cartier Affair, A Time to Triumph, Shattered Spirits, Lena: My 100 Children, Dance 'Til Dawn, Shadow of a Doubt, Empty Cradle, If These Walls Could Talk 2, Empire Falls. Series: The Trials of Rosie O'Neill, Significant Others, Time of Your Life, 68, If These Walls Could Talk 2. Mini-series: Drug Wars: The Camarena Story.

ULLMAN, TRACEY
Actress, Comedian, Singer. b. Hackbridge, England, Dec. 29, 1959. m. British TV prod. Allan McKeown. e. won a performance sch. scholarship at 12. Attended the Italia Conti School for 4 years. Soon after appeared on British TV and onstage in Grease and The Rocky Horror Picture Show. Also performed in improvisational play Four in a Million (1981) at the Royal Court Theatre, London (London Theatre Critics Award). Recorded gold-selling album You Broke My Heart in Seventeen Places. Appeared in music video They Don't Know. U.S. TV debut, The Tracey Ullman Show (debuted April, 1987).
THEATRE: NY: The Taming of the Shrew, The Big Love.
PICTURES: Give My Regards to Broad Street, Plenty, Jumpin' Jack Flash, I Love You to Death, Happily Ever After (voice), Robin Hood: Men in Tights, Household Saints, Bullets Over Broadway, Ready to Wear (Pret-a-Porter), Small Time Crooks, C-Scam, Searching For Debra Winger.
TELEVISION: Series: Three of a Kind (BBC), The Tracey Ullman Show (Emmy Awards, 1989, 1990), Visible Panty Lines. Specials: The Best of the Tracey Ullman Show (Emmy Award, 1990), Tracey Ullman—A Class Act. Guest: Love & War (Emmy Award, 1993), Tracey Ullman: Takes on New York (Emmy Award, 1994) Tracey Takes On... (Emmy, Cable Ace Awards, 1997), Ally McBeal (recurring). Movies: Tracey Ullman in the Trailer Tales (also dir, exec.prod., writer).

ULLMANN, LIV
Actress. b. Tokyo, Japan, of Norwegian parents, Dec. 16, 1939. Accompanied parents to Canada when WWII began and later returned to Norway. Was catapulted to fame in a succession of Swedish films directed by Ingmar Bergman. Author: Changing, Choices. Ambassador for UNICEF since 1980. Youngest person to date to receive the Order of St. Olav from the King of Norway. Recipient of 11 honorary doctorates.
THEATRE: U.S.: A Doll's House, Anna Christie, I Remember Mama (musical), Ghosts, Old Times.
PICTURES: Fjols til Fjells (debut, 1957), The Wayward Girl, Tonny, Kort ar Sommaren, De Kalte Ham Skarven, Persona, Hour of the Wolf, Shame, The Passion of Anna, The Night Visitor, Cold Sweat, The Emigrants, Pope Joan, Cries and Whispers, Lost Horizon, Forty Carats, The New Land, Scenes From a Marriage, Zandy's Bride, The Abdication, Leonor, Face to Face, Couleur Chair, A Bridge Too Far, The Serpent's Egg, Autumn Sonata, Players (cameo), Richard's Things, The Wild Duck, Bay Boy, Dangerous Moves, Let's Hope It's a Girl, Gaby—A True Story. Moscow Adieu (Donatello Award, 1987), A Time of Indifference, La Amiga, The Rose Garden, Mindwalk, The Ox, The Long Shadow, Sophie (dir., co-s.p. only), Kristin Lavrandsdatter (dir., s.p. only), Dreamplay, Lumiere and Company, I Am Curious Film, Liv Ullmann scener fra et liv, Light Keeps Me Company, Saraband, Trolösa (dir.).
TELEVISION: Lady From the Sea, Jacobo Timerman: Prisoner Without a Name Cell Without a Number, Indiffirenti Gli, Zorn, Anna, Private Confessions.

ULRICH, SKEET
Actor. r.n. Bryan Ray Ulrich. b. NC, Jan. 20, 1970.
PICTURES: Albino Alligator, Last Dance, The Craft, Boys, Scream, Touch, As Good As It Gets, The Newton Boys, A Soldier's Sweetheart, Takedown, Ride with the Devil, Chill Factor, Kevin of the North, Take Down, Nobody's Baby.
TELEVISION: Miracles.

UNDERWOOD, BLAIR
Actor. b. Tacoma, WA, Aug. 25, 1964. e. Carnegie-Mellon Univ. NY stage: Measure for Measure.
PICTURES: Krush Groove, Posse, Just Cause, Set It Off, The Eighth Day, Gattaca, Deep Impact, Asunder, The Wishing Tree, Rules of Engagement, Free to Dance, Final Breakdown, The Art of Negotiating A Turn, G, Full Frontal, Malibu's Most Wanted.
TELEVISION: Series: One Life to Live, Downtown, L.A. Law, High Incident, City of Angels. Movies: The Cover Girl and the Cop, Heat Wave, Murder in Mississippi, Father & Son: Dangerous Relations (also assoc. prod.), Soul of the Game,

Mistrial, Mama Flora's Family. *Guest*: Scarecrow and Mrs. King, The Cosby Show, Knight Rider, 21 Jump Street.

UNDERWOOD, RON
Director. b. Glendale, CA, Nov. 6, 1953. e. USC, AFI.
PICTURES: Tremors (also co-story), City Slickers, Heart and Souls, Speechless, Mighty Joe Young, The Adventures of Pluto Nash, Stealing Sinatra.
TELEVISION: The Mouse and the Motorcycle (Peabody Award), Runaway Ralph (Emmy nom.). *Series*: Monk.

UNGER, ANTHONY B.
Executive, Producer. b. New York, NY, Oct. 19, 1940. e. Duke U., USC. Prod. ass't Third Man, TV series, 1961. v.p. Unger Productions, Inc., 1964; v.p. Landau-Unger Co., Inc., 1965; v.p. Commonwealth United Entertainment in London, 1968; pres., Unger Prods. Inc., 1978-present.
PICTURES: The Desperate Ones. The Madwoman of Chaillot. The Battle of Neretva, The Magic Christian, Julius Caesar, The Devil's Widow, Don't Look Now, Force Ten From Navarone, The Unseen, Silent Rage, The Dark Side of Hollywood (doc., prod.).

UNGER, STEPHEN A.
Executive. b. New York, NY, May 31, 1946. e. NYU, Grad. Film and Television Instit. Started as independent prod. and dist. of theatrical and TV films. 1978, joined Universal Pictures Intl. Sales as foreign sls. mgr.; named v.p. Universal Theatrical Motion Pictures in 1979, responsible for licensing theatrical or TV features not handled by U.I.P. in territories outside U.S. & Canada and worldwide acquisitions; 1980 joined CBS Theatrical Films as intl. v.p., sls.; 1982-88, pres., Unger Intl. Distributors, Inc.; 1988 joined Korn/Ferry Intl. as exec. v.p., worldwide entertainment div. Promoted to mng. dir., 1989-91. Joined Spencer Stuart Exec. Search Consultants as mng. dir., Worldwide Ent. Div. 1991. Elected Partner, 1994-98. Joined Heidrick & Struggles in 1998 as Managaing Partner Media, Entertainment, and Interactive Content. Elected to Bd. of Dirs. in 1999.

URBANSKI, DOUGLAS
Producer.
PICTURES: Nil By Mouth (BAFTA Award, Outstanding Brit. Film, 1997), Plunkett & MacLeane, The Contender, Nobody's Baby, Tiptoes.

URMAN, MARK
Executive. b. New York, NY, Nov. 24, 1952. e. Union Coll., 1973; NYU, cinema, 1973-74. m. story analyst Deborah Davis. 1973, apprentice publicist, Universal Pictures; 1973-82, United Artists intl. dept. as assoc. publicist, sr. publicist and ultimately asst. to v.p. worldwide ad-pub.; 1982-84, dir., publicity and marketing, Triumph Films (Columbia/Gaumont); 1985-86, exec. dir. East Coast pub., Columbia Pictures; 1986-89, v.p. East Coast pub., Columbia Pictures. Joined Dennis Davidson Associates as v.p., 1989; promoted to sr. v.p., 1991. Member: Motion Picture Academy.

USLAN, MICHAEL E.
Producer, Writer. b. Bayonne, NJ, June 2, 1951. e. Indiana U., A.B., M.S., J.D. Wrote 12 books, including Dick Clark's 1st 25 Years of Rock 'n' Roll; 1976-80 atty. with United Artists; writer of syndicated comic strip Terry and the Pirates; produced with Benjamin Melniker.
PICTURES: Swamp Thing (prod.), The Return of Swamp Thing (prod.), Batman (exec. prod.), Batman Returns (exec. prod.), Batman: The Animated Movie (prod.), Batman Forever (exec. prod), Batman & Robin (exec. prod.), Batman Beyond: Return of the Joker 2000 (direct-to-video), Catwoman.
TELEVISION: Three Sovereigns for Sarah (exec. prod.), Dinosaucers (exec. prod., creator, writer), Swamp Thing (exec. prod. for both live-action and animated series), Fish Police (exec. prod.), South Korea cultural segments NBC Summer Olympics 1988 (exec. prod.), Television's Greatest Bits (prod., creator, writer), 1st National Trivia Quiz (prod., writer), Where On Earth Is Carmen Sandiego? (animated, exec. prod.; Emmy Award), Robin Cook's Harmful Intent (exec. prod.), Little Orphan Annie's Very Animated Christmas (exec. prod., writer), remakes of The Kiss, The Sneeze, The Great Train Robbery, The Barbershop, Streetcar Chivalry, Smashing a Jersey Mosquito (prod., dir.), Doomsday.

USTINOV, SIR PETER
Actor, Writer, Director. b. London, Eng., Apr. 16, 1921. e. Westminster Sch. In Brit. Army, W.W.II. On Brit. stage from 1937. Screen debut 1941 in Brit. picture Mein Kampf, My Crimes. Awards: 3 Emmy Awards (Specials: Life of Samuel Johnson, Barefoot in Athens, A Storm in Summer); Grammy Award for Peter and the Wolf; NY Critics Award and Donaldson Award for best foreign play (The Love of Four Colonels); British Critics Award (Romanoff and Juliet). Chancellor, Durham Univ., 1992. Received Britannia Award from BAFTA, 1992; Critics Circle Award, 1993; German Cultural Award, 1994; German Bambi, 1994; Rudolph Valentino Award, 1995.
THEATRE: Romanoff and Juliet, N.Y., London; and 17 other plays. Dir., acted, Photo Finish; wrote, Life In My Hands, The Unknown Soldier and His Wife, Half Way Up The Tree, King Lear

Beethoven's Tenth, An Evening With Peter Ustinov.
PICTURES: *Actor*: The Goose Steps Out, One of Our Aircraft Is Missing, The Way Ahead (co-s.p.), School for Secrets (wrote, dir. & co-prod. only), Vice Versa (dir., s.p. only), Private Angelo (also adapt., dir., co-prod.), Odette, Quo Vadis (Acad. Award nom.), The Magic Box, Hotel Sahara, The Egyptian, Beau Brummell, We're No Angels, Lola Montez, The Spies, The Man Who Wagged His Tail, School for Scoundrels (adapt. only), The Sundowners, Spartacus (Academy Award, best supporting actor, 1960), Romanoff and Juliet (also prod., s.p.), Billy Budd (also prod., dir., s.p.), Topkapi (Academy Award, best supporting actor, 1964), John Goldfarb Please Come Home, Lady L. (also dir., s.p.), The Comedians, Blackbeard's Ghost, Hot Millions, Viva Max. Hammersmith Is Out (also dir.), Robin Hood (voice), One of Our Dinosaurs Is Missing, Logan's Run, Treasure of Matecumbe, Purple Taxi, The Last Remake of Beau Geste, Doppio Delitto, Death on the Nile, Ashanti, Charlie Chan and the Curse of the Dragon Queen, Grendel Grendel Grendel (voice), The Great Muppet Caper, Evil Under the Sun, Memed My Hawk (also dir., s.p.), Appointment with Death, Lorenzo's Oil, The Phoenix and the Magic Carpet, Stiff Upper Lips, The Bachelor, My Khmer Heart, Majestat brauchen Sonne, Stanley Kubrick: A Life in Pictures, The Will to Resist, Luther.
RECENT TV: The Well Tempered Bach, 13 at Dinner, Deadman's Folly, Peter Ustinov's Russia, World Challenge, Murder in Three Acts, The Secret Identity of Jack the Ripper (host), Around the World in 80 Days, The Mozart Mystique, Ustinov on the Orient Express, Ustinov Meets Pavarotti, Inside the Vatican, The Old Curiosity Shop, Haydn Gala, An Evening With Sir Peter Ustinov, Paths of the Gods, A Royal Birthday Celebration, Planet Ustinov, Alice in Wonderland, Animal Farm, On the Trail of Mark Twain, In 80 Jahren um die Welt, Victoria & Albert, Salem Witch Trials.

V

VACCARO, BRENDA
Actress. b. Brooklyn, NY, Nov. 18, 1939. e. Thomas Jefferson H.S., Dallas; studied two yrs. at Neighborhood Playhouse in N.Y. Was waitress and model before landing first B'way role in Everybody Loves Opal.
THEATRE: Everybody Loves Opal (Theatre World Award), Tunnel of Love (tour), The Affair, Children From Their Games, Cactus Flower (Tony Award, 1965), The Natural Look, How Now Dow Jones (Tony nom.), The Goodbye People (Tony nom.), Father's Day, The Odd Couple, Jake's Women.
PICTURES: Where It's At (debut), Midnight Cowboy, I Love My Wife, Summertree, Going Home, Once Is Not Enough (Acad. Award nom., Golden Globe Award), Airport '77, House by the Lake (Death Weekend), Capricorn One, Fast Charlie the Moonbeam Rider, The First Deadly Sin, Zorro the Gay Blade, Supergirl, Water, Cookie, Heart of Midnight, Masque of the Red Death, Ten Little Indians, Lethal Games, Love Affair, The Mirror Has Two Faces, Sonny.
TELEVISION: *Series*: Sara, Dear Detective, Paper Dolls, Spawn, Johnny Bravo. *Guest*: The F.B.I., The Name of the Game, The Helen Reddy Show, The Shape of Things (Emmy Award, 1974), The Golden Girls, Columbo, Murder She Wrote, Flesh & Blood, Golden Girls (Emmy nom.), Civil Wars, Red Shoe Diaries, Spawn, Friends, Johnny Bravo (voice). *Movies*: Travis Logan D.A., What's a Nice Girl Like You...?, Honor Thy Father, Sunshine, The Big Ripoff, Guyana Tragedy, The Pride of Jesse Hallam, The Star Maker, A Long Way Home, Deceptions, Julius and Ethel Rosenberg: Stolen: One Husband, Red Shoes Diaries, Following Her Heart, When Husbands Cheat, Just A Walk in the Park, Just Desserts.

VAJNA, ANDREW
Executive. b. Budapest, Hungary, Aug. 1, 1944. e. UCLA. Launched career with purchase of m.p. theaters in Far East. Founded Panasia Film Ltd. in Hong Kong. Exhibitor and dist. of feature films since 1970. Formed Carolco Service, Inc. (foreign sls. org.), with Mario Kassar 1976. Founder and Pres., American Film Mkt. Assn., 1982. Resigned from Carolco, 1989; formed independent production co., Cinergi Prods., 1989.
PICTURES: *Exec. Prod.*: The Deadly China Doll, The Silent Partner, The Changeling, Victory, The Amateur, First Blood, Superstition, Rambo: First Blood Part II, Angel Heart, Extreme Prejudice, Rambo III, Red Heat, Iron Eagle II, Deepstar Six, Johnny Handsome, Music Box, Mountains of the Moon, Total Recall, Air America, Narrow Margin, Jacob's Ladder, Medicine Man, Tombstone, Renaissance Man, Color of Night, Die Hard With a Vengeance, Judge Dredd, The Scarlet Letter, The Shadow Conspiracy, Nixon, Evita, Alan Smithee Film: Burn Hollywood Burn, Out of Order, The 13th Warrior, Eyes of the Holocaust, Basic Instinct 2, An American Rhapsody, I Spy, Terminator 3.: The Rise of the Machines

VALENTI, JACK J.
Executive. b. Sept. 5, 1921. e. U. of Houston, B.A., 1946; Harvard U., M.B.A., bus. admin., 1948. Air force pilot in European theatre, W.W.II; adv. and pub. rel. exec. in Houston; special asst. and advisor to Pres. Lyndon B. Johnson, 1963-66, elected pres.,

Motion Picture Association of America, MPEA and AMPTP, since June, 1966. Named Motion Picture Pioneer of the Year, 1988.

VALENTINE, DEAN
Executive. b. Romania, 1954. e. U. of Chicago, English major, honors grad. Began career in journalism at *Time*, *Life* and *The Saturday Review*. Dir., comedy programming, NBC. 1988, joined Walt Disney Television as dir., of TV dev't; 1990, sr. v.p.; appt'd. pres. of WD Television and WD Television Animation. 1997, appointed COO, United Paramount Networks, then chairman & CEO, UPN. Resigned, Jan. 2002.

VALENTINE, KAREN
Actress. b. Sebastopol, CA, May 25, 1947.
PICTURES: Forever Young Forever Free, Hot Lead and Cold Feet, The North Avenue Irregulars.
TELEVISION: *Series*: Room 222 (Emmy Award, 1970), Karen, Our Time (host). *Guest*: My Friend Tony, Hollywood Squares, Laugh-In, The Bold Ones, Sonny and Cher, Mike Hammer, Murder, She Wrote. *Movies*: Gidget Grows Up, The Daughters of Joshua Cabe, Coffee Tea or Me?, The Girl Who Came Gift-Wrapped, The Love Boat (pilot), Having Babies, Murder at the World Series, Return to Fantasy Island, Go West Young Girl, Muggable Mary: Street Cop, Money on the Side, Skeezer, Illusions, Jane Doe, Children in the Crossfire, He's Fired She's Hired, A Fighting Choice, Perfect People. *Special*: The Emancipation of Lizzie Stern (Afterschool Special).

VALLI, ALIDA
Actress. r.n. Alida von Altenburger. b. Pola, Italy, May 31, 1921. e. M.P. Acad., Rome (dramatics); m. Oscar de Mejo, pianist-composer. In Italian m.p.; won Venice Film Festival Award in Piccolo Mondo Antico (Little Old World); to U.S. in 1947, billed simply as Valli.
PICTURES: Vita Ricomincia, Giovanna; The Paradine Case, The Miracle of the Bells, The Third Man, Walk Softly Stranger, The White Tower, Lovers of Toledo, We the Women, Senso, The Stranger's Hand, The Outcry, The Night Heaven Fell, This Angry Age (The Sea Wall), The Horror Chamber of Dr. Faustus, The Long Absence, The Happy Thieves, The Castilian, Ophelia, Oedipus Rex, The Spider's Stratagem, Tender Dracula, La Jeu de Solitaire, The Cassandra Crossing, Suspiria, 1900, The Tempter, Luna, Inferno, Le Jupon Rouge, A Notre Regrettable Epoux, A Month by the Lake.

VAN ARK, JOAN
Actress. b. New York, NY, June 16, 1943. m. NBC news reporter John Marshall. e. Yale U. of Drama. Began career in touring co., then on Broadway and in London in Barefoot in the Park. Also appeared on B'way with the APA-Phoenix Rep. Co. in the 1970s. As a runner has competed in 12 marathons, incl. Boston Marathon. On TV also created voices for animated series Spiderwoman, Thundarr and Dingbat, Dumb and Dumber, Santo Bugito and the Creeps and special Cyrano de Bergerac. Estee Lauder spokesperson.
THEATER: School for Wives (Tony Award nom.; Theatre World Award), The Rules of the Game (Theatre World Award). L.A.: Cyrano de Bergerac, Ring Around the Moon, Chemin de Fer, As You Like It (L.A. Drama Critics Award). Williamstown Theatre Fest.: Night of the Iguana, The Legend of Oedipus, Little Night Music. *Off-B'way & L.A.*: Love Letters, Three Tall Women.
PICTURES: Frogs, Dedication Day (dir. only).
TELEVISION: *Series*: Temperatures Rising, Testimony of Two Men, We've Got Each Other, Dallas, Knots Landing. *Guest*: The F.B.I., The Girl with Something Extra, Quark, Dallas, Quincy, Rockford Files, Rhoda. *Co-host*: Miss USA and Miss Universe Pageants, Battle of the Network Stars, Macy's Thanksgiving Parade, Tournament of Roses Parade. *Movies*: The Judge and Jake Wyler, Big Rose, Shell Game, The Last Dinosaur, Red Flag—The Ultimate Game, Glitter, Shakedown on the Sunset Strip, My First Love, Always Remember I Love You, The Grand Central Murders, Tainted Blood, In the Shadows Someone's Watching (also co-exec. prod.), Moment of Truth: A Mother's Deception, When the Dark Man Calls, Loyal Opposition: Terror in the White House, Tornado Warning .*Special*: Boys Will Be Boys (also dir.). *Mini-series*: Knots Landing: Back to the Cul-de-Sac.

VANCE, COURTNEY B.
Actor. b. Detroit, MI, Mar. 12, 1960. e. Harvard (B.A.), Yale Drama Sch. (M.A.).
THEATRE: *B'way*: Fences (Theatre World & Clarence Derwent Awards; Tony nom.), Six Degrees of Separation (Tony nom.). *Off-B'way*: My Children My Africa (Obie Award), Romeo and Juliet, Temptation. *Regional*: A Lesson From Aloes, Rosencrantz and Guildenstern Are Dead, Hamlet, Butterfly, Jazz Wives Jazz Lives, Geronimo Jones.
PICTURES: Hamburger Hill, The Hunt for Red October, The Adventures of Huck Finn, Holy Matrimony, Panther, Dangerous Moves, The Last Supper, The Preacher's Wife, Blind Faith, Ambushed, Love and Action in Chicago (also co-prod.), Cookie's Fortune, Space Cowboys, The Acting Class, Eye See You, D-Tox.
TELEVISION: *Movies*: Percy and Thunder, Race to Freedom, Tuskegee Airmen, The Affair, Black Tuesday, 12 Angry Men, Naked City: Justice with a Bullet, Naked City: A Killer Christmas, Parting the Waters, Whitewash: The Clarence Brandley Story. *Series*: Boston Public, Law & Order: Criminal Intent.

VAN DAMME, JEAN-CLAUDE
Actor. r.n. Jean-Claude Van Varenberg. b. Brussels, Belgium, Apr. 1, 1961. Former European karate champion, began studying martial arts at 11 yrs. old. Won the European Professional Karate Association's middleweight championship. As teen established the California Gym in Brussels; also worked as a model before coming to U.S. in 1981. Resumed career teaching martial arts before landing first film role.
PICTURES: No Retreat No Surrender, Bloodsport, Black Eagle, Cyborg, Kickboxer (also co-story), Death Warrant, Lionheart (also co-s.p., story), Double Impact (also co-prod., co-s.p., co-story, fight choreog.), Universal Soldier, Nowhere to Run, Last Action Hero (cameo), Hard Target, Timecop, Street Fighter, Sudden Death, The Quest (also dir. & story), Maximum Risk, Double Team, Legionnaire (also s.p., prod.), Knock Off, Inferno, Universal Soldier: The Return (also prod.), Replicant, The Order, Derailed, The Monk, Abominable.

VAN DER BEEK, JAMES
Actor. b. Cheshire, CT, March 8, 1977
PICTURES: Angus, I Love You I Love You Not, Castle in the Sky (voice), Varsity Blues, Harvest, Scary Movie, Storytelling, Jay and Silent Bob Strike Back, Texas Rangers, The Rules of Attraction.
TELEVISION: *Series*: As the World Turns, Dawson's Creek, Total Access 24/7. *Guest*: Clarissa Explains It All.

VAN DEVERE, TRISH
Actress. b. Englewood Cliffs, NJ, March 9, 1945. e. Ohio Wesleyan U. m. late actor George C. Scott. On B'way in Sly Fox, Tricks of the Trade.
PICTURES: The Landlord (debut, 1970), Where's Poppa?, The Last Run, One Is a Lonely Number, Harry in Your Pocket, The Day of the Dolphin, The Savage Is Loose, Movie Movie, The Changeling, The Hearse, Uphill All the Way, Hollywood Vice Squad, Messenger of Death.
TELEVISION: *Series*: Search for Tomorrow, One Life to Live. *Movies*: Stalk the Wild Child, Beauty and the Beast, Sharon: Portrait of a Mistress, Mayflower—The Pilgrim's Adventure, Beauty and the Beast, Stalk the Wild Child, Columbo: Make Me a Perfect Murder, All God's Children, Haunted, Curacao.

VAN DOREN, MAMIE
Actress. r.n. Joan Lucille Olander. b. Rowena, SD, Feb. 6, 1933. e. Los Angeles H.S. Secy. law firm, L.A.; prof. debut as singer with Ted Fio Rita orch.; debuted in films as Joan Olander.
PICTURES: His Kind of Woman (debut, 1951), Forbidden, The All-American, Yankee Pasha, Francis Joins the WACs, Ain't Misbehavin', The Second Greatest Sex, Running Wild, Star in the Dust, Untamed Youth, The Girl in Black Stockings, Teacher's Pet, Guns Girls and Gangsters, High School Confidential, The Beat Generation, The Big Operator, Born Reckless, Girls' Town, The Private Lives of Adam and Eve, Sex Kittens Go to College, College Confidential, Vice Raid, The Sheriff Was a Lady, The Candidate, Three Nuts in Search of a Bolt, The Navy vs. the Night Monsters, Las Vegas Hillbillies, You've Got to Be Smart, Voyage to the Planet of the Prehistoric Women, The Arizona Kid, Boarding School (Free Ride), Slackers.

VAN DYK, NICOLAS
Executive. e. B.A., political science (Phi Beta Kappa), UCLA, M.B.A., Harvard Business School. Served as consultant, LEK Partnership, where he worked on strategies for clients in the media & entertainment industries; manager, The Walt Disney Co., where he was responsible for technology-related acquisitions and strategies for business such as ABC, ESPN, Disney Regional Entertainment, and Disney Interactive, as well as the acquisition of Dream Quest Images. Became v.p. of strategic planning, Artisan Entertainment, 1997, helping to acquire LIVE Entertainment. Currently executive v.p. & CSO, Artisan, and president, Artisan Digital Media. Oversees company-wide business development, strategic planning, mergers & acquisitions, and corporate finance, as well as all strategic and operational aspects of Artisan's Internet initiatives, including the management of iArtisan, LLC, an Internet investment vehicle.

VAN DYKE, DICK
Actor. b. West Plains, MO, Dec., 13, 1925. Brother is actor Jerry Van Dyke. Son is actor Barry Van Dyke. Served in USAF, WWII. After discharge from service, opened advertising agency in Danville, IL. Teamed with friend in nightclub act called Eric and Van, The Merry Mutes, and for 4 yrs. toured country doing a routine in which they pantomimed and lip-synched to records. 1953 hosted local TV show in Atlanta, then New Orleans. 1955 to NY as host of CBS Morning show.
THEATRE: *NY*: The Girls Against the Boys (Theatre World Award), Bye Bye Birdie (Tony Award, 1961), The Music Man (revival).
PICTURES: Bye Bye Birdie (debut, 1963), What a Way to Go!, Mary Poppins, The Art of Love, Lt. Robin Crusoe USN, Divorce American Style, Fitzwilly, Chitty Chitty Bang Bang, Some Kind of a Nut, The Comic, Cold Turkey, The Runner Stumbles, Dick Tracy.
TELEVISION: *Series*: The Morning Show (host), CBS Cartoon Theatre (host), The Chevy Showroom, Pantomime Quiz, Laugh

Line (emcee), The Dick Van Dyke Show (3 Emmy Awards: 1964, 1965, 1966), The New Dick Van Dyke Show, Van Dyke and Company (Emmy Award, 1977), The Carol Burnett Show, The Van Dyke Show, Diagnosis Murder. *Guest*: Jake and the Fat Man, Highway to Heaven, Matlock. *Movies*: The Morning After, Wrong Way Kid, Drop-Out Father, Found Money, The Country Girl, Ghost of a Chance, Keys to the Kingdom, Daughters of Privilege, The House on Sycamore Street, A Twist of the Knife, A Town Without Pity, Without Warning, The Gin Game. *Pilot*: Harry's Battles. *Specials*: The Dick Van Dyke Special, Dick Van Dyke and the Other Woman, Julie and Dick in Covent Garden, The Confessions of Dick Van Dyke, CBS Library: The Wrong Way Kid (Emmy Award, 1984), Breakfast With Les and Bess, The Town Santa Forgot (narrator), The People's Choice Awards (host), I Love Christmas.

VAN DYKE, JERRY
Actor. b. Danville, IL, July 27, 1931. Brother is actor Dick Van Dyke. Served in U.S. Air Force before becoming standup comic, banjo player in nightclubs. Guested on The Dick Van Dyke Show, playing Van Dyke's brother.
PICTURES: The Courtship of Eddie's Father (debut, 1963), McLintock!, Palm Springs Weekend, Love and Kisses, Angel in My Pocket, W.A.R.: Women Against Rape, Run If You Can, Annabelle's Wish.
TELEVISION: *Series*: Picture This, The Judy Garland Show, My Mother the Car, Accidental Family, Headmaster, 13 Queens Boulevard, Coach, You Wish, Teen Angel. *Mini-Series*: Fresno. *Movie*: To Grandmother's House We Go. *Pilots*: My Boy Googie, You're Only Young Twice, Merry Christmas, George Bailey.

VANGELIS
Composer, Conductor. r.n. Vangelis Papathanassiou. b. Greece, March 23, 1943. Began composing as child, performing own compositions at 6. Left Greece for Paris by late 1960s. Composed and recorded his symphonic poem Faire que Ton Reve Soit Plus Long que la Nuit, and album Terra. Collaborated with filmmaker Frederic Rossif for whom composed La Cantique des Creatures. Moved to London then to Greece in 1989. Formed band Formynx in Greece; then Aphrodite's Child in Paris.
PICTURES: Chariots of Fire (Academy Award, 1981), Antarctica, Missing, Blade Runner, The Year of Living Dangerously, The Bounty, Wonders of Life, Wild and Beautiful, Nosferatu in Venice, Francesco, 1492: Conquest of Paradise, Bitter Moon, Cavafy, How the Grinch Stole Christmas, Old School, Bruce Almighty.

VANOCUR, SANDER
News Commentator. b. Cleveland, OH, Jan. 8, 1928. e. Northwestern U. Began career as journalist on London staff of Manchester Guardian 1954-5; City staff, NY Times 1956-57. Joined NBC in 1957, hosting First Tuesday series. Resigned in 1971 to be correspondent of the National Public Affairs Center for PBS. TV Critic for Washington Post, 1975-7. In 1977 joined ABC News as v.p., special reporting units 1977-80. Chief overview corr. ABC news, 1980-81; sr. corr. 1981-present. Anchor: Business World.

VAN PALLANDT, NINA
Actress. b. Copenhagen, Denmark, July 15, 1932. e. USC. Returned to Denmark where she was married to Baron Frederik Van Pallandt with whom she appeared as folk singer throughout Europe, as well as making 3 films with him; went on world tour together before divorcing. Has appeared in New York as singer.
PICTURES: The Long Goodbye, Assault on Agathon, A Wedding, Quintet, American Gigolo, Cloud Dancer, Cutter and Bone, Asi Como Habian Sido, The Sword and the Sorcerer, Jungle Warriors, Time Out, O.C. and Stiggs.
TELEVISION: *Movie*: Guilty or Innocent: The Sam Shepherd Murder Case, Diary of a Young Comic, Second Serve.

VAN PATTEN, DICK
Actor. b. New York, NY, Dec. 9, 1928. Sister is actress Joyce Van Patten. Father of actors James and Vincent Van Patten. Began career as child actor with B'way debut at 7 yrs., playing son of Melvyn Douglas in Tapestry in Gray.
THEATRE: The Lady Who Came to Stay, O Mistress Mine, On Borrowed Time, Ah, Wilderness, Watch on the Rhine, The Skin of Our Teeth, Kiss and Tell, Mister Roberts, Thieves.
PICTURES: Reg'lar Fellers (debut, 1941), Psychomania, Charly, Zachariah, Making It, Joe Kidd, Soylent Green, Dirty Little Billy, Westworld, Superdad, The Strongest Man in the World, Gus, Treasure of Matecumbe, The Shaggy D.A., Freaky Friday, High Anxiety, Spaceballs, The New Adventures of Pippi Longstocking, Robin Hood: Men in Tights, A Dangerous Place, Demolition High, Love Is All There Is, The Price of Air, Quiet Kill, Groom Lake, The Sure Hand of God.
TELEVISION: *Series*: Mama, The Partners, The New Dick Van Dyke Show, When Things Were Rotten, Eight Is Enough, WIOU. *Guest*: Arnie, The Rookies, Cannon, Banyon, The Little People, The Streets of San Francisco, Hotel, Growing Pains, Love Boat, Murder She Wrote. *Specials*: Jay Leno's Family Comedy Hour, A Mouse A Mystery and Me, 14 Going On 30. *Movies*: Hec Ramsey (pilot), The Crooked Hearts, The Love Boat (pilot), With This Ring, Diary of a Hitchhiker, Eight Is Enough Reunion, Going to the Chapel, An Eight Is Enough Wedding, Jake Spanner—

Private Eye, The Odd Couple: Together Again, The Gift of Love, Eight Is Enough: The E! True Hollywood Story, Another Pretty Face, The Santa Trap.

VAN PATTEN, JOYCE
Actress. b. New York, NY, March 9, 1935. Brother is actor Dick Van Patten. Mother of actress Talia Balsam.
THEATRE: *NY*: Spoon River Anthology, Same Time Next Year, The Supporting Cast, The Seagull, I Ought to Be in Pictures, Brighton Beach Memoirs, Murder at the Howard Johnson's, Rumors, Jake's Women.
PICTURES: Reg'lar Fellers (debut, 1941), Fourteen Hours, The Goddess, I Love You Alice B. Toklas, Making It, Something Big, Thumb Tripping, The Manchu Eagle Murder Caper Mystery, Mame, The Bad News Bears, Mikey and Nicky, The Falcon and the Snowman, St. Elmo's Fire, Billy Galvin, Blind Date, Trust Me, Monkey Shines, Infinity, Show and Tell.
TELEVISION: *Series*: The Danny Kaye Show, The Good Guys, The Don Rickles Show, Mary Tyler Moore Hour, Unhappily Ever After. *Guest*: Brooklyn Bridge. *Movies*: But I Don't Want to Get Married!, Winter Kill, The Stranger Within, Let's Switch, Winner Take All, To Kill a Cop, Murder at the Mardi Gras, The Comedy Company, Eleanor: First Lady of the World, Another Woman's Child, The Demon Murder Case, In Defense of Kids, Malice in Wonderland, Under the Influence, The Haunted, Maid for Each Other, Breathing Lessons, The Gift of Love, Grandpa's Funeral, Jake's Women. *Mini-Series*: The Martian Chronicles. *Special*: Bus Stop.

VAN PEEBLES, MARIO
Actor, Director, Producer, Writer. b. Mexico D.F., Mexico, Jan. 15, 1957. Father is filmmaker Melvin Van Peebles. e. Columbia U., B.A. economics, 1980. Studied acting with Stella Adler 1983. Served as budget analyst for NY Mayor Ed Koch and later worked as a Ford model. Directed music videos for Kid Creole and the Coconuts, Nighttrain (also prod., cameo) and for film Identity Crisis. Appeared as child in father's film Sweet Sweetback's Baadasssss Song. Dir., prod., wrote and starred in short, Juliet. Exec. prod. of soundtracks for Posse and Gunmen.
THEATRE: Waltz of the Stork (B'way debut, 1984), Take Me Along, The Legend of Deadwood Dick, Champeen, Friday the 13th.
PICTURES: *Actor*: The Cotton Club, Delivery Boys, Exterminator II, 3:15, Rappin' (also wrote and performed 5 songs), South Bronx Heroes, Heartbreak Ridge (also songs), Last Resort, Jaws: the Revenge, Hot Shot, Identity Crisis (also s.p.), New Jack City (also dir.), Posse (also dir.), Gunmen, Highlander: The Sorcerer, Panther (also dir., prod.), Jaws IV: The Revenge, Solo, Los Locos (also s.p., prod., exec. prod.), Stag, Love Kills (also. dir., prod., s.p.), Crazy Six, Raw Nerve, Judgement Day, Blowback, Guardian, Ali, The Hebrew Hammer.
TELEVISION: *Series*: Sonny Spoon, Nude Awakening, Fiona., The Street Lawyer. *Guest*: L.A. Law, One Life to Live, The Cosby Show, The Pat Sajack Show (guest host), In Living Color, Living Single, Outer Limits: Bodies of Evidence. *Movies*: The Cable Car Murder, Sophisticated Gents, Children of the Night (Bronze Halo Award), The Facts of Life Down Under, The Child Saver, Blue Bayou, Triumph of the Heart: The Ricky Bell Story, Stompin' at the Savoy, In the Line of Duty: Street War, Crosscurrents: Cable Car Murder, Full Eclipse, American Masters: A Glory of Ghosts (Emperor Jones, All God's Chillun), Third & Oak: The Pool Hall (CBS play), Strangers: Leave, Gang In Blue, Riot, Gang In Blue (also. co-direct, co-prod.), Valentine's Day, Mama Flora's Family, Killers in the House, Protector, 10,000 Black Men Named George, 44 Minutes: The North Hollywood Shoot-Out, *Director*: Sonny Spoon, 21 Jump Street, Top of the Hill, Wise Guy, Malcolm Takes a Shot (DGA nom.), Gabriel's Fire, Missing Persons, Sally Hemmings: An America Scandal.

VAN PEEBLES, MELVIN
Producer, Director, Writer, Composer, Editor, Actor. b. Chicago, IL, Aug. 21, 1932. e. Ohio Wesleyan U., 1953. Father of actor Mario Van Peebles. Was portrait painter in Mexico, cable car driver in San Francisco; journalist in Paris and (in 1970s) options trader on Wall Street. Dir. Funky Beat music video.
AUTHOR: *Books*: The Big Heart, A Bear for the FBI, Le Chinois de XIV, La Permission (Story of a Three Day Pass) La Fete a Harlem, The True American, Sweet Sweetback's Baadasssss Song, Just an Old Sweet Song, Bold Money, No Identity Crisis (co-author with Mario Van Peebles), Panther.
ALBUMS: *Composer*: Brer Soul, Watermelon Man, Sweet Sweetback's Baadasssss Song, As Serious as a Heart Attack, Don't Play Us Cheap, Ain't Suppose to Die a Natural Death, What the #*!% You Mean I Can't Sing, Ghetto Gothic.
THEATRE: *B'way* (writer, prod., dir.): Ain't Supposed to Die a Natural Death, Don't Play Us Cheap, Waltz of the Stork (also actor). *Off-B'way*: Champeen, Waltz of the Stork, Kickin the Science.
PICTURES: The Story of a Three-Day Pass (dir., s.p., music), Watermelon Man (dir., music), Sweet Sweetback's Baad Asssss Song (prod., dir., s.p., edit., music, actor), Don't Play Us Cheap (prod., dir., s.p., edit., music), Greased Lightning (co-s.p.), America (actor), O.C. and Stiggs (actor), Jaws: The Revenge (actor), Identity Crisis (prod., dir., co-edit., actor), True Identity (actor), Boomerang (actor), Posse (actor), Last Action Hero

(actor), Terminal Velocity (actor), Fist of the North Star (actor), Panther (s.p., actor, prod., co-edit.), Classified X.
TELEVISION: *Writer*: Down Home, Just an Old Sweet Song, The Day They Came to Arrest the Book (Emmy Award). *Actor*: Taking Care of Terrific, Sophisticated Gents, Sonny Spoons (series). *Director*: Nipsey Russell at Harrah's, Vroom Vroom Vroom (also writer; German TV), The Outer Limits, The Shining (mini-), Riot.

VAN SANT, GUS
Director, Writer. b. Louisville, KY, July 24, 1952. Raised in Darien, CT, then moved to Oregon at age 17. e. Rhode Island Sch. of Design, where he studied painting. Went to L.A. in 1976, becoming prod. asst. to dir. Ken Shapiro. Made first low-budget film, Alice in Hollywood, which was never released. Later made commercials for NY ad agency before returning to filmmaking.
PICTURES: Mala Noche, Drugstore Cowboy (Natl. Soc. of Film Critics Awards for best dir. & s.p.; NY Film Critics & L.A. Film Critics Award for s.p.), My Own Private Idaho, Even Cowgirls Get the Blues, To Die For, Ballad of the Skeletons, Good Will Hunting, Psycho, Finding Forrester, Brokeback Mountain, Jay and Silent Bob Stike Back (actor only), Gerry.

VAUGHN, ROBERT
Actor. b. New York, NY, Nov. 22, 1932. e. L.A. State coll., B.S. and M.A. Theatre Arts 1956; USC, Ph.D. Communications, 1970. Gained fame as Napoleon Solo in The Man From U.N.C.L.E. TV series. *Author*: Only Victims, 1972.
PICTURES: The Ten Commandments (debut, 1956), Hell's Crossroads, No Time to Be Young, Teenage Caveman, Unwed Mother, Good Day for a Hanging, The Young Philadelphians (Acad. Award nom.), The Magnificent Seven, The Big Show, The Caretakers, To Trap a Spy, The Spy With My Face, One Spy Too Many, The Glass Bottom Boat (cameo), The Venetian Affair, How to Steal the World, Bullitt, Bridge at Remagen, If It's Tuesday This Must Be Belgium (cameo), The Mind of Mr. Soames, Julius Caesar, The Statue, Clay Pigeon, The Towering Inferno, The Babysitter, Lucifer Complex, Demon Seed (voice), Starship Invasions, Brass Target, Good Luck Miss Wycoff, Hangar 18, Sweet Dirty Tony, Battle Beyond the Stars, Virus, S.O.B., Superman III, Black Moon Rising, The Delta Force, Rampage, Nightstick, Hour of the Assassin, Skeleton Coast, River of Death, Captive Rage, Nobody's Perfect, Fair Trade, Edgar Allan Poe's Buried Alive, That's Adequate, Blind Vision, C.H.U.D. II: Bud the Chud, Transylvania Twist, Going Under, Twilight Blue, Joe's Apartment, Vulcan, The Sender, Motel Blue, Milk and Money, Anakng Bulkan, An American Affair, McCinsey's Island, BASEketball, Cottonmouth, Pootie Tang, Happy Hour, Hoodlum & Son.
TELEVISION: *Series*: The Lieutenant, The Man From U.N.C.L.E., The Protectors, Emerald Point N.A.S., The A-Team, Danger Theatre, As the World Turns, One Life to Live. Mini-Series: Captains and the Kings, Washington: Behind Closed Doors (Emmy Award, 1978), Centennial, Backstairs at the White House, The Blue and the Gray, Evergreen, Tracks of Glory. *Movies*: The Woman Hunter, Kiss Me Kill Me, The Islander, The Rebels, Mirror Mirror, Doctor Franken, The Gossip Columnist, City in Fear, Fantasies, The Day the Bubble Burst, A Question of Honor, Inside the Third Reich, Intimate Agony, The Return of the Man From U.N.C.L.E., International Airport, Murrow, Prince of Bel Air, Desperado, Perry Mason: The Case of the Defiant Daughter, Dark Avenger, Escape to Witch Mountain, Dancing in the Dark. BBC: One of Our Spies is Missing, The Spy in the Green Hat, The Karate Killers, Virtual Obsession, Host. *Guest*: Law and Order.

VAUGHN, VINCE
Actor. b. Minneapolis, MN, March 28, 1970.
PICTURES: For the Boys, Rudy, At Risk, Swingers, Just Your Luck, The Locusts, The Lost World: Jurassic Park, Return to Paradise, Clay Pigeons, A Cool Dry Place, The Cell, Psycho, South of Heaven, West of Hell, The Prime Gig, Zoolander, Made (also prod.), Domestic Disturbance, Dust: An Extraordinary Disturbance, Old School, Starsky & Hutch, Thumbsucker, The Sky Is Green.
TELEVISION: *Guest*: 21 Jump Street, Sex & the City.

VEL JOHNSON, REGINALD
Actor. b. Queens, NY, Aug. 16, 1952. e. Long Island Inst. of Music and Arts, NYU.
THEATRE: *NY*: But Never Jam Today, Inacent Black, World of Ben Caldwell, Staggerlee.
PICTURES: Wolfen (debut, 1981), Ghostbusters, The Cotton Club, Remo Williams, Armed and Dangerous, Crocodile Dundee, Die Hard, Turner & Hooch, Die Hard 2, Posse, Ground Zero, Like Mike.
TELEVISION: *Series*: Perfect Strangers, Family Matters. *Movies*: Quiet Victory: The Charlie Wedemeyer Story, The Bride in Black, Jury Duty: The Comedy, Grass Roots, One of Her Own, Deadly Pursuits.

VENORA, DIANE
Actress. b. Hartford, CT, 1952. e. Juilliard Sch. (BFA degree). Member of Juilliard's Acting Company, Circle Repertory Co. and the Ensemble Studio Theatre.
THEATRE: A Midsummer Night's Dream, Hamlet (New York Shakespeare Festival), Uncle Vanya (at La Mama), Messiah (Manhattan Theatre Club), Penguin Toquet, Tomorrow's Monday (Circle Rep), Largo Desolato, School for Scandal, The Seagull, A Man for All Seasons (Roundabout Theatre Co.), Peer Gynt (Williamstown Fest.), The Winter's Tale, Hamlet (NYSF).
PICTURES: All That Jazz, Wolfen, Terminal Choice, The Cotton Club, F/X, Ironweed, Bird (NY Film Critics Award, 1988; Golden Globe nom.), Heat, Three Wishes, Surviving Picasso, The Subsitute, Romeo and Juliet, The Jackal, Young Girl and the Monsoon, Looking for an Echo, The 13th Warrior, The Joyriders, The Insider, Hamlet, True Crime, Meggido: The Omega Code 2, Heartbreak Hospital.
TELEVISION: *Mini-Series*: A.D. *Movie*: Cook and Peary: The Race to the Pole. *Specials*: Getting There, Rehearsing Hamlet, Hamlet, Race Against Time. *Guest*: Law and Order. *Series*: Thunder Alley, Chicago Hope.

VEREEN, BEN
Singer, Dancer, Actor. b. Miami, FL, Oct. 10, 1946. e. High School of Performing Arts.
THEATRE: *NY*: Hair, Sweet Charity, Jesus Christ Superstar (Theatre World Award), Pippin (Tony Award, 1973), Grind.
PICTURES: Sweet Charity, Gasss, Funny Lady, All That Jazz, The Zoo Gang, Buy and Cell, Friend to Friend, Once Upon a Forest (voice), Why Do Fools Fall in Love, I'll Take You There, The Painting.
TELEVISION: *Movies*: Louis Armstrong—Chicago Style, The Jesse Owens Story, Lost in London, Intruders, Fosse. *Mini-Series*: Roots, Ellis Island, A.D., Feast of All Saints. *Series*: Oz, Ben Vereen... Comin' at Ya, Ten Speed and Brown Shoe, Webster, Zoobilee Zoo, You Write the Songs (host), J.J. Starbuck, Silk Stalkings. *Specials*: Ben Vereen—His Roots, Uptown— A Tribute to the Apollo Theatre.

VERHOEVEN, PAUL
Director. b. Amsterdam, The Netherlands, July 18, 1938. e. U. of Leiden, Ph.D., (mathematics and physics) where he began making films.
PICTURES: Business Is Business, Turkish Delight, Keetje Tippel (Cathy Tippel), Soldier of Orange, Spetters, The Fourth Man, Flesh + Blood, Robocop, Total Recall, Basic Instinct, Showgirls, Starship Troopers, Hollow Man.

VERNON, ANNE
Actress. r.n. Edith Antoinette Alexandrine Vignaud. b. Paris, Jan. 7, 1924. e. Ecole des Beaux Arts, Paris. Worked for French designer; screen debut in French films; toured with French theatre group; first starring role, Le Mannequin Assassine 1948. Wrote French cookbooks. Was subject of 1980 French TV film detailing her paintings, Les Peintres Enchanteurs.
PICTURES: Edouar et Caroline, Terror on a Train, Ainsi Finit La Nuit, A Warning to Wantons, Patto Col Diavolo, A Tale of Five Cities, Shakedown, Song of Paris, The Umbrellas of Cherbourg, General Della Rovere, La Rue L'Estrapade, Love Lottery, Therese and Isabelle.

VERNON, JOHN
Actor. r.n. Adolphus Raymondus Vernon Agopowicz. b. Montreal, Canada, Feb. 24, 1932. e. Banff Sch. of Fine Arts, Royal Acad. of Dramatic Art. Worked on London stage and radio. First film work as voice of Big Brother in 1984 (1956). Daughter is actress Kate Vernon.
PICTURES: 1984 (voice; debut, 1956), Nobody Waved Goodbye, Point Blank, Justine, Topaz, Tell Them Willie Boy is Here, One More Train to Rob, Dirty Harry, Fear Is the Key, Charley Varrick, W (I Want Her Dead), The Black Windmill, Brannigan, Sweet Movie, The Outlaw Josey Wales, Angela, A Special Day, The Uncanny, Golden Rendevzous, National Lampoon's Animal House, It Rained All Night the Day I Left, Crunch, Fantastica, Herbie Goes Bananas, Heavy Metal (voice), Airplane II: The Sequel, Chained Heat, Curtains, Savage Streets, Jungle Warriors, Fraternity Vacation, Doin' Time, Double Exposure (Terminal Exposure), Ernest Goes to Camp, Blue Monkey, Nightstick, Border Heat, Deadly Stranger, Dixie Lanes, Killer Klowns From Outer Space, Bail-Out, I'm Gonna Git You Sucka, Office Party, War Bus Commando, Mob Story, The Naked Truth, Malicious, The Gnomes Great Adventure, You're Still Not Fooling Anybody, Stageghost, Sorority Boys, Warrior Angels, Welcome to America.
TELEVISION: *Series*: Tugboat Annie (Canadian TV), Wojeck (Canadian TV), Delta House, Hail to the Chief. *Movies*: Trial Run, Escape, Cool Million, Hunter, The Questor Tapes, Mousey, The Virginia Hill Story, The Imposter, Swiss Family Robinson, The Barbary Coast, Matt Helm, Mary Jane Harper Cried Last Night, The Sacketts, The Blood of Others, Two Men (Can.), The Woman Who Sinned, The Fire Next Time, The Forget-Me-Not Murders. *Mini-Series*: The Blue and the Gray, Louisiana (Fr.). *Pilots*: B-Men, War of the Worlds. *Guest*: Tarzan, Kung Fu, Faerie Tale Theatre (Little Red Riding Hood), The Greatest American Hero, Fall Guy, Alfred Hitchcock Presents, Knight Rider, Tales From the Crypt.

425

VERONA, STEPHEN
Director, Producer, Writer. b. Illinois, Sept. 11, 1940. e. Sch. of Visual Arts. Directed and wrote some 300 commercials (over 50 award-winners) before turning to feature films in 1972, which he wrote as well. Also dir. award-winning short subjects (featuring Barbra Streisand, The Beatles, Simon and Garfunkle and The Lovin' Spoonful). Also prod., dir. of Angela Lansbury's Positive Moves video. Is an artist whose works have been exhibited at numerous CA and NY galleries. Dir. Acad. Award nom. short subject, The Rehearsal, 1971.
PICTURES: *Director*: The Lords of Flatbush (prod., co-dir., co-s.p.), Pipe Dreams (also prod., s.p.), Boardwalk (also co-s.p.), Talking Walls (also s.p.).
TELEVISION: Class of 1966 (prod. designer, ani. dir.), Diff'rent Strokes, The Music People, Sesame Street, Take a Giant Step, Double Exposure, Flatbush Avenue (pilot, prod., co-s.p.).

VETTER, RICHARD
Executive. b. San Diego, CA, Feb. 24, 1928. e. Pepperdine Coll., B.A., 1950; San Diego State Coll., M.A., 1953; UCLA, Ph.D., 1959. U.S. Navy: aerial phot., 1946-48, reserve instr., San Diego County Schools, 1951-54; asst. prof., audio-vis. commun., U.C.L.A., 1960-63. Inventor, co-dev., Dimension 150 Widescreen Process. 1957-63: formed D-150 Inc., 1963; exec. v.p. mem.: SMPTE, Technical & Scientific Awards Committee, AMPAS.

VIANE, CHUCK
Executive. e. B.S., marketing, De Paul U. Began as film buyer, v.p. & head buyer, General Cinema Theater Corp., 1973-85; v.p. & asst. gen. sales mgr., Buena Vista Pictures, 1986; senior v.p. & gen. sales mgr., Buena Vista Pictures, 1995. Currently president, Buena Vista Pictures Distribution (since 1999), overseeing sales and distribution operations throughout U.S. and Canada for all motion pictures released by Walt Disney, Touchstone, and Hollywood Pictures. His tenure with Buena Vista has seen the company break numerous industry records and finish as the industry leader for six of the last ten years, surpassing the $1 billion mark at the box office for five of the past six years.

VICTOR, JAMES
Actor. r.n. Lincoln Rafael Peralta Diaz. b. Santiago, Dominican Republic, July 27, 1939. e. Haaren H.S., N.Y. Studied at Actors Studio West. Member of Academy of Mo. Pic. Arts & Sciences, Actors Branch. Recipient of Cleo Award, 1975, for Mug Shot; Golden Eagle Award, 1981, for consistent outstanding performances in motion pictures.
THEATRE: Bullfight, Ceremony for an Assassinated Blackman, Latina (Drama-Logue Critics Award, 1980), The Man in the Glass Booth, The M.C. (Drama-Logue Critics, and Cesar best actor awards, 1985), I Gave You a Calendar (Drama-Logue Critics Award, 1983), I Don't Have To Show You No Stinking Badges (Drama-Logue Critics Award, 1986), The Rooster and the Egg, One Hour Without Television, The Red Devil Battery Sign.
PICTURES: Fuzz, Rolling Thunder, Boulevard Nights, Defiance, Losin' It, Borderline, Stand and Deliver, Gunfighter's Moon, Executrive Decision, Love Always.
TELEVISION: *Series*: Viva Valdez, Condo, I Married Dora, Angelica Mi Vida, The New Zorro, Murder She Wrote. Many appearances on specials. *Movies*: Robert Kennedy and His Times, Twin Detectives, Remington Steel, The Streets of L.A., I Desire, Second Serve, Grand Slam, Falcon Crest, The Second Civil War. *Mini-Series*: Streets of Laredo.

VIGODA, ABE
Actor. b. New York, NYU, Feb. 24, 1921.
PICTURES: The Godfather, The Don Is Dead, Newman's Law, The Cheap Detective, Vasectomy - A Delicate Matter, Plain Clothes, Look Who's Talking, Prancer, Joe vs. the Volcano, Sugar Hill, Jury Duty, Good Burger, Just the Ticket.
TELEVISION: *Series*: Dark Shadow, Barney Miller, Fish, One Life to Live. *Movies*: The Devil's Daughter, Tomaa, Having Babies, How to Pick Up Girls, Death Car on the Freeway, Witness to the Mob. *Guest*: Mannix, Kojak, The Rookies, B.J. and the Bear, B.K. Stryker.

VINCENT, JR., FRANCIS T
Executive. b. Waterbury, CT, May 29, 1938. e. Williams Coll. B.A., 1960; Yale Law Sch. LL.B., 1963. Bar, CT 1963; NY, 1964; D.C. 1969. 1969-78, partner in law firm of Caplin & Drysdale, specializing in corporate banking and securities matters; 1978, assoc. dir. of, Division of Corporation Finance of Securities & Exchange Commission; exec. v.p. of the Coca-Cola Company and pres. & CEO of its entertainment business sector. Also chmn. & CEO of Columbia Pictures Industries, Inc.; appt. pres. CEO, 1978; mem. bd. of dir. of The Coca-Cola Bottling Co. of NY. 1987-88; rejoined law firm of Caplin & Drysdale, Washington, D.C., 1988. Trustee of Williams Coll. & The Hotchkiss Sch.

VINCENT, JAN-MICHAEL
Actor. b. Denver, CO, July 15, 1945. e. Ventura City (CA) Coll. as art major. Joined National Guard. Discovered by agent Dick Clayton. Hired by Robert Conrad to appear in his film, Los Bandidos. Signed to 6-mo. contract by Universal, for which made U.S. debut in Journey to Shiloh. Then did pilot TV movie for 20th-Fox based on Hardy Boys series of book. Originally called self Michael Vincent; changed after The Undefeated.
PICTURES: Los Bandidos (debut, 1967), Journey to Shiloh, The Undefeated, Going Home, The Mechanic, The World's Greatest Athlete, Buster and Billie, Bite the Bullet, White Line Fever, Baby Blue Marine, Vigilante Force, Shadow of the Hawk, Damnation Alley, Big Wednesday, Hooper, Defiance, Hard Country, The Return, The Last Plane Out, Born in East L.A., Enemy Territory, Hit List, Deadly Embrace, Demonstone, Hangfire, Raw Nerve, Alienator, Haunting Fear, Gold of the Samurai, The Divine Enforcer, Beyond the Call of Duty, Sins of Desire, Hidden Obsession, Xtro II, Deadly Avenger, Midnight Witness, Ice Cream Man, Abducted II: The Reunion, Red Line, Orbit, Codename: Silencer, Buffalo '66, White Boy, The Thundering 8th, Escape to Grizzly Mountain.
TELEVISION: *Series*: Dangerous Island (Banana Splits Hour), The Survivors, Airwolf. *Movies*: Tribes, The Catcher, Sandcastles, Deliver Us From Evil, Six Against the Rock, Tarzan in Manhattan, The Final Heist, Singapore Sling, Jurassic Women. *Mini-Series*: The Winds of War. *Guest*: Lassie, Bonanza.

VINER, MICHAEL
Producer, Writer. b. 1945. m. actress Deborah Raffin. e. Harvard U., Georgetown U. Served as aide to Robert Kennedy; was legman for political columnist Jack Anderson. Settled in Hollywood, where worked for prod. Aaron Rosenberg, first as prod. asst. on three Frank Sinatra films; then asst. prod. on Joaquin Murietta. In music industry was record producer, manager, executive, eventually heading own division, at MGM. Debut as writer-producer in 1976 with TV special, Special of the Stars. Theatrical film debut as prod.-co-writer of Touched by Love, 1980. Pictures: Wilde (exec. prod.). Television: *Mini-Series*: Memories of Midnight .*Movies:* Willa, Sidney Sheldon's The Sands of Time, Morning Glory, Home Song, Family Blessings, *Exec. Prod.:* Windmills of the Gods , Rainbow Drive, Unwed Father, Futuresport. *President*: Dove Audio.

VITALE, RUTH
Executive. e. Tufts U., B.A.; Boston U., M.S. Prior to motion picture career, worked in advertising and media. Senior v.p., Vestron Pictures then s.v.p. of feature production at United Artists and management at Constantin Film Development before joining New Line. Joined New Line as exec. v.p. of worldwide acquisitions. Currently pres., Fine Line Features, a wholly owned division of New Line Cinema.

VITTI, MONICA
Actress. r.n. Maria Luisa Ceciarelli. b. Rome, Italy, Nov. 3, 1933. Started acting in plays as teen, studying at Rome's Natl. Acad. of Dramatic Arts.
PICTURES: Ridere Ridere Ridere (debut, 1955), Smart Girls, L'Avventura, La Notte, L'Eclipse, Dragees du Poivre (Sweet and Sour), Three Fables of Love, The Nutty Naughty Chateau, Alta Infidelitata (High Infidelity), The Red Desert, Le Bambole (The Dolls), Il Disco Volante, Le Fate (The Queens), Modesty Blaise, The Chastity Belt (On My Way to the Crusades I Met a Girl Who...), Girl with a Pistol, La Femme Ecarlate, The Pizza Triangle, The Pacifist, Teresa la Ladra, Tosca, The Phantom of Liberty, Midnight Pleasures, My Loves, Duck in Orange Sauce, An Almost Perfect Affair, The Mystery of Oberwald, Tigers in Lipstick, The Flirt (also s.p.), When Veronica Calls, Secret Scandal (also dir., co- s.p.).

VOIGHT, JON
Actor. b. Yonkers, NY. Dec. 29, 1938. e. Archbishop Stepinac H.S., White Plains, NY; Catholic U. of Amer., D.C. (B.F.A.) 1960; studied acting at the Neighborhood Playhouse and in private classes with Stanford Meisner, four yrs. Daughter is actress Angelina Jolie.
THEATRE: B'way: The Sound of Music (debut, 1959), That Summer That Fall (Theatre World Award), The Seagull. Off-B'way: A View From the Bridge (1964 revival). *Regional*: Romeo & Juliet, A Streetcar Named Desire, Hamlet.
PICTURES: Hour of the Gun (debut, 1967), Fearless Frank, Midnight Cowboy, Out of It, Catch-22, The Revolutionary, Deliverance, All-American Boy, Conrack, The Odessa File, End of the Game, Coming Home (Acad. Award, 1978), The Champ, Lookin' To Get Out (also co-s.p., prod.), Table for Five (also prod.), Runaway Train, Desert Bloom, Eternity, Heat, Rosewood, U-Turn, Mission Impossible, Anaconda, The Rainmaker, Enemy of the State, The General, A Dog of Flanders, Varsity Blues, Pearl Harbor, Lara Croft: Tomb Raider, Zoolander, Ali, Unleashed, Baby Genuises 2: Superbabies, A Decade Under the Influence, Holes.
TELEVISION: *Movies*: Chernobyl: The Final Warning, The Last of His Tribe, The Tin Soldier (also dir.), Convict Cowboy, The Fixer, Noah's Ark, Second String, Uprising, Jasper Texas. *Mini-Series*: Return to Lonesome Dove, Jack and the Beanstalk: The Real Story. *Special*: The Dwarf (Public Broadcast Lab). *Guest*: Gunsmoke, Naked City, The Defenders, Coronet Blue, NYPD.

VON SYDOW, MAX
Actor. b. Lund, Sweden, April 10, 1929. Theatrical debut in a Cathedral Sch. of Lund prod. of The Nobel Prize. Served in the Swedish Quartermaster Corps two yrs. Studied at Royal Dramatic Theatre Sch. in Stockholm. Tour in municipal theatres. Has appeared on stage in Stockholm, London (The Tempest, 1988), Paris and Helsinki in Faust, The Legend and The Misanthrope. 1954 won Sweden's Royal Foundation Cultural Award. Appeared on B'way in Duet for One.
PICTURES: Bara en Mor (Only a Mother; debut, 1949), Miss Julie, Ingen Mans Kvinna, Ratten att Alska, The Seventh Seal, Prasten i Uddarbo, Wild Strawberries, Brink of Life, Spion 503, The Magician, The Virgin Spring, Brollopsdagen, Through a Glass Darkly, Nils Holgerssons Underbara Resa, Alskarinnen, Winter Light, 4x4, The Greatest Story Ever Told (English-language debut, 1965), The Reward, Hawaii, The Quiller Memorandum, Hour of the Wolf, Here Is Your Life, Svarta Palmkronor, Shame, Made in Sweden, The Kremlin Letter, The Passion of Anna, The Night Visitor, The Touch, The Emigrants, Appelbriget, Embassy, The New Land, The Exorcist, Steppenwolf, Egg! Egg!, Illustrious Corpses, Three Days of the Condor, The Ultimate Warrior, Foxtrot (The Other Side of Paradise), Cuore di Cane, Voyage of the Damned, Les Desert des Tartares, Exorcist II: The Heretic, March or Die, Brass Target, Gran Bolitto, Hurricane, Deathwatch, Venetian Lies, Flash Gordon, Victory, She Dances Alone (voice), Conan the Barbarian, Flight of the Eagle, Strange Brew, Never Say Never Again, Target Eagle, Dreamscape, Dune, Code Name: Emerald, Hannah and Her Sisters, Duet for One, The Second Victory, Wolf at the Door, Pelle the Conqueror (Acad. Award nom.), Katinka (dir.), Cellini: A Violent Life, Awakenings, A Kiss Before Dying, Until the End of the World, Zentropa (narrator), The Bachelor, The Best Intentions, The Ox, Father, Grandfather's Journey, Needful Things, The Silent Touch, Time Is Money, The Atlantic (narrator), Judge Dredd, Needful Things, Jerusalem, Hamsun, What Dreams May Come, Snow Falling on Cedars, Non ho sonno, Vercingétorix, Intact, Minority Report.
TELEVISION: *Movies/Mini-Series*: Samson and Delilah, Christopher Columbus, Kojak: The Belarus File, Brotherhood of the Rose, Hiroshima: Out of the Ashes, Red King White Knight, Radetzky March, Citizen X, A Que Punto E La Notte, Uncle Vanya, Confessions, Hostile Waters, Fantasma Per Caso, Salomone, La Principessa E Il Povero, Nuremberg.

VON TRIER, LARS
Director, Writer, Editor, Actor. r.n. Lars Trier. b. Copenhagen, Denmark, April 30, 1956. e. Danish Film Institute. Attracted international attention with Forbrydelsens Element (The Element of Crime). Is working on a film project taking a 3 minute shot every year from different locations all over Europe for a period of 33 years; begun in 1991, the premiere is expected in the year 2024.
PICTURES: *Director*: Orchidegartneren (1976), Menthe la bienheureuse, Den Sidste detalje, Befrielsesbilleder (also s.p.), The Element of Crime (also actor, s.p.), Epidemic (also actor, s.p., edit.), Medea (also s.p.), Un Monde de Difference (actor only), Zentropa (a.k.a. Europa; also actor, s.p.), The Kingdom (orig. for Danish TV; also s.p.), Breaking the Waves (also s.p.); Grand Jury Prize, Cannes, 1996), The Kingdom 2 (orig. for Danish TV; also s.p.), The Idiots (also s.p.), Dancer in The Dark (also s.p.), Dogville. *Actor*: Orchidefartneren, Menthelabienheureuse, Kaptajn Klyde og hans venner vender tilbage, Forbrydelsens element, Épidemic, En Verden til forskel, Zentropa, The Kingdom, The Kingdom II, Tranceformer - A Portrait of Laws von Trier, Idioterne, De Ydmygede, Lars from 1-10, Morten Korch - Solskin kan man altid finde, Kopisten, Foot On The Moon, De Udstillede, The Name of This Film is Dogme95, Von Trier's 100 Eyes.

VON TROTTA, MARGARETHE
Director, Writer. b. Berlin, Germany, Feb. 21, 1942. e. Studied German and Latin literature in Munich and Paris. Studied acting in Munich and began career as actress. 1970 began collaborating on Schlondorff's films as well as acting in them.
PICTURES: *Actress*: Hands Up!, Madchen zwischen Nacht und Morgen, Schrage Vogel, Brandstifter, Gotter der Pest, Baal, Drucker, Der Amerikanische Soldat, Gods of the Plague, Why Does Herr R. Run Amok?, The Sudden Wealth of the Poor People of Kombach (also co-s.p.), Beware the Holy Whore, Die Moral der Ruth Halbfass, Free Woman (also s.p.), Desaster, Ubernachtung in Tirol, Die Atlantikschwimmer, Bierkampf, Coup de Grace (also co-s.p.), Blaubart. *Dir./ Co-s.p.*: The Lost Honor of Katharina Blum (co-dir., co-s.p., with Schlondorff), The Second Awakening of Christa Klages, Sisters or the Balance of Happiness, Circle of Deceit, Marianne and Julianne, Friends & Husbands, Unerreichbare Nahe, Rosa Luxemburg, Felix, Paura e more (Three Sisters), The African Woman, The Long Silence, The Promise.
TELEVISION: *Dir., Movies*: Dunkle Tage, Beischlaf auf Befehl, Mit fünfzig küssen Männer anders. *Mini-Series*: Jahrestage.

VON ZERNECK, FRANK
Producer. b. New York, NY, Nov. 3, 1940. e. Hofstra Coll., 1962. Has produced plays in New York, Los Angeles and on national tour. Partner, von Zerneck/Sertner Films. Devised Portrait film genre for TV movies: Portrait of a Stripper, Portrait of a Mistress, Portrait of a Centerfold, etc. Past chmn. of California Theatre Council; former officer of League of Resident theatres; member of League of New York Theatres & Producers; Producers Guild of America; chmn's council, the Caucus for Producers, Writers and Directors; Board of Directors, Allied Communications, Inc. Museum of Radio & Television in NYC, Hollywood Television & Radio Society, Acad. of TV Arts & Sciences, Natl. Acad. of Cable Programming. Received American Film Institute Charles Fries Producer of the Year Award.
PICTURE: God's Lonely Man, Living In Oblivion.
TELEVISION: 21 Hours at Munich, Dress Gray, Miracle on Ice, Combat High, Queenie, In the Custody of Strangers, The First Time, Baby Sister, Policewoman Centerfold, Obsessive Love, Invitation to Hell, Romance on the Orient Express, Hostage Flight. *Exec. prod.*: The Proud Men, Man Against the Mob, To Heal a Nation, Lady Mobster, Maybe Baby, Full Exposure: the Sex Tapes Scandal, Gore Vidal's Billy the Kid, Too Young to Die, The Great Los Angeles Earthquake, The Court-Martial of Jackie Robinson, White Hot: The Mysterious Murder of Thelma Todd, Survive the Savage Sea, Opposites Attract, Menu for Murder, Battling for Baby, Woman With a Past, Jackie Collins' Lady Boss, Danger Island, The Broken Chain, Beyond Suspicion, French Silk, The Corpse Had a Familiar Face, Robin Cook's Mortal Fear, Take Me Home Again, The Other Woman, Seduced and Betrayed, Robin Cook's Virus, The West Side Waltz, Crazy Horse, Robin Cook's Terminal, She Said No, Terror In the Family, My Son Is Innocent, Tornado!, Border Music, No One Would Tell, Robin Cook's Invasion, Nightscream, Mother Knows Best, Dying To Belong, Still Holding on: The Legend of Cadillac Jack, Two Came Back, Murder Live!, Holiday in Your Heart, Virtual Obsession, Don't Look Down, Too Rich: The Secret Life of Doris Duke, Fatal Error, Silent Predators, A Murder On Shadow Mountain, Mr. Rock and Roll, Nowhere to Land, Inside the Osmonds, Within These Walls, After Amy, Three Days, We Were the Mulvaneys, Scared Silent, Just a Walk in the Park, They Shoot Divas, Don't They?, Heart of a Stranger, Tempted, See Jane Date.

W

WADLEIGH, MICHAEL
Director. b. Akron, OH, Sept. 24, 1941. e. Ohio State U., B.S., B.A., M.A., Columbia Medical Sch.
PICTURES: Woodstock (dir.), Wolfen (dir., co-s.p.), Out of Order, The Village at the End of the Universe (dir., s.p.).

WAGGONER, LYLE
Actor. b. Kansas City, KS, April 13, 1935. e. Washington U., St. Louis. Was salesman before becoming actor with road co. prod. of Li'l Abner. Formed own sales-promo co. to finance trip to CA for acting career in 1965. Did commercials, then signed by 20th-Fox for new-talent school.
PICTURES: Love Me Deadly, Journey to the Center of Time, Catalina Caper, Surf II, Murder Weapon, Dead Women in Lingerie, Gypsy Angels.
TELEVISION: *Series*: The Carol Burnett Show, The Jimmie Rodgers Show, It's Your Bet (host), Wonder Woman. *Movies*: Letters from Three Lovers, The New Original Wonder Woman, The Love Boat II, The Gossip Columnist, Gridlock, Return to the Batcave: The Misadventures of Adam and Burt.

WAGNER, JANE
Writer, Director, Producer. b. Morristown, TN, Feb. 26, 1935. e. attended Sch. of Visual Arts, NY. Worked as designer for Kimberly Clark, created Teach Me Read Me sheets for Fieldcrest.
THEATRE: *B'way*: Appearing Nitely (dir., co-writer), The Search for Signs of Intelligent Life in the Universe (dir., writer; NY Drama Desk Award & Special NY Drama Critics Award), both starring Lily Tomlin.
PICTURES: Moment by Moment (s.p., dir.), The Incredible Shrinking Woman (s.p., exec. prod.), The Search for Signs of Intelligent Life in the Universe (s.p., exec. prod.).
TELEVISION: *Specials*: Exec. prod./writer: J.T. (Peabody Award), Lily (prod., co-writer; Emmy & WGA Awards, 1974), Lily Tomlin (also prod.; Emmy Award for writing, 1976), People (also prod.), Lily—Sold Out (co-writer; Emmy Award for producing, 1981), Lily for President? (co-writer), The Edith Ann Show, Edith Ann: A Few Pieces of the Puzzle, Edith Ann: Homeless Go Home, Edith Ann's Christmas: Just Say Noel (Peabody Award). *Mini-Series*: The Question of Equality.

WAGNER, LINDSAY
Actress. b. Los Angeles, CA, June 22, 1949. Appeared in school plays in Portland, OR; studied singing and worked professionally with rock group. In 1968 went to L.A. Signed to Universal contract in 1971.
PICTURES: Two People, The Paper Chase, Second Wind, Nighthawks, High Risk, Martin's Day, Ricochet, Frog and Wombat, The Fourth Horseman, A Light in the Forest. TELEVISION: *Series*: The Bionic Woman (Emmy Award, 1977), Jessie, Peaceable Kingdom. *Guest*: The F.B.I., Owen Marshall:

Counselor at Law, Night Gallery, The Bold Ones, Marcus Welby M.D., The Six Million Dollar Man. *Movies*: The Rockford Files (pilot), The Incredible Journey of Dr. Meg Laurel, The Two Worlds of Jennie Logan, Callie and Son, Memories Never Die, I Want to Live, Princess Daisy, Two Kinds of Love, Passions, This Child Is Mine, Child's Cry, Convicted, Young Again, Stranger in My Bed, The Return of the Six Million Dollar Man and the Bionic Woman, Student Exchange, Evil in Clear River, The Taking of Flight 847, Nightmare at Bitter Creek, From the Dead of Night, The Bionic Showdown: The Six-Million Dollar Man and the Bionic Woman, Shattered Dreams, Babies, Fire in the Dark, She Woke Up, Treacherous Crossing, To Be the Best, A Message From Holly, Nurses on the Line: The Crash of Flight 7, Danielle Steel's Once in a Lifetime, Bionic Ever After?, Fighting for My Daughter, Their, Second Chance, Contagious, Sins of Silence, A Mother's Instinct, Voyage of Terror, Frog and Wombat.

WAGNER, RAYMOND JAMES
Producer. b. College Point, NY, Nov. 3, 1925. e. Middlebury Coll., Williams Coll. Joined Young & Rubicam, Inc., as radio-TV commercial head in Hollywood, 1950-59. Head of pilot devt., Universal Studios, 1960-65. V.P. of prod. (features) for MGM, 1972-79. Presently indt. prod.
PICTURES: *Prod.*: Petulia, Loving (exec. prod.), Code of Silence, Rent-a-Cop, Hero and the Terror, Turner and Hooch, Run, Fifty Fifty, Snow Day.
TELEVISION: *Movies*: Maniac Magee.

WAGNER, ROBERT
Actor. b. Detroit, MI, Feb. 10, 1930. e. Saint Monica's H.S. m. actress Jill St. John. Signed contract with 20th Century-Fox, 1950.
PICTURES: The Happy Years (debut, 1950), The Halls of Montezuma, The Frogmen, Let's Make It Legal, With a Song in My Heart, What Price Glory?, Stars and Stripes Forever, The Silver Whip, Titanic, Beneath the 12-Mile Reef, Prince Valiant, Broken Lance, White Feather, A Kiss Before Dying, The Mountain, Between Heaven and Hell, The True Story of Jesse James, Stopover Tokyo, The Hunters, In Love and War, Say One for Me, All the Fine Young Cannibals, Sail a Crooked Ship, The Longest Day, The War Lover, The Condemned of Altona, The Pink Panther, Harper, Banning, The Biggest Bundle of Them All, Don't Just Stand There, Winning, The Towering Inferno, Midway, The Concorde—Airport '79, Trail of the Pink Panther, Curse of the Pink Panther, I Am the Cheese, Delirious, The Player, Dragon: The Bruce Lee Story, Austin Powers: International Man of Mystery, Wild Things, Something to Believe In, No Vacancy, The Kidnapping of Chris Burden, Austin Powers: The Spy Who Shagged Me, Crazy in Alabama, Play It To The Bone, Love and Fear, Forever Fabulous, Sol Goode, The Calling, Nancy & Frank: A Manhattan Love Story, Austin Powers in Goldmember, Hollywood Homicide, El Padrino.
TELEVISION: *Series*: It Takes A Thief, Colditz (UK), Switch, Hart to Hart, Lime Street. *Movies*: How I Spent My Summer Vacation, City Beneath the Sea, The Cable Car Murder, Killer by Night, Madame Sin (also exec. prod.), Streets of San Francisco (pilot), The Affair, The Abduction of St. Anne, Switch (pilot), Death at Love House, To Catch a King, There Must Be a Prey, Love Among Thieves, Windmills of the Gods, Indiscreet, This Gun for Hire, False Arrest, Daniel Steel's Jewels, Deep Trouble, Hart to Hart Returns (also co-exec. prod.), Hart to Hart: Home is Where the Hart Is, Hart to Hart: Crimes of the Hart, Hart to Hart: Old Friends Never Die, Parallel Lives, Hart to Hart: Secrets of the Heart, Fatal Error, Becoming Dick, Rocket's Red Glare, The Retrievers. *Mini-Series*: Pearl, Around the World in 80 Days, Heaven & Hell: North and South Book III, Camino de Santiago.

WAHL, KEN
Actor, Producer. b. Chicago, IL, Feb. 14, 1957. No acting experience when cast in The Wanderers in 1978.
PICTURES: The Wanderers (debut, 1979), Fort Apache The Bronx, Race to the Yankee Zephyr, Jinxed, The Soldier, Purple Hearts, The Omega Syndrome, The Taking of Beverly Hills (also co-exec. prod.), The Favor, Back in the U.S.A.
TELEVISION: *Movies*: The Dirty Dozen: The Next Mission, The Gladiator, Search for Grace, Wise Guy. *Series*: Double Dare, Wiseguy.

WAITE, RALPH
Actor. b. White Plains, NY, June 22, 1929. e. Bucknell U.; Yale U. Social worker, publicity dir., assistant editor and minister before turning to acting. Founder of the Los Angeles Actors Theatre.
THEATRE: *B'way*: Hogan's Goat, The Watering Place, Trial of Lee Harvey Oswald. *Off-B'way*: The Destiny of Me, The Young Man From Atlanta. *Regional*: Hometown Heroes.
PICTURES: Cool Hand Luke, A Lovely Way to Die, Last Summer, Five Easy Pieces, Lawman, The Grissom Gang, The Sporting Club, The Pursuit of Happiness, Chato's Land, The Magnificent Seven Ride, Trouble Man, Kid Blue, The Stone Killer, On theNickel (also dir., prod., s.p.), Crash and Burn, The Bodyguard, Cliffhanger, Sioux City, Homeward Bound II: Lost in San Francisco, Spirit, Second Change, Sunshine State.
TELEVISION: *Series*: The Waltons, The Mississippi, All My Children, Murder One, Orleans, Carnivàle. *Movies*: The Secret

Life of John Chapman, The Borgia Stick, Red Alert, Ohms, Angel City, The Gentleman Bandit, A Wedding on Waltons Mountain, Mother's Day on Waltons Mountain, A Day for Thanks on Waltons Mountain, A Good Sport, Crime of Innocence, Red Earth White Earth, A Walton Thanksgiving Reunion, Sin and Redemption, A Season of Hope, A Walton Wedding, The Third Twin, The President's Man, Spirit. *Mini-Series*: Roots.

WAITE, RIC
Cinematographer. b. Sheboygan, WI, July 10, 1933. e. Univ. of CO. Photographed more than 40 movies-of-the-week for TV, 1979-83.
PICTURES: The Other Side of the Mountain (debut, 1975), Defiance, On the Nickel, The Long Riders, The Border, Tex, 48 Hrs., Class, Uncommon Valor, Footloose, Red Dawn, Volunteers, Summer Rental, Brewster's Millions, Cobra, Adventures in Babysitting, The Great Outdoors, Marked for Death, Out for Justice, Rapid Fire, On Deadly Ground, Truth or Consequences—N.M.
TELEVISION: Nakia, The November Plan, Captains and the Kings (Emmy Award, 1977), Tail Gunner Joe (Emmy nom.), Huey P. Long (Emmy nom.), The Initiation of Sarah, And Baby Makes Six, Revenge of the Stepford Wives, Baby Comes Home, Dempsey, Police Story: Burnout, Scam, Last Light, Andersonville, Money Plays, Hope, Andersonville (Emmy nom.), Last Stand at Saber River, Heart Full of Rain, Absence of the Good, Ratz, The Triangle.

WAITS, TOM
Singer, Composer, Actor. b. Pomona, CA, Dec. 7, 1949. Recorded numerous albums and received Acad. Award nom. for his song score of One from the Heart. Composed songs for On the Nickel, Streetwise, Paradise Alley, Wolfen, American Heart, Dead Man Walking, Night on Earth (score). Featured songs in Smoke and Things to Do in Denver When You're Dead. Has starred in Chicago's Steppenwolf Theatre Co.'s Frank's Wild Years (also co-wrote, wrote the music) and Los Angeles Theatre Co.'s Demon Wine. Wrote songs and music for opera The Black Rider (1990). Co-wrote songs and music for opera Alice by Robert Wilson. Received Grammy Award for album, Bone Machine, 1992.
PICTURES: *As actor*: Paradise Alley, Poetry in Motion, The Outsiders, Rumble Fish, The Cotton Club, Down by Law (also music), Ironweed, Candy Mountain, Big Time (also co-s.p.), Cold Feet, Bearskin, Night On Earth (music only), The Two Jakes, Queens Logic, The Fisher King, At Play in the Fields of the Lord, Bram Stoker's Dracula, Short Cuts, Luck, Trust & Ketchup: Robert Altman In Carver Country, Coffee and Cigarettes III, Guy Maddin: Waiting for Twilight, Mystery Men, Freedom Highway. *As composer*: Léolo, American Heart, Smoke, Twelve Monkeys, Dead Man Walking, Fight Club, Liberty Heights, Gun Shy, Keeping the Faith, The Perfect Storm, Pollock, Big Bad Love.

WAJDA, ANDRZEJ
Director, Writer. b. Suwalki, Poland, March 6, 1926. e. Fine Arts Academy, Krakow, Poland, 1945-48; High School of Cinematography, Lodz, Poland, 1950-52. 1940-43, worked as asst. in restoration of church paintings. 1942, joined Polish gov. in exile's A.K. (Home Army Resistance) against German occupation. 1950-52, directed shorts (While You Sleep; The Bad Boy, The Pottery of Ilzecka) as part of film school degree; 1954, asst. dir. to Aleksander Ford on 5 Boys from Barska Street. 1981, concentrated on theatrical projects in Poland and film prods. with non-Polish studios. 1983, gov. dissolved his Studio X film prod. group. 1984, gov. demanded Wajda's resignation as head of filmmakers' assoc. in order to continue org.'s existence. 1989, appt. artistic dir. of Teatr Powszechny, official Warsaw theater. Also leader of the Cultural Comm. of the Citizen's Committee. 1989, elected senator. Short films: While You Sleep, The Bad Boy, The Pottery of Ilza, I Go to the Sun. Received Honorary Academy Award, 1998.
PICTURES: *Dir.-Writer*: A Generation (debut, 1957), Kanal, Ashes and Diamonds, Lotna, Innocent Sorcerers, Samson, Siberian Lady Macbeth (Fury Is a Woman), Love at 20 (Warsaw Poland episode), Ashes, Gates to Paradise, Everything for Sale, Hunting Flies, Landscape After the Battle, The Wedding, Promised Land, Shadow Line, Man of Marble, Without Anesthetic, The Girls From Wilko, The Orchestra Conductor, Man of Iron (Golden Palm Award, Cannes, 1981), Danton, A Love in Germany, Chronicle of Love Affairs, The Possessed, Korczak, The Ring with a Crowned Eagle, Nastasja, Holy Week, Miss Nobody, Pan Nikt, Pan Tadeusz, Zemsta.
TELEVISION: Roly-Poly, The Birch Wood, Pilate and the Others, The Dead Class, November Night, Crime and Punishment, Wyrok na Franciszka Klosa, Broken Silence.

WALD, MALVIN
Writer, Producer. b. New York, NY, Aug. 8, 1917. e. Brooklyn Coll., B.A., J.D. Woodland U. Coll. of Law; grad. work Columbia U., NYU, USC. Newspaper reporter, editor, publicist, social worker, radio actor. Screenplays and original stories for Columbia, 20th-Fox, UA, MGM, WB. U.S. Air Force tech. sgt., wrote 30 doc. films for film unit. Exec. prod., 20th Century Fox tv doc. unit, 1963-64. Writer-prod. U.S.I.A., 1964-65. Writer-prod., Ivan Tors Films, 1965-69. Prof., USC Sch. of Cinema, TV, 1956-96. Bd. of

dir., Writer's Guild of America; 1983-85, Trustee, Writers Guild Foundation. Edit. bd. WGA Journal, 1996; editorial bd., Creative Screenwriting, 1996. Acad. of Motion Picture Arts and Sciences, co-author of book, Three Major Screenplays. Contributor to books, American Screenwriters, The Search for Reality, Close-Ups, Henry Miller: A Book of Tributes, Tales From the Casting Couch. Published s.p., Naked City. Consultant, Natl. Endowment for Humanities and Corp. for Public Broadcasting. Visiting professor, Southern Illinois Univ., Univ of PA. Pre-selection judge, Focus writing awards. Media & prod. consultant, Apache Mountain Spirit (PBS). Playwright, ANTA-West, Actors Alley, Rep. Theatre. Co-author, L.A. Press Club 40th Anniversary Show, 1987. Mag. articles published in Film Comment, Journal of Popular Film & TV, Journal of Writers Guild of America, American Heritage, Creative Screenwriting, Directors Guild Magazine, Hollywood: Then and Now, Writers Digest, Producers Guild Magazine, 1991-. Shorts: An Answer, Employees Only (Acad. Award nom.), Boy Who Owned a Melephant (Venice Children's Film Fest. gold medal), Unarmed in Africa, The Policeman, James Weldon Johnson, Me an Alcoholic?, Problem Solving, Managerial Control, UFO—Fact or Fiction? Was admitted to Producers Guild Hall of Fame, 1996.
PICTURES: The Naked City (Acad. Award nom., best story), Behind Locked Doors, The Dark Past, Ten Gentlemen from West Point, The Powers Girl, Two in a Taxi, Undercover Man, Outrage, On the Loose, Battle Taxi, Man on Fire, Al Capone, Venus in Furs, In Search of Historic Jesus, Mysteries From Beyond Earth.
TELEVISION: Many credits including Playhouse 90, Marilyn Monroe, Hollywood: The Golden Years, The Rafer Johnson Story, D-Day, Project: Man in Space, Tales of Hans Christian Andersen, John F. Kennedy, Biography of A Rookie, Alcoa-Goodyear Hour, Climax Mystery Theatre, Shirley Temple Storybook, Life of Riley, Peter Gunn, Perry Mason, Dobie Gillis, Combat!, Moonport (U.S.I.A.; prod., writer), Daktari (assoc. prod.) Primus, California Tomorrow (prod.), Mod Squad, Untamed World, Around the World of Mike Todd, The Billie Jean King Show, Life and Times of Grizzly Adams, Mark Twain's America, Greatest Heroes of the Bible, Littlest Hobo, Rich Little's You Asked For It, Hugh Hefner's Bunny Memories, Hollywood Commandoes, Visiting with Huell Howser, Have Gun Will Travel, The Legend of Sleepy Hollow, Naked City: Justice with a Bullet, Naked City: A Killer Christmas.

WALKEN, CHRISTOPHER
Actor. r.n. Ronald Walken b. Astoria, NY, Mar. 31, 1943. Began career in off-B'way play J.B. billed as Ronnie Walken. Appeared in Madonna video Bad Girl.
THEATRE: NY: Best Foot Forward (Clarence Derwent Award), Kid Champion (Obie Award), High Spirits (B'way debut, 1964), The Lion in Winter (Clarence Derwent Award). The Rose Tattoo (Theatre World Award), Hurlyburly (B'way), Him (also author). NY Shakespeare Festival: Coriolanus, Othello.
PICTURES: The Anderson Tapes (debut, 1971), The Happiness Cage, Next Stop Greenwich Village, The Sentinel, Annie Hall, Roseland, The Deer Hunter (Academy Award, best supporting actor, 1978), Last Embrace, Heaven's Gate, The Dogs of War, Shoot the Sun Down, Pennies from Heaven, Brainstorm, The Dead Zone, A View to a Kill, At Close Range, Deadline, The Milagro Beanfield War, Biloxi Blues, Puss in Boots, Homeboy, Communion, King of New York, The Comfort of Strangers, McBain, All-American Murder, Batman Returns, Mistress, Le Grand Pardon, Day of Atonement, True Romance, Wayne's World 2, A Business Affair, Pulp Fiction, Search and Destroy, The Prophecy, The Addiction, Wild Side, Things to Do in Denver When You're Dead, Nick of Time, The Funeral, Last Man Standing, Touch, Excess Baggage, Suicide Kings, Mouse Hunt, Trance, The Prophecy II, New Rose Hotel, Illuminata, Antz (voice), Vendetta, The Prophecy III: The Ascent, The Opportunists, Kiss Toledo Goodbye, Blast from the Past, Sleepy Hollow, Inside Job, Joe Dirt, The Papp Project, America's Sweethearts, Scotland PA, The Affair of the Necklace, Poolhall Junkies, Stuart Little 2 (voice), Down and Under, Plots With A View, The Country Bears, Catch Me If You Can, Gigli, Helldorado, Kangaroo Jack, Envy, The Rundown, Man on Fire, The Stepford Wives.
TELEVISION: Movies: Barefoot in Athens, Who Am I This Time?, Sarah: Plain and Tall, Scam, Sarah, Plain and Tall: Skylark, Sarah, Plain and Tall: Winter's End, Vendetta. Mini-Series: Caesar. Special: Saturday Night Live 25th Anniversary.

WALKER, KATHRYN
Actress. b. Philadelphia, PA, Jan. 9, 1943. e. Wells Coll., Harvard. m. singer-songwriter James Taylor. Studied acting at London Acad. of Music and Dramatic Art on Fulbright Fellowship. Stage roles include part in Private Lives with Elizabeth Taylor and Richard Burton, and Wild Honey with Ian McKellen.
PICTURES: Slap Shot, Rich Kids, Neighbors, D.A.R.Y.L., Dangerous Game, Emma and Elvis, The Fringe Dwellers.
TELEVISION: Series: Beacon Hill, Another World. Movies: The Winds of Kitty Hawk, Too Far to Go, FDR: The Last Year, A Whale for the Killing, Family Reunion, Special Bulletin, The Murder of Mary Phagan, Private Sessions, Mrs. Delafield Wants to Marry, Uncle Tom's Cabin. Mini-Series: The Adams Chronicles (Emmy Award, 1976).

WALKER, SHIRLEY
Composer.
PICTURES: Composer: The End of August, Touched, Violated, Ghoulies, The Dungeonmaster, Batman (mus. conductor only), Immediate Family (mus. conductor only), Strike It Rich, Chicago Joe and the Showgirl, Nightbreed, Days of Thunder, Born to Ride, Memoirs of an Invisible Man, A League of Their Own (mus. conductor only), Batman: Mask of the Phantasm, John Carpenter's Escape from L.A., Turbulence (also mus. conductor), Mystery Men, White Fang, Final Destination, Ritual, Final Destination 2, Willard. Orchestration: Children of a Lesser God, The Accused, Black Rain, Immediate Family, Teenage Mutant Ninja Turtles, Bird on a Wire, Arachnophobia, Edward Scissorhands, Defending Your Life, The Butcher's Wife, Backdraft (also mus. conductor), True Identity, Article 99, Toys, Johnny Mnemonic (also mus. conductor), Fear.
TELEVISION: Movie: The Flash, Majority Rule, Rasputin, (mus. conductor), The Garbage Picking Field Goal Kicking Philadelphia Phenomenon, The Haunting of Seacliff Inn, The Adventures of Captain Zoom in Outer Space, Rasputin, It Came from Outer Space II, The Crying Child, Superman: The Last Son of Krypton, Asteroid, The Love Bug, Baby Monitor: Sound of Fear, Batman/Superman Adventures: World's Finest, Batman Beyond: The Movie, Disappearance. Series: Falcon Crest, China Beach, The Flash, Batman: The Animated Series, Space: Above and Beyond, Superman, Spawn, Batman Beyond, The Others. Mini-series: Asteroid.

WALLACE, MIKE
TV Commentator, Interviewer. b. Brookline, MA, May 9, 1918. e. U. of Michigan, 1939. Night Beat, WABD, N.Y., 1956; The Mike Wallace Interview, ABC, 1956-58; newspaper col., Mike Wallace Asks, N.Y. Post, 1957-58; News Beat, WNTA-TV, 1959-61; The Mike Wallace Interview, WNTA-TV, 1959-61; Biography, 1962; correspondent, CBS News, 1963, CBS Radio; Personal Closeup, Mike Wallace at Large; Co-editor, 60 Minutes (Emmy Awards, 1971, 1972, 1973), CBS News, Host, 20th Century, 1994, Breaking the News, 2001.

WALLACH, ELI
Actor. b. Brooklyn, NY, Dec. 7, 1915. e. U. of TX. m. actress Anne Jackson. Capt. in Medical Admin. Corps during WWII. After college acting, appeared in summer stock. Charter member of the Actors Studio.
THEATRE: Skydrift (B'way debut, 1945), Antony & Cleopatra, The Rose Tattoo (Tony Award, 1951), Mademoiselle Colombe, Camino Real, The Teahouse of August Moon (also London), Major Barbara, Rhinoceros, Luv, Twice Around the Park, Cafe Crown, The Price, In Persons (Off-B'way), The Flowering Peach, Visiting Mr. Green.
PICTURES: Baby Doll (debut, 1956; BFA Award), The Line Up, The Magnificent Seven, Seven Thieves, The Misfits, Hemingway's Adventures of A Young Man, How the West Was Won, The Victors, Act One, The Moonspinners, Kisses for My President, Lord Jim, Genghis Khan, How to Steal a Million, The Good the Bad and the Ugly, The Tiger Makes Out, How to Save a Marriage and Ruin your Life, MacKenna's Gold, A Lovely Way to Die, Ace High, The Brain, Zigzag, The People Next Door, The Angle Levine, The Adventures of Gerard, Romance of a Horse Thief, Cinderella Liberty, Crazy Joe, Stateline Motel, Don't Turn the Other Cheek, The Sentinel, Nasty Habits, The Deep, The Domino Principle, Girlfriends, Movie Movie, Circle of Iron, Firepower, Winter Kills, The Hunter, The Salamander, Sam's Son, Tough Guys, Nuts, Funny, The Two Jakes, The Godfather Part III, Article 99, Mistress, Night and the City, Two Much, The Associate, Keeping the Faith, Cinerama Adventure, Advice and Dissent, Broadway; The Golden Age by the Legends Who Were There, Mystic River, The Pursuit of Happiness.
TELEVISION: Series: Our Family Honor. Guest: Studio One, Philco Playhouse, Playhouse 90, The Poppy Is Also a Flower (Emmy Award, 1967), Law & Order. Movies: Cold Night's Death, Indict and Convict, Seventh Avenue, The Pirate, Fugitive Family, Pride of Jesse Halam, Skokie, The Wall, Anatomy of an Illness, Murder: By Reason of Insanity, Something in Common, Executioner's Song, Christopher Columbus, Embassy, The Impossible Spy, Vendetta: Secrets of a Mafia Bride, Legacy of Lies, Teamster Boss: The Jackie Presser Story, Vendetta 2: The New Mafia, Naked City: Justice with a Bullet, The Bookfair Murders, Monday Night Mayhem.

WALLACH, GEORGE
Producer, Writer, Director. b. New York, NY, Sept. 25, 1918. e. SUNY-Westbury. Actor in theater & radio 1936-45. U.S. Navy 1942-45. Supvr. radio-TV Div. of American Theatrical Wing, 1946-48. Dir., WNEW, 1946-48. Prod./dir., Wendy Barrie Show, 1948-49. Prod.-dir. for WNBC-WNBT, 1950; dir., news, spec. events WNBT-WNBC, 1951-52; prod. mgr., NBC Film Div. 1953-56, appt. TV officer, U.S.I.A., 1957. Film-TV officer American Embassy, Bonn, 1961; Film-TV officer American Embassy, Tehran, 1965-66. MoPix Prod. Officer, JUSPAO, American Embassy, Saigon, 1966. Prod., dir.,writer, Greece Today, 1967-68. Exec. prod.,dir., George Wallach Productions, spec. doc., travel, and industrial films. Chmn., Film-TV Dept., N.Y. Institute of Photography, 1968-75. Prof. film-TV-radio, Brooklyn Coll., 1975-80. Dir., special projects, DGA 1978-88. Presently: intl. rep. for

Denver Film Festival; U.S. Contact for Moscow Film Festival; U.S. prod. for A Native of Beijing in NY, a series of 20 1 hr. programs for Beijing TV.
PICTURES: It Happened in Havana, Bwana Devil.
TELEVISION: *NBC producer*: Inner Sanctum, The Falcon, His Honor Homer Bell, Watch the World. *Dir.*: Wanted.

WALLMAN, KATHLEEN
Attorney. e. Catholic U. of America, BA; Georgetown U, MS, JD. Clerked for various judges on the U.S. Court of Appeals, District of Columbia & Federal Circuits, 1984-86. Became assoc., Arnold & Porter, 1987-92; partner, 1992-94. In 1994, became Deputy Chief, FCC Cable Services Bureau. Chief, FCC Common Carrier Bureau, 1994-95. Deputy Counsel to the President, 1995-97. Deputy Asst. to the Pres. for Economic Policy/Chief of Staff, National Economic Council, 1997.

WALSH, DYLAN
Actor. b. Nov. 17, 1963. Raised in Africa, Indonesia, India, Washington D.C. e. Univ. of VA. On D.C. stage with Arena Stage and Studio Theatre, Heritage Rep. Co. Appearing in A Midsummer Night's Dream, Curse of the Starving Class, Romeo & Juliet, Death of a Salesman.
PICTURES: Loverboy, Where the Heart Is, Betsy's Wedding, Arctic Blue, Nobody's Fool, Congo, Eden, Changing Habits, Men, Final Voyage, Chapter Zero, Jet Boy, Deadly Little Secrets, We Were Soldiers, Par 6, Blood Work, Power Play.
TELEVISION: *Series*: Gabriel's Fire, Brooklyn South, Nip/Tuck . *Guest*: Kate and Allie. *Movies*: When We Were Young, Chameleons, Telling Secrets, The Almost Perfect Bank Robbery, Radio Inside, The Lone Ranger, Divided by Hate, More Than Meets the Eye: The Joan Brock Story.

WALSH, M. EMMET
Actor. r.n. Michael Emmet Walsh. b. Ogdensburg, NY, Mar. 22, 1935. e. Clarkson Col. (B.B.A., 1958), American Academy of Dramatic Arts (1959-61).
THEATRE: *B'way*: Does the Tiger Wear a Necktie?, That Championship Season. *Off-B'way*: Shepherds of the Shelf, The Old Glory, The Outside Man, Death of the Well Loved Boy, Three From Column 'A', Are You Now or Have You Ever Been, Marathon '93. Extensive summer stock and regional theatre.
PICTURES: End of the Road, Midnight Cowboy, Alice's Restaurant, Stiletto, Loving, They Might Be Giants, The Traveling Executioner, Little Big Man, Escape from the Planet of the Apes, Get to Know Your Rabbit, The Gambler, The Prisoner of 2nd Avenue, What's Up Doc?, Kid Blue, The Fish That Saved Pittsburgh, Serpico, Mikey and Nicky, Cold Turkey, At Long Last Love, Nickelodeon, Bound for Glory, Airport '77, Slap Shot, Straight Time, The Jerk, Raise the Titanic, Brubaker, Ordinary People, Reds, Back Roads, Fast-Walking, The Escape Artist, Cannery Row, Blade Runner, Silkwood, Blood Simple, Scandalous, (Raw) Courage, Grandview USA, The Pope of Greenwich Village, Back to School, Critters, Missing in Action, Fletch, Wildcats, The Best of Times, Raising Arizona, Harry and the Hendersons, The Milagro Beanfield War, No Man's Land, Sunset, War Party, Clean and Sober, Catch Me If You Can, Thunderground, Sundown: The Vampire in Retreat, Chattahoochee, Red Scorpion, The Mighty Quinn, Narrow Margin, Killer Image, The Naked Truth, White Sands, Equinox, Wilder Napalm, The Music of Chance, Bitter Harvest, Cops and Robbersons, Relative Fear, The Glass Shield, Probable Cause, Dead Badge, Camp Nowhere, Panther, Free Willy 2: The Adventure Home, Criminal Hearts, Portraits of a Killer, Albino Alligator, The Killing Jar, A Time to Kill, Romeo & Juliet, Retroactive, Carrot Top–Chairman of the Board, My Best Friend's Wedding, Legal Tender, Twilight, Me and Will, Iron Giant, Jack of Hearts, Eyeball Eddie, Wild Wild West, Random Hearts (cameo), Jack of Hearts, Baggage, Poor White Trash, Eyeball Eddie, Christmas In The Clouds, Snow Dogs.
TELEVISION: *Series*: The Sandy Duncan Show, Dear Detective, Unsub, The Mind of the Married Man. *Movies*: Sarah T.—Portrait of a Teenage Alcoholic, Crime Club, Invasion of Johnson County, Red Alert, Superdome, A Question of Guilt, No Other Love, The Gift, Skag, City in Fear, High Noon Part II, Hellinger's Law, Night Partners, The Deliberate Stranger, Resting Place, Broken Vows, Hero in the Family, The Abduction of Kari Swenson, Murder Ordained, Brotherhood of the Rose, Love and Lies, Fourth Story, Wild Card, Four Eyes and Six-Guns, From the Mixed-Up Files of Mrs. Basil E. Frankweiler, The Lottery, Dogs, Monster., Tracey Ullman in the Trailer Tales. *Mini-Series*: The French-Atlantic Affair, East of Eden. *Guest*: Julia, Amy Prentiss, The Jimmy Stewart Show, Bonanza, All in the Family, Rockford Files, Baretta, The Waltons, Nichols, Starsky & Hutch, Amazing Stories, Twilight Zone, The Flash, Jackie Thomas Show, Tales From the Crypt, Home Improvement, The Outer Limits, The X Files.

WALTER, JESSICA
Actress. b. Brooklyn, NY, Jan. 31, 1944. m. actor Ron Leibman. e. H.S. of the Performing Arts. Studied at Bucks County Playhouse and Neighborhood Playhouse. Many TV performances plus lead in series, For the People. Broadway debut in Advise and Consent, 1961. Also, Photo Finish (Clarence Derwent Award), Night Life, A Severed Head, Rumors.

PICTURES: Lilith (debut, 1964), The Group, Grand Prix, Bye Bye Braverman, Number One, Play Misty for Me, Goldengirl, Going Ape, Spring Fever, The Flamingo Kid, Tapeheads, Ghost in the Machine, PCU, Dark Goddess, Slums of Beverly Hills, Dummy.
TELEVISION: *Series*: For the People, Love of Life, Amy Prentiss (Emmy Award, 1975), Bare Essence, Aaron's Way, Dinosaurs (voice), The Round Table, One Life to Live, Oh Baby, Arrested Development. *Movies*: The Immortal (pilot), Three's a Crowd, They Call It Murder, Women in Chains, Home for the Holidays, Hurricane, Having Babies, Victory at Entebbe, Black Market Baby, Wild and Wooly, Dr. Strange, Secrets of Three Hungry Wives, Vampire, She's Dressed to Kill, Miracle on Ice, Scruples, Thursday's Child, The Return of Marcus Welby M.D., The Execution, Killer in the Mirror, Leave of Absence, Mother Knows Best, Doomsday Rock. *Mini-Series*: Wheels. *Guest*: Just Shoot Me.

WALTER, TRACEY
Actor. b. Jersey City, NJ, Nov. 25, 1942.
PICTURES: Goin' South, Blue Collar, Hardcore, The Hunter, The Hand, Raggedy Man, Honkytonk Man, Timerider, Rumble Fish, Conan the Destroyer, Repo Man, At Close Range, Something Wild, Malone, Mortuary Academy, Married to the Mob, Under the Boardwalk, Out of the Dark, Batman, Homer and Eddie, Young Guns II, The Two Jakes, Pacific Heights, The Silence of the Lambs, City Slickers, Delusion, Amos and Andrew, Philadelphia, Mona Must Die, Destiny Turns on the Radio, Wild America, Road to Ruin, Dorothy Day, Junior, Amanda, Larger Than Life, Matilda, Desperate Measures, Playing God, Kiss the Girls, Beloved, Mighty Joe Young, Man on the Moon, Facade, Drowning Mona, Erin Brokovich, Blast, The Man From Elysian Fields, How High, Face Value, Imposter, Death to Smoochy, Ted Bundy, Masked and Anonymous, Duplex.
TELEVISION: *Series*: Best of the West, On the Air, Nash Bridges. *Movies*: Ride With the Wind, In the Line of Duty: Kidnapped, Buffalo Girls, Bill On His Own, Mad Bull, Out of this World, Tell Me No Secrets, The Devil's Child, Monster Makers.

WALTERS, BARBARA
Broadcast Journalist. b. Boston, MA, Sept. 25, 1931. e. Sarah Lawrence Coll. Daughter of Latin Quarter nightclub impressario Lou Walters. Began working in TV after graduation. Joined The Today Show in 1961 as writer-researcher, making occasional on-camera appearances. In 1963, became full-time on camera. In April, 1974, named permanent co-host. Also hosted own synd. prog., Not for Women Only. In 1976, joined ABC-TV Evening News, (host, 1976-78), correspondent World News Tonight (1978); corresp. 20/20 (1979-present). Host of The Barbara Walters Specials (1979-present). Author: How to Talk with Practically Anybody About Practically Anything (1970). Recipient of numerous awards including Emmy, Media, Peabody. Named one of women most admired by American People in 1982 & -84 Gallup Polls. Inducted into the Television Academy Hall of Fame, 1990. 1994, co-anchor of Turning Point, co-host of The View.

WALTERS, JULIE
Actress. b. Birmingham, England, Feb. 22, 1950. Trained for 2 years to be a nurse before studying drama at Manchester Polytechnic, followed by year at Granada's Stables Theatre. Joined Everyman Theatre, Liverpool. Also toured Dockland pubs with songs, dance and imitations.
THEATRE: Breezeblock Park, Funny Perculiar, The Glad Hand, Good Fun, Educating Rita, Jumpers, Fool for Love, When I Was a Girl I Used to Scream and Shout, Frankie and Johnnie in the Claire de Lune, Macbeth, Having a Ball, The Rose Tattoo, Jumpers, Fool for Love, When I Was a Girl I Used to Scream and Shout, Frankie and Johnny.
PICTURES: Educating Rita (debut, 1983; Acad. Award nom.), She'll be Wearing Pink Pyjamas, Car Trouble, Personal Services, Prick Up Your Ears, Buster, Mack the Knife, Killing Dad, Stepping Out, Wide Eyed and Legless, The Summer House, The Wedding Gift, Just Like a Woman, Sister My Sister, Bath Time, Girls' Night, Titanic Town, Billy Elliot, All Forgotten, Harry Potter and the Sorcerer's Stone, Before You Go, Harry Potter and the Chamber of Secrets, Harry Potter and the Prisoner of Azkaban.
TELEVISION: Unfair Exchanges, Talent, Nearly a Happy Ending, Family Man, Happy Since I Met You, The Secret Diary of Adrian Mole (series), Wood and Walters (series), Say Something Happened, Intensive Care, The Boys from the Black Stuff, Talking Heads, Victoria Wood As Seen on TV (series & special), The Birthday Party, Her Big Chance, Nearly a Happy Ending, Julie Walters & Friends (special), GBH (series), The All-Day Breakfast Show (special), Murder, Strange Relations, We Know Where You Live.

WALTERS, MELORA
Actress. b. Saudi Arabia, Oct. 21, 1968.
PICTURES: Dead Poets Society, Underground, Beethoven, Twenty Bucks, Ed Wood, Cabin Boy, America's Deadliest Home Video, All Tied Up, Eraser, American Strays, Hard Eight, Boogie Nights, Los Locos, Magnolia, Desert Saints, Speaking of Sex, Wisegirls, Rain, Matchstick Men, Cold Mountain, The Runaway Jury, The Butterfly Effect, The Big Empty.
TELEVISION: *Movies*: How to Murder a Millionaire, Telling

Secrets, Dead Man's Revenge, Midnight Run for Your Life, Twice Upon a Time. *Series:* Roseanne, L.A. Doctors, Threat Matrix. *Guest:* NYPD Blue, Seinfeld, The Wonder Years, Murphy Brown, Walker, Texas Ranger, Bakersfield, P.D., The Marshal, Picket Fences, Dream On, Nash Bridges.

WANG, WAYNE
Director. b. Hong Kong, Jan. 12, 1949. e. came to U.S. to study photography at College of Arts and Crafts, Oakland, CA. m. actress Cora Miao. With a Master's Degree in film and television, returned to Hong Kong. Worked on TV comedy series. First dir. work, as asst. dir. for Chinese sequences of Golden Needle. First film was A Man, A Woman and a Killer. Won grant from AFI and National Endowment for the Arts, used to finance Chan is Missing (1982) which cost $22,000.
PICTURES: Chan is Missing (also s.p., editor, prod.), Dim Sum: A Little Bit of Heart (also prod., story), Slam Dance, Eat a Bowl of Tea, Life is Cheap... But Toilet Paper is Expensive (also exec. prod., story), The Joy Luck Club, Smoke, Blue in the Face (also co-s.p.), Chinese Box (also prod., s.p.), Anywhere But Here, Center of the World, Maid in Manhattan.

WARBECK, STEPHEN
Composer.
PICTURES: Sister My Sister, Skallagrigg, O Mary This London, Nervous Energy, Brothers in Trouble, Different for Girls, Element of Doubt, Mrs. Brown, My Son the Fanatic, Shakespeare in Love, Heart, Mystery Men, Fanny and Elvis, Billy Elliot, Quills, Captain Corelli's Mandolin, Birthday Girl, Charlotte Gray.
TELEVISION: *Movies:* Prime Suspect, Femme Fatale, The Mother, The Changeling, Bambino mio, Prime Suspect 4: The Lost Child, Prime Suspect 4: inner Circles, Devil's Advocate, Truth or Dare, Bright Hair, The Student Prince, A Christmas Carol, The Prince of Hearts. *Mini-series:* Prime Suspect 2, Prime Suspect 3, Prime Suspect 5: Errors of Judgement.

WARD, DAVID S.
Writer, Director. b. Providence, RI, Oct. 24, 1947. Raised in Cleveland. e. Pomona Col. (BA), UCLA (MFA).
PICTURES: *Writer:* Steelyard Blues, The Sting (Academy Award, 1973), Cannery Row (also dir.), The Milagro Beanfield War (co-s.p.), Major League (also dir.), King Ralph (also dir.), Sleepless in Seattle (co-s.p.; Acad. Award nom.), The Mask of Zorro, Smoke & Mirrors, Jumanji 2. *Director:* Major League II (also s.p., prod.), Down Periscope, The Program (also s.p.), The Best Man (also s.p.).

WARD, FRED
Actor. b. San Diego, CA, Dec. 30, 1943. Raised in Louisiana and Texas. Studied at Herbert Berghof Studio. Moved to Rome to work in experimental theatre. Returned to U.S. to appear on San Fransico stage with Sam Shepard's Magic Theatre in Inacoma and Angel City. Additional stage work in The Glass Menagerie, One Flew Over the Cuckoo's Nest, Domino Courts, Simpatico.
PICTURES: Escape From Alcatraz (debut, 1979), Tilt, Carny, Southern Comfort, Timerider, The Right Stuff, Silkwood, Uncommon Valor, Swing Shift, Uforia, Secret Admirer, Remo Williams: The Adventure Begins, Off Limits, Big Business, The Prince of Pennsylvania, Tremors, Miami Blues (also co-exec. prod.), Henry and June, Thunderheart, The Player, Bob Roberts, The Dark Wind, Equinox, Short Cuts, Naked Gun 33 1/3: The Final Insult, Two Small Bodies, The Blue Villa, Chain Reaction, Best Men, Dangerous Beauty, Circus, All the Fine Lines, The Crow: Salvation, Ropewalk, Road Trip, The Chaos Factor, Joe Dirt, Summer Catch, Corky Romano, Enough, A.K.A. Birdseye, Sweet Home Alabama, Abandon, Masked and Anonymous, Hairy Tale.
TELEVISION: *Movies:* Belle Starr, Noon Wine, Florida Straits, Cast a Deadly Spell, Backtrack, Four Eyes and Six-Guns, ...First Do No Harm, Wild Iris, Coast to Coast. *Mini-Series:* Invasion: Earth, Jackie Bouvier Kennedy Onassis, Dice, 10.5. *Special:* Noon Wine (Amer. Playhouse). *Series:* Georgetown.

WARD, RACHEL
Actress. b. London, Sept. 12, 1957. m. actor Bryan Brown. Top fashion and TV commercial model before becoming actress. Studied acting with Stella Adler and Robert Modica.
PICTURES: Night School (debut, 1981), The Final Terror, Sharky's Machine, Dead Men Don't Wear Plaid, Against All Odds, The Good Wife, Hotel Colonial, How to Get Ahead in Advertising, After Dark My Sweet, Christopher Columbus: The Discovery, Wide Sargasso Sea, The Ascent, Harry Potter and the Chamber of Secrets, Underworld.
TELEVISION: *Minis:* The Thorn Birds, Shadow of the Cobra (U.K.), Seasons of Love, Johnson County War. *Movies:* Christmas Lillies of the Field, Fortress, And the Sea Will Tell, Black Magic, Double Jeopardy, My Stepson My Lover, On the Beach, And Never Let Her Go, Bobbie's Girl. *Series:* In the Name of Love.

WARD, SELA
Actress. b. Meridian, MS, July 11, 1956.
PICTURES: The Man Who Loved Women, Rustler's Rhapsody, Nothing in Common, Steel Justice, Hello Again, The Fugitive, My Fellow Americans, The Reef, 54, Runaway Bride, The Day After Tomorrow, Dirty Dancing: Havana Nights.
TELEVISION: *Series:* Emerald Point N.A.S., Sisters (Emmy Award, 1994), Once and Again, The Badge. *Movies:* Almost Golden: The Jessica Savitch Story (Cable Ace Award, 1996), The Haunting of Sarah Hardy, Rainbow Drive, Child of Darkness, Child of Light, Bridesmaids, Killer Rules, Double Jeopardy, Rescuers: Stories of Courage: Two Women , Passion's Way, Catch a Falling Star, The Badge.

WARD, SIMON
Actor. b. London, England, Oct. 19, 1941. Ent. ind. 1964.
PICTURES: If... (debut, 1969), Frankenstein Must Be Destroyed, I Start Counting, Quest for Love, Young Winston, Hitler—The Last Ten Days, The Three Musketeers, The Four Musketeers, Deadly Strangers. Aces High, Children of Rage, Battle Flag, The Chosen, Dominique, Zulu Dawn, La Sabina, The Monster Club, L'Etincelle, Supergirl, Leave All Fair, Double X, Wuthering Heights.
TELEVISION: Spoiled, Chips with Everything, The Corsican Brothers, All Creatures Great and Small, Dracula, Valley Forge, The Last Giraffe (Raising Daisy Rothschild), Around the World in 80 Days, Ruth Rendell: The Strawberry Tree.

WARD, VINCENT
Director, Writer. b. New Zealand, 1956. e. Ilam Sch. of Art. At 21 dir. & co-wrote short film A State of Siege (Hugo Award, Chicago Film Fest.)
PICTURES: In Spring One Plants Alone (Silver Hugo, Chicago Film Fest.), Vigil (Grand Prix Awards, Madrid & Prades Film Fests), The Navigator (Australian Film Awards for Best Picture & Director), Alien³ (story only), Map of the Human Heart, Leaving Las Vegas (actor only), The Shot (actor only), One Night Stand (actor only), What Dreams May Come, The Last Samurai (exec.prod.).

WARDEN, JACK
Actor. r.n. Jack Warden Lebzelter. b. Newark, NJ, Sept. 18, 1920. Started with Margo Jones theatre in Dallas (rep. co.).
THEATRE: *B'way:* Golden Boy, Sing Me No Lullaby, Very Special Baby, Cages (Obie Award), A View from the Bridge, The Man in the Glass Booth, The Body Beautiful. *Repertory:* Twelfth Night, She Stoops to Conquer, The Importance of Being Earnest, Summer and Smoke, The Taming of the Shrew, etc.
PICTURES: You're in the Navy Now (U.S.S. Teakettle; debut, 1951), The Frogmen, The Man With My Face, Red Ball Express, From Here to Eternity, Edge of the City, 12 Angry Men, The Bachelor Party, Darby's Rangers, Run Silent Run Deep, The Sound and the Fury, That Kind of Woman, Wake Men When It's Over, Escape From Zahrain, Donovan's Reef, The Thin Red Line, Blindfold, Bye Bye Braverman, The Sporting Club, Summertree, Who Is Harry Kellerman?, Welcome to the Club, Billy Two Hats, The Man Who Loved Cat Dancing, The Apprenticeship of Duddy Kravitz, Shampoo (Acad. Award nom.), All the President's Men, The White Buffalo, Heaven Can Wait (Acad. Award nom.), Death on the Nile, The Champ, Dreamer, Beyond the Poseidon Adventure, And Justice for All, Being There, Used Cars, The Great Muppet Caper, Chu Chu and the Philly Flash, Carbon Copy, So Fine, The Verdict, Crackers, The Aviator, September, The Presidio, Everybody Wins, Problem Child, Problem Child 2, Passed Away, Night and the City, Toys, Guilty As Sin, Bullets Over Broadway, While You Were Sleeping, Things to Do in Denver When You're Dead, Mighty Aphrodite, Ed, The Island of Dr. Moreau, Chairman of the Board, Bulworth, Dirty Work, A Dog of Flanders, The Replacements.
TELEVISION: *Series:* Mr. Peepers, Norby, The Asphalt Jungle, The Wackiest Ship in the Army, N.Y.P.D., Jigsaw John, The Bad News Bears, Crazy Like a Fox. *Guest:* Philco Goodyear Producer's Showcase, Kraft, Norm. *Movies:* The Face of Fear, Brian's Song (Emmy Award, 1972), What's a Nice Girl Like You...?, Man on a String, Lt. Schuster's Wife, Remember When, The Godchild, Journey From Darkness, They Only Come Out at Night, Raid on Entebbe, Topper, A Private Battle, Hobson's Choice, Helen Keller: The Miracle Continues, Hoover vs. The Kennedys, The Three Kings, Dead Solid Perfect, Judgment, Problem Child 3: Junior in Love. *Mini-Series:* Robert Kennedy and His Times, A.D.

WARNER, DAVID
Actor. b. Manchester, England, July 29, 1941. e. Royal Acad. of Dramatic Art. Made London stage debut in Tony Richardson's version of A Midsummer Night's Dream (1962). Four seasons with Royal Shakespeare Co. Theater includes Afore Night Comes, The Tempest, The Wars of the Roses, The Government Inspector, Twelfth Night, I Claudius.
PICTURES: Tom Jones (debut, 1963), Morgan!, The Deadly Affair, A King's Story (voice), Work Is a Four Letter Word, A Midsummer's Night Dream, The Bofors Gun, The Fixer, The Seagull, Michael Kolhaus, The Ballad of Cable Hogue, Perfect Friday, Straw Dogs, A Doll's House, From Beyond the Grave, Little Malcolm (and His Struggle Against the Eunuch), Mr. Quilp,

The Omen, Providence, The Disappearance, Cross of Iron, Silver Bears, Nightwing, The Concorde—Airport '79, Time After Time, The 39 Steps, The Island, The French Lieutenant's Woman, Time Bandits, Tron, The Man With Two Brains, The Company of Wolves, Hansel and Gretel, My Best Friend Is a Vampire, Waxworks, Mr. North, Silent Night, Office Party, Hanna's War, Pulse Pounders, Keys to Freedom, Star Trek V: The Final Frontier, S.P.O.O.K.S., Tripwire, Mortal Passions, Teenage Mutant Ninja Turtles II: The Secret of the Ooze, Star Trek VI: The Undiscovered Country, Blue Tornado,
Drive, Unnameable II, Dark at Noon, In the Mouth of Madness, Ice Cream Man, Final Equinox, Felony, Beastmaster III: The Eye of Braxus, Seven Servants, The Leading Man, Money Talks, Titanic, Scream 2, The Little Unicorn, The Last Leprechaun, Wing Commander, Shergar, Back to the Secret Garden, The Code Conspiracy, Planet of the Apes, Superstition, Straight Into Darkness, Pulse Pounders, Avatar.
TELEVISION: Movies: S.O.S. Titantic, Desperado, A Christmas Carol, Hitler's SS—Portrait in Evil, Perry Mason: The Case of the Poisoned Pen, The Secret Life of Ian Fleming, Cast a Deadly Spell, The House on Sycamore Street, Perry Mason: The Case of the Skin-Deep Scandal, John Carpenter Presents Body Bags, Danielle Steel's Zoya, Rasputin, Houdini, Cinderella, Hornblower: Mutiny, Hornblower: Retribution, The Investigation, Dr. Jekyll and Mr. Hyde, Hearts of Gold. Mini-Series: Holocaust, Masada (Emmy Award, 1981), Marco Polo, Wild Palms, Signs and Wonders, The Choir, In the Beginning. Specials: Love's Labour's Lost, Uncle Vanya. Series: Spider-Man (voice), Men in Black: The Series (voice), Three, Toonsylvania (voice).

WARNER, JULIE
Actress. b. New York, NY, Feb. 9, 1965. e. Brown Univ., B.A. in Theatre Arts.
PICTURES: Doc Hollywood (debut, 1991), Mr. Saturday Night, Indian Summer, The Puppet Masters, Tommy Boy, White Lies, Wedding Bell Blues.
TELEVISION: Series: Pride and Joy, Family Law. Guest: Star Trek: The Next Generation, 21 Jump Street, The Outsiders. Movies: Stolen: One Husband, Mr. Murder.

WARNER, MALCOLM-JAMAL
Actor. b. Jersey City, NJ, Aug. 18, 1970. Raised in Los Angeles.
THEATRE: Three Ways Home (off-B'way debut, 1988).
PICTURE: Drop Zone (debut, 1994), Restaurant.
TELEVISION: Series: The Cosby Show (also dir. episode), Here and Now, Magic School Bus (voice), Malcolm & Eddie. Movies: The Father Clements Story, Mother's Day, Tyson, The Tuskegee Airmen. Special: Kids Killing Kids (host).

WARREN, JENNIFER
Actress, Producer. b. New York, NY, Aug. 12, 1941. e. U. of Wisconsin, Madison, B.A. Graduate work at Wesleyan U. Studied acting with Uta Hagen at HB Studios. As part of AFI Women's Directing Workshop, directed Point of Departure, short film which received Cine Golden Eagle and Aspen Film Festival Awards. Formed Tiger Rose Productions, indep. film-TV prod. co., 1988. Exec. prod., You Don't Have to Die (Acad. Award, doc. short, 1989). Dir., The Beans of Egypt Maine, 1994. Recipient of 2 Spirit Awards.
THEATRE: Scuba Duba (off-B'way debut, 1967), 6 RMS RIV VU (Theatre World Award), Harvey, P.S., Your Cat Is Dead, B'way: Saint Joan, Volpone, Henry V (Guthrie Theatre).
PICTURES: Night Moves (debut, 1975), Slapshot, Another Man Another Chance, Ice Castles, Fatal Beauty.
TELEVISION: Series: Paper Dolls. Pilots: Double Dare, Knights of the Kitchen Table. Guest: Kojak. Movies: Banjo Hackett: Roamin' Free, Shark Kill, First You Cry, Steel Cowboy, Champions: A Love Story, Angel City, The Choice, The Intruder Within, Freedom, Paper Dolls (pilot), Confessions of a Married Man, Amazons, Full Exposure: The Sex Tape Scandal, Dying to Belong. Mini-Series: Celebrity.

WARREN, LESLEY ANN
Actress. b. New York, NY, Aug. 16, 1946. Studied acting under Lee Strasberg. Big break came in Rodgers and Hammerstein's 1964 tv prod. of Cinderella, where she was seen by Disney scout. Broadway debut in 110 in the Shade (1963, Theatre World Award), followed by Drat! The Cat! Appeared in Aerosmith video Janie's Got a Gun.
PICTURES: The Happiest Millionaire (debut, 1967), The One and Only Genuine Original Family Band, Pickup on 101, Harry and Walter Go to New York, Victor/Victoria (Acad. Award nom.), A Night in Heaven, Songwriter (Golden Globe nom.), Choose Me, Race to the Yankee Zephyr, Clue, Burglar, Cop, Worth Winning, Life Stinks, Pure Country, Color of Night, Bird of Prey, The First Man, Going All the Way, Love Kills, Twin Falls Idaho, Trixie, Teaching Mrs. Tingle, Spoken in Silence, The Limey, All of It, Secretary, Alexander the Great.
TELEVISION: Series: Mission: Impossible. Mini-Series: 79 Park Avenue (Golden Globe Winner), Pearl, Evergreen, Family of Spies, Joseph. Movies: Seven in Darkness, Love Hate Love, Assignment Munich, The Daughters of Joshua Cabe, The Letters, The Legend of Valentino, Betrayal, Portrait of a Stripper, Beulah Land, Portrait of a Showgirl, A Fight for Jenny, Apology, Baja Oklahoma (Ace Award nom.), A Seduction in Travis County,

In Sickness and in Health, Willing to Kill: The Texas Cheerleader Story, A Mother's Revenge, Family of Spies (Emmy nom.), Murderous Intent, 27 Wagons Full of Cotton, Natural Enemy., Wolf Girl , Recipe for Disaster . Specials: The Saga of Sonora, It's a Bird It's a Plane It's Superman, A Special Eddie Rabbit, The Dancing Princess, 27 Wagons Full of Cotton (Ace Award nom.), Willie Nelson: Big Six-O. Guest: Will & Grace.

WARRICK, RUTH
Actress. b. St. Joseph, MO, June 29, 1916. Started as radio singer. Autobiography: The Confessions of Phoebe Tyler (1980).
PICTURES: Citizen Kane (debut, 1941), Obliging Young Lady, The Corsican Brothers, Journey Into Fear, Forever and a Day, Perilous Holiday, The Iron Major, Secret Command, Mr. Winkle Goes to War, Guest in the House, China Sky, Song of the South, Driftwood, Daisy Kenyon, Arch of Triumph, The Great Dan Patch, Make Believe Ballroom, Three Husbands, Let's Dance, One Too Many, Roogie's Bump, Ride Beyond Vengeance, The Great Bank Robbery, Deathmask, The Returning, The Battle Over Citizen Kane.
TELEVISION: Movie: Peyton Place—The Next Generation. Series: Peyton Place, As the World Turns, All My Children. Guest: Studio One, Robert Montgomery Presents, Lux Star Playhouse. Special: Sometimes I Don't Love My Mother.

WARZEL, PETER C.
Executive. b. Buffalo, NY, May 31, 1952. e. Univ. of Rochester, Canisius Col. Joined Tele-Communications Inc., 1982, also serving as v.p. of industrial relations at Community Tele-Communications Inc., a TCI subsidiary. 1988, became sr. v.p. of United Artists Entertainment Co.; 1990, promoted to pres. & CEO of United Artists Theatre Circuit. 1992, was party to management buy-out of UATC as pres. & COO.

WASCO, DAVID
Production Designer.
PICTURES: Goldy: The Last of the Golden Bears, Smooth Talk, Student Confidential, Stacking, Rachel River, The Wash, Twister, In A Shallow Grave, Reservoir Dogs, Where the River Flows North, Killing Zoe, Pulp Fiction, Oleanna, Bottle Rocket, Touch, She's So Lovely, Jackie Brown, Rushmore, Bounce, The Heist, The Royal Tenenbaums, Kill Bill: Volume 1, Kill Bill: Volume 2.
TELEVISION: Traveling Man, A Life in the Theater.

WASHBURN, DERIC
Writer. b. Buffalo, NY. e.Harvard U., English lit. Has written number of plays, including The Love Nest and Ginger Anne.
PICTURES: Silent Running (co-s.p.), The Deer Hunter (co-s.p.), The Border, Extreme Prejudice.

WASHINGTON, DENZEL
Actor. b. Mt. Vernon, NY, Dec. 28, 1954. e. Fordham U., B.A., journalism. Studied acting with American Conservatory Theatre, San Francisco.
THEATRE: When the Chickens Come Home to Roost (Audelco Award), Coriolanus, Spell #7, The Mighty Gents, Ceremonies in Dark Old Men, A Soldier's Play, Checkmates, Richard III.
PICTURES: Carbon Copy (debut, 1981), A Soldier's Story, Power, Cry Freedom (Acad. Award nom.), The Mighty Quinn, For Queen and Country, Glory (Academy Award, best supporting actor, 1989; Golden Globe Award), Heart Condition, Mo' Better Blues, Ricochet, Mississippi Masala, Malcolm X (NY Film Critics Award; Acad. Award nom.), Much Ado About Nothing, Philadelphia, The Pelican Brief, Crimson Tide, Virtuosity, Devil in a Blue Dress, Courage Under Fire, The Preacher's Wife, Fallen, He Got Game, The Siege, The Hurricane, The Bone Collector, Remember the Titans, Training Day (Academy Award), John Q, Antwone Fisher (also dir.), Out of Time, Man on Fire.
TELEVISION: Movies: Wilma, Flesh and Blood, License to Kill, The George McKenna Story. Series: St. Elsewhere.

WASSERMAN, DALE
Writer, Producer. b. Rhinelander, WI, Nov. 2, 1917. Stage: lighting designer, dir., prod.; dir. for. attractions, S. Hurok; began writing, 1954. Founding member & trustee of O'Neill Theatre Centre; artistic dir. Midwest Playwrights Laboratory; member, Acad. M.P. Arts & Sciences; awards include Emmy, Tony, Critics Circle (Broadway), Outer Circle; Writers Guild.
PICTURES: Cleopatra, The Vikings, The Sea and the Shadow, Quick Before It Melts, Mister Buddwing, A Walk with Love and Death, Man of La Mancha, One Flew Over the Cuckoo's Nest.
TELEVISION: The Fog, The Citadel, The Power and the Glory, Engineer of Death, The Lincoln Murder Case, I Don Quixote, Elisha and the Long Knives, and others.PLAYS: Livin' the Life, 998, One Flew Over the Cuckoo's Nest, The Pencil of God, Man of La Mancha, Play With Fire, Shakespeare and the Indians, Mountain High, Western Star, Green.

WASSERMAN, LEW
Executive. b. Cleveland, OH, March 15, 1913. Natl. dir. advertising and pub., Music Corporation of Amer. 1936-38; v.p. 1938-39; v.p. motion picture div. 1940; chmn. of the bd., CEO, MCA, Inc., Universal City, CA. Named chmn. emeritus of MCA in 1995. Received Jean Hersholt Humanitarian Award, 1973; awarded Presidential Medal of Freedom, 1995.

WASSON, CRAIG
Actor. b. Ontario, OR, March 15, 1954. Also musician/songwriter.
THEATRE: Godspell, All God's Chillun Got Wings, Death of a
Salesman (also wrote incidental music), Jock, Children of Eden,
M. Butterfly, Skin of Our Teeth, The Sisters (Pasadena
Playhouse). Wrote incidental music for prod. of The Glass
Menagerie and Death of a Salesman.
PICTURES: Rollercoaster, The Boys in Company C (also wrote
and performed song Here I Am), Go Tell the Spartans, The
Outsider, Carny, Schizoid, Ghost Story, Four Friends, Second
Thoughts (also wrote and performed music), Body Double, The
Men's Club, A Nightmare on Elm Street 3, The Trackers, Midnight
Fear (co-s.p.), Malcolm X, Bum Rap (also wrote and performed
music), Velocity Trap, The Debt, Father, The Image Maker, The
Outfitters.
TELEVISION: Series: Phyllis (also wrote and performed orig.
songs), Skag, For Jenny with Love, One Life to Live. Guest:
M*A*S*H, Baa Baa Black Sheep, Rockford Files, Hart to Hart,
L.A. Law, Kung Fu: The Legend Continues, Dr. Quinn Medicine
Woman, Murder She Wrote, Walker Texas Ranger, Deep Space
Nine, Dangerous minds, Profiler, The Practice, Touched By an
Angel. Movies: The Silence, Mrs. R's Daughter, Skag, Thornwell,
Why Me?, Strapped, Trapped in Space, The Calvin Mire Story,
The Becky Bell Story, Sister in Law, The Tomorrow Man, Epoch
, Harvest of Fire, Deep Family Secrets, Seed. Specials: A More
Perfect Union, Innocents Abroad.

WATANABE, GEDDE
Actor. b. Ogden, UT, June 26, 1955. Trained for stage at
American Conservatory Theatre, San Francisco. Appeared with
N.Y. Shakespeare Fest. Shakespeare in the Park series and with
Pan Asian Repertory Theatre, N.Y.
THEATER: Pacific Overtures (debut, as Tree Boy, B'way and on
tour, 1976), Bullet Headed Birds, Poor Little Lambs, Dispatches,
Music Lesson, Good Person.
PICTURES: Sixteen Candles (debut, 1984), Gremlins 2: The
New Batch, Volunteers, Gung Ho, Vamp, UHF, Boys on the Side,
That Thing You Do!, Nick and Jane, Booty Call, Mulan (voice),
Guinevere, EDtv, Slackers.
TELEVISION: Series: Gung Ho, Sesame Street, ER. Movie: Miss
America: Behind the Crown. Guest: The Simpsons (voice).

WATERHOUSE, KEITH
Writer. b. Leeds, England, Feb. 6, 1929. Early career as journal-
ist, novelist. Author: There is a Happy Land, Billy Liar, Jubb, The
Bucket Shop. Ent. m.p. ind. 1960.
PICTURES: Writer (with Willis Hall): Whistle Down the Wind, A
Kind of Loving, Billy Liar, Man in the Middle, Pretty Polly, Lock Up
Your Daughters, The Valiant, West Eleven.
TELEVISION: Series: Tonight, That Was the Week That Was,
BBC 3, The Frost Report, Inside George Webley, Queenie's
Castle, Budgie, The Upper Crusts, The Upchat Line, Worzel
Gummidge, Billy Liar, There is a Happy Land, Charters and
Caldicott, West End Tales, The Happy Apple, Worzel Gummidge
Down Under, Andy Capp. Movies: A Deadly Game, Worzel
Gummidge: A Cup 'o Tea and a Glass 'o Milk, This Office Life .

WATERS, JOHN
Director, Writer. b. Baltimore, MD, April 22, 1946. First short film
Hag in a Black Leather Jacket (1964) shot in Baltimore, as are
most of his films. Other shorts include Roman Candles, Eat Your
Makeup. Feature debut, Mondo Trasho. Appeared as actor in
films Something Wild, Homer and Eddie. On tv in Homicide: Life
on the Streets.
PICTURES: Director/Writer/Prod.: Mondo Trasho (also photo.,
edit.), Multiple Maniacs (also ed., sound), Pink Flamingos (also
photo., edit.), Female Trouble (also photo.), Desperate Living,
Polyester, Hairspray (also co-prod., actor), Cry-Baby, Serial
Mom, Pecker, Cecil B. Demented. Actor: Divine Trash, Anthem,
Pecker, Home Movie on John Waters, Sweet & Lowdown,
Forever Hollywood, Cecil B. Demented, Pie in the Sky: The Brigid
Berlin Story, Welcome to Hollywood, In Bad Taste, Memories of
Oz, The Cockettes, Blood Feast 2: All U Can Eat, Each Time I Kill.
TELEVISION: Guest: The Simpsons (voice). Numerous specials.

WATERSTON, SAM
Actor. b. Cambridge, MA, Nov. 15, 1940. e. Yale U. Spent jr. year
at Sorbonne in Paris as part of the Amer. Actors' Workshop run
by American dir. John Berry. Broadway debut in Oh Dad Poor
Dad ... (1963). Film debut, The Plastic Dome of Norma Jean
(made 1965; unreleased). TV debut Pound (Camera Three). Has
worked in New York Shakespeare Festival prods. since As You
Like It (1963).
THEATRE: N.Y. Shakespeare Festival: As You Like It, Ergo,
Henry IV (Part I & II), Cymbeline, Hamlet, Much Ado About
Nothing, The Tempest. Off-B'way: The Knack, La Turista, Waiting
for Godot, The Three Sisters. B'way: The Paisley Convertible,
Halfway Up the Tree, Indian, Hay Fever, The Trial of Cantonsville
Nine, A Meeting by the River, Much Ado About Nothing (Drama
Desk and Obie Awards), A Doll's House, Lunch Hour,
Benefactors, A Walk in the Woods, Abe Lincoln in Illinois.
PICTURES: Fitzwilly, Three, Generation, Cover Me Babe,
Mahoney's Estate, Who Killed Mary What's 'er Name?, Savages,
The Great Gatsby, Journey Into Fear, Rancho Deluxe, Sweet
Revenge, Capricorn One, Interiors, Eagle's Wing, Sweet William,

Hopscotch, Heaven's Gate, The Killing Fields, Warning Sign,
Hannah and Her Sisters, Just Between Friends, A Certain
Desire, The Devil's Paradise, September, Welcome Home,
Crimes and Misdemeanors, The Man in the Moon, Mindwalk, A
Captive in the Land, Serial Mom, The Journey of August King
(also co-prod.), The Proprietor, The Shadow Conspiracy, Le
Divorce.
TELEVISION: Specials: Pound, Robert Lowell, The Good
Lieutenant, Much Ado About Nothing, Oppenheimer, A Walk in
the Woods. Movies: The Glass Menagerie, Reflections of Murder,
Friendly Fire, Games Mother Never Taught You, In Defense of
Kids, Dempsey, Finnegan Begin Again, Love Lives On, The Fifth
Missile, The Room Upstairs, Terrorist on Trial: The United States
vs. Salim Ajami, Gore Vidal's Lincoln, Lantern Hill, The Shell
Seekers, Assault at West Point: The Court-Martial of Johnson
Whittaker, David's Mother, The Enemy Within, Miracle at
Midnight, Exiled: A Law & Order Movie, A House Divided, The
Matthew Shepard Story. Mini-Series: The Nightmare Years, The
Civil War (voice), Thomas Jefferson, Lewis & Clark. Series:
Q.E.D., I'll Fly Away, Law & Order. Guest: Amazing Stories.

WATKIN, DAVID
Director of Photography. b. Margate, England, March 23, 1925.
Entered British documentary ind. in Jan., 1948. With British
Transport Films as asst. cameraman, 1950 -55; as cameraman,
1955 -61. Feature film debut The Knack beginning long creative
relationship with director Richard Lester.
PICTURES: The Knack... and How to Get It (debut, 1965), Help!,
Marat/Sade, How I Won the War, The Charge of the Light
Brigade, The Bed-Sitting Room, Catch-22, The Devils, The
Boyfriend, The Homecoming, A Delicate Balance, The Three
Musketeers, The Four Musketeers, Mahogany, To the Devil a
Daughter, Robin and Marian, Joseph Andrews, Hanover Street,
Cuba, That Summer, Endless Love, Chariots of Fire, Yentl, The
Hotel New Hampshire, Return to Oz, White Nights, Out of Africa
(Academy Award, 1985), Moonstruck, Sky Bandits, Masquerade,
The Good Mother, Last Rites, Journey to the Center of the Earth,
Memphis Belle, Hamlet, The Object of Beauty, Used People, This
Boy's Life, Bopha!, Milk Money, Jane Eyre, Bogus, Night Falls on
Manhattan, Obsession, Critical Care, Gloria, Tea with Mussolini.

WATROS, CYNTHIA
Actress. b. Sept. 2, 1968.
PICTURES: Cafe Society, His and Hers, Mercy Streets.
TELEVISION: Series: Guiding Light (Emmy Award, 1998),
Another World, Titus, The Drew Carey Show. Guest: Spin City.

WATSON, BARRY
Actor. r.n. Michael Barret Watson. b. Traverse City, MI, April 23,
1974.
PICTURES: Teaching Mrs. Tingle, Ocean's Eleven, Sorority
Boys, Boogeyman.
TELEVISION: Movies: Fatal Deception: Mrs. Lee Harvey
Oswald, Attack of the 50 Ft. Woman, Co-ed Call Girl. Series:
7th Heaven. Guest: Malibu Shores.

WATSON, EMILY
Actress. b. London, England, Jan. 14, 1966.
PICTURES: Breaking the Waves (Acad. Award nom., 1997;
Golden Globe nom.; NY Society of Film Critics Award; Nat'l
Society of Film Critics Award;), Mill on the Floss, Metroland, The
Boxer, Hilary and Jackie (Acad. Award nom.), Trixie, The Luzhin
Defence, Gosford Park, The Cradle Will Rock, Angela's Ashes,
Punch-Drunk Love,Red Dragon, Equilibrium.
TELEVISION: Movies: The Life and Death of Peter Sellers.

WAX, MORTON DENNIS
Public Relations Executive. b. New York, NY, March 13, 1932.
e. Brooklyn Coll., 1952. President of Morton Dennis Wax &
Assoc., Inc., p.r. and marketing firm servicing int'l creative marketplace, established 1956. Recent PR & Marketing for foreign
films: Hungarian Fairy Tale, December Bride, Eden Valley.
Contrib. writer to Box Office Magazine, Film Journal. Recent arti-
cles: Creativity (Advertising Age), Rolling Stone's Marketing
Through Music, Words & Music, Campaign Magazine,
Songwriters Guild of America National Edition. As sect. of VPA,
conceptualized int'l Monitor Award, an annual event, currently
under auspices of ITS. Public relations counsel to London Int'l
Advertising Awards. Member of The Public Relations Society of
America, Nat'l Academy of TV Arts & Sciences, Nat'l Acadrmy of
Recording Arts & Sciences, Publishers Publicity Association.
Morton Dennis Wax & Assocs. in NY was awarded the first EPM
Entertainment Marketing Cause Event Award for creating, devel-
oping and promoting a nat'l fund raising campaign to combat
homelessness, called Brother Can You Spare a Dime Day.

WAYANS, DAMON
Actor, Writer, Producer. b. New York, NY, Sept. 4, 1960.
Brothers are comedian-actors Keenen Ivory Wayans and Marlon
Wayans. Started as stand up comedian.
PICTURES: Beverly Hills Cop (debut, 1984), Hollywood Shuffle,
Roxanne, Colors, Punchline, I'm Gonna Git You Sucka, Earth
Girls Are Easy, Look Who's Talking Too (voice), The Last Boy
Scout, Mo' Money (also s.p., co-exec. prod.), Last Action Hero
(cameo), Blankman (also co-s.p., exec. prod.), Major Payne

(also co-s.p., co-exec. prod.), The Great White Hype, Bulletproof, Harlem Aria, Goosed, Bamboozled, All Jokes Aside, Marci X.
TELEVISION: *Series*: Saturday Night Live (1985-6), In Living Color (also writer), 413 Hope St., (also prod.), Damon, My Wife and Kids. *Special*: The Last Stand? (HBO).

WAYANS, KEENEN IVORY
Actor, Director, Writer. b. NYC, June 8, 1958. e. Tuskegee Inst. Began as stand-up comic at The Improv in NYC and L.A. Brothers are comedian-actors Damon Wayans, Marlon Wayans. PICTURES: Star 80 (debut, 1983), Hollywood Shuffle (also co-s.p.), Eddie Murphy Raw (co-prod., co-s.p. only), I'm Gonna Git You Sucka, The Five Heartbeats (co-s.p. only), A Low Down Dirty Shame (dir., writer), The Glimmer Man, America's Most Wanted, Scary Movie, Scary Movie 2 (dir. only), Scary Movie 3: Episode 1—Lord of the Brooms (dir., s.p.), The Incredible Shrinking Man (dir., s.p.).
TELEVISION: *Series*: For Love and Honor, In Living Color (also exec. prod. & writer; Emmy Award 1990), Keenen Ivory Wayans Show (also exec. prod., writer), My Wife and Kids (writer, creator, exec. prod.) *Guest*: Benson, Cheers, CHiPS, A Different World. *Special*: Partners in Crime (also co-writer).

WAYANS, MARLON
Actor, Producer, Writer. b. NYC, July 23, 1972. E. School of Performing Arts, NY and Howard U. Brothers are comedian-actors Damon and Keenan-Ivory Wayans.
PICTURES: I'm Gonna Git You Sucka, Mo'Money, Above the Rim, Don't Be a Menace to South Central While Drinking Your Juice in the Hood (also exec. prod, s.p.), The Sixth Man, Senseless, Requiem for a Dream, Scary Movie (also prod., s.p.), The Tangerine Bear, Dungeons & Dragons, Scary Movie 2 (also co-exec prod., s.p.), Scary Movie 3: Episode 1—Lord of the Brooms.
TELEVISION: *Series*: In Living Color, The Wayans Brothers (also prod., writer).

WAYNE, JOEL
Executive. Began career with Grey Advertising; in 17 years won many awards (60 Clios, 25 N.Y. Art Director Club Awards, etc.). Was exec. v.p. & creative dir. of agency when left in 1979 to join Warner Bros. as v.p., creative adv. 1987, named sr. v.p., worldwide creative adv., then exec. v.p. worldwide creative adv. & publicity.

WAYNE, MICHAEL A.
Executive. r.n. Michael A. Morrison. b. Los Angeles, CA, Nov. 23, 1934. Father was late actor John Wayne. e. Loyola H.S.; Loyola U., B.B.A. Asst. dir., various companies, 1955-56; asst. dir., Revue Prods., 1956-57; pres. Batjac Prods, and Romina Prods., 1961.
PICTURES: *Asst. to producer*: China Doll, Escort West, The Alamo (asst. to prod.). *Prod.*: McLintock!, Cast Giant Shadow (co- prod.), The Green Berets, Chisum (exec. prod.), Big Jake, The Train Robbers, Cahill; U.S. Marshal, McQ (exec. prod.), Brannigan (exec. prod.).

WAYNE, PATRICK
Actor. b. Los Angeles, July 15, 1939. e. Loyola U, 1961, BS in biology. Father was late actor John Wayne. Made film debut at age 11 in Rio Grande with father.
PICTURES: The Long Gray Line, Mister Roberts, The Searchers, The Alamo, The Comancheros, McClintock, Donovan's Reef, Cheyenne Autumn, Shenandoah, An Eye for an Eye, The Green Berets, The Deserter, Big Jake, The Gatling Gun, Beyond Atlantis, The Bears and I, Mustang Country, Sinbad and the Eye of the Tiger, The People Time Forgot, Rustler's Rhapsody, Young Guns, Her Alibi, Blind Vengeance, Deep Cover.
TELEVISION: *Series*: The Rounders, Shirley, The Monte Carlo Show (host), Tic Tac Dough. *Movies*: Sole Survivor, Yesterday's Child, Flight to Holocaust, The Last Hurrah, Three on a Date. *Guest*: Frank's Place.

WEATHERS, CARL
Actor. b. New Orleans, LA, Jan. 14, 1948. e. San Diego State U.
PICTURES: Bucktown (debut, 1975), Friday Foster, Rocky, Close Encounters of the Third Kind, Semi-Tough, Force Ten From Navarone, Rocky II, Death Hunt, Rocky III, Rocky IV, Predator, Action Jackson, Hurricane Smith, Happy Gilmore, Little Nicky, Eight Crazy Nights (voice).
TELEVISION: *Series*: Fortune Dane, Tour of Duty, Street Justice, In the Heat of the Night, For the People (dir.) *Movies*: The Hostage Heart, The Bermuda Depths, Breaker, Dangerous Passion, In the Heat of the Night: A Matter of Justice, In the Heat of the Night: Who Was Geli Bendl?, In the Heat of the Night: By Duty Bound, Tom Clancy's Op Center, In the Heat of the Night: Grow Old With Me, Assault on Devil's Island, Assault on Death Mountain, The Defiant Ones, Shadow Warriors, Shadow Warriors II. *Director*: Silk Stalkings (7 episodes), Renegade (1 episode).

WEAVER, DENNIS
Actor, Director. b. Joplin, MO, June 4, 1925. e. U. of Oklahoma, B.A., fine arts, 1948.

PICTURES: Horizons West (debut, 1952), The Raiders, The Redhead From Wyoming, The Lawless Breed, Mississippi Gambler, Law and Order, It Happens Every Thursday, Column South, The Man From the Alamo, The Golden Blade, The Nebraskan, War Arrow, Dangerous Mission, Dragnet, Ten Wanted Men, The Bridges at Toko-Ri, Seven Angry Men, Chief Crazy Horse, Storm Fear, Touch of Evil, The Gallant Hours, Duel at Diablo, Way... Way Out, Gentle Giant, Mission Batangas, A Man Called Sledge, What's the Matter With Helen?, Walking After Midnight, Two Bits & Pepper, Escape From Wildcat Canyon, The Virginian, Submerged.
TELEVISION: *Series*: Gunsmoke (Emmy Award, 1959), Kentucky Jones, Gentle Ben, McCloud, Stone, Emerald Point NAS, Buck James, Lonesome Dove: The Outlaw Years., Watching Ellie. *Movies*: McCloud: Who Killed Miss USA?, The Forgotten Man, Duel, Rolling Man, Female Artillery, The Great Man's Whiskers, Terror on the Beach, Intimate Strangers, The Islander, Ishi: The Last of His Tribe, The Ordeal of Patty Hearst, Stone (pilot), Amber Waves, The Ordeal of Dr. Mudd, The Day the Loving Stopped, Don't Go to Sleep, Cocaine: One Man's Seduction, Bluffing It, Disaster at Silo 7, The Return of Sam McCloud (also co-exec. prod.), Greyhounds, Seduction in a Small Town, Stolen Women, Captured Hearts,The Virginian, High Noon. *Mini-Series*: Centennial, Pearl. *Special*: Mastergate.

WEAVER, FRITZ
Actor. b. Pittsburgh, PA, Jan. 19, 1926. e. U. of Chicago.
THEATRE: The Chalk Garden (Theatre World Award), Miss Lonelyhearts, All American, A Shot in the Dark, Baker Street, Child's Play (Tony, 1970), The Price, The Crucible, The Professional, etc.
PICTURES: Fail Safe (debut, 1964), The Guns of August (narrator), The Maltese Bippy, A Walk in the Spring Rain, Company of Killers, The Day of the Dolphin, Marathon Man, Demon Seed, Black Sunday, The Big Fix, Jaws of Satan, Creepshow, Power, The Thomas Crown Affair.
TELEVISION: *Series*: All My Children. *Movies*: The Borgia Stick, Berlin Affair, Heat of Anger, The Snoop Sisters, Hunter, The Legend of Lizzie Borden, Captains Courageous, The Hearst and Davies Affair, A Death in California, My Name is Bill W, Ironclads, Citizen Cohn, Blind Spot, Pointman, Spring Awakening, Broken Trust, Rescuers: Stories of Courage: Two Women. *Mini-Series*: Holocaust, The Martian Chronicles, Dream West, I'll Take Manhattan.

WEAVER, SIGOURNEY
Actress. r.n. Susan Weaver. b. New York, NY, Oct. 8, 1949. e. Stanford U., Yale U. Daughter of Sylvester (Pat) Weaver, former NBC pres. Mother, actress Elizabeth Inglis (one-time contract player for Warner Bros.). After college formed working partnership with fellow student Christopher Durang for off-b'way improv. productions. First professional appearance on stage in 1974 in The Constant Wife with Ingrid Bergman. Formed Goat Cay Prods.
THEATRE: *Off-Off-B'way*: The Nature and Purpose of the Universe. *Off-B'way*: Titanic/Das Lusitania Songspiel (also co-writer), Gemini, Marco Polo Sings a Solo, New Jerusalem, The Merchant of Venice, Beyond Therapy. *B'way*: Hurlyburly.
PICTURES: Madman (Israeli; debut, 1976), Annie Hall, Alien, Eyewitness, The Year of Living Dangerously, Deal of the Century, Ghostbusters, One Woman or Two, Aliens (Acad. Award nom.), Half Moon Street, Gorillas in the Mist (Acad. Award nom.), Working Girl (Acad. Award nom.), Ghostbusters II, Alien 3 (also co-prod.), 1492: Conquest of Paradise, Dave, Death and the Maiden, Jeffrey, Copycat, The Ice Storm (BAFTA Award, Best Supporting Actress, 1997), Alien: Resurrection (also co-prod.), Snow White, A Map of the World, Get Bruce, Galaxy Quest, Company Man, Speak Truth to Power, Heartbreakers, Big Bad Love, Tadpole, The Guys, Holes, The Wedding Contract, Happily N'Ever After.
TELEVISION: *Series*: The Best of Families (PBS), Somerset. *Special*: The Sorrows of Gin.

WEBB, CHLOE
Actress. b. New York, NY, 1960. e. Boston Conservatory of Music and Drama. On stage with Boston Shakespeare Co., Goodman Theatre in Chicago and Mark Taper Forum, L.A., improv. groups Imagination Theatre Co., Paul Sills Theatre.
THEATRE: Forbidden Broadway (Off-B'way and L.A.), Addiction, Family Album, The Model Apartment (LA Critics Circle & Dramalogue Awards), House of Blue Leaves (Dramalogue Award), School Talk, A Midsummer Night's Dream.
PICTURES: Sid and Nancy (debut, 1986; Natl. Society of Film Critics Award), Twins, Heart Condition, The Belly of an Architect, Queens Logic, A Dangerous Woman, Love Affair, She's So Lovely, The Newton Boys, Practical Magic.
TELEVISION: *Series*: Thicke of the Night, China Beach. *Special*: Who Am I This Time? *Movies*: China Beach, Lucky Day, Silent Cries, The Ballad of Lucy Whipple. *Mini-Series*: Tales of the City. *Guest*: Remington Steele, China Beach (pilot).

WEBER, STEVEN
Actor. b. March 4, 1961. e. Purchase Col. Acted with Mirror Rep. Co. Off-B'way.
THEATRE: *NY:* Paradise Lost, The Real Thing (B'way debut, 1985), Something About Baseball. *Regional:* Made in Bangkok, Come Back Little Sheba, Naked at the Coast, Death of a Salesman.
PICTURES: The Flamingo Kid, Flanagan, Hamburger Hill, Les Anges, Single White Female, The Temp, Jeffrey, Dracula: Dead and Loving It, I Woke Up Early the Day I Died, The Breakup, Sour Grapes, At First Sight, Timecode, Sleep Easy Hutch Rimes.
TELEVISION: *Series:* Wings, All Dogs Go to Heaven, Hercules, Cursed, Once and Again. *Mini-Series:* The Kennedys of Massachusetts, The Shining. *Movies:* In the Company of Darkness, In the Line of Duty: The Undercover Murders, Deception: A Mother's Secret, Betrayed by Love, Take Out the Beast, Stories From the Edge, Thanks of a Grateful Nation, Love Letters, Late Last Night, Common Ground, Club Land. *Special:* Pudd'nhead Wilson.

WEDGEWORTH, ANN
Actress. b. Abilene, TX, Jan. 21, 1935. e. U. of Texas. On stage in Thieves, Blues for Mr. Charlie, Chapter Two (Tony Award, 1978).
PICTURES: Andy, Bang the Drum Slowly, Scarecrow, The Catamount Killing, Law and Disorder, Dragonfly (One Summer Love), Birch Interval, Thieves, Handle With Care, No Small Affair, Sweet Dreams, The Men's Club, Made in Heaven, A Tiger's Tale, Far North, Miss Firecracker, Steel Magnolias, Green Card, Hard Promises, Love and a .45, The Whole Wide World.
TELEVISION: *Series:* The Edge of Night, Another World, Somerset, Three's Company, Filthy Rich, Evening Shade. *Movies:* The War Between the Tates, Bogie, Elvis and the Beauty Queen, Killjoy, Right to Kill?, A Stranger Waits, Cooperstown, A Burning Passion: The Margaret Mitchell Story, Fight for Justice: The Nancy Conn Story. *Pilot:* Harlan & Merleen.

WEILL, CLAUDIA
Director. b. New York, NY 1947. e. Radcliffe, B.A., 1969. Teacher of acting, Cornish Institute, 1983; guest lecturer on film directing, NYU and Columbia U. Winner of Donatello Award, best director, 1979; Mademoiselle Woman of the Year, 1974; AFI Independent Filmmakers Grant, 1973. Worked as prod. asst. on doc., Revolution.
THEATRE: An Evening for Merlin Finch (debut, 1975, Williamstown), Stillife, Found a Peanut, The Longest Walk.
PICTURES: *Doc. shorts:* This Is the Home of Mrs. Levant Grahame, Roaches' Serenade, Joyce at 34. *Director:* The Other Half of the Sky—A China Memoir (also photog., edit.), Girlfriends (also prod., story), It's My Turn.
TELEVISION: *Series:* The 51st State, Sesame Street, Joyce at 34, The Great Love Experiment, thirtysomething, Birdland, My So-Called Life, Chicago Hope, Once and Again. *Movie:* Face of a StrangerA Child Lost Forever: The Jerry Sherwood Story, Critical Choices, Giving Up the Ghost.

WEINBLATT, MIKE
Executive. b. Perth Amboy, NJ, June 10, 1929. e. Syracuse U. Served in Army as counter-intelligence agent, mostly in Japan, 1952-53. Joined NBC in 1957; has headed two major TV network functions—talent/program admin. & sls.; joined network business affairs dept. in 1958 as mgr., business affairs, facilities operations; rose to post of director, pricing & financial services before moving to sales in 1962, as mgr., participating program sales; named v.p., eastern sales, NBC-TV, 1968; named v.p., talent & program admin., 1968; promoted to v.p. sales, 1973; 1975 named sr. v.p., sales; later became exec. v.p.; appointed exec. v.p. & gen. mgr. of NBC TV network, 1977; appointed Pres., NBC Entertainment, 1978; 1980, joined Showtime/Movie Channel as pres. & COO; 1984, pres., Multi Media Entertainment; 1990, chmn. Weinblatt Communications Co. Inc. 1991, mng. dir. Interequity Capital Corp.

WEINGROD, HERSCHEL
Writer, Producer. b. Milwaukee, WI, Oct. 30, 1947. e. U. of Wisconsin, 1965-69; London Film Sch., 1969-71.
PICTURES: *Co-writer* with Timothy Harris: Cheaper to Keep Her, Trading Places (BAFTA nom.), Brewster's Millions, My Stepmother Is An Alien, Paint It Black, Twins, Kindergarten Cop, Pure Luck, Falling Down (prod. only), Space Jam (co-s.p.).
TELEVISION: Street of Dreams (exec. prod.).

WEINSTEIN, BOB
Executive. With brother Harvey founded distribution company Miramax Films in 1979. Company branched into feature production in 1989 with film Scandal. Serves as Miramax co-chairman.
PICTURES: Light Years (Bob: prod.), Harvey: dir. of U.S. version). *Co-Executive Producers:* Scandal, The Lemon Sisters, Hardware, A Rage in Harlem, The Miracle, Crossing the Line, The Night We Never Met, Benefit of the Doubt, True Romance, Into the West, Mother's Boys, Pulp Fiction, Ready to Wear (Pret-a-Porter), The Englishman Who Went Up a Hill But Came Down a Mountain, Smoke, The Crossing Guard, The Journey of August King, Last of the High Kings, Addicted to Love, Air Bud, Cop Land, The English Patient, Scream , Wishful Thinking, The

Wings of the Dove, She's So Lovely, Mimic, Good Will Hunting, Scream 2, Jackie Brown, Velvet Goldmine, Shakespeare in Love (Acad. Award for Best Picture), Rounders, The Prophecy II, A Price Above Rubies, Playing by Heart, The Mighty, Little Voice, Heaven, Halloween H20: Twenty Years Later, The Faculty, B. Monkey, Phantoms, Senseless, Ride, Wide Awake, Nightwatch, 54, Talk of Angels, The Yards, Teaching Mrs. Tingle, Outside Providence, My Life So Far, Music of the Heart, Mansfield Park, Holy Smoke, Guinevere, The Cider House Rules, Allied Forces, She's All That, In Too Deep, Scream If You Know What I Did Last Halloween, Reindeer Games, The Yards, Boys and Girls, Scary Movie, Highlander: Endgame, Backstage, Chocolat, The Lord of the Rings: The Fellowship of the Ring, Scary Movie 2, Daddy and Them, The Others, Jay and Silent Bob Strike Back, Waking Up in Reno, Texas Rangers, Kate & Leopold, The Shipping News, Ritual, The Art of Negotiating a Turn, Alone In The Dark, Alice, Below, The Great Raid, Bad Santa, Spy Kids 2: The Island of Lost Dreams.
TELEVISION: *Series:* Wasteland, Clerks: The Animated Series, Glory Days.

WEINSTEIN, HARVEY
Executive. With brother Bob founded distribution company Miramax Films in 1979. Company branched into feature production in 1989 with film Scandal. Serves as Miramax co-chairman. (For list of films see Bob Weinstein.)

WEINSTEIN, PAULA
Producer. b. Nov. 19, 1945. e. Columbia U. Daughter of late prod. Hannah Weinstein. Raised in Europe. Partnered with Gareth Wigan in WW Productions at Warner Brothers. Started as theatrical agent with William Morris and ICM. With Warner Brothers, 1976-78 as production v.p.; left to go to 20th Century-Fox in same capacity; named Fox sr. v.p., worldwide prod; 1980, appointed v.p., prod., the Ladd Company; 1981, joined United Artists as pres., m.p. div.; 1983, began own prod. company at Columbia Pictures, also serving as a consultant for Columbia; 1987, joined MGM as exec. consultant; With late husband Mark Rosenberg formed Spring Creek Prods.
PICTURES: *Prod.:* American Flyers, A Dry White Season, The Fabulous Baker Boys, Fearless,The House of the Spirits, Flesh and Bone, With Honors, Something to Talk About, The Incredible Mr. Limpet, Analyze This, Liberty Heights, The Perfect Storm, An Everlasting Piece, Possession, Bandits, Analyze That, Deliver Us from Eva, Looney Tunes: The Movie, ID, Envy, Looney Tunes: Back in Action.
TELEVISION: *Movies:* Bejewelled, The Rose and the Jackal, Citizen Cohn, Truman (Emmy Award, 1996), The Cherokee Kid, First-time Felon, Cloned, Giving Up the Ghost, If You Believe, Crossed Over. *Mini-Series:* Salem Witch Trials.

WEINTRAUB, FRED
Executive, Producer. b. Bronx, NY, April 27, 1928. e. U. of PA, Wharton Sch. of Bus. Owner of The Bitter End Coffeehouse to 1971. Personal management, Campus Coffee House Entertainment Circuit; TV Production Hootenanny, Popendipity; syndicated TV show host: From The Bitter End; motion picture prod.; v.p., creative services, Warner Bros. 1969; exec. in chg. Woodstock; prod. motion pictures, Weintraub-Heller Productions, 1974; then Fred Weintraub Productions, which became Weintraub/Kuhn Prods. in 1990.
PICTURES: Enter the Dragon, Rage, Black Belt Jones, Truck Turner, Golden Needles, Animal Stars, Hot Potato, The Ultimate Warrior, Dirty Knights Work, Those Cuckoo Crazy Animals, Crash, Outlaw Blues, The Pack, The Promise, Tom Horn, Battle Creek Brawl, Force Five, High Road to China, Out of Control, Gymkata, Princess Academy, Born to Ride.
TELEVISION: *Movies:* Triplecross, The Devil's Arithmetic, Trouble Bound, Dead Wrong, JFK Assassination (doc.), The Bruce Lee Story (doc.), *Series:* The New Adventures of Robin Hood (exec. prod.). *Mini-Series:* Really Naked Truth (exec. prod.), La Femme Musketeer.

WEINTRAUB, JERRY
Producer. b. New York, NY, Sept. 26, 1937. m. former singer Jayne Morgan. Sole owner and chmn. of Management Three, representing entertainment personalities, including John Denver, John Davidson, Frank Sinatra, Neil Diamond, etc. Also involved with Intercontinental Broadcasting Systems, Inc. (cable programming) and Jerry Weintraub/Armand Hammer Prods. (production co.). 1985, named United Artists Corp. chmn. Resigned, 1986. 1987: formed Weintraub Entertainment Group.
PICTURES: Nashville, Oh God!, Cruising, All Night Long, Diner, The Karate Kid, The Karate Kid Part II, The Karate Kid Part III, Pure Country, The Firm (actor), The Next Karate Kid, The Specialist, National Lampoon's Vegas Vacation, The Avengers, Soldier, The Independent, Ocean's Eleven, Full Frontal (actor), Confessions of a Dangerous Mind (actor), Ocean's Twelve.

WEIR, PETER
Director, Writer. b. Sydney, Australia, Aug. 21, 1944. e. Scots Coll. and Sydney U. Briefly worked selling real estate, traveled to England 1965. Entered Australian TV industry as stagehand 1967 while prod. amateur revues. *Dir. shorts:* Count Vim's Last Exercise, The Life and Times of Reverend Buck Shotte,

Homeside, Incredible Floridas, What Ever Happened to Green Valley? 1967-73.
PICTURES: *Director*: Three to Go (debut, 1970; segment: Michael), The Cars That Ate Paris (also s.p., co-story; a.k.a. The Cars That Eat People), Picnic at Hanging Rock, The Last Wave (also s.p.), The Plumber (also s.p.; tv in Australia). Gallipoli (also story), The Year of Living Dangerously (also co-s.p.), Witness (Academy Award nom.), The Mosquito Coast, Dead Poets Society (Academy Award nom.), Green Card (also prod., s.p.; Academy Award nom.), Fearless, The Truman Show (Acad. Award nom. for dir.), Lumumba (actor), Master and Commander: The Far Side of the World.

WEISS, STEVEN ALAN
Executive. b. Glendale, CA, Oct. 19, 1944. e. Los Angeles City Coll., A.A., 1964; USC, M.S., 1966; Northwestern U., B.S., 1967; LaSalle Extension U., J.D., 1970. U.S. Navy-San Diego, Great Lakes, Vallejo & Treasure Island, 1966-67; shipyard liaison officer, Pearl Harbor Naval Shipyard, U.S. Navy, 1967-70; gen. mgr., Adrian Weiss Prods., 1970-74; organized Weiss Global Enterprises with Adrian Weiss 1974 for production, acquisition & distribution of films. Purchased with Tom J. Corradine and Adrian Weiss from the Benedict E. Bogeaus Estate nine features, 1974. Sec./Treas. of Film Investment Corp. & Weiss Global Enterprises which own, control or have dist. rights to over 300 features, many TV series, documentaries, etc. CFO/COO Flo-Fowes, a full service telecommunications corp., 1992-present. Member of the Nat'l Assn. of TV Program Executive Int'l, National Cable TV Assn., AFI.

WEISWASSER, STEPHEN A.
Executive. e. Wayne St. Univ., John Hopkins Univ., Harvard Law School. Partner at Wilmer Cutler & Pickering law firm until he joined Capital Cities/ABC in 1984 as sr. v.p. Aug. 1993 became pres. of Capital Cities/ABC Multimedia Group until Oct. 1995. Nov. 1995, became pres. & CEO of Americast.

WEITZNER, DAVID
Executive. b. New York, NY, Nov. 13, 1938. e. Michigan State U. Entered industry in 1960 as member Columbia Pictures adv. dep't; later with Donahue and Coe as ass't exec. and Loew's Theatres adv. dep't; later with Embassy Pictures, adv. mgr.; dir. of adv. and exploitation for Palomar Pictures Corp.; v.p. in charge of adv., pub., and exploitation for ABC Pictures Corp.; v.p., entertainment/leisure div., Grey Advertising; v.p., worldwide adv., 20th Century Fox; exec. v.p. adv./pub./promo., Universal Pictures; exec. v.p., mktg. & dist., Embassy Pictures; 1985, joined 20th Century-Fox Films as pres. of mktg. 1987, pres., mktg., Weintraub Entertainment Group; 1988 joined MCA/Universal as pres. worldwide marketing, MCA Recreation Services.

WELCH, RAQUEL
Actress. r.n. Raquel Tejada. b. Chicago, IL, Sept. 5, 1940. e. La Jolla H.S. Theatre arts scholarship San Diego State Coll. Worked as model before landing bit parts in films. Broadway debut, Woman of the Year, 1981.
PICTURES: A House Is Not a Home (debut, 1964), Roustabout, Do Not Disturb, A Swingin' Summer, Fantastic Voyage, Shoot Loud Louder... I Don't Understand, One Million Years B.C., Fathom, The Oldest Profession, Bedazzled, The Biggest Bundle of Them All, Le Fate (The Queens), Bandolero, Lady in Cement, 100 Rifles, Flare Up, The Magic Christian, Myra Breckinridge, Restless, Hannie Caulder, Kansas City Bomber, Fuzz, Bluebeard, The Last of Sheila, The Three Musketeers, The Four Musketeers, The Wild Party, Mother Jugs and Speed, Crossed Swords, L'Animal, Naked Gun 33 1/3: The Final Insult, Tortilla Soup, Legally Blonde.
TELEVISION: *Series*: American Family, Central Park West. *Specials*: Really Raquel, Raquel, FY2K: Graham Norton Live, 2000 Hispanic Heritage Awards (host). *Movies*: The Muppets Go Hollywood, The Legend of Walks Far Woman, Right to Die, Scandal in a Small Town, Trouble in Paradise, Tainted Blood, Judith Krantz's Torch Song, Hollyrock-a-Bye Baby (voice), Central Park West *Guest*: Cher, The Muppet Show.

WELD, TUESDAY
Actress. r.n. Susan Weld. b. New York, NY, Aug. 27, 1943. m. violinist Pinchas Zuckerman. e. Hollywood Professional Sch. Began modeling at 4 yrs.
PICTURES: Rock Rock Rock (debut, 1956), Rally 'Round the Flag Boys! The Five Pennies, Because They're Young, High Time, Sex Kittens Go to College, The Private Lives of Adam and Eve, Return to Peyton Place, Wild in the Country, Bachelor Flat, Soldier in the Rain, I'll Take Sweden, The Cincinnati Kid, Lord Love a Duck, Pretty Poison, I Walk the Line, A Safe Place, Play It As It Lays, Looking for Mr. Goodbar (Acad. Award nom.), Who'll Stop the Rain, Serial, Thief, Author! Author!, Once Upon a Time in America, Heartbreak Hotel, Falling Down, Feeling Minnesota, Chelsea Walls.
TELEVISION: *Series*: The Many Loves of Dobie Gillis (1959-60). *Movies*: Reflections of Murder, F. Scott Fitzgerald in Hollywood, A Question of Guilt, Mother and Daughter: The Loving War, Madame X, The Winter of Our Discontent, Scorned and Swindled, Circle of Violence, Something in Common.

WELLER, PETER
Actor. b. Stevens Point, WI, June 24, 1947. Acting since 10 years old. e. North Texas State U. Studied at American Acad. of Dramatic Arts with Uta Hagen. Member, Actor's Studio.
THEATRE: Sticks and Bones (moved up from understudy, B'way debut), Full Circle, Summer Brave, Macbeth, The Wool-Gatherer, Rebel Women, Streamers, The Woods, Serenading Louie, Daddy Wolf.
PICTURES: Butch and Sundance: The Early Years (debut, 1979), Just Tell Me What You Want, Shoot the Moon, Of Unknown Origin, The Adventures of Buckaroo Banzai Across the 8th Dimension, Firstborn, Robocop, Shakedown, A Killing Affair, Leviathan, The Tunnel, Robocop 2, Cat Chaser, Naked Lunch, Fifty Fifty, Sunset Grill, The New Age, Screamers, Mighty Aphrodite, Beyond the Clouds, Top of the World, Enemy of My Enemy, Diplomatic Siege, Shadow Hours, Ivansxtc, Falling Through, The Contaminated Man, Styx, The Sin Eater, The Order
TELEVISION: *Movies*: The Man Without a Country, The Silence, Kentucky Woman, Two Kinds of Love, Apology, Women & Men: Stories of Seduction (Dust Before Fireworks), Rainbow Drive, The Substitute Wife, The Road to Ruin, Decoy, Gold Coast (dir.), Lakota Woman: Siege at Wounded Knee, End of Summer, The Sands of Time, Dark Prince: The True Story of Dracula, Odyssey 5. *Guest*: Lou Grant, Exit 10. *Special*: Partners (also dir., cowriter). *Series*: Odyssey 5, Homicide: Life on the Street (dir.), Michael Hayes (dir.). *Mini-Series*: Mourning Becomes Electra.

WENDERS, WIM
Director, Writer. b. Dusseldorf, Germany, August 14, 1945. Studied film 1967-70 at Filmhochschule in Munich. Worked as film critic 1968-70 for Filmkritik and Die Suddeutsche Zeitung. 1967 made first short films (Schauplatze) and three others before first feature, Summer in the City.
PICTURES: *Director-Writer*: Summer in the City (debut, 1970; also prod., actor), The Scarlet Letter, The Goalie's Anxiety at the Penalty Kick, Alice in the Cities, Wrong Move (dir. only), Kings of the Road (also prod.), The American Friend, Lightning Over Water (also actor), Chambre 66 (dir., actor), Hammett (dir. only), The State of Things, Paris Texas (dir. only), I Played It for You (dir., actor only), Tokyo-Ga (also edit.), Wings of Desire (also prod.), Notebooks on Cities and Clothes (also photog.), Until the End of the World, Faraway So Close! (also prod.), Lisbon Story, Beyond the Clouds (co-dir. & co-s.p. with Michelangelo Antonioni), The End of Violence (also prod.), City of Angels (s.p. only), The Million Dollar Hotel (also prod.), Buena Vista Social Club, Vill Passiert, Ten Minutes Older: The Trumpet. *Actor:* Long Shot, King Kong's Faust, Helsinki Napoli All Night Long, Motion and Emotion.
TELEVISION: *Mini-Series*: The Blues.

WENDKOS, PAUL
Director. b. Philadelphia, PA, Sept. 20, 1926. e. Temple U., Columbia, the New School.
PICTURES: The Burglar, Tarawa Beachhead, Gidget, Face of a Fugitive, Battle of the Coral Sea, Because They're Young, Angel Baby, Gidget Goes to Rome, Miles to Terror, Guns of the Magnificent Seven, Cannon for Cordova, The Mephisto Waltz, Special Delivery.
TELEVISION: Hawaii 5-0 (pilot), Fear No Evil, The Brotherhood of the Bell, Travis Logan D.A., A Tattered Web, A Little Game, A Death of Innocence, The Delphi Bureau, Haunts of the Very Rich, Footsteps, The Strangers in 7-A, Honor Thy Father, Terror on the Beach, The Underground Man, The Legend of Lizzie Borden, Death Among Friends, The Death of Ritchie, Secrets, Good Against Evil, Harold Robbins' 79 Park Avenue, A Woman Called Moses, The Ordeal of Patty Hearst, Act of Violence, Ordeal of Doctor Mudd, A Cry for Love, The Five of Me, Golden Gate, Farrell for the People, Cocaine: One Man's Seduction, Intimate Agony, The Awakening of Candra, Celebrity, Scorned and Swindled, The Execution, The Bad Seed, Picking Up the Pieces, Rage of Angels: The Story Continues, Sister Margaret and the Saturday Night Ladies, Six Against the Rock, Right to Die, The Taking of Flight 847: The Uli Derickson Story, The Great Escape II: The Untold Story (co-dir.), From the Dead of Night, Cross of Fire, Blind Faith, Good Cops Bad Cops, The Chase, White Hot: The Murder of Thelma Todd, Guilty Until Proven Innocent, Trial: The Price of Passion,The Trail, Bloodlines: Murder in the Family, Message from Nam, A Match Made in Heaven, Crimes of Passion: Edna Buchanan's Nobody Lives Forever, A Wing and a Prayer, Different.

WENDT, GEORGE
Actor. b. Chicago, IL, Oct. 17, 1948. e. Rockhurst Col. Joined Second City's acting troupe in 1973. Appeared in NBC pilot Nothing but Comedy.
PICTURES: My Bodyguard, Somewhere in Time, Airplane II: The Sequel, Jekyll & Hyde Together Again, The Woman in Red, Dreamscape, Thief of Hearts, No Small Affair, Fletch, House, Gung Ho, Plain Clothes, Guilty by Suspicion, Forever Young, The Little Rascals, Man of the House, Spice World, Anarchy TV, Space Truckers, The Lovemaster, Rupert's Land, Outside Providence.
TELEVISION: *Series*: Making the Grade, Cheers, The George Wendt Show, The Naked Truth, Sabrina, the Teenage Witch.

Guest: Alice, Soap, Taxi, Hart to Hart, Seinfeld, The Simpsons (voice). *Movies*: Oblomov (BBC), The Ratings Game, Hostage for a Day, Shame II: The Secret, Bye Bye Birdie, Alien Avengers, Alien Avengers II, The Price of Heaven, Alice in Wonderland, The Pooch and the Pauper, Strange Relations.

WERNER, PETER
Producer, Director. b. New York, NY, Jan. 17, 1947. e. Dartmouth Coll., AFI. Received Academy Award for short subject, In the Region of Ice, 1976.
PICTURES: Don't Cry It's Only Thunder, No Man's Land.
TELEVISION: *Movies: Director*: Battered, William Faulkner's Barn Burning, Sins of the Father, Aunt Mary, No Man's Land, Women in Song, No Man's Land, LBJ: The Early Years. Men (exec. prod., dir.; Emmy nom.), The Image (Ace Award), Hiroshima: Out of the Ashes (D.G.A. nom.), The Good Policeman, Doorways, Middle Ages (co-exec. prod.), Substitute Wife, The Four Diamonds, The Unspoken Truth, Inflammable, Almost Golden: The Jessica Savitch Story (D.G.A. nom.), For the Love of Zachary, On the Edge of Innocence, Tempting Fate, Mama Flora's Family, Parallels, Hefner: Unauthorized, After Amy Ruby's Bucket of Blood, Call Me Claus,We Were the Mulvaneys, The Pact. *Series*: Family , Moonlighting (Emmy & D.G.A. nom.), Outlaws (also pilot), Hooperman, The Wonder Years, D.E.A. (pilot), Ned Blessing (pilot), Nash Bridges (also pilot), The Expert, Grounded for Life, Maybe It's Me, Philly, For the People, Boomtown, *Mini-Series:* House of Frankenstein 1997, The '70s.

WERTHEIMER, THOMAS
Executive. b. 1938. e. Princeton U., B.A. 1960; Columbia U., LLB, 1963. V.p. business affairs subs. ABC 1964-72; joined MCA Inc, 1972; v.p. Universal TV dir.; corp. v.p. 1974 -83; exec. v.p 1983-; chmn., MCA Television and Home Entertainment Groups. Consultant, 1996-present

WERTMULLER, LINA
Director, Writer. b. Rome, Italy, Aug. 14, 1928. m. sculptor-set designer Enrico Job. e. Acad. of Theatre, Rome, 1951. Began working in theatre in 1951; Prod.-dir. avant-garde plays in Italy 1951-52; member puppet troupe 1952-62; actress, stage mgr., set designer, publicity writer, for theater, radio & TV, 1952-62. Began film career as asst. to Fellini on 8 1/2 in 1962. Following year wrote and directed first film, The Lizards. Had big TV success with series called Gian Burasca and then returned to theatre for a time. 1988, named Special Commissioner of Centro Sperimentale di Cinematografia. Was the first woman to be nominated for an Acad. Award for Best Director (Seven Beauties, 1976).
PICTURES: *Director-Writer*: The Lizards (dir. debut, 1963), Let's Talk About Men, The Seduction of Mimi (Cannes Film Fest Award, 1972), Love and Anarchy, All Screwed Up, Swept Away... By an Unusual Destiny in the Blue Sea of August, Seven Beauties (Acad. Award noms. for dir. & s.p., 1976), The End of the World in Our Usual Bed in a Night Full of Rain, Blood Feud, A Joke of Destiny (Lying in Wait Around the Corner Like a Bandit), A Complex Plot About Women, Sotto Sotto (Softly Softly), Summer Night With Greek Profile Almond Eyes and a Scent of Basil, The Tenth One in Hiding, On a Moonlit Night, Saturday Sunday Monday, Ciao Professore!, The Nymph, Metalmeccanico e parrucchiera in un turbine di sesso e di politica, 12 registi per 12 citta, Ferdinando e Carolina, An Interesting State, Francesa e Nunziata, Swept Away (2002, s.p. only).
TELEVISION: Rita the Mosquito, Il Decimo Clandestino (Cannes Fest. Award).

WEST, ADAM
Actor. r.n. William West Anderson. b. Walla Walla, WA, Sept. 19, 1929. e. Whitman Col. (B.A.), Stanford Univ. Created classic Batman role. Appeared in interactive short film Ride for Your Life, and CD-ROM The Golden Nugget.
PICTURES: The Young Philadelphians, Geronimo, Soldier in the Rain, Tammy and the Doctor, Robinson Crusoe on Mars, The Outlaws Is Coming!, Mara of the Wilderness, Batman, The Girl Who Knew Too Much, Marriage of a Young Stockbroker, The Specialist, Hell River, Hooper, The Happy Hooker Goes to Hollywood, Blonde Ambition, One Dark Night, Young Lady Chatterly, Hell Raiders, Zombie Nightmare, Doin' Time on Planet Earth, Mad About You, John Travis: Solar Survivor, Maxim Xul, Night of the Kickfighter, The New Age, Not This Part of the World, Bigger Than Watermelon, An American Vampire Story.
TELEVISION: *Series*: The Detectives, Batman, Tarzan and the Super 7, The Last Precinct, Danger Theatre, The Clinic, The Adventures of Pete & Pete, The Secret Files of the SpyDogs (voice), Family Guy (voice), Black Scorpion. *Movies*: The Eyes of Charles Sands, For the Love of It, I Take These Men, Nevada Smith, Poor Devil, The Last Precinct, Lookwell, Return to the Batcave: The Misadventures of Adam and Burt. *Mini-Series:* Partizani, Achieving the Glow (host). *Guest:* Hawaiian Eye, 77 Sunset Strip, Bonanza, The Outer Limits, Petticoat Junction, Bewitched, The Big Valley, Love American Style, Night Gallery, Mannix, Alice, Murder She Wrote, Hope and Gloria, Lois and Clark, Burke's Law, The Simpsons (voice), The Critic (voice), Batman (animated series; voice), Politically Incorrect, Weird Science, Rugrats (voice), Animaniacs (voice), Murphy Brown, Wayans Brothers, MTV's Singled Out. *Pilots:* Reel Life, Doc Holliday, Burnett, Johnny Cinderella, Alexander the Great.

WEST, TIMOTHY
Actor. b. Yorkshire, England, Oct. 20, 1934. m. actress Prunella Scales. e. John Lyon Sch. Harow. Ent. ind. 1960. Began acting 1956 after two years as recording engineer. Worked in regional repertory, London's West End and for Royal Shakespeare Company. Dec., 1979 appointed artistic controller of Old Vic. Has directed extensively in the theatre.
PICTURES: Twisted Nerve, The Looking Glass War, Nicholas and Alexandra, The Day of the Jackal, Hedda, Joseph Andrews, The Devil's Advocate, Agatha, The Thirty Nine Steps, Rough Cut, Cry Freedom, Consuming Passions.
TELEVISION: Edward VII, Hard Times, Crime and Punishment, Henry VIII, Churchill and the Generals, Brass, The Monocled Mutineer, The Good Doctor Bodkin Adams, What the Butler Saw, Harry's Kingdom, The Train, When We Are Married, Breakthrough at Reykjavik, Strife, A Shadow on the Sun, The Contractor, Blore, m.p., Survival of the Fittest, Oliver Twist, Why Lockerbie, Framed, Smokescreen, Eleven Men Against Eleven, Cuts, The Place of the Dead.

WESTON, JAY
Producer. b. New York, NY, March 9, 1929. e. New York U. Operated own pub. agency before moving into film prod. In 1965 launched Weston Production; sold orig. s.p., The War Horses, to Embassy Pictures; acquired and marketed other properties. Became prod. story exec. for Palomar-ABC Pictures in 1967.
THEATRE: Does a Tiger Wear a Necktie? (co-prod.).
PICTURES: For Love of Ivy (co-prod.), Lady Sings the Blues (co-prod.), W.C. Fields and Me, Chu Chu and the Philly Flash, Night of the Juggler, Buddy Buddy, Side Out.
TELEVISION: Laguna Heat (exec. prod.), Invisible Child.

WETTIG, PATRICIA
Actress. b. Cincinnati, OH, Dec. 4, 1951. m. actor Ken Olin. e. Temple Univ. Studied at Neighborhood Playhouse. Began acting career with NY's Circle Repertory Company appearing in The Wool Gatherer, The Diviners and A Tale Told. Other theatre work includes The Dining Room, Talking With (LA), Threads, Innocent Thoughts, My Mother Said I Never Should.
PICTURES: Guilty by Suspicion, City Slickers, Veronica & Me, City Slickers II: The Legend of Curly's Gold, Dancer, Texas Pop. 81.
TELEVISION: *Series*: Police Story: Cop Killer, St. Elsewhere, thirtysomething (2 Emmy Awards), Courthouse, Alias. *Movies*: Silent Motive, Taking Back My Life: The Nancy Ziegenmeyer Story, Parallel Lives, Nothing But the Truth, Kansas. *Mini-Series:* Stephen King's The Langoliers.

WEXLER, HASKELL
Cinematographer, Director. b. Chicago, IL June 2, 1922. Photographed educational and industrial films before features. Documentaries as cinematographer include: The Living City, The Savage Eye, T. for Tumbleweed, Stakeout on Dope Street, Brazil—A Report on Torture, Interviews With Mai Lai Veterans, Interview—Chile's President Allende, Introduction to the Enemy. Elected by AMPAS to Bd. of Governors, Cinematographers Branch. 1991, elected by AMPAS to bd. of govs., Cinematographers Branch; 1993, received lifetime achievement award from American Society of Cinematographers.
PICTURES: *Cinematographer*: Studs Lonigan, Five Bold Women, The Hoodlum Priest, Angel Baby, A Face in the Rain, America America, The Best Man, The Bus (also dir., prod.), The Loved One (also co-prod.), Who's Afraid of Virginia Woolf? (Academy Award, 1966), In the Heat of the Night, The Thomas Crown Affair, Medium Cool (also dir., co-prod., s.p.), Trial of Catonsville Nine, American Graffiti, One Flew Over the Cuckoo's Nest, Bound for Glory (Academy Award, 1976), Coming Home, Days of Heaven (addit. photog.), No Nukes (also co-dir.), Second Hand Hearts, Richard Pryor: Live on the Sunset Strip, Lookin' to Get Out, The Man Who Loved Women, Matewan (Oscar nom.), Colors, Latino (dir., writer only), Three Fugitives, Blaze (Oscar nom.), Through the Wire, Other People's Money, Rolling Stones at the MAX, The Babe, The Secret of Roan Inish, Canadian Bacon, The Sixth Sun: Mayan Uprising in Chiapas, Mulholland Falls, The Rich Man's Wife, Mexico, Stakeout on Dope Street, Limbo, Bus Rider's Union, Good Kurds Bad Kurds, The Man on Lincoln's Nose.
TELEVISION: Steve McQueen: The King of Cool, 61*.

WHALEY, FRANK
Actor. b. Syracuse, NY, July 20, 1963. e. SUNY, Albany. With his brother formed rock band the Niagaras. Member of Malaparte Theatre Co. in NY.
THEATRE: *NY*: Tigers Wild (debut, 1986), Face Divided, The Indian Wants the Bronx, The Years, Good Evening, Hesh, The Great Unwashed.
PICTURES: Ironweed (debut, 1987), Field of Dreams, Little Monsters, Born on the Fourth of July, The Freshman, Cold Dog Soup, The Doors, Career Opportunities, JFK, Back in the U.S.S.R., A Midnight Clear, Hoffa, Swing Kids, Pulp Fiction, I.Q., Swimming With Sharks, Homage, Cafe Society, Broken Arrow, Retroactive, Glam, When Trumpets Fade, Went to Coney Island on a Mission from God...Be Back By Five, The Wall, Curtain Call, Pursuit of Happiness.
TELEVISION: *Specials*: Soldier Boys, Seasonal Differences.

Movies: Unconquered, Flying Blind, Fatal Deception: Mrs. Lee Harvey Oswald, To Dance With the White Dog, The Desperate Trail, Dead Man's Gun, Shake, Rattle, and Roll: An American Love Story, When Trumpets Fade. *Pilot*: Flipside. *Guest*: Spenser: For Hire.

WHALLEY-KILMER, JOANNE
Actress. b. Manchester, England, Aug. 25, 1964. Began stage career while in teens including season of Edward Bond plays at Royal Court Theatre (Olivier Award nom.) and The Three Sisters, The Lulu Plays. *NY*: What the Butler Saw (Theatre World Award).
PICTURES: Dance with a Stranger, No Surrender, The Good Father, Willow, To Kill a Priest, Scandal, Kill Me Again, Navy SEALS, Crossing the Line, Shattered, Storyville, Mother's Boys, The Secret Rapture, Trial by Jury, A Good Man in Africa, The Man Who Knew Too Little, Texas Funeral, Run the Wild Fields, The Guilty.
TELEVISION: *Series:* Coronation Street, Emmerdale Farm , A Kind of Loving. *Mini-Series:* Reilly: Ace of Spies, The Singing Detective, A TV Dante, A Quiet Life, Edge of Darkness, A Christmas Carol, Save Your Kisses, Will You Love Me Tomorrow, Scarlett, Jackie Bouvier Kennedy Onassis, 40.

WHEATON, WIL
Actor. r.n. Richard William Wheaton III. b. Burbank, CA, July 29, 1972. Began acting in commercials at age 7. Graduated L.A. Professional H.S., June, 1990.
PICTURES: The Secret of NIMH (voice), The Buddy System, Hambone and Hillie, The Last Starfighter, Stand by Me, The Curse, Toy Soldiers, December, The Liars' Club, Pie in the Sky, Trekkies, Tales of Glamour and Excess, Flubber, Fag Hag, The Girls' Room, Foreign Correspondents, Star Trek: Nemesis.
TELEVISION: *Series*: Star Trek: The Next Generation, Arena . *Pilots*: Long Time Gone, 13 Thirteenth Avenue, The Man Who Fell to Earth. *Movies*: A Long Way Home (debut, 1981), The Shooting, The Defiant Ones, Young Harry Houdini, The Man Who Fell to Earth, Star Trek: The Next Generation - Encounter at Farpoint, The Last Prostitute, Mr. Stitch, The Day Lincoln Was Shot, The Flintstones: On the Rocks, It Was Him or Us, Book of Days. *Specials*: Lifestories (A Deadly Secret). *Guest*: St. Elsewhere, Family Ties, Tales From the Crypt, Outer Limits.

WHEDON, JOSS
Writer. b. June 23, 1964. e. Wesleyan University.
PICTURES: Buffy the Vampire Slayer, Speed, Waterworld, Toy Story, Twister, Alien Resurrection, Titan A.E, Atlantis: The Lost Empire.
TELEVISION: *Series:* Roseanne, Parenthood, Angel (dir. and prod. only), Buffy the Vampire Slayer (also prod. and dir.), Angel: The Series, Boy Meets World (prod. and dir. only), Ripper (creator), Buffy The Animated Series exec. prod. and creator), Firefly.

WHITAKER, FOREST
Actor, Director. b. Longview, TX, July 15, 1961. Raised in Los Angeles. e. Pomona Col., studying music; USC, studying opera and drama. Prof. debut in prod. of The Beggar's Opera. Directed Whitney Houston's "Exhale (Shoop Shoop)" video.
THEATRE: Swan, Romeo and Juliet, Hamlet, Ring Around the Moon, Craig's Wife, Whose Life Is It Anyway?, The Greeks (all at Drama Studio London); School Talk (LA), Patchwork Shakespeare (CA Youth Theatre), The Beggar's Opera, Jesus Christ Superstar. *Dir.*: Look Back in Anger, Drums Across the Realm.
PICTURES: Tag: The Assassination Game (debut, 1982), Fast Times at Ridgemont High, Vision Quest, The Color of Money, Platoon, Stakeout, Good Morning Vietnam, Bloodsport, Bird (Cannes Film Fest. Award, 1988), Johnny Handsome, Downtown, Rage in Harlem (also co-prod.), Article 99, Diary of a Hit Man, Body Snatchers, Consenting Adults, The Crying Game, Article 99, Bank Robber, Body Snatchers, Blown Away, Jason's Lyric, Ready to Wear (Prêt-à-Porter), Smoke, Species, Phenomenon, The Split, Ghost Dog: The Way of the Samurai, Four Dogs Playing Poker, Light It Up, Battlefield Earth: A Saga of the Year 3000, Clint Eastwood: Out of the Shadows, American Storytellers, The Panic Room, Green Dragon, The Fourth Angel, Phone Booth. *Dir.*: Waiting to Exhale, Hope Floats.
TELEVISION: *Movies*: Hands of a Stranger, Criminal Justice, Last Light, Strapped (dir. only), Last Light, Lush Life, The Enemy Within, Door to Door (co-exec.prod.), Rebound: The Legend of Earl 'The Goat' Manigault, Witness Protection, Deacons for Defense. *Guest*: Amazing Stories, Hill Street Blues, Cagney and Lacey, Trapper John M.D., The Fall Guy, Different Strokes. *Mini-Series*: North and South Parts I & II, Feast of All Saints. *Series*: The Twilight Zone.

WHITE, BETTY
Actress. b. Oak Park, IL, Jan. 17, 1924. Graduated from Beverly Hills H.S. Performed on radio beginning in early 1940's on such shows as Blondie, The Great Gildersleeve, This Is Your FBI. Became local L.A. tv personality in early 1950's prior to starring in her first series to be seen nationwide, Life With Elizabeth, in 1953. Was married to late tv host Allen Ludden. Inducted into Academy of Television Arts & Sciences Hall of Fame, 1994. Recipient of Comedy Lifetime Achievement Award.

AUTHOR: Betty White's Pet Love (1983), Betty White In Person (1987), The Leading Lady: Dinah's Story (1991), Here We Go Again: My Life in Television (1995).
PICTURES: Hard Rain, Holy Man, Lake Placid, The Story of Us , Advise and Consent, The Flood, Bringing Down the House.
TELEVISION: *Series*: Life With Elizabeth, Make the Connection (panelist), Date With the Angels, The Betty White Show (1958), The Jack Paar Show, The Pet Set, The Mary Tyler Moore Show (2 Emmy Awards: 1975, 1976), Match Game PM. (panelist), Liar's Club (panelist), The Betty White Show (1977-78), Just Men (host; Emmy Award, 1983), Mama's Family, The Golden Girls (Emmy Award, 1986), The Golden Palace, Bob, Maybe This Time, Ladies Man. *Movies*: Vanished, With This Ring, The Best Place to Be, Before and After, The Gossip Columnist, Chance of a Lifetime, Eunice , A Weekend in the Country, The Story of Santa Claus, The Retrievers, The Wild Thornberrys: The Origin of Donnie, Return to the Batcave: The Misadventures of Adam and Burt. *Host*: Macy's Thanksgiving Parade for 10 yrs, Tournament of Roses Parade (20 yrs.). *Guest*: The Millionaire, U.S. Steel Hour, Petticoat Junction, The Odd Couple, Sonny and Cher, The Love Boat, Hotel, Matlock, The John Laroquette Show (Emmy Award, 1996), Suddenly Susan.

WHITE, ROY B.
Executive, Exhibitor. b. Cincinnati, OH, July 30, 1926. e. U. of Cincinnati. U.S. Air Force during WWII; sales department of 20th Century-Fox, 1949-52; began in exhibition, 1952; past pres., Mid-States Theatres; chmn. R. M. White Management, Inc.; past president, National Association of Theatre Owners, past Chairman of the Board, NATO, Board of Trustees—American Film Inst.; bd.of dirs. NATO of Ohio, Motion Picture Pioneers Foundation; Will Rogers Hospital, Nat'l. Endowment for Arts.

WHITELAW, BILLIE
C.B.E., D.Litt.: Actress. b. Coventry, England, June 6, 1932. Acted on radio and television since childhood. Winner of the TV Actress of the Year and 1972, Guild Award, Best Actress, 1960. British Acad. Award 1969; U.S. National Society of Film Critics Award best supp. actress, 1968. Evening News, Best Film Actress, 1977; best actress Sony Radio Radio Award 1987, 1989. 1988 Evening Standard Award for Best Actress.
THEATRE: England Our England (revue), Progress to the Park, A Touch of the Poet, Othello; 3 yrs. with Natl. Theatre of Great Britain; Trelawney of the Wells, After Haggerty, Not I, Alphabetical Order, Footfalls, Molly, The Greeks, Happy Days, Passion Play, Rockaby (also in N.Y. and Adelaide Festival), Tales from Hollywood, Who's Afraid of Virginia Woolf?
PICTURES: The Fake (debut, 1953), Companions in Crime, The Sleeping Tiger, Room in the House, Small Hotel, Miracle in Soho, Gideon of Scotland Yard, Carve Her Name With Pride, Bobbikins, Mania, Hell Is a City, Make Mine Mink, No Love for Johnnie, Mr. Topaze (I Like Money), Payroll, The Devil's Agent, The Comedy Man, Charlies Bubbles, The Adding Machine, Twisted Nerve, Start the Revolution Without Me, Leo the Last, Eagle in a Cage, Gumshoe, Frenzy, Night Watch, The Omen, Leopard in the Snow, The Water Babies, An Unsuitable Job for a Woman, The Dark Crystal (voice), Tangier, Slayground, Shadey, The Chain, Murder Elite, Maurice, The Dressmaker, Joyriders, The Krays, Freddie as F.R.O.7 (voice), Deadly Advice, Jane Eyre, Quills.
TELEVISION: Over 100 leading roles including: *Series*: Dixon of Dock Green, Time Out for Peggy, The Sextet, Born to Run. *Mini-Series*: Napoleon and Love, Private Schulz, Imaginary Friends, Firm Friends, Changing Stages. *Movies*: No Trams to Lime Street, Lena, O My Lena, Lady of the Camelias, Resurrection, Beyond the Horizon, Anna Christie, You and Me, A World of Time, Dr. Jekyll and Mr. Hyde, Poet Game, Sextet (8 plays for BBC), Wessex Tales, The Fifty Pound Note, Supernatural (2 plays), Four plays by Samuel Beckett, Eustace and Hilda, The Oresteia of Aeschylus, The Haunted Man, Jamaica Inn, Happy Days, Camille, The Secret Garden, The Picnic, A Tale of Two Cities, The Fifteen Streets, Three Beckett plays, Lorna Doone, Duel of Love, A Murder of Quality, The Cloning of Joanna May, Merlin, Shooting the Past, The Entertainer, The Last of the Blonde Bombshells, A Dinner of Herbs.

WHITEMORE, HUGH
Writer. b. England, 1936. Studied acting at Royal Acad. of Dramatic Art. Has since written for television, film, theatre.
THEATRE: Stevie, Pack of Lies, Breaking the Code, The Best of Friends, It's Ralph.
PICTURES: All Neat in Black Stockings, All Creatures Great and Small, Stevie, The Return of the Soldier, 84 Charing Cross Road, Utz, Jane Eyre.
TELEVISION:*Series*: Thirty-Minute Theatre, Midsomer Murders . *Mini- Series*: Elizabeth R (Emmy Award, 1971), A Fall of Eagles , Shoulder to Shoulder, David Copperfield, I Remember Nelson , Boy in the Bush, A Dance to the Music of Time. *Movies*: Angus Slowly Sinking?, Macready's Gala, Final Demand, Frankenstein Mark II, Amerika, Too Many Cooks, Act of Betrayal, The Adventures of Don Quixote, Cider With Rosie (Writers' Guild Award 1971), Country Matters (Writers' Guild Award, 1972), Dummy (RAT—Prix Italia, 1979), Rebecca, All For Love, A Dedicated Man, Down at the Hydro, A Bit of Singing and Dancing, Concealed Enemies (Emmy & Neil Simon Awards,

1984), Pack of Lies, The Final Days, The Best of Friends, The Turn of the Screw, The Rector's Wife, The Haunting of Helen Walker, Breaking the Code, The Gathering Storm, My House in Umbria.

WHITMAN, STUART
Actor. b. San Francisco, CA., Feb. 1, 1928. Army Corp. of Engineers (1945-1948), at Fort Lewis, WA; while in army, competed as light heavyweight boxer. Studied drama under G.I. Bill at Ben Bard Drama Sch. and L.A. City Coll. Performed in Heaven Can Wait and became member of Michael Chekhov Stage Society and Arthur Kennedy Group. Entered films in early 1950's. TV debut on 26 episodes of Highway Patrol.
PICTURES: When Worlds Collide, The Day The Earth Stood Still, Rhapsody, Seven Men From Now, War Drums, Johnny Trouble, Darby's Rangers, Ten North Frederick, The Decks Ran Red, China Doll, The Sound and the Fury, These Thousand Hills, Hound Dog Man, The Story of Ruth, Murder Inc., Francis of Assisi, The Fiercest Heart, The Mark (Acad. Award nom.), The Comancheros, Convicts 4, The Longest Day, The Day and the Hour (Fr./It.), Shock Treatment, Rio Conchos, Those Magnificent Men In Their Flying Machines, Sands of the Kalahari, Signpost to Murder, An American Dream, The Invincible Six, The Last Escape, Captain Apache (U.S./Sp.), Night Of The Lepus, Welcome To Arrow Beach (Tender Flesh), Crazy Mama, Call Him Mr. Shatter, Assault on Paradise (Maniac/Ransom), Mean Johnny Barrows, Las Vegas Lady, Eaten Alive!, Tony Saitta/Tough Tony (It.), Strange Shadows In An Empty Room, Ruby, The White Buffalo; Delta Fox, Thoroughbred (Run for the Roses), Oil (It. as Red Adair), La Murjer de la Tierra Caliente (Sp./It.); Guyana: Cult of the Damned, Cuba Crossing, Jamaican Gold, The Monster Club, Demonoid, Butterfly, Treasure of The Amazon, John Travis: Solar Survivor, Deadly Reactor, Moving Target, Mob Boss, Private Wars, Trail by Jury, Improper Conduct, Land of Milk and Honey, Second Chances.
TELEVISION: Series: Cimarron Strip, Roughcuts, Superboy , Knots Landing, Shaunessy (pilot). Guest: The Crowd Pleaser (Alcoa-Goodyear), Highway Patrol, Dr. Christian, Hangman's Noose (Zane Grey), Walker Texas Ranger, Adventures of Brisco County Jr., Time Trax, Courthouse. Mini-Series: The Last Convertible, Hemingway, Women in White, The Seekers. Movies: The Man Who Wanted to Live Forever, City Beneath the Sea, Revenge, The Woman Hunter, The Man Who Died Twice, Cat Creature, Go West Young Girl, The Pirate, Condominium, Beverly Hills Cowgirl Blues, Stillwatch, Once Upon a Texas Train, Wounded Heart, Shaughnessy, The President's Man.

WHITMORE, JAMES
Actor. r.n. James Allen Whitmore, Jr. b. White Plains, NY, Oct. 1, 1921. e. Yale U. In Yale Drama Sch. players; co-founder Yale radio station, 1942; U.S. Marine Corps, W.W.II; in USO, in American Wing Theatre school, in stock. Broadway debut in Command Decision, 1947.
THEATRE: Give 'em Hell Harry, Will Rogers USA, Almost an Eagle.
PICTURES: The Undercover Man (debut, 1949), Battleground (Acad. Award nom.), The Asphalt Jungle, The Next Voice You Hear, Mrs. O'Malley and Mr. Malone, The Outriders, Please Believe Me, Across the Wide Missouri, It's a Big Country, Because You're Mine, Above and Beyond, The Girl Who Had Everything, All the Brothers Were Valiant, Kiss Me Kate, The Command, Them!, Battle Cry, The McConnell Story, The Last Frontier (Savage Wilderness), Oklahoma!, Crime in the Streets, The Eddie Duchin Story, The Deep Six, Face of Fire, Who Was That Lady?, Black Like Me, Chuka, Waterhole No. 3, Nobody's Perfect, Planet of the Apes, Madigan, The Split, Guns of the Magnificent Seven, Tora! Tora!, Chato's Land, The Harrad Experiment, Where the Red Fern Grows, Give 'em Hell Harry (Acad. Award nom.), The Serpent's Egg, Bully, The First Deadly Sin, The Adventures of Mark Twain (voice), Nuts, Old Explorers, The Shawshank Redemption, The Relic, Old Hats, Here's to Life!, The Majestic.
TELEVISION: Series: The Law and Mr. Jones, Survival, My Friend Tony, Temperature's Rising, Comeback, Mister Sterling. Movies: The Tenderfoot, The Challenge, If Tomorrow Comes, I Will Fight No More Forever, All My Sons, Rage, Mark I Love You, Glory! Glory!, Sky High, Swing Vote, A Ring of Endless Light. Mini-Series: The Word, Celebrity, Favorite Son.

WHITTON, MARGARET
Actress. b. Baltimore, MD, Nov. 30, 1950. Raised in Haddonfield, NJ. Has written articles for Village Voice, The National.
THEATRE: NY: Nourish the Beast (Off-B'way debut, 1973), Another Language, The Art of Dining, Chinchilla, Othello, One Tiger to a Hill, Henry IV Part 1, Don Juan, Steaming, Aunt Dan and Lemon, Ice Cream/Hot Fudge. Regional: Hamlet, Camille, Time and the Conways, The House of Blue Leaves.
PICTURES: National Lampoon Goes to the Movies (debut, 1981), Love Child, The Best of Times, 9-1/2 Weeks, The Secret of My Succe$s, Ironweed, Major League, Little Monsters, Big Girl Don't Cry... They Get Even, The Man Without a Face, Major League 2, Trial by Jury.
TELEVISION: Series: The Doctors, Search for Tomorrow, Hometown, A Fine Romance, Good and Evil, Cutters. Movies: Summer My Father Grew Up, Menendez: A Killing in Beverly Hills.

WIDMARK, RICHARD
Actor. b. Sunrise, MN, Dec. 26, 1914. e. Lake Forest U. Was drama instructor, 1936, before going to NY where he acted on many radio dramas, then stage.
PICTURES: Kiss of Death (debut, 1947), Road House, Street With No Name, Yellow Sky, Down to the Sea in Ships, Slattery's Hurricane, Night and the City, Panic in the Streets, No Way Out, Halls of Montezuma, The Frogmen, Red Skies of Montana, Don't Bother to Knock, O. Henry's Full House, My Pal Gus, Destination Gobi, Pickup on South Street, Take the High Ground, Garden of Evil, Hell & High Water, Broken Lance, Prize of Gold, The Cobweb, Backlash, Run for the Sun, The Last Wagon, Saint Joan, Time Limit, The Law and Jake Wade, The Tunnel of Love, The Trap, Warlock, The Alamo, The Secret Ways, Two Rode Together, Judgment at Nuremberg, How the West Was Won, Flight from Ashiya, The Long Ships, Cheyenne Autumn, The Bedford Incident, Alvarez Kelly, The Way West, Madigan, Death of a Gunfighter, A Talent for Loving, The Moonshine War, When The Legends Die, Murder on the Orient Express, The Sell Out, To the Devil a Daughter, Twilight's Last Gleaming, The Domino Principle, Rollercoaster, Coma, The Swarm, Dinero Maldito, Bear Island, National Lampoon Goes to the Movies, Hanky Panky, Who Dares Wins, The Final Option, Against All Odds, True Colors, Wild Bill: Hollywood Maverick.
TELEVISION: Series: Madigan. Movies: Vanished, Brock's Last Case, The Last Day, Mr. Horn, All God's Children, A Whale for the Killing, Blackout, A Gathering of Old Men, Once Upon a Texas Train, Cold Sassy Tree. Special: Benjamin Franklin.

WIESEN, BERNARD
Producer, Director, Writer, Executive. b. New York, NY. e. City Coll. of New York, B.A.; Pasadena Playhouse Coll. of Theatre, Master of Theatre Arts; Dramatic Workshop of New School.
THEATRE: First Monday in October (B'way, co. prod).
PICTURES: Producer-Director: Fear No More. Asst. Dir.: The King and I, The Left Hand of God, The Rains of Ranchipur, To Catch a Thief, The Trouble with Harry.
TELEVISION: Director: How to Marry a Millionaire, Valentine's Day. Assoc. Producer: Valentine's Day, Three on an Island, Cap'n Ahab, Sally and Sam. Assoc. Prod.: Daniel Boone. Producer/Director: Julia, Co-Producer-Director: The Jimmy Stewart Show. Prod. Exec.: Executive Suite (pilot). Exec. Paramount TV, director of current programming. Writer: Love 4 Love, The Grand Turk.

WIEST, DIANNE
Actress. b. Kansas City, MO, March 28, 1948. e. U. of Maryland. Studied ballet but abandoned it for theatre. Did regional theatre work (Yale Repertory, Arena Stage), performed with NY Shakespeare Festival, toured with American Shakespeare Co.
THEATRE: Regional: Arena Stage (DC): Heartbreak House, Our Town, The Dybbuk, Inherit the Wind. Yale Rep.: Hedda Gabler, A Doll's House. NY: Ashes (NY debut, 1977, at Public Theatre), Agamemnon, Leave It to Beaver Is Dead, The Art of Dining (Obie & Theatre World Awards), Bonjour La Bonjour, Frankenstein (B'way), Three Sisters, Othello, Beyond Therapy, Other Places, Serenading Louie (Obie Award), After the Fall, Not About Heroes (dir.; also at Williamstown Fest.), Hunting Cockroaches, Square One, In the Summer House, Blue Light, The Shawl (Off B'way), One Flea Spare (NY Public Theatre).
PICTURES: It's My Turn (debut, 1980), I'm Dancing as Fast as I Can, Independence Day, Footloose, Falling in Love, The Purple Rose of Cairo, Hannah and Her Sisters (Acad. Award, supporting actress, 1986), Radio Days, The Lost Boys, September, Bright Lights Big City, Parenthood (Acad. Award nom.), Cookie, Edward Scissorhands, Little Man Tate, Cops and Robbersons, The Scout, Bullets Over Broadway (Academy Award, best supporting actress, 1994; also Golden Globe, NY Film Critics, LA Film Critics, Natl. Bd. of Review Awards), Drunks, The Birdcage, The Associate, Practical Magic, The Horse Whisperer, I Am Sam, Not Afraid Not Afraid, Portofino.
TELEVISION: Specials: Zalman or the Madness of God, Out of Our Father's House. Movies: Bigfoot, The Wall, The Face of Rage, The Simple Life of Noah Dearborn. Guest: Avonlea (Emmy Award, 1997). Series: Law and Order. Mini-Series: The 10th Kingdom.

WIGAN, GARETH
Executive. b. London, England. e. Oxford U.. Began career in the industry as theatrical agent and film producer. v.p. of production, Twentieth Century Fox, 1975-79; partner & producer, The Ladd Co. (Warner Communications), 1979-83; producer, American Flyers, produced by his own company with Paula Weinstein under Warner Bros;, 1983-87; consultant, exec. of production, exec. v.p., Columbia Pictures, 1987-97. Currently co-vice chairman, Columbia TriStar Motion Picture Group.

WILBY, JAMES
Actor. b. Rangoon, Burma, Feb. 20, 1958. Lived a nomadic childhood moving from Burma to Ceylon, then Jamaica and finally England. e. Durham U. Trained at Royal Acad. of Dramatic Art where he played Shakespearean roles and landed a part in Oxford Film Foundation's Privileged (1982). West End stage debut Another Country. Also acted in regional theater. 1988: The Common Pursuit.

PICTURES: Privileged (debut, 1982), Dreamchild, Maurice, A Handful of Dust, A Summer Story, Immaculate Conception, Howards End, Behind the Lines, The Chess Game, Une Partie d'Echec, Regeneration: Tom's Midnight Garden, Cotton Mary, Gosford Park.
TELEVISION: Series: Original Sin. Movies: Dutch Girls, Tell Me That You Love Me, Adam Bede, Lady Chatterly, You Me + It , Treasure Seekers, Witness Against Hitler, The Woman in White, The Dark Room, Trial & Retribution IV, Bertie and Elizabeth. Mini-Series: A Tale of Two Cities, Mother Love, Crocodile Shoes, Adrian Mole: The Cappuccino Years.

WILDE, ARTHUR L.
Publicist. b. San Francisco, CA, May 27. S.F. Daily News; Matson Lines; pub. dept., Warner Bros., 1936; photo editor at Columbia Pictures, RKO Pictures, Universal Pictures; dir. exploitation, CBS; pub. dir., Hal Wallis Prod.; pub. dept., Paramount; pub. Hecht-Hill-Lancaster; v.p., Arthur Jacobs, public rel.; Blowitz-Maskell Publicity Agency; pub. dir., C. V. Whitney Pictures; gen. v.p., 1958; owner, pub.-ad. agency, The Arthur L. Wilde Co., 1961-65; freelance publicist, 1965-66; pub. rel. consultant, Marineland of Florida 1965; unit publicity dir., United Artists, National General, Paramount, 1966-69; freelance publicity, 1971; unit publicist, MGM, Paramount, United Artists, 1972-74; staff position; Features Publicity at Paramount Pictures, 1973. Freelance unit publicist again in 1976 at Universal, Paramount and Lorimar Productions. 1978-79, Columbia Pictures & Universal Studios; 1980, Marble Arch. Prods. & Northstar Intl. Pictures; 1981, studio pub. mgr. 20th Century-Fox; recently staff unit publicist for 20th-Fox; 1984-89; currently freelance unit publicist for feature films.
PICTURES: ...And Justice for All, Coal Miner's Daughter. Unit: Raise the Titanic, The Postman Always Rings Twice.

WILDER, GENE
Actor, Director, Writer. r.n. Jerry Silberman. b. Milwaukee, WI, June 11, 1935. e. U. of Iowa. Joined Bristol Old Vic company in England, became champion fencer; in NY, worked as chauffeur, fencing instructor, etc. before NY off-B'way debut in Roots. Co-founder of Gilda's Club, a cancer support center in Manhattan.
THEATRE: B'way: The Complacent Lover, Mother Courage, Luv, One Flew Over the Cuckoo's Nest.
PICTURES: Bonnie and Clyde (debut, 1967), The Producers (Acad. Award nom.), Start the Revolution Without Me, Quackser Fortune Has a Cousin in the Bronx, Willy Wonka and the Chocolate Factory, Everything You Always Wanted to Know About Sex* But Were Afraid to Ask, Rhinoceros, Blazing Saddles, The Little Prince, Young Frankenstein (also co-s.p.), The Adventure of Sherlock Holmes' Smarter Brother (also dir., s.p.), Silver Streak, The World's Greatest Lover (also dir., s.p., prod.), The Frisco Kid, Stir Crazy, Sunday Lovers (also dir. & s.p.; episode: Skippy), Hanky Panky, The Woman in Red (also dir., s.p.), Haunted Honeymoon (also dir., s.p., prod.), See No Evil Hear No Evil (also co-s.p.), Funny About Love, Another You, Stuart Little (voice).
TELEVISION: Series: Something Wilder. Specials: The Man Who Refused to Die, Death of a Salesman (1966), The Scarecrow, Acts of Love—And Other Comedies, Annie and the Hoods, The Trouble With People, Marlo Thomas Special. Movies: The Scarecrow, The Berk, Thursday's Game, Murder in a Small Town, Alice in Wonderland, The Lady in Question. Guest: Will & Grace.

WILKINSON, TOM
Actor. b. UK, Dec. 12, 1948.
PICTURES: A Pocketful of Rye, Wetherby, Sylvia, Sharma and Beyond, Paper Mask, In the Name of the Father, Priest, All Things Bright and Beautiful, Business Affair, Sense and Sensibility, The Ghost and the Darkness, Wilde, Smilla's Sense of Snow, The Full Monty (BAFTA Award, Best Supporting Actor, 1997), Oscar and Lucinda, The Governess, Rush Hour, Shakespeare in Love, Molokai: The Story of Father Damien, Ride with the Devil, The Patriot, Essex Boys, Chain of Fools, In the Bedroom, Another Life, Black Knight, The Importance of Being Earnest, Before You Go, An Angel for May, Girl with a Pearl Earing.
TELEVISION: Movies: Sakharov, Shake Hands Forever, The Woman He Loved, The Attic: The Hiding of Anne Frank, First and Last, Prime Suspect, Resnick: Lonely Hearts, Eskimo Day, Interview Day, Crossing the Floor, Cold Enough for Snow, David Copperfield ,The Gathering Storm. Mini-series: Spyship, Martin Chuzzlewit.

WILLENBORG, GREGORY H.
Producer. b. Miami, FL, Feb. 18, 1959. e. Geroge Washington U., B.B.A. 1981; UCLA M.B.A. Marketing & Strategic Planning 1983. During grad. school, worked at the political fundraising firm of Lynn, Bryan & Associates. In 1983, he formed Willenborg & Associates, a consulting grp. specializing in marketing and fundraising. Raised 25 million for the Bob Hope Cultural Center in Palm Desert, CA.
TELEVISION: America's Hope Awards (creator), America's Dance Awards (creator), America's Hope Award Honoring Bob Hope, America's All-Star Tribute to Elizabeth Taylor, Ray Charles: 50 Years in Music, An All-Star Tribute to Oprah Winfrey, Jerry Herman's Broadway at the Hollywood Bowl.

WILLIAMS, ANDY
Singer, Performer. b. Wall Lake, IA, Dec. 3, 1927. Sang as teen with brothers, performing on radio in Des Moines, Chicago, and Los Angeles. William Brothers were back up singers on Bing Crosby's hit recording of Swinging on a Star. Andy dubbed singing voice of Lauren Bacall in To Have and Have Not. Went solo after group disbanded in early 1950's.
PICTURES: Something to Sing About, I'd Rather Be Rich.
TELEVISION: Series: The College Bowl, Tonight (with Steve Allen; 1954-57), The Andy Williams and June Valli Show, The Chevy Showroom, The Andy Williams Show (1958), The Andy Williams Show (1962-67, 1969-71), The Andy Williams Show (synd.: 1976-77). Specials: Love Andy, Kaleidoscope Company, Magic Lantern Show Company, The NBC Kids Search for Santa, The NBC Kids Easter in Rome, NBC 75th Anniversary Celebration, many Christmas specials.

WILLIAMS, BILLY DEE
Actor. b. New York, NY, April 6, 1937. e. National Acad. of Fine Arts and Design. Studied acting with Paul Mann and Sidney Poitier at actor's workshop in Harlem. Was child actor in the Firebrand of Florence with Lotte Lenya; Broadway adult debut in The Cool World in 1961.
THEATRE: A Taste of Honey, Hallelujah Baby, I Have a Dream, Fences.
PICTURES: The Last Angry Man (debut, 1959), The Out-of-Towners, The Final Comedown, Lady Sings the Blues, Hit!, The Take, Mahogany, The Bingo Long Travelling All-Stars and Motor Kings, Scott Joplin, Star Wars: Episode V-The Empire Strikes Back, Nighthawks, Star Wars: Episode VI-Return of the Jedi, Marvin and Tige, Fear City, Number One with a Bullet, Deadly Illusion, Batman, The Pit and the Pendulum, Driving Me Crazy, Giant Steps, Alien Intruder, Steel Sharks, The Prince, Moving Target, Mask of Death, Woo, The Contract, Fear Runs Silent, The Visit, The Ladies Man, The Last Place on Earth, Good Neighbor, Undercover Brother.
TELEVISION: Series: Another World, The Guiding Light, Double Dare, Dynasty, Code Name: Eternity, 18 Wheels of Justice. Mini-Series: Chiefs. Movies: Lost Flight, Carter's Army, Brian's Song, The Glass House, Christmas Lilies of the Field, Children of Divorce, Shooting Stars, Time Bomb, The Hostage Tower, The Imposter, Courage, The Return of Desperado, Oceans of Fire, The Right of the People, Dangerous Passion, The Jacksons: An American Dream, Marked for Murder, Percy & Thunder, Message from Nam, Heaven & Hell: North and South Book III, Falling for You, Triplecross, Il Quarto re, Hard Time. Guest: The F.B.I., The Interns, Mission Impossible, Mod Squad, Dynasty, In Living Color.

WILLIAMS, CARA
Actress. r.n. Bernice Kamiat. b. Brooklyn, NY, June 29, 1925. e. Hollywood Professional Sch. Ent. ind., 20th Century Fox, child actress.
PICTURES: The Happy Land (debut, 1943), Something for the Boys, In the Meantime Darling, Boomerang!, Don Juan Quilligan, Sitting Pretty, The Saxon Charm, Knock on Any Door, The Girl Next Door, Monte Carlo Baby, The Great Diamond Robbery, Meet Me in Las Vegas, The Helen Morgan Story, Never Steal Anything Small, The Defiant Ones (Acad. Award nom.), The Man from the Diners' Club, Doctors' Wives, The White Buffalo.
TELEVISION: Series: Pete and Gladys, The Cara Williams Show, Rhoda. Guest: Alfred Hitchcock Presents, Desilu Playhouse, The Jackie Gleason Show, Henry Fonda Special.

WILLIAMS, CARL W.
Executive. b. Decatur, IL, March 9, 1927. e. Illinois State Normal U., B.S.; 1949; UCLA, M.A., 1950. dir. adv. photo., Clark Equipment Co., 1951-54; film dir. WKAR-TV, E. Lansing, MI, 1954-56; Prod., dir., Capital Films, E. Lansing, MI, 1957; dir. A-V Laboratory, U.C.L.A., 1957-63; co-dev. Dimension 150 Widescreen process, 1957; formed D-150 Inc., 1963; Filbert Co., 1970, v.p., 1977; v.p., Cinema Equipment Sales of Calif., Inc., 1986; pres. 1992. Member: AMPAS, SMPTE, AFI.

WILLIAMS, CINDY
Actress. b. Van Nuys, CA., Aug. 22, 1947. e. Los Angeles City Coll. Appeared in high school and college plays; first prof. role in Roger Corman's film Gas-s-s-s.
PICTURES: Gas-s-s-s (debut, 1970), Beware! the Blob, Drive He Said, The Christian Licorice Store, Travels With My Aunt, American Graffiti, The Conversation, Mr. Ricco, The First Nudie Musical, More American Graffiti, UFOria, Rude Awakening, Big Man on Campus, Bingo!, Father of the Bride II (co-prod. only), Meet Wally Sparks.
TELEVISION: Series: The Funny Side, Laverne and Shirley, Normal Life, Getting By. Guest: Barefoot in the Park, My World and Welcome to It, Love American Style, Nanny and the Professor, Getting Together, Lois and Clark. Movies: The Migrants, Helped Wanted: Kids, Save the Dog, Tricks of the Trade, The Leftovers, Perry Mason: The Case of the Poisoned Pen, Menu for Murder (Murder at the PTA Luncheon), Earth Angel, The Patty Duke Show: Still Rockin' in Brooklyn Heights, Escape From Terror: The Teresa Stamper Story, The Stepford Husbands, Entertainment Tonight Presents: Laverne and Shirley Together Again, Intimate Portrait: Kathy Ireland. Pilot: Steel Magnolias, The Neighbors.

WILLIAMS, CLARENCE, III
Actor. b. New York, NY, Aug. 21, 1939. B'way stage: Slow Dance on the Killing Ground (Tony nom.; Theatre World Award), The Great Indoors, Night and Day.
PICTURES: Rituals, The End, Judgment, Road to Galveston, Purple Rain, 52 Pick-Up, Tough Guys Don't Dance, I'm Gonna Git You Sucka, My Heroes Have Always Been Cowboys, Deep Cover, Dead Fall, Sugar Hill, Tales From the Hood, The Immortals, Ritual, The Brave, Sprung, Hoodlum, Starfucker, Frogs for Snakes, Half Baked, The Legend of 1900, Life, The Day October Died, The General's Daughter, Reindeer Games, Blue Hill Avenue, Impostor.
TELEVISION: *Series*: The Mod Squad, Crazy Love. *Guest*: The Nasty Boys, Miami Vice, Twin Peaks, Uptown Undercover, Cosby Mysteries. *Movies*: The Return of the Mod Squad, House of Dies Drear, The Last Innocent Man, Father & Son: Dangerous Relations, Against the Wall, Road to Galveston, Encino Woman, Rebound: The Legend of Earl 'The Goat' Manigault, George Wallace, The Love Bug, Ali: An American Hero.

WILLIAMS, ELMO
Film Editor, Director, Producer. b. Oklahoma City, OK, Apr. 30, 1913. Film editor 1933-39, with British & Dominion Studio, England. Since then with RKO-Radio as film editor for numerous major productions; mgr.; dir., 20th Century Fox Prod. Ltd. v.p., worldwide production, 20th Century-Fox Film 1971. President Ibex Films. Exec. v.p., Gaylord Prods., 1979; promoted to pres., worldwide prods.
PICTURES: High Noon (edit; Academy Award, 1952), Tall Texan (dir., edit.), The Cowboy (prod., dir., edit.), 20,000 Leagues Under the Sea (edit.), Apache Kid (dir.), The Vikings (2nd unit dir., film ed.), The Big Gamble (2nd unit dir.), The Longest Day (assoc. prod.), Zorba the Greek (exec. prod.), Those Magnificent Men in Their Flying Machines (exec. prod.), The Blue Max (exec. prod.), Tora! Tora! Tora! (prod.), Sidewinder One (edit.), Caravans (edit.), Man Woman and Child (prod.), Ernest Goes to Camp.
TELEVISION: Tales of the Vikings (co-prod., dir.).

WILLIAMS, ESTHER
Actress, Swimmer. b. Los Angeles, CA, Aug. 8, 1923. e. USC. Swimmer at San Francisco World's Fair Aquacade; professional model. Signed to movie contract by MGM. Voted one of Top Ten Money-Making Stars in M.P. Herald-Fame poll, 1950.
PICTURES: Andy Hardy's Double Life (debut, 1942), A Guy Named Joe, Bathing Beauty, Thrill of a Romance, Ziegfeld Follies, The Hoodlum Saint, Easy to Wed, Fiesta, This Time for Keeps, On an Island With You, Take Me Out to the Ball Game, Neptune's Daughter, Pagan Love Song, Duchess of Idaho, Texas Carnival, Callaway Went Thataway (cameo), Skirts Ahoy!, Million Dollar Mermaid, Dangerous When Wet, Easy to Love, Jupiter's Darling, The Unguarded Moment, Raw Wind in Eden, The Big Show, The Magic Fountain, That's Entertainment III.
TELEVISION: *Specials*: Esther Williams in Cypress Gardens, Live From New York, Esther Williams Aqua Spectacular.

WILLIAMS, JO BETH
Actress. b. Houston, TX, Dec. 6, 1948. m. director John Pasquin. e. Brown U. One of Glamour Magazine's top 10 college girls, 1969-70. Acted with rep. companies in Rhode Island, Philadelphia, Boston, Washington, DC, etc. Spent over two years in New York-based daytime serials, Somerset and The Guiding Light.
THEATRE: Ladyhouse Blues (1979), A Coupla White Chicks Sitting Around Talking, Gardenia.
PICTURES: Kramer vs. Kramer (debut, 1979), Stir Crazy, The Dogs of War, Poltergeist, Endangered Species, The Big Chill, American Dreamer, Teachers, Desert Bloom, Poltergeist II, Memories of Me, Welcome Home, Switch, Dutch, Stop Or My Mom Will Shoot, Me Myself & I, Wyatt Earp, Jungle 2 Jungle, Little City.
TELEVISION: *Movies*: Fun and Games, The Big Black Pill, Feasting with Panthers, Jabberwocky, The Day After, Adam, Kids Don't Tell, Adam: His Song Continues, Murder Ordained, Baby M, My Name is Bill W, Child of the Night, Bump in the Night (co-exec. prod. only), Victim of Love, Jonathan: The Boy Nobody Wanted, Sex Love and Cold Hard Cash, Chantilly Lace, Final Appeal, Parallel Lives, Voices From Within, A Season of Hope, Ruby Jean and Joe, Breaking Through, A Chance of Snow, It Came From the Sky, Jackie's Back: Portrait of a Diva, Backlash, Trapped in a Purple Haze, Frankie & Hazel (dir.), The Ponder Heart. *Series*: Somerset, The Guiding Light, Fish Police (voice), John Grisham's The Client, Stories from My Childhood (voice), Payne, Night Visions. *Mini-Series*: From the Earth to the Moon.

WILLIAMS, JOHN
Composer. b. New York, NY, Feb. 8, 1932. e. UCLA, Juilliard Sch. Worked as session musician in '50s; began career as film composer in late '50s. Considerable experience as musical director and conductor as well as composer. Since 1977 conductor of Boston Pops.
PICTURES: I Passed for White, Because They're Young, The Secret Ways, Bachelor Flat, Diamond Head, Gidget Goes to Rome, The Killers, None But the Brave, John Goldfarb Please Come Home, The Rare Breed, How to Steal a Million, The Plainsman, Not with My Wife You Don't, Penelope, A Guide for

the Married Man, Fitzwilly, Valley of the Dolls, Daddy's Gone A-Hunting, Goodbye Mr. Chips (music supvr. & dir.), The Reivers, Fiddler on the Roof (musc. dir.; Acad. Award, 1971). The Cowboys, Images, Pete 'n' Tillie, The Poseidon Adventure, Tom Sawyer (musc. supvr.), The Long Goodbye, The Man Who Loved Cat Dancing, The Paper Chase, Cinderella Liberty, Conrack, The Sugarland Express, Earthquake, The Towering Inferno, The Eiger Sanction, Jaws (Acad. Award, 1975), Family Plot, The Missouri Breaks, Midway, Black Sunday, Star Wars: Episode IV-A New Hope (Acad. Award, 1977), Raggedy Ann & Andy, Close Encounters of the Third Kind, The Fury, Jaws II, Superman, Meteor, Quintet, Dracula, 1941, Star Wars: Episode V-The Empire Strikes Back, Raiders of the Lost Ark, Heartbeeps, E.T.: The Extra-Terrestrial (Acad. Award, 1982), Yes Giorgio, Monsignor, Star Wars: Episode VI-Return of the Jedi, Indiana Jones and the Temple of Doom, The River, SpaceCamp, The Witches of Eastwick, Empire of the Sun, The Accidental Tourist, Indiana Jones and the Last Crusade, Born on the Fourth of July, Always, Stanley & Iris, Presumed Innocent, Home Alone, Hook, JFK, Far and Away, Home Alone 2: Lost in New York, Jurassic Park, Schindler's List (Acad. Award, 1993), Sabrina., The Lost World: Jurassic Park, Seven Years In Tibet, Amistad, Rosewood, Stepmom, Saving Private Ryan, Angela's Ashes, The Patriot, Star Wars: Episode I-The Phantom Menace, Memoirs of a Geisha, A.I., Star Wars: Episode II-Attack of the Clones, Minority Report, Star Wars: Episode III, Harry Potter and the Sorcerer's Stone, Catch Me If You Can, Harry Potter and the Prisoner of Azkaban, Terminal, Indiana Jones 4.
TELEVISION: Once Upon a Savage Night, Jane Eyre (Emmy Award), Sergeant Ryker, Heidi (Emmy Award), The Ewok Adventure. *Series themes*: Checkmate, Alcoa Premiere, Wide Country, Lost in Space, The Time Tunnel, NBC News Theme, Amazing Stories.

WILLIAMS, KENNETH S.
Executive. b. Tulsa, OK, Dec. 31, 1955. e. Harvard Coll., B.A. 1978; Columbia U., M.S. 1985. Began as team leader of Chase Manhattan's motion picture lending group 1978-81. Joined Sony Pictures Entertainment in Jan. 1982 as director of corporate finance, was promoted to assistant treas. Oct. 1982. He became treas. in Feb. 1984 and named assistant v.p. in Nov. 1984. Served as v.p. & treas. of both Columbia Pictures Industries, Inc. and the Entertainment Business Sector of the Coca-Cola Co. (Sony Pictures previous parent co.), 1986-87. 1987-90, corporate v.p. & treas. of Sony Pictures Entertainment and was then promoted to senior v.p., Corporate Operations. Was named executive v.p. of Sony Pictures Entertainment in Aug. 1995. Named pres. of Digital Division of Sony Pictures in Jan. 1997.

WILLIAMS, MICHELLE
Actress. b. Kalispell, MT, Sept. 9, 1980.
PICTURES: Lassie, Species, Timemaster, A Thousand Acres, Halloween H20: Twenty Years Later, Dick, But I'm a Cheerleader, Me Without You.
TELEVISION: *Series*: Raising Caines, Dawson's Creek. *Movies*: My Son Is Innocent, Killing Mr. Griffin, Kangaroo Palace, If These Walls Could Talk 2. *Guest*: Home Improvement.

WILLIAMS, PAUL
Actor, Composer. b. Omaha, NE, Sept. 19, 1940. Began career at studios as set painter and stunt parachutist. Bit and character parts in commercials followed. Became song writer, collaborating briefly with Biff Rose and later with Roger Nichols, with whom wrote several best-sellers, including We've Only Just Begun, Rainy Days and Mondays, Just an Old-Fashioned Love Song.
PICTURES: *Actor*: The Loved One (debut, 1965), The Chase, Watermelon Man, Battle for the Planet of the Apes, Phantom of the Paradise (also songs), Smokey and the Bandit, The Cheap Detective, The Muppet Movie (also songs), Stone Cold Dead, Smokey and the Bandit II, Smokey and the Bandit 3, Zombie High, The Chill Factor, The Doors, Solar Crisis (voice), A Million to Juan, Headless Body in Topless Bar, The Gospel According to Philip K. Dick, The Rules of Attraction. *Songs for Films*: Cinderella Liberty, Bugsy Malone (also vocals), Lifeguard, A Star Is Born (co-composer; Academy Award for best song: Evergreen, 1976), One on One, The End, Agatha, Ishtar, The Muppet Christmas Carol, The Sum of All Fears (lyricist).
TELEVISION: *Series*: Sugar Time! (songs, music spvr.), The Love Boat (theme song), Another Day (theme song), The Paul Williams Show, Batman: The Animated Series, Phantom 2040 (voice), Batman: Gotham Knights (voices), *Movies (actor)*: Flight to Holocaust, The Wild Wild West Revisited, Rooster, The Night They Saved Christmas, People Like Us, Hart to Hart Returns.

WILLIAMS, PAUL
Director. b. New York, NY, Nov. 12, 1943. e. Harvard (Phi Beta Kappa), 1965). First gained attention as director of film short, Girl, which won Golden Eagle award, made in collaboration with producer Edward R. Pressman, with whom he formed Pressman-Williams Enterprises. Now with Fulcrum Productions. In Rose Against the Odds, tv movie.
PICTURES: Out of It (also s.p.), The Revolutionary, Dealing: or the Berkeley-to-Boston Forty-Brick Lost-Bag-Blues (also s.p.), Nunzio, Miss Right (also story), The November Men (also actor), Mirage (also actor), Men (prod.).

WILLIAMS, RICHARD
Producer, Painter, Film Animator. b. March, 1933, Toronto, Canada. Entered industry in 1955. Founded Richard Williams Animation Ltd. in 1962, having entered films by producing The Little Island (1st Prize, Venice Film Festival) in 1955. His company produces TV commercials for England, America, France and Germany, entertainment shorts and animated films. Designed animated feature titles/sequences for What's New Pussycat?, A Funny Thing Happened On The Way To The Forum, Casino Royale, The Charge of the Light Brigade, A Christmas Carol (Academy Award for best animated short, 1972), Who Framed Roger Rabbit (dir. of animation), Arabian Knight (dir., prod., co-s.p.). Awards: at Festivals at Venice, Edinburgh, Mannheim, Montreal, Trieste, Melbourne, West Germany, New York, Locarno, Vancouver, Philadelphia, Zagreb, Hollywood, Cork, Los Angeles. 1989, Academy Award, BAFTA Award, AMPAS Award, special effects, also Special Achievement Awards for work over 30 years, esp. Roger Rabbit by both BAFTA and AMPAS, Arabian Knight (dir./writer).

WILLIAMS, ROBIN
Actor, Comedian. b. Chicago, IL, July 21, 1951. e. Claremont Men's Coll. (CA), Coll. of Marin (CA), studying acting at latter. Continued studies at Juilliard with John Houseman in New York augmenting income as a street mime. As San Francisco club performer appeared at Holy City Zoo, Intersection, The Great American Music Hall and The Boardinghouse. In Los Angeles performed as stand-up comedian at The Comedy Store, Improvisation, and The Ice House. First TV appearance on 1977 Richard Pryor series followed by The Great American Laugh Off. Guest on Happy Days as extraterrestrial Mork from Ork, led to own series.
PICTURES: Can I Do It...Til I Need Glasses? (debut, 1977), Popeye, The World According to Garp, The Survivors, Moscow on the Hudson, The Best of Times, Club Paradise, Good Morning Vietnam (Acad. Award nom.), The Adventures of Baron Munchausen, Dead Poets Society (Acad. Award nom.), Cadillac Man, Awakenings, Dead Again, The Fisher King (Acad. Award nom.), Hook, Shakes the Clown, FernGully... The Last Rainforest (voice), Aladdin (voice), Toys, Mrs. Doubtfire (also co-prod.), Being Human, Nine Months, To Wong Foo—Thanks for Everything—Julie Newmar, Jumanji, Birdcage, Jack, Hamlet, Good Will Hunting (Acad. Award, Best Supporting Actor, 1997), Flubber, What Dreams May Come, Patch Adams, Jakob the Liar, Get Bruce, Bicentennial Man, A.I. (voice), One Hour Photo, Insomnia, Death to Smoochy, House of D.
TELEVISION: Series: The Richard Pryor Show (1977), Laugh-In (1977-78 revival; later aired as series in 1979), Mork and Mindy, Shakespeare: The Animated Tales (host). Guest: America Tonight, Ninety Minutes Live, The Alan Hamel Show. Specials: An Evening With Robin Williams, E.T. & Friends, Faerie Tale Theatre (The Frog Prince), Carol Carl Whoopi and Robin (Emmy Award, 1987), Free To Be... a Family, Dear America: Letters Home from Vietnam (reader), ABC Presents a Royal Gala (Emmy Award, 1988), In Search of Dr. Seuss. Movie: Seize the Day.

WILLIAMS, ROGER
Pianist, Concert, Film, TV Personality. b. Omaha, NE, Oct. 1, 1924. e. Drake U., Idaho State Coll. Hon. Ph.D. Midland and Wagner Colls. Served U.S. Navy WWII. Appeared as guest artist in number of films. Public debut on TV's Arthur Godfrey Talent Scouts and Chance of a Lifetime. Other TV appearances include Ed Sullivan, Hollywood Palace, Kraft Summer Series, Celanese Special. Recorded 75 Albums, Kapp (now MCA) Records, with sales over 15 million albums.

WILLIAMS, TREAT
Actor. r.n. Richard Williams. b. Rowayton, CT, Dec. 1, 1952. e. Franklin and Marshall Coll. Landed role on B'way in musical, Over Here! also played leading role in Grease on B'way.
THEATRE: Over Here, Bus Stop (Equity Library Theatre), Once in a Lifetime, The Pirates of Penzance, Some Men Need Help, Oh Hell, Oleanna.
PICTURES: Deadly Hero (debut, 1976), The Ritz, The Eagle Has Landed, Hair, 1941, Why Would I Lie?, Prince of the City, The Pursuit of D. B. Cooper, Once Upon a Time in America, Flashpoint, Smooth Talk, The Men's Club, Dead Heat, Sweet Lies, Heart of Dixie, Night of the Sharks, Russicum, Beyond the Ocean, Where the Rivers Flow North, Hand Gun, Things to Do in Denver When You're Dead, Mulholland Falls, The Phantom, The Devil's Own, Deep Rising, The Deep End of the Ocean, The Circle, Hollywood Ending.
TELEVISION: Series: Eddie Dodd, Good Advice, Everwood. Mini-Series: Drug Wars: The Camarena Story, Guilty Hearts. Movies: Dempsey, A Streetcar Named Desire, Some Men Need Help, J. Edgar Hoover, Echoes in the Darkness, Third Degree Burn, Max and Helen, Final Verdict, The Water Engine , Deadly Matrimony, Bonds of Love, Parallel Lives, Vault of Horror I, In the Shadow of Evil, Johnny's Girl, The Late Shift, Escape: Human Cargo, The Substitute 2: School's Out, 36 Hours to Die, The Substitute 3: Winner Takes All, Journey to the Center of the Earth.

WILLIAMS-JONES, MICHAEL
Executive. b. England, June 3, 1947. Joined United Artists as trainee, 1967; territorial mgr., South Africa, 1969; territorial mgr., Brazil, 1971; territorial mgr., England, 1976; appt. v.p., continental European mgr., 1978; sr. v.p. foreign mgr., 1979; 1982 joined United Intl. Pictures as sr. v.p. intl. sls., based in London. 1984, named pres. UIP motion picture group; 1986, named pres. & CEO. In Dec. 96, retired from UIP to create own production co., Merlin Angelsey U.K. Ltd.

WILLIAMSON, FRED
Actor, Director, Producer, Writer. b. Gary, IN, March 5, 1937. e. Northwestern U. Spent 10 yrs. playing pro football before turning to acting.
PICTURES: M*A*S*H (debut, 1970), Tell Me That You Love Me Junie Moon, Fist of Fear Touch of Death, Taxi Killer (prod.), The Legend of Nigger Charlie, Hammer, That Man Bolt, The Soul of Nigger Charlie, Hell Up in Harlem, Black Caesar, Three Tough Guys, Three Days to a Kill (also dir., s.p.), Justice Done (also dir.), Soda Cracker (also dir., prod.), Three the Hard Way, Crazy Joe, Black Eye, 'Boss Nigger, Death Journey (also dir., prod.), Bucktown, The Black Bounty Killer (also prod.), Adios Amigo (also dir., prod., s.p.), Take a Hard Ride, Mean Johnny Barrows (also dir., prod.), Joshua, No Way Back (also dir., prod., s.p.), Quel Maledetto Treno Blindato, Mr. Mean (also dir., prod.), Hell's Heroes, Blind Rage, Express to Terror, Fist of Fear Touch of Death, Vigilante, Warriors of the Wasteland, One Down Two to Go (also dir., prod.), The Last Fight (also dir., s.p.), Warriors of the Year 2072, The Big Score (also dir.), 1990: The Bronx Warriors, Warrior of the Lost World, White Fire, Deadly Impact, Foxtrap (also dir., prod.), Delta Force Commando, The Black Cobra, Deadly Intent, Taxi Killer (prod. only), The Kill Reflex (also dir.), Detective Malone, Steele's Law (also dir.), Critical Action (also dir.), Delta Force Commando II: Priority Red One, South Beach (also dir., prod.), Silent Hunter (also dir.), From Dusk Till Dawn, Original Gangstas (also prod.), Full Tilt Boogie, Ride, Whatever It Takes, The Independent, Starsky & Hutch.
TELEVISION: Series: Julia, Monday Night Football, Half Nelson, Fast Track. Guest: Police Story, The Rookies, Lou Grant. Movies: Deadlock, 3 Days to a Kill, Half Nelson, Carmen: A Hip Hopera . Mini-series: Wheels.

WILLIAMSON, KEVIN
Writer. b. New Bern, NC, March 14, 1965.
PICTURES: Scream, I Know What You Did Last Summer, Scream 2 (also exec. prod., actor), Halloween H20: Twenty Years Later (also co-exec. prod.), The Faculty, Teaching Mrs. Tingle (also dir.), Scream 3 (also prod.), Her Leading Man (also prod & dir.), Cursed (also prod.).
TELEVISION: Series: Another World, Kidsongs, Dawson's Creek (exec. prod., creator), Wasteland (exec. prod.), Glory Days (writer, creator, exec. prod.).

WILLIAMSON, NICOL
Actor. b. Hamilton, Scotland, Sept. 14, 1938. Has played many classical roles with Royal Shakespeare Co., including Macbeth, Malvolio, and Coriolanus. Starred on Broadway in Inadmissible Evidence, Rex (musical debut), Macbeth, I Hate Hamlet. London: Jack.
PICTURES: Inadmissible Evidence (debut, 1968), The Bofors Gun, Laughter in the Dark, The Reckoning, Hamlet, The Jerusalem File, The Monk, The Wilby Conspiracy, Robin and Marian, The Seven Percent Solution, The Goodbye Girl (cameo), The Cheap Detective, The Human Factor, Excalibur, Venom, I'm Dancing as Fast as I Can, Return to Oz, Black Widow, The Exorcist III, The Hour of the Pig, Apt Pupil, The Advocate, The Wind in the Willows, Spawn.
TELEVISION: Movies: Of Mice and Men, Columbo: How to Dial a Murder, Macbeth, Sakharov, Passion Flower. Mini-Series: Lord Mountbatten: The Last Viceroy, The Word, Christopher Columbus. Specials: I Know What I Meant.

WILLIAMSON, PATRICK
Executive. b. England, Oct. 1929. Joined Columbia Pictures London office 1944—career spanned advertising & publicity responsibilities until 1967 when appt. managing dir. Columbia Great Britain; also mng. dir. on formation of Columbia-Warner; promoted to exec. position in Columbia's home office, NY, 1973, and pres. of intl. optns. 1974; v.p., Coca-Cola Export Corp., 1983; exec. v.p. Columbia Pictures Industries, 1985; director, CPI, 1985; exec. v.p., Coca-Cola Entertainment Business Sector, 1987; promoted to special asst. to pres. & CEO of Coca-Cola Entertainment Business Sector, 1987; served on boards of Tri-Star Pictures, RCA/Columbia Home Video, RCA/ Columbia Int'l. Video; 1987, named pres. Triumph Releasing Corp., a unit of Columbia Pictures Entertainment; Consultant to Sony Pictures Entertainment, 1989. 1994, dir. & co-founder, Sports Alliance Intl. TV.

WILLIS, BRUCE
Actor. r.n. Walter Bruce Willis. b. Germany, March 19, 1955. Moved to New Jersey when he was 2. After graduating high school, worked at DuPont plant in neighboring town. First entertainment work was as harmonica player in band called Loose Goose. Formed Night Owl Promotions and attended Montclair

State Coll. NJ, where he acted in Cat on a Hot Tin Roof. *NY stage debut:* Heaven and Earth. Member of Barbara Contardi's First Amendment Comedy Theatre; supplemented acting work by doing Levi's 501 jeans commercials and as bartender in NY nightclub, Kamikaze. Appeared as extra in film The First Deadly Sin. Star on the Hollywood Walk of Fame, 1998.
THEATRE: Fool for Love.
PICTURES: Blind Date, Sunset, Die Hard, In Country, Look Who's Talking (voice), That's Adequate, Die Hard 2, Look Who's Talking Too (voice), The Bonfire of the Vanities, Mortal Thoughts, Hudson Hawk (also co-story), Billy Bathgate, The Last Boy Scout, The Player, Death Becomes Her, National Lampoon's Loaded Weapon 1 (cameo), Striking Distance, North, Color of Night, Pulp Fiction, Nobody's Fool, Die Hard With a Vengeance, Twelve Monkeys, The Fifth Element, Last Man Standing, Mercury Rising, Armageddon, The Jackal, Mercury Rising, The Siege, The Sixth Sense, Breakfast of Champions, Franky Goes to Hollywood, The Story of Us, The Kid, The Whole Nine Yards, Unbreakable, Hart's War, Bandits, Hart's War, The Crocodile Hunter: Collision Course (exec. prod.), Man of War, Tears of the Sun, Rugrats Go Wild!, Charlie's Angels: Full Throttle, The Whole Ten Yards, Hostage.
TELEVISION: *Series:* Moonlighting (Emmy Award, Golden Globe Award, 1987), Bruno the Kid (exec. prod. lyricist, singer, theme song). *Guest:* Hart to Hart, Miami Vice, Twilight Zone, Friends (Emmy Award, 2000).

WILLIS, GORDON
Cinematographer. Acted two summers in stock at Gloucester, MA, where also did stage settings and scenery. Photographer in Air Force; then cameraman, making documentaries. In TV did commercials and documentaries.
PICTURES: End of the Road, Loving, The Landlord, The People Next Door, Little Murders, Klute, The Godfather, Bad Company, Up the Sandbox, The Paper Chase, The Parallax View, The Godfather Part II, The Drowning Pool, All the President's Men, Annie Hall, Interiors, September 30, 1955, Comes a Horseman, Manhattan, Stardust Memories, Pennies from Heaven, A Midsummer Night's Sex Comedy, Zelig, Broadway Danny Rose, The Purple Rose of Cairo, Perfect, The Money Pit, The Pick-Up Artist, Bright Lights Big City, Presumed Innocent, The Godfather Part III, Malice, The Devil's Own. *Director:* Windows (1980; debut).
TELEVISION: *Movie:* The Lost Honor of Kathryn Beck.

WILSON, ELIZABETH
Actress. b. Grand Rapids, MI, April 4, 1921.
THEATRE: *B'way:* Picnic (debut, 1953), The Desk Set, The Tunnel of Love, Little Murders, Big Fish Little Fish, Sheep on the Runway, Sticks and Bones (Tony Award, 1972), Uncle Vanya, Morning's at Seven, Ah! Wilderness, The Importance of Being Earnest, You Can't Take It With You, A Delicate Balance.
Off-B'way: Sheep on the Runway, Token in Marriage (Drama Desk Award), Three Penny Opera, Salonika, Ante Room, Eh?, All's Well That Ends Well. *Tour:* The Cocktail Hour.
PICTURES: Picnic (debut, 1955), Patterns, The Goddess, The Tunnel of Love, Happy Anniversary, A Child is Waiting, The Birds, The Tiger Makes Out, The Graduate, Jenny, Catch-22, Little Murders, Day of the Dolphin, Man on a Swing, The Happy Hooker, The Prisoner of Second Avenue, Nine to Five, The Incredible Shrinking Woman, Grace Quigley, Where Are the Children?, The Believers, Regarding Henry, The Addams Family, Quiz Show, Nobody's Fool, Rocky Road.
TELEVISION: *Series:* East Side West Side, Doc, Morningstar/ Eveningstar, Delta. *Movies:* Miles to Go Before I Sleep, Once Upon a Family, Million Dollar Infield, Sanctuary of Fear, Morning's at Seven, Nutcracker: Money Madness and Murder (Emmy nom.), Conspiracy of Love, Skylark, In the Best of Families: Marriage Pride & Madness, Bitter Blood, In the Best Families, Spring Awakening, Journey to Mars. *Mini-Series:* Queen, Scarlett, Promised Land, Delaventure. *Specials:* Patterns, Happy Endings, You Can't Take It With You. *Guest:* U.S. Steel Hour, Maude, All in the Family, Love Sidney, Murder She Wrote, The Boys Next Door.

WILSON, HUGH
Producer, Director, Writer. b. Miami, FL, Aug. 21, 1943. e. Univ. of FL., 1965. Gained fame for creating, writing, producing and directing TV series. Feature film dir. debut with Police Academy (1984).
PICTURES: *Director &/or Writer:* Stroker Ace, Rough Riders, Police Academy, Rustler's Rhapsody, Burglar, Guarding Tess (also voice), Down Periscope (co-s.p.), Blast From the Past, The First Wives Club, Dudley Do-Right.
TELEVISION: *Series:* The Tony Randall Show, WKRP in Cincinnati, Frank's Place, The Famous Teddy Z. *Movies:* Rough Riders.

WILSON, LUKE
Actor. b. Dallas, TX, Sept. 21, 1971. Brother is actor-writer Owen Wilson. Debuted in short film Bottle Rocket, which was later expanded to a feature.
PICTURES: Bottle Rocket, Telling Lies in America, Best Men, Scream 2, Rushmore, Home Fries, Dog Park, Bongwater, My Dog Skip, Kill the Man, Committed, Blue Streak, Preston tylk,

Charlie's Angels, Soul Survivors, The Third Wheel, Legally Blonde, The Royal Tenenbaums, The Third Wheel, Charlie's Angels: Full Throttle, Loosely Based On a True Love Story, Old School, Legally Blonde 2: Bigger, Bolder, Blonder, Around the World in 80 Days.
TELEVISION: *Guest:* The X Files.

WILSON, OWEN
Actor. b. Nov. 18, 1968. Brother is actor Luke Wilson. Debuted in short film Bottle rocket, which he co-wrote and later expanded to feature.
PICTURES: Bottle Rocket (also co-s.p.), The Cable Guy, Anaconda, As Good As It Gets (assoc. prod. only), Rushmore (also co-s.p., exec. prod.), Permanent Midnight, Armageddon, The Minus Man, The Haunting, Breakfast of Champions, Shangai Noon, Kingdom of the Sun (voice), Meet the Parents, Zoolander, Behind Enemy Lines, I Spy, The Royal Tenenbaums (also exec. prod., s.p.), Shanghai Knights, The Big Bounce, Starsky & Hutch, Around the World in 80 Days.
TELEVISION: *Movies:* Heat Vision and Jack (voice).

WILSON, ROYCE
Executive. b. Rison, AR, Feb. 19, 1957. e. U. of Arkansas, BS/BA, 1980. Sales mgr., Viacom: 1980-83. Sales mgr., KATV Little Rock, 1983-84. VP (southwest), Paramount TV, 1984-87. East. reg. mgr., 1987-90. SVP, syndication, Columbia TriStar Domestic TV, 1990-94. Founder, MaXaM, 1994-96. Pres., Eyemark Entertainment, CBS Entertainment Division, CBS, Inc., 1996-.

WILSON, SCOTT
Actor. b. Atlanta, GA, March 29, 1942. Was college athlete on basketball scholarship when injured and had to leave school. Moved to L.A. and enrolled in local acting class.
PICTURES: In the Heat of the Night (debut, 1967), In Cold Blood, The Gypsy Moths, Castle Keep, The Grissom Gang, The New Centurions, Lolly Madonna XXX, The Great Gatsby, Twinkle Twinkle Killer Kane (The Ninth Configuration), The Right Stuff, The Aviator, On the Line, A Year of the Quiet Sun, Blue City, Malone, Johnny Handsome, The Exorcist III, Young Guns II, Femme Fatale, Pure Luck, Flesh and Bone, Geronimo: An American Legend, Tall Tale, Judge Dredd, The Grass Harp, Dead Man Walking, Shiloh, Shiloh 2: Shiloh Season, South of Heaven, West of Hell, G.I. Jane, Our God's Brother, Clay Pigeons, Pride, The Way of the Gun, The Animal, Pearl Harbor, The Last Samurai.
TELEVISION: *Movies:* The Tracker, Jesse, Elvis and the Colonel, Soul Survivors, The Jack Bull, California Quartet.

WINCER, SIMON
Director. b. Australia. Directed over 200 hours of dramatic programs for Australian TV, including Cash and Company, Tandarra, Ryan, Against the Wind, The Sullivans, etc. Exec. prod. of The Man from Snowy River, then the top-grossing theatrical film in Australia.
PICTURES: Snapshot (The Day After Halloween), Harlequin, Phar Lap, D.A.R.Y.L., The Lighthorsemen (also co.-prod.), Quigley Down Under, Harley Davidson and the Marlboro Man, Free Willy, Lightning Jack (also co-prod.), Operation Dumbo Drop, The Phantom, Flash, Crocodile Dundee in Los Angeles.
TELEVISION: *Movies:* The Haunting of Hewie Dowker, The Last Frontier, Bluegrass, Flash, Lonesome Dove (Emmy Award, 1989), The Girl Who Spelled Freedom, Escape: Human Cargo, The Echo of Thunder, Murder She Purred: A Mrs. Murphy Mystery, Louis L'Amour's 'Crossfire Trail', Monte Walsh. *Series:* Homicide (prod.) Matlock Police, The Box, Cash & Company, Tandarra, The Sullivans, Young Ramsey, Chopper Squad, Prisoner, The Young Indiana Jones Chronicles, Ponderosa. *Mini-series:* Against the Wind, Lonesome Dove, P.T. Barnum.

WINCHELL, PAUL
Actor, Ventriloquist. b. New York, NY, Dec. 21, 1922. e. Sch. of Industrial Arts. At 13 won first prize Major Bowes Radio Amateur Hour; signed by Ted Weems; created dummies Jerry Mahoney and Knucklehead Smiff. On radio as host of his own show in 1940's. In the news in 1975 as inventor of an artificial heart.
PICTURES: Stop! Look! and Laugh! (actor), Winnie the Pooh and the Blustery Day (short; voice), The Aristocats (voice), Which Way to the Front? (actor), Winnie the Pooh and Tigger Too (short; voice), The Fox and the Hound (voice).
TELEVISION: *Series:* The Bigelow Show, The Paul Winchell-Jerry Mahoney Spiedel Show (also prod., writer), Jerry Mahoney's Club House (also writer), What's My Name?, Circus Time (ringmaster), Toyland Express (also prod.), The Paul Winchell Show (1957-60), Banana Splits Adventure Hour (voice), Runaround. *Voices for series:* The Wacky Races, Cartoonsville, Dastardly and Mutley, Help It's the Hair Bear Bunch, Goober and the Ghost Chaser, The Oddball Couple, Clue Club, The C.B. Bears, Wheelie and the Chopper, Heathcliff and Marmaduke Show, The Smurfs, Winnie the Pooh Hour, various Dr. Seuss specials, Smurf specials. *Movie:* The Treasure Chest. *Guest:* Pat Boone Show, Polly Bergen Show, The Lineup, Candid Camera, The Beverly Hillbillies, 77 Sunset Strip, Donna Reed Show, Perry Mason, Dick Van Dyke Show, Lucy Show, Love American Style, Brady Bunch, many others.

WINCOTT, MICHAEL
Actor. b. Canada, Jan. 6, 1959. Studied acting at Juilliard. NY stage incl. Talk Radio, States of Shock.
PICTURES: Wild Horse Hank (debut, 1979), Circle of Two, Ticket to Heaven, Curtains, The Sicilian, Talk Radio, Suffering Bastards, Bloodhounds of Broaway, Born on the Fourth of July, The Doors, Robin Hood: Prince of Thieves, 1492: Conquest of Paradise, The Three Musketeers, Romeo Is Bleeding, The Crow, Panther, Strange Days, Dead Man, Basquiat, Alien: Resurrection, Metro, Gunshy, Before Night Falls, Along Came a Spider, The Count of Monte Cristo, Treasure Planet (voice), The Assassination of Richard Nixon.
TELEVISION: Movies: An American Christmas Carol, Tragedy of Flight 103: The Inside Story, The Darkest Day, The Red Phone, Remembering Charlie. Guest: Miami Vice, Crime Story, The Equalizer. Special: High School Narc.

WINDOM, WILLIAM
Actor. b. New York, NY, Sept. 28, 1923.
PICTURES: To Kill a Mockingbird (debut, 1962), Cattle King, For Love or Money, One Man's Way, The Americanization of Emily, Hour of the Gun, The Detective, The Gypsy Moths, The Angry Breed, Brewster McCloud, Fool's Parade, Escape From the Planet of the Apes, The Mephisto Waltz, The Man, Now You See Him Now You Don't, Echoes of a Summer, Mean Dog Blues, Separate Ways, Last Plane Out, Grandview U.S.A., Prince Jack, Space Rage, Funland, Pinocchio and the Emperor of the Night (voice), Planes Trains and Automobiles, She's Having a Baby, Sommersby, Miracle on 34th Street, True Crime.
TELEVISION: Series: The Farmer's Daughter, My World and Welcome to It (Emmy Award, 1970), The Girl With Something Extra, Brothers and Sisters, Murder She Wrote, Parenthood., Sky Commanders, Sonic the Hedgehog (voice). Movies: Seven Times Monday, Prescription: Murder, U.M.C., The House on Greenapple Road, Assault on the Wayne, Escape, A Taste of Evil, Columbo: Short Fuse, Marriage: Year One, The Homecoming, Second Chance, A Great American Tragedy, Pursuit, The Girls of Huntington House, The Day the Earth Moved, The Abduction of St. Anne, Journey from Darkness, Guilty or Innocent: The Sam Sheppard Murder Case, Bridger, Richie Brockelman: Missing 24 Hours, Hunters of the Reef, Portrait of a Rebel: Margaret Sanger, Leave 'Em Laughing, Side Show, Desperate Lives, The Rules of Marriage, Why Me?, Off Sides, Velvet, Surviving, There Must Be a Pony, Dennis the Menace, Chance of a Lifetime, Attack of the 50 Ft. Woman, Fugitive X: Innocent Target. Mini-Series: Once an Eagle, Seventh Avenue, Blind Ambition. Guest: Robert Montgomery Presents, Ben Casey, Lucy Show, The FBI,
Gunsmoke, Partridge Family, That Girl, The Rookies, Streets of San Francisco, Barney Miller, Kojak, Police Woman, Love Boat, St. Elsewhere, Newhart, Night Gallery, Twilight Zone, Star Trek.

WINFIELD, PAUL
Actor. b. Los Angeles, CA, May 22, 1940. e. attended U. of Portland 1957-59, Stanford U., L.A. City Coll, and UCLA. Inducted in Black Filmmakers Hall of Fame.
THEATRE: Regional work at Dallas Theatre Center (A Lesson From Aloes), Goodman Theatre (Enemy of the People), Stanford Repertory Theatre and Inner City Cultural Center, L.A.; At Lincoln Center in The Latent Heterosexual, and Richard III. B'way: Checkmates, Othello, Merry Wives of Windsor.
PICTURES: The Lost Man (debut, 1969), R.P.M., Brother John, Sounder (Acad. Award nom.), Trouble Man, Gordon's War, Conrack, Huckleberry Finn, Hustle, Twilight's Last Gleaming, The Greatest, Damnation Alley, A Hero Ain't Nothin' But a Sandwich, High Velocity, Carbon Copy, Star Trek II—The Wrath of Khan, White Dog, On the Run, Mike's Murder, The Terminator, Blue City, Death Before Dishonor, Big Shots, The Serpent and the Rainbow, Presumed Innocent, Cliffhanger, Dennis the Menace, Original Gangstas, Mars Attacks!, Strategic Command, Relax...It's Just Sex, Catfish in Black Bean Sauce, Assignment Berlin, Knockout.
TELEVISION: Series: Julia, Livin', The Charmings, Wiseguy, 227, Built to Last, Gargoyles, Spider-Man (voice) Teen Angel, City Confidential. Movies: The Horror at 37,000 Feet, It's Good to Be Alive (The Fight), Green Eyes, Angel City, Key Tortuga, The Sophisticated Gents, Dreams Don't Die, Sister Sister, For Us the Living, Go Tell It on the Mountain, Under Siege, The Roy Campanella Story, Guilty of Innocence: The Lenell Geter Story , Mighty Pawns, Women of Brewster Place, Back to Hannibal: The Return of Tom Sawyer and Huckleberry Finn, 83 Hours 'Til Dawn, Irresistible Force, Roots: The Gift, Back to Hannibal, Breathing Lessons, Tyson, White Dwarf, Stolen Memories: Secrets From the Rose Garden, The Assassination File, Strange Justice, Sounder . Mini-Series: King, Backstairs at the White House, The Blue and the Gray, Roots: The Next Generations, Queen, Scarlett.

WINFREY, OPRAH
TV Talk Show Hostess, Actress, Producer. b. Kosciusko, MS, Jan. 29, 1954. e. Tennessee State U. Started as radio reporter then TV news reporter-anchor in Nashville. Moved to Baltimore in same capacity, later co-hosting successful morning talk show. Left for Chicago to host own show AM Chicago which became top-rated in only a month; expanded to national syndication in

1986. Formed own production co., Harpo Productions, Inc. in 1986 which assumed ownership and prod. of The Oprah Winfrey Show in 1988. Named Broadcaster of the Year by Intl. Radio and TV Soc., 1988. Purchased Chicago movie and TV production facility, 1988; renamed Harpo Studios. National Daytime Emmy Award, 1987, Outstanding Talk/Service Program Host. Was given Emmy Lifetime Achievement Award in 1998, and then permanently withdrew her name from annual award consideration. Received Honorary National Book Award, 1999. Launched magazine "O" in 2000.
PICTURES: The Color Purple (debut, 1985; Acad. Award nom.), Native Son, Throw Momma From the Train (cameo), Listen Up: The Lives of Quincy Jones, Malcolm X, Beloved.
TELEVISION: Movies: (as actress), The Women of Brewster Place (actress, co-exec. prod.), There Are No Children Here, Lincoln (voice), Before Women Had Wings, About Us: The Dignity of Children, (as exec.prod./prod), Overexposed, The Wedding, David and Lisa, Tuesdays with Morrie, Amy & Isabelle. Series: The Oprah Winfrey Show (many Emmy Awards), Brewster Place (also exec. prod.), Use Your Life. Special: Pee-wee's Playhouse Christmas Special, Scared Silent: Ending and Exposing Child Abuse, Lincoln, Quincy Jones... The First 50 Years, A Celebration: 100 Years of Great Women, Our Friend, Martin, A Prayer for America: Yankee Stadium Memorial, The Kennedy Center Honors: A Celebration of the Performing Arts, Unchained Memories: Readings from the Slave Narratives.

WINGER, DEBRA
Actress. b. Cleveland, OH, May 16, 1955. e. California State U. Began career on TV series Wonder Woman.
PICTURES: Slumber Party '57 (debut, 1977), Thank God It's Friday, French Postcards, Urban Cowboy, Cannery Row, An Officer and a Gentleman (Acad. Award nom.), Terms of Endearment (Acad. Award nom.), Mike's Murder, Legal Eagles, Black Widow, Made in Heaven, Betrayed, Everybody Wins, The Sheltering Sky, Leap of Faith, Wilder Napalm, A Dangerous Woman, Shadowlands (Acad. Award nom.), Forget Paris., Rumi: Poet of the Heart, Big Bad Love, Searching for Debra Winger, Radio, Eulogy.
TELEVISION: Movie: Special Olympics, Guest: Wonder Woman, James at 16. Specials: The Wizard of Oz in Concert: Dreams Come True, In the Wild: Pandas.

WINITSKY, ALEX
Producer. b. New York, NY, Dec. 27, 1924. e. NYU, BS, LLB, JD. In partnership as attorneys in L.A. for 20 years with Arlene Sellers before they turned to financing and later production of films.
PICTURES: Co-prod. with Sellers: End of the Game, The White Dawn, The Seven-Per-Cent Solution, Cross of Iron, Silver Bears, The Lady Vanishes, Cuba, Blue Skies Again, Irreconcilable Differences, Scandalous, Swing Shift, Bad Medicine, Stanley & Iris, Circle of Friends.
TELEVISION: Movies: Ford—The Man and the Machine. Series: Cadets.

WINKLER, HENRY
Actor, Producer, Director. b. New York, NY, Oct. 30, 1945. e. Emerson Coll., Yale Sch. of Drama, MA. Appeared with Yale Repertory Co.; returned to N.Y. to work in radio. Did 30 TV commercials before starring in The Great American Dream Machine and Masquerade on TV. Formed Fairdinkum Productions with Ann Daniel.
PICTURES: Actor: Crazy Joe (debut, 1974), The Lords of Flatbush, Heroes, The One and Only, Night Shift, Scream, The Waterboy, P.U.N.K.S, Dill Scallion, Ugly Naked People, Down To You, Holes. Exec. Prod: The Sure Thing, Sightings 6 Years, Dead Man's Gun. Director: Memories of Me, Cop and a Half.
TELEVISION: Series (actor): Happy Days, Monty, Clifford's Puppy Days. Series: (dir.): Joanie Loves Chachi, Dave's World , Too Something, Clueless, Sabrina, the Teenage Witch. (prod.): Ryans Four (co-prod.), Mr. Sunshine (co-exec. prod.), McGyver, A Life Apart, WinTuition, Young MacGyver (exec. prod.). Guest: The Mary Tyler Moore Show, The Bob Newhart Show, The Paul Sand Show, Rhoda, Laverne & Shirley, The Larry Sanders Show. Specials: Henry Winkler Meets William Shakespeare, America Salutes Richard Rodgers, A Family Again (exec. prod.), Two Daddies (voice, exec. prod.), So Weird, Hollywood Squares (2002-). Movies: Katherine, An American Christmas Carol, Absolute Strangers, The Only Way Out, Truman Capote's One Christmas, A Child Is Missing, Dad's Week Off, Detention: The Siege at Johnson High, Director: A Smoky Mountain Christmas (movie), All the Kids Do It (also actor, exec. prod.; Emmy Award as exec. prod., 1985). Exec. prod.: Who Are the DeBolts and Where Did They Get 19 Kids?, Scandal Sheet, When Your Lover Leaves, Starflight, Second Start, Morning Glory (pilot), MacGyver: Lost Treasure of Atlantis, MacGyver: Trail to Doomsday, Sightings: Heartland Ghost.

WINKLER, IRWIN
Producer, Director. b. New York, NY, May 28, 1934. e. NYU.
PICTURES: Producer: Double Trouble, Blue, The Split, They Shoot Horses Don't They?, The Strawberry Statement, Leo the Last, Believe in Me, The Gang That Couldn't Shoot Straight, The Mechanic, The New Centurions, Up the Sandbox, Busting,

S*P*Y*S, The Gambler, Breakout, Peeper, Rocky (Academy Award for Best Picture, 1976), Nickelodeon, New York New York, Valentino, Comes a Horseman, Uncle Joe Shannon, Rocky II, Raging Bull, True Confessions, Rocky III, Author! Author!, The Right Stuff, Rocky IV, Revolution, 'Round Midnight, Betrayed, Music Box, GoodFellas, Rocky V, The Juror. *Director*: Guilty by Suspicion (also s.p.), Night and the City, The Net (also co-s.p., co-prod.), At First Sight (also s.p., prod.,), Life As A House, The Shipping News, Enough, .
TELEVISION: *Series*: The Net (exec. prod/writer).

WINNER, MICHAEL
Producer, Director, Writer. b. London, England, Oct. 30, 1935. e. Cambridge U. Ent. m.p. ind. as columnist, dir., Drummer Films. *Presenter*: Michael Winner's True Crimes. *Actor*: For the Greater Good, Decadence, Calliope, Kenny Everett Show, The Full Wax, Birds of a Feather.
PICTURES: *Writer*: Man With A Gun. *Dir.-Writer*: Haunted England (also prod.), Shoot to Kill, Swiss Holiday, Climb Up the Wall, Out of the Shadow, Some Like It Cool, Girls Girls Girls, It's Magic, Behave Yourself, The Cool Mikado, You Must Be Joking, West 11 (dir. only). *Dir./Prod.*: The System (The Girl-Getters), I'll Never Forget What's 'is Name, The Jokers, Hannibal Brooks (also s.p.), The Games, Lawman, The Nightcomers, Chato's Land, The Mechanic (dir. only), Scorpio (also s.p.), The Stone Killer, Death Wish, Won Ton Ton the Dog Who Saved Hollywood, The Sentinel (also s.p.), The Big Sleep (also s.p.), Firepower (also s.p.), Death Wish II, The Wicked Lady (also s.p.), Scream for Help, Death Wish III (dir. only), Appointment With Death (also s.p.), A Chorus of Disapproval (also s.p.), Bullseye (also s.p.), Dirty Weekend (also s.p.), Parting Shots (also s.p., ed.).
TELEVISION: *Series*: White Hunter, Dick and the Duchess, , Camcorder.

WINNINGHAM, MARE
Actress. r.n. Mary Megan Winningham. b. Phoenix, AZ, May 16, 1959. TV debut at age 16 as a singer on The Gong Show. Debut solo album What Might Be released in 1992.
PICTURES: One-Trick Pony, Threshold, St. Elmo's Fire, Nobody's Fool, Made in Heaven, Shy People, Miracle Mile, Turner and Hooch, Hard Promises, Teresa's Tattoo, Wyatt Earp, The War, Georgia (Indep. Spirit Award, Best Supporting Actress, 1996), The Deliverance of Elaine, Bad Day on the Block.
TELEVISION: *Series*: The Brotherhood of Poland, New Hampshire. *Mini-Series*: The Thorn Birds, Studs Lonigan, Too Rich: The Secret Life of Doris Duke. *Movies*: Special Olympics, The Death of Ocean View Park, Amber Waves (Emmy Award, 1980), Off the Minnesota Strip, The Women's Room, Freedom, A Few Days in Weasel Creek, Missing Children: A Mother's Story, Helen Keller: The Miracle Continues, Single Bars Single Women, Love Is Never Silent, Who is Julia, A Winner Never Quits, Eye on the Sparrow, God Bless the Child, Love and Lies, Crossing to Freedom, Fatal Exposure, She Stood Alone, Those Secrets, Intruders, Better Off Dead, Betrayed by Love, Letter to My Killer, The Boys Next Door, The Deliverance of Elaine, George Wallace (Emmy Award, 1998), Little Girl Fly Away, Everything That Rises, The Poet, Everything That Rises.

WINSLET, KATE
Actress. b. Reading, England, Oct. 5, 1975. Began studying drama at age 11.
THEATER: *U.K. Regional*: Adrian Mole, Peter Pan, What the Butler Saw, A Game of Soldiers.
PICTURES: Heavenly Creatures, Sense and Sensibility (BAFTA, Screen Actors Guild Awards, Academy Award nom. 1996), A Kid In King Arthur's Court, Jude, Hamlet, Titanic, Hideous Kinky, Plunge, Holy Smoke, Faeries (voice), Quills, Therese Raquin, Enigma, Christmas Carol: The Movie (voice), Iris, The Life of David Gale, Eternal Sunshine of the Spotless Mind, J.M. Barrie's Neverland.
TELEVISION: *Series*: Casualty, Dark Season, Get Back. *Movies*: Anglo Saxon Attitudes.

WINSTON, STAN
Makeup and Special Effects Artist. b. 1946. e. UofVA. Started in business in 1970 as apprentice to Robert Schiffer at makeup dept. of Walt Disney Studios. Established Stan Winston Studio in Van Nuys, CA.
PICTURES: W.C. Fields and Me, The Wiz, Dead and Buried, Heart Beeps, The Thing, The Entity, Something Wicked This Way Comes, The Terminator, Starman, Invaders From Mars, Aliens (Academy Award for Visual Effects, 1986), Predator, The Monster Squad, Alien Nation, Pumpkinhead (dir. debut), Leviathan, Predator 2, Edward Scissorhands, Terminator 2: Judgment Day (2 Academy Awards: Visual Effects and Makeup, 1991), A Gnome Named Gnorm (dir.), Batman Returns, Jurassic Park (Academy Award for Visual Effects, 1993), Interview With the Vampire, Tank Girl, Congo, Ghosts (dir.), The Ghost and the Darkness, The Relic, The Lost World: Jurassic Park, Mouse Hunt, Paulie, Small Soldiers, End of Days, Inspector Gadget, Galaxy Quest, Instinct, Lake Placid, Pearl Harbor, Artificial Intelligence: AI (animatronics designer), Jurassic Park III, Darkness Falls, Wrong Turn, Terminator 3: Rise of the Machines, Big Fish.

TELEVISION: *Movies*: Gargoyles (Emmy Award for Makeup, 1972), The Autobiography of Miss Jane Pittman (Emmy Award for Makeup, 1974), The Phantom of the Opera, Chiller, Earth vs. the Spider (prod.), How to Make a Monster (prod.), Roots, The Day the World Ended, She Creature, Teenage Caveman. *Specials*: Masquerade, Pinocchio, An Evening With Diana Ross.

WINTER, ALEX
Actor. b. London, England, July 17, 1965. e. NYU. At age 4 began studying dance. Played opposite Vincent Price in St. Louis Opera production of Oliver! Co-founder of Stern-Winter Prods. Produced videos for Red Hot Chili Peppers, Human Radio, Ice Cube, etc. Co-directed TV special Hard Rock Cafe Presents: Save the Planet.
THEATRE: *B'way*: The King and I (1977 revival), Peter Pan (1979 revival). *Off-B'way*: Close of Play.
PICTURES: Death Wish III, The Lost Boys, Haunted Summer, Bill & Ted's Excellent Adventure, Rosalie Goes Shopping, Bill & Ted's Bogus Journey, Freaked (also co-dir., co-s.p., co-prod.), Fever (dir., s.p.).
TELEVISION: *Movie*: Gaugin the Savage. *Series*: Bill & Ted's Excellent Adventures, Idiot Box (also co-creator, co-dir., co-writer).

WINTERS, DAVID
Choreographer, Actor, Director. b. London, April 5, 1939. Acted in both Broadway and m.p. version of West Side Story (as A-rab). Directed and acted in number of TV shows. Pres., A.I.P. Distribution, A.I.P. Productions and A.I.P. Home Video, 1989, formed Pyramid Distributors.
PICTURES: *Choreographer*: Viva Las Vegas, Billie, Send Me No Flowers, Bus Riley's Back In Town, Tickle Me, Pajama Party, Girl Happy, The Swinger, Made in Paris, Easy Come, Easy Go, The Island of Doctor Moreau, Roller Boogie, A Star is Born, Blame It on the Night. *Director*: Welcome to My Nightmare, Racquet, The Last Horror Show, The Last Horror Film (also prod., s.p., act.), Thrashin', Rage to Kill, The Mission... Kill, Space Mutiny (also prod.), Code Name Vengeance. *Producer*: Young Lady Chatterley, Future Force, Raw Nerve, Operation Warzone, Raw Justice, Good Cop Bad Cop, The Dangerous, Codename: Silencer, Rapid Fire, Chase, Battleground, Born Killer, Firehead, Night Wars, Center of the Web, Blood on the Badge, Armed for Action, Body Count,Rhythm & Blues, Devil's Harvest. *Actor*: Rock Rock Rock, West Side Story, The Crazy-Quilt, Welcome 2 Ibiza (also prod.), Invasion Force (writer).
TELEVISION: *Choreographer*: *Series*: Hullabaloo, Shindig, Donny and Marie Osmond, The Big Show, and Steve Allen Show. *Specials starring*: Joey Heatherton, Nancy Sinatra, Diana Ross, Raquel Welch, Ann Margret, Lucille Ball. *Movies*: Firehead, Raw Nerve, Center of the Web, Double Vision.

WINTERS, DEBORAH
Actress. b. Los Angeles, CA. e. Professional Children's Sch., New York; began studying acting at Stella Adler's with Pearl Pearson. at age 13 and Lee Strasberg at 16. Acting debut at age 5 in TV commercials. Casting dir.: Aloha Summer (asst.), Breakdancers From Mars (assoc. prod., casting dir.), Into the Spider's Web, The Hidden Jungle, Haunted, Broken Spur, Behind the Mask (also assoc. prod.).
PICTURES: Me Natalie, Hail Hero!, The People Next Door, Kotch, Class of '44, Blue Sunshine, The Lamp, The Outing.
TELEVISION: *Special*: Six Characters in Search of an Author. *Guest*: Matt Houston, Medical Center. *Movies*: Lottery, Gemini Man. *Tarantulas*: The Deadly Cargo, Little Girl Lost, Space City. *Mini-Series*: The Winds of War.

WINTERS, JONATHAN
Actor. b. Dayton, OH, Nov. 11, 1925. e. Kenyon Coll.; Dayton Art Inst., B.F.A. Disc jockey, Dayton and Columbus stations; night club comedian performing at Blue Angel and Ruban Bleu (NY), Black Orchid (Chicago), Flamingo, Sands, Riviera (Las Vegas), then on B'way in John Murray Anderson's Almanac.
Author: Mouse Breath, Conformity and Other Social Ills, Winters Tales, Hang Ups (book on his paintings). Recorded 7 comedy albums. Won Grammy Award for "Crank Calls" comedy album, 1996.
PICTURES: Alakazam the Great! (voice), It's a Mad Mad Mad Mad World, The Loved One, The Russians Are Coming the Russians Are Coming, Penelope, Oh Dad Poor Dad Mama's Hung You in the Closet and I'm Feeling So Sad, Eight on the Lam, Viva Max, The Fish That Saved Pittsburgh, The Longshot, Say Yes, Moon Over Parador, The Flintstones, The Shadow, Arabian Knight (voice), Santa vs. the Snowman, The Adventures of Rocky & Bullwinkle.
TELEVISION: *Series*: And Here's the Show, NBC Comedy Hour, The Jonathan Winters Show (1956-57), Masquerade Party (panelist), The Andy Williams Show, The Jonathan Winters Show (1967-69), Hot Dog, The Wacky World of Jonathan Winters, Mork and Mindy, Hee Haw, The Smurfs (voice of Papa Smurf), The Completely Mental Misadventures of Ed Grimley (voices), Davis Rules (Emmy Award, 1991), Fish Police (voice). *Guest*: Steve Allen Show, Garry Moore Show, Jack Paar, Omnibus, Twilight Zone, Bob Hope specials, Tonight Show, Hollywood Squares. *Specials*: The Jonathan Winters Special, The Jonathan Winters Show (1964, 1965), Jonathan Winters Presents 200

Years of American Humor, 'Tis the Season to Be Smurfy (voice). *Movies*: Now You See It—Now You Don't, More Wild Wild West, Jonathan Winters: On the Loose.

WINTERS, SHELLEY
Actress. r.n. Shirley Schrift. b. St. Louis, MO, Aug. 18, 1922. e. Wayne U. Clerked in 5 & 10 cent store; in vaudeville, chorus girl in night clubs; NY stage (Conquest, Night Before Christmas, Meet the People, Rosalinda, A Hatful of Rain, Girls of Summer, Minnie's Boys, One Night Stand of a Noisy Passenger. (Off-B'way).
AUTHOR: Shelley Also Known as Shirley (1981), Shelley II: The Middle of My Century (1989).
PICTURES: What a Woman! (debut, 1943), Nine Girls, Sailor's Holiday, Knickerbocker Holiday, Cover Girl, A Double Life, Cry of the City, Larceny, Take One False Step, Johnny Stool Pigeon, The Great Gatsby, South Sea Sinner, Winchester '73, Frenchie, A Place in the Sun, He Ran All the Way, Behave Yourself, The Raging Tide, Phone Call From a Stranger, Meet Danny Wilson, Untamed Frontier, My Man and I, Tennessee Champ, Executive Suite, Saskatchewan, Playgirl, To Dorothy a Son (Cash on Delivery), Mambo, Night of the Hunter, I Am a Camera, Big Knife, Treasure of Pancho Villa, I Died a Thousand Times, The Diary of Anne Frank (Academy Award, best supporting actress, 1959), Odds Against Tomorrow, Let No Man Write My Epitaph, Young Savages, Lolita, Chapman Report, The Balcony, Wives and Lovers, Time of Indifference, A House Is Not a Home, A Patch of Blue (Academy Award, best supporting actress, 1965), The Greatest Story Ever Told, Harper, Alfie, Enter Laughing, The Scalphunters, Wild in the Streets, Buona Sera Mrs. Campbell, The Mad Room, How Do I Love Thee?, Bloody Mama, Flap, What's the Matter with Helen?, Who Slew Auntie Roo?, The Poseidon Adventure, Cleopatra Jones, Something to Hide, Blume in Love, Diamonds, Journey Into Fear, That Lucky Touch, Next Stop Greenwich Village, The Tenant, Tentacles, Pete's Dragon, King of the Gypsies, The Magician of Lublin, The Visitors, City on Fire, S.O.B., Over the Brooklyn Bridge, Ellie, Witchfire (also assoc. prod.), Deja Vu, Very Close Quarters, The Delta Force, The Order of Things, Purple People Eater, An Unremarkable Life, Touch of a Stranger, Stepping Out, Weep No More My Lady, The Pickle, The Silence of the Hams, Heavy, Jury Duty, Portrait of a Lady.
TELEVISION: *Special*: Bob Hope Chrysler Theatre: Two Is the Number (Emmy Award, 1964). *Movies*: Revenge, A Death of Innocence, The Adventures of Nick Carter, The Devil's Daughter, Big Rose, The Sex Symbol, The Initiation of Sarah, Elvis, Alice in Wonderland, Mrs. Munck. *Mini-Series*: The French Atlantic Affair.

WINTMAN, MELVIN R.
Theatre Executive, b. Chelsea, MA. e. U. of Massachusetts, Northeastern U., J.D. Major, infantry, AUS, W.W.II. Attorney. Now consultant & dir., General Cinema Corp.; formerly exec. v.p., GCC and press., GCC Theatres, Inc., Boston. Dir. Will Rogers Memorial Fund. Former pres. Theatre Owners of New England (1969-70); past dir. NATO (1969-70); treas., Nat'l Assoc. of Concessionaires (1960).

WISDOM, NORMAN
O.B.E. Actor, Singer, Comedian. b. London, England, Feb. 4, 1915. Awarded Order of the British Empire (O.B.E.), 1995. Many London West End stage shows including royal command performances. N.Y. B'way shows include Walking Happy and Not Now Darling.
PICTURES: A Date With a Dream (debut, 1948), Meet Mr. Lucifer, Trouble in Store, One Good Turn, As Long as They're Happy, Man of the Moment, Up in the World, Just My Luck, The Square Peg, Follow a Star, There Was a Crooked Man, The Bulldog Breed, The Girl on the Boat, On the Beat, A Stitch in Time, The Early Bird, Press for Time, The Sandwich Man, The Night They Raided Minsky's, What's Good for the Goose, Double X.
TELEVISION: *Series*: Norman, Music Hall, Nobody Is Norman Wisdom, A Little Bit of Wisdom. *Movies*: Androcles and the Lion, Dalziel and Pascoe: Mens Sana, Between the Sheets, Five Children and It.

WISE, ROBERT
Director, Producer. b. Winchester, IN, Sept. 10, 1914. e. Franklin Coll., Franklin, IN. Ent. m.p. ind. in cutting dept. RKO, 1933; sound cutter, asst. edit.; film edit., 1938; edited Citizen Kane, Magnificent Ambersons; 1944, became dir.; to 20th Century-Fox, 1949; ass'n. Mirisch Co. independent prod. 1959; assn. MGM independent prod., 1962; assn. 20th Century Fox Independent Prod. 1963. Partner, Filamakers Group, The Tripar Group. Amer. Film Inst. Life Achievement Award, 1998.
PICTURES: Curse of the Cat People (debut as co-dir., 1944), Mademoiselle Fifi, The Body Snatcher, A Game of Death, Criminal Court, Born to Kill, Mystery in Mexico, Blood on the Moon, The Set-Up, Three Secrets, Two Flags West, The House on Telegraph Hill, The Day the Earth Stood Still, The Captive City, Something for the Birds, Destination Gobi, The Desert Rats, So Big, Executive Suite, Helen of Troy, Tribute to a Bad Man, Somebody Up There Likes Me, Until They Sail, This Could Be the Night, Run Silent Run Deep, I Want to Live!, Odds Against

Tomorrow (also prod.), West Side Story (co-dir., prod.; Acad. Awards for Best Picture & Director, 1961), Two For the Seesaw, The Haunting (also prod), The Sound of Music (also prod.; Acad. Awards for Best Picture & Director, 1965), The Sand Pebbles (also prod.), Star! (also prod.), The Andromeda Strain (also prod.), Two People (also prod.), The Hindenburg (also prod.), Audrey Rose, Star Trek: The Motion Picture, Wisdom (exec. prod only), Rooftops, The Stupids (as actor).
TELEVISION: A Storm in Summer.

WISEMAN, FREDERICK
Documentary Filmmaker, Producer, Director & Editor. b. Boston, MA, Jan. 1, 1930. e. Williams College, B.A., 1951; Yale Law Sch., L.L.B., 1954. Member: MA Bar. Private law practice, Paris, 1956-57. Lecturer-in-Law, Boston U. Law Sch., 1959-61; Russell Sage Fndn. Fellowship, Harvard U., 1961-62; research assoc., Brandeis U., dept. of sociology 1962-66; visiting lecturer at numerous universities. Author: Psychiatry and Law: Use and Abuse of Psychiatry in a Murder Case (American Journal of Psychiatry, Oct. 1961). Co-author: Implementation (section of report of President's Comm. on Law Enforcement and Administration of Justice). Fellow, Amer. Acad. of Arts & Sciences, 1991; John D. and Catherine T. MacArthur Foundation Fellowship, 1982-87; John Simon Guggenheim Memorial Foundation Fellowship, 1980-81. Films are distributed through his Zipporah Films, located in Cambridge, MA. Awards include 3 Emmys, Peabody Award, Intl. Documentary Assn. Career Achievement Award, 3 Columbia Dupont Awards for Excellence in Broadcast Journalism, among others.
PICTURES: Titicut Follies, High School, Law and Order, Hospital, Basic Training, Essene, Juvenile Court, Primate, Welfare, Meat, Canal Zone, Sinai Field Mission, Manoeuvre, Model, Seraphita's Diary, The Store, Racetrack, Deaf, Blind, Multi-Handicapped, Adjustment and Work, Missile, Near Death, Central Park, Aspen, Zoo, High School II, Ballet, La Comedie Francaise, Public Housing, Belfast, Maine, Cinéma Vérité: Defining the Moment, Domestic Violence, The Last Letter, Domestic Violence 2.

WISEMAN, JOSEPH
Actor. b. Montreal, Canada, May 15, 1918.
THEATRE: King Lear, Golden Boy, The Diary of Anne Frank, Uncle Vanya, The Last Analysis, Enemies, Detective Story, Three Sisters, Tenth Man, Incident at Vickey, Marco Williams, Unfinished Stories, many others.
PICTURES: Detective Story (debut, 1951), Viva Zapata, Les Miserables, Champ for a Day, The Silver Chalice, The Prodigal, Three Brave Men, The Garment Jungle, The Unforgiven, Happy Thieves, Dr. No, Bye Bye Braverman, The Counterfeit Killer, The Night They Raided Minsky's, Stiletto, Lawman, The Valachi Papers, The Apprenticeship of Duddy Kravitz, Journey Into Fear, The Betsy, Buck Rogers in the 25th Century, Jaguar Lives.
TELEVISION: *Mini-Series*: QB VII, Masada, Rage of Angels. *Movies*: Pursuit, Murder at the World Series, Seize the Day, Lady Mobster, Ghost Writer. *Series*: Crime Story.

WITHERS, GOOGIE
Actress. b. Karachi, India, Mar. 12, 1917. Trained as a dancer under Italia Conti, Helena Lehmiski & Buddy Bradley; stage debut Victoria Place in Windmill Man, 1929. Best Actress Award, Deep Blue Sea, 1954. Began screen career at 18. TV also. Theatrical tours Australia, Sun Award, Best Actress, 1974. Awarded officer of the Order of Australia (A.O.) 1980. U.S. ACE Cable award, best actress for Time After Time, 1988.
THEATRE: *Britain*: Winter Journey, Deep Blue Sea, Hamlet, Much Ado About Nothing. *Australia*: Plaza Suite, Relatively Speaking, Beckman Place, Woman in a Dressing Gown, The Constant Wife, First Four Hundred Years, Roar Like a Dove, The Cherry Orchard, An Ideal Husband. *London*: Getting Married, Exit the King. *New York*: The Complaisant Lover. Chichester Festival Theatre and Haymarket, London, in The Circle, The Kingfisher, Importance of Being Earnest, The Cherry Orchard, Dandy Dick, The Kingfisher (Australia and Middle East), Time and the Conways (Chichester), School for Scandal (London), Stardust (UK tour). 1986: The Chalk Garden, Hay Fever, Ring Round the Moon, The Cocktail Hour (UK, Australian tour), High Spirits (Aus. tour), On Golden Pond (UK tour).
PICTURES: Haunted Honeymoon, Jeannie, One of Our Aircraft Is Missing, On Approval, Dead of Night, It Always Rains on Sunday, Miranda, Traveler's Joy, Night and the City, White Corridors, Lady Godiva Rides Again, Derby Day, Devil on Horseback, Safe Harbor, Nickel Queen, Country Life, Shine.
TELEVISION: *Series*: Within These Walls, Time After Time, *Movies*: Hotel Du Lac, Northanger Abbey, Ending Up.

WITHERS, JANE
Actress. b. Atlanta, GA, April 12, 1927. By 1934 attracted attention as child player on screen, after radio appearance in Los Angeles and experimental pictures parts, in 1934 in Fox production Bright Eyes, Ginger; thereafter to 1942 featured or starred in numerous 20th-Fox prod. Voted Money-Making Star M.P. Herald-Fame Poll, 1937, 1938. Starred as Josephine the Plumber in Comet tv commercials. TV Movie: All Together Now.
PICTURES: Handle With Care (debut, 1932), Bright Eyes, Ginger, This Is the Life, The Farmer Takes a Wife, Paddy O'Day, Pepper, Gentle Julia, Little Miss Nobody, Can This Be Dixie?,

Wild and Woolly, The Holy Terror, Checkers, Angel's Holiday, Forty-Five Fathers, Always in Trouble, Rascals, Keep Smiling, Arizona Wildcat, Pack Up Your Troubles, Chicken Family Wagon, Boy Friend, Shooting High, High School, Youth Will Be Served, The Girl From Avenue A, Golden Hoofs, A Very Young Lady, Her First Beau, Small Town Deb, Young America, The Mad Martindales, Johnny Doughboy, The North Star, My Best Gal, Faces in the Fog, The Affairs of Geraldine, Danger Street, Giant, The Right Approach, Captain Newman M.D., The Hunchback of Notre Dame (voice), The Hunchback of Notre Dame II (voice).
TELEVISION: *Series:* Mickey Mouse Works, House of Mouse. *Movies:* All Together Now.

WITHERSPOON, REESE
Actress. r.n. Laura Jean Reese Witherspoon. b. Nashville, TN, March 22, 1976. m. actor Ryan Phillippe.
PICTURES: The Man in the Moon, Jack the Bear, A Far Off Place, S.F.W., Fear, Freeway, Pleasantville, Overnight Delivery, Twilight, Cruel Intentions, Election, Best Laid Plans, American Psycho, Little Nicky, The Trumpet of the Swan, Slow Motion, Legally Blonde, Sweet Home Alabama, The Importance of Being Ernest, Legally Blonde 2: Bigger, Bolder, Blonder.
TELEVISION: *Movies:* Wildflower, Desperate Choices: To Save My Child, Return to Lonesome Dove.

WITT, PAUL JUNGER
Producer. b. New York, NY, Mar. 20, 1941. e. Univ. of VA. Was assoc. prod., prod. and dir. for Screen Gems, starting in 1965; prod. for Spelling-Goldberg Prods., 1972; Prod.-exec. prod. for Danny Thomas Prods., 1973. With Tony Thomas became co-founder, exec. prod. of Witt/Thomas Prods., 1975.
PICTURES: Firstborn, Dead Poets Society, Final Analysis, Mixed Nuts, Three Kings, Insomnia.
TELEVISION: *Series:* Here Come the Brides, The Partridge Family, The Rookies, Soap, Benson, It's a Living, I'm a Big Girl Now, It Takes Two, Condo, Hail to the Chief, The Golden Girls (Emmy Awards: 1986, 1987), Beauty and the Beast, Empty Nest, Blossom, Good and Evil, Herman's Head, Nurses, Woops, Golden Palace, The John Larroquette Show, Brotherly Love, Minor Adjustments, Common Law, Pearl, Local Heroes, The Secret Lives of Men, Everything's Relative. *Movies:* Brian's Song (Emmy Award: 1972), No Place to Run, Home for the Holidays, A Cold Night's Death, The Letters, Blood Sport, Remember When, The Gun and the Pulpit, Satan's Triangle, Griffin and Phoenix, High Risk, Trouble in High Timber Country, Radiant City.

WOLF, DICK
Producer, Writer. b. New York, NY, Dec. 20, 1946. e. Univ. of PA. Started in advertising winning three Clio Awards for excellence.
PICTURES: *Prod./Writer:* Skateboard, Gas, No Man's Land, Masquerade (exec. prod., writer, actor), School Ties (story only).
TELEVISION: *Series (exec. prod.):* Miami Vice (also writer), Gideon Oliver (also writer), Christine Cromwell (also creator), Nasty Boys (also creator, writer), H.E.L.P (also creator, writer), Law and Order (also creator, writer), Mann and Machine (also writer), The Human Factor, Crime and Punishment (also creator), South Beach (also creator), New York Undercover (also creator), The Wright Verdicts (also creator), FEDS (creator), Players (prod.), D.C. , Law & Order: Special Victims Unit, Deadline, Arrest & Trial (exec.prod. also writer, creator), Law & Order: Criminal Intent, Law & Order: Crime & Punishment (exec.prod.), Dragnet (also writer, creator).

WOLF, EMANUEL L.
Executive b. Brooklyn, NY, Mar. 27, 1927. e. Syracuse U., B.A., 1950; Maxwell Sch., Syracuse U., M.A. 1952; Maxwell Scholar in Public Admin.-Economics; Chi Eta Sigma (Econ. Hon.). 1952-55. Management consultant, exec. office of Secretary of Navy & Dept. of Interior, Wash, DC, 1956; pres. E.L. Wolf Assocs., Washington, DC, 1961-65; Kalvex, Inc., treas: 1962, dir.: 1963, pres./chmn. of

WOO, JOHN
Director. r.n. Yusen Wu. b. Guangzhou, China, May 1, 1948. e. Matteo Ricci Col, Hong Kong. Started making experimental 16 mm films in 1967. Joined film industry in 1969 as prod. asst. for Cathay Film Co., then asst. dir. 1971 joined Shaw Brothers working as asst. dir. to Zhang Che.
PICTURES: The Young Dragons (debut, 1973), The Dragon Tamers, Countdown in Kung Fu, Princess Chang Ping, From Riches to Rags, Money Crazy, Follow the Star, Last Hurrah for Chivalry, To Hell With the Devil, Laughing Times, Plain Jane to the Rescue, Sunset Warriors (Heroes Shed No Tears), The Time You Need a Friend, Run Tiger Run, A Better Tomorrow, A Better Tomorrow II, Just Heroes, The Killer, Bullet in the Head, Once a Thief, Hard Boiled, Hard Target (U.S. debut, 1993), Cinema of Vengeance (act. only), Broken Arrow, Face/Off, The Big Hit (exec. prod. only), The Replacement Killers (exec. prod. only), King's Ransom, Mission: Impossible 2, The Devil's Pale Moonlit Kiss (prod. only), Windtalkers (also prod.), King's Ransom, Bulletproof Monk (prod. only), Paycheck (also prod.).
TELEVISION: *Series:* Once a Thief. *Movie:* John Woo's Once a Thief (prod.), Black Jack (also prod.), Red Skies.

WOOD, ELIJAH
Actor. b. Cedar Rapids, IA, Jan. 28, 1981. Started in commercial modeling. Landed first acting job in Paula Abdul video Forever Your Girl.
PICTURES: Back to the Future Part II (debut, 1989), Internal Affairs, Avalon, Paradise, Radio Flyer, Forever Young, The Adventures of Huck Finn, The Good Son, North, The War, Flipper, The Ice Storm, The Faculty, Deep Impact, The Bumblebee Flies Away, Black and White, The Adventures of Tom Thumb and Thumbelina (voice), The Lord of the Rings: The Fellowship of the Ring, Ash Wednesday, The Lord of the Rings: The Two Towers, Spy Kids 3-D: Game Over, Eternal Sunshine of the Spotless Mind, The Lord of the Rings: The Return of the King.
TELEVISION: *Movies:* Child of the Night, Day-O, Oliver Twist.

WOODARD, ALFRE
Actress. b. Tulsa, OK, Nov. 8, 1953. e. Boston U., B.A. Soon after graduation landed role in Washington, D.C. Arena Stage theater in Horatio, and Saved.
THEATRE: A Christmas Carol, Bugs Guns, Leander Stillwell, For Colored Girls Who Have Considered Suicide/When the Rainbow Is Enuf, A Map of the World, A Winter's Tale, Two By South.
PICTURES: Remember My Name, Health, Cross Creek (Acad. Award nom.), Extremities, Scrooged, Miss Firecracker, Grand Canyon, The Gun in Betty Lou's Handbag, Passion Fish, Rich in Love, Heart and Souls, Blue Chips, Crooklyn, How to Make an American Quilt, Primal Fear, Star Trek: First Contact, Follow Me Home, Mumford, Down in the Delta, Dinosaur, Brown Sugar, What's Cooking?, Love & Basketball, K-PAX , Searching for Debra Winger, The Wild Thornberrys Movie (voice), The Core, Radio.
TELEVISION: *Series:* Tucker's Witch, Sara, St. Elsewhere. *Guest:* Palmerstown USA, What Really Happened to the Class of '65?, Hill Street Blues (Emmy Award, 1984), L.A. Law (Emmy Award, 1987), People's Century: 1900-1999 (narrator). *Mini-series:* Cadillac Desert, A Wrinkle in Time. *Movies:* Freedom Road, Sophisticated Gents, The Ambush Murders, Go Tell It on the Mountain, Sweet Revenge, L.A. Law, Unnatural Causes, The Killing Floor, Mandela, A Mother's Courage: The Mary Thomas Story, The Child Saver, Blue Bayou, Race to Freedom: The Underground Railroad, Aliens for Breakfast, The Piano Lesson, Gulliver's Travels, The Wizard of Oz in Concert: Dreams Come True, Member of the Wedding, Funny Valentines, Miss Evers' Boys (Golden Globe Award, 1998). *Specials:* For Colored Girls Who Have Considered Suicide/When the Rainbow Is Enuf, Trial of the Moke, Words by Heart.

WOODS, JAMES
Actor. b. Vernal UT, Apr. 18, 1947. e. Massachusetts Inst. of Technology (appeared in 36 plays at MIT, Harvard and Theatre Co. of Boston). Left college to pursue acting career in New York.
THEATRE: Borstal Boy (B'way debut, 1970), followed by Conduct Unbecoming (off-B'way, Obie Award), Saved, Trial of the Catonsville Nine, Moonchildren (Theatre World Award), Green Julia (off-B'way), Finishing Touches.
PICTURES: The Visitors (debut, 1971), Hickey and Boggs, The Way We Were, The Gambler, Distance, Night Moves, Alex and the Gypsy, The Choirboys, The Onion Field, The Black Marble, Eyewitness, Fast-Walking, Split Image, Videodrome, Against All Odds, Once Upon a Time in America, Cat's Eye, Joshua Then and Now, Salvador (Acad. Award nom.), Indept. Film Project Spirit Award, 1986), Best Seller, Cop (also co-prod.), The Boost, True Believer, Immediate Family, The Hard Way, Straight Talk, Diggstown, Chaplin, The Getaway, The Specialist, For Better or Worse, Casino, Nixon, Killer: A Journal of Murder, Ghosts of Mississippi, Hercules (voice), Contact, Another Day in Paradise, John Carpenter's Vampires, The Virgin Suicides, True Crime, Any Given Sunday, The General's Daughter, Race to Space, Play it to the Bone, Final Fantasy (voice), Riding In Cars With Boys, Scary Movie 2, John Q, Stuart Little 2 (voice), The Return to the Onion Field, Northfork.
TELEVISION: *Movies:* Footsteps, A Great American Tragedy, Foster and Laurie, F. Scott Fitzgerald in Hollywood, The Disappearance of Aimee, Raid on Entebbe, Billion Dollar Bubble, The Gift of Love, The Incredible Journey of Dr. Meg Laurel, And Your Name Is Jonah, Badge of the Assassin, Promise (Emmy & Golden Globe Awards, 1987), In Love and War, My Name is Bill W. (Emmy Award, 1989), Women & Men: Stories of Seduction (Hills Like White Elephants), The Boys, Citizen Cohn, Jane's House, Next Door, Curse of the Starving Class, Indictment: The McMartin Trial, The Summer of Ben Tyler, Dirty Pictures, Hercules: Zero to Hero (voice), Founding Brothers, Rudy: The Rudy Giuliani Story. *Specials:* All the Way Home, Crimes of Passion (host), Wildfire (host), Mobs and Mobsters (host), Fallen Angels, A Salute to Martin Scorcese, America's Endangered Species: Don't Say Goodbye (narrator), World's Deadliest Earthquakes. *Mini-series:* Holocaust. *Guest:* Kojak, Rockford Files, Streets of San Francisco, The Rookies, Police Story, Dream On, The Simpsons (voice).

WOODWARD, EDWARD
O.B.E.: Actor, Singer. b. Croydon, England, June 1, 1930. e. Royal Acad. of Dramatic Art. As singer has recorded 11 LPs. 2 Gold Discs. Television Actor of the Year, 1969-70; also Sun Award, Best Actor, 1970-72. Has received 15 national & international awards.
THEATRE: With Royal Shakespeare Company, 1958-59; Cyrano, 20 West End plays and musicals, including The Art of Living, The Little Doctor, A Rattle of a Simple Man (West End/B'way), The High Bid, The Male of the Species, High Spirits (B'way musical), The Best Laid Plans, On Approval, The Wolf, Richard III, The Assassin.
PICTURES: Where There's a Will (debut, 1955), Becket, File on the Golden Goose, Incense for the Damned, Young Winston, Sitting Target, Hunted, Wicker Man, Callan, Stand Up Virgin Soldiers, Breaker Morant, The Appointment, The Final Option (Who Dares Wins), Champions, King David, Mister Johnson, Deadly Advice.
TELEVISION: Series: Callan, Nice Work, The Equalizer (4 Emmy noms.), Golden Globe Award), Over My Dead Body, In Suspicious Cirumstances, Common As Muck, CI5: The New Professionals, Dark Realm. Movies/Specials: Sword of Honour, Bassplayer and Blonde (mini-series), Saturday, Sunday, Monday, Rod of Iron, The Trial of Lady Chatterly, Wet Job–Callan Special, Churchill: The Wilderness Years, Blunt Instrument, Killer Contract, Arthur the King, Uncle Tom's Cabin, A Christmas Carol, Codename: Kyril, Hunted, The Man in the Brown Suit, Hands of a Murderer, World War II, Suspicious Circumstances, The Shamrock Conspiracy, Common as Muck, Gulliver's Travels, Harrison: Cry of the City, Messiah, Night Flight.

WOODWARD, JOANNE
Actress. b. Thomasville, GA, Feb. 27, 1930. m. Paul Newman. e. Louisiana State U. Studied at Neighborhood Playhouse Dramatic Sch. and the Actors Studio. Appeared in many TV dramatic shows.
THEATRE: Picnic, The Lovers, Baby Want a Kiss, Candida, The Glass Menagerie (Williamstown, The Long Wharf), Golden Boy (dir., the Blue Light Theatre Company).
PICTURES: Count Three and Pray (debut, 1955), A Kiss Before Dying, Three Faces of Eve (Academy Award, 1957), No Down Payment, The Long Hot Summer, Rally 'Round the Flag Boys, The Sound and the Fury, The Fugitive Kind, From the Terrace, Paris Blues, The Stripper, A New Kind of Love, Signpost to Murder, A Big Hand for the Little Lady, A Fine Madness, Rachel Rachel (Acad. Award nom.), Winning, WUSA, They Might Be Giants, The Effect of Gamma Rays on Man-in-the-Moon Marigolds, Summer Wishes Winter Dreams (Acad. Award nom.), The Drowning Pool, The End, Harry and Son, The Glass Menagerie, Mr. and Mrs. Bridge (Acad. Award nom.), The Age of Innocence (narrator), Philadelphia, Even If A Hundred Ogres (voice), Remembering the Kindertransports.
TELEVISION: Specials: Broadway's Dreamers: The Legacy of The Group Theater (host, co-prod.; Emmy Award, 1990), Family Thanksgiving Special (dir. only). Movies: Sybil, Come Back Little Sheba, See How She Runs (Emmy Award, 1978), A Christmas to Remember, The Streets of L.A., The Shadow Box, Crisis at Central High, Passions, Do You Remember Love? (Emmy Award, 1985), Foreign Affairs, Blind Spot (also co-prod.), Breathing Lessons, James Dean: A Portrait, Our Town (exec. prod.), Empire Falls.

WOOLDRIDGE, SUSAN
Actress. b. London, England. e. Central Sch. of Speech & Drama/Ecole/Jacques LeCoq. Paris. Ent. ind. 1971.
THEATER: Macbeth, School for Scandal, Merchant of Venice, The Cherry Orchard, Look Back in Anger, 'night Mother, Map of the Heart.
PICTURES: The Shout, Butley, Loyalties, Hope and Glory, How to Get Ahead in Advertising, Bye Bye Blues, Twenty-One, Afraid of the Dark, Just Like a Woman, The Hummingbird Tree.
TELEVISION: The Naked Civil Servant, John McNab, The Racing Game, The Jewel in the Crown, The Last Place on Earth, Hay Fever, Time and the Conways, Dead Man's Folly, The Devil's Disciple, The Dark Room, Pastoralcare, The Small Assassin, A Fine Romance, Ticket to Ride, Changing Step, Pied Piper, Crimestrike, Broke, Miss Pym's Day Out, An Unwanted Woman, The Humming Bird Tree, Inspector Alleyn Mysteries, Tracey Ullman Show, Bad Company, Under the Hammer, All Quiet on the Preston Front, Wycliffe, The Writing Game. Guest: The Ray Bradbury Theatre.

WOPAT, TOM
Actor. b. Lodi, WI, Sept. 9, 1951. e. U. of Wisconsin. Left school to travel for two years with rock group as lead singer and guitarist. Spent two summers at Barn Theater in MI. Came to New York; Off-B'way in a Bistro Car on the CNR. On B'way in I Love My Wife, City of Angels, Guys and Dolls.
TELEVISION: Series: The Dukes of Hazzard, Blue Skies, A Peaceable Kingdom, Cybill, Prime Time Country (host), All My Children. Movies: Christmas Comes to Willow Creek, Burning Rage, Just My Imagination, Contagious, The Dukes of Hazzard: Reunion!, Meteorites.

WORKMAN, CHUCK
Director, Writer, Producer. b. Philadelphia, PA. June 5. e. Rutgers U., B.A.; Cornell U. Pres., International Documentary Assoc. 1987-88; Member: Directors Guild of America, National Board. Lecturer, U. of Southern California. Pres. Calliope Films, Inc. Winner Clio Award, 1969, 1970. Acad. Award, 1987; ShowEast Achievement Award, 1996; Cable Ace Award, 1996.
THEATRE: Bruno's Ghost (1981, writer, dir.), Diplomacy (writer, dir.), The Man Who Wore White Shoes (writer), Bloomers (writer).
PICTURES: Monday's Child (1967, editor), Traitors of San Angel (editor), The Money (dir., s.p.), Protocol (dir., media sequences), Stoogemania (dir., co-s.p.), Precious Images (Acad. Award, Best Live Action Short, 1986; Gold Hugo Award, Cannes Film Fest., N.Y. Film Fest.), Words (Best Short, Houston Fest., N.Y. Film Fest., 1988), Pieces of Silver, Superstar (dir.-prod.), The First 100 Years (dir., prod.), The Source.
DOCUMENTARIES: The Making of the Deep (prod., dir., writer), The Director and the Image (CINE Golden Eagle Award, 1980), The Game, The Best Show in Town (CINE Golden Eagle), And the Winner Is..., The Keeper of the Light.

WORONOV, MARY
Actress. b. Brooklyn, NY, Dec. 8, 1946. e. Cornell. On NY stage in In the Boom Boom Room (Theatre World Award).
PICTURES: The Chelsea Girls, Kemek: It's Controlling Your Mind, Sugar Cookies, Seizure, Cover Girl Models, Death Race 2000, Cannonball, Jackson County Jail, Hollywood Boulevard, Bad Georgia Road, Mr. Billion, The One and Only, The Lady in Red, Rock 'n' Roll High School, National Lampoon Goes to the Movies, Angel of H.E.A.T., Heartbeeps, Eating Raoul, Get Crazy, Night of the Comet, Hellhole, My Man Adam, Nomads, Movie House Massacre, Chopping Mall, Terrorvision, Black Widow, Scenes From the Class Struggle in Beverly Hills, Let It Ride, Mortuary Academy, Dick Tracy, Watchers II, Warlock, Club Fed, Where Sleeping Dogs Lie, Motorama, Good Girls Don't, Hell-Rollers, Grief, Sweet Jane, Looney Tunes: Back in Action.
TELEVISION: Series: Somerset, Flying Blind, Women: Stories of Passion (dir. writer many episodes). Movies: In the Glitter Palace, Challenge of a Lifetime, A Bunny's Tale, Eyes of a Stranger, Shake, Rattle and Rock!, Here Come the Munsters , Acting on Impulse.

WOWCHUK, HARRY N.
Actor, Stunts, Writer, Photographer, Producer, Executive. b. Philadelphia, PA. Oct. 16, 1948. e. Santa Monica City Coll., UCLA, theater arts, 1970. Started film career as actor, stunt-driver-photographer. T.V. and commercial credits include: TV Guide, Seal Test, Camel Cigarettes, Miller High Life, American Motors, Camera V, AW Rootbeer. Former exec. v.p. International Cinema, in chg. of prod. and distribution; V.P. J. Newport Film Productions; pres., United West Productions.
PICTURES: The Lost Dutchman, Las Vegas Lady, This Is a Hijack, Tidal Wave, Tunnel Vision, Incredible 2-Headed Transplant, Jud, Bad Charleston Charlie, Some Call It Loving, Summer School Teachers, Five Minutes of Freedom, Pushing Up Daisies, Money-Marbles-Chalk, The Models, Love Swedish Style, Up-Down-Up, Sunday's Child, Soul Brothers, Freedom Riders, Perilous Journey, Claws of Death, Georgia Peaches, The Pom Pom Girls, The Last American Virgin, Up the Creek, Murphy's Law, Sister, Sister, License to Drive, Phantasm II, Alien Nation, Messenger of Death, See No Evil, Hear No Evil, Robocop 2, Marked for Death,The Hard Way, Deep Cover, The Cowboy Way, Die Hard: With a Vengeance, The Usual Suspects, Batman Forever, Assassins, Carpool, Chain Reaction, Set It Off, City of Industry, Volcano,The End of Violence, Air Force One, Conspiracy Theory, An Alan Smithee Film: Burn Hollywood Burn, The Replacement Killers, The Gingerbread Man, Bulworth, Lethal Weapon 4, Without Limits, Magnolia, The Adventures of Rocky & Bullwinkle, Rush Hour 2,Jay and Silent Bob Strike Back, Bandits, Frailty, Ocean's Eleven, Red Dragon, Star Trek: Nemesis, S.W.A.T., The Last Shot.

WOWCHUK, NICHOLAS
Executive, Producer, Writer, Editor, Financier. b. Philadelphia, PA. e. St. Basil's Coll., UCLA. Founder-publisher: All-American Athlete Magazine, Sports and Health Digest, The Spectator. Former sports writer: Phila. Evening Public Ledger; Phila. Daily Record; Phila. Inquirer. Founder & bd. chmn.: Mutual Realty Investment Co.; Mutual Mortgage Co., Beverly Hills, CA. President: Mutual General Films, Bev. Hills, CA; Abbey Theatrical Films, NY; Mutual Film Distribution Co.; Mutual Recording & Broadcasting Enterprises.
PICTURES: Exec. Prod.: Perilous Journey, The Incredible 2-Headed Transplant, Pushing Up Daisies, Money-Marbles-Chalk, Five Minutes of Freedom, The Campaign, Claws of Death. Prod.: Scorpion's Web, Pursuit, Brave Men, Sea of Despair, Cossacks in Battle, The Straight White Line, Tilt, Rooster, To Live... You Gotta Win.

WRAY, FAY
Actress. b. Alberta, Canada, Sept. 15, 1907. On stage in Pilgrimage Play, Hollywood, 1923; m.p. debut in Gasoline Love; thereafter in many m.p. for Paramount to 1930; then in films for various Hollywood and Brit. prod. Autobiography: On the Other Hand (1989).
PICTURES: Streets of Sin, The Wedding March, The Four Feathers, The Texan, Dirigible, Doctor X, The Most Dangerous Game, The Vampire Bat, The Mystery of the Wax Museum, King Kong, The Bowery, Madame Spy, The Affairs of Cellini, The Clairvoyant, They Met in a Taxi, Murder in Greenwich Village, The Jury's Secret, Smashing the Spy Ring, Navy Secrets, Wildcat Bus, Adam Had Four Sons, Melody for Three, Not a Ladies' Man, Small Town Girl, Treasure of the Golden Condor, Queen Bee, The Cobweb, Hell on Frisco Bay, Crime of Passion, Rock Pretty Baby, Tammy and the Bachelor, Summer Love, Dragstrip Riot, Frank Capra's American Dream, Off the Menu: The Last Days of Chasen's, Broadway: The Golden Age By the Legends Who Were There.
TELEVISION: Series: Pride of the Family. Movie: Gideon's Trumpet.

WRIGHT, AMY
Actress. b. Chicago, IL, Apr. 15, 1950. e. Beloit Col. Studied acting with Uta Hagen; 1976, joined Rip Torn's Sanctuary Theatre. B'way in Fifth of July, Noises Off, Mrs. Klein.
PICTURES: Not a Pretty Picture, Girlfriends, The Deer Hunter, Breaking Away, The Amityville Horror, Heartland, Wise Blood, Stardust Memories, Inside Moves, Off Beat, The Telephone, Crossing Delancey, The Accidental Tourist, Miss Firecracker, Daddy's Dyin', Deceived, Love Hurts, Hard Promises, Josh and S.A.M., Tom and Huck, Where the Rivers Flow North, The Scarlet Letter, Joe Henry, Besotted.
TELEVISION: Movies: Trapped in Silence, Settle the Score, Vaclav Havel's 'Largo Desolato', In the Line of Duty: Manhunt in the Dakotas, Final Verdict, To Dance With the White Dog, Amy & Isabelle. Special: Largo Desolato. Pilot: A Fine Romance.

WRIGHT, ROBERT C.
Executive. b. Hempstead, NY, April 23, 1943. e. Coll. Holy Cross, B.A. history, 1965; U. of Virginia, LLB 1968. Mem. NY, VA, MA, NJ Bar. 1969, joined General Electric; lawyer in plastics div. Later moved into product & sls. management in plastics div. 1980, moved to Cox Cable as pres. Returned to GE 1983 heading small appliances div.; moved to GE Financial Services & GE Credit Corp. as pres., which posts he held when named head of NBC following purchase of NBC's parent RCA by GE. Pres. and CEO, National Broadcasting Co. (NBC), 1986-. Humanitarian Award from Foundation Fighting Blindness, 1995.

WRIGHT, TERESA
Actress. b. New York, NY, Oct. 27, 1918. e. Columbia H.S., Maplewood, NJ, 1938.
THEATRE: Mary Mary, Tchin-Tchin, The Effect of Gamma Rays on Man-in-the-Moon Marigolds, Noel Coward in Two Keys, The Master Builder. Regional: Long Day's Journey into Night, You Can't Take It With You, All The Way Home, Wings. NY: Life with Father, Dark at the Top of the Stairs, I Never Sang for My Father,
Death of a Salesman, Ah Wilderness!, Morning's at Seven (also London), On Borrowed Time.
PICTURES: The Little Foxes (debut, 1941), Pride of the Yankees, Mrs. Miniver (Academy Award, best supporting actress, 1942), Shadow of a Doubt, Casanova Brown, The Best Years of Our Lives, The Trouble With Women, Pursued, Imperfect Lady, Enchantment, The Capture, The Men, Something to Live For, California Conquest, Steel Trap, Count the Hours, The Actress, Track of the Cat, The Search for Bridey Murphy, Escapade in Japan, The Restless Years, Hail Hero, The Happy Ending, Roseland, Somewhere in Time, The Good Mother, The Red Coat, The Rainmaker.
TELEVISION: Specials: The Margaret Bourke-White Story, The Miracle Worker, The Golden Honeymoon, The Fig Tree, A Century of Women. Movies: Crawlspace, The Elevator, Flood, Bill—On His Own, Perry Mason: The Case of the Desperate Deception, Lethal Innocence, Diamonds on the Silver Screen. Mini-series: A Century of Women. Guest: The U.S. Steel Hour, Climax, The Alcoa Hour, Playhouse 90, Picket Fences.

WUHL, ROBERT
Actor, Writer. b. Union, NJ, Oct. 9, 1951. e. Univ. of Houston. Worked as stand-up comedian and joke writer. Was story editor on series Police Squad! Appeared in 1988 Academy Award winning short Ray's Male Heterosexual Dance Hall.
PICTURES: The Hollywood Knights (debut, 1980), Flashdance, Good Morning Vietnam, Bull Durham, Batman, Blaze, Wedding Band, Hollywood Mistress, The Bodyguard, A Kiss Goodnight, Blue Chips, Cobb, Dr. Jekyll and Ms. Hyde, Open Season (also dir., s.p.), Good Burger.
TELEVISION: Series: Police Squad!, Sledge Hammer!, Arli$$. Pilots: Rockhopper, Sniff. Guest: Tales from the Crypt, Moonlighting, L.A. Law, Falcon Crest. Specials: The Big Bang (also dir.), Comic Relief IV, The Earth Day Special, The Real Deal. Movies: Percy & Thunder, The Last Don, The Last Don II,

A Kiss Goodnight, Writer: Police Squad, Sledge Hammer, Grammy Awards (1987-89), Academy Awards (Emmy Award, 1991).

WYATT, JANE
Actress. b. Campgaw, NJ, Aug. 12, 1910. e. Miss Chapin's Sch.; Barnard Coll. m. Edgar B. Ward. Joined Apprentice Sch., Berkshire Playhouse, Stockbridge, Mass. Understudied in Tradewinds and The Vinegar Tree. Appeared in Give Me Yesterday and the Tadpole. In 1933 succeeded Margaret Sullavan in Dinner at Eight.
THEATRE: The Autumn Garden (NY), The Bishop Misbehaves, Conquest, Eveningsong, The Mad Hopes, Hope for the Best, The Joyous Season For Services Rendered, Driving Miss Daisy, Love Letters.
PICTURES: One More River (debut, 1934), Great Expectations, We're Only Human, The Luckiest Girl in the World, Lost Horizon, The Girl From God's Country, Kisses for Breakfast, Hurricane Smith, Weekend for Three, Army Surgeon, The Navy Comes Through, The Kansan, Buckskin Frontier, None But the Lonely Heart, Strange Conquest, The Bachelor's Daughters, Boomerang!, Gentleman's Agreement,
Pitfall, No Minor Vices, Bad Boy, Canadian Pacific, Task Force, House By the River, Our Very Own, My Blue Heaven, The Man Who Cheated Himself, Criminal Lawyer, Interlude, Two Little Bears, Never Too Late, Treasure of Matecumbe, Star Trek IV: The Voyage Home.
TELEVISION: Series: Father Knows Best (1954-59; 3 Emmy Awards: 1957, 1958, 1959), Confidential For Women. Guest: Bob Hope Chrysler Theater, The Virginian, Wagon Train, U.S. Steel Hour, Bell Telephone Hour, My Father My Mother, Barefoot in the Park, The Ghost and Mrs. Muir, Here Come the Brides, Love American Style, Fantasy Island, Love Boat. Movies: Katherine, Tom Sawyer, Father Knows Best Reunion, A Love Affair, Amelia Earhart, Superdome, The Nativity, The Millionaire, Missing Children—A Mother's Story, Legacy of the Hollywood Blacklist, Amityville: The Evil Escapes, Neighbors, Ladies of the Corridor, Star Trek, Frank Capra's American Dream, Simisola.

WYMAN, THOMAS H.
Executive. b. 1931. Joined CBS, Inc. in 1980 as pres. & chief exec. Then chmn until 1986. William H. Donaldson Faculty Fellow at Yale School of Mgmt., 1987. Prior career as chief exec. of Green Giant Co.; became v. chmn. to 1988, of Pillsbury Co. when it acquired Green Giant in 1979. Chairman of Bd., Amherst College. Trustee, Ford Foundation.

WYNN, TRACY KEENAN
Writer. b. Hollywood, CA, Feb. 28, 1945. e. UCLA Theatre Arts Dept., BA in film/TV division, 1967. Fourth generation in show business: son of actor Keenan Wynn, grandson of Ed Wynn, great-grandson of Frank Keenan, Irish Shakespearean actor who made B'way debut in 1880.
PICTURES: The Longest Yard, The Drowning Pool (co-s.p.), The Deep (co. s.p.), Robinson Crusoe, Mean Machine.
TELEVISION: Series: The Net. Movies: The Glass House, Tribes (also assoc. prod.: Emmy & WGA Awards, 1971), The Autobiography of Miss Jane Pittman (Emmy Award & WGA Awards, 1974), Hit Lady (dir. only), The Quest, The Quest: The Longest Drive, In the Line of Duty: The F.B.I. Murders, Bloody Friday (also co-prod.), Capone in Jail, Carolina Skeletons.

Y

YABLANS, FRANK
Executive. b. Brooklyn, NY, Aug. 27, 1935. Entered m.p. ind. as Warner Bros. booker, 1957. Warner Bros. salesman in N.Y., Boston, Milwaukee, Chicago, 1957-59. Milwaukee br. mgr. Buena Vista, 1959-66. Midwest sales mgr., Sigma III, 1966. Eastern sales mgr., 1967, sales v.p. 1968. V.P. general sales mgr., Paramount Pic. Corp., 1969; v.p.-dist., 1970; sr. v.p.-mkt., 1970; exec. v.p., 1971; named pres. 1971. 1975, became an indep. prod. for his company, Frank Yablans Presentations Inc. 1983, MGM/UA Entertainment Co. as bd. chmn. & CEO. Held titles of bd. chmn. & CEO with both MGM and UA Corp when resigned, 1985. Same year teamed with PSO Delphi to form Northstar Entertainment Co.; 1986, non-exclusive deal with Empire Entertainment; 1988, non-exclusive 3-year deal with Columbia Pictures; 1989, pres. Epic Prods., pres., CEO Nova Intl. Films Inc.
PICTURES: Producer: Silver Streak (exec. prod.), The Other Side of Midnight, The Fury, North Dallas Forty (also co-s.p.), Mommie Dearest (also co-s.p.), Monsignor (co.-prod), Star Chamber, Kidco, Buy and Cell, Lisa, Congo (exec. prod.), A Dog of Flanders.

YABLANS, IRWIN
Executive. b. Brooklyn, NY, July 25, 1934. Began career in industry at WB in 1956 after two-yr. stint with U.S. Army in Germany. Held m.p. sales posts in Washington, DC, Albany, Detroit, Milwaukee and Portland. In 1962 joined Paramount as L.A. mgr.; in 1964 made western sales mgr. In 1972 entered

production as assoc. prod. on Howard W. Koch's Badge 373. Pres. of Compass Int'l. Pictures. Exec. v.p., low budget films, Lorimar Productions. Resigned June, 1984. In 1985 named chmn., Orion Pictures Distributing Corp. 1988: named chmn. and CEO of newly formed Epic Pictures.
PICTURES: The Education of Sonny Carson. *Exec. prod.*: Halloween, Roller Boogie (also story), Fade To Black (also story), Seduction (prod.), Halloween II, Halloween III: Season of the Witch, Parasite, Tank, Hell Night, Prison Arena, Why Me?, Men at Work.

YATES, PETER
Producer, Director. b. Ewshoot, England, July 24, 1929. e. Royal Acad. of Dramatic Art. Entered m.p. ind. as studio mgr. and dubbing asst. with De Lane Lea. Asst. dir.: The Entertainer, The Guns of Navarone, A Taste of Honey, The Roman Spring of Mrs. Stone. Stage dir.: The American Dream, The Death of Bessie Smith, Passing Game, Interpreters. Received Acad. Award noms.for Best Director/Picture (Producer): Breaking Away, The Dresser.
PICTURES: Summer Holiday, One Way Pendulum, Robbery (also co-s.p.), Bullitt, John and Mary, Murphy's War, The Hot Rock, The Friends of Eddie Coyle, For Pete's Sake, Mother Jugs and Speed (also prod.), The Deep, Breaking Away (also prod.), Eyewitness (also prod.), Krull, The Dresser (also prod.), Eleni, Suspect, The House on Carroll Street (also prod.), An Innocent Man, Year of the Comet (also co-prod.), Needful Things (exec. prod. only), Roommates, The Run of the Country (also co-prod.).
TELEVISION: *Series:* Danger Man (Secret Agent), The Saint. *Movies:* Koroshi, Nunsense, Don Quixote, A Separate Peace.

YELLEN, LINDA
Producer, Director, Writer. b. New York, NY, July 13, 1949. e. Barnard Coll., B.A.; Columbia U., M.F.A., Ph.D. Lecturer Barnard Coll.; Yale U.; asst. professor, City U. of N.Y. Member: exec. council, DGA.
THEATRE: Chantilly Lace (dir., prod., writer), Parallel Lives (dir., prod. writer).
PICTURES: The End of Summer (dir., prod., s.p.), Looking Up (prod., dir.), Prospera, Come Out Come Out, Everybody Wins (prod.).
TELEVISION: *Movies:* Mayflower: The Pilgrims' Adventure (prod.), Playing for Time (exec. prod.; Emmy, Peabody & Christopher Awards, 1980), Hardhat and Legs (prod.), The Royal Romance of Charles and Diana (exec. prod., co-writer), Prisoner Without a Name Cell Without a Number (prod., dir., co-writer; Peabody & WGA Awards), Second Serve (exec. prod.), Liberace: Behind the Music (exec. prod.), Sweet Bird of Youth (exec. prod.), Rebound (dir., co-writer), Chantilly Lace (prod., dir., writer, story), Parallel Lives (prod., dir., writer, story), End of Summer (exec. prod., dir., written by), Northern Lights (dir.).

YEOH, MICHELLE
Actress. r.n. Yeoh Chu-Kheng. b. Ipoh, Malaysia, August 6, 1962. Has acted under the name Michelle Khan.
PICTURES: In the Line of Duty, Magnificent Warriors, The Heroic Trio, Police Story 3: Supercop, Butterfly Sword, Heroic Trio 2: Executioners, Seven Maidens, Tai-Chi, Wing Chun, The Stunt Woman, The Soong Sisters, Tomorrow Never Dies, Moonlight Express, Crouching Tiger, Hidden Dragon, The Touch.

YORDAN, PHILIP
Writer. b. Chicago, IL, April 1, 1914. e. U. of Illinois, B.A., Kent Coll. of Law, LL.D. Was attorney, then author, prod., playwright (Anna Lucasta). Began screen writing 1942 with collab. s.p. Syncopation.
PICTURES: Syncopation, The Unknown Guest, Johnny Doesn't Live Here Anymore, When Strangers Marry, Dillinger, Whistle Stop, Suspense, The Chase, Reign of Terror, Bad Men of Tombstone, Anna Lucasta, House of Strangers, Edge of Doom, Drums in the Deep South, Detective Story, Mutiny, Mara Maru, Man Crazy, Houdini, Blowing Wild, The Naked Jungle, Broken Lance, Johnny Guitar, Joe MacBeth, Conquest of Space, The Big Combo, Man from Laramie, The Last Frontier, The Harder They Fall, No Down Payment, Gun Glory, Four Boys and a Gun, Men in War, The Fiend Who Walked the West, The Bravados, God's Little Acre, Day of the Outlaw, The Bramble Bush, Studs Lonigan, King of Kings, El Cid, The Day of the Triffids, 55 Days at Peking, Fall of the Roman Empire, Circus World, Battle of the Bulge, Royal Hunt of the Sun, Captain Apache, Bad Man's River, Night Train to Terror, Fort Saganne, Bloody Wednesday, Cry Wilderness, The Unholy.
(d. March 24, 2003).

YORK, MICHAEL
Actor. r.n. Michael York-Johnson. b. Fulmer, England, March 27, 1942. Early career with Oxford U. Dramatic Society and National Youth Theatre; later Dundee Repertory, National Theatre. Chmn., California Youth Theatre. 1992 *Autobiography*: Accidentally on Purpose (Simon & Schuster).
THEATRE: Any Just Cause, Hamlet, Ring Round the Moon (Los Angeles), Cyrano de Bergerac, Ira Gershwin At 100. B'way: Outcry, Bent, The Little Prince and the Aviator, Whisper in the Mind, The Crucible, Someone Who'll Watch Over Me, Nora.
PICTURES: The Taming of the Shrew, Accident, Red and Blue,

Smashing Time, Romeo and Juliet, The Strange Affair, The Guru, Alfred the Great, Justine, Something for Everyone, Zeppelin, La Poudre D'Escampette, Cabaret, England Made Me, Lost Horizon, The Three Musketeers, Murder on the Orient Express, The Four Musketeers, Conduct Unbecoming, Logan's Run, Seven Nights in Japan, The Last Remake of Beau Geste, The Island of Dr. Moreau, Fedora, The Riddle of the Sands (also assoc. prod.), Final Assignment, The White Lions, The Weather in the Streets, Success Is the Best Revenge, Dawn, Lethal Obsession (Der Joker), The Return of the Musketeers, Phantom of Death, Megiddo, The Secret of the Sahara, Midnight Cop, The Wanderer, The Long Shadow, Wide Sargasso Sea, Rochade, Discretion Assured, The Shadow of a Kiss, Gospa, Goodbye America, Austin Powers: International Man of Mystery, Dark Planet, The Treat, Perfect Little Angels, Wrongfully Accused, 54, Austin Powers: The Spy Who Shagged Me, The Omega Code, The Haunting of Hell House, Puss in Boots, Borstal Boy, Megiddo: The Omega Code 2, In Search of Peace (doc. voice), Austin Powers: Goldmember.
TELEVISION: *Series:* The Forsyte Saga, Knots Landing, The Human Adventure, Liberty's Kids. *Mini-Series:* Jesus of Nazareth, A Man Called Intrepid, Au nom de tous les miens, Il Segreto del Sahara, Till We Meet Again, La Nouvelle tribu, The Great War and the Shaping of the 20th Century, Founding Fathers, La Femme Musketeer. *Specials:* The Forsyte Saga, Rebel in the Grave, True Patriot, Much Ado About Nothing. *Series:* Knots Landing. *Guest:* Seaquest, The Naked Truth, Babylon 5, Sliders. *Movies:* Great Expectations, The Phantom of the Opera, The Master of Ballantrae, Space, For Those I Loved, The Far Country, Dark Mansions, Sword of Gideon, Four Minute Mile, The Lady and the Highwayman, The Heat of the Day, Till We Meet Again, Night of the Fox, A Duel of Love, The Road to Avonlea, Charles Dickens' David Copperfield (voice), Fall from Grace, Tek War: Tek Lab, September, A Young Connecticut Yankee in King Arthur's Court, Not of This Earth, The Out of Towner, Danielle Steel's The Ring, True Women, The Ripper, Perfect Little Angels, A Knight in Camelot, Glory, Glory .Host: The Hunt for Stolen War Treasure, The Magic Paint Brush, Gardens of the World.

YORK, SUSANNAH
Actress. b. London, England, Jan. 9, 1941. Ent. tv 1959; m.p. 1960. Author: In Search of Unicorns, Lark's Castle.
THEATRE: A Cheap Bunch of Flowers, Wings of the Dove, Singular Life of Albert Nobbs, Man and Superman, Mrs. Warren's Profession, Peter Pan, The Maids, Private Lives, The Importance of Being Earnest, Hedda Gabler (N.Y.), Agnes of God, The Human Voice, Penthesilea, Fatal Attraction, The Apple Cart, Private Treason, Lyric for a Tango, The Glass Menagerie, A Streetcar Named Desire, September Tide. Produced The Big One, a variety show for peace, 1984.
PICTURES: Tunes of Glory (debut, 1960), There Was a Crooked Man, Greengage Summer (Loss of Innocence), Freud, Tom Jones, The Seventh Dawn, Sands of the Kalahari, Kaleidoscope, A Man for All Seasons, Sebastian, Duffy, The Killing of Sister George, Oh What a Lovely War, The Battle of Britain, Lock Up Your Daughters, They Shoot Horses Don't They? (Acad. Award nom.), Brotherly Love (Country Dance), Zee & Co. (X Y & Zee), Happy Birthday Wanda June, Images, The Maids, Gold, Conduct Unbecoming, That Lucky Touch, Sky Riders, The Silent Partner, Superman, The Shout, Falling in Love Again, The Awakening, Superman II, Loophole, Yellowbeard, Land of Faraway, Superman IV (voice), Prettykill, Bluebeard Bluebeard, A Summer Story, American Roulette, Diamond's Edge, Melancholia, En Hanfull Tio, Fate, Pretty Princess.
TELEVISION: *Movies:* The Crucible, The Rebel and the Soldier, The First Gentleman, The Richest Man in the World, Slaughter of St. Teresa's Day, Kiss On A Grass Green Pillow, Fallen Angels, Prince Regent, Second Chance, Betjeman's Briton, We'll Meet Again, Jane Eyre, A Christmas Carol, Star Quality, Macho, Return Journey, After the War, The Man From the Pru, The Haunting of the New, Devices and Desires, Boon, Little Women, Illusions. *Series:* Second Chance, We'll Meet Again,Trainer, Holby City . *Mini-Series:* Prince Regent, After the War, Devices and Desires.

YORKIN, BUD
Producer, Director. r.n. Alan Yorkin. b. Washington, PA, Feb. 22, 1926. e. Carnegie Tech., Columbia U. U.S. Navy, 1942-45. Began career in tv in NBC's engineering dept. Moved into prod., first as stage mgr., then assoc. dir. of Colgate Comedy Hour (Martin and Lewis) and dir. of Dinah Shore Show. Formed Tandem Productions with Norman Lear; 1974 formed own production co.
PICTURES: Come Blow Your Horn (dir., co-prod., adapt.), Never Too Late (dir.), Divorce American Style (dir.), The Night They Raided Minsky's (exec. prod.), Inspector Clouseau (dir.), Start the Revolution Without Me (prod., dir.), Cold Turkey (exec. prod.), Thief Who Came to Dinner (prod., dir.), Deal of the Century (prod.), Twice in a Lifetime (prod., dir.), Arthur 2 on the Rocks (dir.), Love Hurts (prod., dir.), For the Boys (actor), Intersection (co-prod.).
TELEVISION: *Series dir:* Songs at Twilight, Martin & Lewis Show, Abbott and Costello Show, Spike Jones Show, The Soldiers, Tony Martin Show (also prod., writer), The Colgate Comedy Hour , George Gobel Show, The Ford Show Starring

Tennesse Ernie Ford (also prod.), The Andy Williams Show , Specials (dir.): An Evening with Fred Astaire (Emmy Award, 1959), Another Evening with Fred Astaire, The Jack Benny Hour Specials (Emmy Award, 1960), Henry Fonda and the Family, We Love You Madly with Duke Ellington, TV Guide Awards Show, Bobby Darin and Friends, Danny Kaye Special, Where It's At with Dick Cavett, Many Sides of Don Rickles, Robert Young and the Family, Owner. Series co-prod.: All In The Family, Sanford and Son, Maude, Good Times, What's Happening!, Carter Country, Sanford Arms, Diff'rent Strokes, Archie Bunker's Place, One in a Million. Movies: I Love Liberty.

YOUNG, ALAN
Actor. r.n. Angus Young. b. North Shield, Northumberland, England, Nov. 19, 1919. First acted as monologist for 13 years in Canada; radio comedian 10 yrs. in Canada and U.S. Served in Canadian Navy as sub-lt. 1942-44. Wrote, dir. and acted in comedy broadcasts.
AUTHOR: Mister Ed and Me.
PICTURES: Margie (debut, 1946), Chicken Every Sunday, Mr. Belvedere Goes to College, Aaron Slick from Punkin Crick, Androcles and the Lion, Gentlemen Marry Brunettes, Tom Thumb, Baker's Hawk, The Cat from Outer Space, The Great Mouse Detective (voice), Duck Tales: The Movie (voice), Beverly Hills Cop III, The Time Machine.
TELEVISION: Series: The Alan Young Show (Emmy Award, 1950), Saturday Night Revue, Mr. Ed, Coming of Age. Movies: Earth Angel, Hart to Hart: Home is Where the Hart Is.

YOUNG, BURT
Actor, Writer. b. New York, NY, April 30, 1940. Worked at variety of jobs (boxer, trucker, etc.) before turning to acting and joining Actor's Studio. Appeared in off-B'way plays which led to Hollywood career. On B'way in Cuba and His Teddy Bear.
PICTURES: The Gang that Couldn't Shoot Straight, Carnival of Blood, Across 110th Street, Cinderella Liberty, Chinatown, The Gambler, Murph the Surf, You Can't Steal Love, The Killer Elite, Rocky (Acad. Award nom.), Harry & Walter Go to New York, Twilight's Last Gleaming, The Choirboys, Uncle Joe Shannon (s.p. only), Convoy, Uncle Joe Shannon (also s.p.), Rocky II, Blood Beach, ...All the Marbles, Rocky III, Lookin' To Get Out, Amityville II: The Possession, Over the Brooklyn Bridge, Once Upon a Time in America, The Pope of Greenwich Village, Rocky IV, Back to School, Bandini, Going Overboard, Blood Red, Beverly Hills Brats, Last Exit to Brooklyn, Medium Rare, Betsy's Wedding, Wait Until Spring Bandini, Diving In, Backstreet Dreams, Rocky V, Bright Angel, Red American, Club Fed, Excessive Force, North Star, Red Blooded American Girl II, The Undertaker's Wedding, She's So Lovely, Kicked in the Head, Heaven Before I Die, Firehouse, The Deli, The Mouse, Mickey Blue-Eyes, Loser Love, The Florentine, Blue Moon, The Adventures of Pluto Nash.
TELEVISION: Series: Roomies, Alternate Realities. Guest: M*A*S*H, The Rockford Files, Miami Vice, The Equalizer, Alfred Hitchcock Presents, Tales From the Crypt, Miami Vice, The Equilizer, Law & Order, Walker Texas Ranger, The Outer Limits, Law & Order. Movies: The Great Niagara, Hustling, Serpico: The Deadly Game, Woman of the Year, Daddy I Don't Like It Like This (also s.p.), Murder Can Hurt You, A Summer to Remember, Vendetta: Secrets of a Mafia Bride, Double Deception, Vendetta 2: The New Mafia, Before Women Had Wings, Greener Fields. Mini-series: The Maharaja's Daughter, Crocodile Shoes, The Last Don.

YOUNG, CHRIS
Actor. b. Chambersburg, PA, April 28, 1971. Stage debut in college production of Pippin, followed by On Golden Pond.
PICTURES: The Great Outdoors (debut, 1988), Book of Love, December, The Runestone, Warlock: The Armageddon, PCU, Deep Down, Falling Sky, The Brave Little Toaster Goes to Mars (voice).
TELEVISION: Series: Max Headroom, Falcon Crest, Live-In, Married People, The Adventures of A.R.K. (dir.), The New Adventures of A.R.K. (exec. prod. dir.). Pilot: Jake's Journey. Movies: Dance 'Til Dawn, Breaking the Silence, MacShayne: The Final Roll of the Dice, Runaway Daughters, Killing Mr. Griffin. Special: Square One. Guest: Crime & Punishment.

YOUNG, KAREN
Actress. b. Pequonnock, NJ, Sept. 29, 1958. Trained at Image Theatre/Studio in NYC.
THEATRE: A Lie of the Mind, 3 Acts of Recognition, Five of Us, Mud People.
PICTURES: Deep in the Heart (debut, 1983), Almost You, Birdy, 9-1/2 Weeks, Heat, Jaws the Revenge, Torch Song Trilogy, Criminal Law, Night Game, The Boy Who Cried Bitch, Hoffa, Love & Human Remains, The Wife, Daylight, Pants on Fire, Pleasant View Avenue, Joe Henry.
TELEVISION: Movies: The Execution of Raymond Graham, The 10 Million Dollar Getaway, The Summer My Father Grew Up, Drug Wars: The Cocaine Cartel, On the Edge of Innocence. Guest: The Equalizer.

YOUNG, ROBERT M.
Director. b. New York, NY, Nov. 22, 1924. e. Harvard.
PICTURES: Nothing But a Man (prod., co-s.p.), The Plot Against Harry (co-prod., photog.), Short Eyes, Rich Kids, One-Trick Pony, The Ballad of Gregorio Cortez (also s.p. adapt.), Alambrista! (also s.p., photog.), Extremities, Saving Grace, Dominick and Eugene, Triumph of the Spirit, Talent for the Game, American Me (co-prod. only), Children of Fate (exec. dir. & exec. prod. only), Roosters, Caught, China: The Panda Adventure.
TELEVISION: Series: Visions, Tales of the Unexpected (writer). Specials: Sit-In, Angola—Journey to a War (Peabody Award), The Inferno (Cortile Cascino; also prod., writer, edit.), Anatomy of a Hospital, The Eskimo: Fight for Life (Emmy Award, 1971). Movie: J.T., Solomon and Sheba, We Are the Children, Slave of Dreams.

YOUNG, SEAN
Actress. r.n. Mary Sean Young. b. Louisville, KY, Nov. 20, 1959. e. Interlochen Arts Acad., MI, studied dance, voice, flute and writing. After graduating, moved to N.Y., and signed with ICM. Shortly after signing with ICM debuted in Jane Austen in Manhattan. On L.A. Stage in Stardust.
PICTURES: Jane Austen in Manhattan (debut, 1980), Stripes, Blade Runner, Young Doctors in Love, Dune, Baby: The Secret of the Lost Legend, No Way Out, Wall Street, The Boost, Cousins, Fire Birds, A Kiss Before Dying, Love Crimes, Once Upon a Crime, Hold Me Thrill Me Kiss Me, Forever,Fatal Instinct, Ace Ventura: Pet Detective, Even Cowgirls Get the Blues, Mirage, Dr. Jekyll and Ms. Hyde, The Proprietor, Motel Blue, Exception to the Rule, The Invader, Men, Out of Control, Special Delivery, Poor White Trash, The Amati Girls, Sugar & Spice, In the Shadow of the Cobra.
TELEVISION: Series: A Force of One. Special: Under the Biltmore Clock. Mini-Series: Tender Is the Night, Kingpin. Movies: Blood and Orchids, Under the Biltmore Clock, The Sketch Artist, Blue Ice, Witness to the Execution, Model by Day, Evil Has a Face, Barbara Taylor Bradford Trilogy: Everything to Gain, The Cowboy and the Movie Star, Secret Cutting, 1st to Die, The King and Queen of Moonlight Bay, Before I Say Goodbye.

YU, JESSICA
Director. b. 1966. e. Yale University.
PICTURES: Sour Death Balls, Breathing Lessons: The Life and Work of Mark O'Brien (also edit., prod., s.p.; Academy Award), Better Late, The Living Museum (also edit.; nom. Grand Jury prize, Sundance Film Fest.).
PICTURES: Picture Bride, Maya Lin: A Strong Clear Vision.
TELEVISION: Series: ER, The West Wing, The Guardian.

YULIN, HARRIS
Actor. b. Los Angeles, Nov. 5, 1937. On B'way in Watch on the Rhine, A Lesson from Aloes, etc. Founder of the Los Angeles Classic Theatre.
THEATRE: Numerous productions including: The Little Foxes, Who's Afraid of Virginia Woolf?, Becket, The Entertainer, Uncle Vanya, Tempest, Timon of Athens, The Seagull, A Midsummer Night's Dream, Hamlet, Julius Caesar, Tartuffe, Henry V, The Visit (B'way), Arms and the Man, It's a Mad Mad World, Arts and Leisure, Diary of Anne Frank, The Visit. Director: Baba Goya, The Front Page, The Guardsman, Sheba, The Man Who Came to Dinner, Guns of Carrar, Cuba Si, Candida, Don Juan in Hell, Jitta's Atonement, As You Like It, The Rehearsal, After the Fall, Winterplay, Last Meeting of the Knights of the White Magnolia.
PICTURES: End of the Road, Doc, The Midnight Man, Night Moves, Steel, Scarface, The Believers, Fatal Beauty, Candy Mountain, Bad Dreams, Judgement in Berlin, Another Woman, Ghostbusters II, Narrow Margin, Final Analysis, There Goes the Neighborhood, Clear and Present Danger, Stuart Saves His Family, The Baby-sitters Club, Looking for Richard, Multiplicity, Loch Ness, Bean,Cradle Will Rock, The Hurricane, The Million Dollar Hotel, Rush Hour 2, American Outlaws, Training Day, Chelsea Walls, The Emperor's Club.
TELEVISION: Specials/Movies: Melvin Purvis: G-Man, The Greatest Gift, Alvin Karpis: Public Enemy No. 1, The Kansas City Massacre, The Americans, Victory at Entebbe, The Thirteenth Day—The Story of Esther, The Night Rider, When Every Day Was the Fourth of July, Missiles of October, Conspiracy: Trial of the Chicago Seven, Last Ride of the Dalton Gang, Robert Kennedy and His Times, Tailspin: Behind the Korean Airlines Tragedy, Daughter of the Streets, Face of a Stranger, The Heart of Justice, The Last Hit, Incident at Vichy, How the West Was Won, Truman, If These Walls Could Talk, Hostile Waters, The Virginian. Series: As the World Turns, WIOU, Frasier, Mister Sterling.

YUN-FAT, CHOW
Actor. b. May 18, 1955, Nam Nga Island, Hong Kong. Has won several awards in Asia, including Hong Kong Best Actor Award 3 times, Taiwan Golden Horse Best Actor Award twice, and Asian Pacific Festival Best Actor Award. CineAsia, the Asian Theatre Owners Convention, named him the Star of the Decade.
PICTURES: Massage Girls, Heroic Cops, Miss O, See-Bar, Patrol Horse, Woo Yuet's Story, Blood Money, Shanghai Beach, Shanghai Beach 2, The Head Hunter, Flower City, Love in a

Fallen City, The Occupant, Waiting for Daybreak, Woman, Witch from Nepal, The Story of Rose, The Phantom Bride, The Seventh Curse, A Better Tomorrow, A Hearty Response, 100 Ways to Murder Your Wife, You Will I Will, Dream Lovers, Lunatic's True Story, Love Unto Waste, The Missed Date, Blacklist, A Better Tomorrow II, Heroic Hero, Scared Stiff, City on Fire, An Autumn's Tale, Dragon and Tiger Fight, Drifter Love, Prison Turbulence, The Romancing Star, Goodbye My Friend, Legend of Yu Ta Fu,City War, Tiger Goes on the Beat, The Greatest Lover, Diary of a Big Man, Fractured Follies, The Eighth Happiness, All About Ah-Long, A Better Tomorrow III, Brotherhood, The Inside Story, The Fun The Luck and the Tycoon, God of Gamblers, The Killer, Wild Search, Once a Thief, Black Vengeance, Prison on Fire II, Full Contact, Now You See Love Now You Don't, Hard-Boiled, All for the Winner, Treasure Hunt, God of Gamblers Returns, The Peach Hotel, The Replacement Killers, The Corruptor, Anna and the King, Crouching Tiger, Hidden Dragon, King's Ransom, Bulletproof Monk.
TELEVISION: *Movies:* The Reincarnation.

Z

ZAENTZ, SAUL
Producer. b. Passaic, NJ. Feb. 28, 1921. Irving R. Thalberg Award, 1997.
PICTURES: One Flew Over the Cuckoo's Nest (Acad. Award: Best Picture, 1975), Three Warriors, The Lord of the Rings, Amadeus (Acad. Award: Best Picture, 1984), The Mosquito Coast (exec. prod.), The Unbearable Lightness of Being, At Play in the Fields of the Lord, The English Patient (Acad. Award: Best Picture, 1996).

ZAHN, STEVE
Actor. b. Marshall, MN, Nov. 13, 1968.
PICTURES: Rain Without Thunder, Reality Bites, Crimson Tide, That Thing You Do!, Race the Sun, SubUrbia, The Object of My Affection, Out of Sight, Safe Men, You've Got Mail, Hamlet, Freaks Talk About Sex, Forces of Nature, Happy Texas, Stuart Little (voice), Hamlet, Chain of Fools, Squelch, Saving Silverman, Dr. Dolittle 2 (voice), Joy Ride, Chelsea Walls Riding in Cars with Boys, Stuart Little 2 (voice), National Security, Daddy Day Care.
TELEVISION: *Movies:* Subway Stories: Tales from the Underground, From the Earth to the Moon. *Guest:* Friends.

ZAILLIAN, STEVEN
Writer. Director. b. Jan. 30, 1951.
PICTURES: Kingdom of the Spiders (editor), The Falcon and the Snowman, Awakenings, Jack the Bear, Searching for Bobby Fischer (also dir.), Schindler's List (Acad. Award, 1993; WGA & Golden Globe Awards), Clear and Present Danger (co-s.p.), Mission: Impossible (co-s.p.), Amistad, A Civil Action, Hannibal, Gangs of New York.

ZANE, BILLY
Actor. b. Chicago, IL, Feb. 24, 1966. Sister is actress Lisa Zane. Studied acting at American School in Switzerland. To Hollywood in 1984 landing small role in Back to the Future. On stage in American Music (NY), The Boys in the Backroom (Actors' Gang, Chicago).
PICTURES: Back to the Future (debut, 1985), Critters, Dead Calm, Back to the Future Part II, Megaville, Memphis Belle, Blood & Concrete: A Love Story, Millions, Femme Fatale, Sniper, Posse, Orlando, Flashfire, Tombstone, The Silence of the Hams, Cyborg Agent, Only You, Tales From the Crypt Presents Demon Knight, Reflections in the Dark, Danger Zone, The Phantom, Titanic, This World—Then the Fireworks, Head Above Water, Susan's Plan, I Woke Up Early the Day I Died, Taxman, Morgan's Ferry, Claim, The Believer, C.Q.
TELEVISION: *Series:* Twin Peaks, Sole Survivor. *Movies:* Brotherhood of Justice, Police Story: Monster Manor, The Case of the Hillside Stranglers, Lake Consequence, Running Delilah, The Set Up, Cleopatra, Howard Hughes: His Women and His Movies, Hendrix, Invincible, Deep Attack.

ZANE, DEBRA
Casting Director.
PICTURES: Days of Thunder, Cadillace Man, Delirious, The Addams Family ,My Cousin Vinny, Whitesands, Hoffa, Joshua Tree, Addams Family Values, Mr. Wonderful, Ghost in the Machine, The War, The Firm, Disclosure, The Last Supper, Get Shorty, The Truth About Cats & Dogs, Men In Black, Washington Square, Wag the Dog, Red Meat, A Cool, Dry Place, Home Fries, Pleasantville, The Limey, American Beauty, Liberty Heights, Stuart Little, Galaxy Quest, The Legend of Bagger Vance, Traffic, K-PAX, Ocean's Eleven, Dragonfly, Road to Perdition, Full Frontal, Solaris, Catch Me If You Can, Terminal.
TELEVISION: *Movies:* The Nightman, The Last Seduction, David and Lisa. *Series:* Maximum Bob.

ZANUCK, LILI FINI
Producer, Director. b. Leominster, MA, April 2, 1954. e. Northern VA Community Coll. Worked for Carnation Co. in LA prior to entering film business. Joined Zanuck/Brown Company in 1978 working in development and various phases of production; 1984-present, prod. Made directorial debut in 1991 with Rush. Named Producer of the Year (1985) by NATO, along with Richard D. Zanuck and David Brown; Producer of the Year (1989) by Producers Guild of America, with Zanuck.
PICTURES: Cocoon, Cocoon: The Return, Driving Miss Daisy (Academy Award, Golden Globe & Natl. Board of Review Awards for Best Picture 1989), Rush (dir.), Rich in Love, Clean Slate, Wild Bill, Mulholland Falls, The Double, True Crime, Reign of Fire.
TELEVISION: *Movies:* Rush, Into Thin Air. *Mini-series:* From the Earth to the Moon.

ZANUCK, RICHARD DARRYL
Executive. b. Los Angeles, CA, Dec 13, 1934. e. Stanford U. 1952-56. Father was exec. Darryl Zanuck. Story dept., 20th Century Fox, 1954; NY pub. dept., 1955; asst. to prod.: Island in the Sun, The Sun Also Rises, The Longest Day; v.p. Darryl F. Zanuck Prods. 1958; first credit as prod. Compulsion (1959); president's prod. rep., 20th Century Fox Studio, 1963; v.p. charge prod., 20th Fox; pres., 20th Fox TV exec. v.p. in charge of prod.; 1968 Chmn. of Bd., Television div., 20th Century Fox, 1969 Pres., 20th Century Fox Film Corp. Joined Warner Bros., 1971, as sr. exec. v.p.; resigned 1972 to form Zanuck-Brown Production Company, Universal Pictures. Joined 20th Century-Fox, 1980-83. To Warner Bros., 1983. To MGM Entertainment, 1986. 1988, dissolved 16-year partnership with David Brown. Formed The Zanuck Company, 1989. Recipient: Irving Thalberg Award (1991).
PICTURES: Compulsion, The Chapman Report, Ssssssss, The Sting (Acad. Award for Best Picture, 1973), The Sugarland Express, Willie Dynamite, The Black Windmill, The Girl from Petrovka, The Eiger Sanction, Jaws, MacArthur, Jaws 2, The Island, Neighbors, The Verdict, Cocoon, Target, Cocoon: The Return, Driving Miss Daisy (Acad. Award for Best Picture, 1989), Rush, Rich in Love, Clean Slate, Wild Bill, Mulholland Falls, Chain Reaction, Deep Impact, True Crime, Rules of Engagement, Planet of the Apes, Reign of Fire, Road to Perdition, Big Fish.

ZEFFIRELLI, FRANCO
Director, Writer. b. Florence, Italy, Feb. 12, 1923. e. Florence Univ. Was stage director before entering film industry. Set designer 1949 -52 for Visconti plays (A Streetcar Named Desire, The Three Sisters). Worked as asst. dir. on La Terra Trema, Bellissima, Senso. Director of operas.
PICTURES: *Dir./Writer:* The Taming of the Shrew (also co-prod.), Romeo and Juliet (also exec. prod.), Brother Sun Sister Moon, The Champ (dir. only), Endless Love (dir. only), La Traviata (also prod. design), Othello, Young Toscanini (also story), Hamlet, Jane Eyre, Tea with Mussolini (also story), Callas Forever.
TELEVISION: *Mini-Series:* Jesus of Nazareth. *Movies:* Much Ado About Nothing, Tosca.

ZELLWEGER, RENÉE
Actress. b. Katy, TX, April 25, 1969. e. Univ. of Texas, Radio-Television-Film major, 1991. Much-nominated actress whose recent performances have garnered Golden Globes, SAG and BAFTA nods.
PICTURES: A Taste for Killing, My Boyfriend's Back, Murder in the Heartland, Shake-Rattle and Rock!, The Return of the Texas Chainsaw Massacre, The Low Life, 8 Seconds, Reality Bites, Love and a .45, Empire Records, Jerry Maguire, The Whole Wide World, A Price Above Rubies, Liar, One True Thing, Nurse Betty (Golden Globe, 2001), Me, Myself, and Irene, Bridget Jones' Diary (BAFTA, Academy Award nominations), White Oleander, Chicago (Golden Globe, SAG cast award and best perf. by female actor, 2003; Acad. Award nom. for best actress) Down With Love, Cold Mountain, Sharkslayer (voice), Bridget Jones: The Edge of Reason.

ZELNICK, STRAUSS
Executive. b. Boston, MA, June 26, 1957. e. Wesleyan U. B.A., 1979 (Summa Cum Laude); Harvard Grad. School of Business Administration, M.B.A., 1983; Harvard Law School, J.D., 1983 (Cum Laude). 1983-86, VP Int'l. TV for Columbia Pictures. 1988-89, pres. & COO, Vestron, Inc.; 1989-93, pres. & COO, 20th Century Fox. CEO, Crystal Dynamics, pres. & CEO of BMG Entertainment North America, 1994-1998, pres.& CEO of BMG Entertainment Bd. member BMG Entertainment and Recording Industry Association of America, Founder of ZelnickMedia to present.

ZEMECKIS, ROBERT
Director, Writer. b. Chicago, IL, May 14, 1951. e. U. of Film Awards sponsored by M.P. Academy of Arts & Sciences, plus 15 intl. honors. m. actress Mary Ellen Trainor. Has film editing background, having worked as cutter on TV commercials in Illinois. Also cut films at NBC News, Chicago, as summer job. After schooling went to Universal to observe on set of TV series, McCloud. Wrote script for that series in collab. with Bob Gale. Turned to feature films, directing I Wanna Hold Your Hand and co-writing s.p. with Gale.
PICTURES: Director: I Wanna Hold Your Hand (also co-s.p.), Used Cars (also co-s.p.), Romancing the Stone, Back to the Future (also co-s.p.), Who Framed Roger Rabbit, Back to the Future II (also story), Back to the Future III (also story), Death Becomes Her (also co-prod.), Forrest Gump (Acad. Award, Golden Globe & DGA Awards, 1994), Contact (also prod.), House on Haunted Hill (prod.), What Lies Beneath (also prod.), Cast Away (also prod.), Macabre (also prod.), Thir13en Ghosts (prod. only), Revelation (prod. only), Clink, Inc. (prod. only), Ritual, Ghost Ship (prod.) Gothika (prod.), The Polar Express (prod. also dir.). Co-Writer: 1941, Trespass. Exec. Prod.: The Public Eye, Tales From the Crypt Presents Demon Knight, The Frighteners, Tales From the Crypt Presents Bordello of Blood, Matchstick Men.
TELEVISION: Amazing Stories, Tales From the Crypt (exec. prod.; also dir., All Through the House, You Murderer).

ZERBE, ANTHONY
Actor. b. Long Beach, CA, May 20, 1936. Studied at Stella Adler Theatre Studio.
THEATRE: NY: Solomon's Child, The Little Foxes.
PICTURES: Cool Hand Luke, Will Penny, The Liberation of L.B. Jones, The Molly Maguires, The Call Me Mister Tibbs, Cotton Comes to Harlem, The Omega Man, The Life and Times of Judge Roy Bean, The Strange Vengeance of Rosalie, The Laughing Policeman, Papillon, The Parallax View, Farewell My Lovely, Rooster Cogburn, The Turning Point, Who'll Stop the Rain, The First Deadly Sin, The Dead Zone, Off Beat, Opposing Force, Private Investigation, Steel Dawn, Listen to Me, See No Evil Hear No Evil, Licence to Kill, Touch, Star Trek: Insurrection, True Crime, The Matrix Reloaded.
TELEVISION: Series: Harry-O (Emmy Award, 1976), The Young Riders. Movies: The Priest Killer, The Hound of the Baskervilles, Snatched, She Lives, The Healers, In the Glitter Palace, KISS Meets the Phantom of the Park, Child of Glass, Attica, The Seduction of Miss Leona, Rascals and Robbers: The Secret Adventures of Tom Sawyer and Huck Finn, A Question of Honor, The Return of the Man from U.N.C.L.E., One Police Plaza, Independence, Baja Oklahoma, Onassis: The Richest Man in the World, Columbo: Columbo Goes to the Guillotine, To Save a Child, Treasure Island: The Adventure Begins, Memories of Manon, The Craft, On Seventh Avenue, Jack Reed: Death and Vengeance, Asteroid. Mini-Series: Once an Eagle, How the West Was Won, Centennial, The Chisholms, George Washington, A.D., North and South II, Dream West.

ZETA-JONES, CATHERINE
Actress. b. Swansea, Wales, Sept. 25, 1969. m. actor Michael Douglas. Starred in the Yorkshire Television comedy/drama series "Darling Buds of May" (1991). The show was a smash hit and made Jones one of the United Kingdom's most popular television actresses.
PICTURES: Les 1001 Nuits, Out of the Blue, Christopher Columbus: The Discovery, Splitting Heirs, Blue Juice, The Phantom, The Mask of Zorro, The Haunting, Entrapment, High Fidelity, Traffic, America's Sweethearts, Chicago, Intolerable Cruelty, Sinbad: Legend of the Seven Seas, Terminal, Smoke & Mirrors.
TELEVISION: Movies: Out of the Blue, The Cinder Path, Katharina die Große, The Return of the Native, Catherine the Great, Titanic. Series: Darling Buds of May. Guest: The Young Indiana Jones Chronicles.

ZIDE, LARRY M.
Executive. b. Flushing, NY, Oct. 16, 1954. 3rd generation in mp. industry. Started 1972 with American Intl. Pictures in sls. & adv.; 1973, named branch sls. mgr., Memphis. 1975, joined Dimension Pictures as print controller; 1978, formed Zica Films Co. serving m.p. industry; 1985, Zica merged with Filmtreat Intl. Corp; named pres., newly formed Filmtreat West Corp.

ZIDE, MICHAEL (MICKEY)
Executive. b. Detroit, MI, May 31, 1932. Joined m.p. ind. with American Intl. Pictures as print controller; 1962, promoted to asst. gen. sls. mgr. Named v.p., special projects; 1970; 1972, joined Academy Pictures as v.p. of prod. Later went with Zica Film Co.; 1985, named exec. v.p., Filmtreat West Corp.

ZIEFF, HOWARD
Director. b. Chicago, IL. e. Art Center School in Los Angeles. Started as artist and photographer, working as newsreel photographer for L.A. TV station. Went to N.Y. to still photography; became top photo artist in advertising. Turned to film direction with Slither.
PICTURES: Slither (debut, 1973), Hearts of the West, House Calls, The Main Event, Private Benjamin, Unfaithfully Yours, The

Dream Team, My Girl, My Girl 2.

ZIMBALIST, JR., EFREM
Actor. b. New York, NY, Nov. 30, 1923. e. Fay Sch., Southboro, MA; St. Paul's, Concord, NH; Yale. Son of violinist Efrem Zimbalist and soprano Alma Gluck. Daughter is actress Stephanie Zimbalist. Studied drama, Neighborhood Playhouse. N.Y. Stage debut, The Rugged Path. Shows with American Repertory Theatre; Henry VIII, Androcles and the Lion, What Every Woman Knows, Yellow Jack, Hedda Gabler, Fallen Angels. Co-prod., The Medium, The Telephone, The Consul. Gave up acting after death of his wife and served as asst. to father, Curtis Inst. of Music for 4 years. Returned to acting, stock co., Hammonton, NJ, 1954.
PICTURES: House of Strangers (debut, 1949), Bombers B-52, Band of Angels, The Deep Six, Violent Road, Girl on the Run, Too Much Too Soon, Home Before Dark, The Crowded Sky, A Fever in the Blood, By Love Possessed, The Chapman Report, The Reward, Harlow, Wait Until Dark, Airport 1975, Elmira, Hot Shots!, Batman: Mask of the Phantasm (voice).
TELEVISION: Series: Concerning Miss Marlowe (daytime serial), Maverick, 77 Sunset Strip, The FBI, Remington Steele, Hotel, Streets, Zorro, Prince Valiant (voice), Batman: The Animated Series (voice), Spiderman the Series, The Marvel Action Hour: Iron Man, Batman: Gotham Knights, A Year to Remember (host). Guest: Philco, Goodyear Playhouse, U.S. Steel Hour. Movies: Who Is the Black Dahlia?, A Family Upside Down, Terror Out of the Sky, The Best Place to Be, The Gathering Part II, Baby Sister, Shooting Stars, Batman/Superman Adventures: World's Finest, Cab to Canada. Host: You Are the Jury, The Tempest. Mini-Series: Trade Winds, Scruples.

ZIMBALIST, STEPHANIE
Actress. b. New York, NY, Oct. 8, 1956. Father is actor Efrem Zimbalist Jr.; grandparents: violinist Efrem Zimbalist and soprano Alma Gluck; aunt: novelist Marcia Davenport.
THEATRE: LA: Festival, The Tempest, American Mosaic, Love Letters, The Baby Dance, The Crimson Thread, AdWars, Sylvia. Williamstown Theatre Festival: Barbarians, Summer and Smoke, Threepenny Opera. Tours: My One and Only, Carousel. Regional: The Philadelphia Story, The Cherry Orchard, The Baby Dance.
PICTURES: The Magic of Lassie, The Awakening.
TELEVISION: Series: Remington Steele. Mini-Series: Centennial. Movies: Yesterday's Child, In the Matter of Karen Ann Quinlan, The Gathering, The Long Journey Back, Forever, The Triangle Factory Fire Scandal, The Best Place to Be, The Baby Sitter, The Golden Moment—An Olympic Love Story, Elvis and the Beauty Queen, Tomorrow's Child, Love on the Run, A Letter to Three Wives, Celebration Family, The Man in the Brown Suit, Caroline?, Personals, The Killing Mind, The Story Lady, Some Kind of Love, Breaking the Silence, Sexual Advances, Jericho Fever, Incident in a Small Town, Voices From Within, The Great Elephant Escape, Whose Daughter Is She? Stop the World—I Want to Get Off, Dead Ahead, Prison of Secrets.

ZIMMER, HANS
Composer. b. Germany, Sept. 12, 1957. Member of the Buggles, producing hit song Video Killed the Radio Star. Pioneered use of digital synthesizers with computer technology and traditional orchestras.
PICTURES: Burning Secret, A World Apart, Rain Man, Paperhouse, Wonderland, Black Rain, Driving Miss Daisy, Bird on a Wire, Days of Thunder, Pacific Heights, Green Card, Thelma & Louise, Backdraft, Radio Flyer, The Power of One, K-2, A League of Their Own, Toys, Younger and Younger, True Romance, Cool Runnings, I'll Do Anything, The House of the Spirits, Renaissance Man, The Lion King (Acad. Award, Golden Globe, 1994), Drop Zone, Crimson Tide, Nine Months, Something to Talk About, Beyond Rangoon, Muppet Treasure Island, Broken Arrow, The Preacher's Wife, Smilla's Sense of Snow, The Peacemaker, As Good As It Gets, The Thin Red Line, The Prince of Egypt, The Last Days, Gladiator, Chill Factor, The Road to El Dorado, Mission Impossible II, The Pledge, Hannibal, Pearl Harbor, Invincible, Riding in Cars With Boys, Black Hawk Down, Spirit: Stallion of the Cimarron, The Ring, Tears of the Sun, Pirates of the Caribbean: The Curse of the Black Pearl, Matchstick Men, The Last Samurai, Collateral, King Arthur.
TELEVISION: Series: Space Rangers, Iron Chef, The Critic, High Incident, Fame L.A., Die Motorrad-Cops: Hart am Limit , El Candidato, What About Joan, Threat Matrix. Mini-Series: First Born. Movies: Wild Horses, Comeback, Die Motorrad-Cops: Hart am Limit, Live From Baghdad.

ZINNEMANN, TIM
Producer. b. Los Angeles, CA. e. Columbia U. Son of dir. Fred Zinnemann. Entered m.p. ind. as film editor; then asst. dir. on 20 films. Production mgr. for 5 projects; assoc. prod. on The Cowboys and Smile. Prod., Straight Time for Warners with Stanley Beck.
PICTURES: Carnal Knowledge (assist. dir.), The Cowboys, A Small Circle of Friends, The Long Riders, Tex, Impulse, Fandango, Crossroads, The Running Man, Pet Sematary (exec. prod.), Street Fighter, The Island of Dr. Moreau.
TELEVISION: Series: Miami Vice, The Jericho Mile, Lies of the Twins.

ZISKIN, LAURA
Producer. e. USC Cinema School. Worked as game show writer, development exec. before joining Jon Peters' prod. co. where she worked on A Star is Born, Eyes of Laura Mars (assoc. prod.). Formed Fogwood Films with Sally Field. Became pres. of company Fox 2000 Pictures.
PICTURES: Murphy's Romance, No Way Out, D.O.A., The Rescue, Everybody's All American, Pretty Woman (exec. prod.), What About Bob?, The Doctor, Hero (also co-story), To Die For, Courage Under Fire, As Good As It Gets, Spider-Man, Spider-Man II.
TELEVISION: *Series:* Tarzan, The Spaces. *Movies:* Fail Safe, Dinner with Friends.

ZSIGMOND, VILMOS
Cinematographer. b. Szeged, Hungary, June 16, 1930. e. National Film Sch. Began career photographing Hungarian Revolution of 1956. Later escaped from Hungary with friend Laszlo Kovacs, also a cinematographer. Winner of Academy Award and British Academy Award for cinematography, also several int'l and domestic awards as dir. of TV commercials.
PICTURES: The Time Travelers (1964), The Sadist, The Name of the Game Is Kill, Futz, Picasso Summer, The Monitors, Red Sky at Morning, McCabe and Mrs. Miller, The Hired Hand, The Ski Bum, Images, Deliverance, Scarecrow, The Long Goodbye, Cinderella Liberty, The Sugarland Express, The Girl From Petrovka, Sweet Revenge, Death Rides, Obsession, Close Encounters of the Third Kind (Academy Award, 1977), The Last Waltz, The Deer Hunter (BAFTA Award; Acad. Award nom.), Winter Kills, The Rose, Heaven's Gate, Blow Out, The Border, Jinxed, Table for Five, No Small Affair, The River (Acad. Award nom.), Real Genius, The Witches of Eastwick, Fat Man and Little Boy, The Two Jakes, Journey to Spirit Island, The Bonfire of the Vanities, The Long Shadow (dir.), Sliver, Intersection, Maverick (also actor), The Crossing Guard, Assassins, The Ghost and the Darkness (A.S.C. Award nom.), Playing by Heart, The Body, Life as a House, Jersey Girl.
TELEVISION: *Mini-Series:* The Mists of Avalon. *Movies:* Flesh and Blood, Stalin (Emmy Award, ACE Award, ASC Award).

ZORADI, MARK
Executive. e. B.A. economics and sociology, Westmont College, 1976. M.B.A., Marketing & Finance, UCLA Graduate School of Management, 1980. Mktg. mgr., Walt Disney Home Video. Participated in Home Video and Disney Channel start-ups in the early 1980s, and growth of Buena Vista Pictures Distribution in the mid 1980s; mktg. dir., The Disney Channel, 1983-85; dir. of sales, establishing national advertsting sales division generating $100 million in first-yr. sales, Buena Vista Pictures Distribution, 1985-87; senior v.p. & gen. mgr., Buena Vista Television, 1987-92; president, Buena Vista Intl., 1992-99. Currently president, Buena Vista Intl. (BVI) and Buena Vista Home Entertainment (BVHE) Intl. Named to head BVI & BVHE Intl. Distribution groups, combining groups to generate over $1.5 billion in revenue. Currently member, Los Angeles chapter of Young Presidents Org. and board of trustees, Westmont College.

ZUCKER, DAVID
Producer, Director, Writer. b. Milwaukee, WI, Oct. 16, 1947. e. U. of Wisconsin, majoring in film. With brother, Jerry, and friend Jim Abrahams founded the Kentucky Fried Theatre in Madison in 1971 (moved theater to L.A. 1972); later wrote script for film of that name released in 1977.
PICTURES: The Kentucky Fried Movie (co-s.p., actor), Airplane! (co-s.p., co-dir., actor), Top Secret (co-s.p., co-dir., co-prod.), Ruthless People (co-dir.), The Naked Gun: From the Files of Police Squad! (exec. prod., dir., co-s.p.), The Naked Gun 2 1/2: The Smell of Fear (dir., exec. prod., co-s.p., actor), Brain Donors (co-exec. prod.), The Naked Gun 33 1/3: The Final Insult (prod., co-s.p., actor), A Walk in the Clouds (co-prod.), High School High (prod., s.p.), BASEketball, For Goodness Sake, Santa Claus Conquers the Martians (prod. only), Phone Booth (prod. only), My Boss's Daughter (dir.), Scary Movie 3, Scary Movie 4.
TELEVISION: *Series:* Police Squad, Absolutely True. Our Planet Tonight (special). *Movies:* H.U.D.

ZUCKER, JERRY
Producer, Director. Writer. b. Milwaukee, WI, March 11, 1950. e. U. of Wisconsin. With brother, David, and friend Jim Abrahams founded the Kentucky Fried Theatre in Madison in 1970 and wrote script for film of that name released in 1977.
PICTURES: The Kentucky Fried Movie (co-s.p., actor), Airplane! (co-dir., co-s.p.), Top Secret (co-dir., co-s.p.), Ruthless People (co-dir.), The Naked Gun (exec. prod., co-s.p.), Ghost (dir.), The Naked Gun 2-1/2 (exec. co-prod.), Brain Donors (co-exec. prod.), My Life (co-prod.), Naked Gun 33-1/3 (co-exec. prod.), First Knight (dir., co-prod.), A Walk in the Clouds (co-prod.), First Knight, My Best Friend's Wedding, Toddlers, Imagining Nathan, Unconditional Love (prod.), Rat Race (prod.).
TELEVISION: *Series:* Police Squad! (co-exec. prod., dir.; co-wrote first episode). Our Planet Tonight (special).

ZUNIGA, DAPHNE
Actress. b. Berkeley, CA, October 28, 1962. e. UCLA.
PICTURES: Pranks (debut, 1982), The Dorm That Dripped Blood, The Initiation, Vision Quest, The Sure Thing, Modern Girls, Spaceballs, Last Rites, The Fly II, Gross Anatomy, Staying Together, Eight Hundred Leagues Down the Amazon, Cityscrapes: Los Angeles, Charlie's Ghost Story, Stand-ins, Naked in the Cold Sun, Enermies of Laughter, Artificial Lies.
TELEVISION: *Movies:* Quarterback Princess, Stone Pillow, Prey of the Chameleon, Pandora's Clock, Loss of Faith., Ghost Dog: A Detective Tail. *Series:* Melrose Place, Stories from My Childhood. *Mini-Series:* Degree of Guilt. *Guest:* Family Ties, Nightmare Classics (Eye of the Panther).

ZWICK, EDWARD
Writer, Producer, Director. b. Chicago, IL, Oct. 8, 1952. e. Harvard U., B.A., 1974; AFI Advanced Film Studies, M.F.A., 1976. Editor and feature writer, The New Republic and Rolling Stone, 1972-74. Author: Literature and Liberalism (1975). Formed Bedford Falls Production Co. with Marshall Herskovitz.
PICTURES: *Director:* About Last Night... (debut, 1986), Glory (Golden Globe nom.), Leaving Normal, Legends of the Fall (also co-prod., Golden Globe nom.), Courage Under Fire, Against All Enemies, The Siege (also prod.). *Prod.:* Shakespeare in Love (Acad. Award for Best Picture, BAFTA award), Dangerous Beauty, Executive Search, Traffic, I Am Sam, Lone Star State of Mind, Abandon, The Last Samurai.
TELEVISION: *Series:* Family (writer, then story editor, dir., prod., Humanitas Prize Award, 1980), thirtysomething (co-exec. prod.; Emmy Award, 1988), Dream Street (exec. prod.), My So-Called Life (also ep. dir.), Relativity, Once and Again (exec.prod), Ooph!. *Movies (dir.):* Paper Dolls, Having It All, Special Bulletin, Extreme Close-Up (also co-exec. prod., co-story), Relativity (pilot), Women vs. Men.

ZWICK, JOEL
Director. b. Brooklyn, NY, Jan. 11, 1942. e. Brooklyn Coll., M.A.
THEATRE: Dance with Me, Cold Storage, Esther, Cafe La Mama.
PICTURES: *Producer:* Can't Be Heaven. *Director:* My Big Fat Greek Wedding.
TELEVISION: *Series:* Happy Days, Laverne and Shirley, Mork and Mindy, Makin' It, It's a Living, Bosom Buddies, America 2100, Goodtime Girls, Hot W.A.C.S. (also exec. prod.), Little Darlings, Joanie Loves Chachi, The New Odd Couple (also supv. prod.), Webster, Street Hawk, Brothers (supv. prod.), Perfect Strangers (also pilot), Full House (also pilot), Family Matters, Step by Step, Getting By (also prod.), The Trouble with Larry, On Our Own, Kirk, Meego, The Wayans Brothers, The Parent 'Hood, The Love Boat: The Next Wave, Two of a Kind, Guys Like Us. *Pilots:* Angie, Bosom Buddies, Struck by Lightning, Family Matters, Adventures in Babysitting, Morning Glory, Star of the Family, Up to No Good, Going Places, Hangin' With Mr. Cooper, Life Happens, On Our Own, Making Out, Nowhere Fast. *Movies:* Adventures in Babysitting.

Obituaries

(Sept. 15, 2002 - Sept. 30, 2003)

Milton Altman ....July 6, 2003
Rod Amateau ....June 29, 2003
Robert Anthony ....March 12, 2003
Royce Applegate ....Jan. 1, 2003
Roone Arledge..Dec. 5, 2002
Howard 'Louie Bluie' Armstrong ....July 30, 2003
Leslie G. Arries Jr. ....Dec. 1, 2002
George Axelrod ....June 21, 2003
Tareq Ayoub ....April 8, 2003
Hilary Bader ....Nov. 7, 2002
Parley Baer..Nov. 22, 2002
Winthrop Patterson Baker Jr. ....June 7, 2003
Anant Balani ....Aug. 28, 2003
Nina Elias Bamberger ....Nov. 20, 2002
Juan Antonio Bardem ....Oct. 30, 2002
Elaine Barrie ....March 1, 2003
Marina Berti ....Oct. 29, 2002
Jack Barton ....Oct. 28, 2002
Robert M. Batscha..July 4th, 2003
Janine Bazin ....May 31, 2003
Anne Belle ....June 18, 2003
Fred Berger..May 23, 2003
Barbara Berjer ....Oct. 20, 2002
Imogene Bliss..Jan. 14, 2003
Ed Bliss ....Nov. 25, 2002
David Bloom ....April 6, 2003
Robert F. Blumofe ....July 22, 2003
Haskell 'Buzz' Boggs ....May 30, 2003
Michel Boisrond ....Nov. 10, 2002
Margaret Booth ....Oct. 28, 2002
Mel Bourne..Jan. 14, 2003
Eddie Bracken..Nov. 14, 2002
Ben Brady ....March 20, 2003
Stan Brakhage ....March 9, 2003
Mary Brian ....Dec. 30, 2002
David Brinkley ....June 11, 2003
Jack Brodsky..Feb. 18, 2003
Charles Bronson ....Aug. 30, 2003
Rand Brooks..Sept. 1, 2003
Horst Buchholz...March 3, 2003
Stan Burns...Nov. 5, 2002
Fritzi Burr ....Jan. 17, 2003
Steve Carlin ....Feb. 4, 2003
Dick Carroll ....March 13, 2003
Bill Carruthers..March 2, 2003
Benny Carter..July 13, 2003
Nell Carter...Jan. 23, 2003
Anthony Caruso ....April 4, 2003
June Carter Cash ....May 15, 2003
Johnny Cash..Sept. 12, 2003
David Charnay..Oct. 2, 2002
Norma Lee Clark...Nov. 8, 2002
Russell Clark..Nov. 12, 2002
Lana Clarkson..Feb. 3, 2003
James Coburn..Nov. 18, 2002
Fielder Cook...June 20, 2003
Jose Couso ....April 8, 2003
Richard Crenna ....Jan. 17, 2003
Hume Cronyn ....June 15, 2003
Celia Cruz ....July 16, 2003
Keene Curtis ....Oct. 13, 2002
John L. "Jack" Dales ....Jan. 16, 2003
Pamela Danova ....Sept. 24, 2002
Andre de Toth ....Oct. 27, 2002
Winston 'Buddy' Deane ....July 17, 2003
Andre Delvaux..Oct. 4, 2002
Jacques Deray..Aug. 9, 2003

Irene Diamond..Jan. 21, 2003
Larry Dobkin..Oct. 28, 2002
Carlos Eduardo Dolabella...................................May 26, 2003
Lonnie Donegan...Nov. 3, 2002
Henry Droz...March 27, 2003
Dean Dunlavey...June 28, 2003
Charles Dupuis ....Nov. 14, 2002
Manfred Durniok ....March 7, 2003
Buddy Ebsen..July 6, 2003
Anthony Eisley..Jan. 29, 2003
Alaa Wally Eldeen ....Feb. 11, 2003
Jules Engel..Sept. 6, 2003
Nick Enright ....March 30, 2003
Howard Fast...March 12, 2003
William A.G. "Bill" Feeder ....Feb. 28, 2003
David B. Fein ....Sept. 5, 2003
Mel Ferber...June 19, 2003
Marjorie Fowler...July 8, 2003
Cedric Francis ....April 7, 2003
Fed Freiberger ....March 2, 2003
Bernard Fresson ....Oct. 20, 2002
Kinji Fukasaku ....Jan. 12, 2003
Chris Fuller ....Nov. 9, 2002
Mark Ganzel...Oct. 24, 2002
Jackie Gayle ....Nov. 23, 2002
Edward Gaylord ....April 26, 2003
Daniel Gelin ....Nov. 29, 2002
Maurice Gibb..Jan. 12, 2003
Arnold Glassman...Feb. 19, 2003
Sidney Glazier ....Dec. 14, 2002
Trevor Goddard...June 8, 2003
Linda Goldenberg..Jan. 21, 2003
Ron Goodwin..Jan. 8, 2003
Alex Gordon ....June 24, 2003
Christine Gouze-Renal ....Oct. 25, 2002
Bert Granet..Nov. 15, 2002
Teresa Graves ....Oct. 10, 2002
Adolph Green ....Oct. 24, 2002
David Greene ....April 7, 2003
S. Frederick Gronich..June 22, 2003
Charles Guggenheim..Oct. 9, 2002
Antonio Velasco Gutierrez...................................Aug. 16, 2003
Buddy Hackett..June 30, 2003
Conrad L. Hall ....Jan. 4, 2003
Bill Hargate..Sept. 12, 2003
John Harris...July 20, 2003
Jonathan Harris ....Nov. 3, 2002
Richard Harris ....Oct. 25, 2002
Anthony Havelock-Allan ....Jan. 11, 2003
Andrew Heiskell...Juky 6, 2003
Luther Henderson ....July 29, 2003
Tomas Henriquez...Dec. 24, 2002
George Henshaw ....Aug. 20, 2003
Katharine Hepburn ....June 29, 2003
Frankie Hewitt ....Feb. 28, 2003
George Roy Hill ....Dec. 27, 2002
Wendy Hiller ....May 14, 2003
Gergory Hines ....Aug. 9, 2003
Thora Hird...March 15, 2003
Al Hirschfeld..Jan. 20, 2003
Morag Hood ....Oct. 5, 2002
Bob Hope...July 27, 2003
Larry Hovis ....Sept. 9, 2003
Ellen Idelson..Sept. 19, 2003
Leigh Jackson ....March 27, 2003
Sebastien Japrisot ....March 4, 2003
Walter 'Matt' Jefferies ....July 21, 2003

Adele Jergens .... Nov. 22, 2002
Michael Jeter .... March 30, 2003
Gordon Jump .... Sept. 22, 2003
Nathan Juran .... Oct. 23, 2002
Leon Kaplan .... July 18, 2003
Beverly Bailis Karp .... May 10, 2003
Lee H. Katzin .... Oct. 30, 2002
Stacy Keach Sr. .... Feb. 13, 2003
William Kelley .... Feb. 3, 2003
Michael Kelly .... April 4, 2003
Rachel Kempson .... May 24, 2003
Zvi Kolitz .... Sept. 29, 2002
Leslie Cheung Kwok-wing .... April 1, 2003
Kevin Laffan .... March 11, 2003
Jean-Luc Lagardere .... March 14, 2003
Henry Lange .... Oct. 25, 2002
Jack Lee .... Oct. 15, 2002
Ernest Leiser .... Nov. 26, 2002
Christian Leonhardt .... Aug. 23, 2003
Buddy Lester .... Oct. 4, 2002
Alfred Levitt .... Nov. 16, 2002
Jules Levy .... May 24, 2003
Robert P. Lieb .... Sept. 28, 2002
Christian Liebig .... April 7, 2003
Lo Lieh .... Nov. 2, 2002
Vincent Liff .... Feb. 25, 2003
Terry Lloyd .... March 22, 2003
Harold Loeb .... May 17, 2003
Charles Longenecker .... Dec. 10, 2002
Florence Segal Lowe .... Nov. 14, 2002
Klaus Lowitsch .... Dec. 3, 2002
John Meredyth Lucas .... OCt. 19, 2002
Gisele MacKenzie .... Sept. 5, 2003
Ian MacNaughton .... Dec. 10, 2002
John Mantley .... Jan. 14, 2003
Antonio Margheriti .... Nov. 4, 2002
William Marshall .... June 11, 2003
Susan Marx .... Dec. 22, 2002
Lin McCarthy .... Nov. 23, 2002
Thomas J. McCarthy .... Aug. 1, 2003
John Reagan 'Tex' McCrary .... Aug. 27, 2003
Maurice McEndree .... May 17, 2003
Kathie Browne McGavin .... April 8, 2003
John Glenn McQueen .... Oct. 29, 2002
Barbara Miller .... Aug. 24, 2003
George Miller .... March 5, 2003
Marvin Mirisch .... Nov. 17, 2002
Paul Monash .... Jan. 14, 2003
Paul Moran .... March 22, 2003
Peggy Moran .... Oct. 25, 2002
Mlchael Morris .... June 20, 2003
John Morris .... April 19, 2003
Brianne 'Bri' Murphy .... Aug. 20, 2003
Bernard Myerson .... Nov. 13, 202
N!xau .... July 2, 2003
David Newman .... June 26, 2003
Cliff Norton .... Jan. 25, 2003
Elliot Norton .... July 20, 2003
Shirley O'Hara Krims .... Dec. 13, 2002
Felice Orlandi .... May 21, 2003
Norman Panama .... Jan. 13, 2003
Julio Anguita Parrado .... April 7, 2003
Philip L. Parslow .... July 29, 2003
Dennis Patrick .... Oct. 13, 2002
Gregory Peck .... June 12, 2003
Edwin Perlstein .... July 12, 2003
Chris Petersen .... May 9, 2003
Margaret "Peg" Phillips .... Nov. 7, 2002

Maurice Pialat .... Jan. 12, 2003
Sidney Pink .... Oct. 12, 2002
Wolfgang Preiss .... Nov. 27, 2002
Taras Protsyuk .... April 8, 2003
Glenn Quinn .... Dec. 3, 2002
Beulah Quo .... Oct. 23, 2002
Karel Reisz .... Nov. 25, 2002
Sheldon Reynolds .... Jan. 25, 2003
Leni Riefenstahl .... Sept. 8, 2003
John Ritter .... Sept. 11, 2003
Carlos Rivas .... June 16, 2003
Jose Tamayo Rivas .... March 26, 2003
Kenneth Rive .... Dec. 30, 2002
Arthur E. Rockwell .... July 18, 2003
Robert Rockwell .... Jan. 25, 2003
Fred Rogers .... Feb. 27, 2003
Frank P. Rosenberg .... Oct. 18, 2002
Lois Fried Rosenfield .... May 25, 2003
Edward Rothman .... July 20, 2003
Gunnar Rugheimer .... Feb. 21, 2003
Al Rush .... Jan. 14, 2003
Merlin Santana .... Nov. 9, 2002
Walter Scharf .... Feb. 24, 2003
Edgar J. Scherick .... Dec. 2, 2002
Tex Schramm .... July 15, 2003
Martha Scott .... May 28, 2003
Benjamin H. Segal .... Dec. 27, 2002
Billie Bird Sellen .... Nov. 27, 2002
Stefan Sharff .... May 12, 2002
Lloyd Shirley .... March 5, 2003
Serge Silberman .... July 22, 2003
Johnny Silver .... Feb. 1, 2003
Richard 'Dick' Simmons .... Jan. 11, 2003
Jack Smight .... Sept. 1, 2003
Jerry Sohl .... Nov. 4, 2002
Jack Solomon .... Nov. 8, 2002
Alberto Sordi .... Feb. 24, 2003
Bernard Spear .... May 9, 2003
Robert Stack .... May 14, 2003
Don Stanley .... Jan. 20, 2003
Paul Stojanovich .... March 15, 2003
Peter Stone .... April 26, 2003
Marv Sugarman .... July 20, 2003
George E. Swink .... Aug. 22, 2003
Daniel Taradash .... Feb. 22, 2003
Edward C. Ternes .... Sept. 10, 2003
Henry Peter Tewksbury .... Feb. 20, 2003
Peter Tinniswood .... Jan. 9, 2003
Leopoldo Trieste .... Jan. 25, 2003
Marie Trintignant .... Aug. 6, 2003
Raf Vallone .... Oct. 31, 2002
Eliot Wald .... July 12, 2003
Alexander Walker .... July 14, 2003
Michael Wayne .... April 2, 2003
Roger Webb .... Dec. 19, 2002
David Webster .... Aug. 6, 2003
Keith Wester .... Nov. 1, 2002
Romney Wheeler .... Dec. 7, 2002
Barry White .... July 4, 2003
Tony Williams .... Oct. 15, 2002
Ralph S. Wilshin .... Sep. 14, 2003
Lionel Wilson .... April 30, 2003
Rod B. Wilson .... Feb. 22, 2003
Lee Winfrey .... March 31, 2003
Sheb Wooley .... Sept. 16, 2003
Thomas H. Wyman .... Dec. 15, 2002
Philip Yordan .... March 24, 2003

YOUR PARTNERS IN HEALTH

Since 1936, the Memorial Fund has been caring for employees, and their immediate families, of the entertainment industry by providing them with health services.

Our representative can put you in touch with expert medical care, and your first consultation with one of our nationwide pulmonary specialists is absolutely free.

For more information, please contact

Will Rogers Memorial Fund at 888.994.3863

MOTION PICTURES

■

This list includes motion pictures from major studios and independents. Many release dates are review or festival release dates.

ABANDON
A Paramount release of a Paramount, Spyglass Entertainment presentation of a Lynda Obst production. Producers: Obst, Edward Zwick, Roger Birnbaum, Gary Barber. Executive producer: Richard Vane. Co-producers: Elizabeth Joan Hooper, Shannon Burke. Director/Writer: Stephen Gaghan, suggested by the book "Adam's Fall" by Sean Desmond. Camera: Matthew Libatique. Editor: Mark Warner. Music: Clint Mansell. In Deluxe color, Panavision widescreen. Release date: Oct. 15, 2002. MPAA Rating: PG-13. Running time: 99 Min.
Cast: Katie Holmes, Benjamin Bratt, Charlie Hunnam, Zooey Deschanel, Gabrielle Union, Gabriel Mann, Mark Feuerstein, Melanie Jayne Lynskey, Will McCormack, Philip Bosco, Tony Goldwyn, Fred Ward.

ADAM SANDLER'S EIGHT CRAZY NIGHTS
A Sony Pictures Entertainment release of a Columbia Pictures presentation of a Happy Madison production. Producers: Adam Sandler, Jack Giarraputo, Allen Covert. Executive producer: Ken Tsumura. Co-producer: Brooks Arthur. Director: Seth Kearsley. Screenplay: Brooks Arthur, Allen Covert, Brad Isaacs, Adam Sandler. Editor: Amy Budden. Music: Ray Ellis, Marc Ellis, Teddy Castellucci. In Technicolor, Deluxe prints. Release date: Nov. 25, 2002. MPAA Rating: PG-13. Running time: 86 Min. Animated.
Voices: Adam Sandler, Jackie Titone, Austin Stout, Kevin Nealon, Rob Schneider, Norm Crosby, Jon Lovitz.

ADAPTATION
A Sony Pictures Entertainment release of a Columbia Pictures presentation in association with Intermedia Films of a Magnet/Clinica Estetico production. Producers: Edward Saxon, Vincent Landay, Jonathan Demme. Executive producers: Charlie Kaufman, Peter Saraf. Director: Spike Jonze. Screenplay: Charlie Kaufman, Donald Kaufman, based on the book "The Orchid Thief" by Susan Orlean. Camera: Lance Acord. Editor: Eric Zumbrunnen. Music: Carter Burwell. In FotoKem color, Deluxe prints. Release date: Nov. 5, 2002. MPAA Rating: R. Running time: 114 Min.
Cast: Nicolas Cage, Meryl Streep, Chris Cooper, Tilda Swinton, Cara Seymour, Brian Cox, Judy Greer, Maggie Gyllenhaal, Ron Livingston, Jay Tavare, Stephen Tobolowsky, Peter Jason, Curtis Hanson.

AGENT CODY BANKS
An MGM release of a Splendid Pictures, Maverick Films, Dylan Sellers production. Producers: David C. Glasser, Andreas Klein, Guy Oseary, Sellers, David Nicksay. Executive producers: Madonna, Jason Alexander, Jennifer Birchfield-Eick, Kerry David, Danny Gold, Michael Jackman, Mark Morgan, Bob Yari. Co-producer: Robert Meyer Burnett. Director: Harald Zwart. Screenplay: Ashley Edward Miller, Zack Stentz, Scott Alexander, Larry Karaszewski. Story: Jeffrey Jurgenson. Camera: Denis Crossan. Editor: Jim Miller. Music: John Powell. In Deluxe color, Panavision widescreen. Release date: March 1, 2003. MPAA Rating: PG. Running time: 102 Min.
Cast: Frankie Muniz, Hilary Duff, Angie Harmon, Keith David, Cynthia Stevenson, Arnold Vosloo, Daniel Roebuck, Ian McShane, Darrell Hammond, Martin Donovan.

ALEX & EMMA
A Warner Bros. release of a Franchise Pictures presentation of a Reiner-Greisman/Escape Artists production. Producers: Rob Reiner, Jeremy Leven, Alan Greisman, Todd Black, Elie Samaha. Executive producers: Peter Guber, Jeffrey Stott, Steve Tisch, Jason Blumenthal. Co-producers: Joseph Merhi, James Holt, Adam Scheinman. Director: Rob Reiner. Screenplay: Jeremy Leven. Camera: Gavin Finney. Editors: Robert Leighton, Alan Edward Bell. Music: Marc Shaiman. In Technicolor. Release date: June 10, 2003. MPAA Rating: PG-13. Running time: 96 Min.
Cast: Kate Hudson, Luke Wilson, Sophie Marceau, David Paymer, Rob Reiner, Francois Giroday, Lobo Sebastian, Chino XL, Cloris Leachman, Rip Taylor.

ALL THE REAL GIRLS
A Sony Pictures Classics release of a Jean Doumanian production. Producers: Lisa Muskat, Doumanian. Director/Writer: David Gordon Green. Story: Green, Paul Schneider. Camera: Tim Orr. Editors: Zene Bakel, Steven Gonzales. Music: David Wingo, Michael Linnen. In Deluxe color, widescreen. Release date: Jan. 24, 2003. Running time: 108 Min.
Cast: Paul Schneider, Zooey Deschanel, Patricia Clarkson, Maurice Compte, Danny McBride, Benjamin Mouton, Shea Wingham.

ALMA MATER
A Yonder Light Films production. Producers: Hans Canosa, Kwesi Collisson, G.L. Zevin. Director: Hans Canosa. Screenplay by G.L. Zevin; story, Zevin, Canosa. Camera: Tom Robotham. Editor: Rich Protnor. Music: John Turner. In color, super-16mm-to-HDV. Release date: Oct. 19, 2002. Running time: 80 Min.
Cast: Will Lyman, Cady McClain, Alexander Chaplin, Kate Super, Andrew van den Houten, Faran Krentcil, Michael Bederman.

AMERICAN MULLET
A Party in the Back Prods. presentation. Producers: Jennifer Arnold, Allison Hebble. Executive producers: Dorka Keehn, Tom Gorai. Director/Writer: Jennifer Arnold. Camera: Patti Lee. Editors: Arnold, Zach Fine. Music: Adam Cohen. In color, video. Release date: Oct. 16, 2002. Running time: 52 Min. Documentary.

AMERICAN SPLENDOR
An HBO Films presentation of a Good Machine production. Producer: Ted Hope. Directors/Writers: Shari Springer Berman, Robert Pulcini, based on the "American Splendor" comics by Harvey Pekar and "Our Cancer Year" by Pekar and Joyce Brabner. Camera: Terry Stacey. Editor: Robert Pulcini. Music: Mark Suozzo. In Deluxe color. Release date: Jan. 20, 2003. Running time: 100 Min.
Cast: Paul Giamatti, Harvey Pekar, Shari Springer Berman, Earl Billings, James Urbaniak, Judah Friedlander, Robert Pulcini, Toby Radloff, Hope Davis, Joyce Brabner, Donal Logue, Molly Shannon, James McCaffrey, Madylin Sweeten, Danielle Batone.

AMERICAN WEDDING
A Universal release of a Zide/Perry-Liveplanet production. Producers: Warren Zide, Craig Perry, Chris Moore, Adam Herz, Chris Bender. Executive producers: Paul Weitz, Chris Weitz, Louis G. Friedman. Director: Jesse Dylan. Screenplay: Adam Herz, based on characters created by Herz. Camera: Lloyd Ahern. Editor: Stuart Pappe. Music: Christophe Beck. In Deluxe color, Panavision widescreen. Release date: July 29, 2003. MPAA Rating: R. Running time: 97 Min.
Cast: Jason Biggs, Alyson Hannigan, January Jones, Thomas Ian Nicholas, Seann William Scott, Eddie Kaye Thomas, Fred Willard, Eugene Levy, Deborah Rush, Eric Allen Kramer, Molly Cheek, Angela Paton, Jennifer Coolidge.

ANALYZE THAT
A Warner Bros. release presented in association with Village Roadshow Pictures and NPV Entertainment of a Baltimore Spring Creek Pictures, Face/Tribeca production. Producers: Paula Weinstein, Jane Rosenthal. Executive producers: Billy Crystal, Barry Levinson, Chris Brigham, Len Amato, Bruce Berman. Co-producer: Suzanne Herrington. Director: Harold Ramis. Screenplay: Peter Steinfeld, Ramis, Peter Tolan, based on characters created by Kenneth Lonergan, Tolan. Camera: Ellen Kuras. Editor: Andrew Mondshein. Music: David Holmes. In Technicolor. Release date: Nov. 25, 2002. MPAA Rating: R. Running time: 95 Min.
Cast: Robert De Niro, Billy Crystal, Lisa Kudrow, Joe Viterelli, Reg Rogers, Cathy Moriarty-Gentile, John Finn, Kyle Sabihy, Callie Thorne, Pat Cooper, Frank Gio, Donnamarie Recco.

ANGELS CREST
A Coast 2 Coast Films production. Producer: David Chilewich. Executive producers: Salvatore Albanese, Larry Jackson. Director: J. Michael Couto. Screenplay: Couto, Grant Holly. Camera: (FotoKem color), Cameron Cutler. Editors: Robert Komatsu, Vanessa Newel. Music: Fuzzbee Morse. Release date: April 19, 2003. Running time: 82 Min.
Cast: Chris Bauer, Currie Graham, J. Michael Couto.

ANGER MANAGEMENT
A Sony Pictures Entertainment release of a Revolution Studios presentation of a Happy Madison production. Producers: Jack Giarraputo, Barry Bernardi. Executive producers: Adam Sandler, Allen Covert, Tim Herlihy, Todd Garner, John Jacobs. Co-producers: Michael Ewing, Allegra Clegg, Derek Dauchy. Director: Peter Segal. Screenplay: David Dorfman. Camera: Donald M. McAlpine. Editor: Jeff Gourson. Music: Teddy Castellucci. In Technicolor, Panavision widescreen. Release date: April 8, 2003. MPAA Rating: PG-13. Running time: 106 Min.
Cast: Adam Sandler, Jack Nicholson, Marisa Tomei, Luis Guzman, Allen Covert, Lynne Thigpen, Kurt Fuller, Jonathan Loughran, Krista Allen, January Jones, Woody Harrelson, John Turturro.

ANIMAL ATTRACTION
A Video Data Bank presentation of an Animals With Attitude production. Producer/Director: Kathy High. Camera: High, Mary Patierno, Tara Matiek. Editor: Patierno. Music: Mary Feaster. In color, vid. Release date: June 22, 2003. Running time: 60 Min. Documentary.

ANNE B. REAL
A Reve Entertainment Group presentation of an Urban Dream production. Producers: Josselyne Harman-Saccio, Luis Moro, Jeanine Rohn. Executive producers: Lenny Bier, Moro, Herman-Saccio. Co-producers: Felice Schachter, Michael Saccio, Lisa France. Co-executive producers: David Cera, Antonio Macia Sr., Jackie Martling, Nancy Sirianni. Director: Lisa France. Screenplay: Antonio Macia, France. Screen story: Luis Moro. Story: Macia. Camera: Stefan Forbes. Editor: Doug Forbes. Music: Dean Parker. In color. Release date: Feb. 16, 2003. Running time: 91 Min.
Cast: Janice Richardson, Carlos Leon, Sherri Saum, Eric Smith, Jackie Quinones, Geronimo Frias, Antonio Macia, Ernie Hudson.

ANONYMOUSLY YOURS

An Aerial Production. Producer/Director: Gayle Ferraro. Camera: Jill Tufts. Editor: Keiko Deguschi. Music: Claudio Ragazzi. In color, digital video. Release date: Nov. 10, 2002. Running time: 87 Min. Documentary.

ANYTHING ELSE

A DreamWorks Pictures release and presentation, in association with Gravier Prods. of a Perdido production. Producer: Letty Aronson. Executive producer: Stephen Tenenbaum. Co-producer: Helen Robin. Co-executive producers: Jack Rollins, Charles H. Joffe. Director/Writer: Woody Allen. Camera: Darius Khondji. Editor: Alisa Lepselter. In Technicolor, widescreen. Release date: Aug. 27, 2003. Running time: 108 Min.
Cast: Woody Allen, Jason Biggs, Christina Ricci, Danny DeVito, Stockard Channing, KaDee Strickland, Jimmy Fallon, Erica Leerhsen, William Hill, David Conrad, Adrian Grenier, Diana Krall.

ASSISTED LIVING

A MomoDog Production in association with Economic Projections, Inc. Producers: Alan Oxman, Archie Borders, Elliot Greenebaum. Director/Writer: Elliot Greenebaum. Camera: Marcel Cabrera. Editors: Paul Frank, Adriana Pacheco. Music: Hub Moore. In color, Super 16mm. Release date: Jan. 19, 2003. Running time: 77 Min.
Cast: Michael Bonsignore, Maggie Riley, Nanci Jo Boone, Mallory Jo Boone, Clint Vaught, Gail Benedict, Jose Albovias.

ATTITUDE

A Tenderloin yGroup presentation of a 9 @ Night production. Producers: Terry Forgette, Chikara Motomura, Kevin Winterfield, Rob Nilsson. Executive producers: David and Carol Richards. Director: Rob Nilsson. Story: Nilsson. Camera: Steve Burns, Mickey Freeman. Editor: Chikara Motomura. Music: Daniel Feinsmith. In B&W, HD vid. Release date: May 19, 2003. Running time: 102 Min.
Cast: Michael Disend, Robert Viharo, Edwin Johnson, Selana Allen, Marion Christian, Vernon Medeiros, David Fine.

BACHELORMAN

A Films on Tap presentation. Producers: Karen Bailey, Rodney Lee Conover, Helen Woo. Executive producer: Tad Lebeck. Co-producers: John Putch, Jerry P. Jacobs, Jeffrey C. Hause. Director: John Putch. Screenplay: Rodney Lee Conover, Jeffrey C. Hause, David Hines. Camera: Keith J. Duggan. Editor: Randy Carter. Music: Steve Bauman, J. Lynn Duckett. In color, DV. Release date: July 26, 2003. Running time: 90 Min.
Cast: David DeLuise, Missi Pyle, Rodney Lee Conover, Karen Bailey, Carol Locatell, Clyde Kusatsu.

BAD BOYS II

Bad Boys II
A Sony Pictures Entertainment release of a Columbia Pictures presentation of a Don Simpson/Jerry Bruckheimer production. Producer: Bruckheimer. Executive producers: Mike Stenson, Chad Oman, Barry Waldman. Director: Michael Bay. Screenplay: Ron Shelton, Jerry Stahl. Story: Marianne Wibberley, Comac Wibberley, Shelton, based on characters created by George Gallo. Camera: Amir Mokri. Editors: Mark Goldblatt, Thomas A. Muldoon, Roger Barton. Music: Trevor Rabin. In Technicolor, Panavision widescreen. Release date: July 9, 2003. MPAA Rating: R. Running time: 146 Min.
Cast: Martin Lawrence, Will Smith, Jordi Molla, Gabrielle Union, Peter Stormare, Theresa Randle, Joe Pantoliano, Michael Shannon, Jon Seda, Yul Vazquez, Jason Manuel Olazabal, Otto Sanchez, Henry Rollins.

BASIC

A Sony Pictures Entertainment release of a Columbia Pictures and Intermedia Films presentation of a Phoenix Pictures production. Producers: Mike Medavoy, Arnie Messer, James Vanderbilt, Michael Tadross. Executive producers: Moritz Borman, Nigel Sinclair, Basil Iwanyk, Jonathan Krane. Co-producers: Andy Given, Louis Philips, Lee Nelson, Dror Soref. Co-executive producer: Bradley J. Fischer. Director: John McTiernan. Screenplay: James Vanderbilt. Camera: Steve Mason. Editor: George Folsey Jr. Music: Klaus Badelt. In Technicolor, Deluxe prints; Panavision widescreen. Release date: March 18, 2003. MPAA Rating: R. Running time: 98 Min.
Cast: John Travolta, Connie Nielsen, Samuel L. Jackson, Giovanni Ribisi, Brian Van Holt, Tim Daly, Cristian de la Fuente, Dash Mihok, Taye Diggs, Roselyn Sanchez, Harry Connick Jr.

THE BATTLE OF SHAKER HEIGHTS

A Miramax Films release of a LivePlanet production. Producers: Chris Moore, Jeff Balis. Executive producers: Ben Affleck, Matt Damon, Rick Schwartz, Joel Hatch. Directors: Kyle Rankin, Efram Potelle. Screenplay: Erica Beeney. Camera: Thomas E. Ackerman. Editor: Richard Nord. Music: Richard Marvin. In Fotokem color and prints. Release date: Aug. 18, 2003. MPAA Rating: PG-13. Running time: 78 Min.
Cast: Shia LaBeouf, Elden Henson, Amy Smart, Billy Kay, Kathleen Quinlan, Shiri Appleby, William Sadler, Ray Wise, Philipp Karner , Anson Mount.

THE BEAT

A Tripped Out Prods. and Symbolic Entertainment production. Producers: Brandon Sonnier, Jason Peterson, Ryan Seashore, Scott Speer. Executive producers: Ken and Ruth Arnold. Director/Writer: Brandon Sonnier. Camera: Graham Futerfas. Editor: John Randle. In color.
Release date: Jan. 19, 2003. Running time: 86 Min.
With: Rahman Jamaal, Michael Colyar, Steve Connell, Jazmin Lewis, Keith Ewell, Coolio.

BEAUTIFUL KID

An MC production. Producers: Patrick McCullough, Michael Carty. Executive producers: Peter Newman, Greg Johnson, Colum McCann. Director: Colum McCann, Michael Carty. Screenplay: Carty. Camera: James Capria. Editor: Carty. In color, DV. Release date: March 22, 2003. Running time: 104 Min.
With: Frank McCourt, Malachy McCourt, Arthur French, Dan Brennan, Javier Pire, John "the Terror" Carty, Kate Forsatz, Christie Myers, Halley Wegryn-Gross.

BED: THE BED THAT EATS

A Cult Epics release. Producer: George Barry. Co-producer: Maureen Petrucci. Director/Writer: George Barry. Camera: Robert Fresco. Editor: Ron Medfico. Music: Cyclobe. In color, 16mm. Release date: Feb. 15, 2003. Running time: 77 Min.
With: Demene Hall, Rusty Russ, Julie Ritter, Linda Bond, Patrick Spence-Thomas, Dave Marsh, Rosa Luxemburg, Ed Oldani.

BEYOND THE SEA

A Gato Media production. Producer: Lisandro Perez-Rey. Executive Producer: Perez-Rey. Director/Editor: Perez-Rey. Camera: Perez-Rey. Music: Juan Montoya, Karl Ferrari. In color, DV. Release date: June 18, 2003. Running time: 80 Min. Documentary.

BIKER BOYZ

A DreamWorks release of an 3 Arts production. Producers: Stephanie Allain, Gina Prince-Bythewood, Erwin Stoff. Executive producer: Don Kurt. Director: Reggie Rock Bythewood. Screenplay: Craig Fernandez, Bythewood, based on the New Times article by Michael Gougis. Camera: Gregory Gardiner. Editors: Terilyn A. Shropshire, Caroline Ross. Music: Camara Kambon. In Technicolor. Release date: Jan. 28, 2003. MPAA Rating: PG-13. Running time: 110 Min.
Cast: Laurence Fishburne, Derek Luke, Orlando Jones, Djimon Hounsou, Lisa Bonet, Brendan Fehr, Larenz Tate, Kid Rock, Rick Gonzalez, Meagan Good, Salli Richardson-Whitfield.

BITTER JESTER

A Bitter Jester Prods., Mc Belz Enterprises and Panacea Entertainment presentation. Producer: Kenneth R. Simmons. Executive producers: Richard Belzer, Eric Gardner. Co-producers: Ron DiGiorgio, David Klingman, Thomas Chestaro. Director/Editor: Maija DiGiorgio. Camera: Jody Del Giorno. In color, Digital Beta. Release date: March 9, 2003. Running time: 91 Min. Documentary.
With: Maija DiGiorgio, Richard Belzer, Kenneth R. Simmons, Joy Behar, Peter Boyle, George Carlin, Chevy Chase, Norm Crosby, Phyllis Diller, Whoopi Goldberg, Gilbert Gottfried, DL Hughley.

BLACK CADILLAC

An Artists View Entertainment presentation of a Painting Entertainment production. Producers: John Murlowski, Kenneth Burke, Steven Douglas Smith. Co-producers: Miriam Flynn, John Lind. Director: John Murlowski. Screenplay: Will Aldis, Story: Murlowski. Camera: Smith. Editors: John Gilbert. In color. Release date: April 21, 2003. Running time: 93 Min.
Cast: Randy Quaid, Shane Johnson, Josh Hammond, Jason Dohring.

BLOOD FEAST 2: ALL U CAN EAT

A Queso Grande Prods. presentation. Producer: Jacky Lee Morgan. Executive producer: David F. Friedman. Co-producers: W. Boyd Ford, Penelope Helmer, Melissa Morgan, Brian Pitt, Jimi Woods. Director: Herschell Gordon Lewis. Screenplay: W. Boyd Ford. Camera: Chris W. Johnson. Editor: Steven Teagle. Music: Southern Culture on the Skids. In color, DV. Release date: July 9, 2003. Running time: 99 Min.
With: J.P. Delahoussaye, John McConnell, Mark McLachlan, Toni Wynne, Kristi Polit, Christi Brown, Christina Cuenca, Michelle Miller, Jill Rao, Cindy Roubal, Veronica Russell, John Waters.

BLUE COLLAR COMEDY TOUR: THE MOVIE

A Warner Bros. release presented in association with Pandora of a Gaylord Films/Parallel Entertainment production. Producers: Alan C. Blomquist, J.P. Williams, Hunt Lowry, Casey La Scala. Executive producer: E.K. Gaylord II. Director: CB Harding. Camera: Bruce Finn. Editor: Tony Hayman. Music: James S. Levine. In Deluxe color, digital HD video. Release date: March 20, 2003. MPAA Rating: PG-13. Running time: 105 Min. Documentary.
With: Jeff Foxworthy, Bill Engvall, Ron White, Larry the Cable Guy, David Alan Grier, Chris Cagle, Heidi Klum.

BLUE HILL AVENUE

An Artisan Entertainment release in association with Cahoots Prods./Asiatic Associates/Glen Shaffer/Den Pictures. Producers: Mike Erwin, J. Max Kirishima, Brian "Killa B" Hinds. Executive producers: Rand Chortkoff, Craig Ross Jr., Mark Holdom. Co-producer: Ronn Roberts. Director/Writer/Editor: Craig Ross Jr. Camera: Carl Bartles. Music: Jan Pomerans, Cruel Timothy. In Deluxe color. Release date: Sept. 19, 2003. MPAA Rating: R. Running time: 128 Min.
Cast: Allen Payne, Angelle Brooks, William Johnson, Aaron D. Spears, Andrew Divoff, Clarence Williams III, William Forsythe, Michael "Bear" Taliferro, Myquan Jackson, Marlon Young, Richard Lawson.

BLUE WILD ANGEL: JIMI HENDRIX AT THE ISLE OF WIGHT

An MLF Prods. & Experience Hendrix LLC presentation. Producers: Janie Hendrix, John McDermott. Director: Murray Lerner. Camera: Andy Carchrae, Jack Hazen, Nic Knowland, Norman Langley, Lerner, Richard Stanley, Charles Stewart, Mike Whittaker. Editor: Einar Westerlund. In color. Release date: Oct. 16, 2002. Running time: 101 Min. Documentary.

BOAT TRIP

An Artisan Entertainment release of a Motion Picture Corp. of America, presentation of an Intl. West Pictures, ApolloMedia, Brad Krevoy, Gemini Films production. Producers: Brad Krevoy, Gerhard Schmidt, Frank Huebner, Andrew Sugerman. Executive producer: Sabine Mueller. Director: Mort Nathan. Screenplay: Nathan, William Bigelow. Camera: Shawn Maurer. Editor: John Axness. Music: Robert Folk. In Deluxe color. Release date: March 18, 2003. MPAA Rating: R. Running time: 94 Min.
Cast: Cuba Gooding, Jr., Horatio Sanz, Roselyn Sanchez, Vivica A. Fox, Maurice Godin, Roger Moore, Lin Shaye , Victoria Silvstedt.

BOMB THE SYSTEM

A Drops Entertainment production. (International sales: The Film Sales Company, New York.) Producers: Ben Rekhi, Sol Tryon. Executive producers: Kanwal Rekhi, Mark Webber. Co-executive producer: Rob Bethge. Co-producers: Smriti Mundhra, Theo Sena. Director/Writer: Adam Bhala Lough. Camera: Ben Kutchins. Editor: Jay Rabinowitz. Music: El-P. In Technicolor. Release date: May 9, 2003. Running time: 91 Min.
Cast: Mark Webber, Gano Grills, Jade Yorker, Jaclyn DeSantis, Joey Dedio, Stephen Buchanan, Al Sapienza, Bonz Malone.

BOOKIES

A Motion Picture Corp. of America presentation of an Intl. West Pictures, Intl. Arts Entertainment and Gemini Film production. Producers: Alan Greenspan, Paul Greenstone, Sabine Mueller. Executive producers: Gerhard Schmidt, Andrea Kreuzhage, Brad Krevoy. Director: Mark Illsley. Screenplay: Michael Bacall. Camera: Brendan Galvin. Editor: Norman Buckley. Original music: Christopher Tyng. In color, HD-to-35mm. Release date: Jan. 19, 2003. Running time: 88 Min.
Cast: Nick Stahl, Lukas Haas, Johnny Galecki, Rachael Leigh Cook, David Proval, John Diehl, Zuri Williams.

BOOK OF DANNY

A Fingerprint Films presentation of a Yaffe/Diamond production. Producers: Lalou Diamond, Michael Young. Executive producer: Malya Penchik. Director/Writer: Adam Yaffe. Camera: Peter Agliata. Editor: Ben Slatkin. Music: John Kimbrough. In color. Release date: June 19, 2003. Running time: 54 Min.
Cast: Daniel Randell, Larry Block, Marcia Jean Kurtz, Elaina Erika Davis, Madison Arnold, Maria Tucci, Adam Busch.

BORN RICH

A Wise and Good Film production. Producers: Jamie Johnson, Nick Kurzon, Dirk Wittenborn. Co-producer: Bingo Gubelman. Director: Jamie Johnson. Camera: Nick Kurzon. Editors: Steve Pilgrim, Jason Zemlicka, Kurzon. Music: Joel Goodman. In color, HD. Release date: Jan. 21, 2003. Running time: 75 Min. Documentary.
With: Georgina Bloomberg, Ivana Trump, Si Newhouse IV, Juliet Hartford, Carlo von Zeitschel, Stephanie Ercklentz, Christina Floyd, Josiah Hornblower, Cody Franchetti, Luke Weil.

BOUGHT AND SOLD

A Pawnshop Pictures production. Producers: Bergen Swanson, Michael Tolajian. Co-producers: Rene Tolajian, Mark Kossick. Director/Writer: Michael Tolajian. Camera: Kip Bogdahn. Editors: Seth Anderson, Michael Tolajian. Music: Joe Delia. In color, super 16 mm-2-35 mm. Release date: May 2, 2003. Running time: 92 Min.
Cast: Rafael Sardina, David Margulies, Joe Grifasi, Marjan Neshat, Frank Harts, Christina Ablaza, Anthony Chisholm.

A BOY'S LIFE

An HBO presentation of a Moxie Firecracker production. Producers: Liz Garbus, Rory Kennedy. Director: Rory Kennedy. Co-director: Nick Doob. Camera: Doob. Editors: Charlton McMillan. Music: Joel Goodman. In color, DV. Release date: April 24, 2003. Running time: 77 Min. Documentary.

BREAK A LEG

A Catchlight Films presentation. Producers: Jeanette Volturno, Trey Wilkins. Executive producer: Charles Lee. Co-producers: John Cassini, Ric Wolfe. Director: Monika Mitchell. Screenplay: Frank Cassini, John Cassini. Camera: Eric J. Goldstein. Editors: Donald J. Paonessa, Lawrence Maddox. Music: Roger Bellon. In CFI color. Release date: June 16, 2003. Running time: 97 Min.
Cast: John Cassini, Rene Rivera, Molly Parker, Jennifer Beals, Kevin Corrigan, Frank Cassini, Sandra Oh, J.J. Johnston, Eric Roberts.

BREAKFAST WITH HUNTER

Producer: Wayne Ewing. Executive producer: Andrew Ewing. Director/Editor: Wayne Ewing. Camera (color, digital video), Ewing, Mark Muhein, Steve York; associate producer, Jennifer Erskine. Reviewed at Cinevegas Film Festival, Las Vegas, Release date: June 17, 2003. Running time: 91 Min. Documentary.
Cast: Hunter S. Thompson, Johnny Depp, Benicio Del Toro, PJ O'Rourke, John Cusack, Terry Gilliam, Alex Cox, Todd Davies, Jann Wenner, Terry McDonald, Matt Dillon, George Plimpton, Ralph Steadman.

BRINGING DOWN THE HOUSE

A Buena Vista release of a Touchstone Pictures presentation in association with Hyde Park Entertainment of a David Hoberman/Ashok Amritraj production. Producers: Hoberman, Amritraj. Executive producers: Jane Bartelme, Queen Latifah. Co-producer: Todd Lieberman. Director: Adam Shankman. Screenplay: Jason Filardi. Camera: Julio Macat. Editor: Jerry Greenberg. Music: Lalo Schifrin. In Technicolor, Panavision widescreen. Release date: Feb. 19, 2003. MPAA Rating: PG-13. Running time: 105 Min.
Cast: Steve Martin, Queen Latifah, Eugene Levy, Joan Plowright, Jean Smart, Missi Pyle, Kimberly J. Brown, Steve Harris, Betty White.

BROADWAY: THE GOLDEN AGE

An Albert M. Tapper presentation. Producers: Albert M. Tapper, Jamie deRoy, Anne L. Bernstein. Director/Editor: Rick McKay. Camera: McKay. In color, DV. Release date: June 24, 2003. Running time: 109 Min. Documentary.
Cast: Edie Adams, Beatrice Arthur, Elizabeth Ashley, Alec Baldwin, Kaye Ballard, John Barrowman, Bryan Batt, Jim Borstelmann, Tom Bosley, Betty Buckley, Carol Burnett, Kitty Carlisle, Carol Channing, Betty Comden, Barbara Cook, Carole Cook, Hume Cronyn.

BROTHER OUTSIDER: THE LIFE OF BAYARD RUSTIN

A Question Why Films LLC production in association with Independent Television Service, National Black Programming Coalition. Producers: Nancy Kates, Bennett Singer. Executive producer: Sam Pollard. Co-producer: Mridu Chandra. Associate producer: Heather Seldes. Directors: Nancy Kates, Bennett Singer. Camera: Robert Shepard. Editors: Veronica Selver, Rhonda Collins. Music: B. Quincy Griffin. In color, HD video. Release date: Jan. 12, 2003. Running time: 82 Min. Documentary.

THE BROWN BUNNY

A Kinetique presentation of a Vincent Gallo production. (International sales: Wild Bunch, Paris.) Producer: Gallo. Director/Writer/Editor: Vincent Gallo. Camera: Gallo. Music: Ted Curson, Jeff Alexander, Gordon Lightfoot, Jackson C. Franck. Release date: May 21, 2003. Running time: 119 Min.
Cast: Vincent Gallo, Chloe Sevigny, Cheryl Tiegs.

BRUCE ALMIGHTY

A Universal Pictures release of a Spyglass Entertainment presentation of a Shady Acres/Pit Bull production. Producers: Tom Shadyac, Jim Carrey, James D. Brubaker, Michael Bostick, Steve Koren, Mark O'Keefe. Executive producers: Gary Barber, Roger Birnbaum, Steve Oedekerk. Director: Tom Shadyac. Screenplay: Steve Koren, Mark O'Keefe, Steve Oedekerk. Story: Steve Koren, Mark O'Keefe. Camera: Dean Semler. Editors: Scott Hill. Music: John Debney. In Deluxe color. Release date: May 20, 2003. MPAA Rating: PG-13. Running time: 101 Min.
Cast: Jim Carrey, Morgan Freeman, Jennifer Aniston, Philip Baker Hall, Catherine Bell, Lisa Ann Walter, Steven Carell, Nora Dunn.

BUKOWSKI: BORN INTO THIS

A Pictures From Earth production. Producer: John Dullaghan. Co-producers: Diane Markow, John McCormick. Director: John Dullaghan. Camera: Matt Mindlin, Bill Langley. Editor: Victor Livingstone; music/sound designer, Jennifer Boyd. In color/B&W, HD cam. Release date: Jan. 22, 2003. Running time: 130 Min. Documentary.

BULLETPROOF MONK

An MGM release of a Lion Rock production and a Flypaper Press production in association with Lakeshore Entertainment and Mosaic Media Group. Producers: Charles Roven, Douglas Segal, Terrence Chang, John Woo. Executive producers: Kelley Smith-Wait, Michael Yanover, Gotham Chopra, Caroline Macaulay. Co-producers: Brent O'Connor, Alan G. Glazer, Mark Paniccia. Director: Paul Hunter. Screenplay: Ethan Reiff, Cyrus Voris, based on the Flypaper Press comic book. Camera: Stefan Czapsky. Editor: Robert K. Lambert. Music: Eric Serra. In Deluxe color, Clairmont widescreen. Release date: April 4, 2003. MPAA Rating: PG-13. Running time: 103 Min.
Cast: Chow Yun-Fat, Seann William Scott, Jaime King, Karel Roden, Victoria Smurfit, Marcus Jean Pirae, Mako, Roger Yuan.

CAMERA OBSCURA

A Fish Eye Films production. Producer: Tassos G. Kazinos. Executive producer: Albertino Abela. Director/Writer: Hamlet Sarkissian. Camera: Haris Zambarloukos. Editor: Andrea Zondler. Music: Tigran Mansurian. In Deluxe colro/B&W. Release date: Sept. 21, 2003. Running time: 99 Min.
Cast: Adam Trese, Ariadna Gil, Cully Fredricksen, VJ Foster, Kirk Ward.

CAMP

An IFC Films release of an IFC Prods. presentation of a Jersey Films, Killer Films, Laughlin Park Pictures production. Producers: Katie Roumel, Christine Vachon, Pamela Koffler, Danny DeVito, Michael Shamberg, Stacey Sher, Jonathan Weisgal. Executive producers: John Wells, Richard Klubeck, Jonathan Sehring, Caroline Kaplan, Holly Becker. Co-producers: Allen Bain, Dan Levine. Director/Writer: Todd Graff. Camera: Kip Bogdahn. Editor: Myron Kerstein. Music: Stephen Trask. In DuArt color. Release date: Jan. 21, 2003. Running time: 114 Min.
Cast: Daniel Letterle, Joanna Chilcoat, Robin De Jesus, Tiffany Taylor, Sasha Allen, Alana Allen, Anna Kendrick, Don Dixon.

CANDY VON DEWD

A Massacre at Central Hi presentation in association with Cosmic Hex Archive and Werepad Enterprises. Producer: Jacques Boyreau. Executive producer: Scott Moffett. Director/Writer: Jacques Boyreau. Camera: Boyreau, Scott Moffett, Lorelei David, Soren Ragsdale. Editor: Anton Herbert. Music: Zonetech, Brian Hock, Billy Bates. In color, DV. Release date: March 27, 2003. Running time: 54 Min.
With: Katie Birrell, Pandemonium, Scott Moffett, James Patrik, Chuck Mignacco, Phillip Mauro, Brian Saxsenmeier, Patrick Fisher.

CAPTURING THE FRIEDMANS

A Hit the Ground Running Films presentation. Producers: Andrew Jarecki, Marc Smerling. Director: Andrew Jarecki. Camera: Adolfo Doring. Editor: Richard Hankin. Music: Andrea Morricone. In Duart color. Release date: Jan. 17, 2003. Running time: 107 Min. Documentary.
With: Arnold Friedman, Elaine Friedman, David Friedman, Seth Friedman, Jesse Friedman, Howard Friedman, John McDermott, Detective Frances Galasso, Anthony Sgueglia, Joseph Onorato.

CARANDIRU

A Sony Pictures Classics release (in U.S.) of a Sony Pictures Classics and HB Filmes in association with Columbia TriStar do Brasil, Globo Filmes and Br Petrobas presentation. (International sales: Columbia TriStar Film Distributors Intl.) Producer: Hector Babenco. Co-produced by Flavio R. Tambellini, Fabiano Gullane. Director: Hector Babenco. Screenplay: Victor Nava, Babenco, Fernando Bonassi, based on the book "Carandiru Station" by Drauzio Varella. Release date: May 18, 2003. Running time: 148 Min. Brazilian.

Cast: Luiz Carlos Vasconcelos, Milhem Cortaz, Milton Goncalves, Ivan de Almeida, Ailton Graca, Maria Luisa Mendonca, Aida Lerner, Rodrigo Santoro, Gero Camilo.

CARRY ME HOME

A Showtime presentation of a Saturday Pictures/Soup Kitchen Films production. Producers: Anna Ryan Hansen, Sean Hewitt. Executive producer: Matthew S. Hansen. Director: Jace Alexander. Screenplay: Christopher Fay. June 20, 2003. Running time: 97 Min.

Cast: Penelope Ann Miller, Kevin Anderson, David Alan Basche, Ashley Rose Orr, Jane Alexander, Leo Burmester, Nicholas Braun, Harrison Chad.

CASA DE LOS BABYS

An IFC Films release of a Syvan/Springall production. Producers: Lemore Syvan, Alejandro Springall. Executive producers: Alison Bourke, Jonathan Sehring, Caroline Kaplan. Director/Writer/Editor: John Sayles. Camera: Mauricio Rubinstein. Music: Mason Daring. In color. Release date: July 14, 2003. Running time: 95Min.

Cast: Maggie Gyllenhaal, Marcia Gay Harden, Daryl Hannah, Susan Lynch, Mary Steenburgen, Lili Taylor, Rita Moreno, Vanessa Martinez.

CATCH ME IF YOU CAN

A DreamWorks release from Amblin Entertainment of a Kemp Co. and Splendid Pictures production and a Parkes/MacDonald production. Producers: Steven Spielberg, Walter F. Parkes. Executive producers: Barry Kemp, Laurie MacDonald, Michel Shane, Tony Romano. Coproducer: Devorah Moos-Hankin. Co-executive producer: Daniel Lupi. Director: Steven Spielberg. Screenplay: Jeff Nathanson, based on the book by Frank W. Abagnale with Stan Redding. Camera: Janusz Kaminski. Editor: Michael Kahn. Music: John Williams. In Technicolor. Release date: Dec. 9, 2002 MPAA Rating: PG-13. Running time: 140 Min.

Cast: Leonardo DiCaprio, Tom Hanks, Christopher Walken, Martin Sheen, Nathalie Baye, Amy Adams, James Brolin, Brian Howe, Frank John Hughes, Steve Eastin, Chris Ellis, John Finn, Jennifer Garner.

THE CEMENT BALL OF EARTH, HEAVEN, AND HELL

A Trent Harris (Salt Lake City) production. Producer/Director/Writer/Editor: Trent Harris. Camera: Trent Harris. In color, DigiBeta. Release date: June 11, 2003. Running time: 60 Min. Documentary.

A CERTAIN KIND OF DEATH

A New Box presentation. Producer/Director:Editor: Blue Hadaegh, Grover Babcock. Camera: Hadaegh, Babcock. In color, DVCam. Release date: Jan. 20, 2003. Running time: 69 Min.

CHARLIE: THE LIFE AND ART OF CHARLES CHAPLIN

A Warner Home Video release of a Lorac Prods. production. (International sales: MK2, Paris.) Producer: Richard Schickel. Director/Writer: Richard Schickel. Editors: Brian McKenzie. Release date: May 21, 2003. Running time: 132 Min. Documentary.

Cast: Woody Allen, Johnny Depp, Robert Downey Jr., Milos Forman, Marcel Marceau, Richard Attenborough, Martin Scorsese, Norman Lloyd, Michael Chaplin, Geraldine Chaplin, Sydney Chaplin, David Raksin, Claire Bloom, David Thomson, David Robinson, Bill Irwin, Jeffrey Vance, Andrew Sarris, Jeanine Basinger. Narrator: Sydney Pollack.

CHARLIE'S ANGELS: FULL THROTTLE

A Sony Pictures Entertainment release of a Columbia Pictures presentation of a Leonard Goldberg Production in association with Flower Films and Tall Trees Prods./Wonderland Sound and Vision. Producers: Leonard Goldberg, Drew Barrymore, Nancy Juvonen. Executive producers: Jenno Topping, Patrick Crowley. Director: McG. Screenplay: John August, Cormac and Marianne Wibberley, based on a story by John August. Camera: Russell Carpenter. Editors: Wayne Wahrman. Music: Edward Shearmur. In Deluxe color, Panavision widescreen. Release date: June 18, 2003. MPAA Rating: PG-13. Running time: 111 Min.

Cast: Cameron Diaz, Drew Barrymore, Lucy Lu, John Forsythe, Bernie Mac, Crispin Glover, Justin Theroux, Robert Patrick, Demi Moore, Radrigo Santara, Shia LaBeouf, Matt LeBlanc, Luke Wilson, John Cleese, Ja'net DuBois, Robert Forster, Eric Bogosian, Carrie Fisher.

CHASING PAPI

A 20th Century Fox release of a Fox 2000 presentation of a Spirit Dance Entertainment production. Producers: Forest Whitaker, Tracey Trench, Laura Angelica Simon. Executive producer: Tajamika Paxton. Co-producers: Elaine Dysinger, Nellie Nugiel. Director: Linda Mendoza. Screenplay: Laura Angeica Simon, Steven Antin, Alison Balian, Elizabeth Sarnoff, from a story by Simon, Antin. Camera: Xavier Perez Grobet. Editor: Maysie Hoy. Music: Emilio Estefan, Jr. In Deluxe color. Release date: April 14, 2003. MPAA rating: PG. Running time: 80 Min.

Cast: Roselyn Sanchez, Sofia Vergara, Jaci Velasquez, Eduardo Verastegui, Lisa Vidal, Freddy Rodriguez, D.L. Hughley, Maria Conchita Alonso, Ian Gomez.

CHICAGO

A Miramax release of a Producer Circle Co. production. Producer: Martin Richards. Executive producers: Craig Zadan, Neil Meron, Sam Crothers, Bob Weinstein, Meryl Poster. Co-producer: Don Carmody. Co-executive producers: Julie Goldstein, Jennifer Berman. Director: Rob Marshall. Screenplay: Bill Condon, based on the musical play by Bob Fosse, Fred Ebb, based on the play by Maurine Dallas Watkins. Camera: Dion Beebe. Editor: Martin Walsh. Music: John Kander. In Deluxe color. Release date: Dec. 3, 2002. MPAA Rating: PG-13. Running time: 113 Min.

Cast: Catherine Zeta Jones, Renee Zellweger, Richard Gere, Queen Latifah, John C. Reilly, Christine Baranski, Lucy Liu, Taye Diggs, Colm Feore, Dominic West.

COCK & BULL STORY

A Pantheon Entertainment, Bailey/Hayes Prods. and Hawkemedia presentation. Producer: R.S. Bailey. Executive producers: Dennis Woods-Doderer, Brian A. Green, Greg H. Sims. Co-producer: David Toma. Director/Writer: Billy Hayes, based on the play by Richard Crowe, Richard Zajdlic. Camera: Ben Kufrin. Editor: Gregory Plotkin. Music: Pierpaolo Tiano. In color. release date: June 23, 2003. Running time: 102 Min.

With: Brian A. Green, Bret Roberts, Wendy Fowler, Greg Mullavey, John Prosky, Sam Scarber, P. Darin Heames, Christian Payne, David Spates, Jason Boggs, Murray Robert Miano, Jennifer Rebecca Bailey, "King" Ipitan, Kurt Caceres, Luke Massy, Elias McCabe, Kay Lenz.

COFFEE AND CIGARETTES

A Smokescreen Inc. production in association with Asmik ACE (Japan)/BIM Distribuzione (Italy). (International sales: Fortissimo Film Sales, Amsterdam.) Producers: Joana Vicente, Jason Kliot. Co-producers: Stacey Smith, Gretchen McGowan. Director/Writer: Jim Jarmusch. Camera: Federick Elmes, Ellen Kuras, Robby Muller, Tom DiCillo. Editors: Jay Rabinowitz, Melody London, Terry Katz, Jarmusch. In B&W. Release date: Sept. 4, 2003. Running time: 96 Min.

With: Roberto Benigni, Steven Wright, Joie Lee, Cinque Lee, Steve Buscemi, Iggy Pop, Tom Waits, Joe Rigano, Vinny Vella, Vinny Vella Jr., Renee French, E. J. Rodriguez, Alex Descas, Isaach De Bankole, Cate Blanchett, Meg White, Jack White, Alfred Molina, Steve Coogan, Gza, Rza, Bill Murray, Bill Rice, Taylor Mead.

COLD CREEK MANOR

A Buena Vista release of a Touchstone Pictures presentation of a Red Mullet production. Producers: Annie Stewart, Mike Figgis. Executive producers: Lata Ryan, Richard Jefferies. Director: Mike Figgis. Screenplay: Richard Jefferies. Camera: Declan Quinn. Editor: Dylan Tichenor. Music: Figgis. In Technicolor. Release date: Sept. 17, 2003. MPAA Rating: R. Running time: 119 Min.

Cast: Dennis Quaid, Sharon Stone, Stephen Dorff, Juliette Lewis, Kristen Stewart, Ryan Wilson, Dana Eskelson, Christopher Plummer.

THE COLD WAR AND BEYOND

A Chronicles Group presentation. Producer: Jim Thebaut. Executive producers: Edsel Dunford, Thebaut. Director: Jim Thebaut. Screenplay: Thebaut, Edsel Dunford. Camera: Anna Kouranova, Michael Ford, Maury Dahlen, Reggie Lafrance, Vic Losick, Brain Pratt. Editor: William Rotberg. Music: Pace James Music Group. In color, video. Release date: Oct. 6, 2002. Running time: 130 Min. Documentary.

With: Robert McNamara, Georgy Arbatov, Robert Gates, Valentine Berezhkov, Roland Timerbaev, Dr. Zbigniew Brezinski, Gen. Andrew Goodpaster, Nikolai Leonoy, Adolph K. Thiel, Peter Bird Swiers, Henry Kissinger, Gen. Brent Scowcroft, Dr. Edward Teller, Dr. Sergei Rogov.

COMEDIAN

A Miramax Films release of a New Material presentation of a Bridgnorth Films production. Producer: Gary Streiner. Executive producer: Jerry Seinfeld. Director: Christian Charles. Camera: Charles, Gary Streiner, Mark Plumber. Editor: Chris Franklin. In color, video-to-35mm. Release date: Oct. 8, 2002. MPAA Rating: R. Running time: 81 Min. Documentary.

With: Jerry Seinfeld, Greg Geraldo, Sherrod Small, Jim Norton, Godfrey Danchimah, Allan Havey, Colin Quinn, Cynthia Koury, Orny Adams, George Wallace, Eddie Ifft, Robert Klein, Mario Joyner, T. Sean Shannon, Gary Greenberg, Shawn Seymour, Bill Cosby.

CONFESSIONS OF A DANGEROUS MIND

A Miramax release of a Mad Chance production in association with Section Eight. Producer: Andrew Lazar. Executive producers: Steven Soderbergh, Rand Ravich, Bob Weinstein, Harvey Weinstein, Jonathan Gordon, Stephen Evans. Co-Executive producer: Far Shariat. Co-producer: Jeffrey Sudzin. Director: George Clooney. Screenplay: Charlie Kaufman, based on the book by Chuck Barris. Camera: Newton Thomas Sigel. Editor: Stephen Mirrione. Music: Alex Wurman. In Deluxe color, Panavision widescreen. Release date: Dec. 3, 2002. MPAA Rating: R. Running time: 113 Min.

Cast: Sam Rockwell, Drew Barrymore, George Clooney, Julia Roberts, Rutger Hauer, Maggie Gyllenhaal, Kristen Wilson, Jennifer Hall.

CONFIDENCE

A Lions Gate release of a Lions Gate Films presentation in association with Cinerenta of an Ignite Entertainment, Cinewhite production. Producers: Marc Butan, Michael Paseornek, Michael Burns, Michael Ohoven. Executive producers: Eric Kopeloff, Marco Mehlitz, Eberhard Kayser, Scott Bernstein. Director: James Foley. Screenplay: Doug Jung. Camera: Juan Ruiz-Anchia. Editor: Stuart Levy. In color, widescreen. Release date: Jan. 20, 2003. Running time: 98 Min.

Cast: Ed Burns, Rachel Weisz, Andy Garcia, Dustin Hoffman, Paul Giamatti, Donal Logue, Luis Guzman, Brian Van Holt, Frankie G, Morris Chestnut, Robert Forster.

THE COOLER

A Lions Gate Films release (in N. America) of a ContentFilm and Gryphon Films presentation of a Pierce-Williams/Furst Films and Dog Pond Films production. Producers: Sean Furst, Michael Pierce. Executive producers: Edward S. Pressman, John Schmidt, Alessandro Camon, Brett Morrison, Robert Gryphon, Joe Madden. Co-producers: Elliot Lewis Rosenblatt, Bryan Furst. Director: Wayne Kramer. Screenplay: Frank Hannah, Kramer. Camera: James Whitaker. Editor: Arthur Coburn. Music: Mark Isham. In Deluxe color, Panavision widescreen. Release date: Jan. 17, 2003. Running time: 101 Min.
Cast: William H. Macy, Alec Baldwin, Maria Bello, Shawn Hatosy, Ron Livingston, Paul Sorvino, Estella Warren, Arthur J. Nascarella, M.C. Gainey, Ellen Greene, Joey Fatone, Don Scribner, Tony Longo, Richard Israel, Timothy Landfield, T.J. Gioia, Jewel Shepard.

CORAL REEF ADVENTURE

A MacGillivray Freeman Films production in association with National Science Foundation, Museum of Science, Boston, National Wildlife Federation, Lowell, Blake & Associates and Museum Film Network. Producer: Greg MacGillivray, Alec Lorimore. Executive producers: Charlton Reynders, Christopher Palmer. Director: Greg MacGillivray. Writers: Stephen Judson, Osha Gray Davidson. Narration: Jack Stephens. Camera: Howard Hall (underwater), Brad Ohlund (topside). Editor: Judson. Music: Crosby, Stills & Nash. In color, 15/70 large format. Release date: April 8, 2003. Running time: 45 Min. Documentary. IMAX.
With: Michele and Howard Hall, Rusli Valakoro, Richard Pyle, Jean-Michel Cousteau. Narrator: Liam Neeson.

CRADLE 2 THE GRAVE

A Warner Bros. release of a Silver Pictures production. Producer: Joel Silver. Executive producers: Herbert W. Gians, Ray D. Copeland. Co-producers: Susan Levin, Melina Kevorkian. Director: Andrzej Bartkowiak. Screenplay: John O'Brien, Channing Gibson. Story: O'Brien. Camera: Daryn Okada. Editor: Derek G. Brechin. Music: John Frizzell, Damon "Grease" Blackman. In Technicolor, Panavision widescreen. Release date: Feb. 20, 2003. MPAA Rating: R. Running time: 99 Min.
Cast: Jet Li, DMX, Anthony Anderson, Kelly Hu, Tom Arnold, Mark Dacascos, Gabrielle Union, Michael Jace, Drag-On, Paige Hurd.

CYPHER

A Miramax release of a Pandora presentation of a Gaylord Films production. (International sales: Pandora, Burbank, Calif.) Producers: Hunt Lowry, Paul Federbush, Casey La Scala, Wendy Grean. Executive producer: Shebnem Askin. Director: Vincenzo Natali. Screenplay: Brian King. Camera: Derek Rogers. Editor: Bert Kish. Music: Michael Andrews. In color. Release date: July 16, 2003. Running time: 90 Min.
Cast: Jeremy Northam, Lucy Liu, Nigel Bennett, Timothy Webber.

DADDY COOL

A Catrack Films presentation. Producer: Brady Lewis. Executive producers: David Rosenberg. Co-producer: Susan Howard. Director/Writer: Brady Lewis. Camera: Mark Knobil. Editor: Lewis. Music: Lou Stellute. In color and B&W, 16mm-to35mm. Release date: July 15, 2003. Running time: 84 Min.
With: Streeter Nelson, Larry John Meyers, John Amplas, Conrad Waite, Mae Hignett, Gerrard Spencer, Holly Thurma, Alice Eisner.

DALLAS 362

A Sunlion Films presentation of a Gregory K. Sabatino/Konwiser Brothers production. Producers: Greg Sabatino, Kip Konwiser, Chad Marshall. Executive producers: Brian Williamson, Beau Flynn. Director/Writer: Scott Caan. Camera: Phil Parmet. Editor: Andy B. In FotoKem color, Panavision widescreen. Release date: June 16, 2003. Running time: 95 Min.
Cast: Scott Caan, Jeff Goldblum, Shawn Hatosy, Kelly Lynch, Heavy D, Bob Gunton, Marley Shelton, Val Lauren, Selma Blair, Isla Fisher.

THE DANCE

A Haynes/Geadelmann Pictures production in association with Casa Grande Entertainment. Producers: Eric A. Geadelmann, John Darling Haynes, Scott Mayo. Director: John Darling Haynes. Camera/Editor: Scott Mayo. In color, digital video. Release date: April 5, 2003. Running time: 70 Min. Documentary.

DANGEROUS LIVING: COMING OUT IN THE DEVELOPING WORLD

An After Stonewall production. Producers: Dan Hunt, Janet Baus. Executive producer: Reid Williams. Director: John Scagliotti. Camera: Dan Hunt, John Hanlon, Shayla Sellars, Wendy Wallas, Anat Salomon, Michael Hanish, Adnan Ali, Liz Miller, Adriana Pacheco, Jayashree. Editors: Hanish, Richard Davis, Salomon. Music: Don DiNicola. In color, video. Release date: June 28, 2003. Running time: 70 Min. Documentary.

DAREDEVIL

A 20th Century Fox release of a 20th Century Fox and Regency Enterprises presentation in association with Marvel Enterprises of a New Regency/Horseshoe Bay production. Producers: Arnon Milchan, Gary Foster, Avi Arad. Executive producers: Stan Lee, Bernie Williams. Co-producers: Kevin Feige, Becki Cross Trujillo. Director/Writer: Mark Steven Johnson. Camera: Ericson Core. Editors: Dennis Virkler, Armen Minasian. Music: Graeme Revell. In Deluxe color, widescreen. Release date: Feb. 11, 2003. MPAA Rating: PG-13. Running time: 104 Min.
Cast: Ben Affleck, Jennifer Garner, Michael Clarke Duncan, Colin Farrell, Joe Pantoliano, Jon Favreau, David Keith, Erick Avari, Paul Ben-Victor, Derrick O'Connor, Leland Orser, Scott Terra.

DARK BLUE

An MGM (U.S.)/CDI (Italy) release of an Intermedia Films, United Artists presentation in association with Im Film Produktion of an Alphaville production in association with Cosmic Pictures. Producers: Caldecot Chubb, David Blocker, James Jacks, Sean Daniel. Executive producers: Moritz Borman, Guy East, Nigel Sinclair. Director: Ron Shelton. Screenplay: David Ayer. Story: James Ellroy. Camera: Barry Peterson. Editor: Paul Seydor. Music: Terence Blanchard. In FotoKem color. Release date: Jan. 10, 2003. MPAA Rating: R. Running time: 113 Min.
Cast: Kurt Russell, Brendan Gleeson, Scott Speedman, Michael Michelle, Lolita Davidovich, Ving Rhames, Dash Minok, Kurupt.

DARKNESS FALLS

A Sony Pictures Entertainment release of a Columbia Pictures and Revolution Studios presentation of a Distant Corners/Blue Star Pictures production. Producers: John Hegeman, John Fasano, William Sherak, Jason Shuman. Executive producers: Derek Dauchy, Lou Arkoff. Director: Jonathan Liebesman. Screenplay: John Fasano, James Vanderbilt, Joe Harris, from a story by Harris. Camera: Dan Laustsen. Editors: Steve Mirkovich, Tim Alverson. Music: Brian Tyler. In DeLuxe color. Release date: Jan. 21. 2003. MPAA Rating: PG-13. Running time: 85 Min.
Cast: Chaney Kley, Emma Caulfield, Lee Cormie, Grant Piro, Sullivan Stapleton, Steve Mouzakis, Peter Curtin, Kestie Morassi, Jenny Lovell, Peter Stanton, Angus Sampson, Joshua Anderson, Emily Browning, Rebecca McCauley.

DARK ROOTS: THE UNAUTHORIZED ANNA NICOLE

A Showtime presentation of a World of Wonder production. Producers/Directors/Writers: Fenton Bailey, Randy Barbato, Gabriel Rotello. Camera: Teo Maniaci. Editor: Blake West. In color, DV. Release date: June 27, 2003. Running time: 89 Min. Documentary.

DEATH OF A DYNASTY

A Roc-A-Fella Films/R&B FM production in association with Intrinsic Value Films and Entertainment Funding Group. Producers: Damon Dash, Steven C. Beer. Executive producers: Ron Rothholz, Lisa Fragner. Co-producers: Isen Robbins, Aimee Schoof. Director: Damon Dash. Screenplay: Mr. Blue. Camera: Dave Daniel. Editors: Chris Fiore. Music: Big Chuck, Theron Feemster. In color. Release date: May 7, 2003. Running time: 91 Min.
Cast: Ebon Moss-Bachrach, Devon Aoki, Capone, Robert Stapleton, Rashida Jones, Kevin Hart, Gerald Kelly.

A DECADE UNDER THE INFLUENCE

An IFC Films release of an IFC presentation of a Written in Stone, Constant Communications production of a Demme/LaGravenese film. Producers: Gini Reticker, Jerry Kupfer, Richard LaGravenese, Ted Demme. Executive producers: Alison Bourke, Caroline Kaplan, Jonathan Sehring. Directors: Richard LaGravenese, Ted Demme. Camera: Clyde Smith, Anthony Janelli. Editor: Meg Reticker. Music: John Kimbrough. In color. Release date: Jan. 19, 2003. Running time: 109 Min. Documentary.
With: Martin Scorsese, Francis Ford Coppola, Robert Altman, Peter Bogdanovich, Ellen Burstyn, Julie Christie, Dennis Hopper, Sidney Lumet, Milos Forman, Robert Towne, Sydney Pollack, Paul Schrader, Pam Grier, William Friedkin, Bruce Dern.

THE DECAY OF FICTION

A Lookout Mountain Films production. Producers: Pat O'Neill, Rebecca Hartzell. Director/Writer: Pat O'Neill. Camera: George Lockwood. Editor: O'Neill. In color/B&W. Release date: Jan. 29, 2003. Running time: 71 Min.
With: Wendi Winburn, William Lewis, Julio Leopold, Amber Lopez, Jack Conley, John Rawling, Patricia Thielemann, Dan Bell, Kane Crawford, Damon Colazzo, Jacqueline Humbert.

DELIVER US FROM EVA

A Focus Features release of a Baltimore/Spring Creek Pictures production. Producers: Len Amato, Paddy Cullen. Executive producers: Paula Weinstein, Barry Levinson. Director: Gary Hardwick. Screenplay: James Iver Mattson, B.E. Brauner, Hardwick. Camera: Alexander Gruszynski. Editor: Earl Watson. Music: Marcus Miller. In Technicolor. Release date: Jan. 16, 2003. MPAA Rating: R. Running time: 105 Min.
Cast: LL Cool J, Gabrielle Union, Duane Martin, Essence Atkins, Robinne Lee, Meagan Good, Mel Jackson, Dartanyan Edmonds, Kym Whitley, Royale Watkins, Matt Winston, Ruben Paul.

DETECTIVE FICTION

A Ten Ten Films and Farnam Street Ltd. presentation. Producer: Paul Johnson. Executive producer: Michael McHugh. Director/Writer: Patrick Coyle, based on his play. Camera: Gregory R. Winter. Editor: Jeffrey Stickles. Music: Jimi Englund, Greg Herzenach. In Alpha-Cine color. Release date: Jan. 20, 2003. Running time: 102 Min.
Cast: Mo Collins, Patrick Coyle, Sarah Agnew, Brent Doyle.

DICKIE ROBERTS: FORMER CHILD STAR

A Paramount release of a Happy Madison production of a Sam Weisman film. Producers: Adam Sandler, Jack Giarraputo. Executive producer: Fred Wolf. Co-producer: Blair Breard. Director: Sam Weisman. Screenplay: Fred Wolf, David Spade. Camera: Thomas E. Ackerman. Editor: Roger Bondelli. Music: Christophe Beck, Waddy Wachtel. In DeLuxe color. Release date: Aug. 14, 2003. MPAA Rating: PG-13. Running time: 99 Min.
Cast: David Spade, Mary McCormack, Jon Lovitz, Craig Bierko, Jenna Boyd, Scott Tessa, Alyssa Milano, Doris Roberts, Rob Reiner, Edie McClurg, Leif Garrett, Brendan Fraser, Emmanuel Lewis.

DIE ANOTHER DAY

An MGM release of an Albert R. Broccoli's Eon Prods. Ltd. presentation. Producers: Michael G. Wilson, Barbara Broccoli. Executive producer: Anthony Waye. Co-producer: Callum McDougall. Director: Lee Tamahori. Screenplay: Neal Purvis, Robert Wade. Camera: David Tattersall. Editor: Christian Wagner. Music: David Arnold. In Deluxe color, Panavision widescreen. Release date: Nov. 8, 2002. MPAA Rating: PG-13. Running time: 130 Min.

Cast: Pierce Brosnan, Halle Berry, Toby Stephens, Rosamund Pike, Rick Yune, Judi Dench, John Cleese, Michael Madsen, Kenneth Tsang, Will Yun Lee, Emilio Echevarria, Samantha Bond, Colin Salmon, Michael Gorevoy, Lawrence Makoare.

DIE MOMMIE DIE!

An Aviator Films, Ken Kenwright Ltd. presentation. Producers: Dante Di Loreto, Anthony Edwards, Bill Kenwright. Executive producer: Lony Dubrofsky. Co-producer: Frank Pavich. Co-executive producer: Neil Ellman. Director: Mark Rucker. Screenplay: Charles Busch, based on his stage play. Camera: Kelly Evans. Editor: Philip Harrison. Music: Dennis McCarthy. In color. Release date: Jan. 20, 2003. Running time: 90 Min.

Cast: Charles Busch, Natasha Lyonne, Jason Priestley, Frances Conroy, Philip Baker Hall, Stark Sands, Victor Raider-Wexler, Nora Dunn.

DILDO DIARIES

An IA Films, RoadTrip Prods. presentation. Producers: Laura Barton, Judy Wilder. Executive producer: Bill Kirkner. Directors/Editors: Laura Barton, Judy Wilder. Camera: Barton, Wilder, James Eiland. In color, Beta SP. Release date: June 19, 2003. Running time: 63 Min. Documentary.

DISCHORD

An Artistic License release of an Ivy Media Group production. Producer: Mark Wilkinson. Director/Writer/Editor: Mark Wilkinson. Camera: Ernst Kubitza. Music: John McCarthy. In color, widescreen. Release date: March 2, 2003. Running time: 105 Min.

With: Thomas Jay Ryan, Annunziata Gianzero, Richard Bakalyan, Andrew Borba, Rick Wessler.

DOGVILLE

A Zentropa Entertainments8 APS production in association with Isabella Films Intl., Something Else BV, Memfis Film Intl. AB, Trollhattan Film AB, Pain Unlimited GMBH, Sigma Films Ltd./Zoma Ltd., Slot Machine Sarl/Liberator2 Sarl. (International sales: Trust Film Sales, Copenhagen.) Producer: Vibeke Windelov. Executive producer: Peter Aalbaek Jensen. Co-producers: Gillian Berrie, Bettina Brokemper, Anja Grafers, Els Vandervorst. Director/Writer: Lars von Trier. Camera: Anthony Dod Mantle. Editors: Molly Malene Stensgaard. In color, widescreen. Release date: May 19, 2003. Running time: 178 Min.

Cast: Nicole Kidman, Harriet Anderson, Lauren Bacall, Jean-Marc Barr, Paul Bettany, Blair Brown, James Caan, Patricia Clarkson, Jeremy Davies, Ben Gazzara, Philip Baker Hall, Siobhan Fallon Hogan, John Hurt, Zeljko Ivanek, Udo Kier, Cleo King, Miles Purinton, Bill Raymond, Chloe Sevigny, Shauna Shim, Stellan Skarsgard.

DOMESTIC VIOLENCE 2

A Domestic Violence Films production. (International sales: Zipporah Films, Cambridge, Mass.) Producer/Director/Editor: Frederick Wiseman. Camera: John Davey. In color, 16mm. Release date: June 14, 2003. Running time: 155 Min. Documentary.

DOPAMINE

A Kontent Films presentation. Producers: Tad Fettig, Debbie Brubaker. Executive producer: Eric Kovisto. Co-producers: Liz Decena, Brian Benson, Timothy Breitbach. Director: Mark Decena. Screenplay: Decena, Timothy Breitbach. Camera: Rob Humphreys. Editor: Jess Congdon. Music: Eric Holland. In color, 24P HD video. Release date: Jan. 23, 2003. Running time: 79 Min.

Cast: John Livingston, Sabrina Lloyd, Bruno Campos, Reuben Grundy, Kathleen Antonia, Nicole Wilder.

THE DOUBLE-D AVENGER

A William Winckler Prods. presentation. Producer: Winckler. Executive producers: Patricia Tousicnant, Jim Tousicnant, Elizabeth Sturm. Director/Writer: William Winckler. Camera: Raoul J. Germain, Jr.; editor, Germain, Jr.; music, Don Shore. In color, digital video. Release date: Jan. 14, 2003. Running time: 73 Min.

With: Kitten Natividad, Haji, Raven de la Croix, Forrest J. Ackerman, Mimma Mariucci, Sheri Dawn Thomas, G. Larry Butler, Lunden de'Leon, Gary Canavello, Andrea Ana Persun, Ray Verduzco, Bob Mackey.

DREAMCATCHER

A Warner Bros. release of a Castle Rock Entertainment presentation in association with Village Roadshow Pictures and NPV Entertainment of a Kasdan Pictures production. Producers: Lawrence Kasdan, Charles Okun. Executive producer: Bruce Berman. Co-producers: Stephen Dunn, Casey Grant, Jon Hutman. Director: Lawrence Kasdan. Screenplay: William Goldman, Kasdan, based on the novel by Stephen King. Camera: John Seale. Editors: Carol Littleton, Raul Davalos. Music: James Newton Howard. In Technicolor, Panavision widescreen. Release date: March 7, 2003. MPAA Rating: R. Running time: 131 Min.

Cast: Morgan Freeman, Thomas Jane, Jason Lee, Damian Lewis, Timothy Olyphant, Tom Sizemore, Donnie Wahlberg, Michael O'Neill, Rosemary Dunsmore.

DRUMLINE

A 20th Century Fox release of a Fox 2000 Pictures presentation of a Wendy Finerman production. Producers: Finerman, Timothy M. Bourne, Jody Gerson. Executive producers: Dallas Austin, Greg Mooradian. Director: Charles Stone III. Screenplay: Tina Gordon Chism, Shawn Schepps, based on a story by Schepps. Camera: Shane Hurlbut. Editors: Bill Pankow, Patricia Bowers. Music: John Powell. In DeLuxe color. Release date: Nov. 20, 2002. MPAA Rating: PG-13. Running time: 118 Min.

Cast: Nick Cannon, Zoe Saldana, Orlando Jones, Leonard Roberts, GQ, Jason Weaver, Earl C. Poitier, Candace Carey, Shay Rountree, Miguel A. Gaetan, J. Anthony Brown, Afem Omilami.

DUMB AND DUMBERER: WHEN HARRY MET LLOYD

A New Line Cinema release of a Brad Krevoy/Charles B. Wessler/Steve Stabler and Burg/Koules and Dakota Pictures production. Producers: Oren Koules, Charles B. Wessler, Brad Krevoy, Steve Stabler, Troy Miller. Executive producers: Toby Emmerich, Richard Brener, Cale Boyter, Bennett Yellin. Co-producer: Carl Mazzocone. Director: Troy Miller. Screenplay: Robert Brener, Miller. Story: Brener, based on characters created by Peter Farrelly, Bennett Yellin, Bobby Farrelly. Camera: Anthony Richmond. Editor: Lawrence Jordan. Music: Eban Schletter. In DeLuxe color. Release date: June 11, 2003. MPAA Rating: PG-13. Running time: 85 Min.

Cast: Eric Christian Olsen, Derek Richardson, Rachel Nichols, Cheri Oteri, Luis Guzman, Elden Henson, William Lee Scott, Mimi Rogers, Eugene Levy, Lin Shayne, Shia LaBeouf, Josh Braaten, Teal Redmann, Michelle Krusiec, Brian Posehn.

DUMMY

A Quadrant Entertainment presentation. Producers: Richard Temtchine, Bob Fagan. Director/Writer: Greg Pritikin. Camera: Horacio Marquinez. Editor: Bill Henry. In color. Release date: March 6, 2003. Running time: 90 Min.

Cast: Adrien Brody, Milla Jovovich, Illeana Douglas, Vera Farmiga, Jessica Walter, Ron Leibman, Jared Harris.

DUNSMORE

An Aslan Prods. presentation in association with Valencia Motion Pictures. Producers: Paul Sirmons, Peter Spirer, Michael Andrews. Executive producers: Ralph Clemente, Dorothy Spirer. Co-producers: Eva Strickland, Richard Strickland. Director: Peter Spirer. Screenplay: Michael Andrews. Story: Spirer, Andrews. Camera: Adam Teichman. Editors: Miklos Wright, Robert Gordon. Music: Benedikt Brydern. In Digital Film Technologies color. Release date: April 21, 2003. Running time: 88 Min.

Cast: W. Earl Brown, Kareem Hardison, Jeannetta Arnette, Rus Blackwell, Barry Corbin, Talia Shire, Alicia Lagano, Brain Lally.

DUPLEX

A Miramax Films release of a Red Hour Films/Flower Films production. Producers: Ben Stiller, Stuart Cornfeld, Jeremy Kramer, Nancy Juvonen, Drew Barrymore. Executive producers: Bob Weinstein, Harvey Weinstein, Meryl Poster, Jennifer Wachtell, Richard N. Gladstein, Alan C. Blomquist. Co-producer: Larry Doyle. DirectOR: Danny DeVito. Screenplay: Larry Doyle. Camera: Anastas N. Michos. Editor: Lynzee Klingman. Music: David Newman. In Deluxe color. Release date: Sept. 18, 2003. Running time: 89 Min.

Cast: Ben Stiller, Drew Barrymore, Eileen Essell, Harvey Fierstein, Justin Theroux, Robert Wisdom, Amber Valletta, James Remar, Maya Rudolph, Cheryl Klein, Swoosie Kurtz, Wallace Shawn.

DUST TO DUST

A Michael Brown production. Producer/Director/Writer: Brown. Camera: Kevin Brown. Editor: Kevin Brown. Music: James Gaertner. In color/B&W, video. Release date: Nov. 11, 2002. Running time: 93 Min. Documentary.

DYLAN'S RUN

A Squeak Pictures production. Producers: Steven Johnson, David Rosenthal, Pam Tarr. Executive producers: Tarr, Peter Kellner, Chris Weitz. Directors: Steven Johnson, David Rosenthal. Camera: Rosenthal. Editor: Kate Amend. Music: Daniel Cage, W. Gardner Knight. In color, Beta SP. Release date: Nov. 17, 2002. Running time: 94 Min. Documentary.

EASY RIDERS, RAGING BULLS

A Trio presentation of a Freemantle Corp., Submarine Entertainment production. Producers: Rachel Talbot, Kenneth Bowser. Executive producer: Josh Braun. Executive producer for Trio, Andrew Cohen. Executive producer for BBC, Nick Wave. Supervising producer for Trio, Samuel J. Paul. Director/Writer: Kenneth Bowser, based on the book by Peter Biskind. Camera: Paul Mailman. Editors: Paskal Akesson, Mike Lahaie. In color, video. Release date: Jan. 18, 2003. Running time: 119 Min. Documentary.

With: Dede Allen, Peter Bart, Tony Bill, Karen Black, Peter Bogdanovich, Ellen Burstyn, Roger Corman, Micky Dolenz, Richard Dreyfuss, Peter Fonda, Carl Gottlieb, Jerome Hellman, Monte Hellman, Dennis Hopper, Willard Huyck, Stanley Jaffe.

EAT THIS NEW YORK

Producers/Directers/Writers: Andrew Rossi, Kate Novack. Camera: Rossi. Editor: Rossi. Music: Steve O'Reilly, Matt Anthony of Tammany Hall NYC. In color, DV. Release date: Oct. 18, 2002. Running time: 83 Min. Documentary.

With: John McCormick, Billy Phelps, Daniel Boulud, Sirio Maccioni, , Keith McNally, Danny Meyer, Drew Nieporent, Ruth Reichl, Jean-Georges Vongerichten, Tim Zagat.

EDDIE GRIFFIN: DYSFUNKTIONAL FAMILY

A Dimension Films release presented in association with Gold Circle Films and Heartland Prods. of a Brad Grey Prods., Permut Presentations production. Producers: David Permut, Paul Brooks. Director: George Gallo. Camera: Theo Van De Sande. Editor: Michael R. Miller. In color, 24P HD video. Release date: Feb. 12, 2003. MPAA Rating: R. Running time: 83 Min.

THE EDUCATION OF GORE VIDAL

An American Masters production. Producer: Matt Kapp. Executive producer: Susan Lacy. Director/Writer: Deborah Dickson. Camera: Don Lenzer. Editor: Sakae Ishikawa. In color. Release date: Jan. 31, 2003. Running time: 84 Min. Documentary.
Readers: Anne Jackson, Paul Newman, Tim Robbins, Susan Sarandon, Eli Wallach, Joanne Woodward.

8 MILE

A Universal release of a Universal Pictures and Imagine Entertainment presentation of a Brian Grazer/Curtis Hanson production. Producers: Grazer, Hanson, Jimmy Iovine. Executive producers: Carol Fenelon, James Whitaker, Gregory Goodman, Paul Rosenberg. Co-producer: Stuart Parr. Director: Curtis Hanson. Screenplay: Scott Silver. Camera: Rodrigo Prieto. Editors: Jay Rabinowitz, Craig Kitson. Music: Eminem. In Deluxe color, widescreen. Release date: Oct. 29, 2002. MPAA Rating: R. Running time: 110 Min.
Cast: Eminem, Kim Basinger, Brittany Murphy, Mekhi Phifer, Evan Jones, Omar Benson Miller, Eugene Byrd, De'Angelo Wilson, Anthony Mackie, Taryn Manning, Michael Shannon, Chloe Greenfield, Craig Chandler, Paul Bates.

ELEPHANT

An HBO Films presentation of a Meno Films production in association with Blue Relief. (International sales: HBO Films, London.) Producer: Dany Wolf. Executive producers: Diane Keaton, Bill Robinson. Director/Writer/Editor: Gus Van Sant. Camera: Harris Savides. In FotoKem color, 1.33 aspect ratio. Release date: May 17, 2003. Running time: 81 Min.
Cast: Alex Frost, Eric Deulen, John Robinson, Elias McConnell, Jordan Taylor, Carrie Finklea, Nicole George, Brittany Mountain, Alicia Miles, Kristen Hicks, Bennie Dixon, Nathan Tyson, Timothy Bottoms, Matt Malloy, Ellis E. Williams.

11:14

An MDP Worldwide presentation of a Firm Films production. (International sales: MDP, Los Angeles.) Producers: Beau Flynn, John Morrissey. Executive producers: Mark Damon, Sammy Lee, Stewart Hall, Raju Patel, Tripp Vinson, Hilary Swank, Jeff Kwatinetz, David Scott Rubin. Director/Writer: Greg Marcks. Camera: Shane Hurlbut. Editors: Dan Lebenthal, Richard Nord. Music: Clint Mansell. In color. Release date: Sept. 11, 2003. Running time: 86 Min.
Cast: Henry Thomas, Blake Heron, Barbara Hershey, Clark Gregg, Hilary Swank, Shawn Hatosy, Stark Sands, Colin Hanks, Ben Foster, Patrick Swayze, Rachel Leigh Cook, Jason Segel, Rick Gomez.

EMPATHY

An Amie Siegel production with Three-Legged Cat Prods. Producer/Director/Writer/Editor: Siegel. Release date: Feb. 13, 2003. Running time: 96 Min.
With: Gigi Buffington, Dr. David Solomon, Maria Silvermann, Patricia Donegan, Alix Pearlstein, Aria Wachtel Knee.

END OF THE CENTURY

Producer/Director/Editor: Michael Gramaglia, Jim Fields. Camera: Fields. In color, digital video. Release date: Jan. 21, 2003. Running time: 112 Min. Documentary.
With: Joey Ramone, Johnny Ramone, Dee Dee Ramone, Tommy Ramone, Marky Ramone, C.J. Ramone, Ritchie Ramone, Arturo Vega, Monty Melnick, Danny Fields, Linda Stein, Micky Leigh.

EQUILIBRIUM

A Dimension Films release of a Blue Tulip production. Producers: Jan De Bont, Lucas Foster. Executive producers: Bob Weinstein, Harvey Weinstein, Andrew Rona. Co-producer: Sue Baden-Powell. Director/Writer: Kurt Wimmer. Camera: Dion Beebe. Editors: Tom Rolfe, William Yeh. Music: Klaus Badelt. In color. Release date: Nov. 8, 2002. MPAA Rating: R. Running time: 107 Min.
Cast: Christian Bale, Emily Watson, Taye Diggs, Angus MacFayden, Sean Bean, Matthew Harbour, William Fichtner.

EVENHAND

A Cypress Films production. Producers: Fernando Cano II, Joseph Pierson. Executive producer: Jon Glascoe. Director: Joseph Pierson. Screenplay: Mike Jones. Camera: Tim Orr. Editor: Alex Albanese. Music: Joel Goodman. In Duart color. Release date: Nov. 14, 2002. Running time: 92 Min.
Cast: Bill Sage, Bill Dawes, Io Tillett Wright, Irene Pena, Hector Garcia, Lee Stringer.

FAILURES

A Werner Film presentation. Producer: Kathrin Werner, Felix Werner. Co-producers: Andrew Seklir, Hal Haberman. Director: Tim Hunter. Screenplay: Hal Haberman. Camera: Nancy Schreiber. Music: Brian Ray, Abe Laboriel, Jr. In color, HD video. Release date: May 17, 2003. Running time: 87 Min.
With: Ashley Johnson, Chad Lindberg, Henry Czerny, Seth Adkins, Joseph Reitman, Michael Ironside.

THE FIGHTING TEMPTATIONS

A Paramount Pictures release of an MTV Films/Handprint Entertainment production. Producers: David Gale, Loretha Jones, Jeff Pollack. Executive producers: Van Toffler, Benny Medina. Co-producers: Susan Lewis, Momita Sengupta. Director: Jonathan Lynn. Screenplay: Elizabeth Hunter, Saladin K. Patterson. Story: Hunter. Camera: Affonso Beato. Editor: Paul Hirsch. Music: Jimmy Jam, Terry Lewis, James "Big Jim" Wright. In Deluxe color, widescreen. Release date: Sept. 10, 2003. Running time: 122 Min.
Cast: Cuba Gooding Jr., Beyonce Knowles, Melba Moore, Mike Epps, Shirley Caesar, LaTanya Richardson, Steve Harvey, Montel Jordan.

FINAL DESTINATION 2

A New Line Cinema release of a Zide/Perry production. Producers: Warren Zide, Craig Perry. Executive producers: Toby Emmerich, Richard Brener, Matt Moore, Jeffrey Reddick. Co-producer: Justis Greene. Director: David R. Ellis. Screenplay: J. Mackye Gruber, Eric Bress, based on characters created by Jeffrey Reddick. Story: Gruber, Bress, Reddick. Camera: Gary Capo. Editor: Eric Sears. Music: Shirley Walker. In Alpha Cine color, Deluxe prints. Release date: Jan. 23, 2003. MPAA Rating: R. Running time: 90 Min.
Cast: Ali Larter, A.J. Cook, Michael Landes, T.C. Carson, Jonathan Cherry, Keegan Connor Tracy, Sarah Carter, Lynda Boyd, David Paetkau, Justina Machado, James N. Kirk, Tony Todd.

FINAL DRAFT

A TriBro Pictures presentation of a Scott Rosenfelt production. Producer: Scott Rosenfelt. Executive producer: Erez Goldman. Director/Writer: Oren Goldman, Yariv Ozdoba. Camera: Guy Livneh. Editors: Yoram Tal, William Morris. Music: Sharon Farber. In color-DV. Release date: Feb. 10, 2003. Running time: 96 Min.
With: Michael Weston, Hamish Linklater, Emily Bergl, Laura Jordan, Tristine Skyler, Jeffrey Donovan, Tristine Skyler, Chris Williams, Jimmi Simpson, Michael Irby, Andrew Shaifer, Carl Bressler, David Spielberg.

FINDING NEMO

A Buena Vista release of a Walt Disney Pictures presentation of a Pixar Animation Studios film. Producer: Graham Walters. Executive producer: John Lasseter. Director: Andrew Stanton. Screenplay: Stanton, Bob Peterson, David Reynolds. Original story: Stanton. Camera: Sharon Calahan, Jeremy Lasky. Editors: David Ian Salter. Music: Thomas Newman. In Technicolor. Release date: May 9, 2003. MPAA Rating: PG. Running time: 100 Min. Animated.
Voices: Albert Brooks, Ellen DeGeneres, Alexander Gould, Willem Dafoe, Brad Garrett, Allison Janney, Austin Pendleton, Stephen Root, Vicki Lewis, Joe Ranft, Geoffrey Rush, Andrew Stanton, Elizabeth Perkins, Nicholas Bird, Bob Peterson, Barry Humphries, Eric Bana, Bruce Spence, Bill Hunter, LuLu Ebeling, Jordy Ranft, Erica Beck.

A FINE STATE THIS IS

An Underdog Pictures production. Producers: Valoree Adamski, Jessica Chandler. Executive producer: Jay Silverman. Director: Jessica Chandler. Camera: Robert Richman. In color, digital video. Release date: June 6, 2003. Running time: 55 Min.
With: Deborah Fargo Whitman, Lucille Colin, Donna Newman.

THE FITTEST

A Crook Brothers Prods. presentation. Producer: Angela Grant. Executive producers: Gil Holland, Ilana Sparrow. Co-producers: Andres Baiz, Wendy Coutau. Director/Writer: Joshua Crook, Jeffrey Crook. Camera: John Barrett Ashmore. Editor: Joshua Crook. Music: Wendell Hanes. Release date: June 16, 2003. Running time: 84 Min.
With: Jason Madera, Angela Grant, Chris Ferry, Christina Caparoula, Joshua Crook, Wendy Coutau, Peter Blitzer, Heidi Laughrey, Rob Vroom, Jeffrey Crook, David Pasad, Jessica Mastan, Caroline Barton.

FLAVORS

A dreams2reality/MAUJ Entertainment production. Producers: Amupam Mittal, Raj Nidimoru, DK Krishna. Executive producers: Sita Menon, Siva Atturum Rambabu Gotur, Ramesh Kaika, Sudhaker Medboyina, Amit Mittal, Vinod Nair. Directors/Writers: Raj Nidimoru, DK Krishna. Camera: David Isern. Editor: Frank Reynolds. Music: Lezlie Lewis. In color, DV. Release date: June 29, 2003. Running time: 120 Min.
With: Anjan Srivastava, Bharati Achreker, Reef Karim, Pooja Kumar, Jicky Schnee, Sireesha Katragadda, Guarang Vyas, Anupam Mittal.

THE FOG OF WAR

A Sony Pictures Classics release of a Senart Films & @Radical.Media production in association with Globe Department Store. Producers: Errol Morris, Michael Williams, Julie Ahlberg. Executive producers: Jack Lechner, Jon Kamen, Frank Scherma, Robert Fernandez, Robert May, John Sloss. Director: Errol Morris. Camera: Peter Donahue, Robert Chappell. Editors: Karen Schmeer, Doug Abel, Chyld King. Music: Philip Glass. In color. Release date: May 21, 2003. Running time: 105 Min.
Cast: Robert S. McNamara.

FOREIGN AFFAIR

An Innovation Film Group release (in the U.S.) of a Myriad Pictures presentation of a Black & White Films production in association with Bijker Prods. and Dreamscape Films. Executive producers: Dirk-Jan Bijker, Tonneke Bijker, David J. Bijker, Esli Bijker, David Arquette, Tim Blake Nelson, Geert Heetebrij, Helmut Schleppi. Director: Helmut Schleppi. Screenplay: Geert Heetebrij. Camera: M. David Mullen. Editor: Schleppi. Music: Todd Holden Capps. In color, DV. Release date: June 19, 2003. Running time: 98 Min.
Cast: Tim Blake Nelson, David Arquette, Lois Smith, Allyce Beasley, Larry Pine, Emily Mortimer, Megan Follows.

THE 4TH TENOR

A Wine Women & Song Films presentation of a Joseph Merhi production. Producer: Merhi. Director: Harry Basil. Screenplay: Basil, Rodney Dangerfield. Camera: Ken Blakey. Editor: Tony Lombardo. Music: Christopher Lennertz. In FotoKem color. Release date: Nov. 19, 2002. Running time: 97 Min.

Cast: Rodney Dangerfield, Robert Davi, Annabelle Gurwitch, Anita De Simone, Charles Fleischer, Richard Libertini, Dom Irrera.

FREAKY FRIDAY

A Buena Vista release of a Walt Disney Pictures presentation of a GUNNFilms production. Producer: Andrew Gunn. Executive producer: Mario Iscovich. Co-producer: Ann Marie Sanderlin. Director: Mark Waters. Screenplay: Heather Hach, Leslie Dixon. Based on the novel by Mary Rodgers. Camera: Oliver Wood. Editor: Bruce Green. Music: Rolfe Kent. In Technicolor. Release date: July 18, 2003. MPAA Rating: PG. Running time: 96 Min.

Cast: Jamie Lee Curtis, Lindsay Lohan, Mark Harmon, Harold Gould, Chad Michael Murray, Stephen Tobolowsky, Christina Vidal, Ryan Malgarini, Rosalind Chao, Lucille Soong, Willie Garson, Dina Waters.

FREDDY VS. JASON

A New Line Cinema release of a Sean S. Cunningham production. Producer: Cunningham. Executive producers: Douglas Curtis, Robert Shaye, Stokely Chaffin, Renee Witt. Director: Ronny Yu. Writer: Damian Shannon, Mark Swift, based on characters created by Wes Craven, Victor Miller. Camera: Fred Murphy. Editor: Mark Stevens. Music: Graeme Revell. In color, widescreen. Release date: July 30, 2003. MPAA Rating: R. Running time: 97 Min.

Cast: Robert Englund, Ken Kirzinger, Monica Keena, Jason Ritter, Kelly Rowland, Katharine Isabelle, Christopher George Marquette, Brendan Fletcher, Tom Butler, James Callahan, Lochlyn Munro.

FRIDAY AFTER NEXT

A New Line Cinema release of a New Line Cinema and Cube Vision Prods. presentation of a Cube Vision production. Producer: Ice Cube, Mat Alvarez. Executive producers: Toby Emmerich, Matt Moore, Douglas Curtis. Director: Marcus Raboy. Screenplay: Ice Cube, based on characters created by Ice Cube, DJ Pooh. Camera: Glen McPherson. Editor: Suzanne Hines. Music: John Murphy. In Deluxe color. Release date: Nov. 12, 2002. MPAA Rating: R. Running time: 82 Min.

Cast: Ice Cube, Mike Epps, John Witherspoon, Don "DC" Curry, Anna Maria Horsford, Clifton Powell, BeBe Drake, K.D. Aubert, Sommore, Rickey Smiley, Joel McKinnon Miller, Reggie Gaskins, Terry Crews, Starletta Dupois, Katt Williams, Maz Jobrani.

FROM JUSTIN TO KELLY

A 20th Century Fox release of a 19 Entertainment production. Producers: Gayla Aspinall, John Steven Agoglia. Executive producer: Simon Fuller. Co-producers: Bob Engelman, Niki Boella. Director: Robert Iscove. Screenplay: Kim Fuller. Camera: Francis Kenny. Editors: Casey Rohrs, Tirsa Hackshaw. Music: Michael Wandmacher. In Deluxe color. Release date: June 20, 2003. MPAA Rating: PG. Running time: 81 Min.

Cast: Kelly Clarkson, Justin Guarini, Katherine Bailess, Anika Noni Rose, Greg Siff, Brian Dietzen, Jason Yribar, Theresa San Nicholas, Justin George, Kaitlin Riley, Renee Robertson, Yamil Piedra.

FUNNY HA HA

Producer: Ethan Vogt. Director/Writer/Editor: Andrew Bujalski. Camera: Matthias Grunsky. In color, 16 mm. Release date: May 23, 2003. Running time: 89 Min.

Cast: Kate Dollenmayer, Christian Rudder, Myles Paige, Jennifer L. Schaper, Lissa Patton Rudder, Marshall Lewy, Andrew Bujalski.

GANGS OF NEW YORK

A Miramax release (in North America) of an Alberto Grimaldi production. Producers: Grimaldi, Harvey Weinstein. Executive producers: Michael Ovitz, Bob Weinstein, Rick Yorn, Michael Hausman, Maurizio Grimaldi. Co-producers: Joseph Reidy, Laura Fattori. Co-Executive producers: Graham King, Rick Schwartz, Colin Vaines. Director: Martin Scorsese. Screenplay: Jay Cocks, Steven Zaillian, Kenneth Lonergan. Story: Cocks. Camera: Michael Ballhaus. Editor: Thelma Schoonmaker. Music: Howard Shore. In Technicolor, widescreen. Release date: Dec. 3, 2002. MPAA Rating: R. Running time: 168 Min.

Cast: Leonardo DiCaprio, Daniel Day-Lewis, Cameron Diaz, Liam Neeson, Jim Broadbent, John C. Reilly, Henry Thomas, Brendan Gleeson, Gary Lewis, Stephen Graham, Eddie Marsan, Alec McCowen, David Hemmings, Larry Gilliard Jr., Cara Seymour.

GAY HOLLYWOOD

An American Movie Channel presentation of a World of Wonder production. Producers: Jeremy Simmons, Michael Warwick. Executive producers: Randy Barbato, Fenton Bailey. Director: Jeremy Simmons. Camera: Jesse Phinney, Thaddeus Wadleigh, Jerry Henry. Editor: Rick Weis. Music: Jimmy Henry. In color, video. Release date: July 13, 2003. Running time: 88 Min. Documentary.

With: Lance Black, Allan Brocka, Robert Laughlin, Micah McCain, Benjamin Morgan, Judy Tenuta, Bruce Vilanch, Stuart Krasnow.

GETTING HAL

Producers: Tony Markes, Wonder Fortune Serra, Brad Rowe, Daniel Hassid, Adam Rifkin. Executive producers: James W. Gaffney, Eric Lord. Director/Editor: Tony Markes. Screenplay: Doug Stuart. Story: Pamela Chais, Diana Levitt. Camera: Claudio Rocha. Music: Lars Anderson. In color. Release date: Feb. 15, 2003. Running time: 85 Min.

With: Brian Doyle-Murray, Delicia Lanza, Carlo Glorioso, DeAnna Steele, Jonathan Kay, James Gaffney, Chandra Ray, Doug Stuart.

GHOST SHIP

A Warner Bros. release presented in association with Village Roadshow Pictures and NPV Entertainment of a Dark Castle Entertainment production. Producers: Joel Silver, Robert Zemeckis, Gilbert Adler. Executive producers: Bruce Berman, Steve Richards. Co-producers: Richard Mirisch, Susan Levin. Director: Steve Beck. Screenplay: Mark Hanlon, John Pogue. Story: Hanlon. Camera: Gale Tattersall. Editor: Roger Barton. Music: John Frizzell. In Technicolor. Release date: Oct. 21, 2002. MPAA Rating: R. Running time: 91 Min.

Cast: Julianna Margulies, Ron Eldard, Desmond Harrington, Isaiah Washington, Gabriel Byrne, Alex Dimitriades, Karl Urban, Emily Browning, Francesca Rettondini.

GHOSTS OF THE ABYSS

A Buena Vista Pictures release of a Walt Disney Pictures presentation of an Earthship production in association with Walden Media. Producers: James Cameron, Chuck Comisky, Gig Rackauskas, Janace Tashjian. Creative producer: Ed W. Marsh. Director: James Cameron. Camera: Vince Pace. Editors: Ed W. Marsh, Sven Pape, John Refoua. Music: Joel McNeely. In CFI color, CineAlta HD 3-D, Imax format. Release date: April 7, 2003. MPAA Rating: G. Running time: 60 Min. Documentary. IMAX 3-D.

With: Bill Paxton, Lewis Abernathy, Lori Johnson, Dr. Charles Pellegrino, Don Lynch, Ken Marschall , James Cameron, Mike Cameron, Jeffrey N. Ledda, Genya Chernaiev , Victor Nischeta.

GIGLI

A Sony Pictures Entertainment release of a Revolution Studios presentation of a City Lights Films/Casey Silver production. Producers: Casey Silver, Martin Brest. Executive producer: John Hardy. Director/Writer: Martin Brest. Camera: Robert Elswit. Editors: Billy Weber, Julie Monroe. Music: John Powell. In Deluxe color, Panavision widescreen. Release date: July 27, 2003. MPAA Rating: R. Running time: 124 Min.

Cast: Ben Affleck, Jennifer Lopez, Justin Bartha, Lainie Kazan, Missy Crider, Lenny Venito, Christopher Walken, Al Pacino.

GIRL HOOD

A Moxie Firecracker Films production. Producers: Liz Garbus, Rory Kennedy. Director: Liz Garbus. Camera: Tony Hardman. Editors: Mary Manhardt. In color, DV. Release date: March 24, 2003. Running time: 79 Min. Documentary.

THIS GIRL'S LIFE

A Miracle Mile Films and Muse Films presentation in association with Milkshake Films. Producers: Ash, Boro Yukadinovic, Chris Hanley, David Hillary. Executive producer: Boro Yukadinovic. Co-producers: Daniel M. Berger, Allyson Tang, Douglas Salkin, Clark McCutchen. Co-executive producers: Tim Peternel, Perica Perovic, Jerry Fishman, David Alan Graf. Director/Writer: Ash. Camera: Alessandro Zezza. Editor: Troy Takaki. Music: Agartha, Halou. In color, 24P HD video. Release date: June 16, 2003. Running time: 106 Min.

Cast: James Woods, Juliette Marquis, Kip Pardue, Tomas Arana, Michael Rapaport, Rosario Dawson, Ioan Gruffudd, Cheyenne Silver, Kam Heskin, Natalie Taylor, Isaiah Washington.

GIRLS WILL BE GIRLS

An SRO Pictures production. Producers: Michael Warwick, Richard Ahren. Executive producer: Jack Plotnick. Director/Writer: Richard Day. Camera: Nicoholas Hutak. Editor: Chris Conlee. Music: Steve Edwards. In color, HD. Release date: Jan. 17, 2003. Running time: 79 Min.

Cast: Jack Plotnick, Clinton Leupp, Jeffery Roberson, Ron Mathews, Eric Stonestreet, Hamilton von Watts, Dana Gould, Chad Lindsey.

GODS AND GENERALS

A Warner Bros. release of a Ted Turner Pictures presentation of an Antietam Filmworks production. Producer: Ronald F. Maxwell. Executive producers: Ted Turner, Robert Katz, Robert Rehme, Moctezuma Esparza, Mace Neufeld. Co-executive producer: Ronald G. Smith. Co-producer: Nick Grillo. Director/Writer: Ronald F. Maxwell, based on the book by Jeffrey M. Shaara. Camera: Kees Van Oostrum. Editor: Corky Ehlers. Music: John Frizzell, Randy Edelman. In Technicolor, Panavision widescreen. Release date: Feb. 11, 2003. MPAA Rating: PG-13. Running time: 223 Min.

Cast: Jeff Daniels, Stephen Lang, Robert Duvall, Mira Sorvino, Kevin Conway, C. Thomas Howell, Frankie Faison, Matt Letscher, Jeremy London, William Sanderson, Kali Rocha, Brian Mallon, Mia Dillon.

GO FURTHER

A Sphinx Prods. production in association with Boneyard Entertainment, Cameraplanet and Chum Television. Producer: Ron Mann. Co-producer: Sharon Brooks. Director: Ron Mann. Screenplay: Solomon Vesta. Camera: Robert Fresco. Editors: Robert Kennedy. Music: Guido Luciani. In color. Release date: March 7, 2003. Running time: 80 Min. Documentary.

Cast: Woody Harrelson.

GOING DOWN

A Paia Pictures release in association with Wasatch Screen Partners of a Bill Ferguson production. Producer: Bill Ferguson. Co-producer: Jim Pasternak. Director: Joseph A. Pineda. Screenplay: Joey Velazquez. Story: Velazquez, Wade Warren. Camera: Olivier Donohue. Editor: Yoshio Kohashi. Music: Jeff Cardoni. In CFI color. Release date: April 8, 2003. Running time: 80 Min.

With: Jay Michael Ferguson, Josh Blake, Christine Lakin, Hope Riley, Matthew Carey, Lacey Bullard, Renee Estevez, Pat Thomas, Nicholas Downs, Rachelle Carson, Blake Shields, Dennis Haskins.

GOOD FENCES

A Showtime presentation of a 40 Acres and a Mule Filmworks production. Producers: Whoopi Goldberg, Danny Glover. Executive producers: Spike Lee, Sam Kitt. Director: Ernest Dickerson. Screenplay: Trey Ellis, based on the novel by Ericka Ellis. Camera: Jonathan Freeman. Editor: Stephen Lovejoy. Music: George Duke. In color. Release date: Jan. 29, 2003. Running time: 119 Min.
With: Whoopi Goldberg, Danny Glover, Zachary Simmons Glover, Ryan Michelle Bathe, Ashley Archer, Vincent McCurdy Clark, Mo'Nique.

A GREAT WONDER

A Two Shoes Prods. (Seattle) production, with support from Threshold Foundation, King County Cultural Commission, Loving Friends of the Sudanese. Producer/Director/Writer: Kim Shelton. Camera: Leigh Kimball. Editor: Jennifer Chinlund. Music; Hamza El Din, Todd Boekelheide. In color, DigiBeta. Release date: June 15, 2003. Running time: 65 Min. Documentary.

GREEN CARD FEVER

A Vijay Vaidyanathan presentation of a Net Effect Media production. Producer: Vijay Vaidyanathan. Director/Writer: Bala Rajasekharuni. Camera: Scott Spears. Editors: Robert Komatsu, Robin Lee. Music: Pete Sears. In color. Release date: Aug. 18, 2003. Running time: 100 Min.
Cast: Vikram Dasu, Deep Katdare, Purva Bedi, Robert Lin.

THE GREY

A Dax Prods. and Thick Water presentation. Producer: Mark Boone Junior. Executive producers: Corky Taylor, Hugh Bishop. Co-producer: Ted Baer. Director: Shane Dax Taylor. Screenplay: Taylor, Mark Boone Junior, based on the novel "The Cockfighter" by Frank Manley. Camera: Marcel Cabrera. Editor: Neguine Sanani. Music: David Vaught. In color; film/video. Release date: March 7, 2002. Running time: 86 Min.
Cast: John Quertermous, Mark Boone Junior, Catherine Kellner, Jake LaBotz, Max Perlich, Jesse Rae, Chris Norsworthy, Richard Ross.

GRIND

A Warner Bros. release of a Pandora presentation of a Gaylord Films/Gerber Pictures production in association with 900 Films. Producers: Bill Gerber, Hunt Lowry, Casey La Scala. Executive producers: E.K. Gaylord II, Morgan Stone. Co-producer: Betsy Mackey, Lance Sloane. Director: Casey La Scala. Screenplay: Ralph Sall. Camera: Richard Crudo. Editor: Eric Strand. In color. Release date: Aug. 11, 2003. MPAA Rating: PG-13. Running time: 105 Min.
Cast: Mike Vogel, Vince Vieluf, Adam Brody, Joey Kern, Jennifer Morrison, Jason London, Randy Quaid, Christopher McDonald.

A GUY THING

An MGM release of a David Ladd Films production. Producers: Ladd, David Nicksay. Co-producers: Danielle Sterling, David Kerwin. Director: Chris Koch. Screenplay: Greg Glienna, Pete Schwaba, Matt Tarses, Bill Wrubel. Story: Glienna. Camera: Robbie Greenberg. Editor: David Moritz. Original music: Mark Mothersbaugh. In Deluxe color. Release date: Jan. 13, 2003. MPAA rating: PG-13. Running time: 101 Min.
Cast: Jason Lee, Julia Stiles, Selma Blair, James Brolin, Shawn Hatosy, Lochlyn Munro, Diana Scarwid, David Koechner, Julie Hagerty, Thomas Lennon, Jackie Burroughs.

HALF PAST DEAD

A Sony Pictures Entertainment release of a Screen Gems and Franchise Pictures presentation in association with Modern Media Filmproduktion. Producers: Andrew Stevens, Elie Samaha, Steven Seagal. Executive producers: Christopher Eberts, Uwe Schott, Randall Emmett, George Furla. Co-producers: Phil Goldfine, James Holt. Director/Writer: Don Michael Paul. Camera: Mike Slovis. Editor: Vanick Moradian. Music: Tyler Bates. In Deluxe color. Release date: Nov. 7, 2002. MPAA Rating: PG-13. Running time: 98 Min.
Cast: Steven Seagal, Morris Chestnut, Ja Rule, Nia Peeples, Tony Plana, Kurupt, Michael "Bear" Taliferro, Claudia Christian, Linda Thorson, Bruce Weitz.

HANSEL & GRETEL

An Innovation Film Group release of a Steve Austin and Jonathan Bogner presentation of a Tag Entertainment production in association with Majestic Film Partners IV. Producers: Steve Austin, Jonathan Bogner. Executive producers: Kent Scott. Co-executive producers, David Borg, Peter King, Robin Bains, Scott Schomer. Co-producer: Gary Depew. Director: Gary J. Tunnicliffe. Screenplay: Timothy Dolan, Jonathan Bogner, Tunnicliffe, based on a story by the Brothers Grimm. Camera: Brian Baugh. Editor: Andrew Cohen. Music: Bob Mothersbaugh, Rusty Andrews. In Fotokem color, Arriflex widescreen. Release date: Oct. 18, 2002. MPAA Rating: PG. Running time: 88 Min.
Cast: Taylor Momsen, Jacob Smith, Delta Burke, Howie Mandel, Gerald McRaney, Lynn Redgrave, Alana Austin, Dan Roebuck, Thomas Curtis, Dakota Fanning. Voices: Tom Arnold, Bobcat Goldthwaite, Sinbad.

HARLEM ARIA

A Kintop Pictures/Alive Entertainment/In Motion presentation of a Bent Nail production. Producers: Deeppak Nayar, Philip von Alvensleben. Executive producers: Damon Wayans, Isabell von Alvensleben, Hale Coughlin. Co-producers: Darryl D. Pryor, Linda Moran, Annice Parker. Director/Writer: William Jennings. Camera: Keith Smith. Editor: Sabine Hoffman. Music: Jeff Beal, Fabian Cooke. In Moviecam color. Release date: Feb. 9, 2003. Running time: 100 Min.
Cast: Damon Wayans, Gabriel Casseus, Christian Camargo, Malik Yoba, Paul Sorvino, Kristen Wilson, Eyde Byrde, Nicole Ari Parker.

HARRY POTTER AND THE CHAMBER OF SECRETS

A Warner Bros. release of a Heyday Films/1492 Pictures production. Producer: David Heyman. Executive producers: Mark Radcliffe, Michael Barnathan, Chris Columbus, David Barron. Co-producer: Tanya Seghatchian. Director: Chris Columbus. Screenplay: Steve Kloves, based on the novel by J.K. Rowling. Camera: Roger Pratt. Editor: Peter Honess. Music: John Williams. In Technicolor, Panavision widescreen. Release date: Nov. 4, 2002. MPAA Rating: PG. Running time: 161 Min.
Cast: Daniel Radcliffe, Rupert Grint, Emma Watson, Kenneth Branagh, John Cleese, Robbie Coltrane, Warwick Davis, Richard Griffiths, Richard Harris, Jason Isaacs, Alan Rickman, Fiona Shaw, Maggie Smith, Julie Walters, Shirley Henderson, Julian Glover.

HEAD OF STATE

A DreamWorks release and presentation of a 3 Arts Entertainment production. Producers: Ali LeRoi, Chris Rock, Michael Rotenberg. Executive producer, Ezra Swerdlow. Director: Chris Rock. Screenplay: Rock, Ali LeRoi. Camera: Donald E. Thorin. Editor: Stephen A. Rotter. Music: Marcus Miller, David "DJ Quik" Blake. In DuArt color, Technicolor prints. Release date: March 18, 2003. MPAA Rating: PG-13. Running time: 95 Min.
Cast: Chris Rock, Bernie Mac, Dylan Baker, Nick Searcy, Lynn Whitfield, Robin Givens, Tamala Jones, James Rebhorn, Keith David, Tracy Morgan, Stephanie March, Robert Stanton, Jude Ciccolella, Nate Dogg.

HEART OF THE SEA: KAPOLIOKA'EHUKAI

A Women Make Movies presentation of a Swell Cinema production in association with ITVS, Pacific Islanders in Communications and KHET. Producer: Charlotte Lagarde. Executive producer: Janet Cole. Directors: Lisa Denker, Charlotte Lagarde. Camera: Denker. Editors: Vivien Hillgrove. Music: Miriam Cutler. In color, 16mm/video. Release date: April 27, 2003. Running time: 57 Min. Documentary.

THE HEBREW HAMMER

A Content Film presentation of a Jericho Entertainment, Content Film production. Producers: Josh Kesselman, Sofia Sondervan, Lisa Fragner. Executive producers: Edward R. Pressman, John Schmidt. Director/Writer: Jonathan Kesselman. Camera: Kurt Brabbee. Editor: Dean Holland. Music: Michael Cohen. In color, Panavision widescreen. Release date: Jan. 23, 2003. Running time: 85 Min.
Cast: Adam Goldberg, Judy Greer, Andy Dick, Mario Van Peebles, Peter Coyote, Sean Whalen, Tony Cox, Nora Dunn, Richard Riehle.

HELL'S HIGHWAY

A the Asylum presentation of a Poushay production. Producers: Steve Grabowsky, Susan Wright. Executive producers: David Latt, David Rimawi. Director: S. Lee Taylor. Screenplay: Steve Grabowsky, Taylor. Camera: Cort Fey. Editor: Taylor. Original music: Joey Peters. In color. Release date: Feb. 14, 2003. Running time: 88 Min.
With: Aaron Buer, Ryan DeRouen, Ashley Elizabeth, Jill Jacobs, Jessica Osfar, Brent Taylor, Kelsey Wedeen, Anthony Connell.

HIDDEN IN PLAIN SIGHT

A Raven's Call Prods. (Berkeley, Calif.) production. Producers: Vivi Letsou, John H. Smihula. Co-producer: Andres Thomas Conteris. Director/Writer: John H. Smihula. Camera: Chip Holley. Editor: Andrea Zondler. Music: Luis Peres. In color, Beta SP-NTSC. Release date: June 8, 2003. Running time: 71 Min.
With: Father Roy Bourgeois, Noam Chomsky, Christopher Hitchens, Eduardo Galeano, Sandra Alvarez, Rep. Barbara Lee, Sister Dianna Ortiz. Narrator, Martin Sheen.

HOLES

A Buena Vista release of a Walt Disney Pictures presentation in association with Walden Media of a Chicago Pacific Entertainment/Phoenix Pictures production. Producers: Mike Medavoy, Andrew Davis, Teresa Tucker-Davies, Lowell Blank. Executive producers: Marty Ewing, Louis Phillips. Director: Andrew Davis. Screenplay: Louis Sachar, based on his novel. Camera: Stephen St. John. Editors: Tom Nordberg, Jeffrey Wolf. Music: Joel McNeely. Release date: April 15, 2003. MPAA Rating: PG. Running time: 118 Min.
Cast: Sigourney Weaver, Jon Voight, Patricia Arquette, Tim Blake Nelson, Dule Hill, Shia LaBeouf, Henry Winkler, Nate Davis, Rick Fox, Scott Plank, Roma Maffia, Eartha Kitt, Siobhan Fallon Hogan.

HOLLYWOOD BUDDHA

A YBG.com/Hollywood Buddha production. (International sales: Conquistador, L.A.) Producer/Director/Writer: Philippe Caland. Camera: Lisa Brook. Editors: Lance Cutter, Keiko Deguchi. Music: Claude Chaloub. In color, DV-to-35mm. Release date: June 10, 2003. Running time: 75 Min.
With: Philippe Caland, Theo Cardan, Nikki Stalder, Jim Stewart.

HOLLYWOOD HOMICIDE

A Sony Pictures Entertainment release of a Columbia Pictures/Revolution Studios presentation of a Pitt/Shelton production. Producers: Lou Pitt, Ron Shelton. Executive producers: Joe Roth, David Lester. Co-producers: Robert Souza, Allegra Clegg, Scott Bernstein. Director: Ron Shelton. Screenplay: Robert Souza, Shelton. Camera: Barry Peterson. Editor: Paul Seydor. Music: Alex Wurman. In Deluxe color, Panavision widescreen. Release date: Sept. 5, 2003. MPAA Rating: PG-13. Running time: 115 Min.
Cast: Harrison Ford, Josh Hartnett, Lena Olin, Bruce Greenwood, Isaiah Washington, Lolita Davidovich, Keith David, Master P, Gladys Knight, Lou Diamond Phillips, Meredith Scott Lynn, Tom Todoroff, James MacDonald, Kurupt, Andre Benjamin, Alan Dale, Clyde Kusatsu, Dwight Yoakam, Martin Landau, Eric Idle, Frank Sinatra Jr.

HOME ROOM

A DEJ Releasing release of a DEJ Prods. presentation in conjunction with MOR Pictures of a Benjamin Ormand production. Producer: Ormand. Co-producer: Russ Matthews, Paul F. Ryan. Director/Writer/Editor: Paul F. Ryan. Camera: Rebecca Baehler. Music: Michael Shapiro. In Fotokem color. Release date: Sept. 2, 2003. MPAA Rating: R. Running time: 132 Min.
Cast: Busy Philipps, Erika Christensen, Victor Garber, Holland Taylor, Ken Jenkins, Raphael Sbarge, James Pickens Jr.

HONEYBOY

A Free Range Pictures (Chicago) production. Producer: Kerna Z Bakirci. Executive producers: Jamie M. Taradash, Scott L. Taradash. Director/Writer/Editor: Scott L. Taradash. Camera: Eric C. McKay. Music: David "Honeyboy" Edwards, Willie Foster, others. In color, HiDef. Release date: Oct. 5, 2002. Running time: 82 Min. Documentary.
With: David "Honeyboy" Edwards, Willie Foster, B.B. King.

HORNS AND HALOS

A RumuR Inc. production. (International sales: RumuR Inc., Brooklyn.) Producers: Suki Hawley, Michael Galinsky, David Beilinson. Directors: Suki Hawley, Michael Galinsky. Camera: Hawley, Galinsky, Bob Ray. Editor: Hawley. Music: various. In color, Digital Betacam. Release date: Sept. 10, 2002. Running time: 79 Min. Documentary.
With: Sander Hicks, J.H. Hatfield, Peter Slover, Mark Crispin Miller.

HORROR

An Elite Entertainment release (for DVD) of an LD Media presentation. Producer: Dante Tomaselli. Executive producer: Jack Swain. Co-producer: Maria Tassiello. Director/Writer: Dante Tomaselli. Camera: Tim Naylor. Editor: Marcus Bonilla. Music: Tomaselli. In color. Release date: Feb. 15, 2003. Running time: 76 Min.
With: The Amazing Kreskin, Lizzy Mahon, Danny Lopes, Vincent Lamberti, Christie Sanford, Jessica Pagan, Raine Brown, Kevin Kenney, Chris Farabaugh, Felissa Rose.

THE HOT CHICK

A Buena Vista release of a Touchstone Pictures presentation. Producers: John Schneider, Carr D'Angelo. Executive producers: Adam Sandler, Jack Giarraputo, Guy Riedel. Co-producers: Nathan T. Reimann, Ian Maxtone-Graham. Screenplay: Tom Brady. Screenplay: Brady, Rob Schneider. Camera: Tim Suhrstedt. Editor: Peck Prior. Music: John Debney. In Technicolor, Panavision widescreen. Release date: Nov. 21, 2002. MPAA rating: PG-13. Running time: 101 Min.
Cast: Rob Schneider, Anna Faris, Matthew Lawrence, Eric Christian Olsen, Robert Davi, Melora Hardin, Alexandra Holden, Rachel Mcadams, Maritza Murray, Fay Hauser, Jodi Long, Tia Mowry, Tamera Mowry, Lee Garlington, Angie Stone, Matt Weinberg, Leila Kenzle, Michelle Branch, Michael O'keefe, Adam Sandler.

THE HOURS

A Paramount (in North America) release of a Paramount Pictures and Miramax Films presentation of a Scott Rudin/Robert Fox production. Producers: Rudin, Fox. Executive producer: Mark Huffam. Director: Stephen Daldry. Screenplay: David Hare, based on the novel by Michael Cunningham. Camera: Seamus McGarvey. Editor: Peter Boyle. Music: Philip Glass. In Deluxe color. Release date: Dec. 25, 2002. MPAA Rating: PG-13. Running time: 114 Min.
Cast: Meryl Streep, Julianne Moore, Nicole Kidman, Ed Harris, Toni Collette, Claire Danes, Jeff Daniels, Stephen Dillane, Allison Janney, John C. Reilly, Miranda Richardson, Eileen Atkins, Margo Martindale.

HOUSE OF 1000 CORPSES

A Lions Gate Films release. Producer: Andy Gould. Executive producers: Andy Given, Guy Oseary. Co-producer: Danielle Shilling Lovett. Director/Writer: Rob Zombie. Camera: Tom Richmond, Alex Poppas. Editors: Kathryn Himoff, Robert K. Lambert, Sean Lambert. Music: Zombie, Scott Humphrey. In Technicolor. Release date: April 11, 2003. MPAA Rating: R. Running time: 88 Min.
Cast: Sid Haig, Bill Moseley, Sheri Moon, Karen Black, Chris Hardwick, Erin Daniels, Jennifer Jostyn, Rainn Wilson, Walton Goggins, Tom Towles, Matthew McGrory, Robert Mukes.

HOW TO DEAL

A New Line Cinema release of a Radar Pictures/Golden Mean production. Producers: William Teitler, Erica Huggins. Executive producers: Ted Field, Chris Van Allsburg, Scott Kroopf, David Linde, Toby Emmerich, Michele Weiss. Co-producer: Stephanie Striegel. Director: Clare Kilner. Screenplay: Neena Beber. Based on the novels "Someone Like You" and "That Summer," by Sarah Dessen. Camera: Eric Edwards. Editors: Janice Hampton, Shawna Callahan. Music: David Kitay. In Deluxe color. Release date: July 8, 2003. MPAA Rating: PG-13. Running time: 101 Min.
Cast: Mandy Moore, Allison Janney, Trent Ford, Alexandra Holden, Dylan Baker, Nina Foch, Mackenzie Astin, Connie Ray, Mary Catherine Garrison, Sonja Smits, Peter Gallagher.

HOW TO GET THE MAN'S FOOT OUTTA YOUR ASS!

A Sony Pictures Classics (in U.S.) release of a MVP Filmz presentation of a Bad Aaas Cinema, Inc. production. Producer: Bruce Wayne Gillies. Executive producer: Michael Mann. Co-producers: Dennis Haggerty, G. Marq Roswell. Co-executive producer: Tobie Haggerty. Director: Mario Van Peebles. Screenplay: Van Peebles, Dennis Haggerty, based on the book "Sweet Sweetback's Baadasssss Song" by Melvin Van Peebles. Camera: Robert Primes. Editors: Anthony Miller, Nneka Goforth. Original music: Tyler Bates. In color, HD vid. Release date: Sept. 9, 2003. Running time: 108 Min.
Cast: Mario Van Peebles, Joy Bryant, Terry Crews, Ossie Davis, David Alan Grier, Nia Long, Saul Rubinek, Rainn Wilson.

HOW TO LOSE A GUY IN 10 DAYS

A Paramount Pictures release and presentation of a Robert Evans/Christine Peters production and a Lynda Obst production. Producers: Lynda Obst, Robert Evans, Christine Peters. Executive producer: Richard Vane. Director: Donald Petrie. Screenplay: Kristen Buckley, Brian Regan, Burr Steers, based on the book by Michele Alexander, Jeannie Long. Camera: John Bailey. Editor: Debra Neil-Fisher. Music: David Newman. In Deluxe color. Release date: Jan. 24, 2003. MPAA Rating: PG-13. Running time: 116 Min.
Cast: Kate Hudson, Matthew McConaughey, Adam Goldberg, Michael Michele, Shalom Harlow, Bebe Neuwirth, Robert Klein, Kathryn Hahn, Thomas Lennon, Annie Parisse.

HULK

A Universal release presented in association with Marvel Enterprises of a Valhalla Motion Pictures/Good Machine production. Producers: Gale Anne Hurd, Avi Arad, James Schamus, Larry Franco. Executive producers: Stan Lee, Kevin Feige. Director: Ang Lee. Screenplay: John Turman, Michael France, James Schamus. Story: Schamus, based on the Marvel comicbook character created by Stan Lee, Jack Kirby. Camera: Frederick Elmes. Editors: Tim Squyres. Music: Danny Elfman. In Technicolor. Release date: June 9, 2003. MPAA Rating: PG-13. Running time: 138 Min.
Cast: Eric Bana, Jennifer Connelly, Sam Elliott, Josh Lucas, Nick Nolte.

THE HUMAN STAIN

A Miramax (in U.S.) release of a Lakeshore Entertainment and Miramax Films presentation of a Lakeshore Entertainment/Stone Village production, in association with Cinerenta-Cineepsilon. Producers: Tom Rosenberg, Gary Lucchesi, Scott Steindorff. Executive producers: Bob Weinstein, Harvey Weinstein, Ron Bozman, Andre Lamal, Rick Schwartz, Steve Hutensky, Michael Ohoven, Eberhard Kayser. Co-producer: Mario Ohoven. Director: Robert Benton. Screenplay: Nicholas Meyer, based on the novel by Philip Roth. Camera: Jean Yves Escoffier. Editor: Christopher Tellefsen. Music: Rachel Portman. In Deluxe color, Panavision Widescreen. Release date: Aug. 29, 2003. Running time: 106 Min.
Cast: Anthony Hopkins, Nicole Kidman, Ed Harris, Gary Sinise, Wentworth Miller, Jacinda Barrett, Harry Lennix, Clark Gregg, Anna Deavere Smith, Lizan Mitchell, Kerry Washington, Phyllis Newman, Margo Martindale, Ron Canada, Mili Avital, Danny Blanco Hall, Kristen Blevins, Anne Dudek, Mimi Kuzyk, John Finn.

THE HUNTED

A Paramount release presented in association with Lakeshore Entertainment of a Ricardo Mestres/Alphaville production. Producers: Mestres, James Jacks. Executive producers: David Griffiths, Peter Griffiths, Marcus Viscidi, Sean Daniel. Co-producer: Art Monterastelli. Director: William Friedkin. Screenplay: David Griffiths, Peter Griffiths, Art Montersatelli. Camera: Caleb Deschanel. Editor: Augie Hess. Music: Brian Tyler. In CFI color. Release date: March 10, 2003. MPAA Rating: R. Running time: 94 Min.
Cast: Tommy Lee Jones, Benicio Del Toro, Connie Nielsen, Leslie Stefanson, John Finn, Jose Zuniga, Ron Canada, Mark Pellegrino, Lonny Chapman, Rex Linn, Eddie Velez.

IDENTITY

A Sony Pictures Entertainment release of a Columbia Pictures presentation of a Konrad Pictures production. Producer: Cathy Konrad. Executive producer: Stuart Besser. Director: James Mangold. Screenplay: Michael Cooney. Camera: Phedon Papamichael. Editor: David Brenner. Music: Alan Silvestri. In FotoKem color, Deluxe prints; Panavision widescreen. Release date: April 12, 2003. MPAA Rating: R. Running time: 90 Min.
Cast: John Cusack, Ray Liotta, Amanda Peet, John Hawkes, Alfred Molina, Clea DuVall, John C. McGinley, William Lee Scott, Jake Busey, Pruitt Taylor Vince, Rebecca DeMornay, Carmen Argenziano.

I DON'T KNOW JACK

A David Lynch presentation of a Next Step Studios production. Producers: Richard Green, Donna Du Bain, Wendy De Rycke, Jeffrey Scott McConnell. Executive producers: Richard Green, Donna Du Bain. Director: Chris Leavens. Camera: Alex Szuch. Editor: Michael Wargo. Music: Brantley Kearns. In color, digital video. Release date: Nov. 10, 2002. Running time: 90 Min. Documentary.
With: John Achorn, Leo Bulgarini, Catherine Case, Catherine Coulson, Billy Damota, Donna Du Bain, Wayne Grace, Bob Graham, T Max Graham, Dennis Hopper, Brantley Kearns, David Lindeman, Bobby Logan, David Lynch, Dennis Nance, Richard Nance.

I'LL BE THERE

A Warner Bros. release of a Morgan Creek production, in association with Immortal Entertainment. Producer: James G. Robinson. Executive producer: Guy McElwaine. Co-producers: David C. Robinson, Wayne Morris. Director: Craig Ferguson. Screenplay: Ferguson, Philip McGrade. Camera: Ian Wilson. Editor: Sheldon Kahn. Music: Trevor Jones. In Fujicolor. Release date: June 17, 2003. Running time: 104 Min.
Cast: Craig Ferguson, Jemma Redgrave, Charlotte Church, Joss Ackland, Ralph Brown, Ian McNeice, Imelda Staunton, Anthony Head, Steve Noonan, Marion Bailey, Tom Ellis.

I LOOK UP AT THE SKY NOW

Producer: Barbara M. Bickart, Miriam Yeung. Director: Barbara M. Bickart. Camera: Bickart, others. Editors: Bickart, Cheryl Furjanic, Aurora Maria Aguero. In color/B&W, DV. Release date: June 15, 2003. Running time: 63 Min.
With: An-D, Andy Monk, Anna Goldsznycer, Dexter Asido, G.i.JaEn. HaRdCoRe; Jon Salvator, Kevin Santos, P Concepcion, Sara Wekselblatt, Suraby Yensi, Teaspoon.

INSPECTOR GADGET 2

A Walt Disney Home Video release of a Walt Disney Pictures presentation of a Fountain production. Producers: Charles Hirschhorn, Peter M. Green. Executive producers: Andy Heyward, Jean Chalopin, Roger Birnbaum, Jordan Kerner, David Roessell. Director: Alex Zamm. Screenplay: Ron Anderson, William Robertson, Alex Zamm, based on characters created by Andy Heyward, Jean Chalopin, Bruno Bianchi. Camera: Geoffrey Wharton. Editor: Jimmy Hill. Music: Chris Hajian. In color. Release date: March 23, 2002. MPAA Rating: G. Running time: 88 Min.

Cast: French Stewart, Elaine Hendrix, Caitlin Wachs, Tony Martin, Mark Mitchell, Sigrid Thornton, Bruce Spence, John Batchelor.

INFESTED

A City Block Films production. Producer: Charles X Block. Executive producer: Philip Knowles. Director/Writer: Josh Olson. Camera: M. David Mullen. Editor: David Wilson. Music: Rodney Wittenberg. In color. Release date: Oct. 18, 2002. Running time: 84 Min.

With: Zach Galligan, Lisa Ann Hadley, Daniel Jenkins, Amy Jo Johnson, Nahanni Johnstone, Robert Duncan McNeill, Jack Mulcahy, David Packer, Camilla Overbye Roos, Tuc Watkins, Mark Margolis.

AN INJURY TO ONE

A Travis Wilkerson production. Producer/Director/Editor: Travis Wilkerson. Camera: Wilkerson. Music: Jim O'Rourke, Will Oldham, Dirty Three, If Thousands. In color, HD Cam. Release date: Jan. 20, 2003. Running time: 53 Min. Documentary.

INTERSTATE 60

An IDP Distribution release of a Fireworks Pictures and Peter Hoffman presentation of a Fireworks Pictures production. Producers: Ira Deutchmann, Peter Hoffman, Neil Canton, Peter Bray. Executive producers: Greg Johnson, Hoffman, Eric Sandys, Jay Firestone. Director/Writer: Bob Gale. Camera: Kelly Mason. Editor: Michael Fallavollita. Music: Christophe Beck. In Deluxe Toronto color. Release date: Oct. 6, 2002. Running time: 112 Min.

With: James Marsden, Gary Oldman, Kurt Russell, Michael J. Fox, Chris Cooper, Amy Smart, Ann-Margret, Christopher Lloyd.

INTOLERABLE CRUELTY

A Universal release of a Universal Pictures and Imagine Entertainment presentation of a Brian Grazer production in association with Alphaville. Producers: Ethan Coen, Brian Grazer. Executive producers: James Jacks, Sean Daniel. Co-producers: John Cameron, James Whitaker. Director: Joel Coen. Screenplay: Robert Ramsey, Matthew Stone, Ethan Coen, Joel Coen. Story: Ramsey, Stone, John Romano. Camera: Roger Deakins. Editor: Roderick Jaynes. Music: Carter Burwell. In Technicolor. Relesae date: Sept. 2, 2003. Running time: 100 Min.

Cast: George Clooney, Catherine Zeta-Jones, Geoffrey Rush, Cedric the Entertainer, Edward Hermann, Richard Jenkins, Billy Bob Thornton, Paul Adelstein.

IT RUNS IN THE FAMILY

An MGM release of a Metro-Goldwyn-Mayer Pictures and Buena Vista Intl. presentation of a Further Films production. Producer: Michael Douglas. Executive producers: Fred Schepisi, Kerry Orent. Co-producer: Marcy Drogin. Director: Fred Schepisi. Screenplay: Jesse Wigutow. Camera: Ian Baker. Editor: Kate Williams. Music: Paul Grabowsky. In Deluxe color and prints, Panavision widescreen. Release date: April 16, 2003. MPAA Rating: PG-13. Running time: 109 Min.

Cast: Michael Douglas, Kirk Douglas, Rory Culkin, Cameron Douglas, Diana Douglas, Bernadette Peters, Michelle Monaghan, Geoffrey Arend, Sarita Choudhury, Irene Gorovaia, Annie Golden.

IRISH EYES

A Shooting Spree Films production. Producers: Julian Valdes, David McCarthy. Director/Writer: David McCarthy. Camera: Kristian Bernier. Editor: Lindsay Moffard. Music: Randy Miller. In CFI color. Release date: March 22, 2003. Running time: 112 Min.

Cast: Daniel Baldwin, John Novak, Wings Hauser, Alberta Watson, Torri Higgerson, Eugene Lipinski.

I SPY

A Sony Pictures Entertainment release of a Columbia Pictures presentation of a Tall Trees/C-2 Pictures production in association with Sheldon Leonard Prods. Producers: Jenno Topping, Betty Thomas, Mario Kassar, Andy Vajna. Executive producers: Warren Carr, Marc Toberoff, David R. Ginsburg. Director: Betty Thomas. Screenplay: Marianne Wibberley, Cormac Wibberley, Jay Scherick, David Ronn, based on characters created by Morton Fine and David Friedkin. Story: Marianne Wibberley, Cormac Wibberley. Camera: Oliver Wood. Editor: Peter Teschner. Music: Richard Gibbs. In Alpha Cine color, Deluxe prints. Release date: Oct. 8, 2002. MPAA Rating: PG-13. Running time: 96 Min.

Cast: Eddie Murphy, Owen Wilson, Famke Janssen, Malcolm McDowell, Gary Cole, Phill Lewis, Viv Leacock.

THE ITALIAN JOB

A Paramount release of a De Line Pictures production. Producer: Donald De Line. Executive producers: James R. Dyer, Wendy Japhet, Tim Bevan, Eric Fellner. Director: F. Gary Gray. Screenplay: Donna Powers, Wayne Powers, based on the film written by Troy Kennedy Martin. Camera: Wally Pfister. Editors: Richard Francis-Bruce, Christopher Rouse. Music: John Powell. In Deluxe color, Panavision widescreen. Release date: May 22, 2003. MPAA Rating: PG-13. Running time: 111 Min.

Cast: Mark Wahlberg, Charlize Theron, Edward Norton, Seth Green, Jason Statham, Mos Def, Franky G, Donald Sutherland, Gawtti.

I WITNESS

A Promark Entertainment Group presentation in association with Videal GmbH. Producers: David Bixler, Shelly Strong. Executive producers: Jon Kramer, Paul Desouza. Co-producers: Ed Cathell III, Julia Verdin, Robert Ozn, Colin Greene. Director: Rowdy Herrington. Screenplay: Colin Greene, Robert Ozn. Camera: Michael Wojciechowski. Editors: Pasquale Buba. Music: David Kitay. In Continental Laboratory color, Image Laboratory prints. Release date: April 20, 2003. Running time: 98 Min.

Cast: Jeff Daniels, James Spader, Portia De Rossi, Clifton Collins Jr.

JACKASS THE MOVIE

A Paramount release presented with MTV Films of a Dickhouse production in association with Lynch Siderow Prods. Producers: Jeff Tremaine, Spike Jonze, Johnny Knoxville. Executive producers: Trip Taylor, John Miller, David Gale. Co-executive producers: Michelle Klepper, Jessica Swirnoff. Co-producers: Sean Cliver, Dimitry Elyashkevich. Director: Jeff Tremaine. Camera: Dimitry Elyashkevich. Editors: Liz Ewart, Mark Hansen, Kristine Young. In Deluxe color. Release date: Oct. 24, 2002. MPAA Rating: R. Running time: 84 Min.

With: Johnny Knoxville, Bam Margera, Chris Pontius, Steve-O, Dave England, Ryan Dunn, Jason "Wee Man" Acuna, Preston Lacy, Ehren McGhehey.

JEEPERS CREEPERS 2

An MGM release of a United Artists presentation in association with Myriad Pictures of an American Zoetrope production. Producer: Tom Luse. Executive producers: Francis Ford Coppola, Bobby Rock, Kirk D'Amico, Lucas Foster. Co-executive producer: Philip von Alvensleben. Director/Writer: Victor Salva, based on characters created by Salva. Camera: Don E. FauntLeRoy. Editor: Ed Marx. Music: Bennett Salvay. In Deluxe color, Panavision widescreen. Release date: Aug. 26, 2003. MPAA Rating: R. Running time: 104 Min.

Cast: Ray Wise, Jonathan Breck, Garikayi Mutambirwa, Eric Nenninger, Nicki Aycox, Travis Schiffner, Lena Cardwell, Billy Aaron Brown, Marieh Delfino, Diane Delano, Thom Gossom Jr., Tom Tarantini, Al Santos, Josh Hammond, Kasan Butcher.

JESUS FREAK

A Movie Farm production. Producers: Amy Dawn Anderson, Pete Kuzov. Director: Morgan Nichols. Screenplay: Laura Lee Bahr. Camera: David S. Danesh. Editor: Nichols, Danesh. Music: Dan Adams. In color. Release date: June 17, 2003. Running time: 86 Min.

Cast: Laura Lee Bahr, Regan Forman, Josh Kantor, Pete Kuzov, Oded Gross.

THE JOURNEY

A J F Prods. presentation. Producers: Edwin Avaness, Emy Hovenesyan, Anghela Zograbyan. Executive producer: Krikor B. Tatoyan. Co-producers: Serj Minassians , Matt Terzian. Directors: Edwin Avaness, Emy Hovanesyan. Screenplay: Avaness, Hovanesyan, Anghela Zograbyan. Camera: Avaness. Editor: Avaness. Music: Alan Derian. In color, 24P high-definition video. Release date: July 13, 2003. Running time: 96 Min.

With: Sona Tatoyan, Varduhi Varderesyan, Tigran Nersesyan, Anoush Stepanyan, Roupen Harmandayan , Zenda Tatoyan, Zohrab Bek-Gasparents .

THE JUNGLE BOOK 2

A Buena Vista release of a Walt Disney Pictures presentation produced by DisneyToon Studios. Producers: Mary Thorne, Chris Chase. Director: Steve Trenbirth. Screenplay: Karl Geurs. Editors: Peter N. Lonsdale, Christopher Gee. Music: Joel McNeely. In Technicolor. Release date: Feb. 6, 2003. MPAA Rating: G. Running time: 72 Min.

Voices: John Goodman, Haley Joel Osment, Mae Whitman, Connor Funk, Bob Joles, Tony Jay, John Rhys-Davies, Jim Cummings, Phil Collins.

JUST ANOTHER STORY

A Showtime Networks presentation of a Hart Sharp Entertainment production in association with Q-Brothers Prods. Producers: Robert Kessel, Caroline Jaczko. Executive producers: Michael Hogan, John N. Hart, Jeffrey Sharp. Director/Writer: GQ. Camera: Keith Smith. Editors: Jacob Craycroft, Lee Percy. Music: J.A.Q., Conor O'Brien. In color, HDCam. Release date: May 9, 2003. Running time: 74 Min.

With: GQ, Omar Scroggins, Mylike Davis, Nate Mooney, Jaclyn DeSantis, Fay Wolf.

JUST MARRIED

A Twentieth Century Fox release and presentation in association with Mediastream 1. Prods. of a Robert Simonds production. Producer: Robert Simonds. Director: Shawn Levy. Screenwriter: Sam Harper. Executive producers: Tracey Trench, Josie Rosen, Lauren Shuler Donner. Co-producer: Ira Shuman. Editors: Don Zimmerman, Scott Hill. Music: Christophe Beck. Release date: Dec. 31, 2002. MPAA Rating: PG-13. Running time: 94 Min.

Cast: Ashton Kutcher, Brittany Murphy, Christian Kane, David Mooscow, Monet Mazur, David Rashe, Veronica Cartwright.

KANGAROO JACK

A Warner Bros. release of a Castle Rock Entertainment presentation of a Jerry Bruckheimer production. Producer: Bruckheimer. Executive producers: Mike Stenson, Chad Oman, Barry Waldman, Andrew Mason. Director: David McNally. Screenplay: Steve Bing, Scott Rosenberg. Story: Bing, Barry O'Brien. Camera: Peter Menzies Jr. Editors: John Murray, William Goldenberg. In Technicolor, widescreen. Release date: Jan. 4, 2003. MPAA Rating: PG. Running time: 89 Min.

Cast: Jerry O'Connell, Anthony Anderson, Estella Warren, Michael Shannon, Christopher Walken, Bill Hunter, Marton Csokas.

KILL BILL VOL. 1

A Miramax release of A Band Apart production. Producers: Lawrence Bender, Quentin Tarantino. Executive producers: Harvey Weinstein, Bob Weinstein, Erica Steinberg, E. Bennett Walsh. Director/Writer: Quentin Tarantino. Camera: Robert Richardson. Editor: Sally Menke. Original music: The RZA. In Technicolor, Deluxe prints; Panavision widescreen. Release date: Sept. 24, 2003. MPAA Rating: R. Running time: 110 Min.

Cast: Uma Thurman, Lucy Liu, Vivica A. Fox, Michael Madsen, Daryl Hannah, David Carradine, Sonny Chiba, Chiaki Kuriyama, Gordon Liu Chia-hui, Michael Parks, Julie Dreyfus.

KING OF THE ANTS

An Asylum presentation of an Anthill Prods. (Los Angeles) production, in association with Hecht Prods., Red Hen Prods. Producers: Duffy Hecht, David Michael Latt. Executive producers: David Rimawi, Sherri Strain. Co-producers: Stuart Gordonm, Charlie Higson, George Wendt. Director: Stuart Gordon. Screenplay: Charlie Higson, based on his novel. Camera: Mac Ahlberg. Editor: David Michael Latt. Music: Bobby Johnston. In color. Release date: June 11, 2003. Running time: 101 Min.

Cast: Chris McKenna, Kari Wuhrer, Daniel Baldwin, George Wendt, Tim Sharp, Vernon Wells, Ron Livingston, Lionel Mark Smith.

KISS THE BRIDE

An Imageworks and Empera Pictures presentation of a Replay Pictures production. Producers: Vanessa Parise, Jordan Gertner. Executive producers: David Shoshan, Richard Pepin. Co-producers: Richard Middleton, Daniel Sciortino, Chris Fisher. Director/Writer: Vanessa Parise. Camera: Rob Sweeney. Editors: Sam Citron, Lois Freeman-Fox. Music: Jeremy Parise. In color. Release date: Oct. 16, 2002. Running time: 89 Min.

Cast: Amanda Detmer, Sean Patrick Flanery, Burt Young, Talia Shire, Alyssa Milano, Brooke Langton, Vanessa Parise, Monet Mazur, Jonathan Schaech, Johnny Whitworth.

KLEPTO

A Nucleus Films presentation. Producer: Mark Ean. Executive producers: Thomas Trail, Meredith Bishop. Director/Editor: Thomas Trail. Screenplay: Ethan Gross, Trail. Camera: Peter Rieveschl. Original music: David Delaski. In color, HD-cam. Release date: March 7, 2003. Running time: 80 Min.

With: Meredith Bishop, Jsu Garcia, Leigh Taylor Young, Michael Nouri, Michael Irby, Kirk B.R. Woller, Michael E. Rodgers, Henry Czerny.

KUNG PHOOEY!

A Nakota Films and Kung Phooey Prods. presentation. Producer: Darryl Fong. Executive producers: John Lucasey, Simon Johnson. Director/Writer: Darryl Fong. Camera: Cliff Traiman. Editors: Rick LeCompte, Steve S. Liu. Music: Ryan Kallas, Kent Carter. In color. Release date: May 2, 2003. Running time: 87 Min.

Cast: Michael Chow, Joyce Thi Brew, Karena Davis, Colman Domingo, Darryl Fong, Wallace Choy, Robert Wu, Stuart Yee, Fred Salvallon.

LADY KILLERS

A Delfino Entertainment presentation of a Don Ashley production. Producers: Ashley, Gary Preisler. Executive producers: Leland Preisler, Charles V. Kinstler II. Co-producers: Kami Norton, Howard Houng, Dean Blagg. Director/Writer: Gary Preisler. Story: Preisler, Michael Canale. Camera: Tom Callaway. Editor: Robert Brakey. Music: Chris Horvath. In FotoKem color. Release date: June 15, 2003. Running time: 84 Min.

With: Will Friedle, Chris Owen, Louise Lasser, Renee Taylor.

LARA CROFT TOMB RAIDER: THE CRADLE OF LIFE

A Paramount release of a Paramount Pictures presentation in association with Mutual Film Co. & BBC, Tele-Munchen, Toho-Towa of a Lawrence Gordon/Lloyd Levin production in association with Eidos Interactive. Producers: Lawrence Gordon, Lloyd Levin. Executive producer: Jeremy Heath-Smith. Co-producer: Louis A. Stroller. Director: Jan De Bont. Screenplay: Dean Georgaris. Story: Steven E. De Souza, James V. Hart. Based on the Eidos Interactive game series developed by Core Design. Camera: David Tattersall. Editor: Michael Kahn. Music: Alain Silvestri. In Deluxe color, Panavision widescreen. Release date: July 22, 2003. MPAA Rating: PG-13. Running time: 118 Min.

Cast: Angelina Jolie, Gerard Butler, Ciaran Hinds, Christopher Barrie, Noah Taylor, Djimon Hounsou, Til Schweiger, Simon Yam, Terence Yin.

LAST MAN RUNNING

A Rocket Bread Pictures presentation. Producers: Rudy Callegari, Mary Stuart Masterson, Bob Fagan, Joseph Levy. Co-producers: Taylor Lawrence, Linda Pahlman . Director: Damon Santostefano. Screenplay: Rick Gomez, Santostefano. Camera: Santostefano. Editor: Sam Citron. Music: Emil Millar. In color/B&W, video. Release date: June 25, 2003. Running time: 89 Min.

With: Rick Gomez, Joshua Gomez, Amy Redford, Jenifer Wymore-Gomez, Frank Coraci, Michael Kang, Joe LoTruglio, Dave Weir.

THE LEAGUE OF EXTRAORDINARY GENTLEMEN

A 20th Century Fox release presented in association with Mediastream III of a Don Murphy production. Producers: Murphy, Trevor Albert. Executive producers: Sean Connery, Mark Gordon. Director: Stephen Norrington. Screenplay: James Dale Robinson. Based on the comic books by Alan Moore, Kevin O'Neill. Camera: Dan Laustsen. Editor: Paul Rubell. Music: Trevor Jones. In Deluxe color, Panavision widescreen. Release date: July 8, 2003. MPAA Rating: PG-13. Running time: 110 Min.

Cast: Sean Connery, Shane West, Stuart Townsend, Richard Roxburgh, Peta Wilson, Tony Curran, Jason Flemyng, Naseeruddin Shah, David Hemmings, Max Ryan.

LE DIVORCE

A Fox Searchlight Pictures release of a Merchant Ivory production in association with Radar Pictures. Producers: Ismail Merchant, Michael Schiffer. Executive producers: Ted Field, Scott Kroopf, Erica Huggins. Co-producers: Paul Bradley, Richard Hawley. Director: James Ivory. Screenplay: Ruth Prawer Jhabvala, Ivory. Based on Diane Johnson's novel. Camera: Pierre Lhomme. Editor: John David Allen. Music: Richard Robbins. In color, Panavision widescreen. Release date: July 16, 2003. MPAA Rating: PG-13. Running time: 117 Min.

Cast: Kate Hudson, Naomi Watts, Jean-Marc Barr, Leslie Caron, Stockard Channing, Glenn Close, Romain Duris, Stephen Fry, Samuel Labarthe, Thomas Lennon, Thierry Lhermitte, Daniel Mesguich, Matthew Modine, Bebe Neuwirth, Melvil Poupaud, Nathalie Richard.

LEGALLY BLONDE 2: RED WHITE & BLONDE

An MGM release of a Metro-Goldwyn-Mayer Pictures presentation of a Marc Platt production in association with Type A Films. Producers: Marc Platt, David Nicksay. Executive producer: Reese Witherspoon. Co-producers: Jennifer Simpson, Steve Traxler. Director: Charles Herman-Wurmfeld. Screenplay: Kate Kondell. Story: Eve Ahlert, Dennis Drake, Kondell. Based on characters created by Amanda Brown. Camera: Elliot Davis. Editor: Peter Teschner. Music: Rolfe Kent. In color. Release date: June 23, 2003. MPAA Rating: PG-13. Running time: 94 Min.

Cast: Reese Witherspoon, Sally Field, Regina King, Jennifer Coolidge, Bruce McGill, Dana Ivey, Mary Lynn Rajskub, Jessica Cauffiel, Alanna Ubach, J. Barton, Bob Newhart, Luke Wilson.

LETTERS TO URANUS: THE HIDDEN LIFE OF TEDD BURR

A Just Fooling Around Entertainment presentation. Producer/Director: Lenny Pinna. Camera: Pinna. Editor: Gisela Rosario. In color, digital video. Release date: March 15, 2003. Running time: 114 Min. Documentary.

With: Tedd Burr.

LEVELLAND

A Levelland Sk8 production. Producer: Anne Walker-McBay. Director/Writer: Clark Lee Walker. Camera: Mark Miks. Editor: Mark Coffey. In color, Super 16mm-to-35mm. Release date: April 21, 2003. Running time: 107 Min.

Cast: Matt Barr, Layne McKay, Marie Black, Logan Camp, Jessica Schwartz, Erik Ostos, Jason Juranek, Simon Bingham.

LEVITY

A Sony Pictures Classics (in U.S.) release of a Sony Pictures Classics and StudioCanal presentation of a FilmColony production in association with Echo Lake Prods., Entitled Entertainment and Revelations Entertainment. Producers: Richard N. Gladstein, Adam J. Merims, Ed Solomon. Executive producers: Morgan Freeman, Lori McCreary, Fred Schepisi, Andrew Spaulding, James Burke, Doug Mankoff. Co-producer: Irene Litinsky. Director/Writer: Ed Solomon. Camera: Roger Deakins. Editor: Pietro Scalia. Music: Mark Oliver Everett. In Deluxe color. Release date: Jan. 16, 2003. Running time: 100 Min.

Cast: Billy Bob Thornton, Morgan Freeman, Holly Hunter, Kirsten Dunst, Dorian Harewood, Geoffrey Wigdor, Luke Robertson, Billoah Greene, Catherine Colvey, Manuel Aranguiz.

LIFE AFTER WAR

A Magic Lamp Distribution Services (Tujunga, Calif.) presentation of a Brian Knappenberger production. Producer: Brian Knappenberger. Executive producer: Larry Hart. Co-producers: Marc, Marla Halperin. Director/Writer: Brian Knappenberger. Camera: Knappenberger. Editor: Greg MacDonald. In color, DigiBeta. Release date: June 15, 2003. Running time: 80 Min. Documentary.

With: Sarah Chayes, Quyam Karzai.

THE LIFE OF DAVID GALE

A Universal release of a Universal Pictures and Intermedia Films presentation of a Saturn Films/Dirty Hands production. Producers: Alan Parker, Nicolas Cage. Co-producer: Lisa Moran. Executive producers: Moritz Borman, Guy East, Nigel Sinclair. Co-executive producer: Norm Golightly. Director: Alan Parker. Screenplay: Charles Randolph. Camera: Michael Seresin. Editor: Gerry Hambling. Music: Alex Parker, Jake Parker. In DeLuxe color, widescreen. Release date: Feb. 7, 2003. Running time: 130 Min.

Cast: Kevin Spacey, Kate Winslet, Laura Linney, Gabriel Mann, Matt Craven, Rhona Mitra, Leon Rippy, Elizabeth Gast, Cleo King, Constance Jones, Lee Ritchey, Jim Beaver, Michael Crabtree.

A LITTLE CRAZY

A Paved Prods. presentation. Producers: Jordan Ellis, Alice Ellis. Director: Jordan Ellis. Screenplay: Ellis, James Encinas. Camera: Jeff Baustert. Editors: Jon Vasquez. Music: Bobby Johnston. In color, video. Release date: April 24, 2003. Running time: 81 Min.

Cast: Jack Kerrigan, Kim Gillingham, Sandra Seacat, Mitchell Edmonds, Alice Ellis, Sasha Jenson, Kirk Baltz.

THE LIZZIE MCGUIRE MOVIE

A Buena Vista release of a Walt Disney Pictures presentation of a Stan Rogow production. Producer: Rogow. Executive producers: David Roessel, Terri Minsky. Co-producer: Susan Estelle Jansen. Director: Jim Fall. Screenplay: Susan Estelle Jansen, Ed Decter, John J. Strauss. Camera: Jerzy Zielinski. Editor: Margie Goodspeed. Music: Cliff Eidelman. In Technicolor, Panavision widescreen. Release date: April 26, 2003. MPAA Rating: PG. Running time: 93 Min.

Cast: Hilary Duff, Adam Lamberg, Robert Carradine, Hallie Todd, Jake Thomas, Yani Gellman, Ashlie Brillault, Clayton Snyder, Alex Borstein.

LOCAL BOYS

A First Look Media presentation of a Capstone Media production. (International sales: Overseas Filmgroup, L.A.) Producers: Jennie Lew Tugend, Ron Moler. Executive producers: Jim Parks, Leo David. Co-producers: Patrick McIntire, Ricarda Ankenbrand. Co-executive producer: Peter Brown. Director: Ron Moler. Screenplay: Norman Douglas Bradley, Thomas Matthew Stewart, Moler. Camera: James Glennon. Editor: Terry Blythe. Music: Hal Lindes. In CFI color. Release date: March 8, 2003. Running time: 102 Min.
Cast: Eric Christian Olsen, Stacy Edwards, Jeremy Sumpter, Giuseppe Andrews, Chaka Forman, Mark Harmon, Lukas Behnken.

LOCO LOVE

A Pathfinder Pictures release of a Barnholtz Entertainment presentation in association with Three Springs Prods. and Enigma Entertainment. Producer: Bryan Lewis. Executive producers: Lewis, Charlie Bravo. Director: Bryan Lewis. Screenplay: Steven P. Baer. Camera: Thaddeus Wadleigh. Editor: Sherril Schlesinger. Music: Jon McCallum. In Alpha Cinelabs color. Release date: Aug. 12, 2003. MPAA Rating: PG. Running time: 94 Min.
With: Laura Elena Harring, Roy Werner, Gerardo Mejia, Margaret Scarborough, Frank Gallegos, Victoria Regina, Chi Chi Navarro.

LONG GONE

Producers: Jack Cahill, David Eberhardt. Executive producers: Don Hyde, Amanda White. Co-producers: Ariel Peretz, Nancy Egan. Director: Jack Cahill, David Eberhardt. Camera: Greg Yolen. Senior editor: Manuel Tsingaris. Editors: John Wolfendon, Joe Rubinstein, Eberhardt. Music: Tom Waits, Kathleen Brennan, Charlie Musselwhite. In color/B&W, 16mm/Super 16mm/35mm/digital video. Release date: Jan. 20, 2003. Running time: 100 Min. Documentary.
With: Dog Man Tony, Joshua Long Gone, Horizontal John, New York Slim, Stonie, Jesse, James, Stupid the Dog.

THE LOOK

An Eight Entertainment presentation of a Carmichael Films production. Producers: Christopher Pizzo, Seth D. Carmichael. Director: David Sigal. Screenplay: Jean Mandel. Camera: Mark Smith. Editors: Leah O'Donnell. In color, HD video. Release date: May 6, 2003. Running time: 94 Min.
Cast: Carrie Southworth, Carol Alt, Anderson Gabrych, Callie de Fabry, Neal Dodson, Julia Jones, Theresa Hill, Angie Hsu, Ned Stresen-Reuter, Michelle Ferrera, Al Sapienza, Krysten Ritter, Ashley Shelton, Hedda Lettuce, Kristy Hinze.

THE LORD OF THE RINGS: THE TWO TOWERS

A New Line Cinema release of a Wingnut Films production. Producers: Barrie M. Osborne, Fran Walsh, Peter Jackson. Executive producers: Mark Ordesky, Bob Weinstein, Harvey Weinstein, Robert Shaye, Michael Lynne. Co-producers: Rick Porras, Jamie Selkirk. Director: Peter Jackson. Screenplay: Fran Walsh, Philippa Boyens, Stephen Sinclair, Jackson, based on the book by J.R.R. Tolkien. Camera: Andrew Lesnie. Editors: Michael Horton with Jabez Olssen. Music: Howard Shore. In Deluxe color, widescreen. Release date: Dec. 2, 2002. MPAA Rating: PG-13. Running time: 179 Min.
Cast: Elijah Wood, Ian McKellen, Liv Tyler, Viggo Mortensen, Sean Astin, Cate Blanchett, John Rhys-Davies, Bernard Hill, Christopher Lee, Billy Boyd, Dominic Monaghan, Orlando Bloom, Hugo Weaving, Miranda Otto, David Wenham, Brad Dourif, Andy Serkis, Karl Urban.

LOS ANGELES PLAYS ITSELF

A Burton/Floyd presentation. (International sales: Submarine Entertainment, N.Y.) Producer/ Director/Writer: Thom Andersen. Camera: Deborah Stratman. Editor: Yoo Seung-Hyun. In color, DV. Release date: Sept. 6, 2003. (Also in Vancouver Film Festival.) Running time: 169 Min. Documentary.

LOST BOYS OF SUDAN

An Actual Films and Principe Productions presentation. Producers: John Shenk, Megan Mylan. Executive producer: Frances Reid. Directors: John Shenk, Megan Mylan. Camera: Shenk. Editors: Kim Roberts, Mark Becker. In color, HD vid. Release date: April 25, 2003. Running time: 90 Min. Documentary.

LOST IN TRANSLATION

A Focus Features release of a Focus Features presentation in association with Tohokushinsha of an American Zoetrope/Elemental Films production. Producers: Ross Katz, Sofia Coppola. Executive producers: Francis Ford Coppola, Fred Roos. Co-producer: Stephen Schible. Director/Writer: Sofia Coppola. Camera: Lance Acord. Editor: Sarah Flack. Music: Kevin Shields, Air, Brian Reitzell, Roger Joseph Manning Jr., William Storkson. In color. Release date: July 9, 2003. MPAA Rating: R. Running time: 102 Min.
Cast: Bill Murray, Scarlett Johansson, Giovanni Ribisi, Anna Faris, Fumihiro Hayashi, Catherine Lambert.

LOST JUNCTION

A Bigel/Mailer Films production. (International sales: MGM.) Producers: Michael Mailer, Daniel Bigel. Executive producer: Tom Luse. Co-producers: Jeff Cole, Matt O'Toole. Director: Peter Masterson. Screenplay: Jeff Cole. Camera: Thomas Burstyn. Editor: Peter Frank. Music: Normand Corbeil. In color. Release date: Feb. 14, 2003. Running time: 95 Min.
With: Neve Campbell, Billy Burke, Jake Busey, Charles Powell, Michel Perron, David Gow, Norm Berketta, Mariah Inger, Amy Sloan.

LOVE AND DIANE

A Chilmark production in association with the Independent Television Service and Arte France. Producer: Jennifer Dworkin. Executive producer: Jennifer Fox. Co-producer: Sharon Sklar. Director: Jennifer Dworkin. Camera: Tsuyoshi Kimoto. Editor: Mona Davis. In color/B&W, Beta SP/Hi8/mini-DV/Super 8mm. Release date: Oct. 8, 2002. Running time: 155 Min. Documentary.
With: Love Hazzard, Diane Hazzard, Donyaeh.

LOVE OBJECT

A ContentFilms presentation of a Base 12/Catapult Films production in association with Visionbox Pictures. Producers: Lawrence Levy, Kathleen Haase. Executive producers: Edward R. Pressman, John Schmidt, Alessandro Camon. Director/Writer: Robert Parigi. Camera: Sidney Sidell. Editor: Troy Takaki. Music: Nicholas Pike. In color. Release date: April 21, 2003. Running time: 88 Min.
Cast: Desmond Harrington, Melissa Sagemiller, Udo Kier, Robert Bagnell, Michael Pena, Brad Henke, John Cassini, Rip Torn.

MADNESS AND GENIUS

A Riot Films production. Producer/Director/Writer/Editor: Ryan Eslinger. Camera: Steve Huber. Music: Eslinger. In B&W, HD-cam. Release date: Sept. 13, 2003. Running time: 103 Min.
Cast: Tom Noonan, David James Hayward, David Williams, Christine Meyers, Norm Golden, Gary Lamadore, Rick Spates, Erik Frandsen.

MAID IN MANHATTAN

A Sony Pictures Entertainment release of a Columbia Pictures and Revolution Studios presentation of a Red Om Films production. Producers: Elaine Goldsmith-Thomas, Deborah Schindler, Paul Schiff. Executive producers: Charles Newirth, Benny Medina. Co-producer: Richard Baratta. Director: Wayne Wang. Screenplay: Kevin Wade. Story: Edmond Dantes. Camera: Karl Walter Lindenlaub. Editor: Craig McKay. Music: Alan Silvestri. In Deluxe color, Panavision widescreen. Release date: Nov. 29, 2002. MPAA Rating: PG-13. Running time: 105 Min.
Cast: Jennifer Lopez, Ralph Fiennes, Natasha Richardson, Stanley Tucci, Bob Hoskins, Tyler Garcia Posey, Frances Conroy, Chris Eigeman, Marissa Matrone, Amy Sedaris, Priscilla Lopez.

MAKING ARRANGEMENTS

A 9-10 Prods. presentation. Producers: Melissa Scaramucci, Peter Austin Hermes. Executive producers: Todd Scaramucci, Bud and Marilyn Meade, Jay and Janis Scaramucci. Director/Writer: Melissa Scaramucci. Camera: Peter Austin Hermes. Editor: Dan Pringle. Music supervisor: M. Scaramucci. In color, digital beta. Release date: March 8, 2003. Running time: 105 Min.
With: Randy Colton, Rebecca McCauley, Linda McDonald, W. Jerome Stevenson, Stacy Farley, Dave Shuler.

THE MALDONADO MIRACLE

A Showtime presentation in association with Hallmark Entertainment of an Allegra Films production. Producers: Susan Aronson, Eve Silverman. Executive producer: Salma Hayek. Co-producer: Jose "Pepe" Tamez. Director: Salma Hayek. Screenplay: Paul W. Cooper, based on the novel by Theodore Taylor. Camera: Claudio Rocha. Editor: Luis Colina. Music: Leonardo Heiblum, Jacobo Lieberman. In color, HD vid. Release date: Jan. 20, 2003. Running time: 99 Min.
Cast: Peter Fonda, Mare Winningham, Ruben Blades, Eddy Martin, Bill Sage, Dan Merket, Soledad St. Hilaire, Scott Michael Campbell, Jesse Borrego, Christina Cabot.

MALIBU'S MOST WANTED

A Warner Bros. release of a Karz Entertainment production. Producers: Mike Karz, Fax Bahr, Adam Small. Executive producer: Bill Johnson. Co-producers: Russell Hollander, Josh Etting. Director: John Whitesell. Screenplay: Fax Bahr, Adam Small, Jamie Kennedy, Nick Swardson. Camera: Mark Irwin. Editor: Cara Silverman. Music: John Van Tongeren, Damon Elliott. In Technicolor, Clairmont widescreen. Release date: April 9, 2003. MPAA Rating: PG-13. Running time: 86 Min.
Cast: Jamie Kennedy, Taye Diggs, Anthony Anderson, Blair Underwood, Regina Hall, Damien Dante Wayans, Ryan O'Neal, Snoop Dogg, Bo Derek, Jeffrey Tambor.

A MAN APART

A New Line Cinema release of a Vincent Newman & Tucker Tooley production and Joseph Nittolo Entertainment production. Producers: Tooley, Newman, Nittolo, Vin Diesel. Executive producers: Michael De Luca, Claire Rudnick Polstein, F. Gary Gray. Co-producer: George Zakk. Director: F. Gary Gray. Screenplay: Christian Gudegast, Paul Scheuring. Camera: Jack N. Green. Editors: Bob Brown, William Hoy. Music: Anne Dudley. In FotoKem color, Deluxe prints. Panavision widescreen. Release date: March 27, 2003. MPAA Rating: R. Running time: 109 Min.
Cast: Vin Diesel, Larenz Tate, Timothy Olyphant, Geno Silva, Jacqueline Obradors, Steve Eastin, Juan Fernandez, Jeff Kober.

MANGO KISS

A Sunpallah Prods. presentation. Producers: Erin O'Malley, Joe Mellis, Sascha Rice. Producers: Sascha Rice. Screenplay: Rice, Sarah Brown, based on the stage play "Bermuda Triangles: The Non-Monogamy Experiment" by Brown. Camera: John Pirozzi. Editor: Cindy Parisotto. Music: Matthew Ferraro. In color. Release date: June 13, 2003. Running time: 80 Min.
With: Michelle Wolff, Daniele Ferraro, Sally Kirkland, Shannon Rossiter, Dru Mouser, Tina Marie Murray, Joe Mellis.

MAN OF THE YEAR

A Rewind/Play LLC presentation. Producers: Andrea Mia, Betsy Fels, Andy Goldberg, Richard Mann. Executive producers: Straw Weisman, Debbie Weisman. Co-producers: John Ritter, Steven M. Rubenstein, Camille S. Thien. Director/Conceived: Straw Weisman. Co-directors: Tamara Friedman, Andy Goldberg, David Roy, Jonathan Tydor, Barry Zetlin. Camera: David Roy, Al Satterwhite. Editor: Bill Black. Music: David Kates, Jeffrey Silverman. In color, Mini DV. Release date: Feb. 18, 2003. Running time: 88 Min.

With: Jade Carter, Brian Cousins, Adria Dawn, Idalis DeLeon, Kathleen Gati, Leeza Gibbons, Archie Hahn, Khrystyne Haje, Rebecca Harrell, Amy Hill, Jon Jacobs, Shawnee Free Jones, Clayton Landey, Ivo Lopez-Lewis, Samantha Lloyd, Heidi Mark, Kristen Miller.

MARATHON

An Alphaville NYC production. Producers: Amir Naderi, Reza Namazi. Director/Writer: Amir Naderi. Camera: Michael Simmonds. Editors: Naderi, Donal O'Ceilleachair, Moira Demos. In B&W, 16mm/DV. Release date: April 29, 2003. Running time: 78 Min.

Cast: Sara Paul, Trevor Moore, Voice: Rebecca Nelson.

MARCI X

A Paramount Pictures release of a Scott Rudin production. Producer: Scott Rudin. Executive producers: Steve Nicolaides, Adam Schroeder. Director: Richard Benjamin. Screenplay: Paul Rudnick. Camera: Robbie Greenberg. Editor: Jacqueline Cambas. Music: Mervyn Warren. In color. Release date: Aug. 22, 2003. MPAA Rating: R. Running time: 84 Min.

Cast: Lisa Kudrow, Damon Wayans, Richard Benjamin, Christine Baranski, Paula Garces, Billy Griffith, Jane Krakowski.

MATCHSTICK MEN

A Warner Bros. release of an Imagemovers/Scott Free production in association with Rickshaw Prods. and Liveplanet. Producers: Jack Rapke, Ridley Scott, Steve Starkey, Sean Bailey, Ted Griffin. Executive producer: Robert Zemeckis. Co-producers: Charles J.D. Schlissel, Giannina Facio. Director: Ridley Scott. Screenplay: Nicholas Griffin, Ted Griffin, based on the book by Eric Garcia. Camera (Technicolor, Panavision widescreen), John Mathieson; editor, Dody Dorn; music, Hans Zimmer. In Technicolor, Panavision widescreen. Release date: Aug. 25, 2003. MPAA Rating: R. Running time: 116 Min.

Cast: Nicolas Cage, Sam Rockwell, Alison Lohman, Bruce Altman, Bruce McGill, Sheila Kelley, Beth Grant.

MAYOR OF THE SUNSET STRIP

A Caldera Prods. presentation with Perna Prods. and Questionmark (?) Prods. in association with Kino-Eye American. Producers: Chris Carter, Greg Little, Tommy Perna. Executive producer: Donald Zuckerman. Co-producer: Julie Janata. Director/Writer: George Hickenlooper. Camera: Kramer Morgenthau, Igor Meglic, Hickenlooper, Chris Carter. Music: Anthony Marinelli. In FotoKem color. Release date: June 19, 2003. Running time: 94 Min. Documentary.

MC5: A TRUE TESTIMONIAL

A Zenta L.L.C. presentation of a Future/Now Films production. Producer: Laurel Legler. Executive producers: Jim Roehm, Howard Thompson. Director/Editor: David C. Thomas. Camera: Anthony Allen. Music: MC5. In color, Digital Betacam. Release date: Sept. 7, 2002. Running time: 120 Min. Documentary.

MELVIN GOES TO DINNER

A Phyro-Giant Partners presentation in association with Situation Films, Squaresville Prods./LeFoole Inc. of a DJ Paul production. Producers: Naomi Odenkirk, DJ Paul, Jeff Sussman. Co-producers: Michael Blieden, Bob Odenkirk. Director: Bob Odenkirk. Screenplay: Michael Blieden. Camera: Alex Vendler. Editor: Blieden. Music: Michael Penn. In color, 16mm. Release date: Feb. 2, 2003. Running time: 83 Min.

Cast: Michael Blieden, Stephanie Courtney, Matt Price, Annabelle Gurwitch, Kathleen Roll, Maura Tierney.

A MIGHTY WIND

A Warner Bros. release of a Castle Rock Entertainment production. Producer: Karen Murphy. Director: Christopher Guest. Screenplay: Guest, Eugene Levy. Camera: Arlene Donnelly Nelson. Editor: Robert Leighton. Music/Songs/Guest: Michael McKean, Harry Shearer, Levy, Annette O'Toole, Catherine O'Hara, C.J. Vanston, John Michael Higgins. In Technicolor. Release date: April 3, 2002. MPAA Rating: PG-13. Running time: 90 Min.

Cast: John Michael Higgins, Eugene Levy, Jane Lynch, Michael McKean, Catherine O'Hara, Parker Posey, Harry Shearer, Fred Willard Ed Begley Jr., Jennifer Coolidge, Paul Dooley, Michael Hitchcock.

MILK & HONEY

A P-Kino Films production in association with Concrete Films, Highbrow Entertainment. Producers: Matthew Myers, Thierry Cagianut. Executive producer: Cedric Jeanson. Director/Writer: Joe Maggio. Camera: Gordon Chou. Editor: Seth E. Anderson. Music: Hal Hartley, Yo La Tengo, Fischerspooner. In color, digital video. Release date: Jan. 18, 2003. Running time: 91 Min.

With: Clint Jordan, Kirsten Russell, Anthony Howard, Dudley Findlay Jr., Eleanor Hutchins, Greg Amici.

MILWAUKEE, MINNESOTA

A Framework Entertainment and Empire State Entertainment presentation. Producers: Jeff Kirshbaum, Michael Brody. Director: Allan Mindel. Screenplay: R.D. Murphy. Camera: Bernd Heinl. Editor: David Rawlins. In FotoKem color. Release date: Jan. 9, 2003. Running time: 95 Min.

Cast: Troy Garity, Alison Folland, Randy Quaid, Bruce Dern, Hank Harris, Debra Monk, Josh Brolin, Holly Woodlawn.

MISSING PEACE

Producer/Director: Victoria Bruce, Karin Hayes. Camera: Cesar Pinzon. Editors: Hayes, Bruce. Music supervisor: Matt Scott. In color, digital video. Release date: Jan. 23, 2003. Running time: 82 Min. Documentary.

MMI: A CHRONICLE OF TIME

A John Sanborn production. Producer/DirectorEditor: Sanborn. Camera: Sanborn. Music: Paul Dresher. In color, mini-DV. Release date: Oct. 8, 2002. Running time: 62 Min. Documentary.

MOCKINGBIRD DON'T SING

A Dorian presentation of a Genieworks production. Producers: Harry Bromley-Davenport, Kris Murphy. Executive producers: Jim Hanson, Francis Schwartz. Director: Harry Bromley-Davenport. Screenplay: Daryl Haney. Camera: Jeff Baustert. Music: Mark Hart. In Fotokem color, Clairmont widescreen. Release date: Sept. 19, 2002. Running time: 98 Min.

Cast: Melissa Errico, Joe Regalbuto, Sean Young, Michael Lerner, Kim Darby, Tarra Steele, Laurie O'Brien, Ed Brigadier, Sharon Madden, Jack Betts, Ben Messmer, Lora Criswell, Michael Azria.

MORNING SUN

A Long Bow Group production, in association with TVS, NAATA, BBC, Arte. (International sales: Jane Balfour Films, London.) Producers: Carma Hinton, Geremie R. Barme, Richard Gordon. Co-producer: Jane Balfour. Directors: Carma Hinton, Geremie R. Barme, Richard Gordon. Screenplay: Barme, Hinton. Camera: Gordon. Editor: David Carnochan. Music: Mark Pevsner. In color, PAL DigiBeta. Release date: Feb. 13, 2003. Running time (PAL): 119 Min. Documentary.

With: Huang Yongyu, Li Nanyang, Li Rui, Li Zhensheng, Liu Ting, Luo Xiaohai, Song Binbin, Wang Guangmei, Xu Youyu, Yang Rui, Ye Weili, Yu Luowei, Zhang Zhong. Narrator: David Carnochan.

THE MUDGE BOY

A Showtime presentation of a First Cold Press production. Producers: Elizabeth W. Alexander, Alison Benson, Randy Ostrow. Executive producer: Stanley Tucci. Director/Writer: Michael Burke. Camera: Vanja Cernjul. Editor: Alfonso Goncalves. Music: Marcelo Zarvos. In color. Release date: Jan. 17, 2003. Running time: 94 Min.

Cast: Emile Hirsch, Thomas Guiry, Richard Jenkins, Pablo Schreiber, Zachary Knighton, Ryan Donowho, Meredith Handerhan, Beckie King.

THE MURDER OF EMMETT TILL

An American Experience presentation of a Firelight Media production. Producer: Stanley Nelson. Executive producer: Margaret Drain. Director: Stanley Nelson. Screenplay: Marcia A. Smith. Camera: Robert Shepard. Editor: Lewis Erskine. Music: Tom Phillips. In color, HD video. Release date: Jan. 12, 2003. Running time: 55 Min. Documentary.

MY ARCHITECT

A Louis Kahn Project production. Producers: Susan Rose Behr, Nathaniel Kahn. Executive producers: Behr, Andrew Clayman, Darrell Friedman. Co-executive producers: Robert Guzzardi, Lynne and Harold Honickman. Co-producer: Yael Melamede. Director/Writer/Narrator: Nathaniel Kahn. Camera: Bob Richman. Editor: Sabine Krayenbuehl. Music: Joseph Vitarelli. In color. Release date: March 17, 2003. Running time: 116 Min. Documentary.

MY BOSS'S DAUGHTER

A Dimension Films release of a Dimension Films presentation of a Gil Netter and a John Jacobs production. Producers: Netter, Jacobs. Executive producers: Paddy Cullen, Bob Weinstein, Harvey Weinstein, Andrew Rona, Brad Weston. Co-producer: Ashton Kutcher. Director: David Zucker. Screenplay: David Dorfman. Camera: Martin McGrath. Editors: Patrick Lussier, Sam Craven. Music: Teddy Castellucci. In Deluxe color and prints. Release date: Aug. 22, 2003. MPAA Rating: PG-13. Running time: 86 Min.

Cast: Ashton Kutcher, Tara Reid, Jeffrey Tambor, Andy Richter, Michael Madsen, Jon Abrahams, David Koechner, Carmen Electra, Terence Stamp, Molly Shannon, Kenan Thompson.

MY DINNER WITH JIMI

A Fallout Films & Rhino Entertainment production. Producer: Harold Bronson. Director: Bill Fishman. Screenplay: Howard Kaylan. Camera: Philip Holahan. Editors: Londin Angel Winters, Peter Shelton. Music: Andrew Gross. In color. Release date: Feb. 16, 2003. Running time: 90 Min.

Cast: Justin Henry, Royale Watkins, Jason Boggs, George Wendt, Brett Gilbert, Sean Maysonet, Kevin Cotteleer, George Stanchev, Brian Groh, Quinton Flynn, Ben Bode, Nate Dushku, Lisa Brounstein, John Corbett, Bret Roberts, Allison Lange, Wendie Jo Sperber.

MY FLESH AND BLOOD

An HBO/Cinemax presentation of a Chaiken Film production. Producer: Jennifer Chaiken. Director: Jonathan Karsh. Camera: Amanda Micheli. Editor: Eli Olsson. Music: Hector H. Perez, B. Quincy Griffin. In color, digital video. Release date: Jan. 13, 2003. Running time: 85 Min. Documentary.

MY HOUSE IN UMBRIA

An HBO presentation of a Canine Films/Panorama Films U.K./Italy production. Producer: Anne Wingate. Executive producer: Frank Doelger. Co-producer: Marco Valerio Pugini. Director: Richard Loncraine. Screenplay: Hugh Whitemore, based on the novella by William Trevor. Camera: Marco Pontecorvo. Editor: Humphrey Dixon. Music: Claudio Capponi. In Deluxe color. Release date: March 8, 2003. Running time: 109 Min.

Cast: Maggie Smith, Chris Cooper, Timothy Spall, Benno Furmann, Ronnie Barker, Emmy Clarke, Giancarlo Giannini, Libero de Rienzo.

MY LIFE WITH COUNT DRACULA

A Hungry Jackal production. Producer/Director/Editor: Dustin Lance Black. Camera: Black. Music: Christopher Hoag. In color, video. Release date: July 2, 2003. Running time: 72 Min. Documentary. *With: Dr. Donald A. Reed.*

MYSTIC RIVER

A Warner Bros. release presented in association with Village Roadshow and NPV Entertainment of a Malpaso production. Producers: Robert Lorenz, Judie G. Hoyt, Clint Eastwood. Executive producer: Bruce Berman. Director: Clint Eastwood. Screenplay: Brian Helgeland. Camera: Tom Stern. Editors: Joel Cox. Music: Eastwood. In Technicolor, Panavision widescreen. Release date: May 8, 2003. MPAA Rating: R. Running time: 137 Min.

Cast: Sean Penn, Tim Robbins, Kevin Bacon, Laurence Fishburne, Marcia Gay Harden, Laura Linney, Kevin Chapman, Thomas Guiry, Emmy Rossum, Spencer Treat Clark, Andrew Mackin, Adam Nelson, Robert Wahlberg, Jenny O'Hara.

NAKED PROOF

A Pinwheel Pictures (Seattle) production, in association with Wigglyworld Studios. Producer: Eden Mackay. Director: Jamie Hook. Screenplay: Deborah Girdwood, Hook. Camera: Charles Peterson. Editors: Joe Shapiro, Hook. Music: Amy Denio. In color. Release date: June 13, 2003. Running time: 110 Min.

Cast: Michael Chick, Arlette Del Toro, August Wilson, Matt Smith, Laura Holtz, Kip Fagan, Gina Malvestuto, Sean John Walsh.

NAKED WORLD

An HBO America Undercover presentation of a Juntos Films production. Producers: Helen Hood Scheer, Arlene Donnelly Nelson. Executive producer: David Nelson. Director: Arlene Donnelly Nelson. Camera: David Linstron, Nelson. Editors: Tom Donahue. Music: Leigh Roberts, Chris Hajian. In color, DV. Release date: May 11, 2003. Running time: 77 Min. Documentary.

NATIONAL SECURITY

A Sony Pictures Entertainment release of a Columbia Pictures presentation of an Outlaw/Intermedia/Firm Films production. Producers: Bobby Newmyer, Jeff Silver, Michael Green. Executive producers: Moritz Borman, Guy East, Nigel Sinclair, Martin Lawrence. Director: Dennis Dugan. Screenplay: Jay Scherick, David Ronn. Camera: Oliver Wood. Editor: Debra Neil-Fisher. Music: Randy Edelman. In color. Release date: Jan. 14, 2003. MPAA Rating: PG-13. Running time: 88 Min.

Cast: Martin Lawrence, Steve Zahn, Colm Feore, Bill Duke, Eric Roberts, Timothy Busfield, Robinne Lee, Matt McCoy, Brett Cullen, Cleo King, Stephen Tobolowsky, Joe Flaherty.

NAT TURNER: A TROUBLESOME PROPERTY

Producer: Frank Christopher. Co-producer: Kenneth S. Greenberg. Director: Charles Burnett. Screenplay: Burnett, Frank Christopher, Kenneth S. Greenberg. Camera: John Demps. Editor: Michael Colin, Frank Christopher. Music: Todd Capps. In color, digital video/24P HD video. Release date: Feb. 16, 2003. Running time: 57 Min. Documentary.

Cast: Carl Lumbly, Tom Nowicki, Tommy Hicks, James Opher, Michael LeMelle, Billy Dye, Phillip Miller, Patrick Waller.

NEVERLAND

A New Media Entertainment presentation of a Second Star production. Producers: Damion Dietz, Stephanie Orff. Director/Writer: Damion Dietz. Based on the novel "Peter Pan," by J.M. Barrie. Camera: Derek Dale. Editor: Scott Baldyga. In color, digital video. Release date: June 11, 2003. Running time: 83 Min.

With: Rick Sparks, Melany Bell, Gary Kelley, Kari Wahlgren, Ray Garcia, Marcus Reynaga, Wil Wheaton, Deborah Quayle, David Jahn, Scott Mechlowicz, Kevin Christy, Stephanie Orff.

NEW GUY

A Siete Machos Prods. presentation. Producers: Pavlina Hatoupis, Gary Giambalvo, Bilge Ebiri. Director/Writer: Bilge Ebiri. Camera: Branan Edgens, Chuck Moss. Editor: Cabot Philbrick. Music: Holst, de Falla. In color, digital beta. Release date: March 6, 2003. Running time: 86 Min.

With: Kelly Miller, Scott Janes, Jonathan Uffelman, Johnny Ray, Tobi-Lyn Byers, Hank Prehodka, Harvey Kaufmann, Louis Cancelmi, Kelly McAndrew, Dustin Brown.

NEW SUIT

An Unbridled Pictures presentation of a Hungry Eye Lowlands Pictures production in association with Trillion Entertainment. Producers: Christina and Laurant Zilber. Co-producers: Ricka Kanter-Fisher, Kathryn Tyus-Adair. Director: Francois Velle. Screenplay: Craig Sherman. Camera: David Mullen. Editor: Kris Cole. In color, HD vid. Release date: Oct. 5, 2002. Running time: 94 Min.

With: Jordan Bridges, Marisa Coughlan, Heather Donahue, Mark Setlock, Benito Martinez, Charles Rocket, Paul McCrane, Dan Hedaya, Dan Montgomery, James Marsh, Danny Strong.

NIGHTSTALKER

A Smooth Pictures presentation of an Imperial Fish Co./Silver Nitrate production. Producers: Ash R. Shah, Chris Fisher. Executive producers: Todd King, Phil Knowles. Co-producer: Danny Trejo. Director/Writer: Chris Fisher. Camera: Eliot Rockett. Editor: Daniel R. Padgett. Music: Ryan Beveridge. In color, Super 16mm. Release date: Jan. 23, 2003. Running time: 96 Min.

Cast: Roselyn Sanchez, Bret Roberts, Danny Trejo, Evan Dexter Parke, Derek Hamilton, Brandi Emma.

NIGHT TRAIN

A Metropolis Pictures, Inc. presentation. Producers: Les Bernstein, Anthony Huljev. Director: Les Bernstein. Screenplay: Bernstein, Gary Walkow. Camera: Bernstein, Patrick Melly. Editor: George Lockwood. Music: Marco Aldaco, Calavera, El Mosco. In DuArt prints. Release date: Sept. 16, 2002. Running time: 80 Min.

With: John Voldstad, Barry Cutler, Nikoletta Skarlatos, Pedro Aldana, Donna Pieroni, Dan Shor, Chuck Skull, Tony Cruz, Richard Head, Martin Hugo Valdiva Montes.

NITWIT

A Xan Price Production. Producer/Director/Screenplay/CameraEditor/Music/Production design: Xan Price. In color, digital video. Release date: Feb. 11, 2003. Running time: 94 Min.

With: Agnes Ausborn, Daniel Brantley, Wilder Selzer, Philly, Francine Pado, Xan Price, Michael Cogliantry, Bess Allison, Bonnie Ann Black.

NOBODY NEEDS TO KNOW

A Kick It Over Prods. presentation. Producer/Director/Writer/Editor: Azazel Jacobs. Camera: Daniel Andrade. Music: Victor Axelrod. In B&W, video. Release date: Jan. 31, 2003. Running time: 96 Min.

With: Tricia Vessey, Liz Stauber, Norman Reedus, Alvin Seme, Jonas Print, Azazel Jacobs.

NOISE

A Tenderloin Group and 9 at Night Films production. Producers: Rob Nilsson, Chikara Motomura, Kevin Winterfield. Executive producers: David and Carol Richards. Co-producers: Pacific Rim Media, Rand Crook, Ethan Sing. Director: Rob Nilsson. Screenplay: Nilsson. Camera: Ethan Sing, Billy Corona. Editor: Josh Williams. Music: Daniel Feinsmith. In B&W, HD video. Release date: Oct. 9, 2002. Running time: 81 Min.

With: Robert Viharo, Paige Olson, Sarge, Angela, jen, Lavonne, Gina, Josh Peterson, Bill Ackridge, Don De Fina, Phil Palmer.

NOLA

A Fireworks Pictures presentation of an Archer Entertainment production. Producers: Jill Footlick, Rachel Peters. Director/Writer: Alan Hruska. Camera: Horacio Marquinez. Editors: Peter C. Frank. Music: Edmond Choi. In color. Release date: May 11, 2003. Running time: 97 Min.

Cast: Emmy Rossum, Mary McDonnell, Steven Bauer, James Badge Dale, Thom Christopher, Michael Cavadias.

NORMAL

An HBO Films presentation of an Avenue Pictures production. Executive producers: Cary Brokaw, Lydia Dean Pilcher. Director/Writer: Jane Anderson, based on her play "Looking for Normal." Camera: Alar Kivilo. Editor: Lisa Fruchtman. Music: Alex Wurman. In color. Release date: Jan. 21, 2003. Running time: 111 Min.

Cast: Jessica Lange, Tom Wilkinson, Hayden Panettiere, Clancy Brown, Joe Sikora, Randall Arney, Richard Bull, Mary Seibel.

NORTHFORK

A Paramount Classics release of a Paramount Classics, Romano/Shane Prods., Departure Entertainment presentation. Producers: Mark Polish, Michael Polish. Executive producers: Paul F. Mayersohn, James Woods, Anthony Romano, Michel Shane, Janet Jensen, Damon Martin. Co-producers: Todd King, Paul Torok. Co-executive producers: Bruce E. Jones, Barbara A. Jones, Gil Amaral. Director: Michael Polish. Screenplay: Mark Polish, Michael Polish. Camera: M. David Mullen. Editor: Leo Trombetta. Music: Stewart Matthewman. In Technicolor, Panavision widescreen. Release date: Jan. 21, 2003. Running time: 103 Min.

Cast: James Woods, Nick Nolte, Claire Forlani, Duel Farnes, Mark Polish, Daryl Hannah, Graham Beckel, Josh Barker, Peter Coyote, Jon Gries, Robin Sachs, Ben Foster, Anthony Edwards.

NO SLEEP 'TIL MADISON

A Modern Ping Pong presentation. Producer: Ivo Knezevic. Executive producers: Erik Moe, Peter Rudy, Knezevic, David Fleer. Directors: Erik Moe, Peter Rudy, David Fleer. Screenplay: Moe, Rudy. Camera: Bradley W. Milsap. Editor: Amy L. Frantz. Music: Stephen Edwards. In color. Release date: Feb. 16, 2003. Running time: 89 Min.

With: Jim Gaffigan, Ian Brennan, T.J. Jagodowski, Michael Gilio, Jed Resnik, Rebekah Louise Smith, Molly Glynn Hammond, Jason Wells, Lusia Strus, Tami Sagher. Will Clinger, Susan Messing.

NOSEY PARKER

A Bellwether Films and Nosey Pictures production. Producer: John O'Brien. Co-producers: Molly O'Brien, Stacey Steinmetz. Director/Editor: John O'Brien. Camera: David Parry. Music: the Nosey Parkers. In DuArt color, Aaton 16mm. Release date: July 17, 2003. Running time: 104 Min.

With: George Lyford, Natalie Picoe, Richard Snee, Fred Tuttle, Vida Martin, Reeve Rogers, Kermit Glines, Frank Marshall, Susannah Blachly, Elizabeth O'Brien, Katie O'Brien, Jordan Lyford.

NTV-1

A Left Hook Films presentation and production in association with Ludicrous Prods./Hurricane Entertainment/Caldera Prods. Producers: Justin Hogan, Cameron McIntyre, Damon White. Executive producers: Greg Little, Billy Kaynor Jr., Zach Samios, Sheldon Collins. Co-executive producers: Cathryn Jaymes, Jeff Goldberg. Co-producer: Justin Lazard. Director/Writer: Sheldon Collins. Camera: Kevin Painchaud, Jon Artigo. Editors: Matt Shaver, Chad Meserve, Painchaud. In color, video. Release date: Oct. 5, 2002. Running time: 81 Min.

With: Sheldon Collins, Jon Artigo, Zach Samios, Ryan Holmes, Kevin Painchaud, Jordi Castillo, Giuseppe Carella.

NUDITY REQUIRED

A Nonla Films/Squish Kitty Prods. (Los Angeles) production. Producers: Charlie Nguyen, Steven Boe, Whitney Boe. Director/Editor/Music: Steven Boe. Screenplay: Steven Boe, Whitney Boe. Camera: Nick Mustille. In color, DigiBeta. Release date: June 10, 2003. Running time: 101 Min.

Cast: Keith Andreen, Roberto Raad, Whitney Leigh, Steve Tancora, Marcia Walter, Steve Gibbons, Jayne Trcka , Derek Crabbe.

THE ODDS OF RECOVERY

A Down Stream Prods. presentation. Producer/Director/Editor: Su Friedrich. Camera: Friedrich. In color, vid. and 16mm. Release date: Sept. 23, 2002. Running time: 66 Min. Documentary.

OFF THE CHARTS: THE SONG-POEM STORY

Producers: Jamie Meltzer, Henry S. Rosenthal. Director: Jamie Meltzer. Camera: Bruce Dickson, Meltzer. Editors: Stephanie Mechura Challberg. In color, HD video. Release date: April 20, 2003. Running time: 63 Min. Documentary.

OFF THE MAP

A Holedigger Films presentation. Producers: Campbell Scott, George VanBuskirk. Executive producers: Martin Garvey, David Newman, Jonathan Filley. Director: Campbell Scott. Screenplay: Joan Ackermann, based on her play. Camera: Juan Ruiz Anchia. Editor: Andy Keir. Music: Gary DeMichele. In color. Release date: Jan. 22, 2003. Running time: 108 Min.

Cast: Joan Allen, Valentina de Angelis, Sam Elliott, J.K. Simmons, Jim True-Frost, Amy Brenneman.

OLD SCHOOL

A DreamWorks release of a Montecito Picture Co. production. Producers: Daniel Goldberg, Joe Medjuck, Todd Phillips. Executive producers: Ivan Reitman, Tom Pollock. Co-producer: Paul Deason. Director: Todd Phillips. Screenplay: Phillips, Scot Armstrong. Story: Court Crandall, Phillips, Armstrong. Camera: Mark Irwin. Editor: Michael Jablow. Music: Theodore Shapiro. In Technicolor. Release date: Feb. 12, 2003. MPAA Rating: R. Running time: 90 Min.

Cast: Luke Wilson, Will Ferrell, Vince Vaughn, Jeremy Piven, Ellen Pompeo, Juliette Lewis, Leah Remini, Perrey Reeves, Craig Kilborn, Elisha Cuthbert.

THE OLIVE HARVEST

A Jarmaq Films presentation. Producer: Kamran Elahian. Co-producers: Sharbel Elias, Kayo Hatta. Director/Screenplay: Hanna Elias. Camera: Ofer Harari. Editors: Sabine el Gaymael. Music: Mark Adler. In color, HD vid-to-35mm. Release date: April 25, 2003. Running time: 91 Min.

Cast: Raeda Adon, Maazen Saade, Taher Najeeb, Muhamad Bacri, Arren Umari, Samia Kazmuz.

ONCE UPON A TIME IN MEXICO

A Sony Pictures Entertainment (U.S.)/Miramax Films (international) release of a Columbia Pictures/Dimension Films presentation of a Troublemaker Studios production of a Robert Rodriguez film. (International sales: Miramax Intl., New York.) Producers: Elizabeth Avellan, Carlos Gallardo, Robert Rodriguez. Co-producers: Tony Mark, Luz Maria Rojas, Sue Jett. Director/Writer/Editor: Robert Rodriguez. Camera: Rodriguez. Music: Rodriguez. In Deluxe color, DV-to-35mm, widescreen. Release date: Aug. 27, 2003. MPAA Rating: R. Running time: 101 Min.

Cast: Antonio Banderas, Salma Hayek, Johnny Depp, Mickey Rourke, Eva Mendes, Danny Trejo, Enrique Iglesias, Marco Leonardi, Cheech Marin, Ruben Blades, Willem Dafoe, Gerardo Vigil, Pedro Armendariz Jr.

100 MILE RULE

A Road Rules Prods. presentation of a Honeydo production. Producers: John Nelson, Eric Gustavson. Executive producers: Wendi Lampassi, Isabelle Schenkel. Director: Brent Huff. Screenplay by Drew Pillsbury. Camera: Giovanni Lampassi. Editor: Richard Fields. In color. Release date: Nov. 7, 2002. Running time: 98 Min.

Cast: Jake Weber, Maria Bello, David Thornton, Michael McKean.

101 DALMATIANS II: PATCH'S LONDON ADVENTURE

A Walt Disney Home Video release of a Walt Disney Television Animation production. Producers: Carolyn Bates, Leslie Hough. Director/Writer: Jim Kammerud, Brian Smith, based on the novel "The One Hundred and One Dalmatians" by Dodie Smith. Supervising animation directors: Hiroshi Kawamata, Kenichi Tsuchiya. Editor: Robert E. Birchard. Music: Richard Gibbs. In color. Release date: Feb. 24, 2002. MPAA Rating: G. Running time: 73 Min. ANIMATED.

Voices: Barry Bostwick, Jason Alexander, Martin Short, Bobby Lockwood, Susanne Blakeslee, Samuel West, Maurice LaMarche, Jeff Bennett, Jodi Benson, Tim Bentinck, Kath Soucie, Mary Macleod, Michael Lerner.

ONLY IN AMERICA

A Seventh Art Releasing presentation of a 24/6 Prods. (L.A.) production. Producers: Ann Benjamin, Ron Frank. Executive producer: Larry Rifkin. Director/Writer/Editor: Ron Frank. Camera: Frank, John Kavanaugh, Uri Ackerman, Peter Krajewski, Yuval Shusterman. Music: Paul D. Lehrman. In color, BetaSP. Release date: May 28, 2003. Running time: 72 Min.

With: Joe Lieberman, Hadassah Lieberman, Leon Wieseltier.

ONMYOJI

A Pioneer Entertainment USA release (in U.S.) of a Tohokushinsha Film Corp. /TBS/Dentsu/Kadokawa Shoten Publishing Co., Ltd./Toho Co., Ltd. production. (International sales: Kadokawa Shoten Publishing Co., Ltd., Tokyo.) Producers: Tetsuji Kayashi, Kazuya Hamana, Nobuyuki Tohya . Executive producer: Banjiro Uemura. Co-producers: Takashi Hirano, Wataru Tanaka, Yutaka Okawa. Director: Yojiro Takita. Screenplay: Yasushi Fukuda, Baku Yumemakura, Itaru Era, based on the book by Yumemakura. Camera: Naoki Kayano, Tatsuya Osada. Editor: Isao Tomita. Music: Shigeru Umebayashi. In color. Release date: April 4, 2003. MPAA Rating: R. Running time: 116 Min.

Cast: Mansai Nomura, Hideaki Ito, Hiroyuki Sanada, Kyoko Koizumi, Eriko Imai, Yui Natsukawa, Kenichi Yajima, Sachiko Kokuba, Akira Emoto, Masato Hagiwara, Ittoku Kishibe, Mai Hosho.

OPEN RANGE

A Buena Vista release of a Touchstone Pictures presentation in association with Cobalt Media Group of a Tig production. Producers: David Valdes, Kevin Costner, Jake Eberts. Executive producers: Armyan Bernstein, Craig Storper. Director: Kevin Costner. Screenplay: Craig Storper, based on the novel "The Open Range Men" by Lauran Paine. Camera: James Muro. Editors: Michael J. Duthie, Miklos Wright. Music: Michael Kamen. In Technicolor, Panavision widescreen. Release date: July 31, 2003. MPAA Rating: R. Running time: 138 Min.

Cast: Robert Duvall, Kevin Costner, Annette Bening, Michael Gambon, Michael Jeter, Diego Luna, James Russo, Abraham Benrubi, Dean McDermott, Kim Coates.

THE OPPOSITE SEX: RENE'S STORY

A Showtime presentation of a Hensel/Krasnow production. Producers: Josh Aronson, Linda York, Francine Bergman. Executive producers: Bruce Hensel, Stuart Krasnow. Director: Josh Aronson. Camera: Brett Wiley. Editor: Kate Hirson. Music: Michael Rohaytn. In color, DV. Release date: June 22, 2003. Running time: 73 Min. Documentary.

THE OPPOSITE SEX: JAMIE'S STORY

A Showtime presentation of a Hensel/Krasnow production. Producers: Josh Aronson, Linda York, Francine Bergman. Executive producers: Bruce Hensel, Stuart Krasnow. Director: Josh Aronson. Camera: Brett Wiley. Editor: Janet Swanson. Music: Michael Rohaytn. In color, DV. Release date: June 22, 2003. Running time: 73 Min. Documentary.

THE ORDER

A Twentieth Century Fox release of a Baumgarten Merims production, in association with N1 European Film Produktions. Producers: Craig Baumgarten, Brian Helgeland. Executive producers: Michael Kuhn, Thomas M. Hammel. Co-producer: Giovanni Lovatelli. Director/Writer: Brian Helgeland. Camera (Cinecitta color, Technovision), Nicola Pecorini; editor, Kevin Stitt; music, David Torn. In Cinecitta color, Technovision. Release date: Sept. 5, 2003. MPAA Rating: R. Running time: 102 Min.

Cast: Heath Ledger, Shannyn Sossamon, Benno Furmann, Mark Addy, Peter Weller, Francesco Carnelutti.

OUR HOUSE

A Caesar Prods. presentation. Producers: Sevan Matossian, Bessie Katerina Morris, Greg Shields. Director: Sevan Matossian. Co-director: Greg Shields. Camera: Matosian, Bessie Katerina Morris. Editors: Matossian, Morris, Shields. Music: Eric Brena, Rob Mitchell. In color, digital video. Release date: Feb. 24, 2003. Running time: 83 Min. Documentary.

With: Tim Warinner, Tim Staab, Erik Reitzel, Scott Ryker, Kellee Johnson, Laura Langston, Talin Hagopian.

OUT OF TIME

An MGM release of an Original Film/Monarch Pictures production. Producers: Neal H. Moritz, Jesse B'Franklin. Executive producers: Kevin Reidy, Jon Berg, Damien Saccani, Alex Gartner. Director: Carl Franklin. Screenplay: Dave Collard. Camera: Theo Van de Sande. Editor: Carole Kravetz Aykanian. Music: Graeme Revell. In Fotokem color, Deluxe prints, Panavision Widescreen. Release date: Aug. 25, 2003. MPAA Rating: PG-13. Running time: 105 Min.

Cast: Denzel Washington, Eva Mendes, Sanaa Lathan, Dean Cain, John Billingslay, Robert Baker, Alex Carter.

OVERNIGHT

A Black & White Prods. (Los Angeles) production. Producer: Tony Montana. Director: Mark Brian Smith. Camera: Smith. Editors: Tony Montana, Smith. Music: Troy Duffy, others. In color, DigiBeta. Release date: June 12, 2003. Running time: 115 Min. Documentary.

Cast: Troy Duffy, Jeff "Skunk" Baxter, Willem Dafoe, Billy Connolly.

PAID IN FULL

A Dimension Films release and presentation of a Roc-A-Fella Films production in association with Rat Entertainment/Loud Films. Producers: Damon Dash, Shawn Carter, Brett Ratner. Executive producers: Ron Rotholz, Jesse Berdinka. Co-producer: Lisa Niedenthal. Director: Charles Stone III. Screenplay: Matthew Cirulnick, Thulani Davis. Camera: Paul Sarossy. Editors: Bill Pankow, Patricia Bowers. Music: Vernon Reid, Frank Fitzpatrick. In Deluxe color. Release date: Oct. 21, 2002. MPAA Rating: R. Running time: 97 Min.

Cast: Wood Harris, Mekhi Phifer, Kevin Carroll, Esai Morales, Chi McBride, Cam'ron, Remo Green, Cynthia Martells, Elise Neal, Regina Hall.

PANDORA'S BOX

A Rainforest Films release and presentation of a Willpower production. Producer: William Packer. Executive producer: Brian J. Cavanaugh. Co-producer: Gregory Ramon Anderson. Director: Rob Hardy. Screenplay: Hardy, Gregory Ramon Anderson. Story: Anderson, William Packer. Camera: Matthew McCarthy. Editor: Brian J. Cavanaugh. Music: Steven Gutheinz. In CFI color. Release date: Dec. 8, 2002. MPAA Rating: R. Running time: 103 Min.
Cast: Michael Jai White, Monica Calhoun, Kristoff St. John, Joseph Lawrence, Tyson Beckford, Chrystale Wilson.

PARTICLES OF TRUTH

A Matter production. Producer: Jennifer Elster. Co-producers: Lewis Helfer, Terry Leonard. Director/Writer: Jennifer Elster. Camera: Toshiro Yamaguchi. Editor: Ron Len. In color, HDCam. Release date: April 24, 2003. Running time: 101 Min.
Cast: Jennifer Elster, Gale Harold, Richard Wilkinson, Elizabeth Van Meter, Alan Samulski. Larry Pine, Leslie Lyles, Susan Floyd.

PARTY MONSTER

A ContentFilm presentation in association with Fortissimo Film Sales of a Killer Films/John Wells and World of Wonder production. Producers: Jon Marcus, Bradford Simpson, Christine Vachon, Fenton Bailey, Randy Barbato. Executive producers: Wouter Barendrecht, Michael J. Werner, Edward R. Pressman, John Schmidt, Sofia Sondervan, John Wells. Director/Writer: Fenton Bailey, Randy Barbato from the book "Disco Bloodbath" by James St. James. Camera: Teodoro Maniaci. Editor: Jeremy Simmons. Original music: Jimmy Harry. In color. Release date: Jan. 18, 2003. Running time: 98 Min.
Cast: Macaulay Culkin, Seth Green, Chloe Sevigny, Natasha Lyonne, Justin Hagan, Wilson Cruz, Wilmer Valderrama, Dylan McDermott, Marilyn Manson, Diana Scarwid.

PASSIONADA

A Samuel Goldwyn Films release of a Samuel Goldwyn Films/Fireworks Pictures and Sandyo Prods. presentation of a David Bakalar production. Producer: Bakalar. Executive producer: Jim Jermanok. Co-executive producers: Paul Bernard, James Scura. Director: Dan Ireland. Screenplay: Jim Jermanok, Stephen Jermanok. Story: David Bakalar. Camera: Claudio Rocha. Editor: Luis Colina. Music: Harry Gregson-Williams. In Fotokem color, Panavision widescreen. Release date: July 28, 2003. MPAA Rating: PG-13. Running time: 108 Min.
Cast: Jason Isaacs, Sofia Milos, Emmy Rossum, Theresa Russell, Lupe Ontiveros, Seymour Cassel, Chris Tardio.

PEOPLE I KNOW

A Miramax Films (in U.S.) /Medusa Film-CDI (in Italy) release of a Myriad Pictures presentation of a South Fork Pictures production, in association with Galena/Greenestreet Films, Chal Prods., In-Motion AG, WMF V. Producers: Michael Nozik, Leslie Urdang, Karen Tenkhoff. Executive producers: Robert Redford, Kirk D'Amico, Philip von Alvensleben. Co-producer: Nellie Nugiel. Director: Dan Algrant. Screenplay: Jon Robin Baitz. Camera: Peter Deming. Editor: Suzy Elmiger. Music: Terence Blanchard. In FotoKem color. Release date: Oct. 4, 2002. MPAA Rating: R. Running time: 100 Min.
Cast: Al Pacino, Kim Basinger, Ryan O'Neal, Tea Leoni, Richard Schiff, Bill Nunn, Robert Klein, Mark Webber.

PERSONA NON GRATA

A Wild Bunch/Rule 8 presentation in association with Morena Films of an Ixtlan production. Producer: Fernando Sulichin. Executive producers: Vincent Maraval, Alvaro Longoria. Director: Oliver Stone. Camera: Rodrigo Prieto, Sergei Toshio Saldivar. Editors: Langdon F. Page. In color, B&W/high-definition video, HD Cam. Release date: May 14, 2003. Running time: 67 Min. Documentary.
Cast: Shimon Peres, Benjamin Netanyahu, Ehud Barak, Jasan Yosef, members of Al Aqsa Martyrs' Brigade, Yasser Arafat, Oliver Stone.

PIECES OF APRIL

An InDigEnt, IFC Prods. presentation of an InDigEnt production in association with Kalkaska Prods. Producers: John Lyons, Gary Winick, Alexis Alexanian. Executive producers: Jonathan Sehring, Caroline Kaplan, John Sloss. Co-producers: Lucy Barzun, Lucille Masone Smith. Producer for IFC, Holly Becker. Director/Writer: Peter Hedges. Camera: Tami Reiker. Editor: Mark Livolsi. Music: Stephin Merritt. In color. Release date: Jan. 19, 2003. Running time: 81 Min.
Cast: Katie Holmes, Patricia Clarkson, Oliver Platt, Derek Luke, Alison Pill, John Gallagher Jr., Alice Drummond, Sean Hayes, SisQo, Lillias White, Isiah Whitlock.

PIGLET'S BIG MOVIE

A Buena Vista release of a Walt Disney Pictures presentation. Producer: Michelle Pappalardo-Robinson. Director: Francis Glebas. Screenplay: Brian Hohlfeld, adapted from the works of A.A. Milne. Editor: Ivan Bilancio. Original score: Carl Johnson. In Technicolor prints. Release date: March 6, 2003. MPAA Rating: G. Running time: 75 Min. ANIMATED.
Voices: John Fiedler, Jim Cummings, Andre Stojka, Kath Soucie, Nikita Hopkins, Peter Cullen, Ken Sansom, Tom Wheatley.

THE PILL

An American Experience presentation of a Steward/Gazit Prods., Inc. production. Producer: Chana Gazit. Executive producer: Margaret Drain. Co-producers: David Steward, Hilary Klotz. Associate producer: Amy Brown. Director: Chana Gazit, David Steward. Camera: Joel Shaprio, Stephen McCarthy. Editor: Steward. Music: Tom Phillips. In color, HD video. Release date: Jan. 12, 2003. Running time: 55 Min. Documentary.

PIRATES OF THE CARIBBEAN: THE CURSE OF THE BLACK PEARL

A Buena Vista release of a Walt Disney Pictures presentation in association with Jerry Bruckheimer Films. Producer: Bruckheimer. Executive producers: Mike Stenson, Chad Oman, Bruce Hendricks, Paul Deason. Director: Gore Verbinski. Screenplay: Ted Elliott, Terry Rossio. Screen story: Elliott, Rossio, Stuart Beattie, Jay Wolpert. Based on Walt Disney's "Pirates of the Caribbean." Camera: Dariusz Wolski. Editors: Craig Wood, Stephen Rivkin, Arthur Schmidt. Music: Klaus Badelt. In Technicolor, Panavision widescreen. Release date: July 1, 2003. MPAA Rating: PG-13. Running time: 143 Min.
Cast: Johnny Depp, Geoffrey Rush, Orlando Bloom, Keira Knightley, Jack Davenport, Kevin R. McNally, Zoe Saldana, Jonathan Pryce, Treva Etienne, David Bailie, Lee Arenberg, Mackenzie Crook, Trevor Goddard, Isaac C. Singleton Jr., Brye Cooper.

POWER TRIP

A Paul Devlin production. (International sales: Films Transit Intl., Montreal.) Producer: Paul Devlin. Co-producers: Valery Odikadze, Claire Missanelli. Director/Editor: Paul Devlin. Camera: Devlin, Valery Odikadze. In color, DV. Release date: Feb. 14, 2003. Running time: 85 Min. Documentary.

PREY FOR ROCK AND ROLL

A MAC Releasing presentation of a Prey production. Producers: Donovan Mannato, Gina Resnick, Gina Gershon. Executive producer: Robin Whitehouse. Co-producer: Alexis Magagni-Seely. Director: Alex Steyermark. Screenplay: Cheri Lovedog, Robin Whitehouse, from a play by Lovedog. Camera: Antonio Calvache. Editors: Allyson C. Johnson. In color, 24P. Release date: May 8, 2003. Running time: 103 Min.
Cast: Gina Gershon, Lori Petty, Shelly Cole, Marc Blucas, Ivan Martin.

PRIVATE PROPERTY

A Chiaroscuro Pictures presentation. Producr/Director/Writer/Editor: Elizabeth Dimon. Camera: Goran Pavicevic, Tom Robotham. Music: Cyndi Lauper, Bill Whitman. In Duart color, Super 16mm. Release date: June 14, 2003. Running time: 110 Min.
With: Mirjana Jokovic, David Thornton, Tomas Arana, Richard Parent

THE PROCESS

A Greenberg/Seidler production. Producers: Richard Greenberg, Dudley Saunders, Dennis Sugasawara. Executive producer: Gary Seidler. Director: Richard Greenberg. Camera: Michael K. Maley. Editors: Joseph Conarkov, Neeley Lawson. Music: Billy White Acre. In color, digital video. Release date: March 25, 2003. Running time: 70 Min. Documentary.

PROM NIGHT IN KANSAS CITY

A Golden Pig Production. Producers/Directors: Hali Lee, Peter von Ziegesar. Camera: von Ziegesar. Editor: Dina Guttman. Music: Stephen Thomas Cavit. In color, digital video. Release date: Nov. 10, 2002. Running time: 9 Min. Documentary.

PULSE: A STOMP ODYSSEY

A Honda presentation in association with Walden Media of a Giant Screen Films/Stern/Leve production in association with Yes/No Prods. Producers: Don Kempf, Steve Kempf, Jim Stern, Harriet Leve. Director/Editor: Steve McNicholas, Luke Cresswell. Camera: Christophe Lanzenberg, James Neilhouse. In color, IMAX. Release date: Oct. 16, 2002. Running time: 40 Min. Documentary. IMAX.
With: STOMP, Qwii Music Arts' Trust Khoi San Music, Les Percussions de Guinee, Moremogolo Tswana Traditional Dancers, American Indian Dance Theatre, Kodo, Bayeza Cultural Dancers.

PUT THE CAMERA ON ME

A Transmission Films,Triple Feature Prods. presentation. Producers/Directors/Editors: Darren Stein, Adam Shell. Camera: Stein, Shell. Music: Roddy Bottum, Shell. In color, video. Release date: June 28, 2003. Running time: 70 Min. Documentary.

QUATTRO NOZA

A Fountainhead Films presentation. Producer: Fredric King. Executive producers: King, Kevin Segalla. Co-producers: Joey Curtis, David Murillo, Sau-Yin Wong. Director/Writer: Joey Curtis. Story: Curtis, Albert Hernandez. Camera: Derek Cianfrance. Editors: Curtis, Jim Helton. Music: DJ Spooky. In color, DV. Release date: Jan. 17, 2003. Running time: 121 Min.
Cast: Brihanna Hernandez, Victor Larios, Robert Beaumont, Greg Leone, Fabiola Barrios, Albert Hernandez, Gary Brockette, Gerald Russell, Brian Salemi, Nadja Leone, Ana Hernandez.

RACEHOSS

A Breezeway Entertainment presentation. Producer: Sean Hepburn Ferrer. Co-producer: Wayne Middleton. Director: Sean Hepburn Ferrer. Writer: Albert Race Sample. Camera: Tsuneo Azuma. Editors: Carol Oblath, Harry Dunn. Music: Russ Landau. In color, high definition video. Release date: March 14, 2003. Running time: 118 Min. Documentary.

THE REAL OLD TESTAMENT

A PCH Films presentation. Producers: Curtis Hannum, Paul Hannum. Co-producer: Deanne Sellner. Director/Conceived/Editor: Curtis Hannum, Paul Hannum. Camera: Paul Hannum, Shelly Ryan, K.D. Gulko, Curtis Hannum, David Avallone, Steve Lipscomb, Kara Stephens. Music: Jon Kull. In color, digital video. Release date: Feb. 24, 2003. Running time: 87 Min.
With: Curtis Hannum, Andy Hirsch, Kellee McQuinn, Paul Hannum, Ted Michaels, Harry Hannigan, Sam Lloyd, Kate Connor, Julie Harkness, Brian Strauss, Pamela Alster, Laura Meshell.

THE RECRUIT

A Buena Vista release of a Birnbaum/Barber production of a Touchstone Pictures/Spyglass Entertainment presentation. Producers: Roger Birnbaum, Jeff Apple, Gary Barber. Executive producers: Jonathan Glickman, Ric Kidney. Co-producer: Megan Wolpert. Director: Roger Donaldson. Screenplay: Roger Towne, Kurt Wimmer, Mitch Glazer. Camera: Stuart Dryburgh. Editor: David Rosenbloom. Music: Klaus Badelt. In Technicolor, Panavision widescreen. Release date: Jan. 9, 2003. MPAA Rating: PG-13. Running time: 115 Min.
Cast: Al Pacino, Colin Farrell, Bridget Moynahan, Gabriel Macht, Karl Pruner, Eugene Lipinski.

REESEVILLE

A Pied Piper Films presentation of a Doomed Proportions Ltd. production. Producer: Holly Mosher. Co-producers: Christian Otjen, Jerry Holway. Director/Writer: Christian Otjen. Camera: Jerry Holway. Editor: Stephen Goetsch. Music: Kevin Saunders Hayes. In color. Release date: March 8, 2003. Running time: 99 Min.
With: Brad Hunt, Majandra Delfino, Brian Wimmer, Missy Crider, Mark Hamill, Sally Struthers, Angela Featherstone, Cotter Smith, Lee Ernst.

RETURNING MICKEY STERN

A Metroscape Entertainment release and presentation of a 2 Life! Films production in association with Manticore Films. Producers: Michael Prywes, Jason Akel, Victor Erdos, Joseph Bologna. Executive producers: Barry J. Charles, Joseph Brad Kluge. Director/Writer: Michael Prywes. Camera: Mark Smith. Editor: Suzanne Pillsbury. Music: Jeff Jones. In DuArt color, B&W. Release date: Feb. 2, 2003. MPAA Rating: PG-13. Running time: 91 Min.
With: Joseph Bologna. Tom Bosley, Kylie Delre, Joshua Fishbein, Michael Oberlander, Sarah Schoenberg, John Sloan, Connie Stevens, Brett Tabisel, Renee Taylor.

RHYTHM OF THE SAINTS

A Cynalex Prods. presentation. Producers: Yvette Tomlinson, Cyn Canel Rossi. Executive producer: Alex Rossi. Director: Sarah Rogacki. Screenplay: Cyn Canel Rossi. Camera: Matt Clark. Editor: Steven Gonzales. Music: Andrew Hollander In Duart color. Release date: Jan. 21, 2003. Running time: 83 Min.
With: Sarita Choudhury, Daniella Alonso, Gano Grills, Ryan Donowho, Ivan Martin, Onahoua Rodriguez, Amatus Karim, Bridget Barkan, Prinya Intachai.

RISE ABOVE: THE TRIBE 8 DOCUMENTARY

A Red Hill Pictures production. Producers: Tracy Flannigan, Lilith Simcox, Marupong Chuladul. Director: Tracy Flannigan. Camera: Rinaldo Villani. Editors: Marina Tait, Michelle Harrison, Flannigan. Music: Tribe 8. In color, DV. Release date: June 22, 2003. Running time: 80 Min. Documentary.

THE RISING PLACE

A Flatland Pictures release and presentation. Producers: Tracy A. Ford, Marshall Peck, Tom Rice. Co-producer: Robert Johnston. Director/Writer: Tom Rice, based on "The Rising Place" by David Armstrong. Camera: Jim Dollarhide. Editor: Mary Morrisey. Music: Conrad Pope. In FotoKem color. Release date: Nov. 5, 2002. MPAA Rating: PG-13. Running time: 89 Min.
Cast: Laurel Holloman, Elise Neal, Mark Webber, Liam Aiken, Billy Campbell, Gary Cole, Alice Drummond, Frances Fisher ,Mason Gamble, Beth Grant ,Tess Harper, S. Epatha Merkerson, Scott Openshaw, Frances Sternhagen, Jennifer Holliday.

THE R.M.

A HaleStorm Entertainment, Inc. presentation of a HomeComing production. Producer: Dave Hunter. Executive producers: Kurt Hale, Hunter. Director: Kurt Hale. Screenplay: John E. Moyer, Hale. Camera: Ryan Little. Editor: Wynn Hougaard. Music: Cody Hale. In Deluxe color. Release date: Sept. 4, 2003. Running time: 102 Min.
Cast: Kirby Heyborne, Will Swenson, Britani Bateman, Tracy Ann Evans, Merrill Dodge, Michael Birkeland, Maren Ord, Leroy "Big Budah" Te'o, Curt Doussett.

ROBERT CAPA: IN LOVE AND WAR

An American Masters production in association with Muse Film and Television. Producer: Anne Makepeace. Executive producer: Susan Lacy Co-producer: Joanna Rudnick. Director/Writer: Anne Makepeace. Camera: Nancy Schreiber. Editor: Susan Fanshel. Music: Joel Goodman. In color. Release date: Jan. 31, 2003. Running time: 84 Min. Documentary.
Narrator: Robert Burke

ROBIN'S HOOD

A Filmworks 7 presentation of a Last Chance Films production. Producer/Director: Sara Millman. Screenplay: Millman, Khahtee V. Turner. Camera: Howard Shack. Editor: Millman. In color, DV. Release date: June 18, 2003. Running time: 81 Min.
With: Khahtee V. Turner, Clody Cates, Aaron Grialva, Lee Vogt, Kimberly T. Ridgeway, Dante Robinson, Katherine Bettis.

ROBOT STORIES

A Robot Stories production. Producers: Greg Pak, Kim Ima. Co-producer: Karin Chien. Director/Writer: Greg Pak. Camera: Peter Olsen. Editor: Stephanie Sterner. Music: Rick Knutsen. In color, DV to 35mm. Release date: Oct.18, 2002. Running time: 85 Min.
With: Tamlyn Tomita, James Saito, Wai Ching Ho, Cindy Cheung, Greg Pak, Bill Coelius, Julienne Hanzelka Kim, Sab Shimono, Elsa Davis.

ROLLING KANSAS

A Gold Circle Films release and presentation. Producers: Kerry Li, Jeff Levine, Larry Katz, Paul Brooks. Executive producer: Norm Waitt. Co-executive producer, Scott Niemeyer. Co-producer, Ed Cathell, III. Director: Thomas Haden Church. Screenplay: David Denney, Church. Camera: Nathan Hope. Editors: Sandra Adair, Larry Madaras. Music: Anthony Marinelli. In Fotokem color. Release date: Jan. 24, 2003. Running time: 87 Min.
Cast: Charlie Finn, Sam Huntington, Ryan McDow, Jay Paulson, James Roday, Rip Torn.

RUGRATS GO WILD

A Paramount release of a Paramount Pictures and Nickelodeon Movies presentation of a Klasky Csupo production. Producers: Arlene Klasky, Gabor Csupo. Executive producers: Albie Hecht, Julia Pistor, Eryk Casemiro, Hal Waite. Co-producers: Tracy Kramer, Terry Thoren, Patrick Stapleton. Directors: Norton Virgien, John Eng. Screenplay: Kate Boutilier, based on Rugrats characters created by Arlene Klasky, Gabor Csupo, Paul Germain, and The Wild Thornberrys characters created by Klasky, Csupo, Steve Pepoon, David Silverman, Stephen Sustarsic. Editors: John Bryant, Kimberly Rettberg. Music: Mark Mothersbaugh. In Deluxe color, widescreen. Release date: June 3, 2003. MPAA Rating: PG. Running time: 80 Min. Animated.
Voices: Bruce Willis, Chrissie Hynde, Nancy Cartwright, Kath Soucie, Cheryl Chase, E.G. Daily, Tara Strong, Melanie Chartoff, Jack Riley, Tress MacNeille, Michael Bell, Dionne Quan, Cree Summer, Lacey Chabert, Tim Curry, Danielle Harris, Tom Kane, Michael Balzary, Jodi Carlisle.

THE RUNDOWN

A Universal (in U.S.) release of a Universal Pictures and Columbia Pictures presentation in association with WWE Films of a Misher Films/Strike Entertainment production in association with IM3 Entertainment. Producers: Kevin Misher, Marc Abraham, Karen Glasser. Executive producers: Vince McMahon, Ric Kidney. Director: Peter Berg. Screenplay: R.J. Stewart, James Vanderbilt. Story: Stewart. Camera: Tobias Schliessler. Editor: Richard Pearson. Music: Harry Gregson-Williams. In Deluxe color, Panavision widescreen. Release date: Sept. 11, 2003. MPAA rating: PG-13. Running time: 104 Min.
Cast: The Rock, Seann William Scott, Rosario Dawson, Christopher Walken, Ewen Bremner, Jon Gries, William Lucking, Ernie Reyes Jr., Stuart Wilson.

SADAA E ZAN: VOICES OF WOMEN

A Renegade Films presentation. Producer: Renee Bergan. Co-producer: RAWA Supporters Santa Barbara. Director/Editor: Renee Bergan. Camera: Bergan. Music: Matthew Talmage. In color, DV. Release date: March 8, 2003. Running time: 71 Min. Documentary.
With: Farhat Bokhari, Rahela Hashena, Fatana Gailani, Saman Zia-Zarifi, Addena Niaza, Dr. Abdel Karim, Mary MacMakin.

SAM & JOE

A Z Films and Spun Out Prods. presentation. Producers: Jeffrey Zarnow, Evan Astrowsky, Amy Greenspun. Co-producer: Gina Philips. Director/Writer: Jason Ruscio. Camera: Hisham Abed. Editors: Alexandra Bodner. Music: Josh Hager. In color, video. Release date: April 18, 2003. Running time: 92 Min.
Cast: Petra Wright, Michael T. Ringer, Jeffrey Donovan, Gina Philips, Eugene Blakely, Rod McLachlan, Dawn Cody, Shem Bitterman.

THE SAME RIVER TWICE

A Next Life Films production. Producer/Director: Robb Moss. Camera: Moss. Editor: Karen Schmeer. In color, 16mm/HD-to-HD vid. Release date: Jan. 18, 2003. Running time: 78 Min. Documentary.

THE SANTA CLAUSE 2

A Buena Vista release of a Walt Disney Pictures presentation of a Outlaw Prods./Boxing Cat Films production. Producers: Brian Reilly, Bobby Newmyer, Jeffrey Silver. Executive producers: William W. Wilson III, Rick Messina, Richard Baker, James Miller. Director: Michael Lembeck. Screenplay: Don Rhymer, Cinco Paul, Ken Daurio, Ed Decter, John J. Strauss. Story: Leo Benvenuti, Steve Rudnick, based on characters created by Benvenuti, Rudnick. Camera: Adam Greenberg. Editor: David Finfer. Music: George S. Clinton. In Technicolor. Release date: Oct. 26, 2002. MPAA Rating: G. Running time: 104 Min.
Cast: Tim Allen, Elizabeth Mitchell, David Krumholtz, Eric Lloyd, Judge Reinhold, Wendy Crewson, Spencer Breslin, Liliana Mumy, Danielle Woodman, Art Lafleur, Aisha Tyler, Kevin Pollak, Jay Thomas.

SANTA DOMINGO BLUES

A Mambo Media production in association with Glasseye Pictures. Producer/Director/Editor: Alex Wolfe. Writers: Wolfe, Richard Fleming. Camera: David Hocs, Israel Ramirez. In color, B&W, 16mm and DV. Release date: July 24, 2003. Running time: 74 Min.
With: Luis Vargas, Joan Soriano, Luis Diaz, Luis Segura, Eladio Rodriguez Santos, Jose Manuel Calderon, Arida Ventura, Railin Rodriguez, Ramon Cordero.

SANTA VS. THE SNOWMAN

An Imax Corp. release of a Steve Oederkerk presentation of an O Entertainment production. Producers: Oederkerk, Paul Marshal, John A. Davis, Keith Alcorn. Director/Writer: John A. Davis. Creator: Steve Oederkerk. Editor: Kinsey Beck. Music: Harvey R. Cohen. In Color, 3-D Imax. Release date: Oct. 27, 2002. MPAA Rating: G. Running time: 32 Min. Animated. 3-D IMAX.
Voices: Jonathan Winters, Ben Stein, Victoria Jackson, Mark DeCarlo, David Floyd, Mark DeCarlo. Narrator: Don La Fontaine.

SAVAGE ROSES
A Coast2Coast Prods. presentation. Produced by Joshua Nelson, James Tucker. Directed by James Tucker. Screenplay, Joshua Nelson, based on his stage play "Los Rosas Salvaje." Camera: Ross Jordan, Douglas Rodgers. Editor: Tucker. In color, vid. Release date: June 15, 2003. Running time: 105 Min.
With: Misha Gonzales, Tania Galarza, Aura Vence, Diavanna Zarzuela, Tella Storey, Joshua Nelson, Antonio Tomahawk, Milagros Cepeda, Brendan Rothman-Hicks, Max Goldberg.

THE SCHOOL OF ROCK
A Paramount Pictures presentation of a Scott Rudin production in association with Munich Film Partners, New Century and SOR Prods. Producer: Scott Rudin. Executive producers: Steve Nicolaides, Scott Aversano. Director: Richard Linklater. Screenplay: Mike White. Camera: Rogier Stoffers. Editor: Sandra Adair. Original music: Craig Wedren. In color. Release date: Sept. 9, 2003. MPAA Rating: PG-13. Running time: 108 Min.
Cast: Jack Black, Joan Cusack, Mike White, Sarah Silverman, Jordan-Claire Green, Veronica Afflerbach, Miranda Cosgrove, Joey Gaydos Jr., Robert Tsai, Angelo Massagli, Kevin Clark, Maryam Hassan.

SCREAM QUEEN
A Scream Queen production. Producer: Tatiana Bliss. Co-producers: Abel McHone, Jeff Roe. Director/Writer: Tatiana Bliss. Camera: Kara Stephens. Editors: Jeff Roe, Damon Reeves. In color, DV, Canon X-L1. Release date: July 19, 2003. Running time: 86 Min.
Cast: Liz Lavoie, Nipper Knapp, Jason Boegh, Christopher Neiman.

SEABISCUIT
A Universal release of a Universal Pictures/DreamWorks Pictures/Spyglass Entertainment presentation of a Larger Than Life, Kennedy/Marshall production. Producers: Kathleen Kennedy, Frank Marshall, Gary Ross, Jane Sindell. Executive producers: Gary Barber, Roger Birnbaum, Tobey Maguire, Allison Thomas, Robin Bissell. Co-producer: Patricia Churchill. Director/Writer: Gary Ross, based on the book by Laura Hillenbrand. Camera: John Schwartzman. Editor: William Goldenberg. Music: Randy Newman. In Technicolor, Panavision widescreen. Release date: July 11, 2003. MPAA Rating: PG-13. Running time: 140 Min.
Cast: Tobey Maguire, Jeff Bridges, Chris Cooper, Elizabeth Banks, Gary Stevens, William H. Macy, Kingston DuCoeur, Eddie Jones, Ed Lauter, Michael O'Neill, Michael Angarano, Royce D. Applegate, Annie Corley, Valerie Mahaffey, Narrator - David McCullough.

SEARCHING FOR ASIAN AMERICA
A NAATA (National Asian American Telecommunications Assn.)/KVIE production. Producer: Donald Young. Executive producers: David Hosley, Eddie Wong. In color, DV. Release date: June 21, 2003. Running time: 87 Min. Documentary.
With: Gary Locke, Martin Bautista, Jeffrey Lim,Lela Lee.
THE GOVERNOR
Producer: Donald Young. Camera: Duane Poquis. Editor: Gary Weimberg. Music: Jason Kao Hwang.
OKLAHOMA HOME
Producer: Sapana Sakya. Camera: Duane Poquis. Editor: Gary Weimberg. Music: Jason Kao Hwang.
ANGRY LITTLE ASIAN GIRL
Producer: Kyung Sun Yu. Camera: Vincente Franco. Editor: Gary Weimberg. Music: Jason Kao Hwang.

SECONDHAND LIONS
A New Line release of a David Kirschner/Digital Domain/Avery Pix production. Producers: David Kirschner, Scott Ross, Carey Sienega. Executive producers: Cayle Boyter, Janis Rothbard Chaskin, Kevin Cooper, Mark Kaufman, Karen Loop. Co-producer: Amy Sayres. Director/Writer: Tim McCanlies. Camera: Jack N. Green. Editor: David Moritz. Music: Patrick Doyle. In Deluxe color, widescreen. Release date: Sept. 10, 2003. Running time: 109 Min.
Cast: Michael Caine, Robert Duvall, Haley Joel Osment, Kyra Sedgwick, Nicky Katt, Emmanuelle Vaugier, Christian Kane.

SECRET LIVES: HIDDEN CHILDREN & THEIR RESCUERS DURING WWII
An Aviva Films production. Producer: Aviva Slesin. Co-producer: Toby Appleton Perl. Executive producer: Ann Rubenstein Tisch. Director: Aviva Slesin. Writer: Toby Appleton Perl. Camera: Anthony Forma, Hamar Hader. Editor: Ken Eluto. Music: John Zorn. In color. Release date: Oct. 17, 2002. Running time: 72 Min. Documentary.

SECURITY
A Glass Eye production. Producers: Brien Burroughs, Gerardo Merino. Director: Brien Burroughs. Camera: Gerardo Merino. Editors: Melissa Lawson, Beatriz Lopez. Music: Jason Tubbs. In color. Release date: March 15, 2003. Running time: 95 Min.
Cast: Tim Orr, Stephen Kearin, Regina Saisi, Gerri Lawlor, Tom Wade.

7TH STREET
A Paradise Acres Prods. presentation. Producer: Josh Pais. Executive producer: Catherine Scheinman. Director/Writer: Josh Pais. Camera: Elia Lassy, Pais. Editor: Linda Hattendorf. Music: Marty Beller. In color, video. Release date: Nov. 16, 2002. Running time: 71 Min. Documentary.

SEXLESS
An Our Merry Life Prods. production. Producers: Rosa Lockett, Brian McCormick, Eddie Sykes. Director/Writer: Alex Holdridge. Camera: Brian McCormick. Editors: Sandra Adair. In color, digital video. Release date: March 15, 2003. Running time: 102 Min.
Cast: Alex Holdridge, Brian McGuire, Kelly Dealyn, Camille Chen, Michelle Fairbanks, Sara Simmonds.

SHALOM Y'ALL
A Satchel Entertainment and Buzzbox Films production. Producer: Susan Levitas. Executive producers: Michael Arata, Glenn Solomon. Director: Brian Bain. Camera: Alex Vlacos. Editor: Tim Watson. Music: Jep Epstein. In color, video. Release date: Oct., 18, 2002. Running time: 59 Min. Documentary.
With: Leonard Bain, Julie Koppman, Kinky Friedman, Eli Evans, Andrew Young, Reuben Greenberg, Elliott Levitas.

SHANGHAI KNIGHTS
A Buena Vista release of a Touchstone Pictures and Spyglass Entertainment release of a Birnbaum/Barber production. Producers: Gary Barber, Roger Birnbaum, Jonathan Glickman. Executive producers: Jackie Chan, Willie Chan, Solon So, Stephanie Austin, Ed McDonnell. Director: David Dobkin. Screenplay: Alfred Gough, Miles Millar, based on characters created by Gough, Millar. Camera: Adrian Biddle. Editor: Malcolm Campbell. Music: Randy Edelman. In Technicolor, Panavision widescreen. Release date: Jan. 23, 2003. MPAA Rating: PG-13. Running time: 114 Min.
Cast: Jackie Chan, Owen Wilson, Aaron Johnson, Thomas Fisher, Aidan Gillen, Fann Wong, Donnie Yen, Kim S. Chan, Gemma Jones.

THE SHAPE OF THINGS
A Focus Features and StudioCanal presentation of a Working Title production in association with Pretty Pictures. Producers: Neil LaBute, Gail Mutrux, Philip Steuer, Rachel Weisz. Executive producers: Tim Bevan, Eric Fellner. Director: Neil LaBute. Screenplay: LaBute, based on his stage play. Camera: James L. Carter. Editor: Joel Plotch. In FotoKem color, Panavision widescreen. Release date: Jan. 18, 2002. Running time: 96 Min.
Cast: Gretchen Mol, Paul Rudd, Rachel Weisz, Frederick Weller.

SHATTERED GLASS
A Lions Gate Films release of a Cruise/Wagner and Baumgarten/Merims production in association with Forest Park Pictures. Producers: Craig Baumgarten, Adam Merims, Tove Christensen, Gaye Hirsch. Executive producer: Paula Wagner. Director/Writer: Billy Ray, based on the article by Buzz Bissinger. Camera: Mandy Walker. Editor: Jeffrey Ford. Music: Mychael Danna. In Deluxe color, widescreen. Release date: Aug. 31, 2003. Running time: 95 Min.
Cast: Hayden Christensen, Peter Sarsgaard, Chloe Sevigny, Rosario Dawson, Melanie Lynskey, Steve Zahn, Hank Azaria, Cas Anvar, Ted Kotcheff, Mark Blum, Simone-Elise Girard, Chad Donella.

SINBAD: LEGEND OF THE SEVEN SEAS
A DreamWorks release. Producers: Mireille Soria, Jeffrey Katzenberg. Director: Tim Johnson, Patrick Gilmore. Screenplay: John Logan. Editor: Tom Finan. Music: Harry Gregson-Williams. In Technicolor. Release date: June 12, 2003. MPAA Rating: PG. Running time: 86 Min.
Voices: Brad Pitt, Catherine Zeta-Jones, Michelle Pfeiffer, Joseph Fiennes, Dennis Haysbert, Timothy West, Adriano Giannini.

THE SINGING DETECTIVE
An Icon Prods. presentation of a Haft Enterprises production. Producers: Mel Gibson, Steven Haft, Bruce Davey. Executive producer: Stan Wlodkowski. Co-producers: Jane Potter, Sarah Potter, Robert Potter. Director: Keith Gordon. Screenplay: Dennis Potter, adapted from his original television series. Camera: Tom Richmond. Editor: Jeff Wishengrad. Music supervisor: Ken Weiss. In color. Release date: Jan. 17, 2003. Running time: 109 Min.
Cast: Robert Downey Jr., Robin Wright Penn, Mel Gibson, Jeremy Northam, Katie Holmes, Adrien Brody, Jon Polito, Carla Gugino.

SISTERS IN CINEMA
An Our Film Works presentation. Producer: Yvonne Welbon. Co-producers: Michael Fuller, Alison Duke. Director/Writer: Yvonne Welbon. Camera: Catherine Crouch. Editor: Paul Hill. Music: Joseph Welbon. In color, video. Release date: Feb. 15, 2003. Running time: 60 Min. Documentary.
With: Joy (Shannonb) S'hani Ache, Stephanie Allain, Madeline Anderson, Maya Angelou, Neema Barnette, Julie Dash, Bridgett Davis, DeMane Davis, Zainabu irene Davis, Cheryl Dunye.

SLAVE
A WaiterGoneBad production. (International sales: WaiterGoneBad, Chicago.) Producer: by Noel Olken. Co-producers: Christina Varotsis, Ed Koziarski, Junko Kajino. Director/Writer: Noel Olken. Camera: Pete Biagi. Editor: Chris Boscardin. Music: Steven Gibons. In color, DV. Release date: May 16, 2003. Running time: 76 Min.
With: Erinn Strain, Krissy Shields, Andrew Krukowski.

THE SMITH FAMILY
Producer: Tasha Oldham. Co-producer: Noelle Wright. Director: Tasha Oldham. Camera: Tahlee Booher. Editors: Jeff Werner, Janet Swanson. Music: Matthew Bennett. In color, 16mm/video. Release date: Nov. 8, 2002. Running time: 79 Min. Documentary.
With: Kim Smith, Steve Smith, Tony Smith, Parker Smith, Stan Smith, Terry Smith, Paul Smith, Alice Smith, Don Egginton, Shirley Egginton.

SOLARIS
A 20th Century Fox release of a Lightstorm Entertainment production. Producers: James Cameron, Rae Sanchini, Jon Landau. Executive producer: Gregory Jacobs. Co-producers: Michael Polaire, Charles V. Bender. Director/Writer: Steven Soderbergh, based on the book by Stanislaw Lem. Camera: Peter Andrews. Editor: Mary Ann Bernard. Music: Cliff Martinez. In FotoKem color, Deluxe prints; Panavision widescreen. Release date: Nov. 19, 2002. MPAA Rating: PG-13. Running time: 99 Min.
Cast: George Clooney, Natascha McElhone, Jeremy Davies, Viola Davis, Ulrich Tukur.

SOLDIER'S GIRL
A Showtime presentation of a Bachrach/Gottlieb production. Producers: Linda Gottlieb, Doro Bachrach. Co-producer: Ron Nyswaner. Director: Frank Pierson. Screenplay: Nyswaner. Camera: Paul Sarossy. Editor: Katina Zinner. Music: Jan A.P. Kaczmarek. In color. Release date: Jan. 20, 2003. Running time: 112 Min.
Cast: Troy Garity, Lee Pace, Andre Braugher, Shawn Hatosy.

THE SOUL OF A MAN
A Martin Scorsese presentation of a Vulcan Prods./Road Movies co-production in association with Cappa Prods., Jigsaw Prods. (International sales: Road Sales, Berlin.) Producers: Alex Gibney, Margaret Bodde. Executive producers: Scorsese, Paul G. Allen, Jody Patton, Ulrich Felsberg. Director/Writer: Wim Wenders. Camera: Lisa Rinzler. Editors: Mathilde Bonnedfoy. In Duart B&W, color. Release date: May 15, 2003. Running time: 100 Min. Documentary.
Cast: Keith B. Brown, Chris Thomas King. Featured performers: J.B. Lenoir, Skip James, Beck, T Bone Burnett, Nick Cave, Shemekia Copeland, Eagle Eye Cherry, Crow Jane, Garland Jeffreys, Los Lobos, Bonnie Raitt, Marc Ribot, Lou Reed, Vernon Reid.

SPEEDER KILLS
A BadAss Pictures production in association with C/S Prods. Producer: Faith Radle. Director/Writer: Jim Mendiola. Camera: Fernando S. Cano. Editors: Spencer Parsons, Mendiola. In color, DV/Super 8. Release date: June 16, 2003. Running time: 96 Min.
With: Amalia Ortiz, Xelina Flores , Johnny Hernandez, Melissa Flores, Rick Rios, Kat Perez, Kathryn Alexander, Brian Lieb, Tiffany Mock, Sam Gilliam, Ruby Nelda Perez.

SPY KIDS 3D: GAME OVER
A Dimension Films release of a Troublemaker Studios production. Producers: Elizabeth Avellan, Robert Rodriguez. Executive producers: Bob Weinstein, Harvey Weinstein. Director/Writer/Editor: Robert Rodriguez. Camera: Rodriguez. Music: Rodriguez. In Deluxe color, 3-D/HD video. Release date: July 14, 2003. MPAA Rating: PG. Running time: 89 Min.
Cast: Antonio Banderas, Carla Gugino, Alexa Vega, Daryl Sabara, Ricardo Montalban, Holland Taylor, Sylvester Stallone, Mike Judge, Matt O'Leary, Emily Osment, Cheech Marin, Bobby Edner, Courtney Jines, Ryan James Pinkston, Robert Vito, Danny Trejo.

STANDARD TIME
A Jubilee/Intrinsic Values production. Producers: Aimee Schoof, Isen Robbins. Director: Robert Cary. Screenplay: Isabel Rose, Cary. Camera: Horacio Marquinez. Editor: Robert Reitano. Music: Steven Lutvak, Andrew Hollander. In color. Release date: Nov. 5, 2002. Running time: 102 Min.
With: Isabel Rose, Andrew McCarthy, Cameron Bancroft, Alix Korey, Ilana Levine, Victor Argo, Eartha Kitt.

STANDER
An Odeon Films release (in Canada) of a Seven Arts Pictures presentation in association with Peter and Susan Hoffman of an Imaginarium/Grosvenor Park/Seven Arts co-production in association with Industrial Development Corp. of South Africa. (International sales: Seven Arts, Beverly Hills.) Producers: Chris Roland, Martin F. Katz, Julia Verdin. Executive producers: David E. Allen, Steven Markoff, Izidore Codron, Frank Hubner, Jan Fantl. Co-producer: Bima Stagg. Director: Bronwen Hughes. Screenplay: Bima Stagg, Hughes. Story: Stagg. Camera: Jess Hall. Editor: Robert Ivison. Music: the Free Association, David Holmes, Steve Hilton. In Deluxe color, U.K./Canada). Release date: Sept. 5, 2003. Running time: 116 Min.
Cast: Thomas Jane, Dexter Fletcher, David Patrick O'Hara, Deborah Kara Unger, Ashley Taylor, Marius Weyers.

STAR TREK NEMESIS
A Paramount release of a Rick Berman production. Producer: Rick Berman. Executive producer: Marty Hornstein. Co-producer: Peter Lauritson. Director: Stuart Baird. Screenplay: John Logan. Story: Logan, Rick Berman, Brent Spiner, based upon "Star Trek" created by Gene Roddenberry. Camera: Jeffrey L. Kimball. Editor: Dallas Puett. Music: Jerry Goldsmith. In Deluxe color, Panavision widescreen. Release date: Dec. 4, 2002. MPAA Rating: PG-13. Running time: 117 Min.
Cast: Patrick Stewart, Jonathan Frakes, Brent Spiner, Levar Burton, Michael Dorn, Marina Sirtis, Gates McFadden, Tom Hardy, Ron Perlman, Shannon Cochran, Dina Meyer, Jude Ciccolella, Alan Dale, John Berg, Michael Owen, Kate Mulgrew, Robertson Dean, David Ralphe, J. Patrick McCormack, Wil Wheaton, Majel Barrett Roddenberry.

STATE OF DENIAL
A Lovett Prods. and Curious Pictures production. Producer: Elaine Epstein. Executive producer: Joseph Lovett. Co-producer: Penny Elliott Hays. Co-executive producers: Harriet Gavshon, David Jammy. Director: Elaine Epstein. Camera: Sven Cheatle, Carl Deheer, Brian Green, Eddie Wes. Editor: Penny Elliott Hays. Original music: Thomas Derenzo. In color, HD Cam. Release date: Jan. 22, 2003. Running time: 86 Min. Documentary.

THE STATION AGENT
A Miramax release (in North America) of a SenArt Films production in association with Next Wednesday. (International sales: Cinetic Media, New York.) Producers: Mary Jane Skalski, Robert May, Kathryn Tucker. Co-producer: Joshua Zeman. Director/Writer: Tom McCarthy. Camera: Oliver Bokelberg. Editor: Tom McArdle. Music: Stephen Trask. In color. Release date: Jan. 21, 2003. Running time: 88 Min.
Cast: Peter Dinklage, Patricia Clarkson, Bobby Cannavale, Raven Goodwin, Paul Benjamin, Michelle Williams.

STEP INTO LIQUID
A New Visual Entertainment presentation of a Top Secret production. Producer: John-Paul Beeghly. Executive producers: Bruce Brown, Ray Willenberg Jr. Director/Writer/Editor: Dana Brown. Camera: John-Paul Beeghly. Music: Richard Gibbs. In FotoKem color, Super 16mm/24P HD video. Release date: Jan.22, 2003. Running time: 87 Min. Documentary.
With: Jim Knost, Alex Knost, Dan Malloy, Chris Malloy, Keith Malloy, Laird Hamilton, Rob Machado, Kelly Slater, Dale Webster.

STOKED: THE RISE AND FALL OF GATOR
Producer/Director: Helen Stickler. Camera: Stickler, Peter Sutherland, Dag Yngvesson. Editor: Ana Esterov. Music: David Reid. In color, digital video. Release date: Jan. 19, 2003. Running time: 80 Min. Documentary.
With: Mark "Gator" Rogowski, Tony Hawk, Stacy Peralta, Jason Jessee, Steve Olson, MoFo, Carol Leggett, Ed Templeton, Tod Swank.

STUEY
An ADV Prods. presentation. Producers: A.W. Vidmer, F. A. Miller. Executive producers: A.W. Vidmer, Nancy M. Grinder. Director/Writer/Editor: A.W. Vidmer. Camera: Lawrence Boothby. Music: Starr Parodi, Jeff Eden Fair. In Deluxe color. Release date: June 17, 2003. Running time: 109 Min.
Cast: Michael Imperioli, Renee Faia, Michael Nouri, Joe LaDue, Steven R. Schirripa, Todd Susman, Peggy Walton-Walker, Pat Morita, Jonathan Press, Michael Pasternak, Vincent Van Patten, Cynthia Brimhall, Ransom Gates.

SUNSET STORY
An ITVS presentation of a Gabbert/Libresco production. Producers: Laura Gabbert, Caroline Libresco. Co-producer: Eden Wurmfeld. Director: Laura Gabbert. Camera: Shana Hagan. Editor: William Haugse. Music: Peter Golub. Release date: June 5, 2003. Running time: 73 Min.
Cast: Irja Lloyd , Lucille Alpert, Priscilla Yablon, Phil Way, Paul Alpert.

SUSPENDED ANIMATION
A Filmacres production. Producers: Robert J. Hiler, John Hancock. Executive producer: Carey Westberg. Co-producers: Dean Jacobson, Ken Kitch. Director: John Hancock. Screenplay: Dorothy Tristan. Camera: Misha Suslov. Editor: Dennis O'Connor. Music: Angelo Badalementi. In color, HDV. Release date: Oct. 19, 2002. Running time: 114 Min.
With: Alex McArthur, Laura Esterman, Sage Allen, Rebecca Harrell, Maria Cina, Fred Meyers.

S.W.A.T.
A Sony Pictures Entertainment release of a Columbia Pictures presentation of an Original Film/Camelot Pictures/Chris Lee production. Producers: Neal H. Moritz, Dan Halsted. Executive producer: Louis D'Esposito. Co-executive producer: Todd Black. Co-producers: George Huang, Amanda Cohen. Director: Clark Johnson. Screenplay: David Ayer, David McKenna, based on characters created by Robert Hammer. Story: Ron Mita, Jim McClain. Camera: Gabriel Beristain. Editor: Michael Tronick. Music: Elliot Goldenthal. In Fotokem color, Deluxe prints, Arriflex widescreen. Release date: Aug. 4, 2003. MPAA Rating: PG-13. Running time: 116 Min.
Cast: Samuel L. Jackson, Colin Farrell, Michelle Rodriguez, James Todd Smith aka LL Cool J, Josh Charles, Jeremy Renner, Brian Van Holt, Olivier Martinez, Reginald E. Cathey, Larry Poindexter.

SWIMMING UPSTREAM
A Hoyts Distribution (Australia) release of a Crusader Entertainment production. (Intl. Sales: Summit Films, Los Angeles). Producers: Howard Baldwin, Karen Baldwin, Andrew Mason, Paul Pompian. Co-producer: Nick Morton. Executive Producers, William J. Immerman, Anthony Fingleton. Director: Russell Mulcahy. Screenplay: Anthony Fingleton, based on the book by Anthony and Diane Fingleton. Camera: Martin McGrath. Editor: Marcus D'Arcy. Music: Johnny Klimek, Reinhold Heil. In Atlab color. Release date: Oct 31, 2002. Running time: 114 Min.
Cast: Geoffrey Rush, Judy Davis, Jesse Spencer ,Tim Draxl, David Hoflin, Craig Horner, Brittany Byrnes, Deborah Kennedy, Mark Hembrow, Mitchell Dellevergin, Thomas Davidson, Kain O'Keefe, Robert Quinn, Keeara Byrnes.

TATTOO: A LOVE STORY
A Tattoo Prods., LLC presentation. Producers: Stephen F. Davies, Michael Vukas. Executive producer: Frederick L. Davies. Co-producers: Dave Yasuda, Richard W. Bean. Director: Richard W. Bean. Screenplay: Bean, Gregg Sacon. Camera: David Klein. Editor: Brian Murphy. Music: Pete Droge. In DuArt color. Release date: Oct. 15, 2002. Running time: 94 Min.
Cast: Megan Edwards, Benjamin J. Burdick, Virgil Mignanelli.

TEARS OF THE SUN
A Sony Pictures Entertainment release from Columbia Pictures of a Revolution Studios presentation of a Michael Lobell production/Cheyenne Enterprises production. Producers: Lobell, Arnold Rifkin, Ian Bryce. Executive producer: Joe Roth. Co-producer: Steve P. Saeta. Director: Antoine Fuqua. Screenplay: Alex Lasker, Patrick Cirillo. Camera: Mauro Fiore. Editor: Conrad Buff. Music: Hans Zimmer. In Technicolor, Deluxe prints; Panavision widescreen. Release date: Feb. 26, 2003. MPAA Rating: R. Running time: 118 Min.
Cast: Bruce Willis, Monica Bellucci, Cole Hauser, Eamonn Walker, Nick Chinlund, Fionnula Flanagan, Malick Bowens, Tom Skerritt, Johnny Messner, Paul Francis, Chad Smith, Akosua Busia.

THE TECHNICAL WRITER
A Damage Control Prods., Mill Ridge Films and Susie O Prods. presentation. Producers: Scott Saunders, Michael Harris, Jim Calabrese, Susan Leber, David W. Leitner. Executive producers: Michael Yanko, Lisa Green. Director: Scott Saunders. Screenplay: Saunders, Michael Harris. Camera: David W. Leitner. Editor: David Leonard. Music: Stephen Cullo. In color, HD-to-35mm. Release date: Jan. 21, 2003. Running time: 96 Min.
With: Michael Harris, Tatum O'Neal, William Forsythe, Pamela Gordon, Oksana Lada, Natalia Novikova, John Lanzillotto.

TERMINATOR 3: RISE OF THE MACHINES
A Warner Bros. release of a Mario F. Kassar and Andrew G. Vajna presentation of an Intermedia/IMF production in association with C2 Pictures and Mostow/Lieberman productions. Producers: Kassar, Vajna, Joel B. Michaels, Hal Lieberman, Colin Wilson. Executive producers: Moritz Borman, Guy East, Nigel Sinclair, Gale Anne Hurd. Director: Jonathan Mostow. Screenplay: John Brancato, Michael Ferris. Story: Brancato, Ferris, Tedi Sarafian. Camera: Don Burgess. Editors: Neil Travis, Nicolas de Toth. Music: Marco Beltrami. In Deluxe color, Panavision widescreen. Release date: June 13, 2003. MPAA Rating: R. Running time: 110 Min.
Cast: Arnold Schwarzenegger, Nick Stahl, Claire Danes, David Andrews, Kristanna Loken, Mark Famiglietti.

THEY (WES CRAVEN PRESENTS: THEY)
A Dimension Films release of a Dimension Films/Focus Features, Wes Craven presentation of a Radar Pictures production. Producers: Scott Kroopf, Tom Engelman. Executive producers: Ted Field, David Linde. Co-producers: Barbara Kelly, Tony Blain. Director: Robert Harmon. Screenplay: Brendan William Hood. Camera: Rene Ohashi. Editor: Chris Peppe. Music: Elia Cmiral. In color, widescreen. Release date: Nov. 25, 2002. MPAA Rating: PG-13. Running time: 89 Min.
Cast: Laura Regan, Marc Blucas, Ethan Embry, Dagmar Dominczyk, Jon Abrahams, Alexander Gould.

THIRTEEN
A Fox Searchlight release of a Michael London Prods. presentation in association with Working Title Films of an Antidote Film production. Producers: Jeffrey Levy-Hinte, London. Executive producers: Tim Bevan, Eric Fellner, Liza Chasin, Holly Hunter. Co-producer: Rosemary Marks. Director: Catherine Hardwicke. Screenplay: Hardwicke, Nikki Reed. Camera: Elliot Davis. Editor: Nancy Richardson. Music: Mark Mothersbaugh. In FotoKem color. Release date: Jan. 18, 2003. Running time: 100 Min.
Cast: Holly Hunter, Evan Rachel Wood, Nikki Reed, Jeremy Sisto, Brady Corbett, Deborah Kara Unger, Kip Pardue, Sarah Clarke, D.W. Moffett, Vanessa Anne Hudgens, Jenicka Carey.

THIS SO-CALLED DISASTER
An IFC Prods. presentation of a Keep Your Head production. Producers: Callum Greene, Anthony Katagas. Executive producers: Jonathan Sehring, Caroline Kaplan, Holly Becker, John Sloss. Director: Michael Almereyda. Camera: Amber Lasciak, Andy Black, Adam Keker, Michael McDonnough. Editor: Kate Williams. In color, digital video. Release date: Jan. 29, 2003. Running time: 87 Min. Documentary.
With: T Bone Burnett, James Gammon, Woody Harrelson, Cheech Marin, Anne Militello, Nick Nolte, Sean Penn, Sam Shepard., Sheila Tousey.

TIBET: CRY OF THE SNOW LION
An Earthworks Films/Zambuling Pictures production. Producers: Maria Florio, Victoria Mudd, Tom Peosay, Sue Peosay. Director: Tom Peosay. Screenplay: Sue Peosay, Victoria Mudd. Camera: Tom Peosay. Editor: Kathryn Himoff. Music: Jeff Beal, Nawang Khechog. In color, digital video. Release date: March 3, 2003. Running time: 104 Min. Documentary.
With: Lhasang Tsering, Robert Ford, the 14th Dalai Lama, Stephen Batchelor, Palden Gyatso, Robert Thurman, Gendun Rinchen, Adhe Tapontsang, Ngawang, Wei Jingsheng. Narrator: Martin Sheen.

TIME CHANGER
A Five & Two pictures release and presentation in association with Christiano Film Group. Producers: Rich Christiano, Kevin Downes. Executive producer: Paul Crouch. Co-producers: Bobby Downes, Geoff Ludlow. Director/Writer: Rich Christiano. Camera: Philip Hurn. Editor: Jeffrey Lee Hollis. Music: Jaspar Randall. In Deluxe color. Release date: Oct. 26, 2002. MPAA Rating: G. Running time: 98 Min.
Cast: D. David Morin, Gavin MacLeod, Hal Linden, Jennifer O'Neill, Paul Rodriguez, Richard Riehle, John Valdetero, Brad Heller, Ruben Madera, Kevin Downes, Paige Peterson, Alana Curry.

TIPTOES
A Mars Distribution release (in France) of a Langley Prods. presentation, in association with StudioCanal, of a Langley, Muse, Blacklist, Brad Wyman production, in association with SE8. (International sales: Wild Bunch, Paris.) Producers: Fernando Sulichin, Chris Hanley, John Langley, Elie Cohn, Brad Wyman, Douglas Urbanski. Executive producer: Maggie Langley. Co-executive producer: Daryl Marshak. Director: Matthew Bright. Screenplay: Bill Weiner. Camera: Sonja Rom. Editor: Wendy Grace Briemont. Music: Curt Sobel. In color. Release date: Sept. 8, 2003. Running time: 91 Min.
Cast: Gary Oldman, Matthew McConaughey, Kate Beckinsale, Patricia Arquette, Peter Dinklage.

TOM DOWD & THE LANGUAGE OF MUSIC
A Language of Music Films production. Producers: Mark Moormann, Scott Gordon, Mark Hunt. Executive producer: Juan Carlos Lopez. Director: Mark Moormann. Camera: Patrick Longman. Editors: Tino Wohlwend, Moormann. In color. Release date: Jan. 22, 2003. Running time: 92 Min. Documentary.
With: Tom Dowd, Ray Charles, Eric Clapton, the Allman Brothers Band, Les Paul, Lynyrd Skynyrd, Aretha Franklin, Joe Bonnamassa, Ahmet Ertegun, Phil Ramone, Mike Stoller, Arif Mardin, Al Schmitt, Tito Puente Jr.

TOTALLY SEXY LOSER
A Michael Bodie production. Producers: Jason Schafer, Bodie. Executive producer: Eric D'Arbeloff. Director/Writer: Jason Schafer. Camera: Lisa Wiegand. Editor: Patrick Griffin. Music: Roddy Bottum. In color, DV. Release date: June 26, 2003. Running time: 75 Min.
With: Chad Lindsey, Mark DeWhitt, Craig Young, Amy Gollnick, Jesslyn Hoeft, Terrance Elton, Amber Poklar.

TREASURE PLANET
A Buena Vista release of a Walt Disney Pictures presentation. Producers: Roy Conli, John Musker, Ron Clements. Directors: John Musker, Ron Clements. Screenplay: Clements, Musker, Rob Edwards, adapted from the novel "Treasure Island" by Robert Louis Stevenson. Animation story: Clements, Musker, Ted Elliott, Terry Rossio. Editor: Michael Kelly. Original score: James Newton Howard. In Technicolor. Release date: Nov. 20, 2002. MPAA Rating: PG. Running time: 95 Min. Animated.
Voices: Joseph Gordon-Levitt, Brian Murray, David Hyde Pierce, Emma Thompson, Michael Wincott, Martin Short, Laurie Metcalf, Patrick McGoohan, Dane A. Davis, Roscoe Lee Browne, Corey Burton, Michael McShane, Austin Majors. Narrator: Tony Jay.

THE TRUTH ABOUT CHARLIE
A Universal release presented in association with Mediastream Film of a Clinica Estetico production. Producers: Jonathan Demme, Peter Saraf, Edward Saxon. Executive producer: Ilona Herzberg. Co-producers: Neda Armian, Mishka Cheyko. Director: Jonathan Demme. Screenplay: Demme, Steve Schmidt, Peter Joshua, Jessica Bendinger, based on the "Charade" screenplay by Peter Stone. Camera: Tak Fujimoto. Editor: Carol Littleton. Music: Rachel Portman. In Deluxe color, Panavision widescreen. Release date: Oct. 11, 2002. MPAA Rating: PG-13. Running time: 104 Min.
Cast: Mark Wahlberg, Thandie Newton, Tim Robbins, Joong-Hoon Park, Ted Levine, Lisa Gay Hamilton, Christine Boisson, Stephen Dillane, Simon Abkarian, Frederique Meininger, Charles Aznavour, Anna Karina, Magali Noel, Sakina Jaffrey, Olga Sekulic, Pierre Carre.

TRY SEVENTEEN
A Millennium Films presentation of a Michele Weisler, Capital Arts Entertainment, Flirt Pictures production. (International sales: Millennium Films, Los Angeles.) Producers: Randall Emmett, George Furla. Weisler, Mike Elliott, Holly Wiersma. Executive producers: Avi Lerner, Brad Jenkel, Trevor Short, Boaz Davidson, John Thompson. Director: Jeffrey Porter. Screenplay: Charles Kephart. Camera: Blake Evans. Editor: David Richardson. Music: Andrew Gross. In color. Release date: Sept. 11, 2002. Running time: 92 Min.
With: Elijah Wood, Franka Potente, Mandy Moore, Chris William Martin, Deborah Harry, Elizabeth Perkins, Aaron Pearl, Aloma Wright.

25TH HOUR
A Buena Vista release of a Touchstone Pictures presentation of a 40 Acres and a Mule Filmworks, Industry Entertainment, Gamut Films production. Producers: Spike Lee, Jon Kilik, Tobey Maguire, Julia Chasman. Executive producer: Nick Wechsler. Director: Spike Lee. Screenplay: David Benioff, based on his novel. Camera: Rodrigo Prieto. Editor: Barry Alexander Brown. Music: Terence Blanchard. In Technicolor, widescreen. Release date: Dec. 9, 2002. MPAA Rating: R. Running time: 134 Min.
Cast: Edward Norton, Philip Seymour Hoffman, Barry Pepper, Rosario Dawson, Anna Paquin, Brian Cox, Tony Siragusa, Levani, Misha Kuznetsov, Isiah Whitlock Jr., Michael Genet.

21 GRAMS
A Focus Features release of a This is That/Y Prods. production. Producers: Alejandro Gonzalez Inarritu, Robert Salerno. Executive producer: Ted Hope. Director: Alejandro Gonzalez Inarritu. Screenplay: Guillermo Arriaga. Camera: Rodrigo Prieto. Editor: Stephen Mirrione. Music: Gustavo Santaolalla. In Deluxe color. Release date: Sept. 4, 2003. MPAA Rating: R. Running time: 125 Min.
Cast: Sean Penn, Benicio Del Toro, Naomi Watts, Charlotte Gainsbourg, Melissa Leo, Clea DuVall, Danny Huston, Paul Calderon.

2 FAST 2 FURIOUS
A Universal release of a Neal H. Moritz production. Producer: Moritz. Executive producers: Lee R. Mayes, Michael Fottrell. Co-producer: Heather Lieberman. Director: John Singleton. Screenplay: Michael Brandt, Derek Haas. Story: Brandt, Haas, Gary Scott Thompson. Camera: Matthew F. Leonetti. Editors: Bruce Cannon, Dallas Puett. Music: David Arnold. In Technicolor, Panavision widescreen. Release date: May 29, 2003. MPAA Rating: PG-13. Running time: 108 Min.
Cast: Paul Walker, Tyrese, Eva Mendes, Cole Hauser, Chris "Ludacris" Bridges, James Remar, Thom Barry, Michael Ealy, Mark Boone Junior, Devon Aoki, Roberto (Sanz) Sanchez, Matt Gallini, Edward Finlay, Amaury Nolasco, Jin Auyeung, Eric Etebari.

TWO WEEKS NOTICE

A Warner Bros. release of a Castle Rock Entertainment presentation, in association with Village Roadshow Pictures, NPV Entertainment, of a Fortis Films production. Producer: Sandra Bullock. Executive producers: Mary McLaglen, Bruce Berman. Co-producer: Scott Elias. Director/Writer: Marc Lawrence. Camera: Laszlo Kovacs. Editor: Susan E. Morse. Music: Pohn Powell. In Technicolor. Release date: Dec.8, 2002. MPAA Rating: PG-13. Running time: 101 Min.
Cast: Sandra Bullock, Hugh Grant, Alicia Witt, Dana Ivey ,Robert Klein, Heather Burns, David Haig, Dorian Missick.

UNCOMMON COURAGE: PATRIOTISM AND CIVIL LIBERTIES

A KVIE Public Television presentation of a Bridge Media production. Producer/Director/Writer: Gayle K. Yamada. Camera/Editor: Dan Friedman. Music: Dan Kuramoto. In color, video. Release date: March 25, 2003. Running time: 86 Min. Documentary.
With: Harry Fukuhara, George Kanegai, Barry Saiki, Gene Uratsu, Roy Uyehata, Walter Tanaka, Grant Hirabayashi, Steve Yamamoto, Ken Okune, Harry Okune, Shig Kihara. Narrator: Ken Kashiwahara.

UNCONDITIONAL LOVE

A Starz! Pictures/New Line Cinema presentation of a Jerry Zucker/Jocelyn Moorhouse production. Producers: Zucker, Moorhouse, Patricia Whitcher. Executive producers: Michael De Luca, Brian Witten, Gil Netter. Director: P.J. Hogan. Screenplay: Jocelyn Moorhouse, Hogan. Camera: Remi Adefarasin. Editor: Robert C. Jones. Music: James Newton Howard. In color. Release date: June 27, 2003. Running time: 121 Min.
Cast: Kathy Bates, Rupert Everett, Meredith Eaton, Peter Sarsgaard, Lynn Redgrave, Stephanie Beacham, Richard Briers, Marcia Warren, Jake Noseworthy, Dan Wyllie, Dan Aykroyd, Jonathan Pryce.

UNDERMIND

A Vertical Pictures presentation of a double A Films production. (International sales: The Film Sales Co., New York.) Producers: Fred Bernstein, Mark Tarlov. Executive producer: Roger Smith. Director/Writer: Nevil Dwek. Camera: Wolfgang Held. Editor: Andrew Weisblum. Music: Joel Goodman. In Deluxe Color, Moviecam. Release date: July 28, 2003. Running time: 108 Min.
Cast: Sam Trammell, Ian - Erik Jensen, Susan May Pratt, Celia Weston, Jon Devries, Aasif Mandvi, Tara Subkoff, Peter Giles, Ellen Pompeo, Michael Ryan Segal, Jeffrey Emerson, Guillermo Diaz, David Frank, Rocco Sisto, Aliya Campbell, Steven Gevedon.

UNDER THE TUSCAN SUN

A Buena Vista release of a Touchstone Pictures presentation of a Timnick Films/Blue Gardenia production. Producers: Tom Sternberg, Audrey Wells. Executive producers: Laura Fattori, Sandy Kroopf, Mark Gill. Director/Writer: Audrey Wells. Screen story: Wells, based on the book by Frances Mayes. Camera: Geoffrey Simpson. Editors: Andrew Marcus, Arthur Coburn. Music: Christophe Beck. In Technicolor, Panavision widescreen. Release date: Sept. 13, 2003. MPAA Rating: PG-13. Running time: 113 Min.
Cast: Diane Lane, Sandra Oh, Lindsay Duncan, Raoul Bova, Vincent Riotta, Guilia Steigerwalt, Pawel Szajda.

THE UNITED STATES OF LELAND

A Paramount Classics release of a Thousand Words presentation in association with MDP Worldwide of a Trigger Street production. Producers: Kevin Spacey, Bernie Morris, Palmer West, Jonah Smith. Executive producers: Mark Damon, Sammy Lee, Stewart Hall. Director/Writer: Matthew Ryan Hoge. Camera: James Glennon. Editor: Jeff Betancourt. Music: Jeremy Enigk. In color. Release date: Jan. 18, 2003. Running time: 108 Min.
Cast: Don Cheadle, Ryan Gosling, Chris Klein, Jena Malone, Lena Olin, Kevin Spacey, Michelle Williams, Martin Donovan, Ann Magnuson, Kerry Washington, Sherilyn Fenn.

UNPRECEDENTED: THE 2000 PRESIDENTIAL ELECTION

A Robert Greenwald Prods. presentation of a Public Interest Film production. Producers: Joan Sekler, Richard R. Perez. Executive producers: Robert Greenwald, Earl Katz. Directors: Richard R. Perez, Joan Sekler. Screenplay: William Haugse, Perez, Sekler. Camera: Perez. Editors: Haugse, Matt Martin. Music: Bobby Johnston. In color. Release date: Nov. 14, 2002. Running time: 50 Min. Documentary.

UPTOWN GIRLS

An MGM Pictures release of a GreeneStreet Films production. Producers: John Penotti, Fisher Stevens, Allison Jacobs. Executive producers: Joe Caracciolo Jr., Tim Williams, Boaz Yakin. Co-executive producers: Gary Winick, Vicki Cherkas. Director: Boaz Yakin. Screenplay: Julia Dahl, Mo Ogrodnik, Lisa Davidowitz. Story: Allison Jacobs. Camera: Michael Ballhaus. Editor: David Ray. Music: Joel McNeely. In color. Release date: July 30, 2003. MPAA Rating: PG-13. Running time: 93 Min.
Cast: Brittany Murphy, Dakota Fanning, Marley Shelton, Donald Faison, Jesse Spencer, Austin Pendleton, Heather Locklear.

VALLEY OF TEARS

A Seventh Art Releasing release of a David Sandoval & Perry Films presentation. Producer: Hart Perry. Executive producer: David Sandoval. Co-producer: Richard Lowe. Director: Hart Perry. Screenplay: Juan Gonzalez. Camera: Perry. Editor: Richard Lowe. Music: Phil Marsh. In DuArt color, DV. Release date: July 28, 2003. Running time: 86 Min. Documentary.
With: Juanita Valdez, Jesus Moya, Juan Guerra, Marcial Silva, Oscar Correa, Winnie Wetegrove, Paul Whitworth, Tocho Almendarez, Barbara Savage, Norris McGee, Mike Crowell, Larry Spence, Othal Brand, Adriana Flores, Pete Moreno, Fred Klosterman, Quina Flores.

VERONICA GUERIN

A Buena Vista Pictures (in U.S.)/Buena Vista Intl. (UK)(in U.K.) release of a Touchstone Pictures/Jerry Bruckheimer Films presentation. Producer: Bruckheimer. Executive producers: Chad Oman, Mike Stenson, Ned Dowd. Director: Joel Schumacher. Screenplay: Carol Doyle, Mary Agnes Donoghue. Camera: Brendan Galvin. Editor: David Gamble. Music: Harry Gregson-Williams. In Technicolor, Panavision widescreen. Release date: July, 29, 2003. MPAA Rating: R. Running time: 98 Min.
Cast: Cate Blanchett, Gerard McSorley, Ciaran Hinds, Brenda Fricker, Barry Barnes, Joe Hanley, David Murray, David Herlihy, Karl Shiels, Barry McEvoy, Alan Devine, Gerry O'Brien, Don Wycherley, Simon O'Driscoll, Paudge Beehan, Colin Farrell.

VERTICAL FRONTIER

A Peloton Prods. (Mill Valley, Calif.) production. Producer/Director: Kristi Denton Cohen. Writer: Alison Owens. Camera: Josh Helling, Hilary Morgan. Editor: Ben Galland. Music: Jeff Watson. In color/B&W, DigiBetaSP. Release date: June 8, 2003. Running time: 90 Min. Documentary.
Cast: David Brower, Yvon Chouinard, Lynn Hill, Jim Bridwell, Hans Florine, Royal Robbins.

VIEW FROM THE TOP

A Miramax Films release of a Brad Grey Pictures/Cohen Pictures production. Producers: Brad Grey, Matthew Baer, Bobby Cohen. Executive producers: Amy Slotnick, Robbie Brenner, Alan C. Blomquist. Co-producers: Laura Hopper, Francesca Silvestri, Elizabeth Fox Friedman. Director: Bruno Barreto. Screenplay: Eric Wald. Camera: Affonso Beato. Editor: Christopher Greenbury. Music: Theodore Shapiro. In Deluxe color, prints, Panavision widescreen. Release date: March 19, 2003. MPAA Rating: PG-13. Running time: 87 Min.
Cast: Gwyneth Paltrow, Christina Applegate, Mark Ruffalo, Candice Bergen, Joshua Malina, Kelly Preston, Rob Lowe, Mike Myers.

VIRGIN

A Full Moon Films presentation. Producer: Sarah Schenk. Executive producers: Robin Wright Penn, Raye Dowell, Deborah Kampmeier. Co-producer: Carolyn Demerice. Director/Writer: Deborah Kampmeier. Camera: Ben Wolf. Editor: Jane Pia Ambromowitz. In Swete Studios color, digital video. Release date: June 14, 2003. Running time: 113 Min.
With: Elisabeth Moss, Daphne Rubin Vega, Socorro Santiago, Peter Gerety, Stephanie Gatschet, Sam Riley, Charles Socarides, Christopher Wynkoop, Robin Wright Penn.

VOLCANOES OF THE DEEP SEA

An Imax presentation of a Stephen Low Co. and Rutgers U. production. Producers: Pietro Serapiglia, Alexander Low. Executive producer: James Cameron. Director: Stephen Low. Camera: William Reeve. Editor: James Lahti. Music: Michel Cusson. In color, Imax. Release date: Sept. 9, 2003. Running time: 41 Min. Documentary.
Narrator: Ed Harris.

WAKING UP IN RENO

A Miramax Films release of a Ben Myron/Crossfire Sound & Pictures production. Producers: Myron, Robert Salerno, Dwight Yoakam. Executive producers: Bob Weinstein, Harvey Weinstein, Jonathan Gordon, Jeremy Kramer. Co-producer: Bruce Heller. Director: Jonathan Brady. Screenplay: Brent Briscoe, Mark Fauser. Camera: William A. Fraker. Editor: Lisa Zeno Churgin. Music: Marty Stuart. In CFI color, Deluxe prints. Release date: Oct. 22, 2002. MPAA Rating: R. Running time: 91 Min.
Cast: Billy Bob Thornton, Charlize Theron, Natasha Richardson, Patrick Swayze, Holmes Osborne, Chelcie Ross, Penelope Cruz, Tony Orlando.

THE WANNABES

A Hoyts Distribution release of a Macquarie Film Finance, GO Films production. Producers: Nick Giannopoulos, Tom Burstall. Executive producer: Andrew Penney. Directors: Nick Giannopoulos. Screenplay: Giannopoulos, Chris Anastassiades, Ray Boseley. Camera: Dan Burstall. Editors: Peter Carrodus. Music: David Hirschfelder. In color. Release date: May 6, 2003. Running time: 94 Min.
Cast: Nick Giannopoulos, Russell Dykstra, Isla Fisher, Michael Carmen, Tony Nikolakopoulos, Lena Cruz, Costas Kilias.

WANT

A Slant Rhyme Entertainment presentation of a God Shaped Hole production. Producer: Michael Wohl, Divi Crocket, Brian Benson. Director/Writer: Michael Wohl. Camera: Robin McLeod. Editor: Wohl. Original music: Ledenhed, Sorry. In color, HD vid. Release date: Feb. 2, 2003. Running time: 98 Min.
With: Barry Alan Levine, Olin Hyde, Gillian Chadsey, Joan Bernier, Michael Wohl.

THE WEATHER UNDERGROUND

An Independent Television Service and KQED San Francisco presentation. Producers: Sam Green, Bill Siegel, Carrie Lozano, Marc Smolowitz. Executive producers: Christian Ettinger, Mary Harron, Sue Ellen McCann. Director: Sam Green, Bill Siegel. Camera: Andrew Black, Federico Salsano. Editors: Green, Dawn Logsdon. Music: Dave Cerf, Amy Domingues. In color/B&W, super 8mm/super 16mm/digital video. Release date: Jan. 22, 2003. Running time: 92 Min. Documentary.
With: Bernadine Dohrn, Mark Rudd, Brian Flanagan, David Gilbert, Bill Ayers, Naomi Jaffe, Todd Gitlin, Laura Whitehorn, Don Strickland, Kathleen Cleaver. Narrators: Lili Taylor, Pamela Z.

WEST BANK BROOKLYN

Producers: Ghazi Albuliwi, Christine Purcell. Director/Writer: Ghazi Albuliwi. Camera: Mitch Gross. Editor: Robert Tate. Music: Naseer Shamma. In color, Super-16. Release date: Nov. 11, 2002. Running time: 82 Min.

With: Charles Daniel Sandoval, Bronson Picket, Hany Kamal, Ghazi Albuliwi, Anil Kumar, Matt Conley, Sian Heder, Peter Coriaty, Denia Brache, Lissette Taveras, Stacie Linardos, Carlos Molina, Larry Marx.

WESTENDER

A MOB Prods. (Corvallis, Ore.) production. (International sales: Harris Tulchin and Assoc., Los Angeles.) Producers: Hans Hlawaty, Brock Morse. Director/Editor: Brock Morse. Screenplay: Jefferson Brassfield. Camera: Matt Molitor. Music: Rob Simonsen. In color, DigiBeta. Release date: June 9, 2003. Running time: 105 Min.

Cast: Blake Stadel, Rob Simonsen, John Rankin, Darlene Dadras, Kari Gjone, Rod James.

WHAT A GIRL WANTS

A Warner Bros. release presented in association with Gaylord Films of a Di Novi Pictures/Gerber Pictures production. Producer: Denise Di Novi, Bill Gerber, Hunt Lowry. Executive producers: E.K. Gaylord II, Alison Greenspan, Casey La Scala. Co-producer: Steven Harding. Director: Dennie Gordon. Screenplay: Jenny Bicks, Elizabeth Chandler, based on the screenplay and play "The Reluctant Debutante" by William Douglas Home. Camera: Andrew Dunn. Editor: Charles McClelland. Music: Rupert Gregson-Williams. In Technicolor, Panavision widescreen. Release date: March 25, 2003. MPAA Rating: PG. Running time: 95 Min.

Cast: Amanda Bynes, Colin Firth, Kelly Preston, Eileen Atkins, Anna Chancellor, Jonathan Pryce, Oliver James, Christina Cole.

WHAT ALICE FOUND

A Factory Films presentation in association with Highland Entertainment. Producer: Richard Connors. Executive producers: Don Wells, J.C. Chmiel. Director/Writer: A. Dean Bell. Camera: Richard Connors. Editor: Chris Houghton. In color, DV. Release date: Jan. 7, 2003. Running time: 96 Min.

Cast: Judith Ivey, Bill Raymond, Emily Grace, Jane Lincoln Taylor, Justin Parkinson, Michael C. Maronna, Katheryn Winnick, David Rose, John Knox, Tim Hayes, Lucas Papaelias, Clint Jordan.

WHERE'S THE PARTY YAAR?

An MM Films release of a Farid Virani presentation. Producer: Sunil Thakkar. Executive producers: Sandhya Thakkar, Farid Virani, Asha Virani. Director: Benny Mathews. Screenplay: Sunil Thakkar, Mathews, Soham Mehta, Rikesh Patel. Camera: Anthony Fennel. Editor: Shimit Amin. In Fotokem color. Release date: Aug. 26, 2003. Running time: 107 Min.

Cast: Kal Penn, Sunil Malhotra, Prem Shah, Serena Varghese.

WHOLE

A Frozen Feet Independent Prods. presentation. Producer/Director: Melody Gilbert. Camera: Gilbert. Editor: Charlie Gerszowski. Music: CXR. In color, DV. Release date: June 23, 2003. Running time: 55 Mln. Documentary.

THE WILD THORNBERRY'S MOVIE

A Paramount release of a Paramount Pictures, Nickelodeon Movies presentation of a Klasky Csupo production. Producers: Arlene Klasky, Gabor Csupo. Executive producers: Albie Hecht, Julia Pistor, Eryk Casemiro, Hal Waite. Co-producers: Tracy Kramer, Terry Thoren, Norton Virgien, Sean Lurie. Directors: Jeff McGrath, Cathy Malkasian. Screenplay: Kate Boutilier, based on characters created by Arlene Klasky, Gabor Csupo, Steve Pepoon, David Silverman, Stephen Sustarsic. Editor: John Bryant. Music: Drew Neumann. In Deluxe color, widescreen. Release date: Nov. 30, 2002. MPAA Rating: PG. Running time: 85 Min. Animated.

Voices: Lacey Chabert, Tom Kane, Tim Curry, Lynn Redgrave, Jodi Carlisle, Danielle Harris, Rupert Everett, Marisa Tomei, Melissa Greenspan, Kevin Michael Richardson, Obba Babatunde.

WILLARD

A New Line Cinema release of a Hard Eight Pictures production. Producers: James Wong, Glen Morgan. Executive producers: Bill Carraro, Toby Emmerich, Richard Brener. Director/Writer: Glen Morgan, based on a screenplay by Gilbert Ralston, based on the book "Ratman's Notebooks" by Stephen Gilbert. Camera: Robert McLachlan. Editor: James Coblentz. Music: Shirley Walker. In Alpha Cine color, Deluxe prints; Clairmont Camera: Systems widescreen. Release date: March 6, 2003. MPAA Rating: PG-13. Running time: 100 Min.

Cast: Crispin Glover, R. Lee Ermey, Laura Elena Harring.

WONDERLAND

A Lions Gate Films release of a Holly Wiersma/Lions Gate Films production. (International sales: Lions Gate Films Intl., Marina del Rey, Calif.) Producers: Wiersma, Michael Paseornek. Executive producers: Julie Yorn, Peter Kleidman, Randall Emmett, George Furla, Tom Ortenberg, Peter Block, Marc Butan, Michael Burns. Co-producers: Ali Forman, Scott Putnam. Director: James Cox. Screenplay: Cox, Captain Mauzner, Todd Samovitz, D. Loriston Scott. Camera: Michael Grady. Editor: Jeff McEvoy. Music: Cliff Martinez. In color. Release date: Sept. 9, 2003. MPAA Rating: R. Running time: 99 Min.

Cast: Val Kilmer, Kate Bosworth, Lisa Kudrow, Josh Lucas, Tim Blake Nelson, Dylan McDermott, Christina Applegate, Eric Bogosian, Carrie Fisher, Franky G., M.C. Gainey, Janeane Garofalo, Ted Levine.

WRONG TURN

A 20th Century Fox release of a Summit Entertainment and Constantin Film presentation of a Constantin Film/Summit Entertainment/McOne/Stan Winston production in association with Newmarket Capital Group. Producers: Erik Feig, Robert Kulzer, Stan Winston, Brian Gilbert. Executive producers: Mitch Horwits, Patrick Wachsberger, Don Carmody, Aaron Ryder. Co-executive producers: Sven Ebeling, Hagen Behring. Director: Rob Schmidt. Screenplay: Alan McElroy. Camera: John S. Bartley. Editor: Michael Ross. Music: Elia Cmiral. In Deluxe color. Release date: May 30, 2003. MPAA Rating: R. Running time: 84 Min.

Cast: Desmond Harrington, Eliza Dushku, Emmanuelle Chriqui, Jeremy Sisto, Kevin Zegers, Lindy Booth, Julian Richings, Garry Robbins, Ted Clark, Yvonne Gaudry, Joel Harris, David Huband.

YEAR OF THE BULL

An Animus Films presentation with LaSu Prods. Producers: Todd Lubin, Shelly Clippard, Susan Ehrhart, Jim Young. Director: Todd Lubin. Camera: Patrick Longman. Editor: Emir Lewis. Music: Dan the Automator, Trevor Pryce. In color, Super 16mm. Release date: June 15, 2003. Running time: 85 Min. Documentary.

THE YEAR THAT TREMBLED

A Kingdom County Prods. release of a Novel City Pictures production. Producers: Tyler Davidson, Scott Lax. Executive producers: Andrew Rayburn, Dennis Johnson. Director/Writer: Jay Craven, based on the novel by Scott Lax. Camera: John Foster, Jeff Barklage. Editor: Beatrice Sisul. Music: Jeff Claus, Judy Hyman. In Fuji Vision. Release date: Sept. 18, 2003. MPAA Rating: R. Running time: 104 Min.

Cast: Jonathan Brandis, Meredith Monroe, Marin Hinkle, Jonathan M. Woodward, Charlie Finn, Sean Nelson, Jay R. Ferguson, Kiera Chaplin, Fred Willard, Martin Mull, Lucas Ford, Henry Gibson.

YOU STUPID MAN

A New Legend Media/Artists Production Group presentation of an Apollo Media/YSM Filmproduktion GmbH production. Producers: Cathy Schulman, Alex Campbell, Rick Yorn, Tom Berry, Franck Hubner. Executive producers: Al Munteanu, Peter Popp, Gerald Schubert, Brian Burns. Director/Writer: Brian Burns. Camera: David Herrington. Editor: Bill Henry. Music: David Schwartz. In color. Release date: Oct. 18, 2002. Running time: 95 Min.

Cast: David Krumholtz, Milla Jovovich, Denise Richards, William Baldwin, Dan Montgomery Jr., Deborah Odell.

ZERO DAY

An Avatar presentation of a Professor Bright Films production. Producer: Ben Coccio. Executive producers: Richard Abramowitz, Adam Brightman. Director: Ben Coccio. Writer: Ben and Chris Coccio. Camera: Ben Coccio. Editor: Ben Coccio, David Shuff. In color, DV. Release date: Aug. 31, 2003. Running time: 92 Min.

With: Andre Keuck, Calvin Robertson, Rachel Benichak, Chris Coccio, Gerhard and Johanne Keuck, Pam and Steve Robertson.

FOREIGN FEATURE FILMS

(OCTOBER 1, 2002—SEPTEMBER 30, 2003)

Many of the following films have been released in a limited fashion at film festivals or other similar venues but have not yet been nationally distributed. Distribution company, director in parentheses, release date, running time, country and cast.

ABEL FERRARA: NOT GUILTY
(Rafi Pitts) Aug. 7, 2003. Running time: 80 Min. French. Abel Ferrara, Echo Danon, Frank DeCurtis, Pamela Tiffin. Documentary.

ACT NATURAL
(Pierre Olivier) June 8, 2003. Running time: 94 Min. French. Alice Carel, Pierre Olivier, Lawrence Collins, Caroline Gillain.

THE ACTORS
Momentum Pictures (in U.K.)/Miramax (in U.S.). (Conor McPherson) May 6, 2003. Running time: 90 Min. British-German. Michael Caine.

ADDICTED (JUNGDOK)
Showbox. (Park Yeong-hun) Nov. 14, 2002. Running time: 112 Min. South Korean. Lee Byeong-heon, Lee Mi-yeon, Lee Eul.

AFTERMATH: THE REMNANTS OF WAR
(Daniel Sekulich) Oct. 6, 2002. Running time: 73 Min. Canadian. Guy Momper, Henri Belot, Valery Shtrykov. Documentary.

THE AGE OF TERROR
(Jon Blair, Polly Williams, Dan Korn) Oct. 11, 2002. Running time: 200 Min. British. Narrator: Tim Piggot-Smith. Documentary.

THE AGRONOMIST
(Jonathan Demme) Aug. 5, 2003. Running time: 90 Min. U.S.-Haiti. Jean Dominique, Michele Montas. Documentary.

AILEEN: LIFE AND DEATH OF A SERIAL KILLER
(Nick Broomfield, Joan Churchill) May 1, 2003. Running time: 89 Min. Documentary. British.

ALEIJADINHO: PASSION, GLORY AND TORMENT
(Geraldo Santos Pereira) Nov. 29, 2002. Running time: 100 Min. Brazilian. Mauricio Goncalves, Maria Ceica, Antonio Naddeo.

ALEXANDRA'S PROJECT
Palace Films. (Rolf de Heer) Jan 28, 2003. Running time: 103 Min. Australian. Gary Sweet, Helen Buday, Bogdan Koca.

ALEXEI AND THE SPRING
(Seiichi Motohashi) May 9, 2003. Running time: 105 Min. Documentary. Japanese.

ALL I'VE GOT
(Keren Margalit) June 1, 2003. Running time: 69 Min. Israeli. Lea Szlanger, Nathan Gogan, Igal Naor.

ALL THE FINE PROMISES
(Jean-Paul Civeyrac) Aug. 9, 2003. Running time: 85 Min. French. Jeanne Balibar, Bulle Ogier, Eva Truffaut, Renaud, Valerie Crunchant.

ALL TOMORROW'S PARTIES
(Yu Lik-wai) May 16, 2003. Running time: 96 Min. French. Jo Yeong-weon, Diao Yi'nan, Zhao Weiwei, Na Ren.

ALMODOU
(Amadou Thior) Dec. 8, 2002. Running time: 85 Min. Senegal. Doudou Guillaume Faye, Ndeye Fatou Dione.

ALMOST ORDINARY STORY
(Milos Petricic) July 11, 2003. Running time: 78 Min. Serbia-Montenegro. Milica Zaric, Vuk Toskovic, Hristina Popovic.

AMAZING STORY
(Masahiro Kobayashi) Aug. 11, 2003. Running time: 103 Min. Japanese. Kazuki Kitamura, Keiko Oginome, Jiro Sato.

AMERICAN COUSINS
Hollywood Classic Entertainment. (Donald Coutts) July 6, 2003. Running time: 89 Min. British. Danny Nucci, Shirley Henderson, Gerald Lepkowski, Vincent Pastore, Dan Hedaya.

ANA AND THE OTHERS
(Celina Murga) April 21, 2003. Running time: 80 Min. Argentine. Camila Toker.

ANATOMY 2
Columbia TriStar Germany. Feb. 10, 2003. Running time: 101 Min. German. Barnaby Metschurat, Herbert Knaup, Heike Makatsch.

ANDAAZ
(Raj Kanwar) June 12, 2003. Running time: 152 Min. Indian. Akshay Kumar, Lara Dutta, Priyanka Chopra, Aman Verma, Johny Lever.

AN ANGEL FOR MAY
(Harley Cokeliss) Oct. 3, 2002. Running time: 99 Min. British. Matthew Beard, Tom Wilkinson, Charlotte Wakefield.

AN ANGEL IN CRACOW
Kino SwiatIntl. (Artur Wiecek) May 18, 2003. Running time: 84 Min. Polish. Krzysztof Globisz, Ewa Kaim, Jerzy Trela.

ANGST (DER ALTE AFFE ANGST)
Warner Bros. (Oskar Roehler) Feb. 14, 2003. Running time: 92 Min. German. Andre Hennicke, Marie Baumer, Vadim Glowna.

ANITA & ME
Icon. (Metin Huseyin) Nov. 28, 2002. Running time: 93 Min. British. Chandeep Uppal, Anna Brewster, Sanjeev Bhaskar.

ANTENNA
(Kazuyoshi Kumakiri) Aug. 30, 2003. Running time: 117 Min. Japanese. Ryo Kase, Akemi Kobayashi, Daisuke Kizaki.

ANY WAY THE WIND BLOWS
(Tom Barman) Aug. 7, 2003. Running time: 127 Min. Belgian. Natali Broods, Frank Vercruyssen, Diane de Belder, Eric Kloeck.

THE ARCHANGEL'S FEATHER
(Luis Manzo) Jan. 10, 2003. Running time: 95 Min. Venezuela. Ivan Tamayo, Roque Valero, Elaiza Gil.

ARDOR (MILAE)
Cinema Service. (Byeon Yeong-ju) Nov. 15, 2002. Running time: 109 Min. South Korean. Kim Yun-jin, Lee Jong-weon, Gye Seong-yong.

THE ARM OF JESUS
(Andre van der Hout) Jan. 24, 2003. Running time: 69 Min. Dutch. Ferry Heijne, Frank van den Bops, Huug van Tienhoven.

ASAKUSA KID
(Makoto Shinozaki) Sept. 27, 2002. Running time: 111 Min. Japanese. Hakase Suidobashe, Sujitarou Tamabukuro, Saburou Ishikura.

THE ASSASSINATED SUN
(Abdelkrim Bahloul) Aug. 27, 2003. Running time: 85 Min. French-Belgian-Tunisian-Algerian. Charles Berling, Mehdi Dehbi.

AT FIVE IN THE AFTERNOON
(Samira Makhmalbaf) May 15, 2003. Running time: 106 Min. Iranina-French. Agheleh Rezaie, Abdolgani Yousefrazi, Razi Mohebi.

AT THE END OF THE NIGHT
Minerva Pictures. (Salvatore Piscicelli) June 13, 2003. Running time: 90 Min. Italian. Ennio Fantastichini, Elena Sofia Ricci, Ida Di Benedetto, Ricky Tognazzi, Stefania Orsola Garello, Anna Ammirati.

ARAGAMI
(Ryuichi Kitamura) June 13, 2003. Running time: 82 Min. Japanese. Takao Oswa, Masaya Kato, Kanae Uotani.

ARMAAN
(Honey Irani) May 17, 2003. Running time: 153 Min. Indian. Amitabh Bachchan, Anil Kapoor, Preity Zinta, Gracy Singh, Aamir Bashir, Randhir Kapoor, Arun Bali, Ahmed Khan, Prithvi Zutsi.

AYURVEDA: THE ART OF BEING
Kino International (in U.S.)/Mongrel Media. (Pan Nalin) Oct. 1, 2002. Running time: 102 Min. German-Swiaa. Documentary.

BABIJ JAR
(Jeff Kanew). Feb. 11, 2003. Running time: 112 Min. German-Belarus. Michael Degen, Barbara De Rossi, Katrin Sass.

BABUSYA
(Lidia Bobrova) July 6, 2003. Running time: 95 Min. Russian. nina Shubina, Olga Onishenko, Anna Ovsyannikova.

BAD BOYS - A TRUE STORY
Buena Vista Intl. (Aleksi Makela). May 14, 2003. Running time: 119 Min. Finnish. Jasper Paakkonen, Lauri Nurkse, Peter Franzen, Niko Saarela, Vesa-Matti Loiri, Elsa Saisio, Risto Tuorila.

BAD EGGS
Roadshow Films (TOny Martin) July 3, 2003. Running time: 98 Min. Austrian. Mick Molloy, Bob Franklin, Judith Lucy, Bill Hunter.1

BAGHDAD ON/OFF
Vents du Sud Prods. (Saad Salman) March 10, 2003. Running time: 86 Min. French. Documentary. *Salah Al Hamdani, Saad Salman.*

BALLROOM
(Patrick Mario Bernard, Xavier Brillat, Pierre Trividic) April 23, 2003. Running time: 96 Min. French. Patrick Mario Bernard, Pierre Trividic, Peter Bonke, Jean-Yves Jouannais.

BANK BAN
Bunyik Entertainment. (Csaba Kael) Nov. 1, 2002. Running time: 118 Min. Hungarian. Atilla Kiss B., Sandor Solymon, Kolos Kovats.

THE BARBECUE PEOPLE
(David Ofek, Yossi Madmoni) May 18, 2003. Running time: 102 Min. Israeli. Victor Ida, Dana Ivgi, Raymonde Abecassis, Makram Khouri.

THE BARONESS AND THE PIG
(Michael Mackenzie). Sept. 9, 2002. Running time: 95 Min. Canadian. Patricia Clarkson, Caroline Dhavernas, Colm Feore.

BASTONI - THE STICK HANDLERS
There's Enterprise Inc. (Kazuhiko Nakamura) Sept. 18, 2002. Running time: 102 Min. Japanese. Shunsuke Matsuoka, Yuka Kojima.

THE BASQUE GAME, SKIN AGAINST STONE
Golem Distribution. (Julio Medem) Sept. 21, 2003. Running time: 115 Min. Spanish. Documentary.

B.B. AND THE CORMORANT
Medusa Film. (Edoardo Gabbriellini) May 23, 2003. Running time: 89 Min. Italian. Edoardo Gabbriellini, Carolina Felline, Selen.

BEAR'S KISS
Istituto Luce. (Sergei Bodrov) Sept. 3, 2002. Running time: 99 Min. German-Swedish-Russian-Spanish-French-Italian. Rebecka Liljeberg.

BEAUTY QUEEN OLIVIA
(Federica Sparano) Oct. 7, 2002. Running time: 96 Min. Italian. Carolina Felline, Eleonora Materazzo, Manrico Gammarota.

BED AND BREAKFAST
Mars Distribution. (Claude Duty) Aug. 5, 2003. Running time: 107 Min. French. Marina Fois, Philippe Harel, Annie Gregorio, Julie Depardieu.

BEIJING SUBURB
(Hu Ze). Nov. 24, 2002. Running time: 84 Min. Chinese. Wang Chuyu, Zhao Junzhi, Lu Lin, Xu Ruotao, Hu Ze, Zhou Qing, Liu Kejia.

BELLEVILLE RENDEZ-VOUS
Diaphana. (Sylvain Chomet) May 17, 2003. Running time: 82 Min. Animated. French-Belgian-Canadian. Animated. Character voices: Jean-Claude Donda, Michel Robin, Monica Viegas.

BELLISSIMA
(Artur Urbanski). Sept. 5, 2002. Running time: 61 Min. Polish. Maria Goralczyk, Ewa Kasprzyk, Pawel Wilczak, Maria Morin-Kieler.

BELOVED SISTER (FAHR ZUR HOLLE, SCHWESTER!)
(Oskar Rohler). Jan. 29, 2003. Running time: 87 Min. German. Iris Berben, Hannelore Elsner, Anton Rattinger, Wolfgang Joop.

BERLIN SYMPHONY
(Thomas Schadt) Jan. 11, 2003. Running time: 79 Min. German. Documentary.

THE BEST OF YOUTH
(Marco Tullio Giordana) May 19-20, 2002. Running time: 358 Min. Italian. Luigi Lo Cascio, Alessio Boni, Adriana Asti, Sonia Bergamasco.

BETTER THAN SEX
(Su Chao-pin, Lee Feng-bor) July 16, 2003. Running time: 93 Min. Taiwanese. Michael Wong, Bobby Chen, Ginny Liu, Leon Dai.

BETTING ON LOVE
(Didier Aufort) Feb. 14, 2003. Running time: 101 Min. Ivory Coast. Isabelle Beke, Djedje Apali, Virgile M'Fioulou, Aissatou Thiam.

BETWEEN LAND AND SKY
Lantia. (Giuseppe Ferlito) April 19, 2003. Running Time: 95 min. Italian. Davide Gemmani, Antonella D'Arcangelo, Fabio Fulco.

BEYOND RE-ANIMATOR
Filmax. (Brian Yuzna) July 22, 2003. Running time: 93 Min. Spanish. Jeffrey Combs, Jason Barry, Elsa Pataky, Enrique Arce.

BHAVUM: EMOTIONS OF BEING
(Satish Menon) May 28, 2003. Running time: 111 Min. Indian. Mita Vasisht, Murali Menon, Jyothirmayee.

BHOOT
(Ramgopal Varma) June 12, 2003. Running time: 115 Min. Indian. Ajay Devgan, Urmila Matondkar, Nana Patekar, Rekha, Fardeen Khan.

A BIG GIRL LIKE YOU
(Christophe Blanc) Feb. 9, 2003. Running time: 90 Min. French. Mercedes Cecchetto, Laura Locatelli, Sarah Zidhane.

BIG GIRLS DON'T CRY
Columbia TriStar Film (Germany). (Maria von Heland) Sept. 22, 2002. Running time: 87 Min. German. Anna Maria Muhe, Karoline Herfurth.

THE BIRCH-TREE MEADOW
(Marceline Loridan-Ivens) Feb. 14, 2003. Running time: 91 Min. French-German-Polish. Anouk Aimee, August Diehl, Marilu Marini.

BITTER SWEAT
(Sonia Valentin) Feb. 11, 2003. Running time: 114 Min. Puerto Rico. Domingo Quinones, Alba Nydia Diaz, Sonia Valentin, Yamaris Latorre.

A BIZARRE LOVE TRIANGLE
(Lee Moo-Young) June 26, 2003. Running time: 92 Min. South Korean. Kong Hyo-Jin, Cho Eun-Ji, Choi Kwang-Il.

BLACKBALL
Icon Film Distribution. (Mel Smith) Aug. 5, 2003. Running time: 94 Min. British. Paul Kaye, James Cromwell, Alice Evans.

BLACK TAPE: A TEHRAN DIARY - THE VIDEOTAPE FARIBORZ KAMBARI FOUND IN THE GARBAGE
(Fariborz Kamkari) Sept. 7, 2002. Running time: 83 Min. Iranian. Shilan Rahmani, Parviz Moasese, Farzin Saboni, Shokhan Ghafari.

BLESS YOU, PRISON
K. Films Amerique. (Nicolae Margineanu) Sept. 3, 2003. Running time: 88 MIn. Romanian. Maria Ploae, Dorina Lazar, Ecaterina Nazarie.

BLIND SHAFT
(Li Yang) Feb. 12, 2003. Running time: 92 Min. German-Hong Kong. Li Yixiang, Wang Shuangbao, Wang Baoqiang, An Jing, Bao Zhenjiang.

BL,.M
(Sean Walsh) June 13, 2003. Running time: 111 Min. Irish. Stephen Rea, Angeline Ball, Hugh O'Conor, Patrick Bergin, Alan Devlin.

THE BLONDS
(Albertina Carri) April 23, 2003. Running time: 83 Min. Analia Couceyro.

BLUE
(Hiroshi Ando) Sept. 10, 2002. Running time: 116 Min. Japanese. Mikako Ichikawa, Manami Konishi, Asami Imajuku, Jun Murakami.

BLURRED
Becker Entertainment. (Evan Clarry) Oct 1, 2002. Running time: 95 Min. Australian. Matthew Newton, Craig Horner, Kristian Schmid.

BODYSONG
(Simon Pummell) Jan. 30, 2003. Running time: 81 Min. British.

BODY TO BODY
Pathe Distribution. (Francois Hanss) April 17, 2003, Running time: 98 Min. French. Emmanuelle Seigner, Philippe Torreton.

BOLA DE NIEVE
(Jose Sanchez-Montes) Feb.17, 2003. Running time: 73 Min. Spanish-Cuban-Mexican. Documentary.

BOLLYWOOD/HOLLYWOOD
Mongrel Media. (Deepa Mehta) Sept. 7, 2002. Running time: 105 Min. Canadian. Rahul Khanna, Lisa Ray, Moushumi Chatterjee.

BOLLYWOOD QUEEN
(Jeremy Wooding) Jan. 20, 2003. Running time: 89 Min. British. Preeya Kalidas, James McAvoy, Ciaran McMenamin, Kat Bhathena.

BON VOYAGE
ARP Selection. (Jean-Paul Rappeneau) April 16, 2003. Running time: 114 Min. French. Isabelle Adjani, Gerard Depardieu, Virginie Ledoyen.

A BOOKSHELF ON TOP OF THE SKY: TWELVE STORIES ABOUT JOHN ZORN
(Claudia Heuermann) Dec. 20, 2002. Running time: 82 Min. German. Documentary.

THE BOOKSHOP
(Nawfel Saheb-Ettaba) Feb. 10, 2003. Running time: 102 Min. Tunisian-French. Hend Sabri, Ahmed El-Haffiene, Martine Gafsi.

BORDER LINE
(Lee Sang-Il). Oct. 9, 2002. Running time: 117 Min. Japanese. Tetsu Sawaki, Ayaka Maeda, Yumi Asou, Ken Mitsuishi, Jun Murakami.

THE BOTTOM OF THE SEA
(Damian Szifron) April 30, 2003. Running time: 96 Min. Argentine. Daniel Hendler, Dolores Fonzi, Anibal - Gustavo Garzon.

THE BOYS FROM COUNTY CLARE
(John Irvin) Sept. 12, 2003. Running time: 90 Min. Irish-British-German. Colm Meaney, Bernard Hill, Andrea Corr.

THE BOY WHO WANTED TO BE A BEAR
Gebeka Films. (Jannik Hastrup) Dec. 28, 2002. Running time: 76 Min. Danish-French. Animation.

A BREACH IN THE WALL
Sonet Film. (Jimmy Karlsson) Dec. 4, 2002. Running time: 98 Min. Swedish. Magnus Krepper, Sverrir Gudnason.

BREAKING UP
(Domingos De Oliveira) May 20, 2003. Running time: 116 Min. Brazilian. Domingos De Oliveira, Priscila Rozembaum.

BREAK OF DAWN (ENTRE CHIENS ET LOUPS)
Metropolitan Filmexport. (Alexandre Arcady) Sept. 15, 2002. Running time: 110 Min. French. Richard Berry, Said Taghmaoui.

BREAK OUT
Cinema Service. (Jang Hang-jun) Dec. 14, 2002. Running time: 102 Min. South Korean. Kim Seung-woo, Cha Seung-weon.

BRIGHT FUTURE
(Kiyoshi Kurosawa) May 19, 2003. Running time: 92 Min. Japanese. Joe Odagiri, Tadanobu Asano, Tatsuya Fuji, Takashi Sasano.

BRIGHT YOUNG THINGS
Icon Film Distribution. (Stephen Fry) Sept. 6, 2003. Running time: 105 Min. British. Emily Mortimer, Stephen Campbell Moore.

BROKEN WINGS
Sony Pictures Classics (in N. America). (Nir Bergman) Feb. 9, 2003. Running time: 83 Min. Israeli. Orli Zilberschatz-Banai, Maya Maron.

BUDDY
Sandrew-Metronome. (Morten Tyldum) July 6, 2003. Running time: 0 Min. Norwegian. Nicolai Cleve Broch, Aksel Hennie, Pia Tjelta.

BULGARIAN LOVERS
(Eloy de la Iglesia) Feb. 13, 2003. Running time: 101 Min. Spanish. Fernando Guillen Cuervo, Dritan Biba, Pepon Nieto, Anita Sinkovic.

BULLIT AND RIPER
Gaumont. (Eric Lartigau) June 16, 2003. Running time: 89 Min. French. Kad Olivier , Gerard Darmon, Jean-Paul Rouve.

BUNGALOW
(Ulrich Kohler) Oct. 9, 2002. Running time: 100 Min. German. Lennie Burmeister, Tryne Dyrholm, David Striesow, Nicole Glaser.

BUS 174
(Jose Padilha) Oct. 8, 2002. Running time: 133 Min. Brazilian. Documentary.

THE BUTTERFLY
(Philippe Muyl) Jan. 1, 2002. Running time: 80 Min. French. Michel Serrault, Claire Bouanich, Nade Dieu.

CABIN FEVER (NAR NETTENE BLIR LANGE)
(Mona J. Hoel) Jan. 26, 2001. Running time: 102 Min. Norwegian. Gorild Mauseth, Svein Scharfenberg, Kari Simonsen.

CALA, MY DOG
(Lu Xuechang) Feb. 12, 2003. Running time: 101 Min. Chinese. Ge You, Ding Jiali, Li Bin, Li Qinqin, Xia Yu, Li Min, Fu Biao, Pang Yuemin.

CALENDAR GIRLS
Buena Vista Intl. (in U.K.)/Touchstone Pictures (in U.S.). (Nigel Cole) July 29, 2003. Running time: 107 Min. British. Helen Mirren, Julie Walters, John Alderton, Linda Bassett, Annette Crosbie, Philip Glenister, Ciaran Hinds, Celia Imrie, Geraldine James, Penelope Wilton, George Costigan, Graham Crowden, John Fortune.

CALIXTO THE LANDLORD
(Sami Kafati) May 8, 2003. Running time: 110 Min. Honduras. Jose Luis Lopez, Marisela Bustillo, Saul Toro, Educard Bahr.

CAPE NORTH
Thule Film. (Carlo Luglio) March 7, 2003. Running time: 102 Min. Italian. Emanuele Valente, Francesco Vitiello, Alberto Cretara.

CARLOS AGAINST THE WORLD
(Chiqui Carabante) Sept. 24, 2002. Running time: 91 Min. Spanish. Julian Villagran, Victoria Mora, Juanma Lara, Silvia Rey, Manolo Solo.

THE CARPENTER'S PENCIL
Warner Sogefilms. (Anton Reixa) March 26, 2003. Running time: 106 Min. Spanish. Tristan Ulloa, Luis Tosar, Maria Adanez.

THE CAT RETURNS
Gaumont Buena Vista Intl. (Hiroyuki Morita) Aug. 11, 2003. Running time: 75 Min. Japanese. Animated.

CAUCASIAN ROULETTE
(Fyodor Popov) July 6, 2003. Running time: 83 Min. Russian. Nina Usatova, Tatyana Mesherkina, Anatoly Goryachev, Sergei Garmash.

CECILIA
Pablo. (Antonio Morabito) Apr. 28, 2003. Running time: 85 min. Italian. Pamela Villoresi, Gianni Grima, Anna Terzano, Erika Manni.

THE CENTURY OF THE SELF
(Adam Curtis) April 18, 22. Running time: 240 Min. Biritsh. Documentary.

CHALTE CHALTE
Eros Intl. (Aziz Mirza) June 13, 2003. Running time: 165 Min. Indian. Shah Rukh Khan, Rani Mukherjee, Jas Arora, Satish Shah, Jayshree T, Rajiv Verma, Lillette Dubey, Johny Lever, Aditya Pancholi.

THE CHAMELEON
01 Distribution. (Luca Barbareschi) June 8, 2003. Running time: 111 Min. Italian. Luca Barbareschi, Rocco Papaleo, Luigi Maria Burruano.

CHAMPION
(Kwak Kyung-taek) Sept. 6, 2002. Running time: 117 Min. South Korean. Yu Oh-seong, Chae Min-seo, Yun Seung-weon.

CHANDNI BAR
(Madhur Bhandarkar) Jan. 14, 2003. Running time: 125 Min. Indian.

CHEKHOV'S MOTIFS
(Kira Moratova) Oct. 9, 2002. Running time: 121 Min. Russian-Ukraian. Sergei Bekhterev, Nina Ruslanova, Natalya Buzko.

CHILDREN OF LOVE
(Geoffrey Enthoven) Oct. 21, 2002. Running time: 87 Min. Belgian. Nathalie Stas, Winnifred Vigilante, Michael Philpot, Olivier Ythier.

THE CHILD I NEVER WAS
(Kai S. Pieck) Feb. 9, 2003. Running time: 86 Min. German. Tobias Schenke, Sebastian Urzendowsky, Ulrike Bliefert.

CHILL OUT!
Warner Sogefilms. (Felix Sabroso) July 9, 2003. Running time: 98 Min. Spanish. Pepon Nieto, Candela Pena, Loles Leon, Ruben Ochandiano.

CHINESE ODYSSEY 2002
(Jeff Lau) Oct. 5, 2002. Running time: 105 Min. Hong Kong. Tony Leung, Faye Wong, Vicki Zhao Wei, Chang Chen, Rebecca Pan.

THE CHOICE OF HERCULES
(Harada) Nov. 9, 2002. Japanese. Koji Yakusho, Ryudo Uzaki, Yuki Amami, Masatoh Eve, Makoto Fujita.

CHOKHER BALI: A PASSION PLAY
(Rituparno Ghosh) Aug. 8, 2003. Running time: 170 Min. Indian. Lily Chakrabarti, Prosenjit Chatterjee, Tota Raychaudhuri.

CHOROPAMPA: THE PRICE OF GOLD
(Ernesto Cabellos) July 23, 2003. Running time: 75 Mln. Peru. Documentary. Lot Saavedra, Juana MArtinez, Santiago Garcia.

CHOUCHOU
Warner Bros. Transatlantic. (Merzak Allouache) March 19, 2003. Running time: 101 Min. French. Gad Elmaleh, Alain Chabat.

CHRISTMAS
(Gregory King) Aug. 11, 2003. Running time: 86 Min. New Zealand. David Hornblow, Helen Pearse Otene, Darien Takle.

CHRISTMAS ON THE NILE
Filmauro. (Neri Parenti) Dec. 23, 2002. Running time: 110 Min. Italian-Spanish-British. Christian De Sica, Massimo Boldi, Enzo Salvi.

THE CLASH: WESTWAY TO THE WORLD
3DD Entertainment. (Don Letts) July 15, 2003. Running time: 80 Min. British. Documentary. Terry Chimes, Nicky Headon.

THE CLASSIC
Cinema Service. (Kwak Jae-yong) April 18, 2003. Running time: 132 Min. South Korean. Son Ye-jin, Jo Seung-woo, Jo In-seong.

CLAUDE SAUTET, OR THE INVISIBLE MAGIC
(N.T. Binh) May 22, 2003. Running time: 83 Min. Documentary. French-German. Bertrand Tavernier, Philippe Sarde, Jean-Paul Rappeneau, Graziella Sautet, Jose Giovanni, Jean-Louis Livi, Jean-Loup Dabadie.

CLAY DOLLS (ARAIS AL TEIN)
(Nouri Bouzid) Feb. 1, 2003. Running time: 99 Min. Tunisian-French-Morocco. Hend Sabri, Ahmed Hafiane, Oumeya Ben Hafsia.

CLEANING UP!
(Rostislav Aalto) June 7, 2003. Running time: 80 Min. Finnish. Documentary.

CLEAN SWEEP
(Oded Davidoff) May 18, 2003. Running time: 90 Min. Israeli. Yael Hadar, Alon Abutbul, Gal Zaid, Shmulik Calderone, Dalit Kahan.

CLOSE, CLOSING, CLOSURE
(Ram Loevy) Jan. 16, 2003. Running time: 53 Min. Isreal-French. Documentary.

CLOSE TO LEO
(Christophe Honore) July 29, 2003. Running time: 90 Min. French. Yannis Lespert, Pierre Mignard, Marie Bunel, Rodolphe Pauly.

CLOWN IN' KABUL
(Enzo Balestrieri, Stefano Moser) Sept. 6, 2002. Running time: 58 Min. Italian. Hunter "Patch" Adams, Leonardo Spina. Documentary.

CLUB LE MONDE
ScreenProjex. (Simon Rumley) Oct. 4, 2002. Running time: 79 Min. British. Dawn Steele, Allison McKenzie, Brad Gorton.

THE COAST GUARD (HAEANSEON)
(Kim Ki-duk) Nov. 14, 2002. Running time: 92 Min. South Korean. Jang Dong-geon, Park Ji-ah, Kim Jeong-hak, Yu Hae-jin.

CODE 46
United Artists. (Michael Winterbottom) Sept. 3, 2003. Running time: 85 Min. British. Tim Robbins, Samantha Morton, Jeanne Balibar.

COFFEE, TEA OR ME?
(Brita McVeigh) Oct. 5, 2002. Running time: 70 Min. New Zealand. Documentary.

A COLD SUMMER
(Paul Middleditch) June 14, 2003. Running time: 86 Min. Australian. Teo Gebert, Olivia Pigeot, Susan Prior.

THE COLORS OF MUSIC
(Maryte Kavaliauskas, Seth Schneidman) June 8, 2003. Running time: 85 Min. French. Documentary. David Hockney, Max Charruyer.

THE COLOUR OF HAPPINES
(Jozsef Pacskovszky) Feb. 3, 2003. Running time: 87 Min. Hungarian. Anna Gyorgyi, Ildiko Bacsa, Margit Foldessy, Erik Desfosses.

COMANDANTE
(Oliver Stone) Jan. 13, 2003. Running time: 99 Min. U.S.-Spanish. Documentary.

COMING AND GOING
(Joao Cesar Monteiro) May 15, 2003. Running time: 180 Min. Portugese-French. Joao Cesar Monteiro, Rita Pereira Marques.

COMPANY
(Ram Gopal Varma) Feb. 9, 2003. Running time: 155 Min. Indian. Ajay Devgan, Vivek Oberoi, Manisha Koirala, Mohanlal. Documentary.

THE COMPANY
Sony Pictures Classics (in U.S.). (Robert Altman) Sept. 8, 2003. Running time: 112 Min. U.S.-German. Neve Campbell, Malcolm McDowell, James Franco, Barbara Robertson, William Dick.

COMRADE BOYKENZHAYEV
(Yusup Razykov) July 9, 2003. Running time: 74 Min. Uzbekistan. Farkhod Abdullayev, O'lmes Allxo'jayev, Matluba Allmova.

CONCENT
(Shun Nakahara) July 14, 2003. Running time: 110 Min. Japanese. Miwako Ichikawa, Jun Murakami, Miho Tsumiki.

CONDOR: AXIS OF EVIL
(Rodrigo Vazquez) May 19, 2003. Running time: 89 Min. Documentary. French. Manuel Contreras, Juan Arrom, Carlos Alfredo Lobo, Osvaldo Romo, Enrique Gorriaran Merlo, Martin Almada.

CONEY ISLAND BABY
(Amy Hobby) June 30, 2003. Running time: 93 Min. U.S.-Irish. Karl Geary, Laura Fraser, Hugh O'Conor, Tom Hickey.

CONSPIRACY OF SILENCE
(John Deery) June 9, 2003. Running time: 86 Min. British. Jonathan Forbes, Jason Barry, Brenda Fricker, Hugh Bonneville, John Lynch.

THE COST OF LIVING
Pathe Distribution. (Philippe Le Guay) July, 1, 2003. Running time: 109 Min. French. Vincent Lindon, Fabrice Luchini, Geraldine Pailhas.

COPACABANA
BR Distribution. (Carla Camurati) March 1, 2003. Running time: 94 Min. Brazilian. Marco Nanini, Laura Cardoso, Walderez de Barros.

THE CORDON
(Goran Markovic) Aug. 30, 2003. Running time: 87 Min. Serbian-Montengro. Marko Nikolic, Dragan Petrovic, Nenad Jezdic.

CORN IN PARLIAMENT
Vega Distribution. (Jean-Stephane Bron) Aug. 8, 2003. Running time: 90 Min. Swiss. Maya Graff, Josef Kunz. Documentary.

COUNSELOR DE GREGORIO
01. (Pasquale Squitieri) Feb. 4, 2003. Running time: 104 Min. Italian. Giorgio Albertazzi, Ciro Capano, Anna Tognetti, Gabriele Ferzetti.

COWARDS BEND THE KNEE
(Guy Maddin) May 11, 2003. Running time: 64 Min. Canadian. Darcy Fehr, Melissa Dionisio, Amy Stewart, Tara Birtwhistle, Luis Negin.

A COURTESAN
(Nia diNata) Jan. 14, 2003. Running time: 120 Min. Indonesian. Ferry Salim, Lola Amaria, Ninik L. Karim, Robby Tumewu, Lulu Dewayanti.

CRACKERJACK
Roadshow Films. (Paul Moloney) Oct. 22, 2002. Running time: 92 Min. Australian. Mick Molloy, Bill Hunter, Frank Wilson, Monica Maughan.

CRAVAN VS. CRAVAN
Sherlock Films. (Isaki Lacuesta) Nov. 21, 2002. Running time: 99 Min. Spanish. Frank Nicotra, Eduardo Arroyo. Documentary.

CRAZY ABOUT PARIS
(Pago Balke, Elke Besuden) Jan. 11, 2003. Running time: 90 Min. German. Wolfgang Goettsch, Frank Grabski, Corinna Harfouch.

CRIMSON GOLD
Wellspring. (Jafar Panahi) May 24, 2003. Running time: 95 Min. Iranian. Hussein Emadeddin, Kamyar Sheissi.

CRUDE
(Paxton Winters) June 16, 2003. Running time: 83 Min. U.S.-Turkish. Paul Schneider, David Connolly, Yigit Ozsener, Ipek Deger.

THE CRUELEST DAY
(Ferdinando Vincentini) Sept. 1, 2003. Running time: 100 Min. Italian. Giovanna Mezzogiorno, Rade Sherbedgia, Angelo Infanti.

CRY NO MORE
(Narjiss Nejjar) May 5, 2003. Running time: 116 Min. Moroccan-French. Siham Assif, Khalid Benchegra, Raouia, Rafiqua Belhaj.

DAFT PUNK & LEIJI MATSUMOTO'S INTERSTELLA 5555: THE 5TORY OF THE 5ECRET 5TAR SYSTEM
(Kazuhisha Takenouchi) May 20, 2003. Running time: 67 Min. Animated. Japanese-French.

DALKEITH
High Point Films & Television. (Leigh Sheehan) Oct 5, 2002. Running time: 93 Min. Australian. Ray Barrett, Gus Mercurio, Judy Banks.

THE DAMNED AND THE SACRED (DANS, GROZNY, DANS)
(Jos de Putter) Jan. 31, 2003. Running time: 79 Min. Dutch. Documentary.

DANCING IN THE DUST
(Asghar Farhadi) May 21, 2003. Running time: 95 Min. Iranian. Faramarz Gharibian, Yousef Khodaparast, Baran Kosari.

DANGEROUS SUMMER
(Aigars Grauba) July 6, 2003. Running time: 105 Min. Latvian. Uldis Dumpis, Arturs Skrastins, Inese Cauna, Janis Reinis.

DANNY DECKCHAIR
20th Century Fox (Jeff Balsmeyer) June 24, 2003. Running time: 101 Min. Austrian. Rhys Ifans, Mirando Otto, Justine Clarke.

DARK CITIES (CIUDADES OSCURAS)
(Fernando Sarinana) Sept. 25, 2002. Running time: 113 Min. Mexican. Alejandro Tommasi, Alonso Echanove, Bruno Bichir, Demian Bichir.

DARKNESS
Filmax (in Spain)/Dimension Films (in U.S.). (Jaume Balaguero) Sept. 10, 2002. Running time: 102 Min. Spanish-U.S. Anna Paquin.

DARK WOODS
Oro A/S Film (Norway). (Pal Oie) May 15, 2003. Running time: 84 Min. Norwegian. Bjorn Floberg, Kristoffer Joner, Eva Rose, Marko Kanic.

DARNA MANA HAI
(Prawaal Raman) July 30, 2003. Running time: 118 Min. Indian. Vivek Oberoi, Saif Ali Khan, Boman Irani, Nana Patekar.

DAY OF THE WACKO
Vision Film Distribution Co. (Poland). (Marek Koterski) Feb. 9, 2003. Running time: 93 Min. Polish.

DEADLY OUTLAW: REKKA
(Takashi Miike) Jan. 24, 2003. Running time: 96 Min. Japanese. Riki Takeuchi, Ryosuke Miki, Kenichi Endo, Mika Katsumura.

DEAD MAN'S MEMORIES
(Markus Heltschl) July 5, 2003. Running time: 88 Min. Sylvie Testud, Miguel Guilherme, Ana Bustorf, Rita Blanco.

THE DEATH OF KLINGHOFFER
(Penny Woolcock) Jan. 24, 2003. Running time: 120 Min. British. Sanford Sylvan, Christopher Maltman, Yvonne Howard, Tom Randle.

DEATHWATCH
Pathe Pictures. (Michael J. Bassett) Dec. 9, 2002. Running time: 95 min. German-British. Jamie Bell, Ruaidhri Conroy, Laurence Fox.

DEEP BREATH
(Parviz Shahbazi) May 21, 2003. Running time: 86 Min. Iranian. Mansour Shahbazi, Maryam Palyzban, Saeed Amini.

DEEWANGEE
(Anees Bazmee) April 12, 2003. Running time: 168 Min. Indian. Ajay Devgan, Akshaye Khanna, Urmila Matondkar, Vijayendra Ghatge.

DEKADA 70
(Chito S. Rono) June 28, 2003. Running time: 128 Min. Filipino. Vilma Santos, Christopher De Leon, Piolo Pascual, Marvin Augustin.

DESIRE
Lolafilms Distribucion. (Gerardo Vera) Oct. 27, 2002. Running time: 106 Min. Spanish. Leonor Watling, Leonardo Sbaraglia, Cecilia Roth.

DESTINY HAS NO FAVORITES
(Alvaro Velarde) July 24, 2003. Running time: 87 Min. Peru. Angie Cepeda, Monica Steuer, Paul Vega, Tatiana Astengo, Rebeca Raez.

THE DEVIL KNOWS WHY
(Roman Vavra) Feb. 12, 2003. Running time: 104 Min. Czech-Slovakian. Tatiana Pauhofova, Iva Janzurova, Stepan Kubista.

DEVOT
(Igor Zaritzki) Feb. 12, 2003. Running time: 89 Min. German. Annett Renneberg, Simon Boer, Tomek Piotrowski, Sophia Littkopf.

DIL KA RISHTA
(Naresh Malhotra) Jan. 18, 2003. Running time: 149 Min. Indian. Aishwarya Rai, Arjun Rampal, Raakhee, Priyanshu Chatterjee.

DISSONANCES
(Jerome Cornuau) June 7, 2003. Running time: 110 Min. French. Jacques Gamblin, Berenice Bejo, Didier Flamand.

DISTANT
(Nuri Bilge Ceylan) May 16, 2003. Running time: 109 Min. Turkish. Muzaffer Ozdemir, Mehmet Emin Toprak, Zuhal Gencer Erkaya.

DISTANT LIGHTS
Prokino. (Hans-Christian Schmid) Feb. 11, 2003. Running time: 104 Min. German. Ivan Shvedov, Sergei Frolov.

DIVAN
(Pearl Gluck) May 11, 2003. Running time: 77 Min. Documentary. U.S.-Hungarian.

DOCUMENTARIST
(Harutyun Khachatryan) July 9, 2003. Running time: 60 Min. Armenian. Suren Babayan.

DO I LOVE YOU?
(Lisa Gornick) June 21, 2003. Running time: 73 Min. British. Lisa Gornick, Raquel Cassidy, Ruth Posner, Brendan Gregory.

THE DOG'S CALLED FIAT 128
SE TIL VENSTRE, DER ER EN SVENSKER
Nordisk Film Biografdistribution. (Natasha Arthy) Jan. 27, 2003. Running time: 92 Min. Danish. Sidse Babett Knudsen, Bjorn Kjellmann.

DOG DAYS (CANICULA)
UIP. (Alvaro Garcia-Capelo) Aug. 10, 2002. Running time: 113 Min. Spanish. Sergi Calleja, Farid Fatmi, Aitor Merino, Elvira Minguez.

DOG HEADS (HUNDSKOEPFE)
(Karsten Laske) Nov. 2, 2002. Running time: 93 Min. German. Arnd Klawitter, Esther Esche, Simon Werner, Axel Prahl, Marko Brautigam.

DOGVILLE CONFESSIONS
(Sami Saif) May 23, 2003. Running time: 55 Min. Documentary. Danish. Nicole Kidman, Lars von Trier, Stellan Skarsgard, Ben Gazzara, Lauren Bacall, Paul Bettany, James Caan.

DOING TIME (KIMUSHO NO NAKA)
(Yoichi Sai) Oct. 8, 2002. Running time: 92 Min. Japanese. Tsutomu Yamazaki, Teruyuki Kagawa, Tomoro Taguchi, Yutaka Matsushige.

DON'T WORRY, IT'S JUST A PHASE
Folkets Bio. (Cecilia Neant-Falk) Jan. 30, 2003. Running time: 74 Min. Swedish. Documentary.

DOT THE I
(Matthew Parkhill) Jan. 19, 2003. Running time: 92 Min. British-Spanish. Gael Garcia Bernal, Natalia Verbeke, James D'Arcy, Tom Hardy.

DOUBLE AGENT
Showbox. (Kim Hyeon-jeong) May 15, 2003. Running time: 123 Min. South Korean. Han Seok-gyu, Goh So-yeong, Cheon Ho-jin.

DOWN BY LOVE
(Tamas Sas) Jan. 31, 2003. Running time: 92 Min. Hungarian. Patricia Kovacs, Gabor Mate, Jozsa Hacser, Rita Tallos, Imre Csuja.

DREAM CUISINE
(Li Ying) June, 8, 2003. Running time: 134 Min. Chinese-Japanese. Documentary.

THE DREAMERS
Fox Searchlight. (Bernardo Bertolucci) Aug. 31, 2003. Running time: 116 Min. French-Italian-British. Michael Pitt, Eva Green, Louis Garrel.

DRIFTERS
(Wang Xiaoshuai) May 20, 2003. Running time: 120 Min. Hong Kong. Duan Long, Shu Yan, Zhao Yiwei, Tang Yang, Jin Peizhu, Ke Da, Huang Yiqun, Zheng Jianlun, Liu Juyong, Su Youjie, Zeng Meijuan.

DRIVE
(Sabu) Feb. 10, 2003. Running time: 100 Min. Japanese. *Shinichi Tsutsumi, Ko Shibasaki, Ren Osugi, Masanobu Ando.*

DROWNED OUT
(Franny Armstrong) April 28, 2003. Running time: 75 Min. Indian-British. Documentary.

DRY WOOD FIERCE FIRE
Mandarin Films. (Wilson Yip) July 13, 2002. Running time: 91 Min. Hong Kong. Louis Koo, Miriam Yeung, Flora Chen, Wyman Wong.

EAGER BODIES
Pan Europeenne. (Xavier Giannoli) May 7, 2003. Running time: 90 Min. French. Laura Smet, Nicolas Duvauchelle, Marie Denarnaud.

ECHELON: THE SECRET POWER
(David Korn-Brzoza) Jan. 26, 2003. Running time: 82 Min. French. Documentary. *Narrator: Francois Devienne.*

EDI
(Piotr Trzaskalski) Dec. 7, 2002. Running time: 100 Min. Polish. Henryk Golebiewski, Jacek Braciak, Jacek Lenartowicz.

E = MC2
(Benjamin Fry) Jan. 7, 1996. Running time: 100 Min. British. Jeremy Piven, Kelli Williams, Liza Walker, James Villiers.

800 BULLETS
Warner Sogefilms. (Alex de la Iglesia) Oct. 25, 2002. Running time: 124 Min. Spanish. Sancho Gracia, Angel de Andres Lopez.

18 YEARS LATER
Bac Films. (Coline Serreau) Feb. 5, 2003. Running time: 89 Min. French. Andre Dussollier, Michel Boujenah, Roland Giraud.

8:17 P.M. DARLING STREET
(Bernard Emond) May 20, 2003. Running time: 101 Min. Canadian. Luc Picard, Guylaine Tremblay, Diane Lavallee.

EL ALAMEIN: THE LINE OF FIRE
Medusa Film. (Enzo Monteleone) Oct. 31, 2002. Running time: 117 Min. Italian. Paolo Briguglia, Pierfrancesco Favino, Luciano Scarpa.

ELDRA
(Tim Lyn) Jan. 19, 2003. Running time: 93 Min. British-Wales. Iona Wyn Jones, Rhys Richards, Leisa Mereid, John Ogwen.

ELENA DIMITRIEVNA DIAKONOVA: GALA
Nirvana Films. (Silvia Munt) July 13, 2003. Running time: 108 Min. Spainish. Documentary. Tatiana Pigariova, Jeff Fenholt.

EL LEYTON: UNTIL DEATH DO US PART
(Gonzalo Justiniano) Sept. 25, 2002. Running time: 96 Min. Chilean-French. Juan Pablo Saez, Siboney Lo, Luis Wigdorsky.

ELIANA, ELIANA
(Riri Riza) Oct. 10, 2002. Running time: 86 Min. Indonesian. Rachel Sayidina, Jajang C. Noer, Henidar Amroe, Arswendi Nasution.

ELINA AS IF I WASN'T THERE
Sonet Film. (Klaus Haro) Nov. 4, 2002. Running time: 77 Min. Swedish-Finnish. Natalie Minnevik, Bibi Andersson, Marjaana Maijala.

ELSEWHERE
(Nicolaus Geyrhalter) Sept 6, 2002. Running time: 240 Min. Austrian. Mohamed Bada, Abardagh Kalka, Boula Kalka. Documentary.

ENDGAME
TLA. (Gary Wicks) Jan. 11, 2003. Running time: 113 Min. British. Daniel Newman, Corey Johnson, Toni Barry, Mark McGann.

ENTER THE CLOWNS (CHOUJUE DENGCHANG)
(Cui Zi'en) Oct. 9, 2002. Running time: 82 Min. Chinese. Chen Bing, Na-ren-qi-mu-ge, Yu Bo, Yu Xiaoyu, Jia Ge.

EPOCA: THE MAKING OF HISTORY
(Andreas Hoessli, Isabella Huser) Oct. 7, 2002. Running time: 90 Min. Swiss.

EPSTEIN'S NIGHT
(Urs Egger) Jan. 28, 2003. Running time: 86 Min. German-Swiss. Mario Adorf, Bruno Ganz, Otto Tausig, Gunter Lamprecht.

ERIC CLAPTON AND FRIENDS
(Jana Bokova) Oct. 4, 2002. Running time: 80 Min. British. Eric Clapton, Andy Fairweather Low, Steve Gadd. Documentary.

EROICA
(Simon Cellan Jones) Aug. 20, 2003. Running time: 84 Min. British. Ian Hart, Tim Piggott-Smith, Frank Finlay, Claire Skinner, Jack Davenport.

EROTIC TALES
Music
(Amos Kollek) Aug. 31, 2003. Running time: 30 Min. German. Dallas Roberts, Lara Harris, Tara Culp, Victor Argo, Anjelica Torn.
NR. 23 or How the Honey Spoon Got Between the Sheets
(Bernd Heiber) Aug. 31, 2003. Running time: 30 Min. German. Sabine Vitua, Marc Richter.
The Gallery
(Jos Stelling) Aug. 31, 2003. Running time: 27 Min. German. Gene Bervoets, Anouska.

THE EVENT
(Thom Fitzgerald) Jan. 19, 2003. Running time: 110 Min. Canadian. Parker Posey, Olympia Dukakis, Don McKellar, Sarah Polley.

EVERYONE LOVES ALICE
Sonet Film. (Richard Hobert) May 30, 2002. Running time: 116 Min. Swedish. Lena Endre, Marie Richardson, Mikael Persbrandt.

EVIL
(Mikael Hafstrom) May 16, 2003. Running time: 113 Min. Swedish. Andreas Wilson, Henrik Lundstrom, Gustaf Skarsgard, Linda Zilliacus, Marie Richardson, Johan Rabeus, Kjell Bergqvist, Magnus Roosman.

THE EXAM
(Nasser Refaie) Sept. 6, 2002. Running time: 80 Min. Iranian. Raya Nassiri, Farzin Aghaie, Aghdas Khoshmou, Nahid Refaie.

EXTREME OPS
Paramount. (Christian Duguay) Nov. 26, 2002. MPAA Rating: PG-13. Running time: 93 Min. German-British. Devon Sawa, Bridgette Wilson-Sampras, Rupert Graves, Rufus Sewell, Heino Ferch, Joe Absolom.

EXXXORCISMS
(Jaime Humberto Hermosillo) Sept. 11, 2002. Running time: 77 Min. Mexican. Alberto Estrella, Jose Juan Meraz, Patricia Reyes Spindola.

EYES OF A BEAUTY
(Guan Hu) Nov. 8, 2002. Running time: 125 Min. Chinese. Ma Yili, Huang Yiqun, Yang Qianqian, Liu Juyong, Lei Junshen, Hu Xiaoguang.

FACING THE TRUTH (AT KENDE SANDHEDEN)
Nordisk Film Biografdistribution. (Nils Malmros) Aug. 23, 2002. Running time: 98 Min. Danish. Jens Albinus, Soren Ostergaard.

FALLING ANGELS
(Scott Smith) Sept. 10, 2003. Running time: 101 Min. Canadian. Miranda Richardson, Callum Keith Rennie, Katherine Isabelle.

FALLING SKY
(Gunnar Vikene) Jan. 27, 2003. Running time: 83 Min. Norwegian. Kristoffer Joner, Maria Bonnevie, Kim Bodnia, Hildegun Riise.

FAMILY
(Sami Martin Saif, Phie Ambo-Nielsen) Sept. 25, 2002. Running time: 90 Min. Danish.

FANFAN LA TULIPE
EuropaCorp Distribution. (Gerard Krawczyk) May 14, 2003. Running time: 97 Min. French. Vincent Perez, Penelope Cruz, Didier Bourdon.

FAR FROM HOME
(Yu Zhong) Jan. 18, 2003. Running time: 99 Min. Chinese. Liu Xuan, Xu Jinglei, Daniel Chan, Cui Lin, Ding Cheng, Ailiya, Law Kar-ying.

FATHER AND SON
Wellspring. (Alexander Sokurov) May 24, 2003. Running time: 83 Min. German. Andrei Shetinin, Alexei Neimyshev, Alexander Rasbash.

FATHER AND SONS
Gaumont (in France)/Allied Atlantis Vivafilm (in Canada). (Michel Boujenah) Aug. 23, 2003. Running time: 97 Min. French-Canadian. Philippe Noiret, Charles Berling, Bruno Putzulu, Pascal Elbe.

FAT PIZZA
Roadshow. (Paul Fenech) March 25, 2003. Running time: 96 Min. Austrian. Paul Fenech, Paul Nakad, Johnny Boxer, Tahir Bilgic.

FEAR AND TREMBLING
Bac Distribution. (Alain Corneau) March 12, 2003. Running time: 107 Min. French. Sylvie Testud, Kaori Tsuji, Taro Suwa, Bison Katayama.

FEAR X
(Nicolas Winding Refn) Jan. 20, 2003. Running time: 91 Min. Danish-British-Canadian. John Turturro, Deborah Kara Unger.

FEATHERS IN MY HEAD
(Thomas de Thier) May 6, 2003. Running time: 118 Min. Belgian-French. Sophie Museur, Francis Renaud, Ulysse De Swaef.

FEDERICO FELLINI-THROUGH THE EYES OF OTHERS
(Eckhart Schmidt) July 6, 2003. Running time: 89 Min. German. Documentary. Anouk Amiee, Dino De Laurentiis, Anita Akberg.

THE FIFTH REACTION
(Tahmineh Milani) May 18, 2003. Running time: 106 Min. Iranian. Niki Karimi, Jamshid Hashempour, Merila Zareie.

FILM IST. (7-12)
(Gustav Deutsch) Sept. 29, 2002. Running time: 93 Min. Austrian. Documentary.

THE FINAL CURTAIN
UIP (in U.K.)/Universal (in U.S.). (Patrick Harkins) Jan. 30, 2003. MPAA rating: R. Running time: 84 Min. British. Peter O'Toole.

FINE DEAD GIRLS
(Dalibor Matanic) Jan. 14, 2003. Running time: 80 Min. Crotatian. Olga Pakalovic, Nina Violic, Inge Appelt, Kresimir Mikic, Ivica Vidovic.

FIREDANCER
(Jawed Wassel) Feb. 2, 2003. Running time: 79 Min. U.S.-Afghanistan. Baktash Zaher, Yasmine Weiss, Sophia Cameron, Yunis Azizi.

THE FIRST AMENDMENT
(Song Gyeong-shik) june 10, 2003. Running time: 107 Min. South Korean. Ye Ji-weon, Im Seong-min.

THE FIVE OBSTRUCTIONS
(Jorgen Leth, Lars von Trier) Aug. 29, 2003. Running time: 91 Min. Danish-Belgian- Swiss-French. Jorgen Leth, Lars von Trier, Jacqueline Arenal, Daniel Hernandez Rodriguez. Documentary.

FIX: THE STORY OF AN ADDICTED CITY
(Nettie Wild) Sept. 10, 2002. Running time: 92 Min. Canadian. Documentary.

FLASH OF A DREAM
(Robert Fox) Aug. 12, 2002. Running time: 59 Min. Danish. Documentary.

THE FLOWER OF EVIL
MK2. (Claude Chabrol) Jan. 7, 2003. Running time: 105 Min. French. Nathalie Baye, Benoit Magimel, Suzanne Flon, Bernard Le Coq.

FLOWERS OF BLOOD
Alta Films. (Myriam Mezieres, Alain Tanner) June 9, 2003. Running time: 100 Min. Swiss-French-Spanish. Myriam Mezieres, Tess Barthes, Louise Szpindel, Bruno Todeschini, Anne Fassio.

FOOLS
(Tom Schreiber) June 11, 2003. Running time: 93 Min. German. Christoph Bach, Victoria Deutschmann, Hannelore Lubeck.

THE FORCED MARCH
Artes Prods. (Nikolai Stambula) Feb. 11, 2003. Running time: 116 Min. Russian. Vladimir Volga, Olga Chursina, Eugene Kosirev.

FORD TRANSIT
(Hany Abu-Assad) June 19, 2003. Running time: 84 Min. Dutch. Documentary. Rajai, Azmi Bishara, Hanan Ashrawi.

FOREST
(Benedek Fliegauf) Jan. 31, 2003. Running time: 91 Min. Hungarian. Rita Braun, Barbara Csonka, Edit Lipcsei, Katalin Meszaros, Ilka Sos.

THE FOREST
(Didier Ouenangare, Bassek ba Kobhio) May 19, 2003. Running time: 93 Min. Central African. Eriq Ebouaney, Nadege Beausson-Diagne.

FOREST WALKERS
Spin Film. (Ivan Vojnar) Jan. 24, 2003. Running time: 95 Min. Czech-Slovakian-French. Jiri Schmitzer, Zdenek Novak, Jitka Prosperi.

FOR MY CHILDREN
Women Make Movies. (Michal Aviad) April 27, 2003. Running time: 65 Min. Israeli. Documentary.

FOR ONE MORE HOUR WITH YOU
(Alina Marazzi) Jan. 17, 2003. Running time: 55 Min. Italian. Documentary.

FOR SHE'S A JOLLY GOOD FELLOW
Ad Vitam. (Siegrid Alnoy) May 16, 2003. Running time: 102 Min. French. Sasha Andres, Carlo Brandt, Catherine Mouchet., Eric Caravaca, Pierre-Felix Graviere, Jacques Spiesser, Mireille Roussel.

FOUL KING
(Do Minh Tuan) Jan. 18, 2003. Running time: 101 Min. Vietnamese. Nguyen Bich Ngoc, Vo Hoai Nam, Tran Hanh, Cuong Tuc.

FREE RADICALS
(Barbara Albert) Aug. 9, 2003. Running time: 120 Min. Austrian-German-Swiss. Kathrin Resetarits, Ursula Strauss, Georg Friedrich.

FRESCOES
(Alexander Gutman) Jan. 25, 2003. Running time: 96 Min. Russian-German. Documentary.

FUSE
(Pjer Zalica) Aug. 10, 2003. Running time: 111 Min. Bosnian-Herzegovina-Austrian-Turkish-French. Enis Beslagic, Bogdan Diklic.

GABRIEL OROZCO
(Juan Carlos Martin) June 6, 2003. Running time: 78 Min. Mexican. Gabriel Orozco, Pablo Soler Frost, Robert Storr, Ann Temkin, Kasper Konig. Documentary.

GACACA, LIVING TOGETHER IN RWANDA?
(Anne Aghion) June 26, 2003. Running time: 55 Min. French-U.S. Documentary.

GALINDEZ
(Ana Diez) Sept. 26, 2002. Running time: 85 Min. Spanish-Cubian. Documentary.

GALLANT GIRLS
(Barbara Teufel) June 27, 2003. Running time: 95 Min. German. Jana Straulino, Ursula Renneke, Katja Danowski, Mieke Schymura.n

GAMBLING, GODS AND LSD
Odeon. (Peter Mettler) Oct. 1, 2002. Running time: 180 Min. Canadian-Swiss. Documentary.

GAME OVER: KASPAROV AND THE MACHINE
Odeon Films. (Vikram Jayanti) Sept. 5, 2003. Running time: 87 Min. Canadian. Garry KAsparov, Frederic Friedel. Documentary.

GAZ BAR BLUES
Alliance Atlantis Vivafilm. (Louis Belanger) Aug. 27, 2003. Running time: 115. Canadain. Serge Theriault, Gilles Renaud.

GEORGIE GIRL
(Annie Goldson, Peter Wells) Nov. 2, 2002. Running time: 70 Min. Documentary. New Zealand.

GINOSTRA
(Manuel Pradal) Sept. 13, 2002. Running time: 138 Min. French. Harvey Keitel, Andie MacDowell, Harry Dean Stanton.

GIRAFFES
(Tzahi Grad) May 18, 2003. Running time: 115 Min. Israeli. Meital Dohan, Liat Glick, Tinkerbell, Micha Selektar, Gal Zaid.

GIRLIE
(Benjamin Tucek) Release date: Feb. 1, 2003. Running time: 83 Min. Cast: Dorota Nvotova, Jana Hubinska. Czech-Slovenian.

GIRL WITH A PEARL EARRING
Lions Gate Films (in U.S.). (Peter Webber) Aug. 31, 2003. Running time: 99 Min. British-Luxembourgs. Colin Firth, Scarlett Johansson.

THE GLOW
(Igal Bursztyn) March 17, 2003. Running time: 86 Min. Israeli. Tinkerbell, Asi Dayan, Rivka Michaeli, Yair Rubin.

GOD IS AFRICAN
Ster-Kinekor. (Akin Omotoso) Feb. 7, 2003. Running time: 90 Min. South African. Hakeem Kae Kazim, Sami Sabiti, Esmeralda Bihi.

GOD IS BRAZILIAN
(Carlos Diegues) Sept. 9, 2003. Running time: 110 Min. Brazilian. Antonio Fagundes, Paloma Duarte, Wagner Moura.

GOLDFISH MEMORY
(Liz Gill) March 22, 2003. Running time: 88 Min. Irish. Flora Montgomery, Sean Campion, Fiona Glascott, Keith McErlean.

GOMEZ & TAVARES
SND. (Gilles Paquet-Brenner) April 10, 2003. Running time: 109 Min. French. Stomy Bugsy, Titoff, Elodie Navarre, Jean Yanne.

GOODBYE, DRAGON INN
(Tsai Ming-liang) Aug. 28, 2003. Running time: 81 Min. Taiwanese. Lee Kang-sheng, Chen Shiang-chyi, Kiyonobu Mitamura.

GOOD BYE LENIN!
Warner Bros. Germany. (Wolfgang Becker) Feb. 8, 2003. Running time: 121 Min. German. Daniel Bruehl, Katrin Sass, Maria Simon.

A GOOD LAWYER'S WIFE
(Im Sand-soo) May 20, 2003. Running time: 105 Min. South Korean. Mun So-ri, Hwang Jeong-min, Yun Yeo-jeong.

GOOD MORNING, NIGHT
01 Distribution. (Marco Bellocchio) Sept. 3, 2003. Running time: 106 Mln. Italian. Maya Sansa, Luigi Lo Cascio, Roberto Herlitzka.

THE GOSPEL OF JOHN
(Philip Saville) Sept. 12, 2003. Running time: 180 Mln. Canadian-British. Henry Ian Cusick, Christopher Plummer, Daniel Kash.

GO WEST!
Cineclassic. (Philippe Ramos) Jan. 29, 2003. Running time: 84 Min. French. Anne Azoulay, Philippe Garziano, Frederic Bonpart.

GO WEST, YOUNG MAN!
(Peter Delpeut, Mart Dominicus) Feb. 1, 2003. Running time: 79 Min. Dutch. John Milius, William Fraker, Annie Proulx. Documentary.

GOZU
(Takashi Miike) May 17, 2003. Running time: 130 Min. Japanese. Hideki Sone, Sho Aikawa, Kimika Yoshino, Shohei Hino, Keiko Tomita.

THE GREAT DANCE: A HUNTER'S STORY
Ster-Kinekor. (Craig Foster, Damon Foster) Release date: March 1, 2003. Running time: 53 Min. Nqate Xqamxebe, Karoha "Pro" Langwane. South African. Documentary.

THE GREAT GATO
Hispano Foxfilm. (Ventura Pons) Jan. 23, 2003. Running time: 105 Min. Spanish. Carmen Alvarez, Jaume Sosa. Documentary.

A GREAT LITTLE BUSINESS
Rezo Films. (Eric Veniard) Jan. 7, 2003. Running time: 87 Min. French. Denis Podalydes, Clovis Cornillac, Axelle Laffont, Husky Kihal.

GRIMM
A-Film Distribution. (Alex van Warmerdam) Sept. 10, 2003. Running time: 104 Min. Canadian. Halina Reijn, Jacob Derwig, Carmelo Gomez, Elvira Minguez, Ulises Dumont. Documentary.

GULPILIL: ONE RED BLOOD
(Darlene Johnson) Feb. 28, 2003. Running time: 56 Min. Australian. David Gulpilil, Phillip Noyce, Jack Thompson. Documentary.

THE GUY IN THE GRAVE NEXT DOOR
Sonet Film. (Kjell Sundvall) June 10, 2002. Running time: 94 Min. Swedish. Elisabet Carlsson, Michael Nyquist, Annika Olsson.

H
A Line. (Lee Jong-hyeok) June 8, 2003. Running time: 106 Min. South Korean. Yeom Jeong-ah, Ji Jin-heui.

HACKER
MGE. (Janusz Zaorski) April 27, 2003. Running time: 86 Min. Polish. Bartosz Obuchowski, Katarzyna Smutniak, Piotr Miazga, Pawel Wilczak, Boguslaw Linda, Pawel Delag.

1/2 THE RENT
(Marc Ottiker) Jan. 27, 2003. Running time: 92 Min. German. Stephan Kampwirth, Doris Schretzmayer, Natascha Bub, Alexander Beyer.

THE HANDCUFF KING
(Arto Koskinen) June 11, 2003. Running time: 90 Min. Finish-Swedish. Miikka Enbuske, Emil Lundberg.

HANDFUL OF BULLETS
(Una Celma) July 7, 2003. Running time: 87 Min. Latvian-Swedish. Janis Murnieks, Harijs Spanovskis, Kristine Nevarauska.

HAPPINESS COSTS NOTHING
Lucky Red. (Mimmo Calopresti) Feb. 11, 2003. Running time: 95 Min. Italian-French-Swiss. Mimmo Calopresti, Vincent Perez.

HAPPY BIRTHDAY!
(Csaba Fazekas) Feb. 2, 2003. Running time: 100 Min. Hungarian. Gergely Kocsis, Eszter Onodi, Judit Hernadi, Gabor Mate.

HAVANA SUITE
Nirvana. (Fernando Perez) Sept. 15, 2003. Running time: 80 Min. Spanish-Cubian.

HEADNOISE
(Andrej Kosak) Jan. 13, 2003. Running time: 90 Min. Slovenian. Jernej Sugman, Ksenija Misic, Uros Potocnik, Radko Polic, Petar Arsovski.

THE HEART IS ELSEWHERE
01 Distribution. (Pupi Avati) Feb. 9, 2003. Running time: 107 Min. Italian. Neri Marcore, Giancarlo Giannini, Vanessa Incontrada.

HEART OF AMERICA: HOMEROOM
(Uwe Boll) Feb. 13, 2003. Running time: 87 Min. Canadian-German. Jurgen Prochnow, Elisabeth Rosen, Michael Belyea, Clint Howard.

THE HEART OF ME
(Thaddeus O'Sullivan) Sept. 8, 2002. Running time: 95 Min. British. Helena Bonham Carter, Olivia Williams, Paul Bettany, Eleanor Bron.

THE HEART OF MEN
Bac Films. (Marc Esposito) March 5, 2003. Running time: 106 Min. French. Gerard Darmon, Jean-Pierre Darroussin, Bernard Campan.

HELP I'M A BOY!
(Oliver Dommenget) Sept. 17, 2002 Running time: 95 Min. German. Sarah Hannemann , Nick Seidensticker, Philipp Blank, Pinkas Braun.

HERO
Beijing New Picture Film Co. (in China)/Edko Films (in H.K.)/Miramax (in U.S.). (Zhang Yimou) Dec. 30, 2002. Running time: 93 Min. Chinese-Hong Kong. Jet Li, Tony Leung Chiu-wai, Maggie Cheung.

THE HERO: LOVE STORY OF A SPY
(Anil Sharma) April 16, 2003. Running time: 183 Min. Indian. Sunny Deol, Preity Zinta, Priyanka Chopra, Kabir Bedi, Amrish Puri.

THE HEXER (WIEDZMIN)
(Marek Brodzki) Nov. 2, 2002. Running time: 129 Min. Polish. Michal Zebrowski, Zbigniew Zamachowski, Maciej Kozlowski.

H.I.J.O.S. SPLIT SOUL
(Carmen Guarini, Marcelo Cespedes) Jan. 28, 2003. Running time: 78 Min. Argentine. Documentary.

HIS BROTHER
(Patrice Chereau) Feb. 11, 2003. Running time: 88 Min. French. Bruno Todeschini, Eric Caravaca, Nathalie Boutefeu, Catherine Ferran.

THE HONOURABLE WALLY NORMAN
Becker Entertainment. (Ted Emery) June 6, 2003. Running time: 87 Min. Australian. Kevin Harrington, Alan Cassell, Shaun Micallef.

HOPE SPRINGS
Buena Vista Intl. (in U.K.)/Buena Vista (in U.S.). (Mark Herman) April 15, 2003. MPAA Rating: PG-13. Running time: 90 Min. British-U.S. Colin Firth, Heather Graham, Minnie Driver, Mary Steenburgen.

HORSE FEVER: THE MANDRAKE STING
Warner Bros. Italia. (Carlo Vanzina) Oct. 30, 2002. Running time: 104 Min. Italian. Gigi Proietti, Nancy Brilli, Rodolfo Lagana.

HORSEPLAY
Buena Vista Intl. (Stavros Kazantzidis) Sept. 30, 2002. Running time: 92 Min. Australian. Marcus Graham, Tushka Bergen, Jason Donovan.

HOTEL DANUBIO
Columbia TriStar Spain. (Antonio Gimenez-Rico) May 2, 2003. Running time: 93 Min. Spanish. Santiago Ramos, Carmen Morales, Mariola Fuentes, Maria Asquerino, Jose Sazatornil.

HOTELS
(Aldo Paparella) April 23, 2003. Running time: 95 Min. Argentine. Noemi Amaya, Fernando Carballo, Anahi Paz, Jorge Richter.

THE HOURS OF THE DAY
(Jaime Rosales) May 5, 2003. Running time: 101 Min. Spanish. Alex Brendemuhl, Agata Roca, Maria Antonia Martinez, Pape Monsoriu.

HOUSE OF THE DEAD
(Uwe Boll) Feb. 15, 2003. Running time: 90 Min. German-U.S.-Canadian. Jonathan Cherry, Tyron Leitso, Clint Howard, Ona Grauer.

THE HOUSE ON TURK STREET
CDI Compagnia Distribuzione Internazionale-Medusa Film. (Bob Rafelson) Oct. 29, 2002. Running time: 103 Min. Canadian-U.S.-German. Samuel L. Jackson, Milla Jovovich, Stellan Skarsgard.

HOW IT ALL WENT DOWN
(Silvio Pollio) Sept. 3, 2003. Running time: 90 Min. Canadian. Silvio Pollio, Daniela Evangelista, Franco Valenti, Paige Gray.

HUNGARIAN BEAUTY
(Peter Gothar) Feb. 3, 2003. Running time: 112 Min. Hungarian. Gabor Mate, Dorottya Udvaros, Gabi Hamori, Agi Szirtes, Anna Szandtner.

A HUNGARIAN PASSPORT
(Sandra Kogut) Dec. 21, 2002. Running time: 74 Min. French-Hungarian-Brazilian-Belgian. Documentary.

HURRICANES
(Enrique Colina) May 15, 2003. Running time: 122 Min. Cubian-Spanish-French. Mijail Mulkay, Indira Valdes, Mario Balmaseda, Klara Badiola, Renny Arozarena, Yaima Torres, Raul Pomares.

I AM EMMA
Istituto Luce. (Francesco Falaschi) Nov. 5, 2002. Running time: 87 Min. Italian. Cecilia Dazzi, Marco Giallini, Pierfrancesco Favino.

I CAPTURE THE CASTLE
(Tim Fywell) Jan. 11, 2003. Running time: 111 Min. British. Romola Garai, Rose Byrne, Henry Thomas, Marc Blucas, Bill Nighy.

I, CESAR
EuropaCorp Distribution. (Richard Berry) April 13, 2003. Running time: 97 Min. French. Jules Sitruk, Jean-Philippe Ecoffey.

IDENTITY KILLS
(Soren Voigt) Feb. 9, 2003. Running time: 81 Min. German. Brigitte Hobmeier, Daniel Lommatzch, Mareike Alscher, Julia Blankenburg.

I DON'T KNOW WHAT YOUR EYES DID TO ME
(Lorena Munoz, Sergio Wolf) April 21, 2003. Running time: 64 Min. Documentary. Argentine. Ada Falcon, Anibal Ford, Rolando Goyaud, Jose Martinez Suarez, Miguel Ciacci, Oscar Del Priore.

THE IGUAZU EFFECT
Cre-Accion Films. (Pere Joan Ventura) Jan. 27, 2003. Running time: 89 Min. Spanish. Adolfo Jimenez, Valeriano Aragones. Documentary.

IF I SHOULD FALL FROM GRACE: THE SHANE MACGOWAN STORY
Pop Twist Entertainment. (Sarah Share) Aug. 13, 2003. Running time: 93 Min. Irish. Shane MacGowan, Victoria Clarke, Maurice and Terese MacGowan, Aunty Monica, Philip Chevron. Documentary.

IF I WERE A RICH MAN
UGC Distribution. (Michel Munz, Gerard Bitton) Dec. 6, 2002. Running time: 105 min. French. Jean-Pierre Darroussin, Valeria Bruni-Tedeschi, Richard Berry, Francois Morel, Zinedine Soualem.

IF I WERE YOU
(Giulio Manfredonia) Nov. 22, 2002. Running time: 101 Min. Italian. Emilio Solfrizzi, Gioele Dix, Paola Cortellesi, Fabio de Luigi.

I'LL SLEEP WHEN I'M DEAD
Paramount Classics. (Mike Hodges) Aug. 21, 2003. Running time: 102 Min. British-U.S. Clive Owen, Charlotte Rampling, Jonathan Rhys Meyers, Malcolm McDowell, Jamie Foreman, Ken Stott, Sylvia Syms.

I LOVE YOU (WO AI NI)
Asia Union Film. (Zhang Yuan) Nov. 16, 2002. Running time: 98 Min. Chinese. Xu Jinglei, Tong Dawei, Wang Xuebing, Du Peng, Pan Juan.

IMAGINING ARGENTINA
(Christopher Hampton) Aug. 31, 2003. Running time: 107 Min. British-Spanish. Antonio Banderas, Emma Thompson, Ruben Blades.

I'M NOT SCARED
Medusa Film. (Gabriele Salvatores) Feb. 3, 2003. Running time: 110 Min. Italian-Spanish-British. Aitana Sanchez Gijon, Dino Abbrescia.

IN MY SKIN
Rezo Films. (Marina de Van) Sept. 27, 2002. Running time: 93 Min. French. Marina de Van, Laurent Lucas, Lea Drucker.

INFERNAL AFFAIRS
Media Asia Distribution. (Andrew Lau, Alan Mak) Jan. 11, 2003. Running time: 100 min. Hong Kong. Tony Leung Chiu-wai, Andy Lau.

INGMAR BERGMAN: INTERMEZZO
(Gunnar Bergdahl) Aug. 15, 2002. Running time: 40 Min. Swedish. Ingmar Bergman, Gunnar Bergdahl. Documentary.

THE INHERITANCE (A PARTILHA)
Columbia TriStar Pictures Intl. (Daniel Filho) Nov. 10, 2002. Running time: 95 Min. Brazilian. Gloria Pires, Andrea Beltrao, Paloma Duarte,.

INNER SENSES
(Lo Chi-leung) June 10, 2003. Running time: 100 Min. Hong Kong. Leslie Cheung, Karena Lam, Valerie Chow, Waise Lee.

THE INTENDED
IFC Films. (Kristian Levring) Sept. 6, 2002. Running time: 112 Min. British-Denmark. Janet McTeer, Olympia Dukakis, Brenda Fricker.

INTERMISSION
Buena Vista Intl. (in U.K.)/IFC Films (in U.S.). (John Crowley). Aug. 18, 2003. Running time: 103 Min. Irish-British. Colin Farrell, Shirley Henderson, Kelly Macdonald, Colm Meaney, Cillian Murphy.

IN THE CUT
Sony Pictures Entertainment. (Jane Campion) Sept. 8, 2003. Running time: 118 Min. U.S.-Australian. Meg Ryan, Mark Ruffalo, Jennifer Jason Leigh, Nick Damici, Sharrieff Pugh.

IN THIS WORLD
(Michael Winterbottom) Nov. 8, 2002. Running time: 88 Min. British. Jamal Udin Torabi, Enayatullah, Imran Paracha, Hiddayatullah.

INVESTIGATION INTO THE INVISIBLE WORLD
(Jean Michel Roux) July 9, 2003. Running time: 85 Min. French. Documentary.

IRAN IS MY HOME
(Fariborz David Diaan) June 20, 2003. Running time: 79 Min. U.S.-Iranian. Documentary.

IRAN, VEILED APPEARANCES
(Thierry Michel) Jan. 18, 2003. Running time: 91 Min. Belgian-French. Documentary.

THE ISLAND
Istituto Luce. (Costanza Quatriglio) May 21, 2003. Running time: 103 Min. Italian. Veronica Guarrasi, Ignazio Ernandes, Marcello Mazzarella, Erri De Luca, Anna Ernandes, Francesco Vasile.

I-SAN SPECIAL
(Mingmongkol Sonakul) Oct. 9, 2002. Running time: 112 Min. Thai. Mesini Kaewratri, Mark Salmon, Phurida Vichitphan.

IT'S ABOUT TIME
(Ayelet Menahemi) May 28, 2003. Running time: 54 Min. Israeli. Yakov Cohen, Jacky Levi, Aviv Tsidon, Moshe Amsalem.

IT'S ALL ABOUT LOVE
(Thomas Vinterberg) Jan. 19, 2003. Running time: 105 Min. Danish. Joaquin Phoenix, Claire Danes, Sean Penn, Douglas Henshall.

IT'S EASIER FOR A CAMEL...
Gemini Films. (Valeria Bruni Tedeschi) April 4, 2003. Running time: 108 Min. French-Italian. Valeria Bruni Tedeschi, Chiara Mastroianni.

I WAS A RAT
(Laurie Lynd) Oct. 5, 2002. Running time: 98 Min. Canadian-British. Tom Conti, Brenda Fricker, Calum Worthy, Katie Blake, James Millard.

IXIEME, DIARY OF A PRISONER
(Pierre-Yves Borgeaud, Stephane Blok) Aug. 12, 2003. Running time: 105 Min. Swiss. Louis-Charles Finger, Celine Bolomey.

JACKIE KENNEDY: WHAT JACKIE KNEW
(Patrick Jeudy) June 7, 2003. Running time: 55 Min. French. Documentary. Narrator: Christine Gagnieux.

JAGODA IN THE SUPERMARKET
(Dusan Milic) Feb. 7, 2003. Running time: 83 Min. Yugoslavian-German-Italian. Branka Katic, Srdjan Todorovic, Dubravka Mijatovic.

JAIL BREAKERS (GWANGBOKJEOL TEUKSA)
Cinema Service. (Kim Sang-jin) Nov. 20, 2002. Running time: 118 min. South Korean. Seol Gyeong-gu, Cha Seung-weon, Song Yun-ah.

JAMES' JOURNEY TO JERUSALEM
(Ra'anan Alexandrowicz) May 19, 2003. Running time: 90 Min. Israeli. Siyabonga Melongisi Shibe, Arie Elias, Salim Daw.

JANIS AND JOHN
Mars Distribution. (Samuel Benchetrit) Aug. 20, 2003. Running time: 104 Min. French. Sergi Lopez, marie Trintignant, Francois Cluzet.

JAPANESE STORY
Palace Films (Australia). (Sue Brooks) May 1, 2003. Running time: 105 Min. Australian. Toni Collette, Gotaro Tsunashima, Matthew Dyktynski, Lynette Curran, Yumiko Tanaka, Kate Atkinson, John Howard.

JEALOUSY IS MY MIDDLE NAME
(Park Chan-ok) Nov. 15, 2002. Running time: 123 Min. South Korean. Park Hae-il, Bae Jong-ok, Mun Seong-geun, Seo Yeong-heui.

JEANS
(Nicolette Krebitz) Jan. 11, 2003. Running time: 83 Min. German. Oskar Melzer, Marc Hosemann, Angie Ojciec, Nicolette Krebitz.

JENIN DIARY
(Gil Mezuman) June 1, 2003. Running time: 65 Min. Israeli. Documentary.

JESUS, YOU KNOW
(Ulrich Seidl) July 5, 2003. Running time: 87 Min. Australian. Documentary. Elfriede Ahmad, Waltraute Bartel.

JISM
Worldwide Entertainment Group. (Amit Saxena) May 2, 2003. Running time: 136 Min. Indian. Bipasha Basu, John Abraham, Gulshan Grover, Vinay Pathak, Ranvir Shorey, Anahita Uberoi, Sheeba Chadha.

JOHAN PADAN AND THE DISCOVERY OF THE AMERICAS
Mikado. (Giulio Cingoli) Sept. 8, 2002. Running time: 83 Min. Italian. Animated. Voice: Rosario Fiorello.

JOHNNY ENGLISH
UIP (in U.K.)/Universal (in U.S.). (Peter Howitt) March 23, 2003. MPAA rating: PG. Running time: 86 Min. Britiah-U.S. Rowan Atkinson, John Malkovich, Natalie Imbruglia, Ben Miller, Douglas McFerran.

JOHNNY VANG
UIP. (Jens Lien) Feb. 8, 2003. Running time: 85 Min. Norwegian. Aksel Hennie, Laila Goody, Fridtjov Saheim, Marit A. Andreassen.

A JOURNEY CALLED LOVE
01 Distribution. (Michele Placido) Sept. 3, 2002. Running time: 96 Min. Italian. Laura Morante, Stefano Accorsi, Alessandro Haber.

JOURNEY OF THE GREY MEN
(Amir Shahab Razavian) Jan. 25, 2003. Running time: 105 Min. Iranian-Japanese. Reza Sheikh Ahmad Khamesh, Ahmad Bigdeli.

THE JOY OF MADNESS
(Hana Makhmalbaf) Aug. 27, 2003. Running time: 73 Min. Iranian. Samira Makhmalbaf, Agheleh Rezaei. Documentary.

JULIA, ALL IN ME
(Ivonne Belen) Aug. 10, 2003. Running time: 102 Min. Puerto Rican. Grechen Colon, Teofilo Torres, Virianai Rodriguez.

JULIE WALKING HOME
(Agnieszka Holland) Sept. 4, 2002. Running time: 118 Min. Miranda Otto, William Fichtner, Lothaire Bluteau, Ryan Smith, Bianca Crudo.

JUNE MOON
(Hanno Hackfort) Feb. 14, 2003. Running time: 92 Min. German. Oliver Mommsen, Laura Tonke, Stephan Kampwirth, Teresa Harder.

KAANTE
(Sanjay Gupta) Dec. 20, 2002. Running time: 154 Min. Indian. Amitabh Bachchan, Sanjay Dutt, Sunil Shetty, Kumar Gaurav.

KADDIM WIND-MOROCCAN CHRONICLE
(David Benchetrit) June 23, 2003. Running time: 255 Min. Israeli. Documentary. Rabbi Arieh Deri, Ezer Bitton, Reuven Abergel.

KAMCHATKA
Hispano Foxfilm. (Marcelo Pineyro) Nov. 30, 2002. Running time: 104 min. Argentine-Spanish. Ricardo Darin, Cecilia Roth, Hector Alterio.

KARAMUK
(Sulbiye V. Gunar) Jan. 31, 2003. Running time: 97 Min. German. Julia Mahnecke, Adnan Maral, Anne Kasprik, Buket Yeni, Burak Gulgen.

KAT
(Martin Schmidt) Oct. 20, 2002. Running time: 85 Min. Danish. Liv Corfixen, Charlotte Munck, Martin Brygmann, Soren Pilmark.

THE KEY FOR DETERMINING DWARFS OR THE LAST TRAVEL OF LEMUEL GULLIVER
(Martin Sulik) July 6, 2003. Running time: 58 Min. Czech Republic. Marek Juracek, Edita Leva, Julie Ritzingerova.

KILLING WORDS
Filmax. (Laura Mana) May 1, 2003. Running time: 89 Min. Spanish. Dario Grandinetti, Goya Toledo, Fernando Guillen, Eric Bonicatto.

KILL ME TENDER
Buena Vista Intl. Spain. (Ramon de Espana) May 2, 2003. Running time: 98 Min. Spanish. Ingrid Rubio, Alberto San Juan, Emilio Gutierrez Caba, Manuel Manquina, Chusa Barbero, Agata Lys.

THE KING (O VASILIAS)
(Nikos Grammatikos) Dec. 25, 2002. Running time: 137 Min. Greek. Vangelis Mourikis, Marilita Lambropoulou, Minas Hatzisavvas.

THE KING'S BEARD
(Tony Collingwood) Oct. 10, 2002. Running time: 73 Min. British. Voices: Jim Broadbent, Robin Edwards, Maria Darling. Animated.

KISS OF LIFE
(Emily Young) May 21, 2003. Running time: 86 Min. British-French. Ingeborga Dapkunaite, Peter Mullan, David Warner, Millie Findlay.

KITCHEN STORIES
(Bent Hamer) May 15, 2003. Running time: 95 Min. Norwegian-Swedish. Joachim Calmeyer, Tomas Norstrom, Bjorn Floberg.

THE KITE
(Randa Chahal Sabbag) Aug. 29, 2003. Running time: 78 Min. French-Lebanon. Flavia Behara, Maher Bsaibes, Ziad Rahbani.

KOI...MIL GAYA
Yash Raj Films. (Rakesh Roshan) Aug. 23, 2003. Running time: 172 Min. Indian. Hrithik Roshan, Preeity Zinta, Rekha, Johny Lever.

KOKTEBEL
(Boris Khlebnikov) July 11, 2003. Running time: 144 Min. Russian. Igor Chernevich, Gleb Puskepalis, Agrippina Stekhlova.

KOPS
Sonet Film. (Josef Fares) Jan. 20, 2003. Running time: 91 Min. Swedish. Fares Fares, Torkel Petersson, Goran Ragnerstam.

KUNPAN: LEGEND OF THE WARLORD
Mongkol. (Thanit Jitnukul) Nov. 21, 2002. Running time: 89 Min. Thai. Watchara Tangkaprasert, Bongkoo Kongmalai.

LA BEUZE
Pathe Distribution. (Francois Desagnat, Thomas Sorriaux) Jan. 14, 2003. Running time: 93 Min. French. Michael Youn, Vincent Desagnat.

LABYRINTH
Vans. (Miroslav Lekic) Jan. 12, 2003. Running time: 119 Min. Yugoslavian. Dragon Nikolic, Maja Sabljic, Katarina Radivojevic.

THE LANDLORDS (MILLE MILLIEMES)
Diaphana. (Remi Waterhouse) Aug. 21, 2002. Running time: 90 Min. French. Patrick Chesnais, Jean-Pierre Darroussin, Albert Delpy.

THE LAND OF THE OGRES
(Sami Kafati) May 15, 2003. Running time: 107 Min. Honduras-French. Jose Luis Lopez, Saul Toro, Daniel Vasquez, Marisela Bustillo.

LA PETITE LILI
Pyramide. (Claude Miller) May 22, 2003. Running time: 104 Min. French-Canadian. Nicole Garcia, Bernard Giraudeau, Jean-Pierre Marielle, Ludivine Sagnier, Robinson Stevenin, Julie Depardieu.

THE LAST JUST MAN
(Steven Silver) Oct. 19, 2002. Running time: 70 Min. Canadian. Brig. Gen. Romeo Dellaire, Col. Luc Marchal. Documentary.

LAST LIFE IN THE UNIVERSE
(Pen-ek Ratanaruang) Aug. 29, 2003. Running time: 108 Min. Thai-Japanese. Tadanobu Asano, Sinitta Boonyasak.

THE LAST MINUTE
(Stephen Norrington) Nov. 9, 2002. Running time: 104 Min. British. Max Beesley, Emily Corrie, Tom Bell, Jason Isaacs, Kate Ashfield.

LAST SCENE
(Hideo Nakata) Release date: Feb. 14, 2003. Running time: 99 Min. South Korean. Hidetoshi Nishijima, Yumi Aso, Kumiko Aso.

THE LAST SNOW (NAGORI YUKI)
(Nobuhiko Obayashi) Nov. 8, 2002. Running time: 112 Min. Japanese. Tomokazu Miura, Atsuko Sudo, Keiko Tsushima, Takahito Sorita.

LAST STOP (HLEMMUR)
(Olafur Sveinsson) Jan. 28, 2003. Running time: 85 Min. German. Documentary.

THE LAST SUPPER (SHAAM-E-AKHAR)
Iranian Film Society and NEJ Intl. Pictures. (Fereydoun Jeyrani) Nov. 13, 2002. Running time: 96 Min. Iranian. Katayoun Riahi, Mohammad Reza Golzar, Sorayya Ghasemi, Atila Pesiani, Haniye Tavassoli.

THE LAST ZAPATISTAS, FORGOTTEN HEROES
(Francesco Taboada Tabone) July 23, 2003. Running time: 69 Min. Documentary.

LAUGHTER AND PUNISHMENT
EuropaCorp Distribution. (Isabelle Doval) Feb. 10, 2003. Running time: 90 Min. French. Jose Garcia, Isabelle Doval, Laurent Lucas.

LEAVE YOUR HANDS ON MY HIPS
ARP Selection. (Chantal Lauby) March 7, 2003. Running time: 107 Min. French. Chantal Lauby, Jean-Pierre Martins, Rossy de Palma.

LEAVING IN SORROW
(Vincent Chui) Oct. 20, 2002. Running time: 89 Min. Hong Kong. Tony Ho, Duncan Lai, Crystal Lui, Ivy Ho, Shawn Yu, Sheung Ming-fai.

LE BISON (AND HIS NEIGHBOR DORINE)
Pathe. (Isabelle Nanty) June 17, 2003. Running time: 93 Min. French. Isabelle Nanty, Edouard Baer, Martin Laval, Juliette Duval.

THE LEGEND OF AL, JOHN AND JACK
Medusa Film. (Aldo, Giovanni & Giacomo, Massimo Venier) Dec. 29, 2002. Running time: 95 Min. Italian. Aldo Baglio, Giacomo Poretti.

LEMMY
(Peter Sempel) Sept. 20, 2002. Running time: 112. German. Lemmy Kilmister, Phil Campbell, Mikkey Dee, Ozzy Osbourne. Documentary.

LENT
(Jose Alvaro Morais) May 18, 2003. Running time: 95 Min. Portudese-French. Beatriz Batarda, Filipe Cary, Rita Durao, Ricardo Aibeo, Laura Soveral, Paula Guedes, Teresa Madruga.

LEO
(Mehdi Norowzian) Sept. 11, 2002. Running time: 102 Min. U.S.-British. Joseph Fiennes, Elisabeth Shue, Justin Chambers.

LES COTELETTES
EuropaCorp Distribution. (Bertrand Blier) May 23, 2003. Running time: 87 Min. French. Philippe Noiret, Michel Bouquet, Farida Rahouadj.

LES SENTIMENTS
(Noemie Lvovsky) Aug. 31, 2003. Running time: 96 Min. French. NAthalie Baye, Jean-Pierre Bacri, Isabelle Carre.

LESTER JAMES PERIES: CINEASTE FROM ANOTHER TIME
(Julien Plantureux) May 20, 2003. Running time: 56 Min. French. Documentary.

LET'S HAVE THE TRUTH ABOUT LOVE
(Francesco Apolloni) Nov. 24, 2002. Running time: 106 Min. Italian. Elda Alvigini, Francesco Apolloni, Pierfrancesco Favino, Beatrice Fazi.

LET'S LOVE HONG KONG
(Yau Ching) Nov. 10, 2002. Running time: 86 Min. Chinese. Wong Chung-Ching, Erica Lam, Colette Koo, Maria Cordero.

LETTER FROM THE MOUNTAIN
(Takashi Kozumi) Sept. 23, 2002. Running time: 127 Min. Japanese. Akira Terao, Kanako Higuchi, Hisashi Igawa, Tanie Kitabayashi.

LETTERS IN THE WIND
Lucky Red. (Edmond Budina. June 3, 2003. Running time: 84 Min. Italian. Edmond Budina, Yllka Mujo. Bujar Asquriu.

LIFE MARKS
Alta Films. (Enrique Urbizu) March 25, 2003 (In Malaga Film Festival, competing.) Running time: 107 Min. Spanish. Jose Coronado, Zay Nuba, Juan Sanz.

LIFE ON THE TRACKS
(Ditsi Carolino) June 21, 2003. Running time: 69 Min. British-Filipino. Documentary. Eddie and Pen Renomeron.

LILLY'S STORY
(Robert Manthoulis) Sept. 6, 2002. Running time: 130 Min. Greek-French-Slovenian. Juliette Andrea, Yorgo Vogiatzis.

A LITTLE BIT OF FREEDOM
(Yuksel Yavuz) May 6, 2003. Running time: 100 Min. German. Cagdas Bozkurt, Necmettin Cobanoglu, Leroy Delmar, Sunay Girisken.

LITTLE GIRL BLUE
(Anna Luif) Aug. 29, 2003. Running time: 84 Min. Swiss. Muriel Neukom, Andreas Eberle, Bernarda Reichmuth, Sabine Berg.

LITTLE MEN
(Nariman Turebayev) Aug. 14, 2003. Running time: 92 Min. Erjan Bekmuratov, Oleg Kerimov, Lyazat Dautova.

LIVE FOREVER
Helkon SK. (John Dower) March 4, 2003. Running time: 84 Min. British. Damon Albarn, Ozwald Boateng, James Brown. Documentary.

LIVING KILLS
(Nicolas Echevarria) Jan. 17, 2003. Running time: 92 Min. Mexican. Daniel Gimenez Cacho, Susana Zabaleta, Alejandra Gollas.

LOCAL ANGEL
(Udi Aloni) Sept. 10, 2002. Running time: 69 Min. U.S.-Israeli. Udi Aloni, Shulamit Aloni, Hanan Ashwari, Yasser Arafat. Documentary.

A LONG WEEKEND IN PEST AND BUDA
(Karoly Makk) Feb. 1, 2003. Running time: 88 Min. Hungarian. Ivan Darvas, Mari Torocsik, Eszter Nagy-Kalozy, Eileen Atkins.

LOS
A James Benning production. Producer/Director/Editor: Benning. Camera: Benning. In color, 16mm. Release date: April 30, 2003. Running time: 90 Min. Documentary.

THE LOST FILM
(Joana Hadjithomas, Khalil Joreige) Jan. 26, 2003. Running time: 42 Min. Lebanon-French. Documentary.

LOST THINGS
Cinema Vault Releasing. (Martin Murphy) May 17, 2003. Running time: 83 Min. Australian-Canadian. Leon Ford, Lenka Kripac.

LOVE IS NOT A SIN
(Doug Kin-Tak) June 21, 2003. Running time: 83 Min. Macao. Moon Man, Manman Lam, Chaoebe Chao, Sheila Un, Cherry Vong.

LOVE ME IF YOU DARE
A Mars Distribution (in France)/Cineart (in Belgium). (Yann Samuell) June 28, 2003. Running time: 95 Min. French-Belgian. Guillaume Canet, Marion Cotillard, Thibault Verhaeghe, Josephine Lebas Joly.

A LOVE MOVIE
(Julio Bressane) May 5, 2003. Running time: 100 Min. Brazilian. Bel Garcia, Josi Antello, Fernando Eiras.

LUCIA, LUCIA
20th Century Fox. (Antonio Serrano) July, 2003. Running time: 109 Min. Mexican-Spanish. Cecilia Roth, Carlos Alvarez Nova.

LUPARELLA
(Giuseppe Bertolucci) Sept. 6, 2002. Running time: 75 Min. Italian. Isa Danieli, Giuliana Colzi, Anna Ferrigno, Franco Coni.

LUTHER
(Eric Till) Aug. 19, 2003. Running time: 120 Min. German. Joseph Fiennes, Alfred Molina, Jonathan Firth, Claire Cox, Peter Ustinov.

THE MAGIC BOX (SANDOUK AJAB/LA BOITE MAGIQUE)
(Ridha Behi) Aug. 31, 2002. Running time: 88 Min. French-Tunisian. Marianne Basler, Abdelatif Kechiche, Hichem Rostom, Lotfi Bouchnak, Medhi Rebii.

MAGNIFICO
(Maryo J. de los Reyes) July, 11, 2003. Running time: 121 Min. Filipino. Jiro Manio, Albert Martinez, Lorna Tolentino.

MAIN PREM KI DIWANI HOON
Yash Raj Films. (Sooraj R. Barjatya) July 3, 2003. Running time: 96 Min. Indian. Hrithik Roshan, Kareena Kapoor, Abhishek Bachchan, Johny Lever.

MAKIBEFO
Epicentre Films. (Alexander Abela) Feb. 9, 2003. Running time: 75 Min. British-French-Madagascar. Martin, Noeliny, Gilbert Laumord.

MAMBO ITALIANO
An Equinoxe Films (Canada)/Samuel Goldwyn Films (U.S.). (Emile Gaudreault) June 5, 2003. Running time: 88 Min. Canadian. Luke Kirby, Ginette Reno, Paul Sorvino, Mary Walsh, Claudia Ferri.

A MAN, A REAL ONE
Haut & Court. (Arnaud Larrieu, Jean-Marie Larrieu) Apr. 14, 2003. Running time: 120 Min. French. Helene Fillieres, Mathieu Amalric.

MANGO YELLOW
(Claudio Assis) Oct. 4, 2002. Running time: 103 Min. Brazilian. Matheus Nachtergaele, Jonas Bloch, Leona Cavalli, Dira Paes.

MANSION BY THE LAKE
(Lester James Peries) May 8, 2003. Running time: 109 Min. Sri Lankan. Malini Fonseka, Vasanthi Chaturani, Ravindra Randeniya.

THE MAORI MERCHANT OF VENICE
(Don C. Selwyn) Nov. 9, 2002. Running time: 158 Min. New Zealand. Waihoroi Shortland, Ngarimu Daniels, Scott Morrison.

THE MARBLE ROAD (DIE MARMORSTRASSE)
(Michael Trabizsch) Oct. 2, 2002. Running time: 82 Min. German-Swiss. Documentary.

MARGARETTE'S FEAST
Panda Filmes. (Renato Falcao) Oct. 8, 2002. Running time: 80 Min. Brazilian. Hique Gomez, Ilana Kaplan, Carmem Silva, Pedro Gil.

MARIA
(Peter Netzer) Aug. 12, 2003. Running time: 97 Min. Romanian-German-French. Diana Dumbrava, Horatiu Malaele, Serban Ionescu.

MARRYING THE MAFIA (GAMUNEUI YEONGGWANG)
Cinema Service. (Jeong Heung-sun) Dec. 1, 2002. Running time: 112 Min. South Korean. Jeong Jun-ho, Kim Jeong-eun, Yu Dong-geun.

THE MARSH
(Kim Nguyen) Sept. 7, 2002. Running time: 83 Min. Canadian. Gregory Hlady, Paul Ahmarani, Gabriel Gascon, Jennifer Morehouse.

MARTHA'S NEW COAT
(Rachel Ward) July 27, 2003. Running time: 52 Min. Australian. Matilda Brown, Alycia Debnam-Carey, Lisa Hensley, Daniel Wyllie.

MARVELOUS LIGHT
Alta Films. (Miguel Hermoso) Feb. 6, 2003. Running time: 105 Min. Spanish. Alfredo Landa, Nino Manfredi, Kiti Manver.

MARY'S CITY
(Enrique Ballande) Oct. 8, 2002. Running time: 85 Min. Argentine. Documentary.

MASKED AND ANONYMOUS
Sony Pictures Classics. (Larry Charles) Jan. 22, 2003. Running time: 112 Min. U.S.-British. Bob Dylan, Jeff Bridges, Penelope Cruz.

MASTER BUILDING
(Eduardo Coutinho) April 19, 2003. Running time: 110 Min. Documentary. Brazilian.

MATANZA
(Grupo Documental) Feb. 12, 2003. Running time: 73 Min. Argentine. Documentary.

THE MEDALLION
Sony Pictures Entertainment. (Gordon Chan) Aug. 19, 2003. Running time: 88 Min. Hong Kong-U.S. Jackie Chan, Lee Evans, Claire Forlani, Julian Sands, Jonathan Rhys-Davies, Anthony Wong, Christy Chung.

MEMORIES OF A FORGOTTEN WAR
(Camilla Benolirao Griggers, Sari Lluch Dalena) Dec. 23, 2002. Running time: 61 Min. Filipino-U.S. Documentary.

MERCANO THE MARTIAN
Distribution Co. July 21, 2003. Running time: 72 Min. Argentine. Graciela Borges, Roberto Carnaghi, Damian Dreizik.

MERCI DOCTEUR REY
(Andrew Litvack) Sept. 20, 2002. Running time: 91 Min. French-U.S. Dianne Wiest, Jane Birkin, Stanislas Merhar, Bulle Ogier.

METAMORPHOSIS
(Valery Fokin) May 18, 2003. Running time: 82 Min. Russian. Igor Kvasha, Tatiana Lavrova, Avangard Leontyev.

MIFFO
Sonet Film. (Daniel Lind-Lagerlof) July 31, 2003. Running time: 100 Min. Swedish. Jonas Karlsson, Livia Millhagen, Ingvar Hirdwall.

MIKE BRANT: LAISSE-MOI T'AIMER
(Erez Laufer) June 10, 2003. Running time: 104 Min. Israeli-French. Documentary. Alan Banon, Hubert Baumann.

THE MIRACLE OF BERN
Senator. (Soenke Wortmann) Aug. 10, 2003. Running time: German. Louis Klamroth, Peter Lohmeyer, Johanna Gastdorf, Mirko Lang.

MISS ENTEBBE
(Omri Levy) June 11, 2003. Running time: 80 Min. Israeli. Merav Abrahami, Igal Naor, Meyrav Gruber.

THE MISSING GUN (XUN QIANG)
(Lu Chuan) Sept. 2, 2002. Running time: 90 Min. Chinese. Jiang Wen, Ning Jing, Wu Yujuan, Liu Xiaoning, Wei Xiaoping, Shi Liang.

MISTER V.
(Emilie Deleuze) Aug. 10, 2003. Running time: 92 Min. French. Mathieu Demy, Aure Atika, Patrick Catalifo, Fabien Luciarini.

MODEL EMPLOYEE
(Jacques Otmezguine) Aug. 10, 2003. Running time: 90 Min. French. Francois BErleand, Delphine Rollin, Nicole Calfan, Francois Morel.

MODEL STUDENT
(Stefano Mordini) April 24, 2003. Running time: 60 Min. Documentary. Italian.

MOLLY & MOBARAK
(Tom Zubrycki) June 16, 2003. Running time: 85 Min. Australian. Documentary.

MONIQUE
Pan-Europeenne. (Valerie Guignabodet) Sept. 15, 2002. Running time: 91 Min. French. Albert Dupontel, Marianne Denicourt.

MONKEY BUSINESS
(Ricardo Carrasco Farfan) Feb. 15, 2003. Running time: 96 Min. Chilean. Sergio Hernandez, Luis Dubo, Emilio Garcia.

MONSIEUR IBRAHIM AND THE FLOWERS OF THE KORAN
Lucky Red. (Francois Dupeyron) Aug. 28, 2003. Running time: 94 Min. French. Omar Sharif, Pierre Boulanger, Gilbert Melki

MONSIEUR N.
Mars Distribution. (Antoine de Caunes) Jan. 13, 2003. Running time: 128 Min. French-British. Philippe Torreton, Richard E. Grant.

MOON CHILD
Shochiku Co. (Takahisa Zeze) July 14, 2003. Running time: 115 Min. Japanese. Hyde, Gackt, Wang Lee-hom, Taro Yamamoto,

MOONLIGHT
A-Film Distribution. (Paula van der Oest) Sept. 26, 2002. Running time: 91 Min. Dutch-British-Luxembourgors-German. Laurien van den Broeck, Hunter Bussemaker, Johan Leysen, Jemma Redgrave.

MORTADELO & FILEMON: THE BIG ADVENTURE
Warner Sogefilms. (Javier Fesser) Feb. 11, 2003. Running time: 105 Min. Spanish. Benito Pocino, Pepe Viyuela, Dominique Pinon.

MOSCOW GOLD
Columbia TriStar Spain. (Jesus Bonilla) Jan. 31, 2003. Running time: 108 Min. Spanish. Jesus Bonilla, Santiago Segura, Alfredo Landa.

MOSKU-THE LAST OF HIS KIND
Columbia TriStar Nordisk Film. (Tapio Suominen) June 12, 2003. Running time: 133 Min. Finish. Kai Lehtinen, Maria Jarvenhelmi.

MOST PEOPLE LIVE IN CHINA
SF Norge. Aug. 25, 2002. Running time: 95 Min. Norwegian.
1. Lasses drom
(Thomas Robsahm) Trond Hovik, Marit Pia Jacobsen, Henrik Mestad.
2. Dressman - Hoyre
(Sven Nordin) Sven Nordin, Siv Charlotte Klynderud, Martin Slaatto.
3. Grenselos kjaerlighet - Kristelig folkeparti
(Sara Johnsen) Agot Sendstad, Gjertrud Jynge, Dani Aso Ahmad.
4. Heimat - Senterpartiet
(Arild Frohlich) Kristin Skogheim, Trond Hovik, Steinar Hammer.
5. Den lille bedriften - Venstre
(Ingebjorg Torgersen) Ingrid Jorgensen, Marianne Ulrichsen.
6. Redd barna - Fremskrittspartiet
(Terje Rangnes) Rosa Engebrigtsen Bye, Luis Engebrigtsen Bye.
7. Pokemon Power - Rod valgallianse
(Magnus Martens) Sampda Sharma, Edvardt Schultheiss.
8. Passasjerene - Sosialistisk venstreparti
(Martin Asphaug) Sverre Anker Ousdal, Lasse Valdal.
9. De beste gar forst - Arbeiderpartiet
(Hans Petter Moland) Ole Jorgen Nilsen, Rolf Brandt.

MOTHER
(Miklos Gimes) April 18, 2003. Running time: 100 Min. Documentary. Swiss.

THE MOTHER
(Roger Michell) May 17, 2003. Running time: 111 Min. British. Anne Reid, Daniel Craig, Steven Mackintosh, Cathryn Bradshaw, Oliver Ford Davies, Anna Wilson Jones, Peter Vaughn.

MOVE ME
(Morten Arnfred) Jan. 30, 2003. Running time: 97 Min. Danish. Birthe Neumann, Jesper Lohmann, Ditte Grabol, Asger Reher, Niels Olsen.

MRS. CALDICOT'S CABBAGE WAR
Arrow Film Distributors. (Ian Sharp) Oct. 10, 2002. Running time: 109 Min. British. Pauline Collins, Peter Capaldi, Anna Wilson-Jones.

MUD
(Dervis Zaim) Aug. 26, 2003. Running time: 98 Min. Italian-Turkish-Cypriot. Mustafa Ugurlu, Yelda Reynaud, Taner Birsel.

MUSIC FOR WEDDINGS AND FUNERALS
SF Norge. (Unni Straume) Aug. 22, 2002. Running time: 97 Min. Norwegian. Lena Endre, Bjorn Floberg, Rebecka Hemse.

MUSICAL CHAIRS
(Ana Katz) Sept. 23, 2002. Running time: 93 Min. Argentine. Raquel Bank, Diego de Paula, Ana Katz, Luciana Lifschitz, Veronica Moreno.

MUTT BOY
Show East. (K.T. Kwak) July 17, 2003. Running time: 97 Min. South Korean. Jeong Woo-seong, Kim Kab-su, Eom Ji-weon, Kim Tae-uk.

MY BROTHER-IN-LAW
(Alessandro Piva) Aug. 9, 2003. Running time: 90 Min. Italian. Sergio Rubini, Luigi Lo Cascio, Mariangela Arcieri, Alessandra Sarno.

MY CAMERA DOESN'T LIE
(Solveig Klassen, Katharina Schneider-Roos) June 12, 2003. Running time: 92 Min. Chinese-German-Australian. Documentary.

MY CHILDREN ARE DIFFERENT
Ocean Distribution. (Denis Dercourt) June 4, 2003. Running time: 82 Min. French. Richard Berry, Mathieu Amalric.

MY LIFE WITHOUT ME
Sony Pictures Classics (in N. America). (Isabel Coixet) Feb. 10, 2003. Running time, 106 Min. Spanish-Canadian. Sarah Polley.

MY NAME IS TANINO
Cecchi Gori Distribuzione/Medusa Film. (Paolo Virzi) Sept. 5, 2002. Running time: 124 Min. Italian. Corrado Fortuna, Rachel McAdams.

MY NAME WAS SABINA SPIELREIN
(Elisabeth Marton) Jan. 12, 2003. Running time: 93 Min. Swedish-Swiss-Danish-Finnish. Eva Osterberg, Lasse Almeback. Documentary.

MY ROAST CHICKEN
(Iwona Siekierzynska) May 20, 2003. Running time: 63 Min. Polish. Agata Kulesza, Adam Nawojczyk, Maja Maj.

MY RUSSIA
Polyfilm. (Barbara Graftner) Jan. 20, 2003. Running time: 93 Min. Austrian. Andrea Nurnberger, Natalia Baranova, Holger Schober.

MY SISTER MARIA
(Maximilian Schell) Jan. 18, 2003. Running time: 90 Min. Austrian. Maria Schell, Maximilian Schell. Documentary.

MY TEACHER, MR. KIM
Dimension Films. (Jang Gyu-seong) May 3, 2003. Running time: 113 Min. South Korean. Cha Seung-weon, Byun Heuibong.

MY TERRORIST
(Yulie Gerstel) April 27, 2003. Running time: 58 Min. Documentary. Israeli.

MY TUTOR FRIEND (DONGGABNAEGI GWAWIHAGI)
CJ Entertainment. (Kim Gyeong-hyeong) March 28, 2003. Running time: 113 Min. South Korean. Kim Ha-neul, Gweon Sang-woo.

THE MYSTERY OF THE YELLOW ROOM
UFD-UGC Distribution. (Bruno Podalydes) June 4, 2003. Running time: 119 Min. French-Belgian. Denis Podalydes, Sabine Azema, Michael Lonsdale, Pierre Arditi, Claude Rich, Olivier Gourmet.

NAKED
(Doris Dorrie) Sept. 2, 2002. Running time: 100 Min. German. Heike Makatsch, Benno Furmann, Alexandra Maria Lara, Jurgen Vogel.

NAKED WEAPON
Media Asia Distribution. (Tony Ching) Jan. 16, 2003. Running time: 90 Min. Hong Kong. Maggie Q, Anya, Daniel Wu, Jewel Lee.

NAMES IN MARBLE
Columbia TriStar Egmont. (Elmo Nuganen) June 10, 2003. Running time: 93 Min. Estonian-Finish. Priit Voigemast, Alo Korve, Hele Kore.

NEAREST TO HEAVEN (AU PLUS PRES DU PARADIS)
(Tonie Marshall) Aug. 30, 2002. Running time: 100 Min. French-Spanish-Canadian. Catherine Deneuve, William Hurt.

NED
Icon (Australia). (Abe Forsythe) May 8, 2002. Running time: 81 Min. Australian. Abe Forsythe, Felix Williamson, Nick Flint.

NED KELLY
UIP (Australia). Release date: March 13, 2003. Running time: 109 Min. Cast: Heath Ledger, Orlando Bloom, Naomi Watts. Australian-British.

THE NEGRO (LE NEG')
Christal Films. (Robert Morin) Sept 9, 2002. Running time: 91 Min. Canadian. Robin Aubert, Emmanuel Bilodeau, Vincent Bilodeau.

NEOPOLITAN HEART
(Paolo Santoni) Sept. 9, 2002. Running time: 95 Min. Italian. Peppe Barra, Jimmy Roselli, Jerry Vale, Rita Berti, John Gentile. Documentary.

NEVER TOO YOUNG TO DREAM
(Gustavo Loza) Oct. 5, 2002. Running time: 101 Min. Mexican. Hector Suarez, Lumi Cavazos, Plutarco Haza, Luis Felipe Tovar.

NEWS FROM A PERSONAL WAR
(Joao Moreira Salles, Katia Lund) Sept. 28, 2002. Running time: 60 Min. Brazilian. Documentary.

NICKEL AND DIME
Mars Distribution. (Sam Karmann. July 1, 2003. Running time: 98 Min. French. Gerard Lanvin, Jacques Gamblin, Clovis Cornillac.

NIGHT OF THE SHOOTING STARS
(Shin Togashi) Feb. 10, 2003. Running time: 106 Min. Japanese. Yuko Takeuchi, Yu Yoshizawa, Kazuya Takahashi, Mami Nakamura.

THE NIGHT WE CALLED IT A DAY
Icon Film Distribution. (Paul Goldman) Aug. 6, 2003. Running time: 96 Min. Australian-British. Joel Edgerton, Rose Byrne, Dennis Hopper., Melanie Griffith, Portia De Rossi, David Hemmings, David Field.

NIKI AND FLO
(Lucian Pintile) May 18, 2003. Running time: 99 Min. French-Romanian. Victor Rebengiuc, Razvan Vasilescu, Coca Bloos, Micaela Caracas, Serban Pavlu, Dorina Chiriac, Marius Galea, Andreea Bibiri.

NILOFAR IN THE RAIN
(Homayoun Karimpour) April 22, 2003. Running time: 97 Min. Afghanistan-French. Mamnoun Maqsoudi, Niki Zischka, Afrouz Nikzad, Maimouna Ghezal, Qader Farokh, Asad Tajzai.

9 DEAD GAY GUYS
TLA. (Ky Mo Lab) Jan. 10, 2003. Running time: 83 Min. British. Glen Mulhern, Brendan Mackey, Simon Godley, Steven Berkoff.

19 MONTHS
(Randall Cole) Sept. 26, 2002. Running time: 78 Min. Canadian. Benjamin Ratner, Angela Vint, Kari Matchett, Sergio DiZio.

NO BIG DEAL
Pathé. (Bernard Rapp) Feb. 24, 2003. Running time: 103 Min. French-Belgian-Spanish. Sami Bouajila, Romain Duris, Jean-Michel Portal.

NOBODY'S LIFE
Warner Sogefilms. (Eduard Cortes) Feb. 5, 2003. Running time: 103 Min. Spanish. Jose Coronado, Adriana Ozores, Marta Etura.

NOI ALBINOI
(Dagur Kari) Jan. 26, 2003. Running time: 90 Min. Icelandic-German-British-Danish. Tomas Lemarquis, Throstur Leo Gunnarsson.

NO ONE'S ARK
(Nobujiro Yamashita) Sept. 28, 2002. Running time: 117 Min. Japanese. Hiroshi Yamamoto, Tomoko Kotera, Yuko Hosoe.

NOORA (THE KISS OF LIFE)
(Mahmoud Shoolizadeh) June 9, 2003. Running time: 86 Min. Iranian. Mohammad Abbasi, Masoomeh Yousefi.

NO PASARAN, SOUVENIR ALBUM
Shellac. (Henri-Francois Imbert) May 17, 2003. Running time: 70 Min. Documentary. French. Narrator: Henri-Francois Imbert.

NO REST FOR THE BRAVE
(Alain Guiraudie) May 20, 2003. Running time: 104 Min. French-Australian. Thomas Suire, Thomas Blanchard, Laurent Soffiati.

NOT FOR OR AGAINST
Bac Films. (Cedric Klapisch) Feb. 19, 2003. Running time: 113 Min. French. Marie Gillain, Vincent Elbaz, Zinedine Soualem.

NOTHING TO LOSE (NEUNG BUAK NEUNG PEN SOON)
Film Bangkok. (in Thailand)/Raintree Pictures (in Singapore). (Danny Pang) Nov. 16, 2002. Running time: 94 min. Thai-Singapore. Pierre Png, Fresh, Yvonne Lim, Niponth Chaisirikul.

NOW OR NEVER
(Lucio Pellegrini) Aug. 7, 2003. Running time: 92 Min. Italian. Jacopo Bonvicini, Violante Placido, Edoardo Gabbriellini, Elio Germano.

AN OCEAN TOO DEEP
(Pan Kuang Yuan, Yeh Chi Ku) Nov. 5, 2002. Running time: 98 Min. Taiwanese. Wang Tong, Wang Chi-Tsan, Christopher Downs.

OCTANE
(Marcus Adams) June 14, 2003. Running time: 90 Min. British-Luxembourgors. Madeline Stowe, Norman Reedus.

OCTAVIA
Golem. (Basilio Martin Patino) Sept. 9, 2002. Running time: 130 Min. Spanish-French. Miguel Angel Sola, Margarita Lozano.

OF MEN AND GODS
Documentary Education Resources. (Anne Lescot, Laurence Magliore) July 12, 2003. Running time: 52 Min. Haiti. Blondine, Innocente, Madsen, Fritzner, Erol, Denis. Documentary.

OGU AND AMAPATO IN RAPA NUI
(Alejandro Rojas) Jan. 12, 2003. Running time: 75 Min. Chilean. Animated.

OGYA
(Fujiro Mitsuishi) Nov. 8, 2002. Running time: 97 Min. Japenese. Aya Okamoto, Ryosuke Mura, Kimiko Yo, Ken Mitsuishi, Yoshinori Hiruma.

OLD MEN IN NEW CARS AKA IN CHINA THEY EAT DOGS II
(Lasse Spang Olsen) Aug. 24, 2002. Running time: 95 Min. Danish. Kim Bodnia, Tomas Villum Jensen, Nikolaj Lie Kaas, Iben Hjejle.

THE OLD TESTAMENT
(Cui Zien) Feb 12, 2003. Running time: 104 Min. Chinese. Yu Bo, Yang Qing, Ma Ran, Zhao Zheng Yang, Do Hua Nan, Meng Hao, Yu Xiao Yu.

OLGA'S CHIGNON
Diaphana. (Jerome Bonnell) Jan. 28, 2003. Running time: 95 Min. French. Hubert Benhamdine, Nathalie Boutefeu, Serge Riaboukine.

ON THE SEVEN SEAS (AUF ALLEN MEEREN)
(Johannes Holzhausen) Oct. 1, 2002. Running time: 95 Min. Austrian. Documentary.

THE ONE & ONLY
Pathe (in U.K.)/TFM (in France). (Simon Cellan Jones) Oct. 4, 2002. Running time: 89 Min. British-French. Richard Roxburgh.

ONE LOVE
(Rick Elgood, Don Letts) May 18, 2003. Running time: 100 Min. British-Norwegian. Ky-mani Marley, Cherine Anderson, Idris Elba.

ONE NIGHT HUSBAND
(Pimpaka Towira) Feb. 15, 2003. Running time: 117 Min. Thai. Nicole Theriault, Siriyakorn Pukkavesa, Pongpat Vachirabanjong.

ONE-WAY TICKET TO MOMBASA
Columbia TriStar Egmont Film Distributors. (Hannu Tuomainen) Aug. 23, 2002. Running time: 88 Min. Finnish. Antti Tarvainen.

OPEN HEARTS
(Susanne Bier) Aug. 24, 2002. Running time: 113 Min. Danish. Sonja Richter, Nikolaj Lie Kaas, Mads Mikkelsen, Paprika Steen.

OPEN MY HEART (APRIMI IL CUORE)
Lucky Red. (Giada Colagrande) Aug. 27, 2002. Running time: 93 Min. Italian. Giada Colagrande, Natalie Cristiani, Claudio Botosso.

THE ORIGINAL MERMAID
(Michael Cordell) June 11, 2003. Running time: 52 Min. Australian-Dutch. Documentary. Esther Williams, Tara Morice.

ORLAN-CARNAL ART
Myriapodus Films. (Stephen Oriach) June 2, 2003. Running time: 76 Min. French. Documentary.

OSAMA
(Siddiq Barmak) May 20, 2003. Running time: 82 Min. Afghanistan-Japanese-Irish. Marina Golbahari, Arif Herati, Zubaida Sahar.

THE OTHER BOLEYN GIRL
(Philippa Lowthorpe) June 10, 2003. Running time: 90 Min. British. Natascha McElhone, Jodhi May, Jared Harris.

THE OTHER FINAL
(Johan Kramer) June 7, 2003. Running time: 78 Min. Dutch-Japanese-Italian. Documentary.

OUR PRECIOUS CHILDREN
Pyramide Distribution. (Benoit Cohen) July 8, 2003. Running time: 83 Min. French. Mathieu Demy, Romane Bohringer, Laurence Cote, Julien Boisselier.

OUR TROPICAL ISLAND (MARI DEL SUD)
(Marcello Casena) Nov. 3, 2002. Running time: 94 min. Italian. Diego Abatantuono, Victoria Abril, Chiari Sani, Stefano Scandaletti.

THE OVER-EATER
TFM Distribution. (Thierry Binisti) July 19, 2003. Running time: 88 Min. French. Eric Cantona, Rachida Brakni, Caroline Silhol.

OVER THE RAINBOW
(Gonzalo Lopez-Gallego) May 1, 2003. Running time: 86 Min. Spanish. Luis Callejo, Isabelle Stoffel, Emily Behr, Martha Fessehatzion, J.F. Sebastian.

OWNING MAHOWNY
Sony Pictures Classics. (Richard Kwietniowski) Jan. 23, 2003. MPAA rating: R. Running time: 104 Min. Canadian-British. Philip Seymour Hoffman, Minnie Driver, Maury Chakin, John Hurt, Sonja Smits.

O-YO
(Ikuo Sekimoto) Nov. 8, 2002. Running time: 118 Min. Japanese. Tatsuya Kumakawa, Aki Shibuya, Naoto Takenaka, Kohtaro Satomi.

OYSTERS AT NAM KEE'S
UIP. (Pollo de Pimentel) Sept. 27, 2002. Running time: 110 Min. Dutch-German. Egbert-Jan Weeber, Katja Schuurman, Stefan Jurgens.

PARADISE
Svensk Filmindustri. (Colin Nutley) Feb. 24, 2003. Running time: 116 Min. Swedish. Helena Bergstrom, Niklas Hjulstrom, Orjan Ramberg.

PARADISE IS SOMEWHERE ELSE
(Abdolrasoul Golbon) July 5, 2003. Running time: 77 Min. Iranian. Yar-Mohammad Damanipour, Jan mohammad Tajik.

PASSIONATE PEOPLE (APASIONADOS)
Manga Films. (Juan Jose Jusid) Sept. 3, 2002. Running time: 98 Min. Argentine-Spanish. Pablo Echarri, Nancy Duplaa, Natalia Verbeke.

THE PASSION OF MARIA ELENA
(Mercedes Moncada Rodriguez) Jan. 22, 2003. Running time: 76 Min. Mexican. Documentary.

THE PASTRY GIRL
Iranian Film Society. (Iraj Tahmasb) Feb. 5, 2003. Running time: 101 Min. Iran. Fatemeh Motamed Aria, Soraya Ghasemi, Hamid Jebelli.

PATER FAMILIAS
Istituto Luce. (Francesco Patierno) March 11, 2003. Running time: 90 Min. Italian. Luigi Iacuzio, Federica Bonavolonta, Francesco Pirozzi.

THE PATH TO LOVE
(Remi Lange) June 16, 2003. Running time: 69 Min. French-Algerian. Karim Tarek, Sihem Benemoune, Abdellah Taia, Mustapha Dhadar.

A PECK ON THE CHEEK
(Mani Ratnam) Sept. 7, 2002. Running time: 135 Min. Indian. Madhavan, Simran, Prakashraj, Nandita Das.

A PERFECT MATCH (JOHEUN SARAM ISSEUMYEON JOGAE SHIKYEOJWEO)
Cinema Service. (Moh Ji-eun) Jan. 18, 2003. Running time: 99 Min. South Korean. Shin Eun-gyeong, Jeong Jun-ho, Gong Hyeong-jin.

PERFECT STRANGERS
20th Century Fox. (Gaylene Preston) July 28, 2003. Running time: 96 Min. New Zealand. Sam Neill, Rachael Blake, joel Tobeck.

THE PETER SELLERS STORY -- AS HE FILMED IT
(Anthony Wall, Peter Lydon) British. April 23, 2003. Running time: 88 Min. Documentary.

PHONE
Buena Vista Intl. Korea. (Ahn Byeong-gi) Dec. 3, 2002. Running time: 102 min. South Korean. Ha Ji-weon, Kim Yu-mi, Choi Woo-jae.

PHOOEY ROAS!
(Rosa von Praunheim) July 19, 2003. Running time: 70 Min. German. Rosa von Praunheim, Rene Krummenacher. Documentary.

PICKPOCKET
(Linton Semage) Jan. 25, 2003. Running time: 80 Min. Sri Lanka. Linton Semage, Dilhani Ekanayake.

PIGS WILL FLY
(Eoin Moore) Sept. 27, 2002. Running time: 102 Min. German. Andreas Schmidt, Thomas Morris, Laura Tonke, Kirsten Block.

PING PONG
(Sori) Oct. 7, 2002. Running time: 114 Min. Japanese. Yosuke Kubozuka, Arata, Sam Lee, Shidou Nakamura, Koji Ohkura.

PINOCCHIO
Medusa Film/Cecchi Gori Group (in Italy)/Miramax Films (in U.S.). (Roberto Benigni) Oct. 4, 2002. Running time: 108 Min. Italian-U.S. Roberto Benigni, Nicoletta Braschi, Mino Bellei, Carlo Giuffre.

PINOCHET'S CHILDREN (VOLVER A VERNOS)
(Paula Rodriguez) Sept. 24, 2002. Running time: 83 Min. Documentary. German. Alejandro Goic, Enrique Paris, Carolina Toha.

A PLACE AMONG THE LIVING
(Raoul Ruiz) Aug. 26, 2003. Running time: 107 Min. French. Christian Vadim, Thierry Gibault, Valerie Kaprisky, Cacile Bois.

PLAYING 'IN THE COMPANY OF MEN'
(Arnaud Desplechin) May 15, 2003. Running time: 121 Min. French. Sami Bouajila, Jean-Paul Roussillon, Wladimir Yordanoff.

PLOTS WITH A VIEW
Miramax. (Nick Hurran) Oct. 4, 2002. Running time: 94 Min. British. Brenda Blethyn, Alfred Molina, Christopher Walken, Naomi Watts.

POKEMON HEROES: LATIOS & LATIAS
Miramax. (Kunihiko Yuyama) May 13, 2003. MPAA Rating: G. Running time: 71 Min. Animated. Japanese-U.S. Voices: Veronica Taylor, Rachael Lillis, Eric Stuart, Maddie Blaustein, Ikue Otani, Lisa Ortiz.

PONIENTE
Araba Films. (Chus Gutierrez) Aug. 1, 2002. Running time: 96 Min. Spanish. Cuca Escribano, Jose Coronado, Antonio Dechent.

POWER AND TERROR: NOAM CHOMSKY IN OUR TIME
First Run Features. (John Junkerman) Nov. 18, 2002. Running time: 71 Min. Japanese. Documentary.

THE POWER OF THE PAST
Istituto Luce. (Piergiorgio Gay) Sept. 5, 2002. Running time: 98 Min. Italian. Sergio Rubini, Bruno Ganz, Sandra Ceccarelli.

PRESENCE
Triangelfilm. (Jan Troell) Feb. 1, 2003. Running time: 83 Min. Swedish. Documentary.

PRESERVATION
(Sofya Gollan) June 12, 2003. Running time: 54 Min. Australian. Jacqueline McKenzie, Jack Finsterer, simon Burke.

PRETTY BIG FEET
(Yang Yazhou) Jan. 25, 2003. Running time: 103 Min. Chinese. Ni Ping, Yuan Quan, Sun Haiying, Xu Yajun, Ge Zhijun, Yang Tiahe.

THE PRINCIPLES OF LUST
(Penny Woolcock) Jan. 29, 2003. Running time: 108 Min. British. Alec Newman, Sienna Guillory, Marc Warren, Lara Clifton, Julian Barratt.

THE PROFESSIONAL
(Dusan Kovacevic) Sept. 2, 2003. Running time: 104 Min. Serbian-Montengro. Bora Todorovic, Branislav Lecic, Natasa Ninkovic.

THE PROMISED LIFE
Bac Distribution. (Olivier Dahan) Running time: 94 Min. French. Isabelle Huppert, Pascal Greggory, Maud Forget, Fabienne Babe.

PROVENCE UNITED
(Ori Inbar) June 1, 2003. Running time: 88 Min. Israeli. Ze'ev Ravach, Itay Turgeman, Eli Eltonyo, Osnat Hakim.

PTU
Mei Ah. (Johnnie To) Feb. 10, 2003. Running time: 87 Min. Hong Kong. Simon Yam, Lam Suet, Ruby Wong, Maggie Shiu, Ko Hung.

PUBLIC AFFAIRS
(Mathieu Amalric) May 21, 2003. Running time: 85 Min. French. Jean-Quentin Chatelain, Anne Alvaro, Michele Laroque.

PUBLIC TOILET (RENMIN GONGCHE)
(Fruit Chan) Aug. 30, 2002. Running time: 105 Min. Hong Kong-South Korean. Tsuyoshi Abe, Zhe Ma, Hyuk Jang, Insung Cho, Yanghee Kim.

PUPENDO
Falcon. (Jan Hrebejk) April 1, 2003. Running time: 126 Min. Czech. Bolek Polivka, Jaroslav Dusek, Eva Holubova, Vilma Cibulkova.

PURIFIED
(Jesper Jargil) Aug. 12, 2002. Running time: 68 Min. Danish. Documentary. Lars von Trier, Thomas Vinterberg.

PURPLE BUTTERFLY
(Lou Ye) May 21, 2003. Running time: 127 Min. Chinese-French. Zhang Ziyi, Liu Ye, Feng Yuanzheng, Toru Nakamura, Li Bingbing.

THE PYTHON
Laila Pakalnina) Sept. 3, 2003. Running time: 91 Min. Latvian. Mara Kimele, Juris Grave, Januss Johansons, Ilze Pukinska.

RABID DOGS
(Mario Bava) Feb. 16, 2003. Running time: 96 Min. Italian. Riccardo Cucciolla, Lea Lander, Maurice Poli, George Eastman, Aldo Caponi.

RAGE
Gaumont. (Karim Dridi) Feb. 16, 2003. Running time: 106 Min. French. Samuel Le Bihan, Yu Nan, Yann Tregouet, Bounsy Luang Phinith.

THE RAGE IN PLACID LAKE
Palace Films. (Tony McNamara) May 7, 2003. Running time: 89 Min. Australian. Ben Lee, Rose Byrne, Miranda Richardson.

RAID
Columbia TriStar Nordisk Film Distributors. (Tapio Piirainen) Jan. 27, 2003. Running time: 124 Min. Finnish. Kai Lehtinen, Oiva Lohtander.

THE RAIN CHILDREN
(Philippe Leclerc) June 30, 2003. Running time: 86 Min. French-South Korean. Animated.

THE RAIN FALLS ON OUR SOULS
(Vlado Balco) Nov. 3, 2002. Running time: 83 Min. Slovakian. Kristina Svarinska, Erik Olle, Stano Danciak, Alexandra Zaborska.

RAINING COWS
Pablo. (Luca Vendruscolo) April 7, 2003. Running time: 92 Min. Italian. Alessandro Tiberi, Massimo De Lorenzo, Luca Amorosino.

RAJA
(Jacques Doillon) Aug. 27, 2003. Running time: 115 Mln. French-Morrocco. Pascal Greggory, Najat Benssallem, Hassan Khissal.

THE RASHEVSKI TANGO
Rezo Films. (Sam Gabarski) Aug. 20, 2003. Running time: 100 Min. Belgian-French-Luxembourgors. Hippolyte Girardot, Ludmila Mikael.

REAL TIME
(Fabrizio Prada) Feb. 11, 2003. Running time: 87 Min. Mexican. Jorge Carillo, Enrique Rendon, Raul Ranstamariia, Leticia Valenzuela.

RECONSTRUCTION
(Christoffer Boe) May 5, 2003. Running time: 91 Min. Danish. Nikolaj Lie Kaas, Maria Bonnevie, Krister Henriksson.

RECONSTRUCTION
(Irene Lusztig) Oct. 3, 2002. Running time: 90 Min. U.S.-Romanian. Documentary.

RED & BLUE
Academy Films. (Rudolf Thome) July 10, 2003. Running time: 109 Min. German. Hannelore Elsner, Serpil Turhan, Hanns Zischler.

THE RED KNIGHT
Diaphana. (Helene Angel) Aug. 15, 2003. Running time: 106 Min. French. Daniel Auteuil, Nicolas Nollet, Sergi Lopez.

RED PASSPORT
(Albert Xavier) Feb. 16, 2003. Running time: 93 Min. U.S.-Dominican Republic. Frank Molina, Maite Bonilla, Frank Medrano.

REGINA
(Maria Sigudardottir) Aug. 24, 2002. Running time: 92 Min. Icelandic. Sigurbjorg Alma Ingolfsdottir, Benedikt Clausen, Baltasar Kormakur.

REMEMBER ME
Medusa Films. (Gabriele Muccino) Jan. 29, 2003. Running time: 124 Min. Italian-French-British. Fabrizio Bentivoglio, Laura Morante.

REMEMBRANCES
(Marcela Arteaga) June 11, 2003. Running time: 86 Min. Mexican. Luis Frank, Miriam Frank, Jose Frank, Max Kerlow, Genoveva Arteaga.

RESURRECTION OF THE LITTLE MATCH GIRL
CJ Entertainment. (Jang Sun-woo) Nov. 22, 2002. Running time: 121 min. South Korean. Im Eun-gyeong, Kim Hyeon-seong, Kim Jin-pyo.

THE RETURN
(Andrei Zvyagintsev) Sept. 2, 2003. Running time: 110 Min. Russian. Ivan Dobronravov, Vladimir Garin, Konstantin Lavronenko.

THE RETURN OF CAGLIOSTRO
Istituto Luce. (Daniele Cipri) Aug. 30, 2003. Running time: 100 Min. Italian. Robert Englund, Luigi Maria Burruano, Pietro Giordano.

REVERSAL OF FORTUNE
Cinema Service. (Park Yong-woon) July 13, 2003. Running time: 104 Min. South Korean. Kim Seung-woo, Ha Ji-weon, Kang Sung-jin.

THE REVOLUTION WILL NOT BE TELEVISED
(Kim Bartley, Donnacha O'Briain) July 17, 2003. Running time: 74 Min. Irish-British-Dutch-German. Documentary.

RIDING THE TIGER
01 Distribution. (Carlo Mazzacurati) Oct. 23, 2002. Running time: 98 Min. Italian. Fabrizio Bentivoglio, Tuncel Kurtiz, Paola Cortellesi.

RINALDO
(Tamas Toth) Feb. 3, 2003. Running time: 83 Min. Hungarian. Janos Ban, Peter Scherer, Lajos Kovacs, Bence Matyasi, Vilmos Kun.

ROAD TO LADAKH
(Ashvin Kumar) May 4, 2003. Running time: 50 Min. British. Irfan Khan, Koel Purie, Milan Moudgill, Amit Vasisht, Sardaji.

ROBINSON'S CRUSOE
(Lin Chen-sheng) May 21, 2003. Running time: 91 Min. Taiwanese. Leon Dai, Yang Kuei-Mei, Chen Shiang-Chyi, Chang Feng-shu, Lee Sin-Je, Wu Kuei Chuen.

ROCCO
(Houchang Allahyari) Jan. 30, 2003. Running time: 76 Min. Austrian. Morteza Tavakoli, Anna Franziska Srna, Ronald Rudoll.

ROCK MY WORLD
Cinemavault Releasing. (Sidney J. Furie) Nov. 2, 2002. Running time: 106 Min. Canadian-British. Peter O'Toole, Joan Plowright.

ROKHSAREH
Atlantis Enterprises. (Amir Ghavidel) Sept. 18, 2002. Running time: 94 Min. Iranian. Mitra Hajjar, Shahab Hosseini, Mohammad Ali Sepanloo.

ROOM 36
(Jim Groom) Oct. 5, 2002. Running time: 89 Min. British. Paul Herzberg, Portia Booroff, Brian Murphy, Norman Mitchell.

ROOM TO LET
(James Lee) June 22, 2003. Running time: 118 Min. Malaysian. Berg Lee, Kiew Suet Kim, Andrew Low, Ling Tan, Chong Sheon Wei.

ROSENSTRASSE
(Margarethe von Trotta) Aug. 30, 2003. Running time: 135 Min. German-Dutch. Katja Riemann, Maria Schrader, Martin Feifel.

ROUND 1
Asmik Ace Entertainment. (Daiki Yamada) Nov. 17, 2002. Running time: 104 Min. Japanese. Takanori Hatakeyama, Song Seon-mi.

ROUND TRIP
(Shahar Rosen) June 1, 2003. Running time: 95 Min. Israeli. Anat Waxman, Nathati Moshesh, Eyal Rozales, Nathan Zahavi.

ROYAL BON BON
K Films Amerique. (Charles Najman) Sept 8, 2002. Running time: 89 Min. French-Canadian-Haiti. Dominique Battraville, BenjiAnne-Louise Mesadieux, Erol Josue, Alain Thompson.

RUB & TUG
Les Films Seville. (Soo Lyu) Sept. 10, 2002. Running time: 89 Min. Canadian. Don McKellar, Lindy Booth, Tara Spencer-Nairn.

RUNAWAY MUMMY
Warner Bros. Intl. (Erdal Murat Aktas) Oct. 6, 2002. Running time: 115 Min. Turkish. Selami Sahin, Teoman, Nurgul Yesilcay, Nurseli Idiz.

SAATHIYA
(Shaad Ali) Dec. 23, 2002. Running time: 137 Min. Indian. Rani Mukherji, Vivek Oberoi, Sandhya Mridul, Tanuja, Satish Shah.

THE SADDEST MUSIC IN THE WORLD
TVA Films (Canada)/IFC Films (U.S.). (Guy Maddin) Aug. 30, 2003. Running time: 99 Min. Canadian. Mark McKinney, Isabella Rossellini, Maria de Medeiros, David Fox, Ross McMillan.

SALAMINA SOLDIERS
UIP. (David Trueba) Release date: March 21, 2003. Running time: 121 Min. Spanish. Ariadna Gil, Ramon Fontsere, Joan Dalmau.

SALAM IRAN: A PERSIAN LETTER
(Jean-Daniel Lafond) Oct. 7, 2002. Running time: 72 Min. Canadian. Documentary. Narrator: Christian Allard.

SALT
(Bradley Rust Gray) Feb 15, 2003. Running time: 86 Min. Icelandic. Brynja Thora Gudnadottir, David Orn Halldorsson.

SAMMY AND ME
Lauren Films. (Eduardo Milewicz) Oct. 12, 2002. Running time: 88 Min. Argentine. Ricardo Darin, Angie Cepeda, Alejandra Flechner.

SANSA
(Siegfried) May 5, 2003. Running time: 116 Min. French-Spanish. Roschdy Zem, Ivry Gitlis, Emma Suarez, Valentina Cervi, Rita Durao, Silke, Ayako Fujitani, George Abes, Bassem Samra.

SAUDADE: LONGING
A GMfilms (Germany)/TLA Releasing. (Jurgen Bruning) June 14, 2003. German. Hendrik Scheider, Aldri D'Anunciacao.

SAVE THE GREEN PLANET!
CJ Entertainment. (Jang Jun-hwan) April 11, 2003. Running time: 116 Min. South Korean. Shin Ha-gyun, Baek Yun-shik, Hwang Jung-min.

SAVING MY HUBBY (GUDSEORA GEUMSUNA)
Korea Pictures. (Hyeon Nam-seob) Nov. 18, 2002. Running time: 92 Min. South Korean. Bae Du-na, Kim Tae-woo, Lee Chan-min.

SAYEW
Sahamongkol Film Intl. (Kongdej Jaturanrasmee) June 10, 2003. Running time: 117 Min. Thai. Pimpaporn Leenutapong.

SCENT OF LOVE
Cinema Service. (Lee Jeong-uk) May 3, 2003. Running time: 106 Min. South Korean. Jang Jin-yeong, Park Hae-il, Song Sun-mi.

SCENT OF TIME
(Naoto Akikawa) Nov. 10, 2002. Running time: 77 Min. Japanese. Kazue Fukiishi, Takumi Saito, Hiromi Kitigawa, So Yamanaka.

SCHULTZA GETS THE BLUES
(Michael Schorr) Sept. 1, 2003. Running time: 113 Min. German. Horst Krause, Harald Warmbrunn, Karl-Fred Muller, Ursula Schucht.

THE SEA
(Baltasar Kormakur) Sept. 8, 2002. Running time: 109 Min. Icelandic-French. Gunnar Eyjolfsson, Hilmir Snaer Gudnason.

SEASON IN THE SUN
Aura Entertainment (Lee Min-yeong) July 11, 2003. Running time: 102 Min. South Korean. Jang Mi-heui, Park Yeong-gyu, Cha In-pyo.

THE SEA WATCHES
(Kei Kumai) Sept. 22, 2002. Running time: 119 Min. Japanese. Misa Shimizu, Nagiko Tohno, Masatoshi Nagase, Hidetaka Yoshioka.

SECOND NAME
Filmax. (Paco Plaza) Nov. 13, 2002. Running time: 98 Min. Spanish. Erica Prior, Denis Rafter, Frank O'Sullivan, John O'Toole.

SECRET THINGS
Rezo Films. (Jean-Claude Brisseau) Oct. 29, 2002. Running time: 113 Min. French. Coralie Revel, Sabrina Seyvecou, Roger Mirmont.

SEDUCER
Warner Bros. (Andrea Sedlackova) Feb. 8, 2003. Running time: 88 Min. Czech. Ivana Chylkova, Jan Kraus, Ivan Trojan.

SEDUCING DOCTOR LEWIS
Alliance Atlantis Vivafilm. (Jean-Francois Pouliot) May 23, 2003. Running time: 108 Min. Canadian. Raymond Bouchard, David Boutin, Benoit Briere, Bruno Blanchet, Pierre Collin, Lucie Laurier.

SEEING DOUBLE
Columbia TriStar. (Nigel Dick) April 14, 2003. Running time: 91 Min. British-U.S. Hannah Spearitt, Jo O'Meara, Rachel Stevens, Jon Lee, Bradley McIntosh, Tina Barrett, Joseph Adams, David Gant.

THE SENTIMENTAL TEASER
Nirvana Films. (Cristian Galaz) Jan. 29, 2003. Running time: 88 Min. Chilean. El Rumpy (Roberto Artiagoitia), Daniel Munoz, Lorene Prieto.

SEPTEMBER
(Max Faerberboeck) May 22, 2003. Running time: 109 Min. German. Catharina Schuchmann, Justus von Dohnanyi, Nina Proll, Jorg Schuttauf, Moritz Rinke, Solveig Arnarsdottir, Stefanie Stappenbeck.

SEPTEMBER FLOWERS
(Pablo Osores, Roberto Testa, Nicolas Wanszelbaum) April 20, 2003. Running time: 111 Min. Documentary. Argentine.

SERGEANT SHAKESPEARE (KOMSER SEKSPIR)
(Sinan Cetin) Oct. 27, 2002. Running time: 113 Min. Turkish. Kadir Inanir, Mujde Ar, Okan Bayulgen, Ozkan Ugur, Pelin Batu.

THE SETTLERS
(Ruth Walk) Jan. 16, 2003. Running time: 58 Min. Israel. Documentary.

SEVEN DAYS, SEVEN NIGHTS
(Joel Cano) Sept. 20, 2003. Running time: 106 Min. French-Italian. Ludmila Alonso-Yodu, Mercedes Morales, Eruadye Muniz.

7 YEARS OF MARRIAGE
UGC Distribution. (Didier Bourdon) June 27, 2003. Running time: 93 Min. French. Didier Bourdon, Catherine Frot, Jacques Weber, Yan Duffas.

SHANGHAI WOMEN
Shanghai Film Studio. (Peng Xiaolian) Jan. 18, 2003. Running time: 94 Min. Chinese. Lu Liping, Zhou Wenqian, Sun Haiying, Zheng Zhenyao.

SHANGRI-LA (TOGENKYO NO HITOBITO)
(Takashi Miike) Sept. 26, 2002. Running time: 109 Min. Japanese. Sho Aikawa, Shiro Sano, Yo Tokui, Midoriko Kimura, Shugeru Muroi.

SHARA
Pyramide Distribution. (Naomi Kawase) May 24, 2003. Running time: 99 Min. Japanese. Kohei Fukunaga, Yuka Hyoudo, Naomi Kawase, Katsuhisa Namase, Kanako Higuchi.

SHATTERED GLASS
(Chris Kraus) Nov. 11, 2002. Running time: 101 Min. German. Jurgen Vogel, Margit Carstensen, Nadja Uhl, Peter Davor.

SHOOTING BOKKIE
(Rob de Mezieres) Jan. 29, 2003. Running time: 74 Min. South African. Christo Davids, Charlton George.

SILENT GRACE
(Maeve Murphy) Oct. 17, 2002. Running time: 86 Min. Irish. Orla Brady, Cathleen Bradley, Cara Seymour, Dawn Bradfield.

SILENT WATERS
(Sabiha Sumar) Aug. 14, 2003. Running time: 100 Min. Pakistan-French-German. Kirron Kher, Aamir Malik, Arshad Mahmud.

SILVIA'S GIFT
Lolafilms. (Dionisio Perez Galindo) May 2, 2003. Running time: 91 Min. Spanish-Chilean-Portugese. Barbara Goenaga, Luis Tosar, Victor Clavijo, Adriana Dominguez, Maria Bouzas, Pablo Galan.

SIMON, AN ENGLISH LEGIONNAIRE
(Martin Huberty) Jan. 18, 2003 MPAA: PG. Running time: 90 Min. British. Paul Fox, Tom Hardy, Aitor Merino, Felicite du Jeu.

SINCE OTAR LEFT
Haut et Court (France). (Julie Bertuccelli) May 20, 2003. Running time: 103 Min. French-Belgian. Esther Gorintin, Nino Khomassouridze, Dinara Droukarova, Temour Kalandadze, Roussoudan Bolkvadze.

SINGARAVVA
(T.S. Nagabharana) July 10, 2003. Running time: 169 Min. Indian. Prema, Avinash, Akhila, Shivadwai, Sharath Lohithashwa.

SINGLES
Big Blue. (Gweon Chil-in) July 15, 2003. Running time: 107 Min. South Korean. Jang Jin-yeong, Lee Beom-su, Eom Jeong-Hwa.

16 YEARS OF ALCOHOL
Metro Tartan. (Richard Jobson) Aug. 7, 2003. Running time: 97 Min. British. Kevin McKidd, Laura Fraser, Susan Lynch, Stuart Sinclair Blyth, Jim Carter, Ewen Bremner.

66 SEASONS
Czech TV. (Peter Kerekes) July 10, 2003. Running time: 84 Min. Slovakian-Czech. Documentary.

SKAGERRAK
Egmont Entertainment. (Soren Kragh-Jacobsen) March 11, 2003. Running time: 104 Min. Danish-British. Iben Hjejle, Bronagh Gallagher, Martin Henderson, Ewen Bremner, Gary Lewis.

SKINHEAD ATTITUDE
(Daniel Schweizer) Aug. 7, 2003. Running time: 93 Min. Swiss-German-French. Karole, Laurel Aitken. Documentary.

SLEEP TIGHT
(Claire Doyon) May 23, 2003. Running time: 77 Min. French. Lisa Lacroix, Marie Felix, Guillaume Gouix.

SLEEPING WITH THE DEAD
(Wai-Man Cheng) Feb. 16, 2003. Running time: 88 Min. Hong Kong. Jordan Chan, Kelly Lin, Sharon Chan, Simon Lui, Paul Wong.

SMALL CUTS
(Pascal Bonitzer) Feb. 12, 2003. Running time: 95 Min. French-British. Daniel Auteuil, Kristin Scott Thomas, Ludivine Sagnier.

SNAPSHOTS
A-Film Distribution. (Rudolf van den Berg) Sept. 26, 2002. Running time: 93 Min. Ducth-U.S. Burt Reynolds, Carmen Chaplin.

SNOWBOARDER
Mars Films Distribution. (Olias Barco) March 31, 2003. Running time: 109 Min. French-Swiss. Nicolas Duvauchelle, Gregoire Colin.

SO CLOSE
Columbia Pictures. (Cory Yuen) Nov. 6, 2002. Running time: 110 Min. Hong Kong. Shu Qi, Zhao Wei, Karen Mok, Song Seung-heon.

SO FAR AWAY
Alta Films. (Juan Carlos Tabio) June 25, 2003. Running time: 98 Min. Indian. Antonio Valero, Mirtha Ibarra, Barbaro Marin, Laura Ramos.

SOLID AIR
Momentum Pictures. (May Miles Thomas) Aug. 22, 2003. Running time: 115 Min. British. Maurice Roeves, Brian McCardie, Kathy Kiera Clarke, Gary Lewis.

SOLINO
(Fatih Akin) Feb. 10, 2003. Running time: 124 Min. German. Barnaby Metschurat, Moritz Bleibtreu, Antonella Attili, Gigi Savoia.

SOME SECRETS
(Alice Nellis) Sept 21, 2002. Running time: 100 Min. Czech. Iva Janzurova, Theodora Remundova, Igor Bares, Sabina Remundova.

SOMEWHERE OVER THE DREAMLAND
(Cheng Wen-tang) Sept. 2, 2002. Running time: 92 Min. Taiwanese. Yu Lao Yu Gan, Muo Tsi-yi, Wu Yi-ting.

SONG FOR A RAGGY BOY
(Aisling Walsh) Jan. 19, 2003. Running time: 98 Min. Irish-Danish-British-Spanish. Aidan Quinn, Iain Glenn, Marc Warren.

THE SOUL KEEPER
Medusa. (Roberto Faenza) Jan. 15, 2003. Running time: 90 Min. Italian-French-British. Iain Glen, Emilia Fox, Caroline Ducey.

SOLE SISTERS
Bae Films. (Pierre Jolivet) May 20, 2003. Running time: 87 Min. French. Sandrine Kiberlain, Francois Berleand.

THE SOUL'S PLACE
01 RAI Cinema/Studio Canal Distribution. (Riccardo Milani) June 24, 2004. Running time: 105 Min. Italian. Michele Placido, Silvio Orlando, Claudio Santamaria, Paola Cortellesi.

SOUTHEAST
(Sergio Bellotti) Sept. 24, 2002. Running time: 98 Min. Argentine. Javier Locatelli, Luis Ziembrowsky, Claudio Escobar, Bernardo Perco.

SOUTH FROM GRANADA
Warner Sogefilms/Sogepaq. (Fernando Colomo) Dec. 5, 2002. Running time: 111 Min. Spanish. Matthew Goode, Veronica Sanchez.

SOUTH OF THE CLOUDS
Monopole Pathe. (Jean-Francois Amiguet) Aug. 7, 2003. Running time: 77 Min. Swiss-French. Bernard Verley, Francois Morel.

SPARE PARTS
(Damjan Kozole) Feb. 13, 2003. Running time: 87 Min. Slovenian. Peter Musevski, Aljosa Kovacic, Primoz Petkovsek, Valter Dragan.

THE SPEAKING DRUM
(Sumantra Ghosal) May 29, 2003. Running time: 104 Min. Documentary. Indian. Ustad Zakir Hussain, Ustad Alla Rakha , Bavi Begum Alla Rakha , Pandit Jasran, Khursheed Aulia.

SPRING SUBWAY
(Zhang Yibai) Jan. 23, 2003. Running time: 93 Min. Chinese. Xu Jinglei, Geng Le, Zhang Yang.

SPRING, SUMMER, FALL, WINTER...AND SPRING
(Kim Ki-duk) Aug. 13, 2003. Running time: 102 Min. South Korean-German. Oh Yeong-su, Kim Ki-duk, Kim Yeong-min.

STARKISS - CIRCUS GIRLS IN INDIA
(Chris Relleke, Jascha de Wilde) Jan. 31, 2003. Running time: 77 Min. Dutch. Documentary.

STORM SEASON
UIP. (Pedro Olea) April 26, 2003. Running time: 86 Min. Spanish. Maribel Verdu, Jorge Sanz, Dario Grandinetti, Maria Barranco.

STORMY WEATHER
Diaphana release (in France). (Solveig Anspach) May 18, 2003. Running time: 91 Min. French-Icelandic-Belgian. Elodie Bouchez, Didda Jonsdottir, Baltasar Kormakur, Ingvar E. Sigurdsson.

STORMY WEATHER: THE MUSIC OF HAROLD ARLEN
(Larry Weinstein) Feb. 8, 2003. Running time: 78 Min. Canadian. Paul Soles, Kim Bubbs, Ranee Lee, Debbie Harry, Little Jimmy Scott.

STORY OF A KISS
Columbia-Tristar Pictures (Spain). (Jose Luis Garci) Nov. 10, 2002. Running time: 105 Min. Spanish. Alfredo Landa, Ana Fernandez.

A STORY THAT BEGINS AT THE END
(Murali Nair) May 18, 2003. Original title: Arimpara. Running time: 90 Min. Indian-Japanese. Nedumudi Venu, Sona Nair, Bharathan Njarakkal, Rajan Sithara, Master Bhagyanath.

STRANGE
(Santiago Loza) Feb. 1, 2003. Running time: 81 Min. Argentine-French. Julio Chavez, Valeria Bertucelli, Raquel Albeniz.

STRANGE GARDENS
UFD. (Jean Becker) March 6, 2003. Running time: 97 Min. French. Jacques Villeret, Andre Dussollier, Thierry Lhermitte.

STRAYED
Mars Distribution (France). (Andre Techine) May 16, 2003. Running time: 95 Min. French-British. Emmanuelle Beart, Gaspard Ulliel, Gregoire Leprince-Ringuet, Clemence Meyer, Jean Fornerod.

STRONG AS A LION
Sonet Film. (Manne Lindwall) Dec. 16, 2002. Running time: 89 Min. Swedish. Lisa Lindgren, Magnus Krepper, Eric Lager, Linus Nord.

STRUGGLE
(Ruth Mader) May 18th, 2003. Running time: 76 Min. Australian. Aleksandra Justa, Gottfried Breitfuss.

S21: THE KHMER ROUGE KILLING MACHINE
(Rithy Panh) May 16, 2003. Running time: 105 Min. Documentary. French. Vann Nath, Chum Mey, Kim Houy, Prak Khan, Sours Thi.

SQUINT YOUR EYES
Zair. (Andrzej Jakimowski) Jan. 19, 2003. Running time: 88 Min. Polish. Zbigniew Zamachandowski, Ola Proszynska, Rafal Guzniczak.

THE SUIT
Alta Films. (Alberto Rodriguez) Sept. 17, 2002 Running time: 102 Min. Spanish. Eugenio Jose Roca, Manuel Moron, Vanesa Cabeza.

THE SUIT
(Bakhtiyar Khudoinazarov) Feb. 21, 2003. Running time: 92 Min. Russian-German-Italian-French. Alexander Yatsenko, Artur Povolotsky, Ivan Kokorin, Ingeborga Dapkunaite, Andrei Panin.

SUMMER, DREAM (SHIDING DE XIATIAN)
(Cheng Yu-Chieh) Oct. 7, 2002. Running time: 61 Min. Taiwanese. Huang Chien-Wei, Manon Garceau, Li Hsiu, Hsieh Chun-Hui.

SUMO EAST AND WEST
(Ferne Pearlstein) June 13, 2003. Running time: 87 Min. U.S. Japanese. Wayne Vierra, Akebono, Konishiki.

SUPERPRODUCTION
MGE. (Juliusz Machulski) May 18, 2003. (Running time: 94 Min. Polish. Rafal Krolikowski, Piotr Fronczewski, Janusz Rewinski, Anna Przybylska, Marta Lipinska, Magda Schejbal, Krzysztof Globisz.

SWEPT AWAY
Screen Gems. (Guy Ritchie) Oct. 8, 2002. MPAA rating: R. Running time: 89 Min. British. Madonna, Adriano Giannini, Jeanne Tripplehorn, Bruce Greenwood, Elizabeth Banks, David Thornton.

SWIMMING ALONE
(Ezequiel Acuna) April 19, 2003. Running time: 102 Min. Argentine. Nicolas Mateo, Santiago Pedrero, Antonella Costa.

SWIMMING POOL
Focus Features (U.S.)/Mars Films Distribution (France). (Francois Ozon) May 18, 2003. MPAA Rating: R. Running time: 102 Min. French-British. Charlotte Rampling, Ludivine Sagnier, Charles Dance.

SWITCHBLADE ROMANCE
EuropaCorp. (Alexandre Aja. June 30, 2003. Running time: 89 Min. French. Cecile de France, Maiwennm Philippe Nahon.

SWORD IN THE MOON
Shinabro Entertainment. (Kim Eui-seok) July 17, 2003. Running time: 94 Min. South Korean. Choi Min-su, Jo Jae-hyeon, Kim Bo-gyeong.

TAKE MY EYES
Alta Films. (Iciar Bollain) Sept. 12, 2003. Running time: 106 Min. Spanish. Laia Marull, Luis Tosar, Candela Pena, Rosa Maria Sarda.

A TALE OF TWO SISTERS
Big Blue Film. June 30, 2003. Running time: 114 Min. South Korean. Im Su-jeong, Yeom Jeong-ah, Kim Gab-su, Mun Geun-yeong.

A TALKING PICTURE
(Manoel de Oliveira) Aug. 30, 2003. Running time: 96 Min. Portugese-French-Italian. Leonor Silveira, Filipa de Almeida.

TASTY BITS
(Sasha Valenti) June 2, 2003. Running time: 85 Min. Russian. Julia Muranova, Tatiana Alyokhina, Roman Erykalov, Igor Avrov.

TAXI 3
ARP Selection. (Gerard Krawczyk) Feb. 4, 2003. Running time: 84 Min. French. Samy Naceri, Frederic Diefenthal, Emma Sjoberg.

TEENAGE HOOKER BECAME KILLING MACHINE IN DAEHAKROH
(Nam Ki-woong) Oct. 20, 2002. Running time: 60 Min. South Korean. Lee So-woon, Kim Ae-tong, Bae Soo-back, Kim Ho-kyum.

TEN MINUTES OLDER: THE CELLO
Release date: Sept. 3, 2002. Running time: 106 Min. German-British-Spanish.
History of Water
(Bernardo Bertolucci) Amit Arroz, Valeria Bruni Tadeschi.
About Time 2
(Mike Figgis) Mark Long, Alexandra Staden, Dominic West.
One Moment
(Jiri Menzel) Rudolf Hrusinsky.
Ten Minutes After
(Istvan Szabo) Ildiko Bansagi, Gabor Mate.
Towards Nancy
(Claire Denis) Jean-Luc Nancy, Ana Samardzija, Alex Descas.
The Enlightenment
(Volker Schlondorff) Bibiana Beglau, Irm Hermann, Mario Irrek.
Addicted To The Stars
(Michael Radford) Daniel Craig, Charles Simon, Roland Gift.
In The Darkness of Time
(Jean-Luc Godard)

TERRORISTS-THE KIDS THEY SENTENCED
Folkets Bio. (Stefan Jarl) June 23, 2003. Running time: 85 Min. Sweden. Documentary.

THANK GOD I'M IN THE FILM BUSINESS!
(Lothar Lambert) Feb. 8, 2003. Running time: 79 Min. German. Documentary. Eva Ebner.

THAT DAY
(Raoul Ruiz) May 14, 2003. Running time: 105 Min. French-Swiss. Bernard Girardeau, Elsa Zylberstein, Jean-Luc Bideau, Christian Vadim.

THERE AND BACK
(Wojciech Wojcik) Nov. 2, 2002. Running time: 103 Min. Polish. Janusz Gajos, Jan Frycz, Olaf Lubaszenko, Miroslaw Baka, Edyta Olszowka.

THEY'RE WATCHING US
Columbia TriStar. (Norberto Lopez Amado) Sept. 16, 2002. Running time: 105 Min. Spanish-Italian. Carmelo Gomez, Iciar Bollain.

THEY'VE GOT KNUT
(Stefan Krohmer) Feb. 8, 2003. Running time: 107 Min. German-Austrian. Hans-Jochen Wagner, Valerie Koch, Markus Sieber.

THINK IT OVER
(Katerina Evangelakou) Dec. 22, 2002. Running time: 99 Min. Greek. Mania Papadimitriou, Yvonne Maltezou, Hristos Steryoglou.

3RD WORLD HERO
(Mike de Leon) Nov. 2, 2002. Running time: 93 Min. Filipino. Joel Torre, Ricky Davao, Cris Villanueva, Ed Rocha, Joonee Gamboa.

THE THIRTEEN STEPS
Pony Canyon. (Masahiko Nagasawa) Jan. 13, 2003. Running time: 122 Min. Japanese. Takashi Sorimachi, Tsutomu Yamazaki, Kankuro Kudo.

THE 13TH HOUSE
(Shane McNeil) June 16, 2003. Running time: 58 Min. Australian. Damon Gameau, Shaum Micallef, Rebecca Havey.

THIS VERY MOMENT
(Christoph Hochhausler) Feb. 10, 2003. Running time: 94 Min. German. Judith Engel, Horst-Guenther Marx, Miroslav Baka.

THOMAS PYNCHON: A JOURNEY INTO THE MIND OF [P.]
(Fosco Dubini, Donatello Dubini) Oct. 7, 2002. Running time: 89 Min. German-Swiss. Documentary. Richard Lane, George Plimpton.

A THOUSAND CLOUDS OF PEACE FENCE THE SKY, LOVE; YOUR BEING LOVE WILL NEVER END
(Julian Hernandez) Feb. 15, 2003. Running time: 82 Min. Mexican. Juan Carlos Ortuno, Juan Torres, Perla de la Rosa, Salvador Alvarez.

A THOUSAND MONTHS
MK2. (Faouzi Bensaidi) May 16, 2003. Running time: 124 Min. Moroccan-French-Belgian. Fouad Labied, Nezha Rahil.

THREE
Oct. 4, 2002. Running time: 129 Min. South Korean-Thai-Hong Kong.
1. Memories
(Kim Jee-Woon) Running time: 40 Min. South Korean. Kim Hye-Soo.
2. The Wheel
(Nonzee Nimibutr) Running time: 36 Min. Thai. Komgich Yuttiyong.
3. Coming Home
(Peter Ho-Sun Chan) Running time: 52 Min. Hong Kong. Leon Lai.

THE THREE THOUSAND
(Dominique Abel) Feb. 16, 2003. Running time: 105 Min. Spanish-French. Emilio Caracafe, Ramon Quilate, Luis de los Santos.

3 WALLS
(Nagesh Kukunoor) May 29, 2003. Running time: 116 Min. Indian. Naseeruddin Shah, Jackie Shroff, Juhi Chawla, Nagesh Kukunoor, Gulshan Grover, Bannerjee, Nageraj, Aditya Lakha.

THE TICCERS
(Philippe Locquet) April 16, 2003. Running time: 87 Min. French. Mathieu Lagarrigue, Nelly Amado, Anne Pauleau-Gauthier.

TIE XI QU: WEST OF THE TRACKS
(Wang Bing) Jan. 28-31, 2003. Running time: 556 Min. Documentary. Chinese.

TIME OF THE WOLF
(Michael Haneke) May 20, 2003. Running time: 113 Min. French-Austrian-German. Isabelle Huppert , Maurice Benichou, Lucas Biscombe, Patrice Chereau, Beatrice Dalle, Anais Demoustier.

TINY SNOWFLAKES
(Ali Reza Amini) Aug. 13, 2003. Running time: 76 Min. Iranian. Mohsen Tanabandeh, Majid Bahrami.

TIRESIA
Haut et Court. (Bertrand Bonello) May 19, 2003. Running time: 116 Min. French-Canadian. Clara Choveaux, ThiagoTeles Terranova, Laurent Lucas, Celia Catalifo, Lou Castel.

TITAN IN THE RING
(Viviana Cordero) Jan. 29, 2003. Running time: 111 Min. Ecuador. Toty Rodriguez, Norbert Stimpfig, Marta Ormaza, Juana Garderas.

TODAY AND TOMORROW
(Alejandro Chomski) May 22, 2003. Running time: 87 Min. Argentine-Spanish. Antonella Costa, Manuel Navarro, Romina Ricci, Carlos Duranona, Ricardo Merkin, Horacio Acosta.

TO KILL A KING
Pathe. (Mike Barker) May 9, 2003. Running time: 102 Min. British-German. Tim Roth, Dougray Scott, Rupert Everett, Olivia Williams.

TOO LATE TOMORROW
(Laya Giourgou) Dec. 23, 2002. Running time: 93 Min. Alexis Georgoulis, Marina Kaloyirou, Odysseas Papaspiliopoulos.

TORREMOLINOS 73
Buena Vista Intl. (Pablo Berger) May 6, 2003. (In Malaga Film Festival, competing.) Running time: 93 Min. Spainsh-Danish. Javier Camara, Candela Pena, Juan Diego, Thomas Bo Larson, Fernando Tejero.

TOTAL KHEOPS
Pyramide. (Alain Beverini) July 23, 2002. Running time: 90 Min. French. Richard Bohringer, Marie Trintignant, Daniel Duval.

THE TOUCH (TIAN MAI CHUANQI)
Gala Film Distribution (in Hong Kong)/Miramax (in U.S.). (Peter Pau) Sept. 9, 2002. Running time: 102 Min. Hong Kong-Taiwanese-Chinese. Michelle Yeoh, Ben Chaplin, Richard Roxburgh.

TOUCHED BY LOVE
(Jiang Ping, Liu Xin) Nov. 3, 2002. Running time: 97 Min. Chinese. Niu Ben, Qiang Gao, Keyu Guo, Xie Yuxin.

TOUCHING THE VOID
IFC (in U.S.). (Kevin Macdonald) Aug. 30, 2003. Running time: 107 Min. British. Brendan Mackey, Nicholas Aaron, Joe Simpson.

TRACES OF A DRAGON: JACKIE CHAN AND HIS LOST FAMILY
(Mabel Cheung) Feb. 7, 2003. Running time: 94 Min. Hong Kong. Documentary. Narrator: Ti Lung.

THE TRANSPORTER
20th Century Fox. (Cory Yuen) Oct. 7, 2002. MPAA Rating: PG-13. Running time: 92 Min. French. Jason Statham, Shu Qi.

TRASH
Bonton Film. (Karel Spevacek) July 9, 2003. Running time: 85 Min. Czech. Jan Skultety, Jan Plouhar, Ondrej Nosalek.

TRAVELLERS AND MAGICIANS
(Khyentse Norbu) Sept. 3, 2002. Running time: 107 Min. Bhutan. Tshewang Dendup, Lhakpa Dorji, Sonam Kinga.

TRAVELLING LIGHT
Dendy Films. (Kathryn Millard) July 31, 2003. Running time: 88 Min. Australian. Pia Miranda, Sacha Horler, Brett Stiller, Tim Draxl.

THE TRIGGER
(Alex Yang) Oct. 8, 2002. Running time: 102 Min. Taiwanese. Ni Ming Ran, Kelly Ko, Cai Xing Hong, Xu Hui Ni, Tao Chuan Zheng.

TRIO
(alexander Proshkin) July 9, 2003. Running time: 102 Min. Russian. Andrei Panin, Mikhail Porechenka, Maria Zvonareva.

TRISTAN
EuropaCorp Distribution. (Philippe Harel) April 10, 2003. Running time: 100 Min. French. Mathilde Seigner, Jean-Jacques Vanier, Jean-Louis Loca, Adina Cartianu, Daniel Cohen, Nicole Garcia.

THE TRUCE
(Alfonso Rosas Priego) June 12, 2003. Running time: 115 Min. Mexican. Gonzalo Vega, Adriana Fonseca.

THE TRUE MEANING OF PICTURES: SHELBY LEE ADAMS' APPALACHIA
(Jennnifer Baichwal) Jan. 17, 2003. Running time: 70 Min. Canadian. Documentary.

TSUI HARK'S VAMPIRE HUNTERS
Destination Films. (Wellson Chin) May 13, 2003. MPAA Rating: R. Running time: 90 Min. Hong Kong-Japanese-Netherlands. Chan Kwok Kwan, Ken Chang, Lam Suet, Michael Chow Man-Kin, Ji Chun Hua.

TUBE
Tube Entertainment. (Baek Woon-hak) May 15, 2003. Running time: 112 Min. South Korean. Kim Seok-hun, Bae Du-na.

THE TULSE LUPER SUITCASES
(Peter Greenaway) May 24, 2003. Running time: 127 Min. British-Spanish-Luxembourgors-Hungarian-Italian-German-Russian. JJ Feild, Valentina Cervi, Drew Mulligan, Nigel Terry, Raymond J. Barry.

THE TULSE LUPER SUITCASES: EPISODE 3
(Peter Greenaway) Aug. 31, 2003. Running time: 108 Mln. British-Spanish-Luxembourgors-Hungarian-Italian-German-Russian. JJ Field, Valentina Cervi, Drew Mulligan, Caroline Dhavernas.

28 DAYS LATER
20th Century Fox. (Danny Boyle) Oct. 9, 2002. Running time: 112 Min. British-U.S. Cillian Murphy, Noah Huntley, Naomie Harris.

TWENTYNINE PALMS
Tadrart Films. (Bruno Dumont) July 31, 2003. Running time: 119. French-German. Katia Golubeva, David Wissak.

TWILIGHT
Iranian Film Society and N.E.J. Intl. Pictures. (Hassan Hedayat) Aug. 13, 2003. Running time: 100 Min. Iranian. Ezzatollah Entezami Darbandi, Ahmad Najafi, Behnaz Moharrar.

THE TWILIGHT
(Mohammad Rasoulof) Oct. 7, 2002. Running time: 79 Min. Iranian. Ali-Reza Shalikaran, Fatemeh Bijan, Ali-Reza Mahdaviyan.

THE TWILIGHT SAMURAI
Shochiku Co. (Yoji Yamada) Feb. 13, 2003. Running time: 129 Min. Japanese. Hiroyuki Sanada, Rie Miyazawa, Nenji Kobayashi, Ren Osugi.

TWIN SISTERS
RCV Film Distribution. (Ben Sombogaart) Jan. 27, 2003. Running time: 129 Min. Dutch. Thekla Reuten, Nadja Uhl, Ellen Vogel.

THE TWINS EFFECT
Emperor Multimedia Group. (Dante Lam) Sept. 18, 2003. Running time: 90 Min. Hong Kong. Charlene Choi, Gillian Chung, Ekin Cheng.

TWIST
(Jacob Tierney) Aug. 28, 2003. Running time: 97 Min. Canadian. Nick Stahl, Joshua Close, Gary Farmer, Michele-Barbara Pelletier.

TWO ANGELS
(Mamad Haghighat) May 21, 2003. Running time: 80 Min. Iranian-French. Siavoush Lashgari, Mehran Rajabi, Golshifte Farahani.

TWO LOST IN A DIRTY NIGHT
(Jose Joffily) Oct. 4, 2002. Running time: 100 Min. Brazilian. Debora Falabella, Roberto Bomtempo.

TWO MEN WENT TO WAR
Guerilla Films. (John Henderson) Oct. 28, 2002. Running time: 108 Min. British. Kenneth Cranham, Leo Bill, Derek Jacobi.

TWO SUMMERS
(Jorge Furtado) Oct. 7, 2002. Running time: 74 Min. Brazilian. Andre Arteche, Ana Maria Manieri, Pedro Furtado, Julia Barth.

TWO TOUGH GUYS
Buena Vista Intl. (Juan Martinez Moreno) May 2, 2003. Running time: 99 Min. Spanish. Antonio Resines, Elena Anaya, Maria Rosa Sarda.

TWO YEARS LATER
(Agnes Varda) Oct. 20, 2002. Running time: 67 Min. French. Documentary.

UNCLE GHOST
(Sai Paranjpye) Oct. 7, 2002. Running time: 82 Min. Indian. Nedumudy Venu, Vinay Katore, Arun Homekar, Anil Bhagwat.

UNDEAD
Imagine Entertainment (Australia) (Peter and Michael Spierig) June 13, 2003. Running time: 104 Min. Australian. Felicity Mason, Mungo McKay, Rob Jenkins, Lisa Cunningham.

UNDER ANOTHER SKY (LES CHEMIN DE L'OUED)
(Gael Morel) Oct. 5, 2002. Running time: 78 Min. French-Algerian. Nicolas Cazale, Amira Casar, Mohammed Majd, Kheireddine Defdaf.

UNDERWORLD
Sony Pictures Entertainment. (Len Wiseman) Sept. 7, 2003. MPAA Rating : R. Running time: 121 Mln. British-German-Hungarian-U.S. Kate Beckinsale, Scott Speedman, Michael Sheen, Shane Brolly, Bill Nighy, Erwin Leder, Sophia Myles, Robbie Gee, Wentworth Miller.

UNDYING LOVE: TRUE STORIES OF COURAGE AND FAITH
(Helene Klodawsky) Jan. 12, 2003. Running time: 88 Min. Canadian. Documentary. David and Zenia Rybowski, Bluma Klodawski.

THE UNINVITED
CJ Entertainment. (Lee Soo-youn) Sept. 23, 2003. South Korean. Park Shin-yang, Jeon Ji-hyeon, Yu Seon, Kim Yeo-jin, Jeong Uk.

UPSWING
(Johanna Vuoksenmaa) May 17, 2003. Running time: 98 Min. Finish. Tiina Lymi, Petteri Summanen, Antti Virmavirta.

UTOPIA
Hispano Foxfilm. (Maria Ripoll) March 28, 2003. Running time: 104 Min. Spanish-French. Leonardo Sbaraglia, Najwa Nimri, Tcheky Karyo, Jose Garcia, Emma Vilarasau, Fele Martinez.

VAGABOND
(Gyorgy Szomjas) Feb. 1, 2003. Running time: 99 Min. Hungarian. Peter Simon, Kata Horvath, Graci Benke, Robert Kerenyi.

VALENTIN
Cinemien (in Netherlands)/Miramax (in U.S.). (Alejandro Agresti) Sept. 27, 2002. Running time: 86 Min. Dutch-Argentine. Rodrigo Noya, Carmen Maura, Alejandro Agresti, Julieta Cardinali.

VALENTIN
(Juan Luis Iborra) June 13, 2003. Running time: 119. Spanish. Lluis Homar, Inaki Font, Armando Del Rio.

VENGEANCE FOR SALE (SUKEDACHIYA SUKEROKU)
(Kihachi Okamoto) Nov. 9, 2002. Running time: 88 Min. Japanese. Hiroyiki Sanada, Kyoka Suzuki, Tatsuya Nakadai, Takehiro Murata.

VENUS & MARS
Innovation Film Group. (Harry Mastrogeorge) April 14, 2003. MPAA Rating: R. Running time: 93 Min. German. , Daniela Amavia, Julie Bowen, Michael Weatherly, Fay Masterson, Ryan Hurst.

THE VERY MERRY WIDOWS
Mars Distribution. (Catherine Corsini) July 9, 2003. Running time: 99 Min. French-Belgian. Jane Birkin, Emilie Dequenne, Pierre Richard.

VILLA DES ROSES
Miracle. (Frank Van Passel) Oct. 4, 2002. Running time: 114 Min. Belgian-British-Dutch-Luxembourgors. Julie Delpy, Shaun Dingwall.

VIOLIN (XIAO TI QING)
(Jiang Cheng) March 7, 2003. Running time: 100 Min. Chinese. Gu Jing Lin, Annie Wu, Cheng Qi.

THE VIRGIN OF LUST
(Arturo Ripstein) Aug. 30, 2002. Running time: 140 Min. Spanish-Mexican-Portugese. Luis Felipe Tovar, Ariadne Gil.

VIRGINIA'S RUN
Constellation Entertainment (U.S.)/Alliance Atlantis Motion Picture Distribution Group. (Peter Markle) Jan. 12, 2003. MPAA Rating, PG. Running time: 102 Min. U.S.-Canadian. Gabriel Byrne, Joanne Whalley, Lindze Letherman, Kevin Zegers, Rachel Skarsten.

VISIBLE SECRET II
Media Asia Distribution. (Abe Kwong) Sept. 21, 2002. Running time: 98 Min. Hong Kong. Eason Chan, Jo Kuk, Cherrie Ying, David Lee.

VODKA LEMON
(Hiner Saleem) Sept. 4, 2003. Running time: 90 Min. French-Swiss-Armenian-Italian. Romik Avinian, Lala Sarkissian, Ivan Franek.

VON WERRA
(Werner Swiss Schweizer) April 21, 2003. Running time: 103 Min. Documentary. Swiss-German. Hardy Kruger, Marthe Rey-Von Werra, Therese Wildhaber-Von Werra, Hans Von Werra, James Leasor.

WAKE UP, MATE, DON'T YOU SLEEP
Budapest Film. (Miklos Jancso) Jan. 31, 2003. Running time: 85 Min. Hungarian. Ildiko Toth, Zoltan Mucsi, Peter Scherer, Miklos Jancso.

WALKERS
(Fernando Leon de Aranoa) Feb. 17, 2003. Running time: 57 Min. Spanish-Mexican. Documentary. Juan Chavez Alonso, Guadalupe Samaniego, Juan Romero Orozco, Ignacio Romero.

WARMING UP YESTERDAY'S LUNCH
(Kostadin Bonev) Jan. 14, 2003. Running time: 98 Min. Bulgarian. Svetlana Yancheva, Biliana Kazakova, Galin Stoev, Roussi Tshanev.

WARM WINTER
(Wu Tiange) June 29, 2003. Running time: 96 Min. Chinese. Wang Xuebing, Wang Ji, Ding Jiayuan.

WAR TAKES
(Patricia Castano, Adelaida Trujillo) June 26, 2003. Running time: 78 Min. Colobian. Documentary.

WATERMARK
(Georgina Willis) May 24, 2003. Running time: 78 Min. Australian. Jai Koutrae, Sandra Stockley, Ruth McDonald, Ellouise Rothwell.

WE
(Zauberland (Martin Gypkens) July 5, 2003. Running time: 101 Min. German. Knut Nerger, Oliver Bokern, Patrick Gueldenberg.

WELCOME TO DESTINATION SHANGHAI
(Andrew Cheng) Jan. 31, 2003. Running time: 86 Min. Chinese. Yang Zhiying, Cui Zien, Zhou Yi.

WELCOME TO HADASSAH HOSPITAL
(Ramon Gieling) June 15, 2003. Running time: 55 Min. Ducth. Documentary.

WELCOME TO THE ROZES
TFM Distribution. (Francis Palluau) March 26, 2003. Running time: 88 Min. French. Carole Bouquet, Andre Wilms, Jean Dujardin.

WELCOME TO THE WAKS FAMILY
(Barbara Chobocky) May 20, 2003. Running time: 58 Min. Australian. Documentary. Zephania and Haya Waks.

WESTEND
(Markus Mischkowski, Kai Maria Steinkuehler) Jan. 15, 2003. Running time: 89 Min. German. Markus Mischkowski, Kai Maria Steinkuehler.

WET DREAMS (MONGJEONGGI)
A-Line. (Jeong Cho-shin) Nov. 16, 2002.Running time: 97 Min. South Korean. Lee Beom-su, Kim Seon-ah, Noh Hyeong-uk.

WHAT ARE YOU LOOKING FOR (QUELLO CHE CERCHI)
(Marco S. Puccioni) Nov. 19, 2002. Running time: 99 Min. Italian. Marcello Mazzarella, Stefania Orsola Garello, Antal Nagy.

WHAT FAULT IS IT OF OURS?
Warner Bros. Italia. (Carlo Verdone) Dec. 17, 2002. Running time: 114 Min. Italian. Carlo Verdone, Margherita Buy, Anita Caprioli.

WHAT THE EYE DOESN'T SEE
(Francisco J. Lombardi) Sept. 11, 2003. Running time: 149 Min. Peru. Gianfranco Brero, Gustavo Bueno, Patricia Pereyra, Paul Vega.

WHAT'S WITH LOVE
(Rudy Soejarwo) Nov. 5, 2002. Running time: 112 Min. Indonesian. Dian Sastrowardoyo, Nicholas Saputra, Ladya Cheryll, Titi Kamal.

WHEN RUOMA WAS SEVENTEEN (RUOMA DE SHIQI SUI)
(Zhang Jiarui) Dec. 7, 2002. Running time: 89 Min. Chinese. Li Min, Yang Zhigang, Li Cui, Zhulinyuan, Ma Jie, Sang Yi, Li Long, Gao Rui.

WHEN YOU COME DOWN TO EARTH
Les Films du Losange. (Eric Guirado) March 31, 2003. Running time: 97 Min. French-Belgian. Benoit Giros, Serge Riaboukine.

WHERE IS MADAME CATHERINE?
(Marc Recha) May 9, 2003. Running time: 106 Min. French-Spanish. Dominique Marcas, Eduardo Noriega, Mireille Perrier, Pierre Berriau, Jeremie Lippman, Olivier Gourmet, Eulalia Ramon, Luis Hostalot.

WHO KILLED BAMBI?
Haut et Court. (Gilles Marchand) May 17, 2003. Running time: 126 Min. French. Laurent Lucas, Sophie Quinton, Catherine Jacob.

WILBUR WANTS TO KILL HIMSELF
(Lone Scherfig) Jan. 27, 2003. Running time: 106 Min. Danish-British. Jamie Sives, Adrian Rawlins, Shirely Henderson, Lisa McKinlay.

WILD BERRIES
(Miwa Nishikawa) March 18, 2003. Running time: 108 Min. Japanese. Hiroyuki Miyasako, Miho Tsumiki, Sei Hiraizumi, Naoko Otani.

WILD CARD
Cinema Service. (Kim Yu-jin) May 19, 2003. Running time: 112 Min. South Korean. Jeong Jin-yeong, Yang Dong-geun.

WINDOW OF THE SOUL
Copacabana Films. (Joao Jardim, Walter Carvalho) Jan. 18, 2003. Running time: 73 Min. Brazilian. Documentary. Eugen Bavcar, Antonio Cicero, Arnaldo Godoy, William Lima Jr., Hermeto Pascoal.

WINNING TICKET
(Sandor Kardos, Illes Szabo) Jan. 31, 2003. Running time: 100 Min. Hungarian. Sandor Gaspar, Mariann Szalay, Agi Szirtes.

THE WINTER SONG
(Farhad Mehranfar) Sept. 21, 2002. Running time: 90 Min. Iranian. Nazbanu Mohammadyari, Simin Amidi, Musa Alijani.

WISDOM OF THE PRETZEL
(Ilan Heitner) June 1, 2003. Running time: 100 Min. Israeli. Guy Loel, Osnat Hakim, Yoram Sachs, Benni Avni, Shay Werker.

WISHING STAIRS (YEOGO GOIDAM SEBEONJJAE IYAGI: YEOWU GYEDAN)
Cinema Service. (Yun Jae-yeon) July 19, 2003. Running time: 97 Min. South Korean. Song Ji-hyo, Park Han-byeol.

WITH BEAK AND CLAW
(Krystian Matysek) April 26, 2003. Running time: 53 Min. Documentary. Polish.

WITH LOVE, LILLY
(Larisa Sadilova) Jan. 29, 2003. Running time: 98 Min. Russian. Marina Zubanova, Viktor Uralsky Valentina Berezutskaya.

WITHOUT MY DAUGHTER
(Alexis Kouros, Kari Tervo) Jan. 28, 2003. Running time: 93 Min. Finnish. Documentary. Sayed Bozorg Mahmoody, Alice Sharif.

WITNESSES
(Vinko Bresan) July 30, 2003. Running time: 88 Min. Croatian. Mirjana Karanovic, Leon Lucev, Alma Rica, Kresimir Mikic.

WOLFSBURG
(Christian Petzold) Feb. 13, 2003. Running time: 90 Min. German. Benno Fuermann, Nina Hoss, Antje Westermann, Astrid Meyerfeldt.

WOMAN OF WATER (MIZU NO ONNA)
(Hidenori Sugimori) Sept. 4, 2002. Running time: 115 Min. Japanese. Ua, Tadanobu Asano, Hikaru, Mayumi Ogawa.

THE WOMAN WHO BELIEVED SHE WAS PRESIDENT OF THE UNITED STATES
(Joao Botelho) May 16, 2003. Running time: 92 Min. Portugese. Alexandra Lencastre, Rita Blanco.

A WOMAN'S WORK (TRAVAIL)
(Kentaro Otani) Oct. 20, 2002. Running time: 118 Min. Japanese. Asaka Seto, Shinya Tsukamoto, Mikako Ichikawa, Jun Murakami.

WOMEN'S PRISON (ZENDAN-E ZANAN)
(Manijeh Hekmat) Sept. 5, 2002. Running time: 106 Min. Iranian. Roya Nonahali, Roya Taymourian, Pegah Ahangarani.

WONDERFUL DAYS
Aura. (Kim Mun-saeng) May 15, 2003. Running time: 91 Min. Animated. South Korean.

WONDROUS OBLIVION
Momentum Pictures. (Paul Morrison) July 30, 2003. Running time: 106 Min. British-German. Sam Smith, Delroy Lindo, Emily Woof. Stanley Townsend, Angela Wynter, Leonie Elliott, Naomi Simpson.

WORK HARD PLAY HARD
(Jean-Marc Moutout) Aug. 8, 2003. Running time: 100 Min. French-Belgiam. Jeremie Renier, Laurent Lucas, Cylia Malki, Olivier Perrier.

THE WORLD AGAIN
(Nikos Cornilios) Dec. 25, 2002. Running time: 112 Min. Greek-French. Niki Miha, Fotini Mourati, Sokratis Androulidakis.

THE WORLD'S GREATEST MONSTER
(Goran Rusinovic) July 31, 2003. Running time: 72 Min. Croatian. Goran Susljik, Mirta Haramina, Slobodan Milovanovic, Ivica Vidovic.

YES NURSE! NO NURSE!
(Pieter Kramer) Feb. 11, 2003. Running time: 100 Min. Dutch. Loes Luca, Paul R. Kooij, Paul de Leeuw, Tjitske Reidinga.

YMCA BASEBALL TEAM
(Kim Hyun-Seok) Nov. 1, 2002. Running time: 104 Min. South Korean. Song Kang-Ho, Kim Hye-Su, Kim Joo-Hyuk, Hwang Jeong-Min.

YOSSI & JAGGER
Strand Releasing. (Eytan Fox) Feb. 10, 2003. Running time: 67 Min. Israeli. Yehuda Levi, Ohad Koller, Assi Cohen, Aia Steinovits-Koren.

YOU CAN'T STOP THE MURDERS
Miramax/BVI. (Anthony Mir) Feb. 19, 2003. Running time: 99 Min. Australian. Gary Eck, Akmal Saleh, Anthony Mir, Richard Carter.

YOU'LL GET OVER IT
(Fabrice Cazeneuve) July 27, 2003. Running time: 86 Min. French. Julien Baumgartner, Julie Maraval, Francois Comar.

YOUNG ADAM
Warner Bros. Pictures UK (in U.K.)/StudioCanal (in France). (David Mackenzie) May 16, 2003. Running time: 98 Min. British-French. Ewan McGregor, Tilda Swinton, Peter Mullan, Emily Mortimer, Jack McElhone, Therese Bradley, Ewan Stewart, Stuart McQuarrie.

YOU'RE MY HERO
Yedra Film. (Antonio Cuadri) May 2, 2003. Running Time: 103 Min. Spanish. Manuel Lozano, Toni Canto, Felix Lopez, Antonio Dechent, Carmen Navarro, Juan Fernandez, Alfonso Mena, Pablo Acosta.

YVES SAINT LAURENT - TIME REGAINED
(David Teboul) Oct. 25, 2002. Running time: 77 Min. French. Documentary. Yves Saint Laurent, Lucienne Mathieu Saint Laurent.

YVES SAINT LAURENT 5, AVENUE MARCEAU 75116 PARIS
(David Teboul) Oct. 26, 2002. Running time: 85 Min. Documentary. French. Yves Saint Laurent, Anne-Marie Munoz, Catherine Deneuve.

ZATOICHI
Shochiku. (Takeshi Kitano) Sept. 1, 2003. Running time: 115 Min. Japanese. Beat Takeshi, Tadanobu Asano, Michiyo Ogusu.

ZHOU YU'S TRAIN
(Sun Zhou) Feb. 13, 2003. Running time: 92 Min. Chinese-Hong Kong. Gong Li, Tony Leung Kar-fai, Sun Honglei, Li Zhixiong, Shi Chunling.

FEATURE FILMS

JANUARY 1, 1998 – SEPTEMBER 30, 2002

In the following listings, the distributor is followed by the release date, country of origin, the director (in parentheses), and cast.

A
"A" PRODUCTION COMMITTEE. Feb., 1999. Japanese. (Mori Tatsua). Documentary.

AANKHEN
April, 2002. Indian. (Vipul Amrutlal Shah) Amitabh Bachchan, Akshay Kumar, Sushmita Sen, Arjun Rampal.

ABANDONED
BUDAPEST FILMSTUDIO-DUNA TV. Feb., 2001. Hungarian. (Arpad Sopsis) Tamas Meszaros, Szabolcs Csizmadia, Attila Zsilak, Pal Macsai, Laszlo Galffy.

ABC AFRICA
May, 2001. Iranian. (Abbas Kiarostami) Abbas Kiarostami, Seifollah Samadian.

ABCD
LAXMI PICTURES/THE BUSINESS. Nov., 1999. (Krutin Patel) Madhur Jaffrey, Faran Tahir, Sheetal Sheth, Aasif Andvi, David Ari, Jennifer Dorr White, Adriane Forlana Erdos, Rex Young.

THE ABDUCTION CLUB
PATHE. July, 2002. British-French-Irish. (Stefan Schwartz) Alice Evans, Daniel Lapaine, Sophia Myles, Matthew Rhys, Liam Cunningham, Edward Woodward, Patrick Malahide.

ABERDEEN
NORSK FILM /FREEWAY FILMS. July, 2000. Norwegian-British. (Hans Petter Moland) Stellan Skarsgard, Lena Headey, Ian Hart, Charlotte Rampling.

ABILENE
CLEAR STREAM PICTURES. Sept., 1999. (Joe Camp III) Ernest Borgnine, Kim Hunter, James Morrison, Wendell Pierce, Park Overall, Adrian Richard, Alan North, Zouanne Leroy, Mary Jo Catlett, Rance Howard.

ABOUT A BOY
UIP. (IN U.K.)/UNIVERSAL (IN U.S.) Feb., 2002. British-U.S. (Paul and Chris Weitz) Hugh Grant, Toni Collette, Rachel Weisz, Nicholas Hoult, Isabel Brook, Sharon Small, Victoria Smurfit, Augustus Prew.

ABOUT ADAM
MIRAMAX/HAL FILMS/BBC FILMS. Jan., 2000. British-Irish. (Gerard Stembridge) Stuart Townsend, Kate Hudson, Frances O'Connor, Charlotte Bradley, Rosaleen Linehan, Tommy Tiernan, Alan Maher.

ABOUT JULY
RICE FILM. Oct., 1999. Taiwanese. (Wei Te-Sheng) Wan En-Yong, Si-ma San-San, Dong Wai-Xiu, Zeng Mian, Zhang Long.

ABOUT SCHMIDT
NEW LINE CINEMA. Dec., 2002. (Alexander Payne) Jack Nicholson, Hope Davis, Dermot Mulroney, Kathy Bates, Len Criou, Howard Hesseman, June Squibb.

ABOVE FREEZING
COOLER PICTURES. June, 1998. (Frank Todaro) Mike O'Malley, Jill Tracy, J. K. Simmons, Phyllis Somerville.

ABSOLUMENT FABULEUX
BAC DISTRIBUTION. Aug., 2001. French. (Gabriel Aghion) Josiane Balasko, Nathalie Baye, Marie Gillain, Vincent Elbaz, Glaude Gensac, Yves Renier.

ABSOLUT WARHOLA
PEGASOS. June, 2002. German. (Stanislaw Mucha) Michal Warhola, Janko Zavacky, Maria Warhola, Eva Prevtova, Dr. Michal Bycko.

ACCELERATOR
FLASHPOINT. May, 1999. British-Irish. (Vinny Murphy) Stuart Sinclair Blyth, Gavin Kelty, Aisling O'Neill, Mark Dunne, Georgina McKeritt.

THE ACCIDENT
JOSEPH LOVETT PICTURES. June, 1999. (Joseph Lovett). Documentary.

ACCIDENTAL SAINT (JOJO LA FRITE)
MOVIE DA. June, 2002. French. (Nicolas Cuche) Didier Becchetti, Fred Saurel, Melanie Thierry, Bernard Campan, Jean-Christophe Bouvet, Jean-Francois Gallotte, Jean-Paul Rouve, Marina Fois, Pascal Vincent.

THE ACCIDENTAL SPY
GOLDEN HARVEST (IN HONG KONG)/DIMENSION FILMS (IN U.S.). June, 2001. Hong Kong. (Teddy Chen) Jackie Chan, Eric Tsang, Vivian Hsu, Kim Min-jeong, Wu Hsing-kuo, Alfred Cheung.

ACCORDING TO MATTHIEU
WHY NOT PRODS./LES FILMS ALAIN SARDE. Sept., 2000. French. (Xavier Beauvois) Benoit Magimel, Nathalie Baye, Antoine Chappey, Fred Ulysse, Jean-Marie Winling, Francoise Bette, Melanie Leray.

THE ACID HOUSE
PICTURE PALACE NORTH/UMBRELLA PRODS. May, 1998. Scottish. (Paul McGuigan) Stephen McCole, Maurice Roeves.

ACROSS A GOLD PRAIRIE
PRIME PICTURES. Feb., 2000. Japanese. (Isshin Inudo) Yusuke Iseya, Chizuru Ikewaki, Masatoshi Matsuo, Miako Tadano.

(AN ACT OF...) SABOTAGE
Big Head/ZDF. Nov. 1999. U.S.-German. (Christopher Anderson) Bettina Hurzner, Rehane Abrahams, Ross Campbell, Kevin Evensen.

ACTORS
BAC/LES FILMS ALAIN SARDE/PLANETE A/TF1/LE STUDIO CANAL PLUS. Apr., 2000. French. (Bertrand Blier) Pierre Arditi, Josiane Balasko, Jean-Paul Belmondo, Francois Berleand, Dominique Blanc, Bertrand Blier, Gerard Depardieu.

ACTS OF WORSHIP
MANIFESTO FILMS. Jan., 2001. (Rosemary Rodriguez) Ana Reeder, Michael Hyatt, Nestor Rodriguez, Christopher Kadish.

ADANGGAMAN
IMTM FILMS/RENARDES PRODS (FRANCE)/AMKA FILMS PRODS. (SWITZERLAND)/ABYSSA FILM (IVORY COAST)/DIRECTION NATIONALE DE LA CINEMATOGRAPHIE (BURKINA FASO). Aug., 2000. French-Swiss-Ivory Coast-Burkina Faso. (Roger Gnoan M'Bala) Rasmane Ouedraogo, Albertine N'Guessan.

ADDRESS UNKNOWN
Aug., 2001. South Korean. (Kim Ki-Duk) Yang Dong-Kun, Kim Young-Min, Ban Min-Yung, Cho Jae-Hyun, Pang Eun-Jin, Myung Kye-Nam, Lee In-Ock, Mitch Malum.

ADELA
IN VITRO FILMS. Sept., 2000. Spanish-Argentine. (Eduardo Mignogna) Eulalia Ramon, Gregoire Colin, Martin Lamotte.

ADIEU BABYLONE
MARS FILMS. April, 2001. French. (Raphael Frydman) Isild Le Besco, Emmanuel Faventines, Stephane Touly, Catherine Oudin, Frederic Epaud, Raphael Frydman.

AN ADOLESCENT
Aug., 2001. Japanese. (Eiji Okuda) Eiji Okuda, Mayu Ozawa, Shoji Akira, Mari Natsuki, Hideo Murota.

ADOLPHE
Sept., 2002. French. (Benoit Jacquot) Isabelle Adjani, Stanislas Merhar, Jean Yanne, Romain Duris, Jean-Louis Richard, Anne Suarez, Jean-Marc Stehle, Maryline Even.

THE ADOPTED
NATIONAL FILM DEVELOPMENT CORP. May, 2001. Indian. (Gul Bahar Singh) Rajit Kapur, Anjan Srivastava, A.K. Hangal, Kritika Desai.

THE ADOPTED SON
KIRGIZFILM/NOE PRODS. Aug., 1998. Kirghizian-French. (Aktan Abdykalykov) Mirlan Abdykalykov, Albina Imasheva.

ADRENALINE DRIVE
ADRENALINE DRIVE COMMITTEE/KINDAI EIGA KYOKAI CO./GAGA COMMUNICATIONS/THERE'S ENTERPRISE/NIPPON SHUPPAN HANBAI. Mar., 1999. Japanese. (Shinobu Yaguchi) Hikari Ishida.

THE ADVENTURES OF ALIGERMAA
MANDEN MED CAFAEN/MIGMA FILMS. Oct., 2000. Danish. (Andrea Lasmanis) Documentary.

THE ADVENTURES OF ELMO IN GROUCHLAND
SONY/COLUMBIA PICTURES/JIM HENSON PICTURES/CHILDREN'S TELEVISON WORKSHOP. Sept., 1999. (Gary Halvorson) Kevin Clash, Fran Brill, Stephanie, D'Abruzzo, Dave Goelz, Joseph Mazzarino, Jerry Nelson (voices). Animated.

THE ADVENTURES OF PLUTO NASH
WARNER BROS. Aug., 2002. (Ron Underwood) Eddie Murphy, Randy Quaid, Rosario Dawson, Joe Pantoliano, Jay Mohr, Luis Guzman, James Rebhorn, Peter Boyle, Burt Young, Miguel A. Nunez Jr., Pam Grier, John Cleese, Victor Varnado.

THE ADVENTURES OF ROCKY AND BULLWINKLE
UNIVERSAL/CAPELLA/KC MEDIEN/TRIBECA. June, 2000. (Des McAnuff) Rene Russo, Jason Alexander, Piper Perabo, Randy Quaid, Robert De Niro, Janeane Garofalo, Jonathan Winters, John Goodman.

THE ADVENTURES OF SEBASTIAN COLE
PARAMOUNT CLASSICS. Sept. 1998. (Tod Williams) Adrian Grenier, Clark Gregg, Aleska Palladino, Margaret Colin.

ADULT BEHAVIOR: IT'S ALL IN THE MIND
SVENSK FILMINDUSTRI/SVT/FLAB/FLX COMEDY. Sept., 1999. Swedish. (Fredrik Lindstrom, Felix Herngren) Felix Herngren, Karin Bjurstrom, Cecilia Ljung, Mikael Persbrandt, Kalla Bie.

THE ADVENTURES OF GOD
CQ3 FILMS/ESTUDIOS DARWIN/XL FILMS. Sept., 2000. Argentine. (Eliseo Subiela) Pasta Dioguardi, Flor Sabatella, Daniel Freire

THE ADVERSARY
BAC DISTRIBUTION. May, 2002. French-Swiss-Spanish. (Nicole Garcia) Daniel Auteuil, Geraldine Pailhas, Francois Cluzet, Emanuelle Devos, Bernard Fresson, Francois Berleand.

ADWA: AN AFRICAN VICTORY
NEGOD GWAD/ZDF/ARTE. Sept. 1999. Ethiopian-U.S. Italian. (Haile Gerima). Documentary.

AN AFFAIR
NINE FILM. Sept., 1998. South Korean. (E J-Yong) Lee Mi-suk, Lee Jeong-jae.

THE AFFAIR OF THE NECKLACE
WARNER BROS. Oct., 2001. (Charles Shyer) Hilary Swank, Jonathan Pryce, Simon Baker, Adrien Brody, Brian Cox, Joely Richardson, Christopher Walken.

AFRAID OF EVERYTHING
FLORIDA PICTURES AND LOCUS STOTUS. Jan., 1999. (David Barker) Nathalie Richard, Sarah Adler, Daniel Aukin.

AFTER FREEDOM
April, 2002. (Vahe Babaian) Mic Tomasi, Sophie Chahinan, Greg Stamian, Shant Benjanian.

AFTERIMAGE
INTERMEDIA FILMS. Jan., 2001. (Robert Manganelli) John Mellencamp, Terrylene, Louise Fletcher, Billy Burke, Michael Zelniker, Michael Twaine.

AFTER LIFE
TV MAN UNION/ENGINE FILM. Sept., 1998. Japanses. (Hirokazu Koreeda) Erika Oda, Susumu Terajia, Takashi Naito, Kei Tani.

AFTER THE END OF THE WORLD
META BM-4/SAXONIA MEDIA. Feb., 1999. Bulgarian-Greek-German. (Ivan Nichev) Katerina Didaskalo, Stefan Danalyov, Zlatil Davidov, Zhana Dakovska, Vasil Michailov.

AFTER THE FALL
UMBRELLA. Apr., 2000. German-U.S. (Frauke Sandig, Eric Black). Documentary.

AFTER THE RAIN
CAPELLA INTL. June, 1999. South African. (Ross Kettle) Raul Bettany, Louise Lombard, Ariyon Bakare, Hakeem Kae-Kazim.

AFTER THE RECONCILIATION
VELVET FILMS. Jan., 2001. French-Swiss. (Anne-Marie Mieville) Claude Perron, Anne-Marie Mieville, Jacques Spiesser.

AFTER THE TRUTH
HELKON FILMVERLEIH. July, 1999. German. (Roland Suso Richter) Kai Wiesinger, Goetz George, Karoline Eichhorn, Doris Schade, Peter Roggisch.

AFTER WAR (JEONJAENG KEU IHU)
Aug., 2002. South Korean. (Nobuhiro Suwa) Kim Ho-jeong, Nobuhiro Suwa, Mashu Suwa.
Survival Game
(Moon Seung-wook) Jung Eun-pyo.
The New Year
(Wang Xiashuai) Taozi, Shi Jie'en

THE AFTERNOON OF A TORTURER
Sept., 2001. French-Romanian. (Lucian Pintilie) Gheorghe Dinica, Radu Beligan, Ioana Macaria, Coca Bloos.

AGATHA
ALPHA PLUS/STUDIO VIRTUAL. Dec. 22, 1999. Czech. (Dan Krames) Eva Salzmannova, David Prachar, Jiri Ornest.

AGNES BROWNE
OCTOBER FILMS. May, 1999. (Angelica Huston) Angelica Huston, Marion O'Dwyer, Niall O'Shea, Ciaran Owens.

AGUJETAS, CANTAOR
IDEALE AUDIENCE/IMALYRE-GROUP FRANCE TELECOM/LA SEPT ARTE/TVE. Apr., 2000. French. (Dominique Abel). Documentary.

A.I. ARTIFICAL INTELLIGENCE
WARNER BROS. June, 2001. (Steven Spielberg) Haley Joel Osment, Jude Law, Frances O'Connor, Brendan Gleeson, Sam Robards.

AIKI
Aug., 2002. Japanese. (Daisuke Tengan) Haruhiko Kato, Rie Tomosaka, Ryo Ishibashi.

AIMEE & JAGUAR
SENATOR FILM. Feb., 1999. German. (Max Faerberboeck) Maria Schrader, Juliane Koehler, Heike Makatsch, Johanna Wokalek.

AINSI SOIT-IL
LEO & CIE. Aug. 1999. French. (Gerard Blain). Paul Blain, Sylvie Ollivier, Marie Allanioux, Delphine Dalbin, Michel Subor.

AIR BUD: GOLDEN RECEIVER
MIRAMAX. Aug., 1998. (Richard Martin) Kevin Zegers, Cynthia Stevenson, Gregory Harrison, Nora Dunn, Perry Anzilotti.

AJAX–HARK THE HERALD ANGELS SING
RCV FILM DISTRIBUTION. Jan., 2001. Dutch. (Roel van Dalen) Documentary.

AKA
June, 2002. British. (Duncan Roy) Matthew Leitch, George Asprey, Lindsey Coulson, Diana Quick, Peter Youngblood Hills.

A.K.A. BIRDSEYE
Aug., 2002. Swiss. (Stephen Beckner) Fred Ward, Fred Koehler, Stefan Kurt, Amy Hathaway, Johnny Whitworth, Jaimz Woolvett.

AKSUAT
TOO EAST CINEMA. Feb., 1999. Kazakh-Japanese. (Serik Aprymov) Sabit Kurmanbekov, Erschan Aschim, Erbolat Ospankulov, Inessa Radinova, Nurschuman Ichtymbaev.

A LA PLACE DU COEUR
Agat Films. Sept., 1998. French. (Robert Guediguian) Ariane Ascaride, Christine Bruecher, Jean-Pierre Darroussin, Gerard Meylan.

ALASKA.DE
FILMVERLAG DER AUTOREN/ARTHAUS. Sept., 2000. German. (Esther Gronenborn) Jana Pallaske, Frank Droese, Toni Blume.

ALCATRAZ AVENUE
LATHER RINSE REPEAT. OCT., 2000. (Tom Edgar) Jeff Feher, Brian Casey, Judy Leedom Tyrer, Bill Krauss, Megan Casey, Michelle Green.

ALCATRAZ IS NOT AN ISLAND
DIAMOND ISLAND PRODS. JAN., 2001. (James M. Fortier) DOCUMENTARY.

THE ALCHEMIST AND THE VIRGIN
MAGYAR TV-DIALOG STUDIO-EUROFILM STUDIO-TOR FILM STUDIO. Feb., 1999. Hungarian-Polish. (Zoltan Kamondi) Mariusz Bonazewski, Eszter Onodi, Danuta Zaflarska, Norbert Novenyi.

ALEGRIA
OVERSEAS FILMGROUP. Jan., 1999. Canadian-French-Dutch. (Franco Dragone) Renee Bazinet, Frank Langella, Julie Cox, Heathcote Williams, Clipper Miano.

ALEX IN WONDER
DOG FILMS ON SOLDIER LAND. MAR., 2001. (Drew Ann Rosenberg) Angela gots, Robert Hays, Ellen Greene, Sean Flynn, Danny Masterson, Alison Lohman, Soleil Moon Frye.

ALGIERS-BEIRUT: A SOUVENIR
CINETEVE/DJINN HOUSE PRODS. Aug., 1998. French-Lebanese. (Merzouk Allouache) Fabienne Babe, Georges Corraface, H. Choutri.

ALI
SONY PICTURES ENTERTAINMENT Dec., 2001. (Michael Mann) Will Smith, Jamie Foxx, Jon Voight, Mario Van Peebles, Ron Silver, Jeffrey Wright, Mykelti Williamson, Jada Pinkett Smith, Nona Gaye, Michael Michele, Joe Morton, Paul Rodriguez.

ALI AZOUA
PLAYTIME/REMSTAR/ALEXIS FILMS/ALI'N. Aug., 2000. French-Moroccan-Belgian. (Nabil Ayouch) Maunim Kbab.

ALICE AND MARTIN
LES FILMS ALAIN SARDE, FRANCE 2 CINEMA, FRANCE 3 CINEMA)/VERTIGO FILMS. Oct., 1998. French-Spanish. (Andre Techine) Juliette Binoche, Alexis Loret, Carmen Maura, Mathieu Amalric, Pierre Maguelon.

ALIEN ADVENTURE
NWAVE/IWERKS/MOVIDA/TRIX. Aug., 2000. Belgian-U.S. (Ben Stassen Phil "Bouli" Lanners, Pierre "Lele" Lebecque (voices.)

ALIENS TO THEMSELVES
CERO EN CONDUCTA. Oct., 2000. Spanish. (Lopez Linares, Rioyo) Documentary.

ALI FARKA TOURE: SPRINGING FROM THE ROOTS
LES FILMS DU VILLAGE (PARIS). Sept., 2000. French. (Yves Billon, Henry Lecomte) Ali Farka Toure.

ALI G INDAHOUSE
UIP (IN U.K.)/UNIVERSAL (IN U.S.). March, 2002. British-U.S. (Mark Mylod) Sacha Baron Cohen, Michael Gamdon, Charles Dance, Kellie Bright, Martin Freeman, Rhona Mitra, Barbara New, Ray Panthaki.

ALIVE
Jan., 2002. French. (Sandrine Ray) Vahina Giocante, Samuel Jouy, Francois Berleand, Fanny Cottencon, Pierre Cassignard.

ALL ABOUT LILY CHOU-CHOU
Sept., 2001. Japanese. (Shunji Iwai) Hayato Ichihara, Shugo Oshinari, Ayumi Ito, Yu Aoi.

ALL ABOUT MY FATHER
Jan., 2002. Norwegian-Danish. (Even Benestad) Documentary.

ALL ABOUT MY MOTHER
WARNER SOGEFILMS/SONY. Apr., 1999. Spanish-French. (Pedro Almodovar) Cecilia Roth, Eloy Azorin, Marisa Paredes, Penelope Cruz, Candela Pena.

ALL ABOUT THE BENJAMINS
NEW LINE CINEMA. March, 2002. (Kevin Bray) Ice Cube, Mike Epps, Eva Mendes, Tommy Flanagan, Carmen Chaplin, Valarie Rae Miller, Roger Guenveur Smith, Anthony Michael Hall, Lil Bow Wow, Anthony Giaimo.

ALL THE LOVE YOU CANNES!
TROMA TEAM. May, 2002. (Sean McGrath, Gabriel Friedman, Lloyd Kaufman) Documentary.

ALL THE QUEEN'S MEN
Oct., 2001. U.S.-Austrian-German-Hungarian. (Stefan Ruzowitzky) Matt LeBlanc, Eddie Izzard, James Cosmo, Nicolette Krebitz, Udo Kier, David Birkin, Oliver Korittke, Karl Markovics.

ALL ACCESS: FRONT ROW. BACKSTAGE. LIVE! PRESENTED BY CERTS
IMAX CORP. March, 2001. (Martyn Atkins) Sting, Cheb Mami, George Clinton & Parliament Funkadelic, Mary J. Blige, Kid Rock, Sheryl Crow, B.B. King, Trey Anastasio & the Roots. Music Documentary-Imax.

ALL FOR ONE
QUO VADIS CINEMA. May, 1998. French-Belgian. (Bruno Bontzolakis) Alexandre Carriere, Nicolas Ducron, Florence Masure.

ALL IS BRAZIL
TUPANA FILMS. May, 1998. Brazilian. (Rogerio Sganzerla) documentary with Richard Wilson, Robert Wise, Bill Krohn, Edmar Morel.

ALL MY LOVED ONES
IN FILM PRAHA/EURIMAGES. Jan., 2000. Slovak-Czech-Polish-German. (Matej Minac) Josef Abrham, Jiri Bartoska.

ALL OF IT
BLOOMFIELD PARTNERS. Sept., 1999.(Jody Podolsky).Alanna Ulbach, Lesley Ann Warren, James Rebhorn.

ALL OF US, EFFENDI
Greek Film Centre. Nov., 1998. Greek. (Leonidas Vardaros) Vassilis Kolovos, Perikles Moustakis, Antonis Vlissidis, Antonis Maibatzis, Yannis Tsikis.

ALL OVER THE GUY
LIONS GATE FILMS. MAY, 2001. (Julie Davis) Dan Bucatinsky, Richard Ruccolo, Adam Goldberg, Sasha Alexander, Christina Ricci.

ALL THE KNOWLEDGE IN THE WORLD
NUVOLA FILM. Feb., 2001. Italian. (Eros Puglielli) Giovanna Mezzogiorno, Marco Bonini, Glaudio Guain, Girogio Albertazzi.

ALL THE LITTLE ANIMALS
RECORDED PICTURES CO. May, 1998. British. (Jeremy Thomas) John Hurt, Christian Bale, Daniel Benzali, James Faulkner.

ALL THE LOVE THERE IS
CECCHI GORI/CGG. Mar., 2000. Italian. (Sergio Rubini.) Damiano Russo, Michele Venitucci, Francesco Cannito, Pierluigi Ferrandini.

ALL THE PRETTY HORSES
MIRAMAX (IN U.S.)/SONY PICTURES ENTERTAINMENT (FOREIGN). DEC., 2000. (Billy Bob Thornton) Matt Damon, Henry Thomas, Lucas Black, Penelope Cruz, Ruben Blades, Robert Patrick.

ALL THE RAGE
MUTUAL FILM CO./SCANBOX ENTERTAINMENT/NEWMARKET FILM CO./SCREENLAND PICTURES. Sept., 1999. (James D. Stern) Joan Allen, Andre Braugher, Josh Brolin, Jeff Daniels, Robert Forster, Anna Paquin, Giovanni Ribisi, David Schwimmer, Gary Sinise.

ALL THE MORON'S MEN
MEDUSA FILM/PALOMAR/GIALAPPA'S BAND FILM. Dec., 1999. Italian. (Paolo Costella) Claudia Gerini, Paolo Hendei.

ALL THE WAY
IMAR FILM CO. Jan., 2001. Chinese. (Shi Runjiu) Karen Muk, Jiang Wu, Chang Cheng-yu, Guan Yue, Qi Zhi,Zhuo Kui.

ALL YOU NEED
JOURNEY ENTERTAINMENT CORP. March, 2001. (Randy Ser) Kellie Martin, Kayren Ann Butler, Amy Raymond, Janet Carroll, Robert Pine, Gloria LeRoy, Sean Patrick Murphy.

ALMOST A WOMAN
July, 2002. (Betty Kaplan) Wanda De Jesus, Miriam Colon, Cliff DeYoung, Ana Maria Lagasca, Francesco Quinn, Luis Garcia.

ALMOST BLUE
CECCHI GORI DISTRIBUZIONE. Nov., 2000. Italian. (Alex Infascelli) Lorenza Indovina, Claudio Santamaria, Rolando Ravello, Andrea Di Stefano, Dario D'Ambrosi, Marco Giallini, Benedetta Buccellato.

ALMOST ELVIS
SEVENTH ART. Aug., 2001. (John Paget) Doug Church, Quentin Flagg, Robert Washington, Irv Cass, Johnny Thompson, Steve Sogura, James Lowrey, Rich Andrews. Documentary.

ALMOST FAMOUS
DREAMWORKS/ VINYL FILMS. Aug., 2000. (Cameron Crowe) Billy Crudup, Frances McDormand, Kate Hudson, Jason Lee, Patrick Fugit, Anna Paquin, Fairuza Balk, Noah Taylor, Zooey Deschanel.

ALMOST HEROES
WARNER BROS. May, 1998. (Christopher Guest) Chris Farley, Matthew Perry, Eugene Levy, Kevin Dunn, Bokeen Woodbine.

ALMOST NOTHING
MORENA/FILMANIA. Aug., 2000.Brazilian-Mexican. (Sergio Rezende) Genesio de Barros, Denise Weinberg, Augusto Pompeu.

ALMOST PEACEFUL (UN MONDE PRESQUE PAISIBLE)
Sept., 2002. French. (Michel Deville) Simon Abkarian, Zabou Breitman, Denis Podalydes, Vincent Elbaz, Lubna Azabal, Stanislas Merhar, Clotilde Courau, Julie Gaynet.

ALONE
MAESTRANZA FILMS. Feb., 1999. Spanish. (Benito Zambrano) Ana Fernandez, Maria Galiana, Carlos Alvarez-Novoa.

ALONG CAME A SPIDER
PARAMOUNT PICTURES. March, 2001. (Lee Tamahori) Morgan Freeman, Monica Potter, Michael Wincott, Dylan Baker, Mika Boorem, Anton Yelchin, Kim Hawthorne, Jay O. Sanders, Billy Burke.

ALWAYS A BRIDESMAID
NINA DAVENPORT/CINEMAX/CHANNEL FOUR. Mar., 2000. (Nina Davenport). Documentary.

AMARGOSA
TRIPLE PLAY PICTURES. Mar., 2000. (Todd Robinson) Marta Becket, Tom Willet, Ray Bradbury, Paul Lyday. Documentary.

THE AMATEUR
ALEPH. Sept., 2000. Agrentine (Juan Bautista Stagnaro) Mauricio Dayub, Vando Villamil, Juan Verdaguer, Cacho Espindola, Walter Santa Ana, Alejandra Puy, Roly Serrano.

THE AMATI GIRLS
PROVIDENCE ENTERTAINMENT. Jan., 2001. (Anne DeSalvo) Mercedes Ruehl, Paul Sorvino, Cloris Leachman, Sean Young, Dinah Manoff, Lily Knight, Lee Grant, Mark Harmon.

AMATO: A LOVE AFFAIR WITH OPERA
INSIGNIA FILMS. March, 2001. (Stephen Ives) Tony and Sally Amato, Richard Cerullo, Mignon Dunne, Richard Leighton, Jack Blackhall, Allen Vail, Chester Ludgin. Documentary.

AMAZING WOMEN BY THE SEA
KINOPRODUCTION. Aug., 1998. Finnish. (Claes Olsson). Marika Krook, Asa Karlin, Nicke Lignell, Onni Thulesius.

AMAZON
BAC/LES FILMS ALAIN SARDE/TF1 FILMS/PHF. June, 2000. (Philippe de Broca) Jean-Paul Belmondo, Arielle Dombasle, Patrick Bouchitey, Thylda Bares, Andre Penvern.

AMBUSH
MATILA & ROHR PRODS. Feb., 1999. Finnish. (Olli Saarela) Peter Franzen, Irina Bjorklund, Kari Heiskanen, Taisto Reimaluoto.

AMELIA
CRYSTAL CINEMATOGRAFICA. May, 2001. Brazilian. (Ana Carolina) Miriam Muniz, Camila Amado, Beatrice Agenin, Alice Borges, Betty Goffman, Marilia Pera.

AMELIE FROM MONTMARTRE
MIRAMAX (IN U.S.)/UFD. March, 2001. French-German. (Jean-Pierre Jeunet) Audrey Tautou, Mathieu Kassovitz, Rufus, Yolande Moreau, Artus Penguern, Urbain Cancellier, Dominique Pinon.

AMEN.
Feb., 2002. French. (Costa-Gavras) Ulrich Tukur, Mathieu Kassovitz, Ulrich Muhe, Michel Duchaussoy, Ion Caramitru, Marcel Iures, Friedrich von Thun.

THE AMERICAN ASTRONAUT
BNS PRODUCTION Jan., 2001. (Cory McAbee) Cory McAbee, Rocco Sisto, Gregory Russell Cook, Annie Golden, James Ransone, Joshua Taylor, Tom Aldredge.

AMERICAN BABYLON
COURT TV/RS/COURT TV. May, 2000. (Robert Stone) Jeff Fauntleroy, Lonell Jones. Documentary.

AMERICAN BEAUTY
DREAMWORKS PICTURES. Sept., 1999. (Sam Mendes) Kevin Spacey, Annette Bening, Thora Brich, Wes Bentley.

AMERICAN CHAI
FUSION FILMS. Jan., 2001. (Anurag Mehta) Aalok Mehta, Paresh Rawal, Sheetal Sheth, Josh Ackerman, Ajay Naidu, Aasif Mandvi.

AMERICAN CUISINE
POLYGRAM. Aug., 1998. French. (Jean-Yves Pitoun) Eddy Mitchell, Irene Jacob, Jason Lee, Thibault de Montalembert, Michel Muller.

AMERICAN DESI
EROS ENTERTAINMENT. APRIL, 2001. (Piyush Dinker Pandya) Deep Katdare, Purva Bedi, Ronobir Lahri, Rizwan Manji, Kal Penn, Anil Kumar, Sunita Param, Eric Axen.

AMERICAN GUN
June, 2002. (Alan Jacobs) James Coburn, Barbara Bain, Virginia Madsen, Alexandra Holden.

AMERICAN GYPSY: A STRANGER IN EVERYBODY'S LAND
LITTLE DUST. Apr., 2000. (Jasmine Dellal). Documentary.

AMERICAN HISTORY X
NEW LINE. Oct., 1999. (Tony Kaye) Edward Norton, Edward Furlong, Fairuza Balk, Beverly D'Angelo.

AMERICAN HOLLOW
HBO. Jan., 1999. (Rory Kennedy) Documentary.

AN AMERICAN LOVE STORY
AMERICAN PLAYHOUSE AND INDEPENDENT TELEVISION SERVICE. Jan. 1999. (Jennifer Fox) Documentary.

AMERICAN MOVIE
SONY. Jan. 1999. (Chris Smith) Documentary.

AMERICANOS: LATINO LIFE IN THE UNITED STATES
OLMOS PRODS./BAK PRODS./REFLECTIONS JOINT VENTURE. Jan., 2000. (Susan Todd, Andrew Young). Documentary.

AMERICAN OUTLAWS
WARNER BROS. Aug., 2001. (Les Mayfield) Colin Farrell, Scott Caan, Ali Larter, Gabriel Macht, Gregory Smith, Harris Yulin, Kathy Bates, Timothy Dalton, Will McCormack, Ronny Cox, Terry O'Quinn.

AMERICAN PIE
UNIVERSAL June, 1999. (Paul Weitz) Jason Biggs, Shannon Elizabeth, Alyson Hannigan, Chris Klein, Natasha Lyonne.

AMERICAN PIE 2
UNIVERSAL PICTURES. Aug., 2001. (J.B. Rogers) Jason Biggs, Shannon Elizabeth, Alyson Hannigan, Chris Klein, Natasha Lyonne.

AMERICAN PIMP
UNDERWORLD ENTERTAINMENT Jan., 1999. (Allen and Albert Hughes) Rosebudd, Schauntte, Bradley, C-Nolte, Ken Ivy.

AMERICAN PSYCHO
LIONS GATE/EDWARD R. PRESSMAN FILM CORP. Jan., 2000. (Mary Harron) Christian Bale, Willem Dafoe, Jared Leto, Reese Witherspoon, Samantha Mathis, Chloe Sevigny, Justin Theroux.

AN AMERICAN RHAPSODY
PARAMOUNT CLASSICS (IN U.S.). July, 2001. (Eva Gardos) Nastassja Kinski, Scarlett Johansson, Tony Goldwyn, Kelly Endresz Banlaki, Agi Banfalvy, Zsuzsa Czinkoczi, Balazs Galko.

THE AMERICAN TAPESTRY
SHOWTIME/EL NORTE. Feb., 2000. (Gregory Nava, Barbara Martinez-Jitner). Documentary.

AMERICA SO BEAUTIFUL
April, 2001. (Babak Shokrian) Mansour, Fariborz David Diaan, Alain deSatti, Houshang Touzie, Akbar Moazezi, Atossa Leoni, Diane Gaidry.

AMERICA'S SWEETHEARTS
SONY PICTURES ENTERTAINMENT. July, 2001. (Joe Roth) Julia Roberts, Billy Crystal, Catherine Zeta-Jones, John Cusack, Hank Azaria, Stanley Tucci, Christopher Walken, Alan Arkin, Seth Green.

AM I BEAUTIFUL?
ATLAS INTL. Sept., 1998. German. (Doris Dorrie) Senta Berger, Gottfried John, Otto Sander, Franka Potente, Anica Dobra.

AMNESIA
A-FILM DISTRIBUTION. Jan., 2001. Dutch. (Martin Koolhoven) Fedja van Huet, Carice van Houten, Sacha Bulthuis, THeo Maassen, Cas Enklaar, Eva van der Gucht.

AMNESIA
MEDUSA FILM. Feb., 2002. Italian-Spanish. (Gabriele Salvatores) Diego Abatantuono, Sergio Rubini, Martina Stella, Juanjo Puigcorbe, Ruben Ochandiano.

AMONG GIANTS
CAPITOL FILMS. May, 1998. British. (Sam Miller) Pete Postlethwaite, Rachel Griffiths, James Thornton, Lennie James, Andy Serkis.

AMY
VILLAGE ROADSHOW. May, 1998. Australian. (Nadia Tass) Alana De Roma, Rachel Griffiths, Ben Mendelsohn, Nick Barker.

AMY'S ORGASM
SERIOUS DAN/WITHOUT A BOX. MARCH, 2001. (Julie Davis) Julie Davis, Nick Chinlund, Jeff Cesario, Mitchell Whitfield, Jennifer Bransford, Caroline Aaron, Mark Brown.

ANACARDIUM
Dec., 2001. (Scott Thomas) Frank John Hughes, Richard Ruccolo, Laura Cayouette, Bob Rumnock, Sean Masterson, Courtney Thomas, Tony Cannata.

AN ANGEL
UIP. July, 2001. French. (Miguel Courtois) Richard Berry Elsa Zylberstein, Pascal Greggory, Bernard Le Coq, Vincent Martinez, Virginie Lanoue, Nicolas Silberg.

ANAK
STAR CINEMA PRODS. March, 2001. Filipino. (Rory B. Quintos) Vilma Santos, Claudien Barretto, Joel Torre, Baron Geisler, Sheila Mae Alvero, Amy Austria, Cherrie Pie Picache.

ANALYZE THIS
WARNER BROS. Feb., 1999. (Harold Ramis) Robert De Niro, Billy Crystal, Lisa Kudrow, Joe Vierelli, Chazz Palminteri.

ANANSI
Aug., 2002. German. (Fritz Baumann) George Quaye, Naomie Harris, Jimmy Akingbola, Maynard Eziashi, Chrys Koomson, Danny Sapani.

ANARCHISTS
MOKEP/SZINHAZ FILMMUVESZETI. Feb., 2001. Hungarian. (Tamas Toth) Szabolcs Thuroczy, Eva Csatari, Istvan Gyuricza, Hedi Temessy.

ANARCHISTS
MIRAE ASSET CAPITAL AND CHINA EASTERN. Feb., 2001. Korean-Chinese. (Yu Young-shik) Jang Dong-gun, Jung Joon-ho, Kim Sang-joong, Lee Bum-soo, Kim In-kwon, Ye Ji-won.

ANATOMY
SONY/COLUMBIA TRISTAR/DEUTSCHE COLUMBIA/CLAUSSEN & WOEBKE. July, 2000. German. (Stefan Ruzowitzky) Franka Potente, Benno Fuermann, Anna Loos Holger Speckhahn.

AND NOW...LADIES AND GENTLEMEN
SND RELEASE (IN FRANCE)/PARAMOUNT CLASSICS (IN U.S.). May, 2002. French-British. (Claude Lelouch) Jeremy Irons, Patricia Kaas, Thierry Lhermitte, Alessandra Martines, Jean-Marie Bigard, Ticky Holgado, Yvan Attal.

ANDRE THE MAGNIFICENT
UFD/NOE PRODS./ANDRE PRODS. Apr., 2000. French. (Emmanuel Silvestre, Thibault Staib) Michel Vuillermoz, Patrick Ligardes, Isabelle Candelier, Jean-Luc Porraz, Loic Houdre.

AND THEY CALL THIS SPRING?
DIAPHANA. Jan., 2001. French. (Herve Le Roux) Marilyne Canto, Maryse Cupaiolo, Marie Matheron, Bernard Ballet, Pierre Berriau, Michal Bompoli, Antoine Chappey.

...AND THEY DARED TO DREAM
July, 2002. Indian. (Subrata Sen) Subrata Dutta, Firdous Ahmed, Nilanjana Sharma, Deepankar De, Baisaki Marjito, Haradhan Bandopadhyay.

AND YOUR MOTHER TOO
IFC FILMS (IN NORTH AMERICA)/20TH CENTURY FOX (IN MEXICO). June, 2001. Mexican. (Alfonso Cuaron) Maribel Verdu, Gael Garcia Bernal, Diego Luna, Diana Bracho, Emilio Echevarria, Ana Lopez Mercado, Maria Aura, Andres Almeida.

ANGELA'S ASHES
PARAMOUNT/UNIVERSAL PICTURES INTL./DAVID BROWN/SCOTT RUDIN/DIRTY HANDS Nov., 1999. (Alan Parker) Emily Watson, Robert Carlyle, Joe Breen, Ciaran Owens, Michael Legge, Ronnie Masterson.

ANGEL EYES
WARNER BROS. May, 2001. (Luis Mandoki) Jennifer Lopez, Jim Caviezel, Sonia Braga, Terrence Howard, Jeremy Sisto, Victor Argo, Monet Mazu, Shirley Knight.

ANGEL EXIT
FALSON. July, 2001. Czech Republic. (Vladimir Michalek) Jan Cechticky, Klara Issova, Zuzana Stivinova, Vojtech Pavlicek, Pavel Landovsky, Eva Holubova.

ANGEL FACE
PABLO TORRE. Feb., 1999. Argentine. (Pablo Torre) Virginia Innocenti, Mario Pasik, Enrique Pinti, Mariano Marini.

ANGEL OF THE NIGHT
WISE GUY PRODS. Feb., 1999. Danish. (Shaky Gonzalez) Maria Karlsen, Mette Louise Holland, Tomas Villum Jensen, Ulrich Thomsen.

ANGEL ON MY SHOULDER
A D.D. PRODS. Feb. 1998. (Donna Deitch), Documentary.

ANGEL ON THE RIGHT
HAUT ET COURT. May, 2002. Italian-Swiss-French-Tajikistani. (Djamshed Usmonov) Uktamoi Miyasarova.

ANGELOS' FILM
LUMEN FILM/VPRO TELEVISION. May, 2000. Dutch. (Peter Forgacs). Documentary. Caroline Bodoczky, Peter Forgacs, Johanna Ter Steege, Charlotte Van Dijk, Ad Van Kempen (voices).

ANGELS!
DIET ANGELS. July, 2000. (Rico Martinez) Ruben Zambrano, John Stapleton, Raja, Monty Freeman, Christian Campbell.

ANGEL'S DANCE
PROMARK ENTERTAINMENT GROUP Feb., 1999. (David L. Corley) James Belushi, Sheryl Lee, Kyle Chandler, Frank John Hughes.

ANGELS OF THE UNIVERSE
ICELANDIC FILM CORP./FILMHUSET/PETER ROMMEL PRODS./ SDF-ARTE, ORB/SVT/ZENTROPA PRODS. Jan., 2000. Icelandic-Norwegian-German-Swedish-Danish. (Fridrik Thor Fridriksson) Ingvar E. Sigurdsson, Baltasar Kormakur, Bjorn Jorundur Fridbjornsson.

ANGELUS
Jan., 2002. Polish. (Lech Majewski) Jan Siodlaczek, Pawel Steinert, Jacenty Jedrusik, Malgorzata Madejowska, Marian Makula, Andrzej Mastalerz, Elzbieta Okupska.

THE ANGRY EYE
Nov., 2001. (Susan A Golenbock, William Talmadge, Denis O'Keefe) Documentary. Jane Elliott.

ANGST
UIP/AUSTRALIAN FILM FINANCE CORP/GREEN LIGHT/NSW FILM & TV OFFICE/AUSTRALIAN FILM COMMISSION. July, 2000. Australian. (Daniel Nettheim) Sam Lewis, Jessica Napier, Justin Smith, Abi Tucker, Luke Lennox, Lara Cox.

ANIMA
TANGENT FILMS/OTHER PICTURES. MAY, 1998. (Craig Richardson) George Bartenieff, Jacqueline Bertrand, Bray Poor, Geoffrey Cantor.

ANIMAL
VIBUS PRODUCCIONES. April, 2001. Argentine. (Sergio Bizzio) Carlo Roffe, Cristina Banegas, Carolina Fal, Walter Quiros, Pepe Monje.

THE ANIMAL
SONY PICTURES ENTERTAINMENT. May, 2001. (Luke Greenfield) Rob Schneider, Colleen Haskell, John C. McGinley, Edward Asner, Michael Caton, Louis Lombardi, Guy Torry.

ANIMAL FACTORY
FRANCHISE PICTURES/PHOENICIAN ENTERTAINMENT/ INDUSTRY ENTERTAINMENT/ARTS PRODUCTION CORP. Jan., 2000. (Steve Buscemi) Willem Dafoe, Edward Furlong, Seymour Cassel, Mickey Rourke, Steve Buscemi, Tom Arnold, John Heard.

ANIMAL FARM
HALLMARK/TNT. Sept., 1999. (John Stephenson) Pete Postlethwaite, Kelsey Grammer, Ian Holm, Julia Louis-Dreyfus, Julia Ormond, Paul Scofield, Patrick Stewart, Peter Ustinov (voices).

ANIMALS (AND THE TOLLKEEPER)
MAGNOLIA MAE FILMS. Jan., 1998. (Michael Di Giacomo) Tim Roth, Mili Avital, Rod Steiger, Mickey Rooney, John Turturro, Jacques Herlin.

ANIMALS CROSSING THE ROAD
THULE. Sept., 2001. Italian. (Isabella Sandri) Enrica Maria Modugno, Francesca Rallo, Salvatore Grasso, Andrea Renzi, Antonio Pennarella, Cristina Donadio.

ANITA TAKES A CHANCE
LAUREN FILMS. Jan., 2001. Spanish. (Ventura Pons) Rosa Maria Sarda, Jose Coronado, Maria Barranco, Jordi Dauder, Albert Forner.

ANNA AND THE KING
20TH CENTURY FOX/FOX 2000 PICTURES/LAWRENCE BENDER. Nov., 1999. (Andy Tennant) Jodie Foster, Chow Yun-Fat, Bai Ling, Tom Felton, Syed Alwi, Randall Duk Kim, Lim Kay Siu, Melissa Campbell.

ANNALUISE AND ANTON
BUENA VISTA INTL. Feb., 1999. German. (Caroline Link) Elea Geissler, Max Felder, Juliane Koehler, August Zirner, Meret Becker.

ANNA MAGDALENA
UNITED FILMMAKERS ORGANISATION. Sept., 1998. Hong Kong. (Yee Chung-man) Takeshi Kaneshiro, Aaron Kwok, Kelly Chen, Leslie Cheung, Anita Yuen.

ANNA'S SUMMER
INTEGRAL FILM (GERMANY)/MALENA FILMS (GERMANY)/FS (GREECE)/EL IMAN (SPAIN)/WDR (GERMANY)/ERT (GERMANY). Aug., 2001. German-Greek-Spanish. (Jeanine Meerapfel) Angela Molina, Herbert Knaup, Dimitris Katalifos, Rosana Pastor.

ANNA WUNDER
Nov., 2001. German. (Ulla Wagner) Alice Deekeling, Renee Soutendijk, Stephan Dellgrunn, Gotz Schubert, Hanspeter Muller, Marlon Kittel, Imogen Kogge.

ANNE FRANK'S DIARY OF A YOUNG GIRL
GLOBE TROTTER NETWORK/ANIMATION PRODUCTION MULTIMEDIA INVESTISSEMENT/ASSOCIATED STUDIOS GLOBAL TOON NETWORK/BROOKFIELD BS/CLEEVE STUDIOS. OCT., 1999. Frech-British-Irish. (Julian Y. Wolf). Animated.

THE ANNIHILATION OF FISH
PAUL HELLER Sept., 1999. (Charles Burnett Lynn Redgrave, James Earl Jones, Margot Kidder.

THE ANNIVERSARY PARTY
FINE LINE FEATURES. May, 2001. (Jennifer Jason Leigh, Alan Cumming) Alan Cumming, Jennifer Jason Leigh, Jane Adams, Mina Badie, Jennifer Beals, Phoebe Cates, John Benjamin Hickey.

ANOOSH OF THE AIRWAVES
PACIFIC MOTION PICTURE CO. Aug., 1999. (James Westby) Melik Malkasian, Steven Clark Pachosa, Barbara Niven.

ANOTHER BATTLE
TOEI CO. Oct., 2000. Japanese. (Junji Sakamoto) Etsushi Toyokawa, Tomoyasu Hotei, Show Aikawa, Ittoku Kishibe, Koichi Sato.

ANOTHER DAY IN PARADISE
TRIMARK PICTURES. Sept. 1998. (Larry Clark) James Woods, Melanie Griffith, Vincent Kartheiser, Natasha Gregson Wagner.

ANOTHER LIFE
WINCHESTER FILMS DISTRIBUTION. June, 2001. British. (Philip Goodhew) Natasha Little, Nick Moran, Ioan Gruffudd, Imelda Staunton, Rachael Stirling, Tom Wilkinson, Diana Coupland, Michael Bertenshaw.

ANOTHER PLANET
DOMINO FILM & TELEVISION/SYNCOPATED PRODS. Oct., 1999. Canadian. (Christene Browne) Sandy Daley, Kevin White, Marcia Brown, Daniel Levesque, Monique MacDonald, Tiemoko Simaga.

ANTIGUA, MY LIFE
ALTAFILMS. Feb. 6, 2002. Argentine-Spanish. (Hector Olivera)

ANTILLES-SUR-SEINE
OCEAN FILMS. Jan., 2001. French. (Pascal Legitimus) Med Hondo, Chantal Lauby, Thierry Desroses, Edouard Montoute, Pierre-Olivier Mornas, Theo Legitimus, Georges Mathieu.

ANTITRUST
MGM. Jan., 2001. (Peter Howitt) Ryan Phillippe, Rachael Leigh Cook, Claire Forlani, Tim Robbins, Douglas McFerran, Richard Roundtree, Tygh Runyan.

THE ANTO WAR
CECCHI GORI. Oct., 1999. Italian. (Riccardo Milani) Flavio Pistilli, Paolo Setta, Danilo Mastracci, Federico Di Flauro, Regina Orioli.

ANTS IN THE PANTS
CONSTANTIN FILM PRODUKTION. PRODUCTION. July, 2000. German (Marc Rothemund) Tobias Schenke, Axel Stain, Luise Helm, Bjorn Kirschniok, Mina Tander, Nicky Kantor, Tom Lass.

ANTWONE FISHER
FOX SEARCHLIGHT. SEPT., 2002. (Denzel Washington) Derek Luke, Joy Bryant, Denzel Washington, Salli Richardson, Earl Billings, Kevin Connolly, Viola Davis, Rainoldo Gooding, Novella Nelson, Yolonda Ross, Kente Scott.

ANTZ
DREAMWORKS. Sept., 1998. (Eric Darnell, Tim Johnson) Woody Allen, Dan Aykroyd, Anne Bancroft, Jane Curtin, Danny Glover.

ANY GIVEN SUNDAY
WARNER BROS/IXTLAN/THE DONNERS' CO. Dec., 1999. (Oliver Stone) Al Pacino, Cameron Diaz, Dennis Quaid, James Woods, Jamie Foxx, LL Cool J, Matthew Modine, Jim Brown, Charlton Heston, Ann-Margret.

ANYWHERE BUT HERE
20TH CENTURY FOX. Sept., 1999. (Wayne Wang) Susan Sarandon, Natalie Portman, Eileen Ryan, Ray Baker.

APARTMENT 5C
May, 2002. French-Israeli-U.S. (Raphael Nadjari) Tingerbell, Richard Edson, Ori Pfeffer, Jeff Ware, Olga Merediz.

APOCALYPSE NOW REDUX
MIRAMAX (IN U.S.). May, 2001. (Francis Coppola) May 3, 2001. Marlon Brando, Robert Duvall, Martin Sheen, Frederic Forrest, Albert Hall, Sam Bottoms, Larry Fishburne, Dennis Hopper, G.D. Spradlin.

APOLLO 13: THE IMAX EXPERIENCE
Sept., 2002. IMAX.

APPASSIONATA
UNIVERSAL. Sept., 1999. Italian. (Tonino de Bernardi) Anna Bonaiuto, Ines de Medeiros, Iaia Forte, Galatea Ranzi, Isabel Ruth.

APRIL
CONSORTIUM FILM. May, 2000. Georgian. (Otar Iosseliani) Tania Tchantouria, Guia Tchirakadze.

APRIL
Feb., 2002. Russian. (Konstantin Murzenko) Yevgeny Stychkin, Denis Burgazliev, Sasha Kulikova, Yury "Gosha" Kutsenko, Mikhail Krug, Olga Suslova.

THE APRIL CHILDREN
INTER NATIONALES/VENTURA FILMS/ZERO FILM/ZDF. Jan., 2000. German. (Yuksel Yavuz) Erdal Yildiz, Inga Busch, Bulent Esrungun, Senem Tepe, Serif Sezer, Cemel Yavuz, Kaan Emre.

APRIL STORY
ASIAN FILM LIBRARY/ROCKWELL EYES. Aug., 1998. Japanese. (Noboru Shinoda) Takako Matsu, Seiichi Tanabe, Kaori Fujii, Rumi.

APRILIE
TANDEM DISTRIBUZIONE. March, 1998. Italian. (Nanni Moretti) documentary with Nanni Moretti, Silvio Orlando, Silvia Nono.

APT PUPIL
SONY PICTURES ENTERTAINMENT. Aug, 1998. (Bryan Singer) Ian McKellen, Brad Renfro, Bruce Davison, Elias Koteas, Joe Morton.

ARACHNID
FILMAX. July, 2001. Spanish. (Jack Sholder) Alex Reid, Chris Potter, Pepe Sancho, Neus Asensi, Ravil Isyanov, Roqueford Allen.

ARARAT
MIRAMAX (IN U.S.)/ALLIANCE ATLANTIS (IN CANADA)/ARP (IN FRANCE). May, 2002. Canadian. (Atom Egoyan) David Alpay, Charles Aznavour, Eric Bogosian, Marie-Josee Croze, Bruce Greenwood.

ARCHIBALD THE RAINBOW PAINTER
EMPTY BOX. Aug., 1998. (Les Landau) Dorian Harewood, Michael McKean, Patti D'Arbanville.

ARIAN'S JOURNEY
MONTJUIC ENTERTAINMENT. Sept., 2000. Spanish. (Eduard Bosch) Ingrid Rubio, Abel Folk, Silvia Munt, Carlos Manuel Diaz.

ARISMAN: FACING THE AUDIENCE
March, 2002. (Tony Silver) Marshall Arisman, Bruce Arisman, Paul Theroux, Steven Heller. Documentary.

ARLINGTON ROAD
SONY. Mar. ,1999. (M Bobby Bukowski) Jeff Bridges, Tim Robbins, Joan Cusack, Hope Davis.

ARMAGEDDON
BUENA VISTA. June, 1998. (Michael Bay) Bruce Willis, Billy Bob Thornton, Liv Tyler, Ben Affleck, Will Patton, Peter Stormare.

ARO TOLBUKHIN IN THE MIND OF A KILLER
LAUREN FILMS. Sept., 2002. Spanish-Mexican. (Agusti Villaronga, Lydia Zimmermann, Isaac P. Racine). Daniel Gimenez Cacho, Carmen Beato, Zoltan Jozan, Mariona Castillo, Aram Gonzalez, Eva Fortea.

AROUND THE PINK HOUSE
MILLE ET UNE PRODS. Apr., 2000. French-Canadian-Lebanese. (Joana Hadjithomas, Khalil Joreige) Joseph Bon Nassar, Mireille Safa, Chadi El Zein, Hassan Mrad, Ziad Said, Rabih Mroue, Aline Aoun.

ARTISTS IN EXILE: A STORY OF MODERN DANCE IN SAN FRANCISCO
RAPT PRODS. Sept., 2000. (Austin Forbord, Shelley Trott) Anna Halprin, Terry Sendgraff, Tumbleweed, Mangrove, Margaret Jenkins, Brenda Way, K.T. Nelson, ODC/San Francisco, the Wallflower Collective, Drissy Keefer, Dance Brigade Documentary.

ART MUSEUM BY THE ZOO
CINE 2000. MAY, 1999. South Korean. (Lee Jeong-hyang) Shim Eun-ha, Ahn Sung-ki, Lee Seong-jae, Song Seon-mi.

THE ART OF DYING
AURUM/TVE/CANAL PLUS. Mar., 2000. Spanish. (Alvaro Fernandez Armero) Fele Martinez, Maria Esteve, Gustavo Salmeron.

THE ART OF WAR
WARNER BROS/MORGAN CREEK PRODS/FRANCHISE PICTURES/AMEN RA FILMS. Aug., 2000. (Christian Duguay) Wesley Snipes, Anne Archer, Maury Chaykin, Cary-Hiroyuki Tagawa, Donald Sutherland, Michael Biehn.

THE ART OF WOO
Sept., 2001. Canadian. (Helen Lee) Sook-Yin Lee, Adam Beach, Jel Keller, Alberta Watson, John Gilbert, Kelly Harms, Sarah Brown, Siu Ta, Damien Atkins.

ASAKO IN RUBY SHOES
CINEMA SERVICE (SOUTH KOREA). May, 2001. South Korean-Japanese. (Lee Jae-yeong) Lee Jeong-jae, Misato Tachibana, Ren Osugi, Kim Min-heui, Urara Awata.

AS A MAN
MILLE ET UNE PRODS. Aug., 2001. (Alain Gomis) Djolof Mbengue, Delphine Zingg, Samir Guesmi, Theophile Moussa Sowie, Thierno Ndiaye Doss, Bass Dhem.

AS FAR AS MY FEET WILL CARRY ME
CASCADEUR FILMPRODUKTION. MAY, 2001. GERMAN. (Hardy Martins) Bernhard Bettermann, Andre Hennicke, Michael Mendl, Irina Pantayeva, Iris Boehm, Hans-Uwe Bauer, Hans-Peter Hallwachs.

ASH WEDNESDAY
May, 2002. IFC FILMS. (Edward Burns) Edward Burns, Elijah Wood, Rosario Dawson, Oliver Platt, Pat McNamara, James Handy.

AS I WAS MOVING AHEAD OCCASIONALLY I SAW BRIEF GLIMPSES OF BEAUTY
JONAS MEKAS. Feb., 2001. (Jonas Mekas) Documentary.

ASK ME IF I'M HAPPY
MEDUSA. Dec., 2000. Italian. (Aldo, Giovanni & Giacomo, Massimo Venier) Aldo Baglio, Giovanni Storti, Giacomo Poretti, Marian Massironi, Silvana Fallisi, Antonio Catania, Giuseppe Battiston.

ASOKA
ARCLIGHTZ & FILMS. Sept., 2001. Indian. (Santosh Sivan) Shah Rukh Khan, Dareena Kapoor, Danny Denzongpa, Ajit, Rahul Dev, Hrishitaa Bhatt.

ASPHALT
ALTA FILMS/JOSE MARIA LARA P.C/ALBARES PRODS./SUR FILMS/TVE/CANAL PLUS/ETB. Feb., 2000. Spanish. (Daniel Calparsoro) Najwa Nimri, Juan Diego Botto, Gustavo Salmeron.

ASSASSINATION TANGO
Sept., 2002. UNITED ARTISTS. (Robert Duvall) Robert Duvall, Ruben Blades, Kathy Baker, Luciana Pedraza, Julio Oscar Mechoso, James Keane, Frank Gio, Katherine Micheaux Miller, Frank Cassavetes, Michael Corrente, Raul Outeda.

AS SEEN ON TV
SVENSK FILMINDUSTRI. Sept., 2001. Swedish. (Fredrik Lindstrom) Johan Rheborg, Alexandra Rapaport, Kristian Luuk, Pia Johansson, Gerd Hegnell, Martian Haag, Pernilla Stalfelt.

ASTERIX & OBELIX VS. CAESAR
AMLF DISTRIBUTION. Jan., 1999. French-German-Italian. (Claude Zidi) Christian Clavier, Gerard Depardieu, Roberto Benigni, Michel Galabru, Claude Pieplu.

ASTORIA
MAREVAN PICTURES/ASTORIA PARTNERS. Mar., 2000. (Nick Efteriades) Paige Turco, Rick Stear, Ed Setrakain, Joseph D'Onofrio, Geraldine Librandi, Steven J. Christofer, Yianni Sfinias, Gregory Sims.

THE ASTRONAUT'S WIFE
New Line. Aug., 1999. (Rand Ravich) Johnny Depp, Charlize Theron, Joe Morton, Clea DuVal.

ASUNDER
OBSIDIAN PRODS./WORLD INTL. NETWORK. Oct., 1999. (Tim Reid) Blair Underwood, Michael Beach, Debbi Morgan, Marva Hicks, Desiree Marie Velez, Ira Hawkins, Alene Dawson, Wendy Moore.

AS WHITE AS IN SNOW
SVENSK FILMINDUSTRI. Feb., 2001. Danish-Swedish. (Jan Troell) Amanda Ooms, Rikard Wolff, Bjorn Granath, Bjorn Kjellman, Stina Ekblad, Shanti Roney, Hans Palsson, Antti Reini.

THE ASYLUM
NUNHEAD FILMS. Nov., 2000. British. (John Stewart) Steffanie Pitt, Nick Waring, Ingrid Pitt, Patrick Mower, Robin Askwith, Colin Baker, Chloe Annett, Paul Reynolds, Jean Boht.

ATANARJUAT THE FAST RUNNER
IGLOOLIK ISUMA PRODS. May, 2001. Canadian-Canadian Inuit. (Zacharias Kunuk) Natar Ungalaaq, Sylvia Ivalu, Peter Henry Arnatsiaq, Lucy Tulugarjuk, Pakkak Innushuk, Madeline Ivalu.

AT FIRST SIGHT
METRO-GOLDWYN-MAYER. Jan., 1999. (Irwin Winkler) Val Kilmer, Mira Sorvino, Kelly McGillis, Steven Weber.

AT FULL GALLOP
NIRVANA. July, 2001. Spanish. (Julio Suarez) Ana Alvarez, Aitor Merino, Ramon Langa, Africa Gozalbes,Kiti Manver, Sancho Gracia.

ATILANTO FOR PRESIDENT
CINE CO. Sept., 1998. Spanish. (La Cuadrilla) Manuel Manquina, Ramon Barea, Laura Conejero, Fernando Vivanco, Carlos Lucas.

AT MIDNIGHT AND A HALF
SUDAKA FILMS/FUTURO FILMS. June 5, 2000. Venezuelan-Peruvian. (Marite Ugas, Mariana Rondon) Salvador Del Solar.

ATILANO FOR PRESIDENT
CINE CO. Sept., 1998. Spanish. (Luis Guridi, Santiago Aguilar) Manuel Manquina, Ramon Barea, Laura Conejero, Fernando Vivanco.

ATLANTIS: THE LOST EMPIRE
BUENA VISTA. June, 2001. (Gary Trousdale, Kirk Wise) Michael J. Fox, James Garner, Cree Summer, Leonard Nimoy, Don Novello, Claudia Christian, Jacqueline Obradors.

THE ATROCITY EXHIBITION
THE BUSINESS. June, 2000. (Jonathan Weiss) Victor Slezak, Anna Juvander, Michael Kirby, Mariko Takai, Rob Brink, Diane Grotke, Caroline McGee, Robert Morgan, Tom Constantine, Jeremy Graham.

AT SATCHEM FARM
ITASCA PICTURES. Sept., 1998. (John Huddles) Rufus Sewell, Nigel Hawthorne, Minnie Driver, Amelia Heinie, Michael E. Rodgers.

ATTACK OF THE BAT MONSTERS
ATTACK PRODS. June., 2000. (Kelly Greene) Michael Dalmon, Fred Ballard, Casie Waller, Ryan Wickerham, Douglas Taylor, Robert Graham, Bill Wise, Rob Bassetti.

ATTACK THE GAS STATION!
CINEMA SERVICE/FUN & HAPPINESS. Oct., 1999. South Korean. (Kim Sang-jin.) Lee Seong-jae, Yu Oh-seong, Kang Seong-jin.

AT THE FIRST BREATH OF WIND
ISTITUTO LUCE. Aug., 2002. Italian. (Franco Piavoli) Primo Gaburri, Mariella Fabbris, Ida Carnevali, Alessandra Agosti, Bianca Galeazzi, Lucky Ben Dele, Guglielmo Dal Corso.

AT THE HEIGHT OF SUMMER
LAZENNEC/STUDIO CANAL PLUS/ARTE FRANCE CINEMA/HANG PHIM TRUYEN. May, 2000. French-Vietnamese. (Tran Anh Hung) Than Nu Yen Khe, Nguyen Nhu Quynh, Le Khanh, Ngo Quang Hai.

AT THE RIGHT MOMENT
CECCHI GORI DISTRIBUZIONE. Oct., 2000. Italian. (Giorgio Panariello, Gaia Gorrini) Giorgio Panariello, Kasia Smutniak, Luisa Corna, Giovanni Cacioppo, Carlo Pistarino, Evelina Gori, Athina Cenci.

THE ATTIC EXPEDITIONS
TSE TSE FLY. JUNE, 2001. (Jeremy Kasten) Andras Jones, Seth Green, Jeffry Combs, Wendy Robie, Ted Raimi, Beth Bates, Shannon Hart Cleary, Alice Cooper.

ATTRACTION
TRIMARK PICTURES/KRAUSS-DEGRAZIER/CAPITAL ARTS. Sept., 2000. (Russell DeGrazier) Samantha Mathis, Gretchen Mol, Tom Everett Scott, Matthew Settle.

AUDITION
OMEGA PROJECT. Oct., 1999. Japanese. (Takashi Miike). Ryo Ishibashi, Eihi Shiina, Miyuki Matsuda, Renji Ishibashi.

AUGGIE ROSE
ROXIE RELEASING. May, 2001. (Matthew Tabak) Jeff Goldblum, Anne Heche, Timothy Olyphant, Nancy Travis, Richard T. Jones, Joe Santos, Kim Coates.

AUGUSTIN, KING OF KUNG-FU
PATHE DISTRIBUTION/ALAIN SARDE PRODS/CINE B/CINEA, FRANCE 2/BOCABOCA PRODUCCIONES/CANAL PLUS/ SOFINERGIE 5. August, 1999. French-Spanish. (Anne Fontaine) Jean-Chretien Sibertin-Blanc, Maggie Cheung, Darry Cowl.

AUGUST: A MOMENT BEFORE THE ERUPTION
June, 2002. Israeli-French. (Avi Mograbi) Mograbi, Adi Ezroni, Meital Dohan, Tchelet Semel.

AUGUST 32ND ON EARTH
MAX FILMS. May, 1998. Canadian. (Denis Villeneuve) Pascale Bussieres, Alexis Martin, Richard S. Hamilton.

AUSTIN POWERS IN GOLDMEMBER
NEW LINE CINEMA. July, 2002. (Jay Roach) Mike Myers, Beyonce Knowles, Seth Green, Michael York, Robert Wagner, Mindy Sterling, Verne Troyer, Michael Caine.

AUSTIN POWERS: THE SPY WHO SHAGGED ME
NEW LINE. June, 1999. (Jay Roach) Mike Myers, Heather Graham, Michael York, Robert Wagner,·Rob Lowe, Seth Green.

THE AUTEUR THEORY
THEORETICAL FILMS. Nov., 1999. (Evan Oppenheimer) Alan Cox, Natasha Lyonne, Angeline Ball, Rachel True, Armin Shimerman, Ian McNeice, Jeremy Sisto, Garrett Wang, Dana Lee.

AUTO FOCUS
SONY PICTURES CLASSICS. Aug., 2002. (Paul Schrader) Greg Kinnear, Willem Dafoe, Rita Wilson, Maria Bello, Ron Leibman, Kurt Fuller, Ed Begley Jr., Michael Rodgers.

AUTUMN
BIM DISTRIBUZIONE/DODICI DICEMBRE/RAI RADIOTELEVISIONE ITALIANA/TELEPIU. Aug., 1999. (Nina di Majo) Giovanni Bruno, Francesca Caracciolo, Marco Mario De Notaris.

AUTUMN BLOSSOMS
CINEQUANON/NIKKATSU. Sept., 1999. Japanese. (Shunsaku Ikehata.) Ken Ogata, Jijiri Kojima, Yoshi Oida.

THE AUTUMN HEART
FILM CELLAR. Jan., 1999. (Steven Maler) Tyne Daly, Ally Sheedy, Jack Davidson, Davidlee Willson.

AUTUMN IN NEW YORK
MGM/LAKESHORE ENTERTAINMENT/GARY LUCCHESI/AMY ROBINSON. Aug., 2000. (Joan Chen) Richard Gere, Winona Ryder, Anthony LaPaglia, Elaine Stritch, Vera Farmiga, Sherry Stringfield, Jill Hennessy.

AUTUMN TALE
LES FILMS DU LOSANGE. Aug., 1998. French. (Eric Rohmer) Marie Riviere, Beatrice Romand, Alain Libolt, Didier Sandre, Alexia Portal.

AVALANCHE
PM ENTERTAINMENT GROUP. May, 1999.(Steve Kroschel) Thomas Ian Griffith, Caroleen Feeney, R. Lee Ermey, C. Thomas Howell.

AVALON
MIRAMAX. May, 2001. Japanese. (Mamoru Oshii) Malgorzata Foremniak, Wladyslaw Kowalski, Jerzy Gudejko, Dariusz Biskupski, Bartek Swiderski, Katarzyna Bargiettowska.

AVEC MON MARI
MUTO KIICHI OFFICE/NEW CINEMA WORKSHOP/CINEMAN BRAIN. Dec., 1999. Japanese. (Kentaro Otani) Hirofumi Kobayashi, Yuka Itaya, Kaori Tsuji, Ren Osugi, Kentaro Otani, Mayumi Terashima.

AVE MARIA
LESTES FILMS, IMCINE AND MANGA FILMS. Mexican-Spanish. Nov., 1999. (Eduardo Rossoff) Tere Lopez Tarin, Damian Alcazar, Demian Bichir, Ana Torrent, Juan Diego Botto.

THE AVENGERS
WARNER BROS. Aug., 1998. (Jeremiah Chechick) Ralph Fiennes, Uma Thurman, Sean Connery, Patrick Macnee, Jim Broadbent.

AVENGING ANGELO
WARNER BROS. Sept, 2002. (Martyn Burke) Sylvester Stallone, Madeleine Stowe, Raoul Bova, Anthony Quinn, Harry Van Gorkum, Billy, Gardell.

AWAY FROM HOME
HAYLAZZ. May, 2001. Turkish. (Semih Kaplanoglu) Tolga Cevik, Erol Keskin, Anna Bielska.

AWAY WITH WORDS
TIMEWARP. May, 1999. Japanese. (Christopher Doyle)Cast: Tadano Asano, Kevin Sherlock, Mavis Xu, Christa Hughes, Georgina Dobson.

AZZURRO
A C-FILMS/TSI/ALHENA FILMS/MACHINASSOU/PCT CINEMA & TELEVISION//GAM FILM/TECHNOVISUAL. Aug., 2000. Swiss-French-Italian. (Denis Rabaglia) Paolo Villaggio, Francesca Pipoli, Marie-Christine Barrault, Jean-Luc Bideau, Renato Scarpa, Julien Boisselier.

B

BAADER
PROKINO. Feb., 2002. German. (Christopher Roth) Frank Giering, Laura Tonke, Vadim Glowna, Birge Schade, Jana Pallaske, Michael Sideris, Sebastian Weberstein.

BABAR: KING OF THE ELEPHANTS
ALLIANCE ATLANTIS. Mar., 1999. Canadian-French-German. (Raymond Jafelice). Animated.

BABEL
IMA FILM/ALLEGRO FILM. Apr., 1999. French-Canadian. (Gerard Pullicino) Mitchell David Rothpan, Maria de Medeiros, Tcheky Karyo, Michel Jonasz.

BABE: PIG IN THE CITY
UNIVERSAL. Nov., 1999. (George Miller) Magda Szubanski, James Cromwell, Mary Stein, Mickey Rooney, Julie Godfrey.

BABY BOY
SONY PICTURES ENTERTAINMENT. JUNE, 2001. (John Singleton) Tyrese Gibson, Omar Gooding, A.J. Johnson, Taraji P. Henson, Snoop Dogg, Tarama LaSeon Bass, Ving Rhames.

BABY GENIUSES
SONY. Mar. 1999. (Bob Clark) Kathleen Turner, Christopher Lloyd, Kim Cattrall, Peter MacNicol.

BABY, IT'S YOU
ITVS. Jan., 1998. (Anne Makepeace), Documentary.

BABYFACE
STABLE FILMS. May, 1998. Canadian. (Jack Blum) Lenore Zann, Elisabeth Rosen, Shawn Doyle, James Gallanders, William Dunlop.

BABYMOTHER
FILM FOUR DISTRIBUTORS. July, 1998. British. (Julian Henriques) Anjela Lauren Smith, Wil Johnson, Caroline Chikezie, Jocelyn Esien.

THE BACHELOR
NEW LINE/LLOYD SEGAN CO/ GEORGE STREET PICTURES. Nov., 1999. (Gary Sinyor) Chris O'Donnell, Renee Zellweger, Hal Holbrook, James Cromwell, Artie Lange, Edward Asner, Marley Shelton.

THE BACK COUNTRY
MARS FILMS. May, 1998. French. (Jacques Nolot) Jacques Nolot, Henri Gardey, Mathilde Mone.

BACK DOOR
IDEEFIXE/GREEK FILM CENTRE/ALPHA TV/ROSEBUD SA/NETMED/ JBA/FILMEX/TNT. MAY, 2000. Greek. (Yorgos Tsemberopoulos) Constantinos Papadimitriou, Alexandriani Kikelianou, Haris Sozos, Ierkolis Michallides, Antonis Kafetzopoulos..

THE BACK OF THE WORLD
ELIAS QUEREJETA PC. Sept., 2000. Spanish. (Javier Corcuera) Guinder Rodriguez, Mehdi Zana, Thomas Miller-El, Tomas Rangel. Documentary.

THE BACK OF GOD
NIRVANA. June, 2001. Spanish. (Pablo Llorca) Isabel Ampudia, Alberto Jimenez, Pedro Casablanc.

BACKROADS
OFFLINE ENTERTAINMENT. Jan., 2000. (Shirley Cheechoo) Renae Morriseau, Sheila Tousey, Shirley Cheechoo, Greta Cheechoo.

BACKSTAGE
DIMENSION FILMS/ ROC-A-FELLA RECORDS/ISLAND DEF JAM MUSIC GROUP. Sept., 2000. (Chris Fiore) Jay-Z, DMX, Method Man, Redman, Beanie Sigel, Memphis Bleek, DJ Clue, Amil, Ja Rule. Documentary.

THE BACKYARD
May, 2002. (Paul Hough) Documentary.

BAD CITY BLUES
BAD CITY PICTURES/MICHAEL STEVENS. Oct., 1999. (Michael Stevens) Michael Massee, Michael McGrady, Judith Hoag, Jim Metzler, Simon Billig, Earl Holliman, Dennis Hopper, Ruth Livier, Scott MacDonald.

BAD COMPANY
J-MOVIE WARS 5/WOWOW/BANDAI VISUAL. Feb., 2001. Japanese. (Tomoyuki Furumaya) Yamato Okitsu, Ryosuke Takahashi, Yuta Nakajima, Ken Mitsuishi, Asako Yashiro, Mikio Shimizu.

BAD COMPANY
UNIVERSAL PICTURES/PAN-EUROPEENNE PROD./LES FILMS ALAIN SARDE/M6 FILMS/CANAL PLUS/SOFYGRAM 3/PFP PRODS. Oct, 1999. French. (Jean-Pierre Ameris) Maud Forget, Lou Doillon, Micheline Presle, Ariane Ascaride, Robinson Stevenin.

BAD COMPANY
BUENA VISTA. May, 2002. (Joel Schumacher) Anthony Hopkins, Chris Rock, Matthew Marsh, Gabriel Macht, Kerry Washington, Adoni Maropis, Peter Stormare, Garcelle Beauvais-Nilon, Dragan Micanovic.

BADDING
FENNADA FILMI/YLE TV2 DRAMA. Jan., 2001. Finnish. (Markku Polonen) Janne Reinikainen, Karoliina Blackburn, Peter Franzen, Puntti Valtonen, Ilkka Koivula, Pertti Koivula, Vappu Jurkka.

BAD GENRES
PYRAMIDE DISTRIBUTION. Aug., 2001. Belgian-French. (Francis Girod) Richard Bohringer, Robinson Stevenin, Stephane Metzger, Micheline Presle, William Nadylam, Frederic Pellegeay.

BAD GIRL TRILOGY
CENTRAL MOTION PICTURE CO. Mar., 2000. Taiwanese. (Yan-Ting Wen, Jin-Jie Lin, Ying-Yu Chan) Rui-Jun Fan, Chi-Yao Chang, Tsan-De Tsai, Jing-Wen Jia, Han-Liang Chung, Pei-Wen Huang.

BAD GUY
Nov., 2001. South Korean. (Kim Ki-duk) Jo Jai-hyeon, Seo Weon.

BAD GUYS
MAGIC MEDIA/MEDIEN & TELEVISION MUNCHEN/HBO/MTV. Feb., 2000. Hungarian-German. (Tamas Sas) Viktor Bodo, Zoltan Rajkai, Andras Stohl, Anna Palmai, Andrea Fullajtar, Laszlo Banszky.

BAD LUCK LOVE
GNU FILMS. Feb., 2001. Finnish. (Olli Saarela) Jorma Tommila, Tommi Eronen, Maria Jarvenhelmi, Elmeri Karlsson, Rauno Juvonen, Ikka Koivula, Tarja-Tuulikki Tarsala.

BAD MONEY
RED SKY ENTERTAINMENT/SECURITY FILM CORP. Sept., 1999. Canadian. (John Hazlett) Graham Greene, Karen Sillas, Stephen Spender, Alison Down, Tamsin Kelsey.

BAD TIMES
UNIVERSIDAD DEL CINE Y ARTES AUDIOVISUALES. Nov., 1998. Argentine. (Nicolas Saad, Mariano De Roas, Salvador Roselli, Rodrigo Moreno) Pablo Vega, Daniel Valenzuela, Nicolas Leivas, Diego Peretti, Virginia Innocenti.

BAIT
WARNER BROS./CASTLE ROCK ENTERTAINMENT. Aug., 2000. (Antoine Fuqua) Jamie Foxx, David Morse, Doug Hutchison, Robert Pastorelli, Kimberly Elise, David Paymer, Mike Epps, Jamie Kenned.

BALALAIKA
TMC FILM. May, 2001. Turkish. (Ali Ozgenturk) Ugur Yucel, Cem Davran, Ozan Guven, Yekaterina Rednikova, Anna Voronova.

BALKAN BAROQUE
REGARDS PRODS./INSTITUT NATIONAL DE L'AUDIOVISUEL/WEGA FILM/SCARABEE/ARTE-WDR/ORF. Sept., 1999. French. (Pierre Coulibeuf) Marina Abramovic, Ulay, Michel Butor, Sean Kelly. Documentary.

BALKAN INVENTORY
BIENNALE DI VENEZIA CINEMA SECTION. Nov., 2000. Italian. (Yervant Gianikian, Angela Ricci Lucchi) Documentary.

THE BALLAD OF BERING STRAIT
June, 2002. U.S.-Japanese. (Nina Gilden Seavey) Documentary.

THE BALLAD OF RAMBLIN' JACK
PLANTAIN FILMS/CRAWFORD COMMUNICATIONS. Jan., 2000. (Aiyana Elliott). Documentary.

THE BALLAD OF THE WINDSHIELD WASHERS
MIKADO. Sept., 1998. Italian. (Peter Del Monte) Olek Mincer, Agara Buzek, Kim Rossi Stuart, Andrzej Grabowski, Grazyna Wolszak.

BALL IN THE HOUSE
June, 2002. (Tanya Wexler) Jonathan Tucker, Jennifer Tilly, David Strathairn, Dan Moran, Deirdre O'Connell, Ethan Embry, Larry Neumann Jr.

BALLISTIC: ECKS VS. SEVER
WARNER BROS. Sept., 2002. (Kaos) Antonio Banderas, Lucy Liu, Gregg Henry, Ray Park, Talisa Soto, Miguel Sandoval, Terry Chen, Roger R. Cross, Sandrine Holt.

BALLISTIC KISS
CRASH MEDIA. Oct., 1998. Hong Kong. (Donnine Yen) Donnie Yen, Annie Wu, Jimmy Wong, Simon Lui, Yu Rongguang.

BALSEROS
LAUREN FILM (IN SPAIN). July, 2002. Spanish. (Carles Bosch, Josep M. Domenech) Documentary.

BAMBOOZLED
NEW LINE CINEMA. Sept., 2000. (Spike Lee) Damon Wayans, Savion Glover, Jada Pinkett-Smith, Tommy Davidson, Michael Rapaport.

BANDITS
MGM. Sept., 2001. (Barry Levinson) Bruce Willis, Billy Bob Thornton, Cate Blanchett, Troy Garity, Brian F. O'Byrne, Stacey Travis, Bobby Slayton, January Jones.

BANG, BANG, YOU'RE DEAD
June, 2002. (Guy Ferland) Tom Cavanagh, Ben Foster, Randy Harrison, Janel Moloney, Jane McGregor, Gillian Barber, Kristian Ayre, Brent Glenen, Eric Johnson, David Paetkau, Eric Keenleyside, Glynis Davies.

BANG BOOM BANG: A DEAD-CERT THING
SENATOR. June, 1999. German. (Peter Thorwarth) Oliver Korittke, Markus Knuefken, Ralf Richter, Diether Krebs.

THE BANGER SISTERS
UFD (IN FRANCE)/FOX SEARCHLIGHT (IN U.S.) Sept., 2002. (Bob Dolman) Goldie Hawn, Susan Sarandon, Geoffrey Rush, Erika Christensen, Eva Amurri, Robin Thomas, Matthew Carey.

BANG RAJAN
FILM BANGKOK. May, 2001. Thai. (Thanit Jitnukul) Winai Kraibutr, Bin Bunluerit, Jaran Ngamdee, Chumphorn Thepphithak, Attakorn Suwannaraj, Bongkoj Khongmalai.

THE BANK
AUSTRALIAN FILM FINANCE CORP. April, 2001. Australian-Italian. (Robert Connolly) David Wenham, Anthony LaPaglia, Sibylla Budd, Steve Rodgers, Mitchell Butel, Mandy McElhinney, Greg Stone.

BANKRUPT
LA VIE EST BELLE FILMS ASSOCIES/LES FILMS EN HIVER/ELISON/HORIZON MARS/LES PRODUCTIONS DE L'AMOUR FOU. Feb., 2000. French. (Antoine Desrosiers) Mathieu Demy, Gwennola Bothorel, Zinedine Soualem, Antoine Chappey.

BAR
Dec., 2001. Cypriot-Greek. (Aliki Danezi-Knutsen). Stela Fyrogeni, Achileas Grammatikopoulos, Yannis Stankoglou, Michael McKell, Maria Colombatti, Keith James.

BARAN
Feb., 2001. Iranian. (Majik Majidi) Hossein Abedini, Zahra Bahrami, Mohammad Reza Naji.

BARBARA
PER HOLST FILM/SVENSK FILMINDUSTRI. Feb., 1998. Danish-Swedish-Norwegian. (Nils Malmros) Anneke von der Lippe, Lars Simonsen, Helene Egelund, Trond Hovik, Peter Hesse Overgaard.

BARBECUE-PEJO
TABOU-TABAC FILMS (BEMIN)/45 RDLE (FRANCE). Oct., 2000. French. (Jean Odoutan) Jean Odoutan, Laurentine Milebo, Didier Dorlipo, Adama Kouyate.

THE BARBER OF SIBERIA
MICHEL SEYDOUX. May, 1999. Russian-French-Italian-Czech. (Nikita Mikhalkov) Julia Ormond, Oleg Menshikov, Richard Harris

BARBERSHOP
METRO-GOLDWYN-MAYER. Aug., 2002. (Tim Story) Ice Cube, Anthony Anderson, Cedric the Entertainer, Sean Patrick Thomas, Eve, Troy Garity, Michael Ealy, Leonard Earl Howze, Keith David, Jazsmin Lewis, Lahmard Tate, Tom Wright.

BARBIE IN THE NUTCRACKER
ARTISAN HOME ENTERTAINMENT Sept., 2001. (Owne Hurley)

BARENAKED IN AMERICA
NETTFILMS. Sept., 1999. Canadian. (Jason Priestley) The Barenaked Ladies, Jon Steward, Jason Priestley, Moses Znaimer.

BARK!
Jan., 2002. (Kasia Adamik) Lee Tergesen, Heather Morgan, Lisa Kudrow, Vincent D'Onofrio, Hank Azaria, Mary Jo Deschanel, Scott Wilson, Aimee Graham, Wade Andrew Williams.

BARKING DOGS NEVER BITE
CINEMA SERVICES. Sept., 2000. South Korean. (Bong Joon-ho) Lee Sung-jae, Bae Doo-na.

BARNEY'S GREAT ADVENTURE
POLYGRAM FILMS. March, 1998. (Steve Gomer) George Hearn, Shirley Douglas, Trevor Morgan, Kyla Pratt, Diana Rice, David Joyner.

BARNIE'S MINOR ANNOYANCES
BAC DISTRIBUTION. March, 2001. French. (Bruno Chiche) Fabrice Luchini, Nathalie Baye, Marie Gillain, Hugo Speer, Serge Hazanavicius, Melanie Bernier.

507

BARRACKS
VGTRK/DAR CINEMATOGRAPHIC CO.. Aug., 1999. Russian. (Valeri Ogorodnikov) Irina Senotova, Yulia Svezhakova.

BARRIO
WARNER SOGEFILMS. Sept., 1998. Spanish. (Fernando Leon de Aranoa) Crispulo Cabezas, Timy, Eloi Yebra, Marieta Orozco.

BARTLEBY
PARKER FILM CO. March, 2001. (Jonathan Parker) David Paymer, Crispin Glover, Glenne Headly, Joe Piscopo, Maury Chaykin, Seymour Cassel, Carrie Snodgrass, Dick Martin.

BARTOK THE MAGNIFICENT
20TH CENTURY FOX/GARY GOLDMAN. Nov., 1999. (Don Bluth, Gary Goldman) Hank Azaria, Kelsey Grammer, Andrea Martin, Catherine O'Hara, Tim Curry, Jennifer Tilly. Animated.

BASED ON THE NOVEL
DKP AMSTERDAM. Jan. 1999. Dutch. (Eddy Terstall) Dirk Seelenberg, Nadja Hupscher, Femke Lakerveld, Alette Dirkse.

BASEKETBALL
UNIVERSAL PICTURES. July, 1998. (David Zucker), Trey Parker, Matt Stone, Yasmine Bleeth, Jenny McCarthy, Robert Vaughn.

THE BASEMENT AND THE KITCHEN
DRAMA 3/4. June, 1999.(David Frickas) David Frickas, Pam Cook, Mo Gaffney, Ric Barbera.

THE BASKET
NORTH BY NORTHWEST ENTERTAINMENT. May, 1999.(Rich Cowan) Peter Coyote, Karen Allen, Robert Karl Burke.

BASTARDS IN PARADISE
LATINORDISK/CORFO. Sept., 2000. Swedish-Chilean. (Luis R. Vera) Lotta Kalge, Camilo Alanis, Daniel Ojala, Maria E. Cavieres.

BATANG WEST SIDE
July, 2002. Filipino-U.S. (Lav Diaz) Joel Torre, Yul Servo, Gloria Diaz, Priscilla Almeda, Arthur Acuna, Rubem Tizon.

BATS
DESTINATION FILMS. Oct., 1999. (Louis Morneau) Lou Diamond Phillips, Dina Meyer, Bob Gunton, Leon, Carlos Jacott, David Shawn McConnell, Marcia Dangerfield, Oscar Rowland.

BATTLEFIELD EARTH
WARNER BROS./MORGAN CREEK/FRANCHISE PICTURES/JONATHAN D. KRANE/JTP FILMS. May, 2000. (Roger Christian) John Travolta, Barry Pepper, Forest Whitaker, Kim Coates, Richard Tyson, Sabine Karsenti, Michael Byrne, Sean Hewitt, Michel Perron, Shaun Austin-Olsen.

BATTLE FOR LIFE
VERBASCUM/CZECH TV. June, 2001. Czech Republic. (Miroslav Janek, Vit Janacek, Roman Vavra) Documentary.

BATTLE ROYALE
TOEI CO.Jan., 2001. Japanese. (Tatsuya Fujiwara, Aki Maeda, Taro Yamamoto, Masanobu Ando, Kou Shibasaki, Chiaki Kuriyama.

BAY OF LOVE AND SORROWS
Aug., 2002. Canadian. (Tim Southam) Peter Outerbridge, Jonathan Scarfe, Joanne Kelly, Christopher Jacot, Elaine Cassidy, Zachary Bennett.

BAYSIDE SHAKEDOWN
TOHO. May, 1999. Japanese. (Katsuyuki Motohiro) Yuji Oda, Toshiro Yanagiba, Eri Fukatsu, Miki Mizuno, Kyoko Koizumi.

THE BEACH
20TH CENTURY FOX/FIGMENT FILM. Feb., 2000. (Danny Boyle) Leonardo DiCaprio, Tilda Swinton, Virginie Ledoyen, Guillaume Canet, Paterson Joseph, Robert Carlyle, Peter Youngblood Hills.

THE BEACH AT TROUVILLE
TRANS-FILM/TIME FILMVERLEIH. Feb., 1999. German. (Michael Hofmann) Boris Aljinovic, Antje Westermann, Katja Zinsmeister, Karin Krawczyk, Christoph Zapatka.

BEACH CAFÉ
Sept., 2001. French. (Benoit Graffin) Jacques Nolot, Ouassini Embarek, Leila Belarbi, Dalia Amrani, Meriem Serbah.

BEAR WITH ME
BLUE BEAR PRODS. II. Sept., 2000. Canadian. (Paul Ziller) Kaitlyn Burke, Michael Ontkean, Helen Shaver, Kimberley Warnat, Gordon Tootoosis, Eric Johnson, Alan Thicke, Kristian Ayre.

BEASTCOPS
Media Asia Films. May, 1998. Hong Kong. (Gordon Chan) Michael Fitzgerald Wong, Anthony Wong, Kathy Chau, Roy Cheung, Sam Lee.

BEAT
SHOCHIKU. Sept., 1998. Japanese. (Amon Miyamoto) Claude Maki, Yuki Uchida, Dean Stapleton, Naoto Harata, Judy Motomura.

BEAT
MILLENNIUM PICTURES/PFILMCO/DONALD ZUCKERMAN/PENDRAGON FILM/WALKING PICTURES/MARTIEN HOLDING/BACKGROUND PRODS. Jan., 2000. (Gary Walkow) Courtney Love, Norman Reedus, Ronn Livingston, Kiefer Sutherland, Daniel Martinez, Kyle Secor, Sam Trammell.

THE BEATING OF THE BUTTERFLY'S WINGS
LES FILMS DES TOURNELLES/LES FILMS DES TOURNELLES/LES FILMS EN HIVER PRODUCTION/GIMAGES/CANAL PLUS. July, 2000. French. (Laurent Firode) Audrey Tautou, Faudel, Eric Feldman, Eric Savin, Lysiane Meis, Francoise Bertin, Irene Ismailoff, Said Ferrai.

BEAUTIFUL
DESTINATION FILMS/FLASHPOINT/PROSPERITY PICTURES/2 DRIVERS/FOGWOOD FILMS. Sept., 2000. (Sally Field) Minnie Driver, Joey Lauren Adams, Hallie Kate Eisenberg, Kathleen Turner, Leslie Stefanson, Bridgette Wilson, Kathleen Robertson.

BEAUTIFUL CREATURES
UIP/UNIVERSAL/DNA FILMS/UNITED PICTURES INTL./ARTS COUNCIL OF ENGLAND/SNAKEMAN. Aug., 2000. British. (Bill Eagles) Rachel Weisz, Susan Lynch, Alex North, Iain Glen.

BEAUTIFUL MEMORIES
Aug., 2001. French. (Zabou Breitman) Isabelle Carre, Bernard Campan, Bernard Le Coq, Dominique Pinon, Anne Le Ny, Isabelle Nanty, Aude Briant, Zabou Breitman.

A BEAUTIFUL MIND
UNIVERSAL. Dec., 2001. (Ron Howard) Russell Crowe, Ed Harris, Jennifer Connelly, Paul Bettany, Adam Goldberg, Judd Hirsch, Josh Lucas, Anthony Rapp, Christopher Plummer, Austin Pendleton, Jason Gray-Stanford.

A BEAUTIFUL NEW WORLD
IMAR FILM. Feb., 1999. Chinese. (Shi Runjiu) Jiang Wu, Tao Hong, Chen Ning, Ren Xianqi, Wu Pai.

A BEAUTIFUL SECRET (EL SECRETO DE ESPERANZA)
July, 2002. Mexican. (Leopoldo Laborde) Katy Jurado, Imanol Landeta, Ana de la Reguera, Maria Karunna, Michel Corral, Roberto Cobo, Jaime Aymerich, Amparo Garrido, Mariana Gaja, Gustavo Laborde, Roberto Trujillo.

BEAUTIFUL SUMMER
KIEV STUDIO. Aug., 2000. Soviet Union–1950. (Boris Barnet) Nikolai Kryuchkov, Nina Arkhipova, Mikhail Kuznetsov, Marina Bebutova, Viktor Dobrovolsky.

BEAUTIFUL SUNDAY
JJ-PHONE. Sept., 1998. Japanese. (Tetsuya, Nakashima) Masatoshi Nagase, Momoki Bitoh, Kumiko Nakamura, Mamako Yoneyama, Kyoko Endoh.

BEAUTOPIA
FOX LORBER. Jan., 1998. (Katharina Otto) Documentary.

BEAUTY
MARGIN FILMS. Feb., 1999. Hong Kong-Chinese. (Manshih Yonfan): Stephen Fung, Daniel Wu, Jason Tsang, Terence Yiin, Shu Qi.

BEAUTY AND THE BEAST: SPECIAL EDITION
BUENA VISTA. Dec., 2001. (Gary Trousdale, Kirk Wise) Animation.

THE BEAVER TRILOGY
STRAND RELEASING. Jan., 2001. (Trent Harris)
THE BEAVER KID (1979)
(Trent Harris) Groovin' Gary.
BEAVER KID 2 (1981)
(Trent Harris) Sean Penn.
THE ORKLY KID (1985)
(Trent Harris) Crispin Glover, Stefan Arngrim, John Bluto, Ken Butler, Lila Waters, Shane McCabe, Elizabeth Daily.

BECK–REVENGE
COLUMBIA TRISTAR (SWEDEN). May, 2001. Swedish-Danish. (Kjell Sundvall) Peter Haber, Mikael Persbrandt, Sophie Tolstoy, Marie Goransson, Ingvar Hirdwall, Rebecka Hemse, Shanti Roney.

THE BED
BARRANDOV BIOGRAFIA. May, 1998. Czech. (Oskar Reif) Micheal Przebinda, Stanslava Jachnicka, Jana Hruskova, Martin Stavel.

BEDAZZLED
20TH CENTURY FOX. Oct., 2000. (Harold Ramis) Brendan Fraser, Elizabeth Hurley, Frances O'Connor, Miriam Shor, Orlando Jones.

BEDROOM & COURTROOM
Cinema Service Co. Sept., 1998. South Korean. (Kang Wu-seok) Ahn Sung-ki, Mun Seong-keun, Hwang Cine, Shim Hye-jin.

BEDROOMS & HALLWAYS
PANDORA CINEMA. May, 1998. British. (Rose Troche) Kevin McKidd, Hugo Weaving, Jennifer Ehle, Simon Callow, Harriet Walter.

BEDTIME FAIRY TALES FOR CROCODILES
July, 2002. Mexican. (Ignacio Ortiz Cruz) Arturo Rios, Luisa Huertes, Ana Graham, Mayra Serbulo, Dagoberto Gama.

BEEFCAKE
EMOTION PICTURE/ALLIANCE INDEPENDENT FILMS/CHANNEL FOUR/ODEON FILMS/MIKADO FILMS/LA SEPT ARTE. JAN., 1999. Canadian. (Thom Fitzgerald) Daniel MacIvor, Josh Peace, Carroll Godsman, Jonathan Torrens, Jack Griffin Mazeika.

BEFORE NIGHT FALLS
FINE LINE/GRANDVIEW PICTURES/EL MAR PICTURES. Sept., 2000. (Julian Schnabel) Javier Bardem, Olivier Martinez, Andrea Di Stefano, Johnny Depp, Sean Penn, Michael Wincott, Najwa Nimri, Hector Babenco, Olatz Lopez Garmendia, Vito Maria Schnabel.

BEFORE SUNSET
CECCHI GORI GROUP. Aug., 1999. Italian. (Stefano Incerti) Said Taghmaoui, Vincenzo Peluso, Ninni Bruschetta, Gigi Savoia.

BEFORE THE STORM
ILLUSION FILM/FILM I VAST/FELICIA FILM/PER HOLST FILM/NORSK FILM. Sept., 2000. Swedish. (Reza Parsa) Per Graffman, Maria Lundqvist, Sasha Becker, Anni Ececioglu, Emil Odepark.

BEFORE YOU GO
ENTERTAINMENT FILM DISTRIBUTORS. June, 2002. British. (Lewis Gilbert) Julie Walters, Tom Wilkinson, John Hannah, Joanne Whaley.

BEHIND ENEMY LINES
20TH CENTURY FOX. Nov., 2001. (John Moore) Owen Wilson, Gene Hackman, Gabriel Macht, Charles Malik Whitfield,Joaquim de Almeida, David Keith, Olek Krupa.

BEHIND GOD'S BACK
LA CICATRIZ/CAMERA OBSCURA PELICULAS. Jan., 2001. Spanish. (Pablo Llorca) Isabel Ampudia, Alberto Jimenez, Luis Miguel Cintra, Pedro Casablanc, Guillermo Toledo, Leonor Watling.

BEHIND THE SUN
VIDEOFILMES (BRAZIL)/HAUT ET COURT, BAC FILMS (FRANCE)/DAN VALLEY FILM (SWITZERLAND). Sept., 2001. (Walter Salles) Jose Dumont, Rodrigo Santoro, Rita Assemany, Luis Carlos Vasconcelos, Ravi Ramos Lacerda, Flavia Marco Antonio.

BEIJING BICYCLE
SONY PICTURES CLASSICS. Feb., 2001. Taiwanese-French. (Wang Xiaoshuai) Cui Lin, Li Bin, Zhou Xun, Gao Yuanyuan, Li Shuang.

BEIJING TOCKS
MEDIA ASIA. Nov., 2001. Hong Kong. (Mabel Cheung) Daniel Wu, Shu Qi, Geng Le, Richard Ng, Faye Yue.

BEING CLAUDINE
BEING CLAUDINE PRODS. July, 2002. (I-Fan Quirk) Justine Litchman, Musashi Alexander, Jordan Cael, Russ Vigilante, James Bowman, Rose Arrick, Reggi Wyns.

BEING JOHN MALKOVICH
USA FILMS/UNIVERSAL. Sept., 1999. British-U.S. (Spike Jonze) John Cusak, Cameron Diaz, Catherine Keener, Mary Kay Place, John Malkovich.

BEING LIGHT
REZO FILMS. Dec., 2001. French. (Jean-Marc Barr, Pascal Arnold) Jean-Marc Barr, Romain Duris, Elodie Bouchez, Isabelle Candelier.

BEJART INTO THE LIGHT
Sept., 2002. Swiss-French-Belgian. (Marcel Schupbach) Documentary.

BEL AIR
PLASTERCITY PRODS./MORGAN DIGITAL STUDIOS. Mar., 2000. (Chris Coppol) Marc Coppola, Barbara Bain, Jennifer Rubin, Esteban Powell, Lou Rawls, Charles Fleischer, Ernie Mirich, Brad Wyman, Noah Blake.

THE BELIEVER
PETER HOFFMAN. Jan., 2001. (Henry Bean) Ryan Gosling, Summer Phoenix, Glenn Fitzgerald, Theresa Russell, Billy Zane, Garret Dillahunt, Kris Eivers.

BELLA CIAO
June, 2001. French. (Stephane Giusti) Jacques Gamblin, Yael Abecassis, Jalil Lespert, Serge Hazanavicius, Isabelle carre, Vahina Giocante, Oceane Mozas.

BELLA CIAO: GENOA SOCIAL FORUM 'ANOTHER WORLD IS POSSIBLE'
May, 2002. Italian. (Marco Giusti, Roberto Torelli) Documentary.

BELLARIA - AS LONG AS WE LIVE!
June, 2002. German-Austrian. (Douglas Wolfsperger) Documentary.

BELLINI'S DRIVE
NEVERTHERE PRODS. Sept., 1998. Canadian. (Jeff Stephenson) Paul Bellini, Shania Twain.

BELLY
ARTISAN. Nov., 1999.(Hype Williams) Nas, DMX, Taral Hicks, Tionne "T-Boz" Watkins, Method Man.

BELLYFRUIT
INDEPENDENT WOMEN ARTISTS. Apr., 1999. (Kerri Lee) Tamara LaSeon Bass, Tonatzin Mondragon, Kelly Vin.

BELLYFUL
EURIPIDE/HAVAS IMAGE/LES VOLEURS D'OMBRES PRODS./HARLENKIJN/KRO-TV/ACCOLADE PICTURES/CANAL PLUS/CNC. June, 2000. French-Dutch. (Melvin Van Peebles) Andrea Ferreol, Jacques Boudet, Meiji U Tum'si, Claude Perron.

BELLEVILLE
RAI CINEMAFICTION. Sept., 1998. Italian.(Marco Turco) Ennio Fantastichini, Isabella Ferrari, Massimo Bellinzoni.

BELOVED
BUENA VISTA. Sept., 1998. (Jonathan Demme) Oprah Winfrey, Danny Glover, Thandie Newton, Kimberly Elise, Beah Richards.

BELOVED FRIEND
LAUREN FILMS. Jan., 1999. Spanish. (Ventura Pons): Josep Maria Pou, Rosa Maria Sarda, Mario Gas, David Selvas.

BELOW
DIMENSION FILMS. Oct., 2002. (David Twohy) Matt Davis, Bruce Greenwood, Olivia Williams, Holt McCallany, Scott Foley, Zach Galifianakis, Jason Flemyng, Dexter Fletcher, Nick Chinlund, Andrew Howard, Christopher Fairbank.

BELPHEGOR: PHANTOM OF THE LOUVRE
BAC DISTRIBUTION. March, 2001. French. (Jean-Paul Salome) Sophie Marceau, Michel Serrault, Frederic Diefenthal, Julie Christie, Jean-Francois Balmer, Patachou, Lionel Abelanski.

BEMANI/TO STAY ALIVE
Feb., 2002. Iranian. (Dariush Mehrjui) Masoumeh Bakhshi, Shadi Heydari, Neda Aghayi.

BE MY STAR
POLYFILM. Aug., 2001. Austrian. (Valeska Grisebach) Nicole Glaesner, Tina Sanoke, Christopher Schoeps, Sebastian Rinka, Monique Glaeser, Jeanine Glaeser.

A BENCH IN THE PARK
ALTA FILMS/FERNANDO COLOMO PC/ALTA FILMS/CANAL PLUS. Sept., 1999. Spanish. (Agusti Vila) Alex Brendemuhl, Victoria Freire, Monica Lopez, Aitor Merino, Gary Piquer, Francesco Garrido.

BEND IT LIKE BECKHAM
HELKON SK FILM DISTRIBUTION. March, 2002. U.S.-British-German. (Gurinder Chadha) Parminder Nagra, Keira Knightley, Jonathan Rhys Meyers, Anupam Kher, Archie Panjabi, Shaznay Lewis, Frank Harper, Juliet Stevenson.

BENJAMIN SMOKE
COWBOY BOOKING INTL./C-HUNDRED FILM CORP./COWBOY BOOKING INTL./GRAVITY HILL FILMS/PUMPERNICKEL. Feb., 2000. (Jem Cohen, Peter Sillen) Benjamin, Tim Campion, Brian Halloran, Coleman Lewis, Bill Taft, Todd Butler, Will Fratesi.

BEOWULF
CTV INTL. May, 1999. (Graham Baker) Christopher Lambert, Rhona Mitra, Oliver Cotton, Goetz Otto, Layla Roberts.

BERESINA OR THE LAST DAYS OF SWITZERLAND
T&C FILM)/PANDORA FILM/PRISMA FILM. May, 1999. Swiss-German-Austrian. (Daniel Schmid) Elena Panova, Geraldine Chaplin, Martin Benrath, Ulrich Noethen, Ivan Darvas.

BERLIN-CINEMA
LES FILMES DE LA TERRASSE/LA SEPT-ARTE/LES FILMS DE LA TERRASSE. Sept., 1999. Swiss-French. (Samira Gloor Fadel) Wim Wenders, Jean Nouvel, Thomas, Jean-Luc Godard (voice), Rudiger Vogler (voice).

BERLIN IS IN GERMANY
LUNA-FILM. Feb., 2001. German. (Hannes Stohr) Jorg Schuttauf, Julia Jager, Robin Becker, Edita Malovic, Tom Jahn, Oscar Martinez, Robert Lohr.

BESAME MUCHO
EUROSTAR 95. Jan., 1999. Italian. (Maurizio Ponzi) Toni Bertorelli, Giuliana De Sio, Elena Russon, Duccio Giordano, Francesco Stella.

BESAME MUCHO
TERZP MONDO. July, 2000. Israeli. (Joseph Pitchhadze) Ryan Early, Carmel Betto, Eli Danker, Ayala Verete, Ezra Kafri, Moni Moshonov.

BESEIGED
FINE LINE CINEMA. Sept., 1998. Italian. (Bernardo Bertolucci) Thandie Newton, David Thewlis, Claudio Santamaria.

BESIDE MYSELF
PABLO DISTRIBUZIONE/PUPKIN. Nov., 1999. Italian. (Gianni Zanas) Paolo Sassanelli, Lorenzo Viaconzi, Marit Nissen, Dino Abbrescia.

BEST
OPTIMUM RELEASING/IAC FILM/SKY FILMS/ISLE OF MAN FILM COMMISSION/SMOKE & MIRRORS FILM PRODS./PEMBRIDGE PICTURES. May, 2000. British. (Mary McGuckian) John Lynch, Ian Bannen, Jerome Flynn, Ian Hart, Patsy Kensit, Cal Macaninch.

BEST IN SHOW
WARNER BROS/CASTLE ROCK. Sept., 2000. (Christopher Guest) Bob Balaban, Jennifer Coolidge, Christopher Guest, John Michael Higgins, Michael Hitchcock, Eugene Levy, Jane Lynch, Michael McKean, Catherine O'Hara, Parker Posey, Fred Willard, Patrick Cranshaw.

BEST LAID PLANS
20TH CENTURY FOX. June, 1999. (Mike Barker) Alessandro Nivola, Reese WItherspoon, Josh Brolin, Rocky Carroll.

THE BEST MAN
OCTOBER FILMS. Jan., 1998. Italian. (Pupi Avati) Diego Abantantuono, Ines Sastre, Dario Cantarelli, Cinia Mascoli.

THE BEST MAN
UNIVERSAL. Sept., 1999. (Malcolm D. Lee) Taye Diggs, Nia Long, Morris Chestnut, Harold Perrineau, Terrence Howard.

BEST MEN
FILM FOUR DISTRIBUTORS. March, 1998. (Tamra Davis) Dean Cain, Andy Dick, Sean Patrick Flanery, Luke Wilson, Fred Ward.

THE BEST OF TIMES (MEILI SHIGUANG)
Sept., 2002. Taiwanese-Japanese. (Chang Tso-Chi) Fan Wing, Gao Meng-Jie, Tien Mao-Ying, Wu Yu-Chih, Yu Wan-Mei, Chang Shang-Ting, Lin Hen-Bao, Zeng Yi-Tse, Tsai Ming-Hsiu.

BETELNUT BEAUTY
ARC LIGHT FILMS (TAIPAI)/PYRAMIDE PRODS. (PARIS). Feb., 2001. Taiwanese-French. (Lin Cheng-sheng) Chang Chen, Sinje, Tsai Chen-nan, Kao Ming-chun, Kelly Kuo, Leon Dai, Tsai Chao-yi, Sun Yu-hui, Ko I-cheng.

BE THERE OR BE SQUARE
BEIJING FORBIDDEN CITY/BEIJING FILM STUDIO. Dec., 1998. Chinese. (Feng Xiaogeng) Ge You, Xu Fan.

BETTER LIVING
GOLDHEART PICTURES. Nov. 1998. (Max Mayer) Olympia Dukakis, Roy Scheider, Edward Herrmann, Cathrine Corpeny.

BETTER LIVING THROUGH CIRCUITRY
Cleopatra Pictures. April 1999. (Jon Reiss) The Crystal method, Roni Size, DJ Spooky, Electric.

BETTER LUCK TOMORROW
Jan., 2002. (Justin Lin) Parry Shen, Jason Tobin, Sung Kang, Roger Fan, John Cho, Karin Anna Cheung, Jerry Mathers.

BETTER THAN SEX
SAMUEL GOLDWYN FILMS/NEW VISION/NEW SOUTH WALES FILM & TV OFFICE/FRANCE TELEVISION DISTRIBUTION-MEERCAT FILMS. June, 2000. Australian-French. (Jonathan Teplitzky) David Wenham, Susie Porter, Catherine McClements, Kris McQuade, Simon Bossell.

BETTY FISHER AND OTHER STORIES
UFD (IN FRANCE)/ALLIANCE ATLANTIS VIVAFILM (IN CANADA). Sept., 2001. French-Canadian. (Claude Miller) Sandrine Kiberlain, Nicole Garcia, Mathilde Seigner, Luck Mervil, Edouard Baer, Stephane Freiss, Roschdy Zem, ALexis Chatrian, Arthur Setbon.

BETWEEN STRANGERS
MEDUSA FILM. Aug., 2002. Canadian-Italian. (Edouardo Ponti) Sophia Loren, Mira Sorvino, Deborah Kara Unger, Pete Postlethwaite, Klaus Maria Brandauer, Gerard Depardieu.

BETWEEN YOUR LEGS
COLUMBIA TRISTAR. Jan., 1999. Spanish-French. (Manuel Gomez Pereira) Victoria Abril, Javier Bardem, Carmelo Gomez, Juan Diego, Sergio Lopez.

BEWARE OF GREEKS BEARING GUNS
PALACE FILMS/AUSTRALIAN FILM FINANCE CORP./MEDIA WORLD FEATURES/MYTHOS PRODS./FILM VICTORIA/MEGA CHANNEL/THE GREEK FILM CENTER. Mar., 2000. Australian-Greek. (Tatoulis) Lakis Lazopoulos, Zoe Carides, John Bluthal, Claudia Buttazzoni, Tasso Kavvadia, Noni Ionannidou.

BEWARE OF MY LOVE
REZO FILMS. Aug., 1998. French. (Jeanne Labrune) Nathalie Baye, Daniel Duval, Hubert Saint Macary.

BEYOND
THURA FILM/BECH FILM/DANISH FILM INSTITUTE/TV2//NORDIC SCREEN/SVENSKA FILMKOMPANIET/SVT DRAMA. Aug., 2000. Danish-Swedish. (Ake Sandgren) Robert Hansen, Ralf J. Hollander, Otto Brandenburg, Baard Owe, Jesper Asholt, Laura Aagaard.

BEYOND FORGIVIN'
MAGNA PICTURES/FIVE STAR. Oct., 1999. Thai.(Manop Udomdej) Dom Hetrakul, Nuchnart Saichompoo, Juthamas Chantasorn.

BEYOND OUR DREAMS
UGC INTL./LES FILMS DU RIVAGE/MK2 DIFFUSION/CANAL PLUS. Aug., 2000. French-Armenian-Italian. (Hiner Saleem) Olivier Sitruk, Roasanna Vite Mesropian, Ramen Avinian, Edik Bagdassarian.

BEYOND PARADISE
KAMA'AINA FILM PARTNERS. Oct., 1998. (David L. Cunningham) Roy Newton, David Schultz, Lorenzo Callender, Daryl Bonilla.

BEYOND REASON: A FRIEND ON DEATH ROW
SCARBEE FILMPRODUCTIES NEDERLAND BV (AMSTERDAM). Oct., 2000. Dutch. (Marijke Jongbloed) Gea Knol, Bryan Jennings, Bart Stapert, Margaret Danna, Greetje Bijma, Donna Clement, Suezann Bosler, Cynthia Barlow.

BEYOND THE OCEAN
GO EAST PRODS./INTRINSIC VALUE/PERSISTENCE OF VISION FILMS. Jan., 2000. U.S.-Russian-Austrian. (Tony Pemberton) Dasha Volga, Rik Nagel, Donovan Barton, Sage, Tatiana Kuznetsova.

BEYOND THE PALE
CLARKE/ALVINO. July, 1999.George Bazala) Patrick Clarke, Conn Horgan, Beverley Elder, Malachy McCourts.

B-52
COFILM (HUMBURG)-BIG SKY FILM (U.S.)-DSCHOINT VENTSCHR FILMPRODUKTION (ZURICH). Feb., 2001. German-Swiss (Hartmut Bitomsky) Documentary.

BHOPAL EXPRESS
HIGHLIGHT FILMS/KINTOP PICTURES/ALIVE ENTERTAINMENT. Mar., 2000. Indian. (Mahesh Mathai) Kay Kay, Nethra Raghuraman, Naseeruddin Shah, Zeenat Aman, Vijay Raaz.

BICENTENNIAL MAN
BUENA VISTA/TOUCHSTONE/COLUMBIA PICTURES/1492 PICTURES/LAURENCE MARK PRODS./RADIANT PRODS. Dec. 1999. (Chris Columbus) Robin Williams, Sam Neill, Embeth Davidtz, Oliver Platt, Wendy Crewson, Hallie Kate Eisenberg, Stephen Root, Lynne Thigpen.

BICHUNMOO
CINEMA SERVICE. Sept., 2000. South Korean. (Kim Yeong-jun) Shin Hyeon-jun, Kim Heui-seon, Jeong Jin-yeong, Jang Dong-jik, Kim Hakcheol, Bang Hyo-up.

THE BIG ANIMAL
TELEWIZJA POLSKA. July, 2000. Polish. (Jerzy Stuhr) Anna Dymna, Jerzy Stuhr, Dominika Dednarczyk, Blazej Wojcik, Rubio.

BIG BAD LOVE
PIEFACE/ROCKING S. May, 2001. (Arliss Howard) Arliss Howard, Debra Winger, Paul Le Mat, Rosanna Arquette, Angie Dickinson, Michael Parks, Alex Van.

THE BIG BANG
CECCHI GORI. Apr., 2000. Italian. (Leone Pompucci) Carlo Buccirosso, Emilio Solfrizzi, Alessandro Di Carlo, Gennaro Nunziante.

BIG DADDY
SONY. June, 1999. (Dennis Dugan) Adam Sandler, Joey Lauren Adams, Jon Stewart, Cole Sprouse.

BIG EDEN
CHAIKEN FILMS. Apr., 2000. (Thomas Bezucha) Arye Gross, Eric Schweig, Tim DeKay, Louise Fletcher, George Coe, Nan Martin, O'Neal Compton, Corinne Bohrer, Veanne Cox.

BIG FEELINGS
FAMA FILM DISTRIBUTION. Aug., 1999. Swiss-Luxembourgeois. (Christof Schertenleib) Anne Weber, Stefan Suske, Manuela Biedermann, Markus Wolff, Delia Mayer.

BIGGER THAN TINA
PALACE FILMS/BACKYARD PRODS./PALACE FILMS/FILM VICTORIA. Nov., 1999. Australian. (Neil Foley) Michael Dalley, Sally Lightfoot, Barry Friedlander, Dobe Newton, Phillipa Chapple.

THE BIG HIT
SONY PICTURES ENTERTAINMENT. April, 1998. (Che-Kirk Wong) Mark Wahlberg, Lou Diamond Phillips, Christina Applegate.

THE BIG KAHUNA
LIONS GATE. Sept. 1999. (John Swanbeck) Kevin Spacey, Danny DeVito, Peter Facinelli.

THE BIG LEBOWSKI
GRAMERCY. March, 1998. (Joel Coen) Jeff Bridges, John Goodman, Julianne Moore, Steve Buscemi, Peter Stormare, Flea, Sam Elliott.

BIG MAMA
NIKKATSU CORP. Sept., 2001. Japanese. (Kon Ichikawa) Keiko Kishi, Ryuji Harada, Shoichi Ozawa, Kanae Katsuno, Tsuyoshi Ujiki, Masaki Iizumi, Yuta Yamazaki, Hiroya Konno.

THE BIG MAMBO
KINOWELT. Feb., 1998. German. (Michael Gwisdek) Corinna Harfouch, Michael Gwisdek, Juergen Vogel, Uwe Kokisch.

BIG MOMMA'S HOUSE
20TH CENTURY FOX /FOX AND REGENCY ENTERPRISES/DAVID T. FRIENDLY/RUNTELDAT ENTERTAINMENT/TAURUS FILM. May, 2000. (Raja Gosnel) Martin Lawrence, Nia Long, Paul Giamatti, Terrence Howard, Anthony Anderson, Ella Mitchell, Jascha Washington.

BIG SHOT'S FUNERAL
Feb., 2002. Hong Kong-Chinese. (Feng Xiaogang) Ge You, Rosamund Kwan, Donald Sutherland, Ying Da, Paul Mazursky, He Ping, Fu Biao.

THE BIG SPLIT
KRAMER/TORNELL/CROSSROADS FILMS. Oct., 1999. (Martin Hynes) Martin Hynes, Judy Greer, Darryl McCane, Rachel True, Maggie Baird, Casey Lee, Lindsay Price.

THE BIG TEASE
WARNER BROS. Aug., 1999. (Kevin Allen).Craig Ferguson, Frances Fisher, Chris Langham, Mary McCormack.

BIG TROUBLE
BUENA VISTA. Sept., 2001. (Barry Sonnenfeld) Tim Allen, Rene Russo, Stanley Tucci,Tom Sizemore, Johnny Knoxville, Dennis Farina, Jack Kehler, Janeane Garofalo, Patrick Warburton, Ben Foster, Zooey Deschanel.

BILALIAN
Feb., 2002. (Aminah Bakeer Abdul-Jabbaar) Donald Bakeer, Ameerah Abdul-Mujeeb, Haaziq Muhammad, Imam Saadiq Saafir, Daaimah Jordan, Warith Deen Muhammad, Dafer Dakhil, Aminah Bakeer Abdul-Jabbaar (narrator).

BILLY'S HOLLYWOOD SCREEN KISS
REVOLUTIONARY EYE LLC. Jan., 1998. (Tommy O'Haver) Sean P. Hayes, Brad Rowe, Richard Ganoung, Meredith Scott Lynn.

BIMBOLAND
LEGENDE ENTREPRISES/GAUMONT/TF1 FILMS. May, 1999. French. (Ariel Zeitoun) Judith Godreche, Aure Atika, Gerard Depardieu, Sophie Forte, Armelle.

BINGO: THE DOCUMENTARY
JEFFCOAT FILMS. June, 1999. (John Jeffcoat.) Documentary.

BIO COPS
Feb., 2002. Hong Kong. (Wai-Man Cheng) Stephen Fung, Sam Lee, Alice Chan, Wai Ming Chan, Benny Lai, Shiu Hung Hui, Chi Hung Hg, Sammuel Leung.

THE BIRD PEOPLE OF CHINA
SEDIC INT'L. April, 1998. Japanese. (Takashi Miike) Masahiro Motoki, Renji Ishibashi, Mako, Wang Li Li.

BIRDCAGE INN
BOOGUI CINEMA. Sept. 1998. South Korean. (Kim Ki-deok) Lee Ji-eun, Lee Hye-un.

THE BIRD THAT STOPS IN THE AIR
DONGNYUK FILM. SEPT., 1999. South Korean. (Jeon Soo-il) Sul Kyung-gu, Kim So-hee, Lee Chung-in.

THE BIRDWATCHER
CINEMA PUBLIC FILMS. Jan., 2001. French-Portuguese. (Gabriel Auer) Thom Hoffman, Ines de Medeiros, Catherine de Seynes, Javier Cruz, Diane Bellego, Hans Meyer, Carlos Andreu, Diego Asensio.

BIRTHDAY
NAKED EYE. June, 2001. German. (Stefan Jager) Bibiana Beglau, Tamara Simunovic, Claudio Cailo, Harald Koch.

THE BIRTHDAY
SONET FILM/CIMBRIA FILM/SVT DRAMA MALMO/FILM PA OSTERLEN. Jan., 2000. Swedish. (Richard Hobert) Camilla Lunden, Goran Stangertz, Lena Endre, Pernilla August, Sven Lindberg.

BIRTHDAY GIRL
PORTOBELLO PICTURES/MIRAMAX FILMS/FILMFOUR/MIRAGE ENTERPRISES. Sept., 2001. British-U.S. (Jez Butterworth) Nicole Kidman, Ben Chaplin, Vincent Cassel, Mathieu Kassovitz.

BITTERSWEET MOTEL
IMAGE ENTERTAINMEN/AVIVA ENTERTAINMENT/LITTLE VILLA FEATURES/STANGER THAN FICTION/BITTERSWEET FILMS. Aug., 2000. (Todd Phillips). Documentary.

A BIZARRE ROMANCE: RURAL DECAMERON
GO FILM. Feb., 2001. Hungarian. (Dezso Zsigmond) Lajos Kovacs, Jozsef Szarvas, Edit Soos, Aniko Kiss, Karoly Safranek.

BLACK & GOLD
BIG NOISE FILMS. Jan., 2001. (Jacqueline Soohen, Richard Rowley) Documentary.

BLACK AND WHITE
NEW VISION FILMS (AUSTRALIA). June, 2002. Austrlian-British. (Craig Lahiff) Robert Carlyle, Charles Dance, Kerry Fox, Colin Friele, Ben Mendelsohn, David Ngoombujarra, Roy Billing.

BLACK & WHITE IN COLOR
CZECH TELEVISION/ARCIMBOLDO. Aug., 1999. Czech. (Mira Erdevicki-Charap). Documentary.

BLACK ANGEL VOL. 2
SHOCHIKU. Feb., 1999. Japanese. (Takashi Ishii) Yuki Amami, Takeshi Yamato, Reiko Kataoka, Yozaburo Ito, Daisuku Iijima.

THE BLACK BEACH
GEMINI FILMS. May, 2001. French-Portuguese-Swiss-Polish. (Michel Piccoli) Jerzy Radziwilowicz, Dominique Blanc, Jade Fortineau, Teresa Buszisz-Krzyanowska, Ignacy Gogolewski.

BLACKBOARDS
MAKHMALBAF FILM HOUSE/FABRICA CINEMA/RAICINEMA/T-MARK. May, 2000. Iranian-Italian. (Samira Makmalbaf) Bahman Ghobadi, Said Mohamadi, Behnaz Jafari.

BLACK CAT, WHITE CAT
OCTOBER FILMS/GOLDWYN FILMS. Sept., 1998. French-German-Yugoslav. (Emir Kusturica) Bajram Severdzan, Florijan Ajdini.

BLACK DAYS
ARTFUL DODGER AND JONX/DOTTIE THE DOG PRODS. Jan., 2001. (Ari Margolis, James Morley III) S. Greg Gardner, Shiva Rose, D. Reynolds, Nick Roye, Matthew Winberg, William Knight, Sarah Silverman.

BLACK DOG
UNIVERSAL. April, 1998. (Kevin Hooks), Patrick Swayze, Meat Loaf, Randy Travis, Gabriel Casseus, Brian Vincent, Brenda Strong.

BLACK EYED DOG
AISLING WORKS. Sept. 1999. (Richard O'Connell) Paul Barnett, Dermot Carroll, Lorcan Keating, Clive Worsley, Kevin Kearns, Suzanne Nece, Bernadette McCarthy, Pamela Wylie.

BLACK HAWK DOWN
SONY PICTURES ENTERTAINMENT. Dec., 2001. (Ridley Scott) Josh Hartnett, Ewan McGregor, Tom Sizemore, Eric Bana, William Fichtner, Ween Bremner, Sam Shepard, Gabriel Casseus, Kim Coates, Hugh Dancy, Ron Eldard.

BLACK HOLE
CINEROCK PICTURES. Oct. 16, 1999. South Korean. (Kim Kuk-hyeong) Ahn Sung-ki, Kim Min, Sa Hyun-jin, Bang Eun-jin.

THE BLACK HOUSE
ASMIK ACE ENTERTAINMENT. Feb., 2000. Japanese. (Yoshimitsu Morita) Shinobu Otake, Masaki Uchino, Masahiko Nishimura.

BLACK KNIGHT
20TH CENTURY FOX. Nov., 2001. (Gil Junger) Martin Lawrence, Marsha Thomason, Tom Wilkinson, Vincent Regan, Kevin Conway, Jeannette Weegar.

THE BLACK METEOR
MATTHIJS VAN HEIJNINGEN. June, 2001. Dutch. (Guido Pieters) Jet Novuka, Erik Van Der Horst, Gijs Scholten Van Aschat, Peter Tuinman, Thekla Reuten, Angelique De Bruijne.

BLACK OUT
PAUSILYPON FILMS/MACT PRODS./ ANIMATOGRAFO PRODUCAO DES FILMES. Nov., 1998. Greek-French-Portuguese. (Menelaos Karamaghiolis) Alkis Kourkoulos, Myrto Alikaki, Cleon Grigoriadis, Hanna Schygulla, Karyofilia Karabeti.

THE BLACKSHEEP AFFAIR
EASTERN FILM CO. Aug., 1998. Hong Kong. (Allun Lam) Zhao Wenzhuo, Shu Qi, Andrew Lin, Ken Wong, Kent Tseng.

BLACK TAR HEROIN: THE DARK END OF THE STREET
HBO/FARALLON/FILMS/IMAGINEER CO/TAPESTRY INTL. Nov., 1999.(Steven Okazaki). Documentary.

BLACK TEARS
RYNIKS FILMS BV. April, 1998. Dutch. (Sonia Herman Dolz) La Vieja Trova Santiaguera.

BLACK TEARS
ALTA FILMS. Nov., 1998. Spanish. (Ricardo Franco) Ariadne Gil, Fele Martinez, Ana Risueno, Elena Anaya, Elvira Minguez.

BLACKWOODS
VELOCITY ENTERTAINMENT. May, 2002. German-Canadian. (Uwe Boll) Patrick Muldoon, Keegan Connor Tracy, Michael Pare, Clint Howard, Ben Derrick, Will Sanderson.

BLADE
NEW LINE CINEMA. Aug., 1998. (Stephen Norrington) Wesley Snipes, Stephen Dorff, Kris Kristofferson, N'Bushe Wright.

BLADE II
NEW LINE CINEMA. 2002. (Guillermo del Toro) Wesley Snipes, Kris Kristofferson, Norman Reedus, Leonor Varela, Luke Goss, Ron Perlman, Matt Schulze.

THE BLAIR WITCH PROJECT
ARTISAN. Jan., 1999. (Daniel Myrick, Eduardo Sanchez) Heather Donahue, Michael Williams, Joshua Leonard, Sandra Sanchez.

BLAME IT ON THE KING
ALTA FILMS/PEDRO COSTA PC/ENRIQUE CEREZO PC/CANAL PLUS/TVE. Feb., 2000. Spanish. (Jose Antonio Quiros) Antonio Resines, Adriana Ozores, Jesus Bonilla, Manuel Alexandre.

BLAME IT ON VOLTAIRE
FLACH FILM. Sept., 2000. French. (Abdel Kechiche) Sami Bouajila, Elodie Bouchez, Aure Atika, Bruno Lochet, Virginie Darmon.

BLANK PAGE
Feb., 2002. Iranian. (Naser Taghvai) Hedye Tehrani, Khosro Shakibaie.

BLAST FROM THE PAST
NEW LINE. Feb. 1999. (Hugh Wilson) Brendan Fraser, Alicia Silverstone, Christopher Walken Sissy Spacek.

BLEEDER
SCANBOX ENTERTAINMENT. May, 1999. Danish. (Nicolas Winding) Kim Bodnia, Mads Mikkelsen, Rikke Louise Andersson, Liv Corfixen, Levino Jensen.

BLEEDER
POST MEDIDIAN CINEMA-CENTRO NACIONAL AUTONOMO DE CINEMATOGRAFICA-CINEMA SURE. Sept., 2000. (Leonardo Henriquez)

THE BLEEP BROTHERS
BLEEP BROTHERS INC. Jan., 2001. Japanese. (Yoshiyasu Fujita) Kentaro Seagal, Zenjiro, Mireiyu, Teruyuki Kagawa, Ittoku Kishibe.

BLESSED ARE THOSE WHO THIRST
NORDIC SCREEN PROD. Aug., 1998. Norwegian. (Carl Jorgen Kionig) Kjersti Elvik, Lasse Kolsrud, Anne Ryg, Bjorn Sundquist, Nils Ole Oftebro.

BLESSED ART THOU
YUCCA STREET PRODS. Jan., 2000. (Tim Disney) Bernard Hill, Paul Guilfoyle, Daniel von Bargen, Naveen Andrews, Joe Spano, M.E. Hackett, Michael Cudlizt, David Thornton, Brent Hinkley.

BLESS THE CHILD
PARAMOUNT/ICON PRODS./MACE NEUFELD. Aug., 2000. (Chuck Russell) Kim Basinger, Jimmy Smits, Holliston Coleman, Rufus Sewell, Angela Bettis, Christina Ricci, Michael Gaston, Ian Holm.

BLINDFOLDED
DADA/FILMI OY. May, 1999. Finnish. (Matti Ijas) Martti Suosalo, Walter Grohn, Mikko Vanhala, Turo Rannema.

BLINDGUYS
MEGAFILM, RTL KLUB, NATIONAL EURENT. Feb., 2001. Hungarian. (Peter Timar) Jeno Csiszar, Yvette Bozsik, Judit Mataek, Attila Magyar, Aron Ocsvari, Monika Berke, Agnes Fodor, Anna Nage.

BLINDNESS
PARK AVENUE. Aug., 1998. (Anna Chi) Vivian Wu, Joe Lando, Lisa Lu, Chin Han.

BLIND SPOT
Aug., 2002. Slovenian. (Hanna A. W. Slak) Manca Dorrer, Kolja Saksida, Lotus Vincenc Sparovec, Jozica Avbelj, Silva Cusin, Uros Furst.

BLIND SPOT: HITLER'S SECRETARY
Feb., 2002. Austrian. (Andre Heller, Othmar Schmiderer) Documentary.

BLIND SPOT: MURDER BY WOMEN
ALLIE LIGHT AND IRVING SARAF. Nov., 2000. (Irving Saraf, Allie Light, Julia Hilder) Documentary.

BLINK
THOMPSON PRODS. (SAN FRANCISCO). (Elizabeth Thompson) Susan Stone. Documentary.

BLISSFULLY YOURS
May, 2002. Thai-French. (Apichatpong Weerasethakul) Kanokporn Tongaram, Min Oo, Jejira Jansuda.

BLOOD, GUTS, BULLETS & OCTANE
LIONS GATE. Jan., 1998. (Joe Carnahan) Dan Leis, Joe Carnahan, Dan Harlan, Ken Rudulph, Hugh McCord, Mark S. Allen.

BLOOD WORK
WARNER BROS. July, 2002. (Clint Eastwood) Clint Eastwood, Jeff Daniels, Anjelica Huston, Wanda De Jesus, Tina Lifford, Paul Rodriguez, Dylan Walsh, Mason Lucero, Gerry Becker, Rick Hoffman, Alix Koromzay, Igor Jijikine.

BLOODY ANGELS
UNITED MEDIA. May, 1999. Norwegian. (Karin Julsrud) Reidar Sorensen, Gaute Skjegstad, Trond Hovik, Laila Goody. Reyes.

BLOODY MALLORY
MARS FILMS DISTRIBUTION. July, 2002. French. (Julien Magnat) Olivia Bonamy, Adria Collado, Jeffrey Ribier, Laurent Spielvogel, Valentina Vargas, Julien Boisselier, Tylda Bares.

BLOSSI/810551
ICELANDIC FILM CO. May, 1998. Icelandic-Danish. (Julius Kemp) Pall Banine, Thora Dungal, Finnur Johannsson.

BLOSSOMS OF FIRE
INTREPIDAS PROD. Apr., 2000. (Maureen Gosling, Ellen Osborne. Documentary.

BLOW
NEW LINE CINEMA. March, 2001. (Ted Demme) Johnny Depp, Penelope Cruz, Jordi Molla, Franka Potente, Rachel Griffiths, Ray Liotta, Ethan Suplee.

BLOW DRY
MIRAMAX FILMS. March, 2001. U.S.-British. (Paddy Breathnach) Alan Rickman, Natasha Richardson, Rachel Griffiths, Rachael Leigh Cook, Josh Hartnett, Bill Nighy, Warren Clarke.

BLUE CAR
MIRAMAX FILMS. Jan., 2002. (Karen Moncrieff) David Strathairn, Agnes Bruckner, Margaret Colin, Frances Fisher, A.J. Buckley, Regan Arnold, Sarah Beuhler.

BLUE CLEAR ACROSS TO AMERICA
NORIA FILMS/LITTLE BIG FILMS/ALTA LOMA FILMS/MACT PRODS./LE STUDIO CANAL PLUS/ARTE FRANCE CINEMA. Dec., 1999. French. (Sarah Levy) Samuel Jouy, Marion Cotillard, Albert Dupontel, Claude Perron, Zabou Breitman, Feodor Atkine.

BLUE CRUSH
UNIVERSAL. Aug., 2002. (John Stockwell) Kate Bosworth, Matthew Davis, Michelle Rodriguez, Sanoe Lake, Mika Boorem, Chris Taloa, Kala Alexander, Ruben Tejada, Kaupena Miranda, Asa Aquino, Faizon Love, George Veikoso.

BLUE DINER
BLUE DINER FILMS. April, 2001. (Jan Egleson) Lisa Vidal, Miriam Colon, Jose Yenque, William Marquez, Jack Mulcahy, Fidel Vicioso, Jaime Tirelli, Virginia Rambal.

BLUE END
EXTRA FILM. Aug., 2000. Swiss. (Kaspar Kasics). Documentary.

BLUE FISH
TONPU CO., LTD. Feb., 1998. Japanese. (Yosuke Nagagawa) Mari Ouchi, Keigo Heshiki, Yoshino Tamaki.

BLUE GATE CROSSING
May, 2002. Taiwanese-French. (Yee Chih-yen) Chen Bo-lin, Guey Lun-mei, Liang Shu-hui, Joanna Chou.

THE BLUE MONK
ZENTROPA ENTERTAINMENTS/KOLLEKTIV FILM. Feb., 1999. Danish. (Christian Braad Thomsen) Helle Ryslinge, Ole Meyer, Bent Conradi, Claus Nissen, Jarl Forsmann.

BLUE MOON
BLUE MOON FILMS. Nov,. 1998. Taiwanese. (Ko Yi-cheng) Tarcy Su, Leon Dai, David Wang, Chang Han, Teddy Lo.

BLUE MOON
PARADISE PICTURES/BLUE MOON. Jan., 2000. (John Gallagher) Ben Gazzara, Rita Moreno, Alanna Ubach, Brian Vincent, Shawn Elliot, David Thornton, Burt Young, Vincent Pastore, Heather Matarazzo.

BLUE MOON
Aug., 2002. Australian. (Andrea Maria Dusl) Josef Hader, Viktoria Malektorovych, Detlev W. Buck, Ivan Laca, Peter Aczel, Andrea Karnasova, Emoke Vinczeova, Orest Ogorodnik.

BLUES BROTHERS 2000
UNIVERSAL. Feb., 1998. (John Landis) Dan Aykroyd, John Goodman, Joe Morton, J. Evan Bonifant, Nia Peeples, Kathleen Freeman.

BLUE SPRING
Feb., 2002. Japanese. (Toshiaki Toyoda) Ryuhei Matsuda, Hirofumi Arai, Sosuke Takaoka, Yusuke Ohshiba, Yuta Yamazaki, Shogo Oshinari, Mame Yamada.

B. MONKEY
BUENA VISTA INTL./MIRAMAX. Nov., 1998. British-U.S. (Michael Radford) Asia Argento, Jared Harris, Rupert Everett, Jonathan Rhys Meyers.

BO A BU
HORUS & BASTET. Nov. 1998. Italian-French-Uzbeck. (Ali Khamraev) Arielle Dombasle, Abdrashid Abdrakhmanov, Djavakhir ZaKhirov.

BOATMAN
SINEVIZYON FILM/MARATHON FILMS, HYPERION PRODS./ADELA MEDIA. Apr., 1999. Turkish-Greek-Bulgarian. (Biket Ilhan) Memet Ali Alabora, Katerina Mousatsos, Mustafa Avkran, Elina Phillippa.

BOBBY G. CAN'T SWIM
CINEBLAST!. Mar., 1999. (John-Luke Montias) John-Luke Montias, Susan Mitchell, Vincent Vega, Norman Milton.

BOCAGE, THE TRIUMPH OF LOVE
Cinema do Seculo XXI. Jan., 1998. Brazilian. (Djalma Limongi Batista) Victor Wagner, Francisco Farinelli, Vietia Rocha, Majo de Castro.

THE BODY
AVALANCHE FILMS. April, 2001. (Jonas McCord) Antonio Banderas, Olivia Williams, John Shrapnel, Derek Jacobi, Jason Flemyng, John Wood, Makhram J. Khoury.

BODY COUNT
POLYGRAM. April, 1998. (Robert Patton-Spruill) David Caruso, Linda Fiorentino, John Leguizamo, Ving Rhames, Donnie Wahlberg.

BODY DROP ASPHALT
AICHI ARTS CENTER (TOKYO). Oct., 2000. Japanese. (Junko Wada) Sayuri Oyamada, Makoto Ogi, Yoji Tanaka, Yuicho Kishino, Kenichi Okubo, Makoto Tezuka, Takuji Suzuki, Hiroto Ojiro.

BODYWORK
GUERILLA FILMS. Oct., 2000. British. (Gareth Rhys Jones) Hans Matheson, Charlotte Coleman, Peter Ferdinando, Beth Winslet, Lynda Bellingham, Clive Russell, Michael Attwell.

BOESMAN & LENA
PATHE/PRIMEDIA PICTURES/CANAL PLUS/LA SEPT-ARTE. Apr., 2000 French. (John Berry) Danny Glover, Angela Bassett.

BOILER ROOM
NEW LINE/TEAM TODD. Jan., 2000. (Ben Younger) Giovanni Ribisi, Vin Diesel, Nia Long, Nicky Katt, Scott Caan, Ron Rifkin, Jamie Kennedy, Taylor Nichols, Bill Nichols, Tom Everett Scott, Ben Affleck.

BOLIVIA
IACAM. May, 2001. Argentine. (Israel Adrian Caetano) Freddie Flores, Rosa Sanchez, Oscar Bertea, Enrique Liporace, Marcelo Videla.

BOLLYWOOD BOUND
July, 2002. Canadian. (Nisha Pahuja) Ruby Bhatia, Vikram Dhillon, Vekeana Dhillon, Neehru Bajwa. Documentary.

BOMBAY BOYS
KISMET TALKIES. Sept., 1998. Indian. (Kaizad Gustad) Naveen Andrews, Rahul Bose, Alexander Giffor, Naseeruddin Shah.

BOMBAY EUNUCH
GIDALYA PICTURES. June, 2001. Documentary.

BONANZA
April, 2001. Argentine. (Ulises Rosell). Bonanza Muchinsci, Norberto Muchinsci, Veronica Muchinsci. Documentary.

THE BONE COLLECTOR
UNIVERSAL. Aug., 1999. (Phillip Noyce) Denzel Washington, Angelina Jolie, Queen Latifah, Michael Rooker.

BONGJA
NEXT FILMS. Oct., 2000. South Korean. (Park Chul-soo) Seo Kap-suk, Kim Jin-ah, Kim Il-woo.

BONGWATER
ALLIANCE INDEPENDENT FILMS. April, 1998. (Richard Sears) Luke Wilson, Alicia Witt, Amy Locane, Andy Dick, Jeremy Sistos.

THE BOOK OF LIFE
COLLECTION 2000. May, 1998. French. (Hal Hartley) Martin Donovan, P. J. Harvey, Thomas Jay Ryan, Dave Simonds.

BOOK OF SHADOWS: BLAIR WITCH 2
ARTISAN ENTERTAINMENT AND HAXAN ENTERTAINMENT. Oct., 2000. (Joe Berlinger) Jeff Donovan, Tristen Skyler, Stephen Barker Turner, Erica Leerhsen, Kim Director, Lanny Flaherty.

THE BOOK OF STARS
SHOWCASE ENTERTAINMENT. June, 2001. (Michael Miner) Mary Stuart Masterson, Jena Malone, Delroy Lindo, Karl Geary, D.B. Sweeney.

THE BOOKS AND THE NIGHT
UNIVERSIDAD NACIONAL GENERAL SAN MARTIN/CANAL PLUS. Feb., 2000. Argentine (Tristan Bauer) Walter Santa Ana, Hector Alterio, Lorenzo Quinteros.

THE BOOK THAT WROTE ITSELF
SIAR A RACHAS MIUID PRODS. Sept., 1999. Irish. (Liam O'Mochain) Liam O'Mochain, Antoinette Guiney, Marco Van Belle, Kristen Marken.

BOOMERANG
Feb., 2002. Yugoslavian-Canadian. (Dragan Marinkovic) Lazar Ristovski, Paulina Manov, Nebojsa Glogovac, Dragan Jovanovic, Petar Bozovic, Milena Dravic, Zoran Cvijanovic.

BOOM: THE SOUND OF EVICTION
Dec., 2001. (Francine Cavanaugh, A. Mark Liiv, Adams Wood, Jeff Taylor) Documentary.

BOONDOCK SAINTS
INDICAN PICTURES/FRANCHISE PICTURES/BROOD SYNDICATE/FRIED FILMS/THE LLOYD SEGAN CO./CHRIS BRINKER PRODS. Jan., 2000. (Troy Duffy) Willem Dafoe, Sean Patrick Flanery, Norman Reedus, David Della Rocco, Bob Marley.

BOOTLEG FILM
MONKEY TOWN PRODS. May, 1999. Japanese. (Masahiro Kobayashi) Akira Emoto, Kippei Shiina, Maika, Wakaba Nakano.

BOOTMEN
20TH CENTURY FOX/FOX SEARCHLIGHT/AUSTRALIAN FILM FINANCE CORP./BOOTMEN PRODS. July, 2000. Australian-U.S. (Dein Perry) Adam Garcia, Sophie Lee, Sam Worthington, William Zappa, Richard Carter, Susie Porter, Anthony Hayes.

BORICUA'S BOND
USA FILMS/OCTOBER FILMS/ROGUE PICUTRES/MINDZ IN ACTION. June, 2000. (Val Lik) Frankie Negron, Val Lik, Ramses Ignacio, Jorge Gautier, Jesglar Cabral, Geovanny Pineda, Erica Torres, Kaleena Justiniano.

BORN IN ABSURDISTAN
EPO-FILM. Jan., 2001. Austrian. (Houchang Allahyari) Karl Markovics, Julia Stemberger, Ahmet Ugurlu, Meltem Cumbul.

BORN OF A STORK
MONDO FILMS/PRINCES FILM/CANAL PLUS. Dec., 1999. French. (Tony Gatlif) Romain Duris, Rona Hartner, Ouassini Embarek.

BORN ROMANTIC
BBC FILMS/HARVEST PICTURESK Sept., 2000. British. (David Kane) Craig Ferguson, Ian Hart, Jane Horrocks, Adrian Iester, Catherine McCormack Jimi Mistry, David Morrissey, Olivia Williams.

BORN TO LOSE: THE LAST ROCK 'N' ROLL MOVIE
KW FILMWORKS. Sept., 2000. (Lech Kowalski) Dee Dee Ramone, Johnny Thunders, Willy DeVille, John Spacely, Stiv Bators, Cheetah Chrome, Wayne Kramer, Sylvain Sylvain, Chris Spedding.

BORN UNDER LIBRA
IRANIAN FILM SOCIETY AND NEJ PICTURES. Aug., 2001. Iranian. (Ahmad Reza Darvish) Mohammad Reza Foroutan, Mitra Hajjar, Mahmoud Azizi, Hossein Razi, Farshid Zareie Fard.

BORSTAL BOY
HELL'S KITCHEN/DAKOTA FILMS/BSKYB/IRISH FILM BOARD/RTE/AFULL SCHILLING INVESTMENTS. July, 2000. Irish-British. (Peter Sheridan) Shawn Hatosy, Danny Dyer, Michael York, Lee Ingleby, Robin Laing, Eva Birthistle.

BOSSA NOVA
SONY/COLUMBIA TRISTAR/LC BARRETO/FILMES DO EQUADOR/GLOBO FILMES. Feb., 2000. Brazilian. (Bruno Barreto) Amy Irving, Antonio Fagundes, Alexandre Borges, Debora Bloch, Drica Moraes, Giovanna Antonelli, Rogerio Cardoso.

THE BOTTLE
LIONS GATE. Sept., 2000. Canadian. (Alain DesRochers) Real Bosse, Francois Papineau, Jean Lapointe, Helene Loiselle, Pascale Bussieres, Didier Lucien, Sylvie Moreau, Louis Champagne.

BOUNCE
DENDROBIUM FILMS. Oct., 1999. Walter Velasquez, Jamal Mackey, L. Vee Anduze, Anthony Young, Pamela Johnson.

BOUNCE
MIRAMAX. Nov., 2000. (Don Roos) Ben Affleck, Gwyneth Paltrow, Joe Morton, Natasha Henstridge, Tony Goldwyn, Johnny Galecki, Alex D. Linz.

BOUNCE: BEHIND THE VELVET ROPE
STICK FIGURES. Apr., 2000. (Steven Cantor) Lenny "The Guv'nor" McLean, Terence "The Black Prince" Buckley, Mike and Frank DeMaio, Jordan Maldonado, Alan Crosley, Homer "Omar" Cook.

THE BOURNE IDENTITY
UNIVERSAL June, 2002. (Doug Liman) Matt Damon, Franka Potente, Chris Cooper, Clive Owen, Brian Cox, Adewale AkinnuoyeAgbaje, Julia Stiles, Josh Hamilton.

BOWFINGER
UNIVERSAL. Aug., 1999. (Frank Oz) Steve Martin, Eddie Murphy, Heather Graham, Christine Baranski.

BOWLING FOR COLUMBINE
May, 2002. Canadian. (Michael Moore) Documentary.

BOX 507
WARNER SOGEFILMS. Aug., 2002. Spanish. (Enrique Urbizu) Antonio Resines, Jose Coronado, Goya Toledo, Dafne Fernandez, Juan Fernandez, Miriam Montilla, Sancho Gracia.

BOXHEAD REVOLUTION
Aug., 2002. (Mark Christensen) Adam Cooper, Jenny Kim, Amy Davenport, Dan Farren, Heather Watsom, Mark Christensen, James Berry.

BOX LUNCH
HOT PICTURES. Feb. 2000. Japanese. (Shungo Kaji) Saki Shiratori, Shungo Kaji, Chocoball Mukai.

THE BOXER
UNIVERSAL. JAN., 1998. (Jim Sheridan) Daniel Day-Lewis, Emily Watson, Brian Cox, Ken Stott, Gerard McSorley, Eleanor Methven.

A BOY AND A GIRL ON THE 14TH FLOOR
MONDO FILMS/LE POISSON VOLANT/LES FILMS DU ROND-PONT /CNC. Nov., 1999. French. (Sophie Blondy) Sophie Blondy, Paul Tang.

BOYHOOD LOVES
OCEAN FILMS DISTRIBUTION. May, 2001. French. (Yves Caumon) Mathieu Amalric, Lauryl Brossier, Fabrice Cals, Michele Gary.

THE BOYS
GLOBE FILMS. Feb., 1998. Australian. (Rowan Woods) David Wenham, Toni Collette, Lynette Corran, John Poison, Anthony Hayes.

THE BOYS II
LIONS GATE. Dec., 1998. Canadian. (Louis Saia) Marc Messier, Remy Girard, Patrick Huard, Serge Theriault, Paul Houde.

BOYS AND GIRLS
MIRAMAX/DIMENSION FILMS/PUNCH 21. June, 2000. (Robert Iscove) Freddie Prinze Jr., Claire Forlani, Jason Biggs, Amanda Detmer, Heather Donahue, Alyson Hannigan, Raquel Beaudine.

BOY'S CHOIR
SUNCENT CINEMAWORKS/WOWOW/BANDAI VISUAL. Feb., 2000. Japanese. (Akira Ogata) Atsushi Ito, Sora Toma, Teruyuki Kagawa.

BOYS FROM MADRID
MANCHEGO FILMS. July, 2001. (Carlo Gustaff) Theo Pagones, Jesse Harper, Christopher Jacobs, Elan James, Betsy Monroe, Vance Strickland.

BOYS LIFE 3
STRAND RELEASING. Nov., 2000. (Various directors).

MAJORETTES IN SAPCE
(David Fourier) Cleo Delacruz, Aurelien Bianco, Jean-Marc Delacruz, Elise Laurent, Olivier Laville, Philippe Bianco.

HITCH
(Bradley Rust Gray) Drew Wood, Jason Herman.

INSIDE OUT
(Jason Gould) Jason Gould, Alexis Arquette, Jon Polito, Katie Asner, Charlie Brill, Christina Crawford, Anne DeSalvo, Steve Flynn.

JUST ONE TIME
(Lane Jange) Joelle Carter, Guillermo Diaz, Jennifer Esposito, Lane Janger.

$30
(Gregory Cooke) Erik MacArthur, Greg Itzin, Sara Gilbert.

BOYS DON'T CRY
FOX SEARCHLIGHT. Aug., 1999. (Kimberly Peirce) Hilary Swank, Chloe Sevigny, Peter Sarsgaard, Brendan Sexton III.

BRAIN DRAIN
FERNANDO MUSA PRODUCCIONES. Sept., 1998. Argentine. (Fernando Musa) Nicolas Cabre, Luis Quiroz, Roberto Carnaghi.

BRAINSTORM
DEZENOVE SOM & IMAGENS (BRAZIL)/FABRICA CINEMA (ITALY). Aug., 2001. Brazilian-Italian. (Lais Bodanzky) Rodrigo Santoro, Othon Bastos, Cassia Kiss, Jairo Matos, Caco Coicler, Luis Miranda.

BRAKHAGE
ZEITGEIST. Jan. 1999. (Jim Shedden) Benerjee, Maradan Benerjee, Soumitra Chatterjee. Documentary.

THE BRANDON TEENA STORY
BLESS BLESS PRODS. Feb., 1998. (Susan Muska, Greta Olafsdottir) Documentary.

BRATS (SMRADI)
ARTCAM. July, 2002. Czech. (Zdenek Tyc) Petra Spalkova, Ivan Trojan, Lukas Rejsek, Jan Cina, Tomas Klouda, Zdenek Dusek, Jaroslava Pokorna, Oldrich Kohout.

BRAVE NEW LAND
RIOFILME. Sept., 2000. Brazilian. (Lucia Murat) Diogo Infante, Floriano Peixoto, Luciana Rigueira, Leonardo Villar, Buza Ferraz, Murilo Grossi, Sergio Mamberti.

BRAZILERO
Dec., 2001. Greek. (Sotiris Goritsas) Stelios Mainas, Ivano Marescotti, Rufus Beck, Maria Kehayoglou, Panayotis Sapounakis, Anna Mascha, Maria Protopapa, Elissavet Moutafi, Gerasimos Skiadapesis.

BREAD AND MILK
VERTIGO/EMOTIONFILM. Sept., 2001. Slovenian. (Jan Cvitkovic) Peter Musevski, Sonja Savic, Tadej Troha, Perica Rodonijic-Peri.

BREAD AND ROSES
PARALLAX PICTURES/ROAD MOVIES VIERTE/TORNASOL/ALTA FILMS/BRITISH SCREEN/BSKYB/BAC FILMS/BIM DISTRIBUZIONE/ CINEART/FILM CO-OPERATIVE/ZURICH/FILM FOUR/WDR/ ARTE/ LA SEPT CINEMA, ARD/DEGETO FILM//FILMSTIFTUNG NORDHEIN-WESTFALEN. May, 2000. British-German-Spanish. (Ken Loach) Pilar Padilla, Adrien Brody, Elpidia Carrillo, Jack McGee, George Lopez, Alonso Chavez, Monica Rivas, Frank Davila.

BREAD AND TULIPS
ISTITUTO LUCE/MONOGATARI/RAI/AMKA FILMS/TELEVISIONE SVIZZERA ITALIANA. Feb. 2000. Italian-Swiss. (Silvio Soldini) Licia Maglietta, Bruno Ganz, Giuseppe Battiston, Marina Massironi, Antonio Catania.

BREAD DAY
HIGHER COURSES FOR SCRIPTWRITERS/SERGEI DVORTSEVOY. Jan., 2000. Russian. (Sergei Dvortsevoy) Documentary.

BREAK EVEN
DEUTSCHEN FILM AND FERNSEHAKADEMIE BERLIN. Sept., 1998. German. (Eoin Moore) Andreas Schmidt, Tamara Simunovic.

A BREAKFAST CHRONICLE
ESCARABAJA, IMCINE, TABASCO FILMS, ARGOS CINE, TITAN PRODUCCIONES. Oct., 2000. Mexican. (Benjamin Cann) Maria Rojo, Bruno Bichir, Jose Alonso, Fabiana Perzabal, Miguel Santana.

BREAKING THE SILENCE
ASIA UNION FILM & ENTERTAINMENT/ZHUJIANG FILM CO./GUANGDONG SANJIU FILM CO. Feb., 2000. Chinese. (Sun Zhou) Gong Li, Gao Xin, Shi Jingming, Guan Yue, Yue Xiuqing, Li Chengru, Lu Liping.

BREAKING OUT
SONET FILMS. Feb., 1999. Swedish. (Daniel Lind Lagerlof) Bjorn Kjellman, Peter Haber, Viveca Seldahl, Thomas Hanzon.

BREATH CONTROL: THE HISTORY OF THE HUMAN BEAT BOX
April, 2002. (Joey Garfield) Documentary.

BREATHE IN BREATHE OUT
B PRODS./DUNE/ZDF/DAS KLEINE FERNSEHSPIEL/TV 10 ANGERS/BLOW UP PICTURES. Jan., 2000. U.S.-German. (Beth B.). Documentary.

BREATHING HARD
SPARKHILL. May 2001. (Eric Neal Young) John Rafter Lee, June Claman, John Billingsley, Laura D'Arista, Taylor Gilbert, Patrick Egan, Tony Abatemarco.

BREATH OF LIFE
EGM PRODUCCIONES/DIRECCION DE CINEMATOGRAFIA DEL MINISTERIO DE CULTURA DE COLOMBIA/CENTRO NACIONAL DE CINEMATOGRAFIA/FONDS SUD, FRANCE. Oct., 2000. Columbian. (Luis Ospina) Fernando Solorzano, Flora Martinez, Robinson Diaz, Constanza Duque, Cesar Mora, Alvaro Ruiz, Alvaro Rodriguez.

BREATHTAKING
IAC FILM/SKY PICTURES/THE TELEVISION CO./SEPTEMBER FILMS. May, 2000. British. (David Green) Joanne Whalley, Lorraine Pilkington, Jame Foreman, Cal Macaninch, Neil Dudgeon.

THE BRIAN EPSTEIN STORY
ARENA/BBC WORLDWIDE/A&E. June, 2000. British. (Anthony Wall).With: Paul McCartney, Gerry Marsden, Billy J. Kramer, Peter Brown, Alistair Taylor, Stella Epstein, Simon Napier-Bell. Documentary.

BRIDE OF CHUCKY
UNIVERSAL. Oct., 1999. (Ronnie Yu) Jennifer Tilly, Katherine Heigl, Nick Stabile, John Ritter.

THE BRIDE OF FIRE
THIRD EYE. May, 2000. Iranian. (Khosro Sinai) Pasal Soremi, Saeed Poursamimi, Mahdi Ahmadi, Salimeh Rangzan, Hamid Forrokhnezhad, Ghazal Saremi.

BRIDE OF THE WIND
PARAMOUNT CLASSICS. May, 2001. (Bruce Beresford) Sarah Wynter, Jonathan Pryce, Vincent Perez, Simon Verhoeven, Gregor Seberg, Dagmar Schwarz, Wolfgang Hubsch.

A BRIDGE BETWEEN TWO SHORES
AMLF. Apr., 1999. French. (Gerard Depardieu, Frederic Auburtin) Carole Bouquet, Gerard Depardieu, Charles Berling, Stanislas Crevillen, Dominique Reymond.

BRIDGET JONES'S DIARY
MIRAMAX FILMS. March, 2001. (Sharon Maguire) Renee Zellweger, Colin Firth, Hugh Grant, Gemma Jones, Jim Broadbent, Embeth Davidtz, Shirley Henderson.

BRIGHAM CITY
EXCEL ENTERTAINMENT GROUP. March, 2001. (Richard Dutcher) Richard Dutcher, Matthew A. Brown, Wilford Brimley, Carrie Morgan, Jon Enos, Tayva Patch.

BRIGHTER THAN THE MOON
VIRGIL WIDRICH FILM/MULTIMEDIPRODUKTIONS. Jan. 2000. Austrian. (Virgil Widrich) Christopher Buchholz, Piroska Szekely, Lars Rudolph, Gerhard Liebmann, Werner Prinz, Alexander Ebeert.

BRINGING OUT THE DEAD
PARAMOUNT/TOUCHSTONE/SCOTT RUDIN-CAPPA/DE FINA. Oct., 1999. (Martin Scorcese) Nicolas Cage, Patricia Arquette, John Goodman, Ving Rhames, Tom Sizemore, Marc Anthony, Mary Beth Hurt.

BRING IT ON
UNIVERSAL/BEACON PICTURES. Aug., 2000. (Peyton Reed) Kirsten Dunst, Eliza Dushku, Jesse Bradfor, Gabrielle Union, Glare Kramer, Nicole Bilderback, Tsianina Joelson, Rini Bell.

BROKEDOWN PALACE
20TH CENTURY FOX. Aug., 1999. (Jonathan Kaplan) Claire Danes, Kate Beckinsale, Bill Pullman, Jacqueline Kim.

BROKE EVEN
BROKE EVEN PRODS. Apr., 2000. (David Feldman) Kevin Corrigan, Elizabeth Berridge, Mick Cunningham, Michael Lowry, Michael Kenneth Williams, Mary Diveny, Austen Pendleton.

BROKEN BRIDGES
ARAZ GOLDEN GATE. Jan., 1999. Azerbaijani-U.S. (Rafigh Pooya) Peter Reckell, Rebeccah Bush, Behrouz Vossoughi, Fatima Ibragimbekov.

BROKEN HEARTS
PRODUCCIONES VOLCAN, IMCINE, FONDO PARA LA PRODUCCION CINEMATOGRAFICA DE CALIDAD, FONDO DE FOMENTO A LA CALIDAD CINEMATOGRAFICA, RENTA IMAGEN. March, 2001. Mexican. (Rafael Montero) Veronica Merchant, Rafael Sanchez Navarro, Carmen Montejo, Odiseo Bichir, Cristina Michaus, Lorena Rojas, Francisco de la O.

BROKEN SILENCE
ALTA FILMS. April, 2001. Spanish. (Montxo Armendariz) Lucia Jimenez, Juan Diego Botto, Mercedes Sampietro, Alvaro de Luna, Maria Botto, Joseba Apaolaza, Jordi Bosch, Helio Pedrigal.

BROKEN VESSELS
ZIEHL AND ZAL. April, 1998. (Scott Ziehl) Todd Field, Jason London, Roxana Zal, Susan Traylor, James Hong, Patrick Cranshaw.

BRONX-BARBES
HACHETTE PREMIERE/ FILM D'ICI/ARTE/FRANCE 3 CINEMA/ CNRS IMAGES-MEDIA. Aug., 2000. French. (Eliane de Latour) Antony Koulehi Diate, Loss Sylla Ousseni, Edwige Dogo.

BROOKLYN BABYLON
ARTISAN ENTERTAINMENT. Jan., 2001. (Marc Levin) Tariq Trotter, Karen Goberman, David Vadim, Bonz Malone, Joanne Baron.

BROTHER
SONY/RECORDED PICTURE CO/FILM FOUR/BAC FILMS. Aug., 2000. Japanese-British. (Takeshi Kitano) Beat Takeshi, Claude Maki, Omar Epps, Masaya Kato, Ren Ohsugi, Susumu Terajima, Ryo Ishibashi.

BROTHERHOOD OF THE WOLF
METROPOLITAN FILMEXPORT. Jan., 2001. French. (Christophe Gans) Samuel Le Bihan, Mark Dacascos, Emilie Dequenne, Vincent Cassel, Monica Bellucci, Jeremie Renier, Jean Tanne.

BROTHERS
PARADISE FILMS/BROTHERS FILMS. June, 2000. British. (Martin Dunkerton) Justin Brett, Daniel Fredenburgh, Rebecca Cardinale, Daren Jacobs.

THE BROTHERS
SONY PICTURES ENTERTAINMENT. March, 2001. (Gary Hardwick) Morris Chestnut, D.L. Hughley, Bill Bellamy, Shemar Moore, Gabrielle Union, Tatyana Ali, Jenifer Lewis.

BROTHER 2
CTB FILM CO. Aug., 2000. Russian. (Alexei Balabanov) Sergei Bodrov, Victor Sukhorukov, Sergei Makovetsky, Irina Saltykova, Kirill Pirogov, Alexander Diachenko, Darya Lesnikova.

BROWN'S REQUIEM
J&T PRODS. Nov., 1998. (Jason Freeland) Michael Rooker, Tobin Bell, Selma Blair, Jack Conley, Kevin Corrigan.

BROWN SUGAR
FOX SEARCHLIGHT. Sept., 2002. (Rick Famuyiwa) Taye Diggs, Sanaa Lathan, Mos Def, Nicole Ari Parker, Boris Kodjoe, Queen Latifah, Erik Weiner, Reggi Wyns, Wendell Pierce.

BROWNSVILLE BLACK AND WHITE
July, 2001. (Richard Broadman) Documentary.

BRUNO
J & M ENTERTAINMENT. Apr., 2000. (Shirley MacLaine) Alex D. Linz, Shirley MacLaine, Gary Sinise, Kathy Bates, Stacey Halprin, Kiami Davael, Joey Lauren Adams, Jennifer Tilly.

BRUISER
LE STUDIO CANAL PLUS/ BEN BARENHOLTZ/ROMERO-GRUNWALD PRODS. Feb., 2000. French. (George A. Romero) Jason Flemyng, Peter Stormare, Leslie Hope, Nina Garbiras.

BRUTE
BOJE BUCK FILM/DOUEK PRODS. Feb., 1998. Polish. (Maciej Dejczer) Wojciech Brzezinski, John Hurt, Ida Jablonska.

BUBBA HO-TEP
June, 2002. (Don Coscarelli) Bruce Campbell, Ossie Davis.

BUBBLE BOY
BUENA VISTA. Aug., 2001. (Blair Hayes) Jake Gyllenhaal, Swoosie Kurtz, Marley Shelton, Danny Trejo, John Carroll Lynch, Stephen Spinella, Verne Troyer.

BUDDHA HEADS
PATHFINDER PICTURES. Aug., 2002. (Brian T. Maeda) Eddie Mui, Calvin Jung, Helen Ota, Kipp Shiotani, Paul Hughes, Art Lai, Jack Lam, Ken Narasaki, Louise Mita.

BUDDY BOY
INDEPENDENT PICTURES. Sept., 2000. (Mark Hanlon) Aiden Gillen, Emmanuelle Seigner, Susan Tyrrell, Mark Boone Junior, Harry Groener, Hector Elias, Jon Huertas, Richard Assad.

BUENA VISTA SOCIAL CLUB
ROAD MOVIES FILMPRODUKTION. Feb., 1999. German-U.S. (Wim Wenders) Ry Cooder, Compay Segundo, Ruben Gonzalez, Ibrahim Ferrer, Eliades Ochoa.

BUFFALO 66
LIONS GATE FILMS/CINEPIX. Jan., 1998. (Vincent Gallo) Vincent Gallo, Christina Ricci, Anjelica Huston, Ben Gazzara, Mickey Rourke, Rosanna Arquette.

BUFFALO SOLDIERS
MIRAMAX (IN U.S.). British-German. (Gregor Jordan) Joaquin Phoenix, Ed Harris, Scott Glenn, Anna Paquin, Gabriel Mann, Leon Robinson, Sheik Mahumd-Bey, Michael Pena.

BUFO & SPALLANZANI
Jan, 2002. Brazilian (Flavio R. Tambellini) Jose Mayer, Tony Ramos, Isabel Gueron, Zeze Polessa, Gracindo Junior, Maite Proenca, Matheus Nachtergaele.

A BUG'S LIFE
BUENA VISTA. Oct., 1998. (John Lasseter) Animated.

THE BUILDING
GIAI PHONG FILM STUDIO/GIAI PHONG/LE BUREAU. Sept., 1999. Vietnamese-French. (Viet Linh) Mai Thanh, Hong Anh, Don Duong, Minh Trang, Quyen Linh, Kim Xuan, Le Binh, Huu Tien, Chi Cuong, Hoang Anh, Cam Ha, Ngoe.

BULLET BALLET
KAIJYU THEATER CO. Sept., 1998. Japanese. (Shinya Tsukamoto) Shinya Tsukamoto, Kirina Mano, Tatsuya Nakamura, Takahiro Murase.

BULLET ON A WIRE
PROVISIONAL. Nov., 1998. (Jim Sikora) Jeff Strong, Lara Phillips, David Yow, Paula Killen, Richard Kern.

BULLETS OVER SUMMER
BRILLIANT IDEA GROUP/MEI AH. Sept., 1999. Hong Kong. (Wilson Yip) Francis Ng, Louis Koo, Michelle Alicia Saram, Stephanie Lin, Helena Law, Lai Yiu-cheung, David Lee, Lo Mong, Joe Lee.

BULLY
LIONS GATE FILMS. July, 2001. (Larry Clark) Brad Renfro, Rachel Miner, Nick Stahl, Bijou Phillips, Michael Pitt, Kelli Garner, Daniel Franzese, Leo Fitzpatrick.

BULWORTH
20TH CENTURY FOX. May, 1998. (Warren Beatty) Warren Beatty, Halle Berry, Don Cheadle, Oliver Platt, Paul Sorvino, Jack Warden.

THE BUMBLEBEE FLIES ANYWAY
SHOOTING GALLERY/HAFT ENTERTAINMENT. Sept., 1999. (Martin Duffy) Elijah Wood, Janeane Garofalo, Rachel Leigh Cook, Roger Rees.

BUNDLED
BLACK & WHITE. March, 2001. Taiwanese. (Chen Hsin-hsuan) Yun Mu-tsuen, Chen Li-te, Zhang Yui-wei, Lin Zhong-ying, Lee Jien, Juan Ping, Lin Tsung-hsi, Wu Hsin-ru.

BUNJEE JUMPING OF THEIR OWN
KTB NETWORK/WON FILM. Feb., 2001. South Korean. (Kim Dae-seung) Lee Byung-hun, Lee Eun-ju, Yae Hyun-soo, Hong Su-hyun, Kim Kab-su, Lee Bum-soo.

BUNNY
GIRLS WITH NO GLASSES. Aug., 2000. (Mia Trachinger) Petra Tikalova, Edyk Dratver, Elizabeth Liebel, Eugene Alper, Brian Morri.

BUNUEL AND KING SOLOMON'S TABLE
FILMAX. Sept., 2001. Spanish-German-Mexican. (Carlos Saura) El Gran Wyoming, Pere Arquillue, Ernesto Alterio, Adria Collado, Valeria Marini, Amira Casar, Jean-Claude Carriere.

BUNUEL'S PRISONERS
PIETER VAN HUYSTEE FILM & TV. Feb., 2000. Dutch. (Ramon Gieling). Documentary.

BURIED COUNTRY
FILM AUSTRALIA/SBS INDEPENDENT. June, 2000. Australian. (Andy Nehl). Documentary.

BURLESK KING
SEIKO FILMS. Sept., 1999. Filipino. (Mel Chionglo) Rodel Velayo, Nini Jacinto, Leonardo Litton, Raymond Bagsting, Elizabeth Oropesa

BURNING IN THE WIND
01 DISTRIBUTION Jan., 2001. Italian-Swiss. (Silvio Soldini) Ivan Franek, Barbara Lukesova, Ctirad Gotz, Caroline Baehr, Cecile Pallas, Petr Forman, Zuzana Maurery, Pavel Andel.

BURNING MAN: THE BURNING SENSATION
ALEX NOHE & ALAN ROBERTS. Mar., 2000. (Alex Nohe). Documentary.

BURNING MONEY
ALTA FILMS. Sept., 2000. Argentine-Spanish-Uruguayan. (Marcelo Pineyro) Eduardo Noriega, Leonardo Sbaraglia, Pablo Echarri, Leticia Bredice, Ricardo Bartis, Dolores Fonzi, Carlos Roffe, Hector Alterio.

THE BURNING WALL
Feb., 2002. (Hava Kohav Beller) John Dildine (narrator). Documentary.

BURN WITH ME
AURUM Jan., 2002. Spanish. (Miguel Angel Sanchez) Cristina Silva, Daniel Cabello, Manuel de Blas, Julieta Serrano, Enrique Villen.

BURY ME IN KERN COUNTY
KRANK. Aug., 1998. (Julien Nitzberg), Mary Sheridan, Judson Mills, Mary Lynn Rajskub, Johnny Strong, Thom Rachford, Sandra Tucker.

THE BUSINESS OF STRANGERS
I5 FILMS. Jan., 2001. (Patrick Stettner) Stockard Channing, Julia Stiles, Frederick Weller.

BUS RIDERS UNION
HASKELL WEXLER. Mar., 2000. (Haskell Wexler, Johanna Demetrakas). Documentary.

BUT FOREVER IN MY MIND
MIKADO. Aug., 1999. Italian. (Gabriele Muccino) Silvio Muccino, Giuseppe Sanfelice di Monteforte, Giula Steigerwalt, Giulia Carmignani.

BUT I'M A CHEERLEADER
FINE LINE. Sept., 1999. (Jamie Babbit) Natasha Lyonne, Cathy Moriarty, Bud Cort, Mink Stole, Ru Paul Charles.

BUT I WAS A GIRL: THE STORY OF FREIDA BELINFANTE
FIRST RUN/ICARUS FILMS/A FRAME MEDIA AND HPS. Apr., 2000. (Toni Boumans). Documentary.

THE BUTTERFLY
D-PRODUCTION CO. Aug., 2001. South Korean. (Moon Seung-wook) Kim Ho-jung, Kang Hea-jung, Jang Hyun-sung.

BUTTERFLY SMILE
Sept. 25, 2001. Chinese. (He Jianjun) Ge You, Jiang Weiwei, Sun Chun.

THE BUTTERFLY'S TONGUE
WARNER SOGEFILMS/SOGETEL/LAS PRODUCCIONES DEL ESCORPION/GRUPO VOZ/CANAL PLUS/TVG. Sept., 1999. Spanish. (Jose Luis Cuerda) Fernando Fernan Gomez, Manuel Lozano, Uxia Blanco, Gonzalo Martin Uriarte, Alexis de Los Santos.

BYE BYE AFRICA
LES PRODUCTIONS DE LA LANTERNE. May, 2000. Chad-French. (Mahamet-Saleh Haroun) Mahamet-Saleh Haroun, Garba Issa, Aicha Yelena, Mahamat-Saleh Abakar.

BY HOOK OR BY CROOK
STEAKHAUS PRODS. July, 2001. (Harry Dodge, Silas Howard) Silas Howard, Harry Dodge, Stanya Kahn, Carina Gia, Joan Jett.

BY MY SIDE AGAIN
WARNER SOGEFILMS/SOGETEL/ELIAS QUEREJETA/ALBARES PRODS./BLUE CINEMATOGRAFICA/ESICMA, CONTINENTAL/TVE/CANAL PLUS/TELE PLUS/TVG. July, 2000. Spanish-French-Italian. (Gracia Querejeta, Elias Querejeta) Mercedes Sampietro, Jorge Perugorria, Julieta Serrano.

BY PLAYER
KINDAI EIGA KYOKAI CO./DRAGON FILM CO.Aug., 2000. Japanese. (Kaneto Shindo) Naoto Takenaka, Yoko Oginome, Hideko Yoshida, Nobuko Otowa.

C

THE CABBIE
CENTRAL MOTION PICTURE CORP./CITY FILMS. Feb., 2001. Taiwanese. (Chang Hwa-kun, Chen Yi-wen) Rie Miyazawa, Chu Chung-heng, Cheung Ka-nin, Cheng Hsiu-ying, Tsai Tsan-de, Su Zhao-bin, Bao Tai.

CABIN FEVER
FREEDOM FROM FEAR UNLIMITED. Jan., 2001. Norwegian. (Mona J. Hoel) Gorild Mauseth, Svein Scharfenberg, Kari Simonsen, Bjarte Hjelmeland, Benedicte Linbeck, Turid Gunnes.

A CAB FOR THREE
Sept., 2001. Chilean. (Orlando Lubbert) Alejandro Trejo, Fernando Gomez-Rovira, Daniel Munoz, Juan Rodriguez, Ivonne Becerra, Elsa Poblete, Cristian Quezada.

CAFE OLE
EQUINOX FILMS. Sept., 2000. Canadian. (Richard Roy) Andrew Tarbet, Laia Marull, Dino Tavarone, Stephanie Morgenstern, Sheena Larkin, Harry Standjofski, Dorothee Berryman.

THE CAGE
Aug., 2002. French. (Alain Raoust) Caroline Ducey, Roger Souza, Beppe Clerici, Maryvonne Shiltz.

CAHOOTS
CHEWING SCHOOL (MONTANA). Feb., 2001. (Dirk Benedict) Keith Carradine, David Keith, Wendie Malick, Janet Gunn, Jan Triska, Bill Erwin, Anne Lockhart, Jim Hanks, Tony Pierce.

CAIMAN'S DREAM
ALTA FILMS. Sept., 2001. Mexican-Spanish. (Beto Gomez) Daniel Guzman, Kandido Uranga, Rafael Velasco, Miguel Fomero, Patricia Reyes Spindola, Roberto Espejo, Roberto Cobo.

CALLAS FOREVER
MEDUSA (IN ITALY)/BAC DISTRIBUTION (IN FRANCE). Sept., 2002. Italian-British-French-Romanian-Spanish. (Franco Zeffirelli) Fanny Ardant, Jeremy Irons, Joan Plowright, Jay Rodan, Gabriel Garko.

THE CALL OF THE OBOE
IMAGICA/RIO FILME/SKYLIGHT CINEMA/QUANTA/ARA FILMS. Oct., 1999. Brazilian-Paraguayan. (Claudio MacDowell) Paulo Betti, Leticia Vota, Mario Lozano, Arturo Fleitas, Graciela Canepa.

CALMNESS
KTC May, 2001. Indian. (Jayaraaj) K.P.A.C. Lalitha, Seema Biswas, I.M. Vijayan.

CAMARATE
Jan., 2002. Portuguese. (Luis Filipe Rocha) Maria Joao Luis, Filipe Ferrer, Virgilio Castelo, Candido Ferreira, Ana Nave, Carlos Quintas, Alexandra Leite.

CAMEL(S)
Nov., 2001. South Korean. (Park Ki-yong) Lee Dae-yeon, Park Myeong-shin.

THE CAMP OF FALLEN WOMEN
STUDIO KOBILA. Feb., 1998. Slovakian-German-Czech. (Laco Halama) Juraj Kukura, Dana Dinkova, Stefan Kvietik.

CAMP SCOTT LADIES
MTV NEWS AND DOCS. June, 2001. (Susan Koch, Jeff Werner) Documentary.

CAMPUS
CONSTANTIN FILM. Feb., 1998. German. (Soenke Wortmann) Heiner Lauterbach, Axel Milberg, Sibylle Canonica, Barbara Rudnik.

CAMP X
VICTORY MOTION PICTURES. Jan., 2001. Canadian. (Jeremy McCormack) Documentary.

CANONE INVERSO–MAKING LOVE
CECCHI GORI/FIN.MA.VI. May, 2000. Italian. (Ricky Tognazzi) Hans Matheson, Melanie Thierry, Lee Williams, Gabriel Byrne, Ricky Tognazzi, Peter Vaughn, Nia Roberts, Adriano Pappalardo.

CAN'T HARDLY WAIT
SONY PICTURES ENTERTAINMENT. June, 1998. (Deborah Kaplan) Jennifer Love Hewitt, Ethan Embry, Charlie Korsmo, Lauren Ambrose.

CAN'T STOP DANCING
PM ENTERTAINMENT. Jan., 1999. (Stephen Falick, Ben Zook) Ben Zook, Melanie Hutsell, Margaret Cho, Bruce DanielsDouglas, Taylor Negron.

CAPTAIN CORELLI'S MANDOLIN
UNIVEAL (IN U.S.)/BUENA VISTA INTL. (IN U.K.). March, 2001. U.S.-British. (John Madden) Nicolas Cage, Penelope Cruz, John Hurt, Christian Bale, David Morrissey, Irene Pappas, Piero Maggio.

CAPTAIN JACK
WINCHESTER FILMS. May, 1998. British. (Robert Young) Bob Hoskins, Peter McDonald, Sadie Frost, Jemma Jones.

CAPTAIN PANTOJA AND THE SPECIAL SERVICE
AMERICA/INCA FILMS AND TORNASOL FILM/ VIA DIGITAL. Feb., 2000. Peruvian. (Francisco J. Lombardi) Salvador Del Solar, Angie Cepeda, Monica Sanchez, Pilar Bardem, Gianfranco Brero.

THE CAPTAIN'S DAUGHTER
NTV PROFIT/ROISSY FILMS/LE PONT/CANAL PLUS/GLOBUS FILM STUDIO/ORENBURG REGION ADMINISTRATION. Feb., 2000. Russian-French. (Aleksandr Proshkin) Vladimir Mashkov, Karolina Gruszka, Mateusz Damiecki, Sergei Makovetsky, Vladimir Ilyin.

CAPTAINS OF APRIL
JBA/MUTANTE FILME/ALIA FILMES (LISBON) PRODUCTION IN ASSOCIATION WITH ALIA FILM. May, 2000. French-Portuguese. (Maria de Medeiros) Stefano Accorsi, Maria de Medeiros, Joaquim de Almeida, Frederic Pierrot.

THE CAPTIVE
GEMINI FILMS/ARTE FRANCE CINEMA/PARADISE FILMS/CANAL PLUS/CENTRE NATIONAL DE LA CINEMATOGRAPHIE/GIMAGES 3. May, 2000. French-Belgian. (Chantal Akerman) Stanislas Merhar, Sylvie Testud, Olivia Bonamy, Liliane Rovere, Francoise Bertin, Aurore Clement.

CAPTIVE AUDIENCE
CORPORATE SUCKER FILMS. July, 1999. (Mike Gioscia, Kurt St. Thomas) Michael Kevin Walker, Daniel Haas, Mike Gioscia, Kat Corbett.

CARESSES
LAUREN FILMS. Feb., 1998. Spanish. (Ventura Pons) David Selvas, Laura Conejero, Julieta Serrano, Montserrat Salvador.

CARLO GIULIANI, BOY
May, 2002. Italian. (Francesca Ceomecini) Documentary.

CARMAN: THE CHAMPION
8X ENTERTAINMENT. March, 2001. (Lee Stanley) Carman, Michael Nouri, Patricia Manterola, Jeremy Williams, Jed Allan, Romeo Fabian, Betty Carvalho.

CARNAGE
DIAPHANA DISTRIBUTION. May, 2002. French-Belgian-Spanish-Swiss. (Delphine Gleize) Chiara Mastroianni, Angela Molina, Jeanne Lucia Sanchez, Esther Gorintin, Maryline Even, Clovis Cornillac.

CARNIVALE
TERRAGLYPH. July, 1999. Irish. (Deane Taylor). Animated.

CAROL'S JOURNEY (EL VIAJE DE CAROL)
Aug., 2002. Spanish. (Imanol Uribe) Clara Lago, Juan Jose Ballesta, Alvaro de Luna, Maria Barranco, Rosa Maria Sarda, Carmelo Gomez, Alberto Jiminez.

CARRIED AWAY
HYSTERIA FILMS. June, 1998. (Paul Kostick) Christian Ryser, Susan Tate, Matt Riedy.

THE CARRIERS ARE WAITING
K-STAR/RTBF/CAB PRODS. May, 1999. Belgian-French-Swiss. (Benoit Mariage) Benoit Poelvoorde, Morgane Simon, Bouli Ianners, Dominiue Baeyens.

CASCABEL
WARNER SOGEFILMS/ALMA ATA/GALIARDO/XALOC/CANAL PLUS. Feb., 2000. Spanish. (Daniel Cebrian) Irene Visedo, Pilar Punzano, Antonio Dechent, Chete Lera, Javier Albala.

CASCADEUR: THE AMBER CHAMBER
CASCADEUR FILMPRODUKTION/PROSIEBEN/FIMA. May, 1998. German. (Hardy Martins) Hardy Martins, Regula Grauwiller.

CAST AWAY
20TH CENTURY FOX. Dec., 2000. (Robert Zemeckis) Tom Hanks, Helen Hunt, Nick Searcy, Lari White, Michael Forest, Viveka Davis.

CASTING
July, 2002. French. (Emmanuel Finkiel) Documentary.

CATCHING OUT
June, 2002. (Sarah George) Switch, Baby Girl, Jessica, Lee. Documentary.

CATFISH IN BLACK BEAN SAUCE
BLACK HAWK ENTERTAINMENT. Apr., 1999. (Chi Muoi Lo.) Paul Winfield, Mary Alice, Chi Muoi Lo, Lauren Tom.

CATS & DOGS
WARNER BROS. June, 2001. (Lawrence Guterman) Jeff Goldblum, Elizabeth Perkins, Miriam Margolyes.

THE CAT'S MEOW
LIONS GATE FILMS. Aug., 2001. German-British. (Peter Bogdanovich) Kirsten Dunst, Cary Elwes, Edward Herrmann, Eddie Issard, Joanna Lumley, Victor Slezak, Jennifer Tilly.

CAUGHT UP
LIVE ENTERTAINMENT. Feb., 1998. (Darin Scott) Bokeem Woodbine, Cynda Williams, Joseph Lindsay, Clifton Powell, LL Cool J.

THE CAVE
GET REEL PRODS. Aug., 2001. Dutch. (Martin Koolhoven) Benja Bruijning, Floris Drost, Gwen Eckhaus, Brendan Fletcher, Porgy Franssen, Marcel Hensema, Kim Huffman, Fedja van Huet.

THE CAVEMAN'S VALENTINE
UNIVERSAL FOCUS. Jan., 2001. (Kasi Lemmons) Samuel L. Jackson, Colm Feore,Ann Magnuson, Aunjanue Ellis, Rodney Eastman, Tamara Tunie, Jay Rodan.

CECIL B. DEMENTED
ARTISAN/LE STUDIO CANAL PLUS/POLAR ENTERTAINMENT. May, 2000. (John Waters) Melanie Griffith, Stephen Dorff, Alicia Witt, Larry Giliard Jr., Maggie Gyllenhall, Eric M. Barry, Zenzele Uzoma, Erika Lynn Rupli, Harriet Dodge, Adrian Grenier, Ricki Lake.

THE CELL
NEW LINE/CARO-MCLEOD/RADICAL MEDIA. Aug., 2000. (Tarsem) Jennifer Lopez, Vince Vaughn, Vincent D'Onofrio, Jake Weber, Dylan Baker, Marianne Jean-Baptiste, James Gammon, Tara Subkoff.

THE CELEBRATION
OCTOBER FILMS. May, 1998. Danish. (Thomas Vinterberg) Ulrich Rhomsen, Henning Moritzen, Thomas Bo Larsen.

CELEBRITY
MIRAMAX. Aug., 1998. (Woody Allen) Hank Azaria, Kenneth Branaugh, Judy Davis, Leonardo DiCaprio, Melanie Griffith, Famke Janssen.

THE CENTER OF THE WORLD
ARTISAN ENTERTAINMENT. March, 2001. (Wayne Wang) Peter Sarsgaard, Molly Parker, Carla Gugino, Balthazar Getty, Shane Edelman, Karry Brown, Alisha Klass, Mel Gorham.

CENTER STAGE
SONY/COLUMBIA PICTURES/LAURENCE MARK. May, 2000. (Nicholas Hytner) Amanda Schull, Zoe Saldana, Susan May, Peter Gallagher, Donna Murphy, Debra Monk, Ethan Stiefel, Sascha Radetsky.

CENTRAL STATION
SONY PICTURES CLASSICS. Jan., 1998. Brazilian-French. (Walter Salles) Fernanda Montenegro, Marilia Pera, Vinicius de Oliveira.

CENTURY HOTEL
TVA INTL. Oct., 2001. Canadian. (David Weaver) Lindy Booth, Colm Feore, Earl Pastko, Mia Kirshner, Tom McCamus, Sandrine Holt, Russell Yuen, Albert Chung, David Hewlett.

A CENTURY'S END
MIRAE ASSET CAPITAL/TAEHUNG PICTURES. Sept., 2000. South Korean. (Song Neung-han) Kim Kap-su, Lee Jae-un, Cha Seung-won.

CHA CHA CHA
Sogepaq. July, 1998. Spanish. (Antonio del Real) Eduardo Noriega, Ana Alvarez, Maria Adanez, Jorge Sanz.

CHAIN CAMERA
CINEMAX REEL LIFE. Jan., 2001. (Kirby Dick) Documentary.

CHAIN OF FOOLS
WARNER BROS. March, 2001. (Traktor) Steve Zahn, Salma Hayek, Jeff Goldblum, Lara Flynn Boyle, Tom Wilkinson, David Cross, Elijah Wood, David Hyde Pierce.

CHAIRMAN OF THE BOARD
TRIMARK PICTURES. March, 1998. (Alex Zamm) Carrot Top, Courtney Thorne-Smith, Larry Miller, Raquel Welch, Mystro Clark.

A CHANCE TO DIE
BURNING PRODS., TEAM OKAYAMA. Sept., 2000. Taiwanese-Japanese. (Yiwen Chen) Miki Mitsuno, Chun-Hao Duan, jack Kao, Mingjun Gao, Li-Chun Lee, Winnie Ho, Zhaoxiong Lin.

CHANGE MY LIFE
PAN-EUROPEENNE. Dec., 2001. French. (Liria Begeja) Fanny Ardant, Roschdy Zem, Fanny Cottencon, Sami Bouajila, Olivier Cruveiller, Arie Elmaleh.

CHANGING LANES
PARAMOUNT. April, 2002. (Roger Michell) Ben Affleck, Samuel L. Jackson, Toni Collette, Sydney Pollack, William Hurt, Amanda Peet, Richard Jenkins, Kim Staunton, John Benjamin Hickey, Jennifer Dundas Lowe, Dylan Baker, Matt Malloy.

CHANNELLING BABY
OCEANIA PARKER LTD. May, 1999. New Zealand. (Christine Parker) Danielle Cormack, Kevin Smith, Anber Sainsbury, Joel Tobeck.

CHAOS
BAC DISTRIBUTION. Sept., 2001. French. (Coline Serreau) Catherine Frot, Vincent Lindon, Rachida Brakni, Line Renaud, Aurelien Wilk, Wojtek Pszoniak, Ivan Franek.

CHAOS AND DESIRE (LA TURBULENCE DES FLUIDES)
ALLIANCE ATLANTIS VIVAFILM (IN CANADA)/EUROPA CORP. (IN FRANCE). Aug., 2002. Canadian-French. (Manon Briand) Pascale Bussieres, Julie Gayet, Jean-Nicolas Verreault, Genevieve Bujold, Vincent Bilodeau, Ji-yan Seguin.

THE CHARCOAL PEOPLE
ZAZEN. Jan., 2000. Brazilian. (Nigel Noble). Documentary.

CHARGE!
DIAPHANA DISTRIBUTION/AGAT FILM & CIE./DIAPHANA/TF1 FILMS/CANAL PLUS. Apr., 2000. French. (Robert Guediguian) Ariane Ascaride, Pierre Banderet, Frederique Bonnal, Patrick Bonnel.

CHARISMA
NIKKATSU CORP./KING RECORDS CO./TOKYO THEATERS CO. May, 1999. Japanese. (Kiyoshi Kurosawa) Koji Yakusho, Hiroyuki Ikeuchi, Ren Osugi, Yoriko Doguchi, Jun Fubuki.

CHARLOTTE GRAY
WARNER BROS. Nov., 2001. British-Australian. (Gillian Armstrong) Cate Blanchett, Billy Crudup, Michael Gambon, Rupert Penry-Jones, Anton Lesser, James Fleet, Ron Cook, Jack Shepherd.

CHARLOTTE SOMETIMES
June, 2002. (Eric Byler) Michael Idemoto, Jacqueline Kim, Eugenia Yuan, Matt Westmore, Shizuko Hoshi, Kimberly Rose.

CHARMING BILLY
BEECH HILL FILMS/SLEDGEHAMMER MFA FILMS/ MOHAWK FILMS. Oct., 1999. (William R. Pace) Michael Hayden, Sally Murphy, Tony Mockus, Chelcie Ross, Bernadette O'Malley, Adam Tanguay.

CHARMING FELLOW
CARLOTTA FILMS. March, 2001. French. (Patrick Chesnais) Patrick Chesnais, Alexandra Vandernoot, Jean-Francois Balmer, Bernard Crombey, Samuel Labarthe, Micheline Presle.

CHASING SLEEP
TVA INTL/GLASKI PRODS./FORENSIC FILMS/LE STUDIO CANAL PLUS. Sept., 2000. (Michael Walker) Jeff Daniels, Emily Bergl, Gil Bellows, Zach Grenier, Julian McMahon, Ben Shenkman, Molly Price.

THE CHATEAU
GREENESTREET FILMS. Jan., 2001. (Jesse Peretz) Paul Rudd, Sylvie Testud, Romany Malco, Didier Flamand, Philippe Mahon, Maria Verdi, Nathalie Jouen, Donal Logue.

CHEAP SMOKES
BAD MOVIES. Nov., 2000. Greek. (Renos Haralambidis) Renos Haralambidis, Anna Maria Papaharalambous, Michalis Iatropoulos, Costas Tsakonas.

CHECK AND MATE
ARCHIPELAGO CINEMATOGRAFICA AND GIANNI SCHETTINI. Jan., 2001. Italian. (Claudia Florio) Barbara Bobulova, Tony Bertorelli, Ettore Bassi, Massimo De Rossi, Felice Andreasi, Valleria D'Obici.

CHECKPOINT
ORT-STW FILM CO. Feb., 1999. Russian. (Alexander Rogoshkin) Andrei Krasko, Alexei Buldakov, Zoya Burjak, Roman Romancov.

CHELSEA WALLS
LIONS GATE. May, 2001. (Ethan Hawke) Kevin Corrigan, Rosario Dawson, Vincent D'Onofrio, Kris Kristofferson, Robert Sean Leonard, Natasha Richardson, Uma Thurman, Mark Webber, Tuesday Weld.

CHEN MO AND MEITING
Feb., 2002. Chinese. (Liu Hao) Wang Libo, Du Hau'nan.

CHERISH
Jan., 2002. (Finn Taylor) Robin Tunney, Tim Blake Nelson, Brad Hunt, Liz Phair, Jason Priestley, Nora Dunn, Lindsay Crouse, Ricardo Gil, Kenny Kwong.

CHERRY
CYPRESS FILMS. Apr., 1999. (John Glascoe, Joseph Pierson) Shalom Harlow, Jake Weber, Isaach de Bankole, Laurel Holloman.

CHERRY FALLS
ENTERTAINMENT FILM DISTRIBUTORS RELEASE (IN U.K.). Sept, 2000. (Geoffrey Wright) Michael Biehn, BrittanyMurphy, Jay Mohr, Gabriel Mann, Joe Inscoe, Keram Malicki-Sanchez, Natalie Ramsey.

THE CHERRY ORCHARD
MELANDA FILM PRODS. Sept., 1999. Greek-French-Cypriot. (Michael Cacoyannis) Charlotte Rampling, Alan Bates, Katrin Cartlidge, Owen Teale, Frances de la Tour.

THE CHERRY TREE
OBERON CINEMATOGRAFICA, S.A. Feb., 1999. Spanish. (Marc Recha) Pere Ponce, Diana Palazon, Jordi Dauder, Isabel Rocatti.

CHICAGO CAB
GFT ENTERTAINMENT. March, 1998. (Mary Cybulski, John Tintori) Paul Dillon, Michael Ironside, Laurie Metcalf, John C. Reilly, Gillian Anderson, John Cusack, Julianne Moore.

CHICKEN HEART
May, 2002. Japanese. (Hiroshi Shimizu) Hiroyuki Ikeuchi, Kiyoshiro Imawano, Suzuki Matsuo, Nobuyoshi Araki.

CHICKEN POETS
Aug., 2002. Chinese. (Meng Jinghui) Chen Jianbin, Qin Hailu, Liao Fan, Chen Minghao, Yang Ting.

CHICKEN RICE WAR
SHAW ORGANIZATION. Dec., 2000. Sinapore. (Cheah Chee-kong) Pierre Png, Lum May-yee, Catherine Sng, Gary Yuen, Kevin Murphy, Kelvin Ng, Teh Su-ching, Cheong Wuiseng, Irene Ong.

CHICKEN RUN
DREAMWORKS/PATHE/AARDMAN. June, 2000. U.S. British. (Peter Lord, Nick Park) Mel Gibson, Julia Sawalha, Miranda Richardson, Jane Horrocks, Lynn Ferguson, Imedlda Staunton (voices). Animated.

CHICKEN SKIN
LAUREN FILM. Jan., 2002. Spanish. (Javier Maqua) Karra Elejalde, Anabel Alonso, Nathalie Sesena, Amparo Valle, Txema Blasco, Maxi Rodriguez, Isabel Ordaz.

CHICO
HUNNIA STUDIO (HUNGARY)/ZDF-ARTE (GERMANY)/MAXIMA FILM (CROATIA)/ROOS FILM (CHILE). July, 2001. Hungarian-German-Croatian-Chilean. (Ibolya Fekete) Eduardo Rozsa Flores, Sergio Hernandez, Richie Varga.

CHI GIRL
TRISHORE ENTERTAINMENT. Jan., 1999. (Heidi Van Lier) Heidi Van Lier, Joe Kraemer, Scott Benjaminson, Phil Smith.

CHIHWASEON
May, 2002. South korean. (Im Kwon-Taek) Choi Min-Sik, Ahn Sung-Ki, You Ho-Jeong, Kim-Yeo-Jin.

THE CHILD
PRABHAVI NIRMITEE. Oct., 2000. Iadian. (Shrabani Deodkar) Sania, Nimish Kathale,Sachin Khedekar, Mrinal Kulkarni.

THE CHILD AND THE SOLDIER
FARABI CINEMA FOUNDATION. May, 2000. Iranian. (Seyyed Reza Mir-Karimi) Mehdi Lotfi, Rouhallah Hosseini, Mehran Rajabi.

CHILDREN: KOSOVO 2000
ENGRAM FILM. Feb., 2001. Hungarian. (Ferenc Moldovanyi) Documentary.

THE CHILDREN OF CHABANNES
PERENNIAL PICTURES/WETHERELL & ASSOCIATES. June, 1999. (Lisa Gossels) Documentary.

CHILDREN OF PETROLEUM
Feb., 2001. Iranian. (Ebrahim Forouzesh) Milad Rezai, Azar Khosravi, Nasrin Boustan, Hamide Bakhtiari, Parinaz Khoshe, Milad Shadi.

THE CHILDREN OF THE CENTURY
BAC FILMS. Sept. 1999. French. (Diane Kurys)Juliette Binoche, Benoit Magimel, Stefano Dionisi, Robin Renucci.

CHILDREN OF THE MARSHLAND
UGC. Apt., 1999. French. (Jean Becker) Jacques Villeret, Jacques Gamblin, Andre Dussollier, Michel Serrault.

THE CHILDREN OF RUSSIA
NIRVANA. Jan., 2002. Spanish. (Jaime Camino) Ernesto Vega de la Iglesia, Araceli Sanchez, Juanita Prieto.

CHILDREN'S PLAY
MARS FILMS. July, 2001. French. (Laurent Tuel) Karin Viard, Charles Berling, Ludvine Sagnier, Camille Vatel, Alexandre Bongibault.

CHILDREN UNDERGROUND
BELZBERG FILMS. Jan. 2001. (Edet Belzberg) Mihai Tudose, Cristina, Ana, Marian, Macarena, Angi Preda, Sister Mary Murphy. Documentary.

CHILL FACTOR
WARNER BROS. Aug., 1999. (Hugh Johnson) Cuba Gooding, Jr., Skeet Ulrich, Peter Firth, David Paymer.

CHILLICOTHE
BLUE YONDER FILMS. Jan., 1999. (Todd Edwards) Todd Edwards, Peter Bedgood, Cory Edwards, Brad Knull.

CHILL OUT
JOST HERING/ZDF. Feb., 2000. German. (Andreas Struck) Sebastian Blomberg, Tatjana Blacher, Barnaby Metschurat.

CHIMERA
MIKADO. April, 2001. Italian. (Pappi Corsicato) Iaia Forte, Tommaso Ragno, Tomas Arana, Marit Nissen, Cristina Donadio, Fabio Sartor, Branko Tesanovic, Franco Nero.

THE CHIMP
HAUT & COURT. March, 2001. French-Kirgizstanian-Japanese. (Aktan Abdykalykov) Mirlan Abdykalykov, Sergei Golovkin, Dzylkycy Dzakypov, Alexandra Mitrokhina, Yuri Sokolov, Salynbek Sarymsakov.

CHINA: THE PANDA ADVENTURE
IMAX CORP. Sept., 2001. (Robert M. Young) Maria Bello, Xander Berkeley, Yu Xia.

CHINESE COFFEE
20TH CENTURY FOX/FOX SEARCHLIGHT/CHAL PRODS/ SHOOTING GALLERY. Sept., 2000. (Al Pacino) Al Pacino, Jerry Orbach, Susan Floyd, Ellen McElduff.

CHINESE DEFENSE
OBJEKTIV FILMSTUDIO-MAGYAR TV-COVI DESIGN FILM. FEB., 1999. Hungarian-Romanian. (Gabor Tompa) Emil Gyorgy, Ivan Dengyei, Victor Rebengiuc, Maia Morgenstern.

A CHINESE IN A COMA
CECCHI GORI. Feb., 2000. Italian. (Carlo Verdone) Carlo Verdone, Beppe Fiorello, Marit Nissen, Anna Safroncik, Zanni Tamma.

CHIN UP!
DIAPHANA. May, 1999. French-Belgain. (Solveig Anspach) Karin Viard, Laurent Lucas, Julien Cottereau, Philippe Duclos.

CHIYOKO: MILLENNIUM ACTRESS
Nov., 2001. Japanese. (Satoshi Kon) Animated.

CHLOE
J WORKS. Feb., 2001. Japanese. (Go Riju) Masatoshi Nagase, Rie Tomosaka, Shinya Tsukamoto, Miyuki Matsuda, Shinji Aoyama.

CHOCOLAT
MIRAMAX FILMS. Dec., 2000. (Lasse Hallstrom) Juliette Binoche, Lena Olin, Johnny Depp, Judi Dench, Alfred Molina, Peter Stormare, Carrie-Anne Moss, Leslie Caron, John Wood.

CHOCOLATE FOR BREAKFAST
ASPECT RATIO. Apr., 1999. (Emily Baer) Isabel Gillies, Brooke Hailey, Marin Hinkle, Callie Thorne.

CHOLERA STREET
OZEN FILM. May, 1998. Turkish-Hungarian-French. (Mustafa Altioklar) Okan Bayulgen, Mujde Ar, Savas Dincel, Burak Sergen.

CHOPPER
PALACE FILMS/AUSTRALIAN FILM FINANCE CORP./Mushroom Pictures/Pariah Films. June, 2000. Australian. (Andrew Dominik) Eric Bana, Vince Colosimo, Simon Lyndon, Kate Beahan, David Field.

CHOP SUEY
JUST BLUE FILMS. Feb., 2001. (Bruce Weber) Documentary.

CHRISTMAS CAROL: THE MOVIE
PATHE (IN U.K.). British. (Jimmy T. Murakami) Simon Callow, Kate Winslet, Nicolas Cage, Michael Gambon, Jane Horrocks, Rhys Ifans, Juliet Stevenson. Animated.

CHRISTMAS IN AUGUST
ILSHIN INVESTMENT CO. May, 1998. Korean. (Hur Jin-Ho) Suk-Kyu, Shim Eun-Ha, Shin Koo, Oh Ji-Hae, Lee Han-Wi.

CHRISTMAS VACATION 2000
FILMAURO. Jan., 2000. Italian. (Carlo Vanzina) Christian De Sica, Massimo Boldi, Magan Gale, Nino D'Angelo, Monica Scattini.

CHRONICALLY UNFEASIBLE
NEW YORKER FILMS. Brazilian. (Sergio Bianchi) Daniel Dantas, Betty Gofman, Umberto Magnani, Dira Paes, Dan Stulbach.

CHRONICLE OF AN AMERICAN SUBURB
Feb., 2002. (H. James Gilmore) Documentary.

CHUCK & BUCK
ARTISAN/BLOW UP PICTURES/FLAN DE COCO. Jan., 2000. (Miguel Arteta) Mike White, Chris Weitz, Lupe Ontiveros, Beth Colt, Paul Weitz, Maya Rudolph, Mary Wigmore, Paul Sand, Gino Buccola.

CHUMP CHANGE
Oct., 2000. (Stephen Burrows) Stephen Burrows, Tim Matheson, Traci Elizabeth Lords, Jerry Stiller, Anne Meara, Fred Willard, A.J. Benza.

CHUNHYANG
TAENUNG PICTURES/MIRAE ASSET CAPITAL COCJ ENTERTAINMENT/SAEHAN INDUSTRIES. May, 2000. South Korean. (Im Kwon Taek) Yi Hyo Jeong, Cho Seung Woo, Kim Sung Nyu, Lee Jung Hun, Kim Hak Yong.

CIAO AMERICA
Sept., 2002. (Frank Ciota) Anthony Di Nanno, Antonio Navarro, Eddie Malavarca, Vittorio Amandola, Maurizio Nichetti, Michele Bertelli, Anthony DeSando, Umberto Franchini, Violante Placido.

THE CIDER HOUSE RULES
MIRAMAX. Sept., 1999 (Lasse Hallstrom) Tobey Maguire, Charlize Theron, Delroy Lindo, Paul Rudd, Michael Caine.

CINEMANIA
June, 2002. German. (Angela Christlieb, Stephen Kijak) Jack Angstreich, Roberta Hill, Bill Heidbreder, Harvey Schwartz, Eric Chadbourne. Documentary.

CINEMATOGRAPHY 3: REVENGE OF IRIS
DAIEI. May, 1999. Japanese. (Shusuke Kaneko) Shinobu Nakayama, Ai Mada, Ayako Fujitani, Senri Yamasaki.

CINEMA VERITE: DEFINING THE MOMENT
NATIONAL FILM BOARD, TORONTO/TELEFILM CANADA. Oct., 1999. Canadian. (Peter Wintonick) D.A. Pennebaker, Richard Leacock, Wolf Koenig, Al Maysles, Hope Ryden. Documentary.

CINERAMA ADVENTURE
Aug., 2002. (David Strohmaier) Debbie Reynolds, Carroll Baker, Eli Wallach, Russ Tamblyn, Leonard Maltin, Joe Dante, Kevin Brownlow, Rudy Behlmer. Documentary.

THE CIRCLE
MIKADO/JAFAR PANAHI FILM/MIKADO/LUMIERE & CO. Sept., 2000. Iranian-Italian. (Kambozia Partovi) Maryiam Parvin Almani, Nargess Mamizadeh, Fereshteh Sadr Orafai, Monir Arab, Elham Saboktakin.

CIRCLING
VON VIETINGHOFF FILMPRODUKTION. Jan., 2001. German. (Jacob Hilpert) Cornelius Schwalm, Matthias Zelic, Jakob Matschenz, Willem Veerkamp, Ronnie Wechselberger.

CIRCUIT
SNEAK PREVIEW ENTERTAINMENT. July, 2001. (Dirk Shafer) Jonathan Wade Drahos, Andre Khabazzi, Kiersten Warren.

CIRCUS
COLUMBIA TRISTAR/SONY//FILM DEVELOPMENT CORP. May, 2000. British-U.S. (Rob Walker) John Hannah, Famke Janssen, Peter Stormare, Eddie Izzard, Fred Ward, Brian Conley, Tiny Lister, Amanda Donohoe.

THE CIRCUS
MOSFILM. Aug., 2000. Soviet Union–1936. (Grigori Aleksandrov) Lyubov Orlova, Evgenia Melnikova, Vladimir Volodin, Sergei Stoliarov.

CIRCUS BAOBAB
MONDO FILMS. French. (Laurent Chevallier) The Acrobatic Circus of Guinea (Le Cirque Acrobatique de Guinee) aka Circus Baobab. Documentary.

CIRCUS PALESTINA
TRANSFAX FILM PRODS. Sept., 1999. Israeli. (Eyal Halfon) Yoram Hatav, Evgenia Dudina, Amos Lavi, Basaam Zuamot.

CIRQUE DU SOLEIL: JOURNEY OF MAN
SONY/CIRQUE DU SOLEIL/MOTION INTL. Jan., 2000. (Keith Melton) Ian McKellan, Nicky Dewhurst, Brian Dewhurst, Anait Karagyezyan, Mikhail Matorin, Chris Van Wagenen, Kenny Raskin, Cully Smoller.

THE CISTERN
Dec., 2001. Greek. (Hristos Dimas) Yota Festa, Themis Bazaka, Yorgos Marinos, Mihalis Evripiotis.

CITIES OF THE PLAIN
LES FILMS DU PARADOXE. Jan., 2001. French. (Robert Kramer) Ben, Amelie Desrumaux, Bernard Trolet, Nathalie Sarles.

CITIZEN JAMES
DOUG E. DOUG WORLD INC./DOUG E. DOUG MOVING PICTURE CO. Mar., 2000. (Doug E. Doug) Doug E. Doug, Kayinde Harris, Tyrone Jefferson, Albert Shiver Jr.

CITIZEN TOXIE: THE TOXIC AVENGER IV
TROMA TEAM. May, 2001. (Lloyd Kaufman) David Mattey, Keidi Sjursen, Clyde Lewis Debbie Rochon, Ron Jeremy, Paul Kyrmse.

CITY BY THE SEA
WARNER BROS. Aug., 2002. (Michael Caton-Jones) Robert De Niro, Frances McDormand, James Franco, Eliza Dushku, William Forsythe, George Dzundza, Patti Lupone, Anson Mount, John Doman, Brian Tarantina.

THE CITY
NORTH STAR FILMS. Sept., 1998. (David Riker), Fernando Reyes, Marcos Martinez Garcia, Moises Garcia, Anthony Rivera.

CITY LOOP
AUSTRALIAN FILM COMMISSION/PACIFIC FILM & TV COMMISSION/SBS /SHOWTIME AUSTRALIA/NHK/RED MOVIES. June, 2000. Australian. (Belinda Chayko) Sullivan Stapleton, Ryan Johnson, Megan Dorman, Kellie Jones, Brendan Cowell.

CITY OF ANGELS
WARNER BROS. March, 1998. (Brad Silberling), Nicolas Cage, Meg Ryan, Andre Braugher, Dennis Franz, Colm Feore, Robin Bartlett.

CITY OF DREAMS
FILM AUSTRALIA/AUSTRALIAN BROADCASTING CORP. July, 2000. Australian. (Belinda Mason). Documentary.

CITY OF GHOSTS
UNITED ARTISTS. Sept., 2002. (Matt Dillon) Matt Dillon, James Caan, Natascha McElhone, Gerard Depardieu, Sereyvuth Kem, Stellan Skarsgard, Rose Byrne, Shawn Andrews, Chalee Sankhavesa, Christopher Curry.

CITY OF GLASS
GOLDEN HARVEST. Dec., 1998. Hong Kong. (Mabel Cheung) Leon Lai, Shu Qi, Nicola Cheung, Daniel Wu, Enson Chan.

THE CITY OF LOST SOULS
TOKUMA SHOTEN, DAIEI CO. Oct., 2000. Japanese. (Takashi Miike) Teah, Michelle Reis, Patricia Manterola, Mitsuhiro Oikawa, Koji Kikkawa, Ren Osugi, Akaji Maro, Anatoli Krasnov.

CITY OF M
GUSTAV SANCHEZ GARCIA. Sept., 2000. Peruvian. (Felipe Degregori) Santiago Magill, Christian Meier, Jorge Madueno.

THE CITY OF MARVELS
FILMAX. June, 1999. Spanish-French-Portuguese. (Mario Camus) Olivier Martinez, Emma Suarez, Francois Marthouret, Joaquin Diaz.

THE CITY OF NO LIMITS
Dec., 2002. Spanish-Argentine. (Antonio Hernandez) Leonardo Sbaraglia, Fernando Fernan-Gomez, Geraldine Chaplin, Ana Fernandez, Adriana Ozores.

CITY OF PEACE
CABIN JOHN. April, 1998. (Susan Koch) Documentary.

A CIVIL ACTION
BUENA VISTA. Dec., 1998. (Steven Zaillian) John Travolta Robert Duvall, Tony Shalhoub, William H. Macy, Zeljko Ivanbeck.

CIVIL BRAND
June, 2002. (Neema Barnette) LisaRae, Mos Def, N'Bushe Wright, Monica Calhoun, Da Brat, MC Lite, Clifton Powell, Lark Voorhies, Reed McCants, Tichina Arnold.

THE CLAIM
MGM. Nov., 2000. British-Canadian. (Michael Winterbottom) Peter Mullan, Wes Bentley, Milla Jovovich, Nastassja Kinski, Sarah Polley, Julian Richings, Sean McGinley.

CLAIRE
June, 2002. (Milford Thomas) Toniet Gallego, Mish P. DeLight, James Ferguson, Anna May Hirsch, Allen Jeffrey Rein, Katherine Moore.

CLAMS AND MUSSELS
BUENA VISTA INTL. SPAIN. Oct., 2000. Spanish-Argentine. (Marcos Carnevale) Jorge Sanz, Leticia Bredice, Antonio Gasalla, Loles Leon.

THE CLANDESTINE MARRIAGE
UNIVERSAL/PORTMAN ENTERTAINMENT/BBC FILMS/BRITISH SCREEN/GUNNER & STABLES GROUP/MILESIAN FILMS. Dec., 1999. British. (Christopher Miles) Nigel Hawthorne, Joan Collins, Timothy Spall, Tom Hollander.

CLASSIC
SPUTNIK OY. Feb., 2001. Finland. (Kari Vaananen) Martti Suosalo, Janne Hyytiainen, Matti Onnismaa, Pertti Sveholm, Pirkka-Pekka Petelius, Arvi Lind, Minna Koskela.

CLASS TRIP
LES FILMS DE LA BOISSIERE. May, 1998. French. (Claude Miller) Clement Van Den Bergh, Lokman Nalcakan, Francoise Roy.

CLAUDE JUTRA, AN UNFINISHED STORY
Aug., 2002. Canadian. (Paule Baillargeon) Claude Jutra, Michel Brault, Bernardo Bertolucci, Genevieve Bujold, Saul Rubinek. Documentary.

CLAUDINE'S RETURN
JAZZ PICTURES. April, 1998. (Antonio Tibaldi) Christina Applegate, Stefano Dionisi, Matt Clark, Tony Torn, Gabriel Mann, Perry Anzilotti.

THE CLAY BIRD
AN MK2 DIFFUSION. French-Bangladeshi. (Tareque Masud) Nuril Islam Bablue, Russell Farazi, Jayanto Chattopadhyay.

CLAY PIGEONS
GRAMERCY PICTURES. Sept., 1998. (David Dobkin) Vince Vaughn, Janeane Garofalo, Joaquin Phoenix, Georgina Cates, Phil Morris.

THE CLEAN AND NARROW
DEL MAR/SNEAK PREVIEW ENTERTAINMENT. Jan., 2000. (William Katt) Jack Noseworthy, Laura Keighton, Wings Hauser, Paul Francis, Wes Culwell, William Katt, Sondra Locke.

CLEMENT
PYRAMIDE. May, 2001. French. (Emmanuelle Bercot) Olivier Gueritee, Emmanuelle Bercot, Kevin Goffette, Remi Martin.

CLEOPATRA'S SECOND HUSBAND
CUCOLORIS FILMS. April, 1998. (Jon Reiss) Paul Hipp, Boyd Kestner, Bitty Schram, Rhada Mitchell, Alexis Arquette.

THE CLIMB
WORLD WIDE PICTURES. Feb., 2002. (John Schmidt) Jason George, Ned Vaughn, Dabney Coleman, Clifton Davis, Kyli Santiago, Todd Bridges.

CLINT EASTWOOD: OUT OF THE SHADOWS
WARNER HOME VIDEO/RHAPSODY FILMS/AMERICAN MASTERS/ BBC FILMS. Aug., 2000. U.S.-British. (Bruce Ricker) Clint Eastwood, Martin Scorsese, Gene Hackman, Meryl Streep, Forest Whitaker. Documentary.

CLOCKSTOPPERS
PARAMOUNT. March, 2002. (Jonathan Frakes) Jesse Bradford, Paula Garces, French Stewart, Michael Biehn, Robin Thomas, Garikayi Mutambirwa, Julia Sweeney.

CLOSED WARD
YEE-HA FILMS. Sept., 2000. Japanese. (Susumu Fukahara) Saki Kamiryo, Yoshitaka Zushi, Yasufumi Hayashi, Katsuo Nakamura, Rikiya Yasuoka, Junko Miyashita, Ineko Arima, Morio Kazama, Takehiro Murata.

THE CLOSER YOU GET
FOX SEARCHLIGHT/REDWAVE. Feb., 2000. Irish-British. (Aileen Ritchie) Ian Hart, Sean McGinley, Niamh Cusack, Ruth McCabe, Ewan Stewart, Pat Shortt, Cathleen Bradley, Sean McDonagh.

THE CLOSET
GAUMONT BUENA VISTA INTL. Dec., 2000. French. (Francis Veber) Daniel Auteuil, Gerard Depardieu, Thierry Lhermitte, Michele Laroque, Michel Aumont, Jean Rochefort, Alexandra Vandernoot.

CLOSE TO HOME
GRQ PRODS. March, 2001. (Georg Hartmann) Abe Baron, Betty Deutsch, Karl-Dieter Hartmann, William Kirban. Documentary.

CLOSE TO LOVE
HUNNIA STUDIO/MAFILM AKTIV STUDIO. Feb., 1999. Hungarian. (Andras Salamon) Ferenc Hujber, Tsuyu Shimizu, Nimrod Antal, Janos Gyuriska, Karoly Gesztesi.

CLOSE TO THE BORDER
OPERA PRIMA. Nov., 2000. Argentine. (Rodolfo Duran) Claudio Gallardou, Ulises Dumont, Leonor Manso, Victor Laplace, Alberto Benegas, Mirna Suarez, Paula Pourtale.

THE CLOUD
CINESUR/LES FILMS DU SUD. Sept., 1998. Argentine-French-Italian-German. (Fernando E. Solanas) Eduardo Pavlovsky, Angela Correa, Franklin Caicedo, Carlos Perez, Leonor Manso.

CLOUDS: LETTERS TO MY SON
MAN'S FILMS PRODS. (BELGIUM)/PEGASOS FILMS (GERMANY). May, 2001. Belgian-German. (Marion Hansel) Documentary.

CLOUDS OF MAY
NBC AJANS. Feb., 2000. Turkish. (Nuri Bilge) Muzaffer Ozdemir, M. Emin Ceylan, Fatma Ceylan.

THE CLOWN SMILES
EUROZOOM. June, 1999. French. (Eric Besnard) Ticky Holgado, Vincent Elbaz, Francois Berleand, Bruno Putzulu.

THE COAST IS CLEAR
UFD. Feb., 1998. French. (Stephane Clavier) Francois Cluzet, Philippine Leroy-Beaulieu, Emma de Caunes, Eric Caravaca.

COCONUT HEADS
MEDUSA FILM. Nov., 2000. Italian. (Ugo Fabrizio Giordani) Alessandro Gassman, Gian Marco Tognazzi, Manuela Arcuri, Marco Messeri, Phillipe Leroy, Marisa Merlini, Greta Vaillant.

CODE UNKNOWN: INCOMPLETE TALES OF SEVERAL JOURNEYS
MK2 DIFFUSION/LES FILMS ALAIN SARDE/ ARTE FRANCE CINEMA/FRANCE 2 CINEMA/BAVARIA FILM/ZDF/ROMANIAN CULTURE MINISTRY/FILMEX ROMANIA/CANAL PLUS. May, 2000. French. (Michael Haneke) Juliette Binoche, Thierry Neuvic, Luminita Gheorghiu, Ona Lu Yenke, Helene Diarra, Sepp Bierbichler.

COFFEE & LANGUAGE
C&L PRODS. (SAN FRANCISCO). Feb., 2001. (J.P. Allen) Chopper Bernet, Janis DeLucia Allen, J.P. Allen, Chris Pflueger.

COFFIN JOE: THE STRANGE WORLD OF JOSE MOJICA MARINS
PRATICAMENTE FILMS. Jan., 2001. (Andre Barcinski, Ivan Finotti).

COINCIDENCE IN PARADISE
T&C FILM AG (ZURICH). Sept., 2000. Swiss. (Matthias von Gunten) Kamoya Kimeu, Maeve Leakey, Elisabeth Vrba. Documentary.

COLD AROUND THE HEART
20TH CENTURY FOX. Nov., 1998. (John Ridley) David Caruso, Kelly Lynch, Stacey Dash, Chris Noth, John Spencer, Pruitt Taylor Vince.

COLD IS THE BREATH OF EVENING
SENATOR. Aug., 2000. German. (Rainer Kaufmann) Heinz Bennent, Gisela Trowe, August Diehl, Fritzi Haberlandt, Ingo Naujoks, Andre Hennicke, Elisabeth Trissenaar, Vadim Glowna.

COLD LANDS
MERCURE DISTRIBUTION/AGAT FILMS/LA SEPT ARTE. Sept., 1999. French. (Sebastien Lifshitz) Yasmine Belmadi, Bernard Verley, Sebastien Charles, Valerie Donzelli, Eric Savin.

THE COLOR OF COURAGE
STUDIOS USA PICTURES. Oct., 1998. (Lee Rose) Linda Hamilton, Lynn Whitfield, Bruce Greenwood, Roger Guenveur Smith.

THE COLOR OF GOD
VARAHONAR CO. Feb., 1999. Iranian. (Majid Majidi) Mohsen Ramezani, Hossein Mahjub, Salime Feizi, Elham Sharifi.

THE COLOR OF LIES
MK2 DIFFUSION. Jan., 1999. French. (Claude Chabrol) Sandrine Bonnaire, Jacques Gamblin, Valeria Bruni-Tedeschi, Antoine de Caunes.

COLOURFUL
NHK ENTERPRISES 21. Sept., 2000. Japanese. (Shun Nakahara) Koki Tanaka, Sawako Agawa, Kanako Magara, Asuka Komayu.

COME AT NIGHT
REFUGE PRODS. Sept., 1998. (Lindy Laub) Elpidia Carrillo, Barbara Williams, Trevor O'Brien, Sabrina Weiner, Romeo Romero Fabian.

COMEDIA INFANTIL
TORROMFILM/PROLE FILME/AVENIDA PRODUCOES. Feb., 1998. Swedish-Mozambican-Portuguese. (Solveig Nordlund) Sergio Titos, Joao Manja, Joaquina Odete, Jaime Julio, Avelino Manhica.

COMEDIAN
VEGA FILM Aug., 2000. Swiss. (Markus Imboden) Beat Schlatter, Patrick Frey, Brigitte Beyeler, Stephanie Glaser.

COMEDIAN HARMONISTS
MIRAMAX. Feb., 1998. German. (Joseph Vilsmaier) Ben Becker, Heino Ferch, Ulrich Noethen, Heinrich Schafmeister, Max Tidof.

COME, SWEET DEATH
DOR FILM. Jan., 2001. Austrian. (Wolfgang Murnberger) Josef Hader, Barbara Rudnik, Nina Proll, Simon Schwarz, Michael Schonborn.

THE COMET
INSTITUTO MEXICANO DE CINEMATOGRAPHIA/FONDO DE FOMENTO A LA CALIDAD CINEMATOGRAFICA/FONDO SUD . Jan., 1999. Mexican. (Marisa Sistach, Jose Buil) Diego Luna, Ana Claudia Talancon, Carmen Maura, Gabriel Retes.

COME TOGETHER
Oct., 2001. Canadian. (Jeff MacPherson) Tygh Runyan, Eryn Collins, Laura Harris, Russell Porter, Jamie Bell, Tanya Macpherson, Juliana Wimbles.

COME UNDONE
PICTURE THIS! ENTERTAINMENT. July, 2001. French. (Sebastien Lifshitz) Jeremie Elkaim, Stephane Rideau, Marie Matheron, Dominique Reymond, Laetitia Legrix, Nils Ohlund, Rejane Kerdaffrec.

COMEUPPANCE
CHINA STAR ENTERTAINMENT. Feb., 2001. Hong Kong. (Derek Chiu) Jordan Chan, Sunny Chan, Patrick Tam, Wu Hsing-kuo.

COMING SOON
KEY ENTERTAINMENT. May, 1999. (Colette Burson) Tricia Vessey, Gaby Hoffman, Bonnie Root, James Roday, Mia Farrow.

COMING TO LIGHT: EDWARD S. CURTIS AND THE NORTH AMERICAN INDIANS
ANNE MAKEPEACE PRODS./THIRTEEN/WNET FOR AMERICAN MASTERS. Jan., 2000. (Anne Makepeace). Documentary.

THE COMMISSIONER
METROPOLIS FILMPRODUKTION/NEW ERA VISION/SAGA FILM. Feb., 1998. German-British-Belgian. (George Sluizer) John Hurt, Rosana Pastor, Alice Krige, Armin Mueller-Stahl, Johan Leysen.

COMMITTED
MIRAMAX/DEAN SILVERS/MARLEN HECHT. Jan., 2000. (Lisa Krueger) Heather Graham, Casey Affleck, Luke Wilson, Goran Visnjic, Patricia Velasquez, Alfonso Arau, Mark Ruffalo, Kim Dickens, Clea Duvall.

COMMON PLACES
AN ALTA CLASSICS. Sept., 2002. Spanish-Argentine. (Adolfo Aristarain) . Federico Luppi, Mercedes Sampietro, Arturo Puig, Carlos Santamaria, Yael Barnatan.

COMMON WEALTH
LOLAFILMS DISTRIBUCION. Sept., 2000. Spanish. (Alex de la Iglesia) Carmen Maura, Eduardo Antuna, Jesus Bonilla.

COMPANY MAN
PARAMOUNT CLASSICS/UFD/INTERMEDIA FILMS/FOUNDRY FILM PARTNERS/UGC. May, 2000. (Douglas McGrath, Peter Askin) Douglas McGrath, Sigourney Weaver, John Turturro, Anthony LaPaglia, Ryan Phillippe, Denis Leary, Woody Allen, Alan Cumming.

COMPENSATION
WIMMIN WITH A MISSION PRODS. Jan., 2000. (Zeinabu Irene Davis) John Earl Jelks, Michelle A. Banks, Christopher Smith.

THE COMPENSATION
BENN FILMS CREATION HOUSE. Aug., 2001. Sri Lankan. (Bennett Rathnayake) Joe Abeywickrama, Jackson Anthoney, Ravindra Randeniya, Sangeetha Weerrarathna, Mahendra Perera.

COMPLICITY
J&M ENTERTAINMENT/ENTERTAINMENT FILM DISTRIBUTORS/ CARLTON FILMS/TALISMAN FILMS. July, 2000. British. (Gavin Millar) Jonny Lee Miller, Brian Cox, Keeley Hawes.

COMRADES
PIREJ FILM AND K#300. Feb., 2001. Macedonian-U.S. (Mitko Panov) Documentray.

CONAMARA
BAVARIA FILM. June, 2001. German-Irish. (Eoin Moore) Ellen Ten Damme, Darragh Kelly, Andreas Schmidt, Rosaleen Linehan, Garrett Keogh, Mairtin Jamsie, Maighread Ni Chonghaile.

CONCERTO OF LIFE
BEIJING FILM STUDIO. June, 1998. Chinese. (Xia Gang) Wang Luoyong, Da Shichang, Yan Xiaopin, Shi Ke, Wang Bozhao, Zhang Xi.

THE CONDEMNATION OF FRANCISZEK KLOS
Feb., 2002. Polish. (Andrzej Wajda) Miroslaw Baka, Maja Komorowska, Grazyna Blecka-Kolska, Andrzej Chyra, Krzysztof Globisz, Artur Zmijewski.

CONDO PAINTING
USA FILMS. Aug., 1999. (John McNaughton) George Condo, William S. Burroughs, Allen Ginsberg, John Sampas.

THE CONFESSION
May, 2002. Turkish. (Zeki Demirkubuz) Taner Birsel, Basak Koklukaya, Iskender Altin, Mirac Eronat.

CONFESSIONS OF A PICK-UP ARTIST
REZO FILMS. July, 2001. French. (Alain Soral) Said Taghmaoui, Thomas Dutronc.

CONFESSIONS OF A SEXIST PIG
PIZZA PRODS. March, 1998. (Sandy Tung) Edward Kerr, Traylor Howard, Michael Trucco, Lauren Graham, Anneliza Scott, Sal Viscuso.

CONFLICT
NATIONAL FILM DEVELOPMENT CORP./SHYAM BENEGAL. Aug., 2000. Indian. (Shyam Benegal) Rajeshwari Schdev, Rajit Kapur, Ravi Jhankal, Raghubir Yadav, Kishore Kadam, Seem Biswas, Divya Dutta.

CONFUSION OF GENDERS
HAUT & COURT. Nov., 2000. French. (Ilan Duran Cohen) Pascal Greggory, Nathalie Richard, Vincent Martinez, Alain Bashung, Julie Gayet, Gyrille Thouvenin.

CONJUGATION
TANG FILMS. Aug., 2001. Hong Kong. (Emily Tang) Qian Yu, Zhao Hong, Tian Yu, Huang Wei, Zhang Qi.

CONNECTED TO FATE
TAIWAN FILM CENTER. Sept., 1998. Taiwanese. (Wan Jen) Tsai Cheng-nan, Chang Cheng-yu, Chang Fei-chun, Chen Chiou-yen.

THE CONTACT
MYUNG FILM CO./KIID. Sept., 1998. South Korean. (Jang Yun-hyeon) Han Seok-kyu, Jeon Do-yeon, Park Yong-su, Chu Sang-mi.

THE CONTENDER
DREAMWORKS/CINERENTA/CINECONTENDER/BATTLEGROUND /SE8 GROUP. Aug., 2000. (Rod Lurie) Joan Allen, Gary Oldman, Jeff Bridges, Sam Elliott, Christian Slater, William Petersen.

THE CONVENT
ALPINE PICTURES. Jan., 2000. (Mike Mendez) Adrienne Barbeau, Joanna Canton, Megahn Perry, Dax Miller, Richard Trapp, Coolio, David Gunn, Jim Golden, Liam Kyle Sullivan.

CONVERGENCE
WHITE ROCK FILM. Feb., 1999. Canadian. (Gavin Wilding) Christopher Lloyd, Cynthia Preston, Adrian Paul,' Blu Mankuma.

A CONVERSATION WITH GREGORY PECK
TURNER CLASSIC MOVIES/ON TOUR PRODS./CABIN CREEK FILMS. Oct., 1999. (Barbara Kopple). Documentary.

CONVICTS
MOSFILM. Aug., 2000. Soviet Union 1936. (Evgeni Chervyakov) Mihail Astangov, Aleksandr Cheban, Mikhail Yanshin, Boris Dobronravov, Vera Yanukova, Nadezhda Ermakovich.

COOKERS
PACESETTERS PICTURES INTL. AND FINGERPRINT FILMS. April, 2001. (Dan Mintz) Brad Hunt, Cyia Batten, Patrick McGaw, Ashley Ann Lapan, Karole Nellis, Frankie Ray,.Paul Banashek.

COOKIE'S FORTUNE
OCTOBER FILMS. Jan., 1999. (Robert Altman) Glenn Close, Julianne Moore, Liv Tyler, Chris O'Donnell, Charles S. Dutton.

COOL AND CRAZY
NORSK FILM, BARENTSFILM (NORWAY)/GIRAFFILM (SWEDEN). Feb., 2001. Norwegian-Swedish. (Knut Erik Jensen) Members of the Berlevag Male Choir. Documentary.

A COOL, DRY PLACE
20TH CENTURY FOX. Feb., 1999. (John N. Smith) Vince Vaughn, Joey Lauren Adams, Monica Potter.

COPYCAT KILLER (MOHO HAN)
TOHO CO. Aug., 2002. Japanese. (Yoshimitsu Morita) Masahiro Nakai, Takashi Fujii, Kanji Tsuda, Yoshino Kimura, Tsutomu Yamazaki.

THE COQ IS DEAD
OBJEKTIV FILM. June, 1999. German. (Hermine Huntgebruth) Gisela Schneeberger, August Zirner, Renate Kroessner, Nikolaus Paryla.

CORKY ROMANO
BUENA VISTA. Oct., 2001. (Rob Pritts) Chris Kattan, Vinessa Shaw, Peter Falk, Peter Berg, Chris Penn, Fred Ward, Richard Roundtree, Matthew Glave, Roger Fan.

THE CORNDOG MAN
CORNDOG PRODS. Jan., 1999. (Andrew Shea) Noble Willingham, Jim Holmes.

CORONATION
ANDREA FILMS. Sept., 2000. Chilean. (Silvio Caiozzi) Julio Jung, Maria Canepa, Adela Secall, Gabriela Medina, Jaime Vadell.

*CORPUS CALLOSUM
Aug., 2002. Canadian. (Michael Snow) Kim Plate, Greg Hermanovic, John Massey, Joanne Tod, John Penner, Tom Sherman.

CORRUPTED HANDS
IRANIAN FILM SOCIETY. June, 2001. Iranian. (Cyprus Alvandi) Abolfazi Pour-Arab, Hedieh Tehrani, Asel Badiie, Amin Hayayi, Elham Imani, Shahab Asgari, Saied Pirdoust.

THE CORRUPTOR
NEW LINE. Mar., 1999. (James Foley) Chow Yun-Fat, Mark Wahlberg, Ric Young, Paul Ben-Victor.

COSY DENS
Czech TV/Pavel Borovan Creative Group/Total HelpArt/Studio Barrandov. Sept., 1999. Czech. (Jan Hrebejk) Michal Beran, Miroslav Donutil, Jiri Kodet, Kristyna Novakova, Simona Stasova.

COTTON MARY
UIP/MERCHANT IVORY. Nov., 1999. British. (Ismael Merchant) Greta Scacchi, Madhur Jaffrey, James Wilby, Nina Gupta, Sakina Jaffrey.

THE COUNCIL OF EGYPT
KEY FILMS. March, 2002. Italian-French-Hungarian. (Emidio Greco) Silvio Orlando, Tommaso Ragno, Renato Carpentieri, Marine Delterme, Giancarlo Giannini, Yann Collette, Antonio Catania.

COUNT ME OUT
ICELANDIC FILM CORP/FILMHUSET/PETER ROMMEL FILM-PRODUKTION/ ZENTROPA. May, 1998. Icelandic-Norwegian-German-Danish. (Ari Kristinsson) Bergthora Aradottir, Freydis Kristofersdottir.

COUNTRY
PANDORA. Sept., 2000. Irish. (Kevin Liddy) Lisa Harrow, Des Cave, Gary Lyndon, Marcella Plunkett, Pat Laffan, Laurence Kinlan.

THE COUNTRY BEARS
BUENA VISTA. July, 2002. (Peter Hastings) Christopher Walken, Stephen Tobolowsky, Daryl "Chill" Mitchell, M.C. Gainey, Diedrich Bader, Alex Rocco, Meagen Fay, Eli Marienthal, Queen Latifah, Krystal Marie Harris, Don Henley, Wyclef Jean, Elton John, Willie Nelson, Bonnie Raitt, Brian Setzer, Don Was, Xhibit.

COUNTY KILBURN
@RADICAL.MEDIA/WATERMARK FILM/BREAKNECK FILMS. Aug., 2000. (Elliot Hegarty) Ciaran Mcmenamin, Rick Warden, John Bowe, Georgia Mackenzie, Patrick Duggan, Kay D'Arcy, Norman Rodway.

THE COURTYARD
Studio Uljana Kim. May, 1999. Lithuanian-French. (Valdas Navasaitas) Donatas Banionis, Richardas Vitkaitas, Albinas Keleris, Tatjana Liutajeva.

COUSIN BETTE
FOX SEARCHLIGHT. June, 1998. (Des McAnuff) Jessica Lange, Elisabeth Shue, Bob Hoskins, Hugh Laurie, Kelly Macdonald.

COVENTRY
CHIMBORAZO PICTURES. Feb., 1998. (J. Trumbull Foster) Ryan Gibson, Felicity Jones, Clint Jordan, Lynn Jordan, Tia Hunnicut.

COWBOYS AND ANGELS
SMOKIN' DAWGS. Apr., 2000. (Gregory C. Haynes) Adam Trese, Mia Kirshner, Radha Mitchell, Hamilton Von Watts, Carmen Llywellyn, Steve Lisk, Duane Stephens, Alissa Rice.

COWBOY BEBOP - THE MOVIE
SONY PICTURES ENTERTAINMENT. Aug., 2002. Japanese. (Shinichiro Watanabe) Koichi Yamadera, Unsho Ishizuka, Megumi Hayashibara, Aoi Tada, Tsutomu Isobe, Ai Kobayashi, Mickey Curtis. Animated.

COYOTES
COYOTE MOON. Jan., 1999. (Kevin McCarey) Leo Gannan, Kristen Carmody, Lina Gallegos, Louis Caracas.

COYOTE UGLY
BUENA VISTA/TOUCHSTONE/JERRY BRUCKHEIMER FILMS. July, 2000. (David McNally) Piper Perabo, Adam Garcia, Maria Bello, John Goodman, Melanie Lynskey, Izabella Miko, Bridget Moynahan.

CQ
MGM. May, 2001. (Roman Coppola) Jeremy Davies, Angela Lindvall, Elodie Bouchez, Gerard Depardieu, Giancarlo Giannini.

CRACKERS
SHARMILL/BEYOND FILMS. Feb., 1998. Australian. (David Swann) Warren Mitchell, Daniel Kellie, Peter Rowsthorn, Susan Lyons.

CRADLE WILL ROCK
BUENA VISTA. May, 1999. (Tim Robbins) Hank Azaria, Ruben Blades, Joan Cusack, John Cusack.

CRANE WORLD
CINEMATOGRAFICA SARGENTINA. Sept., 1999. Argentine. (Pablo Trapero) Luis Margani, Adriana Aizemberg, Daniel Valenzuela, Roly Serrano, Federico Esquerro, Graciana Chironi, Alfonso Rementeria.

CRASHING EDEN
AXIOM FILMS. Mar., 1999. (Dean Alioto) Paul Ghiringhelli, Jodi Verdu, Rick Williams, Alecia Derwin.

CRASH LANDING
SHANGHAI FILM STUDIO. Feb., 2001. Chinese, (Zhang Jianya) Shao Bing, You Yong, Xu Fan, Chi Huaqiong, Zhang Kanger, Wei Zongwan, Bai Mu, Zhao Shenzhi, Lin Dongpu.

CRAZY
PIETER VAN HUYSTEE FILM & TV/VPRO. Feb., 2000. Dutch. (Heddy Honigmann). Documentary.

CRAZY
CONSTANTIN/CLAUSSEN & WOEBKE. June, 2000. German. (Hans-Christian) Robert Stadlober, Tom Schilling, Oona-Devi Liebich, Julia Hummer, Can Taylanlar, Christoph Ortmann, Willy Rachow.

CRAZY AS HELL
Feb., 2002. (Eriq La Salle) Michael Beach, Eriq La Salle, Ronny Cox, John C. McGinley, Tia Texada, Sinbad, Chracy Pettit.

CRAZY/BEAUTIFUL
BUENA VISTA. June, 2001. (John Stockwell) Kirsten Dunst, Jay Hernandez, Bruce Davison, Lucinda Jenny, Taryn Manning.

CRAZY ENGLISH
XI'AN FILM STUDIO. Aug., 1999. Chinese. (Zhang Yuan). Documentary.

CRAZY IN ALABAMA
SONY. Aug., 1999. (Antonio Banderas) Melanie Griffith, David Morse, Lucas Black, Cathy Moriarty, Meat Loaf Aday.

THE CREATOR
REZO FILMS. Apr., 1999. French. (Albert Dupontel) Albert Dupontel, Calude Perron, Philippe Uchan, Michel Vuillermoz.

CREATURE
GRAPEVINE FILMS. June, 1999. (Parris Patton) Stacey"Hollywood" Dean, Butch Dean, Dusty Dean, Filberto "Barbarella" Ascencio. Documentary.

CREMASTER 2
GLACIER FIELD/GLACIER FIELD. Oct., 1999. (Matthew Barney) Norman Mailer, Mathew Barney, Lauren Pine, Scot Ewalt, Patty Griffin, Michael Thompson, Dave Lombardo, Bruce Steele, Steve Tucker, Cat Kubic.

CREMASTER 3
May, 2002. (Matthew Barney) Richard Serra, Matthew Barney, Aimee Mullins, Paul Brady

THE CREW
BUENA VISTA/TOUCHSTONE PICTURES/GEORGE LITTO PICTURES/ SONNENFELD/JOSEPHSON WORLDWIDE ENTERTAINMENT. Aug., 2000. (Michael Dinner) Richard Dreyfuss, Burt Reynolds, Dan Hedaya, Seymour Cassel, Carrie-Anne Moss, Jennifer Tilly, Lainie Kazan, Miguel Sandoval, Jeremy Piven, Casey Siemaszko.

CRIME + PUNISHMENT IN SUBURBIA
MGM/UNITED ARTISTS/KILLER FILMS. Jan., 2000. (Rob Schmidt) Monica Keena, Vincent Kartheiser, Ellen Barkin, Jeffrey Wright, James DeBello, Michael Ironside, Christian Payne, Conchata Ferrell, Marshall Teague, Nicki Aycox, Brad Greenquist, Lucinda Jenney.

A CRIME IN PARADISE
UFD. March, 2001. French. (Jean Becker) Jacques Villeret, Josiane Balasko, Andre Dussollier, Suzanne Flon, Gerard Hernandez, Roland Magdane, Valerie Mairesse.

THE CRIME OF FATHER AMARO
Sept., 2002. Mexican-Spanish-Argentine-French. (Carlos Carrera) Gael Garcia Bernal, Sancho Gracia, Ana Claudia Talancon, Damian Alcazar, Angelica Aragon, Luisa Huertas, Ernesto Gomez Cruz.

CRIME SCENES
REZO FILMS FILMS/LA CHAUVE-SOURIS/LE STUDIO CANAL PLUS/TELFRANCE/M6 FILMS. Mar., 2000. French. (Frederic Schoendoerffer) Charles Berling, Andre Dussollier, Eva Darlan.

THE CRIMINAL
DOWNTOWN PICTURES. Oct., 2000. British. (Julian Simpson) Steven Mackintosh, Bernard Hill, Eddie Izzard, Natasha Little, Yvan Attal, Holly Aird, Jana Carpenter, Barry Stearn, Norman Lovett.

CRIMINAL LOVERS
MARS FILMS. July, 1999. French-Japanese. (Francois Ozon). Natacha Regnier, Jeremie Renier, Miki Manojlovic, Salim Kechiouche.

THE CRIMINAL OF BARRIO CONCEPCION
GOOD HARVEST UNLIMITED /REGAL FILMS. Sept., 1999. Filipino. (Lav Diaz) Raymond Bagatsing, Anna Capri, Angel Aquino.

THE CRIMSON RIVERS
GAUMONT BUENA VISTA INTL. (IN FRANCE). Sept., 2000. French. (Mathieu Kassovitz) Jean Reno, Vincent Cassel, Nadia Fares, Dominique Sanda, Karim Belkhadra, Jean-Pierre Cassel.

CRIMSON SAILS
ARTCAM. July, 2002. Czech. (Miroslav Janek).

CROCODILE DUNDEE IN LOS ANGELES
PARAMOUNT (IN U.S.)/UIP (IN AUSTRALIA). April, 2001. U.S.-Australian. (Simon Wincer) Paul Hogan, Linda Kozlowski, Jere Burns, Jonathan Banks, Serge Cockburn, Paul Rodriguez, Aida Turturro.

THE CROCODILE HUNTER: COLLISION COURSE
MGM. June, 2002. Australian. (John Stainton) Steve Irwin, Terri Irwin, Magda Szubanski, David Wenham, Lachy Hulme, Aden Young, Kenneth Ransom, Kate Beahan.

CROOKED EARTH
Nov., 2001. New Zealand. (Sam Pillsbury) Temuera Morrison, Lawrence Makoare, Jaime Passier-Armstrong, Quinton Hita, Nancy Brunning, Sydney Jackson

CROSSFIRE
GEE PEE FILMS. Feb., 1998. Indian. (Rituparno Ghosh) Suchitra Mitra, Indrani Haldar, Rituparna Sengupta, Abhishek Chatterjee.

CROSS FIRE
TOHO CO. Nov., 2000. Japanese. (Shusuke Kaneko) Akiko Yada, Hideaki Ito, Ryuji Harada, Masami Nagasawa, Yu Yoshizawa, Hidenori Tokuyama, Toshiyuki Nagashima, Kaori Momoi.

CROSS-HARBOUR TUNNEL
BILLY'S OUTGROWTH WORKSHOP. Jan., 2000. Hong Kong. (Lawrence Wong) Syna Lee, Martin Kam, Anthony Teoh, Pauline Yam.

THE CROSSING
Isabella Films/Tatfilm/Zentropa/NPS Television/ZDF/Arte. Sept., 1999. Dutch-German-Danish. (Nora Hoppe) Behrouz Vossoughi, Johan Leysen, Viviane de Muynck, Mil Seegers, Juan Carlos Tajes.

THE CROSSING
Siglo. Feb., 2000. Japanese. (Yoichi Higashi): Michitaka Tsutsui, Takahito Hosoyamada, Miho Tsumiki, Yoichiro Aoi, Akemi Omori.

THE CROSSING
ADVITAM. May, 2001. French. (Sebastien Lifshitz) Stephane Bouquet. Documentray.

CROSSMAHEART
LEXINGTON FILMS. May, 1998. British. (Henry Herbert) Gerard Rooney, Maria Lennon, Desmond Cave, Tim Sloane.

CROUCHING TIGER, HIDDEN DRAGON
SONY/UNITED CHINA VISION/COLUMBIA PICTURES FILM PRODUCTION ASIA/GOOD MACHINE INTL./EDKO FILMS/ZOOM HUNT/CHINA FILM CO-PRODUCTION CORP./ASIA UNION FILM & ENTERTAINMENT LTD. May, 2000. Hong Kong. (Ang Lee) Chow Yun-fat, Michelle Yeoh, Zhang Ziyi, Chang Chen, Lung Sihung, Cheng Pei-pei, Li Fazeng, Gao Xian, Hai Yan, Wang Deming.

CROUPIER
CHANNEL FOUR FILMS. Feb., 1998. British-German. (Mike Hodges) Clive Owen, Kate Hardie, Alex Kingston, Gina Mckee, Nicholas Ball.

THE CROW: SALVATION
SND/IMF/PACIFIC FILM/ED PRESSMAN/IMF/JEFF MOST PRODS. June, 2000. (Bharat Nalluri) Kirsten Dunst, Eric Mabius, Jodi Lyn O'Keefe, William Atherton, Fred Ward, Debbie Fan, Grant Shaud, David Stevens, Dale Midkiff, Bill Mondy, Walton Goggins, Tim DeKay.

CRUEL INTENTIONS
SONY. Feb., 1999. (Roger Kumble) Sarah Michelle Gellar, Ryan Phillippe, Reese Witherspoon, Selma Blair.

THE CRUISE
CHARTER FILMS. April, 1998. Documentary.

CRUSH
FILMFOUR DISTRIBUTORS. May, 2001. British. (John McKay) Andie MacDowell, Imelda Staunton, Anna Chancellor, Kenny Doughty, Bill Paterson, Caroline Holdaway, Joe Roberts, Josh Cole.

CRYING HEART
CHARLES HEUNG & IMPERIAL INTL. LTD./SUNDY PRODUCTION CO. LTD. Aug., 2000. Hong Kong. (Jing Wong) Deanie Ip, Patrick Tam, Suki Kwan, Sau Leung, Emotion Cheung, Joe Lee, Jimmy Wong Ga Lok.

CRY WOMAN
May, 2002. Canadian-South Korean. (Liu Bingjian) Liao Qin, Wei Xingkun, Shu Jiayue, Li Longjun, Wen Qing.

CUBA FELIZ
PYRAMIDE DISTRIBUTION/ADR/LE STUDIO CANAL PLUS/EL MOVIMENTO NACIONAL DE VIDEO DE CUBA/CNC/CANAL PLUS. May, 2000. French. (Karim Dridi) Miguel Del Morales (El Gallo), Pepin Vaillant, Mirta Gonzales, Anibal Avila, Alberto Pablo.

THE CUBAN GAME
June, 2002. Spanish. (Manuel Martin Cuenca) Omar Linares, Leonardo Padura, Fabio Ruiz, Luis Albert Garcia; Mercedes Sampietro, narrator. Documentary.

CUBBYHOUSE
AUSTRALIAN FILM FINANCE CORP. May, 2001. Australian. (Murray Fahey) Joshua Leonard, Belinda McClory, Jerome Ehlers.

THE CUCKOO
May, 2002. Russian. (Alexander Rogozhkin) Wille Haapsalo, Anni-Kristina Usso, Viktor Bychkov.

THE CUP
PALM PICTURES. May, 1999. Australian. (Khyentse Norbu) Jamyang Lodro, Orgyen Tobgyal, Neten Chokling.

CULTUREJAM: HIJACKING COMMERCIAL CULTURE
Sept., 2001. Canadian. (Jill Sharpe) Documentary.

CUNNAMULLA
RONIN FILMS. Nov., 2000. Australian. (Dennis O'Rourke) Documentary.

CURE
DAIEI CO. Feb., 1998. Japanese. (Kiyoshi Kurosawa) Koji Yakusho, Tsuyoshi Ujiki, Anna Nakagawa.

THE CURSE OF THE JADE SCORPION
DREAMWORKS PICTURES. Aug., 2001. (Woody Allen) Woody Allen, Dan Aykroyd, Elizabeth Berkley, Helen Hunt, Brian Markinson.

CUT
UIP/BEYOND FILMS/MBP/MUSHROOM PICTURES/BEYOND FILMS/SOUTH AUSTRALIAN FILM CORP. Jan., 2000. Australian. (Kimble Rendall) Molly Ringwald, Jessica Napier, Sarah Kants, Kylie Minogue, Simon Bossell, Geoff Revell, Frank Roberts, Sam Lewis.

THE CUT RUNS DEEP
ILSHIN INVESTMENT CO./ALBUS FILMS INTL. Oct., 1999. South Korean. (John H. Lee) Alexandre Manning, David L. McInnis, Gio Park,.

CYBERWORD
INTEL. Sept., 2000. (Colin Davies, Elaine Despins) Jenna Elfman, Matt Frewer, Robert Smith, Dave Foley.

D

DADDY & PAPA
Jan., 2002. (Johnny Symons) Documentary.

DADDY AND THEM
MIRAMAX (IN U.S.)/ALLIANCE ATLANTIS VIVAFILM (IN CANADA). Aug., 2001. (Billy Bob Thornton) Jeff Bailey, Brenda Blethyn, Laura Dern, Daniel Steven DiVito, Walton Goggins, Andy Griffith, Billy Bob Thornton, Jim Varney, Jamie Lee Curtis, Ben Affleck.

DAD SAVAGE
POLYGRAM FILMED ENTERTAINMENT. June, 1998. British. (Betsan Morris Evans) Patrick Stewart, Kevin McKidd, Helen McCrory.

DAGON, SECT OF THE SEA
FILMAX. Nov., 2001. Spanish. (Stuart Gordon) Ezra Godden, Francisco Rabal, Raquel Merono, Macarena Gomez, Brendan Price, Birgit Bofarull.

DAGS
COVENTRY-WINFALZ-NEW OZ. Nov., 1998. Australian. (Murray Fahey) Tanya Bulmer, David Callan, Daniel Cordeaux, Sheena Crouch, Penny Cooper.

DAHMER
PENINSULA FILMS. June, 2002. (David Jacobson) Jeremy Renner, Bruce Davison, Artel Kayaru, Matt Newton, Dion Basco, Kate Williamson.

DAMN YOU! MOSQUITO
NEUROPA FILM/TV2, MMK, ORTT, NKA, MTV, DUNA TV. Feb., 2000. Hungarian. (Miklos Jancso) Zoltan Mucsi, Peter Scherer, Emese Vasvari, Miklos B. Szekeley.

DANCE CHALLENGE (LE DEFI)
EURIPIDE DISTRIBUTION. June, 2002. French. (Blanca Li) Blanca Li, Amanda Lear, Marco Prince, Benjamin Chaouat, Sofia Boutella, Christophe Salengro.

DANCED
RADIO TELEVISION SERBIA/VIKTORIJA FILM. Feb., 1998. Serbian. (Purisa Djordjevic) Ana Sofrenovic, Ljuba Tadic, Dragan Micanovic.

DANCEMAKER
WALTER SCHEUER. June, 1998. (Matthew Diamond) Documentary.

DANCE ME TO MY SONG
VERTIGO. April, 1998. Australian. (Rolf de Heer.) Heather Rose, Joey Kennedy, John Brumpton, Rena Owen, Phil Macpherson.

DANCE OF DUST
RASANEH-E-AMA. Aug., 1998. Iranian. (Abolfazl Jalili) Mahmood Khosravi, Limua Rahi.

DANCER
UNIVERSAL PICTURES/WORKING TITLE FILMS/BBC FILMS/ARTS COUNCIL OF ENGLAND/TIGER ASPECT PICTURES/WT2.. May, 2000. British. (Stephen Daldry) Julie Walters, Jamie Bell, Jamie Driven, Gary Lewis, Jean Heywood, Stuart Wells, Nicola Blackwell.

THE DANCER
ARP/LEELOO PRODS./TF1 PROD. June, 2000, French. (Fred Garson) Mia Frye, Garland Whitt, Rodney Eastman, Josh Lucas, Feodor Atkine, DJ Atomic.

DANCER IN THE DARK
FINE LINE/ZENTROPA ENTERTAINMENTS/TRUST FILM SVENSKA/FILM I VAST/LIBERATOR PRODS./FRANCE 3 CINEMA/ARTE FRANCE CINEMA/PAIN UNLIMITED FILMPRODUKTION. May, 2000. Danish-Swedish-French. (Lars Von Trie) Bjork, Catherine Deneuve, David Morse, Peter Stormare.

THE DANCER UPSTAIRS
Jan., 2002. U.S.-Spanish. (John Malkovich) Javier Bardem, Juan Diego Botto, Laura Morante, Elvira Minguez, Alexandra Lencastre, Oliver Cotton, Abel Folk, Marie-Anne Verganza.

DANCE WITH ME
SONY PICTURES. June, 1998. (Randa Haines) Vanessa Williams, Chayanne, Kris Kristopherson, Joan Plowright, Jane Krakowski.

DANCER, TEXAS POP. 81
SONY PICTURES ENTERTAINMENT. March, 1998. (Tim McCanlies) Breckin Meyer, Peter Facinelli, Eddie Mills, Ethan Embry.

DANCING AT LUGHNASA
SONY PICTURES CLASSICS. Sept., 1998. (Pat O'Connor) Meryl Streep, Michael Gambon, Catherine McCormack, Kathy Burke.

DANCING AT THE BLUE IGUANA
MOONSTONE ENTERTAINMENT. Sept., 2000. (Michael Radford) Charlotte Ayanna, Daryl Hannah, Sheila Kelley, Elias Koteas, Vladimir Mashkov, Sandra Oh, Jennifer Tilly.

DANCING IN SEPTEMBER
WEECAN FILMS/STARRISE ENTERTAINMENT. Feb., 2000. (Reggie Rock Bythewood) Isaiah Washington, Nicole Ari Parker, Vicellous Reon Shannon, Jay Underwood, Marcia Cross, Jenifer Lewis, James Avery, Michael Cavanaugh, Malinda Williams.

DANDY
Feb., 2002. French. (Francois Armanet) Mathieu Simonet, Cecile Cassel, Alice Taglioni, Aurelien Wiik, Laurent Pialet, Matthias Van Khache, Marie Ravel, Thierry Lhermitte.

DANDY DUST
HANS SCHEIRL. June, 1998. British-Austrian. ((Hans Scheirl) Hans Scheirl, Suzie Krueger, Leonora Rogers-Wright, Tre Temperilli.

DANGEROUS BEAUTY
WARNER BROS. Jan., 1998. (Marshall Herskovitz) Catherine McCormack, Rufus Sewell, Jacqueline Bissett, Oliver Platt.

DARESALAM
LA SEPT ARTE, PIERRE JAVAUX PRODS., PARENTHESE FILMS. Feb., 2001. French. (Issa Serge Coelo) Haikail Zakaria, Abdoulaye Ahmat, Youssouf Djaoro.

DARK BLUE WORLD
BIOGRAF JAN SVERAK (CZECH REP.)/PORTOBELLO PICTURES (U.K.). May, 2001. Czech Republic-British. (Jan Sverak) Ondrej Vetchy, Krystof Hadek, Tara Fitzgerald, Oldrich Kaiser, Hans-Jorg Assmann, Charles Dance, Anna Massey.

DARK CITY
NEW LINE CINEMA. Feb., 1998. (Alex Proyas), Rufus Sewell, Kiefer Sutherland, Jennifer Connelly, William Hurt, Richard O'Brien.

DARK DAYS
PICTURE FARM. Jan., 2000. (Marc Singer). Documentary.

THE DARKEST LIGHT
PATHE DISTRIBUTORS. Aug., 1999. British. (Bille Eltringham) Stephen Dillane, Kerry Fox, Keri Arnold, Kavita Sungha, Jason Walton.

DARK HARBOR
HART SHARP ENTERPRISES. June, 1998. (Adam Coleman) Alan Rickman, Polly Walker, Norman Reedus.

DARKNESS AND LIGHT
CHANG TSO-CHI FILM STUDIO. May, 1999. Taiwanese. (Chang Tso-chi) Lee Kang-i, Tsai Ming-shiou, Shie Bau-huei, He Huang-ji.

DARKNESS IN THE LIGHT
NIKKATSU CORP. Feb., 2001. Japanese. (Kei Kumai) Kiichi Nakai, Akira Terao, Naomi Hosokawa, Nagiko Tono, Yukiya Kitamura, Takayuki Kato, Renji Ishibashi, Kazuo Kitamura.

THE DARK ROOM
PARNASSE INTL./BLUE FILMS)/DELUX PRODS)/ GAM FILMS/CNC/CANAL PLUS. May, 2000. French-Luxembourgois-Italian. (Marie-Christine Questerbert) Caroline Ducey, Melvil Poupaud.

THE DARK SIDE OF DAREN
MOMENTUM FILM. Feb., 2001. German. (Maximilian Moll).

THE DARK SIDE OF THE HEART 2
Aug., 2001. Argentine-Spanish. (Eliseo Subiela) Dario Grandinetti, Ariadna Gil, Nacha Guevara, Sandra Ballesteros, Manuel Bandera.

DARK SUMMER
CINERENTA & MARIE HOY FILMS. May, 1999. Canadian. (Gregory Marquette) Jean-Hughes Anglade, Connie Nielsen, Mia Kirshner, Robert Culp, Anne Archer.

DARK WATER
TOHO. Feb., 2002. Japanese. (Hideo Nakata) Hitomi Kuroki, Rio Kanno, Mirei Oguchi, Asami Mizukawa.

DATE WINE
MISR INTL. FILMS. Aug., 1998. Egyptian. (Radwan el-Kashef) Sherihan, Abla Kamel, Hamdy Ahmed, Mohamed Nagati.

DAUGHTER FROM YAN'AN
July, 2002. Japanese. (Kaoru Ikeya).

DAUGHTER OF SUICIDE
HBO/DAUGHTER ONE PRODS. June, 2000. (Dempsey Rice). Documentary.

DAUGHTERS OF LUCK
STUDIO DOM, TV POLSKI/BUDAPEST FILMSTUDIO-LENGYEI TV/MANFRED DURNIOK PRODS. Feb., 1999. Polish-Hungarian-German. (Marta Meszaros) Olga Drozdowa, Jan Nowicki, Masha Petraniuk, Olaf Lubashenko, Ewa Telega.

DAUGHTERS OF THE SUN
FARABI CINEMA FOUNDATION. Aug., 2000. Iranian. (Maryam Shahriar) Altinary Ghelich Taghani, Soghra Karimi, Zahra Mohamadi, Habib Haddad.

DAVIDE'S SUMMER
RAI CINEMAFICTION. Aug., 1998. Italian. (Carlo Mazzacurati) Stefano Campi, Patrizia Piccinini, Tony Bertorelli, Semsudin Mujic.

DAVID HOCKNEY: SECRET KNOWLEDGE
Jan., 2002. (Randall Wright) David Hockney.

DAY AFTER DAY
AGAV FILMS/CINEMA FACTORY. Sept., 1998. Israeli-French. (Amos Gitai) Moshe Ivgi, Hanna Maron, Juliano Merr, Dalit Kahan.

DAYBREAK
SUEDDEUTSCHER RUNDFUNK/MARAN FILM. May, 1998. German.

DAYBREAK
SCOTTISH ARTS COUNCIL LOTTERY FUND/FILMFOUR/ STARHAUS/BASILISK COMMUNICATIONS/TRAUMWERK. (Bernard Rudden) Diane Bell, Flash, Gaynor Purvis, Jean-Philippe Ecoffey, Shauna Macdonald.

DAYDREAM BELIEVER
IN THE RAW PRODS. Jan., 2001. (Debra Eisenstadt) Sybil Kempson, Gladden Schrock, Wendy Lawrence, Andrew Hernon, Louis Puopolo, Sherri Parker Lee, Jacqueline Knapp.

DAYDRIFT
DAYDRIFT PRODS./TELEFILM CANADA. Sept., 1999. Canadian. (Ryan Bonder) Jed Rees, Enuka Okuma, Jim Thorburn, Jillian Fargey, Megan Leitch, Kurt Max Runte, Christine Anton. (Oliver Storz) Stefan Kurt, Karoline Eichhorn, Bruno Ganz.

THE DAY I BECAME A WOMAN
MAKHMALBAF FILM HOUSE. Sept., 2000. Iranian. (Marziyeh Mashkini) Fatemeh Cherag Akhar, Shabnam Toloui, Azizeh Sedighi.

A DAY IN BLACK AND WHITE
JON GOLD AND DESMOND HALL. Mar., 1999. (Desmond Hall) Harold Perrineau, Anthony DeSando, Francie Swift, Joseph Siravo.

THE DAY NEIL ARMSTRONG WALKED ON THE MOON
TALKING HEADS. Nov., 2000. Australian. (Michael Rivette) Rob Steele, Scott Ferguson.

THE DAY OF BIRTH
NATIONAL FILM DEVELOPMENT CORP. Feb., 1999. Indian. (Suma Josson) Nandita Das, Surekha Sikri.

DAY OFF
EURIPIDE DISTRIBUTION. March, 2001. French. (Pascal Thomas) Vincent Lindon, Victoria Lafaurie, Olivier Gourmet, Isabelle Carre, Clara Navarro, Christian Morin, Catherine Frot.

DAY OF THE FULL MOON
KURIER STUDIOS. SEPT., 1998. Russian. (Karen Shakhnazarov) Vladimir Ilyin, Valeri Premykhov, Valeri Storozhik, Anna Germ.

DAYS (GIORNI)
June, 2002. Italian. (Laura Muscardin) Thomas Trabacchi, Riccardo Salerno, Davide Bechini, Riccardo de Filippis, Monica Rametta, Paola Gassman, Bruna Rossi.

THE DAYS BETWEEN
NOVEMBER FILM/ZDF/HFF KONRAD WOLF. Jan., 2001. German. (Maria Speth) Sabine Timoteo, Hiroki Mano, Florian Muller-Mohrungen, Sabine Riedel, Nicole Marischka, Guntram Brattia.

THE DAY SILENCE DIED
PEGASO PRODUCCIONES/SANDKORN FILMPRODUKTION/RED ATB. Jan., 2000. Bolivian-German. (Paolo Agazzi) Dario Grandinetti, Gustavo Angarita, Maria Laura Garcia.

DAYS LIKE THIS
SONET FILM. Nov., 2001. Swiss. (Mikael Hafstrom) Kjell Bergqvist, Christian Fiedler, Lia Boysen, Fares Fares, Eva Fritjofson, Carina M. Johansson, Staffan Kihlbom, Ulla-Britt Norrman.

DAYS OF BREAD AND HEAVEN.
FILMAX. July, 2001. Spanish. (Juan Luis Iborra) Maria Adanez, Carlos Fuentes, Charo Lopez, Veronica Forque, Roberto Alvarez, Nuria Prims, Elisa Matilla.

DAYS OF GRACE
METROPOLIS FILMS. Aug., 2001. Italian. (Glaver Salizzato) Daniele Lotti, Liberto Rabal, Mandala Tyde, Sarah Miles, Ricky Tognazzi, Ugo Pagliai. Riccardo Salerno, Francesco Venditti.

THE DAY THE PONIES COME BACK
TVA INTL./LAZENNEC PRODS./RIVER QUEST ENTERTAINMENT. Aug., 2000. French. (Jerry Schatzberg) Guillaume Canet, Burt Young, Monica Trombetta, Nick Sandow, Jay Rivera, Tony Lo Bianco.

DEAD AVIATORS
ACCENT ENTERTAINMENT/TEMPLE STREET. Apr., 1999. Canadian. (David Wellington) Lothaire Bluteau, Marsha Mason, Michel Monty.

DEAD BABIES
REDBUS FILM DISTRIBUTION. Jan., 2001. British. (Willaim Marsh) Paul Bettany, Katy Carmichael, Hayley Carr, Charlie Condou, Alexandra Gilbreath, William Marsh, Kris Marshall, Andy Nyman.

DEAD BY MONDAY
BUENA VISTA (IN SWITZERLAND). May, 2001. Swiss-German. (Curt Truninger) Helen Baxendale, Tim Dutton, Guylaine St-Onge.

DEAD DOGS
ONE EIGHT FIVE FILMS. May, 1999. (Clay Eide) Joe Reynolds, Jay Underwood, Margot Demeter, John Durbin.

DEAD END
LIONS GATE. Mar., 1999. Canadian. (Richard Ciupka) Luc Picard, Julien Poulin, Michel Goyette, Serge Houde, Lorne Brass.

DEAD LEAVES
RED LION TAMARIS. Oct.,1998. (Constantin Werner) Haim Abramski, Elisabeth Gondek.

DEAD LETTER OFFICE
POLYGRAM FILMED ENTERTAINMENT. May, 1998. Australian. (John Ruane) Miranda Otto, George DelHoyo, Nicholas Bell, Syd Brisbane.

DEAD MAN ON CAMPUS
PARAMOUNT PICTURES. Aug., 1998. American. (Alan Cohn) Tom Everett Scott, Mark-Paul Gosselaar, Poppy Montgomery, Lochlyn Munro.

DEAD MAN'S CURVE
ALAN SIRITZKY/HOPE STREET ENTERTAINMENT. Jan., 1998. (Dan Rosen), Matthew Lillard, Michael Vartan, Randall Batinkoff.

DEAD OR ALIVE
DAIEI CO./TOEI VIDEO CO. Jan., 2000. Japanese. (Takashi Miike) Riki Takeuchi, Show Aikawa, Renji Ishibashi, Hitoshi Ozawa, Shingo Turumi, Kaoru Sugita, Dankan, Hirotaro Honda.

DEAD OR ALIVE: FINAL
Aug., 2002. Japanese. (Takashi Miike) Riki Takeuchi, Show Aikawa, Terence Yin, Josie Ho, Maria Chen, Kenneth Lo, Tony Ho, Jason Chu, Bonnie Lai, Rachel Ngan.

DEALER
ZDF/TRANS-FILM. Feb. 1999. German. (Thomas Arslan) Tamer Yigit, Idil Uner, Birol Unel, Hussi Kutlucan, Lea Stefane

DEAR CLAUDIA
UNITED INTL. PICTURES. Jan., 1999. Australian. (Chris Cudlipp) Bryan Brown, Aleksandra Vujcic, Rel Hunt, Deborah Mailman, Kim Hillas.

DEAR FIDEL: MARITA'S STORY
Sept., 2001. German. (Wilfried Huismann) Documentary.

DEATH: A LOVE STORY
HARKEN. Jan., 1999. (Michelle Le Brun). Documentary.

DEATH IMPACT
PARAMOUNT.May, 1998. (Mimi Leder) Robert Duvall, Tea Leoni, Elijah Wood, Vanessa Redgrave, Morgan Freeman, James Cromwell.

THE DEATH OF A COMPOSER: ROSA, A HORSE DRAMA
KASANDER FILM CO./NPS-TELEVISION, DE NEDERLANDSE OPERA/NVC ARTS. Sept., 2000. Dutch. (Peter Greenaway) Lyndon Terracini, Marie Angel, Miranda van Kralingen, Roger Smeets.

DEATH ON A FULL MOON DAY
PRASANNA VITHANAGE PRODS./JAPAN BROADCASTING. Oct., 1998. Sri Lankan-Japanese. (Prasanna Vithanage) Joe Abeywickrama, Nayana Hettiarachchi, Priyanka Samarawerera.

DEATHROW
Sept., 2001. Filipino. (Joel Lamangan) Eddie Garcia, Cogie Domingo, Jaclyn Jose, Archie Adamos, Richard Arellano, Alvin Bernales, Nonie Buencamino, Mon Confiado.

DEATH TO SMOOCHY
WARNER BROS. March, 2002. (Danny DeVito) Robin Williams, Edward Norton, Catherine Keener, Danny DeVito, Jon Stewart, Harvey Fierstein, Pam Ferris, Michael Rispoli.

THE DEBT
ZEBRA FILM/CANAL PLUS POLAND/ITI. Cinema Feb., 2000. Polish. (Krzysztof Krauze) Robert Gonera, Jacek Boruch, Andrzej Chyra, Joanna Szurmiej, Cezary Kosinski, Agnieszka Warchulska.

THE DEBT COLLECTOR
FILMFOUR DISTRIBUTORS. Feb., 1999. British. (Anthony Neilson) Billy Connolly, Ken Stott, Francesca Annis, Iain Robertson, Annette Crosbie.

THE DEBUT
5 CARD PRODS. AND CELESTIAL PICTURES. Feb., 2001. (Gene Cajayon) Dante Basco, Eddie Garcia, Tirso Cruz III, Gina Alajar, Darion Basco, Dion Basco, Derek Basco, Bernadette Balagtas.

DECEIT
ADRIANA CHIESA ENTERPRISES/FILM MASTER FILM. Sept., 1999. Italian. (Claudia Florio) Jonathan Pryce, Susan Lynch, Claudia Gerini, Enrico Silvestrio, Alessandra Aciai, Brian Prothroe.

DECEMBER 1-31
ZDF/MAINZ/ABBILDUNGSZENTRUM. Aug., 1999. German. (Jan Peters). Documentary.

THE DECLINE OF WESTERN CIVILIZATION PART III
SPHEERIS FILMS. Jan., 1998. (Penelope Spheeris), Documentary.

DEEP BLUE SEA
WARNER BROS. July, 1999. (Renny Harlin) Thomas Jane, Saffron Burrows, Samuel L. Jackson, Jacqueline McKenzie.

THE DEEP END
I5 PICTURE. Jan., 2001. (Scott McGehee, David Siegel) Tilda Swinton, Goran Visnjic, Jonathan Tucker, Raymond Barry, Josh Lucas, Peter Donat, Tamara Hope, Jordan Dorrance.

THE DEEP END OF THE OCEAN
SONY. Feb., 1999. (Ulu Grosbard) Michelle Pfeiffer, Treat Williams, Whoopi Goldberg, Jonathan Jackson.

DEEP IMPACT
PARAMOUNT PICTURES. May., 1998. (Mimi Leder) Robert Duvall, Tea Leoni, Vanessa Redgrave, Elijah Wood, Morgan Freeman.

DEEP INSIDE CLINT STAR
NATIONAL FILM BOARD, CANADA. Oct., 1999. Canadian. (Clint Alberta). Documentary.

DEEP IN THE WOODS
PATHE/FIDELITE PRODS./LE STUDIO CANAL PLUS/GLOZEL DIFFUSION/CANAL PLUS/GIMAGES 3/STUDIO IMAGES 6/ COFIMAGE 11/CNC. Aug., 2000. French. (Lionel Delplanque) Clotilde Courau, Clement Sibony, Alexia Stresi, VIncent Lecoeur.

DEEPLY
VIF FILMPRODUKTION/BELLWOOD STORIES PROD./TIME FILMPRODUKTION/MEG MEDIA GROUP. May, 2000. German-Canadian. (Sheri Elwood) Kirsten Dunst, Lynn Redgrave, Alberta Watson, Julia Brendler, Brent Carver, Peter Donaldson, Tara Rosling.

DEEP RISING
BUENA VISTA. Jan., 1998. (Stephen Sommers) Treat Williams, Famke Janssen, Anthony Heald, Kevin J. O'Connor, Wes Studi.

THE DEER'S ROOM
TELEWIZJA POLSKA. Oct., 1998. Polish. (Lech Majewski) Rafal Olbrychski, Elzbieta Mazur, Mieczyslaw Czepulonis, Agnieszka Wroblewska.

DEE SNIDER'S STRANGELAND
RAUCOUS RELEASING. Oct., 1998. (John Pieplow) Dee Snider, Kevin Gage, Brett Harrelson, Elizabeth Pena.

DEJA VU
RAINBOW FILM CO./REVERE ENTERTAINMENT. Oct., 1998. (Henry Jaglom) Stephen Dillane, Victoria Foyt, Vanessa Redgrave.

DE L'AMOUR
MARS FILMS. April, 2001. French. (Jean-Francois Richet) Virginie Ledoyen, Yazid Ait, Mar Sodupe, Stomy Bugsy, Jean-Francois Stevenin, Bruno Putzulu, Karim Attia, Jean-Marc Thibault.

DELBARAN
OFFICE KITANO AND BANDAI VISUAL. Aug., 2001. Iranian-Japanese. (Abolfazl Jalili) Kaim Alizadeh, Rahmatollah Ebrahimi, Hossein Hashemia, Ahmad Mahdavi.

DELIVERED
BANNER ENTERTAINMENT. May, 1998. (Guy Ferland) David Strickland, Ron Eldard, Leslie Stefanson, Scott Bairstow, Nicky Katt.

DELIVERING MILO
LAKESHORE ENTERTAINMENT. Jan., 2001. (Nick Castle) Bridget Fonda, Albert Finney, Anton Yelchin, Campbell Scott, Lesley Ann Warren, Douglas Spain.

THE DEMOLITION MAN
Aug., 2002. Indian. (Gul Bahar Singh)Chiranjeet, Debasree Roy, Rajit Ka-poor, Sumitra Mookherjee, Dulal Lahiri, Monu Mukherjee, Manjushree, Chandan Sen.

DEMONLOVER
May, 2002. French. (Olivier Assayas) Connie Nielsen, Charles Berling, Chloe Sevigny, Gina Gershon.

DEMON OF THE DERBY
Nov., 2001.(Sharon Marie Rutter). Documentary.

DENIAL
KUSHNER-LOCKE/TAPESTRY FILMS. June, 1998. (Adam Rifkin), Jonathan Silverman, Leah Lail, Ryan Alosio, Amy Yasbeck.

DEPARTURE
TAYHOO TOKYO CO. Feb., 2001. Japanese. (Yosuke Nakagawa) Keigo Heshiki, Haru Kawazu, Tomoyuki Otsuka, Hirokazu Kagawa, Kumi Fujita, Rumi.

DERRIDA
Jan., 2002. (Kirby Dick, Amy Ziering Kofman) Documentary.

THE DERVISH
MIKADO. Aug., 2001. Italian-Turkish. (Alberto Rondalli) Antonio Buil Puejo, Cezmi Baskin, Haldun Boysan, Basak Koklukaya, Erdem Ozipek, Ruhi Sari, Soner Agin.

DESERT BLUE
SAMUEL GOLDWYN CO. Sept., 1998. (Morgan J. Freeman) Brendan Sexton III, Kate Hudson, Christina Ricci, John Heard, Lucinda Jenney.

THE DESERTED STATION (ISTGAH-MATROUK)
Aug., 2002. Iranian. (Alireza Raisian) Leila Hatami, Nezam Manouchehri, Mehran Rajabi, Mahmoud Pak Neeyat.

THE DESERTED VALLEY
Aug., 2002. Vietnamese. (Pham Nhue Giang) Nguyen Hau, Hong Anh, Tuyet Hanh, Thu Trang, Trung Dung, Giang A Phai.

DESERT MOON
SUNCENT CINEMAWORKS/GAGA COMMUNICATIONS/ YOSHIMOTO KOGYO/RENTRAK JAPAN/KOBI/CYBRO. May, 2001. Japanese. Hiroshi Mikami, Maho Toyota, Shuji Kashiwabara, Yukiko Ikari, Isao Natsuyagi, Kumiko Akiyoshi, Kenichi Hagiwara.

DESI
PUBLICFILM. Feb., 2001. Dutch. (Maria Ramos) Documentary.

DESIGN
Jan., 2002. (Davidson Cole) Daniel J. Travanti, Jennifer Morrison, Edward Cunningham, Mary Kay Cook, Davidson Cole, Taylor Miller.

DESIRE
REMSTAR DISTRIBUTION. Sept., 2000. Canadian-German. (Colleen Murphy) Katja Riemann, Zachary Bennett, Elizabeth Shepher.

DESI'S LOOKING FOR A NEW GIRL
MARY GUZMAN. June, 2000. (Mary Guzman) Desi del Valle, Yesenia Aguirre, Sandra Carola, Rosa Medina, Michelle T. Cordero.

DESPERADO SQUARE (KIKAR HA-HALOMOT)
July, 2002. Israeli. (Benny Torati) Yona Elian, Mohammed Bacri, Yosef Shiloah, Uri Gabrielle, Barouh Sason, Yonatan Dani, Y.R Morad.

DESPERATE ACQUAINTANCES
Mefistofilm AS . Feb., 1999. Norwegian. (Svend Wam) Anders Dale, Bjarte Hjelmeland, Bjornar Teigen.

DETAINED
Aug., 2002. Israeli. (Anat Even, Ada Ushpiz) Documentary.

DETECTIVE RIKO
KADOKAWA SHOTEN. Sept., 1998. Japanese. (Satoshi Isaka) Ryoko Takizawa, Toshiya Nagasawa.

DETENTION
ANDERSONFILM. Dec., 1999. (Andy Anderson) John Davies, Marsha Dietlein, Susana Gibb, Meason Wiley, Rebecca Sanabria.

DETROIT ROCK CITY
NEW LINE. Aug., 1999. (Adam Rifkin) Edward Furlong, Giuseppe Andrews, James De Bello, Sam Huntington.

DEUCE BIGALOW: MALE GIGOLO
BUENA VISTA/TOUCHSTONE/HAPPY MADISON/OUT OF THE BLUE ENTERTAINMENT. Dec., 1999. (Mike Mitchell) Rob Schneider, William Forsythe, Eddie Griffin, Arija Bareikis, Oded Fehr, Gail O'Grady, Richard Riehle, Jacqueline Obradors, Big Boy, Amy Poehler).

DEVDAS
May, 2002. Indian. (Sanjay Leela Bhansali) Shah Rukh Khan, Madhuri Dixit, Aishwarya Rai, Jackie Shroff, Kiron Kher, Smita Jayakar.

THE DEVIL AND MS. D
CONSTANTIN FILM. Feb., 2001. German. (Bernd Eichinger) Til Schweiger, Corinna Harfouch, Thomas Heinze, Sonja Kerskes.

THE DEVILS
May, 2002. French-Spanish. (Christophe Ruggia) Adele Haenel, Vincent Rottiers.

THE DEVIL'S ADVOCATE
WARNER BROS. Oct., 1998. (Taylor Hackford), Keanu Reeves, Al Pacino, Charlize Theron, Jeffrey Jones, Judith Ivey, Connie Neilsen.

THE DEVIL'S BACKBONE
WARNER SOGEFILMS. April, 2001. Spanish-Mexican. (Guillermo del Toro) Marisa Paredes, Eduardo Noriega, Federico Luppi.

DEVILS ON THE DOORSTEP
ASIAN UNION FILM & ENTERTAINMENT/CHINA FILM CO-PRODUCTION CORP./CMC XIANDAI TRADE CO./BEIJING ZHONGBO-TIMES FILM PLANNING/HUAYI BROTHERS ADVERTISING. May, 2000. Chinese. (Jiang Wen) Jiang Wen, Jiang Hongbo, Teruyuki Kagawa, Yuan Ding.

DEVIL'S PLAYGROUND
Jan., 2002. (Lucy Walker) Documentary.

DIAL H FOR HITCHCOCK
UNIVERSAL TELEVISION ENTERPRISE/ENCORE MEDIA GROUP /ROCKET SCIENCE LABORATORIES. Oct., 1999. (Ted Haimes) Jonathan Demme, Joseph Stefano, John Michael Hayes, Janet Leigh, Brian De Palma, Curtis Hanson, Pat Hitchcock O'Connell, Norman Lloyd. Documentary.

DIAMOND MEN
DMC FILMS. Nov., 2000. (Dan M. Cohen) Robert Forster, Donnie Wahlberg, Bess Armstrong, Jasmine Guy, George Coe, Kristin Minter.

DIAMONDS
MIRAMAX. Sept. 1999. U.S. German. (John Asher) Kirk Douglas, Dan Aykroyd, Corbin Allred, Lauren Bacall, Kurt Fuller.

DIAMONDS AND RUST
NEW ISRAEL FOUNDATION FOR CINEMA AND TELEVISION. April, 2001. Israeli. (Adi Barash, Ruthie Shatz) Documentary.

DIARY OF A CITY PRIEST
INDEPENDENT TELEVISION SERVICE. Jan., 2001. (Eugene Martin) David Morse, John Ryan, Philip Goodwin, Ana Reeder, Robert Sella, Judy Bauerlin, Mary Louise Burke.

DICK
SONY. July, 1999. (Andrew Fleming) Kirsten Dunst, Michelle Williams, Jim Breuer, Will Ferrell, Dave Foley.

DIE BAD
CNP ENTERTAINMENT. Oct., 2000. South Korean. (Ryoo Seung-wan) Park Seong-bin, Ryu Seung-beom, Bae Jung-shik.

DIGGING TO CHINA
MOONSTONE ENTERTAINMENT. Jan., 1998. (Timothy Hutton) Kevin Bacon, Mary Stuart Masterson, Cathy Moriarty, Evan Rachel Wood.

DIGIMON: THE MOVIE
20TH CENTURY FOX. Sept., 2000. Japanese. (Mamoru Hosoda, Shigeyasu Yamauchi) Lara Jill Miller, Joshua Seth, Colleen O'Shaughnessy, Philece Sampler, Bob Glouberman, Animated.

THE DILAPIDATED DWELLING
ILLUMINATIONS FILMS (LONDON). Oct., 2000. British. (Patrick Keiller) Tilda Swinton.

DILL SCALLION
PEDESTRIAN FILMS. Jan., 1999. (Jordan Brady) Billy Burke, Peter Berg, Lauren Graham, Kathy Griffin, David Koechner.

THE DINNER
MEDUSA. Nov., 1998. Italian. (Ettore Scola) Fanny Ardent, Vittorio Gassman, Stefania Sandrelli, Lea Gramsdorff.

DINNER AND A MOVIE
HIPPIE CHICK FLIX. Feb., 2001. (Lisa Kors) Marianne Hagan, Dave Gibbs, Mike Dooly, Paul Bartel, Anita Gillette, Barbara Gulan.

THE DINNER GAME
GAUMONT BUENA VISTA INTL. April, 1998. French. (Francis Weber) Jacquest Villeret, Thierry Lhermitte, Francis Huster.

DINNER RUSH
GIRALDI SUAREZ DIGIAIMO. Sept., 2000. (Bob Giraldi) Danny Aiello, Edoardo Ballerini, Vivian Wu, Michael McGline, Kirk Acevedo, Sandra Bernhard, John Corbett.

DINOSAUR
BUENA VISTA/ WALT DISNEY PICTURES. May, 2000. (Ralph Zondag, Eric Leighton) D.B. Sweeney, Alfre Woodard, Ossie Davis, Max Casella, Hayden Panettiere, Samuel E. Wright, Julianne Margulies, Peter Siragusa, Joan Plowright, Della Reese (voices). Animated.

THE DINOSAUR HUNTER
CREDO RELEASING/INDEPENDENT MOVING PICTURES. Aug., 2000. Canadian. (Rick Stevenson) Alison Pill, Bill Switzer, Simon McCorkindale, Christopher Plummer, Enuka Okuma.

THE DIPLOMAT
Film Australia/Emerald Films/SBS Independent/Australian Film Commission/NSW Film & TV Office. June, 2000. Australian. (Tom Zubryck). Documentary.

DIRT
CANNED PICTURES. April, 2001. (Michael Covert, Trace Fraim) Michael Covert, Trace Fraim, Patrick Warburton, Tara Chocol, Olivia Rosewood, Luke Perry, Jennifer Tilly.

DIRT BOY
COOL BLUE PICTURES. June, 2001. (Jay Frasco) Jacon Lee Hedman, Luca Bercovici, Arthur J. Walsh, Michelle Cuthrie, Lonnie Framer, Fran Devasto, Maybeth Holland, Mike Zammitto.

DIRTY
DIRTY/STEPHEN HEGYES. Jan., 1998. Canadian. (Bruce Sweeney) Tom Scholte, Babz Chula, Benjamin Ratner, Nancy Sivak.

DIRTY DEEDS
NINE FILMS AND TELEVISION. June, 2002. Australian. (David Caesar) Bryan Brown, Toni Collette, John Goodman, Sam Neill, Sam Worthington, Felix Williamson, Kestie Morassi, William McInnes.

DIRTY LINEN
CDI. Jan. 1999. Italian. (Mario Monicelli) Mechele Placido, Mariangela Melato, Paolo Bonacelli, Alessandro Haber, Marina Confalone.

DIRTY PRETTY THINGS
MIRAMAX FILMS. Sept., 2002. British. (Stephen Frears) Chiwetel Ejiofor, Audrey Tautou, Sergi Lopez, Sophie Okonedo, Benedict Wong, Sotigui Kouyate, Abi Gouhad, Jean-Philippe Ecoffey.

DIRTY WORK
MGM. June, 1998. (Bob Saget) Norm MacDonald, Jack Warden, Artie Lange, Traylor Howard, Don Rickles, Chevy Chase.

DISCO PIGS
RENAISSANCE FILMS. Jan., 2001. Irish-British. (Kirsten Sheridan) Elaine Cassidy, Cillian Murphy, Geraldine O'Rawe, Eleanor Methven, Brian O'Byrne, Darren Healy, Tara Lynne O'Neill, Michael Rawley.

THE DISH
WORKING DOG. Sept., 2000. Australian. (Rob Sitch) Sam Neill, Kevin Harrington, Tom Long, Patrick Warburton, Genevieve Mooy, Tayler Kane, Bille Brown, Roy Billing.

DISH DOGS
FILMWAVE PICTURES. May, 1998. (Robert Kubilos) Sean Astin, Matthew Lillard, Brian Dennehy, Shannon Elizabeth, Maitland Ward.

DISNEY'S THE KID
BUENA VISTA /WALT DISNEY PICTURES/JUNCTION ENTERTAINMENT. June, 2000. (Jon Turteltaub) Bruce Willis, Spencer Breslin, Emily Mortimer, Lily Tomlin, Chi McBride, Jean Smart, Dana Ivey, Daniel von Bargen.

DISPARUS
PERSONA FILMS/LES FILMS DE L'ATALANTE/LES PRODUCTIONS CRITTIN & THIEBAUD/LA TELEVISION SUISSE ROMANDE/CANAL PLUS/LE CENTRE NATIONAL DE LA CINEMATOGRAPHE/L'OFFICE FEDERAL DE LA CULTURE/LA FONDATION GAN POUR LE CINEMA/PROCIREP. Oct., 1999. French. (Gilles Bourdos) Gregoire Colin, Anouk Grinberg, Xavier Beauvois, Frederic Pierrot.

DISTANCE
TV MAN UNION, ENGINE FILM, JAPAN RENTAL SUPPLY SHOP. May, 2001. Japanese. (Hirokazu Kore-eda) Tadanobu Asano, Arata, Yusuki Iseya, Yui Natsukawa, Susumu Terajima.

DISTURBING BEHAVIOR
MGM. July, 1998. (David Nutter) James Marsden, Katie Holmes, Nick Stahl, Stever Railsback, Bruce Greenwood, William Sadler.

DITTO
HANMAC. Oct., 2000. South Korean. (Kim Jeong-kweon) Kim Ha-neul, Yoo Ji-tae, Park Yong-woo, Ha Ji-weon, Kim Min-ju.

DIVA DOLOROSA
FILMMUSEUM (AMSTERDAM). Oct., 2000. Dutch. (Peter Delpeut) Lyda Borelli , Pina Meichelli, Francesca Bertini, Soava Gallone, Helena Makowska. Documentary.

DIVAS: LOVE ME FOREVER
June, 2002. Canadian. (Edimburgo Cabrera) Michelle Ross, Chris Edwards, Jackae Baker, Stephanie Stevens, Matti Dinah, Duchess. Documentary.

THE DIVER
BUENA VISTA INTL. /FILMFABRIKEN, FILM I VAST/SMILE ENTERTAINMENT/NORDIC SCREEN. Jan., 2000. Swedish-Danish. (Erik Gustavson) Stefan Sauk, Izabella Scorupco, Bjorn Floberg, Klaus Maria Brandaue.

DIVERTIMENTO
ALTA FILMS. Oct., 2000. Spanish. (Jose Garcia Hernandez) Francisco Rabal, Federico Luppi, Pastor Rodriguez Feal, Sonia Castelo.

DIVIDED WE FALL
TOTAL HELPART THA/CZECH TELEVISION. Aug., 2000. Czech. (Jan Hrebejk) Boleslav Polivka, Csongor Kassai, Jaroslav Dusek.

DIVINE BODY
UNDERWORLD FILMS. April, 1998. Belgian-Benin. (Dominique Loreau) Alphonse Atacolodjou, Szymon Zaleski, Fidele Gbegnon.

THE DIVINE RYANS
RED SKY/IMAGEX LTD./WIC/VISION TV/TMN/ ENTERPRISE NEWFOUNDLAND & LABRADOR CORP. Sept. 1999. Canadian. (Stephen Reynolds) Jordan Harvey, Robert Joy, Peter Postlethwaite, Wendel Meldrum, Mary Walsh, Richard Boland, Marguerite McNeil.

DIVINE SECRETS OF THE YA-YA SISTERHOOD
WARNER BROS. June, 2002. (Callie Khouri) Sandra Bullock, Ellen Burstyn, Fionnula Flanagan, James Garner, Cherry Jones, Ashley Judd, SHirley Knight, Angus MacFadyen, Maggie Smith, Jacqueline McKenzie.

DIVINE TRASH
STRATOSPHERE. Jan., 1998. (Steve Yeager) Documentary.

DIVORCE IRANIAN STYLE
TWENTIETH CENTRY VIXEN. Aug., 1998. British. (Kim Longinotto, Ziba Mir-Hosseini). Documentary.

DIVORCING JACK
BBC FILMS/WINCHESTER FILMS. May, 1998. British-French. (David Caffrey) David Thewlis, Rachel Griffiths, Robert Lindsay.

DJOMEH
BEHNEGAR FILMS/LUMEN FILMS. May, 2000. Iranian-French. (Hassan Yektapanah) Jalil Nazari, Mahmoud Behraznia Rashid Akbari

THE DOE BOY
EASTON LTD. PARTNERS. Jan., 2001. (Randy Redroad) James Duval, Kevin Anderson, Andrew J. Ferchland, Jeri Arredondo, Jade Herrera, Jim Metzler, Gordon Tootoosis.

DOG DAYS
ALLEGRO FILM PRODUKTION. Sept., 2001. Austrian. (Ulrich Seidl) Maria Hofstatter, Christine Jirku, Victor Hennemann, Georg Friedrich, Alfred Mrva, Erich Finsches, Gerti Lehner.

DOG EAT DOG
FILM FOUR. June, 2001. British-German. (Moody Shoaibi) Gary Kemp, Mark Tonderai, Crunski, David Oyelowo, Melanie Blatt, Nathan Constance.

DOG FOOD
LVN PICTURES. Sept., 2000. Filipino. (Siguion-Reyna) Ricky Davao, Glydel Mercado, Dante Rivero, Alessandra de Rossi.

A DOG OF FLANDERS
WARNER BROS. Aug., 1999. (Kevin Brodie): Jack Warden, Jeremy James Kissner, Jesse James, Jon Voight, Cheryl Ladd.

DOG PARK
LIONS GATE FILMS. Sept., 1998. Canadian. (Bruce McCulloch) Natasha Henstridge, Luke Wilson, Kathleen Robertson, Janeane Garofalo.

A DOG'S DAY
May, 2001. Indian. (Murali Nair) Krishna Kaimal, Thomas, Lakshmi Raman, Sudhas Thayat, Vinu Prasad, Lakshmi Raman.

DOGS' HOME
ADY FILMS (BULGARIA). Feb., 2001. Bulgarian. (Stefan Komandarev)

DOG SOLDIERS
PATHE. British-Luxembourgois. (Neil Marshall) Sean Pertwee, Kevin McKidd, Emma Cleasby, Liam Cunningham, Darren Morfitt, Chris Robson, Leslie Simpson.

DOG STORY
DOG STORY FILMS/SHOVEL GUY MOVIE. June, 2000. (Jian Hong Kuo) Adam Golomb, Maria Cina, Lyle Schwarz, Kevin Cahill, ALice Lentz, Paul Wadleigh, James Servais, Emmett

A DOG'S WILL
GLOBO FILMES. May, 2001. Brazilian. (Guel Arraes) Matheus Nachtergaele, Selton Mello, Luis Melo, Mauricio Goncalves, Fernanda Montenegro, Diogo Vilela, Virginia Cavendish.

DOGTOWN AND Z-BOYS
VANS OFF THE WALL. Jan., 2001. (Stacy Peralta) Documentary.

THE DOGWALKER
March, 2002. (Jacques Thelemaque) Diane Gaidry, Pamela Gordon, Lyn Vaus, Lisa Jane Persky, Alan Gelfant, John Nielsen, Kerry Bishop, Alan DeSatti.

THE DOGWALKER
RITA FILMS/SOUNDELUX ENTERTAINMENT GROUP/BOUQUET MULTIMEDIA. Jan., 2000. (Paul Duran) Will Stewart, Stepfanie Kramer, Tony Todd, John Randolph, Allan Rich, Stacey Williams, Carol Gustafson, Nicki Aycox.

DOG YEARS
AGIT JACK FILM. March, 1998. (Robert Loomis) R. Michael Caincross, Ted Parks, Veronica Loomis, Shawn Smith, Charlie Rivers.

DO IT
Oct., 2001. Swiss. (Sabine Gisiger, Marcel Zwingli) Documentary.

DOLCE
BEREG PRODS. (ST. PETERSBURG)/QUEST TOKYO. Sept., 2000. Russian-Japanese. (Alexander Sokurov) Miho Shimao, Maya Shimao. Documentary.

DOLCE FAR NIENTE
MACT PRODS/FRANCE 2 CINEMA/SINTRA, K2/TELEPIU/CANAL PLUS. Jan., 2000. French-Italian. (Nae Caranfil) Francois Cluzet, Giancarlo Giannini, Isabella Ferrari, Margherita Buy.

DOLE
CE.NA.CI. (GABON)/DIRECT & DIFFERE (FRANCE). Oct., 2000. Gabonese-French. (Imunga Ivanga) David N'Guema-N'Koghe, Emile Mepango, Roland Nkeyi, Evrard Elle.

DOLLS
Sept., 2002. Japanese. (Takeshi Kitano) Miho Kanno, Hidetoshi Nishijima, Tatsuya Mihashi, Chieko Matsubara, Kyoko Fukada, Tsutomu Takeshige.

DOLPHINS
MACGILLVRAY FREEMAN FILMS. Oct., 2000. (Greg MacGillvray) Kathleen Dudzinski, Dean Bernal, Alejandro Acevedo-Gutierrez, Bernd Wursig, Dr. Louis Herman. Documentary.

DOMENICA
MIKADO. Feb., 2001. Italian. (Wilma Labate) Claudio Amendola, Annabella Sciorra, Valerio Binasco, Peppe Servillo.

DON
CMI. May, 1998. Iranian. (Abolfazi Jalili) Farhad Bahremand, Bakhtiyar Bahremand, Farzad Heliili.

DONNIE DARKO
PANDORA. Jan., 2001. (Richard Kelly) Jake Gyllenhaal, Jena Malone, Drew Barrymore, James Duval, Maggie Gyllenhaal, Mary McDonnell, Holmes Osborne.

DON'S PLUM
POLO PICTURES ENTERTAINMENT. Feb., 2001. Amber Benson, Scott Bloom, Kevin Connolly, Leonardo DiCaprio, Jenny Lewis, Tobey Maguire, Heather McComb.

DON'T BREATHE...LOVE IS IN THE AIR
FILMAX/ASTROLABIO PRODUCCIONES/ SOGEDASA/ALMA ATA/DIGITAL. Oct., 1999. Spanish. (Juan Potau) Oscar Ladoire, Carlos Fuentes, Leonor Watling, Ana Risueno.

DON'T CRY GERMAINE
LAURENFILM/COOPERATIVE NOUVEAU CINEMA/Y.C. ALIGATOR/STUPID/OBERON CINEMATOGRAFICA/TCHIN TCHIN PRODS./RTBF. Aug., 2000. Belgian-French-Spanish. (Alain de Halleux) Rosa Renom, Dirk Roofthooft, Cathy Grosjean.

DON'T GO BREAKING MY HEART
POLYGRAM. Jan. 1999. British. (Willi Patterson) Anthony Edwards, Jenny Seagrove, Charles Dance, Jane Leeves, Lynda Bellinghaml.

DON'T LET ME DIE ON A SUNDAY
PROGRAM 33. Sept., 1998. French. (Didier Le Pecheur) Elodie Bouchez, Jean-Marc Barr, Martin Petitguyot, Patrick Catalifo, Gerard Loussine.

DON'T LOOK BACK
EURO SPACE/THE FILM SCHOOL OF TOKYO. Aug., 1999. Japanese. (Akihiko Shiota) Yusaki Suzuki, Shingo Mizuno, Yuria Haga, Yuuya Suzuki.

DON'T MAKE TROUBLE!
GEBEKA FILMS. Dec., 2000. French. (Various Directors)

DON'T SAY A WORD
20TH CENTURY FOX. Sept., 2001. (Gary Fleder) Michael Douglas, Sean Bean, Brittany Murphy, Skye McCole Bartusiak, Guy Torry.

DON'T TELL ANYONE
LOLAFILMS DISTRIBUCION. Sept., 1998. Spanish-Peruvian. (Fransicso J. Lombardi) Santiago Magill, Lucia Jimenez, Christian Meier, Carmen Elias, Hernan Romero, Giovanni Ciccia.

DOORS OF GLORY
MARS FILMS. July, 2001. French. (Christian Merret-Palmair, Benoit Poelvoorde) Benoit Poelvoorde, Julien Boisselier, Michel Duchaussoy.

DORA-HEITA
TOHO/DORA-HEITA PROJECTS/NIKKATSU CORP./YOMIKO ADVERTISING CO./MAINICHI BROADCASTING SYSTEM/EIZO KYOTO FILM CO. Feb., 2000. Japanese. (Kon Ichikawa) Koji Yakusho, Yuko Asano, Bunta Sugawara, Ryudo Uzaki, Tsurutaro Kataoka.

DOUBLE JEOPARDY
PARAMOUNT PICTURES. Sept., 1999. (Bruce Beresford) Tommy Lee Jones, Ashley Judd, Bruce Greenwood, Annbeth Gish.

DOUBLE PACK
PROKINO/CATAPULT FILM/CINE MEDIA FILM. June, 2000. German. (Matthia Lehmann) Markus Knuefken, Eckhard Preuss, Margret Voelker, Jeanne Tremsal, Jochen Nichel, Edgar Selge.

DOUBLE PARKED
FIERCE FILMS/44TH STREET FILM. Mar., 2000. (Stephen Kinsella) Callie Thorne, William Sage, Noah Fleis, Rufus Read, P.J. Brown, Michelle Hurd, Eileen Galindo, Anthony De Sando.

DOUBLE TAKE
BUENA VISTA. Jan., 2001. (George Gallo) Orlando Jones, Eddie Griffin, Edward Hermann, Jarrett Gary Grubbs, Shawn Elliott.

DOUBLE TAP
GOLDEN HARVEST/GH PICTURES CHINA/FILM UNLIMITED. Aug., 2000. Hong Kong. (Law Chi Leung) Lelie Cheung, Alex Fong, Ruby Wong, Monica Chan.

DOUBLE VISION
May, 2002. Taiwanese-Hong Kong. (Chen Kuo-fu) David Morse, Tony Leung Kar-fai, Rene Liu, Leon Dai.

DOUBLE WHAMMY
LIONS GATE. Jan., 2001. (Tom DiCillo) Denis Leary, Elizabeth Hurley, Steve Buscemi, Luis Guzman, Victor Argo, Chris Noth, Keith Knobbs.

DOUG'S 1ST MOVIE
BUENA VISTA. Mar., 1999. (Maurice Joyce). Animated.

DOWN & OUT WITH THE DOLLS
WHYTE HOUSE PRODS. July, 2001. (Kurt Voss) Zoe Poledouris, Kinnie Starr, Nicole Barrett, Melody Moore, Coyote Shivers, Brendan O'Hara, Shawn Robinson.

DOWN FROM THE MOUNTAIN
MIKE ZOSS PRODS. Aug., 2001. (Nick Doob, Chris Hegedus, D.A. Pennebaker) John Hartford, Dr. Ralph Stanley, Terry Bulger, T-Bone Burnett, Ethan Coen, Joel Coen, the Cox Family. Documentary.

DOWNHILL CITY
LUNA FILM, ZDF, DFFB/TALENT HOUSE, TV 4. June, 1999. Finnish. (Hannu Salonen) Franka Potente, Teemu Aromaa, Andreas Brucher, Michaela Rosen, Sebastian Rudolph.

DOWN IN THE DELTA
MIRAMAX. Sept., 1998. (Maya Angelou) Alfre Woodard, Al Freeman, Jr., Mary Alice, Esther Rolle, Loretta Devine, Wesley Snipes.

DOWN TIME
JOINT PRODS. Jan., 2001. (Sean Wilson) WIlliam Van Nolan, Peter Quartaroli, Sam McBride, Joy Garner, James Cotton, David Fine, David Burkson.

DOWN TO EARTH
PARAMOUNT. Feb., 2001. (Chris Weitz, Paul Weitz) Chris Rock, Regina King,Chazz Palminteri, Eugene Levy, Frankie Faison, Marck Addy Greg Germann, Jennifer Coolidge.

DOWNTOWN 81
NEW YORK BEAT FILMS. May, 2000. (Edo Bertoglio) Jean Michel Basquiat, Anna Schroeder, Giorgio Giomelsky, Marshall Chess, Danny Rosen.

DOWN TO YOU
MIRAMAX/OPEN CITY FILM. Jan., 2000. (Kris Isacsson) Freddie Prinze Jr., Julia Stiles, Selma Blair, Shawn Hatosy, Zak Orth, Ashton Kutcher, Rosario Dawson, Henry Winkler, Lucie Arnaz.

DOWN WITH DEATH!
LES FILMS DU LOSANGE. May, 1999. French. (Romain Goupil) Romain Goupil, Marianne Denicourt, Anne Alvaro, Christine Murillo.

DRACULA, PAGES FROM A VIRGIN'S DIARY
Aug., 2002. Canadian. (Guy Maddin) Zhang Wei-Qiang, Tora Birthwhistle, David Moroni, Cindy Marie Small, Johnny Wright.

DRAFTEDODGING
June, 2002. (Wendall Adams) Anson Scoville, Hugh Eaton, Josh Gross, Georgia Lyman, Sara Spraker, Barbara Mather, Melanie Prud'homme.

DRAGONFLY
UNIVERSAL. Feb., 2002. (Tom Shadyac) Kevin Costner, Joe Morton, Ron Rifkin, Linda Hunt, Susanna Thompson, Jacob Vargas, Kathy Bates, Robert Bailey Jr., Jacob Smith, Jay Thomas, Lisa Banes, Matt Craven.

DRAGONLAND
SCHRAMM FILM/ZDF. Jan., 2000. German. (Florian Gartner) Marek Harloff, Peggy Lukac, Julia Richter, Matthias Matz, Inga Busch.

DR. AKAGI
IMAMURA PRODUCTIONS/TOEI CO. May, 1998. Japanese. (Shohei Imamura) Akira Emoto, Kumiko Aso, Jyuro Kara, Masanori Sera.

DR. DOLITTLE
20TH CENTURY FOX. June, 1998. (Betty Thomas) Eddie Murphy, Ossie Davis, Oliver Platt, Peter Boyle, Richard Schiff, Kristen Wilson.

DR. DOLITTLE 2
20TH CENTURY FOX. June, 2001. (Steve Carr) Eddie Murphy, Kristen Wilson, Jeffrey Jones, Kevin Pollak, Raven-Symone.

DREAM
May, 2001. Swedish. (Mikael Hylin) Sinead Cusack, Philip Martin Brown, Joe Absolom, Kelly Harrison, Amita Dhiri, Carmen Dusautoy.

DREAM CAR
MESEART. Feb., 2001. Hungarian. (Barna Kabay) Andreas Stohl, Eszter Onodi, Imre Bajor, Andreas Kern, Zoltan Bezeredi, Judit Pogany, Piroska Molnar.

DREAMERS
AMERICAN ANVIL/DARK LANTERN PICTURES. June, 2000. (Ann Lu) Jeremy Jordan, Mark Ballou, Courtney Gains, Paul Bartel, Brian Krause, Portia Dawson, Ruth de Sosa.

DREAMING OF JOSEPH LEES
20TH CENTURY FOX/FOX SEARCHLIGHT. July, 1999. British- U.S. (Eric Styles) Samantha Morton, Lee Ross, Rupert Graves, Holly Aird, Miriam Margolyes, Frank Finlay.

A DREAM IN HANOI
June, 2002. (Tom Weidlinger) Lorelle Browning, Doan Hoang Giang, Allen Nause, Do Ky, Anh Dung, Doug Miller, Ngan Hoa, Kristen Martha Brown, Quang Thai, Tran Thach, F. Murray Abraham (narrator) Documentary.

THE DREAM IS GONE
AVANTI-FILM. Feb., 2001. German. (Christoph Schuch) Documentary.

DRIFT
A-FILM DISTRIBUTION. Jan., 2001. Dutch. (Michiel van Jaarsveld) Chistel Oomen, Dragan Bakema, Hans Hoes, Bert Luppes.

DRIFT
MARGIN FILMS. May, 2001. Canadian. (Quentin Lee) R.T. Lee, Greyson Dayne, Jonathon Roessler, Desi del Valle, Sebastien Guy, T. Jerram Young, Michel Choban, Marcus Teo.

DRIVE ME CRAZY
20TH CENTURY FOX/AMY ROBINSON. Sept., 2000. (John Schultz) Melissa Joan Hart, Adrian Grenier, Susan May Pratt, Kris Park, Mark Webber, Ali Larter, Stephen Collins, Gabriel Carpenter, Mark Metcalf.

DRAGON TOWN STORY
CHINA STAR ENTERTAINMENT. March, 1998. Hong-Kong-Chinese. (Yang Fengliang) Wu Chien-lien, You Yong, Huang Zhongqiu.

DREAM
MOSFILM. Aug., 2000. Soviet Union–1943. (Mikhail Romm) Elena Kusmina, Vladimir Solovyov, V. Scheglov, Faina Ranevskaya.

THE DREAMLIFE OF ANGELS
BAGHEERA/DIAPHANA/FRANCE 3 CINEMA. May, 1998. French. (Erick Zonca) Elodie Bouchez, Natacha Regnier, Gregoire Colin.

DREAMS IN THE MIDDLE WORLD
PRODUCTORA GRUPO ALYAZ. Sept. 1999. Ecuadorian-Spanish. (Carlos Naranjo Estrella) Hector Alterio, Concha Cuetos, Oscar ladoire, Maria Kosty, Santiago Naranjo, Claudia Gravi, Mirta Mille.

DREAMTRIPS
MUNKFILMS/KINO GEDANKEN EXPERIMENTS. Mar., 2000. Hong Kong-Canadian. (Kal Ng) Jennifer Chan, Wayne Kwok, Gary Sze, WanChi Hong, Jamie Lau, Jane Show, Kal Ng, Damon Mason.

DRESDEN
Jan., 1999. (Ben Speth) Anne Lobst, Erik Kraus, Carol Schneider, Jeff Taylor.

DR. K
FREE CINEMA. Nov., 1999. South Korean. (Kwak Kyeong-taek) Ja In-pyo, Kim Hye-su, Kim Ha-neul, Yu In-chon.

DRIBBLING FATE
DAVID & GOLIAS /INSTITUTO CINEMA CABOVERDIANO/ACT. Feb., 1998. Portuguese-Cape Verdian-French. (Fernando Vendrell) Carlos Germano, Betina Lopes, Paulo Miranda, Daniel Martinho0.

DRIVEN
WARNER BROS. April, 2001. (Renny Harlin) Sylvester Stallone, Burt Reynolds, Kip Pardue, Stacy Edwards, Til Schweiger, Gina Gershon, Estella Warren.

DROP BACK TEN
E FILMS. Jan., 2000. (Stacy Cochran) James LeGros, Amber Valletta, Desmond Harrington, Josh Lucas, Jodie Markell, Laila Robins, Penny Balfour, Ilana Levine, Kelly De Martino, Eddie Kaye.

DROP DEAD GORGEOUS
NEW LINE. June, 1999. (Michael Patrick) Kirsten Dunst, Ellen Barkin, Allison Janney, Denise Richards, Kirstie Alley.

DROPPING OUT
FLEMINGTON PICTURES/BAD CLAMS. Mar., 2000. (Mark Osborne) Kent Osborne, David Koechner, Vince Vieluf, Adam Arkin, John Stamos, Jennifer Elise Cox, Dylan Haggerty.

DROWNING MONA
DESTINATION FILMS/NEVERLAND FILMS/JERSEY SHORE. Feb., 2000. (Nick Gomez) Danny DeVito, Bette Midler, Neve Campbell, Jamie Lee Curtis, Casey Affleck, William Fichtner, Marcus Thomas.

DROWNING ON DRY LAND
CINEVILLE/UNAPIX ENTERTAINMENT. Oct., 1999. (Carl-Jan Colpaert) Barbara Hershey, Naveen Andrews, Carol Lynley, John Joe, Steven Polk.

DR. SEUSS' HOW THE GRINCH STOLE CHRISTMAS
UNIVERSAL. Nov., 2000. (Ron Howard) Jim Carrey, Jeffrey Tambor, Christine Baranski, Bill Irwin, Molly Shannon, Clint Howard, Taylor Momsen, Anthony Hopkins.

DR. T & THE WOMEN
ARTISAN ENTERTAINMENT/SANDCASTLE 5. Aug., 2000. (Robert Altman) Richard Gere, Helen Hunt, Farrah Fawcett, Laura Dern, Shelley Long, Tara Reid, Kate Hudson, Liv Tyler, Robert Hays.

DRYLONGSO
NATION SACK FILMWORK. Oct., 1998. (Cauleen Smith) Toby Smith, April Barnett, Will Power, Channel Schafer, Salim Akil.

D-TOX
UIP. Feb., 2002. (Jim Gillespie) Sylvester Stallone, Tom Berenger, Charles S. Dutton, Sean Patrick Flanery, Christopher Fulford, Dina Meyer, Robert Patrick, Robert Prosky, Courtney B. Vance, Polly Walker, Jeffrey Wright, Kris Kristofferson.

DUDE, WHERE'S MY CAR?
20TH CENTURY FOX. Dec., 2000. (Danny Leiner) Ashton Kutcher, Seann William Scott, Kristy Swanson, Jennifer Garner, Marla Sokoloff, David Herman.

DUDLEY DO-RIGHT
UNIVERSAL PICTURES. Aug., 1999 (High Wilson) Brendan Fraser, Sarah Jessica Parker, Alfred Molina, Eric Idle.

DUETS
BUENA VISTA/ HOLLYWOOD PICTURES/SEVEN ARTS PICTURES/BEACON PICTURES/KEVIN JONES. Sept., 2000. (Bruce Paltrow) Maria Bello, Andre Braugher, Paul Giamatti, Huey Lewis, Gwyneth Paltrow, Scott Speedman, Kiersten Warren, Angie Dickinson.

THE DUKE
KEYSTONE PICTURES/GONE FISHING PRODS. Oct., 1999. Canadian. (Philip Spink) John Neville, James Doohan, Courtnee Draper, Jeremy Maxwell, Oliver Muirhead, Sophie Heyman.

DUMBARTON BRIDGE
BRIDGE PARTNERS. Mar., 1999. (Charles Koppelman) Tom Wright, Esperanza Catubig, Daphne Ashbrook, Leo Burmester.

DUNGEONS & DRAGONS
NEW LINE CINEMA. Dec., 2000. (Courtney Solomon) Justin Whalin, Marlon Wayans, Zoe McLellan, Thora Birch, Bruce Payne, Jeremy Irons, Kristen Wilson, Richard O'Brien.

DURIAN DURIAN
GOLDEN NETWORK, NICE TOP ENTERTAINMENT/FILMS STUDIO CANAL. Sept., 2000. Hong Kong-French. (Fruit Chan) Qin Hailu, Mak Wai Fan, Biao Xiao Ming, Yung Wai Yiu.

DURVAL DISCOS
Sept., 2002. Brazilian. (Anna Muylaert) Ary Franca, Etty Fraser, Marisa Orth, Leticia Sabatella, Isabela Guasco, Rita Lee, Andre Abujamra, Theo Werneck, Tania Boldezan.

DUST
FILM CONSORTIUM. AUG., 2001. British-German-Italian-Macedonian. (Milcho Manchevski) Joseph Fiennes, David Wenham, Adrian Lester, Anne Brochet, Nikolina Kujaca, Rosemary Murphy.

DUST OF NAPLES
FULVIO LUCISANO. May, 1998. Italian. (Antonio Capuano) Gigio Morra, Antonio Iuorio, Gianni Ferreri, Alan De Luca.

DUST TO DUST
ALTAVISTA FILMS. Sept., 2000. Mexican. (Juan Carlos de Llaca) Osvaldo Benavides, Rodrigo Cachero, Ana de la Reguera, Otto Sirgo, Rosa Maria Bianchi, Pilar Ixquic Mata, Alejandro Tomassi.

THE DUTCHMAN'S ISLAND
LAUREN FILM. Sept., 2001. Spanish. (Siegfried Monleon) Pere Ponce, Cristina Plazas, Feodor Atkine, Juli Mira, Roger Casamajor, Francesc Garrido.

DWM (DIVORCED WHITE MALE)
ARC ANGEL FILMS. July, 1999. (Lou Volpe) Lou Volpe, Lauren Bailey, Lydia De Luccia, Veronica Dipippo.

DYING OF LAUGHTER
LOLAFILMS. Mar., 1999. Spanish. (Alex de la Iglesia) Santiago Segura, El Gran Wyoming, Alex Angulo, Carla Hidalgo.

EARTH
BEHAVIOR/MGM. Sept., 1998. Indian-Canadian. (Deepa Mehta) Aamir Khan, Nandita Das, Rahul Khanna, Maia Sethna, Kitu Gidwani.

EAST OF A
SPAN PRODS. Mar., 2000. (Amy Goldstein) Patrick Breen, Nadine van der Velde, David Alan Grier, Glen Chin, Adam Arkin, Mary McCormack, Melanie Mayron, Camryn Manheim.

EASTSIDE
HOLLYWOOD INDEPENDENTS/CANDLELIGHT FILMS. June, 2000. (Lorena David) Mario Lopez, Elizabeith Bogush, Mark D. Espinoza, Efrain Figueroa, Maurice Compte, Richard Lynch.

EAST-WEST
UFD DISTRIBUTION. Aug., 1999. French-Russian-Spanish-Bulgarian. (Regis Wargnier) Sandrine Bonnaire, Oleg Menshikov, Catherine Deneuve, Sergei Bodrov, Jr. Ruben Tapiero.

EATING AIR
UIP/YTC PICTURES/MULTI-STORY COMPLEX/YELLOW RIVER NETWORK. Jan., 2000. Singapore. (Kelvin Tong, Jasmine Ng) Benjamin Heng, Joseph Cheong, Alvina Toh, Ferris Yeo.

EAT, SLEEP, NO WOMEN
Aug., 2002. German. (Heiner Stadler) Documentary.

EBAN AND CHARLEY
MONQUI FILMS/HARCAMONE FILMS. June, 2000. (James Bolton) Brent Fellows, Giovanni Andrade, Ellie Nicholson, Drew Zeller, Pam Munter, Ron Upton, Nolan V. Chard.

EDEN
Sept., 2001. French-Italian-Israeli. (Amos Gitai) Samantha Morton, Thomas Jane, Luke Holland, Daphna Kastner, Danny Huston.

THE EDEN MYTH
TUESDAY NIGHT MOVIES. Feb, 1999. (Mark Edlitz) Rebecca Boyd, Julia Dyon, Justin Kirk, Zohra Lampert.

EDGE CITY
CITY STORY PICTURES. April, 1998. (Eugene Martin) Charlie Hofheimer, Heather Gottlieb, Isidra Vega, Ryan Carmony, Todd Berry.

ED GEIN
FIRST LOOK PICTURES. April, 2001. (Chuck Parello) Steve Railsback, Carrie Snodgrass, Sally Champlin, Carol Mansell, Nancy Linehan Charles, Pat Skipper, Travis McKenna.

EDGE OF NIGHT
MARIANNA FILMS, GREEK FILM CENTRE, ERT, D.P. SKOURAS (GREECE)/LUMIERES. Feb., 2001. Greek-Cypriot. (Nikos Panayotopoulos) Nikos Kouris, Athina Maximou, Zoe Nalbandi, Kostas Markopoulos, Thanasis Viskadourakis, Yannis Rozakis.

EDGE OF SEVENTEEN
BLUE STREAK FILMS/LUNA PICTURES. June, 1998. (David Moreton) Chris Stafford, Tina Holmes, Andersen Gabrych, Stephanie McVay.

EDGES OF THE LORD
MILLENNIUM FILMS. May, 2001. (Yurek Bogayevicz) Haley Joel Osment, Willem Dafoe.

EDTV
UNIVERSAL. Mar., 1999. (Ron Howard) Matthew McConaughey, Jenna Elfman, Woody Harrelson, Sally Kirkland.

EENY MEENY
POZITIV/CZECH TELEVISION. Apr., 2000. Czech. (Alice Nellis) Iva Janzurova, Leos Sucharipa, Theodora Remundova, Eva Holubova,.

THE EGG
CORE IMAGE. Sept., 2000. Taiwanese. (Kuo Tin-Tin, Marc Chen, Peter Ho, Ho-Fong Lin, Ivan Chang, Dean Andrea, Tim Lowry.

8 1/2 WOMEN
WOODLINE PRODUCTIONS LTD./MOVIE MASTERS/DELUX PRODUCTIONS/CONTINENT FILM. May, 1999. British-Dutch-Luxembourgeois-German.(Peter Greenaway) John Standing, Matthew Delamere, Vivian Wu, Shizuka Inoh, Barbara Sarafian.

EIGHT LEGGED FREAKS
WARNER BROS. July, 2002. (Ellory Elkayem) David Arquette, Kari Wuhrer, Scott Terra, Scarlett Johansson, Doug E. Doug, Rick Overton, Leon Rippy, Matt Czuchry, Jay Arlen Jones, Eileen Ryan, Riley Smith, Matt Holwick.

8MM
SONY. Feb., 1999. (Joel Schumacher) Nicolas Cage, Joaquin Phoenix, James Gandolfini, Peter Stormare, Anthony Heald.

EISENSTEIN
VIF 2 AND AMERIQUE FILM. Sept., 2000. German-Canadian. (Renny Bartlett) Simon McBurney, Raymound Coulthard, Jacqueline McKenzie.

EL BONAERENSE
May, 2002. Argentine-Chilean. (Pablo Trapero) Jorge Roman, Dario Levy, Mimi Arduh, Hugo Anganuzzi.

ELECTION
PARAMOUNT. Apr., 1999. (Alexander Payne) Matthew Broderick, Reese Witherspoon, Chris Klein, Jessica Campbell.

ELECTRIC DRAGON 80,000 V
SUNCENT CINEMAWORKS/TAKI CORP. Jan., 2001. Japanese. (Sogo Ishii) Takenori Asano, Masatoschi Nagase.

ELEPHANT JUICE
MIRAMAX. Aug., 1999. British-U.S. (Sam Miller) Emmanuelle Beart, Sean Gallagher, Daniel Lapaine, Daniela Nardini, Mark Strong.

11'09'01 SEPTEMBER 11
BIM. Sept., 2002. French.
Episodes in order of appearance:
1. (Samira Makhmalbaf) Maryam Karimi.
2. (Claude Lelouch) Emmanuelle Laborit, Jerome Horry.
3. (Youssef Chahine) Nour el-Cherif, Ahmed Seif Eldine.
4. (Danis Tanovic) Dzana Pinjo, Aleksandar Seksan, Tatjana Sojic.
5. (Idrissa Ouedraogo) Lionel Zizreel Guire, Rene Aime Bassinga, Lionel Gael Folikoue, Rodrigue Andre Idani, Alex Martial Traore.
6. (Ken Loach) Vladimir Vega.
7. (Alejandro Gonzalez Inarritu)
8. (Amos Gitai) Keren Mor, Liron Levo, Tomer Russo.
9. (Mira Nair) Tanvi Azmi, Kapil Bawa, Taleb Adlah.
10. (Sean Penn) Ernest Borgnine.
11. (Shohei Imamura) Tomorowo Taguchi, Kumiko Aso, Akira Emoto, Mitsuko Baisho, Tetsuro Tanba.

THE ELEVENTH CHILD
PARIS NEW YORK. Sept., 1998. French-Canadian-Vietnamese. (Dai Sijie) Akihiro Nishida, Tapa Sudana, Nguyen Minh Chau.

ELISKA LOVES IT WILD
BONTON FILM/M.D.M./S PRO ALFA FILM/CZECH TELEVISION. July, 2000. Czech. (Otakaro Schmidt) Bolek Polivka, Zuzana Stivinova, Veronika Zilkova, Martin Dejdar, Jiri Labus, Petr Cyvrtnicke.

ELIZABETH
GRAMERCY/POLYGRAM FILMED ENTERTAINMENT. Sept., 1998. British. (Shekhar Kapur) Cate Blanchett, Geoffrey Rush, Christopher Eccleston, Joseph Fiennes, Richard Attenborough, Fanny Ardant.

ELLES
ARTEMIS. Jan., 1998. Luxembourgeois. (Luis Galvao Teles) Miou-Miou, Carmen Maura, Marthe Keller, Marisa Berenson, Guesch Patti.

ELLING
UIP (NORWAY). Aug., 2001. Norwegian. (Petter Naess) Per Christian Ellefsen, Sven Nordin, Per Christensen, Jorgen Langhelle, Marit Pia Jacobsen, Hilde Olausson, Ola Otnes.

EL REY DE ROCK 'N' ROLL
NOW OR NEVER. Feb., 2001. (Marjorie Chodorov) Documentary.

EL VALLEY CENTRO
JAMES BENNING. Jan., 2000. (James Benning). Documentary.

ELVIRA'S HAUNTED HILLS
June, 2002. (Sam Irvin) Cassandra Peterson, Richard O'Brien, Mary Scheer, Scott Atkinson, Mary Jo Smith, Heather Hopper, Gabriel Andronache.

ELVIS & MERILIN
ISTITUTO LUCE. May, 1998. Italian. (Armando Manni) Edyta Olszowka, Goran Navojec, Giorgio Faletti, Toni Bertorelli.

ELVIS GRATTON II-MIRACLE IN MEMPHIS
LIONS GATE. July, 1999. Canadian. (Pierre Falardeau) Julien Poulin, Yves Trudel, Barry Blake, Jacques Theriault.

ELZE'S LIFE
LIETUVOS KINO STUDIO/Q&Q MEDIA. Feb., 2000. Lithuanian-German. (Algimantas Puipa) Egle Jaselskyte, Andrius Paulavicius, Kostas Smoriginas, Janina Lapinskaite, Eduardas Pauliukonis.

EMIL AND THE DETECTIVES
BAVARIA FILM-UND PRODUKTIONS. May, 2001. German. (Tobias Retzlaff, Anja Sommavilla, Jurgen Vogel, Maria Schrader, Kai Wiesinger, Maximilian Befor, David Klock, Tim Hansen.

THE EMPEROR AND THE ASSASIN
SONY. May, 1999. Japanese-Chinese-French. (Chen Kaige) Gong Li, Zhang Fengyi, Li Xuejian, Sun Zhou, Wang Zhiwen.

THE EMPEROR'S CLUB
UNIVERSAL PICTURES. Sept., 2002. (Michael Hoffman) Kevin Kline, Steven Culp, Embeth Davidtz, Patrick Dempsey, Joel Gretsch, Edward Herrmann, Emile Hirsch, Rob Morrow, Harris Yulin, Paul Dano, Jesse Eisenberg, Rishi Mehta, Roger Rees.

THE EMPEROR'S NEW CLOTHES
FILMFOUR DISTRIBUTORS. Aug., 2001. British. (Alan Taylor) Ian Holm Iben Hjelje, Tim McInnerny, Tom Watson, Nigel Terry, Hugh Bonneville, Murray Melvin, Eddie Marsan, Clive Russell.

THE EMPEROR'S NEW GROOVE
BUENA VISTA. Dec., 2000. (Mark Dindal) Animated. David Spade, John Goodman, Eartha Kitt, Patrick Warburton, Wendie Malick, Kellyann Kelso, Eli Russell Linnetz.

EMPIRE
Jan., 2002. (Franc Reyes) John Leguizamo, Peter Sarsgaard, Denise Richards, Vicent Laresca, Delilah Cotto, Sonia Braga, Isabella Rossellini.

EMPTY DAYS
ADR PRODS. Sept., 1999. French. (Marion Vernoux) Valeria Bruni Tedeschi, Patrick Dell'Isola, Sergi Lopez, Florence Thomassin.

EMPTY EYES
Nov., 2001. Italian. (Andrea Porporati) Fabrizio Gifuni, Valeria Mastandrea, Delia Boccardo, Emanuela Macchniz, Gianni Cavina.

THE ENCHANTED INTERLUDE
OCEAN FILMS/DACIA FILMS/FRANCE 2 CINEMA/PERSONA FILMS/CANAL PLUS/CNC. Apr., 2000. French. (Michel Spinosa) Clotilde Courau, Vincent Elbaz, Geraldine Pailhas, Karin Viard.

ENCOUNTER IN THE THIRD DIMENSION
NWAVE. Mar., 1999. (Ben Stassen): Stuart Pankin, Elvira, Harry Shearer, Andrea Thompson.

TO END ALL WARS
June, 2002. British-Thai. (David L. Cunningham) Ciaran McMenamin, Robert Carlyle, Kiefer Sutherland, Mark Strong, Yugo Saso.

ENDGAME
CHANNEL FOUR INTL. Sept., 2000. Irish. (Conor McPherson) Michael Gambon, David Thewlis, Charles Simon, Jean Anderson.

END OF INNOCENCE
MOONSTONE ENTERTAINMENT. May, 1999. (James Rowe) Peter Facinelli, Jay R. Ferguson, Rodney Eastman, Chris Isaak, Amy Irving.

THE END OF THE AFFAIR
SONY/COLUMBIA PICTURES/STEPHEN WOOLLEY. Nov., 1999. British. (Neil Jordan) Ralph Fiennes, Julianne Moore, Stephen Rea, Ian Hart, Samuel Bould, Jason Isaacs, James Bolam.

END OF DAYS
UNIVERSAL/BEACON PICTURES. Nov., 1999. (Peter Hyams) Arnold Schwarzenegger, Gabriel Byrne, Kevin Pollack, Robin Tunney, C.C.H. Pounder, Rod Steiger, Derrick O'Connor.

THE END OF THE ROAD
SLOW LORIS FILMS/JOINT PRODS. Aug., 2000. (Brent Meeske).Bob Weir, Phil Lesh, Mickey Hart, Bill Kruetzmann, Marl Saunders, Wavy Gravy, Babatunde Olatunji. Documentary.

ENDURANCE
BUENA VISTA. Sept., 1998. (Leslie Woodhead, Bud Greenspan) Haile Gebrselassie, Shawananness Gebrselassie, Yonas Zergaw.

THE ENDURANCE: SHACKLETON'S LEGENDARY ANTARCTIC EXPEDITION
MORGAN STANLEY DEAN WITTER. Sept. 2000. (George Butler) Documentary.

ENEMIES OF LAUGHTER
ETERNITY PICTURES/SFERRAZZA PRODS. Nov., 2000. (Joey Travolta) David Paymer, Judge Reinhold, Rosalind Chao, Bea Arthur, Peter Falk, Vanessa Angel, Christina Fulton, Kathy Griffin.

ENEMY AT THE GATES
PARAMOUNT (IN U.S.)/CONSTANTIN FILM (IN GERMANY). Feb., 2001. British-German-Irish. (Jean-Jacques Annaud) Jude Law, Joseph Fiennes, Rachel Weisz, Bob Hoskins, Ed Harris, Ron Perlman, Gabriel Marshall-Thomson, Eva Mattes.

ENEMY OF MY ENEMY
TRIMARK PICTURES. May, 1999. (Gustavo Graef-Marino) Peter Weller, Daryl Hannah, Tom Berenger, Adrian Pintea

ENGEL & JOE
PROKINO. Aug., 2001. German. (Vanessa Jopp) Robert Stadlober, Jana Pallaske, Sabine Berg, Mirko Lang, Steffi Muehlhan, Nadja Bobyleva, Oliver Wolter, Heike Trinker.

ENGINEER KOCHIN'S ERROR
MOSFILM. Aug., 2000. Soviet Union–1939. (Aleksandr Macheret) M. Zharov, S. Nikonov, Lyubov Orlova, N. Dorokhin, B. Petker.

ENGLAND!
TOSSELL PICTURES/ZDF/STUDIO BABELSBERG INDEPENDENTS/GERMAN FILM & TV ACADEMY BERLIN. June, 2000. German. (Achim von Borries) Ivan Shvedoff, Merab Ninidze, Anna Geislerova, Chulpan Khamatova, Maxim Kowalewski,.

ENIGMA
INTERMEDIA FILMS/SENATOR ENTERTAINMENT. Jan., 2001. (Michael Apted) Dougray Scott, Kate Winslet, Saffron Burrows, Jeremy Northam, Nikolaj Coster Waldau, Tom Hollander.

ENLIGHTENMENT GUARANTEED
CONSTANTIN FILM/BERND EICHINGER/MEGAHERZ. Jan., 2000. German. (Doris Dorrie) Uwe Oschsenknecht, Gustav Peter Wohler, Anica Dobra, Ulrike Kriener, Heiner Lauterbach.

ENNUI
GEMINI FILMS/IMA FILMS. Sept., 1998. French. (Cedric Kahn) Charles Berling, Sophie Guillemin, Arielle Dombasle.

ENOUGH
SONY PICTURES ENTERTAINMENT. May, 2002. (Michael Apted) Jennifer Lopez, Billy Campbell, Juliette Lewis, Dan Futterman, Fred Ward, Bill Cobbs, Tessa Allen, Noah Wyle.

ENOUGH ALREADY
WOLFEBORO FILMS. May, 1998. (Tom Keenan) Alanna Ubach, David Wheir, Rick Gomez, Brad Beyer, Paul Wagner.

ENTER: A FILM ABOUT LOS ANGELES
TRUE PICTURES/VERISMO FILM/VEIT BASTIAN. Feb., 2000. German. (Veit Bastian) Edwin Vela, Jim South, Bola Akinwole, Stoo Mundel.

ENTHUSIASM
CINE XXI/PARAISO PRODUCTION DIFFUSION/CARTEL. May, 1999. Chilean-French-Spanish. (Ricardo Larrain) Maribel Verdu, Carmen Maura, Alvaro Escobar, Alvaro Rudolphi, Gianfranco Lebrini.

ENTRAPMENT
20TH CENTURY FOX. Apr., 1999. (Jon Amiel) Sean Connery, Catherine Zeta-Jones, Ving Rhames, Will Patton, Maury Chaykin.

ENTROPY
TRIBECA FILMS. Apr., 1999. (Phil Joanou) Stephen Dorff, Judith Godreche, Kelly Macdonald, Lauren Holly.

ENVY
ADELPHI. Sept., 1999. Australian. (Julie Money) Linda Cropper, Jeff Truman, Anna Lise Phillips, Wade Osborne, Scott Major.

THE ENVY OF GODS
MOSFILM STUDIOS, GENRE FILM STUDIO, GOSKINO OF RUSSIA. Oct., 2000. Russian. (Vladimir Menshov) Vera Alentova, Anatoly Lobotsky, Aleksandr Feklistov, Gerard Depardieu.

EPHEMERAL TOWN
NOTOS FILM PRODS./GREEK FILM CENTER/BAD MOVIES/TELEFILM/G.M. LAZARIDIS. Nov., 2000. Greek. (Giorgos Zafiris) Girogos Dialegmenos, Maria Skoula, Maria Kehayioglou.

ERASABLE YOU
DORIAN. Aug., 1998. (Harry Bromley-Davenport) Timothy Busfield, Jennifer Grant, Melora Hardin, M. Emmet Walsh.

ERIN BROCKOVICH
UNIVERSAL/COLUMBIA PICTURES/JERSEY FILMS. Feb., 2000. (Steven Soderbergh) Julia Roberts, Albert Finney, Aaron Eckhart, Cherry Jones, Marg Helgenberger, Veanne Cox, Conchata Ferrell.

EROTIC TALES
Aug., 2002. German.
An Erotic Tale
(Dito Tsintsadze) Silvina Buchbauer, Lasha Bakradze, Tobias Oertel.
Porn.com
(Bob Rafelson) Rafelson, Fabienne Babe, Trevor Griffiths, Andreas Schmidt, Thomas Morris.
On Top Down Under
(Fridrik Thor Fridriksson)

THE ESCAPE
WANDA VISION/NIRVANA. Sept., 2001. Argentine-Spanish. (Eduardo Mignogna) Miguel Angel Sola, Ricardo Darin, Alberto Jimenez, gerardo Romano, Patricio Contreras, Inez Estevez, Manuel Andres.

ESCAPE TO LIFE: THE ERIKA AND KLAUS MANN STORY
JEZEBEL FILMS/ZERO FILM. Feb., 2001. German-British. (Andrea Weiss, Wieland Speck) Conny Appenzeller, Albrecht Becker, Sol Bondy, Thomas Bronner, Michael Callahan, Dorothee von Diepenbroick, Cora Frost.

ESCAPE TO PARADISE
Sept., 2001. Swiss. (Nino Jacusso) Duzgun Ayhan, Fidan Firat, Nurettin Yildiz, Walo Luond,Domenico Pecoraio, Hasret Yeniyol.

THE ESCAPIST
May, 2002. British. (Gillies MacKinnon) Jonny Lee Miller, Andry Serkis, Gary lewis, Jodhi May, Paloma Baeza, Vas Blackwood.

THE ESCORT
PATHE/CLAUDE BERRI/RENN PRODS./FRANCE 3 CINEMA/PATHE PRODS. /CANAL PLUS/CNC. Oct., 1999. French-British. (Michel Blanc) Daniel Auteuil, Stuart Townsend, Liza Walker, Noah Taylor.

ESPN'S ULTIMATE X
BUENA VISTA. May, 2002. (Bruce Hendricks) Documentary.

ESSEX BOYS
PATHE/GRANADA FILM. Mar., 2000. British. (Terry Winsor) Sean Bean, Alex Kingston, Charlie Creed-Miles, Tom Wilkinson.

ESTHER KAHN
WHY NOT PRODS./LES FILMS ALAIN SARDE/FRANCE 2 CINEMA/FRANCE 3 CINEMA/ZEPHYR FILMS/ARTS COUNCIL OF ENGLAND/BSKYB/BRITISH SCREEN . May, 2000. French-British. (Arnaud Desplechin) Summer Phoenix, Ian Holm, Fabrice Desplechin.

ETERNITY AND A DAY
THEO ANGELOPOULOS FILMS, GREEK FILM CENTRE, GREEK TV/PARADIS FILMS, LA SEPT CINEMA/INTERMEDIAS. May, 1998. Greek-French-Italian. (Theo Angelopoulos) Bruno Ganz, Isabelle Renauld, Achileas Skevis, Despina Bebedeli, Iris Chatziantoniou.

ETOILES: THE PARIS OPERA BALLET COMPANY
Sept., 2001. French. (Nils Tavernier) Documentary.

EUREKA
J WORKS/SUNCENT CINEMAWORKS/LES FILMS DE L'OBSERVATOIRE,/DENTSU/IMAGICA/SUNCENT CINEMAWORKS/TOKYO THEATERS. May, 2000. Japanese. (Shinji Aoyama) Koji Yakusho, Aoi Miyazaki, Masaru Miyazaki, Yohichiroh Saitoh.

EUROPA EXPRESS
BEST HOLLYWOOD. Feb., 1999. Hungarian. (Csaba Horvath) Andras Stohl, Kata Dobo, Ivan Kamaras, Tibor Szilagyi, Zoltan Ratoti.

EURO PUDDING (L'AUBERGE ESPAGNOLE)
Bac Films. May, 2002. French-Spansih. (Cedric Klapisch) Romain Duris, Cecile Defrance, Judith Godreche.

EVA & ADAM: FOUR BIRTHDAYS AND A FIASCO
SVENSK FILMINDUSTRI. March, 2001. Swedish. (Catti Edfeldt) Ellen Fjaestad, Carl-Robert Holmer-Karell, Ulrika Bergman.

EVAGORAS' VOW
Dec., 2001. Cypriot-Greek-Bulgarian. (Andreas Pantzis) Georges Corraface, Valeria Golino, Yannis Voglis, Ilias Aletras, Tania Kazandjieva, Neoklis Neokleous, Andreas Vasileiou.

EVA'S EYE
NORTHERN LIGHTS/NRK/NORDISK FILM. Feb., 2000. Norwegian-Danish. (Berit Nesheim) Andrine Saether, Bjorn Sundquist, Gisken Armand, Sverre Anker Ousdal, Linda Tomine Coles.

EVELYN
UNITED ARTISTS. Sept., 2002. Irish-British. (Bruce Beresford) Pierce Brosnan, Aidan Quinn, Julianna Margulies, Stephen Rea, Sophie Vavasseur, Alan Bates.

EVER AFTER
20TH CENTURY FOX. July, 1998. (Andy Tennant) Drew Barrymore, Anjelica Huston, Dougray Scott, Patrick Godfrey, Megan Dodds.

EVER CHANGING WATERS
DIGIART. Feb., 1998. Argentine. (Marcos Loayza) Jorge Marrale, Marcos Woinski, Noemi Frenkel, Mariano Bertolini.

AN EVERLASTING PIECE
DREAMWORKS (IN U.S.)/SONY PICTURES ENTERTAINMENT (FOREIGN). Dec., 2000. (Barry Levinson) Barry McEvoy, Brian F. O'Byrne, Anna Friel, Colum Convey, Billy Connolly. Pauline McLynn.

EVEREST
MACGILLIVRAY FREEMAN FILMS. March, 1998. (Greg MacGillivray, David Breashears, Stephen Judson) Documentary.

EVER SINCE THE WORLD ENDED
EPIDEMIC FILMS. March, 2001. (Calum Grant) Calum Grant, Adam Savage, Mark Routhier, Angie Thieriot, Josiah Clark, Jessica Viola, Dan Plumlee, Linda Noveroske.

EVERYBODY FAMOUS!
OTOMATIC (BRUSSELS)/GET REEL PRODS. (AMSTERDAM)/LES FILMS DES TOURNELLES (PARIS). Aug., 2000. Belgian-Dutch-French. (Dominique Deruddere) Josse De Pauw, Eva van der Gucht, Werner De Smedt, Thekla Reuten, Viktor Low, Gert Portael.

EVERYBODY LOVES-SUNSHINE
LION'S GATE/IAC HOLDINGS LTD./ISLE OF MAN FILM COMMISSION /BV FILMS INTL./GOTHIC. Nov., 1999. British. (Andrew Goth) Goldie, Andrew Goth, David Bowie, Rachel Shelley, Clint Dyer, Sarah Shackleton, David Baker, Paul Hawkyard.

EVERYBODY SAYS I'M FINE!
Sept., 2001. Indian. (Rahul Bose) Rehaan Engineer, Kowl Purie, Pooja Bhatt, Anahita Uberoi.

EVERYDAY HEROES
Oct., 2001. (Rick Goldsmith, Abby Ginzberg) Documentary.

EVERY DUMPED BOYFRIEND IS LOST
COLUMBIA TRISTAR. Jan., 2001. Italian. (Piero Chiambretti) Piero Chiambretti, Gretha Cavazzoni, Antonio Catania, Vanessa Asbert, Annalisa Bugliani, Carlo Ferrari, Tiberio Fusco, Aldo Izzo.

EVERY NIGHT
TECUMSEH.WORKS. April, 2001. French. (Eugene Green) Alexis Loret, Adrien Michaux, Christelle Prot.

EVERYONE'S HAPPY
Dec., 2001. British. (Frances Lea) Holly de Jong, Alit Kreiz, Anton Mirfo, David Taylor, Mark Vegh.

EVERYTHING FOR A REASON
ASIA MINOR PICTURES. Oct., 2000. (Vlas Parlapanides) Dominic Comperatore, Erin Neill, Matthew Aibel, Hogan Gorman, Tiffany J. Shepis, Mina Manantee, Mike Woodbridge.

EVERYTHING HAPPENS TO ME
Iris Star. July, 2000. Spanish. (Miguel Garcia Borda) Javier Albala, Lola Duenas, Mariam Alamany, Jordi Collet, Christian Brondo.

EVERYTHING PUT TOGETHER
FURST FILMS. Jan., 2000. (Marc Forster) Radha Mitchell, Megan Mullally, Justin Louis, Catherine Lloyd Burns, Alan Ruck, Michele Hicks, Matt Malloy.

EVERYTHING'S FINE (WE'RE LEAVING)
REZO FILMS PRODS/FRANCE 2 CINEMA/REZP FILMS/RHONE-ALPES CINEMA PROD./LA REGION RHONE-ALPES, CENTRE NATIONAL DE LA CINEMATOGRAPHIE/CANAL PLUS/FRANCE 2/SOFICA SOFINERGIE 5, LA PROCIREP. May, 2000. French. (Claude Mourieras) Michel Piccoli, Miou Miou, Sandrine Kiberlain.

EVERYTHING'S GONNA BE GREAT
FILMA-CASS. Feb., 1999. Turkish-Hungarian. (Omer Vargi) Cem Yilmaz, Mazhar Alanson, Selim Nasit Ozcan, Ceyda Duvenci.

EVERYTHING IN PLACE
A NIRVANA/WANDA VISION. May, 2002. Spanish. (Cesar Martinez Herrada) Santiago Ramos, Daniel Guzman, Miguel Rellan.

EVERYTHING'S JAKE
BLACKJACK ENTERTAINMENT/CHRISTOPHER FETCHKO/BOZ PRODS. Mar., 2000. (Matthew Miele) Ernie Hudson, Graeme Malcolm, Debbie Allen, Lou Myers, Robin Givens, Willis Burks II, Stephen Furst, Lou Rawls.

EVERYTHING WILL BE FINE
NDR DONIS J. HEINZE. July, 1998. German. (Angelina Maccarone) Viati Studemann, Chantal de Freitas, Isabella Pavkinson.

EVIL
ROSA FILMES/RADIOTELEVISAO PORTUGUESA/ METROPOLITAN FILMS /CAMELOT PELIS/QUIMERA FILMES. Sept., 1999. Portuguese-Irish-Spanish-Brazilian. (Alberto Seixas Santos) Pauline Cadell, Rui Morrisson, Alexandre Pinto, Maria Santo.

EVOLUTION
DREAMWORKS PICTURES (IN U.S.)/COLUMBIA PICTURES (INTERNATIONAL). June, 2001. (Ivan Reitman) David Duchovny, Orlando Jones, Seann WIlliam Scott, Julianne Moore, Ted Levine, Ethan Suplee, Katherine Towne.

THE EXAM (DADDY'S LAST RUN)
SHOCHIKU/KADOKAWA/HUMAN DREAM. Nov., 2000. Japanese. (Yojiro Takita) Eikichi Yazawa, Yuko Tanaka, Natsumi Ohira.

THE EXECUTION OF WANDA JEAN
Jan., 2002. (Liz Garbus) Wanda Jean Allen, David Presson, Steven Presson, Mary Allen, Ruby Wilson, Rev. Robin Meyers, Rev. Bill Allen, Sandra Howard.

EXECUTIVE PROTECTION
SONET FILM. July, 2002. Swedish. (Anders Nilsson) Jakob Eklund, Samuel Froler,Lia Boysen, Alexandra Rapaport.

EXILED
GAELIC ARTISTS PRODS. July, 1999. (Bill Muir) Paul Ronan, Ronan Carr, Jenny Conroy, Paul Anthony McGraine.

EXILES IN PARADISE
WESLEY LOWE PRODS. June, 2001. Canadian. (Wesley Lowe) Dmitri Boudrine, Benita Ha, JR Bourne, Tatiana Chekhova, Larissa Blajko, Lindsay Bourne.

EXISTENZ
MIRAMAX. Feb., 1999. Canadian-British. (David Cronenberg) Jennifer Jason Leigh, Jude Law, Willem Dafoe, Ian Holm, Callum Keith Rennie.

EXISTO
HOMETOWN PRODS. Apr., 1999. (Coke Sams) Bruce Arnston, Jackie Welch, Jim Varney, Gailard Sartain.

EXIT TO HEAVEN
BAVARIA FILM INTL. Feb., 2001. German. (Brigitte Muller) Frank Giering, Steffen Wink, Catherine Flemming, Uwe Steimle.

EXIT WOUNDS
WARNER BROS. March., 2001. (Andrzej Bartkowiak) Steven Seagal, DMX, Isaiah Washington, Antony Anderson, Michael Jai White, Bill Duke, Jill Hennessy, Tom Arnold, David Vadim.

EXPECTING
Aug., 2002. Canadian. (Deborah Day) Valerie Buhagiar, Angela Gei, Derwin Jordan, Debra McGrath, Tom Melissis, Colin Mochrie.

EXPECT THE UNEXPECTED
MILKYWAY IMAGE. Sept., 1998. Hong Kong. (Patrick Yau) Lau Ching-wan, Simon Yam, Ruby Wong, Hui Shiu-hung, Raymond Wong.

EXPLODING OEDIPUS
FD FILMS (SAN FRANCISCO). June, 2001. (Mark Lafia) Bruce Ramsay,Charlotte Chatton, Tania Meneguzzi, Michael Jacob, James Cotton, Juliana Hatfield, John Detwiler.

EXPULSION FROM PARADISE
BONTON FILM. July, 2001. Czech Republic. (Vera Chytilova) Boleslav Polivka, Vera Havelkova, J.A. Pitinsky, Chantal Poullain, Milan Steindler, Otakar Schmidt, Petr Vacek.

EXTRAORDINARY VISITOR
CINEMA ESPERANCA. Sept., 1998. Canadian. (John W. Doyle) Mary Walsh, Andy Jones, Raoul Bhaneja, Jordan Canning, Rick Boland.

EXTRAS
SAMBOO FINANCE. Sept., 1998. South Korean. (Shin Seung-Soo) Lim Chang-Jeong, Na Han-Il, Park Joon-Hee, Kim Won-Hee.

EXTREMEDAYS
PROVIDENCE ENTERTAINMENT. Sept., 2001. (Eric Hannah) Dante Basco, Ryan Browning, A.J. Buckley, Derek Hamilton.

THE EYE
SONET FILM. Aug., 1998. Swedish. (Richard Hobert) Lena Endre, Samuel Froler, Goran Stangertz, Camilla Lundin.

THE EYE (GIN GWAI)
May, 2002. Hong Kong. (Pang Brothers) Lee Sin-Je , Lawrence Chou, Chutcha Rujinanon, Candy Lo.

EYE BALL
EUROPAFILM/NORSK FILM/FELICIA FILM/PER HOLST FILM. Jan., 2000. Norwegian-Swedish-Danish. (Catrine Telle) Laila Goody, Bjornar Teigen, Marit A. Andreassen, Kristin Kajander, Kjersti Holmen.

EYE OF THE BEHOLDER
BEHAVIOUR WORLDWIDE/VILLAGE ROADSHOW/AMBRIDGE FILM PARTNERSHIP/HIT & RUN/FILMLINE INTL./EYE OF THE BEHOLDER LTD. Sept., 1999. Canadian. (Stephan Elliott) Ewan McGregor, Ashley Judd, Patrick Bergin, k.d. lang, Jason Priestley.

EYE OF THE DAY (DE STAND VAN DE ZON)
June, 2002. Dutch. (Leonard Retel Helmrich) Rumidja, Barkti, Dwi, Ibu Sum and Tani.

THE EYES OF TAMMY FAYE
LIONS GATE/WORLD OF WONDER/CINEMAX. Jan., 2000. (Fenton Bailey, Randy Barbain). Documentary.

THE EYES OF THE HOLOCAUST
STEVEN SPIELBERG. Oct., 2000. (Janos Szasz)

EYES OF THE SPIDER
DAIEI CO. Aug., 1999. Japanese. (Kiyoshi Kurosawa). Sho Aikawa, Dankan, Ren Osugi, Shun Sugata.

EYES WIDE SHUT
WARNER BROS. July, 1999. (Stanley Kubrick) Tom Cruise, Nicole Kidman, Sydney Pollack, Marie Richardson.

FACE
TOKYO THEATRES CO./SHOCHIKU/EIGA GEKIJO/KUHO. Sept., 2000. Japanese. (Junji Sakamoto) Naomi Fujiyama, Etsushi Toyokawa, Michio Ookusu, Kankuro Nakamura, Ittoku Kishibe, Hiroyuki Sato.

FACE
Jan., 2002. (Bertha Bay-Sa Pan) Bai Ling, Kristy Wu, Kieu Chinh, Treach, Will Yun Lee, Tina Chen, Ken Leung.

THE FACES OF THE MOON
IMCINE, FONDO PARA LA PRODUCCION CINEMATOGRAFICA DE CALIDAD, PRODUCCIONES ARTE NUEVA, ARGOS CINE. March, 2001. Mexican. (Guita Schyfter) Carola Reyna, Geraldine Chaplin, Ana Torrent, Carmen Montejo, Diana Bracho, Haydee de Lev.

FACE TO FACE
ROFILM/ARTIS FOUNDATION. Aug., 1999. Romanian. (Marius Theodor Barna) Maia Morgenstern, Serban Ionescu, Serban Pavlu,.

FACE TO FACE
GIANTS ENTERTAINMENT AND DAVID DADON. April, 2001. (Ellie Kanner) Dean Stockwell, Alex Rocco, Joe Viterelli, Thomas Calabro, Scott Baio, Carlo Imperato, Madchen Amick.

FACING
CINEMANE FILM/CARRERE/M6 FILMS/CANAL PLUS. Feb., 2000. French. (Mathias Ledoux) Jean-Hugues Anglade, Clotilde Courau, Christine Boisson, Jose Garcia, Jean Benguigui, Emmanuel Salinger.

FACING THE FOREST
CANAAN GALIL PRODS. (HAIFA). March, 2001. Israeli. (Daniel Wachsmann) Gal Zayad, Yisrael Poliakov, Oved Zaituvi, Tamara Dayan, Said Wahib, Adi Shmueli, Aryeh Buber, Ofer Levy.

FACING THE MUSIC
RONIN FILMS. June, 2001. Australian. (Bob Connolly, Robin Anderson) Documentary.

THE FACULTY
Dimension Films. Dec., 1998. (Robert Rodriguez) Jordana Brewster, Clea DuVall, Laura Harris, Josh Harnett, Shawn Hatosy.

FADING LIGHT
ATTIKA. Feb., 2001. Greek. (Vasilis Douros) Alekos Alexandrakis, Viki Volioti, Vladimir Goloskinski, Elissavet Naslidou, Dimitris Mavropoulos, Babis Hatzidakis, Stella Yanni.

FAG HAG
POTENKIN. July, 1998. (Damion Dietz) Stephanie Orff, Damion Dietz, Sasha Cardona, Darryl Therise, Wil Wheaton, Jaush Way.

FAG HAG
TROMA TEAM/LLOYD KAUFMAN/MICHAEL HERZ. May, 2000. (Damion Dietz) Damion Dietz, Stephanie Orff, Saadia Billman, Wil Wheaton.

FAILAN
TUBE ENTERTAINMENT. May, 2001. South Korean. (Song Hae-seong) Choi Min-shik, Cecilia Cheung, Son Byeong-ho, Kong Hyeong-jin.

FAIRY HILL
VATTATYUK-HUNNIA FILMSTUDIO-MAGIC MEDIA. Feb., 2001. Hungarian. (Andras Szokes) Balazs Csuzdi, Eszter Sarosdi, Szilvia Makai, Andras Szokes, Balazs Galko, Sandor Fabry, Miklos Szuts.

FAITHLESS
SVT DRAMA/AB SVENSK FILMINDUSTRI/NRK/CLASSIC SRL/RAI/ZDF/SWEDISH FILM INSTITUTE/NORDIC FILM & TV FUND. May, 2000. Swedish. (Liv Ullmann) Lena Endre, Erland Josephson, Krister Henriksson, Thomas Hanzon, Michelle Gylemo.

THE FAITH OF THE VOLCANO
VIADA PRODUCCIONES. April, 2001. Argentine. (Ana Poliak) Monica Donay, Jorge Prado.

FALCONS
Sept., 2002. Icelandic-British-Norweigian-German-French. (Fridrik Thor Fridriksson) Keith Carradine, Margret Vilhjalmsdottir, Ingvar E. Sigurdsson.

THE FALL
ALLIANCE. Feb., 1999. British-Canadian-Hungarian. (Andrew Piddington) Craig Sheffer, Helen de Fourgerolles, Jurgen Prochnow.

FALLEN ANGELS' PARADISE
ART. May, 1999. Egyptian. (Oussama Fawzi) Mahmoud Hamida, Lebleba.

FALLEN ARCHES
SARAGHINE FILM CO./PEMDOLA PRODS. Jan., 2000. (Ron Cosentino) Carmine D. Giovinazzo, Justin Louis, Karen Black, Peter Onorati, Richard Portnow.

FALLING LIKE THIS
FROZEN MOTION PICTURES. June, 2001. (Dani Minnick) Brian Vaughan, Megan Wilson, Patricia Clarkson, John Diehl, Elizabeth Ruscio, Harley Venton, Karen Young.

FALLEN
WARNER BROS. Jan., 1998. (Gregory Hoblit) Denzel Washington, John Goodman, Donald Sutherland, Embeth Davidtz.

THE FALLING
SODONA ENTERTAINMENT. Oct., 1998. Canadian. (Raul Sanchez Inglis) Christopher Shyer, Nicole Oliver, Rob Lee, John Cassini

FALLING BODIES
JBA. Aug., 1998. French-German-Haitian. (Raoul Peck) Geno Lechner, Jean-Michel Martial, Bob Meyer, Israel Horovitz.

FALLING INTO THE EVENING
SHOCHIKU CO. Feb., 1998. Japanese. (Naoe Gozu) Tomoyo Harada, Atsuro Watanabe, Miho Kanno, Midori Kiuchi, Ren Osugi.

THE FALSE SERVANT
PYRAMIDE/DACIA FILMS/ LES FILMS DU CAMELIA/CANAL PLUS. Apr., 2000. French. (Benoit Jacquot) Isabelle Huppert, Sandrine Kiberlain, Pierre Arditi, Mathieu Amalric, Alexandre Soulie.

FAME WHORE
APATHY PRODS./BLURCO. Oct., 1998. (Jon Moritsugu) Peter Friedrich, Amy Davis, Victor of Aquitaine, Jason Rail.

FAMILY
AZERBAIJAN FILM STUDIO-AZERKINOVIDEO/IBRUS FILM. Feb., 1999. Azerbaijan-Russian. (Rustam Ibragimbekov) Gasanaga Turabov, Sijavush Kerimi, Svetlana Metkina, Rafiq Aliev, Tachmina Mamedova.

A FAMILY AFFAIR
ATTA GIRL PRODS. July, 2001. (Helen Lesnick) Helen Lesnick, Erica Shaffer, Arlene Golonka, Michele Greene, Michael Moerman.

FAMILY FUNDAMENTALS
Jan., 2002. (Arthur Dong) Documentary.

THE FAMILY MAN
UNIVERSAL PICTURES. Nov., 2000. (Brett Ratner) Nicolas Cage, Tea Leoni, Don Cheadle, Jeremy Piven, Saul Rubinek, Josef Sommer, Makenzie Vega.

FAMILY PACK
BANANA FILMS (BELGIUM)/RENDEZ-VOUS PROD. (FRANCE)/LES FILMS VISION 4 (CANADA)/CAB PRODS. (SWITZERLAND). Oct., 2000. Belgian-French-Canadian-Swiss. (Chris Vander Stappen) Marie Bunel, Helene Vincent, Tsilla Chelton, Mimie Mathy, Macha Grenon.

FAMILY SECRET
Blinding Light/Morgane Production/La Sept Arte. Feb., 2000. U.S.-French. (Pola Rapaport). Documentary.

FAMILY SECRETS
SVENSK FILMINDUSTRI. Jan., 2001. Swedish. (Kjell-Ake Andersson) Rolf Lassgard, Maria Lundqvist, Erik Johansson, Emma Engstrom, Linue Nord, Mats Blomgren, Rebecka Ostergren.

FAMILY TREE
INDEPENDENT ARTISTS/WARNERVISION FILMS/CURB ENTERTAINMENT. Apr, 2000. (Duane Clark) Robert Forster, Naomi Judd, Cliff Robertson, Andy Laurence, Matthew Laurence.

FAMOUS
STELLA MARIS FILMS/DOLLY HALL/GREENESTREET FILMS/ SIDNEY KIMMEL ENTERTAINMENT/LONGFELLOW PICTURES. May, 2000. (Griffin Dunne) Laura Kirk, Nat De Wolf, Daniel London, Griffin Dunne, L.M. Kit Carson, Buck Henry, Sandra Bullock, Carrie Fisher, Linda Blair, Spike Lee, Penelope Ann Miller, Charles Sheen, Mira Sorvino.

FANCY DANCING
Aug., 2002. Canadian-British. (Brock Simpson) Jason Priestley, Tanya Allen, Ewen Bremner, Dave Foley, Deborah Odell, Dave Thomas, Connor Price, Dan Chameroy.

FANDANGO
BUENA VISTA INTL./CALYPSO FILMPRODUKTION/BVI/BAVARIA FILM. Feb., 2000. German. (Matthias Glasner) Nicolette Krebitz, Moritz Bleibtreu, Richy Mueller, Lars Rudolph, Ill-Young Kim.

FANNY AND ELVIS
UIP/SCALA PRODS./FILM CONSORTIUM/IMA Films. Oct., 1999. British-French. (Kay Mellor) Kerry Fox, Ray Winstone, David Morrissey, Ben Daniels, Jennifer Saunders, Colin Salmon.

FANS
FILMAURO. Oct., 1999. Italian. (Neri Parenti) Massimo Boldi, Christian De Sica, Diego Abatantuono, Enzo Iacchetti, Nino D'Angelo.

THE FANTASTICKS
UNITED ARTISTS FILMS. Sept., 2000. (Michael Ritchie) Joel Grey, Barnard Hughes, Jean Louisa Kelly, Joe McIntyre, Jonathon Morris, Brad Sullivan, Teller.

FANTOZZI 2000: THE CLONING
CECCHI GORI/ITALIAN INTL. FILM. Dec., 1999. Italian. (Domenico Saverni) Paolo Villaggio, Milena Vukotic, Anna Mazzamauro.

FARA
ABA STUDIO/NATIONAL PRODUCTION CENTER, REPUBLIC OF KAZAKHSTAN/RUSSIAN STATE COMM. OF CINEMATOGRAPHY. Feb., 2000. Russian-Kazakhstan. (Abai Karpykov) Farkhat Abdraimov, Kristina Orbakaite.

FAR AWAY
UGC IMAGES/CINE B/VERTIGO FILMS. Sept., 2001. French-Spanish. (Andre Techine) Stephane Rideau, Lubna Azabal, Mohamed Hamaidi, Yasmina Reza, Jack Taylor.

FARDA
Aug., 2002. Iranian-Japanese. (Setsuo Nakayama) Osman Mohammadparast, Kai Shishido, Akiko Oshidary.

THE FAREWELL
NOVOSKOP FILM/WDR/ORB/SWR/ARTE/STUDIO BABELSBERG INDEPENDENTS/ARTHUR HOFER/FILMFORFRUNG HAMBURG/ FILMBOARD BERLIN/EUROPEAN SCRIPT/KULTURSTIFTUNG DER DEUTSCHEN BANK. May, 2000. German. (Jan Schutte) Josef Bierbichler, Monica Bleibtreu, Margit Rogall, Jeanette Hain, Samuel Fintzi, Elfriede Irrall.

FAREWELL PAVEL
STUDIO NIEUWE GRONDEN. Feb., 1999. Dutch. (Rosemarie Blank) Valery Kuchareschin, Boris Khvoles, Isil Zabludowskij, Vlatka Simac, Maria Pliatskovskaya.

FAREWELL, TERRA FIRMA!
PIERRE GRIS PRODS./CARAC FILM/ALIA FILM/ISTITUTO LUCE . May, 1999. French-Swiss-Italian. (Otar Iosseliani) Nico Tarielashvili, Lily Lavina, Philippe Bas, Stephanie Hainque, Mirabelle Kirkland.

FAREWELL TRAVELLING PLAYER
LES FILMS DU SUD. Oct., 1998. Moroccan. (Daoud Aoulad-Syad) Abdellah Didane, Med Bastaoui, Hassen Essaklli, Nezha Rahile.

FAR FROM HEAVEN
FOCUS FEATURES. Sept., 2002. (Todd Haynes) Julianne Moore, Dennis Quaid, Dennis Haysbert, Patricia Clarkson, Viola Davis, James Rebhorn, Celia Weston.

FAR FROM SIGHT
MADRAGOA FILMES/GEMINI FILMS. Sept., 1998. Portuguese-French. (Joao Mario Grillo) Cano E Castro, Francisco Nascimento, Henrique Viana, Zita Duarte, Ria Blance.

A FARE TO REMEMBER
BENT TREE. Mar., 1999. (Jim Yukich) Malcolm Jamal Warner, Challen ates, Stanley Kamel, Tracee Ellis Ross.

THE FARM: ANGOLA, USA
GABRIEL FILMS. Jan., 1998. (Jonathan Stack, Liz Garbus) Documentary.

FAROUGH FARROUKHZAD
Feb., 2002. Iranian. (Nasser Saffarian) Narrators: Shahid Yadegarpour, Behnaz Jafari. Documentary.

FASHIONABLY L.A.
GLAM SLAM PRODS. Nov. 1999. (Tamara Olson) Tamara Olson, Darienne Arnold, Holly Laningham, Miranda Gibson, Jenya Lano.

FASSBINDER'S WOMEN
DIE ZEIT TV. June, 2001. German. (Rosa von Praunheim) Irm Hermann, Peer Raben, Ursula Stratz, Hanna Schygulla, Doris Mattes, Harry Baer, Michael Balhaus, Peter Beling.

THE FAST AND THE FURIOUS
UNIVERSAL. June, 2001. (Rob Cohen) Paul Walker, Vin Diesel, Michelle Rodriguez, Jordana Brewster, Rick Yune, Chad Lindberg, Johnny Strong, Matt Schulze, Ted Levine.

FAST FOOD
TWIN PICTURES/FAST FOOD FILMS. May, 1998. British. (Stewart Sugg) Douglas Henshall, Emily Woof, Miles Anderson, Gerard Butler.

FAST FOOD, FAST WOMEN
OCEAN/LUMEN/BIM/PANDORA/PARADIS/ORLY. May, 2000. French-U.S. (Amos Kollek) Anna Thomson, Jamie Harris, Louise Lasser, Robert Modica, Lonette McKee, Victor Argo, Angelica Torn.

FAST SOFA
SNEAK PREVIEW ENTERTAINMENT/NOEL GAY MOTION PICTURES CO. June, 2001. (Salome Breziner) Jake Busey, Crispin Glover, Jennifer Tilly, Natasha Lyonee, Adam Goldberg, Bijou Phillips, Eric Roberts.

FA TALAI JONE
AICHI ARTS CENTER (TOKYO). Oct., 2000. Thai. (Wisit Sasanatieng) Chartchai Ngamsan, Stella Malucchi, Supakorn Kitsuwon, Arawat Ruangvuth, Sombatl, Pairoj Jaisingha, Naiyana Sheewanun.

FATAL DECISION
SHANGHAI FILM STUDIO. Dec., 2000. Chinese. (Yu Benzheng) Wang Qingxiang, Liao Jingsheng, Zuo Ling, Wang Zhenrong.

FATE
May, 2002. Turkish. (Zeki Demirkubuz) Serdar Orcin, Zeynep Tokus, Demir Karahan, Engin Gunaydin.

FATE AS A RAT
Feb., 2002. Bulgarian-Macedonian. (Ivan Pavlov) Ivaylo Hristov, Hristo Garbov, Alexander Doynov.

FAT GIRL
FLACH PYRAMIDE INTL. Feb., 2001. French-Italian. (Catherine Breillat) Anais Reboux, Roxane Mesquida, Libero de Rienzo, Arsinee Khanjian, Romain Goupil, Laura Betti, Albert Goldberg.

FATHER
BEIJING FILM STUDIO/BEIJING SHANHE YINGSHI YISHU/BEIJING GOOD DREAMS. Aug., 2000. Chinese. (Wang Shuo) Feng Xiaogang, Hu Xiaopei, Xu Fan, Qin Yan, Wang Weining, Ye Qing, Yuan Yuan.

FATHER DAMIEN
KINEPOLIS FILM DISTRIBUTION. Mar., 1999. Belgian-Dutch. (Paul Cox) David Wenham, Kate Ceberano, Chris Haywood, Derek Jacobi.

FATHERLESS
JAPANESE ACADEMY OF MOVING IMAGES. Aug., 1999. Japanese. (Yoshihisa Shigeno). Documentary.

FATHERS
Sept., 2001. Chinese. (Lou Jian) Lu Qi, Jin Zhao, Zhu Lei, Li Mengnan, Liu Xin, Liu Tianchi.

FATMA
MK2 DIFFUSION. May, 2001. Tunisian-French. (Khaled Ghorbal) Awatef Jendoubi, Nabila Guider, Bagdidi Aoum, Amel Safta.

FAT WORLD
POLYGRAM FILMED ENTERTAINMENT GMBH. Aug., 1998. British. (Jan Schuette) Juergen Vogel, Julia Filiminow, Stefan Dietrich.

FAUST 5.0
Aug., 2001. Spanish. (Isidro Ortiz, Alex Olle, Carlos Padrissa) Miguel Angel Sola, Eduard Fernandez, Najwa Nimri, Juan Fernandez, Raquel Gonzalez, Irene Montala, Pep Molina.

FAUST, LOVE OF THE DAMNED
LIONS GATE FILMS (IN U.S.)/FILMAX (IN SPAIN). Jan., 2001. Spanish. (Brian Yuzna) Mark Frost, Isabel Brook, Jeffrey Combs, Monica Van Campen, Junix Inocian, Andrew Divoff.

FEAR AND LOATHING IN LAS VEGAS
UNIVERSAL. May, 1998. (Terry Gilliam) Johnny Depp, Benicio Del Toro, Craig Bierko, Ellen Barkin, Gary Busey, Cameron Diaz, Flea.

FEARDOTCOM
WARNER BROS. U.S.-British-German-Luxembourgois. (William Malone) Stephen Dorff, Natascha McElhone, Stephen Rea, Udo Kier, Amelia Curtis, Jeffrey Combs, Nigel Terry, Gesine Cukrowski.

FEBRUARY 15, 1839
LIONS GATE FILMS. Jan., 2001. Canadian. (Pierre Falardeau) Mario Bard, Yvon Barrette, Denis Trudel, Luc Prouix, Stephen F. Jacques, Benoit Dagenais, Jean Guy, Jean-Francois Blanchard.

FEELING SEXY
NICHE PICTURES. Aug., 1999. Australian. (Davida Allen) Susie Porter, Tamblyn Lord, Amanda Muggleton, John Donatiu.

FELICE...FELICE...
NFM DISTRIBUTIE. Jan., 1998. Dutch. (Peter Delpeut) Johan Leysen, Toshie Ogura, Rina Yasima, Noriko Sasaki, Kumi Nakamura.

FELICIA'S JOURNEY
ARTISAN. May, 1999. British-Canadian. (Atom Egoyan) Bob Hoskins, Elaine Cassidy, Arsinee Khanjian, Peter McDonald, Gerard McSorley.

FELIX AND LOLA
PATHE. Feb., 2001. French. (Patrice Leconte) Charlotte Gainsbourg, Philippe Torreton, Alain Bashung, Philippe du Janerand, Ahmed Guedayia, Philippe Soutan.

FELLINI NARRATES–A DISCOVERED SELF-PORTRAIT
RAI/RAI-TECHE/RAI TRADE. Sept., 2000. Italian. (Paquito Del Bosco) Federico Fellini. Documentary.

FEMALE COACH & MALE PLAYER
TIANJIN FILM STUDIO/CCTV MOVIE CHANNEL. Aug., 2000. Chinese. (Qi Jian) Jiang Wenli, Liu Qiang, Chen Baoguo.

FEMALE COMPANY
ODEON/GREEK FILM CENTER/A-SKY/MYTHOS/NIKOS PERAKIS. Feb., 2000. Greek. (Nikos Perakis) Maria Yorgiadou, Smaragda Diamantidou, Sofi Zanninou, Christina Theodoropoulou.

FEMALE2 SEEKS HAPPYEND
BAVARIA FILM. Feb., 2001. German. (Edward Berger) Ben Becker, Isabella Parkinson, Catrin Striebeck, Nicolas von Wacherbarth, Nele Muller-Stofen, Stefan Kurt, Michael Gwisdek.

FEMININE, SINGULAR
PASO DOBLE. Oct., 1999. Italian. (Claudio Del Punta) Cristina Moglia, Danny Quinn, Valentina Chico, Vincenzo Peluso, Lorenza Indovina.

FERDINAND AND CAROLINA
MEDUSA. Mar., 1999. Italian-French. (Lina Wertmuller) Sergio Assisi, Gabriella Pession, Silvana De Santis, Mario Scaccia, Isa Danieli.

FEROCIOUS SAINT LORD OF GOBI
NYAMGAVAA. Jan., 2000. Mongolian. (Ichinmorloo Nyamgavaa) Dogmid Sosorbaram, O. Baigal. N. Dolgor, L. Jamsranja.

THE FESTIVAL
CINEWALLA. April, 2001. Indian. (Rituparno Ghosh) Madhabi Mukherjee, Pradeep Mukherjee, Alakananda Roy, Arpita Pal.

FEVER
SUNLIGHT PICTURES. May, 1999. British. (Alex Winter) Henry Thomas, David O'Hara, Bill Duke, Teri Hatcher, Sandor Tecsy.

FIBER OPTICS
CONSEJO NACIONAL PARA LA CULTURA Y LAS ARTES/ INSTITUTO MEXICANO DE LA CINEMATOGRAFIA/HUBERT BAL FUND. Feb., 1998. Mexican. (Francisco Athie) Roberto Sosa, Lumi Cavazos.

FIDELITY
GEMINI FILMS/FRANCE 3 CINEMA/CANAL PLUS. Apr., 2000. French. (Andrzej Zulawski) Sophie Marceau, Guillaume Canet, Pascal Greggory, Michel Subor, Magali Noel, Edith Scob, Aurelien Recoing.

FIFI MARTINGALE
Sept., 2001. French. (Jacques Rozier) Jean Lefebvre, Lili Vonderfeld, Yves Afonso, Francois Cattot, Jacques Francois, Alexandra Stewart.

FIFTEEN
Aug., 2001. Japanese. (Yoji Yamada) Yuta Kanai, Hidekazu Akai, Rei Asami, Selko Takada, Nenji Kobayashi, Yoko Akino, Takashi Sasano.

MR. FIFTEEN BALLS
MEDUSA. Sept., 1998. Italian. (Francesco Nuti) Francesco Nuti, Sabrina Ferilli, Novello Novelli, Antonio Pertrocelli, Giulia Weber.

15 AMORE
MAURICE MURPHY & FRIENDS/MTXM. Apr., 2000. Australian. (Maurice Murph) Lisa Hensley, Steve Bastoni, Domenic Galati, Tara Jakszewicz, Gertraud Ingeborg, Rhiana Griffith, Joel Pieterse.

15 MINUTES
NEW LINE CINEMA. Feb., 2001. (John Herzfeld) Robert De Niro, Edward Burns, Kelsey Grammer, Avery Brooks, Melina Kanakaredes, Karel Roden, Oleg Taktarov.

THE FIFTH SET: AUSTRALIA AND THE DAVIS CUP
FILM AUSTRALIA. July, 2000. Australian. (Sue Thompson). Documentary.

THE 51ST STATE
A MOMENTUM PICTURES (IN U.K.)/SCREEN GEMS (IN U.S.)/ALLIANCE ATLANTIS (IN CANADA). Dec., 2001. British-Canadian. (Ronny Yu) Samuel L. Jackson, Robert Carlyle, Emily Mortimer, Rhys Ifans, Meatloaf, Sean Pertwee, Ricky Tomlinson, Paul Barber.

54
MIRAMAX. Aug., 1998. (Mark Christopher) Ryan Phillippe, Salma Hayek, Neve Campbell, Mike Myers, Sela Ward, Breckin Meyer.

FIGHT CLUB
20TH CENTURY FOX. Sept., 1999. (David Fincher) Brad Pitt, Edward Norton, Helena Bonham Carter, Meat Loaf Aday, Jared Leto.

FIGHTER
NEXT WAVE FILM. Apr., 2000. (Amir Bar-Lev) Jan Wiener, Arnost Lustig. Documentary.

A FIGHT TO THE FINISH: STORIES OF POLIO
MANDEL/HERRING/TEXAS SCOTTISH RITE HOSPITAL FOR CHILDREN. June, 2000. (Ken Mandel). Documentary.

FIGHT TO THE MAX
SEVENTH ART. NOV., 2001. (Simeon Soffer) Clifford Ettienne, Preston "Spider" George, Fanon Smith, Donald Valere, Willie "Big Toe" Baker, Donald Dickerson, Patrick Stelly, Cornell Stubbs, Ronnie Gaulliet. Documentary.

FILM
LUCKY RED/BROSFILM. July, 2000. Italian. (Laura Betti) Laura Morante, Monica Scattini, Maddalena Crippa, Naike Rivelli.

FILM...
FILMPLUS/MMK/ORTT/TV2.. Feb., 2000. Hungarian. (Andras Suranyi) Ivan Darvas, Hedi Temessy, Peter Haumann, Juli Basti.

THE FILM BIKER
CROWN SEVEN VENTURES. Sept., 2000. Filipino. (Mel Chionglo) Piolo Pascual, Vanna Victoria.

FILM NOIR
MONKEY TOWN. May, 2000. Japanese. (Masahiro Kobayashi) Ryo Ishibashi, Nene Otsuka, Ken Ogata.

FILM 1
LUNA/FLANDERS FILM FUND/CANAL PLUS. Oct., 1999. Belgian. (Willem Wallyn) Peter van den Begin, Herbert Flack, Frank Vander Linden, David Steegen, Carl Ridders, Luc Wallyn, Syliva Kristel.

THE FILTH AND THE FURY
Fine Line/Film-Four/Sex Pistols/Jersey Shore/Nitrate Film. Jan., 2000. British-U.S. (Julien Temple) the Sex Pistols. Documentary.

THIS FILTHY EARTH
FILMFOUR DISTRIBUTORS. Aug., 2001. British. (Andrew Kotting) Rebecca Palmer, Shane Attwooll, Demelza Randall, Xavier Tchili, Dudley Sutton, Ina Clough, Peter Hugo-Daly.

FINAL
INDEPENDENT FILM CHANNEL PRODS.June, 2001. (Campbell Scott) Denis Leary, Hope Davis, Maureen Anderman, Jim Gaffigan, Earl Hindman, Christina Kirk, J.C. Mackenzie.

FINAL CUT
FUGITIVE FEATURES. Nov., 1998. British. (Dominic Anciano) Ray Winstone, Jude Law, Sadie Frost, Holly Davidson, John Beckett.

FINAL DESTINATION
NEW LINE/WAREN ZIDE/CRAIG PERRY. Mar., 2000. (James Wong) Devon Sawa, Ali Larter, Kerr Smith, Kristen Cloke, Daniel Roebuck, Chad E. Donella, Roger Guenveur Smith, Seann William Scott.

FINAL FANTASY: THE SPIRITS WITHIN
SONY PICTURES ENTERTAINMENT. July, 2001. (Hironobu Sakaguchi) ANIMATED. Ming-Na, Alec Baldwin, Ving Rhames, Steve Buscemi, Peri Gilpin, Donald Sutherland, James Woods, Keith David.

THE FINAL LESSON (L'ULTIMA LEZIONE)
June, 2002. Italian. (Fabio Rosi) Roberto Herlitzka, Ignazio Oliva, Chiara Conti, Luciano Federico, Paolo De Vita, Paolo Sassanelli.

FINAL RINSE
POLYVINYL FILM. June, 1999. (Robert Tucker) Terence Goodman, David Cale, Jennifer Regan, Michael Hannon, Frank Gorshin.

FINDER'S FEE
Shavick Entertainment. June, 2001. (Jeff Probst) Erik Palladino, James Earl Jones, Matthew Lillard, Ryan Reynolds, Dash Mihok, Carly Pope, Robert Forster, Francis Bay.

FINDING FORRESTER
SONY PICTURES ENTERTAINMENT. Dec., 2000. (Gus Van Sant) Sean Connery, Rob Brown, F. Murray Abraham, Anna Paquin, Busta Rhymes, April Grace.

FINDING GRACELAND
TCB PRODS. Sept., 1998. (David Winkler) Harvey Keitel, Johnathon Schaech, Bridget Fonda, Gretchen Mol.

FINDING NORTH
REDEEMABLE FEATURES. Jan., 1998. (Tanya Wexler) Wendy Makkena, John Benjamin Hickey, Jonathan Walker.

A FINE DAY
PICKPOCKET ZERO FILM, ZDF. Feb., 2001. German. (Thomas Arslan) Serpil Turhan, Bilge Bingul, Florian Stetter, Seida Kaya.

FINISTERRE (WHERE THE WORLD ENDS)
ALTA FILMS. Oct., 1998. Spanish. (Xavier Villaverde) Nancho Novo, Elena Anaya, Enrique Alcides, Geraldine Chaplin, Chete Lera.

FIONA
AM KO PRODS. Sept., 1998. (Amos Kollek) Anna Thomas, Felicia Maguire, Alyssa Mulhern, Anna Grace, Bill Dawes.

FIRE-EATER
MARKO ROHR PRODS./AQUAVITE FILM & MEDIA AB, SVT DRAMA. May, 1998. Finnish-Swedish. (Pirjo Honkasalo) Elina Hurme, Tiina Weckstrom, Elena Leeve, Elsa Saisio, Vappu Jurkka.

FIREFLY DREAMS
100 METER FILMS. July, 2001. Japanese. (John Williams) Maho Ukai, Yoshie Minami, Tsutomu Niwa, Etsuko Kimata, Atsushi Ono, Chie Miyajima, Kyoko Kanemoto, Sadayasu Yamakawa.

FIRESTORM
20TH CENTURY FOX. Jan., 1998. (Dean Semler) Howie Long, Scott Glenn, William Forsythe, Suzy Amis, Christianne Hirt. Rena Tanaka, Mieko Harada, Mitsuru Hirate, Hiroyuki Sanada.

FIRST, LAST AND DEPOSIT
HECHT CO. Apr., 2000. (Peter Hyoguchi) Jessica White, Sara Wilcox, Don Margolin, Alanna Learned, Alison Coutts-Jordan, Glen Phillips, Jason Hallows.

FIRST LIGHT OF DAWN
CAVIAR. Feb., 2000. Italian. (Lucio Gaudino) Gianmarco Tognazzi, Francesco Giuffrida, Laura Morante, Roberto Nobile.

FIRST LOVE
ENGINE NETWORK/TOKYO BROADCASTING/BANDAI VISUAL/KADOKAWA SHOTEN PUBLISHING CO./DENTSU/DYNASTY. July, 2000. Japanese. (Tetsuo Shinohara)

FIRST LOVE: THE LITTER ON THE BREEZE
BLOCK 2/AMUSE GROUP/JET TONE. Feb., 2000. Hong Kong-Japanese. (Eric Kot) Takeshi Kaneshiro, Karen Mok, Eric Kot, Lee Wai-wai, Vincent Kuk, Lan Sin, Cheung Tik-lung.

THE FIRST NIGHT
A GRUPO TELEVISA FILM PRODUCTIONS. March, 1998. Mexican. (Alejandro Gamboa) Osvaldo Benavides, Mariana Avila.

FIRST OF THE NAME
OGNON/JMH/CANAL PLUS/CNC/EURIMAGES/COMMUNAUTE URBAINE DE STRASBOURG/SCAM. May, 2000. French-Swiss. (Sabine Franel) Philippe Blachais, Albert Blin. Documentary.

FIRST ON THE ROPE
MC4 DISTRIBUTION. July, 1999. French-Italian-Swiss. (Edouard Niermans, Pierre-Antoine Hiroz) Silvia de Santis, Frederic Gorny, Andrea Ferreol, Giuliano Gemma, Didier Bienaime.

FIRST PERSON PLURAL
INDEPENDENT TELEVISION SERVICE/NATIONAL ASIAN AMERICAN TELECOMMUNICATIONS ASSN. Jan., 2000. (Deann Borshay Liem). Documentary.

THE FIRST TIME
MEDUSA FILM . Apr., 1999. Italian. (Massimo Martella) Alessia Fugardi, Valentina Limongelli, Marco Vivio, Costantino Meloni.

THE FIRST $20 MILLION IS ALWAYS THE HARDEST
20TH CENTURY FOX. June, 2002. (Mick Jackson) Adam Garcia, Rosario Dawson, Jake Busey, Enrico Colantoni, Ethan Suplee, Anjul Nigam, Gregory Jbara, Dan Butler, Linda Hart.

F. IS A BASTARD
FILMCOOPERATIVE. Aug., 1998. Swiss-French. (Marcel Gisler) Frederic Andrau, Vincent Branchet, Urs-Peter Halter, Martin Schenkel.

THE FISH IN LOVE
CECCHI GORI. Dec., 1999. Italian. (Leonardo Peraccioni) Leonardo Peraccioni, Yamila Diaz, Paolo Hendel, Patrizia Loreti.Sergio Forconi.

FISHES IN AUGUST
NHK DRAMA PROGRAMS DIVISION. Sept., 1998. Japanese. (Yoichiro Takahashi) Kenji Mizuhashi, Ayumi Ito, Yoshiki Sekino, Ryuzo Hayashi, Tomoko Mayumi.

THE FISHING TRIP
RESOUNDING PICTURES. Sept., 1998. Canadian. (Amnon Buchbinder) Jhene Erwin, Melissa Hood, Anna Henry, Jim Kinney, Dian Tabak.

FISHING WITH GHANDI
VIDEOACTIVE RELEASING. Nov., 1998. (Gabe Weisert) John Reichmuth, James Reichmuth, Dan Klein, Gabe Weisert.

A FIT OF RAGE
RAVINA FILMES. Feb., 1999. Brazilian. (Aluizio Abranches) Alexandre Borges, Julia Lemmertz, Linneu Dias.

THE FIVE SENSES
ALLIANCE ATLANTIS. May, 1999. Canadian (Jeremy Podeswa) Mary-Louise Parker, Philippe Volter, Gabrielle Rose, Daniel MacIvor.

FIXING FRANK
MAXIMUM VACUUM. July, 2001. (Michael Selditch) Dan Butler, Andrew Elvis Miller, Paul Provenza.

FLAMES OF PARADISE
ICELANDIC FILM/LEIKNAR MYNDIR/VIKING FILM/FILMHUSET/PETER ROMMEL. Feb., 2000. Icelanic-Swedish. (Hrafn Gunnlaugsson) Hilmir Snaer Gudnason, Sara Gogg Magnusdottir, Hallgrimur H. Helgason.

THE FLATS
June, 2002. (Kelly Requa, Tyler Requa) Chad Lindberg, Sean Christensen, Jade Herren, Cristen Coppen, Luc Reynaud, Danny Pickering, Lindsay Beamish, Greg Fawcett, Swil Kanim, Brian Sattler, Leif Johnson, Brittany Wedner.

FLAT TYRE
HMC. Oct., 1999. Taiwanese. (Huang Min-Chuan) Ding Ning, Yang Ming-hsuing, Zeng Bodo.

FLAWLESS
MGM/TRIBECA. Nov. 1999. (Joel Schumacher) Robert De Niro, Philip Seymour Hoffman, Barry Miller, Chris Bauer, Skipp Sudduth, Wilson Jermaine Heredia, Bashom Benjamin, Scott Allen Cooper.

FLEEING BY NIGHT
ZOOM HUNT INTL., CENTRAL MOTION PICTURE CORP., BROADBAND FILMS. Oct., 2000. Taiwanese. (Hsu Li-kong, Yin Chi) Rene Liu, Huang Lei,Yin Chao-te, Tai Li-jen, Shi Yaoxuan.

A FLEETING PASSAGE TO THE ORIENT
AICHHOLZER. July, 2000. Austrian. (Ruth Beckermann). Documentary.

FLICKERING LIGHTS
M&M. Jan., 2001. Danish. (Anders Thomas Jensen) Soren Pilmark, Ulrich Thomsen, Mads Mikkelsen, Nikolaj Lie Kaas, Sofie Grabol, Iben Hjejle, Frits Helmuth, Ole Thestrup.

FLIGHT OF THE BEE
Nov., 1998. Tajik.(Jamshed Usmonov, Min Biong Hun) Muhammadjon Shodi, Mastura Ortik, Tahjoymurod Rozik, Fakhriddin Fakhriddin.

THE FLINTSTONES IN VIVA ROCK VEGAS
UNIVERSAL/HANNA-BARBERA/AMBLINE ENTERTAINMENT. Apr., 2000. (Brian Levant) Mark Addy, Stephen Baldwin, Kristen Johnston, Jane Krakowski, Thomas Gibson, Joan Collins, Alan Cumming.

THE FLIP SIDE
PURO PINOY. Jan., 2001. (Rod Pulido) Verwin Gatpandan, Jose Saenz, Ronalee Par, Abe Pagtama, Ester Pulido, Clint Labrador.

FLOWER & GARNET
ODEON FILMS. Aug., 2002. Canadian. (Keith Behrman) Callum Keith Rennie, Jane McGregor, Colin Roberts, Dov Tiefenbach.

FLOWER ISLAND
Sept., 2001. Korean-French. (Son Il Gon) Joo-hee Seo, Yoo-jin Im, Hye-na Kim.

FLOWER OF MANILA
VIVA FILMS. Sept., 2000. Filipino. (Joel Lamangan) Christopher De Leon, Jomari Yllana, Angelu De Leon.

FLOWER SEASON, RAIN SEASON
SHENZHEN FILM CO./SHENZHEN MUNICIPAL PUBLICITY DEPT. Nov., 1998. Chinese. (Qi Jian) Yan Danchen, Yangzi Baiyun, Li Chen, Liu Yin, Cao Peng.

FLOWERS FROM ANOTHER WORLD
IGUANA/ALTA FILMS. May, 1999. Spanish. (Iciar Bollain) Lissete Mejia, Luis Tosar, Marilin Torres, Jose Sancho.

FLOWERS OF SHANGHAI
SHOCHICKU CO. May, 1998. Taiwanese-Japanese. (Hou Hsiao-hsien) Tony Leung Chiu-wai, Michiko Hada, Michele Reis, Carina Liu.

THE FLUFFER
FLUFF AND FOLD. Feb., 2001. (Richard Glatzer, Wash West) Scott Gurney, Michael Cunio, Roxanne Day, Taylor Negron, Richard Riehle, Deborah Harry, Robert Walden.

FLUFFY RHAPSODY
MI-PIX. Oct., 2000. Tawianese. (Wu Mi-sen)Chang Chia-hui, Tsai Cheng-liang, Yeh Shao-hu, Yi Chih-yen, Juan Wen-ping.

FLUSH
LITTLE BELLY PRODS. July, 2001. (Jeffrey Maccubbin) Tai Little, Brett Coy, Arlene Cooney, Shawn Quinlan, William Byrne, Richardson Jones, A Leslie Kies.

FLYING FLYING
DRAGON FILMS. Feb., 2001. Japanese. (Li Ying) Liao Yi-wu, Mang Ke, Zhang Yi.

FLY LOW
SION FILM. Jan., 1999. South Korean. (Kim Sion) Kang Tae-Young, Lee jong-Woo, Jung Jae-Wook, Lim Ji-Eun, Lee Ah-Youngg.

FOCUS
WATERLINE PICTURES. March, 2001. (Roger Roth) Brandon Karrer, Trent Cameron, Gary Gray, Jennifer Joslyn.

FOCUS
PARAMOUNT CLASSICS. Sept., 2001. (Neal Slavin) William H. Macy, Laura Dern, David Paymer, Meat Loaf Aday, Kay Hewtrey, Michael Copeman, Kenneth Welsh.

FOGBOUND
July, 2002. Dutch-British. (Ate de Jong) Luke Perry, Ben Daniels, Orla Brady, Jeroen Krabbe, Ali Hames, Meg Kubota.

FOND MEMORIES OF CUBA
June, 2002. Australian. (David Bradbury) Documentary.

FOOD OF LOVE
LAUREN FILM. Feb., 2002. Spanish-German. (Ventura Pons) Juliet Stevenson, Paul Rhys, Allan Corduner, Kevin Bishop.

FOOLISH
ARTISAN ENTERTAINMENT. Apr., 1999. (Dave Meyers) Eddie Griffin, Master P, Amy Petersen, Frank Sivero.

FOOLISH HEART
HB FILMS/OSCAR KRAMER S.A./FLACH FILM. May, 1998. Brazilian-Argentine-French. (Hector Babenco) Miguel Angel Sola, Mari Luisa Mendonca, Walter Quiroz, Xuxa Lopes, Norma Aleandro.

THE FOOLISH POMEGRANATE TREE
Budapest Filmstudio/Kvali/Grusi/BBSA/MMK/NKA/ORTT. Feb., 2000. Hungarian-Georgian. (Peter Meszaros) Slava Gasparov, Vahtang Komahidze, Magda Anikasvili, Peter Meszaros.

FOOLS GOLD
JANGER. Jan., 1999. (Lane Janger) Blair Singer, Billy Gallo, J.E. Freeman, Camryn Manheim.

FORBIDDEN ENCOUNTERS
FILMAURO/AURELIA CINEMATOGRAFICA. Sept., 1998. Italian. (Alberto Sordi) Alberto Sordi, Valeria Marini, Franca Faldini.

FORBIDDEN GRASS (EVERYTHING YOU WANTED TO KNOW ABOUT CANNABIS BUT THEY NEVER TOLD YOU)
LUCKY RED DISTRIBUZIONE. May, 2002. Italian. (Alberto Amato, Bortone, Georges Bottos, Candida TV, Renato Ciunfrini, Vincenzo Cusumano, Nicola Condemi, Roberto De Franceschi, Juan Gambino, Davide Gaudenzi, Francesco Menghini, Daniele Mazzocca, Arturo Menichetti, Aliocha Merker, Giandomenico Michilin, Marco Onorato, Gianni Russo, Guido Votnao) Documentary.

A FORCE MORE POWERFUL
SANTA MONICA PICTURES /PETER ACKERMAN-YORK ZIMMERMAN. Nov., 1999. (Steve York) Prof. Devavrat Pathak, Alyque Padamsee, Rev. James Lawson, John Lewis, Diane Nash. Documentary.

FORCES OF NATURE
DREAMWORKS. Mar., 1999. (Bronwen Hughes) Sandra Bullock, Ben Affleck, Maura Tierney, Steve Zahn, Blythe Danner.

FOREIGN FIELDS
BALBOA 2/EXITFILM/ZENTROPA. Feb., 2000. Danish. (Aage Reis) Pelle Hvenegaard, Nicolaj Coster-Waldau, John Widerberg.

FOREIGN SISTER
Dan Wolman. July, 2000. Israeli. (Dan Wolman) Tamar Yerushalmi, Askala Marcus, Avi Salton, Miriam Nevo, Neli Tagar, Yosi Asafa.

FOREVER AND EVER
EMPEROR MOVIE GROUP. Feb., 2001. Hong Kong. (Raymond To) Sylvia Chang, Josie Ho, Chris Lee, Chatman To, Joe Cheung, Perry Chin, Lau Tin-chi, Ann Hui, Chin Lau, Fredric Mao, Koo Tin-lung.

FOREVER FEVER
SHAW ORGANISATION/MIRAMAX. July, 1998. Singaporean. (Glen Goei) Adrian Pang, Medlaine Tan, Anna Belle Francis, Pierre Png.

FOREVER HOLLYWOOD
KODAK/AMERICAN CINEMATHEQUE/ESPLANADE PRODS. Dec., 1999. (Todd McCarthy, Arnold Glassman) Warren Beatty, Annette Bening, Jeff Bridges, Andre de Toth, Michael Douglas, Clint Eastwood, Mel Gibson, Salma Hayek, Charlton Heston, Samuel L. Jackson.

FOREVER LULU
MILLENIUM FILMS/CINERENTA/GREEN MOON PRODS./ABRA EDELMAN. July, 2000. (John Kaye) Melanie Griffith, Patrick Swayze, Penelope Ann Miller, Joseph Gordon-Levin, Richard Schiff, Annie Corley.

FOREVER MINE
J&M ENTERTAINMENT. Sept., 1999. British-U.S. (Paul Schrader) Esquema/Alan, Joseph Fiennes, Ray Liotta, Gretchen Mol, Vincent Laresca.

FORGET AMERICA
ARTHAUS FILMVERLEIH/AVISTA FILM/BRAINPOOL TV/KINOWELT/WDR. June, 2000. German. (Vanessa Jopp) Marek Harloff, Franziska Petri, Roman Knizka, Rita Feldmeier, Andreas Schmidt-Schaller, Gerd Lohmeyer.

FORGET BAGHDAD -- JEWS AND ARABS: THE IRAQI CONNECTION
Aug., 2002. Swiss-German. (Samir) Sami Michael, Moussa Houry, Samir Naqqash, Shimon Ballas, Ella Shohat. Documentary.

FORGIVE AND FORGET
SCOTTISH TELEVISION. June, 2000. British. (Aisling Walsh) John Simm, Steven John Shepherd, Laura Fraser, Maurice Roeves.

FORGIVE ME
PHANTA VISION FILM INTL./STICHTING FILMKRACHT. Jan., 2001. Dutch. (Cyrus Frisch) Nico, Chiquita, Peter, Achmed, Verhoef, Astrid, Ellen ten Damme, Sylvie Kristel, Marien Jongewaard.

FORGIVE ME FATHER
MYRIAD ENTERTAINMENT GROUP. May, 2002. (Ivan Rogers) Ivan Rogers, Charles Napier, Alexander Hill, Chris Elbert, Stephen Jon Cohen, Rich Komenich, Rebecca O'Gorman, Jeff Bass.

THE FORGOTTEN ONES
GIOVANNI SCHETTINI. Jan., 2000. Italian. (Piero Livi) Sandro Ghiani, Alex Partexano, Lucio Salis.

FOR LOVE OF THE GAME
UNIVERSAL. Sept., 1999. (Sam Raimi) Kevin Costner, Kelly Preston, John C. Reilly, Jena Malone, Brian Cox.

THE FORSAKEN
SONY PICTURES ENTERTAINMENT. April, 2001. (J.S. Cardone) Kerr Smith, Brendan Fehr, Izabella Miko, Phina Oruche, Simon Rex, Carrie Snodgress, Johnathon Schaech.

FOR SALE
PYRAMIDE. May, 1998. French. (Laetitia Masson) Sandrine Kiberlain, Sergio Castellitto, Jean-Francoise Stevenin.

FORTUNA (MY SISTER)
SHELEG. Aug., 2000. Isreali. (Timna Rosenheimer). Documentary.

FORTUNE TELLERS AND MISFORTUNE
OCEAN DISTRIBUTION. April, 2001. French. (Emmanuelle Beart, Dieudonne, Anemone Zinedine Soualem, Serge Hazanavicius, Valerie Bonneton.

THE FOUR FEATHERS
PARAMOUNT (IN N. AMERICA)/MIRAMAX (INTERNATIONAL). Sept., 2002. U.S.-British. (Shekhar Kapur) Heath Ledger, Wes Bentley, Kate Hudson, Djimon Hounsou, Michael Sheen.

THE FOURTH ANGEL
CINEVA FILMS (IN FRANCE)/ARTISAN HOME ENTERTAINMENT (IN U.S.). Aug., 2001. Canadian-British. (John Irvin) Jeremy Irons, Forest Whitaker, Charlotte Rampling, Jason Priestley, Ian McNeice.

40 DAYS AND 40 NIGHTS
MIRAMAX (IN U.S.)/UNIVERSAL (FOREIGN). Feb., 2002. (Michael Lehmann) Josh Hartnett, Shannyn Sossamon, Vinessa Shaw, Paulo Costanzo, Maggie Gyllenhaal, Michael Maronna, Glenn Fitzgerald, Mary Gross, Stanley Anderson, Adam Trese, Barry Newman, Griffin Dunne, Monet Mazur.

42 UP
FIRST RUN/GRANADA TELEVISION/BBC FILMS. Oct., 1999. British. (Michael Apted). Documentary

THE FOUL KING
B.O.M. FILM/KM CULTURE INVESTEMENT/CINEMA SERVICE. May, 2000. South Korean. (Kim Jee-soon) Song Kang-ho, Jang Jin-yeong, Jang Hang-seon, Park Sang-myeon, Song Yeong-chang.

FOUR CORNERS
JAMES BENNING. Oct., 1998. (James Benning). Documentary.

FOUR DAYS
BEHAVIOUR DISTRIBUTION/CITE-AMERIQUE/GREG DUMMETT FILMS/CANADIAN TV/TELEFILM CANADA/SODEC/HAROLD GREENBERG FUND/TMN-THE MOVIE NETWORKCITY-TV. Sept., 1999. Canadian. (Curtis Wehrfritz) Kevin Zegers, Lolita Davidovich, Colm Meaney, William Forsythe, Anne-Marie Cadieux, Patrick Goyette.

FOUR DOGS PLAYING POKER
HALF MOON ENTERTAINMENT/NEW MOON PRODS. June, 2000. (Paul Rachman) Olivia Williams, Balthazar Getty, Stacy Edwards, Daniel London, Tim Curry, Forest Whitaker, George Lazenby.

FOUR FOR VENICE
BUENA VISTA INTL. May, 1998. German. (Vivian Naefe) Heino Ferch, Aglaia Szyszkowitz, Gedeon Burkhard, Hilde van Nieghem.

4 SEASONS IN ESPIGOULE
REZO FILMS. Mar., 1999. French. (Christian Philibert) The residents of "Espigoule."

14 DAYS TO LIFE
MIL FILM ART & ENTERTAINMENT. May, 1998. German. (Roland Suso Richter) Kai Wiesinger, Michael Mendl, Katharina Meinecke.

FOUR WOMEN
FOLKETS RIO. Feb., 2001. Swedish. (Baker Karim) Monika Miheller, Annette Johnson, Karen Helene Haugaard, Malin Bjorklund, Josef Saterhagen, Urban Gustavson, Erik Olsson.

FRAGMENTS * JERUSALEM
RON AND JACQUELINE HAVILIO. Sept., 1998. Israeli. (Ron Havilio) Documentary.

FRAGMENTS OF LIFE
ZALA'MEN/PBC PICTURES. Feb., 2000. Cameroon-Belgian. (Francois L. Woukoache) Tshilombo Lubambu, Deneuve Djobong, Jean Bediebe, Helene Beleck, Jerome Bolo, Therese Ngo Ngambi.

FRAILTY
LIONS GATE FILMS. Feb., 2002. (Bill Paxton) Bill Paxton, Matthew McConaughey, Powers Boothe, Matt O'Leary, Luke Askew, Jeremy Sumpter, Derk Cheetwood, Melissa Crider, Alan Davidson, Cynthia Ettinger, Vincent Chase.

FRIDA
MIRAMAX (IN U.S.). Aug., 2002. (Julie Taymor) Salma Hayek, Alfred Molina, Geoffrey Rush, Ashley Judd, Antonio Banderas, Edward Norton, Valeria Golino, Mia Maestro, Roger Rees, Patricia Reyes Spindola, Saffron Burrows.

THE FRAME
SUPER VISION/ASMIK ACE/KINEMA JUNPOSHA/ENVIRONMENT ART LABORATORY/FORWARD GROUP. Feb., 2000. Japanese. (Satoshi Isaka) Hitomi Kuroki, Tetsuo Yamashita, Toshio Kakei, Takanori Jinnai, Akira Shirai, Saburo Shinoda, Takeo Nakahara.

FRANCE, HERE WE COME!
Lotus. July, 2000., Austrian. (Michael Glawogger). Documentary.

FRANCESCA AND NUNZIATA
MEDIATRADE. Aug., 2001. Italian. (Lina Wertmuller) Sophia Loren, Giancarlo Giannini, Claudia Gerini, Raoul Bova, Carmen Femiano, Domenico Orsini, Vanessa Sabet.

FRANK LLOYD WRIGHT
FLORENTINE FILMS. Jan., 1998. (Ken Burns, Lynn Novick) Documentary.

FRANK SPADONE
CINE B/LES FILMS ALAIN SARDE/HACHETTE. Sept., 1999. French. (Richard Bean) Monica Bellucci, Stanislas Mehrar, Carlo Brandt, Antoine Fayard, Christophe Le Masne, Jean-Claude Lecas.

FREAKS, GLAM GODS AND ROCK STARS...THE NYC STORY
Ryanisland Films. Aug., 2001. (John T. Ryan) Kevin Aviance, Jayne County, Theo Kogan, Sami Yaffa, Karmen Guy, Kembra Phaler, Sean, Donovan Leitch, Laurel Barclay. Documentary.

FREAK TALKS ABOUT SEX
NEW SKY COMMUNICATIONS/LATENT IMAGE ENTERTAINMENT. June, 1999. (Paul Todisco): Josh Hamilton, Steve Zahn, Heather McComb, Arabella Field, David Kinney.

FREAK WEATHER
SPARRING PARTNERS I/HKM FILMS/BLURCO. Sept., 1999. (Mary Kuryla) Jacqueline McKenzie, Aida Turturro, John Carroll Lynch, Jacob Chase, Jerry Adler, Robert Wisdom, Justin Pierce, John Heard.

FREDDY GOT FINGERED
20TH CENTURY FOX. April, 2001. (Tom Green) Tom Green, Rip Torn, Marisa Coughlan, Eddie Kaye Thomas, Harland Williams, Anthony Michael Hall, Julie Hagert.

FREEDOM
4L. April, 2001. Argentine. (Lisandro Alonso) Misael Saavedra, Humberto Estrada, Rafael Estrada, Omar Didino, Javier Didino. Documentary.

FREE ENTERPRISE
MINDFIRE ENTERTAINMENT. Oct., 1998. (Robert Meyer) Rafer Weigel, Eric McCormack, Audie England, Patrick Van Horn.

THE FREELANCERS
LES FILMS A UN DOLLAR. Sept., 1998. French. (Denis Dercourt) Pierre Lacan, Marc Citti, Philippe Clay, Henri Garcin, Marie-Christine Laurent.

FREESTYLE
ORGANIC FILMS. Apr., 2000. (Kevin Fitzgerald) Mos Def, the Last Poets, Freestyle Fellowship, Pharoahe Monch, Medusa, Divine Styler, Supernatural, Cut Chemist.

FREE THE FISH
MEDUSA FILM/CATTLEYA/CINERITMO. Jan., 2000. Italian. (Cristina Comencini) Laura Morante, Francesco Paolantoni, Michele Placido.

FREE TIBET
SHOOTING GALLERY. Aug., 1998. (Sarah Pirozek) Documentary.

FREEWHEELING
CECCHI GORI DISTRIBUZIONE. Dec., 2000. Italian. (Vincenzo Salemme) Vincenzo Salemme, Sabrina Ferilli, Carlo Buccirosso, Manuela Arcuri, Massimo Ceccherini, Maurizio Casagrande.

FRENCH DRESSING
DAIEI CO. Feb., 1998. Japanese. (Hisashi Saito) Munehisa Sakurada, Miako Tadano, Hiroshi Abe, Rumi, Shuuhei Minami.

THE FRENCHMAN'S SON
PATHE/FILM PAR FILM/TF1 FILM/TPS/COFIMAGE 10. Jan. 2000. French. (Gerard Lauzier) Josiane Balasko, Fanny Ardant, Thierry Fremont, David-Alexandre Parquier, Luca Barbareschi, George Aguilar.

FREQUENCY
NEW LINE. Apr., 2000. (Gregory Hoblit) Dennis Quaid, Jim Caviezel, Andre Braugher, Elizabeth Mitchell, Noah Emmerich, Shawn Doyle, Jordan Bridges, Melissa Errico.

FRESH AIR
R.B. FILMS/AUSTRALIAN FILM COMMISSION/SBS INDEPENDENT/PREMIUM MOVIE PARTNERSHP. Jan., 1999. Australian.(Neil Mansfield) Nadine Garner, Bridie Carter, Marin Mimica, Tony Barry, Julie Hamilton.

FRESHMEN
STODDARD TEMPLE. Feb., 2000. (Tom Huang) N.D. Brown, Tom Huang, Kurt Kohler, Margaret Scarborough, Wendy Speake, Mary Chen, Richard Guiton, Jake White, Sonya Leslie, Partick Gorman.

FREUD'S 2ND LAW
GORILLA FILMS. MArch, 2001. (Ian Gamazon) Amy Shelton-White, Tim Duquette, Lee Smith, Earle Dittebrandt, J.D. Karas.

FRIDAY NIGHT (VENDREDI SOIR)
BAC DISTRIBUTION. Aug., 2002. French. (Claire Denis) Valerie Lemercier, Vincent Lindon,Helene de Saint Pere, Helene Fillieres.

FRIEND
KOREA PICTURES. May, 2001. South Korean. (Kwak Kyung-taek) Yu Oh-seong, Jang Dong-keon, Seo Tae-hwa, Jeong Un-taek, Im Bo-kyeong, Ju Hyeon, Ki Ju-bong.

FRIENDLY FIRE
DEZENOVE SOM E IMAGENS. Sept., 1998. Brazilian. (Beto Brant) Leonardo Villar, ZeCarlos Machados, Caca Amaral, Genesio de Barros.

FRIENDLY PERSUASION: IRANIAN CINEMA AFTER THE REVOLUTION
JAM-HI PRODS. Aug., 2000. (Jamsheed Akrami) Abbas Kiarosami, Mohsen Makhmalbaf, Dariush Mehrjui, Bahram Bayzai, Masoud Kimiai, Rakhshan Bani Etemad, Ebraheem Hatami Kia. Documentary.

FRIENDS AND FAMILY
CHARLESON PICTURES. July, 2001. (Kristen Coury) Christopher Gartin, Greg Lauren, Rebecca Creskoff, Brian Lane Green, Tony Lo Bianco, Beth Fowler, Frank Pellegrino.

FRIENDS & LOVERS
LIONS GATE. Apr., 1999. (George Haas) Stephen Baldwin, Danny Nucci, George Newbern, Claudia Schiffer.

FRIENDS HAVE REASONS
TORNASOL FILMS. Sept., 2000. Spanish. (Gerardo Herrero) Marta Belaustegui, Sergi Calleja, Joel Joan, Lola Duenas, Jose Tome.

FRIENDS IN HIGH PLACES
Feb., 2002. German-Swiss. (Lindsey Morrison) Documentary.

FROG AND WOMBAT
PIGTAIL PRODS. Oct., 1998. (Laurie Agard) Katie Stuart, Emily Lipoma, Ronny Cox, Lindsay Wagner.

FROGS FOR SNAKES
SHOOTING GALLERY. Feb., 1998. (Amos Poe) Barbara Hershey, Robbie Coltrane, Harry Hamlin, Ian Hart, John Leguizamo, Lisa Marie.

FROM HELL
20TH CENTURY FOX. Sept., 2001. (Allen Hughes and Albert Hughes) Johnny Depp, Heather Graham, Ian Holm, Robbie Coltrane, Ian Richardson, Jason Flemyng, Katrin Cartlidge, Terence Harvey.

FROM RUSSIA TO HOLLYWOOD: THE 100-YEAR OSYSSEY OF CHEKHOV AND SHDANOFF
KEEVE PRODS. Aug., 1999. (Frederick Keeve) John Berry, Dorothy Bridges, Lloyd Bridges, Leslie Caron. Documentary.

FROM THE EDGE OF THE CITY (APO TIN AKRI TIS POLIS)
MYTHOS. Nov., 1998. Greek. (Constantinos Giannaris) Stathis Papadopoulos, Dimitris Papadoulidis, Theodora Tzimou, Costas Cotsianidis.

FROM THE HEART
BHARAT SHAH. Feb., 1999. Indian. (Mani Ratnam) Shahrukh Khan, Manisha Koirala, Preity Zinta, Raghuvir Yadav, Zora Sehgal.

FROM THE OTHER SIDE
May, 2002. French. (Chantal Akerman) Documentary.

FROM THE QUEEN TO THE CHIEF EXECUTIVE
CHINA STAR. Feb., 2001. Hong Kong. (Herman Yau) Stephen Tang, Ai Jin, David Li, Tam Kam-ming, Urfule Wong, Chu Chi-yee, Sam Wong, Alson Wong, Jeffrey Lam, To Chi-man.

FROM ZERO TO TEN
MEDUSA FILM. Feb., 2002. Italian. (Luciano Ligabue) Massimo Bellinzoni, Elisabetta Cavallotti, Pierfrancesco Favino.

FRONTIERS OF DREAMS AND FEARS
Oct., 2001. Lebanese. (Mai Masri) Documentary.

FROZEN HEART: A FILM ABOUT ROALD AMUNDSEN
Motlys/ NRK/SVT/YLE/Epidem/ORB/Final Cut/Czech TV/Norwegian Film Institute. Oct., 1999. Norwegian. (Stig Andersen, Kenny Sanders). Sidsel Endresen, Espen Skjonberg, Terje Stromdal, Bjarte Hjelmeland, Thomas Seltzer. Documentary.

FUCKING AMAL
SONET FILM. Oct., 1998. Swedish. (Lukas Moodysson) Alexandra Dahlstrom, Rebecca Liljeberg, Erica Carlson, Mathias Rust.

FUCKIT
NORA PROD. GROUP/RTV SLOVENIA. Apr., 2000. Slovenian. (Miha Hocevar) Polona Juh, Matej Druznik, David Furlan, Marko Miladinovic, Jure Sotlar, Gorazo Obersnel, Damijan, Skafar, Peter Hvalica.

FUCKLAND
ATOMICFILMS. Nov., 2000. Argentine. (Jose Luis Marques) Fabain Stratas, Camilla Heaney.

FUEHRER EX
MIKADO. Aug., 2002. German. (Winfried Bonengel) Christian Bluemel, Aaron Hildebrand, Jule Flierl, Luci von Org, Harry Baer.

FUGITIVES
WARNER SOGEFILMS. Oct., 2000. Spanish. (Miguel Hermoso, Oscar Plasencia, Raul Brambilla) Laia Marull, Beatriz Coronel, Juan Diego, Maria Galiana, Miguel Hermoso Arnao, Roberto Cairo, Jesus Olmedo.

FULL BLAST
ASKA/LES FILMS DE L'ISLE/TRANSMAR. Sept., 1999. Canadian. (Rodrigue Jean) David La Haye, Martin Desgagne, Louise Portal, Marie-Jo Therio, Patrice Godin.

FULL BLOSSOM: THE LIFE OF POET/ACTOR ROBERTS BLOSSOM
ATOMIC MUSE AND FILMSIGHT PRODS. Oct., 2000. (James Brih Abee) Documentary.

FULL FRONTAL
MIRAMAX FILMS. July, 2002. (Steven Soderbergh) David Duchovny, Nicky Katt, Catherine Keener, Mary McCormack, David Hyde Pierce, Julia Roberts, Blair Underwood.

FULL MONTYS WANTED
COLUMBIA TRISTAR. July, 1999. Spanish. (Alex Calvo-Sotelo) Antonio Molero, Guillermo Toledo, Sonia Javaga.

FULL MOON
A T&C FILM/PANDORA FILM/ARENA FILMS. Aug., 1998. Swiss. (Fredi M. Murer) Hanspeter Muller, Lilo Bauer, Benedict Freitag.

FULLTIME KILLER
TEAMWORK MOTION PICTURES. Sept., 2001. Hong Kong. (Jonnie To, Wai Ka-fai)Andy Lau, Takashi Sorimachi, Simon Yam, Kelly Lin, Cherri Ying, Lam Suet.

FUNKYTOWN
DRUMMER BOY PICTURES. March, 1998. (Steven Greenberg) Documentary.

FUNNY FELIX
ARTE FRANCE CINEMA/PYRAMIDE/ LES FILMS PELLEAS/ GIMAGES/CANAL PLUS. Feb., 2000. French. (Olivier Ducastel, Jacques Martinuea) Sami Bouajila, Patachou, Ariane Ascaride, Pierre-Loup Rajot, Charly Sergue, Maurice Benichou.

FURIA
ALEXANDRE FILMS/FRANCE 2 CINEMA/LE STUDIO CANAL PLUS. June, 1999. French. (Alexandre Aja) Stanislas Merhar, Marion Cotillard, Wadek Stanczak, Pierre Vaneck, Carlo Brandt.

GABRIELA
POWER POINT FILMS. March, 2001. (Vincent Jay Miller) Jaime P. Gomez, Seidy Lopez, Zach Galligan, Troy Winbush, Lupe Ontiveros, Stacy Haiduk, Evelina Fernandez.

GABRIEL & ME
PATHE DISTRIBUTION. Aug., 2001. British. (Udayan Prasad) Iain Glen, David Bradley, Sean Landless, Rosie Rowell, Billy Connolly, Ian Cullen, Jordan Routledge.

GAEA GIRLS
VIXEN/BBC BRISTOL. Aug., 2000. British. (Kim Longinotto, Jano Williams) Chigusa Nagayo, Meiko Satomura, Saika Takeuchi, Yuka Sugiyama. Documentary.

GAJA GAMINI
DASHAKA FILMS. Feb., 2001. Indian. (Maqbool Fida Husain) Madhuri Dixit, Shabana Azmi, Shahrukh Khan, Shilpa Shirodkar, Naseeruddin Shah, Indra Kumar, Farida Jalal.

GALAPAGOS
IMAX FILM/IMAX/SMITHSONIAN INSTITUTION. Nov., 1999. (Al Giddings, David Clark). Documentary.

A GALAXY FAR, FAR AWAY
MORNING STAR PRODS.March., 2001. (Tariq Jalil) Christopher Vogler, Roger Corman, Jam Master Jedi, Meat Loaf,Joe Pesci. Documentary.

GALAXY QUEST
DREAMWORKS/MARK JOHNSON. Dec., 1999. (Dean Parisot) Tim Allen, Sigourney Weaver, Alan Rickman, Tony Shalhoub, Sam Rockwell, Daryl Mitchell, Enrico Colantoni, Robin Sachs.

GAMERA 3: REVENGE OF IRIS
DAIEI. May, 1999. Japanese. (Shusuke Kaneko) Shinobu Nakayama, Ai Maeda, Ayako Fujitani, Senri Yamasaki.

GANGLAND
NEOFILMS. Sept., 1998. Philippine. (Peque Gallaga) Ryan Eigenmann, Jason Salcedo, Junell Hernando, Jesus Simoy, Blakdyak.

GANGSTER
JOSEFINE/WDR/ARTE. May, 2000. German. (Volker Einrauch) Frank Giering, Laura Tonke, Saskia Vester, Dietmar Mues, Andreas Schmidt, Jochen Nickel, Christian Redl, Stefan Kurt.

GANGSTER NO. 1
FILMFOUR/PAGODA/ROAD MOVIES/BRITISH SCREEN/BSKYB/ FILMBOARD BERLIN BRANDENBURG/NFH/LITTLEBIRD. June, 2000. British-German. (Paul McGuigan) Malcolm McDowell, David Thewlis, Paul Bettany, Saffron Burrows, Kenneth Cranham, Jamie Foreman, Razaaq Adoti.

GANGSTERS
UIP. Feb., 2002. French-Belgian. (Olivier Marchal) Richard Anconina, Anne Parillaud, Gerald Laroche, Francois Levantal, Francis Renaud, Jean-Louis Tribes, Alexandra Vandernoot.

GANG TAPES
LIONS GATE FILMS. Feb., 2001. (Adam Ripp) Trivell, Darontay McClendon, Darris Love, Don Cambell, Vi Reasons, Sonja Marie.

GARAGE DAYS
20TH CENTURY-FOX. July, 2002. Australian. (Alex Proyas) Kick Gurry, Maya Stange, Pia Miranda, Russell Dykstra, Brett Stiller.

GARAGE OLIMPO
CLASSIC PARADIS FILMS NISARGA. May, 1999. Italian-French-Argentine. (Marco Bechis) Antonella Costa, Carlos Echeverria, Dominique Sanda, Chiara Caselli, Enrique Pineyro.

THE GARDEN ON EDEN
MEDUSA FILM. Sept., 1998. Italian. (Alessanro D'Alatri) Kim Rossi Stuart, Said Taghmaoui, Boris Terral, Kassandra Voyagis.

GAS ATTACK
HART RYAN SCOTLAND. Aug., 2001. British. (Kenny Glenaan) Sherko Zen-Aloush, Benae Hassan, Robina Qureshi, Laurie Ventry, Morag Caulder.

GASOLINE
STRAND. Sept., 2002. Italian. (Monica Lisa Stambrini) Maya Sansa, Regina Orioli, Mariella Valentini, Luigi Maria Burruano, Chiara Conti, Marco Quaglia, Pietro Ragusa.

GAUDI AFTERNOON
LOLAFILMS. May, 2001. Spanish. (Susan Seidelman) Judy Davis, Marcia Gay Harden, Lili Taylor, Juliette Lewis, Courtney Jines, Christopher Bowen, Maria Barranco.

GAZA STRIP
Aug., 2002. (James Longley) Documentary.

GEMINI
SEDIC INTL./MARUBENI/KAIJYU THEATER. Sept., 1999. Japanese. (Shinya Tsukamoto) Masahiro Motoki, Tyo, Yasutaka Tsutsui, Shiho Fujimura, Akaji Maro, Naoto Takenaka, Renji Ishibashi, Tadanobu Asano.

GENDERNAUTS
HYENA FILMS. Feb., 1999. German. (Monika Treut) Sandy Stone, Jordy Jones, Susan Stryker, Stafford, Texas Tomboy.

GENESIS
KORA FILMS. May, 1999. French-Mali. (Cheick Oumar) Sotigui Kouyate, Salif Keita, Balla Moussa Keita, Fatoumata Diawara.

GEORGICA
A Q-FILM. June, 1998. Estonian. (Sulev Keedus) Evald Aavik, Mait Marekulski, Ulle Toming.

THE GENERAL'S DAUGHTER
PARAMOUNT. June, 1999. (Simon West) John Travolta, Madeleine Stowe, James Cromwell, Timothy Hutton.

THE GENTLEMAN BANDIT
PATHFINDER PICTURES. Feb., 2002. (Jordan Alan) Ed Lauter, Peter Greene, Justine Miceli, Charlie Mattera, Kristina Malota, Ryan O'Neal.

GEOGRAPHY OF FEAR
BLIND SPOT/YTV1/ZENTROPA/WUSTE/NDR/ARTE. Feb., 2000. Finnish-Danish-German. (Auli Mantila) Tanjalotta Raikka, Leena Klemola, Pertti Sveholm, Kari Sorvali, Anna-Elina Lyytikainen.

GEORGE WALLACE: SETTIN' THE WOODS ON FIRE
BIG HOUSE/MIDNIGHT FILMS FOR THE AMERICAN EXPERIENCE. Jan., 2000. (Daniel McCabe, Paul Steckler). Documentary.

GEORGE WASHINGTON
YOUANDWHATARMY FILMED CHALLENGES/BLUE MOON FILM PRODS./DOWN HOME ENTERTAINMENT. Feb., 2000. (David Gordon Green) Candace Evanofski, Donald Holden, Curtis Cotton III, Eddie Rouse, Paul Schneider, Damian Jewan Lee, Rachel Handy, Jonathan Davidson.

GEPPETTO
EDUARDO R. CALCAGNO PROD. Jan., 2000. Argentine. (Eduardo R. Calcagno) Ulises Dumont, Malena Figo, Nicolas Cabre.

GERRY
Jan., 2002. (Gus Van Sant) Casey Affleck, Matt Damon.

GERRY HUMPHRYS: THE LOVED ONE
SUNRISE. July, 2000. Australian. (Nigel Buesst). Documentary.

GET A LIFE
MADRAGOA FILMES/GEMINI FILMS. May, 2001. Portuguese-French. (Joao Canijo) Rita Blanco, Adriano Luz, Teresa Madruga, Alda Gomes, Olivier Leite, Luis Rego.

GET A WAY
Feb., 2002. French. (Noah Nuer) Agnes Roland, Maxine Desmons, Josy Bernard, Julian Lambroschini, Christian Sinniger, Chantal Bronner, Alain Rimoux.

GET BRUCE!
MIRAMAX. Jan., 1999. (Andrew J. Kuehn) Bruce Vilanch, Bette Midler, Billy Crystal, Robin Williams, Whoopi Goldberg.

GET CARTER
WARNER BROS. Oct., 2000, (Stephen Kay) Sylvester Stallone, Miranda Richardson, Rachael Leigh Cook, Alan Cumming, Mickey Rourke, John C. McGinley.

GET OVER IT
MIRAMAX FILMS. March, 2001. (Tommy O'Haver) Kirsten Dunst, Ben Foster, Melissa Sagemiller, Sisqo, Shane West, Colin Hanks, Swoosie Kurtz, Ed Begley Jr.

GET REAL
DISTANT HORIZON. Aug., 1998. British. (Simon Shore) Ben Silverstone, Brad Gorton, Charlotte Brittain, Stacy A. Hart.

GETTING OFF
CINEBLAST! Sept., 1998. (Julie A. Lynch) Christine Harnos, Brooke Smith, Bill Sage, David Marshall Grant.

GETTING TO KNOW YOU
SHOWDOWCATCHER ENTERTAINMENT-SEARCH PARTY. Jan., 1999. (Lisanne Skyler) Heather Matarazzo, Zach Braff, Michael Weston, Bebe Neuwirth.

GHETTOKIDS
Aug., 2002. German-French. (Christian Wagner) Ioannis Tsialas, Toni Osmani, Barbara Rudnik, Gunther Maria Halmer, Renate Becker, Julia Dietze, Marian Losch, Neza Selbuz.

GET YOUR STUFF
REVISION FILMS/WEY-MAN PRODS./PEOPLES PRODS. June, 2000. (Max Mitchell) Cameron Watson, Anthony Meindl, Elaine Hendrix, Patience Cleveland, Grady Hutt, Blyan Barbosa, Kimberly Scott, Kelly Packard.

GHISLAIN LAMBERT'S BICYCLE
BAC DISTRIBUTION. Sept., 2001. French-Belgian. (Philippe Harel) Benoit Poelvoorde, Antoine De Caunes, Jose Garcia, Daniel Ceccaldi, Sacha Bourdo, Emmanuel Quatra, Jean-Baptiste Iera.

GHOST DOG: THE WAY OF THE SAMURAI
JVC/BAC FILMS/LE STUDIO CANAL PLUS. May, 1999. U.S.-French. (Jim Jarmusch) Forest Whitaker, John Tormey, Cliff Gorman, Henry Silva, Isaach de Bankole.

THE GHOST OF MARSHAL TITO
INTERFILM/HRT. Feb., 2000. Croatian. (Vinko Bresan) Drazen Kuhn, Linda Begonja, Ilja Ivezic, Ivo Gregurevic, Boris Buzancic.

THE GHOST OF ROGER CASEMENT
June, 2002. Irish. (Alan Gilsenan) Documentary.

GHOST WORLD
MGM. June, 2001. (Terry Zwigoff) Thora Birch, Scarlett Johansson, Steve Buscemi, Brad Renfro, Illeana Douglas, Bob Balaban, Teri Garr.

GIBTOWN
DECOY FILMS. Feb., 2001. (Melissa Shachat) Documentary.

GIDEON
BALDWIN/COHEN PRODS. May, 1999. (Claudia Hoover) Christopher Lambert, Shelley Winters, Charlton Heston, Carroll O'Connor, Shirley Jones.

THE GIFT
PARAMOUNT CLASSICS. Dec., 2000. (Sam Raimi) Cate Blanchett, Giovanni Ribisi, Keanu Reeves, Katie Holmes, Greg Kinnear, Hilary Swank, Michael Jeter.

GIGANTIC
X FILME CREATIVE POOL/NORDDEUTSCHE RUNDFUNK/ARTE. Oct., 1999. German. (Sebastian Schipper) Frank Giering, Florian.

GIGANTIC: A TALE OF TWO JOHNS
June, 2002. (A.J. Schnack) They Might Be Giants, Frank Black, Dave Eggers, Joe Frankllin, Janeane Garofalo, Ira Glass, Mark Hoppus, Josh Kornbluth.

GILDED YOUTH
MK2. May, 2001. French. (Zaida Ghorab-Volta) Alexandra Jeudon, Alexandra Laflandre.

GINGER SNAPS
TVA INTL. Sept., 2000. Canadian. (John Fawcett) Emily Perkins, Katharine Isabelle, Dris Lemche, Mimi Rogers, Jesse Moss, Danielle Hampton, Peter Keleghan, John Bourgeois.

THE GIRAFFE
Jugendfilm. Sept., 1998. German-Austrian. (Dani Levy) Maria Schrader, Dani Levy, David Strathairn, Nicole Heesters.

GIRL
KUSHNER-LOCKE. May, 1998. (Jonathan Kahn) Dominique Swain, Sean Patrick Flanery, Summer Phoenix, Tara Reid, Selma Blair.

THE GIRL
ARTISTIC LICENSE FILMS. Sept., 2000. (Sande Zeig) Claire Keim, Agathe de la Boulaye, Cyril Lecomte, Sandra N'Kake, Ronald Guttman, Cyrille Hertel, Pascal Cervo.

GIRLFIGHT
SCREEN GEMS/INDEPENDENT FILM CHANNEL/GREEN/RENZI. Jan., 2000. (Karyn Kusama) Michelle Rodriguez, Jaime Tirelli, Paul Calderon, Santiago Douglas, Ray Santiago, Elisa Bocanegra.

GIRL, INTERRUPTED
SONY/COLUMBIA PICTURES/RED WAGON. Dec., 1999. (James Mangold) Winona Ryder, Angelina Jolie, Clea Duvall, Brittany Murphy, Elisabeth Moss, Jared Leto, Jeffrey Tambor, Vanessa Redgrave, Whoopi Goldberg, Mary Kay Place.

THE GIRL IN THE SNEAKERS
ART BUREAU/MILAD. June, 2000. Iranian. (Rassul Sadr) Pegah Ahangarani, Majid Hajizadeh, Akram Mohammadi, Abdolreza Akbari, Mahmud Jafari.

A GIRL IS A GIRL
SHAVICK/MASCULINE-FEMININE FILMS/CITYTV/BRITISH COLUMBIA FILM. Sept., 1999. Canadian. (Reginald Harkema) Andrew McIntyre, Paige Morrison, Laurie Baranyay, Aeryn Twidle, Jo-Ann MacDonald, Keir MacPherson, David Pauls.

THE GIRL NEXT DOOR
INDICAN PICTURES /CAFE SISTERS/BERNS BROTHERS Prods. Apr., 2000. (Christine Fugate). Documentary.

THE GIRL OF YOUR DREAMS
LOLA FILMS. Nov., 1998. Spanish. (Fernando Trueba): Penelope Cruz, Antonio Resines, Neus Asensi, Jesus Bonilla, Liles Leon.

THE GIRL ON THE BRIDGE
UFD. Mar., 1999. French. (Patrice Leconte) Daniel Auteuil, Vanessa Paradis, Demetre Georgalas, Isabelle Petit-Jacques, Frederic Pfluger.

GIRLS CAN'T SWIM
SEPIA PROD./YMC PRODS. Sept., 2000. French. (Anne-Sophie Birot) Isild Le Besco, Karen Alyx, Pascale Bussieres, Pascal Elso, Marie Riviere, Yelda Reynaud, Sandrine Blancke, Julien Cottereau.

GIRLS CAN GET AWAY WITH ANYTHING
April, 2002. French. (Charlotte Silvera) Thylda Bares, Nora Rotman, Agnes Soral, Roland Bertin.

GIRLS' NIGHT
GRANADA. Jan., 1998. British. (Nick Hurran) Brenda Blethyn, Julie Walters, Kris Kristofferson, James Gaddas, George Costigan.

GIRL'S NIGHT OUT
SAMSUNG PICTURES. Sept., 1998. South Korean. (Im Sang-su) Kang Su-yeon, Jin Heui-kyeong, Kim Yeo-jin.

THE GIRLS' ROOM
Mar., 2000. (Irene Turner) Soleil Moon Frye, Wil Wheaton, Cat Taber, Gary Wolf, Michelle Brookhurst, Crystall Carmen, Malinda Williams.

A GIRL'S SECRET
ARAB CO. FOR CINEMA PRODUCTION & DISTRIBUTION. Oct., 2001. Egyptian. (Magdy Ahmed Aly) Maya Sheiha, Ezzat Abou Aouf, Dalal Abdel Aziz, Sawasan Badr.

GLADIATOR
DREAMWORKS/UNIVERSAL/DOUGLAS WICK/SCOTT FREE PRODS. Apr., 2000. (Ridley Scott) Russell Crowe, Joaquin Phoenix, Connie Nielsen, Oliver Reed, Derek Jacobi, Djimon Hounsou, Richard Harris, David Schofield, John Shrapnel, Tomas Arana, Ralf Moeller.

GLADIATORS: A REPORT ON ITALIAN HARDCORE CINEMA
TELEPIU. Nov., 2000. Italian. (Maria Martinelli) Luca Damiano, Federica Gori, Alex Mantegna, Francesco Malcom, Gianfranco Romagnoli, Anita Rinaldi, Max Bellocchio. Documentary.

GLADYS
PRODUCTIONS LA FETE. June, 1999. (Vojtech Jasny). Documentary.

GLAMOUR
MAGYAR TELEVIZIO/FOCUSFILM/ILOONA GRUNDMAN/ARTS & FUTURE FILM FABRIK. Feb., 2000. Hungarian-German-Swiss. (Frigyes Godros) Karoly Eperjes, Eszter Onodi, Gyorgy Barko, Antal Cserna, Katinka Cseke, Lajos Szucs, Janos Szirtes, Tamas Jakab.

THE GLASS HOUSE
SONY PICTURES ENTERTAINMENT. Sept. 2001. (Daniel Sackheim) Leelee Sobieski, Diane Lane, Stellan Skarsgard, Bruce Dern, Kathy Baker, Trevor Morgan, Chris Noth, Michael O'Keefe, Rita Wilson, Gavin O'Connor, Vyto Ruginis.

THE GLASS JAR
STERLING PACIFIC FILMSMCABOY/WADSWORTH. Sept., 2000. (Gil Wadsworth) Anthony Crivello, John Kasir, C. Thomas Howell.

GLASS MARBLES
41T-MARIO KRASTEV/BOYANA FILM CO./BULGARIAN NATIONAL TELEVISION, NATIONAL FILM CENTER OF BULGARIA. Feb., 2000. Bulgarian. (Ivan Cherkelov) Ivan Ivanov, Jana Karaivanova, Rumen Traikov, Georgi Cherkelov.

GLASS TEARS
MEI AH. May, 2001. Hong Kong. (Carol Lai) Zey Kwok, Law Lit, Chi Tien-you, Tats Lau, Carrie Ng.

THE GLASS TIGER
FILMPARTNERS CO. Feb., 2001. Hungarian. (Peter Rudolf, Ivan Kapitany) Peter Fudolf, Gabor Reviczky, Imre Csuja, Jozsef Szarvas, Otto L. Horvath, Sandor Gaspar, Ferenc Killac.

THE GLEANERS AND I
CANAL PLUS/CINE TAMARIS/CENTRE NATIONAL DE LA CINEMATOGRAPHIE/PROCIREP. May, 2000. French. (Agnes Varda). Documentary.

GLITTER
20TH CENTURY FOX RELEASE (IN U.S.). Sept., 2001. (Vondie Curtis-Hall) Mariah Carey, Max Beesley, Da Brat, Tia Texada, Valarie Pettiford, Ann Magnuson, Terrence Howard, Dorian Harewood.

GLISSANDO
Feb., 2002. (Chip Hourihan) Paul Frediani, Petra Wright, Chris Van Strander, Ned Van Zandt.

GLOOMY SUNDAY
UNIVERSAL PICTURES GERMANY/STUDIO HAMBURG/ POLYGRAM/ DOM FILM/FOCUS FILM/WDR/PREMIERE/ ARTE/MTV2. Feb., 2000. German-Hungarian. (Rolf Schuebel) Joachim Krol, Stefano Dionisi, Ben Becker, Erika Marozsan, Sebastian Koch, Laszlo I. Kish, Wanja Mues, Ulrike Grote.

GLORIA
COLUMBIA. Jan., 1999. (Sidney Lumet) Sharon Stone, Jean-Luke Figueroa, Jeremy Northam, Cathy Moriarty, George C. Scot.

GLORIA
ROSA FILMES/CARO-LINE PRODS./CAMELOT PELIS. Feb., 1999. Portuguese-French-Spanish. (Manuela Viegas) Jean-Christophe Bouvet, Raquel Marques, Francisco Relvas, Ricardo Aibeo, Paul So.

GLOWING EYES
April, 2002. French. (Jacques Nolot) Jacques Nolot, Vittoria Scognamiglio, Sebastien Viala.

GLOWING GROWING
Oct., 2001. Japanese. (Kei Horie) Masahiro Toda, Ryo Murashima, Asumi Miwa, Amiko Kanaya, Kunihiko Oshida, Masahi Endo.

GLUE SNIFFER
UNITY FILMS/CNAC/TANGO BRAVO/CREDESCA/FILMART P.C. Jan., 2000. Argentine. (Elia Schneider) Jose G. Rivas, Luis Campos, Alfredo Medina, Adolfo Cubas, Pedro Lander, Laureano Olivarez.

G-MEN FROM HELL
SAWMILL ENTERTAINMENT CORP. Feb., 2001. (Christopher Coppola) William Forsythe, Tate Donovan, Bobcat Goldthwait, Barry Newman, Zach Galligan, Vanessa Angel, Paul Rodriguez.

GO
SONY. Jan., 1999. (Doug Liman) Desmond Askew, Taye Diggs, William Fichtner, J.E. Freeman, Sarah Polley.

THE GOALKEEPER
LOLAFILMS DISTRIBUCION. Sept., 2000. Spanish. (Gonzalo Suarez) Carmelo Gomez, Maribel Verdu, Roberto Alvarez, Eduard Fernandez, Elvira Minguez, Abel Viton, Julio Velez, Adrian Ramirez.

GOAT ON FIRE & SMILING FISH
MARTINI/JORDAN. Sept., 1999. (Kevin Jordan) Derick Martini, Christa Miller, Steven Martini, Bill Henderson.

GODASS
HELL'S BELLS. June, 2000. (Esther Bell) Nika Feldman, Preston Miller, Arik Roper, Julianne Nicholson, George Crowley, Fred Schneider, David Ilku, Tina Holmes, Lola Labelle.

THE GODDESS OF 1967
FANDANGO/ AUSTRALIAN FILM FINANCE CORP./NSW FILM & TV OFFICE. Sept., 2000. Australish. (Clara Law) Rose Byrne, Rikiya Kurokawa, Nicholas Hope, Elise McCredie.

GOD IS GREAT, I'M NOT
MARS FILMS. Sept., 2001. French. (Pascale Bailly) Audrey Tautou, Edouard Baer, Julie Depardieu, Catherine Jacob, Philippe Laudenbach, Cathy Verney, Anna Koch.

GODMOTHER
GRAMCO FILMS. Aug., 1999. Indian. (Vinay Shukla) Shabana Azmi, Milind Gunaji, Nirmal Pandey. Gonvind Namdev, Raima Sen.

GOD SAID, HA!
OH BROTHER. March, 1998. (Julia Sweeney) Julia Sweeney, Quentin Tarantino.

GODS AND MONSTERS
REGENT ENTERTAINMENT. Jan., 1998. (Bill Condon) Ian McKellen, Brendan Fraser, Lynn Redgrave, Lolita Davidovich, Kevin J. O'connor.

GOD'S ARMY
ZION FILMS. May, 2000. (Richard Dutcher) Richard Dutcher, Matthew Brown, DeSean Terry, Michael Buster, Luis Robledo.

GOD'S BANKERS
COLUMBIA TRISTAR FILMS ITALIA. March, 2002. Italian. (Giuseppe Ferrara) Omero Antonutti, Pamela Villoresi, Rutger Hauer, Giancarlo Giannini, Alessandro Gassman, Pierpaolo Capponi, Vincenzo Peluso.

GOD'S CHILDREN
Feb., 2002. Japanese. (Hiroshi Shinomiya) Documentary.

GOD'S WEDDING
MADRAGOA FILMES/GEMINI FILMS. May, 1999. Portuguese-French. (Joao Cesar Monteiro) Joao Cesar Monteiro, Joana Azevedo, Rita Durao, Jose Airosa, Manuela de Freitas.

GODZILLA
SONY. May., 1998. (Roland Emmerich) Matthew Broderick, Jean Reno, Maria Pitillo, Hank Azaria, Kevin Dunn, Michael Lerner.

GODZILLA 2000
SONY/TRISTAR/TOHO. Aug., 2000. Japanese. (Takao Okawara) Takehiro Murata, Shiro Sano, Hiroshi Abe, Naomi Nishida, Mayu Suzuki, Tsutomu Kitagawa.

GO FOR BROKE
ZHU YONGDE. Feb., 2001. Chinese. (Wang Guangli) Zhou Yuhua, Gu Longxiang, Wang Jianxin, Zhang Jia Gang, Xu Mei Jiang.

GO FOR BROKE
June, 2002. (Jean Claude Lamarre) Pras, Michael Goorjian, LisaRae, Bobby Brown, Jean Claude Lamarre, Ed Lauter, Glenn Plummer.

GOING BY
Feb., 2002. Iranian. (Iraj Karimi) Fariba Kamran, Mehran Rajabi, Shahrokh Foroutanian, Mehrdad Mohtashami, Nazanin Farahani.

GOING TO KANSAS CITY
MANDART ENTERTAINMENT LTD. Oct., 1998. Canadian-Finnish. (Pekka Mandart). Mikko Nousiainen, Melissa Galianos, Michael Ironside.

GOING TO SCHOOL WITH DAD ON MY BACK
BEIJING FORBIDDEN CITY FILM COMPANY. Aug., 1998. Chinese. (Zhou Youchao) Zhao Qiang, Jiang Hualin, Yukui, Yan Danchen.

THE GOLD CUP
FULL CIRCLE FILMS. Oct., 2000. (Lucas Reiner) Wood Harris, Jim Haynie, Sarah Lasez, O-Lan Jones, Tsai Chin, Michael McShane.

THE GOLDEN BOWL
MIRAMAX/MERCHANT IVORY/TF1 INTL./MIRAMAX FILMS. May, 2000. U.S.-French-British. (James Ivory) Uma Thurman, Jeremy Northam, Kate Beckinsale, Nick Nolte, Anjelica Huston, James Fox, Madeleine Potter, Peter Eyre.

GO MOAN FOR MAN
REAL FILMS. Nov., 2000. (Doug Sharples) DOCU-DRAMA. Bill Mabon, Steve Marsden, Geoffrey Gray-Lobe, Lonnie Fischer, Joseph Barnett, Ivan Barnett.

GONE IN SIXTY SECONDS
BUENA VISTA/TOUCHSTONE/JERRY BRUCKHEIMER FILMS. June, 2000. (Dominic Sena) Nicolas Cage, Angelina Jolie, Giovanni Ribisi, Delroy Lindo, Will Patton, Christopher Eccleston, Chi McBride, Robert Duvall, Scott Caan, Timothy Olyphant, William Lee Scott.

GONE WITH THE FISH
PER HOLST FILM/DANISH FILM INSTITUTE/DR-TV/NORSK FILM/FELICIA FILM/TV1000/SVT/SWEDISH FILM INSTITUTE/NORDIC FILM & TV FUND. Feb., 2000. Danish-Norwegian-Swedish. (Lotte Svendsen) Henrik Lykkegaard, Sofie Stougaard, Michelle Bjorn Andersen, Helle Dolleris, Thomas Bo Larsen.

GOODBYE CHARLIE BRIGHT
METRODOME. May, 2001. British. (Nick Love) Paul Nicholls, Roland Manookian, Phil Daniels, Jamie Foreman, Danny Dyer, Dani Behr, Richard Driscoll, David Thewlis.

GOODBYE FROM THE HEART
ALTA/ALMA ATA/GALIARDO/GAILA/RAFAEL AZCONA/ANTENA 3 TV/CANAL PLUS. June, 2000. Spanish. (Jose Luis Garcia Sanchez) Juan Luis Galiardo. Laura Ramos, Jesus Bonilla, Neus Asensi, Maria Luisa San Jose, Teresa Gimpera, Juan Echanove.

GOODBYE TOMORROW
RH POLITIC PRODS. INTL./EUROFILM STUDIO/ FRP. Apr., 1999. Turkish-Hungarian-French. (Reis Celik).

GOODBYE, 20TH CENTURY!
MIRCO & SLAVCO FIRST PARTISAN. Feb., 1999. Macedonian. (Aleksandar Popovski) Lazar Ristovski, Mikola Ristanovski, Vlado Jovanovski, Sofija Kunovska, Dejan Acimovic.

THE GOOD GIRL
Jan., 2002. (Miguel Arteta) Jennifer Aniston, Jake Gyllenhaal, John C. Reilly, Tim Blake Nelson, Zooey Deschanel, Mike White, Deborah Rush.

GOOD HANDS
Feb., 2002. Estonian-Latvian. (Peeter Simm) Rezija Kalnina, Leonarda Klavina, Tiit Sukk, Maija Apine, Atis Tenbergs, Lembit Ulfsak, Tonu Kark, Gert Raudsepp.

GOOD HOUSEKEEPING
MODERNICA. Feb., 2000. (Frank Novak) Bob Mills, Petra Westen, Tacey Adams, Zia, Andrew Eichner, Maeve Kerrigan, Scooter Stephan, Al Schuermann, Jerry O'Connor, Doug Duane, Borma Barbour.

GOOD KURDS, BAD KURDS: NO FRIENDS BUT THE MOUNTAINS
ACCESS. Feb., 2000. (Kevin McKiernan). Documentary.

A GOOD LAD
ALMA ATA. Aug., 2000. Soviet Union–1943. (Boris Barnet) E. Grigorev, O. Yakunina, Elena Sipavina, Nikolai Bogolyubov, Viktor Dobrovolsky.

THE GOOD OLD NAUGHTY DAYS
May, 2002. French.

THE GOOD THIEF
Sept., 2002. French-British-Irish. (Neil Jordan) Nick Nolte, Tcheky Karyo, Said Taghmaoui, Gerard Darmon, Emir Kusturica, Marc Lavoine, Ouassini Embarek, Mark Polish.

THE GOOD WAR
ITLIAN INTERNATIONAL FILM. April, 2002. Italian. (Georgio Serafini) Roy Scheider, Luca Zingaretti, Vincent Ruitta, Sue Cremin.

GOOD WORK
LA SEPT ARTE/PATHE TELEVISION/S.M. FILMS. Sept., 1999. French. (Claire Denis) Denis Lavant, Michel Subor, Gregoire Colin.

GOREVILLE, U.S.A.
LEANING SILO. Aug., 1998. (Seth Henrikson, Dave Sarno, Rob Shields). Documentary.

GORGEOUS
GOLDEN HARVEST. July, 1999. Hong Kong. (Vincent Kuk) Jackie Chan, Shu Qi, Tony Leung Chiu-wai, Emil Chow, Jen Hsien-chi.

GOSFORD PARK
USA FILMS. Oct., 2001. U.S.-British. (Robert Altman) Eileen Atkins, Bob Balaban, Alan Bates, Charles Dance, Stephen Fry, Michael Gambon, Richard E. Grant, Tom Hollander, Derek Jacobi.

GOSHOGAOKA
SHARON LOCKHART. Jan., 1998. (Sharon Lockhart). Documentary.

GOSSIP
WARNER BROS./VILLAGE ROADSHOW PICTURES/NPV ENTERTAINMENT/OUTLAW . Apr., 2000. (Davis Guggenheim) James Marsden, Lena Headey, Norman Reedus, Kate Hudson, Joshua Jackson, Marisa Coughlan, Edward James Olmos, Sharon Lawrence, Eric Bogosian.

GOSSIP
SVENSK FILMINDUSTRI. Dec., 2001. Swedish. (Colin Nutley) Pernilla August, Helena Bergstrom, Lena Endre, Stina Ekblad.

GOSTANZA DA LIBBIANO
Arsenali Medicei. Aug., 2000. Italian. (Paolo Benvenuti) Lucia Poli, Valentino Davanzati, Renzo Cerrato, Paolo Spaziani, Lele Biagri, Nadia Capocchini, Teresa Soldaini.

GO TIGERS!
IFC FILMS. Jan., 2001. (Kenneth A. Carlson) DOCUMENTRAY.

THE GOVERNESS
SONY PICTURES CLASSICS. June, 1998. British. (Sandra Goldbacher) Minnie Driver, Tom Wilkinson, Florence Hoath.

GOYA IN BORDEAUX
LOLAFILMS. Sept., 1999. Spanish-Italian. (Carlos Saura) Francisco Rabal, Jose Coronado, Dafne Fernandez.

GRADUATE OF INSANITY
MINE FILM/MACT PRODS./OBJEKTIV FILMSTUDIO. Apr., 1999. Turkish-French-Hungarian.(Tunic Basaran) Ayda Aksel, Selcuk Yontem, Guler Okten, Meric Basaran, Gokham Mete.

THE GREATEST THING
EGMONT COLUMBIA TRISTAR. Aug., 2001. Norwegian-Danish. (Thomas Robsahm) Herborg Krakevik, Thomas Hanzon, Kirsti Stubo, Jesper Langberg, Mads Ousdal, Henrik Mestad, Oyvind Gran.

THE GRANDFATHER
COLUMBIA TRISTAR. Nov., 1998. Spanish. (Jose Luis Garcia) Fernando Fernan-Gomez, Rafael Alonso, Cayetana Guillen-Cuervo, Agustin Gonzalez.

GRAN PARADISO
WARNER BROS./LETTERBOX/MONTY FILMGESELLSCHAFT/ CINEMEDIA. Aug., 2000. German. (Miguel Alexandre) Ken Duken, Regula Grauwiller, Gregor Torzs, Max Herbrechter, Frank Giering, Erhan Emre, Alexander Horbe, Antje Westermann.

GRASS
LIONS GATE . Sept., 1999. Canadian. (Ron Mann). Documentary.

THE GREAT BAGAROZY
CONSTANTIN FILM July, 2000. German. (Bernd Eichinger) Til Schweiger, Corinna Harfouch, Thomas Heinze, Christine Neubauer, Sonja Kerskes, Patricia Lueger, Neza Selbuz.

GREAT DAY IN HAVANA
CINEMBARGO FILMS. March, 2001. (Laurie Ann Schag, Casey Stoll) Tania Bruguera, Israel del Monte, Pedro "Pulido" Gonzalez, Eloy Machado, Elio Ruiz, Asela Diaz, Carlos Alfonso. Documentary.

GREAT IDEA
VERTIGO/PAN-EUROPEENNE/STELLA FILMS/M6. Jan., 2001. French. (Jerome Levy) Ludivine Sagnier, Veronique Balme, Marie Gili-Pierre, Thomas Blanchard, Pascal Reneric, Roland Giraud.

GREED
TURNER CLASSIC MOVIES. Sept., 1999. (Rick Schmidlin). Restoration.

GREEN DESERT
BUENA VISTA INTL. June, 1999. German. (Anno Saul) Tatjana Trieb, Robert Gwisdek, Martina Gedeck, Ulrich Noethen, Heino Ferch.

GREEN DRAGON
FRANCHISE PICTURES/FRANCHISE CLASSICS. Jan., 2001. (Timothy Linh Bui) Patrick Swayze, Forest Whitaker, Don Duong, Heip Thi Le, Billinjer Tran, Long Nguyen, Phuoc Quan Nguyen.

GREEN LIGHTS
July, 2002. (Robert H. Lieberman) John FitzGibbon, Daniel Dresner, Shawn Randall, Joel Leffert, Mimi Bensinger, Karen Rockower, Tim True, Sam Harris, Jim Burne.

THE GREEN MILE
WARNER BROS./CASTLE ROCK/DARKWOODS. Nov., 1999. (Frank Darabont) Tom Hanks, David Morse, Bonnie Hunt, Michael Clarke Duncan, James Cromwell, Michael Jeter, Graham Greene.

GREEN STONES
FLORES DEL VALLE. Jan., 2001. Mexican. (Angel Flores Torres) Vanessa Bauche, Osvaldo Benavides, Juan Claudio Retes.

GREGOIRE MOULIN VERSUS HUMANITY
UIP. Oct., 2001. French. (Artus De Penguern) Artus De Penguern, Pascale Arbillot, Didier Benureau.

GREGORY'S TWO GIRLS
FILMFOUR. Aug., 1999. British. (Bill Forsyth) John Gordon Sinclair, Carly McKinnon, Maria Doyle Kennedy, Kevin Anderson, Martin Schwab.

GRETA
CHARLES STEWART MOTT FOUNDATION/ EUROPEAN CULTURAL FOUNDATION/SOROS DOCUMENTARY FUND OF THE OPEN SOCIETY INSTITUTE/INTERNEWS.Aug., 1999. (Haris Pasovic). Documentary.

GREY OWL
REMSTAR/BEAVER PRODS./ALLIED FILMMAKERS/TRANSFILM. Sept., 1999. British-Canadian. (Richard Attenborough) Pierce Brosnan, Annie Galipeau, Nathaniel Arcand, Vlasta Vrana, David Fox, Charles Powell, Stephanie Cole, Graham Greene.

THE GREY ZONE
LIONS GATE FILMS. Sept., 2002. (Tim Blake Nelson) David Arquette, Daniel Benzali, Steve Buscemi, David Chandler, Allan Corduner, Harvey Keitel, Natasha Lyonne, Mira Sorvino, Michael Stuhbarg, Lisa Benavides, Brian O'Byrne.

GRILL POINT
Feb., 2002. German. (Andreas Dresen) Steffi Kuehnert, Gabriela Maria Schmeide, Thorsten Merten, Axel Prahl.

GRIPSHOLM
KINOWELT. Oct., 2000. German-Austrian-Swiss. (Xavier Koller) Ulrich Noethen, Heike Makatsch, Jasmin Tabatabai, Marcus Thomas, Sara Foettinger, Inger Nilsson.

GRIZZLY ADAMS AND THE LEGEND OF DARK MOUNTAIN
MARK OF THE BEAR PARTNERSHIP. May, 1999. (John Huneck) Tom Tayback, Lindsay Bloom, Jennifer Waldman, Selina Jayne.

GRIZZLY FALLS
PROVIDENCE /BEHAVIOUR WORLDWIDE/ NORSTAR FILMED ENTERTAINMENT/LE SABRE. Jan., 2000. Canadian-British. (Stewart Raffill) Daniel Clark, Bryan Brown, Tom Jackson, Oliver Tobias, Richard Harris, Brock Simpson, Chantal Dick, Trevor Lowden.

GROOVE
SONY PICTURES CLASSICS/415.COM. Jan., 2000. (Greg Harrison) Lola Glaudini, Hamish Linklater, Denny Kirkwood, MacKenzie Firgens, Rachel True, Steve Van Wormer, Nick Offerman, Ari Gold, DJ Dmitri.

GROUP
June, 2002. (Marilyn Freeman) Carrie Brownstein, Kari Fillipi, S. Ann Hall, Vicki Hollenberh, Tracy Kirkpatrick, Nomy Lamm.

GUARDIANS OF THE EARTH
HRISHIKESH FILMS. Aug., 2001. Indian. (Subrahmaniam Santakumar) Manikandan, Beena Antony, Viplavan Balan, Seema G. Nair.

THE GUERRILLA OF MEMORY
ALTA FILMS. March, 2002. Spanish. (Javier Corcuera) Esperanza Martinez, Remedios Montero, Florian Garcia, jose Murrillo. Documentary.

THE GUEST
FILM DAEDALUS. Feb., 1999. Italian. (Alessandro Colizzi) Elodie Treccani, Anita Zagria, Umberto Orsini, Ignazio Oliva, Maddalena Maggi, Lorenzo Lavia. Yoon C. Joyce.

GUEST HOUSE PARADISO
UNIVERSAL INTL. PICTURES. Dec., 1999. British. (Adrian Edmondson) Rik Mayall, Adrian Edmondson, Vincent Cassel, Helene Mahieu.

GUESTS
ARCHIMEDE PRODUZIONE. Sept., 1998. Italian. (Matteo Garrone) Julian Sota, Llazar Sota, Corrado Sassi, Pasqualino Mura, Paola Rota.

THE GUILTY
SND/J&M ENTERTAINMENT/DOGWOOD PICTURES/MUSE ENTERTAINMENT. July, 2000. British-Canadian. (Anthony Waller) Bill Pullman, Gabrielle Anwar, Devon Sawa, Angela Featherstone, Joanne Whalley, Ken Tremblett, Jaimz Woolvet.

GUINEVERE
MIRAMAX. Jan., 1999.(Audrey Wells) Stephen Rea, Sarah Polley, Jean Smart, Gina Gershon, Paul Dooley.

GUNBLAST VODKA
KOBA FILMS DISTRIBUTION. Aug., 2001. French. (Jean-Louis Daniel) Goetz Otto, Angie Everhart, Jurgen Prochnow, Mariusz Pujszo, Anja Kruse, Alain Figlarz, Agnieszka Mursiala, Piotr Wyrwas.

THE GUN IN BETTY LOU'S HANDBAGGUNS AND ROSES
FALCO FILM. Feb., 1999. Italian. (Carla Apuzzo) Anna Ammirati, Duccio Giordano, Luigi Petrucci, Cristina Donadio, Lello Serao.

GUNS & TALKS
CINEMA SERVICE. Nov., 2001. South Korean. (Jang Jin) Shin Hyeon-jun, Jung Jae-yeong, Shin Ha-gyun, Weon Bin.

GUNSHY
PERISCOPE PICTURE. March, 1998. (Jeff Celentano) William Petersen, Michael Wincott, Diane Lane, Kevin Gage, Michael Byrne.

GUN SHY
BUENA VISTA/HOLLYWOOD PICTURES/FORTIS FILMS. Feb., 2000. (Eric Blakeney) Liam Neeson, Oliver Platt, Sandra Bullock, Jose Zuniga, Richard Schiff, Andy Lauer, Mitch Pileggi, Paul Ben-Victor, Mary McCormack, Frank Vincent, Gregg Daniel.

THE GURU
UIP. June, 2002. British-U.S.-French. (Daisy von Scherler Mayer) Heather Graham, Marisa Tomei, Jimi Mistry, Michael McKean, Christine Baranski, Rob Morrow, Malachy McCourt, Sanjeev Bhaskar.

GURU IN SEVEN
RATPACK FILMS. April, 1998. British. (Shani Grewal) Nitin Chandra Ganatra, Saeed Jaffrey, Jacqueline Pearce, Antony Zaki.

GUTS
C.V. LEF. Sept., 1999. Dutch. (Ron Termaat) Viggo Waas, Alice Reys, Rick Engelkes, Victor Reinier, Eric Van Sauers, Ineke Veenhooven.

THE GUYS
FOCUS FEATURES. Sept., 2002. (Jim Simpson) Sigourney Weaver, Anthony LaPaglia.

GYPSY
WARNER SOGEFILMS. Sept., 2000. Spanish. (Manuel Palacios) Joaquin Cortes, Laetitia Casta, Marta Belaustegui, Gines Garcia Millan, Jose Manuel Lorenzo, Manuel de Blas, Jose Luis Gomez.

GYPSY BOYS
ANOTHER B.S. PRODUCTION. Dec., 1999. (Brian Shepp) Adam Gavzer, Robert Hampton, Tom McCann, Jud Parker, Alberto Rosas, Zeke Wheeler, Andrew Abelson, Matt Boucher.

GYPSY 83
VELVET FILMS. July, 2001. (Todd Stephens) Sara Rue, Kett Turton, Karen Black, John Doe, Anson Scoville, Paulo Costanzo.

H

HAIKU TUNNEL
SONY PICTURES CLASSICS. Jan., 2001. (Jacob Kornbluth) Josh Kornbluth, WarrenKeith, Helen Shumaker, Amy Resnick, Brian Thorstenson, June A. Lomena, Sarah Overman.

HAIR SHIRT
LUNATIC PRODS. Sept., 1998. (Dean Paras) Dean Paras, Katie Wright, Neve Campbell, Kimberly Huie, Stefan Brogren.

HAIR UNDER THE ROSES
MAGOURIC. Jan., 2001. French-Luxembourgois. (Agnes Obadia, Jean-Julien Chervier) Julie Durand, Alexis Roucout, Alice Houri, Jean-Baptiste Penigault, Nicolas Duvauchelle.

HALF A CHANCE
UFD. March, 1998. French. (Patrice Leconte) Jean-Paul Belmondo, Alain Delon, Vanessa Paradis, Eric Defosse, Alexandre Iakovlev.

HALF OF HEAVEN
FILM PAR FILM. Sept., 2000. French. (Alain Mazars) Caroline Sihol, Ying Bing, Shiangchyi Chen, Xiaoxing Cheng, Jessica Mazars.

HALLELUJAH! RON ATHEY: A STORY OF DELIVERANCE
AUBIN PICTURES. Feb., 1998. (Catherine Saalfield). Documentary.

HALLOWEEN: H2O
DIMENSION FILMS. July, 1998. (Steve Miner) Jamie Lee Curtis, Adam Arkin, Josh Hartnett, Michelle Williams, Adam Hann-Byrd.

HALLOWEEN: RESURRECTION
DIMENSION FILMS. July,, 2002. (Rick Rosenthal) Jamie Lee Curtis, Brad Loree, Busta Rhymes, Bianca Kajlich, Sean Patrick Thomas, Daisy McCrackin, Katee Sackhoff, Luke Kirby, Thomas Ian Nicholas, Ryan Merriman, Tyra Banks, Rick Rosenthal.

HAMLET
MIRAMAX/DOUBLE A FILMS. Jan., 2000. (Michael Almereyda) Ethan Hawke, Kyle MacLachlan, Sam Shepard, Diane Verona, Bill Murray, Liev Schreiber, Julia Stiles, Karl Geary, Paula Malcomson).

HAMLET
HALLMARK ENTERTAINMENT. June, 2001. (Campbell Scott) Campbell Scott, Blair Brown, Jamey Sheridan, Roscoe Lee Browne, Lisa Gay Hamilton, Roger Guenveur Smith, Sam Robards.

A HANDFUL OF GRASS
KINOWELT/MTM CINETEVE/BAVARIA FILM/WDR/MILAD FILM. June, 2000. German. (Roland Suso Richter) Oliver Korittke, Arman Inci, Ercan Durmaz, Lisa Martinek.

HAND IN GLOVE
LAUREN FILMS. Oct., 2000. Spanish. (Josecho San Mateo) Unax Ugalde, Pilar Lopez de Ayala, Juan Diaz, Benjamin Seva, Fede Celada, Beatriz Sanchez, Beatriz Arguello, Carlos Kaniowski.

HAND OF FATE
LUMINOUS FILMS. June, 1999 (Scott Morgan) Neela Baba, Colette Baron Reid, Thubten Ngodup, Rita Rogers, Frank Andrews.

HANGING UP
SONY PICTURES ENTERTAINMENT/COLUMBIA PICTURES/NORA EPHRON & LAURENCE MARK. Feb., 2000. (Diane Keaton) Meg Ryan, Diane Keaton, Lisa Kudrow, Walter Matthau, Adam Arkin, Duke Mooseokian, Ann Bortolotti, Cloris Leachman, Maree Cheatham, Myndy Crist.

HANG THE DJ
ASKA FILM. Sept., 1998. Canadian. (Marco La Villa, Mauro La Villa). Junior Vasquez, Q-Bert, Roger Sanchez, A-Trak. Documentary.

HANNIBAL
MGM (IN NORTH AMERICA)/UNIVERSAL (FOREIGN). Jan., 2001. (Ridley Scott) Anthony Hopkins, Julianne Moore, Ray Liotta,Frankie R. Faison, Giancarlo Giannini, Francesca Neri, Zeljko Ivanek.

HANS STADEN
LAPFILME DO BRASIL/JORGE NEVES. May, 2000. Brazilian-Portuguese. (Luiz Alberto Pereira) Carlos Evelyn, Beto Simas, Ariana Messias, Clauda Liz, Stenio Garcia.

HANS WARNS–MY 20TH CENTURY
GORDIAN MAUGG. Sept., 1999. German. (Gordian Maugg) Florian Hober, Shenja Lacher, Klaus Kirchner, Fred Angerstein, Julia Jessen, Leonor Quinteros Ochoa, Albert Hetterle.

HANUMAN
GAUMONT BUENA VISTA INTL/BOREALIES & VISUAL EYES. Oct., 1999. French-Indian. (Fred Fougea) Robert Cavanah, Tabu, Nathalie Auffret, Khalid Thiabji, Sydney Kean, Javed Jaffrey, William Doherthy.

HAPPINESS
OCTOBER FILMS. May, 1998. (Todd Solondz) Jane Adams, Dylan Baker, Lara Flynn Boyle, Ben Gazzara, Jared Harris.

HAPPINESS IS A WARM GUN
VEGA DISTRIBUTION. Aug., 2001. Swiss. (Thomas Imbach) Linda Olsansky, Herbert Fritsch, Angelika Waller, Sir Henry, Ingrid Sattes, Stefan-Hyun Wanner, Serge Assongmo Tessa.

HAPPINESS STREET
BEIJING FILM STUDIO. June, 1998. Chinese. (Li Shaohong) Song Dandan, Wang Xueqi, Lu Wenzheng, Gao Jun.

HAPPY ACCIDENTS
INDEPENDENT FILM CHANNEL/ACCIDENTAL. Jan., 2000. (Brad Anderson) Marisa Tomei, Vincent D'Onofrio, Nadia Dajani, Tovah Feldshuh, Holland Taylor, Richard Portnow, Sean Gullette, Cara Buono, Liana Pai, Tamara Jenkins, Jose Zuniga.

HAPPY BIRTHDAY
CINEMA SUPPORT FOUNDATION. Feb., 1999. Russian. (Larisa Sadilova) Gulya Stolyarova, Irina Prosyina, Eugene Turkina, Lyuba Starkova, Masha Kuzmina.

HAPPY BIRTHDAY, MR. MOGRABI
AVI MOGRABI. Feb., 1999. Israeli. (Avi Mograbi) Shachar Degal. Daoud Koutab, Ephraim Stan, Gidi Dar, Roni Pisker.

HAPPY CAMPERS
NEW LINE CINEMA. Jan., 2001. (Daniel Waters) Brad Renfro, Dominique Swain, Emily Bergl, James King, Jordan Bridges, Justin Long, Keram Malicki-Sanchez.

HAPPY DAYS
BLUE ANGELS FILMS/TYRONE PRODUCTIONS. Aug., 2000. Irish. (Patricia Rozema) Rosaleen Linehan, Richard Johnson.

HAPPY END
SANDREW METRONOME. Aug., 1999. Swedish. (Christina Olofson) Par Ericson, Med Reventberg, Elin Gradin, Axel Widegren, Bengt Bostrom.

HAPPY END
CJ ENTERTAINMENT/KOOKMIN FINANCE/MYUNG FILM/SEOUL MOVIES. May, 2000. South Korean. (Jung Ji-woo) Choi Min-shik, Chun Do-yeon, Joo Jin-mo, Hwang Mi-sun, Joo Hyun, Huh Yae-in.

HAPPY FUNERAL DIRECTOR
CJ ENTERTAINMENT/KUKMIN INVESTMENT. Aug., 2000. South Korean. (Jang Mun-il) Im Chang-jeong, Oh Hyeon-kyeong, Kim Chang-wan, Jeong Eun-pyo, Choe Kang-heui, Jeon I-da.

HAPPY HERE AND NOW
June, 2002. (Michael Almereyda) Karl Geary, Shalom Harlow, Clarence Williams III, Ally Sheedy, Josephine Martin, Gloria Reuben, David Arquette.

HAPPY MAN
INDEKS FILM STUDIO. Nov., 2000. Polish. (Malgorzata Szumowska) Jadwiga Jankowska-Cieslak, Piotr Jankowski, Malgorzata, Chajewska-Krzysztofik, Roman Gancarczyk.

HAPPY MEN
ALTA FILMS. June, 2001. Spanish. (Roberto Santiago) Aitana Sanchez-Gijon, Sergi Lopez, Maria Esteve, Pepon Nieto, Carlos Hipolito, Mary Carmen Ramirez.

HAPPY NOW
DISTANT HORIZON AND BBC FILMS. Aug., 2001. British. (Philippa Collie-Cousins) Ioan Gruffudd, Susan Lynch, Om Puri, Emmy Rossum Paddy Considine, Richard Coyle, Robert Pugh, John Henshaw.

HAPPY, TEXAS
MARKED ENTERTAINMENT. Jan., 1999. (Mark Illsley) Jeremy Northam, Steve Zahn, William H. Macy, Ally Walker, Illeana Douglas.

HAPPY TIMES
SONY PICTURES CLASSICS. May, 2001. Chinese. (Zhang Yimou) Zhao Benshan, Dong Jie, Li Xuejuan, Dong Lifan, Leng Qibin, Niu Ben, Fu Biao, Gong Jinghua, Zhang Hongie.

HARAM SUARE
MEDUSA FILM. May, 1999. Italian-French-Turkish. (Ferzan Ozpetek) Marie Gillain, Alex Descas, Lucia Bose, Valeria Golina, Malick Bowens.

HARD
MPH PRODUCTION. June, 1998. (John Huckert) Noel Palomeria, Malcom Moorman, Charles Lanyer, Michael Waite, Arron Zeffron.

HARDBALL
PARAMOUNT PICTURES. Sept., 2001. (Brian Robbins) Keanu Reeves, Diane Lane, John Hawkes, Bryan C. Hearne, Julian Griffith, Michael Jordan, A. Delon Ellis Jr., Kristopher Lofton.

HARD GOODBYES: MY FATHER
Aug., 2002. Greek-German. (Penny Panayotopoulou) Yorgos Karayannis, Stelios Mainas, Ioanna Tsirigouli, Hristos Steryoglou, Hristos Bouyotas, Despo Diamantidou.

HARDIHOOD
QUEENBEA PRODS. June, 2001. (Nicole Hahn) Documentary.

HARD-OFF
PATHE/KATHARINE/RENN PRODS./FRANCE 2 CINEMA/CANAL PLUS/CNC. Oct., 1999, French. (Claude Berri, Arlette Langmann) Claude Berri, Fanny Ardant, Claude Brasseur, Alain Chabat, Daniele Lebrun, Brigitte Bemol, Olga Grumberg. Badia Barentin.

HARD RAIN
PARAMOUNT. Jan., 1998. (Mikael Salomon) Morgan Freeman, Christian Slater, Randy Quaid, Minnie Driver, Ed Asner.

HARDSHIP TEST (HAERTETEST)
JUGENFILM. Feb., 1998. German. (Janek Rieke) Janek Reieke, Lisa Martinek, Gerhard Garber, Katrin Sass.

THE HARD WORD
ROADSHOW. March, 2002. Australian-British. (Scott Roberts) Guy Pearce, Rachel Griffiths, Robert Taylor, Joel Edgerton, Damien Richardson, Rhondda Findleton, Kate Atkinson.

THE HAREM OF MADAME OSMANE
OCEAN FILMS/FRANCE 3 CINEMA/ASTORIA FILMS/CANAL PLUS/TORNASOL/PHF/ZILIS. May, 2000. French-Spanish-Moroccan. (Nadir Mokneche) Carmen Maura, Biyouna, Myriam Amarouchene.

THE HARMONIUM IN MY MEMORY
ILSHIN INVESTMENT. May, 1999. South Korean. (Lee Young-jae) Lee Byung-heon, Jeon Do-yeon, Lee Mi-yeon, Jeon Mu-song.

HARRISON'S FLOWER
7 FILMS CINEMA/STUDIO CANAL/-FRANCE 2 CINEMA. Sept., 2000. French. (Elie Chouraqui) Andie MacDowell, David Strathain, Elias Koteas, Adrien Brody, Brendan Gleeson, Alun Armstrong.

HARRY, HE'S HERE TO HELP
DIAPHANA FILMS. May, 2000. French. (Dominik Moll) Laurent Lucas, Sergi Lopez, Mathilde Seigner, Sophie Guillemin, Liliane Rovere, Dominique Rozan, Michel Fau.

HARRY POTTER AND THE SORCERER'S STONE
WARNER BROS. Nov., 2001. (Chris Columbus) Daniel Radcliffe, Rupert Grint, Emma Watson, John Cleese, Robbie Coltrane, Warwick Davis, Richard Griffiths, Richard Harris, Ian Hart, John Hurt, Alan Rickman, Fiona Shaw, Maggie Smith.

HARVARD MAN
KUSHNER-LOCKE CO. May, 2001. (James Toback) Adrian Grenier, Sarah Michelle Gellar, Joey Lauren Adams, Eric Stoltz, Rebecca Gayheart, Ray Allen.

HARVEST
GOLDHEART PICTURES. April, 1999. (Stuart Burkin) Mary McCormack, John Slattery, Jeffrey DeMunn.

HARVEST TIME
INTERARTES GMBH. Oct., 1998. German. (Stefan Schneider) Lucie Adelus, Jacques Bourgaux, Pascal Gravat, Gil Grillo, Katharine Sehnert.

HATHI
PRODUCTIONS LA FETE. Sept., 1998. Canadian. (Philippe Gautier) Jamedar Sabu Saab, Kawadi Makbul, Noorullah, Pyare Jan.

HAUNTED CASTLE
NWAVE PICTURES. Feb., 2001. Belgian-U.S. (Ben Stassen) Jasper Steverlinck, Kyoko Baertsoen, Harry Shearer.

THE HAUNTING
DREAMWORKS PICTURES. July, 1999. (Jan De Bont) Liam Neeson, Catherine Zeta-Jones, Owen Wilson, Lili Taylor, Bruce Dern.

HAVANA QUARTET
LIDER FILMS. June, 1999. Spanish. (Fernando Colomo) Ernesto Alterio, Mirtha Ibarra, Javier Camara, Laura Ramos, Daisy Granados.

HAWAIIAN GARDENS
LEORA FILMS. May, 2001. U.S.-German. (Percy Adlon) Andre Eisermann, Valeria Hernandez, Richard Bradford.

HAZY LIFE
MIDNIGHT CHILD THEATER. Oct., 1999. Japanese. (Nobuhiro Yamashita) Hiroshi Yamamoto, Teppei Uda, Hiromichi Maeda, Ko Riran, Maki Imaeda.

A HEAD FOR BUSINESS
BAC/ALAIN SARDE/CINE VALSE/LE STUDIO CANAL PLUS/AFCL/STUDIO IMAGES. Aug., 2000. French. (Guy-Philippe Bertin) Feodor Atkine, Claire Keim, Albert Delpy, Guy-Philippe Bertin, Patrice Bornand, Dominique Compagnon, Claude Koener.

HEAD ON
PALACE FILMS. May, 1998. Australian. (Ana Kokkinos) Alex Dimitriades, Paul Capsis, Julian Garner, Tony Nikolakopoulos.

HEAD OVER HEELS
UNIVERSAL PICTURES. Jan., 2001. (Mark Waters) Monica Potter, Freddie Prinze Jr., Shalom Harlow, Ivana Milicevic, Sarah O'Hare, Tomiko Fraser, China Chow.

HEALING BY KILLING
NEW YORKER FILMS. April, 1998. Israeli. (Nitzan Aviram) documentary.

HEART
FEATURE FILM CO. June, 1999. British. (Charles McDougall). Christopher Eccleston, Saskia Reeves, Kate Hardie, Rhys Ifans, Anna Chancellor.

HEARTBREAKERS
MGM. March, 2001. (David Mirkin) Sigourney Weaver, Jennifer Love Hewitt, Ray Liotta, Jason Lee, Anne Bancroft, Jeffrey Jones, Gene Hackman, Nora Dunn.

HEARTBREAK HOSPITAL
Sept., 2002. (Ruedi Gerber) Chelsea Altman, Patricia Clarkson, Diane Venora, John Shea, Demian Bichir.

HEARTLANDS
MIRAMAX (IN U.S.)/BUENA VISTA INTL. (IN U.K.). Aug., 2002. British-U.S. (Damien O'Donnell) Michael Sheen, Mark Addy, Jim Carter, Celia Imrie, Ruth Jones, Philippa Peak, Jane Robbins, Paul Shane, Mark Strong, Jade Rhodes.

HEART OF LIGHT
ASA FILM AS. May, 1998. Danish. (Jacob Gronlykke) Rasmus Lyberth, Vivi Nielsen, Anda Kristiansen, Niels Platou.

HEART OF THE SUN
DANCING STONES FILM. Aug., 1998. Canadian. (Francis Damberger) Christianne Hirt, Shaun Johnston, Michael Riley.

THE HEART OF THE WARRIOR
ALTAFILMS/TORNASOL/CARTEL/VIA DIGITAL/TVE. Jan., 2000. Spanish. (Daniel Monzon) Fernando Ramallo, Neus Asensi, Joel Joan, Santiago Segura, Javier Aller, Adria Collado, Jaime Barnatan.

HEARTS IN ATLANTIS
WARNER BROS. Aug., 2001. (Scott Hicks) Anthony Hopkins, Anton Yelchin, Hope Davis, Mika Boorem, David Morse, Alan Tudyk, Tom Bower, Celia Weston.

THE HEART'S ROOT
SUMA/LES FILMS DE L'ATLANTE. Aug., 2000. Portuguese-French. (Paulo Rocha) Luis Miguel Cintra, Joana Barcia, Melvil Poupaud.

HEATER
MARBLE ISLAND PICTURES/TELEFILM CANADA/VISION TV/WIC. Oct., 1999. Canadian. (Terrance Odette) Gary Farmer, Stephen Ouimette, Tina Keeper, Jan Skene.

HEAVEN
MIRAMAX FILMS. Sept., 1998. New Zealand. (Scott Reynolds) Martin Donovan, Danny Edwards, Richard Schiff, Joanna Going.

HEAVENLY GRASSLAND (TIANSHANG CAOYUAN)
Aug., 2002. Chinese. (Saifu, Mailisi) Narenhua, Ning Cai, Turmen.

HEAVEN'S PATH
Feb., 2002. Iranian-German. (Mahmoud Behraznia) Documentary.

HEAVY METAL 2000
EUROZOOM/COLUMBIA TRISTA/CINEGROUPE ANIMATION/ LIONS GATE/HELKON MEDIA/DAS WERK. Apr., 2000. Canadian-German. (Michel Lemire, Michael Coldewe) Michael Ironside, Julie Strain Eastman, Billy Idol, Pierre Kohn, Sonja Ball (voices). Animated.

HE DIED WITH A FELAFEL IN HIS HAND
NOTORIOUS FILM (AUSTRALIA)/FANDANGO (ITALY). May, 2001. Australian-Italian. (Richard Lowenstein) Noah Taylor, Emily Hamilton, Romane Bohringer, Alex Menglet, Brett Stewart, Damian Walshe-Howling, Torqui Neilson, Sophie Lee.

HEDWIG AND THE ANGRY INCH
FINE LINE FEATURES. Jan., 2001. (John Cameron Mitchell) John Cameron Mitchell, Andrea Martin, Michael Pitt, Alberta Watson, Stephen Trask, Rob Campbell.

HE GOT GAME
BUENA VISTA. April, 1998. (Spike Lee) Denzel Washington, Ray Allen, Mila Jovovich, Rosario Dawson, Hill Harper, Zelda Harris.

HEIDI M.
BAVARIA FILM INTL. Aug., 2001. German. (Michael Klier) Katrin Sass, Dominique Horwitz, Franziska Troegner, Ulrike Krumbiegel, Kurt Naumann, Julia Hummer, Martin Goeres.

THE HEIGHT OF THE SKY
GOOD GIRL FILMS. July, 1999. (Lyn Clinton) Jennifer Weedon, Jackie Stewart, Tom Crone, Grant Moninger, Evan Palazzo.

HEIST
WARNER BROS. Aug., 2001. (David Mamet) Gene Hackman, Danny De Vito, Delroy Lindo, Sam Rockwell, Rebecca Pidgeon, Ricky Jay.

HEJAR
OZEN FILM. April, 2002. Turkish-Greek-Hungarian. (Handan Ipekci) Sukran Gungor, Dilan Ercetin, Furun Demirel, Ismail Hakki Sen.

HELD UP
TRIMARK/MINDS EYE PICTURES/NEIL H. MORITZ. May, 2000. (Steve Rash) Jamie Foxx, Nia Long, Barry Corbin, Eduardo Yanez, John Cullum, Jake Busey, Michael Shamus Wiles, Sarah Paulson.

HELLHOUNDS ON MY TRAIL: THE AFTERLIFE OF ROBERT JOHNSON
NON FICTION FILMS/MUG-SHOT PRODS. Oct. 1999. (Robert Mugge) Bob Weir, Rob Wasserman, Keb' Mo', Robert Lockwood Jr., Joe Louis Walker, Billy Branch, Sonny Landreth. Music Documentary.

HELL HOUSE
Sept., 2001. (George Ratliff) Documentary.

HELL'S KITCHEN N.Y.C.
HK FILM CORP. Sept., 1998. (Cinciripini) Mekhi Phifer, Rosanna Arquette, William Forsythe, Angelina Jolie, Johnny Whitworth.

HE LOVES ME...HE LOVES ME NOT
UGC DISTRIBUTION. March, 2002. French. (Laetitia Colombani) Audrey Tautou, Samuel Le Bihan, Isabelle Carre, Clement Sibony, Sophie Guillemin, Eric Savin, Michele Garay, Elodie Navarre.

HELP!!!
CHINA STAR ENTERTAINMENT GROUP. Nov., 2000. Hong Kong. (Johnnie To, Wai Ka-fai) Ekin Cheng, Jordan Chan, Cecilia Cheung, Raymond Wong, Hui Siu-hung, Lam Suet, Bonnie Wong, Lam Kau.

HELP! I'M A FISH
FILM OFFICE (IN FRANCE)/NORDISK (IN DENMARK). March, 2001. Danish-German-French. (Stefan Fjeldmark) Animated.

HEMINGWAY: A PORTRAIT
OGDEN ENTERTAINMENT. Sept., 1999. (Erik Canuel). Animated.

HEMLOCK
IRANIAN FILM SOCIETY. April, 2001. Iranian. (Behrooz Afkhami) Fariborz Arab-Nia, Hedieh Tehrani, Hamid Reza Afshar, Rozita Ghafari, Manoucher Sadeghpour, Mohammad Saleh Allah.

HENRY HILL
HENRY HILL LLC. Oct. 1999. (David G. Kantar) Moira Kelly, Jamie Harrold, Susan Blommaert, Eden Riegel, John Griesemer, Michael Kimbal.

HENRY JAMES' THE GHOSTLY RENTAL
NEW CONCORDE. May, 1999. (Mitch Marcus) Michael York, Andrew Bowen, Claudia Christian, Aideen O'Donnell.

THE HERD
NATIONAL FILM BOARD/ONTARIO CENTRE. Sept., 1998. Canadian. (Peter Lynch) Colm Feore, David Hemblen, Mark McKinney, Don McKellar, Jim Allodi. Documentary.

HERE ON EARTH
20TH CENTURY FOX/FOX 200/DAVID T. FRIENDLY. Mar., 2000. (Mark Piznarsk) Chris Klein, Leelee Sobieski, Josh Hartnett, Michael Rooker, Annie Corley, Bruce Greenwood, Annette O'Toole.

HERE'S TO LIFE
RED SKY (CANADA). Sept., 2000. Canadian. (Arne Olsen) Eric McCormack, James Whitmore, Kim Hunter, Ossie Davis, Marya Delver, Margaret Ryan, Tyler Labine, Sarah Hayward.

HERE TO WHERE
HOLY COW FILMS, MAXIMUM FILMS (U.K.)/PREMIERE HEURE (FRANCE). Aug., 2001. British-French. (Glen Luchford) Paul Berczeller, Alfred Merhan, Abbas Baktiari, Mai Pexton.

HERE WE ARE WAITING FOR YOU
MARCELO MASAGAO. Jan., 2000. Brazilian. (Marcelo Masagao). Documentary.

HER MAJESTY
Oct., 2001. New Zealand. (Mark J. Gordon) Sally Andrews, Vicky Haughton, Mark Clare, Liddy Holloway, Craig Elliott, Anna Sheridan, Alison Routledge, Cameron Smith.

HEROES AND OTHER COWARDS
JUGENDFILM. Feb., 1999. German. (Dennis Satin) Ralf Bauer, Carin C. Tietze, Edgar M. Boehlke, Andreas Wisniewski, Peter Nottmeier.

HEROES IN LOVE
PCC SKYHORSE/EMPEROR MULTIMEDIA GROUP. Aug., 2001. Hong Kong. (Various directors)
KIDNAP
(Shya Wing) Chang Tze-hin, Elegant Tong, Gloria Cheng.
MY BELOVED
(Nicholas Tse, Stephen Fung) Wu Por.
OH G!
(GC Goo-bi) Charlene Choi, Lawrence Chou.
TBC
(Jan Lamb)

HEROES IN THE TYROL
PROGRESS FILM. Feb., 1999. Austrian-Swiss-German. (Niki List) Christian Schmidt, Elke Winkens, Christian Pogats, I. Stangl, Gregor Seberg.

A HERO NEVER DIES
FILM CITY. Dec., 1998. Hong Kong. (Johnnie To) Leon Lai, Lau Ching-wan, Fiona Leung, Yo Yo Mung, Fong Ping.

THE HERO ZHENG CHENGGONG
XIAOXIANG FILM STUDIO/FUJIAN FILM STUDIO. Aug., 2001. Chinese. (Wu Ziniu) Zhao Wenzhuo, Shui Ling, Du Zhiguo, Yoko Shimada, Jiang Qinqin, Zhang Shan.

HER WAY
SOVKINO. Aug., 2000. Soviet Union–1929. (Aleksandr Strizhak) Emma Tserarskaya, Aleksandr Zhukov, Karl Gurniak, A. Otradin. Silent.

HEY ARNOLD! THE MOVIE
PARAMOUNT. May, 2002. (Tuck Tucker) Spencer Klein, Francesca Marie Smith, Jamil Walker Smith, Dan Castellaneta, Tress MacNeille, Paul Sorvino, Jennifer Jason Leigh, Christopher Lloyd. Animation.

HEY, HAPPY!
BIG DADDY BEER GUTS. Jan., 2001. Canadian. (Noam Gonick) Jeremie Yuen, Craig Aftanas, Clayton Godson, Johnny Simone, Dita Vendetta, Chelsey Perfanick, Sylvia Dueck, Lola Wong.

HEY! RAM
RAAJKAMAL FILMS INTL. Jan., 2001. Indian. (Kamal Haasan) Kamal Haasan, Shah Rukh Khan, Rani Mukharjee, Atul Kulkarni, Arun Bali, Vasundra Das.

THE HIDDEN HALF
ARTA FILM. Feb., 2001. Iranian. (Tahmine Milani) Niki Karimi, Mohammad Nikbin, Atilla Pesiani, Soghra Abissi, Akbar Moazezi, Afarin Obeisi.

A HIDDEN LIFE (UMA VIDA EM SEGREDO)
Aug., 2002. Brazilian. (Suzana Amaral) Sabrina Greve, Caca Amaral, Eliane Giardini, Eric Novinsky, Neusa Borges.

HIDDEN WHISPER
CENTRAL MOTION PICTURE CORP. May, 2000. Taiwanese. (Vivian Chang) Hsiao Shu-shen, Hsia Ching-ting, Huang Pin-hsuan.

HIDEOUS KINKY
AMLF. Oct., 1998. British-French. (Gillies MacKinnon) Kate Winslet, Said Taghmaoui, Bella Riza, Carrie Mullan, Pierre Clementi.

THE HIDING PLACE
UNLEASHED PICTURE. June, 2000. (Douglas Green) Kim Hunter, Timothy Bottoms, Kim Greist, Katie Hagan.

HI, DHARMA
Nov., 2001. South Korean. (Park Cheol-kwan) Park Shin-yang, Jeong Jin-Yeong, Park Sang-myeong, Kang Seong-jin, Kim Su-ro, Hong Kyeong-in, Kim In-mun, Lee Weon-jong.

HIGH ART
OCTOBER FILMS. Jan., 1998. (Lisa Cholodenko) Ally Sheedy, Radha Mitchell, Patricia Clarkson, Tammy Grimes, Gabriel Mann, Bill Sage.

HIGH CRIMES
20TH CENTURY FOX. March, 2002. (Carl Franklin) Ashley Judd, Morgan Freeman, Jim Caviezel, Adam Scott, Amanda Peet, Bruce Davison, Tom Bower, Carlos Hernandez.

HIGH FIDELITY
BUENA VISTA/TOUCHSTONE/WORKING TITLE FILMS/DOGSTAR FILMS/NEW CRIME PRODS. Mar., 2000. (Stephen Frears) John Cusack, Iben Hjejle, Todd Louiso, Jack Black, Lisa Bonet, Catherine Zeta-Jones, Tim Robbins, Chris Rehmann, Ben Carr., Lili Taylor.

HIGH HEELS AND LOW LIFES
BUENA VISTA INTL. (IN U.K.)/BUENA VISTA (IN U.S.) July, 2001. British-U.S. (Mel Smith) Minnie Driver, Mary McCormack, Kevin McNally, Mark Williams, Danny Dyer, Kevin Eldon, Michael Gambon, Len Collin, Darren Boyd.

HIGHLANDER: ENDGAME
MIRAMAX/DIMENSION FILMS/DAVIS/PANZER PROD. Aug., 2000. (Douglas Aarniokoski) Christopher Lambert, Bruce Payne, Lisa Barbuscia, Donnie Yen, Jim Byrnes, Peter Wingfield, Damon Dash.

A HIGH SKY SUMMER
Feb., 2002. Chinese. (Li Jixian) Wei Zhilin, Cheng Taisheng, Li Wanquan.

HIGHWAY MELODY
UIP/PLAYTIME/FRANCE 2 CINEMA/TPS CINEMA. June, 2000. French. (Thierry Boscheron) Sacha Bourdo, Aure Atika, Philippe Nahon, Marc Berman.

HIGHWAY SOCIETY
MARIETTE RISSENBEEK/MARIANNA FILMS/NDR. Nov., 1999. German-Finnish. (Mika Kaurismaki) Kai Wiesinger, Marie Zielcke, Jochen Nickel, Hannes Hellmann, Michaela Rosen.

HIGHWAY 395
FRED DRYER PRODS. Nov., 2000. (Fred Dryer) Fred Dryer, Greg Crooks, Diane Delano, Shawn Huff, Christopher Neame, Steve Reevis, Tim Thomerson.

HILARY AND JACKIE
INTERMEDIA FILMS/FILM FOUR. Sept., 1998. British. (Anand Tucker) Emily Watson, Rachel Griffiths, James Frain.

HILDEGARDE
July, 2002. Australian. (Di Drew) Richard E. Grant, Tom Long, Tara Morice, Sam Geer, Dayne Hudson, Gezelle Byrnes, Paul Goddard, John Dommett, David Hannay.

HI-LIFE
LION'S GATE. Oct., 1998. (Roger Hedden): Katrin Cartlidge, Charles Durning, Daryl Hannah, Moira Kelly. Peter Reigert.

THE HI-LINE
BOYLE/TAYLOR PRODS. Jan., 1999. (Ron Judkins) Rachael Leigh Cook, Ryan Alosio, Tantoo Cardinal, Margot Kdder, Stuart Margolin.

THE HI-LO COUNTRY
GRAMERCY PICTURES. Dec., 1999. (Stephen Frears) Woody Harrelson, Billy Crudup, Patricia Arquette, Cole Hauser.

HIMALAYA
JACQUES PERRIN. Aug., 1999. French-Swiss. (Eric Valli) Thilen Lhondup, Lhapka Tsamchoe, Gurgon Kyap, Karm Tensing Nyama Lama.

HIPHOPBATTLE.COM: HIPHOP FOR LIFE
Jan., 2002. (David Velo Stewart) Q-Nice, Danielle Green, Da Boogie Man, Suave Gotti, Blacknile, George Baynard Jr.

HIPPOLYT
CINEMASTAR/EUROPA 2000/RTL KLUB. Feb., 2000. Hungarian. (Barna Kaba) Karoly Eperjes, Robert Koltai, Judit Pogany, Agi Szirtes.

HIS MASTER'S VOICE
LOLAFILMS DISTRIBUCION. Sept., 2001. Spanish. (Emilio Martinez-Lazaro) Eduard Fernandez, Silvia Abascal, Joaquim de Almeida, Imanol Arias, Ana Otero, Alicia Agut.

HIS MOST SERENE HIGHNESS
IMCINE, FOPROCINE, SERENISIMA FILMS. Feb., 2001. Mexican. (Felipe Cazals) Alejandro Parodi, Ana Bertha Espin, Rodolfo Arias, Pedro Armendariz, Blanca Guerra, Ana Ofelia Murguia.

HISTORY IS MADE AT NIGHT
J&M/SCALA/IMA/SMILE ENTERTAINMENT/HELKON MEDIA/CANAL PLUS. Sept, 1999. British. (.Ilkka Jarvilaturi): Bill Pullman, Irene Jacob, Bruno Kirby, Glenn Plummer, Udo Kier, Andre Oumansky.

HISTORY LESSONS
BARBARA HAMMER. June, 2000. (Barbara Hammer) Ann Maguire, Kaja Aman, Antonio Caputo, Denise Coles, Elvis Herselvis, Cambrea Ezell, Dred, Coco Feliciano, Mo Fisher. Documentary.

HIS WIFE'S DIARY
MINISTRY OF CINEMATOGRAPHY OF RUSSIA-STUDIO ROCK. July, 2000. Russian. (Alexey Uchitel) Andrey Smirnov, Galina Tyunina, Olga Budina, Yevgeny Mironov.

HIT AND RUNWAY
MIRADOR FILMS. Apr., 1999. (Christopher Livingston) Michael Parducci, Peter Jacobson, Judy Prescott, Kerr Smith, Joyt Richards.

HITCHCOCK, SELZNICK AND THE END OF HOLLYWOOD
AMERICAN MASTERS. Jan., 1999. (Michael Epstein). Documentary.

HITEBOYS
FOX SEARCHLIGHT. Aug., 1999. (Marc Levin) Danny Hoch, Dash Mihok, Mark Webber, Piper Perabo, Eugene Bird.

HI TESSA
POLISH TELEVISION. July, 2001. Polish. (Robert Glinski) Aleksandra Gietner, Karoline Sobczak, Zbigniew Zamachowski, Malgorzata Rozniatowska, Krzysztof Kiersznowski.

THE HITMAN
FLEA MARKET. Aug., 1998. Hong Kong. (Tung Wai) Jet Li, Eric Tsang, Simon Yam, Gigi Leung, Keiji Sato.

HOCHELAGA
CINEMA LIBRE. Sept., 2000. Canadian. (Michel Jette) Dominic Darceuil, David Boutin, Ronald Houle, Jean-Nicolas Verreault, Michel Charette, Deano Clavet, Claudia Hurtubise.

HOLD BACK THE NIGHT
FILM CONSORTIUM/FILMFOUR. May, 1999. British. (Phil Davis) Christine Tremarco, Stuart Sinclair Blyth, Sheila Hancock.

HOLD-UP
ALLEGRO. Aug., 2000. Australian. (Florian Flicker) Roland Dueringer, Joachim Bissmeier, Josef Hader, Birgit Doll, Sonja Romei, Ulrike Beimpold, Klaus Ortner, Klaus Haendl.

THE HOLD-UP
COLUMBIA TRISTAR (SPAIN). May, 2001. Spanish. (Eva Lesmes) Adriana Ozores, Carmen Maura, Maribel Verdu, Malena Alterio, Jaime Pujol, Juan Gea, Joaquin Clement.

HOLD YOU TIGHT
GOLDEN HARVEST. Feb., 1998. Hong Kong. (Stanley Kwan) Chingmy Yau, Sunny Chan, Eric Tsang, Ko Yu-lun, Sandra Ng.

THE HOLE
PATHE FILM DISTRIBUTION. April, 2001. British. (Nick Hamm) Thora Birch, Desmond Harrington, Embeth Davidtz, Daniel Brocklebank, Laurence Fox, Keira Knightley, Steven Waddington.

HOLE IN THE SKY
PIA CORP./FLAMINGO/BEAM ENTERTAINMENT. Jan., 2001. Japanese. (Kazuyoshi Kumakiri) Susumu Terajima, Yuriko Kilkuchi, Bunmei Tobayama, Syunsuke Sawada, Syunsuke Gondo.

HOLIDAY
LES FILMS DES TOURNELLES (IN FRANCE). March, 2001. French. (Yves Hanchar) Luc Picard, Luigi Diberti, Didier De Neck, Jeremy Lippmann, Nicolas Scellier, Florence Giorgetti, Catheine Hosmalin.

HOLLOW MAN
SONY PICTURES ENTERTAINMENT/COLUMBIA PICTURES/ DOUGLAS WICK. July, 2000. (Paul Verhoeven) Kevin Bacon, Elisabeth Shue, Josh Brolin, Greg Grunberg, Mary Jo Randle, Steve Altes.

HOLLYWOOD ENDING
DREAMWORKS. May, 2002. (Woody Allen) Woody Allen, Tea Leoni, George Hamilton, Debra Messing, Mark Rydell, Tiffani Thiessen, Treat Williams, Lu Yu, Isaac Mizrahi.

HOLLYWOOD, HONG KONG
CAPITOL FILMS. Aug., 2001. Hong Kong-Japanese-French-British. (Fruit Chan) Zhou Xun, Glen Chin, Wong You-nam, Ho Sai-man, Leung Sze-ping, Wan Kam-li, Hu Wei-wen, Fong Wai-hung.

THE HOLY LAND
April, 2001. (Eitan Gorlin) Oren Rehany, Tchelet Semel, Saul Stein, Albert Illooze, Arie Moskuna.

HOLY MAN
BUENA VISTA. Oct., 1998. (Stephen Herek) Eddie Murphy, Jeff Goldblum, Kelly Preston, Robert Loggia, Jon Cryer.

HOLY SMOKE
MIRAMAX FILMS. Sept., 1999. (Jane Campion) Kate Winslet, Harvey Keitel, Pam Grier, Julie Hamilton, Sophie Lee.

HOLY TONGUE
MEDUSA FILM/RODEO DRIVE/TELEPIU. Sept., 2000. Italian. (Carlo Mazzacurati) Antonio Albanese, Fabrizio Bentivoglio, Toni Bertorelli.

HOMEBOYS ON THE BEACH
AFMD. June, 1999. French. (Djamel Bensalah) Jamel Debbouze, Stephane Soo Mongo, Lorant Deutsch, Julien Courbey.

HOMECOMING: LITTLE BUT TOUGH PART 2
MAFILM AKTIV STUDIO/DUNA TV, HUNNIA STUDIO. Feb., 1999. Hungarian. (Ferenc Grunwalsky) Sandor Gaspar, Agnes Csere, Janos Ban, Jacint Juhasz, Jozsef Szarvas Dorottya Udvaros.

HOME FRIES
WARNER BROS. Sept., 1998. (Dean Parisot) Drew Barrymore, Luke Wilson, Catherine O'Hara, Jake Busey, Shelley Duvall, Kim Robillard.

HOME GAME
QUINTE/ARTE, GOETHE INSTITUTE. Feb., 2000. German. (Pepe Danquart). Documentary.

HOMEGROWN
SONY PICTURES ENTERTAINMENT. April, 1998. (Stephen Gyllenhaal) Billy Bob Thornton, Hank Azaria, Kelly Lynch, Ryan Phillippe, Jon Bon Jovi, John Lithgow, Ted Danson.

HOMELAND
PHILOMATH FILMS. Oct., 2000. (Jilann Spitzmiller, Hank Rogerson) Documentary.

HOME MOVIE
INDEPENDENT MEDIA. Jan., 2001. (Chris Smith) Documentary.

HOME PAGE
COPACETIC PICTURES/CINEMAX/ZDF-ARTE. Jan., 1999. (Doug Block). Documentary.

HOMESICK
MOVER'S ENTERTAINMENT. Feb., 2000. Japanese. (Hineki Mito) Kiminobu Okumura, Aki Onobara, Hana Yamanashi, Masato Kondo, Hiroshi Komiyama, Shingo Tsurumi.

HOME SOUR HOME
SONET FILM. Jan., 2001. Swedish. (Dan Ying) Mats Blomgren, Lars Varinger, Anna Bjelkerud, Anna Eidem, Fredrik Nilsson, Katarina Weidhagen, Michalis Koutsogiannakis.

HOMETOWN BLUE
ARP. May, 1999. French. (Stephane Brize) Florence Vignon, Mathilde Seigner, Antoine Chappey, Philippe Duquesne, Jenny Alpha.

HOMO HEIGHTS
LEHMANN-MOORE PRODS. Feb., 1998. (Sara Moore) Quentin Crisp, Lea DeLaria, Stephen Sorrentino, David Fenley, Emil Herrera.

HONEST
PATHE/SEVEN DIALS. May, 2000. (David A. Stewart) Peter Facinelli, Nicole Appleton, Melanie Blatt, James Cosmo, Jonathan Cake, Corin Redgrave, Rick Warren, Annette Badland, Paul Rider, Sean Gilder.

HONEY FOR OSHUN
ICAIC/EL PASO. Aug., 2001. Cuban-Spanish. (Humberto Solas, Sergio Benvenuto) Jorge Perugorria, Isabel Santos, Mario Limonta, Saturnino Garcia.

HONEY, I SENT THE MEN TO THE MOON
COSTA BRAVA FILMS S.L. June, 1998. Spanish. (Marta Balletbo-Coll, Ana Simon Cerezo) Cookie Rufino, Claudia Carasso, Marta Balletbo-Coll.

HONOLULU
ODEON. March, 2002. German. (Uschi Fersti, Florian Gallenburger, Saskia Jell, Vanessa Jopp, Mattias Lehmann, Beryl Schennen, Sandra Schmidt) Stefan Maass, Jochen Nickel, Chiara Schoras, Daniel Bruehl, Anna Thalbach, Markus Knuefken, Alexandra Maria Lara, Mehdi Moinzadeh, Shira Fleisher, Mina Tander.

HONOLULU BABY
MIKADO. March, 2001. Italian. (Maurizio Nichett) Maruizio Nichetti, Maria de Medeiros, Jean Rochefort, Paulina Galvez, Giulia Weber, Massimo Wertmuller, Renato Scarpa.

HONOUR OF THE HOUSE
UMBIFILM/PEGASUS/GOTAFILM/FILM I VAST/NORDISK FILM PROD. Feb., 2000. Icelandic-Swedish-Danish. (Gudny Halldorsdottir) Ragnhildur Gisladottir, Tinna Gunnlaugsdottir, Egil Olafsson, Rurik Haraldsson, Agneta Ekmanner, Reine Brynolfsson.

HOOVER
PAMPLIN-FISHER CO. Dec., 2000. (Rick Pamplin) Ernest Borgnine, Cartha D. "Deke" Deloach.

HOPE FLOATS
20TH CENTURY FOX. May, 1998. (Forest Whitaker) Sandra Bullock, Larry Connick Jr., Gena Rowlands, Mae Whitman, Michael Pare.

HOPELESS
KAHUKURA/NEW ZEALAND FILM COMMISSION. May, 2000. New Zealand. (Stephen Hickeye) Phil Pinner, Mia Taumoepeau.

THE HORSE WHISPERER
BUENA VISTA. April, 1998. (Robert Redford) Robert Redford, Kristin Scott Thomas, Sam Neill, Dianne Wiest, Scarlett Johansson.

HOTARU
DENTSU/IMAGICA/SUNCENT CINEMAWORKS/TOKYO THEATRE/LES FILMS DE L'OBSERVATOIRE. Aug., 2000. Japanese. (Naomi Kawase) Yuko Nakamura, Tashiya Nagasawa.

HOTEL
MOONSTONE ENTERTAINMENT. Sept., 2001. British-Italian. (Mike Figgis) Rhys Ifans, Saffron Burrows, David Schwimmer, Salma Hayek, Burt Reynolds, Julian Sands, Danny Huston, Lucy Liu.

HOTEL ROOM
ALTA FILMS. Sept., 1998. Spanish-U.S.. (Cesc Gay) Barbara Boudon, Eric Kraus, Paris Kiely, Xaier Domingo.

HOTEL SPLENDIDE
FILMFOUR/TOC/RENEGADE. Feb., 2000. British-French. (Terence Gross) Toni Collette, Daniel Craig, Stephen Tompkinson, Katrin Cartlidge, Hugh O'Conor, Helen McCrory, Peter Vaughan.

THE HOTEL UPSTAIRS
March, 2001. (Daniel Baer) Errol Cooper, Fanny Renoir, Richard Wilburn, Jack Hirschman, Agneta Falk, the Pineda family, John Chen. Documentary.

HOTOKE
SONY PICTURES. June, 2001. Japanese. (Jinsei Tsuji) Shinji Takeda, Ryuichi Oura, Yuma, Shouki Jo, Kanji Tsuda.

HORSES: THE STORY OF EQUUS
Aug., 2002. Australian. (Michael Caulfield) IMAX.

HOUSE!
PATHE/LIVE WIRE/CF1/SOUTH WALES FILM COMMISSION/ VICTOR FILM/BRITISH SCREEN/ARTS FILM COUNCIL OF ENGLAND. Jan., 2000. British. (Julian Kemp) Kelly Macdonald, Freddie Jones, Miriam Margolyes, Jason Hughes, Mossie Smith.

HOUSEBOUND
REARVIEW MIRROR. Sept., 2000. (Mari Kornhauser) Katharina Wressnig, Peter Sarsgaard, Angeline Ball, Geoffrey Lower, Liz Stauber, Ann Magnuson.

A HOUSE BUILT ON WATER
Feb., 2002. Iranian. (Bahman Farmanara) Reza Kianian, Ezat Entezami, Mehdi Safavi, Hedye Tehrani, Bita Farahi, Behnaz Jafari.

A HOUSE DIVIDED
SHOWTIME/PARAMOUNT NETWORK TV/AVNET/KERNER CO./ATKINSON WAY. Jan., 2000. (John Kent Harrison) Jennifer Beals, Lisa Gay Hamilton, Sam Waterston, Tim Daly, Ron White.

A HOUSEKEEPER
PATHE DISTRIBUTION. May, 2002. French. (Claude Berri) Jean-Pierre Bacri, Emilie Dequenne, Brigitte Catillon, Jacques Frantz, Axelle Abbadie, Catherine Breillat.

HOUSE OF ANGELS
WARNER BROS. (TURKEY). Feb., 2001. Turkish-Hungarian-Romanian. (Omer Kavur) Talat Bulut, Aytac Arman, Arslan Kacar, Haldun Hoysan.

THE HOUSE OF CAIN
GREEK FILM CENTRE-NET-GREEK TV-STEFI FILMS. Feb., 2001. Greek. (Christos Karakepelis) Documentary.

HOUSE OF FOOLS (DOM DURAKOV)
BAC FILMS. Sept., 2002. Russian-French. (Andrei Konchalovsky) Bryan Adams, Julia Vysotsky, Sultan Islamov, Stanislav Varkki, Vladas Bagdonas, Eugeny Mironov, Elena Fomina.

HOUSE OF LUK
DISTINCT FEATURES. Jan., 2001. (Derek Diorio) Pierre Brault, Dan Lalande, John Ng, Michaek Moriarty, Pat Morita, Lorraine Ansell, Linda Goodwin, Elaine Klimasko.

HOUSE OF MEMORIES
SURAVI. July, 2000. Indian. (Aparna Sen) Soumitra Chatterjee, Aparna Sen, Rituparna Sengupta, Sohini Haldar, Sailee Sengupta.

THE HOUSE OF MIRTH
FILMFOUR/GRANADA/THREE RIVERS/ARTS COUNCIL OF ENGLAND/SCOTTISH ARTS COUNCIL/SHOWTIME NETWORK/ GLASGOW FILM FUND/DIAPHANA/PROGRES/KINOWELT. Aug., 2000. British. (Terence Davies) Gillian Anderson, Eric Stoltz, Dan Aykroyd, Eleanor Bron, Terry Kinney, Anthony LaPaglia, Elizabeth McGovern.

HOUSE OF ORGIES
KLUSFILM. Sept., 2000. Swiss. (Mathiew Seiler) Gustavo Salami, Vanessa Augustin, Barbara-Magdalena Ahren, Frank Demenga, Norbert Schwientek, Wanda Vyslouzilova.

THE HOUSE OF THE DEAD
MEZHRABPOMFILM. Aug., 2000. Soviet Union–1932. (Vasili Fyodorov) Nikolai Khmelyov, Nikolai Podgorny, Nikolai Vitovtov, Nikolai Radin, Vladimir Belokurov, Vasili Kovrigin.

A HOUSE ON A HILL
CALLIOPE FILMS. April, 2001. (Chuck Workman) Philip Baker Hall, Laura San Giacomo, Shirley Knight, Rebecca Staab, Henry Rollins, James Karen, Domenica Scorsese.

HOUSE ON HAUNTED HILL
WARNER BROS./DARK CASTLE ENTERTAINMENT. Oct. 1999. (William Malone) Geoffrey Rush, Famke Janssen, Taye Diggs, Peter Gallagher, Chris Kattan, Ali Larter, Bridgette Wilson, Max Perlich.

HOW HARRY BECAME A TREE
CATTLEYA. Aug., 2001. Irish-Italian-British-French. (Goran Paskaljevic) Colm Meaney, Adrian Dunbar, Cilliam Murphy, Kerry Condon, Pat Laffan, Gail Fitzpatrick, Maighread Ni Conghaile.

HOW HIGH
UNIVERSAL. Dec., 2001. (Jesse Dylan) Method Man, Redman, Obba Babatunde, Mike Epps, Anna Maria Horsford, Fred Willard, Jeffery Jones, Hector Elizondo, Lark Voorhies, Al Shearer, Chuck Davis.

HOW SAMIRA MADE 'THE BLACKBOARD'
MAKHMALBAF FILM HOUSE. Sept., 2000. Iranian. (Maysam Makhmalbaf) Documentary.

HOW SILLY WE ARE TO GROW UP
ABSURDOFILM. Sept., 2000. Argentine. (Roly Santos) Gustavo Garzon, Laura Melillo, Leo Masliah, Jean Pierre Reguerraz, Ginger Poujoulet, Victoria de Elizalde, Claudio Pazos, Martin Kalwill.

HOW STELLA GOT HER GROOVE BACK
20TH CENTURY FOX. Aug., 1998. (Kevin Rodney Sullivan) Angela Bassett, Taye Diggs, Regina King, Whoopi Goldberg.

HOW THE WAR STARTED ON MY LITTLE ISLAND
HRT PRODUCTION. June, 1998. Croatian. (Vinko Bresan) Vlatko Dulic, Ljubomir Kerekes, Ivan Brkic, Predrag Vuovic-Predjo.

HOW TO KILL YOUR NEIGHBOR'S DOG
MILLENNIUM FILMS/CINERENTA/SOUTH FORK PICTURES/ LONSDALE PICTURES. May, 2000. (Michael Kalesniko) Kenneth Branagh, Robin Wright Penn, Jared Harris, Johnathon Schaech, Peter Riegert, Lynn Redgrave.

HOW TO MAKE A MARTINI
Nov., 2001. Italian. (Kiko Stella) Adriana Asti, Flavio Bucci Antonio Catania, Ivano Marescotti, Elena Sofia Ricci. Flavio Bonacci, Giulio Brogi, Bruno Armado.

HOW TO MAKE THE CRUELEST MONTH
FUGUE STATE/MAGNET. Jan., 1998. (Kip Koenig) Clea DuVall, Gabriel Mann, Mary Kay Place, Marianne Jean-Baptiste.

HS
OCEAN FILMS. July, 2001. French-Belgian. (Jean-Paul Lilienfeld) Dieudonne, Lambert Wilson, Francois Berleand, Lorant Deutsch, Jackie Berroyer, Stephan Guerin-Tillie, Pascal Leguennec.

H STORY
DENTSU-IMAGICA-SUNCENT CINEMAWORKS-TOKYO THEATERS. May, 2001. Japanese. (Nobuhiro Suwa) Beatrice Dalle, Kou Machida, Hiroaki Umano, Nobuhiro Suwa, Caroline Champetier, Michiko Yoshitake, Motoko Suhama.

HUMANITY
TADRART FILMS. May, 1999. (Bruno Dumont) Emmanuel Schotte, Severine Caneele, Philippe Tullier.

THE HUMAN BODY
NWAVE PICTURES DISTRIBUTION. Oct., 2001. (Peter Georgi) Dr. Robert Wilson (narrator) Documentary-IMAX.

THE HUMAN RACE
TELL THE TRUTH PICTURES. June, 1998. (Bobby Houston). Documentary.

HUMAN NATURE
FINE LINE FEATURES (IN U.S.). May, 2001. U.S.-French. (Michel Gondry) Tim Robbins, Patricia Arquette, Rhys Ifans, Miranda Otto, Robert Forster, Mary Kay Place, Miguel Sandoval, Toby Huss, Peter Dinklage, Rosie Perez.

HUMAN RESOURCES
LA SEPT ARTE/HAUT ET COURT/CENTRE NATIONAL DE LA CINEMATOGRAPHIE/PROCIREP/BBC FILMS. Sept., 1999. French. (Laurent Cantet) Jalil Lespert, Jean-Claude Vallod, Chantal Barre, Veronique de Pandelaere, Michel Begnez, Lucien Longueville.

HUMAN TRAFFIC
METRODOME. June, 1999. British-Irish. (Justin Kerrigan) John Simm, Lorraine Pilkington, Shaun Parkes, Danny Dyer, Nicola Reynolds.

THE HUMILIATED
Jesper Jargil/Danish Film Institute/DRTV/Danish Ministry of Education. Sept., 1999. Danish. (Jesper Jargil). Documentary.

HUMRAAZ
July, 2002. Indian. (Abbas-Mustan) Bobby Deol, Akshaye Khanna, Amisha Patel, Johnny Lever.

THE HUNDRED STEPS
ISTITUTO LUCE/TITTI FILM/RAI. Aug., 2000. Italian. (Marco Tullio Girodana) Luigi Lo Cascio, Luigi Maria Burruano, Lucia Sardo, Paolo Briguglia, Tony Sperandeo, Pippo Montalbano, Ninni Bruschetta.

HUNGER
MARKET STREET PRODS. Jan., 2001. (M. Giese) Joseph Culp, Kathleen Luong, Redmond Gleason, James Quill, T. Henry Amitai, Casper Andreas, V. Ray Bodie, Robert Culp.

HUNGER—ADDICTED TO LOVE
BUENA VISTA INTL. Feb., 1998. German. (Dava Vavrova) Catherine Flemming, Kai Wiesinger, Christiane Horbiger, Jurgen Schornagel.

HUNGER AND THIRST
CECCHI GOR. MAR., 1999. Italian. (Antonio Albanese) Antonio Albanese, Lorenza Indovina, Aisha Cerami, Lucia Guzzardi, Rosa Pianeta.

THE HUNGRY BACHELOR'S CLUB
MAMA'S BOYS PRODS./TAGGART TRANSCONTINENTAL/MANAGED PASSION FILMS. Nov., 1999. (Gregory Ruzzin) Candice Azzara, Michael Des Barres, Jorja Fox, Katherine Kendall, Suzanne Mara, Peter Murnik.

THE HUNT
HUNGRY EYE PICTURES. Feb., 1998. Dutch. (Niek Koppen) documentary.

THE HUNTER
UIP. May, 1998. Turkish-Hungarian. (Erden Kiral) Jale Arikan, Ahmet Ugurlu, Fikret Kuskan.

HUNTERS IN THE SNOW
WEGA. Feb., 2000. Austrian. (Michael Kreihsl) Ulrich Tukur, Julia Filiminow, Johannes Silberschneider, Sophia Gorgi, Claudia Martini.

HUNTER'S MOON
MPC & ASSOCIADOS. Feb., 2000. Brazilian. (Alberto Graca) Marcello Antony, Barbara Schulz, Paulo Vespucio, Jean-Louis Tribes.

THE HURDY-GURDY MAN
TIMBERLAKE. Feb., 1999. U.S.-Hungarian. (Gabe Von Dettre) Brad Dourif, Kathleen Gati, William Hickey, Wallace Shawn, Meat Loaf.

HURLYBURLY
FINE LINE. Sept., 1998. (Anthony Drazan) Sean Penn, Kevin Spacey, Robin Wright-Penn, Chazz Palminteri, Garry Shandling, Meg Ryan.

THE HURRICANE
UNIVERSAL/BEACON PICTURES/AZOFF FILMS/RUDY LANGLAIS. Nov., 1999. (Norman Jewison) Denzel Washington, Vicellous Reon Shannon, Deborah Kara Unger, Liev Schreiber, John Hannah, Dan Hedaya.

HURT
AUSTRALIAN FILM INSTITUTE/BIG HART/OMNI GROUP/ARTS NORTHWEST/OUTBACK ARTS/TRUSTEES OF CASINO DEVELOPMENT FUND/NSW MINISTRY OF ARTS/STEPHEN GRANT/OUTSIDER. July, 2000. Australian. (Philip Crawford, Matthew Priestley & 250 young Australians).

HUSH
SONY PICTURES ENTERTAINMENT. March, 1998. (Jonathan Darby) Jessica Lange, Gwyneth Paltrow, Johnathon Schaech, Nina Foch.

HUSH!
FORTISSIMO FILM SALES. May, 2001. Japanese. (Ryosuke Hashiguchi) Seiichi Tanabe, Kazuya Takahashi, Reiko Kataoka.

HYBRID
PICTURE. Oct., 2000. (Monteith McCollum) Documentary.

HYGIENE DE L'ASSASSIN
MFD. Feb., 1999. French. (Francois Ruggieri) Jean Yanne, Barbara Schulz, Sophie Broustal, Catherine Hiegel, Eric Prat.

HYPNOSIS
TOHO/TBS. Dec., 1999. Japanese. (Masayuki Ochiai) Goro Inagaki, Miho Kanno, Ken Utsui, Takeshi Sho, Yuki Watanabe, Shigemitsu Ogi, Kenta Satori, Akira Shirai, Ren Osugi.

HYPNOTIZED AND HYSTERICAL (HAIRSTYLIST WANTED)
MARS DISTRIBUTION. May, 2002. French. (Claude Duty) Amira Casar, Marina Gois, Olivia Bonamy, Charles Berling, Sergi Lopez.

HYSTERIC
LEGEND PICTURES/VENTURE FILM. Aug., 2000. Japanese. (Takahisa Zeze) Hijiri Kojima Koji Chihara, Shingo Tsurumi, Jun Murakami.

I

I AM AN S+M WRITER
A YFC TAIYOTOSHO. Oct., 2000. Japanese. (Ryuichi Hiroki) Ren Osugi, Yoko Hoshi, Jun Murakami, Eri Yamazaki, William Brian Churchill.

I AM DINA
COLUMBIA TRISTAR. Feb., 2002. Danish-Norwegian. (Ole Bornedal) Maria Bonnevie, Gerard Depardieu, Christopher Eccleston, Pernilla August, Bjorn Floberg, Hans Matheson, Jorgen Langhelle.

I AM JOSH POLONSKI'S BROTHER
FRAMED/FILMAKER. Feb., 2001. U.S.-French. (Raphael Nadjari) Richard Edson, Jeff Ware, Meg Hartig, Arnold Barkus, Yvan Martin, Etta Barkus.

I AM SAM
NEW LINE CINEMA. Nov., 2001. (Jessie Nelson) Sean Penn, Michelle Pfeiffer, Dakota Fanning, Dianne Wiest, Loretta Devine, Richard Schiff, Laura Dern, Brad Allan Silverman.

I AM TRYING TO BREAK YOUR HEART
COWBOY PICTURES. June, 2002. (Sam Jones) Jeff Tweedy, John Stirratt, Leroy Bach, Glenn Kotche, Jay Bennett, Tony Margherita, Greg Kot, David Fricke, Howie Klein.Documentary.

ICE AGE
20TH CENTURY FOX. Feb., 2002. (Chris Wedge) Ray Romano, John Leguizamo, Denis Leary, Goran Visnjic, Jack Black, Tara Strong, Stephen Root,Diedrich Bader, Alan Tudyk, Lorri Bagley, Jane Krakowski, Chris Wedge. Animation.

ICE CREAM, CHOCOLATE AND OTHER CONSOLATIONS
Oct., 2001. Canadian. (Julie Hivon) Isabelle Brouillette, Danny Gilmore, Jacinthe Rene, Dorothee Berryman, France Castel, Serge Theriault, Claude Pregent.

THE ICELANDIC DREAM
ICELANDIC FILMCOMPANY. Jan., 2001. Icelandic. (Robert I Douglas) Thorhallur Sverrisson, Jon Gnarr, Hafdis Huld, Matt Keeslar, Laufey Bra Jonsdottir, Gunnar Eyjolfsson.

ICHI THE KILLER
OMEGA PROJECT/OMEGA MICOTT. Sept., 2001. Japanese. (Takashi Miike) Tadanobu Asano, Nao Omori, Shinya Tsukamoto, Alien Sun, Sabu.

I COULDN'T CARE LESS
COLUMBIA TRISTAR SPAIN/ENRIQUE CEREZO PC/CR FILMS/TVE/CANAL PLUS. Aug., 2000., Spanish. (David Gordon) Alejandro Cano, Maria Jurado, Alvaro Gallegos, Fernando Cayo.

I COULD READ THE SKY
ARTS COUNCIL OF ENGLAND/IRISH FILM BOARD/CHANNEL FOUR/BRITISH FILM INSTITUTE/REAL WORLD RECORDS. Aug., 1999. British-Irish. (Nichola Bruce) Dermot Healy, Maria Doyle Kennedy, Brendan Coyle, Stephen Rea, Jake WIlliams.

I.D.
FILMS SUD, VIDEOCAM/PETROUCHKA FILMS/SOL'OEIL FILMS. Sept., 1998. Belgian-French-Congolese. (Mweze Ngangura) Gerard Essomba, Herbert Flack, Jean-Louis Daulne, Dominique Mesa.

AN IDEAL HUSBAND
PATHE/MIRAMAX. Apr., 1999. (Oliver Parker) Rupert Everett, Julianne Moore, Jeremy Northam, Cate Blanchett, Minnie Driver.

I DIDN'T KNOW TURURU
JANDAIRA PRODUCOES ARTISTICAS/RODERAF PRODUCOES. Sept., 2000. Brazilian. (Florinda Bolkan) Maria Zilda Bethlem, Florinda Bolkan, Ingra Libertao, Suzana Goncalves, Valentina Vicario, Fernando Alvez Pinto, Herson Capri.

IDITAROD...A FAR DISTANT PLACE
MINERAL KING PRODS. June, 2000. (Alice Dungan Bouvrie). Documentary.

IDLE HANDS
SONY. Apr., 1999. (Rodman Flender) Devon Sawa, Seth Green, Elden Henson, Jessica Alba, Christopher Hart.

THE IDOL (L'IDOLE)
Aug., 2002. French. (Samantha Lang) Leelee Sobieski, James Hong, Jean-Paul Roussillon, Jalil Lespert, Marie Loboda.

I'D RATHER BE...GONE
RAGAMUFF. June, 2001. (Maria Breaux) Maria Breaux, Amy Kelly, Csilla Horvath, June Sparagna, Sarah Fatemi, Marisol McIlvain, Aaron McIlvain, Bob Martinez.

I DREAMED OF AFRICA
SONY PICTURES ENTERTAINMENT/COLUMBIA PICTURES/JAFFILMS. Apr., 2000. (Hugh Hudson) Kim Basinger, Vincent Perez, Liam Aiken, Garrett Strommen, Eva Marie Saint, Daniel Craig, Lance Reddick.

I FOLLOW IN MY FATHER'S FOOTSTEPS
POLYGRAM. Apr., 1999. French. (Remi Waterhouse) Jean Yanne, Guillaume Canet, Laurence Cote, Yves Renier.

IF YOU ONLY KNEW
MOONSTONE/ ETERNITY PICTURES/CINERENTA/CINEFIRST/TWO STICKS PRODS. Mar., 2000. U.S.-German (David Snedeker) Jonathan Schaech, Alison Eastwood, James LeGros, Gabrielle Anwar, Lainie Kazan.

IF YOU ONLY UNDERSTOOD
LUNA LLENA. Jan., 1999. Cuban-Spanish. (Rolando Diaz). Documentary.

IGBY GOES DOWN
MGM. Sept., 2002. (Burr Steers) Kieran Culkin, Susan Sarandon, Jeff Goldblum, Claire Danes, Ryan Phillippe, Bull Pullman, Amanda Peet, Jared Harris, Rory Culkin.

IGNORANT FAIRIES
MEDUSA FILM. Feb., 2001. Italian-French. (Ferzan Ozpetek) Margherita Buy, Stefano Accorsi, Serra Yilmaz, Andrea Renzi, Gabriel Garko, Erica Blanc, Rosaria De Cicco, Lucrezia Valia.

I GOT THE HOOK-UP
DIMENSION FILMS. May, 1998. (Michael Martin) Master P, A. J. Johnson, Gretchen Palmer, Frantz Turner, Tommy Lister, Jr.

IKINAI
NIPPON HERALD/OFFICE KITANO. Aug., 1998. Japanese. (Hiroshi Himizu) Dankan, Nanako Okoucki, Toshinori Omi, Ippei Soda.

IKINGUT
Aug., 2001. Icelandic. (Gisli Snaer Erlingsson) Hjalti Runar Jonsson,Hans Tittus Nakinge, Palmi Gestsson, Magnus Ragnarsson.

I KNOW I'LL SEE YOUR FACE AGAIN
CORRIDOR. Jan., 2001. Belgian. (Alex Stockman) Stefan Perceval, Stefanie Bodien, Senne Rouffaer, Jacqueline Bir, Marie Bulte.

I KNOW WHO YOU ARE
CONTINENTAL PRODUCCIONES/TORNASOL/ZARLEK. Feb., 2000. Spanish-Argentine. (Patricia Ferreira) Miguel Angel Sola, Ana Fernandez, Roberto Enriquez, Ingrid Rubio, Manuel Manquna.

I.K.U.
UPLINK. Jan., 2000. Japanese. (Shu Lea) Tokitoh Ayumu, Zachery Nataf, Akechi Denki, Yumeno Maria, Sasaki Yumeka, Ariga Miho.

IL CIELO IN UNA STANZA
FILMAURO. Mar., 1999. Italian. (Carlo Vanzina) Elio Germano Gabriele Mainetti, Francesco Venditti, Alessandro Cianfione, Ricky Tognazzi.

ILES FLOTTANTES
A-FILM DISTRIBUTION. Jan., 2001. Dutch. (Nanouk Leopold) Maria Kraakman, Manja Topper, Halina Reijn, Kuno Bakker, Jacob Derwig, Leopold Witte.

I'LL BE HOME FOR CHRISTMAS
BUENA VISTA. Nov., 1998. (Arlene Sanford) Jonathan Taylor Thomas, Jessica Biel, Adam LaVorgna, Gary Cole, Eve Gordon.

ILL GOTTEN GAINS
SPATS FILMS. Sept., 1998. (Joel Ben Marsden) Djimon Hounsou, Akousa Busia, De'Aundre Bonds, Eartha Kitt, Reg E. Cathey.

I'LL MAKE YOU HAPPY
AMPLE FILMS. May, 1999. New Zealand. (Athina Tsoulis) Jodie Rimmer, Carl Bland, Ian Hughes, Michael Hurst, Jennifer Ward-Lealand.

I'LL REMEMBER APRIL
FLASHPOINT/REGENT ENTERTAINMENT. Jan., 2000. (Bob Clark) Trevor Morgan, Pam Dawber, Mark Harmon, Pat Morita, Haley Joel Osment, Yuji Okumoto.

I'LL TAKE YOU THERE
JIM STARK/HOLLYWOOD PARTNERS. Sept., 2000. (Adrienne Shelly) Ally Sheedy, Reg Rogers, Lara Harris, John Pyper-Ferguson.

I'LL WAIT ON YOU HAND AND FOOT
FILMAKADEMI BADEN-WUERTTEMBERG. Aug., 2001. German. (Iain Dilthey) Eva Loebau, Dirk Waanders, Sigrid Skoetz, Manfred Kranich, David Steffen, Maximilian Hummler.

IL MARE
UNIKOREA. Oct., 2000. South Korean. (Lee Hyeon-seung) Lee Jeong-jae, Jeon Ji-hyeon.

I LOVE ANDREA
UNIVERSAL PICTURES ITALY/FRANCESCANDREA/TELEPIU. Jan., 2000. Italian. (Francesco Nuti) Francesco Nuti, Francesca Neri, Agathe de la Fontaine, Marina Giulia Cavalli, Francesca De Rose.

I LOVE BEIJING
EURASIA COMMUNICATIONS/HAPPY VILLAGE. Jan., 2001. Chinese. (Ning Ying) Yu Lei, Zuo Baitao, Tao Hong,Gai Yi, Liu Miao.

I LOVE BUDAPEST
FILMPLUS. Feb., 2001. Hungarian. (Agnes Incze) Gabriella Hamori, Martina Kovacs, Sandor Csanyi, Tamas Lengyel.

I LOVE YOU
ALL JAPAN FILM CENTER. Sept., 2000. Japanese. (Yutaka Osawa, Akihiro Yonaiyama) Akiko Oshidari, Minoru Tanaka, Ai Okazaki, Manasaku Fuwa, Sachiko Takano, Atom Sunada, Chisato Seki.

I LOVE YOU, EUGENIO
Jan., 2002. (Francisco J. Fernandez) Giancarlo Giannini, Giuliana De Sio, Jacques Perrin, Chiara De Bonis, Giada Colonna, Alfredo Scarlata.

IMAGINE: SURFING AS SADHANA
GAIA CO-OP/KOKO PRODS. Apr., 2000. (Marshall K. Hattori). Documentary.

IMAGINE SURFING AS SADHANA
GAIA CO-OP PRODS. July, 2001. (Marshall K. Hattori) Christian Enns, Veronica Kay, Stephen Slater, Rob Machado, Garth Dickenson, Documentary.

I'M ALIVE AND I LOVE YOU
CINEMA PUBLC FILMS. Nov., 1998. French-Belgian-Hungarian. (Roger Kahane) Jerome Deschamps, Dorian Lambert, Agnes Soral, Yvette Merlin.

I'M GOING HOME
MADRAGOA FIMES/GEMINI FILMS/FRANCE2 CINEMA. May, 2001. Portuguese-French. (Maoel de Oliveira) Michel Piccoli, Antoine Chappey, Catherine Deneuve, John Malkovich, Leonor Baldaque.

I'M LOSING YOU
LIONS GATE FILMS. Sept., 1998. (Bruce Wagner) Rosanna Arquette, Amanda Donohoe, Buck Henry, Frank Langella, Andrew McCarthy.

I'M NOT AFRAID OF LIFE
PATHE. Aug., 1999. French-Swiss. (Noemie Lvovsky) Magali Woch, Ingrid Molinier, Julie-Marie Parmentier.

THE IMPATIENT ALCHEMIST
ALTA CLASSIC. May, 2002. Spanish-Argentine. (Patricia Ferreira) Ingrid Rubio, Roberto Enriquez, Chete Lera, Adriana Ozores, Miguel Angel Sola, Jordi Dauder, Nacho Vidal.

THE IMPORTANCE OF BEING EARNEST
MIRAMAX. May, 2002. U.S.-British. (Oliver Parker) Rupert Everett, Colin Firth, Frances O'Connor, Reese Witherspoon, Judi Dench, Tom Wilkinson, Anna Massey.

AN IMPOSSIBLE CRIME
COLUMBIA/TRISTAR FILMS ITALIA. May, 2001. Italian. (Antonello Grimaldi) Carlo Cecchi, Angela Molina, Ivano Marescotti, Lino Capolicchio, Rinaldo Rocco, Sante Maurizi, Giancarlo Monticelli.

IMPOSTOR
DIMENSION FILMS. Dec., 2001. (Gary Fleder) Gary Sinise, Madeleine Stowe, Vincent D'Onofrio, Tony Shalhoub, Tim Guinee, Mekhi Phifer, Lindsay Crouse, Elizabeth Pena.

THE IMPOSTORS
FOX SEARCHLIGHT. May, 1998. (Stanley Tucci) Oliver Platt, Stanley Tucci, Teagle F. Bougere, Steve Buscemi, Billy Connolly.

I'M THE FATHER (VAETER)
Aug., 2002. German. (Dani Levy) Sebastian Blomberg, Maria Schrader, Ezra Valentin Lenz, Christiane Paul, Ulrich Noethen, Rolf Zacher, Marion Kracht.

I'M THE ONE THAT I WANT
CHO TAUSSIG PRODS. June, 2000. (Lionel Coleman) Margaret Cho.

IMUHAR: A LEGEND
M.P. PRODUCTION. Oct., 1998. French-Nigerian. (Jacques Dubuisson) Ibrahim Paris, Mohamed Ixa, Mohamed Ichika, Rhali.

I'M WITH LUCY
GAUMONT BUENA VISTA INTL. (IN FRANCE)/COLUMBIA PICTURES (IN U.S.). Aug., 2002. (Jon Sherman) Monica Potter, Julianne Nicholson, John Hannah, Gael Garcia Bernal, Anthony LaPaglia, Henry Thomas, David Boreanaz.

IN AMERICA
FOX SEARCHLIGHT. Sept., 2002. Irish-British. (Jim Sheridan) Samantha Morton, Paddy Considine, Sarah Bolger, Emma Bolger, Djimon Hounsou.

IN ALL INNOCENCE
BAC FILMS. Nov., 1998. French. (Pierre Jolivet) Gerard Lanvin, Virginie Ledoyen, Carole Bouquet, Guillaume Canet, Aurelie Verillon.

IN A SAVAGE LAND
MOTION INTL/AUSTRALIAN FILM FINANCE/HOLLYWOOD PARTNERS/SHOWTIME AUSTRALIA/STRAND/NEW OZ/POLYGRAM. Oct., 1999. Australian. (Bill Bennet) Maya Stange, Martin Donovan, Rufus Sewell, Max Cullen.

IN BED WITH SANTA
SONET/FILMLANCE/YELLOW/COTTAGE/KINOPRODUCTION/SAN DREW METRONOME/TV1000/CHIMNEY POT. Oct., 1999. Swedish-Norwegian-Finnish. (Kjell Sundvall) Katarina Ewerlof, Peter Haber, Leif Andree, Jessica Zanden.

IN CHINA THEY EAT DOGS - DON'T THEY?
STEEN HERDEL. May, 1999. Danish. (Lasse Spang Olsen). Dejan Cukie, Kim Bodnia, Trine Dyrhol, Nikolaj Lie Kaas, Tomas Villum Jensen.

INCH'ALLAH SUNDAY
ARP SELECTION. Dec., 2001. French. (Yamina Benguigui) Fejria Deliba, Zinedine Soualem, Marie-France Pisier, Mathilde Seigner, Rabia Mokedem, France Darry, Jalil Lespert.

INCIDENTAL JOURNEY
June, 2002. Taiwanese. (Jofei Chen) Wan-Jung Wang, Su-Li Wu, Vicky Chiang, Dung-Ning Hsieh, Man-Nung Chou.

THE IN CROWD
WARNER BROS./MORGAN CREEK PROD. July, 2000. (Mary Lambert) Lori Heuring, Susan Ward, Daniel Hugh Kelly, Matthew Settle, Nathan Bexton, Laurie Fortier, Kim Murphy, Ethan Erickson.

THE INDEPENDENT
UNITED LOTUS. Mar., 2000. (Stephen Kessler) Jerry Stiller, Janeane Garofalo, Max Perlich, Ginger Lynn Allen, Billy Burke, Andy Dick, Fred Dryer, Ethan Embry, Jonathan Katz, Anne Meara, Ben Stiller.

IN DREAMS
DREAMWORKS. Jan., 1999. (Neil Jordan) Annette Bening, Aidan Quinn, Robert Downey Jr., Paul Guilfoyle, Dennis Boutsikaris.

IN EFREN'S PARADISE
GOOD HARVEST. Apr., 2000. Filipino. (Maryo J. Delos Reyes) Anton Bernardo, Allan Paule, Ynez Veneracion, Ana Capri.

INERTIA
Sept., 2001. Canadian. (Sean Garrity) Jonas Chernick, Sarah Constible, Gordon Tanner, Micheline Marchildon.

IN GOD'S HANDS
SONY PICTURES ENTERTAINMENT. April, 1998. (Zalman King) Patrick Shane Dorian, Matt George, Matty Liu, Shaun Thompson.

IN GOOD COMPANY
Feb., 2001. Greek. (Nikos Zapatinos) Yorgos Kimoulis, Nikos Kalogeropoulos, Evelina Papoulia, Mimis Hrisomallis, Maria Protopappa, Anastasios Vasiliou.

IN HEAVEN
FRAMES FILMPRODS.. Jan., 1999. Austrian. (Michael Bindlechner) Sylvie Testud, Xaver Hutter, Merab Ninidse.

INHERITANCE
ROJO FILM. Aug., 2001. Argentine. (Paula Hernandez) Rita Cortese, Adrian Witzke, Martin Adjemian, Hector Anglada.

IN JULY
SENATOR. Ju;y, 2001. German. (Fatih Akin) Moritz Bleibtreu, Christiane Paul. Mehmet Kurtulus, Idil Uner, Jochen Nickel, Branka Katic, Sandra Borgmann.

INNOCENCE
SHARMILL/STRAND/NEW OZ/SHOWTIME AUSTRALIA/SOUTH AUSTRALIAN FILM CORP./ILLUMINATION FILMS/CINETE/ CINEMEDIA CORP. Apr., 2000. Australian. (Paul Cox) Julia Blake, Charles Tingwell, Terry Norris, Robert Menzies, Marta Dusseldorp.

THE INNOCENT
FUJI/TEZUKA PRODS. Sept., 1999. Japanese. (Macoto Tezka) Tadanobu Asano, Miyako Koda, Reika Hashimoto, Masao Kusakari, Syunji Fujimura, Kyoko Enami, Anji, Yasutaka Tsutsui.

THE INNOCENTS
STYOPA. July, 1999. (Katherine Griffin) Kama Lee, Katherine Griffin, Joe Kellogg, Brad Carroll, Monte Jenkins.

INNOWHERELAND
WARNER BROS. TURKEY. May, 2002. Turkish-German. (Tayfun Pirselimoglu) Zuhal Olcay, Michael Mendl, Parkan Ozturan, Meral Okay.

IN PRAISE OF LOVE
PERIPHERIA. May, 2001. Swiss. (Jean-Luc Godard) Bruno Putzulu, Cecile Camp, Jean Davy, Francoise Verney.

INQUIETUDE
MADROGOA FILMES/GEMINI FILMS/WANDA FILMS/LIGHT NIGHT. May, 1998. Portuguese-French-Spanish-Swiss. (Manoel de Oliveira) Jose Pinto, Luis Miguel Cintra, Isabel Ruth, Leonor Silveira.

IN SEARCH OF PEACE–PART ONE: 1948-1967
SEVENTH ART RELEASING. Aug., 2001. (Richard Trank) Documentary.

IN SEARCH OF THE PAPIN SISTERS
ARP SELECTION. Dec., 2000. French. (Claude Ventura) Documentary.

INSEPARABLE
REZO FILMS/LES FILMS BALENCIAGA PRODS. CERCLE BLEU/ARTE FRANCE CINEMA/TELFRANCE/RFK/CRRAV/RENNCN PRODS./CANAL PLUS/SOFICA GIMAGES 2. Dec., 1999. French. (Michel Couvelard) Jean-Pierre Daroussin, Catherine Frot, Fabienne Babe, Herve Pierre, Sami Bouajila, Brigitte Rouan, Marie Mergey.

IN SEARCH OF KUNDUN WITH MARTIN SCORCESE
COMPAGNIE PANOPTIQUE. Aug., 1998. French. (Michael Henry Wilson) documentary.

THE INSIDE STORY
June, 2002. Australian. (Robert Sutherland) Kate Oliver, Andrew Curry, Charles "Bud" Tingwell, Michael Angus, Kristian Pithie, Simone Oliver.

THE INSIDER
BUENA VISTA/TOUCHSTONE/MANN/ROTH/FORWARD PASS PICTURES. Sept., 2000. (Michael Mann) Al Pacino, Russell Crowe, Christopher Plummer, Dianne Venora, Philip Baker Hall, Lindsay Crouse, Debi Mazar, Stephen Tobolowsky

INSOMNIA
COLUMBIA TRISTAR ESPANA. Feb., 1998. Spanish. (Chus Gutierrez) Cristina Marcos, Candela Pena, Ernesto Alterio, Maria Pujalte.

INSOMNIA
WARNER BROS. May, 2002. (Christopher Nolan) Al Pacino, Robin Williams, Hilary Swank, Maura Tierney, Martin Donovan, Nicky Katt, Paul Dooley, Jonathan Jackson, Larry Holden.

INSPECTOR GADGET
BUENA VISTA. July, 1999. (David Kellogg) Matthew Broderick, Rupert Everett, Joely Fisher, Michelle Trachtenberg, Andy Dick.

INSTINCT
BUENA VISTA. May, 1999. (Jon Turteltaub): Anthony Hopkins, Cuba Gooding Jr., Donald Sutherland, Maura Tierney, George Dzundza.

INSTRUMENT: TEN YEARS WITH THE BAND FUGAZI
LAL/GRAVITY HILI. Oct., 1999. (Jem Cohen, Fugazi). Documentary.

INTACT
WARNER SOGEFILMS. Nov., 2001. Spanish. (Juan Carlos Fresnadillo).

INTERN
MOONSTONE ENTERTAINMENT/GIVEN FILMS. Jan., 2000. (Michael Lange) Dominique Swain, Ben Pullen, Peggy Lipton, Joan Rivers, Kathy Griffin.

INTERSTATE 84
POP. 403 ENTERTAINMENT CO. Sept. 2000. (Ross Partridge) Kevin Dillon, John Littlefield, Megan Dodds, John Doman, Harley Cross, Joel Garland, Clifton James.

INTERVIEW
CINE2000. Oct., 2000. South Korean. (Daniel H. Byun) Lee Jeong-jae, Shim Eun-ha, Jo Jae-hyeon, Kweon Min-jung, Iim Jeong-hyeon, Yan Eun-yong, Lee Deok-jin, Jang Ho-il.

THE INTER-VIEW
BKA-KUNSTSEKTION. Aug., 2000. Austrian. (Jessica Hausner) Klaus Handl, Milena Oberndorfer, Birgit Doll, Nica Steinbauer.

INTERVIEW WITH THE ASSASSIN
MAGNOLIA PICTURES. May, 2002. (Neil Burger) Raymond J. Barry, Dylan Haggerty, Renee Faia, Kelsey Kemper, Dennis J. Lau, Jared McVay.

IN THE BATHTUB OF THE WORLD
March, 2001. (Caveh Zahedi) Caveh Zahedi, Amanda Field, Thomas Logoreci. Documentary.

IN THE BEDROOM
MIRAMAX. Jan., 2001. (Todd Field) Sissy Spacek, Tom Wilkinson, Nick Stahl, Marisa Tomei, William Mapother, William Wise, Celia Weston, Karen Allen.

IN THE BEGINNING THERE WAS UNDERWEAR
MEDUSA FILM. Feb., 1999. Italian. (Anna Negri) Teresa Saponangelo, Stefania Rocca, Bebo Storti, Filippo Timi, Monica Scattini.

IN THE FLESH
CAPE TOWN FILMS. June, 1999. (Ben Taylor) Dane Ritter, Ed Corbin, Adele Phares, Philip Solomon, Adrian Roberts.

IN THE MIRROR OF MAYA DEREN
June, 2002. Austrian-Swiss-German. (Martina Kudlacek) Stan Brakhage, Chao-Li Chi, Katherine Dunham, Graeme Ferguson, Alexander Hammid, Jonas Mekas, Andre Pierre. Documentary.

IN THE MOOD FOR LOVE
USA FILMS/BLOCK 2 PICTURES/PARADIS FILMS/JET TONE. May, 2000, Hong Kong (Wong Kar-wai) Tony Leung Chiu-wai, Maggie Cheung Man-yuk, Lai Chin.

IN THE NAVEL OF THE SEA
GMA FILMS/NEPTUNE FILMS. Feb., 1998. Philippine. (Marilou Diaz-Abaya) Jomari Yllana, Elizabeth Oropesa, Chin Chin Gutierrez.

IN THE SHADOWS OF THE CITY
NOUR PRODS. (LEBANON)/CINE-SUD (FRANCE). Oct., 2000. Lebanese-French. (Jean Khalil Chamoun) Majki Machmouchi, Christine Choueiri, Ammar Chalak.

IN THE WAKE
ERICA JORDAN. Nov., 2000. (Eric Jordan) Julia D'Orazio, Timothy Rodriguez, Ted Herzberg, Patricia Jiron, Michael Meyers, John Stevenson, Karen Schub.

IN THE WEEDS
GLATZER. June, 2000. (Michael Rauch) Joshua Leonard, Molly Ringwald, Ellen Pompeo, Michael Buchman Silver, Sam Harris, J.P. Pitoc, Bonnie Root, Kirk Acevedo, Peter Riegert, Eric Bogosian.

IN THE WINTER DARK
GLOBE FILM. May, 1998. Australian. (James Bogle) Brenda Blethyn, Ray Barrett, Richard Roxburgh, Miranda Otto.

INTIMACY
CHARLES GASSOT. Jan., 2001. French. (Patrice Chereau) Mark Rylance, Kerry Fox, Timothy Spall, Alastair Galbraith, Philippe Calvario, Marianne Faithfull, Susannah Harker.

AN INTIMATE FRIENDSHIP
FILLING THE GAP. June, 2001. (Angela Evers Hughey) Lisel M. Gorell, Stacy Marr, Rini Starkey, Tim McMillan, Kerry Leigh LePage, Angela Evers Hughey.

INTO MY HEART
MARS FILMS. Sept., 1998. (Sean Smith, Anthony Stark) Rob Morrow, Claire Forlani, Jake Weber, Jayne Brook.

IN TOO DEEP
DIMENSION FILMS. Aug., 1999. (Michael Rymer) Omar Epps, LL Cool J, Nia Long, Stanley Tucci, Hill Harper.

INTO THE ARMS OF STRANGERS: STORIES OF THE KINDERTRANSPORT
WARNER BROS./SABINE FILMS/U.S. HOLOCAUST MEMORIAL MUSEUM. Aug., 2000. (Mark Jonathan Harris). Documentary.

THE INTRUDER
GFT KINGSBOROUGH/STEVE WALSH PRODS./STUDIO EIGHT. Oct., 1999. Canadian-British. (David Bailey) Charlotte Gainsbourg, Charles Powell, Nastassja Kinski, Molly Parker, John Hannah.

INUGAMI
ASMIK ACE ENTERTAINMENT. Feb., 2001. Japanese. (Masato Harada) Yuki Amami, Atsuro Watabe, Kazuhiro Yamaji, Kanako Fukaura, Eugene Harada, Makoto Togashi, Shion Machida.

IN VANDA'S ROOM
CONTRACOSTA/PANDORA/ VENTURA/ZDF/RTSI. Aug., 2000. Portuguese-German-Swiss. (Pedro Costa) Vanda Duarte, Zita Duarte, Lena Duarte, Manuel Gomes Miranda, Diogo Pires Miranda.

INVASION
COMBINED STUDIO (ALMA-ATA). Aug., 2000. Soviet Union–1945. (Abram Room) V. Gremin, Olga Zhizneva, Oleg Zhakov, Lyudmila Glazova, Zinaida Morskaya, Lyudmila Shabalina, V. Valersky.

THE INVENTION OF LOVE
REMSTAR. Sept., 2000. Canadian. (Claude Demers) David La Haye, Pascale Montpetit, Delphine Brodeur, Andreas Apergis.

INVESTIGATING SEX
GEMINI FILMS. June, 2001. German-U.S. (Alan Rudolph) Dermot Mulroney, Alan Cumming, Neve Campbell, Robin Tunney, Nick Nolte, Tuesday Weld, Julie Delpy, Jeremy Davies.

THE INVESTIGATION MUST GO ON
TRANSFIX. July, 2000. Israeli. (Marek Rozenbaum) Moshe Ivgi, Aki Avni, Osnat Fishman, David Danino, Assi Levy, Itzik Juli.

INVINCIBLE
FILMFOUR. Sept., 2001. British-German. (Werner Herzog) Tim Roth, Jouko Ahola, Anna Gourari, Max Raabe, Jacob Wein, Gustav Peter Wohler, Udo Kier, Herbert Golder, Tina Bordihn.

THE INVISIBLE
SONET FILM. Jan., 2001. Swedish. (Joel Bergvall, Simon Sandquist) Gustaf Skarsgard, Tuva Novotny, Li Bradhe, Thomas Hedengran, Jennie Ulving, David Hagman.

INVISIBLE CHILDREN
Nov., 2001. Columbian-Venezuelan. (Lisandro Duque Naranjo) Guillermo Castaneda, Juvenal Camacho, Gustavo Angarita, Acielo Ingrid Ospina.

THE INVISIBLES
ZERO PICTURES. JAN., 1999. (Noah Stern) Michael Goorjian, Portia de Rossi, Terry Camilleri.

THE INVISIBLE CIRCUS
FINE LINE FEATURES. Jan., 2001. (Adam Brooks) Jordana Brewster, Christopher Eccleston, Cameron Diaz, Blythe Danner, Patrick Bergin, Camilla Belle, Mortiz Bleibtreu.

AN INVITED GUEST
PICTURE ME ROLLIN PRODS. Oct., 1999. (Timothy Wayne Folsome) Mekfi Phifer, Mel Jackson, Mari Morrow, Malinda Williams, Wayna Morris, Kim Fields.

IONE, FLY UP TO HEAVEN
ZINE ZERO/TVE/ETB. . June, 2000. Spanish. (Joseba Salegi) Kike Diaz de Rada, Martxelo Rubio, Anabel Arrainza, Mario Pardo, Klara Badiola, Esther Esparza.

I PREFER THE SOUND OF THE SEA
MIKADO/BIANCAFILM/RAI/ARCAPIX/CANAL PLUS. Mar., 2000. Italian-French. (Mimmo Calopresti) Silvio Orlando, Michele Raso, Fabrizia Sacchi, Mimmo Calopresti, Francesca Occhipinti, Enrica Rosso.

IRAN IS MY HOMELAND
Feb., 1999. Iranian. (Parviz Kimiavi) Rehzad Khodaveysi, Saeed Pur-Samimi, Parviz Shahin-Khoo, Mehdi Faqih, Qasem-Pur-Sattar.

I REMEMBER ME
ZEITGEIST. 2002. (Kim A. Snyder) Documentary.

IRENE
SND. July, 2002. French. (Ivan Calberac) Cecile de France, Bruno Putzulu, Olivier Sitruk, Estelle Larrivaz, Evelyne Buyle, Agathe de la Boulaye, Patrick Chesnais.

IRIS
ARANCIA CINEMA. Oct., 2000. Italian. (Aurelio Grimaldi) Arancia Cecilia Grimaldi, Guja Jelo, Salvatore Lazaro, Beatrice Gallo, Francesco Di Lera.

IRIS
MIRAMAX (IN U.S.)/BUENA VISTA INTL. (IN U.K.). Nov., 2001. British-U.S. (Richard Eyre) Judi Dench, Jim Broadbent, Kate Winslet, Hugh Bonneville, Penelope Wilton, Juliet Aubrey, Samuel West.

THE IRON HEEL OF THE OLIGARCHY
DEBOSHIR FILM. Sept., 1998. Russian. (Alexandre Bashirov) Alexander Bashirov, Rita Margo, Elena Yudanova, Inna Volkova.

THE IRON LADIES
FORTISSIMO/TAI ENTERTAINMENT. Sept., 2000. Taiwanese. (Yongyoot Thongkongtoon) Jessadaporn Pholdee, Sahapap Virakamin, Ekachai Buranapanit, Giorio Maiocchi.

THE IRREFUTABLE TRUTH ABOUT DEMONS
FIRST SUN/NEW ZEALAND FILM COMM. May, 2000. New Zealand. (Glenn Standring) Karl Urban, Katie Wolfe, Sally Stockwell.

IRREVERSIBLE
MARS FILM. May, 2002. French. (Gaspar Noe) Monica Bellucci, Vincent Cassel, Albert Supontel, Philippe Nahon, Jo Prestia.

IS IT CLEAR, MY FRIEND?
DA FILM/CROATIA FILM/GAMA STUDIO. Nov., 2000. Croatian. (Dejan Acimovic) Rade Servedzija, Milan Plestina, Milivoj Beader, Mustafa Madarevic, Ivo Gregurevic, Bozidar Oreskovic.

ISLAND, ALICIA
BEAR HAND FILMS. May, 1998. (Ken Yunome) Jeff Miller, Jne Jepson, Cherly Aden, Ed Bicarri, Kim Beuche, Pony Wilde.

ISLAND OF THE SHARKS
IMAX. Apr., 1999. (Howard Hall). Documentary.

THE ISLAND TALES
THE ISLAND TALES SEISAKU/KWAN'S CREATIVE WORKSHOP. Feb., 2000. Japanese-Hong Kong. (Stanley Kwan) Takao Osawa, Shu Qi, Michele Reis, Julian Cheung, Kaori Momoi, Elaine Jin, Gordon Liu.

THE ISLE
CJ ENTERTAINMENT/MYUNG FILM. May, 2000. South Korean. (Kim Ki-duk) Seoh Jung, Kim Yu-seok, Park Sung-hee, Jang Hang-sun, Jo Jae-hyun.

ISLE OF DARKNESS
NORSK FILM. May, 1998. Norwegian.(Trygve Allister Diesen) Sofie Grabol, Paul-Ottar Haga, Sina Langfeldt, Martin Slaatto.

ISN'T SHE GREAT
UNIVERSAL/MUTUAL FILM CO./LOBELL/BERGMAN. Jan., 2000. (Andrew Bergman) Bette Midler, Nathan Lane, Stockard Channing, David Hyde Pierce, John Cleese, John Larroquette. Amanda Peet.

I STILL KNOW WHAT YOU DID LAST SUMMER
SONY. Nov., 1998. (Danny Cannon) Jennifer Love Hewitt, Freddie Prinze, Jr., Brandy, Mekhi Phifer, Muse Watson.

ITALIAN FOR BEGINNERS
MIRAMAX. Feb., 2001. Danish. (Lone Scherfig) Anders W. Berthelsen, Anette Stovelbaek, Peter Gantzler, Ann Eleonora Jorgensen, Lars Kaalund, Sara Indrio Jensen.

IT ALL STARTS TODAY
LES FILMS ALAIN SARDE/LITTLE BEAR/TF1 FILMS. Jan., 1999. French. (Bertrand Tavernier) Philippe Torreton, Mria Pitarresi.

I, TARANEH, AM FIFTEEN
Feb., 2002. Iranian. (Rasul Sadr-Ameli) Taraneh Alidoosti, Hossein Mahjub, Mahtab Nasirpour.

IT HAPPENED IN HAVANA
IGELDO KOMUNIKAZIOA AND KINOWELT FILMPRODUKTION. July, 2001. Spanish-German-Cuban. (Daniel Diaz Torres) Peter Lohmeyer, Enrique Molina, Coralia Veloz, Ketty de la Iglesia, Mijail Mulkay, Rogelio Blain, Idelfonso Tamayo.

THE ITEM
TRILLION ENTERTAINMENT. Jan., 1999. (Dan Clark) Dawn Marie Velasquez, Dan Clark, Dave Pressler, Dan Lake, Ron Fitzgerald.

IT'S A LONG ROAD
ALCO FILM/GREEK FILM CENTRE. Feb., 1998. Greek. (Pantelis Voulgaris) Dimitris Katalifos, Thanassis Vengos, Giorgos Armenis.

IT'S ALL BOB
HELKON MEDIA. June, 1999. German-Danish-Austrian. (Otto Alexander Jahrreiss) Martina Gedeck, Gregor Torzs, Dieter Landuris, Hasan Ali Mete, Tonio Arango.

IT SHOULD HAVE BEEN NICE AFTER THAT
Oct., 2001. German. (Karin Jurschick) Narrators: Eva Mattes, Reinhart Firchow. Documentary.

IT'S MY LIFE
FIRST RUN/ICARUS FILMS. July, 2002. South Afirican. (Brian Tilley) Documentary.

IT'S YOUR TURN, LAURA CADIEUX
ALLIANCE. Oct., 1998. Canadian. (Denise Filatrault) Ginette Reno, Pierette Robitaille, Denis Dubois, Adele Reinhardt, Mireille Thibault, Danielle Lorain.

IT TAKES ALL KINDS
PATHE/TELEMA/LES FILMS A4/FRANCE 2 CINEMA/CANAL PLUS. Mar., 2000. French. (Agnes Jaoui) Jean-Pierre Bacri, Anne Alvaro, Agnes Jaoui, Gerard Lanvin, Alain Chabat, Brigitte Catillon, Christiane Millet, Wladimir Yordanoff.

IT WILL END UP IN TEARS
Gonen Glaser. July, 2000. Israeli. (Gonen Glaser). Documentary.

IVANSXTC. (TO LIVE AND DIE IN HOLLYWOOD)
RHINO FILMS/ENOS/ROSE/ALTERNATIVE INVESTMENTS OF MICHIGAN. Sept., 2000. (Bernard Rose) Danny Huston, Peter Weller, Lisa Enos, Joanne Duckman, Angela Featherstone, Caroleen Feeney, Valeria Golino.

I WANT IT ALL
UIP/LES FILMS ALAIN SARDE/L'ARBRE & LA COLOMBE/M6 FILMS/CANAL PLUS. Dec., 1999. French. (Guila Braoude) Elsa Zylberstain, Frederic Diefenthal, Alain Bashung, Elisabeth Vitali, Sonia Vollereaux, Patrick Braoude, Smadi Wolfman.

I WANT YOU
POLYGRAM FILMED ENTERTAINMENT. Feb., 1998. British. (Michael Winterbottom) Rachel Weisz, Alessandro Nivola, Luka Petrusic.

I WILL SURVIVE
AURUM/EL PASO/PELICULAS FRENETICAS/VIA DIGITAL/ANTENA 3. Nov., 1999. Spanish. (Alfonso Albacete, David Menkes) Emma Suarez, Juan Diego Botto, Mirtha Ibarra, Rosana Pastor.

I WISH I HAD A WIFE
CINEMA SERVICE. May, 2001. South Korean. (Park Heung-shik) Seol Kyeong-gyu, Jeon Do-yeon, Jin Hee-kyung.

I WOKE UP EARLY THE DAY I DIED
MUSE PRODS./CINEQUANON PICTURES INTL. Sept., 1998. (Aris Iliopulos) Billy Zane, Sandra Bernhard, Ron Perlman, Tippi Hedren.

I WONDER WHO'S KISSING YOU NOW
BUENA VISTA. Feb., 1999. Danish. (Henning Carlsen) Tommy Kenter, Marika Lagercrantz, Morten Grunwald, Lars Knutsen, Henrik Larsen.

I WON'T GO BACK HOME
MANDRAGORA. Apr., 2000. Argentine. (Albertina Carri) Margara Alonso, Manuel Callau, Martin Churba, Analia Couceyro, Fabiana Falcon, Marta Lubos, Ricardo Merkin.

I WON'T LET YOU DOWN
COLUMBIA TRISTAR (Spain). March, 2001. Spanish. (Manuel Rios San Martin) Eva Santolaria, Antonio Hortelano, Fernando Guillen Cuervo, Sancho Gracia Julian Gonzalez, Melani Olivares.

J

JACK & JILL
ALLIANCE. Sept., 1998. Canadian. (John Kalangis) John Kalangis, Shauna MacDonald, Kathryn Zenna, Scott Gibson, Tara Johnson.

JACK FROST
WARNER BROS. Dec., 1998. (Troy Miller) Michael Keaton, Kelly Preston, Mark Addy, Joseph Cross.

JACKPOT
SONY PICTURES CLASSICS. June, 2001. (Michael Polish) John Gries, Garrett Morris, Daryl Hannah, Kool Mo Dee, Ricky Trammell, Peggy Lipton, Anthony Edwards, Crystal Bernard.

JACKS OR BETTER
TRIPS TO WIN. June, 2000. (Robert Sidney Mellette) Jack Wallace, Nathan Anderson, Matt Landers, Vincent Guastaferro, Meshach Taylor, Garthering Marbet.

JACK THE DOG
JUNG N RESTLESS. Jan., 2001. (Bobby Roth) Nestor Carbonell, Barbara Williams, Andrew J. Ferchland, Travis Fine, Micole Mercurio, Elizabeth Barondes.

JACKY
A-FILM/MOTEL FILMS/VPRO TV. Feb., 2000. Dutch. (Fow Pyng Hu, Brat Ljatifi) Fow Pyng Hu, Eveline Wu, Gary Guo, Xuan Wei Zhou.

JADVIGA'S PILLOW
MAFILM/ORTT/MMK. Feb., 2000. Hungarian. (Krisztina Deak) Ildiko Toth, Viktor Bodo, Roman Luknar, Mari Csomos, Eszter Onodi, Bela Fesztbaum, Djoko Rosic, Marian Labuda.

JAILS, HOSPITALS & HIP-HOP
STRATOSPHERE ENTERTAINMENT. Nov., 2001. (Mark Benjamin, Danny Hoch) Danny Hoch, Susan Blommaert, Lynn Schlansky Hoch, Gina Brooke, Pablo Herrera, Hector Arias Boz Malone.

JAIME
JANI THILTGES/CLAUDE WARINGO/SAMSA/FADO FILMES,/SIC/VIDEOFILMES. Sept., 1999. Luxembourgois-Portuguese-Brazilian. (Antonio-Pedro Vasconcelos) Saul Fonseca, Fernanda Serrano, Joaquim Leitao, Sandro Silva.

JAIZKIBEL
Sept., 2001. Spanish. (Ibon Cormenzana) Alfredo Villa, Susana Martin, Susana Garcia, Idoia Bilbao.

JAKOB THE LIAR
SONY. Aug., 1999. (Peter Kassovitz) Robin Williams, Alan Arkin, Bob Balaban, Hannah Taylor Gordon, Michael Jeter.

JALLA! JALLA!
SONET FILM. Dec., 2000. Swedish. (Josef Fares) Fares Fares, Torkel Petersson, Tuva Novotny, Laleh Pourkarim, Leonard Terfelt, Jan Fares, Sofi Ahlstrom Helleday, Benyam Eriksson.

JAM
UNITED SODA FILMS/CHEN YIWEN FILM PRODS./LITTLE MORE CO. Sept.n 1998. Taiwanese. (Chen Yiwen) Cai Xinghung, June Cai, Vina Xu, Gao Minjun, Jine Shijie.

JAMES ELLROY'S FEAST OF DEATH
Sept., 2001. (Vikram Jayanti) Documentary.

JAM SESSION: OFFICIAL BOOTLEG OF KIKUJIRO
OFFICE KITANO. Aug., 1999. Japanese. (Makoto Shinozaki) . Documentary.

JAN DARA
Oct., 2001. Thai-Hong Kong. (Nonzee Nimibutr) Suwinit Panjamawat, Eakarat Sarsukh, Santisuk Promisiri, Christy Chung, Vipavee Charoenpura, Pataravarin Timkul.

JANE AUSTEN'S MAFIA!
BUENA VISTA. July, 1998. (Jim Abrahams) Jay Mohr, Billy Burke, Christina Applegate, Pamela Gidley, Olympia Dukakis, Lloyd Bridges.

THE JANG SUN-WOO VARIATIONS
TUBE ENTERTAINMENT. Jan., 2001. British-Korean. (Tony Rayns) Jang Sun-Woo, Park Joong-Hoon, Moon Sung-Keun. Documentary.

JANICE BEARD
FILM CONSORTIUM. May, 1999. British. (Clare Kilner) Eileen Walsh, Rhys Ifans, Patsy Kensit, David O'Hara, Sandra Voe.

JAPANESE DEVILS
Sept., 2001. Japanese. (Minoru Matsui) Documentary.

JASON X
NEW LINE CINEMA. April, 2002. (Jim Isaac) Lexa Doig, Lisa Ryder, Chuck Campbell, Jonathan Potts, Peter Mensah, Melyssa Ade.

JAWBREAKER
SONY. Jan., 1999. (Darren Stein) Rose McGowan, Rebecca Gayeart, Julie Benz, Judy Greer, Chad Christ.

JAY AND SILENT BOB STRKE BACK
DIMENSION FILMS. Aug., 2001. (Kevin Smith) Ben Affleck, Jeff Anderson, Deidrich Bader, Eliza Dushku, Shannon Elizabeth, Will Ferrell, Mark Hammill, Ali Larter.

JEANNE AND THE PERFECT GUY
LES FILMS DE REQUIN. Feb., 1998. French. (Olivier Ducastel) Virginie Ladoyen, Mathieu Demy, Jacques Bonnaffe, Valerie Bonneton.

JEEPERS CREEPERS
MGM. Aug., 2001. (Victor Salva) Gina Phillips, Justin Long, Jonathan Breck, Patricia Belcher, Brandon Smith, Eileen Brennan.

JERKS
ALLIED ENTERTAINMENT GROUP/CINEMA ARTS MAGIC. Jan., 2000. (Ted Grouya) Emmanuel Xuereb, Francis Fallon, Patrick Sheehan.

JEROME
JET FILM CO. Aug., 1998. (Thomas Johnston, David Elton, Eric Tignini) Drew Pillsbury, Wendie Malick, Scott McKenna.

JESUS IS A PALESTINIAN
WARNER BROS.. Jan., 1999. Dutch. (Lodewijk Crijns) Hans Teeuwen, Dijn Blom, Kim van Kooten, Peer Mascini.

JET LAG (DECALAGE HORAIRE)
BAC FILMS (IN FRANCE)/MIRAMAX (IN U.S.). Sept., 2002. French-British. (Daniele Thompson) Juliette Binoche, Jean Reno, Sergi Lopez.

JET SET
BAC/MANDARIN FILMS/TF1/FILMART/CANAL PLUS. June, 2000. French-Spanish. (Fabien Onteniente) Samuel Le Bihan, Lambert Wilson, Ornella Muti, Ariadna Gil.

JEW-BOY LEVI
ZERO FILM. Mar., 1999. German-Swiss-Austrian. (Didi Danquart) Bruno Cathomas, Caroline Ebner, Ulrich Noethen, Martina Gedeck.

JEWS, MOVIES AND THE AMERICAN DREAM
ASSOCIATED PRODUCERS. Feb., 1998. Canadian. (Simcha Jacobovici) documentary with Bernard Avishai, Judith Balaban.

JIANG HU–'THE TRIAD ZONE'
CHINA STAR ENTERTAINMENT GROUP. Nov., 2000. Hong Kong. (Dante Lam) Tony Leung Kar-fai, Sandra Ng, Anthony Wong, Eason Chan, Lee San-san, Lee Siu-kay, Jo Koo, Roy Cheung.

JIMMY ZIP
INCENDIARY ARTS. Aug., 1999. (Robert McGinley) Brendan Fletcher, Ike Gingrich, Adrienne Frantz, Zia, John Truong,.

JANANI
BADARUDEEN. Jan., 2000. Indian. (Thankamaniamma Rajeevnath) Latiff, Kavitha, Rosline, Santhakumari, Rukmini.

JIM BROWN: ALL AMERICAN
40 ACRES AND A MULE. March, 2002. (Spike Lee) Hank Aaron, Dr. Walter Beach, Jim Brown, Bernie Casey, Johnnie L. Cochran, Joe Frazier, Art Modell, Bill Russell, Stella Stevens. Oliver Stone, James Toback. Documentary.

JIMMY NEUTRON: BOY GENIUS
PARAMOUNT. Dec., 2001. (John A. Davis) Megan Cavanagh, Mark DeCarlo, Debi Derryberry, Jeff Garcia, Bob Goen, Mary Hart, Carolyn Lawrence, Andrea Martin, Candi Milo, Rob Paulsen, Crystal Scales. Animation.

JIMMY SCOTT: IF YOU ONLY KNEW
April, 2002. (Matthew Buzzell) Documentary.

JINNAH
AKBAR AHMED. Sept., 1998. Pakistanian-British. (Jamil Dehlavi) Christopher Lee, James Fox, Maria Aitken, Shashi Kapoor, Richard Lintern.

JIN-ROH: THE WOLF BRIGADE
BANDAI VISUAL CO. May, 1999. Japanese. (Hiroyuki Okiura). Animated.

JOE DIRT
SONY PICTURES ENTERTAINMENT. April, 2001. (Dennie Gordon) David Spade, Dennis Miller, Brittany Daniel, Kid Rock, Adam Beach, Erik Per Sullivan, Jaime Pressly, Christopher Walken.

JOE GOULD'S SECRET
USA FILMS/OCTOBER FILMS/FIRST COLD PRESS/CHARLES WEINSTOCK. Jan., 2000. (Stanley Tucci) Ian Hom, Stanley Tucci, Patricia Clarkson, Hope Davis, Steve Martin, Susan Sarandon, Patrick Tovatt, Celia Weston.

JOE SOMEBODY
20TH CENTURY FOX. Dec., 2001. (John Pasquin) Tim Allen, Julie Bowen, Kelly Lynch, Hayden Panettiere, Jim Belushi, Greg Germann, Robert Joy, Patrick Warburton.

JOE THE KING
49TH PARALLEL, FORENSIC/291 FILMS,LOWER EAST SIDE FILMS . Jan., 1999. (Frank Whaley) Noah Fleiss, Val Kilmer, Karen Young, Ethan Hawke, John Leguizamo.

JOHN CARPENTER'S GHOSTS OF MARS
SONY PICTURES ENTERTAINMENT. Aug., 2001. (John Carpenter) Ice Cube, Natasha Henstridge, Jason Statham, Clea Duvall, Pam Grier, Joanna Cassidy, Richard Cetrone, Rosemary Forsyth.

JOHN JOHN IN THE SKY
TIME WARP/JJSKY. June, 2001. (Jefferson Davis) Matt Letscher, Christian Craft, Rusty Schwimmer, Randy Travis, Romy Rosemont, Aunjanue Ellis, Gemini Bartlett.

JOHNNIE GREYEYES
NEPANTLA/RAVENHEAD PRODS. Jan., 2000. Canadian. (Jorge Manzano) Gail Maurice, Jonathan Fisher, Columpa C. Bobb, Gloria May Eshkibok, Marion Devries, Shirley Cheechoo, Georgina Lightning.

JOHNNY SKIDMARKS
CINEPIX FILM PROPERTIES. Jan., 1998. (John Raffo) Peter Gallagher, Frances McDormand, John Lithgow, Geoffrey Lower.

JOHNNY THE PARTISAN
FANDANGO. Sept., 1998. Italian. (Guido Chiesa) Stefano Dionisi, Andrea Prodan, Fabrizio Gifuni, Giuseppe Cederna, Alberto Gimignani, Claudio Amendola, Chiara Muti.

THE JOLLY BOYS' LAST STAND
JOLLY PRODS. July, 2000. British. (Christopher Payne) Milo Twomey, Yolande Davis, Andy Serkis, Rebecca Craig.

JONAH AND LILA, TILL TOMORROW
FILMOGRAPH/CAB PRODS./GEMINI FILMS/TELEVISION SUISSE ROMANDE/WESTDEUTSCHER RUNDFUNK KOLN. Sept., 1999. Swiss-French. (Alain Tanner) Jerome Robart, Aissa Maiga, Natalia Dontcheva, Jean-Pierre Gos, Cecile Tanner, Philippe Demarle.

JONAH: A VEGGIETALES MOVIE
FHE PICTURES. Sept., 2002. (Phil Vischer, Mike Nawrocki, Marc Vulcano) Phil Vischer, Mike Nawrocki, Tim Hodge, Lisa Vischer, Dan Anderson, Kristin Blegen, Shelby Vischer, Jim Poole, Ron Smith. Animation.

JOSEPH: KING OF DREAMS
DREAMWORKS HOME ENTERTAINMENT. Nov., 2000. (Robert Ramirez, Rob LaDuca) Animated-Video.

JOSE RIZAL
GMA NETWORK. Feb., 1999. Philippine. (Marilou Diaz-Abaya) Cesar Montano, Joel Torre, Jaime Fabregas, Gloria Diaz, Gardo Versoza.

JOSIE AND THE PUSSYCATS
UNIVERSAL PICTURES (IN U.S.) AND METRO-GOLDWYN-MAYER (FOREIGN). April, 2001. (Deborah Kaplan, Harry Elfont) Rachael Leigh Cook, Tara Reid, Rosario Dawson, Alan Cumming, Parker Posey, Gabriel Mann, Paulo Costanzo.

JOUR DE NUIT
BALZLI & FAHRER. Sept., 2000. Swiss. (Dieter Fahrer, Bernhard Nick) Peter Bergman, Monie Meziane, Bruno Netter, Teatro Gioco Vita. Documentary.

JOURNEY INTO AMAZING CAVES
MACGILLIVRAY FREEMAN FILMS. March, 2001. (Steve Judson) IMAX– Documentary.

THE JOURNEYMAN
Feb., 2002. (James Crowley) Brad Hunt, Daniel Lapaine, Dash Mihok, Arie Verveen, Barry Corbin, Assumpta Serna,Burton Gilliam, John Beasley.

JOURNEYS WITH GEORGE
March, 2002. (Alexandra Pelosi) George W. Bush, Alexandra Pelosi, R.G. Ratcliffe, Wayne Slater, Richard Wolffe, Trent Gegax. Documentary.

JOURNEY TO A HATE-FREE MILLENNIUM
NEW LIGHT MEDIA. Apr., 2000. (Martin Bedgone, Brent Scarpo). Documentary.

THE JOURNEY TO KAFIRISTAN
DUBINI FILMPRODUKTION, ARTE-ZDF (GERMANY)/TRE VALLI FILMPRODUKTION (SWITZERLAND)/ARTCAM (NETHERLANDS). AUG., 2001. GERMAN-SWISS-DUTCH. (Fosco Dubini, Donatello Dubini) Jeanette Hain, Nina Petri, Matthew Burton, Hassan Darweesh, Ozlen Soydan, Abbul Karim Qawasmi.

THE JOURNEY TO PARIS
MARS FILMS. May, 1999., French. (Marc-Henri Dufresne) Olivier Broche, Francois Morel, Micheline Presle, Marina Tome, Valentin Morel.

JOURNEY TO THE SUN
ISTINAI FILMLER & REKLAMAS/FABRICA. Feb., 1999. Turkish-Dutch-german. (Yesim Ustaoglu) Newroz Bax, Nazmi Qirix, Mizgin Kapazan, Nigar Aktar, Iskender Bagcilar.

JOYFUL PARTAKING IN THE SORROWS OF LIFE (OR ONE DAMN THING AFTER ANOTHER)
July, 2002. (William Moreing) John Procaccino, Elizabeth Huddle, Jennifer Sue Johnson, Jane Jones, Kit Harris, Barbara Dirickson, George Catalano, Andrew Heffernan, Bridget O'Neill, Orion Orellana, Peter Yang, Nan Hu.

JOY RIDE
20TH CENTURY FOX. Aug., 2001. (John Dahl) Steve Zahn, Paul Walker, Leelee Sobieski, Jessiva Bowman, Stuart Stone, Basil Wallace, Brian Leckner.

THE JOYS OF SMOKING
VERGING PRODS. June, 1999. (Nik Katasapetses) Matthew Rozen, Steven Sorenson, Deborah Cordell, Carrie Mogan, Jon Prutow.

JUAN, I FORGOT, I DON'T REMEMBER
LA MEDIA LUNA. Mar., 1999. Mexican. (Juan Carlos Rulfo). Documentary.

JUBAKU–SPELLBOUND
TOEI/KADOKAWA SHOTEN/ASMIK ACE ENTERTAINMENT. Feb., 2000. Japanese. (Masato Harada) Koji Yakusho, Tatsuya Nakadai, Jun Fubuki, Kippei Shiina, Mayumi Wakamura, Kenichi Endo.

JUDGMENT IN FLAMES
GOLDEN NETWORK. May, 1998. Taiwanese. (James Chia-ming Liu) Rachel Chang, Yin Chiao-the, Jackson Lou.

JUDY BERLIN
CARUSO/MENDELSOHN. Jan., 1999. (Eric Mendelsohn) Barbara Barrie, Bob Dishy, Edie Falco, Carlin Glynn, Aaron Harnick.

JUHA
SPUTNIK OY. Feb., 1999. Finnish. (Aki Kaurismaki) Sakari Kuosmanen, Kati Outinen, Andre Wilms, Markku Peltola, Elina Salo.

JULIE JOHNSON
SHOOTING GALLERY. Jan., 2001. (Bob Gosse) Lili Taylor, Courtney Love, Spalding Gray, Noah Emmerlich, Mischa Barton, Gideon Jacobs, Patrick Fitzgerald.

JULIEN DONKEY-BOY
FINE LINE. Sept., 1999. (Harmony Korine) Ewen Bremner, Chloe Sevigny, Werner Herzog, Evan Neumann, Joyce Korine.

JULIE'S SPIRIT
Aug., 2001. German. (Bettina Wilhelm) Sylvie Testud, Julia Richter, Fritz Karl, Arno Frisch, Svetlana Schoenfeld, Henryk Baranowski, ALexander Hoerbe.

JULIET IN LOVE
BRILLIANT IDEA GROUP. Oct., 2000. Hong Kong. (Wilson Yip) Sandrea Ng, Francis Ng, Eric Kot, Simon Yam, Tats Lau, Angela Tong, Heung Hoi, Tai Pik-chi, Lam Suet, Adam Chan.

JULIETTE OF THE HERBS
MABINOGION FILMS. Apr., 1999. (Tish Streeten). Documentary.

JULIO AND HIS ANGEL
ANGEL FILMS. Oct., 1998. Mexican. (Jorge Cervera, Jr.). Eduardo Saul Martinex, Jorge Cervera, Jr. Carmen del Valle.

JULY RAIN
MOSFILM. Aug., 2000. Soviet Union–1967. (Marlen Khutsiev) Evgeniya Uralova, Aleksandr Belyavsky, Yuri Vizbor, Aleksandr Mitta, Alla Pokrovskaya.

JUMP
(GIVEN) FILMS. Apr., 1999. (Justin McCarthy) Peter Appel, Jessica Hecht, James LeGros, Michael, McGlone, Amanda Peet.

JUMP TOMORROW
IFC FILMS. Jan., 2001. (Joel Hopkins) Tunde Adebimpe, Hippolyte Girardot, Natalia Verbeke, James Wilby, Patricia Mauceri, Isiah Whitlock Jr., Kaili Vernoff.

JUNG (WAR) IN THE LAND OF THE MUJAHEDDIN
HUMAN RIGHTS WATCH INTL. Oct., 2001. Italian-Afghan. (Alberto Vendemmiati, Fabrizio Lazzaretti) Gino Strada, Kate Rowlands, Ettore Mo. Documentary.

JUNK
PIECEMEAL FILMS/FALLEN CINEMA. Feb., 2000. (Roddy Bogawa) William Schefferine, Tara Milutis, Tommy Bigelow, Lazar Stojanovic, Michael Joo, Gloria Park, Victor Bloom.

THE JUNK FOOD GENERATION
URBAN ENTERTAINMENT/OTWO 99. Oct., 1999. Japanese. (Shinobu Sakagami, Hideo Baba) Shinobu Sakagami, Amiko Kanaya, Nathan Ginn, David Adams, Lisa Noelle, Angel Powers, D.C. Warren.

JURASSIC PARK III
UNIVERSAL. July, 2001. (Joe Johnston) Sam Neill, William H. Macy, Tea Leoni, Alessandro Nivola, Trevor Morgan, Michael Jeter, John Diehl, Bruce A. Young.

JURIJ
Nov., 2001. Italian. (Stefano Gabrini) Rajmund Onokj, Charles Dance, Eszter Mazany, Sarah Miles, Fabrizia Sacchi, Fabio Bussotti.

JUST A KISS
PARAMOUNT CLASSICS. June, 2002. (Fisher Stevens) Ron Eldard, Kyra Sedgwick, Patrick Breen, Marisa Tomei, Marley Shelton, Taye Diggs, Sarita Choudhury.

JUST DO IT
CINEMA SERVICE. June, 2001. South Korean. (Park Dae-yeong) Ahn Seok-hwan, Song Ok-suk, Park Sang-myeon, Park Jin-heui, Jeong Jun, Lee Beom-su.

JUST FOR TODAY
UNIVERSIDAD DEL CINE. Feb., 2001. Argentine. (Ariel Rotter) Sergio Boris, Aili Chen, Damian Dreizik, Federico Esquerro.

JUST THE BEGINNING
SENATOR. May, 2001. German. (Pierre Franckh) Julia Richter, Rene Hofschneider, Dieter Landuris, Clelia Sarto, Martin Armknecht, Chris Hohenester, Heinrich Schafmeister.

JUST A LITTLE HARMLESS SEX
PHAEDRA CINEMA. June, 1999. (Rick Rosenthal) Alison Eastwood, Robert Mailhouse, Rachel Hunter, Kimberly Williams, Lauren Hutton.

JUSTIFIABLE HOMICIDE
May, 2002. (Jon Osman) Documentary.

JUST LOOKING
JEAN DOUMANIAN. Oct., 1999. (Jason Alexander) Ryan Merriman, Joseph Franquinha, Peter Onorati, Gretchen Mol, Amy Braverman, Ilana Levine, Richard V. Licata, Patti LuPone, John Bolger.

JUST MARRIED
MOANA-FILM/GMBH. Sept., 1998. German. (Rudolf Thome) Laura Maori Tonke, Herbert Frisch, Marquard Bohm, Johannes Herschmann, Valeska Hanel.

JUST MELVIN
JAMES RONALD WHITNEY/PRODUCTION 920. Jan, 2000. (James Ronald Whitney). Documentary.

JUST MESSING ABOUT
NEXT FILM. Feb., 2000. German. (Jochen Kuhn) Maximilian Schell, Edgar Selge, Tonio Arango, Alexandra Maria Lara, Neza Selbuz, Marianne Schubert, Desiree Nick, Horst Krause.

JUST ONE TIME
ALLIANCE ATLANTIS/DANGER FILMWORKS. Sept., 1999. (Lane Janger) Lane Janger, Joelle Carter, Guillermo Diaz, David Lee Russek, Jennifer Esposito.

JUST RUN
ALTAFILMS/CARTEL/LA FIERA CORRUPIA/FANDANGO/ALIEN PRODS./TVE/VIA DIGITAL. May, 2000. Spanish-Italian-Danish. (Saura Medrano) Fele Martinez, Silke, Patxi Freytez, Aitor Merino, Alberto Escobar, Santiago Etombayambo, Geraldine Chapline.

JUST THE TICKET
MGM. Feb., 1999. (Richard Wenk) Andy Garcia, Andie MacDowell, Richard Bradford, Laura Harris, Andre Blake.

JUST VISITING
BUENA VISTA. April, 2001. (Jean-Marie Gaubert) Jean Reno, Christina Applegate, Christina Clavier, Matthew Ross, Tara Reid, Bridgette Wilson-Sampras.

JUST WRITE
CURB ENTERTAINMENT INTL. Sept., 1998. (Andrew Gallerani) Sherilyn Fenn, Jeremy Piven, JoBeth Williams, Wallace Shawn.

JUWANNA MANN
WARNER BROS. 2002. (Jesse Caughan.) Miguel A. Nunez Jr., Vivica A. Fox, Kevin Pollak, Tommy Davidson, Kim Watans, Jennifer Lewis, Ginuwine.

K

KAATERSKILL FALLS
WHISKEY OUTPOST. April, 2001. (Josh Apter, Peter Olsen) Hilary Howard, Mitchell Riggs, Anthony Leslie.

KABALA
May, 2002. French-Mali. (Assan Kouyate) Modibo Traore, Djeneba Kone, Fily Traore, Hammadoun Kassogue, Siaka Diarra.

KABBARLI
March, 2002. Austrian. (Andrew G. Taylor) Lynne Murphy, Mary Regan.

KABHI KHUSHI KABHIE GHAM
YASH RAJ FILMS. Dec., 2001. Indian. (Karan Johar) Amitabh Bachchan, Jaya Bachchan, Shah Rukh Khan, Kajol, Hrithik Roshan, Kareena Kapoor, Rani Mukherji, Simone Singh.

K.A.F.KA FRAGMENT
HAMMEL FILM & VIDEOPRODUKTION VIENNA/ KONRADFROSCHFILM (BERLIN). Jan., 2001. Austrian-German. (Christian Frosch) Lars Rudolph, Ursula Ofner.

KAKASHI
EMG, PLANET, MI-PIC, BEAM ENTERTAINMENT. June, 2001. Japanese-Hong Kong. (Norio Tsuruta) Maho Nonami, Kou Shibasaki, Grace Ip, Shunsuke Matsuoka, Lily, Kenzo Kawarazaki.

KANAK ATTACK
CONCORDE FILM CLASSIC/BECKER & HAEBERLE/ZDF/ARTE. June, 2000. German. (Lars Becker) Luke Piyes, David Scheller, Tyron Ricketts, Oezlem Cetin, Nadeshda Brennicke, Ercan Durmaz.

KANDAHAR
MARS FILMS. May, 2001. Iranian-French. (Mohsen Makhmalbaf) Niloufar Pazira, Hassan Tantai, Sadou Termouri.

KAPUTT MUNDI
RAI TRADE/INSTITUTO LUCE/SORPASSO/CINECITTA. Sept., 1999. Italian. (Marco Risi) Monica Bellucci, Alessandro Haber, Francesca D'Aloja, Marco Giallini, Ricky Memphis, Giorgio Tirabassi, Natale Tulli.

KARAKUM
EUROARTS INTL. Oct., 1999. German-Turkmenistanian. (Arend Agthe) Max Kullman, Murat Orasov, Pjotr Olev, Neidhart Niedel, Alexander Potapov.

KARAOKE FEVER
SPUTNIK PICTURES. April, 2001. (Arthur Borman, Steve Danielson) Keith "K.B." Allen, Arianna, Adolph "A.D." Barley, Gherlie Dancel, Eric Draven, Spencer Haas, Dui, Julian Moreno. Documentary.

KARMA LOCAL
KLLC PRODS.. Mar., 1999. Indian. (Dharshan Bhagat) Dharshan Bhagat, Josh Pais, Bairaj, Uppal, Mariusz Szczech.

KARMEN
Sept., 2001. French-Senegal-Canadian. (Joseph Gai Ramaka). Jeinaba Diop Gai, Magaye Adama Niang, Stephanie Biddle.

KARNAVAL
MK2. Feb., 1999. French-Belgian-Swiss. (Thomas Vincent) Amar Ben Abdallah, Sylvia Testud, Clovis Cornillac, Martine Godart,.

KATE & LEOPOLD
MIRAMAX FILMS. (James Mangold) Meg Ryan, Hugh Jackman, Liev Schreiber, Breckin Meyer, Natasha Lyonee, Bradley Whitford, Paxton Whitehead, Spalding Gray, Philip Bosco.

KAZA-HANA
CINEQUEEN. Sept., 2000. (Shinji Somai)

KEBAB CONNECTION
AMLF. May, 1998. French. (Hiner Saleem) Georges Corraface, Marina Kobakhidze, Stephanie Lagarde, Tuncel Kurtiz, Fatah Solanti.

KEDMA
MARS FILMS. May, 2002. French-Israeli-Italian. (Amos Gitai) Andrei Kahskar, Helena Yaralova, Yussef Abu Warda, Moni Moshonov, Juliano Merr, Menachem Lang.

KEEPERS OF THE FRAME
MOUNT PILOT PRODS. Mar., 1999. (Mark McLaughlin) Alan Alda, Laurence Austin, Stan Brakhage, Leonard Maltin, Roddy McDowall. Documentary.

KEEPING THE FAITH
BUENA VISTATOUCHSTONE/SPYGLASS ENTERTAINMENT. Mar., 2000. (Edward Norton) Ben Stiller, Edward Norton, Jenna Elfman, Anne Bancroft, Eli Wallach, Ron Rifkin, Milos Forman, Holland Taylor, Lis Edelstein, Rena Sofer, Ken Leung, Brian George.

KEEP RUNNING
MK2 DIFFUSION/LES FILMS DU BOIS SACRE/MK2 PRODS./ARTE FRANCE CINEMA. Dec., 1999. French. (Dante Desarthe) Clemont Sibony, Rona Hartner, Isaac Sharry, Emmanuelle Devos, Gilbert Levy.

KEEP THE RIVER ON YOUR RIGHT: A MODERN CANNIBAL TALE
NEXT WAVE FILMS. Apr., 2000. (David Shapiro, Laurie Gwen Shapiro), Tobias Schneebaum, Norman Mailer, Charlie Rose, Mike Douglas. Documentary.

KEIHO
SHOCHIKU. Feb., 1999. Japanese. (Yoshimitsu Morita) Kyoka Suzuki, Shinichi Tsutsumi, Ittoku Kishibe, Hideko Yoshida, Mirai Yamamoto.

KENNEDY AND I
PATHE/ELIZABETH FILMS/LES FILMS A4/FRANCE 2 CINEMA/ ROISSY FILMS/PRIMA/TELEMA/CANAL PLUS/GIMAGES 2/ COFIMAGE 10. Jan., 2000. French. (Sam Karmann) Jean-Pierre Bacri. Nicole Garcia, Patrick Chesnais, Sam Karmann, Francois Chattot, Eleonore Gosset, Lucas Bonnifait.

KENOMA
A.F. CINEMA E VIDEO. Sept., 1998. Brazilian. (Eliane Caffe) Jose Dumont, Enrique Diaz, Jonas Bloch, Mariana Lima, Matheus Natchergaelle.

KEN PARK
Aug., 2002. U.S.-Dutch-French. (Larry Clark, Ed Lachman) James Ransome, Tiffany Limos, Stephen Jasso, James Bullard.

KESTREL'S EYE
FIRST RUN/PICAFILMS. Jan., 2000. Swedish. (Mikael Kristersson). Documentary.

KESWA, THE LOST THREAD
LES FILMS DE LA MOUETTE/MORGANE PROD./MPS. Oct., 1998. (Kalthoum Bornaz) Rim Turki, Nouna Noureddine, Ali Mosbah, Ahmed El Hafian.

KEVIN & PERRY GO LARGE
ICON/TIGER ASPECT/FRAGILE FILMS. Apr., 2000. British. (Ed Bye) Harry Enfield, Kathy Burke, Rhys Ifans, Laura Fraser, James Fleet, Louisa Rix, Tabith Wady, Paul Whitehouse, Natasha Little.

THE KEY
TOHOKUSHINSHA FILM CO. March, 1998. Japanese. (Toshiharu Ikeda) Naomi Kawashima, Akira Emoto, Mikio Osawa, Kaori Tsuji.

KHRUSTALIOV, MY CAR!
POLYGRAM FILM DISTRIBUTION. May, 1998. French-Russian. (Alexei Guerman) Y. Tsurilo, N. Ruslanova, M. Dementiev, A. Bachirov.

KICHIKU
ONI PROD. Feb., 1998. Japanese. (Kazuyoshi Kumakiri) Sumiko Mikami, Syunsuke Sawada, Shigeru Bokuda, Toshiyuki Sugihara.

KICK
BEYOND FILMS. May, 1999. Australian. (Lynda Heys) Russell Page, Rebecca Yates, Martin Henderson, Radha Mitchell, Paul Mercurio.

THE KID FROM CHAABA
AFMD. Feb., 1998. French. (Christpher Ruggia) Bouzid Negnoug, Mohamed Fellag, Francois Morel, Amina Medjoubi, Nabil Ghalem.

KIDS WORLD
DAYBREAK PACIFIC FILMS, BLUE STEEL. Dec., 2001. New Zealand. (Dale G. Nagan) Christopher Lloyd, Blake Foster, Michael Purvis, Anton Tennet, Todd Emerson, Olivia Tennet.

KIKI'S DELIVERY SERVICE
BUENA VISTA. June, 1998. (Hayao Miyazaki) Voices: Kirsten Dunst, Phil Hartman, Janeane Garofolo, Matthew Lawrence.

KIKUJIRO
SONY. May, 1999. Japanese. (Takeshi Kitano) Beat Takeshi, Yusuke Sekiguchi, Kayoko Kishimoto, Yuko Daike, Kazuko Yoshiyuiki.

KILL BY INCHES
CINEBLAST! Sept, 1999. (.Diane Doniol-Valcroze, Arthur Flam) Emmanuel Salinger, Myriam Cyr, Marcus Powell, Christopher Zach.

KILLER
ARTCAM INTL./KADAM. May, 1998. French-Kazakh. (Darezhan Omirbaev) Talgat Assetov, Roksana Abouova.

KILLER ME
April, 2002. (Zachary Hansen) George Foster, Christina Kew, Garth Wilton, Kirk B.R. Woller.

KILLER STORY
HANMAC ENTERTAINMENT. Sept., 1998. South Korean. (Yeo Kyundong) Hwang Cine, Mun Seong-keun, Lee Kyeong-yeong.

KILLER TATTO
Nov., 2001. Thai. (Yuthlert Sippapak) Somchai Khemglad, Pailin Pichitumphol.

KILLING MAD DOGS
SILKROAD PRODUCTION. Feb., 2001. Iranian-French. (Bahram Bayzai) Mojdeh Shamsai, Majid Mozaffari, Reza Kianian, Mitra Hajar, Dariush Arjmand, Ahmad Najafi, Enayat Bakhshi.

KILLING ME SOFTLY
MGM. March, 2002. (Chen Kaige) Heather Graham, Joseph Fiennes, Natascha McElhone, Ulrich Thomsen, Ian Hart, Jason Hughes, Helen Grace.

THE KILLING YARD
SHOWTIME AND PARAMOUNT NETWORK TELEVISION. Sept., 2001. (Euzhan Palcy) Alan Alda, Morris Chestnut, Rose McGown, Arthur Holden, Robert B. Kennedy, Benz Antoine, Chip Chuipka.

KILL ME LATER
LIONS GATE. March, 2001. Selma Blair, Max Beesley, Brendan Fehr, Lochlyn Munro, O'Neal Compton, D.W. Moffett.

KILL THE MAN
SEATTLE PACIFIC INVESTMENTS/SUMMIT ENTERTAINMENT. Jan., 1999. (Tom Booker) Luke Wilson, Joshua Malina, Paula Devicq, Phil LaMarr, Phillip Rhys.

KIMBERLY
MOONSTONE. Sept., 1999. U.S.-German. (Frederic Golchan) Gabrielle Anwar, Sean Astin, Jason Lewis, Robert Mailhouse, Chris Rydell.

KIN
BARD ENTERTAINMENTS/BSKYB/BRITISH SCREEN/ARTS COUNCIL OF ENGLAND/N-NET. July, 2000. British. (Elaine Proctor) Miranda Otto, Isaiah Washington, Chris Chameleon, Moses Kandjoze, Ndondoro Hevita, Susan Coetzer, Martin Stefanus.

A KIND OF HUSH
CAPITOL FILMS. Sept., 1998. British. (Brian Stirner) Harley Smith, Marcella Plunkett, Ben Roberts, Paul Williams, Nathan Constance.

A KIND OF HUSH
CAPITOL FILMS. Sept., 1998. British. (Brian Stirner) Harley Smith, Marcella Plunkett, Ben Roberts, Paul Williams, Nathan Constance.

THE KING AND I
WARNER BROS. Mar., 1999. (Richard Rich) Miranda Richardson, Christiane Noll, Martin Vidnovic.

KINGDOM COME
FOX SEARCHLIGHT. April, 2001. (Doug McHenry) LL Cool J, Jada Pinkett Smith, Vivica A. Fox, Loretta Devine, Anthony Anderson, Toni Braxton, Cedric the Entertainer, Darius McCrary, Whoopi Goldberg.

KINGDOM OF SKINFLINTS
E.D. DISTRIBUTION. April, 2001. French. (Michel Vignaud) Gael Bordier, Charles Aivar, Virginie Aster, Patrick Athenor.

THE KING IS ALIVE
NEWMARKET/GOOD MACHINE INTL./ZENTROPA ENTERTAINMENTS 5/DANISH BROADCASTING CORP. /SVT DRAMA/DANISH FILM INSTITUTE/NORDIC FILM & TV FUND. May, 2000. Danish. (Kristian Levring) Miles Anderson, Romane Bohringer, David Bradley, David Calder, Bruce Davison, Brion James, Peter Kubheka.

THE KING IS DANCING
UFD. Nov., 2000. French-German-Belgian. (Gerard Corbiau) Benoit Magimel, Boris Terral, Tcheky Karyo, Colette Emmanuelle, Cecile Bois, Claire Keim, Johan Leysen.

KING OF COMEDY
STAR OVERSEAS. July, 1999. Hong Kong. (Li Lik-chi, Stepphen Chiau) Stephen Chiau, Karen Mok, Cecilia Cheung, Jackie Chan.

KING OF THE JUNGLE
BOMBO SPORTS & ENTERTAINMENT/FORENSIC FILMS/MEDIA VENTURES PROD. Apr., 2000. (Seth Zvi Rosenfeld) John Leguizamo, Rosie Perez, Julie Carmen, Cliff Gorman, Michael Rapaport, Marisa Tomei, Justin Pierce, Annabella Sciorra.

THE KING'S DAUGHTERS
UIP/ ARCHIPEL 35/LICHTBLICK FILMPRODUKTION/ENTRE CHIEN ET LOUP/ARTE FRANCE CINEMA/FRANCE 2 CINEMA/WDR/FMB FILMS/ACCAAN/LES FILMS DU CAMELIA/CINEART/SOFINERGIE 5/SOFYGRAM 2/COFIMAGE 10/UGC INTL/CANAL PLUS/CNC. May, 2000. French. (Patricia Mazuy, Yves Thomas) Isabelle Huppert, Jean-Pierre Kalfon, Simon Reggiani, Jean-Francois Balmer, Anne Marev, Nina Meurisse, Morgane More.

KIPPUR
MP PRODS./AGAV HAFAKOT/LE STUDIO CANAL PLUS/ARTE FRANCE CINEMA/R & C PRODUZIONI/CANAL PLUS/TELAD/ ELDAN/TELE PLUS. May, 2000. Israeli-French. (Amos Gita) Liron Levo, Tomer Ruso, Uri Ran Klauzner, Yoram Hattab, Juliano Merr, Ran Kauchinsky, Kobi Livne, Liat Glick Levo.

KIRIKOU AND THE SORCERESS
GEBEKA FILMS. Dec., 1998. French-Belgian-Luxembourgeois. (Michel Ocelot). Animated.

KISMET
HELKON. June, 1999. German. (Andreas Thiel) Steffen Wink, Fatih Akin, Jule Ronstedt, Axel Milberg, Lilo Wanders.

KISS AND TELL
BASE PRODS. May, 1999. (John Brenkus) James McCauley, Bryan Callen, Kerr Smith, Daniel Cosgrove, Bridget Ann White Wimme.

KISS, CUDDLE AND CELEBRATE
ALMA FILMS. July, 1998. German. (Peter Kern) Documentary.

KISSES AND HUGS
CECCHI GORI. Jan., 1999. Italian. (Paolo Virzi) Francesco Paolantoni, Massimo Gambacciani, Piero Gremigni, Samuele Marzi.

KISSES FOR EVERYONE
WARNER SOGEFILMS. Dec., 2000. Spanish. (Jaime Chavarri) Emma Suarez, Eloy Azorin, Roberto Hoyas, Chusa Barbero, Pilar Lopez de Ayala, Inaki Font, Monica Cano, Beatriz Bergamin.

KISSING JESSICA STEIN
EDEN WURMFELD FILMS AND BRAD ZIONS FILMS. April, 2001. (Charles Herman-Wurmfeld) Jennifer Westfeldt, Heather Juergensen, Scott Cohen, Tovah Feldshuh, Jackie Hoffman, Michael Mastro.

KISS KISS (BANG BANG)
Dec., 2001. British. (Stewart Sugg) Stellan Skarsgard, Chris Penn, Paul Bettany, Sienna Guillory, Allan Corduner, Martine McCutcheon.

KISS ME SO LONG I CAN'T BREATHE
ZONE. Feb., 2000. Japanese. (Kim Taegwan) Atsuki Kato, Toshiya Nakamatsu, Ikkoh Suzuki.

KISSING A FOOL
UNIVERSAL. Feb., 1998. (Doug Ellin) David Schwimmer, Jason Lee, Mili Avital, Bonnie Hunt, Vanessa Angel, Kari Wuhrer.

THE KITE
K. Sept., 1999. Filipino. (Gil M. Portes) Ricky Davao, Lester Llansang, Jennifer Sevilla, Mark Gil, Sining Blanco, Daryl Reyes, Connie Lauigan-Chua, Nanding Josef.

THE KITE (ZMEJ)
Sept., 2002. Russian. (Alexei Muradov) Viktor Solovyov, Nadezhda Ozerova, Pavel Zolotilin.

KM.O
UNIVERSAL PICTURES SPAIN/CUARTETO PC. June, 2001. Spanish. (Yoland Garcia Serrano, Juan Luis Iborra) Concah Velasco, Georges Corraface, Silke, Carlos Fuentes, Merce Pons, Armando Del Rio, Tristan Ulloa, Jesus Cabrero.

K-19:THE WIDOWMAKER
PARAMOUNT. July, 2002. (Kathryn Bigelow) Harrison Ford, Liam Neeson, Peter Sarsgaard, Joss Ackland, John Shrapnel, Donald Sumpter, Tim Woodward, Steve Nicholson, Ravil Isyanov, Christian Camargo.

KNIGHTS OF THE QUEST
20TH CENTURY FOX ITALY. March, 2001. Italian-French. (Pupi Avait) Edward Furlong, Raoul Bova, Marco Leonardi, Thomas Kretschmann, Stanislas Merhar, Edmund Purdom, Carlo Delle Piane.

A KNIGHT'S TALE
SONY PICTURES ENTERTAINMENT. April, 2001. (Brian Helgeland) Heath Ledger, Mark Addy, Rufus Sewell, Paul Bettany, Shanynn Sossamon, Alan Tudyk, Laura Fraser, Berenice Beso.

KNOCKAROUND GUYS
NEW LINE CINEMA. Nov., 2001. (Brian Koppelman, David Levien) John Malkovich, Dennis Hopper, Vin Diesel, Barry Pepper, Seth Green, Andrew Davoli, Tom Noonan.

KNOCK OFF
TRISTAR PICTURES. Aug., 1998. (Tsui Hark) Jean-Claude Van Damme, Rob Schneider, Lela Rochon, Paul Sorvino, Carmen Lee.

KNOCKOUT
SVENSK FILMINDUSTRI/GIRAFF FILM/SVENSK FILMINDUSTRI/ SVT FILMPOOL NORD/SF NORGE. Feb., 2000. Swedish-Norwegian. (Agneta Fagerstrom-Olsson) Orjan Landstrom, Reine Brynolfsson, Ludmila Varfolomeyeva, Igor Chernovich, Kirill Ulyanov, Mikhail Wasserbaum, Aleksei Shulin.

KNOCKOUT
RENEGADE PICTURES/CEO FILMS/DMG ENTERTAINMENT. Jan., 2000. (Lorenzo Doumani) Sophia-Adella Hernandez, Eduardo Yanez, Tony Plana, Paul Winfield, William McNamara, Maria Conchita Alonso.

THE KNOT
Studio Nadezha. Oct., 1999. Russian. (Alexander Sokurov). Documentary.

KOMODO
SCANBOX ASIA PACIFIC. May, 1999. Australian. (Michael Lantieri) Jill Hennessy, Billy Burke, Kevin Zegers, Paul Gleeson, Nina Landis.

KRAMPACK
ALTA/MESSIDOR FILMS. May, 2000. Spanish. (Cesc Gay) Fernando Ramallo, Jordi Vilches, Marieta Orozco, Esther Nubiola, Chisco Amado, Ana Gracia, Myriam Mezieres.

KRAPP'S LAST TAPE
RTE. Sept., 2000. Irish. (Atom Egoyan) John Hurt.

KRIPPENDORF'S TRIBE
BUENA VISTA. Feb., 1998. (Todd Holland) Richard Dreyfuss, Jenna Elfman, Natasha Lyonne, Gregory Smith, Elaine Stritch, Tom Poston.

KT
Feb., 2002. Japanese-South Korean. (Junji Sakamoto) Koichi Sato, Kim Kab-soo, Kim Byong-se, Yoshio Harada, Choi Il-hwa, Michitaka Tsutsui, Yang Eun-yong, Teruyuki Kagawa.

KUROSAWA
Nov., 2001. U.S.-British-Japanese. (Adam Low) Narrator: Sam Shepard, Voice of Kurosawa: Paul Scofield. Documentary.

KURT GERRON'S KARUSSELL
TV-VENTURES. Feb., 1999. German. (Ilona Ziok). Documentary.

KUSAH HAKWAAN
ALASKAN NOMAD. July, 1999. (Sean Morris) Paul Asicksik, Don Savage, Gary Waid, Diane E. Benson, Kuth Ka.

KWIK STOP
RACFHEL TENNER/MICHAEL GILIO. APRIL, 2001. (Michael Gilio) Lara Phillips,Michael Gilio, Karin Anglin, Rick Komenich.

L

LA BELLE
EUN-SUK FILM. Oct., 2000. South Korean. (Yeo Kyun-dong) Lee Ji-hyeon, Oh Ji-ho.

LA BOMBA
MEDUSA FILM. Apr., 1999. (Giulio Base) Alessandro Gassman, Enrico Brignano, Rocco Papaleo, Lola Pagnani, Vittorio Gassman.

LA BOSTELLA
PATHE/LA COMPAGNIE PANOPTIQUE/LES PRODUCTIONS EN CABINE/LE STUDIO CANAL PLUS/SYLICONE. July, 2000. French. (Edouard Baer) Edouard Baer, Rosine Favey, Gilles Gaston-Dreyfus, Jean-Michel Lahm, Pierre-Louis Lanier, Philippe Laudenbach.

THE LABYRINTH OF TRUTH
ELECTRA MEDIA/KAKOSEOS. Jan., 2001. Swedish. (Nitza Kakoseos) Documentary.

LA CARBONARA
LION PICTURES/LETIZIA CINEMATOGRAFICA/RAI. Feb., 2000. Italian. (Luigi Magni) Lucrezia Lante Della Rovere, Nino Manfredi, Valerio Mastrandrea, Fabrizio Gifuni, Claudio Amendola.

LA CARNADA
KUSI FILMS/ZDF ARTE/BRUSSELS AVE. May, 1999. Peruvian-German-belgian. (Marianne Eyde) Monica Sanchez, Gabriela Velasquez, Miguel Medina, Orlando Felices, Ana Cecilia.

LA COMMUNE (PARIS 1871)
Sept., 2001. French. (Peter Watkins)

LA CUCARACHA
FLASHPOINT LTD. May, 1998. (Jack Perez) Eric Roberts, Joaquim De Almeida, Victor Rivers, Jack McManus, Tara Crespo.

THE LADIES MAN
PARAMOUNT PICTURES. Oct., 2000. (Reginald Hudlin) Tim Meadows, Karyn Parsons, Bill Dee Williams, Will Ferrell, Lee Evans, Tiffani Thiessen, John Witherspoon.

LADIES ROOM
MOTION INTL./CINE-ROMAN/LAUREM PRODS./TRANSFILM/- SMALLRAIN. Sept., 1999. Canadian-British. (Gabriella Christiani) John Malkovich, Lorraine Bracco, Greta Scacchi, Veronica Ferres, Molly Parker, Greg Thomey, Nanette Workman, Alan Fawcett.

LA DILETTANTE
GOUTTE D'OR. June, 1999. French. (Pascal Thomas) Catherine Frot, Bernard Verley, Barbara Schulz, Didier Bezace, Marie-Christine Barrault.

THE LADY
SAHARA CULTURAL-FILM INSTITUTE/AMA. Feb., 1999. Iranian. (Dariush Mehrjui) Bita Farrahi, Khosro Shakibai, Ezzatollah Entezami.

THE LADY AND THE DUKE
PATHE (IN FRANCE)/SONY PICTURES CLASSICS (IN U.S.). July, 2001. French. (Eric Rohmer) Lucy Russell, Jean-Claude Dreyfus, Francois Marthouret, Leonard Cobiant, Caroline Morin, Alain Libolt, Helena Dubeil.

LADY AND THE TRAMP II: SCAMP'S ADVENTURE
WALT DISNEY HOME VIDEO. Feb., 2001. (Darrell Rooney) ANIMATED (direct-to-video).

LADY IN THE BOX
DOOMED PRODS. Feb., 2001. (Christian Otjen) Darren E. Burrows, Robert Kneppler, Paige Rowland, Mark Sheppard, Robert Glen Keith, Apesanahkwat, Selena Green-Qualls.

THE LADY OF HAMRE
ZENTROPA ENTERTAINMENT S3/TV2/SCANBOX. Feb., 2000. Danish. (Katrine Wiedeman) Bodil Jorgensen, Bjarne Henriksen, Rikke Louise Andersson, Nikolaj Kopernikus, Bodil Lassen, Regitze Estrup, Tommy Kenter.

THE LADY OF THE HOUSE
J. RADICAL ENTERTAINMENT/PRIVATE. Feb., 2000. Indian. (Rituparno Ghosh) Kiron Kher, Chiranjeet Chakraborty, Sudipta Chakraborty, Surya Chatterjee, Rupa Ganguly, Abhishek Chatterjee.

LAGAAN: ONCE UPON A TIME IN INDIA
SET PICTURES. July, 2001. Indian. (Ashutosh Gowariker) Aamir Khan, Gracy Singh, Rachel Shelley, Paul Blackthorne, Suhasini Mulay, Kulbhushan Kharbanda, Raghuveer Yadav.

LAISSEZ-PASSER
BAC DISTRIBUTION. Nov., 2001. French-German-Spanish. (Bertrand Tavernier) Jacques Gamblin, Denis Podalydes, Christian Berkel, Marie Gillain, Charlotte Kady, Marie Desgranges, Maria Pitarresi.

THE LAKE
SONET. JAN., 1999. Swedish. (Hans Ake Gabrielsson) Regina Lund, Mats Rudal, Bjorn Gedda, Fredrik Hammar, Maria Lundquist.

LAKEBOAT
OREGON TRAIL FILMS/ONE VIBE ENTERTAINMENT. Apr., 2000. (Joe Mantegna) Charles Durning, Peter Falk, Robert Forster, J.J. Johnson, Denis Leary, Jack Wallace, George Wendt, Tony Mamet.

LAKE PLACID
20TH CENTURY FOX. July, 1999. (David E. Kelley) Bill Pullman, Bridget Fonda, Oliver Platt, Brendan Gleeson, Betty White.

LALEE'S KIN: THE LEGACY OF COTTON
HBO. Jan., 2001. (Froemke, Deborah Dickson, Albert Maysles) Laura Lee Wallace, Reggie Barnes, Cassandra Wallace, Gregory Wallace, Antonio Wallace, Robert Jamison. Documentary.

L'AMOUR L'ARGENT L'AMOUR
PHILIP GROENING//BALZLI & FAHRER/SOLERA & CIE. Aug., 2000. German-Swiss-French. (Philip Groening) Sabine Timoteo, Florian Stetter, Michael Schech, Dierk Prawdzik, Marquardt Bohm.

LAND FOR A FOREIGNER
GENERAL CINEMA ORGANIZATION. Oct., 2000. Syrian. (Bassam Koussa, Najwa Kandakji, Rayez Abou Dan, Iman Al-Ghouri.

THE LAND GIRLS
GRAMERCY PICTURES. Jan., 1998. (David Leland) Catherine McCormack, Rachel Weisz, Anna Friel, Steven Mackintosh.

LAND OF FEAR
ARAB SOCIETY FOR ADVERTISING & CULTURAL PRODUCTION. Sept., 2000. Egyptian. (Daoud Abdel Sayed) Ahmed Zaki, Farah, Hamdi Ghayth, Abdel Rahman Abou Zahra.

THE LAND OF THE DEAF
GORKY FILMSTUDIO. Feb., 1998. Russian. (Valery Todorovsky) Chulpan Khamatova, Dina Korzun, Maxim Sukhanov, Nikita Tiunin.

LAND OF THE SINGING DOG
May, 2002. French. (Yann Dedet) Katsuko Nakamura, Gen Shimaoka, Dominique Piard, Jules Dedet-Granel.

THE LAND OF THE WANDERING SOULS
INA/LA SEPT-ARTE. Aug., 2000. French. (Rithy Panh). Documentary.

L + R
FISCHER FILM. Jan., 2000. Austrian. (Edgar Honetschlager). Documentary.

LANGMUIR'S WORLD
ROGER R. SUMERHAYES. Jan., 1999. (Roger R. Summerhayes). Documentary.

LANI LOA: THE PASSAGE
FRANCIS FORD COPPOLA/WAYNE WANG. Sept., 1998. (Sherwood Hu) Angus MacFadyen, Carlotta Chang, Ray Bumatai, Chris Tashima.

LANSDOWN
TABLE ROUND FILMS. Feb. 2001. (Tom Zuber) Paul Shields, Jennifer Carlson, Chris Baran, D.W. Warren, Marc Krinsky, Jesse Schein, Chris Stewart, Patrick Louis.

LANTANA
PALACE FILMS. June, 2001. Australian-German. (Ray Lawrence) Anthony LaPaglia, Geoffrey Rush, Barbara Hershey, Kerry Armstrong, Rachael Blake, Vice Colosimo, Daniela Farinacci, Peter Phelps, Leah Purcell, Glenn Robbins, Russell Dykstra, Nicholas Cooper.

LAN YU
OMICO INTL. May, 2001. Hong Kong. (Stanley Kwan) Hu Jun, Kiu Ye, Su Jin, Li Huatong, Lu Fang, Zhang Yongning, Li Shuang.

LARA CROFT: TOMB RAIDER
PARAMOUNT. June, 2001. (Simon West) Angelina Jolie, Jon Voight, Noah Taylor, Iain Glen, Daniel Craig, Christopher Barrie, Julian Rhind-Tutt, Richard Johnson.

THE LARAMIE PROJECT
HBO FILMS. Jan., 2002. (Moises Kaufman) Dylan Baker, Stephen Belber, Tom Bower, Clancy Brown, Steve Buscemi, Nestor Carbonell, Kathleen Chalfant, Jeremy Davies, Clea Duvall, Michael Emerson, Noah Fleiss, Peter Fonda, Ben Foster, Janeane Garofalo, Amanda Gronich.

LARGE
PATHE. May, 2001. British. (Justin Edgar) Luke de Woolfson, Melanie Gutteridge, Ema Catherwood, Lee Oakes, Simon Lowe, Zita Sattar, Lucy Voller, Mirren Delaney.

LARGER THAN LIFE
REGAL FILMS. Aug., 2001. Filipino. (Jeffrey Jeturian) Ina Raymundo, Irma Adlawan, Nante Montreal, Raymond Nieva, Klaudia Koronel, Jaclyn Jose, Dante Rivero, Eric Parilla.

LA SPAGNOLA
NEW VISION. June, 2001. Australian. (Steve Jacobs) Lola Marceli, Alice Ansara, Lourdes Bartolome, Alex Dimitriades, Simon Palomare, Silvio Ofria, Gabrielle Marsella.

LAST BALL
SUGAR POND FILMS. June, 2001. (Peter Callahan) Charlie Hofheimer, Laurel Holloman. Leo Fitzpatrick, Avery Glymph, Thomas Lyons, James Rebhorn, Karen Shallo.

THE LAST BEST SUNDAY
LAST BEST. June, 1999. (Don Most) Douglas Spain, Angela Bettis, William Lucking, Kim Darby, Daneil Beer,.

THE LAST BIG ATTRACTION
HOPWOOD. June, 1999. (Hopwood DePree) Hopwood DePree, Christine Elise, Victoria Haas, Richard Speight, Jr. Brenda Ballard.

LAST CALL
ROOS FILM S.A. Aug., 1999. Chilean. (Christine Lucas) Peter Coyote, Elizabeth Berkley, Garret Dillahunt, Elizabeth Rossa.

THE LAST CASTLE
DREAMWORKS PICTURES. Oct., 2001. (Rod Lurie) Robert Redford, James Gandolfini, Mark Ruffalo, Delroy Lindo, Clifton Collins Jr., Steve Burton, Brian Goodman.

THE LAST CIGARETTE
NEW YORKER FILMS. Aug., 1999. (Kevin Rafferty). Documentary.

THE LAST DANCE
EURO AMERICAN FILMS/PANAVAM. May, 1999. French-Indian. (Shaji Karun) Mohanlal, Suhasini, Mattanoor Shankara Marar, Kukku Parameshwaram, Venmani Haridas.

THE LAST DAY
URBAN INC./PUG POINT Sept., 1999. Japanese. (Takumi Kimizuka) Nae Yuuki, Kazuya Takahashi, Kazuhiko Kanayama, Noriko Nagi, Masahiro Kiyota, Senjyaku Nakamura, Haruko Mabuchi.

THE LAST DAYS
OCTOBER FILMS. Oct., 1998. (James Moll). Documentary.

THE LAST DAYS OF DISCO
GRAMERCY. April, 1998. (Whit Stillman) Chloe Sevigny, Kate Beckinsale, Chris Eigeman, Matt Keeslar, Mackenzie Astin.

THE LAST ENEMY
YONA PRODS/PERES CENTER FOR PEACE/PALESTINIAN CENTER FOR REGIONAL STUDIES. Feb., 2000. Israeli. (Nitzan Gilady)Jim Mirrione, Achim Nowak, Achsen Tourkia.

THE LAST GREAT WILDERNESS
FEATURE FILM CO. Aug., 2002. British. (David Mackenzie) Alastair Mackenzie, Jonny Phillips, David Hayman, Ewan Stewart, Victoria Smurfit, Louise Irwin, John Comerford.

THE LAST KISS
MEDUSA FILM. Feb., 2001. Italian. (Gabriele Muccino)Stefano Accorsi, Giovanna Mezzogiorno, Stefania Sandrelli, Marco Cocci, Pierfrancesco Favino, Sabrina Impacciatore.

THE LAST LETTER
AD VITAM. May, 2002. French-U.S. (Frederick Wiseman) Catherine Samie.

THE LAST MAHADEVI
BILDERWERK FILMPRODUKTION. Oct., 2000. German. (Dirk Szuszies, Karin Kaper) Documentary.

THE LAST MAN
ID FILMS. Oct., 1999. (Harry Ralston) David Arnott, Jeri Ryan, Dan Montgomery.

LAST NIGHT
CINEPLEX. May, 1998. Canadian. (Don McKellar) Don McKellar Sandra Oh, Callum Keith Rennie, Sarah Polley.

LAST ORDERS
WINCHESTER FILMS. Sept., 2001. British. (Fred Schepisi) Michael Caine, Bob Hoskins, Tom Courtenay, David Hemmings, Ray Winstone.

LAST PRESENT
CINEMA SERVICE. June, 2001. South Korean. (Oh Ki-hwan) Lee Jeong-jae, Lee Yeong-ae, Kyeon Hae-hyo, Lee Mu-hyun, Kong Hyeong-jin.

LAST RESORT
BBC FILMS. Aug., 2000. British. (Paul Pawlikowski) Dina Korzun, Artiom Strelnikov, Paddy Considine, Lindsey Honey, Dave Bean, Perry Benson, Adrian Scarborough.

THE LAST RIDE
NATIONAL FILM DEVELOPMENT CORP. May, 2001. Indian. (Nabyendu Chatterjee) Arun Mukhopadhyay, Raisal Islam Asad.

THE LAST SEPTEMBER
TRIMARK. May, 1999. Irish-British-French. (Deborah Warner) Maggie Smith, Michael Gambon, Jane Birkin, Fiona Shaw, Lambert Wilson.

THE LAST SHOT
LES PIERIDES. Aug., 1999. Belgian. (Benoit Peeters) Florin Piersic, Jr., Manuela Servais, Mihai Dinvale, Pierre Arditi, Jean-Michel Jarre.

THE LAST STATION
DANIEL ZUTA FILMPRODUKTION/FILMEX ROMANIA/CDI. May, 1999. German-Romanian-Italian. (Bogdan (Dumitrescu) Dreyer) Sergio Rubini, Marion Kracht, Darel Visan.

LAST STOP PARADISE
MK2 DIFFUSION. Aug., 1998. French-Romanian. (Lucian Pintilie) Costel Cascaval, Dorina Chiriac, Gheorghe Visu, Victor Rebengiuc.

LAST SUPPER AT THE ARABIAN GREY HORSE
NEUROPA FILM. Feb., 2001. Hungarian. (Miklos Jancso) Zoltan Mucsi, Peter Scherer, Emese Vasvari, Eniko Borcsok, Jozsef Szarvas, Roland Raba, Kornel Mundruczo, Laura Ruttkay, Judit Schell.

LAST WEDDING
LAST WEDDING PRODS. (VANCOUVER). Sept. 2001. (Bruce Sweene). Benjamin Ratner, Frida Betrani, Tom Scholte, Nancy Sivak, Vincent Gale, Molly Parker, Babz Chula.

LAST WITNESS
Nov., 2001. South Korean. (Bae Chang-ho) Lee Jeong-jae, Lee Mi-yeon, Ahn Seong-ki, Jeong Jun-ho.

THE LAST YELLOW
SCALA PRODS./CAPITOL FILMS/HOLLYWOOD PARTNERS. Aug., 1999. British-German. (Julian Farino) Mark Addy, Charlie Creed-Miles, Samantha Morton, Kenneth Cranham, James Hooton.

LATE AUGUST, EARLY SEPTEMBER
POLYGRAM. Sept., 1998., French. (Olivier Assayas) Mathieu Amalric, Virginie Ledoyen, Francois, Cluzet, Jeanne Balibar, Alex Descas.

LATE MARRIAGE
DIAPHANA. May, 2001. Israeli-French. (Dover Kosashvili) Lior Louie Ashkenazi, Ronit Elkabetz, Moni Moshonov, Lili Kosashvili, Sapir Kugman, Aya Steinovits Laor, Rozina Cambos.

LATE NIGHT TALKS WITH MOTHER
FACETS MULTI-MEDIA. Oct., 2001. Czech. (Jan Nemec) Karel Roden, Jan Nemec, Zuzana Stivinova, Marta Kubisova, Jan Melicher, Ester Krumbachova. Documentary.

LATE SHOW
CONSTANTIN FILM. Feb., 1999. German. (Helmut Dietl) Thomas Gottschalk, Harald Schmidt, Veronica Ferres, Jasmin Tabatabai, Olli Dittrich, Sabine Orleans.

LATE NIGHT SHOPPING
FILMFOUR DISTRIBUTORS. Feb., 2001. British. (Saul Metzstein) Luke de Woolfson, James Lance, Kate Ashfield, Enzo Cilenti.

LATITUDE ZERO
OLHAR IMAGINARIO-RIOFILME. Feb., 2001. Brazilian. (Toni Venturi) Debora Duboc, Claudio Jaborandy.

LAUGHING DEAD
ISHI ENTERTAINMENT. July, 1998. (Patrick Gleason) Patrick Gleason, John Hamond, Fern Finer Rico Cymone.

LAUGHTER ON THE 23RD FLOOR
SHOWTIME NETWORKS AND PARAMOUNT TELEVISION. Jan., 2001. (Richard Benjamin) Nathan Lane, Mark Linn-Baker, Victor Garber, Saul Rubinek, Peri Gilpin, Dan Castellaneta, Richard Portnow.

LAUNDRY
LAUNDRY PARTNERS (ROBOT, MEDIA FACTORY, NHK ENTERPRISES21, HAKUHODO, IMAGICA). Aug., 2001. Japanese. (Junichi Mori) Yosuke Kubozuka, Koyuki, Takashi Naito.

LAURA CADIEUX...THE SEQUEL
ALLIANCE ATLANTIS/CINEMAGINAIRE. Dec., 1999. Canadian. (Denise Filiatrault) Ginette Reno, Pierrette Robitaille, Denise Dubois, Pauline Lapointe, Daniele Lorain, Dominique Michel, Adele Reinhardt.

LAUTREC
LES FILMS DU LOSANGE. Aug., 1998. French-Spanish. (Roger Planchon) Regis Royer, Elsa Zylberstein, Anemone, Claude Rich.

LAVENDER
GOLDEN HARVEST. Feb., 2001. Hong Kong. (Ip Kam-hung) Takeshi Kaaaaneshiro, Kelly Chen, Eason Chan.

L.A. WITHOUT A MAP
DAN FILMS/EURO AMERICAN FILMS/MARIANNA FILMS. Sept., 1998. British-French-Finnish. (Mika Kaurismaki) David Tennant, Vinessa Shaw, Julie Delpy, Vincent Gallo, Cameron Bancroft.

THE LAWLESS HEART
OVERSEAS FILMGROUP. Aug., 2001. British. (Neil Hunter, Tom Hunsinger) Douglas Henshall, Tom Hollander, Bill Nighy, Clementine Celarie, Josephine Butler, Ellie Haddington, Stuart Laing.

THE LAW OF ENCLOSURES
ALLIANCE ATLANTIS AND ODEON FILMS. Sept., 2000. Canadian. (John Greyson) Sarah Polley, Brendan Fletcher, Diane Ladd, Sean McCann, Kristin Thomson, Rob Stefaniuk, Shirley Douglas.

LAZARO DE TORMES
LOLAFILMS DISTRIBUCION. Jan., 2001. Spanish. (Fernando Fernan-Gomez) Rafael Alvarez, Karra Elejalde, Beatriz Rico, Francisco Algora,Juan Luis Galiardo, Alvaro de Luna, Jose Lifante.

L'CHAYIM, COMRADE STALIN!
BLACKSTREAM FILMS. Aug., 2002. (Yale Strom). Documentary.

LEAF ON A PILLOW
CHRISTINE HAKIM FILM. May, 1998. Indonesian. (Garin Nugroho) Kancil, Heru, Sugeng, Christine Hakim, Kabri Wali, Denny Christantra.

THE LEAFBLOWER
BLACK SHOE FILMS. March, 1998. (Dominic J. DeJoseph) Jon Hyrns, Marco Giudice, Charles Langley, Jeanne Foss, Paul Yates.

LEAK
C-FILMS. Feb., 2001. Dutch. (Jean van de Velde) Cas Jansen, Ricky Koole, Victor Low, Thomas Acda.

THE LEARNING CURVE
MOTION PICTURE CORP. OF AMERICA. Aug., 1999. (Eric Schwab) Carmine Giovinazzo, Monet Mazur, Vincent Ventresca, Steven Bauer, Majandra Delfino.

LEAVE A LITTLE ONE
A LA SEPT/ARTE, AGAT FILMS & CIE. May, 1998. French. (Zaida Ghorab-Volta) Andree Damant, Aurelia Petit, Lise Payen.

LEAVE IT TO LUCIE!
LES FILMS PELLEAS/FRANCE 3 CINEMA. Aug., 2000. French. (Emmanuel Mouret) Marie Gillain, Emmanuel Mouret, Dolores Chaplin, Delphine Zentout, Georges Neri, Arnaud Simon.

LEAVING
SHOCHIKU CO. Feb., 1998. Japanese. (Masato Harada) Hitomi Sato, Yasue Sato, Yukiko Okamoto, Jun Murakami, Shin Yazawa.

LEAVING BY THE WAY (PA CELAM AIZEJOT)
July, 2002. Latvian. (Viesturs Kairiss) Davis Bergs, Elita Klavina, Guna Zarina, Andris Keiss, Janis Paukstello, Eriks Vilsons, Baiba Broka.

LEAVING METROPOLIS
Aug., 2002. Canadian. (Brad Fraser) Troy Ruptash, Vincent Corazza, Lynda Boyd, Cherilee Taylor, Thom Allison.

LEAVING NO TRACE
TABASCO FILMS, ALTAVISTA FILMS (MEXICO)/TORNASOL FILMS (SPAIN). Sept., 2000. Mexican-Spanish. (Maria Novaro) Aitana Sanchez-Gijon, Tiare Scanda, Jesus Ochoa, Martin Altomaro.

LE DERRIERE
AMLF. Mar., 1999. French. (Valerie Lemercier) Valerie Lemercier, Claude Rich, Dieudonne, Marthe Keller, Patrick Catalifo.

LEFT BEHIND
CLOUD TEN PICTURES. Jan., 2001. (Vic Sarin) Kirk Cameron, Brad Johnson, Janaya Stephens.

LEFT LUGGAGE
TRIDENT. Feb., 1998. (Jeroen Krabbe) Laura Fraser, Isabella Rossellini, Maximilian Schell, Jeroen Krabbe, Marianne Sagebrecht.

LEFT OVERS
TROMA TEAM/DEADBEAT PRODS./ANDRE'S WORLD INC./ MONTEGO FILMS. Apr., 2000. (Jason Phillips) Mark Fite, Jason Oliver, Todd Stanton, Timothy DiPri, Cyndy Preston, Jason Cross, Christina Karras, Miranda Viscoli, Jack Moore, David Dickerson, Marine Palmier-Gonzalez.

THE LEFT SIDE OF THE FRIDGE
FILM TONIC. Oct., 2000. Canadian. (Philippe Falardeau) Paul Ahmarani, Stephane Demers, Genevieve Neron, Jules Philippe, Alexandrine Agostini, Marie-Andree Corneille, Khan Hua, Sylvain Bellemare, Elizabeth Walling, Robert Morin, Daniel Briere.

LEGACY
NOMADIC PICTURES. Jan., 2000. (Todd S. Lending). Documentary.

THE LEGACY: MURDER & MEDIA, POLITICS & PRISON
PORCH LIGHT. Jan., 1999. (Michael J. Moore). Documentary.

LEGALLY BLONDE
MGM. June, 2001. (Robert Luketic) Reese Witherspoon, Luke Wilson, Selma Blair, Matthew Davis, Victor Garber, Jennifer Coolidge.

THE LEGEND OF BAGGER VANCE
DREAMWORKS PICTURES (IN U.S.)/20TH CENTURY FOX (FOR-EIGN). Oct., 2000. Will Smith, Matt Damon, Charlize Theron, Bruce McGill, Joel Gretsch, Lane Smith, Harve Presnell, J. Michael Moncrief.

THE LEGEND OF BHAGAT SINGH
June, 2002. Indian. (Rajkumar Santoshi) Ajay Devgan, Sushant Singh, Santosh, Farida Jalal, Amrita Rao, Akhilendra Mishra, Raj Babbar, Mukesh Tiwari, Jonathan Ryan.

THE LEGEND OF DRUNKEN MASTER
DIMENSION FILMS. Oct., 2000. Hong Kong. (Lau Kar-Leung) Jackie Chan, Ti Lung, Anita Mui, Felix Wong, Lau Kar-leung, Low Houi-kang.

THE LEGEND OF LOVE
Aug., 2000. Iranian. (Farhad Mehranfar) Maryam Moqadam, Yusef Moradian, Hawass Palouk.

THE LEGEND OF TEDDY EDWARDS
ROUGH SEA PRODS. Feb., 2001. (Don McGlynn) Teddy Edwards, Ernie Andrews, James B. Smith, Kirk Silsbee, Dan Morgenstern, Clora Bryant, James B. Smith. Documentary.

THE LEGENDS OF RITA
ARTHAUS/BABELSBERG/MITTELDEUTSCHES FILMKONTOR/
MDR TV. Feb., 2000. German. (Volker Schlondorf) Bibiana Beglau,
Martin Wuttke, Nadja Uhl, Harald Schrott, Alexander Beyer, Jenny
Schily, Mario Irrek, Thomas Arnold.

THE LEGEND OF SURIYOTHAI
SONY PICTURES CLASSICS. Sept., 2002. Thai-U.S. (Chatrichalerm
Yukol)

LEILA
FARAZMAND. Feb., 1998. Iranian. (Dariush Mehrjui) Leila Hatami, Ali
Mosaffa, Jamileh Sheikhi, Mohammad Reza Sharifinia.

LENA
ALTA FILMS. May, 2001. Spanish-Portuguese. (Gonzalo Tapia)
Manuel Manquna, Marta Larralde, Roberto Alvarez, Vitor Norte, Luis
Tosar, Anton Reixa.

LENNY BRUCE: SWEAR TO TELL THE TRUTH
WHYADUCK. Oct., 1998. (Robert B. Weide). Documentary.

LEO
EL IMAN. Sept., 2000. Spanish. (Jose Luis Borau) Iciar Bollain, Javier
Batanero, Valeri Jevlinski, Rosana Pastor, Luis Tosar, Charo Soriano.

LEO & CLAIRE
ODEON FILM. Aug., 2001. German. (Joseph Vilsmaier) Michael
Degen, Franziska Petri, Suzanne von Borsody, Alexandra Maria Lara,
Axel Milberg, Jochen Nickel, Andrea Sawatzki.

LES DESTINEES SENTIMENTALES
PATHE/ARENA FILMS/TF1/CAB PRODS./CANAL PLUS/COFIMAGE
11/ARCADE/CNC/PROCIREP/OFFICE FEDERAL DE LA CULTURE/
TELEVISION SUISSE ROMANDE. May, 2000. French-Swiss. (Olivier
Assayas) Emmanuelle Beart, Charles Berling, Isabelle Huppert,
Olivier Perrier, Dominique Reymond, Andre Marcon.

LES SIESTES GRENADINE
HASSAN DALDOUL/LUC DARDENNE/TOUZA PRODS.
(FRANCE)/TOUZA FILMS/LES FILMS DU FLEUVE/CANAL PLUS
HORIZONS TUNISIA/ERTT/CNC. Nov., 1999. French-Tunisian-
Belgian. (Mahmoud Ben Mahmoud.) Hicham Rostom, Yasmine Bahri,
Loubna Azabaal.

LESS IS MORE
AURUM. Aug., 2000. Spanish. (Pascal Jongen) Vanessa Saiz, Sergio
Peris-Mencheta, Elsa Pataky, Miguel Sitjar, Luis Fernando Alves.

LETHAL WEAPON 4
WARNER BROS. July, 1998. Mel Gibson, Danny Glover, Joe Pesci,
Rene Russo, Chris Rock, Jet Li, Steve Kahan, Kim Chan.

LET IT COME DOWN: THE LIFE OF PAUL BOWLES
MONGREL MEDIA/REQUISITE PRODS. Oct., 1999. Canadian.
(Jennifer Baichwal). Documentary.

LET'S GET LOST
PER HOLST FILM. Feb., 1998. Danish. (Jonas Elmer) Sidse Babett
Knudsen, Bjarne Henriksen, Troels Lyby.

LET'S NOT CRY! (YIRLAMA, BARI YAKHSHI!)
June, 2002. South Korean-Uzbekistan. (Min Boung-hun) Muhammad
Rahimo, Diaz Rakhmanitov, Dilvar Ekramova, Erkin Kamilrov.

LET'S TALK ABOUT SEX
FINE LINE FEATURES. Sept., 1998. (Troy Beyer) Troy Beyer, Paget
Brewster, Randi Ingerman, Joseph C. Phillips, Michaline Babich.

THE LETTER
MADRIAGIA FILMES. May, 1999. Portuguese-French-Spanish.
(Manoel de Oliveira): Chiara Mastroianni, Pedro Abrunhosa, Antoine
Chappey, Leonor Silveira, Francoise Fabian.

LETTER TO AMERICA
KLAS FILM (SOFIA)-PHANTA VISION (AMSTERDAM)-BUDAPEST
FILMSTUDIO (BUDAPEST). Feb., 2001. Bulgarian-Dutch-Hungarian.
(Iglika Triffonova) Peter Antonov, Philip Avramov, Ana Papadopulu.

LETTERS IN THE WIND
Sept., 2002. Iranian. (Ali Reza Amini) Taghi Husshemi.

LET THE DEVIL WEAR BLACK
TRIMARK. Jan., 1999. (Stacy Title) Jonathan Penner, Jacqueline
Bisset, Mary-Louise Parker, Jamey Sheridan, Philip Baker Hall.

LET THERE BE LIGHT
AFMD. July, 1998. French. (Arthur Joffe) Helene de Fougerolles,
Tcheky Karyo, Ticky Holgado.

L5: FIRST CITY IN SPACE
IMAX. Nov., 1999. (Toni Myers) Colin Fox, Rachel Walker, Denis
Akiyama, Genevieve Langlois, Martha Henry.

LIAM
BB/LIAM FILMS/ROAD MOVIES/MIDA/DIAPHANA/BIM/WDR/ARTE/
ARD/DEGETO Film. Sept., 2000. British-German. (Stephen Frears)
Ian Hart, Claire Hackett, Anthony Borrows, David Hart, Megan Burns,
Anne Reid, Julia Deakin, Andrew Schofield, Bernadette Shortt.

LIAR'S POKER
NORTH BRANCH/SAVINO BROTHERS. Oct., 1999. (Jeff Santo)
Richard Tyson, Caesar Luisi, Jimmy Blondell, Flea, Neith Andrina,
Pamela Gidley, Amelia Heinle, Colin Partrick Lynch.

LIBERA ME
CINEMA SERVICE. Feb., 2001. South Korean. (Yan Yun-ho) Choi Min-
su, Cha Seung-weon, Yu Ji-tae, Park Sang-myeon, Jeong Jun, Kim
Syu-ri, Kim Su-ro.

LIBERTE-OLERON
UFD. July, 2001. French. (Bruno Podalydes) Denis Podalydes,
Guilaine Londez, Bruno Podalydes, Patrick Pineau, Eric Elmosnino,
Marie-Armelle Deguy, Marie Diot.

THE LIBERTINE
PATHE/TF1/BEL OMBRE/MOSCA/JOSY FILMS/SANS CONTREFACON/
CANAL PLUS. Feb., 2000. French. (Gabriel Aghion) Vincent Perez,
Fanny Ardant, Josiane Balasko, Michel Serrault, Arielle Dombasle,
Christian Charmetant, Francoise Lepine.

LIBERTY HEIGHTS
WARNER BROS./BALTIMORE/SPRING CREEK PICTURES. Nov.,
1999. (Barry Levinson) Adrien Brody, Ben Foster, Orlando Jones,
Bebe Neuwirth, Joe Mantegna, Rebekah Johnson, David Krumholtz,
Richard Kline, Vincent, Guastaferro, Justin Chambers.

LICENSE TO LIVE
DAIEI CO.. Feb., 1999. Japanese. (Kiyoshi Kurosawa) Hidetoshi
Nishijima, Koji Yakusho, Shun Sugata, Lily, Kumiko Asou.

L.I.E.
ALTER EGO/BELLADONNA. Jan., 2001. (Michael Cuesta) Brian Cox,
Paul Franklin Dano, Billy Kay, Bruce Altman, James Costa,Tony
Donnelly, Walter Masterson, Marcia DeBonis.

LIES
SHINCINE COMMUNICATIONS. Sept., 1999. South Korean. (Jang
Sun Woo) Lee Sang Hyun, Kim Tae yeon, Jeon Hye Jin.

LIFE
UNIVERSAL. Apr., 1999. (Ted Demme) Eddie Murphy, Martin
Lawrence, Obba Babatunde, Ned Beatty, Bernie Mac.

LIFE AFTER LOVE
ALLIANCE ATLANTIS/MAX FILMS/CANADIAN TELEVISION
FUND/TELEFILM CANADA/QUEBEC TAX CREDIT/SODEC/
RESEAU TVA. July, 2000. Canadian. (Gabriel Pelletie) Michel Cote,
Sylivie Leonard, Patrick Huard, Yves Jacques, Norman Helms.

THE LIFE AND ASCENSION OF YURAZ BRATCHIK
BELARUSFILM. Aug., 2000. Soviet Union–1968. (Vladimir Bychkov,
S. Skvortsov) L. Durov, I. Rutberg, L. Krugly, A. Smirnov, R. Kormunin.

THE LIFE AND TIMES OF HANK GREENBERG
CIESLA FOUNDATION. June, 1999. (Aviva Kempner). Documentary.

LIFE AS A FATAL SEXUALLY TRANSMITTED DISEASE
TELEWIZJA POLSKA/STUDIO FILMOWE "TOR". Oct., 2000. Polish.
(Krysztof Zanussi) Zbigniew Zapasiewicz, Krystyna Janda, Tadeusz
Bradecki, Monika Krzywkowska, Jerzy Radzowilowicz.

LIFE AS A HOUSE
NEW LINE CINEMA. Aug., 2001. (Irwin Winkler) Kevin Kline, Kristin
Scott Thomas, Hayden Christensen, Jena Malone, Mary Steenburgen,
Mike Weinberg, Scotty Leavenworth.

LIFE BLOOD
MIKADO/PABLO/SIDECAR FILMS & TV. May, 2000. Italian. (Edouardo
Winspeare) Pino Zimba, Lamberto Probo, Claudio Giangreco,
Alessandro Valenti, Ivan Verardo, Lucia Chiuri, Addolorata Turco.

LIFE HURTS
FILMCONTRACT/TVP/AGENCJA PRODUKCJI FILMOWEJ
KOMITETU KINEMATOGRAFI. Jan., 2000. Polish. (Lech Majewski)
Krzysztof Siwczyk, Dominika Ostalowska, Elzbieta Okupska, Andrzej
Mastalerz.

LIFE IS THE MAIN THING
UFA FERNSEHPRODUKTION. May, 1999. German. (Connie Walther)
Renee Soutenkijk, Hans-Werner Meyer, Huub Stapel, Isabel Trimborn,
Rebecca Hessing.

LIFE IS WHISTLING
NIRVANA. JULY, 1999. Cuban-Spanish. (Fernando Perez) Luis Alberto
Garcia, Coralia Veloz, Claudia Rojas, Bebe Perez, Isabel Santos.

LIFE, LOVE & CELLULOID
RAINER WERNER FASSBINDER FOUNDATION. Feb., 1998.
German. (Juliane Lorenz) documentary.

LIFETIME GUARANTEE: PHRANC'S ADVENTURES IN PLASTIC
ROADSIDE ATTRACTIONS. June, 2001. (Lisa Udelson)
Documentary.

THE LIFE OF THE JEWS IN PALESTINE
JERUSALEM FILM ARCHIVE / ARCHIVES DU FILM OF CENTRE
NATIONAL DE LA CINEMATOGRAPHIE/BOIS D'ARCY/
CINEMATHEQUE FRANCAISE/ISRAEL FILM ARCHIVE/HAMIZRAH
SOCIETY. July, 2000. Russian. (Noah Sokolovsky). Documentary.
Archival.

LIFE ON EARTH
A HAUT ET COURT DISTRIBUTION. May, 1998. French. (Abderrahmane
Sissako) Abderrahmane Sissako, Nana Baby, Mohamed Sissako.

LIFE OR SOMETHING LIKE IT
20TH CENTURY FOX. April, 2002. (Stephen Herek) Angelina Jolie, Edward Burns, Tony Shalhoub, Christian Kane, Melissa Errico, Stockard Channing.

LIFE SHOW (SHENGHUO XIU)
Aug., 2002. Chinese. (Huo Jianqi) Tao Hong, Tao Zeru, Pan Yueming, Yang Yi, Luo Deyuan, Zhang Shihong, Wu Ruixue, Li Xiaochen, Liu Min, Jiang Mingxiao, Zheng Meiju, Guan Jiangge.

THE LIFESTYLE
GOOD MACHINE. Apr., 1999. (David Schisgall). Documentary.

LIFE TASTES GOOD
LIFE TASTES GOOD PRODS. Jan. 1999. (Philip Kan Gotanda) Sab Shimono, Julia Nickson, Tamlyn Tomita, Greg Watanabe.

LIFE WITHOUT DEATH
FRANK COLE. Sept., 2000. Canadian. (Frank Cole) Documentary.

LIFT
HART SHARP ENTERTAINMENT. Jan., 2001. (DeMane Davis, Khari Streeter) Kerry Washington, Lonette McKee, Eugene Byrd, Barbara Montgomery, Sticky Fingaz, Samantha Brown, Todd Williams.

LIGHT DROPS (O GOTEJAR DA LUZ)
Aug., 2002. Mozambique-Portugese. (Fernando Vendrell) Luis Sarmento, Filipe Carvalho, Amaral Matos, Alexandra Antunes, Alberto Magassela, Marco de Almeida.

LIGHT IT UP
20TH CENTURY FOX/FOX 2000 PICTURES/EDMONDS ENTERTAINMENT. Nov., 1999. (Craig Bolotin) Usher Raymond, Forest Whitaker, Rosario Dawson, Robert Richard, Judd Nelson, Fredro Starr, Sara Gilbert, Clifton Collins Jr., Glynn Turman, Vic Polizos, Vanessa L. Williams.

LIGHTMAKER
YELLO MUSIC & MOTION PICTURES. Feb., 2001. U.S.-Swiss. (Dieter Meier) Zbigniew Zamachowski, Cornelia Grolimund, Dieter Meier, Malgorzata Potocka, Rod Steiger, Johnny Melville.

LIGHT OF MY EYES
01 DISTRIBUTION. Sept., 2001. Italian. (Giuseppe Piccioni) Luigi Lo Cascio, Sandra Ceccarelli, Silvio Orlando, Barbara Valente.

LIKE A FISH OUT OF WATER
SOCIETE NOUVELLE DE DISTRIBUTION/CLT-UFA. May, 1999. French. (Herve Hadmar) Tcheky Karyo, Monica Bellucci, Dominque Pinon, Michel Muller, Mehmet Ulusoy.

LIKE FATHER
AMBER FILMS. MArch, 2001. British. (Richard Grassick, Ellin Hare, Sirkka-Liisa Konttinen, Murray Martin, Pat McCarthy, Lorna Powell, Peter Roberts) Joe Armstrong, Ned Kelly, Jonathan Dent, Anna Gascoigne, Derek Walmsley, Willie Ross, Brian Hogg, Ashley Gutsell.

LIKE IT IS
DANGEROUS TO KNOW. May, 1998. British. (Paul Oremland) Roger Daltrey, Dani Behr, Ian Rose, Steve Bell.

LIKE MIKE
20TH CENTURY FOX. June, 2002. (John Schultz) Lil' Bow Wow, Morris Chestnut, Jonathan Lipnicki, Robert Forster, Crispin Glover, Eugene Levy, Brenda Song, Jesse Plemons, Julius Charles Ritter, Anne Meara.

LIGHT KEEPS ME COMPANY
BELUGA/SANDREW METRONOME/SVENSK FILMINDUSTRI/SVT. Feb., 2000. Swedish-Danish. (Carl-Gustaf Nykvist). Documentary.

LIKE A MAGNET
MARS/WHY NOT PRODS/ LE STUDIO CANAL PLUS/ESKWAD/LA SOCIETE 361. June, 2000. French. (Kamel Saleh, Akhenaton) Kamel Saleh, Houari Djerir, Brahim Aimad, Sofiane Madjid Mammeri.

LILA LILI
GEMINI FILMS/LA SEPT CINEMA. Feb., 1999. French. (Marie Vermillard) Alexia Monduit, Genevieve Tenne, Simon Abkarian, Zinedine Soualem, Antoine Chappey.

LILITH ON TOP
Oct., 2001. Canadian. (Lynne Stopkewich) Sarah McLachlan, Sheryl Crow, the Pretenders, Dixie Chicks, Indigo Girls, Bif Naked. Documentary.

LILO & STITCH
BUENA VISTA. June, 2002. (Chris Sanders, Dean DeBlois). Daveigh Chase, Chrstopher Michael Sanders, Tia Carrere, David Ogden Stiers, Kevin McFonald, Ving Rhames. Animated.

LILYA 4-EVER
SONET FILM. Aug., 2002. Swedish. (Lukas Moodysson) Oksana Akinshina, Artiom Bogucharski, Elina Benenson, Liliya Shinkaryova, Pavel Ponomaryov, Tomas Neumann, Lyubov Agapova.

LILY FESTIVAL
Aug., 2002. Japanese. (Sachi Hamano) Kazuko Yoshiyuki, Mickey Curtis, Utae Shoji, Kazuko Shirakawa, Sanae Nakahara, Chisako Hara, Hisako Okata.

LIMBO
SONY. May, 1999. (John Sayles) Mary Elizabeth Mastrantonio, David Strathairn, Vanessa Martinez, Kris Kristofferson.

A LINGERING FACE
BEIJING FILM STUDIO/CHINA FILM/CENTER FOR SATELLITE BROADCASTING. Aug., 2000. Chinese. (Lu Xuechang) Ma Xiaoqing, Pan Yueming, Li Min, Ge Yaming, He Xi.

THE LION KING II: SIMBA'S PRIDE.
BUENA VISTA. Oct., 1998. (Darrell Rooney).Animated.

LISA
AB DROITS AUDIOVISUELS. May, 2001. French. (Pierre Grimblat) Benoit Magimel, Jeanne Moreau, Marion Cotillard, Sagamore Stevenin, Michel Jonasz, Denise Chalem, Julia Vaidis-Bogard.

LISBON
ALTA FILMS. June, 1999. Spanish-Argentine. (Antonio Hernandez).

LISE AND ANDRE
LES FILMS A UN DOLLAR. May, 2001. French. (Denis Dercourt) Isabelle Candelier, Michel Duchaussoy, Aissa Maiga.

LITHIUM
CARAVAN. Aug., 1999. Swedish. (David Flamhole) Agnieszka Doson, Fredrik Dolk, Johna Widerberg, Pierre Boutros, Yvonne Lombard.

THE LITTLE BIG GIRL
Aug., 2002. Danish. (Morten Kohlert) Sarah Juel Werner, Peter Jeppe Hansen, Lisbet Dahl, Erik Wedersoe, Birthe Neumann, Bent Mejding.

A LITTLE BIRD BOY
Feb., 2002. Iranian. (Rahbar Qanbari) Reza Naji, Mehdi Shahabi, Sylva Andranian, Nasrin Nakisa, Samira Aalaie.

LITTLE BROTHERS
MK2 DIFFUSION. Feb., 1999. French. (Jacques Doillon) Stephanie Touly, Ilies Sefraoui, Mustapha Goumane, Nassim Izem, Rachid Mansouri.

LITTLE CHEUNG
METEOR INDEPENDEN/NHK JAPAN BROADCASTING. Nov., 1999. Hong Kong-Japanese. (Fruit Chan) Yiu Yuet-ming, Mak Wai-fan, Mak Yuet-man, Chu Sun-yau.

THE LITTLE CHINESE SEAMSTRESS
BAC DISTRIBUTION. May, 2002. French. (Dai Sijie) Ziiou Xun, Chen Kun, Wang Shuangbao, Chung Zhijun.

LITTLE CRUMB
SHOOTING STAR FILMCOMPANY. Jan., 2001. Dutch. (Maria Peters) Ruud Feltkamp, Thekla Reuten, Hugo Haenen, Jan Decleir, Gilles Van Welzen, Benten Wijnen, Sacha Bulthuis.

LITTLE DARLING
TADRART FILMS/3B PRODS./ARTE FRANCE CINEMA/OGNON PICTURES/CANAL PLUS/GAN CINEMA FOUNDATION. May, 2000. French. (Anne Villaceque) Corinne Debonniere, Jonathan Zaccai, Laurence Fevrier, Patrick Prejean.

LITTLE GIRLS
ARENA FILMS. LA SEPT ARTE. Nov., 1998. French. (Noemie Lvovsky) Magalie Woch, Ingrid Molinier, Julie-Marie Parmentier, Camille Rousselet, Jean Luc Bideau.

THE LITTLE GIRL WHO SOLD 'THE SUN'
MAAG DAAN/WAKA FILMS/RENARDES PRODS. Feb., 1999. Senegalese-Swiss-French. (Dijibril Diop Mambety) Lissa Balera.

LITTLE MEN
LEGACY. May, 1998. (Rodney Gibbons) Michael Caloz, Mariel Hemingway, Ben Cook, Ricky Mabe, Chris Sarandon, Gabrielle Boni.

THE LITTLE MERMAID II: RETURN TO THE SEA
WALT DISNEY HOME VIDEO. Sept., 2000. (Jim Kammerud) Jodi Benson, Samuel E. Wright, Tara Charendoff, Pat Carroll, Buddy Hackett, Kenneth Mars, Max Casella, Stephen Furst (voices). Animated.

LITTLE MIRACLES
SPANISH TELEVISION SERVICES. April, 1998. Argentine. (Eliseo Subiela) Julieta Ortega, Antonio Birabent, Monica Galan, Paco M.

LITTLE NICKY
NEW LINE CINEMA. Nov., 2000. (Steven Brill) Adam Sandler, Patricia Arquette, Harvey Keitel, Rhys Ifans, Tommy "Tiny" Lister Jr., Robert Smigel, Allen Covert.

THE LITTLE PRINCE'S RAP AGAINST THE WICKED SOULS
RIOFILME. Aug., 2000. Brazilian. (Paulo Caldas, Marcelo Luna) Documentary.

THE LITTLE REPUBLIC
Aug., 2002. Indian. (Anwar Jamal) Alka Amin, Harvinder Chatterji, Mandakini Goswami, Rajendra Gupta.

LITTLE SECRETS
SAMUEL GOLDWYN FILMS. Aug., 2002. (Blair Treu) Evan Rachel Wood, Michael Angarano, David Gallagher.

LITTLE SENEGAL
TADRAT FILMS. Feb., 2001. French-German-Algerian. (Rachid Bouchareb) Sotigui Kouyate, Sharon Hope, Roschdy Zem, Karim Koussein Traore, Adetoro Makinds, Adja Diarra, Malaaika Lacario.

LITTLE TEACHERS
CECCHI GORI DISTRIBUZIONE. Aug., 1998. Italian. (Daniele Luchetti) Stefano Accorsi, Stefania Montorsi, Giorgio Pasotti.

LITTLE THIEVES, BIG THIEVES
ALEJANDRO SADERMAN PRODS., CNAC, CINEMATERIALES, POST HOUSE/LICHTBLICK/TNT AMERICA LATINA. Sept., 1998. Venezuelan-German-U.S. (Alejandro Saderman) Orlando Urdaneta, Daniel Lugo.

LITTLE TONY
WARNER BROS. May, 1998. Dutch. (Alex van Warmerdam) Annet Malherbe, Ariane Schluter, Alex van Warmerdam.

LITTLE TROPICANA
ICAIC/BMG INTL. Sept., 1998. Cuban-Spanish-German. (Daniel Diaz Torres) Peter Lohmeyer, Vladimir Cruz, Corina Mestre, Thais Vlades.

THE LITTLE VAMPIRE
NEW LINE/ICON/COMETSTONE/COMET FILM/STONEWOOD COMMUNICATIONS/AVRORA MEDIA/PROPAGANDA FILMS. Aug., 2000. German-Dutch. (Uli Edel) Jonathan Lipnicki, Richard E. Grant, Jim Carter, Alice Krige, Rollo Weeks, John Wood, Pamela Gidley, Tommy Hinkley.

LITTLE VILMA: THE LAST DIARY
DIALOG STUDIO/EUROARTS/AKSON STUDIO/CANAL PLUS. Feb., 2000. Hungarian-German-Polish. (Marta Meszaros) Jan Nowicki, Barbara Hegyi, Kitty Keri, Lukas Nowiczki, Cleo Ladanyi, Lili Monori.

THE LITTLE VOYAGE
ZSEBCSELEK CSOPOR/MMK/ORTT/MAFSZ. Feb., 2000. Hungarian. (Mihaly Buzas) Jozsef Gyabronka, Arnold Farkas, Jozsef Szikra, Imola Gaspar, Nora Cseszarik, Erzsebet Dozsa.

LIVE IN PEACE
PEARL RIVER FILM STUDIO. June, 1998. Chinese. (Hu Bingliu) Pan Yu, Bai Xueyun, Sun Min, Wang Hong, Huang Jinchang. "T.C." Carson, Lisa Arrindell, Blanche Baker.

LIVE NUDE GIRLS, UNITE!
QUERY? Apr., 2000. (Julia Query, Vicky Funari). Documentary.

LIVES
LES FILMS DE L'ASTROPHORE. Jan., 2001. French. (Alain Cavalier) Yves Pouliquen, Jean-Louis Faure, Francoise Widhoff. Documentary.

LIVE VIRGIN
GRANITE RELEASING/ VERTIGO PRODS./M6 FILMS/TPS. June, 2000. French. (Jean-Pierre Marois) Bob Hoskins, Robert Loggia, Mena Suvari, Sally Kellerman, Lamont Johnson, Gabriel Mann, Bobbie Phillips, Esai Morales.

LIVING IN PARADISE
3B PRODS./ALINEA FILM/EXPOSED FILMS/WFE. Sept., 1998. French-Belgian-Norwegian-Algerian. (Bourlem Guerdjou) Roschdy Zem, Fadila Belkebla, Omar Bekhaled, Farida Rahouadj.

LIVING IN MISSOURI
ASTHEY GO PRODS. Feb., 2002. (Shaun Peterson) Ian McConnel, Christina Puzzo, Connor Ratliff, Holmes Osborne, Greta Ratliff, Louise McCabe.

LIVING IT UP
COLUMBIA TRISTAR. Sept., 2000. Spanish. (Antonio Cuadri) Salma Hayek, Carmelo Gomez, Tito Valverde, Alicia Agut, Miguel Ayones, Eusebio Lopez.

THE LIVING MUSEUM
LIVING FILMWORKS. Jan. 1999. (Jessica Yu). Documentary.

LIVING OUT LOUD
NEW LINE CINEMA. Sept., 1998. (Richard LaGravenese) Holly Hunter, Danny DeVito, Queen Latifah, Martin Donovan, Elias Koteas.

LIVING THE LIFE
RICHARD AND ESTHER SHAPIRO ENTERTAINMENT. July, 2001. (Alex Munoz) Katrina Marie Gibson, Melida Prado, Abel Soto, Yvette Cruise, Jay Hernandez, Roger Velasco, Roberto Alvarez.

LOCKDOWN
PALM PICTURES. Sept. 2000. (John Luessenhop) Richard T. Jones, Gabriel Casseus, De'Aundre Bonds, Melissa De Sousa, Bill Nunn, Clifton Powell, Master P.

LOCK, STOCK AND TWO SMOKING BARRELS
POLYGRAM FILMED ENTERTAINMENT. July, 1998. British. (Guy Ritchie) Jason Flemyng, Dexter Fletcher, Nick Moran, Jason Statham.

LOCO FEVER
Sept., 2001. Chilean-Spanish-Mexican. (Andres Wood) Emilio Bardi, Loreto Moya, Luis Dubo, Tamara Acosta, Maria Izquierdo, Julio Marcone, Luis Margani,Carmen Barros.

LOLA + BILIDIKID
ZERO FILM. Feb., 1999. German. (Kutlug Ataman) Gandi Mukli, Erdal Yildiz, Baki Davrak, Inge Keller, Celal Perk.

LOLA COME HERE
FILMAX. May, 2002. Spanish. (Llorenc Soler) Cristina Brondo, Miguel "El Toleo," Carmen Munoz, Antonio Reyes, Mercedes Porras.

THE LONELINESS OF THE CROCODILES
Aug., 2001. German. (Jobst Oetzmann) Janek Rieke, Thomas Schmauser, Rosemarie Fendel, Julia Jaeger, Arndt Schwering-Sohnrey, Renate Krossner, Ernst Stotzner.

LONERS
CINEMART/LUCKY MAN/CINEMART/CZECH TV/E-MOTION FILM. July, 2000. Czech. (David Ondricek) Labina Mitevska, Jitka Schneiderova, Sasa Rasilov, Jiri Machacek, Ivan Trojan, Miki Kren, Dana Sedlakova.

THE LONGEST SUMMER
TEAM WORK PRODUCTION HOUSE. Feb., 1999. Hong Kong. (Fruit Chan) Tony Ho, Sam Lee, Jo Kuk, Chan Sang, Pang Yick-wai,.

LONG HELLO AND SHORT GOODBYE
WARNER BROS.. June, 1999. German. (Rainer Kaufmann) Nicholette Krebitz, Marc Hosemann, Sunnyi Melles, Axel Milberg, Dietrich Hollinderbaumer.

THE LONG HOLIDAY
PUBLIC FILM/PIETER VAN HUYSTEE FILM & TV. Feb., 2000. Dutch. (Johan van der Keuken). Documentary.

THE LONGING (DAS VERLANGEN)
Aug., 2002. German. (Iain Dilthey) Susanne-Marie Wrage, Klaus Gruenberg, Robert Lohr, Heidemarie Rohweder, Manfred Kranich, Peter Lerchbaumer.

THE LONG JOURNEY
GIAI PHONG FILMS STUDIO. Jan., 1998. Vietnamese. (Le Hoang) Moc Mien, Cong Minh, My Duyen.

LONG LIVE LIFE
BHAVE-SUKTHANKAR. Sept., 1998. Indian. (Sumitra Bhave, Sunil Sukthankar) Om Puri, Meeta Vashishta, Milind Gunaji, Uttara Baokar.

LONG LIVE US!
GEMINI FILMS/FELIX FILMS/FRANCE 2 CINEMA/CANAL PLUS/CNC. Feb., 2000. French. (Camille de Casabianca) Dieudonne, Camille de Casabianca, Michele Bernier, Daniel Prevost, Emmanuelle Devos, Thibault de Montalembert, Pascal Elbe.

A LONG LONG LONG NIGHT OF LOVE
LANTIA. Feb., 2001. Italian. (Luciano Emmer) Giancarlo Giannini, Marie Trintignant, Isabelle Pasco, Eljana Popova, Marina Confalone, Gloria Sirabella, Ornella Muti, James Thierree, Silvia De Santis.

LONG NIGHT'S JOURNEY INTO DAY
REID/HOFFMAN. Jan., 2000. (Frances Reid, Deborah Hoffmann Desmond Tutu, Glenda Wildschut, Mary Burton, Pumla Gobodo-Madikizela, Jann Turner, Tony Weaver. Documentary.

LONG TIME DEAD
UIP (IN U.K.)/UNIVERSAL FOCUS (IN U.S.). Dec., 2001. British. (Marcus Adams) Joe Absolom, Lara Belmont, Melanie Gutteridge, Lukas Haas, James Hillier, Alec Newman, Mel Raido.

LONG TIME SINCE
LUCIUS FILMS/BERGMAN LUSTIG. Sept., 1998. (Jay Anania) Paulina Porizkova, Julian Sands, Julianne Nicholson.

LONG WAY HOME
SAMUEL GOLDWYN FILMS, FIREWORKS PICTURES (IN U.S.). (Peter Sollett) Victor Rasuk, Judy Marte, Melonie Diaz, Altagracia, Guzman, Silvestre Rasuk.

LOOK AT ME
FILMAURO/LUIGI & AURELIO DE LAURENTIIS/TRIO FILM. Sept.,1999. Italian. (Davide Ferrario) Elisabetta Cavallotti, Stefania Orsola Garello. Flavio Insinna, Gianluca Gobbi, Claudio Spadaro, Anglica Ippolito, Luigi Diberti.

LOOKING FOR ALIBRANDI
ROADSHOW/AUSTRALIAN FILM FINANCE/MIALL & KERSHAW/SHOWTIME AUSTRALIA/NSW FILM & TV OFFICE/BEYOND FILMS. Apr., 2000. Australian. (Kate Woods) Pia Miranda, Greta Scaachi, Anthony LaPaglia, Elena Cotta, Kerry Walker, Kick Gurry, Matthew Newton, Leanne Carlow.

LOOKING FOR AN ECHO
STEVE TISCH/PAUL KURTA. Oct., 1999. (Martin Davidson) Armand Assante, Diane Venora, Joe Grifasi, Tom Mason, Tony Denison, Johnny Williams, Edoardo Ballerini, Christy Romano.

LOOKING FOR ANGEL
PISS FACTORY. Sept., 2000. Japanese. (Akihiro Suzuki) Koichi Imaizumi, Akira Suehiro, Hotaru Hazuki, Akira Kuroiwa, Koichi Fujisima, Tho Ogura, Keiko Suzuki, Yusui Kawasaki.

LOOK OUT HASKELL, IT'S REAL! THE MAKING OF 'MEDIUM COOL'
STICKING PLACE FILMS. Aug., 2001. British. (Paul Cronin) Haskell Wexler, David Sterritt, David Farber, Studs Terkel, Todd Gatlin, Steven North, Verna Bloom, Paul Golding. Documentary.

LOOSE ENDS
FRAMELINE. Apr., 1999. German. (Sandra Nettelbeck) Regula Grauwiller, Jasmin Tabatabai, Natascha Bub, Andreas Herde.

THE LORD OF THE RINGS: THE FELLOWSHIP OF THE RING
NEW LINE CINEMA. Dec., 2001. (Peter Jackson) Elijah Wood, Ian McKellen, Liv Tyler, Viggo Mortensen, Sean Astin, Cate Blanchett, John Rhys-Davies, Billy Boyd.

THE LORD'S LANTERN IN BUDAPEST
KREATIV MEDIA MUHELY/3J+1BT. Feb., 1999. Hungarian. (Miklos Jancso) Zoltan Mucsi, Peter Scherer, Miklos Jancso, Gyula Hernadi, Emese Vasvari.

LOSER
SONY PICTURES ENTERTAINMENT/COLUMBIA PICTURES. July, 2000. (Amy Heckerling) Jason Biggs, Mena Suvari, Zak Orth, Tom Sadoski, Jimmi Simpson, Greg Kinnear, Dan Aykroyd, Twink Caplan, Bobby Slayton, Robert Miano, Mollee Israel, Colleen Camp, Andy Dick.

LOS ENCHILADAS!
EXPAND PRODS. Jan., 1999. (Mitch Hedberg) Mitch Hedberg, Jana Johnson, Brian Malow, Dave Attell, Marc Maron.

LOSING IT
GREYTAK PRODS. March, 2001. (Sharon Greytak) Fyodor Krasov, Laris Tokareva, Marcelo Paiva,Edith Mok, Edna Maria Pacheco, Marino Crivellari, Carol Roberson. Documentary.

THE LOSS OF SEXUAL INNOCENCE
SONY. Jan., 1999. (Mike Figgis) Julian Sands, Saffron Burrows, Stefano Dionisi, Johnathan Rhys-Meyers, Kelly MacDonald.

LOST AND DELIRIOUS
SEVILLE PICTURES. Jan.,2001. Canadian. (Lea Pool) Piper Perabo, Jessica Pare, Mischa Barton, Jackie Burroughs, Graham Greene, Mimi Kuzyk, Luke Kirby.

LOST & FOUND
WARNER BROS. APR., 1999. (Jeff Pollack) David Spade, Sophie Marceau, Patrick Bruel, Artie Lange, Mitchell Whitfieldk.

LOST AND FOUND
ML PRODS. June, 1998. (Ron Burrus) Michael Landes, Hedy Burress, Dina Spybey, Lane Smith, Geoffrey Blake, Lenny Clarke, John Shea.

LOST HORIZON
SAMPIERI PRODUCTIONS. Jan., 2001. Argentine. (Luis Sampieri) Eusebio Poncela, Micky Ruffa, Graciela Pal, Elio Lacier.

LOST IN LA MANCHA
Feb., 2002. British. (Keith Fulton, Louis Pepe) Narrator: Jeff Bridges. Documentary.

LOST IN SPACE
NEW LINE CINEMA. April, 1998. (Stephen Hopkins) William Hurt, Mimi Rogers, Heather Graham, Gary Oldman, Matt LeBlanc.

LOST IN THE PERSHING POINT HOTEL
PIERREPONT PRODS. AND PERSHING POINT PRODS. May, 2000. (Julia Jay Pierrepoint II) Leslie Jordan, Erin Chandler, Mark Pellegrino, Carlos Gomez, Luke Eberl, John Ritter, Marilu Henner, Michelle Phillips.

LOST KILLERS
HOME RUN PICTURES/ROMMEL FILM/MFG BADEN-WURTTEMBERG/ BKM/FILMBOARD BERLIN-BRANDENBERG/ZDF/ ARTE. May, 2000. German. (Dito Tsintsadze) Nicole Seelig, Misel Maticevic, Lasha Bakradze.

THE LOST LOVER
MIKADO/JEAN VIGO ITALIS//STEEL PICTURES/RAI TELEVISION/ BRITISH SCREEN/BRITISH SKY BROADCASTING/TELEPIU. Oct., 1999. Italian-British. (Roberto Faenza) Ciaran Hinds, Juliet Aubrey, Stuart Bunce, Phyllida Law, Erick Vazquez, Clara Bryant.

THE LOST SKELETON OF CADAVRA
FRAGMIGHTY ENTERTAINMENT. Oct., 2001. (Larry Blamire) Larry Blamire, Fay Masterson, Brian Howe, Jennifer Blaire, Susan McConnell, Andrew Parks, Dan Conroy, Robert Deveau.

THE LOST SON
BAC FILMS/UIP-THE FILM CONSORTIUM. Apr., 1999. British-French. (Chris Menges) Daniel Auteuil, Natassja Kinski, Katrin Cartlidge, Ciaran Hinds, Marianne Denicourt.

LOST SONS
EGOLI/STORY. March, 2001. German-Swedish. (Fredrik von Krusenstjerna) Hans Canje, Ingo Hasselbach, Burkhard Schroder, Kurt Goldstein, Werner Handler, Jens Pfannschmidt. Documentary.

LOST SOULS
NEW LINE CINEMA. Oct., 2000. Winona Ryder, Ben Chaplin, Sarah Wynter, Philip Baker Hall, John Hurt, Elias Koteas, Brian Reddy, John Beasley.

LOST WINGS
KOPPFILM/ERF EDGAR REITZ FILMPRODUKTION/SIC!FILM (MUNICH). Sept., 2000. German. (Wolfgang Scholz) Gudrun Okras, Peter Franke, Roy Helbig, Christel Peters.

LOTUS LANTERN
SHANGHAI ANIMATION FILM STUDIO/SHANGHAI TV. Aug., 2000. Chinese. (Chang Guangxi) Jiang Wen, Xu Fan, Ning Jing, Chen Peisi, Ge You, CoCo Lee, Liu Xin, Zhang Xinzhe.

LOUDER THAN BOMBS
July, 2002. Polish. (Przemyslaw Wojcieszek) Sylwia Juszczak, Rafal Mackowiak, Grazyna Krukowna, Magdalena Schejbal, Andrzej Galla.

LOUISE (TAKE 2)
INITIAL PRODS./STUDIO CANAL PLUS/CINE VALSE. June, 1998. French. Elodie Bouchez, Roschdy Zem, Gerald Thomassin.

LOUIS PRIMA: THE WILDEST!
BLUE SEA PRODS./HISTORIC FILMS. Oct., 1999. (Don McGlynn). Documentary.

A LOVE
PABLO/GIANLUCA ARCOPINTO/RAI. Feb., 2000. Italian. (Gianluca Maria Tavarelli) Lorenza Indovina, Fabrizio Gifuni, Luciano Federico, Roberta Lena, Riccardo Montanaro, Ezio Sega, Benedetta Francardo.

LOVE AND ACTION IN CHICAGO
FLASHPOINT/GOLD/BASULTO Entertainment/Prosperity Pictures. Sept., 2000. (Swayne Johnson-Cochran) Courtney B. Vance, Regina King, Jason Alexander, Kathleen Turner, Edward Asner.

LOVE AND BASKETBALL
NEW LINE/40 ACRES AND A MULE FILMWORKS. Jan., 2000. (Gina Prince-Bythewood) Sanaa Lathan, Omar Epps, Alfre Woodard, Dennis Haysbert, Debbie Morgan, Harry J. Lennix, Kyla Pratt.

LOVE & CRIME
KINOPRODUCTION OY. Feb., 1999. Finnish. (Pekka Milonoff) Kai Lehtinen, Tiina Lymi, Tomi Salmela, Maija Junno Pekka Valkeejarvi.

LOVE AND HATE
MEZHRABPOM. Aug., 2000. Soviet Union–1935. (Albert Gendelstein) Emma Tsesarskaya, A. Chistyakov, V. Maretskaya, N. Kryuchkov, V. Stanitsyn, M. Kedrov, V. Popova, Boris Barnet.

LOVE & RAGE
J&M/ISLE OF MAN FILM COMM./NOVA FILMS/IRISH FILM BOARD/CATHAL BLACK PRODS. Aug., 1999. British-Irish-German. (Cathal Black) Greta Scacchi, Daniel Craig, Stephen Dillane, Valerie Edmond.

LOVE & SEX
BEHAVIOUR WORLDWIDE/BOGART/WYMAN. Jan., 2000. (Valerie Breiman) Famke Janssen, Jon Favreau, Noah Emmerich, Ann Magnuson, Cheri Oteri, Josh Hopkins, Robert Knepper.

LOVE AT FIRST HICCOUGH
REGNER GRASTEN/V2/DENMARK/DANISH FILM INSTITUTE. Feb., 2000. Danish. (Tomas Villum Jensen) Sofie Lassen Kahlke, Robert Hansen, Karl Bille, Mira Wanting.

LOVE AT FIRST SIGHT
CECCHI GORI. Oct., 1999. Italian. (Vincenzo Salemme) Vincenzo Salemme, Mandala Tayde, Carlo Buccirosso, Naurizio Casagrande, Nando Paone, Biagio Izzo, Tosca D'Aquino.

LOVE BANDITS
COLIFILMS DISTRIBUTION. May, 2001. French. (Pierre Le Bret) Florence Loiret, Vincent Ozanon, Marc Chapiteau, Gerard Blain, Remy Ventura, Philippe Herisson, Elizabeth Leguillon.

LOVE BITES
BAC DISTRIBUTION. March, 2001. French. (Antoine de Caunes) Guillaume Canet, Gerard Lanvin, Asia Argento, Gilbert Melki, Jean-Marie Winling, Jose Garcia, Vincent Perez, Orazio Massaro.

LOVE COME DOWN
EQUINOX (IN CANADA). Sept., 2000. Canadian. (Clement Virgo) Larenz Tate, Deborah Cox, Martin Cummins, Rainbow Sun Francks, Peter Williams, Barbara Williams, Kenneth Welsh, Sarah Polley.

LOVE, CURIOSITY, PROZAC AND DOUBT
WARNER SOGEFILMS. June., 2001. Spanish. (Miguel Santesmases) Pilar Punzano, Rosa Mariscal, Silvia Marso, Guillaume Depardieu, Guillermo Toledo, Nancho Novo, Esther Ortega.

LOVE = ME^3
OUTSKIRTS PROD. June, 2001. (Agustin) Agustin, Evly Pacheco, Angelica Ordonez, Greyson Steele, Victor Argo.

LOVE FOOLS
SONET. Oct., 1998. Swedish. (Leif Magnusson) Tomas von Bromssen, Anna Wallander, Ia Langhammer, Mikael Persbrandt, Matar Samba.

LOVE FROM GROUND ZERO
SANDBOX FILMS. Oct., 1998. (Stephen Grynberg) Pruitt Taylor-Vince, Simon Baker-Denny, Jacqueline McKenzie, Kathryne Erbe.

LOVE GO GO
CENTRAL MOTION PICTURE CORP./SPRING CINEMA AGENCIES/ ZOOM HUNT INTL.. Sept., 1998. Taiwanese. (Chen Yu-hsun) Tang Na, Eli Shih, Chen Cheng-hsin, Liao Hui-jen, Huang Tsi-chiao.

LOVE HAPPENS
CURB ENTERTAINMENT. June, 1999. (Tony Cookson) Megyn Price, Ken Marino, Jenica Bergere, Ryan Bollman, Elizabeth Lackey.

LOVE, HONOUR AND OBEY
UIP/BBC FILMS/FUGITIVE. Jan. 2000. British. (Dominic Anciano, Ray Burdis) Sadie Frost, Ray Winstone, Jonny Lee Miller, Jude Law.

LOVE INC.
QUIMERA FILMES. Feb., 1998. Brazilian. (Helvecio Ratton) Marco Nanini, Patricia Pillar, Alexandre Borges.

LOVE IN THE MIRROR
FACTORY/G.M.F. Sept., 1999. Italian. (Salvatore Maira) Anna Galiena, Peter Stormare, Simona Cavallari, Jacques Sernas, Maurizio Micheli.

LOVE IN THE TIME OF MONEY
Jan., 2002. (Peter Mattei) Vera Farmiga, Domenick Lombardozzi, Jill Hennessy, Malcolm Gets, Steve Buscemi, Rosario Dawson, Carol Kane, Michael Imperioli.

LOVE INVENTORY
Muse/Noga Communications/JCS Content. July, 2000. Israeli. (David Fisher). Documentary.

LOVE IS THE DEVIL
STRAND RELEASING (U.S.)/ARTIFICAL EYE (U.K.). May, 1998. British. (John Maybury) Derek Jacobi, Daniel Craig, Tilda Swinton.

LOVE/JUICE
CINE BAZAR. Oct., 2000. Japanese. (Kaze Shindo) Mika Okuno, Chika Fujimura, Toshiya Nagasawa, Hidetoshi Nishijima.

LOVE KILLS
TRIDENT. May, 1998. (Mario Van Peebles) Mario Van Peebles, Lesley Ann Warren, Daniel Baldwin, Donovan Leitch, Alexis Arquette.

THE LOVE LETTER
DREAMWORKS. May, 1999. (Peter Ho-Sun) Kate Capshaw, Blythe Danner, Ellen DeGeneres, Geraldine McEwan, Julian Nicholson.

LOVELY & AMAZING
BLOW UP PICTURES. Aug., 2001. (Nicole Holofoener) Catherine Keener, Brenda Blethyn, Emily Mortimer, Raven Goodwin, Aunjaue Ellis, Clark Gregg, Jake Gyllenhaal, James LeGros, Michael Nouri.

LOVELY RITA
COOP 99 FILMPRODUKTION, ESSENTIAL FILMPRODUKTION, PRISMA FILM. May, 2001. Austrian. (Jessica Hausner) Barbara Osika, Christoph Bauer, Peter Fiala, Wolfgang Kostal, Karina Brandlmayer.

THE LOVE MACHINE
CRYSTAL PICTURES. Apr., 1999. (Gordon Ericksen) Marlene Forte, Gary Perez, Tomo Omori, Jun Suenaga, Elizabeth Wunsch.

A LOVE OF BLUENESS
Aug., 2001. Chinese. (Huo Jianqi) Pan Yueming, Yuan Quan, Dong Yong, Zhang Xiaojun.

THE LOVER (LUBOVNIK)
Sept., 2002. Russian. (Valery Todorovsky) Oleg Yankovskiy, Sergei Garmash, Vera Voronkova, Andrey Smirnov, Yulia Rytikova.

LOVERS
TOLODA & BAR-NOTHING. May, 1999. French. (Jean-Marc Barr) Elodie Bouchez, Sergei Trifunovic, Genevieve Page, Dragan Nicolic, Thibault de Montalembert.

LOVERS & LEAVERS
Aug., 2002. Finnish. (Aku Louhimies) Minna Haapkyla, Peter Franzen, Laura Malmivaara.

LOVER'S GRIEF OVER THE YELLOW RIVER
SHANGHAI PARADISE FILM & TV GROUP. Jan., 2000. Chinese. (Feng Xiaoning) Ning Jing, Paul Kersey, Wang Xinjun, Tu Men.

THE LOVERS OF SAN FERNANDO
FOLKETS BIO. Jan., 2001. Swedish-Finnish. (Peter Torbiornsson) Documentary.

THE LOVERS OF THE ARCTIC CIRCLE
SOGETEL. July, 1999. Spanish. (Julio Medem) Najwa Nimri, Fele Martinez, Nancho Novo, Maru Valdiviesio, Peru Medem.

LOVE'S A BITCH
ALTA VISTA/ZETA FILM. May, 2000. Mexican. (Alejandro Gonzalez Inarritu) Emilio Echevarria, Gael Garcia Bernal, Goya Toledo.

LOVE SCENES FROM PLANET EARTH
BUENA VISTA INTL. Feb., 1999. German. (Marc Rothemund) Christoph Waltz, Ann-Kathrin Kramer, Heio von Stetten, Michaela May, Anica Dobra, Dieter Landuris.

LOVE'S LABOUR'S LOST
PATHE/MIRAMAX/INTERMEDIA/ARTS COUNCIL OF ENGLAND/LE STUDIO CANAL PLUS/SHAKESPEARE FILM CO. Feb., 2000. British. (Kenneth Branagh) Alessandro Nivola, Alicia Silverstone, Natascha McElhone, Kenneth Branagh, Carmen Ejogo, Matthew Lillard, Adrian.

LOVE STINKS
INDEPENDENT ARTISTS. Sept. 1999. (Jeff Franklin) French Stewart, Bridgette Wilson, Bill Bellamy, Tyra Banks, Steve Hytner.

LOVE STORY
WOMEN MAKING MOVIES/BRITISH BROADCASTING. Jan., 2000. British. (Catrine Clay). Documentary.

LOVE TANGLES
AB FILMS DISTRIBUTION. Feb., 1998. French-Swiss-Spanish. (Olivier Peray) Bruno Putzulu, Smadi Wolfman, Vincent Elbaz.

LOVE THE HARD WAY
VIF INTL. PRODS. Aug., 2001. German. (Peter Sehr) Adrien Brody, Charlotte Ayanna, Jon Seda, August Diehl, Pam Grier.

LOVE TORN IN DREAM
MADRAGOA/GEMINI FILMS/CANAL PLUS/RADIOTELEVISAO PORTUGUESA/INSTITUTO DO CINEMAAUDIOVISUAL E MULTIMEDIA FUNDACAO CULTURSINTRACAMERA MUNICIPAL DE SINTRA/QUINTA REGALEIRA. Aug., 2000. Chilean-Portuguese-French. (Raoul Ruiz) Melvil Poupaud, Elsa Zylberstein, Lambert Wilson, Christian Vadim, Diogo Doria, Rogerio Samora.

LOVE WILL TEAR US APART
TONY LEUNG PRODS.. May, 1999. Hong Kong. (Nelson Yu Lik-wai) Tony Leung Kar-fai, Lu Liping, Wang Ning, Rolf Chow.

LOVE YOUR NEIGHBOR!
DELPHI FILMVERLEIH. May, 1999. German. (Detlev Buck) Moritz Bleibtreu, Lea Mornar, Heike Makatsch, Marc Hosemann.

A LOVING FATHER (AIME TON PERE)
UGC DISTRIBUTION. Aug., 2002. French-Canadian-British-Swiss. (Jacob Berger) Gerard Depardieu, Guillaume Depardieu, Sylvie Testud, Julien Boisselier, Noemie Kocher, Hiam Abbass, Frederic Polier, Pierre-Alexandre Crevaux, Pippa Schallier, Johanna Mohs.

LOVING JEZEBEL
STARZ!/BET MOVIES/DAVID LANCASTER PROD. Oct., 1999. (Kwyn Bader) Hill Harper, Nicole Ari Parker, Laurel Holloman, Sandrine Holt, David Moscow, Andre Blake, John Doman, Elisa Donovan, Phylicia Rashad.

LOW ALTITUDE
Feb., 2002. Iranian. (Ebrahim Hatamikia) Hamid Farrokhnezhad, Leila Hatami, Gohar Kheirandish, Mohammad Ali Inanloo.

THE LOW DOWN
FILMFOUR/BRITISH SCREEN/BOZIE/OIL FACTORY/SLEEPER FILMS. Aug., 2000. British. (Jamie Thraves) Aidan Gillen, Kate Ashfield, Kean Lennox Kelly, Tobias Menzies, Rupert Proctor, Samantha Powers, Deanna Smiles.

LOW SELF ESTEEM GIRL
BLUE CURTAIN. June, 2000. Canadian. (Blaine Thurier) Corrina Hammond, Rob McBeth, Ted Dave, Cindy Wolfe.

LUBOV AND OTHER NIGHTMARES
DREAMSCANNER. Jan., 2001. Russian. (Andrei Nekrasov) Olga Konskaia, Ekaternina Urvantseva, Angelika.

LUCIGNOLO
CECCHI GORI. Mar., 1999. Italian. (Massimo Ceccherini) Massimo Ceccherini, Claudia Gernin, Alessandro Paci, Flavio Bucci, Cosetta Mercatelli.

LUCINDA'S SPELL
ZERO PICTURES. May, 1998. (Jon Jacobs) Jon Jacobs, Christina Fulton, Shannah Battz, Leon Herbert, Angie Green, Alex Koromzay.

LUCKY BREAK
PARAMOUNT (IN U.S.)/FILMFOUR DISTRIBUTORS (IN U.K.). June, 2001. British. (Peter Cattaneo) James Nesbitt, Olivia Williams, Timothy Spall, Bill Nighy, Lennie James, Frank Harper, Raymond Waring, Christopher Plummer.

LUCKY NUMBERS
PARAMOUNT. Oct., 2000. (Nora Ephron) John Travolta, Lisa Kudrow, Tim Roth, Ed O'Neill, Michael Rapaport, Daryl Mitchell, Bill Pullman, Richard Schiff.

LUCK OR COINCIDENCE
FILM 13/TF1 FILMS/UGC IMAGES/NEUILLY/SDA. Sept., 1998. French-Canadian. (Claude Lelouch) Alessandra Martines, Pierre Arditi, Marc Hollogne, Geoffrey Holder, Laurent Hilare.

LUCKYTOWN
PLUS ENTERTAINMENT. Aug., 2000. (Paul Nicholas) Kirsten Dunst, Vincent Kartheiser, James Caan, Luis Guzman, Robert Miano, Jennifer Gareis.

LULU
ARTEDIS. June, 2002. French. (Jean-Henri Roger) Jean-Pierre Kalfon, Elli Medeiros, Gerard Meylan, Bruno Putzulu, Tony Gatlif, Matthieu Amalric.

LULU KREUTZ'S PICNIC
LES FILMS DU LOSANGE/JM COMPAGNIE/FRANCE 3 CINEMA/RHONE ALPES CINEMA/CANAL PLUS/CNC/PROCIREP. Feb., 2000. French. (Didier Martiny) Philippe Noiret, Carole Bouquet, Niels Arestrup, Stephane Audran, Michel Aumont, Judith Magre, Johan Leysen.

LULU ON THE BRIDGE
CAPITOL FILMS. May, 1998. (Paul Auster) Harvey Keitel, Mira Sorvino, Willem Dafoe, Gina Gershon, Mandy Patinkin, Vanessa Redgrave.

LUMINOUS MOTION
FIONA FILMS. Aug., 1998. (Bette Gordon) Eric Lloyd, Deborah Kara Unger, Terry Kinney, Jamey Sheridan, James Berland.

LUMUMBA
OCEAN/CINELUX/JBA PRODS./ENTRE CHIEN ET LOUP/
ESSENTIAL FILMPRODUKTION/VELVET S.A./ARTE FRANCE
CINEMA/RTBF. May, 2000. French-Belgian-German-Haitian. (Raoul
Peck) Eriq Ebouaney, Alex Descas, Theophile Moussa Sowie.

LUNA'S GAME
ENRIQUE CEREZO, IBEROAMERICANA FILMS, LOLAFILMS. July,
2001. Spanish. (Monica Laguna) Ana Torrent, Carlos Kaniowsky, Jose
Pedro Carrion, Manuel San Martin, Jorge De Juan, Gara Munoz.

THE LUNATICS' BALL
PLATINUM GLASS STUDIOS. Jan., 2000. New Zealand. (Michael
Thorp) Russel Walder, Jane Irwin, Sara Ashworth, Alan De
Malmanche, Jamie Martin.

LUNCH WITH CHARLES
HOLIDAY. Jan., 2001. Canadian-Hong Kong. (Michael Parker) Sean
Lau, Nicholas Lea, Theresa Lee, Bif Naked, Philip Granger, Tom
Scholte, Francoise Yip, Peter Wilds, Simon Kendall.

LUSH
I5 PICTURE. Jan., 2000. (Mark Gibson) Campbell Scott, Jared Harris,
Laurel Holloman, Laura Linney, Nick Offerman, Kimo Wills, James R.
Hall Jr., Don Hood, Joe Chrest, David Sellars, Michael Cahill.

LUSTER
June, 2002. (Everett Lewis) Justin Herwick, Shane Powers, b. Wyatt,
Pamela Gidley, Susanna Melvoin, Jonah Blechman, Sean Thibodeau,
Willie Garson.

LUST FOR LIFE
ARTHAUS FILMVERLEIH. Feb., 1999. German. (Oskar Roehler)
Jasmin Tabatabai, Richy Mueller, Gregor Toerzs, Nele Mueller-
Stoefen, Eva Hassmann.

THE LUZHIN DEFENCE
ENTERTAINMENT FILM/SONY/RENAISSANCE/CLEAR BLUE SKY
PRODS./CE3/LANTIA CINEMA/MAGIC MEDIA/FRANCE 2 CINEMA.
Aug., 2000. British-French. (Marleen Gorris) John Turturro, Emily
Watson, Stuart Wilson, Christopher Thompson, Fabio Sartor, Peter
Blythe, Orla Brady, Mark Tandy.

MAANGAMIZI—THE ANCIENT ONE
Aug., 2001. U.S.-Tanzanian. (Ron Mulvihill, Martin Mhando) Amandina
Lihamba, Barbara O, Mwanajuma Ali Hassan, Waigwa Wachira,
Thecla Mjatta, Adam S. Mwambile, Kasaka.

MACARTHUR PARK
WIRTHWHILE. Jan., 2001. Thomas Jefferson Byrd, Brandon Adams,
Tami Anderson, B-Real, Bad Azz, Ellen Cleghorne, Keno Deary.

MACBETH IN MANHATTAN
AMBER WAVES. Mar., 1999. (Greg Lombardo) Gloria Reuben, David
Lansbury, Nick Gregory, John Glover, Harold Perrineau.

MACHIN: A FULL LIFE
ALTA FILMS. July, 2002. Spanish-Cuban. (Nuria Villazan) Antonio
Machin, Sara Montiel, Joan Manuel Serrat, Joaquin Sabina, Antonio
Gala, Botafogo, Antonio Canales.

MAD ABOUT MAMBO
USA FILMS/GRAMERCY PICTURES/PHOENIX PICTURES/FIRST
CITY/PLURABELLE FILMS. Aug., 2000. (John Forte) William Ash,
Keri Russell, Brian Cox, Theo Fraser Steele, Rosaleen Linehan,
Maclean Stewart, Tim Loane, Julian Littman, Russell Smith, Joe Rea,
Aingeal Grehan, Jim Norton.

MADAME BROUETTE
Aug., 2002. Canadian-Senegal-French. (Moussa Sene Absa) Rokhaya
Niang, Aboubacar Sadikh Ba, Kadiatou Sy, Ndeye Seneba Seck,
Ousseynou Diop, Akela Sagna, Ibramhima Mbaye.

MADAME SATA
MARS FILMS DISTRIBUTION. May, 2002. Brazilian-French. (Karim
Ainoux) Lazaro Ramos, Marcelia Cartaxo, Flavio Bauraqui, Felippe
Marques, Emiliano Querioz.

MAD COWS
ENTERTAINMENT FILM/CAPITOL FILMS/FEWMARKET CAPITAL
GROUP/FLASHLIGHT FILMS. Oct., 1999. British. (Sara Sugarman)
Anna Friel, Joanna Lumley, Anna Massey, Phyllida Law, Greg Wise,
John Standing, Nicholas Woodeson, Prunella Scales.

MADE
ARTISAN ENTERTAINMENT. June, 2001. (Jon Favreau) Jon Favreau,
Vince Vaughn, Sean Combs, Famke Janssen, Faizon Love, David
O'Hara, Vincent Pastore, Peter Falk.

MADELINE
SONY PICTURES ENTERTAINMENT. June, 1998. (Daisy von
Scherler Mayer) Frances McDormand, Nigel Hawthorne, Hatty Jones.

MADEMOISELLE
REZO FILMS. March, 2001. French. (Philippe Lioret) Sandrine
Bonnaire, Jacques Gamblin, Isabelle Candelier, Zinedine Soualem.

MADE-UP
SISTER FILMS. March, 2002. (Tony Shalhoub) Brooke Adams, Lynne
Adams, Eva Amurri, Kalen Conover, Light Eternity, Jim Issa, Lance
Krall, Tony Shalhoub.

MADNESS OF LOVE
WARNER SOGEFILMS. Sept., 2001. Spanish-Italian-Portuguese.
(Vicente Aranda) Pilar Lopex de Ayala, Daniele Liotti, Manuela Arcuri,
Eloy Azorin, Rosana Pastor, Giuliano Gemma, Roberto Alvarez.

THE MAD SONGS OF FERNANDA HUSSEIN
TRAVELING LIGHT. April, 2001. (John Gianvito) Thia Gonzales,
Dustin Scott, Robert Perrea, Sherri Goen, Carlos Stevens.

MAELSTROM
ALLIANCE ATLANTIS/MAX FILMS/TELEFILM CANADA/SODEC.
Aug., 2000. Canadian-Norwegian. (Denis Villeneuve) Marie-Josee
Croze, Jean-Nicholas Verreault, Stephanie Morgenstern, Pierre
LeBeau, Marc Gelinas, Klimbo, Bobby Beshro.

THE MAGDALENE SISTERS
Aug., 2002. British. (Peter Mullan) Geraldine McEwan, Anne-Marie
Duff, Nora-Jane Noone, Dorothy Duffy, Eileen Walsh, Mary Murray.

THE MAGIC OF MARCIANO
LUMIERE FILMS INTL./LILA CAZES. Apr., 2000. (Tony Barbieri)
Nastassja Kinski, Robert Forster, Cody Morga, Jason Cairns.

THE MAGIC PUDDING
20TH CENTURY FOX (AUSTRALIA). Aug., 2000. Australian. (Karl
Zwicky) John Cleese, Geoffrey Rush, Sam Neill, Hugo Weaving, Toni
Collette, Jack Thompson, Dave Gibson, John Laws, Mary Coustas.
Animated.

MAGIK AND ROSE
KAHUKURA PRODS./NEW ZEALAND FILM COMM. May, 2000. New
Zealand. (Vanessa Alexander) Alison Bruce, Nicola Murphy, Oliver
Driver, Simon Ferry.

THE MAGNETIST'S FIFTH WINTER
COMUMBIA TRISTAR. Jan., 1999. Danish-Norwegian-Swedish.
(Morten Henriksen) Ole Lemmeke, Rolf Lassgard, Johanna Sallstrom,
Gard B. Eidsvold, Robert Skjaerstad.

MAGNOLIA
NEW LINE/JOANNE SELLAR/GHOULARDI FILM. Nov., 1999. (Paul
Thomas Anderson) Jason Robards, Julianne Moore, Tom Cruise,
Philip Seymour Hoffman, John C. Reilly, Melora Walters, Jeremy
Blackman, Michael Bowen, William H. Macy, Philip Baker Hall.

MAIDEN WORK
EASTLINE. Oct., 1998. Chinese. (Wang Guangli) Ye You, Lou Ming, He
Xiaipei, Meng Jinghiu, Liu Bo.

MAIDS
O2 FILMES. Jan., 2001. Brazilian. (Fernando Meirelles, Nando Olival)
Claudia Missura, Grazielle Moretto, Lena Roque, Olivia Araujo.

MAI'S AMERICA
Feb., 2002. (Marlo Poras). Documentary.

A MAJOR INCONVENIENCE
SND/LES FILMS DE LA BOISSIERE/FRANCE 3 CINEMA produc-
tion/Canal Plus. Feb., 2000. French. (Bernard Stora) Jalil Lespert,
Mireille Perrier, Chantal Banlier, Clement Sibony.

THE MAJESTIC
WARNER BROS. Dec., 2001. (Frank Darabont) Jim Carrey, Martin
Landau, Laurie Holden, David Ogden Stiers, James Whitmore, Jeffrey
DeMunn, Ron Rifkin, Hal Holbrook, Bob Balaban, Brent Briscoe,
Gerry Black.

MAJOR LEAGUE: BACK TO THE MINORS
WARNER BROS. April, 1998. (John Warren) Scott Bakula, Corbin
Bernsen, Dennis Haysbert, Takaaki Ishibashi, Jensen Daggett.

MAKING BABIES
SONET FILM. Jan., 2001. Swedish. (Daniel Lind Lagerlof) Jonas
Karlsson, Johanna Sallstrom, Ralph Carlsson, Shanti Roney, Michalis
Koutsogiannakis, Lisa Lindgren, Michael Nyqvist.

THE MAKING OF A NEW EMPIRE
LAVA FILM/STICHTING JURA FILM/NPS. Sept., 1999. Dutch. (Jos
de Putter). Documentary.

THE MAKING OF STEEL
BEIJING FILM STUDIO. May, 1998. Chinese. (Lu Xuechang) Zhu
Hongmao, Zhe Jie, Yin Shoujie, Luo Jun, Tian Zhuangzhuang.

MAKING VENUS
June, 2002. Australian. (Gary Doust) Documentary.

MALLBOY
BUENA VISTA/AUSTRALIAN FILM COMM./SBS INDEPENDENT/
SHOWTIME AUSTRALIA/TWENTY 20. May, 2000. Australian.
(Vincent Giarrusso) Kane McNay, Nell Feeney, Brett Swain, Brett
Tucker.

MALLI
CHILDREN'S FILM SOCIETY, INDIA. Sept., 1999. Indian. (Santosh
Sivan) Swetha, Vanitha, Janakraj, Parameshwaran, Baby Amma.

MALOU MEETS INGMAR BERGMAN AND ERLAND JOSEPHSON
TV4. May, 2000. Swedish. Ingmar Bergman, Erland Josephson, Malou von Sivers.

MALRAUX, THE DARING DREAMER
GO FILM. Aug., 2001. French. (Michele Rosier) Philippe Clevenot, Jerome Robart, Isabelle Ronayette, Vanessa Larre, Marion Beulque, Raphael Personnaz, Francois Lebrun.

MAMA
STUDIO RUSSIAN PROJECT/NTV-PROFIT FILM CO. May, 1999. Russian. (Denis Yevstigneev) Nonna Mordukova, Oleg Menshikov, Vladimir Mashkov, Alexei Kravchenko, Mikhail Krylov.

MAMADRAMA: THE JEWISH MOTHER IN CINEMA
SHARMILL DISTRIBUTORS. Oct., 2001. Australian. (Monique Schwarz) Documentary.

MAMBI
CARTEL/RIOS TV .Sept., 1998. Spanish. (Teodoro and Santiago Rios) Carlos Fuentes, Gretel Pequeno, Alvaro de Luna, Aitor Merino, Carlos Quintana.

A MAN AND HIS DOG
GOUTTE D'OR DISTRIBUTION . Mar., 1999. Dutch. (Annette Apon) Ramsey Nasr, Viviane de Muynck, Monic Hendrickx, Nina Deuss, Truus te Selle.

A MAN CALLED HERO
GOLDEN HARVEST/GH PICTURES/CENTRO DIGITAL/BOB & PARTNERS CO./SIL-METROPOLE ORG./CHINA FILM/SHANGHAI FILM Studio. Nov., 1999. Hong Kong (Andrew Lau) Ekin Cheng, Shu Qi, Kristy Yang, Nicholas Tse, Yuen Biao, Jerry Lamb, Dion Lam, Anthony Wong, Elvis Tsui, Harold Low, Grace Yip, Francis Ng.

MANHOOD AND OTHER MODERN DILEMMAS
BLUE DAHLIA/FRANCE 3 CINEMA/CANAL PLUS/STUDIO IMAGES 6. June, 2000. French. (Ronan Girre) Bruno Putzulu, Estelle Skornik, Emmanuelle Meyssignac, Sandrine Le Berre, Olga Sekulic, Philippe Nahon, Yse Tran.

MANIC
NEXT WAVE FILMS. Jan., 2001. (Jordan Melamed) Joseph Gordon-Levitt, Michael Bacall, Zooey Deschanel, Cody Lightning, Elden Henson,Sara Rivas, Don Cheadle.

MANILA
SENATOR/PANTERA FILM/COBRA/SENATOR FILM. Aug., 2000. German. (Romuald Karmakar) Juergen Vogel, Michael Degen, Chin-Chin Gutierrez, Ana Capri, Peter Ruehring, Margit Carstensen, Manfred Zapatka, Sky Du Mont.

THE MAN I LOVE (L'HOMME QUE J'AIME)
June, 2002. French. (Stephane Giusti) Jean-Michel Portal, Marcial Di Fonzo Bo, Mathilde Seigner, Vittoria Scognamiglio, Jacques Hansen, Stephane Leveque.

THE MAN IN HER LIFE
STAR CINEMA. Feb., 1998. Philippine. (Carlos Siguion-Reyna) Rosanna Roces, Ricky Davao, Gardo Versoza, Alan Paule.

THE MAN IN THE IRON MASK
MGM. March, 1998. (Randall Wallace.) Leonardo DiCaprio, Jeremy Irons, John Malkovich, Gerard Depardieu, Gabriel Byrne

MAN IS A WOMAN
POLYGRAM FILM DISTRIBUTION. March, 1998. French. (Jean-Jacques Zilbermann) Antoine de Caunes, Elsa Zylberstein.

A MAN IS MOSTLY WATER
DOG PARK PRODS. April, 2001. (Fred Parnes) Mark Curry, Michele Harris, Paulina Mielech, Fred Parnes, Heather Roop, Chris Rydell.

MANITO
Jan., 2002. French. (Eric Eason) Franky G., Leo Minaya, Manuel Cabral, Julissa Lopez, Jessica Morales, Hector Gonzalez, Panchito Gomez.

MANITOU'S SHOE
CONSTANTIN FILM. Nov., 2001. German. (Michael "Bully" Herbig) Michael "Bully" Herbig, Christian Tramitz, Sky Dumont, Marie Baumer, Hilmi Sozer, Rick Kavanian, Tim Wilde, Siegfried Terpoorten.

MAN OF STEEL
VCKJ/FAVOURITE FILMS. Oct., 1999. Belgian. (Vincent Ba) Ides Meire, Charlotte de Ruyter, Peter Gorissen.

MANOLITO GAFOTAS
FILMAX INTL. June, 1999. Spanish. (Miguel Albaladejo) Savid Sancheza del Rey, Adriana Ozores, Roberto Alvarez, Antonio Gamero.

MAN ON THE MOON
UNIVERSAL/MUTUAL FILM CO./JERSEY FILMS/CINEHAUS. Nov., 1999. (Milos Forman) Jim Carrey, Danny DeVito, Courtney Love, Paul Giamatti, Vincent Schiavelli, Peter Bonerz, Jerry Lawler, Gerry Becker.

THE MAN ON THE TRAIN
Sept., 2002. French. (Patrice Leconte) Jean Rochefort, Johnny Hallyday, Jean-Francois Stevenin, Charlie Nelson, Pascal Parmentier, Isabelle Petit-Jacques.

MANSFIELD PARK
MIRAMAX. Aug., 1999. British-U.S. (Patricia Rozema) Embeth Davidtz, Jonny Lee Miller, Alessandro Nivola, Frances O'Connor, Harold Pinter.

MAN'S GENTLE LOVE
MAGOURIC DISTRIBUTION. Feb., 2002. French. (Jean Paul Civeyrac) Renaud Becard, Calire Perot, Marie-Josephine Crenn, Serge Bozon, Raphael Bianchin, Marie Rousseau.

THE MAN WHO CRIED
UNIVERSAL FOCUS/WORKING TITLE/ADVENTURE PICTURES/PIE/STUDIO CANAL PLUS. Sept., 2000. British-French. (Sally Potter) Christina Ricci, Cate Blanchett, John Turturro, Johnny Depp, Harry Dean Stanton, Claudia Lander-Duke, Oleg Yankovsky.

THE MAN WHO DROVE WITH MANDELA
JEZEBEL PRODS. Aug., 1998. British. (Greta Schiller) documentary with Corin Redgrave.

THE MAN WHO SAW TOO MUCH
NEXT FILM (SEOUL). Sept., 2000. South Korean. (Jae-Gon son) Sang-Hon Kim, Shin-Song Kim, Kyo-Yong Lee, So-Yong Chong.

THE MAN WHO WASN'T THERE
USA FILMS (IN U.S.). May, 2001. (Joel Coen) Billy Bob Thornton, Frances McDormand, Michael Badalucco, James Gandolfini, Katherine Borowitz, Jon Polito, Scarlett Johansson, Richard Jenkins.

THE MAN WHO WALKED ON SNOW
MONKEY TOWN PRODS. May, 2001. Japanese. (Masahiro Kobayashi) Ken Ogata, Teruyuki Kagawa, Yasufumi Hayashi, Nene Otsuka, Fusako Urabe, Sayoko Ishii.

THE MAN WHO WOULD LIVE FOREVER
FINAL CUT PRODS./POINT OF NO RETURN PRODS. Jan., 1999. Danish. (Torben Skjodt Jensen) Ghita Norby, Lars Simonsen, Anita Ekblad, Claus Flygare, Torben Zeller.

THE MAN WITHOUT A PAST
May, 2002. Finnish-German-French. (Aki Kaurismaki) Markku Peltola, Kati Outinen, Juhani Niemela, Kaija Pakarinen, Sakari Kuosmanen.

THE MAN WITH RAIN IN HIS SHOES
HANDMADE FILMS/PARAGON ENTERTAINMENT CORP. Feb., 1998. Spanish-British. (Maria Ripoll) Douglas Henshall, Lena Headey.

MAN OF THE CENTURY
SUN-TELEGRAM PICTURES. Mar., 1999. (Adam Abraham) Gibson Frazier, Susan Egan, Cara Buono, Brian Davies, Swight Ewell.

THE MAO GAME
RENAISSANCE ROAD. June, 1999. (Joshua Miller) Joshua Miller, Piper Laurie, Kirstie Alley, Jeffrey Tambor, Jodi Leesley.

A MAP OF THE WORLD
OVERSEAS FILMGROUP. Sept., 1999. (Scott Elliott) Sigourney Weaver, Julianne Moore, David Strathairn, Ron Lea, Arliss Howard.

MARAL
SHIRAZ FILM. April, 2001. Iranian. (Faramarz Sedighi, Soraya Ghasemi, Hadis Fouladvand, Majid Hajizadeh, Mahtaj Nojoumi.

MARARIA
ALTA FILMS. Oct., 1998. Spanish.(Antonio Jose Betancor) Carmelo Gomez, Ian Glen, Goya Toledo, Mirta Ibarra, Jose Manuel Cervino.

THE MARCORELLE AFFAIR
EURIPE PRODS./RHONE-ALPES CINEMA/CANAL PLUS/RHONE-ALPES REGION/CNC. Apr., 2000. French. (Serge Le Peron) Jean-Pierre Leaud, Irene Jacob, Mathieu Amalric, Philippe Khorsand, Dominique Reymond, Helene Surgere.

MARCH OF HAPPINESS
GREEN APPLE FILMS/FORMOSA TV. May, 1999. Taiwanese. (Lin Cheng-sheng) Lim Giong, Hsiao Shu-shen, Leon Dai, Chen Kun-chang, Grace Chen.

MARCUS GARVEY: LOOK FOR ME INTHE WHIRLWIND
AMERICAN EXPERIENCE. Jan., 2001. (Stanley Nelson) Documentary.

MARGARITA HAPPY HOUR
PASSPORT PICTURES AND SUSIE Q PRODS. Jan., 2001. (Ilya Chaiken) Eleanor Hutchins, Larry Fessenden, Holly Ramos, Jonah Leland, Barbara Sicuranza, Amanda Vogel, Macha Ross.

MARIE-JO AND HER 2 LOVES
DIAPHANA DISTRIBUTION (FRANCE). May, 2002. French. (Robert Guediguian) Ariane AScaride, Hean-Pierre Darroussin, Gerard Meyland, Julie-Marie Parmentier, Jacques Boudet.

MARIE-LINE
REZO FILMS. Jan., 2001. French. (Mehdi Charef) Muriel Robin, Fejria Deliba, Valerie Stroh,Yan Epstein, Aissa Maiga, Selma Kouchy, Antonia Malinova, Veronica Novak.

MARIE'S SONS
May, 2002. Canadian-French. (Carole Laure) Carole Laure, Jean-marc Barr, Felix Lajeunesse-Guy, Danny Gilmore.

MARIGOLDS IN FLOWER
LENFILM/STUDIO BARMALE/PK SLOVO/ROSKOMKINO. Feb., 1999. Russian. (Sergei Sneshkin) Era Siganshina, Marine Saloptshenko, Ksenya Rappoport, Julia Sharikova, German Orlov.

MARINE LIFE
ODEON FILMS/ALLIANCE ATLANTIS. Sept., 2000. (Anne Wheeler) Cybill Shepherd, Peter Outerbridge, Alexandra Purvis, Gabrielle Miller, Michael Hogan.

MARIO MONICELLI, THE VIAREGGIO CRAFTSMAN
Aug., 2002. Italian. (Marco Porru) Documentary.

MARK TWAIN'S AMERICA IN 3D
SONY PICTURES CLASSICS. June, 1998. (Stephen Low) Documentary. Narrator: Anne Bancroft.

THE MARKUS FAMILY
MIRA FILMPRODUKTION. Jan., 2001. German. (Elfi Mikesch) Documentary.

MARLENE
SENATOR FILM/TREBITSCH PRODUKTION INTL./PERATHON/ ZDF/RAI/STUDIO BABELSBERG. May, 2000. German. (Joseph Vilsmaier) Katja Flint, Herbert Knaup, Heino Ferch, Hans-Werner Meyer, Christiane Paul, Suzanne von Borsody, Armin Rhode.

MARLENE DIETRICH: HER OWN SONG
Feb., 2002. German-U.S. (J. David Riva) Maria Riva, Burt Bacharach, Volker Schlondorff, Rosemary Clooney, Hildegarde Knef, Nicholas von Sternberg, A.C. Lyles.

THE MARRIAGE CERTIFICATE
Nov., 2001. Chinese. (Huang Jianxin) Feng Gong, Lu Liping, Li Xiaoming, Luo Xiangjin, Niu Zhenhua, Feng Xiaogang.

MARRIAGE PREP
LIGHTED PATHWAY. Feb., 2000. (Donahue Tuitt) Donahue Tuitt, Temple Parker, Skip Mullen, Darlene Rene, Thomas Iazare, Sonya Leslie, Joel Kindrick, Roe Williams, Baron Jay, Alicia Mallory.

MARRIAGES
FILMAURO. Oct., 1998. Italian-French. (Cristina Comencini) Francesca Neri, Diego Abatantuono, Stefania Sandrelli, Claude Brasseur.

MARRIAGES
FILM TONIC. Aug., 2001. Canadian. (Catherine Martine) Marie-Eve Bertrand, Guylaine Tremblay, Mirianne Brule, Helene Loiselle, Markita Boies, David Boutin, Raymond Cloutier.

MARRY ME
Gaumont/Buena Vista Intl. Aug., 2000. French. (Harriet Marin) Michele Laroque, Vincent Perez, Miki Manojlovic, Arnaud Giovaninetti.

MARSINAH
Nov., 2001. Indonesian. (Slamet Rahardjo Djarot) Megarita, Dyah Arum, Intarti, Tosan Wiryawan.

MARTA AND SURROUNDINGS
ALTA FILM/CLAVE/EPC/CHEROKEE LUZ/CANAL PLUS. Jan., 2000. Spanish. (Nacho Perez de la Paz, Jesus Ruiz) Marta Belaustegui, Tristan Ulloa, Lola Duenas, Roberto Enriquez, Maria Jose Millan, Nieve de Medina, Sergi Calleja.

MARTHA
OGNON PICTURES. May, 2001. French. (Sandrine Veysset) Valerie Donzelli, Yann Goven, Lucie Regnier, Lydia Andrei, Severine Vincent, Javier Cruz, Pierre Pezon.

MARTHA— MEET FRANK, DANIEL AND LAURENCE
FILM FOUR DISTRIBUTORS/MIRAMAX. March, 1998. British. (Nick Hamm) Monica Potter, Rufus Sewell, Tom Hollander, Joseph Fiennes.

MARTIN LAWRENCE LIVE: RUNTELDAT
PARAMOUNT. July, 2002. (David Raynr). Martin Lawrence.

THE MARTINS
ICON. July, 2001. British. (Tony Grounds) Lee Evans, Kathy Burke, Linda Bassett, Eric Byrne, Terri Dumont, Frank Finlay, Lennie James, Jack Shepherd, Mark Strong.

MARTYR-IN-LOVE, BOOTA SINGH
SAIN PRODS. Sept., 1999. Indian. (Manoj Punj) Gurdas Mann, Divya Dutta, Aroon Bakshi, Raghubeer Yadav, Yograj Chedda, Darshan Aulakh, Hari Om Jalota, Gurkitan.

MARYAM
STREETLIGHT FILMS. Apr., 2000. (Ramin Serry) Mariam Parris, David Ackert, Shaun Toub, Shohreh Aghdashloo, Maziyar Jobrani.

MASCARA
PHAEDRA CINEMA. May, 1999. (Linda Kandel) Ione Skye, Lumi Cavazos, Amanda de Cadenet, Steve Schub, Steve Jones.

MASHENKA
MOSFILM. Aug., 2000. Soveit Union–1942. (Yuli Raizman) Valentina Karavayeva, Mikhail Kuznetsov, D. Pankratova, Vera Altaiskaya.

MASK OF DESIRE
MILO PRODS./NHK. Apr., 2000. Nepalese-Japanese. (Twering Rhitar Sherpa) Gauri Malla, Mithila Sharma, Ratan Subedi, Nirmal Pyakurel, Rama Thapalia.

THE MASK OF ZORRO
SONY PICTURES ENTERTAINMENT. June, 1998. (Martin Campbell) Antonio Banderas, Anthony Hopkins, Catherine Zeta-Jones.

MASSOUD THE AFGHAN
AFMD. Dec., 2001. French. (Christophe de Ponfilly) Documentary.

THE MASTER OF DISGUISE
July, 2002. (Perry Andelin Blake) Dana Carvey, Jennifer Esposito, Harold Gould, James Brolin, Brent Spiner, Edie McClurg, Maria Canals, Austin Wolff.

THE MATCH
UNIVERSAL, AUG., 1999. British-U.S. (Mick Davis) Max Beesley, Isla Blair, James Cosmo, Laura Fraser, Richard E. Grant.

THE MATING HABITS OF THE EARTHBOUND HUMAN
EARTHBOUND HUMAN PRODS. Sept., 1999. (Jeff Abugov) Mackenzie Astin, Carmen Electra, Markus Redmond, Lucy Liu.

THE MATRIX
WARNER BROS. Mar., 1999. (Wachowski Brothers) Keanu Reeves, Laurence Fishburne, Carrie-Anne Moss, Hugo Weaving.

MATRONI AND ME
ALLIANCE ATLANTIS/MAX FILMS. Oct., 1999. Canadian. (Jean-Philippe Duval) Alexis Martin, Guylaine Tremblay, Gary Boudreault, Pierre Lebeau, Maude Guerin, Pierre Curzi, Daniel Briere.

MAU MAU SEX SEX
7TH PLANET. Apr., 2000. (Ted Bonnitt) David Friedman, Dan Sonney, Frank Henenlotter, Mike Vraney, Carol Friedman. Documentary.

MAX
LIONS GATE FILMS. Sept., 2002. Hungarian-Canadian-British. (Menno Meyjes) John Cusack, Noah Taylor, Leelee Sobieski, Molly Parker, Ulrich Thomsen, David Horovitch, Janet Suzman.

MAX & BOBO
ARTEMIS. Jan. 1999. Belgian. (Frederic Fonteyne) Alfredo Pea, Jan Hamenecker.

MAXIMUM PENALTY
Danish. (Tomas Gislason) Documentary.

MAXIMUM VELOCITY (V-MAX)
MEDUSA. Aug., 2002. Italian. (Daniele Vicari) Valerio Mastandrea, Cristiano Morroni, Alessia Barela, Ivano De Matteo.

MAX KEEBLE'S BIG MOVE
BUENA VISTA. Oct., 2001. (Tim Hill) Alex D. Linz, Larry Miller, Jamie Kennedy, Zena Grey, Josh Peck, Nora Dunn, Robert Carradine, Clifton Davis.

MAYA
LES FILMS SEVILLE. Aug., 2001. (Digvijay Singh) Nitya Shetty, Anant Nag, Mita Vasisht, Shilpa Navalkar.

MAY
LIONS GATE FILMS. Jan., 2002. (Lucky McKee) Angela Bettis, Jeremy Sisto, Anna Faris, James Duval, Nichole Hiltz, Kevin Gage, Merle Kennedy, Chandler Hecht.

MAYBE
WARNER BROS./VERTIGO PRODS./PECF/M6/TPS CINEMA. Nov., 2000. French. (Cedric Klapisch) Romain Duris, Jean-Paul Belmondo, Geraldine Pailhas, Vincent Elbaz, Riton Liebman, Julie Depardieu.

MAYBE BABY
REDBUS/USA FILMS/PANDORA/BBC FILMS/PHIL MCINTYRE. June, 2000. British-French. (Ben Elton) Hugh Laurie, Joely Richardson, Adrian Lester, James Purefoy, Tom Hollander, Joanna Lumle, Dawn French.
FLASHPOINT. Oct., 2001. (Rob Morrow, Bradley White) Rob Morros, Laura Linney, Craig Sheffer, Rose Gregorio, Robert Hogan.

ME & ISAAC NEWTON
PAUL G. ALLEN/CLEAR BLUE SKY PRODS. Sept., 1999. (Michael Apted) Gertrude Elion, Ashok Gadgil, Michio Kaku, Maja Mataric, Steven Pinker, Karol Likora, Patricia C. Wright. Documentary.

MEAN MACHINE
A PARAMOUNT (IN U.S.)/UIP (IN U.K.). Dec., 2001. (Barry Skolnick) Vinnie Jones, Jason Statham, David Kelly, David Hemmings, Vas Blackwood, Jason Flemyng, Danny Dyer, Robbie Gee, John Forgeham, Andrew Grainger, Stephen Walters, Omid Djalili.

THE MECHANICS OF WOMEN
REZO FILMS. Nov., 2000. French. (Jerome de Missolz) Remi Martin, Christine Boisson, Fabienne Babe, Christine Loiret-Caille, Severine Paquier, Florence Denou.

THE MECHANISM
HORIZON 2000/CENTAR FILM. Sept., 2000. Yugoslavian. (Djordje Milosavljevic) Ivana Mihic, Nikola Kojo, Andrej Sepetkovski.

THE MEDICINE SHOW
MEDICINE SHOW PRODS. Nov., 2001. (Wendell Morris) Jonathan Silverman, Natasha Gregson Wagner, Greg Gunberg, Kari Wuhrer, Annabelle Gurwitch, Maz Jobani, Patricia McCormack.

MEET THE PARENTS
UNIVERSAL/DREAMWORKS. Sept., 2000. (Jay Roach) Robert De Niro, Ben Stiller, Blythe Danner, Teri Polo, James Rebhorn, Jon Abrahams, Phyllis George, Kali Rocha, Tom McCarthy, Nicole DeHuff.

MEETING DADDY
MIKE SAYLES AND MATT SALINGER. Oct., 1998. (Peter Gould) Josh Charles, Alexandra Wentworth, Lloyd Bridges, Beau Bridges.

MEETING PEOPLE IS EASY
SEVENTH ART RELEASING. Mar., 1999. British. (Grant Gee) Radiohead (Thom Yorke, Jonny Greenwood, Phil Selway, Ed O'Brien, Colin Greenwood.). Documentary.

MEET JOE BLACK
UNIVERSAL. Oct., 1998. (Martin Brest) Brad Pitt, Anthony Hopkins, Claire Forlani, Jake Weber, Marica Gay Harden.

MEET THE DEEDLES
BUENA VISTA. March 21, 1998. (Steve Boyum) Steve Van Wormer, Paul Walker, A.J. Langer, John Ashton, Dennis Hopper, Eric Braeden.

MEGA CITIES: 12 STORIES OF SURVIVAL
LOTUS FILM/FAMA FILM. Aug. 1998. Austrian-Swiss. (Michael Glawogger). Documentary.

MEGIDDO
8X ENTERTAINMENT. Sept., 2001. (Brian Trenchard-Smith) Michael York, Michael Biehn, Diane Venora, R. Lee Ermy, Udo Kier, Franco Nero, Jim Metzler, Noah Huntley, Michael Paul Chan, Gil Colon.

MEKTOUB
SHEM'S/PLAYTIME. Jan., 1998. Moroccan-French. (Nabil Ayouch) Rachid El Ouali, Amal Chabli, Mohamed Miftah, Faouzi Bensaidi.

MELVIN VAN PEEBLES' CLASSIFIED X
LES FILMS D'ICI/YEAH INC./ECOUTEZ VOIE/LA SEPT ARTE. Jan., 1998. French-U.S. (Mark Daniels) Documentary.

MEMENTO
NEWMARKET. Sept., 2000. (Christopher Nolan) Guy Pearce, Carrie-Anne Moss, Joe Pantoliano, Mark Boone Jr., Stephen Tobolowsky, Harriet Sansom Harris, Callum Keith Rennie, Russ Fega.

MEMENTO MORI
CINE 2000/CINEMA SERVICE. Feb., 2000. South Korean. (Kim Tae-yong, Min Kyu-dong) Kim Min-seon, Park Ye-jin, Lee Yeong-jin.

MERE YAAR KI SHAADI HAI
YASH RAJ FILMS. June, 2002. Indian. (Sanjay Gadhvi) Uday Chopra, Jimmy Shergill, Sanjana, Bipasha Basu, Alok Nath, Neena Kulkarni, Bindu.

MEMORIES UNLOCKED
LIONS GATE. Aug., 1999. Canadian. (Jean Beaudin) James Hyndman, Pascale Bussieres. Pierre-Luc Brillant.

MEMORY & DESIRE
NEWMARKET CAPITAL GROUP/GOLDWYN FILMS. May, 1998. New Zealander. (Niki Caro) Yuri Kinugawa, Eugene Nomura, Yoko Narahashi.

ME, MY OWN BOSS
CULT FILM. Feb., 2001. Australian. (Niki List) Christian Polser, Christa Polster, Robert Polster. Documentary.

ME, MYSELF & IRENE
20TH CENTURY FOX/CONUNDRUM ENTERTAINMENT. June, 2000. (Bobby Farrelly, Peter Farrelly) Jim Carrey, Renee Zellweger, Chris Cooper, Robert Forster, Richard Jenkins, Rob Moran, Traylor Howard, Daniel Greene, Zen Gesner, Tony Cox, Anthony Anderson, Mongo Brownlee.

ME MYSELF I
SONY. Sept., 1999. Australian-French. (Pip Karmel) Rachel Griffiths, David Roberts, Sandy Winton, Yael Stone, Shaun Loseby.

MEN AND WOMEN
APSARAS FILM & TV. Aug., 1999. Chinese. (Liu Bingjian) Yang Qing, Yu Bo, Zhang Kang, Yu Mengjie, Wei Jiangang.

MEN CRY BULLETS
IDIOT FILMS. March, 1998. (Hernandez) Steven Nelson, Honey Lauren, Jeri Lynn Ryan.

MEN BEHIND BARS
ADRIANA CHIESE ENTERPRISES. Sept., 1998. Italian. (Giancarlo Planta) Massimo De Francovich, Gianni Cavina, Chiara Muti, Said Taghnaoui, Franco Castellano.

MEN IN BLACK II
SONY PICTURES ENTERTAINMENT. June, 2002. (Barry Sonnenfeld) Tommy Lee Jones, Will Smith, Rip Torn, Lara Flynn Boyle, Rosario Dawson, Tony Shalhoub, Patrick Warburton, Johnny Knoxville, Jack Kehler, David Cross, Colombe Jacobsen.

MEN OF HONOR
20TH CENTURY FOX/FOX 2000 PICTURES/STATE STREET PICTURES. Sept., 2000. (George Tillman Jr) Robert De Niro, Cuba Gooding Jr., Charlize Theron, Aunjanue Ellis, Hal Holbrook, David Keith, Michael Rapaport, Powers Boothe, Joshua Leonard, David Conrad, Glynn Turman.

MEN ON WINGS
MOSFILM. Aug., 2000. Soviet Union–1935. (Yuli Raisman) Boris Shchukin, Ivan Koval-Samborsky, Evgenia Melnikova.

MEN WITH BROOMS
ALLIANCE ATLANTIS. March, 2002. Canadian. (Paul Gross) Paul Gross, Molly Parker, Peter Outerbridge, Jed Rees, James Allodi, Leslie Nielsen, Polly Shannon, Michelle Nolden, Kari Matchett.

MEN WITH GUNS
NORSTAR ENTERTAINMENT. Feb., 1998. Canadian. (Kari Skogland) Donal Logue, Gregory Sporleder, Callum Keith Rennie, Max Perlich.

MENAGE A TROIS
MIRABELLA FILM. Feb., 1998. Russian. (Pyotr Todorovsky) Elena Yakovleva, Sergei Makovetsky, Yevgeni Sidikhin.

MENSAKA
ALTA FILMS. May, 1998. Spanish. (Salvador Garcia Ruiz) Gustavo Salmeron, Tristan Ulloa, Adria Collado, Laia Marull, Maria Esteve.

MERCI MON CHIEN
BAC FILMS. May, 1999. French. (Philippe Galland) Atmen Kelif, Jean Benguigui, Yolande Moreau, Laurent Olmedo, Abbes Zahmani, Geno Lechner, Faiza Kaddour.

MERCURY RISING
UNIVERSAL March, 1998. (Harold Becker) Bruce Willis, Alec Baldwin, Miko Hughes, Chi McBride, Kim Dickens, Bodhi Pine Elfman.

MERCY
FRANCHISE PICTURES/JAZZ PICTURES. Feb., 2000. (Damian Harris) Ellen Barkin, Wendy Crewson, Peta Wilson, Karen Young, Julian Sands, Stephen Baldwin, Marshell Bell, Beau Starr.

MERCY STREETS
PROVIDENCE ENTERTAINMENT. Nov., 2000. (Jon Gunn) David White, Eric Roberts, Cynthia Watros, Shiek Mahmud-Bey, Robert La Sardo, Stacy Keach.

MERLIN: THE RETURN
PEAKVIEWING RELEASING. Dec., 2000. British. (Paul Matthews) Rik Mayall, Patrick Bergin, Craig Sheffer, Tia Carrere, Adrian Paul, Julie Hartley, Byron Taylor.

MERRY CHRISTMAS
BENDERCINE. Sept., 2000. Argentine. (Lucho Bender) Luis Machin, Gaston Pauls, Silke, Pablo Cedron, Carlos Belloso.

MESSAGE IN A BOTTLE
WARNER BROS. Feb., 1999. (Luis Mandoki) Kevin Costner, Robin Wright Penn, Paul Newman, John Savage, Illeana Douglas.

MESSENGERS
TOHO/FUJI TV NETWORK/PONY CANYON/SHOGAKUKAN/PREMIER INTL. Nov., 1999. Japanese. (Yasuo Baba) Naoko Iijima, Tsuyoshi Kusanagi, Hiroyuki Yabe, Kotomi Kyono, Yuzo Kayama.

THE MESSENGER: THE STORY OF JOAN OF ARC
SONY/COLUMBIA PICTURES/GAUMONT. Oct., 1999. French. (Luc Besson) Milla Jovovich, John Malkovich, Faye Dunaway, Dustin Hoffman, Pascal Greggory, Vincent Cassel, Tcheky Karyo.

MESSIAH
REZO/KUIV/FRANCE 2 CINEMA/RAI/SACEM ACTION FUND/CANAL PLUS/SOFICA GIMAGES/MISSION TO CELEBRATE 2000 IN FRANCE/PROCIREP. Dec., 1999. French. (William Klein) Daniel Edinger, Sebastian Gutierrez, Nicholas Savalas, Arjun Spinner.

METADE FUMACA
MEDIA ASIA/UNITED FILMMAKERS Org. Nov., 1999. Hong Kong. (Riley Ip [[Ip Kamhung]]) Eric Tsang, Nicholas Tse, Shu Qi, Kelly Chen, Sandra Ng, Anthony Wong, Terence Yin, Stephen Fung, Sam Lee, Eleaine Jin.

METAL
21ST CENTURY PICTURES GROUP/UBUNTU FILMWORKS. Sept., 1999. (Christopher E. Brown) Wedrell James, Venieta Porter, Khafre James, R. Tyrone Fields, Thea-Marie Perkins, Andre C. Andre.

METROPOLIS
TOHO CO. Aug., 2001. Japanese. (Shigeyuki Hayashi) Animated.

ME WITHOUT YOU
MOMENTUM PICTURES, ROAD MOVIES, ISLE OF MAN FILM COMMISSION. Sept., 2001. British. (Sandra Goldbacher) Anna Friel, Michelle Williams, Kyle MacLachlan, Oliver Milburn, Trudie Styler, Marianne Denicourt, Nicky Henson, Allan Corduner.

THE MEXICAN
DREAMWORKS PICTURES. Feb., 2001. (Gore Verbinski) Brad Pitt, Julia Roberts, James Gandolfini, Bob Balaban, J.K. Simmons, David Krumholtz, Richard Coca, Michael Cerveris, Sherman Augustus.

MEXICO
SOL FILM. Feb., 2000. (Lorena M. Parlee). Documentary.

ME, YOU, THEM
SONY/CONSPIRACAO FILMES/COLUMBIA PICTURES. May, 2000. Brazilian. (Andrucha Waddington) Regina Case, Lima Duarte, Stenio Garcia, Luis Carlos Vasconcelos, Nilda Spencer.

MICHAEL JORDAN TO THE MAX
GIANT SCREEN SPORTSMVP.COM. May, 2000. (James D. Stern, Don Kempf) Michael Jordan, Phil Jackson, Doug Collins, Bob Greene, Bob Costas, Dean Smith, Deloris Jordan, Fred Lynch. Documentary.

MICKEY BLUE EYES
WARNER BROS. Aug., 1999. (Kelly Makin) Hugh Grant, James Caan, Jeanne Tripplehorn, Burt Young, James Fox.

MIDDLEMEN
WEASELMAN PRODS. (VANCOUVER). Oct., 2000. Canadian. James Hutson, Kirsten Robek, Byron Lucas, Philip Maurice Hayes, Jay Brazeau, Blu Mankumka.

THE MIDDLE OF NOWHERE
BAVARIA FILM INTL. Aug., 2001. German. (Nathalie Steinbart) Tamara Simunovic, Florian Panzner, Oliver Brocker, Vadim Glowna, Horst-Gunter Marx, Hendrik Arnst, Marc Richter.

THE MIDDLE PASSAGE
KREOL PRODS. Sept., 2000. Martinique. (Guy Deslauriers) Maka Koto.

MIDNIGHT
HAUT & COURT, LA SEPT-ARTE/VIDEOFILMES, RIOFILME. Aug., 1998. French-Brazilian. (Walter Salles, Daniela Thomas) Fernanda Torres, Luis Carlos Vasconcellos, Carlos Vereza.

MIDNIGHT TEST
GEMINI FILMS. Dec., 1998. French. (Daniele Dubroux) Francois Cuzet, Serge Riaboukine, Julie Depardieu.

MIFUNE
SONY. Feb., 1999. Danish. (Soren Kragh-Jacobsen) Anders W. Berthelsen, Iben Hjejle, Jesper Asholt, Emil Tarding, Anders Hove.

MIGHTY JOE YOUNG
BUENA VISTA. Dec., 1998. (Ron Underwood) Charlize Theron, Bill Paxton, Rade Sherbedgia, Peter Firth, David Paymer.

MIGUEL/MICHELLE
FOREFRONT FILMS. Aug., 1998. Filipino. (Gil M. Portes) Romnick Sarmenta, Gloria Diaz, Ray Ventura, Cris Villanueva, Mylene Dizon.

THE MIGRATION OF THE ANGEL
Jan., 2002. Georgian. (Nodar Managadze) Amiran Chichinadze, Dimitri Djaiani , Nino Koridze, Zurab Kandelaki, Gvantsa Maisuradze.

MIKE BASSETT: ENGLAND MANAGER
ENTERTAINMENT FILM DISTRIBUTORS. Sept., 2001. British. (Steve BaronRicky Tomlinson, Amanda Redman, Philip Jackson, Bradley Walsh, Phill Jupitus, Ulrich Thomsen, Robert Putt, Martin Bashir.

MILK
SKY PICTURES/REMIL & ASSOCIATES/CINEQUANON/ARCANE PICTURES. Oct., 1999. British. (Bill Brookfield) James Fleet, Phyllida Law, Joss Ackland, Clotilde Coureau, Peter Jones, Francesca Annis.

THE MILK OF HUMAN KINDNESS
REZO FILMS (IN FRANCE)/CINEART (IN BELGIUM). Aug., 2001. French-Belgian. (Dominique Cabrera) Patrick Bruel, Marilyne Canto, Dominique Blanc, Sergi Lopez, Valeria Bruni-Tedeschi.

MILLENNIUM MAMBO
3H PRODS., SINOMOVIE.COM (TAIWAN)/PARADIS FILMS, ORLY FILMS (FRANCE). May, 2001. Taiwanese-French. (Hou Hsiao-hsien) Shu Qi, Jack Gao, Tuan Chun-hao, Jun Takeuchi, Niu Chen-er, Kao Kuo-guang, Chen Yi-hsuan, Jenny Tseng, Tramy Wat.

THE MILLION DOLLAR HOTEL
ICON/ROAD MOVIES/KINTOP PICTURES. Feb., 2000. German-U.S., (Wim Wenders) Jeremy Davies, Milla Jovovich, Mel Gibson, Jimmy Smits, Peter Stormare, Amanda Plummer, Gloria Stuart, Tom Bower.

MINE ALONE
BUENA VISTA INTL. (SPAIN). Oct., 2001. Spanish. (Javier Balaguer.) Sergi Lopez, Paz Vega, Elvira Minguez, Alberto Jimenez, Maria Jose Alfonso, Asuncion Balaguer.

MINIMAL STORIES (HISTORIAS MINIMAS)
Sept., 2002. Argentine-Spanish. (Carlos Sorin) Javier Lombardo, Antonio Benedictis, Javiera Bravo.

MINORITY REPORT
20TH CENTURY FOX. June, 2002. (Steven Spielberg) Tom Cruise, Colin Farrell, Samantha Morton, Max von Sydow, Lois Smith, Peter Stormare, Tim Blake Belson, Steve Harris.

THE MINUS MAN
TSG PICTURES. Jan., 1999. (Hampton Fancher) Owen Wilson, Brian Cox, Mercedes Ruehl, Janeane Garofalo, Dwight Yoakam.

A MINUTE OF SILENCE
REZO FILMS. Sept., 1998. French-German-Belgian. (Florent Emilio Siri) Benoit Magimel, Bruno Putzulu, Rudiger Voegler.

THE MIRACLE MAKER
ICON/S4C FILMS/BRITISH SCREEN/BBC FILMS WALES/CARTWN CYMRU/CHRISTMAS FILMS. Mar., 2000. British-Russion. (Stanislav Sokolov, Derek Hayes). Ralph Fiennes, Michael Bryant, Julie Christie, Rebecca Callard, James Frain, Richard E. Grant, Ian Holm, William Hurt, Miranda Richardson (voices). Animated.

THE MIRACULOUS MANDARIN
MANDARIN FILM-EUROFILM STUDIO. Feb., 2001. Hungarian. (Marta Meszaros) Yvette Bozsik, Zhang Yu Jung, Jan Nowicki, Laszlo Galffy, Ivan Kamaras, Gyozo Szabo, Tamas Vati.

MIRANDA
FILMFOUR LTD. Jan., 2002. British. (Marc Munden) Christina Ricci, John Simm, Kyle MacLachlan, John Hurt, Julian Rhind-Tutt, Cavan Clerkin, Matthew Marsh.

MIRKA
MIKADO/FILMART/BONGIORNO PRODS./DAVID PRODS./DD PRODS./ENRIQUE CEREZO PC PROD/RAI/CANAL PLUS/ ARCAPIX/ CAPITOL FILMS. Mar., 2000. Italian-French-Spanish. (Rachid Benhad) Karim Benhadj, Barbora Bobulova, Vanessa Redgrave, Gerard Depardieu, Sergio Rubini, Franco Nero.

MIRROR IMAGE
CHANG SHU A&V PRODUCTION/SINO-MOVIE.COM. May, 2001. Taiwanese. (Hsiao Ya-chuan) Lee Jiunn-jye, Fan Hsiao-fan, Era Wang, Yang Li-wei, Chu Dei-yuan.

THE MISADVENTURES OF MARGARET
TF1 INTL./GRANADA. Jan., 1998. British-French. (Brian Skeet) Parker Posey, Jeremy Northam, Craig Chester, Elizabeth McGovern.

MISERABLE LIFE
TRI PICTURES. Nov., 2000. Spanish. (Fernando Huertas) Santiago Ramos, Manuel Alexandre, Luisa Martin, Jorge Bosch.

LES MISERABLES
SONY PICTURES ENTERTAINMENT. April, 1998. (Bille August) Liam Neeson, Geoffrey Rush, Uma Thurman, Claire Danes.

MISFORTUNES OF BEAUTY
BAC FILMS . Aug., 1999. French. (John Lvoff) Arielle Dombasle, Maria de Medeiros, Thibault de Montalembert, Jean-Philippe Ecoffey.

MISS CONGENIALITY
WARNER BROS. Dec., 2000. (Donald Petrie) Sandra Bullock, Michael Caine, Benjamin Bratt, William Shatner, Candice Bergen.

THE MISSING
ROADSHOW/JIM STARK & LYNDA HOUSE/AUSTRALIAN FILM FINANCE CORP/HOLLYWOOD PARTNERS/UPSIDE DOWN FILMS-UND FILM PRODUKTION/FILM VICTORIA. Oct., 1999. Australian-German. (Manuela Alberti) Fabrizio Bentivoglio, David Ngoombujarra, John Moore, Rebecca Frith, David Franklin, Fiorenzio Fiorentini.

THE MISSING BOY
TALATTA/SWEDISH NATIONAL TV. Apr., 2000. Swedish. (Tove Torbiornsson). Documentary.

MISSING YOUNG WOMAN
Sept., 2001. (Lourdes Portillo). Documentary.

THE MISSION
INTL. FILMS/MILKYWAY IMAGE. Nov., 1999. Hong Kong. (Johnnie To) Anthony Wong, Francis Ng, Jackie Lui, Roy Cheung, Lam Suet, Simon Yam, Wong Tin-lan, Ko Hung, Elaine Eca Da Silva, Keiji Sato.

MISSION
LOREN MARSH. June, 2001. (Loren Marsh) Chris Coburn, Joshua Leonard, Bellamy Young, Sandrine Holt, Evan Arnold, Adam Arkin.

MISSION: IMPOSSIBLE 2
PARAMOUNT. May, 2000. (John Woo) Tom Cruise, Dougray Scott, Thandie Newton, Ving Rhames, Richard Roxburgh, John Polson, Brendan Gleeson, Rade Sherbedgia, Anthony Hopkins.

MISSION TO MARS
BUENA VISTA/TOUCHSTONE/JACOBSON CO. Mar., 2000. (Brian De Palma) Gary Sinise, Tim Robbins, Don Cheadle, Connie Nielsen, Jerry O'Connell, Kim Delaney, Elise Neal, Peter Outerbridge, Jill Teed.

MISS JULIE
MGM/UA. Sept., 1999. British. (Mike Figgis) Saffron Burrows, Peter Mullan, Maria Doyle Kennedy.

MISS MONDAY
LAKESHORE INTL. May, 1998. (Benson Lee) Andrea Hart, James Hicks, Alex Giannini, Louise Barrett, Julie Alanagh-Brighten.

MISS WONTON
DREAMCHAMBER FILMS. Jan., 2001. (Meng Ong) Amy Ting, Ben Wang, James Burns, Chyna Ng, Sakura Ting, Scott Chan.

MISTER FEDERMANN
JOST HERING/ZDF. Aug., 1999. German. (Christian Diedrichs) Christian Redl, Adelheid Arndt, Teresa Harder, Rolf Zacher.

THE MISTRESS
WILD HORSE PRODS. May, 2000. Hong Kong. (Crystal Kwok [Kwok Kamyan])) Ray Lui, Moses Chan, Vicky Chen, Jacqueline Peng.

MIXING NIA
ARROWHEAD PICTURES. April, 1998. (Alison Swan) Karyn Parsons, Eric Thal, Isaiah Washington, Diego Serrano, Rosalyn Coleman.

MODERN COMFORTS
KEY LIGHT/CNC/CANAL PLUS. June. 2000. French. (Dominique Choisy) Nathalie Richard, Valerie Mairesse, Jean-Jacques Vanier.

MODERN LIFE
GEMINI FILMS/LE STUDIO CANAL PLUS/LES FILMS DU CAMELIA/LIGHT NIGHT PRODS./CANAL PLUS/CNC/COFIMAGES 10/OFFICE FEDERAL DEL AL CULTURE, TV SUISSE ROMANDE. Mar., 2000. French-Swiss. (Laurence Ferreira Barbosa) Isabelle Huppert, Frederic Pierrot, Lolita Chammah, Juliette Andrea.

THE MOD SQUAD
MGM. Mar., 1999. (Scott Silver) Claire Danes, Giovanni Ribisi, Omar Epps, Dennis Farina, Josh Brolin.

MODULATIONS
CALPIRINHA PRODS. Jan., 1998. (Lara Lee) Documentary.

MOLLY
MGM/COCKAMAMIE/ABSOLUTE ENTERTAINMENT. Oct., 1999. (John Duigan) Elisabeth Shue, Aaron Eckhart, Jill Hennessy, Thomas Jane, D.W. Moffett, Elizabeith Mitchell, Robert Harper, Elaine Hendrix, Michael Paul Chan, Lucy Liu.

MOLOCH
LENFILM/ZERO FILM. May, 1999. Russian-German-French. (Alexander Sokurov) Elena Rufanova, Leonid Mosgovoi, Leonid Sokol.

MOMMY'S A FOOL
DIORAMA. May, 1999. Spanish. (Santiago Lorenzo) Jose Luis Lago, Faustina Camacho, Eduardo Antuna, Cristina Marcos, Gines Garcia Millan.

MOMO, THE CONQUEST OF TIME
CECCHI GORI GROUP. Dec., 2001. Italian-German. (Enzo D'Alo) Erica Necci, Giancarlo Giannini, Diego Abatantuono, Sergio Rubini. Animated.

MONARCH
HOURGLASS PRODS. Oct., 2000. British. (John Walsh) T.P. McKenna, Jean Marsh, James Coombes, Peter Sowerbutts, George Stains, Peter Miles, Mark Montgomerie.

MONDAY
CINEROCKET/MEDIA FACTORY/CINEQUANON/MME. Feb., 2000. Japanese. (Sabu) Shinichi Tsutsumi, Yasuko Matsuyuki, Ren Osugi, Masanobu Ando, Hideki Noda.

MONDAY MORNING
Feb., 2002. French-Italian. (Otar Iosseliani) Jacques Bidou, Arrigo Mozzo, Anne Kravz-Tamavsky, Narda Blanchet, Dato Tarielashvili, Anna Lamour-Flori, Adrien Pachod.

MONDAYS IN THE SUN
Sept., 2002. Spanish-French-Italian. (Fernando Leon de Aranoa) Javier Bardem, Luis Tosar, Jose Angel Egido, Nieve De Medina, Enrique Villen, Celso Bugallo, Joaquin Climent, Aida Folch.

MONDIALITO
CARAVAN/ADR. Aug., 2000. Swiss-French. (Nicolas Wadimoff) Moussa Maaskri, Antoine Maulini, Emma de Caunes, Anton Kouznetsov, Carlo Brandt.

MONKEY LOVE
June, 2002. (Mark Stratton) Amy Stewart, Jeremy Renner, Seamus Dever, Neala Cohen, Mary Margaret Robinson, Jesse Vint, Oleg Vidov, Marion Calvert, Eve Brenner, William Sanderson, Woong-ki Min.

MONGOLAND
MUZ, DEADLINE FILM, TRES COJONES. Feb., 2001. Norwegian. (Arild Ostin Ommundsen) Pia Tjelta, Kristoffer Joner, Vegar Hoel, Reidar Wayne Ewing.

MONKEYBONE
20TH CENTURY FOX. Jan., 2001. (Henry Selick) Brendan Fraser, Bridget Fonda, Whoopi Goldberg, Chris Kattan, Dave Foley, Giancarlo Esposito, Rose McGowan.

MONKEYS LIKE BECKY
ELS QUATRE GATS. Sept., 2000. Spanish. (Joaquin Jorda, Nuria Villazan) Joao Maria Pinto, Marian Varela, Petra Alcantara.

THE MONKEY'S MASK
TVA INTL. Sept., 2000. Australian. (Samantha Lang) Susie Porter, Kelly McGillis, Marton Csokas, Deborah Mailman.

MON-RAK TRANSISTOR
May, 2002. Thai. (Pen-ek Ratanaruang) Suppakorn Kitsuwan, Siriyakorn Pukkavesa, Black Pomtong.

MONSIEUR BATIGNOLE
BAC DISTRIBUTION. March, 2002. French. (Gerard Jugnot) Jules Sitruk, Gerard Jugnot, Michele Garcia, Jean-Paul Rouve, Alexia Portal, Gotz Burger, Sam Karmann, Ticky Holgado.

MONSOON WEDDING
USA FILMS (IN U.S.). Aug., 2001. U.S.-Indian. (Mira Nair) Neseeruddin Shar, Lillete Dubey, Shefali Shetty, Vasundhara Das, Parvin Dabas, Vijay Raaz, Tilotama Shome, Rajat Kapoor.

MONSTER'S BALL
LION'S GATE FILMS. Nov., 2001. (Marc Forster) Billy Bob Thornton, Heath Ledger, Halle Berry, Sean Combs, Mos Def, Will Rokos, Milo Addica, Coronji Calhoun.

MONTANA
INITIAL ENTERTAINMENT GROUP. Jan., 1998. (Jennifer Leitzes) Kyra Sedgwick, Stanley Tucci, Robbie Coltrane, Robin Tunney.

MONUMENT AVE.
FILMLINE INTL./PHOENICIAN FILMS/CLINICA ESTETICO/ TRIBECO. Jan., 1998. (Ted Demme) Denis Leary, Jason Barry, Billy Crudup.

MOOKIE
AMLF. Dec., 1998. French. (Herve Palud) Jacques Villeret, Eric Cantona, Emiliano Suarez, Victor Sanchez Ramirez.

MOON FATHER
PANDORA/PRISMA FILM/THOMAS KOERFER/NTV-PROFI/LES FILMS DE L'OBSERVATOIRE/EURO SPACE/VISS/TAKJIK. Sept., 1999. German-Austrian. (Bakhtiar Khudojnazarov) Chulpan Khamatova, Moritz Bleibtreu, Merab Ninidze.

MOONFISH
PAULO BRANCO/MADRAGOA FILMES/GEMINI FILMS/PARIS/ MADRAGOA FILMES/ALCOCHETE/PORTUGAL. Aug., 2000. Portuguese-French-Spanish. (Jose Alvaro Morais) Beatriz Batarda, Marcello Urgeghe, Ricardo Aibeo, Luis Miguel Cintra, Isabel Ruth, Assuncion Balaguer.

MOONLIGHT WHISPERS
NIKKATSU CORP. Aug., 1999. Japanese. (Akihiko Shiota) Kenji Mizuhashi, Tsugumi, Kota Kusano Kota Inoue.

MOONCALF
REZO FILMS May, 1998. French. (Claude Mourieras) Muriel Mayette, Frederic Pierrot, Vincent Deneriaz, Cedric Vieira, Julien Charpy.

MOONLIGHT MILE
BUENA VISTA PICTURES. Aug., 2002. (Brad Silberling) Jake Gyllenhaal, Dustin Hoffman, Susan Sarandon, Holly Hunter, Ellen Pompeo, Richard T. Jones, Dabney Coleman.

MORE THAN YESTERDAY
MOVIMENTO, RHONE-ALPES CINEMA, LA SEPT CINEMA. Feb., 1999. French. (Laurent Achard) Martin Mihelich, Laetitia Legrix, Mireille Roussel.

MORNING
DOWN HOME ENTERTAINMENT. Feb., 2001. (Ami Canaan Mann) Kieran Mulroney, Annabeth Gish, J.R. Richards, Pat Hingle, Steven Schub, Andrea Atkins, Laurel Holloman.

MORTAL TRANSFER
UFD. Jan., 2001. French-German. (Jean-Jacques Beineix) Jean-Hugues Anglade, Helene de Fougerolles, Denis Podalydes, Miki Manojlovic, Yves Renier, Robert Hirsch.

MORVERN CALLAR
MOMENTUM PICTURES. May, 2002. British-Canadian. (Lynne Ramsay) Samantha Morton, Kathleen McDermott, Raife Patrick Burchell, Dan Cadan, Carolyn Calder, Jim Wilson, Dolly Wells.

MOSCOW
STUDIO TELEKINO. Sept., 2000. Russian. (Alexander Zeldovich) Ingeborga Dapkunaite, Tatiana Drubich, Natalia Koliakanova, Alexander Baluev, Viktor Gvozditsky, Stanislav Pavlov.

MOSCOW SQUARE
HUNNIA FILMSTUDIO. Feb., 2001. Hungarian. (Ferenc Torok) Gabor Karalyos, Erzsi Papai, Vilmos Csatlos, Andras Rethelyi, Simon Szabo, Bence Javor, Imre Csujha, Zsolt Kovacs, Eszter Balla, Ilona Beres.

THE MOST FERTILE MAN IN IRELAND
ALIBI FILMS INTL./SKY PICTURES. Sept., 2001. Irish. (Dudi Appleton) Kris Marshall, Kathy Kiera Clarke, Bronagh Gallagher, James Nesbitt, Kenneth Cranham, Tara Lynne O'Neill.

MOSTLY MARTHA
PANDORA FILM PRODUKTION. Sept., 2001. German-Austrian-Swiss-Italian. (Sandra Nettelbeck) Martina Gedeck, Sergio Castellito, Maxime Foerste, August Zirner, Ulrich Thomsen, Sibylle Canonica, Katja Studt.

MOST PROMISING YOUNG ACTION
UFD/RF2K/NOVO ARTURO FILMS/LES FILMS ARIANE/TF1 FILMS PROD./CANAL PLUS. Apr., 2000. French. (Gerard Jugnot) Gerard Jugnot, Berenice Bejo, Antoine Dulery, Sabine Haudepin, Mohamed Hicham, Chantal Lauby, Ticky Holgado.

MOTHER
SUNCENT CINEMAWORKS. MAY, 1999. Japanese. (Nobuhiro Suwa) Tomokazu Miura, Makiko Watanabe, Ryudai Takahashi.

MOTHER CHRISTIAN
CINE 9. Sept., 1998. French. (Myriam Boyer) Myriam Boyer, Bruno Boeglin, Maryline Even, Clovis Cornillac, Lorraine Bouchet.

THE MOTHMAN PROPHECIES
SONY PICTURES ENTERTAINMENT. Jan., 2002. (Mark Pellington) Richard Gere, Laura Linney, Will Patton, Debra Messing, Lucinda Jenney, Alan Bates, David Eigenberg, Ann McDonough.

MOULIN ROUGE
20TH CENTURY FOX. May, 2001. U.S.-Australian. (Baz Luhrmann) Nicole Kidman, Ewan McGregor, John Leguizamo, Jim Broadbent, Richard Roxburgh, Garry McDonald, Jacek Koman, Matthew Whittet.

THE MOUNTAIN HAWK (EL GAVILAN DE LA SIERRA)
Aug., 2002. Mexican. (Juan Antonio de la Riva) Guillermo Larrea, Juan Angel Esparza, Claudia Goytia, Abel Woolrich, Mario Almada.

MR. ACCIDENT
ROADSHOW/UNITED ARTISTS/SERIOUS. Aug., 2000. Australian-U.S., (Yahoo Serious) Yahoo Serious, Helen Dallimore, David Field, Grant Piro.

MR. BONES
Aug., 2002. South African. (Gray Hofmeyr) Leon Schuster, David Ramsey, Faizon Love, Robert Whitehead, Jane Benney.

MR. DEATH: THE RISE AND FALL OF FRED A. LEUCHTER JR.
LIONS GATE/INDEPENDENT FILM Channel/Channel 4, of a Fourth Floor/Scout. Sept., 1999. (Errol Morris). Documentary.

MR. DEEDS
SONY PICTURES ENTERTAINMENT. June, 2002. (Steven Brill) Adam Sandler, Winona Ryder, Peter Gallagher, Jared Harris, Allen Covert, Erick Avari, John Turturro, Peter Dante, Conchata Ferrell, Harve Presnell, Steve Buscemi.

MR. FIFTEEN BALLS
MEDUSA. Sept., 1998. Italian. (Francesco Nuti) Francesco Nuti, Sabrina Ferilli, Novello Novelli, Antonio Perocelli, Giulia Weber.

MR. NAPHTALI
PATHE. Aug, 1999. French. (Olivier Schatzky) Elie Kakou, Gilbert Melki, Isabelle Ferron, Alice Evans, Jena-Marie Lamour.

MR. RICE'S SECRET
NEW CITY PRODS. June, 2000. Canadian. (Nicholas Kendall) David Bowie, Bill Switzer, Garwin Sanford, Teryl Rothery, Zachary Lipovsky, Jason Anderson, Tyler Thompson.

MR. ROOKIE
Aug., 2002. Japanese. (Satoshi Isaka) Kazushige Nagashima, Mayu Tsuruta, Jun Kunimura, Mirai Yanamoto, Tamao Sato, Mitsuru Fukikoshi, Takeo Nakahara.

MRS. RETTICH, CZERNY AND ME
JUGENDFILM. May, 1998. German. (Markus Imboden) Iris Berben, Marina Gedeck, Jeanette Hain, Olli Dittrich, Thomas Heinze.

MR. ZHAO
BEIJING ZHANG TIAN CULTURE & MEDIA CENTER/NAM KWONG DEVELOPMENT. Aug., 1998. Chinese. (Lu Yue) Shi Jingming, Zhang Zhihua, Chen Yinan, Jiang Wenli.

MUCH ADO ABOUT SOMETHING
AUSTRALIAN FILM FINANCE CORP. Sept., 2001. Australian. (Michael Rubbo) Documentary.

MUGGERS
REP/AUSTRALIAN FILM FINANCE CORP./WINCHESTER FILMS-CLOCK END FILMS/FILM VICTORIA/AUSTRALIAN FILM COMM. Apr., 2000. Australian-British. (Dean Murphy) Matt Day, Jason Barry, Petra Yared, Marshall Napier.

MUJHSE DOSTI KAROGE!
YASH RAJ FILMS. Aug., 2002. Indian. (Kunal Kohli) Hrithik Roshan, Rani Mukherjee, Satish Shah, Kareena Kapoor, Uday Chopra, Kiran Kumar, Sachin Khedekar, Smita Jayakar.

MULAN
BUENA VISTA. May, 1998. (Barry Cook, Tony Bancroft) Ming-Na Wen, Lea Salonga, Eddie Murphy, B. D. Wong, Donny Osmond (voices).

MULE SKINNER BLUES
SOLARIS. June, 2001. (Stephen Earnhart) Beanie Andrew, Steve Walker, Miss Jeannie, Larry Parrot, Ricky Lix, Annabelle Lea Usher. Documentary.

MULHOLLAND DRIVE
BAC DISTRIBUTION (IN FRANCE). May, 2001. (David Lynch) Justin Theroux, Naomi Watts, Laura Elena Harring, Ann Miller, Dan Hedaya, Mark Pellegrino, Brian Beacock.

MULLET
GLOBE FILM CO. AND DENDY FILMS. Dec., 2001. Australian. (David Caesar) Ben Mendelsohn, Susie Porter, Andrew S. Gilbert, Belinda McClory, Tony Barry, Kris McQuade, Peta Brady, Wayne Blair.

MUMFORD
BUENA VISTA. Sept., 1999. (Lawrence Kasdan) Loren Dean, Hope Davis, Jason Lee, Alfre Woodard, Mary McDonnell.

THE MUMMY
UNIVERSAL PICTURES. May, 1999. (Stephen Sommers) Brendan Fraser, Rachel Weisz, John Hannah, Arnold Vosloo.

THE MUMMY RETURNS
UNIVERSAL. April, 2001. (Stephen Sommers) Brendan Fraser, Rachel Weisz, John Hannah, Arnold Vosloo, Oded Fehr, Patricia Velasquez, Freddie Boath, The Rock, Alun Armstrong, Adewale Akinnuoye-Agbaje.

MUMU
MOSFILM. June, 1999. Russian. (Yuri Grymov) Lyudmilla Makasakova, Alexander Baluev, Vladimir Steklov.

MUPPETS FROM OUTER SPACE
SONY. July, 1999. (Tim Hill) Dave Goelz, Steve Whitmire, Bill Barretta, Jerry Nelson, Brian Henson.

MURATTI AND SAROTTI-THE HISTORY OF GERMAN ANIMATION FILM 1920-1960
ANIGRAF FILMPRODUKTION. Aug., 1999. German. (Gerd Gockell). Documentary.

MURDER BY NUMBERS
WARNER BROS. April, 2002. (Barbet Schroeder) Sandra Bullock, Ryan Gosling, Michael Pitt, Agnes Bruckner, Chris Penn, R.D. Call, Ben Chaplin.

THE MURDER IN CHINA BASIN
GERARD FILMS. July, 1999. (Norman Gerard) Elizabeth Rossa, Chris Byrne, Jennifer Starr, Noel Harrison, Derek Sitter.

MURDER IN FEBRUARY
LAUREN FILMS. May, 2001. Spanish. (Eterio Ortega) Natividad Rodriguez, Begona Elorza, Angel Diez, Bernardo Elorza.

MURDEROUS MAIDS
ARP SELECTION. Dec., 2000. French. (Jean-Pierre Denis) Sylvie Testud, Julie-Marie Parmentier, Isabelle Renauld, Dominique Labourier, Jean-Gabriel Nordmann, Marie Dunnio.

MUSA
CJ ENTERTAINMENT. Sept., 2001. South Korean. (Kim Sung-su) Ahn Sung-ki, Jung Woo-sung, Ju Jin-mo, Zhang Ziyi, Yu Rongguang, Park Jung-hak, Park Yong-woo, Lee Du-il, Yu Hae-jin.

THE MUSE
USA FILMS. Aug., 1999. (Albert Brooks) Albert Brooks, Sharon Stone, Andie MacDowell, Jeff Bridges, Mark Feuerstein.

MUSIC OF THE HEART
MIRAMAX. Sept., 1999. (Wes Craven) Meryl Streep, Aidan Quinn, Angela Bassett, Cloris Leachman, Gloria Estefan.

THE MUSKETEER
UNIVERSAL. Sept., 2001. (Peter Hyams) Catherine Deneuve, Mena Suvari, Stephen Rea, Tim Roth, Justin Chambers, Bill Treacher, Daniel Mesguich, David Schofield.

MUTANT ALIENS
PLYMPTOONS. Jan., 2001. (Bill Plympton) Animated

MUTANTS
Feb., 2002. German. (Katalin Godros) Karoline Teska, Jacob Matschenz, Sabine Timoteo, Peter Lohmeyer, Barbara Philipp.

THE MUTANTS
JBA. Feb., 1999. French-Portuguese. (Teresa Villaverde): Ana Moreira, Alexandre Pinto, Nelson Varela.

MVP: MOST VALUABLE PRIMATE
KEYSTONE RELEASING. Oct., 2000. (Robert Vince) Bernie, Mac, Louie, Kevin Zegers, Jamie Renee Smith, Russell Ferrier, Rick Ducommun, Oliver Muirhead, Lomax Study.

MVP2: MOST VERTICAL PRIMATE
KEYSTONE ENTERTAINMENT. Jan., 2002. (Robert Vince) Richard Karn, Cameron Bancroft , Robert Costanzo, Oliver Muirhead, Troy Ruptash, Scott Goodman, Bob Burnquist.

MY AMERICAN VACATION
SANTA MONICA PICTURES. Apr., 1999. (V V Dachin) Tsai Chin, Kim Miyori, Deborah Nishimura, Dennis Dun.

MY BEAUTIFUL DAYS
CINEMA SERVICE. Aug., 2001. South Korean. (Im Jong-jai) Kim Hyun-sung. Byun Eun-jeong, Pang Eun-jin, Myung Kye-nam.

MY BEST FIEND
WERNER HERZOG FILMPRODUKTION/CAFE PRODUCTION/ ZEPHIR FILM. May, 1999. German. (Werner Herzog).

MY BEST FRIEND
LL PRODS./MEGA CHANNEL/FILMNET/GREEK FILM CENTER. Aug., 2001. Greek. (Lakis Lazopoulos) Lakis Lazopoulos, Antonis Kafetzopoulos, Vera Krushka, Smaragda Karydi, Maria Kavoyianni.

MY BIG FAT GREEK WEDDING
April, 2002. (Joel Zwick) Nia Vardalos, John Corbett, Michael Constantine, Lainie Kazan, Andrea Martin, Joey Fatone, Gia Carides, Louis Mandylor, Bess Meisler, Fiona Reid, Bruce Gray, Ian Gomez.

MY BROTHER AND I
GREEK FILM CENTER-HYPERION-GREEK TELEVISION ERKTONIKON-SPENTZOS FILM. May, 1998. Greek. (Antonis Kokkinos) Vangelis Germanos, Demosthenes Papadopoulos, Pemy Zouni.

MY BROTHER TOM
FILMFOUR. Jan., 2001. British. (Dom Rotheroe) Jenna Harrison, Ben Whishaw, Adrian Rawlins, Jonathan Hackett, Richard Hope, Judith Scott, Honeysuckle Weeks.

MY CAMERA: AND ME
REZO FILMS. June, 2002. French. (Christophe Loizillon) Zinedine Soualem, Julie Gayet, Julien Collet, Isabelle Grare, Juliette Andrea.

MY DEAREST FRIENDS
CECCHI GORI DISTRIBUZIONE. April, 1998. Italian. (Alessandro Benvenuti) Alessandro Benvenuti, Eva Robin's, Athina Cenci.

MY DETOX
GAGSTONES/MILK & HONEY FILMS/CZECH TELEVISION/SPACE FILMS. July, 2000. Czech. (Victor Taus) Viktor Taus, Mikulas Kren, Vanda Hybnerova, Milan Hlavsa.

MY DOG SKIP
WARNER BROS./ALCON ENTERTAINMENT/MARK JOHNSON/ JOHN LEE HANCOCK. Jan., 2000. (Jay Russell) Frankie Muniz, Diane Lane, Like Wilson, Kevin Bacon, Caitlin Wachs, Bradley Coryell, Daylan Honeycutt, Cody Linley, Peter Crombie, Clint Howard, Harry Connick Jr.

MY FAMILY'S HONOR
3.B. PRODS./LA SEPT CINEMA. Feb., 1998. French. (Rachid Bouchareb) Seloua Hamse, Karole Rocher, Roschdy Zem.

MY FATHER, MY MOTHER, MY SISTER AND MY BROTHERS...
SND. July, 1999. French-Spanish. (Charlotte de Turckheim) Victoria Abril, Charlotte de Turckheim, Alain Bashung, Philip Giangreco.

MY FATHER'S ANGEL
RANFILM. Sept., 1999. Canadian. (Davor Marjanovic) Tony Nardi, Timothy Webber, Tygh Runyan, Brendan Fletcher, Asja Pavlovic, Lynda Boyd, Vanessa King.

MY FATHER SAVED MY LIFE
BAC FILMS DISTRIBUTION. April, 2001. French. (Jose Giovanni) Bruno Cremer, Vincent Lecoeur, Rufus, Michele Goddet, Nicolas Abraham, Eric Defosse, Cedric Chevalme.

MY FATHER'S SON
June, 2002. (Ben Van Hook) John Blalock, Jeanne Walter, John Carroll, Janos Ivanitch, Rodrick Maring, Jim Disney, Martin Banish, Patrick Laurita, Sarah Kostrub, Todd Hardy. Documentary.

MY FATHER'S WORDS
MIKADO. May, 2001. French. (Francesca Comencini) Fabrizio Rongione, Chiara Mastroianni, Claudia Coli, Camille Dugay Comencini, Viola Graziosi, Mimmi Calopresti, Toni Bertorelli.

MY FATHER, THE GENIUS
Jan., 2002. (Lucia Small) Glen Howard Small, Lucia Small, Greg Davis, Jan Mardian, John Harris, Michael Rendler, John Johansen, Milica Dedijer, Allen Nelson, Rose Nelson, Joanne Small-Eggert.

MY FAVORITE MARTIAN
BUENA VISTA. Feb., 1999. (Donald Petrie) Christopher Lloyd, Jeff Daniels, Elizabeth Hurley, Daryl Hannah, Wallace Shawn.

MY FIRST MIRACLE
Aug., 2002. German. (Anne Wild) Henriette Confurius, Leonard Lansink, Juliane Koehler, Gabriela Maria Schmeide, David Striesow.

MY FIRST MISTER
PARAMOUNT CLASSICS. Jan., 2001. (Christine Lahti) Albert Brooks, Leelee Sobieski, Desmond Harrington, Carol Kane, Mary Kay Place, Michael McKean, John Goodman.

MY FRIEND PAUL
FIVE POINTS PICTURES. Mar., 1999. (Jonathan Berman). Documentary.

MY GENERATION
Mikado/Cabin Creeks/Polygram/Road Movies Filmproduktion/ Schulberg Prods./Solaris. Sept., 2000. U.S.-Italian.-German. (Barbara Kopple, Tom Haneke). Documentary.

MY HEART
BAE CHANGHO PROD/KOREAN FILM COMM. Oct., 1999. South Korean. (Bae Chang-ho) Kim Yu-mi, Kim Myeong-kon, Yun Yu-seon, Nam Jeong-hi, Jeong In-ha, Choi Suk-jin.

MY KHMER HEART
Sir Peter Ustinov/iCandy. Aug., 2000. Australian. (Janine Hosking) Geraldine Cox, Hun Sen, Prince Norodom Ranariddh, Peter Ustinov. Documentary.

MY KINGDOM
SKY PICTURES. May, 2001. British. (Don Boyd) Richard Harris, Lynn Redgrave, Tom Bell, Emma Catherwood, Aidan Gillen, Louise Lombard, Paul McGann, Jimi Mistry, Reece Noi.

MY LIFE AS A TROLL
STARFIRE PRODS. July, 2001. (Dominick Brascia) Dominick Brascia, David Chisum,Tava Smiley, Kevin Castro, Damon Shalit, Kerri Kasem, Bobby Johnston.

MY LIFE SO FAR
MIRAMAX. May, 1999. British. (Hugh Hudson): Colin Firth, Mary Elizabeth Mastrantonio, Rosemary Harris, Irene Jacob, Tcheky Karyo.

MY LITTLE BUSINESS
BAC FILMS. Aug., 1999. French. (Pierre Jolivet) Vincent Lindon, Francois Berleand, Roschdy Zem, Zabou Breitman, Albert Dray.

MY LITTLE DEVIL
ROCK DEMERS. April, 2001. Canadian-Indian. (Gopi Desai) Om Puri, Pooja Batra, Rushach Patni, Satyajit Sharma.

MY LITTLE EYE
MOMENTUM PICTURES (IN U.K.)/UNIVERSAL FOCUS (IN U.S.). July, 2002. British-U.S.-French. (Marc Evans) Sean CW Johnson, Kris Lemche, Stephen O'Reilly, Laura Regan, Jennifer Sky, Bradley Cooper, Nick Mennell.

MY MOTHER HAD FOURTEEN CHILDREN
SWEDISH FILM INSTITUTE. May, 2001. Swedish. (Lars-Lennart Forsberg) Documentary.

MY MOTHER FRANK
UIP/BEYOND FILMS/AUSTRALIAN FILM FINANCE CORP. /INTREPID FILMS/SHOWTIME AUSTRALIA/NSW FILM AND TV OFFICE/AUSTRALIAN FILM COMM./CHANNEL 4. Feb., 2000. Australian. (Mark Lamprell) Sinead Cusak, Sam Neill, Matthew Newton, Rose Byrne, Sacha Horler, Joan Lord, Melissa Jaffer, Lynette Curran.

MY MOTHER'S EARLY LOVERS
OFF THE GRID PRODS. June, 2001. (Nora Jacobson) Sue Ball, George Woodard, Molly Hickok, Gilman Rood, Dudley Rood, Kim Meredith, Kathy Blume, Jacob Crumbine.

MY NAME IS JOE
PARALLAX PICTURES/ROAD MOVIES VIERTE PROD. May, 1998. French-German-British. (Ken Loach) Peter Mullan, Louise Goodall.

MY NAME IS ROCKY
Oct., 2001. Canadian-Iranian. (Moshar) Documentary.

MY NAME IS SARA
FILMAX. May, 1999. Spanish. (Dolores Payas) Elvira Minguez, Francois Eric Gendron, Jeannine Mestre, Elena Castells.

MY SASSY GIRL
CINEMA SERVICE. Nov., 2001. South Korean. (Kwak Jae-yong) Jeon Ji-hyeon, Cha Tae-hyeon.

MYSTERIOUS OBJECT AT NOON
9/6 CINEMA FACTORY/THAI FILM FOUNDATION/HUBERT BALS FOUNDATION. Feb., 2000. Thai. (Apichatpong Weerasethakul) Duangjai Hiransri, Kongkeirt Komsiri, Saisiri Xoomsai.

MYSTERY, ALASKA
BUENA VISTA. Oct., 1999. (Jay Roach) Russell Crowe, Hank Azaria, Mary McCormack, Burt Reynolds, Colm Meaney.

MYSTERY MEN
UNIVERSAL. July, 1999. (Kinka Usher) Hank Azaria, Janeane Garofalo, William H. Macy, Del Mitchell, Paul Reubens.

THE MYSTERY OF PAUL
AGAT FILMS & CO. July, 2000. French. (Abraham Segal, Frederic Boyer) Didier Sandre. Documentary.

THE MYSTIC MASSEUR
Oct., 2001. (Ismail Merchant) Om Puri, James Fox, Aasif Mandvi, Sanjeev Bhaskar, Ayesha Dharker, Jimi Mistry, Zohra Segal Sakina Jaffrey, Grace Maharaj.

MY SWEETHEART
NIRVANA. May, 2001. Spanish. (Jesus Mora) Aitana Sanchez-Gijon, Barbara Goenaga, Santiago Ramos, Unax Ugalde, Arianna Puello, Mario Cocci.

MY SWEET HOME
PEGASOS. Feb., 2001. German-Greek. (Filippos Tsitos) Harvey Friedman, Nadja Uhl, Monika Hansen, Mario Mentrup, David Monteiiro, Mehdi Nebbou, Eleftheria Sapountzis, Peter Lewan.

MY TREASURE
FUERTE APACHE/INCAA. Sept., 1999. Argentine. (Sergio Bellotti) Gabriel Goity, Edda Bustamente, Victoria Onetto.

MY TRUE SWEDISH FRIEND
CECCHI GORI. Jan., 1999. Italian. (Vincenzo Salemme) Vincenzo Salemme, Eva Harzigova, Carlo Buccirosso, Maurizio Casagrande, Nando Paone.

MY VOICE (NHA FALA)
Aug., 2002. Portugese-French-Luxembourgois. (Flora Gomes) Fatou N'Diaye, Jean-Christophe Dolle, Angelo Torres, Bia Gomes.

MY VOYAGE TO ITALY
MEDIATRADE. May, 2001. Italian. (Martin Scorsese) Documentary.

MY WEST
CECCHI GORI. Dec., 1998. Italian. (Giovanni Veronesi) Leonardo Pieraccioni, Harvey Keitel, David Bowie, Sandrine Holt, Alessia Marcuzzi.

MY WIFE IS A GANGSTER
KOREA PICTURES (IN SOUTH KOREA)/MIRAMAX (IN U.S.). Nov., 2001. South Korean. (Jo Jin-gyu) Shin Eun-gyeong, Park San-myeong, Ahn Jae-mo, Kim In-gweon, Shim Weon-cheol.

MY WIFE IS AN ACTRESS
SONY PICTURES CLASSICS (IN U.S.). Sept., 2001. French. (Yvan Attal) Charlotte Gainsbourg, Yvan Attal, Terence Stamp, Noemie Lvovsky, Laurent Bateau, Ludivine Sagnier, Keith Allen.

MY WIFE'S NAME IS MAURICE
WARNER BROS. FRANCE. Sept., 2002. French-German. (Jean-Marie Poire) Alice Evans, Regis Laspales, Philippe Chevallier, Gotz Otto, Anemone, Martin Lamotte, Virginie Lemoine, Guy Marchand, Urban Chancelier, Stephane Audran, Jean-Pierre Castaldi.

N

NADIA AND THE HIPPOS
DIAPHANA. May, 1999. French. (Dominique Cabrera) Ariane Ascaride, Marilyne Canto, Thierry Fremont, Philippe Fretun, Najd Hamou-Medja.

NADRO
ARTEMESIA. Oct., 1998. French. (Ivana Massetti). Documentary.

NAILED
SANFORD-PILLSBURY. April, 2001. (Joel Silverman) Harvey Keitel, Brad Rowe, Rachel Blanchard, Mary Kay Place, Dash Mihok, Lori Heuring, Richard Voll, Gina Philips.

THE NAKED EYE (LA MIRADA DEL OTRO)
COLUMBIA TRISTAR ESPANA. Feb., 1998. Spanish. (Vicente Aranda) Laura Morante, Jose Coronado, Miguel Angel Garcia.

NAKED STATES
JUNTOS FILMS. Oct., 2000. (Arlene Donnelly) Spencer Tunick, Ron Kuby, Fraya Berg, David Silver, Tanysha Marbury, Dan Speers, Deborah Berman, Ken Q. Fine. Documentary.

NAKED UNDER THE MOON
GOOD HARVEST/REGAL ENTERTAINMENT. Feb., 2000. Filipino. (Lav Diaz) Klaudia Koronel, Elizabeth Oropesa, Joel Torre, Julio Diaz, Isabel Granada, Ronnie Lazaro, Richard Joson.

THE NAMELESS
FILMAX/JOAN GINARD PC/SOGEDASA/ VIA DIGITAL/TVC. Nov., 1999. Spanish. (Jaime Balaguero) Emma Vilarasau, Karra Elejalde, Tristan Ulloa, Pep Tosar.

NANG NAK
TAI ENTERTAINMENT/BUDDY FILMS & VIDEO. Sept., 1999. Thai. (Nonzee Nimbutr) Intira Jaroenpura, Winai Kraibutr, Pramote Suksatit, Pracha Thawongfia, Manit Meekaewjaroen.

THE NANNY
ISTITUTO LUCE. May, 1999. Italian. (Marco Bellocchio) Fabrizio Bentivoglio, Valeria Bruni Tedeschi, Maya Sansa, Jacqueline Lustig, Pier Giorgio Bellocchio.

NAQOYQATSI
MIRAMAX. Sept., 2002. (Godfrey Reggio) Documentary.

NARC
LIONS GATE FILMS. Jan., 2002. (Joe Carnahan) Ray Liotta, Jason Patric, Chi McBride, Busta Rhymes, Anne Openshaw, Richard Chevolleau, John Ortiz.

NASTY NEIGHBOURS
IPSO FACTO/GLENRINNES FILM/MPCE. Sept., 1999. British. (Debbie Isitt) Ricky Tomlinson, Marion Bailey, Phil Daniels, Rachel Fielding, Hywel Bennett, Nick Whitfield, Debbie Isitt.

NATIONAL LAMPOON'S VAN WILDER
ARTISAN ENTERTAINMENT. March, 2002. (Walt Becker) Ryan Reynolds, Tara Reid, Tim Matheson, Kal Penn, Teck Holmes, Daniel Cosgrove, Deon Richmond, Alex Burns, Emily Rutherfurd, Paul Gleason, Erik Estrada, Jason Winer.

NATIONAL 7 (UNEASY RIDER)
REZO FILMS. Jan., 2001. French. (Jean-Pierre Sinapi) Nadia Kaci, Olivier Gourmet, Lionel Abelanski, Chantal Neuwirth, Julien Boisselier, Nadine Marcovici, Said Taghmaoui.

THE NATURAL HISTORY OF THE CHICKEN
MARK LEWIS RADIO PICTURES. Jan., 2001. (Mark Lewis) Documentary.

NATURALLY NATIVE
RED-HORSE NATIVE. Jan., 1998. (Jennifer Wynne Farmer, Valerie Red-Horse) Valerie Red-Horse, Irene Bedard, Kimberly Norris Guerrero.

THE NATURE OF NICHOLAS
Aug., 2002. Canadian. (Jeff Erbach) Jeff Sutton, David Turnbull, Ardith Boxall, Tom McCamus, Robert Huculak, Katherine Lee Raymond.

THE NAVIGATORS
PARALLAX PICTURES (LONDON)/ROAD MOVIES FILMPRODUKTION (BERLIN)/TORNASOL FILMS (MADRID). Sept., 2001. British-German-Spanish. (Ken Loach) Dean Andrews, Tom Craig, Joe Duttine, Steve Huison.

NEEDING YOU...
CHINA STAR ENTERTAINMENT GROUP. Nov., 2000. Hong Kong. (Johnnie To, Wai Ka-fai) Andy Lau, Sammi Cheng, Fiona Leung, Raymond Wong.

NEGATIVE SPACE
LLUMINATIONS. Feb., 2001. (Chris Petit) Manny Farber, Dave Hickey, Chris Petit. Documentary.

THE NEGOTIATOR
WARNER BROS. July, 1998. (F. Gary Gray) Samuel L. Jackson, Kevin Spacey, David Morse, Ron Rifkin, John Spencer, J. T. Walsh.

NEJISHIKI: WIND-UP TYPE
BITTERS END/ISHII PROD. June, 2000. Japanese. (Teruo Ishii) Tadanobu Asano, Miki Fujitani, Kazuhiko Kanayama, Tetsuro Tanba, Nijiko Kiyokawa, Yuko Fujimori, Tsugaumi, Mutsumi Fujita.

NEITHER FISH, NOR FOWL
June, 2002. German. (Matthias Keilich) Ill-Young Kim, Ju Youn Kim, Lisa Kreuzer, Christian Steyer, Jurgen Lehmann, Sun-Chai Chung.

THE NEPHEW
IRISH DREAMTIME/WORLD 2000 ENTERTAINMENT. May, 1998. Irish. (Eugene Brady) Hill Harper, Aislin McGuckin, Pierce Brosnan.

THE NEST
PATHE DISTRIBUTION. Feb., 2002. French. (Florent-Emilio Siri) Samy Naceri, Benoit Magimel, Nadia Fares, Pascal Greggory, Sami Bouajila, Anisia Uzeyman, Richard Sammel.

NEUTRAL
NAVARRO FILMS. Aug., 2001. Swiss. (Xavier Ruiz) Robert Bestazzoni, Olivier Iglesias, Lambert Bastar, Gaspard Boesch, Miami Themo, Nicholas Michel, Julien George, Jeff Samartin.

NEVER AGAIN
MOVIE CO. March, 2001. (Eric Schaeffer) Jeffrey Tambor, Jill Clayburgh, Michael McKean, Caroline Aaron, Sandy Duncan, Bill Duke.

NEVER BEEN KISSED
20TH CENTURY FOX. Mar., 1999. (Raja Gosnell) Drew Barrymore, David Arquette, Michael Vartan, Molly Shannon, John C. Reilly.

NEVER GET OUTTA THE BOAT
Sept., 2002. (Paul Quinn) Lombardo Boyar, Darren Burrows, Thomas Jefferson Byrd, Nick Gillie, Devon Gummersall, Harry J. Lennix.

NEW BEST FRIEND
SONY PICTURES ENTERTAINMENT. April, 2002. (Zoe Clarke-Williams) Mia Kirshner, Meredith Monroe, Dominique Swain, Scott Bairstow, Rachel True, Taye Diggs, Glynnis O'Connor.

NEW BLOOD
LIONS GATE/SCREENLAND PICTURES. May, 1999. British-Canadian. (Michael Hurst) John Hurt, Nick Moran, Carrie-Anne Moss, Shawn Wayans, Joe Pantoliano.

THE NEWCOMER
SKY PLANNING/HORI PRO/CITY OF KYOTO. Sept., 1999. Japanese. (Isao Morimoto) Edward Atterton, Honami Suzuki, Yoshiko Nakata, Tetsu Watanabe, Sokyu Fujita, Keizo Kanie.

THE NEW COUNTRY
SONET FILM. Nov., 2000. Swedish. (Geir Hansteen Jorgensen) Mike Almaheyu, Michalis Koutsogiannakis, Lia Noysen, Lars Varinger, Niklas Riesbeck, Evert Lindqvist, Inga Alenius, Jan Astrom.

NEW DAWN
HAUT ET COURT . May, 1999. French. (Emilie Deleuze) Samuel Le Bihan, Marcial De Fonzo Bo, Catherine Vinatier.

THE NEW EVE
Gemini. Jan. 1999. French. (Catherine Corsini) Karin Viard, Pierre-Loup Rajot, Catherine Frot, Sergi Lopez, Mireille Roussel.

THE NEW GUY
SONY PICTURES ENTERTAINMENT. May, 2002. (Ed Decter) DJ Qualls, Eliza Dushku, Zooey Deschanel, Lyle Lovett, Jerod Mixon, Illieana Douglas, Parry Shen, Kurt Fuller, Julius Carry.

THE NEW JEAN-CLAUDE
PATHE DISTRIBUTION. July, 2002. French. (Didier Tronchet) Mathieu Demy, Clotilde Courau, Richard Berry, Darry Cowl, Benoit Tachiores, Michele Garcia, Veronique Boulanger.

NEW MOON (BAGONG BUWAN)
July, 2002. Filipino. (Marilou Diaz-Abaya) Cesar Montano, Amy Austria, Caridad Sanchez, Carlo Quino, Jericho Rosales, Nonie Buencamino, Jhong Hilario, Ronnie Lazaro.

NEW ROSE HOTEL
EDWARD R. PRESSMAN FILM CORP. Sept., 1998. (Abel Ferrara) Christopher Walken, Willem Dafoe, Asia Argento, Yoshitaka Amano, Annabella Sciorra, Gretchen Mol, John Lurie.

THE NEWTON BOYS
20TH CENTURY FOX. March, 1998. (Richard Linklater) Matthew McConaughey, Skeet Ulrich, Ethan Hawke, Vincent D'Onofrio, Julianna Margulies, Dwight Yoakam.

NEW WATERFORD GIRL
ODEON. Sept., 1999. Canadian. (Allan Moyle) Liane Balaban, Tara Spencer Nairn, Andrew McCarthy, Mary Walsh, Nicholas Campbell.

THE NEW WOMEN
INTERZONE. July, 2001. (Todd Hughes) Mary Woronov, Jaime Tolbert, Sandra Kinder, Jane Ray, Roma Maffia, Jenny Shimizu.

NEW YEAR'S DAY
FLASHPOINT/ALCHYMIE/ECF/LIBERATOR PRODS/CANAL PLUS. Jan., 2000. British. (Suri Krishnamma) Andrew Lee Potts, Robby Barry, Marianne Jean-Baptiste, Jacqueline Bisset, Anatasia Hille.

THE NEXT BEST THING
PARAMOUNT//LAKESHORE ENTERTAINMENT. Feb., 2000. (John Schlesinger) Rupert Everett, Madonna, Benjamin Bratt, Michael Vartan, Josef Sommer, Lynn Redgrave, Malcolm Stumpf, Neil Patrick Harris, Illeana Douglas, Mark Valley, Suzanne Krull, Stacy Edwards.

NEXT FRIDAY
NEW LINE/CUBEVISION. Jan., 2000. (Steve Carr) Ice Cube, Mike Epps, Justin Pierce, John Witherspoon. Don "DC" Curry, Jacob Vargas, Lobo Sebastian, Rolando Molina, Lisa Rodriguez, Tommy "Tiny" Lister Jr., Kym E. Whitley, Amy Hill, Tamala Jones, Robin Allen.

NEXT STOP WONDERLAND
MIRAMAX. Jan., 1998. (Brad Anderson) Hope Davis, Alan Gelfant, Victor Argo, Jon Benjamin.

NEXT TIME
ALHONDIGA PICTURES. Aug., 1998. (Alan Fraser) Christian Campbell, Jonelle Allen.

NEXXT: FRAU PLASTIC CHICKEN SHOW
INTERCOM. Feb., 2001. Hungarian. (Arpad Schilling) Dorottya Udvaros, Zoltan Mucsi, Viktor Bodo, Sandor Terhes, Annamaria Lang, Borbala Peterfy, Sandor Csanyi Zsolt Nagy, Gergely Banki.

NIGHT AT THE GOLDEN EAGLE
SHANGRI-LA. April, 2002. (Ada Rifkin) Vinny Argiro, Donnie Montemarano, Vinne Jones, Ntasha Lyonne, Ann Magnuson, Nicole Jacobs, James Cahn.

A NIGHT AT THE ROXBURY
PARAMOUNT PICTURES. Sept., 1998. (John Fortenberry) Will Ferrell, Chris Kattan, Molly Shannon, Dan Hedaya, Richard Grieco.

NIGHTCAP
MK2 DIFFUSIONMK2 PRODS./CAB PRODS./FRANCE 2 CINEMA/TELEVISION SUISSE ROMANDE/YMC PRODS./CANAL PLUS/OFFICE FEDERAL DE LA CULTURE/SUISSE SUCCES CINEMA/TELECLUB. Aug., 2000. French-Swuss. (Claude Chabrol) Isabelle Huppert, Jacques Dutronc, Anna Mouglalis, Rodolphe Pauly, Michel Robin, Brigitte Catillon, Mathieu Simonet.

NIGHTFALL
MEDIOPOLIS/FILMES DO TEJO/WESTDEUTSCHER RUNDFUNK. Sept., 1999. German-Portuguese. (Fred Kelemen) Wolfgang Michael, Verena Jasch, Adolfo Assor, Isa Hochgerner.

NIGHT FLIER
NEW LINE CINEMA. Feb., 1998. (Mark Pavia) Miguel Ferrer, Julie Entwisle, Dan Monahan, Merton H. Moss, John Bennes.

THE NIGHT LARRY KRAMER KISSED ME
FILMNEXT/JOHN TILLEY/FILMNEXT/MONTROSE PICTURES. July, 2000. (Tim Kirkman) David Drake

NIGHTMARE
TUBE INVESTMENT/TUBE ENTERTAINMENT. Oct., 2000. South Korean. (Ahn Byeong-ki) Kim Kyu-ri, Ha Ji-weon, Yu Ji-tae, Choe Jeong-yun, Yu Jun-sang, Jeong Jun, Jo Hye-yeong.

NIGHT OF DESTINY
LES FILMS DU PLACE. Feb., 1999. French. (Abdelkrim Bahloul) Philippe Volter, Boris Terral, Gamil Ratib, Sonia Mankai, Marie-Jose Nat.

A NIGHT ON THE TOWN
BUENA VISTA INTL./HAGER MOSS/SEVEN PICTURES. June, 2000. German. (Soenke Wortmann) Benno Fuermann, Kathleen Gallego Zapata, Armin Rohde, Maruschka Detmers, Axel Milberg, Oliver Stokowski, Florian Lukas.

NIGHTS
MADRAGOA FILMES. Sept., 2000. Portuguese. (Claudia Tomaz) Joao Pereira, Claudia Tomaz, Ana Bustorff, Joao D'Avila, Isabel Ruth.

NIGHTS OF CONSTANTINOPLE
April, 2002. Spanish. (Orlando Rojas) Liberto Rabal, Veronica Lynn, Francisco Rabal, Marisabel Diaz, Rosa Fornes, Zulema Clares.

NIGHT SERVICE STATION
FILMAKADEMIE BADEN/LILION FILM/SN FILM. Feb., 2000. German. (Samir Nasr). Documentary.

NIGHT SHAPES
PETER ROMMEL PRODS. Feb., 1999. German. (Andreas Dresen) Meriam Abbas, Dominique Horwitz, Oliver Bassler, Susanne Bornmann, Michael Gwisdek.

NIGHTSHIFT
LAZENNEC. Feb., 2001. French. (Philippe Le Guay) Gerald Laroche, Marc Barbe, Bernard Ballet, Alexandre Carriere, Jean-Francois Lapalus, Sabri Lahmer, Luce Mouchel.

NIGHT TIME
AVISTA/ROXY FILM/LUGGI WALDLEITNER/PROSIEBEN. Mar., 2000. German. (Peter Fratzscher) Jan Josef Liefers, Ulrich Muhe, Marie Baumer, Christoph Waltz.

NIGHT TRAIN
ALTERNATIVE CINEMA CO. Sept., 1998. Irish. (John Lynch) John Hurt, Brenda Blethyn, Pauline Flanagan, Rynagh O'Grady, Peter Caffrey.

NIGHT WALTZ: THE MUSIC OF PAUL BOWLES
OWSLEY BROWNE PRESENTS/TELEFILM CANADA. Oct., 1999. (Owsley Browne III). Paul Bowles, Allen Ginsberg, William S. Burroughs. Documentary.

NIGHTWATCH
MIRAMAX FILMS. April, 1998. (Ole Bornedal) Ewan McGregor, Nick Nolte, Josh Brolin, Patricia Arquette, Alix Koromzay, Brad Dourif.

NIGHTWATCHMAN
EAGLE PICTURES/DIGITAL FILM/RAI/TELEPIU. Mar., 2000. Italian. (Francesco Calogero) Diego Abatantuono, Anna Safroncik, Flavio Insinna, Marco Messeri, Simona Caramelli, Antonio Petrocelli.

NIGHT WIND
MARS FILMS. Jan., 1999. French-Swiss-Italian. (Philippe Garrel) Catherine Deneuve, Daniel Duval, Xavier Beauvois, Jacques Lasalle.

A NIGHT WITH SABRINA LOVE
PATAGONIK FILM GROUP. Jan., 2001. Argentine. (Alejandro Agresti) Cecilia Roth, Fabian Vena, Tomas Fonzi, Giancarlo Giannini, Julieta Cardinali, Mario Paolucci, Carlos Roffe, Norma Aleandro.

NINA HAGEN = PUNK + GLORY
BLACK SUN FLOWER. Feb., 1999. German. (Peter Sempel). Documentary.

9
May, 2002. Turkish. (Umit Unal) Ali Poyrazoglu, Cezmi Baskin, Fikret Kuskan, Ozan Guven.

900 WOMEN
WOMEN MAKE MOVIES. Jan., 2001. (Laleh Khadivi) Documentary.

THE NINE LIVES OF TOMAS KATZ
GEISSENDORFER FILMS/G2/STRAWBERRY VALE. Aug., 2000. British-German. (Ben Hopkins) Thomas Fisher, Ian McNeice, Tim Barlow, Janet Henfrey.

NINE QUEENS
SONY PICTURES CLASSICS (IN U.S.). Sept., 2001. Argentine. (Fabian Bielinsky) Ricardo Darin, Gaston Pauls, Leticia Bredice, Tomas Fonzi.

19
GAGA COMMUNICATIONS. Sept., 2000. Japanese. (Kazushi Watanabe) Kaijiro Kawaoka, Kazushi Watanabe, Takeo Noro, Ryo Shinmyo.

1999
SACRED POOLS. April, 1998. (Nick Davis) Dan Futterman, Jennifer Garner, Matt McGrath, Amanda Peet, Steven Wright, Sandrine Hold.

1999 MADELEINE
PLAYTIME/CLIMAX. Aug., 1999. French. (Laurent Bouhnik) Vera Briole, Manuel Blanc, Anouk Aimee, Jean-Michel Fete, Jean-Francois Galotte.

THE NINTH GATE
BAC FILMS/ARTISAN. Aug., 1999. French-Spanish. (Roman Polanski) Johnny Depp, Frank Langella, Lena Olin, Emmanuelle Seigner, Barbara Jefford.

NINTH STREET
Hodcarrier Films. Jan., 1999. (Tim Rebman) Don Washington, Devin WIllmott, Nadine Griffith, Byron Myrick, Isaac Hayes.

90 MILES
90 MILES LLC. Mar., 2001. (Juan Carlos Zaldivar) Juan Carlos Zaldivar, Pachuco Zaldivar, Nilvi Zaldivar. Documentary.

NO BLOOD NO TEARS
CINEMA SERVICE. May, 2002. South Korean. (Ryu Seungowan) Jeon Do-yeon, Lee Hye-yeong, Jeong Jae-yeong, Ryu Seung-beom, Shin Gu.

NOBODY KNOWS ANYBODY
WARNER SOGEFILMS/SOGETEL/MAESTRANZA FILMS/DMBV/CANAL PLUS/CANAL SUR TV. Nov., 1999. Spanish-French. (Mateo Gil) Eduardo Noriega, Jordi Molla, Natalia Verbeke, Paz Vega, Pedro Alvarez Osorio.

NOBODY'S BABY
MILLENNIUM FILMS. Jan., 2001. (David Seltzer) Skeet Ulrich, Gary Oldman, Radha Mitchell, Mary Steenburgen, Gordon Tootoosis, Anna Gunn, Peter Greene.

NOBODY SOMEDAY
UIP. Jan., 2002. British. (Brian Hill) Documentary.

NO COFFEE, NO TV, NO SEX
LATKE FILMS/LA TELEVISION SUISSE ROMANDE. Apr., 2000. Swiss. (Romed Wyder) Vincent Coppey, Alexandra Tidemann, Pietro Musillo, Nalini Selvadoray.

NO DEPOSIT, NO RETURN
ISTITUTO LUCE. Feb., 1999. Italian. (Massimo Costa) Giancarlo Giannini, Silvia De Santis, Max Malatesta.

NO LOOKING BACK
GRAMERCY/20TH CENTURY FOX. March, 1998. (Edward Burns) Lauren Holly, Edward Burns, Jon Bon Jovi, Blythe Danner.

NO MAN'S LAND
OCEAN RILMS. May, 2001. (Danis Tanovic) Brancko Djuric, Rene Bitorajac, Filip Sovagovic, Geroges Siatidis, Katrin Cartlidge, Simon Callow, Serge-Henri Valcke.

NO MAPS FOR THESE TERRITORIES
MARK NEALE PRODS. (LONDON). Oct., 2000. British. (Mark Neale) William Gibson, Bono, the Edge. Documentary.

NO MORE MONKEYS JUMPIN' ON THE BED
JUMPIN' ON THE BED PRODS. (VANCOUVER). Sept., 2000. Canadian. (Ross Weber) Tom Scholte, Nancy Sivak, Can Cronin, Sophie Yendole, Erik Whittaker, Frida Betrani, Babz Chula.

NO NEWS FROM GOD
LAUREN FILMS. Dec., 2001. Spanish-French-Italian-Mexican. (Agustin Diaz Yanes) Victoria Abril, Penelope Cruz, Demian Bechir, Fanny Ardant, Gael Garcia Bernal, Juan Echanove, Bruno Bichir, Emilio Gutierrez Caba, Luis Tosar, Cristina Marcos.

A NON-VIOLENT LIFE
ISTITUTO LUCE/FILM 7 INTL./RAI. Nov., 1999. Italian. (David Emmer) Yuri Gugliucci, Ninetto Davoli, Jacqueline Lustig, Gianluca Angelini, Gianfranco Mattioli, Adriana Asti.

NO ONE SLEEPS
GALERIA ALASKA PRODS./HAMBURGER FILMFORDERUNG/ MEDIEN-UND FILMGESELLSCHAFT BADEN-WURTTEMBERG/ FILMSTIFTUNG NORDRHEIN-WESTFALEN/WDR/ARTE. Feb., 2000. German. (Jochen Hick) Tom Wlaschiha, Irit Levi, Jim Thalman, Richard Thalman, Richard Conti, Kalene Parker, Charles Shaw Robinson.

NO ONE WRITES TO THE COLONEL
PRODS. AMARANTA, GARDENIA PRODS., TORNASOL/DMVB/ INSTITUTO MEXICANO DE CINEMATOGRAFIA/ FONDO PARA LA PRODUCCION CINEMATOGRAFICA DE CALIDAD. Apr., 1999. Mexican-Spanish-French. (Arturo Ripstein) Fernando Lujan, Marisa Paredes, Salma Hayek.

NO PAIN, NO GAIN
ALTA FILMS. July, 2001. Spanish. (Victor Garcia Leon) Biel Duran, Barbara Lennie, Manuel Lozano, Fernando Conde, Asuncion Planas, Pilar Duque, Maria Galiana, Enrique San Francisco.

NO PLACE TO GO
DISTANT DREAMS/ZDF/GEYER WERKE BERLIN. May, 2000. German. (Oskar Orehler) Hannelore Elsner, Vadim Glowna, Jasmin Tabatabai, Lars Rudolph, Michael Gwisdek, Nina Petri, Tonio Arango.

NORA
ALLIANCE ATLANTIS/NATURAL NYLON ENTERTAINMENT/IAC HOLDINGS/VOLTA FILMS/ROAD MOVIES/VIERTE PRODUKTIONEN/ GAM FILM/METROPOLITAN FILMS. Feb. 2000. British. (Pat Murphy) Ewan McGregor, Susan Lynch, Peter McDonald, Aedin Moloney, Roberto Citran.

NORIEGA: GOD'S FAVORITE
SHOWTIME/REGENCY ENTERPRISES/NANCY HARDIN/ INDUSTRY ENTERTAINMENT. Mar., 2000. (Roger Spottiswoode) Bob Hoskins, Jeffrey Demunn, Rosa Blasi, Luis Avalos, Denise Blasor, Nestor Carbonell, Tony Plana, John Verea, Richard Masur, David Marshall Grant.

NORMA JEAN, JACK, AND ME
NEW PATH PICTURES/MAURICE SINGER. Mar.., 2000. (Cyrus Nowrasteh.) Sally Kirkland, Michael Murphy, Kai Lennox, Dan Mandehr, David De Vos.

NOROC
VERSATILE/TELEFILM CANADA. Oct., 1999. Canadian. (Marc Retailleau) Peter La Croix, Gina Chiarelli, Jay Brazeaau, Babz Chula.

NORTH BEACH
FUR BOAT FILMS. Jan., 2001. (Jed Mortenson, Richard Speight Jr.) Casey Peterson, Jennifer Milmore, Gabrielle Anwar, Richard Speight Jr., Jim Hanna, Barrow Davis.

NORTH BY NORTH
BBSA/DOLMENFILM. Feb., 1999. Hungarian. (Csaba Bollok) Laura Ruttkay, Zsolt Trill, Barnabas Marton, Nelli Szucs.

NORTHERN SKIRTS
POLYFILM. Sept., 1999. Austrian-German-Swiss. (Barbar Albert) Nina Proll, Edita Malovcic, Michael Tanczos, Tudor Chirila.

NO SCANDAL
CINE B/IMA. Sept., 1999. French. (Benoit Jacquot) Fabrice Luchini, Isabelle Huppert, Vincent Lindon, Vahina Giocante, Sophie Aubry.

NO SHAME
ALTA FILMS. July, 2001. (Joaquin Oristrell) Veronica Forque, Daniel Gimenez Cacho, Candela Pena, Carmen Balague, Elvira Lindo, Rosa Maria Sarda, Jorge Sanz.

NO SUCH THING
MGM. May, 2001. (Hal Hartley) Sarah Polley, Robert John Burke, Helen Mirren, Julie Christie, Baltasar Kormakur, Paul Lazar.

NOT A DAY GOES BY
July, 2002. (Joe G.M. Chan) Larry Chin, Joey Chin, Joey Garfield, Kenneth Hawkins Chin, Brenda Chan, Mona Chiang, Michael Harner, John Quincy Lee.

NOT ANOTHER TEEN MOVIE
SONY PICTURES ENTERTAINMENT. Dec., 2001. (Joel Gallen) Chyler Leigh, Chris Evans, Jaime Pressly, Eric Christian Olsen, Mia Kirshner, Deon Richmond, Eric Jungmann, Ron Lester, Cody McMains, Sam Huntington, Riley Smith.

NOTES FOR A STORY
LIDER FILMS. Sept., 1998. Argentine-Spanish. (Jana Bokova) German Palacios, Silke, Ines Estevez, Hector Alterio.

NOT FORGOTTEN
BITTERS END. Oct., 2000. Japanese. (Makoto Shinozaki) Tatsuya Mihashi, Minoru Oki, Keiko Utsumi, Tomio Aoki, Saburo Shinoda.

NOTHING
TELEWIZJA POLSKA/KID FILM/AGENCJA PRODUKCJI FILMOWEJ/ LODZKIE CENTRUM FILMOWE. Mar., 1999. Polish. (Dorota Kedzierzawska); Anita Kuskowska-Borkowska, Janusz Panasewicz.

NOTHING BUT THE TRUTH
MARK STEVEN SHEPHERD. Oct., 1998. (Mark Steven Shepherd). Documentary.

NOTHING IN THE FRIDGE
COLUMBIA TRISTAR. Oct., 1998. Spanish. (Alvaro Fernandez Armero) Maria Esteve, Coque Malla, Roberto Alvarez, Laura Aparicio, Itziar Miranda.

NOTHING SO STRANGE
Jan., 2002. (Brian Flemming) David James, Laurie Pike, Steve Wilcox, Steve Sires, Philip Anthony Traylor, Sarah Stanley.

NOT OF THIS WORLD
MIKADO. Mar., 1999. Italian. (Giuseppe Piccioni) Margherita Buy, Silvio Orlando, Carolina Freschi.

NOT ONE LESS
COLUMBIA. Sept., 1999. Chinese. (Zhang Yimou) Wei Minzhi, Zhang Huike, Tian Zhenda, Gao Enman.

NO TRAINS NO PLANES
WARNER BROS. Feb., 1999. Dutch. (Jos Stelling) Dirk van Dijck, Ellen ten Damme, Henri Garcin, Gene Bervoets, Dominique Horwitz.

NO TURNING BACK
ZOKALO ENTERTAINMENT. Aug., 2001. U.S.-Spanish. (Jesus Nebot) Jesus Nebot, Chelsea Rendon, Lindsay Price, Vernee Watson Johnson, Susan Haskell, Robert Vestal, Paul Ganus, Joe Estevez.

NOT WITH A BANG
IMBARCO PER CITERA. Sept., 1999. Italian. (Mariano Lambeerti) Paola Pitagora, Nello Mascia, Mariano D'Amora, Giovanna Giuliani, Carlo Giuliano, Rita Montes, Elena Cannella.

NOT AFRAID TO SAY...
UNTITLED PRODS./FREEWHEEL PRODS. July, 1999. (Adam Vetri) Adam Vetri Chelsea Lago, Monica Trombetta, Jason Beck.

NOTORIOUS C.H.O.
WELLSPRING ENTERTAINMENT. (Lorene Machado) Margaret Cho.

NO VACANCY
ERNEST KOSKIN. Apr., 1999. (Marius Balchunas Ryan Bollman, Lolita Davidovich, Joaquim de Almeida, Olek Krupa, Gabriel Mann.

NOVOCAINE
ARTISAN ENTERTAINMENT. Sept., 2001. (David Atkins) Steve Martin, Helena Bonham Carter, Laura Dern, Elias Koteas, Scott Caan, Keith David, Lynne Thigpen.

NOW & FOREVER
Aug., 2001. Canadian. (Bob Clark) Mia Kirshner, Adam Beach, Gordon Tootoosis, Theresa Russell, Gabriel Olds, Callum Keith Rennie, Simon Baker, Alexandra Purvis.

NOW & THEN: FROM FROSH TO SENIORS
GELLER/GOLDFINE PRODS. Sept., 1999. (Daniel Geller, Dayna Goldfine). Documentary.

NOW CHINATOWN
DARQUE PICTURES. Nov., 2001. (Steven Dunning) Lianne X. Hu, Steven Dunning, Michael Minh, Benjamin Lum, Jack C. Huang, Peggy Lu, June Kyoko Lu, Debi Parker.

NOWHERE IN AFRICA
CONSTANTIN. Feb., 2002. German. (Caroline Link) Juliane Koehler, Merab Ninidze, Matthias Habich, Sidede Onyulo, Lea Kurka.

NOWHERE TO GO
KEVIN J. FOXE. March, 1998. (John Caire) Tricia Vessy, John Shea, Marianne Jean-Baptiste, Carroll Baker, Jacob Smith, Ryan Francis

NOWHERE TO HIDE
CINEMA SERVICE/TAEWON ENTERTAINMEN/KOOKMIN VENTURE CAPITAL/SAMBOO FINANCE ENTERTAINMENT/FOX VIDEO KOREA. Oct., 1999. South Korean. (Lee Myeong-se) Ahn Sung-ki, Park Jung-hun, Jang Dong-keon, Choe Ji-woo.

NOW OR NEVER
LICHBLICK/MR. BROWN ENTERTAINMENT/SENATOR FILM. Jan., 2001. German. (Lars Buchel) Christel Okras, Elisabeth Scherer, Christel Peters, Martin Semmelrogge, Thierry van Werveke, Vladimir Weigl.

'N SYNC: BIGGER THAN LIVE
REALLY BIG FILM CORP. March, 2001. N Sync (Lance Bass, Joshua "J.C." Chasez, Joey Fatone, Chris Kirkpatrick, Justin Timberlake). Documentary-Imax.

NUCLEAR DYNAMITE
NATIONAL FILM BOARD (VANCOUVER). Oct., 2000. Canadian. (Gary Marcuse) Edward Teller, Barry Commoner, Ursula Franklin, Victor Mikhailkov, Keith Lawton. Documentary.

THE NUGGET
Sept., 2002. Australian. (Bill Bennett) Eric Bana, Stephen Curry, Dave O'Neil, Peter Moon, Alan Brough, Vince Colosimo, Belinda Emmett.

NUMERO BRUNO
HOODWINK/NEW ZEALAND ON AIR/TV ONE/TELECOM. July, 2000. New Zealand. (Steve La Hood). Documentary.

NURSE BETTY
USA FILMS/GRAMERCY PICTURES/PACIFICA FILM DISTRIBUTION/ PROPAGANDA FILMS/AB'-STRAKT PICTURES/IMF. May., 2000. (Neil LaBute) Renee Zellweger, Morgan Freeman, Chris Rock, Greg Kinnear, Aaron Eckhart, Tia Texada, Crispin Glover, Pruitt Taylor Vince, Allison Janney, Kathleen Wilhoite, Harriet Sanson Harris, Laird Macintosh.

NUTS FOR LOVE
ZARLEK. Sept., 2000. Argentine-Spanish. (Alberto Lecchi) Ariadna Gil, Gaston Pauls, Nicolas Pauls, Malena Solda, Nancy Duplaa, Gabriel Goity.

NUTTY PROFESSOR II: THE KLUMPS
UNIVERSAL PICTURES/IMAGINE ENTERTAINMENT/BRIAN GRAZER. July., 2000. (Peter Segal) Eddie Murphy, Janet Jackson, Larry Miller, John Ales, Richard Gant, Anna Maria Horsford, Melinda McGraw, Jamal Mixon.

NUYORICAN DREAM
BIG MOUTH PRODS./JOHN LEGUIZAMO/JELLYBEAN BENITEZ. Jan.., 2000. (Laurie Collyer). Documentary.

O
LIONS GATE FILMS. June, 2001. (Tim Blake Nelson) Mekhi Phifer, Josh Hartnett, Julia Stiles, Elden Henson, Andrew Keegan, Rain Phoenix, John Heard.

OASIS
Sept., 2002. Korean. (Lee Chang-dong) Sol Kyung-gu, Moon So-ri, Ahn Nae-sang, Ryoo Seung-wan, Chu Gui-jeong, Kim Jin-jin, Sohn Byung-ho, Yoon Ga-hyun.

OBAACHAN'S GARDEN
Dec., 2001. Canadian. (Linda Ohama) Documentary.

OBERWASSER - BY U BOAT TO AMERICA
NEUW BERLINER FILMGESELLSCHAFT. Sept., 1998. German. (Wolfram R. Bauer). Documentary.

THE OBJECT OF MY AFFECTION
20TH CENTURY FOX. April, 1998. (Nicholas Hytner) Jennifer Aniston, Paul Rudd, Alan Alda, Nigel Hawthorne, John Pankow, Tim Daly.

O BROTHER, WHERE ART THOU?
BUENA VISTA/UNIVERSAL/TOUCHSTONE. May., 2000. (Joel Coen) George Clooney, John Turturro, Tim Blake Nelson, Charles Durning, John Goodman, Michael Badalucco, Holly Hunter.

OCCASIONAL COARSE LANGUAGE
ROADSHOW. Nov., 1998. Australian. (Brad Hayward Sara Browne, Astrid Grant, Nicholas Bishop.

OCCIDENT
May, 2002. Romanian. (Cristian Mungiu) Alexandru Papdopol, Anea Androne, Tania popa, Coca Bloos.

OCEAN OASIS
SUMMERHAYS FILMS. June 25, 2001. (Soames Summerhays) Exequiel Ezcurra, Iliana Ortega Bacmeister, Mercedes Eugenia Guerrero-Ruiz, Enriquetta Velarde. Documentray-Imax

OCEAN'S ELEVEN
WARNER BROS. Nov., 2001. (Steven Soderbergh) George Clooney, Matt Damon, Andy Garcia, Brad Pitt, Julia Roberts, Casey Affleck, Scott Caan, Don Cheadle, Elliott Gould, Eddie Jemison, Bernie Mac, Shaobo Qin,Carl Reiner.

OCTOBER SKY
UNIVERSAL. Feb., 1999. (Joe Johnston) Jake Gyllenhaal, Chris Cooper, Laura Dern, Chris Owen, William Lee Scott.

THE OCTOPUS
BAC FILMS. Sept., 1998. French. (Guillaume Nicloux) Jean-Pierre Darroussin, Clotilde Courau, Stephane Boucher, Julie Delarme.

THE ODD COUPLE II
PARAMOUNT PICTURES. March, 1998. (Howard Deutch) Jack Lemmon, Walter Matthau, Christine Baranski, Barnard Hughes.

ODE TO COLOGNE: A ROCK 'N' ROLL
Feb., 2002. German. (Wim Wenders) BAP (Sheryl Hackett, Werner Kopal, Helmut Krumminga, Michael Nass, Wolfgang Niedecken, Jens Streifling, Juergen Zoeller), Marie Baumer, Joachim Krol, Willi Laschet, Anger 77, Wolf Biermann.

ODE TO THE POET
VERTIGO/E-MOTION FILM. July, 2001. Slovenian. (Martin Srebotnjak) Martin Srebotnjak, Barbara Cerar, Gregor Cusin, Brane Grubar, Barbara Zefran, Gasper Tlc, Tomi Janezic, Avone Coh.

OF CIVIL WRONGS & RIGHTS: THE FRED KOREMATSU STORY
PUSHTAN PRODS. June., 2000. (Eric Paul Fournier) Fred Korematsu, Rosa Parks, Bill Clinton. Documentary.

OFFICERS' WARD
ARP SELECTION. May, 2001. French. (Francois Dupeyron) Eric Caravaca, Denis Podalydes, Gregori Derangere, Sabine Azema, Andre Dussollier, Isabelle Renauld, Geraldine Pailhas.

OFF TO THE REVOLUTION BY A 2CV
SINTRA/PANTER FILM. Aur., 2001. Italian. (Maurizio Sciarra) Adriano Giannini, Gwenaelle Simon, Andoni Gracia, Oscar Ladoire, Georges Moustaki, Francisco Rabal.

OH BABY, A BABY
DOR FILM. June, 2001. Australian. (Wolfgang Murnberger) Nicole Ansari, Eva Herzig, Ralf Bauer, Peter Matic, Viktoria Schubert, Sigrid Hauser, Alexander Pschill, Michael Gampe.

OI! WARNING
SCHLAMMTACHER-FILM. June, 1999. German. (Dominik and Bejamin Reding) Sascha Backhaus, Simon Goerts, Sandra Borgmann, Jens Veith, Britta Dirks.

OKAY
May, 2002. Danish. (Jesper W. Nielsen) Paprika Steen, Troels Lyby, Ole Ernst.

OKIE NOODLING
LITTLE LEAGUE PICTURES. March, 2001. (Bradley Beesley) Documentary.

OFFICE SPACE
20TH CENTURY FOX. Feb., 1999. (Mike Judge) Ron Livingston, Jennifer Aniston, David Herman, Ajay Naidu, Diedrich Bader.

OF WOMEN AND MAGIC
LA SEPT ARTE/LES FILMS DE LA BOISSIERE/TELECIP/LES FILMS DE LA BOISSIERE/TELECIP/LA SEPT ARTE. Feb., 2000. French. (Claude Miller) Anne Brochet, Mathilde Seigner, Annie Noel, Yves Jacques, Eduard Baer, Jacques Mauclair, Edith Scob, Marc Cennelier.

O.K. GARAGE
TALANA PRODS./RIALTO FILM. April, 1998. (Brandon Cole) John Turturro, Lili Taylor, Will Patton, Gemma Jones, Joe Maher.

THE OLD MAN AND THE SEA
OGDEN ENTERTAINMENT. Sept., 1999. (Alexander Petrov). Animated.

OLD MAN RIVER
PINK PLASTIC PRODS. Feb., 1999. (Allan Holzman). Documentary.

THE OLD MAN WHO READ LOVE STORIES
FILDEBROC (PARIS)/MAGNETIC HALL (ADELAIDE)/KINO VISION (MADRID)/ODUSSEIA FILMS (AMSTERDAM). July, 2001. French-Australian-Spanish-Dutch. (Rolf de Heer) Richard Dreyfuss, Timothy Spall, Hugo Weaving, Cathy Tyson, Victor Bottenbley, Frederico Celada, Luis Hostalot, Guillermo Toledo.

OLD SCHOOL
OPENING/SCARLA FILMS/TANKA PRODS./GLORINDA PRODS. June, 2000. French. (Kader Ayd, Karim Abbou) Fabienne Babe, Julien Courbey, Kader Ayd, Hocine Ossoukine, Stephane Soo Mongo.

OMAR 2000
SHOAA. Jan., 2001. Egyptian. (Ahmed Atef) Khaled Al Nabawi, Mona Zaki, Ahmed Helmi, Monalisa, Ahmed Fouad Selim.

THE OMEGA CODE
PROVIDENCE ENT./TBN FILMS/GENER8XION ENT. Oct., 1999. (Rob Marcarelli) Casper Van Dien. Michael York, Catherine Oxenberg, Michael Ironside, Jan Triska, Gregory Wagrowski.

ON BOARD
YENI SINEMACILIK. Apr., 1999. Turkish. (Serdar Akar) Erkan Can, Haldun Boysan, Yildiray Sahinler.

ONCE AND FUTURE QUEEN
BANGOR FILMS. March, 2001. (Todd Verow) Philly, Jim Dwyer, Rich Fowler, Tia Sprocket, Eric Sapp, Little Nick, Brenda Velez.

ONCE IN A LIFETIME
SONET FILM. Oct., 2000. Danish-Swedish. (Susanne Bier) Helena Bergstrom, Jonas Karlsson, Thomas Hanzon, Bjorn Kjellman, Johan Ulveson, Katarina Ewerlof, Regina Lund.

ONCE UPON AN ANGEL (PEAU D'ANGE)
EUROPA CORP. DISTRIBUTION. Aug., 2002. French. (Vincent Perez) Morgane More, Guillaume Depardieu, Magalie Woch, Karine Silla, Helene de Saint Pere, Stephane Boucher, Olivier Gourmet.

ONCE UPON ANOTHER TIME
CINEMA INDIE GROUP/ATLANTICO/TVG. June, 2000. Spanish. (Juan Pinzas) Monti Castineiras, Pilar Saavedra, Vicente de Souza, Mara Sanchez, Victor Mosquiera, Isabel Vallejo, Marcos Orsi

A ONE AND A TWO...
1+2 SEISAKU IINKAI/ATOM/PONY CANYON/OMEGA PROJECT. May, 2000. Taiwanese-Japanese. (Edward Yang) Wu Nien-jen, Elaine Jin, Issey Ogata, Kelly Lee, Jonathan Chang, Chen Hsi-sheng, Ko Su-yun, Michael Tao, Hsaio Shu-shen.

ONE DAY IN SEPTEMBER
HBO/PASSION PICTURES/ARTHUR COHN. Sept., 2000. (Kevin McDonald). Documentary.

ONE DAY IN THE LIFE OF ANDREI ARSENEVITCH
AMIP/La Sept Arte/INA/Arkeion Films. Feb., 2000. French. (Chris Marker) Marina Vlady, Alexandra Stewart (narrators). Documentary.

ON EDGE
Nov., 2001. (Karl Slovin) Jason Alexander, John Glover, Scott Hamilton, Chris Hogan, A.J. Langer, Wallace Langham, Wendie Malick.

O-NEGATIVE
GRAMMY FILM CO. Nov., 1998. Thai. (Paiboon Damrongchaithan) Amita (Tata) Young, Shawekrit Yamnam, Ray MacDonald.

ONEGIN
SEVEN ARTS INTL.. Sept., 1999. British. (Martha Fiennes) Ralph Fiennes, Liv Tyler, Toby Stephens, Lena Heady, Martin Donovan.

101ST KILOMETER (101ST KILOMETRE)
June, 2002. Russian. (Leonid Maryagin) Piotr Fedorov, Glafira Sotnikova, Oleg Zhukov, Yevgeny Kozyrov, Larissa Shatilo, Olga Litvinova, Sergei Kaplunov, Denis Kravstov, Sergei Yushkeviol.

101 RENT BOYS
CINEMAX/WORLD OF WONDER. June, 2000. (Randy Barbato, Fenton Bailey). Documentary.

101 REYKJAVIK
101 LTD./ZENTROP/LIBERATOR PRODS./FILMHUSET/ICELANDIC FILM FUND. Aug., 2000. Icelandic-Danish. (Baltasar Kormakur) Victoria Abril, Hilmir Snaer Gudnason, Hanna Maria Karlsdottir, Baltasar Kormakur, Olafur Darri Olafsson.

100 DAYS
Sept., 2001. British. (Nick Hughes) Cleophas Kabasita, Mazimpaka Kennedy, Davis Kagenza, Davis Dwizera, David Mulwa, Denis Nsanzamahoro.

102 DALMATIONS
BUENA VISTA. Nov., 2000. (Kevin Lima) Glenn Close, Ioan Gruffudd, Alice Evans, Tim McInnerny, Ian Richardson, Gerard Depardieu.

ONE DAY IN AUGUST
Jan., 2002. Greek. (Constantine Giannaris) Kostas Kotsianidis, Eleni Kastani, Akylas Karazisis, Amalia Moutouzi, Aimilios Heilakis, Theodora Tzimou, Mihalis Iatropoulos.

ONE FINE SPRING DAY
Nov., 2001. South Korean-Japanese-Hong Kong. (Hur Jin-ho) Yu Ji-tae, Lee Yeong-ae, Baek Seong-heui, Park In-hwan, Shin Sin-ae.

ONE HOUR PHOTO
20TH CENTURY FOX. Jan., 2002. (Mark Romanek) Robin Williams, Connie Nielsen, Michael Vartan, Gary Cole, Dylan Smith, Eriq La Salle, Erin Daniels.

ONE HUNDRED YEARS OF FORGIVENESS
GRUPO S.U. pSept., 2000. Argentine. (Jose Glusman) Margara Alonso, Pompeyo Audivert, Noemi Frenkel, Jose Glusman, David Szneck, Helena Tritec.

ONE LEG KICKING
UIP. March, 2002. Singapore. (Eric Khoo, Wei Koh). Gurmit Singh, Mark Lee, Sharon Au, Moe Alkaff, Robin Leong, Siva Choy, Hossan Leong, Lim Kay-tong, Fiona Xie, Jack Neo.

ONE LIFE STAND
ELEMENTAL FILMS. Aug., 2000. British. (May Miles Thomas) Maureen Carr, John Kielty, Gary Lewis, Archie Lal, Alyson Orr, Rohanna Law, Ros McCue.

ONE MAN'S CEILING
April, 2002. (Richard LaPorta) Robert LaPorta, Alexa Fischer, David Engel, Richard LaPorta.

ONE MORE DAY
CIMA. Feb., 2000. Iranian. (Babak Payam) Ali Hosseini, Leila Saadi.

ONE MORE KISS
METRODOME/MOB FILMS/JAM/FREEWHEEL INTL. Nov., 1999. British. (Vadim Hean) Gerry Butler, James Cosmo, Valerie Edmond, Valerie Gogan, Danny Nussbaum, Carl Proctor.

ONE MAN'S HERO
MGM. Sept., 1999. (Lance Hool) Tom Berenger, Joaquim De Almeida, Daniela Romo, Mark Moses, Stuart Graham.

ONE NIGHT
YEREVAN STUDIOS. Aug., 2000. Soviet Union–1945. (Boris Barnet) Irina Radchenko, Boris Andreyev, I. Kuznetsov, B. Leonov, A. Judin, V. Viazemsky, Boris Barnet.

ONE NIGHT AT MCCOOL'S
USA FILMS. April, 2001. (Harald Zwart) Liv Tyler, Matt Dillon, John Goodman, Paul Reiser, Michael Douglas, Richard Jenkins, Reba McEntire, Andrew Silverstein.

ONE OF THE HOLLYWOOD TEN
MORENA FILMS (SPAIN). Sept., 2000. Spanish-British. (Karl Francis) Jeff Goldblum, Greta Scacchi, Angela Molina, Christopher Fulford, Antonio Valero, John Sessions, Geraint Wyn Davies.

ONE PIECE!
PIA FILM FESTIVAL. Sept., 1999. Japanese. (Shinobu Yaguchi, Takuji Suzuki) Youji Tanaka, Nao Nekota, Satoru Jitsunashi, Masumi Kiuchi, Keiko Shionoya, Miako Tadano, Yoko Chosokabe, Tsurumi Komatsu.

ONE MAN UP
KEY FILMS. July, 2001. Italian. (Paolo Sorrentino) Toni Servillo, Andrea Renzi, Nello Mascia, Ninni Bruschetta, Angela Goodwin, Enrica Rosso, Peppe Lanzetta.

ONE'S OWN SHADOW
LENFILM. March, 2001. Russian. (Olga Narutskaya) Valentina Korotayeva, Evdokiya Germanova, Aleksandr Feklistov, Boris Lekhman, Viktor Shevtzov.

ONE SWALLOW BROUGHT SPRING
MARS FILMS. July, 2001. French. (Christian Carion) Michel Serrault, Mathilde Seigner, Jean-Paul Roussillon, Frederic Pierrot, Marc Berman, Francoise Bette.

ONE THOUSAND AND ONE VOICES
Sept., 2001. French-Belgian. (Mahmoud Ben Mahmoud) Documentary.

ONE THOUSAND WOMEN LIKE ME
IRANIAN FILM SOCIETY. July, 2002. Iranian. (Niki Karimi, Fariburz Arabnia, Faramarz Sadighi, Nikoo Kheradmand, Yasaman Malek Nasr.

ONE THOUSAND YEARS
Feb., 2002. (Gabriel Fleming) Mara Gerstein, Soren Gray, Abby Paige, Phil Young, Nancy Stone, Maura Madden.

ONE TOUGH COP
STRATOSPHERE ENTERTAINMENT. Sept., 1998. (Bruno Barreto) Stephen Baldwin, Chris Penn, Mike McGlone, Gina Gershon, Paul Guilfoyle, Amy Irving, Victor Slezak, Luis Guzman.

ONE TRUE THING
UNIVERSAL PICTURES. Aug., 1998. (Carl Franklin) Meryl Streep, Rene Zellweiger, William Hurt, Tom Everett Scott, Lauren Graham.

ONE WEEK
FILM LIFE. Oct., 2001. (Carl Seaton) Kenny Young, Saadiqa Muhammed, Eric Lane.

ONE WINTER BEHIND GOD'S BACK
MAGIC MEDIA/47EME PARALELLE/MAGELLAN PRODUCTION/ NEIKA FILMS. Feb., 1999. Hungarian-French-Belgian-Slovak. (Togay Can) Matej Matejka, David Szabo, Karoly Eperjes.

ON-LINE
Dec., 2001. (Jed Weintrob) Josh Hamilton, Harold Perrineau, Isabel Gillies, John Fleck, Vanessa Ferlito, Eric Millegan.

ON THE BEACH BEYOND THE PIER
ADRIANA CHIESA/C.E.P/RADIOTELEVISIONE ITALIANA. May, 2000. Italian. (Giovanni Fago) Lorenza Indovina, Stephane Freiss, Andrea Renzi, Laurent Terzieff, Ludovica Modugno, Omero Antonutti, Eros Pagni.

ON THE BUS
SOCK PUPPET ENTERPRISES. June, 2001. (Dustin Lance Black) Documentary.

ON THE HEIGHTS ALL IS PEACE
MUSEO STORICO IN TRENTO, COMUNE DI ROVERETO, FONDAZIONE CADUTI IN GUERRA DI ROVERETO. Feb., 1999. Italian. (Yervant Gianikian, Angela Ricci Lucchi). Documentary.

ON THE LINE
MIRAMAX FILMS. Oct., 2001. (Eric Bross) Lance Bass, Joey Fatone, Emmanuelle Chriqui. GQ, James Bulliard, Al Green, Tamala Jones, Richie Sambora.

ON THE NOSE
SUBOTICA ENT. (IRELAND)/HIGHWIRE ENT. (CANADA). May, 2001. Canadian-Irish. (David Caffrey) Robbie Coltrane, Brenda Blethyn, Dan Aykroyd, Eanna MacLiam, Zara Turner.

ON THE OLD ROMAN ROAD
DON FILM. Jan., 2001. Armenian-Dutch. (Don Askarian) Pavel Sahakyantz, Anna Bassentyan, Ohan Askarian.

ON THE ROPES
HIGHWAY FILMS/LEARNING CHANNEL. Jan., 1999. (Nanette Burstein). Documentary.

ON THE RUN, AN AMAZING COUPLE, AFTER LIFE
MERCURE DISTRIBUTION. (Lucas Belvaux) Ornella Muti, Francois Morel, Dominique Blanc, Gilbert Melki, Lucas Belvaux, Catherine Frot, Patrick Descamps, Valerie Mairesse.

ON THE TIPS OF HER FINGERS
OCEAN FILMS DISTRIBUTION. June, 2002. French. (Yves Angelo) Marina Hands, Anne-Sophie Latour, Martine Chevallier, Thierry Hancisse, Pierre Charras.

ON TIPTOE: THE MUSIC OF LADYSMITH BLACK MAMBAZO
NOMA FILMS/ON TIP TOE PRODS. June, 2000. (Eric Simonson) Ladysmith Black Mambazo, Paul Simon, Patrick Bhutelezi. Documentary.

OPERA FANATIC
PARS MEDIA. Jan., 2000. German. (Jan Schmidt-Garre) Stefan Zucker, Leyla Gencer, Gigliola Frazzoni, Iris Adami Corradetti, Giulietta Simionato, Magda Olivero, Gina Cigna.

THE OPERA LOVER
GIFTHORSE. Oct., 1999. (Ron Lazzeretti, Venturino Liberatore) Tom Bastounes, Monica Zaffarano, Dean Bastounes, Nick Bastounes, Coren Caldwell, Tom White, Robert Altman.

THE OPERATOR
BLACK WOLF PRODS. Mar., 2000. (Jon Dichter) Michael Laurence, Christa Miller, Brion James.

THE OPPONENT
EDGEWOOD FILMS. Oct., 2000. (Eugene Jarecki) Erika Eleniak, James Colby, Aunjanue Ellis, John Doman, Harry O'Reilly.

THE OPPORTUNISTS
EUREKA FILMS/CLINICA ESTETICO/KALKASKA FILMS. Jan., 2000. (Myles O'Connel) Christopher Walken, Peter McDonald, Cyndi Lauper, Donal Logue, Vera Farmiga, Jose Zuniga, Anne Pitoniak.

THE OPTIMISTS
COMFORTY MEDIA CONCEPTS, CHAMBON FOUNDATION. Feb., 2001. (Jacky Comforty) Documentary.

ORANGE COUNTY
PARAMOUNT. Jan., 2001. (Jake Kasdan) Colin Hanks, Jack Black, Catherine O'Hara, Schuyler Fisk, John Lithgow, Harold Ramis, Jane Adams, Garry Marshall, Dana Ivey, Chevy Chase, Lily Tomlin, George Murdock, Leslie Mann.

ORATOR
UZBEKINO. June, 2000. Uzbekistanian. (Yusup Razykov) Bosh Rollarda, Bahodir Odilov, Lola Eltoeva, Jahovir Zukirov, Asal Alijuheva, Nargiza, Rahmonova, Shohsanam Khamrokulova.

ORDINARY BOLSHEVISM
INTL. ASSN. OF BUSINESS AND CULTURAL COOPERATION. Oct., 2000. Russian. (Evgeny Tsymbal) Documentary.

ORDINARY DECENT CRIMINAL
ICON/MIRAMAX/LITTLE BIRD/TATFILM/TRIGGER STREET PRODS./IRISH FILM BOARD/GREENLIGHT FUND/FILMSTIFTUNG NRW. Mar., 2000. Irish-British. (Thaddeus O'Sullivan) Kevin Spacey, Linda Fiorentino, Peter Mullan, Stephen Dillane, Helen Baxendale.

ORDINARY HEROES
GOLDEN HARVEST. Feb., 1999. Hong Kong. (Ann Hui) Rachel Lee, Lee Kang-sheng, Anthony Wong, Tse Kwan-ho.

ORDINARY MADNESS
LEGENDARY PRODS. Feb., 2000. (Bernardo Gigliotti) Ron Carlson, Denise Gentile, Mariah O'Brien, Gary D. Mosher, Robert Musgrave, Alan Gelfant, Mark Boone Jr., Steve Richard Harris, Pat Cocran.

ORIENTATIONS–CHRISTOPHER DOYLE: STIRRED NOT SHAKEN
AUSTRALIAN FILM FINANCE CORP./PAGAN/NSW FILM & TV OFFICE/SBS INDEPENDENT/AUSTRALIAN FILM COMM. June, 2000. Australian. (Rick Farquharson). Documentary.

ORIGINAL DINER GUYS
BALTIMORE/SPRING CREEK PRODS. Oct., 1999. (Barry Levinson). Documentary.

THE ORIGINAL KINGS OF COMEDY
MTV FILMS/LATHAM ENTERTAINMENT/40 ACRES AND A MULE FILMWORKS. Aug., 2000. (Spike Lee) Steve Harvey, D.L. Hughley, Cedric the Entertainer, Bernie Mac. Documentary.

ORIGINAL SIN
MGM (IN U.S.)/EUROPA DISTRIBUTION (IN FRANCE). July, 2001. (Michael Cristofer) Antonio Banderas, Angelina Jolie, Thomas Jane, Jack Thompson, Gregory Itzin, Allison Mackie, John Pringle.

THE ORIGIN OF MAN
MYSTERIOUS OFFSHORE HOLDINGS. June, 2000. (Stuart Hynson Culpepper) Gabe Anderson, Phil Beaumont, Lou Seitchik, Stuart Hynson Culpepper, Kitty Culpepper, Nakissa Eternad.

ORIUNDI
LAZ AUDIOVISUAL LTDA. Sept., 1999. Brazilian. (Ricardo Bravo) Anthony Quinn, Leticia Spiller, Paulo Betti, Gabriela Duarte, Marly Bueno, Raquel Rizzo, Paulo Autran, Lorenzo Quinn, Tiago Real.

ORPHAN
CA.THAR.TIC FILMWORKS. March, 2001. (Richard Moos) Marty Maguire, Charis Michaelson, Robert Wahlberg, Karen MacDonald, Alisa Besher, Charlie Broderick.

THE ORPHAN MUSES
FILM TONIC. Nov., 2000. Canadian. (Robert Favreau) Marina Orsini, Celine Bonnier, Fanny Mallette, Stephane Demers, Louise Portal, Patrick Labbe, Eric Hoziel, Paul Dion.

THE ORPHAN OF ANYANG
May, 2001. Chinese. (Wang Chao) Zhu Jie, Sun Guilin, Yue Senyi, Liu Tianhao, Miao Fuwen.

ORSON WELLES IN THE LAND OF DON QUIXOTE
CANAL PLUS (SPAIN). Nov., 2000. Spanish. (Carlos F. Heredero, Esteve Riambau) Documentary.

OSAKA STORY
KINDAI EIGA KYOKA. Oct., 1999. Japanese. (Jun Ichikawa) Chizuru Ikewaki, Kenju Sawada, Yuko Tanaka.

OSKAR AND LENI
BASIS FILM. Feb., 1999. German. (Petra Katharina Wagner) Christian Redl, Anna Thalbach, Elisabeth Trissenaar, Reiner Heise.

OSMOSIS JONES
WARNER BROS. Aug., 2001. (Piet Kroon, Tom Sito) Animated. Bill Murray, Molly Shannon, Chris Elliott, Elena Franklin, Danny Murphy.

OTESANEK
ATHANOR (CZECH RE.) ILLUMINATIONS FILMS (U.K.). Sept., 2000. Czech Republic-British. (Jan Svankmajer) Veronika Zilkova, Jan Hartl.

THE OTHER
MISR INTERNATIONAL. MAY, 1999. French-Egyptian. (Youssef Chahine) Nabila Ebeid, Mahmoud Hemeida, Hanane tork, Hani Salama, Lebleba.

THE OTHER CONQUEST
CARRASCO & DOMINGO FILMS/SECRETARIA DE DESARROLLO SOCIAL/CONACULTA/FONCA/IMCINE/TABASCO FILMS. May, 1999. Mexican. (Salvador Carrasco) Damian Delgado, Jose Carlos Rodriguez, Elpidia Carrillo, Inaki Aierra, Honorato Magaloni.

OTHER GIRLS
REZO FILMS/TS PRODS. Apr., 2000. French. (Caroline Vignal) Julie Leclercq, Benoite Sapim, Caroline Baehr, Jean-Francois Gallotte, Bernard Menez.

THE OTHERS
DIMENSION FILMS. July, 2001. (Alejandro Amenabar) Spanish-U.S. Nicole Kidman, Christopher Eccleston, Fionnula Flanagan, Elaine Cassidy, Eric Sykes, Alakina Mann, James Bentley.

THE OTHER SIDE
ALTAFILMS. Sept., 2000. Spanish. (Salvador Garcia Ruiz) Alex Casanovas, Jorge Alcazar, Alberto Ferreiro, Pepa Pedroche.

THE OTHER SIDE OF THE TRACKS
FRANCE 2/LITTLE BEAR. Oct., 1998. French. (Bertrand Tavernier). Documentary.

THE OTHER SISTER
BUENA VISTA. FEB. 1999. (Garry Marshall) Juliette Lewis, Diane Keaton, Tom Skerritt, Giovanni Ribisi, Poppy Montgomery.

OTHER STORIES
RIOFILME. May, 1999. Brazilian. (Pedro Bial) Paulo Jose, Walderez De Barros, Caca Carvalho, Chico Neto, Juca De Oliveira.

OTHER VOICES
UNAPIX ENTERTAINMENT/CHARNY/STRONG/REDWOOD COMM./PHANTOM LIMBS PLAYS & PICTURES. Jan., 2000. (Dan McCormack) Mary McCormack, David Aaron Baker, Campbell Scott, Rob Morrow, Stockard Channing, Peter Gallagher, Ricky Aiello.

OTHER WORLD
Aug., 2001. French-Algerian. (Merzak Allouache) Marie Brahimi, Karim Bouaiche, Nazim Boudjenah, Michelle Moretti, Abdelkrim Bahloul.

OTOMO
FILMGALERIE 451/ZDF MAINZ. Jan., 2000. German. (Frieder Schlaich) Isaach de Bankole, Eva Mattes, Hanno Friedrich, Barnaby Metschurat, Lara Kugler, Sigrid Burkholder.

OT: OUR TOWN
April, 2002. (Scott Hamilton Kenedy) Documentary.

OUCH
PIERRE GRISE PRODS./FMB/CANAL PLUS/CNC. Aug., 2000. French. (Sophie Fillieres) Andre Dussollier, Helene Fillieres, Emmanuelle Devos, Anne Le Ny, Lucienne Hamon, Alain Rimou.

OUR AMERICA
Jan., 2002. (Ernest Dickerson) Josh Charles, Vanessa Williams, Roderick Pannell, Brandon Hammond, Mykelti Williamson, Peter Paige, Irma P. Hall.

OUR FATHER
May, 2002. French-Chad. (Mahamat-Saleh Haroun) Ahidjo Mahamat Moussa, Hamza Moctar Aguid, Zara Haroun.

OUR HAPPY LIVES
MARS FILMS. May, 1999. French. (Jacques Maillot) Marie Payen Cecile Richard Camille Japy, Sami Bouajila, Eric Bonicatto.

OUR ISLAND IN THE SOUTH PACIFIC
SENATOR FILM. May, 1999. German. (Thomas Bahmann) Herbert Knaup, Andrea Sawitzki, Alexandra Maria Lara.

OUR LADY OF THE ASSASSINS
LES FILMS DU LOSANGE/LE STUDIO CANAL PLUS/VERTIGO FILMS/TUCAN /CANAL PLUS. Sept., 2000. French-Colombian. (Barbet Schroeder) German Jaramillo, Anderson Ballesteros, Juan David Restrepo, Manuel Busquets.

OUR LOVE
HUNNIA FILMSTUDIO/GAMBI/TV POLSKA/MMK/RTL/KLUB/ORTT/ MTV. Feb., 2000. Hungarian-Polish. (Jozsef Pacskovszky) Melinda Major, Lajos Bartok, Erik Desfosses, Jan Kidawa-Blonski.

OUR SONG
INDEPENDENT FILM CHANNEL/BEECH HILL FILMS/JOURNEYMAN PICTURES/C-HUNDRED FILM CORP. Jan., 2000. (Jim McKay) Kerry Washington, Anna Simpson, Melissa Martinez, Marlene Forte, Ray Anthony Thomas, Rosalyn Coleman, Carmen Lopez.

OUR TIMES
Feb., 2002. Iranian. (Bani-Etemad) Documentary.

OUR YEARS
PABLO DISTRIBUZIONE. Nov., 2000. Italian. (Daniele Gaglianone) Virgilio Biei, Piero Franzo, Giuseppe Boccalatte, Massimo Miride, Enrico Saletti, Luigi Salerno, Diego Canteri.

OUT COLD
BUENA VISTA. Nov., 2001. (Brendan and Emmett Malloy) Jason London, Lee Majors, Willie Garson, Zach Galifianakis.

THE OUTFITTERS
PORCHLIGHT. Jan., 1999. (Reverge Anselmo) Danny Nucci, Del Zamora, Sarah Iassez, Dana Delany, Jerry Haynes.

AN OUTGOING WOMAN
MARS FILMS/SUNDAY MORNING PRODS./RHONE ALPES CINEMA/GROUPE TS/CNC/CANAL PLUS/SOFIGA/GIMAGES 2. Feb., 2000. French. (Christophe Blanc) Agnes Jaoui, Serge Riaboukine, Sarah Haxaire, Richard Morgieve.

OUTLAW
COLUMBIA TRISTAR. Apr., 1999. Italian. (Enzo Monteleone) Stefano Accorsi, Giovanni Esposito, Eilio Solfrizzi.

OUT OF CONTROL
Aug., 2002. British. (Dominic Savage) David Morrissey, Tamzin Outhwaite, Jamie Foreman, Frank Harper, Danny Young, Leo Gregory.

OUT OF DEPTH
REDBUS FILMS. May, 1999. British. (Simon Marshall) Sean Maguire, Danny Midwinter, Nicholas Ball, Phil Cornwall, Josephine Butler.

OUT OF SIGHT
UNIVERSAL PICTURES. June, 1998. (Steven Soderbergh) George Clooney, Jennifer Lopez, Ving Rhames, Don Cheadle, Dennis Farina.

OUT OF THE BLACK
DIVERSA FILMS. July, 2001. (Karl Kozak) Tyler Christpher, Sally Kirkland, Dee Wallace Stone, Jack Conley, Jacqueline Aries, Jason Widener, Sally Struthers.

OUT OF THE CITY
FALCON. July, 2001. Czech Republic. (Tomas Vorel) Tomas Hanak, Barbora Nimcova, Michal Vorel.

OUT OF THE CLOSET, OFF THE SCREEN: THE WILLIAM HAINES STORY
WORLD OF WONDER. June, 2001. (Fenton Bailey, Randy Barbato) Christopher Lawford, Chris Allen, Herb Gore, Bob WIldman, Stockard Channing. Documentary.

OUT OF THE COLD
OLD TOWN. Aug., 1999. Estonian-Russian. (Sasha Buravsky) Keith Carradine, Mia Kirschner, Brian Dennehy, Judd Hirsch, Mercedes Ruehl.

OUT OF TIBET
LICHTBLICK. Jan., 2001. German. (Solveig Klaben) Documentary.

THE OUT-OF-TOWNERS
PARAMOUNT. Mar., 1999. (Sam Weisman) Steve Martin, Goldie Hawn, Mark McKinney, John Cleese, Oliver Hudson.

OUTSIDE OZONA
SONY. Dec. 1998. (J. S. Cardone) Robert Forster, Kevin Pollak, Sherlyn Fenn, David Paymer, Penelope Ann Miller.

OUTSIDE PROVIDENCE
MIRAMAX. July, 1999. (Michael Corrente) Shawn Hatosy, Jon Abrahams, Tommy Bone, Jonathan Brandis, Jack Ferver.

THE OUTSKIRTS
MORNING OF THE XXI CENTURY STUDIO/GOSKINO OF RUSSIA. Oct., 1998. Russian. (Petr Lutsik) Yuri Dubrovin, Nikolai Olyalin, Alexei Pushkin, Alexei Vanin, Rimma Markova.

OUTTAKES
Jan., 2000. (Katherine Brooks, Karen Klopfenstein) Katherine Brooks, Karen Klopfenstein, Sean Carlos Larkin.

OUTTA TIME
PATHFINDER PICTURES. April, 2002. (Lorena David) Mario Lopez, Emma Cross - Tava Smiley, Carlos Mencia, Ali Landry, Richard Cox, Gary Cervantes, Dyana Ortelli, Nancy O'Dell.

OVER THE RAINBOW
ARSENAL FILMVERLEIH/LE VISION/FERNSEHPRODUKTION/ MITTELDEUTSCHER RUNDFUNK. July, 2000. German. (Jan Peter) Mareike Fell, Annett Renneberg, Mina Tander, Pascal Ulli.

OWLS' CASTLE
TOHO/OWLS' CASTLE PROJECT/FUJI TELEVISION/HYOGENSHA. May, 2000. Japanese. (Masahiro Shinoda) Kiichi Nakai, Mayu Tsuruta.

OWNED
May,, 2002. (Jennifer Read) Documentary.

P

PACHITO REX–I'M LEAVING BUT NOT FOR GOOD
CENTRO DE CAPACITACION CINEMATOGRAFICA, IMCINE, CONACULTA, ESTUDIOS CHURUBUSCO AZTECA. March, 2001. Mexican. (Fabian Hofman) Jorge Zarate, Ernesto Gomez Cruz, Ana Ofelia Murguia, Fernando Torre Lapham, Damian Alcazar, Arturo Rios, Lisa Owen.

PAIN IS...
Les Films d'Ici/Urbane Ltd./ZDF/Arte. Oct., 1998. French-German-British. (Stephen Dwoskin). Documentary.

A PAINTING FOR LOVE
FARABI CINEMA FOUNDATION. May, 1999. Iranian. (Hosseinali Lialastani) Farrokh Nemati, Jahangir Almasi, Fateme Goudarzi, Jamshid Layegh.

PALERMO WHISPERS
SOLOFILM. Aug., 2001. Italian. (Wolf Gaudlitz) Mimmo Cuticchio, Francesco Di Gangi, Simone Genovese, Sergio Lo Verde, Giuseppe La Licata, Toti Palma, Donatella Febraro.

PALMER'S PICK-UP
WINCHESTER FILMS. Mar., 1999. (Christopher Coppola) Robert Carradine, Richard Hillman, Patrick Kilpatrick, Neil Guintoli.

PANDAEMONIUM
BBC FILMS/MARINER FILMS/ARTS COUNCIL OF ENGLAND/ MOONSTONE. Sept., 2000. British. (Julien Temple) Linue Roache, John Hannah, Samantha Morton, Emily Woof, Emma Fielding, Andy Serkis, Samuel West.

THE PANDORA PROJECT
CINE/TEL. May, 1998. (Jim Wynorski, John Terlesky) Daniel Baldwin, Erika Eleniak, Richard Tyson, Tony Todd, Jeff Yagher, Bo Jackson.

PANDORA'S BEAUTY
ALLIANCE ATLANTIS/CITE-AMERIQUE/SODEC/TELEFILM CANADA/ CANADIAN TELEVISION FUND/SOCIETE RADIO-CANADASUPER ECRAN. Feb., 2000. Canadian. (Charles Biname) Pascale Bussieres, Jean-Francois Casabonne, Maude Guerin, Gary Boudreault, Pascale Montpetit, Annick Bergeron.

PANDORA'S BOX
RAINFOREST FILMS. June, 2002. (Rob Hardy) Monica Calhoun, Michael Jai White, Kristoff St. John, Tyson Beckford, Joey Lawrence, Chrystale Wilson.

PANIC
BAC FILMS/VAULT/MAD CHANCE. Sept., 2000. (Henry Bromell) William H. Macy, John Ritter, Neve Campbell, Donald Sutherland, Tracey Ullman, Barbara Bain, David Dorfman.

PANIC ROOM
SONY PICTURES ENTERTAINMENT. March, 2002. (David Fincher) Jodie Foster, Kristen Stewart, Forest Whitaker, Dwight Yoakam, Jared Leto, Patrick Bauchau, Ann Magnuson.

PAN TADEUSZ
HERITAGE FILMS/LES FILMS DU LOSANGE/CANAL PLUS POLAND/LE STUDIO CANAL PLUS/VISION FILM//APOLLO FILM /FILM ART/MAX FILM/NEPTUNE FILM/ODRA FILM/SILESIA Film. Feb., 2000. Polish-French. (Andrzej Wajda) Boguslaw Linda, Daniel Olbrychski, Andrzej, Seweryn.

PAPARAZZI
FILMAURO. Jan., 1999. Italian. (Neri Parenti). Christian De Sica, Massimo Boldi, Diego Abatantuono, Roberto Brunetti, Nin D'Angelo.

PAPER
DB. Jan., 2000. Chinese. (Ding Jiancheng) Chen Ying, Dan Da, Zhou Zhe, Cong Zhijun, Zhou Yunpeng.

PAPERBACK HERO
POLYGRAM. Feb., 1999. Australian. (Antony J. Bowman) Claudia Karvan, Hugh Jackman, Angie Milliken.

PARADISE FALLS
MECEO PRODS. Aug., 1998. (Nick Sercy) Sean Bridgers, Christopher Berry, Nick Searcy, Sonny Shroyer, Claire Eye.

A PARADISE UNDER THE STARS
ICAIC/WANDA/IBSERMEDIA/SPANISH TV. Jan., 2000. Cuban-Spanish. (Gerardo Chijona) Thais Valdes, Vladimir Cruz, Ampoaro Munoz, Enrique Molina.

PARADISO–SEVEN DAYS WITH SEVEN WOMEN
MOANA-FILM. Feb., 2000. German. (Rudolf Thome) Hanns Zischler, Cora Frost, Adriana Altaras, Sabine Bach, Khyana El Bitar, Irm Hermann, Isabel Hindersin, Amelie zur Muhlen.

PARAGRAPH 175
TELLING PICTURES. Jan., 2000. (Rob Epstein, Jeffrey Friedman). Documentary.

PARALLEL WORLDS
TOSARA/CZECH TV/ARTCAM. Aug., 2001. Czech Republic-Dutch. (Petr Vaclav) Lenka Vlasakova, Karel Roden, Jitka Schneiderova, Gabina Skrabakova, Marek Daniel, Petra Ernyeiova.

A PARALYZING FEAR:
THE STORY OF POLIO IN AMERICA
BELLEVUE FILMS. Feb., 1998. (Nina Gilden Seavey) Nina Dickens, Lillian Folley, Hermine Douglas, Alan Douglas, Anisa Dickens.

PARANOID
PORTMAN/SKY PICTURES/ISLE OF MAN FILM COMM./PAUL TRIJBITS/GARETH NEAME. May, 2000. British. (John Duigan) Jessica Alba, Iain Glen, Jeanne Tripplehorn, Ewen Bremner, Kevin Whately, Oliver Milburn, Amy Phillips, Gary Love, David Fahm.

THE PARENT TRAP
BUENA VISTA. July, 1998. (Nancy Meyers) Lindsay Lohan, Dennis Quaid, Natasha Richardson, Elaine Hendrix, Lisa Ann Walter.

PARIAH
NOSY BE. April, 2001. French. (Nicolas Klotz) Cyril Troley, Gerald Thomassin, Didier Berestelsky, Morgane Hainaux, Aristide Demonico, Nouredine Barour, Emel Ghomari.

PARIS
DOUBLE D COPYRIGHT FILMS. Aug., 1998. French. (Raymond Depardon) Sylvie Peyre, Luc Delahaye, Emilie Lafarge, Barbara Jung, Metilde Weyergans.

PARIS, MY LITTLE BODY IS AWEARY
OF THIS GREAT WORLD
OGNON PICTURES/GALATEE FILMS. Aug., 1999. French. (Franssou Prenant) Manuel Cedron, Cecile Garcia Fogel, Franssou Prenant

PARIS: XY
Sept., 2001. French. (Zeka Laplaine) Sylvia Vaudano, Zeka Laplaine, Pilou Ioua, Lisa Edmonson, Moussa Sene Absa.

PARK
HIGH-HAT FILMS. Aug., 2000. Irish. (John Carney, Tom Hall) Des Nealon, Jayne Snow, Claudia Terry, Pat Laffin, Aidan Walshe.

PARK DAY
CLANDESTINE ENTERTAINMENT. Nov., 1998. (Sterling Macer, Jr.) Hill Harper, Monica Calhoun, Lande Scott, Brock Peters.

THE PAROLE OFFICER
UIP (IN U.K.)/UNIVERSAL FOCUS (IN U.S.). July, 2001. British. (John Duigan) Steve Coogan, Lena Headey, Stephen Dillane, Om Puri, Steven Waddington, Ben Miller, Jenny Agutter, Emma Williams.

PARSLEY DAYS
A.D. PICTURES (HALIFAX). Oct., 2000. Canadian. (Megan Dunlop, Mike Le Blanc, Marla MacLean, Kenneth Harrington, Marcia Connolly, Shannon Cunningham.

PARTNERS OF THE HEART
June, 2002. (Andrea Kalin) Documentary.

THE PARTY CRASHERS
CINEMA ARTS. Feb. 1999. (Phil Leirness) John Saxon, Max Parrish, Peter Murnik, Shawnee Smith, Phil Leirness.

PARTY MONSTER
WORLD OF WONDER. Feb., 1998. (Fenton Bailey, Randy Barbato) Documentary.

PARTY 7
INTRINSIC. Nov., 2000. Japanese. (Katsuhit Ishii) Masatoshi Nagase, Keisuke Horibe, Toshinori Okada, Akemi Kobayashi, Tadanobu Asano, Yoshio Harada, Tatsuya Gasyuin.

THE PASSENGERS
LES FILMS DU LOSANGE. Apr., 1999. French. (Jean-Claude Guiguet) Fabienne Babe, Philippe Garziano, Bruno Putzulu, Stephane Rideau, Gwenaelle Simon.

PASSING DARKNESS
KOMMUNENES FILMSENTRAL/BARENTSFILM/NORSK FILM/BV FILM. Jan., 2000. Norwegian. (Knut Erik Jensen) Stig Henrik Hoff, Snorre Tindberg, Gunnel Lindblom, Gorild Mauseth, Nicholas Hope.

PASSING STONES
PASSING STONES. Jan., 2001. (Roger Majkowski) Roger Majkowski, Tom Ellis, Thomas Majkowski, Orlagh Cassidy, Elizabeth Van Meter, Anita Keel, Jed Zion.

PASSING SUMMER
PERIPHER FILMVERLEIH. Feb., 2001. German. (Angela Schanelec) Ursina Lardi, Andreas Patton, Anne Tismer, Wolfgang Michael, Sophie Aigner, Clara Enge, Nina Weniger, Devid Striesow.

PASSION
REP. June, 1999. Australian-U.S. (Peter Duncan) Barbara Hershey, Richard Roxburgh, Emily Woof, Claudia Karvan, Simon Burke.

PASSIONATELY
OCEAN/FILM PAR FILM/FRANCE 3 CINEMA/TPS/COFIMAGE 10. June, 2000. French. (Bruno Nuytten) Gerard Lanvin, Charlotte Gainsbourg, Eric Ruf, Liliane Rovere, Tania Da Costa, Berenice Bejo, Catherine Sola, Angelica Chaves.

PASSION BOULEVARD
ROI STUDIO. Feb., 2000. Russian. (Vladimir Khotinenko) Sergei Koltakov, Nina Usatova, Vladimir Ilyin, Sergei Garmash, Sergei Parshin, Elena Starodub.

THE PASSION OF AYN RAND
SHOWTIME. Jan., 1999. (Christopher Menaul) Helen Mirren, Eric Stoltz, Julie Delpy, Peter Fonda, Tom McCamus.

PASSION OF MIND
PARAMOUNT CLASSIC/LAKESHORE ENTERTAINMENT/RON BASS PRODS. Apr., 2000. (Alain Berline) Demi Moore, Stellan Skarsgard, William Fichtner, Sinead Cusack, Peter Riegert, Joss Ackland, Eloise Eonnet.

PASSPORT
DUNA TV/TV2. Feb, 2001. Hungarian. (Peter Gothar) Eniko Borcsok, Gergely Kocsis, Mari Nagy, Eva Feher, Istvan Medgyesi, Gabor Kocso.

THE PAST
WORLD CIRCLE/CZECH TV/UNION OF THE DEAF & HARD OF HEARING , CZECH REP. Aug., 1999. Czech. (Ivo Trajkov) Karel Zima, Klara Melisova, Peter Georgiev.

PATCH ADAMS
UNIVERSAL. Dec., 1998. (Tom Shadyac) Robin Williams, Daniel London, Monica Potter, Philip Seymour Hoffman, Bob Gunton.

PATHOS
HARVEST FILMS (KERALA). Sept., 2000. Indian. (Jayaraaj) Vavachan, Eliyamma, Biju Menon, Madambu, K.K. Jacob.

PATHS IN THE NIGHT
O-FILM/ZDF. May, 1999. German. (Andreas Kleinert) Hilmar Thate, Cornelia Schamus, Henriette Heinze.

PATRIOT
SONY PICTURES ENTERTAINMENT/COLUMBIA PICTURES/ MUTUAL FILM CO./CENTROPOLIS ENTERTAINMENT. June, , 2000. (Roland Emmerich) Mel Gibson, Heath Ledger, Joely Richardson, Jason Isaacs, Chris Cooper, Tcheky Karyo.

PAUL AND HIS BROTHER
LAUREN FILMS. April, 2001. Spanish-French. (Marc Recha) David Selvas, Nathalie Boutefeu, Marieta Orozco, Luis Hostalot.

PAULINE AND PAULETTE
SONY PICTURES CLASSICS (IN U.S.). May, 2001. Belgian-French-Dutch. (Lieven Debrauwer) Dora van der Groen, Ann Petersen.

PAUL IS DEAD
X FILME CREATIVE POOL. Jan., 2001. German. (Hendrik Handloegten) Sebastian Schmidtke, Vasko Scholz, Martin Reinhold, Myriam Abeillon, Ian T. Dickinson, Rainer Egger.

PAULIE
DREAMWORKS PICTURES. April, 1998. (John Roberts) Gena Rowlands, Tony Shalhoub, Cheech Marin, Bruce Davison, Jay Mohr, Trini Alvarado, Buddy Hackett.

PAULINA
CINEMAMAS. March, 1998. (Vicky Funari) Paulina Cruz Suarez, Mathyselene Heredia Castillo, Mariam Manzano Duran.

PAVILION OF WOMEN
UNIVERSAL PICTURES. April, 2001. (Yim Ho) Willem Dafoe, Luo Yan, Shek Sau, John Cho, Yi ding, Koh Chieng Mun, Anita Loo, Amy Hill, Kate McGregor-Stewart.

PAYBACK
PARAMOUNT. Feb., 1999. (Brian Helgeland) Mel Gibson, Gregg Henry, Maria Bello, Deborah Kara Unger, David Paymer.

PAY IT FORWARD
WARNER BROS. Oct., 2000. (Mimi Leder) Kevin Spacey, Helen Hunt, Haley Joel Osment, Jay Mohr, James Caviezel, Jon Bon Jovi, Angie Dickinson, David Ramsey.

PAZ!
MIKADO. Feb., 2002. Italian. (Renato De Maria) Claudio Santamaria, Flavio Pistilli, Max Mazzotta, Fabrizia Sacchi, Cristiano Callegaro, Matteo Taranto.

PEACHES
ABBEY FILMS. Nov., 2000. Irish. (Nick Grosso) Matthew Rhys, Kelly Reilly, Justin Salinger, Matthew Dunster, Sophie Okonedo, Emily Hillier, Stephanie Bagshaw.

PECKER
FINE LINE. July, 1998. (John Waters) Edward Furlong, Christina Ricci, Mary Kay Place, Martha Plimpton, Mink Stole, Lili Taylor.

PEDESTRIAN
PEDESTRIAN PRODS. June, 2000. (Jason Kartalian) Jeffrey Stubblefield, Melissa Marie Lewis, Joe Seely, Krikor Satamian, Jerry Corley, Buck Kartalian, Jack Sanderson, Kevin E. West, Peter Onorati.T
TESELA. Aug., 2000. Spanish. (Achero Manas) Juan Jose Ballesta, Pablo Galan, Alberto Gimenez, Manuel Maron, Ana Wagener.

THE PENITENT'S TREE
COLUMBIA TRISTAR SPAIN/KANZAMAN PRODUCTION/VIA DIGITAL. Apr., 2000. Spanish. (Jose Maria Borell) Javier Manrique, Elena Anaya, Alfredo Landa, Ildefonso Tamayo.

THE PENKNIFE
BOS BROS. Oct., 1998. Dutch. (Ben Sombogaart) Olivier Tuinier, Genio de Groot, Adelheid Roosen, Verno Romney.

PEOPLE IN SWIMSUITS AREN'T (NECESSARILY) SHALLOW
OCEAN FILM. Jan., 2001. French. (Eric Assous) Isabelle Gelinas, Serge Hazanavicius, Agnes Soral, Veronique Boulanger, Gad Elmaleh, Yasmine Belmadi, Maher Kamoun.

PEOPLE WHO LOVE EACH OTHER
BLUE DAHLIA PROD., LE STUDIO CANAL PLUS, FRANCE 3 CINEMA, JCT PRODS./ARTEMIS PROD./SAMSA FILM/TORNASOL FILMS. June, 1999. French-Belgian-Luxembourgois. (Jean-Charles Tacchella) Richard Berry, Jacqueline Bisset, Jule Gayet, Bruno Putzulu, Marie Collins.

PEPE GUINDO
ALTA FILMS. Aug., 1999. Spanish. (Manuel Iborra) Fernando Fernan-Gomez, Veronica Forque, Antonio Resines, Jorge Sanz, Yael Barnatan.

PEPPERMINT CANDY
UNIKOREA/DREAM VENTURE CAPITAL/EAST FILM/NHK. Oct., 1999. South Korean-Japanese. (Lee Chang-dong) Seol Kyeong-gu, Mun So-ri, Kim Yeo-jin.

PEP SQUAD
TROMA ENTERTAINMENT. May, 1998. (Steve Balderson) Jennifer Dreiling, Brooke Balderson, Amy Kelly, Adrian Pejol.

PERFECT BLUE
PALM PICTURES/MANGA/REX ENTERTAINMENT. Oct., 1999. Japanese. (Satoshi Kon). Animated.

THE PERFECT EDUCATION
SHOCHIKU CO. LTD. Aug., 1999. Japanese. (Ben Wada) Naoto Takenaka, Hijiri Kojima, Eriko Watanabe, Kazuki Kitamura.

A PERFECT MURDER
WARNER BROS. May, 1998. (Andrew Davis) Michael Douglas, Gwyneth Paltrow, Vigo Mortensen, David Suchet, Sarita Choudhury.

PERFECT SITE
BAVARIA FILM INTL. Jan., 2001. German. (Soren Voigt) Ill Young Kim, Henriette Heinze, Paul Faanact, Astrid Meyersfeldt, Fritz Roth, Julia Hummer, Samuel Fintzi, Michi Fanselow.

THE PERFECT SON
EQUINOX ENTERTAINMENT. Sept., 2000. Canadian. (Leonard Farlinger) Com Feore, David Cubitt, Chandra West, John Boylan.

THE PERFECT STORM
WARNER BROS./BALTIMORE SPRING CREEK PICTURES/RADIANT PRODS. June, 2000. (Wolfgang Petersen) George Clooney, Mark Wahlberg, John C. Reilly, Diane Lane, William Fichtner, John Hawkes, Allen Payne, Mary Elizabeth Mastrantonio.

PERFUME
LIONS GATE FILMS. Jan., 2001. (Michael Rymer) Joanne Baron, Angela Bettis, Sonia Braga, D.W. Brown, Coolio, Carmen Electra.

PERMANENT MIDNIGHT
ARTISAN ENTERTAINMENT. Sept., 1998. (David Veloz) Ben Stiller, Elizabeth Hurley, Maria Bello, Owen Wilson, Lourdes Benedicto.

THE PERSONALS
EDKO FILMS. Dec., 1998. Taiwanese. (Chen Kuo-fu) Rene Liu, Chen Chao-jung, Wu Pai, Chin Shih-chieh, Ku Pao-ming,.

PERSONALS
THE PERSONALS CO. Oct., 1999, (Mike Sargent) Malik Yoba, Stacey Dash, Monteria Ivey, Rhoda Ross Kendrick, Sheryl Lee Ralph, Jim Gaffigan, Rosalyn Coleman, Delilah Cotto, Angela Bullock.

PERSONAL VELOCITY: THREE PORTRAITS
Jan., 2002. (Rebecca Miller) Narrator: Jon Ventimiglia.

PETTSON AND FINDUS
Svensk Filmindustri/Happy Life/TMO-ToonLand Film. Dec., 1999. Swedish-German. (Albert Hanan Kaminski.). Animated.

PETTY CRIMES
VELVET FILMS. March, 2002. French. (Michel Ferry) Jeremie Covillault, Sarah Zoe Canner, Andrew Pang, Ann Hu.

PHANTOM
ROSA FILMES/RADIOTELEVISAO PORTUGUESA/ICAM/MC. Sept., 2000. Portuguese. (Joao Pedro Rodrigues) Ricardo Meneses, Beatriz Torcato, Andre Barbosa.

PHANTOM BEIRUT
GH FILMS, IDEA PRODS/OPTIMA. Oct., 1998. French-Lebanese. (Ghassan Salhab) Aouni Kawas, Darina Al Joundi, Rabih Mroue.

THE PHANTOM OF THE OPERA
MEDUSA. Nov., 1998. Italian. (Dario Argento). Julian Sands, Asia Argento, Andrea Di Stefano, Nadia Rinaldi, Coralina Cataldi-Tassoni.

PHANTOM, THE SUBMARINE
Ilshin Investment/Uno Films. Oct., 1999. South Korean. (Min Byeong-cheon) Choe Min-su, Cheong Wu-seong, Yun Ju-sang.

PHILANTHROPY
SWIFT DISTRIBUTION. June, 2002. Romanian-French. (Nae Caranfil) Mircea Diaconu, Gheorghe Dinica, Mara Nicolescu, Viorica Voda.

PHOENIX
LAKESHORE ENTERTAINMENT. May, 1998. (Danny Cannon) Ray Liotta, Anthony La Paglia, Anjelica Huston, Daniel Baldwin, Jeremy Piven, Giancarlo Espositio.

PHONE BOOTH
20TH CENTURY FOX. Sept., 2002. (Joel Schumacher) Colin Farrell, Kiefer Sutherland, Forest Whitaker, Radha Mitchell, Katie Holmes, Richard T. Jones, Keith Nobbs, John Enos III.

THE PHOTOGRAPH
MESOPOTAMIA CULTURE CENTRE (CINEMA DEPT.). May, 2002. Turkish. (Kazim Oz) Feyyaz Duman, Nazmi Kirik, Mizgin Kapazan, Muhlis Asan.

PHOTOGRAPHER
SEVENTH ART. Dec., 1998. Polishi-French. (Darius Jablonski). Documentary.

THE PHOTOGRAPHER
PHOTOGRAPHER CO. Apr., 2000. (Jeremy Stein) Reg Rogers, Rob Campbell, Chris Bauer, Kristen Wilson, Maggie Gyllenhaal,.

PHOTOS TO SEND
March, 2002. (Dierdre Lynch) Michael Kenneally, Michael Patsy Flanagan, Kitty Quinn, Bridie Kenneally, Nancy Keane, Bridie Power, Seamus Quinn, Dan Dixon.

THE PIANIST
MASSA D'OR PRODS./TORNASOL. Sept., 1998. Spanish. (Mario Gas) Jordi Molla, Pere Ponce, Paulina Galvez, Laurent Terzieff, Serge Reggiani.

THE PIANIST
BAC DISTRIBUTION (IN FRANCE)/FOCUS (IN U.S.). May, 2002. French-Polish-German-British. (Roman Polanski) Adrien Brody, Thomas Kretschmann, Frank Finlay, Maureen Lipman, Emilia Fox, Ed Stoppard, Julia Rayner.

THE PIANO TEACHER
MK2. May, 2001. Austrian-French. (Michael Haneke) Isabelle Huppert, Annie Girardot, Benoit Magimel, Anna Sigalevitch, Susanne Lothar.

PICASSO FACE
CECCHI GORI DISTRIBUZIONE. Oct., 2000. Italian. (Massimo Ceccherini) Massimo Ceccherini, Alessandro Paci, Marco Giallini, Bianca Guaccero, Yuliya Mayarchuk, Chiara Conti.

PICKAXE
PICKAXE PRODS.Oct., 2000. (Tim Ream, Tim Lewis) Documentary.

PICKPOCKET
ART PORT/EISEI GEJKO CO. Aug., 2000. Japanese. (Kazuo Kuroki) Yoshio Harada, Jun Fubuki, Kirina Mano, Shuji Kashiwabara, Renji Ishibashi, Mituru Hirata, Eruyuki Kagawa, Atushi Kawashima.

PICTURE CLAIRE
ALLIANCE ATLANTIS. Sept. 2001. Canadian. (Bruce McDonald) Juliette Lewis, Gina Gershon, Callum Keith Rennie, Kelly Harms, Camilla Rutherford, Mickey Rourke.

PICTURES DEEP IN ONE'S EYES
WUNDERKAMMER. Sept., 2000. (Giuseppe Rocca) Giusi Saija, Andrea Refuto, Mariagrazia Galasso, Antonio Pennarella, Nuccia Fumo, Olimpia Di Maio, Antonella Stefanucci.

A PIECE OF EDEN
FILMACRES. Oct., 2000. (John Hancock)Marc Grapey, Rebecca Harrell, Robert Breuler, Tyne Daly, Jeff Puckett, Irma St. Paule, Frederic Forrest, Tristan Rogers.

A PIECE OF SKY
VITAM. April, 2002. French-Belgian-Luxembougeois. (Benedicte Lienard) Severine Caneele, Sofia Leboutte, Josiane Stoleru, Naima Hireche, Annick Keusterman, Yolande Moreau.

PIE IN THE SKY: THE BRIGID BERLIN STORY
VINCENT FREMONT ENTERPRISES. Sept., 2000. (Vincent Fremont, Shelly Dunn Fremont) Brigid Berlin, John Waters, Patty Hearst, Paul Morissey, Taylor Mead, Larry Rivers. Documentary.

PIER PAOLO PASOLINI AND THE REASON OF A DREAM
Aug., 2001. Italian-French. (Laura Betti) Documentary.

PIGEONHOLED
ECLIPSE PICTURES. Oct., 1999. (Michael Swanhaus) Justin Pierce, Allison Folland, Galaxy Craze, Tom Lock, Andrea Ciannavei, Jon Abrahams, Chris Noth, Rosanna Arquette.

THE PIG'S RETRIBUTION
SUNCENT CINEMA WORKS. Aug. 1999. (Yohichi Sai) Yukiyoshi Ozawa, Yoshie Hayasaka, Michiko Ameku, Mayumi Ueda.

PILGRIMAGE
Feb., 2002. Indian. (G.R. Kannan) Jayaram, Suhasini, B.R. Prasad, Joshy, Appu, Ashwati, Sreelatha, Swapna Ravi, Radha.

THE PILGRIMAGE OF STUDENTS PETER AND JACOB
CINEART/CZECH TV/SLOVAK TV/KVARTFILM/KRATKY FILM/ MARGO FILMS. July, 2000. Czech-Slovak-French. (Drahomira Vihanova) Adrian Jastraban, Gustav Reznicek, Zuzana Stivinova.

THE PILGRIM FACTOR
TESELA/SEISDEDOS. Aug., 2000. Spanish. (Santi Amoedo, Alberto Rodriguez) Alex O'Dogherty, Enrico Vecchi, Jons Pappila, Simon Edwards, Howard Nightingall, Paul Rattee, Kevin Brock, Jane Paul.

PINERO
MIRAMAX. Aug., 2001. (Leon Ichaso) Benjamin Bratt, Giancarlo Esposito, Talisa Soto, Nelson Vasques, Michael Irby, Michael Wright, Rita Moreno, Jaime Sanchez, Rome Neal, Mandy Patinkin.

PINK PUMPKINS AT DAWN
Jan., 2000. (Rick Onorato) Chris Gunn, Dominique Debroux, Robert Brown, John Stonehill, Rick Onorato, Jeb Eastman, Glory Gallo.

PIN-PON–THE FILM
LIONS GATE/VISION 4/CANADIAN TV FUND/TELEFILM CANADA/ SODEC/QUEBEC & CANADIAN GOV'T./SUPER ECRAN/TELE-QUEBEC. Dec., 1999. Canadian. (Ghyslaine Cote) Thomas Graton, Yves Soutiere, Philippe Lambert, Julien Poulin, Anastassia Fomina, Melven Gilbert, Mireille Levesque.

P.I.N.S.
Cinemedia/Film Victoria/Australian Film Comm./Australian Broadcasting. July, 2000. Australian. (Garth Davis). Documentary.

PISCES
J&J. Feb., 2001. South Korean. (Kim Hyung-tae) Lee Mi-yeon, Choe Woo-je, Yun Ji-hye, Park Kwang-jeong, Park Sun-cheon, Kwak Seung-nam, Lee Jae-kyeong.

PISTOL OPERA
April, 2002. Japanese. (Seijun Suzuki) Makiko Esumi, Sayoko Yamaguchi, Kan Hanae, Masatoshi Nagase.

PIT AND THE PENDULUM
JGM/FULL MOON. May, 1991. (Stuart Gordon) Lance Henriksen, Rona De Ricci, Jonathan Fuller.

PITCH BLACK
USA FILM/GRAMERCY PICTURES/INTERSCOPE COMMUNICATION. Jan., 2000. (David Twohy) Radha Mitchell, Vin Diesel, Cole Hauser, Lewis Fitz-Gerald, Claudia Black, Rhiana Griffith, John Moore, Simon Burke.

PITCH PEOPLE
SJPL FILMS. Oct., 2000. (Stanley Jacobs) Documentary.

PIZZA, BOOZE, SMOKES
PALO Y A LA BOLSA CINE. Sept., 1998. Argentine. (Bruno Stagnaro) Hector Anglada, Jorge Sesan, Pamela Jordan.

PIZZAMAN
Jan., 2002. Hungarian. (Gyorgy Balogh) Andras K. Kovacs, Eva Kreiter, Denes Bernath, Ildiko Incze, Eva Timar, Eniko Detar, Laszlo Szacsvay, Peter Haumann, Karoly Rekasi.

PIZZA WARS: THE MOVIE
Feb., 2002. (Babak Sarrafan) Omar Miller, Andy Sims, Elliot Peele, charisse Loriaux, Chris Murphy, Terrance Camilleri, Heather Rae Gavin.

A PLACE NEARBY
NORDISK FILM/TV2 DENMARK/BG FUND/DANISH FILM INSTITUTE. Feb., 2000. Danish. (Kaspar Rostrup) Ghita Norby, Frits Helmuth, Henning Moritzen, Thure Lindhardt.

A PLACE ON EARTH
ABA STUDIO-MINISTRY OF CULTURE (RUSSIA). May, 2001. Russian. (Artur Aristakisjan) Anna VErdi, Vitaly Khaev.

THE PLACE THAT WAS PARADISE
ALTA FILMS. Jan., 2002. Spanish-Argentine-Brazilian-German. (Gerardo Herrero) Federico Luppi, Elena Ballesteros, Gaston Pauls, Paulina Galvez, Gianfranco Brero, Villanueva Cosse.

PLACIDO RIZZOTTO
ISTITUTO LUCE/ARBASH/RAI. Aug., 2000. Italian. (Pasquale Scimeca.) Marcello Mazzarelli, Gioia Spaziani, Arturo Todaro,.

PLAITS
HERACLES. Nov., 2000. Moroccan. (Jillali Ferhati) Salima Belmoumen, Mohamed Miftah, Ramzi, Fawzi Bensaidi, Salwa Restragui, Mahmoud Ostour.

PLANET ALEX
DE.FLEX-FILM. Jan., 2001. (Uli M. Schuppel) Marusha, Marie Zielcke, Nadeshda Brennicke, Baki Davrak, Ben Becker.

PLANET OF THE APES
20TH CENTURY FOX. July, 2001. (Tim Burton) Mark Wahlberg, Tim Roth, Helena Bonham Carter, Michael Clarke Duncan, Paul Giamatti, Estella Warren, Cary-Hiroyuki Tagawa.

PLASTER CASTER
FRAGMENT FILMS. May, 2001. (Jessica Villines) Documentary.

PLATFORM
HU-TONG COMMUNICATION/T-MARK/ARTCAM INTL./OFFICE KITANO/BANDAI VISUAL. Sept., 2000. Hong Kong-Japanese-French. (Jia Zhang-ke) Wang Hong-wei, Zhao Tao, Liang Jing-dong.

PLAY DEAD
HEADSTRONG ENTERTAINMENT. Jan., 2001. (Jeff Jenkins) Diva Zappa, Nathan Bexton, Sherrie Rose, Jesssica Stone, Jason Hall.

THE PLAYERS CLUB
NEW LINE CINEMA. April, 1998. (Ice Cube) Lisa Raye, Bernie Mac, Monica Calhoun, A.J. Johnson, Ice Cube, Alex Thomas, Jamie Foxx.

PLAY FOR ME
MATEINA PRODS. Feb., 2001. Argentine. (Rodrigo Furth) Hermes Gaido, Laura Frigerio, Alejandro Fiore, Bernardo Perco, Emilio Urdapilleta, Oscar Alegre, Cristian Pinkiewicz.

PLAYING BY HEART
MIRAMAX. Dec., 1998. (Willard Carroll) Gillian Anderson, Angelina Jolie, Madeleine Stowe, Anthony Edwards, Ryan Phillipe.

THE PLAY OF GOD
NEW GENERATION CINEMA. Oct., 1998. Indian. (Jayaraaj) Jatin Bora, Ashish Vidyarthi, Debashree Roy, Nipon Gowami, Mridhula Barua.

PLEASANTVILLE
NEW LINE CINEMA. Sept., 1998. (Gary Ross) Tobey Maguire, Jeff Daniels, Joan Allen, William H. Macy, J. T. Walsh, Reese Witherspoon.

THE PLEDGE
WARNER BROS. Jan., 2001 (Sean Penn) Jack Nicholson, Patricia Clarkson, Benicio Del Toro, Dale Dickey, Aaron Eckhart, Costas Mandylor, Helen Mirren, Tom Noonan, Robin Wright Penn.

PLENILUNE
WARNER SOGEFILMS. Sept., 2000. Spanish. (Imanol Uribe) Miguel Angel Sola, Adriana Ozores, Juan Diego Botto, Fernando Fernan-Gomez, Chete Lera, Charo Lopez.

PLUM BLOSSOM
CINEMA SERVICE. Oct., 2000. South Korean. (Jin Heui-kyeong) Kim Jeong-hyeon, Bae Du-na, Kim Rae-weon, Yun Ji-hye.

PLUMP FICTION
LEGACY. May, 1998. (Bob Koherr) Tommy Davidson, Julie Brown, Paul Dinello, Sandra Bernhard, Dan Castellaneta, Colleen Camp.

PLUNKETT & MACLEANE
POLYGRAM/GRAMMERCY. Mar., 1999. (Jake Scott) Robert Carlyle, Jonny Lee Miller. Liv Tyler, Ken Stott, Michael Gambon.

A POET
S.E.T. AUDIOVISUAL WORKSHOP. Jan., 2001. Indonesian. (Garin Nugroho) Ibrahim Kadir, Berliana Fibrianti, Jose Rizal Manua, Ella Gayo, Fuat Idris.

THE POET AND THE CON
POET PRODS. Sept., 1999. (Eric Trules). Documentary.

POISONS, OR THE WORLD HISTORY OF POISONING
MOSFILM CINEMA CONCERN/COURIER FILM STUDIO. July, 2001. Russian. (Karen Shakhnazarov) Ignat Akrachkov, Oleg Basilashvili, Shanna Dudanova, Aleksandr Bashirov, Olga Tumaikina.

POKEMON 4EVER
MIRAMAX FILMS. Oct., 2002. Japanese. (Kunihiko Yuyama) Veronica Taylor, Rachael Lillis, Eric Stuart, Maddie Blaustein, Ikue Otani, Tara Jayne, Dan Green. Animated.

POKEMON: THE FIRST MOVIE
WARNER BROS./KIDS WB!/PIKACHU PROJECT '98-SHOGAKUKAN/4KIDS ENTERTAINMENT. Nov., 1999. Japanese. (Kunihiko Yuyama) Veronica Taylor, Philip Bartlett, Rachael Lillis, Eric Stuart, (voices).

POKEMON THE MOVIE 2000: THE POWER OF ONE
WARNER BROS./KIDS WB!/PIKACHU PROJECT '99-SHOGAKUKAN/ 4KIDS ENTERTAINMENT. July, 2000. (Kunihiko Yuyama, Michael Haigney). Veronica Taylor, Rachael Lillis, Addie Blaustein, Eric Stuart (voices). Animated.

POKEMON 3 THE MOVIE: SPELL OF THE UNOWN
WARNER BROS. FAMILY ENTERTAINMENT. March, 2001. Japanese. (Kunihiko Yuyama) Veronica Taylor, Rachael Lillis, Eric Stuart.

POLA X
PATHE. May, 1999. French-German-Japanese-Swiss. (Leos Carax) Guillaume Depardieu, Katerina Golubeva, Catherine Deneuve, Delphine Chuillot, Petruta Catana.

POLES APART
LEAD DOG PRODS. July, 2000. (Greg Stiever) Ann Bancroft, Sunniva Sorby, Anne Dal Vera, Sue Giller. Documentary.

POLICEWOMAN
WESTDEUTSCHE UNIVERSUM-FILM/WESTDEUTSCHE RUNDFUNKS. June, 2000. German. (Andreas Dresen) Gabriela Maria Schmeide, Axel Prahl, Paul Grubba, Yevgeni Sitokhin, Katrin Sass, Horst Krause.

POLISH WEDDING
FOX SEARCHLIGHT. July, 1998. (Theresa Connelly) Lena Olin, Gabriel Byrne, Claire Danes, Adam Trese, Mili Avital.

THE POLITICS OF FUR
June, 2002. (Laura Nix) Katy Selverstone, Brynn Horrocks, T. Jerram Young, Carolyn Mignini, Craig Villarubia, Jonathan Bierner.

POLLOCK
SONY PICTURES CLASSICS/BRANT-ALLEN/ZEKE FILMS/ED HARRIS/FRED BERNER FILMS. Sept., 2000. (Ed Harris) Ed Harris, Marcia Gay Harden, Amy Madigan, Jennifer Connelly, Jeffrey Tambor, Bud Cort, John Heard, Val Kilmer.

POP & ME
RICHARD AND CHRIS ROE. Apr., 1999. (Chris Roe). Documentary.

POPCORN
FIM PLUSS KFT. Feb., 1999. Hungarian. (Peter Gabor) Tamas J. Toth, Ferenc Karsai, Zsolt Gonda, Sarolta Zoldhegyi.

POP IN REYKJAVIK
101 LTD. Mar., 2000. Icelandic. (Agust Jakobsson) Bang Gang, Bellatrix, Botnleoja, Curver, DJ Addi, Ensimi, Gus Gus, Hringir, Magga Stirina, Maus, Moa, Pall Oskar & Casino.

POOLHALL JUNKIES
June, 2002. (Mars Callahan) Chazz Palminteri, Rick Schroder, Rod Steiger, Michael Rosenbaum, Mars Callahan, Alison Eastwood, Christopher Walken.

POOR WHITE TRASH
KINGSIZE ENTERTAINMENT. June, 2000. (Michael Addis) Sean Young, William Devane, Jason London, Tony Denman.

POOTIE TANG
PARAMOUNT. June, 2001. (Louis C.K.) Lance Crouther, Jennifer Coolidge, Wanda Sykes, Robert Vaughn, Chris Rock, Dave Attell, Reg E. Cathey, JB Smoove.

PORNO FILM
E-MOTION FILM/TV Slovenia production. July, 2000. Slovernian. (Damjan Kozole) Matjaz Latin, Natalia Danilova, Primoz Petkovsek.

THE PORNOGRAPHER
INTEGRITY PICTURES. Mar., 1999. (Doug Atchison) Michael DeGood, Craig Wasson, Monique Parent, Katheryn Cain, Todd Feder.

THE PORNOGRAPHER
HAUT & COURT. April, 2001. French-Canadian. (Bertrand Bonello) Jean-Pierre Leaud, Jeremie Renier, Dominique Blanc, Thibault De Montalembert, Andre Marcon, Catherine Mouchet.

A PORNOGRAPHIC AFFAIR
FINE LINE FEATURES. Sept., 1999. Belgian-French. (Frederic Fonteyne) Nathalie Baye, Sergi Lopez.

PORNOSTAR
LITTLE MORE CO. Dec., 1999. Japanese. (Toshiaki Toyoda) Koji Chihara, Onimaru, Rin Ozawa, Tetta Sugimoto, Akaji Maro, Reona Hirota.

PORTRAIT OF GOD
Aug., 2001. Danish. (Jon Bang Carlsen) Documentary.

PORTLAND STREET BLUES
EVERWIDE. Oct., 1998. Hong Kong. (Raymond Yip) Sandra Ng, Kristy Yeung, Alex Fong, Vincent Wan, Shu Q.

THE PORT OF LAST RESORT
Pinball Films/Estrafilm/Home Box Office. Oct., 1999. Austrian. (Joan Grossman, Paul Rosdy) Fred Fields, Ernest Heppner, Illo Heppner, Siegmar Simon. Documentary.

PORTUGUESE
HUNNIA FILM STUDIO. Feb., 2000. Hungarian. (Andor Lukats) Imre Csuja, Reka Pelsoczy, Agi Szirtes, Ferenc Lengyel, Zoltan Varga, Jozsef Kelemen, Zsolt Kovacs, Viktor Nagy, Eszter Onodi.

POSSESSED
ZENTROPA ENTERTAINMENTS/DRTV DANISH BROADCASTING CORP./SVT. May, 1999. Danish. (Anders Ronnow-Klarlund) Udo Kier, Ole Lemmeke, Kirsti Eline Torhaug, Ole Ernst, Neils Anders Thorn, Jesper Langberg.

POSSESSION
FOCUS FEATURES. April, 2002. U.S.-British. (Neil LaBute) Gwyneth Paltrow, Aaron Eckhart, Jeremy Northam, Jennifer Ehle, Lena Headey, Toby Stephens, Tom Hickey, Trevor Eve.

POSSIBLE LOVES
20TH CENTURY FOX BRAZIL. Jan., 2001. Brazilian. (Sandra Werneck) Murilo Benicio, Carolina Ferraz, Emilio de Mello.

POSSUMS
HSX FILMS/KUSHNER-LOCKE. June, 1998. (J. Max Burnett) Mac Davis, Cynthia Sikes, Gregory Coolidge, Andrew Prine.

POST CONCUSSION
DANIEL D. YOON. Oct., 1999. (Daniel Yoon) Daniel Yoon, Jennifer Welch, Michael Hohmeyer, Niloufar Talebi, C.B. Yoon, Kristy Bright, Felecia Faulkner, Dr. Lester Luz.

POSTHUMOUS MEMORIES
CINEMATOGRAFICAN SUPERFILMES. Feb., 2001. Brazilian-Portuguese. (Andre Klotzel) Reginaldo Faria, Petronio Gontijo, Vietia Rocha, Sonia Bragaa, Otavio Muller, Marcos Caruso.

POSTMAN BLUES
SUPLEX INC. Nov., 1998. Japanese. (Sabu) Shinichi Tsutsumi, Keiko Tohyama, Ren Ohsugi, Keisuke Horibe.

POSTMARK PARADISE
ENTERTAINMENT PARADISE GROUP. Oct., 2000. (Thompson Clay) Natalia Nazarova, Tantoo Cardinal, Vincent Angelini, Randall Godwin.

POST MORTEM
FILM TONIC. Aug., 1999. Canadian. (Louis Belanger) Gabriel Arcand, Sylvie Moreau, Helene Loiselle, Sarah Lecompte-Bergeron.

POTESTAD
Aug., 2002. Argentine. (Luis Cesar D'Angiolillo) Pavlovsky, Lorenzon Quinteros, Luis Machin, Noemi Frenkel, Alejo Garcia Pintos, Susy Evans, Maria Victoria Biscay.

P.O.V.–POINT OF VIEW
Sept., 2001. Danish. (Tomas Gislason) Trine Dyrholm, Gareth Williams, Ulrich Thomsen.

POWDER
TRIANGELFILM. Jan., 2001. Swedish. (Marie-Louise Ekman) Gosta Ekman, Orjan Ramberg, Dan Ekborg, Lena Nyman, Rolf Skoglund, Tova Magnusson Norling, Alexander Bard.

THE POWER OF GOOD -- NICHOLAS WINTON
MULTIKINO 93 (IN CZECH REPUBLIC)/MENEMSHA FILMS (IN U.S.). July, 2002. Czech-Slovakian. (Matej Minac) Documentary.

THE POWER OF KANGWON PROVINCE
MIRACIN KOREA FILM CO. Sept., 1998. South Korean. (Hong Sang-soo) Baek Jong-hak, Oh Yun-hong, Kim Yu-seok, Chun Jae-hyun, Park Hyun-yeong.

THE POWERPUFF GIRLS MOVIE
WARNER BROS. June, 2002. (Craig McCracken) Catherine Cavadini, Tara Strong, E.G. Daily, Roger L. Jackson, Tom Kane, Tom Kenny, Jennifer Hale, Jennifer Martin. Animated.

PRACTICAL MAGIC
WARNER BROS. Oct., 1998. (Griffin Dunne) Sandra Bullock, Nicole Kidman, Dianne Wiest, Stockard Channing, Aidan Quinn.

PRAGUE STORIES
SIRENA FILM. Jan., 1999. Czech. (Artermio Benki, Michaela Pavlatova, Martin Sulik, Petr Vaclav, Vladimir Michalek): Laurence Cote.

THE PRAYING MANTIS
FILMLADEN. Feb., 2001. Austrian. (Paul Harather) Christiane Hoerbiger, Udo Kier, Jan Niklas, Simon Schwarz, Ursula Koban.

PRESENCE OF MIND
COLUMBIA TRISTAR FILMS DE ESPANA. Sept., 2000. Spanish. (Antoni Aloy) Sadie Frost, Lauren Bacall, Harvey Keitel, Nilo Mur.

THE PRESS SECRETARY
May, 2001. (Theodore Bogosian) Joe Lockhart, Helen Thomas, Mark Knoller, Bob Deans, Susan Page, Claire Shipman, Sonya Ross. Documentary.

PRESTON TYLK
NEXT GENERATION/CUTTING EDGE ENTERTAINMENT. June, 2000. (Jon Bokenkamp) Luke Wilson, Norman Reedus, Dennis Farina, Mili Avital, Vincent kartheiser, T.J. Thyne, Larry Boothby.

PRESUMED GUILTY
March, 2002. (Pamela Yates) Documentary.

PRETEND I'M NOT HERE
OCEAN FILMS/CINEART/QUO VADIS CINEMA/ARTE FRANCE CINEMA/MIKADO/BIANCA FILMS. May, 2000. French-Italian. (Olivier Jahan) Jeremie Renier, Aurore Clement, Johan Leysen.

PRETTY DEVILS/
LES FILMES DU LOSANGE/OCELOT/FILDEBROC/NEF/CANAL PLUS. Nov., 1999. French. (Serge Meynard): Olivia Bonamy, Audrey Tautou, Axelle Ade-Pasdeloup.

PRETTY THINGS
HUGO FILMS, M6 FILMS, CAPAC. June., 2001. French. (Gilles Paquet-Brenner) Marion Cotillard, Stomy Bugsy, Patrick Bruel, Titoff, Ophelie Winter.

THE PRICE
CINE CITTA/SINTRA. Nov., 1999. Italian. (Rolando Stefanelli) Stefano Dionisi, Chiara Caselli, Alessandro Repossi.

A PRICE ABOVE RUBIES
MIRAMAX. Jan., 1998. (Boaz Yakin) Rene Zellweiger, Christopher Eccleston, Glenn Fitzgerald, Allen Payne, Julianna Margulies.

THE PRICE OF AIR
ARTISTIC LICENSE. Sept., 2000. (Josh Evans) Josh Evans, Charis Michelson, Michael Madsen, Dick Van Patten, Michelle Phillips, Sticky Fingaz, Goldie, Allison Lange.

THE PRICE OF FORGIVENESS
Sept., 2001. French-Senegalese. (Mansour Sora Wade) Hubert Kounde, Rokhaya Niang, Gora Seck.

PRICE OF GLORY
NEW LINE/ESPARZA-KATZ/ARTHUR E. FRIEDMAN PRODS. Mar., 2000. (Carlos Avila) Jimmy Smits, Jon Seda, Clifton Collins Jr., Maria del Mar, Sal Lopez, Louis Mandylor, Danielle Camastra.

THE PRICE OF MILK
LOT 47 FILMS/JOHN SWIMMER/NEW ZEALAND FILM COMM. May, 2000. New Zealand. (Harry Sinclair) Danielle Cormack, Karl Urban.

PRIDE AND PERIL
PARADIDDLE PICTURES. Apr., 2000. (Tony Mortillaro) Bernie Sparago, Catherine McGoohan, Brian Whitman, Tony Mortillaro, James O'Leary, Heather McClurg, Sparkle, Sofia Milos.

PRIMARY COLORS
UNIVERSAL. March, 1998. (Mike Nichols) John Travolta, Emma Thompson, Billy Bob Thornton, Kathy Bates, Adrian Lester, Larry Hagman, Diane Ladd.

THE PRIME GIG
FINE LINE/INDEPENDENT PICTURES. Sept., 2000. (Gregory Mosher) Vince Vaughn, Julia Ormond, Ed Harris, Rory Cochrane, Wallace Shawn, George Wendt, Stephen Tobolowsky.

THE PRINCE OF CENTRAL PARK
SEAGAL/NASSO. May, 1999. (John Leekley) Kathleen Turner, Danny Aiello, Cathy Moriarty, Frankie Nasso, Harvey Keitel.

THE PRINCE OF EGYPT
DREAMWORKS. Dec., 1998. (Brenda Chapman). Animated.

THE PRINCE OF LIGHT: THE LEGEND OF RAMAYANA
SHOWCASE ENTERTAINMENT. Nov., 2001. Japanese-Indian-U.S. (Yugo Sako) Bryan Cranston, Edie Mirman, Richard Cansino, Michael Sorich, Mike L. Reynolds, Tony Pope, Mari Devon. Animated.

THE PRINCE OF THE PACIFIC
UFD. Dec., 2000. French. (Alain Corneau) Thierry Lhermitte, Patrick Timsit, Marie Trintignant, Francois Berleand, Anituavau.

PRINCESA
PARALLAX PICTURES (LONDON)/BIM DISTRIBUZIONE (ROME)/ ROAD MOVIES FILMPRODUKTIOON (BERLIN). Jan., 2001. British-Italian-German. (Henrique Goldman) Ingrid de Souza, Cesare Bocci, Lulu Pecorari, Mauro Pirovano, Biba Lerhue.

PRINCES AND PRINCESSES
LES ARMATEURS/LA FABRIQUE/STUDIO O/GEBEKA FILMS. Sept., 2000. French. (Michel Ocelot) Arlette Mirapeau, Philippe Cheytion, Yves Barsacq. Animated.

THE PRINCE'S MANUSCRIPT
WARNERS ITALIA/SCIARIO. Mar., 2000. Italian. (Roberto Ando) Michel Bouquet, Jeanne Moreau, Paolo Briguglia, Girogio Lupano, Laurent Terzieff, Massimo de Francovich.

THE PRINCESS AND THE WARRIOR
SONY/X FILME CREATIVE POOL. Sept., 2000. German. (Tom Tykwer) Franka Potente, Benno Furmann, Joachim Krol, Marita Breuer, Jurgen Tarrach, Lars Rudolph, Melchior Beslon, Ludger Pistor

PRINCESS-D
MEDIA ASIA DISTRIBUTION. June, 2002. Hong Kong-Taiwanese. (Sylviu Chang, Alan Yuen) Daniel Wu, Edison Chen, Angelica Lee, Anthony Wong, Patricia Ha, Wong Yiklam, Jonathan Lee.

THE PRINCESS DIARIES
BUENA VISTA. July, 2001. (Garry Marshall) Julie Andrews, Anne Hathaway, Hector Elizondo, Heather Matarazzo, Mandy Moore, Caroline Goodall, Robert Schwartzman, Erik Von Detten.

PRISONERS IN PARADISE
June, 2001. (Camilla Calamandrei) Mario Alfonsi, Anna Alfonsi, Novaro Bagnoli, Armando Boscolo. Documentary.

PRIVATE LIES
BERND BURGEMEISTER/TV-60 FILMPRODUKTION MUNICH/ BR/NDR/WDR/ORF/SF DRS. June, 2000. German. (Sherry Hormann) Martina Gedeck, Vyto Ruginis, John Corbett, Marianne Saegerbrecht, Rosemarie Fendel, Margaret Colin.

THE PRIVATE LIFE OF PYOTR VINOGRADOV
MOSKINOKOMBIANAT. Aug., 2000. Soviet Union–1935. (Aleksandr Macheret) Boris Livanov, V. Chishevsky, Konstantin Gradopolov.

PROBABLY LOVE
ISTITUTO LUCE. Aug., 2001. Italian-Swiss. (Giuseppe Bertolucci) Sonia Bergamasco, Rosalinda Celentano, Fabrizio Gifuni, Teco Celio.

THE PROF
Rezo FILMS/ALTER FILMS/LE STUDIO CANAL PLUS/FRANCE 2 CINEMA/CANAL PLUS. Apr., 2000. French. (Alexandre Jardin) Jean-Hughes Anglade, Yvan Attal, Helene de Fougerolles, Odette Laure.

THE PROFESSION OF ARMS
MIKADO. May, 2001. Italian-French-German. (Ermanno Olmi) Hristo Jivkov, Sergio Grammatico, Dimitar Ratchkov, Fabio Giubbani.

PROFESSOR ALBEIT
MEGAFILM/RTL KLUB. Feb., 1999. Hungarian. (Robert Koltai) Robert Koltai, Kata Dobo, Ferenc Kallai, Gabor Reviszky, Judit Hernadi.

PROGENY
FRIES FILM GROUP. May, 1998. (Brian Yuzna) Arnold Vasloo, Jillian McWhirther, Brad Dourif, Lindsay Crouse, Wilford Brimley.

PROMISES
PROMISE FILM PROJECT. Feb., 2001. (Justine Shapiro, B.Z. Goldberg, Carlos Bolado) Documentary.

THE PROMPTER
WILDHAGEN PRODS. May, 1999. Norwegian. (Hilde Heier): Hege Schoyen, Sven Nordin, Philip Zanden, Sigrid Huun.

PROOF OF LIFE
WARNER BROS. Nov., 2000. (Taylor Hackford) Meg Ryan, Russell Crowe, David Morse, Pamela Reed, David Caruso, Anthony Heald, Stanley Anderson.

THE PROPOSITION
POLYGRAM FILMS. March, 1998. (Lesli Linka Glatter) Kenneth Branagh, Madeleine Stowe, William Hurt, Neil Patrick Harris, Robert Loggia, Josef Sommer, Blythe Danner.

THE PROTAGONISTS
MEDUSA FILM/MASSIMO VIGLIAR/SURF FILM/MEDUSA FILM/TELEPIU. Aug., 1999. Italian. (Luca Guadagnino) Tilda Swinton, Fabrizia Sacchi, Andrew Tiernan, Claudio Gioe.

PROTECTION
THOUGHTCRIME PRDS./RED STORM PRODS. Aug., 2000. Canadian. (Bruce Spangler) Nancy Sivak, Jillian Fargey.

PROTEST
IRAN FILM SOCIETY AND NEJ PICTURES. Nov., 2000. Iranian. (Massoud Kimiayi) Dariush Arjmand, Mohammad Reza Foroutan.

PROZAC NATION
MILLENNIUM FILMS. Sept., 2001. (Erik Skjoldbjaerg) Christina Ricci, Jason Biggs, Anne Heche, Michelle Williams, Jonathan-Rhys-Meyers, Jessica Lange, Nicholas Campbell, Lou Reed, Sheila Paterson.

PSYCHO
UNIVERSAL. Dec., 1998. (Gus Van Sant) Vince Vaughn, Anne Heche, Julianne Moore, Viggo Mortensen, William H. Macy.

PSYCHO BEACH PARTY
STRAND/NEW OZ/RED HORSE FILMS. Jan., 2000. (Robert Lee King) Lauren Ambrose, Thomas Gibson, Nicholas Brendon, Kimberly Davies, Matt Keeslar, Charles Busch, Beth Broderick, Danni Wheeler.

P.S. YOUR CAT IS DEAD!
June, 2002. (Steve Guttenberg) Steve Guttenberg, Lombardo Boyar, Cynthia Watros, Shirley Knight, A.J. Benza, Paul Dillon, Tom Wright, Kenneth Moskow.

P. TINTO'S MIRACLE
WARNER SOGEFILMS. Dec., 1998. Spanish. (Javier Fesser) Luis Ciges, Silvia Casanova, Pablo Pinedo, Javier Aller, Emilio Gaviria.

PUBLIC ENEMY
ARCHIPEL 33/EGOLI FILM/KINOTAR OY. Sept., 1999. French-German. (Jens Meurer) Bobby Seale, Jamal Joseph, Kathleen Cleaver, Nile Rodgers.

PUBLIC ENEMY
CINEMA SERVICE. March, 2002. South Korean. (Kang Woo-seok) Seol Gyeong-gu, Jee Seong-jae, Kang Shin-il, Kim Jeong-hak, Do Yong-gu, Ahn Nae-sang, Lee Mun-shik, Sung Ji-ru, Yu Hae-jin.

PUCKOON
June, 2002. British-Irish. (Terence Ryan) Sean Hughes, Elliott Gould, Daragh O'Malley, John Lynch, Griff Rhys-Jones, Nickolas Grace.

PULSE
TOHO. May, 2001. Japanese. (Kiyoshi Kurosawa) Haruhiko Kato, Kumiko Aso,Koyuki, Kurume Arisaka, Masatoshi Matsuo.

PUMPKIN
MGM. Jan., 2002. (Adam Larson Broder, Tony R. Abrams) Christina Ricci, Hank Harris, Brenda Blethyn, Dominique Swain, Marisa Coughlan, Sam Ball, Harry Lennix, Nina Foch, Caroline Aaron.

PUNCH-DRUNK LOVE
SONY PICTURES ENTERTAINMENT. May, 2002. (Thomas Anderson) Adam Sandler, Emily Watson, Philip Seymour Hoffman, Luis Guzman, Mary Lynn Rajskub.

THE PUNISHMENT
NOVOTNY & NOVOTNY. July, 2001. (Goran Rebic) Zivota Neimarevic, Dragan Jovanovic, Nebojsa Glogovac, Biljana Srbljanovic, Tijana Mandic, Vlado Gavrilovic. Documentary.

PUNITIVE DAMAGE
RONIN FILMS. June, 1999. New Zealand. (Annie Goldson). Documentary.

PUNKS
E2 FILMWORKS/TALL SKINNY BLACK BOY. Jan., 2000. (Patrik-Ian Polk), Seth Gilliam, Dwight Ewell, Rockmond Dunbar, Jazzmun, Renoly Santiago, Loretta Devine, Vanessa Williams, Devon O'Dessa.

PUPS
TEAM OKUYAMA/TBD. Apr., 1999. (Ash) Cameron Van Hoy, Mischa Barton, Burt Reynolds.

PURE
Sept., 2002. British. (Gillies MacKinnon) Molly Parker, David Wenham, Harry Eden, Geraldine McEwan, Keira Knightley, Kate Ashfield.

PURELY BELTER
FILM FOUR/MUMBO JUMBO. May, 2000. British. (Mark Herman) Chris Beattie, Greg McLane, Charlie Hardwick, Jody Baldwin.

PURE MOMENT OF ROCK 'N' ROLL
UNIVERSAL/MP PRODS./BREGUET PRODS./HAVAS IMAGES/ CENTRE NATIONAL DU CINEMA/CANAL PLUS/SOFINERGIE V. Sept., 1999. French. (Manuel Boursinhac) Vincent Elbaz, Nicolas Abraham, Samy Naceri, Laurence Cote.

PURPLE STORM
MEDIA ASIA/JACKIE CHAN. Nov., 1999. Hong Kong. (Teddy Chen) Daniel Wu, Kam Kwok-leung, Emil Chow, Josie Ho, Joan Chen.

PURPLE SUNSET
SHANGHAI PARADISE FILM & TV GROUP CORP./BEIJING FORBIDDEN CITY FILM CO. Aug., 2001. Chinese. (Feng Xiaoning) Fu Dalong, Anna Dzenilalova, Chie Mięta, Wang Xuewei.

PUSHING TIN
20TH CENTURY FOX. Apr., 1999. (Mike Newell) John Cusack, Billy Bob Thornton, Cate Blanchett, Angelina Jolie, Vicki Lewis.

QUAND ON SERA GRAND
OCEAN FILMS. Sept., 2000. French. (Renaud Cohen) Mathieu Demy, Amira Casar, Maurice Benichou, Louise Benazeraf, Marie Payen.

QUANTUM PROJECT
SIGHTSOUND.COM/METAFILMICS. May, 2000. (Eugenio Zanetti) Stephen Dorff, Fay Masterson, John Cleese, Russell Brown.

QUARTET
SONY PICTURES ENTERTAINMENT (JAPAN). Aug., 2001. Japanese. (Joe Hisaishi) Yoshihiko Hakamada, Sachiko Sakurai, Nao Ohmuri, Kaoru Kukita, Shunji Fujimura, Tomokazu Miura.

QUARTET
LANTIA CINEMA & AUDIOVISIVI. Dec., 2001. Italian. (Beatrice Fazi, Anna Ammirati, Maddalena Maggi, Raffaella Ponoz, Valeria Cavalli, Ida Di Benedetto, Armando De Razza.

QUARTET FOR TWO
SHOCHIKU CO. Feb., 2001. Japanese. (Naoto Takenaka) Naoto Takenaka, Yuki Amami, Keika Fukitsuka, Yuta Minowa.

QUASIMODO D'EL PARIS
BAC FILMS. Mar., 1999. French. (Patrick Timsit) Patrick Timsit, Richard Berry, Melanie Thierry, Vincent Elbaz, Didier Flamand.

QUEENIE IN LOVE
PYRAMIDE (IN FRANCE). May, 2001. French-U.S. (Amos Kollek) Victor Argo, Valerie Geffner, Louise Lasser, Mark Margolis, Austin Pendleton, Kris Carr, David Wike, Jose Grifasi.

QUEEN ISABEL IN PERSON
HARDY FILMS. Nov., 2000. Spanish. (Rafael Gordon) Isabel Ordaz.

QUEEN OF THE WHOLE WIDE WORLD
April, 2001. (Roger Hyde) Kris Andersson, Scott Lan, Dan Gibson, Oscar Quintero, Darryl Keith Roach, Worthis Meacham, Charles Herrera. Documentary.

QUEEN: THE MAKING OF AN AMERICAN BEAUTY
ANIMA PRODS. July, 2000. (Mimi Riley) Angela McCulley, Tara Watson, Joe Wilmouth, Jack Newsom, Mike Graham.

QUEST FOR CAMELOT
WARNER BROS. April, 1998. (Frederick Du Chan) Jessalyn Gilsig, Andrea Corr, Cary Elwes, Bryan White, Gary Oldman, Eric Idle, Don Rickles, Jane Seymour, Celine Dion.

QUESTIONING FAITH
June, 2002. (Macky Alston) Documentary.

A QUESTION OF TASTE
PYRAMIDE/CDP/LE STUDIO CANAL PLUS/FRANCE 3 CINEMA/RHONE-ALPES CINEMA/CANAL PLUS/CNC. Apr., 2000. French. (Bernard Rapp) Bernard Giraudeau, Jean-Pierre Lorit, Florence Thomassin, Jean-Pierre Leaud, Artus de Penguern.

THE QUICKIE
PYRAMIDE DISTRIBUTION. July, 2001. German-British. (Sergei Bodrov) Vladimir Mashkov, Jennifer Jason Leigh, Dean Stockwell.

THE QUIET AMERICAN
MIRAMAX. Sept., 2002. Australian-U.S. (Phillip Noyce) Michael Caine, Brendan Fraser, Do Thi Hai Yen, Rade Sherbedgia.

THE QUIET FAMILY
MYUNG FILM. Sept., 1998. South Korean. (Kim Ji-un) Song Kang-ho, Park In-hwan, N Mun-heui, Choe Min-sik, Lee Yeon-sung.

QUILLS
20TH CENTURY FOX/FOX SEARCHLIGHT PICTURE/INDUSTRY ENTERTAINMENT/A WALRUS & ASSOCIATES/HOLLYWOOD PARTNERS. Sept., 2000. (Philip Kaufman) Geoffrey Rush, Kate Winslet, Joaquin Phoenix, Michael Caine, Billie Whitelaw.

QUITTING
IMAR (IN CHINA)/SONY PICTURES CLASSIC (IN U.S.). Aug., 2001. Chinese. (Zhang Yan) Jia Hongsheng, Jia Fengsen, Chai Xiurong, Wang Tong, Shun Xing, Li Jie,Zhang Yang, Yu Baoshan.

QUO VADIS
Jan., 2002. Polish. (Jerzy Kawalerowicz) Pawel Delag, Magdalena Mielcarz, Boguslaw Linda, Michal Bajor, Jerzy Trela, Franciszek Pieczka, Krzysztof Majchrzak.

RAAZ
June, 2002. Indian. (Vikram Bhatt) Dino Morea, Bipashi Basu, Malini Sharma, Shruti Ulfat.

RABBIT-PROOF FENCE
BECKER ENTERTAINMENT (IN AUSTRALIA)-MIRAMAX (IN U.S.). Jan., 2002. Austrian-British. (Phillip Noyce) Everlyn Sampi, Tianna Sansbury, Laura Monaghan, David Gulpilil, Kenneth Branagh, Deborah Mailman, Jason Clarke.

THE RACE
GAUMONT BUENA VISTA INTL. March, 2002. French. (Djamel Bensalah) Josiane Balasko, Helene de Fougerolles, Gerard Jugnot, Julien Courbey, Lorant Deutsch, Atmen Kelif, Roschdy Zem.

THE RACE TO SAVE 100 YEARS
WARNER BROS./TURNER ENTERTAINMENT. March, 1998. (Scott Benson) Documentary.

RACE TO SPACE
LIONS GATE FILMS. March, 2002. (Sean Patrick McNamara) James Woods, Annabeth Gish, Alex D. Linz, William Devane, William Atherton, Wesley Mann, Patrick Richwood, Mark Moses.

RACHIDA
May, 2002. French-Algerian. (Yamina Bachir) Ibtissem Djouadi, Bahia Rachedi, Hamis Remas.

RADIATION
RADIATION PICTURES. Jan., 1999. (Suki Stetson Hawley) Unai Fresnedo, Katy Petty, Ignacio Fernandez, Thalia Zedek, Chris Brokaw.

RADIO FREE STEVE
UGH FILMS. Jan., 2001. (Jules Beesley) Ryan Junell, Jessy Schwartz, Chris Sykes, Dean Haglund, Joy Gohring,Johanna Stein, Dave Kendall, Kris McGaha.

RAGE
GRANITE FILMWORKS. Sept., 1999. British. (Newton I. Aduaka) Fraser Ayres, Shaun Parkes, John Pickard, Shango Baku.

THE RAGE: CARRIE 2
MGM. Mar., 1999. (Katt Shea): Emily Bergl, Jason Lodon, Dylan Bruno, J. Smith-Cameron, Amy Irving.

RAGE: 20 YEARS OF PUNK ROCK WEST COAST STYLE
SEVENTH ART RELEASING OF A CLASSIFIED FILMS. June, 2001. (Michael Bishop, Scott Jacoby) Jack Grisham, Keith Morris, Duane Peters, Gitane Demone, Don Bolles, Jello Biafra. Documentary.

RAIN
ROSE ROAD/COMMUNICADO. May, 2001. New Zealand. (Christine Jeffs) Alicia Fulford-Wierzbicki, Sarah Peirse, Marton Csokas, Alistair Browning, Aaron Murphy.

RAIN
MARTIN SCORCESE. Sept., 2001. U.S.-Spanish-German. (Katherine Lindberg) Melora Walters, Kris Park, Jo Anderson, Diane Ladd, Jamey Sheridan, Ellen Muth, Adrian Johansson.

RAINBOW TROUT
PARK CHONG-WON PROD./TROUT PRODS./CINEMA SERVICE. Sept., 1999. SouthKorean. (Park Chong-won) Kan Su-yeon, Hwang In-sung, Sul Kying-gu, Kim Sae-dong.

RALPH BUNCHE: AN AMERICAN ODYSSEY
SOUTH CAROLINA EDUCATIONAL TELEVISION AND SCHOMBURG CENTER FOR RESEARCH IN BLACK CULTURE. JAN., 2001. (William Greaves) Documentary.

RALPH ELLISON: AN AMERICAN JOURNEY
Jan., 2002. (Avon Kirkland) Andre Braugher, John Amos, Paul Benjamin, Jacques C. Smith. Documentary.

RAM DASS: FIERCE GRACE
Feb., 2002. (Mickey Lemle) Documentary.

RANCID ALUMINIUM
ENTERTAINMENT FILM/EFD/FICTION FACTORY. Jan., 2000. British. (Ed Thomas) Joseph Fiennes. Rhys Ifans, Tara Fitzgerald.

RANCOR
ALTA FILMS, June, 2002. Spanish. (Miguel Albaladejo) Lolita, Jorge Perugorria, Elena Anaya, Mar Regueras, Geli Albaladejo.

RANDOM ACTS OF VIOLENCE
GUTTER BROTHERS. July, 1999. (Drew Bell): Esteban Powell, A.J. Buckley, Alex Solowitz, Brain Klugman, Rainbow Borden.

RANDOM HEARTS
SONY PICTURES ENTERTAINMENT/COLUMBIA PICTURES/RASTAR/MIRAGE ENTERPRISES. Sept. 1999. (Sydney Pollack) Harrison Ford, Kristin Scott Thomas, Charles S. Dutton, Bonnie Hunt, Dennis Haysbert, Sydney Pollack, Richard Jenkins, Paul Guilfoyle.

RAPE ME
PAN-EUROPEENNE/TOUTE PREMIERE FOIS/PHILIPPE GODEAU/CANAL PLUS. June, 2000. French. (Virginie Despentes, Coralie Trinh Thi) Raffaela Anderson, Karen Bach.

RARE BIRDS
LIONS GATE FILMS. Sept., 2001. Canadian. (Sturla Gunnarsson) William Hurt, Andy Jones, Molly Parker, Cathy Jones, Vicky Hynes, Greg Malone, Maggie Myer, Lawrence Barry, Sheila McCarthy.

RAT
LES FILMS A UN DOLLAR. Aug., 2000. French. (Christophe Ali, Nicolas Bonilauri) Marcel Fix.

RATCATCHER
PATHE PICTURES/BBC FILMS. May, 1999. British. (Lynne Ramsay) William Eadie, Tommy Flanagan, Mandy Matthews.

RATED X
SHOWTIME/ DISTRICT. Jan., 2000. (Emilio Estevez) Charlie Sheen, Emilio Estevez, Rafer Weigel. Tracy Hutson, Megan Ward, Terry O'Quinn, Danielle Brett, Peter Bogdanovich.

A RATHER ENGLISH MARRIAGE
WALL TO WALL TELEVISION. Nov., 1998. British. (Paul Seed) Albert Finney, Tom Courtenay, Joanna Lumley, John Light, Katie Carr.

RAT RACE
PARAMOUNT PICTURES. July, 2001. (Jerry Zucker) Rowan Atkinson, John Cleese, Whoopi Goldberg, Cuba Gooding Jr., Seth Green, Jon Lovitz, Breckin Meyer, Kathy Najimy, Amy Smart.

RATS
ZOO PRODS. Sept. 1999. (James M. Felter). Documentary.

RAVE
TWELVE CORNERS ENTERTAINMENT. Feb., 2001. (Ron Krauss) Douglas Spain, Aimee Graham, Nicholle Tom, Dante Basco, Franco Vega, Shaun Weiss, Lela Lee, Steven Bauer.

RAVENOUS
20TH CENTURY FOX. Jan., 1999. (Antonio Bird) Guy Pearce, Robert Carlyle, Jeremy Davies, Jeffrey Jones, John Spencer.

RAW DEAL: A QUESTION OF CONSENT
ARTISAN ENTERTAINMENT. Jan., 2001. (Billy Corben) Documentary.

RAY: LIFE AND WORK OF SATYAJIT RAY
Satyajit Ray Archive/Orchid Films/Ford Foundation. Sept., 1999. Indian. (Goutam Ghose). Documentary.

RAZING APPALACHIA
June, 2002. (Sasha Waters) Documentary.

RAZOR BLADE SMILE
PALM PICTURES/MANGA LIVE. Oct., 1998. British. (Jake West) Eileen Daley, Christopher Adamson, Kevin Howarth, Jonathan Coote, David Warbeck.

REACH THE ROCK
GRAMMERCY. Oct., 1998. (William Ryan) William Sadler, Alessandro Nivola, Bruce Norris, Karen Sillas, Brooke Langton.

READ MY LIPS
PATHE. Sept., 2001. French. (Jacques Audiard) Vincent Cassel, Emmanuelle Devos, Olivier Gourmet, Olivia Bonamy, Olivier Perrier, Bernard Alane, Cecile Samie.

READY TO RUMBLE
WARNER BROS./BEL-AIR ENTERTAINMENT/OUTLAW/TOLLIN/ROBBINS PRODS. Apr., 2000. (Brian Robbins) David Arquette, Oliver Platt, Scott Caan, Bill Goldberg, Rose McGowan.

READY WILLING & ABLE
UNITED CREW FILMS. July, 1999. (Jenni Gold) Christopher Templeton, Rus Blackwell, Steve DuMouchel, Mike Kalvoda.

REAL FICTION
SAEROM ENTERTAINMENT. May, 2001. South Korean. (Kim Ki-duk) Ju Jin-mo, Kim Jin-ah, Son Min-seok, Lee Je-rak, Kim Ki-yeon.

REAL MCCOY
BOMBO SPROTS & ENTERTAINMENT. April, 2001. (Daniel Carey) Documentary.

THE REAL MCCOY
KINOFINLANDIA. Finnish-British-Swdish-Indian.1999 (Pekka Lehto) Andy McCoy, Angela Nicoletti, Michael Monroe.

REAL WOMEN HAVE CURVES
Jan., 2002. (Patricia Cardoso) America Ferrera, Lupe Ontiveros, Ingrid Oliu, George Lopez, Brian Sites.

A REAL YOUNG LADY
REZO FILMS/CB FILMS/ARTEDIS/CNC/GNCR. June, 2000. French. (Catherine Breillat) Charlotte Alexandra, Hiram Keller, Rita Meiden.

A REASONABLE MAN
PANDORA CINEMA. Aug., 1999. South African-French. (Gavin Hood) Gavin Hood, Nigel Hawthorne, Janine Eser, Vusi Kunene, Ken Gampu.

REBELS BY CHANCE
Nov., 2001. Italian. (Vincenzo Terraciano) Antonio Catania, Giovanni Esposito, Franco Javarone, Renato Scarpa, Tiberio Murgia, Antonio Petrocelli, Gea Martire.

REBELS WITH A CAUSE
SHIRE FILMS. June, 2000. (Helen Garvey) Tom Hayden, Cathy Wilkerson, Todd Gitlin, Carl Ogelsby, Junius Williams.

RECESS: SCHOOL'S OUT
BUENA VISTA. Feb., 2001. (Chuck Sheetz) Animated. Rickey D'Shon Collins, Jason Davis, Ashley Johnson, Andy Lawrence, Courtland Mead, Pam Segall.

RECKLESS INDIFFERENCE
UTOPIA FILMS AND OPEN EDGE MEDIA. Oct., 2000. (William Gazecki) Judie Farris, Jim Farris Sr., Tony Miliotti, Jeff Semow, Alan Dershowitz, Patrick Sullivan, Robert Derham. Documentary.

RECONCILED
TECNOVISUAL. Feb., 2001. Italian. (Rosalia Polizzi) Beatriz Spelzini, Franco Castellano, Emilio Bonucci, Lorenzo Majnoni, Paola Pitagora.

RED BEAR
May, 2002. Argentine-French-Spanish. (Israel Adrian Caetano) Julio Chavez, Soledad Villamil, Luis Machin, Rene Lavand.

RED DEER
FOUR BY FOUR FILMS. Sept., 2000. Canadian. (Anthony Couture) Amber Rothwell, James Hutson, Loreya Montayne, Awaovieyi Agie.

RED DIRT
SWEET TEA. Apr., 2000. (Tag Purvi) Karen Black, Dan Montgomery, Aleksa Palladino, Walton Goggins.

RED DRAGON
UNIVERSAL. Sept., 2002. (Brett Ratner) Anthony Hopkins, Edward Norton, Ralph Fiennes, Harvey Keitel, Emily Watson, Mary-Louise Parker, Philip Seymour Hoffman, Anthony Heald, Bill Duke, Ken Leung, Stanley Anderson, Azura Skye.

RED DUST
INTERFILM/CROATION TV. Sept., 1999. Croation. (Zrinko Ogresta) Josip Kusan, Marko Matanovic, Ivo Gregurevic.

RED INK
KRESCENT FILMS. Feb., 2000. (Jerry A. Henry) Davi Jay, Clarence Whitmore, Diego Villareal Garcia, Errol Wilks, Deborah Flowers.

RED INK
AMERICA PRODUCCIONES (PERU)/TORNASOL FILMS (SPAIN)/PRODUCCIONES INCA FILMS (PERU). Sept., 2000. Peruvian-Spanish. (Francisco Lombardi) Gianfranco Brero, Giovanni Ciccia.

RED MOON
DANIA FILM/VIP MEDIA. Sept., 2001. Italian. (Antonio Capuano) Carlo Cecchi, Licia Maglietta, Tony Servillo, Antonino Iuorio.

THE RED ONE: TRIUMPH
INTERCINEMA-ART AGENCY. Sept., 2000. Russian. (Loeg Pogodin, Vladimir Alenikov) Petr Ulianov, Ekaterina Cherepukhina, Aram Gevorkhyan.

RED PLANET
WARNER BROS. Oct., 2000. (Antony Hoffman) Val Kilmer, Carrie-Anne Moss, Tom Sizemore, Benjamin Bratt, Simon Baker.

RED RAIN
LOLA FILMS. June, 2000. (Laura Plotkin). Documentary.

THE RED RIBBON
VARAHONAR CO. Feb., 1999. Iranian. (Ebrahim Hatamikia) Azita Hajiyan, Parviz Parastuyi, Reza Kianian.

RED, WHITE & YELLOW
NORTHERN LIGHTS POST. Oct., 1998. (Marshall Dostal, Mark Littman). Documentary.

REEF HUNTERS
GMA NETWORK FILMS. Oct., 2000. Filipino. (Marilou Diaz-Abaya) Cesar Montano, Pen Medina, Jhong Hilario, Amy Austria.

REGRET TO INFORM
SUN FOUNTAIN. 1999. (Barbara Sonneborn). Documentary.

REINDEER GAMES
DIMENSION FILMS/MARTY KATZ. Feb., 2000. (John Frankenheimer) Ben Affleck, Gary Sinise, Charlize Theron, Dennis Farina, James Frain, Donal Logue, Danny Trejo, Isaac Hayes.

REIGN OF FIRE
BUENA VISTA. July, 2002. (Rob Bowman) Christian Bale, Matthew McConaughey, Izabella Scorupco, Gerald Butler, Scott James Moutter, David Kennedy, Alexander Siddig, Ned Dennehy, Rory Keenan, Terence Maynard, Ben Thornton.

RELATIVE VALUES
ALLIANCE ATLANTIS/MIDSUMMER FILMS/ISLE OF MAN FILM COMM. June, 2000. British. (Eric Styles) Julie Andrews, Sophie Thompson, Edward Atterton, Jeanne Tripplehorn, William Baldwin.

RELAX... IT'S JUST SEX
ATLAS ENTERTAINMENT. Jan., 1998. (P.J. Castellaneta) Jennifer Tilly, Mitchell Anderson, Cynda Williams, Lori Petty, Serena Scott Thomas.

REMBRANDT
PYRAMIDE/OGNON/FRANCE 2 CINEMA/PAIN UNLTD.FILMS-TIFTUNG NORDRHEIN-WESTFALEN/ARGUS FILM/TROIS TV/ COBO FUND/CANAL PLUS/CNC. Sept. 1999. French-German-Dutch. (Charles Matton) Klaus Maria Brandauer, Romane Bohringer, Jean Rochefort, Johanna ter Steege, Jean-Philippe Ecoffey.

REMEMBER THE TITANS
BUENA VISTA. Sept., 2000. (Boaz Yakin) Denzel Washington, Will Patton, Donald Faison, Wood Harris, Ryan Hurst, Ethan Suplee.

RENDEZVOUS IN SAMARKAND
SAMARKAND PICTURES. Oct., 1999. (Tim Bridwell) John Littlefield, Marie Ravel, Tsuyu Shimizu, Miho Mikaido, Lyes Salem.

RENDING
Sept., 2001. Portuguese-French. (Raquel Freire) Ricardo Aibeo, Ana Teresa Carvalhosa, Isabel Ruth, Ana Brandao, Paula Marques, Ana Moreira, Susana Vidal.

RENE
Aug., 2002. French. (Alain Cavalier) Joel Lefrancois, Thomas Duboc, Guy-Francois Malbranche, Nathalie Grandcamp.

RENNIE'S LANDING
FRANCHISE PICTURES. June, 2001. (Marc Fusco) Peter Facinelli, Ethan Embry, Scott Foley, Charlotte Ayanna, Annalouise Paul.

RENT-A-FRIEND
A FILM/JORDAAN FILM/BNN-TV/FU WORKS. Feb., 2000. Dutch. (Eddy Terstall) Marc van Uchelen, Rifka Lodeizen, Nadja Hupscher.

THE REPENTANT
ARP SELECTION. April, 2002. French. (Laetitia Masson) Isabelle Adjani, Sami Frey, Samy Naceri, Aurore Clement.

THE REPLACEMENT KILLERS
SONY. Jan., 1998. (Antoine Fuqua) Chow Yun-Fat, Mira Sorvino, Michael Rooker, Jurgen Prochnow, Kenneth Tsang, Til Schweiger.

THE REPLACEMENTS
WARNER BROS./BEL AIR ENTERTAINMENT/DYLAN SELLERS. July, 2000. (Howard Deutch) Keanu Reeves, Gene Hackman, Orlando Jones, Jon Favreau, Brooke Langton, Rhys Ifans.

REPLAY
PYRAMIDE. May, 2001. French-Canadian. (Catherine Corsini) Emmanuelle Beart, Pascale Bussieres, Dani Levy.

REPLICANT
METROPOLITAN FILMS. July, 2001. (Ringo Lam) Jean-Claude Van Damme, Michael Rooker, Catherine Dent, Ian Robison.

REPLY WITH PHOTO
SONET FILMS. Aug., 1999. Swedish-Latvian. (Una Celma) Samuel Froler, Baiba Broka, Lennart Jahkel, Eva-Lena Bjorkman

REQUIEM FOR A DREAM
ARTISAN ENTERTAINMENT/THOUSAND WORDS. May, 2000. (Darren Aronofsky) Ellen Burstyn, Jared Leto, Jennifer Connelly, Marlon Wayans, Christopher McDonald, Louise Lasser, Keith David.

REQUIEM FOR A ROMANTIC WOMAN
TIME. May, 1999. German. (Dagmar Knoepfel) Janina Sachau, Sylvester Groth, Jeanette Hain, Felix von Manteuffel.

RESIDENT EVIL
SONY PICTURES ENTERTAINMENT. March, 2002. German-British. (Paul W.S. Anderson) Milla Jovovich, Eric Mabius, Michelle Rodriguez, James Purefoy, Martin Crewes, Colin Salmon.

RESISTING REMEMBRANCE
SUNDAY MORNING PRODS. May, 2000. French. (Orso Miret) Yann Goven, Olivier Gourmet, Brigitte Catillon, Martine Audrain.

A RESPECTABLE MAN
CDI/BUENA VISTA INTL. ITALIA/CLEMI CINEMATOGRAFICA/ MEDIATRADE. Sept., 1999. Italian. (Maurizio Zaccaro) Michele Placido, Stefano Accorsi, Marianegla Melato, Giovanna Mezzogiorno.

RESTAURANT
PALISADES PICTURES. April, 1998. (Eric Bross) Adrien Brody, Elise Neal, David Moscow, Malcolm Jamal Warner.

RESTLESS
SCITECH CULTURE CO./CELESTIAL PICTURES. Nov., 1998. (Jule Gilfillan) Catherine Kellner, David Wu, Sarita Choudhury, Geng Le.

RESURRECTION
Oct., 2001. Italian-French-German. (Paolo and Vittorio Taviani) Stefania Rocca, Timothy Peach, Giulio Scarpati, Marina Vlady, Antonella Ponziani, Marie Baumer, Cecile Bois, Eva Christian.

RETURN IN AUTUMN
Aug., 2001. Czech. (George Agathonikiadis) Jiri Bartoska, George Velendzas, Olga Tournaki-Diamantopoulou, Vilm Cibulkova.

RETURN OF THE IDIOT
CINEMART. Sept., 1999. Czech. (Sasa Gedeon) Pavel Liska, Tatiana Vilhelmova, Anna Geislerova, Jiri Langmajer, Jiri Machacek.

RETURN TO ALGIERS
BAC FILMS/ALEXANDRE FILMS/CANAL PLUS/LE STUDIO CANAL PLUS/STUDIO IMAGES 6. Mar., 2000. French. (Alexandre Arcady) Antoine de Caunes, Nozha Khouadra, Samy Naceri, Said Amadis.

RETURN TO GO!
O-FILMPRODUKTION/ZDF. Feb., 2000. German. (Pierre Sanoussi-Bliss) Pierre Sanoussi-Bliss, Matthias Freihof, Dieter Bach, Bart Klein.

RETURN TO ME
MGM/JLT. Mar., 2000. (Bonnie Hunt) David Duchovny, Minnie Driver, Carroll O'Connor, Robert Loggia, Bonnie Hunt, David Alan Grier, Joely Richardson.

RETURN TO PARADISE
POLYGRAM FILMS. July, 1998. (Joseph Ruben) Vince Vaughn, Anne Heche, Joaquin Phoenix, David Conrad, Vera Farmiga, Nick Sandow.

RETURN TO PONTIANAK
PHAEDRA CINEMA. Aug., 2001. Singapore. (Dijinn) Hiep Thi Le, Fadzlinda Mohammed Shafie, Eleanor Lee, Steve Banks, Victor Khong, Fadali, Jaffar Aris, Pak Rahman.

RETURN WITH HONOR
SANDERS & MOCK. Oct., 1998. (Freida Lee Mock, Terry Sanders) . Documentary.

THE REUNION
GOOD MEDICINE/ASYLUM PICTURES/ESQUIRE FILMS. Jan., 2000. (Larry Eudene) Tim Devlin, Elizabeth P. McKay, Patrick Ferraro, Leila Sbatini, Jack Mulcahy, Mimi Langeland.

REUNION (DOGME #17)
O'HARA/KLEIN. Feb., 2001. (Leif Tilden) Dwier Brown, Marlene Forte, Andres Faucher, Corey Glover, Rainer Judd, Jennifer Rubin.

REVENGE
WOOD PRODS./SOMBRERO VERDE/ARAUCO. Sept., 1999. Chilean. (Andres Wood) Tamara Acosta, Willy Semler, Maria Izquierdo, Belgica Castro, Patricia Lopez, Daniel Munoz, Aldo Parodi.

REVENGERS TRAGEDY
Aug., 2002. British. (Alex Cox) Christopher Eccleston, Eddie Izzard, Derek Jacobi, Diana Quick, Carla Henry, Andrew Schofield.

REVOLUTIONARY GIRL UTENA: THE MOVIE
June, 2002. Japanese. (Kunihiko Ikuhara) Tomoko Kawakami, Yuriko Fuchizaki, Takehito Koyasu, Kotono Mitsuishi, Aya Hisakawa, Takeshi Kusao, Kumiko Nishihara. Animated.

REVOLUTION #9
CINEBLAST!. APRIL, 2001. (Tim McCann) Michael Risley, Adrienne Shelly, Spalding Gray, Callie Thorne, Michael Rodrick, Sakina Jaffrey.

REVOLUTION OS
SEVENTH ART RELEASING. Feb., 2002. (J.T.S. Moore) Linus Torvalds, Richard Stallman, Eric Raymond, Larry Augustin, Bruce Perens, Michael Tiemann, Brian Behlendorf. Documentary.

REWIND
ALTA FILMS. July, 1999. Spanish. (Nicolas Munoz) Daniel Guzman, Maria Adanez, Enrique Simon, Paz Gomez, Tristan Ulloa.

REYKJAVIK GUESTHOUSE -- RENT A BIKE
Aug., 2002. Icelandic. (Bjorn Thors, Unnur Osp Stefansdottir) Hilmir Snaer Guonason, Kristjorg Kjeld, Stefan Eiriksson, Margret Vilhjalmsdottir, Bjorn Hylnur Hinriksson, Kjartan Guojondottir.

RHAPSODY IN BLOOM
BECKER ENTERTAINMENT. May, 1998. (Craig Saavedra) Penelope Ann Miller, Ron Silver, Craig Sheffer, Caroline Goodall.

RHYTHM & BLUES
EQUATOR/LIFE ON MARS. Sept., 1999. British. (Stephen Lennhoff) Angus McInnes, Ian Henderson, Paul Blackthorne, Gary Fairhall.

RICHTER, THE ENIGMA
WARNER VISION. Sept., 1998. French. (Bruno Monsaingeon) Sviatoslav Richter. Documentary.

RIDE
DIMENSION FILMS. March, 1998. (Millicent Shelton) Malik Yoba, Melissa De Sousa, John Witherspoon, Frendro Starr.

THE RIDE
WORLD WIDE PICTURES. March, 1998. (Michael O. Sajbel) Michael Biehn, Brock Pierce, Jennifer Blanc, Chris Owen, Clarence Felder.

RIDER OF THE FLAMES
PROGRESS FILM-VERLEIH. Jan., 1999. German. (Nina Grosse) Martin Feifel, Marianne Denicourt, Ulrich Matthes, Ulrich Muhe, Nina Hoss.

RIDERS
SND. May, 2002. French-Canadian-British. (Gerard Pires) Stephen Dorff, Natasha Henstridge, Bruce Payne, Steven Berkoff, Cle Bennet, Steven McCarthy.

RIDE WITH THE DEVIL
USA FILMS. Aug., 1999. (Ang Lee) Skeet Ulrich, Tobey Maguire, Jewel, Jeffrey Wright, Simon Baker.

RIDING IN CARS WITH BOYS
SONY PICTURES ENTERTAINMENT. Oct., 2001. (Penny Marshall) Drew Barrymore, Steve Zahn, Brittany Murphy, Adam Garcia, Lorraine Bracco, James Woods, Sara Gilbert, Desmond Harrington, David Moscow, Maggie Gyllenhall, Peter Facinelli.

RIEN SUR ROBERT
REZO FILMS. Feb., 1999. French. (Pascal Bonitzer) Fabrice Luchini, Sandrine Kiberlain, Valentina Cervi, Michel Piccoli, Bernadette Lafont.

THE RIFLEMAN OF THE VOROSHILOV REGIMENT
NTV-PROFIT. Feb., 2000. Russian. (Stanislav Govoruchin) Michail Uljanov, Anna Sinjakina, Aleksandr Porochosikov, Irina Rozanova.

RIGHT UNDER MY EYES (SOUS MES YEUX)
June, 2002. French. (Virginie Wagon) Valerie Donzelli, Jean-Baptiste Montagut, Hugh Bonneville, Damien Ricourt, Mark Downey.

THE RING
KADOKAWA SHOTEN PUBLISHING CO. July, 1999. Japanese. (Hideo Nakata) Nanko Matsushima, Hiroyuki Sanada, Miki Nakatani, Yuko Takeuchi, Hitomi Sato.

THE RING
DreamWorks Pictures. Sept., 2002. (Gore Verbinski) Naomi Watts, Martin Henderson, David Dorfman, Brian Cox, Jane Alexander, Lindsay Frost, Pauley Perrette, Amber Tamblyn, Rachael Bella, Sara Rue, Shannon Cochran, Daveigh Chase.

RING 0: THE BIRTHDAY
TOHO CO. June, 2001. Japanese. (Norio Tsuruta) Yukie Nakama, Seiichi Tanabe, Kumiko Aso, Yoshiko Tanaka.

THE RING 2
KADOKAWA SHOTEN PUBLISHING CO. July, 1998. Japanese. (Hideo Nakata) Miki Nakatani, Hitomi Sato, Kyoko Fukada.

RINGMASTER
ARTISAN. Nov., 1998. (Neil Baramson) Jerry Springer, Jaime Pressly, Molly Hagan, Michael Dudikoff, Ashley Holbrook.

RIPLEY'S GAME
FINE LINE FEATURES. Sept., 2002. Italian-British. (Liliana Cavani) Dougray Scott, Ray Winstone, Lena Headey, Chiara Caselli.

RISK
ROADSHOW FILM DISTRIBUTORS. Sept., 2000. Australian. (Alan White) Bryan Brown, Tom Long, Claudia Karvan, Jason Clarke, Brian Meegan, Bob Baines, Kim Knuckey, Thomas Clunie, Sharin Contini.

RISOTTO
PAPANDREOU, ANTENNA TV, PLENMAN ENTERPRISES, A MANIATIS, GREEK FILM CENTRE. Feb., 2001. Greek. (Olga Malea) Dimitra Matsouka, Anna Mascha, Konstantinos Markoulakis.

RITES OF PASSAGE
WORLD INTL.. June, 1999. (Victor Salva) Dean Stockwell, Jason Behr, Robert keith, Jaimz Woolvett, James Remar.

RITUAL
GOTHAM ENTERTAINMENT/RASLAN CO. OF AMERICA. July, 2000. (Stanley Bennett Clay) Clarence Williams III, Denise Nicholas, Shawn Michael Howard, Angelle Brooks, Gerrie Ellis.

RITUAL
TOKUMA INTL. Feb., 2001. Japanese. (Hideaki Anno) Shunji Iwai, Ayako Fujitani, Jun Murakami, Shinobu Otake.

THE RIVER
Sept., 2001. Finnish. (Jarmo Lampela) Sanna Hietala, Antti, Ikkala, Jyri Ojansivu, Antti Mikkola, Jari Virman, Liisa Vuori, Elina Hoffren.

RIVER RED
DRILLING FILMS. Jan., 1998. (Eric Drilling) Tom Everett Scott, David Moscow, Cara Buono, David Lowery, Denis O'Hare, Michael Kelly.

RIVERS OF BABYLON
MARIAN URBAN/ALEF FILM & MEDIA GROUP/CESKA TELEVIZE/ATELIERY ZLIN/POKIUM/TV MARKIZA. Sept., 1999. (Vlado Balco) Andrej Hryc, Ady Hajdu, Diana Morova.

RIVIERA HOTEL
PIETER VAN HUYSTEE FILM & TV. Oct., 1998. Dutch. (Bernie Ijdis). Documentary.

THE ROAD
KADAM-T, KAZAKHFILM AIMONOV (KAZAKHSTAN)/ARTCAM INTL. (FRANCE)/NHK (JAPAN). May, 2001. Kazakhstanian-French-Japanese. Djamshed Usmonov, Saoule Toktibaeva, Alnour Tourgambaeva, Magiane Omirbaev, Valeria Gouliaeva.

ROADBLOCKS
FILMODE/GREEK FILM CENTER. Nov., 2000. Greek. (Stavros Ioannou) Hussein Abdullah, Falaha Hassan, Ahmet Guli, Zirek Mizuri.

ROAD DOGS
Feb., 2000. (Detdrich McClure) Glenn Plummer, Chris Spencer, J. Lamont Pope.

THE ROAD HOME
SONY/COLUMBIA PICTURES FILM PROD. ASIA/GUANGXI FILM STUDIO/BEIJING NEW PICTURE DISTRIBUTION. Feb., 2000. Chinese. (Zhang Yimou) Zhang Ziyi, Sun Honglei, Zheng Hao, Zhao Yuelin, Li Bin, Chang Guifa, Sung Wencheng, Liu Qi, Ji Bo.

ROAD KILL
RICMAR PRODS. Mar., 1999. (Matthew Leutwyler) Jennifer Rubin, Erik Palladino, Billy Jayne, Tony Denison, Jon Polito.

ROADS AND BRIDGES
Apr., 2000. (Abraham Lim) Gregory Sullivan, Abraham Lim, Matt Malloy, Soon-Tek Oh, Jim Akman, Emmet Brennan, Joe Michaelski.

THE ROAD TO EL DORADO
DREAMWORKS. Mar., 2000. (Eric "Bibo" Bergeron, Don Paul) Kevin Kline, Kenneth Branagh, Rosie Perez, Armand Assante, Edward James Olmos, Elton John (voices). Animated.

ROAD TO PERDITION
DREAMWORKS (IN NORTH AMERICA)/20TH CENTURY FOX (INTERNATIONAL). June, 2002. (Sam Mendes) Tom Hanks, Paul Newman, Jude Law, Jennifer Jason Leigh, Stanley Tucci, Daniel Craig, Tyler Hoechlin, Liam Aiken, Dylan Baker, Ciaran Hinds.

ROAD TO REDEMPTION
WORLD WIDE PICTURES. Feb., 2001. (Robert Vernon) Jule Condra, Pat Hingle, Leo Rossi, Jay Underwood, Tony Longo, Wes Studi.

ROAD TRIP
DREAMWORKS/MONTECITO PICTURE CO. Apr., 2000. (Todd Phillips) Breckin Meyer, Seann William Scott, Amy Smart, Paulo Costanzo, D.J. Qualls, Rachel Blanchard, Anthony Rapp, Fred Ward.

ROBERTA
MOVING PARTS. Jan. 1999. (Eric Mandelbaum) Kevin Corrigan, Daisy Rojas, Amy Ryan, Bill Sage, Brian Tarantina.

ROBERTO SUCCO
DIAPHANA DISTRIBUTION. May, 2001. French. (Cedric Kahn) Stefano Cassetti, Isild Le Besco, Patrick Dell'Isola, Vincent Deneriaz.

ROBERT LOUIS STEVENSON'S THE SUICIDE CLUB
NEW CONCORDE. Jan., 2000. (Rachel Samuels) David Morrissey, Jonathan Pryce, Catherine Siggins, Paul Bettany, Neil Stuke.

ROCK OPERA
CRASHCAM CINEPRODUCTIONS. Jan., 2000. (Bob Ray) Jerry Don Clark, Ted Jarrell, Chad Holt, Paul Wright, Luis Olmeda, Rob Gasper.

ROCK STAR
WARNER BROS. Aug., 2001. (Stephen Herek) Mark Wahlberg, Jennifer Aniston, Jason Flemyng, Timothy Olyphant, Timothy Spall.

RODENTS
CABEZA HUECA PRODS. Sept., 1999. Ecuadorian. (Sebastian Cordero) Carlos Valencia, Marco Bustos, Irina Lopez, Simon Brauer.

RODGER DODGER
April, 2002. (Dylan Kidd) Campbell Scott, Jesse Eisenberg, Isabella Rossellini, Elizabeth Berkley, Jennifer Beals, Ben Shenkman, Mina Badle.

ROGUE TRADER
PATHE. June, 1999. British. (James Dearden) Ewan McGregor, Anna Friel, Yves Beneyton, Betsy Brantley, Carole Langrishe.

ROLLERCOASTER
GIRAFFE/CANADIAN TV FUND/TELEFILM CANADA/CANADIAN BROADCASTING CORP./TMN-THE MOVIE NETWORK/BRITISH COLUMBIA FILM. Sept., 1999. Canadian. (Scott Smith) Brendan Fletcher, Kett Turton,. Crystal Buble, Brent Glenen, Seam Amsing.

ROMAN AND LULU
BAC DISTRIBUTION. April, 2001. French. (Pierre-Olivier Scotto) Thierry Lhermitte, Claire Keim, Patrick Bouchitey, Pierre-Olivier Scotto, Cyrielle Clair.

ROMANCE
FLACH FILM, CB FILMS, ARTE-FRANCE CINEMA. Feb., 1999. French. (Catherine Brellat) Caroline Ducey, Sagamore Stevenin.

ROMAN SUMMER
ISTITUTO LUCE. Aug., 2000. Italian. (Matteo Gaudioso) Rossella Or, Monica Nappo, Salvatore Sansone, Victor Cavallo, Simone Carella.

ROMEO MUST DIE
WARNER BROS./SILVER PICTURES. Mar., 2000. (Andrzej Bartkowiak) Jet Li, Aaliyah, Isaiah Washington, Russell Wong, DMX.

RONIN
MGM. Aug., 1998. (John Frankenheimer) Robert De Niro, Jean Reno, Natascha McElhone, Stellan Skarsgard, Sean Bean, Skipp Sudduth.

THE ROOKIE
BUENA VISTA PICTURES. March, 2002. (John Lee Hancock) Dennis Quaid, Rachel Griffiths, Jay, Hernandez, Beth Grant, Angus T. Jones, Brian Cox, Rick Gonzalez.

A ROOM FOR ROMEO BRASS
Alliance Atlantis. Aug., 1999. British. (Shane Meadows) Andrew Shim, Ben Marshall, Paddy Considine, Frank Harper, Julia Ford.

ROOM TO RENT
UIP. Oct., 2000. British-French. (Khaled Al Haggar) Said Taghmaoui, Juliette Lewis, Rupert Graves, Anna Massey, Clementine Celarie.

THE ROOSTER
CECCHI GORI. Oct., 1998. Italian. (Carlo Verdone) Carlo Verdone, Regina Orioli, Paolo Triestino, Ines Nobili, Enrica Rosso.

ROSENZWEIG'S FREEDOM
SWR TELEVISION. Aug., 1999. German. (Liliane Targownik) Benjamin Sadler, Christoph Gareissen, Peter Roggisch, Gertrud Roll.

ROSETTA
USA FILMS. May, 1999. Belgian-French. (Luc and Jean-Pierre Dardenne) Emilie Dequenne, Fabrizio Rongione, Anne Yernaux.

ROUNDERS
MIRAMAX. Aug., 1998. (John Dahl) Matt Damon, Edward Norton, John Turturro, Gretchen Mol, Famke Janssen, John Malkovich, Martin Landau.

ROUTE 9
MOTION PICTURE CORP. OF AMERICA/PFG ENTERTAINMENT . May, 1999. (David Mackay) Kyle MacLachlan, Peter Coyote, Roma Maffia, Miguel Sandoval, Wade Andrew Williams.

ROW YOUR BOAT
GULLANE PICTURES/49TH PARALLEL PRODS./PREFERRED FILMS/WATER STREET PICTURES. Apr., 2000. (Sollace Mitchell) Jon Bon Jovi, Bai Ling, William Forsythe, Jill Hennessy, Peter Kwong.

THE ROYAL TENENBAUMS
BUENA VISTA. Oct., 2001. (Wes Anderson) Gene Hackman, Anjelica Huston, Ben Stiller, Gwyneth Paltrow, Luke Wilson, Own Wilson, Danny Glover, Bill Murray, Seymour Cassel, Kumar Pallana, Alec Baldwin, Grant Rosenmeyer, Jonah Meyerson.

RUDOLF THE RED-NOSED REINDEER: THE MOVIE
LEGACY. Oct., 1998. (Bill Kowalchuk). Animated.

RUE DU RETRAIT
CINEMA PUBLIC FILMS. April, 2001. French. (Rene Feret) Dominique Marcas, Marion Held.

RUGRATS IN PARIS: THE MOVIE
PARAMOUNT. Nov., 2000. (Stig Bergqvist, Paul Demeyer) ANIMATED. E.G. Daily, Christine Cavanaugh, Michael Bell, Susan Sarandon, Cheryl Chase, Julia Kato, Jack Riley, John Lithgow.

THE RUGRATS MOVIE
PARAMOUNT. Nov., 1998. (Norton Virgien, Igor Kovalyov. Animated.

THE RUINATION OF MEN
FILMANIA, GARDENIA PRODUCCIONES (MEXICO)/CANAL PLUS ESPANA, WANDA VISION (SPAIN). Sept., 2000. Mexican-Spanish. (Arturo Ripstein) Patricia Reyes Spindola, Rafael Inclan, Luis Felipe Tovar, Carlos Chavez, Leticia Valenzuela, Alejandra Montoya.

THE RULES OF ATTRACTION
LIONS GATE FILMS. Sept., 2002. (Roger Avary) James Van Der Beek, Ian Somerhalder, Shannyn Sossamon, Jessica Biel, Kip Pardue, Thomas Ian Nicholas, Kate Bosworth, Fred Savage, Eric Stoltz, Clifton Collins Jr., Faye Dunaway, Swoosie Kurtz.

RULES OF ENGAGEMENT
PARAMOUNT/SEVEN ARTS PICTURES/RICHARD D. ZANUCK/ SCOTT RUDIN. Mar., 2000. (William Friedkin) Tommy Lee Jones, Samuel L. Jackson, Guy Pearce, Bruce Greenwood, Blair Underwood,

Philip Baker Hall, Anne Archer, Ben Kingsley.

RUM AND COKE
RUM AND COKE/ESCOBEDO/GHERARDI. Feb., 2000. (Maria Escobedo) Diana Marquis, Juan Carlos Hernandez, Christopher Marazzo, Kevin A. King, Jacqueline Torres, Rosa Nino.

A RUMOR OF ANGELS
CINETEL FILMS. Sept., 2000 (Peter O'Fallon) Vanessa Redgrave, Ray Liotta, Catherine McCormack, Trevor Morgan, Ron Livingston.

RUNAWAY
VIXEN FILMS. Aug., 2001. British. (Kim Longinotto, Ziba Mir-Hosseini) Documentary.

RUNAWAY BRIDE
PARAMOUNT. July, 1999. (Garry Marshall) Julia Roberts, Richard Gere, Joan Cusack, Hector Elizondo, Rita Wilson.

A RUN FOR MONEY
WARNER BROS/ATLANTIK FILM. June, 2000. Turkish. (Reha Erdem) Taner Birsel, Bennu Yildirimlar, Zuhal Gencer, Engin Alkan.

THE RUNNER
ASPECT RATIO FILMS. May, 1999. (Ron Moler): Ron Eldard, Courteney Cox, Joe Mantegna, Bokeem Woodbine, John Goodman.

RUNNING BLUE
Nov., 2001. South Korean. (Kim Yu-min) Ha Ri-su, Shin Yi, Mo Hong-jin, Yun Chan.

RUNNING FREE
SONY PICTURES ENTERTAINMENT/COLUMBIA PICTURES/ REPERAGE. May, 2000. (Sergei Bodrov) Chase Moore, Jan Decleir.

RUNNING ON THE SUN: THE BADWATER 135
MEL STUART/GALAXY ENTERTAINMENT/QUALCOMM. Aug., 2000. (Mel Stuart). Documentary.

RUNNING OUT OF TIME
CHINA STAR/MILKYWAY IMAGE/WIN'S ENTERTAINMENT. Nov., 1999. Hong Kong. (Johnnie To) Andy Lau, Lau Ching-wan, YoYo Mung, Lee Chi-hung, Hui Shiu-hung, Lam Suet, Ruby Wong.

RUNNING OUT OF TIME 2
CHINA STAR ENTERTAINMENT GROUP. Feb., 2002. Hong Kong. (To, Law Wingcheong) Lau Ching-wan, Ekin Cheng, Kelly Lin, Hui Shiu-hung, Lam Suet, Ruby Wong, Ding Yuin-shan.

RUN RONNIE RUN!
NEW LINE CINEMA. Jan., 2002. (Troy Miller) David Cross, Bob Odenkirk, Nikki Cox, E.J. De La Pena, R. Lee Ermey, M.C. Gainey, Thomas J. Kenney, David M. Koechner.

RUSH HOUR
NEW LINE CINEMA. Aug., 1998. (Brett Ratner) Jackie Chan, Chris Tucker, Tom Wilkinson, Elizabeth Pena, Philip Baker Hall.

RUSH HOUR 2
NEW LINE CINEMA. July, 2001. (Brett Ratner) Jackie Chan, Chris Tucker, John Lone, Zhang Ziyi, Roselyn Sanchez, Harris Yulin.

RUSHMORE
BUENA VISTA. Sept., 1998. (Wes Anderson) Jason Schwartzman, Bill Murray, Olivia Williams, Seymour Cassel, Brian Cox, Mason Gamble.

RUSSIAN ARK
May, 2002. Russian-German. (Alexander Sokurov) Sergei Dreiden, Maria Kuznetsova, Leonid Mozgovoy.

RUSSIAN DOLL
LOT 47 FILMS. April, 2001. Australian. (Stavros Kazantzidis) Hugo Weaving, Natalia Novikova, David Wenham, Rebecca Frith, Sacha Horler, Helen Dallimore.

RUSSIAN MEAT
HRVATSKA RADIO TELEVISZIJA. Aug., 1998. Croation. (Luka Nola) Ivo Gregurevic, Barbara Nola, Goran Grgic, Kristijan Ugrina, Bojan Navojec.

RUSTEM'S NOTES WITH ILLUSTRATIONS
CENTER FOR FILM PRODUCTION, REPUBLIC OF KAZAKHSTAN. Feb., 1999. Kazakhstani. (Ardak Armikulov) Erzhan Rustembekov, Assel Shaimukhammedova.

RUSTIN
GRABBA-BAT FILMS. June, 2001. (Rick Johnson) Rick Johnson, Meat Loaf Aday, Ashley Johnson, Zachery Ty Bryan, Shawn Weatherly, Michael Papajohn, Dean Biasucci.

RUSTLING LANDSCAPES
Aug., 2002. Slovenian. (Janez Lapajne) Barbara Cerar, Rok Vihar, Gregor Zorc, Masa Derganc, Mateja Koleznik, Val Furst, Miha Brajnik.

RUTHIE & CONNIE: EVERY ROOM IN THE HOUSE
June, 2002. (Deborah Dickson) Documentary.

'R XMAS
STUDIOCANAL. May, 2001. French. (Abel Ferrara) Drea de Matteo, Lillo Brancato Jr., Ice-T, Victor Argo, Naomi Morales, Lisa Valens.

S.
FLANDERS IMAGE. June, 1999. Belgian. (Guido Henderickx) Natali Broods, Kristine van Pellicom, Inge Paulussen, Isnel Da Silveira, Katelijne Damen.

SABOTAGE!
UIP (SPAIN)/ARABA. Nov., 2000. Spanish-French-British. (Esteban Ibarretxe, Jose Miguel Ibarretxe) Stephen Fry, David Suchet, Dominique Pinon, Alexandra Vandernoot, Santiago Segura.

SACHS' DISEASE
PATHE/ELEFILM/RENN PRODS./KATHARINA/FRANCE2 CINEMA/ CANAL PLUS. Sept., 1999. French. (Michel Deville) Albert Dupontel, Valerie Dreville, Dominique Reymond, Martine Sarcey.

SACRED
OCEAN FILMS. May, 1999. Israeli-French. (Amos Gitai) Yael Abecassis, Yoram Hattab, Meital Barda, Uri Ran Klauzner.

SACRED FLESH
GOTHICA/SALVATION FILMS/400 CO. Apr., 2000. British. (Nigel Wingrove) Sally Tremaine, Moyna Cope, Simon Hill, Kristina Bill.

SADE
OCEAN FILMS/ALICELIO/TF1 FILMS PROD./COFIMAGE 11/CANAL PLUS. Aug., 2000. French. (Benoit Jacquot) Daniel Auteuil, Marianne Denicourt, Jeanne Balibar, Gregoire Colin, Isild Le Besco.

A SAD FLOWER IN THE SAND
Nov., 2001. Dutch. (Jan Louter) Joyce Fante, Robert Towne, Stephen Cooper, Jim Fante, Dan Fante, John Martin. Documentary.

SAFE MEN
ANDELL ENTERTAINMENT. Jan., 1998. (John Hamburg) Sam Rockwell, Steve Zahn, Paul Giamatti, Michael Schmidt.

SAFE SEX
PAPANDREOU S.A.-MEGA CHANNEL/TASSOS PAPANDREOU. Feb., 2000. Greek. (Thanassis Papathanassiou, Michalis Reppas) Mina Adamaki, Alexandros Antonopoulos, Kostas Grekas.

THE SAFETY OF OBJECTS
CLEAR BLUE SKY/RENAISSANCE FILMS. Sept., 2001. (Rose Troche) Glenn Close, Dermot Mulroney, Jessica Campbell, Patricia Clarkson, Joshua Jackson, Moira Kelly Robert Klein.

SAGITTARIUS
LAUREN FILMS. June, 2001. Spanish. (Vicente Molina Foix) Angela Molina, Eusebio Poncela, Enrique Alcides, Daniel Freire, Maria Isasi.

SAILING HOME
SACHER DISTRIBUZIONE. Aug., 2001. Italian. (Vincenzo Marra) Aniello Scotto D'Antuono, Salvatore Iaccarino, Giovanni Iaccarino, Abdel Aziz Azouz, Roberta Papa.

SAINT BERNARD
COLUMBIA TRISTAR FILMS DE ESPANA. Aug., 2000. Spanish. (Joan Potau) Alberto San Juan, Patricia Velasquez, Ana Risueno.

SAINT JUDE
SEVILLE PICTURES. Oct., 2000. Canadian. (John L'Ecuyer) Liane Balaban, Nicholas Campbell, Raymond Cloutier, Victoria Sanchez.

THE ST. FRANCISVILLE EXPERIMENT
TRIMARK. Apr., 2000. (Tim Baldini) Tim Baldini, Madison Charap, Ryan Larson, Paul Palmer.

SAINT JEROME
RIO FILME/TB PRODUCOES. Sept., 1999. Brazilian. (Julio Bressane) Everaldo Pontes, Hamilton Vaz Pereira, Balduino Lellis.

THE SALESMAN
MONTI PALLIDI FILM-CLEMART. Feb., 2001. Italian. (Francesco Dal Bosco) Claudio Bigagli, Maddalena Crippa, Carlo Croccolo, Valentia Emeria, Katia Pietrobelli.

SALLY MARSHALL IS NOT AN ALIEN
UIP. June, 1999. Australian-Canadian. (Mario Andreacchio) Helen Neville, Natalie Vansier, Thea Gumbert, Glenn McMillan, Danielle de Grossi.

SALOME
Aug., 2002. Spanish. (Carlos Saura) Aida Gomez, Pere Arquillue, Paco Mora, Carmen Villena, Javier Toca, Dos y Danza Dance Co.

THE SALTON SEA
WARNER BROS. Feb., 2002. (D.J. Caruso) Val Kilmer, Vincent D'Onofrio, Adam Goldberg, Luis Guzman, Doug Hutchison, Anthony LaPaglia, Glenn Plummer, Peter Sarsgaard, Deborah Kara Unger, Chandra West, B.D. Wong, R. Lee Ermey, Shalom Harlow.

SALTWATER
IRISH FILM BOARD/BBC FILMS/TREASURE FILMS. Feb., 2000. Irish-British. (Conor McPherso) Peter McDonald, Brian Cox, Conor Mullen, Laurence Kinlan, Brendan Gleeson, Eva Birthistle, Valerie Spelman, David O'Rourke.

SALUZZI, COMPOSITION FOR BANDONEON AND THREE BROTHERS
DANIEL ROSENFELD. Apr., 2000. Argentine (Daniel Rosenfeld). Documentary.

THE SAME LOVE, THE SAME RAIN
WARNER BROS./JORGE ESTRADA MORA PRODS. Apr., 2000. Argentine. (Juan Jose Campanella) Ricardo Darin, Soledad Villamil, Eduardo Blanco, Ulises Dumont, Graciela Tenebaum.

SAMIA
OGNON PICTURES/ARTE FRANCE CINEMA. Sept., 2000. French. (Philippe Faucon) Lynda Benahouda, Mohamed Chaouch, Kheira Oualhaci, Lakhdar Smati, Nadia El Koutei.

SAMPLE PEOPLE
REP/SOUTH AUSTRALIAN FILM CORP./LIVING MOTION PICTURES/SCANBOX ASIA PACIFIC. Mar., 2000. Australian. (Clinton Smith) Kylie Minogue, Ben Mendelsohn, Simon Lyndon.

SAMOURAI
PATHE. July, 2002. French. (Giordano Gederlini) Cyril Mourali, Mai Anh Le, Yasuaki Kurata, Said Serrari, Santi Sudaros, Pascal Gentil, Omar Sy, Dara-Indo Oury.

SAMSARA
MIRAMAX (IN U.S.). July, 2002. German. (Pan Nalin) Shawn Ku, Christy Chung, Neelesha BaVora, Lhakpa Tsering, Tenzin Tashi, Jamayang Jinpa, Sherab Sangey, Kelsang Tashi.

SAMURAI FICTION
PONY CANYON/JUNGLE/DIGITAL GARAGE . May, 1999. Japanese. (Hiroyuki Nakano) Morio Kazama, Mitsuru Fukikoshi, Tomoyasu Hotei, Tamaki Ogawa, Mari Natsuki.

SANAM
VELVET FILMS. Oct., 2001. French. (Rafi Pitts) Roya Nonahali, Ismail Amani.

SANCTIMONY
REGENT ENTERTAINMENT/1ST BOLL KINO BETEILIGUNGS. May, 2000. German-U.S. (Uwe Boll) Casper Van Dien, Michael Pare, Eric Roberts, Catherine Oxenburg, Jennifer Rubin, Michael Rasmussen.

THE SANDMEN
LES FILMS DU LOSANGE/AGAT FILMS & CO./LES FILMS PELLEAS/CNC/SOFICA/GIMAGES 2/GIMAGES DEVELOPPEMENT/ LA SEPT/ARTE. July, 2000. French. (Pierre Salvadori) Robert Castel, Mathieu Demy, Serge Riaboukine, Guillaume Depardieu.

SANDSTORM
SMRITI PICTURES. Feb., 2001. Indian. (Jagmohan) Nandita Das, Raghuvir Yadav, Deepti Naval, Rahul Khanna, Laila Rouass.

SANTA MARADONA
MIKADO. Italian. (Marco Ponti) Stefano Accorsi, Anita Caprioli, Libero De Rienzo, Mandala Tayde.

SARA AMERIKA
BLACKWOOD CONNECTION/HELKON MEDIA FILMPRODUCTION. Oct., 1999. German. (Roland Suso Richter) Dennenesch Zoude, Thomas Heinze, Gregor Torzs, Oliver Korittke.

SASHA ENTERS LIFE
MOSFILM. Aug., 2000. Soviet Union–1957. (Mikhail Shveitser) Viktor Avdyushko, Oleg Tabakov, Nikolai Sergeyev, Ivan Pereverzev.

SATURDAY
Aug., 2001. Argentine. (Juan Villegas) Gaston Pauls, Daniel Hendler, Camila Toker, Mariana Anghileri, Leonardo Murua, Eva Sola.

SATURDAY NIGHT
LATE SATURDAY FILMS/AUSTRALIAN FILM COMM. Mar., 2000. Australian. . (James Balian) Alison Whyte, Aaron Pederson.

SAUDATE FOR THE FUTURE
LATERIT PRODS/COBRA FILMS/LX FILMES/AF CINEMA & VIDEO/RTBF LIEGE/VOYAGE/MEZZO. Aug., 2000. Brazilian-French. (Cesar Paes). Documentary.

SAUSALITO
STAR EAST/BOB & PARTNERS CO. May, 2000. Hong Kong. (Andrew Lau) Leon Lai, Maggie Cheung, Eric Kot, Richard Ng.

SAVAGE HONEYMOON
STEVE SACHS. Jan. 2000. New Zealand. (Mark Beasley) Nicholas Eadie, Perry Piercy, Elizabeth Hawthorne.

SAVAGES
ALTA FILMS. Spanish. (Carlos Molinero) Marisa Paredes, Imanol Arias, Manuel Moron, Roger Casamajor, Maria Isasi, Alberto Ferreiro, Jose Luis Alcobendas.

SAVAGE SOULS
MDI PRODS.-LES FILMS DU LENDEMAIN. May, 2001. French-Belgian. (Raul Ruiz) Laetitia Casta, Frederic Diefenthal, Arielle Dombasle, John Malkovich, Charles Berling, Johan Leysen.

SAVE ME
FLACH PYRAMIDE INTL., FRANCE INFO AND PYRAMIDE DISTRIBUTION. April, 2001. French. (Christian Vincent) Roschdy Zem, Rona Hartner, Karole Rocher, Jean-Roger Milo.

SAVE THE LAST DANCE
PARAMOUNT. Jan., 2001. (Thomas Carter) Julia Stiles, Sean Patrick Thomas, Kerry Washington, Fredro Starr, Terry Kinney, Bianca Lawson, Vince Green.

SAVING GRACE
FINE LINE/PORTMAN ENTERTAINMENT/SKY PICTURES/WAVE PICTURES/HOMERUN. Jan., 2000. British. (Nigel Cole) Brenda Blethyn, Craig Ferguson, Martin Clunes, Tcheky Karyo.

SAVING PRIVATE RYAN
DREAMWORKS PICTURES/PARAMOUNT. July, 1998. (Steven Spielberg) Tom Hanks, Edward Burns, Tom Sizemore, Jeremy Davies, Adam Goldberg, Barry Pepper, Giovanni Ribisi, Matt Damon.

SAVING SILVERMAN
SONY PICTURES ENTERTAINMENT. Jan., 2001. (Dennis Dugan) Jason Biggs, Steve Zahn, Jack Black, Amanda Peet, R. Lee Ermey, Amanda Detmer, Neil Diamond, Lillian Carlson.

SAVIOR
FIRST INDEPENDENT. June, 1998. (Peter Antonijevic) Dennis Quaid, Nastassja Kinski, Stellan Skarsgard. Natasa Ninkovic.

SAY IT ISN'T SO
20TH CENTURY FOX. March, 2001. (J.B. Rogers) Chris Klein, Heather Graham, Orlando Jones, Sally Field, Richard Jenkins, John Rothman, Jack Plotnick Eddie Cibrian.

SAY YOU'LL BE MINE
EAGLE BEACH PRODS. June, 1999. (Brad Kane) Nicky Katt, Libby Langdon, Daniel Lapaine, Megan Ward, Justine Bateman.

SCARFIES
ESSENTIAL FILMS. May, 1999. New Zealand. (Robert Sarkies) Willa O'Neill, Neill Rea, Taika Cohen, Ashleigh Seagar, Charlie Bleakley.

SCARLET DIVA
MINERVA/DARIO ARGENTO/CLAUDIO ARGENTO/OPERA FILM/ GIANLUCA & STEFANO CURT/ADRIANA CHIESA DI PALMA. May, 2000. Italian. (Asia Argento) Asia Argento, Jean Shepherd, Herbert Fritsch, Joe Coleman, Francesca d'Aloja, Vera Gemma.

SCARRED CITY
MILLENNIUM FILMS. May, 1998. (Ken Sanzel) Stephen Baldwin, Chazz Palminteri, Tia Carrere, Gary Dourdan, Michael Rispoli.

SCARS
INSTITUTO NACIONAL DE CINE & ARTES AUDIOVISUALES/JUAN CARLOS FISNER & ASOCIADOS. Apr., 2000. Argentine. (Patricio Coll) Omar Fantini, Raul Kreig, Pablo Di Crocce, Monica Galan.

SCARS
May, 2002. Norwegian. (Lars Berg) Eirik Evjen, Marin Jonny Raaen Eidissen, Eirik Stigar.

SCARY MOVIE
DIMENSION PICTURES/WAYANS BROS. ENT./GOLD-MILLER/ BRAD GREY PICTURES. June, 2000. (Keenen Ivory Wayans) Shawn Wayans, Marlon Wayans, Cheri Oteri, Shannon Elizabeth, Anna Faris, Jon Abrahams, Lochlyn Munro.

SCARY MOVIE 2
DIMENSION PICTURES. July, 2001. (Keene Ivory Wayans) Shawn Wayans, Marlon Wayans, Anna Faris, Regina Hall, Chris Masterson, Kathleen Robertson, David Cross, James Woods, Tim Curry.

SCENERY
YAN CHEN. Jan., 1999. Chinese. (Zhao Jisong): Lin Peng, Sun Fengyiin, Zhao Yunyun.

SCENES OF THE CRIME
CINERENTA, BATTLE PLAN PRODS.Sept., 2001. (Dominique Forma) Jeff Bridges, John Abrahams, Noah Wyle, Morris Chestnut, Madchen Amick, Peter Greene, Bob Gunton.

THE SCENT OF THE NIGHT
FILMAURO. Sept., 1998. Italian. (Claudio Caligari) Valerio Mastandrea, Marco Giallini, Giorgio Tirabassi, Alessio Fugardi.

SCHPAAA
EUROPAFILM. Feb., 1999. Norwegian. (Erik Poppe) Maikel Andressen Abou-Zelof, Jalal Zahedjekta, Sharjil Arshed Vaseer.

SCOOBY-DOO
WARNER BROS. June, 2002. (Raja Gosnell) Freddie Prinze Jr., Sarah Michelle Gellar, Matthew Lillard, Linda Cardellini, Rowan Atkinson, Isla Fisher.

THE SCORE
PARAMOUNT PICTURES. July, 2001. (Frank Oz) Robert De Niro, Edward Norton, Marlon Brando, Angela Bassett, Gary Farmer.

SCORN
ALLIANCE-ATLANTIS. Sept., 2000. Canadian. (Sturla Gunnarsson) Eric Johnson, Brendan Fletcher, Bill Switzer, Emily Hampshire.

SCOTLAND, PA.
ABANDON PICTURES. Jan., 2001. (Billy Morrissette) James LeGros, Maura Tierney, Christopher Walken, Kevin Corrigan, James Rebhorn, Thomas Guiry, Amy Smart.

SCOTTSBORO: AN AMERICAN TRAGEDY
SOCIAL MEDIA PRODS./AMERICAN EXPERIENCE. Jan., 2000. (Barak Goodman, Daniel Anker). Documentary.

THE SCOUNDREL'S WIFE
March, 2002. (Glen Pitre) Tatum O'Neal, Julian Sands, Tim Curry, Lacey Chabert, Eion Bailey, Patrick McCullough.

SCOUT-MAN
GOLD VIEW. Sept., 2000. Japanese. (Masato Ishioka) Miku Matsumoto, Hideo Nakaizumi, Yuka Fujimoto, Akihito Yoshiie, Yuri Komuro, Shiro Shimomoto.

SCOUT'S HONOR
INDEPENDENT TELEVISION SERVICE. Jan., 2001. (Tom Shepard) Documentary.

SCRAPBOOK
FRAGILE ENTERTAINMENT. Jan., 1999. (Kurt Kuenne) Justin Urich, Eric Balfour, Chadwick Palmatier, Keili Lefkowitz, Jed Rhein.

SCRATCH
RIDGEWAY ENTERTAINMENT. Jan., 2001. (Doug Pray) Qbert, Invisibl Skratch Piklz, Rob Swift and the X-ecutioners, DJ Shadow, Steve Dee, Cut Chemist & NuMark, DJ Craze. Documentary.

SCRATCHES IN THE TABLE
EGMOND FILM & TV/VPRO TV. Jan., 2000. Ductch. (Ineke Houtman) Madelief Vereist, Rijk de Gooijer, Margo Dames, Freek Bom.

SCREAM 3
DIMENSION FILMS/KONRAD PICTURES/CRAVEN/MADDALENA FILMS. Feb., 2000. (Wes Craven) David Arquette, Neve Campbell, Courteney Cox Arquette, Patrick Dempsey, , Lance Henriksen, Matt Keeslar, Jenny McCarthy, Emily Mortimer, Parker Posey.

SCREENPLAY
SCREENPLAY LIMITED PARTNERS. July, 1999. (Adam Winston) Sean Gavigan, David Coburn, Kathryn Morris, Kristofer Linquist.

SCREEN QUOTA IN KOREA
UNIKOREA/DREAM VENTURE CAPITAL/SCREEN QUOTA WATCHERS/SEOUL VISUAL COLLECTIVE. Oct., 1999. South Korean. (Cho Jae-hong) Myung Kay-nam, Lee Cheon-yeon, Kim Hae-jin, Chung Ji-yeong, Mun Sung-keun, Ahn Sung-ki. Documentary.

SCREWED
UNIVERSAL PICTURES/ROBERT SIMONDS/BRAD GREY. May, 2000. (Scott Alexander, Larry Karaszewski) Norm Macdonald, Dave Chappelle, Elaine Stritch, Danny DeVito, Daniel Benzali.

THE SEA
MASSA D'OR PRODS./COFUC/TVE/TVC. Feb., 2000. Spanish. (Agusti Villaronga) Bruno Bergonzini, Roger Casamajor, Antonia Torrens, Angela Molina, Simon Andreu, Juli Mira, Hernan Gonzalez.

THE SEAGULL'S LAUGHTER (MAVAHLATUR)
July, 2002. Icelandic-German-British. (Agust Gudmundsson) Margret Vilhjalmsdottir, Ugla Egilsdottir, Heino Ferch, Hilmir Snaer Gudnason, Kristbjorg Kjeld, Edda Bjorg Eyjolfsdottir.

SEALED WITH A KISS
MEI AH/MILKYWAY IMAGE. Nov., 1999. Hong Kong. (Derek Chiu) Louis Koo, Yo Yo Mung, Raymond Wong, Siu Au.

SEANCE
KANSAI TELECASTING/TWINS JAPAN. Aug., 2000. Japanese. (Kiyoshi Kurosawa) Koji Yakusho, Jun Fubuki, Tsuyoshi Kusanagi.

THE SEARCH FOR JOHN GISSING
Nov., 2001. (Mike Binder) Mike Binder, Janeane Garofalo, Alan Richman, Sonya Walger, Juliet Stevenson, Allan Corduner.

SEARCHING FOR DEBRA WINGER
May, 2002. (Rosanna Arquette) Patricia Arquette, Emanuelle Beart, Laura Dern, Roger Ebert, Jane Fonda, Teri Garr, Whoopi Goldberg, Melanie Griffith, Daryl Hannah, Holly Hunter, Diane Lane, Frances McDormand. Documentary.

SEASIDE
PYRAMIDE. May, 2002. French. (Julie Lopes-Curval) Jonathan Zaccai, Bulle Ogier, Ludmilla Mikael, Liliane Rovere, Helene Fillieres.

SEASIDE, DUSK
KEP-ARNYEK/HAZARD/MMK/NKA/TV2/ORTT/DUNA TV. Feb., 2000. Hungarian-German. (Andras Fesos) Gyozo Szabo, Andrea Takats, Laszlo Keszeg, Maria Schuster.

THE SEASON OF GUAVAS
YOUTH STUDIO/LES FILMS D'ICI/MINISTRY OF CULTURE & TOURISM /VIETNAM CINEMA OFFICE. Aug., 2000. Vietnamese. (Dan Nhat Minh) Bui Bai Binh, Nguyen Lan Huong, Pham Thu Thuy.

THE SEASON OF MEN
APPOLO DISTRIBUTION/LES FILMS DU LOSANGE/ MAGHREBFILMS CARTHAGE/ARTE FRANCE CINEMA. May, 2000. Tunisian-French. (Moufida Tlatli) Rabiaa Ben Abdallah, Sabah Bouzouita, Ghalia Ben Ali, Hend Sabri, Ezzedine Gennoun.

THE SEA THAT THINKS
A-FILM DISTRIBUTION. Jan., 2001. Dutch. (Gert de Graaff) Bart Klever, Rick de Leeuw, Don Duyns, Devia Strooker.

SECOND CLASS CITIZENS
MINISTRY OF CULTURE & ART OF UKRAINE. Feb., 2001. Ukrainian. (Kira Muratova) Natalia Buzko, Sergei Chetvertkov, Nikola Sadnev, Jean Daniel.

SECOND COMING
COLONY FILMS. June, 2001. (Darren Campbell, Steve Rees) Darren Campbell, Jay Boyer, J.J. Donier, Lucie Laurier, Billy Brown, Arthur Rouidoulas, Anthony Joseph, Ortrud Swanson.

SECOND GENERATION
SECOND GENERATION FILMS. Nov., 2000. British. (Shane O'Sullivan) Hanayo, Shigetomo Yutani, Saeed Jaffrey, Nitin Ganatra.

SECOND SKIN
LOLAFILMS DISTRIBUCION/VIA DIGITAL/ANTENA 3 TV. Jan., 2000. Spanish. (Gerardo Vera) Javier Bardem, Jordi Molla, Ariadna Gil.

THE SECOND WIFE
CECCHI GORI. Aug., 1998. Italian. (Ugo Chiti) Maria Grazia Cucinotta, Lazar Ristovski, Girogio Noe, Jessica Auriemma, Patrizia Corti.

THE SECOND WIND
NUVISION. April, 2001. Mexican. (Fernando Sarinana) Jesus Ochoa, Lisa Owen, Jorge Poza, Ximena Sarinana.

SECRET
TOKYO BROADCASTING. Dec., 1999. Japanese. (Yojiro Takita) Ryoki Hirosue, Kaoru Kobayashi, Kayoko Kishimoto, Ken Kaneko.

THE SECRET
LES PRODS. BAGHEERA/FRANCE 3 CINEMA/DIAPHANA FILMS/CANAL PLUS/LE CENTRE NATIONAL DE LA CINEMATOGRAPHIE/LA PROCIREP/SOFICA S. May, 2000. French. (Virginie Wagon) Anne Coesens, Michel Bompoil, Tony Todd, Quentin Rossi.

SECRET BALLOT
SONY CLASSICS PICTURES. Sept., 2001. Italian-Iranian-Canadian-Swiss. (Babak Payami) Nassim Abdi, Cyrus Abidi, Youssef Habashi, Farrokh Shojaii, Gholbahar Janghali.

THE SECRET LAUGHTER OF WOMEN
OPTIMUM RELEASING/PARAGON ENT./HANDMADE FILMS/EUROPEAN CO-PRODUCTION FUND/BSKYB/ARTS COUNCIL OF ENGLAND/ELBA/PARAGON. Nov., 1999. British-Canadian. (Peter Schwabach) Colin Firth, Nia Long, Fissy Roberts, Caroline Goodall.

THE SECRET LIFE OF GIRLS
OVERSEAS FILM GROUP. June, 1999. (Holly Goldberg) Linda Hamilton, Eugene Levy, Majandra Delfino, Meagan Good.

THE SECRET LIVES OF DENTISTS
MANHATTAN PICTURES. Sept., 2002. (Alan Rudolph) Campbell Scott, Hope Davis, Denis Leary, Robin Tunney, Gianna Beleno, Cassidy Hinkle, Lydia Jordan, Jon Patrick Walker, Kevin Carroll, Kate Clinton.

SECRET LOVE
T&C FILM. Aug., 2001. Swiss. (Christoph Schaub) Emmanuelle Laborit, Lars Otterstetd, Renate Becker, Wolfram Berger, Renate Steiger, Roeland Wisnekker.

SECRET SOCIETY
ENA FILM (GERMANY)/FOCUS FILMS PRODS. (U.K.). Nov., 2000. German-British. (Imogen Kimmel) Charlotte Brittain, Lee Ross, Annette Badland, James Hooton.

SECRETS OF SILICON VALLEY
SNITOW-KAUFMAN PRODS. April, 2001. (Alan Snitow, Deborah Kaufman) Documentary.

SECRET TEARS
CINEMA SERVICE. Oct., 2000. South Korean. (Park Ki-hyeong) Kim Seung-woo, Yun Mi-jo, Jeong Hyeon-woo, Park Eun-suk.

SEED
WORKING PICTURES. Apr., 2000. (Bobby Sheehan) John Michael Bolger, Chuck Negron.

SEE HOW THEY RUN (EMBRASSEZ QUI VOUS VOUDREZ)
UFD-UGC DISTRIBUTION. Aug., 2002. French-British-Italian. (Michel Blanc) Charlotte Rampling, Jacques Dutronc, Carole Bouquet, Michel Blanc, Karin Viard, Denis Podalydes, Clotilde Courau, Vincent Elbaz.

SEE JANE RUN
ORCHID WENDLE PICTURES AND EOXON ENTERTAINMENT. Feb., 2001. (Sarah Thorp) Clea Du Vall, Kevin Corrigan, Jennifer Aspen, Richmond Arquette, Terry Kiser, Stanley DeSantis.

SEE JULIE AGAIN
FILM TONIC. Oct., 1998. Canadian. (Jeanne Crepeau) Dominique Leduc, Stephanie Morgenstern, Marcel Sabourin, Muriel Dutil, Lucille Belair.

SEE SPOT RUN
WARNER BROS. Feb., 2001. (John Whitesell) David Arquette, Michael Clarke Duncan, Leslie Bibb, Joe Viterelli, Angus T. Jones, Steven R. Schirripa.

SEE YA LATER, POLLUX (A+POLLUX)
MAGOURIC DISTRIBUTION. July, 2002. French. (Luc Pages) Gad Elmaleh, Cecile De France, Nathalie Boutefeu, Jean-Marie Galey, Marina Golovine, Marilu Marini, Pierre Berriau.

SEE YOU
ISTITUTO LUCE/TANGRAM FILM/INSTITUTO LUCE/RAI RADIOTELEVISIONE ITALIANA. Sept., 1999. Italian. (Gianni Zanasi) Stefania Rivi, Andrea Corneti, Wilson Saba, Paolo Sassanelli.

SEE YOU OFF TO THE EDGE OF TOWN
June, 2002. U.S.-Hong Kong. (Ching C. Ip) Zhu Xi Juan, K.K. Wong, Yvonne Teoh, Jo Chim, Christopher Cheng, Henry Amitai.

THE SELF-DESTRUCTION OF GIA
July, 2002. (JJ Martin) Kathleen Sperr, Sandy Linter, Francesco Scavullo, Jade Hobson Charnin, Diane Von Furstenberg, Nancy Donahue, Robert Hilton, Vera Wang, Zoe Lund, Maurice Tannenbaum, Harry King. Documentary.

SELKIE
UIP/BLUESTONE/AUSTRALIAN FILM COMM./SOUTH AUSTRALIAN FILM CORP./SHOWTIME AUSTRALIA. Mar., 2000. Australian. (Donald Crombie) Shimon Moore, Chelsea Bruland, Bryan Marshall.

SENSITIVE NEW-AGE KILLER
FRISSON. July, 2000. Australian. (Mark Savage) Paul Moder, Kevin Hopkins, Helen Hopkins, Carolyn Bock, Frank Bren.

SENSO '45
EAGLE PICTURES. April, 2002. Italian. (Tinto Brass) Anna Galiena, Gabriel Garko, Franco Branciaroli.

SENSO UNICO
BENGAL TIGER PICTURES. June, 1999. Italian-Indian-British. (Aditya Bhattacharya) Lothaire Bluteau, Laila Rouass.

SERBIA YEAR ZERO
BERNARD-HENRY LEVY. Sept., 2001. French-Tugoslavian. (Goran Markovic) Documentary.

SERENADES
PALACE FILMS (AUSTRALIA). Nov., 2000. Australian. (Mojgan Khadem) Alice Haines, Aden Young, Sinisa Copic, Bille Brown.

SERENDIPITY
MIRAMAX. Sept., 2001. (Peter Chelsom) John Cusack, Kate Beckinsale, Molly Shannon, Jeremy Piven, John Corbett, Bridget Moynahan, Eugene Levy.

SERPENT'S PATH
DAIEI CO. Aug., 1999. Japanese. (Kiyoshi Kurosawa) Sho Aikawa, Teruyuki Kagawa.

THE SERVANT'S SHIRT
ANT CARRY THE MOUNTAIN FILMS. Feb., 1999. Indian-Dutch. (Mani Kaul) Pankaj Sudhir Mishra, Anu Joseph, Om Praksh Dwivedi.

SERVING SARA
PARAMOUNT PICTURES. Aug., 2002. (Reginald Hudlin) Matthew Perry, Elizabeth Hurley, Bruce Campbell, Amy Adams, Vincent Pastore, Cedric the Entertainer, Terry Crews, Jerry Stiller, Joe Viterelli.

SESSION 9
USA FILMS. July, 2001. (Brad Anderson) Peter Mullan, David Caruso, Stephen Gevedon, Josh Lucas, Brendan Sexton III, Paul Guilfoyle.

SET ME FREE
FRANCE FILM. Feb., 1999. Canadian-Swiss-French. (Lea Pool) Karine Vanasse, Alexandre Merineau, Pascale Bussieres.

THE SETTLEMENT
DOGSMILE PICTURES/DAVIS ENTERTAINMENT/CINETEL FILMS . Apr., 1999. (Mark Steilen) John C. Reilly, William Fichtner, Kelly McGillis, David Rasche, Dan Castellaneta.

THE SETTLEMENT
ST. PETERSBURG DOCUMENTARY FILM STUDIO. July, 2001. Russian. (Sergei Loznitsa) Documentary.

SETTLERS
TENFOOT FILMS. Oct., 2000. British. (Sean McAllister) Documentary.

SEVEN AND A MATCH
SMART FILMS AND ROBSON ENTERTAINMENT. April, 2001. (Derek Simonds) Tina Holmes, Eion Bailey, Petra Wright.

SEVEN DAYS IN SEPTEMBER
Sept., 2002. (Steven Rosenbaum) Documentary.

7 DAYS IN TEHRAN (LES BEAUX LENDEMAINS DE TEHERAN)
June, 2002. French-Iranian. (Reza Khatibi) Jean-Philippe Cheru, Sabrina Delarue, Esfandiar Esfandi, Iradj Esmaili, Reza Khatibi.

7 DAYS TO LIVE
SENATOR FILM/INDIGO/BECKER & HAEBERLE/ROOFTOP ENT./EIS PRODS. June, 2000. German. (Sebastian Niemann) Amanda Plummer, Sean Pertwee, Nick Brimble.

SEVEN GIRLFRIENDS
WHITE DWARF PRODS./J. TODD HARRIS/BARRY OPPER. Feb., 2000. (Paul Lazarus) Tim Daly, Olivia D'Abo, Jami Gertz, Melora Hardin, Laura Leighton, Elizabeth Pena, Mimi Rogers.

SEVEN SONGS FROM THE TUNDRA
JORN DONNER. Feb., 2000. Finnish. (Anatasia Lapsui, Markku Lehmuskallio) Vitalina Hudi, Hatjako Yzangi, Gregory Anaguritsi.

17 RUE BLEUE
QUO VADIS CINEMA. Aug., 2001. French. (Chad Chenouga) Lysiane Meis, Abdel Halis, Aimen Ben Hamed, Nassim Sakhoui.

SEVENTEEN YEARS
KEETMAN LTD./XI'AN FILM STUDIO. Aug., 1999. Chinese-Italian. (Zhang Yuan) Liu Lin, Li Bingbing, Le Yeping, Liang Song, Li Jun.

7/25
PALMYLA MOON. May, 1999. Japanese. (Wataru Hayakawa) Isamu Hyuga, Mihoko Umetsu, Junya Nakano, Risa Miyanaga.

75 DEGREES IN JULY
STOCKYARD FILMS. Aug., 2000. (Hyatt Bass) Shirley Knight, William Moses, Karen Sillas, Heidi Swedberg, Harris Yulin.

76 89 03
LA PRODU 90'/ATOMIC FILMS. Sept., 2000. Argentine. (Cristian Bernard, Flavio Nardini) Sol Alac, Sergio Baldini, Gerardo Chendo, Diego Mackenzie, Claudio Rissi.

'73 MODEL
TRESPLANOS CINE. April, 2001. Argentine. (Rodrigo Moscoso) Emmanuel Moscoso, Sebastian Colina, Fernando Belton, Jimena Gonzalez, Andrea Rodriguez, Carolina Terpolili.

THE 7TH SUN OF LOVE
Dec., 2001. Greek-Bulgarian-Turkish. (Vangelis Serdaris) Thodoros Skourtas, Katerina Papadaki, Maria Kavoukidou, Hrysanthos Pavlou, Anastasia Pantazopoulou, Thalia Argyrion.

A SEVERE YOUNG MAN
UKRAINFILM. Aug., 2000. Soviet Union–1936. (Abram Room) Dmitri Dorliak, Olga Zhizneva, Yuri Yurev, Maksim Straukh.

SEX AND LUCIA
WARNER SOGEFILM. Aug., 2001. Apanish. (Julio Medem) Paz Vega Tristan Ulloa, Najwa Nimri, Daniel Freire, Elena Anaya, Silvia Llanos.

SEX IS COMEDY
REX FILMS. May, 2002. French. (Catherine Breillat) Anne Parillaud, Gregoire Colin, Roxane Mesquida, Ashley Wanninger, Dominique Colladant, Burt Binnema.

THE SEX MONSTER
TRIMARK. May, 1999. (Mike Binder) Mariel Hemingway, Mike Binder, Renee Humphrey, Taylor Nichols, Missy Crider.

SEX, SHAME AND TEARS
TITAN & SPL.. Mar., 1999. Mexican. (Antonio Serrano) Demian Bichir, Susana Zabaleta, Monic Dionne, Jorge Salinas.

SEX: THE ANNABEL CHONG STORY
OMNI INTL. AND GREYCAT RELEASING. Jan., 1999. U.S.-Canadian. (Gough Lewis) Grace Quek, Annabel Chong.

SEX OUT OF COMPASSION
FILMAX/SOGEDASA VISUAL GROUP/RESONANCIA PROD./VIA DIGITAL. June, 2000. Spanish-Mexican. (Laura Mana) Elisabeth Margoni, Alex Angulo, Pilar Bardem, Juan Carlos Colombo.

THE SEXUAL LIFE OF THE BELGIANS 4: PLEASURE AND HYSTERIA
TRANSATLANTIC FILMS/DE SMET FILMS. Feb., 2000. Belgian. (Jan Bucquoy), Jan Bucquoy, Evelyne Letwe, Marie Bucquoy.

SEX WITH STRANGERS
Feb., 2002. (Joe and Harry Gantz) Documentary.

SEXY BEAST
FILMFOUR/FOX SEARCHLIGHT/RECORDED PICTURE CO./KANZAMAN. Sept., 2000. British. (Jonathan Glazer) Ray Winstone, Ben Kingsley, Ian McShane, Amanda Redman.

SEXY BOYS
Dec., 2001. French. (Stephane Kazandjian) Julien Baumgartner, Matthias Van Khache, Jeremie Elkaim, Armelle Deutsch, Virginie Lanoue, Sarah Marshall, Violette Palcossian, Laurent Baffie.

SEXY COMEDY
CECCHI GORI DISTRIBUZIONE. Jan., 2001. Italian. (Claudio Begagli) Alessandro Benvenuti, Elena Sofia Ricci, Ricky Tognazzi.

SHACKLETON'S ANTARCTIC ADVENTURE
MORGAN STANLEY DEAN WITTER. Feb., 2001. (George Butler) Documentary-Imax.

SHACKY CARMINE
AURUM/FERNANDO COLOMO P.C./VIA DIGITAL. Sept., 1999. Spanish. (Chema de la Pena) Fernando Cayo, Andres Gertrudix, Pau Colera, Manolo Caro, Rebeca Jimenez, Nathalie Sesena, Patxi Freytez.

THE SHADE
FILMAKER. May, 1999. French. (Raphael Nadjari) Richard Edson, Lorie Marino, Barbara Haas, Jeff Ware.

SHADES OF GRAY
SHADES OF GRAY. June, 2001. (Tim DePaepe) Documentary.

SHADOW BOXERS
SWERVE FILMS. June, 1999. (Katya Bankowsky) Lucia Rijker, Jill Matthews, Freddie Roach. Documentary.

SHADOW HOURS
NEWMARK FILMS. Jan., 2000. (Isaac H. Eaton) Balthazar Getty, Peter Weller, Rebecca Gayheart, Peter Greene, Michael Dorn, Richard Moll, Johnny Whitworth, Corin Nemec.

SHADOW MAGIC
SONY/SCHULBERG PRODS./ROAD MOVIES VEIRTE PRODUKTIONEN/FILMSTIFTUNG NORDRHEIN-WESTFALEN GMBH. Jan., 2000. U.S.-German. (Ann Hu) Jared Harris, Xia Yu, Liu Peiqi, Lu Liping, Xing Yufei, Wang Jingming, Li Yusheng, Zhang Yukui.

THE SHADOW OF CAIN
UIP. July, 1999. Spanish-Portuguese-Dutch. (Paco Lucio) Eusebio Poncela, Laia Marull, Jorge de Juan, Juan Erasmo Mochi.

THE SHADOW OF THE GIANT
CINEMA E SOCIETA/CONSIGLIO DEI MINISTRI/DIPARTIMENTO DELLO SPETTACOLO/ALBA. Feb., 2000. Italian. (Roberto Petrocchi) Margherita Buy, Arnaud Arbessier, Marisa Solinas.

SHADOW OF THE VAMPIRE
LIONS GATE/SATURN/LONG SHOT/BBC FILMS/DELUX. May, 2000. British-U.S. (E. Elias Merhige) John Malkovich, Willem Dafore, Cary Elwes, John Aden Gillet, Eddie Izzard, Udo Kier, Catherine McCormack, Ronan Vibert.

SHADOWS IN THE DARK
VITAL FILMS/NATIONAL FILM DEV. CORP./JBA/HUBERT BALS FUND. Sept., 1999. Indian-French. (Pankaj Butalia) Kitu Gidwani, Subrata Dutta, Srivardhan Trivedi, Ikhlaque Khan.

SHADY GROVE
BITTERS END/BRANDISH. Nov., 1999. Japanese. (Shinji Aoyama) Urara Awata, Arata, Tomohiro Sekiguchi, Wakaba Nakano.

SHAFT
PARAMOUNT PICTURES/SCOTT RUDIN/NEW DEAL. July, 2000. (John Singleton, Shane Salerno) Samuel L. Jackson, Vanessa Williams, Jeffrey Wright, Christian Bale, Busta Rhymes, Dan Hedaya, Toni Collette, Richard Roundtree, Ruben Santiago-Hudson.

SHAKE IT ALL ABOUT (EN KORT EN LANG)
ANGEL FILM DISTRIBUTION. Aug., 2002. Danish-German. (Hella Joof) Mads Mikkelsen, Troels Lyby, Charlotte Munck, Jesper Lohmann, Ditte Grabol, Peter Frodin, Nikolaj Steen, Ellen Hillingso.

SHAKESPEARE IN LOVE
MIRAMAX/UNIVERSAL. Dec., 1998. (John Madden) Joseph Fiennes, Gwyneth Paltrow, Geoffrey Rush, Judi Dench, Simon Callow.

SHANGHAI GHETTO
March, 2002. (Dana Janklowicz-Mann, Amir Mann) Documentary.

SHANGHAI NOON
BUENA VISTA/TOUCHSTONE/SPYGLASS ENTERTAINMENT/ BIRNBAUM/BARBER/JACKIE CHAN FILMS. May, 2000. (Tom Dey) Jackie Chan, Owen Wilson, Lucy Liu, Brandon Merrill, Roger Yuan, Xander Berkeley, Rong Guang Ye, Chi Ya Hi, Eric Chi Cheng Chen.

SHAOLIN SOCCER
STAR OVERSEAS/UNIVERSE ENTERTAINMENT (IN HONG KONG)/MIRAMAX (IN U.S.). Sept., 2001. Hong Kong. (Stephen Chow) Stephen Chow, Zhao Wei, Ng Mang-tat, Patrick Tse, Cecilia Cheung, Karen Mok, Vincent Kok, Li Hui, Wong Yat-fei.

SHAOLIN ULYSSES: KUNGFU MONKS IN AMERICA
June, 2002. (Mei-Juin Chen, Martha Burr) Shi Guolin, Li Peng Zhang, Shi Xing Hao, Shi De Shan, Shi Xing Hong. Narrator: Beau Bridges. Documentary.

SHARK SKIN MAN AND PEACH HIP GIRL
TOHOKUSHINSHA FILM CORP. Sept., 1998. Japanese. (Katsuhito Ishii) Tadanobu Asano, Sie Kohinata, Ittoku Kishibe.

SHATTERED IMAGE
SEVEN ARTS PICTURES/SCHROEDER HOFFMAN. Aug., 1998. (Raul Ruiz) Anne Parillaud, William Baldwin, Lisanne Falk, Graham Greene.

SHE'S ALL THAT
MIRAMAX. Jan., 1999. (Robert Iscove) Freddie Prinze Jr., Rachael Leigh Cook, Matthew Lillard, Paul Walker, Jodi Lyn O'Keefe.

SHIKOKU
TOHO. Aug., 1999. Japanese. (Shunichi Nagasaki) Yui Natsukawa, Michitaka Tsutsui, Chiaki Kuriyama.

SHINER
WISECROFT LTD. Sept., 2000. British. (John Irvin) Michael Caine, Martin Landau, Frances Barber, Claire Rushbrook, Frank Harper, Andy Serkis, Matthew Marsden.

THE SHIPPING NEWS
MIRAMAX FILMS. Dec., 2001. (Lasse Hallstrom) Kevin Spacey, Julianne Moore, Judi Dench, Cate Blanchett, Pete Postlethwaite, Scott Glenn, Rhys Ifans, Gordon Pinsent, Jason Behr, Larry Pine.

SHIPWRECKED ON ROUTE D 17
GEMINI FILMS. June, 2002. French. (Luc Moullet) Patrick Bouchitey, Iliana Lolic, Sabine Haudepin, Mathieu Almaric, Jean-Christophe Bouvet.

SHIRI
SAMSUNG/KAN JE-GYU FILM CO. Oct., 1999. South Korean. (Kand Je-gyu [Jacky Kang]) Han Seok-kyu, Choe Min-shik, Song Kang-ho.

SHIT HAPPENS
BUENA VISTA INTL./S/S FLADEN FILM/SVT DRAMA MALMO/ CANAL PLUS. Jan., 2000. Swedish. (Mans Herngren, Hannes Holm) Josefin Nilsson, Marie Richardson, Cecilia Frode.

SHOCKING TRUTH
MOTHER SUPERIOR FILMS. Jan., 2001. Swedish. (Alexa Wolf) Lisa Nelson, Tim Nelson, Mikko Roth, Marita Ulvskog.

SHOOTING STAR
LITTLE MORE CO. Jan., 2000. Japanese. (Hiromitsu Yamanaka.) Ken Ogata, Yosuke Eguchi, Mami Shimizu, Jun Kunimura, Michio Akiyama.

SHOOTING STARS
BAC DISTRIBUTION. April, 2002. French. (Fabien Onteniente) Gerard Lanvin, Samuel Le Bihan, Lorant Deutsch, Gerard Darmon, Ticky Holgado, Isabelle Nanty.

SHOPPING
PYRAMIDE. Feb., 2002. French-Belgian-Luxembourgois. (Philippe Boon, Laurent Brandenbourger) Albert Dupontel, Marie Trintignant, Bouli Lanners, Serge Lariviere.

SHORES OF TWILIGHT (TA RODINA AKROYIALIA)
GREEK FILM CENTRE. Nov., 1998. Greek. (Efthimios Hatzis) Stefanos Iatridis, Anna-Maria Papaharalambous.

A SHOT AT GLORY
BUTCHERS RUN FILMS. Sept., 2000. Robert Duvall, Michael Keaton, Ally McCoist, Brian Cox , Cole Hauser, Morag Hood, Kirsty Mitchell.

SHOT THROUGH THE HEART
ALLIANCE COMMUNICATIONS, HBO PICTURES, BBC FILMS. Nov., 1998. British-Canadian-Hungarian. (David Attwood) Vincent Perez, Linus Roache, Lia Williams, Lothaire Bluteau, Adam Kotz.

SHOWBOY
June, 2002. (Lindy Heymann, Christian Taylor) Christian Taylor, Lindy Heymann, Marilyn Milgrom, Joe Daley, Erich Miller, Jason Buchtel, Aaron Porter, Adrian Armas.

SHOWER
XI'AN FILM STUDIO/ZHANG PEIMIN. Sept., 1999. Chinese. (Zhang Yang) Zhu Xu, Pu Cunxin, Jiang Wu, Li Ding, Feng Shun.

SHOW ME THE ALIENS!
NO MORE RICE AND BEANS PRODUCTIONS. May, 2000. (Devin Crowley) Devin Crowley, Aaron Rudelson, Kim Reinle, Denny Siegel.

SHOWTIME
WARNER BROS. March, 2002. (Tom Dey) Robert De Niro, Eddie Murphy, Rene Russo, Frankie R. Faison, William Shatner, Drena De Niro, Pedro Damian.

SHREK
DREAMWORKS PICTURES. April, 2001. (Andrew Adamson, Vicky Jenson) Animated. Mike Myers, Eddie Murphy, Cameron Diaz, John Lithgow, Vincent Cassel.

SHRAPNEL IN PEACE
Aug., 2001. Iranian. (Ali Shah-Hatami) Nemat Soltani, Abdolhamid Darchi-Pouran, Faramarz Mehrju, Amir Iranian.

SHUT YER DIRTY LITTLE MOUTH!
Feb., 2002. (Robert Taicher) Gill Gayle, Glenn Shadix, Robert Musgrave, Pat Quinn, Christopher Cameron, John Welty, Rachel Niebur.

SIAM SUNSET
UIP. May, 1999. Australian. (John Polson) Linus Roache, Victoria Hill, Danielle Cormack, Ian Bliss, Roy Billing.

SIA, THE PYTHON'S DREAM
Oct., 2001. French-Burkina Faso. (Dani Kouyate) Sotigui Kouyate, Fatoumata Diawara, Ibrahim Baba Cisse, Habib Dembele.

SICILY!
PIERRE GRISE PRODS./MARTINE MARIGNAC/CENTRE NATIONAL DE LA CINEMATOGRAPHIE/ALIA FILM/ENZO PORCELLI/ ISTITUTO LUCE. May, 1999. French-Italian. (Daniele Huillet).

SIDE STREETS
MERCHANT IVORY PRODS./CEO FILMS. Sept., 1998. (Tony Gerber) Valeria Golino, Shashi Kapoor, Leon, Art Malik, Shabana Azmi.

SIDEWALKS OF NEW YORK
PARAMOUNT CLASSICS. April, 2001. (Edward Burns) Edward Burns, Rosario Dawson, Dennis Farina, Heather Graham, David Krumholtz, Brittany Murphy, Stanley Tucci.

SIEGFRIED & ROY: THE MAGIC BOX
IMAX LTD./L-SQUARED ENTERTAINMENT/LEXINGTON ROAD PRODS./FOUNDRY FILM PARTNERS. Oct., 1999. (Brett Leonard) Siegfried Fischbacher, Roy Uwe, Ludwig Horn, John Summers.

A SIGN FROM GOD
OVER A ROPEMAR., 2000. (Greg Watkins) Laura Macias, Caveh Zahedi, Celia Gamburg, Francesca Schneider, Henry Rosenthal.

SIGNS
BUENA VISTA. July, 2002. (M. Night Shyamalan). Mel Gibson, Joaquin Phoenix, Cherry Jones, Rory Culkin, Abigail Breslin, Patricia Kalember, M. Night Shyamalan.

SILENCE!
WIGGLYWORLD STUDIOS. April, 2001. (Gregg Lachow) Megan Murphy, Michael Chick, Judith Weber, Richard Waugh.

SILENCE (CISZA)
July, 2002. Polish. (Michal Rosa) Kinga Preis, Bartosz Opania, Irena Burawska, Grazyna Walasek, Magdalena Kuta.

SILENCE BROKEN: KOREAN COMFORT WOMEN
DAI SIL. Mar., 1999. (Dai Sil Kim-Gibson) Han Seung Yun, Lee Kwang Sun, Hwang Jin Kyung. Docudrama.

SILENT PARTNER
PALACE FILMS. June, 2001. Australian. (Alkinos Tsilimidos) David Field, Syd Brisbane.

SILVIA PRIETO
LES ATELIERS DES ARCHES. Jan., 1999. Argentine. (Martin Rejtman) Rosario Blefari, Gabriel Fernandez Capello, Mirtha Busnelli.

THE SIMIAN LINE
S.L./DA WA MOVIES. Jan., 2000. (Linda Yellen), Lynn Redgrave, Jamey Sheridan, Cindy Crawford, Samantha Mathis, Dylan Bruno, Monica Keena, Harry Connick Jr., Tyne Daly, William Hurt.

SIMON BIRCH
BUENA VISTA. Aug., 1998. (Mark Steven Johnson) Ian Michael Smith, Joseph Mazzello, Ashley Judd, Oliver Platt, David Strathairn.

SIMONE
NEW LINE CINEMA. July, 2002. (Andrew Niccol) Al Pacino, Catherine Keener, Pruitt Taylor Vince, Jay Mohr, Jason Schwartzman, Stanley Anderson, Evan Rachel Wood.

SIMON MAGUS
HAROM NYUL STUDIO, MTV, EUROFILM STUDIO/ARTCAM INTL. . Feb., 1999. Hungarian-French. (Ildiko Enyedi) Peter Andorai, Julie Delarme, Peter Halasz.

SIMON SEZ
INDEPENDENT ARTISTS. Sept., 1999. (Kevin Elders Dennis Rodman, Dane Cook, Natalia Cigliuti, Filip Nicolic, John Pinette.

SIMPATICO
FINE LINE. Sept., 1999. (Matthew Warchus) Nick Nolte, Jeff Bridges, Sharon Stone, Catherine Keener, Albert Finney.

A SIMPLE PLAN
PARAMOUNT. Sept., 1998. (Sam Raimi) Bill Paxton, Billy Bob Thornton, Brent Briscoe, Bridget Fonda, Jack Walsh, Chelcie Ross.

SIMPLY IRRESISTIBLE
20TH CENTURY FOX. Feb., 1999. (Mark Tarlov) Sarah Michelle Gellar, Sean Patrick Flanery, Patricia Clarkson, Dylan Baker.

SING FASTER: THE STAGEHANDS' RING CYCLE
SING FASTER. Jan., 1999. (Jon Else). Documentary.

SINGING
9 @ NIGHT FILMS. Oct., 2000. (Rob Nilsson) Jim Carpenter, Barbara Jaspersen, Domenique Lozano, Devin Qualls, Josh Peterson, Teddy Weiler, Edwin Johnson.

SINGLE ACTION
KINGSIZE. Sept., 1998. (Carlos Gallardo) Carlos Gallardo, Alejandra Prado, Miguel Gurza, Oscar Castaneda, Manuel Vela.

THE SINGLE DROP OF WATER IN A MIGHTY RIVER
TOHO. Feb., 2002. Japanese. (Seijiro Koyama) Narumi Yasuda, Atsuro Watabe, Sergei Nakariakov, Mitsuko Baisho, Rentaro Mikuni, Yoko Minamino, Kei Yamamoto.

THE SINGLES WARD
Sept., 2002. (Kurt Hale) Will Swenson, Connie Young, Kirby Heyborne, Daryn Tufts, Michael Birkeland, Robert "Bob-o" Swenson, Michelle Ainge, Lincoln Hoppe, Terance Edwards, Sedra Santos, Gretchen Whalley.

THE SINISTER SAGA OF MAKING "THE STUNT MAN"
BART PIERCE AND RICHARD RUSH/FILM ORGANIZATION. Feb., 2000. (Richard Rush) Peter O'Toole, Steve Railsback, Barbara Hershey, Chuck Bail, Sharon Farrell, Mario Tosi. Documentary.

SISTERS
CTB FILM CO. Sept., 2001. Russian. (Sergei Bodrov Jr.) Oksana Akinshina, Katia Gorina, Sergei Bodrov Jr., Andrei Krasko.

SISTER WIFE
May, 2002. (Timna Goldstein, Hadar Kleinman) Documentary.

SIX DAYS IN ROSWELL
BENEVOLENT AUTHORITY/NEO ART AND LOGIC. Oct., 1999. (Tomothy B. Johnson) Richard Kronfeld, Dennis Balthaser. Documentary

SIX DAYS, SEVEN NIGHTS
BUENA VISTA. June, 1998. (Ivan Reitman) Harrison Ford, Anne Heche, David Schwimmer, Jacqueline Obradors, Temuera Morrison.

SIX-STRING SAMURAI
PALM PICTURES. Feb., 1998. (Lance Mungia) Jeffrey Falcon, Justin McQuire, Stephane Gauger, John Sakisian, Gabrielle Pimenter.

THE 6TH DAY
SONY PICTURES ENTERTAINMENT. Nov., 2000. (Roger Spottiswoode) Arnold Schwarzenegger, Tony Goldwyn, Michael Rapaport, Michael Rooker, Sarah Wynter, Wendy Crewson.

6:3
BUDAPEST FILM. Feb., 1999. Hungarian. (Peter Timar) Karoly Eperjes, Ferenc Kallai, Tamas Cseh, Andras Kern, Attila Lote.

THE SIXTH SENSE
BUENA VISTA. July, 1999. (M. Night Shyamalan) Bruce WIllis, Toni Collette, Olivia Williams, Haley Joel Osment, Donnie Wahlberg.

SKELETON WOMAN
SKELETON WOMAN PRODS. Oct., 2000. (Vivi Letsou) Serena Scott Thomas, Daphne Rubin-Vega, Tony Denison, Ria Pavia, J.E. Freeman.

SKIES, SATELLITES
Nov., 2001. Croatian. (Lukas Nola) Filip Nola, Filip Sovagovic,Barbara Nola, Rene Bitorajac.

SKIN OF MAN, HEART OF BEAST
WHY NOT PRODS./ARTE FRANCE CINEMA. Aug., 1999. French. (Angel, Agnes de Sacy) Serge Riaboukine, Bernard Blancan, Pascal Cervo, Maaike Jansen.

A SKIN TOO FEW: THE DAYS OF NICK DRAKE
ROXIE RELEASING. May, 2002. (Jeroen Berkvens) Gabrielle Drake, Joe Boyd, Brian Wells, John Wood, Robert Kirby, Keith Morris, Paul Weller. Documentary.

SKIPPED PARTS
TRIMARK/SKIPPED PARTS. June., 2000. (Tamra Davis) Jennifer Jason Leigh, Bug Hall, Mischa Barton, Peggy Lipton, Brad Renfro, Michael Greyeyes, Alison Pill, Angela Featherstone, Drew Barrymore.

THE SKULLS
UNIVERSAL/ORIGINAL FILM/NEWMARKET CAPITAL GROUP. Mar., 2000. (Rob Cohen) Joshua Jackson, Paul Walker, Hill Harper, Leslie Bibb, Christopher McDonald, Steve Harris, Craig T. Nelson.

THE SKY IS FALLING
STELLARQUEST. Mar., 1999. (Florrie Laurence) Dedee Pfeiffer, Teri Garr, Howard Hesseman, Eric Close, Laura Leighton,.

SKYLINE CRUISERS
GOLDEN HARVEST. Dec., 2000. Hong Kong. (Wilson Yip) Leon Lai, Jordan Chan, Shu Qi, Sam Lee, Michelle Saram, Alex To, Terrence Yin, Patrick Lung, Ken Wong.

THE SKY OVERHEAD
Oct., 2001. Canadian. (Andre Melancon, Genevieve Lefebvre) Arianne Maheu, Marc Messier, Celine Bonnier, Serge Dupire, David Boutin, Daniel Fanego, Maka Kotto, Rosa Zacharie.

SKY. PLANE. GIRL. (NEBO. SAMOLJOT. DEVUSHKA.)
Sept., 2002. Russian. (Vera Storozheva) Renata Litvinova, Dimitri Orlov, Inga Strelkova-Oboldina, Mikhail Efremov, Konstantin Murzenko.

THE SKY WILL FALL
ISTITUTO LUCE/SILVIA D'AMICO BENDICO/ PARUS FILM/VIVA CINEMATOGRAFICA/ISTITUTO LUCE/RAI. June, 2000. Italian. (Andrea & Antonio Frazzi) Isabella Rossellini, Jeroen Krabbe.

THE SLAMMER
MARIE-DOMINIQUE GIRODET. Aug., 1999. French. (Alain Robak) Claude Brasseur, Olivier Martinez, Bernard Le Coq.

SLAP HER, SHE'S FRENCH! (FRECHE BIESTER!)
CONSTANTIN FILM (IN GERMANY)/WINCHESTER FILM DISTRIBUTION (IN U.K.)/THE PREMIERE MARKETING & DISTRIBUTION GROUP (IN U.S.). July, 2002. German. (Melanie Mayron) Piper Perabo, Jane McGregor, Trent Ford, Michael McKean, Julie White, Brandon Smith, Jesse James, Nicki Aycox, Alexandra Adi.

THE SLAUGHTER RULE
Jan., 2002. (Andrew and Alex Smith) Yan Gosling, David Morse, Clea Duvall, David Cale, Eddie Spears, Kelly Lynch, Amy Adams.

SLC PUNK
SONY. Jan., 1999. (James Merendino) Matthew Lillard, Michael Goorjian, Annabeth Gish, Jennifer Lien, Christopher McDonald.

SLEEP EASY, HUTCH RIMES
EMBY EYE. Nov., 2000. (Matthew Irmas) Steven Weber, Swoosie Kurtz, Gail O'Grady, Nina Siemaszko, Gabriel Mann, Stephen Tobolowsky, Gregg Henry.

SLEEP IN A NEST OF FLAMES
SYMBIOSIS FILMS. June, 2001. (James Dowell, John Kolomvakis) James Dowell (narrator), Charles Henri Ford, Paul Bowles, William Burroughs, Mary Lynn Broe, Paul Cadmus, Documentary.

THE SLEEPING WIFE
La 11 Mars Cinematografique. Aug., 2001. Italian. (Silvano Agosti) Franco Nero, Eleonora Brigliadori, Laura Linzi.

SLEEPLESS
MEDUSA. March, 2001. Italian. (Dario Argento) Max von Sydow, Stefano Dionisi, Chiara Caselli, Rosella Falk, Paolo Maria Scalondro.

THE SLEEPWALKER
LA SONAMBULA. Sept., 1998. Argentine. (Fernando Spiner) Eusebio Ponce, Sofia Viruboff, Lorenzo Quintero, Norman Briski.

SLEEPWALKER
SVENSK FILMINDUSTRI. Oct., 2000. Swedish-Norwegian. (Johannes Runeborg) Ralph Carlsson, Tuva Novotny, Ewa Carlsson.

SLEEPY HOLLOW
PARAMOUNT/MANDALAY PICTURES/SCOTT RUDIN/AMERICAN ZOETROPE. Nov., 1999. (Tim Burton) Johnny Depp, Christina Ricci, Miranda Richardson, Michael Gambon, Casper Van Dien.

THE SLEEPY TIME GAL
MUNCH/CHARNY. Jan., 2001. (Christopher Munch) Jacqueline Bisset, Martha Plimpton, Nick Stahl, Amy Madigan, Frankie R. Faison, Carmen Zapata, Peggy Gormley.

SLIDIN'-BRIGHT AND SHINY WORLD
NOVOTNY & NOVOTNY. Jan., 1999. Austrian. (Barbara Albert) Maria Kastner, Cornelia Stastny, Sandra Maria Schoner, Martina Poltl.

A SLIPPING-DOWN LIFE
DVC/RADDON. Jan. 1999. (Toni Kalem): Lili Taylor, Guy Pearce, John Hawkes, Sara Rue, Irma P. Hall.

SLOGANS
LES FILMS DES TOURNELLES. April, 2001. French-Albanian. (Gjergi Xhuvani) Artur Gorishti, Luiza Xhuvani, Agim Qirjaqi, Birce Hasko, Niko Kanxheri, Festim Cela, Robert Ndrenika, Rita Ladi.

THE SLOW BUSINESS OF GOING
CINEMANOMAD (U.S.)/GREEK FILM CENTER (GREECE). Nov., 2000. Nov., 2000. U.S.-Greek. (Athina Rachel Tsangari) Lizzie Martinez, Maria Tsantsanoglou, Gary Price, Kenny Strickland.

SLOW FADE
RYMD INDUSTRIES. Sept., 1999. Hong Kong. (Daniel Chan) Ken Wong, Jimmy Wong, Josie Ho, Roy Cheung.

THE SLURB
KINOWELT FILMVERLEIH (IN GERMANY). Feb., 2002. German. (Ben Verbong) Ulrich Noethen, Christine Urspruch, Aglaia Szyazkowitz, Armin Rohde, Eva Mattes, August Zirner.

SMALL SOLDIERS
DREAMWORKS. July, 1998. (Joe Dante) Kirsten Dunst, Gregory Smith, Jay Mohr, Phil Hartman, Kevin Dunn, Denis Leary.

SMALL TIME CROOKS
DREAMWORKS/SWEETLAND FILMS/JEAN DOUMANIAN. May., 2000. (Woody Allen) Woody Allen, Tracey Ullman, Hugh Grant, George Grizzard, Jon Lovitz, Elaine May, Michael Rapaport.

SMALL TIME OBSESSION
GUERILLA FILMS/SOLO FILMS/SEVENTH TWELFTH COLLECTIVE. June, 2000. British. (Piotr Szkopiak) Alex King, Juliette Caton, Jason Merrells, Oliver Young.

SMELL OF CAMPHOR, FRAGRANCE OF JASMINE
NEW YORKER FILMS (IN U.S.). Sept., 2000. Iranian. (Bahman Farmanara) Bahman Farmanara, Roya Nonahali, Reza Kianian, Valiyollah Shirandami, Parivash Nazarieh, Hossien Kasbian.

SMOKE AND MIRRORS: A HISTORY OF DENIAL
ROSENZWEIG CO./AMERICAN LUNG ASSN. Jan., 2000. (Torrie Rosenzweig). Documentary.

THE SMOKERS
INTL. PROD. CO. March, 2000. (Christina Peters) Dominque Swain, Busy Phillipps, Keri Lynn Pratt, Nicholas Loeb, Oliver Hudson.

SMOKERS ONLY
Sept., 2001. Argentine. (Veronica Chen) Cecilia Bengolea, Leonardo Brezicki, Adrian Fondari, Pablo Razuk, Adrian Blanco, Carlos Issa, Fernando Moumdijian.

SMOKE SIGNALS
MIRAMAX. Jan., 1998. (Chris Eyre) Adam Beach, Evan Adams, Irene Bedard, Gary Farmer, Tantoo Cardinal, Cody Lightning, Simon Baker.

SMOKING CUBAN STYLE
BLOW-UP FILM/KUBA FILM. Oct., 1999. Austrian-German. (Stephan Wagner) Simon Licht, Thomas Morris, Seymour Cassel, Tatjana Alexander, Eva-Maria Straka, Wolfgang S. Zechmayer, Alfons Haider.

SMOKING ROOM
DEA PLANETA. June, 2002. Spanish. (Julio Wallovits, Roger Gual) Antonio Dechent, Juan Diego, Alises Dumont, Eduard Fernansez, Chete Lera, Francese Garrido.

SNAKE EYES
PARAMOUNT/BUENA VISTA INTL. Aug., 1998. (Brian De Palma) Nicolas Cage, Gary Sinise, John Heard, Carla Gugino, Stan Shaw.

A SNAKE OF JUNE (ROKUGATSU NO HEBI)
Sept., 2002. Japanese. (Shinya Tsukamoto) Asuka Kurosawa, Yuji Koutari, Shinya Tsukamoto.

SNAKESKIN
PORTMAN ENTERTAINMENT. May, 2001. New Zealand. (Gilliam Ashurst) Melanie Lynskey, Boyd Kestner, Dean O'Gorman, Oliver Driver, Paul Glover, Charlie Bleakley, Jodie Rimmer, Taika Cohen.

SNAPPED
ILLVILLE PICTURES. Apr., 1999. (Jesse Feigelman) Gaby Hoffman, Johnny Zander, David Wheir, Seymour Cassel.

SNATCH
COLUMBIA/SCREEN GEMS/SKA FILMS/MATTHEW VAUGHN. Sept., 1999. British-U.S. (Guy Ritchie) Benicio Del Toro, Dennis Farina, Vinnie Jones, Brad Pitt.

SNIPES
IN-MOTION. Sept., 2001. (Rich Murray) Sam Jones III, Zoe Saldana, Nelly, Dean Winters, Rashaan Nall, Schoolly D, Joel Garland.

SNOW
WINTER LIGHT FILMS. April, 1998. (Eric Tretbar) Shane Barach, Rose Mailutha, Lara Miklasevics, Erika Remillard, John Crozier

SNOW DAY
PARAMOUNT/NICKELODEON MOVIES. Feb., 2000. (Chris Koch) Chris Elliott, Mark Webber, Jean Smart, Schuyler Fisk, Iggy Pop, Pam Grier, Chevy Chase, John Schneider, Zena Grey.

SNOW DAYS
GIRL AND BOY PRODS./MARCUS BROS. Oct., 1999. (Adam Marcus) Kipp Marcus, Alice Dylan, Bernadette Peters, Henry Simmons, Miriam Shor, Judith Malina, Larry Pine, Debra Sullivan.

SNOW DOGS
BUENA VISTA. Jan., 2002. (Brian Levant) Cuba Gooding Jr., James Coburn, Sisqo, Nichelle Nichols, M. Emmet Walsh, Graham Greene, Brian Doyle-Murray, Joanna Bacalso, Jean-Michel Pare, Michael Bolton.

SNOW FALLING ON CEDARS
UNIVERSAL. Sept., 1999. (Scott Hicks) Ethan Hawke, James Cromwell, Richard Jenkins, James Rebhorn, Sam Shepard.

SNOW ON NEW YEAR'S EVE
BUENA VISTA INTL./UFA/WESTDEUTSCHE UNIVERSUM-FILM/WDR/ARTE. Jan., 2000. German. (Thorsten Schmidt) Jurgen Tarrach, Tamara Simunovic, Hannes Jaenicke, Dieter Landuris.

SNOW WHITE
MADRAGOA FILMES/RTP RADIOTELEVISAO PORTUGUESA. Sept.,2000. Portuguese. (Jaoa Cesar Monteiro) Maria Do Carmo, Reginaldo Da Cruz, Ana Brandao.

SOBIBOR, OCT. 14, 1943, 4 P.M.
WHY NOT PRODS./LES FILMS ALEPH/FRANCE 2 CINEMA. May, 2001. French. (Claude Lanzmann) Yehuda Lerner. Documentary.

SOCCER RULES!
SEVEN X FILMVERLEIH/NOVAMEDIA/HOFMANN & VOGES FILMPRODUKTION/SVEN PICTURES. Feb., 2000. German. (Tomy Wigand) Uwe Ochsenknecht, Ralf Richter, Oscar Ortega Sanchez.

SOFREH IRANI
July, 2002. Iranian. (Kianoosh Ayyari) Noor-Ali Lotfi, Mehrdad Falahatger, Mansoureh Ali-Akbari, Masoumeh Shir-Rafat.

SOFT FOR DIGGING
Dec., 2001. (JT Petty) Edmond Mercier, Sarah Ingerson, Andrew Hewitt, Kate Petty, Wayne Knickel, Joshua Billings, David Huusko, Mia Todd.

SOFT FRUIT
FOX SEARCHLIGHT/20TH CENTURY FOX. June, 1999. Australian. (Christina Andreef) Jeanie Drynan, Linal Haft,Genevieve Lemon.

SOFT HEARTS
VIVA FILM/NEO FILMS/KAIZZ VENTURES. Sept., 1999. Filipino. (Joel Lamangan, Eric Quizon) Lorna Tolentino, Albert Martinez, Eric Quizon, Caridad Sanchez, Jake Roxas, Matthew Mendoza.

SOFT SHELL MAN
FILM TONIC. Oct., 2001. Canadian. (Andre Turpin) David La Haye, Isabelle Blais, Emmanuel Bilodeau, Chantal Giroux, Pascale Desrochers, Charles Turpin.

SOFT TOILET SEATS
PHAEDRA CINEMA/SHIRLEY CRAIG. Mar., 2000. (Tina Valinsky) David Alex Rosen, Alexa Jago, Sammi Davis, Jonathan Aube.

SOGOBI
Feb., 2002. (James Benning) Documentary.

SOLDIERS IN THE ARMY OF GOD
OFFLINE ENTERTAINMENT GROUP. Sept., 2000. (Marc Levin, Daphne Pinkerson) Documentary.

SOLID ONES
ARTISTS' COLONY/S&J ENTERTAINMENT. Mar., 2000. (Brent Florence) Brent Florence, Josh Holland, Tracy Zahoryin, Christian Leffler, Michael Trucco, Tava Smiley, Kenny Luper, June Allyson.

SOLDIER
WARNER BROS. Sept., 1998. (Paul Anderson) Kurt Russell, Jason Scott Lee, Connie Nielsen, Sean Pertwee, Michael Chiklis.

A SOLDIER'S DAUGHTER NEVER CRIES
OCTOBER FILMS. July, 1998. (James Ivory) Kris Kristofferson, Barbara Hershey, Leelee Sobieski, Jesse Bradford, Dominique Blanc.

SOLO FOR CLARINET
SENATOR FILM. Oct., 1998. German. (Nico Hofmann) Gotz George, Corinna Harfouch, Tim Bergmann.

SOLOMON AND GAENOR
FILMFOUR DISTRIBUTORS. Feb., 1999. British. (Paul Morrison) Ioan Gruffudd, Nia Roberts, Sue Jones Davies, William Thomas.

SOLO SHUTTLE
PSYCHOLOGY NEWS. July, 1999. British-French. (David Cohen) Virginie Aster, Jean Yves Berteloot, John Shrapnel, Alex Jennings.

SO MAMBO
MEDUSA. Aug., 1999. Italian. (Luca Pellegrini Luca Bizzarri, Paolo Kessisoglu, Luciana Littizzetto, Maddalena Maggi.

SOME BODY
NEXT WAVE FILMS. Jan., 2001. (Henry Barrial) Stephanie Bennett, Jeramy Guillory, Billy Ray Gallion, Tom Vitorino, Laura Katz.

SOME NUDITY REQUIRED
ONLY CHILD. Jan., 1998. (Odette Springer, Johanna Demetrakas) Documentary.

SOMEONE LIKE YOU
20TH CENTURY FOX. March, 2001. (Tony Goldwyn) Ashley Judd, Greg Kinnear, Hugh Jackman, Marisa Tomei, Ellen Barkin, Catherine Dent. Peter Friedman, Laura Regan.

SOMETHING MORE
ALLIANCE ATLANTIS. Sept., 1999. Canadian. (Rob King) Michael Goorjian, Chandra West, David Lovgren, Thomas Cavanaugh, Jennifer Beals.

SOMETHING ORGANIC
HAUT & COURT. Sept., 1998. French-Canadian. (Bertrand Bonello) Romane Bohringer, Laurent Lucas, Charlotte Laurier.

SOMETHING SWEET
CINEBLAST!. Oct., 2000. (Olivia Pi-Sunyer) Lauren Stamile, Nick Chinlund, Anne Jackson, Daniel J. Travanti, Jan Maxwell.

SOMETHING TO REMIND ME
Jan., 2002. German. (Christian Petzold) Nina Hoss, Andre Hennicke, Sven Pippig, Heinrich Schmieder, Kathrin Angerer.

SOME VOICES
FILMFOUR/BRITISH SCREEN/DRAGON PICTURES. May, 2000. British. (Simon Cellan Jones) Daniel Craig, David Morrissey, Kelly Macdonald, Julie Graham.

SOMEWHERE IN THE NIGHT
CO2 FILMS/MULTIMEDIA CO./ROOS FILM/FONDART/CORFO/J.J. HARTING. Mar., 2000. Chilean. (Martin Rodriguez) Francisco Lopez, Luciano Cruz-Coke, Faride Kaid, Paula Pizarro, Diego Munoz.

THE SON
May, 2002. Belgian-French. (Jean-Pierre and Luc Dardenne) Olivier Gourmet, Morgan Marinne, Isabella Soupart.

SONGCATCHER
RIGAS ENTERTAINMENT/INDEPENDENT FILM PROJECT/ERGOARTS. Jan., 2000. (Maggie Greenwald) Janet McTeer, Aidan Quinn, Pat Carroll, Jane Adams, Gregory Cook, Iris DeMent.

A SONG FOR MARTIN
COLUMBIA TRISTAR (SWEDEN). Jan., 2001. Danish-Swedish. (Bille August) Sven Wollter, Viveka Seldahl, Reine Brynolfsson.

SONG OF THE STORK (VU KHUC CON CO)
Aug., 2002. Singapore. (Jonathan Foo, Nguyen Phan Quang Binh) Tran Van Thuy, Wayne Karlin, Duong Quang Vuong, Luu Quang Vinh, Le Dung Nhi, Ta Ngoc Bao, Trinh Mai Nguyen, Ngo Quang Hai.

SONG OF TIBET
SHANDONG FILM STUDIO, BEIJING FILM STUDIO, BEIJING FOUR SEASONS EVERGREEN FILM & TV CO. Oct., 2000. Chinese. (Xie Fei) Danzengzhuoga, Laqiong, Dawangdui. Renqingdunzhu.

SONGS FROM THE SECOND FLOOR
ROY ANDERSSON FILMPRODUKTION/ SVERIGES TV/DANMARKS RADIO/NORSK RIKSKRINGKASTING/ARTE FRANCE CINEMA/SOCIETE PARISIENNE PRODUCTION/ESSENTIAL FILMPRODUKTION/EASY FILM/ZDF/ARTE-LA SEPT. May, 2000. Swedish. (Roy Andersso) Lars Nordh, Stefan Larsson, Torbjorn Fahlstrom, Sten Andersson, Lucio Vucino, Hanna Eriksson.

THE SONGS OF MY HOMELAND
May, 2002. Iranian. (Nahman Ghobadi) Shahab Ebrahimi, Fa'eq Mohammadi, Alahmorad Rashtiani, Iran Ghobadi.

SONNY
Sept., 2002. (Nicolas Cage) James Franco, Brenda Blethyn, Mena Suvari, Harry Dean Stanton.

SON OF MARY
HI KHANEH HOUSE OF CHILDREN'S LITERATURE & ARTS . Feb., 1999. Iranian. (Hamid Jebelli) Mohsen Falsafin, Rafik Dergabrilian, Hadi Na'iinizade, Seyyed Ali, Seyyad Mehdi.

**SON OF TWO MOTHERS
OR THE COMEDY OF INNOCENCE**
MACT PRODS./TF1 INTL./LES FILMS DU CAMELIA. Sept., 1999. French. (Raul Ruiz) Isabelle Huppert, Jeanne Balibar, Charles Berling, Nils Hugon, Edith Scob, Denis Podalydes.

SONS AND DAUGHTERS
CECCHI GORI DISTRIBUZIONE. Sept., 2001. Italian. (Marco Bechis) Carlos Echevarria, Giulia Sarano, Stefania Sandrelli, Enrique Pineyro.

THE SON'S ROOM
SACHER DISTRIBUZIONE. March, 2001. Italian-French. (Nanni Moretti) Nanni Moretti, Laura Morante, Jasmine Trinca, Giuseppe Sanfelice, Silvio Orlando, Claudia Della Seta, Stefano Accorsi.

SOONER OR LATER
OCEAN FILMS/BLUE DAHLIA PROD./STUDIOCANAL/FRANCE 2 CINEMA. July, 2000. French. (Anne-Marie Etienne) Philippe Torreton, Amira Casar, Laura Del Sol, Anny Duperey, Jacques Webe.

SOPHIIIIE!
Aug., 2002. German. (Michael Hofmann) Katharina Schuettler, Alexander Beyer, Martin Brambach, Ercan Durmaz, Josef Ostendorf, Gerd Wameling, Robert Stadlober.

SORDID LIVES
DEL SHORES/DALY/HARRIS & DAVIS CLASSICS. June, 2000. (Del Shores) Bonnie Bedelia, Delta Burke, Beth Grant, Ann Walker, Leslie Jordan, Rosemary Alexander, Beau Bridges, Kirk Giger.

SORDID LIVES
REGENT ENTERTAINMENT. May, 2001. (Del Shores) Rosemary Alexander, Bonnie Bedelia, Beau Bridges, Earl H. Bullock, Delta Burke, Kirk Geiger, Beth Grant, Sarah Hunley.

SORORITY BOYS
BUENA VISTA. March, 2002. (Wally Wolodarsky) Barry Watson, Michael Rosenbaum, Harland Williams, Melissa Sagemiller, Tony Denman, Brad Beyer, Kathryn Stockwood, Heather Matarazzo.

SORORITY GIRLS' REVENGE
IBEX ENTERTAINMENT. Sept., 2001. (Keith Warn) Stacy Oliver, Kevin Wortman, Kelly Kraeger, Tisha Brown, Nicole Holmes, Nikki Trexler, Keith Warn.

SORRY BABY
FORBIDDEN CITY FILM/HUAYI BROTHERS ADVERTISING/ASIAN FILM UNION/FORBIDDEN CITY FILM. Feb., 2000. Chinese. (Feng Xiaogang) Ge You, Wu Chien-lien, Fu Biao, Ming He.

SORTED
ADVANCED FILM/JOVY JUNIOR ENTERPRISES. June, 2000. British. (Alex Jovy) Matthew Rhys, Sienna Guillory, Tim Curry, Fay Masterson, Jason Donovan, Steven Marcus, Kelly Brook.

SORUM
BUENA VISTA INTL. KOREA. Nov., 2001. South Korean. (Yoon Jong-chan) Kim Myeong-min, Jang Jin-yeong, Ki Ju-bong, Jo Ahn.

SOUL ACHE
EL MECANISMO ENCANTADO/ARTCAM INTL./AXELOTIL FILMS . June, 1999. Spanish-French-Italian. (Fernando Merinero) Martxelo Rubio, Bruno Buzzi, Juan Potau, Nathalie Sesena, Angelica Reverte.

THE SOUL GUARDIANS
POLYVISION. Sept., 1998 South Korean. (K. C. Park) Ahn Sung-ki, Shin Hyeon-jun, Chu Sang-mi, Oh Hyeon-chul.

SOUL MATE (L'ANIMA GEMELLA)
CECCHI GORI DISTRIBUZIONE/MEDUSA FILM. Sept., 2002. Italian. (Sergio Rubini) Valentina Cervi, Violante Placido, Michele Venitucci, Sergio Rubini, Dino Abbrescia, Alfredo Minenna, Rino Diana.

SOUL SQUARE
DISTRIBUTION CO. Sept., 1998. Argentine. (Fernando Diaz) Alejandro Gance, Vera Fogwill, Olga Zubarry, Norman Briski.

SOUL SURVIVORS
ARTISAN ENTERTAINMENT. Sept., 2001. (Steve Carpenter) Melissa Sagemiller, Casey Affleck, Wes Bentley, Eliza Dushku, Angela Featherstone, Luke Wilson, Allen Hamilton, Ken Moreno.

SOUND AND FURY
ARONSON FILM ASSOCIATE/PUBLIC POLICY PRODS., THIRTEEN/ WNET, CHANNEL 4. Jan., 2000. (Josh Aronson). Documentary.

SOUND MAN
MOUNTAINAIR FILMS. Aug., 1998. (Steven Ho) Wayne Pere, Eliane Chappuis, William Forsythe, Wes Studi, Nick Stahl, John Koyama.

SOUND OF THE SEA
LOLAFILMS DISTRIBUCION. June, 2001. Spanish. (Bigas Luna) Jordi Molla, Leonor Watling, Eduard Fernandez.

SOUR GRAPES
SONY. April, 1998. (Larry David) Steven Weber, Craig Bierko, Matt Keeslar, Karen Sillas, Robyn Peterman, Viola Harris, Orlando Jones.

SOUTH
AMIP/PARADISE FILMS/CHEMAH I.S. May, 1999. French-Belgian. (Chantal Akerman). Documentary.

THE SOUTH: ALICE NEVER LIVED HERE
AKEDIA PRODS. Oct., 1999. Israeli. (Senyora Bar David). Documentary.

SOUTHERN COMFORT
Q-BALL PRODS. Jan., 2001. (Kate Davis) Documentary.

SOUTHIE
AMERICAN WORLD PICTURES. June, 1998. (John Shea) Donnie Wahlberg, Rose McGowan, Anne Meara, James Cummings.

SOUTH KENSINGTON
MEDUSA FILM. Dec., 2001. Italian-British-French. (Carlo Vanzina) Rupert Everett, Elle Macpherson, Judith Godreche, Enrico Brignano, Giampaolo Morelli, Max Pisu, Naike Rivelli, Jean Claude Brialy.

SOUTH OF HEAVEN, WEST OF HELL
PHAEDRA CINEMA. Dec., 2000. (Dwight Yoakam) Dwight Yoakam, Vince Vaughn, Billy Bob Thornton, Bridget Fonda, Peter Fonda, Paul Reubens, Bud Cort, Bo Hopkins.

SOUTH OF THE SUN
Sept., 2001. Italian. (Pasquale Marrazzo) Giovanni Brignola, Elisabetta D'Arco, Cristina Donadio, Filippo Venuti, Raffaella Boscolo, Beniamino Bertoldo, Matteo Speroni.

SOUTH PARK
PARAMOUNT/WARNER BROS. June, 1999. (Trey Parker).Animated.

SOUTHPAW
BOARD SCANNAN NA HEIREANN. Jan., 1999. Irish. (Liam McGrath). Documentary.

SOUTH SIDE STORY
ISTITUTO LUCE/GAM FILM. Sept., 2000. Italian. (Roberta Torre) Forstine Ehobor, Roberto Rondelli, Eleonora Teriaca, Rosa D'Alba, Giuseppa Vella, Little Tony (Antonio Ciacci), Mario Merola.

SOUTH WEST NINE
FRUIT SALAD FILMS. July, 2001. British-Irish. (Richard Parry) Wil Johnson, Stuart Laing, Mark Lethern, Amelai Curtis, Orelssa Edwards, Nicole Stapleton, Frank Harper.

SPACE COWBOYS
WARNER BROS./VILLAGE ROADSHOW PICTURES/CLIPSAL FILMS/MALPASO/MAD CHANCE. July, 2000. (Clint Eastwood) Clint Eastwood, Tommy Lee Jones, Donald Sutherland, James Garmer, James Cromwell, Marcia Gay Harden, William Devane, Loren Dean.

SPACE STATION
IMAX. April, 2002. (Toni Myers) Documentary.

SPACE TRAVELERS
TOHO. Nov., 2000. Japanese. (Katsuyuki Motohiro) Takeshi Kaneshiro, Eri Fukatsu, Masanobu Ando, Hiroyuki Ikeuchi, Masatoshi Hamada, Ken Watanabe.

SPANK!
PALACE. June, 1999. Australian. (Ernie Clark) Robert Mammone, Vice Poletto, Victoria Dixon-Whittle, Mario Gamma, Lucia Mastrantone.

SPANISH FLY
MIRAMAX. May, 1998. (Daphna Kastner) Daphna Kastner, Toni Canto, Martin Donovan, Marianne Sagebrecht, Maria de Medeiros.

SPEAKERS OF TRUTH
A-FILM/MOTEL FILMS/NPS TV. Jan., 2000. Dutch. (Karim Traidia) Sid Ahmed Agoumi, Jaap Spijkers, Monic Hendrickx, Mireille Perrier.

SPEAKING IN STRINGS
COUNTERPOINT FILMS. Jan., 1999. (Paola di Florio). Documentary.

SPEAKING OF BUNUEL
NIRVANA FILMS/CERO EN CONDUCTA/ARTE/TVE/AMARANTA. May, 2000. Spanish-Mexican. (Jose Luis Lopez Linares, Javier Rioyo) Jose Bello, Angela Molina, Francisco Rabal, Luis Bunuel.

SPEAK LIKE A CHILD
BFI PRODS./BBC FILMS/LEDA SERENE. Sept., 1998. British. (John Akomfrah) Cal Macaninch, Daniel Newman, Richard Mylan, Fraser Ayres, Rachel Fielding.

SPEAK TO ME OF LOVE (PARLEZ-MOI D'AMOUR)
Aug., 2002. French. (Sophie Marceau) Judith Godreche, Niels Arestrup, Anne Le Ny, Laurence Fevrier, Jean-Marie Frin, Aurelien Wiik.

THE SPECIALIST
Intermedia Arc. Feb., 1999. French. (Eyal Sivan).

THE SPECIALS
REGENT ENT./MINDFIRE ENT./BRILLSTEIN/GREY ENT. Sept., 2000. (Craig Mazin) Rob Lowe, Jamie Kennedy, Thomas Haden Church, Paget Brewster, Kelly Coffield, Judy Greer, James Gunn.

SPECIES II
MGM. April, 1998. (Peter Medak) Michael Madsen, Natasha Henstridge, Marg Helgenberger, Mykelti Williamson, George Dzundza.

SPECTRES OF THE SPECTRUM
OTHER CITY. Sept., 1999. (Craig Baldwin) Sean Kilcoyne, Caroline Koebel, Beth Liseck.

SPEEDWAY JUNKY
MAGIC ENTERTAINMENT. Feb., 1999. Israeli-U.S. (Nickolas Perry) Jesse Bradford, Jordan Brower, Jonathan Taylor Thomas, Daryl Hannah.

SPEEDY BOYS
CARGO CULT PRODS.. Jan., 1999. (James Herbert) Andy Liedilato, Carter Davis, Aline Nari, Alessandra Palma, Kari Malievich.

SPELLBOUND
April, 2002. (Jeff Blitz) Harry Altman, Angela Arenivar, Ted Brigham, April DeGideo. Documentary.

SPENT
REGENT ENTERTAINMENT/TRADEMARK ENTERTAINMENT/THF PICTURES. July, 2000. (Gil Cates Jr.) Jason London, Charlie Spradling, Phill Lewis, Erin Beaux, James Parks, Richmond Arquette.

SPIDERS OF THE NIGHT
April, 2002. French. (Jean-Pierre Mocky) Jean-Pierre Mocky, Patricia Barzyk, Michel Bertay, Francois Tourmarkine, Francoise Michaud.

SPIN THE BOTTLE
CINEBLAST!. Mar., 1999. (Jamie Yerkes): Mitchell Riggs, Kim Winter, Jessica Faller, Heather Goldenhersch, Holter Graham.

SPIRITED AWAY
TOHO. Feb., 2002. Japanese. (Hayao Miyaki). Animation director: Masashi Ando) Rumi Hiiragi, Miyu Irino, Mari Natsuki, Takashi Naito, Yasuko Sawaguchi, Tatsuya Gashuin, Ryunosuke Kamiki, Yumi Tamai, Yo Oizumi, Koba Hayashi, Tsunehiko Kamijo, Takehiko Ono, Bunta Sugawara. Animated.

SPIRITED AWAY (SEN TO CHIHIRO - NO KAMIKAKUSHI)
BUENA VISTA PICTURES DISTRIBUTION. Sept., 2002. Japanese. (Hayao Miyaki). U.S. version: (Kirk Wise) Daveigh Chase, Suzanne Pleshette, Jason Marsden, Susan Egan, David Ogden Stiers, Lauren Holly, Michael Chiklis. Animated.

SPIRITS OF HAVANA
NATIONAL FILM BOARD OF CANADA. July, 2001. Canadian. (Bay Weyman, Luis O. Garcia) Jane Bunnett, Larry Cramer, Bobby Carcasses, Ernesto Gatell, Amado Dedeu, Guillermo Rubalcaba.

SPIRIT: STALLION OF THE CIMARRON
DREAMWORKS. April, 2002. (Kelly Asbury, Lorna Cook) Matt Damon, James Cromwell, Daniel Studi. Animated.

SPLENDOR
SUMMIT ENTERTAINMENT/ NEWMARKET CAPITAL GROUP. Jan., 1999. (Gregg Araki) Kathleen Robertson, Johnathon Schaech, Matt Keeslar, Kelly Macdonald, Eric Mabius.

THE SPLIT
ALFA FILM/ICELANDIC FILM CORP./ARTCAM INTL./TNS PRODS./SCARABEE FILM PRODS.. May, 1999. Icelandic-Turkish. (Canan Gerede) Bennu Gerede, Mahir Gunsiray, Baltasar Kormakur, Rebecca Haas, Sibel Baykam.

SPLIT WIDE OPEN
ADLABS/BMG CRESCENDO/TROPICFILM. Sept., 1999. Indian. (Dev Benegal) Rahul Bose, Laila Rouass, Shivaji Sathem, Ayesha Dharker, Farida Haider Mulla, Shiv Paul, Kiran Nagarkar, Arti Gosavi.

THE SPREADING GROUND
TSUNAMI ENTERTAINMENT/VINE INTL. PICTURES/ALPINE PICTURES/STONELOCK PICTURES/POLSON STREET. Mar., 2000. Canadian. (Derek Vanlint) Dennis Hopper, Leslie Hope, Frederic Forrest, Tom McCamus, Elizabeth Shepherd, Chuck Shamata.

SPRING FORWARD
INDEPENDENT FILM CHANNEL PRODS./C-HUNDRED FILM CORP./CINEBLAST! Jan., 2000. (Tom Gilroy) Ned Beatty, Liev Schreiber, Campbell Scott, Peri Gilpin, Bill Raymond, Catherine Kellner, Hallee Hirsh.

SPRINGTIME IN A SMALL TOWN (XIAO CHENG ZHI CHUN)
Sept., 2002. Chinese-Hong Kong. (Tian Zhuangzhuang) Hu Jingfan, Wu Jun, Xin Baiqing, Ye Xiaokeng, Lu Sisi.

THE SPRING TO COME
MESSAGE FILM. July, 2001. Polish. (Filip Bajon) Mateusz Damiecki, Krystyna Janda, Janusz Gajos, Daniel Olbrychski, Malgorzata Lewinska, Urszula Grabowska.

SPUN
SILVER NITRATE. June, 2002. (Jonas Akerlund) Jason Schwartzman, John Leguizamo, Mena Suvari, Patrick Fugit, Brittany Murphy, Mickey Rourke, Peter Stormare, Alexis Arquette, Deborah Harry, Eric Roberts, Chloe Hunter, Julia Mendoza.

SPY GAME
UNIVERSAL. Nov., 2001. (Tony Scott) Robert Redford, Brad Pitt, Catherine McCormack, Stephen Dillane, Larry Bryggman, Michael Paul Chan, Marianne Jean-Baptiste, Ken Leung, David Hemmings, Matthew Marsh.

SPY KIDS
DIMENSION FILMS. March, 2001. (Robert Rodriguez) Antonio Banderas, Carla Gugino, Alexa Vega, Daryl Sabara, Alan Cumming, Tony Shalhoub, Teri Hatcher, Cheech Marin, Robert Patrick.

SPY KIDS 2: THE ISLAND OF LOST DREAMS
DIMENSION FILMS. July, 2002. (Robert Rodriguez) Antonio Banderas, Carla Gugino, Alexa Vega, Daryl Sabara, Steve Buscemi, Mike Judge, Danny Trejo, Cheech Marin, Matt O'Leary, Emily Osment, Ricardo Montalban, Holland Taylor.

THE SQUALE
CINE NOMINE. Sept., 2000. French. (Fabrice Genestal) Esse Lawson, Tony Mpoudja, Khereddine Ennasri, Stephanie Jaubert.

SRI
MARSELLI SUMARNO. Oct., 1999. Indonesian. (Marselli Sumarno) Rina Ariyanti, RMT, Ronosuripto, Sardono W. Kusumo.

STADIUM COUP
ALTA FILMS. Aug., 1999. Spanish-Italian-Colombain. (Sergio Cabrera) Emma Suarez, Nicolas Montero, Cesar Mora, Raul Sender, Andrea Giordana.

STAKAMAN
Dec., 2001. Greek. (Antonis Kafetzopoulos) Antonis Kafetzopoulos, Dimitris Kallivokas, Spyros Kaloyirou, Dafni Koutsafti.

STAND-BY
DIAPHANA/SALOME/LE STUDIO CANAL PLUS/ARTE FRANCE CINEMA/HAVAS IMAGES/ISTA FILMS/DIAPHANA DISTRIBUTION/CANAL PLUS/STUDIO IMAGES 5. Aug., 2000. French. (Roch Stephanik) Dominique Blance, Roschdy Zem, Patrick Catalifo, Jean-Luc Bideau, Georges Corrafce, Cecile Brune.

STANDING BY YOURSELF
Jan., 2002. (Josh Koury) Josh Siegfried, Adam Koury, Helen Koury, Roselyn Siegfried, Richard Koury Sr., Richard Koury Jr., Brandon Shorey. Documentary.

STANDING IN THE SHADOWS OF MOTOWN
ARTISAN ENTERTAINMENT. May, 2002. (Paul Justman) Andre Braugher.

STANDING ON FISHES
STANDING ON FISHES. Mar., 1999. (Meredith Scott Lynn, Bradford Tatum) Bradford Tatum, Meredith Scott Lynn, Jason Priestley, Lauren Fox.

STANLEY KUBRICK–A LIFE IN PICTURES
WARNER BROS. Feb., 2001. (Jan Harlan) Christiane Kubrick, Woody Allen, Martin Scorsese, Steven Spielberg, Jack Nicholson, Tom Cruise, Nicole Kidman. Documentary.

STANLEY'S GIG
LEFT HOOK FILM/LAMPEDUSA FILMS. June, 2000. (Marc Lazard) William Sanderson, Marla Gibbs, Faye Dunaway, Steven Tobolowsky, Paul Benjamin, Kevin Jackson, Ian Whitcomb.

THE STAR (ZVEZDA)
July, 2002. Russian. (Nikolai Lebedyev) Igor Petrenko, Artem Semakin, Alexei Panin, Alexei Kravchenko, Anatoly Gushchin, Amadu Mamadakov, Yury Laguta, Andrei Yegorov, Ekaterina Vulichenko

STARDOM
ALLIANCE ATLANTIS/SERENDIPITY POINT FILMS/ CINEMAGINAIRE/ CINE B/TELEFILM CANADA/QUEBEC FILM & TV TAX CREDI/ CANADIAN FILM OR VIDEO PROD. TAX CREDIT/MOVIE NETWORK/ SODEC/SUPER ECRAN/GOV'T. OF ONTARIO/CANAL PLUS/ MINISTERE DE LA CULTURE & COMMUNICATION/CENTRE NATIONAL DE LA CINEMATOGRAPHIE. May, 2000. Canadian-French. (Denys Arcand) Jessica Pare, Dan Aykroyd, Charles Berling, Thomas Gibson, Frank Langella, Robert Lepage, Patrick Huard.

STAR KID
TRIMARK. Jan., 1998. (Manny Coto) Joseph Mazzello, Joey Simmrin, Alex Daniels, Arthur Burghardt, Brian Simpson, Corinne Bohrer.

STARRY NIGHT
YELLOW HAT. Aug., 1999. U.S.-British. (Paul Davids) Abbott Alexander, Lisa Waltz, Lou Wagner, Sally Kirkland.

STAR SISTERS
FILMLANCE INTL. Feb., 1999. Swedish. (Tobias Falk) Teresa Niva, Vania Panes Lundmark, Fanny Kivimaki, Tintin Anderzon.

STAR TREK: INSURRECTION
PARAMOUNT. Dec., 1998. (Jonathan Frakes) Patrick Stewart, Jonathan Frakes, Brent Spiner, LeVar Burton, Gates McFadden.

STARTUP.COM
ARTISAN ENTERTAINMENT. Jan., 2001. (Jehane Noujaim, Chris Hegedus) Documentary.

STARVING ARTISTS
PANAORAMA ENTERTAINMENT. Jan., 1999. (Allan Piper) Allan Piper, Bess Wohl, Joe Smith, Sandi Carroll.

STAR WARS: EPISODE I - THE PHANTOM MENACE
20TH CENTURY FOX. May, 1999. (George Lucas) Qui-Gon Jinn, Ewan McGregor, Natalie Portman, Jake Lloyd, Pernilla August.

STAR WARS: EPISODE II–ATTACK OF THE CLONES
20TH CENTURY FOX. May, 2002. (George Lucas) Ewan McGregor, Natalie Portman, Hayden Christensen, Christopher Lee, Samuel L. Jackson, Frank Oz, Ian McDiarmid, Pernilla August, Temuera Morrison, Jimmy Smits, Jack Thompson.

STATE AND MAIN
FINE LINE FEATURES/FILMTOWN ENTERTAINMENT/GREEN-RENZI/EL DORADO PICTURES. Aug., 2000. (David Mamet) Alec Baldwin, Charles Durning, Philip Seymour Hoffman, Patti LuPone, William H. Macy, Sarah Jessica Parker, David Paymer, Rebecca Pidgeon, Julia Stiles.

THE STATE I AM IN
SCHRAMM FILM. Sept., 2000. German. (Christian Petzold) Julia Hummer, Barbara Auer, Richy Muller, Bilge Bingul, Gunther Maria Halmer, Katharina Schuttler.

STATE PROPERTY
LIONS GATE. Feb., 2002. (Abdul Malik Abbott) Beanie Sigel, Omillio Sparks, Memphis Bleek, Damon Dash, Sundy Carter, Tyran "Ty-Ty" Smith, Oskeeno, Jay-Z.

STEAL HAPPINESS
XI'AN FILM STUDIO. Oct., 2000. Chinese. (Yang Yazhou) Feng Gong, Ding Jiali, Qi Ke, Xiao Hui, Jiang Feng, Li Mingqi, Zheng Weili.

STEALING HARVARD
SONY PICTURES ENTERTAINMENT. Sept., 2002. (Bruce McCulloch) Jason Lee, Tom Green, Leslie Mann, Megan Mullally, Dennis Farina, Chris Penn, John C. McGinley, Seymour Cassel.

STEALING THE FIRE
June, 2002. U.S.-German. (John S. Friedman, Eric Nadler) Documentary.

STEAL THIS MOVIE
LIONS GATE/LAKESHORE INTL./GREENLIGHT/ARDENT FILMS. Mar., 2000. (Robert Greenwald) Vincent D'Onofrio, Janeane Garofalo, Jeanne Tripplehorn, Kevin Pollak, Donal Logue, Kevin Corrigan, Alan Van Sprang, Troy Garity, Ingrid Veninger.

STEP BY STEP (UN HONNETE COMMERCANT)
Aug., 2002. Belgian-Luxembourgois. (Philippe Blasband) Benoit Verhaert, Philippe Noiret, Yolande Moreau, Frederic Bodson, Serge Lariviere, Patrick Hastert, Jean-Michel Vovt.

STEPMOM
SONY. Nov., 1998. (Chris Columbus) Julia Roberts, Susan Sarandon, Ed Harris, Jena Malone, Liam Aiken.

THE STERLING CHASE
WEINBERG ENTERTAINMENT/INDYSSEY ENTERTAINMENT/REDWOOD COMMUNICATIONS. Sept., 1999. (Tanya Fenmore) Andrea Ferrell, John Livingston, Irene Ng, Jack Noseworthy.

STEVIE
LIONS GATE. SEPT., 2002. (Steve James) Stephen Dale Fielding, Verna Hagler, Bernice Hagler, Brenda Hickam, Doug Hickam, Tonya Gregory. Documentary.

STICKMEN
PORTMAN ENTERTAINMENT. May, 2001. New Zealand. (Hamish Rothwell) Robbie Magasiva, Scott Wills, Paolo Rotondo.

STIGMATA
MGM. Sept., 1999. (Rupert Wainwright) Patricia Arquette Gabriel Byrne, Jonathan Pryce, Nia Long, Thomas Kopache.

STILL CRAZY
COLUMBIA TRISTAR FILMS/SONY. Oct., 1998. British. (Brian Gibson) Stephen Rea, Billy Connolly, Jimmy Nail, Timothy Spall, Bill Nighy.

STING OF CHANCE
NEW PATH CINEMA. Feb., 2000. (Babak Sarrafan) Mohammad Ali Golabaz, Behzad Maghadam, Mohsen Rastegar-panah.

STIR OF ECHOES
ARTISAN. July, 1999. (David Koepp) Kevin Bacon, Kathryn Erbe, Illeana Douglas, Kevin Dunn, Conor O'Farrell, Jennifer Morrison.

STOCKPILE
WORLDVIEW PICTURES. Aug., 2001. U.S.-Dutch-Swiss. (Stephen Trombley) Paul White, Vladislav N. Mokhor, Mike Burns, Radi I. Il'Kaev, Siegfried S. Hecker, Harold Agner. Documentary.

THE STONECUTTER
FOOTPATH FILMS. March, 1998. (Stephen Erickson) Michael Cavalieri, Trisha Melynkov, Harold Cannon, Karin Argoud-Morrisey.

THE STONERAFT (LA BALSA DE PIEDRA)
Aug., 2002. Spanish-Portugese-Dutch. (George Sluizer) Federico Luppi, Iciar Bollain, Gabino Diego, Ana Padrao, Diogo Infante.

STONES
HISPANO FOXFILM. Feb., 2002. Spanish. (Ramon Salazar) Antonia San Juan, Najwa Nimri, Vicky Pena, Angela Molina, Monica Cervera, Rodolfo de Souza, Daniele Liotti, Nacho Duato, Enrique Alcides.

STONES IN THE SKY
Aug., 2002. Brazilian-Cuban. (Eryk Rocha) Documentary.

STOREFRONT HITCHCOCK
ORION PICTURES. April, 1998. (Jonathan Demme) Documentary.

THE STORM
MISR INTL. FILMS, EGYPTIAN TELEVISION AND OGNON PICTURES. April, 2001. Egyptian-French. (Khaled Youssef) Yousra, Hisham Selim, Hanan Tork, Hani Salama, Mohamed Nagati.

A STORM IN SUMMER
SHOWTIME ORIGINAL PICTURES FOR ALL AGES/HALLMARK PRODS./RENEE VALENTE. Jan., 2000. (Robert Wise) Peter Falk, Aaron Meeks, Natassja Kinski, Andrew McCarthy, Ruby Dee.

THE STORY OF A BAD BOY
SWEET FILMS. June, 1999. (Tom Donaghy) Jeremy Hollingworth, Christian Camargo, Stephen Lang, Julie Kavner, Lauren Ward.

THE STORY OF COMPUTER GRAPHICS
ACM/SIGGRAPH. Aug., 1999. (Frank Foster). Documentary.

STORYTELLING
FINE LINE FEATURES. May, 2001. (Todd Solondz) Selma Blair, Leo Fitzpatrick, Aleksa Palladino, Robert Wisdom, Noah Fleiss.

STRAIGHT CLOWNIN'
July, 2002. (Ifeanyi Njoku) Alex Thomas, Tyra Banks, Jamie Foxx, Shaquille O'Neal, Will Smith, Dr. Dre.

STRAIGHT FROM THE HEART
BHANSALI FILMS (NEW DELHI). Sept., 2000. Indian. (Sanjay Leela) Salman Khan, Aishwarya Rai, Smita Jaykar, Ajay Devgan.

STRAIGHTMAN
BENZFILM GROUP. Apr., 2000. (Ben Berkowitz) Ben Redgrave, Ben Berkowitz, Rachel Tomlinson, Butch Jerinic, Joaquin De La Puente, Victoria Kallay, Scott Holme.

STRAIGHT RIGHT
MARCEL PAGULAYAN, CHRIS DONAHUE, BRENT SMITH. Apr., 2000. (P. David Ebersole) Brent Smith, Lynn Evans, Zeke Rippy, Mary Woronov, Bob Romanus, Mickey Cottrell.

THE STRAIGHT STORY
BUENA VISTA. May, 1999. French-U.S. (David Lynch) Richard Farnsworth, Sissy Spacek, Jane Galloway Heitz, Everett McGill, Jennifer Edwards-Hughes.

THE STRANGE CASE OF SENOR COMPUTER
CORROSIVE LIQUID PRODS. Jan., 2001. (Tom Sawyer) Rick Ziegler, Gladys Hans, Lisa Goodman, Barbara Beneville, Constance Tillotson, David Damico, Will Lewis.

STRANGE FITS OF PASSION
BEYOND FILMS. May, 1999. Australian. (Elise McCredie) Michela Noonan, Mitchell Butel, Samuel Johnson, Steve Adams, Anni Finsterer.

STRANGE FRUIT
June, 2002. (Joel Katz) Abel Meeropol, Billie Holiday, Amiri Baraka, Abbey Lincoln, Farah Jasmine Griffin, Frank Sinatra, Pete Seeger, Don Byron. Documentary.

STRANGE PLANET
NEW VISION. May, 1999. Australian. (Emma-Kate Croghan). Claudia Karvan, Naomi Watts, Alice Garner, Tom Long, Aaron Jeffrey.

THE STRANGER
FILMTEAM WIEN. Sept., 2000. Austrian. (Goetz Spielmann) Goya Toledo, Hary Prinz, Martin Feifel, Nina Proll, Simon Schwarz.

STRANGER INSIDE
HBO FILMS. Jan., 2001. (Cheryl Dunye) Yolonda Ross, Davenia McFadden, LaTonya "T" Hagan, Mary Mara, Rain Phoenix, Marc Vann, Medusa, Ella Joyce.

A STRANGER IN THE KINGDOM
WHISKEYJACK PICTURES/KINGDOM COME PICTURES. Aug., 1998. (Jay Craven) David Lansbury, Ernie Hudson, Martin Sheen.

STRANGERS
CIMA FILM INTL./NORUZ PRODS. May, 2000. Iranian-U.S. (Ramin Bahrani) Ramin Bahrani, Karim Kashani.

STRANGER THAN FICTION
MOONSTONE. May, 1999. (Eric Bross) Mackenzie Astin, Todd Field, Dina Meyer, Natasha Gregson Wagner.

A STRANGE WORLD
IMCINE, CENTRO UNIVERSITARIO DE ESTUDIOS CINEMATOGRAFICOS, FONDO PARA LA PRODUCCION CINEMATOGRAFICA DE CALIDAD. March, 2001. Mexican. (Armando Casas) Victor Hugo Arana, Emilio Guerrero, Ana Serradilla, Jorge Sepulveda, Juan Carlos Vives, Anilu Pardo, Jorge Zarate.

STRAY DOGS
STRAY DOGS. June, 2001. (Catherine Crouch) Guinevere Turner, Bill Sage, Dot-Marie Jones, Ryan Kelley, Zach Gray.

STRAYDOGS
SANDREW METRONOME. Jan., 1999. Swedish. (Daniel Alfredson) Michael Legge, Sarah Jane Potts, Kevin Knapman, Mark Bagnall.

STREETERS
TIEMPO Y TONO FILMS. March, 2001. Mexican. (Gerardo Tort) Luis Fernando Pena, Maya Zapata, Armando Hernandez, Mario Zaragoza.

STREET LOVE
ORIGINAL FILM. Sept., 2000. Swedish. (Asa Faringer) Rosa Zaragoza, Angelica Garcia.

STRICTLY SINATRA
UNIVERSAL FOCUS. June, 2001. British. (Peter Capaldi) Ian Hart, Kelly Macdonald, Alun Armstrong, Brian Cox, Tommy Flanagan, Iain Cuthbertson, Una McLean, Paul Dennan.

STRIKE!
MIRAMAX. Aug., 1998. (Sarah Kernochan) Lynn Redgrave, Gaby Hoffman, Kirsten Dunst, Monica Keena, Heather Matarazzo.

STRIKING BACK
OCTOBER FILMS/MUSIC. Oct., 1998. Taiwanese. (Fu Shan-Fong) Neil Peng, Ku Jung-Kao, Tsan Cheng-Chun, Huang Shih-Wei.

STRIPPED
March, 2001. (Jill Morley) Documentary.

STRIPPED AND TEASED: TALES FROM LAS VEGAS WOMEN
BAL-MAIDEN. Nov., 1998. (Amie Williams). Documentary.

STRIPPERS
HOLLYWOOD INDEPENDENTS/A.J. PRODS. Sept., 2000. (Jorge Ameer) Tony Tucci, John Greenlaw, Kerrie Clark, Jeff Seal, JD Roberto, Linda Graybel, Kirsten Holly Smith, Jane Grogan.

STROKE
9 @ NIGHT FILMS. Oct., 2001. (Rob Nilsson) Edwin Johnson, Teddy Weiler, Omewene, Robert Viharo, Gabriela Maltz Larkin, Peter Richards, Paige Olson.

STRONG LANGUAGE
SIMON RUMLEY. Jan., 2000. British. (Simon Rumley) David Groves, Al Nedjari, Paul Tonkinson, Julie Rice, Charlie De'ath, Kelly Marcel.

THE STRUMA
Sept., 2001. British-Canadian. (Simcha Jacobovici) Documentary.

STRUMPET
BBC FILMS PRODUCTION. AUG., 2001. BRITISH. (Danny Boyle) Christopher Eccleston, Jenna Gee, Stephen Walters, David Crellin, Jonathan Ryland, Stephen Da Costa, Graeme Hawley.

STUART BLISS
PERILOUS PICTURES. Jan., 1998. (Neil Grieve) Michael Zelniker, Dea Lawrence, Hoke Howell, Derek McGrath, Ania Suli, Mark Fite.

STUART LITTLE
SONY PICTURES ENTERTAINMENT/COLUMBIA PICTURES/ DOUGLAS WICK/FRANKLIN-WATERMAN. Nov., 1999. (Rob Minkoff) Geena Davis, Hugh Laurie, Jonathan Lipnicki.

STUART LITTLE 2
SONY PICTURES ENTERTAINMENT. July, 2002. (Rob Minkoff) Geena Davis, Hugh Laurie, Jonathan Lipnicki, Anna Hoelck/Ashley Hoelck, Marc John Jefferies. Voices: Michael J. Fox, Nathan Lane, Melanie Griffith, James Woods, Steve Zahn.

THE STUBBORN ONES
Sept., 2001. Argentine-French. (Torres Manzur) German de Silva, Mario Paolucci, Ernesto Candoni, Leon Dogodny, Natalia de Parseval, Mario Offemhenden.

SUDDENLY (TAN DE REPENTE)
Aug., 2002. Argentine. (Diego Lerman) Tatiana Saphir, Carla Crespo, Veronica Hassan, Beatriz Thibaudin, Maria Merlino, Marcos Ferrante.

STUFF
BRUCE MCDONALD/BULLSEYE FILM. Oct., 1999. Canadian. (James Dunnison) Max Danger, Sanda Guerard, Maureen Burgoyne, Joe Sather, Winston Spear, Art Bergman, Moe Berg, Russell Oliver.

STUFF AND DOUGH
ROFILM. May, 2001. Romanian. (Cristi Puiu) Alexandru Papadopol, Dragos Bucur, Ioana Flora.

SUGAR SWEET
June, 2002. Japanese. (Desiree Lim) Saori Kitagawa, C Snatch Z, Saki, Mao Nakagawa, Iri, Shoko, Sakura Michinogi.

THE SUBURBANS
IGNITE ENTERTAINMENT. Jan., 1999. (Donal Lardner Ward) Craig Bierko, Amy Brenneman, Antonio Fargas, Will Ferrell, Tony Guma.

A SUBURBAN TALE
KINOTAR OY. May, 2001. Finnish. (Skakri Kirjavainen) Taisto Remialuoto, Anna-Maija Valonen, Elena Leeve, Antti Litja.

SUCH A LONG JOURNEY
RED SKY. Sept., 1998. Canadian-British. (Sturla Gunnarsson) Roshan Seth, Soni Razdan, Om Puri, Naseeruddin Shah, Ranjit Chowdhry.

SUCH IS LIFE...
FILMANIA/GARDENIA PRODS./FONDO PARA LA PRODUCCION/ CINEMATOGRAFICA DE CALIDAD/INSTITUTO MEXICANO DE CINEMATOGRAFIA/WANDA VISION/DMVB/PROGRAMA IBERMEDIA. Apr., 2000. Mexican-French-Spanish. (Arturo Ripstein) Arcelia Ramirez, Luis Felipe Tovar, Patricia Reyes Spindola, Ernesto Yanez.

SUICIDE CLUB
Jan., 2002. Japanese. (Sion Sono) Ryo Ishibashi, Masatoshi Nagase, Tamao Sato, Mai Housyou, Takashi Nomura, Rolly, Yoko Kamon, Saya Hagiwara, Kimiko Yo.

SUCKERFISH
GLASS EYE. Mar., 1999., (Brien Burroughs) Dan Donovan, Tim Orr, Gerri Lawlor, Kurt Bodden.

SUCKERS
NEO MOTION PICTURES/NEO ART AND LOGIC. Oct., 1999. (Roger Nygard) Daniel Benzali, Louis Mandylor, Lori Loughlin, David A. Brooks, William Shockley, Michael D. Roberts, Wayne Duvall.

SUNDAY
April, 2002. British. (Charles McDougall) Ciaran McMenamin, Barry Mullan, Paul Campbell, Julieann Campbell, Eva Birthistle, Chrstopher Eccleston.

A SUDDEN LOSS OF GRAVITY
BANGOR FILMS. Feb., 2000. (Todd Verow) Devery Doleman, Jim Dwyer, Aaron Falls, Brenda Velez, Philly, Erma Verow, Leanne Whitney, Craig Bowden, Rebecca Denise, Jesse Manson, Eric Sapp.

SUGAR & SPICE
NEW LINE CINEMA. Jan., 2001. (Francine McDougall) Marley Shelton, James Marsden, Mena Suvari, Marla Sokoloff, Rachel Blanchard, Melissa George, Alexandra Holden.

SUGAR TOWN
OCTOBER FILMS. Jan., 1999. (Allison Anders, Kurt Voss) Jade Gordon, Michael Des Barres, John Taylor, Martin Kemp.

SUGIHARA: CONSPIRACY OF KINDNESS
SEVENTH ART/DENTSU INC./DAVID RUBINSON/CREATIVE PRODUCTION GROUP. Aug., 2000. (Robert Kirk) Hiroki Sugihara, Benjamin Fishoff, Rabbi Moses Zupnik, Susan Bluman. Documentary.

SUICIDE, THE COMEDY
ALIBI ENTERTAINMENT. Aug., 1999. (Glen Freyer) Jamie Harris, Alison Eastwood, Brian Klugman, Josh Fardon, Walter Olkewicz.

SUITS
TENAFLY FILM CO. Jan., 1999. (Eric Weber) Robert Klein, Tony Hendra, Larry Pine, Paul Lazar, Randy Pearlstein.

THE SUM OF ALL FEARS
PARAMOUNT. May, 2002. (Phil Alden Robinson) Ben Affleck, Morgan Freeman, James Cromwell, Liev Schreiber, Bridget Moynahan, Alan Bates, Ciaran Hinds, Philip Baker Hall, Ron Rifkin, Colm Feore.

SUMMER CATCH
WARNER BROS. Aug. 2001. (Mike Tollin) Freddie Prinze Jr., Jessica Biel, Matthew Lillard, Brain Dennehy, Fred Ward, Jason Gedrick, Brittany Murphy.

A SUMMER TALE
SONET FILM/MEMFIS FILM/FILM I VAST/SVT DRAMA GOTHENBURG /ZENTROPA ENTERTAINMENTS/TV1000. Feb., 2000. Swedish-Danish. (Ulf Malmros) Kjell Bergqvist, Cecilia Nilsson, Brasse Brannstrom, Rebecka Scheja, Anastasios Soulis.

SUMO BRUNO
SENATOR FILM. Sept., 2000. German. (Lenard Fritz Krawinkel) Hakan Orbeyi, Oliver Korittke, Julia Richter, Martin Seifert.

SUMMER OF SAM
BUENA VISTA. May, 1999. (Spike Lee) John Leguizamo, Adrien Brody, Mira Sorvino, Jennifer Esposito, Anthony LaPaglia.

SUMMER OF THE MONKEY
BWE. Sept., 1998. Canadian. (Michael Anderson): Michael Ontkean, Leslie Hope, Wilford Brimley.

SUN ALLEY
DELPHI FILMVERLEIH/BOJE BUCK PROD./O-FILMPRODUKTION/ SAT 1. Feb., 2000. German. (Leander Haussmann) Alexander Scheer, Alexander Beyer, Katharina Thalbach, Teresa Weissbach, Detlev Buck, Henry Huebchen, Ignaz Kirchner.

SUNBURN
SWEETLAND FILMS. July, 1999. (Nelson Hume) Cillian Murphy, Paloma Baeza, Barry Ward, Michael Liebmann.

SUNDAY DRIVE
KAIJU THEATER CO. Sept., 1998. Japanese. (Hisashi Saito) Shinya Tsukamoto, Miako Dadano, Takumi Tanji.

SUNDAY'S DREAM
NHK. May, 2000. Japanese. (Yoichiro Takahashi) Kenji Mizuhashi, Yumika Hayashi, Tetsu Watanabe, Liliy, Shinya Tsukamoto.

SUNFLOWER
KSS. Oct., 2000. Japanese. (Isao Yukisada) Kumiko Aso, Aya Kawamura, Yoshihiko Hakamada.

SUNSET STRIP
20TH CENTURY FOX/FOX 2000 PICTURES /LINSON FILMS. Aug., 2000. (Adam Collis) Simon Baker, Anna Friel, Nick Stahl, Rory Cochrane, Adam Goldberg, Tommy J. Flanagan, Jared Leto, Stephanie Romanov.

SUNSHINE
ALLIANCE ATLANTIS. Sept., 1999. Hungarian-German-Canadian-Austraian. (Istvan Szabo) Ralph Fiennes, Rosemary Harris, Rachel Weisz, Jennifer Ehle, Molly Parker, Deborah Kara Unger.

SUNSHINE STATE
SONY PICTURES CLASSICS. May, 2002. (John Sayles) Edie Falco, Angela Bassett, Jane Alexander, Ralph Waite, James McDaniel, Timothy Hutton, Mary Steenburgen.

SUPER CHIEF
IO PICTURES. Oct., 1999. (Nick Kurzon) Darrell "Chip" Wadena, Eugene "Bugger" McArthur, Lowell Bellanger, Erma Vizenor. Documentary.

SUPER 8 STORIES
FANDANGO, PANDORA FILM, RASTA FILMS AND COOPERATIVA EDISON. Feb., 2001. German-Italian. (Emir Kusturica) Dr. Nelle Karajilic, Dejan Sparavalo, Stribor Kusturica, Zoran Marjanovic Ceda, Foran Markovski glava, Nena Gajin Coce. Documentary.

SUPERGUY: BEHIND THE CAPE
July, 2002. (Bill Lae, Mark Teague) Mark Teague, Charles Dierkop, Katherine Victor, Jan Garrett, Christopher Fey, Elizabeth Jaeger-Rydall, Marcello Paz-Pulliam.

SUPERLOVE
PLAYTIME. Apr., 1999. French. (Jean-Claude Janer) Gregoire Colin, Isabelle Carre, Carmen Maura, Luis Rego, Marthe Villalonga.

SUPERNOVA
MGM/SCREENLAND PICTURES/HAMMERHEAD. Jan., 2000. (Thomas Lee) James Spader, Angela Bassett, Robert Forster, Lou Diamond Phillips, Peter Facinelli, Robin Tunney, Wilson Cruz.

SUPERSTARLET A.D.
BIG BROAD. Sept., 2000. (John Michael McCarthy) Starlet Kerine Elkins, Gina Velour, Michelle Carr, Rita D'Albert, Hugh B. Brooks, Jim Townsend, Katherine Greenwood, Kitty Diggins.

SUPER TROOPERS
FOX SEARCHLIGHT PICTURES. Jan., 2001. (Jay Chandrasekhar) Jay Chandrasekhar, Kevin Heffernan, Steve Lemme, Paul Soter, Erik Stolhanske, Brian Cox, Daniel Von Bargen.

SUPPLEMENT (SUPLEMENT)
July, 2002. Polish. (Krzysztof Zanussi) Pavel Okraska, Monika Krzywkowska, Zbigniew Zapasiewicz.

SURFING FOR LIFE
DAVID L. BROWN/SENIORITY INC. Mar., 2000. (David L. Brown). Documentary.

SURIYOTHAI
Nov., 2001. Thai. (Chatrichalerm Yukol) Piyapas Bhirombhakdi, Sarunyoo Wongkrachang, Chatchai Plengpanich, Siriwimol Charoenpura, Johnny Anfone.

SUSPICIOUS RIVER
KEY FILMS. Sept., 2000. Canadian. (Lynne Stopkewich) Molly Parker, Callum Keith Rennie, Joel Bissonette.

SUZHOU RIVER
COPRODUCTION OFFICE/ESSENTIAL FILM/DREAM FACTORY. Jan., 2000. Chinese-German. (Lou Ye) Zhou Xun, Jia Hongsheng, Yao Anlian, Nai An.

SUZIE WASHINGTON
FILMLADEN. Sept., 1998. Austrian. (Florian Flicker) Birgit Doll, August Zirner, Karl Ferdinand Kratzl, Wolfram Berger, Nina Proll.

THE SWAMP
LITA STANTIC AND 4K FILMS. Feb., 2001. Argentine-Spanish. (Lucrecia Martel) Mercedes Moran, Graciela Borges, Martin Adjemian.

SWAMP!
MAGLOO. Sept., 1999. French. (Eric Bu) Satya Esquenazi, Michel Toesca, Thierry Buisson, Carole Frank, Isabelle Leprince, Claude Grinberg, Anne Sylvestre, Jean-Paul Farre.

SWEAT
METROPOLITAN FILMEXPORT. July, 2002. French. (Louis-Pascal Couvelaire) Jean-Hugues Anglade, Joaquim De Almeida, Cyrille Thouvenin, Sagamore Stevenin, Nozha Khouadra, Thierry Ashanti.

THE SWEATBOX
Sept., 2002. British. (John-Paul Davidson, Trudie Styler) Documentary.

SWEET AND BITTER
IMAGO PROD. (TUNISIA)/LES FILM SURE LA PLACE (FRANCE). Oct., 2000. Tunisian-French. (Naceur Ktari) Nourreddine El Ati, Ines Baili, Sonia El Ati, Lamine Nahdi, Zouheir Bornaz, Jelloul Jelassi.

SWEET AGONY
Feb., 1999. Iranian. (Ali Reza Davudnezhad) Reza Davudnezhad, Mona Davudnezhad, Mohammad Reza Davudnezhad, Ehteram Habibian, Shojo-o-Din Habibian.

SWEET DREAMS
ARSMEDIA. Aug., 2001. Slovenian. (Saso Podgorsek) Janko Mandic, Veronika Drolc, Iva Zupancic, Josef Nadj, Marinka Stern, Joze Hrovat.

THE SWEETEST SOUND
CINE-MATRIX. Feb., 2001. (Alan Berliner) Alan Berliner, Alain Berliner, Allen Berliner, Alan S. Berliner. Documentary.

THE SWEETEST THING
SONY PICTURES ENTERTAINMENT. March, 2002. (Roger Kumble) Cameron Diaz, Christina Applegate, Thomas Jane, Selma Blair, Jason Bateman, Parker Posey.

SWEET HOME ALABAMA
BUENA VISTA. Sept., 2002. (Andy Tennant) Reese Witherspoon, Josh Lucas, Patrick Dempsey, Candice Bergen, Mary Kay Place, Fred Ward, Jean Smart, Ethan Embry.

SWEET REPOSE
CINEMATOGRAFICA SARGENTINA PRODUCCIONES. April, 2001. Argentine. (Rodrigo Moreno, Andres Tambornino, Ulises Rosell) Juan Ignacio Machado, Fernando Miasnik, Raul Urtizberea, Jose Palomino Cortez, Javier Lombardo.

A SWEET SCENT OF DEATH
MIRADOR/IVANIA/LOLA/FONDO PARA LA PRODUCCION CINEMATOGRAFICA DE CALIDAD, ALEPH MEDIA, IMCINE, INCAA, VIA DIGITAL. Mar., 1999. Mexican-Spanish-Argentine. (Gabriel Retes) Karra Elejalde, Ana Alvarez, Diego Luna.

SWEET NOVEMBER
WARNER BROS. Feb., 2001. (Pat O'Connor) Keanu Reeves. Charlize Theron, Jason Isaacs, Greg Germann, Liam Aiken, Lauren Graham, Michael Rosenbaum.

SWEET THING
JAM PICTURES. June, 1999. (Mark David). Jeremy Fox, Amalia Stifter, Ev Lunning, Jr., Steven Bruton, Evan Greenwalt.

SWEET UNDERGROUND
FOURTH DENSITY PRODS. April, 1999. (Dorsay Alavi) Matthew Flint, Kevin Walls, Cindy Adkins, Alex Demir, Tracy Grant.

SWIMFAN
20TH CENTURY FOX. Sept., 2002. (John Polson) Jesse Bradford, Erika Christensen, Shiri Appleby, Kate Burton, Clayne Crawford, Jason Ritter, Kia Joy Goodwin, Dan Hedaya.

SWIMMING
OCEANSIDE PICTURES. Feb., 2000. (Robert J. Siegel) Laruen Ambrose, Jennifer Dundas Lowe, Joelle Carter, Jamie Harrold.

SWING
TAPESTRY/KUSHNER-LOCKE. Apr., 1999. British. (Nick Mead) Hugo Speer, Lisa Stansfield, Paul Usher, Tom Bell, Rita Tushingham.

SWING
PYRAMIDE DISTRIBUTION. Feb., 2002. French. (Tony Gatlif) Oscar Copp, Lou Rech, Tchavolo Schmitt, Ben Zimet, Fabiene Mai.

SWORDFISH
WARNER BROS. May, 2001. (Dominic Sena) John Travolta, Hugh Jackman, Halle Berry, Don Cheadle, Vinnie Jones, Sam Shepard, Drea de Matteo, Rudolf Martin.

SYMPATHY FOR MR. VENGEANCE
CJ ENTERTAINMENT. March, 2002. South Korean. (Park Chan-wook) Song Kang-ho, Shin Ha-gyun, Bae Du-na, Im Ji-eun.

T

TABOO
SHOCHIKU CO./BAC FILMS/LE STUDIO CANAL PLUS/RECORDED PICTURE CO./KADOKAWA SHOTEN PUBLISHING CO./IMAGICA/BS ASAHI/EISEI GEKIJO CO. May, 2000. Japanese-French-U.S. (Nagis Oshima) Beat Takeshi, Ryuhei Matsuda, Shinji Takeda.

TACKLE HAPPY
RADIANT INDUSTRIES. June, 2000. Australian. (Mick Molloy Simon Morley, David Friend. Documentary.

TADPOLE
Jan., 2002. (Gary Winick) Sigourney Weaver, Aaron Stanford, John Ritter, Bebe Neuwirth, Robert Iler, Adam Lefevre, Peter Appel, Ron Rifkin, Paul Butler.

TAEKWONDO
MS FILMS/KEYWECKSHIDE. Sept, 1998. Polish-South Korean. (Moon Seung-wook) Ahn Sung-ki, Pawel Burczyk, Ewa Gawryluk.

TAIL LIGHTS FADE
MOTION INTL./CADENCE ENTERTAINMENT/CANADIAN TV FUND/TELEFILM CANADA/CITY-TV/BRITISH COLUMBIA FILM/FILM INCENTIVE B.C./CANADIAN FILM OR VIDEO PROD. TAX CREDIT/HAROLD GREENBERG FUND. Dec., 1999. Canadian. (Malcolm Ingram) Denise Richards, Breckin Meyer, Jake Busey.

THE TAILOR OF PANAMA
SONY PICTURES ENTERTAINMENT. Feb., 2001. U.S.-Irish. (John Boorman) Pierce Brosnan, Geoffrey Rush, Jamie Lee Curtis, Brendan Gleeson, Catherine McCormack, Leonor Varela, Harold Pinter.

TAKE CARE OF MY CAT
Nov., 2001. South Korean. (Jeong Jae-eun) Bai Du-na, Lee Yo-weon, Ok Ji-yeong, Lee Eun-sil, Lee Eun-ju.

TAKING SIDES
MAECENAS FILM & FERNSEH, MBP, STUDIO BABELSBERG (GERMANY)/PALADIN PRODS. (FRANCE). Sept., 2001. German-French. (Istvan Szabo) Harvey Keitel, Stellan Skarsgard, Mortiz Bleibtreu, Birgit Minichmayr, Oleg Tabakov, Ulrich Tukur.

TAKING WING
TNVO. Aug., 2000. French. (Steve Suissa) Clement Sibony, Isabelle Carre, Francis Huster, Christine Citti, Marc Samuel, Leopoldine Serre, Steve Suissa, Corinne Dacla.

TAINA, AN AMAZON ADVENTURE
Oct., 2001. Brazilian. (Tania Lamarca, Sergio Block) Eunice Baia, Caio Romei, Rui Polanah, Jairo Mattos, Branca Camargo, Alexandre Zachia, Luciana Rigueira, Charles Paraventi.

THE TALENTED MR. RIPLEY
PARAMOUNT/MIRAMAX/MIRAGE ENTERPRISES/TIMNICK FILMS. Dec. 1999. (Anthony Minghella) Matt Damon, Gwyneth Paltrow, Jude Law, Cate Blanchett, Philip Seymour Hoffman, Jack Davenport.

A TALE OF A NAUGHTY GIRL (MANDA MEYER UPAKHYAN)
Sept., 2002. Indian. (Buddhadeb Dasgupta) Samata Das, Rituparna Sengupta, Arpan Basar, Tapash Paul, Ramgopal Bajaj.

TALE OF THE SIBERIAN LAND
MOSFILM. Aug., 2000. Soviet Union–1948. (Ivan Pyriev) Vladimir Druzhnikov, Marina Ladynina, Boris Andreyev, Vera Vasileva.

TALK TO HER
WARNER SOGEFILMS (IN SPAIN)/SONY PICTURES CLASSIC (IN U.S). March, 2002. Spanish. (Pedro Almodovar) Javier Camara, Dario Grandinetti, Leonor Watling, Rosario Flores, Geraldine Chaplin.

TALK OF ANGELS
MIRAMAX FILMS. OKCT., 1998. (Nick Hamm) Polly Walker, Vincent Perez, Franco Nero, Marisa Paredes, Leire Berrocal.

TAMARO: STONES AND ANGELS. MARIO BOTTA AND ENZO CUCCHI
IMAGOFILM LUGANO. June, 1999. Swiss. (Villi Hermann). Documentary.

TANGIER- LEGEND OF A CITY
PETER GOEDEL FILMPRODUKTION. Feb., 1998. (Peter Goedel) Armin Muller-Stahl, Martin Kluge, Ulrich Klaus Gunther, Paul Bowles.

TANGO NOTES
April, 2001. Argentine. (Rafael Filippelli) Pablo Bardauil, Elsa Berenguer, Pablo Blitstein, Josefina Darriba, Carlos Fijman.

TANGUY
UFD. Nov., 2001. French. (Etienne Chatiliez) Sabine Azema, Andre Dussolllier, Eric Berger, Helene Duc, Aurore Clement, Jean-Paul Rouve, Andre Wilms.

TANKA THE INNKEEPER
SOVKINO. Aug., 2000. Soviet Union–1929. (Boris Svetozarov) Tania Mukhina, K. Yastrebitsky, L. Nenasheva, A. Antonov.

THE TAO OF STEVE
GOOD MACHINE/THUNDERHEAD PRODS. Jan., 2000. (Jenniphr Goodman) Donal Logue, Greer Goodman, Kimo Wills.

TAPE
INDIGENT. Jan., 2001. (Richard Linklater) Ethan Hawke, Robert Sean Leonard, Uma Thurman.

TAR ANGEL
ALLIANCE ATLANTIS VIVAFILM/ODEON FILMS. Aug., 2001. Canadian. (Denis Chouinard) Zinedine Soualem, Catherine Trudeau, Rabaj Ait Ouyahia, Hiam Abbass, Raymond Cloutier.

THE TARGET SHOOTS FIRST
Feb., 2000. (Christopher Wilcha). Documentary.

TARZAN
BUENA VISTA. June, 1999. (Kevin Lima, Chris Buck). Animated.

TARZAN AND THE LOST CITY
WARNER BROS. April, 1998. (Carl Schenkel) Casper Van Dien, Jane March, Steven Waddington, Winston Ntshona, Rapulana Seiphemo.

TATAWO
LAUREN FILMS. Nov., 2000. Spanish. (Jo Sol) Alexis Valdes, Mercedes Ortega, Paulina Galvez, Miguel Molina.

TATTOO
TOBIS STUDIOCANAL. Feb., 2002. German. (Robert Schwentke) August Diehl, Christian Redl, Nadesha Brennicke, Ilknur Bahadir.

TAURUS
LENFILM. May, 2001. Russian. (Alexander Sokurov) Leonid Mozgovoi, Maria Kuznetsova, Sergei Razhuk.

THE TAVERN
FOOTE SPEED PRODS. July, 1999. (Walter Foote) Cameron Dye, Kevin Geer, Carlo Alban, Kym Austin, Margaret Cho.

TAXI: AN ENCOUNTER
LA COFRADIA NOCTURNA. July, 2001. Argentine. (Gabriela David) Diego Peretti, Miguel Guerberof, Josefina Viton, Pochi Ducasse, Pablo Brichta, Ricardo Diaz Mourelle, Ernesto Torchia.

TAXI DANCER
POWERS PRODS. Sept., 1998. (Sharon Powers) Darlene Reynolds, Bel Hernandez, Robert Nelson, Takayo Fischer, Leigh Kelly.

TAXI 2
ARP/LUC BESSON/LEELOO PRODS./ARP/TF1 FILMS PROD../LE STUDIO CANAL PLUS. Mar., 2000. French. (Gerard Krawczyk) Samy Naceri, Frederic Diefenthal, Emma Sjoberg, Barnard Farcy.

TAXMAN
COUNTERCLOCK PICTURES. May, 1998. (Avi Nesher) Joe Pantoliano, Wade Dominguez, Elizabeth Berkley, Michael Chiklis.

TEACHING MRS. TINGLE
DIMENSION FILMS. Aug., 1999. (Kevin Williamson) Helen Mirren, Katie Holmes, Jeffrey Tambor, Barry Watson, Marisa Coughlan.

TEARS
B.O.M FILM. Oct., 2000. South Korean. (Im Sang-soo) Han Jun, Park Geun-yeong, Bong Tae-gyu, Jo Eun-ji.

TEA WITH MUSSOLINI
UIP/MGM. Mar., 1999. Italian-British. (Franco Zeffirelli) Cher, Judi Dench, Joan Plowright, Maggie Smith, Lily Tomlin.

TED
CHRONIC FILMWORKS. Jan., 1999. (Gary Ellenberg) Daniel Passer, Edie McClurg, Richard Fancy, Jeff Corey, Paul Provenza.

TED BUNDY
METRO TARTAN DISTRIBUTION (IN U.K.)/FIRST LOOK PICTURES RELEASING (IN U.S.). Aug., 2002. British-U.S. (Matthew Bright) Michael Reilly Burke, Boti Ann Bliss, Stefani Brass, Marina Black, Wayne Morse.

TEDDY BEARS' PICNIC
MAGNOLIA PICTURES. March, 2002. (Harry Shearer) John Michael Higgins, Ming Na, Henry Gibson, David Rasche, Brenda Strong, Thom Sharp, Judith Owen, Gilley Grey.

TEESH & TRUDE
July, 2002. Australian. (Melanie Rodriga)Susie Porter, Linda Cropper, Peter Phelps, Jacob Allen, Bill McCluskey, Mason Richardson, Igor Sas, Kazmir Sas, Francoise Sas.

TEETH
CECCHI GORI/COLORADO FILM. Sept., 2000. Italian. (Gabriele Salvatores) Sergio Rubini, Anouk Grinberg, Tom Novembre, Anita Caprioli.

TEKNOLUST
Jan., 2002. (Hershman Leeson) Tilda Swinton, Jeremy Davies, James Urbaniak, Karen Black, Al Nazemian, Josh Kornbluth, Thomas Jay Ryan.

TELLING YOU
MIRAMAX. Aug., 1998. (Robert DeFranco) Peter Facinelli, Dash Mihok, Jennifer Love Hewitt, Frank Medrano, Richard Libertini.

TELL ME SOMETHING
KOO & C FILM CO./CINEMA SERVICE/KOOKMIN VENTURE CAPTIAL. JAN., 2000. SOUTH KOREAN. (Kyong Su-chang, In Eun-ah, Shim Hye-weon, Kim Eun-jeong, Chang) Han Seok-kyu, Shim Eun-ha, Jang Hang-seon, Yeom Jeong-ah, An Seok-hwan.

TEMPORARY REGISTRATION
LEO & CIE., FGF, ARTE FRANCE. Feb., 2001. French. (Gahite Fofana) Fatoumata Kante, Gahite Fofana, Yves Guichard Traore, Ibrahima Sano, Mohamed Dinah Sampil, Alhassane & Alseny Bah.

TEMPS
FIVE SISTERS PRODS. Nov., 1999. (Maria Burton) Gabrielle C. Burton, Robert Perberton, Ursula Burton, Tim Bohn, Katrina Stevens.

TEMPTATION
MGN FILMES/SIC/SKY LIGHT CINEMA. Aug., 1998. Portuguese-Brazilian. (Joaquim Leitao) Joaquim de Almeida, Cristina Camara.

TEMPTED
REP DISTRIBUTORS (AUSTRALIA). Sept., 2001. French-U.S.-Australia. (Bill Bennett) Burt Reynolds, Saffron Burrows, Peter Facinelli, Mike Starr, George DiCenzo, Eric Mabius, Maichel Arata.

TEMPTING HEART
MEDIA ASIA. May, 1999. Hong Kong-Japanese. (Sylvia Chang) Takeshi Kaneshiro, Gigi Leung, Karen Mok, Elaine Jin.

TEN DAYS WITHOUT LOVE
AURUM. Feb., 2001. Spanish. (Miguel Albaladejo) Sergi Lopez, Mariola Fuentes, Maria Jose Alfonso, Emilio Gutierrez Caba, Geli Albaladejo, Marcela Wallerstein, Javier Dorado.

TENEBRAE LESSONS
LES FILMS DE LA CROISADE/CARRE NOIR/RTDF LIEGE/LA REGION HAUTE NORMANDIE/PRESTIGE TV. June, 2000. French. (Vincent Dieutre) Andrzej Burzynski, Hubert Geiger, Vincent Dieutre, Leo Bersani.

TEN THINGS I HATE ABOUT YOU
BUENA VISTA. Mar., 1999. (Gil Junger) Heath Ledger, Julia Stiles, Joseph Gordon-Levitt, Larisa Oleynik, David Krumholtz.

TE QUIERO
DIAPHANA. Feb., 2001. French. (Manuel Poirier) Philippe Bas, Marine Delterme, Patricia Farfan, Maruschka Detmers, Patrick Chenais.

TERMINAL RITE
CUEC/UNAM/IMCINE/FOPROCINE. Sept., 2000. Mexican. (Oscar Urrutia Lazo) Guillermo Larrea, Soledad Ruiz, Angeles, Rafael Velasco, Guillermo Rios, Fabiana Perzabal.

TERNITZ TENNESSEE
THALIA FILM. Jan., 2001. Austrian. (Mirjam Unger) Nina Proll, Sonja Romei, Gerald Votava, Clemens Haipl.

TERRA INCOGNITA
AD VITAM. May, 2002. Lebanese-French. (Ghassan Salhab)Carole Abboud, Abla Khoury, Walid Sadek, Rabih Mroueh.

TERRA NOVA
DENDY FILMS. Aug., 1998. Australian. (Paul Middleditch) Jeanette Cronin. Paul Kelman, Trent Atkinson, Angela Punch McGregor.

TERROR FIRMER
TROMA TEAM. May, 1999. (Lloyd Kaufman) Will Keenan, Alyce LaTourelle, Trent Haaga, Debbie Rochon, Sheri Wenden.

THE TERRORIST
MODERNE GALLERIE/INDIAN IMAGE PRODS. Sept., 1998. Indian. (Santosh Sivan) Ayesha Dharkar, Vishnu Vardhan, Bhanu Prakash.

A TEXAS FUNERAL
DRAGON PICTURES. Mar., 2000. (William Blake Herron) Robert Patrick, Joanne Whalley, Isaiah Washington, Quinton Jones, Jane Adams, Chris Noth, Olivia D'Abo, Martin Sheen.

TEXAS RANGERS
DIMENSION FILMS. Nov., 2001. (Steve Miller) James Van Der Beek, Dylan McDermott, Usher Raymond, Ashton Kutcher, Robert Patrick, Rachael Leigh Cook, Leonor Varela, Randy Travis, Jon Abrahams.

TGV
FLACH FILM, LES FILMS DE LA SAGA/LES FILMS DU CROCODILE. Oct., 1998. French-Senegalese. (Moussa Toure) Makena Diop, Al Hamdou Traore, Bernard Giraudeau.

THAI SAHEBA
Shri Soundarya Arts. Sept., 1999. Indian. (Girish Kasaravalli) Jaimala Ramachandra, Suresh Heblikar, Shivaram, Harish Raju.

THANKS FOR THE GESTURE
MARS FILM/TELEMA/STUDIO CANAL PLUS/FRANCE 2 CINEMA/CANAL PLUS. Dec., 1999. French. (Claude Faraldo) Jacques Hansen, Marie Rousseau, Agathe de la Boulaye.

THAT GIRL FROM RIO
LOLAFILMS DISTRIBUCION. July, 2001. British-Spanish. (Christopher Monger) Hugh Laurie, Vanessa Nunes, Santiago Segura.

THAT OLD DREAM THAT MOVES
MAGOUIRE DISTRIBUTION. Jan., 2002. French. (Alain Guiraudie) Pierre Louis-Calixte, Jean-Marie Combelles, Jean Segani, Yves Dinse, Serge Ribes, Jean-Claude Monteil, Rui Fernandes.

THAT ONE NO ENOUGH
CATHAY ASIA FILMS/OAK 3 FILMS. Dec., 1999. Singapore. (Jack Neo)Jack Neo, Mark Lee, Henry Thua, Hong Hui-fang, Patricia Mok.

THAT'S IT
MIKADO. Nov., 1998. Italian. (Gabriele Muccino) Giorgio Pasotti, Barbora Bobulove, Claudkio Santamaria, Ginevra Colonna, Enrico Silvestrin.

THAT'S JUST LIKE YOU
AGATA FILMS & CIE./LA SEPT ARTE/LE THEATRE NATIONAL DE STRASBOURG . Aug., 2000. French. (Claire Simon) Stephanie Pasquet, Sophie Rodrigues, Marie Eleonore Pourtois

THAT'S LIFE
MEDUSA. Dec., 1998. Italian. (Aldo Baglio, Giovanni Storti, Giacomo Poretti, Massimo Venier) Aldo Baglio, Giovanni Storti.

THAT WOMEN LIVE
BECUE-RENARD. June, 2001. French. (Laurent Becue-Renard) With: Jasmina Dedic, Senard-Hajrija Mumic, Sedina Salcinovic, Fika Ibrahimefendic, Fatima Babic.

THEHEADISSPINNING
KUBLA KHAN/MUNBUT. Feb., 2000. Italian. (Alessandro Piva) Dino Abbrescia, Mino Barbarese, Mimmo Mancini, Dante Marmone, Paolo Sassanelli, Teodosio Barresi, Nicola Pignataro.

THERE'S NO FISH FOOD IN HEAVEN
STORM ENTERTAINMENT. Oct., 1998. (Eleanor E. Gaver) Fairuza Balk, Noah Taylor, Debi Taylor, Tea Leoni, James LeGros.

THERE'S ONLY ONE JIMMY GRIMBLE
PATHE/ARTS COUNCIL OF ENGLAND/LE STUDIO CANAL PLUS/SARAH RADDYCLYFFE PRODS./IMPACT FILMS. July, 2000. British. (John Hay) Robert Carlyle, Ray Winstone, Gina McKee.

THERE'S SOMETHING ABOUT MARY
20TH CENTURY FOX. June, 1998. (Peter Farrelly, Bobby Farrelly) Cameron Diaz, Matt Dillon, Ben Stiller, Lee Evans, Chris Elliott.THEY

THESE MEN OF CONSCIENCE
Sept., 2002. (Carol Ann Francis) Capt. Tom Damore, Lt. Billy Bergen, Steve Marley, Phil Pillet. Documentary.

THICKER THAN WATER
PALM PICTURES/MARSMEDIA/HOO-BANGIN'/PRIORITY FILM. Oct., 1999. (Ernest Nyle Brown) Mack 10, Fat Joe, Ice Cube, MC Eiht, CJ Mac, Big Pun, K-Mack, Tom'ya Bowden, Kidada Jones.

THE THIEF OF SAINT LUBIN
MERCURE FILM/AGAT FILMS/LA SEPT ARTE. Sept., 1999. French. (Calire Devers, Jean-Louis Benoit) Dominique Blanc, Denis Podalydes, Michele Goddet, Fanny Florido.

THIEF OR REALITY
GREEK FILM CENTRE, ERT, TOWN FILM CO. Aug., 2001. Greek. (Antonietta Angelidi) Nikos Pantelidis, Parthenopi Bouzouri, Evrikleia Sofroniadou, Angela Brouskou, Katerina karayanni.

THINGS BEHIND THE SUN
ECHO LAKE PRODS./SIDEKICK ENTERTAINMENT. Jan., 2001. (Allison Anders) Kim Dickens, Gabriel Mann, Don Cheadle, Eric Stolz, Elizabeth Pena, Rosanna Arquette, Alison Folland, Patsy Kensit.

THE THIN RED LINE
20TH CENTURY FOX. Dec., 1998. (Terence Malick) Sean Penn, Adrien Brody, Jim Caviezel, Ben Chaplin, George Clooney.

THINGS YOU CAN TELL JUST BY LOOKING AT HER
MGM/UNITED ARTISTS/JON AVNET/FRANCHISE PICTURES. Jan., 2000. (Rodrigo Garcia) Glenn Close, Cameron Diaz, Calista Flockhart, Kathy Baker, Amy Brenneman, Valeria Golino, Holly Hunter, Matt Craven, Gregory Hines, Miguel Sandoval.

THE THIRD MIRACLE
SONY. Sept., 1999. (Agnieszka Holland) Ed Harris, Anne Heche, Armin Mueller-Stahl, Charles Haid, Michael Rispoli.

THE THIRD PAGE
MAVI FILMCILIK CO. Aug., 1999. Turkish. (Zeki Demirkubuz) Ruhi Sari, Basak Kuklukaya, Cengiz Sezici, Serdar Orcin, Emrah Elciboga.

THE THIRD WHEEL
MIRAMAX FILMS. June, 2002. (Jordan Brady) Luke Wilson, Denise Richards, Jay Lacopo, Ben Affleck, Matt Damon.

THIRD WORLD COP
PALM PICTURES/HAWK'S NEST PRODS. Sept., 1999. Jamaican. (Chris Browne) Paul Campbell, Mark Danvers, Carl Bradshaw, Audrey Reid, Winston Bell, Lenford Salmon.

13 CONVERSATIONS ABOUT ONE THING
FIRST LOOK MEDIA. Sept., 2001. (Jill Sprecher) Matthew McConaughey, John Turturro, Alan Arkin, Clea Du Vall, Amy Irving, Barbara Sukowa, David Connolly, Tia Texada, Frankie Faison.

THIRTEEN DAYS
NEW LINE CINEMA. Nov., 2000. (Roger Donaldson) Kevin Costner, Bruce Greenwood, Steven Culp, Dylan Baker, Michael Fairman, Henry Strozier, Frank Wood.

THE THIRTEENTH FLOOR
COLUMBIA PICTURES. May, 1999. (Josef Rusnak) Craig Bierko, Armin Mueller-Stahl, Gretchen Mol, Vincent D'Onofrio.

THE 13TH WARRIOR
BUENA VISTA. Aug., 1999. (John McTiernan) Antonio Banderas, Diane Venora, Dennis Storhoi, Vladimir Kulich, Omar Sharif.

30 DAYS
ARIELLE TEPPER/ARACA GROUP/ARACA GROUP/ARIELLE TEPPER. Sept., 1999. (Aaron Harnick) Ben Shenkman, Arija Bareikis, Alexander Chaplin, Bradley White, Thomas McCarthy.

30, STILL SINGLE: CONTEMPLATING SUICIDE
TEAM LAN. Mar., 1999. (Gregory J. Lanesky) Christopher May, Terry Gatens, Jill Zimmerman, Jill Kneeland, Rachel Reenstra.

30 YEARS
GEMINI FILMS/CANAL PLUS/CNC/GIMAGES 3. Aug., 2000. French. (Laurent Perrin) Anne Brochet, Laurent Lucas, Gregori Derangere, Nathalie Richard, Arielle Dombasle, Julie Depardieu, Hector Noguera.

30 YEARS TO LIFE
OASIS ENTERTAINMENT. Jan., 2001. (Vanessa Middleton) Erika Alexander, Melissa De Sousa, Tracy Morgan, Paula Jai Parker, Allen Payne, T.E. Russell, Kadeem Hardison

THIS IS ME
PUBLIC FILM/PIETER VAN HUYSTEE FILM & TV/VPRO. Feb., 2000. Dutch. (Sonia Herman). Documentary.

THIS IS MY BODY
GEMINI FILMS (PARIS)-MADRAGOA FILMES (LISBON). May, 2001. French-Portuguese. (Rodolphe Marconi) Louis Garrel, Jane Birkin, Melanie Laurent, Annie Girardot, Elisabeth Depardieu, Didier Flamand, Didier Bezace, Cedric Delsaux.

THIS IS MY FATHER
FILMLINE INTL./HUMMINGBIRD COMMUNICATION. Aug., 1998. (Paul Quinn) Aidan Quinn, James Caan, Stephen Rea, John Cusack.

THIS IS MY MOON
BE-POSITIVE MEDIA GROUP FOR SOCIAL DEVELOPMENT. Nov., 2000. Sri Lankan. (Asoka Handagama) Saumya Liyanage, Dilhani Ekanayake, W. Jayasiri, Somalatha Subasinghe, Hemasiri Liyanage.

THIS IS NOT A LOVE STORY
July, 2002. New Zealand. (Keith Hill) Sarah Smuts-Kennedy, Stephen Lovatt, Peta Rutter, Beryl Te Wiata, Peter Elliott, Stelios Yiakmos.

THIS IS THE GARDEN
LUCKY RED. Sept., 1999. Italian. (Giovanni Davide Maderna) Carolina Fresche, Denis Fasolo, Allesandro Quattro, Emanuela Macchniz, Delia Boccardo, Tiziana Bergamaschi.

THIS IS WHAT DEMOCRACY LOOKS LIKE
INDEPENDENT MEDIA CENTER AND BIG NOISE FILM. Nov., 2000. (Jill Friedberg, Rick Rowley) Documentary.

THIS I WISH AND NOTHING MORE
BUDAPEST FILM. June, 2001. Hungarian. (Kornel Mundruczo) Ervin Nagy, Roland Raba, Martina Kovacs, Imre Csuja, Agi Szirtes.

THIS SPACE BETWEEN US
TSBU/LLC. June, 1999. (Matthew Leutwyler) Jeremy Sisto, Vanessa Marcil, Poppy Montgomery, Clara Bellar, Erik Palladino.

THOMAS AND THE MAGIC RAILROAD
ICON/DESTINATION FILMS/GULLANE PICTURES/ISLE OF MAN FILM COMM. July, 2000. (Britt Allcroft) Peter Fonda, Mara Wilson, Alec Baldwin, Didi Conn, Michael E. Rodgers, Cody McMains.

THE THOMAS CROWN AFFAIR
MGM. July, 1999. (John McTiernan) Pierce Brosnan, Rene Russo, Denis Leary, Ben Gazzara, Frankie Faison.

THOMAS IN LOVE
ENTRE CHIEN & LOUP/JBA PRODS. Sept., 2000. Belgian-French. (Pierre-Paul Renders) Serge Verhaert, Aylin Yay, Magali Pinglaut, Micheline Hardy, Alexandre von Sivers, Frederic Topart.

THOSE FACING US
POM FILMS. Oct., 2001. French. (Jean-Daniel Pollet) Michael Lonsdale, Valentine Vidal, voice of Alain Beigel.

THRANE'S METHOD
SPERANZA FILMS/UNNI STRAUME. Feb. 1999. Norwegian. (Unni Straume) Bjorn Sundquist, Petronella Barker, Nils O. Oftebro, Kai Remlov, Hege Schoyen.

3 A.M.
SHOWTIME NETWORKS. Jan., 2001. (Lee Davis) Danny Glover, Pam Grier, Michelle Rodriguez, Sergej Trifunovic, Sarita Choudhury, Isaach De Bankole, Mike Starr.

THREE BRIDGES OVER THE RIVER
GEMINI/MADRAGOA. Feb., 1999. French-Portuguese. (Jean-Claude Biette) Jeanne Balibar, Mathieu Amalric, Thomas Badek, Andre Baptista, Sara Paz.

THREE BROTHERS
EAST CINEMA. Feb., 2000. Kazakhstanian. (Serik Aprymov) Kasym Zhakibaev, Shakir Vilyoumov, Bulat Mazhagulov, Bahtiyour Kuatbaev.

THREE BUSINESSMEN
EXTERMINATING ANGEL. Oct., 1998. (Alex Cox) Miguel Sandoval, Alex Cox, Robert Wisdom, Isabel Ampudia.

THREE CHINAMEN WITH A DOUBLE BASS
JUGENDFILM. Jan., 2001. German. (Klaus Kraemer) Boris Aljinovic, Jurgen Tarrach, Claudia Michelsen, Ilja Richter, Edgar Selge, Carola Regnier.

THREE-FIVE PEOPLE
Oct., 2001. (Li Lin) Hu Jian, Chen Li, Tian Bo, Li. Documentary.

THREE KINGS
WARNER BROS. Sept., 1999. (David O. Russell) George Clooney, Mark Wahlberg, Ice Cube, Spike Jonze, Nora Dunn.

THE THREE KINGS
PATHE. Dec., 2001. French. (Didier Bourdon, Bernard Campan) Didier Bourdon, Bernard Campan, Pascal Legitimus, Virginie de Clausade, Walid Afkir, Nathalie Roussel, Claude Brusset, Christophe Hemon.

THE THREE MADELEINES
FILMS EQUINOX/FILMO/LA COMPAGNIE FRANCE FILM/HAROLD GREENBERG FUND/CANADIAN ARTS COUNCIL/MAIN FILM/TELEFILM CANADA/NATIONAL FILM OFFICE OF CANADA/QUEBEC COUNCIL OF ARTS & LETTERS. May, 2000. Canadian. (Guylaine Dionne) Sylvie Drapeau, France Arbour, Isadora Galwey, Kathleen Fortin, Maxim Gaudette, Isabelle Blais.

THE THREE MEN OF MELITA ZGANJER
KVADAR. Feb., 2000. Croation. (Snjezana Tribuson) Mirjana Rogina, Goran Navojec, Sanja Vejnovic, Suzana Nikolic, Filip Sovagovic.

3 NINJAS: HIGH NOON ON MEGA MOUNTAIN
SONY. April, 1998. (Sean McNamara) Hulk Hogan, Loni Anderson, Jim Varney, Mathew Botuchis, Michael J. O'Laskey II, J.P. Roeske.

THREE SEASONS
OCTOBER FILMS. Jan., 1999. (Tony Bui) Don Duong, Nguyen Ngoc Hiep, Tran Manh Cuong, Harvey Keitel, Zoe Bui.

THREE SONGS ABOUT LENIN
MEZHRABPOMFILM. Aug., 2000. Soviet Union–1935. (Dziga Vertov). Documentary.

THREE STORIES
IPOTESI CINEMA/RAI. Nov., 1999. Italian. (Piergiorgio Gay with Roberto San Pietro) Stefano Dionisi, Chiara Caselli, Alessandro Repossi, Barbara Lerici, Vittorio Amandola, Fabrizio Mele.

3 STRIKES
MGM/ABSOLUTE ENTERTAINMENT/MOTION PICTURE CORP. OF AMERICA/LITHIUM ENTERTAINMENT GROUP. Mar., 2000. (D.J. Pooh) Brian Hooks, N'Bushe Wright, Faizon Love, E40, Starletta DuPois, George Wallace, David Alan Grier, Dean Norris.

3000 MILES TO GRACELAND
WARNER BROS. Feb., 2001. (Demian Lichtenstein) Kurt Russell, Kevin Costner, Courteney Cox, Christian Slater, Kevin Pollak, David Arquette, Jon Lovitz, Howie Long.

THREE TO TANGO
WARNER BROS./VILLAGE ROADSHOW PICTURES/VILLAGE-HOYTS FILM PARTNERSHIP/OUTLAW. Oct., 1999. (Damon Santostefano) Matthew Perry, Neve Campbell, Dylan McDermott, Oliver Platt, Cylk Cozart, John C. McGinley, Bob Balaban, Deborah Rush.

THREE WIVES
01 DISTRIBUTION. Oct., 2001. Italian-Spanish. (Marco Risi) Francesca d'Aloja, Iaia Forte, Silke, Claudio Gregori.

THROUGH SUNGLASSES
IRANIAN FILM SOCIETY AND NEJ INTL. PICTURES. Nov., 2001. Iranian. (Mohammad Hossein Latifi) Iraj Tahmasb, Fatemeh Motamed Aria, Hassan Shokoohi, Faghiheh Soltani, Azizolah Honaramouz.

THROUGH THE WINDOW
A.F. CINEMA E VIDEO/BIAL CULTURE & ARTS. Feb., 2000. Brazilian. (Tata Amaral) Laura Cardoso, Fransergio Araujo, Ana Lucia Torre, Leona Cavalli, Joao Acaiabe, Antonio Petrin, Debora Duboc.

THUG LIFE IN D.C.
HBO. Feb., 1999. (Marc Levin). Documentary.

THUNDERPANTS
PATHE. April, 2002. British-German. (Pete Hewitt) Bruce Cook, Rupert Grint, Simon Callow, Stephen Fry, Celia Imre, Paul Giamatti, Ned Beatty, Bronagh Gallagher, Victor McGuire.

THURSDAY
GRAMERCY PICTURES. Sept., 1998. (Skip Woods) Thomas Jane, Aaron Eckhart, Paulina Porizkova, James Le Gros, Paula Marshall.

TIERRA DEL FUEGO
ISTITUTO LUCE/SURF FILM/CASTELAO PRODS./BUENAVENTURA FILMS. May, 2000. Italian-Spanish-Chilean. (Miguel Littin) Jorge Perugorria, Ornella Muti, Claudio Santamaria, Nancho Novo, Nelson Villagra, Alvaro Rudolphy.

TIGERLAND
20TH CENTURY FOX/REGENCY ENTERPRISE/HAFT ENT./ NEW REGENCY. Sept., 2000. (Joel Schumacher) Colin Farrell, Matthew Davis, Clifton Collins Jr., Thomas Guiry, Shea Whigham, Russell Richardson Cole Hauser.

THE TIGGER MOVIE
BUENA VISTA PICTURES/WALT DISNEY PICTURES. Feb., 2000. (Jun Falkenstein) Jim Cummings, Nikita Hopkins, Ken Sansom, John Fiedler, Peter Cullen, Andre Stojka, John Hurt. Animated.

THE TIGER OF SANTA JULIA
June, 2002. Mexican. (Alejandro Gamboa) Miguel Rodarte, Iran Castillo, Fernando Lujan, Isaura Espinoza, Adalberto Parra, Cristina Michaus, Ivonne Montero, Anilu Pardo.

THE TIGHT KNOT
MOSFILM . AUg., 2000. Soviet Union–1957. (Mikhail Shveitser) Viktor Avdyushko, Oleg Tabakov, Nikolai Sergeyev, Vladimir Emelyanov.

TILL HUMAN VOICES WAKE US
BECKER ENTERTAINMENT-GLOBE FILM CO. April, 2001. Australian. (Michael Petroni) Helena Bonham Carter, Frank Gallacher, Lindley Joyner, Brooke Harman, Peter Curtin, Margot Knight, Anthony Martin, Dawn Klingberg.

TILT
SALTO DE EJE/ASTROLABIO. Sept., 2001. Spanish. (Juanjo Gimenez Pena) Pepe Pereza, Vicente Gil, Ghamedy M'Baye, Inma Ochoa, Felipe Garcia Velez, Ramon Sala, Alicia Yague.

TIMECODE
SCREEN GEMS/RED MULLET. Apr., 2000. (Mike Figgis) Xander Berkeley, Golden Brooks, Saffron Burrows, Viveka Davis, Richard Edson, Aimee Graham, Salma Hayek, Glenne Headly, Andrew Heckler, Holly Hunter.

A TIME FOR DRUNKEN HORSES
MK2 DIFFUSION/B.H. FILMS. May, 2000. Iranian. (Bahman Ghobadi) Nezhad Ekhtiar-Dini, Amaneh Ekhtiar-Dini, Madi Ekhtiar-Dini, Ayoub Ahmadi, Jouvin Younessi.

TIMELESS, BOTTOMLESS, BAD MOVIE
MIRACIN KOREA. Oct., 1998. South Korean. (Jang Sun-Woo) Kwok Hyok-Sin, Jang Nam-Kyoung, Ducky Kim.

THE TIME MACHINE
DREAMWORKS (IN NORTH AMERICA)/WARNER BROS. (FOREIGN). March, 2002. (Simon Wells) Guy Pearce, Samantha Mumba, Mark Addy, Sienna Guillory, Phyllida Law, Alan Young, Omero Mumba.

TIME OF FAVOR
ISRAEL FILM FUND/YES/CINEMA FACTORY. Jan., 2001. Israeli. (Joseph Cedar) Aki Avni, Tinkerbell, Edan Alterman, Asi Dayan, Micha Selektar, Ammon Wolf, Shimon Mimran, Uri Klausner, Shemuel Kalderon.

THE TIME OF THE BRAVE
COLUMBIA TRISTAR. Dec., 1998. Spanish. (Antonio Mercero) Gabino Diego, Leonor Watling, Adriana Ozores, Luis Cuenca, Hector Colome.

TIME OUT
HAUT ET COURT. Sept., 2001. French. (Laurent Cantet) Aurelien Recoing, Karin Viard, Serge Livrozet, Jean-Pierre Mangeot, Monique Mangeot, Nicolas Kalsch, Marie Cantet.

TIME REGAINED
GEMINI. May, 1999. French-Italian. (Raoul Ruiz) Catherine Deneuve, Emmanuelle Beart, Vincent Perez, John Malkovich, Pascal Greggory.

TIME'S UP!
JOSE MARIA LARA-CECILIA BARRIGA (SPAIN)/CONCEPT BARRIGA (U.S.)/HUALQUI PRODUCCIONES (CHILE). May, 2001. U.S.-Spanish-Chilean. (Cecilia Barriga) Leonor Benedetto, Santiago Douglas, Marvin Starkman, Cristina Hernandez, Ching Valdes-Aran, Susan Levin, Jon Bennett.

A TIME TO LOVE
3 EMME CINEMATOGRAFICA/HUNGRY EYE LOWLANDS/NOE . Aug., 1999. Italian-British-French. (Giacomo Campiotti) Ciaran Hinds, Ignazio Oliva, Juliet Aubrey, Natacha Regnier, Natalia Piatti.

TITAN A.E.
20TH CENTURY FOX/20TH CENTURY FOX ANIMATION/GARY GOLDMAN/DAVID KIRSCHNER PRODS. June, 2000. (Don Bluth, Gary Goldman) Matt Damon, Drew Barrymore, Bill Pullman, John Leguizamo, Nathan Lane, Janeane Garofalo, Ron Perlman.

TO AND FRO
IMCINE/CENTRO DE CAPACITACION CINEMATOGRAFIA. Aug., 2000. Mexican. (Salvador Aguirre) Gerardo Taracena, Ricardo Esquerra, Tiare Scanda.

TO BE OR NOT TO BE
FARABI CINEMA. Feb., 1999. Iranian. (Kianoosh Ayyari) Asal Badi'ie, Farhad Sharifi, Hossein Ilbeygi, Maryam Bubani, Nur-Ali Lotfin.

TOBIA AL CAFFE
AB FILM/FACTORY PRODUZIONI CINEMATOGRAFICHE. July, 2000. Italian. (Gianfranco Mingozzi) Roberto Citran, Nicola Russo, Candice Hugo, Federico Galante.

TODAY OR NEVER
REMSTAR. Oct., 1998. Canadian. (Jean Pierre Lefebvre) Marcel Sabourin, Jean-Pierre Ronfard, Claude Blanchard, Julie Menard, Micheline Lanctot.

TO DIE (OR NOT)
LAUREN FILMS/ELS FILMS DE LA RAMBLA/CANAL PLUS/TVE/TVC. Jan., 2000. Spanish. (Ventura Pons) Lluis Homar, Carmen Elias, Roger Coma, Marc Martinez, Anna Azcona.

TOGETHER
SONET FILM/MEMFIS FILM/FILM I VAST/SVT DRAMA GOTHENBURG/ZENTROPA/KEYFILMS ROMA/TV 1000. Aug., 2000. Swedish-Danish-Italian. (Luka Moodysson) Lisa Lindgren, Mikael Nyqvist, Gustaf Hammarsten.

TOGETHER (HE NI ZAIYIQI)
UNITED ARTISTS. Sept., 2002. Chinese-South Korean. (Chen Kaige) Tang Yun, Liu Peiqi, Chen Hong, Wang Zhiwen, Chen Kaige, Cheng Qian, Zhang Qing, Kim Hye-ri, Liu Bing.

TOKYO RAIDERS
GOLDEN HARVEST. Sept., 2000. Hong Kong. (Jingle Ma) Tony Leung, Chiu-wai, Ekin Cheng, Kelly Chen, Cecilia Cheung.

TO LOVE, TOO MUCH
BUENA VISTA INTL. March, 2001. Mexican-Spanish. (Ernesto Rimoch) Karina Gidi, Ari Telch, Martin Altomaro, Daniel Martinez.

TOMCATS
SONY PICTURES ENTERTAINMENT. March, 2001 (Gregory Poirier) Jerry O'Connell, Shannon Elizabeth, Jake Busey, Horatio Sanz, Jaime Pressly, Bernie Casey, David Ogden Stiers.

TOMORROW
WARNER BROS. ITALIA. Jan., 2001. Italian. (Francesca Archibugi) Marco Baliani, Ornella Muti, Valerio Mastrandrea, Ilaria Occhini.

TOMORROW LA SCALA!
May, 2002. British. (Francesca Joseph) Jessica Stevenson, Samantha Spiro, Shaun Dingwall, Kulvinder Ghir, Kard Johnson, Dudley Sutton.

TOMORROW'S ANOTHER DAY
BAC FILMS/CINE VALSE/ART LIGHT PRODS./FRANCE 2 CINEMA/LE STUDIO CANAL. Aug., 2000. French. (Jeanne Labrune) Nathalie Baye, Jeanne Balibar, Jean-Pierre Darroussin.

TOMORROW NIGHT
CIRCUS KING. Jan., 1998. (Louis C.K.) Chuck Sklar, Martha Greenhouse, Heather Morgan, Rick Shapiro, J.B. Smoove.

TOM'S MIDNIGHT GARDEN
HYPERION. June, 1999. British. (Willard Carroll) Greta Saachi, James Wilby, Joan Plowright, Anthony Way, David Bradley.

TOO MUCH FLESH
TOLODA & BARNOTHING. Sept., 2000. French. (Jean-Marc Barr, Pascal Arnold) Rosanna Arquette, Elodie Bouchez, Jean-Marc Barr, Ian Vogt, Ian Brennan.

TOO TIRED TO DIE
DREAM SEARCH ENTERTAINMENT. Jan., 1998. (Wonsuk Chin) Takeshi Kaneshiro, Mira Sorvino, Jeffrey Wright, Michael Imperioli.

TOO YOUNG TO DIE
May, 2002. South Korean. (Park Jin-pyo) Park Chi-gyu, Lee Sun-ye.

TOP OF THE FOOD CHAIN
RED SKY/UPSTART PICTURES/BEDARD/LALONDE AMUSEMENTS/ VICTOR FILM CO./ONTARIO FILM DEV. CORP./SPACE: THE IMAGINATION STATION. Sept., 1999. Canadian. (John Paizs) Campbell Scott, Fiona Loewi, Tom Everett Scott, Hardee T. Lineham, Bernard Behrens, Nigel Bennett.

TOPS & BOTTOMS
BaRKING AT MOON/TVONTARIO, ARTE, SHOWCASE TV/ WOMEN'S TV NETWORK/KNOWLEDGE NETWORK/CANADIAN FILM BOARD WOMEN'S EQUITY PROGRAM. Sept., 1999. Canadian. (Christine Richey). Documentary.

TOPSY-TURVY
OCTOBER FILMS/PATHE. Sept., 1999. British. (Mike Leigh) Jim Broadbent, Allan Corduner, Lesley Manville, Eleanor David, Ron Cook.

TORO
REGAL ENTERTAINMENT CORP./AVAILABLE LIGHT. Mar., 2000. Filipino. (Jose Javier Reyes) Paolo Rivero, Anna Capri, Klaudia Koronel, Hazel Espinosa.

TORRENTE 2: MISSION IN MARBELLA
LOLAFILMS DISTRIBUCION. March, 2001. Spanish. (Santiago Segura) Santiago Segura, Gabino Diego, Tony Leblanc, Jose Luis Moreno, Ines Sastre, Arturo Valls.

TORTILLA SOUP
SAMUEL GOLDWYN FILMS. July, 2001. (Maria Ripoll) Hector Elizondo, Jacqueline Obradors, Elizabeth Pena, Tamara Mello, Nikolai Kinski, Raquel Welch, Joel Joan.

TOSCA
EURIPEDE PRODS. (PARIS)-VERADIA FILM (ROME)-INTEGRAL FILM (BERLIN)-AXIOM FILMS (LONDON). Aug., 2001. French-Italian-German-British. (Benoit Jacquot) Angela Gheorghiu, Roberto Alagna, Ruggero Raimondi, David Cangelosi, Sorin Coliban, Enrico Fissore, Maurizio Muraro.

TOSCA: A TALE OF LOVE AND TORTURE
FILM AUSTRALIA/AUSTRALIAN BROADCASTING CORP. June, 2000. Australian. (Trevor Graham). Documentary.

TOTAL LOSS
WARNER BROS./LEMMING FILM/V-PRO TV/MAJADE FILM/HEINO DECKERT. Aug., 2000. Dutch-German. (Dana Nechushtan) Franky Ribbens, Roef Ragas, Yorick van Wageningen.

TOTAL LOVE
CINEMA FACTORY. Nov., 2000. Israeli. (Gur Bentwich) Maor Cohen, Tinkerbel, Gur Bentwich, Zohar Dinar, Teodora, Herman Brood.

TOTALLY CONFUSED
MURRAY SHUMAN. June, 1998. (Gary Rosen, Greg Pritikin) Greg Pritikin, Gary Rosen, Jackie Katzman, Heather Donaldson.

TOTALLY IRRESPONSIBLE
KILLER BUD FILMS/PROSPERITY PICTURES. Feb., 2000. (Karl Hirsch) Corin Nemec, David Faustino, Caroline Keenan.

TOTALLY FLAKY
LES FILMS DU LOSANGE. April, 2001. French. (Jacques Doillon) Lou Doillon, Caroline Ducey, Guillaume Saurrel, Camille Clavel, Xavier Villeneuve, Hafed Benotman, Joshua Phillips, Antoine Chain.

TOTAL WESTERN
UFD/LAZENNEC/UGC IMAGES/CANAL PLUS,/STUDIO IMAGES 6,/GIMAGES. July, 2000. French. (Eric Rochant) Samuel Le Bihan, Jean-Pierre Kalfon, Jean-Francois Stevenin, Kahena Saighi.

TO THE HORIZON AND BEYOND
PROGRESS. Feb., 1999. German. (Peter Kahane) Wolfgang Stumph, Corinna Harfouch, Nina Petri, Gudrun Okras, Heinrich Schafmeister.

TO THE LEFT OF THE FATHER
Aug., 2001. Brazilian. (Luiz Pernando) Selton Mello, Raul Cortez, Juliana Carneiro da Cunha, simone Spoladore, Leonardo Medeiros.

TO THE SOUTH AND BACK
FEATURE FILM CO. NO. 1 (HANOI). Feb., 2001. Vietnamese. (Phi Tien Son) Le Hong Quang, Vu Phuong Thanh.

TO THOSE WHO LOVE
ALTA. Oct., 1998. Spanish-French. (Isabel Coixet) Julio Nunez, Patxi Freitez, Olalla Moreno, Monica Bellucci, Christopher Thompson.

TOUCHED
RED SKY/RANFILM. Sept., 1999. Canadian. (Mort Ransen) Lyn Redgrave, Tygh Runyan, Annick Obonsawin, Maury Chaykin, Lolita Davidovich, Ian Tracey, Graham Greene, Gary Farmer.

TOUR ABROAD
MIRA FILM. June, 2001. German. (Ayse Polat) Hilmi Sozer, Ozlem Blume, Ozay Fecht, Martin Glade, Birol Unel, Karen Friescicke.

TO WALK WITH LIONS
KINGSBOROUGH GREENLIGHT. June, 1999. Canadian-British-Kenyan. (Carl Schultz) Richard Harris, John Michie, Ian Bannen, Kerry Fox, High Quarshie.

THE TOWERING MONTPARNASSE INFERNO
UFD. March, 2001. French. (Charles Nemes) Eric Judor, Ramzy Bedia, Marina Fois, Serge Riaboukine.

TOWN & COUNTRY
NEW LINE CINEMA. April, 2001. (Peter Chelsom) Warren Beatty, Diane Keaton, Andie McDowell, Garry Shandling, Jenna Elfman, Nastassja Kinski, Goldie Hawn, Charlton Heston, Marian Seldes.

THE TOWN IS QUIET
MERCURE FILM/AGAT FILMS & CIE-DIAPHANA/CANAL PLUS. Aug., 2000. French. (Robert Guediguian) Ariane Ascaride, Jean-Pierre Darroussin, Gerard Meylan, Alexandre Ogou, Pierre Banderet.

TOY STORY 2
BUENA VISTA/WALT DISNEY PICTURES/PIXAR ANIMATION STUDIOS. Nov., 1999. (John Lasseter, Lee Unkrich, Ash Brannon) Tom Hanks, Tim Allen, Kelsey Grammer, Don Rickles, Jim Varney, Wallace Shawn, John Ratzenberger, Annie Potts (voices). Animated.

THE TRACKER
GLOBE FILMS (AUSTRALIA). March, 2002. Austrian. (Rolf de Heer) David Gulpilil, Gary Sweet, Damon Gameau, Grant Page, Noel Wilton.

TRADE OFF
WRIGHT ANGLE MEDIA. June, 2000. (Shaya Mercer) Mike Dolan, Michael Moore, Jello Biafra, Jerry Mander, Vandana Shiva, Charlene Barshefsky, Bill Clinton, Tom Hayden, Michael Franti.. Documentary.

THE TRIALS OF HENRY KISSINGER
May, 2002. (Eugene Jarecki) Christopher Hitchens, William Safire, Gen. Alexander Haig, Gen. Brent Scowcroft, Seymour Hersch, Daniel Davidson. Documentary.

THE TRAIN GOES EAST
MOSFILM. Aug., 2000. Soviet Uniion–1948. (Yuli Raisman) Lidia Dranovskaya, Leonid Gallis, Maria Yaroskaya, N. Vorobev, K. Sorokin.

TRAINING DAY
WARNER BROS. Aug., 2001. (Antoine Fuqua) Denzel Washington, Ethan Hawke, Scott Glenn, Tom Berenger, Harris Yulin, Raymond J. Barry, Cliff Curtis, Dr. Dre, Snoop Dogg, Macy Gray.

TRAIN TO PAKISTAN
NATIONAL FILM DEVELOPMENT CORP. OF INDIA. Feb., 1999. Indian. (Pamela Rooks) MohanAgashe, Xirmal Pandey, Rajit Kapur, Smriti Mishra, Divya Dutta.

TRAFFIC
USA FILMS. Nov., 2000. (Steven Soderbergh) Michael Douglas, Don Cheadle, Benicio Del Toro, Luiz Guzman, Dennis Quaid, Catherine Zeta-Jones, Steven Bauer, Benjamin Bratt, James Brolin.

THE TRAMP AND THE DICTATOR
Feb., 2002. British-German. (Kevin Brownlow, Michael Kloft) Walter Bernstein, Ray Bradbury, Sydney Chaplin, Al Hirschfeld, Stanley Kauffmann, Sidney Lumet, Ivor Montagu, Nikola Radosevic. Documentary.

TRANS
YID PRADER/DOWN HOME PICTURES. Sept., 1998. (Julian Goldberger) Tyan Daugherty, Justin Lakes, Jon Daugherty, MIchael Gulnac, Stephanie David.

TRANSGRESSION
MASSIMO FERRERO. Jan., 2000. Italian. (Tinto Brass) Yuliya Mayarchuk, Jarno Berardi, Francesca Nunzi, Max Parodi.

TRAP FOR A CAT
PRODUCCIONESJOTA Y JOROPODO. Sept., 1998. Venezuelan. (Manuel de Pedro) Amado Zambrano, Alejandro Faillace, Gregorio Milano. Yasmin Hernandez, Alberto Alcala.

TRAPPED
SONY PICTURES ENTERTAINMENT. Sept., 2002. (Luis Mandoki) Charlize Theron, Courtney Love, Stuart Townsend, Kevin Bacon, Pruitt Taylor Vince, Dakota Fanning, Colleen Camp.

TRAPS
CINEART. Sept., 1998. Czech. (Vera Chytilova): Miroslav Donutil, Zuzana Stivinova, Tomas Hanak.

TRASH
DANCING BABIES ENTERTAINMENT/TODD FELDMAN. Sept., 1999. (Mark Anthony Galluzzo) Jeremy Sisto, Eric Michael Cole, Jaime Pressly, Grace Zabriskie, Jonathan Bank, Charles Venturi, Marisa Ryan.

TRAVELING BIRDS
BAC DISTRIBUTION. Nov., 2001. French-German-Spanish-Italian-Swiss. (Jacques Perrin) Documentary.

TRAVELING SAINTS
INSTITUTO MEXICANO DE CINEMATOGRAFIA. Jan., 1999. Mexican. (Alejandro Springall) Dolores Heredia, Demian Bichir, Alberto Estrella, Roberto Cobo, Ana Bertha Espin.

TREADING WATER
TUNNEL VISION. June, 2001. (Lauren Himmel) Angela Redman, Nina Landey, Annette Miller, Robert Harte, Shawn Nee, Richard Snee, Lysa Apostle, Linda Robinson.

TREASURE ISLAND
KING PICTURES. Jan., 1999. (Scott King) Lance Baker, Nick Offerman, Jonah Blechman, Pat Healy, Suzy Nakamura.

TREASURE ISLAND
FRIES FILM GROUP. June, 2001. British-Canadian. (Peter Rowe) Jack Palance, Patrick Bergen, Kevin Zegers, Walter Sparrow.

THE TREATMENT
BEIJING TV & FILM ART CENTER/HUA YI BROTHERS/TAI HE FILM INVESTMENT CO. LTD./BEIJING FORBIDDEN CITY FILM CO. May, 2001. Chinese. (Zheng Xiaolong) Tony Leung, Zhu Xu, Jiang Wenli, Dennis Zhu, Hollis Huston.

THE TREATY OF CHANCE
PIERRA GRISE. July, 1999. French. (Patrick Mimouni) Eliane Pin Carringhton, Nini Crepon, Laurent Chemda, Bruno Anthony de Trigancei.

THE TREE
UIP (SINGAPORE). June, 2001. Singapore. (Daisy Chan) Francis Ng, Zoe Tay, Phyllis Quek, Tse Kwan-ho, Lau Siu-ming, Edmund Tay, Deng Mao-hui, Dasmond Koh, Lee Eewurn.

THE TREE OF LIFE
IRIB CHANNEL 2, MOHAMMAD-REZA, SARHANGI. Sept., 1998. Iranian. (Farhad Mehranfar) Anis Shakoori, Omid Amiri, Adeleh Shaoori, Jian Amir Rezvani.

A TREE WITHOUT ROOTS (LALSALU)
Aug., 2002. Bangladesh. (Tanvir Mokammel) Raisul Islam Asad, Munira Yusuf Memy, Chandni, Aly Zaker, Rowshan Jamil, Amirul Haque Choudhury, Towquir Ahmed.

TREMBLING BEFORE G-D
SIMCHA LEIB PRODS. AND TURBULENT ARTS. Jan., 2001. (Sandi Simcha DuBowski) Documentary.

THE TRENCH
ENTERTAINMENT FILM DISTRIBUTORS. May, 1999. British-French. (William Boyd) Paul Nichols, Daniel Craig, Julian Rhind-Tutt, Danny Dyer, James D'Arcy.

THE TRESPASSER
Jan., 2002. Brazilian. (Beto Brant) Marco Ricca, Alexandre Borges, Paulo Miklos, Malu Mader.

T-REX: BACK TO THE CRETACEOUS
IMAX. Oct., 1998. (Brett Leonard) Peter Horton, Liz Stauber, Kari Coleman, Laurie Murdoch, Tuck Milligan.

A TRIAL IN PRAGUE
PICK/SPACE FILMS. Aug., 2000. (Zuzana Justman). Documentary.

TRIANGLE SQUARE
CORNERBROOK FILMS. July, 2001. Donny Terranova, Jon Cellini, Down Cochran, Gregory Phelan, Eric Etebari, Ashley Turner, Jessica Randle.

TRIBUTE
Nov., 2001. (Rich Fox, Chris Curry) Andy Kelley, Danny Lopez, Chuck Hartel, Jay Harris, Jeff Richards, Mark Eldridge, Richie Sorenson, Enrique Segura. Documentary.

TRICK
FINE LINE/GOOD MACHINE. Jan., 1999. (Jim Fall) Christian Campbell, John Paul Pitoc, Tori Spelling, Steve Hayes.

TRICKY LICE
Aug., 2001. Uruguayan-Belgian-Spanish-Cuban. (Beatriz Flores Silva) Mariana Santangelo, Silvestre, Josep Linuesa, Andrea Fantoni, Rodrigo Speranza, Agustin Abreu, Fermi Herrero, Augusto Mazzarelli.

TRIFLING WITH FATE
SEPARATE STAR. June, 2000. (Michael Bergmann) Teri Lamm, Ryan Dunn, Bridget Moynahan, Vivienne Benesch, Rob Gerlach, Holter Graham, Robin Dorian, Michael Hayward-Jones.

THE TRIP
June, 2002. (Miles Swain) Larry Sullivan, Steve Braun, Sirena Irwin, Alexis Arquette, Ray Baker, Jill St. John, Julie Brown, David Mixner.

TRIPPIN'
Rogue Pictures. May, 1999. (David Raynr) Deon Richmond, Donald Adeosun Faison, Maia Campbell, Guy Torry, Aloma Wright.

A TRIP TO THE COUNTRY
LES FILMS DU RAPHIA/ZDF/ARTE. Feb., 2000. Cameroon-French-German. (Jean-Marie Teno) Documentary.

THE TRIUMPH OF LOVE
PARAMOUNT CLASSICS. Aug., 2001. Italian-British. (Clare Peploe) Mira Sorvino, Ben Kingsley, Firona Shaw, Jay Rodan, Ignazio Oliva, Rachael Stirling Luis Molteni.

TRIXIE
SONY PICTURES CLASSICS. Jan., 2000. (Alan Rudolph) Emily Watson, Dermot Mulroney, Nick Nolte, Nathan Lane, Brittany Murphy, Lesley Ann Warren, Will Patton, Stephen Lang.

TROIKA
GUARDEZ-BIEN. Nov., 1998. (Jennifer Montgomery) Jenny Bass, Lev Shekhtman, Marina Shterenberg, Valery Manenti, Vitali Baganov.

TROIS
RAINFOREST PRODS./TRF PRODS. July, 2000. (Rob Hardy) Gary Dourdan, Kenya Moore, Gretchen Palmer, Soloman K. Smith, Thom Byrd, Chrystale Wilson, Bryce Wilson.

TROUBLE EVERY DAY
REZO FILMS (IN FRANCE)/LOT 47 (IN U.S.). May, 2001. French. (Claire Denis) Vincent Gallo, Tricia Vessey, Beatarice Dalle, Alex Descas, Florence Loiret-Caille, Nicolas Duvauchelle, Jose Garcia.

TROUBLE-SHOOTERS
BANDAI VISUAL. June, 1999. Japanese. (Masato Harada) Koji Matoba, Leo Morimoto, Hiroko Fukuda, Hajime Asoh.

THE TROUBLE WITH LOU
Jan., 2001. (Gregor) Lou Romano, Katheryn Cain, Tom Winkler, Michelle Maaske, Donne McRea, Michael Ambrosini.

THE TROUBLE WITH MERLE
June, 2002. Australian. (Maree Delofski) Charles Higham. Documentary.

TRUE FRIENDS
2ND GENERATION FILMS. Jan., 1998. (James Quattrochi) James Quattrochi, Loreto Mauro, Rodrigo Botero, Kyle Gibson.

TRUE-HEARTED VIXENS
SOUVENIR PICTURES. July, 2001. (Mylene Moreno) Jany Bolin, Kertria "Moochie" Lofton, Kaylee Alayon, Terry Sullivan, Cynthia "Red" Bryant, John "JT" Turner. Documentary.

TRUE MOMENTS
SANDREW. Aug., 1998. Swedish-Finnish-Danish. (Lena Koppel) Lena Endre, Krister Henriksson, Arne Ukskula, Anita Bjork, Oyana Lugn-Rodriguez.

TRUE STORIES
March, 2002. Azerbaijani-Russian. (Murad Ibragimbekov) Vladimir Steklov, Kristina Orbakaite, Ludmilla Polyakova.

THE TRUE STORY OF MY LIFE IN ROUEN
Aug., 2002. French. (Olivier Ducastel, Jacques Martineau) Jimmy Tavares, Ariane Ascaride, Helene Surgere, Jonathan Zaccai.

TRULY HUMAN
Aug., 2001. Danish. (Ake Sandgren) Nikolaj Lie Kaas, Susan A. Olsen, Peter Mygind, Troels II Munk, Line Kruse, Soren Hauch-Fausboll, Clara Nepper Winther.

THE TRUMAN SHOW
PARAMOUNT. April, 1998. (Peter Weir) Jim Carrey, Laura Linney, Noah Emmerich, Natascha McElhone, Holland Taylor, Ed Harris

A TRUMPET IN THE WADI (HATZOZRA BAVADI)
Aug., 2002. Israeli. (Lina and Slava Chaplin) Aleander Senderovich, Khawlah Hag-Debsy, Raeda Adon, Salwa Nakkara-Hadad, Itzhak Neeman, Imad Gabarin.

THE TRUMPET OF THE SWAN
TRISTAR PICTURES. May, 2001. (Richard Rich, Terry L. Noss) Animated. Jason Alexander, Mary Steenburgen, Reese Witherspoon, Seth Green, Carol Burnett, Joe Mantegna.

THE TRUTH GAME
SCREEN PRODUCTION ASSOCIATES. May, 2001. British. (Simon Rumley) Paul Blackthorne, Tania Emery, Thomas Fisher, Selina Giles, Stuart Laing, Jennifer White, Wendy Wason.

TUBE TALES
SKY PICTURES/HORSEPOWER FILMS. Dec., 1999. British. (Amy Jenkins, Stephen Hopkins, Mehaj Huda, Bob Hoskins, Ewan McGregor, Armando Iannucci, Jude Law, Gaby Dellal, Charles McDougall) Kelly Macdonald, Jason Flemyng, Denise Van Outen, Tom Bell, Stephen Da Costa, Dele Johnson, Ray Winstone, Tom Watson.

TUCK EVERLASTING
BUENA VISTA. Aug., 2002. (Jay Russell) Alexis Bledel, William Hurt, Sissy Spacek, Jonathan Jackson, Scott Bairstow, Ben Kingsley, Amy Irving, Victor Garber.

TUMBLEWEEDS
FINE LINE. Jan., 1999. (Gavin O'Connor) Janet McTeer, Kimberly J. Brown, Gavin O'Connor, Jay O'Sanders, Lois Smith.

THE TUNNEL
BETA FILM. Feb., 2001. German. (Roland Suso Richter) Heino Ferch, Nicolette Krebitz, Sebastian Koch, Alexandra Maria Lara.

THE TURANDOT PROJECT
ALTERNATE CURRENT. Sept., 2000. U.S.-German. (Alan Miller) Documentary.

TURBULENCE
SKYLIGHT CINEMA/ICAIC/D & D. May, 2000. Brazilian-Cuban-Portuguese. (Ruy Guerra) Jorge Perugorria, Bianca Byington, Susana Ribeiro, Leonor Arocha, Xando Graca.

TURN IT UP
NEW LINE. Aug., 2000. (Robert Adetuyi) Pras, Ja Rule, Vondie Curtis-Hall, Tamala Jones, Jason Statham, Eugene Clark, John Ralston, Chris Messina.

TURN OF THE CENTURY
Sept., 2001. Russian. (Konstantin Lopushansky) Svetlana Svirko, Irina Sokolova, Roman Viktyuk, ALexander Baluyev, Dmitry Shevchenko.

TURNING GATE
CINEMA SERVICE. May, 2002. South Korean. (Hong Sang-soo) Kim Sang-gyeong, Chu Sang-mi, Ye Ji-weon, Kim Hak-sun.

TUVALU
VEIT HELMER/BOROUGH FILM/BUENA VISTA INTL/FILMBOARD BERLIN-BRANDENBERG/FFA/SWR/MITTELDEUTSCHER RUNDFUNK. Sept., 1999. German. (Veit Helmer) Denis Lavant, Chulpan Hamatova, Philippe Clary, Terrence Gillespie, EJ Callahan, Djoko Rossich.

THE TUXEDO
DREAMWORKS PICTURES. Sept., 2002. (Kevin Donovan) Jackie Chan, Jennifer Love Hewitt, Jason Isaacs, Debi Mazar, Ritchie Coster, Peter Stormare, Mia Cottet, Romany Malco.

TWEEKED
DUMPSTER FILMS. March, 2001. (Beth Dewey) Darling Narita, Ali Raymer, Gavin Hignight, David Carrera, Alfredo Gasso, Chris D, Jay Dialo, Richmond Arquette.

TWEETY'S HIGH-FLYING ADVENTURE
WARNER HOME VIDEO. Sept., 2000. (James T. Walker) Animated. Joe Alaskey, June Foray.

12
May, 2002. (Lawrence Bridges) Alison Elliott, Tony Griffin, Allen Lulu, Terrence Burton T-Bone.

TWELVE NIGHTS
GOLDEN HARVEST. Oct., 2000. Hong Kong. (Aubrey Lam) Cecilia Cheung, Eason Chan, Candy Lo, Nicola Cheung, Su Au, Vincci Cheuk, Jim Yan, Nicholas Tse.

28 DAYS
SONY PICTURES ENTERTAINMENT/COLUMBIA PICTURES/TALL TREES. Apr., 2000. (Betty Thomas) Sandra Bullock, Viggo Mortensen, Dominic West, Diane Ladd, Elizabeth Perkins, Steve Buscemi.

25 KIDS & ONE DAD
Aug., 2002. Chinese. (Huang Hong) Huang Hong, Li Lin, Lei Kesheng, Siqin Gaowa, Yu Lan, Huang Zhaohan, Li Song, Yu Hao, Zhang Yinghong, Jia Erwa, Zhao Ran, Fan Lei, Zhou Wei.

25 WATTS
CTRL Z FILMS. Jan., 2001. Uruguayan. (Juan Pablo Rebella) Daniel Hendler, Jorge Temponi, Alfonso Tort, Valentin Rivero, Valeria Mendieta.

24 HOURS IN LONDON
BLUE DOLPHIN FILMS/ONE WORLD FILMS. July, 2000. British. (Alexander Finbow) Gary Olsen, Anjela Lauren-Smith, John Benfield, Amita Dhiri, James Oliver, Sara Stockbridge, Richard Graham.

24 HOUR PARTY PEOPLE
PATHE. Feb., 2002. British. (Michael Winterbottom) Steve Coogan, Lennie James, Shirley Henderson, Paddy Considine, Andy Serkis, Sean Harris, John Simm, Ralf Little, Danny Cunningham.

THE 24 HOUR WOMAN
ARTISAN. Jan., 1999. (Nancy Savoca) Rosie Perez, Marianne Jean-Baptiste, Patti LuPone, Karen Duffy, Diego Serrano.

24 NIGHTS
CYNICAL BOY. Mar., 1999. (Kieran Turner) Kevin Isola, Aida Turturro, Stephen Mailer, David Burtka, Mary Louise Wilson.

TWENTY PEACHES IN A BOX
SIDE SHOW FILMS. Jan., 1999. (Carlos Hamill) Cindy Peters, Talitha Peters, Giorgio della Terza, Michele Markarian.

27 MISSING KISSES
JENS MEUER & OLIVER DAMIAN/EGOLI FILMS/LE STUDIO CANAL PLUS/MOCO FILMS/BRITISH SCREEN/STUDIO BABELSBERG INDEPENDENTS/WAVE PICTURES. May, 2000. German-Georgian. (Nana Djordjadze) Nino Kuchanidze, Eugenij Sidichin, Shalva Iashvili.

23RD MARCH 1931: SHAHEED
June, 2002. Indian. (Guddu Dhanoa) Bobby Deol, Sunny Deol, Amrita Singh, Tej Sapru, Rahul Dev, Vicky Ahuja, Viveck Shauq, Deepak Sharma, Suresh Oberoi, Akshay Anand, Shakti Kapoor.

20–VENTI
QUATTROCENTOUNDICI/411/BONGIOMO PRODS./DAVID PRODS. Feb., 2000. Italian. (Marco Pozzi) Cecilia Dazzi, Anita Caprioli.

TWILIGHT
PARAMOUNT. March, 1998. (Robert Benton) Paul Newman, Susan Sarandon, Gene Hackman, Reese Witherspoon, Stockard Channing, James Garner, Giancarlo Esposito.

TWILIGHT: LOS ANGELES
ANNA DEAVERE SMITH/OFFLINE. ENTERTAINMENT GROUP. Jan., 2000. (Marc Levin).

TWIN DRAGONS
DIMENSION. APR., 1999. Hong Kong. (Tsui Hark) Jackie Chan, Maggie Cheung, Nina Li Chi, Anthony Chan, Philip Chan.

TWIN FALLS IDAHO
SONY. Jan. 1999. (Michael Polish) Michael Polish, Mark Polish, Michele Hicks, Jon Gries, Patrick Bauchau.

TWO
May, 2002. French-German-Portuguese. (Werner Schroeter) Isabelle Huppert, Bulle Ogier, Manuel Blanch, Arielle Dombasle, Annika Kuhl, Jean-Francois Stevenin, Robinson Stevenin.

2 BY 4
ELECTRIC HEAD. Jan., 1998. (Jimmy Smallhorne) Jimmy Smallhorne, Chris O'Neill, Bradley Fitts, Joe Holyoake, Terrence McGoff.

TWO CAN PLAY AT THAT GAME
SONY PICTURES ENTERTAINMENT. Aug., 2001. (Mark Brown) Vivica A. Fox, Morris Chestnut, Anthony Anderson, Gabrielle Union, Wendy Raquel Robinson, Tamala Jones, Mo'Nique, Ray Wise.

TWO DRIVERS
July, 2002. Russian. (Alexandr Kott) Pavel Derevyanko, Irina Rakhmanova, Valeri Ivakov, Vladimir Romanovsky, Yulia Butakova.

TWO FAMILY HOUSE
LIONS GATE/FILBERT STEPS. Jan., 2000. (Raymond De Felitta) Michael Rispoli, Kelly Macdonald, Katherine Narducci, Kevin Conway, Matt Servitto, Michele Santopietro, Louis Guss.

TWO FOR TEA
LAUREN FILMS/PRODUCCIONS KILIMANJARO. Aug., 2000. Spanish. (Isabel Gardela) Nuria Prims, Zack Qureshi, Txell Sust, Olalla Moreno, Teresa Gimpera, Moncia Van Campen, Xavier Graset.

TWO FRIENDS
MEDUSA. Aug., 2002. Italian. (Spiro Scimone, Francesco Sframeli) Francesco Sframeli, Spiro Scimone, Felice Andreasi, Sara Bertela, Valerio Binasco, Roberto Citran, Gianfelice Imparato.

TWO HANDS
BEYOND FILMS/AUSTRALIAN FILM FINANCE CORP. Jan., 1999. Australian. (Gregor Jordan) Heath Ledger, Rose Byrne, Bryan Brown, David Field.

TWO LIKE US, NOT THE BEST
ISTITUTO LUCE/METAFILM. Apr., 2000. Italian. (Stefano Grossi) Marcello Sambati, Adel Bakri, Stefania Orsola Garello.

2 MINUTES SILENCE, PLEASE
PUBLIC FILM/PIETER VAN HUYSTEE FILM &TV/NPS. Oct., 1999. Dutch. (Heddy Honigmann). Documentary.

TWO NINAS
KING BROOK ENTERTAINMENT/CASTLEREA FILMS/ ACCIDENTAL PICTURES. Sept., 1999. (Neil Turitz) Cara Buono, Amanda Peet, Bray Poor, Linda Larkin, Ron Livingston, Jill Hennessy.

2000+1 SHOTS
DNA FILMS. Nov., 2000. Greek. (Dimitris Athanitis) Vicky Volioti, Ieronymos Kaletsanos, Maria Protopappa, Dimosthenis Papadopoulos, Marianne Calbari.

TWO STREAMS
DEZENOVE SOM E IMAGENS. Aug., 1999. Brazilian. (Carlos Reichenbach) Carlos Alberto Riccelli, Beth Goulart, Ingra Liberato.

2000 AD
MEDIA ASIA/RAINTREE/MEDIA ASIA FILMS/RAINTREE PICTURES. May, 2000. Hong Kong-Singapore. (Gordon Chan) Aaron Kwok, Daniel Wu, Phyllis Quek, James Lye, Andrew Lin, GiGi Cho.

TWO THOUSAND AND NONE
GALAFILM PRODS./CANADIAN TV FUND/CHUM TV/MOVIE NETWORK/SUPER ECRAN/SUPER CHANNEL. July, 2000. Canadian. (Arto Paragamian) John Turturro, Oleg Kisseliov.

TWO UNKNOWN PHOTOGRAPHERS
STOLEN PICTURES. Jan., 2001. (Kon Pet Moon) Documentary.

TWO WOMEN
ARTA. Feb., 1999. Iranian. (Tahmineh Milani). Niki Karimi, Marila Zare'i, Mohammad Reza Forutan.

TYCOON (OLIGARCH)
Aug., 2002. Russian-French. (Pavel Lounguine) Vladimir Mashkov, Andrei Krasko, Maria Mironova, Sergei Oshkevich, Alexandre Samoilenko, Levani Uchaineshvili.

U

U-571
UNIVERSAL/STUDIO CANAL PLUS/DINO DE LAURENTIIS. Apr., 2000. (Jonathan Mostow) Matthew McConaughey, Bill Paxton, Harvey Keitel, Jon Bon Jovi, Jake Weber, David Keith, T.C. Carson, Jack Noseworth.

THE UGLIEST WOMAN IN THE WORLD
AURUM/CANAL PLUS/TVE. Nov., 1999. Spanish. (Miguel Bardem) Elia Galera, Roberto Alvarez, Hector Alterio, Javivi, Alberto San Juan.

UNBOWED
FILMANTHROPIC. Nov., 1999. (Nanci Russov) Tembi Locke, Jay Tavare, Edward Albert, Orson Bean, Ron Glass, Hattie Winston, Michele Thomas, Mark Abbott, Fran Bennett.

UNBREAKABLE
BUENA VISTA. Nov., 2001. (M. Night Shyamalan) Bruce Willis, Samuel L. Jackson, Robin Wright Penn, Charlayne Woodard, Spencer Treat Clark, James Handy.

THE UNCERTAINTY PRINCIPLE
May, 2002. Portuguese-French. (Manoel de Oliveira) Leonor Baldaque, Leonor Silveira, Isabel Ruth, Ricardo Trepa, Ivo Canelas.

THE UNCLES
FEATURE FILM PROJECT. April, 2001. Canadian. (Jim Allodi) Chris Owens, Tara Rosling, Kelly Harms, Veronika Hurnik, Dino Tavarone, Nicola Lipman, Alan Van Sprang, Walter Anza.

UNCLE SADDAM
JOEL SOLER. Oct., 2000. (Soler) Documentary.

UNCONDITIONAL LOVE
HORNE ENTERTAINMENT, INC. Feb., 1999. (Steven Rush) John Kennedy Horne, Tracey Ross, Henry Silva, Miles O'Keefe.

UNDER CALIFORNIA: THE LIMIT OF TIME
IMCINE/SINCRONIA. Jan., 1999. Mexican. (Carlos Bolado) Damian Alcazar, Jesus Ochoa.

UNDERCOVER BROTHER
UNIVERSAL. May 28, 2002. (Malcolm D. Lee) Eddie Griffin, Chris Kattan, Denise Richards, Anjanue Ellis, Dave Chappelle, Chi McBride, Neil Patrick Harris, Bill Dee Williams.

UNDER HELLGATE BRIDGE
FORTUNE FILMS/CAVU PICTURES/EL-TRAIN. Aug., 2000. (Michael Sergio) Michael Rodrick, Jonathan LaPaglia, Frank Vincent, Jordan Bayne, Brian Vincent, Dominic Chianese, Vincent Pastore.

UNDERSTANDING JANE
SCALA. Nov., 1998. British. (Caleb Lindsay) Kevin McKidd, Amelia Curtis, John Simon, Louisa Milwood Haigh, Carl Proctor.

UNDER SUSPICION
REVELATIONS ENTERTAINMENT/TF1 INTI. May, 2000. U.S.-French. (Stephen Hopkins Le) Morgan Freeman, Gene Hackman,Thomas Jane, Monica Bellucci, Nydia Caro, Angel Suarez.

UNDERTAKER'S PARADISE
BUENA VISTA INTL./CLAUSSEN & WOEBKE. Aug., 2000. German. (M.X. Oberg) Thomas Schmauser, Ben Gazzara, Michael Fitzgerald, Emma Catherwood, Edward Jewesbury, Sally Dexter, Janine Eser.

UNDER THE CITY'S SKIN
Feb., 2001. Iranian. (Rakhshan Bani-Etemad) Golab Adineh, Mohammad Reza Foroutan, Baran Kosari, Ebrahin Sheibani, Mohsen Ghazi Moradi, Homeira Riazi.

UNDER THE MOONLIGHT
Feb., 2001. Iranian. (Seyyed Reza Mir-Karimi) Hossein Pour Sattar, Hamed Rajabali, Mehran Rajabi, Mahmud Nazar-Alian, Fereshteh Sadr-Orafai, Ashar Heidari.

UNDER THE SAND
FIDELITE PRODS./EURO SPACE/HAUT & COURT/ARTE FRANCE CINEMA. Sept., 2000. French. (Francois Ozon) Charlotte Rampling, Bruno Cremer, Jacques Nolot, Alexandra Stewart, Pierre Vernier.

UNDER THE SUN
SVENSK FILMINDUSTRI. Dec., 1998. Swedish. (Colin Nutley) Rolf Lassgard, Helena Bergstrom, Johan Widerberg, Gunilla Roor.

UNDISPUTED
MIRAMAX FILMS. Aug., 15, 2002. (Walter Hill) Wesley Snipes, Ving Rhames, Peter Falk, Michael Rooker, Jon Seda, Wes Studi, Fisher Stevens, Dayton Callie, Amy Aquino, Johnny Williams, Joe D'Angerio, Nils Allen Stewart, Denis Arndt, Rose Rollins.

UNFAIR COMPETITION
MEDUSA FILM. Feb., 2001. Italian-French. (Ettore Scola) Diego Abatantuono, Sergio Castellitto, Gerard Depardieu, Jean-Claude Brialy, Claude Rich, Claudio Bigagli, Anita Zagaria.

THE UNFINISHED SONG
FILM E-EMROOZ. Feb., 2001. Iranian. (Maziar Miri) Ali-Reza Anoushfar, Ghogha Bayat, Hossein Soleimani.

UNFORESEEN
Feb. 23, 2002. (Edward Barkin) Steve Parlavecchio, Lisa Lawrence, David Heymann, Ari Gold, Arthur Nascarella, Kim Director, David Stepkin.

THE UNIVERSAL CLOCK: THE RESISTANCE OF PETER WATKINS
Sept., 2001. Canadian. (Geoff Bowie) Peter Watkins, Sara Louis, Anna Pano, Marie-Josephe Barrere, Kamel Ikachamene, Renaud Bazin. Documentary.

THE UNIVERSAL SOLDIER: THE RETURN
SONY. Aug., 1999. (Mic Rodgers) Jean-Claude Van Damme, Michael Jai White, Heidi Schanz, Xander Berkeley, Justin Lazard.

UNINVITED
FRANCO NERO/FRANCESCO PAPA/BAROLO FILMS/NO LIMIT INTL./MEDIASET. Sept., 1999. U.S.-Italian. (Carlo Gabriel Nero) Kevin Isola, Adam Hann-Byrd, Stephen Mendillo, Patricia Dunnock.

THE UNKNOWN
SANDREW METRONOME. July, 2001. Swedish. (Michael Hjorth) Jacob Ericksson, Marcus Palm, Ann-Sofie Rase, Ingar Sigvardsdotter, Tomas Tivemark.

UNKNOWN PLEASURES
May, 2002. Japanese-Chinese. (Jia Zhang-ke) Zhao Tao, Zhao Wei Wei, Wu Qiong, Zhou Qing Feng, Wang Hong Wei, Rai Ru.

UNDER HEAVEN
BANNER ENTERTAINMENT. Jan., 1998. (Meg Richman) Joely Richardson, Aden Young, Molly Parker, Kevin Phillip.

UNDETECTABLE: THE NEW FACES OF AIDS
April, 2001. (Jay Corcoran) Matilda Garcia, Anibal Castaneda, Belinda Dunn, Carole Miselman, Joe Pennell, David Brudnoy. Documentary.

UNFINISHED SYMPHONY: DEMOCRACY AND DISSENT
NORTHERN LIGHTS. Jan., 2001. (Bestor Cram, Mike Majoros) Documentary.

THE UNKNOWN CYCLIST
TRIDENT RELEASING. June, 1998. (Bernard Salzman) Lea Thompson, Vincent Spano, Danny Nucci, Stephen Spinella.

UNKNOWN FRIEND
MONEYPENNY/ZDF/DFFB. Feb., 2000. German. (Anne Hoegh Krohn) Karoline Eichhorn, Inga Busch, Biroll Uenel, Antonio Wannek.

UNLEADED
REZO FILMS. Aug., 2000. French. (Muriel Teodori) Emma de Caunes, Alexis Loret, Eric Caravaca, Miki Manojlovic, Elvis Costello, Alain Souchon, Michael Maloney, Julian Kerridge.

UNLOVED
SUNCENT CINEMAWORKS. May, 2001. Japanese. (Kunitoshi Manda) Yuko Moriguchi, Toru Nakamura, Shunsuke Matsuoka.

THE UNSAID
REZO FILMS. Sept., 2001. U.S.-Canadian. (Tom McLoughlin) Andy Garcia, Vincent Kartheiser, Linda Cardellini, Trevor Blumas, Teri Polo, Sam Bottoms.

AN UNUSUAL LOVE
BEIJING FILM/BEIJING XINYINGJIA. Aug., 2000. Chinese. (Wu Tianming) Yuan Li, Liu Yunlong, Zhu Daoxian, Han Fuyi, Gong Peixi.

THE UNVEILING
MIASMA FILMS. June, 1998. Documentary.

UP AT THE VILLA
USA FILMS//UIP/UNIVERSAL/INTERMEDIA FILMS/MIRAGE/ STANLEY BUCHTAL. Apr., 2000. U.S.-British. (Philip Haas) Kristin Scott Thomas, Sean Penn, Anne Bancroft, James Fox, Jeremy Davies, Derek Jacobi, Massimo Ghini.

THE UPRISING
CINEMA SERVICE. Aug., 1999. South Korean-French. (Park Kwang-su) Lee Jung-jae, Shim Eun-ha, Myung Kay-nam, Frederic Andrau.

UPSIDE DOWN
AND WHATABOUT US/DE CUERNOS AL ABISMO FILMS. July, 1999. (Mario Mandujano) Chantal Chamandy, Alex Furth.

UP SYNDROME
TRISOMY FILMS. Jan., 2001. (Duane Graves) Rene Moreno, Duane Graves.Documentary.

UP TO THE ANGELS
MEDUSA FILM/DUEA FILM. Dec., 1999. Italian. (Pupi Avati) Gianni Cavina, Valentina Cervi, Carlo Delle Piane, Libero De Rienzo, Eliana Miglio, Chiara Muti, Paola Saluzzi, Mario Maranzana.

URBAN FEEL
URBAN FEEL PRODS. Feb., 1999. Israeli. (Jonathan Sagall) Dafna Rechter, Scharonn Alexander, Jonathan Sagall.

URBANIA
SHEAR/GOLDEN/HARRIS. Jan., 2000. (Jon Shear) Dan Futterman, Alan Cumming, Matt Keeslar, Josh Hamilton, Lothaire Bluteau, Bill Sage, Barbara Sukowa, Paige Turco, Meagan Dodds, Gabriel Olds.

URBAN LEGEND
TRISTAR. Sept., 1998. (Jamie Blanks) Jared Leto, Alicia Witt, Rebecca Gayheart, Michael Rosenbaum, Loretta Devine.

URBAN LEGENDS: FINAL CUT
SONY PICTURES ENTERTAINMENT/COLUMBIA PICTURES/ PHOENIX PICTURES/NEAL H. MORITZ/GINA MATTHEWS. Sept., 2000. (John Ottman) Jennifer Morrison, Matthew Davis, Hart Bochner, Loretta Devine, Joseph Lawrence, Anson Mount, Eva Mendez.

U.S. MARSHALS
WARNER BROS. March, 1998. (Stuart Baird) Tommy Lee Jones, Wesley Snipes, Robert Downey, Jr., Kate Nelligan, Joe Pantoliano, Irene Jacob.

VACUUMING COMPLETELY NUDE IN PARADISE
BBC FILMS PRODUCTION.,Aug., 2001. British. (Danny Boyle) Timothy Spall, Michael Begley, David Crellin, Katy Cavanagh.

VALENTINE
WARNER BROS. Feb., 2001. (Jamie Blanks) David Boreananz, Denise Richards, Marley Shelton, Jessica Capshaw, Jessica Cauffiel, Katherine Heigl.

VALERIE FLAKE
I.E. FILMS. Jan., 1999. (John Putch) Susan Traylor, Jay Underwood, Christina Pickles, Peter Michael Goetz, Rosemay Forsyth.

THE VALLEY
MBC/SUSPECT DEVICE FOR CHANNEL 4. Apr., 2000. British. (Dan Reed). Documentary.

VAMPIRE HUNTER D
URBAN VISION ENTERTAINMENT. Oct., 2000. Japanese. (Yoshiaki Kawajiri). Animated.

VAMPIRES
CTV INTL. April, 1998. (John Carpenter) James Woods, Daniel Baldwin, Sheryl Lee, Thomas Ian Griffith, Tim Guinee, Maximilian Schell.

VANILLA SKY
PARAMOUNT. Nov., 2001. (Cameron Crowe) Tom Cruise, Penelope Cruz, Cameron Diaz, Kurt Russell, Jason Lee, Noah Taylor, Timothy Spall, Tolda Swinton, Alicia Witt, Johnny Galecki, Michael Shannon.

VAN VAN, LET'S PARTY
April, 2002. Argentine-Cuban. (Liliana Mazure, Aaron Vega) Documentary.

VARIOUS POSITIONS
Aug., 2002. Canadian. (Ori Kowarsky) Tygh Runyan, Carly Pope, L. Harvey Gold, Marie Stillin, Michael Suchanek, Terry Chen.

VARSITY BLUES
PARAMOUNT. Jan., 1999. (Brian Robbins) James Van Der Beek, Jon Voight, Paul Walker, Ron Lester, Scott Cann.

VATEL
MIRAMAX/GAUMONT/GAUMONT-LEGENDE ENTERPRISES/ TIMOTHY BURRILL PRODS./NOMAD/RF1 FILMS/CANAL PLUS. May, 2000. French-British. (Roland Joffe) Gerard Depardieu, Uma Thurman, Tim Roth, Julian Glover, Julian Sands, Timothy Spall, Arielle Dombasle.

THE VELOCITY OF GARY
CINEVILLE. Sept., 1998. (Dan Ireland) Salma Hayek, Vincent D'Onofrio, Thomas Jane, Olivia d'Abo, Chad Lindberg, Lucky Luciano.

VELOMA
Jan., 2002. (Marie de Laubier) Patrick Pineau, Julie Depardieu, Thibault Patell, Hery Ranaivo-Rajanoa, Auguste Boleat.

VELVET HANGOVER
Feb., 2002. (Robert Buchar, David Smith) Jaroslav Boucek, Jaroslav Brabec, Vera Chytilova, Sasa Gedeon, Jiri Krejcik, Antonin Masa, Jiri Menzel, Stanislav Milota, Jan Nemec, Ivan Passer, Jan Sverak, Karel Vachek, Drahomira Vihanova, Zuzana Zemanova.

VENIAL SINS
JOSE MARIA LARA PC/ALOKATU PC. Sept., 1998. Spanish. (Ramon Barea) Elena Irureta, Ane Gabarain, Loli Astoreka, Aitzpea Goenaga, Itziar Lazkano.

THE VENICE PROJECT
TERRA FILM-JUNE 99-OZANIT. Sept., 1999. Austrian. (Robert Dornhelm) Lauren Bacall, Dennis Hopper, Linus Roache, Ben Cross.

VENUS BEAUTY INSTITUTE
PYRAMIDE. Jan., 1999. French. (Tonie Marshall) Nathalie Baye, Bulle Ogier, Samuel LeBihan.

VENUS BOYZ
June, 2002. Swiss. (Gabriel Baur) Diane Torr, Dred Gerestant, Del LaGrace Volcano, Bridge Markland, Mo B. Dick, Storme Webber, Shelley Mars, Queen Bee Luscious, Hans Scheirl, Svar Simpson, Judith Halberstam. Documentary.

VENUS TALKING
MOANA-FILM. March, 2001. German. (Rudolph Thome) Sabine Bach, Roger Tebb, Vladimir Weigl, Guntram Brattia.

VERCINGETORIX
LOLISTAR. Jan., 2001. French-Canadian. (Jacques Dorfmann) Christophe Lambert, Klaus Maria Brandauer, Max Von Sydow, Ines Sastre, Bernard-Pierre Donnadieu, Maria Kavardijikova.

VERSUS
Sept., 2001. Japanese. (Ryuhei Kitamura) Tak Sakaguchi, Hideo Sakaki, Chieko Misaka,Kenji Matsuda.

VERTICAL LIMIT
SONY PICTURES ENTERTAINMENT. Nov., 2000. (Martin Campbell) Chris O'Donnell, Bill Paxton, Robin Tunney, Scott Glenn, Izabella Scorupco, Temuera Morrison, Stuart Wilson.

VERY ANNIE-MARY
FILMFOUR DISTRIBUTORS. Jan., 2001. British-French. (Sara Sugarman) Rachel Griffiths, Jonathan Pryce, Ioan Gruffudd.

VERY BAD THINGS
POLYGRAM FILMS. Sept., 1998. (Peter Berg) Christian Slater, Cameron Diaz, Daniel Stern, Jeanne Tripplehorn, Jon Favreau.

VERY MEAN MEN
GIANTS ENTERTAINMENTBAIO/WHITE. June, 2000. (Tony Vitale) Mathew Modine, Martin Landau, Ben Gazzara, Scott Baio, Burt Young, Paul Ben-Victor, Billy Drago, Charles Durning.

VERY OPPOSITE SEXES
K'IEN. June, 2002. French-Belgian. (Eric Assous) Charlotte de Turckheim, Patrick Chesnais, Elisa Tovati, Antoine Dulery, Jean-Noel Broute, Veronique Boulanger, Stephanie Lagarde.

VIA DOLOROSA
BOOTH THEATER/LINCOLN CENTER THEATE/ROYAL COURT THEATER/BRANDMAN PRODS. Jan., 2000. (John Bailey) David Hare.

VIA SATELLITE
SCREEN VISION NZ. NOV., 1998. NEW ZEALAND. (Anthony McCarten) Danielle Cormack, Rima Te Wiata, Jodie Dorday.

VICTIM
MEI AH/BRILLIANT IDEA GROUP. Nov., 1999. Hong Kong. (Ringo Lam) Tony Leung Kar-fai, Lau Ching-wan, Amy Kwok, Lai Yiu-cheung, Colling Chou, Emily Kwan, Shiu Hsiu-hong, David Lee.

VICTIMS AND MURDERERS
WARNER BROS. July, 2001. Czech Republic. (Andrea Sedlackova) Karel Roden, Ivana chylkova, Monika Hilmerova.

VICTOR...WHILE IT'S TOO LATE
PYRAMIDE. Nov., 1998. French. (Sandrine Veysset) Jeremy Chaix, Lydia Andrei, Mathieu Lane

VICTORY SQUARE
Aug., 2002. U.S.-Belarus. (Liza Davitch) Documentary.

VIDOCQ
UFD. Aug., 2001. French. (Pitof) Gerard Depardieu, Guillaume Canet, Ines Sastre, Andre Dussollier, Edith Scob, Moussa Maaskri, Isabelle Renauld.

THE VIGIL
COME AS YOU ARTS. Sept., 1998. Canadian. (Justin MacGregor) Damon Johnson, Donny Lucas, Allan Franz, Trevor White.

VIGO: PASSION FOR LIFE
FILMFOUR DISTRIBUTORS. May, 1999. British-Japanese-French. (Julien Temple) Romane Bohringer, James Frain, Jim Carter, Diana Quick, William Scott-Masson.

VILLA-LOBOS: A LIFE OF PASSION
MAPA FILMES. Oct., 2000. Brazilian. (Zelito Viana) Antonio Fagundes, Andre Ricardo, Leticia Spiller, Ana Beatriz Nogueira, Jose Wilker, Marieta Severo, Othon Bastos.

THE VINEYARD
BUENA VISTA INTL./AURA PRODUCCIONES INTERNACIONALES/ NUEVA IMAGEN. Aug., 2000. Uruguayan-Chilean. (Esteban Schroeder) Danilo Rodriquez, Liliana Garcia, Fernando Kliche.

VIOLET
ALLIANCE ATLANTIS/ VIVA FILM/DARK FLOWERS. Aug., 2000. Canadian. (Mary Sexton) Mary Walsh, Peter MacNeill, Andrew Younghusband, Susan Kent, Berni Stapleton, Janis Spence.

VIOLET PERFUME–NOBODY HEARS YOU
VIDEOCINE. March, 2001. Mexican. (Marysa Sistach) Ximena Ayala, Nancy Gutierriz, Arcelia Ramirez, Maria Rojo.

VIPER
LANTIA CINEMA & AUDIOVISIVI. May, 2001. Italian. (Sergio Citti) Harvey Keitel, Giancarlo Giannini, Elide Melli, Larissa Volpentesta, Annalisa Schettino, Olimpia Carlisi, Goffredo Fofi.

VIRGIL BLISS
CONCRETE FILMS. Jan., 2001. (Joe Maggio) Clint Jordan, Kirsten Russell, Anthony Gorman, Marc Romeo, Greg Amici, Tom Brangle, Rich Bierman.

THE VIRGIN
NANOOK FILMS. Feb., 2000. Austrian. (Diego Donnhofe) Joey Kern, Kristy Hinchcliffe, Glenn Cruz.

VIRGIN STRIPPED BARE BY HER BACHELORS
UNIKOREA/MIRACIN KOREA. May, 2000. South Korean. (Hong Sang-soo) Lee Eun-ju, Jeong Bo-seok, Mun Seong-keun.

VIRTUAL SEXUALITY
COLUMBIA TRISTAR. Apr., 1999. British. (Nick Hurran) Laura Fraser, Rupert Penry-Jones, Luke de Lacey, Kieran O'Brien, Marcelle Duprey.

VIRTUAL VAMPIRE
LUXUS FILM/ZD/DAS KLEINE FERNSEHSPIEL/BURKHARDT ALTHOFF. Mar., 2000. German. (Michael Busch) Inga Busch, Armin Dallpiccola, Rene Hofschneider, Rudiger Kuhlbrodt, Claudia Splitt.

VISIBLE SECRET
MEDIA ASIA DISTRIBUTION. June, 2001. Hong Kong. (Ann Hui) Eason Chan, Shu Qi, Sam Lee, James Wong, Wai Ying-hung.

VISIONARIES
ALTAFILMS. Sept., 2001. Spanish. (Manuel Gutierrez Aragon) Eduardo Noriega, Ingrid Rubio, Emma Suarez, Fernando Fernan-Gomez, Earra, Elejalde, Leire Ucha.

THE VISIT
DAWA MOVIES/JORDAN WALKER-PEARLMAN. June, 2000. (Jordan Walker-Pearlman) Hill Harper, Obba Babatunde, Rae Dawn Chong, Billy Dee WIlliams, Marla Gibbs, Phylicia Rashad, Talia Shire.

THE VISITANT
TERCER MILENIO/ARIES CINEMATOGRAFICA ARGENTINA. Sept., 1999. Argentine. (Javier Olivera) Julio Chavez, Valentina Bassi, Mariano Bertolini, Elsa Berenguer, Alejandro Awada, Silvina Bosco.

A VISITOR FROM THE LIVING
NEW YORKER FILMS/LES FILMS ALEPH/CINETEVE/LA SEPT ARTE. Sept., 1999. French. (Claude Lanzmann). Documentary.

VIVA LAS NOWHERE
FRANCHISE PICTURES (L.A.). June, 2001. (Jason Bloom) Daniel Stern, Patricia Richardson, James Caan, Sherry Stringfield.

VIVA ST. JOHN!
July, 2002. Brazilian. (Andrucha Waddington) Narrator: Gilberto Gil. Documentary.

VIZONTELE
Aug., 2001. Turkish. (Yilmaz Erdogan, O. Faruk Sorak) Yilmaz Erdogan, Demet Akbag, Altan Erkekli, Cem Yilmaz, Cezmi Baskin, Bican Gunalan, Sebnem Sonmez.

A VOICE FROM HEAVEN
CROSSMEDIA COMMUNICATIONS. Oct., 1999. (Giuseppe Asaro) Ustad Nusrat Fateh Ali Khan, Rahat Nusrat Fateh Ali Khan, Farrukh Ali Khan, Dildar Hussein, Rick Rubin, Michael Brook. Documentary.

THE VOICE OF LJUDMILA
TRIANGELFILM. Oct., 2001. Swedish-Danish. (Gunnar Bergdahl) Documentary.

VOICES
BUSKIN FILM AND FACTORY. Aug., 2001. Italian. (Franco Giralki) Valeria Bruni Tedeschi, Miki Manojlovic, Gabriele Lavia, Gabriella Pession, Erica Blanc, Sonia Bergamasco, D. Nigrelli.

VOICES UNHEARD
B PRODUCTIONS. Apr., 1998. Beth B. Documentary.

VOLAVERUNT
AURUM/MATE PROD./MDA FILMS/UGC YM/UGC INTL./TV ESPANOLA/VIA DIGITAL/CANAL PLUS. Sept 1999., Spanish-French. (Bigas Luna) Aitana Sanchez-Gijon, Penelope Cruz.

THE VOLCANO
OTTOKAR RUNZE FILMHERSTELLUNG. Aug., 1999. German. (Ottokar Runze) Nina Hoss, Meret Becker, Christian Nickel.

VOLCANO HIGH (HWASAN GO)
CINEMA SERVICE. June, 2002. South Korean. (Kim Tae-gyun) Jang Hyeok, Shin Min-ah, Heo Jun-ho, Kim Su-ro, Gweon Sang-woo, Gong Hyo-jin, Jung Sang-hun, Kim Hyung-jeong, Jo Sung-ha.

VOYAGES
MK2 DIFFUSION. May, 1999. French. (Emmanuel Finkiel) Shulamit Adar, Liliane Rovere, Esther Gorintin, Nathan Cogan, Moscu Alcalay.

VULCAN JUNCTION
ERAN RIKLIS PRODS./ISRAEL FILM FUND/NCP-RESHET TV. June, 2000. Israeli. (Eran Riklis) Oren Shabo, Sammy Ori, Yael Hadar, Danny Shteg, Tomer Sharon, Gilli Shoshan, Jack Adalist.

VULGAR
LIONS GATE/VIEW ASKEW. Sept., 2000. (Bryan Johnson) Scott O'Halloran, Bryan Johnson, Ralph Lamblase, Scott Mosier.

WAALO FENDO: WHERE THE EARTH FREEZES
AMKA FILMS PRODS. SA. Sept. 1998. Senegalese-Swiss. (Mohammed Soudani) Saidou Moussa Ba, Bara Ngom, Souleymane Ndiaye.

THE WACKOS (LES PERCUTES)
ARTEDIS. Sept., 2002. French-Romanian-Belgian. (Gerard Cuq) Ingrid Chauvin, Christophe Laubion, Tomi Cristin, Denis Karvil.

WAG THE DOG
NEW LINE CINEMA. Dec., 1998. (Barry Levinson) Dustin Hoffman, Robert De Niro, Anne Heche, Woody Harrelson, Denis Leary.

WAIKIKI, IN THE WAKE OF DREAMS
FILMWORKS PACIFIC. March, 2001. (Edgy Lee) Don Ho, Arthur Lyman, Jerry Byrd, Harry Robello, Boyce Rodrigues. Documentary.

WAIT AND SEE
SHOCHIKU. Feb., 1999. Japanese. (Shinji Somai) Koichi Sato, Yuki Saito, Tsutomu Yamazaki, Jyunko Fuji.

WAIT FOR ME
COMBINED STUDIO (ALMA-ATA). Aug., 2000. Soviet Union–1943. (Aleksandr Stolper, Boris Ivanov) Boris Blinov, Valentina Serova, Lev Sverdlin, Mikhail Nasvanov, Nina Zorskaya, Elena Tyapkina.

WAITING FOR A TENOR
SVENSK FILMINDUSTRI. Aug., 1998. Swedish. (Lisa Ohlin) John Hison Kjellgren, Krister Henriksson, Lena B. Erikson.

WAITING FOR HAPPINESS
HAUT ET COURT. May, 2002. Mauritanian. (Abderrahmane Sissako) Khatra Ould Abdel Kader, Maata Ould Mohamed Abeid.

WAITING FOR THE MESSIAH
BURMAN-DUBCOVSKY CINE. Apr., 2000. Argentine. (Daniel Burman) Daniel Hendler, Hector Alterio, Enrique Pineyro.

THE WAITING LIST
TORNASOL FILMS/ICAIC/DMVB/TABASCO FILMS/RODUCCIONES AMARANTA/ ROAD MOVIES/VIA DIGITAL/CANAL PLUS. May, 2000. Spanish-Cuban-French-Mexican. (Juan Carlos Tabio) Vladimir Cruz, Thaimi Alvarino, Jorge Perugorria.

A WAKE IN PROVIDENCE
MISTER P. PRODS./GLADIATOR PICTURES. Sept., 1999. (Rosario Roveto Jr.) Vincent Pagano, Victoria Rowell, Mike Pagano, Adrienne Barbeau, Micole Mercurio, Lisa Raggio, Dan Lauria, Kaye Kingston.

WAKING THE DEAD
USA FILMS/GRAMERCY PICTURES/POLYGRAM FILMED ENTERTAINMEN/EGG PICTURES. Jan., 2000. (Keith Gordon) Billy Crudup, Jennifer Connelly, Molly Parker, Janet McTeer, Paul Hipp, Sandra Oh, Hal Holbrook, Laurence Dane.

WAKING LIFE
INDEPENDENT FILM CHANNEL AND THOUSAND WORDS. Jan., 2001. (Richard Linklater) Wiley Wiggins, Trevor jack Brooks, Lorelei Linklater, Glover Gill, Lara Hicks, Ames Asbell, Leigh Mahoney.

WALKING ACROSS EGYPT
MITCHUM ENTERTAINMENT. Feb., 2000. (Arthur Allan Seidelman) Ellen Burstyn, Jonathan Taylor Thomas, Mark Hamill, Judge Reinhold, Gail O'Grady, Gwen Verdon, Edward Herrmann, Harve Presnell, Pat Corley, James Colman III, Patrick David.

A WALK ON THE MOON
MIRAMAX. Jan., 1999. (Tony Goldwyn) Diane Lane, Liev Schreiber, Anny Paquin, Viggo Mortensen, Tovah Feldshuh.

WALK THE TALK
20TH CENTURY FOX/DREAMWORKS PICTURES/JAN CHAPMAN/ PACIFIC FILM AND TV COMM. Aug., 2000. Australian-U.S. (Shirley Barrett) Salvatore Coco, Sacha Horler, Nikki Bennett, Carter Edwards, Robert Coleby, Skye Wansey, John Burgess.

WALLOWITCH & ROSS: THIS MOMENT
KARMIC RELEASE LTD. Jan., 1999. (Richard Morris). Documentary.

WALTER ROSENBLUM: IN SEARCH OF PITT STREET
DAEDALUS PRODS. Oct., 1999. (Ninam Rosenblum). Documentary.

WANDERLUST
TERRA FILM/VP KREGAR/TERESIANUM. Sept., 2000. Yugoslavian-Slovenian-Hungarian. (Zelimir Zilnik) Giuseppe Pastorchich, Jovan Kiselicki, Gordana Kamenarovic.

WAR (VOINA)
Aug., 2002. Russian. (Alexei Balabanov) Alexei Chadov, Ian Kelly, Ingeborga Dapkunaite, Sergei Bodrov Jr., Evklid Kyurdzidis, Georgi Gurgula.

WAR AND PEACE
March, 2002. Indian. (Anand Patwardhan) Documentary.

WAR BOOTY
ZAFRA CINE DIFUSION/TORNASOL FILMS/TVE/ARTE. Apr., 2000. Argentine. (David Blaustein). Documentary.

THE WAR BRIDE
Dec., 2001. British-Canadian. (Lyndon Chubbuck) Anna Friel, Brenda Fricker, Aden Young, Loren Dean, Julie Cox, Molly Parker, Caroline Cave.

THE WAR IN THE HIGHLANDS
CAB PRODS. Feb., 1999. Swiss-French-Belgian. (Francis Reusser) Marion Cotillard, Yann Tregouet, Francois Marthouret.

WARM WATER UNDER A RED BRIDGE
NIKKATSU INC.-IMAMURA PRODS. May, 2001. Japanese. (Shohei Imamura) Koji Yakusho, Misa Shimizu, Mitsuko Baisho, Mansaku Fuwa, Kazuo Kitramura, Hijiri Kojima.

WAR PHOTOGRAPHER
FIRST RUN ICARUS FILMS. March, 2002. Swiss (Christian Frei) Documentary.

THE WARRIOR
FILMFOUR DISTRIBUTORS. Aug., 2001. British. (Asif Kapadia) Irfan Khan, Puru Chhibber, Mandakini Goswami, Sunita Sharma, Noor Mani Damayanti Marfatia, Firoz Khan.

WARRIORS
WARNER SOGEFILMS. March, 2002. Spanish. (Daniel Calparsoro) Eloy Azorin, Eduardo Noriega, Ruben Ochandiano, Carla Perez, Jordi Vilches.

THE WARRIOR'S BROTHER
BAC DISTRIBUTION. March, 2002. French. (Pierre Jolivet) Vincent Lindon, Guillaume Canet, Melanie Doutey, Francois Berleand, Thierry-Perkins Lyautey, Anne Le Ny, Brunelle Lemmonier.

WAR ZONE
FILM FATALE INC./HANK LEVINE FILM. Feb., 1998. (Maggie Hadleigh-West) Documentary.

WAR WITHOUT IMAGES
COLUMBUS FILM. Aug., 2002. Swiss-French. (Mohammed Soudani) Documentary.

THE WAR ZONE
FILM FOUR. Jan. 1999. British. (Tim Roth) Ray Winstone, Tilda Swubton, Lara Belmont, Freddie Cunliffe, Kate Ashfield.

THE WASH
LIONS GATE FILM. Nov., 2001. (DJ Pooh) Dr. Dre, Snoop Dogg, George Wallace, Angell Conwell, Tommy "Tiny" Lister Jr., Bruce Bruce, Alex Thomas, Shawn Fonteno, Lamount Bentley, Shari Watson, Arif S. Kinchen.

WASHINGTON HEIGHTS
May, 2002. (Aldredo de Villa) Tomas Milian, Manny Perez, Danny Hoch, Andrea Navedo.

WASHINGTON WOLVES
ALTA FILMS. Aug., 1999. Spanish. (Mariano Barroso) Javier Bardem, Eduardo Fernandez, Jose Sancho, Ernesto Alterio, Antonio San Juan.

WATANI: A WORLD WITHOUT EVIL
MH FILMS. June, 1999. French. (Med Hondo) Patrick Poivey, Coumba Awa Tall, Mboup Massyla, Anne Jolivet, James Campbell.

THE WATCHER
UNIVERSAL/INTERLIGHT/LEWITT/EBERTS-CHOI/NIAMI. Sept., 2000. (Joe Charbanic) James Spader, Marisa Tomei, Keanu Reeves, Ernie Hudson, Chris Ellis, Robert Cicchini, Yvonne Niami.

WATCHING THE DETECTIVE
YAGI JUNICHI. Oct., 1998. Japanese. (Yagi Junichi) Oki Eiji, Mabuchi Haruko, Ozawa Miki, Nakamura Horyu, Kato Kanami.

WATCH THE SKY: STELLA, SONIA, SILVIA
IPOTESI CINEMA. Nov., 2000. Italian. (Piergiorgio Gay) Sandra Ceccarelli, Paolo Peirobon, Antonio Latella, Denis Fasolo, Margareta Von Kraus, Lina Bernardi, Raffaele Fallica, Giuseppe Battiston.

THE WATERBOY
BUENA VISTA. Nov., 1998. (Frank Coraci) Adam Sandler, Kathy Bates, Henry Winkler, Fairuza Balk, Jerry Reed.

WATERBOYS
FUJI TELEVISION NETWORK/ALTAMIRA PICTURES/TOHO/ DENTSU. May, 2001. Japanese. (Shinobu Yaguchi) Satoshi Tsumabuki, Hiroshi Tamaki, Akifumi Miura, Kuen Kondo.

WATER DROPS ON BURNING ROCKS
FIDELITE PRODS./LES FILMS ALAIN SARDE/EURO SAGE. Feb., 2000. French. (Francois Ozon) Bernard Giraudeau, Malick Zidi, Ludivine Sagnier.

THE WATERFALL
MAy, 2002. Turkish. (Semir Aslanyurek) Hulya Kocyigit, Tuncel Kurtiz, Aykut Oray, Ali Surmeli.

WAVE
Jan., 2002. Japanese. (Hiroshi Okuhara) Sakutaro Inui, Asako Kobayashi, Chiharu Konno, Tatsushi Oomori.

WAVES
MADRA TALKIES. Feb., 2001. Indian. (Mani Ratnam) Madhavan, Shalini, Jayasudha, Swarnamalya, Vivek, Natarjan.

WAVE TWISTERS
THUD RUMBLE. Jan., 2001. (Syd Garon, Eric Henry) Animated. ODEON FILMS (CANADA). Sept., 2000. Canadian. (Gary Burns) Fabrizio Filippo, Don McKellar, Marya Delver, Gordon Currie, Jennifer Clement, Tammy Isbell, Tobias Godson, James McBurney.

THE WAY HOME
CJ ENTERTAINMENT. May, 2002. South Korean. (Lee Jung-hyang) Kim Eul-bun, Yu Seung-ho, Min Kyung-hun.

THE WAY I KILLED MY FATHER
PATHE. Aug., 2001. French-Spanish. (Anne Fontaine) Michel Bouquet, Charles Berling, Natacha Regnier, Amira Casar, Stephane Guillon, Hubert Kounde, Francois Berleand.

WAY OFF BROADWAY
JUST FOR FUN FILMS. June, 2001. (Daniel Kay) Brad Beyer, Morena Baccarin, Forbes March, Jordan Gelber, Michael Parducci.

THE WAY OF THE GUN
ARTISAN. Aug., 2000. (Christopher McQuarrie) Ryan Phillippe, Benicio Del Toro, James Caan, Juliette Lewis, Taye Diggs, Nicky Katt.

WAYWARD SON
AVENUE PICTURES/MACCABEE PRODS. Sept., 1999. (Randall Harris) Harry Connick Jr., Peter Postlethwaite, Patricia Clarkson, Vinessa Shaw, Michael Gaston.

WEAK AT DENISE
PENINSULA FILMS. Dec., 1999. British. (Julian Nott) Bill Thomas, Chrissie Cotterill, Craig Fairbrass, Tilly Blackwood, Claudine Spiteri.

WE ALL FALL DOWN
ROAD CONE. Oct., 2000. Canadian. (Martin Cummins) Darcy Belsher, Martin Cummins, Francoise Robertson, Helen Shaver.

WE CAN BE HEROES! (BAST I SVERIGE!)
SANDREW METRONOME. July, 2002. Swedish. (Ulf Malmros) Ariel Petsonk, Zamand Hagg, Michael Nyqvist, Anna Pettersson.

THE WEDDING
PYRAMIDE/CDP/FILM STUDIO MOSFILM SERVICE/ARTE FRANCE CINEMA/WDR/LICHTBLICK COLOGNE/CINE B. May, 2000. French-Russian-German. (Pavel Lounguine) Marat Basharov, Maria Mironova, Andrei Panine, Alexandre Semtchev.

THE WEDDING
NRK DRAMA/SF NORGE. Jan., 2001. Norwegian. (Leidulv Risan) Mads Ousdal, Susan Badrkhan, Benaissa Ahssain, Samir Ibrahim Zedan, Narmaa Alward, Jan O. Wiig.

WEDDING BAND
BIRD WOLF. Jan., 1999. (Martin Guigni) Deborah Gibson, Joey Scherr, Martin Gyigui, Kelly Bishop, Les Shenkel.

THE WEDDING COW
SUDWESTRUNDFUNK/FSDRS/ARTE. Mar., 2000. German. (Tomi Streiff) Isabella Parkinson, Oliver Reinhard, Hannah the Cow, Dani Levy, Maria Schrader, Julia Stohl-Palmer.

A WEDDING IN RAMALLAH
June, 2002. Australian. (Sherina Salama) Documentary.

WEDDING MOON
COTUDIC. Oct., 1998. Tunisian. (Taieb Louhichi) Mess Hattou, Mohamed Hedi Moumen, Rym Riahi.

WEDDING NIGHT
SEVILLE PICTURES. Oct., 2001. Canadian. (Emile Gaudreault) Francois Morency, Genevieve Brouillette, Pierette Robitaille, Yves Jacques, Michel Courtemanche.

THE WEDDING PLANNER
SONY PICTURES ENTERTAINMENT. Jan., 2001. (Adam Shankman) Jennifer Lopez, Matthew McConaughey, Bridgette Wilson-Sampras, Justin Chambers, Judy Greer, Alex Rocco, Joanna Gleason.

THE WEDDING TACKLE
VIKING FILMS. July, 2000. British. (Rami Dvir) Adrian Dunbar, James Purefoy, Tony Slattery, Neil Stuke, Leslie Grantham, Victoria Smurfit.

WEDNESDAY'S CHILD
WRITE ANGLES PRODS. July, 1999. (Brad Marlowe) Sommer Knight, David King, Brandon Hiott, Todd Surber, Tom Polanski.

THE WEEKEND
STRAND RELEASING/GRANADA/LUNATICS & LOVERS/ GRANADA FILM. June, 2000. U.S.-British. (Brian Skeet) Deborah Kara Unger, Jared Harris, D.B. Sweeney, Gena Rowlands, Brooke Shields.

A WEEK IN THE LIFE OF A MAN
ZEBRA. Sept., 1999. Polish. (Jerzy Stuhr) Jerzy Stuhr, Gosia Dobrowolska, Danuta Szaflarska.

THE WEIGHT OF WATER
LIONS GATE/STUDIOCANAL/MANIFEST FILM CO./PALOMAR PICTURES/MIRACLE PICTURES. Sept., 2000. (Kathryn Bigelow) Catherine McCormack, Sarah Polley, Sean Penn, Josh Lucas.

WEISER
"TOR" FILM PROD., VEGA FILM AND PROVOBIS FILM. Feb., 2001. Polish-Swiss-German-Danish. (Wojciech Marczewski) Marek Kondrat,Krystyna Janda, Julian Kohler, Teresa Marczewska.

WELCOME TO COLINWOOD
WARNER BROS. Sept., 2002. (Anthony Russo, Joe Russe) Luis Guzman, Michael Jeter, Patricia Clarkson, Andrew Davoli, Isaiah Washington, William H. Macy, Sam Rockwell, Gabrielle Union, Jennifer Esposito, George Clooney.

WE MET ON THE VINEYARD
CAN YOU SPOT ME A TWENTY PICTURES. Oct., 2000. (Ian McCrudden) Julianna Margulies, Ivan Sergi, Kevin Tighe, Dixie Carter, Clayton Rohner, Kathleen York, C.C.H. Pounder.

WENDIGO
GLASS EYE PIC/ANTIDOTE FILMS. Jan., 2001. (Larry Fessenden) Patricia Clarkson, Jake Weber, Erik Per Sullivan, John Speredakos, Christopher Winkoop, Lloyd E. Oxendine.

WE ONLY LIVE ONCE
OBJEKTIV FILMSTUDIO/MAGYAR TELEVIZIO PRODUCTION/ MMK/ORTT/NKA. Feb., 2000. Hungarian. (Gyorgy Molnar) Jozsef Szarvas, Juli Basti, Sandor Gaspar, Mari Csomos, Lujza Orosz.

WERCKMEISTER HARMONIES
GOESS FILM/VON VIETINGHOFF/13 PRODUCTION/MAGYAR MOZGOKEP KOZALAPITVANY/ORTT/MAGYAR TELEVIZIO/ NEMZETI KULTURALIS ALAPPROGRAM/ZDF/ARTE/STUDIO BABELSBERG/RAI-3/FONDAZIONE MONTECINEMAVERITA. May, 2000. Hungariann-German-French. (Bela Tarr) Lars Rudolph, Peter Fitz, Hanna Schygulla, Janos Derzi, Djoko Rossich.

WES CRAVEN PRESENTS: DRACULA 2000
DIMENSION FILMS. Dec., 2000. (Patrick Lussier) Christopher Plummer, Gerard Butler, Jonny Lee Miller, Justine Waddell, Jennifer Esposito, Omar Epps.

WE SOLD OUR SOULS FOR ROCK 'N' ROLL
DIVINE PICTURES. Jan., 2001. (Penelope Spheeris) Ozzy Osbourne, Sharon Osbourne, Black Sabbath, Rob Zombie, Slipknot, Godsmack, Slayer, Primus, Fear Factory, Deftones. Documentray.

WEST
PABLO DISTRIBUZIONE. Nov., 2000. Italian. (Corso Salani) Agnieszka Czekanska, Corso Salani, Fabio Sabbioni, Gianluca Arcopinto, Monica Rametta.

WEST OF HERE
June, 2002. (Peter CB Masterson) Josh Hamilton, Mary Stuart Masterson, Norbert Leo Butz, Tate Donovan, Elisabeth Moss, Guillermo Diaz, John Elsen, Kevin Cooney, Carlin Glynn.

WET HOT AMERICAN SUMMER
EUREKA PICTURES. Jan., 2001. (David Wain) Janeane Garofalo, David Hyde Pierce, Michael Showalter, Marguerite Moreau, Paul Rudd, Zak Orth, Christopher Meloni.

THE WETONKAWA FLASH
GONER PRODS. Nov., 1999. (Boyd Hale, Wendy Hopkins) Mark Boone Jr. Kevin Tighe, Toby Huss, Neil Giutoli, Algie Kirkland, Brian Shoop, Craig Walter, Betty Haynes.

WE WERE SOLDIERS
PARAMOUNT. Feb., 2002. (Randall Wallace) Mel Gibson, Madeleine Stowe, Greg Kinnear, Sam Elliott, Chris Klein, Keri Russell, Barry Pepper, Don Duong, Ryan Hurst, Robert Bagnell, Marc Blucas, Josh Daugherty, Jsu Garcia.

WHALE RIDER
Sept., 2002. New Zealand-German. (Niki Caro) Keisha Castle-Hughes, Rawiri Paratene, Vicky Haughton, Cliff Curtis, Grant Roa.

WHAT ABOUT ME: THE RISE OF THE NIHILIST SPASM BAND
SUB VERSIVE MEDIA ARTS. Sept., 2000. Canadian. (Zev Asher) Documentary.

WHAT BECOMES OF THE BROKEN HEARTED?
POLYGRAM. May, 1999. New Zealand. (Ian Mune) Temuera Morrison, Clint Eruera, Nancy Brunning, Pete Smith, Lawrence Makoare.

WHAT DREAMS MAY COME
POLYGRAM FILMS. Sept., 1998. (Vincent Ward) Robin Williams, Cuba Gooding Jr., Annabella Sciorra, Max von Sydow.

WHATEVER
MARS FILMS/LAZENNEC/LE STUDIO CANAL PLUS. Sept., 1999. French. (Philippe Harel) Philippe Bianco, Phillipe Harel, Jose Garcia, Catherine Mouchet.

WHATEVER HAPPENED TO HAROLD SMITH?
UIP/USA FILMS/INTERMEDIA FILMS /OCTOBER FILMS/ARTS COUNCIL OF ENGLAND/WEST ELEVEN FILMS. Nov., 1999. British. (Peter Hewitt) Tom Courtenay, Stephen Fry, Michael Legge.

WHATEVER IT TAKES
SONY PICTURES ENTERTAINMENT/COLUMBIA PICTURES/PAUL SCHIFF. Mar., 2000. (David Raynr) Shane West, Marla Sokoloff, Jodi Lyn O'Keefe, James Franco, Aaron Paul, Richard Schiff.

WHAT HAPPENED TO TULLY
TELL TALE FILMS. Apr., 2000. (Hilary Birmingham) Anson Mount, Julianne Nicholson, Glenn Fitzgerald, Catherine Kellner, Bob Burrus, Natalie Canerday, John Diehl.

WHAT IF WE TALK ABOUT LOVE
MARS DISTRIBUTION. April, 2002. (Daniel Karlin) Documentary.

WHAT I LIKE ABOUT YOU
MISERY LOVES COMPANY INC./HOCKEYRADO PRODS./TONY HEWET. Mar., 2000. (Jeff Stolhand) Marie Black, Ryan Wickerham, Cameron Johnson, Ben Pascoe, Scott Von Doviak, Tim Curry.

WHAT I SAW IN HEBRON
NOGA COMMUNICATIONS/ISRAELI FILM SERVICE/JERUSALEM CINEMATHEQUE. July, 2000. Israeli. (Dan and Noit Geva). Documentary.

WHAT IS LIFE?
DIAPHANA/SALOME/DIAPHANA/FRANCE 3 CINEMA/CANAL PLUS/CNC. Aug., 2000. French. (Francois Dupeyron) Eric Caravaca, Jacques Dufilho, Isabelle Renauld, Jean-Pierre Darroussin.

WHAT LIES BENEATH
DREAMWORKS/20TH CENTURY FOX/IMAGEMOVER. July, 2000. (Robert Zemeckis) Harrison Ford, Michelle Pfeiffer, Diana Scarwid, Miranda Otto, James Remar, Joe Morton, Amber Valletta, Victoria Birdwell.

WHAT PLANET ARE YOU FROM?
SONY PICTURES ENTERTAINMENT/COLUMBIA PICTURES/BRAD GREY-BERNIE BRILLSTEIN. Feb., 2000. (Mike Nichols) Garry Shandling, Annette Bening, Greg Kinnear, Ben Kingsley, Linda Fiorentino, John Goodman, Richard Jenkins, Caroline Aaron.

WHAT'S COOKING?
FLASHPOINT/JEFFREY TAYLOR'S STAGESCREEN. Jan., 2000. British-U.S. (Gurinder Chadha) Alfre Woodard, Dennis Haysbert, Ann Weldon, Mercedes Ruehl, Victor Rivers, Douglas Spain.

WHAT'S THE WORST THAT COULD HAPPEN?
MGM PICTURES. May, 2001. (Sam Weisman) Martin Lawrence, Danny DeVito, John Leguizamo, Glenne Headly, Carmen Ejogo, Bernie Mac, Larry Miller, Nora Dunn.

WHAT TIME IS IT OVER THERE?
DIAPHANA. May, 2001. French-Taiwanese. Lee Kang-sheng, Chen Shiang-chyi, Lu Yi-ching, Miao Tien, Cecilia Yip, Jean-Pierre Leaud.

WHAT WOMEN WANT
PARAMOUNT. Dec., 2000. (Nancy Meyers) Mel Gibson, Helen Hunt, Marisa Tomei, Mark Feuerstein, Lauren Holly, Ashley Johnson.

WHAT YOU NEVER KNEW
ENRIQUE CEREZO PC/SAMARKANDA. Sept., 2000. Spanish. (Juan Vicente Cordoba) Silvia Munt, Gary Piquer, Andres Gertrudix.

THE WHEEL OF FIRE
FENDA FILMS. Nov., 1999. Spanish. (Raul Veiga) Rosana Pastor, Sergi Lopez, Chete Lera, Maria Bouzas, Miguel Pernas.

WHEN BRENDAN MET TRUDY
COLLINS AVENUE/DEADLY FILMS 2. Sept., 2000. British-Irish. (Kieron J. Walsh) Peter McDonald, Flora Montgomery, Marie Mullen.

WHEN GODS MEET
UIP/BLU CINEMATOGRAFICA/ESICMA/RAI/TELE PLUS/CANAL PLUS. Apr., 2000. Italian-Spanish. (Antonello De Leo) Pere Ponce.

WHEN IT'S OVER
PAPA FILMS. April, 1998. (Richard Mancuso) Troy Ruptash, Vincent Caruso, Renee Rizzo, Shoshana Ami, John Fell, Patrick Ferraro.

WHEN THE DEAD START SINGING
JADRAN. Aug., 1999. Croation. (Krsto Papic) Ivo Gregurevic, Ivica Vidovic, Mirjana Majurec.

WHEN THE EAST MEETS THE WEST
BEJING FILM STUDIO. Nov., 1998. Chinese. (Ding Yinnan). Wang Zhuxia, Zhu Xu, Du Ruiqiu, Rachel Dworsky.

WHEN TRUMPETS FADE
HBO NYC. June, 1998. (John Irvin) Ron Eldard, Zak Orth, Frank Whaley, Dylan Bruno, Martin Donovan, Timothy Olyphant.

WHERE A GOOD MAN GOES
INTL. FILMS INTERI-RISE/MILKYWAY IMAGE (H.K.). Oct., 1999. Hong Kong. (Johnnie To) Lau Ching-wan, Ruby Wong, Lai Yiu-hung.

WHERE ESKIMOS LIVE
Jan., 2002. U.S.-German-Polish. (Tomasz Wiszniewski) Bob Hoskins, Sergiusz Zymelka, Krzystof Majchrak, Lukasz Komosa.

WHERE HAS ETERNITY GONE?
Jan., 2002. British. (Barney Snow) Gerald Polley, Linda Polley, Jesse Torres, Eric Hahn. Documentary

WHERE'S MARLOWE?
PARAMOUNT. Oct., 1998. (Daniel Pyne) Miguel Ferrer, Mos Def, John Livingston, Allison Dean, John Slattery.

WHERE THE HEART IS
20TH CENTURY FOX/WIND DANCER. Apr., 2000. (Matt Williams) Natalie Portman, Ashley Judd, Stockard Channing, Joan Cusack, James Frain, Dylan Bruno, Keith David, Sally Field.

WHERE THE MONEY IS
USA FILMS/GRAMERCY PICTURES/INTERMEDIA FILMS/PACIFIC FILM DISTRIBUTION/SCOTT FREE/IMF. Apr., 2000. (Marek Kanievska) Paul Newman, Linda Fiorentino, Dermot Mulroney.

WHERE THE RAINBOW ENDS
SONET FILM/CIMBRIA FILM/SVT DRAMA MALMO/SONET FILM/FILM OSTERLEN. Oct., 1999. Swedish. (Richard Hobert) Goan Stangertz, Camilla Lindin, Rolf Lassgard, Pernilla August.

WHERE THE SKY MEETS THE LAND
CINE DOK/EUROARTS. Sept., 1999. German. (Frank Hartwig Hendrik Mueller) Bubush Alayeva, Rysbek Jumabayev.

WHERE VIOLENCE ENDS LOVE BEGINS
PRODUKTIONSGRUPPEN WECHSELMANN/WOWAM. Jan., 2000. Swedish-South African. (Maj Wechselmann) Ossi Carp, Nadine Naidoo, Bill Curry, Rafiq Jajbhay, Sivan Pillay, Olivia Stevens.

WHICH SIDE EDEN
LUMAR PRODS. Sept., 1999. Czech-U.S. (Vojtech Jasny). Vladimir Pucholt, Ingrid Timkova, Adam Davidson.

WHIPPED
EMOTION MOTION PICTURES. Feb., 2000. (Iana Porter, Sasha Waters). Documentary.

WHIPPED
DESTINATION FILMS/HI-REZ FILMS. Aug., 2000. (Peter M. Cohen) Armanda Peet, Brian Van Holt, Judah Domke, Zorie Barber, Jonathan Abrahams, Callie Thorne.

WHIRLPOOL
OMEGA MICOTT. Apr., 2000. Japanese. (Higunchinsky) Eriko Hatsune, Fhi Fan, Hinako Saeki, Shin Eun Kyung, Keiko Takahasi.

WHISPERING CORRIDORS
CINE 2000. Oct., 1998. South Korean. (Park Ki-Hyung) Lee Mi-Youn, Park Yong-Su, Lee Yong-Nyuh, Kim Yoo-Suk.

WHISPERING SANDS
Nov., 2001. Indonesian-Japanese. (Nan T. Achnas) SChristine Hakim, Slamet Rahardjo Djarot, Dian Sastrowardoyo.

WHISPERS: AN ELEPHANT'S TALE
BUENA VISTA PICTURES. Oct., 2000. Angela Bassett, Joanna Lumley, Anne Archer, Debi Derryberry, Kevin Michael Richardson, Alice Ghostley. Animated.

THE WHITE
V & R PLANNING. Feb., 2000. Japanese. (Katsuyuki Hirano). Documentary.

WHITE DREAM
Feb., 2002. Iranian. (Hamid Jebelli). Hamid Jebelli, Soghra Karimi, Elizabeth Amini, Yusef Pashandi, Abbas Qadir.

WHITE LIES
TEKNEW MEDIA. March, 2001. Israeli. (Itzhak Rubin) Orna Porat, Sharon Alexander, Gina Lidoni, Smadar Killtchinski.

WHITE OLEANDER
WARNER BROS. Aug., 2002. (Peter Kosminsky) Alison Lohman, Robin Wright Penn, Michelle Pfeiffer, Renee Zellweger, Billy Connolly, Svetlana Efremova, Patrick Fugit, Cole Hauser, Noah Wyle.

THE WHITE SOUND
April, 2002. German. (Hans Weingartner) Daniel Bruhl, Anabelle Lachatte, Patrick Joswig, Michael Schutz.

THE WHITE SUIT
ZILLION FILMS. May, 1999. Yugoslav. (Lazar Ristovski) Lazar Ristovski, Radmila Shchogolyeva, Dragan Nikolic.

WHOAFRAIDWOLF
OMBRA-FILM/BE-PICTURES. Feb., 2000. Swiss-Italian. (Clemens Klopfenstein) Bruno Ganz, Tina Engel, Mathias Gnadinger, Charlotte Heinimann, Stefan Kurt, Norbert Klassen, Doraine Green.

WHO IS BERNARD TAPIE?
GRACEFUL PICTURES. April, 2001. (Marina Zenovich) Documentary.

WHO IS CLETIS TOUT?
PARAMOUNT CLASSICS. July, 2002. (Chris Ver Wiel) Christian Slater, Tim Allen, Portia De Rossi, Richard Dreyfuss, Billy Connolly, Peter MacNeil, Elias Zarou, Richard Chevolleau, Rupaul.

WHO KNOWS?
LES FILMS DU LOSANGE. May, 2001. French-Italian-German. (Jacques Rivette) Jeanne Balibar, Sergio Castellitto, Jacques Bonnaffe, Marianne Basler, Helene de Fougerolles.

THE WHOLE NINE YARDS
WARNER BROS./MORGAN CREEK PRODS./FRANCHISE PICTURES/RATIONAL PACKAGING FILMS/LANSDOWN FILMS. Feb., 2000. (Jonathan Lynn) Bruce Willis, Matthew Perry Rosanna Arquette, Michael Clarke Duncan, Natasha Henstridge.

THE WHOLE SHEBANG
CHRISTAL FILMS. Aug., 2001. Canadian-U.S. (Geroge Zaloom) Stanley Tucci, Bridget Fonda, Giancarlo Giannini, Talia Shire, Anna Maria Alberghetti, Anthony DeSando, Jo Champa.

WHO PLUCKED THE FEATHERS OFF THE MOON?
CINE VALSE/ARTE FRANCE CINEMA/CRRAV. May, 1999. French. (Christine Carriere) Jean-Pierre Darroussin, Garance Clavel.

WHO'S THE CABOOSE?
PILOT SEASON PRODS. June, 1999. (Sam Seder) Sarah Silverman, Sam Seder, Andy Dick, H. Jon Benjamin, David Cross.

WHO THE HELL IS BOBBY ROOS?
June, 2002. (John Feldman) Roger Kabler, Iris Paldiel, John Powers, Anabelle Larson, Jacqui Malouf, Angel Engel, Everett Tebben, Mel Kabler, Tony Faske.

WHY DO FOOLS FALL IN LOVE
WARNER BROS. Aug., 1998. (Gregory Nava) Halle Berry, Vivica A. Fox, Lela Rochon, Larenz Tate, Paul Mazursky, Little Richard.

WHY GET MARRIED THE DAY THE WORLD ENDS
BOOMERANG PICTURES. Feb., 2001. Belgian-Luxembourgois. (Harry Cleven) Elina Lowensohn, Pascal Greggory, Jean-Henri Compere, Lofti Yahya Jedidi, Philippe Martin.

WHY NOT ME?
UFD. Jan., 1999. French-Spanish-Swiss. (Stephane Guisti) Amira Casar, Julie Gayet, Bruno Putzulu.

WICKED
FRANKENSTEIN ENTERTAINMENT. Jan., 1998. (Michael Steinberg) Julia Stiles, William R. Moses, Patrick Muldoon, Vanessa Zima.

THE WICKSBORO INCIDENT
RICHARD LOWRY. Aug., 2001. (Richard Lowry) Bobby Harwell, Dan Brinkle, Kyle Nudo, David Arnold.

WIDE AWAKE
MIRAMAX. FEB., 1998. (M. Night Shyamalan) Joseph Cross, Timothy Reifsnyder, Dana Delaney, Denis Leary, Camryn Manheim.

THE WIDOW OF SAINT-PIERRE
PATHE/EPITHETE FILMS/FRANCE 2/FRANCE 3/CINEIMAGINAIRE. Mar., 2000. French. (Patrice Leconte) Juliette Binoche, Daniel Auteuil, Emir Kusturica, Michel Duchaussoy, Philippe Magnan.

WILBUR FALLS
VEXATIOUS FILMS. Sept., 1998. (Juliane Glantz) Danny Aiello, Sally Kirkland, Shanee Edwards, Jeff Daurey, Cheril Hayres.

WILD ABOUT HARRY
UIP. Oct., 2000. British. (Declan Lowney) Brendan Gleeson, Amanda Donohoe, Adrian Dunbar, James Nesbitt, George Wendt, Henry Deazley, Bronagh Gallagher.

WILD BLUE, NOTES FOR SEVERAL VOICES
LES FILMS. DU SABLIER/LA SEPT ARTE/ARTLINE FILMS/MAN'S FILMS/ NAVIGATOR FILMS/RTBF. May, 2000. Belgian. (Thierry Knauff) Joan Leighton, Neela Bhagwat, Charlene Alenga. Documentary.

THE WILD DOGS
Sept., 2002. Canadian. (Thom Fitzgerald) Anca-Ioana Androne, Rachel Blanchard, Visinel Burcea, Mihai Calota, Marcel Unguriano Catalin, Nelu Dinu, Thom Fitzgerald.

WILDFIRE: FEEL THE HEAT
PRIMESCO COMMUNICATIONS. July, 1999. (Mike Slee). Documentary.

WILDFLOWERS
FRIED FILM GROUP/FILMSMITH. Mar., 2000. (Melissa Painter) Clea DuVall, Daryl Hannah, Tomas Arana, Eric Roberts.

WILD FLOWERS
BONTONFILM. July, 2001. Czech Republic. (F.A. Brabec) Linda Rybova, Dan Barta, Jane Svandova, Vera Galatikova, Alena Miholuva, Boleslav, Polivka, Zuzana Bydzovska, Karel Roden.

WILD INNOCENCE
MARS FILMS. Sept., 2001. French-Dutch. (Philippe Garrel) Julia Faure, Mehdi Belhaj Kacem, Michel Subor,Jerome Huguet, Zsuzsanna Varkonji. Maurice Garrel, Huguette Maillard.

WILD MUSSELS
UPSTREAM PICTURES. Jan., 2001. Dutch. (Erik de Bruyn) Fedja van Huet, Frank Lammers, Freek Brom, Will van Kralingen, Angelique de Bruijne, Josse de Pauw, Martin Dunne.

WILDSIDE
BALBOA 2/ICELANDIC FILM CORP. May, 1998. Danish-Icelandic. (Simon Staho) Nikolaj Coster Waldau, Mads Mikkelsen, Nukaka.

WILD THINGS
SONY. (John McNaughton) Kevin Bacon, Matt Dillon, Neve Campbell, Theresa Russell, Denise Richards, Daphne Rubin-Vega.

WILD WILD WEST
WARNER BROS. June, 1999. (Barry Sonnenfeld) Will Smith, Kevin Kline, Salma Hayek, Ted Levine, M. Emmet Walsh.

WILD ZERO
GAGA COMMUNICATIONS. Sept., 2000. Japanese. (Tetsuro Takeuchi) Guitar Wolf, Drum Wolf, Bass Wolf, Endo Masashi, Inamiya Makoto, Sato Masao, Namiki Shiro, Shitichai Kwancharu.

WILLFULL
LATENT IMAGE PRODS. (SYDNEY). June, 2001. Australian. (Rebel Penfold-Russell) Anna Lise Phillips, Anne Looby, C. Thomas Howell, Charles "Bud" Tingwell, John Gaden, Jennifer Claire, Ellesha Dobbs.

WILLIAMSTOWNE
WOODLEAF. Nov., 1998. (Richard Horian) Deni Delory, Richard Horian, Lynn Britt, Brian Heath, Adisa Bankole.

WILLOW AND WIND
CINA MEDIA INTL./NHK. Aug., 2000. Iranian-Japanese. (Mohammad Ali Talchi) Hadi Alipour, Amir Janfada, Majid Alipour, Mohammad Sharif Ebrahimi.

THE WIMBLEDON STAGE
GEMINI FILMS. Feb. 22, 2002. French. (Mathieu Amalric) Jeanne Balibar, Esther Gorintin, Anna Prucnal, Ariella Reggio, Paul-Jean Franceschini, Anton Petje, Peter Hudson, Claudio Birsa.

WINDHORSE
SHADOW DISTRIBUTION. Sept., 1998. (Paul Wagner) Dadon, Jampa Kelsang, Richard Chang, Taije Silverman, Lu Yu.

WINDTALKERS
MGM. May, 2002. (John Woo) Nicolas Cage, Adam Beach, Peter Stormare, Noah Emmerich, Mark Ruffalo, Brain Van Holt, Martin Henderson, Roger Willie, Frances O'Connor, Christian Slater, Jason Isaacs.

THE WIND WILL CARRY US
MK2 DIFFUSION. Sept., 1999. French-Iranian. (Abbas Kiarostami) Behzad Dourani.

WING COMMANDER
20TH CENTURY FOX. Mar., 1999. (Chris Roberts) Freddie Prinze, Jr., Saffron Burrows, Matthew Lillard, Tcheky Karyo.

WINNING GIRLS THROUGH PSYCHIC MIND CONTROL
June, 2002. (Barry Alexander Brown) Bronson Pinchot, Ruben Santiago-Hudson, Amy Carlson, Chris Murney.

THE WINSLOW BOY
SONY. Apr., 1999. (David Mamet) Nigel Hawthorne, Jeremy Northam, Rebecca Pidgeon, Gemma Jones, Guy Edwards.

THE WINTER OF THE FAIRIES
NIRVANA FILMS/CREACION/AMANDA FILMS/ALMA ATA INTL./TVE/CANAL PLUS. May, 2000. Spanish. (Pedro Telechea) Elena Anaya, Eduardo Noriega, Juan Diego, Elvira Minguez.

WINTER STORIES
BEHAVIOUR DISTRIBUTION. Feb., 1999. Canadian. (Francois Bouvier) Joel Drapeau-Dalpe, Denis Bouchard, Luc Guerin.

WIREY SPINDELL
WINSTAR CINEMA/ FIVE MINUTES BEFORE THE MIRACLE. Sept., 1999. (Eric Schaeffer) Eric Schaeffer, Eric Mabius, Devon Matthews.

WISCONSIN DEATH TRIP
BBC Arena/Cinemax/Hands On production. Apr., 2000. U.S.-British. (James Marsh) Jo Vukelich, Jeffrey Golden, Marilyn White, John Schneider. Documentary.

THE WISDOM OF CROCODILES
ENTERTAINMENT FILM DISTRIBUTORS. Nov., 1998. British. (Po Chih Leong) Jude Law, Elina Lowensohn, Timothy Spall, Kerry Fox.

WISEGIRLS
Jan., 2002. (David Anspaugh) Mira Sorvino, Mariah Carey, Melora Walters, Arthur Nascarella, Saul Stein, Joseph Siravo, Christian Maelen, Anthony Alessandro.

THE WITCH DOCTORS
RAI TRADE. Nov., 2000. Italian. (Anne Riitta Ciccone) Antonella Ponziani, Cecilia Dazzi, Macha Meril, Piero Natoli, Mario De Candia.

WITCHES TO THE NORTH
MEDUSA. Nov. 13, 2001. Italian. (Giovanni Veronesi) Teo Mammucari, Paul Sorvino, Emmanuelle Seigner, Gerard Depardieu, Daniele Liotti.

A WITCH IN THE FAMILY
SONET FILM/FILMLANCE INTL./SONET FILM/CHIMNEY POT, BV FILM/YELLOW COTTAGE/BOGAEUS MANUSKRIPT/HARALD HAMRELL. Jan., 2000. Swedish. (Harald Hamrell) Johan Rheborg, Tintin Anderzon, Margreth Weivers, Karin Bogaeus, Rebecca Scheja.

WITH ALL MY LOVE
CINEVIA. Aug., 2001. French. (Amalia Escriva) Jeanne Balibar, Bruno Todeschini, Dominique Blanc, Dominique Reymond.

WITH CLOSED EYES
MADAVI FILMS. Sept., 2000. Austrian. (Mansur Madavi) Lorenzo Montalban, Felix Alcallaga, Ruben Fernandez, Hans Michael, Diaz Espinosa.

WITH FRIENDS LIKE THESE...
ROBERT GREENHUT/PARKWAY/QUADRANT. Feb., 1998. (Philip Messina) Adam Arkin, Beverly D'Angelo, Elle Macpherson, Amy Madigan, Laura San Giacomo.

WITH GREAT JOY
A-FILM DISTRIBUTION. Feb., 2001. Dutch. (Lodewijk Crijns) Jaap Spijkers, Renee Soutendijk, Jack Wouterse, Camilla Siegertsz, Michel Vermey.

WITH OR WITHOUT YOU
MOUNT CURVE AND WARDENCLYFFE ENTERTAINMENT. April, 1998. (Wendell Jon Andersson) Kristoffer Winters, Marisa Ryan.

WITH OR WITHOUT YOU
MIRAMAX. Sept., 1999. British. (Michael Winterbottom) Christopher Eccleston, Dervla Kirwan, Yvan Attal.

WITHOUT LIMITS
WARNER BROS. March, 1998. (Robert Towne) Billy Crudup, Donald Sutherland, Monica Potter, Jeremy Sisto, Matthew Lillard, Billy Burke.

THE WOGBOY
20TH CENTURY FOX/AUSTRALIAN FILM FINANCE CORP./THIRD COSTA/G.O. FILMS/FILM VICTORIA. Feb., 2000. Australian. (Aleksi Vellis) Nick Giannopolulos, Lucy Bell, Vince Colosimo, Geraldine Turner, Abi Tucker, John Barresi, Tony Nikolakopoulos.

THE WOLF OF THE WEST COAST
Aug. 27, 2002. French-Portugese. (Hugo SantiagoJames Faulkner, Anna Mouglalis, Gerard Watkins, Valerie Dreville, Lizzie Brochere.

THE WOMAN CHASER
DEFINITIVE FILMS/TARMAC FILMS. Oct., 1999. (Robinson Devor) Patrick Warburton, Eugene Roche, Ron Morgan, Emily Newman, Paul Malevitz, Lynette Bennett, Joe Durrenberger, Marilyn Rising.

THE WOMAN EVERY MAN WANTS
TONIC FEATURES. Jan., 2001. (Gabriela Tagliavini) Ryan Hurst, Daniela Lunkewitz, Justin Walker, Alexis Arquette, Michelle Anne Johnson, Pat Crawford Brown.

WOMEN IN FILM
LIONS GATE. Jan., 2001. (Bruce Wagner) Beverly D'Angelo, Marianne Jean-Baptiste, Portia de Rossi.

WOMEN IN THE MIRROR
May 23, 2002. Japanese-French. (Kiju Yoshida) Mariko Okada, Yoshiko Tanaka, Sae Issiki, Hideo Morota, Tokuma Nishioka, Mirai Yamamoto, Miki Sanjo.

A WOMAN OF THE NORTH
HUNGRY EYE LOWLAND. Sept., 1999. Dutch-Italian. (Frans Weisz) Johanna Ter Steege, Massimo Ghini, Anthony Calf.

WOMAN ON A TIN ROOF
GOOD HARVEST FILMS. Oct., 1999. Filipino. (Mario O'Hara,) Nike Magat, Aya Medel, Anita Linda, Frank Rivera, Renzo Cruz.

WOMAN ON TOP
FOX SEARCHLIGHT/UFD/20TH CENTURY FOX INTL. Apr., 2000. (Fina Torres) Penelope Cruz, Murilo Benicio, Harold Perrineau Jr., Mark Feuerstein.

A WOMAN'S A HELLUVA THING
REGENT ENTERTAINMENT. June, 2001. (Karen Leigh Hopkins) Angus MacFadyen, Penelope Ann Miller, Ann-Margret, Kathryn Harrold, Mary Kay Place, Barry Del Sherman.

WOMAN SOUP
GROUP POWER WORKSHOP CO. Jan., 2000. Taiwanese. (Emily Liu) May Chin, Tien Hsin, Elsie Yeh, April Wang, Tony Chang, Andrew, Liu Liang-tso, Khan Lee.

WOMEN'S EXPECTATIONS
TADRART FILMS. SEPT. 26, 2001. ALGERIAN-FRENCH. (Naguel Belouad) Tounes Ait Ali, Sonia Mekkiou, Doudja Achachi, Salima Seddiki, Abdallah Bouzida, Kamel Rouini.

WOMEN'S PARADISE
STATE JOINT STOCK CO., UZBEKISTAN. Jan., 2001. Uzbekistanian. (Yusup Razykov) Bakhtier Zakirov, Fatykh Jalolov, Mokhira Nurmetova, Zebo Nuruzova, Bigora Rakhimova.

WOMEN WITHOUT WINGS
Aug. 28, 2002. Canadian. (Nicholas Kinsey) Katya Gardner, Micheline Lanctot, Lowell Gasoi, Besa Imani.

THE WONDERFUL ICE CREAM SUIT
BUENA VISTA. Jan., 1998. (Stuart Gordon) Joe Mantegna, Esai Morales, Edward James Olmos, Clifton Gonzalez, Gregory Sierra.

WONDERLAND
UNIVERSAL. May, 1999. British. (Michael Winterbottom) Shirley Henderson, Gina McKee, Molly Parker, Ian Hart.

WOO
NEW LINE. April, 1998. (Daisy V.S. Mayer) Jada Pinket Smith, Tommy Davidson, Duane Martin, Michael Ralph, Darrel M. Heath.

THE WOOD
PARAMOUNT. July, 1999. (Rick Famuyiwa) Omar Epps, Sean Nelson, Taye Diggs, Trent Cameron, Richard T. Jones.

THE WOODEN GUN
ZERO PICTURES. June, 2001. (Jon Jacobs, Michael Kastenbaum) Jon Jacobs, Stephen Polk, Michael Kastenbaum, Dawn Kapatos, Haley Gilbert.

WONDER BOYS
PARAMOUNT/MUTUAL FILM CO./SCOTT RUDIN-CURTIS HANSON/BBC/MARUBEN/TOHO-TOWA/TELE MUNCHEN/MFF FEATURE FILM PRODUCTIONS. Feb., 2000. (Curtis Hanson) Michael Douglas, Tobey Maguire, Frances McDormand, Robert Downey Jr., Katie Holmes, Richard Thomas, Rip Torn, Philip Bosco.

WON'T ANYBODY LISTEN
SEVENTH ART RELEASING. Aug., 2001. (Dov Kelemer) Art Aviles, Robert Aviles, Roxanne Aviles, Lori Graves-Bartolini, Mark Billes, Hugo Burnham, Robin Canada, C. Tucker Cheadle. Documentary.

WORD AND UTOPIA
MADRAGOA FILMES (PORTUGAL)/RTP (PORTUGAL)/GEMINI FILMS (FRANCE)/PLATEAU PRODUCOES. (BRAZIL)/WANDA FILMS (SPAIN). Aug., 2000. Portuguese-French-Brazilian-Spanish. (Manoel de Oliveira) Lima Duarte, Luis Miguel Cintra, Ricardo Trepa, Miguel Guilherme, Leonor Silveira, Jeronimo, Renato Di Carmine.

WORD ATTACK
FILMAX/ICONICA/FREEDONIA/VIA DIGITAL, TVV. Mar., 2000. Spanish. (Miguel Albaladejo) Antonia San Juan, Sergi Lopez, Antonio Resines, Fedra Lorente, Adriana Ozores, Roberto Alvarez.

WORK IN PROGRESS
WANDA VISION/NIRVANA. Sept. 12, 2001. Spanish-French. (Jose Luis Guerin) Juana Rodriguez, Ivan Guzman, Juan Lopez, Juan manuel Lopez, Santiago Segde, AbdelAziz el Mountassir, Antonio Atar. Documentary.

WORKERS, FARMERS
PIERRE GRISE DISTRIBUTION. May, 2001. Italian-French. (Danielle Huillet, Jean-Marie Straub) Angela Nugara, Giacinto di Pascoli, Giampaolo Cassarino, Enrico Achilli, Angela Durantini, Martina Gionfriddo.

WORKERS FOR THE GOOD LORD
REZO FILMS/LA SORCIERE ROUGE/EURIPIDE PRODS./ARTE FRANCE CINEMA/RHONE ALPES CINEMA/CANAL PLUS. Apr., 2000. French. (Jean-Claude Brisseau) Stanislas Merhar, Raphaele Godin, Emile Abossolo M'Bo, Coralie Revel, Paulette Dubost.

THE WORKERS' SETTLEMENT
LENFILM. Aug., 2000. Soviet Union–1965. (Vladimir Vengerov) Oleg Borisov, Tatyana Doronina, Viktor Avdyushko, Lyudmila Gurchenko, Nikolai Simonov, Lyubov Sokolova.

THE WORLD IS NOT ENOUGH
MGM/ALBERT R. BROCCOLI'S EON PRODS. LTD. Nov. 1999. (Michael Apted) Pierce Brosnan, Sophie Marceau, Robert Carlyle, Denise Richards, Robbie Coltrane, Judi Dench, Desmond Llewelyn, John Clelese, Maria Grazia Cucinotta, Samantha Bond.

WORLD TRAVELER
ALLIANCE ATLANTIS AND INDEPENDENT FILM CHANNEL. Sept., 2001. U.S.-Canadian. (Bart Freundlich) Billy Crudup, Julianne Moore, Clevant Derricks, David Keith, James Le Gros, Karen Allen, Mary McCormack, Liane Balaban.

WOULD I LIE TO YOU? 2
WARNER BROS.Jan., 2001. French. (Thomas Gilou) Richard Anconina, Jose Garcia, Bruno Solo, Gad Elmaleh, Gilbert Melki, Daniel Prevost, Elisa Tovati, Enrico Macias.

THE WOUNDS
COBRA FILM DEPT./PANDORA. Sept., 1998. Serbian-French. (Srdjan Dragojevic) Dusan Pekic, Milan Maric, Dragan Bjelogrlic.

THE WRESTLERS
BUDDHADEB DASGUPTA PRODS. Aug., 2000. Indian. (Buddhadeb Dasgupta) Jaya Seal, Tapas Pal, Shankar Chakraborty. R.I. Asad, Tapas Adhikari, Saurav Das, Gautam Warshi, Masud Akhtar.

WRESTLING WITH ALLIGATORS
PORTMAN PRODS./HOMEGROWN PICTURES. Jan., 1998. (Laurie Weltz) Aleksa Palladino, Koely Richardson, Claire Bloom.

WRONGFULLY ACCUSED
WARNER BROS. Aug., 1998. (Pat Proft) Leslie Nielson, Richard Crenna, Kelly Le Brock, Melinda McGraw, Michael York.

THE WRONG SIDE OF THE BED
BUENA VISTA INTL. (SPAIN). July 1, 2002. Spanish. (Emilio Martinez-Lazaro) Ernesto Alterio, Paz Vega, Guillermo Toledo, Natalia Verbeke, Alberto San Juan, Maria Esteve, Ramon Barea, Nathalie Poza.

X

X
MANGA ENT./X COMMITTEE CLAMP/KADOKAWA SHOTEN PUBLISHING CO./BANDAI VISUAL CO./MARUBENI CORP./ SHELTY CO./SEGA ENTERPRISES/VICTOR ENT./ ANIMATION STUDIO MAD HOUSE CO/MOVIE CO LTD. Apr., 2000. Japanese. (Rintaro). Animated.

X-MEN
20TH CENTURY FOX/MARVEL ENTERTAINMENT GROUP/ DONNERS' CO./BAD HAT HARRY. July, 2000. (Bryan Singer) Hugh Jackman, Patrick Stewart, Ian McKellan, Famke Janssen, James Marsden, Halle Berry, Anna Paquin, Tyler Mane, Ray Park, Rebecca Romijn-Stamos.

THE X-FILES
20TH CENTURY FOX. June, 1998. (Rob Bowman) David Duchovny, Gillian Anderson, Martin Landau, Armin Mueller-Stahl, Blythe Danner, Mitch Pileggi, William B. Davis.

X-PATRIOTS
April, 2002. (Darien Sills-Evans) Bobby Lyle, Natalie Edwardes, Chimene van Oosterhout.

XXX
SONY PICTURES ENTERTAINMENT. July, 2002. (Rob Cohen) Vin Diesel, Asia Argento, Marton Csokas, Samuel L. Jackson, Danny Trejo, Michael Roof, Tom Everett, Richy Muller, Werner Daehn.

Y

YADO YADEGAR
Oct. 3, 2001. Iranian. (Mostafa R. Karimi, Farhad Varahram) Documentary.

YAMAKASI
EUROPA CORP. DISTRIBUTION. April, 2001. French. (Ariel Aeitoun) Chau Belle Dinh, Williams Belle, Malik Diouf, Yann Hnautra, Guylain N'Guba Boyeke, Laurent Piemontesi, Charles Perriere.

THE YARDS
MIRAMAX/PAUL WEBSTER/INDUSTRY ENTERTAINMENT. May, 2000. (James Gray) Mark Wahlberg, Joaquin Phoenix, Charlize Theron, James Caan, Ellen Burstyn, Faye Dunaway, Chad Aaron, Andrew Davoli, Steve Lawrence, Tony Musante, Victor Argo, Tomas Milian.

YEAR OF THE DEVIL (ROK DABLA)
FALCON. July 4, 2002. Czech. (Peter Zelenka) Jarek Nohavica, Karel Plihal, Jan Prent, Karel Holas, Frantisek Cerny, Radek Poboril, Michal Pavlik, Radek Klucka, Jaz Coleman.

YEAR OF THE DRAG-IN
MAVSURFER FILMS. Dec., 2000. (Curt Myers, Frank Quirarte) Documentary.

THE YEAR OF MARIA
AURUM/ASEGARCE/TVE/VIA DIGITAL/ETB. Aug., 2000. Spanish. (Fernando Guillen Cuervo, Karra Elejalde) Karra Elejalde, Fernando Guillen Cuervo, Manuel Manquina.

YEARNING FOR A LIFE
SVENSK FILMINDUSTRI. Feb., 1999. Swedish. (Christer Engberg) Lotta Ornryd, Mattias Barthelsson, Nina Morin.

YEAR'S LOVE
ENTERTAINMENT FILM DISTRIBUTORS. Feb., 1999. British. (David Kane) Kathy Burke, Jennifer Ehle, Ian Hart, Douglas Henshall, Catherine McCormack.

YELLOW ASPHALT
NEW YORKER FILMS. June 23, 2002. Israeli. (Danny Verete) Sami Samir, Tatjana Blacher, Raida Adon, Motti Katz, Abed Zuabi, Hagit.

YELLOW BRIDE
AZERKINOVIDEO. Nov., 2000. Azerbaijani. (Yaver Rzayev) Dzhamilya Kyamal, Siyavush Kerimi, Gyseymaga Yachyaev.

YELLOW CARD
PATHFINDER INTL./MEDIA FOR DEVELOPMENT TRUST. Sept., 2000. Zimbabwe. (John Riber) Leroy Gopal, Kasamba Mkumba, Ratidzo Mambo, Collin Dube, Pedzisai Sithole, Walter Muparutsa.

YELLOW HAIR
PIKSYEON BAENGKEU/KOREAN MOTION PICTURE PROMOTION CORP. CO., 1999. South Korean. (Kim Yoo-min) Lee Jai-eun, Kim Ki-yeon, Kim Hyeon-cheol, Kim Hyeok-euk.

YES, BUT...
REZO FILMS. April, 2001. French. (Yves Lavandier) Emilie Dequenne, Gerard Jugnot, Cyrille Thouvenin, Alix de Konopka, Vanessa Jarry, Patrick Bonnel.

YESTERDAY CHILDREN
REYNAFILMS. Mar., 2000. Filipino. (Carlos Siguion-Reyna) Ara Mina, Tonton Gutierrez, Patricia Ann Roque, Carlo Aquino, Pen Medina.

YOLNGU BOY
PALACE FILMS (AUSTRALIA). Dec., 2000. Australian. (Stephen Johnson) John Sebastian Pilakui, Sean Mununggurr, Nathan Daniels, Lirrina Mununggurr, Maakuma Yunupingu, Nungki Yunupingu.

YOU ARE FREE
FARABI CINEMA FOUNDATION. Aug., 2001. Iranian. (Mohammad Ali Talebi) Ehsan Ghasemi, Siavash Lashkari, Abdolreza Akbari, Parivash Nazariye.

YOU CAN COUNT ON ME
SHOOTING GALLERY/HART SHARP ENTERTAINMENT. Jan., 2000. (Kenneth Lonergan) Laura Linney, Mark Ruffalo, Rory Culkin, Matthew Broderick, Jon Tenney, V. Smith-Cameron, Kenneth Lonergan.

YOU KNOW MY NAME
TNT. Jan., 1999. (John Kent Harrison) Sam Elliott, Arliss Howard, Carolyn McCormick, James Gammon, R. Lee Erney.

THE YOUNG AND THE DEAD
TAIL SLATE PICTURES. Sept., 2000. (Shari Springer Berman, Robert Pulcini). Documentary.

THE YOUNG GIRL AND THE MONSOON
MONSOON. Mar., 2000. (James Ryan) Terry Kinney, Ellen Muth, Mili Avital, Diane Venora, Tom Guinee.

THE YOUNG UNKNOWNS
WIT'S END PRODS. March, 2001. (Catherine Jelski) Devon Gummersall, Arly Jover Eion Bailey, Leslie Bibb, Dale Godboldo, Simon Templeman.

YOU ONLY LIVE ONCE
CECCHI GORI/BOCCIA FILM. Nov., 1999. Italian. (Eugenio Cappuccio, Massimo Gaudioso, Fabio Nunziata) Eugenio Cappuccio, Massimo Gaudioso, Fabio Nunziata, Anna Scaglione.

YOU OR ME
AXIS PLUSZ/MTV. Feb., 1999. Hungarian. (Tamas Sas) Gabi Gubas, Attila Kiraly, Viktor Bodo, Karina Kecskes.

YOU REALLY GOT ME
4 1/2 PRODUCTION. May, 2001. Norwegian. (Pal Sletaune) Robert Skjaerstad, Bjorn Sundquist, Andrine Saether, Trond Hovik, Berit Boman, Philip Zanden, Per Schaaning.

YOUR FRIENDS & NEIGHBORS
GRAMERCY PICTURES. July, 1998. (Neil LaBute) Amy Brenneman, Aaron Eckhart, Catherine Keener, Nastassja Kinski, Jason Patric, Ben Stiller.

YOU'RE LAUGHING
ISTITUTO LUCE. Aug., 1998. Italian-Spanish-French. (Paolo and Vittorio Taviani) Antonio Albanese, Sabrina Ferilli, Luca Zingaretti.

YOU'RE THE ONE (A STORY OF THE PAST)
COLUMBIA TRISTAR SPAIN. Nov., 2000. Spanish. (Jose Luis Garci) Lydia Bosch, Julia G. Caba, Juan Diego, Ana Fernandez, Manuel Lozano, Inaki Miramon, Carlos Hipolito, Jesus Puente.

YOUR GUARDIAN
JUNEBUG FILMS. Feb., 2001. (Kari Nevil) Irene Bedard, Chad Lowe, Leann Hunley, Jeannetta Arnette, Stephen Heath, Claire Dunlap.

YOU'VE GOT MAIL
WARNER BROS. Dec., 1998. (Nora Ephron): Tom Hanks, Meg Ryan, Parker Posey, Greg Kinnear, Jean Stapleton.

Y2K
PM ENTERTAINMENT GROUP. May, 1999. (Richard Pepin) Louis Gossett, Jr., Jaimz Woolvett, Ed O'Ross, Sarah Chalke.

YOYES
COLUMBIA TRISTAR SPAIN/CIPI CINEMATOGRAFICA/MACT PRODS./MARVEL MOVIES/VIA DIGITAL/TVE/ETB. Apr., 2000. Spanish-French-Italian. (Helena Taberna) Ana Torrent, Ernesto Alterio, Florence Pernel, Ramon Langa, Inaki Aierra, Isabel Ordaz.

YUSHO-RENAISSANCE
JEANS FACTORY. Jan., 1999. Japanese. (Hiroyuki Oki). Toshiko Taniuchi, Ken Morimoto, Riko Kondo, Sawako Goda, Yuko Fukunaga.

Z

ZACHARIA FARTED
WINDOWSHOT. Sept., 1998. Canadian. (Michael Rohl) Colin Cunningham, Benjamin Ratner, Madison Graie.

THE ZERO EFFECT
COLUMBIA. Jan., 1998. (Jake Kasdan), Bill Pullman, Ben Stiller, Ryan O'Neal, Kim Dickens, Angela Featherstone.

THE ZEROS
June, 2001. (John Ryman) Mackenzie Astin, John Ales, Rachel Wilson, Jennifer Morrison, Sam Vlahos, Kyle Gass, John Diehl.

ZERO TOLERANCE
SONET FILM/FILM I VAST/SANDREW METRONOME/TV4/TV1000. Oct., 1999. Swedish. (Anders Nilsson) Jakob Eklund.

ZOE
CURB ENTERTAINMENT AND BILL KENRIGHT FILMS. Jane, 2001. (Deborah Attoinese) Vanessa Zima, Jenny Seagrove, Stephi Lineburg.

ZONZON
MK2 DIFFUSION. Sept., 1998. French. (Laurent Bouhnik) Pascal Greggory, Gael Morel, Jamel Debbouze.

THE ZOOKEEPER
SVENDSEN FILMS (DENMARK). Aug., 2001. Danish-British-Czech Republic-Dutch. (Ralph Ziman) Sam Neill, Gina McKee, Ulrich Thomsen, Om Puri, Javor Loznica, Mikulas Kren.

ZOOLANDER
PARAMOUNT. Sept., 2001. (Ben Stiller) Ben Stiller, Owen Wilson, Christine Taylor, Milla Jovovich, Jerry Stiller, Jon Voight, David Duchovny, Judah Friedlander, Nathan Lee Graham, Alexander Manning, Asio Highsmith, Alexander Skarsgard.

ZOOM
VEGA FILM. Aug., 2000. German. (Otto Alexander Jahrreis) Florian Lukas, Oana Solomon, Albert Kitzl, Goetz Schubert.

ZORA THE VAMPIRE
CECCHI GORI DISTRIBUZIONE. Oct., 2000. Italian. (Manetti Brothers) Toni Bertorelli, Micaela Ramazzotti, Carlo Verdone.

PRODUCTION COMPANIES

■

HISTORIES OF THE MAJOR MOTION PICTURE STUDIOS

COLUMBIA PICTURES
(SONY PICTURES ENTERTAINMENT, INC.)

Columbia Pictures can trace its beginnings to the CBC Films Sales Co., formed in 1920 by Harry Cohn, Jack Cohn and Joe Brandt, all of whom had previously worked together at Universal Studios. CBC was set up to make a series of shorts known as Screen Snapshots, showing the off-screen activities of movie stars to publicize their current pictures. Soon the new company expanded to produce westerns and other comedy shorts and in 1922 produced its first feature, "More To Be Pitied Than Scorned." In 1924, the owners renamed their company Columbia Pictures.

Two years later, Columbia had advanced to the point where it began to open film exchanges of its own instead of selling films outright to theatres for a flat fee and established a studio with two stages and a small office building. Sam Briskin was hired as general manager. In 1929, it produced its first all-talking feature, "The Donovan Affair." This low-budget murder mystery was directed by Frank Capra. By this time, the company had opened a home office in New York where Jack Cohn functioned as vice president and treasurer, while Harry ran the production operation on the West Coast.

In 1931, Brandt sold his interest in Columbia and retired. The next year, Harry Cohn assumed the title of president, while retaining his post as production chief. In 1935, Columbia purchased a 40-acre ranch in Burbank for location filming (later expanded to 80 acres). The company's first big artistic success was in 1934 with Capra's "It Happened One Night," which was not only the top box office draw of 1934, but a winner of five major Academy Awards including Best Picture. Capra followed this with such hits as "Mr. Deeds Goes to Town" (1936), "Lost Horizon" (1937), "You Can't Take It With You" (1938) and "Mr. Smith Goes to Washington" (1939).

Throughout the 40s Columbia prospered and by the end of the decade, it could claim to be one of the industry's major studios. Unlike the other studios, Columbia did not own any theatres and was not affected by the industry's Consent Decrees which forced those studios to divest themselves of their exhibition properties. Commercial hits of the period included "Gilda" (1946), "The Jolson Story" (1946) and "Jolson Sings Again" (1949).

In 1951, Columbia diversified into television by forming Screen Gems, a wholly owned subsidiary set up to make programs and commercials. Founder, Harry Cohn died in 1958. The successor management—headed by veterans of the company Abe Schneider and Leo Jaffe—made major investments in British film production and released "Lawrence of Arabia" (1962), "A Man for All Seasons" (1966) and the musical "Oliver!" (1968). Other hits of the '60s were "Guess Who's Coming to Dinner" (1967) and "To Sir With Love" (1967). The success of these and others was attributable to Mike Frankovich, who became production head in 1954 and was succeeded by Stanley Schneider, whose father, Abe, headed the company at the time. Another son of Abe, Bert, and Bob Rafelson co-produced "Easy Rider" in 1969, one of the biggest hits in Columbia's history.

At the beginning of the '70s, Herbert Allen Jr., a former Wall Street banker, bought control of Columbia and took over as president and CEO. Allen brought in new management headed by Alan Hirschfield and David Begelman, who produced such hits as "Shampoo" (1975)

and "Close Encounters of the Third Kind" (1977). Begelman's successor as production chief was Frank Price (who had previously headed Universal Television) and under his regime the company produced such successful films as "Kramer vs. Kramer" (1979), "Tootsie" (1982) and "Ghostbusters" (1984). In 1982, Columbia was purchased by the Coca-Cola Company. Under its aegis Columbia, Home Box Office and CBS, Inc. joined forces to finance a new production company, TriStar Pictures. At the start, it was emphasized that the new company would be separate from Columbia, with TriStar using Columbia's distribution. Price departed in 1985 and in 1986 David Puttnam, an independent British producer, was signed as chairman. Succeeding him was Dawn Steel, who was named president. In 1989, TriStar was made a unit of Columbia Pictures with Jeff Sagansky, president of TriStar, reporting to Ms. Steel.

Columbia Pictures Entertainment was formed in 1987 by Coca-Cola to restructure its entertainment business. CPE consisted of two film-production companies: Columbia Pictures and TriStar Pictures; two television arms: Columbia Pictures Television, Merv Griffin Enterprises, and Loews Theatre Management Corp.

In September 1989, Columbia Pictures Entertainment was purchased by the Sony Corporation of Japan. Sony previously acquired CBS Records in 1987. Producers Jon Peters and Peter Guber were brought in as co-chairmen. In 1991, Peters resigned from his position as co-chairman, the company was renamed Sony Pictures Entertainment, Inc. and Mark Canton left Warner Bros. to become the new chairman of Columbia Pictures. In June, 1994, Fred Bernstein was put in charge of the motion picture units at Columbia Pictures, TriStar Pictures, Sony Pictures Classics and Triumph Releasing Corporation. Later that summer, the marketing and distribution arms of these divisions were consolidated under the direction of Sid Ganis as president. In September, 1994, Peter Guber announced his resignation as Sony chairman, with Alan J. Levine named as his successor. Sony was forced to write off $3.2 billion in 1995, but the Japanese parent company vowed to maintain its Hollywood commitment. In September of 1996, Canton was removed as chairman of Columbia Pictures, followed in October of that year by the resignation of Levine, who was replaced by John Calley, formerly of MGM/UA. Mr. Canton's removal was accompanied by that of Lisa Henson and Barry Josephson, Columbia Pictures presidents; Marc Platt was ousted as was his successor Robert Cooper, TriStar Pictures president along with Stacey Snider, Tristar production president, Alan Levine, Sony Pictures chairman, and Fred Bernstein, Columbia TriStar president. This was a rather strange turn of events, as the deposed team was responsible for Sony's record $1.3 billion in domestic box office for 1997, having developed such movies as "Jerry Maguire," "Anaconda," "The Fifth Element" and "My Best Friend's Wedding."

Calley reorganized and restructured Sony Pictures Entertainment, closing the TriStar Motion Picture Group and bringing the remaining executives over to Columbia Pictures which became Sony Pictures Entertainment's principal production arm. SPE also resurrected a past label, Screen Gems, to make films in the $4-5 million range.

In 1998, Jeff Sagansky left Columbia to join the newest network, Pax TV. Sony Pictures Classics, the art film distributor arm of Sony Corp., despite a profitable 1998, came under criticism for its co-presidents' insistence on earning a profit on each of their releases and failing to take on more commercial fare. Although its revenues of $20 million for the first seven months of 1998, were twice its 1997 grosses, SPC was surpassed in 1995 by Miramax, a younger arthouse, but one that has taken more financial risks. After a two-year legal battle, Sony lost its claim to the movie rights for the lucrative James Bond franchise. In a settlement with MGM, Sony gave up its claim for a meager $5 million, but ended up with the rights to Spiderman.

In early 1999, Sony Pictures Entertainment signed a groundbreaking deal with 30 screenwriters stating that in exchange for one film each over the next four years, each writer will receive up-front fees as well as 2% of gross receipts.

On October 3, 1999, Sony bade a final farewell to its co-founder, Akio Morita who died at the age of 78.

Currently, Sony Pictures Entertainment, still helmed by Chairman & CEO John Calley, includes the unified production studio, Columbia Pictures, Screen Gems, Sony Pictures Classics (specializing in arthouse films), producers of third-party product (e.g., Phoenix, Centropolis, Jim Henson Productions), and global motion picture production operations. SPE's releasing arms include Sony Pictures Releasing (U.S.) and Columbia TriStar Film Distributors International.

In 2000, Sony continued to struggle, releasing several expensive features that generated little box office interest. What Planet Are You From? cost $50 million and grossed only $6.5 million, while I Dreamed of Africa cost $40 million and brought in $6.5 million. Even the highly anticipated summer films, The Patriot and Hollow Man underperformed at the box office, barely breaking even. John Calley, now 70, has been able to slow the outrageous spending and losses that once plagued the studio but has yet to improve market share (currently 9%) or produce the blockbusters needed to return Sony to its former prominence. In spite of Monday-morning box office woes, Sony Pictures Entertainment has increased overall sales 55% since Calley took over in 1996, in large part due to its pay-tv, video and tv-content businesses.

In 2000, parent Sony restructured, and Sony Pictures Entertainment was placed under the Sony Broadband Entertainment umbrella. That year the company created a digital entertainment unit, Sony Pictures Digital Entertainment, and restructured its top management in preparation for Chairman and CEO John Calley's planned departure in 2003. In a move geared to meet the targeted programming needs of the upcoming broadband decade, Sony Pictures Entertainment (SPE) is consolidating its two domestic television operations into a new division, Columbia TriStar Domestic Television.

Sony's 2000 sales were $6,106 million, showing one year growth of 34.6%.

In 2001, Sony had hits with "The Wedding Planner," "A Knight's Tale," "Ali" and "Not Another Teen Movie" while Sony Pictures Classics continued to enjoy box office and critical success with "Crouching Tiger, Hidden Dragon."

In 2002, Sony sold its stake in exhibitor, Loews Cineplex Entertainment and scored a record breaking year with a number of huge releases, including "Spider-Man," "Men in Black II," and "Stuart Little 2."

Anticipating the retirement of longtime studio head John Calley, Sony Corp. of American chairman & CEO, Howard Stringer renewed his contract and promoted Yair Landau (president, Sony Pictures Digital Entertainment), Amy Pascal (Columbia Pictures chair) and Jeff Blake (president, worldwide marketing and distribution for Columbia TriStar Motion Picture Group) to the co-equal posts of vice-chairmen, Sony Pictures Entertainment. They will replace former COO, Mel Harris, who left the company in September.

While not as huge as 2002, Sony had a big year at the boxoffice in 2003. Meanwhile the electronics coglomerate announced a reduction in 20,000 jobs over the next three years, of which 1,700 will be cut from the studio workforce. Sony now pays 55% of the budgets for Joe Roth's Revolution Studios and is very dependent on them for hit films. In 2003 Revolution delivered hits, such as "Anger Management" and misses like "Gigli." Sony also signed a co-production deal with the very successful Spyglass Productions run by Gary Barber and Roger Birnbaum.

RECENT COLUMBIA/SPE RELEASES

1995:   The Net, Sense and Sensibility.

1996:   The Cable Guy, Donnie Brasco, The Fan, Jerry Maguire.

1997:   Air Force One, Anaconda, The Devil's Own, The Fifth Element, Men in Black.

1998:   Can't Hardly Wait, I Know What You Did Last Night, My Giant, Wild Things.

1999:   Big Daddy, Muppets From Space, Blue Streak, Hanging Up, Girl Interrupted.

2000:   The Patriot, Hollow Man, Random Hearts, 28 Days, I Dreamed of Africa, What Planet Are You From?

2001:   The Wedding Planner, A Knight's Tale, The Anima,America's Sweethearts, Ali.

2002:   Spider-Man, Men in Black II, Stuart Little 2, Swept Away, XXX, I Spy.

2003   Bad Boys II, Anger Management, S.W.A.T., Charlie's Angels: Full Throttle, Once Upon A Time in Mexico

RECENT SONY PICTURES CLASSICS RELEASES

1995:   Shanghai Triad, Safe, Celluloid Closet, Crumb.

1996:   Beautiful Thing, Welcome To the Dollhouse, The Flower of My Secret.

1997:   In the Company of Men, The Myth of Fingerprints, Ma Vie En Rose.

1998:   The Governess, The Opposite of Sex, Henry Fool.

1999:   Run Lola Run, The Dreamlife of Angels, The Winslow Boy, Sweet and Lowdown.

2000:   Crouching Tiger, Hidden Dragon, Bossa Nova, Trixie, Groove, Pollock.

2001:   Pauline and Paulette, Secret Ballot, Haiku Tunnel.

2002:   Sunshine State, Mad Love, Autofocus, Love Liza, My Wife Is an Actress.

2003   Winged Migration, The Tiplets of Bellville, The Fog of War, The Company.

THE WALT DISNEY COMPANY

In 1923, Walt Disney set up an animation studio with his brother Roy. Five years later, he introduced his most famous creation, Mickey Mouse, in a cartoon called "Steamboat Willie." It was an immediate hit and Disney began his series of Silly Symphony cartoons, based on musical themes, the first of which was called "The Skeleton Dance." From 1929 through 1931, Disney distributed his products through Columbia Pictures. In 1932, distribution was through United Artists with about 20 cartoons per year, half of them featuring Mickey Mouse and the others in the Silly Symphony series. Production cost of the cartoons was about $50,000 each. UA paid Disney 60% of rentals received from exhibitors, and his gross income at the time was in the neighborhood of one and a half million dollars per year.

Disney's contract with UA expired in 1937. He switched over to RKO, for whom he produced his first feature-length cartoon, "Snow White and the Seven Dwarfs," followed by "Pinnochio" (1940), "Fantasia" (1940), "Dumbo" (1941), "Bambi" (1942), "Cinderella" (1950) and "Peter Pan" (1953), all released by RKO.

RKO's financial troubles, which led to its demise in 1958, caused Walt Disney Productions to break with it in 1953 and form its own national distribution unit, Buena Vista.

Buena Vista's first release was "The Living Desert" 1953), winner of the Academy Award for feature documentary and an outgrowth of the True-Life Adventure shorts started in 1948. Disneyland in Anaheim, California, opened in 1955.

Rising costs in the production of animation films caused Disney to concentrate on live-action features, such as "20,000 Leagues Under the Sea" (1954) which took in over $11 million in domestic rentals, and "Mary Poppins" (1964) which made more than $45 million.

Walt Disney died in 1966. Roy Disney's death in 1971 left no surviving Disney family members at the studio's helm. Walt Disney World in Central Florida (near Orlando) opened in 1971. In 1983, Ron Miller, Walt's son-in-law, was made chief executive and started Touchstone Pictures, a subsidiary designed to make adult-oriented films. In 1984, Touchstone delivered "Splash." In the same year, a drive for new leadership was spearheaded by Roy Disney, son of Walt's brother of the same name. Frank Wells, former vice chairman of Warner Bros. and Michael Eisner, president of Paramount, were hired in 1984 with Eisner as chairman, Wells as president and Disney serving as vice chairman. Early in 1990, the Company announced a massive, ten-year expansion agenda that would add hundreds of new rides and shows to its existing theme parks, and provide for the building of additional attractions in Southern California and Florida. Euro-Disneyland opened near Paris in 1992.

Disney continued to do well in its motion picture division with "Pretty Woman," "Dick Tracy" and new division Hollywood Pictures' "Arachnophobia" and "The Hand That Rocks the Cradle." The 1991 animated feature "Beauty and the Beast" took in over $145 million in the U.S., and became the first animated feature nominated for Best Picture. This success was followed by 1992's "Aladdin" which became the first Disney release to gross more than $200 million in the U.S.

In 1993, Disney purchased the highly successful independent distributor Miramax, which would continue to operate as a separate company.

1994 saw the death of Frank Wells. "The Lion King" became the highest grossing film in Disney history. Jeffrey Katzenberg, crucial to the revitalization of the company's animation department, resigned as chairman to join Steven Spielberg and David Geffen in their own entertainment company, DreamWorks SKG. David Hoberman was named president of Disney's motion picture divisions. However, his departure after eight months threw the weight of responsibilities over to new chairman of the motion picture group, Joe Roth. The year ended with Disney becoming the first distributor to achieve annual box office revenues of over $1 billion.

The big entertainment news of 1995 was the company's $19 billion purchase of Capital Cities/ABC. Michael Eisner named Creative Artists Agency chairman Michael Ovitz as president of the Walt Disney Company. Ovitz was removed as chairman in November of 1996 (with a severance package rumored to be in excess of $90 million, much to the ire of Disney stock-holders).

Three years later, the dispute between Jeffrey Katzenberg, the former Disney animation chairman, and Michael Eisner, was still bubbling. Katzenberg was allegedly promised 2% share of revenues from projects begun while still at Disney. Mr. Eisner disputed the claim. In November of 1997, Disney attorneys admitted that Katzenberg was owed the money under the terms of his employment contract. The pact was thrown out of court, and handed over to a "rent-a-judge." In light of Mr. Ovitz's settlement in 1996, many speculated that Disney would make a preemptive settlement offer rather than risk the rent-a-judge's decision for an amount that would upset Disney stockholders. Mr. Katzenberg's lawsuit was for $500 million.

Miramax's past two years were good ones, with the Oscar wins in 1997 for "The English Patient" and for "Good Will Hunting" a year later. Dimension also fared well in 1998, increasing its revenue from $14 million in 1993, to $120 million in 1998. In 1997, Dimension made-up 45% of Miramax's total grosses with only 3 releases: "Scream 2," "Operation Condor," and "Mimic." Despite its success, Miramax lost some of its top executives in 1997, and chairmen Bob and Harvey Weinstein had to entrust their key personnel with additional duties. President Richard Sands was promoted to chairman, making him the only executive to have the title besides the Weinsteins.

Miramax scored again in 1998 with "Shakespeare in Love" which was a box office and critical success.

In July of 1999, Disney agreed to settle the suit brought by its former studio chief, Jeffrey Katzenberg, who claimed over $500 million in damages for bonuses he said he was owed. Leaks about the settlement put the figure paid to Katzenberg between $100 million to close to $250 million.

Other financial woes were plaguing the company. Despite box office gross exceeding $500 million in the summers of 1998 and 1999, Disney as a whole had been in a two-year slump, during which earnings dropped 21% through the fiscal third quarter of 1999 (ending June 30) and shares lost an annual average of 1.3%. Eisner had been struggling ever since company president Frank Wells died in a helicopter crash in 1994. Eisner had yet to choose a second-in-command from the ranks of Disney's talented executives. However the motion picture division is one of Disney's most profitable businesses with 1999 box office revenue up by $150 million.

As a result of the drop in revenue, Eisner initiated a review of capital spending. In spite of the studio's profitability, cuts were to be widespread. Eisner slashed development deals and offloaded hundreds of millions of dollars in costs, including staff and production overhead at Miramax and Disney.

Personnel changes at Disney in 1999 included Peter Schneider's promotion to President of Walt Disney Pictures and Robert Iger's selection to head up the newly streamlined operations of Buena Vista International.

In 2000, Peter Schneider began to make his presence felt. Schneider was one of the executives responsible for "Mulan," "Tarzan," "The Lion King" and "Beauty & The Beast" and now wants to make Disney even more family-friendly with dramas such as "Disney's The Kid" and "Remember the Titans." Schneider is also keen to make the most of Disney's franchises, encouraging synergy among the divisions, as evidenced by the upcoming films "Pirates of the Caribbean" and "Country Bears," based on Disneyland rides, "Recess" and "The Tigger Movie" which derive from animated series and the stage production of "The Lion King." Disney will continue to produce adult-oriented fare with Jerry Bruckheimer and others, but recognizes that the road to profit is through multi-division branding and family product.

Also in 2000, Nina Jacobsen became sole president of the Buena Vista Motion Picture Group after Todd Garner left to join Joe Roth and Rob Moore at Revolution.

With theme-park attendance down, investors heard a good deal about the Sept. 11, 2001, effect on Disney's financial health. Travel by American consumers to tourist sites such as Disney's parks was expected to decline after the events of September 11th. Disney's two parks account for a large percentage of total income. Disney had a strong summer season at the box office which helped to offset weak attendance at its theme parks and slowing revenue from its broadcast outlets.

After Peter Schneider's abrupt departure from Disney in June, 2001, Michael Eisner finally promoted Richard Cook to the position of chairman, Walt Disney Studios in February 2002. Eisner had tried to woo talent friendly producers such as Brian Grazer and Armyan Bernstein, but his overtures were rejected. Disney continues to be troubled by a downturn in its theme-park revenues and a slate of movies that limit its market share. Accordingly, analysts downgraded the company's long-term debt several times in 2002. Ironically, Disney's first animated picture Oscar ame for the Japanese anime film, "Spirited Away." Miramax continued its winning ways with "Chicago" surpassing "Good Will Hunting" as its highest grossing film.

2003 set two box office records for Disney with "Finding Nemo," a co-prodution with Pixar, supplanting "Lion King" as their highest grossing film ever and 'The Pirates of the Caribbean: Curse of the Black Pearl," which became the company's highest grossing live action film.and the first PG-13 film released through the Walt Disney Pictures label. Michael Eisner has still not come to terms with Steve Jobs at Pixar for an extension beyond the current deal which given Pixar's track record, will have important implications for the future.

RECENT DISNEY RELEASES

1995:	Crimson Tide, Pocahontas, Toy Story.
1996:	The Hunchback of Notre Dame, Ransom, The Rock.
1997:	ConAir, George of the Jungle, Hercules, Jungle 2 Jungle
1998:	Flubber, Starship Troopers, George of the Jungle, Mr. Magoo.
1999:	Tarzan, Inspector Gadget, The Sixth Sense, The Insider, Toy Story 2
2000:	Dinosaur, Keeping the Faith Disney's The Kid, Coyote Ugly, Gone in Sixty Seconds, Unbreakable.
2001:	Pearl Harbor, The Princess Diaries, The Royal Tenebaums, Atlantis: The Lost Empire.
2002:	Tuck Everlasting, The Santa Clause 2, Lilo & Stitch, Signs, The Rookie, Sweet Home Alabama.
2003	Finding Nemo, Pirates of the Caribbean: The Curse of the Black Pearl, Bringing Down the House, Freaky Friday

RECENT MIRAMAX/DIMENSION RELEASES

1995:	Muriel's Wedding, The Postman.
1996:	The English Patient, Scream, Shine, Sling Blade, Trainspotting.
1997:	Copland, Mimic, She's So Lovely, The House of Yes, Wings of the Dove, Scream 2.
1998:	Good Will Hunting, Jackie Brown.
1999:	An Ideal Husband, Music of the Heart, Princess Mononoke, She's All That, The Faculty, In Too Deep.
2000:	Down to You, The Yards, Scary Movie, Scream 3.
2001:	Chocolat, Spy Kids, Bridget Jones' Diary, The Others, The Shipping News.
2002:	Frida, Spy Kids 2, Ararat, Gangs of New York.
2003	Chicago, Kill Bill: Vol. 1, Scary Movie 3, Spy Kids 3-D: Game Over, Cold Mountain.

DREAMWORKS SKG

Dreamworks SKG was founded in 1994 by director Steven Spielberg, former Disney executive Jeffrey Katzenberg, and record mogul David Geffen. Dreamworks started out with a few dreamy deals including a 10-year, $1 billion HBO licensing agreement with HBO; a $100 million programming partnership with ABC; a $50 million animation studio co-founded with Silicon Graphics; and a $30 million joint venture with Microsoft to produce interactive software. The first release for the infant studio was "The Peacemaker" in September 1997, starring George Clooney. In a surprise move, Dreamworks devised a new distribution paradigm, opting for self-distribution, rather than relying on one of the major studios' distribution arms, and by attempting to book the film theatre-by-theatre in order to optimize grosses.

The fledgling company managed to silence many of its critics, with the success of its movie releases. "Antz,"

proved the highest grossing non-Disney animation film, and the first post-Disney animation film for Mr. Katzenberg. The summer of 1998 brought "Deep Impact" and "Saving Private Ryan" which were the company's first real blockbusters. The company had more of a problem dealing with the development of their new headquarters at Playa Vista, near L.A. Int'l. Airport. The project, announced in December 1995, went stale when Dreamworks began having disagreements with Playa Capital, the owners of the site since 1997. Playa Capital wanted to share some of the proposed studio lot, but Dreamworks opposed the idea. In October, 1998, the two reached an agreement in which Playa Capital surrendered its claim for part of the property.

However, on July 1, 1999, Dreamworks announced that they were pulling out of the deal and temporarily continued to work out of their offices in Universal City.

Jeffrey Katzenberg settled his $500 million suit against Disney for an undisclosed amount somewhere between $100 and $250 million.

DreamWorks enjoyed a good year at the box office in 2000, with two films in the top ten highest grossing movies of the year. Gladiator had an astounding $35 million opening weekend, DreamWorks' strongest to date.

DreamWorks also landed a three-picture distribution deal with Woody Allen, who ended his longtime relationship with Jean Doumanian's Sweetland Films.

The studio scored an early summer hit in 2001 with Shrek, which became that year's highest grossing film with more than $265 million at the box office. Following its release on video, the purchase of 2.5 million "Shrek" DVDs in three days set a record, making it the fastest selling title of the year.

Also in 2001, the company exited its GameWorks venture when the arcades failed to catch on quickly. Burger King formed an ongoing alliance with DreamWorks to promote animated and live-action films, including "Spirit: Stallion of the Cimarron." In other ventures, Imagine Entertainment and DreamWorks SKG planned to team with Microsoft cofounder Paul Allen to launch a web entertainment company that creates and produces Internet-only programming. Called Pop.com, the site would allow users to view short live-action or animation clips, live events, and video on demand. The clips, which the company calls "pops," last one to six minutes per episode

In personnel, Michael De Luca (New Line) became the new President of production at DreamWorks Pictures in 2001.

In 2002, DreamWorks continued to make a strong showing at the box office while signing on new talent like Eddie Murphy and Todd Field to ensure future returns. The studio also secured a $1.5billion in financing to fund production and a third digital animation facility.

Dreamworks continues to produce a reliable slate of a limited number of releases each year. "Catch Me If You Can" did most of its business in 2003, eventually grossing over $100 million in North America. and "Old School" performed well. At year end, Dreamworks announced that it was close to a deal to sell its music unit to Vivendi Universal for $100 million. This marked a narrowing of the focus of the company to a core of motion picture production. Dreamworks had previously scaled back its television plans, its Santa Monica high-tech studio plans never got off the ground, and both Gameworks and an internet site have been abandonned. The company is focusing on both live action and computer animated films such as "Shrek 2" and "Sharkslayer."

DREAMWORKS RELEASES

1997:	Amistad, The Peacemaker, Mouse Hunt.
1998:	Saving Private Ryan, Small Soldiers, Deep Impact, Antz.
1999:	Prince of Egypt, American Beauty, The Haunting,
2000:	Almost Famous, Meet the Parents, Gladiator,

What Lies Beneath.

2001:   Shrek, Evolution, The Last Castle, The Curse
         of the Jade Scorpion.

2002:   The Ring, The Road to Perdition, Spirit: Stallion
         of the Cimarron, The Tuxedo.

2003   Catch Me If You Can, Old School, Head Of State,
         Biker Boyz, House of Sand and Fog.

METRO-GOLDWYN-MAYER/
UNITED ARTISTS, INC.

Metro-Goldwyn-Mayer, Inc. was originally founded by exhibitor Marcus Loew. In 1910, after several years of expansion, Loew organized Loew's Consolidated Enterprises, succeeded the next year by Loew's Theatrical Enterprises. In 1920, Loew's acquired the Metro Pictures Corporation, which later turned out such films as "The Prisoner of Zenda," "Scaramouche" and "The Four Horsemen of the Apocalypse."

In 1924, Loew and his associates, Nicholas and Joseph Schenk and Adolph Zukor, acquired the Goldwyn Company (founded in 1917), and Loew's became the owner of the merged Metro-Goldwyn stock. Loew's then acquired Louis B. Mayer Pictures and the services of Mayer, Irving Thalberg and J. Robert Rubin. The company was renamed Metro-Goldwyn-Mayer.

In 1936 and 1937, legal control of the entire production and distribution organization was vested in Loew's, with Metro-Goldwyn-Mayer used merely as a trade name. On February 6, 1952, the consent decree against Loew's, Inc. provided for a divorce between the producing and distributing phases of the corporation and its domestic exhibition activities and interests. Among notable pictures in the company's history have been "Ben Hur" (silent), "The Thin Man," "Mutiny on the Bounty," "Goodbye Mr. Chips," "Mrs. Miniver," "The Wizard of Oz," "Gone With the Wind," "Meet Me in St. Louis," "King Solomon's Mines," "Ben Hur" (sound), "Doctor Zhivago," "2001: A Space Odyssey" and many more.

In 1973, the company ceased its own distribution and licensed domestic distribution to United Artists and foreign distribution to CIC. In June 1980, the motion picture operations of MGM, Inc. were sold to stockholders as Metro-Goldwyn-Mayer Film Co. United Artists was purchased by the Metro-Goldwyn-Mayer Film Co. in 1981, with the former company becoming a wholly owned subsidiary of the latter. In 1983, the name of the parent company was changed to MGM/UA Entertainment Co.In 1986, Turner Broadcasting System purchased MGM/UA and sold the UA portion to Tracinda Corporation along with MGM motion picture and television production, distribution and the home entertainment division. The MGM lot and lab were sold by Turner to Lorimar-Telepictures. Turner retained only the MGM film library. During this period, MGM-UA produced "Moonstruck," "Rain Man" and "A Fish Called Wanda."

Pathe Communications Corporation acquired MGM/UA in November 1990 with Giancarlo Parretti as chairman. The new company was now renamed MGM-Pathe. In 1991, Parretti was removed as chairman with control given to Alan Ladd Jr., and MGM-Pathe was given a $145 million loan from Credit Lyonnais, allowing them to start film distribution after months of inactivity. Due to loans and transactions totalling $885 million, Pathe was $395 million in debt to Credit Lyonnais. In 1992, Credit Lyonnais bought up 98.5% of MGM, thereby officially disposing of Parretti. Following this move, the company was again renamed Metro-Goldwyn-Mayer, Inc. In July of 1993, Alan Ladd Jr. was replaced by former Paramount Pictures chairman Frank G. Mancuso. In 1994, the distribution arm was once again bearing the title MGM/UA and the revived studio had a major hit with the science-fiction film "Stargate." 1995 proved that Metro-Goldwyn-Mayer was again a major force with a number of critical and financial successes such as "Get Shorty" and "Leaving Las Vegas." Although "The Birdcage" was a big hit, in early 1996 MGM was the target of yet another bidding war. In late July of 1996 MGM was purchased (again) by Kirk Kerkorian and a consortium of investors, including Australian television magnate Kerry Packer, for $1.3 billion.

In 1997, MGM purchased the movie-related business of John Kluge's Metromedia Group, including Orion Pictures.

Less than two years after buying MGM for the third time, Kerkorian put MGM on the auction block again. Faced with a cash crisis, MGM froze television production and made cutbacks in the number of features planned for release.

In October of 1997, MGM, Inc. announced Goldwyn Films, a division specializing in film production that takes on horror pics, oddball comedies and off-beat movies. Not to be confused with Samuel Goldwyn Co., the reincarnation of the company was swallowed up first by Metromedia, then by MGM.

MGM continued to struggle, despite the box office success of "Armageddon" and "Tomorrow Never Dies." By the spring of 1999 however, things were beginning to look up. As part of a plan to revitalize the ailing studio, MGM announced a company-wide restructuring under the new leadership of Alex Yemenidjian, the new chairman & CEO. Through the Orion and PolyGram acquisitions, MGM had the world's largest film library with over 5,000 titles. MGM also won its legal battle with Sony over the rights to the James Bond franchise, negotiated an early termination of its Home Video contract with Warner and signed a multi-picture deal with Miramax.

In October, 1999, MGM posted the results of its first profitable quarter in over three years. A $750 million equity offering was expected to provide funding for new film and television production initiatives while the company turned an eye toward expansion in cable and satellite.

2000 saw the profits continue, with 3rd-quarter results showing improved cash flow and exceeding expectations. Much of the credit went to MGM's film library and aggressive licensing to television and home video and DVD sales though MGM's own distribution channels. MGM also closed several movie-channel deals worldwide for which they can provide current and future content through their film library and new product.

MGM had slated 21 films for 2001 release under new head of production, Alex Gartner and new distribution head, Ian Sutherland. By September of 2001, however, the studio had only released 10 of the 21 films planned, pushing seven releases back to 2002. MGM's biggest successes of the year were "Hannibal," "Bandits" and "Legally Blonde" which helped to offset the disappointing performance of "Original Sin" and "Antitrust."

MGM planned to release a total of 20 films in 2002, mostly at non-peak times in an ongoing effort to pull itself out of the box office doldrums. As it turned out, MGM hit its goal of profitability one quarter earlier than expected. By the third quarter of 2002, in spite of slightly lower than expected box office, the studio was in the black, thanks in part to strong home video performance and tv revenues.

The studio continued to emphasize lower-cost filmmaking, with the production budget for 2003 set at $250 million -- the same level as in 2002, minus costs on the James Bond picture, "Die Another Day." With successes like "Barbershop," which cost only $12 million, the formula seems to be working.

Charman-CEO Alex Yemenidjian continued to stress this theatrical philosophy in 2003, with modestly budgeted films aimed at target demos, with a mix of sequels and remakes such as "Legally Blond 2," "Walking Tall" and "Barbershop 2." Meanwhile, MGM's library continues to generate substantial revenue, with both DVD and home video revenue up over 50% compared to 2002.

RECENT MGM RELEASES

1995:	Get Shorty, Goldeneye, Leaving Las Vegas.
1996:	The Birdcage.
1997:	Hoodlum, Hurricane, Tomorrow Never Dies, Warriors of Virtue.
1998:	The Parent Trap, Armageddon, Mulan, The Horse Whisperer, Six Days Seven Nights.
1999:	Flawless, The World Is Not Enough, Tea With Mussolini, Stigmata, The Thomas Crown Affair.
2000:	Things You Can Tell Just By Looking At Her, Supernova, Original Sin.
2001:	Hannibal, Jeepers Creepers, Legally Blonde, Bandits, No Man's Land, Ghost World.
2002:	Babershop, Die Another Day, Windtalkers, Bowling for Columbine.
2003	Legally Blond 2: Bigger, Bolder, Blonder, Agent Cody Banks, Jeepers Creepers II, Out of Time.

PARAMOUNT PICTURES

Adolph Zukor formed the Engadine Corporation in 1912, which evolved into Famous Players Film Company. W. W. Hodkinson, from General Film Company, formed Paramount Pictures Corporation in 1914, distributing Zukor products and the products of the Jesse L. Lasky Feature Play Company and others. Famous Players-Lasky Corp. was incorporated in 1916. In 1917, twelve production companies merged with it and the corporation integrated production and distribution by acquiring a national distribution system through a merger with Artcraft Pictures and Paramount Pictures. Famous Players-Lasky began acquiring theatres in 1919 with Southern Enterprises, Inc. (135 theatres); followed in later years by New England Theatres, Inc. (50 theatres), the Butterfield Theatre Circuit (70 theatres) and Balaban & Katz (50 theatres). Theatres in the West and Midwest were acquired later.

Paramount's first great star was Mary Pickford. B.P. Schulberg was named head of production in 1925. In April 1927, the corporate name was changed to Paramount Famous Lasky Corporation, and in April of 1930 it became Paramount Publix Corporation, which declared bankruptcy in 1933. Lasky and Schulberg left the company at this point. In 1935, it was reorganized under the name of Paramount Pictures. During this period, the studio's greatest asset was Mae West, whose outrageous hits, "She Done Him Wrong" and "I'm No Angel," caused much furor among censors.

The company regained its footing in the late 1930s and 1940s with such popular stars as Bing Crosby, Bob Hope, Ray Milland and Dorothy Lamour, as well as high-profile films from notable directors Ernst Lubitsch, Preston Sturges, Billy Wilder and Cecil B. DeMille. The 1940s saw such blockbuster hits as "For Whom the Bell Tolls," "Going My Way" and "Samson and Delilah." In 1949, as a result of the Consent Decree, Paramount split into two companies: Paramount Pictures Corp. for production and distribution, and United Paramount Theatres for theatre operation. After WWII, Paramount introduced a new process called VistaVision to compete with 20th Century Fox's Cinema Scope. The first film in the process was the Bing Crosby-Danny Kaye hit musical "White Christmas," followed by Cecil B. DeMille's 1956 remake of "The Ten Commandments."

Paramount merged with Gulf & Western Industries in 1966, with Paramount as a subsidiary retaining its own management. Robert Evans was brought in as production head under Charles Bludhorn, head of Gulf & Western. Bludhorn expanded theatrical film production and increased the company's investment in TV production (an area Paramount had been slow to develop). Evans had great success with "Love Story" (1970) and two Francis Ford Coppola pictures, "The Godfather" (1972) and "The Godfather, Part II" (1974).

With the departure of Evans in 1975, the company moved ahead under Barry Diller as CEO and later under Frank Mancuso, promoted from vice president of distribution to chairman of Paramount Pictures in 1984. The decade of the 1980s brought the company many successes including the "Star Trek" series, the "Indiana Jones" films, "Fatal Attraction," and "Top Gun." Ned Tanen left Universal Pictures to become president of Paramount. In 1989, Gulf and Western changed its name to Paramount Communications, Inc. and Davis began streamlining Paramount Communications in order to focus on entertainment and publishing.

In 1991, Mancuso was replaced by former NBC head Brandon Tartikoff, who resigned in 1992 to be replaced by Sherry Lansing. In the winter of 1994, Viacom, Inc. purchased the company for $9.75 billion. Viacom head Sumner Redstone appointed Jonathan Dolgen, formerly of Sony, to oversee entertainment at both Paramount and Viacom.

Earlier in 1994, the studio soared at the box office with "Forrest Gump" which became the highest grossing movie in Paramount history.

In 1996, Viacom president and CEO Frank Biondi was dismissed with no replacement. That summer, "Mission: Impossible," a remake of the classic television show, became a smash hit, taking in $75 million over the six-day Memorial Day weekend.

Viacom entered 1997 in a slump and with investor confidence low, for the most part due to the poor fortunes of the Viacom-owned Blockbuster Video chain.

In March, 1998, James Cameron's "Titanic" grosses reached a record $1 billion plus, worldwide. Although the revenues of "Titanic" more than covered the $200 million production cost, the hard fact remains that the already phenomenal cost of movie production keeps going up.

Parent company Viacom's fortunes improved dramatically in 1999. Viacom decided to sell a minority stake in the Blockbuster video chain in 1999 and planned to shed the rest over the next year. Viacom agreed to buy TV network CBS in an enormous deal valued at about $35 billion. The acquisition was the biggest media transaction in history to date and catapulted Viacom to the second-largest entertainment firm in the world (behind Time Warner). Chairman Sumner Redstone, who controls 67% of Viacom's voting stock through his privately held company, National Amusements, remained as chairman and CEO of the combined firm. CBS president Mel Karmazin became president and COO.

Like the other studios, Paramount spent 2000 streamlining its operations, ridding itself of costly production deals and creating synergy between broadcast, cable and motion picture divisions for multi-franchise content. In 2001, Paramount joined MGM, Sony Pictures Entertainment, Universal Studios and Warner Bros. in a joint venture to create an on-demand movie service, the first service to offer a broad selection of theatrically-released motion pictures via digital delivery for broadband Internet users in the United States.

The studio enjoyed box office success with "Zoolander," "Rat Race," "Lara Croft: Tomb Raider" and the highly anticipated "Vanilla Sky."

In 2002, Paramount had a few disappointments at the box office. "K-19: The Widowmaker" and "The Four Feathers" underperformed, but were offset by the success of "The Sum of All Fears."

Under the leadership of Sumner Redstone, Viacom has turned into a huge media conglomerate that in addition to Paramount includes; Paramount Television, CBS, MTV, Showtime, Infinity Broadcasting, BET and Blockbuster.

Mel Karmazin is president and COO of Viacom Entertainment Group and Sherry Lansing is chairman of the Motion Picture Group. "The Italian Job" and "How to Lose a Guy in 10 Days" were 2003 hits and "Paycheck" opened at year end.

RECENT PARAMOUNT RELEASES

1996: Mission: Impossible, Star Trek: Resurrection Day.

1997: Event Horizon, Face/Off, The Flood, Howard Stern's Private Parts, Kiss the Girls, The Saint, Titanic (with Fox).

1998: Deep Impact, The Truman Show.

1999: Runaway Bride, Double Jeopardy, The General's Daughter, Angela's Ashes.

2000: Wonder Boys, The Next Best Thing, Mission Impossible 2, Shaft, The Original Kings of Comedy, Rules of Engagement.

2001: What Women Want, Zoolander, Rat Race, Along Came a Spider, Lara Croft: Tomb Raider, Vanilla Sky, Jimmy Neutron.

2002: K-19: The Widowmaker, The Sum of All Fears, Serving Sara, Four Feathers, Narc.

2003 The Italian Job, How to Lose a Guy in 10 Days, Lara Croft Tom Raider: The Cradle of Life, The School of Rock, Paycheck.

TWENTIETH CENTURY FOX

Twentieth Century Fox Film Corporation was started by William Fox, a pioneer in the arcade and nickelodeon business. Fox became a member of the exhibition firm of Fox, Moss and Brill and established the Greater New York Film Rental Company. In 1913, he organized the Box Office Attraction Company, acquiring the services of Winfield Sheehan. On February 1, 1915, the Fox Film Corporation was founded, combining production, exhibition and distribution under one name and with film exchanges in a dozen cities.

In 1917, Fox Films moved into its Sunset Studio in Hollywood. In 1926, Fox introduced Movietone, a sound-on-film process developed by Theodore Case and Earl I. Sponable.

In 1929, Fox began a series of reorganizations and financial deals, principally the purchase by Fox Films of Loew's, Inc. By order of the courts, Fox's ownership of Loew's was later dissolved and various banking interests acquired control of Loew's. During these reorganizations, William Fox's connections with the company were discontinued. Sidney R. Kent became the company's president.

In 1935, The Fox Film Corporation merged with Twentieth Century Pictures, headed by Joseph M. Schenck, and the company assumed its present corporate name. This merger brought Darryl F. Zanuck into the company as vice president in charge of production. Schenck became chairman of the board and continued in that position until his resignation in June 1942, when Wendell L. Wilkie took over the post. Zanuck remained as production head until 1956, when Buddy Adler succeeded him. Upon Adler's death, Robert Goldstein and then Peter G. Levathes took over studio reins. Spyros P. Skouras, a leading theatre operator, became president. On July 25, 1962, Darryl F. Zanuck was elected president and Skouras was named chairman of the board, a position he held until 1969. Richard D. Zanuck was named executive vice president in charge of worldwide production. The Zanucks turned an ailing company into an industry leader. In 1969, Darryl Zanuck was made chairman of the board and CEO and Richard Zanuck was made president.

In 1971, 20th Century Fox Film Corporation weathered a trying proxy fight which had the resounding effect of giving the company added resolve. A new managerial team was elected by the Board of Directors which saw Dennis C. Stanfill succeeding Richard Zanuck as president of the company. Shortly thereafter, Stanfill was elevated to the position of chairman of the board of directors and the studio's CEO. In 1972, Fox's East Coast offices were consolidated with the West Coast offices.

In 1981, Fox merged with a company owned by Marvin Davis. In 1985, Davis sold the company to Rupert Murdoch's News Corporation and Fox, Inc. was formed, consolidating the principal operating units: Twentieth Century Fox Film Corporation, Fox Television Stations, Inc. and Fox Broadcasting Company. In the summer of 1989, revamping signalled a new emphasis on motion pictures. The company appointed Joe Roth, an independent producer and director, as chairman of its major filmmaking unit and renamed it the Fox Film Corporation, marking the first time a film director had run a major studio since Ernst Lubitsch headed Paramount Pictures in 1935. Roth's first picture for Fox, "Die Hard 2," proved to be a hit in the summer of 1990. This was followed by the gigantic success of "Home Alone" which went on to become the second highest grossing film in the studio's history following 1977's "Star Wars." At that time, the science-fiction epic had dethroned the company's previous record-holder, "The Sound of Music."

Roth announced his resignation in December of 1992. His replacement, Peter Chernin, was a Fox television executive. In 1994, Fox released the James Cameron film "True Lies" which reportedly cost in excess of $100 million to produce.

In 1996, "Independence Day" became one of the top-grossing films in history. In the Winter of 1996-97, George Lucas' ground-breaking "Star Wars" trilogy was re-released theatrically, with new state-of-the-art special effects footage added, and all three immediately broke box-office records (again). The 1997 release of James Cameron's "Titanic" was delayed from its scheduled July release until the Fall of 1997, ostensibly due to extensive special-effects re-shooting. With this feature Cameron broke the "Waterworld" record by setting a new negative cost record rumored to be in excess of $200 million. Late in the year, Fox threatened Disney's monopoly on animated musicals, with its own mega-budgeted animated feature release, "Anastasia."

In 1998, Fox, Inc. went public. 20th Century Fox and Fox 2000 now operate under the supervision of Bill Mechanic, chairman of Fox Filmed Entertainment.

In late 1999, Fox Filmed Entertainment promoted Tom Rothman to President of 20th Century Fox Film Group, a newly created executive post charged with overseeing production operations for Twentieth Century Fox and Fox 2000. Elizabeth Gabler replaced Laura Ziskin as head of Fox 2000, which despite failing box office, will continue to produce around 15 pictures per year.

After 1998's record year, box office revenue continued to be healthy in 1999, largely driven by the summer release of "Star Wars Episode 1: The Phantom Menace" which, by Labor Day, had grossed $421 million. It was, however, the only superhit of the year.

2000 brought the blockbusters Big Momma's House and X-Men, though midsummer's Me, Myself and Irene proved to be a disappointment in spite of Jim Carrey's leading role. Earnings for the quarter ending September 30th were $119 million (EBITDA) versus $62 million for the previous year, showing a nice rebound after the post-Titanic doldrums. Fox continues to reap strong returns from its television product. Currently, the company is the largest producer of programming for the U.S. market. Fox began 2001 with "Cast Away," its biggest hit of the year. Other successes included "Dr. Dolittle 2," "Planet of the Apes" and "Moulin Rouge," which was re-released at year's end for Oscar consideration.

2002 was a very successful year for Fox Filmed Entertainment with "Minority Report" and "Star Wars: Episode II-Attack of the Clones," two of the top grossing films of the year.

In 2003 profits for the filmed entertainment division of Fox, Inc. grew more than 40% on contributions from "X2," "Daredevil," "Daddy Day Care" and other films. "Master and Commander: The Far Side of the World" was the year end release. The Studio's successful classic division, Fox Searchlight, also added significantly to the bottom line with hits like, "28 Days Later," Bend It Like Beckham" and 'Antwone Fisher."

RECENT FOX RELEASES

1996:	Broken Arrow, Independence Day.
1997:	Alien Resurrection, Anastasia, Great Expectations, Picture Perfect, Speed II: Cruise Control, Titanic (with Paramount), Volcano.
1998:	The X-Files, Bulworth, Hope Floats, Something About Mary, Dr. Dolittle, Ever After
1999:	Star Wars Episode 1: The Phantom Menace, Anna and the King, Fight Club.
2000:	The Beach, Big Momma's House, Me, Myself and Irene, X-Men, Men of Honor, Cast Away.
2001:	Moulin Rouge, Dr. Dolittle 2, Joe Somebody, Shallow Hal, Planet of the Apes.
2002:	Minority Report, Life or Something Like It, High Crimes, Star Wars: Episode II-Attack of the Clones, Swim Fan.
2003	X2, Daddy Day Care, Daredevil, The League of Extraordinary Gentlemen, Runaway Jury, Master and Commander: The Far Side of the World.

UNIVERSAL PICTURES

Universal Pictures was formed in 1912, when exhibitor Carl Laemmle amalgamated Bison 101, Nestor, Powers and several other organizations, including his own Imp firm. Laemmle had earlier founded Laemmle Film Service and released his first Independent Motion Picture Company feature "Hiawatha" in 1909. Universal launched the star system by hiring Florence Lawrence for $1,000 a week and billing her as "Queen of the Screen." Universal acquired a studio in 1914. In 1915, production was moved to its present site, Universal City. Contracted stars included Wallace Reid, Lon Chaney, Mary Pickford, Rudolph Valentino and Boris Karloff. "Foolish Wives" ("the first million-dollar feature"), "The Hunchback of Notre Dame," "All Quiet On the Western Front" and others were filmed in the decades that followed. On March 16, 1920, Laemmle and R. H. Cochrane assumed complete control of the company.

In 1936, Universal named new management, with J. Cheever Cowdin as chairman of the board and Nate J. Blumberg as president beginning in 1938. Under the new management, Universal embarked upon the policy of developing star values and such stars as Deanna Durbin, Abbott & Costello, Maria Montez, Donald O'Connor and others were put under contract.

In 1946, the company underwent its second transformation, eliminating the production of all so-called "B" pictures, westerns and serials. This followed a merger and acquisition of the assets of International Pictures Corp. of Leo Spitz and William Goetz, who became production heads and the Universal-International trademark emerged. Universal also completed a distribution deal with the J. Arthur Rank organization for the American distribution of British pictures produced by Rank. 1946 also saw the emergence of United World Pictures, a wholly-owned Universal subsidiary, to handle the production and distribution of non-theatrical films including the Bell and Howell Film Library and Castle Films.

1950 saw the resignation of Cowdin with Blumberg assuming full command. Alfred E. Daff, who had been foreign sales manager, assumed the top post in the foreign distribution set-up and then became director of world sales. In 1951, Decca Records acquired approximately 28% of Universal's common stock to make it the largest single stockholder in the company. In 1952, Decca Records became the controlling stockholder of Universal. Milton R. Rackmil, president of Decca Records, was made a member of the Universal board and subsequently elected president of Universal in July, 1952.

In 1962, MCA consolidated with Decca and made Universal Pictures Company the theatrical film producing division of MCA, Inc. In 1964, the creation of the Universal City Studios image started with the separate motion picture and television arms. That same year, the company began its profitable Universal Studios Tour. In 1966, Universal Pictures became a division of Universal City Studios, Inc., a subsidiary of MCA, Inc. The company entered a successful period of high-profile hits including "Thoroughly Modern Millie," "Airport," "American Graffiti," "The Sting," "Earthquake" and Steven Spielberg's "Jaws," which in 1975 became the highest grossing movie to that date.

In 1982, Universal released Steven Spielberg's "E.T.: The ExtraTerrestrial," which became the top-grossing film of all time, racking up over $228 million in film rentals in the domestic market alone. Other recent success have included the "Back to the Future" series, "Field of Dreams," "Born on the Fourth of July," and "Fried Green Tomatoes."

1990 saw two major events in the studio's recent history. A fire swept through the backlot in Universal City destroying acres of sets and causing millions of dollars worth of damage.

MCA Inc. was purchased by the Matsushita Electrical Industrial Company for an estimated $6.6 billion, the most expensive sale of an American company to the Japanese in history. In 1993, Spielberg's "Jurassic Park" grossed over $300 million, placing it as the second highest grossing film of all time right behind "E.T." Spielberg was also responsible for "Schindler's List," the first black-and-white Academy Award winner for Best Picture in 33 years. Seagram Co. purchased 80% of MCA Inc. in 1995 for $5.7 billion, with Seagram's president & CEO Edgar Bronfman Jr. serving as acting chairman of the entertainment company. With this change of ownership, Lew Wasserman stepped down and was named chairman emeritus, and Sid Sheinberg ended his 22-year reign as president. In the summer of 1995, Universal released "Waterworld," which held the dubious distinction of being the most expensive movie ever made to date, with estimates of its cost ranging as high as $175 million. In spite of critical drubbings and a lackluster domestic box office, Waterworld went on to earn money for the company in the international market. "The Lost World," Steven Spielberg's sequel to his mega-hit "Jurassic Park," opened Memorial Day weekend to a record-breaking $90.2 million at approximately 6000 screens (nearly one-quarter of the screens in the United States). Universal also purchased art house distributor October Films in 1997.

The departure of Steven Spielberg and Amblin Entertainment placed the burden on Ron Howard and partner Brian Grazer's Imagine Entertainment as Universal Pictures' major provider. Although the history between Universal and Imagine goes back some ten years, and although the company has accounted for more than $2.6 billion in grosses, Universal's need for Imagine to put out box office hits has deepened in Mr. Spielberg's absence. To fill the hole left by Mr. Spielberg, Universal has also signed production deals with Will Smith, Penny Marshall, Mike Nichols and Danny Devito.

Universal went through some executive cuts in April 1998. Although there were no explanations offered for the restructuring, speculation arose that the changes were the by-product of Edgar Bronfman Jr.'s, dissatisfaction with Universal's performance in 1997-98.

Universal's lagging sales and string of disappointing films in 1998 (such as "Meet Joe Black" and "Babe: Pig in the City") resulted in Universal posting more than $130 million in losses. Universal's film business turned the corner in 1999 thanks to the success of its releases such as "The Mummy," "Notting Hill" and "American Pie." The company's box office grosses for 1999 exceeded $775 million, compared to 1998's $315 million. In addition, the studio's market share grew from 2.4 percent in 1998 to 12.9 percent in 1999, without adding extra movies to its roster.

In 2000, merger-mania hit Universal. In a three-way deal worth $34 billion, Seagram (Universal's 92% owner) was acquired by French companies Vivendi and Canal Plus to create a multinational media giant. The merger was approved by the EC, simplifying the process that has plagued the AOL-TimeWarner merger. The new company, Vivendi Universal, was chaired by Jean-Marie Messier (Vivendi), Pierre Lescure (Canal Plus) and Edgar Bronfman Jr. (Seagram) who offered the Studio executives his assurance that film production would be business-as-usual despite the merger.

Meanwhile, Brian Grazer and Ron Howard's Imagine Entertainment signed on for another five years with Universal after a brief flirtation with DreamWorks, guaranteeing the box-office health of Universal in the near future.

In 2001 the company bought music download site MP3.com for its music group and textbook publisher Houghton Mifflin for its publishing unit. Also in 2001, Vivendi Universal agreed to buy News Corp.'s 50% stake in Stream (Italian pay-TV operator), which it plans to merge with its Telepiu service, and form a new entity. Reducing its reliance on magazine advertising revenue, the company in 2001 agreed to sell its trade and medical publishing businesses to British investment firm Cinven. But the biggest news of the year came when Vivendi Universal announced that it would merge the operations of Universal Studios and French movie company Studio Canal.

Universal's Home Video unit scored with the release of Shrek (DreamWorks) which became the fastest selling DVD of the year, setting a record in its first weekend. Box office was also strong with summer blockbusters "Jurassic Park III" and "The Mummy Returns." These and other hits helped parent company Vivendi to show 30% growth in third-quarter sales.

In 2002, the French media company Vivendi Universal bought the entertainment assets of USA Networks (now named USA Interactive) and created Vivendi Universal Entertainment. VUE's primary holdings include Universal Studios and Universal Television Group. Vivendi Universal owns 93% of VUE; Chairman and CEO Barry Diller's USA Interactive, 6%.

In July, 2002, embattled VUE Chairman Jean-Marie Messier was ousted from the company and later replaced by Jean-Rene Fourtou. While VUE was doing well with its filmed and television entertainment, the parent company VUE faced a debt crisis and made plans to sell off its publishing businesses and restructure its remaining assets.

After a prolonged and sometimes rancorous auction by VUE in 2003 that involved many of the largest media companies, Universal will be acquired by NBC in early 2004. Universal Pictures had a strong year on a comparative basis with releases such as "American Wedding,: "Seabiscuit" and "Bruce Almighty." Interestingly, Nikki

Rocco remains the only woman to ever head a major studios distribution arm.

RECENT UNIVERSAL RELEASES

1996: Dragonheart, Flipper, The Nutty Professor.

1997: Dante's Peak, For Richer For Poorer, The Jackal, Leave It to Beaver, Liar, Liar, The Lost World.

1998: BASEketball, Out of Sight, Primary Colors, Mercury Rising, Meet Joe Black.

1999: The Mummy, Notting Hill, America Pie, The Bone Collector, The Best Man, EDtv.

2000: Meet the Parents, The Nutty Professor II: The Klumps, Erin Brokovich, U-571, Billy Elliot, How the Grinch Stole Christmas, The Family Man, Head Over Heels.

2001: The Fast and the Furious, American Pie 2, Jurassic Park III, The Mummy Returns, Spy Game, A Beautiful Mind.

2002: D-Tox, Dragonfly, The Bourne Identity, Red Dragon, Undercover Brother.

2003 Bruce Almighty, Hulk, Seabiscuit, The Rundown, Dr Seuss' The Cat in the Hat.

WARNER BROS.

Warner Bros. Pictures, Inc. may be said to have its origins in the 90-seat Cascade Theatre set up by Harry Warner and his three brothers, Sam, Albert and Jack in New Castle, PA, in 1905. The brothers soon branched into distribution, establishing film exchanges in Pennsylvania and Virginia. In 1913, they moved into film production with Warner Features. Warner Features' first production was 1918's "My Four Years in Germany." In 1920-22 they averaged only two or three features per year. Warner Bros. was incorporated in 1923 to produce as well as distribute and release 14 pictures, including the first of the famous Rin-Tin-Tin series. Scripts were written by Darryl F. Zanuck, an ambitious writer who soon worked his way up to become the company's production chief under Jack Warner. Harry was president; Albert, treasurer; and Sam shared production responsibilities with Jack. Zanuck stayed until 1933 and was succeeded by Hall Wallis, who held the post for the next decade.

In 1925, Warner acquired Vitagraph, Inc., which operated 34 exchanges in the U.S. and Canada, and two other concerns with foreign exchanges. That same year, the company began its experiments with sound, collaborating with Western Electric to produce a sound-on-disc process (called Vitaphone) for synchronized film sound.

The first Vitaphone program premiered in August 1926, including some musical shorts and the feature "Don Juan" with John Barrymore backed by a full musical and sound-effects track. Owing to this success, the studio released the feature "The Jazz Singer" in October 1927, with dialogue and certain musical numbers in sound and in 1928, "the first 100% all-talking picture—Lights of New York," a one-hour feature that broke box office records. In 1927, Sam Warner died.

The new sound technology brought Warner Bros. to the forefront of the industry. It further expanded its theatre holdings and studio facilities, acquiring the Stanley Company of America theatre circuit in 1928, First National Pictures which had a 135-acre studio and back lot, along with exchanges and theatres, and a number of music publishing companies. Those acquisitions greatly helped in the production of the Warner Bros. musicals including "Forty-Second Street," the "Gold Diggers" series, "Footlight Parade" and others. Along with the other motion picture companies, Warner Bros. suffered in the early days of the Depression. Sales of some assets and theatres, along with drastic cuts in production costs, enabled the company to recover and to take advantage of the boom in the 1940s.

In 1953, the company completed the reorganization it was forced to undergo by the government's Consent Decree. Stockholders approved a plan to separate the company into two entities: the theatres were sold to Fabian Enterprises, Inc., and the company was renamed Stanley Warner Corporation. The "new" production-distribution company remained Warner Bros. Pictures, Inc. In 1956, Harry and Albert sold their shares in the company to an investment group headed by Serge Semenenko and Charles Allen Jr. Jack retained his shares, remaining the largest single stockholder and becoming president of the company. The Warner pre-1948 film library of 850 features and 1,000 shorts was sold to United Artists in 1956.

On July 15, 1967, a subsidiary of Seven Arts Productions Limited (a Canadian-based company headed by Eliot Hyman) acquired substantially all the assets and business of Warner Bros. Pictures, Inc. The company subsequently was called Warner Bros.-Seven Arts Limited. In 1969, Warner Bros.-Seven Arts was acquired by Kinney National Service, Inc., headed by Steven J. Ross, and changed its name in 1971 to Warner Communications, Inc. The studio reverted to the original name of Warner Bros. and appointed Ted Ashley as studio chief. The studio's successes during this period included "Superman," "The Exorcist" and "All the President's Men." Robert A. Daly succeeded Ashley as Warner Bros. chairman and CEO in 1980.

In 1989, Warner Communications was acquired by Time, Inc. in an $18 billion merger that created one of the largest communications and entertainment companies in the world. The new Time-Warner, consisted of Warner and its subsidiaries, Time Publishing, Home Box Office, Cinemax, HBO Video and American Television & Communications Corp. John Peters and Peter Guber were instrumental in aiding Warner to rebound from a two-year box office slump. In the summer of 1989, Peters and Guber produced "Batman," which brought in domestic rentals of over $150 million, making it the fourth top-grossing film of all time to that date.

In early 1991, the company announced a partnership with several European entertainment companies to produce 20 films. Time-Warner continues to hold a 50% interest in Cinamerica Limited Partnership, a company that includes Mann Theatres and Festival Theatres in California, and Trans-Lux Theatres in the East. In October 1991, two Japanese companies, Toshiba Corp. and C. Itoh & Co., paid $500 million each for a combined 12.5% stake in the company. In May 1993, the company created a new division, Warner Bros. Family Entertainment, to release movies aimed at the children's market including the hit "Free Willy."

In the autumn of 1995, Time-Warner began negotiations for the $7.3 billion purchase of the Turner Broadcasting System. These negotiations were the subject of intense FTC scrutiny in 1996, due to the 20% stake cable giant TCI held in Turner, but were finally approved by Warner Bros. stockholders on October 10, 1996. Although Turner-owned New Line Cinema was originally to be auctioned off, in May of 1997 the company was removed from the sale shelf, with no plans for its future by Time-Warner, but with its release schedule and creative autonomy intact.

After 18 stagnant months, New Line scored big with the release of "The Wedding Singer." The success was due to the new formula of releasing quirky, non-studio material such as, "Wag the Dog" and "Boogie Nights." The company is also concentrating on producing movies with potential ancillary value. New Line's arthouse division, Fine Line Features, is going through changes of its own, under the leadership of its new president, Mark Ordesky.

In April of 1998, New Line announced the launching of Fine Line's international and distribution division, Fine Line International, headed by Mr. Ordesky and New Line International president, Rolf Mittweg.

In 1998, New Line's domestic ticket sales climbed 42%, and the studio's 8% market share put it ahead of majors like Universal Pictures, Dreamworks, and MGM for a sixth-place finish at the U.S. box office. New Line grossed over $200 million with "Austin Powers: The Spy Who Shagged Me," continuing its boxoffice success. Sara Risher celebrated her 25th year with New Line Cinema by creating a new in-house production company called ChickFlicks.

In July, 1999, Robert Daly and Terry Semel stunned the entertainment world by telling Time Warner Chairman Gerald Levin and other directors of the studio's parent company that they would not renew their contracts after their 19-year tenure with the company.

Effective October, 1999, Barry Meyer, executive vice president and COO of Warner Bros., was promoted to chairman and CEO, and Alan Horn, chairman and CEO of Castle Rock Entertainment, became president and COO. 1999 box office was favorable, with four films surpassing the $100 million domestic box office mark: "You've Got Mail," "Analyze This," "The Matrix" and "Wild Wild West."

In 2000, Time-Warner agreed to an acquisition by AOL. Gerald Levin became the CEO of the newly merged concern that would likely pursue new opportunities for cable and online distribution.

Both Warner and New Line enjoyed box office success in 2000, with the phenomenal grosses of "The Perfect Storm" and the impressive opening of "The Cell." Its 2000 releases of "Pokemon: The Movie," "The Powerpuff Girls" and "Harry Potter" created synergy with other Time-Warner owned units, especially offering numerous opportunities for tv and consumer-product merchandising

Warner's slate for 2001 included "AI: Artificial Intelligence," "Training Day," the highly anticipated star-studded "Ocean's Eleven" and the first in the Harry Potter franchise which generated an advance ticket-buying frenzy. Warner's future looks bright with the Matrix sequels, a new Batman, and several Harry Potter projects to come. With so many merchandising tie-ins in the pipeline, Warner created a new position for Brad Ball (McDonalds)—Executive Vice President, Domestic Corporate Marketing.

In 2001, New Line scored with "Rush Hour 2" which grossed over $225 million.

America Online acquired Time Warner in 2001, making Warner Bros. part of AOL Time Warner. Following the merger, Warner Bros. transferred its majority interest in the WB Television Network to sister company Turner Broadcasting. It also closed down all of its Warner Bros. Studio Stores citing poor sales and declining interest in movie-related merchandise. Later that year Warner Bros. Pictures released "Harry Potter and the Sorcerer's Stone" which made $93.5 million in domestic box office receipts in its opening weekend, breaking Universal Pictures' $72.1 million record with Jurassic Park: The Lost World. The film went on to become 2001's top-grossing film in domestic box office receipts.

2002 was a very positive year for Warner, with several high-grossing films, and more sequels (The Matrix, Harry Potter) in the pipeline.

Symptomatic of the problems of the company for the last several years, Time Warner planned to remove the "AOL" from its corporate moniker in October 2003. The SEC and the Department of Justice had been looking at the corporations accounting practices since at least the summer of 2002 and both Richard Parson and Steve Case have been subpoenaed in the ongoing probe. However, the filmed entertainment division had an extremely strong year driven by such titles as "The Matrix Reloaded," "The Matrix Revolutions" and "Terminator 3: The Rise of the Machines."

New Line continued to scare up big boxoffice numbers in 2003 with "Freddy V. Jason," "Texas Chainsaw Massacre" and the conclusion to the Tolkien trilogy, "The Lord of the Rings: The Return of the King."

RECENT WARNER BROS. RELEASES

1995:   Ace Ventura: When Nature Calls, Batman Forever, The Bridges of Madison County.

1996:   Eraser, Executive Decision, Space Jam, A Time to Kill, Twister.

1997:   Batman and Robin, Conspiracy Theory, Contact, Father's Day, L.A. Confidential.

1998:   The Negotiator, Lethal Weapon 4, A Perfect Murder, City of Angels, You've Got Mail.

1999:   The Matrix, Deep Blue Sea, Iron Giant, Three Kings, The Green Mile.

2000:   The Perfect Storm, Any Given Sunday, The Art of War, Space Cowboys, Pokemon.

2001:   AI: Artificial Intelligence, Harry Potter and the Sorcerer's Stone, Training Day, Ocean's Eleven, The Lord of the Rings: The Fellowship of the Ring.

2002:   The Adventures of Pluto Nash, Ballistic: Ecks vs. Sever, City by the Sea, The Divine Secrets of the Ya-Ya Sisterhood, Analyze That, Harry Potter and the Chamber of Secrets, Scooby Doo.

2003   The Matrix Reloaded, Terminator 3: Rise of the Machines, Kangaroo Jack, The Matrix Revolutions.

RECENT NEW LINE/FINE LINE RELEASES

1995:   Don Juan DeMarco, Mortal Kombat, Seven.

1996:   The Grass Harp, The Island of Doctor Moreau, Last Man Standing, Michael.

1997:   Austin Powers, Crash, Dark City, Mortal Kombat II: Annihilation, Spawn, Boogie Nights.

1998:   Lost In Space, The Wedding Singer, Woo, Wag the Dog.

1999:   Austin Powers: The Spy Who Shagged Me, The Bachelor, Magnolia.

2000:   Frequency, The Cell, Dancer in the Dark, Saving Grace, State and Main.

2001:   Rush Hour 2, The Lord of the Rings: Fellowship of the Ring, Blow, I Am Sam, Life As A House, Hedwig and the Angry Inch, The Anniversary Party.

2002:   Austin Powers in Goldmember, Mr. Deeds, All About the Benjamins, About Schmidt

2003   The Lord of the Rings: The Two Towers, FreddyVs. Jason, Elf, The Lord of the Rings: The Return of the King.

PROTECT YOUR INDUSTRY.

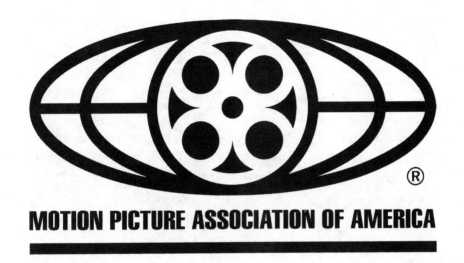

MOTION PICTURE ASSOCIATION OF AMERICA ®

REPORT FILM PIRACY TO THE
MPAA ANTI-PIRACY HOTLINE:

1-800-NO-COPYS

EMAIL: HOTLINE@MPAA.ORG.

MOTION PICTURE
PRODUCERS & DISTRIBUTORS

Also see Large Format Producers, Film Distributors in Key Cities, Non-Theatrical Motion Picture Companies.

ABANDON ENTERTAINMENT
(Motion picture & TV producer)
135 W. 50th St., Ste. 2305, New York, NY 10020. (212) 246-4445. FAX: (212) 397-8361. www.abandonent.com
email: abandonent@abandonent.com
PRESIDENT & CEO
Marcus Ticotin
PRESIDENT, ABANDON PICTURES
Karen Lauder
ASSISTANT V.P. & DIRECTOR, CREATIVE AFFAIRS
Deborah Marinoff

ABILENE PICTURES
Abilene Pictures, PMB #P, 3435 Ocean Park Blvd. Ste. 112, Santa Monica, CA 90405.
DIRECTOR
Gregory Hoblit
V.P., DEVELOPMENT
Beverly Graf
ASSOCIATE PRODUCER
Patricia Graf

ACAPPELLA PICTURES
(Motion picture & TV producer)
8271 Melrose Ave., Ste. 101, Los Angeles, CA 90046. (323) 782-8200. FAX: (323) 782-8210.
PRESIDENT
Charles Evans Jr.
PRODUCTION & DEVELOPMENT
Charmine Parcero

ACE STORYBOARD ON DEMAND
(Storyboards, concepts art & flesh animation)
31455 West St., S. Laguna Beach, CA 90046. (949) 499-9964. FAX: (949) 4999-9964. www.markpacella.com
ART DIRECTOR
Mark Pacella

ACRONYM ENTERTAINMENT
(Talent management; producer)
9350 Wilshire Blvd., Ste. 328, Beverly Hills, CA 90212. (310) 247-9119. FAX: (310) 247-9974. email: ebugg@acronyment.com
PARTNERS
Laina Cohn
Michael Sugar

ORLY ADELSON PRODUCTIONS
(Motion picture & TV producer)
12304 Santa Monica Blvd., Ste. 115, Los Angeles, CA 90025. (310) 442-2012. FAX: (310) 442-2013.
PRESIDENT
Orly Adelson
DIRECTOR, DEVELOPMENT
Jonathan Eskenas

AFFINITY FILMS INTERNATIONAL LTD.
6512 Hayes Dr., Los Angeles, CA 90048. (323) 571-0777.
www.affinityfilms.com
PRODUCERS/DIRECTORS
Mark Hammond
Simon MacCorkindale
PRODUCERS
Ira Besserman

MINDY AFFRIME PRODUCTIONS
1429 Avon Park Terrace, Los Angeles, CA 90026. (323) 661-4481. FAX: (323) 644-0680. email: minaffrime@aol.com
PRESIDENT & PRODUCER
Mindy Affrime

AGAMEMNON FILMS, INC.
(Production)
650 N. Bronson Ave., Ste. B-225, Los Angeles, CA 90004. (323) 960-4066.
PRESIDENT
Fraser C. Heston
VICE PRESIDENT
John Stronach
PRODUCER
Alex Butler

ALCON ENTERTAINMENT, LLC
(Film & tv production)
10390 Santa Monica Blvd., Ste. 250, Los Angeles, CA 90025. (310) 789-3040. FAX: (310) 789-3060. email: info@alconent.com
CO-PRESIDENT & CO-FOUNDER
Broderick Johnson
CO-PRESIDENT & CO-FOUNDER
Andrew A. Kosove
SENIOR V.P. & CFO
Scott Parish
SENIOR V.P., DEVELOPMENT
Steven P. Wegner
DIRECTOR, FINANCE & OPERATIONS
Rodney Quon
DIRECTOR, HUMAN RESOURCES & OPERATIONS
Chris Alexander
V.P., PRODUCTION
Kira Davis
V.P., TELEVISION
Jamie Wager
TV, COORDINATOR
Amy Berg
CREATIVE EXECUTIVE
Christopher Fealy
PRODUCTION CONTROLLER
Yolanda Cochran
EXECUTIVE ASSISTANTS
Dina Delkhah
Greg Rogers
Nathan Moore
Robyn Harwood
Jennifer Petruniak
OFFICE RUNNER
Rudy Darden
RECEPTIONIST
Jessica Soto

ALFA-FILM ENTERPRISES, INC.
(Motion picture & TV producer & distributor)
264 S. La Cienega Blvd., #1138, Beverly Hills, CA 90211. (323) 882-6193. FAX: (323) 882-6103.
email: sidarfov@earthlink.net
PRESIDENT
Anatoly A. Fradis
DEVELOPMENT EXECUTIVE
Felix Kleiman

ALIVE FILMS
(Motion picture producer)
3264 S. Kihei, Kihei, HI 96753. (808) 891-0022. FAX: (808) 879-2734. email: alivewow@maui.net
CHAIRMAN
Shep Gordon

ALLIANCE ATLANTIS COMMUNICATIONS, INC.
(Broadcaster, creator & intl. distributor of filmed entertainment)
121 Bloor St. E., Ste. 1500, Toronto, ON, Canada M4W 3M5. (416) 967-1174. FAX: (416) 960-0971.
www.allianceatlantis.com email: info@allianceatlantis.com
CHAIRMAN & CEO
Michael MacMillan
CEO, MOTION PICTURE DISTRIBUTION GROUP
Victor Loewy
SENIOR EXECUTIVE V.P. & CFO
W. Judson Martin
EXECUTIVE V.P., CORPORATE & PUBLIC AFFAIRS
Heather E. Conway
EXECUTIVE V.P., MOTION PICTURE PRODUCTION
Bill House
EXECUTIVE V.P. & GM, MOTION PICTURE DIST. GROUP
Jim Sherry
PRESIDENT, MOTION PICTURE DISTRIBUTION GROUP
Patrice Théroux
PRESIDENT, PRODUCTION, ENTERTAINMENT GROUP
Seaton McLean
CEO, ENTERTAINMENT GROUP
Peter Sussman
PRESIDENT, DISTRIBUTION, ENTERTAINMENT GROUP
Ted Riley
PRESIDENT, ODEON FILMS
Bryan Gliserman
PRESIDENT, ALLIANCE ATLANTIS VIVAFILM
Guy Gagnon

S.V.P., ACQ. & SALES, ALLIANCE ATLANTIS VIVAFILM
Patrick Roy
S.V.P., PUBLICITY, ENTERTAINMENT GROUP
Pam Wilson
S.V.P., MARKETING & PUBLICITY, ENTERTAINMENT GROUP
Gail Rivett
V.P., PUBLICITY & PROMOTION, MOTION PICTURE
DISTRIBUTION GROUP
Susan Smythe
V.P., MARKETING, MOTION PICTURE DISTRIBUTION
GROUP
Frank Mendicino
MANAGING DIRECTOR, INTL. MOTION PICTURE SALES
Charlotte Mickie
DIRECTOR, PUBLICITY, MOTION PICTURE DIST. GROUP
Carrie Wolfe
808 Wilshire Blvd., Third Flr., Santa Monica, CA 90401. TEL:
(310) 899-8000. FAX: (310) 899-8100.
London: 184-192 Drummond St., 2nd Flr., London, United
Kingdom, NW1 3HP. TEL: (44 207) 391-6900. FAX: (44 207)
383-0404.
Montreal: 5 Place Ville-Marie, Ste. 1435, Montreal, PQ, H3B
2G2, Canada. TEL: (514) 878-2282. FAX: (514) 878-2419.
Dublin: 40 Westland Row, Dublin 2, Ireland. TEL: (353-1) 449-
8400. FAX: (353-1) 449-8470.
Shannon: Block 1, Unit C, Shannon Business Park, Shannon,
Co. Clare, Ireland. TEL: (35 36) 147-2329. FAX: (35 36) 147-
2228.
Edmonton: 3720-76 Ave., Edmonton, AB, Canada, T6B 2N9.
TEL: (780) 440-2022. FAX: (780) 440-3400.
Halifax: 1668 Barrington St., Ste. 500, Halifax, NS, Canada,
B3J 2A2. TEL: (902) 420-1577. FAX: (902) 420-0521.
Sydney: 401 Darling St., Ste. 2, Balmain, Australia NSW 2041.
TEL: (61 29) 810-8922. FAX: (61 29) 810-8966.

ALLIED STARS
(Motion picture producer)
10202 W. Washington Blvd., Lean Bldg., #423, Culver City, CA
90232-3195. (310) 244-5188. FAX: (310) 244-6499.
SENIOR V.P., PRODUCTION
Melissa Henning
V.P., DEVELOPMENT
Kelly Jones

ALPHAVILLE
5555 Melrose Ave., DeMille Bldg., 2nd Flr., Hollywood, CA
90038-3197. (323) 956-4803. FAX: (323) 862-1616.
PRODUCER & PARTNER
Sean Daniel
PRODUCER & PARTNER
Jim Jacks
SENIOR V.P.
Kate Guinzburg
VICE PRESIDENT
Jennifer Moyer
VICE PRESIDENT
Susanna Jolly
PRODUCTION EXECUTIVES
Ty Warren
Rebecca Nelson
STORY EDITOR
Carlo Hart
EXECUTIVE ASSISTANTS
Chris Palmer
Amy Heidish
Andrea Chu
Jody Kay

AMAZING MOVIES
(Motion picture worldwide producer & distributor)
7471 Melrose Ave., Ste. 7, Los Angeles, CA 90046. (323) 852-
1396. FAX: (323) 658-7265. www.amazingpix.com
email: amazingmov@aol.com
PRESIDENT
Douglas C. Witkins
VICE PRESIDENT
Koing Kuoch
PUBLICITY
Matt Giedlinski

AMC ENTERTAINMENT INC.
(For theatres listing see AMC in Theatre Circuits section)
106 W. 14th St., Kansas City, MO 64105. (816) 221-4000.
www.amctheatres.com
CHAIRMAN & CEO
Peter C. Brown
EXECUTIVE V.P. & CFO
Craig R. Ramsey
SENIOR V.P., TREASURY
James V. Beynon
PRESIDENT & COO OF AMERICAN MULTI-CINEMA, INC.
Philip M. Singleton
EXECUTIVE V.P., NORTH AMERICAN OPERATIONS
John D. McDonald

AMC FILM MARKETING, INC.
(Motion picture licensing)
21700 Oxnard St., Ste. 640, Woodland Hills, CA 91367.(818)
587-6400. FAX: (818) 587-6498.
AMC FILM PRESIDENT
Richard M. Fay

AMERICAN NEW WAVE FILMS
(Motion picture, independent film & TV producer)
7775 Sunset Blvd., Ste. 150, Hollywood, CA 90046. (323) 850-
1700. FAX: (323) 850-1788.
WRITER & DIRECTOR & PRODUCER
Norman Thaddeus Vane
LINE PRODUCER
Gus Raner

AMERICAN WORLD PICTURES
6355 Topanga Canyon Blvd., Ste. 428, Woodland Hills, CA
91367. (818) 715-1480. FAX: (818) 715-1081.
email: info@americanworldpictures.com
PRESIDENT
Mark L. Lester
PRESIDENT, PRODUCTION
Dana Duborsky
EXECUTIVE V.P., DISTRIBUTION
Terese Linden-Kohn
V.P., ACQUISITIONS & CO-PRODUCTIONS
Lawrence Silverstein
DIRECTOR, DEVELOPMENT
Rafael Pujals

AMERICAN ZOETROPE
(Motion picture & TV producer)
6747 Milner Rd., Los Angeles, CA 90068. (323) 851-8808.
FAX: (323) 851-8803. www.zoetrope.com
CEO
Jay Shoemaker
SENIOR V.P., PRODUCTION & DEVELOPMENT
Bobby Rock
ASSISTANT
Brendan Kenney

AM PRODUCTIONS & MANAGEMENT
8899 Beverly Blvd., Ste. 713, Los Angeles, CA 90048. (310)
275-9081. FAX: (310) 275-9082. email: bramam@aol.com
ACTOR & EXECUTIVE PRODUCER
Ann-Margret
ACTOR & DIRECTOR & EXECUTIVE PRODUCER
Burt Reynolds
EXECUTIVE PRODUCER
Alan Margulies
EXECUTIVE PRODUCER & WRITER
Roger Smith

AMSELL ENTERTAINMENT, INC.
(Motion picture, TV & video distributor)
12001 Ventura Pl., Ste. 404, Studio City, CA 91604. (818) 766-
8500. FAX: (818) 766-7873. email: amsellent@aol.com
PRESIDENT
Alan Solomon

CRAIG ANDERSON PRODUCTIONS
(Motion picture, independent film & TV producer)
9696 Culver Blvd., Ste.208, Culver City, CA 90232. (310) 841-
2555. FAX: (310) 841-5934. email: info@cappix.com
EXECUTIVE PRODUCER
Craig Anderson
EXECUTIVE V.P., DEVELOPMENT
Phil Kruener
PRODUCTION EXECUTIVE
Kerry Bailey
CREATIVE EXECUTIVE
Noah Jones
DEVELOPMENT ASSOCIATE
Dani de Jesus

ANGEL ARK PRODUCTIONS
(Motion picture & TV producer)
5042 Wilshire Blvd., Ste. 592, Los Angeles, CA 90036. (818)
981-8833. FAX: (818) 981-8412.
CREATIVE PARTNERS
Jason Alexander
Jenny Birchfield-Eick (Features & Television)

ANGEL FILMS/PHOEENIX ORG
(Motion picture & TV series producer; computer generated)
967 Highway 40, New Franklin, MO 65284-9778. (573) 698-
3900. FAX: (573) 698-3900. email: Angelphoeenixorg@aol.com
PRESIDENT
Wilhelm: Lord Du Sackville
CEO & CFO
Joyce L. Chow
V.P., PRODUCTION
Matthew P. Eastman

ANGRY DRAGON ENTERTAINMENT

(Motion picture & TV producer)
10202 W. Washington Blvd., Culver City, CA 90232. (310) 244-6996. FAX:(310) 244-0996.
CONTACTS
Dean Cain
Laura Bass
Mike Carr

APATOW PRODUCTIONS

c/o Revolution Studios, 2900 W. Olympic Blvd., Santa Monica, CA 90404. (310) 255-7026.
PRODUCER & WRITER
Judd Apatow
ASSISTANT TO JUDD APATOW
Adam Karasick

APOSTLE PICTURES

(Motion picture, independent film & TV producer)
The Ed Sullivan Theater, 1697 Broadway, Ste. 906, New York, NY 10019. (212) 541-4323. FAX: (212) 541-4330.
ACTOR & DIRECTOR & PRODUCER
Denis Leary
PRESIDENT, MOTION PICTURES & TV
Jim Serpico
CREATIVE EXECUTIVE
Tom Sellitti

APPLEDOWN FILMS, INC.

(Motion picture, independent film & TV producer)
9687 W. Olympic Blvd., Beverly Hills, CA 90212. (310) 552-1833. FAX: (310) 552-1331.
PRODUCER & WRITER
Larry Spiegel
PRODUCER
Judy Goldstein

AQUARIUS RELEASING, INC./AQUARIUS MEDIA CORP.

(Producer, distributor; exhibition)
P.O. Box 590 Englewood, NJ 07631. (201) 541-1912. FAX: (201) 541-2365.
CEO
Terry Levene
SECRETARY & TREASURER
Sarai Berenstein
PUBLICITY & ADVERTISING DEPARTMENT
Wayne Weil
Irving Russell (NY & Philadelphia branch office)
FOREIGN SALES
Harry Sloan
U.S. SYNDICATION & CABLE
Leon Silverman

MARK ARCHER ENTERTAINMENT

c/o New Hollywood Studios, 6633 E. State Blvd., Ste. 100B, Fort Wayne, IN 46815. (260) 486-8831.
PRESIDENT
Mark Archer

ARCIMAGE FILMS

(Motion picture & TV producer)
12358 Deerbrook Lane, Los Angeles, CA 90049. (310) 440-9596. FAX: (310) 440-2096.
PRODUCERS
Elizabeth Karl
John Roach
John Faunce
EXECUTIVE CONSULTANT
Ronald Suppa

ARIES ENTERTAINMENT, INC.

13547 Ventura Blvd., Ste. 384, Sherman Oaks, CA 91423. (818) 907-0084. email: ariesent@hotmail.com
PRESIDENT
Norbert Meisel

ARROW ENTERTAINMENT

(Motion picture, TV & video distributor)
57 W. 38th St., Ste. 302, New York, NY 10018. (646) 825-8891. FAX: (212) 656-1543. www.arrowfeatures.com
email: johncusimano@arrowfeatures.com
PRESIDENTS
Jessica Glass
Robert Levin
V.P., BUSINESS & LEGAL AFFAIRS/ACQUISITIONS
John Cusimano

ARTISAN ENTERTAINMENT

2700 Colorado Ave., 2nd Flr., Los Angeles, CA 90404. (310) 449-9200. www.artisanent.com
157 Chambers St., 11th Flr., New York, NY 10007. (212) 577-2400.
CEO, ARTISAN ENTERTAINMENT
Amir Malin
PRESIDENT & COO, ARTISAN ENTERTAINMENT
Ken Schapiro
PRESIDENT, PRODUCTION, ARTISAN PICTURES
Richard Saperstein
PRESIDENT, ARTISAN HOME ENTERTAINMENT
Steve Beeks
PRESIDENT, FAMILY HOME ENTERTAINMENT
Glenn Ross
PRESIDENT, SALES & MARKETING, ARTISAN HOME ENTERTAINMENT
Jeff Fink
PRESIDENT, DOMESTIC THEATRICAL DISTRIBUTION, ARTISAN RELEASING
Steve Rothenberg
CFO, ARTISAN ENTERTAINMENT
Greg Arvesen
COO, ARTISAN HOME ENTERTAINMENT
Bob Denton
EXECUTIVE V.P., GENERAL COUNSEL, ARTISAN ENT.
Erin Austin
EXECUTIVE V.P., ARTISAN ENTERTAINMENT
Patrick Gunn
EXECUTIVE V.P., PRODUCTION, ARTISAN PICTURES
Andrew Golov
EXECUTIVE V.P., WORLDWIDE THEATRICAL MARKETING, ARTISAN PICTURES
Amorette Jones
EXECUTIVE V.P., ACQUISITIONS & SALES, ARTISAN TELEVISION DISTRIBUTION
Gary Rubin
EXECUTIVE V.P., SALES & DISTRIBUTION, ARTISAN HOME ENTERTAINMENT
Jed Grossman
EXECUTIVE V.P., RETAIL & BRAND DEVELOPMENT, ARTISAN HOME ENTERTAINMENT
Tim Fournier
SENIOR V.P., MARKETING, ARTISAN HOME ENTERTAINMENT
Hosea Belcher
SENIOR V.P., PUBLICITY & PROMOTIONS, ARTISAN PICTURES
Paul Campbell
SENIOR V.P., ACQUISITIONS & PRODUCTION, ARTISAN PICTURES
Rachel Cohen
SENIOR V.P., HUMAN RESOURCES & ADMINISTRATION, ARTISAN ENTERTAINMENT
Nancy Coleman
SENIOR V.P & CIO, ARTISAN ENTERTAINMENT
Leo Collins
SENIOR V.P., SALES, ARTISAN TELEVISION DISTRIBUTION
Jon Ferro
SENIOR V.P., NATIONAL PROMOTIONS & STRATEGIC PARTNERSHIPS, ARTISAN PICTURES
LeAnne Gayner
SENIOR V.P., BUSINESS & LEGAL AFFAIRS, ARTISAN ENTERTAINMENT
Jim Gladstone
SENIOR V.P., PUBLICITY, ARTISAN ENTERTAINMENT
Sarah Greenberg
SENIOR V.P., NATIONAL SALES W., ARTISAN HOME ENTERTAINMENT
Patrick McDonough
SENIOR V.P., NATIONAL SALES E., ARTISAN HOME ENT.
Dale Moyer
SENIOR V.P., EXHIBITOR RELATIONS & PRINT CONTROL, ARTISAN RELEASING
Mike Polydoros
SENIOR V.P., MUSIC, ARTISAN ENTERTAINMENT
Gwen Riley
SENIOR V.P., SALES W. COAST, ARTISAN RELEASING
David Spitz
SENIOR V.P., POST PRODUCTION & DELIVERY SERVICES, ARTISAN PICTURES
Bob Wenokur

ARTISTIC LICENSE FILMS

(Motion picture distributor)
101 W. 79th St., Ste. 21C, New York, NY 10024. (212) 265-9119. FAX: (212) 877-1949. www.artlic.com
email: info@artlic.com
PRESIDENT
Sande Zeig
DISTRIBUTION MANAGER
Vicky Waldron
FINANCIAL DIRECTOR
Nora Coblence

THE ARTISTS' COLONY

(Motion picture, independent film & TV producer)
256 S. Robertson Blvd., Ste. 1500, Beverly Hills, CA 90211. (310) 720-8300. www.theartisitscolony.com
PRODUCER
Lloyd A. Silverman
DIRECTORS OF DEVELOPMENT
Adam Neal
David Donnelly
Steve Grill
EXECUTIVE ASSISTANT
Caelyn Smith

ASCENT MEDIA GROUP

(Formerly Liberty Livewire Corporation)
520 Broadway, 5th Flr., Santa Monica, CA 90401. (310) 434-7000. FAX: (310) 434-7001.
CHAIRMAN & CEO
William Fitzgerald
COO
Ken Williams
COO, CREATIVE SERVICES
Bob Solomon
PRESIDENT, MEDIA MANAGEMENT SERVICES
Bill Humphrey
PRESIDENT, NETWORK SERVICES
Scott Davis
PRESIDENT, AUDIO SERVICES
Lon Bender
V.P., MARKETING COMMUNICATIONS
Barry Stagg

ASTRON FILMS CORPORATION

(Writers, producers & directors, independent financiers)
360 W. 22 St., New York, NY 10011. (212) 989-6089. FAX: (212) 627-5191.
PRESIDENT & CHAIRMAN
Jack O'Connell
CREATIVE DIRECTOR
Patricia Kay Williams

THE ASYLUM

(Motion picture producer & distributor)
6671 Sunset Blvd, Bldg. 1593, Hollywood, CA 90028. (323) 463-6575. FAX: (323) 463-6299. email: asylumthe@aol.com
PRODUCTION
David Michael Latt
ACQUISITIONS
David Rimawi
INTERNATIONAL SALES
Sherri Strain
HOME ENTERTAINMENT/DISTRIBUTION
Rick Walker

ATA TRADING CORP.

(TV & video distributor)
P.O. Box 307, Massapequa Park, NY 11762. (516) 541-5336. FAX: (516) 541-5336. email: atatr@optonline.net
PRESIDENT
Harold G. Lewis
DIRECTOR OF SALES
M. Beinhacker

ATLANTIC STREAMLINE

(Motion picture producer)
1323A Third St., Santa Monica, CA 90401. (310) 319-9366. FAX: (310) 319-9235.
CEO & PRESIDENT
Marco Weber
SENOR, V.P., PRODUCTION & FINANCE
Fran Lucci
HEAD OF DEVELOPMENT
Vanessa Coifman

ATLAS ENTERTAINMENT

(Motion picture & independent film producer)
9200 Sunset Blvd., 10th Flr., Los Angeles, CA 90069. (310) 786-4900. FAX: (310) 777-2185.
PRODUCER & PARTNER
Charles Roven
PRODUCER & PARTNER
Allen Shapiro
PRESIDENT, PRODUCTION
Rob Guralnick
CEO
Ted MacKinney
V.P., PRODUCTION
George Gatins
V.P., MARKETING & PUBLICITY
Alan Glazer
DIRECTOR, BUSINESS AFFAIRS
Bailey Spencer-Jackson
FEATURE DEVELOPMENT
Gloria Fan
CREATIVE EXECUTIVE
Alex Ankeles
STORY EDITOR
M. Riley
ASSISTANT TO DIRECTOR OF OPERATIONS
Erin Smith

ATMAN ENTERTAINMENT

(Motion picture & TV producer)
7966 Beverly Blvd., 3rd Flr., Los Angeles, CA 90048. (323) 951-4628. FAX: (323) 951-4601. email: rossgraysonbell@aol.com
PRODUCER
Ross Grayson Bell

AUGUST ENTERTAINMENT

(Motion picture distributor)
838 N. Fairfax Ave., Los Angeles, CA 90046. (323) 658-8888. FAX: (323) 658-7654. email: augustent@mindspring.com
PRESIDENT
Gregory Cascante
EXECUTIVE V.P. & CFO
Elizabeth Davis
V.P., OPERATIONS
Colleen McNichols

AURORA PRODUCTIONS

(Motion picture, independent film & TV producer)
8642 Melrose Ave., Ste. 200, Los Angeles, CA 90069. (310) 854-6900. FAX: (310) 854-0583. email: auroraprod@aol.com
PRESIDENT
William Stuart
DIRECTOR, DEVELOPMENT
Anna Griffin

AUTOMATIC PICTURES

(Motion picture producer)
5225 Wilshire Blvd., Ste. 525, Los Angeles, CA 90038. (323) 935-1800. FAX: (323) 935-8040.
email:automaticpictures@hotmail.com
PRODUCER
Frank Beddor
CREATIVE EXECUTIVE
Liz Cavalier

AVALANCHE ENTERTAINMENT

(Motion picture, independent film & TV producer)
11041 Santa Monica Blvd., Ste. 511, Los Angeles, CA 90025. (310) 477-1464. FAX: (310) 552-0549.
PRESIDENT & PRODUCER
Richard Hull

AVENUE PICTURES

(Motion picture, independent film & TV producer)
11111 Santa Monica Blvd., Ste. 525, Los Angeles, CA 90025. (310) 996-6800. FAX: (310) 473-4376. www.avepix.com
CHAIRMAN & CEO
Cary Brokaw
SENIOR V.P. & CFO
Sheri Halfon
CONTROLLER
Judy Geletko
PRODUCTION
Aaron Craig Geller

AVIATOR FILMS, LLC

1531 N. Cahuenga Blvd., Hollywood, CA 90028. (323) 465-4400. FAX: (323) 465-4800.
PARTNERS
Anthony Edwards
Dante di Lorento
ASSOCIATE
Frank Pavich

AXELSON-WEINTRAUB PRODUCTIONS

(TV producer)
4421 Riverside Dr., Burbank, CA 91505. (818) 954-8661. FAX: (818) 954-0468. email: aw-prods@earthlink.net
EXECUTIVE PRODUCER & DIRECTOR
John Axelson
EXECUTIVE PRODUCER
Barbara Weintraub
CREATIVE ASSOCIATE
Rosa Tran

THE BADHAM CO.

(Motion picture, independent film & TV producer)
3344 Clerendon Road, Beverly Hills, CA 90210. (818) 990-9495. FAX: (818) 981-9163. www.badhamcompany.com
DIRECTOR & PRODUCER
John Badham
ASSOCIATE PRODUCER
Vanessa Ruane
PROJECTS MANAGER
Todd Harris (310) 276-7881

BAER ENTERTAINMENT GROUP

(Motion picture producer)
650 Madison Ave., 17th Flr., New York, NY 10022. (212) 371-7300. FAX: (212) 371-3240.
PRODUCER
Thomas Baer
PARTNER
Michael Steinhardt
DIRECTOR, DEVELOPMENT
Mario Acosta

BAKULA PRODUCTIONS, INC.
(TV producer)
5555 Melrose Ave., Hollywood, CA 90038. (323) 960-4005.
CEO & PRODUCER
Scott Bakula
PRESIDENT & PRODUCER
Tom Spiroff
CREATIVE EXECUTIVE
Ron Cortes

BALLPARK PRODUCTIONS
(Motion picture, independent film & TV producer)
P.O. Box 508, Venice, CA 90294. (310) 827-1328. FAX: (310) 577-9626.
PRODUCER
Michael Schiffer
V.P., DEVELOPMENT
Sally Allen

BALLYHOO, INC.
(Motion picture & TV producer)
6738 Wedgewood Pl., Los Angeles, CA 90068. (323) 956-8740, (323) 874-3396. FAX: (323) 883-0265.
email: mbesman@dslextreme.com
PRODUCER
Michael Besman

BALTIMORE/SPRING CREEK PICTURES, LLC
(Production)
4000 Warner Blvd., Burbank, CA 91522. (818) 954-2737. FAX: (818) 954-1210. www.Levinson.com
DIRECTOR & WRITER & PRODUCER
Barry Levinson
PRODUCER
Paula Weinstein
CFO & BUSINESS AFFAIRS
Amy Solan
EXECUTIVE V.P.
Len Amato
VICE PRESIDENT
Naketha Mattocks
CREATIVE EXECUTIVE
Palak Patel

BANNER ENTERTAINMENT
4000 Warner Blvd., Bldg. 138, Ste. 1201, Burbank, CA 91522. (818) 977-7557. FAX: (818) 954-7501.
PRESIDENT & PRODUCER
Mickey Liddell

ALAN BARNETTE PRODUCTIONS
(Motion picture, independent film & TV producer)
100 Universal City Plaza, Bldg. 2352, Rm. A101, Universal City, CA 91608. (818) 733-0993.
EXECUTIVE PRODUCER
Alan Barnette
EXECUTIVE ASSISTANT
Marie Colabelli

BARNHOLTZ ENTERTAINMENT
34133 Mulholland Hwy., Malibu, CA 90265. (818) 879-6500.
FAX: (818) 879-5074. email: bbarnholtz@aol.com
PRESIDENT/CEO
Barry Barnholtz
CFO
Murray Gilden
DIRECTOR, ACQUISITIONS
Matt Cunningham
SENIOR V.P., BUSINESS AFFAIRS
Matthew Fladell

BARNSTORM FILMS
73 Market St., Venice, CA 90291. (310) 396-5937. FAX: (310) 450-4988.
PRODUCER & DIRECTOR
Tony Bill
PRODUCER
Helen Bartlett

BATJAC PRODUCTIONS, INC.
9595 Wilshire Blvd., #610, Beverly Hills, CA 90212-2506. (310) 278-9870. FAX: (323) 272-7381.
PRESIDENT
Mrs. Michael A. Wayne

THE BAUER COMPANY
(Motion picture, independent film & TV producer)
9300 Wilshire Blvd., Penthouse Ste., Beverly Hills, CA 90212.
(310) 247-3880. FAX: (310) 247-3881.
PRODUCERS
Martin R. Bauer
Robert Marsala
Ben Tappan

CAROL BAUM PRODUCTIONS
(Motion picture producer)
8899 Beverly Blvd., Ste. 721, Los Angeles, CA 90048. (310) 550-4575. FAX: (310) 550-2088.
PRODUCER
Carol Baum

BAY FILMS
(Film & TV producer)
631 Colorado Ave., Santa Monica, CA 90401. (310) 319-6565.
FAX: (310) 319-6570.
DIRECTOR & PRODUCER
Michael Bay
VICE PRESIDENT
Matthew Cohan

BEACON PICTURES
(Motion picture producer)
120 Broadway, Ste. 200, Santa Monica, CA 90401. (310) 260-7000. FAX: (310) 260-7050.
CHAIRMAN
Armyan Bernstein
CEO
Charlie Lyons
COO
Michael A. Helfant
DEVELOPMENT & PRODUCTION
Suzann Ellis
EXECUTIVE V.P. & CFO
Cynthia McWethy
PRODUCTION
Nancy Rae Stone

THE BEDFORD FALLS CO.
409 Santa Monica Blvd., Penthouse, Santa Monica, CA 90401.
(310) 394-5022. FAX: (310) 394-5825.
EXECUTIVE PRODUCER & WRITER & DIRECTOR
Marshall Herskovitz
EXECUTIVE PRODUCER & WRITER & DIRECTOR
Edward Zwick
PRESIDENT
Richard Solomon, (310) 394-5643
S.V.P., PRODUCTION
Robin Budd, (310) 394-7461

BELISARIUS PRODUCTIONS
1438 N. Gower St., Bldg. 35, 4th Flr., Hollywood, CA 90028.
(323) 468-4500. FAX: (323) 468-4599.
WRITER & EXECUTIVE PRODUCER & DIRECTOR
Donald P. Bellisario
CO-EXECUTIVE PRODUCER
Chas Floyd Johnson
CO-EXECUTIVE PRODUCER & WRITER
Stephen Zito
CO-EXECUTIVE PRODUCERS
Mark Horowitz
Dana Coen
John Tinker
SUPERVISING PRODUCERS
Don McGill
Doris Egan
PRODUCERS
David Bellisario
Avery Drewe
Julie Watson
Tommy Moran
Mark Schilz
Phil DeGuen
Matt Witten
Jeff Vlaming
Peter Dunne
Joe Lazard
ASSOCIATE PRODUCER
Megan Mascena-Gaspar
SCRIPT COORDINATOR
Barbara Hecht
Geoffrey Cob
Sharon Eldrige

LAWRENCE BENDER PRODUCTIONS
(Producer)
7966 Beverly Blvd., Los Angeles, CA 90048. (323) 951-4600.
FAX: (323) 951-4601.
WRITER & DIRECTOR & PARTNER
Quentin Tarantino
PRODUCER & PARTNER
Lawrence Bender
PRODUCING PARTNER
Kevin Brown
PRODUCERS
Ross Bell
Karen Barber
SENIOR V.P., PRODUCTION
Julie Kirkham
STORY EDITOR
Janet Jeffries
OFFICE MANAGER
Chris Hill

BENDERSPINK

6735 Yucca St., Hollywood, CA 90028. (323) 856-5500. FAX:
(323) 856-5502. www.benderspink.com
email: info@benderspink.com
EXECUTIVES
Brian Spink
Charlie Gogolak
Chris Bender
J.C. Spink
Jill McElroy
Jake Weiner
Courtney Kivowitz
EXECUTIVE ASSISTANTS
Jeff Mahler
Suzanne Wallach

ROBERT BENEDETTI PRODUCTIONS, INC.

2533 6th St., Santa Monica, CA 90405-3707. (310) 664-0912.
PRESIDENT
Robert Benedetti

RICK BERMAN PRODUCTIONS

(Motion picture, independent film & TV producer)
5555 Melrose Ave., Cooper Bldg., Ste. 232, Los Angeles, CA
90038. (323) 956-5037. FAX: (323) 862-1076.
EXECUTIVE PRODUCER
Rick Berman
ASSISTANT
Joanna Fuller
SUPERVISOR, STAR TREK PROJECTS
Dave Rossi

BLUE TULIP PRODUCTIONS

(Motion picture, independent film & TV producer)
1708 Berkeley St., Santa Monica, CA 90404. (310) 582-1587.
FAX: (310) 582-1597.
PRODUCERS
Jan De Bont
Jessika Borsiczky

BOARDWALK ENTERTAINMENT

(Motion picture & TV producer)
210 E. 39th St., New York, NY 10016. (212) 679-3800. FAX:
(212) 679-3816.
email: Boardwalk@infohouse.com
CHAIRMAN
Alan Wagner
PRESIDENT
Susan Wagner

CAROL BODIE ENTERTAINMENT

8942 Wilshire Blvd., ICM, Beverly Hills, CA 90211. (310) 550-
4028, (310) 550-4338.
PRODUCER & CEO
Carol Bodie
ASSISTANT
Mark Mitchell

BONA FIDE PRODUCTIONS

(Motion picture producer)
8899 Beverly Blvd., Ste. 804, Los Angeles, CA 90048. (310)
273-6782. FAX: (310) 273-7821.
PRODUCERS
Albert Berger
Ron Yerxa
STORY EDITOR
Veronica Lemcoff
CREATIVE EXECUTIVES
Ellen Steloff
Carlo Martinelli

BONEYARD ENTERTAINMENT

(Motion picture, TV & internet producer)
863 Park Ave., Ste. 11E, New York, NY 10021. (212) 628-8600.
FAX: (212) 628-8615.
PRESIDENT & CEO
Daniel J. Victor
EXECUTIVE V.P.
Richard M. Victor

BOXING CAT PRODUCTIONS

11500 Hart St., North Hollywood, CA 91605. (818) 765-4870.
FAX: (818) 765-4975.
PRODUCER & ACTOR
Tim Allen
PRESIDENT, PRODUCTION
Matt Carroll

BRICKMAN MARKETING

395 Del Monte Ctr., #250, Monterey, CA 93940. (831) 633-
4444. FAX: (831) 633-4499. www.brickmanmarketing.com
email: brickman@redshift.com
OWNER
Wendy Brickman

BRILLSTEIN-GREY ENTERTAINMENT

9150 Wilshire Blvd., Ste. 350, Beverly Hills, CA 90212. (310)
275-6135. FAX: (310) 275-6180.
FOUNDING PARTNER
Bernie Brillstein
CHAIRMAN & CEO
Brad Grey
CFO
Steve Blume
SENIOR EXECUTIVE V.P.
Sandy Wernick
EXECUTIVE V.P.
Jonathan Liebman
HEAD, MOTION PICTURE DIVISION
Matthew Baer
CO-PRESIDENT, BG MANAGEMENT
Marc Gurvitz
CO-PRESIDENT, BG MANAGEMENT
Cynthia Pett-Dante
CO-PRESIDENT, BGTV
Peter Traugott
CO-PRESIDENT, BGTV
Susie Fitzgerald

BRISTOL CITIES

(Motion picture, independent film & TV producer)
5555 Melrose Ave., Swanson Bldg., Rm. 105, Los Angeles, CA
90038. (323) 956-3513. FAX: (323) 862-1172.
email: BrstlCty@aol.com
PRODUCERS
Jane Leeves
Peri Gilpin
V.P., CREATIVE AFFAIRS
Steve La Rue

BROOKLYN FILMS

3815 Hughes Ave., Culver City, CA 90232. (310) 841-4300.
FAX: (310) 204-4208.
DIRECTOR & PRODUCER
Jon Avnet
EXECUTIVE V.P., FINANCE & ADMINISTRATION
Carol Chacamaty
SENIOR V.P., DEVELOPMENT & PRODUCTION
Marsha Olgseby

BROOKSFILMS LIMITED

(Motion picture producer)
9336 W. Washington Blvd., Culver City, CA 90232. (310) 202-
3292. FAX: (310) 202-3225.
PRESIDENT
Mel Brooks
V.P., PRODUCTION SERVICES
Leah Zappy
DEVELOPMENT
Jennifer Yale

JERRY BRUCKHEIMER FILMS

(Producer)
1631 10th St., Santa Monica, CA 90403. (310) 664-6260. FAX:
(310) 664-6261. www.jbfilms.com
PRODUCER
Jerry Bruckheimer
PRESIDENT
Mike Stenson
PRESIDENT, PRODUCTION
Chad Oman
SENIOR V.P.
Melissa Reid
DIRECTOR OF PRODUCTION
Kristie Anne Reed

THE BUBBLE FACTORY

8840 Wilshire Blvd., 3rd Flr., Beverly Hills, CA 90211. (310)
358-3000. FAX: (310) 358-3299.
PARTNERS
Sid Sheinberg
Bill Sheinberg
Jon Sheinberg
EXECUTIVE V.P., MOTION PICTURES
Mitch Soloman
V.P., FINANCE & OPERATIONS
Kevin D. Forester
DIRECTOR, DEVELOPMENT
Gwen Osborne
MANAGER, MEDIA & CONSUMER PRODUCTS
Cory M. Lidschin

BUENA VISTA PICTURES

(see The Walt Disney Company)

BUNGALOW 78 PRODUCTIONS

(Motion picture, independent film & TV producer)
5555 Melrose Ave., Lasky Bldg. 200, Los Angeles, CA 90038.
(323) 956-4440. FAX: (323) 862-2090.
EXECUTIVE PRODUCER & WRITER
Barry Kemp
EXECUTIVE ASSISTANT
Jill Bowles

BURRUD PRODUCTIONS

(Documentary producer)
16351 Gothard St., Unit D, Huntington Beach, CA 92647. (714) 842-8422. FAX: (714) 842-0433. www.burrud.com
email: info@burrud.com
PRESIDENT & CEO
John Burrud
EXECUTIVE V.P., BUSINESS AFFAIRS
Stanley H. Green
V.P., PRODUCTION
Drew Horton
V.P., ADMINISTRATION & SALES
Linda Karabin
V.P., POST-PRODUCTION
Kurt Porter

BUTCHERS RUN FILMS

(Motion picture producer)
1041 N. Formosa Ave., Santa Monica Bldg. E. 200, W. Hollywood, CA 90046. (323) 850-2703. FAX: (323) 850-2741.
ACTOR & PRODUCER & DIRECTOR
Robert Duvall
PRODUCER
Rob Carliner
DIRECTOR, DEVELOPMENT
Adam Prince

CAMELOT PICTURES

1113 Electric Ave., Ste. 12, Venice, CA 90291. (310) 450-7804.
FAX: (310) 450-8174.
9 Desbrosses St., 2nd Flr, New York, NY 10013. (212) 609-9393. FAX: (212) 609-9394.
PARTNERS
Dan Halsted
Gary Gilbert
CONTACTS
Lia Mijangos
Seth Marshall
Philip Hall

CAPELLA FILMS, INC.

(Motion picture producer & distributor)
9200 Sunset Blvd., Ste. 315, Los Angeles, CA 90069. (310) 247-4700. FAX: (310) 247-4701.
PRESIDENT & CFO
Craig Arrington
PRESIDENT, CAPELLA INTERNATIONAL
Jean-Louis Rubin

CAPPA PRODUCTIONS

(Motion picture, independent film & TV producer)
445 Park Ave., New York, NY 10022. (212) 906-8800.
DIRECTOR
Martin Scorsese
PRODUCER
Barbara De Fina

CARMICHAEL FILMS

(Motion picture producer & developer)
37 W. 28th St., 12th Flr., New York, NY 10001. (212) 803-5880.
FAX: (212) 684-3875. email: info@carmichaelfilms.com
CEO
Seth D. Carmichael
PRESIDENT
Christopher Pizzo

CASTLE HILL PRODUCTIONS, INC.

(Motion picture, independent film, & TV distributor)
36 W. 25th St., New York, NY 10010. (212) 242-1500. FAX: (212) 414-5737.
PRESIDENT
Julian Schlossberg
PRESIDENT, MARKETING & DISTRIBUTION
Mel Maron
V.P., TELEVISION SALES
Barbara Karmel
DIRECTOR, ADVERTISING AND PUBLICITY
Steve Tulchin

CASTLE ROCK ENTERTAINMENT

335 N. Maple Dr., Ste. 135, Beverly Hills, CA 90210-3867.
(310) 285-2300. FAX: (310) 285-2345.
www.castle-rock.warnerbros.com
PRODUCERS & DIRECTORS
Rob Reiner
Andy Scheinman
CHAIRMAN & CEO, CASTLE ROCK ENTERTAINMENT
Martin Shafer
PRESIDENT, CASTLE ROCK PICTURES
Liz Glotzer
EXECUTIVE V.P. CASTLE ROCK ENTERTAINMENT
Jeff Wittenberg
DIRECTOR, BUSINESS AFFAIRS ADMINISTRATION
Margo Meyer
CREATIVE EXECUTIVE
Gaylyn Fraiche

CAVU PICTURES

(Distribution)
630 9th Ave., Ste. 411, New York, NY 10036. (212) 246-6300.
FAX: (212) 246-6086. email: ms@cavupictures.com
PRESIDENT
Michael Sergio

CECCHI GORI PICTURES

(Motion picture, independent film & TV producer, developer & acquisitions)
11990 San Vicente Blvd., Ste. 200, Los Angeles, CA 90049.
(310) 442-4777. FAX: (310) 442-9507. www.cecchigori.com
PRESIDENT
Gianni Nunnari
CFO
Roland Lilavois

CHARTOFF PRODUCTIONS

(Motion picture & film producer)
1250 Sixth St., Ste. 101, Santa Monica, CA 90401. (310) 319-1960.
FAX: (310) 319-3469.
CEO & PRESIDENT
Robert Chartoff
EXECUTIVE V.P.
Lynn Hendee

CHILDREN'S MEDIA PRODUCTIONS

(Producer and distributor)
P.O. Box 40400, Pasadena, CA 91114. (626) 797-5462. FAX: (626) 797-7524. email: glenray@pacbell.com
CONTACT
C. Ray Carlson

THE CINEMA GUILD

(Motion picture, independent film & TV distributor)
130 Madison Ave., 2nd Fl., New York, NY 10016-7038. (212) 685-6242. FAX: (212) 685-4717. www.cinemaguild.com
PRESIDENT
Philip S. Hobel
V.P. & GENERAL MANAGER
Gary Crowdus
VICE PRESIDENT
Mary Ann Hobel

CINEMANSON MARKETING & DISTRIBUTION

(Motion picture marketers & distributors)
36 W. 25th St., Ste. 202, New York, NY 10010. (212) 255-4088.
FAX: (212) 255-4003. email: cinemanson@aol.com
PRESIDENT
Arthur Manson
ADMINISTRATOR DIRECTOR
Patrick Cullert

CINE EXCEL ENTERTAINMENT

(Full service production & post production company)
1102 N. Screenland Dr., Burbank, CA 91505. (818) 848-4478.
FAX: (818) 848-1590. www.cineexcel.com
PRESIDENT
David Huey

CINEMA SEVEN PRODUCTIONS

(Motion picture producer)
154 W. 57th St., Ste. 112, New York, NY 10019. (212) 315-1060. FAX: (212) 315-1085. email: cin7prod@aol.com
144 S. Beverly Dr., Ste. 407, Beverly Hills, CA 90212. (310) 247-1444. FAX: (310) 247-1477.
PRESIDENT
Elliott Kastner
PRODUCER
Dillon Kastner
HEAD, PRODUCTION
Pasquale Botta (NY)
BUSINESS AFFAIRS
James Deyarmin
HEAD, PRODUCTION
Julius Ortiguero (CA)

CINERGI PICTURES ENTERTAINMENT, INC.

(Motion picture & independent film producer)
2308 Broadway, Santa Monica, CA 90404-2916. (310) 315-6000. FAX: (310) 828-0443.
CHAIRMAN & CEO
Andrew Vajna
SENIOR V.P., FINANCE
Samuel Falconello

CINETEL FILMS, INC.

(Motion picture & TV distributor)
8255 Sunset Blvd., Los Angeles, CA 90046. (323) 654-4000.
FAX: (323) 650-6400.
PRESIDENT & CEO
Paul Hertzberg
EXECUTIVE V.P
Lisa Hansen
CFO
Robert Coramanica

636

V.P., INTERNATIONAL DISTRIBUTION
Marcy Rubin
V.P., PRODUCTION
Vicki Sawyer
V.P., CREATIVE AFFAIRS
Neil Elman

CINETEL PICTURES
PRESIDENT
Lisa Hansen

CINEVILLE INTERNATIONAL
3400 Airport Ave., Santa Monica, CA 90405. (310) 397-7150.
FAX: (310) 397-7155. email: cineville@aol.com
OWNER
Christopher Henkel
PRESIDENT
Carl Colpaert
DIRECTOR, DEVELOPMENT
Annabelle Frankl

CINEVISTA, INC.
(Distributors & sales)
2044 Prairie Ave., Miami Beach, FL 33139. (305) 532-3400.
(800) 341-CINE. FAX: (305) 532-0047. www.cinevistavideo.com
PRESIDENT
Rene Fuentes-Chao
VICE PRESIDENT
Susan Morin

COHEN PICTURES
(Motion picture & TV producer)
3000 W. Olympic Blvd., Ste. 2222, Santa Monica, CA 90404.
(310) 264-8120. FAX: (310) 264-8121.
email: bobby_cohen@yahoo.com
PRODUCER
Bobby Cohen

HERMAN COHEN PRODUCTIONS/COBRA MEDIA, INC.
P.O. Box 901, Murrieta, CA 92564. FAX: (603) 825-8133.
EXECUTIVE V.P.
Didier Chatelain

COLISEUM PICTURES CORPORATION
(Motion picture & TV producer)
5073 Avenida Hacienda, Tarzana, CA 91356-4222. (818) 881-1515. FAX: (847) 589-3811. www.coliseumpictures.com
email: robert@coliseumpictures.com
PRODUCERS
Robert Kesler
Robin Lombardo
ASSISTANTS
Cheryl Campbell
Noah Hall

CONSTANTIN FILM DEVELOPMENT, INC.
(European locations; motion picture, independent film & TV producer)
9200 Sunset Blvd., Ste. 730, Los Angeles, CA 90069. (310) 247-0300. FAX: (310) 247-0305.
CONTACTS
Mitch Horwits
Bernd Eichinger
Lisa Kregness
Robert Kulzner
Marsha Metz
Laura Levinson
Johannes Schlichting
Heather Thomas

CONTINENTAL FILM GROUP LTD.
(Motion picture & TV producer & distributor)
15131 Mulholland Dr., Bel Air, CA 90077 (818) 782-4801.
email: acmoviemogul@earthlink.net
PRESIDENT & CEO
Amin Q. Chaudhri
V.P. IN CHARGE OF DEVELOPMENT
Asha N. Chaudhri
ASSISTANT TO THE PRESIDENT & CEO
Dana Caruso
BOARD OF DIRECTORS
Amin Q. Chaudhri
Robert Holof

CONUNDRUM ENTERTAINMENT
(Motion picture producer)
325 Wilshire Blvd., Ste. 201, Santa Monica, CA 90401. (310) 319-2800. FAX: (310) 319-2808.
CONTACTS
Bobby Farrelly
Peter Farrelly
Bradley Thomas
Mark Charpentier
Clemens Franek
Farah Lopez

CPC ENTERTAINMENT
(Independent features producer)
840 N. Larabee St., Ste. 2322, Los Angeles, CA 90069. (310) 652-8194. www.cpcentertainment.com
353 W. 57th St., Ste. 2227, New York, NY 10019. (212) 554-6447.
PRESIDENT
Peggy Chane

THOMAS CRAVEN FILM CORP.
(Motion picture & TV producer)
5 W. 19th St., New York, NY 10011. (212) 463-7190. FAX: (212) 627-4761.
PRESIDENT
Michael Craven
VICE PRESIDENT
Ernest Barbieri

WES CRAVEN FILMS
(Producer)
11846 Ventura Blvd., Ste. 208, Studio City, CA 91604. (818) 752-0197. FAX: (818) 752-1789.
DIRECTOR & PRODUCER
Wes Craven
PRESIDENT & PRODUCER
Marianne Maddalena
V.P., DEVELOPMENT
Alix Taylor

CROWN INTERNATIONAL PICTURES, INC.
8701 Wilshire Blvd., Beverly Hills, CA 90211. (310) 657-6700.
FAX: (310) 657-4489. www.crownintlpictures.com
PRESIDENT & CEO
Mark Tenser
SENIOR V.P.
Scott E. Schwimer
V.P., FINANCE
Willie De Leon
DIRECTOR, PUBLICITY & ADVERTISING
Lisa Agay
EXECUTIVE PRODUCER/PRODUCER
Marilyn J. Tenser

CRUSADER ENTERTAINMENT
(Motion picture, independent film & TV producer)
132B S. Lasky Dr., Beverly Hills, CA 90212. (310) 248-6360.
FAX: (310) 248-6370.
PRESIDENT & CEO
Howard Baldwin
SENIOR EXECUTIVE V.P. & COO
William J. Immerman
EXECUTIVE V.P., FINANCIAL & CFO
Lawrence Bernstein
EXECUTIVE V.P., CREATIVE AFFAIRS
Karen Baldwin
EXECUTIVE V.P.
Nick Ruta
GENERAL COUNSEL
Gloria Ruiz Oster
V.P., CONTROLLER
Gordon Tichell
SENIOR V.P., PHYSICAL PRODUCTION
Vicki Deerock
V.P., DEVELOPMENT
Nick Morton
V.P., MARKETING
Todd Slater
DIRECTOR PR/MARKETING
Erica Stern

CRYSTAL PYRAMID PRODUCTIONS
(Motion picture, independent film & TV producer; stock footage library)
7323 Rondel Ct., San Diego, CA 92119-1530. (619) 644-3000.
FAX: (619) 644-3001. www.crystalpyramid.com
CEO
Mark Schulze
COO
Patty Mooney
V.P., PRODUCTION
Michael Sterner

CRYSTAL SKY, LLC
1901 Ave. of the Stars, Ste. 605, Los Angeles, CA 90067. (310) 843-0223. FAX: (310) 553-9895.
CHAIRMAN
Hank Paul
CO-CHAIRMAN
Dorothy Koster
PRESIDENT
Steven Paul
SENIOR V.P., FINANCE
Joe Inga
V.P., PRODUCTION & DEVELOPMENT
Patrick Ewald
BUSINESS AFFAIRS
Jason Price

CURB ENTERTAINMENT

(Motion picture & film producer & distributor)
3907 W. Alameda Ave., Ste. 200, Burbank, CA 91505. (818) 843-8580. FAX: (818) 566-1719. www.curbentertainment.com
PRESIDENT
Carole Curb
CHAIRPERSON
Mike Curb

C/W PRODUCTIONS

(Motion picture, independent film & TV producer)
5555 Melrose Ave., Hollywood, CA 90038. (323) 956-8199. FAX: (323) 862-1250.
CONTACTS
Paula Wagner
Darren Miller
Gaye Hirsch
Gunnar Clancey
Grady Lee
Joey Shanley
Mia Fenwick
Tricia Gregory
Jeff Buitenveld

DANJAQ, LLC

(Motion picture producer; distribution through MGM)
2401 Colorado Ave., Ste. 330, Santa Monica, CA 90404. (310) 449-3185. FAX: (310) 449-3189.
CO-CHAIRMAN
Dana Broccoli
PRESIDENT & CEO
Michael Wilson
V.P., PRODUCTION & DEVELOPMENT
Barbara Broccoli

ALAN DAVID MANAGEMENT

(Motion picture, independent film & TV producer)
8840 Wilshire Blvd., Ste. 200, Beverly Hills, CA 90211. (310) 358-3155. FAX: (310) 358-3256.
email: adavid@planbproductions.net
PRESIDENT & CEO
Alan David
EXECUTIVE ASSISTANT
Mirian Kravitz

DAVIS ENTERTAINMENT CO.

(Motion picture & TV producer)
2121 Ave. of the Stars, Ste. 2900, Los Angeles, CA 90067. (310) 556-3550. FAX: (310) 556-3688.
CHAIRMAN, DAVIS ENTERTAINMENT CO.
John A. Davis
PRESIDENT, DAVIS ENTERTAINMENT FEATURES
Wyck Godfrey
EXECUTIVE V.P., ADMINISTRATION
Brooke Brooks
EXECUTIVE V.P., FEATURES
Brian Manis
DIRECTOR, DEVELOPMENT, TV
Amy Palmer

DEEP RIVER PRODUCTIONS

(Motion picture producer)
100 N. Crescent Dr., Ste. 350, Beverly Hills, CA 90210. (310) 432-1800. FAX: (310) 432-1801.
PARTNERS
David T. Friendly
Marc Turtletaub
PRESIDENT
Julie Durk
VICE PRESIDENT
Michael McGahey

DIGITAL DOMAIN

(Motion picture & TV producer)
300 Rose Ave., Venice, CA 90291. (310) 314-2800. FAX: (310) 314-2888. www.d2.com
CEO & PRODUCER
Scott Ross
SENIOR V.P., FEATURE VFX PRODUCTIONS
Nancy Bernstein
SENIOR V.P., BUSINESS AFFAIRS & GENERAL COUNSEL
Brad Call
SENIOR V.P., COMMERCIAL PRODUCTION
Ed Ulbrich
V.P., FEATURE FILM DEVELOPMENT
Kevin K. Cooper

DINAMO ENTERTAINMENT

(Motion picture producer)
2001 S. Barrington Ave., Ste. 150, Los Angeles, CA 90025. (310) 473-1311. FAX: (310) 473-8233.
email: dinamo@earthlink.net
PRESIDENT
Morrie Eisenman
V.P., CREATIVE AFFAIRS
Jim Zaphiriou

DINO DE LAURENTIIS COMPANY

(Motion picture producer)
100 Universal City Plaza, Bung. 5195, Universal City, CA 91608. (818) 777-2111. FAX: (818) 866-5566.
CONSULTANT
Dino De Laurentiis
PRESIDENT & PRODUCER
Martha De Laurentiis
BUSINESS AFFAIRS
Stuart Boros

DI NOVI PICTURES

(Motion picture & TV producer)
3110 Main St., Ste. 220, Santa Monica, CA 90405. (310) 581-1355. FAX: (310) 399-0499.
PRODUCER
Denise Di Novi
PRESIDENT
Ed McDonnell

THE WALT DISNEY COMPANY

500 S. Buena Vista St., Burbank, CA 91521. (818) 560-1000. FAX: (818) 840-5737. www.disney.com
CHAIRMAN & CEO
Michael D. Eisner
VICE CHAIRMAN
Roy E. Disney
PRESIDENT & COO
Bob Iger
SENIOR EXECUTIVE V.P. & CFO
Thomas O. Staggs
SENIOR EXECUTIVE V.P. & CSO
Peter E. Murphy
EXECUTIVE V.P. PLANNING & CONTROL
John J. Garand
EXECUTIVE V.P. & GENERAL COUNSEL
Alan Braverman
SENIOR V.P., DEPUTY GENERAL COUNSEL, THE WALT DISNEY COMPANY & WALT DISNEY INTERNATIONAL
Brett Chapman
SENIOR V.P., CORPORATE COMMUNICATIONS
Zenia Mucha
SENIOR V.P. & CIO
Michael Tasooji
V.P., CORPORATE COMMUNICATIONS, DISNEY CONSUMER PRODUCTS
Gary Foster
V.P., CORPORATE COMMUNICATIONS
John Spelich
V.P., CORPORATE COMMUNICATIONS
Dan Wolf
V.P. & GOVERNANCE ADMINISTRATION ASSISTANT SECRETARY
Marsha L. Reed

WALT DISNEY INTERNATIONAL

500 S. Buena Vista St., Burbank, CA 952. (818) 560-1000.
PRESIDENT & MANAGING DIRECTOR, LATIN AMERICA
Diego Lerner
SENIOR V.P. & GENERAL COUNSEL
Jeffrey N. Paule
SENIOR V.P & CONTROLLER
Brian Spaulding

TOUCHSTONE TELEVISION

500 S. Buena Vista St., Burbank, CA 952. (818) 560-5000.
PRESIDENT, TOUCHSTONE TELEVISION
Stephen McPherson
EXECUTIVE V.P., TOUCHSTONE TELEVISION
Howard Davine
SENIOR V.P., COMEDY DEVELOPMENT
Julia Franz
SENIOR V.P., DRAMA
Suzanne Patmore
SENIOR V.P., CASTING
Keli Lee
SENIOR V.P., PRODUCTION
Barry Jossen
V.P., BUSINESS AFFAIRS
Jerry Longarzo
V.P., LEGAL AFFAIRS
David Cohen
V.P., PRODUCTION FINANCE
Joel Hopkins
V.P., MEDIA RELATIONS
Shawn Blake
V.P., CASTING
Stephanie Mangano

WALT DISNEY RECORDS

500 S. Buena Vista St., Burbank, CA 91521. (818) 560-1000.
SENIOR V.P., SALES & MARKETING, WDR
Robert Marick
SENIOR V.P., A&R, WDR
Jay Landers
V.P., PRODUCT DEVELOPMENT, WDR
Ted Kryczko
V.P., MEDIA RELATIONS, WDR
Maria Kleinman
EXECUTIVE DIRECTOR MARKETING
Damon Whiteside

BUENA VISTA PICTURES DISTRIBUTION, INC.
350 S. Buena Vista St., Burbank, CA 91521. (818) 560-1000.
PRESIDENT
Charles Viane
SENIOR V.P., GENERAL COUNSEL
Robert Cunningham
SENIOR V.P., BUENA VISTA NON-THEATRICAL SALES
Linda Palmer
SENIOR V.P., ADMINISTRATION
Gary Weaver
SENIOR V.P., GENERAL SALES MANAGER
Rod Rodriguez
SENIOR V.P., WORLDWIDE SPECIAL EVENTS
Lylle Breier
SENIOR V.P., SALES
Chris LeRoy
V.P., FINANCE
Ruth Walker
V.P., NEW YORK SALES OFFICE
Phil Fortune
V.P., EXHIBITOR RELATIONS
Nancy Kleuter
V.P., DALLAS SALES OFFICE
Jim Nocella
V.P., LOS ANGELES OFFICE
Pat Pade
V.P., CHICAGO SALES OFFICE
Anthony Macina
V.P., ATLANTA SALES OFFICE
Ken Caldwell

BUENA VISTA PICTURES DISTRIBUTION CANADA, INC.
1235 Bay St., Ste. 502, Toronto, ONT M5R 3K4, Canada. (416) 964-9275.
V.P., CANADA
Anthony Macina

BUENA VISTA PICTURES MARKETING
500 South Buena Vista St., Burbank, CA 91521. (818) 560-1000.
PRESIDENT, MARKETING
Oren Aviv
EXECUTIVE V.P., MARKETING & PROMOTIONS
Brett Dicker
SENIOR V.P., STRATEGIC MARKETING
Dexter Fedor
SENIOR V.P., MEDIA
Kristy Frudenfeld
SENIOR V.P., CREATIVE FILM SERVICES
Jim Gallagher
SENIOR V.P., RESEARCH
Dana Lombardo
SENIOR V.P., NATIONAL PROMOTIONS
Cherise McVicar
SENIOR V.P., CREATIVE PRINT SERVICES
John Sabel
SENIOR V.P., CREATIVE FILM SERVICES
David Singh
SENIOR V.P., PUBLICITY
Heidi Trotta
SENIOR V.P., ADMINISTRATION DISTRIBUTION & MARKETING
Gary Weaver
V.P., MEDIA OPERATIONS
Nina Anderson
V.P., CREATIVE SERVICES
John Blas
V.P., MARKETING & SYNERGY
Christine Cadena
V.P., SPECIAL EVENTS
Diane Connors
V.P., PRINT ADVERTISING
Whitney Cookson
V.P., BROADCAST PUBLICITY
Jonathan Garson
V.P., STUDIO COMMUNICATIONS
Howard Green
V.P., PUBLICITY
Sasha Lord
V.P., INTERNATIONAL MARKETING
Deanna McDaniel
V.P., PUBLICITY
Charlie Nelson
V.P., FIELD OPERATIONS
Georgia O'Connor
V.P., EAST COAST PUBLICITY
Joe Quenqua
V.P., CREATIVE FILM SERVICES
Constance Wells
V.P., BROADCAST & NEW MEDIA PUBLICITY
Jay Williams

BUENA VISTA MOTION PICTURES GROUP
CHAIRMAN, THE WALT DISNEY STUDIOS
Richard Cook
PRESIDENT, BUENA MOTION PICTURES GROUP
Nina Jacobson
PRESIDENT, BUENA VISTA PICTURES MARKETING
Oren Aviv

PRESIDENT, DISNEY THEATRICAL PRODUCTIONS, LTD
Thomas Schumacher
PRESIDENT, WALT DISNEY FEATURE ANIMATION
David J. Stainton
PRESIDENT, BUENA VISTA PICTURES DISTRIBUTION
Chuck Viane
PRESIDENT, PHYSICAL PRODUCTION
Bruce Hendricks
EXECUTIVE V.P. & CFO, THE WALT DISNEY STUDIOS
Alan Bergman
EXECUTIVE V.P., BUSINESS & LEGAL AFFAIRS, THE WALT DISNEY STUDIOS
Bernardine Brandis
EXECUTIVE V.P., CREATIVE AFFAIRS, WALT DISNEY FEATURE ANIMATION
Pam Coats
EXECUTIVE V.P., SOUNDTRACK MUSIC
Bill Green
EXECUTIVE V.P., PRODUCTION, WALT DISNEY FEATURE ANIMATION
Phil Lofaro
EXECUTIVE V.P., WORLDWIDE POST PRODUCTION AND OPERATION, THE WALT DISNEY STUDIOS
Jeffrey Miller
EXECUTIVE V.P. DISNEY THEATRICAL PRODUCTIONS, LTD
Stuart Oken
EXECUTIVE V.P., PRODUCTION
Jason T. Reed
EXECUTIVE V.P. & CREATIVE DIRECTOR, MARKETING
Fred Tio
SENIOR V.P., PRODUCTION, WALT DISNEY FEATURE ANIMATION
Robert W. Bacon
SENIOR V.P., LEGAL AFFAIRS
Steve Bardwil
SENIOR V.P., BUSINESS AFFAIRS
Doug Carter
SENIOR V.P., WALT DISNEY FEATURE ANIMATION
Tim Engel
SENIOR V.P., PRODUCTION
Brad Epstein
SENIOR V.P., PARTICIPATIONS & RESIDUALS
Michele Gazica
SENIOR V.P., DEVELOPMENT & PRODUCTION
Karen Glass
SENIOR V.P., PRODUCTION
Whitney Green
SENIOR V.P., MUSIC BUSINESS & LEGAL AFFAIRS, THE WALT DISNEY COMPANY
Scott Holtzman
SENIOR V.P., LABOR RELATIONS, WALT DISNEY PICTURES & TV
Robert W. Johnson
SENIOR V.P., PRODUCTION
Jerry Ketcha
SENIOR V.P., CORPORATE NEW TECHNOLOGY AND DEVELOPMENT
Bob Lambert
SENIOR V.P., & GM, DISNEY THEATRICAL PRODUCTIONS, LTD
Alan Levey
SENIOR V.P., CASTING ADMINISTRATION
Stephanie Mangano
SENIOR V.P., WALT DISNEY PICTURES & TV POST PRODUCTION
David McCann
SENIOR V.P., FINANCE & PLANNING, WALT DISNEY FEATURE ANIMATION
Duncan Orrell-Jones
SENIOR V.P., HUMAN RESOURCES & ADMINISTRATION, THE WALT DISNEY STUDIOS
Marjorie Randolph
SENIOR V.P., VISUAL EFFECTS & PRODUCTION
Art Repola
SENIOR V.P., FEATURES CASTING
Marcia Ross
SENIOR V.P., FEATURE PRODUCTION FINANCE
Paul Steinke
SENIOR V.P., PUBLICITY, THE WALT DISNEY STUDIOS
Heidi Trotta

WALT DISNEY PICTURES & TOUCHSTONE PICTURES
(See Buena Vista Motion Picture Group)

BUENA VISTA INTERNATIONAL
500 S. Buena Vista St., Burbank, CA 91521 (818) 560-1000.
PRESIDENT, BUENA VISTA INTERNATIONAL
Mark Zoradi
EXECUTIVE V.P. & GENERAL MANAGER
Lawrence Kaplan
EXECUTIVE V.P., DISTRIBUTION/ACQUISITIONS
Anthony Marcoly
EXECUTIVE V.P., WORLDWIDE POST PRODUCTION & OPERATIONS, WDS
Jeffrey S. Miller
EXECUTIVE V.P. & GENERAL MANAGER, EUROPE
Stuart Salter
EXECUTIVE V.P., LATIN AMERICA & THE CARIBBEAN
Diego Lerner

639

SENIOR V.P., INTL. MARKETING & CREATIVE MARKETING
Ignacio Darnaude
SENIOR V.P., INTERNATIONAL PUBLICITY
Teri Meyer
SENIOR V.P. & MANAGING DIRECTOR, UK EUROPEAN
ACQUISITIONS DIRECTOR
Daniel Battsek
SENIOR V.P. & GENERAL MANAGER, GERMANY
Wolfgang Braun
SENIOR V.P. & GENERAL MANAGER, SWEDEN
Eric Broberg
SENIOR V.P., SALES & MARKETING, ASIA/PACIFIC
Jeff Forman
SENIOR V.P. & GENERAL MANAGER, SPAIN
Javier Vasallo
SENIOR V.P. & GENERAL MANAGER, BVI/BVHEI, ITALY
Paul Zonderland
SENIOR V.P. & GENERAL MANAGER, JAPAN
Dick Sano
SENIOR V.P., CREATIVE DISNEY CHARACTER VOICES,
DCV INTL.
Rick Dempsey
EXECUTIVE SALES DIRECTOR, LATIN AMERICA
Martin Iraola
V.P., OPERATIONS DISNEY CHARACTER VOICES INTL.
Barrie Godwin
V.P., FINANCE & PLANNING
Jerome Le Grand
V.P., MARKETING, EUROPE
Nic Crawley
V.P., PUBLICITY, EUROPE
Michelle Sewell
V.P., MARKETING & BRAND DEVELOPMENT, LATIN
AMERICA
Laura Rama
V.P. & GENERAL MANAGER, SWITZERLAND
Roger Crotti
V.P. & GENERAL MANAGER, BVI/BVHEI, BENELUX
Eline Danker
V.P. & MANAGING DIRECTOR, AUSTRALIA & NEW
ZEALAND
Alan Finney
V.P., DISTRIBUTION EUROPE
Daniel Frigo
V.P. & GENERAL MANAGER, SOUTH KOREA
S.I. Kim
V.P. & GENERAL MANAGER, AUSTRIA
Ferdinand Morawetz
V.P. & GENERAL MANAGER, TAIWAN
Rudy Tseng
V.P. & GENERAL MANAGER, IRELAND
Brendan McCaul
GENERAL MANAGER, FINLAND
Jussi Makela
GENERAL MANAGER, NORWAY
Inger Warendolph

BUENA VISTA MUSIC GROUP
CHAIRMAN, BVMG
Bob Cavallo
EXECUTIVE V.P. & GM, BVMG
David Agnew
EXECUTIVE V.P., A&R & SOUNDTRACKS, BVMG
Mitchell Leib
SENIOR V.P., FINANCE & ACCOUNTING, BVMG
Cathleen Taff

BUENA VISTA HOME ENTERTAINMENT INTERNATIONAL
350 South Buena Vista St., Burbank, CA 91521. (818) 560-1000.
PRESIDENT, BUENA VISTA INTL. & BVHE
Mark Zoradi
PRESIDENT, BVHEI
Dennis Maguire
SENIOR V.P., SALES & MARKETING, ASIA & PACIFIC
Jeff Forman
SENIOR V.P., WORLDWIDE CREATIVE SERVICES
Andy Siditsky
SENIOR V.P., EUROPE, MIDDLE EAST & AFRICA
Rob Jongmans
V.P., HUMAN RESOURCES & ADMINISTRATION
Chris Menosky
V.P., MARKETING & BUSINESS DEVELOPMENT
Kris Brown
V.P., PUBLICITY
Joel Binder
V.P., OPERATIONS
Bill Segil
V.P., FINANCE & PLANNING, BVI & BVHEI
Jerome Le Grand
V.P., EUROPE MARKETING
Helen Stratton
V.P., EUROPEAN FINANCE & ADMINISTRATION
Adam Castleton
V.P., BUSINESS DEVELOPMENT, EUROPE
Tony Chambers

BUENA VISTA HOME ENTERTAINMENT (DOMESTIC)
350 S. Buena Vista St., Burbank, CA 91521. (818) 560-1000.
PRESIDENT
Robert Chapek
SENIOR V.P., SALES & DISTRIBUTION
Patrick Fitzgerald
SENIOR V.P., OPERATIONS MANAGEMENT & PLANNING
Bill Stellman
SENIOR V.P., PUBLICITY
Heidi Trotta
SENIOR V.P., RESEARCH
Dana Lombardo
SENIOR V.P., ADVERTISING
Kristy Frudenfeld
SENIOR V.P., WORLDWIDE MARKETING SERVICE
Andy Siditsky
SENIOR V.P., BRAND MARKETING
Gordon Ho
V.P., BRAND MARKETING
Lori Macpherson
V.P., BUSINESS & LEGAL AFFAIRS
Kristin McQueen

WALT DISNEY TELEVISION ANIMATION
500 S. Buena Vista St., Burbank, CA 91521. (818) 560-5000.
PRESIDENT
Barry Blumberg
SENIOR V.P., BUSINESS & LEGAL AFFAIRS
Mark Kenchelian
SENIOR V.P., FINANCE
Joanna Spak
SENIOR V.P., MUSIC
Matt Walker
V.P., DIGITAL PRODUCTION & TECHNOLOGY
Karen Ferguson
V.P., CREATIVE AFFAIRS
Jay Fukuto
V.P., PRODUCTION
Lisa Salamone
V.P., POST PRODUCTION
Steve Swofford

DISNEYTOON STUDIOS
500 S. Buena Vista St., Burbank, CA 91521. (818) 560-5000.
EXECUTIVE V.P.
Sharon Morrill
SENIOR V.P., WORLDWIDE PRODUCTION
Lenora Hume
SENIOR V.P., BUSINESS & LEGAL AFFAIRS
Mark Kenchelian
SENIOR V.P., PUBLICITY, WALT DISNEY STUDIOS
Heidi Trotta
SENIOR V.P., MUSIC
Matt Walker
V.P., DIGITAL PRODUCTION & TECHNOLOGY
Karen Ferguson
V.P., VIDEO PREMIERES
Ellen Gurney
V.P., FINANCE
Paul Rappoport
V.P., VIDEO PREMIERES
Brian Snedeker
V.P., POST PRODUCTION
Steve Swofford
V.P., PUBLICITY
Lori Tellez
V.P., PRODUCTION
Michelle Robinson
V.P., VIDEO PREMIERES
Jill Gilbert

DISNEY CHANNEL
3800 W. Alameda Ave., Burbank, CA 91505. (818) 569-7500.
FAX: (818) 588-1241. www.disneychannel.com
PRESIDENT, ABC CABLE NETWORKS GROUP, ABC FAMILY
PRESIDENT, DISNEY CHANNEL WORLDWIDE
Anne Sweeney
PRESIDENT, WALT DISNEY TELEVISION ANIMATION
Barry Blumberg
PRESIDENT, ENTERTAINMENT DISNEY CHANNEL
Rich Ross
EXECUTIVE V.P., WORLDWIDE BRAND STRATEGY
Eleo Hensleigh
EXECUTIVE V.P., LEGAL & BUSINESS AFFAIRS
Frederick Kuperberg
EXECUTIVE V.P., BUSINESS OPERATIONS & DISTRIBUTION
Michael Dean
EXECUTIVE V.P., ORIGINAL PROGRAMMING &
PRODUCTION, DISNEY CHANNEL
Gary K. Marsh
SENIOR V.P. & CFO
Jewell Engstrom
SENIOR V.P. & GENERAL MANAGER/ABC KIDS & TOON
DISNEY
Jonathan Barzilay
SENIOR V.P. & GENERAL MANAGER, SOAPNET
Deborah Blackwell

BUENA VISTA TELEVISION
500 S. Buena Vista St., Burbank, CA 91521. (818) 560-5000.
FAX: (818) 566-7412.
PRESIDENT
Janice Marinelli
EXECUTIVE V.P., PROG. & DEV., BUENA VISTA PRODS.
Holly Jacobs
EXECUTIVE V.P., SALES
John Bryan
SENIOR V.P., DEVELOPMENT, BUENA VISTA PRODS.
Rob Morehaim
EXECUTIVE V.P., CURRENT PROGRAMMING, BUENA
VISTA PRODS.
Mary Kellogg-Joslyn
EXECUTIVE V.P., STRATEGIC RESEARCH
Lloyd Komesar
SENIOR V.P., FINANCE
Tom Malanga
V.P., PROMOTIONS
Jennie Borne
V.P., AFFILIATE RELATIONS
Sandra Brewer
V.P., CREATIVE SERVICES
Blake Bryant
V.P., RESEARCH
George Gubert
V.P., PRESS & PUBLICITY
Kim Harbin
V.P., PRODUCTION, BUENA VISTA PRODS.
Carlos Torres
DIRECTOR, DEVELOPMENT, BUENA VISTA PRODS.
Brooke Bowman

DISNEY INTERACTIVE
PRESIDENT, DISNEY INTERACTIVE, WORLDWIDE
Graham Hopper
CFO
Steve Gilbert
V.P., INTERNATIONAL
Sanjeer Lamba
V.P., BUSINESS & LEGAL AFFAIRS
Chris Drews
V.P., SALES
Todd Steckbeck
DIRECTOR, HUMAN RESOURCES
Tony Gilliard

WALT DISNEY IMAGINEERING
1401 Flower Street, Glendale, CA 91221. (818) 544-6500. FAX:
(818) 544-5080.
VICE CHAIRMAN & PRINCIPAL CREATIVE EXECUTIVE
Martin Sklar
PRESIDENT, WALT DISNEY IMAGINEERING
Donald Goodman
EXECUTIVE V.P., MASTER PLANNING, ARCH. & DESIGN
Wing Chao
EXECUTIVE V.P., STORY, SCRIPT & MEDIA
Thomas Fitzgerald
SENIOR V.P.
Tony Baxter
SENIOR V.P & EXECUTIVE PRODUCER
Barry Braverman
SENIOR V.P. & GENERAL MANAGER WDI FLORIDA
Thomas Dunlap
SENIOR V.P.
John Hench
SENIOR V.P.
Eric Jacobson
SENIOR V.P., ENGINEERING
Thomas McCann
SENIOR V.P., PROJECT MANAGEMENT & MANAGEMENT
CONTROLS
James Thomas
V.P., PROJECT PLANNING/SCHEDULING
Frank Addeman
V.P., PROJECT MANAGEMENT, WDI (FL)
John Blitch
V.P. CONCEPT/SHOW DESIGN
Christopher Carradine
V.P., EXECUTIVE DESIGNER
Timothy Delaney
V.P., DEVELOPMENT MANAGEMENT
Bryan Elliott
V.P., HUMAN RESOURCES
Tami Garcia
V.P., INVESTMENT MANAGEMENT
Richard Harrison
V.P., SHOW QUALITY STANDARD
George Head
V.P., ARCHITECTURE & FACILITIES ENGINEERING
Arthur Henderson
V.P., RESORTS & FACILITIES DEVELOPMENT
Robert Holland
V.P., REAL ESTATE DEVELOPMENT & OPERATIONS
Matthew Kelly
V.P., FINANCE
Martin Shumaker

V.P., PROJECTS
Arthur Kishiyama
V.P., CREATIVE
Kathryn Klatt
V.P., PROJECT MANAGEMENT
Paul La France
V.P., EXECUTIVE PRODUCTION DESIGNER
Oscar Lange, Jr.
V.P., EXECUTIVE PRODUCER
Kathryn Mangum
V.P., SCIENTIFIC SYSTEMS
Nick Mansur
V.P., PLANNING INFRASTRUCTURE
Harold McIntyre
V.P., DESIGN & PRODUCTION
Michael Morris
V.P., EXECUTIVE PRODUCER
Thomas Morris
V.P., EXECUTIVE PRODUCTION DESIGNER
John Olson
V.P., EXECUTIVE PRODUCER
Paul Osterhout
V.P., GENERAL MANAGER CELEBRATION CO.
Perry Reader
V.P., EXECUTIVE DESIGNER
Joseph Rohde
V.P., EXECUTIVE SHOW PRODUCER
Frederick Rothschild
V.P., A&FE MANAGEMENT
Craig Russell
V.P., CREATIVE DEVELOPMENT, TPP
John Solomon
V.P., GENERAL COUNSEL
Peter Steinman
V.P., PROJECT MANAGEMENT
David Todd
V.P., RESEARCH & DEVELOPMENT
Bruce Vanghn
V.P., PROJECT MANAGEMENT HONG KONG DISNEYLAND
John Verity
V.P., ON-LINE & ADVERTISING MEDIA
Scott Watson
V.P. SHOW RIDE ENGINEERING
Michael Withers

DISTANT HORIZON
(Motion picture distributor, South Africa)
8282 Sunset Blvd., Ste. A, Los Angeles, CA 90046. (323) 848-
4140. FAX: (323) 848-4144. www.distant-horizon.com
PRESIDENT
Anant Singh

MAUREEN DONLEY PICTURES
914 Westwood Blvd., Ste. 591, Los Angeles, CA 90024. (310)
441-0834 FAX: (310) 441-1595. email: mcd@mdpix.com
PRODUCER
Maureen Donley
DIRECTOR, DEVELOPMENT
Lauren Sands

THE DONNERS' COMPANY
(Motion picture, independent film & TV producer)
9465 Wilshire Blvd., Ste. 420, Beverly Hills, CA 90212. (310)
777-4600. FAX: (310) 777-4610.
PRODUCER & DIRECTOR
Richard Donner
PRODUCER
Lauren Shuler Donner

DOTSON-WOOLEY ENTERTAINMENT GROUP
123 Walton Ferry Rd., Hendersonville, TN 37075. (615) 824-
1947. FAX: (615) 264-0462. email: dotwool@bellsouth.net.
PARTNER
Linda S. Dotson
PARTNER
Sheb Wooley

DOUBLE FEATURE FILMS
(Motion picture, independent film & TV producer)
10351 Santa Monica Blvd., Ste. 200, Los Angeles, CA 90025.
(310) 203-1000. FAX: (310) 203-1010.
CO-CHAIRMAN
Michael Shamberg
CO-CHAIRMAN
Stacey Sher
CEO
Rich Klubeck
PRESIDENT, JERSEY TELEVISION
John Landgraf
EXECUTIVE V.P.
Carla Santos Shamberg
V.P., PRODUCTION, JERSEY TV
Ellie Hannibal
DIRECTOR, OPERATIONS
Amy Hurdelbrink
CONTROLLER
Karen Willaman
CREATIVE EXECUTIVES
Erin Dicker
David Posamentier

JEAN DOUMANIAN PRODUCTIONS

(Motion picture, independent film & TV producer)
595 Madison Ave., Ste. 2200, New York, NY 10022. (212) 486-2626. FAX: (212) 688-6236.
PRESIDENT
Jean Doumanian
V.P., PRODUCTION & DEVELOPMENT
Eric Falkenstein
V.P., PRODUCTION & DEVELOPMENT
Etan Frankel
V.P., PRODUCTION & DEVELOPMENT
Kim Jose
ASSISTANTS
Stephen Lancellott
Lisa Quintela

DREAMWORKS SKG

(Producer; distribution through Universal)
100 Flower St., Glendale, CA 91201. (818) 695-7000.
PRINCIPALS
Steven Spielberg
Jeffrey Katzenberg
David Geffen
CO-HEAD, MOTION PICTURE DIVISION
Laurie MacDonald
CO-HEAD, MOTION PICTURE DIVISION
Walter Parkes
CO-HEAD, PRODUCTION
Mike DeLuca
COO
Helene Hahn
HEAD, ANIMATION
Ann Daly
HEAD, WW PAY TV
Hal Richardson
CO-HEADS, TV
Justin Falvy
Darryl Frank
CO-HEADS, MUSIC
Michael Ostin
Mo Ostin
Lenoard Waronker
HEAD, CONSUMER PRODUCTS
Brad Globe
HEAD, HOME VIDEO
Kelly Avery
HEAD, FILM MUSIC
Todd Homme
HEAD, THEATRICAL DISTRIBUTION
Jim Tharp
HEAD, MARKETING & PUBLIC RELATIONS
Terry Press

DREYFUSS/JAMES PRDOUCTIONS

(Motion picture & TV producer)
The Lot, 1041 N. Formosa Ave., Mary Pickford Bldg., Ste. 100, Los Angeles, CA 90046. (323) 850-3140. FAX: (323) 850-3141.
OWNER & EXECUTIVE PRODUCER
Richard Dreyfuss
OWNER & EXECUTIVE PRODUCER
Judith James
DIRECTOR, DEVELOPMENT
Greg Szimonisz

THE DRIVE-BY FILM SHOOTING COMPANY

(Motion picture & TV producer)
12830 Rosa Ave., Los Angeles, CA 90066. (310) 390-7308.
www.michaeladdis.com email: ma@michaeladdis.com
WRITER & DIRECTOR
Michael Addis
DIRECTOR, DEVELOPMENT
Phil Shuster

EARTH LION PRODUCTIONS

(Producer)
5460 White Oak Ave., Ste. F303, Encino, CA 91316. (215) 243-3100. FAX: (215) 243-3100.
PRODUCER
Bonnie Rutherford
CREATIVE EXECUTIVES
Sam Franklin
Jeff Chasin

EASTMAN KODAK COMPANY

343 State St., Rochester, NY 14650. (585) 724-4000.
CHAIRMAN & CEO
Daniel A. Carp
PRESIDENT, ENTERTAINMENT IMAGING
Eric G. Rodli
6700 Santa Monica Blvd., Hollywood, CA 90038. (323) 464-6131.www.kodak.com
360 W. 31st St., New York, NY 10001. (212) 631-3400
Atlanta, GA (770) 777-0410.
MOTION PICTURE, ENTERTAINMENT IMAGING
Janet Tiller

EDMONDS ENTERTAINMENT

(Motion picture & TV producer)
1635 N. Cahenga Blvd., 5th Flr., Los Angeles, CA 90028. (323) 860-1550. FAX: (323) 860-1554.
PRESIDENT & CEO
Kenneth "Babyface" Edmonds
PRESIDENT & CEO
Tracey E. Edmonds
V.P., FILM
Steve Lapuk
V.P. TELEVISION
Shelia Ducksworth
CREATIVE EXECUTIVE, FILM DEPARTMENT
Devon FRANKLIN
EXECUTIVE ASSISTANT, TV DEPARTMENT
Emerlynn Lampitoc

EL DORADO PICTURES

(Motion picture & TV producer)
725 Arizona Ave., Ste. 100, Santa Monica, CA 90401. (310) 458-4800. FAX: (310) 458-4802.
PRODUCERS
Alec Baldwin
Jon Cornick

ENTERTAINMENT PRODUCTIONS, INC.

(Motion picture & TV producer for worldwide markets)
2118 Wilshire Blvd., PMB 744, Santa Monica, CA 90403. (310) 456-3143. FAX: (310) 456-8950.
PRESIDENT & PRODUCER
Edward Coe

ENTERTAINMENT VENTURES INTERNATIONAL

(Film, TV, music & video producer; promotion & packaging)
100 S. Doheny Dr., Ste. 402, Los Angeles, CA 90048. (310) 278-2800. FAX: (310) 274-0400. www.smart90.com/evi
email: entventint@cs.com
DIRECTOR OF OPERATIONS
Jim Beatty
V.P., OPERATIONS
Karen Beth Cantrell
FILM & T.V. PACKAGER
Raya Markson
PUBLIC RELATIONS
Joyce Miller

EQUINOX ENTERTAINMENT, LTD.

(Motion picture, TV & direct to video producer & distributor)
15030 Ventura Blvd., #815, Sherman Oaks, CA 91403. (818) 788-2500. FAX: (818) 528-1488.
EXECUTIVE PRODUCER & PRODUCER
Mark Michopoulos
CO-PRODUCER
Bob Manning
DIRECTOR, OPERATIONS
Ben Carpenter
DIRECTOR, DEVELOPMENT
Alex Ellis
DIRECTOR, RESEARCH & ACQUISITIONS
Mandy Goldberg
DIRECTOR, CREATIVE AFFAIRS
Tim Mathos
DIRECTOR, PRODUCTION
Amy Segal
DIRECTOR, BUSINESS AFFAIRS
Samantha Wagner
DIRECTOR, FINANCE & MARKETING & DISTRIBUTION
Lauren Worth
STORY EDITOR
Nick Andraos
ASSOCIATE PRODUCER & DIRECTOR, TALENT & CASTING
Ryan Sahlberg
EXECUTIVE ASSISTANTS
Lisa Logan
Jennifer Mancini
ASSISTANT STORY EDITOR
Evan Cartwright
ASSISTANT, TALENT & CASTING
Sara Palmer
ASSISTANT, DEVELOPMENT
C.J. Pillsbury
ASSISTANT, RESEARCH & ACQUISITIONS
Max Shepherd

ESCAPE ARTISTS

(Motion picture producer)
10202 W. Washington Blvd., Astaire Bldg., 3rd Flr., Culver City, CA 90232. (310) 244-8833.
PARTNERS
David Alper
Todd Black
Jason Blumenthal
Steve Tisch
SENIOR V.P.
Brian Morewitz

EXECUTIVE V.P., BUSINESS & LEGAL AFFAIRS
David Bloomfield
V.P., DEVELOPMENT
Chrissy Blumenthal
CREATIVE ASSISTANT
Chris Coggins
CONTROLLER & MANAGER, ADMINISTRATION & HUMAN
RESOURCES
Kim Skeeters
STORY EDITOR
Lance Johnson
OFFICE MANAGER
Kathy Rowe
ASSISTANT
Lacy Bougn

ETERNITY PICTURES, INC.

(Motion picture producer & distributor)
169 Pier Ave., Second Flr., Santa Monica, CA 90405. (310)
452-7313. FAX: (310) 452-7318.
email: cmiller@eternitypictures.com
PRODUCER
Willi Baer
PRODUCER
Carmen M. Miller

THE ROBERT EVANS CO.

(Motion picture producer)
5555 Melrose Ave., Lubitsch Bldg. #117, Los Angeles, CA
90038-3197. (323) 956-8800. FAX: (323) 862-0070.
CHAIRMAN
Robert Evans
PRESIDENT
Christine Forsyth-Peters
EXECUTIVE V.P.
Robin Guthrie
STORY EDITOR
Samuel Dowe-Sanders
DEVELOPMENT ASSISTANT
James DeJulio

FACE PRODUCTIONS/JENNILIND PRODUCTIONS

335 N. Maple Dr., Ste. 175, Beverly Hills, CA 90210. (310) 205-
2746. FAX: (310) 285-2386.
WRITER, ACTOR, DIRECTOR
Billy Crystal
V.P., DEVELOPMENT, FEATURES
Samantha Sprecher
V.P., DEVELOPMENT, TELEVISION
Cheryl Bloch
ASSISTANT TO MR. CRYSTAL
Carol Sidlow
ASSISTANT TO MS. SPRECHER & MS. BLOCH
Liz Goumas

EDWARD S. FELDMAN CO.

(Motion picture producer)
1041 N. Formosa Ave., W. Hollywood, CA 90046. (323) 956-
5987. FAX: (323) 850-2649. email: winshipper@aol.com
PRESIDENT & PRODUCER
Ed Feldman
V.P., PRODUCTION & CO-PRODUCER
Winship Cook

FGM ENTERTAINMENT

(Motion picture producer)
301 N. Canon Dr., Ste. 328, Beverly Hills, CA 90210. (310)
205-9900. FAX: (310) 205-9909.
PRODUCER & PRESIDENT
Frank Mancuso Jr.
LINE PRODUCER
Vikki Williams

FIFTY CANNON ENTERTAINMENT, LLC

(Motion picture & TV producer)
1950 Sawtelle, Ste. 333, Los Angeles, CA 90025. (310) 481-
9030. FAX: (310) 481-9049.
CHAIRMAN
Mike Newell
PRESIDENT
Cameron Jones
VICE PRESIDENT
William Butler-Sloss

FILM BUFF PRODUCTIONS, INC.

(Motion picture producer)
73 Market St., Venice, CA 90291. (310) 396-5937.
PARTNER & WRITER & DIRECTOR
Andy Tennant
PARTNER & PRODUCER
Wink Mordaunt

FILMS AROUND THE WORLD, INC.

(Motion picture distributor)
417 E. 57th St., Ste. 31B, New York, NY 10022 (212) 599-
9500. FAX: (212) 599-6040.
PRESIDENT
Alexander W. Kogan, Jr.

FINNEGAN-PINCHUK COMPANY

(Motion picture & TV producer)
4440 Vanceboro Crt., Woodland Hills, CA 91364. (818) 508-
5614. FAX: (818) 313-9746.
EXECUTIVE PRODUCERS
Patricia Finnegan
William Finnegan
Sheldon Pinchuk

FIRST KISS PRODUCTIONS

468 N. Camden Dr., Ste. 200, Beverly Hills, CA 90210. (310)
860-5611. FAX: (310) 285-1735.
ACTRESS & PRODUCER
Alicia Silverstone
MANAGER & PRODUCER
Carolyn Kessler
CREATIVE EXECUTIVE
Matt Miranda

FIRST LIGHT

c/o Paramount Pictures, 5555 Melrose Ave., Clara Bldg., Ste.
200, Hollywood, CA 90038. (323) 956-8871. FAX: (323) 862-
2320.
DIRECTOR
Kathryn Bigelow
VICE PRESIDENT
David Markus

FIRST LOOK PICTURES/OVERSEAS FILM GROUP

(Film distribution & acquisition)
8000 Sunset Blvd., E. Penthouse, Los Angeles, CA 90046.
(323) 337-1000. FAX: (323) 337-1037. www.firstlookmedia.com
PRESIDENT
Bill Lischak
CO-CHAIRMAN
Robert Little
CEO & CO-CHAIRMAN
Chris Cooney
COO
Bill Lischak
SENIOR V.P., MARKETING
Steven Demille
V.P., BUSINESS & LEGAL AFFAIRS
Doug McClure

1ST MIRACLE PICTURES

(Motion picture, independent film & TV producer & distributor)
3439 W. Cahuenga Blvd., Hollywood, CA 90068. (323) 874-
6000. FAX: (323) 874-4252.
PRESIDENT
Simon Bibiyan
CEO
Moshe Bibiyan

FIRST RUN FEATURES

(Motion picture, independent film & TV distributor)
153 Waverly Pl., New York, NY 10014. (800) 229-8575. FAX:
(212) 989-7649. www.firstrunfeatures.com
email: info@firstrunfeatures.com
PRESIDENT
Seymour Wishman
VICE PRESIDENT
Marc A. Mauceri

FLOWER FILMS, INC.

(Motion picture producer)
9220 Sunset Blvd., #309, Los Angeles, CA 90069. (310) 285-
0200. FAX: (310) 285-0827.
PARTNERS
Drew Barrymore
Nancy Juvonen
V.P., PRODUCTION
Chris Miller
V.P., DEVELOPMENT
Gwen Stroman
DEVELOPMENT EXECUTIVE
Alan Trezza
OFFICE MANAGER
Barry Johnson
ASSISTANTS
Miri Yoon
Dawn Haber

FORTIS FILMS

(Motion picture producer)
8581 Santa Monica Blvd., Ste. 1, West Hollywood, CA 90069.
(310) 659-4533.
OWNER
Sandra Bullock
PRESIDENT & CEO
John Bullock
EXECUTIVE V.P.
Gesine Bullock
PRODUCTION EXECUTIVE
Maggie Biggar
DIRECTOR, DEVELOPMENT
Lillian Dean

FORTY ACRES & A MULE FILMWORKS

124 Dekalb Ave., Brooklyn, NY 11217. (718) 624-3703. FAX: (718) 624-2008.
8899 Beverly Blvd. Ste. 401, Los Angeles, CA 90048. (310) 276-2116. FAX: (310) 276-2164.
CEO
Spike Lee
PRESIDENT, PRODUCTION
Sam Kitt

44 BLUE PRODUCTIONS, INC.

(TV producer)
4040 Vineland Ave., Ste. 105, Studio City, CA 91604. (818) 760-4442. FAX: (818) 760-1509.
PRESIDENT & EXECUTIVE PRODUCER
Rasha Drachkovitch
EXECUTIVE IN CHARGE OF PRODUCTION
Stuart Zwagil

FORWARD PASS, INC.

(Motion picture producer)
12233 W. Olympic Blvd., Ste. 340, Los Angeles, CA 90064. (310) 571-3443.
WRITER & PRODUCER & DIRECTOR
Michael Mann

1492 PICTURES

4000 Warner Blvd., Bldg. 139, Ste. 18, Burbank, CA 91522. (818) 954-4924.
WRITER & DIRECTOR & PRODUCER & PARTNER
Chris Columbus
PRESIDENT & PRODUCER & PARTNER
Michael Barnathan
PRODUCER & PARTNER
Mark Radcliffe
ASSOCIATE PRODUCER
Paula DuPre-Pesmen

FOX, INC.

(Fox, Inc. is the parent company of Fox Broadcasting Co., Fox Television Stations Inc. & Fox Filmed Entertainment, which includes Twentieth Century Fox Film Corp. & Fox 2000)
10201 W. Pico Blvd., Los Angeles, CA 90035. (310) 369-1000.
1211 Ave. of the Americas 16th Flr., New York, NY 10036. (212) 556-8600. FAX: (212) 556-8606.
www.newscorp.com www.fox.com
23975 Park Sorrento Dr., Ste. 300, Calabasas, CA 91302. (818) 876-7219. FAX: (818) 876-7200.
33 Bloor St E., Ste. 1106, Toronto, ON M4W 3H1. (416) 921-0001. FAX: (416) 921-9062.
CHAIRMAN & CEO, NEWS CORPORATION
Rupert Murdoch
CHAIRMAN & CO-COO, FOX NEWS CORP.
Peter Chernin
CHAIRMAN & CEO FOX GROUP
Chase Carey
EXECUTIVE V.P. & CFO
David F. DeVoe

FOX FILMED ENTERTAINMENT

CHAIRMEN
Tom Rothman
Jim Gianopulos
VICE CHAIRMAN
Robert Harper
DEPUTY GENERAL COUNSEL
Greg Gelfan
EXECUTIVE V.P. & CFO, FINANCE
Dean Hallett

TWENTIETH CENTURY FOX

CHAIRMEN, TWENTIETH CENTURY FOX FILM GROUP
Tom Rothman
Jim Gianopulos
PRESIDENT, PRODUCTION
Hutch Parker
EXECUTIVE V.P., POST-PRODUCTION
Theodore Gagliano
SENIOR V.P., PRODUCTION
Fred Baron
SENIOR V.P., ACQUISITIONS
Tony Safford

MARKETING

CO-PRESIDENT, DOMESTIC THEATRICAL MARKETING
Anthony Sella
CO-PRESIDENT, DOMESTIC THEATRICAL MARKETING
Pam Levine
EXECUTIVE V.P., PUBLICITY & PROMOTIONS
Jeffrey Godsick
SENIOR V.P., MEDIA & CO-OP ADVERTISING
Steve Siskind
SENIOR V.P., THEATRICAL PUBLICITY
Tom Grane
V.P., PUBLICITY
Carol Sewell
V.P., ADVERTISING & MKTG. & CREATIVE ADVERTISING
Christopher Pawlak

DISTRIBUTION

PRESIDENT, DOMESTIC DISTRIBUTION
Bruce Snyder
EXECUTIVE V.P., & GENERAL SALES MANAGER
Richard Myerson
EXECUTIVE V.P., WORLDWIDE NON THEATRICAL SALES AND DIGITAL
Julian Levin
V.P., EXHIBITOR SERVICES
Branden Miller
MANAGER, EXHIBITOR SERVICES
Jill Amerman
V.P., DISTRIBUTION, SOUTHERN DIVISION
Rusty Gautier
V.P., DISTRIBUTION, WESTERN DIVISION
Bert Livingston
V.P., DISTRIBUTION, EASTERN DIVISION MANAGER
Ron Polon
V.P., DISTRIBUTION, MID-WESTERN DIVISION MANAGER
Henri Frankfurter
GENERAL MANAGER, CANADA
Barry Newstead

ADMINISTRATION

EXECUTIVE V.P., LEGAL AFFAIRS
Robert Cohen
COO, DOMESTIC VIDEO THEATRICAL MARKETING
Steven Bersch
EXECUTIVE V.P., LEGAL BUSINESS AFFAIRS
Michael Doodan
EXECUTIVE V.P., BUSINESS AFFAIRS
Mark Resnick
SENIOR V.P., LEGAL & BUSINESS AFFAIRS
Jamie Samson
SENIOR V.P., BUSINESS AFFAIRS LEGAL MUSIC
Lance Grode
SENIOR V.P., HUMAN RESOURCES
Linda Johns
SENIOR V.P., LEGAL AFFAIRS
Randy Kender
SENIOR V.P., INTERNATIONAL TV
Mark Rosenbaum
SENIOR V.P., FINANCE DISTRIBUTION & MARKETING
John Djergian
V.P., CORPORATE COMMUNICATIONS
Florence Grace
V.P., LEGAL AFFAIRS
Joan Hansen
DIRECTOR, FINANCE, DISTRIBUTION
Todd Greenfield

INTERNATIONAL

EXECUTIVE V.P., INTERNATIONAL SALES & DISTRIBUTION
Paul Hanneman
PRESIDENT, INTERNATIONAL DISTRIBUTION
Stephen Moore
PRESIDENT, HEAD OFFICE INTERNATIONAL THEATRICAL
Scott Neeson
SENIOR V.P., CREATIVE ADVERTISING & INTERNATIONAL THEATRICAL DISTRIBUTION
Jim Darbinian
DIRECTOR, INTERNATIONAL SALES
Craig Dehmel

FOX STUDIO OPERATIONS

EXECUTIVE V.P., FOX SPORTS
Gary Ehrlich

FOX 2000

PRESIDENT
Elizabeth Gabler
EXECUTIVE V.P.
Carla Hacken

FOX SEARCHLIGHT

PRESIDENT
Peter Rice
SENIOR V.P., PRODUCTION
Claudia Lewis
SENIOR V.P., DOMESTIC DISTRIBUTION
Steve Gilula
PRESIDENT, MARKETING, FOX SEARCHLIGHT
Nancy Utley

FOX ANIMATION STUDIOS

PRESIDENT
Chris Meldandri

TWENTIETH CENTURY FOX TELEVISION

CO-PRESIDENT
Sandy Grushnow
PRESIDENT, TCF TELEVISION
Gary Newman
PRESIDENT, TCF TELEVISION
Dana Walden
CFO & EXECUTIVE V.P.
Robert Barron
PRODUCER
Charlie Goldstein

EXECUTIVE V.P., BUSINESS & LEGAL AFFAIRS
Howard Kurtzman
SENIOR V.P., TV PRODUCTION
Janie Kleiman
SENIOR V.P., TV PRODUCTION, COMEDY
Joel Hornstock
SENIOR V.P., COMEDY
Brad Johnson
SENIOR V.P., MARKETING
Steven Melnick

FOX HOME ENTERTAINMENT

PRESIDENT, HOME ENTERTAINMENT
Mike Dunn
SENIOR V.P., NATIONAL SALES
Simon Swart

FRANCHISE PICTURES INC.

(Motion picture & independent film producer & distribution)
8228 Sunset Blvd., Ste. 305, Los Angeles, CA 90046. (323) 822-0730. FAX: (323) 822-2165.
CEO
Elie Samaha
PRESIDENT
David Bergstein
PRESIDENT, DEVELOPMENT & ACQUISITIONS
Tracee Stanley
EXECUTIVE V.P., BUSINESS AFFAIRS
Rick Kwak
EXECUTIVE V.P. & CFO
Hans Turner

FRESH PRODUCE MEDIA

115 Brooks Ave., Venice Beach, CA 90291. (310) 399-0905. FAX: (310) 399-5603. email thebigidea@aol.com
CONTACT
Thomas Elliott

FURTHER FILMS

(Motion picture producer & developer)
100 Universal City Plaza, Bldg. 1320/4G, Universal City, CA 91608. (818) 777-6700. FAX: (818) 866-1278.
825 8th Ave., 30th Flr., New York, NY 10019. (212) 333-1421. FAX: (212) 333-8163.
PRODUCER
Michael Douglas
PRESIDENT
Marcy Drogin
SENIOR V.P. (CA)
Lisa Bellomo
DIRECTOR, DEVELOPMENT
James LaVigne
CONTACTS
Corley Thayer (NY)
Michael Lare (CA)
Robert Mitas (CA)

GENERAL MEDIA INTERNATIONAL

(Video producer & distributor)
11 Penn Plaza., 12th Flr., New York, NY 10001. (212) 702-6000. FAX: (212) 702-6262.
CHAIRMAN & CEO
Bob Guccione
VICE CHAIRMAN., PRESIDENT & COO
John Prebich
V.P., INTERNET OPERATIONS
G. VanDerLuen

GHOULDARDI FILM COMPANY

(Motion picture producer)
4121 1/2 Rudford Ave., Studios City, CA 91604. (818) 505-6603. FAX: (818) 505-6604.
WRITER, DIRECTOR
Paul Thomas Anderson
PRODUCER
Joanne Sellar

GMR PRODUCTIONS, INC.

1333 6th Ave., Venice, CA 90291. (310) 401-1400. FAX: (310) 401-1200. email: ginares@earthlink.net
PRODUCER
Gina Resnick

GOAT CAY PRODUCTIONS, INC.

(Motion picture producer)
P.O. Box 38, New York, NY 10150. (212) 421-8293. FAX: (212) 421-8294. email: goatcay@earthlink.net
PRESIDENT & PRODUCER & ACTOR
Sigourney Weaver

THE GOATSINGERS

(Motion picture producer)
177 W. Broadway, 2nd Flr., New York, NY 10013. (212) 966-3045. FAX: (212) 966-4362.
PRESIDENT
Harvey Keitel

FREDERIC GOLCHAN PRODUCTIONS

(Motion picture & independent film producer)
1447 N. Hayworth Ave., West Hollywood, CA 90046. (323) 656-1122. FAX: (323) 656-3366.
PRESIDENT
Frederic A. Golchan
ASSISTANT TO THE PRESIDENT
Aurelia Abate

GOLDEN QUILL

(Motion picture director)
8899 Beverly Blvd., Ste. 702, Los Angeles, CA 90048. (310) 274-5016. FAX: (310) 274-5028.
DIRECTOR & PRODUCER
Arthur Hiller

THE GOLDSTEIN CO.

1644 Courtney Ave., Los Angeles, CA 90046. (310) 659-9511. FAX: (310) 659-8779.
PRODUCER
Gary W. Goldstein

SAMUEL GOLDWYN FILMS, LLC

(Motion picture producer & distributor)
9570 W. Pico Blvd., Ste. 400, Los Angeles, CA 90035. (310) 860-3100. FAX: (310) 860-3195.
1133 Broadway, Ste. 926, New York, NY 10010. (212) 367-9435. FAX: (212) 367-0853.
CHAIRMAN & CEO
Samuel Goldwyn, Jr.
PRESIDENT & COO
Meyer Gottlieb
V.P., ACQUISITIONS (NY)
Tom Quinn
V.P., DEVELOPMENT
Julie Huey
DIRECTOR, DEVELOPMENT
Tasha Cronin
MANAGER, ACQUISITIONS
Peter Goldwyn

GORDON FILMS, INC.

(Motion picture producer & distributor)
119 W. 57th St., Ste. 319, New York, NY 10019. (212) 757-9390. FAX: (212) 757-9392.
PRESIDENT
Richard Gordon
VICE PRESIDENT
Joseph R. Cattuti

GOTHAM METRO STUDIOS, INC.

(Production, development production finance, film distribution, tv & video production)
303 Broadway, Ste. 204, Laguna Beach, CA 92651. (877) 787-8848. www.GothamMetro.com email: ceo@GothamMetro.com
EXECUTIVE PRODUCER
Michael J Lasky

GOTHAM PICTURES

(Motion picture, independent film & TV producer)
1114 Lachman Lane, Pacific Palisades, CA 90272. (310) 306-0120. www.resolutionprod.com email: rgunner@bigfoot.com
PARTNERS
Greg McMurray
Rhonda Gunner

GRACIE FILMS

(Motion picture & TV producer)
10202 W. Washington Blvd., Poitier Bldg., Culver City, CA 90232. (310) 244-4222. FAX: (310) 244-1530.
10201 W. Pico Blvd., Los Angeles, CA 90035.
PRODUCER & WRITER & DIRECTOR
James L. Brooks
PRESIDENT
Richard Sakai
PRESIDENT, MOTION PICTURES
Julie Ansell
EXECUTIVE V.P.
Denise Sirkot

GRAINY PICTURES

75 Main St., Cold Spring, NY 10516. (845) 265-2241. www.grainypictures.com email: info@grainypictures.com
CO-PRESIDENT
Janet Pierson
CO-PRESIDENT
John Pierson

GREENESTREET FILMS, INC.

(Motion picture, independent film & TV producer)
9 Desbrosses St., 2nd Flr., New York, NY 10013. (212) 609-9000. FAX: (212) 609-9099. www.greenestreetfilms.com
email: general@gstreet.com
PARTNER & CEO
John Penotti

PARTNER & CREATIVE EXECUTIVE
Fisher Stevens
GENERAL MANAGER
Debbie Johnson
HEAD, DEVELOPMENT
Jamie Gordon
HEAD, PRODUCTION
Tim Williams
DIRECTOR, DEVELOPMENT
Courtney Potts

GREEN MOON PRODUCTIONS

11718 Barrington Ct., Ste. 827, Los Angeles, CA 90049. (310)
471-8800. FAX: (310) 471-8022.
PRODUCER, DIRECTOR & ACTRESS
Melanie Griffith
PRODUCER & ACTOR
Antonio Banderas
PRESIDENT
Diane Sillan Isaacs

HARGROVE ENTERTAINMENT, INC.

P.O. Box 750338, Forrest Hill, NY 11375-0338. (718) 657-0542.
www.HargroveTV.com email: tvsales@HargroveTV.com
PRESIDENT
Peter M. Hargrove

HARPO FILMS, INC.

345 N. Maple Dr., Ste. 315, Beverly Hills, CA 90210. (310) 278-
5559.
110 N. Carpenter, Chicago, IL 60607. (312) 633-1000.
CHAIRMAN & CEO
Oprah Winfrey
PRESIDENT
Kate Forte
DIRECTOR, MEDIA & CORPORATE RELATIONS
Lisa Halliday
V.P., DEVELOPMENT, TV & FEATURES
Susan Heyer
CREATIVE EXECUTIVE
Melody Fowler

HAVOC, INC.

16 W. 19th St., 12th Flr., New York, NY 10011. (212) 924-1629
& (212) 924-1629. FAX: (212) 924-3105.
PRODUCER & DIRECTOR & WRITER & ACTOR
Tim Robbins

HEARST ENTERTAINMENT

(Made-for-TV-movies, reality & documentary series & specials)
888 Seventh Ave., New York, NY 10019. (212) 455-4000.
FAX: (212) 455-4310.
PRESIDENT
Bruce L. Paisner

JIM HENSON PICTURES

(Motion picture producer)
1416 N. La Brea Ave., Hollywood, CA 90028. (323) 802-1500.
FAX: (323) 802-1825. www.henson.com
PRESIDENT
Lisa Henson
PRODUCTION
Kristine Belson
STORY EDITOR
Kevin Kelly
PRODUCTION COORDINATOR
Melissa Eaton

HOFFLUND POLONE

9465 Wilshire Blvd., Ste. 820, Beverly Hills, CA 90212. (310)
859-1971. FAX: (310) 859-7250.
PARTNERS
Judy Hofflund
Gavin Polone

HOME BOX OFFICE, INC.

(A premium service and subsidiary of Time Warner, Inc.)
1100 Ave. of the Americas, New York, NY 10036. (212) 512-
1000. FAX: (212) 512-5517.
2049 Century Park E., Ste. 4100, Los Angeles, CA 90067-
3215. (310) 201-9200. FAX: (310) 207-9310. www.hbo.com
CHAIRMAN & CEO
Chris Albrecht
PRESIDENT, HBO FILMS
Collin Callender
PRESIDENT, HBO SPORTS
Ross Greenburg
PRESIDENT, HBO HOME VIDEO
Henry McGee
PRESIDENT, HBO INTERNATIONAL
Steve Rosenberg
PRESIDENT, FILM PROGRAMMING, VIDEO & ENTERPRISES
Steve Scheffer
PRESIDENT, SALES & MARKETING
Eric Kessler

HBO FILMS
SENIOR V.P., HBO FILMS
Kerith Putnam
V.P., CASTING, HBO FILMS
Carrie Frazier
V.P., HBO FILMS
Kary Antholis
V.P., HBO FILMS
Jonathan Krauss
V.P., HBO FILMS
Maud Nadler

**ORIGINAL PROGRAMMING/HBO INDEPENDENT
PRODUCTIONS**
EXECUTIVE V.P., ORIGINAL PROGRAMMING
Sheila Nevins
SENIOR V.P., MERCHANDISING & LICENSING, HBO
Russell Schwartz
SENIOR V.P., ORIGINAL PROGRAMMING
Nancy Geller
EXECUTIVE V.P., ORIGINAL PROGRAMMING
Carolyn Strauss
SENIOR V.P., ORIGINAL PROGRAMMING
Anne Thomopoulos
SENIOR V.P., PLANNING & OPERATIONS, ORIGINAL
PROGRAMMING
Susan Ennis
SENIOR V.P., ORIGINAL PROGRAMMING, COMEDY SERIES
Sarah Condon
V.P., ORIGINAL PROGRAMMING, DOCUMENTARIES
Lisa Heller
V.P., ORIGINAL PROGRAMMING, DOCUMENTARIES
Nancy Abraham
V.P., ORIGINAL PROGRAMMING, HBO FAMILY CHANNEL
Dolores Morris
V.P., ORIGINAL PROGRAMMING, PRODUCTION
Bruce Richmond
V.P., ORIGINAL PROGRAMMING, DRAMA SERIES
Miranda Heller

HBO SPORTS
SENIOR V.P. & EXECUTIVE PRODUCER, HBO SPORTS
Rick Bernstein
SENIOR V.P., MARKETING & OPERATIONS, HBO PPV
Mark Taffet
SENIOR V.P., PROGRAMMING, HBO SPORTS
Kery Davis
SENIOR V.P., FINANCE & TALENT, HBO SPORTS
Barbara Thomas
V.P. & SENIOR PRODUCER, HBO SPORTS
David Harmon
V.P., BUSINESS AFFAIRS & GENERAL COUNSEL, TW
SPORTS
Peter Mozarsky
V.P., SPORTS FINANCE, OPERATIONS & TALENT
Bob Zeiss
V.P., SPORTS PRODUCTION
Kirby Bradley
V.P., SPORTS PRODUCTION
John Micale
V.P., SPORTS PROGRAMMING
Xavier James

CORPORATE COMMUNICATIONS
EXECUTIVE V.P.
Richard Plepler
SENIOR V.P., MEDIA RELATIONS
Quentin Schaffer
SENIOR V.P., MEDIA RELATIONS, WEST COAST
Nancy Lesser
V.P., CORPORATE AFFAIRS
Michelle Baas
V.P., MEDIA RELATIONS
Tobe Becker
V.P., MEDIA RELATIONS, WEST COAST
Mara Mikialian
V.P., SPORTS PUBLICITY
Ray Stallone

TALENT RELATIONS
V.P., SPECIAL EVENTS & TALENT
Eileen Rivard
V.P., TALENT RELATIONS, WEST COAST
Daria Overby

FILM PROGRAMMING
SENIOR V.P., CREATIVE AFFAIRS, FILM DEVELOPMENT
Robert Conte
V.P., FILM PROGRAMMING
Doris Casap

BUSINESS AFFAIRS
EXECUTIVE V.P., BUSINESS AFFAIRS
Hal Akselrad
EXECUTIVE V.P., BUSINESS AFFAIRS & PRODUCTION,
WEST COAST
Michael Lombardo
SENIOR V.P., ORIGINAL PROGRAMMING, BUSINESS
DEVELOPMENT & MEDIA
Carmi Zlotnik
SENIOR V.P., BUSINESS AFFAIRS & PRODUCTION, EAST
COAST
Bruce Grivetti

SENIOR V.P., BUSINESS AFFAIRS & PRODUCTION, WEST COAST
Glenn Whitehead
V.P., BUSINESS AFFAIRS, FILM ACQUISITION
Royce Battleman
V.P., EAST COAST PRODUCTION
Bill Chase
V.P., BUSINESS AFFAIRS ADMINISTRATION, EAST COAST
Agnes Letterese
V.P., PRODUCTION, HBO PICTURES
Jay Roewe
V.P., SPORTS PRODUCTION
John Micale
V.P., BUSINESS AFFAIRS, EAST COAST
Sharon Werner
V.P., BUSINESS AFFAIRS, WEST COAST
Beth White
V.P., BUSINESS AFFAIRS, WEST COAST
Suzanne Young
V.P., ORIGINAL PROGRAMMING & PRODUCTION
Michael Hill

LEGAL
EXECUTIVE V.P. & GENERAL COUNSEL
John Redpath
SENIOR V.P. & CHIEF COUNSEL, FILM PROGRAMMING
George Cooke
SENIOR V.P. & CHIEF COUNSEL, ORIGINAL PROGRAMMING
Viviane Eisenberg
SENIOR V.P. & CHIEF COUNSEL, SALES & MARKETING
Tom Woodbury
SENIOR V.P. & SENIOR COUNSEL, WEST COAST
Jeffrey Guthrie
V.P. & CHIEF COUNSEL, NETWORK OPERATIONS & INTL.
Linda Bogin
V.P., & SENIOR COUNSEL, ORIGINAL PROGRAMMING
Peter Rienecker
V.P., SENIOR COUNSEL, SALES & MARKETING
Michelle Gersen
V.P., & SENIOR COUNSEL, LITIGATION
Stephen Sapienza
V.P. & SENIOR COUNSEL, WEST COAST
Molly Wilson
V.P. & SENIOR COUNSEL
Martine Shahar
V.P. & SENIOR COUNSEL, US NETWORKS
Melissa Barnett
V.P. & SENIOR COUNSEL, MARKETING & ORIGINAL PROGRAMMING
Sandra Scott

MARKETING & CREATIVE SERVICES
SENIOR V.P., SUBSCRIBER MARKETING & SPECIAL MARKETS
Olivia Smashum
SENIOR V.P. & GENERAL MANAGER, CREATIVE SERVICES
Chris Spencer
SENIOR V.P., BUSINESS DEVELOPMENT & NEW MEDIA
Sarah Cotsen
V.P., SUBSCRIBER MARKETING & MULTIPLEX
Shelley Wright Brindle
V.P., ON-AIR, ORIGINAL PROGRAMMING
Sue Bailey
V.P., ON-AIR, IMAGE
Marc Rosenberg
V.P., ON-AIR, SPECIAL MARKETS
Elaine Brown
V.P., OPERATIONS
Patrick Manturi
V.P., MARKET STRATEGY & ANALYSIS
Roger Strong

PROGRAM PLANNING
EXECUTIVE V.P., PROGRAM PLANNING
Dave Baldwin
SENIOR V.P., AUDIENCE RESEARCH
Jan Pasquale
V.P., HBO SCHEDULING & ADMINISTRATION
Amy Feldman
V.P., CINEMAX SCHEDULING
Jill Champtaloup
V.P., PRIMARY PROGRAMMING RESEARCH
Kathleen Carroll
V.P., NETWORK PROGRAMMING OPERATIONS
Janet Schwartz

HOME VIDEO
SENIOR V.P. & CFO, HBO HOME VIDEO
Angelo D'Amelio
SENIOR V.P., MARKETING, HBO HOME VIDEO
Cynthia Rhea
SENIOR V.P., SELL-THRU HBO VIDEO
Robert Cowan

HBO INTERNATIONAL
EXECUTIVE V.P., HBO INTERNATIONAL
Bill Hooks
EXECUTIVE V.P., SALES & MARKETING, HBO ASIA
James Marturano
PRESIDENT & CEO, HBO SINGAPORE
Charles "Dan" Murrell
V.P., HBO INTERNATIONAL
Robert Sender
MANAGING DIRECTOR, HBO ROMANIA
Pavel Stantchev
MANAGING DIRECTOR, HBO POLAND
Slawomir Suss

TECHNOLOGY/STUDIO & BROADCAST OPERATIONS
EXECUTIVE V.P., TECHNOLOGY OPERATIONS, CTO
Bob Zitter
SENIOR V.P., STUDIO & BROADCAST OPERATIONS
Dom Serio
SENIOR V.P., TECHNOLOGY OPERATIONS
Barbara Jaffe
SENIOR V.P., BROADCAST OPERATIONS
Charles Cataldo
SENIOR V.P., STUDIO OPERATIONS
Ralph Fumante
V.P., PRODUCTION ENGINEERING
Andres Colpa
V.P., TECHNOLOGY
Craig Cuttner
V.P., TECHNOLOGY OPERATIONS
Elmer Musser
V.P., NETWORK QUALITY CONTROL, OPERATIONS
Debbie Pritchett

INFORMATION TECHNOLOGY
SENIOR V.P., INFORMATION TECHNOLOGY
Michael Gabriel
SENIOR V.P., APPLICATION DEVELOPMENT, NETWORK PROGRAMMING
Elizabeth Flanagan
SENIOR V.P., INFORMATION TECHNOLOGY INFRASTRUCTURE
James Flock
SENIOR V.P., TECHNOLOGY SERVICES
Bruce Probst

INTEGRATED BUSINESS SOLUTIONS
V.P., INTEGRATED BUSINESS SOLUTIONS
Lisa Gussack

FINANCE
COO
Bill Nelson
SENIOR V.P. & CFO
Rob Roth
SENIOR V.P. & ASSISTANT CONTROLLER, WEST COAST
Rich Battaglia
SENIOR V.P., FINANCIAL ANALYSIS
Keith Owitz
SENIOR V.P. & ASST. CONTROLLER, CASH & REVENUE OPERATIONS
Joe Tarulli
V.P & ASST. CONTROLLER, CASH & REVENUE OPERATIONS
Anne Marie Mirabella
V.P., FINANCIAL PLANNING & ANALYSIS
Peter Accettura

HUMAN RESOURCES
EXECUTIVE V.P., HUMAN RESOURCES & ADMINISTRATION
Shelley Fischel
SENIOR V.P., COMPENSATION & BENEFITS
Elly Silverman
SENIOR V.P., STAFFING & DEVELOPMENT
Scott McElhone
SENIOR V.P., HUMAN RESOURCES & FACILITIES, W. COAST
Mary Lou Thomas
V.P., REAL ESTATE & ADMINISTRATION
Michael Morrin

AFFILIATE OPERATIONS
EXECUTIVE V.P., AFFILIATE RELATIONS
Jerry Flavin
SENIOR V.P. & GENERAL MANAGER
Janice Aull
SENIOR V.P. & GENERAL MANAGER
Sandra Mitchell
SENIOR V.P., AFFILIATE OPERATIONS
John High
SENIOR V.P., AFFILIATE OPERATIONS
Matthew Kasman
SENIOR V.P., AFFILIATE OPERATIONS
Jane Moyer
SENIOR V.P., DIRECT TO HOME
John Ovrutsky
V.P., AFFILIATE OPERATIONS
Dan Fobas
V.P., SALES & MARKETING OPERATIONS
Sue Casey
V.P., SPECIAL MARKETS
John Hagerty
REGIONAL VICE PRESIDENTS
Kathy McCarthy
Jocelyn Harris

647

HORSESHOE BAY PRODUCTIONS

10202 W. Washington Blvd., Lean Bldg. Ste. 219, Culver City, CA 90232. (310) 244-3770. FAX: (310) 244-1201.
PRODUCER
Gary S. Foster
WRITER & DIRECTOR & PRODUCER
Mark Steven Johnson
CREATIVE ASSOCIATES
Brian Olson
Amberwren Briskey-Choen

PETER HYAMS PRODUCTIONS, INC.

(Motion picture producer)
1453 3rd St. Promenade, Ste. 315, Santa Monica, CA 90401-2397. (310) 393-1553. FAX: (310) 393-1554.
DIRECTOR & WRITER
Peter Hyams
DIRECTOR, DEVELOPMENT
Jonathan Steinberg

HYDE PARK ENTERTAINMENT

(Motion picture producer)
2450 Broadway St., Ste. 600, Santa Monica, CA 90404. (310) 449-3191. FAX: (310) 449-3356.
CHAIRMAN & CEO
Ashok Amritraj
PRESIDENT
Jon Jashni
V.P., FINANCE
Joe D'Angelo
CREATIVE EXECUTIVE
Ezra Hudson

ICON PRODUCTIONS, INC.

(Motion picture producer)
808 Wilshire Blvd., 4th Flr., Santa Monica, CA 90401. (310) 434-7300. FAX: (310) 434-7377.
PRESIDENT
Bruce Davey
PRODUCER
Steve McEveety
SENIOR V.P., FEATURE FILMS
Kevin Lake

IFM WORLD RELEASING

(Motion picture, independent film & TV producer & distributor)
1328 E. Palmer Ave., Glendale, CA 91205. (818) 243-4976.
FAX: (818) 550-9728. www.ifmfilm.com email: ifmfilm@aol.com
PRESIDENT
Antony I. Ginnane
EXECUTIVE V.P.
Ann Lyons
V.P., INTERNATIONAL
Anthony J. Lyons
SALES EXECUTIVE
David Makhlout

IMAGEMOVERS

100 Universal City Plaza, Bldg. 484, Universal City, CA 91608. (818) 733-8313.
WRITER, DIRECTOR, PRODUCER & PARTNER
Robert Zemeckis (818) 733-8312
PRODUCER & PARTNER
Steve Starkey (818) 733-8335
PRODUCER & PARTNER
Jack Rapke (818) 733-8303
HEAD, CREATIVE AFFAIRS
Bennett Schneir (818) 733-8304

IMAGINE ENTERTAINMENT

(Motion picture, film & TV producer)
9465 Wilshire Blvd., 7th Flr., Beverly Hills, CA 90212. (310) 858-2000. FAX: (310) 858-2020.
www.imagine-entertainment.com
CO-CHAIRMAN
Brian Grazer
CO-CHAIRMAN
Ron Howard
CO-CHAIRMAN, IMAGINE FILMS
Karen Kehela
PRESIDENT, ENTERTAINMENT
Michael Rosenberg
EXECUTIVE V.P., MOTION PICTURES
Jim Whitaker
SENIOR V.P., ADMINISTRATION & OPERATIONS
Robin Barris
SENIOR V.P., MOTION PICTURES
Kim Roth
V.P., MOTION PICTURES
Suzy Barbieri
V.P., MOTION PICTURES
Steve Crystal
V.P., MOTION PICTURES
David Bernardi
CREATIVE EXECUTIVE
Sarah Bowen

CREATIVE EXECUTIVE
Beth Babyak
DIRECTOR, FINANCE
Christy Sterling
STORY EDITOR
Anna Culp

IMMORTAL ENTERTAINMENT

1650 21 St., Santa Monica, CA 90404. (310) 582-8300. FAX: (310) 582-8301.
OWNER
Happy Walters
HEAD, FILM PRODUCTION
Matt Weaver
VICE PRESIDENT
Scott Nemes

INDEPENDENT GROUP (TALENT MANAGEMENT)

Independent Film Group (Film Packaging)
Independent Television Group (TV Packaging)
(Talent Management; Film & Television packaging)
8721 W. Sunset Blvd., Ste. 105, Los Angeles, CA 90069. (310) 854-2300. FAX: (310) 854-2304. email: mail@indygroup.tv
CONTACT
TALENT MANAGEMENT, FILM & TV PACKAGING
Steven Jensen
TALENT MANAGEMENT
Claudine Vacca
FILM & TV PACKAGING
Jeff Davis

INDUSTRY ENTERTAINMENT

(Motion picture, independent film & TV producer)
955 S. Carrillo Dr., 3rd Flr., Los Angeles, CA 90048. (323) 954-9000. FAX: (323) 954-9009.
MANAGING PARTNERS
Nick Wechsler
Keith Addis
Geyer Kosinski
PRODUCTION EXECUTIVES
Nana Greenwald
Jeff Sommerville
TV EXECUTIVES
Emile Levisetti
Helena Heyman

INITIAL ENTERTAINMENT GROUP

(Motion picture & independent production & finance co./foreign distribution)
3000 W. Olympic Blvd., Ste. 1550, Santa Monica, CA 90404. (310) 315-1722. FAX: (310) 315-1723.
PRESIDENT & CEO
Graham King
COO
Colin Cotter

INSIGHT PRODUCTIONS

(Independent film, digital media & music production)
529 W. 42nd St., Ste. 2D, New York, NY 10036. (212) 979-7727.
PRESIDENT
Bradley Latham

INTERAMA, INC.

720 W. End Ave., #416, New York, NY 10025. (212) 222-5525.
FAX: (212) 222-9569. email: interamany@aol.com
PRESIDENT
Nicole Jouve

INTERMEDIA FILMS

(Motion picture finance & distribution)
9350 Civic Center Dr., Ste. 100, Beverly Hills, CA 90210. (310) 777-0007. FAX: (310) 777-0008.
email: info@intermediafilm.com
CHAIRMAN
Moritz Borman
VICE CHAIRMAN
Jon Gumpert
COO
Bahman Naraghi
PRESIDENT, PRODUCTION
Basil Iwanyk
PRESIDENT, PHYSICAL PRODUCTION
Andy Given
PRESIDENT, INTERMEDIA MUSIC GROUP
Joel Sill
SENIOR V.P., CORPORATE COMMUNICATIONS & PUBLICITY
Dennis Higgins

INTERNATIONAL FILM CIRCUIT

(Motion picture distributor)
419 Park Ave. S., 20th Flr., New York, NY 10016 (212) 686-6777 ext. 164. FAX: (212) 545-9931. www.wellspring.com
PRESIDENT
Wendy Lidell

IRISH DREAMTIME

(Motion picture producer)
2450 Broadway, Ste. E-5021, Santa Monica, CA 90404. (310) 449-3411. FAX: (310) 586-8138.
PRODUCER & PARTNER
Pierce Brosnan
PRODUCER & PARTNER
Beau St. Clair
V.P., DEVELOPMENT
Angelique Higgins
CREATIVE EXECUTIVE
Chris Charalambous
PRODUCTION EXECUTIVE
Amanda Scarano

ITALTOONS CORP.

(International producer & distributor of video & film products)
32 W. 40 St., Ste. 2L, New York, NY 10018. (212) 730-0280.
FAX: (212) 730-0313. www.italtoons.com
email: salesinfo@italtoons.com
PRESIDENT
Giuliana Nicodemi
PRODUCTION COORDINATOR
Jane Stewart
PRODUCER
Luisa Rivosecchi

IWERKS ENTERTAINMENT

(Simulation rides, 3D & 2D productions)
4520 Valerio St., Burbank CA 91505. (818) 841-7766. FAX: (818) 840-7462. www.iwerks.com email: dougy@iwerks.com
FOUNDER
Don Iwerks
CHAIRMAN & CEO
Michael Meedham
V.P., FILM PRODUCTION
Scott Shepley
POST-PRODUCTION COORDINATOR
Greg Meader

JUDGE BELSHAW ENTERTAINMENT

4655 Kingswell Dr., Ste 208, Los Angeles, CA 90027. (323) 662-3365. FAX: (323) 662-333.
PARTNERS
George Belshaw
Jonathan M. Judge (NY)

JUNCTION ENTERTAINMENT

(Producer)
500 S. Buena Vista St., Animation 1-B, Burbank, CA 91521-1616. (818) 560-2800. FAX: (818) 841-3176.
Production Office: (818) 560-7570. FAX: (818) 845-6873.
PRODUCER & DIRECTOR
Jon Turtletaub, (818) 560-2070
PRESIDENT & PRODUCER
Christina Steinberg, (818) 560-6020
CREATIVE EXECUTIVE
Victor H. Constantinto, (818) 560-5240
DIRECTOR, DEVELOPMENT
Nikki Reed, (818) 560-5948
CREATIVE ASSOCIATES
Dominique Fichera, (818) 560-7161
Karim Zreick, (818) 560-7113

JUNCTION FILMS

9615 Brighton Way, Ste. 320, Beverly Hills, CA 90210. (310) 246-9799. FAX: (310) 246-3824.
PRESIDENTS
Brad Wyman
Donald Kushner
DIRECTOR, DEVELOPMENT
David Alvarado

JUST SINGER ENTERTAINMENT

(TV producer)
4242 Tujunga Ave., Studio City, CA 91604. (818) 506-2400.
FAX: (818) 506-2409.
EXECUTIVE PRODUCER
Sheri Singer
SENIOR V.P.
Ruth Feinberg
DEVELOPMENT ASSISTANT
Rebecca Verdolino

MARTY KATZ PRODUCTIONS

(Motion picture producer)
3000 Olympic Blvd., Ste. 1471, Santa Monica, CA 90404. (310) 264-3948. FAX: (310) 264-3949.
PRODUCER
Marty Katz
V.P., DEVELOPMENT
Tiffany Tiesiera
DIRECTOR, DEVELOPMENT
Campbell Katz

KELLER ENTERTAINMENT GROUP, INC.

(Producer & distributor)
14225 Ventura Blvd., Sherman Oaks, CA 91423. (818) 981-4950. FAX: (818) 501-6224.
CEO
Max Keller
PRESIDENT
Micheline Keller
VICE PRESIDENT
Kirt Eftekhar
DIRECTOR, DEVELOPMENT
Joshua B. Dasal

KENNEDY-MARSHALL COMPANY

619 Arizona Ave., Santa Monica, CA 90401. (310) 656-8400.
FAX: (310) 656-8430.
PRODUCER
Kathleen Kennedy
PRODUCER & DIRECTOR
Frank Marshall

KILLER FILMS, INC.

(Independent film producer)
380 Lafayette St., Ste. 302, New York, NY 10003. (212) 473-3950. FAX: (212) 473-6152. www.killerfilms.com
email: killer@killerfilms.com
PARTNERS/PRODUCERS
Christine Vachon
Katie Roumel
Pamela Koffler
PRODUCER
Bradford Simpson
DIRECTOR, DEVELOPMENT
Jocelyn Hayes
COORDINATORS
Charles Pugliese
Meghan Wicker

KINGSGATE FILMS, INC.

(Motion picture & TV producer)
8954 W. Pico Blvd., 2nd Flr., Los Angeles, CA 90035. (310) 281-5880. FAX: (310) 281-2633.
email: KG1@kingsgatefilms.com
ACTOR & PRODUCER
Nick Nolte
PRODUCER
Greg Shapiro

KINGS ROAD ENTERTAINMENT, INC.

(Motion picture producer)
12 E. 33rd St., 12th Flr., New York, NY 10016. (212) 252-9519.
FAX: (212) 725-4678.
CHAIRMAN
Michael L. Berresheim

KINO INTERNATIONAL CORP.

(Film distributor)
333 W. 39th St., Ste. 503, New York, NY 10018. (212) 629-6880. FAX: (212) 714-0871. www.kino.com
email: contact@kino.com
PRESIDENT
Donald Krim

THE KONIGSBERG-SMITH CO.

7919 Sunset Blvd., 2nd Flr., Los Angeles, CA 90046. (323) 845-1000. FAX: (323) 845-1020.
EXECUTIVE PRODUCER
Frank Konigsberg
PRODUCER
Drew Smith
ASSOCIATE PRODUCER
Neal Doherty

KOPELSON ENTERTAINMENT

(Motion picture, independent film & TV producer)
8560 Sunset Blvd., Ste. 600, West Hollywood, CA 90069. (310) 360-3200. FAX: (310) 360-3201.
PRODUCER & CO-CHAIRPERSON
Arnold Kopelson, (310) 360-3222
PRODUCER & CO-CHAIRPERSON
Anne Kopelson, (310) 360-3232
EXECUTIVE V.P.
Sherryl Clark, (310) 360-3240
V.P., PRODUCTION
Mark Stein, (310) 360-3270
CREATIVE EXECUTIVE
Erin Newell (310) 360-3255
EXEC. ASST. TO ANNE KOPELSON
Claudia O'Hehir, (310) 360-3244
EXEC. ASST. TO ARNOLD KOPELSON
Elaine Mongeon, (310) 360-3233

KOUF-BIGELOW PRODUCTIONS

10061 Riverside Dr., PMB #1024, Toluca Lake, CA 91602. (818) 508-1010. FAX: (818) 508-1079.
WRITER & DIRECTOR & PRODUCER
Jim Kouf
PRODUCER
Lynn Bigelow-Kouf

KUSHNER-LOCKE CO.

(Motion picture, independent film & TV distributor)
8671 Wilshire Blvd., Ste. 714, Beverly Hills, CA 90211. (310) 659-1508. FAX: (310) 659-2315.
OFFICER
Alice Neuhauser

THE LADD COMPANY

(Motion picture, independent film & TV producer)
9465 Wilshire Blvd., Ste. 910, Beverly Hills, CA 90212. (310) 777-2060. FAX: (310) 777-2061.
PRESIDENT
Alan Ladd Jr.
PRODUCER
Kelliann Ladd
CREATIVE EXECUTIVE
Amanda Lamb

LAKESHORE ENTERTAINMENT CORP.

(Motion picture producer & distributor)
5555 Melrose Ave., Gloria Swanson Bldg., Hollywood, CA 90038. (323) 956-4222. FAX: (323) 862-1190.
CHAIRMAN & CEO
Thomas B. Rosenberg
PRESIDENT, LAKESHORE ENTERTAINMENT
Gary Lucchesi
COO
Eric Reid
CFO
Marc Reid
PRESIDENT, LAKESHORE INTERNATIONAL
Stephanie Denton
EXECUTIVE V.P. & HEAD, PRODUCTION
Richard Wright
SENIOR V.P., BUSINESS & LEGAL AFFAIRS
Robert Benun
SENIOR V.P., DEVELOPMENT
Robert McMinn
V.P., PHYSICAL PRODUCTION
Andre Lamal
V.P., FINANCE
Renee Mancuso
V.P., MUSIC & BUSINESS & LEGAL AFFAIRS
Christine Bucklet
V.P., ACQUISITIONS & CO-PRODUCTIONS
Bic Tran
OFFICE MANAGER
Kjose Elliot

LARGER THAN LIFE PRODUCTIONS

(Motion picture producer)
100 Universal City Plaza, Bldg. 5138, Universal City, CA 91608. (818) 777-4004. FAX: (818) 866-5677.
PRINCIPAL
Gary Ross
PRODUCER
Allison Thomas
PRODUCER
Robin Bissell
DIRECTORS, DEVELOPMENT
Maggie Malone
Michelle Steffes

LEISURE TIME FEATURES

(Motion picture distributor)
40 Worth St., Rm. 817, New York, NY 10013. (212) 267-4501. FAX: (212) 267-4501. www.leisurefeat.com
email bpleisure@aol.com
PRESIDENT
Bruce Pavlow

LEVY-GARDNER-LAVEN PRODUCTIONS, INC.

Wilshire Blvd., Ste. 610, Beverly Hills, CA 90212. (310) 278-9820. FAX: (310) 278-2632.
PRESIDENT
Jules V. Levy
SECRETARY, TREASURER & V.P.
Arthur Gardner
VICE PRESIDENT
Arnold Laven

THE ROBERT LEWIS COMPANY

(Motion picture producer & distributor)
8755 Shoreham Dr., Ste. 303, Beverly Hills, CA 90069. (310) 854-3714. FAX: (310) 659-6932.
PRESIDENT
Robert Lewis

LEWIS MEDIA GROUP

(Producer of large-format & traditional motion pictures)
9300 Wilshire Blvd., Ste. 108, Beverly Hills, CA 90212. (310) 550-1930. FAX: (310) 550-1731.
CEO & CO-FOUNDER
Michael V. Lewis

LIGHTHOUSE PRODUCTIONS

(Motion picture, independent films & TV producer)
120 El Camino Dr., Ste. 212, Beverly Hills, CA 90212. (310) 859-4923. FAX: (310) 859-7511.
email: lighthouse38@hotmail.com
PRODUCERS
Michael Phillips
Juliana Maio
John Frank Rosenblum
DIRECTOR, DEVELOPMENT
Lucy Mukerjee

LIGHTMOTIVE, INC.

(Motion picture & TV producer)
10351 Santa Monica Blvd., #402, Los Angeles, CA 90025. (310) 282-0660. FAX: (310) 282-0990.
PARTNER & CEO
Roland Joffe
V.P., DEVELOPMENT
Dabney Lee

LIGHTSTORM ENTERTAINMENT

919 Santa Monica Blvd., Santa Monica, CA 90401. (310) 656-6100. FAX: (310) 656-6102.
CHAIRMAN & CEO
James Cameron
PRESIDENT & PARTNER
Rae Sanchini
PARTNER
Jon Landau
V.P., DEVELOPMENT & PRODUCTION
Curtis Burch
V.P., DEVELOPMENT & PRODUCTION
Greg Frankovich
CREATIVE EXECUTIVE
Tom Cohen
V.P., PRODUCTION RESOURCES, SVC & TECHNOLOGY
Geoff Burdick
MANAGER, PRODUCTION RESOURCES, SERVICE & TECHNOLOGY
Al Rives
COORDINATOR, PRODUCTION RESOURCES, SERVICES & TECHNOLOGY
Joe Hagg
COORDINATOR, PRODUCTION RESOURCES, SERVICES & TECHNOLOGY
Charlie Palafox

LION ROCK PRODUCTIONS

(Motion picture, independent film & TV producer)
2120 Colorado Ave., Ste. 225, Santa Monica, CA 90404. (310) 309-2980. FAX: (310) 309-6151.
DIRECTOR & PRODUCER
John Woo
PRODUCER
Terrence Chang
SENIOR V.P.
Caroline Macaulay
CREATIVE EXECUTIVE
Annie Hughes

LIONS GATE FILMS PRODUCTION

4553 Glencoe Ave., Ste. 200, Marina Del Rey, CA 90292. (310) 314-2000. FAX: (310) 399-4062. www.lionsgate-ent.com
CEO
Jon Feltheimer
PRESIDENT, LIONS GATE FILMS RELEASING
Tom Ortenberg
PRESIDENT, PRODUCTION
Michael Paseornek
EXECUTIVE V.P.
John J. Dellaverson
EXECUTIVE V.P. & GENERAL COUNSEL
Wayne Levine
PRESIDENT, HOME ENT., ACQUISITIONS AND NEW MEDIA
Peter Block

SI LITVINOFF PRODUCTIONS

(Motion picture, independent film & TV producer; no unsolicited screenplays etc.)
2825 Woodstock Rd., Los Angeles, CA 90046.
email: slitvinoff@aol.com
PRODUCER
Si Litvinoff
CREATIVE AFFAIRS
Paul Madden

LIVEPLANET

(Motion picture & TV producer)
2644 30th St., Santa Monica, CA 90405. (310) 664-2400. FAX: (310) 664-2401. www.liveplanet.com
CEO & PRESIDENT
Larry Tanz
FOUNDERS
Chris Moore
Sean Bailey
Ben Affleck
Matt Damon

LONGBOW PRODUCTIONS, LLC
(Motion picture, independent film & TV producer)
15340 Longbow Dr., Sherman Oaks, CA 91403. (818) 762-6600. FAX: (818) 501-7688. www.longbowfilms.com
email: mail@longbowfilms.com
PARTNERS
Richard Kughn
Ronnie D. Clemmer
Bill Pace

WARREN LOCKHART PRODUCTIONS, INC.
(Multi dimensional film and tv production company)
P.O. Box 11629, Marina Del Rey, CA 90295. (310) 821-1414.
FAX: (310) 301-0536. email: warren@lockhartproductions.com
PRESIDENT
Warren L. Lockhart

LOWSON INTERNATIONAL
P.O. Box 12766, Marina del Rey, CA 90295. (310) 827-6798.
email: lowsonintl@aol.com
CEO & COO
Kathleen Lowson

LUCASARTS ENTERTAINMENT COMPANY
(Video game producer & distributor)
P.O. Box 10307, San Rafael, CA 94912. (415) 472-3400. FAX: (415) 444-2840. www.lucasarts.com
PRESIDENT
Simon Jeffery
DIRECTOR, SALES & MARKETING
Mary Bihr

LUCAS DIGITAL LTD
(Post-production; special effects)
P.O. Box 2459, San Rafael, CA 94912. (415) 448-9000. FAX: (415) 448-9550. www.ilm.com
PRESIDENT
Jim Morris
V.P. & GENERAL MANAGER, SKYWALKER SOUND
Glenn Kiser

LUCASFILM, LTD.
(Motion picture producer)
P.O. Box 10228, San Rafael, CA 94912. (415) 662-1800. FAX: (415) 662-7437. www.lucasfilm.com
CHAIRMAN OF THE BOARD
George W. Lucas, Jr.
COO
Micheline Chan

LUCID MEDIA
(Independent film & promotional producer & distributor)
(818) 362-5170. www.marinocolmano.com
email: contact@marinocolmano.com
PRESIDENT
Marino Colmano

MAD CHANCE
(Motion picture producer)
4000 Warner Blvd., Bung. 3, Burbank, CA 91522. (818) 954-3803. FAX: (818) 954-3447.
PRODUCER
Andrew Lazar
SENIOR V.P., PRODUCTION
Far Shariat
VICEROY, PHYSICAL PRODUCTION
Gym Hinderer
CREATIVE EXECUTIVE
Geoff Moore

MALIBU BAY FILMS
(Motion picture & TV producer)
P.O. Box 17244, Beverly Hills, CA 90209-3244. (310) 278-5056.
FAX: (310) 278-5058. www.adnysidaris.com
PRESIDENT
Andrew Sidaris

MALPASO PRODUCTIONS
(Motion picture producer)
4000 Warner Blvd., Bldg. 81, Burbank, CA 91522-0811. (818) 954-3367. FAX: (818) 954-4803.
PRODUCER & ACTOR & DIRECTOR
Clint Eastwood
EDITOR
Joel Cox

MANDALAY PICTURES
(Motion picture producer & distributor)
4751 Wilshire Blvd., 3rd Flr, Los Angeles, CA 90010. (323) 549-4300. FAX: (323) 549-9824.
CHAIRMAN
Peter Guber
VICE CHAIRMAN
Paul Schaeffer
EXECUTIVE V.P., BUSINESS AFFAIRS
Darrell Walker

EXECUTIVE V.P., PRODUCTION
Ori Marmur
EXECUTIVE V.P., PRODUCTION ADMINISTRATION
David Zelon
EXECUTIVE V.P., CORPORATE OPERATIONS
Shelly Riney
CFO, BUSINESS DEVELOPMENT
Randy Hermann
V.P., BUSINESS AFFAIRS ADMINISTRATION
Michelle DiRaffaele

MANDY FILMS, INC. (PANDA PRODUCTIONS)
(Motion picture & TV producer)
9201 Wilshire Blvd., #206, Beverly Hills, CA 90210. (310) 246-0500. FAX: (310) 246-0350.
PRESIDENT
Leonard Goldberg
V.P., DEVELOPMENT & PRODUCTION
Amanda Goldberg

MANHATTAN PICTURES INTERNATIONAL
369 Lexington Ave., 10th Flr., New York, NY 10017. (212) 453-5055. FAX: (212) 453-5080. www.manhattanpics.com
CHAIRMAN
Paul J. Manafort
CO-CHAIRMAN
Joel Sieden
PRESIDENT & CEO
Paul E. Cohen
SENIOR EXECUTIVE V.P.
TC Rice

MANIFEST FILM COMPANY
(Motion picture producer)
9595 Wilshire Blvd., PH1000, Beverly Hills, CA 90212. (310) 899-5554. FAX: (310) 899-5553. email: manifilm@aol.com
PRODUCER
Janet Yang

LAURENCE MARK PRODUCTIONS
(Motion picture & TV producer)
10202 W. Washington Blvd., Poitier Bldg., Culver City, CA 90232. (310) 244-5239.
PRESIDENT & PRODUCER
Laurence Mark
PRESIDENT, PRODUCTION
Jonathan King
PRESIDENT, TV
Ilene Amy Berg
V.P., CREATIVE AFFAIRS
Terrence Myers

MARVEL STUDIOS
10474 Santa Monica Blvd., Ste. 206, Los Angeles, CA 90025.
(310) 234-8991. FAX: (310) 234-8481. www.marvel.com
PRESIDENT & CEO, MARVEL STUDIOS
Avi Arad
EXECUTIVE V.P., MARVEL STUDIOS
Kevin Feige

MATRIXX ENTERTAINMENT
(Feature films & documentaries)
223 W. Lancaster Ave., Devon, PA 19333. (610) 688-9212.
www.mecfilms.com
DIRECTOR, PUBLIC RELATIONS
Lorraine Sterling

THE MATTHAU COMPANY, INC.
11661 San Vicente Blvd., Ste. 609, Los Angeles, CA 90049.
(310) 454-3300.
PRESIDENT
Charles Matthau
DIRECTOR, CREATIVE AFFAIRS
Lana Morgan

MAVERICK FILMS
9348 Civic Center Dr., 3rd Flr., Beverly Hills, CA 90210. (310) 276-6177. FAX: (310) 276-9477.
CONTACTS
Madonna
Guy Oseary
Mark Morgan
Chris Daniel
Jonathan Schwartz
Brent Emery
Doug Morton
Martina Papinjak
Jay Polstein
Daniel Rosenfeld
Greg Mouradian
Eve La Due
David Faigenblum
Rachel Rothman
Eric Thompson

651

MDP WORLDWIDE

(Motion picture producer & distributor)
1875 Century Park E., Ste. 2000, Los Angeles, CA 90067.
(310) 226-8352. FAX: (310) 226-8350.
email: info@mpdworldwide.com
CHAIRMAN & CEO
Mark Damon
VICE CHAIRMAN
Sammy Lee
BOARD MEMBER
Stewart Hall
PRESIDENT & COO
Richard Kiratsoulis
V.P., STRATEGIC BUSINESS & FINANCIAL PLANNING
Jimmy Li
V.P., FINANCE
Devin Cutler
SENIOR V.P. DISTRIBUTION
Brian O'Shea
SENIOR V.P., MARKETING & PUBLICITY
David Gaynes
V.P., ADMINISTRATIVE AFFAIRS
Tatyana Joffe

BARRY MENDEL PRODUCTIONS

(Motion picture producer; deal with Universal Studios)
100 Universal City Plaza, Bung. 5163, Universal City, CA
91608. (818) 733-3076. FAX: (818) 733-4070.
CONTACTS
Barry Mendel
Sarah Schechter
Molly Cooper
Amina Runyan-Shefa
Billy Rosenberg
Alisa Tager

MERCHANT-IVORY

(Motion picture producer & distributor)
250 W. 57th St., Ste. 1825, New York, NY 10107. (212) 582-
8049. FAX: (212) 459-9201. www.merchantivory.com
CO-PRESIDENT, PRODUCER, DIRECTOR
Ismail Merchant
CO-PRESIDENT, DIRECTOR
James Ivory
EXECUTIVE V.P. & EXECUTIVE PRODUCER, PRODUCER,
DIRECTOR
Richard Hawley
PRODUCTION COORDINATOR
Pierre Proner

METRO-GOLDWYN-MAYER

10250 Constellation Blvd., Los Angeles, CA 90067-6241. (310)
449-3000. FAX: (310) 449-3100.
1350 Ave. of the Americas, New York, NY 10019-4870. (212)
708-0300. FAX: (212) 708-0337. www.mgm.com
CHAIRMAN & CEO
Alex Yemenidjian
VICE CHAIRMAN
Christopher McGurk
PRESIDENT, WORLDWIDE THEATRICAL MKTG.
Peter Adee
PRESIDENT, MGM DISTRIBUTION CO.
Erik Lomis
PRESIDENT, MGM TELEVISION GROUP
Hank Cohen
PRESIDENT, WORLDWIDE TELEVISION DISTRIBUTION
James Griffiths
PRESIDENT & COO, MGM HOME ENTERTAINMENT
David Bishop
EXECUTIVE V.P., MGM MUSIC
Anita Camarato
EXECUTIVE V.P., FINANCE & CORPORATE DEVELOPMENT
Charles E.Cohen
EXECUTIVE V.P., DEPUTY GENERAL COUNSEL
Jay Rakow
EXECUTIVE V.P., INVESTOR RELATIONS & CORPORATE
COMMUNICATIONS
Joseph Fitzgerald
EXECUTIVE V.P., MARKETING & DISTRIBUTION
Daniel J. Rosett
SENIOR V.P., LABOR RELATIONS
Mark Crowley
SENIOR E.V.P. & CFO
Daniel J. Taylor
SENIOR E.V.P. & SECRETARY
William A. Jones
SENIOR V.P., WORLDWIDE PUBLICITY
Eric Kops
SENIOR V.P. & CIO, INFORMATION SERVICES
Kim Spenchian
SENIOR V.P., ADMINISTRATION
Rick Lopez
V.P., TAXES
Deborah J. Arvesen

MGM PICTURES

10250 Constellation Blvd., Los Angeles, CA 90067-6241. (310)
449-3000. FAX: (310) 449-3100.
PRESIDENT, MGM PICTURES
Michael Nathanson
PRESIDENT, ENTERTAINMENT BUSINESS GROUP
Darcie Denkert
EXECUTIVE V.P., WORLDWIDE FEATURE POST-
PRODUCTION
Jeff Coleman
SENIOR V.P., LABOR RELATIONS
Mark Crowley
SENIOR V.P., BUSINESS AFFAIRS ADMINISTRATION
Luba Keske
SENIOR V.P., BUSINESS AFFAIRS
Marla E. Levine
EXECUTIVE V.P., PRODUCTION
Elizabeth Ingold
DIRECTOR, CREATIVE AFFAIRS
Kim Ciliberto

UNITED ARTISTS PICTURES

PRESIDENT, UNITED ARTISTS (NY)
Bingham Ray
SENIOR V.P., PRODUCTION & ACQUISITIONS (CA)
Sara Rose

MGM DISTRIBUTION COMPANY

US
1350 Ave. of the Americas, New York, NY 10019-4870. (212)
708-0300.
1111 Santa Monica Blvd., 3rd Flr., Los Angeles, CA 90025.
(310) 444-1600. FAX: (310) 312-3372. FAX (Sales): (310) 440-
1698.
SENIOR V.P., EASTERN SALES MANAGER
William Lewis
SENIOR V.P., WESTERN SALES MANAGER
Mike Bisio
V.P., CANADIAN DIVISION MANAGER
Phil May
V.P., NON THEATRICAL SALES
Jan Sirridge
V.P., DOMESTIC DISTRIBUTION
Derek Mclay

CANADA
720 King St. W., Ste. 611, Toronto, ONT M5V 2T3, Canada.
(416) 703-9579. FAX: (416) 504-3821.

UNITED KINGDOM
5 Kew Rd., Richmond, Surrey, England TW9 2PR. TEL: (20 89)
39-9300. FAX: (20 89) 39-9430.

MIRACLE PICTURES

(Motion picture & TV producer)
1223 Wilshire Blvd., #916, Santa Monica, CA 90401. (310)
392-3011. FAX: (310) 392-2021.
PRESIDENT
A. Kitman Ho
ADMINISTRATION & DEVELOPMENT
Robb Earnest

MIRAGE ENTERPRISES

(Motion picture producer)
233 S. Beverly Dr., Ste. 200, Beverly Hills, CA 90212. (310)
888-2830. FAX: (310) 888-2825.
PRODUCERS & DIRECTORS
Sydney Pollack
Anthony Minghella

MIRAMAX FILM CORP.

(Subsidiary: Dimension Films)
375 Greenwich St., New York, NY 10013. (212) 941-3800. FAX:
(212) 941-3949. www.miramax.com
8439 Sunset Blvd., West Hollywood, CA 90069. (323) 822-
4100. FAX: (323) 822-4128.
CHAIRMEN
Bob Weinstein
Harvey Weinstein
COO
Rick Sands
EXECUTIVE V.P., FINANCE & OPERATIONS & CFO
Ross Landsbaum
EXECUTIVE V.P., OFFICE OF CO-CHAIRMAN
Charles Layton
EXECUTIVE V.P., CO-HEAD, BUSINESS AFFAIRS
Steve Hutensky
EXECUTIVE V.P., BUSINESS AFFAIRS & GENERAL
COUNSEL
Alan Friedman
EXECUTIVE V.P., CO-HEAD, BUSINESS AFFAIRS
Michael Luisi
EXECUTIVE V.P., MIRAMAX INTERNATIONAL
Stuart Ford
EXECUTIVE V.P., ACCOUNTING & FINANCIAL REPORTING
Irwin Reiter
SENIOR V.P., HUMAN RESOURCES
Paula Simonetti

PRODUCTION
CO-PRESIDENT, PRODUCTION
Meryl Poster
CO-PRESIDENT, PRODUCTION
Robert Osher
EXECUTIVE V.P., EUROPEAN PROD. & DEVELOPMENT
Colin Vaines
EXECUTIVE V.P., PRODUCTION
Jon Gordon
EXECUTIVE V.P., DEVELOPMENT & EUROPEAN PROD.
Julie Goldstein
EXECUTIVE V.P., PHYSICAL & POST-PRODUCTION
Timothy Clawson
EXECUTIVE V.P., MOTION PICTURE & TV PROD. FINANCE
John Hadity
SENIOR V.P., POST-PRODUCTION/V.P., PRODUCTION
Scott Martin
PRESIDENT, MUSIC
Randy Spendlove
ACQUISITIONS
EXECUTIVE V.P., ACQUISITIONS & CO-PRODUCTIONS
Agnes Mentre
EXECUTIVE V.P., DELIVERY & SERVICING
Glaister Kerr
EXECUTIVE V.P. & GENERAL SALES MANAGER
Elliot Slutzky
SENIOR E.V.P., DOMESTIC DISTRIBUTION
Michael Rudnitsky
MARKETING & PUBLICITY
EXECUTIVE V.P., WORLDWIDE PROMOTIONS
Lori Sale
EXECUTIVE V.P., WORLDWIDE PUBLICITY
Amanda Lundberg
EXECUTIVE V.P., MARKETING
Jason Cassidy
EXECUTIVE V.P., MEDIA RELATIONS & CORPORATE COMM.
Paul Pflug
SENIOR V.P., MEDIA MARKETING
Caryn Picker
SENIOR PUBLICITY EXECUTIVE
Cynthia Swartz
SENIOR V.P., CORPORATE COMMUNICATIONS
Matthew J. Hiltzik
SENIOR V.P., CREATIVE ADVERTISING
Stahman, Perry
DIMENSION FILMS
CO-HEAD, PRODUCTION
Brad Weston
CO-HEAD, PRODUCTION
Andrew Rona
EXECUTIVE V.P., BUSINESS & LEGAL AFFAIRS
Andrew Gumpert
EXECUTIVE V.P., PUBLICITY
Elizabeth Clark
SENIOR V.P., MARKETING, DIMENSION
Josh Greenstein
HOME ENTERTAINMENT
EXECUTIVE V.P., MIRAMAX HOME VIDEO
Kevin Kasha
SENIOR V.P., VIDEO BROADCAST & POST-PRODUCTION
Shannon McIntosh

THE MIRISCH CORPORATION OF CALIFORNIA

(Motion picture, independent film & TV producer)
100 Universal City Plaza, Bldg. 1320 #2C, Universal City, CA
91608-1085. (818) 777-1271. FAX: (818) 866-1422.
PRODUCER
Walter Mirisch

THE MONTECITO PICTURE COMPANY

(Motion picture & TV producer)
1482 E. Valley Road, Ste. 477, Montecito, CA 93108. (805)
565-8590. FAX: (805) 565-8661.
9465 Wilshire Blvd., Ste. 920, Beverly Hills, CA 90212. (310)
247-9880.
Ivan Reitman
Tom Pollock
Joe Medjuck
Dan M. Goldberg
Jackie Josephson

MOONSTONE ENTERTAINMENT

(Motion picture producer & distributor)
P.O. Box 7400, Studio City, CA 91614; 3539 Laurel Canyon,
Studio City, CA 91604. (818) 985-3003. FAX: (818) 985-3009.
CEO
Ernst Stroh
PRESIDENT
Yael Stroh
EXECUTIVE V.P.
Luz Moretti
V.P., FINANCE
Greg Majerus
DIRECTOR, PRODUCTION & MARKETING
Michael Grant
MANAGER
Christine Meisner

MORGAN CREEK PRODUCTIONS

(Producer)
4000 Warner Blvd., Bldg. 76, Burbank, CA 91522. (818) 954-
4800. FAX: (818) 954-4811.
CHAIRMAN & CEO
James G. Robinson
CFO
Howard Kaplan
PRESIDENT
Guy McElwaine
SENIOR V.P., DEVELOPMENT
Joe Martino
VICE PRESIDENT
David Robinson
HEAD, PRODUCTION
Braf Luff
INTERNATIONAL
Jonathan Deckter

MOSTOW/LIEBERMAN

100 Universal City Plaza, Bung. 4111, Universal City, CA
91608. (818) 777-4444. FAX: (818) 866-1328.
PARTNERS
Hal Lieberman
Jonathan Mostow

MOTION CITY FILMS

(Film, video & interactive media producer)
501 Santa Monica Blvd., Ste. 150B, Santa Monica, CA 90401.
(310) 434-1272. FAX: (310) 434-1273.

MOTION PICTURE CORP. OF AMERICA

(Motion picture producer & distributor)
1401 Ocean Ave., #301, Santa Monica, CA 90401. (310) 319-
9500. FAX: (310) 319-9501.
CHAIRMAN & CEO
Brad Krevoy

MOVING PICTURES, LTD.

(Motion picture & video support; equipment rentals & sales)
1750 Fortune Rd., Salt Lake City, UT 84104. (801) 973-0632.
FAX: (801) 973-0380. www.movingpics.net
email: mail@movingpics.net
CONTACT
Troy Parkinson

MOZARK PRODUCTIONS

(TV producer)
4024 Radford Ave., Bldg. 5, #104, Studio City, CA 91604. (818)
655-5779. FAX: (818) 655-5129. email: mozark@mptp.com
EXECUTIVE PRODUCER & WRITER
Linda Bloodworth-Thomason
EXECUTIVE PRODUCER & DIRECTOR
Harry Thomason

MR. MUDD

(Motion picture, independent film & TV producer)
5225 Wilshire Blvd., Ste. 604, Los Angeles, CA 90036. (323)
932-5656. FAX: (323) 932-5666.
PRODUCER & DIRECTOR
John Malkovich
PRODUCER
Lianne Halfon
PRODUCER
Russ Smith
CREATIVE EXECUTIVE
Shannon Clark
PRODUCTION ASSISTANT
Shelly Darden

MTV FILMS

(Motion picture producer)
5555 Melrose Ave., Modular Bldg. 213, Los Angeles, CA
90038. (323) 956-8023. FAX: (323) 862-1386. www.mtv.com
PRESIDENT MTV
Van Toffler
EXECUTIVE V.P.
David M. Gale
V.P., PHYSICAL PRODUCTION
Momita Sengupta
VICE PRESIDENT
Susan Lewis
CREATIVE EXECUTIVE
Gregg Goldin
V.P., BUSINESS DEVELOPMENT
Troy Craig Poon

MUSE PRODUCTIONS, INC.

(Motion picture, independent film & TV producer)
15 Brooks Ave., Unit B, Venice, CA 90291. (310) 306-2001.
FAX: (310) 574-2614. www.musefilm.com
PRESIDENT & PRODUCER
Chris Hanley
PRESIDENT & DIRECTOR
Roberta Hanley

MUTANT ENEMY, INC.

P.O. Box 900, Beverly Hills, CA 90213-0900. (310) 369-4540.
CEO
Joss Whedon
PRESIDENT
Chris Buchanan

MUTUAL FILM COMPANY

650 N. Bronson Ave., Clinton Bldg., Los Angeles, CA 90004.
(323) 871-5690. FAX: (323) 871-5689.
PRINCIPALS
Don Granger
Gary Levinsohn
OPERATIONS & ADMINISTRATION, MUTUTAL FILM INTL.
Lesly Gross
INTERNATIONAL SERVICING
Jennifer P. Shepard

NANAS HART ENTERTAINMENT

(Motion picture & TV producer)
14622 Ventura Blvd., Ste. 746, Sherman Oaks, CA 91403.
(818) 342-9800. FAX: (818) 342-1741.
email: mnh319@aol.com
PRODUCER & PERSONAL MANAGER
Scott Hart
PRODUCER & PERSONAL MANAGER
Herb Nanas
ASSISTANT TO MR. NANAS & MR. HART
Fren Messer

JULIUS R. NASSO PRODUCTIONS

(Motion picture, independent film & TV producer)
5824 12th Ave., Brooklyn, NY 11219. (718) 854-1561. FAX:
(718) 972-2355.
PRESIDENT & PRODUCER
Julius R. Nasso

NATIONAL GEOGRAPHIC

(Motion picture & TV producer)
National Geographic Feature Films, 9100 Wilshire Blvd., Ste.
401E, Beverly Hills, CA 90212. (310) 858-5800.
EXECUTIVE V.P,. PRODUCTION & DEVELOPMENT (CA)
Christine Whitaker
DOCUMENTARIES
1145 17th St. N.W., Washington, DC 20036. (202) 775-6147.
FAX: (202) 775-6590. www.nationalgeographic.com/main.html

NATIONAL LAMPOON

(Motion pictures & TV producer)
A subsidiary of J2 Communications, 10850 Wilshire Blvd., Ste.
1000, Los Angeles, CA 90024. (310) 474-5252. FAX: (310)
474-1219. www.nationallampoon.com
CHAIRMAN, PRESIDENT & CEO
James Jimirro
COO & DIRECTOR
Daniel S. Laikin
V.P., MARKETING
Duncan Murray
EXECUTIVE V.P.
Douglas S. Bennett
EDITOR IN CHIEF, NATIONAL LAMPOON.COM
Scott Rubin

MACE NEUFELD PRODUCTIONS

(Motion picture & TV producer)
10202 W. Washington Blvd., Steward Bldg., Ste. 220, Culver
City, CA 90232-3195. (310) 244-2555. FAX: (310) 244-0255.
PRINCIPAL
Mace Neufeld
V.P., DEVELOPMENT
Kel Symons

NEW CANNON, INC.

(Motion picture & film producer & distributor)
304 N. Edinburgh Ave., Los Angeles, CA 90048. (323) 655-
7705, (323) 655-7705. FAX: (323) 655-7706.
www.newcannoninc.com
CHAIRMAN
Menahem Golan
PRESIDENT & CEO
Evgeny Afineevsky

NEW CONCORDE CORP.

(Motion picture & TV producer & distributor)
11600 San Vicente Blvd., Los Angeles, CA 90049. (310) 820-
6733. FAX: (310) 207-6816. www.concorde-newhorizons.com
PRESIDENT & CEO
Roger Corman
PRESIDENT, NEW HORIZONS HOME VIDEO
Gary Jones
EXECUTIVE V.P.
Thomas Krentzin
SENIOR V.P. & PRODUCER
Julie Corman

V.P., DEVELOPMENT
Frances Doel
V.P., FINANCE
Goly Jamshidi
DIRECTOR, CREATIVE AFFAIRS
Sarah Esberg

NEW CRIME PRODUCTIONS

(Motion picture producer)
555 Rose Ave., Venice, CA 90291. (310) 396-2199. FAX: (310)
396-4249. email: newcrime@aol.com
WRITER & PRODUCER & ACTOR
John Cusack
WRITER & PRODUCER
Steve Pink
V.P., PRODUCTION & DEVELOPMENT
Grace Loh
ASSISTANT TO GRACE LOH
Christen McArdle
ASSISTANT TO JOHN CUSACK
Aurelre Levy

NEW LINE CINEMA CORPORATION

888 Seventh Ave., 20th Flr., New York, NY 10106. (212) 649-
4900. FAX: (212) 649-4966. www.newline.com
116 N. Robertson Blvd., 2nd Flr., Los Angeles, CA 90048.
(310) 854-5811. FAX: (310) 854-1824.
CHAIRMAN & CEO
Robert K. Shaye
CHAIRMAN & CFO
Michael Lynne
CFO
Stephen D. Abramson
PRESIDENT, FINE LINE FEATURES
Mark Ordesky
PRESIDENT, TELEVISION
James Rosenthal
EXECUTIVE V.P., PARTICIPATION & CONTRACT
ACCOUNTING
Susannah Juni
EXECUTIVE V.P., ADMINISTRATION
Marsha Hook Haygood
EXECUTIVE V.P., BUSINESS & LEGAL AFFAIRS
Judd Funk
SENIOR EXECUTIVE V.P., FINANCE
Michael Spatt
SENIOR EXECUTIVE V.P., BUSINESS & LEGAL AFFAIRS
Benjamin Zinkin
EXECUTIVE V.P., CONTROLLER
David Eichler
SENIOR V.P., TELEVISION & ANCILLARY
Frank Buquicchio
SENIOR V.P., CORPORATE ACCOUNTING
Raymond Landes
SENIOR V.P., BUSINESS LEGAL AFFAIRS
Amy Goodman
SENIOR V.P., BUSINESS AFFAIRS & ADMINISTRATION
Sonya Thompson
SENIOR V.P., BUSINESS & LEGAL AFFAIRS
Suzanne Rosencranz

THEATRICAL DISTRIBUTION

PRESIDENT, DOMESTIC THEATRICAL DISTRIBUTION
David Tuckerman
EXECUTIVE V.P., GENERAL SALES MANAGER
Robert Kaplowitz
EXECUTIVE V.P., FINE LINE DISTRIBUTION
Steve Friedlander
SENIOR V.P., EASTERN DIVISION MANAGER
Johnathan Beal
SENIOR V.P., SOUTHEASTERN DIVISION MANAGER
Don Osley
SENIOR V.P., SOUTHERN DIVISION MANAGER
John Trickett
SENIOR V.P., WESTERN DIVISION MANAGER
Larry Levy
V.P., NATIONAL PRINT CONTROL
Gisela Corcoran
V.P., EXHIBITOR RELATIONS
Kristina Warner

INTERNATIONAL DISTRIBUTION

CO-CHAIRMAN & PRESIDENT
Rolf Mittweg
PRESIDENT
Camela Galano
EXECUTIVE V.P., SALES & ADMINISTRATION
Nestor Nieves
V.P., INTERNATIONAL MARKETING
Teri Grochowski

MARKETING

PRESIDENT & COO, WORLDWIDE DISTRIBUTION &
MARKETING
Rolf Mittweg
PRESIDENT, DOMESTIC THEATRICAL MARKETING
Russell Schwartz

EXECUTIVE V.P., FINANCE
Robert Kobus
EXECUTIVE V.P., CORPORATE AFFAIRS
Mary Donovan
SENIOR V.P., FIELD & INTERACTIVE
Elissa Greer

PRODUCTION
PRESIDENT, PRODUCTION
Toby Emmerich
CO-PRESIDENT, PHYSICAL PRODUCTION
Paul Prokop
CO-PRESIDENT, PHYSICAL PRODUCTION
Erik Holmberg
EXECUTIVE V.P., MUSIC
Paul Broucek

TELEVISION DISTRIBUTION
PRESIDENT
James Rosenthal
SENIOR E.V.P., TELEVISION DISTRIBUTION
David Spiegelman
SENIOR E.V.P., LICENSING & MERCHANDISING
David Imhoff
SENIOR V.P., SALES ADMINISTRATION
Vicky Gregorian

HOME VIDEO
PRESIDENT
Stephen Einhorn
EXECUTIVE V.P., FINANCE
Rita Chiapetta-Thibault

INFORMATION DISTRIBUTION
EXECUTIVE V.P., INFORMATION SERVICES
Karen Zimmer

NEWMAN/TOOLEY FILMS
(Motion picture & independent film producer)
101 S. Robertson Blvd., #203, Los Angeles, CA 90048. (310) 777-8733. FAX: (310) 777-8730.
email: newmantooley@earthlink.net
PRODUCER & CO-CHAIRMAN
Vincent G. Newman
PRODUCER & CO-CHAIRMAN
Tucker Tooley
PRODUCER
Ronene A. Ettinger
DIRECTOR, PRODUCTION & DEVELOPMENT
Nancy Lanham

NEWMARKET CAPITAL GROUP
(Motion picture & independent film producer)
202 N. Canon Dr., Beverly Hills, CA 90210. (310) 858-7472. FAX: (310) 858-7473.
PARTNERS
Chris Ball
William Tyrer
CFO
Rene Cogan
STORY EDITOR
John Crye
DEVELOPMENT
Carolyn Harris
DISTRIBUTION
Bob Berney
ACQUISITIONS
Linda Hawkins
PRODUCTION
Aaron Ryder

NEW REGENCY PRODUCTIONS
(Motion picture, independent film & TV producer)
10201 W. Pico Blvd., Bldg. 12, Los Angeles, CA 90035. (310) 369-8300. FAX: (310) 969-0470. www.newregency.com
PRODUCER
Arnon Milchan
PRESIDENT & CEO
David Matalon
PRESIDENT, FILMED ENTERTAINMENT
Sanford Panitch
EXECUTIVE V.P. & CFO
Louis Santor
EXECUTIVE V.P., BUSINESS & LEGAL AFFAIRS. & GENERAL COUNSEL
Bill Weiner
SENIOR V.P., PRODUCTION
Peter Cramer
SENIOR V.P., PRODUCTION
Kara Francis
SENIOR V.P., PHYSICAL PRODUCTION
Thomas Imperanto
SENIOR V.P., POST-PRODUCTION
Elissa Loparco
V.P., MARKETING
Michael Brown
V.P., PRODUCTION
Stacy Maes

DIRECTOR, DEVELOPMENT
Alex Amin
PRODUCTION ADMINISTRATOR
Chad Freet
CREATIVE ASSOCIATES
Alex Sundell
STORY EDITOR
Heidi Sherman

NEW YORKER FILMS
(Motion picture distributor)
85 5th Ave., 11th Flr., New York, NY 10023. (212) 645-4600. FAX: (212) 645-3030. www.newyorkerfilms.com
PRESIDENT
Daniel Talbot

NICKELODEON MOVIES
(Motion picture & TV producer)
5555 Melrose Ave., Lubitsch Bldg., #119, Hollywood, CA 90038. (323) 956-8663. FAX: (323) 862-1663.
1515 Broadway, 38th Flr., New York, NY 10036. (212) 258-7500.
PRESIDENT
Albie Hecht
SENIOR V.P.
Julia Pistor
EXECUTIVE ASSISTANT
Niki Williams
DIRECTOR, DEVELOPMENT
Damon Ross
CREATIVE EXECUTIVE
Ali Bell
VICE PRESIDENT
Ramsey Naito
MARKETING COORDINATOR
Michael Zermeno
DEVELOPMENT ASSISTANT
Dean Sameshima

NORTHERN ARTS ENTERTAINMENT
(Motion picture producer & distributor)
P.O. Box 760, Williamsburg, MA 01096. (413) 268-9301.
PRESIDENT
David Mazor
V.P., ACQUISITIONS
Ava Lazar
DIRECTOR, FOREIGN ACQUISITIONS
Andrew Weeks

NUANCE PRODUCTIONS
(TV producer)
9350 Wilshire Blvd., #250, Beverly Hills, CA 90210. (310) 288-9970. FAX: (310) 247-8150.
PARTNER
Paul Reiser
PARTNER
Arthur Spivak

LYNDA OBST PRODUCTIONS
(Motion picture, independent film & TV producer)
5555 Melrose Ave., Bldg. 210, Hollywood, CA 90038. (323) 956-8744. FAX: (323) 862-2287.
PRODUCER
Lynda Obst
SENIOR V.P., PHYSICAL PRODUCTIONS
Elizabeth Hooper

OCTOGRAPH INC.
(Parent company of Showscan Entertainment)
(Producer & distributor of contents for media based attractions; developer & producer of large-format films, feature animation films, CGI & TV programming)
1627 N. Gower St., Unit 3, Los Angeles, CA 90028. (323) 460-5640. FAX: (323) 460-5645. www.octograph.com
SENIOR V.P., SALES & MARKETING
Sue Y. Kim
V.P., WORLDWIDE DISTRIBUTION
Marcelo Floriao

OFFROAD ENTERTAINMENT
(Motion picture, independent film & TV producer)
5555 Melrose Ave., Drier #209, Hollywood, CA 90038. (323) 956-4425.
PRODUCER
Steven L. Bernstein
DIRECTOR, DEVELOPMENT
Pat Bernard
STORY DEPARTMENT
Lucy Baxter

OMEGA ENTERTAINMENT, LTD.
(Motion picture & TV producer & distributor)
8760 Shoreham Dr., Los Angeles, CA 90069. (310) 855-0516. FAX: (310) 652-2044. www.omegapic.com
PRESIDENT & CEO
Nico Mastorakis
EXECUTIVE ASSISTANT
Benjamin Cooke

100% ENTERTAINMENT
(Motion picture & independent film producer)
(323) 461-6360. FAX: (323) 934-0440. www.100percent.com
email: 100percent@iname.com
PRESIDENT & CEO
Stanley Isaacs

ON STILTS PRODUCTIONS
(310) 391-6053. email: PStelzer@aol.com
PRODUCER
Peter Stelzer

OPEN DOOR ENTERTAINMENT
Open Door Entertainment, ul. Kielecka 44, 02-530 Warsaw,
Poland. TEL/FAX: (48 22) 646-0220, Cellular: (48 601)-366-
767. email: kai@opendoorkai.com
CEO & PRESIDENT & PRODUCER
Kai P. Schoenhals

ORIGINAL FILM
(Motion picture producer)
2045 S. Barrington Ave., Los Angeles, CA 90025. (310) 445-
9000. FAX: (310) 445-9191.
PRODUCERS & OWNERS
Neal Moritz
Marty Adelstein
PRESIDENT, ORIGINAL TV
Dawn Parouse
EXECUTIVE V.P., PRODUCTION
Tania Landau
SENIOR V.P., PRODUCTION
Heather Lieberman
V.P., PRODUCTION
Jennifer Linardos
CREATIVE EXECUTIVE
Amanda Cohen
DEVELOPMENT ASSISTANTS
Russ Brown
Elizabeth Buraglio
Keith Dinielli
PRODUCTION ASSISTANT
Jonas Barnes

OUTERBANKS ENTERTAINMENT
(Motion picture, independent film & TV producer)
8000 Sunset Blvd., 3rd Flr., Los Angeles, CA 90046. (323)
654-3700. FAX: (323) 654-3797.
email: firstname@outerbanks-ent.com
WRITER & DIRECTOR & PRODUCER
Kevin Williamson
V.P., DEVELOPMENT & PRODUCTION
Jennifer Ereslow
CREATIVE EXECUTIVE
Sarah Kueserka
DEVELOPMENT ASSISTANT
Eric Altman
ASSISTANT TO KEVIN WILLIAMSON
Jordan Rotter

OUTLAW PRODUCTIONS
(Motion picture producer)
9155 Sunset Blvd., West Hollywood, CA 90069. (310) 777-
2000. FAX: (310) 777-2010. www.outlawfilm.com
email: outlaw@outlawfilm.com
PRODUCER
Robert Newmyer
PRODUCER
Jeffrey Silver
PRESIDENT, PRODUCTION
Scott Strauss
V.P., DEVELOPMENT
Jennifer Eatz
ASSOCIATE PRODUCER
Steve Gaub
STORY EDITOR
Michael Ellenberg
ASSISTANTS TO ROBERT NEWMYER
Mike Glassman
Justin Springer
ASSISTANT TO JEFFREY SILVER
Sarah Johnson
ASSISTANT TO SCOTT STRAUSS
Rene Rigal

OUT OF THE BLUE ENTERTAINMENT
(Motion picture producer)
10202 W. Washington Blvd., Astaire Bldg., Ste.1200, Culver
City, CA 90232-3195. (310) 244-7811. FAX: (310) 244-1539.
CONTACTS
Sid Ganis
Alex Siskin
Mandy Safavi
Nick Crisafi
Mike Johnson
Jill Noel

OVERBROOK ENTERTAINMENT
450 N. Roxbury Dr., 4th Flr., Beverly Hills, CA 90210. (310)
432-2400. FAX: (310) 432-2401.
PARTNER
Will Smith
PARTNER
James Lassiter
GENERAL MANAGER
Jana Babatunde-Bey

OXYGEN MEDIA
75 Ninth Ave., New York, NY 10011. (212) 651-2000. FAX:
(212) 651-2099. www.oxygen.com
FOUNDER & CEO
Geraldine Laybourne
CO-FOUNDER & PARTNER
Marcy Carsey
CO-FOUNDER & PARTNER
Tom Warner
CO-FOUNDER & PARTNER
Caryn Mandabach
CO-FOUNDER
Oprah Winfrey
COO
Lisa Hall
PRESIDENT, PRODUCTION & PROGRAMMING
Geoffrey Darby
PRESIDENT, PROGRAMMING & ON-AIR
Debby Beece
SENIOR V.P., DEVELOPMENT
Jennifer Cotter
GENERAL COUNSEL
Dan Taitz

PACIFICA ENTERTAINMENT, INC.
(Motion picture producer & developer; distribution with
Intermedia)
9350 Civic Center Dr., Beverly Hills, CA 90210. (310) 550-
3800. FAX: (310) 550-3801.
email: info@pacificafilm.com
CHAIRMAN
Moritz Borman
CO-PRESIDENT
Linda Benjamin
CO-PRESIDENT
Chris Dubrow

PARADOX PRODUCTIONS, INC.
(Producer)
801 Tarcuto Way, Los Angeles, CA 90077. (310) 440-8133.
FAX: (310) 472-6467. email: doubledox@aol.com
PRESIDENT
John Pasquin

PARAMOUNT PICTURES
(See Viacom, Inc.)

PARKWAY PRODUCTIONS
(Motion picture producer)
100 Universal City Plz. Bldg. 1320 Ste. 3B, Universal City, CA
91608. (818) 777-3865. FAX: (818) 733-2915.
DIRECTOR
Penny Marshall
PRESIDENT
Sean Corrigan
PRODUCER
Amy Lemisch
DIRECTOR, DEVELOPMENT
Maryann Castronovo

PATCHWORK PRODUCTIONS
(Independent film & documentary producer)
106 Lamplighter Dr., Lewisburg, WV 24901. (304) 645-4998.
CONTACT
B.J. Gudmundsson

PATRIOT PICTURES
(Motion picture & independent film producer & distributor)
9065 Nemo St., West Hollywood, CA 90069. (310) 274-0745.
FAX: (310) 274-0925.
CHAIRMAN & CEO
Michael Mendelsohn
EXECUTIVE ASSISTANT
Samantha Duff

DANIEL L. PAULSON PRODUCTIONS
(Motion picture & TV producer & developer)
9056 Santa Monica Blvd., Ste. 203A, W. Hollywood, CA 90069.
(310) 278-9747. FAX: (310) 278-9751.
PRESIDENT
Daniel L. Paulson
V.P., CREATIVE AFFAIRS
Bob Chmiel
DIRECTOR, ADMINISTRATION
Steve A. Kennedy

PB MANAGEMENT/AFT PRODUCTIONS
(Motion picture, independent film & TV producer)
6449 W. 6th St., Los Angeles, CA 90048. (323) 653-7284. FAX:
(323) 653-5285. email: capnett@hotmail.com
PRESIDENT
Paul Bennett
V.P., DEVELOPMENT
Barbara Caplan

ZAK PENN'S COMPANY
10201 W. Pico, Bldg. 31, Rm. 303, Los Angeles, CA 90035.
(310) 369-7360. FAX: (310) 969-0249.
WRITER & PRODUCER
Zak Penn
DEVELOPMENT
Lance Stockton

PERMUT PRESENTATIONS
(Motion picture & TV producer)
9150 Wilshire Blvd., Ste. 247, Beverly Hills, CA 90212. (310)
248-2792. FAX: (310) 248-2797.
PRODUCER & PRESIDENT
David Permut
V.P., PRODUCTION
Steven A. Longi

LESTER PERSKY PRODUCTIONS, INC.
(Motion picture, independent film & TV producer)
9910 Tower Lane, Beverly Hills, CA 90210-2129. (310) 278-
1995. FAX: (310) 855-1019.
PRESIDENT
Tomlinson Dean
V.P., DEVELOPMENT
Jonas A. Neilson

PET FLY PRODUCTIONS
(Motion picture & TV producer)
3100 W. Burbank Blvd. Ste. 200, Burbank, CA 91505. (310)
234-7256. FAX: (310) 234-7099.
WRITER & EXECUTIVE PRODUCER & DIRECTOR
Danny Bilson
WRITER & EXECUTIVE PRODUCER
Paul De Meo
PRESIDENT
Joe Lauer
PRODUCTION ASSOCIATE
Lisa Beard

DANIEL PETRIE JR. & CO.
(Motion picture & TV producer)
18034 Ventura Blvd., Ste. 445, Encino, CA 91316. (818) 708-
1602. FAX: (818) 774-0345.
DIRECTOR & WRITER & PRODUCER
Daniel Petrie Jr.

STEPHEN PEVNER, INC.
248 W. 73rd St., 2nd Flr., New York, NY 10023. (212) 496-
0474. email: spevner@aol.com
PRODUCER
Stephen Pevner

PFEFFER FILM
(Motion picture producer)
500 S. Buena Vista St., Animation Bldg., 2F-8, Burbank, CA
91521. (818) 560-3177. FAX: (818) 843-7485.
PRODUCER
Rachel Pfeffer
VICE PRESIDENT
Jess Siegler

PHOENIX ENTERTAINMENT
2222 Linstromeberg Rd., Beaufort, MO 63013. (573) 484-3725.
FAX: (573) 484-4599.
CHAIRMAN & CEO
Ed Ascheman

PHOENIX PICTURES
(Motion picture, independent film & TV producer & distributor)
10202 W. Washington Blvd., Frankovich Bldg., Culver City, CA
90232. (310) 244-6100. FAX: (310) 839-8915.
CHAIRMAN & CEO
Mike Medavoy
PRESIDENT & COO
Arnold Messer
CFO
Christopher Trunkey
EXECUTIVE V.P., PRODUCTION, PHOENIX PICTURES
PRODUCTION COMPANY
Matt Bierman
V.P., PRODUCTION, PHOENIX PICTURES DEVELOPMENT
COMPANY
Brad Fischer
DIRECTOR, BUSINESS & LEGAL AFFAIRS
Scott Douglas Sebasty
DIRECTOR, DEVELOPMENT
David Thwaites

PICTURE THIS ENTERTAINMENT
(International distributor)
7471 Melrose Ave., Ste. 7, Los Angeles, CA 90046. (323) 852-
1398. FAX: (323) 658-7265. www.picturethisent.com
email: licensing@picturethisent.com
PRESIDENT
Douglas C Witkins

PLATINUM STUDIOS, LLC
(Motion picture & TV producer)
9744 Wilshire Blvd., Ste. 210, Beverly Hills, CA 90212. (310)
276-3900. FAX: (310) 220-6848. www.platinumstudios.com
email: info@platinumstudios.com
CHAIRMAN & CEO
Scott Mitchell Rosenberg
CREATIVE EXECUTIVES
Joel Revoredo
Aaron Severson

PLATONIC FILMS, INC.
(Independent film producer)
349 Broadway, 4th Flr., New York, NY 10013. (212) 633-2000.
FAX: (212) 966-1676. email: info@platonicfilms.net
PRESIDENT
Kevin Segalla
CREATIVE EXECUTIVE
Benjamin Patton

MARC PLATT PRODUCTIONS
(Motion picture, TV & stage producer)
100 Universal City Plaza, Bung. 5184, Universal City, CA
91608. (818) 777-8811. FAX: (818) 866-6353.
CONTACTS
Marc Platt
Joey Levy
Abby Wolf
Adam Siegal
Nicole Brown

MARTIN POLL FILMS, LTD.
(Motion picture, independent film & TV producer)
P.O. Box 17137, Beverly Hills, CA 90209. (323) 876-8873. FAX:
(323) 876-8892.
PRESIDENT
Martin Poll
EXECUTIVE V.P.
Shirley Mellner

POLYFILM
P.O. Box 4867, Carson, CA 90749. (310) 914-1776. FAX: (978)
334-5539.
CEO & V.P., SALES
Ray Kavandi
PRESIDENT
Zachary Lovas
V.P., PRODUCTION
Jason Lovas

PORCHLIGHT ENTERTAINMENT
(Motion pictures, animation & worldwide distribution)
11777 Mississippi Ave., Los Angeles, CA 90025. (310) 477-
8400. FAX: (310) 477-5555. www.porchlight.com
email: info@porchlight.com
PRESIDENT & CEO
Bruce D. Johnson
EXECUTIVE V.P., COO & CFO
William T. Baumann
SENIOR V.P., WORLDWIDE SALES
Michael D. Jacobs
SENIOR V.P., FILMED ENTERTAINMENT
Joe Broido
V.P., ANIMATION PRODUCTION/PRODUCER
Tom Gleason
V.P. & PRODUCER, CHILDREN'S PROGRAMS
Fred Schaefer
V.P., CONSUMER PRODUCTS DIVISION
Stefanie Tier Friedman
V.P., BUSINESS & LEGAL AFFAIRS
Peggy Lisberger
HEAD, ACQUISITIONS
Zac Reeder

OTTO PREMINGER FILMS, LTD.
(Motion picture & TV producer & distributor)
17 Seth Canyon Dr., Mt. Kisco, NY 10549-9804. (914) 242-
5112. FAX: (914) 666-4553. email: OPFILMS@aol.com
PRESIDENT
Hope B. Preminger
VICE PRESIDENT
Valerie Robins

EDWARD R. PRESSMAN FILM CORP.
(Film producer)
1468 N. Wilcox Ave., Los Angeles, CA 90028. (323) 871-8383.
FAX: (323) 871-1870.
419 Lafeyette St., 7th Flr., New York, NY 10003. (212) 489-
3333. FAX: (212) 489-2103. www.pressman.com
PRESIDENT
Edward R. Pressman

PRETTY PICTURES
(Producer of film & TV)
100 Universal City Plz., Bldg. 2352-A, 3rd Flr., Universal City, CA 91608. (818) 733-0926. FAX: (818) 866-0847.
WRITER, DIRECTOR, PRODUCER
Neil LaBute
PRODUCER
Gail Mutrux
SENIOR V.P., PRODUCTION
Valerie Dean
STORY EDITOR
Guadalupe Rilova
ASSISTANT TO NEIL LABUTE
Tim Harms

PROMARK/ROAD SALES USA
(International producer & distributor)
3599 Cahuenga Blvd. W., 3rd Flr., Los Angeles, CA 90068. (323) 878-0404. FAX: (323) 878-0486.
email: Promark@promarkgroup.com
PRESIDENT
Jonathan M. Kramer
SENIOR V.P., PRODUCTION
Steve Beswick
V.P., INTERNATIONAL SALES
Eric Bernstein
V.P., INTERNATIONAL SALES
Annouchka Leoeur
DIRECTOR, OPERATIONS
Christy Peterson
V.P., PRODUCTION
Shelly Strong
V.P., PRODUCTION
Amy Krell
DIRECTOR, MARKETING & DISTRIBUTION SERVICES
Patrick Caneday

PUNCH PRODUCTIONS
(Motion picture & TV producer)
11661 San Vicente Blvd., Los Angeles, CA 90049. (310) 442-4888.
OWNER
Dustin Hoffman
PRODUCER
Murray Schisgal
DIRECTOR, DEVELOPMENT
Heather Waterman
OFFICE/PROJECT MANAGER
Julie Benson

QUINCE PRODUCTIONS, INC.
(Motion picture, independent film & TV producer)
12400 Ventura Blvd., #371, Studio City, CA 91604. (323) 436-0677. FAX: (323) 436-0246.
PRESIDENT & EXECUTIVE PRODUCER
Edward Asner
EXECUTIVE ASSISTANT
Patricia Egan

RADAR PICTURES
10900 Wilshire Blvd., Ste. 1400, Los Angeles, CA 90024. (310) 208-8525. FAX: (310) 208-1764.
CHAIRMAN & CEO
Ted W. Field
PRESIDENT & COO
Scott Kroopf
PRODUCERS
Erica Huggins
Joe Rosenberg
PRODUCTION EXECUTIVES
Monica Mullens
Sean Gorman
SENIOR V.P., BUSINESS & LEGAL
David Boyle

RAINBOW FILM CO./RAINBOW RELEASING
(Motion picture producer & distributor)
9165 Sunset Blvd., Ste. 300, Los Angeles, CA 90069. (310) 271-0202. FAX: (310) 271-2753. www.rainbowfilms.com
email: rainbow@rainbowfilms.com
PRESIDENT
Henry Jaglom
DIRECTOR, DISTRIBUTION
Sharon Lester Kohn
PRODUCER & DEVELOPMENT
Judith Wolinsky
DEVELOPMENT
Lauren Beck

RANKIN/BASS PRODUCTIONS
24 W. 55 St., New York, NY 10019. (212) 582-4017.
PRESIDENT & CEO
Arthur Rankin, Jr.
SENIOR V.P., PRODUCTION & DEVELOPMENT
Peter Bakalian

MARTIN RANSOHOFF PRODUCTIONS, INC.
(Motion picture producer)
c/o Francis Associates, 501 S. Beverly Dr., 3rd Flr., Beverly Hills, CA 90212. (310) 440-3900. FAX: (310) 440-3920.
PRODUCER
Martin Ransohoff

RAT ENTERTAINMENT/RAT TV
(Motion picture & TV producer & developer)
9255 Sunset Blvd., Ste. 310, Los Angeles, CA 90069. (310) 228-5000. FAX: (310) 860-9251.
DIRECTOR & PRODUCER
Brett Ratner
PRESIDENT, FEATURE DEVELOPMENT
Jay Stern
DIRECTOR, FEATURE DEVELOPMENT
John Cheng

RECORDED PICTURE COMPANY
(Motion picture & independent film producer)
7001 Melrose Ave., Los Angeles, CA 90038. (323) 937-0733. FAX: (323) 936-4913.
24 Hanway St., London W1T 1UH. TEL: (44 207) 636-2251.
PRODUCER & CHAIRMAN
Jeremy Thomas
HEAD, DEVELOPMENT
Hercules Bellville
SENIOR V.P. & HEAD, DEVELOPMENT
Alexandra Stone
HEAD, FINANCE
Stephan Mallmann
HEAD, BUSINESS AFFAIRS
Peter Watson

RED BIRD PRODUCTIONS
(Motion picture, independent film & TV producer)
3623 Hayden Ave., Culver City, CA 90232. (310) 202-1711. FAX: (310) 202-7496.
PRESIDENT & ACTOR & DIRECTOR & PRODUCER
Debbie Allen

REDEEMABLE FEATURES
c/o Studionext, 427 Broadway, 2nd Flr., New York, NY 10013. (212) 334-6398. www.redeemable.com
PRINCIPALS
Ira Deutchman, c/o Emerging Pictures, 245 W. 55th St., 4th Flr., New York, NY 10019. (212) 245-6767. FAX: (212) 202-4984. email: ira@emergingpictures.com
Greg Johnson, c/o Interal, 61 Loomis Pl., New Haven, CT 06511. (203) 776-4429. FAX: (203) 497-8807.
email: greg@redeemable.com
Peter Newman, c/o Peter Newman Prods., 799 Washington St., Rm. 408, New York, NY 10014. (212) 897-3979. FAX: (212) 624-1737. email: peter@redeemable.com
Melissa Chesman, (917) 327-6804. FAX: (253) 550-8481.
email: melissa@redeemable.com
Cara White, (843) 881-1480. email: cara@redeemable.com

RED HOUR FILMS
(Motion picture producer)
193 N. Robertson Blvd., Beverly Hills, CA 90211. (310) 289-2565. FAX: (310) 289-5988.
WRITER & DIRECTOR & PRODUCER
Ben Stiller
PRODUCER
Stuart Cornfeld
DIRECTOR, DEVELOPMENT
Rhoades Rader
STORY EDITOR
Will Klein

RED WAGON PRODUCTIONS
(Motion picture producer)
10202 W. Washington Blvd., Hepburn W. Bldg., Culver City, CA 90232-3195. (310) 244-4466. FAX: (310) 244-1480.
PRODUCER & PRESIDENT
Douglas Z. Wick
PRODUCER
Lucy Fisher
PRESIDENT
Bobby Cohen

REGENT ENTERTAINMENT, INC.
1401 Ocean Ave., Ste. 300, Santa Monica, CA 90401. (310) 260-3333. FAX: (310) 260-3343. www.regententertainment.com
CHAIRMAN & CEO
Stephen P. Jarchow
PRESIDENT
Paul Colichman
PRESIDENT, REGENT WORLDWIDE SALES
Gene L. George
V.P., RELEASING
John Lambert
V.P., BUSINESS AFFAIRS
Judith Merians

REHME PRODUCTIONS
(Motion picture & TV producer)
10956 1/2 Weyburn Ave., Los Angeles, CA 90024. (310) 824-3371. FAX: (310) 824-5459.
PRINCIPAL
Robert Rehme
EXECUTIVE V.P. & PRODUCER
Nick Grillo
DIRECTOR, DEVELOPMENT
Damon O'Daniel

RENAISSANCE PICTURES
(Motion picture, independent film & TV producer)
315 S. Beverly Dr., Ste. 216, Beverly Hills, CA 90212. (310) 785-3900. FAX: (310) 785-9176.
DIRECTOR & EXECUTIVE PRODUCER
Sam Raimi
EXECUTIVE PRODUCER
Robert Tapert
BUSINESS MANAGER
Sue Binder

RENFIELD PRODUCTIONS
(Motion picture, independent film & TV producer)
1041 N. Formosa Ave., Writer's Bldg. 321, West Hollywood, CA 90046. (323) 850-3905. FAX: (323) 850-3907.
PRODUCER & PRESIDENT
Michael Finnell
DIRECTOR
Joe Dante

REVELATIONS ENTERTAINMENT
(Motion picture & TV producer)
301 Arizona Ave., Ste. 303, Santa Monica, CA 90401. (310) 394-3131. FAX: (310) 394-3133. www.revelationsent.com
ACTOR, DIRECTOR, PRODUCER & PRESIDENT
Morgan Freeman
PRESIDENT & CEO
Lori McCreary
EXECUTIVE V.P.
Yvette Taylor
MANAGER, PRODUCTION
Kelly Mendelsohn
BUSINESS CONSULTANT
Stuart Hammer
MANAGEMENT, CONSULTANT
Geanne Frank
PUBLICIST, BIZCUIT (P.R. FOR MORGAN FREEMAN)
Donna Lee

REVOLUTION STUDIOS
(Producer)
2900 W. Olympic Blvd., Santa Monica, CA 90404. (310) 255-7000.
FOUNDER/PARTNER
Joe Roth
PARTNERS
Tom Sherak
Todd Garner
Rob Moore
HEAD, MARKETING & DISTRIBUTION
Terry Curtin
INTERNATIONAL MARKETING & DISTRIBUTION
Geoffrey Bossiere
HEAD, NATIONAL PROMOTIONS & CORP. PARTNERSHIPS
James Costos
HEAD, WORLDWIDE PUBLICITY
Suzanne Fritz
ACQUISITIONS
John Hegeman
Leilani Forby
DEVELOPMENT
Derek Dauchy
Scott Bernstein
Navid McIlharghey

RGH/LIONS SHARE PICTURES, INC.
(Foreign film distributor, co-production; insurance financing)
8831 Sunset Blvd., Ste. 300, West Hollywood, CA 90069. (310) 652-2893. FAX: (310) 652-6237. www.lionssharepictures.com
email: rghlionsharepictures@hotmail.com
CO-CEO & PRESIDENT
Eric Lozil
CO-CEO
Billy Blake
DEVELOPMENT
Gloria Morrison
PRESS RELATIONS
John Howard

RIVER ONE FILMS
(Motion picture, independent film & TV movie producer)
1619 Broadway, Ste. 1109, New York, NY 10019. (212) 956-2455. FAX: (212) 956-1519.
email: BillyGith@riveronefilms.com
PRESIDENT & PRODUCER
Thomas J. Mangan IV
V.P. & PRODUCER
William E. Githens

RKO PICTURES
1875 Century Park E., Ste. 2140, Los Angeles, CA 90067. (310) 277-0707. FAX: (310) 226-2490.
3 E. 54th St., 12th Flr., New York, NY 10022. (212) 644-0600. FAX: (212) 644-0384. www.rko.co email: info@rko.com
CHAIRMAN & CEO
Ted Hartley
VICE CHAIRMAN
Dina Merrill
ADVISOR TO THE CHAIRMAN
Thom Mount
SENIOR V.P., FINANCE & CORPORATE CONTROLLER
Kevin Harris
HEAD, PHYSICAL PRODUCTION
Joe Di Maio
HEAD, STORY DEPARTMENT
Brian Sindell
STRATEGY OFFICER
Jonathan Marshall
ATTORNEY
Ray Reyes
MANAGER, BUSINESS DEVELOPMENT
Sam Marshall

AMY ROBINSON PRODUCTIONS
(Motion picture, independent film & TV producer)
101 5th Ave., Ste. 8R, New York, NY 10003. (212) 645-9811. FAX: (212) 645-9810.
PRODUCER
Amy Robinson
DEVELOPMENT
Gabrielle Cran

HOWARD ROSENMAN PRODUCTIONS
635A Westbourne Dr., Los Angeles, CA 90069. (310) 659-2100. email: BIGzR@aol.com
PRESIDENT
Howard Rosenman

ROUNDTABLE INK
c/o Viacom Productions, 10880 Wilshire Blvd., Ste. 1101, Los Angeles, CA 90024. (310) 234-5085. FAX: (310) 820-9783.
PARTNERS & PRODUCERS
Gina Matthews
Grant Scharbo

ROXIE RELEASING
(U.S. theatrical distributor)
3125 16th St., San Francisco, CA 94103. (415) 431-3611. FAX: (415) 431-2822. www.roxie.com
CEO
Bill Banning
CO-PRESIDENT, DISTRIBUTION
Rick Norris
ACQUISITIONS AND PROGRAMMING
Joel S. Bachar

ROYAL PICTURES
(Motion picture distributor)
19619 E. 17 Pl., Aurora, CO 80011. (303) 367-4948. FAX: (303) 343-6010.
GENERAL MANAGER
James Lowry

SCOTT RUDIN PRODUCTIONS
(Film & theatre producer)
5555 Melrose Ave., DeMille Bldg., #100, Los Angeles, CA 90038. (323) 956-4600. FAX: (323) 862-0262.
120 W. 45th St., 10th. Flr., New York, NY 10036. (212) 704-4600.
PRODUCER
Scott Rudin
PRESIDENT
Scott Aversano
SENIOR V.P.
Mark Roybal
DIRECTOR, DEVELOPMENT
John Delaney

RYSHER ENTERTAINMENT
(For production information call Paramount)
2425 Olympic Blvd., Ste. 6040W, Santa Monica, CA 90404. (310) 309-5200.
PRESIDENT & CEO
Tim Helfet
SENIOR V.P., BUSINESS & LEGAL AFFAIRS
Frank Stewart

SAMUELSON PRODUCTIONS LIMITED
(Motion picture, independent film producer)
10401 Wyton Dr., Los Angeles, CA 90024-2527. (310) 208-1000. FAX: (310) 208-2809. www.oscarwilde.com
email: Petersam@who.net
13 Manette St., London W1V 5LB. TEL: (44 207) 439-4900. FAX: (44 207) 439-4901.
PARTNERS
Peter Samuelson
Marc Samuelson

SANFORD/PILLSBURY PRODUCTIONS

(Motion picture, independent film & TV producer)
2932 Wilshire Blvd., Ste. 202, Santa Monica, CA 90403. (310)
449-4520.
PRODUCER
Sarah Pillsbury
PRODUCER
Midge Sanford
CREATIVE DIRECTOR
Deborah Goodwin

SARABANDE PRODUCTIONS

(Motion picture, independent film & TV producer)
530 Wilshire Blvd., Ste. 308, Santa Monica, CA 90401. (310)
395-4842. FAX: (310) 395-7079.
PRESIDENT
David Manson
EXECUTIVE V.P.
Arla Sorkin Manson
DEVELOPMENT ASSOCIATE
Aaron Graff

ARTHUR SARKISSIAN PRODUCTIONS

(Motion picture, independent film & TV producer)
9255 Sunset Blvd., Ste. 340, W. Hollywood, CA 90069. (310)
385-1486. FAX: (310) 385-1171.
PRODUCER
Arthur Sarkissian
V.P., DEVELOPMENT
Peter Sussman
CREATIVE EXECUTIVE
Tina Sutakanat

SATURN FILMS

(Motion picture producer; deal with Intermedia Films)
9000 Sunset Blvd., #911, Los Angeles, CA 90069. (310) 887-
0900. FAX: (310) 248-2965. www.saturnfilms.com
CEO
Nicolas Cage
PRESIDENT & PRODUCER
Norm Golightly
DIRECTOR, DEVELOPMENT
Seth Schur

SCHERICK ASSOCIATES, INC.

(Motion picture, independent film & TV producer)
1950 Sawtelle Blvd., Ste. 282, Los Angeles, CA 90025. (310)
996-2376. FAX: (310) 996-2392.
CONTACTS
Bradford Scherick
Stephen Abronson
Jamila Dawson

JOEL SCHUMACHER PRODUCTIONS

(Motion picture producer)
Warner Bros. Studios, 4000 Warner Blvd. Bldg. 139, Rm. 26,
Burbank, CA 91522. (818) 954-6100. FAX: (818) 954-4642.
OWNER
Joel Schumacher

SCOTT FREE PRODUCTIONS

(Production)
634 N. La Peer Dr., West Hollywood, CA 90069. (310) 360-
2250. FAX: (310) 360-2251.
CO-CHAIRMAN
Ridley Scott
CO-CHAIRMAN
Tony Scott
PRESIDENT
Lisa Ellzey
V.P., PRODUCTION
Zach Schiff-Abrams
V.P., TELEVISION
David W. Zucker
CREATIVE EXECUTIVES
Anne Lai
Erin Upson

SECTION EIGHT

(Motion picture, independent film & TV producer)
4000 Warner Blvd., Bldg. 15, Burbank, CA 91522. (818) 954-
4840. FAX: (818) 954-4860.
CEO & PARTNER
George Clooney
CEO & PARTNER
Steven Soderbergh
CO-PRESIDENT
Ben Cosgrove
CO-PRESIDENT
Jennifer Fox
PRESIDENT, TELEVISION DIVISION
Grant Heslov

DYLAN SELLERS PRODUCTIONS

4000 Warner Blvd., Burbank, CA 91522. (818) 954-4929.
PRODUCER
Dylan Sellers

SEVEN ARTS PICTURES

(Independent film producer)
9595 Wilshire Blvd., #100W Beverly Hills, CA 90212. (310)
887-3830. FAX: (310) 887-3840.
CEO
Peter M. Hoffman
PRODUCER & PARTNER
Susan Hoffman
CREATIVE EXECUTIVES
Victor Teran
Kate Hoffman
Stephanie Poole
Erik Smith

SEVENTH ART RELEASING

(Motion picture, independent film & TV producer & distributor)
7551 Sunset Blvd., Ste. 104, Los Angeles, CA 90046. (323)
845-1455. FAX: (323) 845-4717. www.7thart.com
EXECUTIVE V.P., ACQUISITIONS & DEVELOPMENT
Stephen Kral
SENIOR V.P., OPERATIONS & P.R.
James Eowan
SENIOR V.P., PRODUCTION & MARKETING
Matt Henderson

SHADY ACRES ENTERTAINMENT

(Motion picture, independent film & TV producer)
100 Universal City Plaza, Bldg. 6111, Universal City, CA
91608. (818) 777-4446. FAX: (818) 866-6612.
CONTACTS
Michael Bostick
Ginny Durkin
Tom Shadyac
Jason Wilson
Jordan Wolfe
Amanda Morgan Palmer
Greta Bramberg

SHOELACE PRODUCTIONS, INC./RED OM FILMS

(Motion picture & TV producer)
16 W. 19th St., 12th Flr., New York, NY 10011. (212) 243-2900.
FAX (212) 243-2973.
ACTOR & PRODUCER
Julia Roberts
PRESIDENT, PRODUCTION & DEVELOPMENT & PRODUCER
Deborah Schindler
ASSISTANTS
Kerry Kane
Maggie Jones

SHONKYTE PRODUCTIONS, INC.

(Motion picture, independent film & TV producer)
11935 Kling St., #10, Valley Village, CA 91607. (818) 505-
1332. FAX: (818) 505-1411. www.seanyoung.org
CEO & ACTRESS & PRODUCER & DIRECTOR
Sean Young
V.P. & PRODUCER & DEVELOPMENT
Stephany Hurkos

SHOWSCAN ENTERTAINMENT

(Specialty & simulation film producer & distributor; media & film
based attractions; specialty & simulations theatres)
1627 N. Gower St., Unit 3, Los Angeles, CA 90028. (323) 460-
5640. FAX: (323) 460-5645.
PRESIDENT
Sue Kim
VICE PRESIDENT
Marcelo Floriao

SHUTT-JONES PRODUCTIONS

(Motion picture producer)
100 Universal City Plaza, Bldg. 6111, Universal City, CA
91608. (818) 777-9619. FAX: (818) 866-5006.
email: shuttjonesproduction@unistudios.com
PRODUCERS
Buffy Shutt
Kathy Jones
STORY EDITOR
Lalo Vasquez

SIGNATURE PICTURES

(Motion picture producer. no unsolicited screenplays etc.)
725 Arizona Ave., Ste. 202, Santa Monica, CA 90401.)310)
394-1000. FAX: (310) 394-1001.
PRODUCER
Art Linson
PRODUCER
Cean Chaffin
DIRECTOR & PRODUCER
David Fincher
PRODUCER
John Linson
EXECUTIVE
John Dorsey
DEVELOPMENT
Kareem Elseify

SILVERFILM PRODUCTIONS, INC.
(Motion picture producer)
510 Park Ave., #9B, New York, NY 10022. (646) 282-0312.
PRESIDENT
Raphael Silver
VICE PRESIDENT
Joan Micklin Silver

SILVERLIGHT ENTERTAINMENT
(Motion picture, independent film & TV producer)
(Music Production): 15490 Ventura Blvd., #220, Sherman
Oaks, CA 91403. (818) 981-4400. FAX: (818) 981-4418.
emial: steve@silverlightent.com
PARTNER & CEO
Stephen Drimmer

SILVERLINE PICTURES
(Motion picture & TV movies)
22837 Ventura Blvd., Ste. 205, Woodland Hills, CA 91364.
(818) 225-9032. FAX: (818) 225-9053.
PRESIDENT
Axel Munch

SILVER LION FILMS
(Motion picture producer)
701 Santa Monica Blvd., Ste. 240, Santa Monica, CA 90401.
(310) 393-9177. FAX: (310) 458-9372.
PRODUCERS
Lance Hool
Conrad Hool

SILVER PICTURES
(Motion picture & TV producer)
4000 Warner Blvd., Bldg. 90, Burbank, CA 91522. (818) 954-
4490. FAX: (818) 954-3237.
CHAIRMAN
Joel Silver
COO
Steve Richard
EXECUTIVE V.P., PRODUCTION
Erik Olsen
SENIOR V.P., PRODUCTION
Susan Levin
SENIOR V.P., TELEVISION
Jennifer Gwartz
SENIOR V.P., TELEVISION
Danielle Stokdyk
V.P. FINANCE
Adam Kuhn

SINGLE CELL PICTURES
(Producer)
1016 N. Palm Ave., West Hollywood, CA 90069. (310) 360-
7600. FAX: (310) 360-7011.
PRODUCER
Michael Stipe
PRODUCER
Sandy Stern

SITTING DUCKS PRODUCTIONS
2578 Verbena Dr., Los Angeles, CA 90068. (323) 461-2095.
FAX: (323) 461-2106.
EXECUTIVE PRODUCERS
Michael Bedard
Elizabeth Daro

SKY POND PRODUCTIONS
(Motion picture & film producer)
12163 W. Sunset Blvd., Los Angeles, CA 90049. (310) 476-
0618. FAX: (310) 476-9492.
PRESIDENT & PRODUCER
John Amicarella

SKYFISH PRODUCTIONS, INC.
(Producer)
10100 Santa Monica Blvd., Los Angeles, CA 90067. (310) 229-
4439. FAX: (310) 284-8503.
ACTRESS
Kim Basinger

SKYLARK ENTERTAINMENT, INC./R&R FILMS
12405 Venice Blvd., Ste. 237, Los Angeles, CA 90066. (310)
390-2659. FAX: (310) 390-2759.
email: jokerose@skylarkfilms.com
PRESIDENT & PRODUCER
Jacobus Rose
CREATIVE EXECUTIVE
John Ross

SKYLARK FILMS, LTD.
(Motion picture, independent film & TV producer, developer &
distributor)
1123 Pacific St., Ste. G, Santa Monica, CA 90405-1525. (310)
396-5753. FAX: (310) 396-5753. email: skyfilm@aol.com
PRODUCER
Bradford Pollack
DEVELOPMENT ASSOCIATE & STORY ANALYST
Annelouise Verboan

SKYLINE PARTNERS
(Motion picture & independent film producer)
10550 Wilshire Blvd., Ste. 1001, Los Angeles, CA 90024. (310)
470-3363. FAX: (310) 470-0060.
email: fkuehnert@earthlink.net
MANAGING PARTNER & PRODUCER
Fred Kuehnert
EXECUTIVE PRODUCER
Robert Birmingham
PRODUCER
Grant Guthrie
DIRECTOR & WRITER & PRODUCER
Gary Chason
EXECUTIVE ASSISTANT
Sandra Chouinard

DANIEL SLADEK ENTERTAINMENT CORP.
8306 Wilshire Blvd., #510, Beverly Hills, CA 90211. (323) 934-
9268. FAX: (323) 934-7362. email: dansladek@aol.com
CEO & PRODUCER
Daniel Sladek

SLOANE/BORDEN PICTURES
4220 W. Newdale Dr., Los Angeles, CA 90027. (323) 665-7700.
PARTNERS
Morgan Sloane
Michael Sweney Borden

ALAN SMITHEE FILMS
(Developer & producer)
7510 Sunset Blvd., Ste. 525, Hollywood, CA 90046. (323) 850-
8926.
DIRECTOR
Fred Smythe
ASSOCIATE DIRECTOR
Michael Runstrom

SNAPDRAGON FILMS, INC.
13428 Maxella Ave., #293, Marina del Rey, CA 90292. (310)
822-2505. FAX: (310) 822-7054.
DIRECTOR & PRODUCER & WRITER
Bonnie Palef

SNEAK PREVIEW ENTERTAINMENT, INC.
(Motion picture, independent film & TV producer)
1604 Vista del Mar St., Hollywood, CA 90028. (323) 962-0295.
FAX: (323) 962-0372.
PRODUCER
Steven J. Wolfe
PRODUCERS & MANAGERS
Michael J. Roth
Brad Warshaw
Josh Silver

SOLO ONE PRODUCTIONS
8205 Santa Monica Blvd., #1279, Los Angeles, CA 90046-
5912. (323) 658-8748. FAX: (323) 658-8749.
email: solo1productions@aol.com
ACTRESS & PRODUCER
Marlee Matlin
PRODUCER
Jack Jason

SONY PICTURES ENTERTAINMENT, INC.
10202 W. Washington Blvd., Culver City, CA 90232. (310) 244-
4000. FAX: (310) 244-2626. www.spe.sony.com
550 Madison Ave., 8th Flr., New York, NY 10022, (212) 833-
8833.
VICE CHAIRMAN
Jeff Blake
VICE CHAIRMAN
Yair Landau
VICE CHAIRMAN
Amy Pascal
EXECUTIVE V.P., CAO
Beth Berke
EXECUTIVE V.P. & CFO
David Hendler
SENIOR V.P. & GENERAL COUNSEL
Leah Weil
SENIOR V.P., HUMAN RESOURCES
Suzanne Criley
SENIOR V.P., CORPORATE COMMUNICATIONS
Susan Tick
V.P. & CORPORATE TREASURER
Simon Baker
VICE PRESIDENT
Karen L. Halby
ASSISTANT SECRETARY
Jared Jussim
ASSISTANT TREASURER
Lynne R. Shulim

COLUMBIA PICTURES

(A Sony Pictures Entertainment Company)
10202 W. Washington Blvd., Culver City, CA 90232. (310) 244-4000. FAX: (310) 244-2626.
CHAIRMAN
Amy Pascal
PRESIDENT, CTMPG, CTHV, DVD DISTRIBUTION
Ben Feingold
PRESIDENT, CTMPG WORLDWIDE MARKETING & DISTRIBUTION
Geoff Ammer
VICE CHAIRMAN, CTMPG
Gareth Wigan
PRESIDENT
Peter Schlessel

PRODUCTION

CO-PRESIDENT, PRODUCTION
Doug Belgrad
CO-PRESIDENT, PRODUCTION
Matt Tolmach
EXECUTIVE V.P., PRODUCTION
Amy Baer
EXECUTIVE V.P., PRODUCTION
Doug Belgrad
EXECUTIVE V.P., PRODUCTION
Matt Tolmach
SENIOR V.P., PRODUCTION
Andrea Giannetti
V.P., PRODUCTION
Rachel O'Connor

COLUMBIA TRISTAR MARKETING GROUP

PRESIDENT, CREATIVE MARKETING
Josh Goldstine
EXECUTIVE V.P., CREATIVE ADVERTISING
Tommy Gargotta
EXECUTIVE V.P., PROMOTIONS
George Leon
EXECUTIVE V.P., CREATIVE ADVERTISING
William Loper
SENIOR V.P., CREATIVE ADVERTISING
Christine Birch
SENIOR V.P., INTERNET MARKETING STRATEGY
Dwight Caines
SENIOR V.P., PUBLICITY
Andre Caraco
SENIOR V.P., MEDIA RELATIONS
Steve Elzer
SENIOR V.P., MARKETING SERVICES
Joseph Foley
SENIOR V.P., RESEARCH
David Kaminow
SENIOR V.P., PUBLICITY/PROMOTIONS
Wendy Lightbourne
SENIOR V.P., MEDIA
Stephanie Napoli
SENIOR V.P., PUBLICITY
Ileen Reich
SENIOR V.P., PUBLICITY
Gigi Semone
SENIOR V.P., ELECTRONIC PRESS KITS
Nancy Tate
V.P., PHOTO SERVICES
Denise Balbier
V.P., SPECIAL EVENTS
Kim Carey
V.P., TRAFFIC SERVICES
Rick Davidson
V.P., MEDIA
Brad Goldberg
V.P., AUDIO VISUAL
Arthur Shapiro
V.P., PRINT ADVERTISING
Mark Walker

OTHER DEPARTMENTS

PRESIDENT, COLUMBIA PRODUCTION ADMINISTRATION
Gary Martin
PRESIDENT, WORLDWIDE MUSIC
Lia Vollack
EXECUTIVE V.P., BUSINESS AFFAIRS & OPERATIONS
Robert Geary
EXECUTIVE V.P., POST-PRODUCTION
James Honore
SENIOR V.P., BUSINESS AFFAIRS
Jon Gobson
SENIOR V.P., BUSINESS AFFAIRS
Alan Krieger
SENIOR V.P., BUSINESS AFFAIRS
John Levy
SENIOR V.P., MUSIC CREATIVE AFFAIRS
Pilar McCurry
SENIOR V.P., POST-PRODUCTION
Russ Paris
SENIOR V.P., MUSIC ADMINISTRATION
Raul Perez

SENIOR V.P., PRODUCTION ADMINISTRATION
Ray Zimmerman
V.P., PRODUCTION ADMINISTRATION
Pete Corral
V.P., BUSINESS AFFAIRS ADMINISTRATION
Mark Horowitz
V.P., MUSIC LICENSING
Donald Kennedy
V.P., BUSINESS AFFAIRS, CTMPG
Pam Kunath
V.P., MUSIC BUSINESS AFFAIRS
Larry Kohorn
V.P., PRODUCTION ADMINISTRATION
Kathy McDermott
V.P., STORY DEPARTMENT
Karen Moy
V.P., BUSINESS AFFAIRS CONTRACT ADMINISTRATION
Thomas Stack
V.P., BUSINESS AFFAIRS
Mark Wyman
V.P., MUSIC PUBLISHING
Rita Zakrzewski

SONY PICTURES CLASSICS

(A Sony Pictures Entertainment Company)
550 Madison Ave., 8th Flr., New York, NY 10022. (212) 833-8833.
CO-PRESIDENT
Michael Barker
CO-PRESIDENT
Tom Bernard
CO-PRESIDENT
Marcie Bloom
SENIOR V.P., ACQUISITIONS
Dylan Leiner
SENIOR V.P., OPERATIONS
Grace Murphy
V.P., ADVERTISING & PUBLICITY
Carmelo Pirrone
V.P., SALES
Tom Prassis
VICE PRESIDENT
Derval Whelan

SCREEN GEMS

(A Sony Pictures Entertainment Company)
10202 W. Washington Blvd., Culver City, CA 90232. (310) 244-4000.
PRESIDENT
Clinton Culpepper
EXECUTIVE V.P., MARKETING
Valerie Van Galder
SENIOR V.P., ACQUISITIONS, CTMPG & CTHV
Benedict Carver
SENIOR V.P., PRODUCTION
Gilbert Dumontet
SENIOR V.P., BUSINESS AFFAIRS
Gilbert Hirsch
SENIOR V.P., PRODUCTION
Stacy Kolker Cramer
SENIOR V.P., MARKETING
Marc Weinstock
V.P., PUBLICITY
Danielle Rosenfeld

SONY PICTURES RELEASING

(A Sony Pictures Entertainment Company)
10202 W. Washington Blvd., Culver City, CA 90232. (310) 244-4000. FAX: (310) 244-2626.
PRESIDENT, CTMPG WORLDWIDE MARKETING & DISTRIBUTION
Jeff Blake
PRESIDENT, SONY PICTURES RELEASING
Rory Bruer
EXECUTIVE V.P. & GENERAL SALES MANAGER
David Garel
EXECUTIVE V.P., MARKETING & DISTRIBUTION, CTMPG
Paul Smith
SENIOR V.P., EASTERN DIVISION
Jim Amos
SENIOR V.P., GM, CANADA
Michael Brooker
SENIOR V.P., PRINT OPERATIONS
Mike Jones
SENIOR V.P., WORLDWIDE THEATRICAL FINANCIAL ADMIN, CTMPG
Eileen Lomis
SENIOR V.P., WESTERN DIVISION
Adrian Smith
SENIOR V.P., SOUTHERN DIVISION
Terry Tharpe
SENIOR V.P., SOUTHERN REGION
Sherman Wood
V.P., SALES ADMINISTRATION
Craig Bartlet
V.P., SALES, CANADA
Tim Bishop
V.P., WORLDWIDE DISTRIBUTION ANALYSIS
John Cacavas

V.P., EXHIBITOR RELATIONS
Ed Clegg
V.P., EXHIBITOR RELATIONS
Ann-Elizabeth Crotty
V.P., MARKETING & DISTRIBUTION, CTMPG
Paula Parker
V.P., ACQUISITIONS & REPERTORY SALES
Michael Schlesinger
V.P., CANADIAN MEDIA & COOP. ADVERTISING
Donna Slack
V.P., DISTRIBUTION SERVICES
Conrad K. Steely

COLUMBIA TRISTAR FILM DISTRIBUTORS INT'L.

10202 W. Washington Blvd., Culver City, CA 90232. (310) 244-4000. FAX: (310) 244-2626.
PRESIDENT, CTMPG WORLDWIDE MARKETING & DISTRIBUTION
Jeff Blake
SENIOR EXECUTIVE V.P.
Mark L. Zucker
SENIOR EXECUTIVE V.P., WORLDWIDE MARKETING
Scott Neeson
SENIOR V.P., SALES & DISTRIBUTION
Ralph Alexander, Jr.
SENIOR V.P., INTERNATIONAL DISTRIBUTION
Stephen Basil-Jones
SENIOR V.P., MARKETING & DISTRIBUTION
Sal Ladestro
SENIOR V.P., INTERNATIONAL OPERATIONS
Jay Sands
SENIOR V.P., INTERNATIONAL PRINT SERVICES
Beverly Starr
SENIOR V.P., PUBLICITY & PROMOTIONS
Susan van der Werff
V.P., SALES EASTERN EUROPE, MIDDLE EAST, AFRICA
Mark Braddel
V.P., INTERNATIONAL DISTRIBUTION
Steve Bruno
V.P., DISTRIBUTION
Mimi Burri
V.P. & MANAGING DIRECTOR, FILM PRODUCTS, ASIA
Barbara Robinson
V.P., INTERNATIONAL POST PRODUCTION
Paul Stapley-Tovey
V.P., MARKETING, LATIN AMERICA
Vittorio Tamburini

COLUMBIA TRISTAR HOME ENTERTAINMENT

(A Sony Pictures Entertainment Company)
10202 W. Washington Blvd., Culver City, CA 90232. (310) 244-4000. FAX: (310) 244-2626.
PRESIDENT, CTMPG, CTHV, DVD DISTRIBUTION
Ben Feingold
SENIOR EXECUTIVE V.P. & GENERAL MANAGER, BUSINESS AFFAIRS
Robin Russell
EXECUTIVE V.P., ASIA & LATIN AMERICA
Adrian Alperovich
EXECUTIVE V.P., NORTH AMERICA
Marshall Forster
EXECUTIVE V.P., WORLDWIDE MARKETING
Lexine Wong
SENIOR V.P., PRODUCTION & BUSINESS AFFAIRS
Gilbert Dumontet
SENIOR V.P., MANUFACTURING & PRODUCTION
Walt Engler
SENIOR V.P., WORLDWIDE PUBLICITY
Fritz Friedman
SENIOR V.P., SALES, RETAIL U.S.
John Reina

DIGITAL STUDIOS DIVISION

(A Sony Pictures Entertainment Company)
10202 W. Washington Blvd., Culver City, CA 90232. (310) 244-4000. FAX: (310) 244-2626.
SENIOR V.P., STRATEGIC TECHNOLOGIES
Dr. Bob Hopkins
SENIOR V.P., DIGITAL DISTRIBUTION
Ribhard O'Hare
SENIOR V.P., OPERATIONS & BUSINESS DEVELOPMENT
Eisuke Tsuyuzaki
V.P., ASSET MANAGEMENT & FILM RESTORATION
Grover Crisp
V.P., INTERNATIONAL SALES SERVICING
Terri Davies
V.P., ADVANCED TECHNOLOGIES
Don Eklund
V.P., POST-PRODUCTION SERVICES
Patricia Furnare
V.P., DVD-DIGITAL VERSATILE
David Sterling

SONY PICTURES DIGITAL AUTHORING CENTER

(A Sony Pictures Entertainment company)
10202 W. Washington Blvd., Culver City, CA 90232. (310) 244-7356. FAX: (310) 244-1518.
SENIOR V.P. & GENERAL MANAGER
James Mercs

WORLDWIDE PRODUCT FULFILLMENT GROUP

(A Sony Pictures Entertainment Company)
10202 W. Washington Blvd., Ste. 209, Culver City, CA 90232. (310) 244-4000. FAX: (310) 244-2626.
SENIOR V.P.
Jeff Hargleroad
VICE PRESIDENT
Bob Billeci
V.P., SUPPORT OPERATIONS
Robert Connolly

FILM & TAPE OPERATIONS

(A Sony Pictures Entertainment Company)
150 Roger Ave., Inwood, NY 11096. (718) 868-5800. FAX: (718) 868-5804.

POST-PRODUCTION FACILITIES

(A Sony Pictures Entertainment company)
PRESIDENT, DIGITAL POST-PRODUCTION FACILITIES
Michael Kohut
EXECUTIVE V.P., SOUND, VIDEO & PROJECTION
Richard Branca
EXECUTIVE V.P., THEATRICAL & TV SOUND EDITORIAL
Tom McCarthy
SENIOR V.P., POST-PRODUCTION SOUND ENGINEERING
Mark Koffman

SONY PICTURES TELEVISION TELEVISION

(A Sony Pictures Entertainment Company)
10202 W. Washington Blvd., Ste. 7th Flr., Culver City, CA 90232. (310) 244- 4000.
Regional Offices: 2859 Paces Ferry Rd., Ste. 1130, Atlanta, GA 30339. (770) 434-5400. FAX: (770) 431-0202.
455 N. Cityfront Plaza Dr., Ste. 3120, Chicago, IL 60611. (312) 644-0770. FAX: (312) 644-0781.
8117 Preston Rd., Ste. 495, Dallas TX 75225. (214) 987-3671. FAX: (214) 987-3675.
550 Madison Ave., 12th Flr., New York, NY 10022. (212) 833-8354. FAX: (212) 833-8360.
PRESIDENT
Steve Mosko
PRESIDENT, PROGRAMMING & PRODUCTION
Russ Krasnoff
EXECUTIVE V.P., ADVERTISER SALES
Bo Argentino
EXECUTIVE V.P., PROGRAMMING
Jeanie Bradley
EXECUTIVE V.P., BUSINESS OPERATIONS
Richard Frankie
EXECUTIVE V.P., PRODUCTION
Edward Lammi
EXECUTIVE V.P., BUSINESS AFFAIRS
Don Loughery
EXECUTIVE V.P., PLANNING & OPERATIONS
David Mumford
EXECUTIVE V.P., MARKETING
Robert Oswaks
EXECUTIVE V.P., MOVIES & MINISERIES
Helen Verno
EXECUTIVE V.P., DISTRIBUTION
John Weiser
SENIOR V.P., MEDIA RELATIONS & PROMOTIONS
Paula Askanas
SENIOR V.P., DISTRIBUTION OPERATIONS
Francine Beougher
SENIOR V.P., ADVERTISER SALES STRATEGY
Richard Burrus
SENIOR V.P., MARKETING
Alan Daniels
SENIOR V.P., DEVELOPMENT
Jamie Erlicht
SENIOR V.P., FAMILY ENTERTAINMENT BUSINESS AFFAIRS
Michael Helfland
SENIOR V.P., MUSIC
Robert Hunka
SENIOR V.P., SOUTHWESTERN REGION
Dirk Johnston
SENIOR V.P., SOUTHEASTERN REGION
Steve Maddox
SENIOR V.P., BUSINESS AFFAIRS
Joanne Mazzu
SENIOR V.P., PRODUCTION
John Morrissey
SENIOR V.P., EASTERN REGION
John Rohrs, Jr.
SENIOR V.P., RESEARCH
Doug Roth
SENIOR V.P., TALENT & CASTING
Dawn Steinberg
SENIOR V.P., TECHNICAL OPERATIONS
Phil Squyres
SENIOR V.P., AD SALES DIRECTV
Joe Tafuri
SENIOR V.P., DEVELOPMENT
Zack Van Amburg
SENIOR V.P., MIDWESTERN REGION
Tom Warner

SENIOR V.P., BUSINESS AFFAIRS, SYNDICATION
Jeff Weiss
SENIOR V.P., MOVIES FOR TELEVISION & MINISERIES
Winifred White Neisser
SENIOR V.P., NORTHEASTERN REGION
Jeff Wolf
SENIOR V.P., NORTHEASTERN REGION
Mark Wurtzel

SONY PICTURES TELEVISION INTERNATIONAL
10202 W. Washington Blvd., Culver City, CA 90232. (310) 244-4000.
PRESIDENT
Michael Grindon
PRESIDENT, COLUMBIA TRISTAR FILMS OF KOREA
Hyuk-Jo Kwon
PRESIDENT, SPTVJ & PRESIDENT, PRODUCTION, EUROPE
Ken Munekata
SENIOR E.V.P., INTERNATIONAL NETWORKS
Andy Kaplan
SENIOR E.V.P. & MANAGING DIRECTOR EUROPE
John McMahon
EXECUTIVE V.P., SALES STRATEGY & PLANNING
Peter Iacono
EXECUTIVE V.P., INTERNATIONAL TV PRODUCTION
Steven Kent
SENIOR V.P., INTERNATIONAL NETWORKS
Darren Childs
SENIOR V.P., SOUTHERN EUROPEAN PRODUCTION
Nathalie Civrais
SENIOR V.P., SALES FOR LATIN AMERICA/CARIBBEAN
John Cuddihy
SENIOR V.P., INTERNATIONAL NETWORKS
Martha Eberts
SENIOR V.P., SALES & MARKETING
Kim Hatamiya
SENIOR V.P. & MANAGING DIRECTOR, ASIA
Dewy Ip
SENIOR V.P., PROGRAMMING
Marie Jacobson
SENIOR V.P., PRODUCTION
Fran McConnell
SENIOR V.P., INTERNATIONAL NETWORKS, ASIA
Todd Miller
SENIOR V.P., SALES PLANNING
Ross Pollack
SENIOR V.P., INTERNATIONAL CHANNELS
T.C. Schultz
SENIOR V.P., INTERNATIONAL AD SALES
Dick Soule

SONY PICTURES DIGITAL
3960 Ince Blvd., Culver City, CA 90232. (310) 840-8676. FAX: (310) 840-8390.
PRESIDENT, DIGITAL ENTERTAINMENT
Yair Landau
EXECUTIVE V.P.
Patrick Kennedy
SENIOR V.P., TECHNOLOGY
Steven Banfield
SENIOR V.P., BUSINESS AFFAIRS
Corii Berg
SENIOR V.P., TECHNOLOGY
Doug Chey
SENIOR V.P., SPDE EUROPE
Ron Geller
V.P., CONTENT SERVICES DEVELOPMENT
Nazir Allibhoy
V.P., OPERATIONS
Andra Anderson
V.P., PRODUCTION OPERATION
Peter Anton
V.P., PRODUCTION SERVICES
Marie Davis
V.P., BUSINESS AFFAIRS
Eric Gaynor
V.P., MEDIA RELATIONS
Don Levy
V.P., ADVANCED PLATFORMS
Shalom Mann
V.P., BUSINESS AFFAIRS
Jim Pickell

SONY PICTURES INTEGRATED NETWORK (SPIN)
(A Sony Pictures Entertainment company)
SENIOR V.P.
Ira Rubenstein
V.P., CUSTOMER RELATIONSHIP MANAGEMENT
Jeremy Barnett
VICE PRESIDENT
Emmanuelle Borde
V.P., MARKETING
Steven Jacobs

SONY PICTURES DIGITAL NETWORKS
3960 Ince Blvd., Culver City, CA 90232. (310) 840-8676. FAX: (310) 840-8390.
SENIOR V.P., STRATEGIC ALLIANCES
Michael Arrieta
SENIOR V.P., ADVANCED PLATFORMS GROUP
Tim Chambers
SENIOR V.P. & GENERAL MANAGER, SOAPCITY
Mary Coller
SENIOR V.P. & GENERAL MANAGER, SCREENBLAST
Andrew Schneider
V.P., WIRELESS SERVICES
Rio Caraeff

SONY PICTURES ANIMATION
9050 W. Washington Blvd., Culver City, CA 90232. (310) 840-8000. FAX: (310) 840-8100.
EXECUTIVE V.P.
Penney Finkelman Cox
EXECUTIVE V.P.
Sandra Rabins
SENIOR V.P., BUSINESS AFFAIRS
Barbara Zipperman
V.P., CREATIVE AFFAIRS
Nate Hopper

IMAGEWORKS
(A Sony Pictures Entertainment Company)
9050 W. Washington Blvd., Culver City, CA 90232. (310) 840-8000. FAX: (310) 840-8100.
PRESIDENT
Tim Sarnoff
SENIOR V.P. & EXECUTIVE PRODUCER, PROD. INFRASTRUCTURE
Debbie Denise
SENIOR V.P., PRODUCTION
Jenny Fulle
SENIOR V.P., OPERATIONS
Thomas Hershey
SENIOR V.P., TECHNOLOGY
George Joblove
SENIOR V.P., ANIMATION PRODUCTION
Barry Weiss
V.P., DIGITAL PRODUCTION
Stanley Szymanski
V.P., TECHNICAL OPERATIONS
William Villarreal

SONY ONLINE ENTERTAINMENT
8958 Terman Court, San Diego, CA 92121. (858) 577-3100. FAX: (858) 577-3200.
PRESIDENT
John Smedley
CTO
Adam Joffe
CCO
Raph Kpster
CFO & SENIOR V.P., FINANCE
John Needham
COO
Russell Shanks
SENIOR V.P., & GENERAL COUNSEL, LEGAL AFFAIRS
Andrew Zaffron
SENIOR V.P., SALES & MARKETING
Donald Vercelli
V.P., MARKETING & PUBLIC RELATIONS
Scott McDaniel

SONY PICTURES CONSUMER PRODUCTS, INC.
10202 W. Washington Blvd., Stewart 3rd Flr., Culver City, CA 90232. (310) 244-7788. FAX: (310) 244-1758.
EXECUTIVE V.P., CONSUMER PRODUCTS
Al Ovadia
SENIOR V.P., DOMESTIC SALES & RETAIL DEVELOPMENT
Juli Boylan
SENIOR V.P., BUSINESS & LEGAL, ASSISTANT GENERAL COUNSEL
Gregory Economos
SENIOR V.P., MARKETING & CLIENT RELATIONS
Michael Malone
SENIOR V.P., OPERATIONS & NEW BUSINESS DEVELOPMENT
Mitch McDiffett
V.P., EUROPEAN LICENSING
Charlotte Hargreaves
V.P., INTERNATIONAL SALES
Lisa Storms

THE CULVER STUDIOS
9336 W. Washington Blvd., Culver City, CA 90232. (310) 202-1234.
PRESIDENT, STUDIO OPERATIONS & ADMINISTRATION
Jack Kindberg
SENIOR V.P., CORP. SECURITY & SAFETY OPERATIONS
Stevan Bernard
SENIOR V.P., OPERATIONS
Jan Kelly

V.P., LOGISTICS
Paul Casella
V.P., STUDIO RELATIONS & INFO MANAGEMENT
April Dmytrenko
V.P., ADMINISTRATION SERVICES
Lucienne Hassler
V.P., TCS STUDIO OPERATIONS
Maria Marill
V.P., STUDIO OPERATIONS
Scott Valentine

SPIKINGS ENTERTAINMENT

1109 Wellesley Ave., Los Angeles, CA 90049. (310) 456-8039.
FAX: (310) 820-1978.
PRESIDENT & OWNER
Barry P. Spikings

SPIRIT DANCE ENTERTAINMENT

(Motion picture, independent film & TV producer)
1023 N. Orange Dr., Los Angeles, CA 90038-2317. (323) 512-7988. FAX: (323) 512-7996.
PRESIDENT
Forest Whitaker
MANAGING DIRECTOR SPIRIT DANCE/NO DANCE FILM FESTIVAL
Michael Connor
V.P., DEVELOPMENT
Arlene Gibbs
DIRECTOR, DEVELOPMENT
Karen Peterkin
DEVELOPMENT ASSISTANT
Chuck Hayward
DIRECTOR, CREATIVE AFFAIRS
Ali Hileman
OFFICE MANAGER
Alysha Augort

SPYGLASS ENTERTAINMENT GROUP

(Motion picture, independent film & TV producer)
500 S. Buena Vista St., Burbank, CA 91521-1855. (818) 560-3458.
CO-CHAIRMAN & CEO
Gary Barber
CO-CHAIRMAN & CEO
Roger Birnbaum
CFO
Paul Schwake
PRESIDENT, PRODUCTION
Jonathan Glickman
EXECUTIVE V.P., WORLDWIDE MARKETING
Karen Sortito
SENIOR V.P., PHYSICAL PRODUCTION
Jeffrey Chernov
V.P., TELEVISION
Megan Wolpert
V.P., PRODUCTION
Derek Evans
V.P., BUSINESS & LEGAL AFFAIRS
Paul Neinstein
VP., POST-PRODUCTION
Rebekah Rudd

STAMPEDE ENTERTAINMENT

(Motion picture, independent film & TV producer)
3000 W. Olympic Blvd., Ste. 1471, Santa Monica, CA 90404.
(310) 552-9977. FAX: (310) 552-9324.
PARTNER, CO-CHAIRMAN & CEO
Nancy Roberts
PARTNERS & CO-CHAIRMEN
S.S. Wilson
Brent Maddock
EXECUTIVE STORY EDITOR
Greg Stevens

STATE STREET PICTURES

(Motion picture, independent film & TV producer)
10201 W. Pico Blvd., Los Angeles, CA 90064. (310) 369-5099.
FAX: (310) 369-8613.
PRODUCER
Robert Teitel
V.P., PRODUCTION
Heather Courtney
DIRECTOR
George Tillman Jr.
DIRECTOR, DEVELOPMENT
Poppy Hanks

THE HOWARD STERN PRODUCTION COMPANY

(Motion picture, independent film & TV producer)
10 E. 44th St., New York, NY 10017. (212) 867-1200. FAX:
(212) 867-2434.
PRESIDENT
Howard Stern
DIRECTOR, DEVELOPMENT
Mark Grande
AGENT
Don Buchwald

STONE VS. STONE

189 Franklin St., 3rd Flr., New York, NY 10013. (212) 941-1200.
PRODUCER & WRITER
Robert Stone, (310) 822-8888
PRODUCER & WRITER
Webster Stone, (212) 334-8228

STRAND RELEASING

(Motion picture, independent film & TV producer & distributor)
1460 4th St., Ste. 302, Santa Monica, CA 90401. (310) 395-5002. FAX: (310) 395-2502. www.strandreleasing.com
email: strand@strandreleasing.com
CO-PRESIDENTS
Jon Gerrans
Marcus Hu

STRATOSPHERE ENTERTAINMENT

(Film distributor; motion picture producer)
767 Fifth Ave., Ste. 4700, New York, NY 10153. (212) 605-1010. FAX: (212) 813-0300. email: stratent@aol.com
V.P., BUSINESS AFFAIRS
Angela Schapiro

STUDIOCANAL (U.S.)

(Distributor & sales)
301 N. Canon Drive, Ste. 207, Beverly Hills, CA 90210. (310)
247-0994. FAX: (310) 247-0998.
CO-PRESIDENTS
Stephane Sperry
Richard Garzilli
CFO
Robert Chamberlain
DIRECTOR, CONTRACT ADMINISTRATION
Barbara DiNallo

STUDIO M

(Producer & distributor)
14225 Ventura Blvd., Sherman Oaks, CA 91423. (818) 981-4950. FAX: (818) 501-6224.
CEO
Max Keller
VICE-CHAIRMAN
Micheline Keller
PRESIDENT
Michael Lloyd
COO
Jack Freedman

SUMMIT ENTERTAINMENT

(Motion picture producer & distributor)
1630 Stewart St., Ste. 120, Santa Monica, CA 90404. (310)
309-8400. FAX: (310) 828-4132.
PRESIDENT & CEO
Patrick Wachsberger
COO
Bob Hayward
EXECUTIVE V.P.
David Garrett
PRESIDENT, PRODUCTION & ACQUISITIONS
Erik Feig
V.P., PRODUCTION & ACQUISITIONS
Adrienne Biddle

SWARTWOUT ENTERPRISES, INC.

(Motion picture producer, giant-screen films)
P.O. Box 20667, Sedona, AZ 86341. (928) 284-3813. FAX:
(928) 284-3571. www.supervue.com
CONTACT
Dave Swartwout

TAPESTRY FILMS, INC.

9328 Civic Center Dr., Beverly Hills, CA 90210. (310) 275-1191.
FAX: (310) 275-1266. email: tapestryfilms@tapestryfilms.com
PRODUCER & PARTNER
Peter Abrams
PRESIDENT, PRODUCTION
Andrew Panay
PRODUCER & PARTNER
Robert L. Levy
PRODUCER
Natan Zahavi
V.P., PRODUCTION
Andrew Panay
POST-PRODUCTION SUPERVISOR
Sherwood Jones

TAURUS ENTERTAINMENT CO.

(Motion picture, independent film & TV producer & distributor)
5831 Sunset Blvd., Hollywood, CA 90028. (323) 860-0807. FAX:
(323) 860-0834. www.taurus-entertainment.com
CHAIRMAN
Stanley Dudelson
PRESIDENT & CEO
James Dudelson
PRESIDENT & COO
Robert Dudelson
V.P., PRODUCTION
Ana Clavell
DIRECTOR, DEVELOPMENT & ACQUISITIONS
Chad Bell

TAYLOR MADE FILMS

(Motion picture, independent film & TV producer)
1270 Stone Canyon, Los Angeles, CA 90077. (310) 472-1763.
FAX: (310) 472-8698. email: tmadefilms@aol.com
PRESIDENT & PRODUCER
Geoffrey Taylor

TEITELBAUM ARTISTS GROUP

(Talent management & production company)
8840 Wilshire Blvd., Beverly Hills, CA 90211. (310) 358-3250.
FAX: (310) 358-3256.
PRESIDENT
Mark Teitelbaum

TELLING PICTURES

(Motion picture, independent film & TV producer & distributor)
2261 Market St., #506, San Francisco, CA 94114. (415) 864-
6714. FAX: (415) 864-4364. www.tellingpictures.com
PRODUCER & DIRECTOR
Rob Epstein
PRODUCER & DIRECTOR
Jeffrey Friedman

3 ARTS ENTERTAINMENT

9460 Wilshire Blvd., 7th Flr., Beverly Hills, CA 90212. (310)
888-3200. FAX: (310) 888-3210.
CONTACTS
Dave Becky
Nick Frenkel
Aron Giannini
Jeff Golenberg
Steven Greener
Howard Klein
Molly Madden
David Miner
Michael Rotenberg
Mark Schulman
Lainie Sorkin
Erwin Stoff
Leonard Torgan
Diane Gordon

BOB THOMAS PRODUCTIONS, INC.

(Motion picture & TV producer)
60 E. 42 St., New York, NY 10165. (212) 221-3602.
2 Franklin Ct., Montville, NJ 07045. (973) 335-9100.
www.bobthomasprods.com
PRESIDENT
Robert G. Thomas

THREE STRANGE ANGELS, INC.

(Motion picture producer)
2450 Broadway St., Santa Monica, CA 90404. (310) 443-5344.
PRODUCER
Lindsay Doran

TIDEWATER ENTERTAINMENT, INC.

320 Mount Holyoke Ave., Pacific Palisades, CA 90272. (310)
393-8591.
PRESIDENT
Bill Unger

TIG PRODUCTIONS, INC.

(Motion picture, independent film & TV producer)
100 Universal City Plaza, Bldg. 1320, Ste. 1B, Universal City,
CA 91608. (818) 777-2737. FAX: (818) 733-5616.
PARTNER
Kevin Costner
PARTNER
Jim Wilson
VICE PRESIDENT
Soraya Delawari Dancsecs
CREATIVE EXECUTIVE
Jasa Abreo

THE STEVE TISCH CO.

(Motion picture producer)
10202 W. Washington Blvd., Astaire Bldg., 3rd Flr., Culver City,
CA 90232. (310) 244-6612.
PRODUCER
Steve Tisch
CREATIVE ASSISTANT
Lacy Boughn
CONTROLLER & MANAGER, ADMINISTRATION FINANCE &
HUMAN RESOURCES
Kim Skeeters

TOTEM PRODUCTIONS

(Motion picture, independent film & TV producer)
8009 Santa Monica Blvd., Los Angeles, CA 90046. (323) 650-
4994. FAX: (323) 650-1961. email: totempro@aol.com
CO-CHAIRMAN
Tony Scott

TRIBECA PRODUCTIONS

375 Greenwich St., 8th Flr., New York, NY 10013. (212) 941-
4000. FAX: (212) 941-4044. www.tribecafilm.com
PARTNER
Robert De Niro
PARTNER
Jane Rosenthal
EXECUTIVE V.P., PRODUCTION
Naomi Despres
V.P., DEVELOPMENT
Hardy Justice
CREATIVE EXECUTIVE
Geoffery Isenman

TRICOR ENTERTAINMENT

1613 Chelsea Rd., Ste. 329, San Marino, CA 91108-1821.
(818) 763-0699. FAX: (626) 441-0033.
PARTNER
Craig Darian
PARTNER
Howard Kazanjian

TRIDENT RELEASING

(Sales agents for motion pictures & TV)
8401 Melrose Pl., 2nd Flr., Los Angeles, CA 90069. (323) 655-
8818. FAX: (323) 655-0515. email: info@tridentreleasing.com
PRESIDENTS
Jean Ovrum
Victoria Plummer

TRILOGY ENTERTAINMENT GROUP

(Motion picture, independent film & TV producer)
2450 Broadway St. Penthouse, Ste. 675, Santa Monica, CA
90404-3061. (310) 449-3095. FAX: (310) 449-3195.
FOUNDERS
Pen Densham
John Watson
EXECUTIVE V.P.
Larry Meyers
DIRECTOR, PRODUCTION & ADMINISTRATION
Jennifer Hare

TROMA ENTERTAINMENT, INC.

(Producer & distributor)
733 Ninth Ave., New York, NY 10019. (212) 757-4555. FAX:
(212) 399-9885. www.troma.com
PRESIDENT
Lloyd Kaufman
VICE PRESIDENT
Michael Herz
DIRECTOR, DOMESTIC AND RETAIL SALES
Megan Powers
DIRECTOR, EVENTS & PUBLICITY
Jonathan Lees
WEBMASTER, TROMA.COM
Edward Havens

UFLAND PRODUCTIONS

(Motion picture, independent film & TV producer)
534 21st St., Santa Monica, CA 90402. (310) 656-3031. FAX:
(310) 656-3073.
PRODUCERS
Harry J. Ufland
Mary Jane Ufland

UNDERGROUND FILMS/MISSION MANAGEMENT

(Feature film production company with First Look deal at
Phoenix; management company)
10202 W. Washington Blvd., Frankovich Bldg., Stes. 115-117,
Culver City, CA 90232. FAX: (310) 842-7530.
PRODUCERS
Nick Osbourne (310) 244-6194
Trevor Engelson (310) 244-6380

UNITED ARTISTS

10250 Constellation Blvd., Los Angeles, CA 90067. (310) 449-
3000. FAX: (310) 586-8358.
PRESIDENT
Bingham Ray
EXECUTIVE V.P., FINANCE
Danny Rosett
SENIOR V.P., ACQUISITIONS & PRODUCTION
Sara Rose

UPA PRODUCTIONS, OF AMERICA (CLASSIC MEDIA)

(Producer & distributor)
8640 Wilshire Blvd., Beverly Hills, CA 90211. (310) 659-6004.
FAX: (310) 659-4599.
PRESIDENT
Eric Ellenbogen

VANGUARD DOCUMENTARIES

(TV & film producer)
P.O. Box 3622, Brooklyn, NY 11202-3622. (212) 517-4333.
www.vanguarddocumentaries.com
PRESIDENT
Charles Hobson

VALHALLA MOTION PICTURES

(Motion picture, independent film & TV producer)
8530 Wilshire Blvd., Ste. 400, Beverly Hills, CA 90211. (310) 360-8530. email: vmp@valhallamotionpics.com
CHAIRMAN & CEO
Gale Anne Hurd
CFO
Julie Thomson
PRESIDENT
Barbara Boyle
SENIOR V.P., PRODUCTION
Jeff Davidson
V.P., DEVELOPMENT
Tracy Mercer
STORY EDITOR
Jacqueline Cruz

VERDON-CEDRIC PRODUCTIONS

(Motion picture, independent film & TV producer)
P.O. Box 2639, Beverly Hills, CA 90213. (310) 274-7253.
PRODUCER & DIRECTOR & WRITER & ACTOR
Sidney Poitier

VIACOM, INC.

1515 Broadway, New York, NY 10036, (212) 258-6000. FAX: (212) 258-6175, (212) 258-6464. www.viacom.com
CHAIRMAN & CEO, VIACOM, INC.
Sumner M. Redstone
CHAIRMAN & CEO, VIACOM ENTERTAINMENT GROUP
Jonathan Dolgen
PRESIDENT, COO & DIRECTOR
Mel Karmazin

PARAMOUNT PICTURES

5555 Melrose Ave., Los Angeles, CA 90038. (323) 956-5000.
CHAIRMAN & CEO, VIACOM ENTERTAINMENT GROUP
Jonathan Dolgen
EXECUTIVE V.P., PARAMOUNT PICTURES
William Bernstein
SENIOR V.P., & CFO
Mark Badagliacca
SENIOR V.P. & TREASURER
Alan J. Bailey
SENIOR V.P., FINANCIAL PLANNING
Stephanie Love
SENIOR V.P., ADMINISTRATION
Rosemary DiPietra
SENIOR V.P. & DEPUTY GENERAL COUNSEL
David Friedman
SENIOR V.P., HUMAN RESOURCES
Louis Gutierrez
SENIOR V.P., INDUSTRIAL RELATIONS
Stephen Koppekin
SENIOR V.P. & GENERAL COUNSEL
Rebecca L. Prentice
SENIOR V.P., FINANCE
Stephen P. Taylor
SENIOR V.P., INFORMATION SYSTEMS & CIO
H. Edgar Trainor
SENIOR V.P., FINANCIAL PLANNING
Stephanie Love
V.P., INFORMATION TECHNOLOGY
S.R. (Stan) Balcomb
V.P., GROUP ACCOUNTING
Chact S. Chu
V.P., CONTRACT ACCOUNTING
Carmen Desiderio
V.P., FINANCE
Michael Masters
V.P., TREASURY MANAGEMENT
Steve Nagan
V.P., HUMAN RESOURCES
Cassandra Thomas
V.P., RESIDUALS
Kathleen Hoops
V.P., EMPLOYEE RELATIONS & SENIOR COUNSEL, EMPLOYEE RELATIONS
Rina Walluck
V.P., LABOR RELATIONS
Louis Shore
V.P., MOTION PICTURE CONTROLLER
Carolyn F. Scott
EXEC. DIRECTOR, GROUP FINANCIAL REPORTING
Stephen Hendry
EXEC. DIRECTOR, CONTRACT ACCOUNTING
Vicente P. Ching

MOTION PICTURE GROUP

CHAIRMAN
Sherry Lansing
VICE-CHAIRMAN & COO, PARAMOUNT PICTURES
Robert Friedman
VICE CHAIRMAN & PRESIDENT, PARAMOUNT PICTURES
John Goldwyn
PRESIDENT, WORLDWIDE MARKETING
Arthur Cohen
PRESIDENT, WORLDWIDE HOME ENTERTAINMENT
Thomas Lesinski
PRESIDENT, MOTION PICTURE DISTRIBUTION
Wayne Lewellen
PRESIDENT, WORLDWIDE PAY TELEVISION
Jack Waterman
SENIOR V.P., IN CHARGE OF BUSINESS AFFAIRS
Richard Fowkes
SENIOR V.P., BUSINESS AFFAIRS
Chris Floyd
SENIOR V.P., LEGAL AFFAIRS
Karen Magid
SENIOR V.P., MUSIC LEGAL AFFAIRS
Linda Wohl
SENIOR V.P., MOTION PICTURE BUSINESS & LEGAL AFFAIRS
Alan Heppel
SENIOR V.P., MUSIC BUSINESS AFFAIRS
Kevin Koloff
SENIOR V.P., INTELLECTUAL PROPERTIES & ASSOCIATE GENERAL COUNSEL
Scott Martin
V.P., INTERNATIONAL (London)
Michael O'Sullivan
V.P., MUSIC
Linda Springer
DISTRICT MANAGER, MOTION PICTURE DISTRIBUTION
Donald Wallace
DISTRICT MANAGERS
Mike Share
Robert Box

DOMESTIC DISTRIBUTION DIVISION, MOTION PICTURE GROUP

PRESIDENT, DISTRIBUTION
Wayne Lewellen
EXECUTIVE V.P., ELECTRONIC CINEMA
Gino Campagnola
EXECUTIVE V.P., SALES OPERATIONS
Steve Rapaport
SENIOR V.P., ASSISTANT GENERAL COUNSEL
Paul Springer
SENIOR V.P. AND GENERAL SALES MANAGER
Clark Woods
SENIOR V.P., CANADIAN DIVISION
Chris Sullivan
SENIOR V.P., SALES ADMINISTRATION
John Hersker
V.P. SOUTHERN DIVISION
Royce Brimage
V.P., EASTERN DIVISION
Mike Share
V.P., WESTERN DIVISION
Robert Weiss
V.P., EXHIBITOR RELATIONS
Mark Mulcahy

DISTRICT BRANCHES AND MANAGERS, MOTION PICTURE GROUP

EASTERN

1633 Broadway, 11th Flr., New York, NY 10019.
DISTRICT MANAGER, NEW YORK
Pam Araujo

SOUTHERN

12222 Merit Dr., Ste. 1700, Dallas, TX 75251.
BRANCH MANAGER, DALLAS & NEW ORLEANS, OKLAHOMA CITY & MEMPHIS
Don Wallace

PUERTO RICO

Miramar Plaza Bldg., 954 Ponce de Leon Avenue, Ste. 201, San Juan, PR 00907.
BRANCH SALES MANAGER
Nestor Rivera

WESTERN

15260 Ventura Blvd., Ste. 1140, Sherman Oaks, CA 91403.
BRANCH MANAGER, LOS ANGELES
Bob Box

MONTREAL

1255 University St., Ste. 921, Montreal, QUE H3B 3W4, Canada.
BRANCH SALES MANAGER
Lise Bertrand

TORONTO

146 Bloor Street West, Toronto, ONT M5S 1M4, Canada.
BRANCH SALES MANAGER, TORONTO
Bob Cowan
BRANCH SALES MANAGER, ST. JOHN & WINNIPEG
Jean White

HOME ENTERTAINMENT DIVISION

PRESIDENT, WORLDWIDE HOME ENTERTAINMENT
Thomas Lesinski

MARKETING DIVISION, MOTION PICTURE GROUP
PRESIDENT, WORLDWIDE MARKETING
Arthur Cohen
EXECUTIVE V.P., WORLDWIDE MARKETING & PROMOTION
Thomas Campanella
EXECUTIVE V.P., CREATIVE ADVERTISING, AUDIO VISUAL
James P. Gibbons
EXECUTIVE V.P., MARKETING & CREATIVE AFFAIRS
Nancy Goliger
EXECUTIVE V.P., WORLDWIDE PUBLICITY
Nancy Kirkpatrick
EXECUTIVE V.P., CREATIVE ADVERTISING & PRINT
Lucia Ludovico
SENIOR V.P., CREATIVE ADVERTISING
William Rus
SENIOR V.P., MEDIA DIRECTOR
Susan Wrenn
SENIOR V.P., MARKETING ADMINSTRATION
Leslie H. Anderson
SENIOR V.P., WORLDWIDE MARKETING PARTNERSHIPS
Lisa Di Marzio
SENIOR V.P., SPECIAL PROJECTS & PHILANTHROPY
Allison Jackson
V.P., NATIONAL PUBLICITY
Susan Ciccone
V.P., BROADCASTING PRODUCTION
Shaylee Dunn
V.P., PRINT PRODUCTION
John Barry
V.P., NATIONAL PUBLICITY
Greg Brilliant
V.P., PLANNING, NATIONAL ADVERTISING
Suki Yamashita
EXEC. DIRECTOR, MARKETING ADMINISTRATION & MEDIA
Fred Manny
EXEC. DIRECTOR, SPOT BROADCASTING
Nicky Shapiro

PRODUCTION DIVISION, MOTION PICTURE GROUP
CO-PRESIDENT
Michelle Manning
CO-PRESIDENT
Karen Rosenfelt
PRESIDENT, FEATURE PROD. MGMT., WORLDWIDE
Fred T. Gallo
EXECUTIVE V.P., PRODUCTION
Brian Witten
PRESIDENT, MOTION PICTURE DIVISION, BVI
Thomas K. Levine
PRESIDENT, MUSIC
Burt Berman
V.P., TELEVISION MUSIC
David Grossman
V.P., CREATIVE AFFAIRS
Bradley Kessell
V.P., MUSIC
Linda Springer
V.P., MUSIC CLEARANCE
Eldridge Walker
V.P., PRODUCTION FINANCE
Brian Wensel
EXEC. DIRECTOR, MUSIC PROD. & CREATIVE AFFAIRS
Steve Londo

POST-PRODUCTION DIVISION, MOTION PICTURE GROUP
EXECUTIVE V.P., POST-PRODUCTION
Paul Haggar
V.P., POST-PRODUCTION
John Wiseman
V.P., POST-PRODUCTION FACILITIES
John Bloechle
V.P., WORLDWIDE TECHNOLOGY
Laverne Williams

PARAMOUNT DIGITAL ENTERTAINMENT
PRESIDENT
Leonard Washington

PARAMOUNT STUDIO GROUP
PRESIDENT
Earl Lestz
SENIOR V.P., VIDEO OPERATIONS
Tom Bruehl
SENIOR V.P., FACILITIES OPERATIONS
Rae Ann Del Pozzo
SENIOR V.P., PLANNING & DEVELOPMENT
Christine Essel
SENIOR V.P., STUDIO ADMINISTRATION
Larry A. Owens
V.P., STUDIO PROTECTION
Thomas G. Hays
V.P., PLANNING & CONSTRUCTION
Michael Romano
V.P., LEGAL SERVICES
Nathan Smith

PARAMOUNT TELEVISION PRODUCTION
PRESIDENT, PARAMOUNT TELEVISION PRODUCTION
Garry Hart
PRESIDENT, VIACOM PRODUCTIONS
Perry Simon
EXECUTIVE V.P., CREATIVE AFFAIRS VIACOM PRODUCTIONS
Steve Gordon
EXECUTIVE V.P., LEGAL, PARAMOUNT PICTURES TV DISTRIBUTION
Milinda McNeely
EXECUTIVE V.P., BUSINESS AFFAIRS
Pamela Weisberg
EXECUTIVE V.P., MARKETING & MEDIA RELATIONS
John A. Wentworth
EXECUTIVE V.P., DRAMA DEVELOPMENT, NETWORK TV
Kathy Lingg
SENIOR V.P., CREATIVE AFFAIRS, VIACOM PRODUCTIONS
Michele Conklin
SENIOR V.P., COMEDY DEVELOPMENT, NETWORK TV
Rose Catherine Pinkney
SENIOR V.P., TELEVISION MUSIC
David Grossman
SENIOR V.P., POST-PRODUCTION, NETWORK TV
Hal Harrison
SENIOR V.P., PRODUCTION & POST PRODUCTION, VIACOM PRODS.
Bruce Kerner
SENIOR V.P., TALENT & CASTING, VIACOM PRODUCTIONS
Beth Klein
SENIOR V.P., BUSINESS AFFAIRS, VIACOM PRODUCTIONS
David Lavin
SENIOR V.P., TALENT & CASTING, NETWORK TV
Sheila Guthrie
SENIOR V.P., CURRENT PROGRAMS, NETWORK TV
Tom Russo
SENIOR V.P., PRODUCTION, NETWORK TV
Reid Shane
V.P., PRODUCTION, NETWORK TV
Ralph Berge
V.P., LONGFORM PROGRAMMING, NETWORK TV
Marshall Coben
V.P., MARKETING & MEDIA RELATIONS
Kim Conant
V.P., BUSINESS AFFAIRS, NETWORK TV
Sandra Delaney
V.P., BUSINESS AFFAIRS, VIACOM PRODUCTIONS
Susan Edelist
V.P., FINANCE & OPERATIONS, VIACOM PRODUCTIONS
Janell Gorham
V.P., DRAMA DEVELOPMENT, NETWORK TV
Andy J. Horne
V.P., CURRENT PROGRAMS, NETWORK TV
Brett King
V.P., PRODUCTION, NETWORK TV
Marilyn Loncar
V.P., BUSINESS AFFAIRS, NETWORK TV
J.R. McGinnis
V.P., MUSIC
Celest Ray
V.P., PRODUCTION FINANCE, VIACOM PRODUCTIONS
Kellie Siemons
V.P., PRODUCTION, VIACOM PRODUCTIONS
Ron Von Schimmelmann
V.P., PRODUCTION FINANCE, NETWORK TV
Mark Weissman
V.P., MEDIA RELATIONS
Manfred Westphal

PARAMOUNT WORLDWIDE TELEVISION DISTRIBUTION
PRESIDENT, PARAMOUNT WORLDWIDE TV DISTRIBUTION
Joel Berman
PRESIDENT, PARAMOUNT ADVERTISING SERVICES
Marc Hirsch
PRESIDENT, INTERNATIONAL TELEVISION
Gary Marenzi
PRESIDENT, PROGRAMMING, DOMESTIC
Greg Meidel
PRESIDENT, PARAMOUNT DOMESTIC TV
John Nogawski
PRESIDENT, WORLDWIDE PAY TV
Jack Waterman
EXECUTIVE V.P., GENERAL SALES MANAGER, DOMESTIC TV
Mark Dvornik
EXECUTIVE V.P., SALES & MARKETING, INTL. TV
Joe Lucas
EXECUTIVE V.P., BUSINESS AFFAIRS & LEGAL, PAY TV
Steven Madoff
EXECUTIVE V.P., INTL. CHANNELS, WORLDWIDE PAY TV
Reed Manville
EXECUTIVE V.P., RESEARCH
Mike Mellon
EXECUTIVE V.P., MARKETING, DOMESTIC TV
Michael Mischler
EXECUTIVE V.P., BUSINESS & LEGAL AFFAIRS, DOMESTIC TV
Bruce Pottash

EXECUTIVE V.P., PROGRAMMING, DOMESTIC TV
Terry Wood
SENIOR V.P., BUSINESS AFFAIRS, INTERNATIONAL TV
Susan Akens
SENIOR V.P., PAY TV
James Brehm
SENIOR V.P., FINANCE & ADMINISTRATION, ADVERTISING
SERVICES
Christopher Callahan
SENIOR V.P., OFF-NETWORK SALES MANAGER,
DOMESTIC TV
Dennis Emerson
SENIOR V.P., CABLE SALES MANAGER, ADVERTISING
SERVICES
Robert H. Friedman
SENIOR V.P., WORLDWIDE SALES INTERNATIONAL TV
James Hurlock
SENIOR V.P., BUSINESS AFFAIRS & LEGAL, DOMESTIC TV
Peter Kane
SENIOR V.P., NATIONAL SALES MANAGER, ADVERTISING
SERVICES
Scott Koondel
SENIOR V.P., ADVERTISING & PROMOTION, DOMESTIC TV
David Lafountaine
SENIOR V.P., BUSINESS SYSTEMS & CONTROLS, PAY TV
Winnie Lun Leung
SENIOR V.P., STRATEGIC PLANNING, ADVERTISING
SERVICES
Jeffrey Manoff
SENIOR V.P., BUSINESS AFFAIRS & LEGAL, DOMESTIC TV
Robert Mendez
SENIOR V.P., GENERAL SALES MANAGER, ADVERTISING
SERVICES
Paul Montoya
SENIOR V.P., PPV, VOD & ANCILLARY SALES, PAY TV
Stephanie V. Morton
SENIOR V.P., TV GROUP OPERATIONS
Phil Murphy
SENIOR V.P., BUSINESS DEVELOPMENT & CO-PROD,
INTERNATIONAL TV
Christopher Ottinger
SENIOR V.P., & SOUTH REGIONAL MANAGER, ADVERTIS-
ING SERVICES
Albert L. Rothstein
SENIOR V.P., TV SYSTEMS & ARCHIVE SERVICES
Bill Weber
SENIOR V.P., CREATIVE AFFAIRS, DOMESTIC TV
John Kohler
SENIOR V.P., MARKETING, INTERNATIONAL TV
Isis Moussa
V.P., SALES, PAY TV
Erica Chung Adler
V.P., CONTRACT ADMINISTRATION
Mallory Baker
V.P., LATIN AMERICA SALES INTERNATIONAL TELEVISION
Susan Bender
V.P., ON-AIR ADVERTISING & PROMOTIONS, DOMESTIC TV
Frank Brooks
V.P., PROGRAMMING, DOMESTIC TV
Linda Carrasquillo
V.P., FINANCE, DOMESTIC TV
Nicole Choper
V.P., RESEARCH, PARAMOUNT ADVERTISING SERVICES
Beth Anne Coleman
V.P., CONTROLLER, PAY TV
Mark Bennett Corbin
V.P., BUSINESS AFFAIRS ADMINISTRATION, DOMESTIC TV
Lynn Fero
V.P., BUSINESS AFFAIRS & LEGAL, DOMESTIC TV
Kim Fitzgerald
V.P., SALES ADMINISTRATION & PROGRAM LINEUPS,
DOMESTIC TV
Lisa Fimiani
V.P., PROGRAMMING & PRODUCTION, DOMESTIC TV
Brad Hart
V.P., ADVERTISING & PROMOTION FINANCE, DOMESTIC
TELEVISION
Tracey Kimball
V.P., WESTERN REGIONAL SALES MANAGER, DOMESTIC
TELEVISION
Deborah K. Bradley
V.P., OFF-NETWORK & SPECIAL PROJECTS, DOMESTIC TV
Cynthia Lieberman
V.P., MIDWEST SALES, PARAMOUNT ADVERTISING
SERVICES
Keith Kuttkus
V.P., SOUTHEAST DIVISION MANAGER, ADVERTISING
SERVICES
John Morrow
V.P., SALES PLANNING & ADMINISTRATION, INTL. TV
Mina Patel
V.P., DEVELOPMENT, DOMESTIC TV
Kristin Peace
V.P., EUROPEAN SALES, INTERNATIONAL TV
William Peck

V.P., EUROPEAN OPERATIONS-ROME, INTERNATIONAL TV
Giovanni Pedde
V.P., BUSINESS & LEGAL AFFAIRS, DOMESTIC TV
Cortez Smith
V.P., DIGITAL MASTERING OPERATIONS
Garrett Smith
V.P., BUSINESS DEVELOPMENT, WORLDWIDE PAY TV
Mara Sternthal
V.P., BUSINESS AFFAIRS, PAY TV
Ron Sufrin
V.P., EUROPEAN SALES, INTERNATIONAL TV
Stephen Tague
V.P., LEGAL, DOMESTIC TV
Cynthia Teele
V.P., BUSINESS & LEGAL AFFAIRS, DOMESTIC TV
David Theodosopoulos
V.P., ADVERTISING & PROMOTION-NY, DOMESTIC TV
Tina Tung-Barisic
V.P., CREATIVE SERVICES & DESIGN, DOMESTIC TV
David Thomas
V.P., SALES, PARAMOUNT ADVERTISING SERVICES
Jessica Wiener
V.P., BUSINESS AFFAIRS & LEGAL DOMESTIC TV
Cary William Clew
V.P., INTERNATIONAL OPERATIONS, INTERNATIONAL TV
Richard Yannich

FAMOUS MUSIC PUBLISHING
10635 Santa Monica Blvd., #300, Los Angeles, CA 90025.
(310) 441-1300.
PRESIDENT
Ira Jaffe

VIEW ASKEW PRODUCTIONS, INC.
(Motion picture producer)
P.O. Box 93339, Los Angeles, CA 90093. (323) 969-9423. FAX:
(323) 969-9008. www.viewaskew.com
PRESIDENT
Kevin Smith
VICE PRESIDENT
Scott Mosier
DEVELOPMENT EXECUTIVE
Gail Stanley

VILLAGE ROADSHOW PICTURES
3400 Riverside Dr., Ste. 900, Burbank, CA 91505. (818) 260-
6000. FAX: (818) 260-6001.
CHAIRMAN & CEO
Bruce Berman
PRESIDENT & COO
Steve Krone
CFO
Reid Sullivan
EXECUTIVE V.P., WORLDWIDE FEATURE PRODUCTION
Michael Lake
HEAD, PRODUCTION
Dana Goldberg
V.P., WORLDWIDE DISTRIBUTION
Alex DeCastro
V.P., DEVELOPMENT
Jordanna Fraiberg
V.P., BUSINESS & FINANCIAL AFFAIRS
Kevin Berg
V.P., BUSINESS & LEGAL AFFAIRS
Joel Goldstein
V.P., ADMINISTRATION & OPERATIONS
Anna Dergan
DIRECTOR, MARKETING & PUBLICITY
Kellie Maltagliati
STORY EDITOR
Fred Klein

VIVENDI UNIVERSAL ENTERTAINMENT
100 Universal City Plaza, Universal City, CA 91608. (818) 777-
1000. www.universalstudios.com
PRESIDENT & COO
Ron Meyer
EXECUTIVE V.P. & GENERAL COUNSEL
Karen Randall
EXECUTIVE V.P., HUMAN RESOURCES
Kenneth L. Kahrs
EXECUTIVE V.P., CFO
Frederick Huntsberry
SENIOR V.P., CORPORATE COMMUNICATIONS & PUBLIC
AFFAIRS
Susan Nahley Fleishman
SENIOR V.P., CORPORATE DEVELOPMENT & STRATEGIC
PLANNING
Diana Schulz

UNIVERSAL OPERATIONS GROUP
PRESIDENT & GENERAL MANAGER
Jim Watters
EXECUTIVE V.P., OPERATIONS & ADMINISTRATION
Michael J. Connor
SENIOR V.P., PRODUCTION SERVICES
Dave Beanes

SENIOR V.P., BUSINESS AFFAIRS
Jerrold E Blair
SENIOR V.P & CFO, FINANCE
Dave Clark
SENIOR V.P., TECHNICAL OPERATIONS
Michael Daruty
SENIOR V.P., SOUND SERVICES
Chris Jenkins
SENIOR V.P., FACILITY SERVICES
Mark Lyrum

UNIVERSAL PICTURES
CHAIRMAN
Stacey Snider
VICE CHAIRMAN
Marc Shmuger
PRESIDENT & COO
Rick Finkelstein
PRESIDENT, FILM MUSIC
Kathy Nelson
EXECUTIVE V.P., BUSINESS & LEGAL AFFAIRS
James M. Horowitz
EXECUTIVE V.P., HUMAN RESOURCES
Laura R. Kessler
EXECUTIVE V.P & CFO
William A. Sutman
SENIOR V.P.
Jeffrey Brauer
SENIOR V.P., CREATIVE ADVERTISING
Frank Chiocchi
SENIOR V.P., BUSINESS AFFAIRS
Jeffrey Goore
SENIOR V.P., BUSINESS DEVELOPMENT & STRATEGIC
PLANNING
Michael Joe
SENIOR V.P., TECHNOLOGY
Jerry Pierce
SENIOR V.P., MARKET RESEARCH
Chuck Gaylord

UNIVERSAL PICTURES PRODUCTION
PRESIDENT, PHYSICAL PRODUCTION
Jim Brubaker
EXECUTIVE V.P., PRODUCTION
Allison Brecker-Schearmur
SENIOR V.P., MUSIC BUSINESS AFFAIRS
Philip Cohen
SENIOR V.P., MUSIC
Harry Garfield
SENIOR V.P., PRODUCTION
Donna Langley
SENIOR V.P., FEATURE POST-PRODUCTION
Greig McRitchie
SENIOR V.P., PRODUCTION TECHNOLOGY
John Swallow
V.P., DEVELOPMENT
Tim O'Hair

UNIVERSAL PICTURES MARKETING
PRESIDENT, MARKETING
Adam Fogelson
CO-PRESIDENT, MARKETING
Edward Egan
SENIOR V.P., NEW MEDIA MARKETING & PUBLICITY
Kevin Campbell
SENIOR V.P., SPECIAL PROJECTS
Hollace Davids
SENIOR V.P., MEDIA & CO-OP ADVERTISING
Anthy Price
EXECUTIVE V.P., THE BRAND GROUP
Beth Goss
SENIOR V.P., PUBLICITY
Stephanie Kluft
SENIOR V.P., PUBLICITY
Michael Moses
SENIOR V.P., CREATIVE ADVERTISING
Maria Pekurovskaya
SENIOR V.P., CREATIVE ADVERTISING OPERATIONS
Dan Wolfe
SENIOR V.P. NATIONAL PROMOTIONS
Kristin Patrick Peterson
V.P., FIELD PUBLICITY & PROMOTIONS
Greg Sucherman

UNIVERSAL PICTURES DISTRIBUTION
PRESIDENT, DISTRIBUTION
Nikki Rocco
EXECUTIVE V.P., NATIONAL SALES MANAGER
Nick Carpou
EXECUTIVE V.P., GENERAL SALES MANAGER
Mark Gaines
SENIOR V.P., DISTRIBUTION & MARKETING
Alan Sutton

FOCUS FEATURES
CO-PRESIDENT
David Linde
CO-PRESIDENT
James Schamus

PRESIDENT, DISTRIBUTION
Jack Foley
EXECUTIVE V.P., MARKETING & PUBLICITY
Adriene Bowles
EXECUTIVE V.P., DISTRIBUTION
Linda Ditrinco
EXECUTIVE V.P., LEGAL & FINANCE
Avy Eschenasy
EXECUTIVE V.P., CREATIVE ADVERTISING
Steve Flynn
EXECUTIVE V.P., DEVELOPMENT & PRODUCTION
Joseph Pichirallo
SENIOR V.P., BUSINESS AFFAIRS
Howard Meyers
SENIOR V.P., ACQUISITIONS & CO-PRODUCTIONS
Amy Kaufman
SENIOR V.P., ADVERTISING
Ron Tsuruda

UNIVERSAL STUDIOS HOME VIDEO
PRESIDENT
Craig Kornblau
EXECUTIVE V.P., OPERATIONS AND LOGISTICS
Larry Hariton
EXECUTIVE V.P., MARKETING
Ken Graffeo
EXECUTIVE V.P., VIDEO SALES, DISTRIBUTION & RETAIL
MARKETING
Richard Longwell
SENIOR V.P., BUSINESS AFFAIRS
Christine Lawton
SENIOR V.P., PUBLICITY
Vivian Mayer
SENIOR V.P., MANUFACTURING & LOGISTICS
Michael Tofolo
SENIOR V.P., CREATIVE SOURCES
Linda Turner

UNIVERSAL PICTURES INTERNATIONAL (VIDEO)
PRESIDENT, INTERNATIONAL VIDEO
Peter J. Smith
PRESIDENT, MARKETING
Mary Daily
PRESIDENT, MARKETING
David Livingstone
SENIOR V.P., LEGAL & BUSINESS AFFAIRS
Andrew Hall
SENIOR V.P., VIDEO DISTRIBUTION
Mike Preece

UNIVERSAL STUDIOS CONSUMER PRODUCTS GROUP
SENIOR V.P., LEGAL & BUSINESS AFFAIRS
Helen Jorda
SENIOR V.P., SALES EUROPE
Bruno Maglione
SENIOR V.P., MERCHANDISING & MARKETING
Tim Rothwell

UNIVERSAL HOME ENTERTAINMENT PRODUCTIONS
EXECUTIVE V.P.
Robert W. Rubin

UNIVERSAL WORLDWIDE HOME
PRESIDENT
Louis A. Feola
EXECUTIVE V.P., PRODUCTION
Suzie Peterson
SENIOR V.P., BUSINESS & LEGAL AFFAIRS
Nancy Eagle
SENIOR V.P., UNIVERSAL CARTOON STUDIOS
Tom Ruzicka

UNIVERSAL PICTURES VISUAL PROGRAMMING
PRESIDENT
Hugh Rees-Parnall
SENIOR V.P., CHILDREN'S PROGRAMMING
Loredana Cunti

UNIVERSAL TELEVISION GROUP
CHAIRMAN
Michael Jackson
COO
David Goldhill
CFO
Steve Brunell
SENIOR V.P., STRATEGIC PLANNING
Michael Bonner
V.P., FINANCE, NETWORKS
Gaspare Benso
V.P., CONTROLLER
Melissa Leffler
V.P.,LEGAL AFFAIRS
Milton Segal

USA CABLE ENTERTAINMENT
PRESIDENT
Angela Mancuso
SENIOR V.P., PROGRAMMING
Paulo De Oliveira
SENIOR V.P., BUSINESS AFFAIRS
Joan Whitehead Evans

UNIVERSAL TELEVISION DISTRIBUTION
CO-PRESIDENT
Belinda Menendez
EXECUTIVE V.P., SALES & NEW BUSINESS
Arthur Hasson
EXECUTIVE V.P., AD SALES, DOMESTIC TELEVISION
Elizabeth Herbst
EXECUTIVE V.P., PROGRAMMING & DEVELOPMENT
Valerie Schaer
SENIOR V.P., NON-THEATRICAL SALES
Phyllis Bagdadi
SENIOR V.P., RESEARCH & PROGRAM STRATEGY
Jeff Dellin
SENIOR V.P., BUSINESS & LEGAL AFFAIRS
Rob Fitzpatrick
SENIOR V.P., NATIONAL SALES MANAGER
Phil Martzolf
SENIOR V.P., BUSINESS & LEGAL AFFAIRS
Andrea Melville
SENIOR V.P., BUSINESS DEVELOPMENT
Elizabeth Minehart
SENIOR V.P., PRODUCTION
Richard Ross
SENIOR V.P., DISTRIBUTION
Bill Vrbanic
SENIOR V.P., WORLDWIDE COMMUNICATIONS
Jim Benson

UNIVERSAL DOMESTIC TELEVISION
PRESIDENT, UNIVERSAL TV ENTERPRISES &
CO-PRESIDENT, UNIVERSAL STUDIOS TV DISTRIBUTION
Steve Rosenberg
EXECUTIVE V.P., DEVELOPMENT
Lisa Hackner
V.P., AFFILIATE RELATIONS & ADVERTISING
Betsy Bergman
V.P., PROGRAMMING
Tracie Wilson
V.P., LEGAL AFFAIRS
Roger Kaplan

UNIVERSAL TELEVISION PRODUCTIONS
PRESIDENT
David Kissinger
EXECUTIVE V.P., PROGRAMMING
Charlie Engel
EXECUTIVE V.P., PRODUCTION
Matt Herman
EXECUTIVE V.P., NETWORK, BUSINESS AFFAIRS
Neil Strum
SENIOR V.P., BUSINESS & LEGAL AFFAIRS
Julianna Carnessale
SENIOR V.P., CASTING
Nancy Perkins
SENIOR V.P., PUBLICITY, ADVERTISING & PROMO
Neil Schubert

USA NETWORK
PRESIDENT
Doug Herzog
EXECUTIVE V.P. & GENERAL MANAGER
Micehele Ganeless
EXECUTIVE V.P., SERIES & LONG FORM PROGRAMMING
Jeff Wachtel
SENIOR V.P., MARKETING
Sarah Beatty
SENIOR V.P., PRODUCTION & SPORTS
Gordon Beck
SENIOR V.P., PROGRAM & ACQUISITIONS
Jane Blaney
SENIOR V.P., MOVIES & MINISERIES
Laurette Hayden
SENIOR V.P., NETWORK PUBLICITY
John Kelley
SENIOR V.P., SERIES PROGRAMMING
Jackie Lyons
SENIOR V.P., ON-AIR PROMOTION
Chris McCumber
SENIOR V.P., REALITY PROGRAMMING & SPECIALS
Chris Sloan

SCI-FI CHANNEL
PRESIDENT
Bonnie Hammer
SENIOR V.P., MARKETING
David Howe
SENIOR V.P., ORIGINAL PROGRAMMING
Ian Valentine
SENIOR V.P., ACQUISITIONS, SCHEDULING & PROGRAM
PLANNING
Thomas Vitale
V.P., PROGRAMMING
Frederick Storey

REVEILLE
CEO
Ben Silverman
V.P., CREATIVE AFFAIRS
Dave Mayer

UNIVERSAL PARKS & RESORTS
CHAIRMAN & CEO
Tom Williams
PRESIDENT, INTERNATIONAL & GLOBAL BUSINESS
AFFAIRS
Glenn J. Gumpel
PRESIDENT, INTERNATIONAL BUSINESS DEVELOPMENT
Frank Stanek
EXECUTIVE V.P. & CFO
Michael Corcoran
EXECUTIVE V.P., SALES
Fred Lounsberry
EXECUTIVE V.P., CMO
Wyman Roberts
SENIOR V.P., INTERNATIONAL MARKETING
Norman Elder
SENIOR V.P., STRATEGIC INSIGHT
Marilyn Franck
SENIOR V.P., BUSINESS DEVELOPMENT
Pete Giacalone
SENIOR V.P., BUSINESS PLANNING & DEVELOPMENT
Lisa Pierozzi
SENIOR V.P., MERCHANDISE & COO, SPENCER GIFTS
Steve Shaiken
EXECUTIVE V.P., HUMAN RESOURCES
John Sprouls
SENIOR V.P., CCO
Mark Woodbury
SENIOR V.P., PUBLICITY & PUBLIC RELATIONS
Jim Yeager

UNIVERSAL STUDIOS HOLLYWOOD
PRESIDENT & COO
Larry Kurzwell
SENIOR V.P. & CFO
Brian Compton
SENIOR V.P., SALES
Heidi Geier
SENIOR V.P., GENERAL MANAGER, UNIVERSAL CITYWALK
OPERATIONS
Ron Herman
SENIOR V.P., MARKETING & RETAIL
Don Skeoch
SENIOR V.P., HUMAN RESOURCES
Kay Straky
SENIOR V.P., GENERAL MANAGER, UNIVERSAL STUDIOS
HOLLYWOOD
Mike Taylor

UNIVERSAL ORLANDO
PRESIDENT & COO
Bob Gault
EXECUTIVE V.P. CFO
Mike Short
SENIOR V.P., OPERATIONS
Rich Costales
SENIOR V.P., GENERAL MANAGER, CITYWALK
Ric Florell
SENIOR V.P., MARKETING
Gretchen Hofmann
SENIOR V.P., FOOD SERVICES
Randy McCann
SENIOR V.P., ENTERTAINMENT
Skip Sherman

UNIVERSAL STUDIOS JAPAN
EXECUTIVE V.P., & COO
Daniel Jensen

UNIVERSAL MEDITERRANEA
MANAGING DIRECTOR
Gregory Miller

JON VOIGHT ENTERTAINMENT
(Motion picture producer)
1901 Ave. of the Stars, Ste. 605, Los Angeles, CA 90067. (310)
843-0223. FAX: (310) 553-9895.
PRESIDENT
Jon Voight
EXECUTIVE V.P., PRODUCTION & DEVELOPMENT
Patrick Ewald
DEVELOPMENT ASSISTANT
Natasha Burr

JEFF WALD ENTERTAINMENT, INC.
(Management producer)
3000 W. Olympic Blvd., Bldg. 2, Ste. 1400, Santa Monica, CA
90404. (310) 264-4156. FAX: (310) 264-4157.
PRESIDENT & CHAIRMAN
Jeff Wald

WARNER BROS. ENTERTAINMENT INC.

(Producer & distributor; a division of AOL Time Warner.)
4000 Warner Blvd., Burbank CA 91522. (818) 954-6000.
1325 Ave. of the Americas, New York, NY 10019. (212) 636-5100.
CHAIRMAN & CEO
Barry M. Meyer
PRESIDENT & COO
Alan Horn
EXECUTIVE V.P., DOMESTIC CORPORATE MARKETING
Brad Ball
EXECUTIVE V.P., ADMINISTRATION & STUDIO OPERATIONS
Gary Credle
EXECUTIVE V.P., INTERNATIONAL
Richard J. Fox
EXECUTIVE V.P., WARNER BROS. TELEVISION GROUP
Bruce Rosenblum
EXECUTIVE V.P. & GENERAL COUNSEL
John A. Schulman
EXECUTIVE V.P. & CFO
Edward A. Romano
EXECUTIVE V.P., CORPORATE BUSINESS DEVELOPMENT
& STRATEGY
Kevin Tsujihara
S.V.P. & CHIEF CORPORATE COMMUNICATIONS OFFICER
Barbara S. Brogliatti
S.V.P., CORPORATE BUSINESS DEVELOPMENT &
STRATEGY
John Calkins
S.V.P. & CHIEF EMPLOYMENT COUNSEL
Leigh Chapman
S.V.P., ASSISTANT CORPORATE CONTROLLER
Michael Goodnight
S.V.P. & CONTROLLER
Reginald Harpur
S.V.P. & CHIEF INFORMATION OFFICER
James L. Halsey
S.V.P., INTELLECTUAL PROPERTY, CORPORATE BUSINESS
DEVELOPMENT & STRATEGY
Dean Marks
S.V.P., CORPORATE BUSINESS DEVELOPMENT & STRATEGY
Gary Meisel
S.V.P. & GENERAL COUNSEL, EUROPE
Steven Mertz
S.V.P. & DEPUTY GENERAL COUNSEL
Zazi Pope
S.V.P. & DEPUTY GENERAL COUNSEL
Sheldon Presser
S.V.P., STUDIO & PRODUCTION AFFAIRS
Lisa Rawlins
S.V.P., WORLDWIDE CORPORATE PROMOTIONS
Bob Schneider
S.V.P., TV FINANCIAL MANAGEMENT
Laura Valan
S.V.P., WORLDWIDE HUMAN RESOURCES
Kiko Washington
S.V.P. & GENERAL COUNSEL, CORPORATE BUSINESS
DEVELOPMENT & STRATEGY
Clarissa Weirick
S.V.P. & DEPUTY GENERAL COUNSEL
Jeremy Williams
V.P., CORPORATE COMMUNICATIONS
Scott Rowe

WARNER BROS. ENTERTAINMENT UK

EXECUTIVE V.P. & MANAGING DIRECTOR
Josh Berger

WARNER BROS. PICTURES

PRODUCTION
PRESIDENT, PRODUCTION
Jeff Robinov
EXECUTIVE.V.P., PRODUCTION
Bob Brassel
EXECUTIVE V.P., PRODUCTION
Kevin McCormick
S.V.P., CASTING
Lora Kennedy
S.V.P., PRODUCTION
Courtenay Valenti
S.V.P., PRODUCTION
Lionel Wigram
V.P., PRODUCTION
Jeffrey Clifford
V.P., THEATRICAL PRODUCTION
Polly Cohen
V.P., PRODUCTION
Jessica Goodman
V.P., PRODUCTION
Dan Lin
V.P., PRODUCTION
Greg Silverman
V.P., PRODUCTION
Aditya Sood
V.P., STORY & CREATIVE ADMINISTRATION
Teresa Wayne

MARKETING
PRESIDENT, DOMESTIC MARKETING
Dawn Taubin
EXECUTIVE V.P., WORLDWIDE CREATIVE ADVERTISING
PROJECTS
Joel Wayne
S.V.P., NEW MEDIA
Don Buckley
S.V.P., CREATIVE ADVERTISING
Jim Fredrick
S.V.P., OPERATIONS & SERVICES DOMESTIC MARKETING
Drew Giordano
S.V.P., PUBLICITY & PROMOTION
Debbie Miller
S.V.P., DOMESTIC MARKETING
Diane Nelson
S.V.P., CREATIVE ADVERTISING
Massey Rafani
S.V.P., MARKETING RESEARCH
Daniel P. Rosen
S.V.P., WORLDWIDE MEDIA
Lynn Whitney
V.P., PUBLICITY
Marc Cohen
V.P., NATIONAL PROMOTIONS, DOMESTIC MARKETING
Erin Corbett
V.P., PUBLICITY
Juli Goodwin
V.P., CREDIT & TITLE ADMINISTRATION
Norma Fuss
V.P., PUBLICITY
Stacy Ivers
V.P., FIELD PUBLICITY & NATIONAL PROMOTION
Ernie Johnson
V.P., PUBLICITY
Maggie Schmidt
V.P., ADMINISTRATION, DOMESTIC MARKETING
Dennis Tange
DOMESTIC DISTRIBUTION (WARNER BROS. DISTRIBUTING
INC.)
PRESIDENT, DOMESTIC DISTRIBUTION
Daniel R. Fellman
EXECUTIVE V.P. & GENERAL SALES MANAGER
Jeff Goldstein
S.V.P. & GENERAL COUNSEL
Connie Minnett
S.V.P., SYSTEMS & SALES OPERATIONS
Don Tannenbaum
S.V.P., ADMINISTRATION
Howard Welinsky
V.P., CANADIAN DISTRICT MANAGER
Florent Boulet
V.P., NON-THEATRICAL SALES
Jeff Crawford
V.P., FINANCIAL ADMINISTRATION & OPERATIONS
Bonnie Fallone
V.P., PRINT CONTROL
Nancy Sams
V.P., SALES OPERATIONS
Richard A. Shiff
PRODUCTION MANAGEMENT
PRESIDENT, PHYSICAL PRODUCTION
Steven Papazian
EXECUTIVE V.P., POST PRODUCTION & VISUAL EFFECTS
Marc Solomon
S.V.P., PHYSICAL PRODUCTION & VISUAL EFFECTS
Chris De Faria
S.V.P., FEATURE PRODUCTION
Frank J. Urioste
S.V.P., FEATURE PRODUCTION
William Young
V.P., FEATURE PRODUCTION
Mark Scoon
MUSIC
PRESIDENT, WORLDWIDE MUSIC
Gary LeMel
PRESIDENT, MUSIC OPERATIONS
Doug Frank
S.V.P., BUSINESS AFFAIRS, MUSIC
Keith Zajic
V.P., MUSIC DEVELOPMENT
Ellen Schwartz
BUSINESS/LEGAL AFFAIRS
EXECUTIVE V.P., WORLDWIDE BUSINESS AFFAIRS
Steve Spira
EXECUTIVE V.P., BUSINESS AFFAIRS
Patti Connolly
S.V.P., FINANCIAL INVESTMENTS & ANALYSIS
Bob Fisher
S.V.P., BUSINESS AFFAIRS
Dan Furie
S.V.P. & GENERAL COUNSEL, LEGAL
Pam Kirsh
S.V.P. & GENERAL COUNSEL, BUSINESS & LEGAL AFFAIRS
David Sagal
V.P., ASSOCIATE GENERAL COUNSEL
Eileen Hale

V.P., BUSINESS AFFAIRS
Jodi Levinson
V.P., BUSINESS AFFAIRS
Virginia Tweedy
INDUSTRIAL RELATIONS
S.V.P., INDUSTRIAL RELATIONS
Alan Raphael
V.P., SENIOR LABOR RELATIONS COUNSEL
Richard Levin
V.P., LABOR RELATIONS
Ted Rubin

WARNER BROS. PICTURES INTERNATIONAL
PRESIDENT, MARKETING
Sue Kroll
PRESIDENT, DISTRIBUTION
Veronika Kwan-Rubinek
EXECUTIVE V.P., OPERATIONS & FINANCE
Angelina Speare
S.V.P., EUROPEAN OPERATIONS
David Brander
S.V.P., DISTRIBUTION
Nancy Carson
S.V.P., EUROPEAN DISTRIBUTION
Monique Esclavissat
S.V.P., LATIN AMERICA
Redo Farah
S.V.P., EUROPEAN THEATRICAL MARKETING
Con Gornell
S.V.P., PUBLICITY
Mic Kramer
S.V.P., MARKETING
Fiona Watts
MANAGING DIRECTOR, SWITZERLAND
Leo Baumgartner
V.P., EUROPEAN PRODUCTION
Simona Benzakein
MANAGING DIRECTOR, FRANCE
Francis Boespflug
V.P., LEGAL & BUSINESS AFFAIRS
Damon Bonesteel
GENERAL MANAGER, BRAZIL
Jose Carlos
V.P., MARKETING
Ling Chan
V.P., EASTERN EUROPE & MIDDLE EAST
Jacques Dubois
MANAGING DIRECTOR, CHINA
Ellen Eliasoph
MANAGING DIRECTOR, INDIA
Blaise Fernandes
MANAGING DIRECTOR, ITALY
Paolo Ferrari
V.P. & MANAGING DIRECTOR, AUSTRIA & GERMANY
Willi Geike
MANAGING DIRECTOR, JAPAN
Bill Ireton
V.P., DISTRIBUTION
Brenda Johns
ACCOUNT MANAGER, CENTRAL AMERICA & MEXICO
Miguel Joseph
MANAGING DIRECTOR, TURKEY
Haluk Kaplanoglu
V.P., MEDIA
Gina Kilberg
V.P., OPERATIONS
Lisa Mundt
V.P., DISTRIBUTION & MARKETING, LATIN AMERICA
Kelley Nichols
V.P., OPERATIONS, ASIA/PACIFIC & LATIN AMERICA
Jack Nguyen
V.P., PROMOTIONS
Juliana Olinka
GENERAL MANAGER, KOREA
Hyo-Sung Park
V.P., EUROPEAN DISTRIBUTION
Sarig Peker
GENERAL MANAGER, POLAND
Arek Praglowski
V.P., MARKETING, CREATIVE ADVERTISING & PRODUCTION
Samantha Reid
V.P., MARKETING & CREATIVE ADVERTISING
Blair Rich
MANAGING DIRECTOR, BELGIUM
Anny Schmit
V.P., EUROPEAN PUBLICITY
Armin Schneider
MANAGING DIRECTOR, UK & IRELAND
Nigel Sharrocks
GENERAL MANAGER, TAIWAN
Eric Shih
V.P., MARKET RESEARCH
Barbara Shuler
MANAGING DIRECTOR, PHILIPPINES
Francis Soliven
JOINT MANAGING DIRECTOR, CZECH REPUBLIC
Dr. Ladislav Stastny

V.P., ASIA
Erlina Suharjono
V.P., AD/PUB SERVICES
Francine Velarde
V.P., PUBLICITY
Lance Volland
V.P., FINANCE
David Williamson
MANAGING DIRECTOR, HOLLAND
Wilco Wolfers

WARNER INDEPENDENT PICTURES
PRESIDENT
Mark Gill
EXECUTIVE V.P., PRODUCTION
Michael Andreen
EXECUTIVE V.P., MARKETING & PUBLICITY
Laura Kim
EXECUTIVE V.P., BUSINESS AFFAIRS & OPERATIONS
Andrew Kramer
S.V.P., PRODUCTION & ACQUISITIONS
Paul Federbush
V.P., PRODUCTION & ACQUISITIONS
Tracey Bing

WARNER BROS. THEATRE VENTURES
EXECUTIVE V.P.
Gregg Maday

WARNER BROS. ANIMATION
PRESIDENT
Sander Schwartz
S.V.P., CREATIVE AFFAIRS
Christopher Keenan
S.V.P. & GENERAL MANAGER
Andy Lewis
S.V.P., ACTION-ADVENTURE PROPERTIES
Roland Poindexter
S.V.P., DOMESTIC PRODUCTION
Howard Schwartz
V.P., CREATIVE AFFAIRS
Kim Christianson
V.P., FEATURE PRODUCTION
Dan Crane
V.P., INTERNATIONAL PRODUCTION
Toshi Hiruma
V.P., POST PRODUCTION
Tim Iverson
V.P., MARKETING
Frank Keating
V.P., BUSINESS & LEGAL AFFAIRS
Peter Steckelman

DC COMICS
PRESIDENT & PUBLISHER
Paul Levitz
S.V.P. & GENERAL COUNSEL
Lillian Laserson

WARNER HOME VIDEO
PRESIDENT
Jim Cardwell
EXECUTIVE V.P. & GENERAL MANAGER
Marsha King
EXECUTIVE V.P., WORLDWIDE FINANCE/SYSTEMS/IT
Ed Byrnes
EXECUTIVE V.P., VIDEO ON DEMAND & PAY PER VIEW
Jeffrey Calman
EXECUTIVE V.P., WORLDWIDE MARKETING
Mark Horak
EXECUTIVE V.P., WORLDWIDE SUPPLY CHAIN MANAGEMENT
John Quinn
EXECUTIVE V.P. & GENERAL MANAGER, UNITED STATES
Ron Sanders
S.V.P., WORLDWIDE BUSINESS AFFAIRS & GENERAL COUNSEL
Beth Baier
S.V.P. & CO-MANAGING DIRECTOR, EUROPE, MIDDLE EAST & AFRICA
Jeff Brown
S.V.P. & CO-MANAGING DIRECTOR, EUROPE, MIDDLE EAST & AFRICA
Philippe Cardon
S.V.P., DOMESTIC SALES
Trevor Drinkwater
S.V.P. & GENERAL MANAGER FOR CANADA
Gordon Edwards
S.V.P., LATIN AMERICA, CANADA, AUSTRALIA & NEW ZEALAND
Marc Gareton
S.V.P., INTERNATIONAL FINANCIAL PLANNING & OPERATIONS
Mark Gillions
S.V.P., INTERNATIONAL MARKETING
Nancy Harris
S.V.P., ASIA PACIFIC
Koji Hase
S.V.P., DOMESTIC FINANCE
Keith Hillyer

S.V.P., NEW MEDIA APPLICATIONS & TECHNOLOGY
Lewis Ostrover
S.V.P., OPERATIONS
Edward Ross
S.V.P., DOMESTIC MARKETING
Mike Saksa
V.P., NON-THEATRICAL FRANCHISE MARKETING
Jeff Baker
MANAGING DIRECTOR, FRANCE
Yves Caillaud
V.P., RESEARCH
Nancy Carberry
GENERAL MANAGER, BRAZIL
Marc Caux
V.P., BUSINESS AFFAIRS & LEGAL
Johnna Cho
V.P., SUPPLY CHAIN MANAGEMENT & CATEGORY
MANAGEMENT, EMEA
Roger Clarke
MANAGING DIRECTOR, PHILIPPINES
Rodolfo Confessor
MANAGING DIRECTOR, SPAIN & IBERIAN PENINSULA
Alex de Muns
V.P., EDITORIAL & PROGRAMMING SERVICES
Mike Finnegan
V.P., REGIONAL FINANCE, ASIA PACIFIC
Moriya Fujita
V.P. & MANAGING DIRECTOR, AUSTRIA & GERMANY
Willi Geike
V.P., FIELD SALES, SELL-THRU
Robert Gerber
V.P., EASTERN MEDITERRANEAN REGION & MANAGING
DIRECTOR, ISRAEL
Ilan Givon
V.P., WORLDWIDE PUBLICITY & COMMUNICATIONS
Pamela Godfrey
MANAGING DIRECTOR & SCANDINAVIAN SUPERVISOR,
SWEDEN
Lars Hakansson
MANAGING DIRECTOR, JAPAN
Takeshi Harada
V.P., BUSINESS AFFAIRS & LEGAL
Jackie Hayes
V.P., FIELD SALES, RENTAL/SELL-THRU
Scott Heiss
V.P., DVD PROGRAMMING
Paul Hemstreet
MANAGING DIRECTOR, SWITZERLAND
Juerg Hofmann
V.P., MANUFACTURING/DISTRIBUTION
Kevin Holden
V.P., INTERNATIONAL OPERATIONS & PLANNING
Charles Itagaki
V.P., BUSINESS AFFAIRS & LEGAL
Julie Jacobson
V.P., INTERNATIONAL CATALOG
Brian Jamieson
V.P., PRE-PRODUCTION/INVENTORY CONTROL
Phil Jarboe
V.P., NEW RELEASE INTERNATIONAL
Monica Juniel
V.P., ASIA ANTI-PIRACY & INTELLECTUAL PROPERTY
Molly Kellogg
V.P., BUSINESS AFFAIRS & LEGAL
Jay Kinn
V.P., CONTROLLER
Mike Kory
V.P., FIELD SALES COMMUNICATION & PROMOTION
Frank Kraus
MANAGING DIRECTOR, TAIWAN
Thomas Kuh
MANAGING DIRECTOR, BENELUX
Ruud Lamers
MANAGING DIRECTOR, HUNGARY
Endre Laczko
MANAGING DIRECTOR, SOUTH KOREA
Harrison Lee
V.P., SPECIAL PROJECTS
Howard Livingston
MANAGING DIRECTOR, HONG KONG
Clarence Lo
MANAGING DIRECTOR, POLAND
Andrzej Ludzinski
V.P., LEGAL & BUSINESS AFFAIRS
Nick Macrae
V.P., INTERNATIONAL BUDGETS & FORECASTS
Robert Mancini
V.P., WORLDWIDE MEDIA & RESEARCH
Vito Mandato
V.P., SALES COMMUNICATION
Christine Martinez
V.P., MARKETING PLANNING & ANALYSIS
Ewa Martinoff
MANAGING DIRECTOR, UK
Neil McEwan
V.P., FINANCE, EMEA
Lauren Miller

V.P., RETAIL DIRECT
Dan Miron
V.P., FINANCIAL PLANNING & ANALYSIS
Peter Morfas
V.P., BUSINESS PLANNING & OPERATIONS
Ken Mueller
MANAGING DIRECTOR, AUSTRALIA
Steve Nickerson
V.P., FINANCIAL PLANNING
Chris Pak
V.P., CREDIT/CUSTOMER OPERATIONS
Rohit Patel
V.P., SUPPLY CHAIN MANAGEMENT & CATEGORY
MANAGEMENT, ASIA PACIFIC
Derek Powell
V.P., THEATRICAL/CATALOG NEW RELEASE
Mike Radiloff
V.P., CATEGORY MANAGEMENT
Jay Reinbold
V.P., WORLDWIDE CREATIVE SERVICES
John Richards
V.P., CREATIVE ADVERTISING
Ardis Rubenstein
V.P., RETAIL BUSINESS DEVELOPMENT
Rodney Satterwhite
V.P., STRATEGIC ALLIANCES & CROSS DIVISIONAL
INTEGRATION
Mimi Slavin
MANAGING DIRECTOR, CZECH REPUBLIC
Dr. Ladislav Stastny
V.P., INT'L FINANCE
Julie Tang
MANAGING DIRECTOR, ITALY
Martin Treu
V.P., MARKETING, EMEA
Tony Vaughan
V.P., THEATRICAL NEW RELEASE
Jim Wuthrich
V.P., CHINA
Francis Yam
V.P. & ADVISOR TO THE PRESIDENT
Adam Yokoi

WARNER BROS. CONSUMER PRODUCTS
PRESIDENT, WORLDWIDE CONSUMER PRODUCTS
Dan Romanelli
EXECUTIVE V.P., DOMESTIC LICENSING
Karen McTier
EXECUTIVE V.P., INTERNATIONAL LICENSING
Mark Matheny
EXECUTIVE V.P., WORLDWIDE MARKETING
Jordan Sollitto
S.V.P., BUSINESS DEVELOPMENT
Marc Choper
S.V.P., RETAIL BUSINESS DEVELOPMENT
Patrick Connor
S.V.P., FINANCE & OPERATIONS
Nairi Gardiner
S.V.P., INTERNATIONAL CONTENT & CREATIVE AFFAIRS
Michael Harkavy
S.V.P., WORLDWIDE PUBLIC RELATIONS & LIVE EVENTS
Karine Joret
S.V.P., INTERNATIONAL RETAIL BUSINESS DEVELOPMENT
Bruce Marshall
S.V.P., BUSINESS & LEGAL AFFAIRS
Gary Simon
S.V.P. & GENERAL MANAGER, EMEA
Pilar Zulueta
V.P., WORLDWIDE PUBLISHING
Paula Allen
MANAGING DIRECTOR, JAPAN
Marcia Aoki
V.P., INTERNATIONAL CONSUMER MARKETING
Grant Besser
V.P., RETAIL BUSINESS DEVELOPMENT
Shari Black
V.P., CATEGORY DEVELOPMENT & SALES,
INTERNATIONAL LICENSING
Bradford Braun
V.P., SOURCING
Jon Brewer
V.P., INTERNATIONAL RETAIL BUSINESS DEVELOPMENT
Michael Brown
V.P., LEGAL AFFAIRS
Ana de Castro
V.P., FINANCIAL PLANNING & BUSINESS ANALYSIS
Steve Chalk
V.P., CREATIVE & IMAGE MARKETING
Brain Deputy
V.P., INTERACTIVE ENTERTAINMENT
Philippe Erwin
V.P., BUSINESS DEVELOPMENT & SALES, INTERNATIONAL
LICENSING
Paul Flett
V.P., BRAND ASSURANCE
Kim Furzer
V.P., TOYS & THEME PARK LICENSING
Kelly Gilmore

V.P., PROMOTIONS & BRANDED FOODS
Dave Hedrick
V.P., GREATER CHINA & SOUTHEAST ASIA
Mickie Leong
GENERAL MANAGER, BRAZIL
Marcus Macedo
V.P., PROPERTY ACQUISITIONS
Karen Miller
V.P., FINANCIAL REPORTING
Donna Raphael
V.P., U.S. SALES
Dave Rupert
V.P., STUDIO LICENSING
Michelle Sucillon
V.P., RETAIL INFORMATION SYSTEMS
Roxane Suurvarik
V.P., LOGISTICS
Michael Tillman
GENERAL MANAGER, MEXICO
Manuel Torres
V.P., APPAREL & ACCESSORIES
Maribeth Towers
V.P., FINANCE
Linda Van Wagner
V.P., LATIN AMERICAN LICENSING
Salvador Viramontes
V.P., RETAIL BUSINESS DEVELOPMENT
Melissa Wong
V.P., MARKETING
Sandy Yi
V.P. & GENERAL MANAGER, TELEVISION LICENSING
Maryellen Zarakas
V.P., WORLDWIDE PUBLIC RELATIONS
Barry Ziehl

WARNER BROS. TELEVISION PRODUCTION

PRESIDENT
Peter Roth
EXECUTIVE V.P.
Craig Hunegs
EXECUTIVE V.P., CREATIVE AFFAIRS
Steve Pearlman
EXECUTIVE V.P., PRODUCTION
Judith Zaylor
S.V.P., CASTING
Mary V. Buck
S.V.P., BUSINESS AFFAIRS
Karen Cease
S.V.P., COMEDY DEVELOPMENT
Leonard Goldstein
S.V.P., CURRENT PROGRAMMING
Melinda Hage
S.V.P., LABOR RELATIONS
Hank Lachmund
S.V.P., TELEVISION MUSIC
Roxanne Lippel
S.V.P., MOVIES & MINI-SERIES
Gregg Maday
S.V.P., PUBLICITY
Sharan Magnuson
S.V.P., ADMINISTRATION
Geriann McIntosh
S.V.P. & GENERAL COUNSEL, LEGAL AFFAIRS
Marjorie Neufeld
S.V.P., BUSINESS AFFAIRS
Brett Paul
S.V.P., DRAMA DEVELOPMENT
Susan Rovner
S.V.P., CURRENT PROGRAMMING
David Sacks
S.V.P., FINANCIAL ADMINISTRATION
Christina Smith
V.P., NETWORK PRODUCTION
Tony Amatullo
V.P., NETWORK RESEARCH
Jeanne Cotton
V.P., COMEDY DEVELOPMENT
Marianne Cracchiolo
V.P., LEGAL AFFAIRS
Nannette Diacovo
V.P., BUSINESS AFFAIRS
Jay Gendron
V.P., BUSINESS AFFAIRS
Adam Glick
V.P., PUBLICITY
Phil Gonzales
V.P., PRODUCTION
Vicky Herman
V.P., PRODUCTION
Henry Johnson
V.P., CURRENT PROGRAMMING
Lisa Lang
V.P., PRODUCTION
Lisa Lewis
V.P., POST-PRODUCTION
Mara Lopez
V.P., LEGAL AFFAIRS
Mimi Magnuson-Carson

V.P. CASTING
Wendi Matthews
V.P., CURRENT PROGRAMMING
Kimberly Metcalf
V.P., BUSINESS AFFAIRS
Sue Palladino
V.P., DRAMA DEVELOPMENT
Andrew Plotkin
V.P., PRODUCTION
Ellen Rauch
V.P., MUSIC
Bronwyn Savasta
V.P., CASTING
Tony Sepulveda
V.P., CASTING
Meg Simon
V.P., CURRENT PROGRAMMING
Adrienne Turner
V.P., LABOR RELATIONS
Sam Wolfson
V.P., LEGAL
Jody Zucker
V.P., LEGAL
Barbara Zuckerman

WARNER BROS. TELEVISION DISTRIBUTION

WARNER BROS. DOMESTIC TELEVISION DISTRIBUTION
PRESIDENT
Dick Robertson
EXECUTIVE V.P.
Jim Paratore
EXECUTIVE V.P., MEDIA RESEARCH
Bruce K. Rosenblum
EXECUTIVE V.P., MEDIA SALES
Michael Teicher
S.V.P., ADMINISTRATION
Leonard Bart
S.V.P., GENERAL SALES MANAGER
Andrew Goldman
S.V.P., SOUTHWEST SALES MANAGER
Jacqueline Hartley
S.V.P., MEDIA RESEARCH
Liz Huszarik
S.V.P., SALES
Bill Marcus
S.V.P., SALES
Rick Meril
S.V.P., PRIMARY RESEARCH
Wayne Neiman
S.V.P., WESTERN SALES
Mark O'Brien
V.P., BUSINESS DEVELOPMENT
Marci Abelow
V.P., MEDIA RESEARCH
Karen Barcheski
V.P., EASTERN SALES
John Buckholtz
V.P., MEDIA SALES
Roseann Cacciola
V.P., RESEARCH, FINANCE & SPECIAL PROJECTS
Keith Friedenberg
V.P., MEDIA SALES RESEARCH
Jean Goldberg
V.P., CONTRACT ADMINISTRATION
Brad Hornor
V.P., WESTERN SALES
Rich Iazzetta
V.P., EASTERN SALES
Michael Kerans
V.P., SOUTHEASTERN SALES
Marlynda Lecast
V.P., CENTRAL SALES
Dan Menzel
V.P., FINANCE
Roxanne Modjallal
V.P., MEDIA SALES
Philip Peters
V.P., SOUTHEASTERN SALES
Chuck Self
V.P., CENTRAL SALES
Ed Seslowsky
V.P., SALES PLANNING & OPERATIONS
Helene Sperling
WARNER BROS. DOMESTIC CABLE DISTRIBUTION
PRESIDENT
Eric Frankel
S.V.P., SALES & MARKETING
Gus Lucas
S.V.P., LEGAL & BUSINESS AFFAIRS
Ron Sunderland
V.P., MARKETING
Linda Abrams
V.P., FINANCE
Donald Putrimas
V.P., SALES PLANNING & PROGRAM INVENTORY
Pam Ritchie
V.P., SALES
Mike Russo

WARNER BROS. INTERNATIONAL TELEVISION DISTRIBUTION

PRESIDENT
Jeffrey R. Schlesinger
EXECUTIVE V.P., INTERNATIONAL SALES & BUSINESS DEVELOPMENT
Malcolm Dudley-Smith
EXECUTIVE V.P., BUSINESS AFFAIRS, OPERATIONS & GENERAL COUNSEL
Ron Miele
S.V.P., SALES & BUSINESS DEVELOPMENT/MANAGING DIRECTOR, EUROPE
Simon Kenny
S.V.P., FINANCE & OPERATIONS
David Camp
S.V.P., BUSINESS AFFAIRS & DEPUTY GENERAL COUNSEL
Renee Wolf
V.P. & MANAGING DIRECTOR, SPAIN & PORTUGAL, WBITV
Jose Abad
V.P., PAY TV CONTRACT ADMINISTRATION
Faye Beland
V.P. & GENERAL MANAGER, CANADA
Robert A. Blair
V.P., FREE TELEVISION CONTRACT ADMINISTRATION
Tony Fricia
V.P. & MANAGING DIRECTOR, MEXICO
David Guerrero
V.P., BUSINESS DEVELOPMENT, LATIN AMERICA
Keith Kohler
MANAGING DIRECTOR, UK
Chris Law
V.P., GENERAL MANAGER, FRANCE
Michel LeCourt
V.P., LEGAL & BUSINESS AFFAIRS-EUROPE
Delyth Fetherston-Dilke
V.P., LEGAL & BUSINESS AFFAIRS
Mark Lieblein
MANAGING DIRECTOR, ITALIAN-SPEAKING EUROPE
Rosario Ponzio
V.P. & MANAGING DIRECTOR, ASIA PACIFIC
Greg Robertson
V.P., BUSINESS DEVELOPMENT
Matthew Robinson
MANAGING DIRECTOR, GERMANY
Sylvia Rothblum
V.P., INTERNATIONAL PRODUCT COORDINATION
June Saitsky
V.P., PUBLICITY & MARKETING SERVICES
Andrew Shipps

TELEPICTURES PRODUCTIONS

PRESIDENT
Jim Paratore
EXECUTIVE V.P. & GENERAL MANAGER
Hilary Estey McLoughlin
EXECUTIVE V.P.
Alan Saxe
S.V.P., PROGRAMMING
David Auerbach
S.V.P., MARKETING & CREATIVE DIRECTOR
Howard Borim
S.V.P., DEVELOPMENT
Stephanie Drachkovitch
S.V.P., PRODUCTION & ADMINISTRATION
Kevin Fortson
V.P., FINANCE & ADMINISTRATION
David Benavente
V.P., PROGRAMMING
Mary Duffy
V.P., DEVELOPMENT
David McGuire
V.P., CONSUMER PUBLICITY
Leslie Oren
V.P., LEGAL & BUSINESS AFFAIRS
Vivienne Vella

WARNER BROS. INTERNATIONAL CINEMAS

PRESIDENT
Millard Ochs
S.V.P., OPERATIONAL FINANCE, INFORMATION SYSTEMS & ADMINISTRATION
David Bent
S.V.P., INTERNATIONAL FILM RELATIONS
Peter Dobson
S.V.P., FINANCE
Paul Miller
S.V.P., WORLDWIDE OPERATIONS
David Pearson
S.V.P., ARCHITECTURAL DESIGN
Ira Stiegler
V.P., BUSINESS & LEGAL AFFAIRS
David Bisoni

WARNER BROS. ONLINE

S.V.P. & GENERAL MANAGER
James Noonan
V.P., INTERNATIONAL
Cathi Cox
V.P., FINANCE & ADMINISTRATION
Robert Genthert

V.P. & GENERAL COUNSEL
Michael Lewis
V.P., STRATEGIC MARKETING
Brian Moreno
V.P., TECHNOLOGY & ENGINEERING
Khalid Oreif
V.P., THEATRICAL PROJECTS
Michael Tritter
V.P., PRODUCTION
Guy W. Vardaman

WARNER BROS. STUDIO FACILITIES

PRESIDENT
Jon Gilbert
EXECUTIVE V.P., STUDIO SERVICES & ADMINISTRATION
Jeff Nagler
S.V.P., POST PRODUCTION SERVICES
Norman Barnett
S.V.P., REAL ESTATE
Michael C. Mason
S.V.P., LABOR RELATIONS & LEGAL AFFAIRS
Michael Messina
S.V.P., OPERATIONS
Bob Pincus
S.V.P., PRODUCTION SERVICES
Ron Stein
S.V.P., FINANCE & PLANNING
Leisa Wu
V.P., STUDIO PROTECTION
Frank O'Donnell

WARNER BROS. TECHNICAL OPERATIONS

PRESIDENT
Chris Cookson
S.V.P., DISTRIBUTION TECHNOLOGIES & OPERATIONS
Darcy Antonellis
S.V.P., TECHNOLOGY
Alan Bell
S.V.P., DISTRIBUTION SERVICES & DUBBING OPERATIONS
Annette Bouso
S.V.P., EMERGING TECHNOLOGIES
Chuck Dages

WARNER BROS. ADVANCED MEDIA SERVICES

S.V.P., PRODUCTION TECHNOLOGIES
Rob Hummel

WARNER BROS. MARKETING & ADVERTISING SERVICES

S.V.P., MARKETING & ADVERTISING SERVICES
Yelena Garofolo
V.P., MARKETING & ADVERTISING SERVICES
Lauren Dansey
V.P., CREATIVE SERVICES
Joel Kaplan
V.P., MARKETING SERVICES
Craig Montgomery

WARNER BROS. TELEVISION CREATIVE SERVICES

S.V.P., TELEVISION CREATIVE SERVICES
Lisa Gregorian

THE WB TELEVISION NETWORK

CHAIRMAN
Garth Ancier
CEO
Jordan Levin
PRESIDENT & COO
Jed Petrick
CO-PRESIDENT, MARKETING
Bob Bibb
CO-PRESIDENT, MARKETING
Lew Goldstein
EXECUTIVE V.P., DRAMA DEVELOPMENT
Carolyn Bernstein
CO-EXECUTIVE V.P., COMEDY DEVELOPMENT
Mike Clements
EXECUTIVE V.P., MARKETING
Suzanne Kolb
EXECUTIVE V.P., CASTING
Kathleen Letterie
EXECUTIVE V.P., CURRENT PROGRAMMING
John Litvack
EXECUTIVE V.P. & GENERAL COUNSEL
John Maatta
EXECUTIVE V.P., MEDIA SALES
Bill Morningstar
EXECUTIVE V.P., FINANCE & OPERATIONS
Mitch Nedick
CO-EXECUTIVE V.P., COMEDY DEVELOPMENT
Tracey Pakosta
EXECUTIVE V.P., BUSINESS AFFAIRS
Michael Ross
EXECUTIVE V.P., NETWORK COMMUNICATIONS
Brad Turell
EXECUTIVE V.P., NETWORK DISTRIBUTION
Ken Werner
S.V.P., ALTERNATIVE PROGRAMMING
Keith Cox
S.V.P., PRINT ADVERTISING & CREATIVE SERVICES
Rick Frey

S.V.P., RESEARCH
Mary Hall
S.V.P., PROGRAMMING, *KIDS' WB!*
John Hardman
S.V.P., THE WB.COM
Nancie Martin
S.V.P., BROADCAST STANDARDS
Rick Mater
S.V.P., MARKETING, *KIDS' WB!*
Betsy McGowen
S.V.P., NETWORK COMMUNICATIONS
Paul McGuire
S.V.P., SCHEDULING/VP, CURRENT PROGRAMMING
Rusty Mintz
S.V.P., ON-AIR PRODUCTION/SPECIAL PROJECTS
Dean Norris
S.V.P., ON-AIR PROMOTION
Russ Popick
S.V.P., DISTRIBUTION DEVELOPMENT
Hal Protter
S.V.P., CURRENT PROGRAMMING
Michael Roberts
S.V.P., CURRENT PROGRAMMING
Chris Sanagustin
S.V.P., SALES PLANNING/ADMINISTRATION
Ira Sperling
S.V.P., NATIONAL SALES
Rob Tuck
V.P., FINANCE & ACCOUNTING
Dana Abel
V.P., INTEGRATED MARKETING
Sonia Borris
V.P., MIDWEST SALES
Cynthia Collins
V.P., BROADCAST STANDARDS
Patricia Gertson Dennis
V.P., EASTERN SALES
Brian Doherty
V.P., BUSINESS AFFAIRS, *KIDS' WB!*
Dennis Dort
V.P., ON-AIR CREATIVE
Matt Fife
V.P., EASTERN SALES
Alida Gaines
V.P., PRINT ADVERTISING
Leigh Anne Gardner
V.P., DRAMA DEVELOPMENT
Maria Grasso
V.P., EASTERN SALES
Michael Guariglia
V.P., AFFILIATE SALES
Lauren Halpern
V.P., CURRENT PROGRAMMING
Janine Jones
V.P., BUSINESS AFFAIRS
Matthew Kearns
V.P., SALES, EASTERN & WESTERN REGIONS
Claudine Lilien
V.P., ON-AIR PRODUCTION/POST PRODUCTION FACILITY
OPERATIONS
Craig MacEachern
V.P., PHOTOGRAPHY
Bonnie Moffet
V.P., PRIME TIME PUBLICITY
Pamela Morrison
V.P., RESEARCH
Jennifer O'Dea
V.P., ON-AIR DESIGN
Karin Rainey
V.P., MUSIC
Leonard Richardson
V.P., MEDIA PLANNING
Melanie Shaw
V.P., BUSINESS AFFAIRS
Kelly Smith
V.P., AFFILIATE MARKETING/BROADCAST SERVICES
Dan Spangler
V.P., DEPUTY GENERAL COUNSEL
Jeremy Sunderland
V.P., INTEGRATED SALES & MARKETING
Alison Tarrant
V.P., AFFILIATE RELATIONS & COMMUNICATIONS
Elizabeth Tumulty
V.P., RESEARCH
Dounia Turrill
V.P., ON-AIR PROMOTION
David Zaccaria
THE WB 100+ STATION GROUP
EXECUTIVE V.P., THE 100+ STATION GROUP
Russ Myerson
S.V.P., PROGRAMMING & DISTRIBUTION
Lynn Stephanian Cartier
S.V.P., MARKETING
Stephen Domier
S.V.P., FINANCE & ADMINISTRATION
Tad Vogels
V.P., ON-AIR PROMOTION
Cris Chavarria

V.P., CREATIVE SERVICES
Andy Crittenden
V.P., PRODUCTION
Maureen Milmore
V.P., TECHNICAL OPERATIONS
Harlan Milton

BRANCH OFFICES

AUSTRALIA & FAR EAST
Warner Bros. Pty. Ltd., Level 6, 116 Military Rd., Neutral Bay,
NSW 2089, Australia. TEL: (612) 9495-3000. FAX: (612) 9908-
5500.
MANAGING DIRECTOR WBA & V.P. OF ASIA PACIFIC WBI
Greg Robertson

BRAZIL
Warner Bros. Brazil, Rua Lauro Muller, 116-S/807, Rio De
Janeiro - RJ, Brazil 22290-160. TEL: (5521) 2543-1155. FAX:
(5521) 2543-2130.
TELEVISION GENERAL MANAGER
Louremberg do Nacimento

CANADA
Warner Bros. International Television, 4576 Yonge St., 2nd Flr.,
Toronto, Ontario M2N 6P1, Canada. TEL: (416) 250-8384. FAX:
(416) 250-8598.
V.P. & GENERAL MANAGER, CANADIAN OPERATIONS
Robert Blair

FRANCE
Warner Bros. International Television, 115-123 Charles de
Gaulle, 92525 Neuilly sur Seine, France. TEL: (331) 7225-
1321. FAX: (331) 7225-1332.
V.P. & GENERAL MANAGER
Michel Lecourt

GERMANY
Warner Bros. International Television Distribution, A Division Of
Warner Home Video GMBH, Prinzegentenstrasse 72, 81675
Munich, Germany. TEL: 49-89-455-7890. FAX: 49-89-455-789-19.
MANAGING DIRECTOR
Sylvia Rothblum

HONG KONG
Warner Bros. International Television Distribution, 33/F, Oxford
House, Taikoo Pl., 979 King's Road, Quarry Bay. TEL: (852)
3128-1617. FAX: (852) 3128-1190.
DIRECTOR, STRATEGIC DEVELOPMENT & SALES
Ted Lai

ITALY
Warner Bros. International TV Italia S.R.L., Via Giuseppe
Avezzana #51, 00195 Roma, Italy. TEL: (39) 06-321-7779.
FAX: (39) 06-321-7278.
MANAGING DIRECTOR
Rosario Ponzio

JAPAN
Warner Entertainment Japan, Hibiya Central Bldg. 15F, 1-2-9
Nishi-Shinbashi, Minato-Ku, Tokyo, 105-0013 Japan. TEL: (81)
3-5251-6440. FAX: (81) 3-5251-6449.
MANAGING DIRECTOR
Akifumi Sugihara

SOUTH AMERICA
Warner Bros. (Mexico), Acapulco 37, Colonea Codesa, Mexico
D.F., 06140 Mexico. TEL: (5255) 5241-5900. FAX: (5255) 5553-
2822.
V.P. & GENERAL MANAGER
David Guerrero

SPAIN
Warner Bros. International Television, Serrano, 38 - 3º Planta,
28001 Madrid, Spain. TEL: (349) 1436-7950. FAX: (349) 1436-
7955.
V.P. & MANAGING DIRECTOR OF SPAIN & PORTUGAL
Jose Abad

**UNITED KINGDOM TERRITORIES, SCANDINAVIA &
BENELUX, AFRICA, MIDDLE EAST**
Warner Bros. International Television, Warner House, 7th. Flr.,
98 Theobald's Rd., London WC1X 8WB, England. TEL: (44)
20-7984-5400. FAX: (44) 20-7984-5401.
EXECUTIVE V.P. & MANAGING DIRECTOR, U.K.
Josh Berger

MD WAX/COURIER FILMS

(Distributor, art films worldwide)
237 Clent Rd., Great Neck, NY 11021. TEL/FAX: (516) 466-
6852. email: mortwax@worldnet.att.net
PRESIDENT
Morton D. Wax

WEED ROAD PICTURES

(Motion picture & TV producer)
4000 Warner Blvd., Bldg. 81, Ste. 115, Burbank, CA 91522.
(818) 954-3771. FAX: (818) 954-3061.
email: weedroad@earthlink.net
PRODUCER
Akiva Goldsman
EXECUTIVE V.P.
Stephanie Gisondi

CREATIVE EXECUTIVE
Anthony Vasto
ASSISTANTS
Linda Hoffman
Jane Kosek
Ryan Swanson

WEEKEND FILMS

(Motion picture producer)
10201 W. Pico Blvd., Bldg. 49, Rm. 123, Los Angeles, CA
90035. (310) 369-0093. FAX: (310) 369-7742.
PRODUCER
Trevor Albert
DIRECTOR DEVELOPMENT
Kym Bye
ASSISTANT TO TREVOR ALBERT
Troy Benjamin

WEST GLEN COMMUNICATIONS, INC.

(TV producer & distributor)
1430 Broadway, 9th Flr., New York, NY 10018. (212) 921-2800.
FAX: (212) 944-9055. www.popcornreport.com
PRESIDENT
Stan Zeitlin

WHITE WOLF PRODUCTIONS

2932 Wilshire Blvd., Ste. 201, Santa Monica, CA 90403. (310)
829-7500. FAX: (310) 586-0717.
PRESIDENT
David S. Ward

WILDWOOD ENTERPRISES, INC.

(Motion picture & independent film producer)
1101 Montana Ave., Ste. E, Santa Monica, CA 90403. (310)
395-5155. FAX: (310) 395-3975.
OWNER
Robert Redford

WINKLER FILMS, INC.

(Motion picture, independent film & TV producer)
211 S. Beverly Dr., #200, Beverly Hills, CA 90212. (310) 858-
5780. FAX: (310) 858-5799.
CEO, PRODUCER & DIRECTOR
Irwin Winkler
PRESIDENT
Rob Cowan

WELLSPRING MEDIA

(Formerly Fox Lorber Associates, Inc; TV & video distributor)
419 Park Ave. S., 20th Flr., New York, NY 10016. (212) 686-
6777. FAX: (212) 685-2625. www.wellspring.com
PRESIDENT
Al Cattabiani
EXECUTIVE V.P., WORLDWIDE SALES
Sheri Levine
DIRECTOR, INTERNATIONAL SALES & CO-PRODUCTIONS
Linda Saetre
HEAD, ACQUISITIONS
Marie Therese Guirgis
DIRECTOR, MARKETING & CREATIVE SERVICES
Julia Panely-Pacetti

WITT-THOMAS FILMS

(Motion picture producer)
11901 Santa Monica Blvd., Ste. 596, W. Los Angeles, CA
90025. (310) 472-6004. FAX: (310) 476-5015.
PARTNERS
Paul Junger Witt
Tony Thomas
Susan Harris
DIRECTOR, DEVELOPMENT
Tony Witt
ASSISTANTS
Richard Seymour
Marlene Fuentes

THE WOLPER ORGANIZATION

(Motion picture & TV producer)
4000 Warner Blvd., Bldg. 14, Rm. X, Burbank, CA 91522-0001.
(818) 954-1421. FAX: (818) 954-1593.
CHAIRMAN
David L. Wolper
PRESIDENT & EXECUTIVE PRODUCER
Mark M. Wolper
V.P., DEVELOPMENT
Kevin Nicklaus
STORY EDITOR
Murad Hussain
OFFICE MANAGER
Laura Cannon

WORKING TITLE FILMS

(Motion picture, independent film & TV producer)
9720 Wilshire Blvd., Beverly Hills, CA 90212. (310) 777-3100.
FAX: (310) 777-5243.
CHAIRMEN
Tim Bevan
Eric Fellner

WORLD FILM SERVICES, INC.

(Motion picture, independent film & TV producer & distributor)
630 Fifth Ave., Ste. 1505, New York, NY 10111. (212) 632-
3456. FAX: (212) 632-3457.
CEO
John Heyman
VICE PRESIDENT
Pamela Osowski
CANADA
Roy Krost

THE WYLE/KATZ COMPANY

(Motion picture, independent film & TV producer)
1041 N. Formosa Ave., Writers Bldg., Ste. 311, West
Hollywood, CA 90046. (323) 850-2777. FAX: (323) 850-2776.
PRODUCER
James Katz
ACTOR & PRODUCER
Noah Wyle
DIRECTOR, DEVELOPMENT
Benjamin Mandelker

SAUL ZAENTZ FILM CENTER

2600 Tenth St., Berkeley, CA 94710. (510) 486-2100. FAX:
(510) 486-2115. www.zaentz.com
PRESIDENT
Saul Zaentz
GENERAL MANAGER
Steve Shurtz
MANAGER
Scott Roberts

THE ZANUCK COMPANY

(Producer, theatrical motion pictures)
9465 Wilshire Blvd., Beverly Hills, CA 90212. (310) 274-0261.
FAX: (310) 273-9217. email: zanuckco@aol.com
PARTNERS
Richard D. Zanuck
Lili Fini Zanuck (310) 274-0209

ZEITGEIST FILMS LTD.

(Distributor, independent films)
247 Centre St., 2nd Flr., New York, NY 10013. (212) 274-1989.
FAX: (212) 274-1644. www.zeitgeistfilm.com
email: mail@zeitgeistfilm.com
CO-PRESIDENTS
Emily Russo
Nancy Gerstman

ZIDE/PERRY ENTERTAINMENT

(Motion picture producer)
9100 Wilshire Blvd., Ste. 615 E., Beverly Hills, CA 90212. (310)
887-2999. FAX: (310) 887-2995. www.inzide.com
PRODUCER & MANAGER
Warren Zide
PRODUCER
Craig Perry
V.P., PRODUCTION & DEVELOPMENT
Sheila Hanahan
MANAGER & DIRECTOR, LITERARY ACQUISITIONS
Jennifer Frankel

ZOLLO/PALEOLOGOS, INC. (ZPI)

(Motion picture producer)
257 W. 52nd St., 2nd Flr., New York, NY 10019. (212) 957-1300.
FAX: (212) 957-1315. www.members.aol.com/zpi/index.html
email: npzpi@aol.com
PRODUCERS
Nicholas Paleologos
Frederick Zollo
CREATIVE AFFAIRS
Jono Gero

ZUCKER PRODUCTIONS

1250 6th St., Ste. 201, Santa Monica, CA 90401. (310) 656-
9202. FAX: (310) 656-9220.
DIRECTOR
Jerry Zucker
PRODUCER
Janet Zucker

ZUCKER/NETTER PRODUCTIONS

(Motion picture producer)
1411 Fifth St., Ste. 402, Santa Monica, CA 90401. (310) 394-
1644. FAX: (310) 899-6722.
PRODUCER & DIRECTOR & WRITER
David Zucker
PRESIDENT
Gil Netter

LARGE FORMAT
PRODUCERS & DISTRIBUTORS

APERTURE FILMS, LTD.
3534 Hayden Ave., Culver City, CA 90232. (310) 202-3939.
FAX: (310) 842-9898. www.aperturefilms.com
MANAGING DIRECTORS
Josh Colover
Chris Blum
OFFICE MANAGER
Ben Lang

ARCLIGHT PRODUCTIONS
6815 W Willoughby Ste. 206, Hollywood, CA 90038. (323) 464-7791. FAX: (323) 464-7406. www.Arclightprods.com
email: info@arclightprods.com
CONTACT
Steven Kochones

ARGENTINE PRODUCTIONS
701 Washington Rd., #2, Pittsburgh, PA 15228. (412) 341-6448. FAX: (412) 341-4410.
email: peter@argentineproductions.com
CONTACT
Peter Argentine

ASCHER PRODUCTIONS, LTD.
293 Terrace Pl., Buffalo Grove, IL 60089-1918. (847) 520-0099.
FAX: (847) 537-7929. www.ascherfilms.com
email: info@ascherfilms.com
CONTACT
Ron Ascher

BLUE MOUNTAIN FILM ASSOCIATES, INC.
(Large-format film producer)
148 Waverly Pl., New York, NY 10014. (212) 645-0745. FAX: (212) 691-1299. email: Bsilleck@aol.com
PRESIDENT
Bayley Silleck

CHUCK DAVIS/TIDAL FLATS, LTD.
1215 Surf Ave., Pacific Grove, CA 93950. (831) 649-1086. FAX: (831) 649-0986. www.Tidalflatsphoto.com
email: cdocean@earthlink.net
CONTACT
Chuck Davis

DCM PRODUCTIONS
1611 19th St., Manhattan Beach, CA 90266. (310) 545-2119.
FAX: (310) 545-5350. email: dcmprods@AOL.com
CONTACT
Doug Merrifield

DESTINATION CINEMA, INC.
(Large-format producer & distributor)
4155 Harrison Blvd., Ste. 210, Ogden, UT 84403. (801) 392-2001. FAX: (801) 392-6703. www.destinationcinema.com
COO
Bob Perkins
DIRECTOR, FILM DISTRIBUTION
Patricia Brandino

DISCOVERY COMMUNICATIONS
(Large-format film producer)
8516 Georgia Ave., Silver Springs, MD 20910. (240) 662-0000.
www.discovery.com

GIANT SCREEN FILMS
500 Davis St., #1005, Evanston, IL 60201. (847) 475-9140.
FAX: (847) 475-9145. email: SKempf@giantscreensports.com
CONTACT
Steve Kempf

GRANDVIEW PRODUCTIONS
(IMAX/large film production)
1016 Fairway Rd., Santa Barbara, CA 93108. (805) 565-3759.
FAX: (805) 565-3769.
email: production@grandviewproductions.com
CONTACT
Michael Cook

GRAPHIC FILMS CORPORATION
3341 Cahuenga Blvd., Hollywood, CA 90068. (323) 851-4100.
FAX: (323) 851-4103 . www.Graphicfilms.com
email: pnovros@graphicfilms.com
CONTACT
Paul Novros

HOWARD HALL PRODUCTIONS
2171 La Amatista Rd., Del Mar, CA 92014-3031. (858) 259-8989. FAX: (858) 792-1467. www.howardhall.com
email: info2@howardhall.com
CONTACT
Howard Hall

HARRAH'S FILM CORP.
(Large-format motion picture producer)
25613 Dollar St., #1, Hayward, CA 94544. (510) 881-4989.
FAX: (510) 881-0448.
CONTACT
Jerry Harrah

HIGH ROAD PRODUCTIONS
1143 Van Buren Ave., Venice, CA 90291. (310) 823-9065. FAX: (800) 886-2991. www.highroadproductions.com
CONTACT
Noah Kadner

IMAX CORPORATION
(Large-format film producer & distributor)
3003 Exposition Blvd., Santa Monica, CA 90404. (310) 255-5500. FAX: (310) 255-5501. www.imax.com
PRESIDENT, FILMED ENTERTAINMENT
Greg Foster
S.V.P., FILMED ENTERTAINMENT
Margaret E.G. Wilson
V.P., FILMED ENTERTAINMENT
Doug Hylton

INFINITY FILMWORKS
(Motion picture producer of large-format features)
19405 Bilmoor Pl., Tarzana, CA 91356. (818) 881-3288.
CONTACT
Keith Melton

LEWIS MEDIA GROUP
(Producer of large-format & traditional motion pictures)
9300 Wilshire Blvd., Ste. 108, Beverly Hills, CA 90212. (310) 550-1930. FAX: (310) 550-1731.
CEO & CO-FOUNDER
Michael V. Lewis

LOBO MEDIA PRODUCTIONS
650 Ward Dr., Ste. I, Santa Barbara, CA 93111-3307. (805) 964-2132. FAX: (805) 964-0737. www.Lobofilms.com
email: info@Lobofilms.com
CONTACT
Mal Wolfe

MACGILLIVRAY FREEMAN FILMS
(Producer & distributor of large-format films)
P.O. Box 205, Laguna Beach, CA 92652. (949) 494-1055. FAX: (949) 494-2079. www.macfreefilms.com
PRESIDENT
Greg MacGillivray

MACHINE AGE FILMS LLC
4048 Benedict Canyon Dr., Sherman Oaks, CA 91423. (818) 906-8008. email: MarkMerrall@Machineagefilms.com
CONTACT
Mark Merrall

METANOIA PRODUCTIONS
11447 Albata St., Ste. 1, Los Angeles, CA 90049. (310) 889-7661. email: doug@metanoiaproductions.com
CONTACT
Douglas Fahleson

DENNIS EARL MOORE PRODUCTIONS, INC.
137 Atlantic Ave., Brooklyn Heights, NY 11201-5504. (718) 875-8024. FAX: (718) 522-4358. email: demp@megapathdsl.net
CONTACT
Dennis Earl Moore

NATIONAL WILDLIFE PRODUCTIONS
11100 Wildlife Center Dr., Reston, VA 20190-5362. (703) 438-6077. FAX: (703) 438-6076.
PRESIDENT & CEO
Christopher Palmer

NOVA LARGE FORMAT FILMS

(Producer, large-format film for museums theaters, cultural institutions & commercial venues worldwide)
WGBH, 125 Western Ave., Boston, MA 02134. (617) 300-2000. www.pbs.org/nova
EXECUTIVE PRODUCER
Susanne Simpson (617) 300-4336

NWAVE PICTURES

(Digital producer, large-format & ride films)
10839 W. Washington Blvd., Culver City, CA 90232. (310) 815-2880. FAX: (310) 845-1716. www.nwave.com
PRESIDENT
Charlotte Huggins
DIRECTOR, MARKETING
Ken Cosci
CFO
Jane Morrison

OCTOGRAPH MEDIA GROUP

(Parent company of Showscan Entertainment)
(Producer & distributor of contents for media based attractions; developer & producer of large-format films, feature animation films, CGI & TV programming)
1627 N. Gower St., Unit 3, Los Angeles, CA 90028. (323) 460-5640. FAX: (323) 460-5645. www.octograph.com
SENIOR V.P., SALES & MARKETING
Sue Y. Kim
V.P., WORLDWIDE DISTRIBUTION
Marcelo Floriao

SBK PICTURES INC.

123 Coulter Ave., Ardmore, PA 19003. (610) 658-5858. FAX: (610) 658-0809. www.sbkpictures.com
email: jeffrey_berry@sbkpictures.com
DIRECTOR/PARTNER
Jeffrey Berry

SHOCONCEPTS

5044 Sunny Slope Ave., Sherman Oaks, CA 91423. (818) 521-5624. FAX: (818) 789-2756. www.shoconcepts.com
email: steve.ryan@shoconcepts.com
EXECUTIVE PRODUCER
Steve Ryan

SLINGSHOT ENTERTAINMENT

4000 W. Burbank, Burbank, CA 91605. (818) 973-2480. FAX: (818) 955-9638. www.slingshotent.com
email: info@slingshotent.com
CONTACT
Christie Smith

VIOLET PICTURES

4000 Via Compesina, Palos Verdes, CA 90247. (310) 378-1202. email: mixryan@earthlink.net
CONTACT
Mix Ryan

WILD CHILD ENTERTAINMENT, LTD.

(Large-format motion picture producer, distributor & consultant)
69 Church St., Seymour, CT 06483-2611. TEL/FAX: (203) 888-2405. email: WildChildEnt@compuserve.com
PRESIDENT
Hans Kummer

NON-THEATRICAL
MOTION PICTURE COMPANIES

Following is a list of producers, distributors and film libraries handling educational, entertainment and advertising pictures for non-theatrical distribution to schools, clubs, civic organizations, and teaching groups, as well as television.

THE AHERN GROUP
(Produces videos for the Federal Government)
3700 Malden Ave., Baltimore, MD 21211. (410) 367-9660. FAX: (410) 367-9661. email: videoahern@aol.com
PRESIDENT/TREASURER
Donald A'Hern

BUENA VISTA NON-THEATRICAL
(Film Distributor)
3900 W. Alameda Ave., #2412, Burbank, CA 91505. (818) 567-5058. FAX: (818) 557-0797.
S.V.P., NON-THEATRICAL
Linda Palmer

CAMERON PRODUCTIONS, INC.
(Corporate films, videos & commercials)
222 Minor Ave. N., Seattle, WA 98109. (206) 623-4103. FAX: (206) 623-7256. email: office@cameronproductions.com
PRESIDENT
R. Scott Cameron

CAROUSEL FILMS, INC.
(Distribution)
250 Fifth Ave., Rm. 204, New York, NY 10001. (800) 683-1660, (212) 683-1660. FAX: (212) 683-1662.
www.carouselfilms.com email: carousel@pipeline.com
PRESIDENT
David Dash

CAVALCADE PRODUCTIONS, INC.
(Clinical training videos for mental health professionals)
P.O. Box 2480, Nevada City, CA 95959-1948. TEL/FAX: (530) 477-0701. www.nccn.net/~cavpro email: cavpro@nccn.net
PRODUCER/DIRECTOR
Bruce McCulley

CIFEX CORPORATION
(Foreign films & productions)
One Peconic Hills Ct., Southampton, NY 11968-1618. (631) 283-9454, FAX: (631) 283-4210. email: cifex@prodigy.net
PRESIDENT
Gerald J. Rappaport

CONTINENTAL FILM PRODUCTIONS CORP.
(Film & video producers/audio visual installations)
4315 North Creek Rd., P.O. Box 5126, Chattanooga, TN 37406. (423) 622-1193. FAX: (423) 629-0853. www.continentalfilm.com
email: cfpc@chattanooga.net
PRESIDENT
James L. Webster

CRAVEN FILM CORPORATION
(Documentaries & industrials, United Nations films)
5 W. 19 St., 3rd Flr., New York, NY 10011-4216. (212) 463-7190. FAX: (212) 627-4761. email: TCFC@aol.com
PRESIDENT
Michael Craven

FILMS FOR EDUCATORS/FILMS FOR TV
(Cardiac angiogram duplication, digital to film, and pre-post production services.)
420 E. 55th St., Ste. 6-U, New York, NY 10022. (800) 722-7340, (212) 486-6577. FAX: (212) 980-9826.
PRESIDENT
Harlan B. DeBell

HARDCASTLE FILMS & VIDEO
(Beta-cam SP production)
7319 Wise Ave., St. Louis, MO 63117. (314) 647-4200. FAX: (314) 647-4201.
DIRECTOR
Jeff Hardcastle

HUGH & SUZANNE JOHNSTON, INC.
(Educational & documentaries)
16 Valley Rd., Princeton, NJ 08540. (609) 924-7505.
email: suzanneandhugh@earthlink.net
PRESIDENT
Hugh Johnston
VICE PRESIDENT
Suzanne Johnston

LEE MENDELSON FILM PRODUCTIONS, INC.
(TV productions)
330 Primrose Rd., Ste 310, Burlingame, CA 94010. (650) 342-8284. FAX: (650) 342-6170.
PRESIDENT
Lee Mendelson

NFL FILMS, INC.
One NFL Plaza, Mt. Laurel, NJ 08054. (856) 222-3500. www.nfl.com
PRESIDENT
Steve Sabol

PENFIELD PRODUCTIONS, INC.
(Film & video production)
35 Springfield St., Agawam, MA 01001. (413) 786-4454. FAX: (413) 789-4240. www.penfieldprod.com
PRESIDENT
Brook Ashby

PLAYHOUSE PICTURES
(Specializes in animated tv commercials)
1401 N. La Brea Ave., Hollywood, CA 90028. (323) 851-2112. FAX: (323) 851-2117. email: playpix@aol.com
PRESIDENT
Ted Woolery

SWAIN FILM & VIDEO
(Industrial and other video productions)
1404 South Tuttle Ave., Sarasota, FL 34239. (941) 365-8433. FAX: (941) 365-5359. email: swain@excelonline.com
PRESIDENT
Tony Swain

SWANK MOTION PICTURES, INC.
(Film & video distributor)
201 S. Jefferson Ave., St. Louis, MO 63103. (314) 534-6300. FAX: (314) 289-2187. www.swank.com
PRESIDENT
Tim Swank

TR PRODUCTIONS, INC.
(Video presentations for corporate communications)
1031 Commonwealth Ave., Boston, MA 02215-1094. (617) 783-0200. FAX: (617) 783-4844.
PRESIDENT
Ross Benjamin

TEL-AIR INTEREST, INC.
(Film producers)
2040 Sherman St., Hollywood, FL 33020. (954) 924-4949. FAX: (954) 924-4980. email: telair@aol.com
PRESIDENT
Grant H. Gravitt, Jr.

VAN VLIET MEDIA
(Digital transfers video-to-film/computer to film/spots, shorts & features/cardiac angiogram dup. for film, digital & video)
(A Film for Educators Company) 420 E. 55th St., Ste. 6-U, New York, NY 10022. (800) 722-7340, (212) 486-6577. FAX: (212) 980-9826.
www.vanvlietmedia.com email: vanvlietmedia@att.net
PRESIDENT
Harlan B. DeBell

WEST GLEN COMMUNICATIONS, INC.
(Film & video producers & distributers specializing in educational)
1430 Broadway, 9th Flr, New York, NY 10018. (212) 921-2800. FAX: (212) 944-9055.
PRESIDENT
Stan Zeitlin

WEXLER FILM PRODUCTIONS, INC.
(Sponsored films: specializing in educational and instructional)
801 N. Seward St., Los Angeles, CA 90038-3601. (323) 462-6671. FAX: (323) 463-5443.

PRODUCTION
SERVICES

■

ADVERTISING & PUBLICITY

ADMARKETING, INC.
1801 Century Park E., Ste. 2000, Los Angeles, CA 90067. (310)
203-8400. FAX: (310) 277-7621. www.admarketing.com
PRESIDENT
Jack Roth

AD PLANET
3952 Main St., Manchester, VT 05254. (800) 288-7678, (802)
366-9145. FAX: (800) 434-3738, (802) 366-8133.
www.adplanet.net email: info@adplanet.net
PRESIDENT
Jon Liebling

ADSPOSURE ADVERTISING SPECIALTIES
209 W. Alameda Ave., Ste. 102, Burbank, CA 91502. (818) 559-
6304. FAX: (818) 563-6423. www.adsposure.com
email: adposureadv@aol.com
PRESIDENT
Mimi Van Horn

AMBERGATE ASSOCIATES
3000 W. Olympic Blvd., Santa Monica, CA 90404. (310) 264-
3970. FAX: (310) 264-3973. www.ambergate.net
CONTACT
Eddie Kalish

**AMERICAN ASSOCIATION OF ADVERTISING AGENCIES,
INC. (A.A.A.A.)**
130 Battery St., Ste. 330, San Francisco, CA 94111. (415) 291-
4999. FAX: (415) 291-4995. www.aaaa.org
email: jerryg@aaaa.org
EXECUTIVE V.P.
Jerry L. Gibbons

AMOROSANO ASSOCIATES
1153 Paseo del Mar., San Pedro, CA 90731. (310) 548-8400.
FAX: (310) 548-1735. email: amorprla@aol.com
CONTACT
Ken Amorosano

THE ANGELLOTTI COMPANY
12423 Ventura Ct., Ste. 200, Studio City, CA 91604. (818) 506-
7887. FAX: (818) 506-8822. email: Tony@angelcopr.com
PRESIDENT
Tony Angellotti
SENIOR PUBLICISTS
Katie Martin
Emmy Chang

ANT FARM
910 N. Sycamore Ave., Los Angeles, CA 90038. (323) 850-
0700. FAX: (323) 850-0777.

APOGEE PRODUCTIONS
10000 Riverside Dr., Ste. 6, Toluca Lake, CA 91602. (818) 762-
6556. FAX: (818) 762-6559.
email: ricko@apogeeproductions.com
PRESIDENT
Rick Ouellette

THE ARENAS ENTERTAINMENT
(Specializing in the Hispanic market)
100 N. Crescent Dr., Garden Level, Beverly Hills, CA 90210.
(310) 385-4401. FAX: (310) 385-4402.
email: info@areasgroup.com
PRESIDENT& CEO
Santiago Pozo

JANE AYER PUBLIC RELATIONS, INC.
3205 Ocean Park Blvd., Ste. 240, Santa Monica, CA 90405.
(310) 581-1330. FAX: (310) 581-1335. email: japr@japr.com

BABLOVE AGENCY, INC.
220 E. Speedway Blvd., Tucson, AZ 85705. (520) 322-9060.
www.bablove.com

BAKER, WINOKUR, RYDER
9100 Wilshire Blvd., 6th Flr., West Tower, Beverly Hills, CA
90212. (310) 550-7776. FAX: (310) 550-1701.
909 Third Ave., 9th Flr., New York, NY 10022. (212) 582-0700.
FAX: (212) 901-3995.

BARCLAY COMMUNICATIONS
3845 N. 44th St., Phoenix, AZ 85018. (602) 277-3550. FAX:
(602) 277-1217.
email: mary_ohanlon@barclaycommunications.com
PRESIDENT
Mary O'Hanlon

BARTEL DESIGN GROUP
2820 Glendale Blvd., Los Angeles, CA 90039. (323) 662-6869.
FAX: (323) 662-2026. www.barteldesign.com
email: jane@barteldesign.com
PRESIDENT & CREATIVE DIRECTOR
Jane Bartel

BBDO LOS ANGELES
10960 Wilshire Blvd., #1600, Los Angeles, CA 90024. (310)
444-4500. FAX: (310) 478-7581. www.bbdo.com

BBDO WORLDWIDE
1285 Ave. of the Americas, New York, NY 10019. (212) 459-
5000.

BEAR ADVERTISING, INC.
32121 Lindero Canyon Rd., Ste. 200, Westlake Village, CA
91361. (818) 865-6464. FAX: (818) 865-6499. www.bearadv.com
email: info@bearadv.com
PRESIDENT
Bruce Bear

BENDER/HELPER IMPACT
11500 W. Olympic Blvd., Ste. 655, Los Angeles, CA 90064.
(310) 473-4147. FAX: (310) 473-7118.
OFFICE MANAGER
Becky Bourn

WALTER BENNETT COMMUNICATIONS
(Motion Picture Distributor)
1787 Sentry Pkwy. W., Bldg. 16, Ste. 450, Blue Bell, PA 19422.
(215) 591-9400. FAX: (215) 591-9420.
SENIOR V.P.
Jack Hibbard

BLOCK-KORENBROT PUBLIC RELATIONS
8271 Melrose Ave., Ste. 200, Los Angeles, CA 90046. (323)
655-0593. FAX: (323) 655-7302. email: press@bk-pr.com

MICHELLE BOLTON & ASSOCIATES
(818) 990-4001. FAX: (818) 990-1540.
email: boltonpr@pacbell.net
CONTACT
Michelle Bolton

BRAGMAN HYMAN CAFARELLI
9171 Wilshire Blvd., Ste. 300, Beverly Hills, CA 90210. (310)
274-7800. FAX: (310) 274-7838.
email: fw@bncpr.com
CONTACT
Felicia Walker

BRAMSON & ASSOCIATES
7400 Beverly Blvd., Los Angeles, CA 90036. (323) 938-3595.
FAX: (323) 938-0852.

BRICKMAN MARKETING
395 Del Monte Ctr., #250, Monterey, CA 93940. (831) 633-4444.
FAX: (831) 633-4499. www.brickmanmarketing.com
OWNER
Wendy Brickman

THE BROKAW COMPANY
9255 Sunset Blvd., #804, Los Angeles, CA 90069. (310) 273-
2060. FAX: (310) 276-4037. email: brokawc@aol.com
PARTNERS
David Brokaw
Sanford Brokaw

BUMBLE WARD & ASSOCIATES
8383 Wilshire Blvd., Ste 340, Beverly Hills, CA 90211. (323)
655-8585. FAX: (323) 655-8844.

LEO BURNETT COMPANY, INC.
35 W. Wacker Dr., Chicago, IL 60601. (312) 220-5959.
FAX: (312) 220-3299. www.leoburnett.com
10900 Wilshire Blvd., Ste. 700, Los Angeles, CA 90024. (310)
443-2000. FAX: (310) 208-5984.

BURSON-MARSTELLER
230 Park Ave. S., New York, NY 10003-1566. (212) 614-4000.
FAX: (212) 614-4084. (Advertising Dept.)
1800 Century Park E., Ste. 200, Los Angeles, CA 90067. (310)
226-3000. FAX: (310) 226-3030.
CO-FOUNDER (NY)
Harold Burson
PRESIDENT &CEO, USA
Chet Burchett
PRESIDENT & CEO, WORLDWIDE
Chris Komisarjevsky

JON BYK ADVERTISING, INC.
140 S. Barrington Ave., Los Angeles, CA 90049. (310) 476-3012. FAX: (310) 476-3016. www.bykadvertising.com
PRESIDENT
Tim Byk

CARAT
Three Park Ave., New York, NY 10016. (212) 252 0050. FAX: (212) 252-1250. www.carat-na.com
email: crutman@carat-na.com
CONTACT
Charlie Rutman

CLICK ACTIVE MEDIA, INC.
2644 30th St., 2nd Flr., Santa Monica, CA 90405. (310) 581-4000. FAX: (310) 581-4004. www.clickmedia.com
email: bizdev@clickmedia.com
V.P., SALES & MARKETING
Cheryl Bennett

CMG WORLDWIDE
10500 Cross Point Blvd., Indianapolis, IN 46256. (317) 570-5000. FAX: (317) 570-5500. www.cmgww.com
FOUNDER
Mark Roesler

COMMUNICATIONS PLUS, INC.
102 Madison Ave. S., 7th Flr., New York, NY 10016. (212) 686-9570. FAX: (212) 686-9687.

CONSOLIDATED ADVERTISING DIRECTORS, INC.
8060 Melrose Ave., Ste. 300, Los Angeles, CA 90046. (323) 653-8060. FAX: (323) 655-9452 email: info@psiemail.com
PRESIDENT
Bentley Morriss

CREATIVE IGNITION
9107 Wilshire Blvd, Mezz, Beverly Hills, CA 90210. (310) 272-1160. FAX: (310) 272-1161. www.creativeignition.com

CREATIVE PRODUCTIONS
4510 E. Pacific Coast Hwy., Ste. 500, Long Beach, CA 90804. (562) 985-1363. FAX: (562) 985-1365.
www.creativeproductions.com
CONTACTS
Robert Peterson
Deborah Castro

CUSHMAN AMBERG COMMUNICATIONS
180 N. Michigan Ave., Ste. 1600, Chicago, IL 60601. (312) 263-2500. FAX: (312) 263-1197.

DAVISELEN ADVERTISING, INC.
865 S. Figueroa St., 12th Flr., Los Angeles, CA 90017. (213) 688-7000. FAX: (213) 688-7288. www.daviselen.com
CEO
Mark Davis
PRESIDENT
Bob Elen

DDB WORLDWIDE, INC.
437 Madison Ave., New York, NY 10022. (212) 415-2000. FAX: (212) 415-3414. www.ddb.com
PRESIDENT & CEO
Ken Kaes

DOREMUS & COMPANY
200 Varick St., 11th Flr., New York, NY 10014. (212) 366-3000. FAX: (212) 366-3060.
530 Bush St., 7th Flr., San Francisco, CA 94108. (415) 398-5699. FAX: (415) 398-0854. www.doremus.com
CONTACT (CA)
Garrett Lawrence
PRESIDENT & CEO (NY)
Carl Anderson

LARRY DORN ASSOCIATES, INC.
(Product placements)
5820 Wilshire Blvd., Ste. 306, Los Angeles, CA 90036. (323) 935-6266. FAX: (323) 935-9523. email: lda_la@msn.com
PRESIDENT
Larry Dorn
CONTACT
Lucy Kohn

EBC ENTERTAINMENT MARKETING
(Consultant)
4465 Nogales Dr., Tarzana, CA 91356. (818) 776-8035. FAX: (818) 776-8108. email: tedlor@aol.com
PRESIDENT
Gene Cofsky

E SQUARED
3335 Deronda Dr., Los Angeles, CA 90068. (310) 278-0669. FAX: (323) 467-1130. www.e2-communications.com
DIRECTOR OF ACCOUNTS
John Ellis

EDELMAN PUBLIC RELATIONS WORLDWIDE
5670 Wilshire Blvd., 22nd Flr., Los Angeles, CA 90036. (323) 857-9100. FAX: (323) 857-9117. www.edelman.com
email: los.angeles@edelman.com
CEO
Richard Edelman
EXECUTIVE V.P./GENERAL MANAGER LOS ANGELES
Gail Becker

MAX EISEN
234 W. 44th St., 7th Flr., Ste. 700, New York, NY 10036. (212) 391-1072. FAX: (212) 391-4004. email: maxeisen@aol.com

11:24 DESIGN ADVERTISING, INC.
322 Culver Blvd., Ste. 211, Playa del Rey, CA 90293. (310) 821-1775. FAX: (310) 821-1972. www.1124design.com
CEO
Art Simms

EMA MULTIMEDIA, INC.
1800 Ave. of the Stars, Ste. 430, Century City, CA 90067. (310) 277-7379. FAX: (310) 277-7378. www.emamulti.com

ENTERTAINMENT COMMUNICATIONS NETWORK
4370 Tujunga Ave., Ste. 210, Studio City, CA 91604. (818) 752-1400. www.ecnmedia.com

EURO RSCG TATHAM PARTNERS
36 E. Grand Ave., Chicago, IL 60611. (312) 337-4400. FAX: (312) 337-2316. www.eurorscgtatham.com
CHIEF CREATIVE
Jim Schmidt

FARON MELROSE
Administrative: 19925 Stevens Creek Blvd., Cupertino, CA 95014. (408) 973-7883.
Creative: 275 Saratoga Ave., Ste. 160, Santa Clara, CA 95050. (408) 615-5777. FAX: (408) 615-5778.
www.faronmelrose.com   email: info@faronmelrose.com
PRESIDENT/ACCOUNT SUPERVISOR
Penny F. Melrose
V.P., MEDIA & RESEARCH
Richard D. Melrose
V.P., CREATIVE & PRODUCTION
Michael Scandling

FELDMAN PUBLIC RELATIONS
13636 Ventura Blvd., #440 Sherman Oaks, CA 91423. (310) 859-9062.

FOOTE, CONE & BELDING COMMUNICATIONS, INC.
101 E. Erie St., Chicago, IL 60611-2897. (312) 425-5000. FAX: (312) 425-5010. CA: (949) 851-3050. NY: (212) 885-3000.
www.fcb.com
PRESIDENT & COO, NORTH AMERICA
Gene Bartley

B. D. FOX & FRIENDS, INC. ADVERTISING
1111 Broadway, Santa Monica, CA 90401. (310) 394-7150. FAX: (310) 393-1569. www.bdfox.com email: info@bdfox.com
PRESIDENT & CEO
Brian D. Fox

FRIES MULTIMEDIA, INC.
1828 Broadway, Santa Monica, CA 90404. (310) 396-3988. FAX: (310) 399-2120. email: dyfries@aol.com
PRESIDENT
Dyanne Fries

GARD AND GERBER
209 S.W. Oak St., Ste. 200, Portland, OR 97204. (800) 800-7132, (503) 221-0100. FAX: (503) 221-6928.
www.gardandgerber.com
PRESIDENT & CEO
Brian Gard
EXECUTIVE V.P.
Duncan Strang

GORDON GELFOND ASSOCIATES
9171 Wilshire Blvd., Ste. 441, Beverly Hills, CA 90210. (310) 205-5534. FAX: (310) 205-5587. email: ggelfond@aol.com
PRESIDENT
Gordon Gelfond

GOLIN/HARRIS COMMUNICATIONS
601 W. 5th St., 4th Flr., Los Angeles, CA 90071. (213) 623-4200. FAX: (213) 895-4745. www.golinharris.com
111 E. Wacker Dr., Chicago, IL 60601. (312) 729-4000.
CHAIRMAN (IL)
Al Golin
CEO (IL)
Rich Jernstedt
GENERAL MANAGER (CA)
Judy Johnson

GREY WORLDWIDE
777 Third Ave., New York, NY 10017. (212) 546-2000. FAX: (212) 546-1495. www.grey.com
6100 Wilshire Blvd., 9th Flr., Los Angeles, CA 90048. (323) 936-6060.
CHAIRMAN & CEO (NY)
Edward H. Meyer

GS ENTERTAINMENT MARKETING GROUP
522 N. Larchmont Blvd., Los Angeles, CA 90004. (323) 860-0270. FAX: (323) 860-0279.
CONTACT
Steven Zeller

GUTTMAN ASSOCIATES
118 S. Beverly Dr., Ste. 201, Beverly Hills, CA 90212. (310) 246-4600. FAX: (310) 246-4601.

HANSON & SCHWAM
9350 Wilshire Blvd., Ste. 315, Beverly Hills, CA 90212. (310) 248-4488. FAX: (310) 248-4499.

BERNARD HODES ADVERTISING
220 E. 42nd St., New York, NY 10017. (212) 999-9299. FAX: (212) 999-9484. CA: (310) 575-4000. FAX: (310) 482-4302.
www.hodes.com email: info@hodes.com
BRANCH MANAGER (NY)
Philip Gentile
BRANCH MANAGER (L.A.)
Susan Edwards

HOFFMAN & ASSOCIATES
429 Santa Monica Blvd., Ste. 620, Santa Monica, CA 90401. (310) 656-3430. FAX: (310) 656-3425.

THE HOLLYWOOD-MADISON GROUP
11684 Ventura Blvd., Ste. 258, Studio City, CA 91604. (818) 762-8008. FAX: (818) 762-8089. www.hollywood-madison.com
PRESIDENT & CEO
Jonathan Holiff

HORIZON MEDIA, INC.
1940 Century Park E., 3rd Flr., Los Angeles, CA 90067. (310) 282-0909. FAX: (310) 277-9692. www.horizonmedia.com

IMAGINARY FORCES
6526 Sunset Blvd., Hollywood, CA 90028. (323) 957-6868. FAX: (323) 957-9577. www.imaginaryforces.com
530 W. 25th St., 5th Flr., New York, NY 10001. (646) 486-6868. FAX: (646) 486-4700.

INFOMERCIAL SOLUTIONS, INC.
5512 Meadow Vista Way, Agoura Hills, CA 91301. (818) 879-1140. FAX: (818) 879-1148. www.infomercialsolutions.com
PRESIDENT
David Schwartz

INITIATIVE MEDIA
5700 Wilshire Blvd., Ste. 400, Los Angeles, CA 90036. (323) 370-8000. FAX: (323) 370-8950. www.im-na.com

INTER/MEDIA ADVERTISING
15760 Ventura Blvd., Ste. 110, Encino, CA 91436. (818) 995-1455. www.intermedia-advertising.com

INTERNET IMPACT
P.O. Box 10207, Beverly Hills, CA 90213. (310) 962-7949. www.internetimpact.com

JENSEN COMMUNICATIONS, INC.
709 E. Colorado, Ste. 220, Pasadena, CA 91101. (626) 585-9575. FAX: (626) 564-8920.

KAISER COMMUNICATIONS, INC
11430 Ventura Blvd., Studio City, CA 91604. (818) 505-6150. FAX: (818) 505-6155. www.kaisercomm.com
PRESIDENT
David Kaiser

KAISER MARKETING
1631 Pontius Ave., Los Angeles, CA 90025. (310) 479-8999. FAX: (310) 479-8006. www.kaisermarketing.com

KAPLAN THALER GROUP, LTD.
Worldwide Plaza, 825 Eighth Ave., New York, NY 10019-7498. (212) 474-5000. FAX: (212) 474-5036.
www.kaplanthalergroup.com
CEO
Linda Kaplan Thaler

BILL LANESE & ASSOCIATES
2164 Hyde St., Ste. 201, San Francisco, CA 94109. (415) 543-8000. FAX: (415) 561-0966.

LEE & ASSOCIATES, INC.
145 S. Fairfax Ave., Ste. 301 Los Angeles, CA 90036. (323) 938-3300. FAX: (323) 938-3305. www.leeassociates.com
CONTACT
Leo Pearlstein

LEVINSON ASSOCIATES
(International marketing support)
1440 Veteran Ave., Ste. 650, Los Angeles, CA 90024. (323) 663-6940. FAX: (323) 663-2820. email: leviinc@aol.com
CONTACT
Jed Leland, Jr.

LIPPIN GROUP INC.
6100 Wilshire Blvd., #400, Los Angeles, CA 90048. (323) 965-1990. FAX: (323) 965-1993. www.lippingroup.com
email: losangeles@lippingroup.com
PRESIDENT
Richard Lippin

LOW WORLDWIDE (FORMERLY BOZELL)
28 W 23rd St., New York, NY 10010. (212) 727-5000. FAX: (212) 645-9262.
CEO
Tom Bernardin

MACY & ASSOCIATES
411 Culver Blvd., Playa del Rey, CA 90293. (310) 821-5300. FAX: (310) 821-8178. www.macyinc.com

MARCUS THOMAS LLC
24865 Emery Rd., Cleveland, OH 44128. (216) 292-4700. FAX: (216) 378-0396. email: askus@marcusthomasad.com
CHAIRMAN EMERITUS
Donald M. Marcus
CHAIRMAN
Harvey L. Scholnick

MARKHAM/NOVELL COMMUNICATIONS, LTD.
211 E. 43rd St., Ste. 1102, New York, NY 10017. (800) 762-4761, (212) 687-1765. FAX: (212) 687-1978.
www.markhamnovell.com email: info@markhamnovell.com
CONTACT
Arthur Novell

MARLIN ENTERTAINMENT GROUP
767 3rd Ave., 14th Flr., New York, NY 10017. (212) 888-5890. FAX: (212) 888-5896. www.marlinent.com
email: marlinet@idt.net

MCCANN-ERICKSON, INC.
622 Third Ave., New York, NY 10017. (646) 865-2000.
6300 Wilshire Blvd., Ste. 2100, Los Angeles, CA 90048. (323) 655-9420. www.mccann.com
CHAIRMAN
James Heekin

MINDSHARE MEDIA
32029 Point Pl., Laguna Beach, CA 92651. (949) 717-6464. FAX: (949) 717-6463.

DAVID MIRISCH
2121 Newcastle Ave., Ste. A, Cardiff, CA 92007. (760) 632-7770. FAX: (760) 632-5408. www.davidmirisch.com

MOMENTUM INTERNATIONAL MARKETING MANAGEMENT
P.O. Box 5889, Sherman Oaks, CA 91413. (818) 752-4500. FAX: (818) 752-4554. email: momentumllc@compuserve.com

MOROCH LEO BURNETT USA
3625 N. Hall St., #1100, Dallas, TX 75219. (214) 520-9700. FAX: (214) 520-5611. www.moroch.com
email: art@moroch.com; action@moroch.com
MANAGING DIRECTOR
Jack Phifer email: jphifer@moroch.com

MOTION PICTURE PLACEMENT
(Product placement and promotional tie-ins)
10625 Chandler Blvd., N. Hollywood, CA 91601. (818) 760-2319. FAX: (818) 760-2904. email: JHenrie@msn.com
PRINCIPAL
Joel Henrie

JULIAN MYERS PUBLIC RELATIONS
5757 W. Century Blvd., Ste. 700, 7th Flr., Los Angeles, CA 90045-6408. (310) 827-9089. FAX: (310) 827-9838.
www.julianmyerspr.com email: julian@julianmyers-pr.com
CEO & OWNER
Julian Myers

NATIONWIDE ADVERTISING SERVICE, INC.
15303 Ventura Blvd., Ste. 1050, Sherman Oaks, CA 91403. (818) 906-3313.

NEALE ADVERTISING ASSOCIATES
10201 Riverside Dr., Ste. 200, Toluca Lake, CA 91602. (818) 508-7003. FAX: (818) 508-3141. email: TEDN236302@aol.com
PRESIDENT
Ted Neale

NEW WAVE ENTERTAINMENT
2660 W. Olive Ave., Burbank, CA 91505. (818) 295-5000. FAX: (818) 295-5001.

OGILVY & MATHER, INC.
309 W. 49th St., New York, NY 10019. (212) 237-4000.
FAX: (212) 237-5123. www.ogilvy.com
3530 Hayden Ave., Culver City, CA 90232. (310) 280-2200.
FAX: (310) 280-2699.
CHIEF MARKETING OFFICER
Eleanor Mascheroni email: eleanor.mascheroni@ogilvy.com
DIRECTOR, BUSINESS DEVELOPMENT
Patrick Keyes email: patrick.keyes@ogilvy.com

DALE C. OLSON & ASSOCIATES
7420 Mulholland Dr., Los Angeles, CA 90046. TEL/FAX: (323)
876-9331. email: dolson2000@aol.com
PRESIDENT
Dale Olson

OLSON BALLARD COMMUNICATIONS
1850 E. Flamingo Rd., Ste. 120, Las Vegas, NV 89119. (800)
864-2792, (702) 836-3000. FAX: (702) 836-3003.

PARROT MEDIA NETWORK
2917 N. Ontario St., Burbank, CA 91504. (818) 567-4700. FAX:
(818) 567-4600. www.parrotmedia.com
PRESIDENT & CEO
Bob Mertz

PASADENA ADVERTISING
51 W. Dayton St., Ste. 100, Pasadena, CA 91105. (626) 584-
0011. FAX: (626) 584-0907. www.pasadenaadv.com
PRESIDENT & CEO
Suzanne Marks
V.P., CREATIVE
J. Anthony Nino

PLA MEDIA WEST
11959 Hatteras St., N. Hollywood, CA 91607. (818) 761-7171.
FAX: (818) 761-7175. www.plamedia.com
email: west-coast@plamedia.com
1303 16th Ave., S. Nashville, TN 37212. (615) 327-0100. FAX:
(615) 320-1061. email: east-coast@plamedia.com

PMK, INC.
8500 Wilshire Blvd., Ste. 700, Beverly Hills, CA 90211. (310)
289-6200. FAX: (310) 289-6677.
650 Fifth Ave., 33rd Flr., New York, NY 10019. (212) 582-1111.
FAX: (212) 582-6666.

THE POLLACK PR MARKETING GROUP
1901 Ave. of the Stars, Ste. 1040, Los Angeles, CA 90067.
(310) 556-4443. FAX: (310) 286-2350. www.ppmgcorp.com
email: info@ppmgcorp.com
PRESIDENT & CEO
Noemi Pollack

PORTER/NOVELLI
10960 Wilshire Blvd., Ste. 1750, Los Angeles, CA 90024. (310)
444-7000. FAX: (310) 444-7004. www.porternovelli.com
GENERAL MANAGER
Bill Kolberg (310) 444-7060 email: bkolberg@porternovelli.com

P.O.V.
11024 Magnolia Blvd., Ste. C, N. Hollywood, CA 91601. (818)
506-3866. FAX: (818) 506-3860. www.povdesign.net
email: dmeltzer@poventdesign.com
PRESIDENT
Duane Meltzer

PR NEWSWIRE
865 S. Figueroa St., Ste. 2500, Los Angeles, CA 90017. (800)
321-8169, (213) 626-5500. FAX: (213) 488-1152.
www.prnewswire.com

PUBLIC RELATIONS ASSOCIATES
557 Norwich Dr., Los Angeles, CA 90048. (310) 659-0380. FAX:
(310) 659-5270.

THE RALEIGH GROUP
Promote Yourself PR & Seminars, P.O. Box 701, Carefree, AZ
85377. (800)249-7322. www.promoteyourself.com
email: raleigh@promoteyourself.com

REGBERG & ASSOCIATES, INC.
10850 Wilshire Blvd., Ste. 301, Los Angeles, CA 90024. (310)
475-5735. FAX: (310) 470-3101.
PRESIDENT
Scott Regberg

MEDIA EDGE CIA
9440 Santa Monica Blvd., Ste 710, Beverly Hills, CA 90210.
(310) 273-2912. FAX: (310) 276-8950.

ROGERS & COWAN
1888 Century Park E., Ste. 500, Los Angeles, CA 90067-1709.
(310) 201-8800. FAX: (310) 788-6611.
640 5th Ave., 5th Flr., New York, NY 10019. (212) 445-8400.
FAX: (212) 445-8290. www.rogersandcowan.com
CEO
Tom Tardio email: ttardio@rogersandcowan.com

STAN ROSENFIELD & ASSOCIATES
2029 Century Park E., Ste. 1190, Los Angeles, CA 90067. (310)
286-7474. FAX: (310) 286-2255.

RUDEHONEY DESIGN GROUP
Corporate: 675 Fairview Dr. Ste. 246, Carson City, NV 89701.
FAX: (775) 882-8924.
2031 Vinca Way, Oxnard, CA 93030. (310) 589-9640. FAX: (818)
540-4251. www.rudehoney.com email: frank@rudehoney.com
V.P., SALES & MARKETING
Frank Celecia

SAATCHI & SAATCHI ADVERTISING
375 Hudson St., New York, NY 10014-3620. (212) 463-2000.
FAX: (212) 463-9855. www.saatchiny.com
CORPORATE COMMUNICATIONS
Chris Traina (212) 463-3647 email: ctraina@saatchiny.com
NEW BUSINESS
Bob McKinnon (212) 463-2613 email: bmckinnon@saatchiny.com
CEO, WORLDWIDE
Kevin Roberts

SAATCHI & SAATCHI LOS ANGELES
3501 Sepulveda Blvd., Torrance, CA 90505. (310) 214-6000.
FAX: (310) 214-6160. www.saatchila.com
PRESIDENT & COO
Rich Anderman

SCREENVISION CINEMA NETWORK
Corporate: 1411 Broadway, New York, NY 10018. (800) 724-
MOVIE, (212) 497-0400. FAX: (212) 497-0500.
3000 Ocean Park Blvd., Ste. 1008, Santa Monica, CA 90405.
(310) 450-2577. www.screenvision.com
PRESIDENT & CEO
Matthew Kearney
COO & CFO
Alan Burge
E.V.P., THEATRE OPERATIONS & EXHIBITOR RELATIONS
Darryl Schaffer
E.V.P., SALES & MARKETING
Todd Siegel
S.V.P. & G.M., SCREENVISION DIRECT
Heather Williams

SCORZA DESIGN & MARKETING
5246 Agnes Ave., Unit 204, Valley Village, CA 91607. (818) 762-
0068. FAX: (818) 762-1806.

NANCY SELTZER & ASSOCIATES
485 7th Ave., Ste. 1011, New York, NY 10018. (212) 307-0117.
FAX: (212) 307-0182.

SGI MARKETING
18034 Ventura Blvd., Ste. 275, Encino, CA 91316. (818) 343-
3669.
PRESIDENT
Brian Scott

SIMONS MICHELSON ZIEVE, INC.
900 Wilshire Dr., Troy, MI 48084-1600. (248) 362-4242. FAX:
(248) 362-2014. www.smz.com
CHAIRMAN
Morton Zieve

SPG
5636 Tujunga Ave., N. Hollywood, CA 91601. (818) 506-7902.

SOUTH BAY STUDIOS
20434 S. Santa Fe Ave., Long Beach, CA 90810. (310) 762-
1360. (310) 639-2055. www.southbaystudios.com
email: info@southbaystudios.com
CONTACT
Rick Gamarra

THE SPARK FACTORY
10 East Colorado Blvd. , Pasadena, CA 91105. (626) 397-2719.
FAX: (626) 397-2732. www.sparkfactory.com
email: tim@sparkfactory.com
PRESIDENT
Tim Street

SPELLING COMMUNICATIONS
2211 Corinth Ave., Ste. 210, Los Angeles, CA 90064. (310) 477-
9500. FAX: (310) 477-9530. www.spellcom.com
email: info@spellcom.com
CEO
Daniel Spelling

SSA PUBLIC RELATIONS
16027 Ventura Blvd., Ste. 206, Encino, CA 91436. (818) 501-
0700. FAX: (818) 501-7216. www.ssapr.com
148 Madison Ave., 16th Flr. PH-1, New York, NY 10016. (212)
679-4750. FAX: (212) 679-4725.
CEO
Steve Syatt

STUDIO CITY
3330 Cahuenga Blvd., Ste. 307, Los Angeles, CA 90068. (818)
557-7777. FAX: (818) 557-6777. www.studiocity.com
Studio City, NY. (212) 777-5755. FAX: (212) 777-5559.
PRESIDENT
Stu Weiss

SUDLER & HENNESSEY, INC.
230 Park Ave. S., 8th Flr., New York, NY 10003. (212) 614-4100.
FAX: (212) 598-6930.
CHAIRMAN & CEO
Jed Beitler

TARGET ENTERPRISES
16501 Ventura Blvd., Ste. 515, Encino, CA 91436. (818) 905-
0005. FAX: (818) 905-1444.

T.G.I.F. COMMUNICATIONS
41 Sea Colony Dr., Santa Monica, CA 90405. (310) 314-1111.
www.tgifproductions.com
CONTACT
Bob Friday

30SIXTY DESIGN, INC.
2801 Cahuenga Blvd. W., Los Angeles, CA 90068. (323) 850-
5311. www.30sixtydesign.com

J. WALTER THOMPSON COMPANY
466 Lexington Ave., New York, NY 10017. (212) 210-7000. FAX:
(212) 210-7770. www.jwt.com
6500 Wilshire Blvd., Ste. 2100, Los Angeles, CA 90048. (323)
951-1500. FAX: (323) 655-3181.
PRESIDENT & CEO
Peter Schweitzer
PRESIDENT (CA)
Jerry McGee

TIERNEY COMMUNICATIONS
200 S. Broad St., Philadelphia, PA 19102. (215) 790-4100. FAX:
(215) 790-4373. www.tierneyagency.com
FOUNDER & CHAIRMAN
Brian P. Tierney
CEO
Scott Franks
PRESIDENT
Mary Stengel Austen
E.V.P. & GENERAL MANAGER, PUBLIC RELATIONS
Steve Albertini

TMG INTERNATIONAL
499 N. Canon Dr., Penthouse, Beverly Hills, CA 90210. (310)
887-7067. FAX: (310) 887-7078.

TRACY-LOCKE PARTNERSHIP
1999 Bryan St., Dallas, TX 75201. (214) 969-9000. www.tlp.com

TRI-ELITE ENTERTAINMENT, LTD.
9244 Wilshire Blvd., Ste. 201, Beverly Hills, CA 90212. (310)
285-9743. FAX: (310) 285-9770.
email: trielite@cs.com
PRESIDENT
Jarvee E. Hutcherson

WESTWAYNE
1170 Peachtree St. N.E., Ste. 1500, Atlanta, GA 30309. (404)
347-8700. FAX: (404) 347-8800. www.westwayne.com
email: jjohnson@westwayne.com
PRESIDENT & CEO
Jeff Johnson

VISTA GROUP
805 S. San Fernando Blvd., Burbank, CA 91502. (818) 840-
6789. FAX: (818) 840-6880. www.vistagroupusa.com
DIRECTOR OF CLIENT SERVICES
Eric C. Dahlquist, Jr.

WANG & WILLIAMS
11400 W. Olympic Blvd., 2nd Flr., Los Angeles, CA 90064. (310)
312-0124. FAX: (310) 312-0082.
CONTACTS
Ming Wang
Denise Williams

MORTON D. WAX & ASSOCIATES
1560 Broadway, Ste. 706, New York, NY 10019. (516) 466-6852.
email: mortwax@worldnet.att.net
PRESIDENT
Morton D. Wax

WHITNEY GROUP
850 3rd Ave., 11th Flr., New York, NY 10022. (212) 508-3500.
CHAIRMAN
Gary Goldstein
PRESIDENT
James H. Feeney

WINWARD ENTERTAINMENT CORPORATION
P.O. Box 2714, Malibu, CA 90265-2714. (310) 456-2627. FAX:
(310) 456-7989. email: WindEntCor@aol.com

WOLF GROUP
215 Park Ave., S., 16th Flr., New York, NY 10003. (212) 596-
0200. www.wolfgroup.com
1350 Euclid Ave., Cleveland, OH 44115. (216) 241-2141. FAX:
(216) 479-2437.
PRESIDENT (NY)
Mike Rogers
PRESIDENT (OH)
Sarah Melamed

WORD OF MOUTH CREATIVE
66 Madison Ave., Ste. 12H, New York, NY 10016. (212) 924-
8359. FAX: (212) 924-8426.
PRESIDENT
Olivia Olkowski

WORTH MENTIONING PUBLIC RELATIONS
8231 De Longpre Ave., Ste. 1, Los Angeles, CA 90046. (323)
650-7121.

YOUNG & RUBICAM, INC.
285 Madison Ave., New York, NY 10017-6486. (212) 210-3000.
FAX: (212) 490-9073. www.yandr.com
CHAIRMAN & CEO
Ann Fudge

ZERO 2 60
121 W. 27th St., Ste. 1204, New York, NY 10001. (212) 807-
7123.

ANIMATION

ANIMATION EQUIPMENT

ANIMATION TOOLWORKS
18484 S.W. Parret Mountain Rd., Sherwood, OR 97140. (877)
625-6438. FAX: (503) 925-0221. www.animationtoolworks.com
email: info@animationtoolworks.com
CONTACT
Howard Mozeico

ASSOCIATES & YAMASHITA
(Formerly Sim Ex Digital Studios. Computer animation,
graphics, digital effects and speciality venue films)
615 Hampton Dr., Ste. D302, Venice, CA 90291. (310) 664-
9500. FAX: (310) 664-9977. www.simexds.com
PRESIDENT
Allen Yamashita

CATALINA GRAPHIC FILMS
27001 Agoura Rd., Ste. 100, Calabasas Hills, CA 91301. (818)
880-8060. FAX: (818) 880-1144. www.catalinagraphicfilms.com
2976 Buford Hwy., Ste. 104, Duluth, GA 30096. (770) 232-1878.
FAX: (770) 232-7133.
870 Greenleaf Ave., Elk Grove Village, IL 60007. (800) 766-
4939, FAX: (212) 806-1340. FAX: (847)806-0296.

CHARACTER BUILDERS, INC.
1476 Manning Pkwy., Powell, OH 43065. (614) 885-2211. FAX:
(614) 885-3873. www.cbuilders.com
PRESIDENT
Jim Kammerud

CHROMACOLOUR INTERNATIONAL
1410 28th St. N.E., Calgary, Alberta T2A 7W6, Canada. (403)
250-5880. FAX: (403) 250-7194. www.chromacolour.com
email: info@chromacolour.com

CINEMA ENGINEERING COMPANY
(New & used equip. Repair & Modify motion picture cameras)
7243 Atoll Ave., Ste. A, N. Hollywood, CA 91605. (818) 765-
5340. FAX: (818) 765-5349.
PRESIDENT
Richard Bennett

DISNEY PRODUCTION SERVICES
Box 10200, Film-TV Dept., Bungalow 2, Lake Buena Vista, FL
32830. (407) 560-5736. FAX: (407) 824-5168.
VICE PRESIDENT
Bob Allen

ALAN GORDON ENTERPRISES
5625 Melrose Ave., Hollywood, CA 90038. (323) 466-3561. FAX:
(323) 871-2193. www.alangordon.com
email: info@alangordon.com
CONTACT
Grant Loucks

INTERGRAPH COMPUTER SYSTEMS
One Madison Industrial Park, Hunstville, AL 35894. (800) 345-
4856, (256) 730-2000. FAX: (256) 730-6445. www.intergraph.com

PIXEL MAGIC
10635 Riverside Dr., Toluca Lake, CA 91602. (818) 760-0862.
FAX: (818) 760-4983. www.pixelmagicfx.com
VICE PRESIDENT
Ray McIntyre, Jr.

QUANTEL, INC.
(Animation equipment)
25 West 43rd St., Ste. 222, New York, NY 10036. (212) 944
6820. FAX: (212) 944 6813. www.quantel.com
199 Elm St., New Canaan, CT 06840. (203) 972-3199. FAX:
(203) 972-3189.
CEO
Ken Ellis email: ken.ellis@quantel.com
REGIONAL SALES MANAGER (NY)
Ron Witko email: ron.witko@quantel.com

OPTICAL EFFECTS & PHOTOGRAPHY, CEL, CLAY AND DIGITAL ANIMATION

A & S ANIMATION
(Character animation & show development)
8137 Lake Crowell Circle, Orlando, FL 32836. (407) 370-2673.
FAX: (407) 370-2602. www.funnytoons.tv
PRESIDENT
Mark Simon

A LUNA BLUE
(Royalty Free Stock Footage and Images)
2163 Vista Del Mar Ave., Los Angeles, CA 90068. (323) 871-
8919. FAX: (323) 464-0502. email: info@alunablue.com;
sales@alunablue.com; raymond@alunablue.com

AARDMAN ANIMATIONS
Gas Ferry Rd., Bristol, Avon BS1 6UN ENGLAND. TEL: (01 17)
984-8485. FAX: (01 17) 984-8486. www.aardman.com
FOUNDERS
David Sproxton
Peter Lord

AARGH! ANIMATION, INC.
(Hand drawn cel and stop-motion animation)
1000 Universal Studios Plaza, Orlando, FL 32819. (407) 224-
5501. FAX: (407) 224-5503.
DIRECTOR
Dave Kallaher

ACE STORYBOARD ON DEMAND
(Storyboards, concept art & flesh animation)
31455 West St., S. Laguna Beach, CA 92677. (949) 499-9964.
FAX: (949) 499-9964. www.markpacella.com
ART DIRECTOR
Mark Pacella

ACME FILMWORKS
6525 Sunset Blvd., Garden Ste. 10, Hollywood, CA 90028. (323)
464-7805. FAX: (323) 464-6614.
www.awm.com/acmefilmworks email: ron@awm.com
EXECUTIVE PRODUCER
Ron Diamond

ACORN ENTERTAINMENT
1800 N. Vine St., Ste. 305, Hollywood, CA 90028. (818) 340-
5272, (310) 568-0781. www.acornentertainment.com
email: thad@acornentertainment.com
PRESIDENT
Thad Weinlein

ANGEL FILMS
(Computer generated)
967 Highway 40, New Franklin, MO 65274. (573) 698-3900.
FAX: (573) 698-3900.
CEO & CFO
Joyce L. Chow
V.P., PRODUCTION
Matthew P. Eastman

ANIMAL MAKERS
(Animatronic animals)
775 East Cochran St., Ste. F, Simi Valley, CA 93065. (805) 527-
6200. FAX: (805) 527-6210. www.animalmakers.com
email: jim@animalmakers.com
CONTACT
Jim Boulden

ANIMATICS & STORYBOARDS, INC.
(Live action & animated storyboards, animatics & web animation)
8137 Lake Crowell Circle, Orlando, FL 32836. (407) 370-2673.
FAX: (407) 370-2602. www.storyboards-east.com
email: mark@FunnyToons.tv
PRESIDENT
Mark Simon

ANIMATION ENTERTAINMENT
(Computer animation)
3830 Valley Centre Dr., Ste. 705, PMB 833, San Diego, CA
92130. (858) 793-1900. FAX: (858) 793-1942.
www.animationtrip.com email: steven@animationtrip.com
PRESIDENT
Steven Churchill

ANIMEKOMIX & ULTIMATE VOCAL CHALLENGE, INC.
(3D, photo realistic and anime style)
590 Hewett Dr., Orlando, FL 32807. (407) 282-5564. FAX: (407)
384-0340. www.animekomix.com
PRESIDENT
Nahid Avaregan

ANIMOTION
501 W. Fayette St., Syracuse, NY 13204. (315) 471-3533. FAX:
(315) 471-2730. www.animotioninc.com
email: info@animotioninc.com
CONTACTS
David Hicock
Larry Royer

ARC SCIENCE SIMULATIONS
306 N. Washington Ave., Box 1955, Loveland, CO 80537. (800)
759-1642, (970) 667-1168. FAX: (970) 667-1105.
www.arcscience.com email: arcmail@arcscience.com
PRESIDENT
Tom Ligon

BAGDASARIAN PRODUCTIONS
1192 E. Mountain Dr., Montecito, CA 93108. (805) 969-3349.
FAX: (805) 969-7466.
CHAIRMAN & CEO
Ross Bagdasarian

BBC WORLDWIDE AMERICAS
747 3rd Ave., New York, NY 10017. (212) 705-9300. FAX: (212)
888-0576.
3500 West Olive Ave., Ste. 110, Burbank, CA 91505. (818) 840-
9770. FAX: (818) 840-9779.
BBC WORLDWIDE LIMITED. Woodlands, 80 Wood Lane,
London W120TT, UK. TEL: 44 (0) 20 8433 2000. FAX: 44 (0) 20
8749 0538. www.bbcworldwide.com
VICE PRESIDENT
Rick Siggelkow

BIFROST LASERFX
(3D animation and laser animation)
6733 Sale Ave., West Hills, CA 91307. (818) 704-0423.
www.howiewood.net email: howie@howiewood.net
OWNER
Howard Shore

BKN INTERNATIONAL, INC.
(Animation in Europe)
41 Madison Ave., 26th Flr., New York, NY 10010. (212) 213-
2700. FAX: (212) 685-8332.
PRESIDENT & CEO
Allen J. Bohbot

BLACK LOGIC
(In the process of consolidating company operations with
Postworks. Still available with this contact informaton.)
216 E. 45th St., 2nd Flr., New York, NY 10017. (212) 557-4949
www.blacklogic.com
CONTACT
Bryan Fitzpatrick

BLUR STUDIO, INC.
589 Venice Blvd., Venice, CA 90291. (310) 581-8848. FAX: (310)
581-8850. www.blur.com

BROADWAY VIDEO DESIGN
1619 Broadway, 10th Flr., New York, NY 10019. (212) 265-7600.
www.broadwayvideo.com email: info@broadwayvideo.com

BRYANT & JOHNSEN, INC.
13351-D Riverside Dr., Ste. 607, Sherman Oaks, CA 91423.
(818) 557-7495. FAX: (818) 764-4949.

BUENA VISTA IMAGING
500 S. Buena Vista St., Burbank, CA 91521. (818) 560-5284.
www.stu-ops.disney.com

BUZZCO ASSOCIATES, INC.
(2D animation)
33 Bleecker St., New York, NY 10012. (212) 473-8800. FAX:
(212) 473-8891.
CONTACT
Candy Kugel

CALABASH ANIMATION
657 West Ohio, Chicago, IL 60610. (312) 243-3433. FAX: (312)
243-6227. www.calabashanimation.com
EXECUTIVE PRODUCER
Monica Kendall

CALICO WORLD ENTERTAINMENT
(Full-service animation company)
10200 Riverside Dr., Ste. 203, N. Hollywood, CA 91602. (818)
755-3800. FAX: (818) 755-4643. www.calicoworld.com
EXECUTIVE DIRECTOR
Tom Burton

CHARACTER BUILDERS, INC.
1476 Manning Pkwy., Powell, OH 43065. (614) 885-2211. FAX:
(614) 885-3873. www.cbuilders.com
email: cbuilders@cbuilders.com
PRODUCER
Leslie Hough

CHIODO BROTHERS PRODUCTIONS, INC.
110 W. Providencia Ave., Burbank, CA 91502. (818) 842-5656.
FAX: (818) 848-0891. www.chiodobros.com
email: klowns@chiodobros.com
PRESIDENT
Steven Chiodo

CHYRON CORP.
5 Hub Dr., Melville, NY 11747. (631) 845-2000. FAX: (631) 845-
3895. www.chyron.com

CINAR CORP.
1055 Rene Levesque East, Ste. 900, Montréal (Québec)
Canada H2L 4S5 (514) 843-7070. FAX: (514) 843-7080.
www.cinar.com email: webmaster@cinar.com

CINEMA CONCEPTS THEATRE SERVICE COMPANY, INC.
2030 Powers Ferry Rd., Ste. 214, Atlanta, GA 30339. (800)
SHOWADS, (770) 956-7460. FAX: (770) 956-8358.
www.cinemaconcepts.com

CLICK 3X
16 W. 22nd St., New York, NY 10010. (212) 627-1900. FAX:
(212) 627-4472. www.click3X.com

CONSOLIDATED FILM INDUSTRIES (CFI)
(Digital)
959 N. Seward St., Hollywood, CA 90038. (323) 960-7444. FAX:
(323) 962-8746.
SALES
Mike Papadaki

CREATIVE CHARACTER ENGINEERING
(Full-service animatronic & digital effects; rental cyclone babies)
16110 Hart St., Van Nuys, CA 91406. (818) 901-0507. FAX:
(818) 901-8417.
CREATIVE DIRECTOR
Andrew Clement

CURIOUS PICTURES
(Computer animation, cel and stop-motion animation)
440 Lafayette, New York, NY 10003. (212) 674-1400. FAX: (212)
674-0081. www.curiouspictures.com
email:info@curiouspictures.com
Cel animation: celjobs@curiouspictures.com
PRESIDENT
Steve Oakes
EXECUTIVE PRODUCER & CFO
Susan Holden

CYBER F/X
615 Ruberta Ave., Glendale, CA 91201. (818) 246-2911. FAX:
(818) 246-3610. www.cyberfx.com
PRESIDENT
Dick Cavdek

DADDY-O PRODUCTIONS
22616 Erwin St., Woodland Hills, CA 91367. (818) 598-8784.
CONTACT
Tom McLaughlin

DEMONSTRATIVES
(Specializes in the production of demonstrative evidence for litigation)
2321 N. Loop Dr., Ames, IA 50010. (877) 480-4060, (515) 296-
6930. FAX: (515) 296-6121. www.demonstratives.com

DIC ENTERTAINMENT, LP
4100 W. Alameda Ave., Burbank, CA 91505. (818) 955-5400.
FAX: (818) 955-5696. www.dicentertainment.com
PRESIDENT
Andy Heyward

DIGISCOPE DIGITAL VISUAL EFFECTS
(Special effects for motion pictures)
2308 Broadway, Santa Monica, CA 90404. (310) 315-6060. FAX:
(310) 828-5856. www.digiscope.com
email: mary@digiscope.com
PRESIDENT
Mary Stuart-Welch

DIGITAL CREATIVE
1112 N. Tamarind Ave., Hollywood, CA 90038. (800) 94M-EDIA,
(323) 993-9570. FAX: (323) 962-3446. www.digitalcreative.com
email: webmaster@digitalcreative.com
PRESIDENT
Brian Patterson

DIGITAL DOMAIN
(Full-service animation company)
300 Rose Ave., Venice, CA 90291. (310) 314-2800. FAX: (310)
314-2888. www.digitaldomain.com
PRESIDENT & CEO
Scott Ross

WALT DISNEY FEATURE ANIMATION
500 S. Buena Vista St., Burbank, CA 91521. (818) 560-1000.
www.disney.go.com
PRESIDENT
David Stainton

WALT DISNEY TELEVISION ANIMATION
500 S. Buena Vista, Burbank, CA 91521. (818) 560-1000.

DLT ENTERTAINMENT, LTD.
31 W. 56th St., New York, NY 10019. (212) 245-4680. FAX:
(212) 315-1132.
CONTACT
John Fitzgerald

DNA PRODUCTIONS, INC.
2201 W. Royal Ln., Ste. 275, Irving, TX 75063. (214) 352-4694.
FAX: (214) 496-9333. www.dnahelix.com
email: dnainfo@dnahelix.com
CONTACT
Keith Alcorn

DREAM THEATER STUDIOS
30699 Russell Ranch Rd., Ste. 190, West Lake Village, CA
91362. (818) 661-1109 FAX: (818) 661-1194.
www.dreamtheater.com email: darren@dreamtheater.com
MANAGER
Darren Chuckry

DREAMWORKS SKG FEATURE ANIMATION
1000 Flower St., Glendale, CA 91201. (818) 733-7000. FAX:
(818) 733-3036.

DUCK SOUP STUDIOS
(Animation for commercials, film and TV titles, multimedia; 2D
and 3D computer animation, cel, character design, digital
compositing, digital ink & paint)
2205 Stoner Ave., Los Angeles, CA 90064. (310) 478-0771.
FAX: (310) 478-0773. www.ducksoupla.com

DYNACS DIGITAL STUDIOS
(Special effects, colorization, restoration and digital ink & paint)
21011 Itasca St., Unit D, Chatsworth, CA 91311. (818) 709-
2450. FAX: (818) 709-8540.

EMA MULTIMEDIA
1800 Ave. of the Stars, Ste. 430, Century City, CA 90067. (310)
277-7379. FAX: (310) 277-7378. www.emamulti.com

ENOKI FILMS U.S.A., INC.
(Japanese animation)
16430 Ventura Blvd., Ste. 308, Encino, CA 91436. (818) 907-
6503. www.enokifilmsusa.com email: info@enokifilmsusa.com

FANTASY II FILM EFFECTS
504 S. Varney St., Burbank, CA 91502. (818) 843-1413. FAX:
(818) 848-2824.
CONTACT
Leslie Huntley

RUSS FARBER
(Blue screen effects, setup, networking & trouble-shooting
computers on location)
19324 Oxnard St., Tarzana, CA 91356. (818) 882-8220.
email: refent@pacbell.net

FARMHOUSE FILMS, INC.
4399 Irvine Ave., Studio City, CA 91604. (818) 760-8700.
PRESIDENT
Fred Calvert

FILM ROMAN, INC.
12020 Chandler Blvd., Ste. 200, N. Hollywood, CA 91607. (818)
761-2544. www.filmroman.com email: info@filmroman.com
PRESIDENT & C.E.O.
John Hyde

FLAMDOODLE ANIMATION, INC.
(2D & 3D animation)
142 Lincoln Ave., Ste. 4C, Santa Fe, NM 87501. (505) 982-
3132. FAX: (505) 982-3172. www.flamdoodle.com
EXECUTIVE PRODUCER
Jeff LaFlamme

FLEISCHER STUDIOS, INC.
10160 Cielo Dr., Beverly Hills, CA 90210. (310) 276-7503. FAX:
(310) 276-1559. email: stanhandman@yahoo.com
PRESIDENT
Mark Fleischer

FLYING FOTO FACTORY, INC.
P.O. Box 1166, Durham, NC 27702. (919) 682-3411. FAX: (919)
402-98576. www.flyingfoto.com
V.P., SALES & MARKETING
Kathy Bennett

F-STOP, INC.
(Opticals & titles)
120 S. Buena Vista St., Burbank, CA 91505. (818) 843-7867.
FAX: (818) 842-7706.

GALAXIE ENTERTAINMENT CO.
P.O. Box 8523, Universal City, CA 91618-8523. (818) 362-6005.
CONTACT
Dave Gregory

JIM GAMBLE PUPPET PRODUCTIONS
(Puppet show and workshops)
6777 Vallon Dr., Rancho Palos Verdes, CA 90275. (310) 541-
1921. FAX: (310) 541-2195. www.jimgamble.com
email: office@jimgamble.com

GRACIE FILMS
(TV animation)
10202 W. Washington Blvd., Sidney Poitier Bldg., 2nd Flr.,
Culver City, CA 90232. (310) 244-4222. FAX: (310) 244-1530.
EXECUTIVE V.P.
Denise Sirkot

GREATEST TALES
22477 MacFarlane Dr., Woodland Hills, CA 91364. (818) 225-
9545.
PRESIDENT
Fred Ladd

GREEN GRASS BLUE SKY COMPANY
10061 Riverside Dr., Ste. 753, Toluca Lake, CA 91602. (818)
787-0024. email: ggbscompany@hotmail.com
WRITER & PRODUCER
Frank Catalano

HALLMARK ENTERTAINMENT
1325 Ave. of the Americas, 21st Flr., New York, NY 10019. (212)
977-9001. FAX: (212) 977-9049. www.hallmarkent.com

JIM HENSON PRODUCTIONS
1416 N. LaBrea Ave., Hollywood, CA 90028. (323) 802-1500.
FAX: (323) 802-1825. www.henson.com

HOUSE OF MOVES MOTION CAPTURE STUDIOS, LLC
(Motion capture)
5318 McConnell Ave., Los Angeles, CA 90066. (310) 306-6131.
FAX: (310) 306-1351. www.moves.com

HYPERION STUDIOS
(Live action and tv animation)
111 N. Maryland Ave., Ste. 300, Glendale, CA 91206. (818) 244-
4704. FAX: (818) 244-4713. www.hyperionpictures.com
email: mail@hyperionpictures.com
PRESIDENT
Tom Wilhite

ICE TEA PRODUCTIONS
160 E. 38th St., #15B, New York, NY 10016. (212) 557-8185.
PRESIDENT
Richard Durkin

ILLUVATAR, LLC
(Rendering and computer consulting)
P.O. Box 8506, Fountain Valley, CA 92728 TEL/FAX: (714) 965-
5918. CELL: (310)753-1774. www.illuvatar.com
email: info@illuvatar.com
CEO
Bill Schortell

IMAGICA USA, INC.
(Large format optical & digital effects)
5320 McConnell Ave., Los Angeles, CA 90066. (310) 305-8081.
FAX: (310) 305-7563. email: chrisr@imagicausa.com
PRESIDENT
Christopher Reyna

INDUSTRIAL LIGHT & MAGIC (ILM)
(A Lucasfilm Ltd. Co. Special effects and post-production)
P.O. Box 2459, San Rafael, CA 94912. (415) 258-2000.
www.ilm.com
S.V.P., PRODUCTION
Chrissie England

THE INK TANK
2 W. 47th St., New York, NY 10036. (212) 869-1630. FAX: (212)
764-4169. email: inktank@inktank.net
DIRECTOR
R.O. Blechman

IN-SIGHT PIX
(CGI animation)
901 Abbot Kinney Blvd., Venice, CA 90291. (310) 399-5670.
www.digitallab.com email: diglab@digitallab.com

JIM KEESHEN PRODUCTIONS
(Pilots, series & specials; pre-visualization specialists)
P.O. Box 251435, Los Angeles, CA 90025. (310) 478-7230. FAX:
(310) 478-5142. email: animatics@aol.com
PRESIDENT
Jim Keeshan

KENIMATION ANIMATION SERVICES
(Titles and computerized moves on photos or artwork to film)
726 N. Cahuenga Blvd., Los Angeles, CA 90038. (323) 462-
2679. email: kenru@attbi.com
CONTACT
Ken Rudolph

GENE KRAFT PRODUCTIONS
29 Calvados, Newport Beach, CA 92657. (949) 721-0609.
OWNER
Gene Kraft

KURTZ & FRIENDS
2312 W. Olive Ave., Burbank, CA 91506. (818) 841-8188. FAX:
(818) 841-6263. email: bobkurtz@aol.com
PRESIDENT
Bob Kurtz
PRODUCER
Boo Kurtz-Lopez

LANDMARK ENTERTAINMENT GROUP
(Motion pictures)
6100 San Fernando Rd., Glendale, CA 91201. (818) 952-6292.
FAX: (818) 949-0312. www.landmarkusa.com

LEPREVOST CORPORATION
6781 Wildlife Rd., Malibu, CA 90265. (310) 457-3742. FAX:
(310) 457-6142. www.leprevost.com email: leprevost@aol.com
EXECUTIVE PRODUCER
John H. LePrevost

JERRY LIEBERMAN PRODUCTIONS
76 Laight St., New York, NY 10013. (212) 431-3452. FAX: (212)
941-8976.
CONTACT
Jerry Lieberman

LIBERTY INTERNATIONAL ENTERTAINMENT, INC.
(Specials and series animation)
1990 Westwood Blvd., Penthouse, Los Angeles, CA 90025.
(800) 576-3431, (310) 474-4456. FAX: (310) 474-7455.
www.libertyinteractive.com email: admin@libertyinteractive.com
PRESIDENT & CEO
Steven Randall Naft
CHAIRMAN
Irv Hollender

LINKER SYSTEMS, INC.
(Computer-assisted 2D char. anim., 3D, image compositing,
film-quality special effects opticals, etc. Win & Mac versions)
13612 Onkayha Circle, Irvine, CA 92620. (949) 552-1904. FAX:
(949) 552-6985. www.linker.com; www.linkersystems.com;
www.animationstand.com email: sales@linker.com

LION'S DEN PRODUCTION
(Cartoon production)
P.O. Box 7368, Northridge, CA 91327. (818) 894-4955.
VICE PRESIDENT
Milton Gray

WILLIAM LITTLEJOHN PRODUCTIONS, INC.
23425 Malibu Colony Dr., Malibu, CA 90265. (310) 456-8620.
FAX: (310) 456-2978.

LIVE WIRE PRODUCTIONS & VFX
(Visual effects animation & compositing; commercial production)
28631 S. Western Ave., Ste. 101, Rancho Palos Verdes, CA
90275. (310) 831-6227. www.livewireprod.com

WARREN LOCKHART PRODUCTIONS, INC.
(Multi dimensional film and tv production company)
P.O. Box 11629, Marina Del Rey, CA 90295. (310) 821-1414.
FAX: (310) 301-0536. email: warren@lockhartproductions.com
PRESIDENT
Warren L. Lockhart

LUMENI PRODUCTIONS, INC.
(Digital and film, titles, graphics, effects)
1632 Flower St., Glendale, CA 91201. (818) 956-2200. FAX:
(818) 956-3298. email: lumeni@aol.com
CONTACT
Carin Janis

MANGA ENTERTAINMENT
(Japanese animation)
727 N. Hudson St., Ste. 100, Chicago, IL 60610. (312) 751-
0020. FAX: (312) 751-2483. www.manga.com/manga

MARVISTA ENTERTAINMENT
(Formerly Whamo Entertainment)
12519 Venice Blvd., Los Angeles, CA 90066. (310) 737-0950.
FAX: (310) 737-9155. email: info@marvista.net

MAVERICK DIGITAL CO.
(Formerly Gear CGI)
(3D animation, digital effects)
9348 Civic Center Dr., Beverly Hills, CA 90210. (310) 276-6177.
FAX: (310) 276-9477. email: dkim@maventertainment.com
EXECUTIVE PRODUCERS
David Kim
Don Kim
Dan Rosenfeld

MAX INK CAFE
(Visual effects, tv, films and games)
2700 Pacific Ave., Venice, CA 90291. (310) 827-5351. FAX:
(310) 827-5651. www.MaxInkCafe.com
email: info@MaxInkCafe.com

MEGA ENTERTAINMENT
150 W. 25th St., Ste. 503, New York, NY 10001. (212) 242-0088.
FAX: (212) 242-0808. email: mega@megaentertainment.com

LEE MENDELSON FILM PRODUCTIONS
330 Primrose Rd., Ste. 310, Burlingame, CA 94010. (650) 342-
8284. FAX: (650) 342-6170.
CONTACT
Glenn Mendelson

METROLIGHT STUDIOS
5724 W. 3rd St., Ste. 400, Los Angeles, CA 90036-3078. (213)
932-0400. FAX: (213) 932-8440. email: info@metrolight.com

METRO3D, INC.
(Formerly Metropolis Digital)
(Game animation)
12 South First St., 10th Flr., San Jose, CA 95113. (408) 286-
2900. (408) 286-2970. www.metro3d.com
S.V.P., SALES & MARKETING
Joe Morici

MODERN CARTOONS
228 Main St., Ste. 12, Venice, CA 90291. (310) 309-4600.
PRODUCER
Aaron Slavin

MOON MESA MEDIA
(Cartoon animation)
14945 Ventura Blvd., Ste. 300, Sherman Oaks, CA 91403. (818)
528-1455. FAX: (818) 528-1467. www.moonmesa.com
C.E.O. & FOUNDER
Sheryl Hardy

MORGAN CREEK PRODUCTIONS
(Motion picture animation)
4000 Warner Blvd., Bldg. 76, Burbank, CA 91522. (818) 954-
4800. www.morgancreek.com
CONTACT
Brian Robinson

MOTION CITY FILMS
(Motion graphics and live action)
501 Santa Monica Blvd., Ste. 150B, Santa Monica, CA 90401.
(800) 719-2812, (310) 434-1272. FAX: (310) 434-1273.
www.motioncity.com email: witt@motioncity.com
CONTACT
G. Michael Witt

M3D STUDIOS, INC.
(3D)
15820 Arminta St., Van Nuys, CA 91406. (818) 785-6662. FAX:
(818) 785-6810. www.planetm3d.com
email: m3d@m3dstudios.com
CEO
Marcel Nottea

MUSIVISION
185 E. 85th St., New York, NY 10028. (212) 860-4420.
CONTACT
Fred Kessler

NELVANA ENTERTAINMENT
(Cartoons for tv)
4500 Wilshire Blvd., 1st Flr., Los Angeles, CA 90010. (323) 549-
4222. FAX: (323) 549-4232. www.nelvana.com

NEST FAMILY ENTERTAINMENT
(Animated videos)
1461 S. Beltline Rd., Ste. 500, TX 75019. (972) 402-7100 FAX:
(972) 629-7181. www.nestfamily.com

NEW HOLLYWOOD, INC.
1302 N. Cahuenga Blvd., Hollywood, CA 90028. (323) 466-
3686. email: newhollywood@hotmail.com

NICKELODEON
1515 Broadway, New York, NY 10036. (212) 258-7500.
www.nick.com

NXVIEW TECHNOLOGIES, INC.
(Custom product configuration & simulation; rich media
interactive 3-D learning & training software systems)
P.O. Box 1429, Cary, NC 27512. (919) 657-3300. FAX: (919)
657-3333. www.nxview.com email: nxsales@nxview.com
CFO & GENERAL MANAGER
William H. Owen

OPTICAM, INC.
(Motion picture titles and end crawls, motion control
downshooter, photo-rotos animation camera service)
810 Navy St., Santa Monica, CA 90405. (800) 345-6394, (310)
396-4665. FAX: (310) 452-0040. email: opcam@aol.com

ORBIT PRODUCTIONS
915 14th St., Modesto, CA 95354. (800) 71-ORBIT, (209) 529-
4835. FAX: (209) 571-2307. www.orbitproductions.com
email: kevin@orbitproductions.com
CONTACT
Kevin Orbit

PEEL ME A GRAPE (TNT MEDIA)
(Formerly Digital Quest)
2330 Pontius Ave., W. Los Angeles, CA 90064. (310) 826-9011.
FAX: (310) 479-9588.
CONTACT
Casey Gelvin

PDI/DREAMWORKS
(3D character animation, visual effects)
3101 Park Blvd., Palo Alto, CA 94306. (650) 846-8100. FAX:
(650) 846-8101. www.pdi.com email: marketing@pdi.com

PERENNIAL PICTURES FILM CORP.
(Character animation)
2102 E. 52nd St., Indianapolis, IN 46205. (317) 253-1519.
www.perennialpictures.com
PRESIDENT
Jerry Reynolds

PHOENIX ENTERTAINMENT GROUP, INC.
2222 Linstromeberg Rd., Beaufort, MO 63013. (573) 484-3725,
(573) 484-4599.
CHAIRMAN & CEO
Ed Ascheman

PIXAR ANIMATION STUDIOS
(Computer animation)
1200 Park Ave., Emeryville, CA 94608. (510) 752-3000. FAX:
(510) 752-3151. www.pixar.com

PIXEL LIBERATION FRONT
1316 1/2 Abbot Kinney Blvd., Venice, CA 90291. (310) 396-
9854. FAX: (310) 396-9874. www.thefront.com
CONTACT
Colin Green

PIXEL MAGIC
(2D and 3D)
10635 Riverside Dr., Toluca Lake, CA 91602. (818) 760-0862.
FAX: (818) 760-4983. www.pixelmagicfx.com
VICE PRESIDENT
Ray McIntyre Jr.

PORCHLIGHT ENTERTAINMENT
(Children's animation)
11777 Mississippi Ave., Los Angeles, CA 90025. (310) 477-
8400. FAX: (310) 477-5555. www.porchlight.com
email: info@porchlight.com

PROTOZOA PICTURES
438 West 37th St., Ste. 5G, New York, NY 10018. (212) 244-
3369. FAX: (212) 244-3735. www.protozoa.com

PUPPET STUDIO
(Puppets)
10903 Chandler Blvd., N. Hollywood, CA 91601. (818) 506-
7374. email: steve@thepuppetstudio.com
CONTACT
Steve Sherman

PYROS CORPORATION
(Computer animation)
3197 Airport Loop Dr., Bldg. A, Costa Mesa, CA 92626. (714)
708-3400. FAX: (714) 708-3500. www.pyros.com
email: gpyros@pyros.com
CONTACT
Greg Pyros

RAINMAKER DIGITAL PICTURES
(2D and 3D visual effects)
50 West Second Ave., Vancouver, B.C. V5Y 1B3 Canada. (604)
874-8700. FAX: (604) 872-2106. www.rainmaker.com
email: info@rainmaker.com
PRESIDENT
Bob Scarabelli

RANKIN/BASS
24 W. 55th St., New York, NY 10019. (212) 582-4017. FAX:
(212) 582-0937. www.rankinbass.com

REALITY CHECK, INC.
(Motion graphics and design, 3D)
6100 Melrose Ave., Los Angeles, CA 90038. (323) 465-3900.
FAX: (323) 465-3600. www.realityx.com
email: info@realityx.com
PRESIDENT
Andrew Heimbold

REMBRANDT FILMS
(Distributor)
34 Cross Pond Rd., Pound Ridge, NY 10576. (888) 205-8778,
(914) 763-5817. www.rembrandtfilms.com
email: info@rembrandtfilms.com
PRESIDENT
Adam Snyder

RENEGADE ANIMATION
204 N. San Fernando Blvd., Burbank, CA 91502. (818) 556-
3395. FAX: (818) 556-3398. www.renegadeanimation.com
EXECUTIVE PRODUCER
Ashley Postlewaite
DIRECTOR
Darrell Van Citters

REZN8 PRODUCTIONS, INC.
(Full-service animation company)
6430 Sunset Blvd., Ste. 100, Hollywood, CA 90028. (323) 957-
2161. FAX: (323) 464-8912. www.rezn8.com
PRESIDENT
Paul Sidlo

RHYTHM & HUES
(Computer animation)
5404 Jandy Place, Los Angeles, CA 90066. (310) 448-7500.
FAX: (310) 448-7600. www.rhythm.com
FILM DIVISION, EXECUTIVE PRODUCER
Lee Berger (310) 448-7727 email: lee@rhythm.com

RICH CREST STUDIO
(2D and 3D)
333 N. Glenoaks Blvd., 3rd Flr., Burbank, CA 91502. (818) 846-
0166.
CONTACT
Tom Tobin

RIOT
702/730 Arizona Ave., Santa Monica, CA 90401. (310) 434-
6000. FAX: (310) 434-6500. www.rioting.com
3399 Peachtree Rd. NE, Ste. 200, Atlanta, GA 30326. (404)
237-9977. FAX: (404)237-3923.
545 Fifth Ave., New York, NY 10017. (212) 687-4000. FAX: (212)
687-2719.
EXECUTIVE PRODUCER
Todd Davidovich (CA)
SALES
Beth Helmer (GA)

RUBY-SPEARS PRODUCTIONS, INC.
213 W. Alameda Ave., Ste. 102, Burbank, CA 91502-3027. (818)
840-1234. FAX: (818) 840-1258. www.rubyspears.com
PRESIDENT
Joe Ruby
VICE PRESIDENT
Ken Spears

SABAN ENTERTAINMENT
(Acquired by Disney)
10960 Wilshire Blvd., 22nd Flr. Los Angeles, CA 90024. (310)
235-5100. FAX: (310)235-5898.
CHAIRMAN & CEO
Haim Saban

SCHOLASTIC ENTERTAINMENT
524 Broadway, 5th Flr., New York, NY 10012. (212) 343-7500.
FAX: (212) 343-7570. www.scholastic.com.
E.V.P. & PRESIDENT, SCHOLASTIC ENTERTAINMENT
Deborah A. Forte
SCHOLASTIC WORLDWIDE HEADQUARTERS & EDITORIAL
557 Broadway, New York, NY 10012. (212) 343-6100.

J.J. SEDELMAIER PRODUCTIONS, INC.
(Commercials and animated shorts)
199 Main St., 10th Flr., White Plains, NY 10601. (914) 949-
7979. FAX: (914) 949-7989. email: sedelmaier@aol.com
PRESIDENT & DIRECTOR
J.J. Sedelmaier

SHERER DIGITAL ANIMATION
(3D animation)
71-956B Magnesia Falls Dr., Rancho Mirage, CA 92270. (760)
346-7234. FAX: (760) 340-3170. www.shererdigital.com
PRESIDENT &CEO
Steve Sherer email: steve@shererdigital.com
V.P., PRODUCTION
Justin Post email: justin@shererdigital.com

SIM EX DIGITAL STUDIOS
(See Associates & Yamashita)

SINGLE FRAME FILMS
(Cut out & stop motion, drawn animation, training, & consultation)
437-1/2 N. Genessee Ave., Los Angeles, CA 90036. (323) 655-2664.
CONTACT
Gary Schwartz

SIX FOOT TWO PRODUCTIONS
(Full-service animation company)
25 Ebbtide Passage, Corte Madera, CA 94925. (415) 927-0880.
FAX: (415) 927-0550. www.sixfoottwo.com
EXECUTIVE PRODUCER
Suzanne Atherly
DIRECTORS
Robbin Atherly
Tom Arndt
Kelly Day
Thomas McKeon
Dan Povenmire

SMITHGROUP COMMUNICATIONS INC.
(Animation for films, commercials and theatrical trailers)
267 S.E. 33rd Ave., Portland, OR 97214. (503) 239-4215. FAX:
(503) 239-1570. www.smithgrp.com
email: smithgrp@smithgrp.com
PRESIDENT
Phil Bevans
OPERATIONS MANAGER/PRODUCER
Georgia Cacy

SONY PICTURES IMAGEWORKS
(Full-service animation company)
9050 W. Washington Blvd., Culver City, CA 90232. (310) 840-
8000. FAX: (310) 840-8100. www.imageworks.com
email: inquiry@imageworks.com

LEONARD SOUTH PRODUCTIONS
11108 Huston St., N. Hollywood, CA 91601. (818) 760-8383.
FAX: (818) 766-8301.

SPECTAK PRODUCTIONS, INC.
(Laser special effects)
222 N. Sepulveda Blvd., Ste. 2000, El Segundo, CA 90245.
(310) 335-2038. FAX: (310) 335-2048. www.spectak.com.au
email: info@spetak.com
PRESIDENT & CEO
Ric Birch (310) 666-2050 email: ricspectak@cs.com

MICHAEL SPORN ANIMATION, LTD.
632 Broadway, 4th Flr., New York, NY 10012. (212) 228-3372.
PRESIDENT
Michael Sporn

SPUMCO, INC.
(Full-service animation company)
10859 Burbank Blvd., Ste. A, N. Hollywood, CA 91601. (818)
623-1955. FAX: (818) 623-1958.
PRESIDENT
John Kricfalusi

ST PRODUCTIONS
(Cel, dimensional, stop motion & CGI, Oxberry & stop motion)
P.O. Box 2449, Hollywood, CA 90078. (323) 960-5622.
email: stprods@mail.com
PRODUCER
Sam Longoria

STARGATE DIGITAL
1001 El Centro St., South Pasadena, CA 91030. (626) 403-
8403. FAX: (626) 403-8403. www.stargatefilms.com
FOUNDER & VISUAL EFFECTS SUPERVISOR & DIRECTOR
OF PHOTOGRAPHY
Sam Nicholson

DAVID STIPES PRODUCTIONS, INC.
45409 Gingham Ave., Lancaster, CA 93535. (818) 243-1442.
PRESIDENT
David Stipes III

STOKES/KOHNE ASSOCIATES, INC.
(Full-service animation company)
742 Cahuenga Blvd., Hollywood, CA 90038. (323) 468-2340.
CONTACT
Dan Kohne

STORYOPOLIS
(Development company)
116 N. Robertson Blvd., Plaza A, Los Angeles, CA 90048. (310)
358-2525. www.storyopolis.com
PRESIDENT
Fonda Snyder

STRIBLING PRODUCTIONS
(Traditional animation)
6528 Camellia Ave., N. Hollywood, CA 91606. (818) 509-0748.
FAX: (818) 509-1966. www.childrenstreasury.com
PRESIDENT
Mike Stribling

SUNBOW ENTERTAINMENT
(A TV Loonland Company)
100 Fifth Ave., 3rd Flr., New York, NY 10011. (212) 893-1600.
FAX: (212) 893-1630.

SUPERCOLOR
979 N. La Brea Ave., Hollywood, CA 90038. (323) 874-2188.
FAX: (323) 436-0588. www.supercolorimaging.com
SALES MANAGER
Ally Chang

TAPE HOUSE TOONS
(In process of consolidating under the Postworks New York
name with all Tapehouse companies and affiliates. Still available
at following address.) 222 E. 44th St., 10th Flr., New York, NY
10017. (212) 557-9611. www.tapehouse.com
EXECUTIVE PRODUCER
David Lipson

THRESHOLD DIGITAL RESEARCH LABS
1649 11th St., Santa Monica, CA 90404. (310) 452-8899. FAX:
(310) 452-0736. www.threshold.tv
PRESIDENT
Larry Kasanoff

TLC ENTERTAINMENT/THE MINI-MOVIE STUDIO
CBS Studios, 4024 Radford Ave., Studio City, CA 91604. (818)
655-6155. FAX: (818) 655-6254. email: TLCE@aol.com

TMS ENTERTAINMENT
(Character and 2D)
15760 Ventura Blvd., Ste. 700, Encino, CA 91436. (818) 905-
8881. FAX: (818) 905-0815.
SALES REPRESENTATIVE
Mitsumoto Sucuki

TOON MAKERS, INC.
16007 Knapp St., North Hills, CA 91343. (818) 895-2995.
email: cartoonmkr@aol.com
EXECUTIVE PRODUCER & CEO
Rocky Solotoff

UNIVERSAL CARTOON STUDIOS
100 Universal City Plaza, Universal City, CA 91608. (818) 777-
1000.
SENIOR V.P., CARTOON STUDIOS
Tom Ruzicka

VIDE-U PRODUCTIONS
9976 W. Wanda Dr., Beverly Hills, CA 90210. (310) 276-5509.
FAX: (310) 276-1183.
CONTACT
Bradly Fridman

VIEW STUDIO, INC.
(Special effects animation)
6715 Melrose Ave., Hollywood, CA 90038. (323) 965-1270. FAX:
(323) 965-1277. www.viewstudio.com
email: info@viewstudio.com
PRODUCER
Terry Whiteside
BUSINESS DEVELOPMENT
Chip McKenney

VIEWPORT IMAGES
109 N. Naomi St., Burbank, CA 91505. (818) 559-8705. FAX:
(818) 559-5453. www.viewportimages.com
PRESIDENT
John Howard

WILL VINTON STUDIOS
(Dimensional computer animation and claymation)
1400 N.W. 22nd Ave., Portland, OR 97210. (503) 225-1130.
FAX: (503) 226-3746. www.vinton.com email: info@vinton.com
1100 Glendon Ave., 17th Flr., Los Angeles, CA 90024. (310)
689-7222. FAX: (310) 689-7244. email: LA@vinton.com
CONTACT
CJ Glazer

VIRTUALMAGIC ANIMATION
4640 Lankershim Blvd., Ste. 201, N. Hollywood, CA 91606.
(818) 623-1866. FAX: (818) 623-1868.
email: don@virtualmagicusa.com
PRESIDENT
Don Spielvogel

VISUAL CONCEPT ENGINEERING
(Digital effects and motion control)
13300 Ralston Ave., Sylmar, CA 91342-7608. (818) 367-9187.
FAX: (818) 362-3490. www.vce.com
PRESIDENT
Peter Kuran

VRSET
(3D and effects; interactive solutions)
940 N. Orange Dr., Ste. 116, Hollywood, CA 90038. (323) 465-
3000. www.vrset.com

WARNER BROS. ANIMATION
15301 Ventura Blvd., Unit E, Sherman Oaks, CA 91403. (800)
286-0868, (818) 977-8700.
PRESIDENT
Sander Schwartz

WRECKLESS ABANDON STUDIOS
(Production company & content provider that produces high
quality clay animation, stop-motion production & 3D-computer
animation)
17 Connecticut South Dr. East Granby, CT 06026. (860) 844-
7090. www.wrecklessabandon.com

WHAMO ENTERTAINMENT
(See Marvista Entertainment. www.whamoentertainment.com)

WILD BRAIN, INC.
(Full-service animation company)
660 Alabama St., San Francisco, CA 94110. (415) 553-8000.
FAX: (415) 553-8009. www.wildbrain.com
email: info@wildbrain.com
1332, 14th St., Ste. B, Santa Monica, CA 90404. (310) 382-6766. FAX: (310) 451-7920.
CONTACT
Andrew Steiner

FRED WOLF FILMS
(Full-service animation company)
4222 W. Burbank Blvd., Burbank, CA 91505. (818) 846-0611.
FAX: (818)845-0979. www.fredwolffilms.com
email: administration@fredwolffilms.com
PRESIDENT
Fred Wolf

WORLD EVENTS PRODUCTIONS, LTD.
One Memorial Dr., Ste. 2000, St. Louis, MO 63102. (314) 345-1000. FAX: (314) 345-1091. www.wep.com

XAOS
(Visual effects and animation)
444 De Haro St., Ste. 211, San Francisco, CA 94107. (415) 643-8637.
PRESIDENT
Arthur Schwartzberg
EXECUTIVE PRODUCER
Christina Scmidlin

MIKE YOUNG PRODUCTIONS
(TV animation)
20335 Ventura Blvd., Ste. 225, Woodland Hills, CA 91364. (818) 999-0062. FAX: (818) 999-0172.
CONTACT
Liz Young

ZOOM CARTOONS ENTERTAINMENT
(Animation studio, 2D and 3D)
c/o Los Angeles Center Studios, 1201 W. 5th St., Ste. M-3000, Los Angeles, CA 90017. (213) 202-5959. FAX: (213) 202-5960.
www.zoomcartoons.com
PRESIDENT & EXECUTIVE PRODUCER
Susan Deming Berstein

CASTING DIRECTORS

ABA PICTURE VEHICLES & CASTING SERVICES
8306 Wilshire Blvd., PMB 900, Beverly Hills, CA 90211. (310) 323-9028. FAX: (310) 323-3144.
CEO
Antoinette Meier
SENIOR V.P.
Warren Taoletti

AKIMA'S CASTING & PRODUCTION SERVICES
(Native American & Latino casting)
P.O. Box 7088, Van Nuys, CA 91409. (818) 988-9168.
CASTING DIRECTOR
Akima Castaneda

AMERICAN INDIANS IN FILM (AMERIND)
(Casting of Native Americans)
65 N. Allen Ave., Ste. 105, Pasadena, CA 91106. (626) 578-0344. FAX: (626) 449-2735.
CEO
Sonny Skyhawk

AQUILA WOOD CASTING
9350 Civic Center Dr., Ste. 110, Beverly Hills, CA 90210. (310) 288-4650. FAX: (310) 288-4658.
CONTACT
Deborah Aquila

ARTZ & COHEN CASTING
c/o Casting Society of America (CSA) 606 N. Larchmont Blvd., #4B, Los Angeles, CA 90004. (323) 463-1925.
CONTACTS
Mary Gail Artz
Barbara Cohen

RISE BARISH CASTING
1216 Fifth St., Santa Monica, CA 90401. (310) 456-9018. FAX: (310) 456-9718.

BARTON G. CREATIVE PRODUCTIONS
3628 NE 2nd Ave., Miami, FL 33137. (305) 576-8888, FAX: (305) 751-0040. www.bartong.com

PAMELA BASKER
Warner Bros. Casting, 300 Television Plaza, Bldg. 140, Rm. #134, Burbank, CA 91505. (818) 506-7348. FAX: (818) 954-7944.

TERRY BERLAND CASTING
2050 S. Bundy Dr., Los Angeles, CA 90025. (310) 571-4141. FAX: (310) 820-5408. www.terryberlandcasting.com

BOSTON CASTING
129 Braintree St., Ste. 107 Allston, MA 02134. (617) 254-1001. FAX: (617) 254-3003. www.bostoncasting.com
DIRECTORS
Angela Peri
Lisa Lobel

BROWN/WEST CASTING
7319 Beverly Blvd., Ste. 10, Los Angeles, CA 90036. (323) 938-2575. FAX: (323) 938-2755.

CATHI CARLTON CASTING
2050 S. Bundy Dr., Los Angeles, CA 90025. (310) 820-9200. FAX: (310) 820-5408.

THE CASTING COMPANY
7461 Beverly Blvd., Penthouse, Los Angeles, CA 90036-2704. (323) 653-1200.

CASTING SOCIETY OF AMERICA
606 N. Larchmont Blvd., #4B, Los Angeles, CA 90004. (323) 463-1925. FAX: (323) 463-5753.
CALIFORNIA MEMBERS
Deborah Aquila, Maureen A. Arata, Patrick Baca, Matthew Barry, Deborah Barylski, Fran Bascom, Pamela Basker, Lisa Beach, Eyde Belasco, Brett Benner, Paul Bens, Amy Jo Berman, Chemin Sylvia Bernard, Juel Bestrop, Sharon Bialy, Tammara Billik, Susan Bluestein, Eugene Blythe, Judith Bouley, Deedee Bradley, Megan Branman, Kate Brinegar, Jackie Briskey, Steve Brooksbank, Mary V. Buck, Perry Bullington, Jackie Burch, Irene Cagen, Akua Campanella, Craig Campobasso, Reuben Cannon, Ferne Cassel, Alice S. Cassidy, Lindsay Chag, Denise Chamian, Sharon Chazin Lieblein, Andrea Cohen, Barbara Cohen, Aisha Coley, Ruth Conforte, Gretchen Rennell Court, Allison Cowitt, Patrick S. Cunningham, Billy Da Mota, Anita Dann, Eric Dawson, Shawn Dawson, Leslee Dennis, Sarah Dalton Donlan, Michael Donovan, Dorian Dunas, Nan Dutton, Susan Edelman, Kathryn Eisenstein, Donna Ekholdt, Felicia Fasano, Mike Fenton, Mali Finn, Sarah Halley Finn, Nancy Foy, Jerold Franks, Carrie Frazier, Lisa Freiberger, Dean Fronk, Jean Sarah Frost, Risa Bramon Garcia, Scott Genkinger, David Giella, Janet Gilmore, Jan Glaser, Laura Gleason, Susan Glicksman, Gail Goldberg, Peter Golden, Carol Goldwasser, Elisa Goodman, Avy Kaufman, Jeff Green-Keyes, Jeff Greenberg, Sheila Guthrie, Milt Hamerman, Theodore Hann, Robert W. Harbin, Natalie Hart, René Haynes, Cathy Henderson-Martin, Nina Henninger, Tory Herald, Dawn Hershey, Richard Hicks, Randi Hiller, Marc Hirschfeld, Janet Hirshenson, Judith Holstra, Vicki Huff, Julie Hutchinson, Donna Isaacson, Jane Jenkins, Liz Jereski, Junie Lowry Johnson, Caro Jones, Christian Kaplan, Tracy Kaplan, Lisa Miller Katz, Sarah Katzman, Peggy Kennedy, Sharon Klein, Thom Klohn, Nancy Klopper, Eileen Mack Knight, Amanda Koblin, Joanne Koehler, Ronna Kress, Carol Kritzer, Jason La Padura, Ruth Lambert, Shana Landsburg, Meredith Layne, Geraldine Leder, Keli Lee, Kathleen Letterie, John Levey, Heidi Levitt, Meg Liberman, Amy Lieberman, Tracy Lilienfield, Amy Lippens, Robin Lippin, Leslie Litt, Lisa London, Molly Lopata, Linda Lowy, Penny Ludford, Bob MacDonald, Francine Maisler, Debi Manwiller, Irene Mariano, Mindy Marin, Elizabeth Marx, Jeanne Mccarthy, Megan Mcconnell, Robert Mcgee, Pat Melton, Jeffery A. Meshel, Joseph Middleton, Barbara Miller, Kenneth Miller, Rick Millikan, Lisa Mionie, Bob Morones, Donna Morong, MichelleMorris-Gertz, Helen Mossler, John Mulkeen, Roger Mussenden, Robin S. Nassif, Nancy Nayor, Bruce H. Newberg, Sonia Nikore, Marjorie Noble, Patricia Noland, Wendy O'brien, Meryl O'loughlin, Gillian O'neill, Lori Openden, Fern Orenstein, Greg Orson, Richard Pagano, Marvin Paige, Mark Paladini, John Papsidera, Cami Patton, Joey Paul, Donald Paul Pemrick, Gayle Pillsbury, Holly Powell, Pamela Rack Guest, Johanna Ray, Robyn Ray, Karen Rea, Cathy Reinking, Barbara Remsen, Debby Romano, Stacey Rosen, Paula Rosenberg, Vicki Rosenberg, Donna Rosenstein, Marcia Ross, Renee Rousselot, Elisabeth Rudolph, Patrick Rush, Mark Saks, Cathy Sandrich Gelfond, Jean Scoccimarro, Kevin Scott, Julie Selzer, Tony Sepulveda, Barbara Shannon, Christine Sheaks, Bill Shepard, Jennifer Shull Clark, Marcia Shulman, Margery Simkin, Melissa Skoff, Mary Jo Slater, Sharon Soble, Dawn Steinberg, Sally Stiner, Andrea Stone, Gilda Stratton, Catherine Stroud, Monica Swann, Judy Taylor, Mark Teschner, Joel Thurm, Mark Tillman, Joy Todd, Elizabeth Torres, Robert J. Ulrich, Nikki Valko, Mary Vernieu, Dava Waite, Alex Wald, Katy Wallin, Samuel Warren Jr., Paul Weber, April Webster, Rosemary Welden, Geri Windsor, Barbara Wright, Ronnie Yeskel, Rhonda Young, Bonnie Zane, Debra Zane, Lisa Zarowin, Gary Zuckerbrod, Dori Zuckerman.
NEW YORK MEMBERS
Robin Joy Allan, Eve Battaglia, Jay Binder, Jeff Block, Jimmy Bohr, Jack Bowdan, Deborah Brown, James Calleri, William Cantler, Jim Carnahan, Aleya Chappelle, Howie Cherpakov, Kathleen Chopin, Amy Christopher, Jodi Collins, Joan D'incecco, Howard Feuer, Alan Filderman, Bonnie Finnegan, Alexa L. Fogel, Paul Fouquet, Alixe Gordin, Judy Henderson, Stuart Howard, Phyllis Huffman, Julie Hughes, Steven Jacobs, Sheila Jaffe, Amanda Mackey Johnson, Geoffrey Johnson, Rosalie Joseph, Avy Kaufman, Stephanie Klapper, Lynn Kressel, Vincent Liff, Julie A. Madison, Jamibeth Margolis, Joe Mcconnell, Pat Mccorkle, Howard Meltzer, Barry Moss, Arnold J. Mungioli, Ellissa Myers, Steven O'neill, Ellen Parks, Marci Phillips, Nancy Piccione, Warren Pincus, Nina Pratt, Shirley Rich, Eleanor Ross, Tara Rubin, Cindi Rush, Suzanne Ryan, Amy Schecter, Sherie Seff, Susan Shopmaker, Mark B. Simon, Meg Simon, Ilene Starger, Irene Stockton, Daniel Swee, Bernard Telsey, Cindy Tolan, Victoria Visgilio, Georgianne Walken, Judy Blye Wilson, Liz Woodman, Andrew Zerman.
Foreign Countries
AUSTRALIA: Mcsweeney, Tom. CANADA: Stuart Aikins, Michelle Allen, John Buchan, Lynne Carrow, Sherry Dayton, Carol Kelsay, Diane Kerbel, Coreen Mayrs. ENGLAND: Carol Dudley. ITALY: Stu Rosen.

THE CASTING STUDIOS
200 S. Labrea, 2nd Flr., Los Angeles, CA 90036. (323) 954-0007. FAX: (323) 954-0933.

CCDA: COMMERCIAL CASTING DIRECTORS ASSOCIATES
c/o Big House Studios, 4420 Lankershim Blvd., N. Hollywood, CA 91602. (818) 752-7100. FAX: (818) 752-7101.
PRESIDENT
Jeff Gerrard

CENTRAL CASTING
Corporate: Entertainment Partners, 2835 N. Naomi St.,
Burbank, CA 90510-7836. (818) 955-6000.
220 S. Flower St., Burbank, CA 91502. (818) 562-2799. FAX:
(818) 260-9806.

CIRCUIT RIDER TALENT & MANAGEMENT
(A division of Dotson-Wooley Entertainment Group: Bookings,
casting, career management)
123 Walton Ferry Rd., Hendersonville, TN 37075. (800) 420-
8568, (615) 824-1947. FAX: (615) 264-0462.
email: dotwool@bellsouth.net
PRESIDENT
Linda Dotson

LORI COBE-ROSS CASTING
2005 Palo Verde Ave., Ste. 306, Long Beach, CA 90815.
(562) 432-7677

ANNELISE COLLINS CASTING
(310) 586-1936. FAX: (310) 586-1100.
email: annelisecast@earthlink.net

COPELAND CREATIVE TALENT
(Talent for commercials, industrials)
4140 1/2 Grand Ave., Des Moines, IA 50312. (515) 271-5970.
FAX: (515) 277-0770. email: copetalent@aol.com
CONTACT
Deb Copeland

PATRICK CUNNINGHAM, CSA
c/o Casting Society of America (CSA), 606 N. Larchmont Blvd.,
Ste. 4B, Los Angeles, CA 90004. (323) 463-1925, (323) 222-
1656. FAX: (323) 225-7815. email: pscrox@aol.com

BILL DANCE CASTING
4605 Lankershim Blvd., Ste. 401, N. Hollywood, CA 91602.
(818) 754-6639 FAX: (818) 754-6643. www.billdancecasting.com

RICHARD DELANCY & ASSOCIATES
4741 Laurel Canyon Blvd., Ste. 100, Valley Village, CA 91607.
(818) 760-3110. www.delancy.com
email: rdelancy@mindspring.com

DIPRIMA CASTING
(TV & film, union & non-union)
1688 Meridian Ave., Ste. 418, Miami Beach, FL 33139. (305)
672-9232. FAX: (305) 672-9020. www.diprimacasting.com
email: barbara@diprimacasting.com
CASTING DIRECTOR
Barbara DiPrima

DIVISEK CASTING & ASSOCIATES
25876 The Old Road, #15, Stevenson Ranch, CA 91381. (323)
655-7766, (661) 253-4590, FAX: 661-253-4592
email: mail@divisekcasting.com
OWNER
Barbara Divisek

PAM DIXON
P.O. Box 672, Beverly Hills, CA 90213. (818) 954-3928.

EDELMAN & ASSOCIATES
12413 Ventura Ct.,Ste. 300, Studio City, CA 91604. (818) 506-
7328.
CONTACT
Susan Edelman

ALICE ELLIS CASTING
P.O. Box 1828, Venice, CA 90294. (310) 314-1488. FAX: (310)
314-2649.
CASTING DIRECTOR
Alice Ellis

STEVEN ERDEK CASTING
2050 S. Bundy Dr., Los Angeles, CA 90025. (310) 820-9200.
FAX: (310) 820-5408.
OWNER
Steven Erdek

SATCHI AGENCY
9868 Main St., Fairfax, VA 22031. (703) 352-7201. FAX: (703)
352-3179. www.satchiagency.com

EXTRAS NETWORK CASTING
(323) 851-9577. FAX: (323) 851-4410. www.extrasnet.com
CASTING DIRECTOR
John Laccetti

MEGAN FOLEY CASTING
11530 Ventura Blvd., Studio City, CA 91604. (818) 286-9350
FAX: (818) 286-9357. email: send2megan@aol.com
OWNER
Megan Foley

EDDIE FOY, III CASTING
11380 Foxglove Ln., Corona, CA 92880. (909) 272-2931. FAX:
(909) 272-2917.

JEFF GERRARD CASTING
(All types of casting)
Big House Studios, 4420 Lankershim Blvd., N. Hollywood, CA
91602. (818) 752-7100. FAX: (818) 752-7101.

DANNY GOLDMAN & ASSOCIATES CASTING
1006 N. Cole Ave., Los Angeles, CA 90038. (323) 463-1600.
FAX: (323) 463-3139.

JEFF GREENBERG CASTING
Paramount Pictures, 5555 Melrose Ave., Marx Brothers Bldg.,
#102, Los Angeles, CA 90038. (323) 956-4886. FAX: (323) 862-
1368.

AARON GRIFFITH CASTING
(Casting for features and television)
8440 Santa Monica Blvd., Ste. 200, Los Angeles, CA 90069.
(323) 654-0033.

A CASTING CONSULTANCY--PATTI HAYES
419 Larchmont Blvd., PMB 249, Los Angeles, CA 90004. (323)
933-0116. FAX: (323) 934-5199.
email: pattisan2@hotmail.com

HISPANIC TALENT CASTING OF HOLLYWOOD
P.O. Box 46123, Los Angeles, CA 90046. (323) 934-6465.
email: billhooey@aol.com

THE HOLLYWOOD MADISON GROUP
(Celebrities Only)
11684 Ventura Blvd., Ste. 258, Studio City, CA 91604. (818)
762-8008. FAX: (818) 762-8089. www.hollywood-madison.com
CONTACT
Jonathan Holiff

DONNA ISAACSON
20th Century Fox, 10201 W. Pico Blvd., Bldg. 12, Rm. 201, Los
Angeles, CA 90035. (310) 369-1824. FAX: (310) 369-1496.

ALEC ISBELL CASTING
16742 Placerita Canyon, Newhall, CA 91321. (661) 255-0097.
FAX: (661) 255-9041.

JAG ENTERTAINMENT
4265 Hazeltine Ave., Sherman Oaks, CA 91423. (818) 905-
5511. FAX: (818) 501-4911. www.jagpr.com
PRESIDENT
Jo-Ann Geffen

DEBORAH KURTZ CASTING
1345 Abbot Kinney Blvd., Venice, CA 90291. (310) 452-6800.
FAX: (310) 314-CAST. email: dkurtz@usfilms.com

ROSS LACY CASTING
200 S. LaBrea, Los Angeles, CA 90036. (310) 358-7558, (323)
954-0007. email: rmmlacy@aol.com

LEAR ENTERPRISES
41 N. Mojave Rd., Las Vegas, NV 89101. (702) 385-9000. FAX:
(702) 438-1333. email: learentertainment@earthlink.net
CEO
Marilee Lear
HEAD, CASTING
Rose Heeter

JOHN LEVEY
(Casting for tv shows)
Warner Bros., 300 Television Plaza, Bldg. 140, Rm. 138,
Burbank, CA 91505. (818) 954-4080.

LIBERMAN PATTON CASTING
4311 Wilshire Blvd., Ste. 606, Los Angeles, CA 90010. (323)
525-1381. FAX: (323) 525-0131.

LIEN COWAN CASTING
7461 Beverly Blvd., Ste. 203, Los Angeles, CA 90036. (323)
937-0411. www.lcc.la

MAGIC CASTING, INC.
1660 Cougar Ridge Rd., Buellton, CA 93427. (805) 688-3702.

MEDIA ACCESS OFFICE
(Casting liaison office for performers with disabilities)
4640 Lankershim Blvd., Ste. 305, N. Hollywood, CA 91602.
(818) 752-1196. FAX: (818) 753-3426.
email: GCastane@edd.ca.gov

MIMI WEBB MILLER
171 Pier Ave., Santa Monica, CA 90405. (310) 452-0863.

MISSING LINK PRODUCTIONS, LLC.
(Cast principals & extras for features, movies of the week,
commercials, music videos & documentaries)
P.O. Box 4137, Rock Hill, SC 29732-6137. (803) 242-0567.
www.maxann.com email: MissingLinkProductions@yahoo.com
OWNER
Maxann Crotts

NEVADA CASTING GROUP, INC.
100 Washington St., Ste. 100, Reno, NV 89503. (775) 322-8187.
FAX: (775) 322-0161. www.nevadacasting.com
email: zak@nevadacasting.com

DAVID O'CONNOR CASTING COMPANY
1017 W. Washington Blvd., Ste. 2A, Chicago, IL 60607. (312)
226-9112. FAX: (312) 226-9921.
email: david@oconnorcasting.tv

MARK HIRSCHFELD
NBC Network, 3000 W. Alameda Ave., Ste. 231, Burbank, CA
91523. (818) 840-3774. FAX: (818) 840-4412.

JEFF OLAN CASTING
11059 McCormick St., Ste. 1, N. Hollywood, CA 91601. (818)
285-5462
OWNER
Jeff Olan

JESSICA OVERWISE
17250 Sunset Blvd., Ste. 304, Pacific Palisades, CA 90272.
(310) 459-2686. FAX: (310) 459-0961.
email: jessicao7@aol.com

MARVIN PAIGE CASTING
P.O. Box 69964, W. Hollywood, CA 90069. (818) 760-3040.

PARADOXE CASTING
P.O. Box 691037, W. Hollywood, CA 90069. (310) 552-8257.
CASTING DIRECTOR
Louis Goldstein

PRIME CASTING
(Extras casting)
6430 Sunset Blvd., Ste. 425, Hollywood, CA 90028. (323) 962-
0377, (323) 962-0378. FAX: (323) 466-4166.
www.primecasting.com email: primecasting@aol.com
CASTING DIRECTOR
Peter Alwazzan

REEL SOUTHERN CASTING
(A division of Dotson-Wooley Entertainment Group)
Talent & Music Casting/Theatrical, TV & Commercial
c/o CRTM-123 Walton Ferry Rd., Hendersonville, TN 37075-
3616. (800) 420-8568. FAX: (615) 264-0462.
email: dotubol@bellsouth.net
PRESIDENT
Linda Dotson

GABRIELLE SCHARY CASTING
1418 Abbot Kinney Blvd., Venice, CA 90291. (310) 450-0835.

TINA SEILER CASTING
P.O. Box 2001, Toluca Lake, CA 91610. (818) 382-7929.
email: tks90046@earthlink.net

LILA SELIK CASTING
(Commercials, films, tv, industrials)
1551 S. Robertson Blvd., Ste. 202, Los Angeles, CA 90035.
(310) 556-2444. FAX: (310) 556-3266.

AVA SHEVITT CASTING
(Village Studio Facility with Teleconference)
Village Studio, 519 Broadway, Santa Monica, CA 90401. (310)
656-4600. FAX: (310) 656-4610.

SHOOTING FROM THE HIP CASTING
c/o Zydeco Studios, 11317 Ventura Blvd., Studio City, CA
91604. (818) 506-0613. FAX: (818) 506-8858.
CASTING DIRECTOR
Francene Selkirk

WEBER & ASSOCIATES CASTING
2400 Broadway, Ste. 340, Santa Monica, CA 90404. (310) 449-
3685. FAX: (310) 449-3685.
CONTACT
Paul Weber

RON SMITH'S PRODUCTIONS
(Celebrity impersonators)
7060 Hollywood Blvd., #1215, Hollywood, CA 90028. (323) 467-
3030. FAX: (323) 467-6720.

LYNN STALMASTER
500 S. Sepulveda Blvd., Ste. 600, Los Angeles, CA 90049.
(310) 552-0983.

STUDIO TALENT GROUP
(Actors and multi-talent)
1328 12th St., Ste. 1 & 3, Santa Monica, CA 90401. (310) 393-
8004. FAX: (310) 393-2473. www.studiotalentgroup.com
email: stgactor@gte.net
PRESIDENT
Phillip L. Brock

MARK TAPER FORUM CASTING/AMY LIEBERMAN CASTING
601 W. Temple St., Ste. 112, Los Angeles, CA 90012. (213) 972-
7374. FAX: (213) 972-7645.
CASTING DIRECTOR
Amy Lieberman
CASTING ASSOCIATE
Paul Dinh-McCrillis
CASTING ASSISTANT
Yasmin Redoblado

SUSAN TYLER CASTING
c/o Chelsea Studios 11530 Ventura Blvd., Studio City, CA
91604. (818) 506-0400. FAX: (818) 762-8449.

VOICECASTER
1832 W. Burbank Blvd., Burbank, CA 91506-1348. (818) 841-
5300. FAX: (818) 841-2085.
OWNER
Huck Liggett

WISE & ASSOCIATES, C.S.A.
18034 Ventura Blvd., Ste. 403, Encino, CA 91316. (818) 535-
7770. email: castwise@aol.com
PRESIDENT
Peter Wise

KEITH WOLFE CASTING
1438 N. Gower, Ste. 39, Hollywood, CA 90028. (323) 469-5595.
FAX: (323) 957-1872. www.hollywoodaccess.com;
www.castingdirector.com

LORI WYMAN CASTING
16499 N.E. 19th Ave., Ste. 203, N. Miami Beach, FL 33162.
(305) 354-3901. FAX: (305) 354-3970.

CONSULTANTS & TECHNICAL ADVISORS

ACCOMMODATING IDEAS, INC.
(Sign-language consultants)
13701 Riverside Dr., Ste. 509, Sherman Oaks, CA 91423. (818)
386-6348. FAX: (818) 386-6352.

ADVANCED FIRE & RESCUE SERVICES
(Fire Rescue Standby, EMT and Fire Personnel; Fire Trucks:
Antique and New)
16205 Lost Canyon Rd., Santa Clarita, CA 91351. (818) 837-
7336, (661) 299-4801. FAX: (661) 298-3069.
www.advancedfire.com
CONTACT
Craig Sanford

AERIAL FOCUS PRODUCTIONS
(Aerial sports, skydiving, base jumps, ultra lights, hang gliding,
stock library.)
P.O. Box 369 Haleiwa, HI 96712 (808) 638-5520.
www.aerialfocus.com email: aerialfcs@aol.com

**ALEXANDER TECHNIQUE/ACTOR'S MOVEMENT
SPECIALIST**
(Movement choreography)
P.O. Box 3194, Beverly Hills, CA 90212. (310) 617-2082.
email: jeanlouisr@aol.com
DIRECTOR OF TRAINING
Jean-Louis Rodrigue

BEE PEOPLE UNLIMITED
(Insect handlers, trainers and research services)
P.O. Box 343, Claremont, CA 91711. (800) 924-3097, (909) 869-
7690. FAX: (909) 869-7391.
CONTACTS
Gregg Manston
Debra Copple

BLACKSTONE MAGIK ENTERPRISES, INC.
(Magic technical advisers, consultants)
12800 Puesta Del Sol, Redlands, CA 92373. (909) 792-1227.
FAX: (909) 794-2737. www.blackstonemagic.com

BRAVO AVIATION
(Aerial technical advisers)
Jack Northrop Field, 12101 S. Crenshaw Blvd., Ste. 2,
Hawthorne, CA 90045. 1-800-77-FLYING, (310) 263-7669. FAX:
(310) 263-7679.
L.A. Port: Ports O' Call Village, Berth 75, San Pedro, CA. (800)
77-FLYING, (310) 337-6701. FAX: (310) 337-6719.
www.bravoair.com email: bravomail@bravoair.com
PRESIDENT
Robert Butler

BRIGHT STRATEGIC DESIGNS
(Identity design & consultants)
4223 Glencoe Ave., Ste. A-100, Marina Del Rey, CA 90292.
(310) 305-2565. FAX: (310) 305-2566. www.brightdesigns.com
CONTACT
Tuire Bright

BROADCAST BUSINESS CONSULTANTS, LTD.
(Talent payment and negotiations)
317 Madison Ave., Ste. 510, New York, NY 10017. (212) 687-
3525. FAX: (212) 949-8143.

PAUL BRONSTON, M.D.
(Medical adviser)
1 Jib St., #202, Marina Del Rey, CA 90292. (310) 301-9426.
FAX: (310) 823-2433. email: drprotec@attbi.com

BUDGETS BY DESIGN
(Schedules & budgets)
428 Spencer St., Glendale, CA 91202. (818) 507-4449. FAX:
(818) 507-4464. www.budgetsbydesign.com
email: info@budgetsbydesign
CONTACT
Robert Schneider

CALIFORNIA HISTORICAL GROUP

WWII LIVING HISTORY ASSOCIATION
(World War II technical advice)
P.O. Box 1950, Costa Mesa, CA 92628. (714) 641-3421. FAX:
(714) 546-9035. www.chgww2.com
CHAIRMAN
Stan Wolcott

CALIFORNIA SAILING ACADEMY
(Boating advisor)
14025 Panay Way, Marina Del Rey, CA 90292. (310) 821-3433.
FAX: (310) 821-4141. email: rufus@ucla.edu
PRESIDENT
Paul Miller

CALL THE COPS
(S.W.A.T. tactics, patrol/homicide procedures)
P.O. Box 911, Agoura Hills, CA 91376. (888) 548-0911.
www.call-the-cops.com
CONTACT
Randy Walker

RICHARD G. CASTANON, M.D., F.A.C.S.
(Medical adviser)
17732 Beach Blvd., Ste. C, Huntington Beach, CA 92647. (714)
848-2222.

THE CHARTER CONNECTION, FILMBOATS, INC.
(Marine coordination & consulting)
5015 Pacific Ave., Marina Del Rey, CA 90292. (800) 242-7877,
(310) 827-4105. FAX: (310) 827-0381. www.filmboats.com
email: Bertram@filmboats.com
CONTACT
Bertram McCann

CHEQUERED FLAG INTERNATIONAL, INC.
(Classic European cars, technical advisers)
4128 Lincoln Blvd., Marina Del Rey, CA 90292. (310) 827-8665.
FAX: (310) 821-1272. www.chequeredflag.com

CURT DECKERT ASSOCIATES, INC.
(Technical management consultants, optical technology
research & development)
18061 Darmel Pl., Santa Ana, CA 92705. (800) 394-0748, (714)
639-0746. FAX: (714) 639-0746.
www.cdeckert.com email: curt@cdeckert.com

EXTREME SPORTS FILMING
(Action sports specialist, marine, air and land; production
facilities, location, equipment, talent and more)
3419 Via Lido, #145, Newport Beach, CA 92663. (714) 235-
7578. email: efilming@mindspring.com

FLORIDA FILM CARS/CLASSIC VEHICLE RENTALS
(Advisers for vehicles for film)
4630 University Dr., Ste. 204, Coral Springs, FL 33067. (954)
340-3013, (954) 340-0117. www.floridafilmcars.com

NINA FOCH STUDIOS
(Creative consultant)
P.O. Box 1884, Beverly Hills, CA 90213. (310) 553-5805. FAX:
(310) 553-6149.
CONTACT
Maud Valot

GOLDEN PARASHOOT ENTERTAINMENT
(Skydiving, hang gliding and aerial stunts)
537 Newport Center Dr., Ste. 645, Newport Beach, CA 92660.
(949) 798-6161.
CONTACT
Craig Le Fronk

IRA A. GREENBERG, PH.D/GROUP HYPNOSIS CENTER
(Hypnosis for problem solving: actors, writers and directors)
8939 S. Sepulveda Blvd., Ste. 318, Los Angeles, CA 90045.
(310) 472-2662.

HANDS-ON BROADCAST
(Search and consulting company)
124 W. 24th St., Ste. 6B, New York, NY 10011. (212) 924-5036.
FAX: (212) 604-9036. email: bgspeed@aol.com
PRESIDENT
Lorraine Bege

LEXINGTON
(Scenery design and fabrication)
12800 Rangoon St., Arleta, CA 91331. (818) 768-5768. FAX:
(818) 768-4217. www.lexingtonscenery.com
email: info@lex-usa.com
OWNERS
Frank Bencivengo
Richard Bencivengo

LIN-DEL ASSOCIATES
(Consultants on period props)
264 S. La Cienega Blvd., Beverly Hills, CA 90211. (310) 453-
0193, (516) 374-0173. FAX: (310) 453-0193.

WARREN LOCKHART CONSULTING
(Film & tv production consultants)
P.O. Box 11629, Marina Del Rey, CA 90295. (310) 821-1414.
FAX: (310) 301-0536. www.lockhartproductions.com
email: warren@lockhartproductions.com
CONTACT
McKenzie Allen

MARSHALL/PLUMB RESEARCH ASSOCIATES
(Legal research, script clearances)
4150 Riverside Dr., # 209, Burbank, CA 91505. (818) 848-7071.
FAX: (818) 848-7702. www.marshall-plumb.com
email: carolyn@marshall-plumb.com

MEDIA CITY TELEPRODUCTION
(Technical advisers for TV production)
2525 N. Naomi St., Burbank, CA 91504. (818) 848-5800. FAX:
(818) 848-6454. www.mediacitystudios.com
email: sales@mediacitystudios.com
V.P., SALES & MARKETING
Carol Noorigian

LARRY MOSS SPEECH & DIALECT SERVICES
(Dialect, diction & speech)
855 3rd St., Ste. 305, Santa Monica, CA 90403. (310) 395-
4284. email: Starcoach@earthlink.net

PANPIPES MAGICKAL MARKETPLACE
(Occult technical advisers)
1641 N. Cahuenga Blvd., Hollywood, CA 90028. (323) 462-
7078. FAX: (323) 462-6700. www.panpipes.com
email: info@panpipes.com

SANTA ANITA PARK
(Technical advisers, horse racing)
285 W. Huntington Dr., Arcadia, CA 91007. (626) 574-7223.
FAX: (626) 446-1456. www.santaanita.com
email: comments@santaanita.com

THE SHINDLER PERSPECTIVE, INC.
(Management consulting for creative, technology & emerging
companies)
P.O. Box 8633, Calabasas, CA 91372-8633. (818) 223-8345.
FAX: (818) 223-8372. www.iShindler.com
email: Marty@iShindler.com
CONTACT
Marty Shindler

THE SIGN LANGUAGE COMPANY
(Sign Language Consultants, Interpreters & Tutors)
14203 Califa St., Van Nuys, CA 91401. (800) 997-2778, (818)
782-6002. FAX: (818) 994-3214.
www.thesignlanguagecompany.com email: scriptla@aol.com
CONTACT
Bill Pugin

THRILLSEEKERS UNLIMITED, INC.
(Extreme sports for film, TV and S.A.G. stuntpersons)
3172 N. Rainbow Blvd., Ste. 321, Las Vegas, NV 89108. (702)
699-5550. Hollywood Stunt Office: (323) 691-8705.
www.thrillseekersunlimited.com
email: stunts@thrillseekersunlimited.com
PRESIDENT & CEO
Rich Hopkins

**MADEMOISELLE IRENE UJDA (YESTERYEARS
DANCERS)**
(Period re-enactment & historical consultant, specializing in 18th
& 19th century dance)
2546 1/2 Corralitas Dr., Los Angeles, CA 90039. (323) 664-
0227, (310) 244-8028.

USHIST HISTORICAL RESOURCES
(Historical production resources)
P.O. Box 26957, Phoenix, AZ 85068-6957. (602) 331-4945. FAX:
(602) 331-8592. www.ushist.com
COORDINATOR
Terrance C. Leavey

MICHAEL WIESE PRODUCTIONS
11288 Ventura Blvd., Ste. 621, Studio City, CA 91604. (818)
379-8799. FAX: (818) 986-3408. www.mwp.com
email: mwpsales@mwp.com

THE WING GALLERY
(Since 1975, a source for Wildlife, Western, Folk, Americana,
Japanese, Fantasy, Cat Art and Collectibles)
13632 Ventura Blvd., Sherman Oaks, CA 91423. (818) 981-
9464. FAX: (818) 981-2787. www.winggallery.com
OWNER
Mark Dietrich

COSTUME & PROP RENTALS

ABC COSTUME SHOP
3704 N.E. 2nd Ave., Miami, FL 33137. (305) 573-5657. FAX:
(305) 573-5658. www.abccostumeshop.com
OWNER
Franco Carretti

ABRAHAM RUGS GALLERY
525 N. La Cienega Blvd., Los Angeles, CA 90048. (800) 222-
RUGS, (310) 652-6520. FAX: (310) 652-6594.
www.abrahamruggallery.com email: abrahamrug@aol.com

ACCU-CAST/ACCU-DENT
(Prosthetic grade alginates, fast to slow setting for prop duplication)
687 Brian Way, Medford, OR 97501. (541) 618-8461. FAX: (541)
618-8460. www.accu-cast.us email: info@accu-cast.us
CONTACT
Lucinda Baker

ACE PROPS
1 West 19th St., New York, NY 10011. (212) 206-1475. FAX:
(212) 929-9082. email: acevideony@aol.com
CONTACT
Tony Cozzi

ADAMM'S STAINED GLASS
1426 4th St., Santa Monica, CA 90401. (310) 451-9390. FAX:
(310) 451-9386. www.adammsgallery.com
CONTACT
Adam Gritlefeld

AERO MOCK-UPS
(Airline cabin interiors)
13110 Saticoy St., Ste. C, N. Hollywood, CA 91605. (818) 982-
7327. FAX: (818) 982-0122. www.aeromockups.com
email: info@aeromockups.com
PRESIDENT
Richard Chan

AGAPE UNIFORM COMPANY
3606 W. Washington Blvd., Los Angeles, CA 90018. (323) 731-
0621. FAX: (323) 731-0690.

AIM PRODUCTIONS, INC.
(Product placement, entertainment promotions)
37-11 35th Ave., Ste. 3B, Astoria, NY 11106. (718) 729-9288.
FAX: (718) 786-0137. email: pattigan@yahoo.com
PRESIDENT
Patricia Ganguzza

AIR HOLLYWOOD
(Aircraft props)
255 Parkside Dr., San Fernando, CA 91340. (818) 365-3700.
FAX: (818) 365-0151. www.airhollywood.com
PRESIDENT
Talaat Captan
GENERAL MANAGER
Robert Shalhoub

AIRPOWER AVIATION RESOURCES
(Antique, civilian and military aircraft)
702 Paseo Vista, Thousand Oaks, CA 91360. (805) 499-0307.
FAX: (805) 498-0357. www.airpower-aviation.com
CONTACT
Michael Patlin

ALLAN UNIFORM RENTAL SERVICE, INC.
121 E. 24th St., 7th Flr., New York, NY 10010. (212) 529-4655.
www.ibuss-allan.com

ALMOST CHRISTMAS PROPSHOP
(Holiday decorations, animated Santas, elves and sleighs)
5057 Lankershim Blvd., N. Hollywood, CA 91601. (818) 285-
9627. FAX: (818) 285-9630. www.christmaslights.com
CONTACT
Cathy Christmas

ALTMAN LUGGAGE
135 Orchard St., New York, NY 10002. (212) 254-7275. FAX:
(212) 254-7663. www.altmanluggage.com

AMERICAN COSTUME CORP.
(Period wardrobe, 1770-1970)
12980 Raymer St., N. Hollywood, CA 91605. (818) 764-2239.
FAX: (818) 765-7614.
PRESIDENT
Diana Foster

ANA SPECIAL EFFECTS
(Glass and props)
7021 Hayvenhurst Ave., Van Nuys, CA 91406. (818) 909-6999.
OWNER
Gladys Nary

ANATOMORPHEX
(Animation creatures, animatronics, characters, makeup effects,
hero props and statues)
8210 Lankershim Blvd., Ste. 14, N. Hollywood, CA 91605. (818)
768-2880. FAX: (818) 768-4808. www.anatomorphex.com
email: anatofx@hotmail.com

ANTIQUARIAN TRADERS
9031 W. Olympic Blvd., Beverly Hills, CA 90211. (310) 247-
3900. FAX: (310) 247-8864. www.AntiquarianTraders.com
email: INFO@AntiquarianTraders.com

AQUAVISION
(Marine props and fabrication)
256 Loma Ave., Long Beach, CA 90803. (562) 433-2863.
www.aquavision.net email: bobanderson@aquavision.net
PRESIDENT
Bob Anderson

BEDFELLOWS
(Contemporary furniture)
12250 Ventura Blvd., Studio City, CA 91604. (818) 985-0500.
FAX: (818) 985-0617.
CONTACT
Barbara Dixon

BRILES WING & HELICOPTER, INC.
16303 Waterman Dr., Van Nuys, CA 91406. (877) TO FLY LA
(863-5952), (818) 994-1445. FAX: (818) 994-1447.
www.toflyla.com email: info@toflyla.com
GENERAL MANAGER
Lance Strumpf

PAT BRYMER CREATIONS
(Custom fantasy walk arounds)
136 N. Avenue 61, Ste. 102, Los Angeles, CA 90042-4263.
(323) 259-0400. FAX: (323) 259-0358. www.pbcreations.com
email: character@pbcreations.com

BUENA VISTA STUDIOS
500 S. Buena Vista St., Burbank, CA 91521. (818) 560-1056.
FAX: (818) 566-8832.
COSTUME DEPARTMENT DIRECTOR
Tom Bronson

CALIFORNIA SAILING ACADEMY
(Antique marine props)
14025 Panay Way, Marina Del Rey, CA 90292. (310) 821-3433.
FAX: (310) 821-4141. www.sailingacademy.com
PRESIDENT
Paul Miller

CALIFORNIA SURPLUS MART
(Military Surplus)
6263 Santa Monica Blvd., Hollywood, CA 90038. (323) 465-
5525.

CAMERA READY CARS
11161 Slater Ave., Fountain Valley, CA 92708. (714) 444-2000,
x511, FAX: (714) 4351008. www.metalcrafters.com

CELEBRITY EYEWORKS
c/o Independent Studio Services, 11907 Wichs St., Sun Valley,
CA 91352. (818) 764-0840. FAX: (818) 768-6320.
CONTACT
Michael Hirsch

CENTRE FIREARMS CO, INC.
10 W. 37th St., New York, NY 10018. (212) 244-4040, (212) 244-
4044. FAX: (212) 947-1233.

CHARISMA DESIGN STUDIO, INC.
(Water-jet cutting, custom prop fabrication, mechanical or steel,
glass & glass etching, foam, plastics, full sign services)
8414 San Fernando Rd. Sun Valley, CA 91352. (818) 252-6611.
FAX: (818) 252-6610. www.charismadesign.com
email: charismads@earthlink.net
CONTACT
Ben Baron

CINTAS CORPORATION
(Uniforms)
460 W. California Ave., P.O. Box 686, Vista, CA 92085. (800)
524-6826, (760) 941-8422. FAX: (760) 941-2685.

C.J.S. FILM STUDIOS
2005 N. 103rd Ave., Avondale, AZ 85323. (602) 264-2539. FAX:
(623) 936-7015. www.cjsstudios.com
email: cjsstudios@earthlink.net
STUDIO MANAGER
Traci Langston

CLASSIC CAR SUPPLIERS
1484 Sunset Plaza Dr., W. Hollywood, CA 90069. (310) 657-7823.

CONTEMPORARY ART RESOURCE
(Custom fine props)
1035 N. Myra Ave., Los Angeles, CA 90029. (323) 665-7566.

CONTINENTAL SCENERY
7802 Clybourn Ave., Sun Valley, CA 91352. (818) 768-8075. FAX: (818) 768-6939. www.continentalscenery.com
OWNER
Frank Pera

COOPER FILM CARS
(Offers photography and special event space)
132 Perry St., New York, NY 10014. (212) 929-3909. FAX: (212) 633-6952. www.cooperclassiccars.com
MANAGER
Noah Levinson

COSTUME ARMOUR, INC.
2 Mill St., Cornwall, NY 12518. (845) 534-9120. FAX: (845) 534-8602. www.costumearmour.com
CONTACT
Michelle Truncale

COSTUME RENTALS CO.
11149 Vanowen St., N. Hollywood, CA 91605. (818) 753-3700. FAX: (818) 753-3737.
CONTACT
Buffy Snyder

ELIZABETH COURTNEY COSTUMES
4019 Tujunga Ave., Studio City, CA 91604. (818) 763-8615. FAX: (818) 506-0772.

CREATIVE COSTUME CO.
242 W. 36th St., 8th Flr., New York, NY 10018. (212) 564-5552. FAX: (212) 564-5613. www.creativecostume.com

CUSTOM CHARACTERS
(Character costuming)
621 Thompson Ave., Glendale, CA 91201-2032. (818) 507-5940. FAX: (818) 507-1619. www.customcharacters.com

DESERT PROPS
42848 150th St. E., Lancaster, CA 93535. (661) 946-1515. FAX: (661) 946-0454. www.waldhaus.com

THE WALT DISNEY STUDIOS
500 S. Buena Vista St., Burbank, CA 91521. (818) 560-1056. FAX: (818) 566-8832. email: tom.bronson@disney.com; kathy.monderine@disney.com

DODGER COSTUME
(Costumes for theatre, tv and film)
601 W. 26th St., Ste. 309, New York, NY 10001. (718) 729-1010. FAX: (212) 243-1534.

DOMSEY INTERNATIONAL SALES CORP.
(Vintage clothing)
431 Kent Ave., Brooklyn, NY 11211. (718) 384-6000. FAX: (718) 782-3962.

DOZAR OFFICE FURNITURE
9937 Jefferson Blvd., Ste. 100, Culver City, CA 90232. (310) 559-9292. FAX: (310) 559-9009. www.dozar.com

E. C. 2 COSTUMES
4019 Tujunga Ave., Studio City, CA 91604. (818) 506-7695. FAX: (818) 506-0772.

E=MC2
(Tv, playback, video and computer props)
710 W. Ivy St., Glendale, CA 91204. (818) 243-2424. FAX: (818) 243-5126. www.emc2visfx.com
CONTACT
Bob Morgenroth

EASTERN COSTUME
7243 Coldwater Canyon, N. Hollywood, CA 91605. (818) 982-3611. FAX: (818) 982-1905. www.easterncostume.com

ECLECTIC ENCORE PROPERTIES, INC.
620 W. 26th St., 4th Flr., New York, NY 10001. (212) 645-8880. FAX: (212) 243-6508. www.eclecticprops.com

ERA AVIATION
6160 Carl Brady Dr., Anchorage, AK 99502. (800) 478-1947, (907) 248-4422. FAX: (907) 266-8350. www.era-aviation.com
email: info@eraaviation.com

EXECUTIVE YACHT MANAGEMENT, INC./FILM SERVICES DIVISION
(Picture and camera boats)
644 Venice Blvd., Marina Del Rey, CA 90291-4801. (310) 306-2555. FAX: (310) 306-1147.

EXTREME MARINE PRODUCTION SERVICES/EXTREME SPORTS FOR FILMING
3419 Via Lido, Ste. 145, Newport Beach, CA 92663. (562) 596-7105. FAX: (562) 596-7125.
PRESIDENT
Miles Flewitt

EYES ON MAIN
(Custom-made eyeglass frames)
3110 Main St., #108, Santa Monica, CA 90405. (888) 287-8177, (310) 399-3302. FAX: (310) 399-7682.

EVENT SOLUTIONS
(Formerly Des Cartes Catering. Full-service events/catering)
3975 Landmark Street, Culver City, CA 90232. (800) 850-9979, (310) 815-2440. FAX: (310) 815-2454. www.eventsolutions.com
email: info@eventsolutions.com

FOAM-TEC, INC.
(Background sets and scenery for tv and film)
11107 Randall St., Sun Valley, CA 91352. (818) 504-7303. FAX: (818) 504-7314.

FUN ANTIQUES & COLLECTIBLES
1101 First Ave., New York, NY 10021. (888) DARROWS, (212) 838-0730. FAX: (212) 838-3617.
email: george@fun-antiques.com

PETER GEYER ACTION PROPS & SETS
(Breakaways, including rubber)
8235 Lankershim Blvd., Ste. G, N. Hollywood, CA 91605. (818) 768-0070.

GLENDALE COSTUMES
746 W. Doran St., Glendale, CA 91203. (818) 244-1161. FAX: (818) 244-8576.
OWNER
Tim Deitlein

GLOBAL EFFECTS, INC.
(Spacesuits and armor)
7115 Laurel Canyon Blvd., N. Hollywood, CA 91605. (818) 503-9273. FAX: (818) 503-9459. www.globaleffects.com

GRAPHIC ILLUSIONS/HOLLYWOOD 2000
(Custom computer props)
4200 Verdant, Unit C, Los Angeles, CA 90039. (818) 840-8333.

GREGORY'S TUX SHOP
12051 Magnolia Blvd., N. Hollywood, CA 91607. (818) 980-5480. FAX: (818) 980-5084. www.tuxedosonline.com
CONTACT
Vrej Gregorian

GROSH SCENIC RENTALS, INC.
4114 Sunset Blvd., Los Angeles, CA 90029. (877) 363-7998, (323) 662-1134. FAX: (323) 664-7526. www.grosh.com
email: info@grosh.com

HAND PROP ROOM, INC.
5700 Venice Blvd., Los Angeles, CA 90019. (323) 931-1534. FAX: (323) 931-2145.

HOLLYWOOD BREAKAWAY
317 Anita St., Redondo Beach, CA 90278. (310) 798-8708. FAX: (310) 798-8144.

HOLLYWOOD GLASS COMPANY
5119 Hollywood Blvd., Los Angeles, CA 90027. (323) 665-8829. FAX: (323) 661-7261.

HOLLYWOOD PICTURE VEHICLES/THE BOSEWS COLLECTION
1028 N. LaBrea Ave., Hollywood, CA 90038. (323) 466-2277. FAX: (323) 466-6541.
CONTACT
Don Thomas

HOLLYWOOD TOYS & COSTUMES
6600 Hollywood Blvd., Hollywood, CA 90028. (888) 760-3330, (323) 464-4444. FAX: (323) 464-4644. www.hollywoodtoys.com
email: info@hollywoodtoys.com

HOUSE OF PROPS
(Fine arts prop rentals)
1117 Gower St., Hollywood, CA 90038. (323) 463-3166. FAX: (323) 463-8302. email: houseprops@aol.com
CONTACT
Norman Balos

IN COSTUME
37 W. 20th St., New York, NY 10011. (212) 255-5502.

INDEPENDENT STUDIO SERVICES
11907 Wicks St., Sun Valley, CA 91352. (818) 764-0840, (818) 768-6320.

INFLATABLE MARKETPLACE
1810 Gillespie Way, Ste. 202, El Cajon, CA 92020. (800) 383-9980, (619) 258-4466. FAX: (619) 258-0732.
www.inflatablemarketplace.com

INTERNATIONAL COSTUME
1423 Marcellina Ave., Torrance, CA 90501. (310) 320-6392.
FAX: (310) 320-3054. email: leticidressu@aol.com
MANAGER
Fritz Sanders

IT'S A WRAP
3315 W. Magnolia Blvd., Burbank, CA 91505. (818) 567-7366.
FAX: (818) 567-0910. www.itsawraphollywood.com
OWNER
Tiara Nappi

IWASAKI IMAGES OF AMERICA
(Food Replicas)
630 Maple Ave., Torrance, CA 90503. Outside CA: (800) 323-9921, (310) 328-7121. FAX: (310) 618-0876.
www.iwasaki-images.com email: mail@iwasaki-images.com

IZQUIERDO STUDIOS
118 W. 22nd St., New York, NY 10011. (212) 807-9757. FAX:
(212) 366-5249.

JULES & JIM CUSTOM ARTWORK
(Design & artwork for props & set dressing, portrait painting)
14740 Cumpston St., Sherman Oaks, CA 91411. (818) 780-3278. FAX: (818) 780-3278.

KREISS COLLECTION
(Upscale home furnishings)
8619 Melrose Ave., Los Angeles, CA 90069-5010. (310) 657-3990.

KUTTNER PROP RENTALS, INC.
601 W. 26th St., 3rd Flr., New York 10001. (212) 242-7969. FAX:
(212) 242-1293.
CONTACT
Barbara Genest

L.A. EYEWORKS
7407 Melrose Ave., Los Angeles, CA 90046. (323) 653-8255.
FAX: (323) 653-8176. email: eyeworksstore@laeyeworks.com
PUBLICITY
Ruth Handel (323) 938-2161 x123

LEXINGTON SCENERY & PROPS
12800 Rangoon St., Arleta, CA 91331. (818) 768-5768. FAX:
(818) 768-4217.

LILLIAN COSTUME CO. OF L.I., INC.
226 Jericho Turnpike, Mineola, NY 11501. (516) 746-6060. FAX:
(516) 746-1058.

THE MANNEQUIN GALLERY
12350 Montague St., Unit E, Pacoima CA 91331. (818) 834-5555. FAX: (818) 834-5558. www.mannequingallery.com
CONTACT
Shelley Wilkey

MED + RENT, INC.
P.O. Box 10248, Burbank, CA 91510. (818) 834-5800. FAX:
(818) 834-5900. www.medrent.com

MODERN PROPS
5500 W. Jefferson Blvd., Los Angeles, CA 90016. (323) 934-3000. FAX: (323) 934-3155. www.modernprops.com
CONTACT
Olivier Albin

MOTION PICTURE COSTUMES & SUPPLIES, INC.
3811 Ve La Halla Dr., Burbank, CA 91505. (818) 557-1247. FAX:
(818) 557-1695.
PRESIDENT
Michelle Archer

MOTION PICTURE MARINE
616 Venice Blvd., Marina Del Rey, CA 90291. (310) 822-1100.
FAX: (310) 822-2679. www.motionpicturemarine.com
PRESIDENT
David Grober

MUSIC PROP SERVICES
(Musical instruments for film & tv)
1609 Cahuenga Blvd., Hollywood, CA 90028. (323) 466-5120.
FAX: (323) 466-5129. www.musicprops.com

NATIONAL HELICOPTER SERVICE
16750 Roscoe Blvd., P.O. Box 17150, Encino, CA 91416. (818) 345-5222. FAX: (818) 782-0466. www.nationalhelicopter.com
CONTACT
Richard Hart

NAUTICAL HERITAGE FILM SERVICES
P.O. Box 545, San Clemente, CA 92674. (949) 369-6773.
CONTACT
Steve Christman

NIGHTS OF NEON
(Prop rental and custom signage)
13815 Saticoy St., Van Nuys, CA 91402. (818) 756-4791. FAX:
(818) 756-4744. www.nightsofneon.com
PRESIDENT
Lisa Schulte

NORCOSTCO, INC.
3606 W. Magnolia Blvd., Burbank, CA 91505. (800) 220-6915,
(818) 567-0753. FAX: (818) 567-1961.wwwnorcostco.com
GENERAL MANAGER
Wayne Thornton

OUR SECRET CREATIONS
(Custom cubic zirconia and jewelry rentals)
246 S. Robertson Blvd., Beverly Hills, CA 90211. (310) 358-8404. FAX: (310) 358-0179.
CONTACT
Anita Reichenberg

PALACE COSTUME & PROP COMPANY
835 N. Fairfax Ave., Los Angeles, CA 90046. (323) 651-5458.
FAX: (323) 658-7133. www.palacecostume.com
CONTACT
Seo Alanzo

PARAMOUNT COSTUME DEPARTMENT
5555 Melrose Ave., Edith Head Bldg., Rm. 200, Hollywood, CA
90038. (323) 956-5288. FAX: (323) 862-2342.

PERIOD PROPS
P.O. Box 6461, Burbank, CA 91510. (818) 848-PROP, (818) 807-6677.
CONTACT
David Inskeep

PETERSEN AVIATION
7155 Valjean Ave., Van Nuys, CA 91406. (800) 451-7270, (818)
989-2300. FAX: (818) 902-9386. www.petersenaviation.com
CONTACT
Tom Magglon

PICTURE CARS EAST, INC.
72 Huntington St., Brooklyn, NY 11231. (718) 852-2300. FAX:
(718) 858-1583.

PROP-ART
(Custom props, including sculpture & mechanized devices)
6189 Sylvan Dr., Simi Valley, CA 93063. TEL/FAX: (805) 584-1797.
CONTACT
John Ramsay

PROP SERVICES WEST, INC.
915 N. Citrus Ave., Los Angeles, CA 90038. (323) 461-3371.
FAX: (323) 461-4571.

PROPS DISPLAYS & INTERIORS, INC.
132 W. 18th St., New York, NY 10011. (212) 620-3840. FAX:
(212) 620-5472.
CONTACT
Stephen Sebbane

PROPS FOR TODAY
330 W. 34th St. New York, NY 10001. (212) 244-9600. FAX:
(212) 244-1053. www.propsfortoday.com
email: info@propsfortoday.com
CONTACT
Jennifer Lehay

QUARTERMASTER UNIFORM COMPANY
P.O. Box 4147, Cerritos, CA 90703. (800) 444-8643. FAX: (562)
304-7335. www.qmuniforms.com

ROCK & WATER CREATIONS, INC.
(Ponds, waterfalls and boulders)
815 5th St., Filmore, CA 93015. (805) 524-5600. FAX: (805)
524-7339. www.rock-n-water.com email: info@rock-n-water.com
PRESIDENT
Roger Embury

RUBIE'S COSTUME CO., INC.
120-08 Jamaica Ave., Richmond Hill, Queens, NY 11418. (718)
846-1008. FAX: (718) 846-6174. www.rubies.com

SCENIC HIGHLIGHTS
4640 Sperry St., Los Angeles, CA 90039. (818) 956-3610. FAX:
(818) 956-3616.

SHELLY'S APPAREL WAREHOUSE
(General costumes)
2089 Westwood Blvd., Los Angeles, CA 90025. (310) 475-1400.
FAX: (310) 470-6125.

SOMPER FURS
301 N. Canon Dr., Beverly Hills, CA 90210. (310) 273-5262.
FAX: (310) 273-7270.

SPORTSROBE
8654 Hayden Pl., Culver City, CA 90232. (310) 559-3999. FAX: (310) 559-4767.

STICKS & STONES
(Specialty props, costume design, custom build only; make-up effects and puppets)
10535 Tujunga Canyon Blvd., Tujunga, CA 91042. (818) 352-9538. FAX: (818) 352-2779. www.sticksandstonesfx.com
CONTACTS
Rob Burman
Jennifer E. McManus

STUDIO PICTURE VEHICLES
(Transportation: police vehicles, armored trucks, ambulances, taxis)
5418 Fair Ave., N. Hollywood, CA 91601. (818) 765-1201, (818) 781-4223. FAX: (818) 506-4789.

THE SWORD & THE STONE
(Period clothing & armour)
723 N. Victory Blvd., Burbank, CA 91502. (818) 562-6548. FAX: (818) 562-6549. www.swordandstone.com
email: tony@swordandstone.com

TRIANGLE SCENERY/DRAPERY/LIGHTING CO.
1215 Bates Ave., Los Angeles, CA 90029. (323) 662-8129. FAX: (323) 662-8120. www.tridrape.com email: info@tridrape.com

MIKE TRISTANO WEAPONS & SPECIAL EFFECTS
(Prop weapons, blank firing weapons, on-set weapons handlers and armorer)
14431 Ventura Blvd., PMB 185, Sherman Oaks, CA 91423. (818) 888-6970. FAX: (818) 888-6447.

20TH CENTURY FOX/FOX PRODUCTION SERVICES: WARDROBE
(Action props and prop construction)
10201 W. Pico Blvd., Bldg. 99, Los Angeles, CA 90035. (310) 369-1897. FAX: (310) 369-2487.

20TH CENTURY FOX/FOX PRODUCTION SERVICES: PROPS
10201 W. Pico Blvd., Bldg. 99, Rm. 342, Los Angeles, CA 90035. (310) 369-2775. FAX: (310) 369-3183.

20TH CENTURY PROPS
(WWII submarine and F-18 fighter jet for rent)
11651 Hart St., N. Hollywood, CA 91605-5802. (818) 759-1190. FAX: (818) 759-0081. www.20thcenturyprops.com

UNITED AMERICAN COSTUME
12980 Raymer St., N. Hollywood, CA 91605. (818) 764-2239. FAX: (818) 765-7614.
MANAGER
Janet Stout

UNIVERSAL FACILITIES RENTAL
100 Universal City Plaza, #4250-3, Universal City, CA 91608. (818) 777-3000. FAX: (818) 866-0293.

USHIST HISTORICAL RESOURCES
(Civil War, Indian Wars, Cowboy costumes)
Box 26957, Phoenix, AZ 85068-6957. (602) 331-4945. FAX: (602) 331-8592. www.ushist.com email: azrahist@ushist.com

WARNER BROS. STUDIOS, FACILITIES/WIG RENTALS
4000 Warner Blvd., Burbank, CA 91522. Costumes: (818) 954-1297. Wigs: (818) 954-2151. FAX: (818) 954-3685.

WESTERN COSTUME CO.
11041 Vanowen St., N. Hollywood, CA 91605. (818) 760-0900. FAX: (818) 508-2190. www.westerncostume.com
email: wccmail@westerncostume.com

WONDERWORKS/ACTION SETS & PROPS
21350 Sherman Way, Canoga Park, CA 91303. (818) 992-8811. FAX: (818) 347-4330. www.wonderworksweb.com
PRESIDENT
Brick Price

ENTERTAINMENT LAWYERS

AKIN, GUMP, STRAUSS, HAUER & FELD, LLP
2029 Century Park E., Ste. 2400, Los Angeles, CA 90067. (310) 229-1000. FAX: (310) 229-1001. www.akingump.com
ATTORNEYS
David A. Braun, P. John Burke, Tuneen Chisolm, Howard D. Fabrick, Steven Fayne, Lev Ginsburg, Peter L. Haviland, Channing D. Johnson, Jason M. Karlov, Lawrence D. Levien, Alissa Morris, Scott H. Racine, Marissa J. Roman, Stephen L. Saltzman, Cecil Schenker, Rebecca C. Schubert, James O. Thoma, Rhonda R. Trotter, Jonathan M. Wight

ANDERSON & ANDERSON LLP
515 S. Flower St., Ste. 3500, Los Angeles, CA 90071-2203. (213) 426-6200. FAX: (213) 623-1533.
ATTORNEY
M. Jan Akre

ALSCHULER, GROSSMAN, STEIN & KAHAN, LLP
The Water Garden, South Tower, 1620 26th St., 4th Flr., Santa Monica, CA 90404. (310) 907-1000. FAX: (310) 907-2000. www.alschuler.com
ENTERTAINMENT LAWYERS
Lucia Coyoca, Marshall Grossman, Bob Kahan, Michael Plonsker, Stanton L. Stein

ARMSTRONG, HIRSCH, JACKOWAY, TYERMAN & WERTHEIMER
1888 Century Park East, 18th Flr., Los Angeles, CA 90067-1722. (310) 553-0305. FAX: (310) 553-5036.
ATTORNEYS
Arthur O. Armstrong (of counsel), Karl R. Austen, Ronald J. Bass (of counsel), Jeffrey A. Bernstein, Joseph D'Onofrio, Alan Epstein, Howard A. Fishman, Andrew Galker, Robert Getman, George T. Hayum, Geraldine S. Hemmerling (of counsel), Barry L. Hirsch, Myreon M. Hodur, James R. Jackoway, Chris F. Kerns, James C. Mandelbaum, David J. Matlof, Marcy Morris, Michele M. Mulrooney, Geoffry Oblath, Kate E. Phillips, Paul Reese, Robert Stulberg, Darren M. Trattner, Barry Tyerman, Robert Wallerstein, Eric Weissler, Alan S. Wertheimer, Leon Liu, Andrea S. Matiauda

ARNOLD & PORTER
777 S. Figueroa St., 44th Flr., Los Angeles, CA 90017-2513. (213) 243-4000. FAX: (213) 243-4199.
1900 Ave. of the Stars, Ste. 1700, Los Angeles, CA 90067. (310) 552-2500. FAX: (310) 552-1191.

ARTISAN LEGAL SERVICES
1925 Century Park E., Ste. 500, Los Angeles, CA 90067. (310) 289-5447. FAX: (310) 289-5486. www.yourcounselor.com
email: gonzo555@aol.com
ATTORNEY
Bryan T. Gonzales

ASHERSON, KLEIN & DARBINIAN
9150 Wilshire Blvd., Ste. 210, Beverly Hills, CA 90212. (310) 247-6070. FAX: (310) 278-8454.
GENERAL PARTNERS
Neville Asherson, Anna Darbinian

MARTIN J. BARAB & ASSOCIATES
9606 Santa Monica Blvd., 3rd Flr., Beverly Hills, CA 90210. (310) 859-6644. FAX: (310) 859-6650.
MANAGING PARTNER
Martin Barab

STEPHEN BARON
1299 Ocean Ave., Ste. 312, Santa Monica, CA 90401. (310) 260-6060. FAX: (310) 260-6061.

BEHR, ABRAMSON & KALLER
2049 Century Park E., Ste. 2690, Los Angeles, CA 90067. (310) 556-9200.

BELDOCK, LEVINE & HOFFMAN
99 Park Ave., Ste. 1600, New York, NY 10016-1503. (212) 490-0400. email: jgreenberg@blhny.com
ATTORNEYS
Carolyn Allen, Jeff Greenberg

BERGER, KAHN
4215 Glencoe Ave., 2nd Flr., Marina Del Rey, CA 92092. (310) 821-9000. FAX: (310) 578-6178. www.bergerkahn.com
DIRECTOR, ENTERTAINMENT DEPARTMENT
Leon Gladstone

BERKOWITZ & BLACK
9401 Wilshire Blvd., Ste. 1100, Beverly Hills, CA 90212-2924. (310) 275-3600. FAX: (310) 724-8340. www.bbzlaw.com
ATTORNEYS
Howard Apple, Eric Berkowitz, Jeffrey Berkowitz, Daniel Black, Daniel Leon, Laura Meltzer, Jonathan Panzer, Roy Silva, Jody Simon, Sherry Spees, Larry Verbit, Michael Weiss, Richard Wirick

BERKOWITZ & ASSOCIATES
468 N. Camden Dr., Ste. 200, Beverly Hills, CA 90210. (310) 276-9031. FAX: (310) 276-9272.
CONTACT
Barbara Berkowitz

GREG S. BERNSTEIN
Law Offices of Greg Bernstein, A Professional Corporation, 9601 Wilshire Blvd., Ste. 300A, Beverly Hills, CA 90210-5288. (310) 247-2790. FAX: (310) 247-2791. www.thefilmlaw.com
ATTORNEY
Greg S. Bernstein

STUART BERTON PROFESSIONAL CORP.
12400 Ventura Blvd., #661, Studio City, CA 91604. (818) 509-8113. FAX: (818) 985-1527. email: stuartberton@earthlink.net
ATTORNEY
Stuart Berton

BLAIN & ASSOCIATES
117 N. Robertson Blvd., Los Angeles, CA 90048. (310) 205-9660. FAX: (310) 205-9669.
ATTORNEYS
Tony Blain, Francine Bellach

BLOOM, HERGOTT, DIEMER & COOK, LLP
150 S. Rodeo Dr., 3rd Flr., Beverly Hills, CA 90212. (310) 859-6800. FAX: (310) 859-2788.
ATTORNEYS
Jacob A. Bloom, Leigh Brecheen, Stephen F. Breimer, Ralph Brescia, Eric M. Brooks, Thomas B. Collier, John Diemer, David B. Feldman, Lawrence H. Greaves, Candice S. Hanson, Alan S. Hergott, Thomas F. Hunter, Jr., Tina J. Kahn, Patricia M. Knapp, John LaViolette, Leif W. Reinstein, Stuart Rosenthal, Robyn Roth, Michael Schenkman, Richard D. Thompson

CHRISTENSEN, MILLER, FINK, JACOBS, GLASER, WEIL & SHAPIRO LLP
10250 Constellation Blvd., 19th Flr., Los Angeles, CA 90067. (310) 553-3000. FAX: (310) 556-2920.
ATTORNEYS
Patricia Glaser, Robert Shapiro

CLARK & GOLDBERG
3250 Ocean Park Blvd., Ste. 350, Santa Monica, CA 90405. (310) 314-8660. FAX: (310) 314-8662.
ATTORNEYS
Roger Clark, Robert Goldberg

CARROLL, GUIDO, GROFFMAN, LLP
9111 Sunset Blvd., Los Angeles, CA 90069-3106. (310) 271-0241. FAX: (310) 271-0775.
ATTORNEY
Rosemary Carroll

COUNTRYMAN & MCDANIEL
5933 W. Century Blvd., Ste. 1111, Los Angeles, CA 90045. (310) 342-6500. FAX: (310) 342-6505. www.cargolaw.com
ATTORNEYS
Byron Countryman, Michael McDaniel.

COWAN, DeBAETS, ABRAHAMS & SHEPPARD, LLP
41 Madison Ave., 34th Flr., New York, NY 10010. (212) 974-7474. FAX: (212) 974-8474.
ATTORNEYS
Anne C. Baker (Also admitted in Louisiana), Frederick P. Bimbler, Judith A. Bresler, Toby M.J. Butterfield, Al J. Daniel, Jr., Timothy J. DeBaets, Lisa K. Digernes, Robert I. Freedman, Jerrold B. Gold, Albert Gottesman, Sabrina Hillson-Chosed, Roger A. Kass, Ellis B. Levine, Mitchell D. Remer, Robert L. Seigel, J. Stephen Sheppard, Adam W. Snukal, Ralph J. Sutton, Kenneth N. Swezey, David B. Wolf

DEL, SHAW, MOONVES, TANAKA & FINKELSTEIN
2120 Colorado Ave., Ste. 200, Santa Monica, CA 90404. (310) 979-7900. FAX: (310) 979-7999.
ATTORNEY
Nina Shaw

THE LAW OFFICE OF JUDITH C. DORNSTEIN, INC.
1925 Century Park E., Ste. 500, Los Angeles, CA 90067. (310) 278-5568. FAX: (310) 278-2271. email: jdornstein@adelphia.net

ERVIN, COHEN & JESSUP
9401 Wilshire Blvd., 9th Flr., Beverly Hills, CA 90212. (310) 273-6333. FAX: (310) 859-2325. www.ecjlaw.com
ATTORNEY
Gary Freedman

ESQ. MANAGEMENT
Box 16194, Beverly Hills, CA 90209. (310) 252-9879.
www.esqmanagement.biz
PERSONAL MANAGER & ATTORNEY
Patricia Lee

FRANKFURT, GARBUS, KURNIT, KLEIN & SELZ, P.C.
488 Madison Ave., 9th Flr., New York, NY 10022. (212) 980-0120. FAX: (212) 593-9175. www.fgkks.com
ENTERTAINMENT PARTNERS
Lisa E. Davis, Michael P. Frankfurt, Richard B. Heller, Richard Hofstetter, Candice Kersh, Stuart Kleinman, Brain Murphy, Amy Cibinic Ondreyka, Edward Rosenthal, Thomas Selz, Gerald E. Singleton, Jerrold B. Spiegel, Michael Williams

FREDRICKS & VON DER HORST
12121 Wilshire Blvd., Ste. 900, Los Angeles, CA 90025. (310) 820-3600. FAX: (310) 820-1832.
CONTACT
Dennis F. Fredricks, Esq.

FREEDMAN & TAITELMAN, LLP
1901 Ave. of the Stars, Ste. 500, Los Angeles, CA 90067. (310) 201-0005. FAX: (310) 201-0045. email: freedtait@ftllp.com
ATTORNEYS
Bryan Freedman, Michael Taitelman, John Guerrini, David Marmorstein, Brandon Krueger

GAGE TEEPLE
9255 Towne Centre Dr., Ste. 500, San Diego, CA 92121. (858) 622-7878. FAX: (858) 622-0411. www.gageteeple.com
PARTNER
Ben Gage

GARVIN & BENJAMIN, LLP
9200 Sunset Blvd., Penthouse 25, Los Angeles, CA 90069. (310) 278-7300. FAX: (310) 278-7306. email: trom@gbllp.com
CONTACT
Thomas Garvin

GENDLER & KELLY
450 N. Roxbury Dr., Penthouse 1000, Beverly Hills, CA 90210. (310) 285-6400. FAX: (310) 275-7333.
PARTNERS
Michael Gendler, Kevin M. Kelly
ATTORNEYS
Marc Golden, Paul Swanson

GERDES & ASSOCIATES
8950 W. Olympic Blvd., Ste. 382, Beverly Hills, CA 90211. (310) 385-9501. FAX: (310) 858-6703. www.gerdeslaw.com
ATTORNEY
Ted Gerdes

GIBSON, DUNN & CRUTCHER, LLP
2029 Century Park E., Ste. 4000, Los Angeles, CA 90067. (310) 552-8500. FAX: (310) 551-8741.

GIPSON, HOFFMAN & PANCIONE
1901 Ave. of the Stars, Ste. 1100, Los Angeles, CA 90067. (310) 556-4660. FAX: (310) 556-8945.
ATTORNEYS
Lawrence R. Barnett, Jeff M. Boren, Robert Gipson, G. Raymond Gross, Kenneth Sidle, Norm D. Sloan, Corey J. Spivey, Robert Steinberg

GLICKFELD, FIELDS & JACOBSON
9460 Wilshire Blvd., Ste. 500, Beverly Hills, CA 90212. (310) 550-7222. FAX: (310) 550-6222.
ATTORNEYS
Michael Glickfeld, Craig M. Fields, Larry Jacobson

GRAKAL, ROOT & ROSENTHAL, LLP
1541 Ocean Ave., Ste. 200, Santa Monica, CA 90401. (310) 260-1055. FAX: (310) 260-1058.
ATTORNEY
Richard Rosenthal

JEFFREY L. GRAUBART
1900 Ave. of the Stars, Ste. 1425, Los Angeles, CA 90067. (310) 788-2650. FAX: (310) 788-2657.

GREENBERG, GLUSKER, FIELDS, CLAMAN, MACHTINGER & KINSELLA LLP
1900 Ave. of the Stars, Ste. 2100, Los Angeles, CA 90067. (310) 553-3610. FAX: (310) 553-0687. www.ggfirm.com
ATTORNEYS
Hillary S. Bibicoff, Bertram Fields, Matt Galsor, E. Barry Haldeman, Robert F. Marshall, Carla M. Roberts

GREENWALD, PAULY FOSTER & MILLER
1299 Ocean Ave., Ste. 400, Santa Monica, CA 90401. (310) 451-8001. FAX: (310) 395-5961.

HALL, DICKLER, KENT, GOLDSTEIN & WOOD, LLP
9665 Wilshire Blvd., Ste. 1050, Beverly Hills, CA 90212. (310) 887-4000. FAX: (310) 887-1820. www.halldickler.com
ATTORNEYS
Fredric W. Ansis, Ted Bro, Joseph T. Gauthier, Alfred Kim Guggenheim, Jeremy T. Kenik, Stephen E. Sessa, Roy Z. Silva, Lawrence Steinberg

HALLORAN LAW CORP.
1925 Century Park E., Ste. 850, Los Angeles, CA 90067. (310) 553-5880. FAX: (310) 553-0880.
ATTORNEY
Mark E. Halloran

HANSEN, JACOBSEN, TELLER, HOBERMAN, NEWMAN, WARREN, SOLOANE & RICHMOND
450 N. Roxbury Dr., 8th Flr., Beverly Hills, CA 90210. (310) 271-8777. FAX: (310) 276-8310.

IRELL & MANELLA, LLP
1800 Ave. of the Stars, Ste. 900, Los Angeles, CA 90067-4276. (310) 277-1010. FAX: (310) 203-7199. www.irell.com
PARTNERS
Richard L. Bernacchi, Norman E. Brunell, Joan Lesser, David Nimmer, Clark Siegel, Juliette Youngblood
ASSOCIATES
Christopher Abramson, Marc A. Fenster, Richard G. Frenkel, Lee Liedecke, Lawrence Liu, Phil Miller

ISAACMAN, KAUFMAN & PAINTER
8484 Wilshire Blvd., Ste. 850, Beverly Hills, CA 90211. (323) 782-7700. FAX: (323) 782-7744.
email: fischer@ikplaw.com
ATTORNEYS
Neil Fischer, Chuck Hurewitz, Steven Lowy, Andrew Zucker

IVERSON, YOAKUM, PAPIANO & HATCH
One Wilshire Bldg., 27th Flr., 624 S. Grand Ave.,Los Angeles, CA 90017. (213) 624-7444. FAX: (213) 629-4563. www.iyph.com
PARTNER
Neil Papiano
ENTERTAINMENT ATTORNEY
Adam Burke

JACOBSON & COLFIN, P.C.
19 W. 21st St. #603A, New York, NY 10010. (212) 691-5630. FAX: (212) 645-5038. www.thefirm.com
email: thefirm@thefirm.com
ATTORNEYS
Bruce E. Colfin, Jeffrey E. Jacobson.

JEFFER, MANGELS, BUTLER & MARMARO
1900 Ave. of the Stars, 7th Flr., Los Angeles, CA 90067. (310) 203-8080. FAX: (310) 203-0567. www.jmbm.com
PARTNER
Michael S. Sherman
OF COUNSEL
John E. Mason

JOHNSON & RISHWAIN, LLP
12121 Wilshire Blvd., Ste. 1201, Los Angeles, CA 90025. (310) 826-2410. FAX: (310) 826-5450. www.jrllp.com
ATTORNEYS
Neville L. Johnson, Brian Rishwain, James Ryan, Douglas Johnson

KATTEN, MUCHIN, ZAVIS & ROSENMAN
2029 Century Park E., Ste. 2600, Los Angeles, CA 90067. (310) 788-4400. FAX: (310) 788-4471. www.kmzr.com
ENTERTAINMENT ATTORNEYS
Darin Chavez, Deidre Downes, Harrison Dossick, Samantha Freedman, Alan L. Friel, Susan A. Grode, David Halberstadter, John Hendrickson, Kristin Holland, Marsha Houston, Joyce S. Jun, Katherine L. McDaniel, Zia F. Modabber, Charles M. Stern, Gail Migdal Title, Rik J. Toulon

KATZ, GOLDEN & SULLIVAN, LLP
2001 Wilshire Blvd., Ste. 400, Santa Monica, CA 90403. (310) 998-9200. FAX: (310) 998-9177.
ATTORNEY
Steven B. Katz

KEHR, SCHIFF & CRANE
12400 Wilshire Blvd., Ste. 1300, Los Angeles, CA 90025-1030. (310) 820-3455. FAX: (310) 820-4414.

KENOFF & MACHTINGER
1901 Ave. of the Stars, Ste. 1050, Los Angeles, CA 90067. (310) 552-0808. FAX: (310) 277-0653.
PARTNERS
Jay S. Kenoff, Leonard S. Machtinger

JEFFREY G. KICHAVEN
555 W. 5th St., Ste. 3000, Los Angeles, CA 90013-1010. (213) 996-8465. FAX: (213) 996-8475. www.jeffkichaven.com
email: jk@jeffkichaven.com

JONATHAN KIRSCH
1875 Century Park E., Ste. 1700, Los Angeles, CA 90067. (310) 785-1200. FAX: (310) 286-9573.

KIRTLAND & PACKARD
2361 Rosecrans Ave., 4th Flr., El Segundo, CA 90245. (310) 536-1000. FAX: (310) 536-1001. www.kirtland-packard.com
ATTORNEYS
Robert Churella, Michelle Moyer, Derek Whitman

KLEINBERG, LOPEZ, LANGE, CUDDY & NEDEL, LLP
2049 Century Park E., Ste. 3180, Los Angeles, CA 90067. (310) 286-9696. FAX: (310) 277-7145. www.kllbc.com

LEONARD, DICKER & SCHREIBER
9430 Olympic Blvd., Ste. 400, Beverly Hills, CA 90212. (310) 551-1987. FAX: (310) 277-8050.

LEWIS, BRISBOIS, BISGAARD & SMITH LLP
221 N. Figueroa, Ste. 1200, Los Angeles, CA 90012. (213) 250-1800. FAX: (213) 250-7900.
ATTORNEYS
Robert Lewis, Jana Lubert, Gary Rattet, Glen Umeda

LICHTER, GROSSMAN, NICHOLS, ADLER & GOODMAN
9200 Sunset Blvd., Ste. 1200, Los Angeles, CA 90069. (310) 205-6999.

LOEB & LOEB, LLP
10100 Santa Monica Blvd., Ste. 2200, Los Angeles, CA 90067. (310) 282-2000. FAX: (310) 828-2200. www.loeb.com
345 Park Ave., New York, NY 10154. (212) 407-4000. FAX: (212) 407-4990.
ATTORNEYS
Kenneth Anderson, Rogers M. Arar, David Byrnes, David Carlin, Marc Chamlin, Craig Emanuel, Kenneth Florin, John T. Frankenheimer, Seth Gelblum, Jim Goodkind, Michael A. Mayerson, Nigel Pearson, Steven Pena, Robert Reich, Terri Seligman, Rebel Steiner, James Taylor, Irwin Tenenbaum, Susan Z. Williams

MANATT, PHELPS & PHILLIPS, LLP
Trident Center, East Tower, 11355 W. Olympic Blvd., Los Angeles, CA 90064. (310) 312-4000. FAX: (310) 312-4224. www.manatt.com
ATTORNEYS
Gerald A. Margolis, Laurence M. Marks, L. Lee Phillips, J. Gunnar Erickson, Brad Small

MAYOR, GLASSMAN, & GAINES
11726 San Vicente Blvd., Ste. 400, Los Angeles, CA 90049-5006. (310) 207-0007. FAX: (310) 207-3578.

MENES LAW CORPORATION
1801 Century Park E., Ste. 1560, Los Angeles, CA 90067. (310) 286-2349. FAX: (310) 556-5695.
ATTORNEYS
Paul Menes, Barry Menes

MITCHELL, SILERBERG & KNUPP, LLP
11377 W. Olympic Blvd., Los Angeles, CA 90064. (310) 312-2000. FAX: (310) 312-3100. www.msk.com
ATTORNEYS
Phillip Davis, Harold Friedman, James Guerra, Kim H. Swartz, Robert M Wise

MORRISON & FOERSTER
1925 Century Park E., Ste. 2200, Los Angeles, CA 90067. (310) 203-4000. FAX: (310) 203-4040. www.mofo.com

MYMAN, ABELL, FINEMAN, GREENSPAN & LIGHT, LLP
11601 Wilshire Blvd., Ste. 2200, Los Angeles, CA 90025. (310) 231-0800. FAX: (310) 207-2680.

NELSON FELKER, LLP
10880 Wilshire Blvd., Ste. 2070, Los Angeles, CA 90024-4101. (310) 441-8000. FAX: (310) 441-8010.
ATTORNEYS
George M. Davis, Patti C. Felker, Peter Martin Nelson, Fred Toczek, Eric Suddleson

LOUISE NEMSCHOFF
1801 Ave. of the Stars, 6th Flr., Los Angeles, CA 90067. (310) 274-4627. FAX: (310) 274-5039.

NOVIAN & NOVIAN, LLP
1801 Century Park E., Ste. 1201, Los Angeles, CA 90067. (310) 553-1222. FAX: (310) 553-0222.
CONTACT
Farhad Novian

JAAK OLESK
345 N. Maple Dr., Ste. 284, Beverly Hills, CA 90210. (310) 288-0693. FAX: (310) 288-0863.

O'MELVENY & MYERS
1999 Ave. of the Stars, 7th Flr., Los Angeles, CA 90067-6035. (310) 553-6700. FAX: (310) 246-6779. www.omm.com
PARTNER
Christopher C. Murray

ORRICK, HERRINGTON & SUTCLIFFE
777 S. Figueroa, Ste. 3200, Los Angeles, CA 90017. (213) 629-2020. FAX: (213) 612-2499. www.orrick.com
666 Fifth Ave., 2nd Flr., New York, NY 10103. (212) 506-5000. FAX: (212) 506-5151.
Washington Harbour, 3050 K. St. N.W., Washington, DC 20007. (202) 339-8400. FAX: (202) 339-8500.

PASCOTTO & GALLAVOTTI
1800 Ave. of the Stars, Ste. 600, Los Angeles, CA 90067. (310) 203-7515. FAX: (310) 284-3021. email: apascotto@mcimail.com
ATTORNEY
Alvaro Pascotto

PILLSBURY WINTHROP, LLP
725 S. Figueroa, Ste. 2800, Los Angeles, CA 90017. (213) 488-7100. FAX: (213) 629-1033. www.pillsburywinthrop.com
PARTNER
M. Katharine Davidson

PROSKAUER ROSE, LLP
2049 Century Park E., 32nd Flr., Los Angeles, CA 90067-3206. (310) 557-2900. FAX: (310) 557-2193. www.proskauer.com
ENTERTAINMENT ATTORNEYS
Howard D. Behar, Sandra A. Crawshaw, Paul H. Epstein, William M. Hart, Jeffrey A. Horwitz, Christopher M. Jaskiewicz, Steven M. Kalb, Andrew L. Lee, Carla M. Miller, Charles B. Ortner, Lawrence I. Weinstein, Scott P Cooper, Bert H. Deixler

HUGH DUFF ROBERTSON
1125 Gayley Ave., Los Angeles, CA 90024. (310) 824-0467. FAX: (310) 208-3854. email: hdr@lawhdr.com
CONTACT
Hugh Robertson

ROSENFELD, MEYER & SUSMAN, LLP
9601 Wilshire Blvd., 4th Flr., Beverly Hills, CA 90210-5288. (310) 858-7700. FAX: (310) 860-2430. www.rmslaw.com
ENTERTAINMENT ATTORNEYS
Ron Dolecki, Renee A. Farrell, Lawrence Kartiganer, Marvin B. Meyer, Elena Muravina, Jerry Nagin, Michelle Raffel

SEYFARTH, SHAW
One Century Plaza, Ste. 3300, 2029 Century Park E., Los Angeles, CA 90067-3063. (310) 277-7200. FAX: (310) 201-5219. www.seyfarth.com

SHELDON & MAK
225 S. Lake Ave., 9th Flr., Pasadena, CA 91101. (626) 796-4000. FAX: (626) 795-6321. www.usip.com
email: daniel@usip.com
ATTORNEY
Daniel J. Coplan

SHEPPARD, MULLIN, RICHTER & HAMPTON
333 S. Hope St., 48th Flr., Los Angeles, CA 90071. (213) 620-1780. FAX: (213) 620-1398. www.sheppardmullin.com

SHUMAKER, STECKBAUER, WEINHART & SRAGOW, LLP
300 S. Grand Ave., Ste. 1400, Los Angeles, CA 90071-3124. (213) 229-2868. FAX: (213) 229-2870.

SIDLEY, AUSTIN, BROWN & WOOD LLP
1501 K St. N.W., Washington, D.C. 20005. (202) 736-8000. FAX: (202) 736-8711. www.sidley.com
555 W. Fifth St., Ste. 4000, Los Angeles, CA 90013. (213) 896-6000. FAX: (213) 896-6600.
ATTORNEYS
Jennifer Tatel, Thomas Van Wazer, Clark Wadlow, Steven A. Ellis (CA)

SKADDEN, ARPS, SLATE, MEAGHER & FLOM, LLP
300 S. Grand Ave., Ste. 3400, Los Angeles, CA 90071. (213) 687-5000. FAX: (213) 687-5600. www.skadden.com
PARTNERS
Douglas B. Adler, John A. Donovan, Jason D. Russell

SLOSS LAW OFFICE
555 W. 25th St., 4th Flr., New York, NY 10001. (212) 627-9898. FAX: (212) 627-9498. www.slosslaw.com
email: office@slosslaw.com
ATTORNEYS
Paul Brennan, Jacqueline Eckhouse, Jennifer Gaylord, John Sloss

SOMMER & BEAR
9777 Wilshire Blvd., Ste. 512, Beverly Hills, CA 90212. (310) 858-4989. FAX: (310) 858-0775.
ATTORNEY
Paul Sommer

SONNENSCHEIN, NATH & ROSENTHAL, LLP
1221 Ave., of the Americas, New York, NY 10020-1089. (212) 768-6700. FAX: (212) 768-6800. www.sonnenschein.com
601 S. Figueroa St., Ste. 1500, Los Angeles, CA 90017. (213) 623-9300. FAX: (213) 623-9924.
ENTERTAINMENT ATTORNEYS
David R. Baum, Laura Becker (CA), Howard S. Bonfield, Jeannie Costello, Martin R. Gold, Jacob Inwald, Christine Lepera, Paul V. LiCalsi, Robert P. Mulvey, Michael Ring (CA), Lewis M. Schwartz, Jane G. Stevens, Howard H. Weller

STANBURY FISHELMAN
9200 Sunset Blvd., Penthouse 30, Los Angeles, CA 90069-3607. (310) 278-1800. FAX: (310) 278-1802.
ATTORNEY
Bruce C. Fishelman

STANKEVICH GOCHMAN, LLP
9777 Wilshire Blvd., Ste. 550, Beverly Hills, CA 90212. (310) 859-8825. FAX: (310) 859-8830.
ATTORNEYS
Mark Gochman, Mark Stankevich

KATHY L. TANNEN
P.O. Box 55004, Sherman Oaks, CA 91413. (818) 501-7517.

THELEN, REID & PRIEST, LLP
875 Third Ave., New York, NY 10022-6225. (212) 603-2000.
FAX: (212) 603-2001. www.thelenreid.com
333 S. Hope St., Ste. 2900, Los Angeles, CA 90071-3048. (213)
576-8000. FAX: (213) 576-8080.
ENTERTAINMENT ATTORNEYS
Deborah L. Ander, James C. Cesare, Ezra J. Doner, Michael S.
Elkin, Jonathan D. Fuhrman, Andrew P. Kransdorf, Shari
Markowitz, H. Joseph Mello, Harvey K. Newkirk

TISDALE & NICHOLSON LLP
2029 Century Park E., Ste. 900, Los Angeles, CA 90067. (310)
286-1260. FAX: (310) 286-2351. www.T-NLaw.com
ENTERTAINMENT ATTORNEYS
Jeffrey A. Tisdale
Marc R. Staenberg

HARRIS TULCHIN & ASSOCIATES
11377 W. Olympic Blvd., 2nd Flr., Los Angeles, CA 90064. (310)
914-7979. FAX: (310) 914-7927. www.medialawyer.com
email: entesquire@aol.com
ATTORNEY
Harris Tulchin

LAWRENCE J. TURNER
9200 Sunset Blvd., Ste. 701, Los Angeles, CA 90069. (310)
273-4858. FAX: (310) 273-1869.

SUZANNE VAUGHAN APC
6848 Firmament Ave., Van Nuys, CA 91406. (818) 988-5599.
FAX: (818) 988-5577. www.suzyvaughan.com
email: svaughan@suzyvaughan.com

A. CHANDLER WARREN, JR.
7715 W. Sunset Blvd., Ste. 208, Los Angeles, CA 90046. (323)
876-6400. FAX: (323) 876-3170. email: achandlerwarren@aol.com

WEIL, GOTSHAL & MANGES
767 5th Ave., New York, NY 10053. (212) 310-8000. Fax: (212)
310-8007. www.weil.com

DONALDSON & HART
9220 Sunset Blvd., Ste. 224, Los Angeles, CA 90069-3501.
(310) 273-8394. FAX: (310) 273-5370. www.donaldsonhart.com
email: joe@donaldsonhart.com, mcd@donaldsonhart.com
ATTORNEYS
Michael C. Donaldson
Joseph F. Hart

WEISSMANN, WOLF, BERGMAN, GROIDIN & EVALL
9665 Wilshire Blvd., Ste. 900, Beverly Hills, CA 90212. (310)
858-7888. FAX: (310) 550-7191.

WILION, KIRKWOOD KESSLER, & HOFFMAN, LLP
(Employment contracts for the entertainment industry)
6500 Wilshire Blvd., Ste. 1600, Los Angeles, CA 90048. (323)
653-3600. FAX: (323) 653-3604.
CONTACT
Allan Wilion

WILSON, ELSER, MOSKOWITZ, EDELMAN & DICKER LLP
1055 W. 7th St., Ste. 2700, Los Angeles, CA 90017. (213) 624-
3044. FAX: (213) 624-8060. www.wemed.com

WOLF, RIFKIN, SHAPIRO & SCHULMAN, LLP
11400 W. Olympic Blvd., 9th Flr., Los Angeles, CA 90064. (310)
478-4100. FAX: (310) 479-1422.
ENTERTAINMENT ATTORNEY
Michael Wolf
Neal K. Tabachnick

ROBERT J. YOUNG
11664 National Blvd., Ste. 441, Los Angeles, CA 90064. (310)
820-2988. FAX: (310) 820-8466.

HELEN YU
1900 Ave. of the Stars, 25th Flr., Los Angeles, CA 90067. (310)
286-7667. FAX: (310) 286-7473.

ZIFFREN & ZIFFREN
1801 Century Park E., Ste. 2400, Los Angeles, CA 90067. (310)
286-9971.
ATTORNEYS
Leo G. Ziffren
Lester Ziffren

ZIFFREN, BRITTENHAM, BRANCA, FISCHER, GILBERT-LURIE & STIFFELMAN
1801 Century Park W., Los Angeles, CA 90067. (310) 552-3388.
FAX: (310) 553-7068.
ATTORNEYS
John G. Branca
Paul Brindze
Harry M. Brittenham
Samuel Fischer
Clifford Gilbert-Lurie
Kathleen Hallberg
Dennis Luderer

FILM PRESERVATION, PROCESSING, REPAIR & STORAGE

AFD/PHOTOGRAD FILM COATING LAB
(Preservation)
738 Cahuenga Blvd., Hollywood, CA 90038. (323) 469-8171.
FAX: (323) 469-0377.

ALLIED/VAUGHN'S NEW INDEPENDENTS LAB
(Negative conforming and 16 to 35mm blow-ups)
6305 N. O'Connor Road, Bldg. 4, #111, Irving, TX 75039. (972)
869-0100. FAX: (972) 869-2117.

ALPHA CINE LABORATORY, INC.
(Processing)
1001 Lenora St., Seattle, WA 98121. (206) 682-8230. FAX:
(206) 682-6649. www.alphacine.com
CONTACT
Don Jensen

ASCENT MEDIA
(Post production)
2901 W. Alameda Ave., Burbank, CA 91505. (818) 840-7000.
FAX: (818) 840-7195.

BONDED SERVICES
(Film Storage)
3205 Burton Ave., Burbank, CA 91504. (818) 848-9766. FAX:
(818) 848-9849. www.bonded.com
SALES MANAGER
Alessandro Higliardi

CHACE PRODUCTIONS, INC.
(Sound restoration and remastering)
201 S. Victory Blvd., Burbank, CA 91502. (818) 842-8346. FAX:
(818) 842-8353. www.chace.com
PRESIDENT
Robert Heiber
GENERAL MANAGER
James Eccles

CINE MAGNETICS FILM & VIDEO
(Video duplication and optical media replication)
100 Business Park Dr., Armonk, NY 10504. (914) 273-7500.
www.cinemagnetics.com
PRESIDENT
Joseph J. Barber, Jr.
VICE PRESIDENT
Robert Orzack
GENERAL MANAGER
Kenneth Wynne

CINE LAB
(Full-service 16mm motion picture lab)
315 Pleasant St., Ste. 11, Fall River, MA 02721. (508) 672-1204.
www.cinelab.com

CINEFILM/CINETRANSFER
(Processing)
2156 Faulkner Rd. N.E., Atlanta, GA 30324. (800) 633-1448,
(404) 633-1448. FAX: (404) 633-3867. www.cinefilmlab.com
CUSTOMER SERVICE MANAGER
Jim Ogburn

CONSOLIDATED FILM INDUSTRIES
2233 Ontario St, Burbank, CA 91501. (818) 260-3839. FAX:
(818) 260-3840. www.technicolor.com
SALES
Mike Papadaki

CONTINENTAL FILM LABS, INC.
(Processing, print and transfers)
1998 N.E. 150 St., N. Miami, FL 33181. (800) 327-8396, (305)
949-4252. FAX: (305) 949-3242. www.flfilmlab.com
CONTACT
Nestor Garcia

CREST NATIONAL/VIDEO & FILM LABORATORIES
(35mm & 16mm lab services, negative processing and prints, color
correction, film, HD video and audio restoration, full DVD services)
1141 N. Seward St., Hollywood, CA 90038. (323) 466-0624,
(323) 462-6696. FAX: (323) 461-8901. www.crestnational.com

CRUSH CREATIVE
(Custom photo lab; creative retouching)
1919 Empire Ave., Burbank, CA 91504. (818) 842-1121.
www.crushcreative.com email: john.davies@crushcreative.com
PRESIDENT & CEO
Guy Claudy
S.V.P, SALES MANAGER
John Davies

DU ART FILM LABORATORIES
(Preservation, processing, repair & storage)
245 W. 55th St., New York, NY 10019. (212) 757-4580.
www.duart.com

DELTA PRODUCTIONS
(Video post production)
3333 Glendale Blvd., Ste. 4, Los Angeles, CA 90039. (323) 663-
8754. FAX: (323) 663-3460.

FILM CRAFT LAB
(Processing, repair, transfers)
23815 Industrial Park Dr., Farmington Hills, MI 48335. (248)
474-3900. FAX: (248) 474-1577. www.filmcraftlab.com
ACCOUNT EXECUTIVE
Patrice Heath

FILM PRESERVE
(Restoration)
2 Depot Plaza, #202-B, Bedford Hills, NY 10507. (914) 242-
9838. FAX: (914) 242-9854.
CONTACT
Robert A. Harris

FILM TECHNOLOGY COMPANY, INC.
(Restoration)
726 N. Cole Ave., Hollywood, CA 90038. (323) 464-3456. FAX:
(323) 464-7439. www.filmtech.com
CONTACT
Denise Casper

FILMACK STUDIOS
(Film lab)
1327 S. Wabash Ave., Chicago, IL 60605-2574. (800) FILMACK,
(312) 427-3395. FAX: (312) 427-4866. www.filmack.com
email: inquiries@Filmack.com
OWNER
Robert Mack

FILMTREAT INTERNATIONAL CORP.
(Film preservation, restoration and repair)
42-24 Orchard St., Long Island City, NY 11101. (718) 784-4040.
FAX: (718) 784-4766
CONTACTS
Y. W. Mociuk
Sam Borodinsky

FILMTREAT WEST CORP.
(Scratch removal)
10810 Cantara St., Sun Valley, CA 91352. (818) 771-5390.

FILMWORKERS-ASTRO LAB
(Processing, transfers & printing)
61 W. Erie St., Chicago, IL 60610. (312) 280-5500. FAX: (312)
280-5510.
CONTACT
Manuela Hung

FORDE MOTION PICTURE LABS
(Processing & printing)
306 Fairview Ave. N., Seattle, WA 98109. (206) 682-2510.
www.fordelabs.com

FORT LEE FILM STORAGE & SERVICE
(Storage)
1 Mt. Vernon St., Ridgefield Park, NJ 07660. (201) 440-6200.
FAX: (201) 440-5799.
OWNER
Jay Bonica

FOTOKEM
(Preservation, processing, repair, storage, transfer)
2801 W. Alameda Ave., Burbank, CA 91505. (818) 846-3101.
FAX: (818) 841-2130. www.fotokem.com
email: sales@fotokem.com
SENIOR V.P., SALES & MARKETING
Tom Ennis
SENIOR V.P., BUSINESS DEVELOPMENT
Jim Hannafin

HIGHLAND LABORATORIES
(All formats of video duplicating)
Pier 96, Administration Bldg., San Francisco, CA 94124. (415)
981-5010. www.highlandlab.com

HOLLYWOOD FILM & VIDEO, INC.
(Processing and print)
6060 Sunset Blvd., Hollywood, CA 90028. (323) 464-2181. FAX:
(323) 464-0893.

HOLLYWOOD FILM CO.
(Restoration)
10909 Tuxford St., Sun Valley, CA 91352. (818) 252-6777. FAX: (818) 252-6770.
CONTACT
Frank Heller

HOLLYWOOD VAULTS, INC.
(Film preservation, off-site storage)
Vault: 742 N. Seward St., Hollywood, CA 90038. (323) 461-6464. FAX: (323) 461-6479.
Corporate office: 1780 Prospect Ave., Santa Barbara, CA 93103. (805) 569-5336. FAX: (805) 569-1657. www.hollywoodvaults.com
email: vault@hollywoodvaults.com
PRESIDENT
David Wexler

ICS SERVICES, INC.
(Film cleaning and rejuvenation)
920 Allen Ave., Glendale, CA 91201. (818) 242-3839. FAX: (818) 242-1566. www.icsfilm.com

INTERMISSION PRODUCTIONS LTD.
(Subsidiary of Cine Dustrial, Inc.)
(Film restoration, DVD release and theatrical)
6179 Knoll Wood Rd., Ste. 306, Willowbrook, IL 60527. (630) 654-0200. FAX: (630) 887-0380. email: interprod1@aol.com
PRESIDENT
Michael Egan
CEO & PRODUCTION MANAGER
Michael Dawson

LAB LINK
(A division of Magno Sound. Features & spot release. 16 & 35mm, processing & print, color & B&W. Cardiac angiogram duplication film, digital & video.)
115 W. 45th St., New York, NY 10036. (212) 302-7373, (212) 575-5159. FAX: (212) 719-1867. email: magnolablink@aol.com
SALES MANAGER
Norma BeBell
LAB MANAGER
Tony Landano

LASER-PACIFIC MEDIA CORP.
(Post production)
809 N. Cahuenga Blvd., Hollywood, CA 90038. (323) 462-6266. FAX: (323) 464-3233. www.laserpacific.com
CHAIRMAN & CEO
James R. Parks

KEN LIEBERMAN LABORATORIES, INC.
(Custom prints and transparencies)
1150 6th Ave., 5th Flr., New York, NY 10036. (212) 633-0500. FAX: (212) 675-8269. www.lieberman-labs.com
email: lieberman@lieberman-labs.com
CONTACT
Ken Lieberman

LIPSNER-SMITH COMPANY
(Film cleaning equipment; negative and print laboratory equipment and planning services)
4700 Chase, Lincolnwood, IL 60712-1689. (800) 323-7520, (847) 677-3000. FAX: (800) 784-6733, (847) 677-1311.
www.lipsner.com email: sales@rtico.com

Unit 6, Swan Wharf Business Center, Uxgridge UB8 2RA, England. TEL: (01895) 7000-78485. FAX: (01895) 274-692. email: email@rtiuk.co.uk

MAGNO SOUND & VIDEO
(Processing)
729 Seventh Ave., New York, NY 10019. (212) 302-2505. FAX: (212) 819-1282. www.magnosoundandvideo.com
VICE PRESIDENT
David Friedman
DIRECTOR
Hada Ruiz

MILLENNIUM FILM WORK SHOP
(Exhibition; film publication & workshop/equipment access & gallery)
66 E. 4th St., New York, NY 10003. (212) 673-0090.
www.millenniumfilm.org
PROGRAM DIRECTOR
Howard Guttenplan

MOTION PICTURE LABORATORIES, INC.
(Mass production)
781 S. Main St., Memphis, TN 38106. (800) 467-5675, (901) 774-4944.

PACIFIC TITLE ARCHIVES
4800 W. San Vicente Blvd., Los Angeles, CA 90019. (323) 938-3711. FAX: (323) 938-6364. www.pacifictitlearchives.com

10717 Vanowen St., N. Hollywood, CA 91605. (818) 760-4223. FAX: (818) 760-1704.
PRESIDENT & CEO
Peter L. Hubbard
CONTROLLER & MANAGER, BUSINESS AFFAIRS
David Weeden

900 Grand Central Ave., Glendale, CA 91201. (818) 547-0090. FAX: (818) 548-7990.
CONTACT
John Bragg

PHOTOBITION BONDED SERVICES
(Film preservation and storage; audio and video storage)
Bonded Services Exec. Office: 520 Main St., Ste. #204, Fort Lee, NJ 07024. (201) 592-8800. FAX: (201) 592-5946.
Bonded Services: 504 Jane St., Fort Lee, NJ 07024. (201) 944-3700. FAX: (201) 592-0727. www.bondednj.com
email: sales@bondednj.com
PRESIDENT
C.W. Preuster
GENERAL MANAGER
Ramona Casanova

PRODUCERS COLOR SERVICE
24242 N. Western Hwy., Southfield, MI 48075. (248) 728-6400.

PRODUCERS FILM CENTER
(Storage)
948 N. Sycamore Ave., Hollywood, CA 90038. (323) 851-1122. FAX: (323) 850-8271. www.filmstorage.net
email: info@filmstorage.net

RGB COLOR LAB
(Processing)
816 N. Highland Ave., Los Angeles, CA 90038. (323) 469-1959.
www.rgbcolorlab.com

RAINMAKER DIGITAL PICTURES
50 W. 2nd Ave., Vancouver, B.C. V5Y 1B3. (604) 874-8700. FAX: (604) 874-1719. email: info@rainmaker.com
PRESIDENT
Bob Scarabelli

TECHNICOLOR, INC.
(Processing)
Professional Film Division, 4050 Lankershim Blvd., N. Hollywood, CA 91604. (818) 769-8500. FAX: (818) 505-5159.
321 W. 44 St., New York, NY 10036. (212) 582-7310. FAX: (212) 265-9089. www.technicolor.com
CEO
Lanny Raimondo

TRACKWISE, INC.
(Preservation and repair)
123 W. 18th St., New York, NY 10011. (212) 627-7700.
MANAGER
Fran Bowen

WARNER BROS. STUDIO FACILITIES
4000 Warner Blvd., Burbank, CA 91522. (818) 954-3000. FAX: (818) 954-2677. www.wbsf.com
email: photolab@warnerbros.com
PHOTO LAB & DIGITAL SERVICES
Greg Dyro (818) 954-7118

FILM STOCK

DR. RAWSTOCK
6150 Santa Monica Blvd., Los Angeles, CA 90038. (323) 960-1781. FAX: (323) 960-1780.
www.drrawstock.com
PRESIDENT
Lowell Kay

EASTMAN KODAK COMPANY
343 State St., Rochester, NY 14650. (585) 724-4000.
1017 N. Las Palmas Ave., Hollywood, CA 90038. (323) 464-6131. FAX: (323) 468-1568.
360 W. 31th St., New York, NY 10001. (212) 631-3400.
3003 Summit Blvd., Ste. 1100, Atlanta, GA 30319-1468. (770) 668-0500. Information: (800) 800-8398; MP Film Orders: (800) 621-FILM.
www.kodak.com
CHAIRMAN & CEO
Daniel Carp
PRESIDENT, ENTERTAINMENT IMAGING
Eric Rodli (CA)

FILM EMPORIUM
(Kodak, Fuji & Ilford film stock, video tape & cameras, production insurance)
274 Madison Ave., Ste. 404, New York, NY 10016. (800) 371-2555, (212) 683-2433. FAX: (212) 683-2740.
www.filmemporium.com
CEO
Laird R. Criner

FUJI PHOTO FILM U.S.A., INC.
(Repair and service)
200 Summit Lake Dr., Valhalla, NY 10595. (800) 755-3854, (914) 789-8100. FAX: (914) 789-8295. www.fujifilm.com
850 Central Ave., Hanover Park, IL 60133. (800) 877-0555, (630) 773-7200. FAX: (630) 773-6266.
1628 W. Crobsy Rd., Ste. 100, Carrollton, TX 75006. (800) 927-3854, (972) 466-9200. FAX: (972) 446-1329.
2450 Satellite Blvd., Duluth, GA 30096. (800) 366-3854, (770) 813-5100. FAX: (770) 813-5166.

ILFORD IMAGING U.S.A., INC.
W. 70 Century Rd., Paramus, NJ 07652. (201) 265-6000.
www.ilford.com

RAW STOCK
1133 Broadway, Rm. 541, New York, NY 10010. (212) 255-0445.
www.raw-stock.com

RESEARCH TECHNOLOGY, INC.
4700 W. Chase Ave., Lincolnwood, IL 60712. (847) 677-3000.
www.rtico.com

EDGEWISE MEDIA FILM & TAPE, INC.
1215 N. Highland, Hollywood, CA 90038. (800) 824-3130.
FAX: (323) 466-6815. www.edgewisemedia.com
630 Ninth Ave., Ste. 800, New York, NY 10036. (800) 444-9330, (212) 977-9330. FAX: (212) 977-9644.

SUPER8 SOUND
2805 W. Magnolia Blvd., Burbank, CA 91505. (818) 848-5522.
www.super8sound.com

FINANCIAL SERVICES

PROJECT FINANCING

ALLEGRA PARTNERS
320 Park Ave., 18th Flr., New York, NY 10022. (212) 277-1526. FAX: (212) 277-1533. www.allegrapartners.com
CONTACTS
Larry J. Lawrence
Richard W. Smith

AMBERGATE ASSOCIATES
3000 W. Olympic Blvd., Santa Monica, CA 90404. (310) 264-3970. FAX: (310) 264-3973. www.ambergate.net
CONTACT
Eddie Kalish

AUSTRALIAN FILM COMMISSION
Level 4, 150 William St., Woolloomooloo, NSW 2011, Australia. TEL: (61 2) 9321-6444. FAX: (61 2) 9357-3737. www.afc.gov.au email: info@afc.gov.au

BANK OF AMERICA NT & SA/COMMERCIAL BANKING ENTERTAINMENT OFFICE
2049 Century Park E., #200, Los Angeles, CA 90067. (310) 785-6062. FAX: (310) 785-6100.
CONTACT
Colleen Garcia

BANK OF NEW YORK
530 Fifth Ave., New York, NY 10036. (212) 852-4099.

BEAR, STEARNS & CO., INC.
1999 Ave. of the Stars, Ste. 3200, Los Angeles, CA 90067-6100. (800) 777-1234, (310) 201-2600. FAX: (310) 201-2755. www.bearstearns.com

BRITISH COLUMBIA FILM
(Production financing)
2225 W. Broadway, Vancouver, BC, V6K 2E4, Canada. (604) 736-7997. FAX: (604) 736-7290. www.bcfilm.bc.ca email: bcf@bcfilm.bc.ca

BRITISH CONNECTION
11955 Missouri Ave., Ste. 10, Los Angeles, CA 90025. (310) 820-7280. FAX: (310) 820-3286. www.britconnection.com email: judy@britconnection.com
PRESIDENT
Judy Hevenly

CAPELLA FILMS, INC. & CONNEXION AMERICAN MEDIA
9200 Sunset Blvd., Ste. 315, Los Angeles, CA 90069. (310) 247-4700. FAX: (310) 247-4701.
PRESIDENT
Craig Arrington

J.P. MORGAN CHASE
(Entertainment financing)
c/o The Chase Manhattan Bank, 1999 Ave. of the Stars, Ste. 2600, 26th Flr., Los Angeles, CA 90067. (310) 860-7000.
CONTACT
Ken Wilson

CITY NATIONAL BANK
Entertainment Division, 400 N. Roxbury Dr., 5th Flr., Beverly Hills, CA 90210. (310) 888-6200. FAX: (310) 888-6157. www.cnb.com/industryexp/entertain
CONTACT
Debbie Gutierrez

COBALT MEDIA GROUP
150 S. Rodeo Drive, Ste. 120, Beverly Hills, CA 90212. (310) 777-6500. FAX: (310) 777-6509.
PARTNER
Hal Sadoff

COMERICA BANK, CALIFORNIA
(Entertainment financing)
9777 Wilshire Blvd., 4th Flr., Beverly Hills, CA 90212. (310) 281-2400. FAX: (310) 205-8331.
PRESIDENT
Morgan Rector

FILM FINANCES, INC.
9000 Sunset Blvd., Ste. 1400, Los Angeles, CA 90069. (310) 275-7323. FAX: (310) 275-1706. www.filmfinances.com email: ffi@ffi.com
PRESIDENT
Richard Soames

FINANCIAL MANAGEMENT ADVISORS, INC.
1900 Ave. of the Stars, Ste. 900, Los Angeles, CA 90067. (310) 229-2940. FAX: (310) 229-2950. www.fma-inc.com
PRESIDENT & CIO
Kenneth D. Malamed

GOTHAMMETRO STUDIOS, INC.
(Production, development production finance, film distribution, tv & video production)
303 Broadway, Ste. 204, Laguna Beach, CA 92651. (877) 787-8848. www.GothamMetro.com email: ceo@GothamMetro.com

HARRIS, NEBITT, GERARD
175 Federal St., 8th Flr., Boston, MA 02110. (671) 960-2355. FAX: (617) 451-1291. www.harrisnesbitt.com
CONTACT
Jeffrey Logsdon

LEWIS HORWITZ ORGANIZATION
1840 Century Park E., Ste. 1000, Los Angeles, CA 90067. (310) 275-7171. FAX: (310) 275-8055.
PRESIDENT
Lewis Horwitz

IANNOTTI FINANCIAL SERVICES
(Manages investments and retirement planning for the entertainment industry)
322 Raymond Ave., Ste. 12, Glendale, CA 91201. (818) 547-1733. FAX: (818) 547-0388. email: saliannotti@att.net
CONTACT
Salvatore Iannotti

KRAMER & KASLOW
23901 Calabasas Rd., Ste. 1078, Calabasas, CA 91302. (310) 553-3838. FAX: (310) 553-3939.

MERCANTILE NATIONAL BANK
Entertainment Industries Division, 1840 Century Park E., 2nd Flr., Los Angeles, CA 90067. (310) 277-2265.
E.V.P., ENTERTAINMENT DIVISION
Melanie Krinsky

MERLIN FILM GROUP
8831 Sunset Blvd., Ste. 201, W. Hollywood, CA 90069. (310) 854-0707. FAX: (310) 854-0757.
CONTACT
Norman Siderow

MORGAN & LASKY
303 Broadway, Ste. 204, Laguna Beach, CA 92651. (949) 376-7600.
CONTACT
Michael Lasky

NATEXIS BANQUES POPULAIRES
1901 Ave. of the Stars, Ste. 1901, Los Angeles, CA 90067. (310) 203-8710. FAX: (310) 203-8720. www.nxbp.com
V.P., GROUP MANAGER
Bennett Pozil

NEUBERGER & BERMAN
1999 Ave. of the Stars, Ste. 2050, Los Angeles, CA 90067. (310) 843-4949. FAX: (310) 843-4944. www.nb.com
SENIOR DIRECTOR
W. Chip Eggers

NEWMARKET CAPITAL GROUP
202 N. Canon Dr., Beverly Hills, CA 90210. (310) 858-7472. FAX: (310) 858-7473.
CONTACTS
William A Tyrer
Chris J. Ball

OPPENHEIMER & CO.
10880 Wilshire Blvd., Los Angeles, CA 90024. (310) 446-7100. FAX: (310) 446-7411.

PACIFIC WESTERN BANK
11150 W. Olympic Blvd., Los Angeles, CA 90064. (310) 996-9100. FAX: (310) 996-9113. www.pacificwesternbank.com
Entertainment Division, 9454 Wilshire Blvd., Beverly Hills, CA 90212. (310) 248-2135.
CONTACT
Debra Bordeaux

THE PULLMAN GROUP
1370 Ave. of the Americas, New York, NY 10019. (212) 750-0210. FAX: (212) 750-0464. www.pullmanbonds.com
FOUNDER/CHAIRMAN/CEO
David Pullman

REGENT ENTERTAINMENT, INC.
1401 Ocean Ave., Ste. 300, Santa Monica, CA 90401. (310) 260-3333. FAX: (310) 260-3343. www.regententertainment.com
PRESIDENT, REGENT WORLDWIDE SALES
Gene George

D. R. REIFF & ASSOCIATES
320 W. 57th St., New York, NY 10019. (800) 827-7363, (212) 603-0231. FAX: (212) 247-0739. www.reiffinsurance.com
CONTACT
Dennis Reiff

AON-ALBERT G. RUBEN
48 W. 25th St., 12th Flr., New York, NY 10010. (212) 627-7400. FAX: (212) 633-1457.

SG COWEN
1221 Ave. of the Americas, New York, NY 10020. (212) 278-5400.

THE SHINDLER PERSPECTIVE, INC.
(Management consulting for creative, technology & emerging companies)
Box 8633, Calabasas, CA 91372-8633. (818) 223-8345. FAX: (818) 223-8372. www.ishindler.com
email: shindler@ishindler.com
CONTACT
Marty Shindler

SMITH BARNEY
10877 Wilshire Blvd., Ste. 500, Los Angeles, CA 90024. (310) 443-0500, (310) 443-0589.

STEREO VISION ENTERTAINMENT
15452 Cabrito Rd., Ste. 204, Van Nuys, CA 91406. (818) 909-7911. FAX: (818) 909-7908. www.stereovision.com
CONTACT
John Honour

TRUST COMPANY OF THE WEST INVESTMENT MANAGEMENT
865 S. Figueroa, Ste. 1800, Los Angeles, CA 90017. (213) 244-0000. FAX: (213) 244-0741. www.tcw.com
CHAIRMAN AND FOUNDER
Robert A. Day

UNION BANK OF CALIFORNIA ENTERTAINMENT GROUP
(Film Financing)
445 S. Figueroa, 16th Flr., Los Angeles, CA 90071. (213) 236-5828. FAX: (213) 236-5852. www.uboc.com
SENIOR V.P. & MANAGER
Christine Ball

THE WALDENVC
(New media financing)
750 Battery St., Ste. 700, San Francisco, CA 94111. (415) 391-7225. FAX: (415) 391-7262. www.waldenvc.com
GENERAL PARTNERS
Art Berliner
Rich LeFurgy
Matt Miller
Phil Sanderson
Steve Eskenazi
Larry Marcus

THEATRE REAL ESTATE FINANCING

ENTERTAINMENT PROPERTIES TRUST
(Real estate financing for movie theatres & destination entertainment)
30 Pershing Rd., Ste. 201, Kansas City, MO 64108. (888) EPR-REIT, (816) 472-1700. FAX: (816) 472-5794. www.eprkc.com
PRESIDENT
David M. Brain
DIRECTOR, CORPORATE COMMUNICATIONS
Jonathan B. Weis

COMPLETION BONDS & INSURANCE

ACORDIA, INC.
(Wholly owned subsidiary of Wells Fargo & Company)
(Entertainment & equine insurance & financial services)
15760 Ventura Blvd., Ste. 1400, Encino, CA 91436-3007. (818) 377-3800. FAX: (818) 377-3899. www.gicins.com
SENIOR V.P. & DIRECTOR, CREATIVE ENTERTAINMENT
Michael Locelso, LL.B.

AIG (AMERICAN INTERNATIONAL GROUP, INC.)
(Entertainment insurance writers)
80 Pine St., 3th Flr., New York, NY 10005. (212) 770-7000. FAX: (212) 809-1533. www.aig.com

AON/ALBERT G. RUBEN INSURANCE SERVICES, INC.
(Insurance for production)
10880 Wilshire Bld., 7th Flr., Los Angeles, CA 90024. (310) 234-6800. FAX: (310) 446-7839. www.albertgruben.aon.com
SENIOR V.P.
John A. Hamby

48 W. 25th St., 12th Flr., New York, NY 10010-2703. (212) 627-7400. FAX: (212) 633-1457. www.aon.com

Pinewood Studios, Pinewood Rd., Iver, Bucks SL0 0NH, England. TEL: (44 175) 365-8200. FAX: (44 175) 365-3152.

AON/RUBEN-WINKLER ENTERTAINMENT INSURANCE BROKERS
20 Bay St., Toronto, ON M5J 2 N9, Canada. (416) 868-2460. FAX: (416) 868-2469. www.aon.ca

BERKETT INSURANCE AGENCY
11150 W. Olympic Bld., Ste. 1100, Los Angeles, CA 90064. (310) 857-5757. FAX: (310) 857-5750.
www.berkettinsurance.com
PRESIDENT & CEO
Jeff Berkett

C&S INTERNATIONAL INSURANCE BROKERS, INC.
19 Fulton St., Ste. 308A, New York. NY 10038. (212) 406-4499. FAX: (212) 406-7588, (212) 406-7584. www.csins.com
PRESIDENT
Deborah Kozee

CHUBB GROUP INSURANCE
801 S. Figueroa St., Ste. 2400, Los Angeles, CA 90017. (213) 612-0880. FAX: (213) 612-5731. www.chubb.com
MANAGER, ENTERTAINMENT
Jay Moore

COLONY WEST FINANCIAL & INSURANCE
(Property, liability & workers compensation)
17602 17th St., Ste. 102, Tustin, CA 92780. (714) 542-4870. FAX: (714) 542-4871. www.colony-west.com
CONTACT
Richard Kaley

COPANS & ASSOCIATES
(Production & cast insurance, medical & employee benefits)
5638 Briarcliff Rd., Los Angeles, CA 90068. (323) 962-2461. FAX: (323) 962-4942.
CONTACT
Jeff Copans

DEWITT STERN GROUP, INC.
(Insurance)
420 Lexington Ave., Ste. 2700, New York, NY 10170. (212) 867-3550. FAX: (212) 949-4435.
MANAGER, ENTERTAINMENT DIVISION
Peter Shoemaker

ENTERTAINMENT BROKERS INTERNATIONAL
(International production insurance, contract coverage)
10940 Wilshire Blvd., 17th Flr., Los Angeles, CA 90024. (310) 824-0111. FAX: (310) 824-5733. www.entbrokersintl.com
PARTNER
Martin Ridgers

FILM FINANCES, INC.
9000 Sunset Blvd., Ste. 1400, Los Angeles, CA 90069. (310) 275-7323. FAX: (310) 275-1706. www.ffi.com

Film Finances Ltd., 14/15 Conduit St., London, England W1S 2XJ. TEL: (44 207) 629-6557. FAX: (44 207) 491-7530.

Film Finances France, 20 Rue Therese, 75001 Paris. TEL: (33 1) 4020-0005. FAX: (331) 4020-0006.

Film Finances. (c/o Samson Productions FSA) 205 Fox Studios Australia, Driver Ave., Moore Park, NSW 1363, Australia. TEL: (61 2) 8353-2600. FAX: (61 2) 8353-2601.

Film Finances Canada Ltd., 27 Yorkville Ave., Ste. 201, Toronto, Ontario M4W 1L1. (416) 929-6763. FAX: (416) 964-3987.

Film Finances Canada Ltd., 3981 Boulevard St. Laurent Cooper Bldg., Ste. 810, Montreal, Quebec H2W 1Y5. (514) 875-6763. FAX: (514) 876-3987.

Film Finances Scandinavia ApS: Langelinie Alle 35 2100 Copenhagen O, Denmark. TEL: (45 33) 91-7323. FAX: (45 72) 27-0027.
CONTACT
Per Neumann

GELFAND, NEWMAN & WASSERMAN
(Production, insurance, D.E.C.E. producers & vendors)
11500 W. Olympic Blvd., Ste. 404, Los Angeles, CA 90064. (310) 473-2522. FAX: (310) 478-8392. www.gnwinsurance.com
CONTACTS
Jeff Newman
Rob DiPallo

GULF INSURANCE GROUP
P.O. Box 131771, Dallas, TX 75313-1771. (972) 650-2800. FAX: (972) 650-3682. www.gulfinsurance.com

ABACUS INSURANCE BROKERS
12300 Wilshire Blvd., Ste. 100, Los Angeles, CA 90025. (310) 207-5432. FAX: (310) 207-8526. www.abacusins.com
CONTACT
Kevin Lewin

EVELYN HUDSON INSURANCE
(Low budget & independent production liability insurance)
1315 Westwood Blvd., Ste. 1, Los Angeles, CA 90024. (310) 477-0568. FAX: (310) 477-0569.
OWNER & BROKER
Evelyn Hudson

INTERNATIONAL FILM GUARANTORS
10940 Wilshire Blvd., Ste. 2010, Los Angeles, CA 90024. (310) 208-4500. FAX: (310) 443-8998. www.nnng.com/entities/ifg
PRESIDENT & COO
Steve Mangel
Studio No. 88, Shepperton Studios, Studios Rd., Shepperton Middlesex TW17 OQD. England. TEL: (011 44) 1932-562611 Ext. 2991. FAX: (011 44) 1932-592524.
CONTACT
Derek Townshend

LA XCESS INSURANCE BROKERS, INC.
7033 Owensmouth Ave., Canoga Park, CA 91303. (714) 562-8500. FAX: (714) 562-9200. www.laxcess.com
V.P. & CIC
Richard Rutkin

ALLEN LAWRENCE & ASSOCIATES
(Entertainment insurance)
7033 Owensmouth Ave., Canoga Park, CA 91303. (818) 704-0700. FAX: (818) 348-5472. www.allenlawrence.com
PRESIDENT
Allen Lawrence

MANAGEMENT BROKERS INSURANCE AGENCY
(Group & individual life & disability)
9301 Wilshire Blvd., Ste. 206, Beverly Hills, CA 90210. (310) 278-5943. FAX: (310) 278-6285.
PRESIDENT
Richard Horowitz

MAROEVICH, O'SHEA & COGHLAN INSURANCE BROKERS
(Insurance & risk management to the theatre industry)
425 Market St., 10th Flr., San Francisco, CA 94105. (800) 951-0600. FAX: (415) 957-0577. www.mocins.com
SENIOR V.P.
Steve Elkins

MARSH RISK & INSURANCE SERVICES
(Liability, entertainment property)
777 S. Figueroa St., Ste. 2200, Los Angeles, CA 90017. (213) 624-5555. FAX: (213) 346-5928. www.marshweb.com
ENTERTAINMENT INSURANCE
Julie Umphries

MARSHALL ENTERTAINMENT INSURANCE, INC.
2000 Universal Studios Plaza, Ste. 625, Orlando, FL 32819. (407) 363-1537. FAX: (407) 352-3308.
www.marshallentertainment.com
email: marshall@marshallentertainment.com
PRESIDENT & CEO
Karen Marshall

THE MOTION PICTURE BOND COMPANY
(Completion guarantee for the film industry)
1801 Ave. of the Stars, #1010, Los Angeles, CA 90067. (310) 551-0371. FAX: (310) 551-0518.
OPERATIONS MANAGER
B.J. Rack

NEAR NORTH INSURANCE BROKERAGE, INC.
(All types of insurance, entertainment & production)
Entertainment Division, 1840 Century Park E., Ste. 1100, Los Angeles, CA 90067-2112. (310) 556-1900. FAX: (310) 556-4702. www.nnng.com
CONTACT
Coriena Baer
International Film Guarantors, 10940 Wilshire Blvd., Ste. 2010, Los Angeles, CA 90024. (310) 208-4500. FAX: (310) 443-8998.
777 Third Ave., 17th Flr., New York, NY 10017. (800) 795-8075, (212) 584-5800. FAX: (212) 702-3333.

PETERSEN INTERNATIONAL UNDERWRITERS
23929 Valencia Blvd., Ste. 215, Valencia, CA 91355. (800) 345-8816, (661) 254-0006. FAX: (661) 254-0604.
www.piu.org email: piu@piu.org

REYNOLDS & REYNOLDS, INC.
(Insurance brokers; movie theatre specialists)
300 Walnut St., Ste. 200, Des Moines, IA 50309-2244. (515) 243-1724. FAX: (515) 243-6664.
email: info@reynolds-reynolds.com
PRESIDENT
Stan Reynolds

SPEARE & COMPANY INSURANCE
(Insurance brokers specializing in film & tv production)
15303 Ventura Blvd., 7th Flr., Sherman Oaks, CA 91403. (818) 464-9300. FAX: (818) 464-9398. www.speare.com
EXECUTIVE V.P.
Tom Alper

TAYLOR & TAYLOR ASSOCIATES, INC.
(Entertainment coverage, film, tv, video & photography)
90 Park Ave., 3rd Flr., New York, NY 10016. (212) 490-8511. FAX: (212) 490-7236. www.taylorinsurance.com
PRESIDENT
Scott Taylor

MAURICE TAYLOR INSURANCE BROKERS, INC.
(Entertainment insurance)
P.O. Box 29127, Los Angeles, CA 90029-0127. (323) 662-9110. FAX: (323) 660-0749. www.mtib.net email: mtinsbkr@aol.com
PRESIDENT
Maurice Taylor

TRAVELERS
c/o Securities Dept., One Tower Sq., Hartford, CT 06183. (860) 277-0111. www.travelers.com

UNION BANK OF CALIFORNIA
Entertainment Division, 9460 Wilshire Blvd., Beverly Hills, CA 90212. (310) 550-6500. FAX: (310) 550-6447.
V.P., MANAGERS
Herold Lewis
Brenda Doby
Brett Martin
Michael Yager

UNITED AGENCIES, INC.
350 W. Colorado Blvd., Ste. 220, Pasadena, CA 91105-1855. (800) 800-5880. FAX: (626) 577-1346. www.unitedagencies.com
email: mail@unitedagencies.com
CONTACT
Jeff Galineau

U. S. BANK
2450 Colorado Ave., Ste. 4000 W., Santa Monica, CA 90404. (310) 315-3346.
CONTACT
Mark Orlando

USI ENTERTAINMENT INSURANCE SERVICES
14140 Ventura Blvd., Ste. 300, Sherman Oaks, CA 91423-2750. (818) 906-3350. FAX: (818) 704-4699.
www.usi-insurance.com
PRESIDENT, ENTERTAINMENT
Shel Bachrach

THE WATKINS GROUP/TWG, LTD.
(Life Insurance, retirement, disability, tax defense, annuities)
5120 W. Goldleaf Cir., Ste. 170, Los Angeles, CA 90056. (323) 782-8991. FAX: (323) 291-4026.
SENIOR PARTNER
Cedric L. Watkins II

MARKET RESEARCH & ANALYSIS

A.C. NIELSEN COMPANY
150 N. Martingale Rd., Schaumburg, IL 60173. (847) 605-5000.
FAX: (847) 605-2000.
11150 W. Olympic, Ste. 1000, Los Angeles, CA 90064. (310)
966-4900.
770 Broadway, 15th Flr., New York, NY 10003. (646) 654-7900.
FAX: (646) 654-8100.
CHAIRMAN & CEO
Gerald S. Hobbs
COO
Thomas A. Mastrelli
SENIOR.V.P. & CFO
Ralph Sherman
SENIOR V.P. & COO
Richard B. Myers

BOZELL
40 W. 23rd St., New York, NY 10010. (212) 727-5000.

BRAMSON & ASSOCIATES
7400 Beverly Blvd., Los Angeles, CA 90036. (323) 938-3595.
FAX: (323) 938-0852.

ROBERT A. BRILLIANT, INC.
(TV, film & promotion research)
13245 Riverside Dr., #530, Sherman Oaks, CA 91423. (818)
386-6600. FAX: (818) 990-9007. email: rabinc@earthlink.net.
PRESIDENT
Robert A. Brilliant

CERTIFIED REPORTS, INC./CERTIFIED MARKETING
(Theatre checking open, blind and trailer checking nationwide)
7 Hudson St., Kinderhook, NY 12106. (518) 758-6400. FAX:
(518) 758-6451. www.certifiedreports.com
CHAIRMAN OF BOARD
Jack J. Spitzer
PRESIDENT
Bill Smith
VICE PRESIDENT
Jim Radcliff
EXECUTIVE V.P.
Frank Falkenhainer

CINEMA CONSULTANTS GROUP
(International sales and marketing)
9903 Santa Monica Blvd., PMB 831, Beverly Hills, CA 90212-
1671. (310) 859-3946. FAX: (310) 859-8327.
email: Goldmanmf@aol.com
PRESIDENT
Michael F. Goldman

CINEMASCORE
8555 W. Sahara Blvd., PMB 106, Las Vegas, NV 89117. (702)
255-9963. FAX: (702) 254-8042. www.cinemascore.com
email: cinemascore@cox.net
CONTACT
Ed Mintz

EXHIBITOR RELATIONS CO., INC.
(Box-office tracking)
15760 Ventura Blvd., Ste. 806, Encino, CA 91436. (818) 784-
2380. FAX: (818) 784-2379. www.exhibitorelations.com
PRESIDENT
Paul Dergarabedian

THE GALLUP ORGANIZATION
502 Carngie Center, Ste. 300, Princeton, NJ 08540. (609) 924-
9600. FAX: (609) 924-0228. www.gallup.com
World Headquarters: 901 F St., N.W., Washington, D.C. 20004.
(202) 715-3030. FAX: (202) 715-3041.

HANOVER SECURITY REPORTS
(Motion picture auditing)
952 Manhattan Beach Blvd., Ste. 250, Manhattan Beach, CA
90266. (800) 634-5560, (310) 545-9891. FAX: (310) 545-7690.
EXECUTIVE V.P.
Nancy Stein

JOAN PEARCE RESEARCH ASSOCS.
(Errors and omissions clearance; legal services)
8111 Beverly Blvd., #308, Los Angeles, CA 90048. (323) 655-
5464. FAX: (323) 655-4770.

KAGAN WORLD MEDIA
(Research and analysis of entertainment, communications and
media industries.)
126 Clock Tower Pl., Carmel, CA 93923-8734. (831) 624-1536.
FAX: (831) 625-3225. www.kagan.com email: info@kagan.com
PRESIDENT
Paul Kagan
CO-COO
Shawn Armbrust

NATIONAL RESEARCH GROUP
5900 Wilshire Blvd., 29th Flr., Los Angeles, CA 90036. (323)
549-5000. FAX: (323) 549-5111. www.nrg.com
email: info@nrg.com
CEO
Joseph Farrell

NEILSEN MEDIA RESEARCH
770 Broadway, New York, NY 10003. (646) 654-8300.
www.nielsenmedia.com

NEXT REALTY
(Market studies, feasibility reports, film zone analysis for
exhibitiors)
1 Northfield Plz., Northfield, IL 60093. (847) 501-6190. FAX:
(847) 501-6195. email: basb1@aol.com
MANAGING PRINCIPAL
Barry A. Schain

OPINION RESEARCH CORP. INTL.
23 Orchard Rd., Skillman, NJ 08558. (908) 281-5100.

RENTRAK CORP.
7700 NE Ambassador Pl., Portland, OR 97220. (503) 284-7581.
FAX: (503) 331-2734. www.rentrak.com
CHAIRMAN & CEO
Paul Rosenbaum
SENIOR VICE PRESIDENT, THEATRICAL
Ron Giambra (818) 936-3550
SENIOR V.P., STUDIO RELATIONS
Marty Graham
SENIOR V.P., SALES & MARKETING
Christopher Roberts

VIDEO MONITORING SERVICES OF AMERICA
(News monitoring, keyword back-searches)
6430 W. Sunset Blvd., #400, Los Angeles, CA 90028. (323) 993-
0111. FAX: (323) 467-7540. www.vmsinfo.com
ADVERTISIGN SERVICES
Wendy Newell
PUBLIC RELATIONS SERVICES
Ashley Griffin

SOUND STUDIOS & SERVICES

AB AUDIO DESIGN STUDIOS
(Audio post-production, sound design, music compostion, editing, non-linear video editing)
3765 Marwick Ave., Long Beach, CA 90808. (562) 429-1042. FAX: (562) 429-2401. www.abaudio.com
email: arlan@abaudio.com
PRESIDENT
Arlan H. Boll
STUDIO MANAGER
Linda Rippee

ALBA DIGITAL RECORDING
(Audio production for the advertising and entertainment industries, including Radio, tv and film)
1648 10th St., Santa Monica, CA 90404. (310) 460-7830. FAX: (310) 460-7845. www.albadigitalrecording.com
CONTACT
Alex Alba

AMERAYCAN RECORDING STUDIOS
5719 Lankershim Blvd., N. Hollywood, CA 91601. (818) 760-8733. FAX: (818) 760-2524. www.paramountrecording.com

ASCENT MEDIA GROUP
(Music composition)
2901 W. Alameda Ave., Burbank, CA 91505. (818) 840-7100. FAX: (818) 840-7195. www.ascentmedia.com
CHAIRMAN & CEO
William R. Fitzgerald

ASSOCIATED PRODUCTION MUSIC (APM)
6255 Sunset Blvd., Ste. 820, Hollywood, CA 90028. (800) 543-4276, (323) 461-3211. FAX: (323) 461-9102.
www.apmmusic.com
PRESIDENT
Adam Taylor
NATIONAL SALES DIRECTOR
George Macias

THE AUDIO DEPARTMENT
(Audio recording & mixing)
119 W. 57th St., 4th Flr., Ste. 400, New York, NY 10019. (212) 586-3503. FAX: (212) 245-1675. www.theaudiodepartment.com

AUDIO MECHANICS
(Sound restoration and noise reduction)
1200 W. Magnolia Blvd., Burbank, CA 91506. (818) 846-5525.
www.audiomechanics.com email: john@audiomechanics.com
CONTACT
John Polito

AUDIO SERVICES COMPANY
(Sound equipment sales, rental & service for film & video production)
353 West 48th St., New York, NY 10036. (212) 977-5151. FAX: (212) 262-5150. www.audioservicesco.com
PRESIDENT
Marva Topham
VICE PRESIDENT
Ron Topham
SERVICE AND REPAIR
Vladimir Tarasov

AVID TECHNOLOGY
(Motion picture film editing equipment)
Avid Technology Park, One Park West, Tewksbury, MA 01876. (978) 640-6789. FAX: (978) 640-1366. www.avid.com
PRESIDENT & CEO
David Krall
SENIOR V.P., WORLDWIDE SALES, MARKETING & SERVICE
Chas Smith
V.P., BUSINESS DEVELOPMENT & CLO
Ethan E. Jacks
GENERAL MANAGER, DIGIDESIGN
David Lebolt
V.P., DEVELOPMENT & OPERATIONS
Joe Bentivegna

THE BAKERY STUDIO
10709 Burbank Blvd., N. Hollywood, CA 91601. (818) 508-7800. FAX: (818) 508-7122.
PRESIDENT
Andrew Watterman
STUDIO MANAGER
Brian Fike

BLUEFIELD MUSIC DESIGN
(Sound recording and pre-production)
1470 Snow Mass Creek Rd., Aspen, CO 81654. (970) 927-9897. email: dblue@sopris.net
OWNER
David Bluefield

CAPITOL STUDIOS
(Recording studio & scoring stage)
1750 N. Vine St., Hollywood, CA 90028. (323) 871-5001. FAX: (323) 871-5058. email: paula@capitolstudios.com
STUDIO DIRECTOR
Paula Salvatore

CHACE PRODUCTIONS, INC.
(Sound restoration and remastering, stereo conversion for DVD)
201 S. Victory Blvd., Burbank, CA 91502. (818) 842-8346. FAX: (818) 842-8353. www.chace.com
PRESIDENT
Robert Heiber
GENERAL MANAGER
James Eccles

CLAY DIGITAL SOUND
(Sound editorial services)
3610 W. Magnolia Blvd., Burbank, CA 91505. (323) 876-3477. FAX: (323) 845-9899.
CONTACT
Paul Clay

CLAY STAHLKA PRODUCTIONS
(Production sound and location recording for video & film, voice-overs, audio restoration services)
1617 Channel Pl., Fort Wayne, IN 46825. (260) 482-3491. FAX: (240) 337-6078. www.claystahlkaproductions.com
CO-OWNER & PRODUCER
Clay Stahlka
CO-OWNER, BUSINESS OFFICE
Marna Stahlka

CORELLI-JACOBS RECORDING, INC.
(Sound studios & services section)
25 W. 45th St., New York, NY 10036. (800) 221-6713, (212) 382-0220. FAX: (212) 382-0278. www.dewolfemusic.com
PRESIDENT
Andrew Jacobs
MANAGER, MUSIC SALES
Jamie Gillespie

CREATIVE MEDIA RECORDING
(Audio post-production for video)
11105 Knott Ave., Ste. G, Cypress, CA 90630. (714) 892-9469.
www.creativemediarecording.com
email: timkeenan@creativemediarecording.com
OPERATIONS DIRECTOR
Tim Keenan
PRODUCTION COORDINATOR
Linda Keenan

CRESCENDO STUDIOS
(Post-production & commercial spots)
615 Battery St., San Francisco, CA 94111. (415) 834-0580. FAX: (415) 834-0599. www.crescendostudios.com
DIRECTOR OF OPERATIONS
Cindy McSherry
COORDINATOR
Jason Plunkett

DB MUSIC
(Post-production for film & tv sound editing)
344 Clybourn Ave., Burbank, CA 91505. (818) 569-0287. FAX: (818) 569-0288. email: bondelev@usc.edu
PRESIDENT
David J. Bondelevitch

DEWOLFE MUSIC
25 W. 45th St., Ste. 801, New York, NY 10036. (800) 221-6713, (212) 382-0220. FAX: (212) 382-0278. www.dewolfemusic.com
email: info@dewolfemusic.com
PRESIDENT
Andrew Jacobs
MANAGER, MUSIC SALES
Jamie Gillespie

DIGITAL THEATER SYSTEMS (DTS)
(Digital sound)
5171 Clareton Dr., Agoura Hills, CA 91301. (800) 959-4109, (818) 706-3525. FAX: (818) 706-1868. www.dtsonline.com
email: info@dtsonline.com
CHAIRMAN
Dan Slusser
PRESIDENT & CEO
Jon Kirchner
DIRECTOR, WORLDWIDE SALES
Jim Murray

DIRECTORS SOUND & EDITORIAL SERVICE
(Post production sound studio specializing in ADR, & sound effects (foley) recording; sound transfers, narration, ADR supervision, & ISDN) 1150 W. Olive Ave., Burbank, CA 91506. (818) 843-0950. FAX: (818) 843-0357. www.dsstudio.com
email: sound@dsstudio.com
OPERATIONS MANAGER
Michael McGee

DOLBY LABORATORIES, INC.
(Movie theatre sound)
3601 W. Alameda Ave., Burbank, CA 91505. (818) 823-2800. FAX: (818) 557-0890.
CONTACT
Karen Greshler-Lewer
100 Portrero Ave., San Francisco, CA 94103. (415) 558-0200. FAX: (415) 863-1373.
175 S. Hill Dr., Brisbane, CA 94005. (415) 715-2500. FAX: (415) 715-2570.
1350 Ave. of the Americas, 28th Flr., New York, NY 10019-4703. (212) 767-1700. FAX: (212) 767-1705.

ECHO SOUND SERVICES, INC.
(Post-production sound)
4119 Burbank Blvd., Burbank, CA 91505. (818) 841-4114. FAX: (818) 563-9358. www.echosound.com
PRESIDENT
Joe Melody
DIRECTOR, SALES
Matt Preble

ALAN ETT MUSIC GROUP
(Music library)
12711 Ventura Blvd., Ste. 110, Studio City, CA 91604. (818) 508-3303. FAX: (818) 508-3314.

FULL HOUSE PRODUCTIONS, INC.
(Full-service audio recording studio)
123 W. 18th St., New York, NY 10011. (212) 645-2228. FAX: (212) 627-2838. www.fullhouseny.com

GLOBUS STUDIOS, INC.
44 W. 24th St., New York, NY 10010. (212) 243-1008.

JOHN HILL MUSIC
527 3rd Ave., #261, New York, NY 10016. (212) 683-2273.
email: jhmusic@mindspring.com

I.D.E.A.S. AT THE DISNEY MGM STUDIOS
(Integrated creative content studio, full-service facility with HD)
P.O. Box 22090, Lake Buena Vista, FL 32830. (407) 560-5600. FAX: (407) 560-2830.
CONTACT
Bob Allen x1070

IF/X PRODUCTIONS
(Interactive effects)
San Francisco, CA. (415) 345-8876. FAX: (415) 345-8905.
PRESIDENT
George Daugherty

INTERACTIVE EFFECTS
(Visual effects)
17351 Sunset Blvd., Ste. 404, Los Angeles, CA 90272. (888) 721-8059, (310) 998-8364. FAX: (310) 998-8233. www.IFX.com
INTERACTIVE EFFECTS WORLDWIDE
Mic Berends

INTERSOUND, INC.
(Post-production, dubbing)
962 N. La Cienega Blvd., Los Angeles, CA 90069. (310) 652-3741. FAX: (310) 652-5973. www.intersound.com
PRESIDENT
Kent Harrison Hayes

INTERWEAVE ENTERTAINMENT, INC.
22723 Berdon St., Woodland Hills, CA 91367. (818) 883-1920. FAX: (818) 883-9650. www.interweaveinc.com
email: iweinc@earthlink.net
CONTACT
Robert Weaver

LASER PACIFIC MEDIA CORP., SOUND SERVICES
809 N. Cahuenga Blvd., Los Angeles, CA 90038. (323) 462-6266. FAX: (323) 466-5047. www.laserpacific.com
email: info@laserpacific.com
PRESIDENT
Emory Cohen
EXECUTIVE V.P.
Leon Silverman

LARSON STUDIOS
(Audio post-production)
6520 Sunset Blvd., Los Angeles, CA, 90028. (323) 469-3986. FAX: (323) 469-8507. www.larson.com
CEO
Michael Perricone
EXECUTIVE V.P.
Jim Henderson
V.P., SALES & MARKETING
Rich Ellis

TODD/SOUNDELUX
7080 Hollywood Blvd., Ste. 1100, Hollywood, CA 90028. (323) 603-3200. FAX: (323) 603-3233. www.soundelux.com
PRESIDENT
Bob Rosenthal

LIVEWIRE STUDIOS (TODD-AO STUDIO WEST)
(Post-production)
3000 W. Olympic Blvd., Bldg. One, Santa Monica, CA 90404. (310) 315-5000. FAX: (310) 315-5018.

THE LOT
(Post-production)
1041 N. Formosa Ave., Bonner Bldg. #12, W. Hollywood, CA 90046. (323) 850-3180. FAX: (323) 850-3535.
CONTACT
Nicolette Bajtay

LUCASFILM THX
1600 Los Gamos Dr., San Rafael, CA 94903. (415) 492-3900. FAX: (415) 492-3988. www.thx.com
V.P., SALES
Ross Portugeis
GENERAL MANAGER
Ivan Fujihara

LEE MAGID PRODUCTION
P.O. Box 532, Malibu, CA 90265. (323) 463-5998. FAX: (310) 457-8891.
PRESIDENT
Lee Magid
VICE PRESIDENT
Adam Magid

CHRIS MANY MUSIC/SILVERSTORM STUDIOS
9441 Vanalden Ave., Northridge, CA 91324. (818) 885-0848. FAX: (818) 885-0488.
PRESIDENT
Chris Many
STUDIO MANAGER
Jim Kee

MARCLAND INTERNATIONAL COMMUNICATIONS
(Foreign language dubbing, subtitling & translation)
P.O. Box 3100, Burbank, CA 91508. (818) 557-6677. FAX: (818) 567-0568. www.marcland.com email: info@marcland.com
CEO
Alfredo Marco Fulchignoni

MEDIA CITY SOUND
(Post-production)
12711 Ventura Blvd., Ste. 110, Studio City, CA 91604. (818) 508-3311. FAX: (818) 508-3314. www.alanettcreativegroup.com
PRESIDENT
Alan Ett
VICE PRESIDENT
Scott Liggett

MOVIE TECH STUDIOS
(Movie production studio and editing services)
832 N. Seward St., Hollywood, CA 90038. (323) 467-8491. FAX: (323) 467-8471. www.movietechstudios.net

MUSIC ROOM PRODUCTIONS
(Film production, post-production, film & video, sound design for interactive toys and games)
525 S. Francisca Ave., P.O. Box 219, Redondo Beach, CA 90277. (310) 316-4551. www.musicroomonline.com
email: mrp@aol.com
PRESIDENT
John Reed

NAMRAC MUSIC
(Music publishing, recording studio & sound stage)
Sound City Center Stage, 15456 Cabrito Rd., Van Nuys, CA 91406. (818) 787-6436. FAX: (818) 787-3981.
www.soundcitycenterstage.com
PRESIDENT
Tommy R. Skeeter

NAVESYNC, INC.
(Video screening editing)
306 W. 38th St., 5th Flr. New York, NY 10018. (212) 244-7177. FAX: (212) 244-5495.
PRESIDENT
Joe Trammell

NOVASTAR DIGITAL SOUND
(Post-production)
6430 Sunset Blvd., #103, Hollywood, CA 90028. (323) 467-5020. FAX: (323) 957-8707. www.novastarpost.com
email: bsky@novastarpost.com
V.P. & GENERAL MANAGER
Bob Sky
MANAGER, CLIENT SERVICES/SCHEDULING
Scott Sonderegger

NT AUDIO'S VIDEO FILM LABS
(Recording and developing optical soundtrack negatives)
1833 Centinela Ave., Santa Monica, CA 90404. (310) 828-1098.
FAX: (310) 828-9737. www.ntaudio.com
email: kk@ntaudio.com
PRESIDENT
Tom McCormick
OPERATIONS MANAGER
Jon Seifert

100% SOUND
(Full service production house, turn key solutions for audio)
114 Catherine St., Saratoga Springs, NY 12866. (518) 584-4431. FAX: (518) 587-9088.

PACIFIC SOUND GROUP
4109 W. Burbank Blvd., Burbank, CA 91505. (818) 845-4100.
FAX: (818) 840-9245.

PARAMOUNT RECORDING STUDIOS
(Analogue-to-digital audio recording & sound mastering)
6245 Santa Monica Blvd., Hollywood, CA 90038. (323) 465-4000. FAX: (323) 469-1905. www.paramountrecording.com
email: info@paramountrecording.com
CONTACTS
Adam L. Beilenson
Michael Kerns

PICTURE HEAD
(Post-production finishing facility)
1132 Vine St., Hollywood, CA 90038. (323) 466-2066. FAX: (323) 466-2717.
PRESIDENT
Darin Kuhlmann

POINT 360
(Formerly VDI MultiMedia) (Post-production services)
1133 N. Hollywood Way, Burbank, CA 91505. (818) 556-5700.
FAX: (818) 556-5748. www.point360.com
SENIOR V.P., SALES & SERVICE
Ben "Ponz" Ponzio

RALEIGH STUDIOS
(Sound editing)
5300 Melrose Ave., Hollywood, CA 90004. (323) 466-3111. FAX: (323) 871-5600. www.raleighstudios.com
GENERAL MANAGER
Mary Fry

RIOT!
(Recording studios, tv post-production)
3399 Peachtree Rd. N.E., Ste. 200, Atlanta, GA 30326. (404) 237-9977. FAX: (404) 237-3923. www.riotatlanta.com
DIRECTOR, SALES & MARKETING
Beth Helmer

SEVEN TORCH MUSIC
(Music composition, post-production sound, sound sweetening & mixing)
5005 Sunnyslope Ave., Sherman Oaks, CA 91423. (818) 789-7568. wwwsteveorich.com
PRESIDENT
Steven Orich

SHORELINE STUDIOS
(Audio post-production)
1316 3rd St., Ste. 109, Santa Monica, CA 90401. (310) 394-4932. FAX: (310) 458-7802. www.shorelinestudios.com

SONY PICTURES STUDIOS
(Post-production)
10202 W. Washington Blvd., Culver City, CA 90232. (310) 244-5789. FAX: (310) 244-4152. www.sonypictures.com
email: megan_costello@spe.sony.com
CONTACT
Megan Costello

SOUND MASTER AUDIO/VIDEO
10747 Magnolia Blvd., Los Angeles, CA 91601. (323) 650-8000.

SOUND THINKING MUSIC RESEARCH
1534 N. Moorpark Rd., #333, Thousand Oaks, CA 91360. (805) 495-3306. FAX: (805) 495-3306. home.earthlink.net/~soundthink
email: soundthink@earthlink.net
CONTACT
Cary Ginell

SOUNDCASTLE RECORDING STUDIO
(Audio recording)
2840 Rowena Ave., Los Angeles, CA 90039. (323) 665-5201.
FAX: (323) 662-4273. www.soundcastle.com
CONTACT
Pat Kane

SOUNDSCAPE PRODUCTIONS
(Dubbing & audio mixing)
3614 Overland Ave., Los Angeles, CA 90034. (310) 202-9989.
FAX: (310) 202-6088. www.dubscape.com
email: dubscape@pacbell.net
CHIEF ENGINEER
Gregg Hall

SOUTHERN LIBRARY OF RECORDED MUSIC
(Music library)
4621 Cahuenga Blvd., Toluca Lake, CA 91602. (818) 752-1530.
FAX: (818) 508-0213.
PRESIDENT
Ralph Peer II
MANAGER
Roy Kohn

STARDUST FILM, INC.
(Production sound for motion pictures)
7510 Sunset Blvd., #240, Hollywood, CA 90046. (310) 288-7889. FAX: (818) 763-5886. www.stardustfilm.com
PRESIDENT
Peter V. Meiselmann, C.A.S.

STUDIO 56
7000 Santa Monica Blvd., Hollywood, CA 90038. (323) 978-0522. FAX: (323) 378-0521. www.56ent.com
PARTNERS
Paul Schwartz
Michael Dumas
Pride Hutchison
STUDIO 56 MANAGER
Chris Muldaur

STUDIO M PRODUCTIONS UNLIMITED
4032 Wilshire Blvd., #403, Los Angeles, CA 90010. (213) 389-7372. FAX: (213) 389-3299. email: studiom@pacbell.net
OWNER
Senator Mike Michaels, C.A.S.

SUNSET SOUND RECORDERS
(Recording studio)
6650 Sunset Blvd., Hollywood, CA 90028. (323) 469-1186. FAX: (323) 465-5579. www.sunsetsound.com
CONTACT
Craig Hubler

SUPERLOOPERS
(Looping)
P.O. Box 341678, Los Angeles, CA 90034. (310) 839-0895, (310) 649-3332. FAX: (310) 839-0896. www.superloopers.com
CONTACTS
DeVera Marcus
Norman Marcus

TECHNICOLOR CREATIVE SERVICES
(Studio sound & dubbing)
2101 St. Catherine St. W., Montreal, QUE, H3H 1M6, Canada.
(514) 939-5060. FAX: (514) 939-5070. www.technicolor.com
PRESIDENT
Claude Gagnon
VICE PRESIDENT
Serge Nadeau
DIRECTOR, MARKETING, SALES & CUSTOMER SERVICE
Pierre Moreau

TODD-AO STUDIOS
(Post-production sound)
900 N. Seward St., Hollywood, CA 90038. (323) 962-4000. FAX: (323) 466-2327. www.ascentmedia.com
CONTACT
George Vorghi

TOM THUMB MUSIC
(Division of Rhythms Productions) (Music composition)
P.O. Box 34485, Los Angeles, CA 90034-0485. (310) 836-4678.
PRESIDENT
Ruth White
EXECUTIVE PRODUCER
David White
ART DIRECTOR
Lotte Cherin

2B PRODUCTIONS
(Full service audio post production facility specializing in sound design and mixing)
1600 Broadway, Ste. 707, New York, NY 10019. (212) 765-8202.
FAX: (212) 765-8234. www.2binc.com

ULTRA STEREO LABS, INC.
(Sound & production equipment)
181 Bonetti Dr., San Luis Obispo, CA 93401. (805) 549-0161.
FAX: (805) 549-0163. www.uslinc.com

UNIVERSAL STUDIOS
(Sound mixing & dubbing, special effects, sound recording for major motion pictures)
100 Universal City Plaza, Bldg. 2315, 2nd Flr., Universal City, CA 91608. (818) 777-0169. FAX: (818) 866-1494.
www.universalstudios.com/studio
S.V.P., SOUND SERVICES
Christopher Jenkins
DIRECTOR, SOUND OPERATIONS
Karen Sebok

UNIVERSAL MASTERING STUDIOS
(Restoration, mastering, CDR duplication, CD enhancing)
5161 Lankershim Blvd., Ste. 201, North Hollywood, CA 91601.
(818) 777-9200. FAX: (818) 777-9235.

WARNER BROS. STUDIOS FACILITIES
4000 Warner Blvd., Bldg. 4, Rm. 101, Burbank, CA 91522. (818)
954-3000. FAX: (818) 954-2677. www.wbsf.com
email: wbsf@warnerbros.com
V.P., SALES & MARKETING, POST-PRODUCTION SERVICES
Daniel R. Chavez (818) 954-2515

WAVES SOUND RECORDERS
(Sound recording)
1956 N. Cahuenga Blvd., Hollywood, CA 90068. (323) 466-
6141. FAX: (323) 466-3751.
SCHEDULING
Cindy Ossello

WESTLAKE AUDIO
(Recording studio, audio service & sales)
7265 Santa Monica Blvd., Los Angeles, CA 90046. (323) 851-
9800. FAX: (323) 851-9386.
8447 Beverly Blvd., Los Angeles, CA 90046. (323) 654-2155.
OWNER
Glen Phoenix
STUDIO MANAGER
Steve Burdick

WORKSHIRT MUSIC
P.O. Box 3945, Hollywood, CA 90078. (323) 466-6046.
OWNER
Chris Anderson

SAUL ZAENTZ FILM CENTER
2600 Tenth St., Berkeley, CA 94710. (800) 227-0466, (510) 486-
2100. FAX: (510) 486-2115. www.zaentz.com
CONTACT
Steve Shurtz

SPECIAL EFFECTS

ANA SPECIAL EFFECTS
(Breakaway glass, mechanical effects-rain, wind & snow)
7021 Hayvenhurst Ave., Van Nuys, CA 91406. (818) 909-6999.
FAX: (818) 782-0635.
CONTACT
Gladys Nary

A.D.2, INC.
(Multimedia design and production)
2118 Wilshire Blvd., Ste. 205, Santa Monica, CA 90403. (310)
394-8379. FAX: (310) 451-0966. www.ad2.com
PRESIDENT
Brad Mooberry

ADVANCED CAMERA SYSTEMS
(Aerial cinematography & vibration/motion-isolating systems)
16117 Cohasset St., Van Nuys, CA 91406. (818) 989-5222.
FAX: (818) 994-8405. www.advancedcamera.com
CONTACT
Russell Ofria

ADVANCED FIRE & RESCUE SERVICES
(Fire rescue standby, EMT and fire personell, fire trucks, antique
and new)
16205 Lost Canyon Rd., Santa Clarita, CA 91351. (818) 837-
7336, (661) 299-4801. FAX: (661) 298-3069.
www.advancedfire.com
CONTACT
Craig Sanford

ALIAS
(Software for special effects)
210 King St. E. Toronto, ON, Canada M5A 1J7. (416) 362-9181.
www.alias.com

AMALGAMATED DYNAMICS
(Special make-up and creature effects design)
20100 Plummer St., Chatsworth, CA 91311. (818) 882-8638.
FAX: (818) 882-7327.
OWNERS
Alec Gillis
Tom Woodruff, Jr.

AMERICAN PAPER OPTICS
6859 Leetsdale Dr., Ste. 202, Denver, CO 80224. (303) 399-
8889. FAX: (303) 399-8881.
CONTACT
Craig T. Jones

ANATOMORPHEX
(Animatronics, miniatures, body casting, & special effects make-up)
8210 Lankershim, Ste. 14, North Hollywood, CA 91605. (818)
768-2880. FAX: (818) 768-4808.
CONTACT
Robert Devine

ANIMAL MAKERS
(Animatronic animals)
775 E. Cochran St., Ste. F, Simi Valley, CA 93065. (805) 527-
6200. FAX: (805) 527-6210. www.animalmakers.com
email: jim@animalmakers.com
CREATIVE DIRECTOR
Jim Boulden

ARTEFFEX
(Animatronics, puppets, specialty costumes, miniatures,
creatures, models & props)
911 Mayo St., Los Angeles, CA 90042. (818) 506-5358. FAX:
(323) 255-4599.
CONTACT
Dann O'Quinn

BIFROST LASERFX
(3D computer animation & laser visual effects)
6733 Sale Ave., West Hills, CA 91307. (818) 704-0423.
www.howiewood.net

BIG FILM DESIGN
(Visual effects & title sequences for feature films)
161 Ave. of the Americas, 11th Flr., New York, NY 10013. (212)
627-3430. FAX: (212) 989-6528. www.bigfilmdesign.com
email: kathyk@bigfilmdesign.com
PRODUCER
Kathy Kelehan

BLACKLIGHT FILMS
12700 Ventura Blvd., 4th Flr., Studio City, CA 91604. (818) 508-
1833. FAX: (818) 508-1253. www.blacklightfilms.com
EXECUTIVE PRODUCER
Louie Schwartzberg
PRODUCER
Vincent Ueber

BLACKSTONE MAGIK ENTRPRISES, INC.
(Magic illusions for special effects)
12800 Puesta Del Sol, Redlands, CA 92373-7408. (909) 792-
1227. FAX: (909) 794-2737. www.blackstonemagic.com

BLUR STUDIO, INC.
(Computer generated effects for games, movies & tv)
159 Venice Blvd., Venice, CA 90291. (310) 581-8848. FAX: (310)
581-8850. www.blur.com email: betty@blur.com
PRESIDENT
Tim Miller
CONTACT
Betty Gaines

BRAIN ZOO STUDIOS
(Visual effects & animation)
16134 Hart St., Ste. 200, Van Nuys, CA 91406. (818) 785-1124.
FAX: (818) 904-1753. www.brainzoostudios.com
email: info@brainzoostudios.com
OWNER
Mohammed Davoudian

BRANAM ENTERPRISES, INC.
(Theatrical rigging & rentals)
28210 Constellation Rd., Santa Clarita, CA 91355. (661) 295-
3300. FAX: (661) 295-3865. www.branament.com
email: branam@branament.com
PRESIDENT
Joe Branam
CONTACT
Randy Haynie

BROOKLYN MODEL WORKS
(Fabrication of miniature & oversize props & prototypes,
architectural models)
60 Washington Ave., Brooklyn, NY 11205. (718) 834-1944. FAX:
(718) 596-8934. www.brooklynmodelworks.com
email: john@brooklynmodelworks.com
PRESIDENT
John Kuntzsch

BURMAN STUDIOS, INC.
(Special make-up effects and prosthetics)
4706 W. Magnolia Blvd., Burbank, CA 91505. (818) 980-6587.
FAX: (818) 980-6589. www.burmanstudio.com
CONTACT
Bari Dreiband-Burman

CAPTIAN DAVE'S MARINE SERVICES, INC.
(Boats, barges, trucks, & submarines for the film industry)
1438 W. 14th St., Long Beach, CA 90813. (562) 437-4772.
Pager: (562) 799-7814.
CONTACT
David W.L. Hilchey

THE CHARACTER SHOP, INC.
(Animatronics)
2296 Agate Court, Simi Valley, CA 93065. (805) 306-9441.
www.character-shop.com
CONTACT & PRESIDENT
Rick Lazzarini

CHIODO BROS. PRODUCTIONS, INC.
110 W. Providencia Ave., Burbank, CA 91502. (818) 842-5656.
FAX: (818) 848-0891.
PRESIDENT
Steve Chiodo

CIMMELLI, INC.
(Mechanical effects, model shop, atmospherics)
16 Walter St., Pearl River, NY 10965. (845) 735-2090. FAX:
(845) 735-1643.
OWNER
Hugo Cimmelli

CINEMA ENGINEERING COMPANY
7243 Atoll Ave., Ste. A, N. Hollywood, CA 91605-4105. (818)
765-5340. FAX: (818) 765-5349. email: CineEng@aol.com

CINESITE, INC.
(Visual effects (London); digital film mastering, scanning &
recording, digital restoration (Hollywood)
1017 N. Las Palmas Ave., Los Angeles, CA 90038. (323) 468-
5742. FAX: (323) 468-4483. www.cinesite.com
Medius House, 2 Sheraton St., London, W1F 8BH. TEL: (44
207) 973-4000. FAX: (44 207) 973-4040.
V.P., MARKETING
Rita Gale

CINEVISION EDITORIAL
(Motion picture editing & trailers)
209 E. Alameda Ave., Burbank, CA 91502. (818) 566-4917. FAX:
(818) 566-6639. email: cinevision2@aol.com
PRESIDENT
Philip Jones

CINNABAR
2840 N. Hollywood Way, Burbank, CA 91505. (818) 842-8190.
FAX: (818) 842-0563. www.cinnabar.com
email: info@cinnabar.com
CONTACTS
Kip Katz
Leslie Crawford
Ann Mitchell

CIS HOLLYWOOD
(Visual effects, 2D and 3D digital effects, all-format compositing)
1144 N. Las Palmas Ave., Hollywood, CA 90038. (323) 463-8811.
FAX: (323) 962-1859. www.cishollywood.com
CEO
Joseph Matza
EXECUTIVE PRODUCER
C. Marie Davis

CREATIVE CHARACTER ENGINEERING
(Computer graphics, animatronics, silicon babies, character-based
visual effects for film & tv)
16110 Hart St., Van Nuys, CA 91406. (818) 901-0507. FAX: (818)
901-8417. email: andyCCE@earthlink.net
CREATIVE DIRECTOR
Andrew Clement

CREATIVE EFFECTS, INC.
(Special effects equipment rental, fabrication, car rigging and
expenables specializing in weather, aptmospheric, pyrotechnic and
fire effects)
760 Arroyo Ave., San Fernando, CA 91340-2222. (818) 365-0655.
FAX: (818) 365-0651. www.creative-effects.com

THE CREATIVE GROUP
(Post-production for tv & cable networks)
305 E. 46th St., 12th Flr., New York, NY 10017. (212) 935-0145.
FAX: (212) 838-0853.

CRUSE & COMPANY, INC.
7000 Romaine St., Hollywood, CA 90038. (323) 851-8814.

DE LA MARE ENGINEERING, INC.
(Electrical apparatus manufacturing for the motion picture
industry)
1908 First St., San Fernando, CA 91340-2610. (818) 365-9208.
FAX: (818) 365-8775.

DIGISCOPE
(Visual digital effects)
2308 Broadway, Santa Monica, CA 90404. (310) 315-6060. FAX:
(310) 828-5856.
www.digiscope.com email: m_stuart@digiscope.com
PRESIDENT
Mary Stuart-Welch

DIGITAL DOMAIN
(Digital visual effects for film, tv, & commercials)
300 Rose Ave., Venice, CA 90291. (310) 314-2800. FAX: (310)
314-2888. www.digitaldomain.com
PRESIDENT
Scott Ross

DIMENSION 3
(Stereoscopic (3D) film & video)
5240 Medina Rd., Woodland Hills, CA 91364-1913. (818) 592-
0999. FAX: (818) 592-0987. www.d3.com email: info@d3.com
PRESIDENT
Daniel Symmes

WALT DISNEY IMAGINEERING
1401 Flower St., P.O. Box 25020, Glendale, CA 91221-5020.
(818) 544-6500.

E=MC² INC.
(Visual effects & 24/30 video playback)
710 W. Ivy St., Glendale, CA 91204. (818) 243-2424. FAX: (818)
243-5126. www.Emc2visfx.com
CONTACT
Bob Morgenroth

EFEX SPECIALISTS
(Atmospheric effects for films and tv)
43-17 37th St., Long Island City, NY 11101. (718) 937-2417.

EFFECTS IN MOTION
(A division of Reelistic FX, Inc.)
21318 Hart St. Canoga Park, CA 91303. (818) 346-2484. FAX:
(818) 346-2710. email: don8@pacbell.net
CONTACT
Don Gray

EFFECTIVE ENGINEERING
(Animatronic control components, mechanical design &
fabrication, servos, pneumatics, linkages & mechanics)
9932 Mesa Rim Rd., Ste. B, San Diego, CA 92121. (858) 450-
1024. FAX: (858) 450-9244.
www.effecteng.com email: mlipsky@effecteng.com
CONTACT
Mark Lipsky

EFILM
(Digital film laboratory)
1146 N. Las Palmas Rd., Hollywood, CA 90038. (323) 463-
7041. FAX: (323) 465-7342. www.efilm.com
email: info@efilm.com
CONTACT
David Hays

ENCORE HOLLYWOOD
(Post-production for episodic tv, film resolution)
6344 Fountain Ave., Los Angeles, CA 90028. (323) 466-7663.
FAX: (323) 467-5539.

ENTERTAINMENT VENTURES INTERNATIONAL
(Film, tv, music & video production, promotion & packaging)
100 S. Doheny Dr., Ste. 402, Los Angeles, CA 90048. (310)
278-2800. FAX: (310) 274-0400. email: entventint@cs.com
OPERATIONS DIRECTOR
Jim Beatty

EUE/SCREEN GEM PRINTS
222 E. 44th St., New York, NY 10017. (212) 867-4030. FAX:
(212) 867-4503.

EXTREME SPORTS FILMING
(Action sports specialist, marine, air and land; production
facilities, location, equipment, talent and more)
3419 Via Lido, #145, Newport Beach, CA 92663. (714) 235-
7578. email: efilming@sbcglobal.net

F-STOP, INC.
(35 & 16mm; special photographic effects, titles, optics and
digital effects; over 30 years experience)
120 S. Buena Vista St., Burbank, CA 91505. (818) 843-7867.
FAX: (818) 842-7706.
CONTACT
Todd Hall

FANTASY II FILM EFFECTS
(Green/blue screen, miniatures, digital special effects)
415 S. Flower St., Burbank, CA 91502. (818) 843-1413. FAX:
(818) 848-2824.
CONTACT
Leslie Huntley

RUSS FARBER
(Blue screen effects, setup, networking & trouble shooting
computers on location)
19324 Oxnard St., Tarzana, CA 91356. (818) 882-8220.
email: refent@pacbell.net

F/X CONCEPTS, INC.
11118 Ventura Blvd., Studio City, CA 91604. (818) 508-1094.

FILMTRIX, INC.
P.O. Box 715, North Hollywood, CA 91603-0715. (818) 981-
8188. FAX: (818) 981-8688. email: filmtrix@mac.com
CONTACT
Kevin Pike

FX & DESIGN
(Visual effects)
2153 Kress St., Los Angeles, CA 90046. (323) 822-1610, (323)
822-1620. email: elanfx@earthlink.net
OWNER
Elan Soltes

GALAXIE ENTERTAINMENT CO.
(Visual & photographic effects, animation)
P.O. Box 8523, Universal City, CA 91618. (818) 362-6005.
CONTACT
Dave Gregory

PETER GEYER ACTION PROPS, INC.
(Rubber & foam props, actor-safety props)
8235 Lankershim Blvd., Ste. G, North Hollywood, CA 91605.
(818) 768-0070. www.actionprops.com
email: petergeyer@earthlink.net

GILDERFLUKE & COMPANY, INC.
205 S. Flower St., Burbank, CA 91502. (800) 776-5972, (818)
840-9484. FAX: (818) 840-9485. www.gilderfluke.com
email: info@gilderfluke.com
CONTACT
Doug Mobley

THE GROUP Y
(Live action effects, models)
180 Varick St., 14th Flr., New York, NY 10014. (646) 732-9197.

HANSARD ENTERPRISES, INC.
(Projected visual effects)
P.O. Box 469, Culver City, CA 90232. (310) 840-5660. FAX: (310) 840-5662.
CONTACT
William Hansard

HBO STUDIO PRODUCTIONS
(Full-service video facility)
120-A E. 23rd St., New York, NY 10010. (212) 512-7800. FAX: (212) 512-7788.
SENIOR V.P.
Ralph Fumante
DIRECTOR, SALES
Paul Brzozowski

HFWD VISUAL EFX
(Creative representation for visual effects directors of photography & supervisors)
394 E. Glaucus St., Leucadia, CA 92024. (760) 944-9525. FAX: (760) 634-5017.
OWNER
Jayelle Sargent

JIM HENSON'S CREATURE SHOP
(Animatronics)
2821 Burton Ave., Burbank, CA 91504. (818) 953-3030. FAX: (818) 953-3039. www.henson.com
CONTACT
David Barrington Holt

HOLOGRAPHIC STUDIOS
(Holographic images & projections)
240 E. 26th St., New York, NY 10010. (212) 686-9397. FAX: (212) 481-8645. www.holostudios.com

I.D.E.A.S. AT THE DISNEY MGM STUDIOS
(Integrated creative content studio, full-service facility with HD)
P.O. Box 22090, Lake Buena Vista, FL 32830. (407) 560-5600. FAX: (407) 560-2830.
CONTACT
Bob Allen x1070

IF/X PRODUCTIONS
San Francisco, CA. (415) 345-8876. FAX: (415) 345-8905.
PRESIDENT
George Daugherty

IMAGE CREATORS, INC.
(Animatronics, puppet creatures, costume characters, prosthetic make-up characters, live-action characters)
2712 6th St., Santa Monica, CA 90405. (310) 392-3583. FAX: (310) 396-6972. www.imagecreators.net
OWNER & CEO
Fred Spencer
CFO
Karen Brooks

IMAGINE THAT
(Custom fabrications for themed environments)
28064 Ave. Stanford, Unit K, Valencia, CA 91355. (661) 294-0061.

INFLATABLE MARKETPLACE
1810 Gillespie Way, Ste. 202, El Cajon, CA 92020. (619) 258-4466. FAX: (619) 449-8299. www.inflatablemarketplace.com
V.P., SALES
Mark Hassett

INTERACTIVE EFFECTS
(Visual effects)
17351 Sunset Blvd., Ste. 404, Los Angeles, CA 90272. (888) 721-8059, (310) 998-8364. email: sales@ifx.com

JEX FX
47 Paul Dr., #9, San Rafael, CA 94903. (415) 488-9788. www.jexfx.com email: gplatek@jexfx.com

KNB EFX GROUP, INC.
(Make-up effects, animatronics)
7535 Woodman Pl., Van Nuys, CA 91405. (818) 901-6562. FAX: (818) 994-4685.
CONTACT
Greg Nicotero
Haward Berger

GENE KRAFT PRODUCTIONS
29 Calvados, Newport Beach, CA 92657. (949) 721-0609.
OWNER
Gene Kraft

L.A. VIDEOGRAMS
3203 Overland Ave., Ste. 6157, Los Angeles, CA 90034. (310) 836-9224. email: LExplore1@aol.com
CONTACT
Larry Rosen

LASER-PACIFIC MEDIA CORP.
(Post-production)
809 N. Cahuenga Blvd., Los Angeles 90038. (323) 462-6266. FAX: (323) 464-3233. www.laserpacific.com
email: info@laserpacific.com
PRESIDENT
Emory Cohen
E.V.P., SALES & MARKETING
Leon Silverman

LEXINGTON SCENERY & PROPS
12800 Rangoon, Arleta, CA 91331. (818) 768-5768. FAX: (818) 768-4217. www.lexingtonscenery.com
email: lexscene@lexingtonscenery.com
C.E.O.
Richard Bencivengo

LIBERTY STUDIOS, INC.
238 E. 26th St., New York, NY 10010. (212) 532-1865. FAX: (212) 779-2207.
CONTACT
John Sawyer

LINKER SYSTEMS
13612 Onkayha Circle, Irvine, CA 92620. (949) 552-1904. FAX: (949) 552-6985. www.linker.com email: linker@linker.com

LIVE WIRE PRODUCTIONS & VFX
28631 S. Western Ave., Ste. 101, Rancho Palos Verdes, CA 90275-0800. (310) 831-6227. www.livewireprod.com
VISUAL EFFECTS PRODUCER
Kris Simmons

LUMENI PRODUCTIONS, INC.
(Computer graphics, animation, special effects for film)
1632 Flower St., Glendale, CA 91201-2357. (818) 956-2200. FAX: (818) 956-3298. www.lumeni.com
PRESIDENT
Tony Valdez

MAGICAL MEDIA INDUSTRIES, INC.
12031 Vose St., North Hollywood, CA 91605. (818) 765-6150.

MAKEUP & EFFECTS LABORATORIES, INC. (M.E.L.)
(Animatronics, props, costumes, special effects make-up)
7110 Laurel Canyon Blvd., Bldg. E, N. Hollywood, CA 91605. (818) 982-1483. FAX: (818) 982-5712.

MAKEUP & MONSTERS
21115 Devonshire St., #109, Chatsworth, CA 91311. (818) 886-6587. FAX: (818) 709-6587. www.makeupandmonsters.com
e-mail: monstermaker@makeupandmonsters.com

MAKING UP
(Make-up & special effects for films, video, tv, & commercials)
6626 Michaeljohn Dr., La Jolla, CA 92037. (858) 459-6063. FAX: (858) 459-6035. Pager: (800) 804-8201. www.dorislew.com
CONTACT
Doris Lew-Jensen

MANEX ENTERTAINMENT
(Visual effects for film)
4751 Wilshire Blvd., Ste. 202, Los Angeles, CA 90010. (323) 936-6822. FAX: (323) 936-7968. www.manexentertainment.com

MANHATTAN TRANSFER
(Post-production)
1111 Lincoln Rd., Ste. 700, Miami Beach, FL 33139. (305) 674-0700. FAX: (305) 674-8900. www.mtmiami.com
VICE PRESIDENT
George O'Neill

MASTERSFX, INC
(Make-up & prosthetic effects)
10312 Norris Ave., Unit D, Arleta, CA 91331. (818) 834-3000. www.mastersfx.com
PRESIDENT
Todd Masters

MATTE WORLD DIGITAL
(Specialists in 2D & 3D environment creations)
24 Digital Dr., Ste. 6, Novato, CA 94949. (415) 382-1929. FAX: (415) 382-1999. www.matteworld.com
email: info@matteworld.com
CONTACT
Krystyna Demkowicz

MAVERICK DIGITAL CO.
(Formerly Gear CGI) (3D animation, digital effects)
9348 Civic Center Dr., 3rd Flr., Beverly Hills, CA 90210. (310) 276-6177. FAX: (310) 276-9477. www.maverickmpg.com
EXECUTIVE PRODUCER
Dan Rosenfeld

MAX INK CAFE
2700 Pacific Ave., Venice, CA 90291. (310) 827-5351. FAX: (310) 827-5655. www.maxinkcafe.com
VICE PRESIDENT
Bob Skibinski

MEDIA FABRICATORS, INC.
(Video & data projection equipment, special effects)
5067 W. Washington Blvd., Los Angeles, CA 90016. (323) 937-3344. FAX: (323) 937-1142. www.mediafab.com
email: mediafab@mediafab.com
PRESIDENT
Barry Fluster

METROLIGHT STUDIOS
(Computer graphic imaging, digital effects, 3D animation)
5724 W. 3rd St., Ste. 400, Los Angeles, CA 90036. (323) 932-0400. FAX: (323) 932-8440. www.metrolight.com
PRESIDENT
James W. Kristoff

MIGRANT FILM WORKERS
6948 Saint Estaban St., Tujunga, CA 91042. (818) 416-8278. www.migrantfilmworker.com email: jveetoo@earthlink.net
CONTACT
John Van Vliet

BILL MILLAR
(Tv visual effects)
116 S. Buena Vista St., Burbank, CA 91505. (818) 848-3300. FAX: (818) 848-3301.

MONSTER MECANIX
(Mechnical design for creature effects)
13958 Huston St., Sherman Oaks, CA 91423. (818) 995-0271. FAX: (818) 783-9014. www.brilligprods.com/efx/efx.html
CONTACT
Jurgen Heimann

NETWORK ART SERVICE
(Graphics for films & tv)
630 S. Mariposa St., Burbank, CA 91506. (818) 843-5078. FAX: (818) 843-2528.
CONTACT
Dan Walker

NEW DEAL STUDIOS
(Miniatures, mechanical effects, visual effects, photography & stage rental)
4105 Redwood Ave., Los Angeles, CA 90066. (310) 578-9929. FAX: (310) 578-7370. email: info@newdealstudios.com
PARTNERS
Matthew Gratzner
Ian Hunter
Shannon Blake Gans

NOVOCOM
(Corporate branding, broadcast corporate design)
4221 Redwood Ave., Los Angeles, CA 90066. (310) 448-2500. FAX: (310) 448-2525. www.novo.com
CREATIVE DIRECTOR
Craig Cleek

JAMES O'NEIL & ASSOCIATES
725 N. Western Ave., Ste. 109, Los Angeles, CA 90029. (323) 464-2995. FAX: (323) 464-2994.
CONTACT
Jim O'Neil

OPTIC NERVE STUDIOS
(Make-up & prosthetics)
9818 Glenoaks Blvd., Sun Valley, CA 91352. (818) 771-1007. FAX: (818) 771-1009. email: opticnervestudios@aol.com
PRESIDENT
John Vulich

OWEN MAGIC SUPREME
(Creator & manufacturer of magical effects)
734 N. McKeever Ave., Azusa, CA 91702. (626) 969-4519. FAX: (626) 969-4614. www.owenmagic.com

PACIFIC ENTERTAINMENT GROUP (ARTISTIC BLACK-LIGHT CREATIONS/DECOR)
(Scenic blacklight, 3D special effects)
100 S. Doheny Dr., Ste. 402, Los Angeles, CA 90048. (310) 278-2800. FAX: (310) 274-0400.
email: capitalizentventabcd@cs.com
OPERATIONS DIRECTOR
Jim Beatty

PACIFIC TITLE
(Visual effects, titles, film opticals)
6350 Santa Monica Blvd., Los Angeles, CA 90038. (323) 464-0121. www.pactitle.com
7215 Santa Monica Blvd., Los Angeles, CA 90046. (323) 769-3700. FAX: (323) 769-3701.
PRESIDENT
Phil Feiner

PDI/DREAMWORKS
1800 Seaport Blvd., Redwood City, CA 94063. (650) 562-9000. FAX: (650) 562-9100. www.pdi.com email: info@pdi.com
MARKETING
Amy Criter

PLAYGROUND
(Special effects)
2415 Michigan Ave., Santa Monica, CA 90404. (310) 264-5511. FAX: (310) 264-5512.

PERPETUAL MOTION PICTURES
(Digital effects & post-production)
27923 Smyth Dr., Valencia, CA 91355-3449. (661) 294-0788. FAX: (661) 294-0786. email: rmpmp@earthlink.net
CONTACT
Richard Malzahn

PIXEL MAGIC (OCS/FREEZE FRAME)
(Digital visual effects & 3D animation)
10635 Riverside Dr., Toluca Lake, CA 91602. (818) 760-0862. FAX: (818) 760-0483. www.pixelmagicfx.com
CONTACT
Ray McIntyre Jr.

PYROS CORPORATION
(3D computer animation, motion capture, environmental design, content creation, visual effects)
3197 Airport Loop Dr., Bldg. A, Costa Mesa, CA 92626. (714) 708-3400. FAX: (714) 708-3500. www.pyros.com
email: gpyros@pyros.com
CONTACT
Greg Pyros

QUANTEL
5670 Wilshire Blvd., Ste. 1777, Beverly Hills, CA 90036. (323) 692-3800. FAX: (323) 549-3424. www.quantel.com
REGIONAL SALES MANAGER
Suzette Ferguson

RACTIVE MEDIA
(Films & corporate interactive media; DVD, CD-ROM & Video)
2401 West Olive Ave. Ste. 250, Burbank, CA 91506. (818) 841-3032. FAX: (818) 841-3039. www. ractivemedia.com
CONTACT
Steve Miller

RAINMAKER DIGITAL PICTURES
(Film & video post production)
50 West 2nd Ave., Vancouver, B.C. V5Y 1B3 Canada. (604) 874-8700. FAX: (604) 872-2106, (604) 874-1719. www.rainmaker.com
PRESIDENT
Bob Scarabelli

RANDO PRODUCTIONS, INC.
(Mechanical special effects; New Ro-Motion RM-36)
7360 Laurel Canyon Blvd., N. Hollywood, CA 91605. (818) 982-4300. FAX: (818) 982-4320. www.rpiefx.com
CONTACT
Joe Rando

REEL EFX
(Full service mechanical effects; special effects product manufacturer sales and rentals; real-time special effects)
5539 Riverton Ave., N. Hollywood, CA 91601. (818) 762-1710. FAX: (818) 762-1734. www.reelefx.com

REELISTIC FX
(Rentals, pyrotechnics, miniatures, motion controlled gimbals and flying devices)
21318 Hart St., Canoga Park, CA 91303. (818) 346-2484. FAX: (818) 346-2710. www.r-fx.com
PRESIDENT
John Gray

RHYTHM & HUES STUDIOS
(Special effects animation)
5404 Jandy Pl., Los Angeles, CA 90066. (310) 448-7500. FAX: (310) 448-7600. www.rhythm.com email: suze@rhythm.com
MEDIA RELATIONS
R. Scot Byrd

RIOT MANHATTAN
(Post-production; Broadcast Design)
545 5th Ave., New York, NY 10017. (212) 907-1200. FAX: (212) 207-1279. www.riotmanhattan.com
MANAGING DIRECTOR
Connie Griffin

S.O.T.A. FX
(Monsters for movies)
7338 Valjean Ave., Van Nuys, CA 91406. (818) 780-1003. FAX: (818) 780-4315.

SAFARI ANIMATION & EFFECTS
10845 Van Owen St., Unit B, North Hollywood, CA 91605. (818) 762-5203. FAX: (818) 762-3709.

SCENIC TECHNOLOGIES
(A Production Resource Group company)
(Scenic props & fabrications)
6050 S. Valley View Blvd., Las Vegas, NV 89118. (702) 942-4774. FAX: (702) 942-4775. www.prg.com
PRESIDENT L.V., PRG
Joe Schenk, Sr.
GENERAL MANAGER, SCENIC TECHNOLOGIES
Carl Townsend

SCREAMING MAD GEORGE, INC.
17939 Chatsworth St #137, Granada Hills, CA 91344. (818) 832-3536. CELL: (818) 601-7603. www.smgfx.com

SIDESHOW, INC.
733 Lakefield Rd., Unit B, Westlake Village, CA 91361. (800) 474-3746, (805) 418-1940. FAX: (805) 418-1971. www.sideshowcollectibles.com

SIGHT EFFECTS
(Visual effects for commercials, telecine)
901 Abbot Kinney Blvd., Venice, CA 90291. (310) 392-0999. FAX: (310) 399-1334.
PRODUCER
Jeff Blodgett

SINGLE FRAME FILMS
(Animation)
437-1/2 N. Genesee Ave., Los Angeles, CA 90036. (323) 655-2664.
CONTACT
Gary Schwartz

SONY PICTURES IMAGEWORKS
(Graphics)
9050 W. Washington Blvd., Culver City, CA 90232. (310) 840-8000. FAX: (310) 840-8100. www.spimageworks.com
CREATIVE TEAM
Rob Legato
John Dykstra
Ken Ralston
Jerome Chen
Sheena Duggal

SPECIAL EFFECTS UNLIMITED, INC.
1005 N. Lillian Way, Hollywood, CA 90038. (323) 466-3361. FAX: (323) 466-5712.

SPECTAK PRODUCTIONS
(Special event production)
222 N. Sepulveda Blvd., Ste. 2000, El Segundo, CA 90245. (310) 335-2038.

STAGE 18
(Special effects equipment rental)
18 Leonard St., Norwalk, CT 06850. (203) 852-8185.

STICKS & STONES
(Make-up effects, costume design, speciality props, puppets-custom build only)
10535 Tujunga Canyon Blvd., Tujunga, CA 91042. (818) 352-9538. FAX: (818) 352-2779. www.sticksandstonesfx.com
CONTACTS
Rob Burman, Jennifer E. McManus

STOKES/KOHNE ASSOCIATES, INC.
(Effects, cinematography, motion control, titles & graphics, animation, tabletop)
742 Cahuenga Blvd., Hollywood, CA 90038. (323) 468-2340.

SUNSET POST, INC.
1813 Victory Blvd., Glendale, CA 91201. (818) 956-7912. FAX: (818) 545-7586.

THIRD DIMENSION EFFECTS
427 W. Alameda Ave., Burbank, CA 91506-3201. (818) 842-5665.

TITLE HOUSE INC./TITLE HOUSE DIGITAL EFFECTS
(Digital visual effects, titles and optical effects)
738 N. Cahuenga Blvd., Hollywood, CA 90038. (323) 469-8171. FAX: (323) 469-0377. www.titlehouse.com
PRESIDENT
Keith Allan
VICE PRESIDENT
Mark Allan
DIRECTOR OF SALES
Ridge Blackwell

TRIBAL SCENERY
(Sets for commercials)
3216 Vanowen St., Burbank, CA 91505. (818) 558-4045. FAX: (818) 558-4356. www.tribalscenery.com
email: tscenery@earthlink.net

TRI-ESS SCIENCES, INC.
(Special effects books, scientific props)
1020 W. Chestnut St., Burbank, CA 91506. (818) 848-7838. FAX: (818) 848-3521. email: science@tri-sssciences.com
CONTACT
Kim Greenfield

MIKE TRISTANO WEAPONS & SPECIAL EFFECTS
(All types of firearms, weapon effects, blood hits, dust hits, spark hits, make-up effects, blood effects)
14431 Ventura Blvd., PMB 185, Sherman Oaks, CA 91423. (818) 888-6970. FAX: (818) 888-6447.

TVA PRODUCTIONS
(Corporate productions & docu-commercials)
3950 Vantage Ave., Studio City, CA 91604. (818) 505-8300. FAX: (818) 505-8370. www.tvaproductions.com
CEO & EXECUTIVE PRODUCER
Jeffrey Goddard

ULTIMATE EFFECTS
(Explosions, weather & atmospheric effects)
723 Sonora Ave., Glendale, CA 91201. (818) 547-4743. www.ultimateeffects.com

VAN VLIET MEDIA
(Digital transfers video-to-film/computer to film/spots, shorts & features/cardiac angiogram dup. for film, digital & video)
(A Film for Educators Company) 420 E. 55th St., Ste. 6-U, New York, NY 10022. (800) 722-7340, (212) 486-6577. FAX: (212) 980-9826. www.vanvlietmedia.com
PRESIDENT
Harlan B. DeBell

VIDEO POST & TRANSFER, INC.
(Film to tape transfer, video online editing, audio, broadcast design, 3D animation, visual effects)
2727 Inwood Rd., Dallas, TX 75235. (214) 350-2676. FAX: (214) 352-1427. www.videopost.com email: roberth@videopost.com
GENERAL MANAGER
Robert Haasz

VIEW POINT STUDIOS
(Full-service special effects)
140 Gould St., Needham, MA 02494. (781) 449-5858. FAX: (781) 449-7272. www.viewpointstudios.com
BROADCAST MARKET COORDINATOR
Amy Coblenz

VIEW STUDIO, INC.
(Computerized special effects)
6715 Melrose Ave., Hollywood, CA 90038. (323) 965-1270. FAX: (323) 965-1277. www.viewstudio.com
OPERATIONS MANAGER
Charlie Stewart

VIEWPORT IMAGES
(Computer animation for broadcast media)
109 N. Naomi St., Burbank, CA 91505. (818) 559-8705. FAX: (818) 559-5453. www.viewportimages.com
PRESIDENT
John Howard

VISUAL CONCEPT ENGINEERING (VCE)
(Special visual effect for film, atomic industry films)
13300 Ralston Ave., Sylmar, CA 91342-7608. (818) 367-9187. FAX: (818) 362-3490. www.vce.com email: vceinc@aol.com
CONTACT
Peter Kuran

WARNER BROS STUDIO FACILITIES
(Mechanical)
4000 Warner Blvd., Burbank, CA 91522. (818) 954-3000. FAX: (818) 954-7829. www.wbsf.com email: wbsf@warnerbros.com

DON WAYNE MAGIC EFFECTS
(Magic illusions)
10929 Hartsook St., N. Hollywood, CA 91601. (818) 763-3192. FAX: (818) 985-4953. email: donwayneinc@earthlink.net

WILDFIRE, INC. LIGHTING & VISUAL EFFECTS
(Manufacturer of ultraviolet blacklights)
5200 W. 83rd St., Los Angeles, CA 90045. (800) 937-8065, (310) 645-7787. FAX: (310) 645-9009. www.wildfire.fx.com
CONTACT
John Berardi

STAN WINSTON STUDIO
(Animatronics)
17216 Saticoy St., P.O. Box 346, Van Nuys, CA 91406. (818) 782-0870. FAX: (818) 782-5367. www.stanwinston.com

WONDERWORKS, INC.
(Models, miniatures, special effects)
21350 Sherman Way, Canoga Park, CA 91303. (818) 992-8811. FAX: (818) 347-4330. www.wonderworksweb.com
PRESIDENT
Brick Price

WUNDERFILM DESIGN
(Main title design)
2276 La Grenada, Hollywood, CA 90068-2724. (323) 845-4100. FAX: (323) 845-4101. www.wunderfilm.com
email: jeff@wunderfilm.com
OWNER
Jeff Wunderlich

KEVIN YAGHER PRODUCTIONS
(Special effects make-up and animatronics)
6615 Valjean Ave., Van Nuys, CA 91406. (818) 374-3210. FAX: (818) 374-3214. www.kevinyagher.com

Stock Shots

ACADEMY OF MOTION PICTURE ARTS & SCIENCES
(Motion picture stills)
333 S. La Cienega Blvd., Beverly Hills, CA 90211. (310) 247-3020, (310) 247-3000. FAX: (310) 657-5193.

AM CAMEO STOCK FILM LIBRARY
(Raw stock, beauty, aerials and military)
10513 Burbank Blvd., N. Hollywood, 91601. (818) 762-7865. FAX: (818) 980-7113. email: amstockca@aol.com
LIBRARIAN
Chris Angelich

AMERICAN FILM INSTITUTE LIBRARY
2021 N. Western Ave., Los Angeles, CA 90027. (323) 856-7600.

AMERICAN STOCK PHOTOGRAPHY
3460 Wilshire Blvd., Ste. 304, Los Angeles, CA 90010. (800) 272-4749, (213) 386-4600. FAX: (213) 365-7171.
www.americanstockphotos.com

ANCHOR EDITORIAL
(Film editing services)
2835 Harmony Pl., La Crescenta, CA 91214. (213) 369-6903. email: swyter@earthlink.net

ARCHIVE FILMS BY GETTY IMAGES
One Hudson Sq., 75 Varick St., 5th Flr., New York, NY 10013. (800) IMAGERY, (646) 613-4000. FAX: (646) 613-4601.
www.gettyimages.com/motion
email: motionrequests@gettyimages.com
DIRECTOR OF SALES, N. AMERICA FILM
Ross Dabrow

CARL BARTH IMAGES
(Representing the Stock House collection and more)
P.O. Box 5325, Santa Barbara, CA 93150-5325. (805) 969-2346, (805) 637-0881. FAX: (805) 969-5057.
CONTACT
Carl Barth

THE BBC WORLDWIDE AMERICAS/THE BBC LIBRARY
(Full selection)
3500 W. Olive Ave., Ste. 110, Burbank, CA 91505. (800) 966-5424, (818) 840-9770. FAX: (818) 840-9781.
www.bbcfootage.com   email: lals@bbcfootage.com

BEST SHOT, INC.
(Full selection)
4726 N. Lois Ave., Ste. A, Tampa, FL 33614. (813) 877-2118. FAX: (813) 874-3655. www.bestshotfootage.com
email: images@bestshotfootages.com
CONTACT
Peter Klein

THE BRIDGEMAN ART LIBRARY INTERNATIONAL
(Full selection)
65 E. 93rd St., New York, NY 10128. (212) 828-1238. FAX: (212) 828-1255. www.bridgeman.co.uk
email: newyork@bridgemanart.com
CONTACT
Ed Whitley

BRITANNICA FILMS
(Full selection)
310 S. Michigan Ave., Chicago, IL 60604. (800) 554-9862, (800) 783-3633, (312) 347-7400, ext. 6512.

BUDGET FILMS
(Vintage and contempory)
4427 Santa Monica Blvd., Los Angeles, CA 90029. (323) 660-0187. FAX: (323) 660-5571. www.budgetfilms.com
CONTACT
Layne Murphy

BUENA VISTA IMAGING (DISNEY)
(Nature, scenics, aerials, contemporary cities)
500 S. Buena Vista St., Burbank, CA 91521. (818) 560-1270. FAX: (818) 842-0532.
CONTACT
Ben F. Hendirks, Jr.

CHERTOK ASSOCIATES, INC. (JAZZ ON FILM)
(Musical performances on film; specializing in jazz performances)
100 S. Main St., New City, NY 10956. (845) 639-4238.

CINENET (CINEMA NETWORK, INC.)
(Film & stock footage library)
1350 Los Angeles Ave., 3rd Flr., Simi Valley, CA 93065. (805) 527-0093. FAX: (805) 527-0305. www.cinenet.com

DICK CLARK MEDIA ARCHIVES
(Rock and roll performances)
3003 W. Olive Ave., Burbank, CA 91505. (818) 841-3003. FAX: (818) 954-8609.

CLASSIC IMAGES
(1900 to contemporary)
469 S. Bedford Dr., Beverly Hills, CA 90212. (800) 949-CLIP, (310) 277-0400, FAX: (310) 277-0412. www.classicimg.com
email: c-images@pacbell.com
PRESIDENT
Marcie Alexander

THE CLIP JOINT FOR FILM
833-B N. Hollywood Way, Burbank, CA 91505. (818) 842-2525. FAX: (818) 842-2644.

CORBIS MOTION
12959 Coral Tree Pl., Los Angeles, CA 90066. (310) 577-2939. FAX: (310) 577-2938. www.corbismotion.com
SALES REPRESENTATIVE
John Brosnan

LARRY DORN ASSOCIATES, INC.
(Film and video libraries; world backgrounds, Cessna aircraft)
5820 Wilshire Blvd., #306, Los Angeles, CA 90036. (323) 935-6266. FAX: (323) 935-9523.
LIBRARIAN
Larry Dorn

EASTMAN KODAK COMPANY
343 State St., Rochester, NY 14650. (800) 242-2424, (800) 621-3456, (585) 724-4000. www.kodak.com

KODAK EPX (DIGITAL IMAGING SYSTEMS)
12100 Rivera Rd., Whittier, CA 90606. (888) 265-6981.

EYEWIREPHOTODISC
601 N. 34th St., Seattle, WA 98103. (800) 661-9410. FAX: (877) 547-4686. www.gettyimages.com/motion
DIRECTOR OF SALES, N. AMERICA FILM
Ross Dabrow

F.I.L.M. ARCHIVES, INC.
(Vintage, contempary, animation, and news/lifestyles)
432 Park Ave. S., Ste. 1007, New York, NY 10016. (212) 696-2616. FAX: (212) 696-0021. www.filmarchivesonline.com
email:info@filmarchivesonline.com
PRESIDENT & CEO
Mark Trost

FILM & VIDEO STOCK SHOTS, INC.
(Full selection)
10442 Burbank Blvd., N. Hollywood, CA 91601-2217. (888) 4-FOOTAGE, (818) 760-2098. FAX: (818) 760-3294.
email: stockshot@mindspring.com
PRESIDENT
Stephanie Siebert

GETTY IMAGES
601 N. 34th St., Seattle, WA 98103. (206) 925-5000. FAX: (206) 925-5001. www.gettyimages.com
CONTACT
Jim Gurke

GREAT WAVES FILM LIBRARY
(Ocean scenes)
483 Mariposa Dr., Ventura, CA 93001-2230. (805) 653-2699.

HOLLYWOOD NEWSREEL SYNDICATE, INC.
(Celebrity)
1622 N. Gower St., Hollywood, CA 90028. (323) 469-7307. FAX: (323) 469-8251. www.hollywoodnewsreel.com

IMAGE BANK FILM BY GETTY IMAGES
One Hudson Sq., 75 Varick St., 5th Flr., New York, NY 10013. (800) IMAGERY. FAX: (646) 613-4601.
www.gettyimages.com/motion
email: motionrequests@gettyimages.com
DIRECTOR OF SALES, N. AMERICA FILM
Ross Dabrow

INTERNATIONAL COLOR STOCK, INC.
(Stock photography, model released people)
1123 Broadway, Ste. 1006, New York, NY 10010. (212) 463-8300. www.stockfoto.com email: fotos@stockfoto.com
CONTACT
Dagmar Fabricius

INTER VIDEO, INC.
(Computer graphics, news, fake news, public domain & tv shows)
1500 W. Burbank Blvd., Burbank, CA 91506-1309. (800) 843-
3626, (818) 843-3624. FAX: (818) 843-6884.
www.intervideo24.com
PRESIDENT
Richard Clark
SALES
Chris Olson

JALBERT PRODUCTIONS, INC.
(US Ski Team; summer and winter mountain sports)
775 Park Ave., Ste. 230, Huntington, NY 11743. (631) 351-5878.
FAX: (631) 351-5875. www.jalbertfilm.com

KESSER STOCK LIBRARY
(Full selection)
21 S.W. 15th Rd., Miami, FL 33129. (305) 358-7900. FAX: (305)
358-2209. www.kesser.com email: kesser@ix.netcom.com

CLAY LACY AVIATION, INC.
7435 Valjean Ave., Van Nuys, CA 91406. (800) 423-2904, (818)
989-2900. FAX: (818) 989-2953. www.claylacy.com
PRESIDENT
Clay Lacy

LIBRARY OF MOVING IMAGES, INC.
(Rare and classic film clips)
6671 Sunset Blvd., #1581, Hollywood, CA 90028. (323) 469-
7499. FAX: (323) 469-7559. email: mylmi@pacbell.net
OWNER
Michael Peter Yakaitis

**AMERICAN MUSEUM OF NATURAL HISTORY SPECIAL
COLLECTIONS**
Central Park W. at 79th St., New York, NY 10024. (212) 769-5418.
FAX: (212) 769-5009. http://library.amnh.org/special/

NBC NEWS ARCHIVES
30 Rockefeller Plaza, Rm. 327W-1, New York, NY 10112. (212)
664-3797. FAX: (212) 703-8558.

NATIONAL GEOGRAPHIC FILM LIBRARY
1145 17th St. N.W., Washington, DC 20036. (202) 828-6605.
FAX: (202) 429-5755. www.ngtlibrarycom
email: sabbott@ngs.org
SALES MANAGER
Steve Abbott

PARAMOUNT PICTURES STOCK FOOTAGE LIBRARY
(Out-takes from paramount features)
5555 Melrose Ave., Hollywood, CA 90038. (323) 956-5510. FAX:
(323) 862-1352.
email: michelle_davidson@paramount.com
HEAD LIBRARIAN
Michelle Davidson

PASSPORT INTERNATIONAL PRODUCTIONS
(Full selection; trailers)
10520 Magnolia Blvd., North Hollywood, CA 91601. (818) 760-
1500. FAX: (818) 760-1532. www.footagehollywood.com
PRESIDENT
Jeanette Pugliese

PRODUCERS LIBRARY SERVICE
(Full selection; hollywood history)
10832 Chandler Blvd., N. Hollywood, CA 91601. (800) 944-
2135, (818) 752-9097. FAX: (818) 752-9196.
www.filmfootage.com email: research@filmfootage.com
OWNER
Jeff Goodman

PYRAMID MEDIA
(Medical and nature/animals)
2801 Colorado Ave., Santa Monica, CA 90404. (310) 828-7577.
FAX: (310) 453-9083. www.pyramidmedia.com
email: info@pyramidmedia.com
PRESIDENT
Randolph Wright

REUTERS MEDIA, INC.
3 Times Square, 18th Flr., New York, NY 10036. (646) 223-
4342. FAX: (646) 223-4390.
CONTACT
Saidah Nash

ROBERTSTOCK.COM/RETROFILE.COM
3460 Wilshire Blvd., Ste 304, Los Angeles, CA 90010. (800)
786-6300. www.robertstock.com; www.retrofile.com

SECOND LINE SEARCH
902 Broadway, 5th Flr., New York, NY 10010. (212) 777-6200.
FAX: (212) 533-4034. email: info@sekani.com
CONTACT
Rick Wysocki

THE SOURCE STOCK FOOTAGE
140 S. Camino Seco, Ste. 308, Tucson, AZ 85710. (520) 298-
4810. FAX: (520) 290-8831. www.sourcefootage.com
email: Requests@sourcefootage.com
LIBRARY MANAGER
Don French

SPECTRAL COMMUNICATIONS
(Celebrity red carpet)
400 S. Victory Blvd., #308, Burbank, CA 91502. (818) 840-0111.
FAX: (818) 840-0618. www.celebcentral.com

STOCK MEDIA
1123 Broadway, Ste. 1006, New York, NY 10010. (212) 463-
8300. www.stockmedia.net email: info@stockmedia.net
CONTACT
Randy Taylor

UCLA FILM & TELEVISION ARCHIVE
(Historical)
1015 N. Cahuenga Blvd., Hollywood, CA 90038. (323) 466-
8559. FAX: (323) 461-6317. www.cinema.ucla.edu
email: footage@ucla.edu
CONTACT
Amy Axvig

UNIVERSAL STOCK FOOTAGE LIBRARY
(Generic scenic footage; US cities)
100 Universal City Plaza, Bldg. 2282, Rm. 242, Universal City,
CA 91608. (818) 777-3000. FAX: (818) 866-0763.
www.universalstudios.com email:john.willison@unistudios.com
HEAD LIBRARIAN
John Willison

VIDEO TAPE LIBRARY, LTD.
1509 N. Crescent Heights Blvd. #2, Los Angeles, 90046. (323)
656-4330. FAX: (323) 656-8746. www.videotapelibrary.com
email: vtl@videotapelibrary.com
PRESIDENT
Melody St. John

WEST GRAND MEDIA, LLC
(Early motown artists)
6255 Sunset Blvd., Ste. 1110, Los Angeles, CA 90028. (323)
856-3500. FAX: (323) 465-4471.
CONTACT
Michael Lovesmith

WISH YOU WERE HERE FILM & VIDEO
(Worldwide images and cultures)
105 W. Alameda Ave., Ste. 217, Burbank, CA 91502. (818) 569-
5876. FAX: (818) 569-5880. www.wywhstock.com
email: noborders@wywhstock.com

STUDIO & EDITING SERVICES & EQUIPMENT RENTALS

ADDRESS ONE POST
662 N. Van Ness Ave., Ste. 301, Los Angeles, CA 90004. (310) 838-7783. FAX: (323) 960-4961. www.addressone.tv
CONTACT
Tess Thompson

AFTERSHOCK DIGITAL
(Post-production editing)
8222 Melrose Ave., Ste. 304, Los Angeles, CA 90046. (323) 658-5700. FAX: (323) 658-5200. www.aftershockdigital.com
email: edit@aftershockdigital.com
CONTACT
Fritz Feick

AMERICAN FILM & TAPE, INC.
(Manufacturer of splicing tape, editorial leaders, dark room custom slitting & perforating)
20928 Osborne St., Unit H, Canoga Park, CA 91304. (818) 885-6641. FAX: (818) 885-6217.
MANAGER
Al Landsdale

AMERICAN ZOETROPE
916 Kearny St., San Francisco, CA 94133. (415) 788-7500. FAX: (415) 989-7910. www.zoetrope.com
CEO
Jay Shoemaker
FACILITIES COORDINATOR
James Levine

ANCHOR EDITORIAL
(Film editing services)
2835 Harmony Pl., La Crescenta, CA 91214. (213) 369-6903.
email: swyter@earthlink.net

ARCHION
(Post-production)
824 N. Victory Blvd., Burbank, CA 91502. (818) 840-0777. FAX: (818) 840-0877. www.archion.com
CONTACTS
James Tucci
Shane Wilhoite

AUTHENTIC DESIGN
(Digital imaging & graphic design)
P.O. Box 310, Malibu, CA 90265. (818) 707-0007.
email: authentic@earthlink.net
OWNER
Stephen Morales

AVID TECHNOLOGY
(Motion picture film editing equipment; no rentals)
Sales: 115 N. 1st St., Ste. 100, Burbank, CA 91502. (818) 557-2520. FAX: (818) 557-2558. www.avid.com
Corporate: Avid Technology, Inc., Avid Technology Park, One Park West, Tewksbury, MA 01876. (978) 640-6789. FAX: (978) 640-1366.
PRESIDENT & CEO
David Krall
SENIOR V.P. & ACTING CFO
Ethan E. Jacks
SENIOR V.P. & GENERAL MANAGER, DIGIDESIGN
David Froker
SENIOR V.P., WORLDWIDE SALES
Chas Smith
CTO, V.P. & GENERAL MANAGER, INTERNET SOLUTIONS GROUP
Mike Rockwell
V.P. & GENERAL MANAGER, MEDIA SOLUTIONS GROUP
Joe Bentivegna

BABYLON POST
(Editing & post-production)
218 Woodbridge Rd., Coventry, TV 06238. (860) 742-8480.
email: babylonpost@earthlink.net
OWNER
Robin Fellows

BAYPOST COMPANY
(Post-production)
8380 Melrose Ave., Ste. 210, Los Angeles, CA 90069. (323) 653-2777. FAX: (323) 653-1531. www.baypost.com
CONTACT
Ben Bayan

BIG TIME PICTURE COMPANY
(Post-production, editing facilities & equipment rentals)
12210-1/2 Nebraska Ave., Los Angeles, CA 90025. (310) 207-0921. FAX: (310) 826-0071. email: bigtimepic@earthlink.net

BOUQUET MEDIA
(Equipment rentals & post-production)
881 Alma Real Dr., Ste. T-8, Pacific Palisades, CA 90272. (310) 573-7394. FAX: (310) 573-2025. www.bouquet.com
email: info@bouquet.com
SALES MANAGER
Matt Radecki x116

CALIFORNIA COMMUNICATIONS, INC. (CCI DIGITAL)
(Post-production)
2921 W. Alameda Ave., Burbank, CA 91505. (818) 562-6300. FAX: (818) 562-8222. www.ccidigital.com
PRESIDENT
Rick Morris

CHARLES AJAR PROJECTOR CO.
(Location equipment rental, distributor for screens and projection equipment and rentals)
(dba Universal Projector Co.) 10510 Burbank Blvd., North Hollywood, CA 91601. (818) 980-1948. FAX: (818) 980-7273.
email: upcajar@aol.com
OWNER
Tammy Ajar

CHACE PRODUCTIONS, INC.
(Audio post-production & sound restoration)
201 S. Victory Blvd., Burbank, CA 91502. (818) 842-8346. FAX: (818) 842-8353. www.chace.com
GENERAL MANAGER
James Eccles

BOB CHENOWETH RENTALS
1860 E. North Hills Dr., La Habra, CA 90631. (562) 691-1652.
email: chenowethrg@msn.com

CHRISTY'S EDITORIAL FILM & VIDEO SUPPLY
(Post-production equipment, editing & video supplies)
3625 W. Pacific Ave., Burbank, CA 91505. (818) 845-1755. FAX: (818) 845-1756. www.christys.net
GENERAL MANAGER
Craig Christy

CINESITE DIGITAL STUDIOS
(Digital effects, digital mastering, 3D editing)
1017 N. Las Palmas Ave., Ste. 300, Hollywood, CA 90038. (323) 468-4400. FAX: (323) 468-4404. www.cinesite.com

CINEVISION EDITORIAL, INC.
(Motion picture editing & trailers)
209 E. Alameda Ave., Burbank, CA 91502. (818) 566-4917. FAX: (818) 566-6639. email: cinevision2@aol.com
PRESIDENT
Philip Jones

CREST NATIONAL DIGITAL MEDIA COMPLEX
(Post-production)
1141 N. Seward St., Hollywood, CA 90038. (323) 462-6696. FAX: (323) 462-5039. www.crestnational.com
FILM ACCOUNT EXECUTIVE
Peter Dana

DELUXE LABORATORIES, INC.
(Film post-production; 35mm motion picture lab)
1377 N. Serrano Ave., Hollywood, CA 90027. (323) 462-6171. FAX: (323) 960-7016.
V.P., SALES
Steve VanAnda

WALT DISNEY STUDIOS POST-PRODUCTION SERVICES
500 S. Buena Vista St., Burbank, CA 91521. (818) 560-1000.
www.stu-ops.disney.com

DISCREET LOGIC
(Post-production, general editing)
2110 Main St., Ste. 207, Santa Monica, CA 90405. (800) 869-3504, (310) 396-1167. FAX: (310) 396-1257. www.discreet.com

EAGLE EYE FILM COMPANY
(Servicing, renting, manufacturer of editing equipment)
824 N. Victory Blvd., Burbank, CA 91502. (818) 506-6100. FAX: (818) 506-4313. www.eagleyedigital.com
CONTACT
Shane Wilhoite

EFILM DIGITAL LABORATORIES
(Digital-to-film lab)
1146 N. Las Palmas Ave., Hollywood, CA 90038. (323) 463-7041. FAX: (323) 465-7342. www.efilm.com
V.P., SALES
David Hays

ELECTRIC PICTURE SOLUTIONS
(Avid/Lightworks editing; rentals/editing suites)
3753 Cahuenga Blvd. W., Studio City, CA 91604. (818) 766-5000. FAX (818) 623-7547. www.picturesolutions.com
email: info@picturesolutions.com
EDITOR & PRESIDENT
David Pincus

ENTERPRISE IMAGE
(AVID nonlinear, Sony, Tascam)
4000 Burbank Blvd., Burbank, CA 91505. (818) 840-8480. FAX: (818) 588-6238. www.enterpriseimage.com
email: info@enterpriseimage.com
GENERAL MANAGER
Craig Minor

ENTERTAINMENT POST
(SyncSound dailies)
3575 Cahuenga Blvd. W., Ste. 103, Los Angeles, CA 90068. (323) 876-5800. FAX: (323) 876-5849. www.entpost.com
GENERAL MANAGER
Glenn Jepson

FPC, INC.
(Film accessories for post-production sound)
6677 Santa Monica Blvd., Hollywood, CA 90038. (323) 468-5774. FAX: (323) 468-5771. www.fpchollywood.com
CEO
Kathy Beckhardt

GOING POSTAL PRODUCTIONS
(Full post-production, production documentaries, streaming media, special edition DVDs & motion picture advertising)
2104 Pisani Pl., Venice, CA 90291. (310) 823-9362. FAX: (310) 823-9562.
CREATIVE DIRECTOR
Wes Rubinstein

GOOD EDIT
(Offline editorial)
417 Canal St., 3rd Flr., New York, NY 10013. (212) 966-8616. FAX: (212) 966-8592.
MANAGER
Janell Fletcher

HAMMER FILMS
(Post-production)
6311 Romaine St., Ste. 7316, Hollywood, CA 90038. (323) 463-9156. FAX: (323) 463-8130. www.hammerfilm.com

HOLLYWOOD FILM COMPANY
(Motion picture equipment manufacturer)
3294 E. 26th St., Los Angeles, CA 90023. (323) 261-3700. FAX: (323) 263-9665. www.hollywoodfilmco.com
CONTACT
Vincent Carabello

LASER PACIFIC MEDIA CORP.
809 N. Cahuenga Blvd., Los Angeles, CA 90038. (323) 462-6266. FAX: (323) 466-5047, (323) 465-6005.
www.laserpacific.com
CHAIRMAN & CEO
James R. Parks
PRESIDENT & COO
Emory Cohen
SENIOR V.P., ENGINEERING
Randolph Blim
V.P. & GENERAL MANAGER
Jane Swearingen
V.P., DEVELOPMENT
Chris Purse
DIRECTOR, OPERATIONS, HOLLYWOOD
Margie Gladden

MAGIC FILM & VIDEO WORKS
(Post-production)
2721 W. Burbank Blvd., Burbank, CA 91505. (818) 845-8781. FAX: (818) 845-4392.

MAGNO SOUND & VIDEO
(Post-production)
729 7th Ave., New York, NY 10019. (212) 302-2505. FAX: (212) 819-1282. www.magnosoundandvideo.com
VICE PRESIDENT
David Friedman

MATCHFRAME VIDEO
(Post-production)
610 N. Hollywood Way, Ste. 101, Burbank, CA 91505. (818) 840-6800. FAX: (818) 840-2726. www.matchframevideo.com
email: info@matchframevideo.com
DIRECTOR, POST-PRODUCTION SERVICES
Michael Levy

MONTANA EDIT
(Rental facility & education center, post-production)
1131 Montana Ave., Santa Monica, CA 90403. (310) 451-9933. FAX: (310) 454-3332. www.montanaedit.com
email: info@montanaedit.com
GENERAL MANAGER
Tony Borton

MY YOU ME PRODUCTIONS
(Shooting & AVID editing, general post-production)
2050 S. Bundy Dr., Ste. 104, West Los Angeles, CA 90025. (310) 820-1772. FAX: (310) 820-1332.
CONTACT
Richard Heene

NEW HOLLYWOOD, INC.
1302 N. Cahuenga Blvd., Hollywood, CA 90028. (323) 466-3686. email: newhollywood@hotmail.com
CONTACT
Ozzie Zornizer

NEWEDIT, INC.
(Post-production)
8300 Beverly Blvd., Los Angeles, CA 90048. (323) 653-3575. FAX: (323) 653-8855. www.newedit.com
CONTACT
Stan Cassio

NITELITE EDITORIAL
(Complete editing services)
10529 Valparaiso St., Ste. 2, Los Angeles, CA 90034. (310) 839-0707. FAX: (310) 839-0149. www.nitelite.org
EXECUTIVE PRODUCER
Harry Lowell

NT AUDIO VIDEO FILM LABS
(Post-production, telecine, optical sound tracks)
1400 N. Cahuenga Blvd., Hollywood, CA 90028. (323) 957-4200. FAX: (323) 957-4212. www.ntaudio.com
ACCOUNT EXECUTIVE
Clarisse Sirianni

ON-TIME OFF-LINE VIDEO
(AVID editing system rentals)
1800 Stanford St., Santa Monica, CA 90404. (310) 828-5662. FAX: (310) 829-9876. www.otvideo.com
CONTACT
Todd Darling

PADDED CELL PRODUCTIONS
3401 Pacific Ave., Ste. 18, Marina Del Rey, CA 90292. (310) 301-9555. email: paddedcell@mediaone.net
CEO
Rich Lewis

PASADENA PRODUCTION STUDIOS
(Studio rentals)
39 E. Walnut St., Pasadena, CA 91103. (626) 584-4090. FAX: (626) 584-4099.
TRAFFIC MANAGER
Kristen Judge

THE GRAPE GROUP & TNT MEDIA SERVICES
(Post production)
2330 Pontius Ave., W. Los Angeles, CA 90064. (310) 479-3877. FAX: (310) 479-9588.

PELICAN PICTURES
(Full production facility)
P.O. Box 1906, Mandeville, LA 70470-1906. (504) 606-8097.
www.pelicanpictures.com
PRODUCER
Bobbie Westerfield

PICTURE HEAD
(Post-production finishing facility)
1132 Vine St., Hollywood, CA 90038. (323) 466-2066. FAX: (323) 466-2717.
PRESIDENT
Darin Kuhlmann

PINNACLE SYSTEMS, INC.
280 N. Bernardo Ave., Mountain View, CA 94043. (650) 526-1600. FAX: (650) 526-1610. www.pinnaclesys.com
PRESIDENT & CEO
J. Kim Fennell

PIVOTAL POST
4142 Lankershim Blvd., North Hollywood, CA 91602-2829. (818) 760-6000. FAX: (818) 760-6012. www.pivotalpost.com
email: jeff@pivotalpost.com
PARTNER
Jeff Buchignani

PLANET VIDEO
(Full-service editing, demo reels)
1956 N. Cahuenga Blvd., Hollywood, CA 90068. (323) 464-6474. www.planet-video.com
CONTACT
D.C. Douglas

PLAYGROUND
Playground (Home Entertainment): 1855 Centinela Ave., Santa Monica, CA 90404. (310) 315-3800. FAX: (310) 315-3801.
SENIOR PRODUCER
Rebecca Jasmine

POST LOGIC STUDIOS
1800 N. Vine St., Ste. 100, Hollywood, CA 90028. (323) 461-7887. FAX: (323) 461-7790. www.postlogic.com
2049 Broadway, Santa Monica, CA 90404. (310) 315-9553. FAX: (310) 315-3073.
PRESIDENT
Barry Snyder

POST PRODUCTION PLAYGROUND
1619 Broadway, 5th Flr., New York, NY 10019. (212) 399-0409.
CONTACT
Eitan Hakami

PRECISION POST
3019 Pico Blvd., Santa Monica, CA 90405. (310) 829-5684. FAX: (310) 315-1757. www.precisionpost.com
POST PRODUCING & CLIENT RELATIONS
Joseph Arnao

PRIME POST
(Post-production)
3500 Caheunga Blvd. W., Los Angeles, CA 90068. (323) 878-0782. FAX: (323) 878-2781. www.primepost.com
email: info@primepost.com
V.P. & COO
Brigitte Prouty

PACIFIC TITLE
(Post-production, visual effects, opticals)
6350 Santa Monica Blvd., Hollywood, CA 90038. (323) 464-0121. FAX: (323) 461-8325.

QUARTERMOON
(Editing for commercials & long-format films, trailors & music videos)
12 Morand Ln., Wilton, CT 06897. (203) 247-5550. FAX: (203) 762-0509. www.quartermoon.com
CREATIVE DIRECTOR
Gary Balionis

RALEIGH STUDIOS
(Film production & editing)
5300 Melrose Ave., Hollywood, CA 90038. (323) 466-3111. FAX: (323) 871-5600. www.raleighstudios.com
GENERAL MANAGER
Mary Fry

RED CAR LOS ANGELES
(Editing for commercials, trailers & promos)
c/o Bergamot Studios, 2415 Michigan Ave., Ste. 200, Bldg. H, Santa Monica, CA 90404. (310) 828-7500. FAX: (310) 828-1245. www.redcar.com

RIOT
(All digital post-production in NTSC and PAL, Telecine HD, Datacine, Inferno, Fire HD, Henry, VYVX capabilities, 3D CGI, scanning and recording, compression & duplication)
Pictures: 730 Arizona Ave., Santa Monica, CA 90401. (310) 434-6300. FAX: (310) 434-6500. www.rioting.com
Colors: 702 Arizona Ave., Santa Monica, CA 90401. (310) 434-6000. FAX: (310) 434-6510.
MANAGING DIRECTOR
Marcie Malooly
DIRECTOR OF SALES
Bill Frazee

RIOT ATLANTA
(Recording studios, tv post-production)
3399 Peachtree Rd. N.E., Ste. 200, Atlanta, GA 30326. (404) 237-9977. FAX: (404) 237-3923. www.riotatlanta.com
email: info@riotatlanta.com
DIRECTOR, SALES & MARKETING
Beth Helmer

ROUNDABOUT ENTERTAINMENT
(Sound, post-production)
3915 Burbank Blvd., Burbank, CA 91505. (818) 842-9300. FAX: (818) 842-9301. www.roundabout.com
email: rndbt@westworld.com
CONTACT
Craig Clark

RUNWAY, INC.
10575 Virginia Ave., Culver City, CA; 90232-3520. (310) 636-2000. www.runway.com
PRESIDENT AND CEO
Roberta Margolis

SDI MEDIA
(Subtitles)
5455 Wilshire Blvd., 12th Flr., Los Angeles, CA 90036. (323) 602-5455. FAX: (323) 602-5460.

SONY PICTURES DIGITAL STUDIOS DIVISION
3960 Ince Blvd., Culver City, CA 90232. (310) 840-8676.
PRESIDENT
Yair Landau

SONY PICTURES STUDIOS POST-PRODUCTION FACILITIES
(Full-service post-production)
10202 W. Washington Blvd., Culver City, CA 90232. (310) 244-5722. FAX: (310) 244-2303.

LEONARD SOUTH PRODUCTIONS
11108 Huston St., North Hollywood, CA 91601. (818) 760-8383.

SUGAR
(Post-production)
Sugar (Commerical): 1855 Centinela Ave., Santa Monica, CA 90404. (310) 315-3888. FAX: (310) 315-3889.
SENIOR PRODUCER
Rebecca Jasmine

TEKTRONIX
(Testing & measuring equipment)
14200 SW Karl Braun Dr., P.O. Box 500, Beaverton, OR 97077. (800) 835-9433, (949) 789-7200. www.tektronix.com

TOTAL DIGITAL PRODUCTIONS
(Full-service production house)
1550 Flower St., Glendale, CA 91201. (818) 241-9792. FAX: (818) 241-9796. www.total-digital.com
PRESIDENT
Hillard Fitzkee

UNIVERSAL STUDIOS
(Full-service editing facility)
100 Universal City Plaza, Bldg. 2313 B, Rm. 101, Universal City, CA 91608. (818) 777-4728. FAX: (818) 866-0763. www.universalstudios.com/studio
CONTACT
Keith Alexander

VAN LING
3217 Overland Av., #8110, Los Angeles, CA 90034. (310) 202-7257. FAX: (310) 202-7388. www.vanlingpro.com
CONATCT
Van Ling

WARNER BROS. STUDIOS FACILITIES
(Post-production)
4000 Warner Blvd., Burbank, CA 91522. (818) 954-2515. FAX: (818) 954-2677. www.wbsf.com
CONTACT
Norman Barnett

XZACTO DIGITAL DYNAMICS
(Film & video post-production, motion graphic design, CGI visual effects)
9325 Browne Rd., Charlotte, NC 28269. (704) 398-8888. www.xzacto.com
PRESIDENT
Ben Griffith, Jr.

THE SAUL ZAENTZ FILM CENTER
2600 10th St., Berkeley, CA 94710. (510) 486-2100. FAX: (510) 486-2115. www.zaentz.com

SUBTITLES & CAPTIONS

BROWNE GLOBAL SOLUTIONS
(Translations & interpretations)
6500 Wilshire Blvd., Ste. 700, Los Angeles, CA 90048. (800) 367-4336. FAX: (323) 866-1001.

CAPTIONMAX
(Closed-captioning, audio description, subtitling)
530 N. Third St., Ste. 210, Minneapolis, MN 55401. (800) 822-3566, (612) 341-3566. FAX: (612) 341-2345.
www.captionmax.com

CAPTIONS, INC.
(Closed-captions, subtitles, translations)
901 W. Alameda Ave., Burbank, CA 91506. (818) 260-2700.
FAX: (818) 260-2850. www.captionsinc.com
SALES MANAGER
Robert Troy

619 W. 54th St., 5th Flr., New York, NY 10019. (212) 489-5705.
FAX: (212) 262-7855.
CONTACT
Mike Rubio

5098 Oaklawn Dr., Cincinnati, OH 45227. (513) 731-4466 FAX: (513) 731-8713.

CINETYP, INC.
(Foreign language and theatrical captions)
843 Seward St., Hollywood, CA 90038. (323) 463-8569. FAX: (323) 463-4129. www.cinetyp.com email: cinetyp@aol.com
CEO & PRESIDENT
John H. Bell
PRODUCTION MANAGER
Dave Margolis

CREST NATIONAL DIGITAL MEDIA COMPLEX
(Foreign language dubbing and subtitling)
1000 N. Highland Ave., Hollywood, CA 90038. (323) 860-1300.
FAX: (323) 461-8901. www.crestnational.com
EXECUTIVE V.P., SALES & MARKETING
John Walker

FOREIGN LANGUAGE GRAPHICS
6180 Laurel Canyon Blvd., Ste. 245, N. Hollywood, CA 91606.
(818) 753-9181. FAX: (818) 753-9617. www.isitrans.com

GLOBAL LANGUAGE SERVICES
2027 Las Lunas St., Pasadena, CA 91107. (626) 792-0862.
FAX: (626) 792-8793. email: aebi@hss.caltech.edu
email: globallang@aol.com
CONTACT
Dr. Andreas Aebi

INTEX AUDIOVISUALS
(Foreign language adaptations, 58 languages)
9021 Melrose Ave., Ste. 205, Los Angeles, CA 90069. (310) 275-9571. FAX: (310) 271-1319. www.intextrans.com

LANGUAGE.NET
(Formerly Language Services International)
804 Main St., Venice, CA 90291. (310) 399-1790. FAX: (310) 399-1901. www.language.net
CONTACT
Melanie Goodman

LASER VIDEO TITLES, INC.
375 Greenwich St., New York, NY 10013. (212) 343-1910. FAX: (212) 965-1338. www.lvt.fr email: lvtnewyork@aol.com
CHAIRMAN
Denis Auboyer

LINGUATHEQUE OF L.A.
(Translations/interpreting)
2219 W. Olive Ave., #261, Burbank, CA 91506. (800) 440-5344, (818) 995-8933. FAX: (818) 995-1228.
www.linguatheque.com email: lingua@linguatheque.com
CONTACTS
Karen Delaney
Eric Laufer

MARCLAND INTERNATIONAL COMMUNICATIONS
P.O. Box 3100, Burbank, CA 91508. (818) 557-6677. FAX: (818) 567-0568. www.marcland.com
CEO
Alfredo Marco Fulchignoni

MASTERWORDS
1512 11th St., #203, Santa Monica, CA 90401-2907. (310) 394-7998. FAX: (310) 394-7954.

MEDIA ACCESS GROUP AT WGBH
(Closed captions, subtitles, video description, mopix)
300 E. Magnolia Blvd., 2nd Flr., Burbank, CA 91502. (818) 562-3344. FAX: (818) 562-3388. www.access.wgbh.org
DIRECTOR, MARKETING
Michelle Maddalena

125 Western Ave., Boston, MA 02134. (617) 300-2000. FAX: (617) 300-1026. www.wgbh.org/caption
MARKETING REPRESENTATIVE
Carl Richardson

545 Fifth Ave., Ste. 609, New York, NY 10017. (212) 490-3677.
MARKETING DIRECTOR
Susan Schneider

NATIONAL CAPTIONING INSTITUTE
(Closed-captioning, subtitlings & translations)
1900 Gallows Rd., Ste. 3000, Vienna, VA 22182. (703) 917-7600. FAX: (703) 917-9853.
www.ncicap.org email: mail@ncicap.org
V.P., MARKETING
Karen O'Conner

303 N. Glenoaks Blvd., Ste. 200, Burbank, CA 91502. (818) 238-0068. FAX: (818) 238-4266.
MARKETING DIRECTOR
Elissa Sarna

333 7th Ave., 10th Flr., New York, NY 10001. (212) 557-7011.
FAX: (212) 557-6975.

PACIFIC TITLE & ART STUDIO
6350 Santa Monica Blvd., Hollywood, CA 90038. (323) 464-0121. FAX: (323) 463-7549. www.pactitle.com

SDI MEDIA
(Subtitles for theatrical, home video & DVD releases)
5455 Wilshire Blvd., 12th Flr., Los Angeles, CA 90036. (323) 602-5455. FAX: (323) 602-5460. www.sdi-media-usa.com
PRESIDENT
Barry Perlstein

STS FOREIGN LANGUAGE SERVICES
(a division of STS Media Services, Inc.)
(Foreign language translations, subtitling, voice-overs)
P.O. Box 10213, Burbank, CA 91510. (818) 563-3004.
www.STSForeignLanguage.com
CONTACT
Spencer Seegrove

SOFTNI CORP.
(Subtitling, dubbing and closed-captions)
11400 W. Olympic Blvd., #200, Los Angeles, CA 90064. (310) 312-9558. FAX: (310) 312-9557. www.softni.com
PRESIDENT
Jose M. Salgado

TITLE HOUSE DIGITAL
738 N. Cahuenga Blvd., Hollywood, CA 90038. (323) 469-8171.
FAX: (323) 469-0377. www.titlehouse.com

TITRA CALIFORNIA, INC.
(Laser subtitles)
733 Salem St., Glendale, CA 91203. (818) 244-3663. FAX: (818) 244-6205. www.titra.com email: lalaser@aol.com
MANAGING DIRECTOR
Robert Dekker

VITAC
(Closed captioning, subtitling in 50 languages)
4605 Lankershim Blvd., Ste. 250, N. Hollywood, CA 91602.
(818) 755-0410. FAX: (818) 755-0411.
email: sales@vitac.com
EXECUTIVE V.P., SALES
Jim Ballard
V.P., SALES
Lorelee Wiseman
V.P., INTL. SUBTITLING
Harlan Collins

TALENT AGENCIES

ABRAMS ARTISTS AGENCY
(Full-service talent agency)
9200 Sunset Blvd., 11th Flr., Los Angeles, CA 90069. (310) 859-0625. FAX: (310) 276-6193.
PRESIDENT, MOTION PICTURES, TV & COMMERCIALS
Harry Abrams
MOTION PICTURES/TV
Eric Emery, Marni Goldman, Gregg Klein, Joe Rice, Lara Nesburn
ON-CAMERA COMMERICALS
Mark Measures, Peter Novick, Lainie Sigesmund, Valerie Chiovetti
YOUTH COMMERICALS
Brad Fiffley
VOICE DEPARTMENT, COMMERICALS
Mark Mea, Mark Quinn
YOUTH DIVISION
Wendi Green, Jennifer Millar, Matt Fletcher
BUSINESS AFFAIRS
Brian Cho, Keith Clemens, Nathan Schwam

275 7th Ave., 26th Flr., New York, NY 10001. (646) 486-4600. FAX: (646) 486-0100.
PRESIDENT, MOTION PICTURES
Harry Abrams
THEATRICAL/MOTION PICTURES/TV
Robert Atterman
TV/MOTION PICTURES/THEATRICAL
Craig Cohen
THEATRICAL/MOTION PICTURES/TV
Jill McGrath, Richard Fisher, Robert Atterman, Paul Reisman
MC'S HOSTS BROADCAST JOURNALISTS
Mark Turner
COMMERICALS ON-CAMERA
Tracey Goldblum, Alison Quartin, Amy Mazur
YOUTH COMMERICALS
Bonnie Saumofsky
YOUTH THEATRICAL
Ellen Gilbert
VOICE DEPARTMENT
Neal Altman, Billy Serow, J.J. Adler, Jonathan Saul

ABOVE THE LINE AGENCY
(Literary agents)
9200 Sunset Blvd., #804, Los Angeles, CA 90069. (310) 859-6115. FAX: (310) 859-6119.
OWNER
Rima Greer
VICE PRESIDENT
Bruce Bartlett

ACME TALENT & LITERARY
(Theatrical, commericals, literary, voice-over, print, kids)
4727 Wilshire Blvd., Ste. 333, Los Angeles, CA 90010. (323) 954-2263. FAX: (323) 954-2262.
875 Ave., of the Americas, # 2108, New York, NY 10001. (212) 328-0388. FAX: (212) 328-0391.
PRESIDENT
Adam Lieblein
AGENT, HEAD OF ADULT THEATRICAL
Stephen Rice
AGENT, ADULT THEATRICAL
Greg Meyer
AGENT, HEAD OF KIDS THEATRICAL
Jackie Lewis
AGENT, HEAD OF ADULT COMMERICAL
Emily Hope
VOICE-OVER
Portia Scott-Hicks
AGENT, HEAD OF THEATRICAL, NY
Nina Shreiber

ACTORS ETC., INC.
(Full-service talent agency)
2620 Fountain View, Ste. 210, Houston, TX 77057. (713) 785-4495. FAX: (713) 785-2641. www.actorsetc.com
AGENTS
Denise Coburn
Jason Wasner

THE AGENCY
(Full-service talent agency)
1800 Ave. of the Stars, Ste. 400, Los Angeles, CA 90067. (310) 551-3000. FAX: (310) 551-1424. email: agencyone@hotmail.com
CHAIRMAN
Jerry Zeitman
TALENT
Frank Gonzales

AGENCY FOR THE PERFORMING ARTS, INC.
9200 Sunset Blvd., Ste. 900, Los Angeles, CA 90069. (310) 273-0744. FAX: (310) 888-4242.
CHAIRMAN & CEO
Roger Vorce
PRESIDENT
Jim Gosnell
EXECUTIVE V.P. & HEAD, PERSONAL APPEARANCE
Nat Burgess
EXECUTIVE V.P., HEAD, LITERARY TV
Lee Dinstman
EXECUTIVE V.P., HEAD, LITERARY/FEATURE
David Saunders
SENIOR V.P., PERSONAL APPEARANCE
Troy Blakely
SENIOR V.P., TALENT
Joel Dean

AGENCY 2 TALENT AGENCY
(Movies, tv & radio commercials, tv series work & print)
1717 Kettner Blvd., Ste. 200, San Diego, CA 92101. (619) 645-7744. FAX: (619) 645-7747. www.agency2.net
AGENTS
Lois Ringe
Terry Ringe
PRINT DIVISION DIRECTOR & SPECIAL EVENTS
Richard Carreon

AGENTS FOR THE ARTS
(Full-service except for children)
203 W. 23rd St., 3rd Flr., New York, NY 10011. (212) 229-2562. FAX: (212) 463-9313.
OWNER
Carole J. Russo

THE ALPERN GROUP
(Literary agency)
15645 Royal Oak Rd., Encino, CA 91436. (818) 528-1111. FAX: (818) 528-1110.

ALVARDO REY AGENCY
(Latino, Hispanic and European)
8455 Beverly Blvd., Ste. 410, Los Angeles, CA 90048-3416. (323) 655-7978.
OWNER/AGENT
Nikkolas Rey

MICHAEL AMATO AGENCY
(Full-service talent agency)
1650 Broadway, Ste. 307, New York, NY 10019. (212) 247-4456.
PRESIDENT
Michael Amato

AMERICAN INTERNATIONAL TALENT AGENCY
(Full-service talent agency)
303 W. 42nd St., Ste. 608, New York, NY 10036. (212) 245-8888. FAX: (212) 245-8926.
CONTACT
Wanza King

AMSEL, EISENSTADT & FRAZIER, INC.
(Actors)
5757 Wilshire Blvd. #510, Los Angeles, CA 90036. (323) 939-1188. FAX: (323) 939-0630.
CO-OWNERS/THEATRICAL AGENTS
Michael Eisenstadt
John Frazier

BEVERLY ANDERSON AGENCY
(Actors, singers & dancers; film, tv and theater)
1501 Broadway, New York, NY 10036. (212) 944-7773. FAX: (212) 944-1034.
OWNER & PRESIDENT
Beverly Anderson

ANDREADIS TALENT AGENCY, INC.
(Talent & commercial)
119 W. 57th St., Ste. 711, New York, NY 10019. (212) 315-0303. FAX: (212) 315-0311.
OWNER & AGENT
Barbara Andreadis

ANIMANAGEMENT
(Literary, specializing in new media, producers, writers & directors)
333 S. Front St., Ste. 206, Burbank, CA 91502. (818) 526-7600. FAX: (818) 526-7606.
PARTNERS
Aaron Berger
Russell Binder
Jim Strader
V.P., PRODUCTION
Rebecca Poole

ARIA MODEL & TALENT MANAGEMENT
(Models, talent and voice-overs)
1017 W. Washington Blvd., Ste. 2-C, Chicago, IL 60607. (312) 243-9400. FAX: (312) 243-9020. www.ariamodel.com
OWNERS
Mary Boncher
Marie Anderson Boyd
David Kronfeld

ARTISTS AGENCY
(Literary; by referral only)
230 W. 55th St., Ste. 29-D, New York, NY 10019. (212) 245-6960. FAX: (212) 333-7420.

ARTIST MANAGEMENT AGENCY
(Models, actors and voice-overs)
835 5th Ave., Ste. 411, San Diego, CA 92101. (619) 233-6655. FAX: (619) 233-5332. www.artistmanagementagency.com
PRESIDENT
Nanci Washburn

ARTIST NETWORK
8438 Melrose Pl., Los Angeles, CA 90039. (323) 651-4244. FAX: (323) 651-4699.
CONTACT
Debra Hope

THE ARTISTS AGENCY
(Literary & talent)
1180 S. Beverly Dr., Ste. 301, Los Angeles, CA 90035. (310) 277-7779. FAX: (310) 785-9338.

ASSOCIATED BOOKING CORP.
(Musical talent)
1995 Broadway, New York, NY 10023. (212) 874-2400. FAX: (212) 769-3649. www.abcbooking.com
PRESIDENT
Oscar Cohen
MARKETING
Lisa Cohen
AGENTS
Jody Wenig, Paul La Monica, Paul Horton, Mike Boheim

RICHARD ASTOR AGENCY
(Actors and singers)
250 W. 57th St. Ste. 2014, New York, NY 10107. (212) 581-1970.

ATKINS ARTISTS
(Actors and writers)
8040 Ventura Canyon Ave., Panarama City, CA 91402. (818) 904-9965.

BADGLEY/CONNOR
9229 Sunset Blvd., #311, Los Angeles, CA 90069. (310) 278-9313. FAX: (310) 278-4128.

BAUMAN REDANTY & SHAUL AGENCY
(Actors)
5757 Wilshire Blvd., Ste. 473, Los Angeles, CA 90036. (323) 857-6666. FAX: (323) 857-0368.
250 W. 57th St., #2223, New York, NY 10019. (212) 757-0098. FAX: (212) 489-8531.

BERZON TALENT AGENCY
(Theater, commericals, print, voiceovers, and literary)
336 E. 17th St., Costa Mesa, CA 92627. (949) 631-5936.
email: mberzon@earthlink.net

THE BOHRMAN LITERARY AGENCY
(Writers)
8899 Beverly Blvd., Ste. 811, Los Angeles, CA 90048. (310) 550-5444.
CEO
Michael Hruska
PRESIDENT
Caren Bohrman

BRADY, BRANNON & RICH
(On-camera and voiceover for commercials only)
5670 Wilshire Blvd., Ste. 820, Los Angeles, CA 90036. (323) 852-9559. FAX: (323) 852-9579.

THE BRANDT COMPANY
(Literary)
15159 Greenleaf St., Sherman Oaks, CA 91403. (818) 783-7747. FAX: (818) 784-6012. email: brandtco@aol.com
CONTACT
Geoffrey Brandt

BREVARD TALENT GROUP, INC.
(Theatrical)
906 Pinetree Dr., Indian Harbour Beach, FL 32937. (321) 773-1355. FAX: (321) 773-1842. www.BrevardTalentGroup.com
email: BrevardTalentGrp@aol.com
PRESIDENT
Traci Danielle

IRIS BURTON AGENCY
(Children to young adults)
1450 Belfast Dr., Los Angeles, CA 90069. (310) 288-0121. FAX: (310) 274-4882.

CAA/CREATIVE ARTISTS AGENCY
(Literary & talent)
9830 Wilshire Blvd., Beverly Hills, CA 90212. (310) 288-4545. FAX: (310) 288-4800. www.caa.com
PRESIDENT
Richard Lovett
CO-CHAIR
Lee Gabler
CO-CHAIR
Rick Nicita
AGENTS
Jenna Adler, Steve Alexander, Rowena Arguelles, Dennis Ashley, Ronald Baird, Jay Baker, Stan Barnett, Martin Baum, Alan Berger, Adam Berkowitz, Heather Berland, Glenn Bickel, Robert Bookman, Michael Camacho, John Campisi, Scott Clayton, Joe Cohen, Kevin Cooper, Erin Culley-LaChapelle, Jill Cutler, Christopher Dalston, Jimmy Darmody, Elie Dekel, Matthew DelPiano, Joshua Donen, Daryl Eaton, Teri Eaton, Rodney Essig, Tony Etz, Roger Fishman, Kelly Flatow, Jeff Frasco, Bryan Geers, Craig Gering, Risa Gertner, Ruth Gonzalez, Boz Graham, Brian Greenbaum, Scott Greenberg, Jeff Gregg, Alix Hartley, Rick Hess, Peter Hess, Jeff Hill, Kim Hodgert, Jared Hoffman, Rand Holston, Laurie Horowitz, John Huie, Kevin Huvane, Kevin Iwashina, Jeffrey Jacobs, Brandt Joel, Nancy Jones, Adam Kanter, Michael Katcher, Rob Kenneally, Carole Kinzel, Rick Kurtzman, Thomas Laffont, Steve Lashever, Matt Leaf, Eunice Lee, James Lefkowitz, Jon Levin, Peter Levine, Josh Lieberman, Byrdie Lifson-Pompan, Rob Light, Tony Lipp, Brett Loncar, Brian Loucks, Bryan Lourd, Brian Manning, Seth Matlins, Allison McGregor, Victoria Metzger, Peter Micelli, Jason Miller,Ted Miller, Don Muller, Darin Murphy, Tracey Murray, Bryan Myers, Andrea Nelson-Meigs, Michael Nilon, Robert Norman, Emanuel Nunez, David O'Connor, Paola Palazzo, Michael Pergtzian, Brian Pike, Jeremy Plager, Scott Pruitt, John Ptak, Jennifer Rawlings, Seth Rodsky, Mitch Rose, Michael Rosenfeld, Sonya Rosenfeld, Rick Roskin, Mark Rousse, Jonathan Ruiz, Carin Sage, Larry Shapiro, Brian Siberell, Chris Simonian, Shari Smiley, Steve Smooke, Matthew Snyder, Fred Specktor, Martin Spencer, Andy Stabile, Brett Steinberg, Beth Stine, Ken Stovitz, David Styne, Mick Sullivan, Elizabeth Swofford, Steve Tellez, David Tenzer, Kelly Tiffan, Jim Toth, Christian Troy, Marlene Tsuchii, Jessica Tuchinsky, Bruce Vinokur, Kathy White, Jeanne Williams, Sally Willcox, Michael Wimer, Allison Winkler

THE CAMPBELL AGENCY
(Fashion and commerical print; tv commericals)
3906 Lemmon Ave., Ste. 200, Dallas, TX 75219. (214) 522-8991.

CARSON ADLER AGENCY, INC.
(Film, tv, commericals, & theater; babies, children & young adults)
250 W. 57th St., Ste. 2030, New York, NY 10107. (212) 307-1882. FAX: (212) 541-7008.
PRESIDENT
Nancy Carson
SENIOR AGENTS
Bonnie Deroski
Shirley Faison

CAVLERI & ASSOCIATES
(Full-service talent agency)
178 S. Victory Blvd., Ste. 205, Burbank, CA 91502. (818) 955-9300. FAX: (818) 955-9399.
OWNER
Ray Cavaleri

CELEBRITY SUPPLIERS
(Celebrities, tv and movies)
2756 N. Green Valley Pkwy., #449, Las Vegas, NV 89014. (702) 451-8090. www.celebritysuppliers.com
PRESIDENT
A.J. Sagman
AGENTS
S. Rosenthal
Deb Manning

CENTURY ARTISTS, LTD.
1187 Coast Village Rd., Ste. One-495, Monte Cito, CA 93108. (805) 969-9344.

THE CHASIN AGENCY
(Theatrical, writers and directors)
8899 Beverly Blvd., Ste. 716, Los Angeles, CA 90048. (310) 278-7505. FAX: (310) 275-6685.
OWNER, AGENT ALL AREAS
Tom Chasin
TALENT
Kelly Duncan
LITERARY
Scott Penney

CIRCLE TALENT AGENCY
(Actors for commercials)
433 N. Camden Dr., #400, Beverly Hills, CA 90210. (310) 285-1585.

CIRCUIT RIDER TALENT MANAGEMENT
123 Walton Ferry Rd., Hendersonville, TN 37075. (615) 824-1947. FAX: (615) 264-0462. email: dotwool@bellsouth.net.
PRESIDENT
Linda S. Dotson

THE CLARK AGENCY
(Actors, children 3-15, seniors 55+, SAG and below-the-line talent)
13415 Ventura Blvd., Ste. 3, Sherman Oaks, CA 91423. (818) 385-0583.
PRESIDENT
W. Randolph Clark
V.P.,TALENT
Arlene Tsurutani

CLI TALENT AGENCY
(Adult commericals; on camera and voice-over)
843 N. Sycamore Ave., Los Angeles, CA 90038. (323) 461-3971. FAX: (323) 461-1134.
PRESIDENT
Leanna Levy
SENIOR AGENTS
Richard Ohanesian

CMT TALENT AGENCY
(Print, commericals and theatrical)
8344-1/2 W. 3rd St., Los Angeles, CA 90048. (323) 658-7072.

COAST TO COAST TALENT GROUP, INC.
(Talent and literary agency)
3350 Barham Blvd., Los Angeles, CA 90068. (323) 845-9200.
FAX: (323) 845-9212.
PRESIDENT
Jeremiah Doryon
V.P. & ADULT THEATRICAL
Elyah Doryon
DIRECTOR, YOUTH DIVISION
Meredith Fine
YOUTH THEATRICAL
Dana Edrick
YOUTH COMMERCIAL
Stephanie Glassberg
Renata Dobrucki
DIRECTOR, ADULT COMMERCIAL
Paula M. Sorenson
CELEBRITY ENDORSEMENTS/PRO SPORTS
Hugh Leon
LITERARY HEAD
Anne McDermott
ADULT THEATRICAL
Kevin Turner
Amber Raitz
YOUTH COMMERICAL
Sydel Lisi

COLLEEN CLER AGENCY
(Babies to teens for print, commercials and theatrical)
178 S. Victory Blvd., #108, Burbank, CA 91502. (818) 841-7943.
FAX: (818) 841-4541.
CONTACT
Colleen Cler

CONTEMPORY ARTISTS
(Producers, writers and directors)
610 Santa Monica Blvd., Ste. 202, Santa Monica, CA 90401.
(310) 395-1800. FAX: (310) 394-3308.

COPELAND CREATIVE TALENT
(Talent agency)
4140 1/2 Grand Ave., Des Moines, IA 50312. (515) 271-5970.
FAX: (515) 277-0770. email: copetalent@aol.com
OWNER
Debra Copeland

CORALIE JR. AGENCY
(Actors)
4789 Vineland Ave., #100, N. Hollywood, CA 91602. (818) 766-9501.
AGENT, ACTORS & ACTRESSES
Stuart Edward
LITERARY AGENT, ACTORS & ACTRESSES
Gary Dean

THE COSDEN MORGAN AGENCY
(Full-service talent agency)
7080 Hollywood Blvd., Ste. 1009, Hollywood, CA 90028. (323) 469-7100.

CUNNINGHAM, ESCOTT, DIPENE TALENT AGENCY
(Adult on camera, voice-over and print; full-service for youth)
10635 Santa Monica Blvd., Ste. 130, Los Angeles, CA 90025-4900. Commercial: (310) 475-2111; Children's: (310) 475-3336.
FAX: (310) 475-1929. www.cedtalent.com
257 Park Ave. S., Ste.900, New York, NY 10010. Commercial:
(212) 477-1666; Children's: (212) 477-6622. FAX: (212) 979-2011.

DADE/SCHULTZ ASSOCIATES
(Theatrical, equity, motion picture and tv)
23905 Plaza Gavilan, Valencia, CA 91355. (818) 760-3100.
FAX: (661) 253-3493.

DH TALENT AGENCY
(Theatrical, commercials and dance)
1800 N. Highland Ave., Ste. 300, Hollywood, CA 90028. (323) 962-6643.

DOUGLAS, GORMAN, ROTHACKER & WILHELM
(Film, tv and theater. By referral only)
1501 Broadway, Ste. 703, New York, NY 10036. (212) 382-2000.
FAX: (212) 719-2878. email: dgrwinc@aol.com

DYTMAN & ASSOCIATES
(Literary agency)
9200 Sunset Blvd., Ste. 809, Los Angeles, CA 90069. (310) 274-8844.

ELITE CASTING
2820 Eagle St., New Orleans, LA 70118. (504) 861-0245.

ENDEAVOR TALENT AGENCY, LLC
9701 Wilshire Blvd., 10th Flr., Beverly Hills, CA 90212. (310) 248-2000. FAX: (310) 248-2020.
BUSINESS AFFAIRS
Rick Olshansky, Tom McGuire, Gary Rosenfeld, Ann Du Vall
PARTNERS
Spencer Baumgarten, Ariel Emanuel, David Greenblatt, John Lesher, David Lonner, Steve Rabineau, Phil Raskind, Rick Rosen, Jason Spitz, Tom Strickler, Brian Swardstrom, Adam Venit, Richard Weitz, Patrick Whitesell
AGENTS
Adriana Alberghetti, Spencer Baumgarten, Bonnie Bernstein, Bryan Besser, Eric Bevans, Jeb Brandon, Leanne Coronel, Sandrine DeClercq, Chris Donnelly, Sean Elliot, Ross Fineman, Hugh Fitzpatrick, Stuart Fry, Cory Gahr, Craig Gartner, Ari Greenburg, Lenny Grossi, Paul Haas, Lisa Harrison, Greg Hodes, Greg Horangic, Lance Klein, Adam Levine, Brian Lipson, Scott Melrose, Jaime Misher, Shelley Morales, Melissa Myers, Tito Oiowu, Sean Perry, Amber Pollard, Philip Raskind, Stephanie Ritz, Rich Rogers, Dawn Saltzman, Rob Sebastian, Elyse Sherz, Greg Siegel, Jason Spitz, Lee Stollman, Jessica Thomas, Kevin Volchok, James Yaffe, Bill Weinstein, Andrew Weitz, Modi Wiczyk

EWCR & ASSOCIATES
(Actors)
311 W. 43rd St., Ste. 304, New York, NY 10036. (212) 586-9110.
FAX: (212) 586-8019.

EXTREME SPORTS FILMING
(Action sports specialist, marine, air and land; production facilities, location, equipment, talent and more)
3419 Via Lido, #145, Newport Beach, CA 92663. (714) 235-7578. email: efilming@sbcglobal.net

FERRAR MEDIA ASSOCIATES
(Commercials)
8430 Santa Monica Blvd., Ste. 220, Los Angeles, CA 90069.
(323) 654-2601. FAX: (323) 654-2979.

THE FIELD CECH AGENCY
(Literary agency; no referrals)
12725 Ventura Blvd., Ste. D, Studio City, CA 91604. (818) 980-2001. FAX: (818) 980-0754.

FILM ARTISTS ASSOCIATES
4717 Van Nuys Blvd., Ste. 215, Sherman Oaks, CA 91403.
(818) 386-9669.
CEO & COMMERCIAL AGENT
Cris Dennis
PRESIDENT & CELEBRITY AGENT
Penrod Dennis
CFO
Martha Dennis

FLASHCAST COMPANIES, INC.
(Computerized casting service specializing in children & infants)
Centrum Towers, 3575 Cahuenga Blvd. W., Ground Floor, Ste. 120, Universal City/Los Angeles, CA 90068.(323) 969-9006.
FAX: (818) 760-6792. www.flashcastkids.com
PRESIDENT & CEO
Carl Carranza

FRONTIER BOOKING INTERNATIONAL
(Children to young adults)
1560 Broadway, Ste. 1110, New York, NY 10036. (212) 221-0220.

THE GAGE GROUP
(Theater, literary, tv, commerical)
14724 Ventura Blvd., Ste. 505, Sherman Oaks, CA 91403. (818) 905-3800. FAX: (818) 905-3322. email: gagegroupla@yahoo.com
315 W. 57 St., Ste. 408, New York, NY 10019. (212) 541-5250.
FAX: (212) 956-7466.

GARBER TALENT AGENCY
(Theater, film and tv)
2 Pennsylvania Plaza, Ste. 1910, New York, NY 10121. (212) 292-4910.

DALE GARRICK INTL. AGENCY
(Motion pictures, tv, soaps and commercials)
8831 Sunset Blvd., #402, W. Hollywood, CA 90069. (310) 657-2661.

GEDDES AGENCY
(Theatrical agency)
8430 Santa Monica Blvd. #200, W. Hollywood, CA 90069. (323) 848-2700.
PRINCIPAL
Ann Geddes
AGENT, THEATRICAL
Ann Geddes

GERLER AGENCY

(Theatrical, motion picture and tv)
3349 Cahuenga Blvd. W., Ste. 1, Los Angeles, CA 90068. (323) 850-7386. FAX: (323) 850-7490.

THE GERSH AGENCY

(Full-service talent agency)
232 N. Canon Dr., Beverly Hills, CA 90210. (310) 274-6611. FAX: (310) 274-4035.
AGENTS
Phil Gersh
David Gersh
Lee Keele
Richard Arlook

130 W. 42nd St., #2400, New York, NY 10036. (212) 997-1818. FAX: (212) 391-8459.
AGENT
Scott Yoselow

GOLD/LIEDKE ASSOCIATES

(Adult and children commercials)
3500 W. Olive, Ste. 1400, Burbank, CA 91505. (818) 972-4300. FAX: (818) 955-6411.

GORFAINE/SCHWARTZ AGENCY, INC.

(Composers)
13245 Riverside, Ste. 450, Sherman Oaks, CA 91423. (818) 461-9600. FAX: (818) 461-9622.

MARY GRADY AGENCY

221 E. Walnut St., Ste. 130, Pasadena, CA 91101. (818) 567-1400.

GREENE & ASSOCIATES

(Tv and film)
526 N. Larchmont Blvd., Ste. 201, Los Angeles, CA 90004. (323) 960-1333. FAX: (323) 960-1330.

LARRY GROSSMAN & ASSOCIATES

(Literary agency)
211 S. Beverly Dr., Ste. 206, Beverly Hills, CA 90212. (310) 550-8127. FAX: (310) 550-8129.

BUZZ HALLIDAY & ASSOCIATES

(Actors, directors and choreographers)
8899 Beverly Blvd., Ste. 715, Los Angeles, CA 90048. (310) 275-6028. FAX: (310) 275-8514.

HANDPRINT ENTERTAINMENT

(Documentaries, motion pictures and tv)
1100 Glendon Ave., Ste. 1000, Los Angeles, CA 90024. (310) 481-4400. FAX: (310) 481-4419.
PARTNERS
Benny Medina
Jeff Pollack
GENERAL MANAGER
Mark Halvorson
HEAD, PRODUCTION
Jane Berliner
HEAD, TV PACKAGING
Evans Weiss
TALENT MANAGEMENT
Michael Baum
Al Onorato
Dannielle Thomas

VAUGHN HART ASSOCIATES

8899 Beverly Blvd., Ste. 815, Los Angeles, CA 90048. (310) 273-7887. FAX: (310) 273-7924.

MICHAEL HARTIG AGENCY, LTD

(Theater, tv and film)
156 Fifth Ave., Ste. 1018, New York, NY 10010. (212) 929-1772.

BEVERLY HECHT AGENCY

(Commercials for children; limited theatrical for adults)
12001 Ventura Pl., Ste. 320, Studio City, CA 91604. (818) 505-1192. FAX: (818) 505-1590.

HENDERSON/HOGAN AGENCY

850 Seventh Ave., Ste. 1003, New York, NY 10019. (212) 765-5190. (212) 586-2855.

THE HOUSE OF REPRESENTATIVES

(Theatrical)
400 S. Beverly Dr., Ste. 101, Beverly Hills, CA 90212. (310) 772-0772. FAX: (310) 772-0998.

HOWARD TALENT WEST

(Commercials and theatrical)
10657 Riverside Dr., Toluca Lake, CA 91602. (818) 766-5300. FAX: (818) 760-3328.

IFA TALENT AGENCY

(Theatrical, actors, tv and film)
8730 Sunset Blvd., #490, Los Angeles, CA 90069. (310) 659-5522. FAX: (310) 659-3344.

INNOVATIVE ARTISTS

(Full-service talent and literary agency)
1505 10th St., Santa Monica, CA 90401. (310) 656-0400. FAX: (310) 656-0456.
(Full-service talent agency)
235 Park Ave. S., 7th Flr., New York, NY 10003. (212) 253-6900. FAX: (212) 253-1198.
OWNER
Scott Harris (LA)

INTERNATIONAL CREATIVE MANAGEMENT

8942 Wilshire Blvd., Beverly Hills, CA 90211. (310) 550-4000. FAX: (310) 550-4100.
CHAIRMAN & CEO
Jeffrey Berg
CO-PRESIDENT & VICE CHAIRMAN
Ed Limato
CO-PRESIDENT
Nancy Josephson
CFO/TREASURER
Robert Murphy
SENIOR V.P. & GENERAL COUNSEL
Richard Levy, Esq.
EXECUTIVE V.P., HEAD OF MOTION PICTURES
John Burnham
EXECUTIVE V.P., HEAD OF INTERNATIONAL OPERATIONS
Ken Kamins
EXECUTIVE V.P., HEAD, OF MOTION PICTURE PRODUCTION
Paul Hook
EXECUTIVE V.P., WORLDWIDE HEAD OF TELEVISION, HEAD OF TV PACKAGING
Bob Levinson
EXECUTIVE V.P., MOTION PICTURE TALENT
Jack Gilardi
EXECUTIVE V.P., HEAD OF MOTION PICTURE TALENT
Eddy Yablans
SENIOR V.P., MOTION PICTURE TALENT
Toni Howard
SENIOR V.P., & HEAD OF TV BUSINESS AFFAIRS
Michael Tenzer
SENIOR V.P., MOTION PICTURE TALENT
Martha Luttrell
SENIOR V.P, MOTION PICTURE TALENT
Risa Shapiro
SENIOR V.P., HEAD OF TV TALENT
Leigh Brillstein
SENIOR V.P., FINANCE & ADMINISTRATION
Don Cannon
SENIOR V.P., HEAD OF MOTION PICTURE BUSINESS AFFAIRS
Pam Brockie
SENIOR V.P., CORPORATE COMMUNICATIONS
David Lux
SENIOR V.P., TV PACKAGES
Scott Arnovitz
SENIOR V.P., HEAD OF VOICEOVER
Jeff Danis
V.P. & HEAD OF OFF-NETWORK PROGRAMMING & NET-WORK SPECIALS, TV SYNDICATION
Steve Wohl
V.P. & HEAD OF COMEDY & MUSIC-WEST COAST CONCERTS
Steve Levine
V.P.,MOTION PICTURE TALENT
Joe Funicello
V.P., TV LITERARY
Dianne Fraser
V.P., BUSINESS AFFAIRS
Anne Pedersen
Janet Kaye
Michael Kernan
V.P., HEAD, SENIOR SUBSIDIARY RIGHTS, MP LITERARY/BOOKS
Ron Bernstein
HEAD OF MOTION PICTURE LITERARY
Robert Newman
HEAD OF TV LITERARY
Matt Solo
HEAD OF THE LONGFORM DIVISION OF TV
Carrie Stein
V.P., HEAD OF NEWS & BROADCASTING, NEWS & PUBLIC AFFAIRS
Babette Perry
HEAD OF CELEBRITY/ENDORSEMENT DEPARTMENT
Karen Sellars

MOTION PICTURE TALENT
Chris Andrews, Carol Bodie, Carter Cohn, Nicole Joel, Richard Konigsberg, Jim Osborne, Jessica Pilch, Scott Schachter, Evan Tripoli, Daisy Wu, Troy Zien

MOTION PICTURE BUSINESS AFFAIRS
Margo Lane, George Ruiz, Michael Runnels

MOTION PICTURE LITERARY/BOOKS
Catherine Brackey, Josie Freedman

MOTION PICTURE LITERARY
Nicole Clemens, Patty Detroit, Jon Huddle, Doug MacLaren, Barbara Mandel, Dan Rabinow, Nick Reed, Brian Sher, Stacey Rosenfelt, Jeff Shumway, Ben Smith, Renee Tab, David Unger
MOTION PICTURE INTERNATIONAL
Shaun Redick, Jeff Shumway
MOTION PICTURE PRODUCTION
Dan Baime, Craig Bernstein, Tad Lumpkin, Tom Marquardt
TV INTERNATIONAL
Eddie Borges
TV TALENT
Tom Burke, Andrew Cohen, Lisa Gallant, Iris Grossman, Michael Jelline, Brain Mann, Scott Simpson
TV SYNDICATION
Cal Boyington
COMMERCIALS/VOICEOVER
Larry Hummel, Kama Nist, Dean Panaro, Natanya Rose, Mike Shallbetter, Jeremy Tefft
TV PACKAGING
Tanya Lopez
TV LITERARY
Greg Cavic, Kevin Crotty, Nancy Etz, Jill Holwager Gillett, Dan Norton, Alan Rautbort, Mike Rizzo, Scott Seidel, Steve Simons
NEW YORK OFFICE
40 W. 57th St., New York, NY 10019. (212) 556-5600. FAX: (212) 556-5665.
SENIOR V.P., CO-HEAD OF THE NY OFFICE & CO-DIRECTOR OF PUBLICATIONS
Esther Newberg
SENIOR V.P., CO-HEAD OF THE NY OFFICE & CO-DIRECTOR OF PUBLICATIONS
Amanda Urban
VICE CHAIRMAN, MOTION PICTURE
Sam Cohn
V.P., HEAD OF MUSIC- EAST COAST, CONCERTS
Terry Rhodes
V.P., NEWS & PA
Helen Shabason
MOTION PICTURE
Will Battersby, Christina Bazdekis, Boaty Boatwright, Andrea Eastman-Wilsker, Sarah Jane Leigh, Paul Martino
BUSINESS AFFAIRS
Maarten Kooij, Marsha Ribon, David Schmerler
CELEBRITY
Gordon Corte, Lisa Roina
COMMERCIALS
David Coakley, Tara Borgaine, David Evans

JACKSON ARTISTS CORP.
(Full-service talent agency)
7251 Lowell Dr., Overland Park, Ste. 200, KS 66204. (913) 384-6688. FAX: (913) 384-6689.
CEO
Dave Jackson

J E TALENT, LLC
(Full-service talent agency specializing in voiceovers)
323 Geary St., Ste. 302, San Francisco, CA 94102. (415) 395-9475. FAX: (415) 395-9301.
OWNER
John J. Erlendson

JORDAN, GILL & DORNBAUM
(Children to early 20's, commercials, tv and film)
1133 Broadway, Ste. 623, New York, NY 10010. (212) 463-8455. FAX: (212) 691-6111.

KAPLAN-STAHLER-GUHMER AGENCY
(Literary agency)
8383 Wilshire Blvd., #923, Beverly Hills, CA 90211. (323) 653-4483.
PARTNERS
Mitchell T. Kaplan
Elliot J. Stahler
Robert Guhmer

KAZARIAN/SPENCER & ASSOCIATES, INC.
(Full-service talent agency)
11365 Ventura Blvd., #100, Studio City, CA 91604. (818) 769-9111. FAX: (818) 769-9840. www.ksawest.com
KSA Inc., Carnegie Plaza, 162 W. 56th St., Ste. 307, New York, NY 10019. (212) 582-7572. FAX: (212) 582-7448.
WEST COAST AGENT
Victoria Morris
EAST COAST AGENT
Lori Swift

KJAR & ASSOCIATES
(Manages established actors)
10153-1/2 Riverside Dr. Ste. 255, Toluca Lake, CA 91602-2313. (818) 760-0321.
CONTACT
Brandon Kjar

THE ERIC KLASS AGENCY
139 S. Beverly Dr., Ste. 331, Beverly Hills, CA 90212. (310) 274-9169.

PAUL KOHNER AGENCY
(Talent & literary agency)
9300 Wilshire Blvd., #555, Beverly Hills, CA 90212. (310) 550-1060. FAX: (310) 276-1083.

THE KRASNY OFFICE
(Commercials and literary)
1501 Broadway, Ste. 1303, New York, NY 10036. (212) 730-8160. FAX: (212) 768-9379.

CANDACE LAKE AGENCY
(Literary, talent, directors, producers and screenwriters)
9200 Sunset Blvd., Ste. 820, Los Angeles, CA 90069. (310) 247-2115. FAX: (310) 247-2116.

LALLY TALENT AGENCY (LTA)
(Actors for tv, theater and film)
630 Ninth Ave., Ste. 800, New York, NY 10036. (212) 974-8718.

LANE AGENCY
(Full-service talent agency)
2700 N. Main St., Ste. 502, Santa Ana, CA 92705. (714) 245-2455. FAX: (714) 245-2335. www.lane-agency.com
email: info@lane-agency.com
PRESIDENT & CEO
Nino Zahrastnik

THE LANTZ OFFICE
(Writers and directors)
200 W. 57th St., #503, New York, NY 10019. (212) 586-0200. FAX: (212) 262-6659.

LIONEL LARNER, LTD.
119 W. 57th St., Ste. 1412, New York, NY 10019. (212) 246-3105. FAX: (212) 956-2851.

JACK LENNY ASSOCIATES
(Choreographers, directors and overseas shows)
9454 Wilshire Blvd., Ste. 600, Beverly Hills, CA 90212. (310) 271-2174. FAX: (310) 246-9883.

BUDDY LEE ATTRACTIONS, INC.
(Booking agency for country music)
38 Music Square E., Nashville, TN 37203. (615) 244-4336. FAX: (615) 726-0429. www.buddyleeattractions.com
CEO
Joey Lee
PRESIDENT
Tony Conway
VICE PRESIDENTS
Paul Lohr
Kevin Neal
Jones Saltel

THE LEVIN AGENCY
(Actors, tv, film, commercials, and equity)
8484 Wilshire Blvd., Ste. 750, Beverly Hills, CA 90211. (323) 653-7073. FAX: (323) 653-0280.

ROBIN LEVY
(Actors and models)
468 N. Camden Dr., Beverly Hills, CA 90210. (310) 278-8748. FAX: (310) 278-8767.

THE LICHTMAN/SALNERS COMPANY
(Adult actors)
12216 Moorpark St., Studio City, CA 91604. (818) 655-9898. FAX: (818) 655-9899.

THE ROBERT LIGHT AGENCY
6404 Wilshire Blvd., Ste. 900, Los Angeles, CA 90048. (323) 651-1777. FAX: (323) 651-4933. email: rlatalent@aol.com

KEN LINDNER & ASSOCIATES, INC.
(News broadcasters and hosts)
2049 Century Park E., Ste. 3050, Los Angeles, CA 90067. (310) 277-9223. FAX: (310) 277-5806. www.kenlindner.com
CEO
Ken Lindner

LOOK TALENT
(Full-service talent agency)
166 Geary St., San Francisco, CA 94108. (415) 781-2841. FAX: (415) 781-5722. www.looktalent.com
DIRECTOR, TALENT & AGENT
Joan Spangler

JANA LUKER TALENT AGENCY
(Actors for film and tv)
1923 1/2 Westwood Blvd., Ste. 3, Los Angeles, CA 90025. (310) 441-2822. FAX: (310) 441-2820.
PRESIDENT
Jana Luker
SENIOR AGENT
Kathy Keeley

LYNNE REILLY AGENCY
10725 Vanowen St., Ste. 113, North Hollywood, CA 91605. (323) 850-1984.

LYONS SHELDON PROSNIT AGENCY
(Specializing in below-the-line talent)
800 S. Robertson Blvd., Ste. 6, Los Angeles, CA 90035. (310) 652-8778. FAX: (310) 652-8772. email: lsagency@aol.com
CONTACTS
Robin Sheldon, Jane Prosnit, Jeannine Angelique, Amiee Rivers

SANDRA MARSH MANAGEMENT
(Below-the-line talent)
9150 Wilshire Blvd., #220, Beverly Hills, CA 90212. (310) 285-0303. FAX: (310) 285-0218.

MARTIN & DONALDS TALENT AGENCY, INC.
(Tv and film)
2131 Hollywood Blvd., Ste. 308, Hollywood, FL 33020. (954) 921-2427. FAX: (954) 921-7635.

JOHNNIE MARTINELLI ATTRACTIONS, INC.
888 8th Ave., New York, NY 10019. (212) 586-0963. FAX: (212) 581-9362.
PRESIDENT
John Martinelli

MCCABE JUSTICE AGENCY
(Actors)
8285 Sunset, Ste. 1, Los Angeles, CA 90046. (323) 650-3738. FAX: (323) 650-6014.

MCQUEENEY MANAGEMENT, INC.
(Movie talent agency)
10279 Century Woods Dr., Los Angeles, CA 90067. (310) 277-1882. FAX: (310) 788-0985.
OWNER/AGENT
Patricia McQueeney

MEDIA ARTISTS GROUP
(Full-service talent agency)
6300 Wilshire Blvd., Ste. 1470, Los Angeles, CA 90048. (323) 658-5050. FAX: (323) 658-7842.

METROPOLITAN TALENT AGENCY
(Actors, writers and directors)
4526 Wilshire Blvd., Los Angeles, CA 90010. (323) 857-4500. FAX: (323) 857-4599.
PRESIDENT
Christopher Barrett

MIRAMAR TALENT AGENCY
(Commercials, theatricals and commercial print)
7400 Beverly Blvd., Ste. 220, Los Angeles, CA 90036. (323) 934-0700.

THE MIRISCH AGENCY
(Specializing in below-the-line talent)
1801 Century Park E., Ste. 1801, Los Angeles, CA 90067. (310) 282-9940. FAX: (310) 282-0702. www.mirisch.com
PRESIDENT
Lawrence A. Mirisch
SENIOR AGENTS
Ann Murtha, Cecilia Banck, Jamie Allen, Paul Ulbrich, Robin Schreer

MONTANA ARTISTS AGENCY
(Full-service below-the-line talent)
625 Montana Ave., 2nd Flr., Santa Monica, CA 90403. (310) 576-3456. FAX: (310) 576-7840.

MOTION ARTISTS AGENCY, INC.
(Storyboard artists, production illustrators, designers and conceptual illustrators)
1400 N. Hayworth Ave., Ste. 36, Los Angeles, CA 90046. (323) 851-7737. FAX: (323) 851-7649. www.motionartists.com
PRESIDENT
Philip Mittell

NAKED VOICES, INC.
(Voiceover)
865 N. Sangamon, Ste. 415, Chicago, IL 60622. (312) 563-0136. FAX: (312) 563-0137. www.nakedvoices.com
CONTACT
Debby Kotzen

OMNIPROP, INC. TALENT AGENCY WEST
(Comedic talent and sketch actors)
10700 Ventura Blvd., Ste. 2C, Studio City, CA 91604. (818) 980-9267. FAX: (818) 980-9371.
55 W. Old Country Rd., Hicksville, NY 11801. (516) 937-6011. FAX: (516) 937-6209.

OSBRINK TALENT AGENCY
4343 Lankershim Blvd., Ste. 100, Universal City, CA 91602. (818) 760-2488. FAX: (818) 760-0991.
CONTACTS
Cindy Osbrink, Scott Wine

OSCARD AGENCY
(Full-service talent agency)
110 W. 40th St., Ste. 1601, New York, NY 10018. (212) 764-1100. FAX: (212) 840-5019.

OTTO MODEL & TALENT AGENCY
(Full-service model and talent agency)
1460 N. Sweetzer Ave., West Hollywood, CA 90069. (323) 650-2200. FAX: (323) 650-1134. www.ottomodels.com
OWNER
Sal Reyes

PAKULA/KING & ASSOCIATES
(Actors for film and tv)
9229 Sunset Blvd., Ste. 315, Los Angeles, CA 90069. (310) 281-4868. FAX: (310) 281-4866.

DOROTHY PALMER TALENT AGENCY, INC.
(Full-service talent agency)
235 W. 56th St., Ste. 24K, New York, NY 10019. (212) 765-4280.

PARADIGM, A TALENT & LITERARY AGENCY
10100 Santa Monica Blvd., 25th Flr., Los Angeles, CA 90067. (310) 277-4400. FAX: (310) 277-7820.
200 W. 57th St., Ste. 900, New York, NY 10019. (212) 246-1030.
LOS ANGELES AGENTS
Alisa Adler, Frank Balkin, Matthew Bedrosian, Jonathan Bluman, Pierre Brogan, Sandi Dudek, Kari Estrin, Sam Gores, James Hess, Debbee Klein, Ra Kumar, Michael Lazo, Katie Mason, Jerry Miko, Judith Moss, Ollie Mossi, Adel Nur, Andy Patman, Valarie Phillips, Pat Quinn, Mark Ross, Joel Rudnick, Andrew Ruf, Jonathan Silverman, Susan Solomon, Lucy Stille, Juanita Tiangco, Susan Tobin, Arthur Toretzky, Bernie Weintraub
NEW YORK AGENTS
Vicki Barroso, Jeb Bernstein, Olivia Catt, Sarah Fargo, Vanessa Gringer, Douglas Kesten, Stacye Mayer, Rosanne Quezada, Richard Schmenner

THE PLAYERS TALENT AGENCY
(Characters, athletic and Hispanic talent)
13033 Ventura Blvd., Ste. N, Studio City, CA 91604. (818) 528-7444.

DIVERSE TALENT GROUP
1875 Century Park E., Ste. 2250, Los Angeles, CA 90067. (310) 201-6565. FAX: (310) 201-6572, (310) 556-0071.

JIM PREMINGER AGENCY
450 N. Roxbury Dr., Beverly Hills, CA 90210. (310) 860-1116.
AGENT
Jim Preminger

PROGRESSIVE ARTISTS AGENCY
(Actors and theatrical)
400 S. Beverly Dr., Ste. 216, Beverly Hills, CA 90212. (310) 553-8561. FAX: (310) 553-4726.

THE MARION ROSENBERG OFFICE
(Actors, screenwriters, directors and authors)
P.O. Box 69826, Los Angeles, CA 90069. (323) 822-2793. FAX: (323) 822-0184.
AGENT
Marion Rosenberg

THE ROTHMAN AGENCY
(Literary agency)
9465 Wilshire Blvd., Ste. 840, Beverly Hills, CA 90212. (310) 247-9898. FAX: (310) 247-9888.

IRV SCHECTER COMPANY
9300 Wilshire Blvd., #400, Beverly Hills, CA 90212. (310) 278-8070. FAX: (310) 278-6058. email: iscagency@aol.com

SCHULLER TALENT
276 Fifth Ave., Ste. 204, New York, NY 10001. (212) 532-6005.

WILLIAM SCHILL AGENCY
(Full-service talent agency)
250 W. 57th St., Ste. 2402, New York, NY 10107. (212) 315-5919. FAX: (212) 397-7366. www.schillagency.com

DON SCHWARTZ & ASSOC.
(Talent for commercials, tv and film)
1604 N. Cahuenga Blvd., #101, Hollywood, CA 90028. (323) 464-4366. FAX: (323) 464-4661.

SEVEN SUMMITS PICTURES & MANAGEMENT
(Full-service agency for film and tv)
8447 Wilshire Blvd., Ste. 200, Beverly Hills, CA 90211. (323) 655-0101.

DAVID SHAPIRA & ASSOCIATES, INC. (DSA)
(Actors for film and tv; writers)
15821 Ventura Blvd., Ste. 245, Encino, CA 91436. (818) 906-0322. FAX: (818) 783-2562.
AGENTS
Donna Gaba, Marc Kamler, David Shapira, Matthew Shapira, Susan Simmons, Doug Warner

MICHAEL SLESSINGER & ASSOCIATES
(Full-service talent agency for actors)
8730 Sunset Blvd., Ste. 270, West Hollywood, CA 90069. (310) 657-7113. FAX: (310) 657-1756.
VICE PRESIDENT
Michael Slessinger

SMS TALENT, INC.
(Adult theatrical)
8730 Sunset Blvd., Ste. 440, Los Angeles, CA 90069. (310) 289-0909. FAX: (310) 289-0990.
PARTNERS
Monty Silver, Donna Massetti, Marilyn Szatmary

SCOTT STANDER & ASSOCIATES
(Film, tv, commericals, theater, national tours, concert, variety acts & comedians)
13701 Riverside Dr., Ste. 201, Sherman Oaks, CA 91423. (818) 905-7000. FAX: (818) 990-0582. www.scottstander.com
AGENT
Scott Stander

SUITE A MANAGEMENT, TALENT & LITERARY AGENCY
(Represents writers, producers and directors; specializing in made for tv movies and low to mid budget features)
1101 S. Robertson Blvd., Ste. 210, Los Angeles, CA 90035. (310) 278-0801. FAX: (310) 278-0807. email: suite-a@juno.com
AGENT PRINCIPAL
Lloyd D. Robinson
ASSISTANTS
Letitia Schuartz, Kevin Douglas

SUTTON, BARTH & VENNARI, INC.
(On camera, commercials and voiceover)
145 S. Fairfax Ave., Ste. 310, Los Angeles, CA 90036. (323) 938-6000. FAX: (323) 935-8671.
PARTNERS
Vic Sutton, Rita Vennari

TALENT TREK AGENCY
(Actors for film and tv)
2021 21st Ave. S., Ste. 102, Nashville, TN 37212. (615) 279-0010. FAX: (615) 279-0013.
AGENTS
Evelyn Foster, Sharon D. Smith, Kara Welker-Ryder

TISHERMAN AGENCY, INC.
(Actors for voiceovers and on-camera commercials only)
6767 Forest Lawn Dr., Ste. 101, Los Angeles, CA 90068. (323) 850-6767. FAX: (323) 850-7340.

TWENTIETH CENTURY ARTISTS
15760 Ventura Blvd., Ste. 700, Encino, CA 91436. (818) 325-3832.
PRESIDENT
Diane Davis
ADULT THEATRICAL MP, TV LITERARY
David Ankrum
ADULT THEATRICAL MP, TV CHILDREN (6 AND UP)
THEATRICAL MP, TV, VIDEO, INDUSTRIALS
Shane Preston

UNITED TALENT AGENCY
9560 Wilshire Blvd., Beverly Hills, CA 90212. (310) 273-6700. FAX: (310) 247-1111.
PRESIDENT, CHAIRMAN & BOARD MEMBER
James Berkus
PARTNER & AGENT
Dan Aloni
PARTNER, AGENT & BOARD MEMBER
Peter Benedek
PARTNER, AGENT & BOARD MEMBER
Gary Cosay
PARTNER, AGENT & BOARD MEMBER
Nick Stevens
PARTNER, AGENT & BOARD MEMBER
Jeremy Zimmer
PARTNER & AGENT
Marty Bowen
PARTNER & AGENT
David Kramer
PARTNER & AGENT
David Guillod
PARTNER & AGENT
Tracey Jacobs
PARTNER & AGENT
Sue Naegle
PARTNER & AGENT
David Schiff
PARTNER & AGENT
Jay Sures
AGENTS
Tobrn Babst, Allison Band, Jeremy Barber, Joel Begleher, Elana Barry, Blair Belcher, Brinda Bhatt, Jason Burns, Andrew Cannava, Sara Chazen, Chris Coelen, Howard Cohen, Pamela Cole, Jummy Cundiff, James Degus, Marissa Devins, Shana Eddy, Donna Fazzari, Charlie Ferraro, Wayne Fitterman, Peter Franciosa, Jay Gassner, Nancy Gates, Richard Green, Lisa Hallerman, Brett Hansen, Jason Heyman, Adam Isaacs, Lisa Jacobsen, Anthony James, Alex Kerr, Keya Khayatian, Bob Kim, Marc Korman, Billy Lazarus, Everly Lee, Martin Lesak, Leslie Maskin, Hayden Meyer, Rob Prinz, Itay Reiss, Matt Rice, Larry Salz, Howard Sanders, Alex Schaffel, Ruthanne Secunda, Amy Shpall, Kevin Stoiper, Ferris Thompson, Nikki Wheeler, Karrie Wolfe

ANNETTE VAN DUREN AGENCY
(Representing writers and animators)
11684 Ventura Blvd., #235, Studio City, CA 91604. (818) 752-6000. FAX: (818) 752-6985. email: avagency@pacbell.net

SHIRLEY WILSON & ASSOCIATES
(Children and adults)
5410 Wilshire Blvd., Ste. 806, Los Angeles, CA 90036. (323) 857-6977. FAX: (323) 857-6980.

WARDLOW & ASSOCIATES
(Writers and directors for film and tv)
1501 Main St., #204, Venice, CA 90291. (310) 452-1292. email: wardlowaso@aol.com
PRINCIPAL & OWNER
David Wardlow
LITERARY AGENT
Jeff Ordway

DONNA WAUHOB AGENCY
(SAG franchised, WGA signatory agent and AFM franchise)
5280 SE Ave., Ste. A3, Las Vegas, NV 89119. (702) 795-1523. FAX: (702) 795-0696.

WILLIAM MORRIS AGENCY
One William Morris Pl., Beverly Hills, CA 90212. (310) 859-4000. FAX: (310) 859-4462.
1325 Ave. of the Americas, New York, NY 10019. (212) 586-5100. FAX: (212) 246-3583.
2100 West End Ave., Ste. 1000, Nashville, TN 37203. (615) 963-3000. FAX: (615) 963-3090.
CHAIRMAN
Norman Brokaw
CO-CEO
Walter Zifkin
CO-CEO & PRESIDENT
James A. Wiatt
COO, WEST COAST
Steven H. Kram
CFO
Irv J. Weintraub
EXCUTIVE V.P. & HEAD, WORLDWIDE MOTION PICTURE DEPARTMENT
David Wirtschafter
EXECUTIVE V.P. & WORLDWIDE HEAD OF TELEVISION
Sam Haskell
HEAD, COMMERCIALS DEPARTMENT
Rick Hersh
HEAD, LITERARY WORLDWIDE
Owen Laster
V.P., SPORTS MARKETING
Jill Smoller
V.P. & HEAD OF HUMAN RESOURCES
Gail Moore
PUBLIC RELATIONS
Amy Elmer

WORLD CLASS SPORTS
(Sports talent for commercial and print; sports consulting, marketing and celebrity appearances)
880 Apollo St., Ste. 337, El Segundo, CA 90245. (310) 535-9120. FAX: (310) 535-9128.
SENIOR AGENTS
Andrew Woolf
Don Franken

WRITERS & ARTISTS AGENCY
8383 Wilshire Blvd., Ste. 550, Beverly Hills, CA 90211. (323) 866-0900. FAX: (323) 866-1899.
PARTNER & HEAD OF TALENT
Norman Aladjem
PARTNER & HEAD OF LITERARY
Marti Blumenthal
PARTNER & TALENT
David Brownstein
V.P., BUSINESS & LEGAL AFFAIRS
Dina Appleton
LITERARY AGENTS
Rick Berg, Angela Cheng-Caplan, Carel Cutler, Jim Ehrich, Richard Freeman, Brandon Stein
TALENT
Cynthia Booth, Sarah Clossey, Carleton Daniels, Todd Eisner, Jason Priluck, Chris Schmidt, Dina Shapiro, Stephen Small
NEW YORK OFFICE
19 W. 44 St., #1000, New York, NY 10036. (212) 391-1112. FAX: (212) 398-9877.
PARTNER & HEAD, NY OFFICE
William Craver
AGENTS, LITERARY
Chris Till
Lydia Wills
AGENTS, TALENT
Sadie Foster
Jason Yarn

DIGITAL PRODUCTION, DISTRIBUTION, EXHIBITION & EQUIPMENT

■

DIGITAL PRODUCTION & MASTERING SERVICES

CAMERAS, LENSES, LIGHTING & MISC. PRODUCTION GEAR

16X9, INC.
(Production equipment)
3605 W. Pacific Ave., Burbank, CA 91505. (866) 800-1699.
FAX: (818) 972-2832. www.16X9inc.com.

ABELCINETECH
(Equipment dealer)
4110 W. Magnolia Blvd., Burbank, CA 91505. (888) 700-4416.
FAX: (818) 972-2673. www.abelcine.com

AMERICAN STUDIO EQUIPMENT
(Camera accessories)
8468 Kewen Ave., Sun Valley, CA 91352. (818) 768-8922. FAX:
(818) 768-0564.

ANGENIEUX SA
(HD and film lenses)
40G Commerce Way, Totowa, NJ 07511. (973) 812-4326. FAX:
(973) 812-9049. www.angenieux.com

ANTON/BAUER
(Batteries and lights)
14 Progress Dr., Shelton, CT 06484. (203) 929-1100. FAX:
(203) 929-9935. www.antonbauer.com

B & H VIDEO
(Dealer)
420 Ninth Ave., New York, NY 10001. (212) 502-6250. FAX:
(800) 947-9003.

BANDPRO FILM/VIDEO, INC.
(Dealer of production and post-production equipment and
accessories)
3403 W. Pacific Ave., Burbank, CA 91505. (818) 841-9655.
FAX: (818) 841-7649. www.bandpro.com

BOGEN CINE
(Support and grip equipment)
565 E. Crescent Ave., P. O. Box 506 Ramsey, NJ 07446. (201)
818-9500. FAX: (201) 818-9177. www.bogenphoto.com

CANON U.S.A.
(HD-EC lenses)
Broadcast Equipment Division: 400 Sylvan Ave., Englewood
Cliffs, NJ 07632. (201) 816-2900. FAX: (201) 816-2909.
www.canonbroadcast.com

CANON U.S.A.
(XL1s and GL1 DV camcorders)
Video Division: One Canon Plz., Lake Success, NY 11042.
(800) 828-4040. www.canondv.com

CARTONI U.S.A.
(Tripods, pedestals, and heads)
4545 INdustrial St., Unit 5B, Simi Valley, CA 93063. (805) 520-
6036. FAX: (805) 520-6949.

CENTURY PRECISION OPTICS
(Special lenses and accessories)
11049 Magnolia Blvd., N. Hollywood, CA 91601. (818) 766-
3715. FAX: (818) 505-9865. www.centuryoptics.com

CHAPMAN/LEONARD STUDIO EQUIPMENT
(Camera support equipment and accessories)
12950 Raymer St., N. Hollywood, CA 91605. (818) 764-6726.
FAX: (888) 502-7263. www.chapman-leonard.com

CHIMERA
(Innovative lighting instruments and accessories)
1812 Valtec Ln., Boulder, CO 80301. (888) 444-1812. FAX:
(303) 444-8303. www.chimeralighting.com

CINEFLEX, LLC
(Gyro-stabilized aircraft camera systems)
13025 Grass Valley Ave., Unit 2, Grass Valley, CA 95945. (530)
477-5862. www.cineflex.com

CINEKINETIC
(Camera support gear)
2 Avon Ct., Thonlie, WA Australia. (618) 9459-3690. FAX: (618)
9493-2168. www.cinekinetic.com

COLORTRAN CORP.
(Gels and lighting accessories)
Leviton-Colortan Division, P. O. Box 2210, Tualatin, OR 97062.
(503) 404-5500. FAX: (503) 404-5600. www.colortran.com

COOL-LUX
(Innovative lighting instruments and batteries)
412 Calle San Pablo, Ste. 200, Camarillo, CA 93012. (805)
482-4820. FAX: (805) 482-0736. www.cool-lux.com

COPTER VISION
(Remote-control camera aircraft)
7625 Havenhurst Ave., No. 41, Van Nuys, CA 91406. (818)
781-64623003. FAX: (818) 782-4070. www.coptervision.com

DESISTI LIGHTING/DESMAR CORP.
(Lighting products)
1109 Grand Ave., N. Bergen, NJ 07047. (201) 3191. FAX: (201)
3104. www.desisti.it

EGRIPMENT USA
(Camera cranes, remote heads, and support gear)
7625 Hayvenhurst Ave., #27, Van Nuys, CA 91408. (818) 787-
4295. FAX: (818) 787-6195. www.egripment.com

EZ FX JIBS
(Camera support equipment)
324 Maguire Rd., Ocoee, FL 34761. (407) 877-2335. FAX:
(407) 877-6603. www.ezfx.com

FAST FORWARD VIDEO
(Digital disk recorders for video-assist)
18200-B W. McDurmott St., Irvine, CA 92614. (949) 852-8404.
FAX: (949) 852-1226. www.ffv.com

MARK FORMAN PRODUCTIONS
(HD production services)
300 West 23rd St., New York, NY 10011. (212) 633-9960.
www.digitalcinematography.com

FORMATT FILTERA
(Camera tilters and related lens products)
Unit 23-27, Aberaman Park Industrial Estate, Aberaman
Aberdare, Mid Glamorgan Wales, CF 44 6DA. UK 44 (0) 20-
8578-7701. FAX: 44 (0) 20-8578-7702. www.formatt.co.uk

FUJI FILM USA
(Digital recording media)
555 Taxter Rd., Elmsford, NY 10523. (914) 789-8100. FAX:
(914) 789-8490. www.fujifilm.com

FUJINON, INC.
(Digital cinema lenses)
Broadcast & Communications Division: 10 High Point Dr.,
Wayne, NJ 07470. (973) 633-5600. FAX: (973) 633-5216.
www.fujinon.com

GAM PRODUCTS
(Lighting equipment and accessories)
4975 W. Pico Blvd., Los Angeles, CA 90019. (323) 935-4975.
FAX: (323) 935-2002. www.gamonline.com

GLIDECAM INDUSTRIES, INC.
(Small camera stabilizers and accessories)
Camelot Industrial Park, 130 Camelot Dr., Bldg. #4, Plymouth,
MA 02360. (508) 830-1414. FAX: (508) 830-1415.
www.glidecam.com

HAMLET
(Digital HD test and measurement equipment)
Tecads Inc, Foothill Ranch, CA (949) 597-1053. FAX: (949)
597-1094. www.hamlet.us.com

HOODMAN
(Monitor and viewfinder hoods)
20445 Gramercy Place Ste. #201, Torrance, CA 90501. (310)
222-8608. FAX: (310) 222-8623. www.hoodmanusa.com

IKEGAMI ELECTRONICS
(Digital HD cameras)
37 Brook Ave., Maywood, NJ 07607. (201) 368-9171. FAX:
(201) 569-1626. www.ikegami.com

INNOVISION OPTICS
(Specialized lenses, support, and motion-control products)
1719 21st Street, Santa Monica, CA 90404. (310) 453-4866.
FAX: (310) 453-4677. www.innovision-optics.com

INTEGRATED LIGHTING SYSTEMS
(Lighting services)
7161 S. Braden Ave., Tulsa, OK 74136. (918) 523-9400. AFX: (918) 523-9401. www.integratedlighting.com

ISCO-OPTIC GMBH
(DLP projection lenses)
Anna-Vandenhoeck-Ring 5, D-37081 Gottingen, Germany. (49 551) 50 58 3. FAX: (49 551) 50 58 410. www.iscooptic.de

JVC PROFESSIONAL PRODUCTS COMPANY
(CineLine digital cinematography cameras)
1700 Valley Rd., Wayne, NJ 07470. (973) 317-5000. FAX: (973) 317-5030. www.jvc.com/pro

K 5600 LIGHTING
(Innovative lighting instruments and accessories)
10434 Burbank Blvd., N. Hollywood, CA 91601. (800) 662-5756. FAX: (818) 762-6629. www.K5600.com

KINO FLO
(Innovative lighting instruments and accessories)
10848 Cantara St., Sun Valley, CA 91352. (818) 767-6528. FAX: (818) 767-7517. www.kinoflo.com

LEADER INSTRUMENTS CORP.
(Digital HD test and measurement equipment)
6484 Commerce Dr., Cypress, CA 90630. (714) 527-9300. FAX: (714) 527-7490. www.leaderusa.com

LOCATION SOUND CORP.
(Location audio equipment)
10639 Riverside Dr., N. Hollywood, CA 91602. (818) 980-9891. FAX: (818) 980-9911. www.locationsound.com

LONG VALLEY EQUIPMENT
(Camera support gear)
165 Fairview Ave., Long Valley, NJ 07853. (908) 876-1022. FAX: (908) 876-1938. www.longvalleyequip.com

LOWEL-LIGHT MANUFACTURING
(Lighting instruments and accessories)
140 58th St., Brooklyn, NY 11220. (800) 334-3426. FAX: (718) 921-0303. www.lowel.com

LTM CORP. OF AMERICA
(Lighting instruments and accessories)
7755 Haskell Ave., Van Nuys, CA 91406. (800) 762-4291. FAX: (818) 780-9828. www.ltmlighting.com

MATTHEWS STUDIO EQUIPMENT (MSE)
(Lighting and grip equipment and accessories)
2405 Empire Ave., Burbank, CA 91504. (800) 843-6715. FAX: (213) 849-1525.

MAXELL CORP. OF AMERICA
(Digital recording media)
Professional/Industrial Sales, 22-08 Rt. 208, Fair Lawn, NJ 07140. (201) 794-5900. FAX: (201) 796-8790.

MICRODOLLY
(Camera support systems)
3110 W. Burbank Blvd., Burbank, CA 91505. (818) 845-8383. FAX: (818) 845-8384. www.microdolly.com

MILLER FLUID HEADS
(Tripods, pedestals and heads)
30 Hotham PDE, Artarmon, Sydney, NSW 2064, Australia. (61 2) 439-6377. FAX: (61 2) 438-2819. www.miller.com.au/

MIRANDA TECHNOLOGIES, INC.
(Downconverters for external monitors)
3499 Douglas B. Floreani, Montreal, QC, H4S 2C6, Canada. (514) 333-1772. FAX: (514) 333-9828. www.miranda.com

MOLE-RICHARDSON
(Lighting, grip, camera accessories, support, and heads)
937 N. Sycamore Ave., Hollywood, CA 90038. (323) 851-0111. FAX: (323) 851-5593. www.mole.com

MOVIE TECH
(Camera support equipment)
2150 Northmont Parkway, Ste.A, Duluth, GA 30096. (678) 417-6352. FAX: (678) 417- 6273. www.movietech.de

MUSCO
(Giant lighting rigs and services)
100 1st. Ave, West, P.O. Box808, Oskaloosa, IA 52577. (800) 825-6020. FAX: (641) 673-4740. www.musco.com/mobile.

NRG RESEARCH
233 Rogue River Hwy., Bldg. 1144, Grants Pass, OR 97527. (541) 479-9433. FAX: (541) 741-6251.

O'CONNER ENGINEERING LAB
(Camera support solutions)
100 Kalmus Dr., Costa Mesa, CA 92626. (714) 979-3993. FAX: (714) 957-8138. www.ocon.com

OPTEX
(Specialized lenses and accessories)
20-28 Victoria Rd., New Barnet, N. London EN4 9PF, U.K. (44 20) 8441-2199. FAX: (44 20) 8441-3646. www.optexint.com

PANASONIC
(HD Cinema cameras and recorders)
6219 De Soto Ave., Woodland Hills, CA 91367. (818) 318-1000. FAX: (818) 316-1101. www.panavision.com

PANTHER GMBH
(Large camera cranes)
Raiffeisenallee 3, 82041 Oberhaching-Munich, Germany. (49 89) 613 900 01. FAX: (49 89) 613 100 0.
www.panther-gmbh.de

PORTA-BRACE (K&H PRODUCTS)
(Field monitor cases)
Box 249, North Bennington, VT 05257. (802) 442-8171. FAX: (802) 442-9118. www.portabrace.com

PROSOURCE/BROADCAST MARKETING, LTD.
(Camera and production accessories)
1515 Black Rock Tpk., Fairfield, CT 06825. (203) 335-2000. FAX: (203) 335-3005. www.prosourceBMI.com

SACHTLER CORP. OF AMERICA
(Tripods, heads, and camera support)
55 N. Main St., Freeport, NY 11520. (516) 867-4900. FAX: (516) 623-6844. www.sachtler.com

SCHNEIDER OPTICS, INC.
(Lenses and optical glass filters)
285 Oser Ave., Hauppauge, NY 11788. (631) 761-5090. FAX: (631) 761-5090. www.schneideroptics.com

SEKONIC DIVISION OF MAMIYA AMERICA
(Light meters)
8 Westchester Plz., Elmsford, NY 10523. (914) 347-3300. FAX: (914) 347-3309. www.sekonic.com

SENNHEISER
(Microphones and professional audio products)
P.O. Box 987, 6 Vista Dr., Old Lyme, CT 06371. (203) 434-9190. FAX: (203) 434-1759. www.sennheiser.com

SHURE BROTHERS, INC.
(Microphones and professional audio products)
5800 W. Touhy Ave. Niles, IL 60714. (847) 600-2000 FAX: (847) 600-1212. www.shure.com

SONY BROADCAST & PROFESSIONAL CO.
(24P HD CineAlta production system)
1 Sony Dr., Park Ridge, NJ 07656. (201) 930-4800. FAX: (201) 930-4752. www.sonyusacinealta.com

SPECTRA CINE
(Light meters)
3605 W. Magnolia Blvd., Burbank, CA 91505. (818) 954-9222. FAX: (818) 954-0016. www.spectracine.com

STRAND LIGHTING LTD.
(Innovative lighting instruments and accessories)
6603 Darin Way, Cypress, CA 90630. (714) 230-8200. FAX: (714) 899-0042. www.strandlight.com

TEKTRONIX, INC.
(Digital HD test, monitoring, and measurement devices)
14200 S.W. Karl Braun Dr., Beaverton, OR 97077. (800) 835-9433. FAX: (503) 222-1542.

THOMSON MULTIMEDIA
(LDK-7000 and 6000 digital cinema cameras)
2255 N. Ontario St., Ste. 150, Burbank, CA 91504. (818) 729-7700. FAX: (818) 729-7777. www.thomsonbroadcast.com

TIFFEN MANUFACTURING CORP.
(Camera accessories; filters, video)
90 Oser Ave., Hauppauge, NY 11788. (631) 273-2500. FAX: (631) 273-2557. www.tiffen.com

TRANSVIDEO
(Flat-panel camera monitors)
10700Ventura Blvd. Ste. 2A, N. Hollywood, CA 91604. (818) 985-4903. FAX: (818) 985-4921. www.transvideointl.com

ULTIMATTE CORP.
(Digital HD blue and grenn screen compositing)
20945 Plummer St., Chatsworth, CA 91311. (818) 993-8007. FAX: (818) 993-3762. www.ultimatte.com

VIDEOTEK, INC.
(Digital HD monitoring products)
243 Shoemaker Rd., Pottstown, PA 19464. (610) 327-2292. FAX: (610) 327-9295. www.videotek.com

DIGITAL DAILIES

ED NET
1 Union St., San Francisco, CA 94111. (415) 274-8800. FAX: (415) 274-8801. www.ednet.com

INTERNET PRO VIDEO (IPV)
(Digital dailies services)
6312 Variel Ave., Woodland Hills, CA 91367. (818) 737-4911. FAX: (818) 598-2698. www.ipv.com

LIVEWIRE TELEVISION GROUP
520 Broadway, 5th Flr., Santa Monica, CA 90401. (310) 434-7000. FAX: (310) 434-7001. www.libertylivewire.com

MEDIA.NET
(Digital dailies service)
840 Apollo Street, Ste #241, El Segundo, CA 90245. (310) 531-1500. FAX: (310) 531-1501. www.media.net

PICTURE PIPELINE
(Digital dailies service)
11400 W. Olympic Blvd., Ste 1020, West Los Angeles, CA 90064. (310) 764-7473. FAX: (310) 445-9439.
email: info@picturepipeline.com

TELESTREAM, INC.
(Internet streaming technologies)
848 Gold Flat Rd., Ste. 1, Nevada City, CA 95959. (530) 470-1300. FAX: (530) 470-1301. www.Telestream.net

GRAPHICS SOFTWARE

5D
(High-end graphics software)
903 Colorado Ave., Ste. 200, Santa Monica, CA 90401. (310) 394-7824. FAX: (310) 934-7924. www.five-d.com

ADOBE SYSTEMS
(Mac and Windows software for digital nonlinear editing, effects and typography)
345 Park Ave., W-16, San Jose, CA 95110. (408) 536-6000. FAX: (408) 537-6000. www.adobe.com

ALIAS/WAVEFRONT
(High-end 3D animation software)
210 King St. E., Toronto Ont. M5A 1J7, Canada. (416) 362-9181. FAX: (416) 369-6140. www.aliaswavefront.com

CAMBRIDGE ANIMATION SYSTEMS
(Digital animation software)
Wellington House, East Road, Cambridge, CB1 1BH, England. 44- (0) 1223-451048. FAX: 44 (0) 1223-451145. www.cambridgeanimation.com

ELECTRIC IMAGE
(High-end 3D animation software)
20770 Hwy 281 North, Ste #108-414, San Antonio, TX. (830) 438-4955. www.electricimage.com

NEWTEK, INC.
(Lightwave 3D aoftware)
5131 Beckwith Blvd, San Antonio, TX 78249. (210) 370-8000. FAX: (210) 370-8001. www.newtek.com

NOTHING REAL
(High-end compositing and effects software)
211 Windward Ave., 2nd Flr., Venice, CA 90291. (310) 664-6152. FAX: (310) 664-6157. www.nothingreal.com

REALVIZ CORP.
(High-end Windows-based image processing software)
350 Toensend Street, Ste #409, San Francisco, CA 94107. (415) 615-9800. FAX: (415) 615-9805. www.realviz.com

HD POST/MASTERING/FILM-OUT/AUDIO POST/FACILITIES

24FPS PRODUCTIONS
(Digital HD production services)
50 W. 23rd St., 7th Flr., New York, NY 10010. (646) 638-0659. FAX: (212) 206-6986. www.24fpsproductions.com

AMERICAN MEDIA GROUP
(Digital HD production and post services)
3350 Scott Blvd., No. 19, Santa Clara, CA 95054. (408) 486-0923. FAX: (408) 486-9826.

AMERICAN PRODUCTION SERVICES, LLC
(Digital HD production and post services)
150 Nims Spring Drive, Fort Mill, SC 29715. (803) 548-2290. FAX: (803) 548-3406. www.apsvideo.com

CFI (CONSOLIDATED FILM INDUSTRIES)
(Digital film out services)
959 Seward St., Hollywood, CA 90038. (323) 960-7444. FAX: (323) 460-4885. www.cfi-hollywood.com

CHACE PRODUCTIONS
(Audio mixing and editing)
201 S. Victory Blvd., Burbank, CA 91502. (818) 842-8346. FAX: (818) 842-8353. www.chace.com

CINERIC
(Digital effects, film out, and titles)
630 Ninth Ave., New York, NY 10036. (212) 586-4822. FAX: (212) 582-3744. www.cineric.com

CINESITE (A KODAK COMPANY)
(Digital production, post-production, digital intermediate, computer graphics, transfer, restoration, and archiving services)
1017 N. Las Palmas Ave., Los Angeles, CA 90038. (323) 468-4400. www.cinesite.com

COLOSSALVISION
(Digital HD production services)
26 Broadway, New York, NY 10004. (212) 269-6333. FAX: (212) 269-4334. www.colossalvision.com

COMPLETE POST
(Full range of services)
6087 Sunset Blvd., Hollywood, CA 90028. (323) 467-1244. FAX: (323) 461-2561. www.completepost.com

CRAWFORD COMMUNICATIONS
(Digital HD post and transfer facility)
3845 Pleasantville Rd., Atlanta, GA 30340. (800) 831-8027. FAX: (678) 421-6715. www.crawford.com

CREST NATIONAL
(Digital film out services)
1141 N. Seward Ave., Hollywood, CA 90038. (800) FLM LABS. FAX: (323) 462-5039. www.crestnational.com

DEMOGRAFX
(Digital compression specialists)
4640 Admirally Way, Ste. 500, Marina Del Rey, CA 90292. (310) 578-7848. FAX: (310) 578-7849. www.demografx.com

DFW (DIGITAL FILM WORKS)
(Full range of services)
3330 Cahuenga Blvd. W., Ste. 300, Los Angeles, CA 90068. (323) 874-9981. www.dfw-la.com

DIGITAL SOUND AND PICTURE
2700 S. La Cienega Blvd., Los Angeles, CA 90034. (310) 836-7688. FAX: (310) 836-4599. www.libertylivewire.com

DUART FILM AND VIDEO
(Film lab, digital film out service, sound mixing, and digital title design)
245 W. 55th St., New York, NY 10019. (212) 757-4580. FAX: (212) 333-7647. www.duart.com

EFILM
(Digital lab/film out)
1146 N. Las Palmas Ave., Hollywood, CA 90038. (323) 463-7041. FAX: (323) 465-7342. www.efilm.com

ENCORE VIDEO
(Digital HD post and mastering)
6344 Fountain Ave., Hollywood, CA 90028. (323) 512-3400. FAX: (323) 512-3567. www.encorevideo.com

FILMLOOK
(Digital image-enhancement technology)
3500 W. Olive Ave., Ate. 1050, Burbank, CA 91505. (818) 955-7082. FAX: (818) 972-4231. www.filmlook.com

FOTOKEM
(Full-service motion picture and video lab)
2801 W. Alameda Ave., Burbank, CA 91505. (818) 846-3101. FAX: (818) 841-2130. www.fotokem.com

HD CINEMA
(Digital HD production and post)
1434 Sixth St., Ste. 2B, Santa Monica, CA 90401. (310) 434-8500. FAX: (310) 434-9600.

HD VISION
(Digital HD production and post)
6305 N. O'Connor Rd., Ste. 126, Irving, TX 75039. (972) 432-9630. FAX: (972) 869-2516. www.hdvision.com

HTV (HIGH TECHNOLOGY VIDEO)
(Digital HD post, intermediate, mastering)
3575 Cahuenga Blvd. W., 4th Flr., Los Angeles, CA 90068. (323) 969-6822. FAX: (323) 969-8860. www.htvinc.net

HOKUS BOGUS
(Digital film out services)
Pilestraede 6, DK 1112, Copenhagen K, Denmark. (45 33) 32 7879. FAX: (45 33) 32 8848. www.hokusbogus.dk

IO FILM
(Digital titles, opticals, and film finishing services)
4640 Lankershim Blvd., Ste. 601, N. Hollywood, CA 91602. (818) 487-2850. FAX: (818) 487-2851. www.iofilm.net

IVC (INTERNATIONAL VIDEO CONVERSIONS)
(Digital transfer and mastering services)
2777 Ontario St., Burbank, CA 91504. (818) 569-4949. FAX: (818) 569-3659. www.ivchd.com

KODAK DIGITAL CINEMA
(Digital cinema mastering, distribution, and projection)
Kodak Imaging Technology Center, 1017 N. Las Palmas Ave., Ste. 201, Los Angeles, CA 90038. (310) 204-7100. FAX: (310) 204-7111. www.kodak.com/go/dcinema.

LASERPACIFIC MEDIA CORP.
(Full digital post-production services)
809 N. Cahuenga Blvd., Hollywood, CA 90038. (323) 462-6266. FAX: (323) 464-3233. www.laserpacific.com

LIBERTY LIVEWIRE
520 Broadway, 5th Flr., Santa Monica, CA 90401. (310) 434-7000. FAX: (310) 434-7001. www.libertylivewire.com

MOVIOLA
(Sales, rentals, education)
1135 N. Mansfield Ave., Los Angeles, CA 90038. (800) 468-3107. www.moviola.com

THE ORPHANAGE
39 Mesa St., Ste. 102-B, San Francisco, CA 94129. (415) 561-2570. FAX: (415) 561-2575. www.theorphanage.com

THE POST GROUP
(Digital HD post, intermediate, mastering)
6335 Homewood Ave., Hollywood, CA 90028. (323) 462-2300. FAX: (323) 462-0836. www.postgroup.com

POSTIQUE
(Digital HD post and transfer facility)
23475 Northwestern Hwy., Southfield, MI 48075. (248) 352-2610. FAX: (248) 352-3708. www.filmcraftlab.com

POST LOGIC STUDIOS
(Digital HD post-production)
1800 N. Vine, Ste. 100, Hollywood, CA 90028. (323) 461-6598. FAX: (323) 461-5919. www.postlogic.com

REALITY CHECK STUDIOS
(Digital design and visual effects studio)
6100 Melrose Ave., Hollywood, CA 90038. (323) 465-3900. FAX: (323) 465-3600. www.realityx.com

ROLAND HOUSE
(HD editing services)
2020 N. 14th St., Arlington, VA 22201. (703) 525-7000. www.rolandhouse.com

SHOOTERS POST & TRANSFER
(Digital HD post and transfer facility)
The Curtis Center, Independence Square W., Ste. 1050, Philadelphia, PA 19106. (215) 861-0100. FAX: (215) 861-0098. email: shooters@shootersinc.com

SOUNDELUX ENTERTAINMENT GROUP
7080 Hollywood Blvd., Ste. 1100, Hollywood, CA 90028. (323) 603-3202. FAX: (800) 849-4970. www.soundelux.com

SUNSET DIGITAL
(Digital HD post-production)
1813 Victory Blvd., Glendale, CA 91201. (818) 956-7912. FAX: (818) 545-7586. www.sunsetpost.com

SWELL, INC.
(Digital HD post and transfer facility)
455 N. City Front Plz. Dr., 18th Flr., Chicago, IL 60611. (312) 464-8000. www.swellinc.com

TAPE HOUSE
(Digital HD transfer and editing)
216 E. 45th St., New York, NY 10017. (212) 557-4949. FAX: (212) 983-4083. www.tapehouse.com

TECHNIQUE
(Digital mastering services)
2233 N. Ontario St., Ste 300, Burbank, CA 91504. (818) 260-3636. FAX: (818) 260-3644. email: technique@technicolor.com

TODDAO CORP.
(Audio post services)
900 N. Seward St., Hollywood, CA 90035. (323) 982-4000. www.toddao.com

VIDFILM INTERNATIONAL DIGITAL
(Mastering for digital cinema release)
1631 Gardena Ave., Glendale, CA 91204. (818) 500-9090. www.vidfilm.com

VTA
(Digital HD post and transfer facility)
1575 Sheridan Rd., N.E., Atlanta, GA 30324. (404) 634-6181. www.vta.com

HD POST/MASTERING TECHNOLOGY

ACCOM
(HD digital disk recording; editing systems)
1490 O'Brien Dr., Menlo Park, CA 94025. (415) 328-3818. FAX: (415) 327-2511. www.accom.com

ADIC (ADVANCED DIGITAL INFORMATION CORP.)
(Stroage area network technology)
11431 Willows Rd., N.E., P.O. Box 97057, Redmond, WA 98073. (800) 336-1233. FAX: (425) 881-2296. www.adic.com

APPLE COMPUTER, INC.
(Digital editing, DVD authoring, and web streaming hardware and software)
One Infinite Loop, Cupertino, CA 95014. (408) 974-0210. FAX: (408) 974-7740. www.apple.com

AVICA TECHNOLOGY
(Compressed and uncompressed digital stroage for production)
1201 Olympic Blvd., Santa Monica, CA 90404. (800) 706-0077, (310) 450-9090. www.avicatech.com

AVID TECHNOLOGY
(Digital nonlinear editing for all applications)
Avid Technology Park, One Park W., Tewksbury, MA 01876. (978) 640-6789. FAX: (978) 851-0418. www.avid.com

BOXX TECHNOLOGIES
(Developer of high-end hardware and software)
9390 Research Blvd., Kaleido II, Ste. 300, Austin, TX 78759. www.boxxtech.com

CIPRICO, INC.
(High performance networked storage solution)
2800 Campus Dr., Plymouth, MN 55441. www.ciprico.com

DIGITAL VISION
(High capacity uncompressed HD disk recorder products)
11835 W. Olympic Blvd., Ste. 1275, Los Angeles, CA 90064. www.digitalvision.se
Discreet
(Film resolution editing, effects, and compositing systems and software)
10 Duke St., Montreal, Que., H3C 2L7, (800) 869-3504. FAX: (514) 393-0110. www.discreet.com

DOREMI LABS, INC.
(Uncompressed HD and MPEG2 disk recorders and the V1 digital media server)
306 E. Alameda Ave., Burbank, CA 91502. (818) 562-1101. FAX: (818) 562-1109. www.doremilabs.com

DVS DIGITAL VIDEO, INC.
(High capacity uncompressed HD disk recorder products)
1756 Flower St., Glendale, CA 91201. (818) 241-8680. FAX: (818) 241-8684. www.digitalvideosystems.com

EMC CORP.
(Digital storage solutions)
80 South St., Hopkinton, MA 01746. (508) 435-1000. FAX: (508) 435-8910. www.emc.com/media

EVERTZ
(HD keyers, converters, and digital film solutions)
5288 John Lucas Dr., Burlington, Ont., L7L 5Z9, Canada. (905) 335-3700. FAX: (905) 335-3573.

LEITCH
(HD signal processing)
920 Corporate Ln., Chesapeake, VA 23320. (757) 548-2300. FAX: (757) 548-0019. www.leitch.com

LIGHTWORKS
(Digital nonlinear edit system designed for filmmakers)
844 N. Seward St., Hollywood, CA 90038. (323) 465-0070. FAX: (323) 465-0080. www.lwks.com

MATHEMATICAL TECHNOLOGIES, INC. (MTI)
(High-end film restoration and post-production software)
209 Angell St., Providence, RI 02906. (401) 831-1315. FAX: (401) 831-1318.

MATROX ELECTRONIC SYSTEMS
(Digital editing products)
Video Products Group, 1055,boul, St. Regis, Dorval, Que., H9P 2T4, Canada. (514) 822-6000. FAX: (514) 822-6292. www. matrox.com

MEDEA
(Digital storage systems)
26707 Agoura Road, Calabasas, CA 91302. (818) 880-0303. FAX: (818) 880-6906. www.medeacorp.com

PANASONIC
(HD cinema cameras, recorders, and related products)
3330 Cahuenga Blvd. W., Los Angeles, CA 90068. (800) 528-8601. www.panasonic.com

PINNACLE SYSTEMS
(CineWave Mac based digital nonlinear 24p HD edit system, radial light film scanner)
280 N. Bernardo Ave., Mountain View, CA 94043. (650) 526-1600. FAX: (650) 526-1601. www.pinnaclesys.com

QUANTEL, INC.
(Digital editing, compositing, effects, and graphics systems)
85 Old Kings Highway N., Darien, CT 06820. (203) 656-3100. FAX: (203) 656-3459. www.quanTel.com

SGI
(IRIX OS based visual workstations and servers)
1600 Amphitheatre Pkwy. Mountain View, CA 94043. (650) 960-1980. FAX: (650) 961-0595. www.sgi.com

SNELL & WILCOX, INC.
(HD 24P production systems)
2225-1 Martin Ave., Santa Clara, CA 95050. (408) 260-1000. FAX: (408) 260-2800. www.snellwilcox.com

SONY BROADCAST & PROFESSIONAL CO.
(24P HD CineAlta production system, digital betacam and DVCAM product lines, XPRI nonlinear editing system)
1 Sony Dr., Park Ridge, NJ 07656. (201) 930-4800. FAX: (201) 930-4801. www.sonyusacinealta.com

STEENBECK, INC.
(Digital and film based editing technologies)
9554 Vassar Ave., Chatsworth, CA 91311. (818) 998-4033. FAX: (818) 998-6992.

SUN MICROSYSTEMS
(Solaris based visual workstations and servers)
901 San Antonio Rd., Palo Alto, CA 94303. (650) 786-8222. FAX: (650) 786-3763. www.sun.com/media

TERANEX
(HD format converters)
7800 Southland Blvd., Ste. 250, Orlando, FL 32809. (407) 858-6000. FAX: (407) 858-6048. www.teranex.com

THOMSON MULTIMEDIA
(Specter 2K digital intermediate system, D-6 VooDoo data and video recorder)
2255 N. Ontario St., Ste. 150, Burbank, CA 91504. (818) 729-7700. FAX: (818) 729-7777. www.thomsongrassvalley.com

SOUND/AUDIO POST TECHNOLOGY

AMEK, HARMAN INTERNATIONAL INDUSTRIES LTD
(Digital audio consoles and signal processors)
Cranborne House, Cranborn Rd., Potters Bar, Herts, EN6, 3JN, UK. 44-(0) 1707-668-047. FAX: 44-(0) 1707-660-482. www.amek.com

DIGIDESIGN
(Digital audio post solutions and systems)
2001 Junipero Serra Blvd., Daly City, CA 94014. (650)-731-6300. www.digidesign.com

EUPHONIX
(Digital audio consoles)
220 Portage Ave., Palo Alto, CA 94306. (650) 855-0400. FAX: (650) 855-0410. www.euphonix.com

FAIRLIGHT DIGITAL SUPPORT GROUP
(Consoles, digital audio workstations)
628 No. Beechwood Dr., Los Angeles, CA 90004. (213) 460-4884. FAX: (213) 460-6120. www.fairlightusa.com

FOSTEX CORP. OF AMERICA
(Audio recording equipment for film and video production and post)
15431 Blackburn Ave., Norwalk, CA 90650. (562) 921-1112. FAX: (562) 802-1964. www.fostex.com

HARRISON BY GLW
(Digital audio consoles)
1024 Firestone Pkwy., La Vergne, TN 37086. (615) 641-7200. FAX: (615) 641-7224. www.glw.com

OTARI CORPORATION, USA
(Digital audio consoles and multitrack recorders)
8236 Remmet Ave., Canoga Park, CA 91304. (800) 877-0577. FAX: (800) 300-3055. www.otari.com

SOLID STATE LOGIC
(Digital post/film audio mixing consoles)
6255 Sunset Blvd., Ste. 1026, Los Angeles, CA 90028. (323) 463-4444. FAX: (323) 463-6568. www.solidstatelogic.com

SONY BROADCAST & PROFESSIONAL CO.
(Digital audio consoles)
1 Sony Dr., Park Ridge, NJ 07656. (201) 930-4800. FAX: (201) 930-4801. www.sonyusacinealta.com

SOUNDCRAFT
8500 Balboa Blvd., Northridge, CA 91329. (818) 920-3212. FAX: (818) 920-3208. www.soundcraft.com

TASCAM
(Audio recording technologies for digital post)
Teac Professional Division, 7733 Telegraph Rd., Montebello, CA 90640. (213) 726. 0303. FAX: (213) 727-7635. www.tascam.com

TELECINE/SCANNERS/COLOR CORRECTION/FILM OUT

ARRI, INC.
(Arri laser film out recorder)
619 W. 54th St., New York, NY 10019. (212) 757-0906. FAX: (212) 713-0075. www.arri.com

CELO
(High resolution film out recorders)
1029 A Trademark St., Rancho Cucamonga, CA 91730. (909) 481-4648. FAX: (909) 481-6899. www.celo.com

CINTEL
(High resolution digital telecines)
25020 Stanford Ave., Valencia, CA 91355. (661) 294-2310. FAX: (661) 294-1019. www.cintel.co.uk

DA VINCI
(HD and SD color enhancement system, uncompressed digital storage and restoration solutions)
4397 NW 124 Ave., Coral Springs, FL 33065. (954) 688-5600. FAX: (954) 575-5936. www.davsys.com

IMAGICA USA
(2K digital film scanners)
5301 Beethoven St., #109, Los Angeles, CA 90066. (310) 306-4180. FAX: (310) 306-2334. www.imagica.com

INNOVATION TK LTD.
(2K Telecine systems)
Scott House, Hagsdell Rd., Hertford, Hertforshire SG13 8BG. (44 1992) 553 533. FAX: (44 1992) 558 879. www.innovation-tk.com

OXBERRY
(Digital film scanners and film out cameras)
180 Broad St., Carlstadt, NJ 07072. (201) 935-3000. FAX: (201) 935-0104. www.oxberry.com

PANDORA USA
(Pogle color correction technology)
3575 Cahuenga Blvd. W., Ste. 370, Los Angeles, CA 90068. (323) 882-1800. FAX: (323) 882-1801. www.pogle.pandora/int.com

PINNACLE SYSTEMS
(Radial light film scanner)
280 N. Bernardo Ave., Mountain View, CA 94043. (650) 526-1600. FAX: (650) 526-1601. www.pinnaclesys.com

SONY BROADCAST & PROFESSIONAL CO.
(Vialta digital telecine)
1 Sony Dr., Park Ridge, NJ 07656. (201) 930-100. FAX: (201) 930-4752. www.sonyusacinealta.com

THOMSON MULTIMEDIA
(Spirit DataCine, Spectar 2K digital intermediate system)
2255 N. Ontario St. Ste. 150, Burbank, CA 91504. (818) 729-7700. FAX: (818) 729-7777 www.thomsongrassvalley.com

DIGITAL DISTRIBUTION & RESOURCES

DIGITAL CINEMA DISTRIBUTION

BOEING DIGITAL CINEMA
(Satellite distribution)
P. O. Box 92919 MC W-R11-M334, Los angeles, CA 90009.
(562) 797-4582. www.boeing.com/saTel:lite

CONSTELLATION 3D
(Distribution via DVD-ROM)
230 Park Ave., Ste. 453, New York, NY 10169. (212) 983-1107.
FAX: (212) 983-1108. www.c-3d.net

ENTRIQ, INC.
(Encryption)
1900 Wright Place, Ste. 200, Carlsbad, CA 92008. (760) 795-2700. FAX: (760) 795-2698. www.entriq.com

GLOBAL CROSSING
(Broadband communications)
Wall Street Plaza, 88 Pine St., New York, NY. 10005.
www.globalcrossing.com

HARMONIC DATA SYSTEMS
(Encryption)
15920 Bernardo Center Dr., San Diego, CA 92127. (858) 675-7797. FAX: (858)675-7798. www.harmonicdata.com

IRDALO ACCESS
(Conditional access technology)
12860 Danielson Court, Ste. B, Poway, CA. 92064. (858) 668-4800. FAX: (858) 668-4808. www.irdetoaccess.com

OMNEON VIDEO NETWORKS
(Digital networking solutions)
965 Stewart Dr., Sunnyvale, CA 94085. (408) 585-5000. FAX:
(408) 585-5001. www.omneon.com

QUANTUM DIGITAL LTD.
26 Granville Street, Aylesbury, Bucks, HP20 2JR, U.K. 44-(0)
1296-429704. FAX: 44-(0) 1296-427875.
www.quantumdigital.co.uk

SIGHTSOUND TECHNOLOGIES
733 Washington Rd., Ste. 400, Mt. Lebanon, PA 15228. (412)
341-1001. FAX: (412) 341-2442. www.sightsound.com

WAMINET
655 Lone Oak Dr., Eagan, MN 55121. (800) 585-3666. FAX:
(651) 256-5578. www.waminet.com

WILLIAMS (VYVX)
(Terrestrial fibre)
1 Williams Center, Tulsa, OK 74172. (918) 573-2000. FAX:
(918) 573-6805. www.williams.com

PRINCIPAL STUDIO CONTACTS

THE WALT DISNEY COMPANY
500 S. Buena Vista St., Mail Code 7716, Burbank, CA. 91521.
(818) 560-1000. www.disney.com
SENIOR V.P., CORPORATE NEW TECHNOLOGY
Bob Lambert

DREAMWORKS, SKG
100 Universal City Plaza, Bldg. 5121, Universal City, CA
91608. (818) 733-7000. www.dreamworks.com
CONTACT
Mark Christiansen

MGM
2500 Broadway St., Santa Monica, CA 90404. (310) 449-3000.
CONTACT Larry Gleason. www.mgm.com

PARAMOUNT
5555 Melrose Ave., Hollywood, CA. 90038. (323) 956-5000.
EXECUTIVE V.P., ELECTRONIC CINEMA
Gino Campagnola www.paramount.com

SONY PICTURES ENTERTAINMENT, INC.
10202 W. Washington Blvd., Culver City, CA 90232. (310) 244-4000. FAX: (310) 244-2626. www.spe.sony.com
PRESIDENT, DIGITAL ENTERTAINMENT
Yair Landau
V.P., DIGITAL DISTRIBUTION
Nazir Allibhoy

TWENTIETH CENTURY FOX
10201 West Pico Blvd., Building 100, 3220, Los Angeles, CA
90035. (310) 369-3716. FAX: (310) 369-8733.
EXECUTIVE VICE PRESIDENT
Julian Levin

VIVENDI UNIVERSAL
100 Universal City Plz., Universal City, CA. 91608. (818) 777-1000. www.vivendiuniversal.com
SENIOR V.P., TECHNOLOGY
Jerry Pierce

WARNER BROS.
4000 Warner Blvd., Burbank, CA. 91522. (818) 954-6000.
www.warnerbros.com
CONTACT
Chris Cookson

RESOURCES

AMERICAN FILM INSTITUTE
(Advancing and preserving the art of the moving image)
2021 N. Western Ave., Los Angeles, CA 90027. (323) 856-7600. FAX: (323) 467-4578. www.afionline.org

AMERICAN SOCIETY OF CINEMATOGRAPHERS
1782 N. Orange Dr., Hollywood, CA 90028. (323) 969-4333.
FAX: (323) 876-4973. www.cinematographer.com

CREATIVEPLANET
(Project management software and entertainment information databases)
5700 Wilshire Blvd., STE.600, Los Angeles, CA 90036. (323)
643-3400. FAX: (323) 634-2615. www.creativeplanet.com

DIGITAL CINEMA CONSORTIUM
(Japanese consortium of leading digital cinema interests)
Pacific Interface, 5351 Hilltop Crescent, Oakland, CA 94618.
(510) 547-2758. FAX: (510) 547-1726.

DIGITAL CINEMA INITIATIVES, LLC
6834 Hollywood Blvd, Ste. 500, Hollywood, CA 90028. (323)
769-2880. FAX: (323) 769-2885. www.dcimovies.com
email: chuck.goldwater@dcimovies.com
PRESIDENT
Chuck Goldwater
CHIEF TECHNOLOGY OFFICER
Walt Ordway

EASTMAN KODAK
(Filmmaker services)
Entertainment Imaging, 1017 N. Las Palmas Ave., Ste. 200,
Hollywood, CA 90038. (323) 982-9053.
www.kodak.com/go/motion

ENTERTAINMENT TECHNOLOGY CENTER (ETC)
(Digital cinema lab)
734 W. Adams Blvd., Los Angeles, CA 90089. (213) 743-1600.
FAX: (213) 743-1803. www.etcinema.org

EXPRESSION CENTER FOR NEW MEDIA
(Education)
6601 Shellmound St., Emeryville, CA 94608. (877) 833-8800.
www.xnewmedia.com

FINAL DRAFT
(Scriptwriting software)
1600 Ventura Blvd., Ste.800, Encino, CA 91436. (818) 995-8995. ext 113. FAX: (818) 995-4422.
email: fairbank@finaldraft.com

FRANCE TELECOM
(Digital cinema research facility)
1270 Avenue of the Americas, New York, NY 10020. (212) 332-2100. FAX: (212) 245-8605. www.francetelecomna.com

INTERNATIONAL CREATIVE ALLIANCE
22 Warwick Street, 3rd Fl, London, W1B 5NF. 44-(0) 20-7434-2950. www.ica-online.com

THE LOS ANGELES FILM SCHOOL
(Digital filmmaking facilities)
6363 Sunset Blvd. Ste. 400, Hollywood, CA 90028. (877) 952-3456. FAX: (323) 634-0044. www.lafilm.com

MOTION PICTURE ASSOCIATION
(Trade association)
15503 Ventura Blvd., Encino, CA 91436. (818) 995-6600. FAX:
(818) 461-1502. www.mpaa.org

NATO (NATIONAL ASSOCIATION OF THEATRE OWNERS)
(Theatre owner's international trade association)
4605 Lankershim Blvd., Ste. 340, N. Hollywood, CA 91602.
(818) 506-1778. FAX: (818) 506-0269.
www.hollywood.com/nato

NIST (NATIONAL INSTITUTE OF STANDARDS & TECHNOLOGY)
(Standards setting body)
U.S. Dept. of Commerce, Mallstop 8951, Bldg. 225, Rm. A258,
Gaithersburg, MD 20899. www.digitalcinema.nist.gov

PRODUCTIONHUB
(Online production guide/search engine)
801 W. Fairbanks Ave., Winter Park, FL 32789. (407) 629-4122.
FAX: (407) 629-8884. www.productionhub.com

QP MEDIA, INC.
(Digital cinema integration and services)
64 Wintergreen Lane, Groton, MA 01450. 978-448-0272. FAX:
978-448-9325. www.qpmedia.com
email: info@qpmedia.com
PRESIDENT
William J. Quigley

SMPTE (SOCIETY OF MOTION PICTURE & TELEVISION ENGINEERS)
(International technical society)
595 W. Hartsdale Ave., White PLains, NY 10607. (914) 761-
1100. FAX: (914) 761-3115. www.smpte.org

VISIONBOX MEDIA GROUP
(Digital production/consulting)
3272 Motor Ave., 2nd Fl, Los Angeles, CA 90034. (310) 204-
4686. FAX: (310) 204-4603. www.visionboxmedia.com

VISUAL EFFECTS SOCIETY
2308 Broadway, Santa Monica, CA 90404. (310) 315-6055.
FAX: (310) 828-6893. www.visual-effects-society.org

DIGITAL CINEMA
EQUIPMENT & SERVICES

DIGITAL CINEMA SERVERS

AVICA TECHNOLOGY
1201 Olympic Blvd., Santa Monica, CA 90404. (310) 450-9090.
FAX: (310) 450-5353. www.avicatech.com

AVID TECHNOLOGY, INC.
(Pluto Technologies server)
Avid Technology Park, One Park W., Tewksbury, MA 01876.
(978) 640-6789. FAX: (978) 640-1366. www.avid.com

DIGITAL VISION
4605 Lankershim Blvd., Ste. 700, N. Hollywood, CA 91602.
(818) 769-8111. FAX: (818) 769-1888. www.digitalvision.se

DVS DIGITAL VIDEO, INC.
300 E. Magnolis Blvd., Ste. 102, Burbank, CA 91502. (818)
846-3600. FAX: (818) 846-3648. www.digitalvideosystems.com

EVS DIGITAL CINEMA
9 Law Drive, Fairfield, NJ 07004. (973) 575-7811. FAX: (973)
575-7812. www.evs-cinema.com
BUSINESS DEVELOPMENT
Steven B. Cohen

GRASS VALLEY GROUP
15655 S.W. Greystone Crt., Beaverton, OR 97006. (503) 526-
8160. FAX: (503) 526-8109. www.grassvalleygroup.com/ad/dc

KODAK DIGITAL CINEMA
Kodak Imaging Technology Center, 1017 N. Las Palmas Ave.,
Ste. 201, Los Angeles, CA 90038. (310) 204-7100. FAX: (310)
204-7111. www.kodak.com/go/dcinema

NEC TECHNOLOGIES, INC.
(HD Cinema Systems)
1250 Arlington Heights Rd., Ste. 500, Itasca, IL 60143. (800)
284-4484, ext. 4740. FAX: (630) 467-4750.
www.tridigitalcinema.com

QUVIS
(QuBit)
2921 Wanamaker Dr., Ste. 107, Topeka, KS 66614. (800) 554-
8116. FAX: (785) 272-3657. www.quvis.com

TECHNICOLOR
(Auditorium Management System)
2233 N. Ontario St., Ste. 300, Burbank, CA 91504. (818) 260-
3700. FAX: (818) 260-3720. www.technicolordigital.com

DIGITAL EXHIBITORS

AMC ENTERTAINMENT, INC.
AMC Theatres, P. O. Box 725489, Atlanta, GA 31139. (877)
262-4450. www.amctheatres.com

BROADCAST CINEMA ASSOCIATION
7605 Carter Ct., Bethesda, MD 20817. (703) 314-4500. FAX:
(301) 365-6292.

BROADCAST TELEVISION NETWORK
268 West 44th St., New York, NY 10036. (212) 471-6084. FAX:
(212) 471-6088. www.broadwayonline.com

EMERGING CINEMAS
(Digital cinema theatres specializing in the performing arts)
304 Hudson St., 6th Flr., New York, NY 10013. (212) 989-9466.
www.emergingcinemas.com

ENTERPRISE BROADCASTING CORP.
(Special-purpose digital cinema theatres)
5900 Butler Ln., Scotts Valley, CA 95066. (831) 461-9000. FAX:
(831) 461-5700. email: info@ebc.cc

FORMAN HIDEFINITION SCREENING ROOM
(HD screening room)
300 West 23rd St., New York, NY 10011. (212) 633-9960. FAX:
(212) 807-0121. www.screeningroom.com

MADSTONE FILMS
(Digital cinema theatres specializing in alternative content)
85 Fifth Ave., 12th Flr., New York, NY 10003. (212) 989-4500.
FAX: (212) 989-7744. www.madstonefilms.com

EXHIBITOR PRODUCTS & SERVICES

C&A ADVERTISING
(In-cinema advertising services)
4725 Marle Hay Rd., Ste. 100, Des Moines, IA 50322. (800)
735-5748. FAX: (515) 334-5226. www.onscreenads.com

CINEQ
(Theatre automation technologies)
1070 Morrison Dr., Ottawa, Ont. K2H 8K7, Canada. (800) 387-
4842. FAX: (613) 820-2729. www.cineq.org

DA-LITE SCREEN CO.
(Projection screens)
3100 N. Detroit St., Warsaw, IN. 46581. (574) 267-8101. FAX:
(574) 267-7804. www.da-lite.com

ELECTRONIC THEATRE CONTROLS
(Lighting controls, consoles, and fixtures)
3030 Laura Ln., Middleton, WI 53562. (608) 831-4116. FAX:
(608) 836-1736. www.etcconnect.com

HARKNESS HALL
(Projection screens)
10 Harkness Blvd., Fredericksburg, VA 22401. (540) 370-1590.
FAX: (540) 370-1592. www.harknesshall.com

HOLLYWOOD SOFTWARE
(Theatrical distribution software)
1604 N. Cahuanga, Ste. 115, Hollywood, CA 90028. (323) 463-
2144. FAX: (323) 463-1319. www.hollywoodsoftware.com

LESNA
(Projection screens)
8487 8th Ave., Montreal, Que. H1Z 2X2, Canada. (514) 721-
6914. FAX: (514) 721-7188. www.lesna.com

MARCEL DESROCHERS, INC.
(Projection screens)
1440 Raoul-Charrette, Joliette, Que. J6E 8S7, Canada. (450)
755-3795. FAX: (450) 755-3122. www.mdicinema.com

NATIONAL CINEMA NETWORK
(Digital theatre distribution system)
1300 E. 104th St., Ste. 100, Kansas City, MO 64131. (816)
942-8411. FAX: (816) 941-8947. www.NCNinc.com

STEWART FILMSCREEN
(Projection screens)
1161 W. Sepulveda Blvd., Torrance, CA 90502. (800) 762-
4999. FAX: (310) 326-6870. www.stewartfilm.com

PROJECTION & DISPLAY

BARCO PROJECTION SYSTEMS
(Texas Instruments DLP cinema equipped digital projectors)
3240 Town Point Dr., Kennesaw, GA 30144. (770) 218-3200.
FAX: (770) 218-3250. www.barco.com/projection_systems

CHRISTIE DIGITAL SYSTEMS
(Texas Instruments DLP cinema equipped digital projectors)
10550 Camden Dr., Cypress, CA 90630. (714) 236-8610. FAX:
(714) 503-3385. www.christiedigital.com

DIGITAL PROJECTION, INC.
55 Chastain Rd., Ste. 115, Kennesaw, GA 30144. (770) 420-
1350. FAX: (770) 420-1360. www.digitalprojection.com

FAROUDJA (A DIVISION OF SAGE)
(Image processing for display)
750 Palomar Ave., Sunnyvale, CA 94085. (408) 735-1492.
FAX: (408) 735-8571. www.faroudja.com

JVC
(D-ILA projection chip)
Digital Image Technology Center, 2310 Camino Vida Roble,
Carlsbad, CA 92009. (760) 929-5490. FAX: (760) 929-5450.
www.jvc.com/pro

KODAK DIGITAL CINEMA
(Kodak Digital Cinema uses JVC D-ILM technology)
1017 N. Las Palmas Ave., Ste. 201, Los Angeles, CA 90038.
(310) 204-7100. FAX: (310) 204-7111.
www.kodak.com/go/dcinema

MIRANDA TECHNOLOGIES, INC.
(Image processing for display)
3499 Douglas-B.-Floreani, Montreal, QC., H4S 2C6. (514) 333-1772. FAX: (514) 333-9828. www.miranda.com

NEC TECHNOLOGIES, INC.
(HD cinema system)
1250 Arlington Heights Rd., Ste. 550, Itasca, IL 60143. (800) 284-4484. ext. 4740. FAX: (630) 467-4750. www.tridigitalcinema.com

PANASONIC
(TI DLP based projectors)
3330 Cahuenga Blvd. W., Los Angeles, CA 90068. (800) 528-8601. www.panasonic.com/hdcinema

SONY BROADCAST & PROFESSIONAL CO.
(DLP and D-ILA projectors)
1 Sony Dr., Park Ridge, NJ 07656. (201) 930-1000. FAX: (201) 930-4752. www.sonyusacinealta.com

TEXAS INSTRUMENTS
(DLP cinema "black chip" projection technologies)
6550 Chase Oaks Blvd., Plano, TX 75023. (888) 357-2984. www.dlpcinema.com

YEM AMERICA, INC.
(Image processing for display)
734 Silver Spur Rd., #203, Rolling Hills Estates, CA 90274. (310) 544-9343. FAX: (310) 544-9363. www.yem.co.jp

THEATRE AUDIO SPEAKERS/SYSTEMS

BGW SYSTEMS
13130 Yukon Ave., Hawthorne, CA 90250. (310) 468-2677. FAX: (310) 676-6713. www.bgw.com

CROWN INTERNATIONAL
P. O. Box 1000, Elkhart, IN 46515. (800) 342-6939. FAX: (219) 294-8329. www.crownintl.com

DOLBY LABORATORIES
100 Potrero Ave., San Francisco, CA 94103. (415) 558-0200. FAX: (415) 863-1373. www.dolby.com

DTS
5171 Clareton Dr., Agoura Hills, CA 91301. (818) 706-3525. FAX: (818) 706-1868. www.dtsonline.com

EASTERN ACOUSTICS WORKS
1 Main St., Whitinsville, MA 01588. (508) 234-6158. FAX: (508) 234-8251. www.eaw.com

ELECTRO-VOICE/EVI AUDIO
12000 Portland Ave. S., Burnsville, MN 55337. (800) 392-3497. FAX: (952) 346-4998. www.electro-voice.com

HIGH PERFORMANCE STEREO
64 Bowen St., Newton, MA 02459. (617) 244-1737. FAX: (617) 244-4390. www.hps4000.com

JBL PROFESSIONAL
8500 N. Balboa Blvd., Northridge, CA 91329. (818) 894-8850. FAX: (818) 830-1220. www.jblpro.com

KLIPSCH AUDIO TECHNOLOGIES
3502 Woodview Trace., Ste. 200, Indianapolis, IN 46240. (317) 860-8100. FAX: (317) 860-9195. www.klipsch.com

KRIX LOUDSPEAKERS PTY LTD.
14 Chapman Rd., Hackham, SA 5163 Australia. (61 883) 843 433. FAX: (61 883) 843 419. email: krix@krix.com.au

MARTIN AUDIO LTD.
P.O. Box 44019, Kitchener, Ont., N2N 3G7, Canada. (519) 747-5853. FAX: (519) 747-3576. www.martin-audio.com

QSC AUDIO PRODUCTS
1675 MacAuthur Blvd., Costa Mesa, CA 92626. (714) 754-6175. FAX: (714) 754-6174. www.qscaudio.com

SONY CINEMA PRODUCTS CORP.
5660 Katella Ave., Cypress, CA 90630. (562) 342-2139. FAX: (562) 342-2220. www.sdds.com

TAD/PIONEER
1925 E. Dominquez St., Long Beach, CA 90810. (800) 872-4159. FAX: (310) 952-2412. www.tad-pioneer.com

THX DIVISION OF LUCASFILM, LTD.
(Alignment certification)
1600 Los Gamos Dr., San Rafael, CA 94903. (415) 492-3900. FAX: (415) 492-3988. www.thx.com

THE EXHIBITION INDUSTRY

■

THEATRE CIRCUITS

Theatre	Address	City	State	Zip	Screens	DMA

ALLEN THEATRES, INC.

22 theatres, 84 screens.
P.O. Drawer 1500, 208B W. Main St., Farmington, NM 87401. (505) 325-9313. FAX: (505) 326-2647. www.allentheatres.com
PRESIDENT
Larry F. Allen
VICE PRESIDENT
Lane E. Allen
SECRETARY-TREASURER
Boyd F. Scott
FILM BUYER
Larry F. Allen

THEATRES

Theatre	Address	City	State	Zip	Screens	DMA
Fiesta Twin	23 W. Main	Cortez	CO	81321	2	790
Cinema 5	3199 N. White Sands	Alamogordo	NM	88310	5	790
Cinema 3	2322 W. Pierce	Carlsbad	NM	88220	3	790
Hilltop 2	#4 Hilltop Plaza	Clovis	NM	88101	2	634
North Plains	2809 N. Prince	Clovis	NM	88101	4	634
Allen 8	1819 20th St.	Farmington	NM	87401	8	790
Animas 4 Theatres	4601 E. Main, Animas Shopping Mall	Farmington	NM	87402	4	790
Apache Drive-In	A1231 W. Apache St.	Farmington	NM	87401	2	790
Cameo	734 W. Broadway	Farmington	NM	87401	1	790
Centennial Twin	3030 E. Main St.	Farmington	NM	87402	2	790
Aztec 5	911 W. Aztec	Gallup	NM	87301	5	790
Red Rock 6	3711 Church Rock St.	Gallup	NM	87301	6	790
Rio West Twin	1300 W. Frontage Rd.	Gallup	NM	87301	2	790
Broadmoor	Broadmoor Shopping Center	Hobbs	NM	88240	1	790
Cinema 3	1609 Joe Harvey Blvd.	Hobbs	NM	88240	3	790
Cinema 4	700 Telshor	Las Cruces	NM	88011	8	765
Telshor Cinemas 12	2811 N. Telshor Blvd.	Las Cruces	NM	88011	12	765
Video 4	1005 S. El Paseo	Las Cruces	NM	88011	4	765
Tower Twin	101 N. Ave.	Portales	NM	88130	2	634
Cinema 4	4501 N. Main	Roswell	NM	88201	4	790
Del Norte Twin	2810 B N. Main	Roswell	NM	88201	2	790
Park Twin	1717 S. Union	Roswell	NM	88203	2	790

ALLIANCE ENTERTAINMENT/GREAT ESCAPE THEATRES

11 theatres, 103 screens.
821 Mt. Tabor Rd., Ste. 306, New Albany, IN 47150. (812) 945-4006. FAX: (812) 945-4076.
PRESIDENT & CEO
Anne Ragains
V.P., FINANCE & CFO
Phil McCauley
V.P., CONSTRUCTION
Jim Marcus
V.P., DEVELOPMENT
Chance Ragains
V.P., OPERATIONS
Steve Menschell

THEATRES

Theatre	Address	City	State	Zip	Screens	DMA
Bedford Great Escape	2929 Great Escaoe Dr.	Bedford	IN	47421	7	527
Madison Great Escape	744 Jefferson Ct.	Madison	IN	47250	6	529
New Albany Great Escape 16	300 Professional Crt.	New Albany	IN	47150	16	
Seymour Great Escape	357 Tanger Blvd., Ste. 401	Seymour	IN	47274	8	529
Bowling Green Great Escape	323 Great Escape Dr.	Bowling Green	KY	42101	12	736
Shelbyville Great Escape 8	Brighton Circle	Shelbyville	KY	40065	8	
Oldham Great Escape	410 S. First St.	LaGrange	KY	40031	8	529
Wilder Great Escape	103 Crossing Dr.	Wilder	KY	41076	14	
Oxford Great Escape	10 N. Beech St.	Oxford	OH	45056	4	515
Clarksville Great Escape 16	1810 Tiny Town Rd.	Clarksville	TN	37042	16	659
Weston Great Escape	100 Market Place Mall #8	Weston	WV	26452	4	598

AMC ENTERTAINMENT INC.

215 theatres, 3,114 screens in U.S.; 236 theatres worldwide total, 3,518 screens worldwide total (Japan: 5 theatres, 79 screens; Hong Kong 1 theatre, 11 screens; Portugal: 1 theatre, 20 screens; Canada 7 theatres, 160 screens; Spain 4 theatre, 86 screens; France: 1 theatre, 14 screens; Sweden: 1 theatre, 18 screens; United Kingdom: 1 theatre, 16 screens.)
Headquarters: 920 Main St., Kansas City, MO 64105. (816) 221-4000. FAX: (816) 480-4617. www.amctheatres.com
CHAIRMAN & CEO, AMC ENTERTAINMENT INC.
Peter C. Brown
PRESIDENT & COO, AMERICAN MULTI-CINEMA, INC.
Philip M. Singleton
EXECUTIVE V.P., & CFO, AMC ENTERTAINMENT INC.
Craig R. Ramsey
EXECUTIVE V.P., AMC ENTERTAINMENT INC. & CHAIRMAN, AMC FILM GROUP
Richard T. Walsh
PRESIDENT, AMC FILM
Richard M. Fay
EXECUTIVE V.P., NORTH AMERICA OPERATIONS, AMERICAN MULTI-CINEMA, INC.
John D. McDonald
EXECUTIVE V.P., NORTH AMERICA OPERATIONS SERVICES, AMERICAN MULTI-CINEMA, INC.
Rolando B. Rodriguez

Theatre	Address	City	State	Zip	Screens	DMA

EXECUTIVE V.P., AMC ENTERTAINMENT INTERNATIONAL, INC.
Mark A. McDonald
SENIOR V.P. & TREASURER, AMC ENTERTAINMENT INC.
James V. Beynon
SENIOR V.P., GENERAL COUNSEL & SECRETARY, AMC ENTERTAINMENT INC.
Kevin M. Connor
SENIOR V.P., CORPORATE COMMUNICATIONS, AMC ENTERTAINMENT, INC.
Richard J. King
SENIOR V.P. HUMAN RESOURCES, AMC ENTERTAINMENT INC.
Kieth Wiedenkeller
V.P. & CAO, AMC ENTERTAINMENT INC.
Chris A. Cox
V.P., FINANCE, AMC ENTERTAINMENT INC.
Craig R. Meegan

THEATRES

Theatre	Address	City	State	Zip	Screens	DMA
AMC Arrowhead 14	7700 W. Arrowhead Dr.	Glendale	AZ	85308	14	753
AMC Mesa Grand 24	1645 S. Stapley	Mesa	AZ	85204	24	753
AMC Ahwatukee 24	4915 E. Ray Rd.	Phoenix	AZ	85044	24	753
AMC Arizona Center 24	455 N. 3rd St.	Phoenix	AZ	85004	24	753
AMC Deer Valley 30	3033 W. Agua Fria Fwy.	Phoenix	AZ	85027	30	753
AMC Desert Ridge 18	21001 N. Tatum Blvd., Ste. 32	Phoenix	AZ	85050	18	753
AMC Esplanade 14	2515 E. Camelback	Phoenix	AZ	85016	14	753
AMC Disney 12	1565 Disneyland Dr.	Anaheim	CA	92802	12	803
AMC Burbank 16	125 E. Palm Ave.	Burbank	CA	91502	16	803
AMC Media Center 8	201 E. Magnolia Blvd.	Burbank	CA	91501	8	803
AMC Media Center North 6	770 N. First St.	Burbank	CA	91501	6	803
AMC Covina 30	1414 N. Azusa Ave.	Covina	CA	91722	30	803
AMC Bay Street 16	5614 Bay St., #220	Emeryville	CA	94608	16	807
AMC Encinitas 8	220 N. El Camino Real	Encinitas	CA	92024	8	825
AMC Fullerton 20	1001 S. Lemon	Fullerton	CA	92832	20	803
AMC Hollywood Galaxy 6	7021 Hollywood Blvd.	Hollywood	CA	90028	6	803
AMC Puente Hills 20	1560 S. Azusa Ave	Industry	CA	91748	20	803
AMC La Jolla Village 12	8657 Villa La Jolla Dr.	La Jolla	CA	92037	12	825
AMC Marina Pacifica 12	6346 E. Pacific Coast Hwy.	Long Beach	CA	90803	12	803
AMC Pine Square 16	245 Pine Ave #100	Long Beach	CA	90802	16	803
AMC Avco Center 4	10840 Wilshire Blvd.	Los Angeles	CA	90024	4	803
AMC Beverly Connection 6	100 N. La Cienega Blvd.	Los Angeles	CA	90048	6	803
AMC Century 14	10250 Santa Monica Blvd.	Los Angeles	CA	90067	14	803
AMC Montebello 10	1475 N. Montebello Blvd.	Montebello	CA	90640	10	803
AMC Norwalk 20	12300 E. Civic Center Dr.	Norwalk	CA	90651	20	803
AMC Ontario Mills 30	4549 Mills Circle	Ontario	CA	91764	30	803
AMC The Block 30	20 City Blvd.	Orange	CA	92868	30	803
AMC Old Pasadena 8	42 Miller Alley	Pasadena	CA	91103	8	803
AMC Galleria South Bay 16	1815 Hawthorne Blvd.	Redondo Beach	CA	90278	16	803
AMC Fashion Valley 18	7037 Friars Rd.	San Diego	CA	92108	18	825
AMC Mission Valley 20	1640 Camino Del Rio	San Diego	CA	92108	20	825
AMC Palm Promenade 24	770 Dennery Rd.	San Diego	CA	92154	24	825
AMC Kabuki 8	1881 Post St.	San Francisco	CA	94115	8	807
AMC Van Ness 14	1000 Van Ness Ave.	San Francisco	CA	94109	14	807
AMC Saratoga 14	700 El Paseo De Saratoga	San Jose	CA	95130	14	807
AMC Mercado 20	3111 Mission College Blvd.	Santa Clara	CA	95054	20	807
AMC Santa Monica 7	1310 3rd St.	Santa Monica	CA	90401	7	803
AMC Rolling Hills 20	2591 Airport Dr.	Torrance	CA	90505	20	803
AMC Promenade 16	21801 Oxnard St.	Woodland Hills	CA	91367	16	803
AMC Seven Hills 10	18605 E. Hampden Ave.	Aurora	CO	80013	10	751
AMC Flatiron Crossing 14	61 W. Flatiron Circle	Broomfield	CO	80021	14	751
AMC Highlands Ranch 24	103 Centennial Rd.	Highlands Ranch	CO	80126	24	751
AMC Westminster Promenade 24	10655 Westminster Blvd.	Westminster	CO	80030	24	751
AMC Mazza Gallerie 7	5300 Wisconsin Ave. N.W.	Washington	DC	20015	7	511
AMC Union Station 9	50 Massachusetts Ave.	Washington	DC	20002	9	511
AMC Altamonte Mall 16	433 E. Altamonte Dr.	Altamonte Springs	FL		16	504
AMC Aventura 24	19501 Biscayne Blvd.	Aventura	FL	33180	24	528
AMC Regency Brandon 20	2496 Brandon Blvd.	Brandon	FL	33511	20	539
AMC Celebration 2	651 Front St.	Celebration	FL	34747	2	534
AMC Tri-City 8	5140 E. Bay Dr.	Clearwater	FL	33764	8	539
AMC Cocowalk 16	3015 Grand Ave.	Coconut Grove	FL	33133	16	528
AMC Ridge Plaza 8	9200 State Rd. 84	Davie	FL	33324	8	528
AMC Volusia Square 8	2455 Volusia Ave.	Daytona	FL	32114	8	534
AMC Coral Ridge 10	3401 N.E. 26th Ave.	Fort Lauderdale	FL	33306	10	528
AMC Sheridan Plaza 12	4999 Sheridan St.	Hollywood	FL	33021	12	528
AMC Regency 24	9451 Regency Square Blvd.	Jacksonville	FL	32225	24	561
AMC Pleasure Island 24	1500 Buena Vista Dr.	Lake Buena Vista	FL	32830	24	534
AMC Merchants Walk 10	3615 S. Florida Ave.	Lakeland	FL	33803	10	539
AMC Lake Square 12	10401-015 U.S. Hwy 441 S.	Leesburg	FL	34788	12	534
AMC Merritt Square 7/12	777 E. Merritt Island Causeway	Merritt Island	FL	32952	6	534
AMC Kendall T and C 10	8400 Mills Dr.	Miami	FL	33183	10	528
AMC Mall Of Americas 14	7795 W. Flager	Miami	FL	33144	14	528
AMC South Dade 8	18591 S. Dixie Hwy.	Miami	FL	33157	8	528
AMC Merchants Crossing 16	15201 N. Cleveland Ave.	N. Ft. Myers	FL	33903	16	571
AMC West Oaks 14	9415 W. Colonial Dr.	Ocoee	FL	34761	14	534
AMC Woodlands Square 20	3128 Tampa Rd.	Oldsmar	FL	34677	20	539
AMC Orange Park 24	1910 Wells Rd.	Orange Park	FL	32073	24	561
AMC Fashion Village 8	735 Herndon Ave.	Orlando	FL	32803	8	534
AMC Sarasota East 7/12	8027 Beneva Rd.	Sarasota	FL	34238	6	539
AMC Sunset Place 24	5701 Sunset Dr.	South Miami	FL	33143	24	528
AMC Tyrone Square 6	6901 22nd Ave	St. Petersburg	FL	33710	6	539
AMC Tallahassee Mall 20	2415 N. Monroe St	Tallahassee	FL	32303	20	530
AMC Veterans Expressway 24	9302 Anderson Rd.	Tampa	FL	33634	24	539
AMC Westshore Plaza 14	210 Westshore Plaza	Tampa	FL	33609	14	539
AMC Indian River 24	6200 20th St.	Vero Beach	FL	32966	24	548
AMC Mansell Crossing 14	7730 N. Point Pkwy.	Alpharetta	GA	30202	14	524

Theatre	Address	City	State	Zip	Screens	DMA
AMC Buckhead Backlot 6	3340 Peachtree Rd.	Atlanta	GA	30326	6	524
AMC Parkway Pointe 15	3101 Cobb Pkwy., Ste. 201	Atlanta	GA	30339	15	524
AMC Phipps Plaza 14	3500 Peachtree Rd.	Atlanta	GA	30326	14	524
AMC North Dekalb Mall 16	2042 Lawrenceville Hwy.	Decatur	GA	30033	16	524
AMC Barrett Commons 24	2600 Cobb Place Ln.	Kennesaw	GA	30144	24	524
AMC Colonial 18	825 Lawrenceville-Suwanee Rd.	Lawrenceville	GA	30245	18	524
AMC Southlake Pavilion	7065 Mount Zion Cir.	Morrow	GA	30260	24	524
AMC River East 21	322 E. Illinois St.	Chicago	IL	60611	21	602
AMC City North 14	2600 N. Western Ave.	Chicago	IL	60647	14	602
AMC Ford City 14	7601 S. Cicero Ave.	Chicago	IL	60652	14	602
AMC Yorktown 18	80 Yorktown Shopping Center	Lombard	IL	60148	18	602
AMC Randhurst 16	101 E. Euclid Ave.	Mount Prospect	IL	60056	16	602
AMC Northbrook Court 14	1525 Lake Cook Rd.	Northbrook	IL	60062	14	602
AMC South Barrington 30	170 Studio Dr.	South Barrington	IL	60010	30	602
AMC Cantera 30	28250 Deihl Rd.	Warrenville	IL	60555	30	602
AMC Greenwood 14	461 S. Greenwood Park	Greenwood	IN	46142	14	527
AMC Castelton Square 3	6135 E. 86th St.	Indianapolis	IN	46250	3	527
AMC Clearwater Crossing 12	4016 E. 82nd St.	Indianapolis	IN	46250	12	527
AMC Eastgate Mall 6	7150 E. Washington St.	Indianapolis	IN	46219	6	527
AMC Southlake Mall 9	2475 Southlake Mall	Merrillville	IN	46410	9	602
AMC Town Center 20	11701 Nall Rd.	Leawood	KS	66211	20	616
AMC Studio 30	12075 S. Stangline Rd.	Olathe	KS	66062	24	616
AMC Oak Park Plaza 6	9747 Quivira	Overland Park	KS	66215	6	616
AMC Newport on the Levee 20	One Levy Way, Ste. 4100	Newport	KY	41071	20	541
AMC Hammond Palace 10	801 C.M. Fagan Dr.	Hammond	LA	70403	10	622
AMC Elmwood Palace 20	1200 Elmwood Park Blvd.	Harahan	LA	70123	20	622
AMC Westbank Palace 16	1151 Manhattan Blvd.	Harvey	LA	70058	16	622
AMC Houma Palace 10	5735 W. Park Ave.	Houma	LA	70364	10	622
AMC Clearview Palace 12	4486 Veterans Memorial Blvd.	Metairie	LA	70006	12	622
AMC Fenway 13	401 Park Dr., Ste. 7.	Boston	MA	02215	13	506
AMC Braintree 10	121 Grandview Rd.	Braintree	MA	02184	10	506
AMC Burlington 10	20 South Ave.	Burlington	MA	01803	10	506
AMC Chestnut Hill 5	27 Boylston St, Ste. B	Chestnut Hill	MA	02467	5	506
AMC Framingham 16	22 Flute Pass	Framingham	MA	01701	16	506
AMC Framingham Premium 1	22 Flute Pass	Framingham	MA	01701	1	506
AMC N. Dartmouth Mall 12	140 N. Dartmouth Mall	N. Dartmouth	MA	02747	12	521
AMC Tyngsboro 12	440 Middlesex Rd.	Tyngsboro	MA	01879	12	506
AMC Security Square 8	1717 Rolling Rd.	Woodlawn	MD	21207	8	512
AMC Academy 6	6228 Greenbelt Rd.	Greenbelt	MD	20770	6	511
AMC Academy 8	6198 Greenbelt Rd.	Greenbelt	MD	20770	8	511
AMC Country Club Mall 6	1280 Volke Rd.	Lavale	MD	21502	6	511
AMC Owings Mills 17	10100 Mill Run Circle	Owings Mills	MD	21117	17	512
AMC Rivertowne 12	6081 Oxon Hill Rd.	Oxon Hill	MD	20745	12	511
AMC City Place 10	8661 Colesville Rd.	Silver Spring	MD	20901	10	511
AMC Towson Commons 8	435 York Rd., Ste. 200.	Towson	MD	21204	8	512
AMC Elmwood Plaza 8	936 Mall Dr.	Lansing	MI	48917	8	551
AMC Laurel Park 10	17310 Laurel Pk Dr.	Livonia	MI	48152	10	505
AMC Livonia 20	19500 Haggerty Rd.	Livonia	MI	48152	20	505
AMC Meridian Mall 6	1999 Central Park Dr.	Okemos	MI	48864	6	551
AMC Forum 30	44681 Mound Rd.	Sterling Heights	MI	48314	30	505
AMC Mall of America 14	401 South Ave.	Bloomington	MN	55425	14	613
AMC Eden Prairie Mall 18	4000 Flying Cloud Dr., Ste. 2400.	Eden Prairie	MN	55344	18	613
AMC Centennial Lakes 8	7311 France Ave. S.	Edina	MN	55435	8	613
AMC Har Mar 1-3	2100 N. Snelling Ave.	Roseville	MN	55113	3	613
AMC Har Mar 4-11	2100 N. Snelling Ave.	Roseville	MN	55113	8	613
AMC Creve Coeur 12	10465 Olive Blvd.	Creve Coeur	MO	63141	12	609
AMC West Olive 16	12657 Olive St.	Creve Coeur	MO	63141	16	609
AMC Independence 20	19200 E. 39th St.	Independence	MO	64057	20	616
AMC Barrywoods 24	8101 Roanridge Rd.	Kansas City	MO	64151	24	616
AMC Parkway 14	8600 Ward Pkwy.	Kansas City	MO	64114	14	616
AMC Crestwood 10	#0248 Crestwood Plaza	St. Louis	MO	63126	10	609
AMC Esquire 7	6706 Clayton Rd.	St. Louis	MO	63117	7	609
AMC Carolina Pavilions 22	9541 S. Blvd.	Charlotte	NC	28273	22	517
AMC Concord Mills 30	8421 Concord Mills Blvd.	Concord	NC	28027	30	517
AMC Oak View 24	3555 S. 140th Plaza	Omaha	NE	68144	24	652
AMC Bridgewater Commons 7	400 Commons Way, Ste. 380	Bridgewater	NJ	08807	7	501
AMC Clifton Commons 16	405 Rte. 3 E.	Clifton	NJ	07014	16	501
AMC Deptford 8	1740 Clements Bridge Rd.	Deptford	NJ	08096	8	504
AMC Deptford Mall 6	1795 Deptford Center Rd.	Deptford	NJ	08096	6	504
AMC Hamilton 24	325 Sloan Ave.	Hamilton	NJ	08619	24	504
AMC Marlton 8	800 N. Rte. 73.	Marlton	NJ	08053	8	504
AMC Essex Green 9	495 Prospect Ave.	West Orange	NJ	07052	9	501
AMC Maple Ridge 8	4276 Maple Rd.	Amherst	NY	14226	8	514
AMC University Mall 8	4100 Maple Rd.	Amherst	NY	14226	8	514
AMC Bay Plaza 13	2110 Barton Ave.	Bronx	NY	10475	13	501
AMC McKinley Mall 6	3701 McKinley Pkwy., Unit 634	Buffalo	NY	14219	6	514
AMC Walden Galleria 12	6 Walden Galleria	Cheektowaga	NY	14225	12	514
AMC Empire 25	234 W. 42nd St.	New York	NY	10036	25	501
AMC West Market Plaza 7	3879 Medina Rd.	Akron	OH	44333	7	510
AMC Ridge Park Square 8	4788 Ridge Rd.	Brooklyn	OH	44144	8	510
AMC Lennox Town Center 24	777 Kinnear Rd.	Columbus	OH	43212	24	535
AMC Easton 30	275 Easton Towne Ctr.	Columbus	OH	43219	30	535
AMC Plaza Chapel Hill 8	500 Howe Ave.	Cuyahoga Falls	OH	44221	8	510
AMC Dublin Village 18	6700 Village Pkwy.	Dublin	OH	43017	18	535
AMC Westgate Mall 6	3200 Linden Rd.	Rocky River	OH	44116	6	510
AMC Westwood Town Center 6	21653 Center Ridge Rd.	Rocky River	OH	44116	6	510
AMC Quail Springs Mall 24	2501 W. Memorial	Oklahoma City	OK	73134	24	650
AMC Southroads 20	4923 E. 41st St.	Tulsa	OK	74135	20	671
AMC Tilghman 8	4608 Broadway	Allentown	PA	18104	8	504
AMC Woodhaven 10	1336 Bristol Pike.	Bensalem	PA	19020	10	504
AMC Neshaminy 24	3900 Rockhill Dr.	Bensalem	PA	19020	24	504
AMC Colonial Commons 9	5114 Jonestown Rd.	Harrisburg	PA	17112	9	566

Theatre	Address	City	State	Zip	Screens	DMA
AMC Hampden Center 8	4902 Carlisle Pike	Mechanicsburg	PA	17055	8	566
AMC Granite Run 8	1067 W. Baltimore Pike	Media	PA	19063	8	504
AMC Franklin Mills 14	1149 Franklin Mills Circle	Philadelphia	PA	19154	14	504
AMC Orleans 8	2274 Bleigh St	Philadelphia	PA	19152	8	504
AMC Plymouth Meeting 12	494 Germantown Pike	Plymouth Meeting	PA	19462	12	504
AMC 309 Cinema 9	Routes 309 & 63	Spring House	PA	19477	9	504
AMC Marple 10	400 S. State St	Springfield	PA	19064	10	504
AMC Painters Crossing 9	112 Wilmington Pike	West Chester	PA	19382	9	504
AMC Citadel Mall 6	2072 Sam Rittenberg Blvd	Charleston	SC	29407	6	519
AMC Dutch Square 14	800 Bush River Rd	Columbia	SC	29210	14	546
AMC Northwoods Mall 8	2181 Northwoods Blvd	N. Charleston	SC	29406	8	519
AMC Parks at Arlington 16	3861 S. Cooper	Arlington	TX	76015	16	623
AMC Barton Creek 14	2901 Capital of Texas Hwy	Austin	TX	78746	14	635
AMC Grand 24	10110 Technology Blvd	Dallas	TX	75220	24	623
AMC Glen Lakes 8	9450 N. Central Expy	Dallas	TX	75231	8	623
AMC The Park 6	200 S. Alto Mesa Dr	El Paso	TX	79912	6	765
AMC Sunland Park 6	750 Sunland Park Dr., Ste. FC1	El Paso	TX	79912	6	765
AMC Palace 9	220 E. Third St	Fort Worth	TX	76102	9	623
AMC Hulen 10	6330 Hulen Bend Blvd	Fort Worth	TX	76132	10	623
AMC Sundance West 11	304 Huston St	Fort Worth	TX	76102	11	623
AMC Stonebriar	2601 Preston Rd	Frisco	TX	74034	24	671
AMC Grapevine Mills 30	3150 Grapevine Mills Pkwy	Grapevine	TX	76051	30	623
AMC Studio 30	2949 Dunvale	Houston	TX	77063	30	618
AMC Meyer Park 16	4730 W. Belfort	Houston	TX	77035	16	618
AMC Gulf Pointe 30	11801 S. Sam Houston Pkwy	Houston	TX	77089	30	618
AMC Willowbrook 24	17145 Tomball Pkwy	Houston	TX	77064	24	618
AMC Deerbrook Mall 24	20131 Highway 59	Humble	TX	77338	24	618
AMC Irving Mall 14	2433 Irving Mall	Irving	TX	75062	14	623
AMC Katy Mills 20	5000 Katy Mills Cir	Katy	TX	77494	20	618
AMC Mesquite 30	19919 I.H. 635	Mesquite	TX	75149	30	623
AMC Rivercenter 9	849 E. Commerce St	San Antonio	TX	78205	9	641
AMC Huebner Oaks 24	11075 1H 10 W	San Antonio	TX	78230	24	641
AMC First Colony 24	3301 Town Center Blvd	Sugarland	TX	77478	24	618
AMC Hoffman 22	206 Swamp Fox Rd	Alexandria	VA	22314	22	511
AMC Courthouse Plaza 8	2150 Clarendon Blvd	Arlington	VA	22201	8	511
AMC Skyline 6	5141 Leesburg Pike	Falls Church	VA	22041	12	511
AMC Hampton Towne Center 24	60 Towne Center Way	Hampton	VA	23666	24	544
AMC Springfield Mall 10	6500 J. Springfield Mall	Springfield	VA	22150	10	511
AMC Lynnhaven 8	2736 N. Mall Dr	Virginia Beach	VA	23452	8	544
AMC Potomac Mills 15	2700 Potomac Mills Cir	Woodbridge	VA	22192	15	511
AMC Renton Village 8	25 S. Grady Way	Renton	WA	98055	8	819
AMC Cinerama 1	2100 Fourth Ave	Seattle	WA	98121	1	819
AMC Pacific Place 11	600 Pine St., Ste. 400	Seattle	WA	98101	11	819
AMC Kitsap 8	P.O. Box 3246, 10055 Kitsap Mall Blvd	Silverdale	WA	98383	8	819
AMC River Park Square 20	808 W. Main	Spokane	WA	99201	20	881
AMC Narrows Plaza 8	2208 Mildred St	Tacoma	WA	98466	8	819
AMC Mayfair 18	2500 N. Mayfair Rd., Ste. M186	Wauwatosa	WI	53226	18	617

AMSTAR ENTERTAINMENT, LLC

6 theatres, 82 screens.
1400 Urban Center Dr., Ste. 420, Vestavia Hills, AL 35242. (205) 970-3930. FAX: (205) 970-9066. www.amstarcinemas.com
PRESIDENT & CEO
Stephen L. Colson, Sr.
DIRECTOR, OPERATIONS SERVICES
Jack Wagner
CONTROLLER
Mollie Whitehead

THEATRES

AmStar Stadium 12	700 Quintard Dr	Oxford	AL	36201	12	630
AmStar Stadium 12	1120 TownPark Ln	Lake Mary	FL	32746	12	534
AmStar Stadium 16	5996 Zebulon Rd	Macon	GA	31210	16	503
AmStar Stadium 14	Brannon Crossing Centre	Nicholasville	KY	40356	12	
AmStar Stadium 14	206 Norman Station Blvd	Mooresville	NC	28117	14	517
AmStar Stadium 14	193 Civic Center Blvd	Anderson	SC	29625	14	567

ATLAS CINEMAS

4 theatres, 32 screens.
22624 Lakeshore Blvd., Euclid, OH 44123. (216) 731-1701. FAX: (216) 731-2138.
PRESIDENT
Albert Saluam

THEATRES

Atlas Avon Lake 4	33487 Lake Rd	Avon Lake	OH	44012	4	510
Atlas Lakeshore 7	22624 Lakeshore Blvd	Euclid	OH	44123	7	510
Atlas Cinemas Diamond Ctr 12	9555 Diamond Centre Dr	Mentor	OH	44060	12	510
Atlas Greatlakes	9550 Mentor Ave	Mentor	OH	44060	9	510

B & B THEATRES

26 theatres, 117 screens.
P.O. Box 171, 114 W. 2nd, Salisbury, MO 65281. (660) 388-5219.
Kansas Office: P.O. Box 388, 210 N. Washington, Iola, KS 66749. (316) 365-5701. FAX: (316) 365-2753.
PRESIDENT & FILM BUYER
Robert Bagby
CHAIRMAN
Elmer Bills

THEATRES

Burford Theatre	118 S. Summit St	Arkansas City	KS	67005	3	678
Chanute Cinema	309 E. Main	Chanute	KS	66720	2	603
Coffeyville Cinema	210 W. 10th St	Coffeyville	KS	67337	2	671

Theatre	Address	City	State	Zip	Screens	DMA
Dodge City Village 8	Village Sq. Mall, 2601 Central	Dodge City	KS	67801	8	678
Independence Cinema	121 Laurel St.	Independence	KS	67301	4	671
Sterling Six	1802 1/2 E. St.	Iola	KS	66749	6	603
Iola 54 Drive-In	1300 2200 St.	Gas City	KS	66749	1	603
McPherson Cinema 4	316 N. Main St.	McPherson	KS	67460	4	678
Winfield Cinema	1007 Main St.	Winfield	KS	67156	3	678
Bolivar Cinema 4	800 E. Aldrich Rd.	Boliver	MO	65613	4	619
Grand 6	2880 N. Grand Dr.	Chillicothe	MO	64601	6	616
Festus Eight	1522 Pkwy	Festus	MO	63028	8	609
Fulton Cinema	613 Court St.	Fulton	MO	65251	2	604
Hannibal Cinema 5	#7 Northport Shopping Center	Hannibal	MO	63401	5	717
Lake West Cinema 5	1651 Hwy. 0, Bldg. C-1	Gravois Mills	MO	65037	5	604
Harrisonville Cinema 6	2727 Cantrell Rd.	Harrisonville	MO	64701	6	616
Ritz 4 Theatre	925 S. Jefferson	Lebanon	MO	65536	4	619
Liberty Cinema 12	2101 W. Kansas	Liberty	MO	64069	12	616
Marshall Cinema	114-120 E. North St.	Marshall	MO	65340	3	616
Moberly Five & Drive	3000 N. Morley	Moberly	MO	65270	6	604
Monett Plaza Five	507 Plaza Dr.	Monett	MO	65708	5	619
Neosho Six	1601 Malcolm Mosby Dr.	Neosho	MO	64850	6	603
Lyric Theatre	110 W. 2nd St.	Salisbury	MO	65281	1	604
Waynesville Cinema 8	City Rte. 66	Waynesville	MO	65583	8	619
Airline Drive-In	1800 W. Highland	Ponca City	OK	74604	1	650
Ponca Plaza Twin	1417 E. Hartford	Ponca City	OK	74604	2	650

BOOKING ACCOUNTS

2 Theatres, 16 Screens.

Great 8	#5 Prairie Dell Plaza	Union	MO	63084	8	609
Down Town Cinema 8	115 N. Elson	Kirksville	MO	63501	8	609

BRENDEN THEATRES

5 theatres, 78 screens.
1985 Willow Pass Rd., Concord, CA 94520. (925) 677-0462. www.brendentheatres.com
OWNER, PRESIDENT & CEO
John Brenden

THEATRES

Concord 14	1985 Willow Pass Rd.	Concord	CA	94520	14	807
Modesto 18	1021 Tenth St.	Modesto	CA	95354	18	862
Pittsburg 16	4085 Century Blvd.	Pittsburg	CA	94565	16	807
Vacaville 16	531 Davis St.	Vacaville	CA	95688	16	862
Las Vegas 14	4321 W. Flamingo Rd.	Las Vegas	NV	89103	14	839

CAMERA CINEMAS

5 theatres, 16 screens.
P.O. Box 720728, San Jose, CA 95172-0728. (408) 998-3022. FAX: (408) 294-3300. www.cameracinemas.com
OWNER
James Zuur
FILM BUYER
Jack NyBlom

THEATRES

Camera 7 Pruneyard	1875 S. Bascom Ave.	Campbell	CA	95008	7	807
Los Gatos	41 N. Santa Cruz Ave.	Los Gatos	CA	95030	2	807
Camera One	366 S. First St.	San Jose	CA	95113	1	807
Camera 3	288 S. Second St.	San Jose	CA	95113	3	807
Towne 3	1433 The Alameda	San Jose	CA	95126	3	807

CAMPBELL PLAZA THEATRES, INC.

6 theatres, 33 screens.
P.O. Box 6395, San Jose, CA 95130-6395. (408) 378-2434. FAX: (408) 378-2785. www.CineLuxTheatres.com
PRESIDENT
Paul D. Gunsky

THEATRES

Plaza 4 Theatres	2501 Winchester Blvd.	Campbell	CA	95008	4	807
Almaden Cinema 5	2306 Almaden Rd., #P	San Jose	CA	95125	5	807
Chabot Cinema	2853 Castro Valley Blvd.	Castro Valley	CA	94546	1	807
New Della Cinema	641 First St.	Brentwood	CA	94513	2	807
Cinema Saver 10	577 E. Calaveras Blvd.	Milpitas	CA	95035	10	807
Tennant Station Stadium 11	750 Tennant Ave.	Morgan Hill	CA	95038	11	807

CARMIKE CINEMAS

303 theatres, 2,248 screens.
1301 First Ave., P.O. Box 391, Columbus, GA 31902-0391. (706) 576-3400. FAX: (706) 576-3880.
CHAIRMAN
C. L. Patrick
PRESIDENT & CEO
Michael W. Patrick
SENIOR V.P., FINANCE, TREASURER & CFO
Martin Durant
SENIOR V.P., FILM
Anthony J. Rhead
SENIOR V.P., OPERATIONS, COO
Fred Van Noy
SENIOR V.P., CONCESSIONS & ASSISTANT SECRETARY
H. Madison Shirley
V.P., ADVERTISING
Marilyn Grant
ASSISTANT V.P. & CONTROLLER
Philip Smitley

DIRECTOR, HUMAN RESOURCES
Sadie Marshall
GENERAL MANAGER, THEATRE OPERATIONS
Gary Krannacker

THEATRES

Theatre	Address	City	State	Zip	Screens	DMA
Carmike Plaza	3416 McClellum Blvd., P.O. Box 204	Anniston	AL	36201	6	646
Carmike Wynnsong	2111 E. University Ave., PO 3461	Auburn	AL	36831	16	522
Carmike	3443 Lorna Ridge Rd.	Birmingham	AL	35216	10	630
Carmike Summit	321 Summit Blvd.	Birmingham	AL	35243	16	630
Carmike Wynnsong	500 Commons Dr.	Birmingham	AL	35209	12	630
Carmike Town Sq.	1644 2nd Ave. S.W., Town Sq Shop. Ctr.	Cullman	AL	35055	3	630
Carmike Century Cinema	607 Fourteenth St. S.E., P.O. Box 988	Decatur	AL	35602	8	691
Carmike Circle West	3120 Ross Clark, Circle W. Shp. Ctr.	Dothan	AL	36303	4	606
Carmike Capri	Cox Creek Hwy., P.O. Box 1017.	Florence	AL	35631	4	691
Carmike Hickory Hills	1946 Florence Blvd., P.O. Box 1017.	Florence	AL	35630	6	691
Carmike	1359 Old Monrovia Rd., P.O. Box 11727	Huntsville	AL	35814	10	691
Carmike	4900 Government Blvd.	Mobile	AL	36616	14	686
Carmike Wynnsong	785 Schillinger Rd., S.	Mobile	AL	36695	16	686
Carmike Eastdale	1755 Eastern Blvd.	Montgomery	AL	36117	8	698
Carmike Wynnsong	3975 Eastern Blvd.	Montgomery	AL	36118	10	698
Carmike Martin	Northgate Shop. Ct., Rte. 1, P.O. Box 42	Talladega	AL	35161	3	630
Carmike Bama	Bama Mall, 2600 McFarland Blvd. E.	Tuscaloosa	AL	35405	6	620
Carmike Sugar Creek	#10 Sugar Creek Center	Bella Vista	AR	72714	10	670
Cinema	3 Faulkner Plaza	Conway	AR	72032	6	693
Carmike	5716 Townson Ave., P.O. Box 6088	Fort Smith	AR	72906	14	670
Carmike Harrison	617 Hwy 62 & 65 N.	Harrison	AR	72601	8	619
Carmike Central City	909 Higdon Ferry Rd.	Hot Springs	AR	71901	10	693
Carmike Riverdale	2600 Cantrell Road.	Little Rock	AR	72202	10	693
Carmike Wynnsong	12200 Westhaven Drive	Little Rock	AR	72211	10	693
Carmike Village	729 E. Hwy 62	Mountain Home	AR	72653	5	619
Carmike Pines Mall	2901 Pines Mall Dr #500.	Pine Bluff	AR	71601	8	693
Carmike Stage	625 E. Main, P.O. Box 12383	Aspen	CO	81612	3	751
Carmike 10	1550 Pulsar Dr., P.O. Box 16100	Colorado Springs	CO	80935	10	752
Carmike Chapel Hills 10-15	1701 Briargate Blvd.	Colorado Springs	CO	80920	6	752
Carmike Chapel Hills 9	1701 Briargate Blvd., Sp#015	Colorado Springs	CO	80920	9	752
Carmike	3636 Manhattan Ave., P.O. Box 272182	Fort Collins	CO	80527	10	751
Carmike Mall	51027 Hwy 6 & 24, P.O. Box 1399.	Glenwood Springs	CO	81601	3	751
Carmike	590 24 1/2 Rd., P.O. Box 3178	Grand Junction	CO	81502	7	773
Carmike	2495 W. 29th St., P.O. Box 5296	Greeley	CO	80634	5	751
Carmike Chief Plaza	813 Lincoln Ave., P.O. Box 775821	Steamboat Springs	CO	80477	4	751
Carmike	US Route 13, Dover Mall	Dover	DE	19901	14	504
Carmike Royal Palm	"2507 53rd Ave. E."	Bradenton	FL	34203	20	539
Carmike Amelia Island	1132 14th St. S., P.O. Box 258	Fernandina Beach	FL	32035	7	561
Carmike Palm Cinema	4226 Old Hwy 37	Lakeland	FL	33812	3	539
Carmike	4049 - W. 23rd	Panama City	FL	32405	10	656
Carmike Mall	HWY 231 & State Rd 77, 2218 N. Cove Blvd.	Panama City	FL	32405	4	656
Carmike	161 E. Nine Mile Rd.	Pensacola	FL	32534	10	686
Carmike Lake Waldon Cinema	220 W. Alexander Street	Plant City	FL	33566	8	539
Carmike Lakeshore	901 US 27 N #120	Sebring	FL	33870	8	539
Carmike University	4080 Goldenrod Rd. (Orlando)	Winter Park	FL	32792	8	534
Carmike Continental Mugs	SE Plaza Shp Ctr., 880 Cypress Gardens Blvd	Winterhaven	FL	33880	2	539
Carmike Wynnsong	"2823 Nottingham Way P.O. Box 4010"	Albany	GA	31707	16	525
Carmike Cinema	1610-D Vienna Rd., P.O. Box 269	Americus	GA	31709	2	522
Carmike	1575 Lexington Rd., P.O. Box 80436	Athens	GA	30608	12	524
Carmike Martin	222 Wallace C. Bryan Pkwy., P.O. Box 278	Calhoun	GA	30703	3	524
Carmike Riverstone	5 Reinhardt College Pkwy.	Canton	GA	30114	15	524
Carmike Plaza	N. Tennessee St. 1129., P.O. Box 683	Cartersville	GA	30120	8	524
Carmike	5301 Sidney Simons Blvd.	Columbus	GA	31904	7	522
Carmike Columbus Sq.	"3100 Macon Road"	Columbus	GA	31907	8	522
Carmike Hollywood Conn.	"1683 Whittlesey Rd"	Columbus	GA	31904	10	522
Carmike Peachtree	"3131 Manchester Expwy"	Columbus	GA	31909	8	522
Carmike Conyers Crossing 16	1536 Dogwood Drive, SE	Conyers	GA	30094	16	524
Carmike Martin	901 E. 16th Ave., P.O. Box 1057	Cordele	GA	31015	3	525
Carmike	2150 E. Walnut Ave., P.O. Box 1424	Dalton	GA	30722	9	575
Carmike Martin	1907 Bowen Mill Rd., P.O. Box 2845	Douglas	GA	31534	2	525
Carmike	2103 Veterans Blvd, Ste. 25, P.O. Box 5007	Dublin	GA	31040	8	503
Carmike Capri	184 Ocilla Hwy., Village Shopping Center	Fitzgerald	GA	31750	2	525
Carmike Wynnsong	7290 Ingersoll St., Bldg 1687, P.O. Box 52618	Fort Benning	GA	31905	10	522
Carmike Southgate	1099 Battlefield Pkwy.	Fort Oglethorpe	GA	30742	5	575
Carmike Griffin Cinema	1671 N. Expway.	Griffin	GA	30223	4	524
Carmike LaGrange	1510 Lafayette Park	LaGrange	GA	30241	6	624
Carmike	2400 N. Columbia St. #39	Milledgeville	GA	31061	6	503
Carmike	87 Newnan Station Rd., P.O. Box 71278	Newnan	GA	30271	10	524
Carmike	511 Stephenson Ave., P.O. Box 14213.	Savannah	GA	31416	10	507
Carmike Wynnsong	1150 Shawnee St., P.O. Box 60158	Savannah	GA	31420	11	507
Carmike	1905 Scenic Hwy Ste. 6000, P.O. Box 504	Snellville	GA	30078	12	524
Carmike Cinema	610 Brannen St., P.O. Box 833	Statesboro	GA	30459	9	507
Carmike Cinema	216 N. Virginia Ave.	Tifton	GA	31794	6	525
Carmike	5245 Northland Cedar Rapids Ave. N.E.	Cedar Rapids	IA	52402	7	637
Carmike Wynnsong	2435 Edgewood Rd. SW, P.O. Box 10136	Cedar Rapids	IA	52404	12	637
Carmike Cobblestone	8501 Hickman Rd., P.O. Box 3630.	Des Moines	IA	50322	9	679
Carmike Southridge	6720 S. E. 14th Ave.	Des Moines	IA	50315	12	679
Carmike Cinema Center	75 J.F. Kennedy Rd.	Dubuque	IA	52002	8	637
Carmike Kennedy Mall	555 J.F. Kennedy Rd.	Dubuque	IA	52002	6	637
Carmike Wynnsong	5233 NW 86th St.	Johnston	IA	50131	12	679
Carmike Plaza	2939 B Hamilton Blvd.	Sioux City	IA	51104	2	624
Carmike Southern Hills	4400 Sergeant Rd.	Sioux City	IA	51106	12	624
Carmike	4031 Poleline Rd., P.O. Box 5430	Chubbuck	ID	83202	7	758
Carmike University	120 N. Farm Rd., P.O. Box 9283	Moscow	ID	83843	4	881
Carmike Alameda Plaza	1010 Yellowstone	Pocatello	ID	83201	3	758
Carmike Holiday Theatre	26 South Center, P.O. Box 640	Rexburg	ID	83440	3	758

Theatre	Address	City	State	Zip	Screens	DMA
Carmike Petite	2002 Mall St., P.O. Box 9.	Collinsville	IL	62234	4	609
Carmike Cinema	306 University Dr., P.O. Box 189	Macomb	IL	61455	2	717
Carmike Seth Childs	2610 Farm Bureau Rd.	Manhattan	KS	66502	12	605
Carmike Greenwood	2625 Scottsville Blvd.	Bowling Green	KY	42101	6	736
Carmike Plaza	600 US 31 W. Bypass, Unit 24, P.O. Box 2150	Bowling Green	KY	42101	6	736
Carmike Cinema	146959 North US Hwy 25E	Corbin	KY	40701	4	557
Carmike Cinema	1594 Houstonville Rd. Ste. 217	Danville	KY	40422	4	541
Carmike Cinema	"Hwy 421 S."	Harlan	KY	40829	4	557
Carmike Martin	4000 Ft. Campbell Blvd., P.O. Box 530	Hopkinsville	KY	42241	5	659
Carmike	3151 Mapleleaf Dr., P.O. Box 55248	Lexington	KY	40509	10	541
Carmike Martin	25 Madison Square Dr., P.O. Box 524	Madisonville	KY	42431	4	649
Carmike Cinema	1579 US Hwy 68.	Maysville	KY	41056	4	515
Carmike Cinema	900 US Hwy 25 E., Middlesboro Mall Box 28.	Middlesboro	KY	40965	4	557
Carmike Alexandria	3820 Alexandria Mall Dr.	Alexandria	LA	71301	6	644
Carmike	5725 Johnston St., P.O. Box 2319	Lafayette	LA	70503	10	642
Carmike North Shores	160 Airport Dr.	Slidell	LA	70460	6	622
Carmike Sun & Surf	14301 Coastal Hwy.	Ocean City	MD	21842	6	576
Carmike Copper	1703 W. Memorial Dr.	Houghton	MI	49931	5	553
Carmike	15630 Cedar Ave., P.O. Box 240-803.	Apple Valley	MN	55124	15	613
Carmike Sterling	1403 First Avenue SW, P.O. Box 777	Austin	MN	55912	3	611
Carmike Cinema	220 Stadium Rd., P.O. Box 1299	Mankato	MN	56002	4	737
Carmike Mall	1640 Mankato Mall, P.O. Box 1299	Mankato	MN	56002	4	737
Carmike Wynnsong	2430 Highway 10	Moundsview	MN	55112	15	613
Carmike Cinema	1 N. German St., P.O. Box 67	New Ulm	MN	56073	3	737
Carmike Oakdale	1188 Helmo Ave., N.	Oakdale	MN	55128	20	613
Carmike Barclay Square	1300 Salem Rd., P.O. Box 845	Rochester	MN	55903	6	611
Carmike Kandi	1605 S. 1st St.	Willmar	MN	56201	6	613
Carmike University	727 N. Charles St.	Warrensburg	MO	64093	8	616
Carmike	2255 Overland Ave., P.O. Box 80245	Billings	MT	59108	7	756
Carmike Cine	925 Broadwater St., P.O. Box 80245	Billings	MT	59108	7	756
Carmike Wynnsong	2456 Central Ave., P.O. Box 80245	Billings	MT	59101	10	756
Carmike Campus Square	1611 S. 11th Ave.	Bozeman	MT	59715	8	754
Carmike Ellen	17 W. Main St.	Bozeman	MT	59715	1	754
Carmike Rialto	10 W. Main St.	Bozeman	MT	59715	1	754
Carmike Plaza	3100 Harrison Ave., P.O. Box 3453	Butte	MT	59701	6	754
Carmike	1601 Marketplace Dr., Ste 75, P.O. Box 1439	Great Falls	MT	59404	10	755
Carmike Cine	1108 Ninth St., S., P.O. Box 1439	Great Falls	MT	59405	4	755
Carmike Circus	3010 N. Montana, P.O. Box 5599	Helena	MT	59601	2	766
Carmike Gaslight	5 W. Broadway, P.O. Box 5599	Helena	MT	59601	3	766
Carmike	"3640 Mullan Rd."	Missoula	MT	59802	10	762
Carmike 10	3640 Mullan Rd.	Missoula	MT	59802	10	762
Carmike Cine	"3601 Brooks St"	Missoula	MT	59801	2	766
Carmike Village	3804 S. Reserve St.	Missoula	MT	59801	6	762
Carmike	299-I Swannanoa River Rd., P.O. Box 9340	Asheville	NC	28805	10	567
Carmike Appalachian	559 West King St., P.O. Box 426	Boone	NC	28607	2	517
Carmike Chalet	290 Boone Heights Dr., P.O. Box 426	Boone	NC	28607	3	517
Carmike Cinema	1018 Fed Station Point Shopping Cntr.	Carolina Bch.	NC	28428	4	550
Carmike Plaza	Dunn Plaza Shopping Cntr, P.O. Box 511	Dunn	NC	28334	2	560
Carmike Willowdale	3823 Guess Rd., Ste. 125.	Durham	NC	27705	8	560
Carmike Wynnsong	1807 Martin Luther King Blvd., P.O. Box 52618	Durham	NC	27717	15	560
Carmike Kingsway	220-L West Kings Hwy., P.O. Box 3161	Eden	NC	27288	4	518
Carmike	Freeway @ Morganton Rd., P.O. Box 40535	Fayetteville	NC	28309	12	560
Carmike Marketfair	1916 Skibo Rd. Ste. 300	Fayetteville	NC	28314	15	560
Carmike Wynnsong	3039 Boone Trail Ext.	Fayetteville	NC	28306	7	560
Carmike Cinema	Tri City Mall, P.O. Box 7886	Forest City	NC	28043	4	567
Carmike Berkley	3101 Cashwell Dr., P.O. Box 10065	Goldsboro	NC	27530	4	560
Carmike	4822 Koger Blvd., P.O. Box 77358	Greensboro	NC	27407	18	518
Carmike	1685 East Fire Tower Rd., P.O. Box 1844	Greenville	NC	27834	12	545
Carmike Cinema	500 McCotter Blvd Hwy 70, P.O. Box 450	Havelock	NC	28532	6	545
Carmike	2000 S.E. Catawba Valley Blvd., P.O. Box 147	Hickory	NC	28603	12	517
Carmike	2705 N. Main St. Ste. 117, P.O. Box 5483	High Point	NC	27262	8	518
Carmike	350 Western Blvd.	Jacksonville	NC	28546	16	545
Carmike Westgate	Westgate Plz. Shop. Ctr. Morganton Blvd.	Lenoir	NC	28645	2	517
Carmike Cinema	235 Talbert Blvd., P.O. Box 1106	Lexington	NC	27292	8	518
Carmike Cinema	1700 N. Aspen St., P.O. Box 356	Lincolnton	NC	28092	8	517
Carmike Cinema	1311 Arendell St., P.O. Box 988.	Morehead City	NC	28557	3	545
Carmike Park Place	9525 Chapel Hill Rd.	Morrisville	NC	27560	16	560
Carmike	5501 Atlantic Springs Rd., P.O. Box 58637	Raleigh	NC	27658	15	560
Carmike Blueridge	600 Blueridge Rd.	Raleigh	NC	27606	14	560
Carmike Kendale Cinema 2	2738 Industrial Drive, Kendale Shop. Ctr.	Sanford	NC	27331	2	560
Carmike Cinema	414 S. Lafayette St.	Shelby	NC	28150	4	517
Carmike Mall	2201 - 4 E. Dixson Blvd.	Shelby	NC	28150	4	517
Carmike Gateway	1203 Free Nancy Rd., P.O. Box 881	Statesville	NC	28677	4	517
Carmike Cinema	Washington Square Mall, P.O. Box 1642	Washington	NC	27889	7	545
Carmike	111 Cinema Dr., P.O. Box 3925	Wilmington	NC	28406	16	550
Carmike Cinema	5335 Oleander Dr., P.O. Box 3925	Wilmington	NC	28406	6	550
Carmike Parkwood	Parkwood Shopping Cntr., P.O. Box 3007	Wilson	NC	27895	3	560
Carmike	3640 Reynolda Rd., P.O. Box 11107	Winston-Salem	NC	27106	10	518
Carmike Wynnsong	1501 Hanes Mall Blvd., P.O. Box 24817.	Winston-Salem	NC	27103	12	518
Carmike	2700 State St., P.O. Box 1622	Bismarck	ND	58502	8	687
Carmike Lake	25 Fourth Street S., P.O. Box 758	Devils Lake	ND	58301	3	724
Carmike Cinema	Hwy. 22 & I-94, Prairie Hills Mall	Dickinson	ND	58601	3	687
Carmike	2306 32nd Ave. S., P.O. Box 13116	Grand Forks	ND	58208	10	724
Carmike Columbia	3100 32nd Ave. S., P.O. Box 13116	Grand Forks	ND	58208	4	724
Carmike Cinema North 1-7	2400 10th St. SW, Ste 15, Dakota Sq. Mall.	Minot	ND	58701	7	754
Carmike Cinema South 8-12.	2400 10th St. SW, Ste. 604, Dakota Sq Mall	Minot	ND	58701	5	754
Carmike Conestoga Mall	3404 W. 13th St. 159, P.O. Box 5014	Grand Island	NE	68802	4	722
Carmike Island	2228 N. Webb Rd.	Grand Island	NE	68802	2	722
Carmike Hilltop Theatre	5037 2nd Ave., P.O. Box 3193	Kearney	NE	68848	4	722
Carmike Mall	1100 S. Dewey St.	North Platte	NE	69101	3	740
Carmike Monument	2302 Frontage Rd.	Scottsbluff	NE	69361	6	759
Carmike Cinema	418 West Main, P.O. Box 1464	Artesia	NM	88210	2	790

Theatre	Address	City	State	Zip	Screens	DMA
Carmike	1875 Cinema Dr Walmart Plz., P.O. Box 15	Olean	NY	14760	8	514
Carmike Ashtabula Mall	3315 N. Ridge E., Ashtabula Mall Unit 400	Ashtabula	OH	44004	6	510
Carmike Findlay	1800 Tiffin Ave. #E-10	Findlay	OH	45840	6	547
Carmike Kingsgate	1300 Park Ave., P.O. Box 2523	Mansfield	OH	44906	4	510
Carmike Ohio Valley Mall	#700 Banfield Ave., P.O. Box 8016	Saint Clairsville	OH	43950	9	554
Carmike Plaza	4314 Milan Rd. Unit #700, P.O. Box 2501	Sandusky	OH	44871	8	510
Carmike Cinema	100 Mall Dr.	Steubenville	OH	43952	6	554
Carmike	2600 W. Broadway, P.O. Box 1207	Ardmore	OK	73402	5	657
Carmike Dunkin Theatre	207 East Broadway, P.O. Box 947	Cushing	OK	74023	1	650
Carmike	1501 Plato Rd., P.O. Box 758	Duncan	OK	73533	6	627
Carmike Video	3517 West Gattiott Rd., P.O. Box 986	Enid	OK	73701	2	650
Carmike	7102 N. W. Cache Rd.	Lawton	OK	73507	8	627
Carmike	2812 West Shawnee By-pass, P.O. Box 1307	Muskogee	OK	74401	6	671
Carmike North Park	800 E. Prospect, P.O. Box 68	Ponca City	OK	74601	4	650
Carmike Cinema Center	3031 North Harrison, P.O. Box 937	Shawnee	OK	74802	8	650
Carmike Hornbeck	125 North Bell, P.O. Box 937	Shawnee	OK	74802	2	650
Carmike	1909 N. Perkins Rd., P.O. Box 277	Stillwater	OK	74076	10	650
Carmike	1700 Catasauqua, P.O. Box 90175	Allentown	PA	18103	16	504
Carmike	600 Logan Valley Mall	Altoona	PA	16602	8	574
Carmike Park Hills Plaza	West Plank Rd.	Altoona	PA	16602	7	574
Carmike Plaza	6800 Big Beaver Blvd.	Beaver Falls	PA	15010	6	508
Carmike Cinema	900 Chambersburg Mall	Chambersburg	PA	17201	7	511
Carmike Cinema	University Dr. Laurel Mall Shop. Center	Connellsville	PA	15425	4	508
Carmike Cranberry Mall	Route 257 & 332, Oil City, Road #1	Cranberry	PA	16319	5	508
Carmike Cranberry Mall	Route 19 & Freedom Rd.	Cranberry Township	PA	16066	8	508
Carmike Wynnsong	401 Vine Street Hollywood Sq., P.O. Box 373	Delmont	PA	15626	12	508
Carmike Cinema	Dubois Mall	Dubois	PA	15801	5	574
Carmike	Rte. 30 Westmoreland Mall Annex	Greensburg	PA	15601	15	508
Carmike Hermitage Plaza Eight	2461 E. State St.	Hermitage	PA	16148	8	536
Carmike Cinema	Indiana Mall	Indiana	PA	15701	4	508
Carmike Cinema	Franklin Village Mall	Kittanning	PA	16201	4	508
Carmike Cinema	500 Hyde Park Rd.	Leechburg	PA	15656	3	508
Carmike Movie World	3944 Brodhead Rd.	Monaca	PA	15061	7	508
Carmike Galleria	1500 Washington Rd.	Mount Lebanon	PA	15228	6	508
Carmike	700 Ft. Couch Rd, S. Hills Village	Pittsburgh	PA	15241	10	508
Carmike Southland	629 Clairton Blvd.	Pleasant Hills	PA	15236	9	508
Carmike Coventry	650 W. Schuylkill Rd.	Pottstown	PA	19464	8	504
Carmike Wyomissing	"800 Brekshire Blvd."	Reading	PA	19610	8	504
Carmike Cinema	116 Heister St., P.O. Box 380	State College	PA	16801	5	574
Carmike Cinema	501 Benner Pike, Rte. 150	State College	PA	16801	6	574
Carmike	1372 W. Main St., Uniontown Mall	Uniontown	PA	15401	6	508
Carmike Maxi Saver	2001 Mountain View Dr.	West Mifflin	PA	15142	12	508
Carmike James Island	1743 Central Park Rd.	Charleston	SC	29412	8	519
Carmike Astro	430 College Ave., P.O. Box 1243	Clemson	SC	29631	3	567
Carmike	"122 Afton Court"	Columbia	SC	29212	14	546
Carmike Wynnsong	5320 Forest Dr., P.O. Box 6855	Columbia	SC	29206	10	546
Carmike Crosscreek Cinemas	420 Bypass 72 NW, Ste. 40.	Greenwood	SC	29646	3	567
Carmike Cinema	118 W Carolina Ave., P.O. Box 817	Hartsville	SC	29550	2	570
Carmike Broadway	1175 Celebrity Circle., P.O. Box 2836	Myrtle Beach	SC	29578	16	570
Carmike Dunes Cinema Eight	4501 N. Kings Hwy., P.O. Box 1388	Myrtle Beach	SC	29577	8	570
Carmike Briarcliffe Cinema Six	Hwy 17 N. #10177, Briarcliffe Mall 77A	N. Myrtle Beach	SC	29582	10	570
Carmike Camelot	2016 Columbia Rd, K-Mart Shop. Ctr.	Orangeburg	SC	29116	4	546
Carmike Cinema	2150 Cherry Rd., P.O. Box 11911	Rock Hill	SC	29731	7	517
Carmike	1985 E. Main St., MR #150	Spartanburg	SC	29307	7	567
Carmike Wynnsong	1640 John B White, Sr. Blvd.	Spartanburg	SC	29301	7	567
Carmike Movies	1016 Broad St.	Sumter	SC	29151	3	546
Carmike	3315 6th Ave. SE, Ste. 4	Aberdeen	SD	57401	9	725
Carmike	230 Knollwood Dr., P.O. Box 3418	Rapid City	SD	57709	7	764
Carmike Rushmore	350 East Disk Dr., P.O. Box 3418	Rapid City	SD	57709	7	764
Carmike	3404 Gateway Blvd., P.O. Box 90310	Sioux Falls	SD	57105	7	725
Carmike Yankton Mall	2101 Broadway Ave., Ste. 5	Yankton	SD	57078	5	725
Carmike Bell Forge	5400 Bell Forge Ln. E.	Antioch	TN	37013	10	659
Carmike Hickory	901 Bell Rd.	Antioch	TN	37011	8	659
Carmike Plaza	1436 Decatur Pike, Athens Shp Ctr.	Athens	TN	37303	2	575
Carmike Bijou	215 Broad St.	Chattanooga	TN	37402	7	575
Carmike Wynnsong	2210 Gunbarrel Rd., P.O. Box 28061	Chattanooga	TN	37424	10	575
Carmike	1955 Madison St., P.O. Box 428	Clarksville	TN	37040	8	659
Carmike Cinema 5	2801 Guthrie Hwy., P.O. Box 428	Clarksville	TN	37040	5	659
Carmike	200 Stuart Rd., P.O. Box 3514	Cleveland	TN	37320	4	575
Carmike Village	Village Shopping Center, P.O. Box 3514	Cleveland	TN	37320	2	575
Carmike Highland	1181 S. Jefferson, P.O. Box 97	Cookeville	TN	38503	10	659
Carmike Capri	Woodmere Mall, Hwy. 127, P.O. Box 157	Crossville	TN	38557	2	557
Carmike	710 US Hwy 51 Bypass W, PMB 600	Dyersburg	TN	38024	9	640
Carmike Thoroughbred	633 Frazier Dr., P.O. Box 682261	Franklin	TN	37068	20	659
Carmike Rivergate	800 Two Mille Pkwy., P.O. Box 229.	Goodlettsville	TN	37070	8	659
Carmike Capri	11 East By-pass, P.O. Box 700	Greenville	TN	37744	2	531
Carmike Northgate	622 Northgate Mall, P.O. Box 289	Hixson	TN	37343	8	575
Carmike Johnson City	1805 N. Roan St.	Johnson City	TN	37601	14	531
Carmike	5020 Millertown Pike, P.O. Box 27408	Knoxville	TN	37917	10	557
Carmike Movies	175 N. Seven Oaks Dr., Bldg. 300	Knoxville	TN	37922	7	557
Carmike Wynnsong	200 North Peters Rd.	Knoxville	TN	37923	16	557
Carmike Movies	2140 Jacksboro Pike.	Lafollette	TN	37766	2	557
Carmike Martin	1447 W. Main St.	Lebanon	TN	37087	3	659
Carmike Foothills	507 Foothills Plaza	Maryville	TN	37801	12	557
Carmike College Square	2250 E. Morris Blvd., P.O. Box 1475	Morristown	TN	37816	9	557
Carmike Wynnsong	2626 Cason Square Blvd.	Murfreesboro	TN	37133	16	659
Carmike Bellevue	120 Belle Forest Circle	Nashville	TN	37221	8	659
Carmike Wynnsong	721 Myatt Dr.	Nashville	TN	37115	10	659
Carmike Oneida Cinema	Hwy 27 N., P.O. Box 4668	Oneida	TN	37841	3	557
Carmike Cinema	718 S. Main St.	Springfield	TN	37172	1	659
Carmike Park Central	3234 S. Clack St.	Abilene	TX	79606	6	662
Carmike	3003 South Expressway #281, P.O. Box 3430	Edinburg	TX	78539	20	636

755

Theatre	Address	City	State	Zip	Screens	DMA
Carmike	9840 Gateway Blvd. N.	El Paso	TX	79924	16	765
Carmike	201 Tall Pines Rd., P.O. Box 9187	Longview	TX	75608	10	709
Carmike Northloop	2531 Judson Rd., P.O. Box 9187	Longview	TX	75606	6	709
Carmike Angelina	3027 John Reddit Dr., P.O. Box 1408	Lufkin	TX	75902	2	709
Carmike Cinema	4600 S. Medford, Lufkin Mall, P.O. Box 1408	Lufkin	TX	75901	4	709
Carmike Town Square	405 N. Timberland Dr.	Lufkin	TX	75901	4	709
Carmike	3801 N. St, Northview Plz. Shop. Ctr.	Nacogdoches	TX	75961	6	709
Carmike Pines Theatre	340 N. 4th St., P.O. Box 1026	Silsbee	TX	77656	1	692
Carmike Century City	4105 Maplewood	Wichita Falls	TX	76308	6	627
Carmike Sikes	238 Sikes Cntr, 3111 Midwestern Pkwy.	Wichita Falls	TX	76308	10	627
Carmike Wynnsong	4925 N. Edgewood Dr.	Provo	UT	84604	12	770
Carmike	1600 West Fox Park Dr.	West Jordan	UT	84088	12	770
Carmike HW Connection	3217 South Decker Lake Dr.	West Valley City	UT	84119	15	770
Carmike	1803 Seminole Trail, P.O. Box 8023	Charlottesville	VA	22901	6	584
Carmike Plaza	2905 Riverside Dr., P.O. Box 1476	Danville	VA	24543	2	573
Carmike	801 Lakeside Dr., P.O. Box 10033	Lynchburg	VA	24506	8	573
Carmike River Ridge	3405 Candlers Mt. Rd., F315 River Ridge Mall	Lynchburg	VA	24502	4	573
Carmike	1100 Alverser Dr., P.O. Box 1185.	Midlothian	VA	23113	10	556
Carmike	4494 Electric Rd. SW	Roanoke	VA	24014	10	573
Carmike Valley	1700 Apperson Dr.	Salem	VA	24153	8	573
Carmike Williamsburg X'ing	5251 John Tyler Hwy. Ste. 13, P.O. Box 2978	Williamsburg	VA	23187	7	544
Carmike Apple Blossom Six	1850 Apple Blossom Dr., Apple Blossom Mall	Winchester	VA	22601	6	511
Carmike Cinema Center	601 E. Jubal Early Dr.	Winchester	VA	22601	6	511
Carmike	1331 Center Park Way	Kennewick	WA	99336	12	810
Carmike Oakwood	4800 Golf Rd. #4.	Eau Claire	WI	54701	12	702
Carmike Valley Theatre	4400 Hwy. 16	Lacrosse	WI	54603	6	702
Carmike Huntington Mall	700 Huntington Mall, P.O. Box 4121.	Barboursville	WV	25504	6	564
Carmike Cinema	Mercer Mall, P.O. Box 7084	Bluefield	WV	24701	8	559
Carmike Meadowbrook	2205 Meadowbrook Mall	Bridgeport	WV	26330	6	598
Carmike Mall	9540 Mall Rd.	Morgantown	WV	26505	8	508
Carmike Cole Square	517 Cole Square Shop. Ctr.	Cheyenne	WY	82001	3	767
Carmike Frontier	1400 Dell Range Blvd.	Cheyenne	WY	82009	6	759

CENTURY THEATRES

79 theatres, 876 screens.
150 Pelican Way, San Rafael, CA 94901. (415) 448-8400. FAX: (415) 448-8358. www.centurytheatres.com
CEO
Raymond W. Syufy
PRESIDENT
Joseph Syufy
COO
David Shesgreen
CFO
Michael Dittmann
EXECUTIVE V.P., BUSINESS AFFAIRS
Mike Plymesser
SENIOR V.P., OPERATIONS
William Hulme
SENIOR V.P., BUSINESS AFFAIRS
Andrew McCullough
SENIOR V.P., FILM
Robert Lenihan
SENIOR V.P., CORPORATE ANALYSIS
Robert McCleskey
SENIOR V.P., CORPORATE DEVELOPMENT
Victor Castillo
V.P., HUMAN RESOURCES
Christi Reddy
V.P., MARKETING
Nancy M. Klasky
V.P., CONSTRUCTION
Blair Walker
V.P.'s, CONCESSIONS
Lisa Rahn
Bob Shimmin
V.P., FACILITIES & PROJECTION
Phil Hacker
V.P., PURCHASING
Chris Duffie
V.P., INFORMATION SERVICES
Damian Wardle

THEATRES

Theatre	Address	City	State	Zip	Screens	DMA
Century 16	301 E. 36th Ave.	Anchorage	AK	99503	16	743
Glendale Drive-In	5650 N. 55th Ave.	Glendale	AZ	85301	9	753
Scottsdale 6 Drive-In	8101 E. Mckellips	Scottsdale	AZ	85256	6	753
Century Park 16	1055 W. Grant Rd.	Tucson	AZ	85705	16	789
Century 20 El Con	3601 E. Broadway	Tucson	AZ	85716	20	789
Century Gateway 12	770 N. Kolb Rd.	Tucson	AZ	85710	12	789
Century 20 Park Place	5870 E. Broadway Blvd.	Tucson	AZ	85711	20	789
Hyatt Cinema 3	1304 Bayshore Hwy	Burlingame	CA	94010	3	807
Solano Drive-In.	1611 Solano Way	Concord	CA	94520	2	807
Century Cinema	41 Tamal Vista Blvd.	Corte Madera	CA	94925	1	807
Century 20 Daly City	1901 Junipero Serra Blvd.	Daly City	CA	94015	20	807
Century 16 Laguna	9349 Big Horn Blvd.	Elk Grove	CA	95758	16	862
Century 14 Folsom	261 Iron Point Rd.	Folsom	CA	95630	14	862
Cinedome 8 East	39153 Fremont Dr.	Fremont	CA	94538	8	807
Century Larkspur Landing	500 Larkspur Landing Cir.	Larkspur	CA	94925	4	807
CineArts at Sequoia	25 Throckmorton Ave.	Mill Valley	CA	94941	2	807
Century 20 Great Mall	1010 Great Mall Dr.	Milpitas	CA	95035	20	807
Century Galaxy 6 Monterey	280 Del Monte Ctr.	Monterey	CA	93940	6	828
Century Cinema 16	1500 N. Shoreline Blvd.	Mountain View	CA	94043	16	807
Cinedome 8	825 Pearl St.	Napa	CA	94559	8	807
Cinedome 7 West	6000 New Park Mall	Newark	CA	94560	7	807

Theatre	Address	City	State	Zip	Screens	DMA
Century 8	12827 Victory Blvd.	N. Hollywood	CA	91606	8	803
Century Rowland Plaza	44 Rowland Way	Novato	CA	94945	8	807
Century Stadium 25	1701 W. Katella Ave.	Orange	CA	92868	25	803
CineArts at Palo Alto Square	3000 El Camino Real, Bldg. 6	Palo Alto	CA	94506	2	807
CineArts at Pleasant Hill 5	2314 Monument Blvd.	Pleasant Hill	CA	94523	5	807
Century 16 Downtown	125 Crescent Dr.	Pleasant Hill	CA	94523	16	807
Century Theatres @ The River	71800 Hwy. 111	Rancho Mirage	CA	92777	12	804
Century Park 12	557 E. Bayshore	Redwood City	CA	94063	12	807
Century 16 Hilltop in Richmond	3200 Klose Way	Richmond	CA	94523	16	807
Century 14 Roseville	1555 Eureka	Roseville	CA	95661	14	862
Sacramento Drive-In	9616 Oates Dr.	Sacramento	CA	95827	6	862
Century Stadium 14	1590 Ethan Way	Sacramento	CA	95825	12	862
Century Downtown Plaza 7	445 Downtown Plaza	Sacramento	CA	95814	7	862
Century 16 Greenback Ln.	6233 Garfield Ave.	Sacramento	CA	95841	16	862
Century 14 Northridge	350 Northridge Shopping Ctr.	Salinas	CA	93906	14	828
Century Park 7	10 Simas St	Salinas	CA	93901	7	828
Empire Cinema	85 W. Portal Ave.	San Francisco	CA	94127	3	807
Presidio	2340 Chestnut St.	San Francisco	CA	94123	1	807
Century Plaza 10	410 Noor Ave.	S. San Francisco	CA	94080	10	807
Capitol Drive-In	3630 Hillcap Ave.	San Jose	CA	95136	6	807
Century Capitol 16	3690 Hillcap Ave.	San Jose	CA	95136	16	807
Century Berryessa	1155 N. Capitol Ave.	San Jose	CA	95132	10	807
Century 21	3161 Olsen Dr.	San Jose	CA	95117	1	807
Century 22	3162 Olsen Ave.	San Jose	CA	95117	3	807
Century 23	3164 Olsen Ave.	San Jose	CA	95117	2	807
Century 24	741 Winchester Blvd.	San Jose	CA	95129	2	807
Century 25	1694 Saratoga Ave.	San Jose	CA	95117	2	807
Century 16 BayFair Mall	350 Bayfair Shopping Ctr.	San Leandro	CA	94578	16	807
Century 12 Downtown	320 E. 2nd Ave.	San Mateo	CA	94401	12	807
Century Northgate	7000 Northgate Dr.	San Rafael	CA	94903	15	807
Century Regency	280 Smith Ranch Rd.	San Rafael	CA	94903	6	807
CineArts at Marin	101 Caledonia	Sausalito	CA	94965	3	807
Century 25	32100 Union Landing Rd.	Union City	CA	94587	25	807
Century 14	109 Plaza Dr., Gateway Plaza Shopping Cntr.	Vallejo	CA	94591	14	807
Century Stadium 16	2875 Elba St.	Ventura	CA	93003	16	803
Century 10 Downtown	555 E. Main St.	Ventura	CA	93001	10	803
Century 14 Downtown	1201 Locust St.	Walnut Creek	CA	94596	14	807
Century 16	14300 E. Alameda Ave.	Aurora	CO	80012	16	751
Century 12 Evanston	1715 Maple Ave.	Evanston	IL	60201	12	602
CineArts 6 Evanston	1715 Maple Ave.	Evanston	IL	60201	6	602
Century 14 Downtown	100 Central Ave., SW	Albuquerque	NM	87102	14	790
Century Rio 24	4901 Pan American Fwy.	Albuquerque	NM	87109	24	790
Cinedome 12	851 So. Boulder Hwy.	Henderson	NV	89015	12	839
Las Vegas Drive-In	4150 W. Carey Ave.	Las Vegas	NV	89032	5	839
Century 18 Sam's Town	5111 Boulder Hwy.	Las Vegas	NV	89122	18	839
Century Stadium 16 Rancho Santa Fe	5101 N. Rainbow Dr.	Las Vegas	NV	89130	16	839
Century 16 Suncoast	9090 Alta Dr.	Las Vegas	NV	89144	16	839
Century Orleans 12	4500 W. Tropicana Blvd.	Las Vegas	NV	89103	12	839
Century 16 Park Lane	210 E. Plum Lane	Reno	NV	89502	16	811
Century 12 Riverside	11 N. Sierra St	Reno	NV	89501	12	811
Century 14 Sparks	1250 Victorian Ave	Sparks	NV	89431	14	811
El Rancho Drive-In	555 El Rancho Dr.	Sparks	NV	89431	4	811
Century 16 Eastport Plaza	4040 S.E. 82nd Ave.	Portland	OR	97266	16	820
Century Stadium 14	2400 S. Carolyn	Sioux Falls	SD	57106	14	725
Century 12 Abilene	3818 John Knox Dr.	Abilene	TX	79606	12	662
Century 16	6685 S. Padre Island Dr.	Corpus Christi	TX	78412	16	600
Century 12	4221 Preston Smith Rd.	Odessa	TX	79762	12	633
Century 16	125 E. 3300	Salt Lake City	UT	84115	16	770

CHAKERES THEATRES

18 theatres, 59 screens.
222 N. Murray St., Box 1200, Springfield, OH 45501. (937) 323-6447. FAX: (937) 325-1100.
PRESIDENT & CEO
Philip H. Chakeres
VICE PRESIDENTS
Harry N. Chakeres
Valerie C. Baker
DIRECTOR OF ADVERTISING
Paul Ramsey
FILM BUYER
Fred Schweitzer
COMPTROLLER
Elden L. Paden

THEATRES

Theatre	Address	City	State	Zip	Screens	DMA
Chakeres Franklin Square 6	161 Franklin Square Shopping Ctr.	Frankfort	KY	40604	6	541
Chakeres Brighton Park	114 Brighton Park Blvd.	Frankfort	KY	40603	2	541
Chakeres University Cinema	159 E. Main St.	Morehead	KY	40351	1	541
Chakeres Bellefontaine Cinema 8	888 E. Sandusky St	Bellefontaine	OH	43311	8	542
Chakeres Celina 5	116 N. Main St.	Celina	OH	45822	5	542
Chakeres Lake Drive-In	8477 State Rte. 703	Celina	OH	45822	1	542
Chakeres Melody 49 Drive-In	State Rte. 49.	Dayton	OH	45322	2	542
Chakeres Kettering Cinema 2	1441 E. Dorothy Ln.	Dayton	OH	45429	2	542
Chakeres Skyborn Drive-In	Rte. 235 & Haddix Rd.	Fairborn	OH	45324	1	542
Chakeres Scioto Breeze Drive-In	State Rte. 23.	Lucasville	OH	45648	2	564
Chakeres Park Layne Drive-In	2550 S. Dayton-Lakeview Rd.	New Carlisle	OH	45344	1	542
Chakeres Sidney 3	101 W. Poplar	Sidney	OH	45365	3	542
Chakeres Melody Cruise-In	4025 E. National Rd.	Springfield	OH	45505	2	542
Chakeres Upper Valley 5	1475 Upper Valley Pike	Springfield	OH	45504	5	542
Chakeres Cinema 10	3115 E. National Rd.	Springfield	OH	45505	10	542
Chakeres Urbana 1 & 2	216 S. Main St.	Urbana	OH	43078	2	542
Chakeres Wilmington Plaza 5	1276 Rombach Ave.	Wilmington	OH	45177	5	515
Chakeres Wilmington Drive-In	1129 N. Rte. 134.	Wilmington	OH	45177	1	515

CINEMA CENTER

5 theatres, 47 screens.
502 S. Market St., Millersburg, PA 17061. (717) 692-4744. FAX: (717) 692-3073. www.cinemacenter.com
PRESIDENT & OWNER
Marvin R. Troutman
EXECUTIVE V.P.
Van Troutman
V.P., CONCESSIONS & MARKETING
Gina Troutman DiSanto
V.P., OPERATIONS & MARKETING
Trudy Withers
FILM BUYER
Al Milgram

THEATRES

Theatre	Address	City	State	Zip	Screens	DMA
Cinema Center of Bloomsburg	1879 Columbia Ave.	Bloomsburg	PA	17815	12	577
Cinema Center of Palmyra	2 N. Londonderry Sq.	Palmyra	PA	17078	12	566
Cinema Center of Selinsgrove	Susquehanna Valley Mall, Ste. T1	Selinsgrove	PA	17870	12	
Cinema Center at Fairgrounds Square	3050 N. Fifth St. Hwy., Ste. A1	Reading	PA	19605	10	504
Sky-Vu Drive-In	Rte. 25	Gratz	PA	17030	1	

CINEMA ENTERTAINMENT CORP.

32 theatres, 232 screens.
Box 1126, St. Cloud, MN 56302. (320) 251-9131. FAX: (320) 251-1003.
PRESIDENT
Robert Ross
VICE PRESIDENT
Tony Tillemans
V.P., FINANCE
Tony Ross
SECRETARY
Dave Ross
DIRECTOR, FILM BUYER & MARKETING
Dwight Gunderson
OPERATIONS
Andy Bergstrom
Greg Carter
Roger Hansen

THEATRES

Theatre	Address	City	State	Zip	Screens	DMA
Mall 8	550 S. Gear Ave., Ste. 3	Burlington	IA	52601	8	682
Cinema 4	6301 University Ave.	Cedar Falls	IA	50613	4	637
Capre 4	218 6th Ave.	Clinton	IA	52732	4	682
Coral Ridge 10	1451 Coral Ridge Ave.	Coralville	IA	52241	10	637
Fort 8	1417 Central Ave.	Ft. Dodge	IA	50501	8	679
Campus III	201 S. Clinton	Iowa City	IA	52240	3	637
Cinema VI	1602 Sycamore St.	Iowa City	IA	52240	6	637
Cinema V Mason City	100 S. Federal	Mason City	IA	50401	5	611
Cinema West 8	4710 4th St. S.W.	Mason City	IA	50401	8	611
Capri V	229 E. Main St.	Ottumwa	IA	52501	5	631
Crossroads 12	2450 Crossroads Blvd.	Waterloo	IA	50702	12	637
Mall Cinema 7	2510 Bridge Ave.	Albert Lea	MN	56007	7	611
Amigo 9	5284 Theatre Ln.	Bemidji	MN	56601	9	613
Cinema 6	320 Minnesota Ave.	Breckenridge	MN	56520	6	724
Cinema 6	200 Western Ave.	Faribault	MN	55021	6	613
Lakes 10	4351 Stebner Rd.	Hermantown	MN	55811	10	676
Cinema 8	4191 Haines Rd.	Hermantown	MN	55811	8	676
Marshall 6	230 W. Lyon	Marshall	MN	56258	6	613
Safari 7	925 S. 30th Ave.	Moorhead	MN	56560	7	724
Cinema 6	7 S. Enterprise Dr.	Mountain Iron	MN	55768	6	676
Parkwood 18	1821 W. Division St.	Waite Park	MN	56387	18	613
Crossroads 6	230 N.E. 3rd Ave.	Waite Park	MN	56387	6	613
Winona 7	70 W. 2nd St.	Winona	MN	55987	7	702
Century 10	3931 9th Ave. S.W.	Fargo	ND	58103	10	724
West Acres 14	4101 17th Ave. S.W.	Fargo	ND	58103	14	724
Center 6	3100 23rd St.	Columbus	NE	68601	6	652
World 2	2318 Central Ave.	Kearney	NE	68847	2	722
Kearney Drive-In	2813 Ave. N.	Kearney	NE	68847	1	722
Norfolk 7	120 S. 3rd.	Norfolk	NE	68701	7	624
Cinema 9	1920 Crestview Dr. #9	Hudson	WI	54016	9	613
Lake 7	1769 County Highway S.	Rice Lake	WI	54868	7	613
Superior 7	69 N. 28th St.	Superior	WI	54880	7	676

CINEMARK USA, INC.

189 U.S. theatres, 2,223 U.S. screens; Foreign holdings: 93 theatres, 826 screens; TOTAL: 282 theatres, 3,049 screens.
3900 Dallas Pkwy., Ste. 500, Plano, TX 75093. (972) 665-1000. FAX: (972) 665-1004. www.cinemark.com
CHAIRMAN & CEO
Lee Roy Mitchell
CFO
Robert Copple
PRESIDENT
Alan Stock
EXECUTIVE V.P.
Tandy Mitchell
SENIOR V.P., OPERATIONS
Robert Carmony
V.P., GENERAL COUNSEL
Mike Cavalier
V.P., PURCHASING
Walter Hebert

Theatre	Address	City	State	Zip	Screens	DMA

V.P., MARKETING & COMMUNICATIONS
Terrell Falk
V.P., CONSTRUCTION
Don Harton
V.P., REAL ESTATE
Margaret Richards
CTO
Jason Rogers
DIRECTOR, CONCESSIONS
Maria Angles

CINEMARK INTERNATIONAL
PRESIDENT
Tim Warner
V.P., HEAD FILM BUYER
Ken Higgins
V.P., CONSTRUCTION
Juan Maldonado
V.P., OPERATIONS
Steve Zuehlke
DIRECTOR, ADVERTISING & MARKETING
James Meredith
V.P. & DIRECTOR, REAL ESTATE
John Hathaway

THEATRES

Theatre	Address	City	State	Zip	Screens	DMA
Tinseltown	17314 I-30	Benton	AR	72015	14	693
Cinemark 6	HWY 65 @ I-40	Conway	AR	72032	6	693
Tandy Movies	4188 E. McCain	Little Rock	AR	72117	10	693
Movies 4	4055 Stockton Hill Rd.	Kingman	AZ	86401	4	753
Cinemark Sierra Vista	2175 El Mercado Loop	Sierra Vista	AZ	85635	10	789
Movies 10	34491 Date Palm Dr.	Cathedral City	CA	92234	10	804
Tinseltown 14	801 E. Ave.	Chico	CA	95926	14	868
Cinemark Movies 8- Chino	5546 Philadelphia St.	Chino	CA	91710	8	803
Blackhawk	4175 Blackhawk Plaza Cir.	Danville	CA	94526	7	807
Movies	136 N. 11th Ave.	Hanford	CA	93230	4	866
Movies 8 Hanford Mall	1669 W. Lacey Blvd.	Hanford	CA	93230	8	866
Movies 12 Lancaster	44790 Valley Central Way	Lancaster	CA	93534	12	803
Movies 1-4	43821 15th St.	Lancaster	CA	93534	4	803
Cinemark 22	2600 W. Ave. I	Lancaster	CA	93536	22	803
Movies 8 Palmdale	2210 Palmdale Blvd.	Palmdale	CA	93550	8	803
Movies 10	1247 W. Ave P	Palmdale	CA	93551	10	803
Movies 8	359 Park Marina Cir.	Redding	CA	96001	8	868
Movies 10	980 Old Alturas Rd.	Redding	CA	96003	10	868
Movies 14	3300 N. Naglee Rd.	Tracy	CA	95376	14	862
Cinemark Victor Valley 10	14470 Bear Valley Rd.	Victorville	CA	92392	10	803
Movies 10	12353 Mariposa Rd.	Victorville	CA	92392	10	803
County Fair Movies 5	1579 A E. St.	Woodland	CA	95776	5	862
Yuba City 8	1410 Whyler Rd.	Yuba City	CA	95993	8	862
Cinemark Carefree Circle	3305 Cinema Point	Colorado Springs	CO	80922	16	752
Tinseltown USA	1545 E. Cheyenne Mountain Blvd.	Colorado Springs	CO	80906	20	752
Tiffany Plaza Movies 6	7400 E. Hampden Ave.	Denver	CO	80231	6	751
Cinemark At Fort Collins	4721 S. Timberline Rd.	Fort Collins	CO	80525	16	751
Tinseltown Pueblo	4140 N. Frwy	Pueblo	CO	81008	14	752
Movies 10	1796 W. Newport Pike	Wilmington	DE	19804	10	504
Tinseltown USA	4535 Southside Blvd.	Jacksonville	FL	32216	20	561
Festival Bay	5150 Orlando Dr.	Orlando	FL	32819	20	534
Movies 8	2810 Sharer #31	Tallahassee	FL	32303	8	530
Movies 10	157 Banks Station	Fayetteville	GA	30214	10	524
Tinseltown	134 Pavilion Pkwy.	Fayetteville	GA	30214	17	524
Movies 12	1317 Buckeye Ave.	Ames	IA	50010	12	679
Varsity II	2412 Lincoln	Ames	IA	50010	2	679
North Grand 5	2801 Grand Ave.	Ames	IA	50010	5	679
Movies 10	1600 N. State, Rte. 50	Bourbonnais	IL	60914	10	602
Movies 8	3101 Hennepin Rd.	Joliet	IL	60435	8	602
Movies 10	2601 Plainfield Rd.	Joliet	IL	60435	10	602
Cinemark 10	1001 W. North Ave.	Melrose Park	IL	60160	10	602
Tinseltown	320 S. Lincoln Way	North Aurora	IL	60542	17	602
Cinemark at Seven Bridges	6500 Rte. 53	Woodridge	IL	60517	17	602
Greentree	717 State Rd. 141	Clarksville	IN	47129	4	529
Greentree	757 A State Rd. 131	Clarksville	IN	47129	10	529
Greenwood	1848 E. Stop 13 Rd.	Indianapolis	IN	46227	8	527
Washington	10455 E. Washington	Indianapolis	IN	46229	8	527
University Park 6	6424 Grape Rd.	Mishawaka	IN	46545	6	588
Movies 14	910 W. Edison.	Mishawaka	IN	46545	14	588
Cinemark -Merriam	5500 Antioch	Merriam	KS	66202	20	616
Town Cinema	400 Winchester Ave.	Ashland	KY	41101	10	564
Man O'war Movies 8	133 N. Locust Hill Dr.	Lexington	KY	40509	8	541
Lexington Green Movies	200 Lexington Green Cir.	Lexington	KY	40503	8	541
Movies 10	425 Codell Dr.	Lexington	KY	40509	10	541
Tinseltown	4400 Towne Center Dr.	Louisville	KY	40241	19	529
Kentucky Oaks	5161 Hinkleville Rd.	Paducah	KY	42001	12	632
Richmond Mall	404 Richmond Mall	Richmond	KY	40475	8	541
Tinseltown	10955 N. Mall Dr.	Baton Rouge	LA	70810	10	716
Cinema 10	4700 Milhaven Rd.	Monroe	LA	71203	10	628
Tinseltown	8400 Millicent Way	Shreveport	LA	71105	17	612
Tinseltown USA	220 Blanchard St.	West Monroe	LA	71291	17	628
Hampshire Mall 12	367 Russell St.	Hadley	MA	1035	12	543
Cinemark 20	3728 Rivertown Pkwy	Grandville	MI	49418	20	563
Movies 16	28600 Dequindre Rd.	Warren	MI	48092	16	505
Movies 8	1850 Adams St.	Mankato	MN	56001	8	737
The Palace Cinemark 14	500 Nichols Rd.	Kansas City	MO	64112	14	616
Cinemark 16	15171 Community Rd.	Gulfport	MS	39503	16	746

Theatre	Address	City	State	Zip	Screens	DMA
Tinseltown USA	411 Riverwind Dr.	Pearl	MS	39208	17	718
Movies 8	1001 Barnes Crossing Rd.	Tupelo	MS	38804	8	673
Brassfield Cinema	2101 New Garden Rd.	Greensboro	NC	27410	10	518
Movies 10.	9508 Northeast Ct	Matthews	NC.	28105	10	517
Tinseltown USA	305 Faith Rd.	Salisbury	NC.	28146	14	517
Movies 8	3205 L St.	Omaha	NE.	68107	8	652
Movies 16.	711 Evesham, Lionshead Plaza	Somerdale	NJ	8083	16	504
Movies 8	4591 San Mateo	Albuquerque	NM	87109	8	790
Movies West	9201 Coors Rd.	Albuquerque	NM	87114	8	790
Tinseltown	2291 Buffalo Rd.	Rochester	NY	14624	17	538
Movies 10.	2613 W. Henrietta Rd.	West Brighton	NY.	14623	10	538
Carnation Cinema	2500 W. State St.	Alliance	OH	44601	5	510
Tinseltown USA	7401 Market St.	Boardman	OH	44512	7	536
Cinema 5	1234 N. Mall St.	Bowling Green	OH	43402	5	547
Movies 4	3911 Everhard Rd.	Canton	OH	44709	4	510
Movie 12	2570 Bethel Rd.	Columbus	OH	43220	12	535
Movies 10.	5275 Westpointe Plaza Dr.	Columbus	OH	43228	10	535
Movies 16.	323 Stoneridge Lane.	Gahanna	OH	43240	16	535
Movies 12.	3773 Ridge Mill Dr.	Hillard	OH	43026	12	535
Cinemark 15.	8161 Macedonia Commons Blvd.	Macedonia	OH	44056	15	510
Cinema 10	498 N. Lexington-Springmill.	Mansfield	OH	44906	10	510
Movies 10.	6284 Dressler Rd.	North Canton	OH	44720	10	510
Tinseltown	4720 Mega St.	North Canton	OH	44720	15	510
Richland III	575 Stumbo Rd.	Ontario	OH	44906	3	510
Miami Valley	987 E. Ash St.	Piqua	OH	43536	6	542
Movies 10.	5500 Milan Rd.	Sandusky	OH	44870	10	510
Cinemark 24.	6001 Canal Rd.	Valley View	OH	44125	24	510
Movies 10.	27613 Chardon Rd.	Willoughby Hills	OH	44092	10	510
Movies 10.	4108 Burbank Rd.	Wooster.	OH	44691	10	510
Movies 8	469 Boardman/Poland Rd.	Youngstown	OH	44512	8	536
Colony Square	3535 N. Maple Ave.	Zanesville	OH	43701	10	596
North Hills	1106 J.A. Richardson Loop	Ada	OK.	74820	6	657
Cinema 8	3812 S. Elm Place	Broken Arrow.	OK.	74011	8	671
Tinseltown 20.	6001 N. M.L.K. Blvd.	Oklahoma City	OK.	73111	20	650
Crossroads Movies 8	7400 South pole Road	Oklahoma City	OK.	73149	8	650
Cinema 8	1112 E. Charles Page Blvd.	Sand Springs.	OK.	74063	8	671
Movies 8	6808 S. Memorial #310.	Tulsa	OK.	74133	8	671
The Tulsa by Cinemark	10802 E. 71st St.	Tulsa	OK.	74133	17	671
Tinseltown	651 Medford Ctr.	Medford	OR	97501	15	813
Movies 12.	2850 Gateway Mall	Springfield	OR	97477	12	801
Cinemark 17.	2900 Gateway.	Springfield	OR	97477	17	801
White City	7501 Crater Lake Hwy	White City	OR	97503	6	813
Movies 17.	1910 Rotunda Dr.	Erie	PA	16509	17	516
Millcreek Cinema	5800 Peast St., Millcreek Mall	Erie	PA	16509	6	516
Cinemark 20.	40 Glenmaura National Blvd.	Moosic	PA	18507	20	577
Movies 8	4488 Ladson Rd.	Summerville	SC	29485	8	519
Tinseltown	755 W. Main St	Oakridge	TN	37830	14	557
Cinemark 16.	9100 Canyon Dr.	Amarillo	TX	79119	16	634
Tinseltown	2815 E. Division St.	Arlington	TX.	76011	9	623
Athens Cinema 4	218 Wood St.	Athens	TX.	75751	4	623
Barton Creek	2224-B Walsh Tarlton Rd.	Austin	TX.	78746	10	635
Dollar Cinema 8	3407 Wells Branch Pkwy.	Austin	TX.	78728	8	635
Tinseltown	5501 IH 35	South Austin	TX.	78744	17	635
Tinseltown	3855 Interstate 10.	Beaumont	TX.	77705	15	692
Movies 10.	3471 Old Hwy 77	Brownsville	TX.	78520	10	636
Cinemark 16.	2370 N. Expressway	Brownsville	TX.	78521	16	636
Cinema 6	1643 W. Henderson.	Cleburne	TX.	76031	6	623
Movies 16.	1401 E. Bypass.	College Station	TX.	77845	16	625
Dollar Cinema	5858 S. Padre Island Dr.	Corpus Christi	TX.	78412	7	600
Tinseltown	5218 Silverberry	Corpus Christi	TX.	78416	16	600
Cinema IV	1803 W. 77th.	Corsicana	TX.	75110	4	623
Cinemark 17.	11819 Webb Chapel Rd.	Dallas	TX.	75234	17	623
Movies 8	2205 Ave. F	Del Rio	TX.	78840	8	641
Tinseltown	11855 Gateway Blvd.	East El Paso	TX.	79936	20	765
Movies 12.	7440 Remcon Circle	El Paso	TX.	79912	12	765
Hollywood USA	4040 S. Shiloh Rd.	Garland	TX.	75041	15	623
Movies 16.	220 Westchester Pkwy	Grand Prairie	TX.	75052	15	623
Tinseltown	911 State Hwy. 114.	Grapevine	TX.	76051	17	623
Movies 10.	629 N. 13th St.	Harlingen	TX.	78550	10	636
Cinemark	601 S. Expy. 83.	Harlingen	TX.	78550	16	636
Tinseltown	12920 N.W. Freeway.	Houston	TX.	77040	16	618
Tinseltown Westchase	3600 W. Sam Houston Pkwy.	Houston	TX.	77042	24	618
Tinseltown	11450 E. Fwy.	Jacinto City	TX.	77029	17	618
Cinemark 19.	1030 W. Grand Pkwy.	Katy	TX.	77449	19	618
Movies 14.	3250 W. Plesant Run Rd.	Lancaster	TX.	75146	14	623
Movies 12.	5412 San Bernardo.	Laredo.	TX.	78041	12	749
Movies 12.	2401 S. Stemmons #1356.	Lewisville.	TX.	75067	12	623
Cinemark 8.	420 Oak Bend Dr.	Lewisville.	TX.	75056	8	623
Movies 16.	5721 58th St.	Lubbock	TX.	79423	17	651
Tinseltown 17.	2535 82nd St.	Lubbock	TX.	79423	17	651
Movies 17.	100 W. Nolana Loop	McAllen	TX.	78504	17	636
Main Place	1800 S. 16th.	McAllen	TX.	78501	6	636
Movies 14.	1701 S. Central Expy.	McKinney	TX.	75069	14	623
Tinseltown	2422 E. Expy. 83.	Mission	TX.	78572	17	636
Movies 8	1225 N. E. Loop 286.	Paris	TX.	75460	8	623
Hollywood USA	2101 E. Beltway 8.	Pasadena	TX.	77503	20	618
Tinseltown	15436 FM 1825	Pflugerville	TX.	78660	20	635
Movies 8	500 N. Jackson.	Pharr	TX.	78577	8	636
Town Centre	1001 I-27 Hwy N. #70	Plainview	TX.	79072	6	651
Movies 10.	1818 Coit Rd.	Plano	TX.	75075	10	623
Tinseltown	3800 Dallas Pkwy.	Plano	TX.	75093	20	623
Cinemark 24.	7201 Central Expy.	Plano.	TX.	75025	24	623

Theatre	Address	City	State	Zip	Screens	DMA
Movies 8	7560 N.E. Loop 820	N. Richland Hills	TX	76180	8	623
Rockwall 8	497 I-30	Rockwall	TX	75032	8	623
Rosenberg 8	5101 Ave. H	Rosenberg	TX	77471	8	618
Movies 8	2132 N. Mays, Ste. 800	Round Rock	TX	78664	8	635
Tinseltown 14	4425 Sherwood Way	San Angelo	TX	76904	14	661
Dollar Movies	5063 Loop 410 N.W.	San Antonio	TX	78229	16	641
Movies 9	4100 New Braufels Ave.	San Antonio	TX	78223	9	641
Cinema 7	2510 Texoma Pkwy.	Sherman	TX	75090	7	657
Midway Movies	4800 Texoma Pkwy.	Sherman	TX	75090	5	657
Cinema 6	2900 W. Washington	Stephenville	TX	76401	6	623
Movies 12	3912 Hampton Rd.	Texarkana	TX	75503	12	612
Movies 12	10000 Emmet F. Lowry Expy.	Texas City	TX	77591	12	618
Victoria Mall	7806 Navarro	Victoria	TX	77904	12	626
Cinema 18	20915 Gulf Fwy.	Webster	TX	77598	18	618
Movies 10	2113 W. Expy. 83.	Weslaco	TX	78596	10	636
Tinseltown	1600 Lake Robbins Dr.	Woodlands	TX	77380	17	618
Tinseltown	720 W. 1500 N.	Layton	UT	84041	17	770
Tinseltown	1010 Newgate Mall	Ogden	UT	84405	14	770
Village Cinema	1776 Park Ave.	Park City	UT	84060	3	770
Movies 8	2424 N. University Pkwy.	Provo	UT	84604	8	770
Cinemark 16	1200 Town Ctr. Blvd.	Provo	UT	84601	16	770
Movies 10	2227 S. Highland Dr.	Salt Lake City	UT	84106	10	770
Movies 9	9539 S. 7th St.	Sandy	UT	84070	9	770
Cinemark 24	7301 S. Jordon Landing	West Jordon	UT	84088	24	770
Valley Fair	3601 S. 2700 W.	West Valley City	UT	84119	9	770
Tinseltown	3004 Linden Dr.	Bristol	VA	24201	14	531
Movies 10	4300 Portsmouth Blvd.	Chesapeake	VA	23321	10	544
Movies 10	3700 Candlers Mountain Blvd.	Lynchburg	VA	24502	10	573
Cinemark at Military Circle	880 N. Military Hwy.	Norfolk	VA	23502	18	544
Tinseltown USA	7101 70th Ct.	Kenosha	WI	53142	14	617

CINEMA WEST THEATRES

10 theatres, 46 screens.
P.O. Box 750595, Petaluma, CA 94975. (707) 762-0990. FAX: (707) 762-3969. www.cinemawest.com
CONTACT
Scott Neff

THEATRES

Theatre	Address	City	State	Zip	Screens	DMA
Angels Theatre	1228 S. Main St.	Angels Camp	CA	95222	3	807
Clearlake Cinemas	3380 Washington St.	Clearlake	CA	95422	2	807
Clover Cinemas	121 E. First St.	Cloverdale	CA	95425	4	807
Fairfax Theatre	9 Broadway.	Fairfax	CA	94930	4	807
Fortuna Theatre	1241 Main St.	Fortuna	CA	95540	7	807
Los Banos Cinemas	San Luis Plaza	Los Banos	CA	93635	6	807
Sebastopol Cinemas	6868 McKinley St.	Sebastopol	CA	95472	9	807
Sonoma Cinemas	200 Siesta Way.	Sonoma	CA	95476	6	807
Tiburon Playhouse	40 Main St.	Tiburon	CA	94920	3	807
Noyo Theatre	57 E. Commerical St.	Willits	CA	95490	3	807

CITY CINEMAS

5 theatres, 22 screens.
189 2nd Ave., Ste. 2S, New York, NY 10003. (212) 871-6840. FAX: (212) 871-9093. www.angelikafilmcenter.com
CHAIRMAN
James J. Cotter
PRESIDENT & CEO
Robert Smerling
COO
Ellen M. Cotter

THEARES

Theatre	Address	City	State	Zip	Screens	DMA
Angelika Film Center	18 W. Houston St.	New York City	NY	10012	6	501
Cinema 1, 2 & 3	1001 3rd Ave.	New York City	NY	10022	3	501
East 86th St. Cinemas	210 E. 86th St.	New York City	NY	10028	4	501
Sutton 1 & 2	205 E. 57th St.	New York City	NY	10022	2	501
Village East Cinemas	181-189 2nd Ave.	New York City	NY	10003	7	501

CINEMAGIC THEATRES

5 theatres, 40 screens.
Midwest Theatres Corporation, 5255 E. River Rd., Ste. 201, Minneapolis, MN 55421-1026. (763) 572-8004 Ext. 107 & Ext. 110. FAX: (763) 572-8005.
www.cinemagictheatres.com
PRESIDENT, COO & FILM BUYER
Steven L. Tripp
CFO & BUSINESS DEVELOPMENT
Bryan J. Sieve
OFFICE MANAGER
Renee L. Strine

THEATRES

Theatre	Address	City	State	Zip	Screens	DMA
Great Lakes Cinema 7	1698 Exchange St.	Okoboji	IA	51355	7	624
CineMagic 7 Theatres	1301 18th Ave. N.W.	Austin	MN	55912	7	611
Century 7 Theatres	766 Century Ave.	Hutchinson	MN	55350	7	613
CineMagic Hollywood Stadium 12	2171 Superior Dr. N.W.	Rochester	MN	55901	12	611
CineMagic Stadium 7 Theatres	2521 Hwy. 25 N.	Menomonie	WI	54751	7	613

CINEMASTAR LUXURY THEATERS, INC.

4 theatres, 61 screens. 2 Mexican theatres, 21 screens. TOTAL: 6 theatres, 81 screens reported.
1949 Avenida Del Oro, Ste. 100, Oceanside, CA 92056. (760) 945-2500. FAX: (760) 945-2510. www.cinemastar.com
CHAIRMAN & CEO
Jack Crosby

Theatre	Address	City	State	Zip	Screens	DMA

CFO
Don Harnois
FILM BUYER
Allen Elrod
COO
Kim Zolna
DIRECTOR OF ADVERTISING & MARKETING
Dan Cahill
DIRECTOR OF INTERNATIONAL OPERATIONS
John Prock

THEATRES

Theatre	Address	City	State	Zip	Screens	DMA
CinemaStar Mission Marketplace 13	431 College Blvd.	Oceanside	CA	92054	13	825
CinemaStar Perris Plaza 10	1688 N. Perris Blvd.	Perris	CA	92571	10	803
CinemaStar Mission Grove 18	121 E. Alessandro	Riverside	CA	92508	18	803
CinemaStar Empire 20	450 N. E St.	San Bernardino	CA	92401	20	803

CLARK THEATRES

5 theatres, 12 screens.
P.O. Box 310570, Enterprise, AL 36331-0570. (334) 347-1129. FAX: (334) 347-8242.
OWNER
Mack Clark, Jr.
GENERAL MANAGER
Walter C. (Charlie) Andrews

THEATRES

Theatre	Address	City	State	Zip	Screens	DMA
Clark Theatre on the Square	Court Square	Andalusia	AL	36420	3	698
Clark Cinemas I & II	608 Boll Weevil Cir.	Enterprise	AL	36330	2	606
Clark Cinemas III & IV	621 Boll Weevil Cir.	Enterprise	AL	36330	2	606
College Cinemas I, II & III	501 Place Pl, Ste. 137	Enterprise	AL	36330	3	606
Clark Twin Cinemas	Hwy 231 & Andrews Ave.	Ozark	AL	36360	2	606

CLASSIC CINEMAS

12 theatres, 84 screens.
(A division of Tivoli Enterprises, Inc.) 603 Rogers St., Downers Grove, IL 60515-3773. (630) 968-1600. FAX: (630) 968-1626. www.classiccinemas.com
PRESIDENT
Willis Johnson
VICE PRESIDENT
Christopher Johnson
CORPORATE SECRETARY
Shirley Johnson
FILM BUYER
Lou Michael
MARKETING MANAGER
Mark Mazrimes

THEATRES

Theatre	Address	City	State	Zip	Screens	DMA
CC Cinema 12 Theatre	100 Besinger Dr.	Carpentersville	IL	60110	12	602
CC Tivoli Theatre	5021 Highland Ave.	Downers Grove	IL	60515	1	602
CC Elk Grove Theatre	1050 Town Ctr.	Elk Grove	IL	60007	6	602
CC York Theatre	150 N. York Rd.	Elmhurst	IL	60126	7	602
CC Fox Lake Theatre	115 Lakeland Plaza	Fox Lake	IL	60020	9	602
CC Lindo Theatre	115 S. Chicago Ave.	Freeport	IL	61032	6	610
CC Meadowview Theatre	55 Meadowview Ctr.	Kankakee	IL	60901	3	602
CC Paramount	213 N. Schuyler Ave.	Kankakee	IL	60901	5	602
CC Ogden 6 Theatre	1227 E. Ogden Ave.	Naperville	IL	60563	6	602
CC Lake Theatre	1022 Lake St.	Oak Park	IL	60301	7	602
CC Charlestowne 18	3740 E. Main St.	St. Charles	IL	60174	18	602
CC Woodstock Theatre	209 Main St.	Woodstock	IL	60098	4	602

CLEARVIEW CINEMA CORP.

55 theatres, 272 screens.
97 Main St., Chatham, NJ 07928 (908) 918-2000. FAX: (973) 377-4303. www.clearviewcinemas.com
SENIOR V.P. & GENERAL MANAGER
Morten Gotterup
V.P., THEATRE OPERATIONS
Doug Oines
DIRECTOR., FACILITIES
Bill Voeltz
V.P., FILM
Craig Zeltner
FILM BUYERS
Rosemarie Devery
Mary Shefford

THEATRES

Theatre	Address	City	State	Zip	Screens	DMA
Clearview Greenwich Cinemas	356 Greenwich Ave.	Greenwich	CT	06830	2	501
Clearview Middlebrook Galleria Cinema 10	1502 Rte. 35 South	Ocean Twnshp.	NJ	07712	10	501
Clearview Bergenfield Cinema 5	58 S. Washington Ave.	Bergenfield	NJ	07621	5	501
Clearview Bernardsville Cinema 3	5 Minebrook Rd., Rte. 202	Bernardsville	NJ	07924	3	501
Clearview Caldwell Cinema 4	317 Bloomfield Ave.	Caldwell	NJ	07006	4	501
Clearview Cinema 23/Cedar Grove	101 Pompton Ave.	Cedar Grove	NJ	07009	5	501
Clearview Chester Cinema 6	Chester Springs Shopping Ctr, 169 Rte. 206	Chester	NJ	07930	6	501
Clearview Allwood Cinema 6	96 Market St.	Clifton	NJ	07012	6	501
Clearview Closter Cinema 4	130 Closter Plaza	Closter	NJ	07624	4	501
Clearview Edison Cinemas	1655 Oak Tree Rd.	Edison	NJ	08818	8	501
Clearview Emerson Quad	344 Kinderkamack Rd.	Emerson	NJ	07630	4	501
Clearview Mansfield Cinema 15	1965 Rte. 57	Hackettstown	NJ	07840	14	501
Clearview Kinnelon 11	25 Kinnelon Rd.	Kinnelon	NJ	07405	11	501

Theatre	Address	City	State	Zip	Screens	DMA
Clearview Madison Cinema 4	14 Lincoln Pl.	Madison	NJ	07940	4	501
Clearview Strathmore Cinema 4	1055 Rte. 34	Aberdeen	NJ	07747	4	501
Clearview Millburn Cinemas	350 Millburn Ave.	Millburn	NJ	07041	4	501
Clearview Clairidge Cinemas	486 Bloomfield Ave.	Montclair	NJ	07042	6	501
Clearview Headquarters 10 Theatres	72 Headquarters Plaza	Morristown	NJ	07960	10	501
Clearview Parsippany Cinema 12	3165 Rte. 46	Parsippany	NJ	07054	12	501
Clearview Red Bank Cinemas	36 White St.	Red Bank	NJ	07701	2	501
Clearview Warner Quad	190 E. Ridgewood Ave.	Ridgewood	NJ	07450	4	501
Clearview Succasunna Cinema 10	21 Sunset Blvd.	Succasunna	NJ	07876	10	501
Clearview Beacon Hill 5	343 Springfield Ave.	Summit	NJ	07901	4	501
Clearview Tenafly Cinema 4	4 1/2 Railroad Ave.	Tenafly	NJ	07670	4	501
Clearview Bellevue Cinema 4	260 Bellevue Ave.	Upper Montclair	NJ	07043	4	501
Clearview Washington Twnshp Cinemas	249 Pascack Rd.	Washington Twnsp.	NJ	07675	3	501
Clearview Wayne Preakness Cinemas	Preakness Shop. Cntr.; Hamburg Tpke.	Wayne	NJ	07470	4	501
Clearview Woodbridge Cinemas	675 Rte. 1 South.	Iselin	NJ	08830	5	501
Clearview Babylon Cinemas	34 Main St.	Babylon	NY	11702	3	501
Clearview Grand Ave. Cinemas	1849 Grand Ave.	Baldwin	NY	11510	5	501
Clearview Bedford Playhouse	633 Old Post Rd.	Bedford	NY	10506	2	501
Clearview Bronxville Cinemas	84 Kraft Ave	Bronxville	NY	10708	3	501
Clearview Franklin Square Cinemas	989 Hempstead Tpke.	Franklin Square	NY	11010	6	501
Clearview Squire Cinemas	115 Middle Neck Rd.	Great Neck	NY	11022	7	501
Clearview Larchmont Playhouse	1975 Palmer Ave.	Larchmont	NY	10538	3	501
Clearview Mamaroneck Playhouse	243 Mamaroneck Ave.	Mamaroneck	NY	10543	4	501
Clearview Manhasset Cinemas	430 Plandome Rd.	Manhasset	NY	11030	3	501
Clearview Mt. Kisco Cinemas	144 Main St.	Mount Kisco	NY	10549	5	501
Clearview New City Cinema 6	202 S. Main St.	New City	NY	10956	6	501
Clearview Herricks Cinema 4	3324 Hillside Ave.	New Hyde Park	NY	11040	4	501
Clearview 59th St. East Cinema	239 E. 59th St.	New York	NY	10022	1	501
Clearview 62nd & Broadway	1871 Broadway	New York	NY	10023	1	501
Clearview Beekman	1254 Second Ave.	New York	NY	10021	1	501
Clearview Chelsea Cinemas	260 W. 23rd St.	New York	NY	10011	9	501
Clearview Chelsea West Cinemas	333 W. 23rd St.	New York	NY	10011	3	501
Clearview First & 62nd Cinemas	400 E. 62nd St.	New York	NY	10021	7	501
Clearview Metro Twin	2626 Broadway	New York	NY	10025	2	501
Clearview Ziegfeld	141 W. 54th St.	New York	NY	10019	1	501
Clearview Port Washington Cinemas	116 Main St.	Port Washington	NY	11050	7	501
Clearview Soundview Cinema	7-9 Soundview Market Place; Shore Rd.	Port Washington	NY	11050	6	501
Clearview Roslyn Cinemas	20 Tower Pl.	Roslyn	NY	11577	4	501
Clearview Rye Ridge Cinema	1 Rye Ridge Pl.	Rye Brook	NY	10573	2	501
Clearview Cinema 100	93 Knollwood Rd.	White Plains	NY	10607	4	501
Clearview Bala Theater	157 Bala Ave.	Bala Cynwyd	PA	19004	3	504
Clearview Anthony Wayne 5	109 W. Lancaster Ave	Wayne	PA	19087	5	504

CLEVELAND CINEMAS

6 theatres, 39 screens.
6200 SOM Center Rd., #C-20, Cleveland, OH 44139. (440) 349-3306. FAX: (440) 349-0210. www.clevelandcinemas.com

THEATRES

Theatre	Address	City	State	Zip	Screens	DMA
Austintown Movies	6000 Mahoning Ave.	Austintown	OH	44515	3	536
Hickory Ridge Cinemas	1055 Pearl Rd.	Brunswick	OH	44212	8	510
Cedar Lee Theatre	2163 Lee Rd.	Cleveland Heights	OH	44118	6	510
Shaker Square Cinemas	13116 Shaker Square	Cleveland	OH	44120	6	510
Tower City Cinemas	230 Huron Road	Cleveland	OH	44113	11	510
Parmatown Cinemas	8141 West Ridgewood Dr.	Parma	OH	44129	5	510

COBB THEATRES

5 theatres, 58 screens.
2100 A SouthBridge Pkwy., Ste. 325, Birmingham, AL 35209. (205) 802-7766. FAX: (205) 802-7771. www.cobbtheatres.com
CONTACT
Judy Sanders

THEATRES

Theatre	Address	City	State	Zip	Screens	DMA
Movies 4	1007 Hwy, 78 West	Jasper	AL	35501	4	630
Dolphin 19 Cinemas	11471 N.W. 12 St.	Miami	FL	33172	19	528
Miami Lakes 17 Cinemas	6711 Main St.	Miami Lakes	FL	33014	17	528
Roxy 10 Cinemas	1553 Palm Bay Rd.	Palm Bay	FL	32905	10	534
Parkway 8 Cinemas	6300 N. Lockwood Ridge Rd.	Sarasota	FL	34243	8	539
Grand 10 Cinemas	920 Spring Lake Sq. NW.	Winter Haven	FL	33881	10	539

COLORADO CINEMA HOLDINGS, LLC

10 theatres, 92 screens.
6696 S. Parker Rd., Aurora, CO 80016. (303) 766-7900. FAX: (303) 766-9865.
PRESIDENT & CEO
Haydn Silleck
V.P. & COO
Cliff Godfrey

THEATRES

Theatre	Address	City	State	Zip	Screens	DMA
Olde Town 14	5550 Wadsworth Blvd.	Arvada	CO	80002	14	751
Arapahoe Crossing 16	6696 S. Parker Rd.	Aurora	CO	80016	16	751
Basemar Twin	2490 Baseline Rd.	Boulder	CO	80305	2	751
Cherry Creek 8	3000 E. 1st Ave.	Denver	CO	80206	8	751
Bergen Park 7	1204 Bergen Pkwy.	Evergreen	CO	80439	7	751
Cinema Saver 6	2525 Worthington Cir.	Ft. Collins	CO	80526	6	751
Bowles Crossing 12	8035 W. Bowles Ave.	Littleton	CO	80123	12	751
Southwest Plaza 5	8501 W. Bowles Ave.	Littleton	CO	80123	5	751
Colony Square 12	1164 Dryer Rd.	Louisville	CO	80027	12	751
20 Mile Village 10	18625 E. StageRun.	Parker	CO	80134	10	751

Theatre	Address	City	State	Zip	Screens	DMA

COMING ATTRACTIONS, INC.

14 theatres, 90 screens.
1644 Ashland St., Ashland, OR 97520. (541) 488-1021. FAX: (541) 482-9290.
OWNER & CEO
John C. Schweiger
SENIOR V.P. & CFO
Larry McLennan
V.P. & GENERAL MANAGER
Don Immenschuh

THEATRES

Theatre	Address	City	State	Zip	Screens	DMA
Crescent City Cinemas	375 M St.	Crescent City	CA	95531	8	802
Mt. Shasta Cinemas	118 Morgan Way.	Mt. Shasta	CA	96067	6	868
Ashland Steel Cinemas	1644 Ashland St.	Ashland	OR	97520	6	813
Varsity Theatre	166 E. Main St.	Ashland	OR	97520	5	813
Astoria Gateway Cinemas	1875 Marine Dr.	Astoria	OR	97103	7	820
Egyptian	229 S. Broadway	Coos Bay	OR	97420	3	801
Movies Six Cinemas	1111 N.E. D St.	Grants Pass	OR	97526	6	813
Southgate Cinemas	1625 S.W. Ringuette St.	Grants Pass	OR	97527	4	813
Pelican Cinemas	2643 Biehn St.	Klamath Falls	OR	97601	10	813
McMinnville Cinemas	2725 N.E. Tanger Dr.	McMinnville	OR	97128	10	820
Pony Village Cinemas	1611 Virginia	North Bend	OR	97459	4	801
Harvard Cinemas	3161 W. Harvard Ave.	Roseburg	OR	97470	3	801
Roseburg Cinemas 7	1750 N.W. Hughwood	Roseburg	OR	97470	8	801
SouthShore Mall Cinemas	1017 South Boone St.	Aberdeen	WA	98520	10	819

CONSOLIDATED THEATRES

12 theatres, 109 screens.
(A subsidiary of Pacific Theatres) 1044 Auahi St., Honolulu, HI 96814. (808) 594-7034. FAX: (808) 594-7030.

THEATRES

Theatre	Address	City	State	Zip	Screens	DMA
Pearlridge West	98-1005 Moanalua Rd.	Aiea	HI	96701	16	744
Kahala	4211 Waialae Ave.	Honolulu	HI	96816	8	744
Koko Marina 8	7192 Kalanianaole Hwy.	Honolulu	HI	96825	8	744
Varsity Twins	1106 University Ave.	Honolulu	HI	96826	2	744
Victoria Ward 16 Cinemas	1020 Auahi St.	Honolulu	HI	96814	16	744
Kaahumanu	275 Kaahumanu St.	Kahului	HI	96732	6	744
Aikahi Twins	25 Kaneohe Bay Dr.	Kailua	HI	96734	2	744
Keauhou 7	78-6831 Alii Dr.	Kailua-Kona	HI	96740	7	744
Ko'olau Stadium 10	47-260 Hui Iwa St.	Kaneohe	HI	96744	10	744
Kapolei 16	890 Kamokila Blvd.	Kapolei	HI	96707	16	744
Kukui Mall 4	1819 S. Kihei Rd.	Kihei	HI	96753	4	744
Mililani 14	95-1249 Meheula Pkwy.	Mililani	HI	96825	14	744

CONSOLIDATED THEATRES

17 theatres, 226 screens.
5970 Fairview Rd., Ste. 600, Charlotte, NC 28210. (704) 554-1695. FAX: (704) 554-1696. www.consolidatedmovies.com
PRESIDENT & CEO
Herman A. Stone
CFO
Chuck Latham
COO
E. Casey Brock
V.P., THEATRE OPERATIONS
Dale Culeman
BOOKING
Ed Kershaw
DIRECTOR, MARKETING
Marie McClaflin

THEATRES

Theatre	Address	City	State	Zip	Screens	DMA
The Majestic	900 Ellsworth Dr. (Opens 4/04)	Silver Spring	MD	20910	20	511
Arboretum Stadium 12	8008 Providence Rd.	Charlotte	NC	28277	12	517
Crossroads 20	501 Caitboo Ave.	Cary	NC	27511	20	560
The Grande	3205 Northline Ave.	Greensboro	NC	27408	10	518
Park Terrace Cinema 6	4289 Park Rd.	Charlotte	NC	28209	6	517
Phillips Place Stadium 10	6911 Phillips Place Ct.	Charlotte	NC	28210	10	517
Raleigh Grande Cinema 16	4840 Grove Barton Rd.	Raleigh	NC	27613	16	560
Southpoint Cinema	8030 Renaissance Pkwy., Ste. 975	Durham	NC	27713	14	560
Union Square Cinema 8	1911 Dickerson Blvd.	Monroe	NC	28110	8	517
Cherrydale 16	3221 Pleasantburg Dr.	Greenville	SC	29609	16	567
Columbiana Grande 14	1250 Bower Pkwy.	Columbia	SC	29212	14	546
Manchester Cinema	1935 Cinema Dr.	Rock Hill	SC	29730	10	517
Palmetto Grande 16	Mt. Pleasant Towne Centre, 1319 Theater Dr.	Mt. Pleasant	SC	29464	16	519
Pastime Pavilion Cinema 8	929 N. Lake Dr.	Lexington	SC	29072	8	546
Commonwealth 20	5001 Commonwealth Centre Pkwy.	Midlothian	VA	23112	20	556
Harbour View Grande	5860 Harbour View Blvd.	Suffolk	VA	23435	16	544
Valley View Grande	4730 Valley View Blvd.	Roanoke	VA	24012	10	573

CROWN THEATRES

16 theatres, 170 screens.
64 N. Main St., South Norwalk, CT 06854. (203) 846-8800. FAX: (203) 846-9828.
PRESIDENT
Daniel M. Crown
V.P., OPERATIONS, CONCESSIONS & MARKETING
Jeremy Welman
FILM ACQUISITION
Chris Dugger
CONTROLLER
Catherine Nonnenmacher

Theatre	Address	City	State	Zip	Screens	DMA

DIRECTOR OF ADVERTISING
Steve Gould
DIRECTOR OF SPECIAL PROJECTS
Thomas Becker

THEATRES

Theatre	Address	City	State	Zip	Screens	DMA
Crown Plaza	2 Railroad Ave	Greenwich	CT	06830	3	501
Crown Royale	542 Westport Ave	Norwalk	CT	06851	6	501
Crown Sono Regent	64 N. Main St.	South Norwalk	CT	06854	8	501
Crown Majestic	118 Summer St.	Stamford	CT	06901	6	501
Crown Landmark Square	5 Landmark Sq.	Stamford	CT	06905	9	501
Crown Marquis	100 Quarry Rd.	Trumbull	CT	06611	16	501
Crown Palace	330 New Park Ave.	W. Hartford	CT	06106	17	533
Crown Abacoa	Abacoa Town Ctr., 4688 Main St.	Jupiter	FL	33458	16	548
Crown Grand	17355 N.W. 59th Ave.	Hialeah	FL	33015	18	528
Crown Village Crossing	7018 Carpenter Rd.	Skokie	IL	60077	18	602
Annapolis Harbour Center	2474 Solomons Island Rd.	Annapolis	MD	21401	9	512
Annapolis Mall	1020 Annapolis Mall	Annapolis	MD	21401	11	512
Eastport Cinemas	919 Chesapeake Ave.	Annapolis	MD	21401	2	512
Crown Block E	600 Hennepin Ave.	Minneapolis	MN	55402	15	613
Crown New York 1 & 2	1271 Second Ave.	New York	NY	10021	2	501
Crown Neonopolis	450 E. Fremont St.	Las Vegas	NV	89101	14	839

DANBARRY CINEMAS

6 theatres, 64 screens.
105 W. 4th St., Ste. 1000, Cincinnati, OH 45202. (513) 784-1521. FAX: (513) 784-1554.
OWNERS
Daniel J. Heilbrunn
Barry A. Kohn
GENERAL MANAGER
Tom Sanders

THEATRES

Theatre	Address	City	State	Zip	Screens	DMA
Danbarry Dollar Saver Cinemas	7650 Turfway	Florence	KY	41042	10	515
Danbarry Dollar Saver Cinemas	5190 Glenncrossing Way	Cincinnati	OH	45238	12	515
Danbarry Dollar Saver Cinemas	4450 Eastgate Blvd.	Cincinnati	OH	45245	8	515
Danbarry Dollar Saver Cinemas	8300 Lyons Ridge Dr.	Dayton	OH	45458	12	515
Danbarry Dollar Saver Cinemas	7650 Waynetowne Blvd.	Huber Heights	OH	45424	12	542
Danbarry Cinemas Middletown	3479 Dixie Hwy.	Middletown	OH	45005	10	515

DEANZA LAND & LEISURE CORP.

7 theatres, 29 screens.
1615 Cordova St., Los Angeles, CA 90007. (323) 734-9951. FAX: (323) 734-2531.
PRESIDENT
William H. Oldknow
SENIOR V.P.
Gerald T. Oldknow

DRIVE-IN THEATRES

Theatre	Address	City	State	Zip	Screens	DMA
De Anza Quad	1401 S. Alvernon Way	Tucson	AZ	85711	4	789
Van Buren Blvd. Triple	3035 Van Buren Blvd.	Arlington	CA	92503	3	803
Mission Quad	4407 State St.	Montclair	CA	91763	4	803
Rubidoux Triple	3770 Opal St.	Riverside	CA	92509	3	803
South Bay Triple	2170 Coronado Ave.	San Diego	CA	92154	3	825
Starlight Six-Plex	2000 Moreland Ave.	Atlanta	GA	30316	6	524
Redwood Six-Plex	3688 S. Redwood Rd.	W. Valley	UT	84119	6	770

DESTINTA THEATRES

6 theatres, 85 screens.
11 Kipp Ave., Lodi, NJ 07644. (973) 473-8002. FAX: (973) 473-8808. www.destinta.com
CEO
Thomas J. Rizzo
CFO
Larry Haber
SENIOR V.P., OPERATIONS
John Spare
CONTROLLER
Jim Cioci
DIRECTOR, PROMOTIONS
Sean Crean
OFFICE MANAGER
Sharon Toth

THEATRES

Theatre	Address	City	State	Zip	Screens	DMA
Metro Square 12	49 College St.	Middletown	CT	06457	12	533
Independence 12	2465 S. Broad St.	Hamilton	NJ	08610	12	504
New Windsor 12	215 Quassaick	New Windsor	NY	12553	12	501
Clarion 7	Clarion Mall, Rd. 3, Box 171	Clarion	PA	16214	7	508
Chartiers Valley 20	1025 Washington Pike	Bridgeville	PA	15017	20	508
Plaza East 22	1701 Lincoln Hwy.	N. Versailles	PA	15137	22	508

DICKINSON THEATRES, INC.

23 theatres, 239 screens.
6801 W. 107th St., Overland Park, KS 66212. (9413) 432-2334. FAX: (913) 432-9507. www.dtmovies.com
PRESIDENT & CEO
John Hartley
EXECUTIVE V.P., FILM & MARKETING
Ron Horton
CFO
Al Lane
CORPORATE SECRETARY
Kevin White

Theatre	Address	City	State	Zip	Screens	DMA

THEATRES

Theatre	Address	City	State	Zip	Screens	DMA
Flinthills 8	1614 Industrial Rd.	Emporia	KS	66801	8	605
Sequoyah 9	1118 Fleming	Garden City	KS	67846	9	678
Mall Hays Theatre	2925 Vine St.	Hays	KS	67601	8	678
Mall 8 Hutchinson	1500 E. 11th St.	Hutchinson	KS	67504	8	678
Plaza 6 Leavenworth	3400 S. 4th St.	Leavenworth	KS	66048	6	616
Great Mall 16	20060 W. 151st St.	Olathe	KS	66061	16	616
Central Mall 8	2259 S. 9th St.	Salina	KS	67402	8	678
Midstates 2	2450 S. 9th St.	Salina	KS	67401	2	678
Westglen 18	16301 Midland Dr.	Shawnee	KS	66217	18	616
Northrock 14	3151 Penstemon	Wichita	KS	67226	14	678
Belton 8	1207 E. North Ave.	Belton	MO	64012	8	616
Blue Springs 8	1901 N. 7 Hwy.	Blue Springs	MO	64015	8	616
Northglen 14	4900 N.E. 80th St.	Kansas City	MO	64119	14	616
Mall 8 Pittsburg	202 Centennial Dr.	Pittsburg	KS	66762	8	508
Eastglen 16	1451 N.E. Douglas St.	Lee's Summit	MO	64086	16	616
Conestoga Mall 8	3404 West 13th St.	Grand Island	NE	68802	8	722
Oakwood Mall Theatre	4125 Owen K. Garriott Rd.	Enid	OK	73703	5	650
Central Mall 12	200 S.W. "C" Ave.	Lawton	OK	73501	12	627
Arrowhead Mall 10	Arrowhead Shopping Ctr.	Muskogee	OK	74401	10	671
Penn Square 10	1901 N.W. Expwy.	Oklahoma City	OK	73118	10	650
Owasso 10	12601 E. 86th St.	Owasso	OK	74055	10	671
Starworld 20	10301 S. Memorial Dr.	Tulsa	OK	74133	20	671
Central Mall 10	3100 Hwy. 365	Port Arthur	TX	77642	10	692

DIPSON THEATRES, INC.

9 theatres, 31 screens.
388 Evans St., Williamsville, NY 14221. (716) 626-9613. FAX: (716) 626-9614. www.dipsontheatres.com
PRESIDENT & CEO
Michael Clement
V.P. & SECRETARY
Bryan Spokane
TREASURER
Connie Tartick

THEATRES

Theatre	Address	City	State	Zip	Screens	DMA
Mall 1 & 2	6 Alva Place W.	Batavia	NY	14020	2	514
Amherst Theatre	3500 Main St.	Buffalo	NY	14226	3	514
North Park Theatre	1428 Hertel Ave.	Buffalo	NY	14216	1	514
Market Arcade Film & Arts Centre	639 Main St.	Buffalo	NY	14203	8	514
Hornell Triple	191 Main St.	Hornell	NY	14843	3	565
Lakewood Cinema 6	171-3 Fairmount Ave.	Lakewood	NY	14750	6	514
Chautauqua Mall 2	500 Chautauqua Mall	Lakewood	NY	14750	2	514
Eastern Hills Cinema	4545 Transit Rd.	Williamsville	NY	14221	3	514
Warren Mall Cinemas	1666 Market St.	Warren	PA	16365	3	514

DOUGLAS THEATRE CO.

12 theatres, 92 screens.
1300 P St., Lincoln, NE 68501. (402) 474-4909. FAX: (402) 474-4914. www.douglastheatres.com
CHAIRMAN
Russell Brehm
CEO & PRESIDENT
David Livingston
VICE PRESIDENT
Deborah Brehm
FILM BOOKER
Frank Rhodes

THEATRES

Theatre	Address	City	State	Zip	Screens	DMA
Twin Creek	3909 Raynor Pkwy.	Bellevue	NE	68123	16	652
Cinema Twin	210 N. 13th St.	Lincoln	NE	68508	2	722
Douglas 3	1300 P St.	Lincoln	NE	68508	3	722
East Park 6	E. Park Plaza, 220 N. 66th	Lincoln	NE	68505	6	722
Edgewood 6	5220 S. 56th St.	Lincoln	NE	68516	6	722
The Lincoln	1145 P St.	Lincoln	NE	68508	3	722
Plaza 4	201 N. 12th St.	Lincoln	NE	68508	4	722
South Pointe Cinema	2920 Pine Lake Rd.	Lincoln	NE	68508	6	722
Starship 9	1311 Q St.	Lincoln	NE	68508	9	722
Cinema Center Complex	2828 S. 82nd Ave.	Omaha	NE	68124	8	652
Q Cinema 9	5505 S. 120th St.	Omaha	NE	68137	9	652
20 Grand	14304 W. Maple Rd.	Omaha	NE	68164	20	652

EASTERN FEDERAL CORP.

21 theatres, 205 screens.
901 E. Blvd., Charlotte, NC 28203-5203. (704) 377-3495. FAX: (704) 358-8427. www.easternfederal.com
PRESIDENT & CEO
Carter Meiselmax
EXECUTIVE V.P.
George Royster
SECRETARY
James I. Stewart
V.P., FILM BUYER
Curtis Fainn
V.P., OPERATIONS
Scott Baldwin
V.P., REAL ESTATE
William Wilson
DIRECTOR, ADVERTISING & MARKETING
Janice Black
SENIOR ENGINEER
Richard McKinney

Theatre	Address	City	State	Zip	Screens	DMA

THEATRES

Theatre	Address	City	State	Zip	Screens	DMA
Sun Plaza Stadium	427 Mary Esther Cutoff	Fort Walton	FL	32549	8	686
Royal Park Stadium	3702 Newberry Rd.	Gainesville	FL	32607	16	592
Regency Eleven	1515 W. 23rd St.	Panama City	FL	32406	11	656
Port Orange Six	1015 Eagle Lake Trail	Port Orange	FL	32129	6	534
Miracle Theatre	1815 Thomasville Rd.	Tallahassee	FL	32303	5	530
Movies @ Governor's Square	1501 Governor's Square Blvd	Tallahassee	FL	32301	12	530
Movies at Timberlyne 6.	120 Banks St.	Chapel Hill	NC	27514	6	560
Plaza Stadium 10	141 Elliott Rd.	Chapel Hill	NC	27514	10	560
Delta Six Theatre	8800 W.T. Harris Blvd.	Charlotte	NC	28212	6	517
Manor Theatre	607 Providence Rd.	Charlotte	NC	28207	3	517
Movies at Crownpoint 12	9630 Monroe Rd.	Charlotte	NC	28270	12	517
Starlight Stadium	11240 N. U.S. Hwy 29	Charlotte	NC	28262	15	517
Movies at the Lake	20310 Chartwell Ctr. Dr.	Cornelius	NC	28031	12	517
Movies at Franklin Square	3778 E. Franklin Blvd	Gastonia	NC	28056	14	704
Movies at Birkdale	16950 Birkdale Commoms Pkwy.	Huntersville	NC	28078	16	517
Town & Country Four	3525 Fayetteville Rd.	Lumberton	NC	28359	4	570
Starlight Cinema	141 Interstate Blvd	Anderson	SC	29621	14	567
Movies at Mt. Pleasant	963 Houston-Northcutt Blvd.	Charleston	SC	29464	12	519
Movies at Polo Road	9700 Two Notch Rd.	Columbia	SC	29223	8	546
Swamp Fox Cinemas	3400 Radio Rd.	Florence	SC	29501	14	570
Movies at Azalea Square	215 Azalea Blvd.	Summerville	SC	29483	16	519

EDWARDS THEATRES

(See Regal Entertainment Group)

ENTERTAINMENT CINEMAS

22 theatres, 167 screens.
7 Central St., South Easton, MA 02375. (508) 230-7600. FAX: (508) 238-1408. www.entertainmentcinemas.com
PRESIDENT
Bill Hanney

THEATRES

Theatre	Address	City	State	Zip	Screens	DMA
Entertainment Cinemas Bloomfield 8	863 Park Ave.	Bloomfield	CT	06002	8	533
Entertainment Cinemas Stratford 14	411 Barnum Ave., Rt 1	Stratford	CT	06614	14	501
Entertainment Cinemas Seymour 12	814 Derby Ave.	Seymour	CT	06483	12	533
Entertainment Cinemas Edgartown 2	65 Main St.	Edgartown	MA	02539	2	506
Entertainment Cinemas Fall River 8	374 William Canning Blvd.	Fall River	MA	02721	8	521
Entertainment Cinemas Leominster 10	45 Sack Blvd., 100 Searstown Mall	Leominster	MA	01453	10	506
Entertainment Cinemas Triboro 14	P.O. Box 2666, 10 Dietsch Blvd. (02763)	Attleboro Falls	MA	02763	14	521
Entertainment Cinemas Stoughton Pub	807 Washington St.	Stoughton	MA	02072	1	506
Entertainment Cinemas Swansea 12	207 Swansea Mall Dr.	Swansea	MA	02777	12	521
Entertainment Cinemas Windham 7	Rte. 302.	N. Windham	ME	04062	7	500
Entertainment Cinemas Wells 7	Wells Shopping Cntr., Rte. 1	Wells	ME	04090	7	500
Entertainment Cinemas Claremont 7	345 Washington St.	Claremont	NH	03743	7	523
Entertainment Cinemas Concord 6	192 Loudon Rd.	Concord	NH	03301	6	506
Entertainment Cinemas Lebanon 6	Rte. 4 Miracle Mile Plz.	Lebanon	NH	03766	6	523
Entertainment Cinemas N. Conway 10	P.O. Box 3068, Mall Theatre, Rte 16 & 302	N. Conway	NH	03860	10	500
Entertainment Cinemas Madison 7	1036 Madison Ave.	Albany	NY	12208	7	532
Entertainment Cinemas Seaford 8	3951 Merrick Rd.	Seaford	NY	11783	8	
Entertainment Cinemas Holiday 8	105 Chase Ln.	Middletown	RI	02842	8	521
Entertainment Cinemas Opera House 3	19 Touro St.	Newport	RI	02840	3	521
Entertainment Cinemas S. Kingston 8	30 Village Sq. Dr.	S. Kingston	RI	02881	8	506
Entertainment Cinemas Brattleboro 6	6 Putney Rd.	Brattleboro	VT	05034	6	506
Entertainment Cinemas W. Dover 3	P.O. Box 2386, Mt. Park Plz., Rte. 100	W. Dover	VT	05356	3	506

FLAGSHIP CINEMAS

7 theatres, 62 screens.
459 Broadway, Ste. 204, Everett, MA 02149. (617) 389-7300. FAX: (617) 389-7304. www.flagshipcinemas.com
PRESIDENT
John J. Crowley, Jr.
VICE PRESIDENT
Andrea K. Cox
CFO
Daniel J. Flynn
FACILITIES DIRECTOR
Paul Wenger
FILM BUYER
Pauline Jandrue

THEATRES

Theatre	Address	City	State	Zip	Screens	DMA
Flagship Cinema New Bedford	500 Kings Hwy., Fieldstone Marketplace	New Bedford	MA	02745	12	521
Flagship Cinemas Quincy	Quincy Fair Mall, 1585 Hancock St.	Quincy	MA	02169	8	506
Flagship Cinemas Wareham	39 Doty St.	Wareham	MA	02576	8	
Flagship Cinema Churchville	2408 Churchville Rd.	Bel Air	MD	21015	7	512
Flagship Cinema Lewiston	855 Lisbon St., Promenade Mall	Lewiston	ME	04240	10	500
Flagship Cinema Oxford	1570 Main St.	Oxford	ME	04270	7	500
Flagship Cinema Rockland	9 Moody Dr.	Thomaston	ME	04861	10	500

FOOTHILLS ENTERTAINMENT COMPANY

7 theatres, 25 screens.
P.O. Box 2549, Kilgore, TX 75663-2549. (903) 758-4749. FAX: (903) 758-0720. email: bmovies@aol.com
PRESIDENT
Byron Berkley

THEATRES

Theatre	Address	City	State	Zip	Screens	DMA
Morley Theatre	701 N. Main St.	Borger	TX	79007	3	
4 Star Cinema	1607 Hwy. 259 S.	Kilgore	TX	75663	4	623
Plaza Cinema 3	1301 Lone Star St.	Henderson	TX	75652	3	623
Orange Cinema 2	3330 Bowling Ln.	Orange	TX	77630	2	618
Star Village 8	3980 Boat Club Dr.	Lake Worth	TX	76135	8	623
Brazos Cinema 3	2801 Hwy. 180 E.	Mineral Wells	TX	76068	3	623
Jackson Cinema 3	1710 S. Jackson St., Box 2421	Jacksonville	TX	75766	3	623

Theatre	Address	City	State	Zip	Screens	DMA

FRIDLEY THEATRES, INC.

34 theatres, 90 screens.
1321 Walnut St., Des Moines, IA 50309. (515) 282-9287. FAX: (515) 282-8310.
OWNER
R. L. Fridley
FILM BUYER
Brian Fridley

THEATRES

Theatre	Address	City	State	Zip	Screens	DMA
Algona Theatre	216 E. State St.	Algona	IA	50511	1	611
The Springwood 9	2829 S. Ankeny Blvd.	Ankeny	IA	50021	9	679
Atlantic	28 W. Fifth St	Atlantic	IA	50022	2	652
Boone Theatre	818 Story St.	Boone	IA	50036	1	679
Carroll 5 Theatre	407 N. Main St.	Carroll	IA	51401	5	679
American	108 E. Main	Cherokee	IA	51012	1	624
Clarion	115 N.E. 1st. Ave.	Clarion	IA	50525	1	679
Strand Theatre	309 W. Adams St.	Creston	IA	50801	1	679
Viking 3	111 N. Mechanic	Decorah	IA	52101	3	637
Riviera Theatre	2209 Main	Emmetsburg	IA	50536	1	624
Grand 3 Theatre	1031 Central Ave.	Estherville	IA	51334	3	737
Cinema Theatre	921 Main St	Grinnell	IA	50112	2	679
Humota	515 Sumner Ave	Humboldt	IA	50548	1	679
Paramount 3	105 S. 1st St.	Indianola	IA	50125	3	679
Metropolitan 2 Theatres	515 Washington Ave.	Iowa Falls	IA	50126	2	679
Sierra Theatre	212 E. State St	Jefferson	IA	50129	1	679
Village 1 & 2 Theatre	212 E. Robinson	Knoxville	IA	50138	2	679
Castle Theatre	112 E. Main	Manchester	IA	52057	1	637
Plaza 5 Theatre	2500 S. Center St.	Marshalltown	IA	50158	5	679
Temple 2	115 N. Main St.	Mt. Pleasant	IA	52641	2	682
Plaza 4	1903 Park Ave.	Muscatine	IA	52761	4	682
Paramount Theatre	26 S. Fredrick Ave.	Oelwein	IA	50662	2	637
Penn Centre Twin	216 2nd Ave.	Oskaloosa	IA	52577	2	679
Grand 3 Theatre	1312 2nd St.	Perry	IA	50220	3	679
Copper Creek 9	1325 Copper Creek Dr.	Pleasant Hill	IA	50317	9	679
Cinema 5	251 N. Main	Sioux Center	IA	51250	5	
Spencer 3	504 Grand Ave.	Spencer	IA	51301	3	624
Vista 3	712 Lake Ave.	Storm Lake	IA	50588	3	624
State Theatre	123 E. Washington St.	Washington	IA	52353	1	637
Webster Theatre	610 2nd St.	Webster City	IA	50595	1	679
Sierra 3 Theatres	1618 22nd St.	W. Des Moines	IA	50265	3	679
Grand	316 W. 3rd St.	Grand Island	NE	68801	1	722
Rivoli 3	528 W. 2nd St.	Hastings	NE	68902	3	722
Cinema 3	224 W. View Plaza	McCook	NE	69001	3	722

GALAXY THEATRE CORPORATION

8 theatres, 21 screens.
7000 Blvd. E., Guttenberg, NJ 07093. (201) 854-6554. www.galaxy-movie-theatre.com
PRESIDENT
Nelson Page
GENERAL MANAGER
Diane Walker

THEATRES

Theatre	Address	City	State	Zip	Screens	DMA
Galaxy Triplex	7000 Blvd. E.	Guttenberg	NJ	07093	3	501
Mall Theatre	215 Mountain Ave.	Hackettstown	NJ	07840	2	501
Hudson Street Cinemas	5 Marine View Plaza	Hoboken	NJ	07030	2	501
Newton Theatre	234 Spring St.	Newton	NJ	07860	2	501
Sparta Theatre	25 Center St.	Sparta	NJ	07871	2	501
Cedar Lane Cinemas	503 Cedar Ln.	Teaneck	NJ	07666	4	501
Valleyview Cinemas	777 Hamburg Tnpk.	Wayne	NJ	07470	2	501
Abby Cinemas	35 D Marshall Hill Rd.	West Milford	NJ	07480	4	501

GALAXY THEATRES LLC

6 theatres, 57 screens.
15060 Ventura Blvd., Ste. 350, Sharman Oaks, CA 91403. (818) 986-9000. FAX: (818) 784-0106. www.galaxytheatres.com
CONTACT
Rafe Cohen

THEATRES

Theatre	Address	City	State	Zip	Screens	DMA
Porterville 9	631 N. Indiana St.	Porterville	CA	93257	9	866
Riverbank 12	2525 Patterson Rd.	Riverbank	CA	95367	12	
Galaxy 10	6700 Middle Fisk Rd.	Austin	TX	78752	10	635
Gateway 8	2501 S. Gateway Center	Federal Way	WA	98003	8	819
Monroe 12	One Galaxy Way	Monroe	WA	98272	12	
Galaxy 6	3102 S. 23nd St.	Tacoma	WA	98402	6	819

GENERAL CINEMA THEATRES

(See AMC Entertainment)

GKC THEATRES (GEORGE KERASOTES CORPORATION)

31 theatres, 268 screens.
755 Apple Orchard St., Springfield IL 62703. (217) 528-4981. FAX: (217) 528-6490. www.gkctheatres.com
PRESIDENT
Beth Kerasotes
CFO & EXECUTVE V.P., FINANCE
Jeffrey A. Cole
EXECUTIVE V.P., FILM & MARKETING
Bryan Jeffries

Theatre	Address	City	State	Zip	Screens	DMA

V.P., CONCESSION
Krystal LaReese
V.P., CONSTRUCTION & DEVELOPMENT
Matt Heissinger
DIRECTOR, THEATRE OPERATIONS & MARKETING
James G. Whitman
DIRECTOR, FILM
Sabrena Campbell

THEATRES

Theatre	Address	City	State	Zip	Screens	DMA
American Cinemas	4690 N. Oracle Rd.	Tucson	AZ	85704	6	789
Parkway Cinemas	2103 N. Veterans Pkwy	Bloomington	IL	61704	8	675
Palace Cinemas	415 Detroit Dr.	Bloomington	IL	61704	10	675
Beverly 18	910 Meijer Dr.	Champaign	IL	61821	18	648
Strand	2360 S. Mt. Zion Rd.	Decatur	IL	62521	10	648
Market Square	2160 Sycamore Rd.	Dekalb	IL	60115	10	602
Hickory Point Cinema	U.S. Highway 51	Forsyth	IL	62535	12	648
Lincoln Cinemas	215 S. Kickapoo St	Lincoln	IL	62656	4	648
Orpheum Cinema	515 W. Gore Rd.	Morris	IL	60450	10	602
University Cinemas	1010 S. Main St.	Normal	IL	61761	8	675
Landmark 12	3225 N. Dries Ln.	Peoria	IL	61604	12	675
Westlake 5	2601 Westlake St.	Peoria	IL	61615	5	675
Peru Mall 8 Cinema	3940 Rte. 251	Peru	IL	61354	8	602
Sauk Valley Cinema	4110 E. 30th St.	Sterling	IL	61081	8	682
Sunnyland 10	Washington Rd.	Washington	IL	61571	10	675
Capri Cinemas	205 Dry Branch Dr	Crawfordsville	IN	47933	8	527
Encore Park 14	2701 Cassopolis St.	Elkhart	IN	46514	14	588
Royal Knights 3	101 S. Second	Alpena	MI	49707	3	583
State Cinema 5	206 N. 2nd St.	Alpena	MI	49707	5	583
Lakeview Square 10	5775 Beckley Rd.	Battlecreek	MI	49015	10	563
Big Rapids 4 Cinemas	213 S. Michigan	Big Rapids	MI	49307	4	540
Birchwood 10	4350 24th St.	Fort Gratiot	MI	48059	10	505
Plaza Cinema	1700 N. Wisner St.	Jackson	MI	49202	8	551
Lyric Cinema 4	208 S. James St.	Ludington	MI	49431	4	540
Delft Cinemas	130 W. Main St.	Marquette	MI	49855	5	553
Royal 10	1351 O'dovero Dr.	Marquette	MI	49855	10	553
Fashion Square Mall 10	4511 Fashion Square	Saginaw	MI	48604	10	513
Varsity Cinema	1098 W. 3 Mile Rd.	Sault Ste Marie	MI	49783	10	540
Grand Traverse Cinema 9	3200 S. Airport Rd.	Traverse City	MI	49684	9	540
Horizon 10	3587 Market Place Cir.	Traverse City	MI	49684	10	540
Pine Tree Cinemas	2727 Cahill Rd.	Marinette	WI	54143	9	658

GEORGIA THEATRE COMPANY II

28 theatres, 265 screens.
500 Sea Island Rd., St. Simons, GA 31522. (912) 634-5192. FAX: (912) 634-5195.
CHAIRMAN & PRESIDENT
William J. Stembler
VICE CHAIRMAN
John H. Stembler
EXECUTIVE V.P.
Aubrey Stone
V.P., OPERATIONS & CONSTRUCTION
Scott Bagwell
VICE PRESIDENT
John H. Stemdler, Jr.
SECRETARY/TREASURER
Dennis P. Merton

THEATRES

Theatre	Address	City	State	Zip	Screens	DMA
Beacon Cinemas 10	1251 Cortez Blvd.	Brooksville	FL	34616	10	539
Beechwood Stadium 11	196 Alps Rd.	Athens	GA	30606	11	524
Georgia Square 5	3700 Atlanta Hwy.	Athens	GA	30606	5	524
Masters 7	2824 Washington Rd.	Augusta	GA	30909	7	520
Movies @ Glynn Place 11	200 Mall Blvd.	Brunswick	GA	31525	11	561
Mall Cinemas 8	First Tuesday Mall	Carrollton	GA	30117	8	524
Gwinnett Place 12	2161 Merchants Way	Duluth	GA	30189	12	524
Venture Value Cinemas 12	3750 Venture Dr.	Duluth	GA	30096	12	524
Heart of Georgia 5	1167 Cochran Hwy.	Eastman	GA	31023	5	
Evans 12 Cinema	4365 Towne Ctr. Dr.	Evans	GA	30809	12	520
Hollywood 15	659 Green Hill Cir.	Gainesville	GA	30501	15	524
Lakeshore Cinemas 4	Lakeshore Mall	Gainesville	GA	30501	4	524
Liberty Cinemas 7	565 W. Oglethorpe Hwy.	Hinesville	GA	31313	7	507
Town Center Cinemas 10	700 Gwinnett Dr.	Lawrenceville	GA	30045	10	524
Merchant's Walk Stadium 12	1301 Johnson Ferry Rd.	Marietta	GA	30068	12	524
Park 12 Cobb	3605 Sandy Plains Rd.	Marietta	GA	30066	12	524
Moultrie Twin	Sunset Plaza	Moultrie	GA	31768	2	525
Kings Bay Cinemas 9	201 City Smitty Dr.	St Marys	GA	31558	9	561
Island Cinemas 7	500 Sea Island Rd.	St Simons	GA	31522	7	561
Gateway Cinemas 7	U.S. 19 S.	Thomasville	GA	31792	7	530
Valdosta Stadium 16	1680 BAgtree Rd.	Valdosta	GA	31602	6	530
Ashley Cinemas 8	2812 N. Ashley St.	Valdosta	GA	31601	8	530
Parkway Cinemas 6	821 Russell Pkwy.	Warner Robins	GA	31088	6	503
Galleria Mall Cinemas 10	2980 Watson Blvd.	Warner Robins	GA	31208	10	503
Mall Cinemas 7	2260 Brunswick Hwy.	Waycross	GA	31503	7	561
Cherokee 16	2295 Towne Lake Pkwy.	Woodstock	GA	30189	16	524
Beacon Cinemas 10	1121 Broad St.	Sumter	SC	29150	10	546
Danville Stadium Cinemas	3601 Riverside Dr.	Danville	VA	24541	12	573

GOODRICH QUALITY THEATERS, INC.

33 theatres, 279 screens.
4417 Broadmoor S.E., Grand Rapids, MI 49512. (616) 698-7733. FAX: (616) 698-7220. www.gqti.com
PRESIDENT & SECRETARY
Robert Emmett Goodrich
V.P. & GENERAL MANAGER
William T. McMannis
CFO
Ross Pettinga
FILM BUYER
Wanda J. Holst
OPERATIONS MANAGER
Martin S. Betz
MARKETING & TRAINING MANAGER
Matthew Johnson
CONCESSIONS MANAGER
Brian Nuffer
DATA ADMINISTRATOR
Darren Pitcher

THEATRES

Theatre	Address	City	State	Zip	Screens	DMA
Randall 16	550 N. Randall Rd.	Batavia	IL	60510	16	602
Kendall 10	95 5th St.	Oswego	IL	60543	10	602
Willow Knolls 14	4100 W. Willow Knolls Dr.	Peoria	IL	61615	14	675
Savoy 16	232 W. Burwash	Savoy	IL	61874	16	648
Applewood 9	1704 E. 60th	Anderson	IN	46013	9	527
Anderson 4	2101 State Rd. 9 S	Anderson	IN	46015	4	527
Huntington 7	350 Hauenstein Rd.	Huntington	IN	46750	7	509
Eastside 10	300 Farabee Dr.	Lafayette	IN	47905	10	582
Lafayette 7	3525 McCarty Ln.	Lafayette	IN	47904	7	582
Wabash Landing 9	300 E. State St.	Lafayette	IN	47906	9	582
Portage 9	5935 U.S. Rte. 6	Portage	IN	46368	9	602
Forum 8	1209 Forum Katy Pkwy.	Columbia	MO	65203	8	604
Capital 8	3550 Country Club Dr.	Jefferson City	MO	65109	8	604
Capital 4	3600 Country Club Dr.	Jefferson City	MO	65109	4	604
Springfield 8	3200 E. Montclair St.	Springfield	MO	65806	8	619
Quality 16	3686 Jackson Rd.	Ann Arbor	MI	48103	16	505
West Columbia 7	2500 W. Columbia	Battle Creek	MI	49015	7	563
Bay City 8	4101 Wilder Rd.	Bay City	MI	48706	8	513
Cadillac 5	202 S. Mitchell St.	Cadillac	MI	49601	5	540
Canton 6	435 Ford Rd.	Canton	MI	48187	6	505
Hampton 6	888 N. Pine Rd.	Essexville	MI	48732	6	513
Grand Haven 9	17220 Hayes St.	Grand Haven	MI	49417	9	563
Hastings 4	213 W. State St.	Hastings	MI	49058	4	563
Holland 7	500 Waverly Rd.	Holland	MI	49423	7	563
Jackson 10	1501 N. Wisner	Jackson	MI	49202	10	551
Kalamazoo 10	820 Maple Hill Dr.	Kalamazoo	MI	49009	10	563
Lansing Mall 6	921 Mall Dr.	Lansing	MI	48917	6	551
Ada Lowell 5	2175 W. Main St.	Lowell	MI	49331	5	563
Novi Town Center 8	26085 Town Ctr. Dr.	Novi	MI	48375	8	505
Oxford 7	48 S. Washington	Oxford	MI	48371	7	505
Krafft 8	2725 Krafft Rd.	Port Huron	MI	48060	8	505
Saginaw 8/The Quad	3250 Kabobel	Saginaw	MI	48604	12	513
Three Rivers 6	120 Enterprise Dr.	Three Rivers	MI	49093	6	563

GREATER HUNTINGTON THEATRE CORP.

4 theatres, 21 screens.
P.O. Box 1957, 401 11th St., Ste. 805, Huntington, WV 25720-1957. (304) 523-0185. FAX: (304) 525-1153. www.ourshowtimes.com
CHAIRMAN
Jack S. Hyman
PRESIDENT
Derek Hyman

THEATRES

Theatre	Address	City	State	Zip	Screens	DMA
Park Place Stadium II	600 Washington St.	Charleston	WV	25301	11	564
Camelot Theatre 2	1030 4th Ave.	Huntington	WV	25701	2	564
Cinema Theatre	1021 4th Ave.	Huntington	WV	25701	4	564
Keith Albee Theatre 4	925 4th Ave.	Huntington	WV	25701	4	564

GULF STATES THEATRES, INC.

(See AMC Entertainment)

HARKINS THEATRES

22 theatres, 259 screens.
7511 E. McDonald Dr., Scottsdale, AZ 85258. (480) 627-7777. (480) 443-0950. www.harkinstheatres.com
PRESIDENT & CEO
Dan Harkins
EXECUTIVE V.P.
Wayne Kullander
CFO
Greta Newell
VICE PRESIDENTS
Timothy Spain
Mike Bowers
V.P. & GENERAL COUNSEL
Dave Farren
DIRECTOR, HUMAN RESOURCES
Gina Browning
FILM BUYER
Lou Lencioni

Theatre	Address	City	State	Zip	Screens	DMA

INTERSTATE AMUSEMENTS INC.

6 theatres, 25 screens.
P.O. Box T, Twin Falls, ID 83301. (208) 734-2402. FAX: (208) 734-8687.
PRESIDENT
John Love
VICE PRESIDENT
Byron Kluth
SECRETARY & TREASURER
Cathy Roper
MANAGING DIRECTOR
Larry Roper

THEATRES

KERASOTES SHOWPLACE THEATRES, LLC

78 theatres, 569 screens.
224 N. DesPlaines, Ste. 200, Chicago, IL 60661-1134. (312) 775-3160. FAX: (312) 258-9943.
104 N. Sixth St., Springfield, IL 62701. (217) 788-5200. FAX: (217) 788-5207. www.kerasotes.com
PRESIDENT & CEO
Tony Kerasotes
EXECUTIVE V.P. & COO
Dean Kerasotes
CFO
Jim DeBruzzi
DIRECTOR, OPERATIONS
Tim Johnson
HEAD FILM BUYER
Pat Rembusch
DIRECTOR, IT
Bill Budig
DIRECTOR, REAL ESTATE
Robert Gallivan
TECHNICAL DIRECTOR/EQUIPMENT BUYER
Fred Walraven
CONCESSION MANAGER
Rob Lehman
ADVERTISING MANAGER
Barry Tester

THEATRES

Theatre	Address	City	State	Zip	Screens	DMA
Showplace 8	400 Potomac	Mt Vernon	IL	62864	8	632
Showplace 14	(Opens 2004)	New Lenox	IL		14	
Showplace 12	1124 Edgewater	Pekin	IL	61554	12	675
Paris Theatre	119 N. Central Ave.	Paris	IL	61944	2	581
Quincy Showcase 6	300 N. 33rd St.	Quincy	IL	62301	6	717
Quincy Mall Cinema	3429 Quincy Mall	Quincy	IL	62301	3	717
Showplace 16	8301 E. State St.	Rockford	IL	61125	16	610
Colonial Village Cinema	4228 Newburg Rd.	Rockford	IL	61125	5	610
North Towne Cinema	890 W. Riverside Blvd.	Rockford	IL	61130	6	610
Movies at Machesney	890 W. Riverside Blvd.	Rockford	IL	61130	10	610
Esquire Theatre	1324 S. MacArthur Blvd.	Springfield	IL	62704	4	648
Parkway Pointe	3025 Lindbergh Blvd.	Springfield	IL	62704	8	648
Showplace	2945 S. Dirksen Pkwy.	Springfield	IL	62704	8	648
Showplace 12	3141 Mercantile Dr.	Springfield	IL	62707	12	648
Cinema	117 W. Main Cross	Taylorville	IL	62568	2	648
River Tree Court	701 N. Milwaukee, Ste. 224	Vernon Hills	IL	60061	8	602
Showplace 8	555 N. Lakeview Pkwy.	Vernon Hills	IL	60061	8	602
College Mall Cinema	1351 College Mall Rd.	Bloomington	IN	47402	4	527
Showplace 11	1351 College Mall Rd.	Bloomington	IN	47408	11	527
Showplace West 12	2929 W. Third St.	Bloomington	IN	47408	12	527
Commons Cinema	395 Courthouse Ctr.	Columbus	IN	47202	2	527
Showplace 12	555 Creekview Court	Columbus	IN	47201	12	527
Stadium 16	5600 Pearl Dr.	Evansville	IN	47719	16	649
Showplace 16	4325 S. Meridian	Indianapolis	IN	46217	16	527
ShowPlace 12	6102 N. Rural St.	Indianapolis	IN	46220	12	527
Kokomo Mall Cinema	1530 E. Blvd.	Kokomo	IN	46902	8	527
Markland Mall Cinema	1201 S. Reed Rd.	Kokomo	IN	46902	5	527
LaPorte Cinema	608 Colfax	LaPorte	IN	46350	4	602
Showplace 12	713 B. Theatre Dr.	Marion	IN	46952	12	527
Marquette Cinema	430 St. John Rd.	Michigan City	IN	46361	3	602
Dunes Plaza Cinema	100 Dunes Plaza, Rte. 20	Michigan City	IN	46361	6	602
Showplace 7	3401 W. Community Dr.	Muncie	IN	47308	7	527
Northwest Plaza Cinema	1907 W. McGalliard	Muncie	IN	47308	8	527
Castle Theatre	221 S. Main St	New Castle	IN	47362	1	527
Eastwood Cinema	663 E. Main St.	Peru	IN	46970	2	527
Princeton Theatre	301 W. Broadway	Princeton	IN	47670	4	649
Dollar Cinema	600 Commerce Rd.	Richmond	IN	47374	10	542
Cinema 11	4713 E. National Rd.	Richmond	IN	47375	11	542
Showplace 16	875 Deercreek Dr.	Schererville	IN	46375	16	602
Showplace 12	(Opens 2004)	Schererville	IN		12	602
Scottsdale Cinema	1290 Scottsdale Mall	South Bend	IN	46614	6	588
Showplace 16	450 Chippewa Dr	South Bend	IN	46614	16	588
Honey Creek West	3131 S. Third St. Pl.	Terre Haute	IN	47802	8	581
ShowPlace 12	3153 S. Third St. Pl.	Terre Haute	IN	47802	12	581
Showplace 8	1495 S. Hart	Vincennes	IN	47591	8	581
Indiana Theatre 2	419 E. Main St.	Washington	IN	47501	2	581
Showplace 16 Coon Rapids	10051 Woodcrest Dr.	Coon Rapids	MN	55433	16	613
Showplace 16	5567 Bishop Ave.	Inver Grove Hts.	MN	55077	16	613
Town Plaza Cinema 5	2136 William St.	Cape Girardeau	MO	63702	5	632
Town & Country Cinema	1618 Business 60	Dexter	MO	63841	2	632
Showplace 4	838 Valley Creek	Farmington	MO	63640	4	609
Kennett Cinema 1	224 First St.	Kennett	MO	63857	1	632
Movies	300 W. Main St.	Park Hills	MO	63601	2	609
Showplace 8	3225 S. Westwood	Poplar Bluff	MO	63902	8	632
Cinemas 10	877 Washington Blvd.	Hamilton	OH	45013	10	515
Showplace 8	Main St.	Hamilton	OH	45013	8	515

KRIKORIAN PREMIERE THEATRES, LLC

6 theatres, 72 screens.
131 Palos Verdes Blvd., Redondo Beach, CA 90277. (310) 791-8688. FAX: (310) 791-1997. www.krikoriantheatres.com
PRESIDENT & CEO
George Krikorian
FILM BUYER
Lou Lencioni (Alamo Theatre Service)
DIRECTOR, OPERATIONS
Todd Cummings

THEATRES

Theatre	Address	City	State	Zip	Screens	DMA
Buena Park Metroplex 18	8290 La Palma Ave.	Buena Park	CA	90620	18	
Chino Marketplace Spectrum 12	3750 Grand Ave.	Chino	CA	91710	12	803
Downey	8200 3rd St.	Downey	CA	90241	10	803
Redlands	340 N. Eureka St.	Redlands	CA	92373	14	803
San Clemente	641-B Camino De Los Mares	San Clemente	CA	92673	6	803
Monrovia Cinema 12	410 S. Myrtle Ave.	Monrovia	CA	91016	12	803

LAEMMLE THEATRES

9 theatres, 39 screens.
11523 Santa Monica Blvd., Los Angeles, CA 90025. (310) 478-1041. FAX: (310) 478-4452.
CHIEF OFFICERS
Robert Laemmle
Gregory Laemmle

THEATRES

Theatre	Address	City	State	Zip	Screens	DMA
Laemmle Music Hall	9036 Wilshire Blvd.	Beverly Hills	CA	90211	3	803
Laemmle's Town Center 5	17200 Ventura Blvd.	Encino	CA	91316	5	803
Laemmle's Fairfax	7907 Beverly Blvd.	Los Angeles	CA	90048	3	803
Laemmle's Grande	345 S. Figueroa St.	Los Angeles	CA	90071	4	803
Laemmle Sunset 5	8000 Sunset Blvd.	Los Angeles	CA	90046	5	803
Laemmle's Royal	11523 Santa Monica Blvd.	Los Angeles	CA	90025	1	803
Laemmle's Playhouse 7	673 E. Colorado	Pasadena	CA	91103	7	803
Laemmle's Monica 4	1332 Second St.	Santa Monica	CA	90401	4	803
Laemmle's Fallbrook 7	6731 Fallbrook Ave.	West Hills	CA	91307	7	803

LAKES & RIVERS CINEMAS

8 theatres, 41 screens.
5255 E. River Rd., Ste. 201, Minneapolis, MN 55421. (763) 572-8004. FAX: (763) 572-8005.
PRESIDENT
James H. Payne
SECRETARY & CASHIER
Shiloy Ziemann
GENERAL MANAGER
Alex Avila
FILM BUYER
Steve Tripp
GENERAL MANAGER, CONCESSIONS
Steve Payne

THEATRES

Theatre	Address	City	State	Zip	Screens	DMA
Washington Square 5	121 W. Front St.	Detroit Lakes	MN	56501	5	724
Fair Lakes 5	1201 N. State St.	Fairmont	MN	56031	5	737
Westridge Cinema 5	2001 W. Lincoln Ave.	Fergus Fails	MN	56537	5	724
Cedar Mall Cinema 6	1929 S. Cedar St.	Owatonna	MN	55060	6	613
Red Wing Cinema 5	160 Tyler Rd.	Red Wing	MN	55066	5	613
Northland Cinema 5	1635 Oxford St.	Worthington	MN	56187	5	725
Watertown Cinema 5	1111 14th St. S.E.	Watertown	SD	57201	5	725
Falls Cinema 5	200 N. Washington	St. Croix Falls	WI	54024	5	613

LANDMARK THEATRES

54 theatres, 185 screens.
2222 S. Barrington Ave., Los Angeles, CA 90064. (310) 473-6701. FAX: (310) 473-8622. www.landmarktheatres.com
PRESIDENT & CEO
Paul Richardson
V.P., MARKETING
Ray Price
V.P., OPERATIONS
Will Fox
DIRECTOR, CONCESSIONS
Sabra Slade
HEAD FILM BUYER
Michael McClellan

THEATRES

Theatre	Address	City	State	Zip	Screens	DMA
Albany Twin	1115 Solano Ave.	Albany	CA	94706	2	807
Act 1 and 2	2128 Center St.	Berkeley	CA	94704	2	807
California Theatre	2113 Kittredge St.	Berkeley	CA	94704	3	807
Shattuck Cinemas	2230 Shattuck Ave.	Berkeley	CA	94704	10	807
Fine Arts	8556 Wilshire Blvd.	Beverly Hills	CA	90211	1	803
La Jolla Village Cinemas	8879 Villa La Jolla Dr.	La Jolla	CA	92037	4	825
Regent Theatre	1045 Broxton Ave.	Los Angeles	CA	90024	1	803
Westside Pavilion Cinemas	10800 Pico Blvd.	Los Angeles	CA	90064	4	803
Nuart Theatre	11272 Santa Monica Blvd.	Los Angeles	CA	90025	1	803
Guild Theatre	949 El Camino Real	Menlo Park	CA	94025	1	807
Piedmont Theatre	4186 Piedmont Ave.	Oakland	CA	94611	3	807
Aquarius Theatre	430 Emerson St.	Palo Alto	CA	94301	2	807
Hillcrest Cinemas	3965 5th Ave.	San Diego	CA	92103	5	825
Ken Theatre	4061 Adams Ave.	San Diego	CA	92116	1	825
Bridge Theatre	3010 Geary Blvd.	San Francisco	CA	94118	1	807
Clay Theatre	2261 Fillmore	San Francisco	CA	94115	1	807
Embarcadero Center Cinemas	1 Embarcadero Ctr., Promenade Level	San Francisco	CA	94111	5	807
Lumiere Theatre	1572 California St.	San Francisco	CA	94109	3	807
Opera Plaza Cinema	601 Van Ness Ave.	San Francisco	CA	94102	4	807
NuWilshire Theatre	1314 Wilshire Blvd.	Santa Monica	CA	90403	2	803
Rialto Theatre	1023 Fair Oaks Ave.	South Pasadena	CA	91030	1	803
Esquire Theatre	590 Downing St.	Denver	CO	80219	2	751
Mayan Theatre	110 Broadway	Denver	CO	80203	3	751
Chez Artiste	4150 E. Amherst Ave.	Denver	CO	80222	3	751
Midtown Art Cinema	931 Monroe Dr.	Atlanta	GA	30308	8	524
Landmark Century Centre Cinema	2828 N. Clark St.	Chicago	IL	60657	7	602
Renaissance Place	1850 2nd St.	Highland Park	IL	60035	5	602
Canal Place Cinema	333 Canal St.	New Orleans	LA	70130	4	622
Kendall Square Cinema	1 Kendall Sq.	Cambridge	MA	02139	9	506
Embassy Cinema	16 Pine St.	Waltham	MA	02154	6	506
Bethesda Row Cinema	7235 Woodmont Ave.	Bethesda	MD	20814	8	511
Maple 3	4135 W. Maple Rd.	Bloomfield	MI	48301	3	505
Main Art Theatre	118 N. Main St.	Royal Oak	MI	48067	3	505
Edina Cinema	3911 W. 50th St.	Edina	MN	55424	4	613
Lagoon Cinema	1320 Lagoon Ave.	Minneapolis	MN	55408	5	613
Uptown Theatre	2906 Hennepin Ave.	Minneapolis	MN	55408	1	613
Hi Pointe Theatre	1005 McCausland Ave.	St. Louis	MO	63117	1	609
Plaza Frontenac	210 Plaza Frontenac	St. Louis	MO	63131	6	609
Tivoli Theatre	6350 Delmar	Universal City	MO	63130	3	609
Sunshine Cinema	143 E. Houston St.	New York	NY	10002	5	501
Dobie Theatre	2021 Guadalupe	Austin	TX	78705	4	635
Inwood Theatre	5458 W. Lovers Ln.	Dallas	TX	75209	3	623
Greenway 3 Theatre	5 Greenway Plaza	Houston	TX	77046	3	618
River Oaks Theatre	2009 W. Gray	Houston	TX	77019	3	618
Crest Cinema Center	16505 5th Ave., N.E.	Seattle	WA	98155	4	819
Egyptian Theatre	801 E. Pine	Seattle	WA	98122	1	819
Guild 45th Theatre	2115 N. 45th	Seattle	WA	98103	2	819
Harvard Exit Theatre	807 E. Roy	Seattle	WA	98105	2	819
Metro Cinemas	4500 8th Ave. N.E., #200	Seattle	WA	98105	10	819
Neptune Theatre	1303 N.E. 45th	Seattle	WA	98105	1	819
Seven Gables Theatre	911 N.E. 50th St.	Seattle	WA	98105	1	819
Varsity Theater	4329 University Way N.E.	Seattle	WA	98105	3	819
Downer Theatre	2689 Downer Ave.	Milwaukee	WI	53211	2	617
Oriental Theatre	2230 N. Farwell Ave.	Milwaukee	WI	53202	3	617

JACK LOEKS THEATRES

8 theatres, 105 screens.
2121 Celebration Dr. N.E., Grand Rapids, MI 49525. (616) 447-4200. FAX: (616) 447-4201.
CHAIRMAN
John D. Loeks
PRESIDENT, CEO & COO
John D. Loeks, Jr.
EXECUTIVE V.P., MARKETING & FILM
Ron Van Timmeren
V.P., OPERATIONS
Roger Lubs
V.P., HUMAN RESOURCES
Steve Forsythe
V.P., IT & TECHNICAL SERVICES
Kenneth Baas
V.P. DIRECTOR, FOOD & BEVERAGE
Kenyon Shane
CFO
Nancy Hagan

THEATRES

Theatre	Address	City	State	Zip	Screens	DMA
Celebration! Cinema	1468 Cinema Way	Benton Harbor	MI	49022	14	588
Celebration Cinema/IMAX Theatre	2121 Celebration Dr.	Grand Rapids	MI	49525	18	563
Studio 28	1350 S.W. 28th St.	Grand Rapids	MI	49509	20	563
Celebration Cinema /IMAX Theatre	200 E. Edgewood Blvd.	Lansing	MI	48911	20	551
Celebration Cinema	4935 E. Pickard	Mt. Pleasant	MI	48858	11	513
Getty Drive-In	920 E. Summit	Muskegon	MI	49441	4	563
Cinema Carousel	4289 Grand Haven Rd.	Muskegon	MI	49441	16	563
Plaza 1 and 2	3450 Henry St.	Muskegon	MI	49441	2	563

LOEWS CINEPLEX ENTERTAINMENT CORP.
(LOEWS, CINEPLEX ODEON, MAGIC JOHNSON & STAR THEATRES)

147 theatres, 1,508 screens (includes 3 IMAX)
Corp. Headquarters: 711 Fifth Ave., New York, NY 10022-3109. (646) 521-6000.
Canadian Headquarters: 1303 Yonge St., Toronto, Ontario M4T 2Y9. (416) 323-6600. 70 Theatres, 609 Screens.
LCE CORPORATE PRESIDENT & CEO
Travis Reid
PRESIDENT, LOEWS CINEPLEX ENTERTAINMENT U.S
Michael P. Norris
SENIOR V.P. & CFO
John J. Walker
DIRECTOR, STRATEGIC DEVELOPMENT
Juan Monroy
SENIOR V.P. & CORPORATE COUNSEL
Michael Politi
SENIOR V.P.. DEPUTY GENERAL COUNSEL
Seymour Smith
SENIOR V.P., MARKETING
John McCauley
SENIOR V.P., FILM BUYER
Steve Bunnell
V.P., AUDITING
Robert Cohen
V.P., FINANCE
Bryan Berndt
SENIOR V.P. & REAL ESTATE COUNSEL
David Badain
V.P., CONCESSIONS
Stuart Holcombe
V.P., FILM
Phil Groves
V.P., HUMAN RESOURCES UNITED STATES
Allan Fox
SENIOR V.P. & CIO MIS
Jim Fagerstrom
DIVISIONAL V.P. OPERATIONS, EAST COAST
Paul Wehrle
DIVISIONAL V.P. OPERATIONS, WEST COAST
Len Westenberg
V.P., PROCUREMENT & STRATEGIS SUPPLY
Thomas Hogan
SENIOR V.P., REAL ESTATE
Alan Benjamin
V.P., SAFETY & SECURITY
Gerry Cieremans
CINEPLEX ODEON CANADA, CHAIRMAN
Allan Karp
SENIOR V.P. & CFO CANADA
Gord Nelson
SENIOR V.P., DEVELOPMENT, DESIGN & CONSTRUCTION & PRESIDENT, CINEPLEX ODEON CANADA
Olga Budimirovic
SENIOR V.P., FILM
Richard Boynton
V.P., MARKETING
Greg Mason
V.P., PURCHASING
Ian Shaw
V.P., OPERATIONS
Colin Smyth

Theatre	Address	City	State	Zip	Screens	DMA

THEATRES

Theatre	Address	City	State	Zip	Screens	DMA
Catalina	2320 N. Campbell Ave.	Tucson	AZ	85719	6	789
Foothills	7401 La Cholla Blvd., Ste. 144	Tucson	AZ	85741	15	789
Beverly Center	8522 Beverly Blvd., Ste. 835	Los Angeles	CA	90048	13	803
Magic Johnson Crenshaw	4020 Marlton Ave.	Los Angeles	CA	90008	15	803
Marina	13455 Maxella Ave., Store #270	Marina Del Rey	CA	90292	6	803
Metreon	101 Fourth St.	San Francisco	CA	94103	15	807
Broadway	1441 3rd St. Promenade	Santa Monica	CA	90401	4	803
Universal Studio Cinemas	100 Universal City Pl.	Universal City	CA	91608	18	803
Danbury	4-6 International Dr.	Danbury	CT	06810	10	501
Plainville	220 New Britain Ave.	Plainville	CT	06062	20	533
Cinema	5100 Wisconsin Ave.	Washington	DC	20016	1	511
Dupont	1350 19th St. N.W.	Washington	DC	20036	5	511
Inner Circle	2301 M St., N.W.	Washington	DC	20037	3	511
Outer Circle	4849 Wisconsin Ave. N.W.	Washington	DC	20016	2	511
Uptown	3426 Connecticut Ave. N.W.	Washington	DC	20008	1	511
Wisconsin	4000 Wisconsin Ave., N.W.	Washington	DC	20016	6	511
Universal Cineplex 20	6000 Universal Blvd.	Orlando	FL	32819	20	534
Magic Johnson Greenbrier	2841 Greenbrier Pkwy. S.W.	Atlanta	GA	30331	12	524
River Oaks 1-6	130 River Oaks Centre	Calumet City	IL	60409	6	602
River Oaks 7-8	70 River Oaks Ctr.	Calumet City	IL	60409	2	602
River Oaks 9-10	300 River Oaks Dr.	Calumet City	IL	60409	2	602
600 North Michigan	600 N. Michigan Ave.	Chicago	IL	60611	9	602
Esquire	58 E. Oak St.	Chicago	IL	60611	6	602
Lincoln Village 1-6	6341 N. McCormick Blvd.	Chicago	IL	60659	6	602
McClurg	330 E. Ohio St.	Chicago	IL	60611	3	602
Pipers Alley	1608 N. Wells	Chicago	IL	60614	4	602
Webster Place	1471 W. Webster Ave.	Chicago	IL	60614	11	602
Chicago Ridge	500 Chicago Ridge Mall	Chicago Ridge	IL	60415	6	602
Country Club Hills	4201 W. 167th St.	Country Club Hills	IL	60478	16	602
Crestwood	13221 Rivercrest Dr.	Crestwood	IL	60445	18	602
Quarry Cinemas	9201 63rd St.	Hodgkins	IL	60525	14	602
Norridge	4520 N. Harlem Ave.	Norridge	IL	60706	10	602
North Riverside	7501 W. Cermak Rd.	N. Riverside	IL	60546	6	602
Oakbrook 5-7	2020 Spring Rd.	Oakbrook	IL	60521	3	602
Streets of Woodfield	601 N. Martingale Rd., Ste. 105	Schaumburg	IL	60173	20	602
Gardens 1-6	220 Old Orchard Ctr.	Skokie	IL	60077	6	602
Gardens 7-13	175 Old Orchard Ctr.	Skokie	IL	60077	7	602
Streamwood	1500 Buttita Dr.	Streamwood	IL	60107	14	602
Rice Lake	301 Rice Lake Sq.	Wheaton	IL	60187	10	602
Woodridge	10000 Woodward Ave.	Woodridge	IL	60517	18	602
College Park	3535 W. 86th St.	Indianapolis	IN	46268	14	527
Merrillville	2360 E. 79th Ave.	Merrillville	IN	46410	10	602
Boston Common	175 Tremont St.	Boston	MA	02111	19	506
Copley Place	100 Huntington Ave., #17	Boston	MA	02116	11	506
Harvard Square 1-5	10 Church St.	Cambridge	MA	02138	5	506
Fresh Pond	168 Alewife Brk. Pkwy.	Cambridge	MA	02138	10	506
Liberty Tree Mall	100 Independence Way.	Danvers	MA	01923	20	506
Methuen	90 Pleasant Valley St.	Methuen	MA	01844	20	660
Natick 1-6	1398 Worcester.	Natick	MA	01760	6	506
Assembly Square 1-12	35 Middlesex Ave.	Somerville	MA	02145	12	506
White Marsh	8141 Honeygo Blvd.	Baltimore	MD	21236	16	512
Center Park	4001 Powder Mill Rd.	Beltsville	MD	20705	8	511
Rio Cinemas	9811 Washingnton Ctr.	Gaithersburg	MD	20878	18	511
Lexington Park 6	21882 FDR Blvd.	Lexington Park	MD	20653	6	511
Marlow	3899 Branch Ave.	Marlow Heights	MD	20748	6	511
Valley Center 9	9616 Reistertown Rd., Ste. 400.	Owings Mills	MD	21117	9	512
White Flint 5	11301 Rockville Pike.	Kensington	MD	20895	5	511
St. Charles Towne Center	11115 Mall Cir.	Waldorf	MD	20603	9	511
Wheaton Plaza 11	11160 Veirs Mill Rd.	Wheaton	MD	20902	11	511
Great Lakes	4300 Baldwin Rd.	Auburn Hills	MI	48326	25	505
Gratiot	35705 S. Gratiot Ave.	Clinton Twp.	MI	48035	21	505
Fairlane	18900 Michigan Ave.	Dearborn	MI	48126	21	505
Grand Rapids	3000 Alpine Ave.	Grand Rapids	MI	49544	18	563
Holland	12271 James St.	Holland	MI	49424	8	563
John R.	32289 John R. Rd.	Madison Heights	MI	48071	15	505
Rochester Hills	200 BArclay Cir.	Rochester Hills	MI	48307	10	505
Southfield	25333 W. 12 Mile Rd.	Southfield	MI	48034	20	505
Taylor	22265 Eureka Rd.	Taylor	MI	48180	10	505
Brick Plaza	3 Brick Plaza	Bricktown.	NJ	08723	10	501
Cherry Hill	2121 Rte. 38.	Cherry Hill	NJ	08002	24	504
East Hanover	145 Rte. 10.	East Hanover.	NJ	07936	12	501
Monmouth Mall	Rte. 35 & 36	Eatontown	NJ	07724	15	501
Menlo Park	390 Menlo Park Mall	Edison	NJ	08837	12	501
Jersey Gardens	651 Kapkowski Pkwy.	Elizabeth	NJ	07201	20	501
Freehold Metroplex	101 Trotters Way.	Freehold	NJ	07728	14	501
Newport Centre	30-300 Mall Dr. W.	Jersey City	NJ	07303	11	501
Mountainside	1021 Rte. 22 E.	Mountainside	NJ	07092	10	501
New Brunswick	17 U.S. Hwy #1.	New Brunswick	NJ	08901	18	501
Paramus Route 4	260 E. Rte. 4.	Paramus	NJ	07652	10	501
Route 17	S-85 Rte. 17.	Paramus	NJ	07652	3	501
Ridgefield Park	75 Challenger Rd.	Ridgefield Park	NJ	07660	12	501
Meadow Six	800 Plaza Dr.	Secaucus	NJ	07094	6	501
Plaza 8	495 Harmon Meadow Blvd.	Secaucus	NJ	07094	8	501
Seacourt 10	Seacourt Pavillion, 635 Bay Ave.	Toms River	NJ	08753	10	501
Wayne	67 Willowbrook Blvd.	Wayne	NJ	07470	14	501
Bay Terrace	211-01 26th Ave.	Bayside	NY	11360	6	501
Alpine	6817 Fifth Ave.	Brooklyn	NY	11220	7	501
Fortway	6722 Fort Hamilton Pkwy	Brooklyn	NY	11219	5	501
Kings Plaza Sixplex	5201 Kings Plaza	Brooklyn	NY	11234	6	501
Cinema #5	183-15 Horace Harding Blvd.	Fresh Meadows	NY	11365	5	501

775

Theatre	Address	City	State	Zip	Screens	DMA
Fresh Meadows	190-02 Horace Harding Blvd.	Fresh Meadows	NY	11365	7	501
Roosevelt Field	Roosevelt Field Mall	Garden City	NY	11530	8	501
Glen Cove Cinemas	5 School St.	Glen Cove	NY	11542	6	501
Shore	37 Wall St.	Huntington	NY	11743	8	501
Nassau Metroplex	3585 Hempstead Tpke.	Levittown	NY	11756	10	501
Galleria Metroplex	1 Galleria Dr.	Middletown	NY	10940	16	501
19th Street East	890 Broadway	New York	NY	10003	6	501
72nd Street	1230 3rd Ave. 72nd St.	New York	NY	10021	1	501
84th Street	2310 Broadway	New York	NY	10024	6	501
Astor Plaza	1515 Broadway	New York	NY	10036	1	501
34th Street	316 W. 34th St.	New York	NY	10001	14	501
E-Walk	247 W. 42nd St.	New York	NY	10036	13	501
Kips Bay Theatre	570 Second Ave.	New York	NY	10016	15	501
Lincoln Square	1998 Broadway	New York	NY	10023	12	501
Loews IMAX	1998 Broadway	New York	NY	10023	1	501
Magic Johnson Harlem	2309 Frederick Douglass Blvd.	New York	NY	10027	9	501
Orpheum	1538 3rd Ave. 86th St.	New York	NY	10028	7	501
State	1540 Broadway	New York	NY	10036	4	501
Village VII	66 3rd Ave. 11th St.	New York	NY	10003	7	501
Fantasy	18 N. Park Ave.	Rockville Centre	NY	11570	5	501
Rockville Centre	340 Sunrise Hwy.	Rockville Centre	NY	11570	2	501
Rotterdam Square Mall Six	93 W. Campbell Rd.	Schenectady	NY	12306	6	532
Stony Brook	2196 Nesconset Highway	Stony Brook	NY	11790	15	501
Loews Towne Square	2425 Vestal Pkwy.	Vestal	NY	13850	9	555
Webster Twelveplex	2190 Empire Blvd.	Webster	NY	14580	12	538
Palisades Center	4403 Palisades Ctr. Dr.	West Nyack	NY	10994	21	501
Roosevelt Raceway	1025 Corporate Dr.	Westbury	NY	11590	10	501
Magic Johnson Randall Park Mall	20801 Miles Rd.	N. Randall	OH	44128	12	510
Richmond Town Square	631 Richmond Rd.	Richmond Heights	OH	44143	20	510
Stroud Mall Seven	Rte 611-160 Stroud Mall	Stroudburg	PA	18360	7	577
Waterfront	300 W. Waterfront Dr.	West Homestead	PA	15120	22	508
20 & 287 6	4930 Little Rd.	Arlington	TX	76016	6	623
Lincoln Square	800 Lincoln Square	Arlington	TX	76011	10	623
Cityplace	2600 N. Haskell	Dallas	TX	75204	14	623
Keystone Park	13933 N. Central Expy.	Dallas	TX	75243	16	623
City View Eightplex	4728 Bryant Irvin Rd.	Fort Worth	TX	76132	8	623
Easton Commons 8	8580 Hwy. 6 N.	Houston	TX	77095	8	618
Magic Johnson Northline	100 Northline Mall	Houston	TX	77022	12	618
Spring Tenplex	20115 Holzwarth Rd.	Spring	TX	77388	10	618
Fountains	11225 Fountain Lake Dr.	Stafford	TX	77477	18	618
Layton Hills 9	728 W. 1425 N.	Layton Hills	UT	84041	9	770
Shirlington 7	2772 S. Randolph St.	Arlington	VA	22206	7	511
Fairfax Square 8	8065 Leesburg Pike	Vienna	VA	22182	8	511
Factoria Cinemas 8	3505 Factoria Blvd. S.E.	Bellevue	WA	98006	8	819
Cascade Mall	200 Cascade Mall Dr.	Burlington	WA	98233	14	819
Lakewood Town Center Cinemas	5721 Main S.W.	Lakewood	WA	98499	12	819
Grand Cinemas Alderwood	18421 Alderwood Mall Pkwy.	Lynnwood	WA	98037	8	819
Redmond Town Center	16451 N.E. 74th St.	Redmond	WA	98052	8	819
Meridian	1501 7th Ave.	Seattle	WA	98101	16	819
Oak Tree Cinemas	10006 Aurora Ave. N.	Seattle	WA	98133	6	819
Uptown Cinemas	511 Queen Ann Ave. N.	Seattle	WA	98109	3	819
Lewis & Clark	15820 Tukwila Int'l Blvd.	Tukwila	WA	98188	7	819
Woodinville	17640 Garden Way N.E.	Woodinville	WA	98072	12	819

LOGAN LUXURY THEATRES

4 theatres, 10 screens.
209 N. Lawler St., Mitchell, SD 57301. (605) 996-9022. FAX: (605) 996-9241. www.loganmovie.com
PRESIDENT
Jeff Logan
VICE PRESIDENT
Linda Logan
BOOKER & FILM BUYER
Jim Wilson

THEATRES

Theatre	Address	City	State	Zip	Screens	DMA
Dells Theatre	511 E. 4th	Dell Rapids	SD	57022	1	725
Huron Cinema 3	215 Dakota Ave.	Huron	SD	57350	3	725
Luxury 5 Cinemas	209 N. Lawler	Mitchell	SD	57301	5	725
Starlite Drive-In	N. Hwy. 37	Mitchell	SD	57301	1	725

MJR THEATRES, INC. (MOVIES JUST RIGHT)

6 theatres, 87 screens.
13691 W. Eleven Mile Rd., Oak Park, MI 48237. (248) 548-8282. FAX: (248) 548-4706.
PRESIDENT
Michael R. Mihalich
V.P. & FILM BUYER
Candi Mihalich
V.P., OPERATIONS
Dennis Redmer
DIRECTOR OF PROMOTIONS
Robin Hansen

THEATRES

Theatre	Address	City	State	Zip	Screens	DMA
Adrian Cinema	3150 N. Adrian Hwy.	Adrian	MI	49221	10	547
Allen Park Cinema	6601 Allen Rd.	Allen Park	MI	48101	5	505
Brighton Town Square Cinema	8200 Murphy Dr.	Brighton	MI	48116	20	505
Chesterfield Crossing	50675 Gratiot Ave.	Chesterfield	MI	48051	16	505
Southgate Cinemas	15651 Trenton Rd.	Southgate	MI	48195	20	505
Waterford Cinema	7501 Highland Rd.	Waterford	MI	48327	16	505

Theatre	Address	City	State	Zip	Screens	DMA

MALCO THEATRES, INC.

35 theatres, 302 screens.
5851 Ridgeway Ctr. Pkwy., Memphis, TN 38120. (901) 761-3480. FAX: (901) 681-2044. www.malco.com
CHAIRMAN
Richard Lightman
PRESIDENT & CEO
Stephen Lightman
EXECUTIVE V.P.
Herbert R. Levy
SENIOR V.P., MARKETING & CORPORATE DEVELOPMENT
Robert Levy
SENIOR V.P., GENERAL MANAGER & OPERATIONS
James Tashie
V.P, CFO & TREASURER
Bill Blackburn
V.P. & HEAD FILM BUYER
Jeff Kaufman
V.P., TECHNICAL SUPPORT
Mike Thompson
V.P., CONCESSIONS OPERATIONS
Larry Etter
V.P. & DISTRICT MANAGER
James Lloyd
OPERATIONS MANAGER
D. Tashie
AREA MANAGER
Don Burchett
AREA MANAGER
Alan Denton
CO-OP ADVERTISING
Jeff Martin
MARKETING & PROMOTIONS COORDINATOR
Jill Freeman

THEATRES

Theatre	Address	City	State	Zip	Screens	DMA
Malco Trio	Hwy. 18 E. At I-55	Blytheville	AR	72315	3	640
Malco Razorback 6	2035 N. College	Fayetteville	AR	72701	6	670
Malco Mall Twin	4201 N. College	Fayetteville	AR	72701	2	670
Malco Cinema 12	1200 Waldron Rd.	Fort Smith	AR	72903	12	670
Malco Mall Trio	5111 Rogers Ave.	Fort Smith	AR	72904	3	670
Malco Cinema 14	2001 E. Highland Dr.	Jonesboro	AR	72401	14	734
Malco Hollywood 12	2407 E. Parker Rd.	Jonesboro	AR	72401	12	734
Malco Hollywood Cinema	120 Dearman Dr.	Monticello	AR	71655	6	693
Malco Plaza Cinema	1725 Paragould Plz.	Paragould	AR	72450	6	734
Malco Town Center 12	621 N. 46th St.	Rogers	AR	72756	16	670
Malco Sunset Cinema 9	2940-G W. Sunset	Springdale	AR	72762	9	670
Malco Cinema 12	5333 Frederica St.	Owensboro	KY	42303	16	649
Malco Trio	1045 E. Malone	Sikeston	MO	63801	3	632
Malco Cinema 3	Hwy. 45 N.	Columbus	MS	39703	3	673
Malco Leigh Mall	Hwy. 45 N.	Columbus	MS	39701	1	673
Malco Twin	219 Alabama St.	Columbus	MS	39701	2	673
Malco Varsity Twin	401 Main St.	Columbus	MS	39703	2	673
Malco DeSoto Cinema 16	7130 Malco Blvd.	Southaven	MS	38671	16	640
Malco Cinema 10	861 Cliff Gookin Blvd.	Tupelo	MS	38801	10	673
Malco Tupelo Cinema	3352 Gloster	Tupelo	MS	38804	10	673
Malco Stage Cinema 12	7930 Stage Rd.	Barlett	TN	38134	12	640
Malco Cordova 16	1080 N. Germantown Pkwy.	Cordova	TN	38018	16	640
Malco Trinity Commons	704 Germantown Pkwy.	Cordova	TN	38018	9	640
Malco Forest Hill	3180 Village Shops Dr.	Germantown	TN	38138	8	640
Malco Collierville Towne Cinema 16	380 Market Blvd.	Bartlett	TN	38017	16	640
Malco Bartlett Cinema 10	2809 Bartlett Blvd.	Memphis	TN	38134	10	640
Malco Highland Quartet	3473 Poplar Ave.	Memphis	TN	38111	4	640
Malco Majestic Theatre	7051 Malco Crossing	Memphis	TN	38115	20	640
Malco Paradiso	584 S. Mendenhall	Memphis	TN	38111	14	640
Malco Raleigh Springs Cinema 12	3384 Austin Peay Hwy.	Memphis	TN	38128	12	640
Malco Ridgeway 4	5853 Ridgeway Ctr. Pkwy.	Memphis	TN	38120	4	640
Malco Studio on the Square	2105 Court St.	Memphis	TN	38104	5	640
Malco Summer Drive-In	5310 Summer Ave.	Memphis	TN	38122	4	640
Malco Winchester Court Cinema	6740 Winchester Rd.	Memphis	TN	38115	8	640
Malco Wolfchase Galleria	2766 N. Germantown Pkwy.	Memphis	TN	38133	8	640

MANN THEATRES OF MINNESOTA

13 theatres, 86 screens.
711 Hennepin Ave. 3rd Flr., Minneapolis, MN 55403. (612) 332-3303. FAX: (612) 332-3305.
PRESIDENT
Stephen Mann
VICE PRESIDENT
Benjie Mann
FILM BUYER & BOOKER
Neil O'Leary

THEATRES

Theatre	Address	City	State	Zip	Screens	DMA
Movies 10 at Westgate	1301 Excelsior Rd.	Baxter	MN	56425	10	613
Westport Theatre	Hwy. 371 & K-Mart Dr.	Baxter	MN	55425	3	613
Champlin Cinema 14	11500 Theatre Dr.	Champlin	MN	55016	14	613
Cottage View Drive-In	9338 E. Point Douglas Rd.	Cottage Grove	MN	55016	1	613
Eagan Cinema 9	1225 Town Centre Dr.	Eagan	MN	55123	9	613
Grand Rapids Cinema	113 S. 21st St.	Grand Rapids	MN	55744	8	676
Irongate Cinema 3	990 W. 41st St.	Hibbing	MN	55746	3	676
Hopkins Cinema 6	1118 Main St.	Hopkins	MN	55343	6	613
Maple Grove Cinema 10	13644 80th Cir.	Maple Grove	MN	55369	10	613
Plymouth Cinema 12	3400 Vicksburg Ln.	Plymouth	MN	55447	12	613
St. Louis Park Cinema	5400 Excelsior Blvd.	St. Louis Park	MN	55416	6	613
Grandview 1 & 2 Theatres	1830 Grand Ave.	St. Paul	MN	55105	2	613
Highland 1 & 2 Theatres	760 S. Cleveland Ave.	St. Paul	MN	55116	2	613

Theatre	Address	City	State	Zip	Screens	DMA

MARCUS THEATRES CORPORATION

46 theatres, 471 screens.
100 E. Wisconsin Ave., 20th Flr., Ste. 2000, Milwaukee, WI 53202-4122. (414) 905-1500. FAX: (414) 905-2189. www.marcustheatres.com
CHAIRMAN
Steve Marcus
PRESIDENT
Bruce J. Olson
EXECUTIVE V.P. & FILM BUYER
Michael Kominsky
SENIOR V.P.
Mark Gramz
V.P., MARKETING, ADVERTISING & CONCESSIONS
Robert Menefee
V.P., FILM
Rick Neals
DIRECTOR, CONSTRUCTION
Gary Berkley
DIRECTOR, HUMAN RESOURCES
Amy Wangerin
DIRECTOR, CONCESSIONS & PURCHASING
Patrick Striebel
DIRECTOR, COMMUNICATIONS & PROMOTIONS
Carlo Petrick
FILM BOOKER
Dave Stawicki

THEATRES

Theatre	Address	City	State	Zip	Screens	DMA
Marcus Cinema Addison	1555 W. Lake St.	Addison	IL	60101	21	602
ICE-Chatham	210 W. 87th St.	Chicago	IL	60620	14	602
ICE-Lawndale	3330 W. Roosevelt St.	Chicago	IL	60624	10	602
ICE-62nd & Western Theatre	2258 W. 62nd St.	Chicago	IL	60636	10	602
Marcus Cinema Chicago Heights	1301 Hilltop Ave.	Chicago Heights	IL	60411	14	602
Marcus Cinema Elgin Fox	111 S. Randall Rd.	Elgin	IL	60123	14	602
Marcus Cinema Gurnee	6144 Grand Ave. Gurnee Mills Mall	Gurnee	IL	60031	20	602
Marcus Cinema Orland Park	16350 S. LaGrange Rd.	Orland Park	IL	60467	14	602
Marcus Cinema Apple Valley	7200 W. 147th St.	Apple Valley	MN	55124	6	613
Marcus Cinema Elk River	Elk River Mall, 570 Freeport Rd.	Elk River	MN	55330	17	613
Marcus Cinema Hastings	1325 S. Frontage Rd.	Hastings	MN	55033	9	613
Marcus Cinema Oakdale	5677 Hadley Ave. N.	Oakdale	MN	55128	16	613
Marcus Cinema Rosemount	15280 Carrousel Way	Rosemount	MN	55068	8	613
Marcus Cinema Shakopee	1116 Shakopee Town Sq.	Shakopee	MN	55379	11	613
Marcus Cinema Crosswoods	200 Hutchinson Ave.	Columbus	OH	43235	17	535
Marcus Cinema Pickerington	1776 Hill Rd. N.	Pickerington	OH	43147	16	535
Marcus Cinema Hollywood	513 N. Westhill Blvd.	Appleton	WI	54914	14	658
Marcus Valley Value Cinemas	1401 Valley Fair Mall	Appleton	WI	54915	6	658
Marcus Cinema Bay Park	755 Willard Dr.	Ashwaubenon	WI	54304	4	658
Marcus Cinema Wisconsin	236 Front St.	Beaver Dam	WI	53916	4	617
Marcus Cinema West Point	20241 W. Bluemound Rd.	Brookfield	WI	53045	8	617
Marcus Cinema Rivoli	W. 62 N. 567 Washington Ave.	Cedarburg	WI	53012	1	617
Marcus Cinema Hillside	2950 Hillside Dr.	Delafield	WI	53018	14	617
Marcus Cinema Green Bay	411 Schoen St.	Green Bay	WI	54302	8	658
Marcus Cinema King	216 S. 7th St.	LaCrosse	WI	54601	3	702
Marcus Cinema LaCrosse	2032 Ward Ave.	LaCrosse	WI	54601	8	702
Marcus Cinema Eastgate	5202 High Crossing Blvd.	Madison	WI	53718	16	669
Marcus Cinema Point	7825 Big Sky Dr.	Madison	WI	53719	16	669
Marcus Cinema Westgate	340 Westgate Mall	Madison	WI	53711	4	669
Marcus Cinema Menomonee Falls	W180 N9393 Premier Lane.	Menomonee Falls	WI	53051	16	617
Marcus Cinema North Shore	11700 N. Port Washington.	Mequon	WI	53092	11	617
Marcus Cinema Northtown	7440 N. 76th St.	Milwaukee	WI	53223	8	617
Marcus Cinema Prospect Mall	2239 N. Prospect Ave.	Milwaukee	WI	53202	3	617
Marcus Cinema Southgate	3330 S. 30th St.	Milwaukee	WI	53215	10	617
Marcus Cinema South Towne	2305 W. Broadway	Monona	WI	53713	5	669
Marcus Cinema Cedar Creek	10101 Market St. Box D20	Mosinee	WI	54455	10	705
Marcus Cinema Ridge	5200 S. Mooreland Rd.	New Berlin	WI	53151	20	617
Marcus Cinema Value Oak Creek	6912 S. 27th St.	Oak Creek	WI	53154	8	617
Marcus Cinema South Shore	7261 S. 13th St.	Oak Creek	WI	53154	16	617
Marcus Cinema Ten	340 S. Koeller Rd.	Oshkosh	WI	54901	10	658
Marcus Cinema Regency	5230 Durand Ave.	Racine	WI	53406	8	617
Marcus Cinema Westgate	5101 Washington Ave.	Racine	WI	53406	5	617
Marcus Cinema Campus	103 Watson St.	Ripon	WI	54971	1	658
Marcus Cinema Sheboygan	3226 Kohler Memorial Dr.	Sheboygan	WI	53081	14	617
Marcus Ho-Chunk Cinema	135 Wittig Rd.	Tomah	WI	54660	6	
Marcus Cinema Westown	2440 E. Moreland Blvd.	Waukesha	WI	53186	9	617
Marcus Cinema Crossroad	306 S. 18th Ave.	Wausau	WI	54401	4	705

MARQUEE CINEMAS

17 theatres, 152 screens.
552 Ragland Rd., Beckley, WV 25801. (304) 255-4036. FAX: (304) 252-0526. www.marqueecinemas.com
PRESIDENT & CEO
Curtis E. McCall
EXECUTIVE V.P.
James M. Cox
CFO
Cindy Ramsden
V.P., PERSONNEL
Toni Y. McCall
DIRECTOR., REAL ESTATE DEVELOPMENT
David Beauregard
DIRECTOR, OPERATIONS
Harry L. Newman

Theatre	Address	City	State	Zip	Screens	DMA

DIRECTOR, MARKETING
Robin A. Shumate
ASSISTANT DIRECTOR
Rob Thompson

THEATRES

Theatre	Address	City	State	Zip	Screens	DMA
Springdale Cinemas	3020 Springdale Mall	Mobile	AL	36626	11	686
Westbrook 12	314 Flatrock Pl.	Westbrook	CT	06498	12	533
Coralwood 10 Cinemas	2301 Del Prado Blvd.	Cape Coral	FL	33990	10	
Highland Cinemas	2400 Happy Valley Rd.	Glasgow	KY	42142	8	736
Mimosa 7	101 Green St.	Morganton	NC	28655	7	517
Barrington 10	140 Barrington Town Sq.	Auora	OH	44202	10	
Consumer Square 14	6530 Tussing Rd.	Reynolds	OH	43068	14	
Tiffin	870 W. Market St.	Tiffin	OH	44883	8	547
Steamtown Mall 8	301 Lackawanna Ave.	Scranton	PA	18503	8	
Fort Henry Cinemas	2101 Fort Henry Dr.	Kingsport	TN	37664	8	531
MacArthur Marketplace 16	8505 Walton Blvd.	Irving	TX	75063	16	
Southpoint Cinemas	5800 Southpoint Blvd.	Fredericksburg	VA	22407	9	511
Showplace Cinemas	1408 N. Eisenhower Dr.	Beckley	WV	25801	7	559
Southridge Cinemas	331 Southridge Blvd	Charleston	WV	25309	12	564
Seneca Showcase	Greenbier Valley Mall	Lewisburg	WV	24901	2	559
Crossroads	22 Crossroads Mall	Mt Hope	WV	25880	6	559
Nicholas Showplace	300 Merchants Walk Plaza	Summersville	WV	26651	4	564

M.E. THEATRES

4 theatres, 6 screens.
P.O. Box 477, Jackson Center, OH 45334-0477. www.metheatres.com

THEATRES

Theatre	Address	City	State	Zip	Screens	DMA
Ada Theatre	215 S. Main St.	Ada	OH	45810	1	568
Elder	106 W. Pike St.	Jackson Center	OH	45334	1	568
Kenton	221 W. Franklin St.	Kenton	OH	43326	3	568
Hi-Road	8059 State Rte. 68 N.	Kenton	OH	43326	1	568

MEGASTAR CINEMAS, LLC

5 theatres, 78 screens.
1660 S. Stemmons Freeway, Ste. 360, Lewisville, TX 75067. (972) 434-8200. FAX: (972) 353-3411. www.megastarcinemas.com
Division offices: 6305 W. 26th Terrace, Overland Park, KS 66209. (913) 322-0315. FAX: (913) 322-6088.
5111 Kent Junction Rd., P.O. Box 1270, Norton, VA 24273. (770) 335-1111. FAX: (276) 679-8406.
CHAIRMAN
Jeff Kiser
PRESIDENT & CEO
James O. McKenna
V.P., CONSTRUCTION & PURCHASING
Lonnie Gillman
DIRECTOR, THEATRE OPERATIONS
Kathleen Gillman
HEAD FILM BUYER
Gary Gibbs

THEATRES

Theatre	Address	City	State	Zip	Screens	DMA
MegaStar Cinemas Stonecrest	8060 Mall Pkwy.	Lithonia	GA	30038	16	524
MegaStar Cinemas Springfield Plaza	1250 Saint James Ave.	Springfield	MA	01104	16	543
MegaStar Cinemas Arbor Lakes	12575 Elm Creek Blvd.	Maple Grove	MN	55369	16	613
MegaStar Cinemas Southdale Center	400 Southdale Ctr.	Edina	MN	55435	16	613
MegaStar Cinemas Chagrin	8200 E. Washington	Chagrin Falls	OH	44023	14	510

METROPOLITAN THEATRES CORP.

15 theatres, 64 screens.
8727 W. Third St., Los Angeles CA 90048. (310) 858-2800 FAX: (310) 858-2860. www.metrotheatres.com
CEO
Bruce C. Corwin
PRESIDENT
David Corwin
V.P., PLANNING & DEVELOPMENT
Bill Hughes
V.P., FILM MARKETING
Alan Stokes
V.P., OPERATIONS & CONCESSIONS
Ralph Breland

THEATRES

Theatre	Address	City	State	Zip	Screens	DMA
Calexico 10 Theatre	2441 Scaroni Rd.	Calexico	CA	92231	10	771
Cinema Twin	6050 Hollister Ave.	Goleta	CA	93117	2	855
Fairview Twin	251 N. Fairview	Goleta	CA	93117	2	855
Camino Real Cinemas	7040 Marketplace Dr.	Goleta	CA	93117	6	855
Park Theatre	6504 Pacific Blvd.	Huntington Park	CA	90255	2	803
Campus Theatre	1020 N. Vermont Ave.	Los Angeles	CA	90029	1	803
Light House Cinemas	525 Light House Ave.	Pacific Grove	CA	93950	4	828
University Village Cinemas	1201A University Ave.	Riverside	CA	92507	10	803
Teatro Fiesta	305-100 E. 4th St.	Santa Ana	CA	92701	2	803
Arlington Theatre	1317 State St.	Santa Barbara	CA	93101	1	855
Fiesta 5 Theatre	916 State St.	Santa Barbara	CA	93101	5	855
Granada Theatres	1216 State St.	Santa Barbara	CA	93101	1	855
Metro 4 Theatre	618 State St.	Santa Barbara	CA	93101	4	855
Paseo Nuevo Cinemas	8 W. De La Guerra Pl.	Santa Barbara	CA	93101	4	855
Plaza De Oro Twin	371 S. Hitchcock Way	Santa Barbara	CA	93105	2	855
Riviera Theatre	2044 Alameda Padre Serra	Santa Barbara	CA	93103	1	855
MetroLux 12 Theatre	1380 N. Denver Ave.	Loveland	CO	80537	12	751

Theatre	Address	City	State	Zip	Screens	DMA

MINI THEATRES

53 theatres, 182 screens.
31 W. Main St., Ste. 310, Patchogue, NY 11772. (631) 758-3456. FAX: (631) 207-0794.
PARTNERS
Marty Goldman
Harold Lager

THEATRES

Theatre	Address	City	State	Zip	Screens	DMA
Norwich Cinema	109 Salem Tnpk.	Norwich	CT	06360	2	533
Diamond State Drive-In	Rte. Box 13	Felton	DE	19943	1	504
Bijou	350 Main St.	Fairhaven	MA	02719	1	521
Gourcester Cinema	74 Essex Ave.	Gloucester	MA	01930	3	506
FineArts	17 Summer St.	Maynard	MA	01754	3	506
Cinema North Adams	Rte. Box # 8	N. Adams	MA	01247	6	532
Route 1	501 E. Washington St.	N. Attelboro	MA	02760	2	506
Island	Circuit Ave.	Oaks Bluff	MA	02557	1	506
Island	Oak Bluffs Ave.	Oaks Bluff	MA	02557	1	506
Strand	Oak Bluffs Ave.	Oaks Bluff	MA	02557	1	506
Cinemagic	6 Merrill St.	Salisbury	MA	01952	9	506
Tower South Hadley	19 College St.	South Hadley	MA	01075	2	543
Capawock	Main St.	Vineyard Haven	MA	02568	1	506
Cinemagic 12	779 Portland Rd.	Saco	ME	04072	12	500
Weirs Drive-In	Rte. 3	Laconia	NH	03246	4	506
Bay Drive-In	Rte. Box 26	Alexandria Bay	NY	13607	2	549
Hollywood Drive-In	9270 Rte. 66	Averill Park	NY	12018	1	532
Fingerlakes Drive-In	Clark St. Rd.	Auburn	NY	13021	1	555
Fingerlakes 4	Rte. 5 & 20	Auburn	NY	13022	4	555
Movieplex	Fingerlakes Mall	Auburn	NY	13021	10	555
Malta Drive-In	R.R. 9	Ballston Spa	NY	12020	1	532
American	98 Main St.	Canton	NY	13617	5	549
Movieplex Carmel	150 Rte. 52	Carmel	NY	10512	8	501
Crandell	Main St.	Chatham	NY	12037	1	532
Park Theater	Main St.	Cobleskill	NY	12043	1	532
Movieplex	10520 Bennett Rd.	Dunkirk	NY	14048	8	514
Movieplex Hudson	350 Fairview Ave.	Hudson	NY	12534	8	532
Hunter Theater	Main St.	Hunter	NY	12442	2	532
Movieplex	371 Hamilton St.	Geneva	NY	14456	8	538
Glen Drive-In	Lake George Rd.	Glens Falls	NY	12801	2	532
Greenville Drive-In	Rte. Box #32	Greenville	NY	12083	1	532
Tamarac Cafe	Rte. Box #28	Inlet	NY	13360	1	532
Movieplex Johnstown	236 N. Comrie Ave.	Johnstown	NY	12095	9	532
Palace	26 Main St.	Lake Placid	NY	12946	4	523
Valley Twin	20 Albany St.	Little Falls	NY	13365	2	526
Town Hall	Shady Ave.	Lowville	NY	13367	1	549
56 Auto Drive-In	Andrews St.	Massena	NY	13662	1	549
Movieplex Massena	Haven Shopping Plaza	Massena	NY	13662	8	549
Hathaway Drive-In	Rte. Box #67	N. Hoosick	NY	12133	1	532
Cinema Twin	Ogdensburg Mall	Ogdensburg	NY	13669	2	549
Strand	Main St.	Old Forge	NY	13420	4	526
Crystal Cinema	94 Victory Hwy.	Painted Post	NY	14870	8	565
Roxy	20 Main St.	Potsdam	NY	13676	4	549
Strand	Main St.	Schroon Lake	NY	12870	1	532
State Theater	Park St.	Tupper Lake	NY	12986	1	523
Unadilla D.I.	Rte. 7	Unadilla	NY	13849	1	526
Munson	310 Guesee St.	Utica	NY	13502	1	526
Valleybrook Drive-In		Lowville	NY	13367	1	526
Pier	3 Beach St.	Narragansett	RI	02882	3	521
Empire	17 Water St.	Block Island	RI	02871	1	521
Plaza	Rutland Plaza	Rutland	VT	05701	9	523
Westway	Westway Mall	West Rutland	VT	05777	4	523
Movieplex	Kocher Dr.	Bennington	VT	05201	3	532

THE MOVIE EXPERIENCE (SANBORN THEATRES, INC.)

6 theatres, 46 screens.
13 Corporate Plaza, Newport Beach, CA 92660. (949) 640-2370. www.movieexperience.com
PRESIDENT
Bruce Sanborn
GENERAL MANAGER
Gary Richardson
FILM BUYER
Pete Cole

THEATRES

Theatre	Address	City	State	Zip	Screens	DMA
Blue Jay Cinema	27315 N. Bay Rd.	Blue Jay	CA	92317	4	803
Movie Experience 17 at California Oaks	41090 California Oaks Rd.	Murrieta	CA	92562	17	803
Town & Country	2253 El Camino Real	Oceanside	CA	92054	4	825
Downtown Centre Cinema	888 Marsh St.	San Luis Obispo	CA	93401	7	855
Movie Experience @ Fremont	1035 Monterey	San Luis Obispo	CA	93401	4	855
Movie Experience 10 at Tower Plaza	27531 Ynez Rd.	Temecula	CA	92591	10	803

MULLER FAMILY THEATRES

7 theatres, 72 screens.
20653 Keokuk Ave., Lakeville, MN 55044. (952) 469-2883. FAX: (952) 985-5643. www.mullerfamilytheatres.com
DIRECTOR, OPERATIONS
Dale Haider

THEATRES

Theatre	Address	City	State	Zip	Screens	DMA
Delano 5 Theatre	4423 US Hwy 12.	Delano	MN	55328	5	613
East Bethel 10 Theatre	18635 Ulysses N.E.	East Bethel	MN	55005	10	613
Lakeville 18 Theatre	20653 Keokuk Ave.	Lakeville	MN	55044	18	613
Monticello 4 Theatre	137 E. Broadway.	Monticello	MN	55362	4	613
WillowCreek 12 Theatre	9900 Schlard Pkwy.	Plymouth	MN	55441	12	613
Waconia 6 Theatre	101 West 1st St.	Waconia	MN	55387	6	613
White Bear Township 17 Theatre	1180 County J Rd.	White Bear Twnshp.	MN	55110	17	613

MUVICO THEATERS

12 theatres, 233 screens.
3101 N. Federal Hwy., 6th Flr., Ft. Lauderdale, FL 33306. (954) 564-6550. FAX: (954) 564-6553. www.muvico.com
PRESIDENT
Hamid Hashemi
CFO
Michael F. Whalen
SENIOR V.P.
Michael Melvin
SENIOR V.P., FILM BUYER
Jerry Gruenberg
V.P., OPERATIONS
Deane Hashemi
DIRECTOR OF MARKETING
Jim Lee
DIRECTOR, FOOD & BEVERAGE
Mark Ciolko
DIRECTOR, OPERATIONS
Chuck DeWitt
V.P., REAL ESTATE
Barry Ruzat
DIRECTOR, DESIGN & CONSTRUCTION
Mike Wilson

THEATRES

Theatre	Address	City	State	Zip	Screens	DMA
Muvico Palace 20	3200 Airport Rd.	Boca Raton	FL	33431	20	548
Muvico Paradise 24	15601 Sheridan St.	Davie	FL	33331	24	528
Muvico Hialeah 14	780 W. 49th St.	Hialeah	FL	33012	14	528
Muvico Pointe 21	9101 International Dr., Ste. 2100	Orlando	FL	32819	21	534
Muvico Palm Harbor 10	37912 U.S. Highway 19N	Palm Harbor	FL	34684	10	539
Muvico Pompano 18	2315 N. Federal Hwy.	Pompano Beach	FL	33062	18	528
Muvico Baywalk 20	151 2nd Ave. N.	St. Petersburg	FL	33701	20	539
Muvico Centro Ybor 20	1600 E. 8th Ave., #A-200	Tampa	FL	33605	20	539
Muvico Starlight 20	18002 Highwoods Preserve Pkwy	Tampa	FL	33647	20	539
Muvico Parisian 20	545 Hibiscus St.	W. Palm Beach	FL	33401	20	548
Muvico Egyptian 24	7000 Arundel Mills Cir., C-1	Hanover	MD	21076	24	512
Muvico Peabody Place 22	150 Peabody Pl., Ste. 300	Memphis	TN	38103	22	640

NATIONAL AMUSEMENTS, INC.

93 U.S. theatres, 1072 U.S. screens; 19 U.K. theatres, 243 U.K. screens; 7 S.A. theatres, 84 screens; Total: 116 theatres, 1,396 screens. 1 US IMAX.
200 Elm St., P.O. Box 9126, Dedham, MA 02026. (781) 461-1600. FAX: (781) 326-1306. www.nationalamusements.com
PRESIDENT
Shari E. Redstone
SENIOR V.P., FINANCE & TREASURER
Jerome Magner
SENIOR V.P., OPERATIONS
William J. Towey
SENIOR V.P., FILM BOOKING
George Levitt
V.P. & GENERAL COUNSEL
Thaddeus Jankowski
V.P., INTERNATIONAL OPERATIONS
John Bilsborough
V.P., REAL ESTATE
William J. Moscarelli
V.P., FILM INTERNATIONAL
Mark Walukevich
V.P., FINANCE & ADMINISTRATION
Richard Sherman
V.P., CONCESSIONS
James Hughes
V.P., MIS
Stephen Sohles
V.P., OPERATIONS
James Murray
V.P., MARKETING & ADVERTISING
Elaine Purdy
V.P., CONSTRUCTION
John Townsend
ASSISTANT V.P. & DEPUTY GENERAL COUNSEL
Patricia Reeser
ASSISTANT V.P., SALES & MARKETING
John Zawalich

THEATRES

Theatre	Address	City	State	Zip	Screens	DMA
The Bridge Cinema DeLux	6081 Center Dr.	Los Angeles	CA	90045	17	803
The Bridge IMAX	6081 Center Dr.	Los Angeles	CA	90045	1	803
Showcase Berlin	19 Frontage Rd.	Berlin	CT	06037	12	533
Showcase Bridgeport	286 Canfield St.	Bridgeport	CT	06605	12	501
S/C East Hartford	936 Silver Ln.	East Hartford	CT	06118	14	533
Showcase East Windsor	171 Bridge St.	East Windsor	CT	06088	12	533
Fairfield Cinemas	40 Black Rock Tpk.	Fairfield	CT	06430	9	501
Showcase Cinemas Buckland Hills	99 Red Stone Rd.	Manchester	CT	06045	16	533
Showcase Milford	230 Cherry St.	Milford	CT	06460	5	533
Milford Quad.	1201 Boston Post Rd.	Milford	CT	06460	4	533
Showcase North Haven	550 Universal Dr.	N. Haven	CT	06473	12	533
Showcase Orange	100 Marsh Hill Rd.	Orange	CT	06477	8	533
Showcase Southington	1821 Meriden Waterbury Tpk.	Southington	CT	06489	12	533
Showcase Cinemas 53 Davenport	I-74 at E. 53rd St. #3601	Davenport	IA	52807	18	682
River Falls Cinemas	951 E. Hwy 131	Clarksville	IN	47129	10	529
Showcase Erlanger	3220 Meadow Ln.	Erlanger	KY	41018	9	515

Theatre	Address	City	State	Zip	Screens	DMA
Florence Cinemas	7685 Florence Mall Rd.	Florence	KY	41042	9	515
Showcase Stonybrook	2745 S. Hurstbourne Pkwy.	Louisville	KY	40220	20	529
Showcase Cinemas Louisville	3408 Bardstown Rd.	Louisville	KY	40218	13	529
Kenwood Drive-In	7001 Southside Dr.	Louisville	KY	40214	1	529
Circle Cinemas	399 Chesnut Hill Ave.	Brookline	MA	02135	7	506
Showcase Cinemas Dedham	950 Providence Hwy.	Dedham	MA	02026	12	506
Showcase Lawrence 1-6	141 Winthrop Ave.	Lawrence	MA	01843	6	506
Showcase Cinemas Lawrence 7-14	141 Winthrop Ave.	Lawrence	MA	01843	8	506
Showcase Cinemas Lowell	32 Reiss Ave.	Lowell	MA	01851	14	506
Showcase Cinemas North Attleboro	640 S. Washington St.	N. Attleboro	MA	02760	12	521
Showcase Cinemas Randolph	Rte 139 73 Mazzeo Dr.	Randolph	MA	02368	16	506
Showcase Cinemas Revere	565 Squire Rd.	Revere	MA	02151	20	506
Showcase Cinmeas Seekonk 1-10	800 Fall River Ave.	Seekonk	MA	02771	10	521
Showcase Seekonk Route 6	100 Commerce Way	Seekonk	MA	02771	10	521
Springfield Cinemas	1060 Wilbraham Rd.	Springfield	MA	01128	12	543
S/C Cinemas At Eastfield Mall	1655 Boston Rd.	Springfield	MA	01129	16	543
S/C West Springfield 1-15	864 Riverdale St.	West Springfield	MA	01089	15	543
Showcase Cinemas Woburn	25 Middlesex Canal Pkwy.	Woburn	MA	01801	14	506
Showcase Cinemas Worcester North	135 Brooke St.	Worcester	MA	01606	18	506
Showcase Flint East	5205 E. Court St.	Burton	MI	48503	14	513
Courtland Center Cinemas	4226 E. Court St.	Burton	MI	48509	6	513
Showcase Dearborn	24115 Michigan Ave.	Dearborn	MI	48126	8	505
Cinema 10 Flint	4425 Lennon Rd.	Flint	MI	48507	10	513
Showcase Flint West	1591 S. Graham Rd.	Flint	MI	48532	14	513
Beacon East Cinemas	19305 Vernier Rd.	Harper Woods	MI	48225	4	505
Showcase Sterling Heights	35100 Van Dyke	Sterling Heights	MI	48312	15	505
Showcase Westland	6800 N. Wayne Rd.	Westland	MI	48185	8	505
Showcase Ann Arbor	4100 Carpenter Rd.	Ypsilanti	MI	48197	20	505
Atco Multiplex	178 White Horse Pike	Atco	NJ	08004	14	504
Town Center Plaza	319 Rte. 30 N.	East Windsor	NJ	08520	15	504
Edgewater Multiplex Cinemas	339 River Rd.	Edgewater	NJ	07020	16	501
Hazlet Multiplex	2821 Hwy. 35	Hazlet	NJ	07730	12	501
All-Jersey Multiplex	104-180 Foundry St.	Newark	NJ	07105	12	501
Amboy Multiplex	U.S. 9 & Rte. 35	Sayreville	NJ	08872	14	501
Concourse Plaza Multiplex	214 E. 161st St.	Bronx	NY	10451	10	501
Whitestone Multiplex	2505 Bruckner Blvd.	Bronx	NY	10465	14	501
Linden Blvd. Multiplex	2784 Linden Blvd.	Brooklyn	NY	11208	14	501
Commack Multiplex	100 Long Island Expy.	Commack	NY	11725	15	501
Farmingdale Multiplex	1001 Broad Hollow Rd.	Farmingdale	NY	11735	14	501
Greenburgh Multiplex Cinemas	320 Saw Mill River Rd.	Greenburgh	NY	10523	10	501
All Westchester Saw Mill Multi	151 Saw Mill River Rd.	Hawthorne	NY	10532	10	501
Broadway Multiplex	955 Broadway Mall	Hicksville	NY	11801	12	501
Island 16 Cinema DeLux	185 Morris Ave.	Holtsville	NY	11742	16	501
Jamaica Multiplex	159-02 Jamacia Ave.	Jamaica	NY	11432	15	501
Green Acres Cinemas	610 W. Sunrise Hwy.	Valley Stream	NY	11581	6	501
Sunrise Multiplex	750 W. Sunrise Hwy.	Valley Stream	NY	11582	14	501
College Point Multiplex	28-55 Ulmer St.	Whitestone	NY	11357	12	501
Cross County Multiplex	Two South Dr.	Yonkers	NY	10704	10	501
Showcase Cross Pointe 12	6751 Loop Rd.	Centerville	OH	45459	12	515
Showcase Cinemas Forest Fair	760 Forest Fair Dr.	Cincinnati	OH	45240	10	515
Showcase Cinemas Springdale	12064 Springfield Pike	Cincinnati	OH	45246	18	515
Showcase Eastgate	4701 Eastgate Blvd.	Cincinnati	OH	45245	7	515
Showcase Cincinnati	1701 Showcase Dr.	Cincinnati	OH	45237	12	515
Showcase Western Hills	5870 Harrison Ave.	Cincinnati	OH	45248	14	515
Kenwood Towne Centre	7875 Montgomery Rd.	Cincinnati	OH	45236	5	515
Super Cinemas Toledo	1301 E. Mall Dr.	Holland	OH	43528	10	547
Showcase Huber Heights 16	7737 Waynetown Blvd.	Huber Heights	OH	45424	16	542
Oakley Drive-In	5033 Madison Rd.	Madisonville	OH	45227	1	515
Showcase Kings Island	5937 Kings Island Dr.	Mason	OH	45040	12	515
Showcase Maumee	1360 Conant St., Rte. 20	Maumee	OH	43537	18	547
Showcase Cinemas Milford	500 Rivers Edge Dr.	Milford	OH	45150	16	515
Franklin Park 6	5001 Monroe St.	Toledo	OH	43623	6	547
Franklin Park Cinemas	5235 Monroe St.	Toledo	OH	43623	5	547
Showcase Toledo	3500 Secor Rd.	Toledo	OH	43606	5	547
Showcase Cinemas Dayton South	195 Mall Woods Dr.	West Carrollton	OH	45449	16	542
The Bridge Cinema DeLux-UPenn	250 S. 40th St.	Philadelphia	PA	19104	6	504
Showcase Cinemas East	3455 Wm. Penn Hwy.	Pittsburgh	PA	15235	10	508
Showcase Cinemas West	Park Manor Dr.	Pittsburgh	PA	15205	12	508
Showcase Cinemas North	9700 Mcknight Rd.	Pittsburgh	PA	15237	11	508
Northway Mall	8000 McKnight Rd.	Pittsburgh	PA	15237	8	508
Apple Valley Cinemas	445 Putnam Pike	Greenville	RI	02828	8	521
Showcase Cinemas Warwick	1200 Quaker Lane	Warwick	RI	02886	15	521
Showcase Cinemas Warwick Mall	400 Bald Hill Rd.	Warwick	RI	02886	12	521
Mt. Vernon Multiplex	7940 Richmond Hwy.	Alexandria	VA	22306	10	511
Centreville Multiplex	6201 Multiplex Dr.	Centerville	VA	22121	12	511
Lee Highway Multiplex	8223 Lee Hwy.	Merrifield	VA	22116	14	511
Reston Multiplex	11940 Market St.	Reston	VA	20195	13	511

NCG (NEIGHBORHOOD CINEMA GROUP)

8 theatres, 68 screens.

314 Comstock, Owosso, MI 48867. (989) 725-5410. FAX: (989) 723-0359. www.ncgmovies.com
CHIEF OFFICERS
Gary Geiger
Steve Smith
GENERAL MANAGER
Mark Henning
FILM BUYER
Shelly Davis

Theatre	Address	City	State	Zip	Screens	DMA

THEATRES

Theatre	Address	City	State	Zip	Screens	DMA
Alma Cinemas	3002 W. Monroe	Alma	MI	48801	6	513
Clio Cinemas	2151 W. Vienna Rd.	Clio	MI	48420	4	513
Coldwater Cinemas	414 N. Willowbrook Rd.	Coldwater	MI	49036	7	563
Greenville Cinemas	1500 N. Lafayette Rd.	Greenville	MI	48828	7	563
Lapeer Cinemas	1650 DeMille Rd.	Lapeer	MI	48445	8	505
Midland Cinemas	6540 Cinema Dr.	Midland	MI	48640	11	513
Owosso Cinemas	314 Comstock	Owosso	MI	48867	7	513
Lansing Cinemas	2205 Lake Lansing Rd.	Lansing	MI	48912	18	551

NORTHEAST CINEMAS LLC

23 theatres, 167 screens.
(Formerly Hoyts Cinemas)
One Exeter Plaza, Boston, MA 02116-2836. (617) 646-5700. FAX: (617) 262-0707.
CEO
Paul Johnson
PRESIDENT & CFO
Terence Moriarty
SENIOR EXECUTIVE V.P., FILM
Jud Parker
SENIOR V.P., OPERATIONS & MARKETING
Daniel Vieira
SENIOR V.P., DEVELOPMENT
Hal Cleveland

THEATRES

Theatre	Address	City	State	Zip	Screens	DMA
Groton Cinemas	Poquonneck Rd.	Groton	CT	06340	6	533
Cinema City	235 Brainard Rd.	Hartford	CT	06114	4	533
Mystic Village 3	Rte. 27, Old Mystic Village	Mystic	CT	06355	3	533
New Canaan Playhouse	89 Elm St.	New Canaan	CT	06840	2	501
Simsbury Commons	530 Bushy Hill Rd.	Simsbury	CT	06070	8	533
Brass Mill Cinemas	Brass Mill Mall	Waterbury	CT	06705	12	533
Wilton Cinemas	Wilton Campus Ctr.	Wilton	CT	06897	4	501
East Bridgewater Cinemas	6 Carriage Crossing	E. Bridgewater	MA	02324	6	506
Salisbury Cinemas	201 Elm St.	Salisbury	MA	01952	6	506
Sharon Cinemas	780 S. Main St.	Sharon	MA	02067	8	506
Towne Mall Cinemas	1301 W. Patrick St.	Frederick	MD	21701	10	511
Auburn Cinemas 10	746 Center St.	Auburn	ME	04210	10	500
Bangor Mall Cinemas	557 Stillwater Ave.	Bangor	ME	04401	10	537
Biddeford Cinemas 8	420 L. Alfred Rd.	Biddeford	ME	04005	8	500
Maine Coast Mall Cinemas	Rte. 1A	Ellsworth	ME	04605	2	537
Aroostook Centre 8	830 Main St.	Presque Isle	ME	04769	8	552
Gilford Cinemas 8	9 Old Lake Shore Rd.	Gilford	NH	03246	8	506
Portsmouth Cinemas	581 Lafayette Rd.	Portsmouth	NH	03801	5	506
Bayshore Cinemas	Lincoln Blvd. & Bayshore Rd.	Cape May	NJ	08204	8	504
Cicero Cinemas	5865 E. Circle Dr.	Cicero	NY	13039	13	555
Sangertown Cinemas	Commercial Dr.	New Hartford	NY	13413	9	526
Riverside Cinemas	Riverside Mall	Utica	NY	13502	8	526
South Burlington 9	10 Fayette Rd.	S. Burlington	VT	05403	9	523

NOVA CINETECH, INC. (THEATRE SERVICE NETWORK, INC.)

17 theatres, 113 screens.
4688 E. 29th Rd., Sandwich, IL 60548. (815) 786-6577. FAX: (815) 786-6337. www.novacinemas.com
PRESIDENT
Albert "Buck" Kolkmeyer
VICE PRESIDENT
George Smiley
EXECUTIVE FILM BUYER
Steve Felperin
DIRECTOR, OPERATIONS
Brandon Jones
SECRETARY/TREASURER
Kara Walker

THEATRES

Theatre	Address	City	State	Zip	Screens	DMA
Nova 9	215 S. McClesky	Boaz	AL	35957	9	691
Nova 8 at Stratford	1755 Eastern Blvd.	Montgomery	AL	36117	8	698
Nova 10 at Haymarket	4353 Merle Hay Rd.	Des Moines	IA	50310	10	679
Nova Cinemas at Sabal Palm	2539 S. Federal Hwy.	Ft. Pierce	FL	34982	4	548
Nova Cinemas at Palm Bay West	Palm Bay W. Shopping Cnt, 160 Malabar Rd. SW	Palm Bay	FL	32907	10	534
Hi-Lite 30 Drive-In	34W 160 Montgomery Rd.	Aurora	IL	60506	1	602
Nova 6	2018 36th Ave.	Moline	IL	61265	6	682
Nova 8	352 S. Rte. 59	Naperville	IL	60540	8	602
Theatres of Georgetown	401 Outlet Center Dr., Ste 175	Georgetown	KY	40324	7	541
Nova 4	1840 West 76 Hwy.	Branson	MO	65616	4	619
Branson Meadows Cinema	4740 Gretna Rd.	Branson	MO	65616	11	619
Tri-Cities Cinemas	354 Shadowtown Rd., Ste. 130-180	Blountville	TN	37617	7	531
Nova Meyerland 8	100 Meyerland Plz.	Houston	TX	77096	8	618
Showboat	2565 Hwy 120 North	Lake Geneva	WI	53147	6	617
Geneva 4 Theatre	244 Broad St.	Lake Geneva	WI	53147	4	617
Paradise Theatre	2014 Pkwy. Dr.	West Bend	WI	53095	6	617
Theatres of Whitewater	151 S. Pearson Ln.	Whitewater	WI	53190	4	617

O'NEIL THEATRES, INC.

10 theatres, 74 screens.
1926 C Corporate Square Dr., Slidell, LA 70458. (985) 641-4720. FAX: (985) 641-5726. www.movie-info.com
PRESIDENT
Tim O'Neil, Jr.
VICE PRESIDENT
Tim O'Neil III

SECRETARY & TREASURER
Betty O'Neil
OFFICE OPERATIONS
C. Jean Bumbieris
FIELD OPERATIONS
Steven L. Moss

THEATRES

Theatre	Address	City	State	Zip	Screens	DMA
O'Neil Promenade Cinema 12	2399 Cobbs Ford Rd.	Prattville	AL	36066	12	698
O'Neil Destin Cinema 10.	759 Hwy 98 E.	Destin	FL	32541	10	686
O'Neil Edgewater Cinema 10	473 B Bechrich Rd.	Panama City Bch.	FL	32407	10	656
O'Neil Holiday Square Cinema 10.	201 N. Hwy 190	Covington	LA	70448	12	622
O'Neil Crowley Cinema IV.	2304 N. Parkerson	Crowley	LA	70526	4	642
O'Neil Causeway Place Cinema 4.	1631 N. Causeway Blvd.	Mandeville	LA	70448	4	622
O'Neil Movies 8 Slidell	139 Gause Blvd.	Slidell	LA	70458	8	622
O'Neil Broadacres Cinema	6661 Hwy 49 N.	Hattiesburg	MS	39401	6	710
O'Neil River Ridge Cinema 4	733 Cooper Rd.	Picayune	MS	39466	4	622
O'Neil Choctaw Cinema 4.	310 Hwy 90	Waveland	MS	39576	4	622

PACIFIC THEATRES

24 theatres, 286 screens.
120 N. Robertson Blvd., Los Angeles, CA 90048. (310) 657-8420. FAX: (310) 659-4315.
BOARD CHAIRMAN
Michael R. Forman
CEO
Christopher Forman
COO
Nora Dashwood
CFO
Gary Marcott
EXECUTIVE V.P., HEAD FILM BUYER
Jerry Pokorski

THEATRES

Theatre	Address	City	State	Zip	Screens	DMA
Valley Plaza 16.	2000 Wible Rd.	Bakersfield	CA	93304	16	800
Winnetka 21.	9201 Winnetka Ave.	Chatsworth	CA	91311	21	803
Commerce 14.	950 Goodrich Blvd.	City of Commerce	CA	90022	14	803
Culver Stadium 12	9500 Culver Blvd.	Culver City.	CA	90232	12	803
Beach Cities 16	831 Nash St.	El Segundo	CA	90245	16	803
Arclight-Hollywood 15.	6360 Sunset Blvd.	Hollywood	CA	90028	15	803
Grossmont Center 10	5500 Grossmont Ctr. Dr.	La Mesa	CA	91942	10	825
Trolley 8	8555 Fletcher Pkwy.	La Mesa	CA	91942	8	825
Lakewood South 9	4821 Del Amo Blvd.	Lakewood	CA	90712	9	803
Lakewood Center 16.	5200 Faculty Ave.	Lakewood	CA	90712	16	803
The Grove 14.	189 The Grove.	Los Angeles	CA	90036	14	803
Manhattan Village 6	3560 Sepulveda Blvd.	Manhattan Beach	CA	90266	6	803
Sweetwater 9	1920 Sweetwater Rd.	National City	CA	91950	9	825
Northridge 10.	19401 Parthenia St.	Northridge	CA	91324	10	803
Fashion Center 10	9400 N. Shirley Ave.	Northridge	CA	91324	10	803
Hastings 8	355 N. Rosemead Blvd.	Pasadena	CA	91107	8	803
Paseo 14	336 E. Colorado Blvd., Ste. B201B	Pasadena	CA	91101	14	807
Rohnert Plaza 16.	555 Rohnert Park Expy. W.	Rohnert Park	CA	94928	16	807
Carmel Mountain 12.	11620 Carmel Mt. Rd.	San Diego	CA	92128	12	825
Cinerama 6	5831 University Ave.	San Diego	CA	92115	6	825
Gaslamp 15	701 5th Ave.	San Diego	CA	92101	15	825
Town Square 14	4665 Clairemont Dr.	San Diego	CA	92117	14	825
Galleria 16	15301 Ventura Blvd., Bldg. A.	Sherman Oaks	CA	91403	16	803
Sherman Oaks 5	14424 Milbank St.	Sherman Oaks	CA	91423	5	803

THE PATRIOT CINEMAS, INC.

6 theatres, 28 screens.
101 Derby St. Ste 202., Hingham, MA 02043. (781) 749-8300. FAX: (781) 749-3953. www.patriotcinemas.com
PRESIDENT
Philip J. Scott
VICE PRESIDENT
David A. Kiolbasa
VICE PRESIDENT
Edith L. Scott
FILM BOOKER & BUYER
David A. Scott

THEATRES

Theatre	Address	City	State	Zip	Screens	DMA
Patriot Cinemas, Hanover Mall	1775 Washington St.	Hanover.	MA	02339	6	506
Patriot Cinemas, Loring Hall	65 Main St.	Hingham	MA	02043	1	506
Patriot Cinemas, Museum Place	2 E. India Sq.	Salem	MA	01970	3	506
Patriot Cinemas, Cameo Theatre	14 Columbian St.	S. Weymouth	MA	02190	2	506
Patriot Cinemas, Nickelodeon 6	One Temple St.	Portland.	ME	04101	6	500
Patriot Cinemas, E. Providence 10	60 Newport Ave.	E. Providence	RI	02916	10	521

POLSON THEATRES

10 theatres, 18 screens.
P.O. Box 999, Polson, MT 59860. (406) 883-5603. FAX: (406) 883-5639.
OWNER
Howard Pickerill
HEAD FILM BUYER
Becky Dupuis

THEATRES

Theatre	Address	City	State	Zip	Screens	DMA
River Cinemas	526 Main St.	Salmon	ID	83467	2	758
Glacier Cinemas	111 E. Main	Cutback.	MT	59427	2	755
Big Sky Cinemas	560 N. Montana	Dillon.	MT	59725	2	754

Theatre	Address	City	State	Zip	Screens	DMA
Valley Cinemas	600 2nd Ave. South	Glasgow	MT	59230	2	755
Havre Cinemas	328 2nd St.	Havre	MT	59501	2	755
Showboat Cinemas	416 Main St.	Polson	MT	59860	2	762
Entertainer Cinema	410 Main St.	Ronan	MT	59864	1	762
Roxy Cinema	189 Main St.	Shelby	MT	59474	1	755
Mountain Cinemas	6475 Hwy. 93	Whitefish	MT	59937	2	762
Prairie Cinemas	314 Main St.	Wolf Point	MT	59201	2	687

R/C THEATRES MANAGEMENT CORP.

23 theatres, 162 screens.
231 W. Cherry Hill Ct., Box 1056, Reisterstown, MD 21136. (410) 526-4774. FAX: (410) 526-6871. www.rctheatres.com
PRESIDENT, CHAIRMAN & CEO
J. Wayne Anderson
EXECUTIVE V.P. & COO
Dennis R. Daniels
CFO
David G. Phillips
DIRECTOR OF FILM
Scott R. Cohen
CONTROLLER
Richard A. Hershel
SENIOR FILM BUYER
Jan S. Anderson
DIVISION MANAGERS
Gerd Jakuszeit (MD, PA)
David Knight (VA & NC)

THEATRES

OceanWalk 10	300 N. Atlantic Ave.	Daytona Beach	FL	32118	10	534
Parkside 16	7200 U.S. Hwy. 19	Pinellas Park	FL	33781	16	539
Carrolltown Movies 6	6405 W. Hemlock Rd.	Eldersburg	MD	21784	6	512
Westview 16	Rte. 85 & Buckystown Pike	Frederick	MD	21701	16	511
Frostburg Cinemas 3	10701 New Georges Creek Rd.	Frostburg	MD	21532	3	511
Valley Mall Movies 16	17301 Valley Mall Rd.	Hagerstown	MD	21740	16	511
M.J. Mall Cinemas 8	250 Noble Blvd.	Carlisle	PA	17013	8	566
Majestic 3	29 Carlisle St.	Gettysburg	PA	17325	3	566
Wilkes-Barres 13	40 S. Washington St.	Wilkes-Barre	PA	18711	13	577
Culpeper Movies 4	210 S. Main St.	Culpeper	VA	22701	4	511

MANAGED THEATRES

Hollywood Cinemas	5509 Oregon Ave.	Arbutus	MD	21227	4	512
Eastpoint Movies	7938 Eastern Blvd.	Baltimore	MD	21224	10	512
Easton Movies	Marlboro Rd.	Easton	MD	21601	4	512
Hatteras Movies	Hwy. 12	Avon	NC	27915	4	544
Corolla Movies	815 E. Ocean Trail	Corolla	NC	27927	4	544
Kitty Hawk Twin	3850 N. Croatan Hwy	Kitty Hawk	NC	27949	2	544
Market Place	110 N. Croatan Hwy	Kitty Hawk	NC	27949	2	544
Kill Devil Hills Movies 10	1803 N. Croatan Hwy.	Kill Devil Hills	NC	27948	10	
Cineplex Movies	2423 S. Croatan Hwy.	Nags Head	NC	27959	4	544
Hanover Movies	380 Eisenhower Dr.	Hanover	PA	17331	9	566
Covington Movies	139 N. Maple Ave.	Covington	VA	24426	3	579
State Cinema 3	12W. Nelson St.	Lexington	VA	24450	3	573
Surf-N-Sand Movies	941 Laskin Rd.	Virginia Beach	VA	23451	8	544

REGAL ENTERTAINMENT GROUP

562 Theatres, 6,119 Screens, 6 IMAX. Alaska: 5 Theatres, 43 Screens.
(Acquired Regal Cinemas, Edwards Theatres and United Artists Theatre Circuits)
7132 Regal Ln., Knoxville, TN 37918. (865) 922-1123. FAX: (865) 922-3188.
CO-CHAIRMAN, REGAL ENTERTAINMENT GROUP
CEO-REGAL ENTERTAINMENT - THEATRE GROUP
Michael L. Campbell
PRESIDENT, COO
Gregory W. Dunn
EXECUTIVE V.P. & CFO
Amy E. Miles
EXECUTIVE V.P., SECRETARY & GENERAL COUNSEL
Peter S. Beandow
EXECUTIVE V.P., FILM
Mike Pade
SENIOR V.P., IT & CIO
J.E. Henry
SENIOR V.P., HUMAN RESOURCE COUNSEL
Randy Smith
SENIOR V.P., PURCHASING & CPO
Rob Del Moro
SENIOR V.P., MARKETING & ADVERTISING
Dick Westerling
SENIOR V.P., FINANCE
David Ownby
SENIOR V.P., OPERATIONS East
Mike Levesque
SENIOR V.P., OPERATIONS WEST
Neal Pinsker
SENIOR V.P., REAL ESTATE
John Roper
SENIOR V.P., CONSTRUCTION/TECH. SERVICE
Ron Reid
SENIOR V.P., FILM EAST
Ted Cooper
SENIOR V.P., FILM WEST
Denise Gurin
SENIOR V.P., FILM SETTLEMENTS
Barry Steinberg

REGAL CINEMEDIA CORPORATION
(A subsidiary of Regal Entertainment Group)
9110 E. Nichols Ave., Ste. 200, Cenntenial, CO 80112. (800) 828-2828, (303) 792-3600.
122 E. 42nd St., Ste. 511, New York, NY 10168. (212) 931-8100.
CEO, REGAL ENTERTAINMENT GROUP
PRESIDENT & CEO, REGAL CINEMEDIA
Kurt C. Hall
EXECUTIVE V.P., PRESIDENT, MARKETING AND SALES (NY)
Cliff Marks
EXECUTIVE V.P., CFO, TREASURER (CO)
David Giesler
EXECUTIVE V.P., BUSINESS DEVELOPMENT (CO)
Ray Nutt
EXECUTIVE V.P., NETWORK OPERATIONS, CTO (CO)
Tom Galley
EXECUTIVE V.P., GENERAL COUNSEL AND SECRETARY (CO)
Gene Hardy
EXECUTIVE V.P., MARKETING & SALES (NY)
Dave Kupiec
SENIOR V.P., BUSINESS DEVELOPMENT (TX)
Stephen Nesbit

THEATRES

Theatre	Address	City	State	Zip	Screens	DMA
Brook Highland Stadium 10	5255 Hwy. 280 S.	Birmingham	AL	35242	10	630
Festival Stadium 18	7001 Crestwood Blvd.	Birmingham	AL	35210	18	630
Galleria 10	3200 Galleria Circle	Birmingham	AL	35216	10	630
Trussville Stadium 16	5895 Trussville Crossings Pkwy.	Birmingham	AL	35235	16	630
Wildwood Stadium 14 Cinemas	275 Lakeshore Pkwy.	Birmingham	AL	35209	14	630
River Oaks Cinema 8	2203 Family Security Place S.W.	Decatur	AL	35603	8	691
Hollywood Stadium 18	3312 S. Memorial Pkwy.	Huntsville	AL	35802	18	691
Madison Square Stadium 12	5905 University Dr.	Huntsville	AL	35806	12	691
Fox 12	900 Skyland Blvd. E.	Tuscaloosa	AL	35405	12	620
Fiesta Square 16	3033 N. College	Fayetteville	AR	72703	16	670
Breckenridge Stadium 12	1200 Breckenridge Dr.	Little Rock	AR	72207	12	693
Cinema Stadium 150	Asher & University Ave.	Little Rock	AR	72204	1	693
Cameo 3	111 N. Jackson	Magnolia	AR	71753	3	612
Lakewood 8	2939 Lakewood Village Dr.	N Little Rock	AR	72116	8	693
Pavilions 11	9090 E. Indian Bend	Scottsdale	AZ	85250	11	753
Sonora Village 10	N. 15512 Pima Rd.	Scottsdale	AZ	85260	10	753
Alhambra Place 5	100 Bay State St.	Alhambra	CA	91801	5	803
Atlantic Palace 10	700 W. Main St.	Alhambra	CA	91801	10	803
Aliso Viejo Stadium 20	26701 Aliso Creek Rd.	Aliso Viejo	CA	92656	20	803
Anaheim Hills 14	8032 E. Santa Ana Canyon Rd.	Anaheim Hills	CA	92808	14	803
Deer Valley Stadium 16	4204 Lone Tree Way	Antioch	CA	94509	16	807
Bakersfield Stadium 14	9000-G Ming Ave.	Bakersfield	CA	93311	14	800
UA East Hills 10	3100 Mall View Rd.	Bakersfield	CA	93306	10	807
Berkeley 7	2274 Shattuck Ave.	Berkley	CA	94704	7	807
Brea Stadium 10 West	155 W. Birch	Brea	CA	92621	10	803
Brea Stadium 12 East	155 W. Birch St.	Brea	CA	92821	12	803
Calabasas Stadium 6	4767 Commons Way	Calabasas	CA	91302	6	803
Camarillo 12	680 Ventura Blvd.	Camarillo	CA	93010	12	803
Canyon Country Stadium 10	18800 Soledad Canyon Rd.	Canyon Country	CA	91351	10	
Cerritos Stadium 10	12761 Towne Center Dr.	Cerritos	CA	90701	10	803
UA Galaxy @ Los Cerritos 11	435 Los Cerritos Center	Cerritos	CA	90703	11	803
El Rey Theatre 1	230 W. 2nd St.	Chico	CA	95928	1	868
Rancho Del Rey Stadium 16	1025 Tierra Del Rey	Chula Vista	CA	91910	16	825
Sunrise 4	5926 Sunrise Mall	Citrus Heights	CA	95610	4	862
Clovis Movies 8	2301 Villa Ave.	Clovis	CA	93612	8	866
Sierra Vista 6	801 Santa Ana Ave.	Clovis	CA	93612	6	866
Corona 15	351 W. Rincon St.	Corona	CA	92880	15	803
Metro Pointe Stadium 12	901 S. Coast Dr.	Costa Mesa	CA	92626	12	803
Triangle Square 8	1870 Harbor Blvd.	Costa Mesa	CA	92627	8	803
Colma Metro Center 6	200 Colma Blvd.	Daly City	CA	94014	6	807
Hacienda Crossings Stadium 20 Plus	5000 Dublin Blvd.	Dublin	CA	94568	21	807
Parkway Plaza Stadium 18	405 Pkwy. Plaza	El Cajon	CA	92020	18	825
Rancho San Diego Stadium 15	2951 Jamacha Rd.	El Cajon	CA	92019	15	825
El Monte 8	10661 Valley Boulevard	El Monte	CA	91731	8	803
Emery Bay Stadium 10	6330 Christie Ave.	Emeryville	CA	94608	10	807
Fairfield Stadium 16	1549 Gateway Blvd.	Fairfield	CA	94533	16	862
Foothill Towne Center Stadium 22	26602 Towne Center Dr.	Foothill Ranch	CA	92610	22	803
Broadway Faire 10	3351 W. Shaw Ave.	Fresno	CA	93711	10	866
Fresno Stadium 21	7750 N. Blackstone Ave.	Fresno	CA	93720	21	866
Garden Grove Stadium 16	9741 Chapman Ave.	Garden Grove	CA	92841	16	803
Del Oro 3	165 Mill St.	Grass Valley	CA	95945	3	862
Hayward 6	24800 Hesperian Blvd.	Hayward	CA	94545	6	862
Hemet Cinema 12	2369 W. Florida Ave.	Hemet	CA	92545	12	803
Charter Centre 5	7822 Warner Ave.	Huntington Beach	CA	92647	5	803
Irvine Spectrum 21	65 Fortune Dr.	Irvine	CA	92618	21	803
Market Place Stadium 10	13728 Jamboree Rd.	Irvine	CA	92602	10	803
Park Place 10	3031 Michelson Dr.	Irvine	CA	92612	10	803
University Town Center 6	4245 Campus Dr.	Irvine	CA	92612	6	803
Westpark 8	3755 Alton Pkwy.	Irvine	CA	92606	8	803
UA La Canada 8	1919 Verdugo Blvd.	La Canada Flintridge	CA	91011	8	803
La Habra Stadium 16	1351 W. Imperial Hwy.	La Habra	CA	90631	16	803
La Verne Stadium 12	1950 E. Foothill Blvd.	La Verne	CA	91750	12	803
Ocean Ranch 7	32401 Golden Lantern St.	Laguna Niguel	CA	92677	7	803
Long Beach Stadium 26	7501 E. Carson Blvd.	Long Beach	CA	90808	26	803
UA Long Beach 6	E. 6601 Pacific Coast Hwy.	Long Beach	CA	90803	6	803
UA Marina Del Rey 6	4335 Glencoe Ave.	Marina Del Rey	CA	90292	6	803
Regency 7	635 Fairfield Dr.	Merced	CA	95340	7	866
Kaleidoscope Stadium 10	27741 Crown Valley Pkwy. Unit 301	Mission Viejo	CA	92691	10	803

Theatre	Address	City	State	Zip	Screens	DMA
State 3 Theatre	417 Alvarado St.	Monterey	CA	93940	3	828
Island 7	999 Newport Center Dr.	Newport Beach	CA	92660	7	803
Newport 6	300 Newport Center Dr. E.	Newport Beach	CA	92660	6	803
Valley Plaza 6	6355 Bellingham Ave.	North Hollywood	CA	91606	6	803
Oceanside Stadium 16	401 Mission Ave.	Oceanside	CA	92054	16	825
Ontario Mountain Village Stadium 14	1575 N. Mountain Ave.	Ontario	CA	91762	14	803
Ontario Palace Stadium 22	4900 E. 4th St.	Ontario	CA	91764	22	803
UA Pasadena 6	64 W. Colorado Blvd.	Pasadena	CA	91105	6	803
Jurupa Stadium 14	8032 Limonite Ave.	Riverside	CA	92509	14	803
Park Sierra 6	3660 Park Sierra Dr.	Riverside	CA	92505	6	803
Terrace Cinema 6	28901 S. Western Ave.	Rnc. Palos Verdes	CA	90275	6	803
Rancho Santa Margarita 6	30632 Santa Margarita Pkwy.	Rnc. Sta Margarita	CA	92688	6	803
Avenues Stadium 13	550 Deep Valley Dr.	Rolling Hills Estates	CA	90274	13	803
Olympus Pointe 12	520 N. Sunrise Ave.	Roseville	CA	95661	12	862
Arden Fair 6	1739 Arden Way	Sacramento	CA	95815	6	862
Laguna Village 12	8755 Center Pkwy Dr.	Sacramento	CA	95823	12	862
Natomas Marketplace Stadium 16	3561 Truxel Rd.	Sacramento	CA	95834	16	862
Mira Mesa Stadium 18	10733 Westview Pkwy.	San Diego	CA	92126	18	825
UA Horton Plaza 14	475 Horton Plaza	San Diego	CA	92101	14	825
Alexandria 3	5400 Geary Blvd.	San Francisco	CA	94121	3	807
Coronet 1	3575 Geary Blvd.	San Francisco	CA	94118	1	807
Galaxy 4	1285 Sutter St.	San Francisco	CA	94109	4	807
Metro 1	2055 Union St.	San Francisco	CA	94123	1	807
Stonestown Twin 2	501 Buckingham Way	San Francisco	CA	94132	2	807
Vogue 1	3290 Sacramento St.	San Francisco	CA	94115	1	807
San Marcos Stadium 18	1180 W. San Marcos Blvd.	San Marcos	CA	92069	18	825
Hutton Centre 8	9 Hutton Centre Dr.	Santa Ana	CA	92707	8	803
South Coast Village 3	1561 W. Sunflower Ave.	Santa Ana	CA	92704	3	803
Valencia Stadium 12	24435 Town Center Dr.	Santa Clarita	CA	91355	12	803
Santa Maria 10	1521 South Bradley Rd.	Santa Maria	CA	93454	10	855
Civic Center Stadium 16	2751 Tapo Canyon Rd.	Simi Valley	CA	93065	16	803
Simi Valley Plaza 10	1457 Los Angeles Ave.	Simi Valley	CA	93065	10	803
South Gate Stadium 20	8630 Garfield Ave.	South Gate	CA	90280	20	803
Temecula Stadium 15	40750 Winchester Rd.	Temecula	CA	92591	15	803
Temple 4	9021 Las Tunas Dr.	Temple City	CA	91780	4	803
UA Thousand Oaks 5	382 W. Hillcrest Dr.	Thousand Oaks	CA	91360	5	803
Tustin Marketplace 6	2961 El Camino Real	Tustin	CA	92782	6	803
West Covina Stadium 18	265 S. Glendora Ave.	West Covina	CA	91790	18	803
Westminster 10	6721 Westminster Blvd.	Westminster	CA	92683	10	803
Village 4	2525 Arapahoe E-65	Boulder	CO	80302	4	751
Colorado Center 9	2000 S. Colorado Blvd.	Denver	CO	80222	9	751
Continental 6	3635 S. Monaco Blvd.	Denver	CO	80237	6	751
Pavilions 15	500 16th St. #310	Denver	CO	80202	15	751
Greenwood Plaza 12	8141 E. Arapahoe Rd.	Englewood	CO	80112	12	751
West Village Stadium 12	14225 W. Colfax Ave.	Golden	CO	80401	12	751
Colorado West 4	2424 Hwy. 6 & 50	Grand Junction	CO	81505	4	773
Teller Arms Twin	2806 C Rd.	Grand Junction	CO	81503	2	773
Bittersweet 4	3760 W. 10TH St.	Greeley	CO	80634	4	751
Cooper Twin	2333 W. 10th St.	Greeley	CO	80632	2	751
Meadows 12	9355 Park Meadows Dr.	Littleton	CO	80124	12	751
Twin Peaks Mall 10	1250 S. Hover Rd.	Longmont	CO	80501	10	751
Thornton Town Center 10	10001 Grant St.	Thornton	CO	80229	10	751
Darien Playhouse 2	1077 Boston Post Rd.	Darien	CT	06820	2	501
Peoples Plaza Cinema Stadium 17	1100 Peoples Plaza	Newark	DE	19702	17	504
Brandywine Town Center 16	3300 Brandywine Pkwy.	Wilmington	DE	19803	16	504
Movies @ Wekiva Riverwalk 8	2141 N. Semoran Blvd.	Apopka	FL	32703	8	534
Shadowood 16	9889 W. Glades Rd.	Boca Raton	FL	33434	16	548
Bonita Springs Stadium 12	25251 Chamber Of Commerce Dr.	Bonita Springs	FL	34135	12	571
Boynton 8 Cinema	2290 N. Congress Ave.	Boynton Beach	FL	33426	8	548
Movies @ Boynton Beach 9	N 244 Congress Ave.	Boynton Beach	FL	33426	9	548
Oakmont 8	4801 Cortez Rd. W.	Bradenton	FL	34210	8	539
Magnolia Place Stadium 16	9645 Westview Dr.	Coral Springs	FL	33067	16	528
Crystal River Mall 9	1801 N.W. Hwy 19	Crystal River	FL	34428	9	539
Delray Beach 18	1660 S. Federal Hwy.	Del Ray Beach	FL	33483	18	548
Las Olas Stadium 23	300 S.W. First Ave. Ste. 205	Ft Lauderdale	FL	33301	23	528
Belltower 20	13499 Belltower Dr.	Ft Myers	FL	33907	20	571
Cypress Creek Station Stadium 16	6415 N. Andrews Ave.	Ft. Lauderdale	FL	33334	16	528
Gainesville Cinema Stadium 14	Butler Plaza	Gainesville	FL	32608	14	592
Oakwood 18	2800 Oakwood Blvd.	Hollywood	FL	33020	18	528
Citrus Cinemas 6	2635 E. Gulf To Lake Hwy.	Inverness	FL	34453	6	539
Avenues Stadium 20	9525 Phillips Hwy.	Jacksonville	FL	32256	20	561
Beach Boulevard Stadium 18	14051 Beach Blvd.	Jacksonville	FL	32250	18	561
Treasure Coast Mall Stadium 16	3290 N. Federal Hwy.	Jenson Beach	FL	34957	16	548
Jupiter Stadium 18	204 N. U.S. 1, Jupiter Mall.	Jupiter	FL	33477	18	548
Cinema Key West 6	3338 N. Roosevelt Blvd.	Key West	FL	33040	6	528
Osceola Square East 6	1821 Armstrong Blvd.	Kissimmee	FL	34741	6	534
Cinema 90 6	Hwy. 90 West	Lake City	FL	32055	6	561
Eagle Ridge Mall 12	955 Eagle Ridge Dr. & Hwy 27	Lake Wales	FL	33853	12	539
Largo Mall 8	10500 Ulmerton Rd. E.	Largo	FL	33771	8	539
Movies @ Lauderhill 13	7800 W. Commercial Blvd.	Lauderhill	FL	33351	13	528
Santa Rosa 10	300 Mary Esther Blvd.	Mary Esther	FL	32569	10	686
Oaks 10	1800 W. Hibiscus Blvd., Ste. 119	Melbourne	FL	32901	10	534
Kendall Nine	12090 S.W. 88 St.	Miami	FL	33186	9	528
Movies @ The Falls 12	9000 S.W. 136th St.	Miami	FL	33176	12	528
Palace 18	11865 S.W. 26th St.	Miami	FL	33175	18	528
South Beach Stadium 18	1120 Lincoln Rd. Mall	Miami Beach	FL	33139	18	528
Hollywood Stadium 20	6006 Hollywood Dr.	Naples	FL	34109	20	571
Hollywood Stadium 16	2801 S.W. 27th Ave.	Ocala	FL	34474	16	534
Marketplace 8	822-4 Saxon Blvd.	Orange City	FL	32763	8	534
Waterford Lakes Stadium 20	541 N. Alafaya Trail	Orlando	FL	32828	20	534
Ormond Beach Cinema 12	215 Williamson Blvd.	Ormond Beach	FL	32174	12	534
Oviedo Marketplace Stadium 22	1500 Oviedo Marketplace Blvd.	Oviedo	FL	32765	22	534

Theatre	Address	City	State	Zip	Screens	DMA
Westfork Stadium 13	15999 Pines Blvd.	Pembroke Pines	FL	33027	13	528
University Mall 11	7171 N Davis Hwy.	Pensacola	FL	32504	11	686
Town Center Stadium 16	1441 Tamiami Trail Unit 701	Port Charlotte	FL	33948	16	571
Hollywood 18, Port Richey	6701 Cinema Dr. (34668)	Port Richey	FL	34668	18	539
Royal Palm Beach Stadium 18	1003 State Rd. 7.	Royal Palm Beach	FL	33411	18	548
Seminole Towne Center	430 Towne Centre Cir.	Sanford	FL	32771	10	534
Hollywood Stadium 20	1993 Main St.	Sarasota	FL	34236	20	539
Spring Hill 8 Cinemas	2955 Commercial Hwy.	Spring Hill	FL	34606	8	539
Mall St Augustine 6	2121 U.S. 1 S, Ponce DeLeon Mall	St Augustine	FL	32086	6	561
Sawgrass Stadium 23	2600 Northwest 136th Ave.	Sunrise	FL	33323	23	528
Channelside Cinemas Stadium 9	601 Channelside Dr.	Tampa	FL	33602	9	539
Citrus Park Stadium 20.	7999 Citrus Park Town Center Mall	Tampa	FL	33625	20	539
University 16	12332 University Mall Ct.	Tampa	FL	33612	16	539
Searstown Mall 10	3550 S. Washington Ave.	Titusville	FL	32780	10	534
Venetian 6	1735 S. Tamiami Trail	Venice	FL	34293	6	539
Movies @ Okee Square 8.	2027 Okeechobee Blvd.	West Palm Beach	FL	33409	8	548
Winter Park Village Stadium 20.	510 N. Orlando Ave.	Winter Park	FL	32789	20	534
North Point Market 8.	6500 N. Point Pkwy.	Alpharetta	GA	30202	8	561
Lenox Square 6	3393 Peachtree Rd.	Atlanta	GA	30326	6	524
Midtown Cinemas 8	931 Monroe Dr.	Atlanta	GA	30308	8	524
Perimeter Pointe 10	1155 Mt. Vernon Hwy.	Atlanta	GA	30338	10	524
Tara Cinemas 4	2345 Cheshire Bridge Rd, N.E.	Atlanta	GA	30324	4	524
Augusta Exchange Stadium 20.	1144 Agerton Ln.	Augusta	GA	30909	20	520
Augusta Village 12	1323 Augusta W. Pkwy.	Augusta	GA	30909	12	520
Regal Stadium 22 @ Austell	2480 E.W. Connector Rd.	Austell	GA	30106	22	524
Mall of Georgia Stadium 20 Plus Imax	3333 A Buford Dr.	Buford	GA	30519	21	524
Hollywood Stadium 24 @ North I-85	3265 N.E. Expwy. Access	Chamblee	GA	30341	24	524
Arbor Place Stadium 18	6600 Douglas Blvd.	Douglasville	GA	30135	18	524
Medlock Crossing Stadium 18	9700 Medlock Bridge Rd., Ste. 170	Duluth	GA	30097	18	524
Town Center Stadium 16	2795 Town Center Dr.	Kennesaw	GA	30144	16	524
Covington Square Cinema 8	2244 Panola Rd.	Lithonia	GA	30058	8	524
Rivergate Cinema 14	245 Tom Hill Sr. Blvd.	Macon	GA	31210	14	503
Delk 10	2854 Delk Rd.	Marietta	GA	30067	10	524
Riverdale Cinema 14	274 Hwy. 138	Riverdale	GA	30274	14	524
Eisenhower Square 6	1100 Eisenhower Dr.	Savannah	GA	31406	6	507
Savannah Stadium 10	1132-34 Shawnee Ave.	Savannah	GA	31419	10	507
Snellville Oaks Stadium 14	2125 E. Main St.	Snellville	GA	30078	14	524
Grand Teton Stadium 14	2707 S. 25th E.	Ammon	ID	83406	14	758
Boise Stadium 21	7709 Overland Rd.	Boise	ID	83709	21	757
Coeur D Alene 5 Cinema	3555 N. Government Way	Coeur D Alene	ID	83814	5	881
Showboat 5 Cinemas	5725 Pioneer Dr.	Coeur D Alene	ID	83814	5	881
Liberty Theatre 1	611 Main St.	Lewiston	ID	83501	1	881
Orchards Tri Cinema.	3323 10th St.	Lewiston	ID	83501	3	881
Nampa Stadium 14.	2001 N. Cassia St.	Nampa	ID	83651	14	757
Showplace 16.	5000 W. Rte. 14	Crystal Lake	IL	60014	16	602
Lake Zurich 12	755 S. Rand Rd.	Lake Zurich	IL	60047	12	602
Lincolnshire Stadium 20 Plus Imax	300 Pkwy. Dr.	Lincolnshire	IL	60069	21	602
Round Lake Beach Stadium 18	550 E. Rollins Rd.	Round Lake Beach	IL	60073	18	602
Shiloh Crossing Stadium 18	10400 E. U.S. 36, Building #800	Avon	IN	46123	18	527
Village Park Cinema Stadium 17.	2222 E. 146th St.	Carmel	IN	46032	17	527
Coldwater Crossing 8	211 W. Washington Center Rd.	Fort Wayne	IN	46825	8	509
Holiday 6	931 Northcrest Shopping Center.	Fort Wayne	IN	46805	6	509
Circle Center 9	49 W. Maryland St.	Indianapolis	IN	46204	9	527
Eagle Highlands 10	4015 Shore Dr.	Indianapolis	IN	46254	10	527
Galaxy Stadium 14.	8105 E. 96Th Ave	Indianapolis	IN	46256	14	527
Hamburg Pavilion Stadium 16.	1949 Starshoot Rd.	Lexington	KY	40509	16	541
Westgate 8.	323 McArthur Dr.	Alexandria	LA	71306	8	644
Washington Square 4.	314 N. Franklin St.	Bastrop	LA	71220	4	628
Citiplace Stadium 11.	2610 Citiplace Dr.	Baton Rouge	LA	70808	11	716
Siegen Village 10	7166 Siegen Ln.	Baton Rouge	LA	70809	10	716
Bossier Corners Cinema 9	2800 Shed Rd.	Bossier City	LA	71111	9	612
Ambassador 10	2315 Kaliste Saloom.	Lafayette	LA	70508	10	642
Northgate 8	100 Castille St.	Lafayette	LA	70501	8	642
Westwood Cinema 1.	2421 W. Congress St.	Lafayette	LA	70596	1	642
Lake Charles 10.	3416 Derek Dr.	Lake Charles	LA	70605	10	643
Lee Hills 6	1350 Boone St.	Leesville	LA	71446	6	644
Bayou Landing 6	1000 Parkview Dr. Bldg. 6A.	New Iberia	LA	70506	6	642
Bel Air Cinema Stadium 14.	409 Constant Friendship Blvd.	Abingdon	MD	21009	14	512
UA Westview Mall 9	5824 Baltimore National Pike	Baltimore	MD	21228	9	512
UA Bethesda 10.	7272 Wisconsin Ave.	Bethesda	MD	20814	10	512
UA Snowden Square Stadium 14	9161 Commerce Center Dr.	Columbia	MD	21046	14	512
Movies @ Marley Station 8.	7900 Governor Richie Hwy.	Glen Burnie	MD	21061	8	512
Rockville Center Stadium 13.	199 E. Montgomery Ave.	Rockville	MD	20850	13	511
West River 9.	30170 Grand River Ave.	Farmington	MI	48336	9	505
Frenchtown Square Mall 8	2121 N. Monroe St.	Monroe	MI	48161	8	505
Crossroads 10	6600 Ring Rd.	Portage	MI	49024	10	563
Commerce Township Stadium 14	3033 Springvale Dr.	Walled Lake	MI	48390	14	505
Eagan Stadium 16	2055 Cliff Rd.	Eagan	MN	55122	16	613
Eden Prairie West 5	1076 Eden Prairie Cntr	Eden Prairie	MN	55344	5	613
Movies @Maplewood II 6	1793 Beam Ave.	Maplewood	MN	55109	6	613
Brooklyn Center Stadium 20	6420 Camden Ave. North	Minneapolis	MN	55430	20	613
Pavilions Place 7	1655 W. County Rd B-2.	Roseville	MN	55113	7	613
Woodbury 10 Theatres	1470 Queens Dr.	Woodbury	MN	55125	10	613
Kansas City Stadium 18 Cinemas.	3200 Ameristar Dr.	Kansas City	MO	64161	18	616
Biloxi 10.	2681 C.T. Switzer Sr. Dr.	Biloxi	MS	39535	10	746
Westbrook 4.	454 Brookway Blvd.	Brookhaven	MS	39601	4	718
Clinton Center 10	201 Clinton Center	Clinton	MS	39056	10	718
Parkway Place Stadium 10.	1075 Pkwy. Blvd.	Flowood	MS	39208	10	718
Singing River 4.	2800 Hwy. 90	Gautier	MS	39553	4	746
Singing River 5.	2800 Hwy. 90	Gautier	MS	39553	5	746
Cinema 4 @ I-82	1541 Hwy One S.	Greenville	MS	38701	4	647
Highland Park 3	604 W. Park Ave.	Greenwood	MS	38935	3	647

Theatre	Address	City	State	Zip	Screens	DMA
Turtle Creek 9	1000 Turtle Creek Dr.	Hattiesburg	MS	39402	9	710
Sawmill Square 5	910 Sawmill Rd.	Laurel	MS	39440	5	710
Camelia Cinema 4	1005 Delaware Ave.	Mccomb	MS	39648	4	718
Bonita Lakes 9	1680 Bonita Lakes Circle	Meridian	MS	39301	9	524
Natchez Mall 4	350 John R. Junkin Dr.	Natchez	MS	39120	4	718
Cine 4 - Oxford Mall	1111 W. Jackson Ave.	Oxford	MS	38655	4	640
North Park Stadium 14	250 Ring Rd.	Ridgeland	MS	39157	14	718
Pemberton Square 4	3505 Pemberton Blvd., Bldg.	Vicksburg	MS	39180	4	718
Eastgate Cinemas 5	Eastgate Shopping Cntr.	Albemarle	NC	28805	5	567
Beaucatcher Cinemas 7	321 Haw Creek Ln.	Asheville	NC	28805	7	567
Biltmore Square 6	800 Brevard Rd.	Asheville	NC	28806	6	567
Hollywood Cinemas 14	1640 Hendersonville Rd.	Asheville	NC	28803	14	567
Boone Cinema 7	210 New Market St. Centre	Boone	NC	28607	7	517
Stonecrest @ Piper Glen Stadium 22	7824 Rea Rd.	Charlotte	NC	28277	22	517
Carolina Mall Cinemas 8	Carolina Mall-U.S. Hwy 29	Concord	NC	28025	8	517
Towne Square 10	2600 Timber Dr.	Garner	NC	27529	10	560
Litchfield Cinemas 4	301 N. Berkeley Blvd.	Goldsboro	NC	27534	4	560
Four Seasons Cinemas	P.O. Box 5098	Hendersonville	NC	28739	4	567
Crown 6 Cinemas	577 U.S. Hwy. 70 S.W.	Hickory	NC	28602	6	517
Oak Hollow Mall 7	931 Eastchester Dr.	High Point	NC	27265	7	518
Mayberry Cinema 5	840 Fowler Rd.	Mount Airy	NC	27030	5	518
College Road Cinemas 6	632 S. College Rd.	Wilmington	NC	28403	6	550
Wilson Cinema 6	1705 Montgomery Dr.	Wilson	NC	27895	6	560
Burlington Stadium 20	250 Bromley Blvd.	Burlington	NJ	08016	20	504
Hudson Mall 7	Rte. 440	Jersey City	NJ	07305	7	501
UA Moorestown Mall 7	Rte. 38 & Lenola Rd.	Moorestown	NJ	08057	7	504
Marlboro Cinema Stadium 8	12 Rte. 9 N.	Morganville	NJ	07751	8	501
Columbia Park 12	3125 Kennedy Blvd.	North Bergen	NJ	07047	12	501
Commerce Center Stadium 18	2399 Rte. 1 S.	North Brunswick	NJ	08902	18	501
Pennsauken Theatre 11	Rte. 73 & 130 N.	Pennsauken	NJ	08110	11	504
Pohatcong 12	1246 Hwy. 22 E.	Phillipsburg	NJ	08865	12	501
Movies @ Market Fair 9	3521 U.S. Rte. 1	Princeton	NJ	08540	9	504
UA Washington Township 14	121 Tuckahoe Rd.	Sewell	NJ	08080	14	504
Hadley Theatre Stadium 16	1000 Corporate Court	South Plainfield	NJ	07080	16	501
Cross Keys Cinema Stadium 12	151 American Blvd.	Turnersville	NJ	08012	12	504
Cumberland Mall Stadium 14	3849 S. Delsea	Vineland	NJ	08360	14	504
Coronado Theatre 6	6401 Upton Blvd. N.E.	Albuquerque	NM	87110	6	790
Cottonwood Theatre Stadium 10	10000 N.W. Coors Blvd.	Albuquerque	NM	87114	10	790
Four Hills Theatre 10	13120 Central S.E.	Albuquerque	NM	87123	10	790
High Ridge Theatre 8	12921 Indian School N.E.	Albuquerque	NM	87112	8	790
Winrock VI	201 Winrock Center	Albuquerque	NM	87110	6	790
Devargas Mall Cinema 6	562 N. Guadalupe	Santa Fe	NM	87501	6	790
UA North 6	4250 Cerrillos Rd.	Santa Fe	NM	87505	6	790
UA South 6	4250 Cerrillos Rd.	Santa Fe	NM	87505	6	790
Green Valley Cinemas 8	4500 E. Sunset Rd.	Henderson	NV	89014	8	839
Green Valley Ranch Stadium 10	2300 Paseo Verde	Henderson	NV	89052	10	839
Sunset Station Stadium 13 Theatre	1301-A W Sunset Rd.	Henderson	NV	89014	13	839
Boulder Station 11 Theatre	4111 Boulder Hwy.	Las Vegas	NV	89121	11	839
Colonnade Stadium 14	8880 S. Eastern Ave.	Las Vegas	NV	89123	14	839
Rainbow Promenade 10	2321 N. Rainbow Blvd.	Las Vegas	NV	89108	10	839
Showcase Theatre 8	3769 S. Las Vegas Blvd.	Las Vegas	NV	89109	8	839
Texas Station Stadium 18	2101 N. Texas Star Ln.	Las Vegas	NV	89030	18	839
Village Square Stadium 18	9400 W. Sahara Ave.	Las Vegas	NV	89117	18	839
Court Street Stadium 12	106 Court St.	Brooklyn	NY	11201	12	501
Sheepshead Bay 14	3907 Shore Pkwy.	Brooklyn	NY	11235	14	501
Elmwood Regal Center 16	2001 Elmwood Ave.	Buffalo	NY	14207	16	514
Coram Theatre 12	3700 Rte. 112	Coram	NY	11727	12	501
Movieworld Douglaston 7	242-02 - 61St Ave.	Douglaston	NY	11363	7	501
East Hampton Cinema 6	30 Main St.	East Hampton	NY	11937	6	501
Meadowbrook Theatre 6	2549 Hempstead Turnpike	Eastmeadow	NY	11554	6	501
UA Farmingdale 10	20 Michael Ave	Farmingdale	NY	11735	10	501
Brandon Cinemas 2	70-20 Austin St.	Forest Hills	NY	11375	2	501
Midway Cinemas Stadium 9	108-22 Queens Blvd.	Forest Hills	NY	11375	9	501
UA Hampton Bays 5	119 W. Montauk Hwy.	Hampton Bays	NY	11946	5	501
Culver Ridge Plaza 16	2255 Ridge Rd. E.	Irondequoit	NY	14622	16	538
Kaufman Astoria Stadium 14	35-30 38th St.	Long Island City	NY	11101	14	501
Lynbrook Theatre 6	321 Merrick Rd.	Lynbrook	NY	11563	6	501
Cortland Town Center Stadium 11	3131 E. Main St.	Mohegan Lake	NY	10547	11	508
New Roc City Stadium 18 Plus Imax	33 Le Count Place	New Rochelle	NY	10801	19	501
Battery Park Stadium 16	102 N. End Ave.	New York	NY	10281	16	501
East 85th Street 1	1629 First Ave.	New York	NY	10028	1	501
UA 64th and 2nd Avenue Expansion 3	1210 Second Ave.	New York	NY	10021	3	501
Union Square Stadium 14	850 Broadway	New York	NY	10003	14	501
Hollywood Stadium 12	720 Builders Way	Niagara Falls	NY	14304	12	514
Quaker Crossing Stadium 18	3450 Amelia Dr.	Orchard Park	NY	14127	18	514
Crossbay Theatre I	94-11 Rockaway Blvd.	Ozone Park	NY	11417	3	501
Crossbay Theatre II	92-10 Rockaway Blvd.	Ozone Park	NY	11417	7	501
Movies @ Patchogue 13	600 Sunrise Hwy.	Patchogue	NY	11772	13	501
Henrietta Cinema Stadium 18	525 Marketplace Dr.	Rochester	NY	14623	18	538
Ronkonkoma Cinema Stadium 9	565 Portion Rd.	Ronkonkoma	NY	11779	9	501
Southampton 4 Theatres	43 Hill St.	Southampton	NY	11968	4	501
Hylan Plaza 5	107 Mill Rd.	Staten Island	NY	10306	5	501
Movies @ Staten Island 14	145 E. Service Rd.	Staten Island	NY	10314	14	501
Staten Island Stadium 16	2474 Forest Ave.	Staten Island	NY	10303	16	501
Eastview Mall 13	70 Eastview Mall Dr.	Victor	NY	14564	13	538
UA Westbury Theatre Stadium 12	7000 Brush Hollow Rd.	Westbury	NY	11590	12	501
Transit Center Stadium 18 Plus Imax	6707 Transit Rd.	Williamsville	NY	14221	19	514
Movieland Yonkers 6	2548 Central Park Ave.	Yonkers	NY	10710	6	501
Movies@Jefferson Valley 8	650 Lee Blvd	Yorktown Heights	NY	10598	8	501
Independence Stadium 10	1210 Independence Ave.	Akron	OH	44310	10	510
Interstate Park Cinema Stadium 18	1089 Interstate Pkwy.	Akron	OH	44312	18	510
Montrose Movies Stadium 12	Market Square at Montrose	Akron	OH	44333	12	510

Theatre	Address	City	State	Zip	Screens	DMA
Hollywood Stadium 20 @ Fairfield Co.	2651 Fairfield Commons	Beavercreek	OH	45431	20	542
Regal 6	2077 Western Ave.	Chillicothe	OH	45601	6	535
Middleburg Town Square Stadium 16	18348 Bagley Rd.	Cleveland	OH	44130	16	535
Severance Town Center Stadium 14	3492 Mayfield Rd.	Cleveland Heights	OH	44118	14	510
Georgesville Square Stadium 16.	1800 Georgesville Square Dr.	Columbus	OH	43228	16	535
Northtowne Cinema 9.	1500 North Clinton St.	Defiance	OH	43512	9	547
Cobblestone Square Stadium 20	5500 Cobblestone Rd.	Elyria	OH	44035	20	510
Hudson Cinema 10	5339 Darrow Rd.	Hudson	OH	44236	10	510
River Valley Mall 10	River Valley Mall	Lancaster	OH	43130	10	535
Lima Center Cinema 3	2720 Elida Rd.	Lima	OH	45805	3	558
Regal Cinema 7	1450 North Cable Rd.	Lima	OH	45805	7	558
Lafayette Center Cinema 7	430 Pike St.	Marietta	OH	45750	7	597
Southland Cinema 7.	1415 Marion-Waldo Rd.	Marion	OH	43302	7	535
Mayfield Heights 10	1345 SOM Center Rd.	Mayfield Heights	OH	44124	10	510
Medina Stadium 16 @ Huntington St.	200 West Reagan Pkwy.	Medina	OH	44256	16	510
New Towne Cinema 8.	400 Mill Ave. S.E., Ste. 703	New Philadelphia	OH	44663	8	510
Boulevard Centre Stadium 14	24 Blvd. Centre	Niles	OH	44446	14	536
Solon Commons Cinema 16	6185 Enterprises Pkwy.	Solon	OH	44139	16	510
Tiffin Movies 4	Tiffin Mall	Tiffin	OH	44883	4	547
Westlake Promenade 11.	30147 Detroit Rd.	Westlake	OH	44145	11	510
Willoughby Commons Stadium 16	36655 Euclid Ave.	Willoughby	OH	44094	16	510
Austintown Plaza 10	6020 Mahoning Ave.	Youngstown	OH	44515	10	536
Cinemasouth Cinema 10	7420 South Ave	Youngstown	OH	44512	10	536
Crossroads Mall Stadium 16.	1211 E. I-240	Oklahoma City	OK.	73149	16	650
Windsor Hills Cinema 10	4625 N.W. 23 RD. St.	Oklahoma City	OK.	73127	10	650
Albany 7 Cinemas	1350 S.E. Waverly Dr.	Albany	OR	97321	7	820
Westgate 5 Theatres	3950 S.W. Cedar Hills Blvd.	Beaverton	OR	97005	5	820
Old Mill Stadium 10	680 S.W. Powerhouse Dr.	Bend	OR	97702	10	821
Pilot Butte 6 Theatres	2717 N.E. Hwy. 20	Bend	OR	97702	6	821
Clackamas Towne Center 5	12000 S.E. 82nd	Clackamas	OR	97266	5	820
Ninth Street 4 Cinemas	1750 N.W. 9th St.	Corvallis	OR	97330	4	801
Cinema World 8 Valley River	1087 Valley River Way.	Eugene	OR	97401	8	801
Stark Street Stadium 10	2929 N.E. Kane Dr.	Gresham	OR	97030	10	820
Evergreen Parkway Stadium 13	2625 N.W. 188th	Hillsboro	OR	97124	13	820
Movies On TV Stadium 16	S.W. 2929 234th Ave.	Hillsboro	OR	97123	16	820
Lincoln City Stadium 6	3755 Southeast High School Dr.	Lincoln Cit	OR	97367	6	820
Newport Tri	130 N.W. 19th St.	Newport	OR	97365	3	820
Hilltop 9 Cinema	325 Beavercreek Rd.	Oregon City	OR	97045	9	820
82nd Avenue 6 Cinemas	9600 S.E. 82nd Ave.	Portland	OR	97266	6	820
Broadway Metro 4 Theatres	1000 S.W. Broadway	Portland	OR	97205	4	820
Division Street Stadium 13	16603 S.E. Division St.	Portland	OR	97236	13	820
Fox Tower Stadium 10	846 S.W. Park Ave	Portland	OR	97205	10	820
Koin Center 6 Cinemas	222 S.W. Columbia	Portland	OR	97205	6	820
Lloyd Center Stadium 10 Cinema	1510 N.E. Multnomah Blvd.	Portland	OR	97232	10	820
Lloyd Mall 8 Cinema	2320 Lloyd Center Mall	Portland	OR	97232	8	820
Lancaster Quad Cinema	831 Lancaster Dr. N.E.	Salem	OR	97301	4	820
Movieland 7	501 Marion St. N.E.	Salem	OR	97301	7	820
Santiam Stadium 11	365 Lancaster Dr. S.E.	Salem	OR	97301	11	820
Sherwood Stadium 10	15995 S.W. Tualatin-Sherwood Rd.	Sherwood	OR	97140	10	820
Tigard 11 Cinemas	11626 S.W. Pacific Hwy.	Tigard	OR	97223	11	820
Wilsonville Stadium 9 Cinema	29300 S.W. Town Center Loop	Wilsonville	OR	97070	9	820
Moraine Pointe Cinema 10	300 Moraine Pointe Plaza	Butler	PA	16001	10	508
UA Capital City Mall Cinemas 6	3594 Capital Mall Dr.	Camp Hill	PA	17011	6	566
Plymouth Meeting 10	1011 W. Ridge Pike	Conshohocken.	PA	19428	10	504
Downingtown Cinema Stadium 16	100 Quarry Rd.	Downingtown	PA	19335	16	504
Barn Plaza Stadium 14.	1745 Easton Rd.	Doylestown	PA	18901	14	504
East Whiteland Stadium 9.	593 W. Lancaster Ave.	East Whiteland	PA	19355	9	504
Northampton Cinema 14.	3720 Easton-Nazareth Hwy.	Easton.	PA	18045	14	504
UA Movies @ Schuylkill Mall 4	Schuylkill Mall.	Frackville	PA	17931	4	577
Macdade Mall Cinemas 4	C/O Macdade Shopping Center.	Holmes	PA	19043	4	504
King Of Prussia Stadium 16.	300 Goddard Blvd.	King Of Prussia	PA	19406	16	504
Manor Stadium 16	1246 Millersville Pike	Lancaster	PA	17603	16	566
Oxford Valley Theatre Stadium 10.	43 Middletown Blvd.	Langhorne.	PA	19047	10	504
Lionville Cinema Stadium 12.	120 Eagleview Blvd.	Lionville	PA	19353	12	504
Main Street Theatre 6.	3720-40 Main St.	Manayunk	PA	19127	6	504
Montgomeryville Theatre 7	Watertower Square Shopping Center	Montgomeryville	PA	18936	7	504
UA Movies @ Lycoming Mall 4	300 Lycoming Mall Circle	Muncy	PA	17756	4	577
Edgmont Square 10	4777 West Chester Pike	Newton Square	PA	19073	10	504
Marketplace @ Oaks Stadium 24	180 Mill Rd.	Oaks	PA	19456	24	504
Riverview Plaza 17	1400 S. Christopher Columbus Blvd	Philadelphia	PA	19147	17	504
UA Grant Plaza 9	1619 Grant Ave.	Philadelphia	PA	19115	9	504
UA Theatre @Cheltenham Square 8	2385 Cheltenham Ave.	Philadelphia	PA	19150	8	504
Richland Crossing 12	185 North West End Blvd	Quakertown	PA	18951	12	504
UA @ Steamtown 8	301 Lackawanna Ave.	Scranton	PA	18503	8	577
UA Scranton 8 Theatre	Rte. 6	Scranton	PA	18508	8	577
Movies @ 69th Street 9	53 South 69Th St.	Upper Darby	PA	19082	9	504
Warrington Crossing Stadium 22	104 Easton Rd., Bldg F.	Warrington	PA	18976	22	504
West Manchester Mall Stadium 13	1800 Loucks Rd.	York	PA	17404	13	566
Aiken Mall 8	300 East Gate Dr.	Aiken	SC	29802	8	520
North Charleston 10	2055 Eagle Landing Blvd.	Charleston	SC	29406	10	519
Columbia Cinema 7	3400 Forest Dr. Ste. 3000	Columbia	SC	29204	7	546
Capri Cinemas 3	840 South Irby St.	Florence	SC	29501	3	570
Julia 4	1110 South Irby St.	Florence	SC	29501	4	570
Hollywood Stadium 20	1025 Woodruff Rd.	Greenville	SC	29607	20	567
Inlet Square 12.	10125 Hwy. 17 By-Pass #12F	Murrels Inlet	SC	29576	12	519
Charles Towne Square Stadium 18	2401 Mall Dr.	North Charleston	SC	29406	18	519
Converse Cinemas 6	1200 E. Main St.	Spartanburg	SC	29302	6	567
Westgate Mall Cinema 8.	205 Blackstock Rd.	Spartanburg	SC	29301	8	567
Hamilton Place 10-17	2000 Hamilton Place Blvd.	Chattanooga	TN	37421	17	575
Hamilton Place Mall Stadium 9	2100 Hamilton Place Mall	Chattanooga	TN	37421	8	575
Indian Lake Cinema 10.	120 Indian lake Blvd.	Hendersonville	TN	37075	10	659
Northgate Crossing 6	5131 Old Hixson Pike	Hixson	TN	37343	6	575

Theatre	Address	City	State	Zip	Screens	DMA
Downtown West Cinema 8	1640 Downtown West Blvd.	Knoxville	TN	37919	8	557
Farragut Towne Square 10	11847 Kingston Pike	Knoxville	TN	37922	10	557
Knoxville Center Stadium 10.	3051 B Knoxville Center Mall	Knoxville	TN	37924	10	557
West Town Mall Stadium 9	7600 Kingston Pike	Knoxville	TN	37919	9	557
Bellevue Cinema Stadium 12	7741 Hwy. 70 South	Nashville	TN	37221	12	659
Green Hills Stadium 16.	3815 Greenhills Village Dr.	Nashville	TN	37215	16	659
Hollywood Stadium 27	719 Thompson Ln.	Nashville	TN	37204	27	659
Opry Mills Stadium 20 Plus Imax	470 Opry Mills Dr.	Nashville	TN	37214	21	659
Tullahoma Cinemas 8.	2221 N. Jackson St.	Tullahoma	TN	37388	8	659
Abilene 10	Mall Of Abilene #1344.	Abilene	TX	79606	10	662
Amarillo Star Stadium 14	8275 Amarillo Blvd West	Amarillo	TX	79106	14	662
Bowen 8.	4255 South Bowen Rd.	Arlington	TX	76015	8	623
Gateway Stadium 16	9700 Stonelake Blvd	Austin	TX	78759	16	635
Metropolitan Stadium 14.	901 Little Texas Ln.	Austin	TX	78745	14	635
Westgate Stadium 11 Theatres	4477 South Lamar Blvd.	Austin	TX	78745	11	635
Bedford 10	2000 Forum Pkwy.	Bedford	TX	76021	10	623
Lakeline Mall 9	11200 Lakeline Mall Dr.	Cedar Park	TX	78613	9	635
Galaxy Theatre Stadium 10	11801 Mccree Rd.	Dallas	TX	75238	10	623
UA Plaza 8.	9330 N. Central Expressway	Dallas	TX	75231	8	623
Denton Mall 5.	2201 Interstate 35E South	Denton	TX	76205	5	623
Golden Triangle 4	2201 Interstate 35 E	Denton	TX	76205	4	623
Fossil Creek Stadium 11.	N. 6100 Freeway	Ft Worth	TX	76137	11	623
Hulen 10	4920 South Hulen St.	Ft Worth	TX	76132	10	623
Las Vegas Trails 8.	8300 I-30 West	Ft Worth	TX	76108	8	623
UA Eastchase Market Stadium 9	8301 Ederville.	Ft Worth	TX	76120	9	623
Northstar 8.	1146 Belt Line Rd.	Garland	TX	75040	8	623
Grand Prairie 10.	510 Westchester	Grand Prairie	TX	75052	10	623
Greenway Grand Palace Stadium 24	3839 Weslayan St.	Houston.	TX	77027	24	618
Houston Marq*E Stadium 23	7600 Katy Freeway	Houston.	TX	77024	23	618
Macarthur Stadium 16	8505 Walton Blvd.	Irving.	TX	75063	16	623
North Creek 10.	7807 San Dario.	Laredo.	TX	78045	10	749
UA Lakepointe 10.	1600 S. Stemmons Freeway	Lewisville	TX	75067	10	623
Live Oak Stadium 18	7901 Pat Booker Rd.	Liveoak	TX	78233	18	641
Alamo Quarry Stadium 14	255 E.Basse.	San Antonio.	TX	78209	14	641
Cielo Vista Stadium 18	2828 Cinema Ridge	San Antonio.	TX	78238	18	641
Crossroads 6 Theatres	4552 Fredericksburg Rd.	San Antonio.	TX	78201	6	641
Fiesta 16 Stadium Theatres	12631 Vance Jackson	San Antonio.	TX	78230	16	641
Northwoods 14.	17640 Henderson Pass.	San Antonio.	TX	78232	14	641
Ballston Common Stadium 12.	671 N. Glebe Rd.	Arlington	VA	22203	12	511
Downtown Mall 6	200 W. Main St.	Charlottesville	VA	22902	6	584
Seminole Square Cinema 4	2306 India Dr.	Charlottesville	VA	22901	4	584
Greenbrier Cinema 13	600 Jarman Rd.	Chesapeake	VA	23320	13	544
Chester Cinemas 6.	13025 Jefferson Davis Hwy.	Chester	VA	23831	6	556
New River Valley 11	400 New River Rd.	Christiansburg	VA	24073	11	573
Southpark Cinema 6.	374 Southpark Mall.	Colonial Heights	VA	23834	6	556
Fairfax Towne Center 10	4110 W Ox Rd.	Fairfax	VA	22033	10	511
Fredericksburg 15.	3301 Plank Rd. Rte. 3W	Fredericksburg.	VA	22401	15	511
Virginia Center Stadium 20.	10091 Jeb Stuart Pkwy.	Glen Allen	VA	23059	20	556
Riverdale Plaza Stadium 12	1044 Von Shilling Dr.	Hampton	VA	23666	12	544
Harrisonburg Stadium 14	381 University Blvd.	Harrisonburg	VA	22801	14	569
Kiln Creek Cinema Stadium 20	100 Regal Way, Victory Center	Newport News	VA	23602	20	544
Macarthur Center Stadium 18.	300 Monticello Ave.	Norfolk.	VA	23510	18	544
Main Gate 10	Bldg CD12 Next to Mall Complex	Norfolk.	VA	23503	10	544
Ridge Cinema 7	1510 East Ridge Rd.	Richmond	VA	23229	7	556
Shortpump Stadium 14.	11650 West Broad St.	Richmond	VA	23233	14	556
UA @ Chesterfield Town Ctr 9	11500 Midlothian Tpk	Richmond	VA	23235	9	556
West Tower Cinemas 10	8998 West Broad St.	Richmond	VA	23229	10	556
Westhampton Cinema 2	5706 Grove Ave.	Richmond	VA	23226	2	556
Aquia 10.	2850 Jefferson Davis Hwy.	Stafford	VA	22554	10	511
Staunton Mall Cinema 6	90 Lee Jackson Hwy., Ste. 196	Staunton	VA	24401	6	556
Countryside Stadium 20	45980 Regal Plaza	Sterling	VA	20165	20	511
Columbus 12	104 Constitution Dr.	Virginia Beach	VA	23462	12	544
Pembroke Cinema 8	4576-76 Virginia Beach Blvd.	Virginia Beach	VA	23462	8	544
Strawbridge Mktplace Stadium 12.	2133 General Booth Blvd.	Virginia Beach	VA	23454	12	544
Auburn Stadium 17 Theatres	1101 Super Mall Way, Ste. 901	Auburn	WA	98001	17	819
Crossroads 8 Cinema	1200 156th Ave. N.E.	Bellevue	WA	98004	8	819
Galleria Stadium 11	550 106th Ave. N.E.	Bellevue	WA	98004	11	819
Bellis Fair 6 Cinema	#5 Bellis Fair Pkwy.	Bellingham	WA	98226	6	819
Sehome 3 Cinemas	3300 Fielding Ave.	Bellingham	WA	98225	3	819
Sunset Square Cinema 6	1135 E Sunset Dr.	Bellingham	WA	98226	6	819
Tall Firs 10	20751 State Rte. 410 E.	Bonneylake	WA	98390	10	819
Cinema 3	2100 N National Ave. Yardbird	Chehalis	WA	98532	3	819
Everett 9 Cinemas	830 S.E. Everett Mall Way	Everett.	WA	98208	9	819
Gig Harbor 3	5401 Olympic Dr. N.W.	Gig Harbor	WA	98335	3	819
Issaquah 9 Theatre.	1490 N.W. 11th Ave.	Issaquah	WA	98027	9	819
Three Rivers Mall 5	1301 Grade St.	Kelso	WA	98626	5	820
Columbia Mall Stadium 8	701 Columbia Center	Kennewick	WA	99336	8	810
Kent 6 Theatres	10116 S.E. 256TH	Kent	WA	98031	6	819
Lakewood Cinema Stadium 15	2410 84th St. S.	Lakewood	WA	98499	15	819
Triangle Quad Cinemas	1228 Washington Way.	Longview	WA	98632	4	820
Alderwood 7 Theatres.	3501 184th St. S.W.	Lynwood	WA	98037	7	819
Marysville Cinema 14	9811 State Ave.	Marysville	WA	98270	14	819
Mount Lake 9 Theatre.	6009 S.W. 244th St.	Mt Lake Terrace	WA	98043	9	819
Capital Mall Cinemas 4	302 Capitol Mall	Olympia	WA	98501	4	819
Lacey 8 Theatres	4431 Martin Way.	Olympia	WA	98516	8	819
South Sound Cinema 10.	1435 Olney Ave. S.E.	Port Orchard	WA	98366	10	819
Poulsbo Stadium 10	N.W. 750 Edvard St.	Poulsbo	WA	98370	10	819
Longston Place Stadium 14	13317 Meridian St. East	Puyallup	WA	98373	14	819
Puyallup 6 Cinemas	1200 Fourth St. N.W.	Puyallup	WA	98371	6	819
South Hill Cinema 6	3500 S Meridian	Puyallup	WA	98373	6	819
Bella Botega Stadium 11 Cinema	8890 N.E. 161st Ave.	Redmond	WA	98052	11	819
East Valley Stadium 13 Cinema	3751 E Rd. Hwy.	Renton	WA	98055	13	819

Theatre	Address	City	State	Zip	Screens	DMA
Uptown Triplex Theatre	1300 Jadwin Ave.	Richland	WA	99352	3	810
Silverdale 4 Theatres	9923 Clear Cr.Rd. N.W.	Silverdale	WA	98383	4	819
Newport Road 8	10404 N Newport Hwy.	Spokane	WA	99218	8	881
Northtown Mall Stadium 12	4750 North Division St.	Spokane	WA	99207	12	881
Spokane Valley Stadium 12	14760 E Indiana Ave.	Spokane	WA	99216	12	881
Parkway Plaza Stadium 12	5910 South 180th St.	Tukwila	WA	98188	12	819
Cascade Stadium 16 Cinemas	1101 S.E. 160th Ave.	Vancouver	WA	98683	16	820
Cinema 99 Stadium 11	9010 N.E. Hwy 99	Vancouver	WA	98665	11	820
City Center Stadium 12	801 C St.	Vancouver	WA	98660	12	820
Vancouver Plaza 10 Cinema	7800 N.E. Fourth Plain	Vancouver	WA	98662	10	820
College Avenue Stadium 16	W3091 Van Roy Rd.	Buchanan	WI	54915	16	658
Grand Central Mall 12	700 Grand Central Mall	Vienna	WV	26105	12	597

REYNOLDS THEATRES ENTERTAINEMNT INC.

4 theatres, 10 screens

122 W. Main St., Box 737, Elmwood, IL 61529. (309) 742-8586. FAX: (309) 742-8587. www.reynoldstheatres.com
PRESIDENT
Vern O. Reynolds

THEATRES

Theatre	Address	City	State	Zip	Screens	DMA
Town Theatre	1029 Second St.	Chillicothe	IL	61523	2	675
Garden Theatre	62 N. Main St.	Canton	IL	61520	2	675
Palace Theatre Elmwood	122 W. Main St.	Elmwood	IL	61529	1	675
Morton Cinema 5	2115 S. Main St.	Morton	IL	61550	5	675

RITZ THEATRE GROUP

4 theatres, 28 screens.

212 Walnut St., Philadelphia, PA 19106. (215) 627-0900. FAX: (215) 627-3295. www.ritzfilmbill.com
OWNER & PRESIDENT
Ramon L. Posel
DIRECTOR, OPERATIONS
Jay Ayrton

THEATRES

Theatre	Address	City	State	Zip	Screens	DMA
Ritz Sixteen	900 Haddonfield-Berlin Rd.	Voorhees	NJ	08043	16	504
Ritz East	125 Samson St. Walkway	Philadelphia	PA	19106	2	504
Ritz Five	214 Walnut St.	Philadelphia	PA	19106	5	504
Ritz at the Bourse	400 Ranstead St.	Philadelphia	PA	19106	5	504

ROGERS CINEMA, INC.

6 theatres, 32 screens.

407 S. Maple, P.O. Box 280, Marshfield, WI 54449. (715) 387-3437. FAX: (715) 387-2165. www.rogerscinema.com
OWNER & PRESIDENT
Paul J. Rogers

THEATRES

Theatre	Address	City	State	Zip	Screens	DMA
Rogers Cinema 7	419 S. Central	Marshfield	WI	54449	7	705
Grand Theatre 4	208 Wolf River Plaza	New London	WI	54961	4	658
Rogers Cinema 4	1601 6th St.	Stevens Point	WI	54481	4	658
Rogers Cinema 6	2825 S. Church St.	Stevens Point	WI	54481	6	658
Rosa Theatre 4	218 S. Main	Waupaca	WI	54981	4	658
Rogers Cinema 7	220 E. Grand Ave.	Wisconsin Rapids	WI	54494	7	705

SANTIKOS THEATRES

8 theatres, 91 screens.

601 Embassy Oaks, Ste. 105, San Antonio, TX 78216. (210) 496-1300. FAX: (210) 496-2720. www.santikos.com
OWNER/PRESIDENT
John Santikos
DIRECTOR, OPERATIONS
Roger Black

THEATRES

Theatre	Address	City	State	Zip	Screens	DMA
Santikos Bijou at Crossroads	At Crossroads Mall	San Antonio	TX	78201	6	641
Santikos Embassy 14	Bitters Rd. at 281 North	San Antonio	TX	78216	14	641
Santikos Galaxy 14	Loop 410 at IH-35N	San Antonio	TX	78218	14	641
Santikos Mayan Palace 14	S.W. Military at IH-35	San Antonio	TX	78221	14	641
Santikos Mission 4 Drive-In	3100 Roosevelt Ave., next to Mission San Jose	San Antonio	TX	78214	4	641
Santikos Northwest 10	Loop 410 at IH-10	San Antonio	TX	78230	10	641
Santikos Silverado 16	Bandera at 1604	San Antonio	TX	78250	16	641
Santikos Westlakes 9	S.W. Loop 410 near Marbach	San Antonio	TX	78227	9	641

SIGNATURE THEATRES

30 theatres, 254 screens.

1600 Broadway, Oakland, CA 94612. (510) 268-9498. FAX: (510) 268-9843. www.signaturetheatres.com
OWNER, CHAIRMAN & PRESIDENT
Philip Harris III
OWNERS
Philip Harris, Sr.
Douglas Stephens
FILM BUYER
Bill Herting

THEATRES

Theatre	Address	City	State	Zip	Screens	DMA
Signature Festival Cinemas 10	1160 W. Branch St.	Arroyo Grande	CA	93420	10	855
Signature Stadium 10	500 Nevada St.	Auburn	CA	95603	10	862
Signature Holiday Cinema	101 F St.	Davis	CA	95616	6	862
Signature Stadium 5	420 G St.	Davis	CA	95616	5	862
Signature Manchester Stadium	2055 E. Shields Ave.	Fresno	CA	93726	16	866
Metro 8	81-725 Hwy. 111.	Indio	CA	90021	8	804
Signature Jackson Cinemas	201 Shopping Dr.	Jackson	CA	95642	4	862

Theatre	Address	City	State	Zip	Screens	DMA
Signature Stadium 10	3969 McHenry Ave.	Modesto	CA	95356	10	862
Jack London Cinema	100 Washington St.	Oakland	CA	94607	9	807
Courtyard 10	777 E. Tahquitz Canyon	Palm Springs	CA	92262	10	804
Signature Placerville 8	337 Placerville Dr.	Placerville	CA	95667	8	862
Rancho 16	72-777 Dinah Short Dr.	Rancho Mirage	CA	92270	16	804
Metro 12	1599 San Jacinto	San Jacinto	CA	92583	12	803
Crow Canyon Cinemas 6	2525 San Ramon Valley Blvd.	San Ramon	CA	94583	6	807
Signature Santa Cruz Cinema 9	1405 Pacific Ave.	Santa Cruz	CA	95060	9	828
Signature Riverfront Twin	155 S. River St.	Santa Cruz	CA	95060	2	828
Signature Stadium 10	901 Sanguinetti	Sonora	CA	95370	10	862
Signature Festival Cinemas, 4-Plex.	6436 Pacific Ave.	Stockton	CA	95207	4	862
Signature Holiday Cinemas 8	6262 W. Ln.	Stockton	CA	95210	8	862
Turlock Stadium 14	2323 W. Main St.	Turlock	CA	95380	14	862
Signature Ukiah 6	612 State St.	Ukiah	CA	95482	6	807
Signature Sequoia Mall 12	3355 S. Mooney Blvd	Visalia	CA	93277	12	866
Signature Stadium 10	120 S. Bridge St.	Visalia	CA	93279	10	866
Signature Dole Cannery	735 B Iwilei Rd.	Honolulu	HI	96817	18	744
Signature Windward Stadium 10	46-056 Kamehemeha Hwy.	Kaneohe	HI	96744	10	744
Signature Pearl Highlands 12	1000 Kam Hwy	Pearl City	HI	96782	12	744
Signature Midway Drive-In	3115 Hwy 40 W.	Columbia Falls	MT	59901	1	762
Signature Gateway Cinema	1275 Hwy. 2 W.	Kalispell	MT	59901	6	762
Signature Liberty Theatre	120 1st Ave. E.	Kalispell	MT	59901	1	762
Signature Strand Theatre	120 2nd St. E.	Kalispell	MT	59901	1	762

SPINELLI CINEMAS

6 theatres, 19 screens.
400 Central Ave., Dover, NH 03820. (603) 749-2555. FAX: (603) 749-0195. www.spinellicinemas.com
PRESIDENT
Michael J. Spinelli, Jr.

THEATRES

Theatre	Address	City	State	Zip	Screens	DMA
Barrington Station Cinema 6	339 Calef Hwy., Rte 125	Barrington	NH	03825	6	506
Strand Theatre	20 Third St.	Dover	NH	03820	3	506
Rialto Theatre	78-82 Main St.	Lancaster	NH	03584	1	506
Merideth Cinema 3	4NH Rte. 25	Merideth	NH	03253	3	506
Plymouth Theatre	39 Main St.	Plymouth	NH	03264	2	506
Lilac Mall Cinema 4	Rte. 125	Rochester	NH	03867	4	506

STAR CINEMA (AGT ENTERPRISES, INC.)

8 theatres, 72 screens.
AGT Enterprises, Inc., P.O. Box 317, Prairie Du Chien, WI 53821. (608) 326-5449. FAX: (608) 326-5382. www.starcinema.com
OWNERS
Bill Adamany
Bill Adamany, Jr.

THEATRES

Theatre	Address	City	State	Zip	Screens	DMA
Star Cinema	3200 23rd Ave.	Council Bluffs	IA	51503	16	652
Star Cinema	Hwy. 18 & PD	Fitchburg	WI	53719	14	669
Star Cinema	420 Village Walk Ln.	Johnson Creek	WI	53038	12	617
Hilldale Theatre	702 N. Midvale Blvd.	Madison	WI	53705	2	669
Star Cinema	Hwy. 18 S.	Prairie Du Chien	WI	53821	6	637
Star Cinema	115 N. Webb Ave.	Reedsburg	WI	53959	6	669
Star Cinema	1010 Maple	Sparta	WI	54656	6	702
Desert Star Cinema	I-90/94 & Hwy. 12	Wisconsin Dells	WI	53940	10	669

STARNET CINEMAS

10 theatres, 57 screens.
P.O. Box 8789, Jacksonville, FL 32239. (904) 251-9957. FAX: (904) 251-9924. www.starnetcinemas.com email: starnetcinemas@aol.com
Booking Office: 4407 Highlands Dr., McKinney, TX 75070. (972) 529-6535.
PRESIDENT
William J. Homer
FILM BUYER
Robert Fulford

THEATRES

Theatre	Address	City	State	Zip	Screens	DMA
Belleview Cinemas	10845 S.E. Hwy. 441	Belleview	FL	34420	2	534
Jax 10 Cinemas	6681 103rd St.	Jacksonville	FL	32210	10	561
Mandarin Corners	10993 San Jose Blvd.	Jacksonville	FL	32223	6	561
Pabio Theatres	1970 S. Third St.	Jacksonville Beach	FL	32250	9	561
Lakeland Square 10 Cinemas	3606 U.S. Hwy. 98 N.	Lakeland	FL	33809	10	539
Leigh Cinema	1201 Taylor Ln. Extension	Lehigh Acres	FL	33936	4	
Marianna Cinemas	4341 Lafayette St.	Marianna	FL	32446	2	656
Palatka Mall Cinemas	400 Hwy. 19 N., #59	Palatka	FL	32177	4	561
Satellite Beach Cinemas	1044 B Hwy. A1A, #136	Satellite Beach	FL	32937	4	534
Bainbridge Mall Cinemas	1400 E. Shotwell St.	Bainbridge	GA	31717	6	530

STARPLEX CINEMAS

7 theatres, 61 screens.
7502 Greenville Ave., Ste. 480, Dallas, TX 75231. (214) 692-6494. FAX: (214) 692-8982. www.starplexcinemas.com
PRESIDENT
J C Mitchell
VICE PRESIDENT
Ken Menard
FILM BUYER
Bill Knight

THEATRES

Theatre	Address	City	State	Zip	Screens	DMA
Mesquite Cinema 10	227 U.S. Hwy. 80 E.	Mesquite	TX	75149	10	623
Irving Cinema 10	4205 W. Pioneer Dr.	Irving	TX	75061	10	623
Brazos Mall 3	110 Hwy. 332 W. #1468	Lake Jackson	TX	77566	3	618

Theatre	Address	City	State	Zip	Screens	DMA
Cinema 10	104 Hwy. 332 E.	Lake Jackson	TX	77566	10	618
Sulphur Springs Cinema 6	500 E. Shannon Rd.	Sulphur Springs	TX	75482	6	
Supersaver 6	410 N. Valley Mills Dr.	Waco	TX	76710	6	625
Waco Galaxy 16	333 S. Valley Mills Dr.	Waco	TX	76710	16	625

SYNDICATE THEATRES, INC.

3 theatres, 10 screens.
870 Mallory Pkwy., Franklin, IN 46131. (317) 736-7144. FAX (317) 736 4299.
PRESIDENT & FILM BUYER
Michael Rembusch
BOOKER
Nancy Gilliland

THEATRES

Theatre	Address	City	State	Zip	Screens	DMA
Canary Creek Cinemas	870 Mallory Pkwy.	Franklin	IN	46131	8	527
13-24 Drive-In Theatre	St. RD. 13 N., 106 W. Market St.	Wabash	IN	46992	1	509
Eagles Theatre	106 W. Market St.	Wabash	IN	46992	1	509

THEATRE MANAGEMENT, INC. (TMI THEATRES)

4 theatres, 27 screens.
P.O. Box 2076, Deland, FL 32721. (386) 736-6830. FAX: (386) 738-2596.
PRESIDENT
Clint DeMarsh
VICE PRESIDENT
Frank DeMarsh

THEATRES

Theatre	Address	City	State	Zip	Screens	DMA
Victoria Square 6	1798 S. Woodland Blvd.	DeLand	FL	32721	6	534
Beacon 12 Theatre	1401 S. Dixie Fwy.	New Smyrna Bch.	FL	32168	12	534
Pioneer Drive-In Theatre	1985 N. Main St.	Butler	PA	16003	5	508
Meadville Cinemas	952 Park Ave.	Meadville	PA	16335	4	516

TRANS-LUX

12 theatres, 62 screens.
433 Paseo de Peralta, Santa Fe, NM 87501. (505) 989-9300. www.transluxmovies.com
SENIOR V.P.
Bryan Mercer
OPERATIONS MANAGER
Nick Sanchez
OPERATIONS SUPERVISOR
Ron Lujan
HUMAN RESOURCES COORDINATOR
Gini Mercer
MARKETING DIRECTOR
Gail Dunn

THEATRES

Theatre	Address	City	State	Zip	Screens	DMA
Trans-Lux Desert Sky Cinema	70 W. Duvall Mine Rd.	Sahuarita	AZ	85629	6	789
Trans-Lux Lake Dillon Cinema	135 Main St, Dillon Ctr.	Dillon	CO	80435	4	751
Trans-Lux Skyline Cinema	312 U.S. Hwy. 6.	Dillon	CO	80435	6	751
Trans-Lux High Five Cinemas	900 Translux Dr.	Durango	CO	81301	5	790
Trans-Lux Gaslight Cinemas	102 E. Fifth St.	Durango	CO	81301	2	790
Trans-Lux Metrolux 12	1380 N. Denver Ave.	Loveland	CO	80537	12	751
Trans Lux Dream Catcher Cinema	33771 S. U.S. Hwy. 285.	Espanola	NM	87532	6	790
Trans-Lux Starlight Cinema	2226 Sun Ranch Village Loop	Los Lunas	NM	87031	8	790
Trans-Lux Jean Cocteau Cinema	418 Montezuma	Santa Fe	NM	87501	1	790
Trans-Lux Loma Theatre	107 Manzanares Ave.	Socorro	NM	87801	1	790
Trans-Lux Storyteller Cinemas	110 Old Talpa Canon Rd.	Taos	NM	87571	7	790
Trans-Lux Fox Theatre	505 S. 20th St.	Laramie	WY	82070	4	751

ULTRASTAR CINEMAS

11 theatres, 81 screens.
6941 El Camino Real, Carlsbad, CA 92009. (760) 431-1996. FAX: (760) 431-8464. www.ultrastarmovies.com
PRESIDENT & CEO
Alan Grossberg
SENIOR V.P. & COO
John Ellison Jr.
V.P., OPERATIONS
Damon Rubio
V.P., MARKETING & ADVERTISING
Julie Bravo
DIRECTOR, CONCESSIONS & TRAINING
Kevin Stengel

THEATRES

Theatre	Address	City	State	Zip	Screens	DMA
UltraStar Galaxy 6	5256 S. Mission Rd.	Bonsall	CA	92003	6	825
UltraStar La Costa 6	6941 El Camino Real	Carlsbad	CA	92009	6	825
UltraStar Chula Vista 10	555 Broadway #2050	Chula Vista	CA	91910	10	825
UltraStar Flower Hill Cinema 4	2630 Via De La Valle	Del Mar	CA	92014	4	825
UltraStar Fontana 8	16741 Valley Blvd.	Fontana	CA	92335	8	803
UltraStar Canyon Springs	12125 Day St., G-301	Moreno Valley	CA	92557	7	803
UltraStar TownGate 8	12625 L Frederick.	Moreno Valley	CA	92553	8	803
UltraStar Poway Creekside Plaza 10	13475 Poway Rd.	Poway	CA	92064	10	825
UltraStar Terra Vista 6	10701 Town Center Dr.	Rancho Cucamonga	CA	91730	6	803
UltraStar Rialto 8	290 W. Baseline Rd.	Rialto	CA	92376	8	803
UltraStar Del Mar Highlands 8	12905 El Camino Real	San Diego	CA	92130	8	825

Theatre	Address	City	State	Zip	Screens	DMA

UNITED ARTISTS THEATRE CIRCUIT, INC.

(See Regal Entertainment Group)

WALLACE THEATER CORPORATION

50 theatres, 425 screens. American Samoa: 1 theatre, 2 screens; Guam: 1 theatre, 14 screens; Saipan: 1 theatre, 8 screens; Marshall Islands: 1 theatre, 3 screens; Micronesia: 1 theatre, 3 screens. Total theatres: 55, Total screens: 455.
(Incorporating Hollywood Theatres)
919 S.W. Taylor St., Ste. 800, Portland, OR 97205. (503) 221-7090. FAX: (503) 796-0229.
CHAIRMAN
Timothy G. Wood
CEO
Scott C. Wallace
VICE CHAIRMAN
Walt Aman
SENIOR V.P., REAL ESTATE & DEVELOPMENT
Tim Reed
V.P., GLOBAL OPERATIONS
Steve Guffey
V.P., OPERATIONS, WESTERN U.S. & PACIFIC RIM
Brett Havlik
V.P., CONCESSIONS & PURCHASING
Robert Perkins
V.P. & HEAD FILM BUYER
Steve Friedstrom
V.P., MARKETING & ADVERTISING
David L. Lyons
CONTROLLER
Lawrence T. Reid

THEATRES

Theatre	Address	City	State	Zip	Screens	DMA
WTC- Stadium/Mobile 18	1230 Satchell Paige Dr.	Mobile	AL	36606	18	686
WTC- Gilbert Stadium Cinemas	1012 S. Gilbert Rd.	Gilbert	AZ	85296	14	753
WTC- New Barstow Cinema 6	1503 E. Main St.	Barstow	CA	92311	6	803
WTC- New Malibu Theatre	3822 Crosscreek Rd.	Malibu	CA	90265	2	803
WTC- Mainplace Stadium Cinemas	403 W. Main St.	Merced	CA	95341	13	866
WTC- Santa Paula Cinema 7	550 W. Main St.	Santa Paula	CA	93060	7	803
WTC- Prince Kuhio Theatre	111 E. Puainako St.	Hilo	HI	96720	9	744
WTC- Kress Cinema 4	174 Kamehameha Ave.	Hilo	HI	96720	4	744
WTC- Restaurant Row 9 Art House	500 Ala Moana Blvd.	Honolulu	HI	96813	9	744
WTC- Maui Mall Megaplex	70 E. Kahnumanu Ave.	Kahului	HI	96732	12	744
WTC- Keolu Center Cinema 4	1090 Keolu Dr.	Kailua	HI	96734	4	744
WTC- Kailua Cinema 2	345 Hahani St.	Kailua	HI	96734	2	744
WTC- Makalapua Stadium Cinemas	74-5469 Kamakacha Ave.	Kailua-Kina	HI	96740	10	744
WTC- Coconut Marketplace 2	4-484 Kuhio Hwy.	Kapa'a	HI	96746	2	744
WTC- Wharf Cinema 3	658 Front St.	Lahaina	HI	96761	3	744
WTC- Front St. Theatre	900 Front St.	Lahaina	HI	96761	4	744
WTC- Lai'e Cinema 2	55-510 Kamehameha Hwy #18	Lai'e	HI	96792	2	744
WTC- Maunaloa Town Cinema 3	1 Maunaloa Hwy.	Maunaloa	HI	96770	3	744
WTC- Village Cinema 3	4805 W. 10th St.	Great Bend	KS	67530	3	678
WTC- Southwind 12	3433 Iowa St.	Lawrence	KS	66046	12	616
WTC- Fox Whitelakes Cinema 4	320 S.W. Croix	Topeka	KS	66611	4	605
WTC- West Ridge 6	1801 S.W. Wanamaker	Topeka	KS	66604	6	605
WTC- West Ridge 8	1727 S.W. Wanamaker	Topeka	KS	66604	8	605
WTC- Stadium 14	2800 Goodwin Pointe Dr.	Columbia	MO	65201	14	604
WTC- Joplin 6	1110 E. 7th St.	Joplin	MO	64801	6	603
WTC- Northstar 14	201 N. Northpark Ln.	Joplin	MO	64801	14	603
WTC- Forum 4	1101 E. 18th St.	Rolla	MO	64502	4	638
WTC- Plaza 8	2219 N. Belt Hwy	St. Joseph	MO	64506	8	638
WTC- Gallatin Mall Cinemas	2825 W. Main St.	Bozeman	MT	59718	9	754
WTC- Northgate 10	2571 N. Carson St.	Carson City	NV	89706	10	811
WTC- Horizon Stadium 8	50 W. Hwy. 50	Stateline	NV	89449	8	811
WTC- Indian Mound 11	771 S. 30th St.	Heath	OH	43506	11	547
WTC- Movies 6	2350 S.E. Washington Blvd.	Bartlesville	OK	74005	6	671
WTC- Cache 8	4908 N.W. Cache Rd.	Lawton	OK	73505	8	627
WTC- Heritage Plaza 5	351 N. Air Dept	Midwest City	OK	73110	5	650
WTC- Spotlight 14	1100 N. Interstate Dr.	Norman	OK	73072	14	650
WTC- Brixton Square 8	7101 N.W. Expy.	Oklahoma City	OK	73132	8	650
WTC- Movies 6	4901 N. Kickapoo	Shawnee	OK	74801	6	650
WTC- Palace 12	4107 S. Yale	Tulsa	OK	74135	12	671
WTC- Crown Center Cinemas	1500 W. Chester St.	Washington	PA	15301	14	508
WTC- Star 12	4455 Dowlen Rd.	Beaumont	TX	77706	12	692
WTC- Movies 14	301 W. Rendon-Crowley Rd.	Burleson	TX	76028	14	623
WTC- Heartland Mall Cinemas	300 Early Blvd.	Early	TX	76802	8	662
WTC- Killeen Stadium 14	2501 E. Central Texas Expy.	Killeen	TX	76543	10	625
WTC- Movies 9	720 U.S. Hwy. 259	Longview	TX	75603	9	709
WTC- Tall City 10	4915 W. Loop 250 N.	Midland	TX	79707	10	633
WTC- Permian Palace 11	4101 E. 42nd St.	Odessa	TX	79762	11	633
WTC- Cinema 7	4325 John Ben Shepperd Pkwy.	Odessa	TX	79762	7	633
WTC- Tyler Rose 14	1250 S.W. Loop 323	Tyler	TX	75701	14	709
WTC- Jewel 16	7200 Woodway Dr.	Waco	TX	76712	16	625

WEHRENBERG THEATRES, INC.

15 theatres, 183 screens.
12800 Manchester Rd., St. Louis, MO 63131. (314) 822-4520. FAX: (314) 822-8032. www.wehrenberg.com
PRESIDENT
Ronald P. Krueger
PRESIDENT, WEHRENBERG, INC.
Ronald Krueger II
V.P. & FILM BUYER
Doug Whitford

Theatre	Address	City	State	Zip	Screens	DMA

DIRECTOR OF FACILITIES
Bill Menke
DIRECTOR OF CONCESSIONS
Larry Mattson

THEATRES

Theatre	Address	City	State	Zip	Screens	DMA
Wehrenberg St. Clair Cine 10	50 Ludwig Dr.	Fairview Heights	IL	62208	10	609
Wehrenberg O'Fallon 15 Cine	1320 Central Park Dr.	O'Fallon	IL	62269	15	609
Wehrenberg Cape West 14 Cine.	247 Siemers Dr.	Cape Girardeau	MO	63703	14	632
Wehrenberg Clarkson 6 Cine	1785 Clarkson Rd.	Chesterfield	MO	63017	6	609
Wehrenberg Eureka 6 Cine	99 Hilltop Village Ctr.	Eureka	MO	63025	6	609
Wehrenberg Jamestown 14 Cine	209 Jamestown Mall	Florissant	MO	63034	14	609
Wehrenberg Osage Village 5 Cine	Factory Outlet Village	Osage Beach	MO	65065	5	619
Wehrenberg Ronnies 20 Cine.	5320 S. Lindbergh Blvd	Sappington	MO	63126	20	609
Wehrenberg Campbell 16 Cine	4005 South Ave.	Springfield	MO	65807	16	619
Wehrenberg Northwest 9 Cine	300 Northwest Pl.	St. Ann	MO	63074	9	609
Wehrenberg St. Charles 18 Cine.	1830 S. 1st Capital Dr. S.	St. Charles	MO	63303	18	609
Wehrenberg Arnold 14 Cine	1912 Richardson Rd.	St. Louis	MO	63131	14	609
Wehrenberg Des Peres 14 Cine	12800 Manchester Rd.	St. Louis	MO	63131	14	609
Wehrenberg Kenrick 8 Cine	7505 Watson Rd.	St. Louis	MO	63119	8	609
Wehrenberg Mid Rivers 14 Cine	I-70 & Midrivers Mall Rd.	St. Louis	MO	63125	14	609

WESTATES THEATRES

24 theatres, 103 screens.
1111 Brickyard Rd., Ste. 106, Salt Lake City, UT 84106. (801) 487-6233. FAX: (801) 487-6633. www.westatestheatres.com

THEATRES

Theatre	Address	City	State	Zip	Screens	DMA
Page Mesa Theatre	42 S. Lake Powell Blvd.	Page	AZ		1	753
Montpelier Centre Theatre	806 Washington	Montpelier	ID	83254	1	758
Elko Cinema 4	1145 Connally.	Elko.	NV	89801	4	811
Elko Crystal 5.	676 Commercial	Elko.	NV	89801	5	811
Virgin River Cinema 4.	115 E. Mesquite Blvd.	Mesquite	NV	89027	4	839
Holladay Center Cinema 6	1945 E. Murray-Holladay Rd.	Salt Lake City	UT	84117	6	770
Trolley Corners Cinemas.	515 S. 700 E.	Salt Lake City	UT	84102	3	770
Water Gardens Cinema 6	912 W. Garden Dr.	Pleasant Grove	UT	84062	3	770
Cache Valley 3	1221 N. 200 E.	Logan	UT	84321	3	770
Logan Cinema 3.	60 W. 100 North	Logan	UT	84321	3	770
Logan Reel Time Theatre	785 N. Main	Logan	UT	84321	1	770
Logan Movies 5	2450 N. Main	Logan	UT	84341	5	770
Providence Stadium 8.	535 W. 100 N.	Providence	UT	84332	8	
Cinema 6	905 S. Main St.	St. George.	UT	84770	6	770
Flood Street	140 N. 400 E.	St. George.	UT	84770	4	770
Movies	214 N. 100 E.	St. George.	UT	84770	3	770
St. George Stadium 8.	1091 N. Bluff St.	St. George.	UT	84770	8	770
Red Cliff Cinemas	1750 Red Cliffs Dr.	St George	UT	84790	4	770
Tooele Cinema 6	1600 Pine Canyon Rd.	Tooele.	UT	84074	6	770
Cedar City Cinema 8	1040 Sage Way	Cedar City.	UT	84720	8	770
Cedar City Twin	33 N. Main St.	Cedar City.	UT	84720	2	770
Cedar City Fiddler 6	170 E. Fiddler Canyon Rd.	Cedar City.	UT	84720	6	770
Thanksgiving Point Stadium 8.	3003 Thanksgiving Way	Lehi.	UT	84043	8	
Evanston Strand Theatre	1028 Main.	Evanston.	WY	82930	1	770

W. F. CINEMA HOLDINGS, L.P. (MANN THEATRES)

22 theatres, 129 screens.
P.O. 20077, Encino, CA 91416-0077; 16530 Ventura Blvd., Ste. 500, Encino, CA, 91436. (818) 784-6266. FAX: (818) 784-8717. www.manntheatres.com
CEO
Ben Barbosa
CFO
John Waterman
V.P., INFORMATION SERVICES
Steve Broudy
DIRECTOR, FILM & MARKETING
Sandy Rodriguez
DIRECTOR, HUMAN RESOURCES
Jason Hebert
DIRECTOR, CONCESSIONS
Sally Basada
DIRECTOR, PURCHASING
Aimee Litel-White
DIRECTOR, REAL ESTATE
Joanne McClellan

THEATRES

Theatre	Address	City	State	Zip	Screens	DMA
Mann Agoura Hills 8 Cinema Center	29045 Agoura Rd.	Agoura Hills	CA	91301	8	803
Mann Culver Plaza 6	9919 Washington Blvd.	Culver City.	CA	90232	6	803
Mann Glendale Exchange 10	128 N. Maryland Ave.	Glendale	CA	91206	10	803
Mann Glendale Marketplace 4	144 S. Brand Blvd.	Glendale	CA	91206	4	803
Mann Granada Hills 9.	16830 Devonshire St.	Granada Hills.	CA	91344	9	803
Mann Grauman's Chinese Theatre	6925 Hollywood Blvd.	Hollywood	CA	90028	1	803
Mann Chinese 6.	6801 Hollywood Blvd., Ste. 335.	Hollywood	CA	90028	6	803
Mann Pierside Pavilion 6	300 Pacific Coast Hwy., Ste. 203.	Huntington Beach	CA	92648	6	803
Mann Rancho Niguel 8.	25471 Rancho Niguel	Laguna Niguel	CA	92677	8	803
Mann Bruin 1	948 Broxton Ave.	Los Angeles	CA	90024	1	803
Mann Festival Westwood 1	10887 Lindbrook Dr.	Los Angeles	CA	90024	1	803
Mann National 1	10925 Lindbrook Dr.	Los Angeles	CA	90024	1	803
Mann Plaza 1	1067 Glendon Ave.	Los Angeles	CA	90024	1	803
Mann Village 1	961 Broxton Ave.	Los Angeles	CA	90024	1	803
Mann Criterion 6.	1313 Third St. Promenade	Santa Monica	CA	90401	6	803
Mann Simi Valley 6	3050 Cochran St.	Simi Valley.	CA	93065	6	803
Mann Valley West 9	8632 Ventura Blvd.	Tarzana	CA	91356	9	803
Mann Janss Marketplace 9	255 N. Moorpark Rd.	Thousand Oaks	CA	91360	9	803

Theatre	Address	City	State	Zip	Screens	DMA
Mann Plant 16	7876 Van Nuys Blvd.	Van Nuys	CA	91402	16	803
Mann Buenaventura 6	1440 Eastman Ave.	Ventura	CA	93003	6	803
Mann Village 8	180 Promenade Way.	Westlake Village	CA	91362	8	803
Mann Green Mountain 6	12344 W. Alameda Pkwy.	Lakewood	CO	80228	6	751

WILDWOOD THEATRES

5 theatres, 54 screens.
557 Cottonwood Ave,. Hartland, WI 53029. (262) 369-1990. FAX: (262) 369-1650. www.wildwoodtheatres.com
COMPANY OFFICERS
Brad Porchetta
Anthony Groh
Hank Furlong

THEATRES

Theatre	Address	City	State	Zip	Screens	DMA
Palm Valley 14	1325 Litchfield Rd.	Goodyear	AZ	85338	14	753
Luxury 10	2799 Cranston Rd.	Beluit	WI	53511	10	669
Movies 10	3100 Deerfield Dr.	Janesville	WI	53546	10	669
Rock Theatres 9	1620 Newport Rd.	Janesville	WI	53546	9	669
Capitol Cinemas 11	1275 Capitol Dr.	Pewaukee	WI	53072	11	617

ZURICH CINEMA CORP.

10 theatres, 58 screens.
5181 Brockway Ln., Fayetteville, NY 13066. (315) 446-9081. FAX: (315) 446-6235.
OWNER, PRESIDENT & FILM BUYER
Conrad Zurich
VICE PRESIDENT
Linda Zurich
DIRECTOR OF OPERATIONS
Jamison Mills

THEATRES

Theatre	Address	City	State	Zip	Screens	DMA
Elmira Drive-In	Rte. 352	Elmira	NY	14903	2	565
Geneva Cinema 5	495 Exchange St.	Geneva	NY	14456	5	538
Hollywood Theatre	2221 Brewerton Rd.	Mattydale	NY	13211	1	555
Glenwood Movieplex 9 of Oneida	Rte. 5 & 46	Oneida	NY	13421	9	555
Southside Oneonta Mall	Rte. 23	Oneonta	NY	13820	9	526
Oswego Cinema 7	138 W. 2nd St.	Oswego	NY	13126	7	555
Pittsford Cinema	3349 Monroe Ave.	Rochester	NY	14618	9	538
Rome Cinemas 8	1122 Erie Blvd. W.	Rome	NY	13440	8	555
West Rome Drive-In	Rte. 69	Rome	NY	13440	2	555
Gateway Cinema Center	75 S. Wymoing Ave.	Edwardsville	PA	18704	6	577

NATO is Exhibition

NATO is Information

NATO is Service

NATO is UNITY

NATO is the Future

NATO is ... You!

(you must be our type)

National Association of Theatre Owners
www.natoonline.org/www.infocusmag.com

CIRCUIT THEATRES IN THE TOP 50 U.S. MARKETS

Listed are national circuit theatres and major regional circuit theatres in the 50 largest U.S. metropolitan markets. The hierarchy used to sort this list is as follows: Market size then alphabetically by circuit name, state (for markets including cities in more than one state), municipality and theatre name. Smaller regional circuits, independent theatres and major national circuits with only one theatre in a market have been excluded. Market regions are determined by broadcast coverage of major television, radio and cable stations and distribution of major newspapers (designated market areas). For futher market information, please see the DMA codes in the Circuit Theatres section of this book.

The top 50 U.S. markets, in order of decreasing size:

1. New York
2. Los Angeles
3. Chicago
4. Philadelphia
5. San Francisco/Oakland/San Jose
6. Boston (Manchester)
7. Dallas/Ft. Worth
8. Washington, DC (Hagerstown)
9. Atlanta
10. Detroit
11. Houston
12. Seattle/Tacoma
13. Tampa/St. Petersburg (Sarasota)
14. Minneapolis/St. Paul
15. Cleveland/Akron (Canton)
16. Phoenix
17. Miami/Ft. Lauderdale
18. Denver
19. Sacramento/Stockton/Modesto
20. Orlando/Daytona Beach/Melbourne
21. Pittsburgh
22. St. Louis
23. Portland
24. Baltimore
25. Indianapolis
26. San Diego
27. Hartford/New Haven
28. Charlotte
29. Raleigh/Durham (Fayetteville)
30. Nashville
31. Milwaukee
32. Cincinnati
33. Kansas City
34. Columbus
35. Greenville/Spartanburg, SC/Asheville, NC/Anderson, SC
36. Salt Lake City
37. San Antonio
38. West Palm Beach/Ft. Pierce
39. Birmingham
40. Norfolk/Portsmouth/Newport News
41. New Orleans
42. Memphis
43. Buffalo
44. Oklahoma City
45. Greensboro/High Point/Winston Salem
46. Providence/New Bedford
47. Albuquerque/Santa Fe
48. Louisville
49. Jacksonville, Brunswick
50. Las Vegas

NEW YORK

AMC ENTERTAINMENT

Bridgewater Commons 7	Bridgewater	NJ
Clifton Commons 16	Clifton	NJ
Essex Green 9	West Orange	NJ
Bay Plaza 13	Bronx	NY
Empire 25	New York	NY

CITY CINEMAS

Angelika Film Center	New York City	NY
Cinema 1, 2 & 3	New York City	NY
East 86th St. Cinemas	New York City	NY
Sutton 1 & 2	New York City	NY
Village East Cinemas	New York City	NY

CLEARVIEW CINEMAS

Greenwich Cinemas	Greenwich	CT
Middlebrook Galleria Cinema 10	Ocean Twnshp.	NJ
Bergenfield Cinema 5	Bergenfield	NJ
Bernardsville Cinema 3	Bernardsville	NJ
Caldwell Cinema 4	Caldwell	NJ
Cinema 23/Cedar Grove	Cedar Grove	NJ
Chester Cinema 6	Chester	NJ
Allwood Cinema 6	Clifton	NJ
Closter Cinema 4	Closter	NJ
Edison Cinemas	Edison	NJ
Emerson Quad	Emerson	NJ
Mansfield Cinema 15	Hackettstown	NJ
Kinnelon 11	Kinnelon	NJ
Madison Cinema 4	Madison	NJ
Strathmore Cinema 4	Aberdeen	NJ
Millburn Cinemas	Millburn	NJ
Clairidge Cinemas	Montclair	NJ
Headquarters 10 Theatres	Morristown	NJ
Parsippany Cinema 12	Parsippany	NJ
Red Bank Cinemas	Red Bank	NJ
Warner Quad	Ridgewood	NJ
Succasunna Cinema 10	Succasunna	NJ
Beacon Hill 5	Summit	NJ
Tenafly Cinema 4	Tenafly	NJ
Bellevue Cinema 4	Upper Montclair	NJ
Washington Twnshp Cinemas	Washington Twnsp	NJ
Wayne Preakness Cinemas	Wayne	NJ
Woodbridge Cinemas	Iselin	NJ
Babylon Cinemas	Babylon	NY
Grand Ave. Cinemas	Baldwin	NY
Bedford Playhouse	Bedford	NY
Bronxville Cinemas	Bronxville	NY
Franklin Square Cinemas	Franklin Square	NY
Squire Cinemas	Great Neck	NY
Larchmont Playhouse	Larchmont	NY
Mamaroneck Playhouse	Mamaroneck	NY
Manhasset Cinemas	Manhasset	NY
Mt. Kisco Cinemas	Mount Kisco	NY
New City Cinema 6	New City	NY
Herricks Cinema 4	New Hyde Park	NY
59th St. East Cinema	New York	NY
62nd & Broadway	New York	NY
Beekman	New York	NY
Chelsea Cinemas	New York	NY
Chelsea West Cinemas	New York	NY
First & 62nd Cinemas	New York	NY
Metro Twin	New York	NY
Ziegfeld	New York	NY
Port Washington Cinemas	Port Washington	NY
Clearview Soundview Cinema	Port Washington	NY
Roslyn Cinemas	Roslyn	NY
Rye Ridge Cinema	Rye Brook	NY
Cinema 100	White Plains	NY

CROWN THEATRES

Plaza	Greenwich	CT
Royale	Norwalk	CT
Sono Regent	South Norwalk	CT
Majestic	Stamford	CT
Landmark Square	Stamford	CT
Marquis	Trumbull	CT
New York 1 & 2	New York	NY

DESTINTA THEATRES

New Windsor 12	New Windsor	NY

ENTERTAINMENT CINEMAS

Stratford 14	Stratford	CT

GALAXY THEATRES

Galaxy Triplex	Guttenberg	NJ
Mall Theatre	Hackettstown	NJ
Hudson Street Cinemas	Hoboken	NJ
Newton Theatre	Newton	NJ
Sparta Theatre	Sparta	NJ
Cedar Lane Cinemas	Teaneck	NJ
Valleyview Cinemas	Wayne	NJ
Abby Cinemas	West Milford	NJ

LANDMARK THEATRES

Sunshine Cinema	New York	NY

LOEWS CINEPLEX

Danbury	Danbury	CT
Brick Plaza	Bricktown	NJ
East Hanover	East Hanover	NJ
Monmouth Mall	Eatontown	NJ
Menlo Park	Edison	NJ
Jersey Gardens	Elizabeth	NJ
Freehold Metroplex	Freehold	NJ
Newport Centre	Jersey City	NJ
Mountainside	Mountainside	NJ
New Brunswick	New Brunswick	NJ
Paramus Route 4	Paramus	NJ
Route 17	Paramus	NJ
Ridgefield Park	Ridgefield Park	NJ
Meadow Six	Secaucus	NJ
Plaza 8	Secaucus	NJ
Seacourt 10	Toms River	NJ
Wayne	Wayne	NJ
Bay Terrace	Bayside	NY
Alpine	Brooklyn	NY
Fortway	Brooklyn	NY
Kings Plaza Sixplex	Brooklyn	NY
Cinema #5	Fresh Meadows	NY
Fresh Meadows	Fresh Meadows	NY
Roosevelt Field	Garden City	NY
Glen Cove Cinemas	Glen Cove	NY
Shore	Huntington	NY
Nassau Metroplex	Levittown	NY
Galleria Metroplex	Middletown	NY
19th Street East	New York	NY
72nd Street	New York	NY
84th Street	New York	NY
Astor Plaza	New York	NY
34th Street	New York	NY
E-Walk	New York	NY
Kips Bay Theatre	New York	NY
Lincoln Square	New York	NY
Loews IMAX	New York	NY
Magic Johnson Harlem	New York	NY
Orpheum	New York	NY
State	New York	NY
Village VII	New York	NY
Fantasy	Rockville Centre	NY
Rockville Centre	Rockville Centre	NY
Stony Brook	Stony Brook	NY
Palisades Center	West Nyack	NY
Roosevelt Raceway	Westbury	NY

MINI THEATRES

Movieplex Carmel	Carmel	NY

NATIONAL AMUSEMENTS

Showcase Bridgeport	Bridgeport	CT
Fairfield Cinemas	Fairfield	CT
Edgewater Multiplex Cinemas	Edgewater	NJ
Hazlet Multiplex	Hazlet	NJ
All-Jersey Multiplex	Newark	NJ
Amboy Multiplex	Sayreville	NJ
Concourse Plaza Multiplex	Bronx	NY
Whitestone Multiplex	Bronx	NY
Linden Blvd. Multiplex	Brooklyn	NY
Commack Multiplex	Commack	NY
Farmingdale Multiplex	Farmingdale	NY
Greenburgh Multiplex Cinemas	Greenburgh	NY
All Westchester Saw Mill Multi	Hawthorne	NY
Broadway Multiplex	Hicksville	NY
Island 16 Cinema DeLux	Holtsville	NY
Jamaica Multiplex	Jamaica	NY
Green Acres Cinemas	Valley Stream	NY
Sunrise Multiplex	Valley Stream	NY
College Point Multiplex	Whitestone	NY
Cross County Multiplex	Yonkers	NY

REGAL ENTERTAINMENT GROUP

Darien Playhouse 2	Darien	CT
Hudson Mall 7	Jersey City	NJ
Marlboro Cinema Stadium 8	Morganville	NJ
Columbia Park 12	North Bergen	NJ
Commerce Center Stadium 18	North Brunswick	NJ
Pohatcong 12	Phillipsburg	NJ
Hadley Theatre Stadium 16	South Plainfield	NJ
Court Street Stadium 12	Brooklyn	NY
Sheepshead Bay 14	Brooklyn	NY
Coram Theatre 12	Coram	NY
Movieworld Douglaston 7	Douglaston	NY
East Hampton Cinema 6	East Hampton	NY
Meadowbrook Theatre 6	Eastmeadow	NY
UA Farmingdale 10	Farmingdale	NY
Brandon Cinemas 2	Forest Hills	NY
Midway Cinemas Stadium 9	Forest Hills	NY
UA Hampton Bays 5	Hampton Bays	NY
Kaufman Astoria Stadium 14	Long Island City	NY
Lynbrook Theatre 6	Lynbrook	NY
New Roc City Stadium 18 Plus Imax	New Rochelle	NY
Battery Park Stadium 16	New York	NY
East 85th Street 1	New York	NY
UA 64th & 2nd Ave. Expansion 3	New York	NY
Union Square Stadium 14	New York	NY

Crossbay Theatre I	Ozone Park	NY
Crossbay Theatre II	Ozone Park	NY
Movies @ Patchogue 13	Patchogue	NY
Ronkonkoma Cinema Stadium 9	Ronkonkoma	NY
Southampton 4 Theatres	Southampton	NY
Hylan Plaza 5	Staten Island	NY
Movies @ Staten Island 14	Staten Island	NY
Staten Island Stadium 16	Staten Island	NY
UA Westbury Theatre Stadium 12	Westbury	NY
Movieland Yonkers 6	Yonkers	NY
Movies@Jefferson Valley 8	Yorktown Heights	NY

LOS ANGELES

AMC ENTERTAINMENT

Disney 12	Anaheim	CA
Burbank 16	Burbank	CA
Media Center 8	Burbank	CA
Media Center North 6	Burbank	CA
Covina 30	Covina	CA
Fullerton 20	Fullerton	CA
Hollywood Galaxy 6	Hollywood	CA
Puente Hills 20	Industry	CA
Marina Pacifica 12	Long Beach	CA
Pine Square 16	Long Beach	CA
Avco Center 4	Los Angeles	CA
Beverly Connection 6	Los Angeles	CA
Century 14	Los Angeles	CA
Montebello 10	Montebello	CA
Norwalk 20	Norwalk	CA
Ontario Mills 30	Ontario	CA
The Block 30	Orange	CA
Old Pasadena 8	Pasadena	CA
Galleria South Bay 16	Redondo Beach	CA
Santa Monica 7	Santa Monica	CA
Rolling Hills 20	Torrance	CA
Promenade 16	Woodland Hills	CA

CENTURY THEATRES

Century 8	N. Hollywood	CA
Century Stadium 25	Orange	CA
Century Stadium 16	Ventura	CA
Century 10 Downtown	Ventura	CA

CINEMARK USA

Cinemark Movies 8- Chino	Chino	CA
Movies 12 Lancaster	Lancaster	CA
Movies 1-4	Lancaster	CA
Cinemark 22	Lancaster	CA
Movies 8 Palmdale	Palmdale	CA
Movies 10	Palmdale	CA
Cinemark Victor Valley 10	Victorville	CA
Movies 10	Victorville	CA

CINEMASTAR LUXURY THEATRES

Perris Plaza 10	Perris	CA
Mission Grove 18	Riverside	CA
Empire 20	San Bernardino	CA

DEANZA LAND & LEISURE CORP.

Van Buren Blvd. Triple	Arlington	CA
Mission Quad	Montclair	CA
Rubidoux Triple	Riverside	CA

KRIKORIAN PREMIERE

Chino Marketplace Spectrum 12	Chino	CA
Downey	Downey	CA
Redlands	Redlands	CA
San Clemente	San Clemente	CA
Monrovia Cinema 12	Monrovia	CA

LAEMMLE THEATRES

Music Hall	Beverly Hills	CA
Town Center 5	Encino	CA
Fairfax	Los Angeles	CA
Grande	Los Angeles	CA
Sunset 5	Los Angeles	CA
Royal	Los Angeles	CA
Playhouse 7	Pasadena	CA
Monica 4	Santa Monica	CA
Fallbrook 7	West Hills	CA

LANDMARK THEATRES

Fine Arts	Beverly Hills	CA
Regent Theatre	Los Angeles	CA
Westside Pavilion Cinemas	Los Angeles	CA
Nuart Theatre	Los Angeles	CA
NuWilshire Theatre	Santa Monica	CA
Rialto Theatre	South Pasadena	CA

LOEWS CINEPLEX

Beverly Center	Los Angeles	CA
Magic Johnson Crenshaw	Los Angeles	CA
Marina	Marina Del Rey	CA
Broadway	Santa Monica	CA
Universal Studio Cinemas	Universal City	CA

METROPOLITAN THEATRES

Park Theatre	Huntington Park	CA
Campus Theatre	Los Angeles	CA
University Village Cinemas	Riverside	CA
Teatro Fiesta	Santa Ana	CA

THE MOVIE EXPERIENCE

Blue Jay Cinema	Blue Jay	CA
Movie Exp. 17 at California Oaks	Murrieta	CA
Movie Exp. 10 at Tower Plaza	Temecula	CA

NATIONAL AMUSEMENTS

The Bridge Cinema DeLux	Los Angeles	CA
The Bridge IMAX	Los Angeles	CA

PACIFIC THEATRES

Winnetka 21	Chatsworth	CA
Commerce 14	City of Commerce	CA
Culver Stadium 12	Culver City	CA
Beach Cities 16	El Segundo	CA
Arclight-Hollywood 15	Hollywood	CA
Lakewood South 9	Lakewood	CA
Lakewood Center 16	Lakewood	CA
The Grove 14	Los Angeles	CA
Manhattan Village 6	Manhattan Beach	CA
Northridge 10	Northridge	CA
Fashion Center 10	Northridge	CA
Hastings 8	Pasadena	CA
Galleria 16	Sherman Oaks	CA
Sherman Oaks 5	Sherman Oaks	CA

REGAL ENTERTAINMENT GROUP

Alhambra Place 5	Alhambra	CA
Atlantic Palace 10	Alhambra	CA
Aliso Viejo Stadium 20	Aliso Viejo	CA
Anaheim Hills 14	Anaheim Hills	CA
Brea Stadium 10 West	Brea	CA
Brea Stadium 12 East	Brea	CA
Calabasas Stadium 6	Calabasas	CA
Camarillo 12	Camarillo	CA
Cerritos Stadium 10	Cerritos	CA
UA Galaxy @ Los Cerritos 11	Cerritos	CA
Corona 15	Corona	CA
Metro Pointe Stadium 12	Costa Mesa	CA
Triangle Square 8	Costa Mesa	CA
El Monte 8	El Monte	CA
Foothill Towne Center Stadium 22	Foothill Ranch	CA
Garden Grove Stadium 16	Garden Grove	CA
Hemet Cinema 12	Hemet	CA
Charter Centre 5	Huntington Beach	CA
Irvine Spectrum 21	Irvine	CA
Market Place Stadium 10	Irvine	CA
Park Place 10	Irvine	CA
University Town Center 6	Irvine	CA
Westpark 8	Irvine	CA
UA La Canada 8	La Canada Flintridge	CA
La Habra Stadium 16	La Habra	CA
La Verne Stadium 12	La Verne	CA
Ocean Ranch 7	Laguna Niguel	CA
Long Beach Stadium 26	Long Beach	CA
UA Long Beach 6	Long Beach	CA
UA Marina Del Rey 6	Marina Del Rey	CA
Kaleidoscope Stadium 10	Mission Viejo	CA
Island 7	Newport Beach	CA
Newport 6	Newport Beach	CA
Valley Plaza 6	North Hollywood	CA
Ontario Mntn. Village Stadium 14	Ontario	CA
Ontario Palace Stadium 22	Ontario	CA
UA Pasadena 6	Pasadena	CA
Jurupa Stadium 14	Riverside	CA
Park Sierra 6	Riverside	CA
Terrace Cinema 6	Rnc. Palos Verdes	CA
Rancho Santa Margarita 6	Rnc. Sta Margarita	CA
Avenues Stadium 13	Rolling Hills Estates	CA
Hutton Centre 8	Santa Ana	CA
South Coast Village 3	Santa Ana	CA
Valencia Stadium 12	Santa Clarita	CA
Civic Center Stadium 16	Simi Valley	CA
Simi Valley Plaza 10	Simi Valley	CA
South Gate Stadium 20	South Gate	CA
Temecula Stadium 15	Temecula	CA
Temple 4	Temple City	CA
UA Thousand Oaks 5	Thousand Oaks	CA
Tustin Marketplace 6	Tustin	CA
West Covina Stadium 18	West Covina	CA
Westminster 10	Westminster	CA

SIGNATURE THEATRES

Metro 12	San Jacinto	CA

ULTRASTAR CINEMAS

Fontana 8	Fontana	CA
Canyon Springs	Moreno Valley	CA
TownGate 8	Moreno Valley	CA
Terra Vista 6	Rancho Cucamonga	CA
Rialto 8	Rialto	CA

WALLACE THEATRE

New Barstow Cinema 6 ....Barstow ....CA
New Malibu Theatre...................Malibu ....CA
Santa Paula Cinema 7 ....Santa Paula ....CA

W.F. CINEMA HOLDINGS (MANN THEATRES)

Agoura Hills 8 Cinema Center......Agoura Hills ....CA
Culver Plaza 6 ....Culver City ....CA
Glendale Exchange 10 ....Glendale ....CA
Glendale Marketplace 4 ....Glendale ....CA
Granada Hills 9 ....Granada Hills ....CA
Chinese 6 ....Hollywood ....CA
Grauman's Chinese Theatre........Hollywood ....CA
Pierside Pavilion 6 ....Huntington Beach ....CA
Rancho Niguel 8 ....Laguna Niguel..................CA
Bruin 1 ....Los Angeles ....CA
Festival Westwood 1 ....Los Angeles ....CA
National 1 ....Los Angeles ....CA
Plaza 1 ....Los Angeles ....CA
Village 1....................................Los Angeles ....CA
Criterion 6.................................Santa Monica ....CA
Simi Valley 6 ....Simi Valley ....CA
Valley West 9 ....Tarzana ....CA
Janss Marketplace 9 ....Thousand Oaks................CA
Plant 16 ....Van Nuys ....CA
Buenaventura 6..........................Ventura ....CA
Village 8....................................Westlake Village...............CA

CHICAGO

AMC ENTERTAINMENT

River East 21 ....Chicago IL
City North 14 ....Chicago IL
Ford City 14 ....Chicago IL
Yorktown 18 ....Lombard IL
Randhurst 16 ....Mount Prospect...............IL
Northbrook Court 14 ....Northbrook.......................IL
South Barrington 30 ....South Barrington IL
Cantera 30 ....Warrenville IL
Southlake Mall 9 ....Merrillville ....IN

CENTURY THEATRES

Century 12 Evanston...................Evanston..........................IL
CineArts 6 Evanston ....Evanston..........................IL

CINEMARK USA

Movies 10 ....Bourbonnais.....................IL
Movies 8 ....Joliet................................IL
Movies 10 ....Joliet................................IL
Cinemark 10 ....Melrose Park....................IL
Tinseltown.................................North Aurora.....................IL
Cinemark at Seven Bridges..........Woodridge IL

CLASSIC CINEMAS

Cinema 12 Theatre ....Carpentersville.................IL
Tivoli Theatre ....Downers Grove IL
Elk Grove Theatre ....Elk Grove IL
York Theatre..............................Elmhurst IL
Fox Lake Theatre ....Fox Lake IL
Lindo Theatre ....Freeport IL
Meadowview Theatre..................Kankakee IL
Paramount ....Kankakee IL
Ogden 6 Theatre.......................Naperville IL
Lake Theatre.............................Oak Park IL
Charlestowne 18 ....St. Charles IL
Woodstock Theatre ....Woodstock IL

CROWN THEATRES

Village Crossing..........................Skokie...............................IL

GKC THEATRES

Market Square ....Dekalb IL
Orpheum Cinema.......................Morris IL
Peru Mall 8 Cinema....................Peru IL

GOODRICH QUALITY THEATRES

Randall 16 ....Batavia IL
Kendall 10.................................Oswego IL
Portage 9..................................Portage ....IN

KERASOTES THEATRES

Showplace 12 ....Bolingbrook......................IL
Lake in the Hills 12 ....Lake in the Hills IL
River Tree Court........................Vernon Hills.....................IL
Showplace 8 ....Vernon Hills.....................IL
LaPorte Cinema ....LaPorte ....IN
Marquette Cinema......................Michigan City ....IN
Dunes Plaza Cinema ....Michigan City ....IN
Showplace 16 ....Schererville......................IN
Showplace 12 ....Schererville......................IN

LANDMARK THEATRES

Landmark Century Centre Cinema Chicago IL
Renaissance Place ....Highland Park IL

LOEWS CINEPLEX

River Oaks 1-6...........................Calumet City IL
River Oaks 7-8...........................Calumet City IL
River Oaks 9-10.........................Calumet City IL
600 North Michigan....................Chicago IL
Esquire ....Chicago IL
Lincoln Village 1-6.....................Chicago IL
McClurg ....Chicago IL
Pipers Alley...............................Chicago IL
Webster Place...........................Chicago IL
Chicago Ridge ....Chicago Ridge..................IL
Country Club Hills ....Country Club Hills IL
Crestwood.................................Crestwood........................IL
Quarry Cinemas ....Hodgkins..........................IL
North Riverside ....N. Riverside IL
Norridge....................................Norridge...........................IL
Oakbrook 5-7.............................Oakbrook IL
Streets of Woodfield..................Schaumburg.....................IL
Gardens 1-6..............................Skokie...............................IL
Gardens 7-13............................Skokie...............................IL
Streamwood...............................Streamwood.....................IL
Rice Lake..................................Wheaton IL
Woodridge ....Woodridge IL
Merrillville.................................Merrillville.........................IN

MARCUS THEATRES

Cinema Addison ....Addison............................IL
ICE-Chatham ....Chicago IL
ICE-Lawndale ....Chicago IL
ICE-62nd & Western Theatre.......Chicago IL
Cinema Chicago Heights..............Chicago Heights...............IL
Cinema Elgin Fox ....Elgin.................................IL
Cinema Gurnee ....Gurnee.............................IL
Cinema Orland Park...................Orland Park IL

NOVA CINETECH

Hi-Lite 30 Drive-In......................Aurora..............................IL
Nova 8 ....Naperville IL

REGAL ENTERTAINMENT GROUP

Showplace 16 ....Crystal Lake.....................IL
Lake Zurich 12 ....Lake Zurich IL
Lincolnshire Stadium 20 Plus ImaxLincolnshire IL
Round Lake Beach Stadium 18 .....Round Lake Beach............IL

PHILADELPHIA

AMC ENTERTAINMENT

Deptford 8.................................Deptford ....NJ
Deptford Mall 6 ....Deptford ....NJ
Hamilton 24 ....Hamilton ....NJ
Marlton 8 ....Marlton ....NJ
Tilghman 8.................................Allentown ....PA
Woodhaven 10 ....Bensalem.........................PA
Neshaminy 24 ....Bensalem.........................PA
Granite Run 8 ....Media ....PA
Franklin Mills 14.........................Philadelphia.....................PA
Orleans 8 ....Philadelphia.....................PA
Plymouth Meeting 12 ....Plymouth Meeting.............PA
309 Cinema 9 ....Spring House....................PA
Marple 10 ....Springfield ....PA
Painters Crossing 9....................West Chester....................PA

CARMIKE CINEMAS

Carmike ....Dover ....DE
Carmike ....Allentown..........................PA
Carmike Coventry ....Pottstown ....PA
Carmike Wyomissing...................Reading............................PA

CINEMA CENTER

Fairgrounds Square.....................Reading............................PA

CINEMARK USA

Movies 10 ....Wilmington ....DE
Movies 16 ....Somerdale ....NJ

CLEARVIEW CINEMA

Bala Theater ....Bala Cynwyd ....PA
Anthony Wayne 5 ....Wayne ....PA

DESTINTA THEATRES

Independence 12 ....Hamilton ....NJ

HOYTS CINEMAS

LOEWS CINEPLEX

Cherry Hill.................................Cherry Hill ....NJ

MINI THEATRES

Diamond State Drive-In................Felton ....DE

NATIONAL AMUSEMENTS

Atco Multiplex ....Atco ....NJ
Town Center Plaza ....East Windsor....................NJ
The Bridge Cinema DeLux-UPenn.Philadelphia ....PA

REGAL ENTERTAINMENT GROUP

Peoples Plaza Cinema Stadium 17	Newark	DE
Brandywine Town Center 16	Wilmington	DE
Burlington Stadium 20	Burlington	NJ
UA Moorestown Mall 7	Moorestown	NJ
Pennsauken Theatre 11	Pennsauken	NJ
Movies @ Market Fair 9	Princeton	NJ
UA Washington Township 14	Sewell	NJ
Cross Keys Cinema Stadium 12	Turnersville	NJ
Cumberland Mall Stadium 14	Vineland	NJ
Plymouth Meeting 10	Conshohocken	PA
Downingtown Cinema Stadium 16	Downingtown	PA
Barn Plaza Stadium 14	Doylestown	PA
East Whiteland Stadium 9	East Whiteland	PA
Northampton Cinema 14	Easton	PA
Macdade Mall Cinemas 4	Holmes	PA
King Of Prussia Stadium 16	King Of Prussia	PA
Oxford Valley Theatre Stadium 10	Langhorne	PA
Lionville Cinema Stadium 12	Lionville	PA
Main Street Theatre 6	Manayunk	PA
Montgomeryville Theatre 7	Montgomeryville	PA
Edgmont Square 10	Newton Square	PA
Marketplace @ Oaks Stadium 24	Oaks	PA
Riverview Plaza 17	Philadelphia	PA
UA Grant Plaza 9	Philadelphia	PA
UA Theatre@Cheltenham Sq. 8	Philadelphia	PA
Richland Crossing 12	Quakertown	PA
Movies @ 69th Street 9	Upper Darby	PA
Warrington Crossing Stadium 22	Warrington	PA

RITZ THEATRES

Ritz Sixteen	Voorhees	NJ
Ritz East	Philadelphia	PA
Ritz Five	Philadelphia	PA
Ritz at the Bourse	Philadelphia	PA

SAN FRANCISCO/OAKLAND/SAN JOSE

AMC ENTERTAINMENT

Bay Street 16	Emeryville	CA
Kabuki 8	San Francisco	CA
Van Ness 14	San Francisco	CA
Saratoga 14	San Jose	CA
Mercado 20	Santa Clara	CA

BRENDEN THEATRES

Concord 14	Concord	CA
Pittsburg 16	Pittsburg	CA

CAMERA CINEMAS

Camera 7 Pruneyard	Campbell	CA
Los Gatos	Los Gatos	CA
Camera One	San Jose	CA
Camera 3	San Jose	CA
Towne 3	San Jose	CA

CAMPBELL PLAZA THEATRES

Plaza 4 Theatres	Campbell	CA
Almaden Cinema 5	San Jose	CA
Chabot Cinema	Castro Valley	CA
New Della Cinema	Brentwood	CA
Cinema Saver 10	Milpitas	CA
Tennant Station Stadium 11	Morgan Hill	CA

CENTURY THEATRES

Hyatt Cinema 3	Burlingame	CA
Solano Drive-In	Concord	CA
Century Cinema	Corte Madera	CA
Century 20 Daly City	Daly City	CA
Cinedome 8 East	Fremont	CA
Century Larkspur Landing	Larkspur	CA
CineArts at Sequoia	Mill Valley	CA
Century 20 Great Mall	Milpitas	CA
Century Cinema 16	Mountain View	CA
Cinedome 8	Napa	CA
Cinedome 7 West	Newark	CA
Century Rowland Plaza	Novato	CA
CineArts at Palo Alto Square	Palo Alto	CA
CineArts at Pleasant Hill 5	Pleasant Hill	CA
Century 16 Downtown	Pleasant Hill	CA
Century Park 12	Redwood City	CA
Century 16 Hilltop in Richmond	Richmond	CA
Century Plaza 10	S. San Francisco	CA
Empire Cinema	San Francisco	CA
Presidio	San Francisco	CA
Capitol Drive-In	San Jose	CA
Century Capitol 16	San Jose	CA
Century Berryessa	San Jose	CA
Century 21	San Jose	CA
Century 22	San Jose	CA
Century 23	San Jose	CA
Century 24	San Jose	CA
Century 25	San Jose	CA
Century 16 BayFair Mall	San Leandro	CA
Century 12 Downtown	San Mateo	CA
Century Northgate	San Rafael	CA
Century Regency	San Rafael	CA

CineArts at Marin	Sausalito	CA
Century 25	Union City	CA
Century 14	Vallejo	CA
Century 14 Downtown	Walnut Creek	CA

CINEMARK USA

Blackhawk	Danville	CA

CINEMA WEST

Angels Theatre	Angels Camp	CA
Clearlake Cinemas	Clearlake	CA
Clover Cinemas	Cloverdale	CA
Fairfax Theatre	Fairfax	CA
Fortuna Theatre	Fortuna	CA
Los Banos Cinemas	Los Banos	CA
Sebastopol Cinemas	Sebastopol	CA
Sonoma Cinemas	Sonoma	CA
Tiburon Playhouse	Tiburon	CA
Noyo Theatre	Willits	CA

LANDMARK THEATRES

Albany Twin	Albany	CA
Act 1 and 2	Berkeley	CA
California Theatre	Berkeley	CA
Shattuck Cinemas	Berkeley	CA
Guild Theatre	Menlo Park	CA
Piedmont Theatre	Oakland	CA
Aquarius Theatre	Palo Alto	CA
Bridge Theatre	San Francisco	CA
Clay Theatre	San Francisco	CA
Embarcadero Center Cinemas	San Francisco	CA
Lumiere Theatre	San Francisco	CA
Opera Plaza Cinema	San Francisco	CA

LOEWS CINEPLEX

Metreon	San Francisco	CA

PACIFIC THEATRES

Paseo 14	Pasadena	CA
Rohnert Park 16	Rohnert Park	CA

REGAL ENTERTAINMENT GROUP

Deer Valley Stadium 16	Antioch	CA
UA East Hills 10	Bakersfield	CA
Berkeley 7	Berkley	CA
Colma Metro Center 6	Daly City	CA
Hacienda Crossings Stadium 20 +	Dublin	CA
Emery Bay Stadium 10	Emeryville	CA
Alexandria 3	San Francisco	CA
Coronet 1	San Francisco	CA
Galaxy 4	San Francisco	CA
Metro 1	San Francisco	CA
Stonestown Twin 2	San Francisco	CA
Vogue 1	San Francisco	CA

SIGNATURE THEATRES

Jack London Cinema	Oakland	CA
Crow Canyon Cinemas 6	San Ramon	CA
Signature Ukiah 6	Ukiah	CA

BOSTON (MANCHESTER)

AMC ENTERTAINMENT

Fenway 13	Boston	MA
Braintree 10	Braintree	MA
Burlington 10	Burlington	MA
Chestnut Hill 5	Chestnut Hill	MA
Framingham 16	Framingham	MA
Framingham Premium 1	Framingham	MA
Tyngsboro 12	Tyngsboro	MA

ENTERTAINEMNT CINEMAS

Edgartown 2	Edgartown	MA
Leominster 10	Leominster	MA
Stoughton Pub	Stoughton	MA
Concord 6	Concord	NH
S. Kingston 8	S. Kingston	RI
Brattleboro 6	Brattleboro	VT
Cinemas W. Dover 3	W. Dover	VT

FLAGSHIP CINEMAS

Quincy	Quincy	MA

HOYTS CINEMAS

LANDMARK THEATRES

Kendall Square Cinema	Cambridge	MA
Embassy Cinema	Waltham	MA

LOEWS CINEPLEX

Boston Common	Boston	MA
Copley Place	Boston	MA
Harvard Square 1-5	Cambridge	MA
Fresh Pond	Cambridge	MA
Liberty Tree Mall	Danvers	MA
Natick 1-6	Natick	MA
Assembly Square 1-12	Somerville	MA

MINI THEATRES

Gourcester Cinema	Gloucester	MA
FineArts	Maynard	MA
Route 1	N. Attelboro	MA
Island	Oaks Bluff	MA
Island	Oaks Bluff	MA
Strand	Oaks Bluff	MA
Cinemagic	Salisbury	MA
Capawock	Vineyard Haven	MA
Weirs Drive-In	Laconia	NH

NATIONAL AMUSEMENTS

Circle Cinemas	Brookline	MA
Showcase Cinemas Dedham	Dedham	MA
Showcase Lawrence 1-6	Lawrence	MA
Showcase Cinemas Lawrence 7-14	Lawrence	MA
Showcase Cinemas Lowell	Lowell	MA
Showcase Cinemas Randolph	Randolph	MA
Showcase Cinemas Revere	Revere	MA
Showcase Cinemas Woburn	Woburn	MA
Showcase Cinemas Worcester N.	Worcester	MA

PATRIOT CINEMAS

Hanover Mall	Hanover	MA
Loring Hall	Hingham	MA
Museum Place	Salem	MA
Cameo Theatre	S. Weymouth	MA

SPINELLI CINEMAS

Barrington Station Cinema 6	Barrington	NH
Strand Theatre	Dover	NH
Rialto Theatre	Lancaster	NH
Merideth Cinema 3	Merideth	NH
Plymouth Theatre	Plymouth	NH
Lilac Mall Cinema 4	Rochester	NH

DALLAS/FT. WORTH

AMC ENTERTAINMENT

Parks at Arlington 16	Arlington	TX
Grand 24	Dallas	TX
Glen Lakes 8	Dallas	TX
Palace 9	Fort Worth	TX
Hulen 10	Fort Worth	TX
Sundance West 11	Fort Worth	TX
Grapevine Mills 30	Grapevine	TX
Irving Mall 14	Irving	TX
Mesquite 30	Mesquite	TX

CINEMARK USA

Tinseltown	Arlington	TX
Athens Cinema 4	Athens	TX
Cinema 6	Cleburne	TX
Cinema IV	Corsicana	TX
Cinemark 17	Dallas	TX
Hollywood USA	Garland	TX
Movies 16	Grand Prairie	TX
Tinseltown	Grapevine	TX
Movies 14	Lancaster	TX
Movies 12	Lewisville	TX
Cinemark 8	Lewisville	TX
Movies 14	McKinney	TX
Movies 8	Paris	TX
Movies 8	N. Richland Hills	TX
Movies 10	Plano	TX
Tinseltown	Plano	TX
Cinemark 24	Plano	TX
Rockwall 8	Rockwall	TX
Cinema 6	Stephenville	TX

FOOTHILLS ENTERTAINMENT CO.

4 Star Cinema	Kilgore	TX
Brazos Cinema 3	Mineral Wells	TX
Jackson Cinema 3	Jacksonville	TX
Plaza Cinema 3	Henderson	TX
Star Village 8	Lake Worth	TX

LANDMARK THEATRES

Inwood Theatre	Dallas	TX

LOEWS CINPLEX

20 & 287 6	Arlington	TX
Lincoln Square	Arlington	TX
Cityplace	Dallas	TX
Keystone Park	Dallas	TX
City View Eightplex	Fort Worth	TX

MARQUEE CINEMAS

MacArthur Marketplace 16	Irving	TX

REGAL ENTERTAINMENT GROUP

Bowen 8	Arlington	TX
Bedford 10	Bedford	TX
Galaxy Theatre Stadium 10	Dallas	TX
UA Plaza 8	Dallas	TX
Denton Mall 5	Denton	TX
Golden Triangle 4	Denton	TX

Fossil Creek Stadium 11	Ft Worth	TX
Hulen 10	Ft Worth	TX
Las Vegas Trails 8	Ft Worth	TX
UA Eastchase Market Stadium 9	Ft Worth	TX
Northstar 8	Garland	TX
Grand Prairie 10	Grand Prairie	TX
Macarthur Stadium 16	Irving	TX
UA Lakepointe 10	Lewisville	TX

STARPLEX CINEMAS

Irving Cinema 10	Irving	TX
Mesquite Cinema 10	Mesquite	TX

WALLACE THEATRE

Movies 14	Burleson	TX

WASHINGTON, DC (HAGERSTOWN)

AMC ENTERTAINMENT

Mazza Gallerie 7	Washington	DC
Union Station 9	Washington	DC
Academy 6	Greenbelt	MD
Academy 8	Greenbelt	MD
Country Club Mall 6	Lavale	MD
Rivertowne 12	Oxon Hill	MD
City Place 10	Silver Spring	MD
Hoffman 22	Alexandria	VA
Courthouse Plaza 8	Arlington	VA
Skyline 6	Falls Church	VA
Springfield Mall 10	Springfield	VA
Potomac Mills 15	Woodbridge	VA

CARMIKE CINEMAS

Carmike Cinema	Chambersburg	PA
Carmike Apple Blossom Six	Winchester	VA
Carmike Cinema Center	Winchester	VA

CONSOLIDATED THEATRES

The Majestic	Silver Spring	MD

LANDMARK THEATRES

Bethesda Row Cinema	Bethesda	MD

LOEWS CINPLEX

Cinema	Washington	DC
Dupont	Washington	DC
Inner Circle	Washington	DC
Outer Circle	Washington	DC
Uptown	Washington	DC
Wisconsin	Washington	DC
Center Park	Beltsville	MD
Rio Cinemas	Gaithersburg	MD
White Flint 5	Kensington	MD
Lexington Park 6	Lexington Park	MD
Marlow	Marlow Heights	MD
St. Charles Towne Center	Waldorf	MD
Wheaton Plaza 11	Wheaton	MD
Shirlington 7	Arlington	VA
Fairfax Square 8	Vienna	VA

MARQUEE CINEMAS

Southpoint Cinemas	Fredericksburg	VA

NATIONAL AMUSEMENTS

Mt. Vernon Multiplex	Alexandria	VA
Centreville Multiplex	Centerville	VA
Lee Highway Multiplex	Merrifield	VA
Reston Multiplex	Reston	VA

R/C THEATRES

Westview 16	Frederick	MD
Frostburg Cinemas 3	Frostburg	MD
Valley Mall Movies 16	Hagerstown	MD
Culpeper Movies 4	Culpeper	VA

REGAL ENTERTAINMENT GROUP

Rockville Center Stadium 13	Rockville	MD
Ballston Common Stadium 12	Arlington	VA
Fairfax Towne Center 10	Fairfax	VA
Fredericksburg 15	Fredericksburg	VA
Aquia 10	Stafford	VA
Countryside Stadium 20	Sterling	VA

ATLANTA

AMC ENTERTAINMENT

Mansell Crossing 14	Alpharetta	GA
Buckhead Backlot 6	Atlanta	GA
Parkway Pointe 15	Atlanta	GA
Phipps Plaza 14	Atlanta	GA
North Dekalb Mall 16	Decatur	GA
Barrett Commons 24	Kennesaw	GA
Colonial 18	Lawrenceville	GA
Southlake Pavilion	Morrow	GA

CARMIKE CINEMAS

Carmike	Athens	GA
Carmike Martin	Calhoun	GA
Carmike Riverstone	Canton	GA
Carmike Plaza	Cartersville	GA
Carmike Conyers Crossing 16	Conyers	GA
Carmike Griffin Cinema	Griffin	GA
Carmike	Newnan	GA
Carmike	Snellville	GA

CINEMARK USA

Movies 10	Fayetteville	GA
Tinseltown	Fayetteville	GA

DEANZA LAND & LEISURE CORP.

Starlight Six-Plex	Atlanta	GA

GEORGIA THEATRE CO.

Beechwood Stadium 11	Athens	GA
Georgia Square 5	Athens	GA
Mall Cinemas 8	Carrollton	GA
Gwinnett Place 12	Duluth	GA
Venture Value Cinemas 12	Duluth	GA
Hollywood 15	Gainesville	GA
Lakeshore Cinemas 4	Gainesville	GA
Town Center Cinemas 10	Lawrenceville	GA
Merchant's Walk Stadium 12	Marietta	GA
Park 12 Cobb	Marietta	GA
Cherokee 16	Woodstock	GA

LANDMARK THEATRES

Midtown Art Cinema	Atlanta	GA

LOEWS CINPLEX

Magic Johnson Greenbrier	Atlanta	GA

MEGASTAR CINEMAS

Stonecrest	Lithonia	GA

REGAL ENTERTAINMENT GROUP

Lenox Square 6	Atlanta	GA
Midtown Cinemas 8	Atlanta	GA
Perimeter Pointe 10	Atlanta	GA
Tara Cinemas 4	Atlanta	GA
Regal Stadium 22 @ Austell	Austell	GA
Mall of GA Stadium 20 Plus Imax	Buford	GA
Hollywood Stadium 24 @ N. I-85	Chamblee	GA
Arbor Place Stadium 18	Douglasville	GA
Medlock Crossing Stadium 18	Duluth	GA
Town Center Stadium 16	Kennesaw	GA
Covington Square Cinema 8	Lithonia	GA
Delk 10	Marietta	GA
Riverdale Cinema 14	Riverdale	GA
Snellville Oaks Stadium 14	Snellville	GA
Bonita Lakes 9	Meridian	MS

DETROIT

AMC ENTERTAINMENT

Laurel Park 10	Livonia	MI
Livonia 20	Livonia	MI
Forum 30	Sterling Heights	MI

CINEMARK USA

Movies 16	Warren	MI

GKC THEATRES

Birchwood 10	Fort Gratiot	MI

GOODRICH QUALITY THEATRES

Quality 16	Ann Arbor	MI
Canton 6	Canton	MI
Novi Town Center 8	Novi	MI
Oxford 7	Oxford	MI
Krafft 8	Port Huron	MI

LANDMARK THEATRES

Maple 3	Bloomfield	MI
Main Art Theatre	Royal Oak	MI

LOEWS CINPLEX

Great Lakes	Auburn Hills	MI
Gratiot	Clinton Twp.	MI
Fairlane	Dearborn	MI
John R.	Madison Heights	MI
Rochester Hills	Rochester Hills	MI
Southfield	Southfield	MI
Taylor	Taylor	MI

MJR THEATRES

Allen Park Cinema	Allen Park	MI
Brighton Town Square Cinema	Brighton	MI
Chesterfield Crossing	Chesterfield	MI
Southgate Cinemas	Southgate	MI
Waterford Cinema	Waterford	MI

NATIONAL AMUSEMENTS

Showcase Dearborn	Dearborn	MI
Beacon East Cinemas	Harper Woods	MI
Showcase Sterling Heights	Sterling Heights	MI
Showcase Westland	Westland	MI
Showcase Ann Arbor	Ypsilanti	MI

NEIGHBORHOOD CINEMA GROUP

Lapeer Cinemas	Lapeer	MI

REGAL ENTERTAINMENT GROUP

West River 9	Farmington	MI
Frenchtown Square Mall 8	Monroe	MI
Commerce Township Stadium 14	Walled Lake	MI

HOUSTON

AMC ENTERTAINMENT

Studio 30	Houston	TX
Meyer Park 16	Houston	TX
Gulf Pointe 30	Houston	TX
Willowbrook 24	Houston	TX
Deerbrook Mall 24	Humble	TX
Katy Mills 20	Katy	TX
First Colony 24	Sugarland	TX

CINEMARK USA

Tinseltown	Houston	TX
Tinseltown Westchase	Houston	TX
Tinseltown	Jacinto City	TX
Cinemark 19	Katy	TX
Hollywood USA	Pasadena	TX
Rosenberg 8	Rosenberg	TX
Movies 12	Texas City	TX
Cinema 18	Webster	TX
Tinseltown	Woodlands	TX

FOOTHILLS ENTERTAINMENT CO.

Orange Cinema 2	Orange	TX

LANDMARK THEATRES

Greenway 3 Theatre	Houston	TX
River Oaks Theatre	Houston	TX

LOEWS CINPLEX

Easton Commons 8	Houston	TX
Magic Johnson Northline	Houston	TX
Spring Tenplex	Spring	TX
Fountains	Stafford	TX

NOVA CINEMAS

Nova Meyerland 8	Houston	TX

REGAL ENTERTAINMENT GROUP

Greenway Grand Plce. Stadium 24	Houston	TX
Houston Marq"E Stadium 23	Houston	TX

STARPLEX CINEMAS

Brazos Mall 3	Lake Jackson	TX
Cinema 10	Lake Jackson	TX

SEATTLE/TACOMA

AMC ENTERTAINMENT

Renton Village 8	Renton	WA
Cinerama 1	Seattle	WA
Pacific Place 11	Seattle	WA
Kitsap 8	Silverdale	WA
Narrows Plaza 8	Tacoma	WA

COMMING ATTRACTIONS

SouthShore Mall Cinemas	Aberdeen	WA

GALAXY THEATRES

Gateway 8	Federal Way	WA
Galaxy 6	Tacoma	WA

LANDMARK THEATRES

Crest Cinema Center	Seattle	WA
Egyptian Theatre	Seattle	WA
Guild 45th Theatre	Seattle	WA
Harvard Exit Theatre	Seattle	WA
Metro Cinemas	Seattle	WA
Neptune Theatre	Seattle	WA
Seven Gables Theatre	Seattle	WA
Varsity Theater	Seattle	WA

LOEWS CINPLEX

Factoria Cinemas 8	Bellevue	WA
Cascade Mall	Burlington	WA
Lakewood Town Center Cinemas	Lakewood	WA
Grand Cinemas Alderwood	Lynnwood	WA
Redmond Town Center	Redmond	WA
Meridian	Seattle	WA
Oak Tree Cinemas	Seattle	WA

Uptown Cinemas ....Seattle ....WA
Lewis & Clark...............................Tukwila ....WA
Woodinville ....Woodinville ....WA

REGAL ENTERTAINMENT GROUP
Auburn Stadium 17 Theatres.........Auburn ....WA
Crossroads 8 Cinema ....Bellevue ....WA
Galleria Stadium 11 ....Bellevue ....WA
Bellis Fair 6 Cinema ....Bellingham ....WA
Sehome 3 Cinemas ....Bellingham ....WA
Sunset Square Cinema 6 ....Bellingham ....WA
Tall Firs 10 ....Bonneylake....................WA
Cinema 3 ....Chehalis ....WA
Everett 9 Cinemas ....Everett...........................WA
Gig Harbor 3 ....Gig Harbor ....WA
Issaquah 9 Theatre ....Issaquah ....WA
Kent 6 Theatres...........................Kent ....WA
Lakewood Cinema Stadium 15 .....Lakewood ....WA
Alderwood 7 Theatres ....Lynwood ....WA
Marysville Cinema 14...................Marysville ....WA
Mount Lake 9 Theatre ....Mt Lake Terrace ....WA
Capital Mall Cinemas 4 ....Olympia ....WA
Lacey 8 Theatres ....Olympia ....WA
South Sound Cinema 10 ....Port Orchard...................WA
Poulsbo Stadium 10 ....Poulsbo ....WA
Longston Place Stadium 14 ....Puyallup ....WA
Puyallup 6 Cinemas ....Puyallup ....WA
South Hill Cinema 6 ....Puyallup ....WA
Bella Botega Stadium 11 Cinema...Redmond........................WA
East Valley Stadium 13 Cinema ....Renton ....WA
Silverdale 4 Theatres ....Silverdale.......................WA
Parkway Plaza Stadium 12...........Tukwila ....WA

TAMPA/ST. PETERSBURG (SARASOTA)

AMC ENTERTAINMENT
Regency Brandon 20....................Brandon ....FL
Tri-City 8 ....Clearwater ....FL
Merchants Walk 10.......................Lakeland ....FL
Woodlands Square 20...................Oldsmar ....FL
Sarasota East 7/12 ....Sarasota.........................FL
Tyrone Square 6...........................St. Petersburg ....FL
Veterans Expressway 24 ....Tampa............................FL
Westshore Plaza 14 ....Tampa............................FL

CARMIKE CINEMAS
Carmike Royal Palm.....................Bradenton ....FL
Carmike Palm Cinema..................Lakeland ....FL
Carmike Lake Waldon Cinema .....Plant City ....FL
Carmike Lakeshore ....Sebring ....FL
Carmike Continental Mugs ....Winterhaven...................FL

COBB THEATRES
Parkway 8 Cinemas ....Sarasota ....FL
Grand 10 Cinemas ....Winter Haven ....FL

GEORGIA THEATRE COMPANY II
Beacon Cinemas 10......................Brooksville ....FL

MUVICO THEATRES
Palm Harbor 10............................Palm Harbor ....FL
Baywalk 20 ....St. Petersburg ....FL
Centro Ybor 20.............................Tampa............................FL
Starlight 20 ....Tampa............................FL

R/C THEATRES
Parkside 16 ....Pinellas Park ....FL

REGAL ENTERTAINMENT GROUP
Oakmont 8 ....Bradenton ....FL
Crystal River Mall 9......................Crystal River..................FL
Citrus Cinemas 6 ....Inverness ....FL
Eagle Ridge Mall 12.....................Lake Wales ....FL
Largo Mall 8.................................Largo..............................FL
Hollywood 18, Port Richey ....Port Richey.....................FL
Hollywood Stadium 20..................Sarasota.........................FL
Spring Hill 8 Cinemas ....Spring Hill ....FL
Channelside Cinemas Stadium 9 ..Tampa............................FL
Citrus Park Stadium 20 ....Tampa............................FL
University 16 ....Tampa............................FL
Venetian 6....................................Venice ....FL

STARNET CINEMAS
Lakeland Square 10 Cinemas ....Lakeland ....FL

MINNEAPOLIS/ST.PAUL

AMC ENTERTAINMENT
Mall of America 14 ....Bloomington ....MN
Eden Prairie Mall 18 ....Eden Prairie ....MN
Centennial Lakes 8 ....Edina..............................MN
Har Mar 1-3 ....Roseville ....MN
Har Mar 4-11................................Roseville ....MN

CARMIKE CINEMAS
Carmike ....Apple Valley....................MN
Carmike Wynnsong ....Moundsview ....MN
Carmike Oakdale ....Oakdale..........................MN
Carmike Kandi ....Willmar...........................MN

CINEMA ENTERTAINMENT CORP.
Amigo 9 ....Bemidji...........................MN
Cinema 6 ....Faribault.........................MN
Marshall 6 ....Marshall ....MN
Parkwood 18 ....Waite Park......................MN
Crossroads 6 ....Waite Park......................MN
Cinema 9 ....Hudson...........................WI
Lake 7..Rice Lake ....WI

CINEMAGIC THEATRES
Century 7 Theatres ....Hutchinson ....MN
CineMagic Stadium 7 Theatres .....Menomonie ....WI

CROWN THEATRES
Crown Block E ....Minneapolis....................MN

KERASOTES THEATRES
Showplace 16 Coon Rapids ....Coon Rapids....................MN
Showplace 16 ....Inver Grove Hts. ....MN

LAKES & RIVERS
Cedar Mall Cinema 6 ....Owatonna ....MN
Red Wing Cinema 5 ....Red Wing ....MN
Falls Cinema 5.............................St. Croix Falls ....WI

LANDMARK THEATRES
Edina Cinema ....Edina..............................MN
Lagoon Cinema ....Minneapolis....................MN
Uptown Theatre............................Minneapolis....................MN

MANN MINNESOTA
Movies 10 at Westgate.................Baxter............................MN
Westport Theatre ....Baxter............................MN
Champlin Cinema 14.....................Champlin ....MN
Cottage View Drive-In ....Cottage Grove................MN
Eagan Cinema 9 ....Eagan.............................MN
Grand Rapids Cinema...................Grand Rapids ....MN
Irongate Cinema 3 ....Hibbing...........................MN
Hopkins Cinema 6........................Hopkins ....MN
Maple Grove Cinema 10................Maple Grove ....MN
Plymouth Cinema 12.....................Plymouth ....MN
St. Louis Park Cinema..................St. Louis Park.................MN
Grandview 1 & 2 Theatres ....St. Paul ....MN
Highland 1 & 2 Theatres ....St. Paul ....MN

MARCUS THEATRES
Apple Valley ....Apple Valley....................MN
Elk River......................................Elk River.........................MN
Hastings.......................................Hastings ....MN
Oakdale ....Oakdale..........................MN
Rosemount ....Rosemount ....MN
Shakopee ....Shakopee ....MN

MEGASTAR CINEMAS
Southdale Center ....Edina..............................MN
Arbor Lakes ....Maple Grove ....MN

MULLER FAMILY THEATRES
Delano 5 Theatre ....Delano............................MN
East Bethel 10 Theatre ....East Bethel.....................MN
Lakeville 18 Theatre ....Lakeville ....MN
Monticello 4 Theatre.....................Monticello ....MN
WillowCreek 12 Theatre ....Plymouth ....MN
Waconia 6 Theatre ....Waconia ....MN
White Bear Township 17 Theatre ...White Bear Twnshp. ....MN

REGAL ENTERTAINMENT GROUP
Eagan Stadium 16 ....Eagan.............................MN
Eden Prairie West 5 ....Eden Prairie ....MN
Movies @Maplewood II 6 ....Maplewood ....MN
Brooklyn Center Stadium 20 ....Minneapolis....................MN
Pavilions Place 7..........................Roseville ....MN
Woodbury 10 Theatres ....Woodbury ....MN

CLEVELAND/AKRON/CANTON

AMC ENTERTAINMENT
West Market Plaza 7 ....Akron..............................OH
Ridge Park Square 8.....................Brooklyn ....OH
Plaza Chapel Hill 8 ....Cuyahoga Falls...............OH
Westgate Mall 6 ....Rocky River ....OH
Westwood Town Center 6.............Rocky River ....OH

ATLAS CINEMAS
Avon Lake 4 ....Avon Lake.......................OH
Lakeshore 7 ....Euclid ....OH
Cinemas Diamond Ctr 12 ....Mentor............................OH
Greatlakes ....Mentor............................OH

CARMIKE CINEMAS

Carmike Ashtabula Mall ....Ashtabula ....OH
Carmike Kingsgate.....................Mansfield ....OH
Carmike Plaza ....Sandusky...........................OH

CINEMARK USA

Carnation Cinema ....Alliance..............................OH
Movies 4 ....Canton...............................OH
Cinemark 15 ....Macedonia ....OH
Cinema 10 ....Mansfield ....OH
Movies 10 ....North Canton ....OH
Tinseltown................................North Canton ....OH
Richland III ....Ontario...............................OH
Movies 10 ....Sandusky...........................OH
Cinemark 24 ....Valley View ....OH
Movies 10 ....Willoughby Hills ....OH
Movies 10 ....Wooster ....OH

CLEVELAND CINEMAS

Hickory Ridge Cinemas................Brunswick ....OH
Cedar Lee Theatre ....Cleveland Heights...............OH
Shaker Square Cinemas ....Cleveland............................OH
Tower City Cinemas ....Cleveland............................OH
Parmatown Cinemas ....Parma.................................OH

LOEWS CINPLEX

Magic Johnson Randall Park Mall .N. Randall.......................OH
Richmond Town Square................Richmond Heights ....OH

MEGASTAR CINEMAS

Chagrin ....Chagrin Falls ....OH

REGAL ENTERTAINMENT GROUP

Independence Stadium 10.............Akron.................................OH
Interstate Park Cinema Stadium 18Akron.................................OH
Montrose Movies Stadium 12 ....Akron.................................OH
Severance Town Ctr. Stadium 14 ...Cleveland Heights...............OH
Cobblestone Square Stadium 20 ....Elyria.................................OH
Hudson Cinema 10 ....Hudson..............................OH
Mayfield Heights 10....................Mayfield Heights ....OH
Medina Stadium 16 @ Huntington St.Medina...............................OH
New Towne Cinema 8...................New Philadelphia................OH
Solon Commons Cinema 16.........Solon.................................OH
Westlake Promenade 11 ....Westlake.............................OH
Willoughby Commons Stadium 16.Willoughby.........................OH

PHOENIX

AMC ENTERTAINMENT

Arrowhead 14............................Glendale.............................AZ
Mesa Grand 24 ....Mesa..................................AZ
Ahwatukee 24 ....Phoenix..............................AZ
Arizona Center 24 ....Phoenix..............................AZ
Deer Valley 30...........................Phoenix..............................AZ
Desert Ridge 18.........................Phoenix..............................AZ
Esplanade 14 ....Phoenix..............................AZ

CENTURY THEATRES

Glendale Drive-In ....Glendale.............................AZ
Scottsdale 6 Drive-In..................Scottsdale ....AZ

CINEMARK USA

Movies 4 ....Kingman ....AZ

HARKINS THEATRES

Chandler Fashion 20...................Chandler ....AZ
Flagstaff 11...............................Flagstaff.............................AZ
Poca Fiesta 4 ....Mesa..................................AZ
Fiesta 5....................................Mesa..................................AZ
Superstition Springs 25...............Mesa..................................AZ
Arrowhead 18............................Peoria................................AZ
Arcadia 8..................................Phoenix..............................AZ
Christown 11.............................Phoenix..............................AZ
Metrocenter 12..........................Phoenix..............................AZ
North Valley 18 ....Phoenix..............................AZ
Paradise Valley Mall 7 ....Phoenix..............................AZ
Scottsdale/101 CineCapri 14........Phoenix..............................AZ
Southwest Plaza 8 ....Phoenix..............................AZ
Prescott Valley 14 ....Prescott Valley ....AZ
Camelview 5 ....Scottsdale ....AZ
Fashion Square 7 ....Scottsdale ....AZ
Shea 14 ....Scottsdale ....AZ
Sedona 6 ....Sedona...............................AZ
Arizona Mills 24 ....Tempe................................AZ
Centerpoint 11 ....Tempe................................AZ
Valley Art Theatre ....Tempe................................AZ

REGAL ENTERTAINMENT GROUP

Pavilions 11 ....Scottsdale ....AZ
Sonora Village 10.......................Scottsdale ....AZ

WALLACE THEATER

Gilbert Stadium Cinemas ....Gilbert................................AZ

WESTATES THEATRES

Page Mesa Theatre.....................Page...................................AZ

WILDWOOD THEATRES

Palm Valley 14 ....Goodyear ....AZ

MIAMI/FT. LAUDERDALE

Paradise 24...............................Davie..................................FL
Hialeah 14 ....Hialeah...............................FL
Pompano 18..............................Pompano Beach ....FL

AMC ENTERTAINMENT

Aventura 24...............................Aventura ....FL
Cocowalk 16 ....Coconut Grove....................FL
Ridge Plaza 8 ....Davie..................................FL
Coral Ridge 10...........................Fort Lauderdale ....FL
Sheridan Plaza 12......................Hollywood...........................FL
Kendall T and C 10 ....Miami.................................FL
Mall Of Americas 14...................Miami.................................FL
South Dade 8 ....Miami.................................FL
Sunset Place 24.........................South Miami........................FL

COBB THEATRES

Dolphin 19 Cinemas ....Miami.................................FL
Miami Lakes 17 Cinemas ....Miami Lakes ....FL

CROWN THEATRES

Crown Grand..............................Hialeah...............................FL

REGAL ENTERTAINMENT GROUP

Magnolia Place Stadium 16..........Coral Springs ....FL
Las Olas Stadium 23...................Ft Lauderdale ....FL
Cypress Creek Station Stadium 16Ft. Lauderdale....................FL
Oakwood 18 ....Hollywood...........................FL
Cinema Key West 6.....................Key West............................FL
Movies @ Lauderhill 13................Lauderhill...........................FL
Kendall Nine ....Miami.................................FL
Movies @ The Falls 12................Miami.................................FL
Palace 18..................................Miami.................................FL
South Beach Stadium 18..............Miami Beach ....FL
Westfork Stadium 13...................Pembroke Pines..................FL
Sawgrass Stadium 23 ....Sunrise...............................FL

DENVER

AMC ENTERTAINMENT

Seven Hills 10 ....Aurora................................CO
Flatiron Crossing 14 ....Broomfield ....CO
Highlands Ranch 24 ....Highlands Ranch ....CO
Westminster Promenade 24 ....Westminster........................CO

CARMIKE CINEMAS

Carmike Stage ....Aspen.................................CO
Carmike ....Fort Collins ....CO
Carmike Mall ....Glenwood Springs ....CO
Carmike ....Greeley...............................CO
Carmike Chief Plaza ....Steamboat Springs ....CO

CENTURY THEATRES

Century 16 ....Aurora................................CO

CINEMARK USA

Tiffany Plaza Movies 6 ....Denver................................CO
Cinemark At Fort Collins ....Fort Collins ....CO

COLORADO CINEMA

Olde Town 14 ....Arvada................................CO
Arapahoe Crossing 16.................Aurora................................CO
Basemar Twin ....Boulder...............................CO
Cherry Creek 8 ....Denver................................CO
Bergen Park 7 ....Evergreen...........................CO
Cinema Saver 6 ....Ft. Collins ....CO
Bowles Crossing 12 ....Littleton..............................CO
Southwest Plaza 5 ....Littleton..............................CO
Colony Square 12 ....Louisville.............................CO
20 Mile Village 10 ....Parker................................CO

LANDMARK THEATRES

Esquire Theatre ....Denver................................CO
Mayan Theatre ....Denver................................CO
Chez Artiste ....Denver................................CO

METROPOLITAN THEATRES

MetroLux 12 Theatre ....Loveland.............................CO

REGAL ENTERTAINMENT GROUP

Village 4....................................Boulder...............................CO
Colorado Center 9......................Denver................................CO
Continental 6 ....Denver................................CO
Pavilions 15 ....Denver................................CO
Greenwood Plaza 12...................Englewood..........................CO
West Village Stadium 12 ....Golden................................CO
Bittersweet 6 ....Greeley...............................CO
Cooper Twin ....Greeley...............................CO
Meadows 12..............................Littleton..............................CO
Twin Peaks Mall 10 ....Longmont ....CO
Thornton Town Center 10 ....Thornton.............................CO

TRANS LUX

Lake Dillon Cinema	Dillon	CO
Skyline Cinema	Dillon	CO
Metrolux 12	Loveland	CO
Fox Theatre	Laramie	WY

W. F. CINEMA (MANN THEATRES)

Green Mountain 6	Lakewood	CO

SACRAMENTO/STOCKTON/MODESTO

BRENDEN THEATRES

Modesto 18	Modesto	CA
Vacaville 16	Vacaville	CA

CENTURY THEATRES

Century 16 Laguna	Elk Grove	CA
Century 14 Folsom	Folsom	CA
Century 14 Roseville	Roseville	CA
Sacramento Drive-In	Sacramento	CA
Century Stadium 14	Sacramento	CA
Century Downtown Plaza 7	Sacramento	CA
Century 16 Greenback Ln.	Sacramento	CA

CINEMARK USA

Movies 14	Tracy	CA
County Fair Movies 5	Woodland	CA
Yuba City 8	Yuba City	CA

REGAL ENTERTAINMENT GROUP

Sunrise 4	Citrus Heights	CA
Fairfield Stadium 16	Fairfield	CA
Del Oro 3	Grass Valley	CA
Hayward 6	Hayward	CA
Olympus Pointe 12	Roseville	CA
Arden Fair 6	Sacramento	CA
Laguna Village 12	Sacramento	CA
Natomas Marketplace Stadium 16	Sacramento	CA

SIGNATURE THEATRES

Stadium 10	Auburn	CA
Holiday Cinema	Davis	CA
Stadium 5	Davis	CA
Jackson Cinemas	Jackson	CA
Stadium 10	Modesto	CA
Placerville 8	Placerville	CA
Stadium 10	Sonora	CA
Festival Cinemas, 4-Plex	Stockton	CA
Holiday Cinemas 8	Stockton	CA
Turlock Stadium 14	Turlock	CA

ORLANDO/DAYTONA BEACH/MELBOURNE

AMC ENTERTAINMENT

Celebration 2	Celebration	FL
Volusia Square 8	Daytona	FL
Pleasure Island 24	Lake Buena Vista	FL
Lake Square 12	Leesburg	FL
Merritt Square 7/12	Merritt Island	FL
West Oaks 14	Ocoee	FL
Fashion Village 8	Orlando	FL

AMSTAR ENTERTAINMENT

Stadium 12	Lake Mary	FL

CARMIKE CINEMAS

Carmike University	Winter Park	FL

CINEMARK USA

Festival Bay	Orlando	FL

COBB THEATRES

Roxy 10 Cinemas	Palm Bay	FL

EASTERN FEDERAL CORP.

Port Orange Six	Port Orange	FL

LOEWS CINPLEX

Universal Cineplex 20	Orlando	FL

MUVICO THEATRES

Muvico Pointe 21	Orlando	FL

NOVA CINEMAS

Nova Cinemas at Palm Bay West	Palm Bay	FL

R/C THEATRES

OceanWalk 10	Daytona Beach	FL

REGAL ENTERTAINMENT GROUP

Movies @ Wekiva Riverwalk 8	Apopka	FL
Osceola Square East 6	Kissimmee	FL
Oaks 10	Melbourne	FL
Hollywood Stadium 16	Ocala	FL
Marketplace 8	Orange City	FL

Waterford Lakes Stadium 20	Orlando	FL
Ormond Beach Cinema 12	Ormond Beach	FL
Oviedo Marketplace Stadium 22	Oviedo	FL
Seminole Towne Center	Sanford	FL
Searstown Mall 10	Titusville	FL
Winter Park Village Stadium 20	Winter Park	FL

STARNET CINEMAS

Belleview Cinemas	Belleview	FL
Satellite Beach Cinemas	Satellite Beach	FL

TMI THEATRES

Victoria Square 6	DeLand	FL
Beacon 12 Theatre	New Smyrna Bch.	FL

PITTSBURGH

CARMIKE CINEMAS

Carmike Plaza	Beaver Falls	PA
Carmike Cinema	Connellsville	PA
Carmike Cranberry Mall	Cranberry	PA
Carmike Cranberry Mall	Cranberry Township	PA
Carmike Wynnsong	Delmont	PA
Carmike	Greensburg	PA
Carmike Cinema	Indiana	PA
Carmike Cinema	Kittanning	PA
Carmike Cinema	Leechburg	PA
Carmike Movie World	Monaca	PA
Carmike Galleria	Mount Lebanon	PA
Carmike	Pittsburgh	PA
Carmike Southland	Pleasant Hills	PA
Carmike	Uniontown	PA
Carmike Maxi Saver	West Mifflin	PA
Carmike Mall	Morgantown	WV

DESTINTA THEATRES

Chartiers Valley 20	Bridgeville	PA
Clarion 7	Clarion	PA
Plaza East 22	N. Versailles	PA

DICKINSON THEATRES

Mall 8 Pittsburg	Pittsburg	KS

LOEWS CINPLEX

Waterfront	West Homestead	PA

NATIONAL AMUSEMENTS

Showcase Cinemas East	Pittsburgh	PA
Showcase Cinemas West	Pittsburgh	PA
Showcase Cinemas North	Pittsburgh	PA
Northway Mall	Pittsburgh	PA

REGAL ENTERTAINMENT GROUP

Cortland Town Center Stadium 11	Mohegan Lake	NY
Moraine Pointe Cinema 10	Butler	PA

TMI THEATRES

Pioneer Drive-In Theatre	Butler	PA

WALLACE THEATRE

Crown Center Cinemas	Washington	PA

ST. LOUIS

AMC ENTERTAINMENT

Creve Coeur 12	Creve Coeur	MO
West Olive 16	Creve Coeur	MO
Crestwood 10	St. Louis	MO
Esquire 7	St. Louis	MO

B & B THEATRES

Festus Eight	Festus	MO

CARMIKE CINEMAS

Carmike Petite	Collinsville	IL

KERASOTES THEATRES

Plaza	Centralia	IL
Eastgate Cinema	East Alton	IL
Showplace 12	Edwardsville	IL
Cottonwood Cinema	Glen Carbon	IL
Nameoki	Granite City	IL
Lory Theatre	Highland	IL
Stadium Theatre	Jerseyville	IL
Showplace 4	Farmington	MO
Movies	Park Hills	MO

LANDMARK THEATRES

Hi Pointe Theatre	St. Louis	MO
Plaza Frontenac	St. Louis	MO
Tivoli Theatre	Universal City	MO

WEHRENBERG THEATRES

St. Clair Cine 10	Fairview Heights	IL
O'Fallon 15 Cine	O'Fallon	IL

Clarkson 6 Cine	Chesterfield	MO
Eureka 6 Cine	Eureka	MO
Jamestown 14 Cine	Florissant	MO
Ronnies 20 Cine	Sappington	MO
Northwest 9 Cine	St. Ann	MO
St. Charles 18 Cine	St. Charles	MO
Arnold 14 Cine	St. Louis	MO
Des Peres 14 Cine	St. Louis	MO
Kenrick 8 Cine	St. Louis	MO
Mid Rivers 14 Cine	St. Louis	MO

PORTLAND

CENTURY THEATRES
| Century 16 Eastport Plaza | Portland | OR |

COMING ATTRACTIONS
| Astoria Gateway Cinemas | Astoria | OR |
| McMinnville Cinemas | McMinnville | OR |

REGAL ENTERTAINMENT GROUP
Albany 7 Cinemas	Albany	OR
Westgate 5 Theatres	Beaverton	OR
Clackamas Towne Center 5	Clackamas	OR
Stark Street Stadium 10	Gresham	OR
Evergreen Parkway Stadium 13	Hillsboro	OR
Movies On TV Stadium 16	Hillsboro	OR
Lincoln City Stadium 6	Lincoln Cit	OR
Newport Tri	Newport	OR
Hilltop 9 Cinema	Oregon City	OR
82nd Avenue 6 Cinemas	Portland	OR
Broadway Metro 4 Theatres	Portland	OR
Division Street Stadium 13	Portland	OR
Fox Tower Stadium 10	Portland	OR
Koin Center 6 Cinemas	Portland	OR
Lloyd Center Stadium 10 Cinema	Portland	OR
Lloyd Mall 8 Cinema	Portland	OR
Lancaster Quad Cinema	Salem	OR
Movieland 7	Salem	OR
Santiam Stadium 11	Salem	OR
Sherwood Stadium 10	Sherwood	OR
Tigard 11 Cinemas	Tigard	OR
Wilsonville Stadium 9 Cinema	Wilsonville	OR
Three Rivers Mall 5	Kelso	WA
Triangle Quad Cinemas	Longview	WA
Cascade Stadium 16 Cinemas	Vancouver	WA
Cinema 99 Stadium 11	Vancouver	WA
City Center Stadium 12	Vancouver	WA
Vancouver Plaza 10 Cinema	Vancouver	WA

BALTIMORE

AMC ENTERTAINMENT
Owings Mills 17	Owings Mills	MD
Towson Commons 8	Towson	MD
Security Square 8	Woodlawn	MD

CROWN THEATRES
Annapolis Harbour Center	Annapolis	MD
Annapolis Mall	Annapolis	MD
Eastport Cinemas	Annapolis	MD

FLAGSHIP CINEMAS
| Flagship Cinema Churchville | Bel Air | MD |

LOEWS CINPLEX
| White Marsh | Baltimore | MD |
| Valley Center 9 | Owings Mills | MD |

MUVICO
| Egyptian 24 | Hanover | MD |

R/C THEATRES
| Carrolltown Movies 6 | Eldersburg | MD |

REGAL ENTERTAINMENT GROUP
Bel Air Cinema Stadium 14	Abingdon	MD
UA Westview Mall 9	Baltimore	MD
UA Bethesda 10	Bethesda	MD
UA Snowden Square Stadium 14	Columbia	MD
Movies @ Marley Station 8	Glen Burnie	MD

INDIANAPOLIS

ALLIANCE ENTERTAINMENT
| Bedford Great Escape | Bedford | IN |

AMC ENTERTAINMENT
Greenwood 14	Greenwood	IN
Castleton Square 3	Indianapolis	IN
Clearwater Crossing 12	Indianapolis	IN
Eastgate Mall 6	Indianapolis	IN

CINEMARK USA
| Greenwood | Indianapolis | IN |
| Washington | Indianapolis | IN |

GKC THEATRES
| Capri Cinemas | Crawfordsville | IN |

GOODRICH QUALITY THEATRES
| Applewood 9 | Anderson | IN |
| Anderson 4 | Anderson | IN |

KERASOTES THEATRES
College Mall Cinema	Bloomington	IN
Showplace 11	Bloomington	IN
Showplace West 12	Bloomington	IN
Commons Cinema	Columbus	IN
Showplace 12	Columbus	IN
Showplace 16	Indianapolis	IN
ShowPlace 12	Indianapolis	IN
Kokomo Mall Cinema	Kokomo	IN
Markland Mall Cinema	Kokomo	IN
Showplace 12	Marion	IN
Showplace 7	Muncie	IN
Northwest Plaza Cinema	Muncie	IN
Castle Theatre	New Castle	IN
Eastwood Cinema	Peru	IN

LOEWS CINPLEX
| College Park | Indianapolis | IN |

REGAL ENTERTAINMENT GROUP
Shiloh Crossing Stadium 18	Avon	IN
Village Park Cinema Stadium 17	Carmel	IN
Circle Center 9	Indianapolis	IN
Eagle Highlands 10	Indianapolis	IN
Galaxy Stadium 14	Indianapolis	IN

SYNDICATE
| Canary Creek Cinemas | Franklin | IN |

SAN DIEGO

AMC ENTERTAINMENT
Encinitas 8	Encinitas	CA
La Jolla Village 12	La Jolla	CA
Fashion Valley 18	San Diego	CA
Mission Valley 20	San Diego	CA
Palm Promenade 24	San Diego	CA

CINEMASTAR LUXURY THEATRES
| Mission Marketplace 13 | Oceanside | CA |

DEANZA LAND & LEISURE CORP.
| South Bay Triple | San Diego | CA |

LANDMARK THEATRES
La Jolla Village Cinemas	La Jolla	CA
Hillcrest Cinemas	San Diego	CA
Ken Theatre	San Diego	CA

THE MOVIE EXPERIENCE
| Town & Country | Oceanside | CA |

PACIFIC THEATRES
Grossmont Center 10	La Mesa	CA
Trolley 8	La Mesa	CA
Sweetwater 9	National City	CA
Carmel Mountain 12	San Diego	CA
Cinerama 4	San Diego	CA
Gaslamp 15	San Diego	CA
Town Square 14	San Diego	CA

REGAL ENTERTAINMENT GROUP
Rancho Del Rey Stadium 16	Chula Vista	CA
Parkway Plaza Stadium 18	El Cajon	CA
Rancho San Diego Stadium 15	El Cajon	CA
Oceanside Stadium 16	Oceanside	CA
Mira Mesa Stadium 18	San Diego	CA
UA Horton Plaza 14	San Diego	CA
San Marcos Stadium 18	San Marcos	CA

ULTRASTAR CINEMAS
Galaxy 6	Bonsall	CA
La Costa 6	Carlsbad	CA
Chula Vista 10	Chula Vista	CA
Flower Hill Cinema 4	Del Mar	CA
Poway Creekside Plaza 10	Poway	CA
Del Mar Highlands 8	San Diego	CA

HARTFORD & NEW HAVEN

CROWN THEATRES
| Crown Palace | W. Hartford | CT |

DESTINTA THEATRES
| Metro Square 12 | Middletown | CT |

ENTERTAINMENT CINEMAS
| Bloomfield 8 | Bloomfield | CT |
| Seymour 12 | Seymour | CT |

LOEWS CINPLEX

Plainville ....Plainville ....CT

MARQUEE CINEMAS

Westbrook 12.............................Westbrook ....CT

MINI THEATRES

Norwich Cinema...........................Norwich ....CT

NATIONAL AMUSEMENTS

Showcase Berlin ....Berlin ....CT
S/C East Hartford.......................East Hartford......................CT
Showcase East Windsor...............East Windsor.......................CT
Showcase Cinemas Buckland Hills.Manchester ....CT
Showcase Milford ....Milford ....CT
Milford Quad ....Milford ....CT
Showcase North Haven................N. Haven ....CT
Showcase Orange......................Orange ....CT
Showcase Southington.................Southington ....CT

CHARLOTTE

AMC ENTERTAINMENT

Carolina Pavilions 22 ....Charlotte...........................NC
Concord Mills 30 ....Concord ....NC

AMSTAR ENTERTAINMENT

Stadium 14 ....Mooresville ....NC

CARMIKE CINEMAS

Carmike Appalachian ....Boone ....NC
Carmike Chalet..........................Boone ....NC
Carmike ....Hickory ....NC
Carmike Westgate......................Lenoir ....NC
Carmike Cinema ....Lincolnton ....NC
Carmike Cinema ....Shelby ....NC
Carmike Mall..............................Shelby ....NC
Carmike Gateway.......................Statesville ....NC
Carmike Cinema ....Rock Hill ....SC

CINEMARK USA

Movies 10 ....Matthews ....NC
Tinseltown USA ....Salisbury...........................NC

CONSOLIDATED THEATRES

Arboretum Stadium 12 ....Charlotte...........................NC
Park Terrace Cinema 6................Charlotte...........................NC
Phillips Place Stadium 10.............Charlotte...........................NC
Union Square Cinema 8...............Monroe ....NC
Manchester Cinema ....Rock Hill ....SC

EASTERN FEDERAL CORP.

Delta Six Theatre ....Charlotte...........................NC
Manor Theatre ....Charlotte...........................NC
Movies at Crownpoint 12.............Charlotte...........................NC
Starlight Stadium ....Charlotte...........................NC
Movies at the Lake......................Cornelius ....NC
Movies at Birkdale......................Huntersville ....NC

MARQUEE CINEMAS

Mimosa 7 ....Morganton ....NC

REGAL ENTERTAINMENT GROUP

Boone Cinema 7 ....Boone ....NC
Stonecrest @ Piper Glen Stadium 22.Charlotte...........................NC
Carolina Mall Cinemas 8 ....Concord ....NC
Crown 6 Cinemas.......................Hickory ....NC

RALEIGH/DURHAM (FAYETTEVILLE)

CARMIKE CINEMAS

Carmike Plaza ....Dunn ....NC
Carmike Willowdale......................Durham ....NC
Carmike Wynnsong ....Durham ....NC
Carmike ....Fayetteville.......................NC
Carmike Marketfair ....Fayetteville.......................NC
Carmike Wynnsong ....Fayetteville.......................NC
Carmike Berkley..........................Goldsboro ....NC
Carmike Park Place ....Morrisville ....NC
Carmike ....Raleigh ....NC
Carmike Blueridge ....Raleigh ....NC
Carmike Kendale Cinema 2.........Sanford ....NC
Carmike Parkwood ....Wilson ....NC

CONSOLIDATED THEATRES

Crossroads 20 ....Cary...........................NC
Southpoint Cinema......................Durham ....NC
Raleigh Grande Cinema 16..........Raleigh ....NC

EASTERN FEDERAL CORP.

Movies at Timberlyne 6 ....Chapel Hill ....NC
Plaza Stadium 10........................Chapel Hill ....NC

REGAL ENTERTAINMENT GROUP

Towne Square 10 ....Garner ....NC
Litchfield Cinemas 4....................Goldsboro ....NC
Wilson Cinema 6.........................Wilson...........................NC

NASHVILLE

ALLIANCE ENTERTAINMENT

Clarksville Great Escape 16..........Clarksville ....TN

CARMIKE CINEMAS

Carmike Martin ....Hopkinsville ....KY
Carmike Bell Forge ....Antioch ....TN
Carmike Hickory.........................Antioch ....TN
Carmike......................................Clarksville ....TN
Carmike Cinema 5 ....Clarksville ....TN
Carmike Highland ....Cookeville ....TN
Carmike Thoroughbred ....Franklin ....TN
Carmike Rivergate ....Goodlettesville ....TN
Carmike Martin ....Lebanon ....TN
Carmike Wynnsong ....Murfreesboro ....TN
Carmike Bellevue ....Nashville ....TN
Carmike Wynnsong ....Nashville ....TN
Carmike Cinema ....Springfield ....TN

REGAL ENTERTAINMENT GROUP

Indian Lake Cinema 10 ....Hendersonville ....TN
Bellevue Cinema Stadium 12 ....Nashville ....TN
Green Hills Stadium 16 ....Nashville ....TN
Hollywood Stadium 27..................Nashville ....TN
Opry Mills Stadium 20 Plus Imax ..Nashville ....TN
Tullahoma Cinemas 8...................Tullahoma...........................TN

MILWAUKEE

AMC ENTERTAINMENT

Mayfair 18...................................Wauwatosa ....WI

CINEMARK USA

Tinseltown USA ....Kenosha ....WI

LANDMARK THEATRES

Downer Theatre ....Milwaukee ....WI
Oriental Theatre ....Milwaukee ....WI

MARCUS THEATRES

Wisconsin ....Beaver Dam ....WI
West Point ....Brookfield ....WI
Rivoli ....Cedarburg ....WI
Hillside ....Delafield ....WI
Menomonee Falls........................Menomonee Falls ....WI
North Shore ....Mequon ....WI
Northtown ....Milwaukee ....WI
Prospect Mall ....Milwaukee ....WI
Southgate ....Milwaukee ....WI
Ridge ....New Berlin ....WI
Value Oak Creek ....Oak Creek ....WI
South Shore ....Oak Creek ....WI
Regency ....Racine ....WI
Westgate.....................................Racine ....WI
Sheboygan ....Sheboygan ....WI
Westown ....Waukesha ....WI

NOVA CINETECH

Showboat ....Lake Geneva ....WI
Geneva 4 Theatre ....Lake Geneva ....WI
Paradise Theatre.........................West Bend...........................WI
Theatres of Whitewater ....Whitewater ....WI

STAR CINEMA

Star Cinema................................Johnson Creek ....WI

WILDWOOD THEATRES

Capitol Cinemas 11.....................Pewaukee...........................WI

CINCINNATI

ALLIANCE ENTERTAINMENT

Oxford Great Escape...................Oxford ....OH

CARMIKE CINEMAS

Carmike Cinema ....Maysville ....KY

CHAKERES

Wilmington Plaza 5 ....Wilmington...........................OH
Wilmington Drive-In.....................Wilmington...........................OH

DANBARRY CINEMAS

Danbarry Dollar Saver Cinemas ....Florence...........................KY
Danbarry Dollar Saver Cinemas ...Cincinnati ....OH
Danbarry Dollar Saver Cinemas ...Cincinnati ....OH
Danbarry Dollar Saver Cinemas ...Dayton ....OH
Danbarry Cinemas Middletown......Middletown ....OH

KERASOTES THEATRES
Cinemas 10................................Hamilton ....OH
Showplace 8 ....Hamilton ....OH

NATIONAL AMUSEMENTS
Showcase Erlanger ....Erlanger ....KY
Florence Cinemas ....Florence ....KY
Showcase Cross Pointe 12.....Centerville ....OH
Showcase Cinemas Forest Fair.....Cincinnati ....OH
Showcase Cinemas Springdale ...Cincinnati ....OH
Showcase Eastgate.......................Cincinnati ....OH
Showcase Cincinnati.....................Cincinnati ....OH
Showcase Western Hills..............Cincinnati ....OH
Kenwood Towne Centre................Cincinnati ....OH
Oakley Drive-In ....Madisonville ....OH
Showcase Kings Island ....Mason ....OH
Showcase Cinemas Milford ....Milford ....OH

KANSAS CITY

AMC ENTERTAINMENT
Town Center 20............................Leawood ....KS
Studio 30 ....Olathe ....KS
Oak Park Plaza 6 ....Overland Park ....KS
Independence 20 ....Independence....................MO
Barrywoods 24 ....Kansas City ....MO
Parkway 14 ....Kansas City ....MO

B & B THEATRES
Grand 6...Chillicothe ....MO
Harrisonville Cinema 6 ....Harrisonville ....MO
Liberty Cinema 12........................Liberty ....MO
Marshall Cinema ....Marshall ....MO

CARMIKE CINEMAS
Carmike University ....Warrensburg.....................MO

CINEMARK USA
Cinemark -Merriam ....Merriam ....KS
The Palace Cinemark 14..............Kansas City ....MO

DICKINSON THEATRES
Plaza 6 Leavenworth....................Leavenworth......................KS
Great Mall 16 ....Olathe ....KS
Westglen 18..................................Shawnee ....KS
Belton 8 ....Belton..................................MO
Blue Springs 8 ....Blue Springs......................MO
Northglen 14.................................Kansas City ....MO
Eastglen 16...................................Lee's Summit ....MO

REGAL ENTERTAINMENT GROUP
Kansas City Stadium 18 Cinemas .Kansas City ....MO

WALLACE THEATRE
Southwind 12 ....Lawrence ....KS

COLUMBUS

AMC ENTERTAINMENT
Lennox Town Center 24................Columbus ....OH
Easton 30 ....Columbus ....OH
Dublin Village 18 ....Dublin ....OH

CINEMARK USA
Movie 12 ....Columbus ....OH
Movies 10 ....Columbus ....OH
Movies 16 ....Gahanna ....OH
Movies 12 ....Hillard................................OH

MARCUS THEATRES
Cinema Crosswoods ....Columbus ....OH
Cinema Pickerington ....Pickerington ....OH

MARQUEE CINEMAS
Consumer Square 14 ....Reynolds ....OH

REGAL ENTERTAINMENT GROUP
Regal 6 ....Chillicothe ....OH
Middleburg Town Sq. Stadium 16 ..Cleveland..........................OH
Georgesville Square Stadium 16 ...Columbus ....OH
River Valley Mall 10.....................Lancaster..........................OH
Southland Cinema 7.....................Marion................................OH

GREENVILLE/SPARTANBURG/ANDERSON/ ASHEVILLE

AMSTAR ENTERTAINMENT
Stadium 14 ....Anderson ....SC

CARMIKE CINEMAS
Carmike ....Asheville ....NC
Carmike Cinema ....Forest City ....NC
Carmike Astro ....Clemson ....SC
Carmike Crosscreek Cinemas ....Greenwood ....SC
Carmike ....Spartanburg ....SC
Carmike Wynnsong ....Spartanburg ....SC

CONSOLIDATED THEATRES
Cherrydale 16 ....Greenville ....SC

EASTERN FEDERAL
Starlight Cinema ....Anderson ....SC

REGAL ENTERTAINMENT GROUP
Eastgate Cinemas 5.....................Albemarle ....NC
Beaucatcher Cinemas 7 ....Asheville ....NC
Biltmore Square 6 ....Asheville ....NC
Hollywood Cinemas 14.................Asheville ....NC
Four Seasons Cinemas ....Hendersonville ....NC
Hollywood Stadium 20.................Greenville ....SC
Converse Cinemas 6.....................Spartanburg ....SC
Westgate Mall Cinema 8 ....Spartanburg ....SC

SALT LAKE CITY

CARMIKE CINEMAS
Carmike Wynnsong ....Provo ....UT
Carmike ....West Jordan.......................UT
Carmike HW Connection ....West Valley City ....UT

CENTURY THEATRES
Century 16 ....Salt Lake City...................UT

CINEMARK USA
Tinseltown.....................................Layton ....UT
Tinseltown.....................................Ogden ....UT
Village Cinema ....Park City ....UT
Movies 8 ....Provo ....UT
Cinemark 16 ....Provo ....UT
Movies 10 ....Salt Lake City...................UT
Movies 9 ....Sandy ....UT
Cinemark 24 ....West Jordan.......................UT
Valley Fair ....West Valley City ....UT

DEANZA LAND & LEISURE CORP.
Redwood Six-Plex ....W. Valley............................UT

LOEWS CINPLEX
Layton Hills 9 ....Layton Hills ....UT

WESTATES THEATRES
Cedar City Cinema 8.....................Cedar City ....UT
Cedar City Twin............................Cedar City ....UT
Cedar City Fiddler 6.....................Cedar City ....UT
Cache Valley 3 ....Logan ....UT
Logan Cinema 3............................Logan ....UT
Logan Reel Time Theatre ....Logan ....UT
Logan Movies 5............................Logan ....UT
Water Gardens Cinema 6.............Pleasant Grove ....UT
Holladay Center Cinema 6 ....Salt Lake City...................UT
Trolley Corners Cinemas ....Salt Lake City...................UT
Red Cliff Cinemas ....St George ....UT
Cinema 6 ....St. George ....UT
Flood Street ....St. George ....UT
Movies ....St. George ....UT
St. George Stadium 8...................St. George ....UT
Tooele Cinema 6 ....Tooele ....UT
Evanston Strand Theatre..............Evanston ....WY

SAN ANTONIO

AMC ENTERTAINMENT
Rivercenter 9 ....San Antonio.......................TX
Huebner Oaks 24 ....San Antonio.......................TX

CINEMARK USA
Movies 8 ....Del Rio ....TX
Dollar Movies ....San Antonio.......................TX
Movies 9 ....San Antonio.......................TX

REGAL ENTERTAINMENT GROUP
Live Oak Stadium 18....................Liveoak ....TX
Alamo Quarry Stadium 14 ....San Antonio.......................TX
Cielo Vista Stadium 18 ....San Antonio.......................TX
Crossroads 6 Theatres ....San Antonio.......................TX
Fiesta 16 Stadium Theatres ....San Antonio.......................TX
Northwoods 14.............................San Antonio.......................TX

SANTIKOS THEATRES
Bijou at Crossroads......................San Antonio.......................TX
Embassy 14 ....San Antonio.......................TX
Galaxy 14 ....San Antonio.......................TX
Mayan Palace 14..........................San Antonio.......................TX
Mission 4 Drive-In ....San Antonio.......................TX
Northwest 10 ....San Antonio.......................TX
Silverado 16 ....San Antonio.......................TX
Westlakes 9 ....San Antonio.......................TX

WEST PALM BEACH/FT. PIERCE

AMC ENTERTAINMENT
Indian River 24.............................Vero Beach ....FL

CROWN THEATRES

Crown Abacoa ....Jupiter ....FL

MUVICO THEATRES

Palace 20....................................Boca Raton.........................FL
Parisian 20..................................W. Palm Beach ....FL

NOVA CINEMAS

Nova Cinemas at Sabal Palm.......Ft. Pierce ....FL

REGAL ENTERTAINMENT GROUP

Shadowood 16 ....Boca Raton........................FL
Boynton 8 Cinema.......................Boynton Beach ....FL
Movies @ Boynton Beach 9.........Boynton Beach ....FL
Delray Beach 18 ....Del Ray Beach....................FL
Treasure Coast Mall Stadium 16 ...Jenson Beach....................FL
Jupiter Stadium 18 ....Jupiter ....FL
Royal Palm Beach Stadium 18 .....Royal Palm Beach...............FL
Movies @ Okee Square 8 ....West Palm Beach ....FL

BIRMINGHAM (ANNISTON & TUSCALOOSA)

AMSTAR ENTERTAINMENT

Stadium 12 ....Oxford ....AL

CARMIKE CINEMAS

Carmike ....Birmingham ....AL
Carmike Summit ....Birmingham ....AL
Carmike Wynnsong ....Birmingham ....AL
Carmike Town Sq. ....Cullman ....AL
Carmike Martin ....Talladega............................AL

COBB THEATRES

Movies 4 ....Jasper ....AL

REGAL ENTERTAINMENT GROUP

Brook Highland Stadium 10...........Birmingham ....AL
Festival Stadium 18......................Birmingham ....AL
Galleria 10 ....Birmingham ....AL
Trussville Stadium 16...................Birmingham ....AL
Wildwood Stadium 14 Cinemas.....Birmingham ....AL

NORFOLK/PORTSMOUTH/NEWPORT NEWS

AMC ENTERTAINMENT

Hampton Towne Center 24 ....Hampton.............................VA
Lynnhaven 8 ....Virginia Beach ....VA

CARMIKE CINEMAS

Carmike Williamsburg X'ing..........Williamsburg......................VA

CINEMARK USA

Movies 10 ....Chesapeake ....VA
Cinemark at Military Circle ....Norfolk...............................VA

CONSOLIDATED THEATRES

Harbour View Grande...................Suffolk ....VA

REGAL ENTERTAINMENT GROUP

Greenbrier Cinema 13..................Chesapeake ....VA
Riverdale Plaza Stadium 12 ....Hampton.............................VA
Kiln Creek Cinema Stadium 20 .....Newport News ....VA
Macarthur Center Stadium 18 ....Norfolk...............................VA
Main Gate 10 ....Norfolk...............................VA
Columbus 12................................Virginia Beach ....VA
Pembroke Cinema 8.....................Virginia Beach ....VA
Strawbridge Mktplace Stadium 12 .Virginia Beach ....VA

NEW ORLEANS

AMC ENTERTAINMENT

Hammond Palace 10.....................Hammond...........................LA
Elmwood Palace 20......................Harahan ....LA
Westbank Palace 16.....................Harvey ....LA
Houma Palace 10.........................Houma...............................LA
Clearview Palace 12.....................Metairie ....LA

CARMIKE CINEMAS

Carmike North Shores..................Slidell ....LA

LANDMARK THEATRES

Canal Place Cinema ....New Orleans.......................LA

O'NEIL THEATRES

Holiday Square Cinema 10............Covington ....LA
Causeway Place Cinema 4...........Mandeville ....LA
Movies 8 Slidell...........................Slidell ....LA
River Ridge Cinema 4 ....Picayune............................MS
Choctaw Cinema 4.......................Waveland...........................MS

MEMPHIS

CARMIKE CINEMAS

Carmike ....Dyersburg ....TN

MALCO THEATRES

Trio ....Blytheville..........................AR
DeSoto Cinema 16.......................Southaven ....MS
Stage Cinema 12 ....Bartlett ....TN
Collierville Towne Cinema 16........Bartlett ....TN
Cordova 16 ....Cordova.............................TN
Trinity Commons ....Cordova.............................TN
Forest Hill ....Germantown ....TN
Bartlett Cinema 10......................Memphis............................TN
Highland Quartet.........................Memphis............................TN
Majestic Theatre ....Memphis............................TN
Paradiso......................................Memphis............................TN
Raleigh Springs Cinema 12..........Memphis............................TN
Ridgeway 4 ....Memphis............................TN
Studio on the Square ....Memphis............................TN
Summer Drive-In ....Memphis............................TN
Winchester Court Cinema ....Memphis............................TN
Wolfchase Galleria ....Memphis............................TN

MUVICO THEATRES

Peabody Place 22 ....Memphis............................TN

REGAL ENTERTAINMENT GROUP

Cine 4 - Oxford Mall....................Oxford ....MS

BUFFALO

AMC ENTERTAINMENT

Maple Ridge 8.............................Amherst ....NY
University Mall 8 ....Amherst ....NY
McKinley Mall 6...........................Buffalo ....NY
Walden Galleria 12 ....Cheektowaga ....NY

CARMIKE CINEMAS

Carmike ....Olean.................................NY

DIPSON THEATRES

Mall 1 & 2 ....Batavia ....NY
Amherst Theatre ....Buffalo ....NY
North Park Theatre.......................Buffalo ....NY
Market Arcade Film & Arts Centre.Buffalo ....NY
Lakewood Cinema 6.....................Lakewood...........................NY
Chautauqua Mall 2.......................Lakewood...........................NY
Eastern Hills Cinema ....Williamsville ....NY
Warren Mall Cinemas ....Warren ....PA

MINI THEATRES

Movieplex....................................Dunkirk ....NY

REGAL ENTERTAINMENT GROUP

Elmwood Regal Center 16............Buffalo ....NY
Hollywood Stadium 12..................Niagara Falls......................NY
Quaker Crossing Stadium 18 ....Orchard Park......................NY
Transit Cntr Stadium 18 Plus Imax Williamsville ....NY

OKLAHOMA CITY

AMC ENTERTAINMENT

Quail Springs Mall 24...................Oklahoma City ....OK

B & B THEATRES

Airline Drive-In ....Ponca City ....OK
Ponca Plaza Twin ....Ponca City ....OK

CARMIKE CINEMAS

Carmike Dunkin Theatre...............Cushing ....OK
Carmike Video ....Enid ....OK
Carmike North Park ....Ponca City ....OK
Carmike Cinema Center ....Shawnee............................OK
Carmike Hornbeck ....Shawnee............................OK
Carmike ....Stillwater ....OK

CINEMARK USA

Tinseltown 20..............................Oklahoma City ....OK
Crossroads Movies 8 ....Oklahoma City ....OK

DICKINSON THEATRES

Oakwood Mall Theatre ....Enid ....OK
Penn Square 10 ....Oklahoma City ....OK

REGAL ENTERTAINMENT GROUP

Crossroads Mall Stadium 16 ....Oklahoma City ....OK
Windsor Hills Cinema 10...............Oklahoma City ....OK

WALLACE THEATRE

Heritage Plaza 5 ....Midwest City ....OK
Spotlight 14.................................Norman ....OK
Brixton Square 8 ....Oklahoma City ....OK
Movies 6 ....Shawnee............................OK

GREENSBORO/HIGH POINT/WINSTON SALEM

CARMIKE CINEMAS

Carmike Kingsway........................Eden..................................NC
Carmike ....Greensboro........................NC

Carmike	High Point	NC
Carmike Cinema	Lexington	NC
Carmike	Winston-Salem	NC
Carmike Wynnsong	Winston-Salem	NC

CINEMARK USA

Brassfield Cinema	Greensboro	NC

CONSOLIDATED THEATRES

The Grande	Greensboro	NC

REGAL ENTERTAINMENT GROUP

Oak Hollow Mall 7	High Point	NC
Mayberry Cinema 5	Mount Airy	NC

PROVIDENCE/NEW BEDFORD

AMC ENTERTAINMENT

N. Dartmouth Mall 12	N. Dartmouth	MA

ENTERTAINMENT CINEMAS

Triboro 14	Attleboro Falls	MA
Fall River 8	Fall River	MA
Swansea 12	Swansea	MA
Holiday 8	Middletown	RI
Opera House 3	Newport	RI

FLAGSHIP CINEMAS

Flagship Cinema New Bedford	New Bedford	MA

MINI THEATRES

Bijou	Fairhaven	MA
Empire	Block Island	RI
Pier	Narragansett	RI

NATIONAL AMUSEMENTS

Showcase Cinemas N. Attleboro	N. Attleboro	MA
Showcase Cinmeas Seekonk 1-10	Seekonk	MA
Showcase Seekonk Route 6	Seekonk	MA
Apple Valley Cinemas	Greenville	RI
Showcase Cinemas Warwick	Warwick	RI
Showcase Cinemas Warwick Mall	Warwick	RI

PATRIOT CINEMAS

Patriot Cinemas, E. Providence 10	E. Providence	RI

ALBUQUERQUE/SANTA FE

ALLEN THEATRES

Fiesta Twin	Cortez	CO
Cinema 5	Alamogordo	NM
Cinema 3	Carlsbad	NM
Allen 8	Farmington	NM
Animas 4 Theatres	Farmington	NM
Apache Drive-In	Farmington	NM
Cameo	Farmington	NM
Centennial Twin	Farmington	NM
Aztec 5	Gallup	NM
Red Rock 6	Gallup	NM
Rio West Twin	Gallup	NM
Broadmoor	Hobbs	NM
Cinema 3	Hobbs	NM
Cinema 4	Roswell	NM
Del Norte Twin	Roswell	NM
Park Twin	Roswell	NM

CARMIKE CINEMAS

Carmike Cinema	Artesia	NM

CENTURY THEATRES

Century 14 Downtown	Albuquerque	NM
Century Rio 24	Albuquerque	NM

CINEMARK USA

Movies 8	Albuquerque	NM
Movies West	Albuquerque	NM

REGAL ENTERTAINMENT GROUP

Coronado Theatre 6	Albuquerque	NM
Cottonwood Theatre Stadium 10	Albuquerque	NM
Four Hills Theatre 10	Albuquerque	NM
High Ridge Theatre 8	Albuquerque	NM
Winrock VI	Albuquerque	NM
Devargas Mall Cinema 6	Santa Fe	NM
UA North 6	Santa Fe	NM
UA South 6	Santa Fe	NM

TRANS LUX

High Five Cinemas	Durango	CO
Gaslight Cinemas	Durango	CO
Lux Dream Catcher Cinema	Espanola	NM
Starlight Cinema	Los Lunas	NM
Jean Cocteau Cinema	Santa Fe	NM
Loma Theatre	Socorro	NM
Storyteller Cinemas	Taos	NM

LOUISVILLE

ALLIANCE ENTERTAINMENT

Madison Great Escape	Madison	IN
Seymour Great Escape	Seymour	IN
Oldham Great Escape	LaGrange	KY

CINEMARK USA

Greentree	Clarksville	IN
Greentree	Clarksville	IN
Tinseltown	Louisville	KY

NATIONAL AMUSEMENTS

River Falls Cinemas	Clarksville	IN
Showcase Stonybrook	Louisville	KY
Showcase Cinemas Louisville	Louisville	KY
Kenwood Drive-In	Louisville	KY

JACKSONVILLE/BRUNSWICK

AMC ENTERTAINMENT

Regency 24	Jacksonville	FL
Orange Park 24	Orange Park	FL

CARMIKE CINEMAS

Carmike Amelia Island	Fernandina Beach	FL

CINEMARK USA

Tinseltown USA	Jacksonville	FL

GEORGIA THEATRE COMPANY II

Movies @ Glynn Place 11	Brunswick	GA
Kings Bay Cinemas 9	St Marys	GA
Island Cinemas 7	St Simons	GA
Mall Cinemas 7	Waycross	GA

REGAL ENTERTAINMENT GROUP

Avenues Stadium 20	Jacksonville	FL
Beach Boulevard Stadium 18	Jacksonville	FL
Cinema 90 6	Lake City	FL
Mall St Augustine 6	St Augustine	FL
North Point Market 8	Alpharetta	GA

STARNET CINEMAS

Jax 10 Cinemas	Jacksonville	FL
Mandarin Corners	Jacksonville	FL
Pabio Theatres	Jacksonville Beach	FL
Palatka Mall Cinemas	Palatka	FL

LAS VEGAS

BRENDEN THEATRES

Las Vegas 14	Las Vegas	NV

CENTURY THEATRES

Cinedome 12	Henderson	NV
Las Vegas Drive-In	Las Vegas	NV
Century 18 Sam's Town	Las Vegas	NV
Century Stadium 16 Rch Santa Fe	Las Vegas	NV
Century 16 Suncoast	Las Vegas	NV
Century Orleans 12	Las Vegas	NV

CROWN THEATRES

Crown Neonopolis	Las Vegas	NV

REGAL ENTERTAINMENT GROUP

Green Valley Cinemas 8	Henderson	NV
Green Valley Ranch Stadium 10	Henderson	NV
Sunset Station Stadium 13 Theatre	Henderson	NV
Boulder Station 11 Theatre	Las Vegas	NV
Colonnade Stadium 14	Las Vegas	NV
Rainbow Promenade 10	Las Vegas	NV
Showcase Theatre 8	Las Vegas	NV
Texas Station Stadium 18	Las Vegas	NV
Village Square Stadium 18	Las Vegas	NV

WESTATES THEATRES

Virgin River Cinema 4	Mesquite	NV

INDEPENDENT THEATRES

The following listing includes U.S. theatres with three or less locations under the same ownership. For exhibitors with four or more theatre locations, please see Circuit Theatres.

Name	Address	City	State	Zip	Phone	Screens

ALABAMA

Name	Address	City	State	Zip	Phone	Screens
Playhouse Cinema 3	1236 Cherokee Rd.	Alexander City	AL	35010-3917	256-234-2509	3
Clark 3 Theatres	109 O'Neal Court	Andalusia	AL	36420	334-222-4761	3
Cinemagic Drive-In Theatre	1702 S. Jefferson St.	Athens	AL	35611	256-233-0402	1
Alabama Theatre	1817 Third Avenue North	Birmingham	AL	35203	205-251-0418	1
McWane Center IMAX	205 19th Street north	Birmingham	AL	35203	205-714-8300	1
Sand Mountain Twin Drive-In	10480 US Highway 431	Boaz	AL	35956-3120	256-593-5599	2
Davis Northside Cinema I	3489 Ross Clark Circle	Dothan	AL	36303	334-793-4999	6
Cinemas I and II	600 US Hwy. 84 Bypass	Enterprise	AL	36330	334-347-3931	
Cinemas III and IV	627 US Hwy 84 Bypass	Enterprise	AL	36330	334-347-3811	2
College Cinema	College Plaza Shopping Center	Enterprise	AL	36330	334-347-4911	3
Starcoast Cinemas-Riviera 12	110 Riviera Blvd.	Foley	AL	36535	251-971-1144	12
Hamilton Theaters	2718 Gault Ave. N.	Fort Payne	AL	35967	256-845-5518	4
Colonial Mall Cinemas	1001 Rainbow Drive	Gadsden	AL	35901	256-547-2660	3
Rainbow Cinema 8	948 Rainbow Dr.	Gadsden	AL	35902	256-546-8812	8
Theatre of Gadsden	310 N. 27th. Street	Gadsden	Al.	35904	256-547-7469	1
Blue Moon Drive-In	4690 US Highway 43	Guin	AL	35563	205-468-8046	1
Dixie Cinema 3	225 Bexar Ave. E.	Hamilton	AL	35570	205-921-3430	3
U.S. Space & Rocket IMAX	1 Tranquility Base	Huntsville	AL	35807	256-837-3400	1
Sumter Theatre	116 Franklin Street	Livingston	AL	35470	205-652-4464	1
IMAX Dome Gulf Coast Exploreum	65 Government Street	Mobile	AL	36602	334-208-6873	1
Capri Theatre	1045 E. Fairview Ave.	Montgomery	AL	36106	334-262-4858	1
Clark Twin Cinema	955 E Andrews Ave.	Ozark	AL	36360	334-774-4224	2
Piedmont Drive-In	1260 US Highway 278 W.	Piedmont	AL	36272	256-447-6521	1
Holiday Twin Cinema	1507 E. Willow Street	Scottsboro	AL	35768	256-259-6246	2
Thomasville Theatre	24 W. Front Street S.	Thomasville	AL	36784	334-636-2807	1
Continental Cinema 5	350 Highway 231 N.	Troy	AL	36081	334-808-4225	5

ALASKA

Name	Address	City	State	Zip	Phone	Screens
Alaska Experience Theatre	705 W. 6th Ave, #200.	Anchorage	AK	99501	907-276-3730	1
Bear Tooth Theatre Pub	1230 W 27th Ave.	Anchorage	AK	99503	907-276-4200	1
Movies for Your Mind	121 West 7th Ave.	Anchorage	AK	99501	907-343-6173	1
Valley River 6 Cinemas	11801 Business Blvd.	Eagle River	AK	99577	907-694-5858	6
The Blue Loon	2999 Parks Highway	Fairbanks	AK	99709	907-457-5666	1
Homer Family Theatre	106 W. Main St.	Homer	AK	99603	907-235-6728	1
20th Century Twin Theatre	222 Front St	Juneau	AK	99801	907-586-4055	2
Back Room Restaurant & Cinema	120 2nd Street	Juneau	AK	99801	907-586-4146	1
Glacier Cinema	9091 Cinema Drive	Juneau	AK	99801	907-789-9191	5
Gold Town Nickelodeon	174 S. Franklin St.	Juneau	AK	99801	907-586-2875	1
Ketchikan Coliseum Theatre	405 Mission St.	Ketchikan	AK	99901	907-225-2294	2
Orpheum Theatre	102 Center Street	Kodiak	AK	99615	907-486-5449	2
Mat-Su 3 Cinema	2430 East Parks Highway	Wasilla	AK	99654	907-373-7003	3

ARIZONA

Name	Address	City	State	Zip	Phone	Screens
Mall Cinema 6	1226 E. Florence Blvd.	Casa Grande	AZ	85222	520-836-5969	6
Cottonwood's Big Show	1389 E Highway 89a	Cottonwood	AZ	86326	928-649-1111	1
Douglas Cinema	1111 San Antonio Ave.	Douglas	AZ	85607	520-364-5000	2
Movies at the Mall	4650 N. Highway 89	Flagstaff	AZ	86004	928-526-3770	2
Apache Drive-In	112 S. Broad Street.	Globe	AZ	85501	928-425-4511	1
Globe 2 Theatre	141 N. Broad St.	Globe	AZ	85501	928-425-5581	2
Palm Valley Cinema	1325 N. Litchfield Rd.	Goodyear	AZ	85338	623-535-4000	14
Grand Canyon IMAX Theatre	Highway 64 & 180	Grand Canyon	AZ	86023	520-638-2203	1
Movies Havasu 6	180 Swanson Ave.	Lake Havasu City	AZ	86403	928-453-7900	6
Lakeside Cinema	20 E White Mountain Blvd	Lakeside	AZ	85929	928-367-3456	2
Fountain Morenci Theatre	Morenci Plaza	Morenci	AZ	85540	520-865-4666	1
Mesa Theatre	42 S. Lake Powell Blvd.	Page	AZ	86040	520-645-9565	1
Sawmill Theaters	201 W Main St	Payson	AZ	85541	520-468-7546	6
Arizona Science Center	600 E. Washington St.	Phoenix	AZ	85004	602-716-2000	1
Fountain Cinema Sapphire	1914 W. Thatcher Blvd.	Safford	AZ	85546-3318	928-428-5571	6
Town Square Theatre	1210 W. Cleveland.	Saint Johns	AZ	85936	520-337-4061	1
Farrelli's Cinema Supper Club	14202 N Scottsdale	Scottsdale	AZ	85254	480-905-7200	2
Winchester 2 Theatre	1850 White Mountain Blvd.	Show Low	AZ	85901	928-367-7469	2
R & M Cinema	300 E. Wilcox Dr.	Sierra Vista	AZ	85635	520-458-6511	3
Uptown 3 Theatres	4341 S. State Highway 92	Sierra Vista	AZ	85650	520-378-2858	3
El Rio Theatre	Springerville	Springerville	AZ	85938	928-333-4590	1
Arizona Mills IMAX	5000 Arizona Mills Circle	Tempe	AZ	85283	480-897-7744	1
Tempe Cinemas	1825 E. Elliot Road	Tempe	AZ	85284	480-345-6461	6
Closed - Silver Screen Twin Cinemas	Highway 160 East, Junction 264	Tuba City	AZ	86045	928-283-5255	2
De Anza Drive-In - Tucson	1401 S. Alvernon Way	Tucson	AZ	85711	520-745-2240	4
Loft 2 Cinemas	3233 E. Speedway Blvd.	Tucson	AZ	85716-3933	520-795-7777	2
Saguaro Theatre	176 E. Wickenburg Way	Wickenburg	AZ	85358	928-684-7189	1
Rex Allen Theatre	150 N. Railroad Ave.	Willcox	AZ	85643-2132	520-384-4244	2
Main Street Cinema	111 South Main St.	Yuma	AZ	85364	928-819-0289	8
Mandarin Cinema	3142 S. Arizona Ave.	Yuma	AZ	85364	928-782-7409	4
Plaza 5 Theatres	1560 S 4th Avenue	Yuma	AZ	85364	928-782-9292	5

Name	Address	City	State	Zip	Phone	Screens

ARKANSAS

Name	Address	City	State	Zip	Phone	Screens
Main Theatre	2075 Main St.	Berryville	AR	72616	870-423-2524	1
Savage Theatre	20 N. Broadway Ave.	Booneville	AR	72927	479-675-3756	1
Silver Screen Theatre	100 Cinema Blvd.	Cabot	AR	72023	501-843-7469	4
Clarksville 4	2424 Clark Rd.	Clarksville	AR	72830	479-754-3520	4
Gateway Twin Theatres	Hwy 65 S.	Clinton	AR	72031	501-745-4004	2
Rialto Theatre	113 East Cedar Street	El Dorado	AR	71730	870-881-8771	3
112 Drive-In	3352 N. Highway 112	Fayetteville	AR	72703	501-442-4542	1
Broadway Cinema	1101 E. Broadway St.	Forest City	AR	72335	870-633-5558	2
Lakeland Twin Cinema	Hwy 25 S. and 6th St.	Heber Springs	AR	72543	501-362-7937	2
Behind The Mall 5 Cinema	4501 Central Ave.	Hot Springs	AR	71901	501-525-0883	5
IMAX @ Aerospace Education Center	3301 East Roosevelt Road	Little Rock	AR	72206	501-376-4629	1
Market Street Cinema	1521 Merrill Drive	Little Rock	AR	72211	501-312-8900	5
Cameo Theater	111 N. Jackson Street	Magnolia	AR	71753	870-234-8722	3
Ritz 2 Theatre	213 S. Main St.	Malvern	AR	72104	501-332-2451	2
Silver Screen Twin Theatre	1200 Pine Ave.	Mena	AR	71953	501-394-2959	2
Twinlake Tri Cinema	1606 Highway 62 East	Mountain Home	AR	72653	870-425-3900	3
Paris Cinema	26 W. Walnut St.	Paris	AR	72855	479-963-3184	1
Cinema City Twin	5259 Highway 67 S.	Pocahontas	AR	72455	870-892-8096	2
Cinema 8	2933 E. Race Street	Searcy	AR	72143	501-268-9420	8
Stuttgart Twin Cinema	806 W. 22nd Street, #F	Stuttgart	AR	72160-6504	870-673-4327	2
Maxie Theatre	Hwy 463 S.	Trumann	AR	72472	870-483-5312	1
Wynne Twin Cinema	1915 North Falls Blvd.	Wynne	AR	72396	870-238-7472	2

CALIFORNIA

Name	Address	City	State	Zip	Phone	Screens
Niles Theatre	127 S. Main Street	Alturas	CA	96101	530-233-5454	1
Cinema City Theatres	5635 E. La Palma Ave.	Anaheim	CA	92807	714-970-6700	13
Angels Theatre	1228 S Main Street	Angels Camp	CA	95222	209-736-6768	1
Aptos Twin	122 Rancho Del Mar Center	Aptos	CA	95003	831-688-6541	2
Arcata Theatre	1036 G St.	Arcata	CA	95521	705-822-3456	1
Minor Theatre	1015 H. St.	Arcata	CA	95521	707-822-3456	3
Fair Oaks Theatre	1007 Grand Ave.	Arroyo Grande	CA	93420	805-489-2364	1
Century Cinemas Atascadero	6905 El Camino Real	Atascadero	CA	93422	805-227-2172	7
Foothill Cinema 10	854 E. Alosta	Azusa	CA	91702-2706	626-334-6007	10
Fox Cineplex	60 W. Ramsey St.	Banning	CA	92220	909-849-3277	3
Skyline Drive-In	31175 US Highway 58	Barstow	CA	92311	760-256-3333	1
Elmwood 3	2966 College Ave.	Berkeley	CA	94705	510-649-0530	3
Fine Arts Cinema	2451 Shattuck Ave.	Berkeley	CA	94704	510-848-1143	2
Pacific Film Archive	2575 Bancroft	Berkeley	CA	94720-2250	510-642-1124	1
Village Theatre	40789 Village Dr.	Big Bear Lake	CA	92315	909-866-5115	2
Village Theatres North	602 Pine Knot Ave.	Big Bear Lake	CA	92315	909-866-5115	3
Bishop Twin	237 N. Main St.	Bishop	CA	93514	760-873-3575	2
All Star Cinemas	691 W. Hobsonway	Blythe	CA	92225	760-921-3117	3
Sonoma Cinemas	200 Siesta Way	Boyes Hot Springs	CA	95431	707-935-1234	4
Captain's Family Theatres Brea 5	453 S. Associated Road	Brea	CA	92821	714-808-0400	5
Delta Cinemas	641 1st St.	Brentwood	CA	94513-1322	925-240-7335	2
Parks Plaza	515 McMurray Rd	Buellton	CA	93427	805-688-7434	5
Mt. Burney Theatre	37030 Main Street	Burney	CA	96013	530-335-2605	1
Camera 7	1875 S. Bascom Ave.	Campbell	CA	95008	408-559-6900	7
Plaza 4 Theatres	2501 S. Winchester Blvd.	Campbell	CA	95008	408-378-2425	4
41st Avenue Playhouse	1475 41st Avenue	Capitola	CA	95010	831-479-3504	3
Carpinteria Plaza Theatre	4916 Carpinteria Ave.	Carpinteria	CA	93013	805-684-4014	1
Chabot Cinema	2853 Castro Valley Blvd.	Castro Valley	CA	94546-5505	510-582-2555	1
Desert IMAX Theatre	68-510 E. Palm Canyon Drive	Cathedral City	CA	92234	760-324-7333	1
Mary Pickford Stadium 14	36850 Civic Center Dr.	Cathedral City	CA	92234	760-328-7100	14
Pageant Theatre	351 E. 6th Street	Chico	CA	95928	530-343-0663	1
Vogue	226 3rd Ave	Chula Vista	CA	91915	619-425-1436	1
Clearlake Twin	15050 Olympic Dr	Clearlake	CA	95422	707-994-7469	2
Clover Cinemas	121 E. 1st Street	Cloverdale	CA	95425	707-894-7920	4
Coalinga Cinemas	122 W. Elm Ave.	Coalinga	CA	93210	559-935-1517	2
Colfax Theatre	49 S. Main Street	Colfax	CA	95713	530-346-8424	1
Colusa Theatre	513 Market Street	Colusa	CA	95932	530-458-8588	1
Brenden Concord 14	1985 Willow Pass Rd.	Concord	CA	94520	925-677-0450	14
Rodger's Theatre	1217 Solano St.	Corning	CA	96021	530-824-1773	1
Red's Showcase Twin Cinemas	369 G Street	Crescent City	CA	95531	707-464-1245	2
Family Twin Cinema	9823 Walker St.	Cypress	CA	90630	714-828-1660	2
Old Town Music Hall	140 Richmond St.	El Segundo	CA	90245	310-322-2592	1
La Paloma	471 S. Coast Highway	Encinitas	CA	92024-3530	760-436-7469	1
Broadway Cinema 8	1223 Broadway St.	Eureka	CA	95501	707-443-1979	8
Movies Bayshore Mall	3300 Broadway	Eureka	CA	95501	707-443-6771	6
Sunrise Drive-In	8149 Greenback Lane	Fair Oaks	CA	95628	916-725-5555	1
Fall River	43118 Hwy 299 East	Fall River Mills	CA	96028	530-336-5030	1
Fillmore Towne Theatre	338 Central Ave.	Fillmore	CA	93015	805-524-3456	1
Coast Cinemas	167 S. Franklin Street	Fort Bragg	CA	95437	707-964-2019	4
Fortuna Theatre	1241 Main Street	Fortuna	CA	95540	707-725-2121	6
Naz 8 Gateway	39160 Paseo Padre Parkway	Fremont	CA	94538	510-797-2000	7
NAZ Cinema	37411 Fremont Blvd.	Fremont	CA	94536-3704	510-797-2000	1
Garberville Theatre	766 Redwood Street	Garberville	CA	95542	707-923-3580	1
Four Star Cinema	12111 Valley View St.	Garden Grove	CA	92845	714-934-6377	4
Gardena Cinema	14948 Crenshaw Blvd.	Gardena	CA	90248	310-217-0505	1
Platinum Theatres	353 E 10th Street	Gilroy	CA	95020	408-846-6843	7
Glendale Cinemas	501 N. Orange.	Glendale	CA	91203	818-549-9950	5
Sierra Cinemas	840 E. Main Street	Grass Valley	CA	95945	530-477-9000	4
Sutton Cinemas	11399 Sutton Way	Grass Valley	CA	95945	530-477-9000	2
Metro 4 Cinemas	123 E. 7th Street	Hanford	CA	93230	559-584-1577	4
Raven Theatre and Film Center	115 North Street	Healdsburg	CA	95448-3805	707-433-5448	5
Granada Discount Theatre	336 5th Street	Hollister	CA	95023	831-637-3116	1

Name	Address	City	State	Zip	Phone	Screens
Premiere Cinemas 5	581-A Mc Cray Street	Hollister	CA	95023	831-638-1800	5
Egyptian Theatre	6712 Hollywood Blvd.	Hollywood	CA	90028	323-466-3456	1
Silent Movie Theatre	611 N. Fairfax Ave.	Hollywood	CA	90036	323-655-2520	1
Vine Theatre	6321 Hollywood Blvd.	Hollywood	CA	90028-6302	323-463-6819	1
Vista	4473 Sunset Blvd.	Hollywood	CA	90020	323-660-6639	1
California Theatre	6528 Pacific Blvd.	Huntington Park	CA	90255	323-581-0777	3
Metropolitan Park Twin	6504 Pacific Blvd.	Huntington Park	CA	90255-4106	323-587-3872	2
Rustic Theatre	54290 N. Circle Drive	Idyllwild	CA	92549	909-659-2747	1
Motor Vu Twin Drive-In	385 W. Aten Rd.	Imperial	CA	92251	760-352-4385	2
Captain's Family Theatres						
A Woodbridge 5	4626 Barranca Parkway	Irvine	CA	92604	949-552-7469	5
King City Cinemas	200 Broadway Street	King City	CA	93930	831-385-9100	4
Lakeport Auto Movies	52 Soda Bay Road	Lakeport	CA	95453	707-263-5011	1
Lakeport Cinema 5	52 Soda Bay Road	Lakeport	CA	95453	707-263-4215	5
Vine Twin Theatre	1722 1st Street	Livermore	CA	94550	925-447-2545	2
Lodi Stadium 12 Cinemas	109 N. School Street	Lodi	CA	95240	209-339-1900	12
Movies Gemini	1028 N. H Street	Lompoc	CA	93436	805-736-1306	2
Movies Of Lompoc	220 W Barton	Lompoc	CA	93436	805-736-1558	4
Art Theatre	2025 E. 4th St.	Long Beach	CA	90814-1001	562-438-5435	1
California Science Center Imax	700 State Drive	Los Angeles	CA	90037	213-744-7400	1
CineSpace	6356 Hollywood	Los Angeles	CA	90028	323-817-3456	1
Flagship University Village 3	3323 S. Hoover St.	Los Angeles	CA	90007-3557	213-748-6321	3
Highland 3 Theatre	5604 Figueroa St.	Los Angeles	CA	90042	323-256-6383	3
Los Angeles County Museum of Art	5905 Wilshire Blvd.	Los Angeles	CA	90036	323-857-6000	1
Los Feliz 3	1822 N. Vermont Ave.	Los Angeles	CA	90027-4213	323-664-2169	3
Majestic Crest Theatre	1262 Westwood Blvd.	Los Angeles	CA	90024-4801	310-474-7866	1
Metropolitan Campus	1020 N. Vermont Ave.	Los Angeles	CA	90029-2620	323-665-5882	2
New Beverly Cinema	7165 Beverly Blvd.	Los Angeles	CA	90036	323-938-4038	1
UCLA Film and TV Archive	1409 Melnitz Hall.	Los Angeles	CA	90095-1622	310-206-8422	1
Los Banos Cinemas	San Luis Plaza	Los Banos	CA	93635	209-826-7469	6
Los Gatos	41 North Santa Cruz Ave.	Los Gatos	CA	95030	408-395-0203	2
Madera 6 Cinema	1140 N Gateway Drive.	Madera	CA	93637	559-661-9121	6
Minaret Cinemas	437 Old Mammoth Road	Mammoth Lakes	CA	93546	760-934-3131	2
Plaza Theatre	569 Old Mammoth Road	Mammoth Lakes	CA	93546	760-934-3131	1
Marketplace Stadium 10	1321 West Yosemite Avenue	Manteca	CA	95336	209-239-3456	10
Contra Costa Cinemas 5	555 Center Avenue	Martinez	CA	94553	925-228-9980	5
Marysville Drive-In Theatre	5575 Chestnut Road	Marysville	CA	95901	530-743-2342	2
Cinema Saver 10	577 E Calaveras Blvd	Milpitas	CA	95035	408-942-7883	10
Brenden Theatres 18	1021 10th Street	Modesto	CA	95354	209-491-7770	18
State Theatre	1307 J Street	Modesto	CA	95354	209-527-4697	1
Mission Drive-In Montclair	10798 Ramona Ave.	Montclair	CA	91763	909-628-0511	1
Rio Theatre	20396 Bohemian Highway	Monte Rio	CA	95462	707-865-0913	1
Mavericks Cinema 3	543 W. Los Angeles Ave	Moorpark	CA	93021	805-552-9154	3
Rheem Theatre	350 Park St.	Moraga	CA	94556	925-988-3411	4
Bay Theatre - Morro Bay	464 Morro Bay Blvd.	Morro Bay	CA	93442	805-772-2444	2
Magic Theatre Nevada City	107 Argall Way	Nevada City	CA	95959	530-265-8262	1
Nevada Theatre	401 Broad Street.	Nevada City	CA	95959	530-265-3456	1
Plaza Theatre	23710 Lyons Ave.	Newhall	CA	91321		1
Met Cinemas	4001 Highway 49.	Oakhurst	CA	93644	559-683-1234	5
Chabot Space & Science Center	10000 Skyline Blvd	Oakland	CA	94619	510-336-7300	1
Paramount	2025 Broadway	Oakland	CA	94612	510-465-6400	1
Parkway Theater	1834 Park Blvd.	Oakland	CA	94606	510-814-2400	2
Ojai Playhouse	145 E. Ojai Ave.	Ojai	CA	93023	805-646-1011	1
Ultrascreen Theatre	1 Mill Circle.	Ontario	CA	91764	909-481-4442	1
A Captain Bloods Village Theatre	1140 N. Tustin Ave.	Orange	CA	92867	714-808-0400	2
Feather River Cinema	2690 Feather River Blvd	Oroville	CA	95965	530-534-1885	6
Channel Islands Cinemas	101 W. Gonzales Road	Oxnard	CA	93030	805-485-0820	5
Spangenberg Theatre	780 Arastradero Road	Palo Alto	CA	94306-3827	650-354-8263	1
Stanford Theatre	221 University Ave.	Palo Alto	CA	94301	650-324-3700	1
Paradise Cinema 7	6701 Clark Rd.	Paradise	CA	95969	530-872-7800	7
Bianchi Paramount 11	7770 E. Rosecrans Ave.	Paramount	CA	90723	562-630-7469	11
Academy 6 Theater	1003 E. Colorado Blvd.	Pasadena	CA	91106	626-229-9400	6
Oakcreek Cinemas	1920 D Creston Road	Paso Robles	CA	93446	805-227-2172	3
Park Cinemas Paso Robles	1100 Pine Street	Paso Robles	CA	93446	805-227-2172	6
Brenden 16 Theatre	4085 Century Blvd.	Pittsburg	CA	94565	925-706-1222	16
Arena Theatre	245 Main Street.	Point Arena	CA	95468	707-882-3456	1
Town Hall Theatre	469 W. Main Street	Quincy	CA	95971	530-283-1140	1
Riverside Plaza	400 S Main Street	Red Bluff	CA	96080	530-529-5491	6
Redondo Beach Cinema 3	1509 Hawthorne	Redondo Beach	CA	90278	310-371-4567	3
Fox Theatre	2215 Broadway	Redwood City	CA	94063	650-369-4119	1
Ridgecrest Cinema	1631 North Triangle Drive	Ridgecrest	CA	93555	760-446-7771	5
Marketplace 6	4040 Vine St.	Riverside	CA	92507	909-682-4040	6
Rubidoux Drive-In	3770 Opal St., Rubidoux	Riverside	CA	92509	909-683-4455	1
Towne Centre Cinema	5225 Canyon Crest Drive.	Riverside	CA	92507	909-788-4445	5
Van Buren Drive-In	3035 Van Buren Blvd.	Riverside	CA	92503	909-688-2360	3
Crest Theatre	1013 K. St.	Sacramento	CA	95814	916-442-7378	2
Esquire IMAX Theatre	1211 K Street	Sacramento	CA	95814	916-443-4629	1
Sterling Cinema 6	2373 N. Sterling Ave.	San Bernardino	CA	92404	909-425-8888	6
Reuben H. Fleet Science Center	1875 El Prado	San Diego	CA	92101	619-238-1233	1
South Bay Drive-In	2170 Coronado Avenue	San Diego	CA	92154	619-423-2727	3
4 Star	2200 Clement St	San Francisco	CA	94121	415-666-3488	3
Alliance Francaise	1345 Bush Street	San Francisco	CA	94109	415-775-7755	1
Balboa Twin	38th & Balboa	San Francisco	CA	94121	415-221-8184	2
Campus All-Male Theatre	220 Jones St.	San Francisco	CA	94102	415-673-3384	1
Castro Theatre	429 Castro St.	San Francisco	CA	94114	415-621-6120	1
Citibank Cinemax	39 Pier	San Francisco	CA	94133	415-956-3456	1
Foreign Cinema	2534 Mission Street.	San Francisco	CA	94110	415-648-7600	1
Sony Metreon Action Theatre	101 Fourth Street	San Francisco	CA	94103	415-307-8491	1
Tearoom Male.	145 Eddy St.	San Francisco	CA	94102	415-885-9887	1
The Red Vic Theatre	1727 Haight	San Francisco	CA	94117	415-668-3994	1

Name	Address	City	State	Zip	Phone	Screens
The Roxie Theatre	3117 16th At Valencia	San Francisco	CA	94103	415-863-1087	1
Victoria Theatre	2961 16th Street	San Francisco	CA	94103	415-863-7576	2
Almaden Cinema Five	2306 Almaden Road	San Jose	CA	95125	408-265-7373	5
Camera 3	288 South Second Street	San Jose	CA	95113	408-998-3300	3
Camera One	366 South First Street	San Jose	CA	95113	408-998-3300	1
Cine 16 at the Agenda Lounge	399 S. First Street	San Jose	CA	95113	408-287-3991	1
Hackworth IMAX Dome	201 South Market Street	San Jose	CA	95113	408-294-8324	2
Towne 3	1433 The Alameda	San Jose	CA	95126	408-287-1433	3
Bringing About Love Theatre	14808 East 14th Street	San Leandro	CA	94578	510-895-8300	1
Palm Theatre 2	817 Palm Street	San Luis Obispo	CA	93401	805-541-5161	2
Sunset Drive-In	255 Elks Lane	San Luis Obispo	CA	93401	805-544-4475	1
Warner Grand Theatre	478 W. Sixth Street	San Pedro	CA	90731	310-548-7672	1
Rafael	1118 Fourth St	San Rafael	CA	94901	415-454-1222	3
Captain's Family Theatres						
A Mainplace 6	2800 N. Main St	Santa Ana	CA	92701	714-808-0400	6
Metropolitan Fiesta Twin	305 E. 4th St	Santa Ana	CA	92701	714-541-4351	2
IMAX Pictorium	2401 Agnew Road	Santa Clara	CA	95054	408-988-1776	1
Del Mar Theatre	1124 Pacific Ave	Santa Cruz	CA	95060-4415	831-426-7500	3
Nickelodeon 4 Theatres	210 Lincoln Street	Santa Cruz	CA	95060	831-426-7500	4
Rio Theatre	1205 Soquel Ave	Santa Cruz	CA	95062	831-423-8209	1
Skyview Drive-In	2260 Soquel Dr	Santa Cruz	CA	95073	831-475-3405	2
Hiway Drive-In	3170 Santa Maria Way	Santa Maria	CA	93455	805-937-3515	1
Airport Cinema 8	409 Aviaiton Way	Santa Rosa	CA	95403	707-522-0330	8
Rialto Cinemas Lakeside	551 Summerfield Rd	Santa Rosa	CA	95405	707-525-4840	6
Roxy Stadium 14	85 Santa Rosa Ave	Santa Rosa	CA	95404	707-522-0330	14
Santee Drive-In	10990 Woodside Ave	Santee	CA	92071-2833	619-448-7447	2
Scotts Valley 6 Cinemas	226 Mount Hermon Road	Scotts Valley	CA	95066	831-438-3260	6
Bay Theatre	340 Main St	Seal Beach	CA	90740	562-431-9988	1
Sebastopol Cinema 9	6868 McKinley St	Sebastopol	CA	95472	707-829-3456	9
Selma Cinema	2705 Mitchell Ave	Selma	CA	93662	209-891-2000	6
Sebastiani Theatre	476 1st St. East	Sonoma	CA	95476	707-996-2020	1
Cameo Cinema	1340 Main St	St. Helena	CA	94574	707-963-3946	1
Sierra Theatre	819 Main St	Susanville	CA	96130	530-257-7469	1
Uptown Cinemas	501 Main St	Susanville	CA	96130	530-257-7469	1
Fox Theatre - Taft	514 Center St	Taft	CA	93304	661-763-1436	3
Cobblestone Cinema Tahoe City	475 N. Lake Boulevard	Tahoe City	CA	96145	530-546-5951	2
Hitching Post Theatre	201 S. Green St	Tehachapi	CA	93561	661-823-7469	4
Temecula Discount Cinema	26463 Ynez Road	Temecula	CA	92591	909-296-9728	6
Martis Village Theatre	Highway 267	Truckee	CA	96161	530-546-5951	2
Smith's Ranch Drive-In	4584 Adobe Road	Twentynine Palms	CA	92277	760-367-7713	1
Universal City IMAX	100 Universal City Plaza	Universal City	CA	91608		1
Brenden Vacaville 16	531 Davis Street	Vacaville	CA	95688	707-469-0180	16
Mooney Drive-In	26672 South Mooney Blvd	Visalia	CA	93291	559-733-0380	2
Fox Theatre	15 Maple St	Watsonville	CA	95076	831-724-1220	3
Green Valley Cinema 6	1125 S Green Valley Road	Watsonville	CA	95076	831-761-8200	6
Trinity Theatre	310 Main	Weaverville	CA	96093	530-623-3555	1
Santa Fe Springs Plaza	13469 Telegraph Road	Whittier	CA	90605	562-903-1910	3
Whittier Village Stadium Cinemas	7038 Greenleaf Ave	Whittier	CA	90602	562-907-3300	8
Noyo Theatre 3	57 E. Commercial Street	Willits	CA	95490	707-459-0280	3
Opus	236 W Sycamore St	Willows	CA	95988	530-934-2959	4
Empire Theatre	6742 Wofford Heights Blvd	Wofford Heights	CA	93285	760-376-3030	1
Woodland State Cinema 3	322 Main Street	Woodland	CA	95695	530-666-3444	3
Sutter Theatre	754 Plumas St	Yuba City	CA	95991	530-673-4297	3
Cinema 6	56401 29 Palms Hwy	Yucca Valley	CA	92284	760-365-9633	4

COLORADO

Name	Address	City	State	Zip	Phone	Screens
Ski Hi 5	7089 W Highway 60	Alamosa	CO	81101	719-589-4471	5
Aurora Plaza 8 Cinemas	777 Peoria St	Aurora	CO	80011	303-364-0726	8
Buckingham Mall Cinema	1390 South Havana	Aurora	CO	80012	303-306-0948	4
Cinema Grill	13682 E. Alameda Ave	Aurora	CO	80013	303-344-3456	3
Boulder Outdoor Cinema	1750 13th Street	Boulder	CO	80302-6226	303-447-9308	1
Boulder Public Library	1000 Canyon Blvd	Boulder	CO	80302	303-441-3197	1
Boulder Theatre	2034 14th St	Boulder	CO	80302	303-786-7030	1
Sands Theatre	211 Clayton St	Brush	CO	80723-2103	970-842-2466	1
Crystal Theatre	427 Main Street	Carbondale	CO	81623	970-963-0633	1
Movieland Cinemas	218 East Valley Rd, Ste 300	Carbondale	CO	81623	970-920-1300	5
Wells Theatre	170 E 1st S	Cheyenne Wells	CO	80810	719-767-5423	1
Kimballs Twin Peak Theatres	115 E. Pikes Peak Ave	Colorado Springs	CO	80903	719-447-1945	2
88 Drive-In Theatre	East 88th Ave. And Rosemary St	Commerce City	CO	80022	303-287-7717	1
Allen Fiesta Theatre	21 W. Main Street	Cortez	CO	81321	970-565-7380	2
West 2 Theatres	29 E. Victory Way	Craig	CO	81625	970-824-2000	2
Majestic 3 Theatres	507 Red Lady Avenue	Crested Butte	CO	81224	970-349-7570	3
Egyptian Theatre	452 Main Street	Delta	CO	81416-1825	970-874-9770	1
Tru Vu Drive-In	1001 Highway 92	Delta	CO	81416	970-874-9556	1
Denver Museum of Nature & Science IMAX	2001 Colorado Boulevard	Denver	CO	80205	303-322-7009	1
Madstone Theaters	7777 E. Hampden Ave	Denver	CO	80231	303-752-3200	6
Rock Island	1614 15th Street	Denver	CO	80202	303-572-7625	1
Starz FilmCenter at the Tivoli	900 Auraria Parkway	Denver	CO	80204	303-893-3456	12
Tiffany Plaza 6	7400 E Hampden Ave	Denver	CO	80231	303-221-1645	6
Rocket Drive-In	26126 Highway 160	Durango	CO	81301	970-247-0833	1
Riverwalk Theatre	34253 US Highway 6	Edwards	CO	81632	970-476-5661	4
Stanley Village 3 Theatres	543 Big Thompson Ave	Estes Park	CO	80517-9651	970-586-4227	3
Holiday Twin Drive-In	2206 S. Overland Trail	Fort Collins	CO	80522	970-221-1244	2
Cover Theatre	314 Main St	Ft. Morgan	CO	80701-2109	970-867-2311	2
Flick Twin Theatres	909 N. Wisconsin	Gunnison	CO	81230	970-349-7570	2
Peerless Movies	212 S Inter Ocean Ave	Holyoke	CO	80734	970-854-3545	1
Lamar Theatre	219 S. Main Street	Lamar	CO	81052	719-336-5737	1
Lincoln Theatre	245 E Ave	Limon	CO	80828	715-775-2114	1

Name	Address	City	State	Zip	Phone	Screens
Elvis Cinemas	6014 S. Kipling	Littleton	CO.	80127	303-948-5555	6
Star Drive-In	2830 US Highway 160	Monte Vista	CO.	81144-9357	719-852-2613	1
Vali Theatre	139 Adams St.	Monte Vista	CO.	81144	970-852-2811	3
Red Rocks Amphitheatre		Morrison	CO.	80465		1
Liberty Theatre	418 N. Pagosa Blvd.	Pagosa Springs	CO.	81147	970-264-4578	1
Paradise Theatre	215 Grand Ave.	Paonia	CO.	81428	970-527-6610	1
Wildlife Experience Iwerks Theater	10035 S. Peoria St.	Parker	CO.	80134	720-488-3300	1
Grand Theatre	405 S Main St.	Rocky Ford	CO.	81067	719-254-6006	1
Storyville Cinema	135 West First Street	Salida	CO.	81201	719-539-7002	1
Cinderella City Drive-In	3400 S. Platte River Dr.	Sheridan	CO.	80236	303-761-8232	2
Capitol Theatre	149 E 9th Ave	Springfield	CO.	81073	719-523-4161	1
Fox 4	313 Poplar St	Sterling	CO.	80751	970-522-1719	4
Starlight Drive-In	16653 Hwy 14	Sterling	CO.	80751	970-522-0211	1
Fox Theatre	423 W. Main St	Trinidad	CO.	81082	719-846-2851	1
Movie Picture Show House	3600 E. Main St.	Trinidad	CO.	81082	719-846-0552	1
Cascade Village Theater	1310 Westhaven Dr.	Vail	CO.	81657	970-476-5661	2
Silver Screen Cinema	Winter Park	Winter Park	CO.	80482	970-726-5390	1
Cliff Theatre	420 Main St.	Wray	CO.	80758-1725	970-332-4337	1

CONNECTICUT

Name	Address	City	State	Zip	Phone	Screens
Bantam Cinema	115 Bantam Lake Road	Bantam	CT	06750	860-567-0006	2
Bethel Cinema	269 Greenwood Ave.	Bethel	CT	06801	203-778-2100	4
Forestville Theatres	815 Pine Street	Bristol	CT	06010	860-583-1223	8
Gallery Cinemas	396 Old Hartford Road	Colchester	CT	06415	860-537-6407	6
Darien Playhouse	1077 Post Rd.	Darien	CT	06820	206-655-7656	2
Community Theatre Foundation	1424 Post Road	Fairfield	CT	06430	203-255-6255	2
Art Cinema	255 Franklin St	Hartford	CT	06114	860-296-1134	2
Atheneum Cinema	600 Main Street	Hartford	CT	06103	860-278-2670	1
Cine Studio Theatre	300 Summit Street	Hartford	CT	06106	860-297-2463	1
Real Art Ways Theatre	56 Arbor Street	Hartford	CT	06106	860-232-1006	1
Madison Art Cinemas	761 Boston Post Road	Madison	CT	06443	203-245-3456	2
Mansfield Drive-In	228 Stafford Rd.	Mansfield	CT	06250	860-423-4441	3
Holiday Meriden 10 Cinemas	61 Pomeroy Ave	Meriden	CT	06450	203-238-4710	10
Cine 1-2-3-4	371 Middletown Ave	New Haven	CT	06513	203-776-5546	4
York Square Cinema 3	55 Broadway	New Haven	CT	06511	203-776-6630	3
Bank Street Theatre	46 Bank Street	New Milford	CT	06776	860-354-2122	2
Edmond Town Hall Theatre	45 Main Street	Newtown	CT	06470-2134	203-426-2475	1
Niantic Cinema	279 Main Street	Niantic	CT	06357	860-739-6929	4
IMAX Maritime Aquarium Norwalk	10 North Water Street	Norwalk	CT	06854	203-866-9202	1
Norwich Cinemas	109 Salem Trnpk.	Norwich	CT	06360	860-886-6843	2
Southington Twin Drive-In	935 Meriden Waterbury Tpk.	Plantsville	CT	06479	860-628-2205	2
Pleasant Valley Drive-In	47 E. River Rd.	Pleasant Valley	CT	06063	860-379-6102	1
Strand Theatre	165 Main Street	Seymour	CT	06483	203-881-5025	1
Cinerom Digital Movieplex Torrington	89 Farley Place	Torrington	CT	06790	860-489-4111	6
Holiday Cinemas 10	117 Sharon Rd.	Waterbury	CT	06702	203-597-1756	10
Country Cinema	523 Main Street	Watertown	CT	06795	860-274-2193	1
Forest Theatre	2 Forest Rd.	West Haven	CT	06513	203-934-0370	1
Cinerom Digital Movieplex	380 New Hartford Road	Winsted	CT	06098	860-738-6501	9
Gilson Theatre	354 Main Street	Winsted	CT	06098	203-379-5108	2

DISTRICT OF COLUMBIA

Name	Address	City	State	Zip	Phone	Screens
American Film Institute	2700 F Street	Washington	DC	20566	202-785-4600	1
National Gallery of Art	3rd Street & Constitution	Washington	DC	20565	202-737-4215	1
Samuel C. Johnson IMAX @ Smithsonian NMNH	10th & Constitution Ave, NW	Washington	DC	20560	202-633-7400	1
Samuel Langley IMAX @ Smithsonian NASM	6th & Independence Ave SW	Washington	DC	20560	202-357-1686	2
Studio Theatre	1333 P Street NW	Washington	DC	20005	202-332-3300	1
The Avalon Theatre	5612 Connecticut Ave. NW	Washington	DC	20015	202-966-6000	2
Visions Cinema & Bistro Lounge	1927 Florida Ave. NW	Washington	DC	20009-1266	202-667-0090	2

DELAWARE

Name	Address	City	State	Zip	Phone	Screens
Clayton Theatre	900 Main St.	Dagsboro	DE	19939	302-732-3744	1
Diamond State Drive-In	9758 S. Du Pont Hwy.	Felton	DE	19943-5613	302-284-8307	1
Everett Theatre	47 W. Main Street	Middletown	DE	19709	302-378-7038	1
F & G Cinema Art House	401 Newark Shopping Center	Newark	DE	19711	302-737-4905	1
F & G Cinema Center 3	401 Newark Shopping Center	Newark	DE	19711	302-737-3720	3
Midway Movies, Rehoboth	29 Midway Shopping Center	Rehoboth Beach	DE	19971-9801	302-645-0200	14
Theatre N at Nemours	11th & Tatnall Streets	Wilmington	DE	19801	302-658-6070	1

FLORIDA

Name	Address	City	State	Zip	Phone	Screens
Altamonte Cinema	8303 E. Altamonte Drive	Altamonte Springs	FL	32701	407-332-1093	8
Arcadia Twin	1340 E Oak Street	Arcadia	FL	34266	863-494-6876	2
Atlantic Theatre	751 Atlantic Blvd	Atlantic Beach	FL	32233	904-246-2030	8
Boynton Cinema	9764 S. Military Trl.	Boynton Beach	FL	33436	561-366-7500	8
Clearwater Cinema Cafe	24095 U.S. Highway 19 North	Clearwater	FL	33763	727-799-3531	2
Main Street Cinemas	27928 US 19N	Clearwater	FL	33761	727-725-0394	6
Clewiston Theatre	100 East Sugarland Highway	Clewiston	FL	33440	863-983-6494	1
Absinthe House Cinematheque	235 Alcazar Ave.	Coral Gables	FL	33134	305-446-7144	1
Bill Cosford Cinema	University of Miami - Memorial Bldg.	Coral Gables	FL	33146	305-284-4861	1
Crestview III Theatre	789 N. Ferdon Blvd.	Crestview	FL	32536	850-682-3201	3
Joylan Drive-In	16414 US Hwy. 301 North	Dade City	FL	33525	352-567-5085	1

Name	Address	City	State	Zip	Phone	Screens
Ruskin Drive-In	5011 US Highway 41 N. in Ruskin	Dade City	FL	33572	813-645-1455	1
N & S Cinema 6	331 Bill France Blvd.	Daytona Beach	FL	32114	386-323-9807	6
Deerfield Cinema 5	2205 W. Hillsboro Blvd.	Deerfield Beach	FL	33442	954-725-4402	5
Delray Square Cinemas	4809 W. Atlantic Ave.	Delray Beach	FL	33445	561-499-9022	5
Movies of Delray	7421 W. Atlantic Ave.	Delray Beach	FL	33446	561-638-0020	5
Blockbuster IMAX	401 SW Second St.	Fort Lauderdale	FL	33312	954-463-4629	1
Cinema Paradiso	503 SE Sixth St.	Fort Lauderdale	FL	33301	954-525-3456	1
Swap Shop Drive-In	3291 W. Sunrise Blvd.	Fort Lauderdale	FL	33311	954-583-7733	11
Northside Drive-In	2521 N. Tamiami Trail	Fort Myers	FL	33903	239-995-2254	1
Suds N Cinema Picture Show	174 S.E. Miracle Strip Pkwy.	Fort Walton Beach	FL	32548	850-244-2484	1
Ft. Myers Beach Theater	6425 Estero Blvd.	Ft. Myers Beach	FL	33931	941-765-9000	4
Hippodrome State Theatre	25 SE 2nd Place Street	Gainesville	FL	32601-6596	352-375-4477	1
Reitz Union Cinema - U of Fl	University of Florida	Gainesville	FL	32611	352-392-1649	2
Clay Theatre	326 Walnut Street	Green Cove Springs	FL	32043-3442	904-284-9012	2
BMC-Greenacres Riverbridge 8	6846 Forest Hills Blvd.	Greenacres	FL	33413	561-304-0015	8
Gulf Breeze Theatre	1175 Gulf Breeze Pkwy	Gulf Breeze	FL	32561	850-934-3435	4
Flipper's Hollywood Cinema 10	7001 Taft St.	Hollywood	FL	33024	954-981-5443	12
Playtime 3 Drive-In	6300 Blanding Rd.	Jacksonville	FL	32244-2816	904-771-2300	3
San Marco Theatre	1996 San Marco Blvd.	Jacksonville	FL	32207	904-396-4845	1
IMAX Theatre 1 & 2	Mail Code:DNPS	Kennedy Space Ctr.	FL	32899	321-452-2121	2
Rialto Villages Town Square	1105 Alonzo Ave	Lady Lake	FL	32159	352-753-8898	8
Lake Worth Drive-In	3438 Lake Worth Rd.	Lake Worth	FL	33461	561-965-4518	1
Movies of Lake Worth	7380 Lake Worth Rd.	Lake Worth	FL	33460	561-968-4545	6
Lakeland Square 10 Cinema	3606 US Highway 98.	Lakeland	FL	33809	863-853-3622	10
Polk Theatre	127 S Florida Ave	Lakeland	FL	33801	863-682-8227	1
Silver Moon Drive-In Theatre	4100 US Highway 92.	Lakeland	FL	33801	941-682-0849	2
Lehigh Cinema	1201 Taylor Lane Ext.	Lehigh Acres	FL	33936	239-339-9955	4
Enzian Cinema Cafe	1300 S. Orlando Ave.	Maitland	FL	32751	407-629-0054	1
Marathon Community Theatre	5101 Overseas Hwy.	Marathon	FL	33050	305-743-0288	1
Marco Movies 4	599 S. COLLIER BLVD.	Marco Island	FL	34145	941-642-1111	4
Premiere Theaters Oaks 10	1800 W. Hibiscus Blvd.	Melbourne	FL	32901	321-953-3200	10
Le Jeune Cinema 6	782 NW Le Jeune Rd.	Miami	FL	33126	305-529-8883	6
Valentino Super Discount	8524 SW Eighth St.	Miami	FL	33144	305-266-2002	3
IFP /Miami at the Shores						
Performing Arts Theater	9806 N.E. Second Ave.	Miami Shores	FL	33139	305-751-0562	1
Naples Drive-In Twin Theatre	7700 E. Davis Blvd.	Naples	FL	34104	941-774-6661	2
Twin Cities Cinema	1047 John Sims Pkwy E	Niceville	FL	32578	850-678-3815	2
California Club 6	850 Ives Dairy Rd.	North Miami Beach	FL	33179	305-249-2345	6
Ocala Drive-In	4850 S. Pine Ave.	Ocala	FL	34480	352-629-1325	1
West Orange 5	1575 Maguire Road	Ocoee	FL	34761	407-877-8111	5
Brahman Theaters 3	1610 S. Parrott Ave.	Okeechobee	FL	34974	863-763-7202	3
Orlando Science Center CineDome	777 E. Princeton St.	Orlando	FL	32803	407-514-2044	1
Sand Lake 7	835 Sand Lake Rd.	Orlando	FL	32809	407-855-6220	7
Universal Studios Florida	1000 Universal Studios Plaza	Orlando	FL	32819	407-363-8000	2
Hollywood Movie Theatre	201 Big Lots Plaza	Palatka	FL	32177	386-329-4009	2
BMC-PGA Cinema 6	4075 PGA Blvd.	Palm Beach Gardens	FL	33410	561-776-4000	6
BMC-Promenade East	9930 Alternate A1A	Palm Beach Gardens	FL	33410	561-624-2664	1
Palm City Cinemas	3150 S.W. Martin Downs Blvd.	Palm City	FL	34990	772-287-7328	4
Picture Show 3	229 St. Joe Plaza Drive	Palm Coast	FL	32164	386-446-6414	3
IMAX Naval Aviation						
Memorial Theater	1750 Radford Ave.	Pensacola	FL	32508	888-627-4629	1
Pensacola Silver Screen	7280 Plantation Rd	Pensacola	FL	32504	850-476-4545	5
Island Cinema	535 Tarpon Bay Road	Sanibel	FL	33957	941-472-1701	2
Burns Court Cinema	506 Burns Lane.	Sarasota	FL	34236	941-955-3456	3
Satellite Beach Cinemas	1044 B. Highway A1A	Satellite Beach	FL	32937	321-777-3778	4
IMAX Theatre at Sunset Place	5701 Sunset Dr.	South Miami	FL	33143	305-663-4629	1
Pot Belly's Cinema Plus	36 Granada Street.	St. Augustine	FL	32084	904-829-3101	3
World Golf Village IMAX	1 World Golf Place	St. Augustine	FL	32092	904-940-4123	1
St. Cloud Theater	1110 10th St.	St. Cloud	FL	34769	407-943-2660	1
Beach Theatre	315 Corey Ave	St. Pete Beach	FL	33706	727-360-6697	1
Florida Twin	101 W. Call St.	Starke	FL	32091	904-964-5451	2
BMC-Regency Square 8	2448 Southeast Federal Hwy	Stuart	FL	34994-4531	772-219-8805	8
Weston 8 Cinemas	1338 SW 160th Ave.	Sunrise	FL	33326	954-385-5858	8
Challenger Learning Center Ima	200 South Duval Street	Tallahassee	FL	32301	850-645-7796	1
Tamarac Cinema 5	10036 W. McNab Rd.	Tamarac	FL	33321	954-726-3500	5
Funlan Drive-In	2302 E. Hillsborough Ave.	Tampa	FL	33610	813-234-2311	3
IMAX Dome at MOSI	4801 E. Fowler Ave.	Tampa	FL	33617	813-987-6100	1
Tampa Pitcher Show	14416 N. Dale Mabry Hwy.	Tampa	FL	33624	813-963-0578	1
Tampa Theatre	711 Franklin St.	Tampa	FL	33602	813-274-8981	1
Tavernier Towne Cinemas	91298 Overseas Hwy.	Tavernier	FL	33070	305-853-7003	5
Maxi's Family Cinema	300 N. Washington Ave.	Titusville	FL	32796	321-269-7552	1
Reel World Wellington Cinema 8	13881 Wellington Trace	Wellington	FL	33414	561-792-4448	8
Silver Screen Cinema Cafe	12795 Forest Hill Blvd.	Wellington	FL	33414	561-793-6657	2
Metro Cinema Cafe	3020 W. New Haven Ave	West Melbourne	FL	32904	321-727-0170	1
Carefree Theatre	2000 S. Dixie Hwy.	West Palm Beach	FL	33401	561-833-7305	1
Aloma Cinema Grill	2155 Aloma Ave.	Winter Park	FL	32792	407-678-8214	2
Park Theatres	501 N. Orlando Ave.	Winter Park	FL	32789	407-644-6000	11
Home Twin Theatre	38521 5th Ave.	Zephyrhills	FL	33540	813-782-8282	2
Zephyrhills Cinema 6	6848 Gall Blvd	Zephyrhills	FL	33541	813-782-2222	6

GEORGIA

Name	Address	City	State	Zip	Phone	Screens
Alps Cinema	191 Alps Road	Athens	GA	30606	706-548-5256	2
Athens-Clarke County Library	2025 Baxter St.	Athens	GA	30606-6331		1
Flicker Theatre and Bar	263 W. Washington	Athens	GA	30601-2754	706-546-0039	1
Georgia Museum of Art	90 Carlton	Athens	GA	30602-1502	706-542-4662	1
Georgia Square 5 Cinemas	3710 Atlanta Highway	Athens	GA	30606	706-548-3426	5
Georgia Theatre	215 Lumpkin Street	Athens	GA	30601-2741	706-549-9918	1
University of Georgia Tate Stu	Baxter St. & Lumpkin St.	Athens	GA	30601	706-583-0200	1

Name	Address	City	State	Zip	Phone	Screens
Cinefest Theatre	66 Courtland Ave.	Atlanta	GA	30303	404-651-2463	1
High Museum of Art	1280 Peachtree Street	Atlanta	GA	30309	404-733-4570	2
Rankin M. Smith IMAX @ Fernbank Museum	767 Clifton Road N.E.	Atlanta	GA	30307	404-370-0019	1
Starlight Drive-In Theatre	2000 Moreland Ave.	Atlanta	GA	30316	404-627-5786	6
Bald Mountain Cinema 3	1650 Backyard Lane	Blairsville	GA	30512	706-745-8222	3
Blue Ridge Twin Theatres	10091 Blue Ridge Dr.	Blue Ridge	GA	30513	706-632-7202	2
Swan Drive-In.	651 Summit St.	Blue Ridge	GA	30513	706-632-5235	1
Zebulon Theatre	209 N. Broad St.	Cairo	GA	31728-2108	229-377-3302	1
Plaza Triple.	P.O. Box 391	Columbus	GA	31907	706-563-3738	3
MNM Movies 400	415 Atlanta Highway	Cumming	GA	30040	678-513-4400	12
Plaza Cinema	Merchants Dr. & Macland Rd.	Dallas	GA	30132	770-445-8888	1
Highway 17 Theatres	2395 Bowman Highway	Dewy Rose	GA	30634	706-213-7693	3
Gwinnett Place 12	2161 Merchants Way	Duluth	GA	30096	678-417-0199	12
Venture Cinema	3750 Venture Dr.	Duluth	GA	30096	678-957-9545	12
East Town Twin Cinema	240 Maddox Dr	Ellijay	GA	30540	706-635-5700	2
Westside Cinemas	403-E US Hwy. 80 West.	Garden City	GA	31405	912-966-9101	2
Jesup Drive-In Theatre	3686 Savannah Highway	Jesup	GA	31545	912-427-7716	2
Strand Cinema Twin	169 W. Cherry St.	Jesup	GA	31545	912-427-8024	2
Spotlight Covington Square 8	2244 Panola Road.	Lithonia	GA	30058	770-593-2600	8
Pal Theatre	134 W Broad St.	Louisville	GA	30434	478-625-9998	1
Marietta Star Cinema	1355 Roswell Road	Marietta	GA	30062-3667	770-971-3131	3
Merchants Walk Cinema	1301 Johnsons Ferry Road	Marietta	GA	30068	678-560-1111	8
Galaxy Cinema @ Green's Corner	4975 Jimmy Carter Blvd.	Norcross	GA	30093	770-931-3456	5
Peachtree Cinema 8	6135 Peachtree Parkway	Norcross	GA	30092	770-448-7002	8
Riverdale Cinemas 14.	274 Hwy 138.	Riverdale	GA	30274	770-473-9674	14
Movies at Berry Square	2820 Martha Berry Hwy. N.E.	Rome	GA	30165-8631	706-235-7799	6
Rome Cinemas.	2535 Shorter Ave.	Rome	GA	30161	706-235-4444	7
Village Theatres	836 Turner McCall Boulevard	Rome	GA	30161	706-235-7799	4
StarTime Roswell Town Center	608 Holcomb Bridge Road.	Roswell	GA	30076-1591	770-993-5411	10
Pastime Theatre	118 S. Harris St.	Sandersville	GA	31082	478-553-0807	1
Bollywood Cinema	5241 Memorial Drive	Stone Mountain	GA	30083	404-292-5277	2
Ritz Theatre	114 S. Church St.	Thomaston	GA	30286	706-647-7022	2
Thomson Twin Cinema	131 Main St.	Thomson	GA	30824	706-595-7317	2
Toccoa Triple Cinema	S. Highway 17	Toccoa	GA	30577	706-886-7346	3
New Pal Theatre	122 Church St.	Vidalia	GA	30475	912-537-3229	1
Sweet Onion Cinema 5	2709 E. First St.	Vidalia	GA	30474	912-537-0789	5

HAWAII

Name	Address	City	State	Zip	Phone	Screens
Honokaa Peoples Theatre	Mamane Street	Honokaa	HI	96727	808-775-0000	1
The Hawaii Experience Domed	824 Front Street	Lahaina	HI	96761	808-661-8314	1
IMAX Polynesia	55-370 Kamehameha Highway	Laie	HI	96762	808-293-3280	1
Waimea Theatre	PO Box 903	Waimea	HI	96796	808-338-2082	1

IOWA

Name	Address	City	State	Zip	Phone	Screens
Lyric Theatre	431 E. Main Street.	Belmond	IA	50421	515-444-7225	1
Majestic Theatre	100 N. 13th St.	Centerville	IA	52544-1706	641-856-6255	2
Charles Theatre	409 N. Main St.	Charles City	IA	50616	515-228-3821	1
Lake Theatre Clear Lake	4 N. 4th St.	Clear Lake	IA	50428	515-357-2414	1
Clinton Cinema 4	214 6th Ave. S.	Clinton	IA	52732-4306	563-242-9315	4
Omni 4 Theatres	300 W. Broadway.	Council Bluffs	IA	51503	712-325-6633	4
Cinema 4 Crawford County	309 Chamberlin Dr.	Denison	IA	51442-2803	712-263-8777	4
Donna Reed Theatre	1303 Broadway	Denison	IA	51442	712-263-3742	1
Merle Hay Mall Cinema.	3800 Merle Hay Road	Des Moines	IA	50310	515-252-0804	1
The Fleur Cinema and Cafe	4545 Fleur Ave.	Des Moines	IA	50306	515-287-4545	4
Varsity Theatre Des Moines	1207 25th Street	Des Moines	IA	50311	515-277-0404	1
Operahouse Theatre Dewitt.	716 6th Ave.	Dewitt	IA	52742	563-659-8213	1
Grand Theatre	1148 Edgington Avenue	Eldora	IA	50627	641-939-3522	1
Co-Ed Theater	119 West Broadway Street.	Fairfield	IA	52556	515-472-3707	2
Forest Theatre	215 N. Clark	Forest City	IA	50436	641-585-2790	1
Windsor Theatre	103 N. Federal St.	Hampton	IA	50441	515-456-4389	1
Harlan 4.	621 Court	Harlan	IA	51537	712-755-2310	4
Bijou	152 Iowa Memorial Union	Iowa City	IA	52240	319-335-3258	1
Royal Twin	33 SW Central Ave.	Le Mars	IA	51031	712-546-4026	2
South Central Iowa Theatre.	208 N. Main St.	Leon	IA	50144	641-446-7800	1
61 Drive-In Maquoketa	Highway 61 South	Maquoketa	IA	52060	563-674-4367	1
Bijou Theater	123 2nd Street SW	Mt. Vernon	IA	52314	319-895-6165	2
Great Lakes Cinema 7	1698 Exchange St.	Okoboji	IA	51355	712-332-7553	7
Grand Theatre	238 Public Square.	Orient	IA	50858	641-743-2182	1
Watts Theatre	714 Main Street.	Osage	IA	50461	515-732-4904	1
Lyric Theatre Osceola.	118 S. Fillmore Street	Osceola	IA	50213	641-342-3004	1
Rialto	324 N. Main St.	Pocahontas	IA	50574		1
Story Theatres	512 Broad St.	Story City	IA	50248	515-733-4318	1
Max Twin	338 9th St.	Sibley	IA	51249	712-754-2672	2
Palace Theatre	210 W. 4th St.	Vinton	IA	52349	319-472-9892	1
Waverly Palace Theatre	90 E. Bremer Ave.	Waverly	IA	50677	319-352-1318	3
Billy Joes Pitcher Show.	1701 25th Street	West Des Moines	IA	50266	515-224-1709	1
New Strand Theatre	111 East 3rd Street	West Liberty.	IA	52776	319-627-2014	1
Iowa Theatre	121 John Wayne Drive.	Winterset	IA	50273	515-462-2979	1

Name	Address	City	State	Zip	Phone	Screens

IDAHO

Name	Address	City	State	Zip	Phone	Screens
Egyptian Theatre	700 Main St.	Boise	ID	83701	208-345-1441	1
Northgate Reel Theatre	6950 W. State Street	BOISE	ID	83703	208-377-2620	6
Overland Park 1-2-3	7051 Overland Rd.	Boise	ID	83709	208-377-3072	3
Burley Century Cinema 5	464 East 5 North	Burley	ID	83318	208-678-7142	5
Linden 3	2312 E Linden St	Caldwell	ID	83605	208-454-8687	3
Spud Too Theatre	190 N Main St.	Driggs	ID	83422	208-354-2727	1
Blue Fox	116 W. Main St.	Grangeville	ID	83530	208-983-1370	10
Liberty Theatre	110 N. Main	Hailey	ID	83333-8410	208-788-3300	1
Coeur d'Alene Discount Cinemas	300 Central	Hayden Lake	ID	83835	208-762-7469	6
Center Theatre	461 Park Avenue	Idaho Falls	ID	83401	208-525-3340	3
Paramount Theatre	2085 Niagara St.	Idaho Falls	ID	83404	208-523-1142	1
Rena Theatre	310 N. Division	Kellogg	ID	83837	208-784-7101	2
Ski Time Cinema	100 E. 2nd St.	Ketchum	ID	83340	208-726-8247	2
Kenworthy 1	508 S Main	Moscow	ID	83843	208-883-3812	1
Take One Cinema	650 West 8 South	Mountain Home	ID	83647	208-587-5338	2
Frontier Cinema	210 S 12th Ave	Nampa	ID	83651	208-467-7469	1
Karcher Reel Theatre	1509 Caldwell Blvd.	Nampa	ID	83651	208-377-2620	2
Parma Motor Vu	29522 Hwy 95	Parma	ID	83660	208-454-8687	6
Cinema 4 West	401 Oak Street	Sandpoint	ID	83864	208-263-5811	4
Sandpoint Cinema	401 Oak St.	Sandpoint	ID	83864	425-488-9318	2

ILLINOIS

Name	Address	City	State	Zip	Phone	Screens
Arlington Theatre	53 South Evergreen	Arlington Heights	IL	60005	847-483-0123	6
Fox Valley Theatre	4001 Fox Valley Center Dr.	Aurora	IL	60504	630-898-8950	2
Hi-Lite 30 Drive-In	34 W. 160 Montgomery Rd.	Aurora	IL	60538	630-898-5888	2
Catlow Theatre	116 W. Main Street	Barrington	IL	60010	847-381-0777	1
Bac Skyview 2 Drive-In	5700 N Belt W.	Belleville	IL	62223	618-233-4400	2
Lincoln Theatre	103 E Main St.	Belleville	IL	62220	618-233-0123	1
Old Red Barn 2	305 N. Hard Rd.	Benld	IL	62009	217-835-2213	2
Bensenville 2 Theater	9 S. Center St.	Bensenville	IL	60106	630-860-7774	2
The Castle Theater	209 E. Washington St.	Bloomington	IL	61701	309-829-4647	1
Marvel Theatre	228 West Main Street	Carlinville	IL	62626	217-854-8016	2
New Art Theatre	126 W. Church Street	Champaign	IL	61820	217-351-7368	1
3 Penny Theatre Chicago	2424 N. Lincoln Avenue	Chicago	IL	60614	773-525-3449	2
Brew & View	3145 N. Sheffield	Chicago	IL	60657	312-618-8439	2
Davis Theatre	4614 N. Lincoln Avenue	Chicago	IL	60625	773-784-0893	4
Doc Films	1212 E. 59th Street	Chicago	IL	60637-1604	773-702-8575	1
Facets Cinematheque	1517 W. Fullerton Ave.	Chicago	IL	60614	773-281-4114	1
Gene Siskel Film Center	164 State Street	Chicago	IL	60601	312-846-2800	1
Henry Crown MSI OMNIMAX	5700 S. Lake Shore Dr.	Chicago	IL	60637	773-684-1414	1
I.C.E. Chatham 14	210 87th Street	CHICAGO	IL	60620	773-783-8711	14
Logan Theatre	2646 N Milwaukee Ave	Chicago	IL	60647	773-252-0628	4
Music Box	3733 N. Southport	Chicago	IL	60613	773-871-6604	2
Navy Pier Imax 1	600 East Grand Ave Ste 115	CHICAGO	IL	60611	312-595-5629	1
Town Theatre	1029 North Second Street	Chillicothe	IL	61523	309-274-3545	2
Avon Theatre	805 W. North St.	Decatur	IL	62522	217-422-8151	1
Midway Drive-In Theatre	Prairiville Rd.	Dixon	IL	61021	815-625-4099	1
Plaza Cinemas 3	1315 N Galena Ave	Dixon	IL	61021	800-852-6802	3
Heart Theatre	133 Jefferson Ave	Effingham	IL	62401	217-342-6161	1
Geneseo Central Theatre	111 N. State Street	Geneseo	IL	61254	309-944-3603	1
Glen Ellyn Art Theatre	540 Crescent Blvd.	Glen Ellyn	IL	60137	630-415-1976	4
Globe Theatre	105 N. 3rd St.	Greenville	IL	62246-1034	618-664-4400	3
Highland Park Theatre	445 Central Avenue	Highland Park	IL	60035	847-458-5050	4
Lorraine	324 E Main Street	Hoopeston	IL	60942	217-283-5311	2
La Grange Theatres	80 S LaGrange Road	LaGrange	IL	60525	708-354-0460	4
Skyview Drive-In	Route 66 North	Litchfield	IL	62056	217-324-4451	2
State Theatre	153 W. Elm St.	Nashville	IL	62263	618-327-8714	1
Fairview Drive-In	16045 E. State Hwy. 33	Newton	IL	62448	618-455-3100	1
Normal Theatre	209 W. North St.	Normal	IL	61761-2533	309-454-9722	1
Arcadia Theatre	238 E. Main Street	Olney	IL	62450	618-393-7777	3
Onarga Theatre	101 W Seminary Ave	Onarga	IL	60955	815-268-9862	1
Roxy Cinema	827 La Salle St.	Ottawa	IL	61350	815-433-8303	6
Roseland Theatre	507 West 3rd St.	Pana	IL	62557	217-562-5141	1
Park Forest Cinemas	116 Centre	Park Forest	IL	60466-2032	708-503-0707	5
Pickwick Theatre	5 S. Prospect Ave.	Park Ridge	IL	60068	847-604-2234	4
Crescent Cinemas	313 W. Madison St.	Pontiac	IL	61764	815-844-3030	2
Hub Triplex Theatres	416 Lincoln Highway	Rochelle	IL	61068	815-562-6424	3
Storefront Cinema	711 N. Main Street	Rockford	IL	61103	815-962-3456	1
Princess Theatre	116 E. Lafayette	Rushville	IL	62681	217-322-2722	1
WoW 7 Cinema	101 Duvick Ave.	Sandwich	IL	60548	815-786-1999	7
Times Theatres	222 Main St.	Savanna	IL	61074	800-542-2594	2
Skokie Theatre	7924 Lincoln Ave.	Skokie	IL	60076	847-673-4214	1
Arcada Theatre	105 E. Main St.	St. Charles	IL	60174	630-845-8900	1
Sycamore Theatre	420 W. State Street	Sycamore	IL	60178	815-895-3549	3
Cicero Drive-In	23500 S. Cicero	University Park	IL	60449	708-712-7469	2
Liberty Theatre	210 S. 4th St.	Vandalia	IL	62471	618-283-1953	1
Twin Cinemas	17 N. Main St.	Villa Grove	IL	61956	217-832-5300	2
Princess Theatre	213 West Walnut	Watseka	IL	60970-1260	815-432-4461	1
Cascade Drive-In	28 W. 741 N. Ave.	West Chicago	IL	60185	630-231-3150	1
Wilmette Theatre	1122 Central Ave.	Wilmette	IL	60091	847-251-7411	2
Hollywood Blvd.	1001 W. 75th Street	Woodridge	IL	60517	630-427-1880	5
Countryside Cinema 1 & 2	550 Countryside Drive	Yorkville	IL	60560	630-553-5021	2

Name	Address	City	State	Zip	Phone	Screens

INDIANA

Name	Address	City	State	Zip	Phone	Screens
Alex Theatre	407 N. Harrison St.	Alexandria	IN	46001	765-724-2292	1
Strand Theatre	51 1/2 Public Square	Angola	IN	46703	219-665-7169	1
Devon Theatre	107 W Mill St.	Attica	IN	47918	765-762-3403	1
Northway Cinemas 1 & 2	500 N. North St.	Auburn	IN	46706		2
Gibson Theatre	107 N. Main	Batesville	IN	47006	812-934-3212	1
Great Escape 7	3215 S Shawnee Dr	Bedford	IN	47421	812-275-8844	7
Ryder Film Series	117 E. 3rd St.	Bloomington	IN	47401	812-339-2002	1
Starlite Drive-In	7630 S. Old State Road 37	Bloomington	IN	47403	812-824-8036	1
Walnut Theatre	24 S. Walnut	Brazil	IN	47834	812-442-0652	1
Brookville Theatre	16 W 5th St.	Brookville	IN	47012	765-647-4421	1
Corydon Cinemas	2025 Edsel Lane NW.	Corydon	IN	47112	812-738-1864	4
Crown Theatre	19 N. Court St.	Crown Point	IN	46307	219-663-1616	1
Showplace Cinema East	1801 Morgan Center Drive.	Evansville	IN	47715	812-479-9732	18
Showplace Cinema North	4200 North Third Avenue	Evansville	IN	47708	812-479-9731	9
Showplace Cinema South	950 South Hebron Ave.	Evansville	IN	47714	812-479-9731	7
Cinema Center Fort Wayne	437 E. Berry Street	Fort Wayne	IN	46802	219-426-3456	1
Georgetown Square 1 & 2	6414 East State Blvd.	Fort Wayne	IN	46815	219-748-7678	2
Northwood Cinema Grill	6069 Stellhorn Road	Fort Wayne	IN	46885-5042	219-492-4234	2
Frankfort Cinemas	1557 E. Wabash St.	Frankfort	IN	46041-2744	765-659-2382	2
Artcraft Theatre	57 N. Main	Franklin	IN	46131	317-738-1041	8
Canary Creek Cinemas	870 Mallory Pkwy.	Franklin	IN	46131	317-736-6611	8
Auburn Garrett Drive-In	1014 State Road 8	Garrett	IN	46738		1
Silver Screen Cinema	111 S. Randolph St.	Garrett	IN	46738	219-357-3345	1
Ridge Plaza Cinemas	5900 W. Ridge Road	Gary	IN	46408	219-923-9100	2
Georgetown Drive-In	8200 State Road 64	Georgetown	IN	47122	812-951-2616	2
Linway Plaza Cinema 9	514 West Lincoln Avenue	Goshen	IN	46526	219-534-8728	9
Ashley Square Cinemas	2 Ashley Square	Greencastle	IN	46135	765-653-5374	2
Legacy	2347 West Main Street	Greenfield	IN	46140	317-462-2006	6
Village Cinema 1 and 2	122 W Main Street	Greenfield	IN	46140	317-462-2006	2
Kennedy Theatre	6735 Kennedy Ave	Hammond	IN	46323	219-845-5336	1
Town Theatre	8616 Kennedy Ave.	Highland	IN	46322	219-838-1222	1
Art Theatre	230 Main St.	Hobart	IN	46342	219-942-1670	1
Huntington Drive-In	1291 Condit Street	Huntington	IN	46750	219-356-5445	1
Greenbriar Cinema Grill	1289 W. 86th Street	Indianapolis	IN	46260	317-254-1995	2
Hollywood Bar & Filmworks	247 S Meridian	Indianapolis	IN	46225	317-231-9250	3
IMAX 3D @ White River State Park.	650 W. Washington St.	Indianapolis	IN	46204	317-233-4629	1
IMAX White River State Park.	650 W. Washington St.	Indianapolis	IN	46204	317-233-4629	1
Key Cinemas	4044 S. Keystone Ave.	Indianapolis	IN	46227	317-784-7454	2
Tibbs Drive-In	480 S Tibbs Ave	Indianapolis	IN	46224	317-243-6666	3
Jasper 8	256 Brucke Strasse	Jasper	IN	47546	812-482-9388	8
Melody Drive-In Theatre	7055 S. US Highway 35	Knox	IN	46534-8210	219-772-2042	2
Walnut Theatre	352 Walnut Street	Lawrenceburg	IN	47025	812-537-0460	1
Pavilion Cinemas	1600 N Lebanon	Lebanon	IN	46052	765-483-1400	8
Linton Cinema 3	Linton Shopping Center	Linton	IN	47441	812-847-2180	3
Skyline Drive-In	1353 N State Rd 17.	Logansport	IN	46947	574-753-4648	2
State Cinemas	321 E. Market St.	Logansport	IN	46947	574-753-4648	2
Ohio Theatre	105 E. Main St.	Madison	IN	47250	812-273-4880	2
Showplace Cinema 2	1910 Morton Ave.	Martinsville	IN	46151	765-342-9797	2
Monon Theatre	421 N Market St	Monon	IN	47959	219-253-7030	1
Twin Lake Cinema 1 & 2	107 S Main Street	Monticello	IN	47960	219-583-9466	2
Mooresville Movies 8	300 S. Bridge Crossing	Mooresville	IN	46151	765-342-9999	8
Skyview Drive-In	1126 County Rd 500 S	New Castle	IN	47362	765-987-8630	2
Showplace Newburgh 7	8099 Bell Oaks Dr.	Newburgh	IN	47630	812-853-6843	9
Village West Theatre	119 W. Main Street	Plainfield	IN	46168	317-839-1191	1
Rees Cinema	100 N. Michigan St.	Plymouth	IN	46563-2133	574-936-2738	1
Showland Theatre	2475 N Oak Road	Plymouth	IN	46563	219-935-0552	3
Tri-Way Drive-In	4400 Michigan Road	Plymouth	IN	46563	219-936-7936	2
Ritz Theatre	202 N Meridian St	Portland	IN	47371	219-726-7489	2
Times 2 Theatre	618 Main St.	Rochester	IN	46975	219-223-2721	2
Holiday Drive-In	US Route 231	Rockport	IN	47635	812-649-2857	1
Ritz Theatre	201 W Ohio St.	Rockville	IN	47872	765-569-0628	1
Great Escape 8	357 Tanger Blvd Ste 401	Seymour	IN	47274	812-524-2417	8
Cinema 3	215 S. Harrison St.	Shelbyville	IN	46176	317-398-7318	3
Skyline Drive-In	3986 E. Michigan Rd.	Shelbyville	IN	46176	317-398-6150	1
Pickwick Theatre	108 W. Main St.	Syracuse	IN	46567	219-457-4160	1
Tell City Twin	120 Hwy 66 East.	Tell City	IN	47586	812-547-5217	4
Indiana Theatre	683 Ohio St.	Terre Haute	IN	47807	812-232-8076	1
Meadows Theatre	Meadows Shopping Plaza #1.	Terre Haute	IN	47803	812-232-5536	2
Mel's Back to the 50s Drive-In.	On State Road 39	Thorntown	IN	46071	765-325-2230	1
Diana Theatre	137 E. Jefferson	Tipton	IN	46072	765-675-4300	1
County Seat Plaza	2849 Calumet/Bell Park	Valparaiso	IN	46383	219-548-8788	6
13-24 Drive-In	106 W. Market St.	Wabash	IN	46992	219-563-3272	1
Eagles Theatre	106 W. Market St.	Wabash	IN	46992	219-563-5338	1
North Pointe Cinemas	1410 Mariner Dr.	Warsaw	IN	46580	219-267-1985	6
Hoosier Theatre	1335 119th St.	Whiting	IN	46394	219-659-0567	1
Airline Drive-In	2870 E State Rd 32.	Winchester	IN	47394	765-584-2545	2

KANSAS

Name	Address	City	State	Zip	Phone	Screens
Anthony Theatre	240 West Main Street	Anthony	KS	67003	620-842-5598	1
Burford Cinemas	118 S Summit St.	Arkansas City	KS	67005	620-442-2270	4
Royal Theatre	612 Commercial St.	Atchison	KS	66002	913-367-0222	3
Augusta Theatre	523 State Street	Augusta	KS	67010	316-775-3661	1
Solomon Valley Cinema	1124 North Highway 14	Beloit	KS	67420	785-738-4800	2
Coffeyville Cinema	210 W 10th St.	Coffeyville	KS	67337	620-251-1164	2
Colby Twin & Arcade.	355 N. Franklin	Colby	KS	67701	785-462-2112	2
Derby Plaza Theatre	1300 North Nelson Drive	Derby	KS	67037	316-789-0114	5

Name	Address	City	State	Zip	Phone	Screens
Cinema Circle	106 Kincaid Street	Dodge City	KS	67801	620-225-1431	2
Dodge Theatre	108 Gunsmoke	Dodge City	KS	67801	620-225-4421	1
South Drive-In	1015 McArt Drive	Dodge City	KS	67801	620-225-4301	2
Village 8 Theatre	2601 Central	Dodge City	KS	67801	620-227-7468	8
Star-Vu Drive-In	RR1	El Dorado	KS	67042	316-321-2444	1
Fredonia Cinema	407 North 6th Street	Fredonia	KS	66736	316-378-4355	2
Sherman Theatre	1203 Main St.	Goodland	KS	67735	785-899-6103	1
Arrow Theatre	729 Oregon St.	Hiawatha	KS	66434	785-742-3706	2
Hoxie Theatre	162 S. Queen Ave.	Hoxie	KS	67740	785-675-3923	1
Kansas Cosmosphere IMAX Theatre	1100 North Plum	Hutchinson	KS	67501	316-662-2305	1
Independence Theatres	121 W. Laurel St	Independence	KS	67301		4
Kanopolis Drive-In Theatre	804 N Kansas Ave.	Kanopolis	KS	67454	785-472-4786	1
Boulevard Drive-In	1051 Merriam Lane	Kansas City	KS	66103	913-262-0392	1
State Theatre	617 Broadway Street	Larned	KS	67550	316-285-7477	1
Liberty Hall Cinema	644 Massachussets Street	Lawrence	KS	66044	785-749-1912	1
Landing 4 Theatres	225 Delaware	Leavenworth	KS	66048	913-651-4646	4
Astro	820 Center St.	Marysville	KS	66508	785-562-3715	3
McPherson Cinema	318 North Main Street	Mc Pherson	KS	67460	620-241-3133	4
Newton Palace Show	601 Southeast 36th Street	Newton	KS	67114	316-283-0555	8
Norton Theatre	215 E Main St.	Norton	KS	67654	785-877-2075	2
Palace	101 Center Avenue	Oakley	KS	67748	785-672-3441	1
Midway Drive-In	29591 W. 327th Old Highway	Osawatomie	KS	66064	913-755-2325	1
Plaza Theatre	209 S. Main	Ottawa	KS	66067	785-242-4650	2
Glenwood Arts Theatre	9575 Metcalf Ave.	Overland Park	KS	66212	913-642-4404	1
Rio Theatre	7204 W. 80th St.	Overland Park	KS	66204	913-383-8500	8
Parsons Theatre	210 N. 17th	Parsons	KS	67357	620-421-4240	5
Majestic Theatre	724 4th St.	Phillipsburg	KS	67661	785-543-2724	2
Barron Theaters	313 S. Main	Pratt	KS	67124	620-672-3031	2
Salina Art Center Cinemas	150 S. Santa Fe	Salina	KS	67401	785-452-9868	1
Seneca	301 Main Street	Seneca	KS	66538	785-336-2512	2
13th Avenue Warren	11611 East 13th St.	Wichita	KS	67206	316-652-8756	10
Cinemas West	9035 West Central	Wichita	KS	67212	316-282-4423	4
Palace Theatre West	535 S. Ridge Rd.	Wichita	KS	67209	316-721-7949	8
Premiere Palace	11010 E. Kellogg St.	Wichita	KS	67230	316-721-7949	10
Royale Towne East Square Mall 2	7700 E. Kellog Dr.	Wichita	KS	67207	316-681-2717	2
The Movie Machine	4600 W. Kellog Dr.	Wichita	KS	67209	316-945-0024	5
Warren Theatre	9150 W. 21st St	Wichita	KS	67205	316-721-9545	18
Winfield Cinema	1007 Main Street	Winfield	KS	67156	316-221-4300	3

KENTUCKY

Name	Address	City	State	Zip	Phone	Screens
Bardstown Twin Theatre	Bardstown Plaza Shopping Ctr.	Bardstown	KY	40004	502-348-9755	2
Keystone Cinemas	2725 E. John Rowan Blvd.	Bardstown	KY	40004	502-350-0130	8
Campbellsville Twin Cinema	Elmhurst Plaza	Campbellsville	KY	42718	502-789-1959	2
Green River Cinema 6	730 Campbellsville Blvd.	Campbellsville	KY	42718	270-789-9600	6
Cinema 3 Theatres Central City	105 N. First Street	Central City	KY	42330-1501	270-754-4228	3
Rohs Opera House	39 East Pike Street	Cynthiana	KY	41031	859-234-9803	1
Movie Palace	1231 Woodland Avenue	Elizabethtown	KY	42701	270-769-1505	8
Franklin Drive-In	6250 Nashville Road	Franklin	KY	42134	877-586-1905	1
Mall Cinema - Hartford	US Highway 231 South	Hartford	KY	42347	270-298-3315	2
Fugate's Cinema	197 Entertainment Dr.	Hazard	KY	41701	606-439-4029	5
Hillside Theater	410 Morton Blvd	Hazard	KY	41701	606-436-2148	4
Old Orchard Cinema	1800 Cinema Drive	Henderson	KY	42420-2617	270-826-6111	5
Kentucky Theatre	214 E. Main Street	Lexington	KY	40507	606-231-6997	2
Reel Deal Cinema	163 Canary Rd	Lexington	KY	40503	859-272-4626	6
Turfland Mall Cinemas 2	2025 Harrodsburg Road	Lexington	KY	40504	859-277-2825	2
Regency 7	1808 Highway 192 West	London	KY	40741	606-877-7775	7
Apex Village 8	4014 Dutchman Lane	Louisville	KY	40207	502-897-1870	8
Broadway Cinemas	1211 W. Broadway	Louisville	KY	40203	502-589-3600	2
Dixie Dozen Cinemas	6801 Dixie Highway	Louisville	KY	40258	502-935-3771	12
Filmworks Baxter Avenue 8 Theatres	1250 Bardstown Road	Louisville	KY	40204	502-459-2288	8
Louisville Science Center IMAX	727 West Main Street	Louisville	KY	40202-2681	502-561-6103	1
Cardinal Drive-In	Hwy 45 South	Mayfield	KY	42066	504-247-4790	1
Judy Drive-In	4078 Mayville Rd.	Mt. Sterling	KY	40353	270-247-8777	1
Tenth Frame Cinemas	930 Camargo Rd.	Mt. Sterling	KY	40353	859-497-2518	6
Cheri Theatre	1008 Chestnut Street	Murray	KY	42071	502-753-3314	7
U.S. Bank IMAX Theatre, Newport on the Levee	1 Levee Way	Newport	KY	41071	859-491-4629	1
Movies 5 - Mayo Plaza	449 N. Mayo Trail	Paintsville	KY	41240	606-789-6352	5
Sipp Theatre	336 Main St.	Paintsville	KY	41240	606-789-9014	1
Riverfill 10	215 Pike Street	Pikeville	KY	41501	606-432-2957	10
Strand 2	102 S. Lake Drive	Prestonsburg	KY	41653-1915	606-886-2696	2
Capitol Theatre 3	203 W Main St	Princeton	KY	42445	270-365-7900	3
Showtime Cinemas	Radcliff Plaza	Radcliff	KY	40160	270-351-1519	3
Showplace 9	4150 S. Hwy. 27	Somerset	KY	42501	606-679-3640	9
Southside 5	390 Southside Mall	South Williamson	KY	41503	606-237-5694	5
Stanford Drive-In Theatre	Hwy 78, 1 Mile West of Stanford	Stanford	KY	40484	606-365-1317	1
Movies 5	925 S Highway 25 W	Williamsburg	KY	40769	606-549-2267	5
Movies 9	40 Winchester Plaza	Winchester	KY	40391	859-745-4900	9

LOUISIANA

Name	Address	City	State	Zip	Phone	Screens
Lafitte Cinema 4	2150 Charity St. #4	Abbeville	LA	70510	337-893-6772	4
Amite Cinemas 4	809 W. Oak St.	Amite	LA	70422	504-748-8114	4
Broadmoor Cinema 4	9810 Florida Blvd.	Baton Rouge	LA	70815-1130	225-926-0068	4
Grand Cinema	15365 George O'Neal Road	Baton Rouge	LA	70817	225-755-8888	8
Magic Cinemas	200 Cumberland St.	Bogalusa	LA	70427	985-732-7770	5
The Queen Cinema	231 W. Walnut Ave.	Eunice	LA	70535	337-457-3283	3
Hollywood Cinemas 9	1401 W. Esplanade Ave.	Kenner	LA	70065-6208	504-464-0990	8

Name	Address	City	State	Zip	Phone	Screens
Charles Cinema 3 Theatre	115 W. Sale Road	Lake Charles	LA	70605	337-477-4500	3
Fairview Cinema	1515 Anthony Street	Morgan City	LA	70380	504-399-7469	3
Lake Cinema Quad	1030 9th Street	Morgan City	LA	70380-1920	504-384-0280	4
735 Nightclub and Bar	735 Bourbon St.	New Orleans	LA	70116	504-581-6740	1
Entergy IMAX Theater	1 Canal Street	New Orleans	LA	70130	504-565-3020	1
Prytania Theatre	5339 Prytania Street	New Orleans	LA	70115	504-486-7722	1
State Palace Theatre	1108 Canal Street	New Orleans	LA	70112	504-522-4435	1
St. Landry Cinema	1277 Heather Drive	Opelousas	LA	70570	337-942-2400	4
Sci-Port IMAX Dome	820 Clyde Fant Parkway	Shreveport	LA	71101	318-424-3466	1

MASSACHUSETTS

Name	Address	City	State	Zip	Phone	Screens
Agawam Twin Cinemas Theatre	866 Suffield Street	Agawam	MA	01001	413-786-8800	2
Allston Cinema Underground	214 Harvard Avenue	Allston	MA	02134	617-912-8626	2
Bombay Cinema 2	214 Howard Ave.	Allston	MA	02134	978-671-9212	2
Stage II Cinema Pub	109 Main Street	Amesbury	MA	01913-2823	978-388-6555	2
Amherst Theatre	30 Amity Street	Amherst	MA	01002	413-253-5426	1
Capitol Theatre	204 Massachussetts Ave.	Arlington	MA	02474	781-648-4340	6
Regent Theatre	7 Medford Street	Arlington	MA	02474	781-646-4849	1
Belmont Studio	376 Trapelo Road	Belmont	MA	02478	617-484-1706	1
Cabot Street Cinema	286 Cabot Street	Beverly	MA	01915	978-927-3677	1
Isabella Stewart Gardner Museum	280 Fenway	Boston	MA	02115-5809	617-566-1401	1
Museum of Fine Arts Film Screenings	465 Huntington Avenue	Boston	MA	02115	617-267-9300	1
Omni Theatre, Museum of Science	1 Science Park	Boston	MA	02114	617-723-2500	
Simons IMAX Theatre New England Aquarium,	Central Wharf	Boston	MA	02110-3399	866-815-4629	1
West End Branch Library	151 Cambridge	Boston	MA	02114	617-523-3957	1
Brookline Public Library	31 Pleasant Street	Brookline	MA	02446	617-730-2380	1
Coolidge Corner Theatre	290 Harvard Ave.	Brookline	MA	02446	617-734-2500	2
Brattle Theatre	40 Brattle Street	Cambridge	MA	02138	617-876-6837	2
Harvard Film Archive	24 Qunicy Street, Harvard University	Cambridge	MA	02141	617-495-4700	1
MIT Film Series	77 Massachusetts Avenue	Cambridge	MA	02139	617-258-8881	1
Strand Theatre	58 High Street	Clinton	MA	01510	978-365-5500	1
Hollywood Hits Theatre	7 Hutchinson Drive	Danvers	MA	01923	617-333-3456	7
Dedham Community Theatre	580 High Street	Dedham	MA	02026	781-326-1463	2
Wellfleet Drive-In	Route 6	Eastham	MA	02663	508-349-7176	1
EMC Edgartown Cinema	65 Main St	Edgartown	MA	02539	508-627-8008	2
Bijou Theatre	350 Main Street	Fairhaven	MA	02719	508-990-8616	1
Cinema World	432 John Fitch Hwy.	Fitchburg	MA	01420	978-345-6700	10
Orpheum Foxborough Theatre	1 School Street	Foxborough	MA	02035-2325	508-543-2787	1
Franklin Zeotrope Theatre	34 East Central St.	Franklin	MA	02038	508-528-0620	3
Gardner Cinemas	34 Parker Street	Gardner	MA	01440	978-632-3544	6
Gloucester Cinema 3	74 Essex Avenue	Gloucester	MA	01930	978-283-9188	3
Triplex Cinema	70 Railroad Street	Great Barrington	MA	01230	413-528-8885	4
Greenfield Cinemas	229 Mohawk Trail	Greenfield	MA	01301	413-772-0298	6
Greenfield Garden Cinemas	361 Main Street	Greenfield	MA	01301	413-774-4881	6
Chunky's Haverhill Cinema & Pub	371 Lowell Avenue	Haverhill	MA	01832	978-372-3456	2
Leicester Drive-In	1675 Main St.	Leicester	MA	01524	508-892-4400	1
Lexington Flick	1794 Massachusetts Ave.	Lexington	MA	02420	781-861-6161	2
Tri-Town Drive-In	3 Youngs Road	Lunenburg	MA	01462	978-345-5062	3
Marlboro's 1-2-3	481 Boston Post Rd.	Marlborough	MA	01752	508-481-8818	3
Fine Arts Theatre	19 Summer St.	Maynard	MA	01754	978-897-8100	3
Mendon Drive-In	35 Milford Street	Mendon	MA	01756	508-473-4958	2
Elm DraughtHouse Theatre	35 Elm Ct.	Millbury	MA	01527	508-865-2850	1
Dreamland Theater	19 S Water St	Nantucket	MA	02554	508-228-5356	1
Gaslight Theater	1 Union Street	Nantucket	MA	02554	508-228-4435	1
Siasconset Casino	New Street	Nantucket	MA	02554	508-257-6661	1
Jordan's IMAX Theatre	1 Underprize Way	Natick	MA	01760	508-424-0088	1
Newburyport Screening Room	82 State Street	Newburyport	MA	01950	978-462-3456	1
North Adams Cinema 8	1665 Curran Highway	North Adams	MA	01247	413-663-5873	8
Triboro Cinema	Triboro Plaza	North Attleboro	MA	02763	508-695-4411	10
Academy of Music Theatre	274 Main Street	Northampton	MA	01060	413-584-8435	1
Pleasant Street Theatre	27 Pleasant Theatre	Northampton	MA	01060	413-586-8686	2
Little Cinema @ Berkshire Museum	39 South Street	Pittsfield	MA	01201	413-443-7171	1
Heritage Theaters	280 Rt. 130	Sandwich	MA	02563	508-833-7777	6
Somerville Theatre	55 Davis Square	Somerville	MA	02144	617-625-5700	5
Tower Theatre	19 College Street	South Hadley	MA	01075	413-533-3456	2
Leominster Tri-Town	52 South Nelson Rd.	Sterling	MA	01564	978-345-5062	1
Cinema Pub Theatres	807 Washington St.	Stoughton	MA	02072	781-344-4566	1
Capawock Theatre	Main Street Ext.	Vineyard Haven	MA	02568	508-696-9200	1
Brandeis Univ. Cinematheque	415 South Street	Waltham	MA	02454	781-736-3040	1
Wellfleet Cinemas	51 Route 6	Wellfleet	MA	02663	508-349-7176	4
West Boylston Cinema	101 West Boylston	West Boylston	MA	01583	508-835-8888	5
West Newton Cinema	1296 Washington Street	West Newton	MA	02465	617-964-6060	3
Images Cinema	50 Spring Street	Williamstown	MA	01267	413-458-5612	1

MARYLAND

Name	Address	City	State	Zip	Phone	Screens
Apex Adult Cinema	110 S. Broadway	Baltimore	MD	21231	410-276-0671	2
Bengies Drive-In Theatre	3417 Eastern Blvd.	Baltimore	MD	21220-2147	410-687-5627	1
Charles	1711 N. Charles St.	Baltimore	MD	21201	410-727-3456	5
IMAX Maryland Science Center	601 Light St.	Baltimore	MD	21230-3899	410-685-5225	1
Senator Theatre	5904 York Rd.	Baltimore	MD	21212	410-435-8338	1
Silver Screen Cinema Beltway 6	7660 Bel Air Rd.	Baltimore	MD	21236	410-882-5911	6
The Rotunda Cinematheque	711 West 40th St.	Baltimore	MD	21211	410-235-4800	2
P and G Montgomery Mall Cinema	7101 Democracy Blvd.	Bethesda	MD	20817	301-767-9555	3
P and G Chester 5 Theatre	21 Washington Square	Chestertown	MD	21620	410-778-2227	5
Hoff Theatre	Univ. of Maryland/Student Union	College Park	MD	20742	301-314-4633	1
National Archives	8601 Adelphi Rd.	College Park	MD	20740	202-501-5000	1

824

Name	Address	City	State	Zip	Phone	Screens
Kentlands Stadium 8	629 Centerpoint Way	Gaithersburg	MD	20878	301-519-6868	8
P and G Old Greenbelt	129 Center Way	Greenbelt	MD	20770	301-474-9744	1
Laurel Cinema	312 Main Street	Laurel	MD	20707	301-490-1993	1
Laurel Town Center	13310 Laurel Bouie Rd	Laurel	MD	20707	301-776-2500	1
Garrett 8	19741 Garrett Highway	Oakland	MD	21550	301-387-2500	8
Fox Gold Coast Mall	11301 Coastal Hwy	Ocean City	MD	21842	410-213-1505	4
Fox White Marlin 5	12641 Ocean Gateway Unit 200	Ocean City	MD	21842	410-213-1505	5
Olney 9 Cinemas	18167 Town Center Dr	Olney	MD	20832	301-744-0018	9
Apex Calvert Village 5	200 W Dares Beach Rd	Prince Frederick	MD	20678	301-855-1147	5

MAINE

Name	Address	City	State	Zip	Phone	Screens
Movie City Cinema	268 Odlin Road	Bangor	ME	04401	207-942-7611	8
Colonial Theatre	163 High Street	Belfast	ME	04915	207-338-1930	3
Casablanca Cinema 4	23 Cross St	Bethel	ME	04217	207-824-8248	4
Magic Lantern Movie Theater	69 Main Street	Bridgton	ME	04009	207-647-5065	2
Evening Star	149 Maine Street	Brunswick	ME	04001	207-729-5486	1
Alamo Theatre	379 Main St	Bucksport	ME	04416	207-469-0924	1
State Cinemas	79 Main St	Calais	ME	04619	207-454-8830	3
Narrow Gauge Cinemas	Front Street	Farmington	ME	04938	207-778-4877	6
Century Theatre	8 Hall St	Ft. Kent	ME	04743	207-834-3107	1
State Cinema	RR 1 Box 293	Harrington	ME	04643-9712	207-454-8830	2
Temple	Market Square	Houlton	ME	04730	207-532-3756	2
Leavitt Fine Arts Theatre 1	41 Main Street	Ogunquit	ME	03907	207-646-3123	1
Spotlight Cinemas	6 Stillwater Ave	Orono	ME	04473	207-827-7411	6
Strand Cinema	339 Main St	Rockland	ME	04861	207-594-7266	2
Saco Drive-In	969 Portland Road Route 1	Saco	ME	04072	207-284-1016	1
Chunky's Sanford Cinema & Pub	1364 Main Street	Sanford	ME	04073	207-490-0000	6
Flagship Cinemas 10	9 Moody Dr	Thomaston	ME	04861	207-594-2100	10
Railroad Square Cinema	17 Railroad Square	Waterville	ME	04901	207-872-5502	3
Wells Five Star Cinema	75 Wells Plaza	Wells	ME	04090	207-646-0500	7
Prides Corner Drive-In	651 Bridgton Rd	Westbrook	ME	04092	207-797-3154	1
Chunky's Cinema Pub	765 Roosevelt Trail	Windham	ME	04062	207-892-4777	2
Windham Mall Cinema	795 Roosevelt Trail, Box 400	Windham	ME	04062	207-892-7000	5

MICHIGAN

Name	Address	City	State	Zip	Phone	Screens
New Bohm 3 Theatre	201 South Superior	Albion	MI	49224	517-629-8881	3
Old Regent Theatre	211 Trowbridge	Allegan	MI	49010	616-673-2737	1
Michigan Theatre	603 E. Liberty Street	Ann Arbor	MI	48107	734-668-8480	2
State Theatre	233 S State Street	Ann Arbor	MI	48104	734-761-8667	2
Cheap Flicks	15375 South Helmer Road	Battle Creek	MI	49015	269-965-1744	8
State Theatre	913 Washington Avenue	Bay City	MI	48708	989-894-2296	1
Gem Theatre	120 N Ross	Beaverton	MI	48612	989-435-2434	1
Bellaire Theatre	219 N. Bridge St	Bellaire	MI	49615	616-533-8725	1
Cinema Hollywood	12280 Dixie Highway	Birch Run	MI	48415	989-624-3456	6
Birmingham 8	211 S. Woodward Rd	Birmingham	MI	48302	248-644-3456	8
Birmingham Palladium 12	250 North Old Woodwards	Birmingham	MI	48009	248-644-3456	12
Boyne Cinema	216 South Lake St	Boyne City	MI	49712	231-582-3212	2
Strand Theatre	101 South State Street	Caro	MI	48723	989-673-3033	1
Cass Theatre	6711 Houghton Street	Cass City	MI	48726	989-872-2252	1
Charlevoix Cinema III	107 Antrim St	Charlevoix	MI	49720	616-547-4353	3
Eaton Theaters	235 S Cochran Street	Charlotte	MI	48813	517-543-2030	3
Bellaire Kingston 5	406 N Main Street	Cheboygan	MI	49721	231-627-5376	5
Ideal Theatre	607 McEwan	Clare	MI	48617	517-386-9968	1
Clinton Theatre	130 W. Michigan Ave	Clinton	MI	49236	517-456-4315	1
Capri Drive-In	1455 West Chicago Road	Coldwater	MI	49036	517-278-5628	1
Loma Theatres	219 North Paw Paw	Coloma	MI	49038	269-468-5662	3
Henry Ford IMAX	20900 Oakwood Blvd	Dearborn	MI	48124	313-271-1570	1
Ford Tel Theatre	23830 Ford Rd	Dearborn Heights	MI	48127	313-278-7469	4
Closed - Olympia Entertainment	2211 Woodward Ave	Detroit	MI	48201	313-965-3595	2
Detroit Institute of Arts	5200 Woodward Ave	Detroit	MI	48202	313-833-3237	1
IMAX Dome Theatre	John Road and Warren	Detroit	MI	48202	313-577-8400	1
Phoenix Theatres @ Bel-Air	10100 E 8 Mile Rd	Detroit	MI	48234	313-438-3494	10
Redford Theatre	17360 Lahser Road	Detroit	MI	48219	313-537-2560	1
5 Mile Drive-In	28190 M 152	Dowagiac	MI	49047	616-782-7879	1
Elk Rapids Cinema Theatre	205 River Street	Elk Rapids	MI	49629	231-264-8601	1
Willow Creek Cinema 8	2701 3rd Ave North	Escanaba	MI	49829	906-789-6234	8
Fenton Cinema	291 Alloy Drive	Fenton	MI	48430	810-629-8900	8
Magic Bag Theatre	22920 Woodward Ave	Ferndale	MI	48220	248-544-3030	1
Garden Theatre	301 Main Street	Frankfort	MI	49635	231-352-7561	1
Fremont Cinemas	1027 W Main St	Fremont	MI	49412	616-924-4524	3
Gaylord Cinema Downtown	115 E Main Street	Gaylord	MI	49735	517-732-5717	2
Grandmarque Sun Theatre	316 Bridge Street	Grand Ledge	MI	48837	517-627-2346	1
Pic Theatre	426 Quincy St	Hancock	MI	49930	906-482-3470	1
Harbor Beach Community Theatre	105 N. Huron Ave	Harbor Beach	MI	48441	989-479-9677	1
Sunset Drive-In	69017 Red Arrow Hwy	Hartford	MI	49057	269-621-4194	1
Knickerbocker Theatre	86 East 8th Street	Holland	MI	49423	616-355-7403	1
Cherrybowl Drive-In	9812 Honor Highway	Honor	MI	49640	231-325-3413	1
Lode Theatre	510 Shelden Ave	Houghton	MI	49931	906-482-0280	1
Cinema III Theatre	543 N. Cedar St	Imlay City	MI	48444	810-724-6571	3
Ionia Theatre	209 West Main Street	Ionia	MI	48846	616-527-3350	1
Plaza	Riverside Plaza	Iron River	MI	49935	906-265-4070	1
Conway Cloverland Cinema Ironw	932 Cloverland Drive	Ironwood	MI	49938	906-932-4424	4
Country Village	1120 Country Lane	Ishpeming	MI	49849	906-486-7469	5
Michigan Theatre - Jackson	124 N. Mechanic	Jackson	MI	49201	517-783-0811	1
Courtyard Cinema	248 S Huron St	Mackinaw City	MI	49701	616-436-7890	5
Vogue Theatre	383 River Street	Manistee	MI	49660	231-723-5555	2
Riverside Cinemas 3	6746 S River Road	Marine City	MI	48039	810-765-1500	3

Name	Address	City	State	Zip	Phone	Screens
Bogar Theatre	223 East Michigan	Marshall	MI	49068	269-781-3511	1
Studio M.	5217 Bay City Rd	Midland	MI	48642	989-496-2530	3
Milford Cinema Theatre	945 E. Summit St.	Milford	MI	48381	248-685-2290	1
Denniston Cinema 1, 2 & 3	6495 N Monroe Street	Monroe	MI	48161	734-241-8700	3
Ready 4 Theatre	420 E Main Street	Niles	MI	49120	269-683-1112	4
Emagine Entertainment Novi	44425 West 12 Mile Road	Novi	MI	48377	248-319-3456	18
Strand Theatre	115 East Michigan	Paw Paw	MI	49079	269-657-2895	1
Gaslight 5	302 Petoskey	Petoskey	MI	49770	616-347-3480	5
M-89 Cinema	392 Cross Oaks Mall	Plainwell	MI	49080	616-685-2121	6
Penn Theatre	760 Penniman Ave	Plymouth	MI	48170	313-453-0870	1
Tri-City Cinema 8	W7700 Hwy US2	Quinnesec	MI	49876	906-774-5808	8
Romeo Theatre	66120 Van Dyke	Romeo	MI	48095	586-752-3455	2
Silver Cinemas - Macomb Mall	32233 Gratiot Ave	Roseville	MI	48066	810-285-8200	8
Michigan 3 Theatres	210 Center	South Haven	MI	49090	616-637-1662	3
South Lyon Cinema	126 E. Lake St.	South Lyon	MI	48178	248-437-4545	1
Shores Theatre	23495 Greater Mack Ave	St Clair Shores	MI	48080	586-775-6800	2
Strand Theatre	217 W Chicago	Sturgis	MI	49091	269-651-5032	1
Bay Theatre	216 N. St. Joseph	Suttons Bay	MI	49682	231-271-3772	1
Vickers Theatre	6 N Elm Street	Three Oaks	MI	49128	616-756-3522	1
Riviera Theatre	50 North Main Street	Three Rivers	MI	49093	269-279-7469	1
West Branch Cinema	210 W. Houghton Ave.	West Branch	MI	48661	517-345-7887	3
Northstar 3 Theatres	8171 White Hall Road	Whitehall	MI	49461	616-894-8864	3
Sun Theatre	150 West Grand River Ave.	Williamston	MI	48895	517-655-1850	1

MINNESOTA

Name	Address	City	State	Zip	Phone	Screens
Orpheum Theatre	305 W Main St	Ada	MN	56510	218-784-7565	1
Rialto Theatre Aitkin	220 N. Minnesota Ave.	Aitkin	MN	56431	218-927-2824	1
Midway Mall	2910 S. Broadway St.	Alexandria	MN	56308	320-762-8204	8
Andover Cinema 10	1836 Bunker Lake Blvd.	Andover	MN	55304	763-754-3000	10
Imation Imax Theatre	12000 Zoo Blvd.	Apple Valley	MN	55124-4623	952-431-4629	1
Tacora Theatre	320 Main St.N.	Aurora	MN	55705	218-229-2670	1
Demarce	1320 Atlantic	Benson	MN	56215	320-842-6871	1
Blackduck Theater	56 NE Main St.	Blackduck	MN	56630	218-835-7775	1
Blaine 65 Drive-In	10100 Central Ave. NE	Blaine	MN	55434		2
Brookdale 8 Discount Theatre	5810 Shingle Creek Pkwy.	Brooklyn Center	MN	55430	763-566-6721	8
Buffalo Cinema	100 First Ave.	Buffalo	MN	55313	612-682-3000	2
Cass Lake Movie Theatre	426 Highland Inn Rd., NE	Cass Lake	MN	56633	218-335-2568	1
Mann Champlin Cinema 14	11500 Theater Drive	Champlin	MN	55316	763-712-9955	14
Chanhassen Cinema	570 Pauly Drive	Chanhassen	MN	55317	952-974-1000	8
Chaska Cinema	511 Walnut St. N.	Chaska	MN	55318	612-448-4218	4
Premiere Theatres	904 Highway 33 S.	Cloquet	MN	55720	218-879-7985	6
Apache 6 Theatre	2101 37th Ave. NE	Columbia Heights	MN	55419	763-788-9079	6
Heights Theatre	3951 NE Central Ave	Columbia Heights	MN	55421	763-788-9079	1
Grand Theatre	124 E. 2nd	Crookston	MN	56716-1711	218-281-1820	2
Delano Theatre	W. Highway 12	Delano	MN	55328	612-777-3456	5
Washington Square Theatre	121 W Front St	Detroit Lakes	MN	56501	218-847-2738	5
Duluth OMNIMAX Theatre	301 Harbor Drive	Duluth	MN	55802	218-727-0022	1
East Bethel 10 Theatres	18635 NE Ulysses	East Bethel	MN	55011	612-777-3456	10
Yorktown Cinema Grill	3313 Hazelton Rd.	Edina	MN	55435	952-841-8419	3
State	238 E. Sheridan St.	Ely	MN	55731	218-365-6311	1
Excelsior Dock Cinema 3	26 Water Street	Excelsior	MN	55331	954-474-6725	3
Fair Lakes Cinema 5	1201 N. State St.	Fairmont	MN	56031	507-235-5336	5
Westridge 5	2001 W Lincoln Ave.	Fergus Falls	MN	56537	218-739-4230	5
Grand Cinema Hinckley	845 Weber Ave. S.	Hinckley	MN	55037	320-384-7999	4
Century Cinema 7	766 Century Ave.,SW	Hutchinson	MN	55350	320-234-6800	8
Cinema 1,2,3	1319 3rd St.	International Falls	MN	56649	218-283-3063	3
Kee Civic Theatre	108 N. Main St.	Kiester	MN	56051	507-294-3410	1
Vali Hi Drive-In	11260 Hudson Blvd.	Lake Elmo	MN	55128	651-436-7464	1
Lakeville 18	20653 Keokuk Ave	Lakeville	MN	55044	952-985-5324	18
Hollywood Theater	210 N. Sibley Ave	Litchfield	MN	55352	320-693-6131	3
Starlite Drive-In	Hwy 12 and 22	Litchfield	MN	55355	320-693-6990	2
Falls Cinema 3	115 S.E. 1st St.	Little Falls	MN	56345	320-632-5646	3
Madelia Theatre	117 W. Main Street	Madelia	MN	56062-1439	507-642-3333	1
Grand Madison	623 W. 3rd st. Po Box 70.	Madison	MN	56256	320-598-7955	2
Coffman Memorial Union Theatre	300 Washington Ave., S.E.	Minneapolis	MN	55455-0396	612-624-4636	1
Minneapolis Institute of Arts	2400 3rd Ave., S.	Minneapolis	MN	55404	612-870-3131	1
Oak Street Cinema	309 SE Oak Street	Minneapolis	MN	55414	612-331-7563	1
Parkway Theatre	4814 Chicago Ave	Minneapolis	MN	55417	612-822-3030	1
U Film Society	17th Ave. S.E. & University Ave. S.E.	Minneapolis	MN	55414	612-331-3134	1
Walker Art Center	725 Vineland Place	Minneapolis	MN	55403	612-375-7619	1
Plaza Theatre	560 1st St. NW	Montevideo	MN	56345	320-269-3135	3
Monti 4 Theatre	137 East Broadway	Monticello	MN	55362	763-257-7388	4
Lake Theatre	318 Elm Ave	Moose Lake	MN	55767	218-485-8060	1
Paradise Theatre	237 South Union	Mora	MN	55058	320-679-3964	1
Morris	12 E. 6th St.	Morris	MN	56267	320-589-2200	2
North Branch Cinema	38573 Tanger Dr	North Branch	MN	55056	651-674-0123	2
Cedar Mall Cinema 6	1929 Cedar Ave S.	Owatonna	MN	55060	507-451-1410	6
Park Theatre, Park Rapids	107 S. Main St.	Park Rapids	MN	56470-1515	218-732-3461	2
Koronis Cinema	209 Washburne Ave	Paynesville	MN	56362	320-243-3500	1
Red Wing Cinema 5	160 Tyler Road North	Red Wing	MN	55066	651-385-8855	5
Redwood Falls Twin	230 E Second St.	Redwood Falls	MN	56283-1604	507-637-5766	2
Chateau Theatres	971 E. Circle Dr. N.E.	Rochester	MN	55906	507-536-7469	14
Flame Theatre	1601 N. Broadway	Rochester	MN	55907	507-553-5713	1
Roseville 4 Theaters	1211 Larpenteur Ave W.	Roseville	MN	55113	651-488-4242	4
Main Street Theatre	319 Main Street	Sauk Centre	MN	56378	320-352-3596	4
Shakopee Town Theater	1116 Shakopee Town Sq	Shakopee	MN	55379	952-445-5300	6
Valleyfair's Pepsi IMAX Cinema	1 Valleyfair Drive	Shakopee	MN	55379	952-445-7600	1
Twin Spin Cinema	151 Progress Circle	Spicer	MN	56288	320-796-5500	2
Princess Theatre Community Center	505 S. 1st Ave.	St. James	MN	56081-1727	507-375-4370	1

Name	Address	City	State	Zip	Phone	Screens
Omnitheatre - Science Museum of Minnesota	120 W. Kellogg Blvd.	St. Paul	MN	55102	651-221-9444	1
St. Paul Student Center	2017 Buford Ave	St. Paul	MN	55108	612-625-9794	1
W Bank Auditorium - U of MN	225 19 Ave S	St. Paul	MN	55108	612-624-7271	1
St. Peter 5	621 South Minnesota Ave	St. Peter	MN	56082	507-931-6631	5
Staples Theatre	204 N.E. 4th Street	Staples	MN	56479	218-894-3818	1
Waconia	101 W. 1st St.	Waconia	MN	55387-1319	651-777-3456	6
Cozy Twin Theatre	223 S. Jefferson St.	Wadena	MN	56482	218-631-1201	2
Gopher	907 Broadway	Wheaton	MN	56296	612-563-4545	1
White Bear Township Theatre	1180 County Road J	White Bear Lake	MN	55110	651-777-3456	17
Woodbury 10 Theatre	1470 Queens Dr.	Woodbury	MN	55125	651-731-0606	10
Northland Cinema 5	1635 Oxford St	Worthington	MN	56187	507-376-4400	5

MISSOURI

Name	Address	City	State	Zip	Phone	Screens
Flick Theatre	105 E Main	Anderson	MO	64831	417-845-6681	1
Princess Theatre	14 W. Olive St.	Aurora	MO	65605	417-678-3441	1
El Teatro Real	117 South 15th Street	Bethany	MO	64424	660-425-7272	2
Bolivar Cinema 4	800 E. Aldrich Rd Suite 10	Bolivar	MO	65613	417-777-7469	4
Branson's IMAX	3562 Shepherd of the Hills Expressway	Branson	MO	65616	800-419-4832	1
The Elite Cinema III	3562 Shepherd of the Hills Expy.	Branson	MO	65616	417-335-3533	3
Starlite Drive-In	Rt 2, Box 2670	Cadet	MO	63630	888-216-6843	1
Grand 6	2880 Grand Avenue	Chillicothe	MO	64601	660-646-7469	6
Missouri 6	431 S. Missouri Ave.	Clinton	MO	64735	660-885-2600	6
Ragtag Cinemacafe	23 N 10th St	Columbia	MO	65201	573-443-4359	3
Melba Theatre	300 S. Main St.	De Soto	MO	63020	636-586-1900	1
Festus 8 Theatres	1522 Parkway West	Festus	MO	63028	636-933-0062	8
Fulton Cinema	613 Court Street	Fulton	MO	65251	573-642-2122	2
Lake West Cinema	1651 Highway O	Gravois Mills	MO	65037	573-372-5554	5
Hannibal Cinema 5	7 Northport Plz	Hannibal	MO	63401	573-221-5038	5
Cinema 6 Harrisonville	2727 Cantrell Road	Harrisonville	MO	64701	816-887-2932	6
Davis Theatre	2208 S. Main Street	Higginsville	MO	64037	660-584-7929	1
Englewood Theatre	10917 Winner Road	Independence	MO	64052	816-252-2463	1
Independence Square Cinema 4	114 W Maple	Independence	MO	64050	816-252-1995	4
Noland Fashion Square 6	13520 Hwy 40	Independence	MO	64055	816-478-2222	6
Twin Drive-In Theatre	1320 N 71 By-Pass	Independence	MO	64137	816-257-2234	2
Ramada 4 Theatres	1614 Jefferson ST.	Jefferson City	MO	65109	573-636-8711	4
Crown Center 6	2450 Grand Ave	Kansas City	MO	64108	816-472-6000	6
I-70 Four Screen Drive-In	8701 E Hwy 40	Kansas City	MO	64129	816-861-0500	4
Red Bridge 4	11118 Holmes Road	Kansas City	MO	64131	816-333-3456	4
Sprint IMAX @ Kansas City Zoo	6800 Zoo Drive	Kansas City	MO	64132	816-513-4629	1
Tivoli Square	4050 Pennsylvania	Kansas City	MO	64111	913-383-7756	3
Downtown Cinema Eight	115 North Elson	Kirksville	MO	63501	660-665-5683	8
Lebanon Ritz 7 Theatre	925 South Jefferson	Lebanon	MO	65536	417-588-9724	7
Liberty Cinema 12	2101 W Kansas	Liberty	MO	64068	816-333-3456	12
Macon Cinema	2218 US Highway 63	Macon	MO	63552	660-385-5550	4
Uptown	104 North Kansas Avenue	Marceline	MO	64658	660-376-2525	1
Marshall Cinema	114-120 E North Street	Marshall	MO	65340	660-886-3616	2
Moberly 5	3000 N. Morley	Moberly	MO	65270	660-263-2000	5
Moberly Drive-In	3000 N. Morley	Moberly	MO	65270	660-263-2000	1
Monett Plaza 5	507 Plaza Dr.	Monett	MO	65708	417-235-0990	5
Century 6	Highway K.	Nevada	MO	64772	417-667-7469	6
Lyric Theatre	110 W 2nd St	Salisbury	MO	65281	660-388-5219	1
State Fair Cinemas	1400 S Limit	Sedalia	MO	65301	660-827-3440	1
Palace Theatre	2220 W. Chesterfield Blvd.	Springfield	MO	65807	417-875-6200	9
St. Andrews 3	2025 Golfway Drive	St. Charles	MO	63301	636-947-1133	3
Arch Odyssey	707 N 1st Street	St. Louis	MO	63102	314-982-1410	1
Chase Park Plaza Cinemas	212 N. Kingshighway Blvd	St. Louis	MO	63108	314-367-0101	5
Galleria 6 Cinemas	#30 St. Louis Galleria	St. Louis	MO	63117	314-725-0808	6
Omnimax @ St. Louis Science Center	5050 Oakland Ave.	St. Louis	MO	63110	314-289-4444	1
Plaza Cinema 4	7 The Plz	Troy	MO	63379	636-528-4647	4
Great Eight Cinema	5 Praire Dell Road	Union	MO	63084	636-583-8889	8
Belle Starr Playhouse and Cinema	112 E. Booneslick	Warrenton	MO	63383	636-456-7937	1
Roxy Theatre	319 Van Buren St.	Warsaw	MO	65355	660-438-6719	2
Cinema 1 Plus	1900 Phoenix Center Drive	Washington	MO	63090	636-239-5056	2
Waynesville Cinema 8.	100 Tremont Ctr.	Waynesville	MO	65583	573-774-6533	8
Glass Sword Cinema	1001 Lanton Rd	West Plains	MO	65775	417-256-8686	3

MISSISSIPPI

Name	Address	City	State	Zip	Phone	Screens
Imperial Palace 6	850 Bayview Avenue	Biloxi	MS	39530	228-432-3292	6
Delta Theatre	11 3rd St.	Clarksdale	MS	39194	662-627-6733	1
Singing River 4	2800 Highway 90.	Gautier	MS	39553	228-497-5895	4
Singing River 5.	2800 Highway 90.	Gautier	MS	39553	228-497-5895	5
Hardy Court Cinema	25 Hardy Court Shopping Center	Gulfport	MS	39507	228-896-8111	9
Beverly Drive-In Theater	Hwy 49	Hattiesburg	MS	39403	601-544-4101	2
Cloverleaf Cinema	5912 US Hwy 49	Hattiesburg	MS	39401	601-544-4400	3
Broadcountry Cinema III	227 2nd Ave SW	Magee	MS	39111	601-849-4800	3
The Movie Reel	720 Coulter Dr.	New Albany	MS	38652	662-534-7300	4
Canal Place Cinema	200 Canal Avenue	Philadelphia	MS	39350	601-656-6843	7
Southaven Cinema	2010 Stateline Rd. W.	Southaven	MS	38671	601-393-0373	8
Cinema 12	Highway 12	Starkville	MS	39759	662-320-9000	5
Hollywood Premier Cinema	101 Hollywood Blvd.	Starkville	MS	39759	662-320-9000	8
Plaza Theatre	K Mart Plaza	Yazoo City	MS	39194	662-746-8902	2

MONTANA

Name	Address	City	State	Zip	Phone	Screens
Washoe Theatre	305 S Main St	Anaconda	MT	59711	406-563-6161	1
Midway Drive-In	Highway 2 & Route 40	Columbia Falls	MT	59912	406-752-7800	1

Name	Address	City	State	Zip	Phone	Screens
Majestic Theatre	215 Dewey Ave	Eureka	MT	59917	406-297-2631	1
Roxy Twin Theatre	120 2nd Street North	Hamilton	MT	59840	406-363-2336	2
Dome Theatre	Mineral Ave	Libby	MT	59923	406-293-2703	1
Empire Twin Theatre	106 N 2nd Ave	Livingston	MT	59047	406-222-0111	2
Montana Theatre	905 Main Street	Miles City	MT	59301	406-232-2957	2
Wilma Theater	131 S Higgins Ave	Missoula	MT	59802	406-728-2521	3
Orpheum Theatre	119 S Main St	Plentywood	MT	59254	406-765-1233	1
Centre Theatre	211 S Central	Sidney	MT	59270	406-488-6377	1
Yellowstone IMAX Theatre	101 S. Canyon St.	West Yellowstone	MT	59758	406-646-4100	1

NEBRASKA

Name	Address	City	State	Zip	Phone	Screens
Geju-Alliance Theatre	410 Box Butte Avenue	Alliance	NE	69301	308-762-4100	3
State Theatre	1221 J. Street	Auburn	NE	68305	402-274-4096	1
Cinema Theatre	615 Court St.	Beatrice	NE	68310	402-223-5124	2
Blair 3 Theatre	West Highway 30	Blair	NE	68008	402-426-4744	3
Eagle Theatre	244 Main St.	Chadron	NE	69337	308-432-2342	4
Rialto Theatre	202 E. 8th St.	Cozad	NE	69130	308-784-3770	1
Isis Theatre	139 W. 13th St.	Crete	NE	68333	402-826-2422	2
Bonham Theatre	519 E Street	Fairbury	NE	68352-0226	402-729-2109	2
Lied Super Screen Theatre	1330 North Burlington Avenue	Hastings	NE	68902-1286	800-508-4629	1
Majestic Theatre	5th and Lincoln	Hebron	NE	68370	402-768-6061	2
Sun Theatre	421 West Ave.	Holdrege	NE	68949	308-995-8201	1
Kearny Drive-In	2318 Avenue N	Kearney	NE	68847	308-237-2783	1
Goodhand Theatre	226 S. Chestnut	Kimball	NE	69145	308-235-2449	1
Cinema Twin	201 N 13th St	Lincoln	NE	68508	402-441-0222	2
Douglas Theatre	1300 P Street	Lincoln	NE	68501	402-441-0222	3
Edgewood 3 Theatre	5220 S 56th St	Lincoln	NE	68516	402-421-0222	3
Joyo	6102 Havelock Ave.	Lincoln	NE	68507-1233	402-464-5696	1
Plaza 4 Theatre	201 N 12th ST	Lincoln	NE	68508	402-441-0222	4
Southpointe Cinema	2920 Pine Lake Road	Lincoln	NE	68516	402-441-0222	6
Star Ship 9	1311 Q Street	Lincoln	NE	68508	402-441-0222	9
The Lincoln	1145 P Street	Lincoln	NE	68508	402-441-0222	3
Nile Theatre	1433 Center Ave.	Mitchell	NE	69357	308-623-2727	1
Pioneer Theater	110 S. 11th St.	Nebraska City	NE	68410	405-873-6487	3
New Moon Theatre	318 Main St.	Neligh	NE	68756	402-887-5584	1
Starlight Drive-In	E. Highway 275	Neligh	NE	68756	402-887-5021	1
Central States Cinemas III	120 S. 3rd St.	Norfolk	NE	68701	402-371-4747	3
Kings Theatre	1000 Riverside Blvd.	Norfolk	NE	68701	402-379-0424	4
Prairie Theatre	208 N. Spruce	Ogallala	NE	69153	308-284-4033	2
Dundee Theatre	4952 Dodge Street	Omaha	NE	68132	402-551-3595	1
Lozier IMAX Theatre	3701 10th Street	Omaha	NE	68107	402-738-8401	2
Westwood 8	2809 S. 125th Ave., Ste 297	Omaha	NE	68144	402-697-1300	8
Rivoli Theatre	533 Main St	Seward	NE	68902	402-643-6195	1
Fox Twin	1120 Illinois St.	Sidney	NE	69162-1648	308-254-3328	2
Crest Theatre	106 W. 5th Street	Superior	NE	68978	402-879-3819	1
Jewel II	710 East Hwy 20	Valentine	NE	69201	406-376-2890	2
March Twin	310 Main Street	Wayne	NE	68787	402-375-1280	2
Sun Theatre	427 N. Lincoln Ave.	York	NE	68467	402-362-7469	3

NEW HAMPSHIRE

Name	Address	City	State	Zip	Phone	Screens
Claremont Cinema Center	345 Washington Street	Claremont	NH	03743	603-542-0400	6
University of NH-MUB	83 Main Street	Durham	NH	03824-2538	603-862-4600	1
Ioka Theatre	55 Water St.	Exeter	NH	03833-2440	603-772-2222	2
Lake Region Cinemas	1387 Lakeshore Rd.	Gilford	NH	03246	603-524-2350	3
Hampton Cinema 6	321 Lafayette Road	Hampton	NH	03842	603-926-5785	6
The Nugget Theatre	57 S. Main Street	Hanover	NH	03755	603-643-2769	4
Colonial Theatre NH	95 Main Street	Keene	NH	03431	603-352-2033	1
Keene Cinemas	121 Key Road	Keene	NH	03431	603-357-5260	6
Lakes Region Cinema 3	1387 Lake Shore Rd.	Laconia	NH	03246-2264	603-524-2350	3
Jax Jr. Cinemas	33 Main Street	Littleton	NH	03561	603-444-5907	2
Apple Tree Mall Cinema 12	16 Orchard View Dr.	Londonderry	NH	03053-3366	603-434-8633	12
Premiere 8	Post Rd Plz.	Merrimack	NH	03054	603-882-5544	8
Milford Drive-In	101 Milford	Milford	NH	03055	603-673-4090	2
Mt. Valley Mall Theatre	Route 16 302	North Conway	NH	03860	603-356-6410	7
North Conway Twin	Main Street N. Conway Village	North Conway	NH	03860	603-356-0263	2
Chunky's Pelham Cinema & Pub	150 Bridge Street	Pelham	NH	03076	603-635-7499	5
The Music Hall	28 Chestnut Street	Portsmouth	NH	03801	603-433-3100	1
Chunky's Cinema Pub - Tilton	630 W. Main St.	Tilton	NH	03276	603-286-4444	6
Wilton Town Theater	40 Main Street, Wilton	Wilton	NH	03086	603-654-9743	2
Meadows Drive-In	Route 135	Woodsville	NH	03785	603-747-2608	1

NEW JERSEY

Name	Address	City	State	Zip	Phone	Screens
Lincoln Cinemas	838 Kearny Ave.	Arlington	NJ	07032	201-997-6873	6
Atlantic Cinema 5	82 First Avenue	Atlantic Highlands	NJ	07716	732-291-0148	5
Montgomery Cinema	1325 Route 206	Belle Mead	NJ	08502	609-924-7444	6
Berkeley Cinema	450 Springfield Ave.	Berkeley Heights	NJ	07922	908-464-8888	1
Roberts Lost Picture Show	562 Bloomfield Ave.	Bloomfield	NJ	07003	973-748-4870	2
Darress Theatre	615 Main Street	Boonton	NJ	07005	973-334-9292	1
Beach Cinema	110 Main St	Bradley Beach	NJ	07720	732-774-9089	1
Roberts Chatham Cinema	641 Shunpike Rd.	Chatham	NJ	07928	973-822-1550	1
Cranford Theatre	25 North Avenue	Cranford	NJ	07016	908-276-3070	5
Dunellen Theatre	458 North Ave.	Dunellen	NJ	08812	732-968-9010	1
MEGA Movies at Brunswick Square	755 Route 18	East Brunswick	NJ	08816	732-257-5555	13
Hyway 6 Theatres	2218 Broadway	Fairlawn	NJ	07410	201-796-1717	6
Americanplace Movies Cinema Plaza 6	240 Routes 202/31	Flemington	NJ	08822	908-782-2777	6
Galaxy Theatre	7000 Blvd. East	Guttenberg	NJ	07093	201-854-6540	3

Name	Address	City	State	Zip	Phone	Screens
Hawthorne 5	300 Lafayette Ave	Hawthorne	NJ	07506	973-427-2828	5
Hillsborough Cinemas	111 Raider Blvd	Hillsborough	NJ	08844	908-874-8181	12
Hudson Street Cinemas	5 Marine View Plaza	Hoboken	NJ	07030	201-795-9996	2
Movies Under the Stars	1 Hudson Place	Hoboken	NJ	07030	201-217-4077	1
IMAX Dome Theatre	251 Phillip Street	Jersey City	NJ	07305-4699	201-200-1000	1
Maplewood Theatre	155 Maplewood Ave.	Maplewood	NJ	07040	973-763-3100	6
Roberts Wellmont Theatre	5 Seymour St.	Montclair	NJ	07042	973-783-9500	3
Rutgers University Film	3 Bartlett St.	New Brunswick	NJ	08903	732-932-8482	2
Newark Screens on Springfield	360-394 Springfield Ave.	Newark	NJ	07103	973-642-5555	6
Newton Twin Theatre	234 Spring Street	Newton	NJ	07860	973-579-9993	2
Cine Plaza 13	2115 69th St.	North Bergen	NJ	07047	201-868-6565	13
Tilton 9 Theatre	331 Tilton Road	Northfield	NJ	08225	609-646-3147	9
Paramus Picture Show	35 Plaza E. 65 Route 4	Paramus	NJ	07652	201-845-6112	1
Pennsville Premier Cinema	245 N. Broadway	Pennsville	NJ	08070	856-678-1781	2
Broadway Theatre	47 South Broadway	Pitman	NJ	08071	609-589-4616	1
Strand Theater	205 E. Front St.	Plainfield	NJ	07060	908-222-8999	1
Towne Theatre in Egg Harbor Tw.	6733 Black Horse Pike	Pleasantville	NJ	08232	609-641-3595	8
Princeton Garden	160 Nassau St.	Princeton	NJ	08542	609-683-7595	2
Union County Arts Center	1601 Irving St.	Rahway	NJ	07065	732-499-8226	1
Ramsey Cinema	125 E. Main Street	Ramsey	NJ	07068	201-825-2090	1
Rialto Arts Cinema - Ridgefield Park	172 Main St.	Ridgefield Park	NJ	07660	201-994-0618	1
Creative Entertainment New Park Cinema	23 W. Westfield Ave	Roselle Park	NJ	07204	908-241-2525	5
Williams Center Cinemas 2	1 Williams Plaza	Rutherford	NJ	07070	201-933-3700	2
Sparta Theatre	25 Centre Street	Sparta	NJ	07871	973-729-5775	2
Cedar Lane Cinemas	503 Cedar Lane	Teaneck	NJ	07666	201-836-3334	4
Union Theaters	990 Stuyvesant Ave & Morris Ave.-	Union	NJ	07083	908-686-4373	7
Summit Quad Theatres	1214 Summit Ave.	Union City	NJ	07087	201-865-2878	4
Ventnor Twin	5211 Ventnor Ave.	Ventnor City	NJ	08406	609-487-5800	2
DeMarco Cinemas	44 W. Landis Ave.	Vineland	NJ	08360-1902	856-692-5566	4
Ritz Sixteen	900 Haddonfield-Berlin Road	Voorhees	NJ	08043	856-770-0600	16
Valley View Twin Theatre	777 Hamburg Turnpike	Wayne	NJ	07470	973-305-4900	2
Abby Cinemas	35D Marshall Hill Rd	West Milford	NJ	07480	973-728-9600	1
Mayfair 3-Plex	6405 Park Ave.	West New York	NJ	07093	201-869-3333	3
Rialto Theatre of Westfield	250 E. Broad St.	Westfield	NJ	07090	908-232-1288	5
Pascack 6	182 Center St.	Westwood	NJ	07675	201-664-3200	6

NEW MEXICO

Name	Address	City	State	Zip	Phone	Screens
Tombaugh IMAX Dome Theatre	New Mexico Hwy 2001	Alamogordo	NM	88310	505-437-2840	1
Dynatheatre	1801 Mountain Road NW.	Albuquerque	NM	87104	505-841-2802	1
Guild Art Theatre	3405 Central Ave. N.E.	Albuquerque	NM	87106-1431	505-255-1848	1
Southwest Film Center	3601 University Blvd SE	Albuquerque	NM	87106	505-277-5608	1
Fiesta Drive-In 3	401 W. Fiesta Dr.	Carlsbad	NM	88220-5454	505-885-4126	3
West Theatre Grants	118 W. Santa Fe Ave.	Grants	NM	87020-2528	505-287-4692	1
Kiva Theater	109 Bridge Street	Las Vegas	NM	87701	505-454-0152	1
Fountain Theatre - Mesilla Valley	2469 Calle de Guadalupe	Mesilla	NM	88046	505-524-8287	1
El Raton 85 Drive-In	115 N. 1st Street	Raton	NM	87740-3859	505-445-3721	1
Sierra Cinema	721 Mechem Dr #D	Ruidoso	NM	88345-6911	505-257-9444	3
Cinematheque At Plan B	1050 Old Pecos Trail	Santa Fe	NM	87501-4562	505-982-1338	1
The Screen	1600 St Michael's Drive	Santa Fe	NM	87505	505-473-6494	1
Pecos Theatre	219 4th	Santa Rosa	NM	88435	505-472-3098	1
Gila Theatre	415 North Bullard Street	Silver City	NM	88061	505-538-5756	1
Real West Cinema II	11585 Highway 180 E.	Silver City	NM	88061-7780	505-538-5659	2
El Cortez Theatre	415 Main St.	Truth/Consequences	NM	87901-2842	505-894-5023	1
Odeon Theatre Tucumcari	123 S. 2nd St.	Tucumcari	NM	88401-2281	505-461-0100	1

NEW YORK

Name	Address	City	State	Zip	Phone	Screens
Madison Theatre	1036 Madison Avenue	Albany	NY	12208	518-489-5431	7
Spectrum 7	290 Delaware Avenue	Albany	NY	12209	518-449-8995	7
Castle Cinema	W. State Rd.	Allegany	NY	14706	716-373-2060	1
Screening Room Cinema Cafe	3131 Sheridan Dr	Amherst	NY	14226	716-837-0376	1
Emerald Amsterdam Theatre	136 Perth Plaza, Route 30.	Amsterdam	NY	12010	518-842-4636	10
Grandview Drive-In	Route 5 and Lake St.	Angola	NY	14006	716-549-2450	2
American Museum of the Moving Image	35 Ave. at 36 Street.	Astoria	NY	11106	718-784-0077	1
Auburn Movieplex 10	Grant Avenue Plaza, Rt 5	Auburn	NY	13021	315-255-4635	10
Fingerlakes Mall Cinemas	0 Fingerlakes Mall	Auburn	NY	13022-7580	315-252-7580	4
Hollywood Drive-In	9254 NY 66.	Averill Park	NY	12018	518-283-4425	1
Vintage Drive-In	1520 W. Henrietta Rd.	Avon	NY	14414	716-226-9290	3
Bellmore Movies	222 Pettit Ave	Bellmore	NY	11710	516-783-7200	1
5 Star Theatres Bellmore Playhouse	525 Bedford Ave.	Bellmore	NY	11710	516-783-5440	5
Mid Island Triplex	4045 Hempstead Turnpike	Bethpage	NY	11801	516-796-7500	3
Brentwood Theatre	1795 Brentwood Road	Brentwood	NY	11717	631-231-8484	1
Strand Theatre	93 Main Street	Brockport	NY	14420	585-637-3310	3
American Theatre	1450 East Ave.	Bronx	NY	10462-7502	718-863-4900	7
Bam Rose Cinemas	30 Lafayette Ave.	Brooklyn	NY	11217	718-623-2770	1
Canarsie Triplex	9310 Ave. L.	Brooklyn	NY	11236-4807	718-251-0700	3
Cobble Hill Cinema	265 Court St.	Brooklyn	NY	11231-4406	718-596-9113	5
Kent Theatre	1170 Coney Island Ave.	Brooklyn	NY	11230-2912	718-338-3371	3
Pavilion Brooklyn Heights Cinema	70 Henry St.	Brooklyn	NY	11201-1727	718-369-0838	2
Pavilion Flatbush	314 Flatbush Ave.	Brooklyn	NY	11238	718-369-0838	2
Pavilion Park Slope	188 Prospect Park W.	Brooklyn	NY	11215	718-369-0838	6
Callicoon Theatre	Acacemy Street	Callicoon	NY	12723	845-887-4460	1
Canandaigua Theatres	3189 Townline Rd.	Canandaigua	NY	14424	585-396-9396	10
American Theatre	96 Main St	Canton	NY	13617	315-386-2981	5
Carmel Movieplex 8	150 Route 52	Carmel	NY	10512	845-228-1666	8
Community Theatre	373 Main Street.	Catskill	NY	12414	518-943-2410	2
Crandell Theatre	46-48 Main Street	Chatham	NY	12037	518-392-3331	1

Name	Address	City	State	Zip	Phone	Screens
Appletree Theatres	34 Appletree Business Park	Cheektowaga	NY	14227	716-681-3100	6
Buffalo Drive-In Theatre	3085 Harlem Rd.	Cheektowaga	NY	14225-2563	716-893-0406	2
Chester Cinema 6	223 Chester Mall	Chester	NY	10918	914-469-5333	6
Clinton Cinema	2 Fountain St.	Clinton	NY	13323	315-853-5553	1
Park Theatre	1 Park Place	Cobleskill	NY	12043	518-234-2771	1
Movieland of Coram	1850 Rt 112	Coram	NY	11727	631-696-4200	8
Queen City Plaza I & II	103-14 Roosevelt Ave.	Corona	NY	11368-2395	718-639-0012	2
Plaza 6 Cinema - Cortland	Tompkins & Glenwood	Cortland	NY	13045	607-753-7386	6
Hi Way Drive-In	Route 9 West	Coxsackie	NY	12037	518-731-8672	1
Dansville Star Theatre	144 Main St	Dansville	NY	14437	716-335-6950	1
State Theatre	128 Front Stret	Deposit	NY	13754	607-467-2727	1
Aurora Theatre	673 Main Street	East Aurora	NY	14052	716-652-1660	1
Elwood Cinema	1950 Jericho Turnpike	East Northport	NY	11740	631-499-7800	2
Queen City Jackson Triplex	40-31 82nd St.	Elmhurst	NY	11373-1304	718-335-0242	3
The Heights Theater	210 E. 14th St.	Elmira Heights	NY	14903	607-733-2533	1
Cinema Saver	19 Madison Ave	Endicott	NY	13760	607-754-6588	4
North Shore Towers	27-10 Grand Central Pkwy.	Floral Park	NY	11005-1109	718-229-7702	2
Cinemart Cinemas	106-03 Metropolitan Ave.	Forest Hills.	NY	11379	718-261-2244	5
IMAX Dome at Cradle of Aviation Museum	1 Davis Ave.	Garden City	NY	11530	516-572-4111	1
Geneseo Square Theatres	4473 Genesee St	Geneseo	NY	14454	716-243-2691	6
Geneva Movieplex 8	371 Hamilton Street.	Geneva	NY	14456	315-789-1653	8
Glen Cove 6	5 School St.	Glen Cove	NY	11542	516-671-2522	6
Jericho Drive-In	Route 9 West	Glenmont	NY	12077	518-767-3398	1
Aimie's Dinner & Movie	190 Glen Street.	Glens Falls	NY	12801	518-792-8181	2
Glen Drive-In	Lake George Rd.	Glens Falls	NY	12801	518-792-0023	1
Village Cinema Greenport	211 Front Street	Greenport	NY	11944	631-477-8600	1
Palace Hamburg	31 Buffalo St.	Hamburg	NY	14075	716-649-2295	1
Hamilton Movie House	7 Lebanon Street.	Hamilton	NY	13346	315-824-2724	3
Capra Cinema	533 West Front St	Hancock	NY	13783	607-637-3456	1
Fairview 3	160 Fairview Ave.	Hudson	NY	12534	518-828-1900	3
Hudson Movieplex	350 Fairview Ave.	Hudson	NY	12534	518-822-1049	8
Hunter Theatre	Main Street	Hunter	NY	12442	518-263-4702	1
Cinema Arts Centre	423 Park Ave.	Huntington	NY	11740	631-423-7653	3
Hyde Park Drive-In	510 Albany Post Rd.	Hyde Park	NY	12538	845-229-4738	1
Roosevelt Cinemas	510 Albany Post Rd.	Hyde Park	NY	12538	845-229-2000	3
Islip 3	410 West Main Street	Islip -LONG I-.	NY	11751-3411	631-581-5200	3
Cinemapolis	171 E State.	Ithaca	NY	14850	607-277-6115	2
Fall Creek Pictures	1201 N. Tioga Street	Ithaca	NY	14850	607-272-1256	4
Park 60 Drive-In	1529 Foote Avenue Exit.	Jamestown.	NY	14701	716-484-6060	2
Holiday Twin Theatre.	Route 30-A @ Arterial Hwy.	Johnstown	NY	12095	518-762-3521	2
Johnstown Movieplex 9.	236 N. Comrie Ave.	Johnstown	NY	12095	518-762-6773	9
Main Street Cinemas	72-66 Main St.	Kew Garden Hills	NY	11367-2421	718-263-4828	6
Kew Gardens Cinemas	81-05 Lefferts Blvd.	Kew Gardens	NY	11415	718-441-9835	5
Palace Theatre	26 Main Street	Lake Placid	NY	12946-1302	518-523-9271	4
Flix Superplex Movie Theatre	4901 Transit Road	Lancaster.	NY	14086	716-668-3549	10
Liberty Theatre	31 S. Main Street	Liberty	NY	12754	845-292-3000	3
Palace Theatre Lockport	2 East Avenue.	Lockport.	NY	14094	716-438-1089	1
Transit Drive-In	6655 Transit Road	Lockport.	NY	14094	716-625-8535	3
Long Beach Cinema	179 East Park Ave.	Long Beach	NY	11561	516-432-0576	2
Thalia Spanish Theater	4117 Greenpoint Ave.	Long Island City	NY	11104	718-729-3880	1
Town Hall Theatre	5428 Shady Ave.	Lowville	NY	13367-9101	315-376-2421	1
West Wayne Theatre.	170 Stafford Rd.	Macedon	NY	14502	315-986-2885	1
Malta Drive-In Theatre	2785 Route 9	Malta	NY	12020	518-587-6077	1
Malverne Cinema 4.	350 Hempstead Ave.	Malverne	NY	11598	516-599-6966	4
Emelin Theatre	153 Library Lane.	Mamaroneck	NY	10543	914-698-0098	1
Manlius Art Cinema	135 East Seneca Street.	Manlius	NY	13104	315-682-9817	1
56 Auto Drive-In	Route 56.	Massena	NY	13662	315-764-1250	1
Massena Movieplex	Rte. 37 &420, Harte Haven Shopping Ctr	Massena	NY	13662	315-769-1268	8
Movieland of Mastic	1708 Montauk Highway	Mastic	NY	11950	631-281-8586	8
Mattituck 8	Route 25.	Mattituck	NY	11952	631-298-7469	8
Merrick Cinemas.	15 Fisher Ave.	Merrick	NY	11566	516-623-1177	4
Sunset Drive-In, Middleport	120 Telegraph Rd.	Middleport	NY	14105	716-735-7372	3
Moviehouse	Main Street	Millerton.	NY	12546	518-789-3408	1
Midway Drive-In	2782 County Route 45.	Minetto	NY	13069	315-343-0211	1
Montauk Movies	3 Edgemere Road.	Montauk.	NY	11954	631-668-2393	1
Mall Quad Cinema	State Highway 42	Monticello	NY	12701	845-794-2600	4
New Paltz Theatre	Route 299.	New Paltz	NY	12561	845-255-0420	4
Anthology Film Archives	32 2nd Ave.	New York	NY	10008	212-505-5110	1
Cinema Classics	332 E. 11th St.	New York	NY	10003	212-677-5368	1
Cinema Village 12th Street	22 E. 12th St.	New York	NY	10003-4403	212-924-3363	1
Film Forum	209 W. Houston St.	New York	NY	10014-4837	212-727-8110	3
Film Society of Lincoln Center	70 Lincoln Center Plaza	New York	NY	10023-6595	212-875-5206	1
Gramercy Theatre.	127 East 23rd Street	New York	NY	10010	212-777-4900	1
LeFrak IMAX Theater	175-208 Central Park Way	New York	NY	10024	212-769-5100	1
Lincoln Plaza Cinemas	30 Lincoln Plaza	New York	NY	10023-7103	212-757-2280	3
Museum of Modern Arts	11 W. 53rd Street	New York	NY	10019	212-708-9480	2
New York Hall of Science	47-01 111th St	New York	NY	10029	718-699-0005	1
NY Public Library Donnell Center	20 West 53rd St.	New York	NY	10019	212-621-0618	1
Paris Theatre	4 W. 58th St.	New York	NY	10019-2515	212-688-3800	1
Quad Cinema	34 W. 13th St.	New York	NY	10011-7911	212-255-8800	4
Screening Room.	54 Varick St.	New York	NY	10013	212-334-2100	1
Strand Wildwood.	3100 Boardwalk	New York	NY	08260	609-523-0288	7
Two Boots Den of Cin.	44 Avenue A	New York	NY	10009	212-254-0800	1
Two Boots Pioneer Theater	155 E 3rd St	New York	NY	10009	212-254-3300	1
Walter Reade Theatre.	70 Lincoln Center Plaza	New York	NY	10023-6548	212-875-5600	4
Whitney Museum of American Art	945 Madison Avenue.	New York	NY	10021	212-621-0618	1
Newark Showplace 6	101 S. Main St.	Newark	NY	14513	315-331-8005	6
Four Seasons Cinema	2429 Military Road	Niagara Falls	NY	14304	716-297-1951	6
Hathaway's Drive-In	Route 67.	North Hoosick	NY	12133	518-686-7768	1

Name	Address	City	State	Zip	Phone	Screens
Colonia Theater	35 S. Broad St.	Norwich	NY	13815	607-334-2135	3
Oceanside Twin	2743 Long Beach Road	Oceanside	NY	11572	516-536-7565	2
Cinema 1 & 2 Ogdensburg	Ogdensburg Mall	Ogdensburg	NY	13669	315-393-6370	2
Strand	Main	Old Forge	NY	13420	315-369-6703	1
Oneonta Theatre 1 & 2	47 Chestnut Street	Oneonta	NY	13820	607-432-2820	2
Crystal Cinemas	88 Victory Highway	Painted Post	NY	14870	607-937-5008	8
Patchogue Theater for Performing Arts	71 East Main Street	Patchogue	NY	11772	631-286-1133	1
Paramount Center	1008 Brown Street	Peekskill	NY	10566	914-737-6068	1
Pelham Picture House	175 Wolf's Lane	Pelham	NY	10803	914-738-3160	1
Lake St. Plaza Theatres-Penn Yan	230A Lake Street Plaza	Penn Yan	NY	14527	315-536-1292	3
Silver Lake Drive-In	7019 Chapman Ave	Perry	NY	14530	716-237-3372	1
Strand Theatre	25 Brinkerhoff Street	Plattsburgh	NY	12901	518-566-7185	2
Jacob Burns Film Center	364 Manville Rd.	Pleasantville	NY	10570	914-747-5555	1
P.J. Cinemas	1068 Route 112	Port Jefferson Station	NY	11776	631-928-3456	7
Roxy Theatre	20 Main Street	Potsdam	NY	13676	315-265-9630	2
Overlook Drive-In	12601 Overlook Road	Poughkeepsie	NY	12538	845-452-3445	1
Lyceum Annex	139 S Broadway	Red Hook	NY	12571	845-758-3311	1
Lyceum Cinemas	139 S Broadway	Red Hook	NY	12571	845-758-3311	7
Upstate Film Theatre	26 Montgomery St.	Rhinebeck	NY	12572	914-876-2515	2
Queen City Ridgewood Theatre	55-27 Myrtle Ave.	Ridgewood	NY	11385-3550	718-821-5993	6
Cinema Theatre Rochester	957 S. Clinton Ave.	Rochester	NY	14620	585-271-1785	1
Little Theatres	240 East Ave.	Rochester	NY	14604	716-232-4699	5
Sag Harbor Cinema	90 Main Street	Sag Harbor	NY	11963	631-725-0010	1
Broadway Joe's Theatre Grille	86 Congress Street	Saratoga Springs	NY	12866	518-587-3456	3
Saratoga Film Forum	320 Broadway	Saratoga Springs	NY	12866	518-584-3456	1
Orpheum Theatre	Main St.	Saugerties	NY	12477	845-246-6561	4
Sayville Theatres	103 Railroad Ave.	Sayville	NY	11715	631-589-0232	4
Fine Arts Theatres	365 Central Avenue	Scarsdale	NY	10583	914-723-6699	1
Proctors Theatre	432 State Street	Schenectady	NY	12301	518-382-3231	2
Scotia Cinema	117 Mohawk Ave.	Scotia	NY	12302	518-346-5055	1
Seaford Cinemas	516 Merrick Road	Seaford	NY	11783	516-409-8703	7
Maveli Twin Cinema 59	57 Kennedy Dr.	Spring Valley	NY	10977	845-578-4000	2
Joylan Theatre	11 W. Main St.	Springville	NY	14141	716-592-7402	1
Atrium Cinema	680 Arthur Kill Rd.	Staten Island	NY	10308-1106	718-317-8300	9
Lafayette Theatre	Route 59	Suffern	NY	10901	845-369-8234	1
Sunnyside Center Cinema	42-17 Queens Blvd.	Sunnyside	NY	11104	718-361-6869	5
Bristol Omnitheatre	500 South Franklin Street	Syracuse	NY	13202	315-425-9068	1
Palace Theatre - Syracuse	2384 James Street	Syracuse	NY	13206	315-463-9240	1
Westcott Cinema	524 Westcott Street	Syracuse	NY	13210	315-479-9911	2
State Theatres	1 Park Avenue	Tupper Lake	NY	12986	518-359-3593	1
Stanley Performing Arts Center	259 Genesee St.	Utica	NY	13501	315-724-4000	3
Uptown Theatres	2014 Genesee St.	Utica	NY	13502	315-797-0020	4
Walton Theatres	Gardiner Place	Walton	NY	13856	607-865-6688	1
Warwick Drive-In	5 Warwick Turnpike	Warwick	NY	10998	845-986-4440	3
South Bay Cinemas	495 W. Montauk Hwy.	West Babylon	NY	11704	631-587-7676	5
Hampton Arts Cinemas	2 Brook Road	W. Hampton Beach	NY	11978	631-288-2602	2
IMAX Theatre @ Palisades Ctr	4270 Palisades Center Drive	West Nyack	NY	10994	845-358-4629	1
Westbury Theatre	250 Post Ave.	Westbury	NY	11030	516-333-1911	2
Westhampton Beach Performing Arts	76 Main St.	Westhampton Beach	NY	11978	631-288-2350	1
Windham Theatre	11 Vets Road	Windham	NY	12496	518-734-6110	1
Wolcott Palace Theatre	61 E. Main St.	Wolcott	NY	14590	315-594-2785	1
Tinker Street Cinema	132 Tinker Street	Woodstock	NY	12498	845-679-6608	2

NEVADA

Name	Address	City	State	Zip	Phone	Screens
BC Cinemas	At the Hacienda Hotel	Boulder City	NV	89005	702-293-7221	1
Cinema 4	1145 Connolly	Elko	NV	89803	775-776-6606	4
Crystal 5 Theatre	676 Commercial St.	Elko	NV	89801	775-738-5214	5
Fallon 2	71 S. Maine St.	Fallon	NV	89406	775-423-6210	2
Incline Cinema	901 Tahoe Blvd.	Incline Village	NV	89451	530-546-5951	1
Brenden Theater 14	4321 W. Flamingo Road	Las Vegas	NV	89103-3903	702-507-4849	14
IMAX 3D Simulator at Caesars Palace	3500 Las Vegas Blvd. South	Las Vegas	NV	89109	702-733-9000	1
Luxor IMAX Theatre	3900 Las Vegas Blvd. S.	Las Vegas	NV	89119	702-262-4555	1
Laughlin Stadium 9	1955 South Casino Drive	Laughlin	NV	89029	702-299-3456	9
Virgin River Cinema	22 Main St	Mesquite	NV	89024	702-346-7700	4
Ironwood Stadium Cinema 8	1760 US Highway 395 N	Minden	NV	89423	775-782-7469	8
Fleischmann SkyDome	1650 N. Virginia St.	Reno	NV	89503	775-784-4811	1
Park Cinemas 2	740 W. Winnemucca Blvd.	Winnemucca	NV	89445	775-623-4454	2

NORTH CAROLINA

Name	Address	City	State	Zip	Phone	Screens
Earl Theatre	127 E Main St.	Ahoskie	NC	27910	252-332-2225	4
Badin Road Drive-In	2411 Badin Road	Albemarle	NC	28001	704-983-4882	1
Fine Arts Theatre	36 Biltmore Avenue	Asheville	NC	28801	828-232-1536	2
Atlantic Station Cinemas	Atlantic Sta Sphg Ctr.	Atlantic Beach	NC	28512	252-247-7016	6
Belmont Drive-In	314 Mc Adenville Road	Belmont	NC	28012	704-825-6044	1
Co-Ed Theatre	101 W. Main St.	Brevard	NC	28712	828-883-2200	1
Carolina Theatre	1088 E Franklin Street	Chapel Hill	NC	27514	919-933-8464	1
Chelsea Theatre	1129 Weaver Dairy Road	Chapel Hill	NC	27514	919-968-3005	3
Lumina Theatre	620 Market St	Chapel Hill	NC	27514	919-932-9000	4
UNC Student Union Auditorium	2 University of NC	Chapel Hill	NC	27514	919-962-2285	1
Varsity Theatre	123 E Franklin Street	Chapel Hill	NC	27514	919-967-8665	2
Observer Omnimax Theatre	301 North Tryon Street	Charlotte	NC	28202	704-372-6261	1
The Palace Cinema @ Kenton Pl	8325 Copley Dr	Cornelius	NC	28036	704-894-0894	12
Carolina Theatre	309 W Morgan Street	Durham	NC	27701	919-560-3040	2
Starlite Drive-In Theatre	2523 E. Club Blvd.	Durham	NC	27704-3533	919-688-1037	1
Eden Drive-In	106 Fireman Club Road	Eden	NC	27288	336-623-9669	2
Taylor Twin	208 South Broad Street	Edenton	NC	27932	252-482-2676	2

Name	Address	City	State	Zip	Phone	Screens
Gateway Cinemas	1417 W. Ehringhaus St.	Elizabeth City	NC	27909	252-338-3937	2
Emerald Plantation Cinemas	8700 Emerald Dr.	Emerald Isle	NC	28594	252-354-5012	5
Cameo Art House Theatre	225 Hay Street	Fayetteville	NC	28301	910-486-6633	1
Ruby Cinemas	2097 Georgia Rd.	Franklin	NC	28734	828-524-2076	4
Graham Cinema	119 N. Main	Graham	NC	27253	336-226-1488	1
Carousel Cinemas	1305 Battleground Ave	Greensboro	NC	27403	336-230-1620	15
Quaker Cinemas 1 & 2	615 Dolly Madison rd.	Greensboro	NC	27410	336-294-1113	2
Sedgefield Crossing $2 Cinemas	4631 High Point Rd.	Greensboro	NC	27407-4239	336-292-7469	7
Market Place Cinema	907 W Beckford Dr	Henderson	NC	27536	252-438-9060	4
Westchester Cinema	2200 Westchester Drive	High Point	NC	27262	336-886-7469	2
Starmount Crossing 5	209 Winston Road	Jonesville	NC	28642	336-526-3456	5
Gem Theatre	111 West 1st Street	Kannapolis	NC	28081	704-932-5111	1
Countryside Cinema Kernersville	631 N. Main Street	Kernersville	NC	27284	336-993-8200	5
Bessemer City Drive-In	1365 Bessemer City Rd.	Kings Mountain	NC	28086	704-739-2150	1
Louisburg Theatre 2	109 West Nash Street	Louisburg	NC	27549	919-496-3460	2
Bright Leaf Drive-In	Hwy. 52 N.	Mt. Airy	NC	27030	336-786-5494	1
Southgate Cinema 6	2806 Trent Rd.	New Bern	NC	28560	252-638-1820	6
State Cinema	117 N. College Ave.	Newton	NC	28658	828-464-2171	2
Colony Theatre	5438 Six Forks Road	Raleigh	NC	27609	919-847-5677	2
IMAX Theater Exploris	201 E. Hargett Street	Raleigh	NC	27601	919-834-4040	1
Mission Valley Cinema	2109 Avent Ferry Road	Raleigh	NC	27605	919-834-8520	5
NC State University Cinema	7306 NC State University	Raleigh	NC	27695	919-515-5146	1
Raleighwood Cinema Grill	6609 Falls of Neuse Road	Raleigh	NC	27615	919-847-0326	2
Rialto Theatre	1620 Glenwood Ave	Raleigh	NC	27608-2320	919-856-8683	1
Six Forks Station Cinema	9500 Forum Drive	Raleigh	NC	27615	919-846-3904	6
Studio	2526-111 Hillsborough Street	Raleigh	NC	27607	919-856-0111	2
Rockingham Theatre	205 Gilmer Street	Reidsville	NC	27320	336-349-5673	1
Roanoke Cinemas	1722 E 10th Street	Roanoke Rapids	NC	27870	252-537-6302	3
Palace Pointe Theater	5050 Durham Rd.	Roxboro	NC	27543	919-226-2300	8
Sunset Drive-In	US 74 West	Shelby	NC	28150	704-434-7782	1
Howell Theatre	141 S 3rd Street	Smithfield	NC	27577	919-934-8202	2
Sand Hills Cinemas 10	104 Brucewood Rd.	Southern Pines	NC	28387	910-695-1100	10
Surf Cinema	4836 Long Beach Rd. S.E.	Southport	NC	28461	910-457-0320	4
Quin Theatre	East Sylva Shopping Center	Sylva	NC	28779	828-586-5918	2
Smokey Moutain Cinema	235 Waynesville Plaza	Waynesville	NC	28786	828-452-9091	1
Cinema 3 Theatre	623 S. Madison St.	Whiteville	NC	28472-4129	910-642-6025	3
Marketplace Mall Theatres	2095 Peters Creek Parkway	Winston Salem	NC	27127	336-727-1787	6

NORTH DAKOTA

Name	Address	City	State	Zip	Phone	Screens
Belfield Theatre	113 1st Ave NW	Belfield	ND	58622	701-575-8140	1
Grand 11 Theatre	1486 Interstate Loop	Bismarck	ND	58501-0567	701-222-1607	11
Botono Theater	511 Main Street	Bottineau	ND	58318	701-228-2674	1
Fargo Theatre	314 Broadway	Fargo	ND	58102	701-239-8385	1
Cinema Twin Theatre	500 7th St. N.E.	Hazen	ND	58545	701-748-6101	2
Bison Twin Theaters	Buffalo Mall	Jamestown	ND	58401	701-252-5688	2
Cinema Twin	James Town Mall	Jamestown	ND	58401	701-252-9220	2
Kenmare Theatre	9 W. Division St.	Kenmare	ND	58746-0251	701-385-4433	1
Regis Theatre	144 S. Main St.	Stanley	ND	58784	701-628-2739	1
Grand Theatre	312 Main St	Williston	ND	58801	701-572-2232	7
Lake Park Drive-In	Highway 2 North	Williston	ND	58801	701-572-9137	1

OHIO

Name	Address	City	State	Zip	Phone	Screens
Ada Theatre	215 S Main St	Ada	OH	45810	419-596-5436	1
Gardner Student Center Theatre	303 Carroll St.	Akron	OH	44325	330-972-6757	1
Highland Theatre	826 W. Market Street	Akron	OH	44303	330-434-3253	1
Linda Theatre	1745 Goodyear Blvd	Akron	OH	44305	330-784-3443	1
Starlite Drive-In Theatre	2255 Beechmont Ave	Amelia	OH	45103	513-734-4001	1
Amherst	260 Church St.	Amherst	OH	44001	440-988-7711	1
Ashland Square Cinemas	214 Center Street	Ashland	OH	44805	419-289-2414	3
Ashtabula Cinemas	3409 North Ridge Road West	Ashtabula	OH	44004	440-992-8711	4
Athena Cinema	20 South Court Street	Athens	OH	45701	740-592-5106	3
Lake Cinema 8	588 W. Tuscarawas Ave.	Barberton	OH	44203	330-848-9100	8
Magic City Drive-In	5602 Cleveland	Barberton	OH	44203	330-825-4333	2
West Theatre	1017 Wooster Road West	Barberton	OH	44203	330-825-6912	1
Midway Theatre	210 W. Plane St.	Bethel	OH	45106	513-734-2278	1
Blanchester Cinemas	115 E. Main St	Blanchester	OH	45107	937-783-3333	3
Shannon Theatre	119 S. Main St.	Bluffton	OH	45817	419-358-1141	1
Cla-Zel Theatre	127 North Main Street	Bowling Green	OH	43402	419-353-1361	1
Bryan Theatre	140 South Lynn Street	Bryan	OH	43506	419-636-3354	3
Capitol Cinema 5	1715 Marion Rd.	Bucyrus	OH	44820-3118	419-563-2525	5
Canton Palace Theatre	605 Market Avenue North	Canton	OH	44702	330-454-8172	1
Esquire 6 Theatre	320 Ludlow Avenue	Cincinnati	OH	45220	513-281-8750	6
Mariemont 3 Theatre	6906 Wooster Pike	Cincinnati	OH	45227	513-272-2002	3
Mount Lookout Cinema Grill	3187 Linwood Ave.	Cincinnati	OH	45208	513-321-3211	2
Parkland Theatre	6550 Parkland Avenue	Cincinnati	OH	45233	513-333-5436	1
Robert D. Lindner Omnimax	1301 Western Avenue	Cincinnati	OH	45203	513-287-7000	1
Cleveland Cinematheque	1141 E. Blvd	Cleveland	OH	44104	216-421-7450	1
Great Lakes Science Center Omnimax	601 Erieside Ave.	Cleveland	OH	44114-1021	216-694-2000	1
Mayfield Drive-In	Rt. 322 at Mayfield Rd.	Cleveland	OH	44114	440-286-7173	1
Memphis 3 Drive-In	10543 Memphis	Cleveland	OH	44144	216-941-2892	3
South Drive-In	3050 South High Street	Columbus	OH	43207	614-491-6771	1
Studio 35 Cinema	3055 Indianola Avenue	Columbus	OH	43202	614-261-1581	1
Conneaut Plaza Theatre	348 W Main Road	Conneaut	OH	44030	440-593-6474	1
Huber Heights Movie Palace	5589 Old Troy Pike	Dayton	OH	45424-5702	937-233-5773	1
IMAX Theatre at the USAF	1 Wright Patterson AFB	Dayton	OH	45433	937-253-4629	1
New Neon Movies	130 E. 5th Street	Dayton	OH	45402	937-222-7469	1

Name	Address	City	State	Zip	Phone	Screens
Delaware Square Movies 5	1141 South Columbus Pike	Delaware	OH	43015	740-363-6634	5
Strand Theatre I, II, III	28 East Winter Street	Delaware	OH	43015	740-363-4914	3
Englewood Cinema	320 W. National Road	Englewood	OH	45322	937-836-0805	1
Paramount Cinema	301 South Front Street	Fremont	OH	43420	419-332-6321	4
Spring Valley 7	1284 Jackson Pike	Gallipolis	OH	45631	740-446-4524	7
Garrettsville Cinema	8001 State Street	Garrettsville	OH	44231	330-527-2026	3
Byjo Theatre	20 N Main	Germantown	OH	45327	937-855-7510	1
Wayne Cinema	538 S. Broadway St.	Greenville	OH	45331-1927	937-548-1410	2
Star Cinema 8-Grove City	2384 Stringtown Rd.	Grove City	OH	43123	614-539-3450	8
Holiday Auto Theatre	1816 Old Oxford Road.	Hamilton	OH	45013	513-929-2999	1
Star Cinema	211 Harry Sauner Rd	Hillsboro	OH	45133	937-393-8400	6
Elder Theatre	106 W. Pike St.	Jackson Center	OH	45334	937-596-6424	1
Kent Plaza Theatres 10	140 Cherry St.	Kent	OH	44240	330-673-4450	10
Hi-Road Drive-In	8059 State Route 68	Kenton	OH	43326	419-675-0922	1
Kenton Theatre 3	221 West Franklin Street	Kenton	OH	43326	937-596-5436	3
Detroit Theatre	16407 Detroit Ave	Lakewood	OH	44107	216-521-2245	2
Colony Square Cinemas 1 & 2	726 E. Main St.	Lebanon	OH	45036-1900	513-932-3456	2
State Theatre	69 S. Main St.	London	OH	43140	740-852-9933	1
Lorain Palace Civic Center	617 Broadway	Lorain	OH	44052	440-245-2323	1
Scioto Breeze Drive-In	9959 US Hwy 23	Lucasville	OH	45648	740-259-2881	2
Sunset Drive-In	4018 Rt. 309	Mansfield	OH	44903	419-529-5514	1
Marysville Cinemas	121 South Main Street	Marysville	OH	43040	937-644-8896	3
Lions Lincoln Theatre	156 Lincoln Way East	Massillon	OH	44646-6634	330-833-2413	1
Mc Arthur Twin Cinema	112 N Market St	Mc Arthur	OH	45651	740-596-2267	2
Atlas Cinemas Great Lakes 9	7850 Mentor Ave.	Mentor	OH	44060	440-974-0764	9
Capitol Theatres	22 W. High St.	Mount Gilead	OH	43338	419-947-3455	1
Movies 10-Nelsonville	14333 US 33 South	Nelsonville	OH	45764	740-753-3400	10
Quaker Cinemas	158 West High Ave	New Philadelphia	OH	44663	330-343-7300	4
USA Cinemas	930 Great East Plaza	Niles	OH	44446	330-652-8726	6
Posh Virginia Theatre	119 North Main	North Baltimore	OH	45872	419-257-4800	1
Aut-O-Rama Twin Drive-In	33395 Lorian Road	North Ridgeville	OH	44039	440-327-9595	2
Fox Woodville 4	3725 Williston Road	Northwood	OH	43616	419-693-8922	4
Starview Drive-In	2083 US Highway 20 W.	Norwalk	OH	44857	419-668-1819	1
Apollo	19 East College Street	Oberlin	OH	44074	440-774-7091	1
Sundance Kid Drive-In	4500 Navarre Avenue	Oregon	OH	43616	419-691-9668	1
Orr Twin Cinema	415 North Main Street	Orrville	OH	44667	330-682-5941	2
Cinema 20	1469 Menter Avenue	Painesville	OH	44077	440-354-6507	1
Parma 3 Theatres	5826 Ridge Road	Parma	OH	44129	440-885-0600	3
Marcus Cinemas - Pickerington	1776 Hill Road N.	Pickerington	OH	43147	614-759-6500	17
Midway Twin Drive-In	2736 State Route 59	Ravenna	OH	44266	330-296-9829	2
Salem Twin Cinema	2350 East State Street	Salem	OH	44460-2577	330-332-0797	2
Act 1 Cinema	11165 Reading Road.	Sharonville	OH	45241	513-733-8214	1
Auto Vue Drive-In	1409 4th Ave.	Sidney	OH	45365	937-492-5909	1
Starlight Drive-In	Rt. 127 & Rt. 119.	St. Henry	OH	45883	419-925-4944	1
Winter Drive-In	400 Luray Ave.	Steubenville	OH	43952	740-266-9020	1
Lynn Auto Theatre	9735 State Route 250 NW.	Strasburg	OH	44680	330-878-5797	2
Strongsville Cinema	14767 Pearl Road	Strongsville	OH	44136	440-572-0134	4
Tiffin Drive-In	4041 Hwy. 53 North	Tiffin	OH	44883	419-447-2551	1
Ohio Theatre	3114 Lagrange St.	Toledo	OH	43608	419-241-6785	1
Mayflower 4 Theatres	9 W Main Street	Troy	OH	45373	937-339-3456	4
Movies 5 - Troy	11 W. Main St.	Troy	OH	45373-3211	937-339-3456	5
Dixie Drive-In	6201 N. Dixie Dr.	Vandalia	OH	45377	937-890-5513	1
Blue Sky Drive-In	959 Broad Street	Wadsworth	OH	44281	330-334-1809	1
Great Oaks Cinema	251 Great Oaks Trail	Wadsworth	OH	44281	330-336-4464	2
Wapa Cinema	15 Willipie St.	Wapakoneta	OH	45895-1968	419-738-3718	1
Elm Road Twin Drive-In	1895 Elm Road	Warren	OH	44483	330-372-9732	2
Wheelersburg 6	8805 Ohio River Rd.	Wheelersburg	OH	45694	740-574-8620	6
Little Art Theatre	247 Xenia Ave.	Yellow Springs	OH	45387	937-767-7671	1

OKLAHOMA

Name	Address	City	State	Zip	Phone	Screens
Heritage Park Theatre	3917 N. Main.	Altus	OK	73521	580-482-0330	5
Rialto Twin Theatre	516 Flynn St	Alva	OK	73717	580-327-1900	2
Valley View Theatre	2505 Valley View Drive	Chickasha	OK	73018	580-482-3443	6
Washita Twin	509 Chickasha Ave.	Chickasha	OK	73023	405-222-1988	2
Palace Twin Theatre	926 W Main St	Duncan	OK	73533	580-255-5588	2
Durant Twin Cinema	915 W Main St	Durant	OK	74701	580-924-2711	2
Kickingbird Cinema	1225 East Danforth Rd	Edmond	OK	73083-3967	405-341-7227	8
Heritage Park Theatre Elk City	2708 W 3rd Street	Elk City	OK	73644	580-243-3545	4
Suburban Cinemas Northridge 8	1950 Highway 64 North	Guymon	OK	73942	580-338-3281	8
McCurtain Cinema	Route 3 Box 138	Idabel	OK	74745	580-286-2220	2
Vaska Theatre	1902 NW Ferris Ave	Lawton	OK	73505	580-353-5000	1
Cinema 69	1116 S. George Nigh Expressway	McAlester	OK	74502	918-423-6969	4
Cinema 69 Drive-In	1116 S. George Nigh Expressway	McAlester	OK	74502	918-423-6969	4
AAFES Base Theatre	3000 S. Douglas Ave.	Oklahoma City	OK	73109	405-734-3400	1
OmniDome Theatre	2100 NE 52nd Street	Oklahoma City	OK	73111	405-602-3663	1
Winchester Drive-In	6930 South Western	Oklahoma City	OK	73139	405-631-8851	1
Orpheum Theatre	210 W. 7th.	Okmulgee	OK	74447	918-756-2270	2
Ponca Plaza Twin	1403 E. Hartford	Ponca City	OK	74604	580-762-0857	2
Poteau Cinema	2214 N Broadway	Poteau	OK	74953	918-647-3606	3
Allred Theatre	418 S Vann St.	Pryor	OK	74361	918-825-2021	3
Admiral Drive-In	7355 E. Easton St.	Tulsa	OK	74115	918-835-5181	2
Eastland Mall Cinema 6	14002 E 21st Street	Tulsa	OK	74134	918-438-1177	6
Super Saver Cinemas 7	5970 E. 31st St, #A	Tulsa	OK	74135	918-665-0808	7
Center Theatre	124 S Wilson.	Vinita	OK	74301	918-256-5097	3
Picture Show Theatre	119 W Main.	Wilburton	OK	74578	918-465-2454	2
Lakeside Theatres	1425 34th St	Woodward	OK	73801	580-256-5798	3

OREGON

Name	Address	City	State	Zip	Phone	Screens
Columbian Theatre	1102 Marine Dr.	Astoria	OR	97103	503-325-3516	2
Eltrym Theatre	1809 1st St	Baker City	OR	97814	541-523-2522	3
Redwood Theatre	621 Chetco Ave.	Brookings	OR	97415	541-469-3701	4
Desert Theatre	68 N. Broadway	Burns	OR	97720	541-573-4220	1
Avalon Cinema Corvallis	160 NW Jackson Avenue	Corvallis	OR	97330-4827	541-752-4161	1
Fox Theatre Dallas OR	166 S.E. Mill St.	Dallas	OR	97338-1908	503-623-9346	1
Motor-Vu Drive-In Dallas	315 S.E. Fir Villa Rd.	Dallas	OR	97338-9200	503-623-4449	1
Bijou Arts Cinemas	492 E. 13th Ave.	Eugene	OR	97401	541-686-2458	2
Forest Theatre	1911 Pacific Avenue	Forest Grove	OR	97116	503-357-5107	1
Mt. Hood Theatre	401 E. Powell Blvd.	Gresham	OR	97030	503-665-0604	1
Hermiston Cinema	355 W Theatre St	Hermiston	OR	97838	541-567-1556	5
Skylight	107 Oak St	Hood River	OR	97031	541-386-4888	2
Granada Theatre	1311 Adams Ave	La Grande	OR	97850	541-963-3866	3
Lake Twin Cinema	106 N State St	Lake Oswego	OR	97034	503-635-5956	2
Alger Theatre	24 S. F St.	Lakeview	OR	97630	541-947-2023	1
Bijou Theatre	1624 NE Highway 101	Lincoln City	OR	97367	541-994-8255	1
Mack Theatre	510 NE 3rd St.	McMinnville	OR	97128	503-472-6225	2
Moonlight Theatre	433 NE 3rd Street	McMinnville	OR	97128	503-434-9515	4
Milwaukie Theatre	11011 SE Main St	Milwaukie	OR	97222	503-653-2222	2
Oak Grove 8 Cinemas	16100 SE McLaughlin Blvd	Milwaukie	OR	97222	503-653-9999	8
99 Indoor Twin	Highway 99W	Newberg	OR	97132	503-538-2738	2
99 West Drive-In	Portland Road	Newberg	OR	97132	503-538-2738	3
Cameo Theatre	304 E. First	Newberg	OR	97132	503-538-4479	1
Pix Theatre	358 S Oregon St.	Ontario	OR	97914	541-889-8788	1
The Reel Theatre 8 Ontario	477 SE 13th Street	Ontario	OR	97914	541-889-0013	8
Pendleton Cinemas	410 Southwest First St	Pendleton	OR	97801	541-278-0482	3
Savoy Theatre	811 Oregon St.	Port Orford	OR	97465	541-332-8105	1
Avalon Theatre	3451 S.E. Belmont Street	Portland	OR	97214	503-238-1617	2
Bagdad Theatre	3702 S.E. Hawthorne Blvd.	Portland	OR	97214	503-669-8754	1
Cine Magic Theatre	2021 S.E. Hawthorne Blvd.	Portland	OR	97214	503-231-7919	1
Cinema 21	616 NW 21st Ave	Portland	OR	97209	503-223-4515	1
Clinton Street Theater	2522 SE Clinton Street	Portland	OR	97202	503-238-8899	1
Fifth Avenue Cinemas	510 Southwest Hall	Portland	OR	97201	503-725-4470	1
Hollywood Theatre	4122 NE Sandy Blvd.	Portland	OR	97212	503-281-4215	3
Kennedy School Theatre	5736 NE. 33rd St.	Portland	OR	97060	503-669-8754	2
Laurelhurst Theatre	2735 E Burnside	Portland	OR	97222	503-232-5511	4
Mission Theatre	1624 NW Glisan	Portland	OR	97209	503-669-8754	1
Moreland Theatre	6712 SE Milwaukie Avenue	Portland	OR	97202	503-236-5257	1
Northwest Film - Guild Theatre	1219 S.W. Park Ave.	Portland	OR	97205	503-221-1156	2
Northwest Film - Whitsell Aud	1219 SW Park Ave	Portland	OR	97205	503-221-1156	1
OMNIMAX @ OR Museum of Science and Industry	1945 SE Water Avenue	Portland	OR	97214-3354	503-797-4000	1
Portlander Cinema	10350 N. Vancover Way	Portland	OR	97217	503-240-5850	1
Roseway Theatre	7229 NE Sandy Blvd.	Portland	OR	97213	503-287-8119	1
St. Johns 1 & 2 Theatre	8704 N Lombard Street	Portland	OR	97203	503-286-1768	2
St. Johns Dome Theater	8203 N. Ivanhoe	Portland	OR	97203	503-225-5555	1
Redmond Theatre	1535 SW Odem Medo Way	Redmond	OR	97756	541-548-1244	1
Salem Cinema	445 High Street SE	Salem	OR	97301-3615	503-378-7676	1
Sandy Cinemas	16605 Champion Way	Sandy	OR	97055	503-826-8100	8
Cannes Cinema Center	1026 12th Ave.	Seaside	OR	97138-7946	503-738-0671	5
Palace Theatre	200 N. Water	Silverton	OR	97381	503-873-2233	1
Columbia Theatre St. Helens	212 S. First Street	St. Helens	OR	97051	503-397-9791	1
Star Cinema	350 North 3rd Avenue	Stayton	OR	97383-1726	503-767-7827	1
Rio Theatre	1439 Main St.	Sweet Home	OR	97386-1618	541-367-5559	1
Cascade Cinema	1410 W 6th St.	The Dalles	OR	97058	541-298-2600	2
Columbia Cinema	2727 W 7th St.	The Dalles	OR	97058	541-296-8081	4
Tigard Joy Theatre	11959 SW Pacific Hwy	Tigard	OR	97223	503-639-1482	1
Coliseum Theatre	310 Main Ave	Tillamook	OR	97141	503-842-6111	1
Edgefield Powerstation Theatre	2126 S.W. Halsey	Troutdale	OR	97060	503-669-8754	1
Tualatin Twin	8345 Nyberg Road	Tualatin	OR	97062	503-692-5000	2

PENNSYLVANIA

Name	Address	City	State	Zip	Phone	Screens
Kane Road Drive-In	2971 Kane Rd.	Aliquippa	PA	15001	724-378-1970	2
19th Street Theatre	527 N. 19th Street	Allentown	PA	18104	610-432-0888	1
Franklin Theater	429 Tilghman Street	Allentown	PA	18102	610-433-3640	1
Ambler Theater	108 E. Butler Avenue	Ambler	PA	19002	215-345-7855	3
Ambridge Family Theatre	645 Merchant Street	Ambridge	PA	15003	724-251-9760	1
Allen's Theatre & MJ's Coffehouse	36 E. Main Street	Annville	PA	17003	717-867-4766	1
Pitt	134 E Pitt St.	Bedford	PA	15522	814-623-7511	1
Garman Opera House Movie Thea	116 E. High St.	Bellefonte	PA	16823	814-353-8803	1
Berwick Theatre	110 E. Front Street	Berwick	PA	18603	570-752-9070	1
Boyd Theatre	30 West Broad Street	Bethlehem	PA	18018	610-866-1521	1
Cinema Center Bloomsburg	1879 New Berwick Highway	Bloomsburg	PA	17815	570-387-8516	12
State Theatre	61 N. Reading Ave.	Boyertown	PA	19512	610-367-4737	1
Bradfor Main Street Movies	123 Main Street	Bradford	PA	16701	814-363-9388	2
Star City Cinemas - S. Fayette 14	100 Hickory Grade Road	Bridgeville	PA	15017	412-221-6789	14
Moonlite Drive-In Theatre	Route 322 West	Brookville	PA	15825	814-849-5588	2
Malden Drive-In	380 Old National Pike Rd.	Brownsville	PA	15417	724-785-5310	1
Bryn Mawr 2 Movie Theater	824 Lancaster Ave.	Bryn Mawr	PA	19010	610-520-7373	2
Clearview Mall Cinemas	101 Clearview Circle; Route 8	Butler	PA	16001	724-283-3884	8
Pioneer Drive-In	1985 N Main Street	Butler	PA	16003	724 284-5003	3
Rialto Theatre	5 E. Main St.	Canton	PA	17724	570-268-7469	2
Carlisle Theatre	44 West High Street	Carlisle	PA	17013	717-258-0666	1
R/C Cinemas 8	250 Noble Blvd.	Carlisle	PA	17013	717-249-5511	8
Skyview Twin Drive-IN	Route 88	Carmichaels	PA		724-966-2364	2
Hi-Way Drive-In	Rt. 219	Carrolltown	PA	15722	814-344-8684	1

Name	Address	City	State	Zip	Phone	Screens
Cheswick Quads	1500 Pittsburgh St.	Cheswick	PA	15024	724-274-6646	6
Ritz Twin	111 E Market	Clearfield	PA	16830	814-765-5835	2
Angela Triplex	113 E Phillips St.	Coaldale	PA	18218	570-645-6204	3
Iris Theatre	157 W. Adams St.	Cochranton	PA	16314	814-425-2900	2
Columbia Drive-In	4061 Columbia Ave	Columbia	PA	17512	717-684-7708	1
Haar's Drive-In	185 Logan Road	Dillsburg	PA	17019	717-432-3011	1
County Theatre	20 E. State St.	Doylestown	PA	18901	215-345-6789	2
Pocono Cinema & Coffee Shop	88 S. Courtland St.	East Stroudsburg	PA	18301	570-421-3456	3
25th Street Cinema	2555 Nazareth Rd. Ste. #107; 25th St.	Easton	PA	18045	610-252-2029	4
Gateway Cinema Center	50 Gateway Shopping Center	Edwardsville	PA	18704	570-287-7200	6
Movietown Theatre	700 N Hanover St	Elizabethtown	PA	17022	717-361-7536	10
Emmaus Cinema	19 S. 4th St.	Emmaus	PA	18049	610-965-2878	1
Main 2 Theatres	128 East Main	Ephrata	PA	17522	717-733-2121	2
Eastway Plaza Cinemas	4050 Buffalo Road	Erie	PA	16510	814-456-9177	2
Plaza Theatre	800 W. Erie Plaza	Erie	PA	16505	814-456-9177	4
West Erie Plaza Cinemas	800 W. Erie Plaza	Erie	PA	16505	814-456-9177	4
Glen Theatre	37 Manchester Street	Glen Rock	PA	17327	717-235-3789	1
Guthrie Theatre	232 S Broad St	Grove City	PA	16127	724-458-9420	1
Hamburg Strand Movie	234 State St.	Hamburg	PA	19526	610-562-4750	1
Value Cinemas	1150 Carlisle Street	Hanover	PA	17331	717-633-6470	6
Midtown Cinema	250 Reily Street	Harrisburg	PA	17102	717-909-6566	4
Whitaker Grass/Rite Aid IMAX	222 Market Street	Harrisburg	PA	17101	717-221-8201	1
Cocoaplex Cinema	1130 Cocoa Ave	Hershey	PA	17033	717-312-1300	7
Cinema 6	Route 6 Plaza	Honesdale	PA	18431	570-251-3456	6
Bargain Cinema Village Mall	Blair Mill Road	Horsham	PA	19044	215-674-1919	2
Huntingdon Cinema Clifton 5	717 Washington St.	Huntingdon	PA	16652	814-643-3310	5
Palace Gardens Drive-In Theatr	225 Indian Springs Rd.	Indiana	PA	15701	724-465-9032	1
Lamp Theatre	220 Main St.	Irwin	PA	15642	724-863-9767	1
Norwin Hills Cinema	8775 Norwin Ave,	Irwin	PA	15642	724-864-7727	10
Baederwood 2 Theatre	1615 The Fairway	Jenkintown	PA	19046	215-887-6310	2
Chas III	212 Old York Rd	Jenkintown	PA	19046	215-886-9800	3
Silver Drive-In	1704 Scalp Ave.	Johnstown	PA	15904	814-266-9177	1
Westfield Mall Cinemas 12	3200 Elton Road	Johnstown	PA	15904	814-266-3133	12
Westwood Plaza Theatre	Westwood Plaza	Johnstown	PA	15905	814-255-2116	3
Family Drive-In Theatre	Route 6 E.	Kane	PA	16735	814-837-9760	1
Strand Theatre	32 N White Oak St.	Kutztown	PA	19530	610-683-8775	2
Cineburger	Route 30 East	Latrobe	PA	15650	724-539-7500	3
Mahoning Drive-In Theatre	Rt. 443	Lehighton	PA	18235	570-645-6201	1
Mahoning Valley 8 Cinema	Rt. 443, Carbon Plaza Mall	Lehighton	PA	18235	610-377-8626	8
Campus Theater	413 Market Street	Lewisburg	PA	17837	570-524-9628	1
Miller Cinema 6	46 W. Market St.	Lewistown	PA	17044	717-248-8654	6
Roxy Theatre Lock Haven	314 E. Main Street	Lock Haven	PA	17745	570-748-5606	1
Foxmoor Cinema 7	Rt. 209, Foxmoor Factory Outlet Ctr.	Marshalls Creek	PA	18335	570-223-7775	7
Tri-State Drive-In	1023 Pennsylvania Ave.	Matamoras	PA	18336	570-491-5000	1
Tristate Indoor	1023 Pennsylvania Ave.	Matamoras	PA	18336	570-491-5000	2
Meadville Cinemas	952 Park Avenue	Meadville	PA	16335	814-336-5696	4
Elks Theatre	Emaus & Union Streets	Middletown	PA	17057	717-944-1981	1
Point Of View Cinema	121 West Frederick Street	Millersville	PA	17551	717-872-4131	1
Montrose Pump N Pantry Theatre	18 Public Ave	Montrose	PA	18801	570-278-3352	1
Dependable Drive In	Moon Township	Moon Township	PA	15108	412-264-7011	3
Dollar Twin Theatre	Pennsbury Plaza	Morrisville	PA	19067	215-736-0771	2
Ritz Theatre	9 N Main St.	Muncy	PA	17756	570-546-3740	1
Narberth Theatre	129 N. Narberth Ave.	Narberth	PA	19072	610-667-0115	2
Westgate Cinema	2000 West State Street	New Castle	PA	16101	724-652-9063	7
West Shore Theatre	317 Bridge Street	New Cumberland	PA	17070	717-774-7160	1
Newtown	120 N. State St.	Newtown	PA	18940	215-968-3859	1
Roxy Theatre	2004 Main Street	Northampton	PA	18067	610-262-7699	1
Oaks Theatre	310 Allegheny River Blvd.	Oakmont	PA	15139	412-828-6311	1
Shankweiler Drive-In	Route 309	Orefield	PA	18069	610-481-0800	1
Cinema Center of Palmyra	2 North Londonderry Square	Palmyra	PA	17078	717-838-4809	12
Cinemagic 3 At Penn	3925 Walnut Street	Philadelphia	PA	19104-3608	215-222-5555	3
International House's Neighbor	3701 Chestnut Street	Philadelphia	PA	19104	215-895-6542	1
Ritz East	204 Walnut St.	Philadelphia	PA	19106	215-925-7900	2
Ritz Theatres Ritz at the Bourse	400 Ramstead Street	Philadelphia	PA	19106-0025	215-925-7900	5
Ritz Theatres Ritz Five	214 Walnut Street	Philadelphia	PA	19106-3904	215-925-7900	5
Roxy Theater	2023 Sanson St.	Philadelphia	PA	19103	215-923-6699	2
Tuttleman Imax Dome Theatre	222 North 20 Street.	Philadelphia	PA	19103	215-448-1200	1
Rowland Theatre Philipsburg	125 N. Front Street	Philipsburg	PA	16866	814-342-0477	1
Colonial Theatre	227 Bridge Street	Phoenixville	PA	19460	610-917-0223	1
Byham Theater	101 Sixth Street	Pittsburgh	PA	15222	412-456-1350	1
Carnegie Museum of Art	4400 Forbes Ave	Pittsburgh	PA	15213-4080	412-622-3212	1
Cinema 4	3075 W. LIBERTY AVENUE	Pittsburgh	PA	15216	412-344-6670	4
Harmar Cinemas	2583 Freeport Road	Pittsburgh	PA	15238	412-826-1960	4
Melwood Screening Room	477 Melwood Ave	Pittsburgh	PA	15213	412-682-4111	1
Pittsburgh Harris Theater	803 Liberty Aveue	Pittsburgh	PA	15222	412-682-4111	1
Plaza Theater 2	4765 Liberty Ave.	Pittsburgh	PA	15224-2039	412-681-0289	2
Rangos OMNIMAX Theater, Carnegie Science Center	1 Allegheny Avenue	Pittsburgh	PA	15212	412-237-3400	1
Regent Square Theatre	1035 S. BRADDOCK AVENUE	Pittsburgh	PA	15218	412-681-5449	1
Waterworks Cinema 10	923 Freeport Rd.	Pittsburgh	PA	15238	412-784-1402	10
Bar Ann Drive-In	1815 S. Main St.	Portage	PA	15963	814-736-9450	1
$2 Movies	240-5 S West End Blvd.	Quakertown	PA	18951	215-536-3830	6
Fox East Theatre	4350 Perkiomen Ave	Reading	PA	19606	610-779-8121	4
Reading Discount Movie	3225 5th Street Hwy	Reading	PA	19605	610-929-0201	4
Cinema 356	718 S. Pike Ave.	Sarver	PA	16055	412-224-7620	4
South Pike Cinemas	718 South Pike Road.	Sarver	PA	16055	724-224-7620	10
Sayre Theatre	205 S. Elmer Ave.	Sayre	PA	18840	570-268-2787	3
Palace Theatre	Route 601 N	Somerset	PA	15501	814-445-3464	1
Broad Theatre	24 W. Broad St.	Souderton	PA	18964	215-723-3444	1
Diamond Theatre	19 N Michael St.	St Marys	PA	15857	814-834-7434	2

Name	Address	City	State	Zip	Phone	Screens
Starlite Drive-In State Colleg	1100 Benner Pike	State College	PA	16801	814-237-0001	1
Keystone	601 Main Street	Towanda	PA	18848-1613	570-268-2787	1
Dietrich Theater	60 E. Tioga Street	Tunkhannock	PA	18657	570-836-1022	2
Lipuma Galaxy Drive-In	Route 66 North	Vandergrift	PA	15690	724-568-5541	1
Becky's Drive-In Theatre	4548 Lehigh Drive	Walnutport	PA	18088	610-767-2249	1
Mall Cinemas	301 Oak Springs Rd	Washington	PA	15301	724-250-7550	8
Watson Theatre	131 Main Street	Watsontown	PA	17777	570-538-1778	1
Waynesboro Theatre	75 Main Street	Waynesboro	PA	17268	717-762-7879	1
Arcadia Theater	50 Main Street	Wellsboro	PA	16901	570-724-4957	4
Kendig Square Movies 6	2600 Willow Street Pike	Willow Street	PA	17584	717-464-7564	6
South York Plaza Cinemas 4	217 Pauline Drive	York	PA	17402	717-741-5409	4

RHODE ISLAND

Name	Address	City	State	Zip	Phone	Screens
Pastime Theater	91 Bradford Ave	Bristol	RI	02809-1908	401-253-2504	2
Holiday Cinemas	105 Chase Lane	Middletown	RI	02842	401-847-3456	1
Narragansett 2 Theatres	3 Beach Street	Narragansett	RI	02882	401-782-2077	2
Jane Pickens Theatre	49 Touro Street	Newport	RI	02840	401-846-5252	1
Opera House 4 Theatres	19 Touro Street	Newport	RI	02840	401-847-3456	4
Rustic Drive-In	Rte 146 Louisquisset Pike	North Smithfield	RI	02896	401-769-7601	3
Avon Cinemas	260 Thayer Street	Providence	RI	02906	401-421-3315	1
Cable Car	204 S Main	Providence	RI	02903	401-272-3970	1
Castle Cinema Cafe	1030 Chalkstone Ave.	Providence	RI	02908	401-528-1976	2
Columbus Theatre	270 Broadway	Providence	RI	02903	401-621-9660	1
Feinstein IMAX Theatre	9 Providence Place Suite R2	Providence	RI	02903	401-453-4629	1
Campus Cinemas	17 Columbia Street	Wakefield	RI	02879	401-783-5972	2

SOUTH CAROLINA

Name	Address	City	State	Zip	Phone	Screens
Hiway 21 Drive-In Beaufort	55 Parker Dr.	Beaufort	SC	29906-8317	843-846-4500	1
American Theater	446 King St.	Charleston	SC	29407	843-722-3456	2
IMAX Theater	360 Concord St.	Charleston	SC	29401	843-725-4629	1
South Windermere	94 Folly Road	Charleston	SC	29407-7551	843-556-1073	2
Terrace	1956 Maybank Hwy.	Charleston	SC	29412-2126	843-762-9494	3
Nickelodeon Theatre	937 Main Street	Columbia	SC	29210-3965	803-254-3433	1
St. Andrews Cinema 5	527 St Andrews Road	Columbia	SC	29210	803-772-7469	5
Colony 2 Theatre	315 W. Main Street	Easley	SC	29640	864-859-9392	2
Easley Cinemas 8.	5065 Calhoun Memorial Hwy.	Easley	SC	29640	864-850-5200	8
Coffee Underground Theatre	1 E. Coffee Street	Greenville	SC	29601	864-298-0494	1
REI Greenwood Cinema 10.	533 Bypass Hwy. 72 NW	Greenwood	SC	29646	864-943-0101	10
Northridge 10.	435 William Hilton Parkway	Hilton Head	SC	29926	843-342-3800	10
Coligny Theatre	1 N. Forest Beach Drive.	Hilton Head Island	SC	29928	838-686-3500	1
Crown Cinema	1041 W. Meeting St.	Lancaster	SC	29720-2205	803-285-5544	2
Monetta Drive-In Theatre	5822 Columbia Highway N.	Monetta	SC	29105	803-685-7949	1
IMAX Discovery Theater	1195 Celebrity Circle.	Myrtle Beach	SC	29577	843-444-3333	1
Seneca Cinema 8	675 Highway 123 Bypass	Seneca	SC	29678	864-882-0000	8
Union Square Cinema.	719 N. Duncan Bypass	Union	SC	29379-8605	864-427-5500	2
Ivanhoe Cinema 4	320 Ivanhoe Rd.	Walterboro	SC	29488	843-549-6400	4

SOUTH DAKOTA

Name	Address	City	State	Zip	Phone	Screens
Showcase Cinema 5.	City Plaza	Brookings	SD	57006	605-692-4412	5
Logan Dells Theatre	511 E 4th Street	Dell Rapids	SD	57022	605-428-3456	1
Geju - Hot Springs Theatre	241 N River St	Hot Springs	SD	57747-1625	605-745-4169	1
Logan Huron Cinema 3.	215 Dakota Ave S	Huron	SD	57350	605-352-6666	3
Mill Theatres 1-2-3	318 S Main St	Milbank	SD	57252-1811	605-432-5772	3
Logan Roxy Cinema 4	209 N Lawler.	Mitchell	SD	57301	605-996-5444	4
Logan Starlite Drive-In	N Hwy 37	Mitchell	SD	57301	605-996-4511	1
Mac Cinema	311 Main.	Mobridge	SD	57601	605-845-2021	1
Pheasant Drive-In Theatre	1 Pheasant Estate.	Mobridge	SD	57601	605-845-2021	1
State 123 Theatre	123 W. Capitol Drive	Pierre	SD	57501	605-224-5858	3
Elks Theatre - Rapid City	512 6th St.	Rapid City	SD	57701-2726	605-341-4149	2
Stargate Theatre.	919 E North St	Rapid City	SD	57701	605-343-8430	2
Northern Hills	1830 North Main Street	Spearfish	SD	57783	605-642-4212	6
Coyote Theatre.	10 E. Main St.	Vermillion	SD	57069	605-624-3331	2
Vermillion Theatre.	4 W. Main St.	Vermillion	SD	57069	605-624-3546	1
Watertown 5.	1111 14th St SE	Watertown	SD	57201	605-886-5000	5

TENNESSEE

Name	Address	City	State	Zip	Phone	Screens
American Cinema of Athens	Whiteway Shopping Center	Athens	TN	37303	423-745-6893	1
Midway Drive-In Theatre	2133 Highway 30 E	Athens	TN	37303	423-263-2632	1
Ajay Hollywood 20 Cinema	6711 Stage Rd.	Bartlett	TN	38134	901-380-1121	20
Twin City Drive-In	2512 Volunteer Parkway	Bristol	TN	37620	423-764-8033	2
IMAX 3D @ Tennessee Aquarium	201 Chestnut Street	Chattanooga	TN	37401	423-266-4629	1
Cinema 1 & 2.	300 Grove Ave. S.W.	Cleveland	TN	37311	423-476-9006	2
Shadybrook 11 Cinemas	1907 Shadybrook Street	Columbia	TN	38401	931-381-7469	11
Broadway Drive-In	3020 Highway 70 East.	Dickson	TN	37055	615-446-2786	1
Roxy 8 Theater	Hwy 46 South	Dickson	TN	37055	615-441-8788	8
Dunlap Drive-In	Hwy 127 South	Dunlap	TN	37327	423-949-3759	1
Bonnie Kate Theatre	115 South Sycamore St.	Elizabethton	TN	37643	423-543-1933	2
The Lincoln Theatre	120 E. College St.	Fayetteville	TN	37334	931-433-1943	2
Franklin Cinema	419 Main St.	Franklin	TN	37064	615-790-7122	1
Ajay Hollywood Cinema 16	575 Vann Drive	Jackson	TN	38305	901-442-3456	16
Real to Reel	130 W. Springbrook Dr.	Johnson City	TN	37604	423-282-2131	2
Halls Cinema	3800 Neal Road	Knoxville	TN	37918	865-922-9095	7
Lafayette Cinema	204 College Street	Lafayette	TN	37083	615-666-6116	1
Macon Drive-In Theater	3570 Scottsville Rd.	Lafayette	TN	37083	615-666-4411	1
Hi Way 50 Drive-In	1584 Fayetteville Highway	Lewisburg	TN	37047	931-270-1591	1

Name	Address	City	State	Zip	Phone	Screens
Three Star	1360 Sparta Street	Mc Minnville	TN	37110	931-473-7600	5
Union Planters IMAX	3050 Central Ave.	Memphis	TN	38111	901-320-6362	1
Crossroads Cinema I & II	6180 Broadway	Merrillville	TN	46410	219-980-0588	2
KUC Theater at MTSU	1301 E Main Street	Murfreesboro	TN	37132	615-898-2551	1
On The Green @ MSU	1301 East Main Street	Murfreesboro	TN	37132	615-898-2454	1
Premiere 6 Theater	810 N.W. Broad St.	Murfreesboro	TN	37129	615-896-4100	6
Agape Fellowship Church	645 Old Hickory Blvd.	Nashville	TN	37202	615-297-7065	1
Belcourt Theatre	2102 Belcourt Ave.	Nashville	TN	37212	615-383-9140	2
Sarratt Cinema	2300 Vanderbilt Place	Nashville	TN	37235	615-322-2425	1
The Frist Center	919 Broadway	Nashville	TN	37203	615-244-3340	1
Watkins Institute	100 Powell Place	Nashville	TN	37204	615-383-4848	1
Newport Cinema 4	424 Heritage Boulevard	Newport	TN	37821	423-625-3429	4
Parisian Theatre	1075 Jim Adams Dr,	Paris	TN	38242	731-644-3006	4
Rogersville Cinema 4	1287 E. Main St.	Rogersville	TN	37857	423-921-9000	4
Movies on the Parkway	713 Winfield Dunn Parkway	Sevierville	TN	37876	865-453-9055	5
Capri Twin Theatre	201 Depot Street	Shelbyville	TN	37144	931-684-7306	2
Hollywood Showcase	1800 W. Reelfoot Ave.	Union City	TN	38261	731-885-5500	6
Mi-De-Ga Theatre	106 W. Court Sq	Waverly	TN	37185	931-296-4500	2
Oldham Theatre	115 1st Ave NE	Winchester	TN	37398	931-967-2515	2

TEXAS

Name	Address	City	State	Zip	Phone	Screens
Westwood Twin Theatre	3440 North 1st	Abilene	TX	79603	915-672-1288	2
Cinema 1 & 2	109 E. HOlland Ave	Alpine	TX	79830	915-837-5111	2
Tascosa Drive-In.	999 Dumas Dr.	Amarillo	TX	79107	806-383-3882	1
Festival Marketplace 6	2900 E Pioneer Parkway	Arlington	TX	76010	817-640-6006	6
Movie Tavern at Green Oaks	5727 West I-20	Arlington	TX	76016	817-563-7469	8
Alamo Drafthouse Downtown	409 Colorado St	Austin	TX	78701	512-867-1839	2
Alamo Drafthouse Lake Creek.	13729 Research Blvd.	Austin	TX	78750	512-476-1320	8
Alamo Drafthouse Village	2700 W. Anderson Lane.	Austin	TX	78757	512-476-1320	4
Bob Bullock IMAX Theatre	1800 N Congress Avenue	Austin	TX	78701	512-936-8746	1
Highland 10	6700 Middle Fiskville Road	Austin	TX	78752	512-467-7305	10
Millennium Theater	1156 Hargrave	Austin	TX	78704	512-472-6932	1
Paramount Theatre	713 Congress Ave.	Austin	TX	78701	512-472-5470	1
Texas Union Theatre	24th & Guadalupe St. Univ. of Texas.	Austin	TX	78701	512-475-6636	1
Plaza Twin - Beeville	N Bypass 181	Beeville	TX	78102	361-358-9373	2
Rio 6	806 E. Houston	Beeville	TX	78102	361-358-9373	6
Ritz	401 S Main	Big Spring	TX	79721	915-263-7480	3
Majestic 6 Theatre	Highway 121 S.	Bonham	TX	75476	903-583-2222	6
Westwood Cinema 3.	2100 Highway 290 W.	Brenham	TX	77833	409-836-7656	3
Palace Theatre	210 Main St	Canadian	TX	79014	806-323-5133	1
Varsity Theatre	2302 4th Ave.	Canyon	TX	79015	806-655-9529	1
Cinema Grill Cafe	2625 Old Denton Rd.	Carrollton	TX	75007	972-389-9968	7
Carthage Twin Theatre	1120 W Panola St	Carthage	TX	75633	903-693-7841	2
Rio Theatre	West Side Square	Center	TX	75935	936-598-3864	1
Lone Star Four Theatre	1900 Avenue G NW.	Childress	TX	79201	940-937-6786	4
Texan Theatre.	102 E Houston St.	Cleveland	TX	77327-4510	281-592-6464	1
Commerce Cineplex	2208 Live Oak St.	Commerce	TX	75428	903-886-8027	4
Pine Hollow Cinema 6.	2000 I-45 North.	Conroe	TX	77305	936-539-4995	6
Cove Theatre	111 W. Ave. D	Copperas Cove	TX	76522	254-547-2210	1
Mission Theatre	409 Denrock Ave.	Dalhart.	TX	79022	806-249-4241	2
Lakewood Theatres.	1825 Abrams Parkway	Dallas	TX	75214	214-827-5253	1
Studio Movie Grill	5405 BeltLine Road.	Dallas	TX	75248	972-991-6684	4
TI Founders IMAX	1318 Second Avenue	Dallas	TX	75210	214-428-5555	1
Plaza 3 Theatre	1510 Hwy 51 South.	Decatur	TX	76234	940-627-5522	3
Evelyn Theatre	705 S. Bliss St.	Dumas	TX	79029	806-935-4005	2
Eagle Pass Cinema 3	455 S. Bibb Ave.	Eagle Pass.	TX	78852	830-773-2035.	3
Majestic Theatre - Eastland.	108 N Lamar St.	Eastland	TX	76448	254-629-1322	1
Showplace 3 Cinema Inc.	904 West Loop	El Campo.	TX	77437	979-543-8182	3
Fort Worth Museum of Science	1501 Montgomery Street	Fort Worth	TX	76107	888-255-9300	1
Ridgmar Movie Tavern	6801 Ridgmar Meadow Rd.	Ft. Worth	TX	76116	817-989-7469	6
IMAX 3D @ Moody Gardens.	1 Hope Blvd.	Galveston	TX	77554	800-582-4673	1
Ganado Theatre	120 South 3rd St.	Ganado	TX	77962	361-771-2164	1
Walnut Theaters	3310 W. Walnut St.	Garland	TX	75042	972-494-6684	1
Last Drive-In Picture Show &	2912 S State Hwy 36.	Gatesville.	TX	76528	254-865-8445	2
National Theatre	522 Oak Street	Graham	TX	76450-3039	940-549-2077	3
Brazos Cinema Drive-In	West Pearl Street	Granbury	TX	76048	817-573-1311	4
Driftwood Theatre 6	1201 Old Cleburne Rd.	Granbury	TX	76048	817-573-6684	6
Majestic 8 Theatres	1401 Joe Ramsey Blvd.	Greenville	TX	75402-7602	903-455-5400	8
Texan Theatre.	110 S Bell St.	Hamilton	TX	76531	254-386-5216	1
Hempstead Theater	740 12th Street	Hempstead	TX	77445	979-826-2981	6
Circle Plaza Cinema 3	1401 Lone Star St.	Henderson	TX	75653	903-957-4217	3
Regent Highland Park Village	32 Highland Park Village	Highland Park	TX	75206	214-526-9668	4
Texas Theatre.	107 S. Waco St.	Hillsboro	TX	76645-3326	254-582-3456	2
Alamo Drafthouse West Oaks	Westheimer & Hwy. 6.	Houston	TX	77082	281-556-5200	6
Aurora Picture Show.	800 Aurora Street	Houston	TX	77009	713-868-2101	1
Fun Plex 3 Cinemas	13700 Beechnut Street	Houston.	TX	77083	281-493-0390	1
IMAX Space Center Houston	1601 NASA Road	Houston	TX	77058	281-244-2100	1
Museum of Fine Arts Houston.	1001 Bissonnet	Houston	TX	77005	713-639-7375	1
North Oaks Cinema 6	4623 FM 1960 West	Houston	TX	77069	832-436-0008	6
Rice Media Center	2030 University Blvd	Houston	TX	77030	713-348-4853	1
Southpoint Dollar Cinema	12813 Gulf Freeway	Houston.	TX	77034	281-481-5942	6
West Bellfort Cinema 5	7703 W. Bellfort	Houston.	TX	77071	713-726-8700	5
Windchimes Cinema 8	13155 Westheimer Road	Houston.	TX	77077	281-920-9900	8
Wortham IMAX.	1 Hermann Circle Drive	Houston.	TX	77030	713-639-4600	2
Cinema 10 Theatre	3027 11 Street	Huntsville.	TX	77340	936-291-0248	10
Everest Theatre	700 Plymouth Park	Irving	TX	75061-1947	972-514-1414	2
Plaza Theatres	110 Plaza Dr.	Kerrville	TX	78028	830-895-4242	6
Four Star Cinema	1607 US Highway 259 N	Kilgore	TX	75663	903-758-4799	4
Starplex Brazos Mall 3	110 Hwy 332.	Lake Jackson	TX	77566	979-480-9620	3

Name	Address	City	State	Zip	Phone	Screens
The Movies at Star Village	3980 Boat Club Road	Lake Worth	TX	76180	817-238-8300	10
Rave Motion Pictures						
Hickory Creek 16	8380 S Stemmons Rd	Lewisville	TX	75067	940-321-2788	16
Lan-Tex Theatre	113 W Main St	Llano	TX	78643	915-247-2524	1
Aviator Theatres	120 Cunningham Dr.	Lockhart	TX	78644	512-398-4100	2
Science Spectrum Omnimax	2579 South Loop 289, Ste. 250	Lubbock	TX	79423	806-745-6299	1
Showplace 6 Theatres	6707 S. University	Lubbock	TX	79413-6303	806-745-3636	6
Driftwood Theatre at Marble Falls	2600 Highway 281 North	Marble Falls	TX	78654	830-798-8463	8
Marble Theatre	218 Main Street	Marble Falls	TX	78645	830-693-4965	1
Marshall Cinema	1901 East Travis Street	Marshall	TX	75670	903-935-5662	5
Odeon Theatre	122 S Moody St	Mason	TX	76856	915-347-9010	1
Lonestar Cinema Towne Crossing 8	3636 Gus Thomasson	Mesquite	TX	75150	972-682-0017	8
Brazos Cinema	2801 Hwy 180 East	Mineral Wells	TX	76068	940-325-4222	3
Southside Cinema 5	1706 S. Jefferson Ave.	Mt Pleasant	TX	75455	903-572 6321	5
Orange Cinema	3330 Bowling Lane	Orange	TX	77630	409-988-0202	2
Schulman Dogwood 6	545 E Palestine Ave	Palestine	TX	75801		6
Pampa Cinema 4	2545 Oerryton Pkwy.	Pampa	TX	79065	806-665-7141	4
State Theater	421 S. Oak St.	Pecos	TX	79772	915-445-7780	1
Ellis Theatre	217 South Main Street	Perryton	TX	79070	806-435-4133	2
Studio Movie Grill	4721 W. Park. #100	Plano	TX	75093	972-596-3999	8
Plestex 3 Theatres	111 W Johnson St.	Pleasanton	TX	78064-3513	830-569-3212	3
Twin Dolphin Cinemas	N Highway 35	Port Lavaca	TX	77979-0989	361-552-6764	2
FunAsia Cinema	1210 E. BeltLine Rd.	Richardson	TX	75081	972-889-8000	6
Cinema 4 - Rockport	2702 Highway 35 N	Rockport	TX	78382	361-729-4448	4
Island Cinema North	4700 Padre Blvd.	S. Padre Island	TX	78597	956-761-7828	5
IMAX Alamo Rivercenter	217 Alamo Plaza	San Antonio	TX	78205	210-247-4629	1
Lone Star Theaters - Starplex	1250 Wonderworld Drive	San Marcos	TX	78666	512-805-8000	12
Showplace Cinema III	321 N. LBJ Dr.	San Marcos	TX	78666	512-353-3555	3
King Ranger Theatres	1373 E Walnut	Seguin	TX	78155	830-379-4884	5
Noret Cinema I & II	1907 College Ave.	Snyder	TX	79549	325-573-7519	2
Lyric Theatre	113 Main St	Spearman	TX	79081	806-659-2812	2
Texas Theatre	114 E Broadway St	Sweetwater	TX	79556	915-235-5441	1
Forum Theatres 6	Highway 90 East	Uvalde	TX	78801	830-278-6618	6
Encore Cinema 6	1105 Wooded Acres	Waco	TX	76710	254-772-4355	6
Starplex Super Saver 6	410 N. Valley Mills Drive	Waco	TX	76710	254-772-1511	6
Movies at Buffalo Creek	507 N. HIGHWAY 77, BLDG. 1300	WAXAHACHIE	TX	75165	972-938-5463	4
Texas Theater	110 West Main	Waxahachie	TX	75165	972-938-5463	1
Weatherford Cinema 10	1000 Cinema Drive	Weatherford	TX	76087	817-341-3232	10
Premiere Nasa Dollar 8	20833 Gulf Freeway	Webster	TX	77598	281-332-4679	8

UTAH

Name	Address	City	State	Zip	Phone	Screens
Towne Cinemas 1 and 2	120 W. Main St.	American Fork	UT	84003	801-756-3181	2
Wayne Theatre	111 East Main Street	Bicknell	UT	84715	435-425-3123	1
Capital Theatre	53 S. Main St.	Brigham City	UT	84302-2526	435-723-3113	2
Walker Cinema IV	1776 S. Highway 89.	Brigham City	UT	84302-4110	435-723-6661	4
Motor Vu Theater	4055 N Highway 36	Erda	UT	84074	435-882-9979	1
Reel Theatre I.	94 S Main St	Heber City	UT	84032	435-654-1181	1
Reel Theatre II	115 N Main	Heber City	UT	84032	435-654-1181	1
Kaysville Theatre	21 N. Main Street	Kaysville	UT	87047	801-546-3400	3
Cinefour	2297 North Main	Logan	UT	84321	435-753-6444	4
Movies 5	2450 North Main	Logan	UT	84341	435-787-9438	5
Utah Theatre	18 West Center	Logan	UT	84321	435-752-3072	1
Reel Theatre Magna	8325 W 3500 South	Magna	UT	84044	801-250-0565	5
Slickrock Cinema 3.	580 Kane Creek Blvd.	Moab	UT	84532	435-259-4441	3
North Pointe Theatre.	1610 North Washington Blvd.	North Ogden	UT	84414	801-782-9822	4
Reel Theatre.	151 12th Street	Ogden	UT	84401	801-392-7474	6
SCERA Theatre	745 S. State St.	Orem	UT	84057	801-225-2560	1
University Mall Cinemas	959 South 700 East Street.	Orem	UT	84097-7246	801-226-1770	4
Huish Theatre.	98 W. Utah Ave.	Payson	UT	84651	801-465-2451	1
Water Gardens Cinema 6	912 West Garden Drive	Pleasant Grove	UT	84062	801-785-3700	6
Huish Reel Theatre.	131 N Main	Richfield	UT	84701	435-896-4400	1
Motor-Vu Drive-In	5368 S. 1050 W.	Riverdale	UT	84405	801-394-1768	4
Roosevelt Twin Theatre	21 S. 200 E.	Roosevelt	UT	84066	435-722-2095	2
Avalon Theatre	3605 S State Street	Salt Lake City	UT	84115	801-266-0258	1
Brewvies 2 Theatre	677 S. 200 WEST	Salt Lake City	UT	84101	801-355-5500	2
Broadway Centre Cinemas	111 East Broadway, #350	Salt Lake City	UT	84111	801-321-0310	6
IMAX Theatre at the Clark Planetarium	110 S. 40 West	Salt Lake City	UT	84101	801-532-7827	1
Megaplex 12 at the Gateway	165 South Rio Grande St.	Salt Lake City	UT	84101	801-304-4636	12
Redwood Drive-In.	3688 S Redwood Road	Salt Lake City	UT	84119	801-973-7088	6
Starship Gateway 8.	206 S. 625 West	Salt Lake City	UT	84104	801-292-7979	8
Tower Theatre.	876 E 900 South	Salt Lake City	UT	84105	801-321-0310	1
Megaplex 17 - Jordon Commons.	9400 S. State Street	Sandy	UT	84070-3213	801-304-4636	17
Spanish 8 Theatre	790 Expressway Lane	Spanish Fork	UT	84660	801-798-9777	8
Zion Canyon Cinemax @ Zion Canyon National Park	145 Zion Park Blvd.	Springdale	UT	84767	888-256-3456	1
Ritz Theatre	111 North Main Street	Tooele	UT	84074	435-882-2273	2
Sunset Drive-In.	1620 W. Hwy 40	Vernal	UT	84078	435-789-6139	1
Vernal Cinema 5.	1400 W. Highway.	Vernal	UT	84078	435-789-6139	5
Vernal Theatre	40 E. Main St.	Vernal	UT	84078	435-789-6139	1
Tu Cine	4140 West 5115 South	West Valley City	UT	84120	801-968-7794. 5

VERMONT

Name	Address	City	State	Zip	Phone	Screens
Paramount Theatre	241 N. Main St.	Barre	VT	05641	802-229-0343	3
Bennington Movieplex	Route 67A, Bennington Plaza	Bennington	VT	05201	802-447-0964	3
Cinema 7 Bennington	319 Northside Drive	Bennington	VT	05201	802-442-8179	7
Kipling Cinemas 6.	Putney Road	Brattleboro	VT	05304	802-258-2275	6

Name	Address	City	State	Zip	Phone	Screens
Latchis Theater	48 Main Street	Brattleboro	VT	05301	802-254-5800	3
Sunset Drive-In	Porters Point Road	Colchester	VT	05446	802-862-1800	4
Essex Outlets Cinema	21 Essex Way, Bldg. 300	Essex Junction	VT	05452	802-879-6543	8
Fairlee Drive-In Theatre	1809 US Route 5 N	Fairlee	VT	05045	802-333-9192	2
Marquis	Main street	Middlebury	VT	05753	802-388-4841	2
Capitol Theatre	100 State St	Montpelier	VT	05602	802-223-4778	5
Bijou Cineplex 4	4 Portland St.	Morrisville	VT	05661	802-888-3293	4
Plaza Movieplex	9 Rutland Street	Rutland	VT	05701	802-775-5500	9
Welden Theatre	104 N Main	Saint Albans	VT	05478-1507	802-527-7888	3
Stowe Cinema 3 Plex	Route 108 Mountain Road	Stowe	VT	05672	802-253-4678	3
West Dover Cinema	Route 100 N	W. Dover	VT	05356	802-464-6447	3
Westway Cinemas	Westway Mall Route 4A	West Rutland	VT	05777	802-775-5500	4
Pentangle Town Hall Theatre	31 The Green	Woodstock	VT	05091	802-457-2620	1

VIRGINIA

Name	Address	City	State	Zip	Phone	Screens
Abingdon Cinemall	721 East Main Street	Abingdon	VA	24210	276-676-0100	8
Moonlite Drive-In Theatre	17555 Lee Hwy.	Abingdon	VA	24210	276-628-7881	1
Foxchase Cinemas	4621 Duke St.	Alexandria	VA	22314	703-370-5565	3
Arlington Cinema 'N' Drafthouse	2903 Columbia Pike	Arlington	VA	22204	703-486-2345	1
Lyric Theatre Blacksburg	135 College Ave.	Blacksburg	VA	24060	540-951-0604	1
Valley Cinema	2275 Beech Ave	Buena Vista	VA	24416	540-261-7292	2
Jefferson Theater	110 E. Main St.	Charlottesville	VA	22902	434-980-1331	2
Vinegar Hill Theatre	220 W. Market Street	Charlottesville	VA	22903	804-977-4911	1
Cinema Cafe	1401 Greenbriar Pkwy Ste 1112	Chesapeake	VA	23320	757-313-8400	4
Island Roxy	4074 S Main Street	Chincoteague	VA	23336	757-336-6301	1
Starlite Drive-In Christiansbg.	365 Starlite Drive	Christiansburg	VA	24073	540-382-9227	1
Cinema Arts Theatre	9650 Main St.	Fairfax	VA	22031	703-978-6991	6
University Mall Theatres	10659 Braddock Road	Fairfax	VA	22032	703-273-7111	3
Royal Cinemas	117 East Main Street	Front Royal	VA	22630	540-622-9997	3
Twin County Cinema 3	957 E Stuart Dr	Galax	VA	24333		3
Hillside 2 Cinema	7321 John Clayton Memorial Hwy.	Gloucester	VA	23061	804-693-2770	2
IMAX Virginia Air & Space Center	600 Settlers Landing Road	Hampton	VA	23669	757-727-0900	1
YRC Riverdale Coliseum 12	1044 Von Schilling Drive	Hampton	VA	23666	757-825-3999	12
Grafton-Stovall Theatre	800 South Main Street	Harrisonburg	VA	22801	540-568-6723	2
The Court Square Theatre	40 N Liberty St	Harrisonburg	VA	22801	540-433-9189	2
York River Crossing	2226 York Crossing Dr.	Hayes	VA	23072	804-642-5999	8
Worldgate 9	13025 Worldgate Drive	Herndon	VA	20170	703-318-9290	9
Tally Ho	19 West Market Street	Leesburg	VA	20176	703-669-8662	2
Manassas Cinemas	8890 Mathis Ave.	Manassas	VA	22210	703-368-9292	4
Movie Town 5	67 Veteran Rd.	Martinsville	VA	24112	276-632-7400	5
Naro Expanded Cinema	1507 Colley Ave.	Norfolk	VA	23517	757-625-6275	1
Roseland Theatre	48 Market Street	Onancock	VA	23417	757-787-2010	1
Commodore Theatre	421 High Street	Portsmouth	VA	23704	757-393-6962	2
Radford Theatre	1043 Norwood Street	Radford	VA	24141	540-639-0772	1
Byrd Theatre	2908 W. Cary St.	Richmond	VA	23222	804-353-9911	1
Ethyl IMAX Dome	2500 W. Broad Street	Richmond	VA	23220	804-864-1400	1
Grandin Theatre	1310 Grandin Road S.W.	Roanoke	VA	24015	540-345-6177	4
The Cinema Cafe	5002 Airport Road	Roanoke	VA	24019	540-527-2233	2
Admira - Classic Drive-In	8086 S. Yale Ave. #288	Springville	VA	23303	918-835-5181	2
Dixie 4 Cinemas	125 E. Beverly Street	Staunton	VA	24401	540-225-6772	4
Essex 5 Cinemas	1653 Tappahannock Blvd.	Tappahannock	VA	22560	804-445-1166	5
Cinema Cafe	758 Independence Blvd.	Virginia Beach	VA	23455	757-499-6165	3
IMAX - V irginia Marine Science Museum	717 General Booth Blvd.	Virginia Beach	VA	23451	757-437-4949	1
Kemps River Crossing 7	1220 Fordham Rd	Virginia Beach	VA	23464	757-578-3435	7
Warrenton Movies 5	627 Frost Avenue	Warrenton	VA	20186	540-341-1894	5
Kimball Theatre	424 Duke Of Gloucester St.	Williamsburg	VA	23185	757-565-8588	1
Millwald Triple Theatre	205 W. Main St.	Wytheville	VA	24382	540-228-5031	3

WASHINGTON

Name	Address	City	State	Zip	Phone	Screens
Olympic Theater	107 N. Olympic Ave.	Arlington	WA	98223	360-435-3939	1
Valley Drive-In	401 49th St. N.E.	Auburn	WA	98002	253-854-1250	6
Bainbridge Cinemas	403 North Madison Avenue	Bainbridge Island	WA	98110	206-855-8173	6
Lynwood Theatre	4569 Lynwood Center Road	Bainbridge Island	WA	98110	206-842-3080	1
Pickford Cinema	1416 Cornwall Ave	Bellingham	WA	98225	360-738-0735	2
Charleston Cinema	333 North Callow Ave	Bremerton	WA	98312-4010	360-373-6093	1
Redwood Cinemas	1500 N.E. Riddell	Bremerton	WA	98310	360-698-6030	4
Liberty Theater	315 N.E. 4th Ave.	Camas	WA	98607	360-834-5038	2
Mount St. Helens Cinedome Theatre	1239 Mt. Saint Helens Way	Castle Rock	WA	98611	360-274-9844	1
Ruby Theatre	135 E. Woodin Ave.	Chelan	WA	98816	509-682-5016	1
Alpine Theatre	112 N. Main St.	Colville	WA	99114	509-684-6119	1
Sunset	102 N. Columbia	Connell	WA	99326	509-234-7811	1
Village Cinema	515 River Dr.	Coulee Dam	WA	99116	509-633-1563	1
Columbia Cinema	470 Grant Rd.	East Wenatchee	WA	98801	509-884-2454	5
Roxy Theatre	115 Marshell Ave.	Eatonville	WA	98328	360-832-7699	1
Edmonds Theater	415 Main Street.	Edmonds	WA	98020	425-778-4554	1
Chalet Theatre	1721 Wells	Enumclaw	WA	98022	360-825-3881	1
Enumclaw Cinema	258 Roosevelt Ave. E.	Enumclaw	WA	98022-8215	360-825-3888	1
Lee Theater	347 Basin St., N.W.	Ephrata	WA	98823	509-754-4566	3
Everett Theatre	2911 Colby Avenue	Everett	WA	98204	425-258-6766	1
Puget Park Drive-In	13020 Meridian Ave. S.	Everett	WA	98208-6422	425-338-5957	1
Kelso Theatre Pub	214 S. Pacific Ave.	Kelso	WA	98632	360-414-9451	1
Kirkland Park Place Cinema 6	404 Park Place	Kirkland	WA	98033	425-827-9000	6
Totem Lake Cinemas	12232 N.E. Totem Lake Way	Kirkland	WA	98033	425-820-5929	3
The Clyde, Langley	213 1st St.	Langley	WA	98260	360-221-5525	1
Neptune Theatre	809 Oceanbeach Blvd. S.	Long Beach	WA	98631	360-642-8888	2
Mossyrock G Theater	106 E. State St.	Mossyrock	WA	98564	360-983-8487	1

Name	Address	City	State	Zip	Phone	Screens
Lincoln Theater	712 1st Street	Mount Vernon	WA	98273	360-336-2858	1
Skagit 5 Mount Vernon	1900 Continental Place	Mount Vernon	WA	98273	360-848-1235	5
Roxy Theater	120 S. Washington Ave.	Newport	WA	99156	509-447-4125	1
North Bend Theatre	125 Bendigo Blvd. N.	North Bend	WA	98045	425-888-1232	1
Blue Fox Drive-In	1403 N. Monroe Landing Rd	Oak Harbor	WA	98277	360-675-5667	1
Oak Harbor Plaza Cinema 3	1321 S.W. Barlow St.	Oak Harbor	WA	98277	360-279-2226	3
Ocean Shores Cinema 3	631 Point Brown Ave. N.W.	Ocean Shores	WA	98569	360-289-2650	3
Capitol Theatre Olympia Film Society	206 5th Ave. S.E.	Olympia	WA	98501	360-754-6670	1
Omak Cinema	108 N. Main St.	Omak	WA	98841	509-826-5521	1
Deer Park Cinemas	96 Deerpark Rd.	Port Angeles	WA	98362	360-452-7176	5
Lincoln Theatre	132 E. 1st St.	Port Angeles	WA	98362	360-457-7997	3
Plaza Twin Cinema	822 Bay St.	Port Orchard	WA	98366	360-876-4021	2
Rodeo Drive-In	7369 State Highway 35 W.	Port Orchard	WA	98367	360-698-6030	3
Rose Theatre	235 Taylor St.	Port Townsend	WA	98368	360-385-1039	2
Uptown Theatre	826 P St.	Port Townsend	WA	98368	360-385-3883	1
Cordova Theatre	135 N. Grand Ave.	Pullman	WA	99163	509-334-1605	1
Raymond Theatre	323 3rd St.	Raymond	WA	98577	360-942-5536	1
The New Ritz Theatre	107 E. Main Ave.	Ritzville	WA	99169	509-659-1247	1
Roslyn Theatre	101 Dakota Ave.	Roslyn	WA	98941	509-649-3155	1
Admiral Twin Theatre	2343 California Avenue S	Seattle	WA	98116	206-938-3456	2
Big Picture	2505 1st Ave.	Seattle	WA	98121	206-256-0572	1
Boeing & Eames IMAX Theatres	200 Second Avenue North	Seattle	WA	98109	206-443-4629	2
Des Moines Cinema	22333 Marina View Dr	Seattle	WA	98198	206-878-1540	1
Frye Art Museum Auditorium	704 Terry Avenue	Seattle	WA	98104	206-622-9250	1
Grand Illusion Theatre	1403 NE 50th Street	Seattle	WA	98105	206-523-3935	1
Laser Fantasy Theater	200 2nd Ave. North	Seattle	WA	98109	206-443-2850	1
Little Theatre	608 19th Avenue E	Seattle	WA	98112	206-675-2055	1
Majestic Bay Theatre	2044 NW Market St.	Seattle	WA	98107	206-781-2229	3
Media Arts Center	117 Yale Avenue North	Seattle	WA	98109	206-682-6552	1
Seattle IMAX Dome	1483 Alaskan Way.	Seattle	WA	98101	206-622-1868	1
Shelton Cinemas	517 W. Franklin St.	Shelton	WA	98584	360-432-0865	2
Skyline Drive-In Theatre	182 S.E Brewer Rd.	Shelton	WA	98584	360-426-4707	1
Garland Dollar Theatre	924 W. Garland	Spokane	WA	99205	509-327-2509	1
Riverfront Park IMAX Theatre	507 N. Howard St.	Spokane	WA	99201	509-625-6686	2
Art Cinema at the Met.	901 W. Sprague.	Sprague	WA	99004		1
Stanwood Cinemas.	6996 265th St. N.W.	Stanwood	WA	98292	360-629-0514	5
Blue Mouse Theatre	2611 N. Proctor St.	Tacoma	WA	98407	253-752-9500	1
Grand Cinema	606 S. Fawcett Ave.	Tacoma	WA	98402	253-593-4474	3
Kiggins Theatre	1011 Main St.	Vancouver	WA	98660	360-737-3161	1
Vashon Theatre	99 SW 178th.	Vashon	WA	98070	206-463-3232	1
Liberty Cinema	1 S. Mission St., #11	Wenatchee	WA	98801	509-662-4567	6
Yelm Cinemas at Prairie Park	201 Prairie Park St., N.E.	Yelm	WA	98597	360-458-8933	8

WEST VIRGINIA

Name	Address	City	State	Zip	Phone	Screens
Raliegh Mall Cinemas	4301 Robert C. Byrd Dr.	Beckley	WV	25801	304-253-2825	2
Star Movie Cinema	137 N. Washington St.	Berkeley Springs	WV	25411	304-258-1404	1
Park Place Stadium Cinemas	600 Washington St. East	Charleston	WV	25301	304-345-6540	7
Elkins Cinema 7	Tygart Valley Mall	Elkins	WV	26241	304-636-3555	6
Tygart Valley Cinema 7	7 Tygart Valley Mall	Fairmont	WV	26554	304-363-3498	7
Warner's Drive-In	H.C. 60 Box 44-B	Franklin	WV	26807	304-358-7610	1
LJH Cinemas - Community Center	Larry Joe Harless Dr.	Gilbert	WV	25621	304-664-2600	3
Grafton Drive-In	RR 3 Box 311	Grafton	WV	26354-9553		1
Ritz Theatre Hinton	211 Ballengee St.	Hinton	WV	25951-2318	304-466-2629	1
Camelot Theatre	30 4th Ave.	Huntington	WV	25701	304-525-4440	2
Cinema 4 Theatre Huntington	401 11th St.	Huntington	WV	25701-2218	304-525-4440	4
Keith Albee 4	925 4th Avenue	Huntington	WV	25701	304-525-4440	4
Lewis Theatre	113 N. Court Street	Lewisburg	WV	24901-1101	304-645-6038	1
Valley Cinema 3	3 New Martinsville Plaza	New Martinsville	WV	26155	304-455-5866	3
Jungle Drive-In	Highway 2	Parkersburg	WV	26101	304-464-4063	1
Mountaineer Cinemas	126 Academy Drive	Ripley	WV	25271	304-372-8209	2
Shepherdstown Opera House	131 W. German St.	Shepherdstown	WV	25443	304-876-3704	1
Putnam Village 3	I-64 & WV34, Exit 39	Teays	WV	25569	304-757-7931	3
Greenbrier Hotel Cinema	300 West Main Street	White Sulphur Springs	WV	24986	800-624-6070	1

WISCONSIN

Name	Address	City	State	Zip	Phone	Screens
Amery Theatre	118 N. Keller Ave.	Amery	WI	54001	715-268-7767	1
Palace Theatre	823 5th Ave.	Antigo	WI	54409	715-623-4570	1
Bay Theatre	420 W Main St	Ashland	WI	54806	715-682-3555	4
Al Ringling Theatre	136 Fourth Ave.	Baraboo	WI	53913	608-356-8864	1
Blaine Theatre	102 E. Oak St.	Boscobel	WI	53805	608-375-4137	1
Chilton Theatre	26 N. Madison St.	Chilton	WI	53014	920-849-9565	1
Cornell Theatre	214 Main St.	Cornell	WI	54732	715-239-6655	1
Durand Theatre	111 E. Main St.	Durand	WI	54736	715-672-3456	1
Conway Vilas Cinema Eagle Rive	218 East Wall Street	Eagle River	WI	54521	715-479-6541	5
Cameo Budget Twin Theatres	315 S. Barstow St.	Eau Claire	WI	54701	715-832-3355	2
London Square Six	3109 Mall Drive	Eau Claire	WI	54701	715-834-1822	6
Fond Du Lac Theatre 8	1131 W. Scott Street	Fond Du Lac	WI	54937	920-907-0954	8
Forest Mall Cinema I & II Fond du Lac	755 W. Johnson Street.	Fond du Lac.	WI	54935	920-921-3000	2
Spector Riverpoint Cinemas	8617 N. Port Washington Rd.	Fox Point	WI	53217	414-540-1302	4
Historic West Theatre	405 W. Walnut St.	Green Bay	WI	54303	920-435-1057	1
Hartford Theatres	2941 Highway 83 S.	Hartford	WI	53027	262-673-7675	8
Hayward Cinema	Highway 27 South	Hayward	WI	54843	715-634-9411	4
Park Theatre	116 East 1st Street	Hayward	WI	54843	715-634-4596	1
Keno Family Drive-In	9102 Sheridan Rd.	Kenosha	WI	53143	262-694-8855	1
Hollywood Theatre	123 S 5th St	La Crosse	WI	54601	608-796-1600	1
Rivoli Theatre	117 N Fourth Street.	La Crosse	WI	54601	608-784-7761	1
Miner Theatre	116 East Miner Avenue	Ladysmith	WI	54848	715-532-7131	1

Name	Address	City	State	Zip	Phone	Screens
Orpheum I & II Theatres	216 State St.	Madison	WI	53703	608-255-8755	2
University Square 4	62 University Square Mall	Madison	WI	53715	608-251-3483	4
Strand Theatre	315 N. 8th St.	Manitowoc	WI	54220	920-684-9291	6
Mariner 2	2000 Ella Ct.	Marinette	WI	54143	715-732-6869	2
Rogers 7 Cinema	419 South Central Avenue	Marshfield	WI	54449	715-387-2566	7
State Cinema 4	639 Broadway Street S.	Menomonie	WI	54751	715-235-5733	4
Humphrey IMAX Dome Theater	710 W. Wells	Milwaukee	WI	53233	414-319-4629	1
Times Cinema	5906 W. Vliet St.	Milwaukee	WI	53208	414-453-3128	1
Mineral Point Opera House	139 High St.	Mineral Point	WI	53565		1
Goetz Sky Vue Drive-In	1936 Highway 69 N.	Monroe	WI	53566	608-325-4200	1
Goetz Theatres 3	1704 11th St.	Monroe	WI	53566	608-325-4545	3
Montello Theatre	30 E. Montello St.	Montello	WI	53949-9701	608-297-7300	1
Rogers Grand Cinema	319 W. North Water St.	New London	WI	54961	920-982-5266	4
New Richmond 6	1261 Heritage Dr.	New Richmond	WI	54017	715-246-4411	6
Cinema North	Highway 13	Phillips	WI	54555	715-339-3605	1
Portage Theatre	322 W. Wisconsin St.	Portage	WI	53901	608-742-6678	7
Bonham Theatre & Video	564 Water St.	Prairie du Sac	WI	53578	608-643-8504	3
Center Cinema-Richland Center	192 S. Central Ave.	Richland Center	WI	53581	608-647-3669	2
Crescent Pitcher Show	220 S. Main St.	Shawano	WI	54166-2746	715-526-2811	1
Shawano Cinema I, II, III, IV	1494 E. Green Bay St.	Shawano	WI	54166	715-524-3636	3
Timbers Theatres	24226 First Ave. North	Siren	WI	54872-8234	715-349-8888	4
Skyway Drive-In Theatre	9990 Highway 57	Sister Bay	WI	54234	920-854-6081	1
Palace Theatre	238 Walnut Street	Spooner	WI	54801	715-635-2936	2
Gard Theatre	111 E. Jefferson St.	Spring Green	WI	53588	608-588-9007	1
Falls Cinema 5	200 N. Washington Ave.	St. Croix Falls	WI	54024	715-483-9785	5
Rogers Cinemas 6	2725 Church St.	Stevens Point	WI	54481	715-341-6161	6
Cinema Cafe 5	255 E. Main St.	Stoughton	WI	53589	608-873-7484	5
Donna Theatre	239 N. 3rd Ave.	Sturgeon Bay	WI	54235-0006	920-746-8371	2
Tomahawk Cinema	17 W. Wisconsin Ave.	Tomahawk	WI	54487	715-453-5414	2
Vernon Square Cinema	1230 N. Main	Viroqua	WI	54665	608-637-0430	3
Towne Cinema Watertown	302 E. Main St.	Watertown	WI	53094	920-261-6201	3
Rogers Rosa Theatre	218 S. Main.	Waupaca	WI	54981	715-258-2510	2
Rosebud Cinema Drafthouse	6823 W. North Ave.	Wauwatosa	WI	53213	414-607-9446	1
West Bend Cinema	125 N. Main St.	West Bend	WI	53095	262-334-5466	3
Fox-Bay Cinema Grill	338 E. Silver Spring Dr.	Whitefish Bay	WI	53217	414-906-9994	3
Big Sky Twin Drive-In	Highway 16	Wisconsin Dells	WI	53965	608-254-6598	1
Rogers Cinema-Wisconsin Rapids	220 East Grand Ave.	Wisconsin Rapids	WI	54494-4361	715-421-3177	7
Elroy Theatre	731 E. Plum Valley Rd.	Wonewoc	WI	53968-9203	608-462-5685	1
Conway Lakeland Cinema Woodruf	1002 2nd Ave	Woodruff	WI	54568	715-356-3404	6

WYOMING

Name	Address	City	State	Zip	Phone	Screens
Big Horn Cinema	2525 Big Horn Avenue	Cody	WY	82414	307-587-8009	2
Cody Theatre	1171 Sheridan Ave.	Cody	WY	82414	307-587-2712	2
Park Drive-In	3127 Big Horn Ave	Cody	WY	82414	307-587-7177	1
Mesa Theatre	104 N. 3rd St.	Douglas	WY	82633-2135	307-358-6209	1
Cinemajik Valley 4 Cinemas	45 East Aspen Grove Road	Evanston	WY	82930	307-789-0522	4
Strand Theatre	1028 Main St.	Evanston	WY	82930	307-789-2974	1
Foothills Twin Theatre	650 N US Highway 14	Gillette	WY	82716	307-682-6766	2
Ski Hi Drive Theater	2201 S. Douglas Hwy.	Gillette	WY	82718	307-682-9948	1
Jackson Hole Twin Cinema	295 W Pearl	Jackson	WY	83001	307-733-4939	2
Movieworks Cinema 4	860 S. Highway 89	Jackson	WY	83001	307-733-4939	4
Teton Theater	120 North Cache	Jackson	WY	83001	307-733-4939	1
Grand Theatre - Lander	250 W. Main St.	Lander	WY	82520-3128	307-332-3300	1
Valley Theatre	110 E Owen	Lyman	WY	82937	307-787-3333	1
Vali Drive-In	1070 Road 9	Powell	WY	82435	307-754-5133	1
Vali Twin Cinema	204 N Bent St	Powell	WY	82435	307-754-4211	2
Acme Theatre	312 E. Main St.	Riverton	WY	82501-4338	307-856-3415	1
Centennial Theatres	36 E. Alger St.	Sheridan	WY	82801-3912	307-672-9811	6
Skyline Drive-In Theatre	1739 E Brundage Lane	Sheridan	WY	82801	307-864-3118	1
The Ritz Theatre - Thermopolis	309 Arapaho St.	Thermopolis	WY	82443-2705	307-864-3118	1
Wyoming Theatre	126 E. 20th Ave.	Torrington	WY	82240-2812	307-532-2226	1
Cinema West Theatre	609 10th Street	Wheatland	WY	82201-2923	307-322-9032	1
Cottonwood Twin Cinemas	101 Pleasant View Dr.	Worland	WY	82401-9777	307-347-8414	2

SPECIALTY & LARGE FORMAT EXHIBITORS

Specialty exhibitors show non-theatrical films, usually in a proprietary format and occasionally involving mechanical simulations or special viewing devices in conjunction with the film, to non-theatrical audiences (usually museum-goers and amusement park attendees). However, traditional exhibitors are installing limited numbers of specialty screens in multiplexes. For equipment & services, please see the section of this book entitled Specialty Exhibitor Equipment & Services.

IMAX CORPORATION

CORPORATE HEADQUARTERS
2525 Speakman Drive, Sheridan Science and Technology Park, Mississauga, ONT L5K 1B1, Canada. (905) 403-6500. FAX: (905) 403-6450. www.imax.com email: info@imax.com
CO-CHAIRMAN & CO-CEO
Richard L. Gelfond
CO-CHAIRMAN & CO-CEO
Bradley J. Wechsler
CFO
Francis T. Joyce
PRESIDENT, FILMED ENTERTAINMENT
Greg Foster
EXECUTIVE V.P., LEGAL AFFAIRS & GENERAL COUNSEL
Robert D. Lister
EXECUTIVE V.P., STRATEGIC PARTNERSHIPS
Ken Howarth
SENIOR V.P. & PRESIDENT DKP/70MM INC.
David Keighley
SENIOR V.P., TECHNOLOGY
Brian Bonnick
SENIOR V.P., HUMAN RESOURCES & ADMINISTRATION
Mary C. Sullivan
SENIOR V.P., IMAX THEATRE OPERATIONS
Brian Hall
SENIOR V.P. THEATRE DEVELOPMENT AND FILM DISTRIBUTION
Larry T. O'Reilly

U.S. IMAX THEATRES

(Most American IMAX theatres are independently owned and operated. Theatres marked with an asterisk have IMAX 3D capability.)

IMAX Dome Theatre	Mcwane Center	Birmingham	AL	(205) 714-8300
Spacedome IMAX Theatre	U.S. Space & Rocket Center	Huntsville	AL	(256) 837-3400
J.L. Bedsole IMAX Dome Theatre	Gulf Coast Exploreum	Mobile	AL	(334) 208-6873
IMAX Theatre	Aerospace Education Center	Little Rock	AR	(501) 371-0331
IMAX Theatre at Arizona Mills*	Arizona Mills	Tempe	AZ	(480) 897-1453
Grand Canyon IMAX Theatre		Tusayan	AZ	(520) 638-2203
Disney's Soarin'.	Disney's California Adventure	Anaheim	CA	NA
The Desert IMAX Theatre*	KESQ-TV3	Cathedral City	CA	(760) 324-7333
Regal IMAX Theatre*	Hacienda Crossing 20	Dublin	CA	(925) 803-4629
Edwards Irvine Spectrum IMAX Theatre		Irvine	CA	(949) 450-4900
Back To The Future–The Ride	Universal Studios	Los Angeles	CA	(818) 622-3855
IMAX Theatre*	California Science Center	Los Angeles	CA	(213) 744-2658
Universal Studios IMAX Theatre*	Citywalk	Los Angeles	CA	(818) 508-0493
IMAX Theatre at The Bridge: Cinema de lux*	Promende at Howard Hughes Cnt.	Los Angeles	CA	(310) 568-3375
Regal IMAX Theatre	Ontario Palace Stadium 22	Ontario	CA	(909) 476-1500
Esquire IMAX Theatre		Sacramento	CA	(916) 446-2333
Reuben H. Fleet Space Theatre	San Diego Space & Sci. Found.	San Diego	CA	(619) 238-1233
Sony IMAX Theatre at Metreon*	Metreon	San Francisco	CA	(415) 369-6201
Hackworth IMAX Dome Theatre	The Tech Museum of Innovation	San Jose	CA	(408) 795-6100
Regal IMAX Theatre	Valencia Grand Palace Stadium 12	Valencia	CA	(661) 287-1740
Cinemark IMAX Theatre*	The Cinemark	Colorado Springs	CO	(719) 596-3212
Lawrence Phipps IMAX Theatre	Denver Museum of Nat. History	Denver	CO	(303) 370-6322
Regal IMAX Theatre	Colorado Center 9	Denver	CO	NA
IMAX Theatre	The Maritime Center	Norwalk	CT	(203) 852-0700
Lockheed Martin IMAX Theatre*	Smithsonian Institute	Washington	DC	(202) 357-1675
Johnson IMAX Theatre*	National Museum of Nat. History	Washington	DC	(202) 633-9049
Blockbuster IMAX 3D Theatre*	Museum of Science & Discovery	Fort Lauderdale	FL	(954) 467-6637
World Golf Village IMAX Theatre	Golf Hall of Fame	Jacksonville	FL	(904) 940-4123
IMAX Theatre #1 & #2*	Kennedy Space Center		FL	(321) 452-2121
IMAX Theatre at Sunset Place*	Sunset Place	Miami	FL	(305) 740-0399
Back To The Future–The Ride*	Universal Studios	Orlando	FL	(407) 363-8000
IMAX Theatre	Ntnl. Museum of Naval Aviation	Pensacola	FL	(850) 453-2025
IMAX Theatre	Challenger Learning Center	Tallahassee	FL	(850) 645-7827
IMAX Dome Theatre	Museum of Science & Industry	Tampa	FL	(813) 987-6300
Channelside Cinemas & IMAX Theatre*	Regal Channelside Cinemas	Tampa	FL	(813) 223-4250
Rankin M. Smith Jr. IMAX Theatre	Fernbank Museum of Nat. History	Atlanta	GA	(404) 929-6368
Regal IMAX Theatre*	Mall of Georgia 20	Mill Creek	GA	(678) 482-9263
IMAX Waikiki Theatre*		Honolulu	HI	(808) 923-4629
IMAX Polynesia	Polynesian Cultural Center	Laie	HI	(808) 293-3280
McLeod/Busse IMAX Dome Theatre	Science Station	Cedar Rapids	IA	(319) 363-4629
IMAX Theatre*	Putnam Museum	Davenport	IA	(563) 324-1933
Regal IMAX Theatre	Bosie Stadium 21	Bosie	ID	(208) 377-1700
Marcus IMAX Theatre*		Addison	IL	(630) 932-4572
Henry Crown Space Center OMNIMAX Theatre	Museum of Science & Industry	Chicago	IL	(773) 684-9844
Loews Cineplex IMAX Theatre*	Navy Pier	Chicago	IL	(312) 595-0090
Pictorium*	Six Flags Great America	Gurnee	IL	(847) 249-2133
Regal IMAX Theatre*	City Park 20	Lincolnshire	IL	(847) 229-9100

Cinemark IMAX Theatre*	Seven Bridges	Woodridge	IL	(630) 663-8894
IMAX 3D Theatre*	White River State Park	Indianapolis	IN	(317) 634-4567
IMAX Theatre	Louisville Science Center	Louisville	KY	(502) 561-6103
Firstar IMAX Theatre*		Newport	KY	(859) 491-4629
IMAX Dome Theatre	KS Cosmosphere & Space Ctr.	Hutchinson	KS	(316) 662-2305
Entergy IMAX Theatre*	Aquarium of the Americas	New Orleans	LA	(504) 565-3020
IMAX Dome Theatre	Sci-Port Discovery Center	Shreveport	LA	(318) 424-3466
Sprint IMAX Theatre	Kansas City Zoo	Kansas City	MO	(816) 513-5800
Mugar OMNI Theatre	Museum of Science	Boston	MA	(617) 589-0100
Simons IMAX Theatre*	New England Aquarium	Boston	MA	(617) 973-5200
Comcast IMAX 3D Theatre	Jordan's Furniture Natick	Natick	MA	(508) 424-0088
IMAX Theatre*	Maryland Science Center	Baltimore	MD	(410) 685-2370
IMAX Theatre, Henry Ford Museum*	Greenfield Village	Dearborn	MI	(313) 982-6100
IMAX Dome Theatre	Detroit Science Center	Detroit	MI	(313) 577-8400
IMAX Theatre Celebration! Village*		Grand Rapids	MI	(616) 474-4231
Duluth OMNIMAX Theatre	Duluth Entertainment Conv. Ctr.	Duluth	MN	(218) 727-0022
Imation IMAX Theatre*	Minnesota Zoo	Minneapolis	MN	(952) 997-9700
IMAX Cinema	Valleyfair Amusement Park	Shakopee	MN	(612) 445-7600
William L. McKnight–3M Omnitheatre	The Science Mus. of Minnesota	St. Paul	MN	(651) 221-9488
Ozarks Discovery IMAX Theatre		Branson	MO	(417) 335-3533
OMNIMAX Theatre	St. Louis Science Center	St. Louis	MO	(314) 289-4400
Yellowstone IMAX Theatre		Yellowstone	MT	(406) 646-4100
Observer OMNIMAX Theatre	Discovery Place	Charlotte	NC	(704) 372-6261
IMAX Theatre Exploris	Exploris	Raleigh	NC	(919) 834-4040
Lozier IMAX Theatre*	Henry Doorly Zoo	Omaha	NE	(402) 733-8401
IMAX Dome Theatre	Liberty Science Center	Jersey City	NJ	(201) 451-0006
Clyde W. Tombaugh Space Theatre	The Space Center	Alamogordo	NM	(505) 437-2840
Luxor IMAX Theatre*	Luxor Hotel	Las Vegas	NV	(702) 262-4500
Race for Atlantis*	Caesars Palace	Las Vegas	NV	(702) 733-9000
Regal IMAX Theatre*	Transit Center 16	Buffalo	NY	(716) 632-4629
IMAX Dome Theatre	Leroy R. and Rose W. Grumman	Garden City	NY	(516) 572-4111
Regal IMAX Theatre*	New Roc City 18	New Rochelle	NY	(914) 235 5106
IMAX Theatre	American Museum of Nat. History	New York	NY	(212) 769-5000
Sony IMAX Theatre*	Sony Theatres at Lincoln Square	New York	NY	(212) 336-5020
Cinemark IMAX Theatre*	Tinseltown	Rochester	NY	(716) 426-2629
Bristol Omnitheatre	M.J. Rubenstein Mus of Sci.& Tech	Syracuse	NY	(315) 425-9068
IMAX Theatre*	Palisades Center	West Nyack	NY	(914) 353-5555
Robert D. Linder Family OMNIMAX Theatre	Mus Cntr at Cincinnati Union Term.	Cincinnati	OH	(513) 287-7000
Cleveland Clinic OMNIMAX Theatre	Great Lakes Science Centre	Cleveland	OH	(216) 694-2020
Marcus IMAX Theatre*	Crossroads Center	Columbus	OH	(614) 840-9800
IMAX Theatre	U.S. Air Force Museum	Dayton	OH	(937) 253-IMAX
Cinemark IMAX Theatre*	The Tulsa	Tulsa	OK	(918) 307-2629
OMNIMAX Theatre	Oregon Museum of Sci.& Industry	Portland	OR	(503) 797-4000
IMAX Theatre*	Whitker Cntr. for Science & Art	Harrisburg	PA	(717) 221-8201
Regal IMAX Theatre	King of Prussia Stadium 16	King of Prussia	PA	NA
Tuttleman IMAX Theatre	Franklin Inst. Science Museum	Philadelphia	PA	(215) 448-1200
Rangos OMNIMAX Theatre	Carnegie Science Center	Pittsburg	PA	(412) 237-3400
Feinstein IMAX Theatre*	Providence Place	Providence	RI	(401) 453-4629
Charleston IMAX Theatre*		Charleston	SC	(843) 725-4630
IMAX Discovery Theatre	Broadway at the Beach	Myrtle Beach	SC	(803) 444-3333
IMAX 3D Theatre*	Tennessee Aquarium	Chattanooga	TN	(423) 265-0695
Union Planters IMAX Theatre	Pink Palace Museum	Memphis	TN	(901) 320-6320
Regal IMAX Theatre*	Opry Mills	Nashville	TN	(615) 514-4633
IMAX Theater*	Bob Bullock Tex. St. His. Mus.	Austin	TX	(512) 936-8746
TI Founders IMAX Theater	The Science Place	Dallas	TX	(214) 428-5555
Cinemark IMAX Theatre*	Cinemark 17	Dallas	TX	(972) 888-2629
Omni Theatre	Museum of Natural History	Fort Worth	TX	(817) 255-9300
IMAX 3D Theatre*	Moody Gardens	Galveston	TX	(409) 744-4673
Regal IMAX Theatre	Marque Stadium 23	Houston	TX	(713) 263-0808
Space Center Theatre	Space Center Houston	Houston	TX	(713) 244-2105
Wortham IMAX Theatre	Houston Museum of Nat. Science	Houston	TX	(713) 639-4601
OMNIMAX Theatre	Science Spectrum	Lubbock	TX	(806) 745-2525
San Antonio IMAX Theatre #1 & #2	Rivercenter	San Antonio	TX	(210) 247-0230
IMAX Theatre	Clark Planetarium	Salt Lake City	UT	(801) 456-7827
IMAX Theatre	Virginia Air & Space Center	Hampton	VA	(757) 727-0900
Ethyl IMAX Dome Theatre	Science Museum of Virginia	Richmond	VA	(804) 367-0000
The Family Channel IMAX 3D Theatre*	Virginia Marine Science Museum	Virginia Beach	VA	(757) 437-4949
Eames IMAX Theatre*	Pacific Science Center	Seattle	WA	(206) 443-2001
Boeing IMAX Theatre	Pacific Science Center	Seattle	WA	(206) 443-2001
Seattle Omnidome	Pier 59 Waterfront Park	Seattle	WA	(206) 622-1869
IMAX Theatre	Riverfront Park	Spokane	WA	(509) 625-6601
Humphrey IMAX Dome Theatre	Milwaukee Public Museum	Milwaukee	WI	(414) 319-4625

INTERNATIONAL LOCATIONS

AUSTRALIA

Panasonic IMAX Theatre*	Darling Harbour	Sydney	NSW	(61 29) 291-1627
Coca-Cola IMAX Theatre	Dreamworld	Coomera	QLD	(61 75) 588-1111
North Queensland IMAX Dome Theatre	Great Barrier Reef Wonderland	Townsville	QLD	(61 89) 328-0600
IMAX Theatre Melbourne*		Melbourne	VIC	(61 9) 656-8623

AUSTRIA

IMAX Wien		Vienna	(43 1) 894-0101

BELGIUM

IMAX Theatre		Brussels	(322)474-2600

CANADA

IMAX Theatre at Eau Claire	Market	Calgary	AB	(403) 974-6400
Famous Players IMAX Theatre*	Chinook Centre	Calgary	AB	(403) 212-8098
IMAX Theatre	Odyssium	Edmonton	AB	(780) 452-9100
Famous Players IMAX Theatre*	Silver City	Edmonton	AB	(780) 484-2400
Famous Players IMAX Theatre*	The Colossus	Langley	BC	(604) 930-4629
Alcan OMNIMAX Theatre	Science World British Coloumbia	Vancouver	BC	(604) 443-7440
CN IMAX Theatre*	Canada Place	Vancouver	BC	(604) 682-2384
National Geographic Theatre	Royal BC Museum	Victoria	BC	(250) 480-4887

IMAX Theatre	Portage Place	Winnipeg	MB	(204) 956-2400
Empire IMAX Theatre*	Empire 12 Cinemas	Halifax	NS	(902) 876-4848
IMAX Theatre	Western Fair	London	ON	(519) 438-7203
Famous Players IMAX Theatre*	The Coliseum	Mississauga	ON	(905) 275 3456
Niagara Falls IMAX Theatre		Niagara Falls	ON	(905) 358-3611
IMAX Theatre	Science North	Subury	ON	(705) 522-3701
Cinesphere IMAX Theatre	Ontario Place	Toronto	ON	(416) 314-9900
Famous Players IMAX Theatre	The Paramount, Festival Hall	Toronto	ON	(416) 368-6089
Shoppers Drug Mart OMNIMAX Theatre	Ontario Science Center	Toronto	ON	(416) 696-1000
Famous Players IMAX Theatre*	The Colossus	Vaughan	ON	(905) 851-6400
CINEPLUS	Can. Museum of Civilization	Hull/Ottawa	PQ	(819) 776-7000
Le Cinema IMAX*	Le Vieux Port de Montreal	Montreal	PQ	(514) 496-IMAX
Famous Players IMAX Theatre*	The Paramount	Montreal	PQ	(514) 842-5828
IMAX Le Theatre*	Les Galeries de la Capitale	Quebec City	PQ	(418) 627-8222
Kramer IMAX Theatre	Saskatchewan Science Center	Regina	SK	(306) 791-7900

CHINA

IMAX Theatre	Shanghai Sci. & Tech. Museum	Shanghai	(86 216) 431-4855
IMAX Dome Theatre	Shanghai Sci. & Tech. Museum	Shanghai	(86 216) 431-4855

CZECH REPUBLIC

Oskar IMAX Theatre	Palace Flora	Prague	(42 25) 574-2021

DENMARK

OMNIMAX Theatre	Tycho Brahe Planetarium	Copenhagen	(453) 311-1124

FRANCE

Gaumont IMAX Cinema*	Centre Thermal et Touristique	Amneville	(33 38) 770-8989
La Geode		Paris	(33 14) 005-7904
Le Kinemax	Futuroscope	Poitiers	(33 54) 949-3000
Le IMAX 3D*	Futuroscope	Poitiers	(33 54) 949-3000
L'OMNIMAX	Futuroscope	Poitiers	(33 54) 949-3000
Magic Carpet	Futuroscope	Poitiers	(33 54) 949-3000
Le Solido	Futuroscope	Poitiers	(33 54) 949-3000
Race for Atlantis*	Futuroscope	Poitiers	(33 54) 949-3000

GERMANY

Discovery IMAX Potsdamer Platz*	Potsdamer Platz	Berlin	(49 302) 592-8210
CineStar IMAX Cinema*	Sony Centre at Potsdamer Platz	Berlin	(49 302) 606-6200
IMAX Filmtheatre*		Bochum	(49 23) 496-1710
Galaxy	Phantasialand	Bruhl	(49) 223-2360
IMAX Filmtheatre*		Frankfurt	(49 691) 338-4821
Formum der Technik*	Deutsches Museum	Munich	(49 892) 112-5184
IMAX am Cinecitta	Multiplex Kinozentrum Cinecitta	Nurnburg	(49 91) 120 6667
IMAX 3D Museum Sinsheim*	Auto & Technik Museum	Sinsheim	(49 72) 619-2990
IMAX Filmtheatre	Technik Museum Speyer	Speyer	(49 62) 327-8844
IMAX Dome Theatre	Technik Museum Speyer	Spever	(49 62) 326-7080
IMAX 'Welton Erleben'*	im Mainfrankenpark	Wuerzburg	(49 930) 293-3933

GREAT BRITAIN

IMAX Theatre at Millenium Point		Birmingham	(44 121) 202-2222
Sheridan IMAX Cinema	Pier Approach	Bournemouth	(44 120) 220 0000
IMAX Cinema*	Ntnl. Mus. of Photog, Film & TV	Bradford, West Yorkshire	(44 127) 420-2030
IMAX Theatre*	At-Bristol	Bristol	(44 117) 909-2000
BFI London IMAX Cinema*	British Film Institute	London	(44 207) 960-3110
Science Museum IMAX Cinema*	Science Museum	London	(44 207) 942-4000
IMAX Cinema @ thefilmworks*	The Printworks	Manchester	(44 870) 588-8999

HONG KONG

Space Theatre	Hong Kong Space Museum	Kowloon	(85 22) 721-0226

INDIA

Gujarat Science City IMAX 3D Theatre		Ahmedabad	NA
IMAX Adlabs Theatre		Mumbai	(91 22) 403-6474

IRELAND

Sheridan IMAX Cinema*	Odyssey Pavilion	Belfast	(44 289) 046-7000

INDONESIA

Keong Emas IMAX Theatre		Jakarta	(62 21) 840-1021

JAPAN

IMAX Theatre	Cinema Hall	Aomori	(81 17) 285-2810
Fujitsu Dome Theatre*	Makuhari System Lab	Chiba	(81 43) 299-3215
OMNIMAX Theatre	Nuclear Exhibition Center	Hamaoka	(81 53) 786-3481
IMAX Dome Theatre	Chiba Museum of Science & Ind.	Ichikawa	(81 47) 379-2000
Space Theatre	Municipal Science Hall	Kagoshima	(81 99) 250-8511
Mercian Karuizawa IMAX Theatre*		Karuizawa	(81 26) 741-2241
Galaxy Theatre	Space World	Kitakyushu	(81 93) 672-3650
Hotaka IMAX Theatre	Azumino	Nagano	(81 26) 383-4800
Ocean Theatre	Port Aquarium	Nagoya	(81 52) 654-7080
Space Theatre	Information Media Culture Center	Omiya	(81 48) 647-0011
IMAX 3D Theatre*	Suntory Museum	Osaka	(81 66) 577-0004
Science Theatre	Science Museum Osaka	Osaka	(81 66) 444-5656
Back To The Future–The Ride	Universal Studios	Osaka	NA
Dome Theatre	Saikai Pearl Sea Center	Sasebo	(81 95) 628-4187
Cambron Theatre	Shima Spain Village	Shima	(81 59) 957-3337
IMAX Experience Theatre	Tokorozawa Aviation Museum	Tokorozawa	(81 42) 996-2225
Merican Shinagawa IMAX Theatre		Tokyo	(81 35) 421-1114
Kirameki Minato Kan*	Tsuruga Port Expo	Tsuruga	(81 77) 020-1100
Space Theatre	Science Center	Yokohama	(81 45) 832-1166

KUWAIT

The Scientific Center IMAX Theatre*		Safat	(965) 242-2439

MALTA

IMAX Vodafone Theatre		St. George's Bay	(35) 637-6401

MEXICO

DOMO IMAX Descubre Museo Interactivo de Ciencia y Tecnologia		Aguascalientes	(52) 13-7012/6746

Explora	Explora Science Center	Leon, Guanajuato	(52 4) 711-6711
Megapantalla IMAX Theatre	Paplota Museo del Niño.	Mexico City	(52 5) 237-1757
Multi-theatre	Centro Cultural Alfa	Monterrey	(52 8) 303-0002
IMAX Dome Theatre	Planetario de Puebla	Puebla	(52 2) 235-2099
Cine Planetario	Centro Cultural Tijuana	Tijuana, Baja Calif. Norte	(52 6) 684-1130
OMNIMAX Theatre	Planetario Tabasco 2000	Villahermosa, Tabasco	(52 9) 312-7436
IMAX Theatre	Museo de Cienca y Tecnologia	Xalapa, Veracruz	(52 2) 812-5110

NETHERLANDS
Omniversum	Sijthoff Planetarium	The Hague	(31 70) 398-0700

NORWAY
Telenor Mobil IMAX Theatre*	Aker Brygge	Oslo	(47 2) 311-6600

POLAND
Panasonic IMAX Krakow		Krakow	(48 12) 290-9080
IMAX Theatre Katowice		Katowice	(48 32) 711-5959
Panasonic IMAX Theatre*	Sadyba Best Mall	Warsaw	(48 22) 550-3993

RUSSIAN FEDERATION
Nescafe IMAX Theatre		Moscow	(70 95) 241-0350

SCOTLAND
IMAX Theatre*	Glasgow Science Center	Glasgow	(44 141) 420-5010

SINGAPORE
Omni-theatre	Singapore Science Center	Singapore	(65) 425-2500
Popular IMAX Theatre		Singapore	NA

SLOVAKIA
Orange IMAX Theatre		Bratislava	(421 2) 4342-3036

SOUTH AFRICA
IMAX Cinema	BMW Pavilion	Cape Town	(27 21) 419-7365
IMAX Theatre	Gateway Shoppertainment World . . .	Durban	(27 83) 619-3374
IMAX Theatre	Menlyn Park Shopping	Pretoria	(27 11) 368-1186

SOUTH KOREA
63 City IMAX Theatre	Daesaeng Corporation	Seoul	(82 2) 789-5505/5882
Earthscape Pavilion	Expo Science Park	Taejon	(82 42) 866-5164

SPAIN
IMAX Port Vell*		Barcelona	(34 3) 225-1111
IMAX Madrid*		Madrid	(34 91) 467-4800
L'Hemisferic	Science and Technology Museum . .	Valencia	(34 96) 335-5330

SWEDEN
Cosmonova	Museum of Natural History	Stockholm	(46 85) 195-5106

SWITZERLAND
IMAX Theatre	Swiss Transport Museum	Lucerne	(41 41) 370-4444

TAIWAN
IMAX 3D Theatre*	Ntnl. Sci. & Tech. Museum	Kaohsiung	(88 67) 380-0089
Space Theatre	Ntnl. Museum of Nat. Science	Taichung	(88 642) 322-6940 x227
IMAX Dome Theatre	Taipei Astronomical Museum	Taipei	(88 622) 831-4551
IMAX Theatre	Taipei Muni. Children's Rec. Ctr	Taipei	(88 622) 593-2211

THAILAND
Krung Tahi IMAX Theatre		Bangkok	(662) 610-9105

TURKEY
Arcelik IMAX Sinemasi*	Migros Alieveris Merkezi	Ankara	(90 312) 541-1333

MEGASYSTEMS
(Full-service provider of products and services for the large-format film industry)
1515 Locust St., Ste. 700, Philadelphia, PA 19102. (215) 546-5300. www.megasystem.com email: info@megasystem.com
PRESIDENT
Cathy Neifeld

U.S. & PUERTO RICO THEATRES
MegaDome at the Chabot Observatory	Oakland	CA
Muvico Pointe 21	Orlando	FL
Douglass Theatre	Macon	GA
Louisiana Arts & Science Center MegaDome	Baton Rouge	LA
MegaDome at Daily Living Science Center	Kenner	LA
Paulucci Space Theater	Hibbing	MN
Russell C. Davis Planetarium MegaSphere	Jackson	MS
Hastings Museum	Hastings	NE
Fleischmann Planetarium	Reno	NV
Strasenburgh Planetarium	Rochester	NY
Muvico Peabody Place 22 Theaters	Memphis	TN
USS Lexington MegaScreen Theatre	Corpus Christi	TX
Cook Center Planetarium	Corsicanna	TX
MegaDome at Central Texas College	Killeen	TX
The Super Screen at Jordan Commons	Salt Lake City	UT
Science Museum of Western VA MegaDome	Roanoke	VA
Experience Music Project (EMP)	Seattle	WA
Sunrise Science Center & Art Museum	Charleston	WV
Caribbean Cinemas MegaScreen	San Juan	PR

INTERNATIONAL THEATRES
City of Durham Millennium Project	City of Durham	England
Rheged: Upland Kingdom Discovery Center	Cumbria	England
The Palladium 4D Theatre in Thorpe Park	London	England
New Lineo Cinemas Israel	Tel Aviv	Israel
Warner Village Torri Bianche	Vimercate	Italy
LMegaDome at the Japan Science Center	Tokyo	Japan
Kreativum MegaDome Theatre	Karlshamn	Sweden
Akva MegaSphere Theatre	Pitea	Sweden

SPECIALTY & LARGE FORMAT
EXHIBITOR SERVICES & EQUIPMENT

The companies below provide equipment, construction, sound, projectors, etc. for large format and special venue exhibition.

ALCORN MCBRIDE, INC.
3300 S. Hiawasee, Bldg. 105, Orlando, FL 32835. (407) 296-5800. FAX: (407) 296-5801. www.alcorn.com
CONTACT
Grace Warfield

ARC LIGHT EFX
(Lighting rental and sales)
9338 San Fernando Rd., Sun Valley, CA 91352. (818) 394-6330. FAX: (818) 252-3486. www.arclightefx.com
OWNER & CEO
Greg Smith
CFO
Kary Smith

BOSTON LIGHT AND SOUND, INC.
(Projection and sound equipment, service and installation)
290 N. Beacon St., Boston, MA 02135-1990. (617) 787-3131. FAX: (617) 787-4257. www.blsi.com
email: info@blsi.com
CONTACT
Chapin Cutler

CAMERA SERVICE CENTER - NEW YORK
(An Arri Group Company)
619 W. 54th St., New York, NY 10019. (212) 757-0906. FAX: (212) 713-0075.

CHRISTIE DIGITAL SYSTEMS
(Manufacturer & distributor of film projections, Xenon consoles, rewinds, bulbs; digital projectors and on-screen advertising)
10550 Camden Dr., Cypress, CA 90630. (714) 236-8610. FAX: (714) 503-3385. www.christiedigital.com
V.P., SALES, LATIN AMERICA
Joe Delgado
CINEMA SALES MANAGER
Scott Freidberg

COBALT ENTERTAINMENT TECHNOLOGIES
12565 Strathern St., N. Hollywood, CA 91605. (818) 759-5551. FAX: (818) 759-5553. www.cobalt3d.com
email: info@cobalt3d.com
FOUNDER & CEO
Steve Schklair

CREST NATIONAL FILM & VIDEOTAPE
(Ultrascan high resolution film to tape scanner for transfer of 65mm, 5, 8, 10, and 15-perf, and 35mm 8-perf Vistavision to digital and analog)
1000 N. Highland Ave., Hollywood, CA 90038. (323) 860-1300. FAX: (323) 461-8901. www.crestnational.com
CONTACTS
Lee Orgel
Jon Truckenmiller

DIGITAL THEATRE SYSTEMS
(DTS 6-track digital playback for theatres; 6-track digital processor w/automation; analog and digital equipment)
5171 Clareton Dr., Agoura Hills, CA 91301. (818) 706-3525. FAX: (818) 706-1868. www.dtsonline.com
DIRECTOR, CINEMA DIVISION
Michael Archer
MANAGER, SPECIAL VENUE PROJECTS
Walter Browski

DOLBY LABORATORIES, INC.
(Cinema sound equipment)
100 Potrero Ave., San Francisco, CA 94103. (415) 558-0200. FAX: (415) 645-4000. www.dolby.com email: info@dolby.com
CONTACT
Patrick Artiaga

ELECTROSONICS
3320 N. San Fernando Rd., Burbank, CA 91504. (818) 566-3045. FAX: (818) 566-4923. www.electrosonic.com

EVANS & SUTHERLAND
(StarRider digital theatres, DigiStar II digital planetarium projection system)
600 Komas Dr., Salt Lake City, UT 84108. (801) 588-1000, (801) 588-7405. FAX: (801) 588-4500. www.es.com
email: jpanek@es.com
CONTACT
Jeri Panek

FUJI PHOTO FILM USA, INC.
(Color negative, intermediate and positve film for large formats)
1141 N. Highland Ave,. Hollywood, CA 90038. (323) 957-8820. FAX: (323) 465-8279. www.fujifilm.com
email: kgrabot@fujifilm.com
CONTACT
Ken Grabot

HARRAH'S THEATRE EQUIPMENT CO.
(Sound, projection, seating, draperies, screens, masking & design services)
25613 Dollar St., Unit #1, Hayward, CA 94544. (510) 881-4989. FAX: (510) 881-0448.
CONTACT
Jerry Harrah

ISCO-OPTIC GMBH
(Manufacturer of cinema projection lenses for all formats, DLP cinema, special venue lenses and LCD projection)
Anna-Vandenhoeck-Ring 5, Gewerbepark Siekhöhe, D-37081 Göttingen, Germany. TEL: (49 551) 505-83. FAX: (49 551) 505-8410. www.iscooptic.de email: info@iscooptic.de
CONTACT
Katja Korzen

IWERKS ENTERTAINMENT
(Provider of high-tech entertainment systems, support services & software ride simulation & specialty venue attractions)
4520 W. Valerio St., Burbank, CA 91505. (818) 841-7766. FAX: (818) 841-7847, (818) 841-6192. www.iwerks.com
COO
Don Stults
CFO
John Choy
V.P., INTERNATIOANL SALES
Fritz Otis

LARGE FORMAT CINEMA ASSOCIATION
28241 Crown Valley Parkway, #401, Laguna Niguel, CA 92677. (949) 831-1142. FAX: (949) 831-4948. www.lfca.org
email: jmoore@lfca.org
EXECUTIVE DIRECTOR
Jeannie Moore
PRESIDENT
Robert Dennis

MEGASYSTEMS
(Full service provider of products and services for large format, including projection systems with state of the art clarity and sound and a compact open-architecture design)
110 Riberia St., St. Augustine, FL 32084. (904) 829-5702. FAX: (904) 829-5070. www.megasystem.com
CONTACTS
Steve Kitten
Mark Adukewicz

PACIFIC TITLE & ART STUDIO
(Optical and digital services)
6350 Santa Monica Blvd., Hollywood, CA 90038. (323) 464-0121. FAX: (323) 461-8325. www.pactitle.com

PEACE RIVER STUDIOS
(Equipment design, including GyroPro camera stabilizers, and TrailRail, a lightweight motion-controlled camera support system that enables multi-axes moves)
9 Montague St., Cambridge, MA 02139. (617) 491-6262. FAX: (617) 491-6703. www.peaceriverstudios.com
CONTACT
John Borden

OTTO NEMENZ INTERNAITONAL, INC.
(Camera rentals, Arriflex, Movie Cam, etc.)
870 N. Vine St., Hollywood, CA 90038. (323) 469-2774. FAX: (323) 469-1217. www.ottonemenz.com
CONTACT
Rick Mervis

PETER CRANE ASSOC.
(Consultants, theatre development)
154 W. San Antonio, San Clemente, CA 92672. (949) 492-0958. FAX: (949) 498-5518. email: Mike4film@aol.com
PRESIDENT
Peter Crane
VICE PRESIDENT
Michael Crane

SHOWPERFECT, INC.
(Manufacturer of large format and special venue electronic projectors)
5620-C Bonsai Ave., Moorpark, CA 93023. (805) 517-1600.
FAX: (805) 517-1604. www.showperfect.com
email: info@showperfect.com
CONTACT
Charles W. Fox

SPITZ, INC.
(Supplier of spherical projection domes for use with large format film, planetarium and other multi-media theaters)
P.O. Box 198, Rte. One, Chadds Ford, PA 19317. (610) 459-5200. (610) 459-3830. www.spitzinc.com
CONTACT
Jon Shaw

STRONG INTERNATIONAL
(Projection & sound equipment; Xenon slide projectors & spotlights)
4350 McKinley St., Omaha, NE 68112. (402) 453-4444. FAX: (402) 453-7238. www.Strong-Cinema.com
email: rboegner@aol.com
CONTACT
Ray Boegner

THORBURN ASSOCIATES, INC.
(Acoustical consulting and audivisual system engineering and design for commercial, corporate, leisure, public and retail industries)
P.O. Box 20399, Castro Valley, CA 94546. (510) 886-7826.
FAX: (510) 886-7828. www. ta-inc.com
CONTACT
Steve Thorburn

USHIO AMERICA, INC.
(Complete line of specialty and projection lamps)
5440 Cerritos Ave., Cypress, CA 90630. (714) 229-3143. FAX: (800) 376-3641. www.ushio.com
CONTACT
Robert Fujihara

VISTATECH LTD.
(Developing a new, super-widescreen movie system, "Vistamorph")
420 Cathcart Rd., Glasgow, Scotland UK G42 7BZ. (44 141) 423-1847 . FAX: (44 141) 423-5500. www.vistamorph.net
email: Vistamorph@aol.com

THEATRE EQUIPMENT & SERVICES

ACOUSTIC AND NOISE CONTROL WALL COVERINGS

ACOUSTIPLEAT CO.
592 Old Sherman Hill Rd., Woodbury, CT 06798. (203) 577-2026. email: acoustiplt@aol.com
PRESIDENT
Diana Peterson

ALPRO ACOUSTICS
(Perforated metal ceiling & wall panels and baffles)
5023 Hazel Jones Rd., Bossier City, LA 71111. (318) 629-2200. FAX: (800) 877-8746.
PRESIDENT
Rand Falbaum

AVL SYSTEMS, INC.
(Acoustical control products)
5540 S.W. 6th Place, Ocala, FL 34474. (800) ACUSTIC. FAX: (904) 854-1278. www.avlonline.com email: info@avlonline.com
PRESIDENT
J. Philip Hale

BREJTFUS THEATRICAL INTERIORS
(Manufacturer & supplier of custom artistic sound panels)
410 S. Madison Dr., Tempe, AZ, 85281. (480) 731-9899. FAX: (480) 731-9469. www.brejtfus.com
email: info@brejtfus
panel.com
PRESIDENT
Michael Regan

CLOUD INDUSTRIES, INC.
(Designer of stage & screen fronts, wall & screen drapery construction; manufacturer of film handling equipment)
P.O. Box 35, Lawson, MO 64062. (816) 296-3354. FAX: (816) 580-3364.
OWNER & PRESIDENT
Mary Shoemaker
V.P., SALES
Chuck Shoemaker

DECOUSTICS CINE-LINE
(Acoustical wall panels)
65 Disco Rd., Toronto, ONT M9W 1M2, Canada. (800) 387-3809, (416) 675-3983. FAX: (416) 675-5546.
www.decoustics.com email: sales@decoustics.com
V.P., SALES
John Balog
CONTACT
Laura Lim

EOMAC
(Manufacture, supply, design and install acoustic wall panels & ceiling systems)
2505 Dunwin Dr., Mississauga, ONT L5L 1T1, Canada. (905) 608-0100. FAX: (905) 608-0103. www.eomac.com
email: eomac@eomac.com
CONTACT
Mark Elliott

G&S ACOUSTICS (GOLTERMAN & SABO), INC.
(Acoustical wall pannels)
3555 Scarlet Oak Blvd., St. Louis, MO 63122. (800) 737-0307. FAX: (636) 225-2966. www.golterman.com
email: ned@golterman.com
V.P. & OPERATIONS MANAGER
Ned Golterman

KINETICS NOISE CONTROL
(Manufacturer of noise control products for all areas of the entertainment and exhibition industrty)
6300 Irelan Place, Dublin, OH 43017-3257. (614) 889-0480. FAX: (614) 889-0540. www.kineticsnoise.com
PRESIDENT & CEO
Virgil Temple
SALES
Jill Skaggs

MAG-TECH ENVIRONMENTAL INC.
(Soundfold/drapery cleaning, screen cleaning, seat cleaning)
710 Season Heather Ct., St. Louis, MO 63021. (636) 394-0414. FAX: (636) 394-0516.
OWNER & PRESIDENT
Don Waldman
VICE PRESIDENT
Lee Waldman

MBI PRODUCTS
(Manufacturer of acoustical products)
5309 Hamilton Ave., Cleveland OH 44114. (216) 431-6400 FAX: (216) 431-9000. www.mbiproducts.com
email: sales@mbiproducts.com
VICE PRESIDENT
Christopher Kysela
SALES MANAGER
Charlie Splain

MDC WALLCOVERINGS
(Acoustical wallcoverings)
1200 Arthur Ave., Elk Grove, IL 60007. (847) 437-4000. FAX: (847) 437-4017. www.mdcwallcoverings.com
EXECUTIVE ASSISTANT
Nancy Camarano

MELDED FABRICS
(Fabrics for trade shows and display booths)
3 Healey Rd., Dandenong, Victoria 3175, Australia TEL: (61 3) 8791-9200. FAX: (61 3) 9706-5481. www.meldedfabrics.com
email: john.hinton@meldedfabrics.com.au
NATIONAL SALES MANAGER
John Hinton

PNC WEST INC
(Manufacture, design, install acoustical wall & ceiling panels)
255 N. Pasadena St., #1, Gilbert, AZ 85233. (480) 917-1999. FAX: (877) 855-3121. www.pncwest.com
email: pncwest@msn.com
PRESIDENT
Cheryl Van Meter

SOUNDFOLD
(Wall carpeting, drapery systems & panels)
9200 N. State Rte. 48, Centerville, OH 45458. (800) 782-8018. FAX: (937) 885-5115. www.soundfold.com
email: kpierson@soundfold.com
VICE PRESIDENT
Thomas Miltner

SOUTHERN SCENIC EQUIPMENT CO.
(Theatre & stage drapery; theatre seat refurbishing; retrofit theatres to stadium seating)
1040 Branch Dr., Alpharetta, GA 30004. (770) 475-0733. FAX: (770) 475-0910.
PRESIDENT
Ted Yarborough

TRIANGLE SCENERY DRAPERY & LIGHTING
(Theatre drapery & rigging)
1215 Bates Ave., P.O. Box 29205, Los Angeles, CA 90029. (323) 662-8129. FAX: (323) 662-8120.
OWNER & PRESIDENT
Terry Miller

TROY SOUND WALL SYSTEMS
(Specialized acoustical materials; accoustical wall & ceiling treatments)
15904 Strathern St. #4, Van Nuys, CA 91406. (800) 987-3306, (818) 376-8490. FAX: (818) 376-8495.
www.troysoundwalls.com
PRESIDENT
Bill Berjiadas

WHISPER WALLS
(Acoustic fabric wall systems)
10957 E. Bethany Dr., Aurora, CO 80014. (303) 671-6696. FAX: (303) 671-0606. www.whisperwalls.com
VICE PRESIDENT
Brad Enter

AISLE AND WALL LIGHTING

ACTION LIGHTING
(Custom theatre lighting design, production & installation)
310 Ice Pond Rd., Bozeman, MT 59715. (800) 248-0076, (406) 586-5105. FAX: (406) 585-3078. www.actionlighting.com
email: action@actionlighting.com
SALES
Don Smith

ALL CINEMA SALES & SERVICE
(Custom wall, step, & aisle lighting installation services, low voltage lighting design)
124 Laurel Rd., East Northport, NY 11731. (631) 754-2510. FAX: (754) 2213.
CONTACT
Jim Kelly

ATLAS SPECIALTY LIGHTING
(Entertainment lighting)
7304 N. Florida Ave., Tampa, FL 33604. (813) 238-6481. FAX: (813) 238-6656. www.asltg2.com email: alicia@asltg2.com
MANAGERS
Ralph Felten Jr.
Bob Ray

CALIFORNIA ACCENT LIGHTING, INC.
(Step, wall and aisle lighting)
2034 E. Lincoln Ave., #431, Anaheim, CA 92806. (714) 535-7900. FAX: (714) 535-7902.
NATIONAL SALES MANAGER
Jaime Nunez

CELESTIAL LIGHTING PRODUCTS
(Architectural and decorative theatre and casino lighting)
14009 Dinard Ave., Santa Fe Springs, CA 90670. (800) 233-3563, (562) 802-8811. FAX: (562) 802-2882
www.celestiallighting.com
NATIONAL SALES MANAGER
Mitch Bronson

CINEMA LIGHTING CORPORATION
(Step & aisle lighting for theatres, auditoriums, and large-scale buildings; UPS backupsystem)
3536 Highland Dr., Hudsonville, MI 49426. (616) 669-5018. FAX: (616) 669-5011. www.cinemalighting.com
CEO
Kirk Campbell
MARKETING DIRECTOR
Wendy Strobel

DAVID TYSON LIGHTING, INC.
(Long-life lighting for theatres)
P.O. Box 1932, Callahan, FL 32011. (800) 385-3148. FAX: (800) 385-3149. www.davidtyson.com
CONTACT
Donna Tyson

EAST COAST LAMP SALES, INC.
(Commercial lighting fixture packages designed for end users)
120 Laurel Rd., East Northport, NY 11731. (631) 754-5655. FAX: (631) 754-2213.
PRESIDENT
James Kelly
VICE PRESIDENT
Thomas Kelly

EMERGENCY LIGHTING SERVICES, INC.
150 Brookside Rd., Waterbury, CT 06708. (800) 225-0263. FAX: (203) 756-6312.
SALES
Dave Cordeau

EVI (ENTERTAINMENT VENTURES INTL.)
(Film, TV, music & video production, promotion & packaging; themed entertainment concept design & creation services)
100 S. Doheny Dr., Ste. 402, Los Angeles, CA 90048. (310) 278-2800. FAX: (310) 274-0400. email: entventint@cs.com
DIRECTOR OF OPERATIONS
Jim Beatty
V.P., OPERATIONS
Karenbeth Cantrell
FILM & TV PACKAGING
Raya Markson
PUBLIC RELATIONS
Joyce Miller-Angus

HIGH END SYSTEMS, INC
(Automated lighting)
2105 Gracy Farms Ln., Austin, TX 78758. (512) 836-2242. FAX: (512) 837-5290. www.highend.com
SALES MANAGER
Dan Rizzoti

LEHIGH ELECTRIC PRODUCTS
(Manufacturer of lighting and dimming controls)
6265 Hamilton Blvd., Allenton, PA 18106. (610) 395-3386. FAX: (610) 395-7735.
PRESIDENT
Lloyd Jones

LIGHTING & ELECTRONIC DESIGN (LED)
(All types of aisle & wall lighting; decorative lighting)
141 Cassia Way, Units B & C, Henderson, NV 89014. (800) 700-5483. FAX: (888) 223-6599. www.ledlinc.com
email: led@ledlinc.com
OWNER
Janie Lynn

MICA LIGHTING COMPANY, INC.
(Fiberoptics & special effects lighting)
717 S. State College Blvd., Ste. L, Fullerton, CA 92831. (714) 738-8448. FAX: (714) 738-7748.
www.micalighting.com email: info@micalighting.com
PRESIDENT
Gayle von Eissler
V.P., OPERATIONS
Francisco Briseno

MICROLITE LIGHTING CONTROL
(Automated lighting control systems)
1150 Powis Rd., W. Chicago, IL 60185. (630) 876-0500. FAX: (630) 876-0580. www.microlite.net
CONTACT
Doug Zabel

PASKAL LIGHTING
(Specializes in all types of lighting for the movie industry)
6820 Romaine St., Hollywood, CA 90038-2433. (323) 466-5233. FAX: (323) 466-1071. www.paskal.com
OWNER & PRESIDENT
Evan Green

PERMLIGHT PRODUCTS
(Decorative lighting, LED aisle lighting, LED wall lighting, LED step lighting)
422 W. Sixth St., Tustin, CA 92780. (714) 508-0729 FAX: (714) 508-0920. www.permlight.com email: sales@permlight.com
PRESIDENT & CEO
Manuel Lynch
DIRECTOR OF SALES
Jim Patalano

QUALITY INSTALLATIONS
215 E. Orangethorpe, Ste. 327, Fullerton, CA 92832. (714) 491-3883. FAX: (714) 491-7514. www.qualityinstallations.org
email: sales@qualityinstallations.org
CONTACT
David Gutierrez

TARGETTI NORTH AMERICA
(Aisle & step lighting)
1513 E. St. Gertrude Place, Santa Ana, CA 92705. (714) 957-6101. FAX: (714) 957-1501. www.tivolilighting.com
SALES
Memo Briseno

TEMPO INDUSTRIES, INC.
(Manufacturer of low-voltage step, aisle & wall lighting for movie theatres; wall graphics and chandeliers)
1961 McGaw Ave., Irvine, CA 92614. (949) 442-1601. FAX: (949) 442-1609. www.tempoindustries.com
email: mail@tempoindustries.com
PRESIDENT
Gregory Smith
SALES
John McAllister

TUBE LIGHTING PRODUCTS
(Aisle & wall lighting specializing in low-voltage products)
1346 Pioneer Way, El Cajon, CA 92020. (619) 442-0577. FAX: (619) 442-0578. www.tubelightingproducts.com
OWNER
Rick Timpkin
SALES
Rodney Ezell

VISTA MANUFACTURING, INC.
(Strip lighting)
8086 Farm Market-2449 E., Ponder, TX 76259. (940) 479-2787. FAX: (940) 479-8139. www.vistamfg.com
email: vistamfg2@sprynet.com
SALES MANAGER
Walter Stevens

WULF INSTALLATIONS
(Aisle lighting installations for stadium & sloped-floor theatres)
54-A Emeraude Pl., Hampton, VA 23666. (757) 871-1439. FAX: (757) 826-8621. www.wulfinstallations.com
PRESIDENT
Karl Brian Wulf

ARCHITECTURE, DESIGN AND CONSTRUCTION

ALY CONSTRUCTION, INC.
(Movie theatre construction)
275 E. Baker St., Ste. A, Costa Mesa, CA 92626. (949) 629-4300. FAX: (949) 629-4310. www.alyconstruction.com
email: ayoungquist@alyconstruction.com
PRESIDENT
Andrew L. Youngquist

ARROWSTREET, INC.
(Large-scale commercial development projects)
212 Elm St., Somerville, MA 02144. (617) 623-5555. FAX: (617) 625-4646. www.arrowstreet.com email: info@arrowstreet.com
PRINCIPAL
John Cole

BEHR BROWERS ARCHITECTS INC
(Large-scale commercial buildings, specializing in motion picture theatres)
340 N. Westlake Blvd., #250, Westlake Village, CA 91362. (805) 496-1101 FAX: (805) 494-1421.
www.behrbrowers.com email: BBAIncArch@aol.com
EXECUTIVE DIRECTOR
Rossana Behr

BENCHMARK DESIGN GROUP
(Furniture for large-scale buildings)
456 Osceola Ave., Jacksonville Beach, FL 32250. (904) 246-5060. FAX: (904) 246-9008. www.benchmarkdesigngroup.com
email: mcarroll@benchmarkdesigngroup.com
PRESIDENT
Mark Carroll

BLAIR DESIGN & CONSTRUCTION
(Commercial buildings)
12021 Plano Rd., Ste. 175, Dallas, TX 75243. (972) 889-0600. FAX: (972) 889-0660.
VICE PRESIDENT
Richard Nelson

CLASSIC INDUSTRIES
(Architectural metal fabrication)
13020 FM 1641, Forney, TX 75126. (972) 564-2192. FAX: (972) 564-2190. www.classicusa.com
email: sales@classicusa.com
CEO
Rick Wilson
V.P., BUSINESS DEVELOPMENT
Gary Byrd

COMMERICAL BLOCK SYSTEMS
(Insulated concrete forms)
P.O. Box 1477, W Jordan, UT 84084. (801) 263-3957. FAX: (801) 263-3958. www.commericalblocksystems.com
PRESIDENT
Michael D. Schwab

CONSTRUCTION SOLUTIONS/STADIUM SEATING
(Large-scale construction, specializing in seating)
6799 Great Oaks Dr., Ste. 207, Memphis, TN 38138. (901) 753-4009. FAX: (901) 752-0720.
OWNERS
Scott Reading
Paul Cartwright

DIMENSIONAL INNOVATIONS
(Thematic architectural elements & signage)
3421 Merriam Ln., Overland Park, KS 66203. (913) 384-3488. FAX: (913) 384-1074. www.dimin.com
PRESIDENT
Jim Baker
VICE PRESIDENT
Tucker Trotter

FIRST IMPRESSIONS
(Design & construction of in-home theatres and custom seating; specializing in 3-D computer-animated design plans)
12564 N.E. 14th Ave., North Miami, FL 33161. (800) 305-7545, (305) 891-6121. FAX: (305) 891-7103.
email: sales@cineloungers.com
PRESIDENT & CEO
Jeffrey W. Smith, C.A.S.

HENRY ARCHITECTS
(Full-service architectural and interior design for multiplex cinemas)
6203 Dayton Ave. N., Seattle, WA 98103. (206) 784-6964. FAX: (206) 784-0837.
PRESIDENT
Rob Henry

IWERKS ENTERTAINMENT
(Specialized theatre manufacturing)
4520 W. Valerio St., Burbank, CA 91505. (818) 841-7766. FAX: (818) 841-7847, (818) 841-6192. www.iwerks.com
COO
Don Stults
CFO
John Choy
V.P., INTERNATIOANL SALES
Fritz Otis

JOHNSON/MCKIBBEN ARCHITECTS
(Large-scale public buildings and movie theatres)
965 Slocum St., Dallas, TX 75207. (214) 745-7070. FAX: (214) 745-1515. www.johnsonmckibben.com
PRESIDENT
Michael L. Johnson

KMD ARCHITECTS
(All types of large-scale building design)
222 Vallejo St., San Francisco, CA 94111. (415) 398-5191. FAX: (415) 394-7158. www.kmd-arch.com
259 W. 30th St., 16th Flr., New York, NY 10003. (212) 253-2272. FAX: (212) 253-2282.

LARGO CONSTRUCTION
(Movie theatre construction)
555 Street Rd., Bensalem, PA 19020. (800) 272-2432, (215) 245-0300. FAX: (215) 638-7933. email: largoconst@aol.com
V.P., THEATRE DIVISION
Jeffrey W. Spence

MARTEK CONTRACTS, LTD.
(Design, manufacture & installation of custom casework & equipment for concessions, box office & lobby)
37 Willow Ln., Mitcham, U.K. CR4 4NA. TEL: (44 20) 8687-8687. FAX: (44 20) 8687-8688. www.martek.co.uk
MANAGING DIRECTOR
Derek Galloway
TECHNICAL DIRECTOR
Martin Preen
OPERATIONS DIRECTOR
David Mansfield
EUROPEAN SALES MANAGER
Edward Eam

MARTEK CRS, INC.
(Design, manufacture & installation of custom casework & equipment for concessions, box office & lobby)
P.O. Box 532, St. Joseph, MI 49085. (616) 982-0031. FAX: (616) 982-8543. www.martek-us.com
email: info@martek-us.com
PRESIDENT
Mike Elliott
INTERNATIONAL SALES DIRECTOR
Derek Galloway

MESBUR & SMITH ARCHITECTS
(Cinema design; rennovation & restoration of old buildings)
148 Kenwood Ave.,Ste. 100, Toronto, ONT M6C 2S3, Canada. (416) 656-5751. FAX: (416) 656-5615. www.mesbursmith.com
email: mail@mesbursmith@on.aibn.com
PARTNER
David Mesbur
PARTNER
Harold Smith

MHB/PARADIGM DESIGN
(Commercial buildings, specializing in movie theatres)
550 3 Mile Rd. N.W., Grand Rapids, MI 49544. (616) 785-5656. FAX: (616) 785-5657. www.mhbparadigm.com
email: paradigm@mhbparadigm.com
VICE PRESIDENT
William H. Brunner

OAKVIEW CONSTRUCTION, INC.
(General contractors for all types of large-scale buildings)
1981 G Ave., Box 450, Red Oak, IA 51566. (712) 623-5561. FAX: (712) 623-5497. www.oakviewconst.com
CONTACT
Ken Rech

PACIFIC CONCESSIONS, INC.
(Concession design; financing for remodeling & construction)
75 Southgate, Daley City, CA 94015. (650) 994-9494. FAX: (650) 994-9490. email: info@pacificconcessions.com
VICE PRESIDENT
Dan Livak

PROCTOR COMPANIES
(Concession design, frabrication & install complete concession packages)
10497 W. Centennial Rd., Littleton, CO 80127-4218. (303) 973-8989. FAX: (303) 973-8884. www.proctorco.com
PRESIDENT
Bruce Proctor

P.P.R. ENTERPRISES
(Concession design)
890 Mariner St., Brea, CA 92821. (714) 529-7863. FAX: (714) 529-1418. email: pprpoul@pacbell.net
PRESIDENT
Poul Rasmussen
VICE PRESIDENT
Peter Rasmussen

RANACK CONSTRUCTORS, INC.
(Design, build & retro-fit construction)
652 S. County Rd. 9E, Ste. 101, Loveland, CO 80537. (970) 667-3698. FAX: (970) 667-3694. www.ranack.com
CONTACT
Doug Shirack

STADIUM SAVERS, LTD.
(System for stadium construction and retro-fitting)
550 3 Mile Rd. N.W., Grand Rapids, MI 49544. (616) 785-5656. FAX: (616) 785-5657. www.stadiumsavers.com
email: stadium@stadiumsavers.com
CONTACTS
Dick Murphy
Dwight Huskey
Bill Brunner

STADIUM SEATING ENTERPRISES/ANDREW L YOUNGQUIST CONSTRUCTION
(All types of construction)
275 E. Baker St., Costa Mesa, CA 92626. (949) 629-4300. FAX: (949) 629-4310. www.alyconstruction.com
CONTACT
Frank Mosen

TK ARCHITECTS
(Specializing in entertainment facilities, cinemas, restaurants)
106 W. 11th St., Ste. 1900, Kansas City, MO 64105. (816) 842-7552. FAX: (816)-842-1302.
www.tkarch.com email: tkapo@tkarch.com
VICE PRESIDENT
Tamra Knapp

BERG, HENNESSY, OLSON
(Planning & design for theatre construction)
50 Front St., Ste. 200, Newburgh, NY 12550. (845) 220-2070.
FAX: (845) 220-2077. email: bho@frontiernet.net
PRINCIPALS
Harvey A. Berg
Andew J. Hennessy
Mark S. Olson

WPH ARCHITECTURE
(Theatre, entertainment, commerical, retail, office and industrial projects)
513 NW 13th Ave., #300, Portland, OR 97209. (503) 827-0505.
FAX: (503) 827-0506. www.wphinc.com
email: office@wphinc.com
PRINCIPALS
Lynn Henderson
Douglas Walton
Steve Pinger
DIRECTOR, BUSINESS DEVELOPMENT
Terri Deskins

ASSISTIVE LISTENING SYSTEMS

ASSOCIATED HEARING INSTRUMENTS
6796 Market St., Upper Darby, PA 19082-2308. (610) 352-0600. FAX: (610) 352-2469. email: asshearing@aol.com
VICE PRESIDENT
Gary Bond

AUDEX, ASSISTIVE LISTENING SYSTEMS
(Infrared & other types of listening systems)
710 Standard St., Longview, TX 75604. (800) 237-0716. FAX: (903) 295-0310. www.audex.com email: cbeatty@audex.com
PRESIDENT
Charles Beatty

NADY SYSTEMS, INC.
6701 Shellmound St., Emeryville, CA 94608. (510) 652-2411.
FAX: (510) 652-5075.
CONTACT
Toby Garten

ODYSSEY PRODUCTS, INC.
(Infrared assistive equipment & support services; all types of booth equipment & supplies)
5845 Oakbrook Parkway, Ste. G, Norcross, GA 30093. (770) 825-0243. FAX: (770) 825-0245.
www.odyssey-products.com
email: odysseyproducts@mindspring.com
PRESIDENT
Eve Miller
CONTACT
Ken Reese

PHONIC EAR
3880 Cypress Dr., Petaluma, CA 94954. (800) 227-0735. FAX: (707) 769-9624. www.phonicear.com
email: marketing@phonicear.com
V.P., MARKETING
Rick Pimentel

SENNHEISER ELECTRONIC CORP.
(Infrared wireless equipment for the hearing-impaired)
1 Enterprise Dr., Old Lyme, CT 06371. (860) 434-9190. FAX: (860) 434-1759. www.sennheiserusa.com
DIRECTOR OF MARKETING
Stefanie Reichert

SOUND ASSOCIATES, INC.
(Distributor of listening systems)
424 W. 45th St., New York, NY 10036. (212) 757-5679. FAX: (212) 265-1250. www.soundassociates.com
V.P., OPERATIONS
Mark Annunziato

WILLIAMS SOUND CORP.
(FM and infrared hearing assistance systems)
10321 W. 70th St., Eden Prairie, MN 55344. (952) 943-2252.
FAX: (952) 943-2174. www.williamssound.com
email: info@williamssound.com
PRESIDENT
Jim Broz
CONTACT
Jeanne Hetland

BOX OFFICE, CONCESSION AND ACCOUNTING SYSTEMS

This listing incorporates both hardware and software.

A.C. NIELSEN EDI
(Box-office tracking and analysis systems)
6255 Sunset Blvd., 20th Flr., Hollywood, CA 90028. (323) 860-4600. FAX: (323) 860-4610.
CEO
Tom Borys
E.V.P., CLIENT SERVICES
Dan Marks

AOL ENTERTAINMENT
565 5th Ave., 8th Flr., New York, NY 10017. (212) 652-6300.
FAX: (212) 652-6301. www.mars-tms.com
MARKETING DIRECTOR
Christine Winston

CARDLOGIX
(Manufacturing & sales of Smart Cards; software for automated ticketing)
16 Hughes St., Ste. 100, Irvine, CA 92618. (949) 380-1312.
FAX: (949) 380-1428. www.cardlogix.com
email: sales@cardlogix.com
PRESIDENT & COO
Bruce Ross
V.P., SALES
Emil Nastri

CREDIT CARD CENTER
(ATM Sales, Service, Processing)
4850 Rhawn St., Philadelphia, PA 19136. (888) 276-0300.
www.ccc-atm.com email: nzullo@ccc-atm.com

EIMS, INC.
(Live ticketing systems and real-time Internet ticketing for cinema, stage, and stadium events)
8801 State Hwy. 16, Ste. A, Gig Harbor, WA 98332. (253) 857-6411. FAX: (253) 857-6461. www.eims-inc.com
CONTACT
Cherlyn Morrell

HURLEY SCREEN CORP./CEMCORP
110 Industry Ln., P.O. Box 296, Forest Hill, MD 21050. (410) 879-3022. FAX: (410) 838-8079.
V.P., OPERATIONS
Gorman White Jr.

INDIANA CASH DRAWER COMPANY
(Manufacturer of cash drawers)
1315 S. Miller St., Shergi, IN 46176. (317) 398-6643. FAX: (317) 392-0958. www.icdpos.com
SALES & MARKETING MANAGER
Catherine Woods

OMNITERM DATA TECHNOLOGY LTD.
(Automated ticketing, concessions, teleticket, ATM and more)
2785 Skymark Ave., #11, Mississauga, ONT L4W 4Y3, Canada. (905) 629-4757. FAX: (905) 629-8590.
www.omniterm.com email: info@omniterm.com
PRESIDENT
Ed Coman

PACER/CATS-CCS
(Specialized POS solutions that include ticketing and remote ticketing options-kiosks, internet, IVR-concessions and merchandise management, advanced reporting and analysis)
355 Inverness Sr. S., Englewood, CO 80112. (303) 649-9818.
FAX: (303) 414-7805. www.pacercats.com
email: sales@pacercats.com
V.P., SALES
Sly Glass

RADIANT SYSTEMS, INC
(Theatre management services for box office, back office, consumer-activated kiosk, ticketing, POS)
3925 Brookside Pkwy., Apharetta, GA 30022. (770) 576-6000. FAX: (770) 754-7790. www.radiantsystems.com

RDS/HOWELL DATA SYSTEMS
(Manufacturer of box office accounting systems & concession stand cash registers)
101 Donly Dr. S., Simcoe, ONT N3Y 4L5, Canada. (888) 737-3282. FAX: (519) 428-0131. www.rdsdata.com
email: info@rdsdata.com
CONTACTS
Brad De Poorter
Paul Howell

READY THEATRE SYSTEMS
(Computer box-office ticketing & concessions software)
8189 Verlynda Dr., Watervliet, MI 49098. (269) 463-5096. FAX: (707) 276-7222. http://rts-solutions.com

RETRIEVER SOFTWARE

(Touch-screen ticketing & concession systems, integrated theatre & labor management, inventory control & reporting)
2525 S. Broadway, Denver, CO 80210. (720) 570-1173. FAX: (720) 570-0620. www.venue-pos.com
V.P., SALES
Phil Norrish

SENSIBLE CINEMA SOFTWARE

(Ticketing & concession inventory software; ticketing printers & blank ticket stock)
7216 Sutton Pl., Fairview, TN 37062. (615) 799-6366. FAX: (615) 799-6367. www.sensiblecinema.com
CONTACT
Rusty Gordon

SYSTEM OPERATING SOLUTIONS, INC.

(Sales, service and support of Pacer ticketing and concession systems)
P.O. Box 1076, Monroe, WA 98272. (800) 434-3098. FAX: (360) 805-0632. www.sosticketing.com
CONTACT
Jason Macomber

TICKETING SYSTEMS.COM

430 State Pl., Ste. B, Escondido, CA 92029. (760) 480-1002. FAX: (760) 480-6830. www.ticketingsystems.com
PRESIDENT
Bruce L. Hall

TICKETPRO SYSTEMS

(Computer software for the theatre industry)
870 Mercury Dr. S.E., Lawrenceville, GA 30045. (770) 682-5485. FAX: (770) 682-8397. www.ticketpro.org
CEO
John Shaw
SYSTEMS INTEGRATOR
Willie Vandenheuvel

VCS TIMELESS

(Box office, concessions, IVR, Web, customer loyalty and head office management systems)
240 Richmond St., W., Toronto, ON M5V 1V6 Canada. (416) 599-8366. FAX: (416) 599-8367. www.vcstimeless.com
email: enquiries@vcstimeless.com
SALES MANAGER
David Wiltshire

CARPETS

BRINTONS U.S. AXMINSTER

(All types of custom & stock carpeting, commercial & residential)
P.O. Box 877, Greenville MS 38702. (662) 332-1581. FAX: (662) 332-1594. www.brintonsusax.com
EXECUTIVE V.P., SALES
Jeff Coveny
SALES
Linda Merrill

DURKAN PATTERNED CARPET

(Specializes in manufacture of patterned carpets)
P.O. Box 1006, 405 Virgil Dr., Dalton, GA 30720. (706) 278-7037. FAX: (706) 279-8451. www.durkan.com
email: sales@durkan.com
CONTACT
Charles Durkan

EAST WEST CARPET MILLS

8507 S. L Cienega Blvd., Inglewood, CA 90301. (310) 559-RUGS (7847). FAX: (310) 559-6357.
CONTACT
Larry Sperling

MASLAND CARPETS, INC.

(All types of carpeting)
P.O. Box 11467, Mobile, AL 36671. (800) 633-0468, (251) 675-9080. FAX: (251) 675-8330. www.maslandcarpets.com
NATIONAL ACCOUNTS MANAGER
Jay Loughran

MILLIKEN CARPET

(Patterned broadloom carpet & carpet tile)
201 Lukken Industrial Dr. W., LaGrange, GA 30240. (706) 880-5154. FAX: (706) 880-5888. www.millikencarpet.com
COMMUNICATIONS MANAGER
Tracy Francis

OMEGA PATTERN WORKS, INC./ARTISANS, INC.

P.O. Box 1059, 716 S. River St., Calhoun, GA 30703. (800) 241-4908. FAX: (706) 629-4247. www.omegaflooring.com
www.artisanscarpet.com
CUSTOMER SERVICE
Joyce Maxwell

CONCESSION EQUIPMENT

ACORTO, INC.

(Manufacturer of espresso machines)
1287 120th Ave. N.E., Bellevue, WA 98005. (425) 453-2800. FAX: (425) 453-2167. www.acorto.com email: info@acorto.com
MARKETING
Niki Primrose

ALL-STAR CARTS AND VEHICLES, INC.

(Manufacturer of concession carts, kiosks, trailers & trucks)
1565 Fifth Industrial Ct., Bayshore, NY 11706. (800) 831-3166. FAX: (631) 666-1319. www.allstarcarts.com
VICE PRESIDENT
Bob Kronrad

AMERICAN CONCESSION SUPPLY, INC.

(Full line of concession equipment & supplies)
3370 Peoria St., Ste. 200, Denver, CO 80010. (303) 361-9337. FAX: (303) 361-9531. www.americanconcessionsupply.com
CONTACT
Jim Walsh

AUTOMATIC BAR CONTROLS/WUNDER-BAR

(Food dispensing systems)
790 Eubanks Rd., Vacaville, CA 95688. (707) 448-5151. FAX: (707) 448-1521. www.wunderbar.com
VICE PRESIDENT
Bret Baker

BAER AND ASSOCIATES

(Complete food service packaging)
P.O. Box 307, 117 Main St., Tarkio, MO 64491. (800) 444-8619. FAX: (660) 736-4832.
OFFICE MANAGER
Jeannine Broerman

BAGCRAFT

(Manufacturers of flexible packaging)
3900 W. 43rd St., Chicago, IL 60632. (773) 254-8000. FAX: (773) 254-8204. www.bagcraft.com
CUSTOMER SERVICE SUPERVISOR
Nancy Chico

BEAVER MACHINE CORP.

(Bulk vending machines)
1341 Kerrisdale Blvd., Newmarket, ON L3Y 7V1, Canada. (800) 265-6772, (905) 836-4700. FAX: (905) 836-4737. www.beavervending.com email: sales@beavervending.com
BUSINESS DEVELOPMENT MANAGER
Matt Miller

BERRY PLASTICS

(Promotional plastic souvenir cups & other vessels)
6917 Tameron Trail, Fort Worth, TX 76132. (817) 423-0424. FAX: (817) 263-9670. www.berryplastics.com
email: davidmeyer@berryplastics.com
CONTACT
David Meyer

C. CRETORS & COMPANY

(Popcorn machines, peanut roasters, cotton candy)
3243 N. California Ave., Chicago, IL 60618. (800) 228-1885. FAX: (773) 588-7141. www.cretors.com
V.P., OPERATIONS
Van Neathery
V.P., SALES & MARKETING
Gino Nardulli
MARKETING DIRECTOR
Beth Cretors

CHART INDUSTRIES/MVE

(Manufacturer of bulk CO2 systems for fountain beverage equipment)
3505 County Rd., 42 W., Burnsville, MN 55306. (800) 247-4446. FAX: (952) 882-5185. www.chart-inc.com
SALES
Dick Mich (515) 317-9729

CINEMA SUPPLY CO.

(Theatre equipment company)
502 S. Market St., Millersburg, PA 17061. (800) 437-5505. FAX: (717) 692-3073. www.cinemasupply.com
OPERATIONS MANAGER
Van Troutman
SALES MANAGER
Gina DiSanto

CONCESSION SUPPLY COMPANY

(New & used concession machines; sales & repair)
1016 Summit St., Toledo, OH 43697. (419) 241-7711. FAX: (419) 241-3219.
OWNER & PRESIDENT
Robert Brockway

FAWN VENDORS
(Snack & drink machines)
8040 University Blvd., Des Moines, IA 50325. (800) 548-1982.
FAX: (515) 274-9256. www.fawnvendors.com
SALES
Gary Bahr

FIELD CONTAINER CO. , LP
(Popcorn containers, theatre trays)
1501 Industrial Park Dr., Tuscaloosa, AL 35401. (205) 333-0333. FAX: (205) 333-9862. www.southfieldcarton.com
V.P., SALES
Richard Burklew

FRYWORKS
(Automatic french-fry cookers)
4640 Admiralty Way, Ste. 310, Marina Del Rey, CA 90292.
(310) 577-4606. FAX: (310) 577-4616 www.fryworks.com
CONTACT
Leila Zold

GABRIELLA IMPORTS
(Espresso & cappuccino machines)
5100 Prospect Ave., Cleveland OH 44103. (216) 432-3651.
FAX: (216) 432-3654. www.gabimports.com
email: info@gabimports.com
OWNER & PRESIDENT
Douglas Friedman

GOLD MEDAL PRODUCTS
(Concession equipment & supplies)
10700 Medallion Dr., Cincinnati, OH 45241-4807. (800) 543-0862, (513) 769-7676. FAX: (800) 542-1496, (513) 769-8500.
www.gmpopcorn.com email: info@gmpopcorn
NATIONAL SALES DIRECTOR
Chris Petroff

HOSHIZAKI NORTH EASTERN
(Ice machines, refrigerators/freezers)
20 Drexel Dr., Bayshore, NY 11706. (800) 281-5249.
ACCOUNT MANAGER
Nick Tippert

IMI CORNELIUS INC.
(Manufacturer of beverage & ice-maker dispensers & slush machines)
One Cornelius Pl., Anoka, MN 55303. (800) 238-3600, (763) 421-6120. FAX: (763) 422-3297. www.cornelius.com

INTEGRATED FOOD SYSTEMS
(Automated frying systems for movie theatres)
11705 Gold Park Ln., Gold River, CA 95670. (916) 852-0556.
FAX: (916) 852-0626. www.ifs.com email: fmathes@home.com
S.V.P.
Forest A. Mathes

JARCO INDUSTRIES
(Custom fabrication of concession stands, box offices, lobby fixtures, display cases and all types of concession equipment)
125 Laser Ct., Hauppauge, NY 11788. (631) 851-9100. FAX:
(631) 851-9101. www.jarcoindustries.com;
www.concessionstands.com
PRESIDENT & CEO
Jeffrey Stein
CONTACT
Justin Stein

LANCER CORP., INC.
(Manufacturer of beverage & ice dispensers)
6655 Lancer Blvd., San Antonio, TX, 78219. (800) 729-1500.
FAX: (210) 310-7242. www.lancercorp.com
CONTROLLER
Mark Feritas

MAINSTREET MENU SYSTEMS
1375 N. Barker Rd., Brookfield, WI 53045. (262) 782-6000.
FAX: (262) 782-6515. www.mainstreetmenu.com
MARKETING MANAGER
Dawn Pankow

MARTEK CONTRACTS, LTD.
(Design, manufacture & installation of custom casework & equipment for concessions, box office & lobby)
37 Willow Ln., Mitcham, U.K. CR4 4NA. TEL: (44 20) 8687-8687. FAX: (44 20) 8687-8688. www.martek.co.uk
email: infor@martek.co.uk
MANAGING DIRECTOR
Derek Galloway
TECHNICAL DIRECTOR
Martin Preen
OPERATIONS DIRECTOR
David Mansfield
EUROPEAN SALES MANAGER
Edward Eam

MARTEK CRS, INC.
(Design, manufacture & installation of custom casework & equipment for concessions, box office & lobby)
9047 US 31, Ste. 1, Berrien Springs, MI 49103. (269) 471-9000. www.martek-us.com email: info@martek-us.com
PRESIDENT
Mike Elliott
INTERNATIONAL SALES DIRECTOR
Derek Galloway

METROPOLITAN PROVISIONS
(Snack bar equipment)
16639 Gale Ave., City of Industry, CA 91745. (626) 330-1414.
SALES DIRECTOR
Ron Naslund

MICHAELO ESPRESSO, INC.
(Espresso machines & grinders; sales & service)
3801 Stone Way N., Seattle, WA 98103-8005. (206) 548-9000.
FAX (206) 695-4951. www.michaelo.com
DISTRICT SALES MANAGER
Bob Cappelletti

MULTIPLEX COMPANY
(A subsidiary of Manitowoc Beverage Equipment)
(Manufacturer of beverage dispensers, soda & beer systems)
2100 Future Dr., Sellersburg, IN 47172. (800) 367-4233. FAX:
(812) 246-9922. www.multiplex-beverage.com
PRODUCT LINE DIRECTOR
Mark Johnson

NATIONAL CINEMA SUPPLY CORPORATION
(Complete line of theatre equipment & supplies, including projection, sound, seating, janitorial, and food service)
CORPORATE HEADQUARTERS
14499 N. Dale Mabry Hwy., Ste. 201, Tampa, FL 33618. (813)
962-2772. FAX: (813) 962-3620. Technical: (800) 776-6271,
(813) 962-0188; Concessions: (800) 733-7278. FAX: (813) 908-6277. www.ncsco.com
PRESIDENT & COO
Barney Bailey
CHAIRMAN & CEO
Daniel P. Miller
REGIONAL SALES MANAGER
Greg Thomas
VICE PRESIDENT
Ron Eiben
V.P., DIRECTOR, MARKETING
Larry Shively
BRANCHES
P.O. Box 206, Castaic, CA 91320-0206. (661) 257-1984. FAX:
(661) 257-1660.
REGIONAL SALES MANAGER
George A. Bruce Jr.
P.O. Box 549, 99 Limestone Rd., Ridgefield, CT 06877. (203)
438-3405, (203) 438-1274. FAX: (203) 438-1419, (203) 438-1542.
V.P. & GENERAL SALES MANAGER
Walter Beatty Jr.
5854 Highland Ridge Dr., Cincinnati, OH 45232. (800) 543-0418, (513) 242-6801. FAX: (513) 242-6931.
VICE PRESIDENT
Barbara Cammack

NATIONAL MAINTENANCE CORPORATION
14499 N. Dale Mabry Hwy., Tampa, FL (813) 739-3308. FAX:
(813) 739-3319.
VICE PRESIDENT
Larry Shively

PACIFIC CONCESSIONS, INC.
(Concession design)
75 Southgate, Daley City, CA 94015. (650) 994-9494. FAX:
(650) 994-9490. www.pacificconcessions.com
email: info@pacificconcessions.com
PRESIDENT
Dan Livak

PACKAGING CONCEPTS
(Manufacturer of theatre popcorn bags & kid's food trays;
represents Sweetheart paper products to the theatre industry)
4971 Fyler Ave., St. Louis, MO 63139. (314) 481-1155. FAX:
(314) 481-6567. www.packagingconceptsinc.com
PRESIDENT
John Irace
VICE PRESIDENT
Tony Irace

PROCTOR COMPANIES
(Supplier & designer of concession stands, popcorn warmers,
box offices and lobby fixtures)
10497 W. Centennial Rd., Littleton, CO 80127-4218. (303) 973-8989. FAX: (303) 973-8884. www.proctorco.com
PRESIDENT
Bruce Proctor

PROMOTIONAL MANAGEMENT GROUP, INC.
(Concession containers & supplies)
925 Wyoming, Ste. 200, Kansas City, MO 64101. (816) 221-3833. FAX: (816) 842-3650.
E.V.P., SALES & MARKETING
James McGuinness

ROBINSON/KIRSHBAUM INDUSTRIES, INC.
(Manufacturer of beverage-dispensing equipment)
261 E. 157th St., Gardena, CA 90248. (310) 354-9948. FAX: (310) 354-9921. email: rkindstry@aol.com
EXECUTIVE VICE PRESIDENT
Bruce Kirshbaum

ROUNDUP FOOD EQUIPMENT
(Manufacturer of commercial food equipment; gas pressure switches, pizza grills)
180 Kehoe Blvd., Carol Stream, IL 60188. (800) 253-2991. FAX: (630) 784-1650. www.ajantunes.com
MARKETING
Thomas Krisch

SANI-SERV
(Ice cream & beverage dispensers)
451 E. County Line Rd., Mooresville, IN 46158. (317) 831-7030. FAX: (317) 831-7036. www.saniserv.com
SALES & MARKETING
Steve Dowling

SERVER PRODUCTS, INC.
(Restaurant & fast-food equipment)
P.O. Box 98, Richfield, WI 53076. (800) 558-8722, (262) 628-5600. FAX: (262) 628-5110. www.serverproducts.com
email: spsales@server-products.com
SALES
Carol Neuser

SOURCE ONE
(Concession equipment; complete booth & sound equipment)
5224 Longview, Shawnee, KS 66218. (913) 441-0664.
OWNER & PRESIDENT
Ryland Cozad

STAR MANUFACTURING INTERNATIONAL
(Restaurant & concession equipment; hot-dog cookers, popcorn/nacho equipment)
P.O. Box 43129, 10 Sunnen Dr., St. Louis, MO 63143. (314) 781-2777. FAX: (314) 781-3636. www.star-mfg.com
V.P., SALES
Tim Gaskill

STEIN INDUSTRIES
(Display cases, concession stands, box offices, popcorn & nacho warmers)
22 Sprague Ave., Amityville, NY 11701. (631) 789-2222. FAX: (631) 789-8888. email: steininc1@aol.com
PRESIDENT
Stuart Stein
VICE PRESIDENT
Andrew Stein

TAYLOR COMPANY
(Manufacturer of ice cream, frozen cocktail & beverage, shake, gourmet, and cooking equipment)
750 N. Blackhawk Blvd., Rockton, IL 61072. (815) 624-8333. FAX: (815) 624-8000. www.taylor-company.com
MARKETING
Tricia Bennett

TURBOCHEF TECHNOLOGIES
(Fast-cook, nonvented ovens)
10500 Metric Dr., #128, Dallas TX 75243. (214) 341-9471. FAX: (214) 340-8477. www.turbochef.com
DIRECTOR, BUSINESS DEVELOPMENT
Pete Ashcraft

2POP
(Concession containers)
171 Pier Ave., #240, Santa Monica, CA 90405. (310) 822-0481. FAX: (310) 822-2322. www.2pop.com
email: sales@2pop.com
CONTACT
P.J. Berjis

WINPAK TECHNOLOGIES, INC.
(Flexible packaging)
85 Laird Dr., Toronto, ON M4G 3T8, Canada. 100 Saulteaux Crescent, Winnipeg, Manitoba R3J 3T3, Canada. (204) 889-1015. FAX: (204) 888-7806. www.winpak.com
DIRECTOR, SALES & MARKETING
Louis de Bellefeuille (416) 421-1750

WESNIC
(Site furnishings)
6000 Bowdendale Ave., Jacksonville, FL 32216. (904) 733-8444. FAX: (904) 733-3736. www.wesnic.com
DIRECTOR OF MARKETING
Bill Gilbert

CROWD CONTROL

ALVARADO MANUFACTURING
(Escort belts)
12660 Colony St., Chino, CA 91710. (909) 591-8431. FAX: (909) 628-1403.
www.alvaradomfg.com email: information@alvaradomfg.com
MARKETING MANAGER
Dale Staton

BRASS SMITH, INC.
(Crowd-control items & sneeze guards)
3880 Holly St., Denver, CO 80207. (800) 662-9595. FAX: (303) 331-8444. www.brasssmith.com
email: bsi@brasssmith.com
SALES MANAGER
Benny Martinez

CROWN INDUSTRIES, INC.
(Ropes and stanchions)
155 N. Park St., East Orange, NJ 07017. (800) GO-CROWN. FAX: (973) 672-7536. www.gocrown.com
email: info@gocrown.com
PRESIDENT
Hugh Loebner

LAVI INDUSTRIES
(Public guidance systems for crowd control)
27810 Ave. Hopkins, Valencia, CA 91355-3409. (800) 624-6225. FAX: (661) 257-4938. www.lavi.com
2 Geneva Rd., Brewster, NY 10509. (877) 213-5284, (845) 278-1766. FAX: (845) 278-1765.
SALES MANAGER
Ed Bradford

LAWRENCE METAL PRODUCTS, INC.
(Guidance system products including portable posts, ropes, railings, turnstiles & gates)
P.O. Box 400-M, Bay Shore, NY 11706. (800) 441-0019, (631) 666-0300. FAX: (631) 666-0336. www.lawrencemetal.com
email: service@lawrencemetal.com
PRESIDENT
David Lawrence
SALES MANAGER
Betty Castro

CURTAINS AND DRAPERY

AUTOMATIC DEVICES COMPANY
(Drapery controls and curtain tracks)
2121 S. 12th St. Allentown, PA 18103-4751. (610) 797-6000. FAX: (610) 797-4088. www.automaticdevices.com
PRESIDENT
John Samuels

CLACO EQUIPMENT AND SERVICE, INC.
(Econo-pleat drapery systems, theatre chairs; complete projection, sound, auditorium equipment & service)
1212 S. State St., Salt Lake City, UT 84111. (801) 355-1250. FAX: (801) 355-1259. www.clacoequipment.com
email: claco@utah-inter.net
PRESIDENT
Clayton Stauffer
SALES
Dennis Lunt

CLOUD INDUSTRIES, INC.
(Designer of stage & screen fronts, wall & screen drapery construction; manufacturer of film handling equipment)
P.O. Box 35, Lawson, MO 64062. (816) 296-3354. FAX: (816) 580-3364.
OWNER & PRESIDENT
Mary Shoemaker
V.P., SALES
Chuck Shoemaker

HALGO SPECIALTIES COMPANY, INC.
(Curtain & drapery systems, stage lighting, auditorium seating, crowd control equipment, signs & displays)
16760 Stagg St., Ste. 209, Van Nuys, CA 91406. (818) 786-4436. FAX (818) 780-3486. email: Halgoone@socal.rr.com
PRESIDENT
Norman Dean Goldstein

S & K THEATRICAL DRAPERIES
(Draperies for large-scale public buildings)
7313 Varna Ave., North Hollywood, CA 91605-4009. (818) 503-0596. FAX: (818) 503-0599. www.sktheatricaldraperies.com
SALES MANAGERS
Beth Russell
Carmela Skogman

TRIANGLE SCENERY DRAPERY & LIGHTING
(Stage drapery & rigging)
P.O. Box 29205, 1215 Bates Ave., Los Angeles, CA 90029-0205. (323) 662-8129. FAX: (323) 662-8120. www.tridrape.com
OWNER & PRESIDENT
Terry Miller

DIGITAL SOUND SYSTEMS

CARDINAL SOUND & MOTION PICTURE SYSTEMS, INC.
(Digital sound systems; 16mm, 35mm, & 70mm equipment)
6330 Howard Ln., Elkridge, MD 21075. (410) 796-5300. FAX:
(410) 796-7995. www.cardinalsound.com
OFFICE MANAGER
Catherine Rockman

DIGITAL THEATER SYSTEMS
(Manufacturer of components for digital sound systems,
including DTS 6-track digital playback & processor with
automation; analog & digital equipment)
5171 Clareton Dr., Agoura Hills, CA 91301. (818) 706-3525.
FAX: (818) 706-1868. www.dtsonline.com
Unit 5, Tavistock Industrial Estate, Ruscombe Ln., Twyford,
Berkshire, England RG10 9NJ. TEL: (44 118) 934-9199. FAX:
(44 118) 934-9198. email: dtsinfo@dtsonline.co.uk
AT Communications KK, 2-14-4 Shinonome, Koto-ku, 135-0062
Tokyo, Japan. email: asano@dstech.co.jp
CHAIRMAN
Dan Slusser
PRESIDENT & CEO
Jon Kirchner
V.P., FINANCE & CFO
Mel Flanigan
V.P., GENERAL COUNSEL
Blake Welcher
V.P., RESEARCH & DEVELOPMENT
Paul Smith
V.P., ENGINEERING
Jan Wissmuller
V.P., OPERATIONS
Andrea Nee
V.P., CONSUMER BUSINESS DEVELOPMENT
Patrick Watson
V.P., MUSIC OPERATIONS
Jeff Skillen
V.P., MARKETING, DTS ENTERTAINMENT
David DelGrosso
V.P., MARKETING DTSE
Brian Caldwell
DIRECTOR, TECHNOLOGY MARKETING
Lorr Kramer
TECHNICAL DIRECTOR, DTS ENTERTAINMENT
Jeff Levison

DOLBY LABORATORIES
(All aspects of sound for motion pictures, consumer
entertainment products, and media, broadcasting, & music
recording)
100 Potrero Ave., San Francisco, CA 94103-4886. (415) 558-
0200. FAX: (415) 863-1373. www.dolby.com
CHAIRMAN & FOUNDER
Ray Dolby
PRESIDENT
Bill Jasper
SENIOR V.P., TECHNOLOGY
David P. Robinson
SENIOR V.P. & GENERAL MANAGER, CONSUMER DIVISION
Ed Schummer
VICE PRESIDENT
Ioan Allen
V.P., OPERATIONS
R. Richard (Dick) Bell
V.P. & CFO
Janet L. Daly
V.P., RESEARCH & DEVELOPMENT
Steven (Steve) E. Forshay
V.P., MANUFACTURING
Jeff Griffith
V.P., LICENSING OPERATIONS
Richard L. Hockenbrock
V.P., BUSINESS AFFAIRS
Martin A. (Marty) Jaffe
V.P. & CHIEF INFORMATION OFFICER
Mina Millett
V.P., PROFESSIONAL DIVISION
Tim Partridge
V.P., EXHIBITOR RELATIONS
Bobby Pinkston

3601 W. Alameda Ave., Burbank, CA 91505-5300. (818) 823-
2800.
V.P., HOLLYWOOD FILM
David Gray

1350 Ave. of the Americas, 28th Flr., New York, NY 10019-
4703. (212) 767-1700. FAX: (212) 767-1705.
V.P., EAST COAST DIVISION
Michael Di Cosimo

Wootton Bassett, Wiltshire SN4 8QJ, England. TEL: (44 179)
384-2100. FAX: (44 179) 384-2101.
MANAGING DIRECTOR
David Watts

DIRECTOR, PRODUCTION
John Blunden
DIRECTOR, FILM PRODUCTION
John Iles
FINANCIAL DIRECTOR
Bruce Nottage
INTERNATIONAL SALES DIRECTOR
Peter Seagger
MARKETING DIRECTOR, TECHNOLOGY
Tony Spath

MARQUEE TECHNICAL SERVICES
(Sound and projection system)
740 Fallowfield Dr., Loganville, GA 30052. (800) 339-1662.
FAX: (770) 554-9844. www.marqueetech.com
email: marquee@america.net
PRESIDENT
Scott Meader
VICE PRESIDENT
Robin Meader

SONY CINEMA PRODUCTS CORPORATION
(All aspects of digital sound production)
10202 W. Washington Blvd., Poitier 3206, Culver City, CA
90232. (310) 244-5777. FAX: (310) 244-2024. www.sdds.com
SALES/MARKETING
Lori Ray (201) 358-4425
SDDS LICENSE AGREEMENTS
Terie Gallo (310) 244-8244
SDDS ORDER PROCESSING
Anna Lopez (562) 342-2139

TECHNICOLOR DIGITAL SERVICES
2233 N. Ontario, Ste. 300, Burbank, CA 91504. (818) 260-
3700. FAX: (818) 260-3720.
www.technicolordigital.com
CEO, TECHNICOLOR DIGITAL CINEMA & TECHNICOLOR
ENTERTAINMENT SERVICES
Dave R. Elliott
CEO, TECHNICOLOR
Lanny Raimondo
PRINCIPAL, FINANCE & BUSINESS DEVELOPMENT,
TECHNICOLOR
Virginia Bushell
PRINCIPAL, TECHNICAL COORDINATION, TECHNICOLOR
DIGITAL CINEMA
Michael Sterling
EXECUTIVE V.P., DISTRIBUTION
Peter Koplik

THX LTD.
(Custom designed sound systems, crossover & systems rack;
digital cinema products)
1600 Los Gamos, Ste. 231, San Rafael, CA 94903. (415) 492-
3900. FAX: (415) 492-3988. www.thx.com
CONTACTS
Ross Portugeis, (415) 492-3940
Kevin Heverin, (415) 492-3916

EXHIBITOR SERVICES

CENTRAL MOTION PICTURE SERVICE
4688 E. 29th Rd., Sandwich, IL 60548. (815) 786-6577. FAX:
(815) 786-6337.
PRESIDENT
George Smiley
VICE PRESIDENT
Albert "Buck" Kolkmeyer

DATA QUEST INVESTIGATIONS, LTD.
(Theatre checkers, headcounts, employment screenings,
undercover operatives, investigations)
667 Boylston St., Ste. 200, Boston, MA 02116. (800) 292-9797.
FAX: (617) 437-0034. www.dataquestonline.com
email: tturgeon@dataquestonline.com
PRESIDENT
Russ Bubas
VICE PRESIDENT
Tracey Turgeon

DIGITAL SPARKS
(Entertainment marketing)
1207 Bridgeway, Ste. I, Sausalito, CA 94965. (415) 332-5555.
FAX: (415) 332-5010. www.digitalsparx.com
CEO
Jon Stern

MAROEVICH, OSHEA & COGHLAN
(Insurance)
425 Market St., # 1030, San Francisco, CA 94105. (800) 951-
0600. (415) 957-0600. FAX: (415) 957-0577.
www.maroevich.com
PRESIDENT & CEO
Ivan Maroevich, Jr.
V.P., ENTERTAINMENT
Steve Elkins

MOVIEAD CORP.
(Distributor of advertising and concession print materials)
3500 N. Andrews Ave., Pompano Beach, FL 33064. (800) 329-4989, (954) 784-6767. FAX: (954) 784-0700. www.moviead.com
PRESIDENT
Emil Noah

NATIONAL CINEMA NETWORK, INC.
(On-screen advertising)
1300 E. 104th St., #100, Kansas City, MO 64131. (800) SCREEN-1. FAX: (816) 942-8418. www.ncninc.com
PRESIDENT
Chuck Battey
SENIOR V.P., SALES
Janice Meyers

P&O NEDLLOYD
(Cinema FF&E logistics)
One Meadowlands Plaza, 14th Flr., E. Rutherford, NJ 07073. (201) 896-6200. FAX: (201) 896-3231. www.ponl.com
DIRECTOR
Barry Williams

TECHNICOLOR CINEMA SERVICES
(Print management & distribution of promotional materials)
2233 Ontario St., Burbank, CA 91504. (818) 260-3700.
3418 State Rte. 73 S., Wilimington, OH 45177. (800) 993-4567.
5491 E. Philadelphia St., Ontario, CA 91761. (909) 974-2030.
PRESIDENT
Tim Maurer
E.V.P., MARKETING
Peter Koplik

WILLIAM TUFT CORP.
(Insurance)
P. O. Box 10167, Peoria, IL 61612-0167. (309) 674-2673, (309) 691-6356. FAX: (309) 691-8340.

MARQUEES, SIGNS AND DISPLAYS

ADAPTIVE MICRO SYSTEMS
(Manufacturer of LED visual communications displays and full featured software programs)
7840 N. 86th St., Milwaukee, WI 53224. (414) 357-2020. FAX: (414) 357-2029. www.adaptivedisplays.com
SALES MANAGER
Christopher Wittmann

BARCO PROJECTION SYSTEMS AMERICA
(High-performance large-screen display systems for theatrical presentations of digitally released films; screen adverstising displays; post-production & outdoor display applications)
3240 Town Point Dr., Kennesaw, GA 30144. (770) 218-3200. FAX: (770) 218-3250.
CONTACT
Lori Bauer

BASS INDUSTRIES
(All types of signage; marquees, lightboxes & boxoffice signs; display cases; cinema home accessories & novelties)
355 N.E. 71st St., Miami, FL 33138-6024. (800) 346-8575, (305) 751-2716. FAX: (305) 756-6165. www.bassind.com
email: sales@bassind.com
OWNER
Robert Baron
VICE PRESIDENT
Eric Finnegan

BUX-MONT SIGNS
(Fabrication & design of flags, banners, pennants, flag poles)
221 Horsham Rd., Horsham, PA 19044. (215) 675-1040. FAX: (215) 675-4443. www.buxmontflagpoles.com
email: buxmont1@verizon.net
OWNER
William Sweigart

CHANGE AD-LETTER COMPANY
(Changeable letters for marquees and signage)
20954 Currier Rd., Walnut, CA 91789. (909) 598-1996. FAX: (909) 598-2251.
OWNER
Beverly Greene

CUSTOM COLOR CORP.
(Graphic solutions for signage)
300 W. 19th Terrace, Kansas City, MO 64108. (816) 474-3200. FAX: (816) 842-1498. www.customcolor.com
CONTACT
Brian Bailey

DAKTRONICS, INC.
(Computer-programmable LED information displays)
331 32nd Ave., Brookings, SD 57006. (605) 697-4000. FAX: (605) 697-4700. www.daktronics.com
COMMERICAL MARKET MANAGER
Sue Almhjeld

DATA DISPLAY U.S.A.
(LED signs)
5004 Veteran's Memorial Hwy., Holbrook, NY 11741. (631) 218-2130. FAX: (631) 218-2140. www.data-display.com
OWNER
Kevin Neville
CONTACT
Staci Greenblatt

EVI (ENTERTAINMENT VENTURES INTL.)
(Film, TV, music & video production, promotion & packaging; themed entertainment concept design & creation services)
100 S. Doheny Dr., Ste. 402, Los Angeles, CA 90048. (310) 278-2800. FAX: (310) 274-0400.
email: entventint@cs.com
DIRECTOR, OPERATIONS
Jim Beatty
V.P., OPERATIONS
Karenbeth Cantrell
FILM & TV PACKAGING
Raya Markson
PUBLIC RELATIONS
Joyce Miller-Angus

FAST-AD, INC.
(Interchangeable letters for signage)
220 S. Center St., Santa Ana, CA. 92703. (714) 835-9353. FAX: (714) 835-4805.
PRESIDENT
Guy Barnes

FILMACK STUDIOS
(On-screen trailers & advertising)
1327 S. Wabash Ave., Chicago, IL 60605. (800) 345-6225. FAX: (312) 427-4866. www.filmack.com
email: inquiries@filmack.com
CONTACT
Robert Mack

GAMMA TECHNOLOGIES
(LED Displays)
6959 N.W. 82nd Ave., Miami, FL 33166. (305) 477-7567. FAX: (305) 477-7637. www.gamma-tech.com
PRESIDENT
Shai Dinari

GEMINI, INC.
(Marquee lettering)
103 Mensing Way, Cannon Falls, MN 55009. (800) 538-8377, (800) LETTERS. FAX: (800) 421-1256, (507) 263-4887. www.signletters.com email: sales@signletters.com
MARKETING
Patty Zimmerman

IMAGE NATIONAL
(Electronic sign manufacturer)
444 E. Amity Rd., Boise, ID, 83716. (208) 345-4020. FAX: (208) 336-9886. www.imagenational.com
555 E. Boeing Ln., Boise, ID 83716.
201 Metro Dr., Terrell, TX 75160.
13210 Cordary Ave., Hawthorne, CA 90250.
GENERAL MANAGER
Doug Bender

MAINSTREET MENU SYSTEMS
(Custom menu boards)
1375 N. Barker Rd., Brookfield, WI 53045. (800) 782-6222, (262) 782-6000. FAX: (262) 782-6515.
www.mainstreetmenus.com
MARKETING MANAGER
Dawn Pankow

MOVIEAD CORP.
(Supplier of ad slicks, title art, concession mylars, interior & exterior signs & displays)
3500 N. Andrews Ave., Pampano Beach, FL 33064. (800) 327-4989. FAX: (954) 784-0700. www.moviead.com
email: etnoahjr@moviead.com
CONTACT
Emil Noah

MOVIE AD MEDIA
(On-screen trailers & advertising)
P.O. Box 307, Johnston, IA 50131. (515) 334-5222. FAX: (515) 334-5226. www.movieadmedia.com
CONTACT
Melissa Jackson

MPO VIDEOTRONICS
(Videowalls; LED displays; electronic signage)
5069 Maureen Ln., Moorpark, CA 93021. (805) 499-8513. FAX: (805) 499-8206. www.mpo-video.com
SALES
Rick Ayeroff

MULTIMEDIA, INC.
(Electronic message displays)
3300 Monier Circle, Ste. 150, Rancho Cordova, CA 95742.
(800) 888-3007, (916) 852-4220. FAX: (916) 852-8325.
www.multimedialed.com
SALES
George White

POBLOCKI AND SONS
(All types of signage & displays)
922 S. 70th St., W. Allis, WI 53214. (414) 453-4010. FAX: (414)
453-3070. www.poblocki.com
CHAIRMAN
Jerry Poblocki
V.P., SALES
Mark Poblocki
NATIONAL ACCOUNTS MANAGER
Rich Nattila
MANAGER, DISPLAYES & DIRECTORIES
Mike Musser

SCHULT DESIGN AND DISPLAY
(All types of signs & displays)
318 Cedar, Pleasant Hill, MO 64080. (800) 783-8998, (816)
540-4798. FAX: (816) 540-4790. www.schult.com
email: sales@schult.com
SALES
Robert Schult
Jeffrey Shult
Bill Lustig
Keith Schult

SUNNYWELL DISPLAY SYSTEMS
(Manufacturer of LED electronic signs)
730 Stimson Ave., City of Industry, CA 91745. (626) 369-7359.
FAX: (626) 369-5739. www.sunnywell.com
email: sales@sunnywell.com
HEAD OF SALES
Mike Yang

TRANS-LUX CORP.
(LED displays; indoor/outdoor programmable signs)
110 Richards Ave., Norwalk, CT 06854. (203) 853-4321. FAX:
(203) 855-8636. www.trans-lux.com
email: sales@trans-lux.com
V.P., CORPORATE SALES
Gene Coyne

Trans-Lux Canada Limited, 320 North Queen St., Ste. 200,
Toronto, ON M9C 5K4. (416) 621-7661. FAX: (416) 621-7055.

Trans-Lux Pty. Limited, 73 Broadmeadow Rd., New Castle
2292, N.S.W. Australia. TEL: (61 2) 4962-3611. FAX: (61 2)
4962-3615.

Trans-Lux Theatres Business Offices, 433 Paseo De Peralta,
Ste. 101, Santa Fe, NM 87501-1941. (505) 989-9300.

TRIMOTION
(Trimotion, internally lit three-sided rotating poster cases)
1515 Palisades Dr., Ste. E, Pacific Palisades, CA 90272. (800)
874-0035, (310) 230-8417. FAX: (310) 230-8418.
www.trimotion.com email: info@trimotion.com
CONTACT
Rick Clemens

WAGNER ZIP CHANGE, INC.
(Manufacturer of letters for signage)
3100 Hirsch St., Melrose Park, IL 60160. (800) 323-0744. FAX:
(800) 243-4924. www.wagnerzip.com
VICE PRESIDENT
Gary Delaquila

MISCELLANEOUS EQUIPMENT

ADVANCED THERMAL TECHNOLOGIES
(Dehumidification/air-processing equipment for improving
air-conditioning systems)
35421 Kanis Rd., Paron, AR 72122. (501) 821-5509. FAX:
(501) 821-4640. email: nkane53797@aol.com
CONTACT
David Kane

BRADLEY FIXTURES CORP.
(Bathroom fixtures & accessories)
W142 N9101 Fountain Blvd., Menomonee Falls, WI 53051.
(262) 251-6000. FAX: (262) 251-0128. www.bradleycorp.com
ASSISTANT MARKETING MANAGER
Lisa Deboer

CADDY CUPHOLDER
(Cup holders)
10501 Florida Ave. S., Minneapolis, MN 55438. (800) 845-
0591, (952) 903-0110. FAX: (952) 903-5020.
www.caddyproducts.com
MANAGING DIRECTOR
Peter Bergin

CARRIER CORPORATION
1838 Elm Hill Pike, Ste. 125, Nashville, TN 37210. (615) 986-
1533. FAX: (615) 883-1335. www.carrier.utc.com
email: bob.furstenberg@carrier.utc.com
CONTACT
Bob Furstenberg

CAWLEY COMPANY
(Name badges)
1544 N. 8th St., Manitowoc, WI 54221. (800) 822-9539. FAX:
(920) 686-7080. www.thecawleyco.com
email: deddies@thecrawleyco.com
SALES REPRESENTATIVE
Debbie Schimmel

CINEMA EQUIPMENT & SUPPLIES
12441 S.W. 130th St., Miami, FL 33186. (305) 232-8182. FAX:
(305) 232-8172. email: sales@cinemaequip.com
CONTACT
Guillermo Younger

CINEMA PRODUCTS INTL.
(Projection booth supplies, splicing tape & splicers; mylar
leader, film cleaners, miniature lamps, xenon bulbs, projection
ports & FM & Drive-In FM Transmeters)
1015 5th Ave. N., Nashville, TN 37219. (800) 891-1031. FAX:
(615) 248-2725. www.cinprod.com email: sales @ cinprod.com
OWNER
Ron Purtee

DURAFORM
(Waste & recycling receptacles, ash urns, benches)
1435 S. Santa Fe Ave., Compton, CA 90221. (800) 823-1121,
(310) 761-1640. FAX: (310) 761-1646.
www.duraformcpi.com email: duraform@earthlink.net
CUSTOMER SERVICES MANAGER
Rick Fingerlut

FANTASY ENTERTAINMENT
(Self-service photo kiosks)
8 Commercial St., Hudson, NH 03051. (603) 324-3240. FAX:
(603) 879-9203. www.fantasyent.com
CONTACT, SALES
Sheri Honeywell

GENERAL THEATRICAL SUPPLY
(Complete theatrical & cinema equipment & supplies)
2181 W. California Ave. Ste. 250, Salt Lake City, UT 84104.
(877) 587-6742, (801) 485-5012. FAX: (801) 485-4365.
www.gtsmarketplace.com.com
PRESIDENT, M.P. DIVISION
David Bevilacaua

GLASSFORM A DIV VANTAGE ASSOCIATES
(Manufacturer of lobby trash receptacles, benches, ash urns &
custom molding. Interior/Exterior use)
199 W. 146th St., Gardena, CA 90248. (800) 842-1121, (800)
995-8322. FAX (630) 761-8859. www.glassformonline.com
email: glassform@aol.com
SALES MANAGER
Cyndi Gardner

GOLDBERG BROTHERS, INC.
(Manufacturer of film shipping, booth & lobby equipment; also
bowling machine replacement parts)
8000 E. 40th Ave., Denver, CO 80207, P. O. Box 17048,
Denver, CO 80217. (303) 321-1099. FAX: (303) 388-0749.
www.goldbergbrothers.bizhosting.com
EXECUTIVE V.P.
Randall Urlik

GREAT WESTERN PRODUCTS CO.
(Manufacturer, processor, & distributor of high quality theatre
supplies & equipment)
P.O. Box 466, Hollywood, AL 35752. (800) 239-2143. FAX:
(256) 259-2939. www.theatreequipment.net
email: greatwesternproducts@yahoo.com

HALGO SPECIALTIES COMPANY
(Curtain & drapery systems, stage lighting, auditorium seating,
crowd control equipment, signs & displays)
16760 Stagg St., Ste. 209, Van Nuys, CA 91406. (818) 786-
4436, (818) 366-0744. FAX: (818) 780-3486.
email: halgoone@socal.rr.com
PRESIDENT
Norman Dean Goldstein

HOLLYWOOD SOFTWARE, INC.
(Theatrical distribution software)
1604 N. Cahuenga Blvd., Ste. 115, Hollywood, CA 90028.
(323) 463-2144. FAX: (323) 463-1319.
www.hollywoodsoftware.com; www.theatricaldistribution.com
www.rightsmart.com
CEO
Dave Gajda

KOALA CORP.
(Child care products)
7881 S. Wheeling Crt., Englewood, CO 80112. (888) 733-3456.
FAX: (303) 539-8399. www.koalabear.com
V.P. & GENERAL MANAGER
Brendan Cherry

LENNOX INDUSTRIES
(Air-conditioning)
2100 Lake Park Blvd., Richardson, TX 75080. (972) 497-5000.
FAX: (972) 497-5112. www.davelennox.com
V.P., NATIONAL MARKETING
Mike Belloli

MANUTECH COMPANY
(High-performance vacuums & blowers for theatre cleaning)
P.O. Box. 51295, 2080 Sunset Dr., Pacific Grove, CA 93950.
(800) 676-2569, (831) 655-8794. FAX: (831) 655-8967.
www.manutech.com
PRESIDENT
Angelo Villucci

MEGASYSTEMS
(Full service provider of products and services for large format,
including projection systems with state of the art clarity and
sound and a compact open-architecture design)
110 Riberia St., St. Augustine, FL 32084. (904) 829-5702. FAX:
(904) 829-5070. www.megasystem.com
CONTACTS
Steve Kitten
Mark Adukewicz

MIRACLE RECREATION EQUIPMENT COMPANY
(Specialzes in outdoor playground equipment)
P.O. Box 420, Monett, MO 65708-0420. (417) 235-6917. FAX:
(417) 235-6816. www.miraclerecreation.com

MODULAR HARDWARE
(Restroom & toilet partition equipment)
P.O. Box 1889, Cortaro, AZ 85652, 6765 W. Ina Rd., Tucson,
AZ 85743. (800) 533-0042. FAX: (800) 533-7942.
www.modularhardware.com
email: sales@modularhardware.com
PRESIDENT
Robert Hotch

NAMCO CYBERTAINMENT
(Amusement equipment, including video & coin-operated
games, simulators, kits & redemption, novelties)
877 Supreme Dr., Bensenville, IL 60106. (630) 238-2200. FAX:
(630) 238-0560. www.namcoarcade.com
V.P., BUSINESS DEVELOPMENT
Sam Dando
CONTACT
Alex Orban

NATION GLASS & GATE SERVICES, INC.
(Emergency repairs & security renovations)
2416 S. Kearney St., Denver, CO 80222. (800) 556-6484, (303)
757-3097. FAX: (303) 691-2052. www.nationalglass.com
WESTERN REGIONAL SALES MANAGER
Kit Filbey

NORCON COMMUNICATIONS, INC.
(Amplified window intercom systems)
510 Burnside Ave., Inwood, NY 11096. (516) 239-0300. FAX:
(516) 239-8915. www.norcon.org
SALES
Ishwar Hariprashad

NOVAR CONTROLS CORP.
(Air-conditioning, lighting, alarm, and ventilation systems)
3333 Copley Rd., Copley, OH 44321. (330) 670-1010. FAX:
(330) 670-1029. www.novar.com
VICE PRESIDENT
Dean Lindstrom

P&O NEDLLOYD
(Cinema FF&E logistics)
One Meadowlands Plaza, 14th Flr., E. Rutherford, NJ 07073.
(201) 896-6200. FAX: (201) 896-3231. www.ponl.com
DIRECTOR
Barry Williams

RAXXESS
(Studio furniture & equipment)
261 Buffalo Ave., Paterson, NJ 07503. (973) 523-5105. FAX:
(973) 523-5106. www.raxxess.com
PRESIDENT
Hyman Peller

R.S. ENGINEERING & MFG.
(Online cinema equipment)
1054 Valley Blvd., Ste. C, Tehachapi, CA 93561. (661) 822-
1488. FAX: (661) 822-1205. www.rsem.com;
www.cinemaparts.com
GENERAL MANAGER
Robert Schultz

TRANE CO.
(Air-conditioning & chilling systems)
2300 Citygate Dr., Ste. 100, Columbus, OH 43219. (614) 473-
3500. FAX: (614) 473-3501.
DISTRICT MANAGER
Al Fullerton

TRI STATE THEATRE SUPPLY CO.
(Complete theatre & concession supply; sales, service &
installation; buyer of used & surplus equipment)
151 Vance, Memphis TN 38103. (800) 733-8249. FAX: (775)
254-6607. www.tristatetheatre.com
email: info@tristatetheatre.com
CONTACT
Fred Blank

UNIVERSAL CINEMA SERVICES
(Distributors of all types of theatre equipment & supplies)
1205 Corporate Dr. E., Arlington, TX 76006. (817) 633-2180.
FAX: (817) 633-2190. email: custserv@goUCS.com
CEO
Jack Panzeca
PRESIDENT
Stan Lamb
CONTACT
Kris Bartlett

VEND TREND
(Complete theatre equipment)
P.O. Box 1056, Reisterstown, MD 21136. (410) 526-4774. FAX:
(410) 526-6871. email: jwarc1@aol.com
CONTACT
David Phillips

WESNIC
(Furniture for theatres including chairs, benches, planters, etc.)
6000 Bowdendale, Jacksonville, FL 32216. (904) 733-8444.
FAX: (904) 733-3736.
CONTACT
Bill Gilbert

WING ENTERPRISES
(Ladder manufacturer; janitorial supplies)
1325 W. Industrial Circle, Springville, UT 84663. (800) 453-
1192. FAX: (801) 489-3685. www.ladders.com
NATIONAL SALES
Doug Wing

WOLFE MERCHANDISING
(Customized point-of purchase displays & menu-board layouts)
6 Dohme Ave.,Toronto, ON M4B 1Y8, Canada. (416) 752-5599.
FAX: (416) 752-8746. www.wolfe-intl.com
ACCOUNTS EXECUTIVE
Kathleen Panos

EDWARD H. WOLK INC.
(All types of theatre supplies & equipment)
606 E. Brook Dr., Arlington Hts., IL 60005. (847) 357-8080.
FAX: (800) 770-1467. www.edwolk.com
email: sales@edwolk.com
GENERAL MANAGER
Juan Urias

PROJECTION ROOM AND FILM HANDLING EQUIPMENT

AVASK
(Feed-safe mechanisms for projectors)
75 W. Forest Ave., Englewood, NJ 07631. (201) 567-7300.
FAX: (201) 569-6285.
PRESIDENT
Robert Bredin
VICE PRESIDENT
Les Kaplan

BALLANTYNE OF OMAHA/STRONG INTERNATIONAL
(Projection equipment, concert spotlights and restaurant
equipment)
4350 McKinley St., Omaha, NE 68112. (402) 453-4444. FAX:
(402) 453-7238. www.strong-cinema.com;
www.ballantyne-omaha.com
PRESIDENT
John Wilmers
VICE PRESIDENT
Ray Boegner

BIG SKY INDUSTRIES
(Manufacturers of projection booth equipment; booth supplies)
1475 Park Ave., Alpha, NJ 08865. (908) 454-6344. FAX: (908)
454-6373. www.bigskyindustries.net
OWNER & PRESIDENT
Mark Smith
CONTACT
Mike Avallone

CINEMA EQUIPMENT SALES OF CA, INC.
(Cinema & screening room projection, sound equipment & parts)
23011 Moulton Pkwy., #I-5, Laguna Hills, CA 92653. (949) 470-0298. FAX: (949) 470-0835. www.cinema-equip.com
SALES
Carl Williams
Mike Smith

CINEMA PRODUCTS INTL.
(Projection booth supplies, splicing tape & splicers; mylar leader, film cleaners, minature lamps, xenon bulbs, projection ports & FM & Drive-In FM Transmeters)
1015 5th Ave. N., Nashville, TN 37219. (800) 891-1031. FAX: (615) 248-2725. www.cinprod.com email: sales @ cinprod.com
OWNER
Ron Purtee

CLACO EQUIPMENT AND SERVICE, INC.
(Econo-pleat drapery systems, theatre chairs; complete projection, sound, auditorium equipment & service)
1212 S. State St., Salt Lake City, UT 84111. (801) 355-1250. FAX: (801) 355-1259. www.clacoequipment.com
email: claco@utah-inter.net
PRESIDENT
Clayton Stauffer
SALES
Dennis Lunt

CLOUD INDUSTRIES, INC.
(Designer of stage & screen fronts, wall & screen drapery construction; manufacturer of film handling equipment)
P.O. Box 35, Lawson, MO 64062. (816) 296-3354. FAX: (816) 580-3364.
OWNER & PRESIDENT
Mary Shoemaker
V.P., SALES
Chuck Shoemaker

DIGITAL PROJECTION
(Ultra-bright, electronic cinema projection systems for large-format video, data, or HDTV imagery in large venues)
55 Chastain Rd., Ste.115, Kennesaw, GA 30144. (770) 420-1350. www.digitalprojection.com email: ccollins@digitalprojection.com
CONTACT
Charles Collins

EPRAD, INC.
(Manufacturer automations, lighting controls, fail-safe devices)
6979 Wales Rd., Northwood, OH 43619. (419) 666-3266. FAX: (419) 666-8109. www.eprad.com
OWNER & MANAGER
Ted Stechschulte
CONTACT
Tom Lewandowski

GOLDBERG BROTHERS, INC.
(Manufacturer of film shipping, booth & lobby equipment; also bowling machine replacement parts)
8000 E. 40th Ave., Denver, CO 80207, P. O. Box 17048, Denver, CO 80217. (303) 321-1099. FAX: (303) 388-0749. www.goldbergbrothers.bizhosting.com
EXECUTIVE V.P.
Randall Urlik

INTERNATIONAL CINEMA EQUIPMENT
(All types of projection room equipment & theatre supplies; consulting & design)
100 N.E. 39th St., Miami, FL 33137-3632. (305) 573-7339. FAX: (305) 573-8101. www.iceco.com email: iceco@aol.com
PRESIDENT & OWNER
Steven Krams

KELMAR SYSTEMS, INC.
(All types of film-handling equipment)
284 Broadway, Huntington Station, NY 11746-1497. (631) 421-1230. FAX: (631) 421-1274. www.kelmarsystems.com
PRESIDENT
Andrew Marglin

KINETRONICS
(Manufactures machines & brushes for dust & static removal)
4363 Independence Crt., Sarasota, FL 34234. (800) 624-3204, (941) 951-2432. FAX: (941) 955-5992. www.kinetronics.com
email: info@kinetronics.com
CONTACT
Bill Stelcher

LEN-D ENTERPRISES
(Distributor & manufacture all types of film-handling equipment; splicing tape & splicers, port glass & projection lenses.)
6080 Okeechobee Blvd., West Palm Beach, FL 33417. (561) 682-3500. FAX: (561) 682-3777.
PRESIDENT
Leonard Dickstein

LUTRON ELECTRONICS
(Visual & environmental controls)
7200 Suter Rd., Coopersburg, PA 18036. (610) 282-3800. FAX: (610)282-6437. www.lutron.com
CONTACT
David Eisenhauer

NATIONAL CINEMA SERVICE
(Equipment sales, maintenance & repairs services for projection booths)
P.O. Box 10799, New Orleans, LA 70181. (504) 734-0707. FAX: (504)734-0700. www.ncservice.com
CONTACT
Charles Achee

NEUMADE PRODUCTS CORP./XETRON DIVISION
(All types of film equipment)
30-40 Pecks Ln., Newtown, CT 06470. (203) 270-1100. FAX: (203) 270-7778. www.Neumade.com
VICE PRESIDENT
Bob Maar

NORCON COMMUNICATIONS, INC.
(Amplified window intercom systems)
510 Burnside Ave., Inwood, NY 11096. (516) 239-0300. FAX: (516) 239-8915. www.norcon.org
SALES
Ishwar Hariprashad

ODYSSEY PRODUCTS, INC.
(All types of booth equipment & supplies)
5845 Oakbrook Pkw., Ste. G, Norcross, GA 30093. (770) 825-0243. FAX: (770) 825-0245. www.odyssey-products.com
PRESIDENT
Eve Miller
CONTACT
Brad Miller

PLASTIC REEL CORP. OF AMERICA
(Manufactures plastic reels & boxes for audio & video tapes)
40 Triangle Blvd., Carlstadt, NJ 07072. (800) 772-4748. FAX: (201) 933-9468.
VICE PRESIDENT
Pat Baccarella

SOURCE ONE
(Concession equipment; complete booth & sound equipment)
5224 Longview, Shawnee, KS 66218. (913) 441-0664.
OWNER & PRESIDENT
Ryland Cozad

SPECTRA CINE, INC.
(Light-measuring equipment)
3607 W. Magnolia Blvd., Burbank, CA 91505. (818) 954-9222. FAX: (818) 954-0016. www.spectracine.com
PRESIDENT
Nasir J. Zaidi

TC COSTIN, LLC
(Distributors of projection room equipment & supplies)
3840 S. Helena St., Aurora, CO 80013-2506. (303) 699-7477. FAX: (303) 680-6071. email: tcostin@worldnet.att.net
OWNER
"TC" Costin

TECHNOLOGY INTERNATIONAL
(CE Marking for European film markets)
715 Twin Ridge Ln., Richmond, VA 23235. (800) 810-9000, (804) 272-5447. FAX: (804) 272-5994. www.techintl.com
GENERAL MANAGER
Wayland Stephenson

TECO
2938 Gladys Fork Rd., Ferguson, NC 28624. (800) 863-8326. FAX: (336) 973-4482.
PRESIDENT
Bob Saunders

PROJECTORS

CHARLES AJAR PROJECTOR FILM & VIDEO CO. (DBA UNIVERSAL PROJECTOR CO.)
10510 Burbank Blvd., North Hollywood, CA 91601. (818) 980-1948. FAX: (818) 980-7273. email: upcajar@aol.com
OWNER
Tammy Ajar

AUDIO SERVICE COMPANY, INC.
(Projection & sound equipment)
P.O. Box 50, Yakima, WA 98907. (509) 248-7041. FAX: (509) 453-3074.

AVICA TECHNOLOGY CORP.
(Digital cinema players & equipment)
1131 Olympic Blvd., Santa Monica, CA 90404. (310) 450-9090. FAX: (310) 450-5353. www.avicatech.com
SALES
Don Bird

BALLANTYNE OF OMAHA/STRONG INTERNATIONAL
4350 McKinley St., Omaha, NE 68112. (402) 453-4444. FAX: (402) 453-7238. www.ballantyne-omaha.com;
www.strong-cinema.com
PRESIDENT
John Wilmers
VICE PRESIDENT
Ray Boegner

859

BARCO PROJECTION SYSTEMS AMERICA
(High-performance large-screen display systems for theatrical presentations of digitally released films; screen adverstising displays; post-production & outdoor display applications)
3240 Town Point Dr., Kennesaw, GA 30144. (770) 218-3200. FAX: (770) 218-3250.
CONTACT
Lori Bauer

CARDINAL SOUND & MOTION PICTURE SYSTEMS, INC.
(Digital sound systems; 16mm, 35mm, & 70mm equipment)
6330 Howard Ln., Elkridge, MD 21075. (410) 796-5300. FAX: (410) 796-7995. www.cardinalsound.com
OFFICE MANAGER
Catherine Rockman

CHRISTIE DIGITAL SYSTEMS U.S.A., INC.
(Manufacturer & distributor of film projectors; Xenon consoles, rewinds, bulbs; digital projectors & on-screen advertising)
10550 Camden Dr., Cypress, CA 90630. (714) 236-8610. FAX: (714) 503-3385. www.christiedigital.com
CINEMA SALES MANAGER
Scott Freidberg
V.P., SALES LATIN AMERICA
Joe Delgado

CINEMECCANICA U.S., INC.
(Projectors, consoles, lamphouses, power supplies & sound systems)
5027 Irwindale Ave., # 800, Irwindale, CA 91706. (626) 939-0811. FAX: (626) 939-8993. www.cinemeccanica-us.com
email: cinemec@earthlink.net
PRESIDENT
Jack Johnston

CINEMEDIA SYSTEMS, LLC
(Digital projection, sound, 35mm digital projection, sales, service and rentals)
445 W. 45th St., New York, NY 10036. (212) 586-2200. FAX: (212) 586-0500. www.cinemediasystems.com
PRESIDENT
Gregg Paliotta

CINETECH, INC.
(35mm & video projection equipment & sound systems)
225 W. Howard St., Stowe, PA 19464. (800) 432-4847. FAX: (610) 323-1664. www.cinetech.net
GENERAL MANAGER
Bruce Fitzsimmons

DLP CINEMA
(Cinema projection technology for use in digital cinema applications)
Texas Instruments, 6550 Chase Oaks Blvd., Plano, TX 75023. (888) 357-2984, (972) 575-2000. www.dlpcinema.com

ERNEMANN CINETEC U.S.A.
(Cinema projectors & platters)
382 Springfield Ave., Summit, NJ 07901. (908) 273-3699. FAX: (908) 273-8995. email: erneanncineusa@aol.com
CONTACT
Roney Weis

HOLLYWOOD THEATRE EQUIPMENT, INC.
(Dealer for all 35mm & 70mm projection & sound equipment)
3300 N. 29th Ave., Ste.104, Hollywood, FL 33020. (954) 920-2832. FAX: (954) 925-3874. email: HWDTHEATRE@aol.com
SALES
Don Gallagher

IWERKS ENTERTAINMENT
(Specialized theatre manufacturing)
4520 W. Valerio St., Burbank, CA 91505. (818) 841-7766. FAX: (818) 841-7847, (818) 841-6192. www.iwerks.com
COO
Don Stults
CFO
John Choy
V.P., INTERNATIOANL SALES
Fritz Otis

JVC PROFESSIONAL
(Digital cinema projectors)
1700 Valley Rd., Wayne, NJ 07470. (973) 317-5000. FAX: (973) 315-5030. www.jvc.com
V.P., DIGITAL SYSTEMS
Jack Faiman

KINOTON AMERICA
(Manufactures & distributes film projectors & sound equipment)
8 Goodenough St., Boston, MA 02135. (617) 562-0003. FAX: (617) 787-4253. www.kinotonamerica.com
email: johng@kinotonamerica.com
SALES
John Gallucci
LARGE FORMAT & CINEMA SALES
Ernie Tracy, (215) 836-9107

KNEISLEY ELECTRIC
P.O. Box 4692, Toledo, OH 43610. (419) 241-1219. FAX: (419) 241-9920.
PRESIDENT
Harry Ewell

MEGASYSTEMS
(Full service provider of products and services for large format, including projection systems with state of the art clarity and sound and a compact open-architecture design)
110 Riberia St., St. Augustine, FL 32084. (904) 829-5702. FAX: (904) 829-5070. www.megasystem.com
CONTACTS
Steve Kitten
Mark Adukewicz

NEC SOLUTIONS
(Cinema-grade digital & electronic projection; all types of projection systems)
10850 Gold Center Dr., Ste. 200, Rancho Cordova, CA 95670. (800) 632-4636, (916) 463-7000. www.nectech.com

PANASONIC BROADCAST & TELEVISION SYSTEMS CO.
(Manufacturers & distributors of projectors & broadcast equipment)
330 Cahuenga Blvd. W., Ste. 100, Los Angeles, CA 90068. (323) 436-3500. FAX: (323) 436-3660.
www.panasonic.com/broadcast
NATIONAL SALES MANAGER
Steve Abend
CONTACT
Dina Macumber

PROJECTOR LAMPS AND LENSES

ADVANCED STROBE
7227 W. Wilson Ave., Harwood Heights, IL 60706. (708) 867-3100, (708) 867-3140. FAX: (708) 867-1103.
www.strobelamps.com email: asp@strobelamps.com

ATLAS SPECIALTY LIGHTING
(Entertainment lighting)
7304 N. Florida Ave., Tampa, FL 33604. (813) 238-6481. FAX: (813) 238-6656. www.asltg2.com email: alicia@asltg2.com
MANAGERS
Ralph Felten Jr.
Bob Ray

CINEMA XENON INTERNATIONAL
(Distributor of projector lamps)
261 Valley Vista Dr., Camarillo, CA 93010. (888) 669-7271. FAX: (805) 389-9611. email: cinexenon@aol.com
PRESIDENT
Dick Stockton

GOLDBERG BROTHERS, INC.
(Manufacturer of film shipping, booth & lobby equipment; also bowling machine replacement parts)
8000 E. 40th Ave., Denver, CO 80207, P.O. Box 17048, Denver, CO 80217. (303) 321-1099. FAX: (303) 388-0749.
www.goldbergbrothers.bizhosting.com
EXECUTIVE V.P.
Randall Urlik

ISCO-OPTIC GMBH
Anna-Vandenhoeck-Ring 5, Gewerbepark Siekhöhe, D-37081 Göttingen, Germany. TEL: (49 551) 505-83. FAX: (49 551) 505-8410. www.iscooptic.de email: info@iscooptic.de
CONTACT
Katja Korzen

BERN LEVY ASSOCIATES
(Lens cleaning)
21 Whippoorwill Ln., Palmyra, VA 22963. (434) 589-2171. FAX: (434) 589-2172.
CONTACT
Bern Levy

L.P. ASSOCIATES, INC.
(Manufacturer of lamp houses, power supply & searchlights; distributor of xenon lamps)
6650 Lexington Ave., Hollywood, CA 90038. (323) 462-4714. FAX: (323) 462-7584.
CORPORATE OFFICER
Leonard Pincus

OSRAM SYLVANIA, INC.
(Osram Xenon lamps)
100 Endicott St., Danvers MA 01923. (978) 777-1900. FAX: (978) 750-2152. www.sylvania.com
V.P. & GENERAL MANAGER, PHOTO-OPTICS
Paul Caramagna

PERKIN ELMER OPTOELECTRONICS
(Complete line of Xenon projection lamps)
44370 Christy St., Fremont, CA 94538-3180. (800) 775-6786, (510) 979-6500. FAX: (510) 687-1140.
CONTACT
Joanne Bakerville

SCHNEIDER OPTICS, INC.
(Projection lenses; port glass)
285 Oser Ave., Hauppauge, NY 11788. (631) 761-5000. FAX:
(631) 761-5090. www.schneideroptics.com
email: info@schneideroptics.com
SENIOR VICE PRESIDENTS
Dwight Lindsey
Ron Leven

SPECIAL OPTICS
(Custom designs for laser & other types of lenses)
315 Richard Mine Rd., Wharton, NJ 07885. (973) 366-7289.
FAX: (973) 366-7407. www.specialoptics.com
email: specopt@aol.com
SALES ASSISTANT
Steven Morales

SUPERIOR QUARTZ PRODUCTS, INC.
(Projection lamps)
404 County Rd. 519, Phillipsburg, NJ 08865-0833. (908) 454-
1700. FAX: (908) 454-4154. email: superior@sqpuv.com
34626 B Camino Capistrano, Capistrano Beach, CA 92624.
(949) 443-0239. FAX: (949) 443-0230. www.sqpuv.com
PRESIDENT & CEO
Dennis Losco
PRESIDENT SQP, WEST
Richard W. Wind
WEST COAST SALES MANAGER
Ernest E. Estrada

VANTAGE LIGHTING, INC.
(Projection booth & studio lamps & lenses)
175 Paul Dr., San Rafael, CA 94903-2041. (800) 445-2677.
(415) 507-0402. FAX: (415) 507-0502. www.vanltg.com
email: vanltg@pacbell.net
PRESIDENT
Marc Allsman

XENONBULBS.COM
(A subsidiary of R.S. Engineering)
(All types of projector bulbs & lamps)
1054 Valley Blvd., Ste. C, Tehachapi, CA 93561. (661) 822-
1488. FAX: (661) 822-1205. www.XenonBulbs.com
GENERAL MANAGER
Robert Schultz

SCREENS AND FRAMES

A&B COMPANY
(Screen, seat, upholstery cleaning; nightly janitorial; carpet &
floor cleaning; pressure wash; fire-protectant application)
6536 Fulton Ave., Van Nuys, CA 91401. (818) 985-7768. FAX:
(818) 763-7914.
CONTACT
Michael Fuss

CINEMA TECHNOLOGY SERVICES, LLC
(All aspects of theatre installation, renovation and technical
services for equipment repair & installation; picture screenings
& special shows)
P.O. Box D-400, Pomona, NY 10970-0484. (845) 354-8563.
FAX: 845-354-9146.
PRINICIPAL
Roger Getzoff

CLACO EQUIPMENT AND SERVICE, INC.
(Econo-pleat drapery systems, theatre chairs; complete
projection, sound, auditorium equipment & service)
1212 S. State St., Salt Lake City, UT 84111. (801) 355-1250.
FAX: (801) 355-1259. www.clacoequipment.com
email: claco@utah-inter.net
PRESIDENT
Clayton Stauffer
SALES
Dennis Lunt

CLOUD INDUSTRIES, INC.
(Designer of stage & screen fronts, wall & screen drapery
construction; manufacturer of film handling equipment)
P.O. Box 35, Lawson, MO 64062. (816) 296-3354. FAX: (816)
580-3364.
OWNER & PRESIDENT
Mary Shoemaker
V.P., SALES
Chuck Shoemaker

DOLCH TOUCH CONTROLS, INC.
(Manufacturer of touch screens)
520 Industrial Way, Fallbrook, CA 92028. (760) 723-7900. FAX:
(760) 723-7910.
DIRECTOR OF MARKETING
Chris McDonald

HARKNESS HALL
(All types of screens & frames, including outdoor air-screens)
10 Harkness Blvd., Fredericksburg VA 22401. (540) 370-1590.
FAX: (540) 370-1592. www.harknesshall.com
email: info@harknesshall.com
SALES MANAGER
Frank Fisher

HURLEY SCREEN CORP./CEMCORP
110 Industry Ln., P.O. Box 296, Forest Hill, MD 21050. (410)
879-3022. FAX: (410) 838-8079.
V.P., OPERATIONS
Gorman White Jr.

INTERNATIONAL CINEMA EQUIPMENT
100 N.E. 39th St., Miami, FL 33137-3632. (305) 573-7339.
FAX: (305) 573-8101. www.iceco.com email: iceco@iceco.com
PRESIDENT & OWNER
Steven Krams

KLIPSCH AUDIO TECHNOLOGIES
(Theatre sound & listening devices)
3502 Woodview Trace, Ste. 200, Indianapolis, IN 46268. (800)
544-1482, (317) 860-8785. FAX: (317) 860-9170.
www.klipsch.com
CONTACT
Christine Pile

MAG-TECH ENVIRONMENTAL INC.
(Soundfold/drapery cleaning, screen cleaning, seat cleaning)
710 Season Heather Ct., St. Louis, MO 63021. (636) 394-
0414. FAX: (636) 394-0516.
OWNER & PRESIDENT
Don Waldman
VICE PRESIDENT
Lee Waldman

MARCEL DESROCHERS, INC. (MDI)
(Screens, progammable masking motors)
1440 Raoul Charrette, Joliette, QUE J6E 8S7, Canada. (450)
755-3795. FAX: (450) 755-3122. www.mdicinema.com
email:sales@mdicinema.com
VICE PRESIDENT
Andrew Lee
PROJECT SUPERVISOR
France Desrochers

MPO VIDEOTRONICS
(Videowalls; LED displays; electronic signage)
5069 Maureen Ln., Moorpark, CA 93021. (805) 499-8513. FAX:
(805) 499-8206. www.mpo-video.com
SALES
Rick Ayeroff

NICK MULONE & SONS, INC.
(Manufacturer of screen frames for movie theatres & public
auditoriums; masking hardware & boards)
100 Highland Ave., Cheswick, PA 15024. (724) 274-3221. FAX:
(724) 274-4808. email: nickmul@aol.com
CONTACT
Dennis Tafi

SELBY PRODUCTS, INC.
(Drive-in screens)
P.O. Box 267, Richfield, OH 44286-0267. (330) 659-6631. FAX:
(330) 659-4112.
CONTACT
Jerry Selby

SOUTHWEST CINEMA PRODUCTS
(Screen cleaning)
P.O. Box 690356, Tulsa, OK 74169-0356. (918) 627-8111. FAX:
(918) 627-9199.
CONTACT
Dennis Hall

STEWART FILMSCREEN CORP.
(Manufacturer of projections screens for movie theatres)
1161 Sepulveda Blvd., Torrance, CA 90502. (800) 762-4999,
(310) 784-5300. FAX: (310) 326-6870. www.stewartfilm.com
VICE PRESIDENT
Don Stewart

TECHNI-BRITE, INC.
(Screen cleaning, licensee of TSII)
1302 La Fiesta, Grand Prairie, TX 75052. (972) 264-4989. FAX:
(972) 264-0319. www.techni-brite.com
email: jatchley@techni-brite.com
PRESIDENT
John Atchley
SENIOR ADVISOR
Ron Leslie

TECHNIKOTE SCREEN CORP.
(Manfacturer of screens & frames)
63 Seabring St., Brooklyn, NY 11231-1697. (718) 624-6429.
FAX: (718) 624-0129.
CONTACT
Mitchell M. Schwam

SEATING AND RE-UPHOLSTERY

A&B COMPANY
(Screen, seat, upholstery cleaning; nightly janitorial; carpet & floor cleaning; pressure wash; fire-protectant application)
6536 Fulton Ave., Van Nuys, CA 91401. (818) 985-7768. FAX: (818) 763-7914.
CONTACT
Michael Fuss

AMERICAN SEATING COMPANY
(Theatres, auditoriums, PAC's & stadium seating)
401 American Seating Central NW, Grand Rapids, MI 49504. (616) 732-6797. FAX: (616) 732-6847.
www.americanseating.com
CONTACT
Mark Wretschko

ASSIGNED SEATING & MANUFACTURING GROUP, INC.
(All types of large-facility seating)
P.O. Box 3206, S. El Monte, CA 91715. (626) 454-4599. FAX: (626) 454-4590. email: seatman1@pacbell.net
PRESIDENT
Chuck Kaplan

BASS INDUSTRIES
(All types of signage; marquees, lightboxes & boxoffice signs; display cases; cinema home accessories & novelties)
355 N.E. 71st St., Miami, FL 33138-6024. (800) 346-8575, (305) 751-2716. FAX: (305) 756-6165. www.bassind.com
email: sales@bassind.com
OWNER
Robert Baron
VICE PRESIDENT
Eric Finnegan

CALIFORNIA SEATING & REPAIR COMPANY, INC.
(New & used theatre seating; repairs & refurbishing)
12455 Branford St., Unit 2 & 3, Arleta, CA 91331. (818) 890-7328. FAX: (805) 581-0226. www.californiaseating.com
CONTACT
Tim McMahan

CAMATIC SEATING
(Stadium-style seating, fixed-back & rocking recliner styles)
2606 Julianne, Belton TX 76513. (254) 939-9392 FAX: (254) 939-9368. www.camatic.com email: cinema@camatic.com
VICE PRESIDENT
Gary Knight

CLACO EQUIPMENT AND SERVICE, INC.
(Econo-pleat drapery systems, theatre chairs; complete projection, sound, auditorium equipment & service)
1212 S. State St., Salt Lake City, UT 84111. (801) 355-1250. FAX: (801) 355-1259. www.clacoequipment.com
email: claco@utah-inter.net
PRESIDENT
Clayton Stauffer
SALES
Dennis Lunt

FIGUERAS INTERNATIONAL SEATING
(Seating)
Crta. Parets a Bigues, km 77, Llica de Munt, Barcelona TEL: (34 93) 844 5050. FAX: (34 93) 844 5061. www.figueras.com
email: tyfigueras@mail.cinet.com
CONTACT
Francisco Gualdo

HUSSEY SEATING COMPANY
(Spectator seating for arenas, stadiums, auditoriums, theatres)
38 Dyer St. Ext., N. Berwick, ME 03906. (800) 341-0401, (207) 676-2271. FAX: (207) 676-2222. www.husseyseating.com
email: rbilodeau@husseyseating.com
NEW BUSINESS DEVELOPMENT MANAGER
Ron Bilodeau

IRWIN SEATING COMPANY
(Auditorium seating)
P.O. Box 2429, Grand Rapids, MI 49501-2429. (616) 574-7400. FAX: (616) 574-7411. www.irwinseating.com
email: dsales@irwin-seat.com
V.P., SALES
Bruce Cohen
CONTACT
Vicki Stein

LINO SONEGO
(Seating)
Via Resel 25, 31010 Pianzano di Godega S.Urbano (TV)-Italy. TEL: (39) 0438-430026. FAX: (39) 0438-430287.
www.linosonego.it email: info@linosonego.it
GENERAL DIRECTOR
Fabio Sonego
CUSTOMER SERVICE
Viviana Favero

MAG-TECH ENVIRONMENTAL INC.
(Soundfold/drapery cleaning, screen cleaning, seat cleaning)
710 Season Heather Ct., St. Louis, MO 63021. (636) 394-0414. FAX: (636) 394-0516.
OWNER & PRESIDENT
Don Waldman
VICE PRESIDENT
Lee Waldman

MANKO SEATING CO.
(Replacement seat coversbacks)
50 W. 36th St., New York, NY 10018-8002. (212) 695-7470. FAX: (212) 563-0840.
CONTACT
Norman Manko

QUINETTE GALLAY
15 rue de la Nouvelle France, 93108 Montreuil Cedex, France. TEL: (33 14) 988-6333. FAX: (33 14) 858-2286.
www.quinette.fr email: info@quinette.fr
MANAGING DIRECTOR
Gilles Ancelin
CONTACT
Brigitte Berty

SEATING CONCEPTS
(Design & manufacture of theatre seating, auditorium seating, and worship seating)
2225 Hancock St., San Diego, CA 92110. (619) 491-3159. FAX: (619) 491-3172. www.seatingconcepts.com
V.P., SALES
John Fennell

SOUTHERN SCENIC EQUIPMENT CO.
(Theatre seat refurbishing; retrofit theatres to stadium seating; theatre & stage drapery)
1040 Branch Dr., Alpharetta, GA 30004. (770) 475-0733. FAX: (770) 475-0910.
PRESIDENT
Ted Yarborough

VISTEON
(Seating)
17000 Rotunda Dr., Dearborn, MI 48120. (800) VISTEON, www.visteon.com
CHAIRMAN & CEO
Peter Pestillo
PRESIDENT & COO
Michael Johnston

CY YOUNG INDUSTRIES, INC.
(Seat renovation; replacement seatcovers, cupholder armrests, cocession trays, booster seats)
16201 W. 110th St., Lenexa, KS 66219. (800) 729-2610, (913) 438-1776. FAX: (913) 888-1774. www.cyyoungind.com
COO
Carrie Young

SECURITY SERVICES

ALCOPS INCORPORATED
(Protective service group; background screening)
6701 W. 64th St., Ste. 221, Overland Park, KS 66202. (800) 345-7347. FAX: (800) 252-4060. www.alcops.com
OWNER
Teri Gitlin

WORLDWIDE SAFE & VAULT
(Cash-handling safes, access-controlled electronic locks, all aspects of physical security hardware)
3660 N.W. 115th Ave., Miami, FL 33178. (305) 477-9266. FAX: (305) 477-9744. www.worldwidesafe.com
OWNER & PRESIDENT
Scott Hirsch

SOUND EQUIPMENT

ACE COMMUNICATIONS
(Audio-visual equipment rental & sound systems)
170 Earle Ave., Lynbrook, NY 11563. (800) 468-7667. FAX: (718) 899-1995. www.aceav.com

AUDIO SERVICE COMPANY, INC.
(Sound & projection equipment)
P.O. Box 50, Yakima, WA 98907. (509) 248-7041. FAX: (509) 453-3074.

BGW SYSTEMS
(Power amplifiers & speakers)
13130 Yukon Ave., Hawthorne, CA 90250. (800) 468-AMPS, (310) 973-8090. FAX: (310) 676-6713. www.bgw.com
email: sales@bgw.com
PRESIDENT
Barbara Wachner

BOSTON LIGHT & SOUND
(Manufacturer & distributor of film projectors & sound equipment; service & installation)
290 N. Beacon St., Boston, MA 02135. (617) 787-3131. FAX: (617) 787-4257. www.blsi.com email: info@blsi.com
CONTACT
Chapin Cutler

CARDINAL SOUND & MOTION PICTURE SYSTEMS, INC.
(Digital sound systems; 16mm, 35mm, & 70mm equipment)
6330 Howard Ln., Elkridge, MD 21075. (410) 796-5300. FAX: (410) 796-7995. www.cardinalsound.com
OFFICE MANAGER
Catherine Rockman

COMPONENT ENGINEERING
(Manufacturer of LED sound readers, sound system accessories, automation equipment and cue detectors)
4237 24th Ave. W., Seattle, WA 98199. (206) 284-9171. FAX: (206) 286-4462. www.componentengineering.com

EVI (ENTERTAINMENT VENTURES INTL.)
(Film, TV, music & video production, promotion & packaging; themed entertainment concept design & creation services)
100 S. Doheny Dr., Ste. 402, Los Angeles, CA 90048. (310) 278-2800. FAX: (310) 274-0400. email: entventint@cs.com
DIRECTOR OF OPERATIONS
Jim Beatty
PUBLIC RELATIONS
Joyce Miller-Angus

HAFLER PROFESSIONAL
(Manufacturer of professional amplifiers & speakers)
600 S. Rockford Dr., Tempe, AZ 85281. (888) 423-5371. FAX: (480) 894-1528. www.hafler.com
NATIONAL SALES MANAGER
Chris Trapp
ADVERTISING & PUBLIC RELATIONS
Charlie Leib

HIGH PERFORMANCE STEREO
(Motion picture sound systems; HPS-4000 systems)
64 Bowen St., Newton, MA 02459-1820. (617) 244-1737. FAX: (617) 244-4390. www.hps4000.com
FOUNDER & PRESIDENT
John Allen

HOLLYWOOD THEATRE EQUIPMENT, INC.
(Dealer for all 35mm & 70mm projection & sound equipment)
3300 N. 29th Ave., Ste.104, Hollywood, FL 33020. (954) 920-2832. FAX: (954) 925-3874. email: HWDTHEATRE@aol.com
SALES
Don Gallagher

INTL. ELECTRICAL WIRE/CABLE
(Manufacturer of electronic wire, audio & video cable, LAN & computer cable, coax & fiber optics)
P.O. Box 958184 Hoffman Estates, IL 60195. (800) 323-0210, (630) 289-2210. FAX: (630) 860-0305.
email: iewcine@comcast.net
SALES MANAGER
Kevin McClure

LOWELL MANUFACTURING CO.
(Speakers, racks & cabinets)
100 Integram Dr., Pacific, MO 63069. (636) 257-3400. FAX: (636) 257-6606. www.lowellmfg.com
PRESIDENT
John J. Lowell

MARTIN AUDIO LIMITED
(Theatre sound & listening devices)
P.O. Box 44019, Kitchener, ON N2N 3G7, Canada. (519) 747-5853. FAX: (519) 747-3576. www.martin-audio.com
email: rhofkamp@martin-audio.com
CONTACT
Robert Hofkamp

MONSTER CABLE PRODUCTS, INC.
(Cabling)
455 Valley Dr., Brisbane, CA 94005. (415) 840-2000. FAX: (415) 468-0311. www.monstercable.com
PRESIDENT
Noel Lee

PANASTEREO, INC.
(Premium sound products & panalogic devices)
5945 Peachtree Corners East, Norcross, GA 30071. (770) 449-6698. FAX: (770) 449-6728. www.panastereo.com
email: cinemasound@panastereo.com
PRESIDENT
Norman Schneider

PROJECTED SOUND, INC.
(Replacement parts for drive-in-theatre speakers)
469 Avon Ave., Plainfield, IN 46168-1001. (317) 839-4111. FAX: (317) 839-2476.
CONTACT
Dick Hilligoss

QSC AUDIO
(Amplifier manufacturing)
1675 MacArthur Blvd., Costa Mesa, CA 92626. (714) 754-6175. FAX: (714) 754-6174. www.qscaudio.com
CEO
Barry Andrews

SMART DEVICES, INC.
(Sound components & systems)
5945 Peachtree Corners East, Norcross, GA 30071. (800) 45-SMART, (770) 449-6698. FAX: (770) 449-6728.
www.smartdev.com email: smart@america.net
PRESIDENT
Norman Schneider

STAGE ACCOMPANY USA
(Speakers using Ribbon Compact drivers, amplifiers, other professional sound equipment)
8917 Shore Ct., Bay Ridge, NY 11209. (800) 955-7474. FAX: (800) 955-9564. www.StageAccompany.com
email: A@StageAccompany.com
SALES & RENTALS
Marcel Vantuyn

THX LTD.
(Custom designed sound systems, crossover & systems rack; digital cinema products)
1600 Los Gamos, Ste. 231, San Rafael, CA 94903. (415) 492-3900. FAX: (415) 492-3988. www.thx.com
CONTACTS
Ross Portugeis (415) 492-3940
Kevin Heverin (415) 492-3916

ULTRA STEREO LABS
(Cinema sound equipment, including processors, booth monitors, crossovers, ADA devices, exciter lamps, test equipment)
181 Bonetti Dr., San Luis Obispo, CA 93401-7310. (805) 549-0161. FAX: (805) 549-0163. www.uslinc.com
VICE PRESIDENT
Felicia Cashin

YAMAHA ELECTRONICS CORP.
(Sound equipment; electronic components & instruments)
P.O. Box 6660, Buena Park, CA 90622. (714) 522-9105. FAX: (714) 670-0108.
ADVERTISING SALES PROMOTIONAL MANAGER
Doan Hoff

SOUND REINFORCEMENT

ASHLY AUDIO, INC.
847 Holt Rd., Webster, NY 14580-9103. (800) 828-6308, (585) 872-0010. FAX: (585) 872-0739. www.ashley.com
MARKETING MANAGER
Jim Stachowski

BGW SYSTEMS
(Power amplifiers & speakers)
13130 Yukon Ave., Hawthorne, CA 90250. (800) 468-AMPS, (310) 973-8090. FAX: (310) 676-6713. www.bgw.com
email: sales@bgw.com
PRESIDENT
Barbara Wachner

CREST AUDIO, INC.
(Amplifiers, consoles, speakers)
16-00 Pollitt Dr., Fair Lawn, NJ 07410-2733. (201) 909-8700. FAX: (201) 909-8744. www.crestaudio.com
PRESIDENT
Hartley D. Peavey

CROWN AUDIO, INC.
(Amplifiers & microphones)
P.O. Box 1000, Elkhart, IN 46515. (574) 294-8200. FAX: (574) 294-8329. www.crownaudio.com
MARKETING
Nicole Kline

HAFLER PROFESSIONAL
(Manufacturer of professional amplifiers & speakers)
600 S. Rockford Dr., Tempe, AZ 85281. (888) 423-5371. FAX: (480) 894-1528. www.hafler.com
NATIONAL SALES MANAGER
Chris Trapp
ADVERTISING & PUBLIC RELATIONS
Charlie Leib

JBL PROFESSIONAL
(Loudspeaker systems)
8400 Balboa Blvd., Northridge, CA 91329. (818) 894-8850. FAX: (818) 830-1220. www.jblpro.com
email: cgoodsell@harman.com
PRESIDENT
Mark Terry
CONTACT
Chuck Goodsell

PEAVEY ARCHITECTURAL ACOUSTICS
(Electronics manufacturer; architectural acoustics)
A division of Peavey Electronics Corp., 711 A St., Meridian, MS
39301. (601) 483-5376. FAX: (601) 486-1154. www.peavey.com
OWNER & CEO
Hartley D. Peavey

QSC AUDIO
(Amplifier manufacturing)
1675 Macarthur Blvd., Costa Mesa, CA 92626. (714) 754-
6175. FAX: (714) 754-6174. www.qscaudio.com
CEO
Barry Andrews

SMART DEVICES, INC
(Manufacturer of cinema sound products)
5945 Peachtree Corners E., Norcross, GA 30071-1337. (800)
457-6278, (770) 449-6698. FAX: (770) 449-6728.
www.smartdev.com
PRESIDENT
Norman Schneider

SOUNDCRAFT USA
(Soundboards & consoles for live and recorded sound)
Harman Pro North America, 8500 Balboa Blvd., Northridge,
CA 91329. (818) 920-3212. FAX: (818) 920-3208.
www.soundcraft.com email: soundcraft-USA@harman.com
NATIONAL SALES MANAGER
Tom Der

SPEAKERS

ALLEN PRODUCTS CO., INC
(Mounting & rigging solutions for speakers and video players)
1635 E. Burnett St., Signal Hill, CA 90755. (562) 424-1100
FAX: (562) 424-3520. www.allenproducts.com
email: pallen@allenproducts.com
PRESIDENT
Paul Allen

CERWIN-VEGA
555 E. Easy St., Simi Valley, CA 93065. (805) 584-9332. FAX:
(805) 583-0865. www.cerwin-vega.com

COMMUNITY PROFESSIONAL LOUDSPEAKERS
333 E. Fifth St., Chester, PA 19013. (610) 876-3400. FAX:
(610) 874-0190. www.loudspeakers.net
CONTACT
Grace Paoli

EAW, INC. (EASTERN ACOUSTIC WORKS)
(Manufacturer of loudspeaker systems for cinemas)
(A subsidiary of Mackie Designs, Inc.) One Main St.,
Whitinsville, MA 01588. (508) 234-6158. FAX: (508) 234-8251.
www.eaw.com email: info@eaw.com
GLOBAL MARKET MANAGER
Paul Carelli

FRAZIER LOUDSPEAKERS
3030 Kintan St., Dallas, TX 75226. (214) 741-7136. FAX: (214)
939-0328.
CONTACT
J. E. Mitchell

HAFLER PROFESSIONAL
(Manufacturer of professional amplifiers & speakers)
600 S. Rockford Dr., Tempe, AZ 85281. (888) 423-5371. FAX:
(480) 894-1528. www.hafler.com
NATIONAL SALES MANAGER
Chris Trapp
ADVERTISING & PUBLIC RELATIONS
Charlie Leib

IRA TEC/PRO AUDIO
(Speaker & professional audio repair)
12315 S.W. 40th St., Yukon, OK 73099. (405) 324-5311. FAX:
(405) 324-5355. www.iratec.50megs.com
OWNER
Ira Rastampour

JBL PROFESSIONAL
(Loudspeaker systems)
8400 Balboa Blvd., Northridge, CA 91329. (818) 894-8850.
FAX: (818) 830-1220. www.jblpro.com
email: cgoodsell@harman.com
PRESIDENT
Mark Terry
CONTACT
Chuck Goodsell

KLIPSCH AUDIO TECHNOLOGIES
(Theatre sound & listening devices)
3502 Woodview Trace, Ste. 200, Indianapolis, IN 46268. (800)
544-1482, (317) 860-8785. FAX: (317) 860-9170.
www.klipsch.com
CONTACT
Christine Pile

KRIX
(Loudspeakers)
14 Chapman Rd., P.O. Box 37, Hackham, South Australia 5163
Australia. TEL: (618) 8384-3433. FAX: (688) 8384-3419.
www.krix.com.au email: krix@krix.com.au
CONTACT
Peter Lawson

MACKIE DESIGNS, INC.
16220 Wood-Red Rd. N.E., Woodinville, WA 98072. (800) 258-
6883, (425) 487-4333. FAX: (425) 487-4337. www.mackie.com
SENIOR V.P., SALES
Frank Loyko

MILLER & KREISEL SOUND CORP.
9351 Deering Ave., Chatsworth, CA 91311. (310) 204-2854.
FAX: (310) 202-8782. www.mksound.com
email: cminto@mksound.com
PRESIDENT
Stephen Powers
EXECUTIVE V.P.
Charles Back
DIRECTOR, M&K PROFESSIONAL
Chris Minto

MISCO/MINNEAPOLIS SPEAKER CO., INC.
(Manufacturer of 2"- 12" speakers)
2637 32nd Ave. S., Minneapolis, MN 55406-1641. (612) 825-1010.
FAX: (612) 825-7010. www.miscospeakers.com
CONTACT
Dan Digre

PEAVEY ARCHITECTURAL ACOUSTICS
(Electronics manufacturer; architectural acoustics)
A division of Peavey Electronics Corp., 711 A St., Meridian,
MS 39301. (601) 483-5376. FAX: (601) 486-1154.
www.peavey.com
OWNER & CEO
Hartley D. Peavey

SOUND RELATED TECHNOLOGIES
(Cinema speaker systems & listening devices)
2680 Production Dr., Ste. 101, Virginia Beach, VA 23454. (757)
463-4300. FAX: (757) 498-3231. www.soundrelatedtech.com
E.V.P. & COO
Don Fisher

TELEX COMMUNICATION, INC.
12000 Portland Ave., S., Burnsville, MN 55337. (952) 884-
4051. FAX: (952) 884-0043. www.electrovoice.com
CONTACT
Mick Whelan

STAGE DESIGN

CALIFORNIA STAGE & LIGHTING
(Stage lighting equipment & supplies)
3211 W. MacArthur Blvd., Santa Ana, CA 92704-6801. (714)
966-1852. FAX: (714) 966-0104. www.calstage.com
email: csl4lights@aol.com
OWNER
Jimmy Ray Hutton

GROSH SCENIC RENTALS, INC
(Backdrop & drapery rental)
4114 Sunset Blvd., Hollywood, CA 90029. (877) 363-7998,
(323) 662-1134. FAX: (323) 664-7526. www.grosh.com
email: Grosh@grosh.com
V.P., MARKETING
Amanda Lindoerfer

LIBERTY THEATRICAL DECOR
22313 Meekland Av., Hayward, CA 94541. (510) 889-1951.
FAX: (510) 889-1602. email: libertyrig@aol.com
OWNER
Don Nethercott

THEATRE CLEANING AND MAINTENANCE

A&B COMPANY
(Nightly janitorial, carpet & floor cleaning, pressure wash,
screen, seat & upholstery cleaning; fire-protectant application)
6536 Fulton Ave., Van Nuys, CA 91401. (818) 985-7768. FAX:
(818) 763-7914.
CONTACT
Michael Fuss

AMPAC THEATRE CLEANING SERVICES
(Janitorial services; screen & carpet cleaning)
P.O. Box 421, Monterey, CA 93942. (831) 372-3728. FAX: (831)
373-3490.
CONTACT
Arnold Meltzer

BRAUN BRUSH COMPANY
(Screen cleaning, all types of brushes, environmentally safe cleaning chemicals, popcorn squeegies)
43 Albertson Ave., Albertson, NY 11507. (800) 645-4111. FAX: (516) 741-6299. www.brush.com email: Sales@brush.com

CINCOM–THE MEGAPLEX CINEMA SPECIALISTS
(Movie-theatre cleaning)
P.O. Box 2533, Salem, NH 03079. (603) 893-4403. FAX: (603) 893-1667. www.cincom.net
PRESIDENT
Matthew W. Sinopoli
DIRECTOR OF CORPORATE OPERATIONS
Lisa Forkey

CLEANNET USA
9861 Broken Land Pkwy., #208, Columbia, MD 21046. (800) 735-8838, (410) 720-6444. FAX: (410) 720-5307.
www.cleannetusa.com

COLGATE-PALMOLIVE COMPANY
(Complete cleaning line & cleaning systems for the theatre and concession industries)
191 E. Hanover Ave., Morristown, NJ 07962. (973) 630-1500. FAX: (973) 292-6021. www.colpalipd.com
MARKETING MANAGER
Barbara Dunn

CREST-TALMADGE
(Janitorial supplies)
1590 Rollins Rd., Burlingame, CA 94010. (650) 692-7378. FAX: (650) 692-8059. email: crestsls@aol.com
VICE PRESIDENT
Mark Talmadge

MAG-TECH ENVIRONMENTAL INC.
(Soundfold/drapery cleaning, screen cleaning, seat cleaning)
710 Season Heather Ct., St. Louis, MO 63021. (636) 394-0414. FAX: (636) 394-0516.
OWNER & PRESIDENT
Don Waldman
VICE PRESIDENT
Lee Waldman

MANUTECH
(Manufacture blowers and vacs for theatres)
2080 Sunset Dr., P.O. Box 51295, Pacific Grove, CA 93950. (800) 676-2569. FAX: (831) 655-8967.
www.manutech.com email: info@manutech.com
OWNER
Angelo Villucci

NATIONAL CINEMA SUPPLY CORPORATION
(Complete line of theatre equipment & supplies, including projection, sound, seating, janitorial, and food service)
CORPORATE HEADQUARTERS
14499 N. Dale Mabry Hwy., Ste. 201, Tampa, FL 33618. (813) 962-2772. FAX: (813) 962-3620. Technical: (800) 776-6271, (813) 962-0188; Concessions: (800) 733-7278. FAX: (813) 908-6277. www.ncsco.com
PRESIDENT & COO
Barney Bailey
CHAIRMAN & CEO
Daniel P. Miller
REGIONAL SALES MANAGER
Greg Thomas
VICE PRESIDENT
Ron Eiben
V.P., DIRECTOR, MARKETING
Larry Shively
BRANCHES
P.O. Box 206, Castaic, CA 91320-0206. (661) 257-1984. FAX: (661) 257-1660.
REGIONAL SALES MANAGER
George A. Bruce Jr.
P.O. Box 549, 99 Limestone Rd., Ridgefield, CT 06877. (203) 438-3405, (203) 438-1274. FAX: (203) 438-1419, (203) 438-1542.
V.P. & GENERAL SALES MANAGER
Walter Beatty Jr.
5854 Highland Ridge Dr., Cincinnati, OH 45232. (800) 543-0418, (513) 242-6801. FAX: (513) 242-6931.
VICE PRESIDENT
Barbara Cammack

PREMIER CHEMICAL PRODUCTS
(Industrial chemical & cleaning products)
5408 N. 59th St., Ste. A, Tampa FL 33610. (800) 790-3090, (813) 740-8611. FAX: (813) 740-8218.
www.premierchemical.com email: premchemical@aol.com
PRESIDENT
George Brydon

PRO STAR INDUSTRIES
(Janitorial equipment for movie theatres)
1590-A N. Harvey Mitchell Pkwy., Bryan, TX 77803. (800) 262-7104, (979) 779-9399. FAX: (979) 779-7616.
www.prostarindustries.com
CONTACT
Dory Howell

PROTOCOL
(Janitorial supplies and equipment)
1370 Mendota Heights Rd., Mendota Heights, MN 55120. (800) 227-5336. FAX: (651) 454-9542. www.air-serb.com
SALES MANAGER
Brett McKay

THEATRE SERVICES INTL.
(Developers of the TS-2 movie-screen cleaning process)
Box 194, 6757 Arapaho Rd., Ste. 711, Dallas, TX 75248. (972) 690-8545. www.theatre-services.com
email: info@theatre-services.com
OWNER & PRESIDENT
David Stuck

THEATRE SPECIALTY COMPANY INC.
(Carpet, seat & floor cleaning)
P.O. Box 2126, Loveland, CO 80538. (970) 669-5407. FAX: (970) 669-1829.
SALES MANAGER
Dave Sizemore

UNITED RECEPTACLE
(Steel, aluminum, fiberglass, concrete & waste receptacles, & smoker's urns)
P.O. Box 870, Pottsville, PA 17901. (800) 233-0314. FAX: (800) 847-8551. www.unitedrecept.com
email: united@unitedrecept.com
SALES & MARKETING
Andy Lesh

BOB WELLS THEATRE PAINTING
1823 Cordova Ave., Cincinnati, OH 45239-4963. (513) 522-9026.
CONTACT
Bob Wells

WINTERS THEATRE CLEANING
(Equipment & janitorial supplies)
P.O Box 15283, Lenexa, KS 66285. (913) 397-7711. FAX: (913) 397-7755. www.theatrecleaning.com
CONTACT
Rob Winters

THEATRE EQUIPMENT DEALERS

AMERICAN CINEMA EQUIPMENT INC.
(All types of motion picture equipment)
1927 N. Argyle St., Portland, OR 97217. (503) 285-7015 FAX: (503) 285-6765. www.cinequip.com email: info@cinequip.com
PRESIDENT
Scott R. Hicks
NATIONAL SALES MANAGER
Doug Sabin

ASC THEATRE EQUIPMENT SALES
(All types of theatre equipment)
7027 Twin Hills, Dallas, TX 75231. (214) 265-9303. FAX: (214) 691-8949.

BIG SKY INDUSTRIES
(Manufacturers of projection booth equipment; booth supplies)
1475 Park Ave., Alpha, NJ 08865. (908) 454-6344. FAX: (908) 454-6373. www.bigskyindustries.net
OWNER & PRESIDENT
Mark Smith
CONTACT
Mike Avallone

BOSTON LIGHT & SOUND
(Manufacturer & distributor of film projectors & sound equipment; service & installation)
290 N. Beacon St., Boston, MA 02135. (617) 787-3131. FAX: (617) 787-4257. www.blsi.com email: info@blsi.com
CONTACT
Chapin Cutler

CARDINAL SOUND & MOTION PICTURE SYSTEMS, INC.
(Digital sound systems; 16mm, 35mm, & 70mm equipment)
6330 Howard Ln., Elkridge, MD 21075. (410) 796-5300. FAX: (410) 796-7995. www.cardinalsound.com
OFFICE MANAGER
Catherine Rockman

CINEMA EQUIPMENT & SUPPLIES
12441 S.W. 130th St., Miami, FL 33186. (305) 232-8181. FAX: (305) 232-8172. email: sales@cinemaequip.com
CONTACT
Guillermo Younger

HARRAH'S THEATRE EQUIPMENT COMPANY
(All types of theatre equipment)
25613 Dollar St., Unit 1, Hayward, CA 94544-2535. (510) 881-4989. FAX: (510) 881-0448.
OWNER
Jerry Harrah

MEGASYSTEMS
(Full service provider of products and services for large format, including projection systems with state of the art clarity and sound and a compact open-architecture design)
110 Riberia St., St. Augustine, FL 32084. (904) 829-5702. FAX: (904) 829-5070. www.megasystem.com
CONTACTS
Steve Kitten
Mark Adukewicz

NATIONAL CINEMA SUPPLY CORPORATION
(Complete line of theatre equipment & supplies, including projection, sound, seating, janitorial, and food service)
CORPORATE HEADQUARTERS
14499 N. Dale Mabry Hwy., Ste. 201, Tampa, FL 33618. (813) 962-2772. FAX: (813) 962-3620. Technical: (800) 776-6271, (813) 962-0188; Concessions: (800) 733-7278. FAX: (813) 908-6277. www.ncsco.com
PRESIDENT & COO
Barney Bailey
CHAIRMAN & CEO
Daniel P. Miller
REGIONAL SALES MANAGER
Greg Thomas
VICE PRESIDENT
Ron Eiben
V.P., DIRECTOR, MARKETING
Larry Shively
BRANCHES

P.O. Box 206, Castaic, CA 91320-0206. (661) 257-1984. FAX: (661) 257-1660.
REGIONAL SALES MANAGER
George A. Bruce Jr.

P.O. Box 549, 99 Limestone Rd., Ridgefield, CT 06877. (203) 438-3405, (203) 438-1274. FAX: (203) 438-1419, (203) 438-1542.
V.P. & GENERAL SALES MANAGER
Walter Beatty Jr.

5854 Highland Ridge Dr., Cincinnati, OH 45232. (800) 543-0418, (513) 242-6801. FAX: (513) 242-6931.
VICE PRESIDENT
Barbara Cammack

RONEY INTERNATIONAL, INC.
(Exporter of 35mm & 70mm equipment, sound & digital equipment & parts)
382 Springfield Ave., Summit, NJ 07901. (908) 273-3696. FAX: (908) 273-8995. email: roneyintl@aol.com
PRESIDENT
Roney Weis

UNIVERSAL CINEMA SERVICES
(Distributors of all types of theatre equipment & supplies)
1205 Corporate Dr. E., Arlington, TX 76006. (817) 633-2180. FAX: (817) 633-2190. email: custserv@goUCS.com
CEO
Jack Panzeca
PRESIDENT
Stan Lamb
CONTACT
Kris Bartlett

WORLDWIDE SAFE & VAULT
(Cash-handling safes, access-controlled electronic locks, all aspects of physical security hardware)
3660 N.W. 115th Ave., Miami, FL 33178. (305) 477-9266. FAX: (305) 477-9744. www.worldwidesafe.com
OWNER & PRESIDENT
Scott Hirsch

THE SAUL ZAENTZ FILM CENTER
(Film editing equipment rental)
2600 10th St., Berkeley, CA 94710. (800) 227-0466, (510) 486-2100. FAX: (510) 486-2115. www.zaentz.com

TICKETS AND TICKET STOCK

ADMIT ONE PRODUCTS
(Complete source for all your admission needs)
1350 Reynolds Ste. 116, Irvine, CA 92614. (949) 756-1089. FAX: (949) 756-8642. www.admitoneproducts.com
V.P., SALES
Steve Turner

AMLON TICKET
(Ticket manufacturer)
254 Helicopter Circle, Corona, CA 92880. (909) 278-8888. FAX: (909) 278-8891. email: amlon@pe.net
SALES
Jason Rogers

DILLINGHAM TICKET COMPANY
(Coupon books, thermal ticketbook, passes & wristbands, admission & reserved-seat tickets)
781 Ceres Ave., Los Angeles, CA 90021-1515. (213) 627-6916. FAX: (213) 623-2758. www.dillinghamticket.com
SALES REPRESENTATIVE
Michael O'Keefe

ECI–WWW.TICKETING SYSTEMS
Electronic Creations Inc., 430 State Pl., Ste. B, Escondido, CA 92029. (760) 480-1002. FAX: (760) 480-6830. www.ticketingsystems.com
email: brucehall@ticketingsystems.com
PRESIDENT
Bruce Hall
SALES MANAGER
Ronn Hall

FANDANGO
(Internet ticketing)
1520 2nd St., Ste. 2, Santa Monica, CA 90401. (800) 326-3264. www.fandango.com
V.P., SALES
Dan Mohler

GLOBE TICKET & LABEL CO.
(Custom printed tickets)
300 Constance Dr., Warminster, PA 18974. (800) 523-5968. www.globeticket.com
COO
Randy Hicks
PRESIDENT
Bob Puleo
NATIONAL SALES MANAGER
Patrick Carter

HOLLYWOOD SOFTWARE
(Ticketing & software)
1604 N. Cahuenga Blvd., Ste. 115, Hollywood, CA 90028. (323) 463-1359. FAX: (323) 463-1319. www.hollywoodsoftware.com
email: davidg@hollywoodsoftware.com
CEO
David Gajda

NATIONAL TICKET COMPANY
(Thermal point-of-sale ticket stock, wristbands, and all other types of theatre tickets)
P.O. Box 547, Shamokin, PA 17872-0547. (570) 672-2900. FAX: (570) 672-2999. www.nationalticket.com
email: ticket@nationalticket.com
V.P., SALES
Timothy Timcoe

OMNITERM DATA TECHNOLOGY LTD.
(Automated ticketing, concessions, teleticket, ATM and more)
2785 Skymark Ave., #11, Mississauga, ON L4W 4Y3, Canada. (905) 629-4757. FAX: (905) 629-8590.
www.omniterm.com email: info@omniterm.com
PRESIDENT
Ed Coman

PACER/CATS-CCS
(Specialized POS solutions that include ticketing and remote ticketing options-kiosks, internet, IVR-concessions and merchandise management, advanced reporting and analysis)
355 Inverness Sr. S., Englewood, CO 80112. (303) 649-9818. FAX: (303) 414-7805. www.pacercats.com
email: sales@pacercats.com
V.P., SALES
Sly Glass

PREMIER SOUTHERN TICKET COMPANY
(Thermal ticket stock; anti-counterfeiting devices for tickets; scratch-off tickets for prizes)
7911 School Rd., Cincinnati, OH 45249. (800) 331-2283. FAX: (513) 489-6867. www.premiersouthern.com
CONTACT
Miranda Lovins

PRACTICAL AUTOMATION
(Manufacturer of high-speed printers for computerized ticketing systems)
45 Woodmont Rd., Milford CT 06460. (203) 882-5640. FAX: (203) 882-5648. www.practicalautomation.com
email: pa@practicalautomation.com
CUSTOMER SERVICE MANAGER
Brian Sikorsky

RADIANT SYSTEMS, INC

(Theatre management services for box office, back office, consumer-activated kiosk, ticketing, POS)
3925 Brookside Pkwy., Apharetta, GA 30022. (770) 576-6000. FAX: (770) 754-7790. www.radiantsystems.com
EXECUTIVE V.P
Carlye Taylor

RDS DATA GROUP

(Manufacturer of box office accounting systems & concession stand cash registers)
101 Donly Dr., S., Simcoe, ON N3Y 4L5, Canada. (519) 428-2500. FAX: (519) 428-0131. www.rdsdata.com
email: info@rdsdata.com
SENIOR MANAGEMENT
Robert Jackson
Steve Jackson
David Kemp
Brad De Poorter

SENSIBLE CINEMA SOFTWARE

(Ticketing & concession inventory software; ticketing printers & blank ticket stock)
7216 Sutton Pl., Fairview, TN 37062. (615) 799-6366. FAX: (615) 799-6367. www.sensiblecinema.com
CONTACT
Rusty Gordon

THEATRE SUPPORT SERVICES, INC.

310 S.W. 66th Terr., Margate, FL 33068. (954) 971-7787. FAX: (815) 352-1625. www.theatresupport.com
email: theogre@theatresupport.com

TICKETPRO SYSTEMS

(Software for theatre ticketing)
870 Mercury Dr. S.E., Lawrenceville, GA 30045. (770) 682-5485. FAX: (770) 682-8397. www.ticketpro.org
CEO
John W. Shaw

WELDON, WILLIAMS & LICK, INC.

(Ticket printing, specializing in number & security printing)
P.O. Box 168, Fort Smith, AR 72902-0168. (800) 242-4995.
FAX: (479) 783-7050. www.wwlinc.com
CONTACTS
Steve Lensing
Greg. W. Slayline

UNIFORMS

CINTAS

5600 W. 73rd St., Chicago, IL 60638. (800) 864-3676. FAX: (800) 864-3888. www.uty.com
V.P., NATIONAL SALES
Bill Riesner

FASHION SEAL UNIFORMS

(All types of uniforms)
10055 Seminole Blvd., Seminole, FL 33772. (727) 397-9611. FAX: (727) 391-5401. www.superioruniformgroup.com
V.P., SALES
Kurt Schauer

FLAVOR WEAR

28425 S. Cole Grade Rd., Valley Center, CA 92082. (800) 647-8372, (760) 749-1332. FAX: (760) 749-6164.
www.flavorwear.com email: flavorwr@ix.netcom.com
CONTACT
Lawrence Schleif

HANOVER UNIFORM COMPANY

(All types of uniforms)
529 W. 29th St., Baltimore, MD 21211-2988. (800) 541-9709, (410) 235-8338. FAX: (410) 235-6071.
www.hanoveruniform.com
CONTACT
John Mintz

PRIORITY MANUFACTURING, INC.

(Hospitality industry uniforms)
571 N.W. 29th St., Miami, FL 33127. (800) 835-5528, (305) 576-3000. FAX: (305) 576-2672. www.customuniforms.com

Concession Suppliers

BEVERAGES

BOYD COFFEE COMPANY
19730 N.E. Sandy Blvd., Portland, OR 97230. (503) 666-4545.
FAX: (503) 669-2223. www.boyds.com
email: info@boyds.com
SENIOR V.P., SALES & MARKETING
Doug McKay
V.P., MARKETING
Marc Bourret

BRAD BARRY CO./CAFFE D'VITA CAPPUCCINO
14020 Central Ave., Ste. 580, Chino, CA 91710. (909) 591-9493. FAX: (909) 627-3747. www.caffedvita.com
email: frank@caffedvita.com
HEAD OF SALES
Frank Abbadessa

CHINA MIST TEA COMPANY
7435 E. Tierra Buena Ln., Scottsdale, AZ 85260. (800) 242-8807, (480) 998-8807. FAX: (480) 596-0811. www.chinamist.com
HEAD OF SALES
Wally Hankins

THE COCA-COLA COMPANY
One Coca-Cola Plaza, Atlanta, GA 30313. (404) 676-2121, (404) 676-7945. FAX: (404) 676-3605. email: kherr@na.ko.com
THEATRE CHANNEL MANAGER
Kristin Herr

DR. PEPPER/SEVEN-UP
5301 Legacy Dr., Plano, TX 75024. (972) 673-7781. FAX: (972) 673-7115. www.drpepper.com, www.seven-up.com
SENIOR PLANNER, CORPORATE TRADE SHOWS
Richard Eisemann

GEHL'S GUERNSEY FARMS, INC.
N116 W15970 Main St., Germantown, WI 53022. (262) 251-8570. FAX: (262) 251-9318. www.gehls.com
HEAD OF SALES
Tracey Propst

THE ICEE COMPANY
4701 Airport Dr., Ontario, CA 91761. (909) 390-4233. FAX: (909) 390-6804. www.icee.com
V.P., MARKETING
Susan Swisher Woods

JUICY WHIP, INC.
15845 Business Center Dr., Irwindale, CA 91706. (800) 501-4558, (626) 338-5339. FAX: (626) 814-8016.
PRESIDENT
Gus Stratton

PARROT-ICE DRINK PRODUCTS OF AMERICA, LTD.
13738 FM 529, Houston, TX 77041. (713) 896-8798. FAX: (713) 896-6676. www.parrot-ice.com
NATIONAL SALES MANAGER
Gus Pasquini

PEPSI-COLA COMPANY
700 Andersonhill Rd., Purchase, NY 10577. (914) 253-3017.
FAX: (914) 249-8224. email: peter.leyh@pepsi.com
SENIOR NATIONAL ACCOUNT SALES MANAGER
Peter Leyh

RIO SYRUP COMPANY, INC.
2311 Chestnut St., St. Louis, MO 63103. (800) 325-7666. FAX: (314) 436-7707. www.riosyrup.com
email: snocones@riosyrup.com
HEAD OF SALES
Phillip Tomber

SIGNATURE BRANDS GROUP
6050 East Hanna Ave., Indianapolis, IN 46203. (800) 362-8714, (317) 791-1900. FAX: (317) 791-1916.
www.signaturebrandsgroup.com
email: sales@signaturebg.com

VICTOR PRODUCTS CO.
328 N. 18th St., Richmond, VA 23223. (804) 643-9091. FAX: (804) 648-3601. www.victorproducts.com
HEAD OF SALES
Mitch Zinder

CANDY & CONFECTIONS

ADAMS & BROOKS
1915 South Hoover St., P.O. Box 7303, Los Angeles, CA 90007. (213) 749-3226. FAX: (213) 746-7614.
www.adams-brooks.com email: info@adams-brooks.com
PRESIDENT
John Brooks
DIRECTOR, SALES & MARKETING
Russell Case

AMERICAN INTERNATIONAL CONCESSION PRODUCTS CORP.
62 Bethpage Rd., Hicksville, NY 11801. (516) 681-1537. FAX: (516) 681-3362. www.aicpcorp.com; www.planetsweets.com
PRESIDENT
Christopher Sciortino
V.P., OPERATIONS
Stephen Sciortino

AMERICAN LICORICE COMPANY
3701 W. 128th Pl., Alsip, IL 60803. (708) 371-1414. FAX: (708) 371-0231. www.americanlicorice.com; www.redvines.com; www.sourpunch.com email: will@americ.com
MARKETING
Will Miller

BANNER CANDY MFG. CORP.
700 Liberty Ave., Brooklyn, NY 11208. (718) 647-4747. FAX: (718) 647-7192.
PRESIDENT
Peter Stone
VICE PRESIDENT
Rose Grunther

CONTINENTAL CONCESSION, LTD
618 Kickapoo Spur, Shawnee, OK 74801. (866) 273-1090.
FAX: (405) 273-1085.
CONTACT
Roger Johnson

DIPPIN' DOTS
5101 Charter Oak Dr., Paduca, KY 42001. (270) 443-8994.
FAX: (270) 443-8997. www.dippindots.com
CONTACT
Marilyn Phillips

EURO-AMERICAN BRANDS, INC.
15 Prospect St., Paramus NJ 07652. (201) 368-2624. FAX: (201) 368-2512. www.euroamericanbrands.com
SALES
Linda Wette

FOLZ VENDING COMPANY
3401 Lawson Blvd., Oceanside, NY 11572. (516) 678-6005.
FAX: (516) 678-3644. email: folzsales@aol.com
CONTACT
Debbie Pugliese

THE FOREIGN CANDY COMPANY, INC.
One Foreign Candy Dr., Hull, IA 51239. (800) 831-8541. FAX: (800) 832-8541. www.megawarheads.com
SALES
Art Zito

GHIRARDELLI CHOCOLATE COMPANY
1111 139th Ave., San Leandro, CA 94578-2631. (800) 877-9338. www.ghirardelli.com

JELLY BELLY CANDY COMPANY
One Jelly Belly Ln., Fairfield, CA 94533. (800) 323-9380. FAX: (707) 428-0819. www.jellybelly.com
PRESIDENT
Robert M. Simpson
V.P., SALES
Andrew Joffer

GOLDENBERG CANDY CO.
7701 State Rd., Philadelphia, PA 19136. (215) 335-4500. FAX: (215) 335-4510. www.goldenbergcandy.com
VICE PRESIDENT
Mindy Goldenberg

HARIBO OF AMERICA, INC.
(Gummy candy)
1825 Woodlawn Dr., Ste. 204, Baltimore, MD 21207. (410) 265-8890. FAX: (410) 265-8898. www.haribo.com
SALES
Elaine Farrar

HERSHEY FOODS
14 E. Chocolate Ave., Hershey, PA 17033. (800) 468-1714, (717) 534-3660. FAX: (717) 534-8718. www.hersheys.com
email: info@hersheypa.com
DIRECTOR, CUSTOMER & INDUSTRY AFFAIRS
Tom Joyce

JUDSON-ATKINSON CANDY CO.
P.O. Box 200669, San Antonio, TX 78220-0669. (800) 962-3984. FAX: (210) 359-8392.
CONTACT
Ken Deecken

JUST BORN, INC.
1300 Stefko Blvd., Bethlehem, PA 18017. (800) 445-5787, (610) 867-7568. FAX: (610) 867-5537.
www.justborn.com email: dpippis@justborn.com
V.P., MARKETING
Matt Petronio
CONTACT
Donna Pippis

MCLANE COMPANY
4747 McLane Pkwy., Temple, TX 76504. (254) 771-7500. FAX: (254) 771-7566. www.mclaneco.com
SALES
Steve Brady

M&M MARS
800 High St., Hackettstown, NJ 07840. (908) 852-1000. FAX: (908) 850-2734. http://gcv.mms.com/us/
CONTACT
Jeanny Zander

NESTLE USA
3450 Dulles Dr., Mira Loma, CA 91752. (800) 367-4449. FAX: (909) 361-0755. www.nestlenewbiz.com
CATEGORY SALES DEVELOPMENT MANAGER
Mike Mosher

NEW ENGLAND CONFECTIONARY
135 American Legion Hwy., Revere, MA 02151. (781) 485-4500. FAX: (781) 485-4509. www.necco.com
CONTACT
Charley Blood

PROMOTION IN MOTION CO., INC./FERRARA PAN CANDY
3 Reuten Dr., Closter, NJ 07624. (201) 784-5800. FAX: (201) 784-1010. www.promotioninmotion.com
email: jscudillo@promotioninmotion.com
PRESIDENT
Michael Rosenburg
V.P., SPECIAL MARKETS
Jeff Scudillo

SARNOW CANDY
1001 S. Oyster Bay Rd., Bethpage, NY 11714. (516) 576-9800. FAX: (516) 576-0730. www.sarnowcandy.com
email: bsmith@sarnowcandy.com
V.P., SALES & OPERATIONS
Bill Smith

SHOWTIME CONCESSIONS
200 S.W. 19th St., Moore, OK 73160. (405) 895-9902.
Contact
Dave Brennan

TOOTSIE ROLL INDUSTRIES, INC.
7401 S. Cicero Ave., Chicago, IL 60629. (800) 877-7655, (773) 838-3400. FAX: (312) 838-3569, (773) 838-3569.
www.tootsie.com
REGIONAL SALES MANAGER
Robert Immen
CONTACT
Cheryl Barko

DAIRY

ALTA-DENA CERTIFIED DAIRY
17637 E. Valley Blvd., City of Industry, CA 91744. (800) 535-1369. FAX: (626) 854-4287. www.altadenadairy.com
CONTACT
Mary Larrowe

ICE CREAM & FROZEN DAIRY PRODUCTS

BEN & JERRY'S HOMEMADE
30 Community Dr., S. Burlington, VT 05403. (802) 846-1500. FAX: (802) 846-1539.
CONTACT
Jeannie Staink

DREYER'S GRAND ICE CREAM
5929 College Ave., Oakland, CA 94618. (510) 652-8187. FAX: (510) 450-4592. www.dreyers.com
V.P., SALES
Tom Delaplane

GOOD HUMOR
909 Packerland Dr., Green Bay, WI 54303. (920) 499-5151. FAX: (920) 497-6582. www.goodhumor.com
V.P., SALES
Joe Colligan

HAAGEN-DAZS
710 Epperson Dr., City of Industry, CA 91748. (626) 935-6017, (626) 935-6018. FAX: (888) 964-2550. www.haagendazs.com
CONTACT
Randy Tripp

NESTLE ICE CREAM
30003 Bainbridge Rd., Solon, OH 44139. (440) 349-5757. FAX: (440) 498-7689. www.nestleusa.com
CONTACT
Cindy Temple

MEAT PRODUCTS

BIL MAR FOODS, INC.
(Sara Lee Corporation)
8300 96th Ave., Zeeland, MI 49464. (616) 875-7711. FAX: (616) 875-7565.
DIVISION MANAGER
Bernie Duignan

EISENBERG GOURMET BEEF FRANKS
3531 N. Elston Ave., Chicago, IL 60618. (773) 588-2882. FAX: (773) 588-0810.
CONTACTS
Ed Weinshenker
Cliff Eisenberg
Howard Eisenberg

HORMEL FOODS, INC.
10550 New York Ave., Urbandale, IA 50322. (515) 334-0500. FAX: (515) 334-0600. www.hormel.com
DISTRICT MANAGER
Craig Drefcinski

KRAFT FOODS/OSCAR MAYER
P.O. Box 7188, Madison, WI 53707. (608) 285-6820.
SENIOR MANAGER, COMMUNICATIONS
Sarah Delea
3 Lakes Dr., Northfield, IL 60093. (847) 646-3845. www.kraft.com
SENIOR MANAGER, COMMUNICATIONS
Alyssa Burns

SARA LEE/BALL PARK FRANKS
10151 Carver, Cincinnati, OH 45242. (888) 317-5867.
www.ballparkfranks.com
REGIONAL SALES MANAGER, MICHIGAN
Brent Beerens

SQUARE H
2731 S. Soto St., Los Angeles, CA 90023. (323) 267-4600. FAX: (323) 261-7350.
V.P., SALES
Mike Polini

PAPER & PLASTIC GOODS

AFFILIATED PAPER COMPANIES, INC.
(Paper, plastic and sanitary supplies)
3468 Mt. Diablo Blvd., Ste. B-301, Lafayette, CA 94549. (510) 283-7513. FAX: (510) 284-2670.
WESTERN DIVISION SALES MANAGER
George Van Fossen

AFFLINK
(Food service and paper distributors and suppliers)
Corporate Headquarters: 1400 Afflink Pl.,Tuscaloosa, AL 35406. (205) 345-4180.
3195 Danville Blvd., #2, Alamo, CA 94507. (925) 855-1065. FAX: (925) 855-1490. www.afflink.com
HEAD, SALES
George Van Fossen

BAGCRAFT PACKAGING
3900 W. 43rd St., Chicago, IL 60632. (800) 621-8468, (773) 254-8000. FAX: (773) 254-8204. www.bagcraft.com
CONTACT
Laura Olson
CONSUMER PRODUCT SPECIALIST
Nancy Chico
DIRECTOR, DISTRIBUTION
Ron Gale

DART CONTAINER CORPORATION
500 Hogsback Rd., Mason, MI 48854. (800) 248-5960. FAX: (517) 676-3883. www.dart.biz

FIELD CONTAINER CO. LP
1501 Industrial Park Dr., Tuscaloosa, AL 35401. (205) 333-0333. FAX: (205) 333-9862. www.fieldcontainer.com
V.P., SALES
Richard Burklew

INTERNATIONAL PAPER FOOD SERVICE
3 Paragon Dr., Montvale, NJ 07645. (201) 391-1776. FAX: (201) 307-6125. www.internationalpaper.com
CONTACT
Tracy Blatt

MAUI CUP
(A Subsidiary of Letica Corp.)
52585 Dequindre Rd., Rochester, MI 48307. (248) 652-0557. FAX: (248) 652-0577.
DIRECTOR, MARKETING
Malcolm McAlpine

MCLANE COMPANY
4747 McLane Pkwy., Temple, TX 76504. (254) 771-7500. FAX: (254) 771-7244. www.mclaneco.com
CONTACT
Steve Brady

PACKAGING CONCEPTS
4971 Fyler Ave., St. Louis, MO 63139. (314) 481-1155. FAX: (314) 481-6567.
CONTACT
Anthony W. Irace

PROMOTIONAL MANAGEMENT GROUP, INC.
(Concession containers & supplies)
925 Wyoming, Ste. 200, Kansas City, MO 64101. (816) 221-3833. FAX: (816) 221-6166.
E.V.P., SALES & MARKETING
James McGuinness

ROYAL PAPER CORP.
8940 Sorensen Ave., Santa Fe Springs, CA 90670. (562) 903-9030. FAX: (562) 944-6000.
CONTACT
Marianne Abi Aad

SHOWTIME CONCESSIONS
200 S.W. 19th St., Moore, OK 73160. (405) 895-9902.
Contact
Dave Brennan

SOLO CUP
1700 Old Deerfield Rd., Highland Park, IL 60035. (847) 831-4800. FAX: (847) 831-0421. www.solocup.com
V.P., SALES
Paul Hulseman

SWEETHEART CUP CO.
10100 Reisterstown Rd., Owings Mills, MD 21117. (410) 363-1111. www.sweetheart.com
V.P., SALES & MARKETING
Mark Karkwood

W.N.A./CUPS ILLUSTRATED, INC.
2155 W. Longhorn Dr., Lancaster, TX 75134. (800) 334-CUPS. FAX: (972) 224 3067. www.cupsillustrated.com
SALES
Tina Daniel

WINCHESTER CARTON
P.O. Box 597, Eutaw, AL 35462. (205) 372-3337. FAX: (205) 372-9226.
GENERAL MANAGER
Dan Williams

WINPAK TECHNOLOGIES INC.
85 Laird Dr., Toronto, Ontario, Canada M4G 3T8. (416) 421-1700. FAX: (416) 421-7957. www.winpak.com
CONTACT
Louis de Bellefeuille

ZENITH SPECIALTY BAG COMPANY, INC.
17625 E. Railroad St., City of Industry, CA 91748. (626) 912-2481. FAX: (626) 810-5136. www.zsb.com
V.P., SALES
Ron Anderson

POPCORN & POPPING OILS

AMERICAN POPCORN COMPANY
P.O. Box 178, Sioux City, IA 51102. (712) 239-1232. FAX: (712) 239-1268. www.jollytime.com email: email@jollytime.com
V.P., SALES
Steve Huisenga

BUNGE NORTH AMERICA (EAST), INC.
11720 Borman Dr., St. Louis, MO 63146. (888) 462-8343, (314) 292-2000. FAX: (314) 292-2110.
www.bungenorthamerica.com

CARGILL
P.O. Box 5697, Minneapolis, MN 55440. (800) 323-6232. FAX: (952) 742-5503. www.cargill.com
CONTACT
Mark Overland

CONAGRA FOODS (SNACK FOODS GROUP)
Vogel Popcorn, 2301 Washington St., Hamburg, IA 51640. (800) 831-5818, (712) 382-2634. FAX: (712) 382-1357. www.vogelpopcorn.com email: info@vogelpopcorn.com
V.P., SALES & MARKETING
Brian Biehn (952) 832-1681

ELLIS POPCORN COMPANY, INC.
101 East Poplar St., Murray, KY 42071. (800) 654-3358, (270) 753-5451. FAX: (270) 753-7002. www.ellispopcorn.com
SALES MANAGER
Dave Roberts

GREAT WESTERN PRODUCTS COMPANY
30290 US Highway 72, Hollywood, AL 35752. (800) 239-2143, (256) 259-3578. FAX: (256) 259-2939.
CONTACT
Mark A. Hamilton

KERNEL SEASONS LLC
(Popcorn seasons)
62 Lakewood Pl., Highland Park, IL 60035. (866) 328-7672. FAX: (773) 326-0869. www.nomorenakedpopcorn.com
email: info@kernelseasons.com
PRESIDENT
Brian Taylor

MCLANE COMPANY
4747 McLane Pkwy., Temple, TX 76504. (254) 771-7500. FAX: (254) 771-7244. www.mclaneco.com
CONTACT
Steve Brady

MORRISON FARMS POPCORN
85824 519th Ave., Clearwater, NE 68726. (402) 887-5335. FAX: (402) 887-4709. www.nebraskapopcorn.com
email: michele@morrisonfarms.com
PRESIDENT
Frank Morrison
CONTACT
Michele Steskal

ODELL'S
1325 Airmotive Way, Ste. 290, Reno, NV 89502.
P.O. Box 11336, Reno, NV 89510-1336. (775) 323-8688. FAX: (775) 323-6532. www.popntop.com
email: odells@popntop.com
PRESIDENT
Arthur Anderson
NATIONAL SALES DIRECTOR
Jim Peterson

PREFERRED POPCORN LLC
1132 9th Rd., Chapman, NE 68827. (308) 986-2526. FAX: (308) 986-2626. email: prefpop@gionline.net
CONTACT
Norm Krug

RAMSEY POPCORN CO., INC.
5645 Clover Valley Rd. N.W., Ramsey, IN 47166. (812) 347-2441. FAX: (812) 347-3336. www.ramseypopcorn.com
CONTACT
Jason Sieg

SHOWTIME CONCESSIONS
200 S.W. 19th St., Moore, OK 73160. (405) 895-9902.
Contact
Dave Brennan

T. MILLER POPCORN CO.
P.O. Box 493, Trenton, MO 64683. (660) 359-6958. FAX: (660) 359-6037. www.tmillerpopcorn.com
CONTACT
Joseph A. DiGirolamo

VENTURA FOODS
P.O. Box 591, Opelousas, LA 70571. (337) 948-6561. FAX: (337) 942-3773. www.venturafoods.com
email: rbiggs@venturafoods.com
VICE PRESIDENT
Richard Biggs

WEAVER POPCORN COMPANY, INC.
P.O. Box 395, Van Buren, IN 46991. (800) 227-6159, (765) 934-2101. FAX: (603) 590-6343. www.popweaver.com
CONTACT
Jim Labas

WORD POPCORN CO.
(A subsidiary of Great Western Products Co.)
30290 US Highway 72, Hollywood, AL 35752. (800) 633-5091. FAX: (205) 574-2116.
CONTACT
Mark A. Hamilton (256) 858-6091

WRIGHT POPCORN & NUT CO.
150 Potrero Ave., San Francisco, CA 94103. (415) 861-0912. FAX: (415) 861-6745. www.wrightpopcorn.com

SNACK FOODS

BRAND CONCESSION
(Manufacturer of full line of prepared pizzas)
P.O. Box 292605, Lewisville, TX 75029. (972) 436-2355. FAX: (972) 436-5813. www.brandconcessions.com
email: russ@brandconcessions.com
PRESIDENT
Russ Vulpitta

CORN POPPERS LLC
P.O. Box 620156, San Diego, CA 92162. (619) 231-2617. FAX: (619) 231-2985. www.cornpoppers.com
EXECUTIVE DIRECTOR OF SALES
Joe Alves

DEAN SPECIALTY FOODS GROUP
(Pickles and cheese sauce)
857-897 School Pl., Green Bay, WI 54307. (920) 497-7131.
CONTACT
Gary Bergsma

FRYWORKS
4640 Admiralty, Ste. 310, Marina del Rey, CA 90292. (310) 577-4606. FAX: (310) 577-4616.
CONTACT
Leila Zold

FUNACHO
2165 Central Pkwy., Cincinnati, OH 45214. (513) 241-9300. FAX: (513) 352-5122.
CONTACT
Mike Grause

GOLD MEDAL PRODUCTS
(Concession equipment, popcorn poppers and supplies)
10700 Medallion Dr., Cincinnati, OH 45241-4807. (513) 769-7676. FAX: (513) 769-8500.
CONTACT
John Evans

HOT COOKIES PRODUCTIONS
5924 S.W. 68th St., South Miami, FL 33143. (305) 667-5577. FAX: (305) 666-5335. email: hotcookies@aol.com
CONTACT
Larry Berrin

J & J SNACKS
5353 Downey Rd., Vernon, CA 90058. (323) 581-0171. FAX: (323) 583-4732. www.jjsnacks.com email: pdebro@jjsnack.com
CONTACT
Portland DeBro

KIM & SCOTT'S GOURMET PRETZELS
2107 W. Carroll Ave., Chicago, IL 60612. (312) 243-9971. FAX: (312) 243-9972. www.kimandscotts.com
CONTACT
Scott Holstein

METROPOLITAN PROVISIONS
16639 Gale Ave., City of Industry, CA 91745. (626) 330-1414. FAX: (626) 336-1455.
CEO
Matt Cook

THE MINUTEMAID CO.
P.O. Box 2079, Houston, TX 77252. (713) 888-5000. FAX: (713) 888-5959. www.minutemaid.com
PRESIDENT
Don Knauss

THE NUTTY BAVARIAN
37 Skyline Dr., Ste. 2106, Lake Mary, FL 32746. (800) 382-4788, (407) 444-6322. FAX: (407) 444-6335.
OWNER
David Brent

PIRYLIS DISTRIBUTORS
(Full service concession wholesale supplier)
221 Sussex Ave., Newark, NJ 07103. (973) 482-9326. FAX: (973) 482-0602. www.pirylis.com email: mike@pirylis.com
SALES CONTACT
Mike

PIZZAS OF EIGHT
1915 Cherokee St., St. Louis, MO 63118-3218. (800) 422-2901, (314) 865-1460. FAX: (314) 865-2449.
www.pizzasofeight.com email: contact@pizzasofeight.com
CONTACT
Chuck McMillen

RICOS PRODUCTS CO., INC.
621 S. Flores, San Antonio, TX 78204. (210) 222-1415. FAX: (210) 227-0907. www.ricos.com email: info@ricos.com
CONTACT
Christine Fellner

SNACKWORKS, INC.
9238 Bally Ct., Rancho Cucamonga, CA 91730. (909) 987-9272. FAX: (909) 987-9252. email: snackworks@aol.com
CONTACT
Josh Schreider

SQUARE H BRANDS, INC./HOFFY HOT DOGS
2731 S. Soto St., Los Angeles, CA 90023. (323) 267-4600. FAX: (323) 261-7350.
V.P., SALES
Mike Polini

SUMMIT FOODS
P.O. Box 141, Dedham, MA 02027. (508) 787-3435. FAX: (508) 787-3439.
CONTACT
Paul Bonfiglio

TASTE OF NATURE
400 S. Beverly Dr., #214, Beverly Hills, CA 90212. (310) 396-4433. FAX: (310) 396-4432. email: doughbites@aol.com
CONTACT
Scott Samet

VISTAR USA
12650 E. Arapahoe Rd., Bldg. D, Englewood, CO 80112. (303) 662-7175. FAX: (303) 662-7550.
email: mikebates@vistarusa.com
CONTACT
Mike Bates

WYANDOT, INC.
135 Wyandot Ave., Marion, OH 43302. (740) 383-4031. FAX: (740) 382-5584. www.wyandotsnacks.com
PRESIDENT
Nick Chilton

TOY VENDING MACHINES

TOMY YUJIN
(Sells bulk toy vending machines)
4695 MacArthur Ct., Newport Beach, CA 92660. (949) 955-1030. FAX: (949) 955-1037.
CONTACT
Amanda Newhard

SCREENING ROOMS

All major studios, producers and distributors have screening rooms for their own use. Major circuits also lease theatres as screening rooms.

ACADEMY OF MOTION PICTURE ARTS AND SCIENCES
8949 Wilshire Blvd., Beverly Hills, CA 90211-1972. (310) 247-3000. FAX: (310) 859-9619.
THEATER OPERATIONS
Moray Greenfield

THE CHARLES AIDIKOFF SCREENING ROOM
150 S. Rodeo Dr., #140, Beverly Hills, CA 90212. (310) 274-0866. FAX: (310) 550-1794. www.aidikoff.tv
CO-OWNERS
Charles Aidikoff
Gregg Aidikoff

AMERICAN FILM INSTITUTE
2021 N. Western Ave., Los Angeles, CA 90027. (323) 856-7600. FAX: (323) 467-4578. www.afi.com
CONTACT
Jonas Wright

BIG TIME PICTURE COMPANY
12210-1/2 Nebraska Ave., W. Los Angeles, CA 90025. (310) 207-0921. FAX: (310) 826-0071.
email: bigtimepic@earthlink.net
PROJECTIONIST
Paul Tani

BROADWAY SCREENING ROOM
1619 Broadway, 5th Flr., New York, NY 10019. (212) 307-0990. FAX: (212) 307-5727. www.mybsr.com
MANAGER
Theresa Herico

CHICAGO FILMMAKERS
5243 N. Clark, 2nd Flr., Chicago, IL 60640. (773) 293-1447. FAX: (773) 293-0575. www.chicagofilmmakers.org
EXECUTIVE DIRECTOR
Brenda Webb

THE CLIP JOINT FOR FILM
833-B N. Hollywood Way, Burbank, CA 91505. (818) 842-2525. FAX: (818) 842-2644.
CONTACTS
Ken Kramer
Kathy Losso

DIRECTORS GUILD OF AMERICA
7920 W. Sunset Blvd., Los Angeles, CA 90046. (310) 289-2000. FAX: (310) 289-5398. www.dga.org
THEATER OPERATIONS MANAGER
Tim Webber

EXPLORATORIUM, MCBEAN THEATER
3601 Lyon St., San Francisco, CA 94123. (415) 563-7337. FAX: (415) 561-0370. www.exploratorium.edu/rentals
CONTACT
Museum Rentals Department

FILMWORKERS/ASTRO LABS, INC.
61 W. Erie St., Chicago, IL 60610. (312) 280-5500. FAX: (312) 280-5510.
GENERAL MANAGER
Manuela Hung

LEONARD H. GOLDENSON THEATER AT ACADEMY OF TELEVISION ARTS & SCIENCES
5230 Lankershim Blvd., N. Hollywood, CA 91601-3109. (818) 754-2825. FAX: (818) 761-8524.
THEATER MANAGER
Vicky Campobasso
DIRECTOR, THEATRE OPERATIONS
Bob Gould

HARMONY GOLD PREVIEW HOUSE
7655 Sunset Blvd., Los Angeles, CA 90046. (323) 851-4900. FAX: (323) 851-5599.
DIRECTOR, THEATRE OPERATIONS
Jud Hudgins

HOLLYWOOD NEWSREEL SYNDICATE, INC.
1622 N. Gower St., Los Angeles, CA 90028. (323) 469-7307. FAX: (323) 469-8251. www.hollywoodnewsreel.com
PRESIDENT
Shirley Eggland Spalla

LOS ANGELES COUNTY MUSEUM OF ART
(Bing Theater provides a fee-for-usage, 600 seat screening room. Brown Auditorium shows rear video)
5905 Wilshire Blvd., Los Angeles, CA 90036. (323) 857-6039. FAX: (323) 857-6021. www.lacma.org
email: events@lacma.org

LOS ANGELES THEATER
615 S. Broadway, Los Angeles, CA 90014. (213) 629-2939. FAX: (213) 629-2999.
DIRECTOR
Don Weiss

MAGNO SOUND & VIDEO
729 Seventh Ave., New York, NY 10019. (212) 302-2505. FAX: (212) 764-1679. www.magnosoundandvideo.com
DIRECTOR
Hada Ruiz

OCEAN AVENUE SCREENING ROOM
1401 Ocean Ave., 1st Flr., Santa Monica, CA 90401. (310) 576-1831. FAX: (310) 319-9501. www.oceanscreening.com
CONTACT
Chris Sutton

PACIFIC FILM ARCHIVE
2625 Durant Ave., Berkeley, CA 94720-2250. (510) 642-1412. FAX: (510) 642-4889. www.bampfa.berkeley.edu
THEATER OPERATIONS MANAGER
Dennis Love (510) 642-5236

RALEIGH STUDIOS
5300 Melrose Ave., Hollywood, CA 90038. (323) 871-5649. FAX: (323) 871-5600. www.raleighstudios.com
DIRECTOR
Mike Donahue
GENERAL MANAGER
Mary Fry

TECHNICOLOR
321 W. 44 St., New York, NY 10036. (212) 582-7310 ext. 124. FAX: (212) 315-4542.
V.P., DAILIES DEPARTMENT
Joe VioLante

TRIBECA FILM CENTER
375 Greenwich St., New York, NY 10013-2338. (212) 941-4000. FAX: (212) 941-3997. www.tribecafilm.com
DIRECTOR
Barry Manasch

VINE THEATER
(600 seats, dolby stereo)
6321 Hollywood Blvd., Hollywood, CA 90028. (310) 444-8955.
MANAGER
Jim Barman

WARNER BROS. STUDIOS FACILITIES
4000 Warner Blvd., Burbank, CA 91522. (818) 954-1625. FAX: (818) 954-4138.
VICE PRESIDENT
Daniel R. Chavez

WRITERS GUILD THEATER
135 S. Doheny Dr., Beverly Hills, CA 90211. (323) 782-4525. FAX: (323) 782-4808.
OPERATIONS ADMINISTRATOR
Caren Mandoyan

SAUL ZAENTZ CO. FILM CENTER
2600 Tenth St., Berkeley, CA 94710. (510) 486-2100. FAX: (510) 486-2115. www.zaentz.com email:info@zaentz.com
GENERAL MANAGER
Steve Shurtz

26 Years of Dedicated Service to the Motion Picture Industry
Prepared and Positioned to Serve the Next Generation

[Theatrical Branding-Policy Trailers, Rolling Stock Ads]
[35mm Duplication & Customized Print Fullfillment]
[Digital Compression for Multimedia, Web & DVD]
[Digital Editing & Visual Effects for HD & 2K]
[Multi-Format Sound Mixing & Recording]
[Award Winning Animation & CGI]
[CD, DVD & Video Duplication]
[Up Conversion to HD & 2K]
[Digital Pre-Show Solutions]
[Digital Screening Facility]
[35mm Screening Room]
[Lobby Video Programs]
[35mm Film Recording]
[HD & 2K Finishing]
[. . . And Much More]

www.cinemaconcepts.com

Preview & Policy Trailers

ALKEMI ENTERTAINMENT
706 N. Citrus Ave., Los Angeles, CA 90038-3402. (323) 525-1155. FAX: (323) 525-1150.
PRESIDENT
Edward Glass

HOWARD A. ANDERSON, CO.
5161 Lankershim Blvd., #120, N. Hollywood, CA 91601. (818) 623-1111. FAX: (818) 623-7761.
PRESIDENT & CEO
Howard Anderson III

BLOOMFILM
P.O. Box 461802, Los Angeles, CA 90046. (323) 850-5575. FAX: (323) 850-7304. email: bloomfilm@attglobal.net
PRESIDENT
Jon Bloom

CINEMA CONCEPTS THEATRE SERVICE COMPANY, INC.
2030 Powers Ferry Rd., Ste. 214, Atlanta, GA 30339. (770) 956-7460, (800) SHOWADS. FAX: (770) 956-8358.
www.cinemaconcepts.com email: info@cinemaconcepts.com
PRESIDENT
Stewart Harnell

CRUSE & CO.
7000 Romaine St., Hollywood, CA 90038. (323) 851-8814.

FILMACK STUDIOS
1327 S. Wabash Ave., Chicago, IL 60605-2574. (800) 345-6225. (800) FILMACK. FAX: (312) 427-4866. www.filmack.com
email: robbie@filmack.com
CONTACT
Robert Mack

HOLLYWOOD NEWSREEL SYNDICATE, INC.
1622 N. Gower St., Los Angeles, CA 90028. (323) 469-7307. FAX: (323) 469-8251. www.hollywoodnewsreel.com
PRESIDENT
Shirley Eggland Spalla

KALEIDOSCOPE FILMS GROUP
8447 Wilshire Blvd., Ste. 300, Beverly Hills, CA 90211. (323) 866-7000. FAX: (323) 866-7001.

LOBBY PREVIEWS
4262 Grand Haven Rd., Muskegon, MI 49441. (800) 861-7675, (231) 799-1133. FAX: (231) 799-1144.
www.pelicanproductions.com
PRESIDENT
Joe Edick

LUMENI PRODUCTIONS
1632 Flower St., Glendale, CA 91201-2357. (818) 956-2200. FAX: (818) 956-3298. www. lumeni.com
email: tvaldez@lumeni.com
PRESIDENT
Marshall "Tony" Valdez

METROLIGHT STUDIOS
5724 W. 3rd St., Ste. 400, Los Angeles, CA 90036. (323) 932-0400. FAX: (323) 932-8440.
PRESIDENT
Jim Kristoff

PIKE PRODUCTIONS, INC.
11 Clarke St., Box 300, Newport, RI 02840. (401) 846-8890. FAX: (401) 847-0070. email: info@pikefilmtrailers.com
OWNER
James A. Pike

PRESHOW PRODUCTIONS
15811 Wolf Creek, San Antonio, TX 78232. (210) 342-2141. FAX: (210) 490-5304. www.preshowproductions.com
e-mail: info@PreShowProductions.com
CONTACT
Doug Willming

QUARTERMOON PRODUCTIONS
228 Saugatuck Ave., Westport, CT 06880. (203) 247-5550.
www.quartermoon.com email: gb@quartermoon.com
CONTACT
Gary Balionis

SMITHGROUP COMMUNICATIONS, INC.
267 S.E. 33rd Ave., Portland, OR 97214. (503) 239-4215. FAX: (503) 239-1570. www.smithgrp.com
email: smithgrp@smithgrp.com
PRESIDENT
Phil Bevans

SSI ADVANCED POST SERVICES
7155 Santa Monica Blvd., Los Angeles, CA 90046. (323) 969-9333. FAX: (323) 850-7189. www.ssi-post.com
7165 Sunset Blvd., Los Angeles, CA 90046.
CONTACT
Stuart Bartell

LEONARD SOUTH PRODUCTIONS
11108 Huston St., N. Hollywood, CA 91601. (818) 760-8383. FAX: (818) 766-8301.
PRESIDENT
Leonard South

VIDE-U PRODUCTIONS
9976 W. Wanda Dr., Beverly Hills, CA 90210. (310) 276-5509. FAX: (310) 276-1183. www.acmetoys.com
email: acmetoys@hotmail.com
PRESIDENT
Bradly Fridman

WEST GLEN COMMUNICATIONS
1430 Broadway, 9th Flr., New York, NY 10018. (212) 921-2800. FAX: (212) 944-9055. www.westglen.com
email: info@westglen.com
PRESIDENT
Stanley Zeitlin

BUYING AND BOOKING SERVICES

ASHURST AGENCY
210 Turnberry Cir., Fayetteville, GA 30215. (770) 461-9851.
FAX: (770) 719-1565.
OWNER
Annette Ashurst

CALIFORNIA BOOKING
P.O. Box 11, Agoura, CA 91376. (818) 991-8593. FAX: (818)
991-8898.
OWNER
Carol Combs

CINEMA BOOKING SERVICE OF NEW ENGLAND
P.O. Box 920827, Needham, MA 02492. (781) 986-2122.
email: stadav@attbi.com
PRESIDENT
Stanton Davis

CINEMA FILM CONSULTANTS
1245 Hancock St., Ste. 11, Quincy, MA 02169. (617) 479-
0138. FAX: (617) 479-4287.
OWNER
Martin Zide

CINEMA SERVICE
8950 N. Central Expwy., #208, Dallas, TX 75231. (214) 692-
7555. FAX: (214) 692-7559. email: tim.csc@flexcomp.com
PRESIDENT
Tim Patton

COMPLETE BOOKING SERVICE
1819 Sabrina Ct., Charlotte, NC 28210. (704) 643-1522.
FAX: (704) 554-0570.
OWNER
Gary Vanderhorst

CONTINENTAL FILM SERVICE
17463 Meadow View Dr., Middletown, CA 95461. (707) 987-
8266. FAX: (707) 987-8270.
OWNERS
Richard Gambogi
Jeanette Gambogi

CO-OPERATIVE THEATRES OF OHIO, INC.
1413 Goldengate Blvd., Rm. 205, Mayfield Heights, OH
44124. (440) 461-2700. FAX: (440) 461-0659.
PRESIDENT
John Knepp
BOOKER
Frances Volan

EDDY G. ERICKSON BOOKING SERVICE
3405 Jubilee Trail, Dallas, TX 75229. (214) 352-3821.
OWNER
Eddy G. Erickson

FILM SERVICE THEATRE GROUP
Ivy Place II, 4700 South 900 East, Ste. 41-D, Salt Lake City,
UT 84117-4938. (801) 281-9694. FAX: (801) 281-9764.
PRESIDENT
David Sharp

FLORIN-CREATIVE FILM SERVICES
125 North Main St., Port Chester, NY 10573. (914) 937-
1603. FAX: (914) 937-8496. email: sflorin33@aol.com
PRESIDENT
Steven Florin

**FLOYD DAVIS BUYING & BOOKING THEATRE
SERVICES**
5809 Lakeside Ave., Ste. GF-1, Richmond, VA 23228. (804)
226-0772. FAX: (804) 226-1071.
CONTACT
Floyd Davis

GUYETT BOOKING SERVICE
P.O. Box 6346, Shawnee Mission, KS 66206. (913) 648-
5189.
FILM BUYER & BOOKER
Harold P. Guyett

INDEPENDENT FILM SERVICES
8900 State Line Rd., Ste. 405, Leawood, KS 66206. (913)
381-5555. FAX: (913) 381-5552.
email: indepfilm@earthlink.net
OWNER
Bradford Bills

INDEPENDENT THEATRE BOOKING
4523 Park Rd., #A-105, Charlotte, NC 28209. (704) 529-1200.
FAX: (704) 529-1201. email: dmovie@netzero.net
PRESIDENT & FILM BUYER
Steve Smith
MANAGER, OPERATIONS
Bryan Smith

LESSER THEATRE SERVICE
110 Greene St., Ste. 701, New York, NY 10012. (212) 925-
4776. FAX: (212) 941-6719.
email: ron@lessertheatreservice.com
PRESIDENT
Ron Lesser
FILM BUYER
Rob Lawinski

MJR THEATRE SERVICE, INC.
13691 West Eleven Mile Rd., Oak Park, MI 48237. (248)
548-8282. FAX: (248) 548-4706. www.mjrtheatres.com
PRESIDENT
Michael R. Mihalich

MARCUS THEATRES CORPORATION
100 E. Wisconsin Ave., Milwaukee, WI 53202. (414) 905-
1500. FAX: (414) 905-2872.
PRESIDENT
Bruce Olson

MESCOP, INC.
P.O. Box 303, Sussex, WI 53089. (262) 251-6808. FAX: (262)
251-9033.
PRESIDENT & BUYER
James Florence
BOOKER
Carol Brown

MORRIS PROJECTS, INC.
P.O. Box 3378, Sarasota, FL 34230. (941) 364-8662 x24.
FAX: (941) 364-8478. www.filmsociety.org
email: mail@filmsociety.org
MANAGING DIRECTOR
Sue Morris

MOTION PICTURE COUNSELING
301 Mt. Shasta Dr., San Rafael, CA 94903-1029. (415) 491-
1234.
OWNER
Ronald Litvin

NORRIS BOOKING AGENCY
P.O. Box 350052, Jacksonville, FL 32235. (904) 641-0019.
FAX: (904) 641-0019.
OWNER
Rex Norris

NORTHWEST DIVERSIFIED ENTERTAINMENT
348 West Olympic Pl., #101, Seattle, WA 98119. (206) 352-4004.
FAX: (206) 352-4008.
OWNER
Benjamin L. Hannah
FILM BUYERS
Victoria Hawker
Bruce Goodnow

PHILBIN CINEMA SERVICE, INC.
4700 S. 900 E., Ste. 9B, Holladay, UT 84117-4938. (801)
263-3725.
OWNER
Tom Philbin

R/C THEATRES BOOKING SERVICE
231 West Cherry Hill Ct., Box 1056, Reisterstown, MD
21136. (410) 526-4774. FAX: (410) 526-6871.
PRESIDENT & CEO
J. Wayne Anderson
PRESIDENT, FILM
Scott R. Cohen
V.P., FILM
Jan S. Anderson

ROXY MANAGEMENT COMPANY, INC.
2004 Main St., Northampton, PA 18067-5514. (610) 262-
7699. FAX: (610) 262-6459.
www.roxytheaternorthampton.com
PRESIDENT
Richard C. Wolfe
VICE PRESIDENT
Todd Lindenmoyer

THEATRE SERVICE NETWORK
4688 E. 29th Rd., Sandwich, IL 60548. (815) 786-6577. FAX:
(815) 786-6337.
PRESIDENT & FILM BUYER
Steve Felperin

EXECUTIVE V.P.
Albert "Buck" Kolkmeyer
FILM BUYERS
Debra Kovacs
Molly Wetzel
Sarah Felperin

TRI-STATE THEATRE SERVICE, INC.
Film Arts Building, 636 Northland Blvd., Cincinnati, OH
45240-3221. (513) 851-5700. FAX: (513) 851-5708.
email: tristatetheatre@cs.com
FILM BUYERS
Florence Groner
Steve Zeiser
Lori Mountcastle

UNITED THEATRE SERVICE
P.O. Box 13153, Mill Creek, WA 98082. (425) 743-6269. FAX:
(425) 743-2246.
email: happymoviequeen@yahoo.com
BOOKER
Dorothea Mayes

REGIONAL DISTRIBUTORS

ATLANTA

NEW LINE CINEMA DISTRIBUTION, INC.
4501 Circle 75 Parkway, Ste. A1270, Atlanta, GA 30339. (770) 952-0056. FAX: (770) 952-9152.
SENIOR V.P. & SOUTHEAST DIVISION MANAGER
Don Osley
V.P. & DISTRICT MANAGER
Maureen Dougherty

BOSTON

CINEMA BOOKING SERVICE OF NEW ENGLAND
P.O. Box 920827, Needham, MA 02492. (781) 986-2122.
email: stadav@attbi.com
PRESIDENT
Stanton Davis

UNIVERSAL PICTURES
95 Broadway, Boston, MA 02116. (617) 426-8760. FAX: (617) 426-5057.
BRANCH MANAGER, BOSTON/NEW HAVEN
Joan Corrado
BRANCH MANAGER, ALBANY/BUFFALO/CINCINNATI
Joe Crimi
SALES MANAGER
David O'Hara
EXHIBITOR RELATIONS
Peter Wright

WARNER BROS. DISTRIBUTING CORP.
35 Braintree Hill, Ste. 110, Braintree, MA 02184. (781) 848-2550. FAX: (781) 849-6270.
BRANCH MANAGER, BOSTON/CINCINNATI
Theresa Craven
SALES MANAGER, BOSTON/CINCINNATI
Margo Connell

ZIPPORAH FILMS
1 Richdale Ave. #4, Cambridge, MA 02140. (617) 576-3603.
FAX: (617) 864-8006. email: info@zipporah.com
DIRECTOR OF DISTRIBUTION
Karen Konicek

BUFFALO

FRONTIER AMUSEMENT
100 Broad St., Ste. 4, Tonawanda, NY 14150. (716) 695-2382.
FAX: (716) 695-2385.
PRESIDENT
Ike Ehrlichmann
VICE PRESIDENT
Mary Beth Lawton
OFFICE MANAGER
Sandra Zavatz

CHICAGO

INDEPENDENT FEATURE PROJECT
33 East Congress Pkwy., Rm. 505, Chicago, IL 60605. (312) 435-1825. FAX: (312) 435-1828. www.ifp.org
email: infoifpmw@aol.com
EXECUTIVE DIRECTOR
Rebekah Cowing

UNITED LEARNING
(Health, education and prevention)
1560 Sherman Ave., #100, Evanston, IL 60201. (800) 323-5448, (847) 328-6700. FAX: (847) 328-6706.
PRESIDENT
Ron Reed

DALLAS

CLARK/MCCRARY FILM
501 Little John Dr., Irving, TX 75061. (972) 313-1738.
BRANCH MANAGER
J.C. McCrary

NEW LINE CINEMA DISTRIBUTION, INC.
6060 N. Central Expwy., Ste. 602, Dallas, TX 75206. (214) 696-0755. FAX: (214) 360-9465.
SOUTHERN DIVISION
SENIOR V.P. & SOUTHERN DIVISION MANAGER
John Trickett
V.P. & DISTRICT MANAGER
Marjorie Stanfield
V.P. & DISTRICT MANAGER
Alan Christian

CENTRAL DIVISION
SENIOR V.P. & CENTRAL DIVISION MANAGER
Scott Huneryager
V.P. & DISTRICT MANAGER
Del Rosa
V.P. & DISTRICT MANAGER
Cai Schmidt

PARAMOUNT FILM DISTRIBUTING CORP.
12222 Merit Dr., Ste. 1700, Dallas, TX 75251. (972) 387-4400.
FAX: (972) 701-8359.
DIVISION V.P.
Royce Brimmage
BRANCH SALES MANAGER, ATLANTA/JACKSONVILLE
Jeff Greenspun
BRANCH SALES MANAGER, DALLAS/NEW ORLEANS/
OKLAHOMA CITY/MEMPHIS
Bob Mueller
BRANCH SALES MANAGER, CHARLOTTE/DES MOINES
Buddy Williams
BRANCH SALES MANAGER, KANSAS CITY/ST. LOUIS
Sue Puhl

SONY PICTURES RELEASING
1300 E. Lookout Dr., Ste. 340A & B, Richardson, TX 75082-4106. (972) 638-1300. FAX: (972) 638-1351, (972) 638-1323.
SOUTHERN DIVISION
SENIOR V.P.
Terry H. Tharpe
VICE PRESIDENT
Juli Mitchell
DISTRICT MANAGER
Gary DiFranco
DISTRICT MANAGER
Jeff Wayne
MIDWEST DIVISION
SENIOR V.P.
Sherm Wood
VICE PRESIDENT
Jim Weiss
DISTRICT MANAGER
Glen Abrams
DISTRICT MANAGER
Karen Calder

TWENTIETH CENTURY FOX FILM CORP.
(please contact the New York office at (212) 556-8600)

UNIVERSAL PICTURES
7502 Greenville Ave., Ste 200, Dallas, TX 75231. (214) 360-0022.
FAX: (214) 360-9003.
V.P./BRANCH MANAGER, DALLAS/OKLAHOMA CITY
Bruce Thompson
BRANCH MANAGER, ATLANTA/CHARLOTTE
James Dixon
BRANCH MANAGER, KANSAS CITY/MEMPHIS NEW
ORLEANS
Dana Poindexter
BRANCH MANAGER, JACKSONVILLE
Doug Coons
BRANCH MANAGER, CHICAGO/MILWAUKEE
Jack Botaro
BRANCH MANAGER, DETROIT/CLEVELAND
Gordon Ward
BRANCH MANAGER, DES MOINES/OMAHA/
INDIANAPOLIS/ST. LOUIS/MINNEAPOLIS
Jim Agliata
SALES MANAGER
Dorrine Kaczmarek
SALES MANAGER
Sharla Van Doorn
EXHIBITOR RELATIONS, FIELD REP. SOUTHERN REGION
Scott Rieckhoff
EXHIBITOR RELATIONS, FIELD REP. MIDWEST REGION
Stephanie Ricks

WARNER BROS. DISTRIBUTING CORP.
8144 Walnut Hill Ln., Ste. 500, Dallas, TX 75231. (214) 691-6101.
FAX: (214) 696-1154.
V.P., SOUTHERN DIVISION MANAGER
Danny Chinich, (214) 360-3043
SOUTHERN DISTRICT MANAGER & BRANCH MANAGER,
DALLAS/OKLAHOMA
Ron MacPhee, (214) 360-3047
BRANCH MANAGER, CHARLOTTE/MEMPHIS
Patsy Lundin, (214) 360-3025

BRANCH MANAGER, ATLANTA/NEW ORLEANS
Stacey Staples-Murphy, (214) 360-3039
BRANCH MANAGER, JACKSONVILLE
Lisa Runa, (214) 360-3014
SALES MANAGER, DALLAS/OKLAHOMA
Danielle Skinner, (214) 360-3028
EXHIBITOR SERVICES REPRESENTATIVE
Danny DiGiacomo, (214) 360-3065
SALES MANAGER/CHARLOTTE
Paula Tucker (214) 360-3028
DIRECTOR, ADMINISTRATION
Barbara Carter (214) 360-3033

LOS ANGELES

BUENA VISTA PICTURES DISTRIBUTION CO. INC.
3800 W. Alameda, 8th Flr., Burbank, CA 91521-6465. (818) 238-1300. FAX: (818) 972-9543.
V.P., WESTERN SALES OFFICE
Patrick Pade
SALES
Steve Getzler
SALES
Brian Hicks
SALES
Chris De Franco
SALES
Jeff Prill
SALES
Kerry Silver
SALES
Steve Schoenburg

CROWN INTERNATIONAL PICTURES, INC.
8701 Wilshire Blvd., Beverly Hills, CA 90211. (310) 657-6700.
DIRECTOR, ACQUISITIONS
Scott Schwimer

FINE LINE FEATURES
(see New Line Cinema Distribution, Inc.)

INDEPENDENT FEATURE PROJECT
8750 Wilshire Blvd., 2nd Flr., Beverly Hills, CA 90211. (310) 432-1200. FAX: (310) 432-1203. www.ifp.org
EXECUTIVE DIRECTOR
Dawn Hudson

LIONS GATE FILMS CORP.
4553 Glencoe Ave., Ste. 200, Marina Del Rey, CA 90292. (310) 314-2000.
REGIONAL SALES MANAGER
Joe Shimer
DIRECTOR, THEATRICAL DISTRIBUTION
Lori Bandazian
GENERAL SALES MANAGER
Jay Peckos

MGM DISTRIBUTION CO.
2500 Broadway St., Santa Monica, CA 90404. (310) 449-3844. FAX: (310) 449-3605.
SENIOR V.P., WESTERN SALES MANAGER
Mike Bisio
V.P., DIVISION MANAGER
Joe Griffin
DISTRICT MANAGER
Jonathan Petrovich
DISTRICT MANAGER
Pam Robb
DISTRICT MANAGER
Dax Mark

MIRAMAX FILMS
8439 Sunset Blvd., West Hollywood, CA 90069. (323) 822-4100.
PRESIDENT, MIRAMAX LOS ANGELES
Bob Osher
EXECUTIVE V.P., MEDIA RELATIONS & CORPORATE COMMUNICATIONS
Paul Pflug
EXECUTIVE V.P., HOME ENTERTAINMENT
Kevin Kasha

NEW LINE CINEMA DISTRIBUTION, INC.
116 N. Robertson Blvd., Los Angeles, CA 90048. (310) 854-5811. FAX: (310) 659-4635.
PRESIDENT, DISTRIBUTION
David Tuckerman
EXECUTIVE V.P. & GENERAL SALES MANAGER
Bob Kaplowitz
SENIOR V.P., EASTERN DIVISION
Jon Beal
SENIOR V.P., SOUTHERN DIVISION
John Trickett
SENIOR V.P., WESTERN DIVISION
Larry Levy
SENIOR V.P., CENTRAL DIVISION
Scott Huneryager
SENIOR V.P., SOUTHERN DIVISION
Don Osley
V.P., EXHIBITOR RELATIONS
Kristina Warner

PARAMOUNT PICTURES
15260 Ventura Blvd,. #1140, Sherman Oaks, CA 91403. (818) 380-7800.
V.P., WESTERN DIVISION
Bob Weiss
DISTRICT MANAGER, LOS ANGELES/DENVER
Bob Box
BRANCH SALES MANAGER/SAN FRANCISCO/SALT LAKE CITY
Jackie Rouleau
BRANCH SALES MANAGER, CHICAGO/MINNEAPOLIS
Sharon Jaeckel
BRANCH SALES MANAGER, SEATTLE/PORTLAND/MILWAUKEE
John Slama

SONY PICTURES RELEASING
(Western division)
10202 W. Washington Blvd., Culver City, CA 90232. (310) 244-4000.
VICE PRESIDENT
Adrian Smith
MANAGING DIRECTOR
Ross Merrin
DISTRICT MANAGER
Patricia Douherty
DISTRICT MANAGER
Kerri Lee

TOHO COMPANY, LTD.
2029 Century Park E., Ste. 1150, Los Angeles, CA 90067. (310) 277-1081. FAX: (310) 277-6351.

TROMA ENTERTAINMENT
733 Ninth Ave., New York, NY 10019. (212) 757-4555. www.troma.com

TWENTIETH CENTURY FOX FILM CORP.
23975 Park Sorrento Dr., Ste. 300, Calabasas, CA 91302. (818) 876-7200.
V.P., WESTERN DIVISION MANAGER
Bert Livingston
BRANCH MANAGER, LOS ANGELES
Cory Ballaban
SALES MANAGER, LOS ANGELES
Matt Garelik
BRANCH MANAGER, SAN FRANCISCO
Brett Resnick
BRANCH MANAGER, DENVER/SALT LAKE CITY
Gary Erickson
BRANCH MANAGER, SEATTLE/PORTLAND
Gavin Smith

UNIVERSAL PICTURES
100 Universal City Plaza, Bldg. 2160, Ste. 7N, Universal City, CA 91608. (818) 777-0002. FAX: (818) 866-3477.
BRANCH MANAGER, LOS ANGELES
Lynne Francis
BRANCH MANAGER, DENVER/SAN FRANCISCO
Robert Taylor
BRANCH MANAGER, PORTLAND/SEATTLE/SALT LAKE CITY
Marji McCormick
SALES MANAGER
Rose Crockett
EXHIBITOR RELATIONS, WESTERN REGION
Scott Carson
Cynthia Orellana

WARNER BROS. DISTRIBUTING CORP.
15821 Ventura Blvd., Ste. 575, Encino, CA 91436. (818) 784-7494. FAX: (818) 986-7559.
V.P., MIDWESTERN DIVISION MANAGER & BRANCH MANAGER, CHICAGO/MILWAUKEE
Allison Fields, (818) 379-1840
V.P., WESTERN DIVISION MANAGER
Scott Forman, (818) 379-1810
DIRECTOR, WESTERN & MIDWESTERN DIVISION ADMINISTRATION
Kim Dimarco, (818) 379-1860
BRANCH MANAGER, SEATTLE/PORTLAND/MINNEAPOLIS
Ralph Albi, (818) 379-1830
BRANCH MANAGER, DENVER/SALT LAKE CITY/ARIZONA
Jennifer Amaya, (818) 379-1841
BRANCH MANAGER, SAN FRANCISCO
Kevin Strick, (818) 379-1871
BRANCH MANAGER, KANSAS CITY/ST. LOUIS/DES MOINES/OMAHA/INDIANAPOLIS
Darla Pierce, (818) 379-1821
DISTRICT MANAGER, WESTERN DIVISION
Michael Viane, (818) 379-1851
SALES MANAGER, LOS ANGELES
Shaun Barber, (818) 379-1835
SALES MANAGER, CLASSICS DIVISION
Linda Evans-Smith, (818) 379-1814
BRANCH MANAGER, LOS ANGELES
Gigi Lestak, (818) 379-1811
EXHIBITOR SERVICES REPRESENTATIVE
William Smith, (818) 379-1813

MIAMI

CINEVISTA, INC./CINEVISTA VIDEO
2044 Prairie Ave., Miami Beach, FL 33139. (305) 532-3400.
FAX: (305) 532-0047. www.cinevistavideo.com
PRESIDENT/CEO
Rene Fuentes-Chao
V.P., MARKETING
Harold Zimmerman
V.P., SALES
Susan Morin

INDEPENDENT FEATURE PROJECT
210 2nd St., Miami, FL 33139. (305) 538-8242.
email: miami@ifp.org
EXECUTIVE DIRECTOR
Joanne Butcher

NEW YORK

BLOSSOM PICTURES
1414 Ave. of the Americas, New York, NY 10019. (212) 486-8880.
PRESIDENT
Jerry Gruenberg

BUENA VISTA PICTURES DISTRIBUTION
(Eastern Division)
1500 Broadway, New York, NY 10019. (212) 536-6400. FAX:
(212) 536-6409.
V.P., SALES, NEW YORK
Phil Fortune
SENIOR MARKETING COORDINATOR
Michael Ricciardi
DIRECTOR, SALES
Leo Fisch
DIRECTOR, SALES
Dennis Meagher
DIRECTOR, SALES
John Molson
SALES MANAGER
Carol Toppin
SAELS MANAGER
Rosemarie Salvo
SALES REPRESENTATIVE
Darrell Smith

CINEMA GUILD
130 Madison Ave., 2nd Flr., New York, NY 10016. (212) 685-6242. email: info@cinemaguild.com

CORINTH FILMS
32 Gansevoort St., New York, NY 10014. (212) 463-0305.

FIRST RUN FEATURES
153 Waverly Place, New York, NY 10014. (212) 243-0600. FAX:
(212) 989-7649. www.firstrunfeatures.com

FOCUS FEATURES
65 Bleecker, 2nd Flr., New York, NY 10012. (212) 539-4000.
FAX: (212) 539-4099.

FOX SEARCHLIGHT PICTURES
1211 6th Ave., 16th Flr., New York, NY 10036. (212) 556-8696.
FAX: (212) 556-8248.
CONTACT
Anna Osso

INDEPENDENT FEATURE PROJECT
104 W. 29th St., 12th Flr., New York, NY 10001. (212) 465-8200. FAX: (212) 465-8525. www.ifp.org
EXECUTIVE DIRECTOR
Michelle Byrd
MARKETING COORDINATOR
Amanda Doss

JACOBS ENTERTAINMENT
26 Alandale Dr., Rye, NY 10580. (914) 925-0099. FAX: (914)
925-9737.
PRESIDENT
Jeffrey Jacobs

KINO INTERNATIONAL
333 W. 39th St., Ste. 503, New York, NY 10018. (800) 562-3330,
(212) 629-6880. FAX: (212) 714-0871. www.kino.com
PRESIDENT
Donald Krim

MGM DISTRIBUTION CO.
1350 Ave. of the Americas, New York, NY 10019-4870. (212)
708-0300. FAX: (212) 708-0337.
SENIOR V.P. & EASTERN SALES MANAGER
William Lewis
V.P. & DIVISION MANAGER
Greg Simi
V.P., EAST COAST PUBLICITY
Debra Nathan

DISTRICT MANAGER
Janice Calamari
DISTRICT MANAGER
Dennis Glenn
DISTRICT MANAGER
John Shahinian
DISTRICT MANAGER
Lisa DiMartino

MIRAMAX FILMS
375 Greenwich St., New York, NY 10013. (212) 941-3800. FAX:
(212) 941-3949.

MUSEUM OF MODERN ART FILM LIBRARY
11 W. 53rd St., New York, NY 10019. (212) 708-9433.

NEW LINE CINEMA
888 Seventh Ave,. New York, NY 10106. (212) 649-4890. FAX:
(212) 956-1944.
SENIOR V.P. & EASTERN DIVISION MANAGER, DISTRIBUTION
Jonathan Beal
V.P. & DISTRICT MANAGER, NY/PHILADELPHIA/BUFFALO
Richard Bonanno
V.P. & DISTRICT MANAGER, BOSTON/NEW HAMPSHIRE/
PITTSBURGH/D.C.
Mary Navarra

NEW YORKER FILMS
16 W. 61st St., 11th Flr., New York, NY 10023. (212) 645-4600.
FAX: (212) 645-3030. www.newyorkerfilms.com
email: info@newyorkerfilms.com

PARAMOUNT PICTURES
1633 Broadway, New York, NY 10019. (212) 654-7000.
V.P., MOTION PICTURE DISTRIBUTION
Jim Orr
DISTRICT MANAGER, BOSTON/NEW HAVEN/PITTSBURGH
Mike Share
DISTRICT MANAGER, NEW YORK/ALBANY
Pam Araujo
BRANCH SALES MANAGER, BUFFALO/CLEVELAND
INDIANAPOLIS
Steve Toback
BRANCH SALES MANAGER, PHILADELPHIA/WASHINGTON
Tom Molen
BRANCH SALES MANAGER, DETROIT/CINCINNATI
Bruce Placke

SONY PICTURES RELEASING
555 Madison Ave., 9th Flr., New York, NY 10022. (212) 833-7623. FAX: (212) 833-6495.
SENIOR V.P.
Jim Amos
VICE PRESIDENT
John Spinello
DISTRICT MANAGER
Adam Bergerman
DISTRICT MANAGER
Janet Murray

TOHO INTERNATIONAL
1501 Broadway, Ste. 2005, New York, NY 10036. (212) 391-9058.

TWENTIETH CENTURY FOX FILM CORP.
1211 Ave. of the Americas, 16th Flr., New York, NY 10036.
(212) 556-8600. FAX: (212) 556-8606.
V.P. & ATLANTIC DIVISION MANAGER
Ron Polon
BRANCH MANAGER, NEW YORK
Lawrence Piller
BRANCH MANAGER, BUFFALO/ALBANY
Shaunda Lumpkin Sutton
BRANCH MANAGER, PHILADELPHIA/PITTSBURGH
Joe Reid
V.P. & EASTERN DIVISION MANAGER
Henri Frankfurther
BRANCH MANAGER, BOSTON/NEW HAVEN
Dan Eckes
BRANCH MANAGER, CINCINNATI/CLEVELAND
Ralph Farnham
BRANCH MANAGER, WASHINGTON D.C.
Jackie Santiago
BRANCH MANAGER, DETROIT/MINNEAPOLIS/OMAHA
Dave Hansen
BRANCH MANAGER, CHICAGO/MILWAUKEE/DES MOINES
Edward Handler

UNIVERSAL PICTURES
825 8th Ave., 30th Flr., New York, NY 10019. (212) 445-3819.
FAX: (212) 445-3809.
V.P., NY METROPOLITAN MANAGER
Gary Rocco
BRANCH MANAGER, WASHINGTON D.C.
Steve Turner

BRANCH MANAGER, PHILADELPHIA/PITTSBURGH
Charles Sampayo
SALES MANAGER
Richard Tabin
EXHIBITOR RELATIONS, FIELD REP. EASTERN REGION
Valerie Raneri
EXHIBITOR RELATIONS, FIELD REP. EASTERN REGION
Paul Francis

USA FILMS
(See Focus Features)

WARNER BROS.
1325 Ave. of the Americas, 29th Flr., New York, NY 10019.
(212) 636-5100. FAX: (212) 636-5237.
V.P. & EASTERN DIVISION MANAGER
Frank Carrol, (212) 636-5220
EASTERN DISTRICT MANAGER
Andy Silverman, (212) 636-5296
METROPOLITAN DISTRICT & NY BRANCH MANAGER
Charles Barcellona, (212) 636-5203
BRANCH MANAGER, CLEVELAND/BUFFALO/ALBANY/
PITTSBURGH
Bruce Blatt, (212) 636-5252
BRANCH MANAGER, WASHINGTON DC
Roberta Peterson, (212) 636-5240
BRANCH MANAGER, PHILADELPHIA/DETROIT
Andy Strulson, (212) 636-5222
SALES MANAGER, NEW YORK
Millie Gautier, (212) 636-5211

PUERTO RICO

COLUMBIA TRISTAR FILMS OF PUERTO RICO
Metro Square Bldg., Ste. G-2, Metro Office Park, Guaynabo,
PR 00968. (787) 793-1500. FAX: (787) 793-2859.
www.columbiapr.com
SENIOR V.P., SOUTHERN DIVISION
Terry Tharpe
MARKETING MANAGER
Annette Monserrate

PARAMOUNT PICTURES
954 Ponce de Leon Ave,. Ste 204-B, San Juan, PR 00907.
(787) 721-2360. FAX: (787) 721-1460.
BRANCH MANAGER
Jack DeCrescente
BOOKER
Carmen Daisy

TWENTIETH CENTURY FOX OF PUERTO RICO, INC.
P.O. Box 19406, Fernandez Juncos Station, San Juan, PR
00910. (787) 723-5081. FAX: (787) 722-8047.
GENERAL MANAGER
Luis Rodriguez

UNIVERSAL PICTURES
P.O. Box 11308, San Juan, Puerto Rico 00910.(787) 725-1353,
(787) 620-5377. FAX: (787) 620-5390.
BRANCH MANAGER
Wilfred Morneau

INTERNATIONAL THEATRE EQUIPMENT ASSOCIATION
770 Broadway, 5th Flr., New York, NY 10003-9595. (646) 654-7680. FAX: (646) 654-7694. www.itea.com
PRESIDENT
Dwight Lindsey
EXECUTIVE DIRECTOR
Robert H. Sunshine
VICE PRESIDENT
Barry Ferrell
TREASURER
Jerry Van de Rydt

LARGE FORMAT CINEMA ASSOCIATION
28241 Crown Valley Pkwy., PMB 401, Laguna Niguel, CA 92677. (949) 831-1142. FAX: (949) 831-4948. www.lfca.org
PRESIDENT
Robert Dennis (818) 260-3841
SECRETARY
Mary Anne Porter (805) 241-5821
EXECUTIVE DIRECTOR
Jean Moore (949) 831-1142
BOARD MEMBERS
Andrew Gellis, Charlotte Huggins, Charlotte Brohi, Christopher Palmer, Christopher Reyna, Chevy Humphrey, David Keighley, Dennis Earl Moore, Jonathan Barker, Mary Kaye Kennedy, Olivier Brunet, Paul Holliman, Rick Gordon, Steve Thorburn.

NATIONAL ASSOCIATION OF CONCESSIONAIRES
35 E. Wacker Dr., Ste. 1816, Chicago, IL 60601. (312) 236-3858. FAX: (312) 236-7809. www.naconline.org
EXECUTIVE DIRECTOR
Charles A. Winans
CHAIRMAN
Gary Horvath, CCM
PRESIDENT
Chris Bigelow
PRESIDENT ELECT
Larry Etter
DIRECTOR, COMMUNICATIONS
Susan Cross
VICE PRESIDENTS
Bruce Proctor, ECM
Wally Helton, ECM
Maria Angles
DIRECTORS, DIVERSIFIED CONCESSION OPERATORS
Scott Baumgartner, CCM
Douglas Drewes
Michael Thompson
Chris Verros
DIRECTOR, THEATRE CONCESSION OPERATORS
Gary Thyer
DIRECTOR, EQUIPMENT MANUFACTURERS
Ken Lapponese
DIRECTOR, SUPPLIERS
Ralph Ferber
DIRECTORS-AT-LARGE
Nick Biello, Eddie Cheyfitz, Randy Collins, ECM, Terry Conlon, ECM, Rob Del Moro, Randy Martin, Krista Schulte, Robert Scribner.
REGIONAL VICE PRESIDENTS
Brian Biehn, Jim Bletner, Lezlie Chesler, ACE, John Evans, Jr., Ron Krueger II, Frank Liberto, Martin Olesen, Robert Perkins, Damian Piza, CCM, Alvin Shandro, Bill Wells, ACE, Gina Troutman DiSanto, CCM, David White.
LIFETIME HONORARY MEMBERS, BOARD OF DIRECTORS
Larry Blumenthal, Sydney Spiegel, Van Myers.

NATIONAL ASSOCIATION OF THEATRE OWNERS, INC.
4605 Lankershim Blvd., Ste. 340, N. Hollywood, CA 91602. (818) 506-1778. FAX: (818) 506-0269. www.natoonline.org
PRESIDENT
John Fithian
CHAIRMAN
Stephen Marcus
TREASURER
William Stembler
SECRETARY
James Murray
VICE PRESIDENT & EXECUTIVE DIRECTOR
Mary Ann Grasso
EXECUTIVE COMMITTEE
J. Wayne Anderson (Reisterstown, MD), Michael Campbell (Knoxville, TN), Jerome Forman (Los Angeles, CA), Kurt Hall (Englewood, CO), Philip Harris, III (Oakland, CA), Stephen Marcus (Milwaukee, WI), Lee Roy Mitchell (Plano, TX), Terence Moriarty (Boston, MA), James Murray, (Dedham, MA), Michael Patrick, (Columbus, GA), Shari Redstone (Dedham, MA), Travis Reid (New York, NY), William Stembler (Atlanta, GA), H. Aubrey Stone, Jr. (Charlotte, NC), Joseph Syufy (San Rafael, CA).
BOARD OF DIRECTORS
Bill Adamany, Sr. (Prairie du Chien, WI), J. Wayne Anderson (Reisterstown, MD), Byron Berkley (Kilgore, TX), Joost Bert (Brusssels, Belgium), Myron N. Blank (Des Moines, IA), Michael Bowers (Scottsdale, AZ), Matt Brandt (N. Hollywood, CA), H. Donald Busch (Philadelphia, PA), Bill Campbell (Sheridon, MD), Michael Campbell (Knoxville, TN), Michael Cavalier (Plano, TX), Hal Cleveland (Boston, MA), Scott Cohen (Reisterstown, MD), Bruce Corwin (Los Angeles, CA), David Corwin (Los Angeles, CA), Daniel Crown (New York, NY), Dennis Daniels (Reisterstown, MD), Nora Dashwood (Los Angeles, CA), Rob Del Moro (Knoxville, TN), Gregory Dunn (Knoxville, TN), Terrell Falk (Plano, TX), Jerome Forman (Los Angeles, CA), Richard Fox (Boca Raton, FL), A. Alan Friedberg (Boston, MA), Jack Fuller, Jr. (Columbia, SC), Darrell Gabel (Lander, WY), Robert Goodrich (Grand Rapids, MI), Jerome Gordon (Hampton, VA), Malcolm Green (Boston, MA), Kurt Hall, (Englewood, CO), Larry Hanson (Northbrook, IL), Dan Harkins (Scottsdale, AZ), Philip Harris, III, (Oakland, CA), Don Harton (Plano, TX), Hamid Hashemi (Ft. Lauderdale, FL), Richard Herring (Bent Mountain, VA), Bryan Jeffries (Springfield, IL), Willis Johnson (Downers Grove, IL), Bess Joyner (Warsaw, IN), Allen Karp (Toronto, Canada), Beth Kerasotes (Springfield, IL), Dean Kerasotes (Chicago, IL), Tony Kerasotes (Chicago, IL), Jeff Kiser (Marrietta, GA), Dan Klusmann (Bozeman, MT), Ronald Krueger, I (St. Louis, MO), Ronald Krueger, II (St. Louis, MO), George Lefont (Atlanta, GA), John Loeks Jr. (Grand Rapids, MI), Jeff Logan (Mitchell, SD), Jerome Magner (Dedham, MA), George Mann (Oakland, CA), Stephen Marcus (Milwaukee, WI), William McMannis (Grand Rapids, MI), Lee Roy Mitchell (Plano, TX), Terence Moriarty (Boston, MA), James Murray (Dedham, MA), R.A. "Skeet" Noret (Lubbock, TX), Michael Norris (New York, NY), Bruce J. Olson (Milwaukee, WI), Mark O'Meara (Fairfax, VA), Millard Ochs (Burbank, CA), Richard Orear (Kansas City, MO), Judson Parker (Boston, MA), Michael Patrick (Columbus, GA), Joe Peixoto (Los Angeles, CA), Nikki Pappas Perakos (Orange, CT), Sperie Perakos (New Britain, CT), Ayron Pickerill (Polson, MT), Howard Pickerill (Polson, MT), Neal Pinsker (Englewood, CO), Shari Redstone (New York, NY), Sumner Redstone (Dedham, MA), Travis Reid (New York, NY), Ron Reid (Knoxville, TN), Michael Rembusch (Franklin, IN), Joel Resnick (Plano, TX), Tony Rhead (Columbus, GA), Paul Richardson (Los Angeles, CA), Paul Rogers (Marshfield, WI), A. Bruce Sanborn (Newport Beach, CA), David Shesgreen (San Rafael, CA), Raymond "Randy" Smith (Knoxville, TN), T. G. Soloman (New Orleans, LA), William Stembler (St. Simon Island, GA), Alan Stock (Plano, TX), Herman Stone, Sr. (Charlotte, NC), H. Aubrey Stone, Jr. (St. Simons Island, GA), Joseph Syufy (San Rafael, CA), Raymond Syufy (San Rafael, CA), Rand Thornsley (Anchorage, AK), William Towey (Dedham, MA), Fred Van Noy (Columbus, GA), Peter Walch (Switzerland), Tim Warner (Plano, TX), Richard Westerling (Knoxville, TN), Roy White (Naples, FL), Russell Wintner (Pepper Pike, OH), Tim Wood (Portland, OR).

ARIZONA THEATRE OWNERS ASSOCIATION
4811 E. Grant Rd., #150, Tucson, AZ 85712. (520) 326-2929. FAX: (520) 326-2691.
PRESIDENT
Kent Edwards
CHAIRMAN
Brian Deveny

NATO OF CALIFORNIA/NEVADA
116 N. Robertson Blvd., Ste. 708, Los Angeles, CA 90048. (310) 652-1093. FAX: (310) 657-4758.
PRESIDENT & CEO
Milton Moritz
CHAIRMAN
Philip Harris

NATO OF COLORADO AND WYOMING
P.O. Box C, Sheriddan, WY 82801. (307) 672-5797. FAX: (603) 388-1546.
PRESIDENT
Bill Campbell
CHAIRMAN
Darrell Gabel

CONNECTICUT ASSOCIATION OF THEATRE OWNERS
3585 Hempstead Trnpk., Levittown, NY 11756. (516) 731-5521. FAX: (516) 731-5413.
PRESIDENT
Ted Maliglowka
VICE PRESIDENT
Nikki P. Perakos

NATO OF FLORIDA
P.O. Box 2076, Deland, FL 32721-2076. (386) 736-6830. FAX: (386) 738-2596.
PRESIDENT
Lee Sparks
VICE PRESIDENT
John Wray

NATO OF GEORGIA
500 Sea Island Rd., St. Simons, GA 31522. (912) 634-5192. FAX: (912) 634-5195.
PRESIDENT
Joe Paletta
VICE PRESIDENTS
John Stembler, Jr.
Norm Shindler
Kip Smiley, Jr.

NATO OF IDAHO
P.O. Box 370, Grangeville, ID 83530. (208) 983-1370.
PRESIDENT
Al Wagner
VICE PRESIDENT
Jeff Bowen
SECRETARY/TREASURER
Karen Cornwell

NATO OF ILLINOIS
603 Rogers St., Downers Grove, IL 60515. (630) 968-1600, x 119. FAX: (630) 968-1626.
PRESIDENT
Willis Johnson
VICE PRESIDENT
Tony Kerasotes

THEATRE OWNERS OF INDIANA
6919 E. 10th St., Ste. B-5, Indianapolis, IN 46219-4811. (317) 357-3660. FAX: (317) 357-3379.
PRESIDENT
David O. Wright
VICE PRESIDENT
Allen Strahl

UMPA (UNITED MOTION PICTURE ASSOCIATION) (MISSOURI & KANSAS)
8900 State Line Rd., Ste. 405, Leawood, KS 66206. (913) 381-5555. FAX: (913) 381-5552.
PRESIDENT
Darryl Smith
VICE PRESIDENT
Richard Durwood

NATO OF MICHIGAN
121 W. Allegan, Lansing, MI 48933. (517) 482-9806. FAX: (517) 482-9934.
PRESIDENT
Nancy Hagan
VICE PRESIDENT
Corey Jacobson

MID-ATLANTIC NATO
(Maryland, Virginia, Washington, D.C.)
P.O. Box 1830, Hampton, VA 23669-1830. (757) 722-5275. FAX: (757) 722-5276.
CHAIRMAN
Ted Pedas
SECRETARY & EXECUTIVE DIRECTOR
Jerome Gordon

MID-STATES NATO
(Kentucky, Ohio, Tennessee, West Virginia)
3982 Powell Rd., #202, Powell, OH 43065. (740) 881-5541. FAX: (740) 881-5390.
EXECUTIVE DIRECTOR
Belinda Judson

MONTANA ASSOCIATION OF THEATRE OWNERS
P.O. Box 999, Polson, MT 59860. (406) 883-5603. FAX: (406) 883-5639.
PRESIDENT
Gary Dupuis
VICE PRESIDENT
Bill Emerson

THEATRE OWNERS OF NEW ENGLAND
One Exeter Plaza, 6th Flr., Boston, MA 02116. (617) 424-8663. FAX: (617) 262-0707.
PRESIDENT
James J. Murray
VICE PRESIDENT
William J. Hanney

NATO OF NEW JERSEY
250 E. Broad St., Westfield, NJ 07090. (908) 232-7100. FAX: (908) 232-7340.
PRESIDENT/SECRETARY
Jesse Y. Sayegh
1ST VICE PRESIDENT & TREASURER
Robert Piechota

NATO OF NEW YORK STATE
770 Broadway, 5th Flr., New York, NY 10003. (646) 654-7680. FAX: (646) 654-7694.
PRESIDENT
Michael Norris
VICE PRESIDENT
Dan Vieira

NORTH CENTRAL STATES NATO
(Minnesota, N. Dakota, S. Dakota, Wisconsin)
209 N. Lawler St., Mitchell, SD 57301. (605) 996-9022. FAX: (605) 996-9241.
PRESIDENT
Jeff Logan
VICE PRESIDENT
Connie Hawley

THEATRE OWNERS OF NORTH & SOUTH CAROLINA
4523 Park Rd., #A-105, Charlotte, NC 28209. (704) 529-1200. FAX: (704) 529-1201.
PRESIDENT
Steve Smith
VICE PRESIDENT & TREASURER
Richard Johnson

NATO OF PENNSYLVANIA
128 Chestnut St., Ste. 303, Philadelphia, PA 19106. (215) 892-0683. FAX: (856) 665-0516.
PRESIDENT
H. Donald Busch
SECRETARY
Gina DiSanto

SOUTH CENTRAL STATES NATO
(Arkansas, Louisiana, Oklahoma, Texas)
P.O. Box 200815, Arlington, TX 76006-0815. (817) 226-1690. FAX: (817) 274-3550.
EXECUTIVE DIRECTOR
Rein Rabakukk

ROCKY MOUNTAIN NATO
(Colorado, Idaho, Montana, Utah, Wyoming)
3 Sunshine Dr., Lander, WY 82520. (307) 332-9117. FAX: (307) 332-6200.
DIRECTORS
Robynn Gabel
Darrell Gabel

NATO OF WISCONSIN & UPPER MICHIGAN
P.O. Box 146, Sussex, WI 53089. (262) 532-0017. FAX: (262) 532-0021.
PRESIDENT
Paul J. Rogers
VICE PRESIDENT
Bruce Olson

PROFESSIONAL AND GOVERNMENT ORGANIZATIONS

■

Motion Picture Organizations

ACADEMY OF MOTION PICTURE ARTS AND SCIENCES
(Organized June, 1927. Membership: approx. 6,000.)
8949 Wilshire Blvd., Beverly Hills, CA 90211-1972. (310) 247-3000. FAX: (310) 859-9351, (310) 859-9619. Library: 333 S. La Cienega Blvd., Beverly Hills, CA 90211. (310) 247-3020.
PRESIDENT
Frank Pierson
FIRST VICE PRESIDENT
Sid Ganis
VICE PRESIDENT
Gilbert Cates
VICE PRESIDENT
Cheryl Boone Isaacs
TREASURER
Kathy Bates
SECRETARY
Don Rogers
EXECUTIVE DIRECTOR
Bruce Davis

BOARD OF DIRECTORS
Dede Allen, Michael Apted, Kathy Bates, Ed Begley, Jr., Carl A. Bell, Charles Bernstein, Jon Bloom, Bruce Broughton, Donn Cambern, Gilbert Cates, Caleb Deschanel, Arthur Dong, Richard Edlund, Jonathan Erland, June Foray, Sid Ganis, Larry Gordon, Douglas Greenfield, Arthur Hamilton, Tom Hanks, Curtis Hanson, J. Paul Huntsman, Cheryl Boone Isaacs, Mark Johnson, Richard Kahn, Fay Kanin, Hal Kanter, Kathleen Kennedy, Jeffrey Kurland, Michael Mann, Marvin March, Bill Mechanic, Freida Lee Mock, Jeannine Oppewall, Frank R. Pierson, Robert Rehme, Donald C. Rogers, Owen Roizman, Tom Rolf, Tom Sherak, Bill Taylor, Haskell Wexler.

ALLIANCE OF MOTION PICTURE AND TELEVISION PRODUCERS
(Membership: Major studios, independent production companies and film processing laboratories.)
15503 Ventura Blvd., Encino, CA 91436-3140. (818) 995-3600. FAX: (818) 382-1798. www.mpaa.org
PRESIDENT
J. Nicholas Counter III
S.V.P., LEGAL & BUSINESS AFFAIRS
Carol A. Lombardini
V.P., LEGAL AFFAIRS
Helayne Antler

AMERICAN CINEMATHEQUE
(Organized 1981. Celebrates the moving picture in all its forms through public film and video exhibition.)
1800 N. Highland Ave., Ste. 717, Hollywood, CA 90028. (323) 461-2020. FAX: (323) 461-9737. Program Information: (323) 466-FILM. www.americancinematheque.com
email: info@americancinematheque.com
CO-CHAIRMEN
Peter J. Dekom
Mike Medavoy
PRESIDENT
Henry Shields, Jr.
EXECUTIVE DIRECTOR
Barbara Zicka Smith
CHAIRMAN EMERITUS
Sydney Pollack
BOARD OF DIRECTORS
Peter Bart, Bill Block, Charles Champlin, Sanford Climan, Wendi L. Doyle, Phil Dusenberry, John S. Farrand, Rick Finkelstein, David Geffen, Jerry Giaquinta, Brian Grazer, Godfrey Isaac, Anne Keshen, Kenneth Kleinberg, Robert Mayson, Chris McGurk, Peter Morton, George E. Moss, Rick Nicita, Sanford P. Paris, Norman J. Pattiz, Elisabeth Pollon, Arnold Rifkin, Lloyd E. Rigler, James G. Robinson, Sigurjon "Joni" Sighvatsson, Steve Tisch, Stephen Unger, J. Kendall Whiting, Saul Zaentz.

THE AMERICAN FILM INSTITUTE
(A national trust dedicated to advancing and preserving the art of the moving image.)
2021 N. Western Ave., P.O. Box 27999, Los Angeles, CA 90027. (323) 856-7600. FAX: (323) 467-4578.
The John F. Kennedy Center for the Performing Arts, Washington, DC. 20566. (202) 416-7815. FAX: (202) 659-1970. www.afi.com
BOARD OF TRUSTEES CHAIR
Howard Stringer
BOARD OF DIRECTORS CHAIRS
Jon Avnet
John F. Cooke

VICE-CHAIRMEN
Mark Conton
Robert A. Daly
Michael Nesmith
Tom Pollock
HONORARY TRUSTEE
Tom Hanks

BOARD MEMBERS
Merv Adelson, Chris Albrecht, Debbie Allen, Gilbert Amelio, John Antioco, Joan Barton, Bob Bennett, Jeff Berg, Allen J. Bernstein, James H. Billington, Richard Brandt, John Calley, Peter Chernin, Henry Cisneros, Martha Coolidge, Suzanne de Passe, John DiBiaggio, Barry Diller, Bill Duke, Jean Picker Firstenberg, Michael Forman, Richard Frank, Stephen O. Frankfurt, Charles W. Fries, Melissa Gilbert, Ina Ginsburg, David Greenblatt, Philip Guarascio, John S. Hendricks, Lawrence Herbert, Marshall Herskovitz, Dawn Hudson, Robert Iger, Gene F. Jankowski, Robert L. Johnson, Fay Kanin, Kathleen Kennedy, James V. Kimsey, Patricia Kingsley, Barbara Kopple, Sherry Lansing, Warren N. Lieberfarb, Suzanne Lloyd, Brad Martin, Marsha Mason, Barry M. Meyer, Ron Meyer, Leslie Moonves, Janet H. Murray, Mace Neufeld, Rick Nicita, Daniel Petrie, Frederick S. Pierce, Tony Ponturo, Robert G. Rehme, Victoria Riskin, Kelly A. Rose, Jill Sackler, Scott Sassa, Robert Shaye, Stacey Snider, Vivian Sobchack, Steven Spielberg, Robert B. Sturm, Jack Valenti, Todd R. Wagner, John E. Warnock, James A. Wiatt, David L. Wolper, Robert C. Wright, Alex Yemenidjian, Bud Yorkin, Ed Zwick.

AMERICAN FILM MARKETING ASSOCIATION (AFMA)
(Organized 1980. Membership: 170 companies engaged in the production and sale of independently produced films and TV programs to the international market. Produces the American Film Market every February.)
10850 Wilshire Blvd., 9th Flr., Los Angeles, CA 90024. (310) 446-1000. FAX: (310) 446-1600.
www.afma.com
email: info@afma.com
CHAIRMAN
Michael Ryan
VICE CHAIRMAN, SECRETARY
Steve Bickel
CHAIRMAN, AFEA
Barbara Mudge
GENERAL VICE CHAIRMAN, NON CA
Nicole Mackey
VICE CHAIRMAN, FINANCE
Howard Kaplan
GENERAL VICE CHAIRMAN
Robert Meyers
GENERAL VICE CHAIRMAN
Rick Sands

BOARD OF DIRECTORS
Wouter Barendrecht (Fortissimo Film Sales), Patrick Binet (TF 1 International), Ehud Bleiberg (Dream Entertainment), Nicolas Chartier (Arclight Films PTY. LTD), Kirk D'Amico (Myriad Pictures), Robert Hayward (Summit Entertainment), Paul Hertzberg (Cinetel Films, Inc.) Lewis Horwitz (The Lewis Horwitz Organization) Lloyd Kaufman (Troma Entertainment, Inc.), David Linde (Focus Features), Mark Lindsay (Miramax International), Robert Little (Overseas Filmgroup/First Look Media), Nick Meyer (Lions Gate Films International), Charlotte Mickie (Alliance Atlantis Communications), Kathy Morgan (Kathy Morgan International (KMI), Antonia Nava Filmax International, Andrew Stevens (Trademark Entertainment, Inc.), Alison Thompson (Pathe International), Michael Weiser (Modern Entertainment), Lisa Wilson (Splendid Pictures).

AMERICAN HUMANE ASSOCIATION
(Organized 1877. Liaison with the television and motion picture industry as supervisors of animal action in television and motion picture production.)
15366 Dickens St., Sherman Oaks, CA 91403. (818) 501-0123. FAX: (818) 501-8725. Hotline: (800) 677-3420.
Film and Television Unit, 15366 Dickens St., Sherman Oaks, CA 91403.
National Headquarters: 63 Inverness Dr. E., Englewood, CO 80112. (800) 227-4645, (303) 792-9900. FAX: (303) 792-5333.
www.ahafilm.org
email: ahawest@aol.com
NATIONAL PRESIDENT
Sharon O'Hara
DIRECTOR
Karen Rosa

AMERICAN SOCIETY OF COMPOSERS, AUTHORS AND PUBLISHERS (ASCAP)

(Organized February 13, 1914. Membership: 120,000 Songwriters and Publishers)
New York: One Lincoln Plaza, New York, NY 10023. (212) 621-6000. FAX: (212) 724-9064. www.ascap.com
Los Angeles: 7920 Sunset Blvd., 3rd Flr., Los Angeles, CA 90046. (323) 883-1000. FAX: (323) 883-1049.
Nashville: Two Music Square W., Nashville, TN 37203. (615) 742-5000. FAX: (615) 742-5020.
Atlanta: PMB 400, 541 Tenth St. N.W., Atlanta, GA 30318-5713. (404) 351-1224. FAX: (404) 351-1252.
Chicago: 1608 N. Milwaukee, Ste. 1007, Chicago, IL 60647. (773) 394-4286. FAX: (773) 394-5639.
Miami: 420 Lincoln Rd., Ste. 385, Miami Beach, FL 33139. (305) 673-3446. FAX: (305) 673-2446.
London: 8 Cork St., London, W1X 1PB, England. (44 207) 439-0909. FAX: (44 207) 434-0073.
Puerto Rico: 654 Ave. Muñoz Rivera, IBM Plaza Ste. 1101 B, Hato Rey, PR 00918. (787) 281-0782. FAX: (787) 767-2805.
PRESIDENT & CHAIRMAN
Marilyn Bergman
CEO
John A. LoFrumento
EXECUTIVE V.P.
Al Wallace
E.V.P., MEMBERSHIP GROUP
Todd Brabec
SENIOR V.P., CREATIVE AFFAIRS
John Alexander
SENIOR V.P., FILM & TV REPERTORY
Nancy Knutsen
SENIOR V.P., MARKETING
Philip Crosland
V.P., MEMBERSHIP
Tom DeSavia
WRITER BOARD MEMBERS
Marilyn Bergman, Elmer Bernstein, Bruce Broughton, Cy Coleman, Hal David, James "Jimmy Jam" Harris III, Wayland Holyfield, Johnny Mandel, Stephen Paulus, Jimmy Webb, Paul Williams, Doug Wood.
PUBLISHER BOARD MEMBERS
Freddy Bienstock, Joanne Boris, Arnold Broido, John L. Eastman, Nicholas Firth, Donna Hilley, Dean Kay, Leeds Levy, Jay Morgenstern, David Renzer, Irwin Z. Robinson, Kathy Spanberger.

ASSOCIATION OF FILM COMMISSIONERS INTERNATIONAL

(Organized 1975. Acts as a liaison between the visual communications industry and local governments or organizations to facilitate on-location production, to stimulate economic benefit for member governments.)
314 N. Main, Ste. 307, Helena, MT 59601. (406) 495-8040. FAX: (406) 495-8039. www.afci.org
CEO
Bill Lindstrom
DIRECTOR OF MEETINGS & EVENTS
Sue Clark Jones

ASSOCIATION OF INDEPENDENT VIDEO & FILMMAKERS, INC. (AIVF)

(AIVF is a membership organization serving independent film and videomakers. AIVF also publishes The Independent Film and Video Monthly, a magazine dedicated to the media field.)
304 Hudson St., 6th Flr. New York, NY 10013. (212) 807-1400. FAX: (212) 463-8519. www.aivf.org
email: info@aivf.org
EXECUTIVE DIRECTOR
Elizabeth Peters
DEVELOPMENT DIRECTOR
Alexander Spencr
PROGRAM DIRECTOR
Sonia Malfa
MEMBERSHIP COORDINATOR
Priscilla Grim
INFORMATION SERVICE ASSOCIATES
Bo Mehrad
James Israel
EDITOR-IN-CHIEF, The Independent
Maud Kersnowski
ADVERTISING DIRECTOR, The Independent
Laura Davis

BMI (BROADCAST MUSIC, INC.)

320 W. 57 St., New York, NY 10019. (212) 586-2000. FAX: (212) 245-8986. www.bmi.com email: newyork@bmi.com
8730 Sunset Blvd., Third Flr. W., Los Angeles, CA 90069. (310) 659-9109. FAX: (310) 657-6947. email: losangeles@bmi.com
10 Music Square E., Nashville, TN 37203. (615) 401-2000. FAX: (615) 401-2707. email: nashville@bmi.com
5201 Blue Lagoon Dr., Ste. 310, Miami, FL 33126. (305) 266-3636. FAX: (305) 266-2442. email: miami@bmi.com

255 Ponce de Leon, East Wing, Ste. A-262, Bank Trust Plaza, Hato Rey, PR 00917. (787) 754-6490. FAX: (787) 753-6765.
84 Harley House, Marylebone Rd., London NW1 5HN, England. (44 207) 486-2036. email: london@bmi.com
PRESIDENT
Ralph N. Jackson
VICE PRESIDENTS
Robbin Ahrold
Gary F. Roth
SECRETARY
Jean Banks
TREASURER
Thomas Curry

COMMUNICATION COMMISSION OF THE NATIONAL COUNCIL OF THE CHURCHES OF CHRIST IN THE USA

475 Riverside Dr., Rm. 852, New York, NY 10115. (212) 870-2574. FAX: (212) 870-2030. www.ncccusa.org
email: redgar@ncccusa.org
GENERAL SECRETARY, NATIONAL COUNCIL OF CHURCHES
The Rev. Dr. Bob Edgar

COUNCIL ON INTERNATIONAL NON-THEATRICAL EVENTS (C.I.N.E.)

(Organized 1957. CINE selects and enters tv documentaries, theatrical short subjects, educational, religious, scientific film and tv products in 120 international film & video competitions.)
1112 16th St. N.W., Ste. 510, Washington, DC 20036. (202) 785-1136. (202) 785-1137. FAX: (202) 785-4114.
EXECUTIVE DIRECTOR
David L. Weiss
DIRECTOR OF COMPETITIONS
Bruce Bucklin

ENTERTAINMENT INDUSTRIES FOUNDATION

11132 Ventura Blvd., Ste. 401, Studio City, CA 91604-3156. (818) 760-7722. FAX: (818) 760-7898. www.eifoundation.org
PRESIDENT & CEO
Lisa Paulsen
EXECUTIVE V.P.
Danielle Guttman
SENIOR V.P & CFO
Merrily Newton
V.P., PROGRAMS
Michael Balaoing
V.P., COMMUNICATIONS
Judi Ketcik
SENIOR ASSOCIATE, CORPORATE RELATIONS
Robert Wilson

FILM SOCIETY OF LINCOLN CENTER

(Organized 1969. Sponsors The New York Film Festival and publishes Film Comment magazine.)
70 Lincoln Center Plaza, 4th Flr. New York, NY 10023-6595. (212) 875-5610. FAX: (212) 875-5636. www.filmlinc.com
CHAIRMAN
Ira M. Resnick
PRESIDENT
Henry McGee
EXECUTIVE DIRECTOR
Claudia Bonn
PROGRAM DIRECTOR
Richard Pena

FILM/VIDEO ARTS

(Organized 1968. Provides independents with training, mentoring and fiscal sponsoring.)
462 Broadway, Ste. 520, New York, NY 10013. (212) 941-8787. FAX: (212) 219-8924. www.fva.com
EXECUTIVE DIRECTOR
Eileen Newman
DIRECTOR OF PUBLIC RELATIONS
Duana C. Butler

FRENCH FILM OFFICE/UNIFRANCE FILM INTERNATIONAL

(Promoting French cinema worldwide.)
424 Madison Ave., 8th Flr., New York, NY 10017. (212) 832-8860. FAX: (212) 755-0629. www.unifrance.org
EXECUTIVE DIRECTOR FOR THE U.S.
Catherine Verret

FRIARS CLUB

57 E. 55th St., New York, NY 10022. (212) 751-7272. FAX: (212) 355-0217. www.friarsclub.com
ABBOT
Alan King
DEAN
Freddie Roman
PRIOR
Sally Jessy Raphael
SCRIBE
Stewie Stone

MOTION PICTURE ASSOCIATION OF AMERICA, INC./ MOTION PICTURE ASSOCIATION

Anti-Piracy Hot Line: 1-800-NO-COPYS
PRESIDENT & CEO, MPAA/CHAIRMAN & CEO, MPA
Jack Valenti
E.V.P., GOVERNMENT RELATIONS & GENERAL COUNSEL, WASHINGTON
Fritz Attaway
E.V.P. & CO-COO
William Murray
E.V.P., CO-COO, GENERAL COUNSEL & SECRETARY
Simon Barsky
S.V.P., CHIEF FINANCIAL OFFICER AND TREASURER
Mark Howe

WASHINGTON, DC
1600 EYE St. N.W., Washington, DC 20006. (202) 293-1966. FAX: (202) 293-7674.
PRESIDENT & CEO, MPAA/CHAIRMAN & CEO, MPA
Jack Valenti
E.V.P., GOVERNMENT RELATIONS & WASHINGTON GENERAL COUNSEL
Fritz Attaway
S.V.P., STATE LEGISLATION AFFAIRS & DOMESTIC TAX
Vans Stevenson
V.P., CONGRESSIONAL AFFAIRS, LEGISLATIVE COUNSEL
Jon Liebowitz
V.P., TRADE & FEDERAL AFFAIRS
Bonnie Richardson
V.P., RETRANSMISSION ROYALTY DISTRIBUTION
Marsha Kessler
V.P., ADMINISTRATION
Nancy Thompson
V.P., INTERNATIONAL COMMERCIAL AFFAIRS
ADMINISTRATION NEW TECHNOLOGY
Jane Saunders
V.P., PUBLIC AFFAIRS
Richard Taylor

ENCINO
15503 Ventura Blvd., Encino, CA 91436. (818) 995-6600. FAX: (818) 382-1799. Anti-Piracy Hot Line: 1-800-NO-COPYS
E.V.P. & CO-COO
William Murray
E.V.P., CO-COO, & GENERAL COUNSEL AND SECRETARY
Simon Barsky
S.V.P., CHIEF FINANCIAL OFFICER AND TREASURER
Mark Howe
S.V.P. & CHIEF TECHNOLOGY OFFICER
Brad Hunt
S.V.P., WORLDWIDE AND DIRECTOR ANTI-PIRACY
Ken Jacobson
V.P. TELEVISION AND VIDEO SYSTEM STANDARDS
Jim Williams
V.P. INTERNET STANDARDS AND TECHNOLOGY
Chris Russell
V.P., DEPUTY GENERAL COUNSEL, AND ASSISTANT SECRETARY
Gregory P. Goeckner
V.P. & DIRECTOR, LEGAL AFFAIRS, WORLDWIDE ANTI-PIRACY
Mark Litvack
V.P., SENIOR COUNSEL, INTERNATIONAL TAX & COMMERCIAL AFFAIRS
Barbara Rosenfeld
V.P. AND SENIOR COUNSEL, COPYRIGHT AFFAIRS
Axel Aus der Muhlen
V.P., COUNSEL/ NEW TECHNOLOGIES
Dan Robbins
V.P. & GENERAL MANAGER, CA GROUP
Melissa Patack
V.P. & MANAGING DIRECTOR, WORLDWIDE ALL MEDIA
Thomas Molter
V.P., FINANCE & ASSISTANT TREASURER
Don McLellan
V.P., MIS
Paul Egge
V.P., CONTROLLER & ASSISTANT TREASURER
Tom Igner
V.P. ADMINISTRATION & DIR., ADVERTISING
Marilyn Gordon
DIRECTOR, HUMAN RESOURCES
Kari Hollinger
CHAIRMAN, CLASSIFICATION & RATING ADMINISTRATION
Joan Graves

EUROPE, MIDDLE EAST & AFRICA OPERATIONS
BRUSSELS
108 rue du Trône, B-1050 Brussels. TEL: (011 322) 778 2711. FAX: (011 322) 778 2700.
S.V.P. AND MANAGING DIRECTOR
Chris Marcich
V.P., WEST EUROPE, AFRICA & MIDDLE EAST
Jimmy Katz
V.P., REGIONAL DIRECTOR
Dara McGreevy

CMPDA
22 St. Clair Ave. E, #1603, Toronto, Ontario, Canada M4T-2S4. TEL: (416) 961-1888. FAX: (416) 968-1016
PRESIDENT, CMPDA, TORONTO
Douglas Frith
V.P., CMPDA & CANADIAN COPYRIGHT & COLLECTIVE
Susan Peacock

CMPDA/FVSO
7900 Taschereau Blvd., Ste. C-210, Brossard, Quebec J4X 1C2. TEL: (450) 672-1990. FAX: (450) 672-1660.
REGIONAL DIRECTOR, ANTI-PIRACY
Serge Corrivea

AUSTRALIA & ASIA
SINGAPORE
08-06 United Sq.e, 101 Thompson Rd., Singapore 307591, Singapore. TEL: (011-65) 6253-1033. FAX: (011-65) 6255-1838.
S.V.P., ASIA PACIFIC
Michael Connors

MPA REGIONAL ANTI-PIRACY OPERATIONS & REGIONAL OPTICAL DISC OPERATIONS
Rm. 2803-2808, 28th Flr., 118 Connaught Rd. West, Western District, Hong Kong, China. TEL: (011 852) 2310 8160. FAX: (011 852) 2310 8160.
V.P., ANTI-PIRACY ASIA/PACIFIC
Michael Ellis

LATIN AMERICA
RIO
Rua Mexico, 31/603, 20031-144 Rio de Janeiro, RJ, Brazil. TEL: (011 55 21) 2240 8340. FAX: (011 55 21) 2524 4416.
S.V.P., LATIN AMERICA
Steve Solot
V.P. & DIRECTOR, ANTI-PIRACY, LATIN AMERICA
Brendan Hudson

MUSEUM OF MODERN ART, DEPT. OF FILM & MEDIA

(Organized May, 1935.)
11 W. 53th St., New York, NY 10019. (212) 708-9500. FAX: (212) 333-1145.
CHAIRMAN EMERITUS
David Rockefeller
PRESIDENT EMERITA
Agnes Gund
CHAIRMAN
Ronald S. Lauder
PRESIDENT
Robert B. Menschel
VICE CHAIRMEN
Sid R. Bass
Mimi Haas
Donald B. Marron
Richard E. Salomon
Jerry I. Speyer
TREASURER
John Parkinson III
DIRECTOR
Glenn D. Lowry
SECRETARY
Patty Lipshutz

NATIONAL ALLIANCE FOR MEDIA ARTS & CULTURE

(NAMAC distributes a newletter to the media arts and information network.)
145 Ninth St., Ste. 250, San Francisco, CA 94103. (415) 431-1391. FAX: (415) 431-1392. www.namac.org
email: namac@namac.org
ACTING NATIONAL DIRECTOR
Jack Walsh
PROGRAM DIRECTOR
Daniel "Dewey" Schott
PROGRAM ASSOCIATE
Amanda Ault

NATIONAL ASIAN AMERICAN TELECOMMUNICATIONS ASSOCIATION (NAATA)

(NAATA supports and distributes Asian Pacific American media productions through national public television broadcasts.)
346 Ninth St., 2nd Flr., San Francisco, CA 94103. (415) 863-0814. FAX: (415) 863-7428. www.naatanet.org
EXECUTIVE DIRECTOR
Eddie Wong
ADMINISTRATIVE DIRECTOR
Ernestine Tayabas-Kim
OFFICE ADMINISTRATOR
Joseph Flores
FINANCIAL MANAGER
Sarah Shang
DEVELOPMENT DIRECTOR
Alina Hua
SPONSORSHIP COORDINATOR
Amina Fazlullah
DISTRIBUTION DIRECTOR
Pear Sintumuang

DISTRIBUTION MARKETING ASSOCIATE
Hieu Ho
EXHIBITION & FESTIVAL DIRECTOR
Chi-hui Yang
SPONSORSHIP COORDINATOR
Mai Le
EXHIBITION & FESTIVAL ASSOCIATE
Taro Goto
MEDIA FUND DIRECTOR
Maritoni Tabora
DIRECTOR OF BROADCAST PROGRAMMING
Donald Young
BROADCAST PROGRAMMING ASSOCIATE
Jimi Choi (Choi Jung Do)
BOARD OF DIRECTORS
Harry Lin (Chair President), Claire Aguilar (Vice Chair), Kai Fujita, Ramsay Liem (Secretary), Marjorie Fujiki, Dipti Ghosh, Stephen Gong, Terry Hong, Lisa Hsia, Michael Hsieh, Sookie Choi Kunst, Jean Tsien, Soon-Chart Yu, Dien S. Yuen.

NATIONAL ASSOCIATION OF THEATRE OWNERS, INC.
(For the NATO board, a complete list of state and regional NATO offices and Directors-at-Large, please see Exhibitor Organizations.)
4605 Lankershim Blvd., Ste. 340, N. Hollywood, CA 91602. (818) 506-1778. FAX: (818) 506-4382.
PRESIDENT
John Fithian
V.P. & EXECUTIVE DIRECTOR
Mary Ann Grasso
ASSISTANT EXECUTIVE DIRECTOR
Elaine Hester
COMMUNICATIONS DIRECTOR
Jim Kozak
FINANCE COMMITTEE & TREASURER
William Stembler
SECRETARY
Jim Murray

NATIONAL FILM PRESERVATION FOUNDATION
(Organized 1997)
870 Market St., Ste. 1113, San Francisco, CA 94102. (415) 392-7291. FAX: (415) 392-7293. www.filmpreservation.org
email: info@filmpreservation.org
DIRECTOR
Annette Melville
ASSISTANT DIRECTOR
Jeff Lambert
PROGRAMS MANAGER
David Wells
OFFICE MANAGER
Rebecca Payne
BOARD OF DIRECTORS
Roger L. Mayer (Chairman), Laurence Fishburne, I. Michael Heyman, The Hon. Robert W. Kastenmeier, Cecilia deMille Presley, John Ptak, Robert G. Rehme, Eric J. Schwartz, Martin Scorsese, James H. Billington (ex officio, The Librarian of Congress).

NATIONAL MUSIC PUBLISHERS' ASSOCIATION, INC.
(NMPA was founded in 1917 and represents more than 800 music publishing companies.)
475 Park Ave. S., 29th Flr., New York, NY 10016. (646) 742-1651. FAX: (646) 742-1779. www.nmpa.org
PRESIDENT & CEO
Edward P. Murphy

NEW YORK FOUNDATION FOR THE ARTS, INC.
(Promotes freedom to develop and create art and provides opportunities for individual artists.)
155 Ave. of the Americas, 14th Flr., New York, NY 10013. (212) 366-6900. FAX: (212) 366-1778. www.nyfa.org
EXECUTIVE DIRECTOR
Theodore Berger
DIRECTOR OF PROGRAMS
Penelope Dannenberg
DIRECTOR OF ADMINISTRATION
Toni Lewis
OFFICE MANAGER
Bill Wagner
OPERATIONS ASSISTANT
Carmen Cuevas-Gomez

NEW YORK STATE COUNCIL ON THE ARTS (NYSCA)
(Funds nonprofit art organizations.)
175 Varick St, 3rd Flr., New York, NY 10014. (212) 627-4455. FAX: (212) 620-5911. www.nysca.org
EXECUTIVE DIRECTOR
Nicolette Clarke
DEPUTY DIRECTOR
Al Berr
DIRECTOR, ELECTRONIC MEDIA & FILM PROGRAM
Karen Helmerson
ASSOCIATE, ELECTRONIC MEDIA & FILM PROGRAM
Claude Meyer
DIRECTOR, INDIVIDUAL ARTISTS PROGRAM
Don Palmer

NEW YORK WOMEN IN FILM & TELEVISION
(Founded in 1978. Dedicated to helping and promoting equity for women in reaching the highest levels of achievement in film, television and other moving-image media.)
6 E. 39th St., 12th Flr., New York, NY 10016-0112. (212) 679-0870. FAX: (212) 679-0899. www.nywift.org
email: staff@nywift.org
PRESIDENT
Linda Kahn
VICE PRESIDENTS
Megan Cunningham
Sylvia Gail Kinard
Barbara Meyer
MJ Sorenson
Jennifer J. Wollan
SECRETARY
Susan Wagner
LEGAL COUNSEL
Marsha S. Brooks
EXECUTIVE DIRECTOR
Terry Lawler
DEVELOPMENT ASSOCIATE
Barbara Nichols
PROGRAM COORDINATOR
Victoria F. Clark
EXECUTIVE ASSISTANT
Nancy Silva
MEMBERSHIP COORDINATOR
Donna Golden

CHAPTERS
U.S.:Arizona (Scottsdale), California (Los Angeles), Georgia (Atlanta), Florida (Orlando), Maryland (Baltimore), New England (Boston, MA), New York (New York), Texas (Dallas and Houston), Washington (Seattle), Washington D.C.

CANADA: Alberta (Calgary), :British Columbia (Vancouver), Ontario (Toronto), Québec (Montreal)

INTERNATIONAL: Africa (Kenya, South Africa, Zimbabwe, Caribbean (Jamaica), Europe (Denmark, France, Germany, Ireland, Italy, Poland, Spain, United Kingdom), Mexico (Mexico City)

OCEANIA: Australia (Queensland, South Australia, Sydney, Victoria), New Zealand (Auckland, Christchurch, Wellington).

ADVISORY BOARD
Marcie L. Setlow, Alayne Baxter, Laverne Berry, Jeanne Betancourt, Grace Blake, Mirra Bank Brockman, Michelle Byrd, Karen Cooper, Beth Dembitzer, Alice Elliott, Harlene Freezer, Pat Herold, Linda Horn, Linda Kahn, Marjorie Kalins, Pat Swinney Kaufman, Wendy Keys, Nancy Littlefield, Susan Margolin, Joy Pereths, Ruth Pomerance, Marquita Pool-Eckert, Wendy Sax, Joan Micklin Silver, Diane Sokolow, Patrizia Von Brandenstein, Dovie F. Wingard, Ellen Zalk.

SESAC, INC.
(A music licensing organization.)
55 Music Square E., Nashville, TN 37203. (800) 826-9996, (615) 320-0055. FAX: (615) 329-9627. www.sesac.com
S.V.P., ADVERTISING/CORPORATE RELATIONS
Pat Rogers
CORPORATE RELATIONS COORDINATOR
Lorie Long
SENIOR V.P., BUSINESS AFFAIRS
Dennis Lord

SOCIETY OF COMPOSERS & LYRICISTS
(Committed to advancing the interests of the film and television music community through information dissemination, education, communication, and workplace enhancement.)
400 S. Beverly Dr., Ste. 214, Beverly Hills, CA 90212. (310) 281-2812. FAX: (310) 284-4861. www.filmscore.org
email: administrator@filmscore.org
PRESIDENT
Dan Foliart
VICE PRESIDENTS
Arthur Hamilton
Mark Adler
CFO
Christopher Farrell
EXECUTIVE DIRECTOR
Laura Dunn
BOARD OF DIRECTORS
Lori Barth, Charles Bernstein, Dennis C. Brown, Harvey Cohen, Miriam Cutler, Sharon Farber, Craig Stuart Garfinkle, Ron Grant, Benoit Grey, Denis M. Hannigan, Ed Kalnins, Lynn Kowal, Julia Lawson, Billy Martin, James McVay, Peter Melnick, Marc Parmet, Harriet Schock, David Schwartz, Garry Schyman.
ADVISORY BOARD
Alan Bergman, Marilyn Bergman, Elmer Bernstein, Bill Conti, Jerry Goldsmith, James Newton Howard, Quincy Jones, Peter Matz, Alan Menken, David Raksin, Lalo Schifrin, Marc Shaiman, Howard Shore, Alan Silvestri, Patrick Williams, Hans Zimmer.

SOCIETY OF MOTION PICTURE AND TELEVISION ENGINEERS
(Organized 1916.)
595 W. Hartsdale Ave., White Plains, NY 10607-1824. (914) 761-1100. FAX: (914) 761-3115. www.smpte.org
EXECUTIVE DIRECTOR
Frederick C. Motts
DIRECTOR OF PUBLICATIONS
David M. Juhren
PUBLICATIONS/PRODUCTION MANAGER
Mathew Kuriakose
MANAGING EDITOR
Dianne Ross Purrier
MEMBERSHIP/COMPUTER SERVICES COORDINATOR
Daureen Matera

UNITED STATES CONFERENCE OF CATHOLIC BISHOPS, DEPARTMENT OF COMMUNICATION—OFFICE FOR FILM & BROADCASTING
(Produces movie and television reviews with the goal of providing information about the moral and artistic values of entertainment programs.)
1011 First Ave., Ste. #13th Flr., New York, NY 10022. (212) 644-1880. FAX: (212) 644-1886. www.usccb.org
email: ofb@email.msn.com
DIRECTOR, OFFICE FOR FILM & BROADCASTING
Gerri Paré
MEDIA OFFICER
David Dicerto

VARIETY INTERNATIONAL- THE CHILDREN'S CHARITY
(Organized October 10, 1927. Membership: 15,000.)
350 Fifth Ave., Ste. 1233, New York, NY 10118-1199. (212) 695-3818. FAX: (212) 695-3857.
www.varietychildrenscharity.com
PRESIDENT
Ory Slonim, Adv.
CHAIRMAN OF THE BOARD
Jody Reynolds
INTERNATIONAL CHAIRMAN
Monty Hall, O.C.
INTERNATIONAL COUNSEL
Robert R. Hall, Q.C.
PAST PRESIDENTS
Jarvis Astaire, Peter J. Barnett, Monty Hall, O.C., Robert R. Hall, Q.C., Salah M. Hassanein, Tony Hatch, Ralph W. Pries, John Ratcliff, Michael J. Reilly, Stanley J. Reynolds, John H. Rowley, Joseph Sinay.
VICE PRESIDENTS
Rob T. Allen, Maureen Arthur-Ruben, Lloyd Barr, F.C.A., Penny Dogherty, Peter S. Drummond, Tom Fenno, Michael R. Forman, Fredrick M. Friedman, Rosalie Gallagher, Julia Morley, Pauline McFedtridge, George W. Pitman, Marsha Rae Ratcliff, Bruce H. Rosen, Neil Sinclair, Matthew Sinopoli.
PRESIDENT'S COUNCIL
Fran Blechman, Louis Lavinthal, Frank Mancuso, Grahame Mapp, A.M., Hank Milgram, Carl Patrick, Frank Strean, John R. Weber, Sr.
AMBASSADORS
Beatrice Arthur, Shirley Bassey, Harry Belafonte, Lance Burton, Michael Caine, Jack Cannons, J. Douglas Clark, Sir Sean Connery, Raymond B. Curtis, Nick Faldo, Richard Freeman, Ilene Graf, G.K. Greidinger, Marilyn Hall, Don Ho, Paul Hogan, David Lapidus, Terry Lee, Peter Legge, John Levy, Dame Vera Lynn, Roger Moore, CBE, Bruce Morrow, James Murray, Mariel Myerson, Gregory Peck, Peter Reveen, Emma Samms, Barbara Stewart, Susan Sullivan, Robert Thorpe, Kirk Tibbetts, Gina Tolleson, Chaim Topol, Jackie Trent, Louis Trepel, Stuart Wagstaff, Clark Woods.
CELEBRITY AMBASSADORS
Beatrice Arthur, Dame Shirley Bassey, Harry Belafonte, Lance Burton, Sir Michael Caine, CBE, Sir Sean Connery, Nick Faldo, Ilene Graf, Don Ho, Paul Hogan, Dame Vera Lynn, Roger Moore, CBE, Bruce Morrow, Emma Samms, Chaim Topol, Stewart Wegstaf.
MEDICAL ADVISOR
Michael LaCorte, M.D.
EXECUTIVE DIRECTOR
Patricia S. Machir
VARIETY INTL.-THE CHILDREN'S CHARITY TENTS
TENT 1: Variety of Pittsburgh, Penn Center W. One, Ste. 411, Pittsburgh, PA 15276. (412) 747-2680. FAX: (412) 747-2681.
www.varietytent1.org
EXECUTIVE DIRECTOR
Celia A. Hindes, CFRE
TENT 4: Variety of St. Louis, 2200 Westport Plaza Dr., St. Louis, MO 63146. (314) 453-0453. FAX: (314) 453-0488.
www.varietystl.com
EXECUTIVE DIRECTOR
Jan Albus
TENT 5: Variety of Detroit, 30161 Southfield Rd., Ste. 301, Southfield, MI 48076. (248) 258-5511. FAX: (248) 258-5575.
www.variety-detroit.com
EXECUTIVE DIRECTOR
Jennie Cascio

TENT 7: Variety of Buffalo, 195 Delaware Ave., Buffalo, NY 14202. (716) 854-7577. FAX: (716) 854-2939.
www.variety.buffnet.net
EXECUTIVE DIRECTOR
Richard Goldstein
TENT 8: Variety of Kansas City, 17 Anchor Dr., Lake Tapawingo, MO 64015. (816) 220-2068. FAX: (816) 224-3734.
www.kcvarietyclub.org
TENT 10: Variety of Indiana, 6919 East 10th St., Ste. B5, Indianapolis, IN 46219. (317) 359-1650. FAX: (317) 357-3379.
EXECUTIVE DIRECTOR
Dave Battas
TENT 13: Variety of Philadelphia, 1520 Locust St., Ste. 900, Philadelphia, PA 19102. (215) 735-0803 FAX: (215) 735-2450. www.varietyphila.org
EXECUTIVE DIRECTOR
Andrew Pack
TENT 14: Variety of Wisconsin, 9000 W. Wisconsin Ave., Ste. 708, Wauwatosa, WI 53226. (414) 266-3812. FAX: (414) 266-2671. www.varietyclub.org
EXECUTIVE DIRECTOR
Joe Natoli
TENT 15: Variety of Iowa, 505 5th Ave., Ste. 310, Des Moines, IA 50309. (515) 243-4660. FAX: (515) 243-5873.
EXECUTIVE DIRECTOR
Sheri McMichael
TENT 17: Variety of N. Texas, 6060 N. Central Expwy., Ste. 308. Dallas, TX 75206. (214) 368-7449. FAX: (214) 696-8765.
www.varietyclub17tx.org
EXECUTIVE DIRECTOR
Maree Grove
TENT 20: Variety of Memphis, 3294 Poplar Ave., Ste. 310, Memphis, TN 38111. (901) 323-2220. FAX: (901) 324-2816.
TENT 21: Variety of Georgia, 2030 Powers Ferry Rd., Ste. 214, Atlanta, GA 30339. (770) 956-7460. FAX: (770) 956-8358.
EXECUTIVE DIRECTOR
Lori Gambaccini
TENT 23: Variety of New England, 27 Tranfaglia Ave., Lynn, MA 01905. (781) 598-0992. FAX: (781) 289-7100.
TENT 25: Variety of Southern California, 8455 Beverly Blvd., Ste. 501, Los Angeles, CA 90048. (323) 655-1547. FAX: (323) 658-7899. www.varietysocal.org
EXECUTIVE DIRECTOR
Maria Schmidt
TENT 26: Variety of Illinois, 1 IBM Plaza, Ste. 2800, Chicago, IL 60611, (312) 822-0660. FAX: (312) 822-0661.
www.variety26.org
EXECUTIVE DIRECTOR
Vince Pagone
TENT 27: Variety of Western Michigan, 2974 28th St. SW #214, Grandville, MI 49418. (616) 531-8600. FAX: (775) 531-7555. www.variety4kids.org
TENT 32: Variety of Northern California, 582 Market St. #101, San Francisco, CA 94104. (415) 781-3894. FAX: (415) 781-4226. www.varietync.org
EXECUTIVE DIRECTOR
Ellen Goodman
TENT 34: Variety of Houston, 1415 N. Loop W., #215, Houston, TX 77008. (713) 426-5437. FAX: (713) 426-6050.
www.varietyclubhouston.org
TENT 35: Variety of New York, 350 Fifth Ave., Ste. 1234, New York, NY 10118. (212) 760-2777. FAX: (212) 760-2779.
www.varietyny.org
EXECUTIVE DIRECTOR
Leslye Schneider
TENT 37: Variety of Colorado, 10497 Centennial Rd., Littleton, CO 80120. (303) 973-1142. FAX: (303) 973-8884.
www.varietyclubco.org
TENT 39: Variety of Southern Nevada, 6950 Via Oliverio, Ste. B, Las Vegas, NV 89117. (702) 383-8466. FAX: (702) 383-1196. www.varietynv.org
TENT 46: Variety of Pacific Northwest, 911 Pine St., #807, Seattle, WA 98101. (206) 812-1159. FAX: (206) 812-1224.
www.varietyclub.com
TENT 50: Variety of Hawaii, P.O. Box 1180, Kaneohe, HI 96744. (808) 955-5106. FAX: (808) 261-7078.
TENT 60: Variety of Utah, 2500 Emigration Canyon Rd., Salt Lake City, UT 84108. (801) 582-0700. FAX: (801) 583-5176.
www.campk.org
EXECUTIVE DIRECTOR
Gary Ethington
TENT 65: Variety of The Palm Beaches, 2875 S. Ocean Blvd., #200, Palm Beach, FL 33480. (561) 585-5561. FAX: (561) 585-7211.
TENT 66: Variety of The Desert, 1729 E. Palm Canyon Dr., Ste. #103. Palm Springs, CA 92264. (760) 320-1177. FAX: (760) 327-2971.
TENT 70: Variety of Orlando, 3905 El Rey Rd., Orlando, FL 32808. (407) 298-2980 ext. 310. FAX: (407) 292-4600.
www.varietycluborlando.org
EXECUTIVE DIRECTOR
Debra Ellen Hartman
TENT 81: Variety of Eastern Tennessee, 7132 Regal Ln., Knoxville, TN 37918. Tel: (865) 925-9539. FAX: (865) 925-

9778.
EXECUTIVE DIRECTOR
Dena Pinsker
TEXTILE DIVISION OF VARIETY
PMB #453, 10645 N. Tatum Blvd., Ste. 200, Phoenix, AZ
85028. (480) 515-1994. FAX: (480) 515-1965.
EXECUTIVE DIRECTOR
Niki Roosma

CANADA
TENT 28: Variety of Ontario, 37 King St. E., Ste. #300,
Toronto, Ontario M5C 1E9 Canada. (416) 367-2828 . FAX:
(416) 367-0028. www.varietyontario.com
EXECUTIVE DIRECTOR
Ed Oliver
TENT 47: Variety of British Columbia, 4300 Still Creek Dr.,
Burnaby, B.C. V5C 6C3 Canada. (604) 320-0505. FAX: (604)
320-0535. www.variety.bc.ca
EXECUTIVE DIRECTOR
Jon Stettner
TENT 58: Variety of Manitoba, 611 Wellington Crescent,
Winnipeg, Manitoba R3M 0A7 Canada. Tel: (204) 982-1058.
FAX: (204) 475-3198.
EXECUTIVE DIRECTOR
Wayne Rogers
TENT 61: Variety of Southern Alberta, Box 56009 RPO AIR-
WAYS, Calgary, Alberta T2E 7C8 Canada. (403) 228-6168.
FAX: (403) 245-9282. www.varietyclub61.ab.ca
TENT 63: Variety of Northern Alberta, #1205 Energy Sq.,
10109 - 106th St., Edmonton, Alberta T5J 3L7 Canada. (780)
448-9544. FAX: (780) 448-9289.
EXECUTIVE DIRECTOR
Sue McEachern
TENT 71: Variety of Ottawa, P.O. Box 533, Ottawa, Ontario
K1C 1S9 Canada. TEL & FAX: (613) 841-6006.
www.varietyclubofottawa.com
EXECUTIVE DIRECTOR
Michael Brennan

MEXICO
TENT 29: Variety of Mexico, General Anaya #198, Col. San
Diego Churubusco, Mexico, D.F. 04120 Mexico. (52 56) 05 52
88. FAX: (52 56) 05 69 80.

LONDON
TENT 36: Variety of Great Britain, Variety Club House, 93
Bayham St., London NW1 0AG, U.K. TEL: (44 207) 428-8100.
FAX: (44 207) 428-8111. www.varietyclub.org.uk

IRELAND
TENT 41: Variety of Ireland, IMC Cinemas Film House, 35
Upper Abbey St., Dublin 2, Ireland. TEL: (3531) 839-3532.
FAX: (3531) 872-1948.

ISRAEL
TENT 51: Variety of Israel, 3, Tvu'ot Ha'arets St., Tel Aviv
69546 Israel. TEL: (972 3) 6447201. FAX: (972 3) 6447203.
www.variety-israel.co.il
EXECUTIVE DIRECTOR
Irit Perlman

UNITED KINGDOM
TENT 52: Variety of Jersey, Maufant Variety Youth Centre,
Grande Route de St. Martin, St. Saviour JE2 6GT, Jersey,
Channel Islands U.K. TEL: (44 1) 534 86937. FAX: (44 1) 534
857097. www.varietyclub52.org.uk

FRANCE
TENT 54: Variety of France, "Soleil d'enfance", 7, boulevard
Exelmans, Paris 75016 France. TEL: (33 146) 47 20 97. FAX:
(33 145) 25 07 37. www.soleildenfance-vci.com
EXECUTIVE DIRECTOR
Guillaume Pires

AUSTRALIA
TENT 56: Variety of New South Wales, 707 Darling St.,
Rozelle, NSW 2039, Australia, TEL: (61 2) 9819 1000. FAX:
61 2 9555 1424. www.varietynsw.org.au
EXECUTIVE DIRECTOR
Fiona Ellis
TENT 74: Variety of Western Australia, 7 Thomas St.,
Sunbiaco, Perth, Western Australia 6008 Australia. TEL: (61
8) 9388 3480. FAX: (61 8) 9388 3482. www.varietywa.asn.au
EXECUTIVE DIRECTOR
Glenn Weiland

TENT 76: Variety of Queensland, 18 Brisbane Rd., Labrador,
Gold Coast, Qld, 4215 Australia. TEL: (61 7) 5537 6376. FAX:
(61 7) 5563 9022.
EXECUTIVE DIRECTOR
Les Riley
TENT 77: Variety of Victoria, 17 Argyle Place S., Carlton,
Victoria 3053, Australia. TEL: (61 3) 9804 3355. FAX: (61 3)
9804 3533. www.variety.org.au
EXECUTIVE DIRECTOR
Norm Hutton
TENT 78: Variety of Tasmania, 1/57 King Street (P.O. Box
893), Sandy Bay, Tasmania, Australia 7005. TEL: (61 3) 6223
1886. FAX: (61 3) 6224 0333.

SOUTH AUSTRALIA
TENT 75: Variety of South Australia, 540 South Rd., Kurralta
Park, Adelaide, S. Australia 5037 Australia. TEL: (61 8) 8293
8744. FAX: (61 8) 8293 8725. www.varietysa.on.net
EXECUTIVE DIRECTOR
Sue Fraser

NEW ZEALAND
TENT 68: Variety of New Zealand, P.O. Box 17276, Greenlane
Auckland 1005, New Zealand. TEL: (64 9) 520 4111. FAX: (64
9) 520 1122. www.varietyclub.org.nz
EXECUTIVE DIRECTOR
Laura Langford

THE NETHERLANDS
TENT 69: Variety of The Netherlands, Wekeromseweg 8,
Arnhein 6816 The Netherlands. TEL: (31 26) 48 38201. FAX:
(31 26) 48 38454. www.bio-kinderrevalidatie.nl
EXECUTIVE DIRECTOR
Willem Van Tuyll

BARBADOS
TENT 73: Variety of The Caribbean (Barbados), Summerland
House, Prospect, St. James, Barbados. TEL: (246) 432-2395.
FAX: (246) 432-0046.
EXECUTIVE DIRECTOR
Ruth Collins

SOUTH AFRICA
TENT 80: Variety of South Africa, c/o Ster-Kinekor Films, P.O.
Box 76461, Wendywood, 2144, South Africa. TEL: (27 11)
445-7760. FAX: (27 11) 445-7765. www.variety-club.com
EXECUTIVE DIRECTOR
Toni Gomes

WILL ROGERS MOTION PICTURE PIONEERS FOUNDATION
10045 Riverside Dr., 3rd Flr., Toluca Lake, CA 91602. (888)
994-3863, (818) 755-2300. FAX: (818) 508-9816.
www.wrinstitute.org; www.wrpioneers.org
CHAIRMAN
Erik Lomis
PRESIDENT
Chuck Viane
VICE PRESIDENTS
Jeff Goldstein, George Levitt, Michael Pade, Travis Reid, Nikki
Rocco, Ted Shugrue, Bruce Snyder, Robert Sunshine, Clark
Woods.
TREASURER
Steve Rapaport
SECRETARY
Richie Fay
EXECUTIVE COMMITTEE
Michael Campbell, Dan Fellman, Jerry Forman, Mary Ann
Grasso, Kurt Hall, Rick Sands, Tom Sherak.
EXECUTIVE DIRECTOR
Todd Vradenburg
HONORARY CHAIRMEN
Salah Hassanein, Wayne Lewellen, Frank Mancuso, Sumner
Redstone, Bud Stone.

WOMEN IN COMMUNICATIONS
780 Ritchie Hwy., Ste. 28-S, Severna Park, MD 21146-4154.
(410) 544-7442. FAX: (410) 544 4640. www.womcom.org
email: info@womcom.org
EXECUTIVE DIRECTOR
Patricia Troy
MEMBERSHIP DIRECTOR
Nancy Badertscher
PUBLIC RELATIONS DIRECTOR
Brenda Gracely

GUILDS AND UNIONS

ACTORS' EQUITY ASSOCIATION
(AAAA AFL CIO CLC)
(Organized May 26, 1913. Membership: 40,000)
National/Eastern Regional Office: 165 W. 46th St. 15th Flr.,
New York, NY 10036. (212) 869-8530. FAX: (212) 719-9815.
Central Regional Office: 125 S. Clark St., Ste. 1500, Chicago,
IL 60603. (312) 641-0393. FAX: (312) 641-6365.
Western Regional Office: 5757 Wilshire Blvd., Ste. One, Los
Angeles, CA 90036. (323) 634-1750. FAX: (323) 634-1777.
San Francisco Office: 350 Sansom St., Ste. 900, San
Francisco, CA 94104. (415) 391-3838. FAX: (415) 391-0102.
Orlando Office: 10319 Orangewood Blvd., Orlando, FL 32821.
(407) 345-8600. FAX (407) 345-1522. www.actorsequity.org
PRESIDENT
Patrick Quinn
ASSISTANT EXECUTIVE DIRECTOR, NATIONAL
ADMINISTRATION & FINANCE
Guy Pace
NATIONAL DIRECTOR, ORGANIZING & SPECIAL
PROJECTS
Flora Stamatiades
CENTRAL REGIONAL DIRECTOR
Kathryn V. Lamkey
WESTERN REGIONAL DIRECTOR
John Holly
EASTERN REGIONAL DIRECTOR
Carol Waaser
EXECUTIVE DIRECTOR
Alan Eisenberg

AMERICAN CINEMA EDITORS
(Organized November 28, 1950. Membership: 500)
100 Universal City Plaza, Ross Hunter Bldg. B, Ste. 202,
Universal City, CA 91608. (818) 777-2900. FAX: (818) 733-
5023. www.ace-filmeditors.org
PRESIDENT
Tina Hirsch
VICE PRESIDENT
Michael Tronick
SECRETARY
Chris Cooke
TREASURER
Doug Ibold
EXECUTIVE DIRECTOR
Jennifer McCormick

AMERICAN FEDERATION OF MUSICIANS (AFL-CIO)
(Organized October, 1896. Membership: 150,000)
1501 Broadway, New York, NY 10036. (212) 869-1330. FAX:
(212) 764-6134. www.afm.com
3550 Wilshire Blvd., Ste. 1900, Los Angeles, CA 90010. (213)
251-4510.
PRESIDENT
Tom F. Lee
VICE PRESIDENT
Harold Bradley, 11 Music Circle, Nashville, TN 37212.
CANADIAN V.P.
David Jandrisch, 75 The Donway West, Ste. 1010, Don Mills,
ONT, Canada M3C 2E9.
SECRETARY-TREASURER
Florence Nelson
EXECUTIVE BOARD
Hal Espinosa, Mark Jones, Bob McGrew, Kenneth B. Shirk,
Edward Ward.

AMERICAN GUILD OF MUSICAL ARTISTS, INC.
(AAAA AFL CIO,)
(Organized 1936. Membership: 5,500)
1430 Broadway, 14th Flr. New York, NY 10018. (212) 265-3687.
FAX: (212) 262-9088. www.musicalartists.org
PRESIDENT
Linda Mays
FIRST V.P.
Tim Jerome
SECOND V.P.
Jimmy Odom
THIRD V.P.
John Coleman
FOURTH V.P.
Colby Roberts
FIFTH V.P.
Burman Timberlake
TREASURER
Lynn A. Lundgren
SECRETARY
Candace Itow
NATIONAL EXECUTIVE DIRECTOR
Alan S. Gordon
NATIONAL MANAGER OF ADMINISTRATION &
OPERATIONS
Gerry Angel

CHICAGO COUNSEL
Barbara J. Hillman
SPECIAL COUNSEL
Gail Lopez-Henriquz
AREA REPRESENTATIVES
NEW ORLEANS: Mary Bertucci, 6216 Marigny St., New
Orleans, LA 70122. (504) 861-8102. NORTHWEST: Cristine
Reynolds, 7304 Alonzo Ave., NW, Seattle, WA 98117. (206) 297-
3716. SAN FRANCISCO: Nora Heiber, (415) 759-7548. MID
ATLANTIC: Eleni Kallas, 16600 Shea Lane, Gaithersburg, MD
20877. (301) 869-8266.

AMERICAN GUILD OF VARIETY ARTISTS
(AAAA AFL-CIO)
(Organized July 14, 1939. Registered Membership: 78,000)
363 7th Ave., New York, NY 10001. (212) 675-1003.
4741 Laurel Canyon Blvd., #208, N. Hollywood, CA 91607.
(818) 508-9984. FAX: (818) 508-3029. email: AGVANY@aol.com
PRESIDENT
Rod McKuen
EXECUTIVE SECRETARY-TREASURER
Frances Gaar
EXECUTIVE V.P.
David J. Cullen
HONORARY PRESIDENT
Phyllis Diller
HONORARY FIRST V.P.
Rip Taylor
REGIONAL VICE PRESIDENTS
Emelise Aleandri
Bobby Brookes
Mary Lynn Cullen
Susanne Doris
Larry Dorn
John Eaden
Wayne Hermans
Elaine Jacovini
Dee Dee Knapp-Brody
Paula Lane
Judy Little
Tina Marie
Victoria Reed
Dorothy Stratton
Dorothy Zuckerman

AMERICAN SOCIETY OF CINEMATOGRAPHERS
1782 N. Orange Dr., Hollywood, CA 90028. (800) 448-0145.
(323) 969-4333. FAX: (323) 882-6391. P.O. Box 2230,
Hollywood, CA 90078. www.cinematographer.com
PRESIDENT
Richard Crudo
VICE PRESIDENT
Owen Roizman
VICE PRESIDENT
John Bailey
VICE PRESIDENT
Laszlo Kovacs
TREASURER
Robert Primes
SECRETARY
Curtis Clark
SERGENT AT ARMS
John C. Hora

ASSOCIATED ACTORS AND ARTISTES OF AMERICA
(AAAA-AFL-CIO)
(Organized July 18, 1919. Membership: 93,000)
165 W. 46th St., New York, NY 10036. (212) 869-0358. FAX:
(212) 869-1746.
PRESIDENT
Theodore Bikel
VICE PRESIDENTS
Carl Harns
Rod McKuen
Greg Hessinger
Paul Borghese
TREASURER
Thomas Jamerson
EXECUTIVE SECRETARY
John T. McGuire

ASSOCIATED MUSICIANS OF GREATER NEW YORK
LOCAL 802 AFM (NEW YORK)
(Organized August 27, 1921. Membership: 15,000)
322 W. 48th St., New York, NY 10036-1308. (212) 245-4802.
FAX: (212) 489-6030.
PRESIDENT
William Moriarity
FINANCIAL V.P.
Tina Hafmeister
RECORDING V.P.
Erwin Price

ASSOCIATION OF TALENT AGENTS
(Organized April, 1937. Official organization of Hollywood talent agents.)
9255 Sunset Blvd., Ste. 930, Los Angeles, CA 90069. (310) 274-0628. FAX: (310) 274-5063.
www.agentassociation.com email: agentassoc@aol.com
EXECUTIVE DIRECTOR
Karen Stuart
ADMINISTRATIVE DIRECT
Shellie Jetton
PRESIDENT
Sandy Bresler
VICE PRESIDENTS
T. J. Escott
Sheldon Sroloff
SECRETARY & TREASURER
Jim Gosnell

AUTHORS GUILD, INC.
31 E. 28th St., 10th Flr., New York, NY 10016. (212) 563-5904. FAX: (212) 564-8363. www.authorsguild.org
email: staff@authorsguild.org
PRESIDENT
Nick Taylor
VICE PRESIDENT
James Gleick
SECRETARY
Pat Cummings
TREASURER
Peter Petre
EXECUTIVE DIRECTOR
Paul Aiken

DIRECTORS GUILD OF AMERICA, INC. (DGA)
7920 Sunset Blvd., Los Angeles, CA 90046. (800) 421-4173, (310) 289-2000. FAX: (310) 289-2029.
110 W. 57th St., New York, NY 10019. (800) 356-3754, (212) 581-0370. FAX: (212) 581-1441.
400 N. Michigan Ave., Ste. 307, Chicago, IL 60611. (888) 600-6975, (312) 644-5050. FAX: (312) 644-5776.
PRESIDENT
Michael Apted
NATIONAL VICE PRESIDENT
Ed Sherin
SECRETARY/TREASURER
Gilbert Cates
ASSISTANT SECRETARY/TREASURER
Scott Berger
FIRST VICE PRESIDENT
Martha Coolidge
SECOND VICE PRESIDENT
Steven Soderbergh
THIRD VICE PRESIDENT
Paris Barclay
FOURTH VICE PRESIDENT
Max Schindler
FIFTH VICE PRESIDENT
Betty Thomas
SIXTH VICE PRESIDENT
Casey Childs

BOARD MEMBERS
Burt Bluestein, LeVar Burton, Gary Donatelli, Cheryl Downey, Taylor Hackford, Alex Hapsas, Victoria Hochberg, Jeremy Kagan, Michael Mann, John Rich, Barbara Roche.

THE DRAMATISTS GUILD OF AMERICA, INC.
1501 Broadway, Ste. 701, New York, NY 10036. (212) 398-9366. FAX: (212) 944-0420. www.dramatistsguild.com
PRESIDENT
John Weidman
VICE PRESIDENT
Marsha Norman
SECRETARY
Arthur Kopit
TREASURER
Christopher Durang
EXECUTIVE DIRECTOR
Christopher C. Wilson
COUNSEL
Cahill, Gordon & Reindel

EPISCOPAL ACTORS' GUILD OF AMERICA, INC.
(Organized 1923. Members: 600)
One E. 29th St., New York, NY 10016. (212) 685-2927. FAX: (212) 685-8793. www.actorsguild.org
EXECUTIVE SECRETARY
Mart Hulswit
PRESIDENT
Sam Waterston
V.P. AND WARDEN
Rev. Dr. Charles Miller
VICE PRESIDENTS
Arthur Anderson
Thomas Barbour
Florence James
Louis Rachow

HOLLYWOOD ENTERTAINMENT LABOR COUNCIL
(Organized September, 1947)
c/o SAG (Yvette Foley) 5757 Wilshire Blvd., 8th Flr., Los Angeles, CA 90036. (323) 549-6613. FAX: (323) 549-6603.
PRESIDENT
Scott Roth
FIRST V.P.
Pamm Fair
SECOND V.P.
Paul Petersen
THIRD V.P.
G. Lynd Bingham
SECRETARY/TREASURER
H. O'Neil Shanks

INTERNATIONAL BROTHERHOOD OF ELECTRICAL WORKERS (AFL-CIO, CFL)
(Organized Nov. 28, 1891. Membership: 775,000)
1125 15th St. N.W., Washington, DC 20005. (202) 833-7000. FAX: (202) 728-7664. www.ibew.org
INTERNATIONAL PRESIDENT
Edwin D. Hill
INTERNATIONAL SECRETARY & TREASURER
Jeremiah J. O'Connor
DISTRICT OFFICES
ALABAMA: Melvin Horton, 100 Concourse Pkwy., Ste. 300, Brimingham, AL 35244. (205) 444-9977. FAX: (205) 444-0306.
CALIFORNIA: Michael Mowrey, 2500 Venture Oaks Way, Ste. 250, Sacramento, CA 95833-4221. (916) 567-0381.
CANADA: Donald Lounds, 1450 Meyerside Dr., Ste. 300, Mississuga, ON L5T 2N5. Canada. (905) 564-5441.
IDAHO: Jon F. Walters, 330 Shoup Ave., Ste. 204, P.O. Box 51216, Idaho Falls, ID 83405. (208) 529-6555.
ILLINOIS: Lawrence P. Curley, 8174 Cass Ave., Darien, IL 60561. (630) 434-1683.
MASSACHUSETTS: Frank J. Carroll, 4 Armstrong Rd., 2nd Flr., Shelton, CT 06484. (203) 402-0490.
MISSOURI: William C. Eads, 300 S. Jefferson, Ste. 300, Springfield, MO 65806. (417) 831-1507.
OHIO: Paul J. Witte, 8260 N. Creek Dr., Ste. 140, Cincinnati, OH 45236. (513) 821-5480.
OKLAHOMA: Jonathan B. Gardner, 320 Westway Pl., Ste. 531, Arlington, TX 76018. (817) 557-1611.
PENNSYLVANIA: Donald C. Siegel, 500 Cherrington Pkwy., Ste. 325, Coraopolis, PA 15108. (412) 269-4963.
TENNESSEE: Robert P. Klein, 5726 Marlin Rd., Ste. 500, Chattanooga, TN 37411-4043. (423) 894-9095.

IBEW, LOCAL 349 (FILM)
1657 N.W. 17th Ave., Miami, FL 33125. (305) 325-1330. FAX: (305) 325-1521.
BUSINESS MANAGER
Art Fernandez

IBEW, LOCAL 40 (FILM)
5643 Vineland Ave., North Hollywood, CA 91601. (818) 762-4239. www.ibewlocal40.com
BUSINESS MANAGER
Rick DesJardins

INTERNATIONAL ALLIANCE OF THEATRICAL STAGE EMPLOYEES & MOVING PICTURE TECHNICIANS, ARTISTS AND ALLIED CRAFTS OF THE U.S., ITS TERRITORIES, AND CANADA (AFL-CIO, CLC)
(Organized nationally, July 17, 1893; internationally, October 1, 1902. The Alliance comprises approximately 500 local unions covering the United States, its territories, Canada and Puerto Rico & Virgin Islands)
1430 Broadway, 20th Flr., New York, NY 10018. (212) 730-1770. FAX: (212) 921-7699. www.iatse.lm.com
INTERNATIONAL PRESIDENT
Thomas C. Short
GENERAL SECRETARY & TREASURER
James Wood
FIRST V.P.
Edward C. Powell
SECOND V.P.
Daniel J. Kerins
THIRD V.P.
Rudy N. Napoleone
FOURTH V.P.
Jean Fox
FIFTH V.P.
Timothy Magee
SIXTH V.P.
Michael J. Sullivan
SEVENTH V.P.
Michael J. Barnes
EIGHTH V.P.
J. Walter Cahill
NINTH V.P.
Thom Davis
TENTH V.P.
Matthew D. Loeb
ELEVENTH V.P.
Anthony DePaulo
TWELFTH V.P.
Mimi Wolch
THIRTEENTH V.P.
Damian Petti

IATSE PRODUCTION

AFFILIATED PROPERTY CRAFTSMEN LOCAL 44 (IATSE-AFL-CIO), HOLLYWOOD
12021 Riverside Dr., N. Hollywood, CA 91607 (818) 769-2500. FAX: (818) 769-1739. www.local44.org
SECRETARY/TREASURER
Walter Keske
BUSINESS AGENT
Stewart McGuire

THE ANIMATION GUILD, LOCAL 839 (IATSE)
4729 Lankershim Blvd., N. Hollywood, CA 91602-1864. (818) 766-7151. FAX: (818) 506-4805. www.mpsc839.org
PRESIDENT
Kevin Koch
BUSINESS REPRESENTATIVE
Steve Hulett
VICE PRESIDENT
George Sukara

ART DIRECTORS GUILD/SCENIC, TITLE & GRAPHIC ARTISTS LOCAL 800 (IATSE)
11969 Ventura Blvd., #200, Studio City, CA 91604. (818) 762-9995. FAX: (818) 762-9997. www.artdirectors.org
EXECUTIVE DIRECTOR
Scott Roth
ASSISTANT EXECUTIVE DIRECTOR
Missy Humphrey

COSTUME DESIGNERS GUILD LOCAL 892
(Founded 1953, Membership: 570)
4730 Woodman Ave., Ste. 430, Sherman Oaks, CA 91423-2400. (818) 905-1557. FAX: (818) 905-1560.
www.costumedesignersguild.com
PRESIDENT
Deborah Nadoolman Landis
EXECUTIVE DIRECTOR
James J. Casey, Jr.

FIRST AID EMPLOYEES, LOCAL 767 (IATSE), LOS ANGELES
243 S. Beachwood Dr., Burbank, CA 91506-2419. FAX: (818) 846-0727, (310) 352-4485.
SECRETARY/TREASURER
Michael A. Kemp
BUSNESS AGENT
Rana Jo Platz Petersen

MOTION PICTURE COSTUMERS, LOCAL 705 (IATSE), HOLLYWOOD
4731 Laurel Canyon Blvd., Ste. 201, Valley Village, CA 91607-3911. (818) 487-5655. FAX: (818) 487-5663.
SECRETARY
Paul DeLucca
BUSINESS REPRESENTIVE
Buffy Snyder

MOTION PICTURE CRAFTS SERVICE & MOTION PICTURE STUDIO GRIPS LOCAL 80 (IATSE)
2520 W. Olive Ave., Burbank, CA 91505. (818) 526-0700. FAX: (818) 526-0719.
BUSINESS REPRESENTATIVE
Thom Davis

MOTION PICTURE EDITORS GUILD, LOCAL 700 (IATSE), LOS ANGELES
7715 Sunset Blvd., Ste. 200, Hollywood, CA 90046. (323) 876-4770. FAX: (323) 876-0861. www.editorsguild.com
EXECUTIVE DIRECTOR
Ronald G. Kutak

MOTION PICTURE EDITORS GUILD, LOCAL 700 (IATSE), NEW YORK
165 W. 46th St., Ste. 900, New York, NY 10036. (212) 302-0700. FAX: (212) 302-1091. www.editorsguild.com
NATIONAL PRESIDENT
Lisa Zeno Churgin
VICE PRESIDENT
Dede Allen

MOTION PICTURE SCRIPT SUPERVISORS AND PRODUCTION OFFICE COORDINATORS, LOCAL 161
630 9th Ave., #1103, New York, NY 10036. (212) 977-9655. FAX: (212) 977-9609.
PRESIDENT
Lynne Twentyman

MOTION PICTURE SET PAINTERS, LOCAL 729 (IATSE), HOLLYWOOD
1811 W. Burbank Blvd., Burbank, CA 91506-1314. (818) 842-7729. FAX: (818) 846-3729.
BUSINESS DIRECTOR & SECRETARY
George A. Palazzo

MOTION PICTURE STUDIO ELECTRICAL LIGHTING TECHNICIANS, LOCAL 728 (IATSE)
14629 Nordhoff St., Panorama City, CA 91402. (818) 891-0728. FAX: (818) 985-5288.
BUSINESS REPRESENTATIVE SECRETARY
Norman Glasser

MOTION PICTURE STUDIO ART CRAFTSMEN, (ILLUSTRATORS AND MATTE ARTISTS) LOCAL 790 (IATSE), HOLLYWOOD
13245 Riverside Dr., Ste. 300-A, Sherman Oaks, CA 91423. (818) 784-6555. FAX: (818) 784-2004.
SECRETARY
Camille Abbott

MOTION PICTURE STUDIO MECHANICS, LOCAL 476 (IATSE), CHICAGO
6309 N. Northwest Hwy., Chicago, IL 60631. (773) 775-5300. FAX: (773) 775-2477.
SECRETARY
J. Paul Oddo

RADIO AND TELEVISION BROADCAST ENGINEERS, LOCAL 1212
225 W. 34th St., Ste. 1120, New York, NY 10122. (212) 354-6770. FAX: (212) 819-9517. www.ibew1212.org
PRESIDENT
Frank Viskup
VICE PRESIDENT
Richard N. Ross
BUSINESS MANAGER/FINANCIAL SECRETARY
Peter Quaranta

SCRIPT SUPERVISORS/CONTINUITY & ALLIED PRODUCTIONS SPECIALISTS GUILD, LOCAL 871 (IATSE)
11519 Chandler Blvd., N. Hollywood, CA 91601. (818) 509-7871. FAX: (818) 506-1555. www.ialocal871.org
BUSINESS AGENT
Lainie Miller

SET DESIGNERS AND MODEL MAKERS, LOCAL 847 (IATSE), HOLLYWOOD
13245 Riverside Dr., Ste. 300-A, Sherman Oaks, CA 91423. (818) 784-6555. FAX: (818) 784-2004.
SECRETARY
Suzanne Feller-Otto

STUDIO MECHANICS, LOCAL 479 (IATSE), ATLANTA
1000 Iris Dr., Ste. G2, Conyers, GA 30094. (404) 885-9134. FAX: (770) 783-0999. www.iatse479.com
email: Local479@mindspring.com
SECRETARY
Suzanne L. Carter
BUSINESS AGENT
Michael Akins

STUDIO MECHANICS, LOCAL 812 (IATSE), DETROIT
20017 Van Dyke St., Detroit, MI 48234. (313) 790-1949. FAX: (313) 368-1151. www.iatse812.org email: tmagee@iatse812.org
BUSINESS AGENT
Tim Magee

STUDIO MECHANICS, LOCAL 52 (IATSE), NEW YORK
326 W. 48th St., New York, NY 10036. (212) 399-0980. FAX: (212) 315-1073. www.iatselocal52.org
SECRETARY
John R. Ford

STUDIO MECHANICS, LOCAL 477 (IATSE), FLORIDA
10705 N.W. 33th St., Ste. 110, Miami, FL 33172. (305) 594-8585. FAX: (305) 597-9278.
SECRETARY
George Cerchiai
BUSINESS AGENT
Joel Humphreys

STUDIO MECHANICS, LOCAL 209 (IATSE), OHIO
1468 W. 9th St., Rm. 435, Cleveland, OH 44113. (216) 621-9537. FAX: (216) 621-3518.
BUSINESS AGENT
Peter Lambros
SECRETARY
Kenneth McCahan

THEATRICAL WARDROBE ATTENDANTS, LOCAL 768 (IATSE), LOS ANGELES
13245 Riverside Dr., Ste. 300, Sherman Oaks, CA 91423. (818) 789-8735. FAX: (818) 789-1928.
SECRETARY
Mary B. Seward
BUSINESS AGENT
William N. Damron, Jr.

THEATRICAL WARDROBE UNION, LOCAL 764 (IATSE), NEW YORK
545 W. 45th St., 2nd Flr., New York, NY 10036. (212) 957-3500. FAX: (212) 957-3232.
SECRETARY/TREASURER
Jenna Krempel
BUSINESS REPRESENTATIVE
James Hurley (television & film)

EXHIBITION

EXHIBITION EMPLOYEES & STAGEHANDS, LOCAL 829 (IATSE), NEW YORK
150 E. 58th St., New York, NY 10022. (212) 752-4427. FAX: (212) 832-2165.
PRESIDENT
John V. McNamee, Jr.

PROJECTIONISTS LOCAL 150
P.O. Box 5143, Culver City, CA 90231-5143. (818) 557-1677.
FAX: (310) 398-9445.
BUSINESS REPRESENTATIVE
Carl Belfor

MOTION PICTURE PROJECTIONISTS, OPERATORS & VIDEO TECHNICIANS, LOCAL 110 (IATSE), CHICAGO
230 W. Monroe St., Ste. 2511, Chicago, IL 60606. (312) 443-1011. FAX: (312) 443-1012.
SECRETARY
Al Brenkus

MOTION PICTURE PROJECTIONISTS, VIDEO TECHNI-CIANS, THEATRICAL EMPLOYEES & ALLIED CRAFTS, LOCAL 306 (IATSE), NEW YORK
545 W. 45th St., 2nd Flr., New York, NY 10036. (212) 956-1306. FAX: (212) 956-9306. www.local306.org
SECRETARY
Martin Unger
BUSINESS REPRESENTATIVES
Joel Deitch
Susan Martin

STAGE EMPLOYEES, LOCAL 4 (IATSE), BROOKLYN
2917 Glenwood Rd., Brooklyn, NY 11210. (718) 252-8777.
FAX: (718) 421-5605.
SECRETARY
Terence Ryan
BUSINESS MANAGER
Peter Fitzpatrick

STAGE EMPLOYEES, LOCAL 2 (IATSE), CHICAGO
20 N. Wacker Dr., Ste. 1032, Chicago, IL 60606. (312) 236-3457. FAX: (312) 236-0701.
SECRETARY
Thomas J. Cleary

STAGE EMPLOYEES, LOCAL 33 (IATSE), LOS ANGELES
1720 W. Magnolia Blvd., Burbank, CA 91506-1871. (818) 841-9233. FAX: (818) 567-1138. www.ia33.org
PRESIDENT
George Blanch

STAGE EMPLOYEES, LOCAL 1 (IATSE), NEW YORK
320 W. 46th St., New York, NY 10036. (212) 333-2500. FAX: (212) 586-2437. www.iatselocalone.org
SECRETARY
David Camus

THEATRE EMPLOYEES, LOCAL B-46 (IATSE), CHICAGO
230 W. Monroe St., Ste. 2511, Chicago, IL 60606. (312) 443-1011. FAX: (312) 443-1012.
SECRETARY
Al Brenkus

TREASURERS AND TICKET SELLERS, LOCAL 750 (IATSE), CHICAGO
446 N. Edgewood, LaGrange Park, IL 60525. (708) 579-4305.
FAX: (708) 579-4313.
SECRETARY
Michael Keenan

TREASURERS AND TICKET SELLERS, LOCAL 857 (IATSE), LOS ANGELES
13245 Riverside Dr., Ste. 300C, Sherman Oaks, CA 91423.
(818) 990-7107. FAX: (818) 990-8287.
SECRETARY
Deirdre Floyd

TREASURERS AND TICKET SELLERS, LOCAL 751 (IATSE), NEW YORK
1430 Broadway, 8th Flr., New York, NY 10018. (212) 302-7300.
FAX: (212) 944-8687.
SECRETARY
Gene McElwain

PRODUCER-WRITERS GUILD OF AMERICA PENSION PLAN
1015 N. Hollywood Way, Burbank, CA 91505. (800) 227-7863, (818) 846-1015. FAX: (818) 566-8445.
ADMINISTRATOR
Thomas Hendricks

PRODUCERS GUILD OF AMERICA
(Founded 1950. Membership: 1,800)
8530 Wilshire Blvd., Ste. 450, Beverly Hills, CA 90211. (310) 358-9020. FAX: (310) 358-9520. www.producersguild.org
email: info@producersguild.org
PRESIDENT
Kathleen Kennedy
VICE PRESIDENT, MOTION PICTURES
Hawk Koch
V.P., TELEVISION
Marshall Nerskovitz
SECRETARY
Pixie Wespiser
TREASURER
Erin O'Malley
EXECUTIVE DIRECTOR
Vance Van Petten

PROFESSIONAL MUSICIANS, LOCAL 47, (AFM, AFL-CIO/CLC)
(Organized October 30, 1894. Membership: 10,000)
817 N. Vine St., Hollywood, CA 90038. (323) 462-2161. FAX: (323) 466-1289. www.promusic47.org
PRESIDENT
Hal Espinosa
VICE PRESIDENT
David Schubach
SECRETARY/TREASURER
Serena Kay Williams

SCREEN ACTORS GUILD (AAAA-AFL-CIO)
(Organized July 1933. Membership: 98,000)
5757 Wilshire Blvd., Los Angeles, CA 90036-3600. (323) 954-1600. FAX: (323) 549-6603.
360 Madison Ave., 12th Flr., New York, NY 10017-7111. (212) 944-1030. FAX: (212) 944-6774. www.sag.org
PRESIDENT
Melissa Gilbert
RECORDING SECRETARY
Elliott Gould
TREASURER
Kent McCord
FIRST V.P.
Mike Farrell (Hollywood Division)
SECOND V.P.
Eileen Henry (New York Division)
THIRD V.P.
Ce Ce DuBois (Regional Branch Division)
NATIONAL EXECUTIVE DIRECTOR/CEO
A. Robert Pisano
SENIOR ADVISOR
John McGuire
ACTING NATIONAL DIRECTOR, COMMUNICATIONS
Ilyanne Kichaven
COUNSEL
Mark Steinberg
DIRECTOR, FINANCE
Franchesca Hickson
NATIONAL DIRECTOR, GOVERNANCE
Michelle Bennett

DISTRICT OFFICES
ARIZONA: 1616 East Indian School Rd., Ste. 330, Phoenix, AZ 85016. (602) 265-2712. FAX: (602) 264-7571.
BOSTON: 535 Boylston St., Boston, MA 02116. (617) 262-8001. FAX: (617) 262-3006.
CHICAGO: One E. Erie St., Ste. 650, Chicago, IL 60611. (312) 573-8081. FAX: (312) 573-0318.
CLEVELAND: 1468 W. 9th St., Ste. 720, Cleveland, OH 44113. (216) 579-9305. FAX: (216) 781-2257.
DALLAS: 6060 N. Central Expwy., Ste. 302, LB 604, Dallas, TX 75206. (214) 363-8300. FAX: (214) 363-5386.
DETROIT: American Center, 27770 Franklin Rd. Ste. 300, Southfield, MI 48034. (248) 213-0272. FAX: (800) 361-3741.
FLORIDA: 7300 N. Kendall Dr., Ste. 620, Miami, FL 33156. (305) 670-7677. FAX: (305) 670-1813.
Southhall Center, 101 Southhall Ln., #405, Maitland, FL 32751. (407) 667-483. FAX: (800) 759-0803.
GEORGIA: Melissa Goodman, 455 E. Paces Ferry Rd. N.E., #334, Atlanta, GA 30305. (404) 239-0131. FAX: (404) 239-0137.
HAWAII: 949 Kapiolani Blvd., Ste. 105, Honolulu, HI 96814. (808) 596-0388. FAX: (808) 305-8146.
HOLLYWOOD: 5757 Wilshire Blvd., Los Angeles, CA 90036. (323) 954-1600. FAX: (323) 549-6603.
HOUSTON: 2020 N. Loop W., #240, Houston, TX 77018. (713) 686-4614. FAX: (713) 688-4369.
MINNEAPOLIS/ST. PAUL: 708 N. First St., Ste. 333, Minneapolis, MN 55401. (612) 371-9120. FAX: (612) 371-9119.
NASHVILLE: 1108 17th Ave. S., Nashville, TN 37212. (615) 371-9120. FAX: (615) 329-2803.
NEVADA: Contact Kathy Morand in Hollywood (702) 737-8818. FAX: (323) 549-6460.
NEW YORK: 360 Madison Ave. 12th Flr., New York, NY 10017. (212) 944-1030. FAX: (212) 944-6774.
NORTH/SOUTH CAROLINA: Tower Place Center, 3340 Peachtree Rd. NE, Ste. 1846, Atlanta, GA 30326. (404) 812-5342.
PHILADELPHIA: 230 S. Broad St., Ste. 500, Philadelphia, PA 19102. (215) 545-3150. FAX: (215) 732-0086.
PORTLAND: 3030 S.W. Moody, Ste. 104, Portland, OR 97201. (503) 279-9600. FAX: (503) 279-9603.
ST. LOUIS: 1310 Papin St., Ste. 103, St. Louis, MO 63103. (314) 231-8410. FAX: (314) 231-8412.
SAN DIEGO: 7867 Convoy Ct., Ste. 307, San Diego, CA 92111. (858) 278-7695. FAX: (858) 278-2505.
SAN FRANCISCO: 350 Sansome St., Ste. 900, San Francisco, CA 94104. (415) 391-7510. FAX: (415) 391-1108.
SEATTLE: 4000 Aurora Ave. N., Ste. 102, Seattle, WA 98103. (206) 270-0493. FAX: (206) 282-7073.
WASHINGTON DC/BALTIMORE: 4340 E. West Hwy., Ste. 204, Bethesda, MD 20814. (301) 657-2560. FAX: (301) 656-3615.

SCREEN COMPOSERS OF AMERICA

2451 Nichols Canyon Rd., Los Angeles, CA 90046-1798. (323) 876-6040. FAX: (323) 876-6041.
PRESIDENT
Herschel Burke Gilbert
VICE PRESIDENT
John Parker
TREASURER
Nathan Scott

THE SONGWRITERS GUILD OF AMERICA

1500 Harbor Blvd., Weehawken, NJ 07086. (201) 867-7603. FAX: (201) 867-7335. www.songwriters.org
1560 Broadway, Ste. 1306, New York, NY 10036. (212) 768-7902. FAX: (212) 768-9048. email songnews@aol.com
6430 Sunset Blvd., Ste. 705, Hollywood, CA 90028. (323) 462-1108. FAX: (323) 462-5430. email: lasga@aol.com
1222 16th Ave. S., Ste. 25, Nashville, TN 37212. (615) 329-1782. FAX: (615) 329-2623.
email: sganash@aol.com
PRESIDENT
Rick Carnes
EXECUTIVE DIRECTOR
Lewis M. Bachman

STUNTMEN'S ASSOCIATION

(Organized 1961)
10660 Riverside Dr., 2nd Flr., Ste. E, Toluca Lake, CA 91602. (818) 766-4334. FAX: (818) 766-5943. www.stuntmen.com
email: info@stuntmen.com

PRESIDENT
Conrad Palmisano
OFFICE MANAGER
Kelly Cunningham

THEATRE AUTHORITY, INC.

(Organized May 21, 1934–Charitable organization for theatrical performers)
729 Seventh Ave., 11th Flr., New York, NY 10019. (212) 764-0156.
V.P. & OPERATIONAL DIRECTOR
Mary Lou Westerfield

WRITERS GUILD OF AMERICA, EAST, INC.

555 W. 57th St., Ste. 1230, New York, NY 10019. (212) 767-7800. FAX: 212) 582-1909.
www.wgaeast.org
PRESIDENT
Herb Sargent
EXECUTIVE DIRECTOR
Mona Mangan

WRITERS GUILD OF AMERICA, WEST, INC.

7000 W. Third St., Los Angeles, CA 90048. (323) 951-4000. FAX: (323) 782-4800. www.wga.org
PRESIDENT
Victoria Riskin
VICE PRESIDENT
Charles Holland
EXECUTIVE DIRECTOR
John McLean

STATE & CITY FILM COMMISSIONS

ALABAMA

ALABAMA FILM OFFICE
401 Adams Ave., Ste. 630, Montgomery, AL 36130. (800) 633-5898, (334) 242-4195. FAX: (334) 242-2077. www.alabamafilm.org
FILM OFFICE COORDINATOR
Brenda Hobbie

CITY OF MOBILE FILM OFFICE
164 Saint Emanuel St., Mobile, AL 36602. (251) 438-7100. FAX: (251) 438-7104.
DIRECTOR
Eva Golson

ARIZONA

ARIZONA FILM COMMISSION
1700 W. Washington, Ste. 220, Phoenix, AZ 85007. (800) 523-6695, (602) 771-1193. FAX: (602) 771-1211.
www.azcommerce.com
DIRECTOR
Robert Detweiler

CITY OF PHOENIX FILM OFFICE
200 W. Washington, 10th Flr., Phoenix, AZ 85003. (602) 262-4850. FAX: (602) 534-2295. www.filmphoenix.com
PROGRAM MANAGER
Luci Fontanilla

CITY OF SCOTTSDALE
7447 E. Indian School Rd., Scottsdale, AZ 85251. (480) 312-7676. FAX: (480) 312-7011.
FILM LIAISON
Robert Henderson

APACHE JUNCTION CHAMBER OF COMMERCE
P.O. Box 1747, Apache Junction, AZ 85217. (800) 252-3141, (480) 982-3141. FAX: (480) 982-3234.
www.apachejunctioncoc.com
email: info@apachejunctioncoc.com
DIRECTOR
Rayna Palmer

COTTONWOOD FILM COMMISSION
1010 S. Main St., Cottonwood, AZ 86326. (928) 634-7593. FAX: (928) 634-7594. http://chamber.verdevalley.com/
DIRECTOR
Peter A. Sesow

FLAGSTAFF FILM COMMISSION
Flagstaff Convention & Visitors Bureau, 211 W. Aspen Ave., Flagstaff, AZ 86001. (800) 217-2367. FAX: (928) 556-1305. www.flagstaffarizona.org email: cvb@ci.flagstaff.az.us
CONTACT
Leslie Connell

GLOBE MIAMI FILM COMMISSION
1360 North Broad St., U.S. 60, Globe, AZ 85502. (928) 425-4495. FAX: (928) 425-3410. www.globemiamichamber.com
email: gmr@cableone.net
DIRECTOR
Gerald Kohlbeck

PAGE/LAKE POWELL FILM COMMISSION
644 N. Navajo Dr., P.O. Box 727, Page, AZ 86040. (928) 645-2741. FAX: (928) 645-3181. www.pagelakepowellchamber.org
email: info@pagelakepowellchamber.org
FILM COMMISSIONER
Joan Nevills Staveley

CITY OF PRESCOTT
P.O. Box 2059, Prescott, AZ 86302. (928) 777-1204. FAX: (928) 771-5870. email: greg.fister@cityofprescott.net
DIRECTOR
Greg Fister

SAFFORD/GRAHAM COUNTY REGIONAL FILM OFFICE
1111 Thatcher Blvd., Safford, AZ 85546. (888) 837-1841, (928) 428-2511. FAX: (928) 428-0744. www.graham-chamer.com
DIRECTOR
Sheldon Miller

SEDONA FILM COMMISSION
P.O. Box 478, Sedona, AZ 86339. (800) 288-7336, (928) 204-1123. FAX: (928) 204-1064. www.sedonachamber.com
CHAIRMAN
Dan Schay

TUCSON FILM OFFICE
Metropolitan Tucson Visitors and Convention Bureau, 100 S. Church Ave., Tucson, AZ 85701. (800) 638-8350, (520) 624-1817. FAX: (520) 884-7804. email: shall@mtcvb.com; pcatalanotte@mtcvb.com
DIRECTOR
Shelli Hall
LOCATION COORDINATOR
Peter Catalanotte (520) 770-2151

WICKENBURG FILM COMMISSION
216 North Frontier St., Wickenburg, AZ 85390. (928) 684-5479. FAX: (928) 684-5470. www.wickenburgchamber.com
DIRECTOR
Julie Brooks

YUMA FILM COMMISSION
850 W. 32nd St., Ste. 6, Yuma, AZ 85364. (928) 341-1616. FAX: (928) 314-9247. www.filmyuma.com
PRESIDENT
Yvonne Taylor

ARKANSAS

ARKANSAS FILM OFFICE
One State Capitol Mall, 4th Flr., Little Rock, AR 72201. (501) 682-7676. FAX: (501) 682-FILM. www.1800arkansas.com/film
email: jglass@1800ARKANSAS.com
FILM COMMISSIONER
Joe Glass

CALIFORNIA

ANTELOPE VALLEY FILM OFFICE
44933 Fern Ave., Lancaster, CA 93534. (661) 723-6090. FAX: (661) 723-5914. www.avfilm.com
email: peast@cityoflancasterca.org
DIRECTOR
Pauline East

BERKELEY FILM OFFICE
2015 Center St., Berkeley, CA 94704-1204. (800) 847-4823, (510) 549-7040. FAX: (510) 644-2052. www.filmberkeley.com
email: filmberkeley@mindspring.com
DIRECTOR
Barbara Hillman

BIG BEAR LAKE FILM OFFICE
39707 Big Bear Blvd., P.O. Box 10000, Big Bear Lake, CA 92315. (909) 878-3040, (909) 866-5831, x 109. FAX: (909) 866-6766. www.citybigbearlake.com/film.html
email: bblfilm@citybigbearlake.com
DIRECTOR
Kresse Armour

CALIFORNIA FILM COMMISSION
7080 Hollywood Blvd., Ste. 900, Hollywood, CA 90028. (800) 858-4PIX. FAX: (323) 860-2972. www.film.ca.gov
email: filmca@commerce.ca.gov
DIRECTOR
Karen Constine

CATALINA ISLAND FILM COMMISSION
125 Metropole Ave., Ste. 103, Avalon, CA 90704. (310) 510-7646. FAX: (310) 510-1646.
DIRECTOR
Shirley Davy

CHICO CHAMBER/BUTTE COUNTY FILM COMMISSION
300 Salem St., Chico, CA 95928. (800) 852-8570, (530) 891-5556 x 326. FAX: (530) 891-3613. www.chicochamber.com
CEO
Jim Goodwin

CITY OF MALIBU FILM COMMISSION
23815 Stuart Ranch Rd., Malibu, CA 90265. (877) 797-4744. FAX: (310) 456-5799. www.ci.malibu.ca.us
email: kim@sws-inc.com
DIRECTOR
Kimberly Collins Nilsson

CITY OF SAN FRANCISCO
San Francisco Film and Video Arts Commission, 1 Dr. Carlton B. Goodlett Place, Rm. #473, San Francisco, CA 94102. (415) 554-6244. FAX: (415) 554-6503
DIRECTOR
Martha Cohen

CITY OF SAN JOSE
San Jose Film & Video Commission, 125 S. Market St., Ste. 300, San Jose, CA 95113. (800) SAN-JOSE, (408) 295-9600. FAX: (408) 295-3937. www.sanjose.org/filmvideo
email: kmanley@sanjose.org
DIRECTOR, VISITOR SERVICES
Kate Manley

CITY OF WEST HOLLYWOOD
8300 Santa Monica Blvd., West Hollywood, CA 90069-4314. (323) 848-6489. FAX: (323) 848-6561.
www.ci.west-hollywood.ca.us
email: wehofilm@ci.west-hollywood.ca.us
DIRECTOR
Terry S. House

CLOVIS FILM OFFICE
325 Pollasky Ave., Clovis, CA 93612. (559) 299-7363. FAX: (559) 299-2969. www.clovischamber.com
email: judith@clovischamber.com
DIRECTOR
Judith Pruss

COUNTY OF LOS ANGELES
Entertainment Industry Development Corp., Los Angeles Film Office, 7083 Hollywood Blvd., Ste. 500, Hollywood, CA 90028. (323) 957-1000. FAX: (323) 463-0613. www.eidc.com
V.P. & GENERAL MANAGER, OPERATIONS
Darryl Seif

EL DORADO/TAHOE FILM & MEDIA OFFICE
542 Main St., Placerville, CA 95667. (800) 457-6279, (530) 621-5885. FAX: (530) 642-1624. www.filmtahoe.com
email: film@eldoradocounty.org
EXECUTIVE DIRECTOR
Kathleen Dodge

HUMBOLDT COUNTY FILM COMMISSION
1034 Second St., Eureka, CA 95501-0541. (800) 338-7352, (707) 444-6633. FAX: (707) 443-5115. www.filmhumboldt.org
email: filmcom@filmhumboldt.org
FILM COMMISSIONER
Barbara Bryant

FRESNO COUNTY OFFICE OF TOURISM & FILM COMMISSION
2220 Tulare St., 8th Flr., Fresno, CA 93721. (559) 262-4271. FAX: (559) 442-6969. email: ggibbs@fresno.ca.gov
DIRECTOR, TOURISM
Gigi Gibbs

IMPERIAL COUNTY FILM COMMISSION
230 S. Fifth St., El Centro, CA 92243. (760) 337-4155. FAX: (760) 337-8235. www.filmhere.com
email: filmhere@earthlink.net
DIRECTOR
Allison Martin

THE INLAND EMPIRE FILM COMMISSION
301 E. Vanderbilt Way, Ste. 100, San Bernardino, CA 92408. (909) 890-1090. FAX: (909) 890-1088.
www.filminlandempire.com email: sdavis@ieep.com
DIRECTOR
Sheri Davis

KERN COUNTY BOARD OF TRADE
2101 Oak St., P. O. Bin 1312, Bakersfield, CA 93302. (800) 500-KERN, (661) 861-2367. FAX: (661) 861-2017.
www.filmkern.com email: kerninfo@co.kern.ca.us
EXECUTIVE DIRECTOR
Barry Zoeller

LAKE COUNTY MARKETING PROGRAM
875 Lakeport Blvd., Lakeport, CA 95453. (800) 525-3743, (707) 263-9562. FAX: (707) 263-1012. www.lakecounty.com
email: info@lakecounty.com
ADMINISTRATIVE OFFICER
Kelly F. Cox

LONG BEACH OFFICE OF SPECIAL EVENTS
1 World Trade Center, Ste. 300, Long Beach, CA 90831. (562) 570-5333. FAX: (562) 570-5335. www.filmlongbeach.com
FILM COORDINATOR
Tasha Day

MADERA COUNTY FILM COMMISSION
41969 Highway 41, Oakhurst, CA 93644. (559) 683-4636. FAX: (559) 683-5697. email: ysvb@sti.net
FILM COMMISSIONER
Dave WoLin

MENDOCINO COUNTY FILM OFFICE
P.O. Box 1141, Fort Bragg, CA 95437. (707) 961-6303. FAX: (707) 964-2056. www.mendocinocoast.com
email: chamber@mcn.org
EXECUTIVE DIRECTOR
Debra Degraw

MONTEREY COUNTY
Monterey County Film Commission, 801 Lighthouse Ave., Ste. 104, Monterey, CA 93940. (831) 646-0910. FAX: (831) 655-9250. www.filmmonterey.org email: filmmonterey@redshift.com
EXECUTIVE DIRECTOR
Greg Robinson

OAKLAND FILM OFFICE
150 Frank H. Ogawa, Ste. 8215, Oakland, CA 94612. (510) 238-4734. FAX: (510) 238-6149. www.filmoakland.com
DIRECTOR
Ami Zins
ASSISTANT FILM COORDINATOR
Janet Austin

ORANGE COUNTY FILM COMMISSION
California State University, Fullerton Center for Entertainment & Tourism, P.O. Box 6850, Fullerton, CA 92834-6850. (714) 278-7569. FAX: (714) 278-7521. www.ocfilm.org
email: jarrington@ocfilm.org
FILM COMMISSIONER
Janice Arrington

PALM SPRINGS DESERT RESORTS CVB/FILM OFFICE
301 E. Vanderbilt Way, Ste. 100, San Bernardino, CA 92408. (909) 890-1090. FAX: (909) 890-1088.
www.filminlandempire.com email: sdavis@ieep.com
DIRECTOR
Sheri Davis

PASADENA FILM OFFICE
175 N. Garfield Ave., Pasadena, CA 91109. (626) 744-3964. FAX: (626)-744-4785. www.filmpasadena.com
email: apenn@ci.pasadena.ca.us
email: jcostner@ci.pasadena.ca.us
FILMING AND SPECIAL EVENTS MANAGER
Ariel Penn
FILMING COORDINATOR
Janet Costner

PLACER-LAKE TAHOE FILM OFFICE
175 Fulweiler Ave., Auburn, CA 95603-4543. (877) 228-3456 (530) 889-4016. FAX: (530) 889-4095. www.placer.ca.gov/films
email: blewis@placer.ca.gov
DIRECTOR
Beverly Lewis

RIDGECREST REGIONAL FILM COMMISSION
139 Balsam St., Ridgecrest, CA 93555. (800)-847-4830, (760) 375-8202. FAX: (760) 375-9850. www.filmdeserts.com
email: racvb@filmdeserts.com
FILM COMMISSIONER
Ray Arthur

SACRAMENTO FILM COMMISSION
1303 J St., Ste. 600, Sacramento, CA 95814. (916) 264-7777. FAX: (916) 264-7788. www.filmsacramento.com
email: lsteffens@cityofsacramento.org
FILM COMMISSIONER
Lucy Steffens

SAN BENITO FILM COUNCIL
650 San Benito St., Ste. 130, Hollister, CA 95023. (831) 637-5315. FAX: (831) 637-1008. www.sanbenitocountychamber.com
email: info@sanbenitocountychamber.com
EXECUTIVE DIRECTOR
Theresa Kiernan

SAN DIEGO FILM COMMISSION
1010 Second Ave, #1500, San Diego, CA 92101-4912. (619) 234-3456. FAX: (619) 234-4631. www.sdfilm.com
FILM COMMISSIONER
Cathy Anderson

SAN LUIS OBISPO COUNTY FILM COMMISSION
1037 Mill St., San Luis Obispo, CA 93401. (805) 541-8000. FAX: (805) 543-9498. www.sanluisobispocounty.com
email: slocvcb@slonet.org
DIRECTOR
Jonni Biaggini

SANTA BARBARA FILM COMMISSION
1601 Anacapa St., Santa Barbara, CA 93101. (805) 966-9222 x110. FAX: (805) 966-1728. www.filmsantabarbara.com
email: martine@filmsantabarbara.com
FILM COMMISSIONER
Martine White

SANTA CLARITA VALLEY FILM OFFICE
23920 Valencia Blvd., Ste. 210, Santa Clarita, CA 91355. (661) 284-1425. FAX: (661) 286-4001. www.filmsantaclarita.com
email: film@santa-clarita.com
DIRECTOR
Jason Crawford

SANTA CRUZ COUNTY FILM COMMISSION
1211 Ocean St., Santa Cruz, CA 95060. (800) 833-3494, (831) 425-1234. FAX: (831) 425-1260. www.santacruzca.org
email: rruble@santacruzca.org
DIRECTOR
Ranee Ruble

SANTA MONICA MOUNTAINS
401 West Hillcrest Dr., Thousand Oaks, CA 91360. (805) 370-2308. FAX: (805) 370-1851. www.nps.gov/samo
email: alice_allen@nps.gov
DIRECTOR
Alice Allen

SHASTA COUNTY FILM COMMISSION
777 Auditorium Dr., Redding, CA 96001. (800) 874-7562, (530)-225-4100. FAX: (530) 225-4354. www.visitredding.org
CONVENTION SALES REP
Sherry Ferguson

SONOMA COUNTY FILM OFFICE
401D College Ave. - EconDevBoard, Santa Rosa, CA 95401. (707) 565-7347. FAX: (707) 565-7231.
www.sonomacountyfilm.com
email: cdeprima@sonoma-county.org
DIRECTOR
Catherine DePrima

TEMECULA VALLEY FILM COUNCIL
27740 Jefferson Ave., Ste. 100, Temecula, CA 92590. (909) 506-1189. FAX: (909) 693-0554.
CONTACT
Maggi Allen

TRI-VALLEY FILM AND VIDEO
260 Main St., Pleasanton, CA 94566. (888) 874-9253, (925) 846-8910. FAX: (925) 846-9502. www.trivalleycvb.com
email: film@trivalleycvb.com
DIRECTOR
Amy Blaschka

TULARE COUNTY FILM COMMISSION
5961 S. Mooney Blvd., Visalia, CA, 93277. (559) 733-4306. FAX: (559) 730-2591. email: jstevens@co.tulare.ca.us
FILM LIAISON
John Stevens

TUOLUMNE COUNTY FILM COMMISSION
P.O. Box 4020, Sonora, CA 95370. (800) 446-1333, (209) 533-4420. FAX: (209) 533-0956. www.tcfilm.org
FILM OFFICE LIAISON
Sandy Esau

VALLEJO/SOLANO COUNTY FILM OFFICE
495 Mare Island Way, Vallejo, CA 94590. (800) 4-VALLEJO, (707) 642-3653. FAX: (707) 644-2206. www.visitvallejo.com/film
email: film@visitvallejo.com
DIRECTOR
Jim Reikowsky

VENTURA COUNTY FILM COUNCIL
1601 Carmen Dr., #215, Camarillo, CA 93010. (805) 384-1800. FAX: (805) 384-1805. www.edc-vc.com
email: dawnbarber@edc-vc.com
EXECUTIVE ASSISTANT
Dawn Barber

COLORADO

COLORADO FILM COMMISSION
1625 Broadway, Ste. 1700, Denver, CO 80202. (800) SCO-UTUS, (303) 620-4500. FAX: (303) 620-4545.
www.coloradofilm.org email: staff@coloradofilm.org
CONTACTS
Stephanie TwoEagles
Adam Clark

BOULDER COUNTY FILM COMMISSION
2440 Pearl St., Boulder, CO 80302. (303) 442-2911. FAX: (303) 938-2098. email: joy@bouldercvb.com
DIRECTOR
Joy Kosanski

CLEAR CREEK COUNTY FILM COMMISSION
P. O. Box 100, Idaho Springs, CO 80452. (800) 882-5278, (303) 567-4660. FAX: (303) 567-0967.
www.clearcreekcounty.org
email: stephanie@clearcreekcounty.org
DIRECTOR
Stephanie Donoho

COLORADO SPRINGS FILM COMMISSION
515 S. Cascade Ave., Colorado Springs, CO 80903. (800) 888-4748 x131, (719) 635-7506 x131. FAX: (719) 635-4968.
www.filmcoloradosprings.com
email: eforeman@filmcoloradosprings.com
FILM COMMISSIONER
Edwina Foreman

FORT COLLINS CONVENTION AND VISITORS BUREAU
3745 E. Prospect Rd., #200 Fort Collins, CO 80525. (800) 274-3678, (970) 491-3388. FAX: (970) 491-3389.
www.ftcollins.com email: rharter@ftcollins.com
DIRECTOR
Richard Harter

FREMONT/CUSTER COUNTY FILM COMMISSION
403 Royal Gorge Blvd., Canon City, CO 81212. (800) 876-7922, (719) 275-2331. FAX: (719) 275-2332.
www.canoncitychamber.com email: chamber@canoncity.com
DIRECTOR
George R. Turner

GREELEY/WELD COUNTY FILM COMMISSION
902 7th Ave., Greeley, CO 80631. (800) 449-3866, (970) 352-3567. FAX: (970) 352-3572. www.greeleycvb.com
email: info@greeleycvb.com
DIRECTOR
Sarah MacQuiddy

NORTHWEST COLORADO FILM COMMISSION /YAMPA VALLEY FILM BOARD
Box 772305, Steamboat Springs, CO 80477. (970) 879-0882. FAX: (970) 879-2543. www.steamboatchamber.com
DIRECTOR
Riley Polumbus

SOUTHWEST COLORADO FILM COMMISSION
P.O. Box HH, Cortez, CO 81321-4059. (970) 565-8227. FAX: (970) 565-1155. www.swcolo.org email: mcedc@swcolo.org
DIRECTOR
Lynn Dyer

TRINIDAD FILM COMMISSION
136 W. Main St., Trinidad, CO 81082. (800) 748-1970, (719) 846-9412. FAX: (719) 846-4550.
www.tsjc.cccoes.edu/tri_film/tri_film.htm
email: tlaced@sensonics.org
DIRECTOR
Joe Tarabino

CONNECTICUT

CONNECTICUT FILM, VIDEO & MEDIA OFFICE
805 Brook St., Bldg. 4, Rocky Hill, CT 06067. (800) 392-2122, (860) 571-7130. FAX: (860) 721-7088. www.CTfilm.com
email: info@CTfilm.com
EXECUTIVE DIRECTOR
Guy Ortoleva
ASSISTANT DIRECTOR
Mark Dixon
PROJECT MANAGER
Judy Schultz

DANBURY FILM OFFICE
P.O. Box 406, Danbury, CT 06813. (800) 841-4488, (203) 743-0546. FAX: (203) 790-6124.
MARKETING DIRECTOR
Molly Curry

NEW MILFORD FILM COMMISSION
Town Hall, 10 Main St., New Milford, CT 06776. (860) 210-2099. FAX: (860) 210-2623. www.filmnewmilfordct.org
HEAD OF COMMISSION
Saun Ellis
Rachel Barton

SOUTHEASTERN CONNECTICUT FILM OFFICE
P.O. Box 89, 470 Bank St, c/o SECT CVB, New London, CT 06320. (888) 657-FILM, (860) 444-2206. FAX: (860) 442-4257. www.sectfilm.com email: film@mysticmore.com
DIRECTOR
Philip Hanson

DELAWARE

DELAWARE FILM OFFICE
Delaware Tourism Office, 99 Kings Hwy., Dover, DE 19901. (302) 739-4271. FAX: (302) 739-5749.

DISTRICT OF COLUMBIA

WASHINGTON DC OFFICE OF MOTION PICTURE AND TELEVISION DEVELOPMENT
441 Fourth St., N.W., Washington, D.C. 20001. (202) 727-6608. FAX: (202) 727-3246. www.film.dc.gov
DIRECTOR
Crystal Palmer

FLORIDA

FORT LAUDERDALE AREA/BROWARD COUNTY
Film & Television Commission, Broward Alliance, 300 S.E. Second St., Ste. 780, Fort Lauderdale, FL 33301. (954) 524-3113. FAX: (954) 524-3167. www.browardalliance.org/film
email: ewentworth@browardalliance.org
DIRECTOR
Elizabeth Wentworth

JACKSONVILLE FILM & TV OFFICE
220 E. Bay St., Ste. 1400, Jacksonville, FL 32202. (904) 630-2522. FAX: (904) 630-2919. www.coj.net
email: film@coj.net
FILM COMMISSIONER
Todd Roobin

FILM COMMISSION OF REAL FLORIDA, INC.
1025 S.W. First Ave., Ste. B, Ocala, FL 34474. (352) 671-1717.
FAX: (352) 671-1482. www.realfla.com
FILM COMMISSIONER
Jude Hagin

FLORIDA KEYS & KEY WEST FILM COMMISSION
1201 White St., Ste. 102, Key West, FL 33040. (800) FILM
KEYS, (305) 293-1800. FAX: (305) 296-0788.
www.filmkeys.com email: keysfilm@fla-keys.com
DIRECTOR
Rita Brown

METRO ORLANDO FILM & TELEVISION COMMISSION
301 E. Pine St., Ste. 900, Orlando, FL 32801. (407) 422-7159.
FAX: (407) 841-9069. www.filmorlando.com
DIRECTORS
Suzy Allen
Jennifer Pennypacker
ASSOCIATE DIRECTOR
Dale Gordon

MIAMI-DADE COUNTY
Miami-Dade Mayor's Office of Film and Entertainment, 111
N.W. 1st St., Ste. 2540, Miami, FL 33128. (305) 375-3288.
FAX: (305) 375-3266. www.filmmiami.org
DIRECTOR
Jeff Peel

NORTHWEST FLORIDA/OKALOOSA FILM COMMISSION
P.O. Box 609, Ft. Walton Beach, FL 32549-0609. (800) 322-
3319, (850) 651-7644. FAX: (850) 651-7149.
www.destin-fwb.com/film

PALM BEACH COUNTY FILM & TV COMMISSION
1555 Palm Beach Lakes Blvd., Ste. 900, West Palm Beach, FL
33401. (800) 745-FILM, (561) 233-1000. FAX: (561) 233-3113.
www.pbfilm.com
FILM COMMISSIONER
Chuck Elderd

SOUTHWEST FLORIDA FILM COMMISSION
2180 W. First St., #100, Fort Myers, FL 33901-3219. (239) 338-
3500, (239) 338-3189. FAX: (239) 334-1106.
DIRECTOR
Nancy Hamilton

SPACE COAST FILM COMMISSION
2725 Judge Jamison Way, Melbourne, FL 32940. (877) 57-
Beach, (321) 637-5483. FAX: (321) 637-5494.
www.space-coast.com email: bkingfilm@aol.com
DIRECTOR
Bonnie King

TAMPA BAY FILM COMMISSION
400 N. Tampa St., Ste. 2800, Tampa, FL 33602. (800) 826-
8358, (813) 342-4058. FAX: (813) 229-6616.
www.visittampabay.com email: eemerald@visittampabay.com
FILM COMMISSIONER
Edie Emerald

GEORGIA

GEORGIA FILM & VIDEO & MUSIC OFFICE
285 Peachtree Center Ave., Ste. 1000, Atlanta, GA 30303.
(404) 656-3591. FAX: (404) 656-3565. www.filmgeorgia.org
email: film@georgia.org
DIRECTOR
Greg Torre

SAVANNAH FILM COMMISSION
P.O. Box 1027, Savannah, GA 31402. (912) 651-3696. FAX:
(912) 238-0872. www.savannahfilm.org
email: jself@ci.savannah.ga.us
FILM COMMISSIONER
Jay M. Self

HAWAII

BIG ISLAND FILM OFFICE
25 Aupuni St., Hilo, HI 96720. Hilo: (808) 961-8366. FAX:
(808) 935-1205. Kona: (808) 326-2663.
www.filmbigisland.com email: film@bigisland.com
FILM COMMISSIONER
Marilyn Killeri

HAWAII FILM OFFICE
P.O. Box 2359, Honolulu, HI 96804. (808) 586-2570. FAX:
(808) 586-2572. www.hawaiifilmoffice.com
email: info@hawaiifilmoffice.com
MANAGER
Donne Dawson

HONOLULU FILM OFFICE
530 S. King St., Ste. 306, Honolulu, HI 96813. (808) 527-
6108. FAX: (808) 527-6102. www.filmhonolulu.com
email: info@filmhonolulu.com
FILM COMMISSIONER
Walea L. Constantinau

KAUAI FILM COMMISSION
4444 Rice St. #200, Lihue, HI 96766. (808) 241-6386. FAX:
(808) 241-6399. www.filmkauai.com
email: info@filmkauai.com
FILM COMMISSIONER
Tiffani Lizama

MAUI FILM OFFICE
200 S. High St., 6th Flr., Wailuku, Maui, HI 96793. (808) 270-
7710. FAX: (808) 270-7995. www.filmmaui.com
email: info@filmmaui.com
FILM COMMISSIONER
Benita Brazier

IDAHO

IDAHO FILM BUREAU
700 W. State St., Box 83720, Boise, ID 83720-0093. (800) 942-
8338. FAX: (208) 334-2631. www.filmidaho.com
DIRECTOR
Peg Owens

ILLINOIS

CHICAGO FILM OFFICE
One N. LaSalle, Ste. 2165, Chicago, IL 60602. (312) 744-6415.
FAX: (312) 744-1378.
DIRECTOR
Richard M. Moskal

ILLINOIS FILM OFFICE
100 W. Randolph, Ste. 3-400, Chicago, IL 60601. (312) 814-
3600. FAX: (312) 814-8874. www.filmillinois.state.il.us
DIRECTOR
Brenda Sexton

INDIANA

INDIANA FILM COMMISSION
1 N. Capitol Ave., Ste. 700, Indianapolis, IN 46204-2288. (317)
232-8829. FAX: (317) 233-6887. www.in.gov/film
DIRECTOR
Jane Rulon

IOWA

CEDAR RAPIDS AREA FILM COMMISSION
119 First Ave. S.E., P.O. Box 5339, Cedar Rapids, IA 52401-
5339. (800) 735-5557 x 127, (319) 398-5383 x 127. FAX: (319)
398-5089. www.cedar-rapids.com
email: mkrug@cedar-rapids.com
DIRECTOR
Matt Krug

IOWA FILM OFFICE
200 E. Grand Ave., Des Moines, IA 50309. (515) 242-4726.
FAX: (515) 242-4718. www.state.ia.us/film
email: filmiowa@ided.state.ia.us
FILM CONSULTANT
Steven Schott

KANSAS

KANSAS FILM COMMISSION
1000 S.W. Jackson St., Ste. 100, Topeka, KS 66612-1354.
(785) 296-2178. FAX: (785) 296-3490. www.filmkansas.com
FILM COMMISSIONER
Peter Jasso

KANSAS III FILM COMMISSION/LAWRENCE CVB
734 Vermont, Ste. 101, Lawrence, KS 66044. (785) 865-4411.
FAX: (785) 865-4400.
DIRECTOR
Judy Billings

WICHITA FILM COMMISSION
100 S. Main, Ste. 100, Wichita, KS 67202. (800) 288-9424,
(316) 265-2800. FAX: (316) 265-0162. www.visitwichita.com
DIRECTOR OF TOURISM
Olivia Reynolds

KENTUCKY

KENTUCKY FILM COMMISSION
Capitol Plaza Tower, 500 Mero St., 22nd Flr., Frankfort, KY
40601. (800) 345-6591. FAX: (502) 564-7588. www.kyfilm.com
DIRECTOR
Jim Toole

LOUISIANA

CITY OF NEW ORLEANS FILM & VIDEO COMMISSION
1515 Poydras St., Ste. 1150, New Orleans, LA 70112. (504)
565-7557. FAX: (504) 565-8108.
email: sdupuy@mayorofno.com
CONTACT
Stephanie Dupuy

JEFF DAVIS PARISH FILM COMMISSION
P.O. Box 1207, Jennings, LA 70546-1207. (337) 821-5534.
www.jeffdavis.org
CONTACT
Kayla Gary

LOUISIANA FILM COMMISSION
P.O. Box 94185, Baton Rouge, LA 70804-4320. (888) 655-
0447, (225) 342-8150. FAX: (225) 342-5349. www.lafilm.org
DIRECTOR
Mark Smith

SHREVEPORT-BOSSIER FILM COMMISSION
P.O. Box 1761, Shreveport, LA 71166. (800) 551-8682, (318)
222-9391. FAX: (318) 222-0056. www.sbctb.org
DIRECTOR
Betty Jo LeBrun-Mooring

MAINE

MAINE FILM OFFICE
59 State House Station, Augusta, ME 04333. (207) 624-7631.
FAX: (207) 287-8070. www.filminmaine.com
email: filmme@earthlink.net
DIRECTOR
Lea Girardin

MARYLAND

BALTIMORE FILM COMMISSION
417 E. Fayette St., Ste. 601, Baltimore, MD 21202. (410) 396-
4550. FAX: (410) 625-4667.
email: rose.greene@baltimorecity.gov
DIRECTOR
Rose Greene

MARYLAND FILM OFFICE
217 E. Redwood St., 9th Flr., Baltimore, MD 21202. (800) 333-
6632, (410) 767-6340. FAX: (410) 333-0044.
www.marylandfilm.org email: filminfo@marylandfilm.org
DIRECTOR
Jack Gerbes

MASSACHUSETTS

MASS FILM BUREAU
198 Tremont St., PMB#135, Boston, MA 02116. (617) 523-
8388. www.massfilmbureau.com
email: MassFilmBureau@aol.com
EXECUTIVE DIRECTOR
Robin Dawson
CHIEF OF STAFF
David Young
ASSISTANT DIRECTOR
Laura Yellen

MICHIGAN

MICHIGAN FILM OFFICE
P.O. Box 30739, Lansing, MI 48909. (800) 477-3456, (517) 373-
0638. FAX: (517) 241-2930. www.michigan.gov
email: jlockwood@michigan.gov
DIRECTOR
Janet Lockwood

MINNESOTA

MINNESOTA FILM & TV BOARD
401 N. Third St., Ste. 460, Minneapolis, MN 55401. (612) 332-
6493. FAX: (612) 332-3735. www.mnfilm.org
EXECUTIVE DIRECTOR
Craig Rice
DIRECTOR OF PRODUCTION
Nicole Hinrichs-Bideau

MISSISSIPPI

CITY OF COLUMBUS
Columbus Film Commission, P.O. Box 789, Columbus, MS
39703. (800) 327-2686, (662) 329-1191. FAX: (662) 329-8969.
www.columbus-ms.org
DIRECTOR
Michael McCalla

CITY OF NATCHEZ
Natchez Film Commission, 640 S. Canal St., Box G, Natchez,
MS 39120. (800) 647-6724, (601) 446-6345. FAX: (601) 442-
0814. www.natchez.ms.us email: ctaunton@bkbank.com
CONTACT
Connie Taunton

GREENWOOD CONVENTION & VISITORS BUREAU
P.O. Drawer 739, Greenwood, MS 38935. (800) 748-9064,
(662) 453-9197. FAX: (662) 453-5526. www.gcvb.com
email: info@gcvb.com
DIRECTOR
Suzy Gordon

MISSISSIPPI FILM OFFICE
P.O. Box 849, Jackson, MS 39205. (601) 359-3297. FAX: (601)
359-5048.
DIRECTOR
Ward Emling

TUPELO FILM COMMISSION
399 East Main St., P.O. Drawer 47, Tupelo, MS 38802. (800)
533-0611, (662) 841-6521. FAX: (662) 841-6558.
www.tupelo.net
FILM COMMISSIONER
Pat Rasberry

VICKSBURG FILM COMMISSION
P.O. Box 110, Vicksburg, MS 39181. (800) 221-3536, (601)
636-9421. FAX: (601) 636-9475. www.vicksburgcvb.org
DIRECTOR
Lynn Foley

MISSOURI

FILM COMMISSION OF GREATER KANSAS CITY
10 Petticoat Ln., Ste. 250, Kansas City, MO 64106. (800)
889-0636, (816) 221-0636. FAX: (816) 221-0189.
www.kcfilm.com email: tway@edckc.com
DIRECTOR
Tiffany Way

MISSOURI FILM OFFICE
301 W. High, Rm. 720, P.O. Box 118, Jefferson City, MO 65102.
(573) 751-9050. FAX: (573) 522-1719.
www.missouridevelopment.org/film
MANAGER
Jerry Jones

MONTANA

**BILLINGS CONVENTION & VISITORS COUNCIL FILM
LIAISON OFFICE**
P.O. Box 31177, Billings, MT 59107. (800) 711-2630, (406)
245-4111. FAX: (406) 245-7333. www.billingscvb.visit.mt.com
DIRECTOR
Rhonda Harms

CITY OF BUTTE FILM LIAISON OFFICE
1000 George St., Butte, MT 59701. (406) 723-3177 FAX: (406)
723-1215. www.butteinfo.org
FILM LIAISON TO STATE COMMISSIONER
Connie Kenney

GREAT FALLS REGIONAL FILM LIAISON
710 1st Ave. N., Great Falls, MT 59401. (406) 761-4434. FAX:
(406) 761-6129. www.greatfallsonline.net
FILM COMMISSIONER
Janet Medina

MONTANA FILM OFFICE
301 S. Park Ave., Helena, MT 59620. (800) 553-4563, (406)
841-2876. FAX: (406) 841-2877. www.montanafilm.com
email: montanafilm@visitmt.com
DIRECTOR
Sten Iverson
LOCATION COORDINATOR
Bill Kuney

NEBRASKA

NEBRASKA FILM OFFICE
P.O. Box 98907, Lincoln, NE 68509. (800) 228-4307, (402)
471-3680. FAX: (402) 471-3026. www.filmnebraska.org
email: info@filmnebraska.org
DIRECTOR
Laurie J. Richards

OMAHA FILM COMMISSION
1001 Farnam St., Ste. 200, Omaha, NE 68102. (402) 444-
7737. FAX: (402) 444-4511. www.filmnebraska.org
email: shootomaha@juno.com
DIRECTOR
Kathy Sheppard

NEVADA

NEVADA FILM OFFICE-LAS VEGAS
555 E. Washington Ave., Ste. 5400, Las Vegas, NV 89101-
1078. (877) 638-3456, (702) 486-2711. FAX: (702) 486-2712.
www.nevadafilm.com email: info@bizopp.state.nv.us
DIRECTOR
Charles Geocaris

NEVADA FILM OFFICE RENO/TAHOE
108 E. Proctor St., Carson City, NV 89701. (800) 336-1600,
(775) 687-1814. FAX: (775) 687-4450. www.nevadafilm.com
email: rhbird@bizopp.state.nv.us
DEPUTY DIRECTOR
Robin Holabird

NEW HAMPSHIRE

NEW HAMPSHIRE FILM & TELEVISION OFFICE
P.O. Box 1856, 172 Pembroke Rd., Concord, NH 03302-1856.
(603) 271-2665. FAX: (603) 271-6870. www.filmnh.org
DIRECTOR
Jay Brenchick

NEW JERSEY

NEW JERSEY MOTION PICTURE & TV COMMISSION
P.O. Box 47023, 153 Halsey St., 5th Flr., Newark, NJ 07101.
(973) 648-6279. FAX: (973) 648-7350. www.njfilm.org
email: njfilm@njfilm.org
DIRECTOR
Joseph Friedman

NEW MEXICO

CITY OF ALBUQUERQUE
Mayors Office, Office of Economic Development, 1 Civic Plaza
NW, Rm. 3047, Albuquerque, NM 87103. (505) 768-3283. FAX:
(505) 768-3280. www.cabq.gov email: alerner@cabq.gov
FILM LIAISON
Ann Lerner

NEW MEXICO FILM OFFICE
1100 St. Francis Dr., Ste. 1200, Santa Fe, NM 87505. (800) 545-
9871, (505) 827-9810. FAX: (505) 827-9799. www.nmfilm.com
email: film@nmfilm.com
DIRECTOR
Frank Zuniga

LAS CRUCES FILM COMMISSION
211 North Water St., Las Cruces, NM 88001. (800) FIESTAS,
(505) 541-2444. FAX: (505) 541-2164. www.lascrucescvb.org
email: cvb@lascrucescvb.org
DIRECTOR
Ted Scanlon

SANTA FE FILM OFFICE
P.O. Box 909, Santa Fe, NM 87504-0909. (800) 984-9984,
(505) 955-6200. FAX: (505) 955-6222. www.santafe.org
CONTACT
Becky Ellis

NEW YORK

CITY OF NEW YORK, MAYOR'S OFFICE OF FILM, THEATRE & BROADCASTING
1697 Broadway, New York, NY 10019. (212) 489-6710. FAX:
(212) 307-6237. www.nyc.gov/film
COMMISSIONER
Katherine Oliver

NASSAU COUNTY FILM OFFICE
Administrative Building, Eisenhower Pack, East Meadow, NY
11554. (516) 571-3168. FAX: (516) 571-5801.
www.longislandfilm.com email: debfilm@aol.com
DIRECTOR
Debra Markowitz

NEW YORK STATE GOVERNOR'S OFFICE FOR MOTION PICTURE & TELEVISION DEVELOPMENT
633 Third Ave., 33rd Flr., New York, NY 10017. (212) 803-2330.
FAX: (212) 803-2339. www.empire.state.ny.us
email: NYFILM@empire.state.ny.us
DEPUTY COMMISSIONER & DIRECTOR
Pat Swinney Kaufman

ROCHESTER/FINGER LAKES FILM & VIDEO OFFICE
45 East Ave., Ste. 400, Rochester, NY 14604. (585) 546-
5490. FAX: (585) 232-4822. www.filmrochester.org
DIRECTOR
June Foster
ASSISTANT DIRECTOR
T.C. Pellett

SARATOGA COUNTY FILM COMMISSION
28 Clinton St., Saratoga Springs, NY 12866. (800) 526-8970,
(518) 584-3255. FAX: (518) 587-0318. www.saratoga.org
email: info@saratoga.org
DIRECTOR
Linda G. Toohey

SUFFOLK COUNTY FILM OFFICE
H. Lee Dennison Bldg., 2nd Flr., 100 Veterans Memorial Hwy.,
Hauppauge, NY 11788. (800) 762-4769, (631) 853-4800. FAX:
(631) 853-4888. www.co.suffolk.ny.us
COMMISSIONER
Judith M. McEvoy
DIRECTOR
Michelle Isabelle-Stark

NORTH CAROLINA

CHARLOTTE REGION FILM OFFICE
1001 Morehead Sq. Dr., Ste. 200, Charlotte, NC 28203. (800)
554-4373, (704) 347-8942. FAX: (704) 347-8981.
www.charlotteusa.com email: bpetty@charlotteregion.com
DIRECTOR
Beth Petty

DURHAM CONVENTION & VISITORS BUREAU
101 E. Morgan St., Durham, NC 27701. (800) 446-8604,
(919) 687-0288. FAX: (919) 680-8353. www.durham-nc.com
DIRECTOR VISITOR SERVICES
Carolyn Carney

NORTH CAROLINA FILM COMMISSION
4317 Mail Service Center, Raleigh, NC 27699-4317. (800)
232-9227, (919) 733-9900. FAX: (919) 715-0151.
www.ncfilm.com email: barnold@nccommerce.com
DIRECTOR
William Arnold

PIEDMONT TRIAD FILM COMMISSION
7614 Business Park Dr., Greensboro, NC 27409. (336) 393-
0001. FAX: (336) 668-3749. www.piedmontfilm.com
email: info@piedmontfilm.com
DIRECTOR
Rebecca Clark

WESTERN NORTH CAROLINA FILM COMMISSION
3 General Avation Dr., Fletcher, NC 28732. (828) 687-7234.
FAX: (828) 687-7552. www.wncfilm.net email: film@awnc.org
CONTACT
Dale Carroll

WILMINGTON REGIONAL FILM COMMISSION
1223 North 23rd St., Wilmington, NC 28405. (910) 343-3456.
FAX: (910) 343-3457. www.wilmington-film.com
email: commish@wilmington-film.com
DIRECTOR
Johnny Griffin

NORTH DAKOTA

NORTH DAKOTA FILM COMMISSION
Century Center, 1600 E. Century Ave., Ste. 2, P.O. Box 2057,
Bismarck, ND, 58502-2057. (800) 435-5663, (701) 328-2525.
FAX: (701) 328-4878. www.ndtourism.com
DIRECTOR
Sara Otte Coleman

OHIO

GREATER CINCINNATI & NORTHERN KENTUCKY FILM COMMISSION
602 Main St., Ste. 712, Cincinnati, OH 45202. (513) 784-1744.
FAX: (513) 768-8963. www.film-cincinnati.org
email: info@film-cincinnati.org
EXECUTIVE DIRECTOR
Kristen Erwin

GREATER CLEVELAND MEDIA DEVELOPMENT CORP.
50 Public Sq., Ste. 825, Cleveland, OH 44113. (888) 746-
FILM, (216) 623-3910. FAX: (216) 623-0876.
www.clevelandfilm.com email: info@clevelandfilm.com
PRESIDENT
Christopher Carmody

OHIO FILM COMMISSION
77 S. High St., 29th Flr., Columbus, OH 43215. (800) 230-
3523, (614) 466-8844. FAX: (614) 466-6744. www.ohiofilm.com
email: scover@odod.state.oh.us
STATE FILM COMMISSIONER
Steve Cover

OKLAHOMA

OKLAHOMA FILM COMMISSION
15 N. Robinson, Ste. 802, Oklahoma City, OK 73102. (800)
766-3456, (405) 522-6760. FAX: (405) 522-0656.
www.oklahomafilm.org email: dlalli@otrd.state.ok.us
DIRECTOR
Dino Lalli

OREGON

OREGON FILM & VIDEO OFFICE
One World Trade Center, 121 S.W. Salmon St., Ste. 1205,
Portland, OR 97204. (503) 229-5832. FAX: (503) 229-6869.
www.oregonfilm.org email: shoot@oregonfilm.org
EXECUTIVE DIRECTOR
Veronica Rinard

PENNSYLVANIA

GREATER PHILADELPHIA FILM OFFICE
Land Title Bldg., 100 S. Broad St., Ste. 600, Philadelphia, PA 19110. (215) 686-2668. FAX: (215) 686-3659. www.film.org email: mail@film.org
EXECUTIVE DIRECTOR
Sharon Pinkenson

PENNSYLVANIA FILM OFFICE
Department of Community and Economic Development, Commonwealth Keystone Bldg., 400 North St., 4th Flr., Harrisburg, PA 17120-0225. (717) 783-3456. FAX: (717) 787-0687. www.filminpa.com
DIRECTOR, DEVELOPMENT
Jane Shecter

PITTSBURGH FILM OFFICE
7 Wood St., 6th Flr., Pittsburgh, PA 15222. (888) 744-3456, (412) 261-2744. FAX: (412) 471-7317. www.pghfilm.org email: info@pghfilm.org
DIRECTOR
Dawn Keezer

RHODE ISLAND

RHODE ISLAND FILM & TV OFFICE
83 Park St., 6th Flr., Providence, RI 02903. (401) 222-3883. FAX: (401) 222-3018. www.rifilm.com
DIRECTOR
Rick Smith

SOUTH CAROLINA

SOUTH CAROLINA FILM OFFICE
P.O. Box 7367, Columbia, SC 29202. (803) 737-0490. FAX: (803) 737-3104. www.scfilmoffice.com
DIRECTOR, BUSINESS DEVELOPMENT
Jeff Monks

SOUTH DAKOTA

SOUTH DAKOTA FILM COMMISSION
711 E. Wells Ave., Pierre, SD 57501. (605) 773-3301. FAX: (605) 773-3256. www.filmsd.com email: chris.hull@state.sd.us
FILM OFFICE COORDINATOR
Chris Hull

TENNESSEE

TENNESSEE FILM, ENTERTAINMENT & MUSIC COMMISSION
312 8th Ave. N., Tennessee Towers, 9th Flr., Nashville, TN 37243. (615) 818-3456, (615) 741-3456. FAX: (615) 741-5554. www.filmtennessee.com
EXECUTIVE DIRECTOR
Pat Ledford-Johnson

EAST TENNESSEE FILM COMMISSION
601 W. Summit Hill Dr., Knoxville, TN 37902-2011. (865) 632-8762. FAX: (865) 524-3863. www.etnfilm.com email: etfc@kacp.com
DIRECTOR
Mona May
OPERATIONS MANAGER
David Bolton

MEMPHIS & SHELBY FILM & TELEVISION COMMISSION
Beale St. Landing, 245 Wagner Pl., Ste. 4, Memphis, TN 38103-3815. (901) 527-8300. FAX: (901) 527-8326. www.memphisfilmcomm.org
FILM COMMISSIONER
Linn Sitler
DEPUTY FILM COMMISSIONER
Sharon Fox O'Guin

NASHVILLE MAYOR'S OFFICE OF FILM
222 2nd Ave. N., Ste. 418, Nashville, TN 37201. (615) 862-4700. FAX: (615) 862-6025. www.filmnashville.com email: jennifer.andrews@nashville.gov
CONTACT
Jennifer Andrews

TEXAS

AMARILLO FILM OFFICE
1000 S. Polk St., Amarillo, TX 79101. (806) 374-1497. FAX: (806) 373-3909. www.amarillofilm.org email: jutta@amarillo-cvb.org
DIRECTOR
Jutta Matalka

AUSTIN FILM OFFICE
201 E. 2nd St., Austin, TX 78701. (512) 583-7230, (512) 583-7229. FAX: (512) 583-7281. www.austinfilmcommission.com
DIRECTOR
Gary Bond

DALLAS FILM COMMISSION
325 N. St. Paul, Ste. 700, Dallas, TX 75201. (214) 571-1000. FAX: (214) 665-2953. www.visitdallas.com/film email: gwoods@dallascvb.com
DIRECTOR
Gary Woods
PROJECT MANAGER
Janis Burklund (214) 571-1053

EL PASO FILM COMMISSION
One Civic Center Plaza, El Paso, TX 79901. (915) 534-0698, (800) 351-6024. FAX: (915) 534-0687. email: elpasofilm@usa.net
FILM COMMISSIONER
Susie Gaines

HOUSTON FILM COMMISSION
901 Bagby, Ste. 100, Houston, TX 77002. (800) 365-7575, (713) 227-3100 x5248. FAX: (713) 223-3816. email: filmhouston@texaswebhost.com
EXECUTIVE DIRECTOR
Rick Ferguson

SAN ANTONIO FILM COMMISSION
203 S. St. Mary's St., 2nd Flr.,San Antonio, TX 78205. (800) 447-3372, (210) 207-6700. FAX: (210) 207-9731. www.sanantoniocvb.com email:filmsa@sanantoniocvb.com
FILM COMMISSIONER
Leighton Chapman

TEXAS ASSOCIATION OF FILM/TAPE PROFESSIONALS
50 B Business Pkwy., Richardson, TX 75081. (972) 231-1608. FAX: (972) 680-9995. www.taftp.com
CONTACT
Molly Brewer

TEXAS FILM COMMISSION
P.O. Box 13246, Austin, TX 78711. (512) 463-9200. FAX: (512) 463-4114. www.governor.state.tx.us/film email: film@governor.state.tx.us
EXECUTIVE DIRECTOR
Tom Copeland

UTAH

CENTRAL UTAH FILM COMMISSION
51 S. University Ave., Ste. 324, Provo, UT 84601. (800) 222-8824, (801) 370-8392. FAX: (801) 343-8096. www.utahvalley.org/film email: ucadm.marilyn@state.ut.us
DIRECTOR
Marilyn Toone

KANAB/KANE COUNTY FILM COMMISSION
78 S. 100 E., Kanab, UT 84741. (800) SEE-KANE, (435) 644-5033. FAX: (435) 644-5923. www.kaneutah.com
DIRECTOR
Stephen Browning

MOAB TO MONUMENT VALLEY FILM COMMISSION
P.O. Box 640 Moab, UT 84532. (435) 259-6388. FAX: (435) 259-1376. www.filmmoab.com
DIRECTOR
Ken Davey

NORTHERN UTAH FILM COMMISSION
160 N. Main, Logan, UT 84321. (800) 882-4433, (435) 752-2161. FAX: (435) 753-5825. www.northernutahfilm.com email: film@tourcachevalley.com
DIRECTOR
Maridene A. Hancock

PARK CITY FILM COMMISSION
P.O. Box 1630, Park City, UT 84060. (800) 453-1360. FAX: (435) 649-4132. www.parkcityfilm.com
COMMISSIONER
Lynn Williams

UTAH FILM COMMISSION
324 S. State St., Ste. 500, Salt Lake City, UT 84111. (800) 453-8824, (801) 538-8740. FAX: (801) 538-8746. www.film.utah.org
EXECUTIVE DIRECTOR
Leigh von der Esch

VERMONT

VERMONT FILM COMMISSION
10 Baldwin St., Drawer 33, Montpelier, VT 05633-2001. (802) 828-3618. FAX: (802) 828-3618. www.vermontfilm.com email: vermontfilm@state.vt.us@dca.state.vt.us
EXECUTIVE DIRECTOR
Danis Regal

VIRGINIA

CENTRAL VIRGINIA FILM OFFICE
15 W. Bank St., Petersburg, VA 23803. (804) 216-2772. FAX: (804) 863-0837. www.cvfo.org email: cvfo@cvfo.org
DIRECTOR
Kenneth W. Roy

CITY OF VIRGINIA BEACH - SPECIAL EVENTS & FILM
2101 Parks Ave., Ste. 502, Virginia Beach, VA 23451. (757) 437-4800. FAX: (757) 437-4737. www.vbgov.com
DIRECTOR
Lisa Bleakley

VIRGINIA FILM OFFICE
901 E. Byrd St., Richmond, VA 23219. (804) 371-8204. FAX: (804) 371-8177. www.film.virginia.org
email: vafilm@virginia.org
DIRECTOR
Rita McClenny
LOCATION MANAGER
Andrew Edmunds

WASHINGTON STATE

CITY OF SEATTLE - MAYOR'S OFFICE OF FILM & MUSIC
700 5th Ave., Ste. 5752, Seattle, WA 98104. (206) 684-5030. FAX: (206) 684-0379. www.seattle.gov/filmoffice
DIRECTOR
Donna James

WASHINGTON STATE FILM OFFICE
2001 Sixth Ave., Ste. 2600, Seattle, WA 98121. (206) 256-6151. FAX: (206) 256-6154. www.filmwashington.com
DIRECTOR
Suzy Kellett

WEST VIRGINIA

WEST VIRGINIA FILM OFFICE
c/o WV Division of Tourism, 90 MacCorkle Ave., SW, South Charleston, WV 25303. (800) 982-3386, (304) 558-2200. FAX: (304) 558-0362.
DIRECTOR
Pam Haynes

WISCONSIN

GREATER MILWAUKEE CVB
101 W. Wisconsin Ave., #425, Milwaukee, WI 53203. (866) 788-3456. FAX: (414) 273-5596. www.milwaukee.org
LIAISON
Vanessa Weller

WISCONSIN FILM OFFICE
201 W. Washington Ave., 2nd Flr., Madison, WI 53703. (800) FILM-WIS. FAX: (608) 266-3403. www.filmwisconsin.org
email: info@filmwisconsin.org
COORDINATOR
Mary Idso

WYOMING

WYOMING FILM OFFICE
I-25 @ College Dr., Cheyenne, WY 82002. (800) 458-6657, (307) 777-3400. FAX: (307) 777-2877. www.wyomingfilm.org
email: info@wyomingfilm.org
COMMISSIONER
Michell Phelan

JACKSON HOLE FILM COMMISSION
P.O. Box 550, Jackson, WY 83001. (307) 733-3316. FAX: (307) 733-5585. www.jacksonholechamber.com
COMMUNICATIONS MANAGER
Chris Henson

CASPER AREA FILM COMMISSION
538 S.W. Wyoming Blvd., P.O. Drawer 848, Mills, WY 82644. (307) 235-9325. FAX: (307) 265-2743. www.filmincasper.net
email: kellye@trib.com
DIRECTOR
Kelly Eastes

CHEYENNE AREA FILM OFFICE
One Depot Sq., Cheyenne, WY 82001. (307) 778-3133. (800) 426-5009. FAX: (307) 778-3190. www.cheyenne.org
email: darren@cheyenne.org
DIRECTOR
Darren Rudloff

U.S. TERRITORIES & PROTECTORATES

PUERTO RICO FILM COMMISSION
Fomento Bldg., 355 F. D. Roosevelt Ave., Ste. 106, San Juan, PR 00918. (787) 758-4747, x 2255. FAX: (787) 756-5706. www.puertoricofilm.com
EXECUTIVE DIRECTOR
Laura A. Velez

U.S. VIRGIN ISLANDS FILM PROMOTION OFFICE
P.O. Box 6400, St. Thomas, U.S.V.I. 00804. (340) 774-8784, (340) 775-1444. FAX: (340) 774-4390. www.usvitourism.vi

Federal Government Offices and Film & Media Services

EXECUTIVE DEPARTMENTS

DEPARTMENT OF AGRICULTURE
BROADCAST MEDIA & TECHNOLOGY CENTER
1400 Indepedence Ave., 1614 South Bldg., USDA,
Washington, DC 20250-1300. (202) 720-6072. FAX: (202) 720-5773. www.usda.gov
DIRECTOR
David Black

DEPARTMENT OF COMMERCE
OFFICE OF PUBLIC AFFAIRS—MEDIA SECTION
Office of the Secretary, 14th St. & Constitution Ave., Rm. 5056,
Washington, DC 20230. (202) 482-5007. FAX: (202) 482-4391.
PRODUCER & DIRECTOR
J.R. Olivero

INTERNATIONAL TRADE ADMINISTRATION—OFFICE OF SERVICE INDUSTRIES
Information Industries Division—International Trade in Film & Recorded Music, 14th St. and Constitution Ave., Rm. H-1124, Washington, DC 20230. (202) 482-4781. FAX: (202) 482-2669.
SENIOR INTERNATIONAL TRADE SPECIALIST
John Siegmund

NATIONAL TELECOMMUNICATIONS AND INFORMATION ADMINISTRATION
Main Commerce Bldg., 1401 Constitution Ave. N.W.,
Washington, DC 20230. (202) 482-1840. FAX: (202) 482-1635.
ASSISTANT SECRETARY
Nancy Victory

NATIONAL TECHNICAL INFORMATION SERVICE
National Audiovisual Center, 5285 Port Royal Rd., Springfield,
VA 22161. (703) 605-6181. FAX: (703) 605-6720.
ASSOCIATE DIRECTOR
Janice Coe

DEPARTMENT OF DEFENSE
AUDIOVISUAL
Office of the Assistant Secretary of Defense (Public Affairs),
Rm. 2E811, The Pentagon, Washington, DC 20301-1400. (703)
695-2936. FAX: (703) 695-1149.
SPECIAL ASSISTANT FOR ENTERTAINMENT MEDIA
DEPARTMENT OF DEFENSE
Philip M. Strub

AUDIOVISUAL DOCUMENTS & FILM
Office of the Assistant Secretary of Defense (Public Affairs),
The Pentagon, Rm. 2E765, Washington, DC 20301. (703) 695-0169. FAX: (703) 697-3501.
DIVISION CHIEF
Terry Mitchell

MILITARY SERVICES
SECRETARY OF THE AIR FORCE
Public Affairs Division, 1690 AF Pentagon, Rm. 4A120,
Washington, DC 20330-1000. (703) 695-9664. FAX: (703) 693-9601.
CHIEF OF DIVISION
Col. Donna Pastor

SECRETARY OF THE ARMY
Media Relations Division, Army Public Affairs, 1500 Army
Pentagon, Rm. 1E475, Washington, DC 20310-1500, (703)
692-2000. FAX: (703) 697-2159.
CHIEF OF DIVISION
Col. Joe Curtin

DEPARTMENT OF THE NAVY
Chief of Information, 1200 Navy Pentagon, Rm. 4B463,
Washington, DC 20350-1200. (703) 697-7391. FAX: (703) 695-5318.
CHIEF OF INFORMATION
Rear Admiral T.L. McCreary

HEADQUARTERS, U.S. MARINE CORPS.
Public Affairs Division, Code PA, The Pentagon, Washington,
DC 20380. (703) 614-8010, (703) 614-1492.
DIRECTOR
BGen. Maryann Krusa-Dossin

DEPARTMENT OF EDUCATION
OFFICE OF PUBLIC AFFAIRS
Audiovisual Division, 400 Maryland Ave. S.W., 7th Flr.,
Washington, DC 20202. (202) 401-1576. FAX: (202) 401-3130.
PUBLIC AFFAIRS SPECIALISTS
Sherry Schweitzer

OFFICE OF SPECIAL EDUCATION AND REHAB. SERVICES
Office of the Asst. Secretary, 330 C St. S.W., Ste. 3006,
Sweitzer Bldg., Washington, DC 20202-2500. (202) 205-5465.
FAX: (202) 205-9252.
DIRECTOR, OFFICE OF SPECIAL ED PROGRAM
Stephanie Lee

DEPARTMENT OF HEALTH AND HUMAN SERVICES
OFFICE OF ASSISTANT SECRATARY PUBLIC AFFAIRS
200 Independence Ave. S.W., HHH Bldg. Rm. 638-E,
Washington, DC 20201. (202) 690-6343. FAX: (202) 690-6247.
DIRECTOR, NEWS DIVISION, OASPA
Campbell Gardett

ADMINISTRATION FOR CHILDREN & FAMILY
370 L'Enfant Promenade S.W., 7th Flr., Washington, DC 20447.
(202) 401-9215. FAX: (202) 205-9688.
VACANT

THE CENTER FOR MEDICARE & MEDICADE SERVICES
200 Independence Ave. S.W., Rm. 314G, Washington, DC
20201. (202) 690-6726. FAX: (202) 690-6262.
ADMINISTRATOR
Thomas A. Scully

SOCIAL SECURITY ADMIN. OFFICE OF COMMUNICATIONS
4200 West High Rise, 6401 Security Blvd., Baltimore, MD
21235. (410) 965-1720. FAX: (410) 965-3903.
DEPUTY COMMISSIONER
James J. Courtney

DEPARTMENT OF HOUSING AND URBAN DEV.
OFFICE OF PUBLIC AFFAIRS
HUD Bldg., 451 7th St. S.W., Rm. 10132, Washington, DC
20410. (202) 708-0980. FAX: (202) 619-8153.
ASSISTANT SECRETARY FOR PUBLIC AFFAIRS
Diane Tomb

DEPARTMENT OF THE INTERIOR
OFFICE OF COMMUNICATIONS, DEPARTMENTAL NEWS & INFORMATION CENTER
1849 C St. N.W., Washington, DC 20240. (202) 208-3771.
BROADCAST OFFICER
Steve Brooks

DEPARTMENT OF JUSTICE
MULTIMEDIA SECTION
950 Pennsylvania Ave. N.W., Washington, DC 20530-0001.
(202) 514-4694. FAX: (202) 514-6741. www.usdoj.gov
SUPERVISOR
Tanya Spann Roche

DEPARTMENT OF LABOR
DIVISION OF AUDIOVISUAL COMMUNICATION SERVICES
200 Constitution Ave. N.W., N-6310, Washington, DC 20210.
(202) 693-5041. FAX: (202) 693-4692.
DIRECTOR/EXECUTIVE PRODUCER
Stan Hankin
STUDIO MANAGER/PRODUCER
Tom Accardi

DEPARTMENT OF STATE
INTERNATIONAL COMM. AND INFORMATION POLICY
Department of State, Rm. 4826, 2201 C St. N.W., Washington,
DC 20520. (202) 647-5212. FAX: (202) 647-5957.
DEPUTY ASSTISTANT SECRETARY
David A. Gross

DIRECTORATE OF DEFENSE TRADE CONTROLS
Bureau of Political Military Affairs, U.S. Department of State,
SA-1, 12th Flr., Washington, DC 20022. (202) 663-2714. FAX:
(202) 261-8264. http://pmdtc.org/
DIRECTOR
Robert Maggi

OFFICE OF PRESS RELATIONS
Department of State, Rm. 2109, Washington, DC 20520. (202)
647-2492. FAX: (202) 647-0244.
ACTING DIRECTOR
Julie Reside

BUREAU OF EDUCATIONAL & CULTURAL AFFAIRS
301 4th St. S.W., Rm. 816, Washington, DC 20547. (202) 203-5107. FAX: (202) 203-5115.
ASSISTANT SECRETARY
Patricia de Stacy Harrison

INTERNATIONAL BROADCASTING BUREAU OF FEDERAL GOVERNMENT
Public Affairs, Voice of America, 330 Independence Ave., S.W., Rm. 3131, Washington, DC 20237. (202) 401-7000. FAX: (202) 619-1241.
DIRECTOR
Joesph O'Connell

DEPARTMENT OF TRANSPORTATION
FEDERAL HIGHWAY ADMINISTRATION AUDIOVISUAL AND VISUAL AIDS
400 7th St. S.W., Rm. 4429, HAIM23, Washington, DC 20590. (202) 366-0481. FAX: (202) 366-7079.
MULTI MEDIA SPECIALIST
Colonel Giles

NATIONAL HIGHWAY AND TRAFFIC SAFETY ADMINISTRATION
Office of Communication & Consumer Information, Media Relations Division, 400 7th St. S.W., Rm. 5236, Washington, DC 20590. (202) 366-9550. FAX: (202) 366-5962.
PUBLIC AFFAIRS SPECIALIST
Liz Neblett

DEPARTMENT OF HOMELAND SECURITY
U.S. COAST GUARD MOTION PICTURE & TELEVISION LIAISON OFFICE
10880 Wilshire Blvd., Ste. 1210, Los Angeles, CA 90024. (310) 235-7817. FAX: (310) 235-7851.
email: uscghollywood@d11.uscg.mil
DIRECTOR
Cmdr. Jeff Loftus

U.S. COAST GUARD MEDIA RELATIONS BRANCH
Public Affairs, 2100 2nd St. S.W., Washington, DC 20593. (202) 267-1587. FAX: (202) 267-4307.
CHIEF OF DEPARTMENT
Lt. Cdr. Jeff Carter

U.S. COAST GUARD IMAGERY BRANCH
2100 2nd Street, S.W., Rm. 3403, G-IPA-1, Washington, DC 20593. (202) 267-0923. FAX: (202) 267-4645.
IMAGERY BRANCH
CWO Lionel Bryant

DEPARTMENT OF TREASURY
OFFICE OF PUBLIC AFFAIRS
1500 Pennsylvania Ave. N.W., Rm. 3442, Washington, DC 20220. (202) 622-2920. FAX: (202) 622-2808.
ASSISTANT SECRETARY
Rob Nichols

EXECUTIVE AGENCIES

BROADCASTING BOARD OF GOVERNORS
WORLDNET TELEVISION AND FILM SERVICE
330 Independence Ave., S.W., Washington, DC 20237. (202) 619-3375. FAX: (202) 690-4952.
ACTING DIRECTOR
Marie Skiba

ENVIRONMENTAL PROTECTION AGENCY
AUDIOVISUAL DIVISION
401 M St. S.W., Rm. B219, North Conference, Washington, DC 20460. (202) 564-8044. FAX: (202) 260-4893.
SPECIALIST
Rolando Hernadez

FEDERAL COMMUNICATIONS COMMISSION
445 12th St. S.W., Washington, DC 20554. (888) 225-5322. FAX: (202) 418-0232. www.fcc.gov email: fccinfo@fcc.gov
OFFICE OF THE CHAIRMAN
445 12th St. S.W., Rm. 8-B201, Washington, DC 20554. (202) 418-1000.
CHAIRMAN
Michael K. Powell
CONFIDENTIAL ASSISTANT
Judith Mann
CHIEF OF STAFF
Marsha J. MacBride
SENIOR LEGAL ADVISOR
Bryan Tramont
COMMISSIONERS
COMMISSIONER
Kathleen Q. Abernathy, (202) 418-2400
CONFIDENTIAL ASSISTANT
Ann Monahan
SENIOR LEGAL ADVISOR
Matthew Brill
COMMISSIONER
Michael Copps, (202) 418-2300
CONFIDENTIAL ASSISTANT
Carolyn Conyers
SENIOR LEGAL ADVISOR
Jordan Goldstein

COMMISSIONER
Kevin J. Martin, (202) 418-2100
CONFIDENTIAL ASSISTANT
Ginger Clark
SENIOR LEGAL ADVISOR
Lisa Zaina

OFFICE OF ADMINISTRATIVE LAW JUDGES
445 12th St. S.W., Rm. 1-C861, Washington, DC 20554.
CHIEF ADMINISTRATIVE LAW JUDGE
Richard L. Sippel, (202) 418-2280
ADMINISTRATIVE LAW JUDGE
Arthur I. Steinberg, (202) 418-2255

OFFICE OF COMMUNICATIONS BUSINESS OPPORTUNITIES
445 12th St. S.W., Washington, DC 20554. (202) 418-0990
DIRECTOR
Carolyn Fleming Williams, (202) 418-0990

OFFICE OF ENGINEERING & TECHNOLOGY
445 12th St. S.W., Rm. 7-C155, Washington, DC 20554. (202) 418-2470.
CHIEF
Ed Thomas
DEPUTY CHIEF
Bruce Franca, (202) 418-2470
DEPUTY CHIEF
Julius P. Knapp, (202) 418-2470
ASSOCIATE CHIEF FOR TECHNOLOGY
Michael J. Marcus, (202) 418-2470
ASSOCIATE CHIEF
Bruce A. Romano
SENIOR ASSOCIATE CHIEF
R. Alan Stillwell

FEDERAL TRADE COMMISSION
Press Office, 6th St. and Pennsylvania Ave. N.W., Washington, DC 20580. (202) 326-2180. FAX: (202) 326-3366.
CHAIRMAN
Timothy J. Muris

LIBRARY OF CONGRESS
U.S. COPYRIGHT OFFICE
101 Independence Ave., LM403, Washington, DC 20540. (202) 707-8350. FAX: (202) 707-8366.
REGISTER OF COPYRIGHTS
Marybeth Peters

COPYRIGHT CATALOGING DIVISION
101 Independence Ave., LM513, Washington, DC 20540. (202) 707-8040. FAX: (202) 707-8049.
CHIEF OF DIVISION
Joanna Roussis

MOTION PICTURE, BROADCASTING AND RECORDED SOUND DIVISION
Madison Bldg., Rm. 338, Washington, DC 20540-4690. (202) 707-5840. FAX: (202) 707-2371.
CHIEF OF DIVISION
Gregory Lukow

NATIONAL AERONAUTICS & SPACE ADMINISTRATION
NASA MEDIA RESOURCE CENTER
NASA LBJ Space Center, 2101 NASA Rd. 1, Bldg. 423/AP32, Houston, TX 77058. (281) 483-4231. FAX: (281) 483-2848.
SUPERVISOR
Mary Wilkerson

NATIONAL ARCHIVES AND RECORDS ADMINISTRATION
MOTION PICTURE, SOUND AND VIDEO BRANCH
700 Pennsylvania Ave. N.W., Washington, DC 20408. (866) 272-6272. www.nara.gov email: inquire@nara.gov
ARCHIVIST OF UNITED STATES
John W. Carlin

PRESIDENTIAL MATERIALS STAFF
700 Pennsylvania Ave. N.W., Rm. 104, Washington, DC 20408. (202) 501-5700. FAX: (202) 501-5709.
DIRECTOR
Nancy Kegan Smith

NATIONAL ENDOWMENT FOR THE ARTS
MEDIA ARTS PROGRAM
1100 Pennsylvania Ave. N.W., Rm. 726, Washington, DC 20506. (202) 682-5400. FAX: (202) 682-5721. www.arts.gov
MEDIA ARTS DIRECTOR
Ted Libbey

NATIONAL ENDOWMENT FOR THE HUMANITIES
HUMANITIES PROJECTS IN MEDIA—DIVISION OF PUBLIC PROGRAMS
1100 Pennsylvania Ave. N.W., Rm. 426, Washington, DC 20506. (202) 606-8269. FAX: (202) 606-8557.
DIRECTOR OF THE DIVISION OF PUBLIC PROGRAMS
Nancy Rogers

SECURITIES AND EXCHANGE COMMISSION
DIVISION OF CORPORATE FINANCE
450 5th St. N.W., Washington, DC 20549. (202) 942-8088.

MOTION PICTURES, RADIO, TV, AND TELEGRAPH
450 5th St. N.W., Washington, DC 20549-0406. (202) 942-1850. FAX: (202) 942-9525. www.sec.gov
ASSISTANT DIRECTOR
Max Webb
TELECOMMUNICATIONS
Barry Summer

SMITHSONIAN INSTITUTION
FILM ARCHIVES
Archives Division, Rm. 3100, MRC 322, National Air and Space Museum, Smithsonian Institution, P.O. Box 37012, Washington, DC 20013-7012. (202) 633-2337. FAX: (202) 786-2835.
FILM ARCHIVIST
Mark Taylor

U.S. INTERNATIONAL TRADE COMMISSION
OFFICE OF THE SECRETARY
500 E St., Rm. 112, Washington, DC 20436. (202) 205-2000. FAX: (202) 205-2104. www.usitc.gov
SECRETARY
Marilyn Abbott

MILITARY FILM LIAISONS

U.S. ARMY, CHIEF OF PUBLIC AFFAIRS
10880 Wilshire Blvd., Ste. 1250, Los Angeles, CA 90024-4101. (310) 235-7621. FAX: (310) 235-6075.
CHIEF OF PUBLIC AFFAIRS
Kathleen Ross
TECHNICAL ADVISOR
Maj. Todd Breasseale

MARINE CORPS PUBLIC AFFAIRS
10880 Wilshire Blvd., Ste. 1230, Los Angeles, CA 90024. (310) 235-7272. FAX: (310) 235-7274.
DIRECTOR
Maj. Brad Bartelt

U. S. AIR FORCE, MOTION PICTURE AND TELEVISION LIAISON OFFICE
10880 Wilshire Blvd., Ste. 1240, Los Angeles, CA 90024. (310) 235-7522. FAX: (310) 235-7500.
CHIEF, ENTERTAINMENT LIAISON
Charles E. Davis

U. S. COAST GUARD, MOTION PICTURE AND TELEVISION OFFICE
10880 Wilshire Blvd., Ste. 1210, Los Angeles, CA 90024. (310) 235-7817. FAX: (310) 235-7851.
LIAISON OFFICERS
Lt. Cmdr. Scott Luftus, CWO Alastair Worden, CWO Dan Waldschmidt

TRADE PUBLICATIONS

ACADEMY PLAYERS DIRECTORY
(Semi-Annual) Academy of Motion Picture Arts & Sciences, 1313 N. Vine St., Hollywood, CA 90028. (310) 247-3000. FAX: (310) 550-5034. www.playersdirectory.com
EDITOR
Keith W. Gonzales

ADVERTISING AGE
(Weekly) 360 N. Michigan Ave., Chicago, IL 60601. (312) 649-5200. 711 3rd Ave., New York, NY 10017. (212) 210-0100.
CHAIRMAN
Keith Crain
PUBLISHING DIRECTOR
David Klein
PUBLISHER
Jill Mannee
PRESIDENT & EDITOR-IN-CHIEF
Rance Crain

THE AMERICAN CINEMATOGRAPHER
(Monthly) Published by American Society of Cinematographers, Inc., P.O. Box 2230, Hollywood, CA 90078. (323) 969-4333. FAX: (323) 876-4973.
PUBLISHER
Jim McCullaugh
EDITOR
Stephen Pizzello
ASSOCIATE EDITOR
Rachael Bosley
CIRCULATION MANAGER
Saul Molina

ANNUAL INDEX TO MOTION PICTURE CREDITS
(Annual compilation of feature film credits) Academy of Motion Picture Arts and Sciences, 8949 Wilshire Blvd., Beverly Hills, CA 90211. (310) 247-3000. FAX: (310) 859-9619.
EXECUTIVE DIRECTOR
Bruce Davis
EDITOR
Torene Svitil

BILLBOARD
(Weekly) 770 Broadway, New York, NY 10003. (646) 654-4400. FAX: (646) 654-4681. www.billboard.com
5055 Wilshire Blvd., Los Angeles, CA 90036-4396. (323) 525-2300. FAX: (323) 525-2394.
49 Music Sq. W., Nashville, TN 37203. (615) 321-4290. FAX: (615) 320-0454.
Endeavor House, 189 Shaftesbury, London WC2H 8TJ. (44 207) 420-6003. FAX: (44 207) 420-6014.
PRESIDENT & PUBLISHER
John Kilcullen
EDITOR-IN-CHIEF
Keith Girard

BOXOFFICE
(Published by RLD.) 155 S. El Molino Ave., Ste. #100, Pasadena, CA 91101. (626) 396-0250. FAX: (626) 396-0248. P.O. Box 269030, Chicago, IL 60625. (773) 338-7007. FAX: (773) 338-1884. www.boxoffice.com
email: editorial@boxoffice.com
PUBLISHER
Robert L. Dietmeier
EDITOR-IN-CHIEF
Kim Williamson
NATIONAL AD DIRECTOR
Robert M. Vale

BROADCASTING & CABLE—THE NEWS WEEKLY OF TELEVISION AND RADIO
(Weekly) 360 Park Ave. South, New York, NY 10010. (646) 746-6400. FAX: (646) 746-7028. www.broadcastingcable.com
1627 K St. NW, 10th Flr., Washington, DC 20036. (202) 463-3711. FAX: (202) 463-3742.
5700 Wilshire Blvd., #120, Los Angeles, CA 90036. (323) 549-4100. FAX: (323) 965-5327.
EDITOR IN CHIEF
Harry A. Jessell
EDITOR
P.J. Bednarski
DEPUTY EDITORS
Steve McClellan
John M. Higgins
REGIONAL SALES MANAGER (NY)
Cheryl Mahon

BROADCASTING & CABLE YEARBOOK
(Annual) R. R. Bowker, 630 Central Ave., New Providence, NJ 07974. (908) 464-6800. FAX: (908) 771-7704.
ASSOCIATE EDITOR
Joe Esser

CELEBRITY SERVICE INTERNATIONAL
Publisher of Celebrity Bulletin (daily), Celebrity Service International Date Book (bi-monthly) and Celebrity Service International Contact Book (semi-annual). 250 W 57th St., Ste. 819, New York, NY 10107. (212) 757-7979. FAX: (212) 582-7701. 8833 Sunset Blvd., Ste. 401, Los Angeles, CA 90069. (310) 652-1700. FAX: (310) 652-9244.
EDITOR, CELEBRITY BULLETIN (NY)
Bill Murray
EDITOR, CELEBRITY BULLETIN (LA)
Maureen Mooney

CINEFEX
(Quarterly) P.O. Box 20027, Riverside, CA 92516. (800) 434-3339, (909) 781-1917. FAX: (909) 788-1793.
www.cinefex.com email: circulation@cinefex.com
PUBLISHER
Don Shay
EDITOR
Jody Duncan

COMING ATTRACTIONS
(Monthly) Connell Communications Inc., 86 Elm St., Peterborough, NH 03458. (603) 924-7271. FAX: (603) 924-7013.
EXECUTIVE PUBLISHER
Jim Connell
EDITOR (HOME ENTERTAINMENT GROUP)
Anna Butler

COMMUNICATIONS DAILY
(Daily) Warren Communications News, Inc., 2115 Ward Ct. N.W., Washington, DC 20037. (202) 872-9200. FAX: (202) 293-3435. www.warren-news.com

CONSUMER ELECTRONICS DAILY
(Daily) Warren Communications News, Inc., 2115 Ward Ct. N.W., Washington, DC 20037. (202) 872-9200. FAX: (202) 293-3435. www.warren-news.com
CHAIRMAN, EDITOR & PUBLISHER
Albert Warren
PRESIDENT & EXECUTIVE PUBLISHER
Paul Warren

COSTUME DESIGNERS GUILD DIRECTORY
(Annual) c/o Costume Designers Guild, 4730 Woodman Ave., Ste. 430, Sherman Oaks, CA 91423. (818) 905-1557. FAX: (818) 905-1560.

DAILY VARIETY
(Daily) 5700 Wilshire Blvd., Ste. 120, Los Angeles, CA 90036. (323) 857-6600. FAX: (323) 857-0494. www.variety.com
V.P. & PUBLISHER
Charles C. Koones
EDITOR-IN-CHIEF
Peter Bart
EXECUTIVE EDITORS
Steven Gaydos
Elizabeth Guider
SPECIAL EDITIONS EDITOR
Michael Speier
MANAGING EDITORS
Tim Gray
Todd Cunningham
NATIONAL SALES MANAGERS
Craig Hitchcock

FILM & VIDEO MAGAZINE
(Monthly) Organized 1983. 2700 Westchester Ave. Ste. 107, Purchase, NY 10577. (800) 800-5474. FAX: (914) 328-7107.
PUBLISHER
Laurie Corn
EDITOR-IN-CHIEF
Alison Johns
EXECUTIVE EDITOR
Bryant Frazer
MANAGING EDITOR
Sharon Kennedy

FILM JOURNAL INTERNATIONAL
(Monthly) 770 Broadway, 5th Flr., New York, NY 10003. (646) 654-7680, FAX: (646) 654-7694. www.filmjournal.com
PUBLISHER & EDITOR
Robert H. Sunshine
CO- PUBLISHER
Jimmy Sunshine
MANAGING EDITOR
Kevin Lally
ASSOCIATE EDITOR/GRAPHIC DESIGNER
Rex Roberts

ASSOCIATE EDITOR
Mitch Neuhauser
ADVERTISING DIRECTOR
Andrew Sunshine

HOLLYWOOD CREATIVE DIRECTORY
(Annual) 1024 N. Orange Dr., Hollywood, CA 90038. (800) 815-0503, (323) 308-3490. FAX: (323) 308-3493. www.hcdonline.com
CEO, IFILM
Adam Frank
SENIOR V.P., IFILM PUBLISHING
Jeff Black

THE HOLLYWOOD REPORTER
(Daily) 5055 Wilshire Blvd., Los Angeles, CA 90036. Editorial: (323) 525-2000. FAX: (323) 525-2377. Advertising FAX: (323) 525-2372. Special Issues FAX: (323) 525-2390. 770 Broadway, New York, NY 10003. (646) 654-5626. FAX: (646) 654-5637. 910 17th St., N.W., Ste. 215, Washington, DC 20006. (202) 833-8845 FAX: (202) 833-8672. www.hollywoodreporter.com
EDITOR-IN-CHIEF & PUBLISHER
Robert J. Dowling
EDITOR
Howard Burns
EDITORIAL DIRECTOR, FEATURES
Paula Parisi
DEPUTY EDITOR
Cynthia Littleton
EXECUTIVE EDITOR
Peter Pryor
EXECUTIVE EDITOR/ELECTRONIC
Glenn Abel
FILM EDITOR
Gregg Kilday
NEWS EDITOR
Harley W. Lond
DIRECTOR, MARKETING
Richard Wilkes
PUBLICITY MANAGER
Lynda Miller

I.A.T.S.E. OFFICIAL BULLETIN
(Quarterly) 1430 Broadway, 20th Flr., New York, NY 10018. (212) 730-1770. FAX: (212) 921-7699. www.iatse-intl.org
EDITOR
James Wood
ASSISTANT EDITOR
Mary Ann Kelly

INSIDE FILM MAGAZINE
(Online) 8421 Wilshire Blvd., Penthouse, Beverly Hills, CA 90211. (323) 852-0434. www.insidefilm.com
PUBLISHER & EDITOR
Susan Royal
ASSISTANT EDITOR
Alyssa Boyle

INTERNATIONAL DOCUMENTARY ASSOCIATION
1201 W. 5th St., Ste. M320, Los Angeles, CA 90017-2015. (213) 534-3600. FAX: (213) 534-3610. www.documentary.org email: info@documentary.org
EDITOR
Tom White

INTERNATIONAL CINEMATOGRAPHERS GUILD MAGAZINE
(Monthly) 7715 Sunset Blvd., Ste. 300, Hollywood, CA 90046. (323) 876-0160. FAX: (323) 878-1180. www.cameraguild.com
EDITOR-IN-CHIEF
George Spiro Dibie, ASC
EDITOR
Neil Matsumodo

INTERNATIONAL MOTION PICTURE ALMANAC
(Quigley Publishing Company, a division of QP Media, Inc.) (Annual) Corporate: P.O. Box 740, Groton, MA 01450. (978) 448-0272. FAX: (978) 448-9325. Editorial & Sales: (800) 231-8239, (860) 228-0247. FAX: (860) 228-0157. www.quigleypublishing.com email: quigleypub@aol.com
PRESIDENT & PUBLISHER
William J. Quigley
EDITOR
Eileen Quigley
ASSOCIATE EDITOR & OPERATIONS MANAGER
Aaron Dior Pinkham

INTERNATIONAL TELEVISION & VIDEO ALMANAC
(Quigley Publishing Company, a division of QP Media, Inc.) (Annual) Corporate: P.O. Box 740, Groton, MA 01450. (978) 448-0272. FAX: (978) 448-9325. Editorial & Sales: (800) 231-8239, (860) 228-0247. FAX: (860) 228-0157. www.quigleypublishing.com email: quigleypub@aol.com
PRESIDENT & PUBLISHER
William J. Quigley
EDITOR
Eileen Quigley
ASSOCIATE EDITOR & OPERATIONS MANAGER
Aaron Dior Pinkham

MARKEE—REGIONAL AMERICA'S MAGAZINE FOR FILM AND VIDEO PRODUCTION
366 E. Graves Ave., Ste. D., Orange City, FL 32763. (386) 774-8881. FAX: (386) 774-8908. www.markeemag.com
PUBLISHER
Janet Karcher
ASSOCIATE PUBLISHER/EDITOR-IN-CHIEF
Jon Hutchinson
ASSOCIATE EDITOR
Christine Bunish

MEDIA WEEK
(Weekly) BPI Communications, 770 Broadway, New York, NY 10003. (646) 654-5115. FAX: (646) 654-5351. www.mediaweek.com
PUBLISHER
Linda D'Adamo
EDITOR
Brian Moran
EXECUTIVE EDITOR
Michael Burgi
NEWS EDITOR
Jim Cooper

MILLIMETER MAGAZINE
(Monthly) Primedia Business Magazines & Media, 249 W. 17th St., 3rd Flr., New York, NY 10011. www.millimeter.com email: cwisehart@primediabusiness.com.
PUBLISHER
Jeff Victor
EDITOR
Cynthia Wisehart

PRODUCERS MASTERGUIDE
60 E. 8th St., 34th Flr., New York, NY 10003. (212) 777-4002. FAX: (212) 777-4101. www.producers.masterguide.com
PUBLISHER
Shmuel Bension

QUIGLEY PUBLISHING COMPANY, A DIVISION OF QP MEDIA, INC.
(Publishers of The International Motion Picture Almanac (Annual) and The International Television and Video Almanac (Annual)).
Corporate: P.O. Box 740, Groton, MA 01450. (978) 448-0272. FAX: (978) 448-9325.
Editorial & Sales: (800) 231-8239, (860) 228-0247. FAX: (860) 228-0157. www.quigleypublishing.com email: info@quigleypublishing.com
CHAIRMAN EMERITUS
Martin S.Quigley
PRESIDENT & PUBLISHER
William J. Quigley
EDITOR
Eileen Quigley
ASSOCIATE EDITOR & OPERATIONS MANAGER
Aaron Dior Pinkham
CONTRIBUTING EDITOR
Dee Quigley, 64 Wintergreen Lane, Groton, MA. 01450. (978) 448-0272.
INTERNATIONAL EDITORIAL
Deborah Tiffen, Editor. Box 720, Port Perry, ONT L9L 1A6, Canada. (905) 986-0050.
Angela Hayes, 9 Fraser Street, London W4 2DA, England

THE REEL DIRECTORY
(Annual) P. O. Box 1910, Boyes Hot Springs, CA 95416. (707) 933-9935. www.reeldirectory.com email: IVISUAL@aol.com.
CONTACT
Lynetta Freeman

SATELLITE WEEK
(Daily) Warren Communications News, Inc., 2115 Ward Ct. N.W., Washington, DC 20037. (202) 872-9200. FAX: (202) 293-3435. www.warren-news.com

SMPTE JOURNAL (SOCIETY OF MOTION PICTURE AND TELEVISION ENGINEERS)
(Monthly) 595 W. Hartsdale Ave., White Plains, NY 10607. (914) 761-1100. FAX: (914) 761-3115. www.smpte.org
EDITORIAL VICE PRESIDENT
Edward P. Hobson

SCREEN ACTOR
(Bi-Monthly) 5757 Wilshire Blvd., Los Angeles, CA 90036. (323) 549-6701. FAX: (323) 549-6656. www.sag.org
EDITOR
Ilyanne Morden Kichaven

SHOOT
(Weekly) 770 Broadway, New York, NY 10003. (646) 654-5500. FAX: (646) 654-5354. 5055 Wilshire Blvd., Los Angeles, CA 90036. (323) 525-2262. FAX: (323) 525-0275.
PUBLISHER
Roberta Griefer
EDITOR
Bob Goldrich

TAPEDISC BUSINESS

(Monthly) PBI Media LLC, 2700 Westchester Ave., Ste. 107, Purchase, NY 10577. (914) 251-4705. FAX: (914) 251-4701. www.m3online.com
SENIOR V.P.
Jim Alkon
EDITOR-IN-CHIEF
Bryant Frazer

TELEVISION & CABLE FACTBOOK

(Annual) Warren Communications News, Inc., 2115 Ward Ct. N.W., Washington, DC 20037. (202) 872-9200. FAX: (202) 293-3435. www.warren-news.com
email: newsroom@warren-news.com
Editorial Office: 276 5th Ave., Rm. 1002, New York, NY 10001. (212) 686-5410. FAX: (212) 889-5097.
CHAIRMAN, EDITOR & PUBLISHER
Albert Warren
MANAGING EDITOR
Michael C. Taliaferro
SENIOR RESEARCH EDITOR
Robert T. Dwyer

TELEVISION QUARTERLY

(Quarterly) National Academy of Television Arts & Sciences, 111 W. 57th St., Ste. 600, New York, NY 10019. (212) 586-8424. FAX: (212) 246-8129. www.emmyonline.org
EDITOR
Federick A. Jacobi
EXECUTIVE V.P.
Alan Benish

TELEVISIONWEEK

(Weekly) 6500 Wilshire Blvd., Ste. 2300, Los Angeles, CA 90048. (323) 370-2400. FAX: (323) 653-4425.
www.emonline.com
MANAGING EDITOR
Tom Gilbert
EDITOR
Alex Ben Block

TOUR GUIDE JOURNAL

(Monthly) Anvil Productions, Inc., 750 Cowan St., Nashville, TN 37207. (615) 256-7006. FAX: (615) 256-7004.
www.tourguidemag.com email: jim@tourguidemag.com
PUBLISHER
Larry Smith
SENIOR EDITOR (LA)
Stann Findelle
MANAGING EDITOR (TX)
Jane Cohen

TV GUIDE

(Weekly) News America Publications, Inc., 1211 6th Ave., New York, 10036. (212) 852-7500. www.tvguide.com
100 Matsonford Rd., Radnor, PA 19088. (610) 293-8500.
EDITOR-IN-CHIEF
Michael Lafavore
PUBLISHER
J. Scott Crystal
EXECUTIVE EDITOR
Steve Sonsky

VARIETY

(Weekly) 5700 Wilshire Blvd., Ste. #120, Los Angeles, CA 90036. (323) 857-6600, (323) 965-4476. FAX: (323) 857-0494. 360 Park Ave. S., New York, NY 10010. (646) 746-7002, (646) 746-7001. FAX: (646) 746-6977. www.variety.com
Washington: (202) 463-3705. FAX: (202) 463-3744.
England: 84 Theobalds Rd., London WC1X 8RR, U.K. (44 207) 611 4580. FAX: (44 207) 611 4581.
Rome: TEL/FAX: (39 6) 3936-6413.
Spain & Portugal: (34 91) 766-1356. FAX: (34 91) 383-8671.
Sydney:(61 2) 9422 8630. FAX: (61 2) 9422-8635.
Latin America: (305) 228-7440. FAX: (305) 228-7436.
V.P. & EDITOR-IN-CHIEF
Peter Bart

EXECUTIVE EDITORS
Steven Gaydos
Elizabeth Guider
MANAGING EDITORS
Timothy M. Gray
Todd Cunningham
PARIS BUREAU CHIEF
Alison James

VIDEO STORE MAGAZINE

(Weekly) 201 E. Sandpointe Ave., Ste. 600, Santa Ana, CA 92707. (800) 854-3112, (714) 513-8400. FAX: (714) 513-8402. www.videostoremag.com www.hive4media.com
PUBLISHER
Don Rosenberg
ASSOCIATE PUBLISHER
Judith McCourt
SENIOR EDITOR/ONLINE EDITOR
Holly Wagner

VIDEO SYSTEMS MAGAZINE

(Monthly) Intertec Publishing, 9800 Metcalf Ave., Overland Park, KS 66212-2215. (913) 341-1300. FAX: (913) 967-1898. www.intertec.com.
EDITORIAL DIRECTOR
Cynthia Wisehart: (818) 563-2647.
SENIOR EDITOR
Michael Goldman: (818) 764-2110.
MANAGING EDITOR
Jared Blankenship: (913) 967-1783.

GREAT BRITAIN

BROADCAST

(Weekly) EMAP Media Ltd., 33-39 Bowling Green Lane, London, EC1R ODA. (44 207) 505 8000. www.produxion.com
ONLINE EDITOR
Luke Satchell

KEMPS FILM, TV & VIDEO HANDBOOK

(Annual) Reed Business Information, Windsor Court, East Grinstead House, E. Grinstead, West Sussex, RH19 1XA. (44 34) 233-2100. www.kftv.com
MARKETING
Jackie Nice
EDITORIAL
Vivien Carne

SCREEN INTERNATIONAL

(Published weekly) Published by EMAP Media, 33-39 Bowling Green Lane, London EC1R 0DA, England. (44 207) 505-8080 New York: 60 Pineapple St., Ste. 6A, Brooklyn, NY 11201. (718) 596 0200. www.screendaily.com
EDITOR-IN-CHIEF
Colin Brown
MANAGING EDITOR
Leo Barraclough

TELEVISUAL

(Published monthly) Centaur Communications, St. Giles House, 50 Poland St., London, W1V 4AX, England. (44 207) 970-6442. (44 207) 439-4222. FAX: (44 207) 970-6733. www.mad.co.uk/publication/tv
PUBLISHER
James Bennett
EDITOR
Mundy Ellis

CANADA

FILM CANADA YEARBOOK

(Annual) Published by Moving Pictures Media
Box 720, Port Perry, ONT L9L 1A6, Canada. (905) 986-0050. FAX: (905) 986-1113. www.filmcanadayearbook.com
email: deborah@filmcanadayearbook.com
PUBLISHER/EDITOR
Deborah Tiffin

THE WORLD MARKET

■

PRODUCTION COMPANIES

ALBERTA

ALBERTA FILMWORKS INC.
1310 – 11th St. S.W., Calgary, AB T2R 1G6
(403) 777-9900, FAX: (403) 777-9914
E-mail: mail@albertafilmworks.com, www.albertafilmworks.com
EXECUTIVE PRODUCERS
Doug MacLeod
Tom Cox
Randy Bradshaw

ALLIANCE ATLANTIS COMMUNICATIONS INC.
3720 – 76 Ave., Edmonton, AB T6B 2N9
(780) 440-2022, FAX: (780) 440-3400
E-mail: info@allianceatlantis.com, www.allianceatlantis.com

See also Ontario.

ANAID PRODUCTIONS INC.
208 – 3132 Parsons Rd., Edmonton, AB T6N 1L6
(780) 413-9285, FAX: (780) 465-0580
E-mail: anaid@anaid.com
CONTACT
Margaret Mardirossian
DIRECTOR OF DEVELOPMENT
Carrie Gour
DIRECTOR OF BUSINESS AFFAIRS
Helen Schmidt, CMA
ASSOCIATE PRODUCER
Erin Berube

TV / drama / documentary / MOWs.

BLACK MEDIA WORKS
534 21st Ave. S.W, Calgary, AB T2S 0H1. (403) 802-0010,
FAX: (403) 802-0012, E-mail: info@blackmediaworks.com,
www.blackmediaworks.com
CONTACT, DIRECTOR, DGC
Darold Black

Script to screen production services.

CANADIAN WILDERNESS VIDEOS & PRODUCTIONS
1010 Larch Place, Canmore, AB T1W 1S7, (403) 678-3795,
FAX: (403) 678-3796, E-mail: crvideo@agt.net
PRODUCER / DIRECTOR / CAMERA
Eric Langshaw
RESEARCHER / CAMERA
Rosemary Power

DB ENTERTAINMENT
Box 51087, Beddington Postal Outlet, Calgary, AB T3K 3V9
(403) 295-8390, FAX: (403) 295-8790.
E-mail: Douglas@DBEntertainment.com,
www.DBEntertainment.com
PRESIDENT / PRODUCTION
Douglas Berquist
Exec. Assistant
ANDREW MOREAU

Specializing in international co-productions.

DINOSAUR SOUP PRODUCTIONS
9353 – 50th St., Unit 13, Edmonton, AB T6B 2L5
(780) 461-9465, FAX: (780) 461-0657,
E-mail: dinosoup@telusplanet.net
PRESIDENT / PRODUCER
Gerri Cook
VICE-PRESIDENT / PRODUCER / MARKETING:
Steve Moore
PROJECTS MANAGER
Pati Olson

Family programming: animation / drama / lifestyle / documentaries.

DMB PRODUCTIONS INC.
9519 42nd St., Edmonton, AB T6E 5R2. (780) 448-0211,
FAX: (780) 425-7235. E-mail: dbenson@dmbproduction.com
www.dmbproduction.com
PRESIDENT / DIRECTOR
David Benson

FRANK'S VIDEO PRODUCTIONS & COPY SERVICES
1420 – 90th Ave. S.W., Calgary, AB T2V 0X2, (403) 252-8075.
OWNER / OPERATOR
Frank Kaufmann

Independent video production / freelance camera.

HBW FILM CORP. / RIVERWOOD PRODUCTIONS
2526 Battleford Ave. S.W., Ste. 232 , Film Services Centre

Calgary, AB T3E 7J4. (403) 228-1900 / (310) 820-0108, FAX:
(403) 259-3860. E-mail: hbw@hbwfilm.com, www.hbwfilm.com
PRINCIPAL
Helene B. White

Services: production / writing / editing

THE IDEA FACTORY!
18520 Stony Plain Rd., Edmonton, AB T5S 1A8.
(780) 439-3985, FAX: (780) 439-4051. E-mail: info@ideafactory.ca
PRESIDENT
Drew Martin
VP, PRODUCTION
Lindsay Speer

IMAGINATION FILM & TELEVISION PRODUCTIONS
10318 – Whyte Ave., 3rd Fl., Edmonton, AB T6E 1Z8
(780) 439-8755, FAX: (780) 430-1871
E-mail: imagi@telusplanet.net, www.imaginationfilm.tv
PRESIDENT / EXECUTIVE PRODUCER
Nicolette Saina

KARVONEN FILMS
2001 – 91 Ave., Edmonton, AB T6P 1L1. (780) 467-7167
FAX: (780) 467-7162. E-mail: films@karvonenfilms.com
PRESIDENT
Albert Karvonen
VICE-PRESIDENT
Pirkko Karvonen
BUSINESS AFFAIRS
Brenda Hennig

Specializing in natural history films / extensive stock footage
library

KING MOTION PICTURE CORPORATION
10104 – 103rd Ave., Ste. 1702, Bell Tower, Edmonton, AB T5J 0H8
(780) 424-2950, FAX: (780) 420-0518.
E-mail: kingpict@planet.eon.net
PRESIDENT
Douglas Hutton

Creates, develops, produces and distributes quality programs
for prime-time television.

MINDS EYE ENTERTAINMENT (ALBERTA)
8925 – 51st Ave., Ste 318, Edmonton, AB T6E 5J3
(780) 944-1055, FAX: (780) 465-0804
www.mindseyepictures.com

Features / TV drama / documentaries. See also British
Columbia & Saskatchewan.

NOMADIC PICTURES
3911 Trasimene Cr. S.W., Calgary, AB T3E 7J6
(403) 240-0444, FAX: (403) 246-0247
E-mail: mfrislev@nomadicpictures.com, www.nomadicpictures.com
PRODUCERS
Mike Frislev
Chad Oakes

PARIAH ENTERTAINMENT GROUP
251 – 90 Ave. S.E., Ste. 82, Calgary, AB T2J 0A4
(403) 230-9474, E-mail: disposablelife@yahoo.ca,
www.pariahville.com
CREATIVE DIRECTOR / CFO
Keith Callbeck
DIRECTOR / COO
Brett Monro
TECHNICAL DIRECTOR
Thomas M. Terashima
PUBLIC RELATIONS
Philip K. Liesemer

PEGASUS PRODUCTIONS LTD.
11313 – 123 St., Edmonton, AB T5K 0G1
(780) 452-8719. E-mail: pegasusproductions@compuserve.com
CONTACT
Marke Slipp

RED DEVIL FILMS LTD.
E-mail: reddevilfilms@sympatico.ca
PRESIDENT
John Hazlett

Theatrical feature films

RIO GRANDE MOTION PICTURES OF CANADA INC.
P.O. Box 1240, Stn. M, Calgary, AB T2P 2L2
(403) 228-9984, FAX: (403) 229-3598
PRESIDENT
Paul Conrad Jackson, conradjackson49@hotmail.com

V.P., FINANCE
Elaine Ethier-Jackson,chiquitapip@canada.com
V.P., DEVELOPMENT & MARKETING
Edmund A. Oliverio, eao@telusplanet.net
LEGAL
Michael R. Birnbaum

Affiliate Company:
Rio Grande Motion Pictures of Mexico, Inc.
Libramiento 100, Unid 623, Apdo 522, Chapala CP 45920
Jalisco, Mexico. TEL: 011-52-376-766-4329

TUSTIAN FILM PRODUCTIONS
10754 – 72nd Ave., Edmonton, AB T6E 1A1
(780) 433-5136, E-mail: jim@tustianfilm.com
www.tustianfilm.com
CONTACT
Jim Tustian, csc

Film / video production & consultation

TVNEWMEDIA.COM
Box 5125, Stn. A, Calgary, AB T2H 1X3. Tel. & FAX: (403)
203-2738. E-mail: tvnew@tvnewmedia.com
www.tvnewmedia.com

WHITE IRON INC.
533, 1201 – 5th St. S.W., Calgary, AB T2R 0Y6
(403) 298-4700, FAX: (403) 233-0528
E-mail: mherringer@whiteiron.tv, www.whiteiron.tv

Full-service film and video production; commercial, corporate
and long form. New media design and production.

DAVID WINNING
(Groundstar Entertainment Corp.)
918 – 16 Ave. N.W., Ste. 4001, Calgary, AB T2M 0K3
(403) 284-2889 / (604) 944-8407, FAX: (403) 282-7797
E-mail: info@davidwinning.com, www.davidwinning.com

Director / producer — features / episodic:
9 features, 16 series, over 70 TV credits
U.S.A.:7336 Santa Monica Blvd., Ste. 710, Los Angeles, CA
90046. (323) 960-5708, FAX: (310) 888-4241
AGENT
Lee Dinstman / APA (310) 888-4283
REP
Don Klein Management (Beverly Hills)
Manager: Don Klein (310) 358-3240

ZOOM COMMUNICATIONS
2509 Dieppe Ave. S.W., Ste. 110, Calgary, AB T3E 7J9
(403) 229-2511, FAX: 403-229-4211.
E-mail: bradshaw@zoomcom.ca, www.zoomcom.ca
PRESIDENT / CEO
Jeff Bradshaw

BRITISH COLUMBIA

THE ACE FILM COMPANY INC.
1152 Mainland St., Ste. 400, Vancouver, BC V6B 4X2
(604) 682-0001, FAX: (604) 682-7346
E-mail: acefilm@acefilm.com, www.acefilm.com
EXECUTIVE PRODUCER
Parker Jefferson
DIRECTOR / CINEMATOGRAPHER
Allen G. Jones

A.K.A. CARTOON
211 Columbia St., Vancouver, BC V6A 2R5
(604) 682-6652, FAX: (604) 682-6259
EXEC. PRODUCER / DIRECTOR
Danny Antonucci
PRODUCER / ACCOUNTANT
Ruth Vincent
PRODUCTION MANAGER
Dan Sioui

ANAGRAM PICTURES
291 E. 2nd Ave., 3rd Fl., Vancouver, BC V5T 1B8
(604) 730-9021, FAX: (604) 730-9042
E-mail: anagram@zoolink.com, www.anagrampictures.ca
CONTACTS
Andrew Currie
Blake Corbet
Trent Carlson
Kevin Eastwood

Feature films.

ARTHUR HOLBROOK PRODUCTIONS INC.
2705 Arbutus Rd., Victoria, BC V8N 1W8
(250) 477-5057, FAX: (250) 477-5447
E-mail: aholbrook@shaw.ca
CONTACT
Arthur Holbrook

Film / video.

ARTSY FARTSY PICTURES
1267 Marineside Cr., Ste. 216, Vancouver, BC V6Z 2X5
(604) 609-0350, FAX: (604) 689-0359
E-mail: e.sanchez@artsyfartsypictures.com
PRODUCER / DIRECTOR
Paul Ziller
WRITER / PRODUCER
Elizabeth Sanchez

ART YOUNG VIDEO PRODUCTIONS
8387 – 13th Ave., Burnaby, BC V3N 2G8
(604) 526-8897, FAX: (604) 526-8814
E-mail: artyoung@telus.net
CONTACT
Art Young

Broadcast / corporate / special events / location sound

ASTERISK PRODUCTIONS LTD.
977 Hampshire Rd., Victoria, BC V8S 4S3
(250) 480-5256, FAX: (250) 598-1299
E-mail: asterisk@islandnet.com, www.asterisk.bc.ca
CONTACTS
David Springbett
Heather MacAndrew

ATOMIC CARTOONS INC.
(604) 734-2866, FAX: (604) 734-2869
E-mail: rob@atomiccartoons.com, www.atomiccartoons.com
CONTACT
Rob Davies

AVANTI PICTURES CORPORATION
410 – 425 Carrall St., Vancouver, BC V6B 6E3
(604) 609-0339, FAX: (604) 609-0336
E-mail: info@avantipics.com, www.avantipics.com
EXEC. PRODUCER / DIRECTOR OF DEVELOPMENT
Cathy Chilco
PRODUCER / DIRECTOR
Tony Papa

Documentaries/dramas/series/children's & music videos/features

BACCHUS ENTERTAINMENT LTD.
1904 W. 16th Ave., Ste. 1, Vancouver, BC V6J 2M4
(604) 732-4804, FAX (604) 408-5177
E-mail: penny@mediatelevision.tv
PRESIDENT
Penny O. Green

Production of multimedia websites and video series for the Internet
including Daxula.com. Specializing in online distribution

BARDEL ENTERTAINMENT
548 Beatty St., Vancouver, BC V6B 2L3. (604) 669-5589,
FAX: (604) 669-9079. E-mail:bardel@bardelentertainment.com
www.bardelentertainment.com
CEO
Delna Bhesania
PRESIDENT
Barry Ward

BIG PICTURE MEDIA CORPORATION
2676 Eton St., Vancouver, BC V5K 1K1. (604) 253-8333
FAX: (604) 253-8355. E-mail: bigpix@thecorporation.tv
DIRECTOR / PRODUCER
Mark Achbar

Documentary / TV / features

BIG RED BARN ENTERTAINMENT
6556 60th Ave., Delta, BC V4K 4E2. (604) 946-6329
FAX: (604) 946-2604. E-mail: ken@brbmg.com
www.brbmg.com
PRESIDENT
Ken Malenstyn
DIRECTOR / PRODUCER / DEVELOPMENT
Alexis Arthur

BLUE SKY PRODUCTIONS INC.
1619 Hampshire Rd., Victoria, BC V8R 5T4. (250) 598-4563
E-mail: cellulloyd@shaw.ca
CONTACTS
Lloyd Chesley
James Fry

Film & video dramas / documentaries / theatre / TV

BRIGHTLIGHT PICTURES
Vancouver Film Studios, 3500 Cornett Rd., Vancouver, BC V5M 2H5
(604) 453-4710, FAX: (604) 453-4711
E-mail: info@brightlightpictures.com
www.brightlightpictures.com
PRODUCERS
Shawn Williamson
Stephen Hegyes
V.P., BUSINESS & LEGAL AFFAIRS
Karyn Edwards
DIRECTOR OF ADMINSITRATION
Dawn Williamson

DIRECTOR OF DEVELOPMENT
Andrew Boutilier

CARSON STREET PRODUCTIONS LTD.
5510 Carson St., Burnaby, BC V5J 2Z2.
Tel. & FAX: (604) 451-1746
CONTACT
Elaine Gans

Television / documentary / educational

CINEMAX FILMS INC.
2222 W. 33rd Ave., Vancouver, BC V6M 1C2
(604) 266-9690
PRODUCER / PRODUCTION MANAGER
Don McLean

Development & production

COAST MOUNTAIN FILMS INC.
8275 Manitoba St., Vancouver, BC V5X 4L8
(604) 437-3740, FAX: (604) 437-3745
PRESIDENT
Rose Lam

COYOTE FILMS LTD.
1423 Howe St., Vancouver, BC V6Z 1R9
(604) 685-1417
PRESIDENT
Ken Kuramoto

Film / TV

CRESCENT ENTERTAINMENT
555 Brooksbank Ave., Bldg. 9, Ste. 330, N. Vancouver, BC V7J
3S5. (604) 983-5992, FAX: (604) 983-5015
CONTACTS
Harold Tichenor, Gordon Mark, Jayme Pfahl, Christine Haebler
PROJECT MANAGER
Karen Cameron
LEGAL & BUSINESS AFFAIRS
Andrea Goodey

Development / independent production / production services

CRONE FILMS LTD.
8175 Pasco Rd., W. Vancouver, BC V7W 2T5. (604) 921-6500
/ (604) 921-6554.
CONTACTS
Robert Crone, csc
David Crone

CULLEN ROBERTSON PRODUCTIONS
408 – 8623 Granville St., Vancouver, BC V6P 5A1
(604) 685-9515, FAX: (604) 685-3987
E-mail: cullenrobertson@shaw.ca
www.cullenrobertson.tv
PRESIDENT
Linda Cullen
SECRETARY
Bob Robertson

DOGWOOD PICTURES
20 Brooksbank Ave., 2nd Fl., N. Vancouver, BC V7J 2B8
(604) 904-5615, FAX: (604) 904-5627. www.muse.ca
PRESIDENT
Lisa Richardson

Features / TV movies & series

EDWARD LEE MULTIMEDIA INC.
15225 – 104th Ave., Ste. 310, Surrey, BC V3R 6Y8
(604) 589-5270, FAX: (604) 588-1555
E-mail: info@elpmedia.com, www.leevideo.com
OWNER
Edward Lee
V.P., MULTIMEDIA
Raymond Lee

Complete video services

FORCE FOUR ENTERTAINMENT
1152 Mainland St., Ste. 310, Vancouver, BC V6B 4X2
(604) 669-4424, FAX: (604) 669-4535
Email: tv@forcefour.com, www.forcefour.com
PRESIDENT
Hugh Beard
V.P., BUSINESS AFFAIRS
Debra Beard
V.P., PRODUCTION
John Ritchie
V.P., DEVELOPMENT & CO-PRODUCTION
Rob Bromley

FORWARD FOCUS PRODUCTIONS LTD.
784 Thurlow St., Ste. 31, Vancouver, BC V6E 1V9
Tel. & Fax: (604) 681-4677. E-mail: mmcewen@sfu.ca
PRESIDENT
Mary Anne McEwen

GENESIS COMMUNICATIONS CORP.
Box 888, Gibsons Landing, BC V0N 1V0
Tel. & FAX: (604) 886-3639
E-mail: devadas@telus.net
President / Producer
Robert Nichol

Educational / TV / entertainment programming

LEN GILDAY, CSC
R.R. #1, B-46, Bowen Island, BC V0N 1G0. (604) 947-2388
FAX: (604) 947-2389

Director / documentaries / cinematographer

GREGORIAN FILMS LTD.
Box 71040, 3552 W. 41st Ave., Vancouver, BC V6N 1W0
Tel. & Fax: (604) 266-1617, E-mail: ckpitts@telus.net
CONTACT
Charles K. Pitts

Film development / production / financing

GRYPHON PRODUCTIONS LTD.
Box 93009, 5331 Headlands Dr., W. Vancouver, BC V7W 3C0
(604) 921-7627, FAX: (604) 921-7626
E-mail: gryphon@telus.net
www.gryphonproductions.com
CONTACT
Peter Von Puttkamer

HADDOCK ENTERTAINMENT INC.
810 – 207 W. Hastings St., Vancouver, BC V6B 1H7
(604) 681-1516, FAX: (604) 684-3530
E-mail: haddock@uniserve.com
EXECUTIVE PRODUCER
Chris Haddock
PRODUCER
Laura Lightbown

Film / TV production

JIM HAMM PRODUCTIONS
2555 Trinity St., Vancouver, BC V5K 1E3. (604) 874-1110
FAX: (604) 874-1124. E-mail: jim.hamm@telus.net
PRESIDENT
Jim Hamm

INFINITY FILMS
873 Beatty St., Ste. 100, Vancouver, BC V6B 2M6
(604) 681-5650, FAX: (604) 681-5664
E-mail: info@infinityfilms.ca, www.infinityfilms.ca
CONTACTS
Shel Piercy
Dan Carriere

H3O FILMED ENTERTAINMENT
1415 West Georgia St., Ste. 1804, Vancouver, BC V6G 3C8
(604) 662-3345, FAX: (604) 662-7720
E-mail: production@h3ofilm.com, www.h3ofilm.com
PARTNERS
John Curtis
Evan Tylor
SENIOR MANAGER
Rod Akizuki, main contact: rakizuki@h3ofilm.com

IN SIGHT FILM & VIDEO PRODUCTIONS LTD.
112 West 6th Ave., Vancouver, BC V5Y 1K6
(604) 623-3369, FAX: (604) 623-3448
E-mail: insight@insightfilm.com
PRESIDENT / PRODUCER
Kirk Shaw
DIRECTOR / WRITER / CREATIVE CONSULTANT
Maryvonne Micale
V.P., DEVELOPMENT
Patti Poskitt

Documentaries for TV, music videos, TV commercials & TV series

INTERNATIONAL ROCKETSHIP LTD.
1338 W. 6th Ave., Ste. 204, Vancouver, BC V6H 1A7
(604) 738-1778, FAX: (604) 738-0009
PRODUCER
Marv Newland

INTREPID FILMS INC. / PETER LHOTKA
315 W. 24th St., N. Vancouver, BC V7M 2C7
Tel. & Fax: (604) 987-5581. E-mail: lhotka@sentry.npsnet.com
PRODUCER
Peter Lhotka

TV / series / features / MOWs

KAMLOOPS PRO VIDEO SERVICES
1318B McGill Rd., Kamloops, BC V2C 6N6
(250) 851-2568, FAX: (250) 851-2921
Website: www.provideo.bc.ca
CONTACTS
Bill Ligertwood
Pat Ebert

KEATLEY MACLEOD PRODUCTIONS LTD.
510 West Hastings St., Ste. 718, Vancouver, BC V6B 1L8
(604) 291-9789, FAX: (604) 291-9759
E-mail: coldsquad@uniserve.com
PRESIDENT
Julia Keatley
SECRETARY
Matt MacLeod
TREASURER
Phillip Keatley

LAISSEZ-FAIRE FILMS INC.
Pier 32, Granville Island, 100 – 1333 Johnston St., Vancouver,
BC V6H 3R9. (604) 689-0880, FAX: (604) 689-3036
WRITER / PRODUCER
Terry Mercer
PRODUCER
Paxton Robertson

LES STANCHUK VIDEO PRODUCTION
1131 Columbia Ave., Trail, BC V1R 1J1. (250) 368-9964,
FAX: (250) 368-9965, Cell: (250) 368-7290
E-mail: lsvp@bigfoot.com

Industrial / commercial video / photographic services

LIONS GATE ENTERTAINMENT CORP.
Three Bentall Centre, 595 Burrard Ave., Ste. 3123, Vancouver,
BC V7X 1J1. (604) 609-6100, FAX:(604) 609-6145
www.lionsgatefilms.com

Develops, produces and distributes a broad range of motion
picture, television and other filmed entertainment content
through its four operation divisions - motion picture, television,
animation, and studio facilities. Trading symbols: AMEX & TSE:
LGF. Majority ownership of CinemaNow Video-On-Demand.
See Also Ontario, Quebec.
U.S.A. OFFICE: 4553 Glencoe Ave., Ste. 200, Marina del Rey,
CA 90292. (310) 314-2000, FAX: (310) 392-0252
E-mail: recep@lgecorp.com
CEO
John Feltheimer
VICE CHAIRMEN
Mark Amin
Michael Burns
CAO/CFO
Jim Keegan
EXECUTIVE. V.P.
John Dellaverson
EXECUTIVE V.P.: LIONS GATE STUDIO
Peter Leitch

THE LUNNY COMMUNICATIONS GROUP
1500 W. Georgia St., 20th Floor, Vancouver, BC V6G 2Z6
(604) 669-0333, FAX: (604) 662-7500
E-mail: lcg@lunny.com, www.lunny.com
PRESIDENT
Shane Lunny
PRODUCTION SUPERVISOR
Tony Dean

Video / film — 35mm / multimedia / studio & post-production
facilities

MAINFRAME ENTERTAINMENT
2025 West Broadway, Ste. 200, Vancouver, BC V6J 1Z6
(604) 714-2600, FAX: (604) 714-2641
E-mail: info@reboot.com
EXECUTIVE PRODUCER
Rick Mischel

MAKE BELIEVE MEDIA
198 East 21st Ave., Vancouver, BC V5N 1P8
(604) 874-9498, FAX: (604) 728-5086
E-mail: lynnb@makebelievemedia.com, www.makebelievemedia.com
PRESIDENT
Lynn Booth

MASSEY PRODUCTIONS LTD.
249 East St. James Rd., N. Vancouver, BC V7N 1L3
(604) 990-9044, FAX: (604) 990-9066
E-mail: mplstudio@cs.com
PRODUCER
Raymond Massey

THE MAY STREET GROUP
Film, Video & Animation Ltd., 4412 Wilkinson Rd.
Victoria, BC V8Z 5B7. (250) 380-6656, FAX: (250) 380-6670
E-mail: maystreet@maystreet.ca
President
Hilary Pryor

Full creative services from concept to release

MEDIAWERKZ PRODUCTIONS LTD.
611 E. Kings Rd., N. Vancouver, BC V7N 1J4. (604) 987-1625
E-mail: zinc@telus.net

Documentary / TV / multimedia / educational / CD-ROM

MILESTONE PRODUCTIONS INC.
740 E. 9th St., N. Vancouver, BC V7L 2B9. (604) 983-2822
FAX: (604) 983-2922. E-mail: ogmilestone@shaw.ca
PRESIDENT
Ogden Gavanski
DIRECTOR OF DEVELOPMENT
Catherine Forbes

Feature films / TV series / documentaries

MINDS EYE PICTURES
1142 Keith Rd., W. Vancouver, BC V7T 1M8
(604) 921-2233, FAX: (604) 925-9595
CONTACT
Andrew Atkins

Features / TV drama / documentaries. See also Alberta &
Saskatchewan.

MOLLY'S REACH PRODUCTIONS INC.
104 – 1260 Lynn Valley Rd., N. Vancouver, BC V7J 2A3
(604) 983-2555, FAX: (604) 983-2558
E-mail: nick@soapboxproductions.ca
EXECUTIVE PRODUCERS
Mark Strange
Jackson Davies
Nick Orchard

MORTIMER & OGILVY PRODUCTIONS LIMITED
1431 Howe St., Ste. 201, Vancouver, BC V6Z 1R9
(604) 408-1693, FAX: (604) 408-1670
Producer
Sharon McGowan
Producer / Writer
Peggy Thompson

Film & TV / development & production

NEW COMMUNICATION CONCEPTS LTD.
5 – 23260 Dyke Rd., Richmond, BC V6V 1E2
(604) 520-0272, FAX: (604) 526-3351. E-mail: cutlerd@look.ca
PRESIDENT
Keith Cutler, kcutler@capcollege.bc.ca
VICE-PRESIDENT
Dixie Cutler

NOVALIS ENTERTAINMENT LTD.
Box 71040, 3552 W. 41st Ave., Vancouver, BC V6N 1W0
Tel. & Fax: (604) 266-1617. E-mail: ckpitts@telus.net
Contact
Charles K. Pitts

Television development / production / financing

O'MARA & RYAN
2337 Nelson Ave., W. Vancouver, BC V7V 2R7
(604) 926-9155, FAX: (604) 926-9152
www.omararyan.com
CONTACTS
James O'Mara
Kate Ryan

Photography / directing / writing / producing

OMNI FILM PRODUCTIONS LTD.
(and Water Street Pictures Ltd.), 111 Water St., Ste. 204
Vancouver, BC V6B 1A7. (604) 681-6543, FAX: (604) 688-
1425. E-mail: omni@omnifilm.com, www.omnifilm.com
PRESIDENT / EXECUTIVE PRODUCER
Michael Chechik

ORCA PRODUCTIONS INC.
3425 W. 2nd Ave., Vancouver, BC V6R 1J3
(604) 732-9387, FAX: (604) 732-3587
E-mail: info@orcaproductions.com, www.orcaproductions.com
PRESIDENT
Nicholas Kendall
PRODUCER / DEVELOPMENT
Abigail Kinch

Feature films / TV drama

PAN PRODUCTIONS
1 – 625 Hillside Ave., Victoria, BC V8T 1Z1. (250) 389-6781
FAX: (250) 383-6514. E-mail: jim@panproductions.com
CONTACT
Jim Eidt

Full-service creative / production. Betacam field crews. Full
digital post facility & closed captioning

PAPERNY FILMS
25 East 2nd Ave., 3rd Fl., Vancouver, BC V5T1B3
(604) 228-1960, FAX: (604) 228-1911. E-mail: info@papernyfilms.com
PRODUCERS / DIRECTORS
David Paperny
Audrey Mehler
PRODUCER
Stacey Offman
DIRECTOR OF DEVELOPMENT
Aynsley Vogel

PEACE ARCH ENTERTAINMENT GROUP INC.
150 West 1st Ave., Ste. 200, Vancouver, BC V5Y 1A4
(604) 681-9308 / (888) 588-3608, FAX: (604) 681-3299
www.peacearch.com

PETERSEN PRODUCTIONS INC.
289 Drake St., Apt.1303, Vancouver, BC V6B 5Z5
(604) 669-8890, FAX: (604) 662-8013
U.S.A. OFFICE: 106 Entrada Dr., Unit 6, Santa Monica, CA
90402. (310) 230-8616
PRESIDENT
Curtis Petersen

See also Ontario.

PICTURES OF LIGHT PRODUCTIONS
701 – 207 West Hastings St., Vancouver, BC V6B 1H7
(604) 603-0705, FAX: (604) 681-7173
E-mail: lightbown@uniserve.com
PRODUCER
Laura Lightbown

PITCAIRN PICTURES INC.
Box 497, Lion's Bay, BC V0N 2E0. (604) 921-8899, FAX: (604)
921-8904. E-mail: jo@pitpix.com
CONTACT
Jo Kirkpatrick & Co.

POINT OF VIEW FILM INC.
3216 W. 2nd Ave., Vancouver, BC V6K 1K8
(604) 734-5035, FAX: (604) 737-0123
E-mail: michellebjornson@excite.com
PRESIDENT
Michelle Bjornson

Drama & documentary: development / production / release

PRISMA LIGHT WEST LTD.
101 – 1184 Denman St. #141, Vancouver, BC V6G 2M9
(604) 801-5256, FAX: (604) 608-3362
E-mail: harry@prismalight.com, www.prismalight.com
TORONTO OFFICE: Prisma Light Ltd., 762 Queen St. W,
Toronto, ON M6J 1E9. (416) 504-4321, FAX: (416) 504-7325
E-mail: info@prismalight.com, www.prismalight.com

PRODUCERS ON DAVIE
520 – 1033 Davie St., Vancouver, BC V6E 1M7
(604) 801-5256, FAX: (604) 801-5286
E-mail: producersondavie@ telus.net
PRODUCERS
Harry Sutherland
Cari Green

P.S. PRODUCTIONS INC.
2871 W. Third Ave., Vancouver, BC V6K 1M8
(604) 730-4700, FAX: (604) 730-4800
E-mail: savath@aol.com
PRESIDENT
Phil Savath

PUDDLE DUCK PRODUCTIONS LTD.
2329 W. 14th Ave., Vancouver, BC V6K 2W2. (604) 734-1103
FAX: (604) 734-1150, Cell: (604) 729-2016
E-mail: puddlesbri@aol.com
PRESIDENT
Brian Schecter

**QUEEN BEE PRODUCTIONS / ROMNEY GRANT
PRODUCTIONS**
1221 West 23rd St., N. Vancouver, BC V7P 2H5
(604) 985-1687, FAX: (604) 985-1667
E-mail: romneygrant@shaw.ca
PRESIDENT
Romney Grant

Children's & information programming

RED LETTER FILMS
4620 Yew St.. Ste. 202, Vancouver, BC V6L 2J6
(604) 737-3657, FAX: (604) 872-0367
E-mail: redletter@axion.net
PRESIDENT
Sylvie Peltier

RED STORM PRODUCTIONS
2558 E. 5th Ave., Vancouver, BC V5M 1M7
(604) 254-1346, FAX: (604) 254-1347
E-mail: redstorm@shaw.ca, Website: www.redstorm.ca
CONTACTS
Erik Paulsson
Arlene Ami

Film / TV

RIVER OF STONE PRODUCTIONS
929 Richards St., Vancouver, BC V6B 3B6
(604) 685-2045, FAX: (604) 685-2024
E-mail: mary@riverofstone.com, www.riverofstone.com
PRESIDENT
Mary Sparacio

SAJO PRODUCTIONS INC.
Box 888, Gibsons Landing, BC V0N 1V0.
Tel. & FAX.: (604) 886-3639. E-mail: devadas@telus.net
PRESIDENT / PRODUCER
Robert Nichol

Features

SAVI MEDIA INC.
2040 W. 12th Ave., Ste. 233, Vancouver, BC V6J 2G2
(604) 734-1550, FAX: (604) 734-1414
E-mail: mail@savi-media.com, www.savi-media.com
PRESIDENT
Alexandra Raffé
DIRECTOR, CREATIVE AFFAIRS
Tara Twigg
TV drama / feature films. See also Ontario

SCINTILLA ENTERTAINMENT INC.
134 Abbott St., 7th Fl., Vancouver, BC V6B 2K4
(604) 688-9818, FAX: (604) 684-2452
E-mail: info@ScintillaEnt.com, www.ScintillaEnt.com
CONTACT
Pindar Azad, TV production

SCREEN SIREN PICTURES INC.
291 East 2nd Ave., Ste. 300, Vancouver, BC V5T 1B8
(604) 687-7591, FAX: (604) 687-4937
E-mail: info@screensiren.ca
PRESIDENT / PRODUCER
Trish Dolman

SEA TO SKY ENTERTAINMENT
Box 3640, Garibaldi Highlands, BC V0N 1T0
Tel. & FAX: (604) 898-5930. E-mail: apolo@shaw.ca
DIRECTORS
Adriane Polo
Mark McConchie
Kathy Daniels
Film / video

SELWYN ENTERPRISES INC.
2917 West 35 Ave., Vancouver, BC V6N 2M5. (604) 731-5257
E-mail: selwyn_jacob@telus.net
EXECUTIVE PRODUCER
Joan Jacob
Film / TV

SHAVICK ENTERTAINMENT
112 West 6th Ave., Vancouver, BC V5Y 1K6
(604) 874-4300, FAX: (604) 874-4305
E-mail: info@shavickentertainment.com
Website: www.shavickentertainment.com
CEO
James Shavick

SOAPBOX PRODUCTIONS INC.
104 – 1260 Lynn Valley Rd., N. Vancouver, BC V7J 2A3
(604) 983-2555, FAX: (604) 983-2558
E-mail: nick@soapboxproductions.ca
EXECUTIVE PRODUCER
Nick Orchard

SOMA: FILM & VIDEO
Box X-26, Bowen Island, BC V0N 1G0
(604) 947-0044, FAX: (604) 947-0049
President
Deepak Sahasrabudhe
Vice-President
Susan Millar

SOMA TELEVISION LTD.
6393 Bruce St., W. Vancouver, BC V7W 2G5
(604) 925-9582, FAX: (604) 925-9436
PRESIDENT
Deepak Sahasrabudhe
VICE-PRESIDENT
Susan Millar

STARVISION ENTERTAINMENT
14027 – 102 Ave., Surrey, BC V3T 1P5
(604) 619-3677, FAX: (604) 930-1878
E-mail: starvisi@intergate.bc.ca
CONTACT
Kenneth W. Meisenbacher

Documentaries, corporate, music, educational and training videos

STUDIO B
600 – 190 Alexander St., Vancouver, BC V6A 1B5
(604) 684-2363, FAX: (604) 602-0208. E-mail: info@studiobproduc-
tions.com, www.studiobproductions.com
CONTACTS
Blair Peters
Chris Bartleman
Rob Simmons
Michael Lahay

TAMARAC FILMWORKS LTD.
3812 W. 14 Ave., Vancouver, BC V6R 2W9. (604) 224-1992
Producer / Writer / Director
Alyson Drysdale

TV dramas / documentaries / shorts

TRIAD COMMUNICATIONS LTD.
2751 Oxford St., Vancouver, BC V5K 1N5. (604) 253-3990
FAX: (604) 253-0770. www.comwave.com
CONTACT
Gay Ludlow

TROIKA PRODUCTIONS
404 – 999 Canada Place, Vancouver, BC V6C 3E2
(604) 990-9020, FAX: (604) 990-9021
E-mail: troika@axion.net
PRESIDENT / PRODUCER
Walter Daroshin

VIDEO PUBLISHING GROUP
1955 Wylie St., 2nd Fl., Vancouver, BC V5Y 3N7
(604) 874-5005 / (800) 667-7718, FAX: (604) 874-5005
E-mail: info@vpgroup.tv
PRESIDENT
Peter Sara
SALES
Ramin Shahidian

Documentaries / corporate / educational

YALETOWN ENTERTAINMENT CORP.
1431 Howe St., Vancouver, BC V6Z 1R9. (604) 669-3543
FAX: (604) 669-5149, www.yaletownentertainment.com
PRESIDENT / EXEC. PRODUCER
Mike Collier
PRODUCTION MANAGER
Lupe Danyluk

Feature film / TV production

MANITOBA

BUFFALO GAL PICTURES INC.
777 – 70 Arthur St., Winnipeg, MB R3B 1G7
(204) 956-2777, FAX: (204) 956-7999
E-mail: info@buffalogalpictures.com
www.buffalogalpictures.com
PRESIDENT
Phyllis Laing

CRITICAL MADNESS PRODUCTIONS
131 Bourkvale Dr., Winnipeg, MB R3J 1P3
(204) 795-7950, FAX: (204) 284-0358
E-mail: jpeeler@mts.net, www.criticalmadness.com
PRESIDENT
Jeff Peeler

EAGLE VISION
509 Century St., Winnipeg, MB R3H 0L8. (204) 772-0368
FAX: (204) 772-0360, E-mail: kyle@midcan.com
www.tipitales.com
PRESIDENT
Lisa Meeches
V.P.
Wayne Sheldon
PRODUCER
Kyle Irving

EDEN II ENTERTAINMENT
137 Scott St., Winnipeg, MB R3L 0K9. (204) 775-4092
FAX: (204) 783-2311. E-mail: info@meritmotionpictures.com
President
Merit Jensen-Carr

FRANTIC FILMS
70 Arthur St., Ste. 300, Winnipeg, MB R3B 1G7
(204) 949-0070, FAX: (204) 949-0050
E-mail: info@franticfilms.com, www.franticfilms.com
PRESIDENT. / CREATIVE DIRECTOR
Christopher Bond
V.P. / PRODUCER
Ken Zorniak
CEO / EXEC. PRODUCER
Jamie Brown

Manitoba's leading visual effects and live-action production
house. Producing Pioneer Quest: Back from the Real West and
Quest for the Bay, History Television's highest-rated series to
date. Both series have received high praise from critics.
Currently in post-production for the next Quest series.

KIZUK PRODUCTIONS
78 Stoneham Cr., Winnipeg, MB R2G 3L8
Tel./Fax: (204) 667-6339, E-mail: kizukvideo@shaw.ca
President
Rick Kizuk

Senior Producer
Hugh McColl

KONO FILMS LTD.
81 Claremont Ave., Winnipeg, MB R2H 1W1. (204) 237-5649
Cell: (204) 782-5939, FAX: (204) 237-1563
E-mail: konosite@shaw.ca
PRESIDENT
Charles Konowal

MEMORIA
200 – 690 St. Joseph St., Winnipeg, MB R2H 3E2
(204) 233-1189, FAX: (204) 233-0811
CONTACT
Romeo Jacobucci

MERIT MOTION PICTURES INC.
137 Scott St., Winnipeg, MB R3L 0K9
(204) 775-4092, FAX: (204) 783-2311
E-mail: info@meritmotionpictures.com
PRESIDENT
Merit Jensen-Carr

NATIVE MULTIMEDIA PRODUCTIONS
7 Evergreen Pl., Ste. 2202, Winnipeg, MB R3L 2T3
(204) 231-1524, FAX: (204) 231-5555
E-mail: donmarks@shaw.ca, www.indiantime3.com
PRESIDENT
Curtis Shingoose Jonnie
V.P.
Don Marks

VONNIE VON HELMOLT FILM
225 Symington Rd., Winnipeg, MB R2C 5J7. (204) 229-9879
FAX: (204) 224-9513. E-mail: vvh@mb.aibn.com
PRESIDENT / PRODUCER
Vonnie Von Helmolt

NEW BRUNSWICK

ABRAMS MEDIA INC.
560 Main St. Ste. 120, Building A, Saint John, NB E2K 1J5
(506) 633-6038, FAX: (506) 633-7493
E-mail: abrams@sonoptic.com
President
Greg Abrams

ACROLECT INTERNATIONAL
155 Topcliffe Cres., Fredericton, NB E3B 4P8
(506) 457-1793 (h & w), FAX: (506) 454-6757
CONTACT
Semra N. Yuksel

ATLANTIC MEDIAWORKS
469 King St., Fredericton, NB E3B 1E5
(506) 458-8806, FAX: (506) 452-2700
E-mail: amw@atlanticmediaworks.com
www.atlanticmediaworks.com
CONTACTS
Bob Miller
Daphne Curtis

FRANCIS BOURQUE
68 MacBeath Ave., Moncton, NB EIC 6Y9
(506) 388-2717, FAX: (506) 388-3766

THE BRISTOL GROUP
720, Main St., 3rd Fl., Moncton, NB E1C 1E4
(506) 383-4000. www.bristolgroup.ca
SECOND LOCATION: One Market Square, Ste. 301N, Saint
John, NB E2L 4Z6. (506) 693-4000

See also Newfoundland, Nova Scotia

CINEFILE PRODUCTIONS INC.
424 Dufferin St., Fredericton, NB E3B 3A7
(506) 455-2344, FAX: (506) 457-1874
E-mail: barrycam@nbnet.nb.ca
President
Barry Cameron

Film, TV, new media and script consultation for writers & producers through Scriptwise Associates

CINIMAGE PRODUCTIONS
8 Belleview Ave., Moncton, NB E1C 4S8
(506) 386-1616, FAX: (506) 855-7025
E-mail: cinimage@rogers.com
CONTACTS
Monique LeBlanc
Michael LeBlanc

CONNECTIONS PRODUCTIONS
91 Driscoll Cr., Moncton, NB E1E 4C8
(506) 382-3984, FAX: (506) 382-3980
CONTACTS
François Savoie, frank@connectionsproductions.com

Michael Savoie, mike@connectionsproductions.com
Development / production / direction

DREAMSMITH ENTERTAINMENT INC.
250 Lutz St., Moncton, NB EIC 5G3. (506) 854-1057
FAX: (506) 382-4144
PRODUCER
Timothy M. Hogan
Cell: (506) 870-0058
E-mail: tmhogan@nbnet.nb.ca
PRODUCER
W. James Hogan
Cell: (506) 545-5744
E-mail: hoganwj@nbnet.nb.ca

FIDDLEHEAD ENTERTAINMENT INC.
250 Lutz St., Moncton, NB EIC 5G3. (506) 854-1057
FAX: (506) 382-4144. E-mail: hoganwj@nbnet.nb.ca
CONTACTS
Sam Grana
W. James Hogan

INNOVATIVE VIDEO SOLUTIONS
76 Princess St., St. John, NB E2L 1K4
Tel. & Fax: (506) 693-4487. E-mail: darrell@videosolutions.ca /
mike@videosolutions.ca. www.videosolutions.ca
CONTACTS
Darrell Bainbridge
Mike Burchill

Documentary, corporate & E.N.G. Betacam SP production
including digital online video and audio post-production.
Complete Betacam SP production, concept to completion.

MAX MEDIA LTD.
849 Barker St., Fredericton, NB E3A 3K4
(506) 474-0006, FAX: (506) 472-1496
E-mail: maxmedia@nbnet.nb.ca
CONTACT
Kevin Matthews

NEW BRUNSWICK FILMMAKERS' CO-OPERATIVE
Box 1537, Fredericton, NB E3B 4Y1
(506) 455-1632, FAX: (506) 457-2006
E-mail: nbfilmco-op@brunnet.net, www.brunnet.net/nbfilm/
CONTACTS
Tony Merzetti
Cathie LeBlanc

PHANTOM PRODUCTIONS INC.
1010 Tamarack Dr., Bathurst, NB E2A 4H4
(506) 547-8984, FAX: (506) 546-7448
CONTACT
Tony Larder

LES PRODUCTIONS DU PHARE EST INC.
CP 517 – 140 rue Botsford, bur. 20, Moncton, NB EIC 8L9
(506) 857-9941, FAX: (506) 857-1806
E-mail: phareest@nbnet.nb.ca
CONTACTS
Cécile Chevrier
Gilles Losier

LES PRODUCTIONS GRANA PRODUCTIONS INC.
880 Main St., Ste. 210, Moncton, NB E1C 1G4
(506) 877-2252, FAX: (506) 877-2255
CONTACT
Sam Grana

PRODUCTIONS LIBRES INC.
14 Church St., Ste. 200, Moncton, NB E1C 4Y9
(506) 853-7889, FAX: (506) 854-5272
E-mail: libres@nbnet.nb.ca
CONTACT
Jocelyn Cyr

Film / video / documentary / post-production / media 100 /
graphic animation

ROWAN RIDGE PRODUCTIONS
175 Chamberlain Rd., Quispamsis, NB E2G 1B7
Tel. & Fax: (506) 847-3185. E-mail: connell@nbnet.nb.ca
CONTACTS
Lynn & Connell Smith

TEL VISION
795 rue Main, 3 étage, bur. 300, Moncton, NB E1C 1E9
(506) 857-1090, FAX: (506) 857-0352
E-mail: telvision@nb.aibn.com
DIRECTEUR GÉNÉRAL
Jean-Claude Bellefeue

WEST STREET PICTURES
97 West St., Moncton, NB E1E 3N8. (506) 382-0487,
FAX: (506) 382-0488. E-mail: weststreetpictures@hotmail.com
PRESIDENT / PRODUCER / DIRECTOR
Rick LeGuerrier

NEWFOUNDLAND

THE BRISTOL GROUP
Fortis Building, P.O. Box 2220 139 Water St., Ste. 100, St.
John's, NL A1C 6E6. (709) 753-7242, FAX: (709) 753-5820
www.bristolgroup.ca

Multimedia production / broadcast. See also Nova Scotia, New
Brunswick

CODLESSCO LTD.
348 Mount Scio Rd., St. John's, NL A1B 4L6
(709) 738-4355, FAX: (709) 738-4360
E-mail: firecrown@roadrunner.nf.net
PRODUCER
Marian Frances White

DARK FLOWERS PRODUCTIONS INC.
683 Water St., 2nd Fl., St. John's, NL A1E 1B5
(709) 739-7922, FAX: (709) 739-9065
E-mail: rhouse@nfld.com
WRITER / DIRECTOR
Rosemary House
PRODUCER
Mary Sexton

MORAG PRODUCTIONS
Box 52, Stn. C, St. John's, NL A1C 5H5
(709) 739-0447, FAX: (709) 739-0467
E-mail: barbara@morag.nf.net
Producer / Director
Barbara Doran

Film / TV

NEW AND IMPROVED FILMS INC.
Box 5581, Stn. C, St. John's, NL A1C 5W4
(709) 739-0270, E-mail: dmcgee@mun.ca
PRESIDENT
Debbie McGee

PASSAGE FILMS
Box 52, Station C, St. John's, NL A1C 5H5
(709) 739-0447, FAX: (709) 739-0467
E-mail: lynne@morag.nf.net
www.randompassage.tv
PRODUCERS
Barbara Doran, Jennice Ripley

PIPERSTOCK PRODUCTIONS LTD.
24 Quarry Rd., Torbay, NL A1K 1A3
Tel. & FAX: (709) 437-1753
E-mail: dorann@roadrunner.nf.net
CONTACT
Dermot O'Reilly

Documentaries

POPE PRODUCTIONS LTD.
114 Water St., St. John's, NL A1C 1A8
(709) 722-7673, FAX: (709) 738-7285
E-mail: ppope@nfld.net
CONTACT
Paul Pope

Feature film / documentary / TV programming

RED OCHRE PRODUCTIONS LIMITED
Bldg. 567, St. John's Place Pleasantville, St. John's, NL A1A
1S2. (709) 739-1711, FAX: (709) 739-0868
PRESIDENT
Ken Pittman

Features / TV drama & children's programming

VIDCRAFT PRODUCTIONS LIMITED
425 Curling St., Cornerbrook, NL A2H 3K4
(709) 637-1157, FAX: (709) 634-8506
E-mail: info@vidcraft.com, www.vidcraft.com
CONTACT
Ron O'Connell

Broadcast video / multimedia / documentaries / commercials

NORTHWEST TERRITORIES / NUNAVUT

YELLOWKNIFE FILMS LTD.
5021 – 53rd St., Yellowknife, NT X1A 1V5. (867) 873-8610
FAX: (867) 873-9405. E-mail: ykfilms@theEdge.ca
CONTACT
Alan Booth

Documentaries / film / video

NOVA SCOTIA

BEAR TRACK PRODUCTIONS
177 Colby, Dartmouth, NS B2V 1K2. (902) 225-2585
FAX: (819) 978-0385
E-mail: brian@wanderingmuse.com, www.beartrackproductions.com
DIRECTOR / EDITOR
Brian W. White

BIG MOTION PICTURES LIMITED
Box 202 – 27 Pleasant St., Chester, NS B0J 1J0
(902) 275-1350, FAX: (902) 275-1353
Contacts
Wayne Grigsby
David MacLeod

Film / TV drama

THE BRISTOL GROUP
Cogswell Tower, 2000 Barrington St., Ste. 800, Halifax, NS B3J 3K1. (902) 429-0900, Fax: (902) 492-3756.
www.bristolgroup.ca

See also Newfoundland, New Brunswick.

CENEX INC.
3600 Kemp Rd., Ste. 202, Halifax, NS B3K 4X8
(902) 446-3775, FAX: (902) 431-4056
E-mail: info@cenex.ca, www.cenex.ca
CONTACT
Scott Westerlaken

Corporate video / commercials

CHRONICLE PICTURES
1657 Barrington St., Ste. 532, Halifax, NS B3J 2A1
(902) 425-4885, FAX: (902) 425-4851
E-mail: info@chroniclepictures.net, www.chroniclepictures.net
PARTNERS
Craig Cameron
Graeme Gunn
Evangelo Kioussis

COLLIDEASCOPE DIGITAL PRODUCTIONS INC.
5212 Sackville St., 4th Fl., Halifax, NS B3J 1K6
(902) 429-8949, FAX: (902) 429-0265
E-mail: info@collideascope.com, www.collideascope.com
CONTACT
Michael-Andreas Kuttner

New media production

CREATIVE ATLANTIC COMMUNICATIONS LIMITED
2085 Maitland St., Halifax, NS B3K 2Z8
(902) 423-1989, FAX: (902) 423-3711
E-mail: info@creativeatlantic.ca
CONTACTS
Janice Evans
Greg Jones

TV comedy / drama / documentaries

DOG'S BREAKFAST PRODUCTIONS
1112 Barrington St., Ste. A, Halifax, NS B3H 2R2
Tel./Fax: (902) 422-8845. E-mail: bamboo@ns.sympatico.ca
www.dogsbreakfastfilms.com
EXEC. PRODUCER / DIRECTOR
Mark Molaro
PRODUCER
Adam Townsend

ECO-NOVA PRODUCTIONS LIMITED
2762 Robie St., Halifax, NS B3K 4P2.
(902) 423-7906, FAX: (902) 423-6226
PRODUCER
John Davis

Documentaries

FOLKUS ATLANTIC INC.
67 Hospital St., Sydney, NS B1P 2H9. (902) 539-3363
FAX: (902) 562-5106. E-mail: folkus@atcon.com
www.folkus.com
CONTACT
Joan Weeks

Video / multimedia. Camera / editing rentals

GLOBAL VIDEO INC.
61 Tacoma Dr., Dartmouth, NS B2W 3E7
Tel. & Fax: (902) 434-7446. E-mail: jverstee@fox.nsgn.ca
Contact
John Versteege

Documentaries

IDLEWILD FILMS
2370 MacDonald St., Halifax, NS B3L 3G4. (902) 545-7866
Fax: (902) 454-7021. E-mail: niven@ns.sympatico.ca
PRODUCER
Bill Niven

IMX COMMUNICATIONS INC.
1190 Barrington St., 4th Fl., Halifax, NS B3H 2R4
(902) 422-4000, FAX: (902) 422-4427
E-mail: imx@imx.ca, www.imxcommunications.com
CHAIRMAN & CEO / EXEC. PRODUCER
Chris Zimmer
PRESIDENT & CFO
Dana Landry

TV & feature films – financing / production

JMCI
170 Thompson Run, Bedford, NS B4B 1T7
(902) 423-5585, FAX: (902) 832-5586
E-mail: jack@inforadiocanada.com
Contact
Jack McGaw

KRIZSAN FILM PRODUCTIONS
23 Fairbank St., Dartmouth, NS B3A 1B9
(902) 456-0948 / 466-8689, FAX: (902) 466-8689
E-mail: krizsan@ns.sympatico.ca
CONTACTS
Les Krizsan, csc,
Corinne Lange

Film / video production

PICTURE PLANT LTD.
983 Kingsburg Beach Rd., R.R. #1, Rose Bay, NS B0J 2X0
(902) 766-0174, FAX: (902) 766-0175
E-mail: info@pictureplant.com, www.pictureplant.com
PRESIDENT
William MacGillivray
VICE-PRESIDENT
Terry Greenlaw

Film and television production

REDSTAR FILMS
1657 Barrington St., Ste. 533, Halifax, NS B3J 2A1
(902) 429-5254, FAX: (902) 429-5256
E-mail: info@redstarfilm.com
PRESIDENT
Paul Kimball

SALTER STREET FILMS LIMITED
1668 Barrington St., Ste. 500, Halifax, NS B3J 2A2
(902) 420-1577, FAX: (902) 425-8260
E-mail: info@salter.com, www.salter.com
EXECUTIVE VICE-PRESIDENT
Charles Bishop
EXECUTIVE PRODUCERS
Michael Donovan
Paul Donovan

See also Ontario. (Alliance Atlantis Communications Inc.)

TOPSAIL ENTERTAINMENT
1583 Hollis St., 2nd Fl., Halifax, NS B3J 1V4
(902) 421-1326, FAX: (902) 423-0484
E-mail: contact@topsailentertainment.com
www.topsailentertainment.com
PRESIDENT / EXECUTIVE PRODUCER
Michael Volpe
EXECUTIVE PRODUCERS
Barry Cowling
Terry Fulmer
DIRECTOR OF CREATIVE DEVELOPMENT
Greg Morris

TV series / MOWs / feature films / documentaries

TRI MEDIA PRODUCTION SERVICES
194 Amaranth Cr., Dartmouth, NS B2W 4B9
(902) 422-8816, FAX: (902) 422-1580
E-mail: whitmantmp@hfx.eastlink.ca
PRESIDENT
F. Whitman Trecartin
CFO
Richard LaBelle
V.P., PRODUCTION
Matthew Trecartin

Documentaries / TV production

VANTAGE COMMUNICATIONS
5657 Spring Garden Rd., Ste. 604, Halifax, NS B3J 3R4
(902) 423-2243, FAX: (902) 425-7866
CEO
Lori Covert
In-house capabilities include film and video production; 3D animation; digital post-production (3 AVID suites); website design, development and hosting; CD-ROM / DVD development and production.

ONTARIO

ABATON PICTURES INC.
214 Rusholme Rd., Toronto, ON M6H 2Y8
(416) 537-2641, FAX: (416) 537-2995
E-mail: ian.mcdougall@pathcom.com
President
Ian McDougall

Features / TV drama

ACCENT ENTERTAINMENT CORPORATION
666B Queen St. W., 2nd Fl., Toronto, ON M6J 1E5
(416) 867-8700, FAX: (416) 867-1764
E-mail: info@accent-entertainment.com
PRESIDENT
Susan Cavan

Features / MOWs / series

AGINCOURT PRODUCTIONS INC.
888 Yonge St., Toronto, ON M4W 2J2. (416) 934-4860,
FAX: (416) 934-4841
CONTACT
Sam Dynes

ALLAN KING ASSOCIATES LIMITED
965 Bay St., Ste. 2409, Toronto, ON M5S 2A3
(416) 964-7284, FAX: (416) 964-7997
PRESIDENT
Allan King
VICE-PRESIDENT
Colleen Murphy

ALLIANCE ATLANTIS COMMUNICATIONS INC.
HEAD OFFICE: 121 Bloor St. E., Ste. 1500, Toronto, ON M4W
3M5. (416) 967-1174, FAX: (416) 960-0971
E-mail: info@allianceatlantis.com, www.allianceatlantis.com
CHAIRMAN & CEO
Michael MacMillan
EXECUTIVE V.P., CORPORATE & PUBLIC AFFAIRS
Heather Conway
CEO, MOTION PICTURE DISTRIBUTION GROUP
Victor Loewy
SENIOR. EXECUTIVE V.P. & CFO
W. Judson Martin
PRESIDENT, PRODUCTION, ENTERTAINMENT GROUP
Seaton McLean
PRESIDENT, DISTRIBUTION, ENTERTAINMENT GROUP
Edward A. Riley
PRESIDENT & COO, BROADCASTING GROUP
Mark Rubinstein
CEO, ENTERTAINMENT GROUP
Peter Sussman
PRESIDENT, MOTION PICTURE DISTRIBUTION GROUP
Patrice Théroux
CEO, BROADCASTING GROUP
Phyllis Yaffe

AAC is a leading vertically integrated broadcaster, creator and
distributor of filmed entertainment with ownership interests in
18 specialty channels, including five established operating
channels. Principal business activities are conducted through
three operating groups: the Broadcast Group, the Motion
Picture Distribution Group and the Entertainment Group.
Headquartered in Toronto, offices are operated in Los Angeles,
London (United Kingdom), Montréal, Dublin and Shannon
(Ireland), Edmonton, Halifax and Sydney (Australia). The
Company's common shares are listed on The Toronto Stock
Exchange — trading symbols AAC.A, AAC.B and on NASDAQ
— trading symbol AACB. See also Alberta, Québec, Nova
Scotia (Salter Street Films Limited).
ALBERTA: 3720 – 76 Ave., Edmonton, AB T6B 2N9
(780) 440-2022
NOVA SCOTIA: 1668 Barrington St., Ste. 500, Halifax, NS B3J
2A2. (902) 420-1577, FAX: (902) 425-8260
QUEBEC: 5 Place Ville-Marie, Ste. 1435, Montréal, QC H3B
2G2. (514) 878-2282, FAX: (514) 878-2419
AUSTRALIA: 401 Darling St., Ste. 2, Balmain, Sydney NSW
2041. (011) 61-2-9810-8922, FAX: (011) 61-2-9810-8966
IRELAND: Block 1, Unit C, Shannon Business Park, Shannon,
Co. Clare. (011) 353-61-472329, FAX: (011) 353-61-472228
SECOND OFFICE: 40 Westland Row, Dublin 2. (011) 353-1-
449-8400, FAX: (011) 353-1-449-8470
UNITED KINGDOM: 184 – 192 Drummond St., 2nd. Fl.,
London NW1 3HP. (011) 44-20-7391-6900,
FAX: (011) 44-20-7383-0404
U.S.A: 808 Wilshire Blvd., 3rd. Fl., Santa Monica, CA 90401
(310) 899-8000, FAX: (310) 899-8100

AMAZE FILM & TELEVISION
6 Pardee Ave., Ste. 104, Toronto, ON M6K 3H5. (416) 588-
7839, FAX: (416) 588-7276. E-mail: info@amazefilm.tv
www.amazefilm.tv

PRODUCERS
Michael Souther ext. 422, michael@amazefilm.tv
Teza Lawrence ext. 423, teza@amazefilm.tv

AMBERWOOD ENTERTAINMENT
987 Wellington St., 2nd Fl., Ottawa, ON K1Y 2Y1
(613) 238-4567, FAX: (613) 233-3857
E-mail: info@amberwoodanimation.com
www.amberwoodanimation.com
PRESIDENT
Sheldon Wiseman
CEO
Mark Edwards

Series Creator: Gerald Tripp

A MUSE PICTURES
3 – 366A Bloor St. W., Toronto, ON M5S 1X2
Tel./Fax: (416) 944-9912. E-mail: princesslarak@hotmail.com
EXEC. DIRECTOR
Lara Kelly
DIRECTOR / PRODUCER
Justin Kelly

ANDRE BENNETT PRODUCTIONS
60 Browning Ave., Toronto, ON M4K 1V9. (416) 977-0123
FAX: (416) 977-7890. E-mail: andre.m.bennett@sympatico.ca
PRODUCER
André Bennett

ANNEX ENTERTAINMENT
332 Dupont St., Toronto, ON M5R 1V9. (416) 929-3939
FAX: (416) 921-1325. E-mail: annexent@aol.com
PRODUCTION / FINANCE
Helder Goncalves

THE "A" PICTURE COMPANY
212 James St., Ottawa, ON K1R 5M7. (613) 230-9769
FAX: (613) 230-6004
CONTACT
Ramona Macdonald

AQUILA FILM & VIDEO INC.
48 Proctor Blvd., Hamilton, ON L8M 2M4
(905) 545-4773, Toronto cellular: (416) 346-5786
DIRECTOR / CAMERAMAN
Jim Aquila, csc

Complete Betacam & Widescreen DVCam camera packages,
lighting, grip

ARLECCHINA PRODUCTIONS INC.
43 Eglinton Ave. E., Ste. 901, Toronto, ON M4P 1A2
(416) 489-9414, FAX: (416) 489-1838
E-mail: arlecchinainfo@yahoo.com
CONTACT
Magie Matulic

Focuses on women-driven projects

ARMEDIA COMMUNICATIONS
3219 Yonge St., Ste. 307, Toronto, ON M4N 2L3
(905) 889-0076, FAX: (905) 889-0078
E-mail: maz@armediacommunications.com
www.armediacommunications.com
CONTACT
David Mazmanian

Audio / video production

ARMSTRONG CASTING & PRODUCTION
554 Carlaw Ave., Toronto, ON M4K 3J7. (416) 877-1746

ARTCORE PRODUCTIONS LTD.
2024 Glenada Cr., Oakville, ON L6H 4M6
(905) 338-3642, FAX: (905) 338-3642
E-mail: artcoreproductions@sympatico.ca
Contact
Vlad Kabelik

Film / TV documentary & educational programming

ARTO-PELLI MOTION PICTURES INC.
124 Cumberland St., 3rd Fl., Toronto, ON M5R 1A6
(416) 928-0164, FAX: (416) 928-3399

Producer: Stavros C. Stavrides

ASSOCIATED PRODUCERS LTD.
110 Spadina Ave., Ste. 1001, Toronto, ON M5V 2K4
(416) 504-6662, Fax: (416) 504-6667
E-mail: general@apdocs.com, www.apdocs.com
CONTACT
Simcha Jacobovici

AUDACINE INC.
68 Hamilton St., Toronto, ON M4M 2C8. (416) 778-4562
PRESIDENT
Mary Jane Gomes

AVP
5004 Timberlea Blvd., Unit 17, Mississauga, ON L4W 5C5
(905) 206-1304, (800) 275-4287, FAX: (905) 206-1170
E-mail: avp@avpinc.ca, www.avpinc.ca
President
Ron Baker
General Manager
Martha Coburn

Television, commercial, video & live event production – specializing in automotive products

AWKWARD FILMS
185 Carlton St., Toronto, ON M5A 2K7. (416) 413-4843
FAX: (416) 323-0388, E-mail: gavin@awkwardfilms.com
www.awkwardfilms.com
EXECUTIVE PRODUCER
Gavin McGarry

BACK ALLEY FILMS
41 Oak Park Ave., Toronto, ON M4C 4M1. (416) 780-0877
FAX: (514) 369-2236. E-mail: bkalley@sprint.ca
www.backalleyfilms.ca
PRODUCER
Janis Lundman
PRODUCER / DIRECTOR
Adrienne Mitchell

BAR HARBOUR FILMS INC.
62 Hazelwood Ave., Toronto, ON M4J 1K5. (416) 778-4491,
FAX: (416) 778-4144, E-mail: barharbour@sympatico.ca
PRODUCER / WRITER / DIRECTOR
Martin Harbury

Documentaries / film / TV

BARNA-ALPER PRODUCTIONS INC.
366 Adelaide St. W., Ste. 700, Toronto, ON M5V 1R9
(416) 979-0676, FAX: (416) 979-7476
E-mail: barnaalper@bap.ca, www.bap.ca
PRESIDENT
Laszlo Barna

TV series / MOWs / documentaries

BERYT PRODUCTIONS INC.
8111 Yonge St., Ste. 1503, Thornhill, ON L3T 4V9
(905) 764-6872, FAX: (905) 764-3615
E-mail: elizh@sprint.ca
PRESIDENT / PRODUCER
Eliza Haddad

Features / television

BIG COAT PRODUCTIONS
145 Front St. E., Ste. L3, Toronto, ON M5A 1E3
(416) 507-9829, FAX: (416) 507-9846
EXECUTIVE PRODUCER
Catherine Fogarty

BIG FISH PRODUCTIONS
42 Burton Ave., Barrie, ON L4N 2R6. (705) 791-9878
FAX: (705) 737-9918. E-mail: bigfishvideo@rogers.com
www.bigfishvideo.com
PRODUCER / DIRECTOR
Peter Olmstead
PRODUCER / WRITER
Carole Wright

BIG STAR ENTERTAINMENT GROUP INC.
13025 Yonge St., Ste. 100, Richmond Hill, ON L4E 1A4
(416) 720-9825 , FAX: (905) 888-5318
E-mail: delucaf@bigstarentertainment.tv
www.bigstarentertainment.tv
PRESIDENT / EXECUTIVE PRODUCER
Frank A. Deluca
V.P. / EXECUTIVE PRODUCER
Giacomo Moncada
PRODUCTION MANAGER
Josie Genovese

Production services for foreign producers / directors / studios

BITS & PIECES PICTURE COMPANY
405 Millwood Rd., Toronto, ON M4S 1K3
(416) 953-8356, FAX: (416) 322-0340
E-mail: bitsandpiecespicture@canada.com
PARTNER, CANADA
Rajiv Maikhuri

BIZNETWORX
1200 Bay St., Ste. 300, Toronto, ON M5R 2A5
(416) 972-1230, FAX: (416) 922-1640
Creative Director
Brian Couch

Videos / commercials / TV programs for North American business, industry and government

BLOKLAND PICTURES CORPORATION
217 St. George St., Unit 44, Toronto, ON M5R 3S7
(416) 975-9259, FAX: (416) 975-8214
E-mail: info@blokland.com, www.blokland.com
WRITER / DIRECTOR
Jim Blokland

Feature films

BLUEMOON PRODUCTIONS INC.
2 Berkeley St., Ste. 400, Toronto, ON M5A 2W3
(416) 955-1855, Fax: (416) 955-0989
E-mail: contact@bluemoonproductions.com
www.bluemoonproductions.com
EXECUTIVE PRODUCERS
John Crampton
June Weber

TV/video/radio – corporate & commercials/documentaries & features

BOOTLEG FILMS
177 Shaw St., Toronto, ON M6J 2W6
(416) 588-5927. E-mail: bootleg@interlog.com
CONTACTS
Milan Cheylov
Lori Lansens

BRAVURA PRODUCTIONS LTD.
One Benvenuto Pl., Ste. 220, Toronto, ON M4V 2L1
(416) 964-7490, FAX: (416) 960-3247
E-mail: bravura@sympatico.ca
PRESIDENT
Bruce Martin

**BREAKTHROUGH FILMS AND TELEVISION INC. /
BREAKTHROUGH ENTERTAINMENT**
122 Sherbourne St., Toronto, ON M5A 2R4. (416) 766-6588
FAX: (416) 769-1436. E-mail: business@breakthroughfilms.com
www.breakthroughfilms.com
EXEC. PRODUCER
Ira Levy
V.P., BUSINESS & LEGAL AFFAIRS
Nghia Nguyen
HEAD OF DEVELOMENT
Sarah Adams

Documentary / drama / lifestyle

BRIAN BOBBIE PRODUCTIONS LTD.
957 Logan Ave., Toronto, ON M4K 3E6
(416) 466-6350. E-mail: people@bbpl.com
CONTACT
Brian Bobbie

BRIDGE FILM PRODUCTIONS INC.
44 Charles St. W., Ste. 2518, Toronto, ON M4Y 1R7
Tel. & Fax: (416) 927-0663. E-mail: bberman@interlog.com
CONTACT
Brigitte Berman

Film / TV production

BROADCAST PRODUCTIONS INC.
77 Huntley St., Ste. 2522, Toronto, ON M4Y 2P3
(416) 961-1776, FAX: (905) 309-0999
E-mail: bpurdy@bserv.com
PRESIDENT
Brian E. Purdy

BUCK PRODUCTIONS
543 Richmond St. W., Ste. 125, Toronto, ON M5V 1Y6
(416) 362-3330, FAX: (416) 362-3336. www.buckproductions.com
EXECUTIVE PRODUCER
Sean Buckley

Corporate video

CAMERA ONE FILMS LIMITED
51 Grant St., Toronto, ON M4M 2H6. Tel./Fax: (416) 461-1383
PRODUCER / DIRECTOR
Elias Petras

CANAMEDIA FILM PRODUCTIONS INC.
1670 Bayview Ave., Ste. 408, Toronto, ON M4G 3C2
(416) 483-7446, FAX: (416) 483-7529. E-mail: canamed@canamedia.com. www.canamedia.com
PRESIDENT / PRODUCER
Les Harris
SECRETARY / TREASURER
Jane Harris
OFFICE ADMINISTRATOR
Céline Senis

CANUCK CREATIONS INC.
401 Richmond St. W., Ste. 111, Toronto, ON M5V 3A8
(416) 979-5687, FAX: (416) 979-5570
E-mail: info@canuckcreations.com, www.canuckcreations.com

CAPITOL J. FILMS
78 Dupont St., Ste. 2, Toronto, ON M5R 1V2. (416) 826-0512

E-mail: info@capitoljfilms.com
EXECUTIVE PRODUCERS
Ryan J. Noth
Jedrzej Jonasz

CATAPULT PRODUCTIONS
477 Richmond St. W., Ste. 101, Toronto, ON M5V 3E7
(416) 504-9876, FAX: (416) 504-6648
E-mail: kim@catapultproductions.com

CCI ENTERTAINMENT
18 Dupont St., Toronto, ON M5R 1V2. (416) 964-8750
FAX: (416) 964-1980. E-mail: cci.production@ccientertainment.com
Website: ccientertainment.com
CEO/PRESIDENT
Arnie Zipursky
CFO
Gord McIlquham

CHESLER / PERLMUTTER PRODUCTIONS INC.
129 Yorkville Ave., Ste. 200, Toronto, ON M5R 1C4
(416) 927-0016, FAX: (416) 960-8447
E-mail: DMP@chesperl.com
CO-CHAIRMAN
David M. Perlmutter
EXEC. ADMINISTRATOR
Roberta Harron

Feature film / TV / series

CHRISTOPHER CHAPMAN LTD.
R.R. #3, Uxbridge, ON L9P 1R3
(905) 852-9136. www.scugog-net.com/chapman
PRESIDENT
Christopher Chapman

CINEMA ESPERANCA INTERNATIONAL INC.
36 Charlotte St., Ste. 1106, Toronto, ON M5V 3P7
(416) 977-0123, FAX: (416) 977-7890
E-mail: andre.m.bennett@sympatico.ca
CHAIRMAN / PRESIDENT / CEO
André Bennett

CINEMILLENNIUM ENTERTAINMENT INC.
400 Walmer Rd., Park Towers E., Ste. 2323, Toronto, ON M5P
2X7. (416) 961-2003. Europe: (011) 36-20-931-8000
E-mail: cinemillennium@aol.com
CONTACT
Bob Schulz

Co-productions

CINENOVA PRODUCTIONS
468 King St. W., 6th Fl., Toronto, ON M5V 1L8
(416) 363-2600, FAX: (416) 363-2609
CHAIRMAN / CEO
David Lint
PRESIDENT
Jane Armstrong
EXECUTIVE DIRECTOR
Christopher Rowley
DEVELOPMENT DIRECTOR
Stephen Hunter

Film / TV / large format series & specials

CITADEL STUDIOS INC.
5100 Timberlea Blvd., Mississauga, ON L4W 2S5
(905) 238-0060 ext. 2225, FAX: (905) 238-9965
E-mail: shelly@citadelstudios.com
CEO
Tony de Pasquale
STUDIO MANAGER
Ken Fraser

A 160,000 sq.ft. studio complex with four production studios,
fully sound proofed, 24 ft. ceilings, two green-screen studios,
wood and metal shop, full make-up, hair and wardrobe facilities, furnished offices with phone systems & T-1 high-speed
Internet, 24-hour security, 150 parking spaces + trailer parking,
14 loading bays + 4 drive-ins, 14 km from Pearson Int'l Airport

CLARE PRODUCTIONS INC.
299 Queen St. W., Toronto, ON M5V 2Z5. (416) 591-7400 ext.
3191, FAX: (416) 351-9241. E-mail: tiinas@clareproductions.com
PRESIDENT
Tina Soomet

CLEARWATER FILMS LIMITED
1255 Yonge St., Ste. 100, Toronto, ON M4T 1W6
(416) 929-7232, FAX: (416) 929-7225
E-mail: info@gcadams.on.ca
PRESIDENT
G. Chalmers Adams

CLOUD TEN PICTURES INC.
1 St. Paul St., Ste. 401, St. Catharines, ON L2R 7L2
(905) 684-5561, FAX: (905) 684-7946. www.cloudtenpictures.com
CEO
Peter Lalonde

COMEDYLAB ENTERTAINMENT
2241 Bloor St. W., Toronto, ON M6S 1N7. (416) 767-3181
E-mail: guyincharge@comedylab.tv, www.comedylab.tv
PRESIDENT / EXEC. PRODUCER
Matthew Robillard
SENIOR V.P., PRODUCTION
Andrew Robillard

COMFY CHAIR PRODUCTIONS
54 Arundel Ave., Toronto, ON M4K 3A4. (416) 405-8809
Cell: (416) 576-8809. E-mail: sskinner@sympatico.ca
CONTACT
Shannon Skinner

COMMUNICADO
156 Marlborough Ave., Ottawa, ON K1N 8G2. (613) 232-6575
FAX: (613) 234-0165. E-mail: macfadjp@magma.ca
CEO / PRESIDENT
Josephine V. MacFadden

COMWEB GROUP
130 Bloor St. W., 5th Fl., Toronto, ON M5S 1N5
(416) 920-7050, FAX: (416) 920-4424
E-mail: paul@comwebmail.com, www.comwebgroup.com
PRESIDENT
Paul Bronfman

See also: Bulloch Entertainment Services Inc. (Financial
Services); Ciné Cité Montréal (Studio); Filmair
International Inc. (Equipment); Protocol Entertainment Inc.
(Production); &
William F. White (Equipment Rentals)

CONDOR PRODUCTIONS
110 The Esplanade, Ste. 511, Toronto, ON M5E 1X9
(416) 362-1740
PRESIDENT / PRODUCER / DIRECTOR
Vladimir Bondarenko

Documentaries / corporate / TV dramas / features

CONQUERING LION PICTURES
18 Gloucester Lane, 4th Fl., Toronto, ON M4Y 1L5
(416) 967-1055, FAX: (416) 923-8580
PRESIDENT
Clement Virgo
VICE-PRESIDENT
Damon D'Oliveira

COOTE COMMUNICATIONS VIDEO/PLUS
568 Caverhill Cr., Milton, ON L9T 5K5. (905) 203-0065
E-mail: gmcoote@hotmail.com
PRESIDENT
G. Morgan Coote
VICE-PRESIDENT
Donald C. Coote
SECRETARY-TREASURER
Morgan Coote

Film / videotape / audio-visual. Production services

C.O.R.E. DIGITAL PICTURES
488 Wellington St. W., Ste. 600, Toronto, ON M5V 1E3
(416) 599-2673, FAX: (416) 599-1212. E-mail: info@coredp.com
www.coredp.com
EXECUTIVE PRODUCER
Samara Melanson

Film & television production

CRAWLEY FILMS LIMITED
Box 11069, Stn. H, Nepean, ON K2H 7T8
(613) 825-2479, FAX: (613) 825-9300
www.crawleyfilms.ca
CONTACT
Bill Stevens Jr.

CRITICAL MASS PRODUCTIONS INC.
77 Mowat Ave., Ste. 110, Toronto, ON M6K 3E3
(416) 538-2535, FAX: (416) 538-3367
E-mail: wa@cmass.ca
PRESIDENT
William Alexander

Feature film / TV production

CROSSROADS CHRISTIAN COMMUNICATIONS INC.
Box 5100, 1295 North Service Rd., Burlington, ON L7R 4M2
(905) 332-6400, FAX: (905) 332-6655. www.crossroads.ca
PRESIDENT
David Mainse
VIDEO PRODUCTION: Crossroads Television System, Box
5321, 1295 North Service Rd., Burlington, ON L7R 4X5
(905) 331-7333. www.ctstv.com
PRESIDENT
Richard Gray

CURLCOM PRODUCTIONS LTD.
365 Colonsay Ct., Oshawa, ON L1J 6H3. (905) 428-6466
FAX: (905) 579-9052
PRESIDENT
E.G. (Ted) Curl

CYCLOPS COMMUNICATIONS CORPORATION
44 Gibson Ave., Toronto, ON M5R 1T5
(416) 926-8981, FAX: (416) 926-9878
E-mail: cyclopscorp@sprint.ca
PRESIDENT / PRODUCER
Samuel C. Jephcott
Feature film / TV / video

DANFORTH STUDIOS
490 Adelaide St. W., Ste. 100, Toronto, ON M5V 1T2
(416) 465-5855, FAX: (416) 504-4843
E-mail:dsl@starhunter.tv
CONTACTS
G. Philip Jackson
Daniel D'or

Independent production / international co-production

DANTE ENTERTAINMENT GROUP
258 Wallace Ave., Ste. 202, Toronto, ON M6P 3M9
(416) 534-6728, FAX: (416) 534-4792
E-mail: info@dante-ent.com, www.dante-ent.com
PRESIDENT & CEO
Jeff Boulton
SUPERVISING PRODUCER, PRODUCTION
Stephen Braund
CONTACT
Lillyann Goldstein

Film, television, web and interactive media production

DARIUS FILMS INC.
1173 Dundas St. E., Ste. 235, Toronto, ON M4M 3P1
(416) 922-0007, FAX: (416) 406-0034
E-mail: darius@dariusfilms.com, www.dariusfilms. com
PRESIDENT / PRODUCER
Nicholas Tabarrok
HEAD OF OPERATIONS
Jonathan Sobol

DECADENCE FILMS
561 Avenue Rd., Ste. 1504
Toronto, ON M4V 2J8
(416) 457-3456
Fax: (416) 352-5026
E-mail: info@decadencefilms.com
Website: www.decadencefilms.com
Exec. Producer: Alec Kinnear
Production Manager: Alexandra Kollo

DECODE ENTERTAINMENT INC.
512 King St. E., Ste. 104, Toronto, ON M5A 1M1
(416) 363-8034, FAX: (416) 363-8919
E-mail: decode@decode-ent.com, www.decode.tv
CONTACTS
John A. Delmage
Steven DeNure
Neil Court
Beth Stevenson

Development / production — family & children's programming

DEE ANDERSON PRODUCTIONS
11 Mansfield Park Ct., Ashburn, ON L0B 1A0. (905) 985-7761
President / Producer
Dee Anderson

DEVINE ENTERTAINMENT CORPORATION
The Berkeley Castle, 2 Berkeley St., Ste. 504, Toronto, ON
M5A 2W3. (416) 364-2282, FAX: (416) 364-1440
E-mail: info@devine-ent.com
www.devine-ent.com / www.devinetime.com
CONTACTS
David Devine
Richard Mozer

Family programming

SIMON CHRISTOPHER DEW
29 Spruce St., Toronto, ON M5A 2H8. (416) 923-3432,
FAX: (416) 923-6007. E-mail: cdew@sympatico.ca

DISTINCT FEATURES INC.
66 Muriel St., The Parking Lot, Ottawa, ON K1S 4E1
(613) 565-7254, FAX: (613) 565-9164
E-mail: info@distinctfeatures.com, www.distinctfeatures.com
PRESIDENT
Derek Diorio
SENIOR PRODUCER
Sarah Fodey

Feature films — production / post-production / writing / directing

DON CARMODY PRODUCTIONS / DCP MYSTERY ARTS PRODUCTIONS
175 Queens Quay E., Ste. 400, Toronto, ON M5A 1B6
(416) 707-4912, FAX: (416) 694-1443
E-mail: don@doncarmody.com
President / Secretary
Don Carmody

Feature films / made-for-televison movies

DOOMSDAY STUDIOS LIMITED
212 James St., Ottawa, ON K1R 5M7. (613) 230-9769
FAX: (613) 230-6004. E-mail: info@doomsdaystudios.com
CONTACT
Ramona Macdonald

DREAMSCAPE VIDEO PRODUCTIONS
645 Manning Ave., Toronto, ON M6G 2W2. (416) 534-7464
FAX: (416) 535-4477. E-mail: bsp@interlog.com
Video Producer / Director
Brock Fricker

DUFFERIN GATE PRODUCTIONS / TEMPLE STREET PRODUCTIONS
20 Butterick Rd., Toronto, ON M8W 3Z8.(416) 255-2260
FAX: (416) 255-7488. E-mail: mail@dufferingate.com
www.dufferingate.com
PRESIDENT
Patrick Whitley
V.P., FINANCE - PRODUCTION
John Weber

See also British Columbia.

EALING FILMS CANADA
313 Richmond St. E., Ste. 864, Toronto, ON M5A 4S7
(416) 504-7557, FAX: (416) 504-7518
E-mail: dbalcon@rogers.com
Exec. Producer
David Balcon

Development, production and distribution of documentary one-offs and series

EGO FILM ARTS
80 Niagara St., Toronto, ON M5V 1C5. (416) 703-2137
FAX: (416) 504-7161, E-mail: questions@egofilmarts.com
www.egofilmarts.com
CONTACTS
Simone Urdl
Atom Egoyan

ELLIS VISION INCORPORATED
(An Ellis Entertainment Company)
1300 Yonge St., Ste. 300, Toronto, ON M4T 1X3.
(416) 924-2186, FAX: (416) 924-6115
E-mail: info@ellisent.com, www.ellisent.com
Chairman
Ralph C. Ellis
President
Stephen Ellis

Natural history, adventure & comedy programming

EPITOME PICTURES INC.
220 Bartley Dr., North York, ON M4A 1G1
(416) 752-7627, FAX: (416) 752-7837
E-mail: info@epitomepictures.com, www.epitomepictures.com
PRESIDENT / PRODUCER
Linda Schuyler
V.P. / PRODUCER
Stephen Stohn

TV production

EQUINOX FILMS INC.
1200 Bay St., Ste 1201, Toronto, ON M5R 2A5
(416) 969-1200, FAX: (416) 969-0301
EXECUTIVE V.P., PRODUCTION
Carlo Liconti
Films for theatrical / video / TV. See also Québec.

EQUUS FILM PRODUCTIONS INC.
174 Fulton Ave., Toronto, ON M4K 1Y3. (416) 429-7399
CONTACT
Keith Lock

ESPRIT FILMS LIMITED
2 Lake St., St. Catharines, ON L2R 5W6
(905) 685-8336
PRESIDENT
Deborah Cartmer

TV / educational / industrial / film / video

EXTENDMEDIA INC.
190 Liberty St., Toronto, ON M6K 3L5
(416) 535-4222, FAX: (416) 535-1201
E-mail: info@extend.com, www.extend.com
PRESIDENT & CEO
Keith Kocho

EYELIGHT INC.
38 Bridgeport Rd. E., Waterloo, ON N2J 2J5
(519) 743-2600. E-mail: info@eyelight.com
PRESIDENT
Ron Repke

FACTORY FILMS INC.
50 Givins St., Toronto, ON M6J 2X8. (416) 530-4328
PRESIDENT
Sari Friedland

FAR WELTERED FILMS
1209 Nottingham Dr., Sarnia, ON N7S 5B1. (519) 336-5745
E-mail: birdman@ebtech.net
CONTACT
Robert Tymstra

Producer / camera operator

FAUST FILMS
438 Markham St., Toronto, ON M6G 2L2
(416) 531-5372, FAX: (416) 531-0929
E-mail: faustfilms@aol.com, www.faustfilms.com
PRODUCER / DIRECTOR / WRITER
Ian Thomson

THE FEATURE FILM PROJECT
2489 Bayview Ave., Toronto, ON M2L 1A8
(416) 445-2890, FAX: (416) 445-3158
E-mail: ffp@cdnfilmcentre.com, www.cdnfilmcentre.com
EXEC. DIRECTOR
Justine Whyte
PROJECT & DEVELOPMENT MANAGER
Erin Burke

FIELDVIEW MOTION PICTURE GROUP
44 Charles St. W., Ste. 1310, Toronto, ON M4Y 1R7
(416) 920-7979. E-mail: david@fieldview.com
www.fieldview.com
PRESIDENT
David Collard

FILM ARTS, INC.
1177 Yonge St., Ste. 608, Toronto, ON M4T 2Y4
(416) 924-4839, FAX: (416) 924-6054
E-mail: wmschultz@rogers.com
Contact
Bill Schultz

Film & TV production

THE FILM FARM
80 Niagara St., Toronto, ON M5V 1C5. (416) 703-7317
FAX: (416) 504-7161. E-mail: thefilmfarm@sympatico.ca
PRODUCERS
Simone Urdl
Jennifer Weiss

FILM ONE
181 Carlaw Ave., Ste. 251, Toronto, ON M4M 2S1
(416) 696-9822, FAX: (416) 696-7901
E-mail: filmonemovies@aol.com
CONTACT
Jalal Merhi

FIRELINE PRODUCTION
210 East Victoria Ave., Ste. 1, Thunder Bay, ON P7C 1A2
(807) 623-5070. E-mail: daustin@tbaytel.net
PRESIDENT
Dennis Austin
V.P.
Rory Macvicar

**FIREWORKS ENTERTAINMENT / CANWEST
ENTERTAINMENT INC.**
(A Canwest Company)
147 Liberty St., Toronto, ON M6K 3G3
(416) 360-4321, FAX: (416) 364-4388
E-mail: info@firecorp.com, www.fireworksentertainment.com
PRESIDENT / CEO CANWEST ENTERTAINMENT
Gerry Noble
PRESIDENT & COO FIREWORKS ENTERTAINMENT
Adam Haight
CFO
Martin Abel
GENERAL COUNSEL
Steve Pasternak

FISHTALES PRODUCTIONS
470 Euclid Ave., Toronto, ON M6G 2S9.
Tel. & Fax: (416) 964-0003. E-mail: fisher@sprint.ca
Director / Writer
Honey Fisher

Video / filmmaker — documentary / corporate / feature / TV

FOREVERGREEN TELEVISION & FILM PRODUCTIONS
181 Carlaw Ave., Ste. 230, Toronto, ON M4M 2S1. (416) 778-9944, FAX: (905) 628-1769
E-mail: foreverg@primus.ca
PRESIDENT
Alan Aylward
VICE-PRESIDENT
Jonathan Welsh

Creative TV / marketing production

49th PARALLEL FILMS
4 Pardee Ave., Toronto, ON M6K 3H5. (416) 516-4950
FAX: (416) 516-1712. E-mail: info@49thparallel.ca
www.49thparallel.ca
PARTNERS
Steve Hoban
Noah Segal
Philip Mellows

FREEDOM FILMS INC.
530 Adelaide St. W., Ste. 204, Toronto, ON M5V 1T5
(416) 778-1358, FAX: (416) 778-1819.
E-mail: info@freedomstudios.com, www.freedomstudios.com
PRESIDENT
Aaron Goldman
V.P., MARKETING & SALES
Deborah MacDonald

TV / commercials / music videos / documentaries

FUNDAMENTALLY FILM INC.
349 St. Clair Ave. W., Ste. 107, Toronto, ON M5P 1N3
(416) 560-6684, FAX: (416) 922-2700
E-mail: info@fundamentallyfilm.com,
www.fundamentallyfilm.com
CONTACT
Joe Green

GAPC ENTERTAINMENT INC.
14 Colonnade Rd., Ste. 180, Ottawa, ON K2E 7M6
(613) 723-3316, FAX: (613) 723-8583
E-mail: kstewart@gapc.com, www.gapc.com
CONTACTS
Ken Stewart
Hoda Elatawi

THE GENERAL COFFEE COMPANY FILM PRODUCTIONS
152 St. Patrick St., Ste. 909, Toronto, ON M5T 3J9
(416) 340-7073. E-mail: general@generalcoffee.com
www.generalcoffee.com
CONTACT
Kent Tessman

GENUINE PICTURES
R.R. #4, 11 Links Dr. S., Ottawa, ON K0A 1B0
(613) 253-2296, FAX: (613) 253-3229
E-mail: office@genuinepictures.com, www.genuinepictures.com
PRESIDENT
Donna Leon

GFT ENTERTAINMENT
124 Merton St., Ste. 407, Toronto, ON M4S 2Z2
(416) 487-0377, FAX: (416) 487-6141
E-mail: judith@gfte.com, www.gfte.com
PRESIDENT
Gary Howsam

GOLDI PRODUCTIONS LTD.
1409 Malibou Terr., Mississauga, ON L5J 4B9
(905) 855-1510. www.goldiproductions.com
CONTACTS
John Goldi, csc,
Joan Goldi

GORDFILM INC.
98 Lawton Blvd., Toronto, ON M4V 2A3. (416) 481-8288
FAX (416) 481-8788
Contact
Ken Gord

GORICA PRODUCTIONS
295 Silverbirch Ave., Toronto, ON M4E 3L6. (416) 324-1332
FAX: (416) 324-9594. E-mail: gorica@interlog.com
www.goricaproductions.com
PRESIDENT
Felice Gorica

GROSSO-JACOBSON PRODUCTIONS INC.
373 Front St. E., Toronto, ON M5A 1G4. (416) 368-9948
FAX: (416) 368-7052
EXEC. PRODUCERS
Larry Jacobson
Sonny Grosso

GUACAMOLE ENTERTAINMENT
Toronto, ON, (416) 939-8795. E-mail: guacreleasing@canada.com
President
Steven Barwin
CEO
Gabriel David Tick

HAMMYTIME
(Includes: Hammytime II Productions, Hammytime III
Productions Inc. / Hammytime Publishing Inc.)
50 Vicora Linkway, Don Mills, ON M3C 1B1
(416) 423-4444, FAX: (416) 423-7070.
E-mail: hammy@hammyhamster.com
www.hammyhamster.com
PRESIDENT
Paul Sutherland
SECRETARY / TREASURER
Glenys Squires
Children's TV

HAZY PICTURES INC.
21 Nassau St., Ste. 313, Toronto, ON M5T 3K6
(416) 597-9948. E-mail: info@hazypictures.com
www.hazypictures.com
Contact
Lisa Hayes
Feature films / short films

HEROIC FILM COMPANY
2 College St., Ste. 301, Toronto, ON M5G 1K3
(416) 922-4303, FAX: (416) 922-9967
E-mail: sayhello@ourhero.tv
EXECUTIVE PRODUCERS
Karen Lee Hall
John May
Suzanne Bolch

HIGHER GROUND PRODUCTIONS
214 Merton St., Ste. 208, Toronto, ON M4S 1A6. (416) 925-
6066, FAX: (416) 925-5923. E-mail: info@higherground.on.ca,
www.higherground.on.ca
PRESIDENT
Chas. Hay
V.P.
Tim Progosh
DIRECTOR OF BUSINESS AFFAIRS
Chris Vokes

HILLS PRODUCTION SERVICES
2440 Industrial St., Burlington, ON L7P 1A5
(905) 335-1146, FAX: (905) 335-1241
E-mail: robhill@hillsvideo.com, www.hillsvideo.com
PRESIDENT
Rob Hill
EXEC. PRODUCER
Gerry Milinkovic
SENIOR EDITOR
John Luff

HOT GLACIER FILMS
33 Eastmount Ave., TH2, Toronto, ON M4K 1V3
(416) 461-8895. E-mail: hotglac@interlog.com
PRODUCER / DIRECTOR
David Gilmour Martin
Dramas / documentaries

HOT SHOTS / F & F PRODUCTIONS
30 Carveth Cres., Newcastle, ON L1B 1N3
(905) 987-3777
CONTACT
Bob Phippard
Video — corporate / broadcast

IMAX CORPORATION
2525 Speakman Dr., Sheridan Park, Mississauga, ON L5K 1B1
(905) 403-6500, FAX: (905) 403-6450
E-mail: info@imax.com, www.imax.com
CHAIRMAN & CO-CEO
Bradley J. Wechsler
VICE-CHAIRMAN & CO-CEO
Richard L. Gelfond
PRESIDENT, FILM
Greg Foster
PRODUCERS
Graeme Ferguson, Toni Myers
U.S.A. OFFICES:
NEW YORK: 110 East 59th St., Ste. 2100, New York, NY
10022. (212) 821-0100.
CALIFORNIA: 3003 Exposition Blvd., Santa Monica, CA
90404. (310) 255-5500, FAX: (310) 255-5640

IMPORTED ARTISTS FILM CO.
49 Spadina Ave., Ste. 100, Toronto, ON M5V 2J1
(416) 971-5915, FAX: (416) 971-7925
E-mail: imported@importedartists.com,
www.importedartists.com
Contact
Christina Ford
Film & TV

INDEPENDENT PICTURES INC.
64 Duncannon Dr., Toronto, ON M5P 2M2. Tel. & FAX: (416)
488-9228. E-mail: ipi@bellnet.ca
PRESIDENT
Peter O'Brian

INSIGHT PRODUCTION COMPANY LTD.
489 King St. W., Ste. 401, Toronto, ON M5V 1K4
(416) 596-8118, FAX: (416) 596-8270
E-mail: insight@idirect.com
EXECUTIVE PRODUCERS
John M. Brunton,
Barbara Bowlby

INTERCOM FILMS LIMITED
34 Colin Ave., Toronto, ON M5P 2B9. (416) 483-3862
FAX: (416) 483-1106
PRESIDENT
Gilbert W. Taylor

ITS – VIDEO AND MULTIMEDIA PRESENTATIONS
Queen's University, McArthur Hall, Rm. B232
Kingston, ON K7L 3N6. (613) 533-6570, FAX: (613) 533-6995
PRODUCER / MANAGER
Richard Webb
Educational / instructional — DVC PRO format

JAMES ROBINSON ASSOCIATES LTD.
884 Queen St. W., Toronto, ON M6J 1G3. (416) 533-3326
Video production

JAMS PRODUCTIONS INC.
1262 Don Mills Rd., Ste. 203, Don Mills, ON M3B 2W7
(416) 449-4844, FAX: (416) 449-4843
Contact
Alan J. Schwarz
SECOND LOCATION: 48 Adelaide St. W., Toronto, ON M5V
1T2. (416) 703-1265, FAX: (416) 504-0329
CONTACT
Paul Jay
TV production / series

JOHN McGREEVY PRODUCTIONS
36 Roxborough St. E., Toronto, ON M4W 1V6
(416) 922-8625, FAX: (416) 922-8624
PRESIDENT
John McGreevy

JOHN M. ECKERT PRODUCTIONS LIMITED
75 Poplar Plains Rd., Toronto, ON M4V 2N1
(416) 960-4961
Contact
John M. Eckert

JOHN VAINSTEIN & ASSOCIATES
173 Heward Ave., Toronto, ON M4M 2T6
(416) 465-9535. E-mail: vainjk@yorku.ca
Documentary / educational / TV

JOHN WALKER PRODUCTIONS LTD.
730 Euclid Ave., 3rd Fl., Toronto, ON M6G 2T9
(416) 532-7442, FAX: (416) 532-8199
E-mail: walkerfilm@sympatico.ca, www.thefairyfaith.com

JUMPPOINT ENTERTAINMENT
1401 Laurin Cr., Orleans, ON K1E 3G9
(613) 255-2325, E-mail: alexpappas@yahoo.com
www.pocketmovies.net
PRODUCER
Alexander Pappas

JUST ONE STEP AT A TIME PRODUCTIONS INC.
118 Castlefield Ave., Toronto, ON M4R 1G4
Tel. & Fax: (416) 484-9671. E-mail: josat@interlog.com
Writer / Director
Peter Gerretsen
Feature films / TV entertainment / workshops

JUTUL FILMS INC.
47 Amiens Rd., West Hill, ON M1E 3S7. (416) 282-4304
FAX: (416) 282-1767. E-mail: jutul@sympatico.ca
CONTACT
Per-Inge Schei
Imax — 2D & 3D

KALEIDOSCOPE PRODUCTIONS
23 Lesmill Rd., Ste. 201, Toronto, ON M3B 3P6
(416) 443-9200, FAX: (416) 443-8685
E-mail: paul@kalent.com
V.P., Production
Paul McConvey
TV / film production — drama / children's / documentary

KATHERINE SMALLEY PRODUCTIONS
368 Brunswick Ave., Toronto, ON M5R 2Y9. (416) 961-8907
Fax: (416) 324-8253
PRESIDENT
Katherine Smalley

KEEP IT IN THE FAMILY PRODUCTIONS
219 Dufferin St., Ste 101A, Toronto, ON M6K 1Y9
(416) 539-9989, FAX: (416) 539-9969
E-mail: claude@keepitinthefamilyproductions.com
www.keepitinthefamilyproductions.com
EXEC. PRODUCER
Claude Barnes
PRODUCER
Karyn Koski

KENSINGTON COMMUNICATIONS INC.
451 Adelaide St. W., Toronto, ON M5V 1T1. (416) 504-9822
FAX: (416) 504-3608. E-mail: info@kensingtontv.com
www.kensingtontv.com
PRESIDENT / PRODUCER
Robert Lang

TV series & documentaries / multimedia

KNIGHT ENTERPRISES
307 – 99 Fifth Ave., Ottawa, ON K1S 5P5. (613) 730-1728
FAX: (613) 730-0182
PRESIDENT
Chris Knight
PRODUCERS
Christine Overvelde
Kathy Doherty

TV programming — food & lifestyle

KNIGHTSCOVE ENTERTAINMENT CORP.
1912 Queen St. E., Toronto, ON M4L 1H5
(416) 691-6655, FAX: (416) 691-8419
E-mail: info@knightscove.com, www.knightscove.com
PRESIDENT / CEO
Leif Bristow

Finances, produces and distributes moderately budgeted ($5M
- $15M), family-oriented feature-length commercial films on an
acquisition production or co-production basis

KUBLACOM PICTURES INC.
126 York St., Ste. 201, Ottawa, ON K1N 5T5. (613) 244-2104
FAX: (613) 244-2105. E-mail: tv@kublacom.ca, www.kublacom.ca
PRESIDENT / PRODUCER
Ed Kucerak

Television programming — youth / educational / documentaries

KUPER PRODUCTIONS LTD.
301 Forest Hill Rd., Toronto, ON M5P 2N7. (416) 782-4553
FAX: (416) 782-4425
CREATIVE DIRECTOR
Jack Kuper
CONTACT
Terry Lee

L&A MOTION PICTURES
155 Marlee Ave., Ste. 911, Toronto, ON M6B 4B5
(416) 783-5159, FAX: (416) 783-7684
E-mail: lamotionpics@yahoo.com
EXEC. PRODUCER
Istvan Luppino

LAWRENCE HERTZOG PRODUCTIONS LIMITED
87 Barton Ave., Toronto, ON M6G 1P7
Tel. & FAX: (416) 531-4670. E-mail: hertzog@rogers.com
PRODUCER
Lawrence Hertzog

Features

LAWRENCE MARSHALL PRODUCTIONS
3348 Bayview Ave., Unit A, North York, ON M2M 3R9
(416) 590-0315, FAX: (416) 590-0317
E-mail: lmp@sympatico.ca
PRESIDENT
Lawrence Marshall

LEDA SERENE FILMS
24 Ryerson Ave., Ste. 206, Toronto, ON M5T 2P3
(416) 598-1410, FAX: (416) 598-1354
E-mail: films@ledaserene.com, www.ledaserene.com
CONTACT
Frances-Anne Solomon

Feature films / TV series

LIFESTYLE MEDIA
67A Portland St., Ste. 1, Toronto, ON M5V 2M9
(416) 977-5575, FAX: (416) 977-5365
E-mail: email@lifestylemedia.ca, www.lifestylemedia.ca
SENIOR PRODUCERS / PARTNERS
Shay Schwartzman
Evan Trestan

LIGHTBOX STUDIOS INC.
422 Dundas St. E., Toronto, ON M5A 2A8
(416) 929-1948, FAX: (416) 323-9295
CONTACT
Mary Young

LINDUM FILMS INC.
73 Robinson St., Peterborough, ON K9H 1E9. (705) 743-6021
FAX: (705) 743-6643. E-mail: lindum@sprint.ca
WRITER / DIRECTOR / PRODUCER
Peter Blow

LIONS GATE ENTERTAINMENT CORP.
2 Bloor St. W., Ste. 1001, Toronto, ON M4W 3E2
(416) 944-0104, FAX: (416) 944-2212
E-mail: info@lgecorp.com, www.lionsgatefilms.com
SR. V.P. BUSINESS & LEGAL AFFAIRS
Laura May
SR. V.P. CANADIAN SALES & DISTRIBUTION
Brad Pelman

See also British Columbia, Quebec.

LIVING IMAGES PRODUCTIONS
36 Park Lawn Rd., 2nd Fl., Toronto, ON M8Y 3H8
Tel./Fax: (416) 503-2227. E-mail: living_images@on.aibn.com
www.livingimagestv.com
PRODUCER / DIRECTOR
Dave Luetjen
WRITER / EDITOR
Kellie Dearman
POST-PRODUCTION SUPERVISOR
Graham Jones

LOCKWOOD FILMS (LONDON) INC.
12569 Boston Drive, R.R. #41, London, ON N6H 5L2
Tel. & Fax: (519) 657-3994.
DIRECTOR / PRODUCER
Mark K. McCurdy, mark.mccurdy@sympatico.ca
PRODUCER/PROGRAM DEVELOPMENT
Nancy C. Johnson, nancycjohnson@hotmail.com

GEORGE LOMAGA
1906 Bough Beeches Blvd., Mississauga, ON L4W 2J7
(905) 629-9207, FAX: (905) 629-9138
Director / producer / DoP

LONE EAGLE ENTERTAINMENT LTD.
26 Soho St., Ste. 401, Toronto, ON M5T 1Z7
(416) 351-9111, FAX: (416) 351-9666
E-mail: info@loneagle.net
PRESIDENT
Mike Geddes
VICE-PRESIDENT
Tom Powers

TV production

LOST MUSIC PRODUCTIONS
39 Ellsworth Ave., Toronto, ON M6G 2K4
Tel. & Fax: (416) 658-3610. E-mail: rgraner@trebnet.com
CONTACT
Ron Graner

Documentaries

LOTEN MEDIA INC.
287 Macpherson Ave., Ste. 304, Toronto, ON M4V 1A4
(416) 598-4699, FAX: (416) 205-1258
E-mail: lotenmedia@sympatico.ca
CONTACT
Wendy Loten

TV series production

LUMANITY PRODUCTIONS
59 Armstrong Ave., Toronto, ON M6H 1V9.
Tel./Fax: (416) 531-9691
E-mail: rbudreau@lumanityproductions.com
www.lumanityproductions.com
President
Robert Budreau

LYNX IMAGES PRODUCTIONS
Box 5961, Stn. A, Toronto, ON M5W 1P4
(416) 925-8422, FAX: (416) 925-8352
E-mail: info@lynximages.com, www.lynximages.com
CONTACTS
Russell Floren
Andrea Gutsche
Barbara Chisholm

Educational / documentary / TV / book publishing

MAC PRODUCTIONS INC.
2169 Denise Rd., Mississauga, ON L4X 1H9. (905) 270-7616
PRODUCER / DIRECTOR
Michael A. Charbon

Specializing in series, TV projects & live sports

MAD CIRCUS FILMS
501 Sutherland Dr., Toronto, ON M4G 1K9
(416) 421-9050, FAX: (416) 421-9483
E-mail: jgoulding@madcircusfilms.com
www.madcircusfilms.com
PRESIDENT
Suzanne Colvin-Goulding
V.P.
Ernie Barbarash
MANAGING DIRECTOR
Jon Goulding

MAKIN' MOVIES INC.
265 Albany Ave., Toronto, ON M5R 3C7. (416) 516-1833
FAX: (416) 920-8130. E-mail: maureen@makinmovies.tv
CONTACT
Maureen Judge

MARBLEMEDIA
50 Richmond St. E., Ste. 400, Toronto, ON M5C 1N7
(416) 646-2711, FAX: (416) 646-0579
E-mail: info@marblemedia.com, www.marblemedia.com
Producers
Mark Bishop
Matt Hornburg

Develops and produces properties delivered across mulitiple
platforms, including broadcast, web, wireless and DVD.

MARKHAM STREET FILMS
516 Markham St., Toronto, ON M6G 2L5
(416) 536-1390, FAX: (416) 536-6405
E-mail: info@markhamstreetfilms.com
CONTACTS
Michael McNamara
Judy Holm

MAXIMA FILM CORPORATION
200 Tiffield Rd., Ste. 101, Toronto, ON M1V 5J1
(416) 449-9400, FAX: (416) 449-9498
DIRECTOR
Allan G. Kent
EXEC. PRODUCER / CEO
J. Gary Gladman

TV programming / underwater documentaries / co-productions

MBZ PRODUCTIONS INC.
30 Rosewell Ave., Toronto, ON M4R 2A1
(416) 567-3418. E-mail: grobisen@interlog.com
PRODUCER
Martin Grobisen

Corporate training & product information

MEDIATIQUE
11 Ontario St., Toronto, ON M5A 4L7
(416) 367-8464, FAX: (416) 367-8466
E-mail: mediatique@mediatique.ca
PRESIDENT
Daniele Caloz

MELK PRODUCTIONS
1053 Bloor St. W., 3rd Fl., Toronto, ON M6H 1M4
(416) 707-3875, FAX: (416) 516-0565
E-mail: heather@hnmag.com
PRESIDENT & EXEC., PRODUCTION
Heather K. Dahlstrom

MERCURY FILMS INC.
56 The Esplanade, Ste. 503, Toronto, ON M5E 1A7
(416) 955-9835, FAX: (416) 955-4556
E-mail: mercfilm@istar.ca
PRODUCER / DOP
Nicholas de Pencier
PRODUCER / DIRECTOR
Jennifer Baichwal

METROPOLIS FILMS INC.
77 Maitland Pl., Ste. 1925, Toronto, ON M4Y 2V6
(416) 368-4593
PRODUCER / DIRECTOR
Robert Buchan
DIRECTOR / CAMERAMAN
Ralph Bongard
PRODUCER
Roxanne Maggiacomo

Commercials / TV / film

MICROTAINMENT PLUS INTERNATIONAL
1 Atlantic Ave., Ste. 103, Toronto, ON M6K 3E7
(416) 537-5004, FAX: (416) 537-8984
E-mail: mail@microtainment.com
CHAIRMAN
Garry Blye
PRESIDENT
Mark Shekter

Full-service film & TV production

MONTE MEDIA MANAGEMENT
38 McAllister Rd., North York, ON M3H 2N2
(416) 398-6114, FAX: (416) 398-7402
E-mail: tino@montemedia.tv, www.montemedia.tv
PRESIDENT
Tino Monte
DIRECTOR OF DRTV OPERATIONS
Linda Brooks

Infomercials / TV info series / multimedia

MORNINGSTAR PRODUCTIONS
23 Cassels Rd. E., Brooklin, ON L1M 1A4
(905) 655-6000, FAX: (905) 655-7307
E-mail: mstar33@aol.com
PRODUCER
Ron Moore

MTR ENTERTAINMENT LTD.
180 Metcalfe St., Ste. 500, Ottawa, ON K2P 1P5
(613) 234-3488, FAX: (613) 234-8704
E-mail: mtr@mtrentertainment.com
PRESIDENT
Merilyn Read
VICE-PRESIDENT
Nicole St. Pierre

TV: comedy, lifestyles, children's and teen programming

MY COUNTRY PRODUCTIONS INC.
3 Hillcrest Ave., Toronto, ON M4X 1W1
(416) 961-6031, FAX: (416) 961-9833
E-mail: elsa.franklin@sympatico.ca
CONTACT
Elsa Franklin

NELVANA LIMITED
(A Corus Entertainment Company)
HEAD OFFICE: 32 Atlantic Ave., Toronto, ON M6K 1X8
(416) 588-5571, FAX: (416) 588-5588. www.nelvana.com
PRESIDENT CORUS TELEVISION AND NELVANA
Paul Robertson
TORONTO, ONTARIO: 42 Pardee Ave., Toronto, ON M6K 3H5
(416) 535-0935, FAX: (416) 530-2832
U.S.A./CALIFORNIA: Nelvana Enterprises, 4500 Wilshire Blvd., 1st
Fl., Los Angeles, CA 90010. (323) 549-4222, FAX: (323) 549-4232
E-mail: all-la@nelvana.ca
CONTACT
Toper Taylor

Animation service production in TV series, specials, features,
interactive CD-ROMs, etc., in children's and family entertainment. Also producer of live action.

NEW WORLD WINE TOUR PRODUCTIONS
181 Carlaw Ave., Ste. 230, Toronto, ON M4M 2S1
(416) 778-9944, FAX: (905) 628-1769
E-mail: foreverg@primus.ca
PARTNERS
Alan Aylward
Jonathan Welsh

TV series (130 episodes)

THE NIGHTINGALE CO.
25 Imperial St., Ste. 200, Toronto, ON M5P 1B9
(416) 656-3797, FAX: (416) 656-8259
E-mail: info@dnightingale.com, www.dnightingale.com
PRESIDENT
Debbie Nightingale

Documentaries / children's programming / MOWs

90TH PARALLEL FILM & TELEVISION PRODUCTIONS LTD.
112 Parliament St., Toronto, ON M5A 2Y8
(416) 364-9090, FAX: (416) 364-0580
PRESIDENT / PRODUCER
Gordon S. Henderson

NORFLICKS PRODUCTIONS
287 MacPherson Ave., Ste. 304, Toronto, ON M4V 1A4
(416) 351-7558, FAX: (416) 205-1258
E-mail: mail@norflicks.com, www.norflicks.com
PRESIDENT
Richard Nielsen
V.P., DEVELOPMENT
Marta Nielsen

NORFOLK INTERNATIONAL LTD.
160 Bloor St. E., Ste. 1220, Toronto, ON M4W 1B9
(416) 921-5100, FAX: (416) 921-8800
E-mail: info@norfolk-international.com, www.norfolk-international.com
PRESIDENT
William Macadam

Film / TV production — drama, movies, documentaries

NORLANE ENTERTAINMENT
240 Williams Point Rd., Caesarea, ON L0B 1E0. (905) 986-
1015. E-mail: norlane@sympatico.ca

www.norlane.net
PRODUCER / CEO
Melanie Arden

NORSTAR FILMED ENTERTAINMENT INC.
148 Yorkville Ave., 2nd Fl., Toronto, ON M5R 1C2
(416) 961-6278, FAX: (416) 961-5608
E-mail: info@norstarfilms.com, www.norstarfilms.com
CHAIRMAN
Peter R. Simpson
V.P., SALES & MARKETING
Agapy Kapouranis
V.P., PRODUCTION & BUSINESS AFFAIRS
Daphne Park Rehdner
EXEC. ASSISTANT
Tina Toffoli

NORTHLAND PICTURES
Box 549, Station Adelaide, Toronto, ON M5C 2J6
(416) 526-3456. E-mail: streamliner@sympatico.ca
CONTACT
Colin Strayer

Drama / documentary / corporate communication / music video
/ television commercial production since 1980.

OASIS INTERNATIONAL
6 Pardee Ave., Ste. 103, Toronto, ON M6K 3H5
(416) 588-6821, FAX: (416) 588-7276
E-mail: info@oasisinternational.com
www.oasisinternational.com
PRESIDENT
Peter Emerson ext. 224, peter@oasisinternational.com
DEVELOPMENT & ACQUISITIONS
Steve Murphy, ext. 222, steve@oasisinternational.com

OMNI MEDIA PRODUCTIONS LIMITED
6 – 235 Martindale Rd., St. Catharines, ON L2W 1A5
(905) 684-9455, FAX: (905) 684-4291
E-mail: tv@omnimedia.com
PRESIDENT
Peter Murray

THE ORIGINAL MOTION PICTURE COMPANY
37 Sussex Ave., Toronto, ON M5S 1J6
(416) 977-7938, FAX: (416) 977-5264
E-mail: sussexprod@sympatico.ca
CONTACT
John Board

PARADIGM PICTURES CORP.
344 Dupont St., Ste. 206, Toronto, ON M5R 1V9
(416) 927-7404, FAX: (416) 927-9839
E-mail: info@paradigmpictures.com
www.paradigmpictures.com
PRESIDENT
Ted Remerowski

TV production – drama, documentary

PASCOE PRODUCTIONS LIMITED
38 Beaufort Rd., Toronto, ON M4E 1M7
(416) 593-0409, FAX: (416) 593-2768
DOP / DIRECTOR
Bob Pascoe

Full-service production company with complete Beta SP video
package & broadcast editing

PATTERSON-PARTINGTON TV PRODUCTIONS
250 Ferrand Dr., Ste. 402, Toronto, ON M3C 3G8
(416) 696-9633 / (800) 305-2999, FAX: (416) 696-9640
CONTACTS
Carol Patterson
Lawrence Partington

PEBBLEHUT PRODUCTIONS INC.
63 Polson St., Ste. 101, Toronto, ON M5A 1B9
(416) 778-6800, FAX: (416) 778-8178
PRESIDENT
Marilyn Stonehouse

PERCH LAKE PICTURES
491 St. John's Rd., Toronto, ON M6S 2L6
(416) 706-8913, FAX: (416) 760-9791
E-mail: gwfilms@sympatico.ca, www.expectingthemovie.com
PRESIDENT
Thomas Mark Walden
V.P., DEVELOPMENT
Angela Gei

PETER ROWE PRODUCTIONS, INC.
180 Pinewood Trail, Mississauga, ON L5G 2L1
(905) 891-9498, FAX: (905) 891-9952
E-mail: prowe@interlog.com

Producer / director / writer

PETERSEN PRODUCTIONS INC.
12 Lewis St., Toronto, ON M4M 2H3. (416) 461-4660
FAX: (416) 461-7471
PRESIDENT
Curtis Petersen
U.S.A. / CALIFORNIA: 106 Entrada Dr., Unit 6, Santa Monica,
CA 90402. (310) 230-8616
See also British Columbia.

PHALANX FILMWORKS INC.
2 Moberly Ave., Toronto, ON M4C 4A8
(416) 690-9981. E-mail:phalanx@istar.ca
ASSISTANT DIRECTOR
Michael Bowman

PHILIP KATES PRODUCTIONS
3 Stonehouse Cres., Toronto, ON M6J 1T4
(416) 535-2103, FAX: (416) 535-3980. www.philipkates.com
DIRECTOR
Philip Kates
HEAD OF DEVELOPMENT
Vanessa Shrimpton

THE PLAYERS FILM CO.
4 Pardee Ave., Toronto, ON M6K 3H5. (416) 516-9110
FAXx: (416) 516-9113. E-mail: work@playfilm.com
www.playersfilm.com
EXECUTIVE PRODUCER / PRESIDENT
Philip Mellows
EXECUTIVE PRODUCER
Derek Sewell
DIRECTOR OF SALES AND MARKETING
Amanda Cohen

PLUM COMMUNICATIONS INCORPORATED
1054 Centre St., Ste.122, Thornhill, ON L4J 8E5
(905) 695-0397. E-mail: bcole@plumcom.ca
www.plumcom.ca
CONTACT
Bruce Cole

Multimedia production / web design / imaging

POLENTA PRODUCTIONS
65 Nello St., St. Catherines, ON L2N 1G5. (416) 995-0575
FAX: (905) 646-7087. E-mail: mmontefiore@canada.com
PRODUCER
Mark Montefiore
DIRECTOR
Vivieno Caldinelli

PORTFOLIO ENTERTAINMENT INC.
110 Eglinton Ave. E., Ste. 602, Toronto, ON M4P 2Y1
(416) 483-9773, FAX: (416) 483-6537.
E-mail: portfolio@portfolio-ent.com
FOUNDERS AND PRESIDENTS
Lisa Olfman
Joy Rosen
SENIOR V.P., DISTRIBUTION
Stephen Kelley
V.P., DEVELOPMENT
Kate Horton
TV programming: quality children's, animation, prime-time TV
movies, lifestyle, travel, sports, documentary and specials

POSTMODERN PRODUCTIONS
80 Carlton St., Ste. 110, Toronto, ON M5B 1L6
(416) 924-0005, FAX: (416) 413-1620
E-mail: postmod@total.net
EXECUTIVE PRODUCER
Susan Papp

POWER PICTURES
21 Elmsthorpe Ave., Toronto, ON M5P 2L5
(416) 485-8293, FAX: (416) 322-5712
E-mail: powerpicturescorp@hotmail.com
PRESIDENT
Julian Marks

PRIMITIVE ENTERTAINMENT
585 Bloor St. W., Ste. 300, Toronto, ON M6G 1K5
(416) 531-3087, FAX: (416) 531-4961
E-mail: office@primitive.net, www.primitive.net

Documentaries

PRISMA-LIGHT LTD.
762 Queen St. W, Toronto, ON M6J 1E9. (416) 504-4321
FAX: (416) 504-7325. E-mail: info@prismalight.com
www.prismalight.com
VANCOUVER/ PRISMA LIGHT WEST LTD.: 101 – 1184
Denman Ste. 141, Vancouver, BC V6G 2M9. (604) 801-5256
FAX: (604) 608-3362. E-mail: harry@prismalight.com
www.prismalight.com

PROSCENIUM FILMS
65 Hilton Ave., Toronto, ON M5R 3E5. (416) 538-3103
PRODUCER
Brian Avery

PROTOCOL ENTERTAINMENT INC.
(Comweb Group)
130 Bloor St. W., 5th Fl., Toronto, ON M5S 1N5
(416) 966-2711, FAX: (416) 920-4424
www.protocolent.com
PRESIDENT
Steve Levitan
CHAIRMAN
Paul Bronfman

Develop, finance, produce / TV & film

PRYCELESS PRODUCTIONS LTD.
59 Pine Cr., Toronto, ON M4E 1L3. (416) 699-6322
FAX: (416) 699-6168
PRODUCER
Craig Pryce

PTV PRODUCTIONS
585 Bloor St. W., 2nd Fl., Toronto, ON M6G 1K5
(416) 531-0100, FAX: (416) 531-3500
E-mail: info@ptvproductions.ca
PRESIDENT
Andrea Nemtin
U.K. DIRECTOR
Bill Nemtin

Documentary and children's animation

RADICAL SHEEP PRODUCTIONS INC.
80 Fraser Ave., Ste. 104, Toronto, ON M6K 3E1
(416) 539-0363, FAX: (416) 539-0496
E-mail: contact@radsheep.com, www.radsheep.com
CONTACT
John Leitch

RAYMOND INTERNATIONAL
33 Hazelton Ave., Ste. 122, Toronto, ON M5R 2E3
(416) 485-3406, FAX: (416) 487-3820
PRESIDENT
Bruce Raymond

REAL TO REEL PRODUCTIONS
3023 Dundas St. W., Toronto, ON M6P 1Z4
(416) 763-0001, FAX: (416) 763-1469
E-mail: annepick@realtoreelproductions.ca
V.P. / EXEC. PRODUCER
Anne Pick

REBELFILMS, INC.
c/o Greenlight Artist Management
244 Bloor St W., 3rd Fl., Toronto, ON M5S 1T8
(416) 963-8692, FAX: (416) 963-8368
E-mail: rebelfilms@sympatico.ca
CONTACT
Charlotte Rose (agent)
PRINCIPAL PRODUCER
Jeremy Podeswa

Feature films / TV

RED APPLE ENTERTAINMENT CORP.
1 St. Clair Ave. W., Ste. 503, Toronto, ON M4V 1K7
(416) 324-8537, FAX: (416) 324-0942
E-mail: redapple@redapple-entertainment.com
www.redapple-entertainment.com
Contact
Tim O'Brien

TV programming

REDMARK MANAGEMENT
2788 Bathurst St., Ste. 303, Toronto, ON M6B 3A3
(416) 256-2941
Exec. Producer
Mark Turkienicz

REVOLVER
53 Ontario St., 4th Fl., Toronto, ON M5A 2V1
(416) 869-0420, FAX: (416) 869-0568
Contacts
Jannie McInnes
Niva Chow

RHOMBUS MEDIA INC.
99 Spadina Ave., Ste. 600, Toronto, ON M5V 3P8
(416) 971-7856, FAX: (416) 971-9647
E-mail: rhombus@rhombusmedia.com, www.rhombusmedia.com
CONTACTS
Niv Fichman
Barbara Willis Sweete
Larry Weinstein
Sheena Macdonald
Daniel Iron

ROBERT BOCKING PRODUCTIONS LTD.
75 Hucknall Rd., Toronto, ON M3J 1W1
(416) 631-9845. E-mail: robert.bocking@sympatico.ca
Website: www.naturefilmfootage.com

TV and educational program producer specializing in natural
history subjects

ROB FRANCIS PRODUCTIONS
10 St. Andrews Ave., Grimsby, ON L3M 3R8. (905) 309-6685
E-mail: robsmi@attcanada.ca
EXECUTIVE PRODUCER
Robert F. Smith

Program consultants and producers of broadcast television
productions. Professional media service provider of electronic
communications dedicated to the integration of traditional
broadcast and new media.

ROGERS PRODUCTIONS
333 Bloor St., 7th Fl., Toronto, ON M4W 1G9
(416) 935-6666. E-mail: rogersproductions@rci.rogers.com
www.rogersproductions.com
CONTACTS
Christa Dickenson
Lisa McLean Stellick

Commercials / documentaries / on-air design / 2D & 3D animation / trailers

ROSEFIRE FILM INC.
77 Huntley St., Ste. 812, Toronto, ON M4Y 2P3. (416) 925-6258
WRITER / PRODUCER / DIRECTOR
David Sobelman

Feature films / documentaries / TV

ROYAL CANADIAN AIR FARCE / AIR FARCE
PRODUCTIONS INC.
250 Front St. W., Ste. 9B 300, Toronto, ON M5V 3G5
(416) 205-3800, FAX: (416) 205-3832
E-mail: mail@airfarce.com, www.airfarce.com
CONTACT
Lucy Stewart

RUSHLIGHT ENTERTAINMENT
110 Robert St., Toronto, ON M5S 2K3. (416) 993-8372
FAX: (416) 960-9368. E-mail: rushlight@sympatico.ca
PRESIDENT / PRODUCER
Michael Currie
PRODUCER / WRITER
Sarah Weight

SAHARA FILMWORKS INC.
915 Queen St. E., Ste. 2, Toronto, ON M4M 1J4
(416) 406-6880, FAX: (416) 406-4478
E-mail: sahara@attcanada.ca
PRESIDENT / PRODUCER
Adam B. Christie
VICE-PRESIDENT / WRITER
Lee Hoverd

Specializing in the development, finance, production and implementation of feature films / TV productions

SAILOR JONES MEDIA
276 Silver Birch Ave., Toronto, ON M4E 3L5
(416) 686-6278, FAX: (416) 946-1889
E-mail: info@sailorjones.com, www.sailorjones.com
PRESIDENT / EXEC. PRODUCER
Barbara Jones

S & S PRODUCTIONS
212 King St. W., Ste. 205, Toronto, ON M5H 1K5
(416) 260-0538, FAX: (416) 260-1628
E-mail: info@ssp.ca, www.ssp.ca
EXECUTIVE PRODUCER
David Smith

TV comedy & magazine series

SARRAZIN COUTURE ENTERTAINMENT INC.
14 Duncan St., Ste. 203, Toronto, ON M5H 3G8
(416) 586-9991, FAX (416) 586-9992
E-mail: sarrazin_couture@hotmail.com
CONTACTS
Pierre Sarrazin
Suzette Couture

SAVI MEDIA INC.
517 College St., Ste. 406, Toronto, ON M6G 4A2
(416) 597-8484, FAX: (416) 597-9596
E-mail: mail@savi-media.com, www.savi-media.com
PRESIDENT
Alexandra Raffé
DIRECTOR, CREATIVE AFFAIRS
Tara Twigg

TV drama / feature films. See also British Columbia.

S. BANKS GROUP INC.
174 Johnston Ave., Toronto, ON M2N 1H3
(416) 224-0296, FAX: (416) 224-8542
PRESIDENT
Sydney Banks

SCHULZ FILMS INC.
400 Walmer Rd., Park Towers E., Ste. 2323, Toronto, ON M5P
2X7. (416) 961-2001, FAX: (416) 961-2003
Europe: (011) 36-20-931-8000
E-mail: cinemillennium@aol.com
CONTACT
Bob Schulz

SCREENLIFE PRODUCTIONS
517 Wellington St. W., Ste 211, Toronto, ON M5V 1G1
(416) 260-2099, FAX: (416) 260-2042

SERENDIPITY POINT FILMS
9 Price St., Toronto, ON M4W 1Z1. (416) 960-0300
FAX: (416) 960-8656. www.serendipitypoint.com
PUBLICITY, MARKETING
Wendy Saffer

Boutique motion picture production cO. formed in 1998 by
Robert Lantos (former Chairman / CEO of Alliance
Communications Corp). Serendipity has since produced,
Ararat, Men with Brooms, Picture Claire, Sunshine, Stardom
and eXistenZ.

SEVENTH MAN FILMS INC.
159 Sheldrake Blvd., Toronto, ON M4P 2B1
(416) 483-3200, FAX: (416) 465-7826
CONTACT
Nicholas Gray

SEVILLE PICTURES INC.
511 King St. W., 4th Fl., Toronto, ON M5V 2Z4
(416) 480-0453, FAX: (416) 480-0501
E-mail: info@sevillepictures.com
CONTACT
Andrew Austin

Film & TV production / distributors. See also Québec

SFA PRODUCTIONS INC.
55 Adelaide St. E., Ste. 300, Toronto, ON M5C 1K6
(416) 214-9900, FAX: (416) 214-9300
E-mail: inquire@sfaproductions.com, www.sfaproductions.com
PRESIDENT / CEO
Sandra Faire
COO
Trisa Dayot
V.P., TALENT & BUSINESS AFFAIRS
Millan Curry-Sharples
V.P., POST-PRODUCTION
Bronwyn Warren

Feature film & TV — comedy / drama / documentary

SHAFTESBURY FILMS
163 Queen St. E., Ste.100, Toronto, ON M5A 1S1
(416) 363-1411, FAX: (416) 363-1428
E-mail: mailbox@shaftesbury.org, www.shaftesbury.org
CHAIRMAN
Christina Jennings
PRESIDENT
Jonathan Barker
VICE-PRESIDENTS
Laura Harbin
Scott Garvie

Film & TV

SHAWNA MCPEEK PRODUCTIONS INC.
74 Indian Rd. Cres., Toronto, ON M6P 2G1. (416) 538-7732
Cell: (416) 520-4666, FAX: (416) 534-2224
E-mail: shawna.mcpeek@sympatico.ca

Freelance agency producer

SHEBANDOWAN FILMS
25 High St. N., Thunder Bay, ON P7A 5R1
Tel./Fax: (807) 345-0221. E-mail: shebafilms@shaw.ca
www.shebafilms.com
PRESIDENT
Kelly Saxberg
VICE PRESIDENT
Ronald Harpelle

SHOES FULL OF FEET
246 Dunview Ave., Toronto, ON M2N 4J2. (416) 512-0084
FAX: (416) 512-0085, E-mail: info@shooesfulloffeet.com
www.shoesfulloffeet.com
PRESIDENT
Kris Booth
CEO
Bryce Mitchell
COO
Raj Panikkar

SHOOTERS INTERNATIONAL INC.
95 Berkeley St., Toronto, ON M5A 2W8
(416) 862-1959, FAX: (416) 862-7189
CONTACT/ EXEC. PRODUCER
Peter Benson, pbenson@shootersfilm.com
EXEC. PRODUCER
Pamela McNamara, pmcnamara@shootersfilm.com

THE SHOOTING EYE
19 Mount Pleasant Dr, Hamilton, ON L8W 3H3. (905) 387-6099
E-mail: info@shootingeye.com, www.shootingeye.com
PRESIDENT
Jeremy Major

SKINNY DIP PRODUCTIONS
3300 Lakeshore Rd. W., Oakville, ON L6L 6S6
(905) 466-2702, FAX: (905) 847-9280
E-mail: nja@cogeco.ca
PRESIDENT
Jennifer Strate
V.P.
Jessica Cowley
CFO
Nicholas Appleton

SMILEY GUY STUDIOS
444 Bathurst St., Studio 2, Toronto, ON M5T 2S6
(416) 979-8800, FAX: (416) 979-2227
E-mail: info@smileyguy.com, www.smileyguy.com
EXEC. PRODUCER
Jonas Diamond
PRODUCERS / DIRECTORS
Adrian Carter
Denny Silverthorne
PRODUCER / WRITER
Jeremy Diamond

SOUND VENTURE PRODUCTIONS
126 York St., Ste. 219, Ottawa, ON K1N 5T5
(613) 241-5111 ext. 250, FAX: (613) 241-5010
E-mail: neil@soundventure.com, www.soundventure.com
PRESIDENT & EXECUTIVE PRODUCER
Neil Bregman
PRODUCER / DIRECTOR
Katherine Jeans

Specializing in documentary, arts and children's programs

SPECTRUM FILMS
79 Lippincott St., Toronto, ON M5S 2P2
(416) 515-1077 / (416) 972-7668, E-mail: spectrum@the-
wire.com, www.the-wire.com/spectrum
CONTACTS
Holly Dale
Janis Cole

SPHINX PRODUCTIONS
24 Mercer St., Toronto, ON M5V 1H3. (416) 971-9131
FAX: (416) 971-6014. E-mail: mann@sphinxproductions.com
www.sphinxproductions.com
CONTACT
Ron Mann

STARGATE STUDIOS
530 Richmond St. W., Rear Bldg., Toronto, ON M5V 1Y4
(416) 504-5335, FAX: (416) 504-4545
PRESIDENT
Wayne Trickett
VICE-PRESIDENT
Robin Trickett

Feature / TV programming — Commercials / music videos

STORM ENTERTAINMENT
314 Dundas St. W., Toronto, ON M5T 1G5
(416) 203-6624, FAX: (416) 203-1572. www.stormentertainment.ca
CONTACTS
Dan Friedman, dfriedman@stormentertainment.ca;
Jack Pepall, jpepall@stormentertainment.ca

Television / multimedia production

STORNOWAY PRODUCTIONS INC.
1200 Bay St., Ste. 304, Toronto, ON M5R 2A5
(416) 923-1104, FAX: (416) 923-1122
E-mail: pmitchell@stornoway.com, www.stornoway.com

Documentaries / drama

STORY CITY
110 Spadina Ave., Toronto, ON M5V 2K4. (416) 367-4997
FAX: (416) 367-9757. E-mail: production@storycity.ca
www.storycity.ca
PRESIDENT
Dave Beatty
V.P., CREATIVE DIRECTOR
Ed Lee
V.P.
Todd Sullivan

STUDIO MAX FILMS
518 Sherbrooke St. E., Montréal, QC H2T 1R8
(514) 282-8444, FAX: (514) 282-9222
E-mail: info@maxfilms.ca
President
Roger Frappier
Producer
Luc Vandal

SULLIVAN ENTERTAINMENT INC.
110 Davenport Rd., Toronto, ON M5R 3R3
(416) 921-7177, FAX: (416) 921-7538
E-mail: inquire@sullivan-ent.com
PRESIDENT
Kevin Sullivan
INTERNATIONAL DEVELOPMENT
Muriel Thomas

SUMMERHILL ENTERTAINMENT INC.
56 Shaftesbury Ave., Toronto, ON M4T 1A3
(416) 967-6503, FAX: (416) 967-1292. www.summerhill.tv
EXECUTIVE PRODUCERS
Ronald Lillie
William Johnston

SUMMER PICTURES
604 Edward Ave., Ste. 2, Richmond Hill, ON L4C 9Y7
(905) 883-5561, FAX: 905-787-1240
E-mail: summer@summerpictures.biz, www.summerpictures.biz
EXEC. PRODUCERS
Tom Strnad
Boris Mojsovski

SUNDOG FILMS
530 Richmond St. W., Rear Bldg., Toronto, ON M5V 1Y4
(416) 504-2555, FAX: (416) 504-4545
E-mail: info@sundogfilms.ca
PRESIDENT
Wayne Trickett
VICE-PRESIDENT
Robin Trickett

SUNRISE FILMS LIMITED
352 Walmer Rd., Toronto, ON M5R 2Y4
(416) 929-7900, FAX: (416) 929-9900
E-mail: sunrise@interlog.com
CONTACT
Paul Saltzman

SUPERFILMS OF CANADA
with Nostalgia Films
236 Millwood Rd., Toronto, ON M4S 1J7. (416) 486-5799
E-mail: wcollins@attcanada.ca
DIRECTOR
Warren Collins

SUPER PEOPLE PRODUCTIONS
21 Windsor Court Rd., Thornhill, ON L3T 4Y4
(416) 579-0652, FAX: (905) 731-1329
E-mail: sidney@sppl.ca, www.sspl.ca
PRODUCER / DIRECTOR
Sidney M. Cohen

SUSSEX PRODUCTIONS LTD.
37 Sussex Ave., Toronto, ON M5S 1J6
(416) 977-5264, FAX: (416) 977-5264
E-mail: sussexprod@sympatico.ca
CONTACT
John Board

TAPESTRY PICTURES INC.
258 Wallace Ave., Ste. 104, Toronto, ON M6P 3M9
(416) 535-7402, FAX: (416) 535-1839
E-mail: tapestrypix@tapestrypictures.com
PRODUCERS
Mary Young Leckie
Heather Goldin

Drama / performing arts / biography

TELEFACTORY
517 College St., Ste. 408, Toronto, ON M6G 1A8
(416) 929-3206, FAX: (416) 929-6200
E-mail: sjepersen@telefactory.ca. www.telefactory.ca
EXEC. PRODUCERS
Arnie Gelbart
Leanna Crouch
Jesse Fawcett

TEMPLE STREET PRODUCTIONS
20 Butterick Rd., Toronto, ON M8W 3Z8
(416) 255-2260, FAX: (416) 255-7488
E-mail: shockin@templestreetproductions.com
PRESIDENT
Patrick Whitley
PRODUCER
Sheila Hockin

THEATRIFILM PRODUCTIONS INC.
34 Colin Ave., Toronto, ON M5P 2B9
(416) 483-3862. FAX: (416) 483-1106
PRESIDENT
Gilbert W. Taylor

3 LEGGED DOG FILMS
9 Tennis Cr., Ste. B19, Toronto, ON M4K 1J4
(416) 406-2208, FAX: (416) 406-0994
E-mail: 3ldfilms@rogers.com, www.3ldfilms.com
DIRECTOR / PRODUCER
Ed Gass-Donnelly

TICKLESCRATCH PRODUCTIONS
575 Gladstone Ave., Toronto, ON M6H 3J3
(416) 535-7737, E-mail: Michael.Glassbourg@humber.ca
CONTACT
Michael Glassbourg

TIMOTHY M WATTS PRODUCTIONS
100 Spruce St., Toronto, ON M4Y 1J2
(416) 816-3658. E-mail: timothymwattsproductions@yahoo.com
PRODUCER
Tim Watts

TORONTO FILMS
300 John St., Ste. 300, Thornhill, ON L3T 5W4
(905) 764-8767, FAX: (905) 764-8640
E-mail: torontofilms@sprint.ca
CONTACTS
Leonard Pearl
Rena Godfrey

Toronto-based film production company — produces documentaries / lifestyles / series / feature films

TORSTAR MEDIA GROUP TV
1 Yonge St., 9th Fl., Toronto, ON M5E 1E6
(416) 869-4700, FAX: (416) 869-4566
E-mail: info@tmgtv.ca, www.tmgtv.ca
V.P. & GENERAL MANAGERS
Don Schafer
Nancy Brown-Dacko

TRANSVISION FILMS
9 Veery Lane, Ottawa, ON K1J 8X4. (613) 741-9292
FAX: (613) 744-3548. E-mail: info@transvisionfilms.com
www.transvisionfilms.com
CONTACT
Rashmi Rekha

Feature films, documentaries, short films, corporate videos /
projects completed in Russia, India, U.S.A. and Canada

TRICORD PICTURES
141 Drakefield Rd., Markham, ON L3P 1G9
(905) 472-0445, FAX: (905) 472-0448
E-mail: windborn@istar.ca
CONTACT
Karen Pascal

Film & TV development / production

TRIPTYCH MEDIA INC.
788 King St. W., 2nd Fl., Toronto, ON M5V 1N6
(416) 703-8866, FAX: (416) 703-8867
E-mail: trip@triptych.on.ca, www.triptych.on.ca
PRODUCERS
Robin Cass
Louise Garfield
Anna Stratton

TRIUNE PRODUCTIONS INC.
111 Wildwood Cr., Toronto, ON M4L 2K9. (416) 686-0467
FAX: (416) 686-0468. E-mail: triune@triune.ca
www.triune.ca
CREATIVE PRODUCER
Michael Witta
PRODUCER / DIRECTOR
John Barclay

Drama / educational programs

BOB TULI
73 – 1588 South Parade Ct., Mississauga, ON L5M 6E7
(905) 273-6855, FAX: (905) 273-7202
E-mail: bobtuli@hotmail.com
CONTACT
Bob Tuli

Motion picture production and production services company

12 TRIBES PRODUCTIONS
300 John St., Ste. 300, Thornhill, ON L3T 5W4.
(905) 764-8767, FAX: (905) 764-8640
E-mail: 12tribes@sprint.ca, www.12tribesproductions.com
CO-PRESIDENTS
Leonard Pearl
Rena Godfrey

TWIN DRAGON FILM PRODUCTIONS LTD.
6347 Yonge St., North York, ON M2M 3X7. (416) 229-1280
FAX: (416) 229-2425. www.twin-dragon.com
PRESIDENT
Michael McNamara
VICE-PRESIDENT
Martin McNamara

Features

UP FRONT ENTERTAINMENT INC.
49 Spadina Ave., Ste. 302, Toronto, ON M5V 2J1
(416) 595-5850, FAX: (416) 595-5851
E-mail: bbarde@upfront.ca
PRESIDENT
Barbara Barde
DIRECTOR OF BUSINESS AFFAIRS
Linda Stregger

UPSTART PICTURES
5951 Ninth Line, R.R. #1, Erin, ON N0B 1T0
(519) 855-4613, FAX: (519) 855-1763
E-mail: sberger@globalserve.net
PRODUCER
Suzanne Berger

VIDEO EFFECTS
2080 Steeles Ave. E., Units 6 & 7, Brampton, ON L6T 5A5
(905) 791-6221, FAX: (905) 791-6412
E-mail: moreinfos@videoscanada.com,
www.videoscanada.com
CONTACT
V.P. Nandrajog

Video production

VILLAGERS MEDIA PRODUCTIONS
110 Cottingham St., Toronto, ON M4V 1C1. (416) 323-3228
FAX: (416) 323-1201. www.villagersmedia.com
CONTACTS
Dawn Deme
Steven Deme

TV drama / documentaries / corporate

VISUAL SERVICES
415 Greenview Ave., Ste. 401, Ottawa, ON K2B 8G5
(613) 828-7342. E-mail: peterdudley@sympatico.ca
PRODUCER / DIRECTOR / RESEARCHER / STILLS
PHOTOGRAPHER
Peter Dudley

VOICE AND THE VOICELESS PRODUCTIONS
538 Glen Forrest Blvd., Waterloo, ON N2J 4R2
(519) 221-0735, E-mail: info@vatv.ca, www.vatv.ca
EXEC. PRODUCER
Matt Brodie
RESEARCH COORDINATOR
Michael Brown
PRODUCER
Mike Hale

LESLIE WASSERMAN
225 Davenport Rd., Ste. 104, Toronto, ON M5R 3R2
(416) 920-0544

Entertainment producer / reporter

WATER PICTURES
2 College St., Ste. 301, Toronto, ON M5G 1K3
(416) 922-4303, FAX: (416) 922-9967
E-mail: info@waterpictures.ca
PRESIDENT
Karen Lee Hall

WAXWORKS CREATIVE
1101 – 60 New Dundee Rd., Kitchener, ON N2P 2N6
(519) 895-2008, (800) 281-9333, FAX: (519) 895-0542
E-mail: waxworks@waxworks.com, www.waxworks.com

Corporate / multimedia

WESTWIND PICTURES
2 Pardee Ave., Ste. 203, Toronto, ON M6K 3H5
(416) 516-4414, FAX: (416) 538-0026
E-mail: clarkdonnelly@westwindpictures.com
Exec. Producer
Clark Donnelly

See also Saskatchewan.

WHATEVER SOLUTIONS & MEDIA
647 Neal Dr., Peterborough, ON K9J 6X7. (705) 749-6325 /
(866) 779-7715, FAX: (705) 742-6129
E-mail: rmorton@whatevermedia.ca,
www.whateversolutions.ca
CONTACT
Robert Morton

TV series, documentaries, animation & post-production,
commercials

WHITE PINE PICTURES
(A division of Investigative Productions Inc.)
822 Richmond St. W., Ste. 200, Toronto, ON M6J 1C9
(416) 703-5580, FAX: (416) 703-1691
E-mail: info@whitepinepictures.com
www.whitepinepictures.com
CONTACTS
Peter Raymont
Lindalee Tracey

Film / video production

WINDBORNE PRODUCTIONS
141 Drakefield Rd., Markham, ON L3P 1G9. (905) 472-0445
FAX: (905) 472-0448. E-mail: karen.windborne@rogers.com
Contact
Karen Pascal

TV & corporate video

WINDSWEPT PRODUCTIONS
241 Victoria Ave., Belleville, ON K8N 2C4. (613) 962-7045
FAX: (613) 966-5461. E-mail: wind@reach.net
www.reach.net/~wind
CONTACT
Doug Knutson

Documentary, educational and promotional video production /
freelance camera & editing

WONDERMENT ENTERTAINMENT INTERNATIONAL INC.
400 Walmer Rd., Park Towers E., Ste. 2323, Toronto, ON M5P
2X7. (416) 961-2001, FAX: (416) 961-2003
CONTACT
Bob Schulz

W. WASIK FILMS & VIDEOS
293 Blue Heron Dr. , Oshawa, ON L1G 6X7
(905) 576-1030, FAX: (905) 576-7364
PRESIDENT
Walter Wasik

Features / studio facilities / 35mm & 16mm / videos

WYNDHAM STUDIOS ENTERTAINMENT
105 Robinson St., Oakville, ON L6H 1G1. (905) 847-9898
E-mail: wse@sympatico.ca
EXEC. PRODUCER
Christian Fennell
V.P., BUSINESS AFFAIRS
Susan White

YAP FILMS
110 Spadina Ave., Ste. 1001, Toronto, ON M5V 2K4
(416) 504-6662, FAX: (416) 504-6667
E-mail: tgreen@acepicturesinc.com
CONTACTS
Elliot Halpen
Jack Rabinovitch

YORKTOWN PRODUCTIONS LTD.
18 Gloucester Lane, 5th Fl., Toronto, ON M4Y 1L5
(416) 923-2787, FAX: (416) 923-8580
E-mail: yorktown@interlog.com
PRESIDENT
Norman Jewison
PERSONAL ASSISTANT
Liz Broden
OFFICE MANAGER
Kim Briggs

YOU AND MEDIA
320 Highfield Rd., Toronto, ON M4L 2V5. (416) 406-5830
FAX: (416) 406-5267. E-mail: info@youandmedia.com
www.youandmedia.com
PRODUCER
Brian Smith

PRINCE EDWARD ISLAND

CELLAR DOOR PRODUCTIONS
90 University Ave., Ste. 406, Charlottetown, PE C1A 4K9
(902) 628-3880, FAX: (902) 628-2088
E-mail: productions@cellardoor.tv, www.cellardoor.tv
PRESIDENT
Gretha Rose

ISLAND IMAGES
274 Salutation Cove Rd., R.R. #1, Bedeque, PE C0B 1C0
(902) 887-3620, FAX: (902) 887-3102
E-mail: islandimages@auracom.com
PRESIDENT
Bill Kendrick
PRODUCTION MANAGER
Richard Games

MEDIA CONCEPTS INC.
Box 593, Cornwall, PE C0A 1H0.. (902) 892-7359
FAX: (902) 368-3798. E-mail: mconcept@isn.net
PRODUCER
Jack MacAndrew

THE TALENT GROUP
3 Malahu Dr., Charlottetown, PE C1A 8A5. (902) 367-3600
FAX: (902) 367-3601. E-mail: lawrie@talentgroup.tv
www.cellardoor.tv
PRESIDENT
Lawrie Rotenberg

Film / TV production

QUÉBEC

ACPAV
1050 boul. René-Lévesque E., bur. 200, Montréal, QC H2L 2L6
(514) 849-2281, FAX: (514) 849-9487. E-mail: info@acpav.ca
PRODUCERS
Marc Daigle
René Gueissaz
Bernadette Payeur

AETIOS PRODUCTIONS
1751 Richardson, bur. 5102, Montréal, QC H3K 1G6
(514) 985-4476, FAX: (514) 985-4453
CONTACTS
Fabienne Larouche
Michel Trudeau

ALLIANCE ATLANTIS COMMUNICATIONS INC.
5 Place Ville-Marie, Ste. 1435, Montréal, QC H3B 2G2
(514) 878-2282, FAX: (514) 878-2419
E-mail: info@allianceatlantis.com, www.allianceatlantis.com
See also Ontario.

AMERIMAGE-SPECTRA
822 rue Sherbrooke est, Montréal, QC H2L1K4
(514) 525-7833, FAX: (514) 525-8033
PRESIDENT / PRODUCER
Pierre L. Touchette

AMERIQUE FILM
507 – 3575 Saint-Laurent, Montréal, QC H2X 2T7
(514) 844-0302, FAX: (514) 844-5184
E-mail: cdemaisoneuve@ameriquefilm.com
VICE-PRESIDENT
P. Martin Paulhus

AQUILON FILM INC.
Box 370, Victoria Stn., Westmount, QC H3Z 2V8
(514) 985-2597, FAX: (514) 982-6894
PRESIDENT
Werner Volkmer

ARTS ET IMAGES PRODUCTIONS
370 Short St., Sherbrooke, QC J1H 2E2. (819) 822-4131
FAX: (819) 822-4132. E-mail: aipi@interlinx.qc.ca
EXEC. PRODUCER / DIRECTOR
Mario Desmarais

AVANTI CINE VIDEO
225 rue Roy est, Ste. 100, Montréal, QC H2W 1M5
(514) 288-7000, FAX: (514) 288-1675
E-mail: productions@avanticinevideo.com
CONTACT
Luc Wiseman

BBR PRODUCTIONS
(Productions Bleu Blanc Rouge)
822 Sherbrooke St. E., Montréal, QC H2L 1K4
(514) 286-2500, FAX: (514) 525-8033
E-mail: bbr@equipespectra.ca, www.bbrproductions.com
PRESIDENT
Suzanne Girard
SUPERVISING DIRECTOR OF PRODUCTION
Debra Kouri
DIRECTOR OF DEVELOPMENT
Kim Segal

CHRISTAL FILMS PRODUCTIONS INC.
375 Victoria Ave, Ste. 300, Montréal, QC H2W 1M5
(514) 336-9696, FAX: (514) 336-6606
PRESIDENT
Christian Larouche
V.P., PRODUCTION
Pierre Gendron

CINAK LTÉE
1313 Chemin Guthrie, Saint-Armand, QC J0J 1T0
(450) 248-3295. E-mail: cinak@bellnet.ca
PRÉSIDENT
Jean-Pierre Lefebvre

CINAR CORPORATION
1055 boul. René Lévesque est., Montréal, QC H2L 4S5
(514) 843-7070, FAX: (514) 843-7080
www.cinar.com
PRESIDENT & CEO
Stuart Snyder
Animation & live-action programming, licensing, merchandising
and educational products for children & families

CINEFLIX INC.
5505 St-Laurent Blvd., Ste. 3008, Montréal, QC H2T 1S6
(514) 278-3140, FAX: (514) 270-3165
E-mail: info@cineflix.com, www.cineflix.com
PRODUCERS
Glen Salzman
André Barro
Katherine Buck
David York
Film / video / multimedia production

CINEGRAPHE PRODUCTIONS
820 rue De Rougemont, Sainte-Foy, QC G1X 2M5
(418) 652-3345, FAX: (418) 652-3353
E-mail: cinegraf@mediom.qc.ca
CONTACTS
Nicholas Kinsey
Andrée Tousignant

CINÉGROUPE
Head Office: 1010, Ste-Catherine St. E., Montréal, QC H2L
2G3. (514) 849-5008, FAX: (514) 849-5001
E-mail: info@cinegroupe.ca, www.cinegroupe.com
PRESIDENT / CEO
Jaques Pettigrew
EXEC. V.P. / COO
Pierre Bernatchez
EXECUTIVE V.P., CREATIVE AFFAIRS:
Michel Lemire
EXECUTIVE V.P., DEVELOPMENT, PRODUCTION
Marie-Claude Beauchamp
EXECUTIVE V.P., DISTRIBUTION, LICENSING AND
MARKETING
Marie-Christine Dufour
Feature film / TV programming / interactive entertainment

U.S.A./CALIFORNIA: 9000 Sunset Blvd., Ste. 715
West Hollywood, CA 90069. (310) 276-7190,
FAX: (310) 276-2976
EXEC. V.P. / HEAD OF U.S. ENTERTAINMENT
Ken Katsumoto

CINÉGROUPE INTERACTIVE
1010 Ste-Catherine E., 5th Fl., Montréal, QC H2L 2G3
(514) 849-5003, FAX: (514) 849-3077
PRESIDENT
Valerie Hénaire
Multimedia and interactive production

CINEMAGINAIRE
5144 St.-Laurent, Montréal, QC H2T 1R8. (514) 272-5505
FAX: (514) 272-9841. E-mail: info@cinemaginaire.com
PRESIDENT
Denise Robert
V.P.
Daniel Louis
DIRECTOR GENERAL
Martin Desroches

CINE QUA NON FILMS
5266 boul. St-Laurent, Montréal, QC H2T 1S1
(514) 271-4000, FAX: (514) 271-4005
PRODUCER
Michel Ouellette
DIRECTOR / PRODUCER
Bernar Hébert
LINE PRODUCER
Sylvie Gagné

CINEVIDEO INC.
CP 48051 CSP du Parc, Montréal, QC H2V 4S8
(514) 272-5077, FAX: (514) 272-3154
E-mail: 283848@sympatico.ca
PRESIDENT / PRODUCER
Justine Héroux
Feature films & TV productions / French & English

CIRRUS COMMUNICATIONS INC.
5100 rue Hutchison, bur. 200, Montréal, QC H2V 4A9
(514) 270-1918, FAX: (514) 270-1825
E-mail: CIRRUS@cirrusprod.qc.ca
PRESIDENT
Jacques Blain
EXECUTIVE IN CHARGE OF FEATURE FILMS
Pierre Even

CITE AMERIQUE CINEMA TELEVISION
5800 boul. St-Laurent, 2nd Fl., Montréal, QC H2T 1T3
(514) 278-8080, FAX: (514) 278-4000
E-mail: info@cite-amerique.com, www.cite-amerique.com
PRESIDENT / PRODUCER
Lorraine Richard
PRODUCERS
Louis Laverdière
Greg Dummett
Luc Martineau
V.P., FINANCE
Vivanne Morin

COMMUNICATIONS CLAUDE HÉROUX PLUS INC.
4984 place de la Savane, Ste. 100, Montréal, QC H4P 1Z6
(514) 738-3737, FAX: (514) 738-3290
E-mail: cherouxx@aol.com
President
Caroline Héroux

Drama / documentaries

COPIE ZERO
19, Cours Le Royer W., Ste. 400
Montréal, QC H2Y 1W4
(514) 284-6565
Fax: (514) 284-0132
E-mail: matt@copiezero.com, katia@copiezero.com
Website: www.copiezero.com
President / Exec. Producer: Matt Zimbel
Exec. Producer: Campbell Webster
Director of Business Affairs: Chrystine Girard
Associate Producer: Katia Clavet

DLI PRODUCTIONS
4301 Avenue de L'Esplande, Montréal, QC H2W 1T1
(514) 272-2220, FAX: (514) 844-2992
E-mail: dliproductions@sympatico.ca, www.dli.ca
PRESIDENT
Abbey Neidik
CHAIRWOMAN
Irene Angelico

DOMINO PRODUCTION LTD.
4002 Grey Ave., Montréal, QC H4A 3P1. (514) 484-0446
FAX: (514) 484-0468. E-mail: jritter@dominofilm.ca
www.dominofilm.ca
PRESIDENT
Jeanne Ritter

EQUINOXE FILMS INC.
505 Sherbrooke St. E., Ste. 2401, Montréal, QC H2L 4N3
(514) 844-0680, FAX: (514) 499-9899
PRESIDENT & CEO
Pierre René
SENIOR VICE-PRESIDENT & COO
Michael Mosca

Films for theatrical / video / TV. See also Ontario

LA FABRIQUE D'IMAGES LTÉE.
318 rue Sherbrooke est, Montréal, QC H2X 1E6
(514) 282-1505, FAX: (514) 282-8784
E-mail: fabinfo@fabimages.com, www.fabimages.com
CONTACTS
Denis Martel
Michel Raymond
Claude Landry
DIRECTORS
Alain DesRochers
Christian Duguay
Alexis Durand-Brault
Jacques Fournier
Maxime Giroux
Marc S. Grenier
Jericho Jeudy
Adam Kimmel
Claude Marchand
Michel Pelletier
Jean-François Pouliot
Jean-Michel Ravon
Jean-François Rivard
Franck Blaess
Frederic Dompierre
DIRECTORS / CINEMATOGRAPHERS
Alexis Durand-Brault
Christian Dugay

FILMO BANDITO PRODUCTIONS INC.
85 – 19th Ave., Lachine, QC H8S 3R7
(514) 937-5091, FAX: (514) 937-1583. E-mail: eagimber@total.net
Producers
Elisabeth-Ann Gimber
Geoff S. Patenaude

LES FILMS VISION 4 INC.
4446 boul. St-Laurent, 7th Fl., Montréal, QC H2W 1Z5
(514) 499-0972, FAX: (514) 844-5498
E-mail: telefiction@login.net
PRODUCERS
Claude Veillet
Jacques Bonin
ASSOCIATE PRODUCER
Lucie Veillet

GALAFILM PRODUCTIONS INC.
5643 rue Clark, Ste. 300, Montréal, QC H2T 2V5
(514) 273-4252, FAX: (514) 273-8689
E-mail: galafilm@galafilm.com, www.galafilm.com
PRESIDENT
Arnie Gelbart
PRODUCERS
Ian Whitehead
Francine Allaire
Sylvia Wilson
DEVELOPMENT
Jamie Gaetz

GLACIALIS PRODUCTIONS
29, Chemin Pealey, Grande-Entree, QC G0B 1H0
(514) 283-1653, Tel./FAX: (418) 986-5960

GO FILMS
400 Avenue Atlantic, Penthouse,10th Fl., Outremont, QC H2V
1A5. (514) 844-0271, FAX: (514) 844-9127
E-mail: info@gofilms.qc.ca
PRESIDENT / PRODUCER
Nicole Robert
SECRETARY / PRODUCER / DIRECTOR
Gabriel Pelletier

GREEN LION PRODUCTIONS
20223 rue Lakeshore, Baie d'Urfe, QC H9X 1P9
(514) 457-5555, FAX: (514) 457-3255
E-mail: cmullins@greenlionfilms.com
PRODUCER
Catherine Mullins

GROUPE CINEMAGINAIRE INTERNATIONAL
5144 boul. Saint-Laurent, Montréal, QC H2T 1R8
(514) 272-5505, FAX: (514) 272-9841
PRESIDENT / PRODUCER
Denise Robert
V.P., PRODUCER
Daniel Louis

Specializing in co-productions / feature films / documentaries

IDEACOM INTERNATIONAL INC.
1000 Amherst, Ste. 300, Montréal, QC H2L 3K5
(514) 849-6966, FAX: (514) 849-0776
E-mail: ideacom@bellnet.ca
CONTACTS
Jacques Nadeau
Josette D. Normandeau

INDO CANADIAN FILMS INTERNATIONAL
4500 boul. de Maisonneuve, bur. 21, Montréal, QC H3Z
1L7. (514) 935-6888, FAX: (514) 935-8588
E-mail: indocdn.films@attglobal.net
PRESIDENT
Gotham Hooja

INFORM-ACTION FILMS INC.
1000 Amherst St., Ste. 301, Montréal, QC H2L 3K5
(514) 284-0441, FAX: (514) 284-0772
E-mail: informaction@bellnet.ca
Contact
Nathalie Barton

Documentary films / series

INFRAME PRODUCTIONS INC.
1744 William St., Ste. 400, Montréal, QC H3J 1R4
(514) 935-7025, FAX: (514) 935-9238
E-mail: info@inframe.com, www.inframeonline.com
Contact
Nick Papadopoli

Documentary / corporates / shorts / DVD / CD

JB MEDIA
4115 rue Sherbrooke W., Ste. 200, Montréal, QC H3Z 1K9
(514) 937-3333, FAX: (514) 937-2338
E-mail: asgreenberg@incendomedia.com
CONTACTS
Jean Bureau
Stephen Greenberg
Anna-Sue Greenberg
Aude Capra

JPL PRODUCTION INC.
1600 de Maisonneuve Blvd. E., Ste. A408, CP 3500, Succ. C
Montréal, QC H2L 4P2. (514) 526-2881 FAX: (514) 598-6024

GENERAL MANAGER & EXEC. PRODUCER:
Real Germaim

KERRIGAN PRODUCTIONS INC.
3877 av. Draper, Montréal, QC H4A 2N9
(514) 486-8456
PRODUCER / DIRECTOR
Bill Kerrigan
WRITER
Louise Roy

LION'S GATE FILMS
376 Victoria Ave., bur. 300, Westmount, QC H3Z 1C3
(514) 336-9696, FAX: (514) 336-6606
www.lionsgatefilms.com

See also British Columbia and Ontario

LOCOMOTION FILMS
318 rue Sherbrooke E., Montréal, QC H2X 1E6
(514) 840-8486, FAX: (514) 840-8844
E-mail: infoloco@locomotionfilms.com
PRESIDENT
Denis Martel

LORENZO ORZARI PRODUCTIONS
6 Libersan, Montréal, QC H9A 2B5
Tel. & Fax: (514) 685-6170. E-mail: lorenzo.orzari@sympatico.ca
www3.sympatico.ca/lorenzo.orzari
WRITER / PRODUCER / DIRECTOR
Lorenzo Orzari

Feature films / TV / books / CD / multimedia

MACUMBA INTERNATIONAL INC.
3862 ave Parc Lafontaine, Montréal, QC H2L 3M6
(514) 521-8303, FAX: (514) 521-0260
E-mail: macumba@macumbainternational.com
PRODUCERS
Robert Cornellier
Patricio Henriquez
Raymonde Provencher

Films / documentaries

MAX FILMS / MAX FILMS TELEVISION
518 Sherbrooke St. E., Montréal, QC H2L 1K1
(514) 282-8444, FAX: (514) 282-9222
E-mail: info@maxfilms.ca
PRESIDENT
Roger Frappier
PRODUCER
Luc Vandal

MEDIA PRINCIPIA INC.
3530 St.-Laurent boul., Ste. 402, Montréal, QC H2X 2V1
(514) 987-7717, FAX: (514) 987-7492
E-mail: info@fondation-langlois.org, www.fondation-langlois.org
PRESIDENT
Daniel Langlois
EXECUTIVE DIRECTOR
Jean Gagnon

Specializing in making films that draw on new digital production technologies

MELENNY PRODUCTIONS INC.
154 Laurier W., Ste. 300, Montréal, QC H2T 2N7
(514) 270-6170, FAX: (514) 270-6988
E-mail: melenny@videotron.ca
CONTACT
Richard Goudreau

MILAGRO FILMS
4446 St. Laurent Blvd., Ste. 806, Montréal, QC H2W 1Z5
(514) 939-9969, FAX: (514) 985-2563
E-mail: info@milagrofilms.ca
PRODUCER
Jean-Marc Felio
DIRECTOR, DEVELOPMENT & SALES
Tom Philpott
CFO
Kamel Benameur

MUSE ENTERTAINMENT ENTERPRISES INC.
4670 St. Catherine St. W., Ste. 200, Montréal, QC H3Z 1S5
(514) 866-6873 (MUSE), FAX: (514) 876-3911
E-mail: mprupas@muse.ca, www.muse.ca
PRESIDENT
Michael Prupas
V.P., PRODUCTION
Irene Litinsky
Features / TV movies & series

OPTIMA PRODUCTIONS INC.
4599 Montcalm Ave., Montréal, QC H4B 2J8
(514) 397-9988, FAX: (514) 954-1237.
 E-mail: jeanzaloum@hotmail.com
President
Jean Zaloum

DIRECTOR
Alain Zaloum

PARK EX PICTURES
4020, rue St. Ambroise, Ste. 200, Montréal, QC H4C 2C7
(514) 939-5755, FAX: (514) 939-7212
E-mail: info@parkexpixtures.ca
PRESIDENT
Kevin Tierney

PGC TELEVISION
4446 boul St-Laurent, Ste. 900, Montréal, QC H2W 1Z5
(514) 849-3999, FAX: (514) 849-8298
E-mail: info@guycloutier.com, www.guycloutier.com
DIRECTOR OF TV DEVELOPMENT
Sonya Theriault

Production / distribution / format rights / world markets

PICTURE THIS PRODUCTIONS
154 Hillcrest St., Lachine, QC H8R 1J4
(514) 484-1145, FAX: (514) 484-3777
E-mail: info@picturethis.ca, www.picturethis.ca
CONTACTS
Maureen Marovitch
David Finch

PRH CREATION IMAGE
836 Bloomfield, Outremont, QC H2V 3S6
(514) 341-3381, FAX: (514) 341-4355
E-mail: info@prh.qc.ca
PRODUCER / DIRECTOR
Roger Heroux
PRODUCTION MANAGER & DEVELOPMENT
Marie-Pierre Rodier

LES PRODUCTIONS DE L'OEIL ENR.
860 Gohier, St-Laurent, QC H4L 3J2
(514) 744-1944, E-mail: mario-b@sympatico.ca
CONTACT
Mario Bonenfant

PRODUCTIONS GRAND NORD QUEBEC INC.
La Maison Premier Plan, Ste. 392, 1600 ave. de Lorimier
Montréal, QC H2K 3W5. (514) 521-7433
FAX: (514) 522-3013. E-mail: imclaren@grandnord.ca
CONTACT
Ian McLaren

PRODUCTIONS IMPEX
480 Chemin Ste-Marie, Lac-Aux-Sables, QC G0X 1M0
(418) 336-3008, FAX: (418) 336-3117
E-mail: impex@videotron.ca
PRESIDENT
Andre Larochelle
PRODUCER
Lucie Tremblay

LES PRODUCTIONS JEAN-PIERRE AVOINE
2 rue de Magog, Blainville, QC J7B 1S1
(450) 437-1802, FAX: (450) 437-8389
E-mail: jpavoine@videotron.ca
Producer / Director
Jean-Pierre Avoine

PRODUCTIONS LA FÊTE INC.
387 rue Saint-Paul ouest, Montréal, QC H2Y 2A7
(514) 848-0417, FAX: (514) 848-0064
E-mail: info@lafete.com
PRESIDENT
Rock Demers
Productions La Fête, headquartered in Montréal, is a private company that develops, produces and distributes feature length drama, documentaries and animated and fiction tv series in English as well as in French and many other languages. Programs are being sold in over 100 countries.

PRODUCTIONS MATCH TV / PRODUCTIONS NEOFILMS
5162 Saint-Laurent, bur. 200, Montréal, QC H2T 1R8
(514) 270-4660, FAX: (514) 270-4465
E-mail: neomatch@neomatch.com
PRODUCERS
Philippe Dussault
Anne-Marie Hetu

LES PRODUCTIONS POINT DE MIRE
154 Laurier Ave. W., Ste 302, Montréal, QC H2T 2N7
(514) 278-8922, FAX: (514) 278-8925.
E-mail: info@pdemire.com
PRESIDENT
Lise Payette
V.P., DRAMA
Jean-François Mercier
V.P., NON-FICTION
Raymond Gauthier
PRODUCER, DRAMA & DEVELOPMENT
Andre Monette

LES PRODUCTIONS SOVIMAGE INC.
1035 Ave. Laurier ouest, 1er étage, Outremont, QC H2V 2L1
(514) 277-6123, FAX: (514) 277-1139
E-mail: productions@sovimage.qc.ca
PRESIDENT / PRODUCER
Vincent Garbriele
PRODUCER
Sophie Deschênes

LES PRODUCTIONS TÉLÉ-ACTION INC.
1324 rue Ste-Catherine est, Montréal, QC H2L 2H5
(514) 524-1118, FAX: (514) 524-2041
E-mail: prodta@videotron.ca
PRODUCER
Claudio Luca

LES PRODUCTIONS VIA LE MONDE
(DANIEL BERTOLINO) INC.
326 ouest rue St-Paul, Montréal, QC H2Y 2A3
(514) 285-1658, FAX: (514) 285-1970
E-mail: berto@vialemonde.qc.ca
CONTACTS
Daniel Bertolino
Catherine Viau

LES PRODUCTIONS VIDEOFILMS LIMITEE
296 ouest rue St-Paul, bur. 400, Montréal, QC H2Y 2A3
(514) 844-8611, FAX: (514) 844-4034
E-mail: videofilms@ca.inter.net
CONTACT
Robert Ménard

Features / TV series

R.C. PRODUCTIONS
132 ave. Kingsley, Dollard des Ormeaux, QC H9B 1M9
(514) 683-2527
DOP
Robert Chammas

Video / film

REMSTAR
85 St. Paul W., Ste. 300, Montréal, QC H2Y 3V4
(514) 847-1136, FAX: (514) 847-1163
E-mail: info@remstarcorp.com, www.remstarcorp.com
Production / distribution / financing

ROONEY PRODUCTIONS
95 Montée Drouin, Lac-des-Loups, QC J0X 3K0
(819) 456-3522, FAX: (819) 456-3551
E-mail: info@rooneyproductions.com
PRODUCER / DIRECTOR
Robert Rooney
PRODUCER
Brenda Rooney

Documentaries

ROSE FILMS INC.
HEAD OFFICE & PRODUCTION OFFICE: C.P. 40, Saint-Paul
d'Abbotsford, QC J0E 1A0. (450) 379-5304
FAX: (450) 379-5742. E-mail: rosefilms@compuserve.com
CONTACTS
Claude Fournier
Marie-José Raymond

ROZON — JUST FOR LAUGHS
2101 boul. St-Laurent, Montréal, QC H2X 2T5
(514) 845-3155, FAX: (514) 845-4140
PRESIDENT
Gilbert Rozon, grozon@hahaha.com
CEO
Bruce Hills, bhills@hahaha.com
DIRECTOR, TELEVISION
Pierre Girard, pgirard@hahaha.com
DIRECTOR, INTERNATIONAL TELEVISION
Nathalie Bourdon, nbourdon@hahaha.com
INTERNATIONAL TELEVISION SALES
Cristos Sorligas, csorlig@hahaha.com

SEVILLE PICTURES INC.
147 St. Paul St. W., 2nd Fl., Montréal, QC H2Y 1Z5
(514) 841-1910, FAX: (514) 841-8030
E-mail: info@sevillepictures.com
CONTACTS
David Reckziegel,
John Hamilton

Film & TV production. See also Ontario.

SLINGSHOT PRODUCTIONS INC.
4599 Montclair Ave., Montréal, QC H4B 2J8
(514) 397-9988, FAX: (514) 954-1237
E-mail: alain.zaloum@sympatico.ca
Director
Alain Zaloum

STONEHAVEN PRODUCTIONS
1310 rue Larivière, Montréal, QC H2L 1M8
(514) 527-2131, FAX: (514) 522-8599
E-mail: m.taylor@stonehaven.ca
PRESIDENT
Michael C. Taylor

TELEFICTION / LES FILMS VISION 4
4446 boul. Saint-Laurent, 7th Fl., Montréal, QC H2W 1Z5
(514) 499-0972, FAX: (514) 844-5498
E-mail: info@telefiction.com
CHAIRMAN & CEO.
Claude Veillet
PRESIDENT
Jacques Bonin
EXEC. VICE-PRESIDENT
Lucie Veillet

TRINOME INC.
1310 Alexandre de Séve, bur. 2, Montréal, QC H2L 2V1
(514) 527-9070 / (877) 527-9070, FAX: (514) 597-1571
E-mail: courrier@trinome.com, www.trinome.com

VENDOME TELEVISION INC.
1751 rue Richardson, Ste. 5.106, Montréal, QC H3K 1G6
(514) 369-4834, FAX: (514) 369-4015
E-mail: productions@vendometelevision.ca
Contacts
Ghislaine Mailhot
André Dubois

TV programming — drama / comedy / documentaries

VENT D'EST INC.
1750 rue Saint-André, Rm. 3028, Montréal, QC H2L 3T8
(514) 523-3163, FAX: (514) 523-4424
E-mail: ventdest@videotron.ca, http://pages.infinit.net/ventdest/
CINÉASTE / SCÉNARISTE / RÉALISATEUR
Richard Boutet
PRODUCTEURS
Bernard Lalonde
Louis Goyer
Richard Boutet

VERSEAU INTERNATIONAL INC.
225 rue Roy est, bur. 200, Montréal, QC H2W 1M5
(514) 848-9814, FAX: (514) 848-9908
PRESIDENT
Aimee Danis

VIDEOGRAPHE PRODUCTION
4550 rue Garnier ,Montréal, QC H2J 3S7. (514) 521-2116
FAX: (514) 521-1676. E-mail: production@videographe.qc.ca
CONTACT
Pierre Brault

Multimedia and video production centre for independent artists
/ digital cameras and editing suites

WHALLEY-ABBEY MEDIA HOLDINGS, INC.
1303 Greene Ave., Ste. 300, Westmount, QC H3Z 2A7
(514) 846-1940, FAX: (514) 846-1550
E-mail: hansr@painted-house.com
CONTACT
H. Rosenstein

Award-winning specialists in lifestyle programs and documentaries

ZONE 3 INC.
1055 René Lévesque boul. est, Ste. 300, Montréal, QC H2L
4S5. (514) 284-5555. FAX: (514) 985-4458
www.zone3.ca
CONTACTS
Michel Bissonnette
Paul Dupont-Hébert
André Larin
Vincent Leduc

SASKATCHEWAN

BIRDSONG COMMUNICATIONS
W.213 – 2440 Broad St., Regina, SK S4P 4A1
(306) 359-3070, FAX: (306) 525-1204
E-mail: birdsong.ltd@sk.sympatico.ca
PRESIDENT / PRODUCER
Don List

Motion picture production services

CAMERA OBSCURA
Box 274, Prince Albert, SK S6V 5R5. (306) 749-2578
PRESIDENT
Patrick Wolfe

Documentary media / film & TV / location scout

CKCK-TV CREATIVE SERVICES
Box 2000, Regina, SK S4P 3E5. (306) 569-2000
FAX: (306) 569-6413. E-mail: ckcknews@ctv.ca, www.ctv.ca
DIRECTOR, CREATIVE SERVICES
Geoff Bradley
PRODUCERS
Craig Farrell
Stacey Euteneier
Paul Chomos

EDGE ENTERTAINMENT INC.
1120 Morgan Ave., Saskatoon, SK S7H 2R7. (306) 374-1207,
FAX: (306) 374-0783. E-mail: edge.ent@edgeentertainment.sk.ca
www.edgeentertainment.sk.ca
PRESIDENT, FILM & TELEVISION
David Doerksen
V.P., FINANCE
Deidre Meeks
V.P., FILM & TELEVISION
Leanne Arnott
BUSINESS AFFAIRS
Linda Davis

Feature & TV films — development / acquisition / production

MINDS EYE PICTURES
HEAD OFFICE: 2440 Broad St., North Block, Regina, SK S4P
4A1. (306) 359-7618, FAX: (306) 359-3466
E-mail: mindseye@mindseyepictures.com
www.mindseyepictures.com
CHAIRMAN /CEO
Kevin DeWalt
V.P., DEVELOPMENT
Josh Miller

Features / TV drama / documentaries. See also British
Columbia & Alberta.

PARTNERS IN MOTION
2704 10th Ave., Regina, SK S4T 1E9. (306) 545-2228,
FAX: (306) 569-9616. E-mail: jstecyk@partnersinmotion.com
www.partnersinmotion.com
CEO
Ron Goetz
PRESIDENT
Chris Triffo
CFO
Linda Goetz
V.P., BUSINESS AFFAIRS
Jeff Stecyk
V.P., PRODUCTION
Nova Herman

STEPHEN ONDA
3035 – 21st Ave., Regina, SK S4S 0T5. (306) 525-6921
FAX: (306) 505-5727. E-mail: onda@sk.sympatico.ca

Producer / writer / feature / TV / documentary

PATRICK WOLFE CAMERA OBSCURA
Box 274, Prince Albert, SK S6V 5R5. (306) 749-2578
PRESIDENT
Patrick Wolfe

Documentary media / film & TV / location scout

THOMEGA ENTERTAINMENT INC.
409 – 135 21st St., Saskatoon, SK S7K 0B4
(306) 244-5503, FAX: (306) 244-5504
E-mail: thomega@sk.sympatico.ca, www.thomega.com
CONTACT
Anthony Towstego

Feature films / TV series/ documentaries

WESTWIND PICTURES
2206 Dewdeny Ave., Ste. 402, Regina, SK S4R 1H3
(306) 777-0160, FAX: (306) 352-8558
E-mail: michaelsnook@westwindpictures.com
EXECUTIVE PRODUCER
Michael Snook
See also Ontario.

PRODUCTION SERVICES

ANIMATION & VISUAL EFFECTS

ALBERTA

GAP PRODUCTIONS
147 RockyRidge Bay N.W., Calgary, AB T3G 4E7
(403) 263-0012, FAX: (403) 263-0016
E-mail: post@gapproductions.com, www.gapproductions.com
3D animation / graphics – full service editorial

BRITISH COLUMBIA

AL SENS ANIMATION LTD.
155 — 1020 Mainland St., Vancouver, BC V6B 2T4
(604) 681-9728, FAX: (604) 681-9758
E-mail: alsensanimation@telus.net
PRESIDENT
Lynka Bélanger

ATOMIC CARTOONS
928 Davie St., Vancouver, BC V6Z 1B8
(604) 734-2866, FAX: (604) 734-2869
www.atomiccartoons.com
CONTACTS
Trevor Bentley, trevor@atomiccartoons.com
Rob Davies, rob@atomiccartoons.com
Character & background design, layout and posing, storyboards, clean-up, slugging, sheet timing, color styling, traditional animation, flash animation, custom webpage design

BARDEL ENTERTAINMENT INC.
548 Beatty St., Vancouver, BC V6B 2L3
(604) 669-5589, FAX: (604) 669-9079
E-mail: bardel@bardelentertainment.com
PRESIDENT
Barry Ward
CEO
Delna Bhesania
Development, production for film / television / direct to video / interactive media / the Internet

BARKING BULLFROG CARTOON COMPANY
1283 Durant Dr., Coquitlam, BC V3B 6K8
(604) 689-0702, www.barkingbullfrog.com
PRESIDENT
Ian Freedman
SUPERVISING PRODUCER
Mark Freedman
Classical animation

ENIGMA STUDIOS INC.
149 E. Pender St., 2nd Fl., Vancouver, BC V6A 1T6
(604) 633-9583, FAX: (604) 633-9582
E-mail: info@enigma3D.com, www.enigma3D.com
Visual effects and animation

FINALE EDITWORKS
201 W. Second Ave., Vancouver, BC V5Y 3V5
(604) 876-7678, FAX: (604) 876-3299
www.finale-editworks.com
PRESIDENT
Don Thompson
Avid non-linear off-line / component digital online edit suites / multi-format duplication / visual effects / post audio

GVFX - GAJDECKI VISUAL EFFECTS
221 E. 10th Ave., Ste. 202, Vancouver, BC V5T 4V1
(604) 736-4839, FAX: 604) 736-4838
E-mail: inquiries@gvfx.com, www.gvfx.com
CONTACT
Ron O'Brien
Effects direction / digital compositing / motion control / models & miniatures / 3-D animation. See also Ontario.

IMAGE ENGINE DESIGN INC.
15 W. 5th Ave., Vancouver, BC V5Y 1H4
(604) 874-5634, FAX: (604) 876-3299
E-mail: design@image-engine.com, www.image-engine.com
PRESIDENT
Christopher Mossman
Computer animation & design / visual effects for video, film or CD-ROM

LOST BOYS STUDIOS
395 Railway St., 3rd Fl., Vancouver, BC V6A 1A6
(604) 738-1805 / (877) 793-0545, FAX:(604) 738-1806
www.lostboys-studios.com
DIGITAL EFFECTS PRODUCER
Roula Lainas
Digital effects design and production for TV series / commercials / video game openers and features. High-end 3D animation and digital compositing

MAINFRAME ENTERTAINMENT INC.
2025 West Broadway, Ste. 500, Vancouver, BC V6J 1Z6
(604) 714-2600, FAX(604) 714-2641
E-mail: info@mainframe.ca, www.mainframe.ca
PRESIDENT
Brett Gannon
CEO
Rick Mischel
Long form CGI – television & film

MERCURY FILMWORKS VANCOUVER
190 Alexander St., Ste. 500, Vancouver, BC V6A 1B5
(604) 684-9117, FAX: (604) 684-8339
E-mail: info@mercuryfilmworks.com
www.mercuryfilmsworks.com
Visual effects & animation for episodic television, feature film, commercials. See also Ontario.

MINDMILL STUDIOS
1601 Yew St., Ste. 200, Vancouver, BC V6K 3E6
(604) 681-1232 / (888) 681-1232, FAX: (604) 739-3006
Email: Reception@MindMillStudios.com
www.MindMillStudios.com
CONTACTS
Verne Andru
Marv Coburn

NORTHWEST IMAGING & F.X.
2339 Columbia St., Ste. 100, Vancouver, BC V5Y 3Y3
(604) 873-9330, FAX: (604) 873-9339. www.nwfx.com
VICE-PRESIDENT
Alex Tkach

PORK & BEANS PRODUCTIONS INC.
1224 Hamilton St., Ste. 200, Vancouver, BC V6B 2S8
(604) 602-6629, FAX: (604) 602-6616
E-mail: info@porkbean.com, www.porkbean.com
CONTACT
Cherish Bryck
Classical & Flash productions – commercials / promos / series work

PRISMA LIGHT WEST LTD.
101 – 1184 Denman St. #141, Vancouver, B.C. V6G 2M9
(604) 801-5256, Fax: (604) 608-3362
E-mail: harry@prismalight.com, www.prismalight.com

RAINMAKER
50 W. 2nd Ave., Vancouver, BC V5Y 1B3
(604) 874-8700, FAX: (604) 874-1719 www.rainmaker.com
PRESIDENT/CEO
Bob Scarabelli
GEN. MANAGER
Barry Chambers
DIRECTOR OF OPERATIONS
K.T. McFadden
LAB GENERAL MANAGER
Rick Cooper
DIRECTOR OF VISUAL EFFECTS
Brian Moylan
LAB MANAGER
George Gliszczynski
Lab, post, visual effects — film, MOWs, TV, commercials, documentaries

STUDIO B PRODUCTIONS
190 Alexander St., Ste. 600, Vancouver, BC V6A 1B5
(604) 684-2363, FAX: (604) 602-0208
Website: www.studiobproductions.com
PARTNERS
Chris Bartleman
Blair Peters

TOYBOX VANCOUVER
(A Division of Command Post & Transfer Corp.)
1090 Homer St., Ste. 500, Vancouver, BC V6B 2W9
(604) 689-1090, FAX: (604) 689-1003
E-mail: lrozon@compt.com, spotter@compt.com
www.compt.com
CONTACTS
Lorraine Rozon
Sherri Potter

Visual effects / 2D & 3D animation & HDTV

MANITOBA

FRANTIC FILMS
70 Arthur St., Ste. 300, Winnipeg, MB R3B 1G7
(204) 949-0070, FAX: (204) 949-0050
E-mail: info@franticfilms.com, www.franticfilms.com
PRESIDENT / CREATIVE DIRECTOR
Christopher Bond
CEO / EXEC. PRODUCER
Jamie Brown
V.P. / PRODUCER:
Ken Zorniak

Cutting edge visual effects, 3D animation & post production

MIDCANADA PRODUCTION SERVICES INC.
509 Century St., Winnipeg, MB R3H 0L8
(204) 772-0368, E-mail: info@midcan.com, www.midcan.com

Flash, 2D, 3D animation, compositing

NEW BRUNSWICK

INNOVATIVE VIDEO SOLUTIONS
76 Princess St., St. John, NB E2L 1K4
Tel. & Fax: (506) 693-4487
E-mail: darrell@videosolutions.ca / mike@videosolutions.ca
www.videosolutions.ca
CONTACTS
Darrell Bainbridge
Mike Burchill

3D animation & graphic design

NEWFOUNDLAND

ANIGRAPH PRODUCTIONS LIMITED
Box 13490, Stn. A, St. John's, NF A1B 4B8
(709) 722-2820, FAX: (709) 739-4801
E-mail: avalon@avint.net
PRESIDENT
C. Anne MacLeod
PRODUCER
Paul G. MacLeod

Animation for film and video / TV / documentaries / corporate / industrial video

NOVA SCOTIA

EVIL CLOWN ANIMATION
5252, Hwy. 332, R.R. #3, Bridgwater, NS B4V 2W2
Tel./Fax: (902) 766-0126
E-mail: mike@evilclownanimation.com
www.evilclownanimation.com
PRODUCER / DIRECTOR / ANIMATOR
Mike Dobson

HELIX DIGITAL INC.
Box 39, Stn. A, 222 George St., Sydney, NS B1P 6Y9
(902) 539-6999, FAX: (902) 539-2181
E-mail: rlorway@helixstudio.com, www.helixstudio.com
CONTACT
Richard Lorway

Digital production services / classical animation

VANTAGE COMMUNICATIONS
5657 Spring Garden Rd., Ste. 604, Park Lane Terraces
Halifax, NS B3J 3R4. (902) 423-2243, FAX: (902) 425-7866
CONTACT
Lori Covert

Vantage is a digitally focused, strategic communications company. Our in-house capabilities include: film and video production; 3D animation; digital post-production (3 AVID suites); website design, development and hosting; CD-ROM/DVD development and production, and multimedia production

WINGIT PRODUCTIONS INC.
1657 Barrington St., Ste. 518, Halifax, NS B3J 2A1
(902) 431-6398. www.wingit.ca
CONTACTS
Brian Howald, (902) 221-4128
Breandan McGrath, (902) 488-4355

Digital video post & effects

ONTARIO

ANIMATION GROUP LIMITED
142 Islington Ave., Ste. 115, Toronto, ON M8V 3B6
(416) 703-7860, FAX: (416) 253-0320
E-mail: agroup@istar.ca
PRESIDENT
Andrew Reid

ANIMETTE CANADA
210 Romfield Circuit, Thornhill, ON L3T 3J1
(905) 881-2099
CONTACTS
Alice & Milo Kubik

Classical 3D animation / children's puppet films

ARDEE PRODUCTIONS COMPUTER ANIMATION
492 Dunkirk Ave., Oshawa, ON L1H 3G7
Tel. & Fax: (905) 438-1947, Cell: (416) 414-9379
E-mail: rick@dolish.com, www.dolish.com
CREATIVE DIRECTOR
Rick Dolishny

AVARD
275 Lancaster St. W., Ste. 202, Kitchener, ON N2H 4V2
(519) 745-5044, FAX: (519) 745-0690
PRESIDENT
Bill Moffatt
CREATIVE DIRECTOR
David Lacey
ARTISTIC DIRECTOR
Paul Watson

Non-linear video / 3D animation / edit & effects / WS Betacam
SP . DVCam camera crew

AVTEL MEDIA COMMUNICATIONS INC.
1020 Brock Rd. S., Unit 1008, Pickering, ON L1W 3H2
(905) 837-9208 / (416) 410-5871 / (888) 522-8835
FAX: (905) 837-9204
PRESIDENT
Fred Pellegrino
V.P., SALES & MARKETING
Mike Allan

Non-linear editing suites / 2D & 3D animation / multimedia

AXYZ
425 Adelaide St. W., Toronto, ON M5V 1S4
(416) 504-0425, FAX: (416) 504-0045. www.axyzfx.com

Full-service digital off-and online / editing / compositing / matte
painting / computer animation

BEEVISION & HIVE PRODUCTIONS INC.
366 Adelaide St. E., Ste. 425, Toronto, ON M5A 3X9
(416) 868-1700 / (888) 868-6511, FAX: (416) 868-9512
www.beevision.com

Animation & web design / Jaleo & AVID suites

BOOMSTONE ANIMATION INC.
290 Picton Ave., Ste. 201, Ottawa, ON K1Z 8P8
(613) 725-3843, FAX: (613) 725-9327
E-mail: info@boomstone.com, www.boomstone.com
PRODUCER / DIRECTOR
Lee Williams
CREATIVE DIRECTOR
Rich Vanatte

CALIBRE DIGITAL PICTURES
65 Heward Ave., Bldg. A, Ste. 201, Toronto, ON M4M 2T5
(416) 531-8383, FAX: (416) 531-8083
E-mail: info@calibredigital.com, www.calibredigital.com
CONTACT
Pete Denomme

2D & 3D computer animation & fx / traditional & stop motion
animation / matte painting / compositing / character design

C.O.R.E. DIGITAL PICTURES
488 Wellington St. W., Ste. 600, Toronto, ON M5V 1E3
(416) 599-2673, FAX: (416) 599-1212
E-mail: info@coredp.com, Website: www.coredp.com
Exec. Producer
Samara Melanson
Pres. & Visual Effects Supervisor
Bob Munroe

Compositing, CGI, 2D / 3D animation, visual effects supervision

CRUSH INC.
439 Wellington St. W., 3rd Fl., Toronto, ON M5V 1E7
(416) 345-1936, FAX: (416) 345-1965
E-mail: joann@crushinc.com, www.crushinc.com
MANAGING DIRECTOR / EXEC. PRODUCER
Jo-ann Cook

Post production / CGI — commercials

DKP EFFECTS INC.
489 Queen St. E., Main Floor, Toronto, ON M5A 1V1
(416) 861-9269, FAX: (416) 363-3301
E-mail: info@dkp.com, www.dkp.com
CONTACTS
Dan Krech
Jackie Lynette
John Morch
Ted Rogers
Linda Gillies
Chad Nixon

EYES POST GROUP
320 King St. E., Toronto, ON M5A 1K6
(416) 363-3073, FAX: (416) 363-6335
E-mail: diane@eyespost.com, www.eyespost.com
PRESIDENT
Izhak Hinitz
V.P., GENERAL MANAGER
Diane Cuthbert
V.P., SALES & MARKETING
Steve Mayhew

Post & effects – commercials / TV / MOWs / features / documentaries / music videos

FILM EFFECTS INC.
21 Phoebe St., 2nd Flr., Toronto, ON M5T 1A8
(416) 598-3456 / (877) 598-3456, FAX: (416) 598-7895
E-mail: inquire@filmeffects.com, www.filmeffects.com
CONTACTS
George Furniotis
Susan Furniotis

Titles / opticals / effects / digital-to-film transfers / digital scanning / recording for 35mm & 16mm

FREELANCE F/X
45 Charles St., Lower Level, Toronto, ON M4Y 1S2
(416) 944-3881 / (905) 404-5423, FAX: (416) 922-9964
E-mail: todd.morgan@freelancefx.com, www.freelancefx.com
OWNER
Todd Morgan

Special effects, animation & graphics — film & TV

FUNBAG ANIMATION STUDIOS
55 Murray St., Ste. 400, Ottawa, ON K1N 5M3
(613) 562-3590, FAX: (613) 562-3518
www.funbag.com
V.P., CORPORATE AFFAIRS
Curtis Crawford
V.P., BUSINESS AFFAIRS
Frank Taylor

GURU ANIMATION STUDIO
Commodore Bldg., 317 Adelaide St. W., Ste. 903
Toronto, ON M5V 1P9. (416) 599-4878
www.gurustudio.com
CONTACT
Anne Deslauriers

HEADGEAR ANIMATION
35 McCaul St., Ste. 301, Toronto, ON M5T 1V7
(416) 408-2020, FAX: (416) 408-2011
www.headgearanimation.com
CONTACTS
Steve Angel
Julian Grey

IMARION INC.
67 Portland St., 2nd Fl., Toronto, ON M5V 2M9
(416) 597-2989, FAX: (416) 596-1344
E-mail: info@imarion.com, www.imarion.com

3D animation / compositing / editorial services

LARRY DOG PRODUCTIONS
2745 4th Ave. W., Owen Sound, ON N4K 6R2
(519) 371-3600, E-mail: wvandyk@bmts.com
CONTACTS
Wilf Van Dyk
Rob McLean

Animation

MAGNETIC NORTH
70 Richmond St. E., Ste. 100, Toronto, ON M5C 1N8
(416) 365-7622 / (800) 624-7678, FAX: (416) 365-2188
E-mail: sales@magpost.com, www.magpost.com
PRESIDENT
Bruce Grant, bgrant@magpost.com
DIRECTOR OF OPERATIONS
Peter Armstrong, parmstrong@magpost.com
SENIOR SALES REPRESENTATIVE
Peter Campbell, pcampbell@magpost.com

3D Studio Max, 2D graphics & effects. Specializing in long form television / design & creation of show openings & promotional pieces / enhancement of location special effects

MATRIX DESIGN & ANIMATION
355 Adelaide St. W., Ste. 2B, Toronto, ON M5V 1S2
(416) 340-7716, FAX: (416) 340-9873
E-mail: sulens@matrixpost.com, www.matrixpost.com
PRESIDENT
Scott Ulens

MERCURY FILMWORKS TORONTO
512 King St. E., Ste. 210, Toronto, ON M5A 1M1
(416) 848-6827 , FAX: (416) 848-6829
www.mercuryfilmworks.com
CONTACT
Michael O'Brien

Visual effects & animation for episodic television, feature film, commercials
See also British Columbia

MR. X INC.
35 McCaul St., Ste. 303, Toronto, ON M5T 1V7
(416) 595-6222, FAX: (416) 595-9122
PRESIDENT / VFX SUPERVISOR
Dennis Berardi
PARTNER / EXEC. PRODUCER
Sylvain Taillon
VFX SUPERVISOR / COMPOSITOR
Aaron Weintraub
VFX PRODUCER
Eric Robertson

Digital studio specializing in animation and visual effects

NELVANA LIMITED
(A Corus Entertainment Company)
42 Pardee Ave., Toronto, ON M6K 3H5
(416) 535-0935, FAX: (416) 530-2832. www.nelvana.com
Animation service production in TV series, specials, features, interactive CD-ROMs, in children's and family entertainment

HEAD OFFICE: 32 Atlantic Ave., Toronto, ON M6K 1X8
(416) 588-5571, FAX: (416) 588-5588
PRESIDENT, CORUS TELEVISION AND NELVANA
Paul Roberston

NOITAMINANIMATION
1500 Merivale Rd., 3rd Fl., Box 5053, Ottawa, ON K2C 3H3
(613) 226-3980, FAX: (613) 226-1851
www.noitaminanimation.com
DIRECTOR
Wade Howie
PRODUCER
Bill Buchanan

PRISMA LIGHT LTD.
762 Queen St. W., Toronto, ON M6J 1E9
(416) 504-4321, FAX: (416) 504-7325
E-mail: info@prismalight.com, www.prismalight.com

2D & 3D animation, full post production facilities

ROGERS PRODUCTIONS
333 Bloor St., 7th Fl., Toronto, ON M4W 1G9
(416) 935-6666, E-mail: rogersproductions@rci.rogers.com
www.rogersproductions.com
CONTACTS
Christa Dickenson
Lisa McLean Stellick

Full-service film and video production house / post-production services and creative concepts / 2D & 3D animation

SPIN PRODUCTIONS
620 King St. W., Toronto, ON M5V 1M6
(416) 504-8333, Fax: (416) 504-3876
E-mail: norm@spinpro.com / cristina@spinpro.com
CHAIRMAN & CEO
Norm Stangl
SALES & MARKETING EXECUTIVE
Cristina Palhares

THE STUDIO UPSTAIRS
(Creative Post Inc.)
510 Front St., Ste. 103, Toronto, ON M5V 1B8
(416) 979-8983, FAX: (416) 979-8246
E-mail: info@thestudioupstairs.com,
www.thestudioupstairs.com
EXEC. PRODUCER
Michael Churchill
VISUAL FX PRODUCER
Debbie Cooke

CGI animation / practical effects / matte painting

SUNDOG FILMS
530 Richmond St. W., Rear Bldg., Toronto, ON M5V 1Y4
(416) 504-2555, FAX: (416) 504-4545
E-mail: info@sundogfilms.ca
PRESIDENT
Wayne Trickett
VICE-PRESIDENT
Robin Trickett

Commercial production / special effects / Flame™

TOPIX / MAD DOG
35 McCaul St., Ste. 200, Toronto, ON M5T 1V7
(416) 971-7711, FAX: (416) 971-9277. www.topix.com
CONTACTS
Chris Wallace
Sylvain Taillon

3D animation / design / Inferno™ / post-production

TOYBOX TORONTO
(A Division of Command Post & Transfer Corp.)
179 John St., 8th Fl., Toronto, ON M5T 1X4
(416) 585-9995, FAX: (416) 979-0428
E-mail: bruce@compt.com, www.compt.com
CONTACT
Bruce Jones

Visual effects / 2D & 3D animation / motion control / HDTV /
digital film services

TRIANGLE
620 King St. W., Toronto, ON M5V 1M6
(416) 204-2880, FAX: (416) 204-2884
E-mail: inbox@trianglestudios.com, www.trianglestudios.com
PRESIDENT
Matthew Bush

VCR / PUREFIRE ACTIVE MEDIA
3055 Lenworth Dr., Mississauga, ON L4X 2G3
(905) 629-2553, FAX: (905) 629-3437
Website: www.vcractive.com / www.purefire.ca
CONTACT
Tony Patafio

Lightwave 3D / 3D Studio Max / green screen — corporate &
broadcast

WARREN-ANIMOTION PRODUCTIONS
31 Alexander St., Ste. 902, Toronto, ON M4Y 1B2
(416) 927-8408. E-mail: clayboy44@hotmail.com
Contact
Neil H. Warren

Clay animation / AV & design

WHATEVER SOLUTIONS & MEDIA
647 Neal Dr., Peterborough, ON K9J 6X7
(705) 749-6325 / (866) 779-7715, FAX: (705) 742-6129
E-mail: rmorton@whatevermedia.ca
www.whateversolutions.ca
CONTACT
Robert Morton

TV series, documentaries, animation &
post-production, commercials

QUÉBEC

BUZZ IMAGE GROUP INC. / GROUPE IMAGE BUZZ INC.
312 Sherbrooke St. E., Montréal, H2X 1E6
(514) 848-0579 / (800) 567-0200, FAX: (514) 848-6371
E-mail: info@buzzimage.com, www.buzzimage.com
PRESIDENT
Michel G. Desjardins
VFX PRODUCER/SUPERVISOR:
Morin
V.P. HD DEVELOPMENT
Pat Cormier

Animation / 2D & 3D visual effects /
E-cinema / video post-production

CINAR ANIMATION
1055 boul. René Lévesque E., Ste. 700, Montréal, QC H2L
4S5. (514) 843-8889, FAX: (514) 843-7488. www.cinar.com
CONTACT
Ken Beaulieu

Children's animated series

CINÉGROUPE
1010 Ste-Catherine E., 6th Fl., Montréal, QC H2L 2G3
(514) 849-5008, FAX: (514) 849-5001
E-mail: info@cinegroupe.ca, www.cinegroupe.com
PRESIDENT & CEO
Jacques Pettigrew
EXEC. V.P., CREATIVE AFFAIRS
Michel Lemire
DIRECTOR, BUSINESS AFFAIRS
Louise Perron St-Louis

Specializing in 2D and 3D animation, CGI and visual effects

MICHAEL MILLS PRODUCTIONS LIMITED
4492 Ste-Catherine St. W., Westmount, QC H3Z 1R7
(514) 931-7117, FAX: (514) 931-7099
PRESIDENT
Michael Mills

Traditional & computer animation

VOODOO ARTS
50 Queen St., Ste. 401, Montréal, QC H3C 2N5
(514) 866-3669, FAX: (514) 866-3683
E-Mail: public@voodooarts.com, www.voodooarts.com

Post-production / CGI animation / visual effects

CONSULTING SERVICES

ALEX FILMS
2684 Beaubien est, Montréal, QC H1Y 1G7
(514) 279-1616, FAX: (514) 279-9492
E-mail: simon.beaudry@alexfilms.com, www.alexfilms.com
PRESIDENT
Simon Beaudry

Provides services such as Québec's box office statistics,
screen tests and marketing research

CINE SOUND & PROJECTION INC.
258 Raleigh Ave., Scarborough, ON M1K 1A8
(416) 269-1066 / (800) 811-3611, FAX: (416) 269-7991
E-mail: cinesound@attcanada.ca
PRESIDENT
Doug Mahaney
TECHNICAL CONSULTING & SERVICE
Chuck Nascimento
CINEMA APPLICATION CONSULTANT
Jim Foote

KING CINEMA SERVICES LTD.
11507 – 120th St., Edmonton, AB T5G 2Y4
(780) 455-1622 / (800) 561-3581, FAX: (780) 455-0663
GENERAL MANAGER
Terry Yushchyshyn
SERVICE MANAGER
Eldon Wilson

SLIDE SCREEN ENTERTAINMENT INC.
61 Renwick Ave., Cambridge, ON N3C 2T5
(519) 658-6920, FAX: (519) 658-5684
E-mail: ibtsl@rogers.com, www.independentbooking.com
PRESIDENT
Barbara Ball
V.P. / SECRETARY-TREASURER
Eric Ball

Management services for independent theatres

LABS / TRANSFERS

ALBERTA

STUDIO POST
5305 Allard Way, Edmonton, AB T6H 5X8
(780) 436-4444, FAX: (780) 438-8520
GENERAL MANAGER
Mark Wood

Film-to-tape / tape-to-tape colour correction
Negative / processing / 16mm / Super 16mm / 35mm

BRITISH COLUMBIA

ALPHACINE
(A Division of Command Post & Transfer Corp.)
916 Davie St., Vancouver, BC V6Z 1B8
(604) 688-7757, FAX: (604) 688-0127
E-mail: darmstrong@compt.com, spotter@compt.com
www.compt.com
CONTACTS
Dave Armstrong
Sherri Potter

A motion picture laboratory providing complete lab services for feature film production, long and short filmmaking and commercials

DIGITAL FILM GROUP INC.
316 1st Ave., 2nd Fl., Vancouver, BC V5T1A9
(604) 879-5800. E-mail: support@digitalfilmgroup.com
www.digitalfilmgroup.com
V.P., Marketing
Patti-Jo Weiss, pj@digitalfilmgroup.net

Digital to film transfer services at an affordable price

RAINMAKER

50 W. 2nd Ave., Vancouver, BC V5Y 1B3
(604) 874-8700, FAX: (604) 874-1719. www.rainmaker.com
PRESIDENT / CEO
Bob Scarabelli
GEN. MANAGER
Barry Chambers
DIRECTOR OF OPERATIONS
K.T. McFadden
LAB GENERAL MANAGER
Rick Cooper
DIRECTOR OF VISUAL EFFECTS
Brian Moylan
LAB MANAGER
George Gliszczynski

Lab, post, visual effects — film, MOWs, TV, commercials, documentaries

ONTARIO

THE ASHLAND VIDEO CORP.

c/o Toronto Film Studios, 629 Eastern Ave., Stage 13
Toronto, ON M4M 1E4. (416) 405-9881, FAX: (416) 405-9941
E-mail: michaelball@ashlandvideo.com
www.ashlandvideo.com
PRESIDENT
Brian Ash
V.P., OPERATIONS
Mike Ball

Video (all formats), CD and DVD replication and DVD authoring.
Editing, standards conversion, duplication, closed captioning,
video transfers and master storage. Web services

AVTEL MEDIA COMMUNICATIONS INC.

1020 Brock Rd. S., Unit 1008, Pickering, ON L1W 3H2
(905) 837-9208 / (416) 410-5871 / (888) 522-8835
FAX: (905) 837-9204
PRESIDENT
Fred Pellegrino
V.P., SALES & MARKETING
Mike Allan

Film transfers / VHS duplication / standards conversion

BLACK & WHITE FILM FACTORY

40 Cawthra Ave., Toronto, ON M6N 5B3
(416) 763-0750, FAX: (416) 763-0847
E-mail: bwff@blackandwhitefilmfactory.com
www.blackandwhitefilmfactory.com
LAB MANAGER
Dragan Stojanovic

Full black & white service / 16mm colour reversal / film to video
transfer

CINE-BYTE IMAGING INC.

543 Richmond St. W., Ste. 126, Box 107
Toronto, ON M5V 1Y6, (416) 504-1010, FAX: (416) 504-9910
E-mail: info@cinebyte.com, www.cinebyte.com
PRESIDENT
Alan Bak

Transfer of digital data to & from film – scanning from original
35mm negative / film finish for commercials / digital opticals /
video to film

DELUXE LABORATORIES — POST PRODUCTION

350 Evans Ave., Etobicoke, ON M9Z 1K5
(416) 364-4321, FAX: (416) 591-6465. www.bydeluxe.com
PRESIDENT
Cyril R. Drabinsky
EXEC. V.P., TORONTO OPERATIONS
Joe Micek, joe.micek@bydeluxe.com
V.P., SALES
Paul Norris, paul.norris@bydeluxe.com
V.P., SALES & CLIENT SERVICES
Stan Ford, stan.ford@bydeluxe.com

THE LAB IN TORONTO

183 Carlaw Ave., Toronto, ON M4M 2S1
(416) 461-8090. www.thelab.on.ca
CONTACTS
Ed Higginson
Al Lindsay

Negative processing

MEDALLION PFA

(Division of Command Post & Transfer Corp.)
111 Peter St., 9th Fl., Toronto, ON M5V 2H1
(416) 593-0556, FAX: (416) 593-7201
E-mail: shippfa@compt.com, www.compt.com
CONTACT
Winston Phillips

Full service film lab / 35mm / 16mm / Super 35 & 16mm color /
35/16mm B&W procesing & complete lab finishing /
Dolby Digital Release Printing

PRECISION TRANSFER TECHNOLOGIES

47 Colborne St., Ste. 49, Toronto, ON M5E 1P8
(416) 366-7525, FAX: (416) 366-7119
E-mail: trevor@precisiontransfer.com,
www.precisiontransfer.com
SALES MANAGER
Trevor Tyre

Standards conversion / broadcast transfer / VHS duplication /
closed-captioning / DVD mastering / CD authoring / new media
CD/DVD replication / custom packaging

OTTAWA OFFICE: 22 Hamilton Ave. N., Ottawa, ON K1V 1B6
(613) 729-8987, FAX: (613) 729-5517
CLIENT SERVICES
Kim Hoffman, kim@precisiontransfer.com

SOHO DIGITAL FILM

26 Soho St., Toronto, ON M5T 1Z7. (416) 591-8408 / (888)
764-6344, FAX: (416) 591-3979. E-mail: britech@inforamp.net
PRESIDENT / DIRECTOR, OPERATIONS
Brian Hunt
V.P., MARKETING & SALES
Nick Paulozza

Digital film lab / film scanning & imaging / video to film

QUÉBEC

GLOBAL VISION / VISION GLOBALE

80 rue Queen, bur. 201, Montréal, QC H3C 2N5
(514) 879-0020 / (800) 667-7690, FAX: (514) 879-0047
www.visionglobale.ca
CHEFS DES VENTES
Paul Bellerose
Jean-Yves Deschênes
DIRECTRICE POTSYNCHRONISATION ET BRUITAGE
Diane Boucher
DIRECTRICE DOUBLAGE
Chantal Pagé
CHEF DE LA COMMUNICATION ET DU MARKETING
Lise-Marie Laporte
RESPONSABLE DU MARCHÉ AMÉRICAIN
Hubert Harel

Standards conversion / broadcast duplication / restoration –
film & video

U.S.A.OFFICE: 630 9th Ave., Ste. 302, New York, NY 10036
(212) 262-0020, FAX: (212) 262-4547

TECHNICOLOR CREATIVE SERVICES
2101 St. Catherine St. W., Ste. 300, Montréal, QC H3H 1M6
(514) 939-5060, FAX: (514) 939-5070
Sales: (514) 933-2200

POST-PRODUCTION FACILITIES

ALBERTA

CINE AUDIO VISUAL LTD.

10251 — 106th St., Edmonton, AB T5J 1H5
(780) 423-5081 / (877) 423-5081, FAX: (780) 424-0309

SECOND LOCATION: 131 – 5655 10th St. N.E., Calgary, AB
T2E 8W9. (403) 777-1070 / (877) 777-1070
FAX: (403) 777-1074. E-mail: post@cineav.com
www.cineav.com

DVD authoring / CDR/DVD replication & packaging / tape to
DVD archiving / non-linear editing / multi-format duplication

THE EDIT SUITE

2526 Battleford Ave. S.W., Ste. 232-234, Calgary, AB T3E 7J4
(403) 249-0601, FAX: (403) 249-0204
E-mail: info@editsuite.ca, www.editsuite.ca

Full service video production / film production / commercials

GAP PRODUCTIONS

147 RockyRidge Bay N.W., Calgary, AB T3G 4E7
(403) 263-0012, FAX: (403) 263-0016
E-mail: post@gapproductions.com, www.gapproductions.com

Online edit suites / animation / graphics / audio

WHITE IRON DIGITAL

1201 – 5th St. S.W., Ste. 533, Calgary, AB T2R 0Y6
(403) 298-4700, FAX: (403) 233-0528
E-mail: bvos@whiteiron.tv, www.whiteiron.tv

Uncompressed DI non-linear editing, graphics, animation, title
design for broadcast

BRITISH COLUMBIA

BLACK TUSK STUDIO
(The Mix Digital Media Group)
3009 Murray St., Unit 2, Port Moody, BC V3H 1X3
(604) 469-0881, FAX: (604) 469-2609
E-mail: btv@istar.ca, www.blacktusk.com
PRESIDENT
Mark Rohmann

Five non-linear editing, computer-based edit suites

COAST MOUNTAIN POST
1168 Hamilton St., Ste. 305, Vancouver, BC V6B 2S2
(604) 682-6578, FAX: (604) 682-3548
E-mail: edit@coastmtnpost.com
EDITORS
Deb Tregale
Ian Jenkins
Melanie Snagg

Editing – commercials / documentaries / music videos. Off-line and online

FINALE EDITWORKS
201 W. Second Ave., Vancouver, BC V5Y 3V5
(604) 876-7678, FAX: (604) 876-3299
www.finale-editworks.com
PRESIDENT
Don Thompson

Avid Non-linear off-line / component digital online edit suites / multi-format duplication / visual effects / post audio

THE LUNNY COMMUNICATIONS GROUP
1500 W. Georgia St., 20th Floor, Vancouver, BC V6G 2Z6
(604) 669-0333 , FAX: (604) 662-7500
E-mail: lcg@lunny.com, www.lunny.com
PRESIDENT
Shane Lunny
PRODUCTION SUPERVISOR
Tony Dean

Video / film — 35mm / multimedia / studio & post-production facilities

NORTHWEST IMAGING & F.X.
2339 Columbia St., Ste. 100, Vancouver, BC V5Y 3Y3
(604) 873-9330, FAX: (604) 873-9339
www.nwfx.com
VICE-PRESIDENT
Alex Tkach

PAN PRODUCTIONS
625 Hillside Ave., Ste. 1, Victoria, BC V8T 1Z1
(250) 389-6781, FAX: (250) 383-6514
E-mail: jim@panproductions.com
CONTACT
Jim Eidt

Full Service creative/production / Betacam field crews / full digital post facility & closed-captioning

RAINMAKER
50 W. 2nd Ave., Vancouver, BC V5Y 1B3
(604) 874-8700, FAX: (604) 874-1719
www.rainmaker.com
PRESIDENT / CEO
Bob Scarabelli
GENERAL MANAGER
Barry Chambers
DIRECTOR OF OPERATIONS
K.T. McFadden
LAB GENERAL MANAGER
Rick Cooper
DIRECTOR OF VISUAL EFFECTS
Brian Moylan
LAB MANAGER
George Gliszczynski

Lab, post, visual effects — film, MOWs, TV, commercials, documentaries

STAR FILM AND VIDEO PRODUCTIONS INC. – STARPOST
25 East 2nd Ave., 2nd Fl., Vancouver, BC V5T 1B3
(604) 879-1777, FAX: (604) 876-1087. www.starpost.tv

Digital Betacam / Betacam SP production / post / duplication

TOYBOX VANCOUVER
(A Division of Command Post & Transfer Corp.)
1090 Homer St., Ste. 500, Vancouver, BC V6B 2W9
(604) 689-1090, FAX: (604) 689-1003
E-mail: spotter@compt.com, djeffrey@compt.com,
mgrady@compt.com, jrobertson@compt.com
www.compt.com
CONTACTS
Sherri Potter
Doug Jeffrey
Michelle Grady
Jon Robertson

Toybox Vancouver offers all data, standard & high definition formats and provides a full range of visual effects and post-production for feature films, television movies, series & commercials

VIDEO PUBLISHING GROUP
1955 Wylie St., 2nd Fl., Vancouver, BC V5Y 3N7
(604) 874-2000 / (800) 667-7718, FAX: (604) 874-5005
E-mail: info@vpgroup.tv
PRESIDENT
Peter Sara
SALES CO-ORDINATOR
Ramin Shahidian

Non-linear off-line / on-line / digital video editing / CD-ROM, DVD-ROM pre-mastering

MANITOBA

FRANTIC FILMS
70 Arthur St., Ste. 300, Winnipeg, MB R3B 1G7
(204) 949-0070 , FAX: (204) 949-0050
E-mail: info@franticfilms.com, www.franticfilms.com
PRES. / CREATIVE DIRECTOR
Christopher Bond
C.E.O. / EXEC. PRODUCER
Jamie Brown
V.P. / Producer: Ken Zorniak

Cutting edge visual effects, 3D animation & post production

MIDCANADA PRODUCTION SERVICES INC.
509 Century St., Winnipeg, MB R3H 0L8
(204) 772-0368 / (800) 772-0368
E-mail: info@midcan.com, www.midcan.com

On-line digital linear & non-linear / HDTV down-conversion

NEW BRUNSWICK

CONNECTIONS PRODUCTIONS
91 Driscoll Cr., Moncton, NB E1E 4C8
(506) 382-3984, FAX: (506) 382-3980
CONTACTS
François Savoie: frank@connectionsproductions.com
Michael Savoie: mike@connectionsproductions.com

Leading-edge post-production services

INNOVATIVE VIDEO SOLUTIONS
76 Princess St., St. John, NB E2L 1K4
Tel. & Fax: (506) 693-4487
E-mail: darrell@videosolutions.ca / mike@videosolutions.ca
www.videosolutions.ca
CONTACTS
Darrell Bainbridge
Mike Burchill

Documentary, corporate & E.N.G. Betacam SP production including digital online video and audio post-production. Complete Betacam SP production, concept to completion

NORTHWEST TERRITORIES

YELLOWKNIFE FILMS LTD.
5021 — 53rd St., Yellowknife, NT X1A 1V5
(867) 873-8610, FAX: (867) 873-9405
E-mail: ykfilms@theEdge.ca
CONTACT
Alan Booth

Non-linear editing / stock footage

NOVA SCOTIA

SALTER STREET DIGITAL
2507 Brunswick St., Halifax, NS B3K 2Z5
(902) 422-6466 , FAX: (902) 423-7046
E-mail: rpower@salter.com, www.salterdigital.com
CONTACT
Rob Power

Full audio & video post-production services — film & television

VANTAGE COMMUNICATIONS
5657 Spring Garden Rd., Ste. 604, Park Lane Terraces
Halifax, NS B3J 3R4. (902) 423-2243, FAX: (902) 425-7866
CONTACT
Lori Covert
Vantage is a digitally focused, strategic communications company, with post services that include in-house 3D anima-tion, digital post (3 AVID suites), CD-Rom & DVD development and production

WINGIT PRODUCTIONS INC.
1657 Barrington St., Ste. 518, Halifax, NS B3J 2A1
(902) 431-6398
CONTACT
Brian Howald (902) 221-4128
Breandan McGrath (902) 488-4355

Digital video post & effects

ONTARIO

AVTEL MEDIA COMMUNICATIONS INC.
1020 Brock Rd. S., Unit 1008, Pickering, ON L1W 3H2
(905) 837-9208 / (416) 410-5871 / (888) 522-8835
FAX: (905) 837-9204
PRESIDENT
Fred Pellegrino
V.P., SALES & MARKETING
Mike Allan

Non-linear editing suites / 2D & 3D animation / multimedia

AXYZ
425 Adelaide St. W., Toronto, ON M5V 1S4
(416) 504-0425, FAX: (416) 504-0045. www.axyzfx.com

Full-service digital off-and online

BARBARA SWIFT NEGATIVE CUTTING INC.
181 Carlaw Ave., Ste. 256, Toronto, ON M4M 2S1
(416) 462-0395, FAX: (416) 462-0612

16 and 35mm editing suites

BEEVISION & HIVE PRODUCTIONS INC.
366 Adelaide St. E., Ste. 425, Toronto, ON M5A 3X9
(416) 868-1700 / (888) 868-6511, FAX: (416) 868-9512
www.beevision.com
Jaleo & AVID suites

BLUE HIGHWAY
26 Soho St., Ste. 303, Toronto, ON M5T 1Z7
(416) 597-2474, FAX: (416) 597-2594
E-mail: mail@bluehighway.ca
EXECUTIVE PRODUCER
Wendy Linton
EDITORS
Andy Attalai
Leo Zaharatos
Joanne Shaw

Creative editorial specializing in television commercials and music videos

BROADCAST CAPTIONING & CONSULTING SERVICES INC. (BCCS)
150 Laird Dr., Ste. 302, Toronto, ON M4G 3V7
(416) 696-1534, FAX: (416) 421-7603
www.closedcaptioning.com
Contact
Brian Hallahan

On-line (real time) / off-line (post-edit) / post display closed captioning

BULLET DIGITAL
219 Dufferin St., Toronto, ON M6K 3J1
(416) 536-9100, FAX: (416) 536-2898
www.bulletdigital.com
PRESIDENT
Rob Engman
DUPLICATION MANAGER
Jason Cook
DIRECTOR OF MEDIA SERVICES
Pat Batrynchuk
EXEC. PRODUCER
Janine Harris

Post-production / duplication / 7 AVID suites / system 7 & 10 / off-line / on-line / DVD authoring / compositing / episodic television series

CFA COMMUNICATIONS LTD.
782 King St. W., Toronto, ON M5V 1N6
(416) 504-5071, FAX: (416) 504-7390
www.cfacommunications.com

Online – non-linear, digital SoftImage, DPS / Off-line – Avid, VHS

CHARLES STREET VIDEO (CSV)
65 Bellwoods Ave., Toronto, ON M6J 3N4
(416) 603-6564, E-mail: csv@charlesstreetvideo.com
CONTACT
Ross Turnbull

A production and post-production access centre with Avid, Pro Tools, mini-DV & Betacam facilities for video, film and video artists.

CREATIVE POST INC.
510C Front St. W., Toronto, ON M5V 1B8
(416) 979-7678, FAX: (416) 979-8246
E-mail: info@creativepostinc.com, www.creativepostinc.com
V.P., OPERATIONS
Ken MacNeil
V.P., MARKETING & SALES
Howie Gold

Film / broadcast / corporate – digital linear and non-linear standard definition suites / hi-definition post

CRUSH INC.
439 Wellington St. W., 3rd Fl., Toronto, ON M5V 1E7
(416) 345-1936, FAX: (416) 345-1965
E-mail: joann@crushinc.com, www.crushinc.com
MANAGING DIRECTOR / EXEC. PRODUCER
Jo-ann Cook

Post production / CGI — commercials

DELUXE LABORATORIES — POST PRODUCTION
424 Adelaide St. E., Toronto, ON M5A 1N4
(416) 364-4321, FAX: (416) 364-0615
www.bydeluxe.com
EXEC. V.P. & GENERAL MANAGER, SOUND & VIDEO
Dan McLellan, daniel.mclellan@bydeluxe.com
V.P., VIDEO
Tony Meerakker, tony.meerakker@bydeluxe.com
V.P., SALES & CLIENT SERVICES
Stan Ford, stan.ford@bydeluxe.com
SOUND SALES EXECUTIVE
Julie Weinstein, julie.weinstein@bydeluxe.com
VIDEO SALES MANAGER
Russ Robertson, russ.robertson@bydeluxe.com

DREAMSCAPE VIDEO EDITING
645 Manning Ave., Toronto, ON M6G 2W2
(416) 534-7464. E-mail: bsp@interlog.com
CONTACT
Brock Fricker

Betacam / VX1000 / Media 100 non-linear editing. Post audio services. See Brock Sound

THE D SQUARED PICTURE COMPANY
1179A King St. W., Ste. 018, Toronto, ON M6K 3C5
(416) 599-4464, FAX: (416) 599-4463
E-mail: info@d2pic.com, www.d2pic.com
EXEC. PRODUCERS
David Taylor,
Dan Kaminsky

Creative post-production services

EYES POST GROUP
320 King St. E., Toronto, ON M5A 1K6
(416) 363-3073, FAX: (416) 363-6335
E-mail: diane@eyespost.com, www.eyespost.com
PRESIDENT
Izhak Hinitz
V.P., GENERAL MANAGER
Diane Cuthbert
V.P., SALES & MARKETING
Steve Mayhew

Post & effects – commercials / TV / MOWs / features / documentaries / music videos

THE FEARLESS FILM & VIDEO CORPORATION
141 Bathurst St., Ste. 202, Toronto, ON M5V 2R2
(416) 504-9694, FAX: (416) 504-9693
PRESIDENT
Al Maciulis
SR. EDITOR
Andrew Mandziuk
OFFICE MANAGER
Delphine Roussel

FLASHCUT EDITING
504 Wellington St. W., 3rd Fl., Toronto, ON M5V 1E3
(416) 977-2401, FAX: (416) 977-4910
GENERAL MANAGER
Mary Beth Odell
EXEC. PRODUCER
Melissa Kahn

Post-production – commercials

HILLS PRODUCTION SERVICES
2440 Industrial St., Burlington, ON L7P 1A5
(905) 335-1146, FAX: (905) 335-1241
E-mail: robhill@hillsvideo.com, www.hillsvideo.com
PRESIDENT
Rob Hill
EXEC. PRODUCER
Gerry Milinkovic
SENIOR EDITOR
John Luff

IMARION INC.
67 Portland St., 2nd Fl., Toronto, ON M5V 2M9
(416) 597-2989, FAX: (416) 596-1344
E-mail: info@imarion.com, www.imarion.com

3D animation / compositing / editorial services

JAZZY POST LIMITED
45 Charles St. E., Lower Level, Toronto, ON M4Y 1S2
(416) 922-9760, FAX: (416) 922-9964
PRESIDENT
Jesse Mills
OFFICE MANAGER
Jo Bradley

Linear & non-linear editing facilities

MAGNETIC NORTH
70 Richmond St. E., Ste. 100, Toronto, ON M5C 1N8
(416) 365-7622 / (800) 624-7678, FAX: (416) 365-2188
E-mail: sales@magpost.com, www.magpost.com
PRESIDENT
Bruce Grant, bgrant@magpost.com
DIRECTOR OF OPERATIONS
Peter Armstrong, parmstrong@magpost.com
SENIOR SALES REPRESENTATIVE
Peter Campbell, pcampbell@magpost.com

Post-production for film & TV – linear & non-linear editing

MANTA DSP / MEDALLION PFA
(Division of Command Post & Transfer Corp.)
49 Ontario St., Toronto, ON M5A 2V1
(416) 364-1422, FAX: (416) 364-7400
E-mail: gracec@compt.com, kevinb@compt.com
www.compt.com
CONTACTS
Grace Carnale-Davis
Kevin Barendregt

Film to videotape transfers / digital editing & compositing / 2D
& 3D animation and effects / transfer / layback & duplication /
high definition / NTSC & PAL

MPI PRODUCTIONS LTD.
37 Madison Ave., Toronto, ON M5R 2S2
(416) 967-1288, FAX: (416) 967-7288
E-mail: mpi@attcanada.ca

On-line & off-line – Avid Media / Film Composer

THE MPSL GROUP
9 Prince Andrew Pl., Toronto, ON M3C 2H2
(416) 449-7614, FAX: (416) 449-9239
E-mail: info@mpsl.com, www.mpsl.com
Betacam SP on-line linear & Pinnacle Reeltime non-linear
online edit suites

PANIC & BOB
312 Adelaide St. W., 2nd Fl., Toronto, ON M5V 1R2
(416) 504-2020, FAX: (416) 504-0266
www.panicandbob.com
EXEC. PRODUCER
Samantha McLaren

Post / creative editorial – commercials

POST PRODUCERS DIGITAL LTD.
111 Berkeley St., Toronto, ON M5A 2W8
(416) 363-4662, FAX: (416) 363-2421
Website: www.ppd.ca
EDITOR / PRESIDENT
Al Mitchell

Non-linear online & offline

PRISMA LIGHT LTD.
762 Queen St. W., Toronto, ON M6J 1E9
(416) 504-4321, FAX: (416) 504-7325
E-mail: info@prismalight.com, www.prismalight.com

2D & 3D animation, full post production facilities

ROCKET DIGITAL POST & SOUND
(A Division of MIJO Corporation)
635 Queen St. E., Toronto, ON M4M 1G4
(416) 778-6852, FAX: (416) 778-9926. www.mijo.ca
V.P., SALES & MARKETING
Cynthia Littler
SALES REPRESENTATIVE
Garth Holding

Digital video editing, digital audio recording & mixing, DVD
authoring & encoding, Quicktime™ video for multimedia web,
extensive sound FX and music libraries

ROGERS PRODUCTIONS
333 Bloor St., 7th Fl., Toronto, ON M4W 1G9
(416) 935-6666. E-mail: rogersproductions@rci.rogers.com
www.rogersproductions.com
CONTACTS
Christa Dickenson
Lisa McLean Stellick

Full-service film and video production house / post-production
services and creative concepts / 2D & 3D animation

SCENE BY SCENE
259 Danforth Ave., Toronto, ON M4K 1N2
(416) 463-5060 / (800) 439-5060, FAX: (416) 463-3324
E-mail: bill@sbys.com, www.sbys.com
CONTACT
Bill Kinnon

Non-linear edit suites / linear digital edit suite (D-Beta) / compositing / animation & effects

SCHOOL
379 Adelaide St. W., 2nd Fl., Toronto, ON M5V 1S5
(416) 907-9070, FAX: (416) 907-9079
www.schoolediting.com
CONTACT
Sarah Brooks
EDITORS
Alison Gordon
Griff Henderson
David Hicks
Mark Morton
Marcus Valentin
Chris Van Dyke

Commercial & music video post-production

SIM POST
One Atlantic Ave., Ste. 110, Toronto, ON M6K 3E7
(416) 979-9958, E-mail: info@simpost.com
www.simpost.com
Editing suites customized to post production requirements

SOUND VENTURE PRODUCTIONS
126 York St. , Ste. 219, Ottawa, ON K1N 5T5
(613) 241-5111 ext. 248, FAX: (613) 241-5010
E-mail: tim@soundventure.com, www.soundventure.com
V.P. POST PRODUCTION SERVICES
Tim Joyce

Video post-production

SUNDOG FILMS
530 Richmond St. W., Rear Bldg., Toronto, ON M5V 1Y4
(416) 504-2555, FAX: (416) 504-4545
E-mail: info@sundogfilms.ca
PRESIDENT
Wayne Trickett
VICE-PRESIDENT
Robin Trickett

Post production / visual effects

TATTERSALL CASABLANCA
(An Alliance Atlantis Company)
22 Boston Ave., Toronto, ON M4M 2T9
(416) 461-2550, FAX: (416) 461-9709
www.tattersallcasablanca.com
CEO
Chuck Ferkranus
SALES DIRECTOR
Mike McConnell
BUSINESS MANAGER
Peter E. Gibson

Recording, sound editing & mixing for feature films, mini-
series, MOWs, television, documentaries

THIRD FLOOR EDITING
410 Adelaide St. W., Ste. 410, Toronto, ON M5V 1S8
(416) 504-6004, FAX: (416) 504-5650
OWNER / EDITOR
Richard Unruh
EXEC. PRODUCER
Jennie Montford

Editing

TOPIX / MAD DOG
35 McCaul St., Ste. 200, Toronto, ON M5T 1V7
(416) 971-7711, FAX: (416) 971-9277
www.topix.com
CO-PRESIDENTS
Chris Wallace
Sylvain Taillon

Post production / animation / compositing

TOYBOX TORONTO
179 John St., 8th Fl., Toronto, ON M5T 1X4
(416) 585-9995, FAX: (416) 979-0428
E-mail: asykes@compt.com, www.compt.com
CONTACT
Andy Sykes

Toybox offers one of Canada's best selections of visual effects
toys with a creative team from around the world. Services
include: visual effects / motion control / HDTV / cinemaHD /
cinemaDI / digital film services / 3D & 2D animation / editorial /
transfer

TRIANGLE
620 King St. W.,Toronto, ON M5V 1M6
(416) 204-2880, FAX: (416) 204-2884
E-mail: inbox@trianglestudios.com, www.trianglestudios.com
PRESIDENT
Matthew Bush

TRINITY SQUARE VIDEO
401 Richmond St. W., Ste. 376, Toronto, ON M5V 3A8
(416) 593-1332, FAX: (416) 593-0958
E-mail: info@trinitysquarevideo.com
www.trinitysquarevideo.com
EXEC. DIRECTOR
Roy Mitchell

TV2GO INC.
250 Ferrand Dr., Ste. 402, Toronto, ON M3C 3G8
(416) 696-9633 / (800) 305-2999, FAX: (416) 696-9640
Mobile Betacam editing / mobile satellite uplink / satellite earth station

VCR / PUREFIRE ACTIVE MEDIA
3055 Lenworth Dr., Mississauga, ON L4X 2G3
(905) 629-2553, FAX: (905) 629-3437
www.vcractive.com / www.purefire.ca
CONTACT
Tony Patafio
Broadcast / documentary / corporate / multimedia editing services

VIDEOGENIC CORP.
431 Richmond St. E., Toronto, ON M5A 1R1
(416) 360-3739, FAX: (416) 360-0750
E-mail: videogenic@bigfilm.ca
CONTACTS
Dave Greenham
Angie Colgoni

QUÉBEC

BUZZ IMAGE GROUP INC. / GROUPE IMAGE BUZZ INC.
312 Sherbrooke St. E., Montréal, H2X 1E6
(514) 848-0579 / (800) 567-0200, FAX: (514) 848-6371
E-mail: info@buzzimage.com, www.buzzimage.com
PRESIDENT
Michel G. Desjardins
V.P., CUSTOMER SERVICE
Joanne Vincelette, joannev@buzzimage.com
POST-PRODUCTION CO-ORDINATOR
Annie Godin, annieg@buzzimage.com
Video post-production / animation / 2D & 3D visual effects

CINÉGROUPE
1010 Ste-Catherine E., 6th Fl., Montréal, QC H2L 2G3
(514) 849-5008, FAX: (514) 849-5001
E-mail: info@cinegroupe.ca, www.cinegroupe.com
PRESIDENT & CEO.
Jacques Pettigrew
EXEC. V.P., CREATIVE AFFAIRS
Michel Lemire
DIRECTOR, BUSINESS AFFAIRS
Louise Perron St-Louis
POST-PRODUCTION DIRECTOR
André-Gilles Gagné
Dubbing studio / sound recording & mixing / film & video editing

COTE POST PRODUCTION LTD.
218 rue St-Paul ouest, Montréal, QC H2Y 1Z9
(514) 284-0674, FAX: (514) 284-6712
PRÉSIDENT
Bob Côté
Video post-production services

GLOBAL VISION / VISION GLOBALE
80 rue Queen, bur. 201, Montréal, QC H3C 2N5
(514) 879-0020 / (800) 667-7690, FAX: (514) 879-0047
www.visionglobale.ca
CHEFS DES VENTES
Paul Bellerose
Jean-Yves Deschênes
DIRECTRICE POTSYNCHRONISATION ET BRUITAGE
Diane Boucher
DIRECTRICE DOUBLAGE
Chantal Pagé
CHEF DE LA COMMUNICATION ET DU MARKETING
Lise-Marie Laporte
RESPONSABLE DU MARCHÉ AMÉRICAIN
Hubert Harel
Post-production services: film services / video editing / translation / closed captioning / video subtitling / restoration / stock footage

U.S.A. OFFICE: 630 9th Ave., Ste. 302, New York, NY 10036
(212) 262-0020, FAX: (212) 262-4547

VIDÉOGRAPHE PRODUCTION
4550 rue Garnier, Montréal, QC H2J 3S7
(514) 521-2116, FAX: (514) 521-1676
E-mail: production@videographe.qc.ca
CONTACT
Marc Fournel
Multimedia and video production centre for independent artists.
Digital cameras and editing suites

VOODOO ARTS
50 Queen St., Ste. 401, Montréal, QC H3C 2N5
(514) 866-3669, FAX: (514) 866-3683
E-Mail: public@voodooarts.com, www.voodooarts.com
Post production / CGI animation / visual effects

WHALLEY-ABBEY DIGITAL STUDIOS, INC.
1303 Greene Ave., Ste. 305, Westmount, QC H3Z 2A7
(514) 846-1940, FAX: (514) 846-1550
E-mail: andy@painted-house.com
CONTACT
Andrew Kemp
Non-linear digital post-production / Avid suites

SASKATCHEWAN

JAVA POST PRODUCTION
2206 Dewdney Ave., Ste. 402, Regina, SK S4R 1H3
(306) 777-0150, FAX: (306) 352-8858
E-mail: jack.javapost@accesscomm.ca
POST SUPERVISOR
Jack Tunnicliffe

PROTRAX DIGITAL
2153 Cameron St., Regina, SK S4T 2V7
(306) 781-7331, FAX: (306) 258-0309
E-mail: butler@protrax.org
CONTACT
Kathy Hanna

SOUND SERVICES

ALBERTA

BETA SOUND RECORDERS LTD.
10534 — 109th St., Edmonton, AB T2H 3B2
(780) 424-3063, FAX: (780) 425-2789
www.betasound.ca
CONTACTS
Gary Koliger, gary@betasound.ca
Jerry Woolsey, jwoolsey@telusplanet.net

BLACKMAN PRODUCTIONS INC.
4004 — 97th St., Ste. 32, Edmonton, AB T6E 6N1
(780) 435-5859, FAX: (780) 436-6234
E-mail: info@blackmanproductions.com
PRESIDENT
Perry Blackman
OFFICE MANAGER
Donna Blackman
Audio post – TV and film

BLT PRODUCTIONS LTD.
112 West 8th Avenue, Vancouver, BC V5Y 1N2
(604) 873-6559, FAX: (604) 873-0122
e-mail: blt@intergate.ca
CONTACTS
Josanne Lovick
Steve Barlow
Voice animation and services in the following areas: casting / dialogue recording / ADR / storyboard sound effects / dialogue confirmation / layouts / production management / music scoring / administration / editing and mag transfer / final audio mix and co-financing

THE EDIT SUITE
2526 Battleford Ave. S.W., Ste. 232-234, Calgary, AB T3E 7J4
(403) 249-0601, FAX: (403) 249-0204
E-mail: info@editsuite.ca, www.editsuite.ca
Full service video production / film production / commercials

GAP PRODUCTIONS
1807 – 18A St. S.W., Calgary, AB T2T 4W1
(403) 263-0012 / (800) 959-2427, FAX: (403) 263-0016
E-mail: post@gapproductions.com www.gapproductions.com
Most audio formats / library of production music, sound effects / announce booth

THE OCEAN SOUND CORPORATION
1758 W. 2nd Ave., Vancouver, BC V6J 1H6
(604) 733-1000, FAX: (604) 733-1500
Email: alext@oceanmedia.com

CONTACT
Alexandra Turner

The Ocean Group of Companies specializes in various aspects of production in both a co-production capacity and as a group of service companies. The Ocean post group specializes in creating audio and video product.

SYNC SPOT DIGITAL AUDIO POST
812A — 16th Ave. S.W., Calgary, AB T2R 0S9
(403) 228-2199, FAX: (403) 228-4579
E-mail: info@syncspot.ca, www.syncspot.ca
Film, video, radio, advertising & multimedia

TWISTED PAIR SOUND
7220 Fisher St., Ste. 360, Calgary, AB T2H 2H8
(403) 258-0207, FAX: (403) 258-0309
E-mail: pat@twistedpairsound.com
www.twistedpairsound.com
CONTACT
Pat Butler

Full service audio – film & video / commercial TV & radio

WOLF WILLOW SOUND INC.
9336 – 49 St., Edmonton, AB T6B 2L7
(780) 448-9653, FAX: (780) 428-3985
E-mail: contact@wolfwillowsound.com
www. wolfwillowsound.com
CONTACTS
Ian Armstrong
John Blerot

Complete audio post, location sound

BRITISH COLUMBIA

AIRWAVES SOUND DESIGN LTD.
25 E. 2nd Ave., 2nd Fl., Vancouver, BC V5T 1B3
(604) 875-0114, FAX: (604) 876-1087
Email:airwaves@smartt.com
CONTACTS
Alex Downie
Derick Cobden

Audio post-production facility specializing in creating customized soundtracks for feature films, movies of the week, documentaries, TV series and animation

BURKEVILLE PRODUCTIONS
34 W. 8th Ave., Vancouver, BC V5Y 1M7
(604) 873-3805, FAX: (604) 873-4295
E-mail: info@burkevilleproductions.com
www.burkevilleproductions.com
CONTACT
Ken Burke

Sound design / audio post for film & television / library music & effects

DICK & ROGER'S SOUND STUDIO LTD.
190 Alexander St., Ste.301, Vancouver, BC V6A 1B5
(604) 873-5777 , FAX: (604) 872-1356
E-mail: info@dickandrogers.com
www.dickandrogers.com
CONTACTS
Dick Abbott
Roger Monk

Dialogue breakdown for animation / 5.1 channel mixing / looping ADR

FINALE EDITWORKS
201 W. Second Ave., Vancouver, BC V5Y 3V5
(604) 876-7678, FAX: 876-3299. www.finale-editworks.com
PRESIDENT
Don Thompson

Avid non-linear off-line / component digital online edit suites / multi-format duplication / visual effects / post audio

GREENHOUSE STUDIOS
3955 Graveley St., Burnaby, BC V5C 3T4
(604) 291-0978, FAX: (604) 291-6909
E-mail: bookings@ greenhouse-studios.com,
www.greenhouse-studios.com
STUDIO MANAGER
Bruce Levens
HEAD OF TECHNICAL DEPT.
Corey Dixon
BUSINESS AFFAIRS
Roger Levens
BOOKING MANAGER
Lindsay Reinelt

Recording for film / video

GRIFFITHS GIBSON & RAMSAY PRODUCTIONS
201 W. 7th Ave., Vancouver, BC V5Y 1L9
(604) 873-3811, FAX: (604) 873-5880. www.ggrp.com
CONTACTS
Gord Lord

Peter Clarke
Brian Griffiths
Miles Ramsay

Music & sound design / audio post

PINEWOOD SOUND
Downtown Studios, 1119 Homer St., Vancouver, BC V6B 2Y1
(604) 669-6900, FAX: (604) 669-0040
E-mail: info@pinewoodsound.com
www.pinewoodsound.com
CONTACT
Jean Turner

Full service audio post production

LIONS GATE STUDIO LOCATION
555 Brooksbank Ave., N. Vancouver, BC V7J 3S5
(604) 983-5200, FAX: (604) 983-5204

POST MODERN SOUND INC.
1720 W. 2nd Ave., Vancouver, BC V6J 1H6
(604) 736-7474, FAX: (604) 738-7768
www.postmodernsound.com
PRESIDENT
Menashe Arbel
V.P. / DIR. OF OPERATIONS
Mark Scott

Audio post / TV & film

THE SOUND KITCHEN INC.
1682 W. 7th Ave., Ste. 100, Vancouver, BC V6J 4S6
(604) 681-6068, FAX (604) 687-2387
E-mail: info@soundkitchenstudios.com
www.soundkitchenstudios.com
PRINCIPALS
Judy Harnett
Paul Airey

Audio post for video, TV series, commercials

WAYNE KOZAK AUDIO PRODUCTIONS
1525 W. 8th Ave., Ste. 300, Vancouver, BC V6J 1T5
(604) 736-8667, FAX: (604) 739-8661
PRODUCER / OWNER
Wayne Kozak
CO-ORDINATOR
Janice Bulger

Audio post / music

MANITOBA

CHANNELS AUDIO & POST PRODUCTION
697 Sargent Ave., Winnipeg, MB R3E 0A8
(204) 786-5578, FAX: (204) 772-5191
ENGINEERS
John Schritt
Howard Rissin
Greg Boboski

MIDCANADA PRODUCTION SERVICES INC.
509 Century St., Winnipeg, MB R3H 0L8
(204) 772-0368. E-mail: info@midcan.com
www.midcan.com

Dolby 5.1 THX certified recording studio / ProTools / ProControl Mix Plus system

NEW BRUNSWICK

INNOVATIVE VIDEO SOLUTIONS
76 Princess St., St. John, NB E2L 1K4
Tel. & Fax: (506) 693-4487
E-mail: darrell@videosolutions.ca / mike@videosolutions.ca
www.videosolutions.ca
CONTACTS
Darrell Bainbridge
Mike Burchill

Documentary, corporate & E.N.G. Betacam SP production including digital online video and audio post-production. Complete Betacam SP production, concept to completion

NOVA SCOTIA

SALTER STREET DIGITAL
2507 Brunswick St., Halifax, NS B3K 2Z5
(902) 422-6466, FAX: (902) 423-7046
E-mail: rpower@salter.com, www.salterdigital.com
CONTACT
Rob Power

Full audio & video post-production services — film & television

ONTARIO

BULLET DIGITAL
219 Dufferin St., Toronto, ON M6K 3J1
(416) 536-9100, FAX: (416) 536-2898
www.bulletdigital.com

PRESIDENT
Rob Engman
DUPLICATION MANAGER
Jason Cook
DIRECTOR OF MEDIA SERVICES
Pat Batrynchuk
EXEC. PRODUCER
Janine Harris

ProTools 5.0 / MIDI production system / isolated recording booth / editing & mixing for film & television soundtracks

BROCK SOUND POST AUDIO
576 Manning Ave., Toronto, ON M6G 2V9
(416) 534-7464, E-mail: bsp@interlog.com
MANAGER / ENGINEER
Brock Fricker

Post audio for video / original music & sound effects for films & TV. Video editing services
See Dreamscape

CFA COMMUNICATIONS LTD.
782 King St. W., Toronto, ON M5V 1N6
(416) 504-5071, FAX: (416) 504-7390
E-mail: info@cfacommunications.com
www.cfacommunications.com

Audio recording, mixing, playback – ProTools

CHERRY BEACH SOUND
33 Villiers St., Toronto, ON M5A 1A9
(416) 461-4224, FAX: (416) 461-4607
E-mail: cherrybeachsound@bellnet.ca
www.cherrybeachsound.com

Dialogue to picture / commercial voice-over / post-audio editing & mixing / sound restoration / custom & stock music

CRUNCH RECORDING
157 Princess St., 3rd Fl., Toronto, ON M5A 4M4
(416) 214-2666, FAX: (416) 214-9912
CONTACTS
Joe Serafini
Steve Pecile

Post audio / music production — commercials / feature films

DELUXE LABORATORIES — POST PRODUCTION
424 Adelaide St. E., Toronto, ON M5A 1N4
(416) 364-4321, FAX: (416) 364-0615
www.bydeluxe.com
EXEC. V.P. & GENERAL MANAGER, SOUND & VIDEO
Dan McLellan, daniel.mclellan@bydeluxe.com
V.P., SALES & CLIENT SERVICES
Stan Ford, stan.ford@bydeluxe.com
SOUND SALES EXECUTIVE
Julie Weinstein, julie.weinstein@bydeluxe.com
VIDEO SALES MANAGER
Russ Robertson, russ.robertson@bydeluxe.com

DESCHAMPS RECORDING STUDIOS
314 Dundas St. W., Toronto, ON M5T 1G5
(416) 977-5050, FAX: (416) 977-6945
E-mail: claude@deschampsstudios.com
CONTACT
Claude Deschamps

Audio post —TV / radio / documentary / film

GAPC — GENERAL ASSEMBLY PRODUCTION CENTRE
14 Colonnade Rd., Ste. 180, Ottawa, ON K2E 7M6
(613) 723-3316 , FAX: (613) 723-8583. www.gapc.com
PRESIDENT
Ken Stewart
FILM & TELEVISION SERVICES
André del Castillo
BROADCAST / ENTERTAINMENT
Hoda Elatawi

Digital audio post production for film & television — sweetening, sound design, music composition

GRAYSON MATTHEWS
468 Queen St. E., Toronto, ON M5A 1T7
(416) 681-9330, FAX: (416) 681-9331
E-mail: elizabeth@graysonmatthews.com
www.graysonmatthews.com
CONTACTS
Elizabeth Taylor
Dave Sorbara
Tom Westin

Music & sound design

JAZZY POST LIMITED
45 Charles St. E., Lower Level, Toronto, ON M4Y 1S2
(416) 922-9760 , FAX: (416) 922-9964
PRESIDENT
Jesse Mills
OFFICE MANAGER
Jo Bradley

Audio post / linear & non-linear editing facilities / animation

KEEN MUSIC VOICE & SOUND DESIGN
119 Spadina Ave., 7th Fl., Toronto, ON M5V 2L1
(416) 977-9845, FAX: (416) 977-4412
www.keenmusic.ca
PRODUCTION MANAGER
Andrea Koziol
CONTACTS
Thomas Neuspiel
Keith Power
Alun Davies
George Spanos

Music / voice / sound design

KINCK SOUND
128 Manville Rd., Unit 22, Toronto, ON M1L 4J5
(416) 288-9766 / (888) 245-4625, FAX: (416) 288-9469
E-mail: info@kincksound.com, www.kincksound.com

Audio post for MOWs, television series & commercials / custom music

KITCHEN SYNC AUDIO DIGITAL
45 Charles St. E., Lower Level 1, Toronto, ON M4Y 1S2
(416) 926-1444, FAX: (416) 926-0259
E-mail: ksync@istar.ca
CONTACT
Russell Walker

Sound editing, mixing, voice-over

KRYSTAL MUSIC & SOUND DESIGN
317 Adelaide St. W., Ste. 401, Toronto, ON M5V 2P9
(416) 217-0488, FAX: (416) 217-0484
E-mail: lisa@krystalmusic.com, www.krystalmusic.com
PRESIDENT
David Krystal
PRODUCTION CO-ORDINATOR
Lisa Cameron

Audio production / original music — film, TV, commercials

MAGNETIC NORTH
70 Richmond St. E., Ste. 100, Toronto, ON M5C 1N8
(416) 365-7622 / (800) 624-7678, FAX: (416) 365-2188
E-mail: sales@magpost.com, www.magpost.com
PRESIDENT
Bruce Grant, bgrant@magpost.com
DIRECTOR OF OPERATIONS
Peter Armstrong, parmstrong@magpost.com
SENIOR SALES REPRESENTATIVE
Peter Campbell, pcampbell@magpost.com

Post-production for film & TV — audio mixing, ADR, audio editorial, music production

MANTA DSP / MEDALLION PFA
(A Division of Command Post & Transfer Corp.)
49 Ontario St., Toronto, ON M5A 2V1
(416) 364-8512, FAX: (416) 364-1585
www.compt.com
CONTACTS
Kevin Evans, kevin@compt.com;
James Porteous, jporteous@compt.com;
Brian White, brianw@compt.com

Full digital post-production sound & music services for feature films, television series & MOWs

MASTER'S WORKSHOP
306 Rexdale Blvd., Suite 7, Toronto, ON M9W 1R6
(416) 741-1312, FAX: (416) 741-1894
E-mail: toronto@mastersworkshop.com
www.mastersworkshop.com
CREATIVE DIRECTOR
Tim Archer
GENERAL MANAGER
Andy Parisien

McCLEAR DIGITAL
225 Mutual St., Toronto, ON M5B 2B4
(416) 977-9740 / (877) 977-9740, FAX: (416) 977-7147
E-mail: instudio@mcclear.com, www.mcclear.com
STUDIO MANAGER
Karen Murphy
SALES & MARKETING
Mike Kelly

Music, audio post & recording studios

MCS RECORDING STUDIOS
(Media Communication Services Limited)
550 Queen St. E., Ste. G-100, Toronto, ON M5A 1V2
(416) 361-1688, FAX: (416) 361-5088. www.mcsrecording.com
PRESIDENT
Wm. (Bill) Walker

Recording & mixing audio for radio / TV industry. Audio duplication / distribution / music production

PIRATE RADIO & TELEVISION / LONESOME PINE STUDIOS
260 King St. E., Ste. 507, Toronto, ON M5A 1K3
(416) 594-3784, FAX: (416) 360-1789
E-mail: linom@pirate.ca, www.pirate.ca
GENERAL MANAGER
Lino Micheli

Sound / music

PRODUCER'S CHOICE
179 John St., Toronto, ON M5T 1X4
(416) 977-1132, FAX: (416) 977-2529
E-mail: staff@producerschoice.ca
PRESIDENT
Steve Hurej
STUDIO MANAGER
Barbara Hurej

Audio post

REVSOUND
25 St. Nicholas. St., Ste. 405, Toronto, ON M4Y 1W5
(416) 410-4146. E-mail: g@revsound.ca
CONTACT
Gary Justice

Original music-to-picture scoring and sound design

ROBERT BOCKING PRODUCTIONS LTD.
75 Hucknall Rd., Toronto, ON M3J 1W1
(416) 631-9845, E-mail: robert.bocking@sympatico.ca
www.naturefilmfootage.com

Stereo digital audio editing for any format / stereo digital audio FX library support / stock shot library / non-linear editing

ROCKET DIGITAL POST & SOUND
(A Division of MIJO Corporation)
635 Queen St. E., Toronto, ON M4M 1G4
(416) 778-6852, FAX: (416) 778-9926
www.mijo.ca
V.P., SALES & MARKETING
Cynthia Littler
SALES REPRESENTATIVE
Garth Holding

Digital audio recording & mixing, digital video editing, DVD authoring & encoding, Quicktime™ video for multimedia web, extensive sound FX and music libraries

ROSNICK MACKINNON WEBSTER
410 Adelaide St. W., Ste. 600, Toronto, ON M5V 1S8
(416) 323-3511, FAX: (416) 323-3647
www.rosmac.net
GENERAL MANAGER & V.P.
Maureen Morris

Audio production – TV & radio commercials / TV series / films, shorts, documentaries

ROUND SOUND STUDIOS INC.
60 Pippin Rd., Units 44 & 45, Concord, ON L4K 4M8
(905) 660-5815
PRESIDENT
Gina Troiano

Music writing & production / audio post-production / audio-video sync

RHYTHM DIVISION
314 Jarvis St., Ste. 102, Toronto, ON M58 2C5
(416) 971-9071, FAX: (416) 971-7871
www.rdiv.com
CONTACTS
Kevan Staples
Jim Longo

Music & audio post / composition / sound design

SCENE BY SCENE
259 Danforth Ave., Toronto, ON M4K 1N2
(416) 463-5060 / (800) 439-5060, FAX: (416) 463-3324
E-mail: bill@sbys.com, www.sbys.com
CONTACT
Bill Kinnon

Audio post

SOUND DOGS
424 Adelaide St. E., Toronto, ON M5A 1N4
(416) 364-4321, FAX: (416) 364-1310
CONTACTS
Nelson Ferriera
Stephen Barden

Sound editing & design for feature films and television

SOUND STROKES STUDIOS
Recording and Production House
154A Main St. N., Markham, ON L3P 1Y3
(905) 472-3168. E-mail: info@soundstrokes.com
www.SoundStrokes.com / www.Canada-Music.com

CONTACTS
Cory T. Paganini
Andrew V. Paganini

Films & TV — original music / sound effects / digital mastering / new media services / creative services

SOUND VENTURE PRODUCTIONS
219 – 126 York St., Ottawa, ON K1N 5T5
(613) 241-5111 ext. 248, FAX: (613) 241-5010
E-mail: tim@soundventure.com, www.soundventure.com
V.P. POST-PRODUCTION SERVICES
Tim Joyce

Audio & video post production

SPENCE-THOMAS AUDIO POST
320 King St. E., Toronto, ON M5A 1K6
(416) 361-6383, FAX: (416) 361-2970
E-mail: info@spence-thomas.com, www.spence-thomas.com
PRESIDENT
Patrick Spence-Thomas

STUDIO 306
17 Central Hospital Lane, Toronto, ON M5A 4N4
(416) 968-2306, FAX: (416) 968-7641
CONTACT
Brian Mitchell

Music / effects / dialogue mixing to picture

TATTERSALL CASABLANCA
(An Alliance Atlantis Company)
22 Boston Ave., Toronto, ON M4M 2T9
(416) 461-2550, FAX: (416) 461-9709
www.tattersallcasablanca.com
CEO
Chuck Ferkranus
SALES DIRECTOR
Mike McConnell
BUSINESS MANAGER
Peter E. Gibson

Recording, sound editing & mixing for feature films, mini-series, MOWs, television, documentaries

TATTOO MUSIC
483 Eastern Ave., Toronto, ON M4M 1C2
(416) 461-3915, FAX: (416) 461-4405
PRESIDENT
Tom Thorney
PRODUCER
Tim Thorney

Music & sound design

TRACKWORKS INC.
324 Prince Edward Dr., Ste. 203, Etobicoke, ON M8Y 3Z5
(416) 463-0036, FAX: (416) 463-3604
E-mail: sound@trackworksinc.com, www.trackworksinc.com
CONTACT
Steve Munro

Sound for feature film, MOWs, documentaries, television & internet media — editing / voice-over / foley / mixing / music composition / sound library

UMBRELLA SOUND
121 Logan Ave., Toronto, ON M4M 2M9
(416) 463-6262, FAX: (416) 469-3730
E-mail: info@umbrellasound.com, www.umbrellasound.com
STUDIO MANAGER
Tara Sales, tara.sales@umbrellasound.com

Audio post & music recording

UP IS LOUD SOUND CO. LTD.
150 Admiral Rd., Ajax, ON L1S 2P1
(905) 428-3528, Cell: (416) 540-7574, FAX: (905) 428-0912
E-mail: post@upisloud.com, www.upisloud.com

VCR / PUREFIRE ACTIVE MEDIA
3055 Lenworth Dr., Mississauga, ON L4X 2G3
(905) 629-2553, FAX: (905) 629-3437
www.vcractive.com / www.purefire.ca
CONTACT
Tony Patafio

Audio post for broadcast, documentary, corporate & multi-media projects

QUÉBEC

AUDIO POST PRODUCTION SPR INC.
640 St-Paul W., Ste. 600, Montréal, QC H3C 1L9
(514) 866-6074, FAX: (514) 866-6147
E-mail: info@studiospr.com, www.studiospr.com

Audio post-production

CINAR STUDIOS
1207 rue St-André, Montréal, QC H2L 3S8
(514) 843-9000, FAX: (514) 843-9587
Dubbing / audio & video recording & mixing / re-packaging / special effects

CINÉGROUPE
1010 Ste-Catherine E., 6th Fl., Montréal, QC H2L 2G3
(514) 849-5008, FAX: (514) 849-5001
E-mail: info@cinegroupe.ca, www.cinegroupe.com
PRESIDENT & CEO
Jacques Pettigrew
EXEC. V.P., CREATIVE AFFAIRS
Michel Lemire
DIRECTOR, BUSINESS AFFAIRS
Louise Perron St-Louis
POST-PRODUCTION DIRECTOR
André-Gilles Gagné
Dubbing studio / sound recording & mixing

GLOBAL VISION / VISION GLOBALE
80 rue Queen, bur. 201, Montréal, QC H3C 2N5
(514) 879-0020 / (800) 667-7690, FAX: (514) 879-0047
www.visionglobale.ca
CHEFS DES VENTES
Paul Bellerose
Jean-Yves Deschênes
DIRECTRICE POTSYNCHRONISATION ET BRUITAGE
Diane Boucher
DIRECTRICE DOUBLAGE
Chantal Pagé
CHEF DE LA COMMUNICATION ET DU MARKETING
Lise-Marie Laporte
RESPONSABLE DU MARCHÉ AMÉRICAIN
Hubert Harel
Sound design / editing / foley / ADR / dubbing

U.S.A. OFFICE: 630 9th Ave., Ste. 302, New York, NY 10036
(212) 262-0020, FAX: (212) 262-4547

IMUSON RECORDING STUDIOS
451 St-Jean St., Montréal, QC H2Y 2R5
(514) 845-4141
STUDIO MANAGER
Mike Matlin
Audio recording — 24 track / studio post-production

TECHNICOLOR CREATIVE SERVICES
2120 Sherbrooke St. E., Montréal, QC H2K 1C3
(514) 526-3668 ext. 421
Sound editing services

SECOND LOCATION: 1500 Papineau St., Montréal, QC H2K 4L9. (514) 527-8671
Original sound mixing

SASKATCHEWAN

TALKING DOG STUDIOS
1212A Winnipeg St., Regina, SK S4R 1J6
(306) 790-4009, FAX: (306) 565-2933
E-mail: talkingdog@talkingdogstudios.com
www.talkingdogstudios.com
PRESIDENT, COMPOSER, PRODUCER
Rob Bryanton
STUDIO MANAGER
Steve Hasiak
AUDIO POST CO-ORDINATOR
Joan Speirs
ProTools digital audio systems / three main control rooms – studios with Dolby 5.1 mixing facility / Foley stage / digital sound effects & music library / theatrical Dolby stereo & surround mixes

TWISTED PAIR SOUND
603B Park St., Regina, SK S4N 5N1
(306) 721-2590, FAX: (306) 721-2055
E-mail: mike@twistedpairsound.com
www.twistedpairsound.com
CONTACT
Mike MacNaughton
Full service audio – film & video, commercial television & radio

STUDIO FACILITIES

ALBERTA

CANWEST STUDIOS
5305 Allard Way, Edmonton, AB T6H 5X8
(780) 438-8444, FAX: (780) 438-8520
CONTACT
Mark Wood

15,000 sq. ft. soundstage / support facilities

CFB STUDIOS
2526 Battleford Ave. S.W., Unit 138, Calgary, AB T2E 7J4
(403) 246-6476, FAX: (403) 686-6624
E-mail: cfb@cfbstudios.com, www.cfbstudios.com
CONTACT
Peggy Telfer
Six studios / production offices / construction area / wardrobe

BRITISH COLUMBIA

AJATAN STUDIOS
1600 E. Railway St., N. Vancouver, BC V7J 1B5
(604) 980-8363. E-mail: ajatan@axion.net
CONTACT
Randy Tan
Two stages / backlot / construction & support facilities

ALL WEST STUDIO
12340 Horseshoe Way, Ste. 280, Richmond, BC V7A 4Z1
(604) 272-2700, FAX: (604) 272-2704
E-mail: bbingham@axion.net
CONTACT
Bruce Bingham
One studio (19,000 sq. ft.) / office & production support space

AM PRODUCTIONS STUDIO
48 E. 6th Ave., Vancouver, BC V5T 1J4
(604) 875-9927, FAX: (604) 875-9971
E-mail: tomk@amproductions.com, www.amproductions.com
CONTACT
Tom Konyves
One studio / post-production facility

ANNEX STUDIO
3144 Thunderbird Cres., Burnaby, BC V5A 3G5
(604) 421-8205. E-mail: annexstudio@telus.net
www.annexstudio.net
CONTACT
Cheryl Taylor
One studio (9,300 sq. ft.) / office & support space

BOUNDARY ROAD STUDIOS
1875 Boundary Rd., Vancouver, BC V5M 3Y4
(778) 772-4019
CONTACT
Gerry McMullin, gerry@boundaryroadstudios.com
94,500 sq. ft. in all / Offices: from 100 – 8,000 sq. ft. /
Warehouse: 17,000 sq. ft., 22 ft. high with loading bays / parking / security system / cafeteria / wardrobe / setdec / props / lockups

THE BRIDGE STUDIOS
2400 Boundary Rd., Burnaby, BC V5M 3Z3
(604) 482-2000, FAX: (604) 482-2007
E-mail: bridgestudios@bcpavco.com, www.bridgestudios.com
CONTACT
Ron Hrynuik
Six soundstages on 15 acres / production offices / wardrobe / props / mill & workshop

THE CROSSING STUDIOS
2058 Alpha Ave., Burnaby, BC V5C 5K7
(604) 296-2622, FAX: (604) 296-2672
E-mail: dian@@crossingstudios.com,
www.crossingstudios.com
CONTACT
Dian Cross
Patricia Sumter
Two studios / one effects studio / digital green screen / production offices & services

FIRST LIGHT STUDIO
3738 Keith St., Burnaby, BC V5J 5B5
(604) 438-9312, FAX: (604) 438-9320
CONTACT
Ben Kikkert
One 9,000 sq. ft. soundstage / green screen, hard-wall cyc

LIONS GATE STUDIOS
555 Brooksbank Ave., N. Vancouver, BC V7J 3S5
(604) 983-5555, FAX: (604) 983-5554
E-mail: pdleitch@lionsgatestudios.com
www.lionsgatestudios.com
GENERAL MANAGER
Peter Leitch
Eight sound stages / long-term & temporary offices / mills & support services

EAGLE CREEK STUDIOS
4210 Phillips Ave., Unit 8, Burnaby, BC V5A 2X2
(604) 983-5555, FAX: (604) 983-5554
E-mail: pdleitch@lionsgatestudios.com
www.eaglecreekstudios.com
CONTACT
Peter Leitch

Two stages / office & support space / backlot

MJA STUDIO
4961 Byrne Rd., Burnaby, BC V5J 3H6
(604) 728-9653, Pager: (604) 735-5241
E-mail: wolfisachsen@hotmail.com, www.mjastudios.com
CONTACT
Wolf Isachsen

One soundstage / office space

PACIFIC NATIONAL EXHIBITION
2900 East Hastings St., Vancouver, BC V5K 4W3
(604) 252-3534, FAX: (604) 251-7761
Website: www.pne.bc.ca
CONTACT
Stephanie Hollingon-Sawyer

Forum Building: 44,579 sq. ft., 40 ft. ceiling (60 ft. peak) / Rollerland Building: Multipurpose / 19,800 sq. ft., 20 ft. ceiling (27 ft. peak) / rooms available for departments, crews, lunchrooms, lockups / construction facilties on-site / high-speed wireless Internet / daily, weekly and monthly rates / full package quotes available

PARAMOUNT STUDIO
2820 Bentall St., Vancouver, BC V5M 4H4
(604) 412-9435 / (604) 868-6140
E-mail: gordfacilities@aol.com
CONTACT
Gord McLeod

Five stages / mill / construction shop / office space equipped with phones & Internet

PORT MANN STUDIOS
14115 – 117th Ave., Surrey, BC V3V 3T2
(604) 580-0251, FAX: (640) 580-1922
CONTACT
Danny Peel

Warehouse: 50,000 sq. ft., 56 ft x 460 ft. x 52 ft. high (mostly clear) / office / workshop areas / additional mezzanine level 24 ft. wide

SHAVICK ENTERTAINMENT / BURNABY STUDIOS
112 West 6th Ave., Vancouver, BC V5Y 1K6
(604) 874-4300 ext. 105, FAX: (604) 874-4305
E-mail: info@shavickentertainment.com
www.shavickentertainment.com
CONTACT
Stephen Cholakis

Enterprise St.: Two studios, production office, carpentry shop McConnell Court: Two studios, production offices, carpentry shop, fenced parking compound

SHOOTERS BROADCAST SERVICES INC.
4010 Myrtle St., Burnaby, BC V5C 4G2
(604) 437-9037 / (800) 567-0037, FAX: (604) 434-0038
E-mail: martin@shooters.ca, www.shooters.ca
CONTACT
Martin Hendricks

One studio (4,000 sq. ft.) / production offices

SUNRISE FILM STUDIO (THE BURNABY STUDIO)
3737 Napier St., Burnaby, BC V5C 3E4
(604) 619-7747
CONTACT
Stephen Cholakis

One studio (8,900 sq. ft.) / production offices / construction space / fenced parking compound / in-house power / 200 amp three phase / clearspan grid at 19 feet

THOMAS STUDIOS
144 Riverside Dr., N. Vancouver, BC V7H 1T9
(604) 929-5455, FAX: (604) 929-6653. www.thomasfx.com
CONTACT
Betty Thomas, email: bettythomas@thomasfx.com

5,000 sq. ft. – blue screen / green screen / 1,750 sq. ft. office space / permanent flying rig / production offices / high-speed Internet / phones / fax / parking / production supplies & equipment rentals on-site

VANCOUVER FILM STUDIOS
3500 Cornett Rd., Vancouver, BC V5N 2H8
(604) 453-5000, FAX: (604) 453-5045
E-mail: info@vancouverfilmstudios.com
www.vancouverfilmstudios.com

CONTACTS
Peter Mitchell
Kim Alexander

Twelve stages, production offices, mill / helipad

MANITOBA

PRAIRIE PRODUCTION CENTRE
1350 Pacific Ave., Winnipeg, MB R3E 1G6
(204) 783-6800, FAX: (204) 480-4447
E-mail: info@prairieproduction.com
www.prairieproduction.com
CONTACT
David Budzak

15,000 sq. ft. sound stage (35' clear span) / production offices equipped with phone & Internet / workshop / production support areas / fenced compound

NOVA SCOTIA

ELECTROPOLIS MOTION PICTURE STUDIOS INC.
5091 Terminal Rd., Halifax, NS B3J 3Y1
(902) 429-1971, FAX: (902) 429-1471
E-mail: greg@electropolis-studios.com
www.electropolis-studios.com
CONTACTS
Rob Power
Greg MacInnis

Four Halifax-waterfront studios / production offices / art department / make-up / wardrobe rooms / actor suites / extra rooms / green room

TOUR TECH EAST
170 Thornhill Dr., Dartmouth, NS B3B 1S3
(902) 468-2800, FAX: (902) 468-8833
E-mail: loril@tourtecheast.com, www.tourtecheast.com
CONTACT
Lori Laderoute

Two studios / production offices / audio & lighting services / support facilities

ONTARIO

@ WALLACE STUDIOS
258 Wallace Ave., Ste. 100, Toronto, ON M6P 3M9
(416) 537-3471, FAX: (416) 532-3132
www.wallacestudios.com
V.P., MARKETING
Lillyann Goldstein

Three sound studios — film / television /video / photography. Car ramps. inside loading docks – truck & ground level loading, free parking, dressing & make-up rooms, kitchen, portable fridges, cafeteria, conference room. Services include casting facilities, production offices, lighting & grip equipment rentals, set construction, web convergence, service production, casting, sound recording, catering and more. Location shooting at the Distillery District, St. Clair, 80 Ward St., and Massey Mansion properties

THE BERKELEY CHURCH
315 Queen St. E., Toronto, ON M5A 1S7
(416) 361-9666, FAX: (416) 361-1849
E-mail: berkeley1871@yahoo.com, www.berkeleyevents.com
CONTACT
Doug Wheler

BERKELEY STUDIO
3250 Bloor St. W., Toronto, ON M8X 2Y4
(416) 232-6024, FAX: (416) 232-3103
E-mail: berkeley@united-church.ca, www.berkeleystudio.org
STUDIO ADMINISTRATOR
Alison Sutherland

Television studio (1,500 sq. ft.) / green screen

CINESPACE STUDIOS
175 Queens Quay E., Toronto, ON M5A 1B6
(416) 364-1964, FAX: (416) 364-3854
E-mail: mail@cinespace.com, www.cinespace.com
CONTACTS
Steve Mirkopoulos
Nick Mirkopoulos

Facilities include: Marine Terminal 28 Studios: four studios / office suites / art department / wardrobe / set storage / production support facilities30 Booth Ave.: four studios / office suites / art department / wardrobe / set storage / production support facilities

Kleinberg Studios: two studios — standing "White House" interior sets / offices / support facilities / wooded backlot
Carlaw Production Centre: two office buildings – production offices / casting / editing suites

CINEVILLAGE
65 Heward Ave., Bldg. B, Toronto, ON M4M 2T5
(416) 461-8750, FAX: (416) 466-9612
E-mail: renato.dumlao@allianceatlantis.com
CONTACT
Renato Dumlao

Production & studio complex

EPITOME PICTURES INC.
220 Bartley Dr., Toronto, ON M4A 1G1
(416) 752-7627, FAX: (416) 752-7837
E-mail: nicole@epitomepictures.com
www.epitomepictures.com
CONTACT
Nicole Hamilton

Three studios / residential backlot / mall & school sets

FAREWELL STUDIOS
2869 Thornton Rd., Oshawa, ON L1H 7K4
(905) 655-3849, Cell: (905) 436-8172
E-mail: film@farewellstudios.com, www.farewellstudios.com
CONTACT
Barb Chupa

One of the largest clearspan studios in Canada. 54K x 85'
high; 42K x 65' high; 12K support space

FREEDOM STUDIOS INC.
350 Adelaide St. W., Unit 204, Toronto, ON M5V 1T5
(416) 778-1358, FAX: (416) 778-1819
E-mail: info@freedomstudios.com, www.freedomstudios.com
CONTACTS
Suzanne Shawyer
Aaron Goldman
V.P., MARKETING & SALES
Deborah MacDonald

3,500 sq. ft. stage / offices / screening lounge

HILLS PRODUCTION SERVICES
2440 Industrial St., Burlington, ON L7P 1A5
(905) 335-1146, FAX: (905) 335-1241
E-mail: studio@hillsvideo.com, www.hillsvideo.com
CONTACTS
Rob Hill
Gerry Milinkovic

Mobile production bus, location packs, studios, edit suites

THE MASONIC TEMPLE / AGINCOURT PRODUCTIONS
(CTV Inc.)
888 Yonge Street, Toronto, ON M4W 2J2
Phone: (416) 332-5272, FAX: (416) 332-6041
CONTACT
Sam Dynes

PYMAN STUDIOS INC.
2196 Dunwin Dr., Mississauga, ON L5L 1C7
(905) 828-7171 ext. 227, FAX: (905) 828-7660
E-mail: charlene@pyman.com
www.pyman.com
PRODUCTION MANAGER
Charlene Newland

Two studios / control rooms / edit suites

SHOOTERS BROADCAST SERVICES INC.
629 Eastern Ave., Toronto, ON M4M 1E4
(416) 405-9977 / (800) 567-0037, FAX: (416) 405-9969

Production studios / 30' broadcast mobile / technical crews /
high definition cameras and accessories / broadcast equipment
rentals

SHOWLINE LIMITED
915 Lakeshore Blvd. E., Toronto, ON M4M 3L5
(416) 778-7379, FAX: (416) 778-7380
www.showlinestudios.com
CONTACTS
Peter Lukas
Richard Lukas

Film / TV sound studios & production offices

Showline Harbourside Studios: three studios / production &
support offices

Showline Oxford-Milton Stages: two stages / support facilities

Showline Trinity Studios: two stages / support facilities

STUDIOASIS MEDIA CORPORATION
793 Pharmacy Ave., Toronto, ON M1L 3K2
(416) 285-1111, FAX: (416) 285-9617
E-mail: studioasis@on.aib.com, www.studioasis.com
STUDIO MANAGER
Gord Brodie

Three studios / production offices / dressing rooms / wardrobe
& make-up rooms / carpentry shop / scissor lift / truck & mobile
bays / screening

STUDIOWORKS / STUDIO 226
611 King St. E., Ste. 801, Toronto, ON M5A 1M6
(416) 214-4886, FAX: (416) 214-4619
E-mail: keithm@studioworks.com, www.studioworks.to
CONTACT
Keith McCully

Stage 1: 17,500 sq. ft. / Stage 2: 8,500 sq. ft.
Production offices & support facilities

SULLIVAN STUDIOS
66 Hymus Rd., Scarborough, ON M1L 2C7
(416) 288-1286, Cell: (416) 254-8995, FAX: (416) 750-1985
E-mail: DanM1968@aol.com
PRODUCTION MANAGER
Dan Matthews

Four studios / backlot with period main street / production
offices / wardrobe / art department

TORONTO FILM STUDIOS
629 Eastern Ave., Toronto, ON M4M 1E4
(416) 406-1235 / (888) 607-1116, FAX: (416) 406-6964
E-mail: info@tfstudios.ca, www.torontofilmstudios.com
CONTACT
Ken Ferguson

Seventeen film / TV stages (1,500 – 40,000 sq. ft.) on a 20-
acre lot. Full services & support — furnished production
offices, wardrobe, set decoration, carpentry shops, editing.
Airplane cabin & cockpit / jail set / luxury New York City apartment set.

TORSTAR MEDIA GROUP TELEVISION / TORONTO STAR
TV
1 Yonge St., 9th Fl., Toronto, ON M5E 1E6
(416) 869-4700 , FAX: (416) 869-4566
E-mail: info@tmgtv.ca, www.tmgtv.ca
ACCOUNT EXECUTIVE
Dave Tyler
EXEC. PRODUCER
Keith Moore

Torstar Media Group Television operates TMGTV productions, a
full-service production facility, which includes Avid editing suites,
an 828 sq. ft. 3D virtual studio, post-production and encoding
services

TRI-LITE TV INC.
2196 Dunwin Dr., Mississauga, ON L5L 1C7
(905) 828-2225, FAX: (905) 828-7660
E-mail: chris@tri-lite.tv, www.tri-lite.tv
TECHNICAL PRODUCER
Chris Priess
PRODUCTION MANAGER
Charlene Newland

Television mobile unit

WHATEVER SOLUTIONS & MEDIA
647 Neal Dr., Peterborough, ON K9J 6X7
(705) 749-6325 / (866) 779-7715, FAX: (705) 742-6129
E-mail: rmorton@whatevermedia.ca
www.whateversolutions.ca
CONTACT
Robert Morton

Music composition – in-house composer / TV series, documentaries, animation & post-production, commercials

QUÉBEC

CINÉ CITÉ MONTRÉAL
(Comweb Group)
4801 rue Leckie, B-121, Saint-Hubert, QC J3Z 1H6
(450) 926-2463, FAX: (450) 926-3937
E-mail: mfontaine@cinecitemontreal.com
www.cinecitemontreal.com
GENERAL MANAGER
Martin Fontaine

Six studios / production offices / wardrobe & dressing rooms /
honeywagon & vehicle rentals / rifle range / outdoor water tanks
/ paint and carpentry shops / fibre-optic video transmission / production financial services / SFX services including animatronics,
miniatures and pyrotechnics / signage and graphic design / set
construction services / filming locations / adjacent airstrip

PMT VIDEO
2600 William Tremblay St., Ste. 20, Montréal, QC H1Y 3J2
(514) 522-5553, FAX: (514) 522-5971
E-mail: isabelle@pmt.qc.ca, www.pmt.qc.ca
CONTACT
Isabelle Gratton

One stage (5,000 sq. ft.) / live broadcast facility / edit suite

STUDIO CENTRE VILLE

(Covitec)
1168 Bishop St., Montréal, QC H3G 2E3
(514) 878-3456 , FAX: (514) 878-9542
E-mail: daniel_martineau@covitec.com, www.covitec.com
CONTACT
Daniel Martineau

Two studios equipped for live television broadcast / fibre-optic link

STUDIO SHANDA

3691 St. Dominique St., Montréal, QC H2X 2X8
(514) 843-8762 / (800) 798-8762, FAX: (514) 843-8706
CONTACT
Dan Shannon

One studio (1200 sq. ft.) / equipment rentals / editing suite

STUDIOS ICESTORM

2595 Place Chassi, Montréal, QC H1Y 2C3
(514) 522-8937 , FAX: (514) 522-7926
E-mail: mfontaine@cinecitemontreal.com,
www.moliflexwhite.com
CONTACT
Martin Fontaine

Four studios / HDTV & digital / VFX / green screen / production offices

STUDIOS LASALLE

(Covitec)
2555 Dollard Ave., LaSalle, QC H8N 3A9
(514) 364-1874, FAX: (514) 364-1594
E-mail: daniel_martineau@covitec.com, www.covitec.com

CONTACT
Daniel Martineau

Three studios / television services / video & audio control rooms

STUDIOS SAINT-MARTIN

4446 St-Laurent, Ste. 1000, Montréal, QC H2N 1Z5
(514) 849-1351, FAX: (514) 849-3350
E-mail: aezerzer@yahoo.com
CONTACT
Albert Ezerzer

Two studios

SASKATCHEWAN

CANADA SASKATCHEWAN PRODUCTION STUDIOS

1831 College Ave., Regina, SK S4P 3V7
(306) 798-3456, FAX: (306) 798-7768
E-mail: frank@saskfilm.com, www.saskfilm.com
CONTACT
Frank Schuurmans

The facility offers four stages with 34,538 sq. ft. of studio space / 40 ft. clear span ceiling heights / 960 sq. ft. recessed tank with a capacity of 67,000 gallons and smoke evacuation capability / complete array of support facilities and services including wardrobe / carpentry / paint / grip / make-up & hair / VIP dressing rooms / 6,000 sq. ft. of production office space and post-production facilities.
The Canada/Saskatchewan Soundstage offers a full-service facility and proper management services through an on-site building manager.

DISTRIBUTION COMPANIES

THEATRICAL

ACTION FILM LIMITEE
4446 boul. St-Laurent, Ste. 20, Montréal, QC H2W 1Z5
(514) 845-5572. FAX: (514) 286-2313
E-mail: actionfilm@qc.aira.com
PRESIDENT
André Monette

35mm / 16mm / vidéo

ALLIANCE ATLANTIS MOTION PICTURE DISTRIBUTION
121 Bloor St. E., Ste. 1500, Toronto, ON M4W 3M5
(416) 967-1174, FAX: (416) 967-0044
Website: www.allianceatlantis.com
CEO, MOTION PICTURE DISTRIBUTION GROUP
Victor Loewy
PRESIDENT, CANADIAN THEATRICAL DISTRIBUTION
Patrice Théroux
PRESIDENT, CANADIAN THEATRICAL DISTRIBUTION
Jim Sherry

Canada's largest producer and distributor of motion pictures.

ALLIANCE ATLANTIS VIVAFILM
5 Place Ville Marie, Ste. 1435, Montréal, QC H3B 2G2
(514) 878-2282. FAX: (514) 878-2419
PRESIDENT
Guy Gagnon

ODEON FILMS
121 Bloor St. E., Ste. 1500, Toronto, ON M4W 3M5
(416) 967-1141, FAX: (416) 934-6999
PRESIDENT
Bryan Gliserman

BBC WORLDWIDE CANADA LTD.
130 Spadina Ave., Ste. 401, Toronto, ON M5V 2L4
(416) 362-3223, FAX: (416) 362-3553
COO CANADA
Hilary Read
V.P., SALES
Mary Egan
MANAGER, PROGRAM ADMINISTRATION
Gwen Jones

BUENA VISTA PICTURES DISTRIBUTION CANADA, INC.
Sales, Simcoe Place
200 Front St. W., Ste. 2900, Toronto, ON M5V 3L4
(416) 964-9275 / (800) 263-2853, FAX: (416) 964-8537
V.P., SALES
Anthony Macina
SALES MANAGER
Tony Schittone
SALES REPRESENTATIVE
Karen Burke
SENIOR MARKETING CO-ORDINATOR
Antonella Zappone

Distributors of Walt Disney Pictures, Touchstone Pictures and Hollywood Pictures

PUBLICITY & PROMOTIONS OFFICE:
21 St. Clair Ave. E., Ste. 701, Toronto ON M4T 1L9
(416) 413-0966, ext 227, FAX: (416) 416-7909
DIRECTOR, PUBLICITY & PROMOTIONS
Jane MacLean

CHRISTAL FILMS DISTRIBUTION INC.
(A division of Lions Gate Films)
376 Victoria Ave., Ste. 300, Montréal, QC H3Z 1C3
(514) 336-9696, FAX: (514) 336-6606
E-mail: info@christalfilms.com, www.christalfilms.com
PRESIDENT
Christian Larouche
DISTRIBUTION & SALES
Sylvain Gagné

CINEMA ESPERANCA INTERNATIONAL INC.
36 Charlotte St., Ste. 1106, Toronto, ON M5V 3P7
(416) 977-0123, FAX: (416) 977-7890
E-mail: andre.m.bennett@sympatico.ca
CHAIRMAN / PRESIDENT / CEO
André Bennett

CINEMAVAULT RELEASING INC.
434 Queen St. E., Toronto, ON M5A 1T5
(416) 363-6060, FAX: (416) 363-2305. www.cinemavault.com
CEO
Nick Stiliadis
V.P., DISTRIBUTION
Amy Beecroft
V.P., BUSINESS AFFAIRS
Kamal Dureja
V.P., PRODUCTION
Steve Arroyave
SR. V.P., ACQUISITIONS & MARKETING
Irene Loewy
DIRECTOR ACQUISITIONS & DEVELOPMENT
Stephen Maynard

CLOUD TEN PICTURES INC.
1 St. Paul St., Ste. 401, St. Catharines, ON L2R 7L2
(905) 684-5561, FAX: (905) 684-7946. www.cloudtenpictures.com
CO-CEO
Peter Lalonde
Paul Lalonde

Producers & distributors of "Left Behind" Christian films

COLUMBIA TRISTAR FILMS OF CANADA
(A division of Columbia Pictures Industries Inc.)
1303 Yonge St., Ste. 100, Toronto, ON M4T 1W6
(416) 922-5740, FAX: (416) 922-3661
SR. V.P. & GENERAL MANAGER, CANADA
Michael Brooker
MANAGING DIRECTOR
Tim Bishop
DISTRICT MANAGERS: DENISE JAMES
Bill Robinson
SALES REPRESENTATIVES
Ellie Munro
Peter Wertelecky
BILLER – EASTERN & WESTERN CANADA
Olga Tavares
COORDINATOR, ADMINSTRATIVE SUPPORT & EXHIBITOR RELATIONS
Srimati Sen

QUÉBEC
c/o Alliance Atlantis Vivafilm
5 Place Ville Marie, Ste. 1435, Montréal, QC H3B 2G2
(514) 878-2282, FAX: (514) 878-2419
GENERAL MANAGER
Claude Chene
BOOKING DIRECTOR
Sylvie Kenny

DOMINO FILM AND TELEVISION INTERNATIONAL LTD.
4002 Grey Ave., Montréal, QC H4A 3P1
(514) 484-0446, FAX: (514) 484-0468
E-mail: jritter@dominofilm.ca, www.dominofilm.ca
PRESIDENT
Jeanne Ritter

Domestic & international distribution of Canadian motion pictures and TV programming

DREAMWORKS DISTRIBUTION CANADA CO.
2 Bloor St. W., Ste. 2510, Toronto, ON M4W 3E2
(416) 513-0312, FAX: (416) 513-0316. www.dreamworks.com
DISTRIBUTION
Don Popow
SALES
Jennifer Hofley
BOOKER
Venka Galic
THEATRICAL MARKETING SERVICES
Harriet Bernstein
ACCOUNTS RECEIVABLE
Lisa Donato

EDGE ENTERTAINMENT INC.
1120 Morgan Avenue, Saskatoon, SK S7H 2R7
(306) 374-1207, FAX: (306) 374-0783
E-mail: edge.ent@edgeentertainment.sk.ca
www.edgeentertainment.sk.ca
PRESIDENT, FILM & TELEVISION
David Doerksen
V.P., FINANCE
Deidre Meeks

V.P., FILM & TELEVISION
Leanne Arnott
BUSINESS AFFAIRS
Linda Davis

Feature & TV films

EQUINOXE FILMS
(A division of La Compagnie France Film Inc.)
505 Sherbrooke St. E., Ste. 2401, Montréal, QC H2L 4N3
(514) 844-0680, FAX: (514) 499-9899
PRESIDENT & CEO
Pierre René
SENIOR VICE-PRESIDENT & COO
Michael Mosca
VICE-PRESIDENT DISTRIBUTION
Yves Dion
DIRECTOR, THEATRICAL DISTRIBUTION
John Xinos

Theatrical, television & video distribution

ONTARIO OFFICE: 1200 Bay St., Ste 1201, Toronto, ON M5R 2A5. (416) 969-1200, FAX: (416) 969-0301

THE FILM CIRCUIT
(A division of the Toronto International Film Festival Group (TIFFG)
2 Carlton St., Ste. 1600, Toronto, ON M5B 1J3
(416) 967-7371, FAX: (416) 967-9477
E-mail: tiffg@torfilmfest.ca, www.bell.ca/filmfest
DIRECTOR (TIFFG)
Piers Handling
MANAGING DIRECTOR (TIFFG)
Michèle Maheux
FILM CIRCUIT DIRECTOR
Cam Haynes
FILM CIRCUIT ASSOCIATE DIRECTOR
Blair Haynes

The Film Circuit, a division of the Toronto International Film Festival Group, was launched in the fall of 1995 to create a broader-based network for Canadian and significant international films. The Film Circuit has launched multiple successful screenings of such films as The Red Violin, Last Night and The Hanging Garden. These films would not have the opportunity to be shown in the smaller-sized centres across Canada without the Circuit. The Circuit is proving to be a viable network for helping to deliver Canadian films to a broader public spectrum. Currently The Film Circuit consists of 90 active communities.

FILMS TRANSIT INTERNATIONAL INC.
402 est rue Notre-Dame, Ste. 100, Montréal, QC H2Y 1C8
(514) 844-3358, FAX: (514) 844-7298
E-mail: info@filmstransit.com, www.filmstransit.com
CEO
Jan Rofekamp

Documentaries

FILM TONIC INC.
5130 boul. St-Laurent, bur. 400, Montréal, QC H2T 1R8
(514) 272-4425, FAX: (514) 274-0214
E-mail: senecal@filmtonic.com, www.filmtonic.com
INTERNATIONAL SALES
Joanne Senécal

FILMWEST ASSOCIATES DISTRIBUTION LTD.
2399 Hayman Rd., Kelowna, BC V1Z 1Z8
(250) 769-3399, FAX: (250) 769-5599
E-mail: info@filmwest.com, www.filmwest.com
CONTACTS
Merrie Christoff, Lynn D'Albertanson
U.S.A. OFFICE
300 W. Second St., Carson City, NV 89703 U.S.A.
(775) 883-8090, FAX: (800) 570-5505
E-mail: sales@filmwest.com
CONTACT
George Christoff

FUNFILM DISTRIBUTION
5146 boul. St-Laurent, Montréal, QC H2T 1R8
(514) 272-4956, FAX: (514) 272-9841
E-mail: funfilm@cinemaginaire.com
CONTACT
Robert Meunier

IMAX CORPORATION
2525 Speakman Dr., Sheridan Park, Mississauga, ON L5K 1B1
(905) 403-6500, FAX: (905) 403-6450
E-mail: Info@imax.com, www.imax.com
CO-CHAIRMAN & CO-CEO
Bradley J. Wechsler
CO-CHAIRMAN & CO-CEO
Richard L. Gelfond
PRESIDENT & COO
John Davison
PRESIDENT, FILM
Greg Foster

Distributing the largest available library of 15/70 films in the industry, including entertainment, space, science and natural history films

INDO CANADIAN FILMS INTERNATIONAL
4500 boul. de Maisonneuve ouest., bur. 21, Montréal, QC H3Z 1L7. (514) 935-6888, FAX: (514) 935-8588
E-mail: indocdn.films@attglobal.net
PRESIDENT
Gotham Hooja

KEYSTONE RELEASING (CANADA) INC.
2339 Columbia St., 3rd Fl., Vancouver, BC V5Y 3Y3
(604) 873-9739, FAX (604) 873-5919
V.P., DISTRIBUTION
Tim Brown
MARKETING CO-ORDINATOR
Malas Thavonesouk

K FILMS AMERIQUE
Box 2, Montréal, QC H2G 3C8, Beaubien Postal Office
(514) 277-2613, FAX: (514) 277-3598
PRESIDENT
Louis Dussault

35mm / home video

KNIGHTSCOVE ENTERTAINMENT CORP.
1912 Queen St. E., Toronto, ON M4L 1H5
(416) 691-6655, FAX: (416) 691-8419
E-mail: info@knightscove.com, www.knightscove.com
PRESIDENT/CEO
Leif Bristow

Finances, produces and distributes moderately budgeted ($5 - $15M), family- oriented, feature-length commercial films on an acquisition, production or co-production basis.

LIONS GATE ENTERTAINMENT CORP.
2 Bloor St. W., Ste. 1001, Toronto, ON M4W 3E2
(416) 944-0104, FAX: (416) 944-2212 (Film) / (416) 944-2843 (Video). www.lionsgatefilms.com
BRITISH COLUMBIA OFFICE:
595 Burrard St., Ste. 3123, Vancouver, BC V7X 1J1
(604) 609-6100, FAX: (604) 609-6149
U.S.A. OFFICE:
4553 Glencoe Ave., Ste. 200, Marina del Rey, CA 90292
(310) 314-9521, FAX: (310) 392-0252

MAXIMA FILM CORPORATION
200 Tiffield Rd., Ste. 101, Toronto, ON M1V 5J1
(416) 449-9400, FAX: (416) 449-9498
DIRECTOR
Allan G. Kent
EXEC. PRODUCER / CEO
J. Gary Gladman

MGM DISTRIBUTION OF CANADA
20 Queen St. W., Ste. 3500, Toronto, ON M5H 3R3
(647) 436-1500.
V.P. / DIVISION MANAGER, CANADA
Phil May
V.P., MEDIA / CO-OP ADVERTISING
Sandra Crann
DISTRICT MANAGER
Danish Vahidy
OFFICE MANAGER
Simone Konieczny
QUÉBEC OFFICE:
1255 Universtity St., Ste 100, Montréal, QC H3B 3W6
(514) 284-5113
DISTRICT MANAGER
Robert Montplaisir
35mm

MONGREL MEDIA INC.
109 Melville Ave., Toronto, ON M6G 1Y3
(416) 516-9775, FAX: (416) 516-0651
E-mail: info@mongrelmedia.com, www.mongrelmedia.com
PRESIDENT
Hussain Amarshi

Theatrical / educational / home video / TV markets

OASIS INTERNATIONAL
6 Pardee Ave., Ste. 103, Toronto, ON M6K 3H5
(416) 588-6821, FAX: (416) 588-7276
E-mail: info@oasisinternational.com
www.oasisinternational.com
PRESIDENT
Peter Emerson, Ext. 224 / E-mail: peter@oasisinternational.com
EXEC. VICE-PRESIDENT
Valerie Cabrera
(310) 260-2548 / E-mail: valerie@oasisinternational.com
V.P., SALES
Steve Murphy

Ext. 222 / E-mail: steve@oasisinternational.com
V.P., FINANCE & OPERATIONS
Brian Barrett, Ext. 226 / E-mail: brian@oasisinternational.com
MANAGER, CLIENT SERVICES
Kristian Grostad, Ext. 229 /
E-mail: kristian@oasisinternational.com
SALES EXECUTIVE
Prentiss Holman, Ext. 228 /
E-mail: prentiss@oasisinternational.com

Film / TV distribution

OASIS SHAFTESBURY RELEASING
6 Pardee Ave., Ste. 103, Toronto, ON M6K 3H5
(416) 588-6821, FAX: (416) 588-7276
CO-PRESIDENT
Peter Emerson
Ext. 224 / E-mail: peter@oasisinternational.com
CO-PRESIDENT
Christina Jennings
E-mail: cjennings@shaftesbury.org

PARAMOUNT PICTURES CANADA
146 Bloor St. W., 6th Floor, Toronto, ON M5S IM4
(416) 969-9901, FAX: (416) 922-0287
OFFICERS / MOTION PICTURE GROUP
PRESIDENT
Gino Campagnola
SR. VICE-PRESIDENT
Don Wallace
VICE-PRESIDENT / CONTROLLER
Anne Shaw

Motion Picture Group / Theatrical 35mm (English & French)

MARKETING
SR. V.P., MARKETING
Greg Ferris
DIRECTOR OF PUBLICITY
Anne Davidson-Muru
DIRECTOR OF ADVERTISING
Leigh Higgins

MANAGERS
District Manager, Calgary / Vancouver / Winnipeg
Chris Sullivan
BRANCH MANAGER, TORONTO
Bob Cowan
BRANCH SALES MANAGER, MONTREAL / SAINT JOHN
Derek Boulet

SALES
SALESPERSON, TORONTO
Perry Persaud
SALES BOOKER, CALGARY / VANCOUVER / WINNIPEG
Anthony Vecchiato

QUÉBEC OFFICE
1255 University Ave., Ste. 912, Montréal, QC H3B 9W4
(514) 866-2010, FAX: (514) 866-2411
BOOKER / CASHIER
Marie Trepanier

PICTURE PLANT RELEASING LTD.
983 Kingsburg Beach Rd., R.R. #1, Rose Bay, NS B0J 2X0
(902) 766-0174, FAX: (902) 766-0175
E-mail: info@pictureplant.com, www.pictureplant.com
PRESIDENT
William MacGillivray
VICE-PRESIDENT
Terry Greenlaw

Feature films & TV

REMSTAR DISTRIBUTION
85 St-Paul St. W., Ste. 300, Montréal, QC H2Y 3V4
(514) 847-1136, FAX: (514) 847-1163
E-mail: info@remstarcorp.com, www.remstarcorp.com
V.P., SALES & ACQUISITIONS
Armand Lafond

Theatrical - domestic & foreign

RHOMBUS INTERNATIONAL
99 Spadina Ave., Ste. 600, Toronto, ON M5V 3P8
(416) 971-7856, FAX: (416) 971-9647
E-mail: rhombus@rhombusmedia.com
www.rhombusmedia.com
PRESIDENT
Sheena Macdonald
VICE-PRESIDENT
Niv Fichman
SALES EXEC.
Sarah Baird

North America's leading distributor of films on the performing arts.
Also representing outside drama and arts productions

THE ROKE ENTERTAINMENT GROUP
522 – 11th Ave. S.W., Calgary, AB T2R 0C8
(403) 264-4660, FAX: (403) 264-6571
CONTACTS
Frank Kettner
Syd Sniderman
Donna Campbell
Ellen Smeltzer

35mm

SEVILLE PICTURES INC.
147 St. Paul St. W., 2nd Fl., Montréal, QC H2Y 1Z5
(514) 841-1910, Fax: (514) 841-8030
CONTACTS
David Reckziegle
John Hamilton

Distribution of feature films / documentaries / TV programs

ONTARIO OFFICE
511 King St. W., 4th Fl., Toronto, ON M5V 2Z4
(416) 480-0453, FAX: (416) 480-0501

SLIDE SCREEN ENTERTAINMENT INC.
1315 Bishop St., Ste. 135, Cambridge, ON N1R 2Z2
(519) 740-1266, FAX: (519) 740-6374
E-mail: ibtsl@rogers.com, www.independentbooking.net
PRESIDENT
Barbara Ball
V.P. / SECRETARY-TREASURER
Eric Ball

North American distributor of Eros Entertainment and other
Indian films

THINKFILM
2300 Yonge St., Ste. 906, Toronto, ON M4P 1E4
(416) 488-0037, FAX: (416) 488-0031
PRESIDENT & CEO.
Jeff Sackman
THEATRICAL DISTRIBUTION (CANADA)
Tamara Shannon, tshannon@thinkfilmcompany.com

U.S.A. OFFICE:
451 Greenwich St., 7th Fl., New York, N.Y. 10013
(646) 214-7908, FAX: (646) 217-7907

TVA FILMS
376 Victoria Ave., Montréal, QC H3Z 1C3
(514) 284-2525, FAX: (514) 985-4461
PRESIDENT
Pierre Lampron
EXEC. V.P., DISTRIBUTION
Marie-Claude Poulin

ONTARIO OFFICE:
2 Bloor St. W., Ste. 1002, Toronto, ON M4W 3E2
(416) 968-0002, FAX: (416) 944-1741
EXEC. DIRECTOR
John Fulton
EXEC. DIRECTOR, TV SALES
Michael Smith

TWENTIETH CENTURY FOX FILM CORPORATION
33 Bloor St. E., Ste. 1106, Toronto, ON M4W 3H1
Sales: (416) 921-0001
Publicity: (416) 515-3365, (800) 668-9927, FAX: (416) 921-9062
VICE-PRESIDENT / GENERAL MANAGER
Barry Newstead
COMPTROLLER
Rosemarie Marshall
BRANCH MANAGER
Damian O'Regan
SALES MANAGER
Darlene Elson
HEAD BOOKER
Jean Paradis
ADVERTISING NEWSPAPER ENGLISH AND FRENCH
Joanna Smith (Ad Express)
(416) 484-5306, FAX: (416) 484-5308
MEDIA
Karen Nayler (Mind Share)
(416) 945-2157, FAX: (416) 484-5308
MANAGER, PUBLICITY & PROMOTION
Julia Perry

UNIVERSAL FILMS CANADA
2450 Victoria Park Ave., Willowdale, ON M2J 4A2
(416) 491-3000, FAX: (416) 502-0323
FAX Publicity: (416) 494-3587
FAX Advertising: (416) 491-5180
SR. VICE-PRESIDENT / GENERAL MANAGER:
EUGENE AMODEO
BRANCH MANAGERS
Gail Shiffman
David Daub

ADMINISTRATIVE / DISTRIBUTION MANAGER
Sharon Irwin
DIVISIONAL CONTROLLER
Linda Allen
DIRECTOR, PUBLICITY & PROMOTION
Janice Luke
EXEC. DIRECTOR, ADVERTISING
Janice Doyle
QUÉBEC OFFICE:
8000 Decarie Blvd., Ste. 601, Montréal, QC H4P 2S4
(514) 987-5233, FAX: (514) 849-8270
BRANCH MANAGER
Louise Palmos

WARNER BROS. CANADA INC.
4576 Yonge St., 2nd Fl., North York, ON M2N 6P1
(416) 250-8384, FAX: (416) 250-1898 (Advertising) /
(416) 250-8930 (Sales)

SR. VICE-PRESIDENT / CANADIAN DIVISION MANAGER
Flo Boulet
SR. V.P., ADVERTISING & PUBLICITY
Dianne Schwalm

QUÉBEC OFFICE:
9900 Cavendish, Ste. 205, Ville Saint-Laurent, QC H4M 2V2
(514) 333-6400, FAX: (514) 333-1460
SALES REP.
Susan Karam

35mm

For Maritimes & Manitoba bookings, refer to Margeret Ramsay
in Toronto office: (800) 263-2876 (35mm)

For British Columbia & Alberta bookings, refer to Adam Dumond
in Toronto office: (800) 668-4961 (35mm)

EXHIBITORS & EXHIBITION SERVICES

EXHIBITORS & CIRCUITS

ALLIANCE ATLANTIS CINEMAS
1788 W. 5th Ave., Ste. 200, Vancouver, BC V6J 1P2
(604) 734-8700, FAX: (604) 734-7489
www.allianceatlantiscinemas.com
DIRECTOR OF NATIONAL OPERATIONS
Jennifer Gee
HEAD OFFICE MANAGER
Owen Cameron

AMC THEATRES OF CANADA
33 William Kitchen Rd., Toronto, ON M1P 5B7
(416) 291-2204, FAX: (416) 291-8173. www.amctheatres.com
FILM BUYER
Eric Bauman
OFFICE MANAGER / ASSISTANT BUYER
Louise Murdoch

A THEATRE NEAR YOU (CANADA) INC.
c/o Dolphin Cinema II
4555 E. Hastings St., N. Burnaby, BC V5C 2K3
Tel. & Fax: (604) 293-0332
Also operating: Hollywood 3 (Surrey, B.C.) and New
Westminster 3 (New Westminster, B.C.)

HEAD OFFICE:
Box 3309, 3813 168th St. N.E.
Arlington, WA 98223 U.S.A.. (360) 653-9899,
FAX: (360) 653-1720
CHAIRMAN
Al Dabestani
PRESIDENT
Sudhir Virendra

BOULEVARD THEATRES
73 Dorland Dr., R.R. #2, Napanee, ON K7R 3K7
(613) 354-6163, FAX: (613) 373-0050
CONTACT
Paul Peterson

Also operating: 1000 Island Cinemas, Picton Drive-In

BROADWAY CINEMAS
518 Broadway N., Tillsonburg, ON N4G 3S7
(519) 688-0923 , FAX: (519) 688-2362
CONTACT
Len Walker

CARNIVAL CINEMAS
5402 – 47 St., Red Deer, AB T4N 6Z4
(403) 341-6565, FAX: (403) 341-4355
www.carnivalcinemas.net
CEO
Bill Ramji

CINEMA CITY INC.
5074 – 130 Avenue, Edmonton, AB T5A 5A9
(780) 472-7922, FAX: (780) 472-7853
Contacts
CEO
Lamar E. Gwaltney
COO
Lamar A. (Andy) GwaltneY

CINEMA GUZZO
1055 Chemin de Coteau, 2 ème étage
Terrebonne, QC J6W 5Y8, (450) 961-2945
FAX: (450) 961-9349
PRÉSIDENT
Angelo Guzzo
VICE-PRÉSIDENT EXÉCUTIF
Vincenzo Guzzo
V.P., FINANCE
Gaetano Iacona
DIRECTEUR DE LA PROGRAMATIO
Vito Franco
DIRECTEUR DES OPERATIONS
Mario Quattrociocche
MARKETING & PROMOTION:
James H.E. Dambrevill
COMPTABILITÉ
Ginette Noiseux

CINEMA PARALLELE
3530 boul. St-Laurent, Montréal, QC H2X 2V1
(514) 847-9272, FAX: (514) 847-0732

DIRECTOR
Caroline Masse
Founded in 1967. A non-profit organization dedicated to the pro-
motion of independent cinema and video in Québec and across
Canada. A 100-seat film and video theatre.

LES CINEMAS CINE-ENTREPRISE
1100 Yzes Blais, La Cheine, QC J6V 1P7
(450) 581-5757, FAX: (450) 581-0594
E-mail: reception@cineentreprise.com
www.cineentreprise.com
PRÉSIDENT
Raffaele Papalia

CINEPLEX ODEON CORPORATION
(An Onex Company)
1303 Yonge St., Toronto, ON M4T 2Y9
(416) 323-6600, FAX: (416) 323-6677
www.cineplex.com
CHAIRMAN
Allen Karp
PRESIDENT
Sam DiMichele
SR. VP, FINANCE
Gord Nelson
SR. VP, FILM
Anthony Cianciotta
V.P., OPERATIONS
Colin Smyth

Operating 64 theatres with more than 560 screens in British
Columbia, Alberta, Saskatchewan, Manitoba, Ontario and
Québec.

CONSKY THEATRES
425 Walmer Rd., Unit 6A, Toronto, ON M5P 2X9
(416) 515-8506
CONTACT
Lou Consky

CRITERION – LUXURY THEATRES CORP.
560 Beatty St., Unit L-100, Vancouver, BC V6B 2L8
(604) 623-3160, FAX: (604) 683-8077
CONTACTS
James Evans
Terry Weir
HEAD BOOKER & FILM BUYER
Eric Ball

DYNASTY THEATRES
Box 1560, Melfort, SK S0E 1A0
(306) 752-5523
CONTACT
Ken Pyrema

EMPIRE THEATRES LIMITED
610 East River Rd., New Glasgow, NS B2H 3S2
(902) 755-7620, FAX: (902) 755-7640
E-mail: empire@empiretheatres.com, www.empiretheatres.com
PRESIDENT
Stuart G. Fraser
V.P., OPERATIONS
Kevin J. MacLeod
DIRECTOR, PURCHASING
Brian MacLeod
COMPTROLLER
Jean Rundle
DIRECTOR, INFORMATION SERVICES
Daron Wong

REGIONAL OFFICE
190 Chain Lake Dr., Halifax, NS B3S 1C5
(902) 876-4848, FAX: (902) 876-4849
DIRECTOR, MARKETING
Dean Leland
BOOKER / BUYER
Greg MacNeil
ADVERTISING
Robert Goguen

FAMOUS PLAYERS INC.
146 Bloor St. W., Toronto, ON M5S 1P3
(416) 969-7800, FAX: (416) 964-1792
Website: www.famousplayers.com

Celebrating its 84th anniversary, Famous Players is Canada's top
grossing theatrical exhibitor. Internationally recognized for its superior
technology and innovation in theatre design and guest services, the
company operates a total of 92 locations with 838 screens
across the country, including theatres in its joint venture witn
IMAX and its partnership with Alliance Atlantis. Famous Players

is a Division of Viacom Canada Inc.

KEY EXECUTIVES
PRESIDENT & CEO
Robb Chase
EXEC. V.P. AND CFO
Michael Borys
SR. V.P., MARKETING, CORPORATE SALES &
CONCESSIONS BUSINESS DEVELOPMENT
Jeff Rush
EXEC. V.P., FILM PROGRAMMING
Michael Kennedy
V.P., FILM PROGRAMMING
Kevin Pasquino
SR. V.P., SECRETARY & GENERAL COUNSEL
Michael Scher
V.P., LEGAL COUNSEL
Wendy Kady
V.P., CORPORATE AFFAIRS
Nuria Bronfman
V.P., HUMAN RESOURCES & INDUSTRIAL RELATIONS
Doug Smith
V.P., CENTRAL OPERATIONS EAST
Nigel Bullers
V.P., OPERATIONS DEVELOPMENT & SUPPORT
David Polny
V.P., FINANCE & CONTROLLER
Lisa Depew
V.P., INFORMATION TECHNOLOGY
Ruta Downey
V.P., DESIGN & CONSTRUCTION
Ronald Rivet

DISTRICT OFFICES:
VANCOUVER
V.P., WESTERN OPERATIONS
Murray Silk
(604) 588-3663, FAX(604) 588-4722

MONTRÉAL
V.P., EASTERN OPERATIONS
Ivars Reiss
V.P., FILM PROGRAMMING EASTERN CANADA
Jean Stinziani
(514) 861-7744, FAX: (514) 861-4969

U.S.A.
SR. EXEC. V.P., FILM
Michael McCartney
California, (818) 808-1607, FAX: (818) 461-9639

FESTIVAL CINEMAS
HEAD OFFICE
2236 Queen St. E., Toronto, ON M4E 1G2
(416) 690-0667, FAX: (416) 690-0755
CONTACT
Jerry Szczur
ACCTS. PAYABLE
Dina Wendler

Festival Cinemas Group/Toronto: Fox Theatre, Kingsway
Theatre, The Music Hall, Revue Cinema, Royal Cinema and
Paradise Cinema.

24-hour movie listings hotline: (416) 690-2600

THE FLICKS CINEMA
Box 154, Stonewall, MB R0C 2Z0. (204) 467-8401
CONTACT
Don Smith

FREDERICK TWIN CINEMAS INC.
516 Innsbruck Place, Waterloo, ON N2V 2N9
(519) 747-4342, FAX: (519) 747-5468. www.fredericktwin.com
CONTACT
Kelly MacLeod, kmacleod@fredericktwin.com

GALAXY ENTERTAINMENT INC.
1303 Yonge St., Ste. 300, Toronto, ON M4T 2Y9
(416) 935-1544, FAX: (416) 935-1422
E-mail: galaxy@galaxycinemas.com, www.galaxycinemas.com
CEO
Ellis Jacob
EXEC. VICE-PRESIDENT
Dan McGrath
CFO
Steve Brown
V.P., OPERATIONS
Brad LaDouceur
V.P., MARKETING
Pat Marshall
FILM BOOKING
Shellie Goldberg

GALLERY CINEMAS (WOODSTOCK) INC.
4351 Morgan Cres., W. Vancouver, BC V7V 2P1
(604) 922-3765, FAX: (604) 922-3725
E-mail: info@gallerycinemas.com, www.gallerycinemas.com
PRESIDENT
Chris Van Snellenberg
FILM BUYER
Eric Ball

GOLDEN THEATRES LTD.
2800 John St., Ste. 16, Markham, ON L3R 0E2
(905) 940-3994, FAX: (905) 940-3997. www.atnymovie.com
CONTACT
Eddie Dehmoubed

HARRIS ROAD ENTERTAINMENT GROUP LTD.
19190 Lougheed Highway, Pitt Meadows, BC V3Y 2H6
(604) 465-0528, FAX: (604) 485-0587
PRESIDENT
Joanne Bondar
GENERAL MANAGER
Bill Bondar
MANAGER, HARRIS RD. 3 CINEMAS
Celia Pink
MANAGER, COTTONWOOD 4 CINEMAS
Julie Ouellette
MANAGER, MISSION CITY CINEMA
Adam Ouellette

HIGHLANDS CINEMAS
Box 85, Kinmount, ON K0M 2A0
(705) 488-2107, Office: (705) 488-2199, FAX: (705) 488-9942
www.highlandscinemas.com
CONTACT
Keith Stata

5 screens

LANDMARK CINEMAS OF CANADA LTD.
HEAD OFFICE – ALL DEPARTMENTS
522 – 11th Ave. S.W., 4th Fl., Calgary, AB T2R 0C8
(403) 262-4255, FAX: (403) 266-1529
DIRECTORS
Philip H. May
Frank Kettner
Charles D.K. May
Barry Myers
Brian F. McIntosh
Stephen H. Ross
OFFICERS
PRESIDENT
Brian F. McIntosh
SECRETARY
Philip H. May
VICE-PRESIDENT
Charles D.K. May
VICE-PRESIDENT
Frank Kettner
VICE-PRESIDENT
Barry Myers
MANAGEMENT
MANAGER, FILM BUYING & BOOKING
Kevin Norman
MANAGER, ADVERTISING & CREATIVE SERVICES
Donald D. Langkaas
ACCOUNTING MANAGER
Ian Harwood
ADMINISTRATION MANAGER
Sherry Chappell
CHIEF OPERATING OFFICER
Neil H. Campbell

MAGIC LANTERN THEATRES
14306 – 115 Ave., Box 3707, Stn. D
Edmonton, AB T5L 4J7. (780) 482-1611, FAX: (780) 482-3520
E-mail: mlt@magiclanterntheatres.ca
PRESIDENT
Tom Hutchinson
SECRETARY
Bill Booth

MAY THEATRES INC.
4905 – 50 Ave., Lloydminster, SK S9V 0P7
(306) 825-3884, FAX: (306) 825-6172
PRESIDENT
Phil May

THE MOVIE MILL INC.
1710 Mayor Magrath Dr. S., Lethbridge, AB T1K 2R6
(403) 381-1251, FAX: (403) 381-1256
E-mail: themill@moviemill.com, www.moviemill.com
PRESIDENT
Leonard Binning

Seven screens

NIAGARA PALACE THEATRES LTD.
Operating Town Cinemas
71 Crestdale Ave., St. Catharines, ON L2T 3B4
Tel. & Fax: (905) 688-0286
CONTACTS
Arthur Lefstein
Betty Lefstein

OAKBURN INVESTMENTS LTD.
Consky Theatres
425 Walmer Rd., Unit 6A, Toronto, ON M5P 2X9
(416) 515-8506
PRESIDENT
Lou Consky

ONTARIO CINEMAS INC.
745 Mt. Pleasant Rd., Toronto, ON M4S 2N4
(416) 481-1186, FAX: (416) 481-5244
PRESIDENT
Norman Stern
EXEC. ASSISTANT TO N. STERN
D. Doody

ONTARIO PLACE CORPORATION
955 Lakeshore Blvd. W., Toronto, ON M6K 3B9
(416) 314-9758 / (416) 318-2523
FAX: (416) 314-9993
CONTACT
David Calado
IMAX theatre

PINETREE 6 CINEMAS
110 – 2991 Pinetree Highway, Coquitlam, BC V3B 6J6
(604) 464-3727, FAX: (604) 464-3712
CONTACT
George Mah

PLAZA THEATRE
8 Castleglen Ct. N.E., Calgary, AB T3J 2B8
(403) 283-2222, FAX: (403) 590-1075
CONTACTS
Mike Brar
Nina Brar

PREMIER OPERATING CORPORATION LIMITED
1262 Don Mills Rd., Ste. 92, Don Mills, ON M3B 2W7
(416) 443-1645, FAX: (416) 443-1760
E-mail: premieroperating@on.aibn.com
PRESIDENT
Madge Allen
V.P. / SECRETARY
Brian Allen

THE PRINCESS CINEMA INC.
6 Princess St., Waterloo, ON N2L 2X8
(519) 885-2950, FAX: (519) 885-1048
www.princess.sentex.net
OWNER
John Tutt
Also operating: Princess Two at 46 King St. N., Waterloo
(opening October 2003)

RAINBOW CINEMAS
3806 Albert St., Regina, SK S4S 3R2
(306) 359-6353, FAX: (306) 359-6362
CONTACT
Wilf Runge

THE RIDGE THEATRE
3131 Arbutus St., Vancouver, BC V6J 3Z3
(604) 732-3352, FAX: (604) 732-3353
E-mail: info@ridgetheatre.com, www.ridgetheatre.com
CONTACT
Ingrid Lae

ROYAL THEATRE – TRAIL
1597 Bay Ave., Trail, BC V1R 4B3
(250) 364-2155, FAX: (250) 364-9311
CONTACT
John Turcotte

RPL FILM THEATRE
Central Library
2311 – 12th Ave., Regina, SK S4P 3Z5
(306) 777-6104, FAX: (306) 949-7260
Website: www.reginalibrary.ca
PROGRAMMER
Belinda New

STINSON THEATRES LTD.
Box 142, Barrie, ON L4M 4S9
(705) 726-8190, FAX: (705) 721-9579
PRESIDENT
Robert Stinson

TARRANT ENTERPRISES LIMITED
350 Davis Dr., Box 95588, Newmarket, ON L3Y 8J8
(905) 898-4072, FAX: (905) 895-7557
PRESIDENT
June Tarrant

TILLSONBURG BROADWAY CINEMAS INC.
518 Broadway North, Tillsonburg, ON N4G 3S7
(519) 688-0923, FAX: (519) 688-2362
E-mail: broadwaycinemastburg@on.aibn.com
PRESIDENT
Len Walker
V.P. & SECRETARY / TREASURER
Kathy VanDenbrink

INDEPENDENT BOOKING COMPANIES

ATLANTIC THEATRE SERVICES LTD.
Box 2419, 114 Dresden Ave., Saint John, NB E2L 3V9
(506) 696-6618, FAX: (506) 696-4472
CONTACT
Don McKelvie

CATHY WATSON BOOKING SERVICES
100 Idlewood Dr., Midhurst, ON L0L 1X1
(705) 727-4007, FAX: (705) 727-7907
E-mail: booker888@rogers.com
CONTACT
Cathy Watson

INDEPENDENT BOOKING & THEATRE SERVICES LTD.
1315 Bishop St., Ste. 135, Cambridge, ON N1R 2Z2
(519) 740-1266, FAX: (519) 740-6374
E-mail: ibtsl@rogers.com, www.independentbooking.net
President
Eric Ball

Booking services for cinemas in Canada

PRAIRIE ALLIED BOOKING ASSOCIATION
(A division of Theatre Agencies Ltd.)
522 – 11th Ave. S.W., Calgary, AB T2R 0C8
(403) 264-4660, FAX: (403) 264-6571
CONTACTS
Syd Sniderman
Frank Kettner
Ellen Smeltzer

DELIVERY SERVICES

AIRDATE TRAFFIC SERVICES
629 Adelaide St. W., Toronto, ON M6J 1A8
(416) 703-5451 / (888) 256-5451, FAX: (416) 703-7833
Duplication / distribution

TECHNICOLOR CINEMA DISTRIBUTION
40 Lesmill Rd., Don Mills, ON M3B 2T5
(416) 449-8597 / (416) 447-5167
CANADIAN GENERAL MANAGER
Karen Davis
GENERAL MANAGER
Paul Dumond

ALBERTA
3904 – 1st St. N.E., Calgary, AB T2E 3E3
(403) 276-6696
MANAGER
Susan Piotrowski

BRITISH COLUMBIA
1644 W. 75th Ave., Vancouver, BC V6P 6G2
(604) 263-2551
Manager
Rick Williston

MANITOBA
2315 Logan Ave., Winnipeg, MB R2R 2S7
(204) 633-1203
MANAGER
Allan Laschuk

NEW BRUNSWICK
55 Bentley St., St. John, NB E2K 1B2
(506) 634-1018
MANAGER
Kevin McDermott

QUÉBEC
708 rue Walnut, Montréal, QC H4C 3E4
(514) 931-6212
MANAGER
Marie-Claude Boudreau

THEATRE ASSOCIATIONS

ASSOCIATION DES PROPRIETAIRES DE CINEMA ET CINE-PARC DU QUEBEC INC.
C.P. 49099, 7275 Sherbrooke est, Montréal, QC H1N 3T6
Tel. & FAX: (514) 356-0800
E-mail: rejean.seguin2@sympatico.ca
PRESIDENT
Raffaele Papalia

ATLANTIC INDEPENDENT THEATRE EXHIBITORS ASSOCIATION
Box 2419, Saint John, NB E2L 3V9
(506) 696-6618
PRESIDENT
Don McKelvie

ATLANTIC MOTION PICTURE EXHIBITORS ASSOCIATION
c/o Empire Theatres Limited
190 Chain Lake Dr., Halifax, NS B3S 1C5
(902) 876-4848, FAX: (902) 876-4849
E-mail: leland@empiretheatres.com
PRESIDENT
Dean Leland

MOTION PICTURE THEATRE ASSOCIATION OF ALBERTA
c/o Cineplex Odeon Corp.
Clareview Town Centre, 4211 – 139th Ave., Edmonton, AB T5Y 2W8. (780) 473-8383
PRESIDENT
Ian Easson
SECRETARY-TREASURER
Ian Harwood

MOTION PICTURE THEATRE ASSOCIATION OF B.C.
5000 Bridge St., Ste. 200, Delta, BC V4K 3X8
(604) 588-3663, FAX: (604) 940-9541
PRESIDENT
Trent Sales

TREASURER
George Man, (604) 853-8600

MOTION PICTURE THEATRE ASSOCIATIONS OF CANADA
146 Bloor St. W., Toronto, ON M5S 1P3
(416) 969-7057, FAX: (416) 964-6007
E-mail: mptac@inforamp.net, www.mptac.ca
EXEC. DIRECTOR
Adina Lebo
PRESIDENT
Robb Chase
SECRETARY
Dean LelandTREASURER
Dan McGrath

MOTION PICTURE THEATRE ASSOCIATION OF MANITOBA
c/o Cinema City Northgate
1399 McPhillips St., Winnipeg, MB R2V 3L4
(204) 334-6189, FAX: (204) 334-6298
E-mail: cinemaservices@shaw.ca
PRESIDENT
Terry Stannard

MOTION PICTURE THEATRES ASSOCIATION OF ONTARIO
21 Dundas Sq., Ste. 906, Toronto, ON M5B 1B7
(416) 368-1139, FAX: (416) 368-1130
PRESIDENT
Norman Stern
SECRETARY-TREASURER
Barry Chapman

MOTION PICTURE THEATRE ASSOCIATION OF SASKATCHEWAN
c/o Rainbow Theatres
3806 Albert St., Golden Mile Centre, Regina, SK S4S 3R2
(306) 359-6353, FAX: (306) 359-6362
PRESIDENT
Wilf Runge

INDOOR THEATRES

Theatres are listed by province, then by the cities within each province. Listings include the theatre name, the licensee/owner, the city's population, and the seat count.

ALBERTA

A

AIRDRIE

Roxy 1	Landmark Cinemas	29,382	250
Roxy 2	Landmark Cinemas		250

B

BANFF

Lux Cinema Centre 1	Landmark Cinemas	7,135	300
Lux Cinema Centre 2	Landmark Cinemas		225
Lux Cinema Centre 3	Landmark Cinemas		125
Lux Cinema Centre 4	Landmark Cinemas		200

BARRHEAD

Roxy	Jim Carnegie	4,213	443

BLAIRMORE

Orpheum	Becky Fabro	1,993	350

BROOKS

Oasis	Landmark Cinemas	11,604	275

C

CALGARY

Moviedome 1	Al Dadani	951,395	116
Moviedome 2	Al Dadani		158
Moviedome 3	Al Dadani		150
Moviedome 4	Al Dadani		156
Moviedome 5	Al Dadani		141
Moviedome 6	Al Dadani		176
Moviedome 7	Al Dadani		176
Moviedome 8	Al Dadani		199
Moviedome 9	Al Dadani		161
Centennial Planetarium	City of Calgary		265
Coliseum 1	Famous Players Inc.		139
Coliseum 2	Famous Players Inc.		157
Coliseum 3	Famous Players Inc.		187
Coliseum 4	Famous Players Inc.		202
Coliseum 5	Famous Players Inc.		202
Coliseum 6	Famous Players Inc.		208
Coliseum 7	Famous Players Inc.		306
Coliseum 8	Famous Players Inc.		316
Coliseum 9	Famous Players Inc.		422
Coliseum 10	Famous Players Inc.		421
Crowfoot Crossing 1	Cineplex Odeon Corp.		162
Crowfoot Crossing 2	Cineplex Odeon Corp.		162
Crowfoot Crossing 3	Cineplex Odeon Corp.		162
Crowfoot Crossing 4	Cineplex Odeon Corp.		181
Crowfoot Crossing 5	Cineplex Odeon Corp.		202
Crowfoot Crossing 6	Cineplex Odeon Corp.		203
Crowfoot Crossing 7	Cineplex Odeon Corp.		183
Crowfoot Crossing 8	Cineplex Odeon Corp.		220
Crowfoot Crossing 9	Cineplex Odeon Corp.		220
Crowfoot Crossing 10	Cineplex Odeon Corp.		220
Crowfoot Crossing 11	Cineplex Odeon Corp.		220
Crowfoot Crossing 12	Cineplex Odeon Corp.		224
Eau Claire 1	Cineplex Odeon Corp.		289
Eau Claire 2	Cineplex Odeon Corp.		293
Eau Claire 3	Cineplex Odeon Corp.		195
Eau Claire 4	Cineplex Odeon Corp.		213
Eau Claire 5	Cineplex Odeon Corp.		468
Globe Cinema 1	Landmark Cinemas		378
Globe Cinema 2	Landmark Cinemas		378
Paramount Chinook 1	Famous Players Inc.		364
Paramount Chinook 2	Famous Players Inc.		469
Paramount Chinook 3	Famous Players Inc.		231
Paramount Chinook 4	Famous Players Inc.		231
Paramount Chinook 5	Famous Players Inc.		160
Paramount Chinook 6	Famous Players Inc.		160
Paramount Chinook 7	Famous Players Inc.		160
Paramount Chinook 8	Famous Players Inc.		160
Paramount Chinook 9	Famous Players Inc.		469
Paramount Chinook 10	Famous Players Inc.		364
Paramount Chinook 11	Famous Players Inc.		231
Paramount Chinook 12	Famous Players Inc.		231
Paramount Chinook 13	Famous Players Inc.		160
Paramount Chinook 14	Famous Players Inc.		160
Paramount Chinook 15	Famous Players Inc.		160
Paramount Chinook 16	Famous Players Inc.		160
Paramount Chinook Imax Plaza	Famous Players Inc. M. Brar / N. Brar		259 370
Silver City Country Hills 1	Famous Players Inc.		341
Silver City Country Hills 2	Famous Players Inc.		157
Silver City Country Hills 3	Famous Players Inc.		227
Silver City Country Hills 4	Famous Players Inc.		157
Silver City Country Hills 5	Famous Players Inc.		227
Silver City Country Hills 6	Famous Players Inc.		157
Silver City Country Hills 7	Famous Players Inc.		157
Silver City Country Hills 8	Famous Players Inc.		443
Silver City Country Hills 9	Famous Players Inc.		443
Silver City Country Hills 10	Famous Players Inc.		157
Silver City Country Hills 11	Famous Players Inc.		157
Silver City Country Hills 12	Famous Players Inc.		227
Silver City Country Hills 13	Famous Players Inc.		157
Silver City Country Hills 14	Famous Players Inc.		227
Silver City Country Hills 15	Famous Players Inc.		157
Silver City Country Hills 16	Famous Players Inc.		341
Sunridge Spectrum 1	Cineplex Odeon Corp.		438
Sunridge Spectrum 2	Cineplex Odeon Corp.		245
Sunridge Spectrum 3	Cineplex Odeon Corp.		161
Sunridge Spectrum 4	Cineplex Odeon Corp.		161
Sunridge Spectrum 5	Cineplex Odeon Corp.		161
Sunridge Spectrum 6	Cineplex Odeon Corp.		209
Sunridge Spectrum 7	Cineplex Odeon Corp.		307
Sunridge Spectrum 8	Cineplex Odeon Corp.		307
Sunridge Spectrum 9	Cineplex Odeon Corp.		209
Sunridge Spectrum 10	Cineplex Odeon Corp.		161
Sunridge Spectrum 11	Cineplex Odeon Corp.		161
Sunridge Spectrum 12	Cineplex Odeon Corp.		161
Sunridge Spectrum 13	Cineplex Odeon Corp.		245
Sunridge Spectrum 14	Cineplex Odeon Corp.		438
Westhills 1	Famous Players Inc.		449
Westhills 2	Famous Players Inc.		323
Westhills 3	Famous Players Inc.		201
Westhills 4	Famous Players Inc.		201
Westhills 5	Famous Players Inc.		201
Westhills 6	Famous Players Inc.		201
Westhills 7	Famous Players Inc.		201
Westhills 8	Famous Players Inc.		201
Westhills 9	Famous Players Inc.		323
Westhills 10	Famous Players Inc.		449

CAMROSE

Duggan 1	Magic Lantern Theatres	14,854	197
Duggan 2	Magic Lantern Theatres		226
Duggan 3	Magic Lantern Theatres		151
Duggan 4	Magic Lantern Theatres		93
Duggan 5	Magic Lantern Theatres		83

CARDSTON

Carriage House	Jamie Quinton	3,475	339

COLD LAKE

Grand Square 1	May Cinemas	27,935	263
Grand Square 2	May Cinemas		211
Grand Square 3	May Cinemas		144
Grand Square 4	May Cinemas		120

D

DRAYTON VALLEY

Cardium	Irvin Janzen	5,801	275

E

EDMONTON

Cinema City 12 - 1	Cinema City	975,477	272
Cinema City 12 - 2	Cinema City		196
Cinema City 12 - 3	Cinema City		196
Cinema City 12 - 4	Cinema City		238
Cinema City 12 - 5	Cinema City		72
Cinema City 12 - 6	Cinema City		84
Cinema City 12 - 7	Cinema City		112
Cinema City 12 - 8	Cinema City		196
Cinema City 12 - 9	Cinema City		196
Cinema City 12 - 10	Cinema City		191
Cinema City 12 - 11	Cinema City		101
Cinema City 12 - 12	Cinema City		112
City Centre 1	Cineplex Odeon Corp.		515
City Centre 2	Cineplex Odeon Corp.		654
City Centre 3	Cineplex Odeon Corp.		310
City Centre 4	Cineplex Odeon Corp.		370
City Centre 5	Cineplex Odeon Corp.		206

Theatre	Operator	Seats
City Centre 6	Cineplex Odeon Corp.	214
City Centre 7	Cineplex Odeon Corp.	262
City Centre 8	Cineplex Odeon Corp.	321
City Centre 9	Cineplex Odeon Corp.	276
Clareview 1	Cineplex Odeon Corp.	126
Clareview 2	Cineplex Odeon Corp.	126
Clareview 3	Cineplex Odeon Corp.	126
Clareview 4	Cineplex Odeon Corp.	155
Clareview 5	Cineplex Odeon Corp.	155
Clareview 6	Cineplex Odeon Corp.	155
Clareview 7	Cineplex Odeon Corp.	205
Clareview 8	Cineplex Odeon Corp.	205
Clareview 9	Cineplex Odeon Corp.	204
Clareview 10	Cineplex Odeon Corp.	206
Garneau	Magic Lantern Theatres	527
Gateway 1	Famous Players Inc.	349
Gateway 2	Famous Players Inc.	328
Gateway 3	Famous Players Inc.	272
Gateway 4	Famous Players Inc.	298
Gateway 5	Famous Players Inc.	234
Gateway 6	Famous Players Inc.	234
Gateway 7	Famous Players Inc.	216
Gateway 8	Famous Players Inc.	298
Movies 12-1	Cinema City	234
Movies 12-2	Cinema City	161
Movies 12-3	Cinema City	119
Movies 12-4	Cinema City	119
Movies 12-5	Cinema City	147
Movies 12-6	Cinema City	237
Movies 12-7	Cinema City	336
Movies 12-8	Cinema City	249
Movies 12-9	Cinema City	147
Movies 12-10	Cinema City	119
Movies 12-11	Cinema City	161
Movies 12-12	Cinema City	189
Paramount	Famous Players Inc.	817
Princess Twin 1	Magic Lantern Theatres	394
Princess Twin 2	Magic Lantern Theatres	98
Silver City West Edm. Mall 1	Famous Players Inc.	446
Silver City West Edm. Mall 2	Famous Players Inc.	347
Silver City West Edm. Mall 3	Famous Players Inc.	242
Silver City West Edm. Mall 4	Famous Players Inc.	446
Silver City West Edm. Mall 5	Famous Players Inc.	197
Silver City West Edm. Mall 6	Famous Players Inc.	197
Silver City West Edm. Mall 7	Famous Players Inc.	242
Silver City West Edm. Mall 8	Famous Players Inc.	242
Silver City West Edm. Mall 9	Famous Players Inc.	230
Silver City West Edm. Mall 10	Famous Players Inc.	242
Silver City West Edm. Mall 11	Famous Players Inc.	197
Silver City West Edm. Mall 12	Famous Players Inc.	347
Silver City W.Edm. Mall Imax	Famous Players Inc.	258
North Edmonton 1	Cineplex Odeon Corp.	446
North Edmonton 2	Cineplex Odeon Corp.	249
North Edmonton 3	Cineplex Odeon Corp.	164
North Edmonton 4	Cineplex Odeon Corp.	164
North Edmonton 5	Cineplex Odeon Corp.	164
North Edmonton 6	Cineplex Odeon Corp.	213
North Edmonton 7	Cineplex Odeon Corp.	308
North Edmonton 8	Cineplex Odeon Corp.	308
North Edmonton 9	Cineplex Odeon Corp.	213
North Edmonton 10	Cineplex Odeon Corp.	164
North Edmonton 11	Cineplex Odeon Corp.	164
North Edmonton 12	Cineplex Odeon Corp.	164
North Edmonton 13	Cineplex Odeon Corp.	249
North Edmonton 14	Cineplex Odeon Corp.	446
South Edmonton 1	Cineplex Odeon Corp.	492
South Edmonton 2	Cineplex Odeon Corp.	213
South Edmonton 3	Cineplex Odeon Corp.	164
South Edmonton 4	Cineplex Odeon Corp.	164
South Edmonton 5	Cineplex Odeon Corp.	164
South Edmonton 6	Cineplex Odeon Corp.	213
South Edmonton 7	Cineplex Odeon Corp.	249
South Edmonton 8	Cineplex Odeon Corp.	307
South Edmonton 9	Cineplex Odeon Corp.	307
South Edmonton 10	Cineplex Odeon Corp.	249
South Edmonton 11	Cineplex Odeon Corp.	213
South Edmonton 12	Cineplex Odeon Corp.	164
South Edmonton 13	Cineplex Odeon Corp.	164
South Edmonton 14	Cineplex Odeon Corp.	164
South Edmonton 15	Cineplex Odeon Corp.	213
South Edmonton 16	Cineplex Odeon Corp.	494
U of A - Myer	University of Alberta Horowitz Theatre	
West Mall 6 - 1	Cineplex Odeon Corp.	241
West Mall 6 - 2	Cineplex Odeon Corp.	243
West Mall 6 - 3	Cineplex Odeon Corp.	235
West Mall 6 - 4	Cineplex Odeon Corp.	236
West Mall 6 - 5	Cineplex Odeon Corp.	232
New West Mall 8 - 1	Cineplex Odeon Corp.	145
New West Mall 8 - 2	Cineplex Odeon Corp.	145
New West Mall 8 - 3	Cineplex Odeon Corp.	159
New West Mall 8 - 4	Cineplex Odeon Corp.	238
New West Mall 8 - 5	Cineplex Odeon Corp.	206

Theatre	Operator	Pop.	Seats
New West Mall 8 - 6	Cineplex Odeon Corp.		414
New West Mall 8 - 7	Cineplex Odeon Corp.		425
New West Mall 8 - 8	Cineplex Odeon Corp.		140
Westmount Centre 1	Famous Players Inc.		498
Westmount Centre 2	Famous Players Inc.		320
Westmount Centre 3	Famous Players Inc.		351
Westmount Centre 4	Famous Players Inc.		256

EDISON
Nova Theatre	Landmark Cinemas	7,585	351

F

FORT MACLEOD
Empress	Film Society	2,990	398

FORT McMURRAY
Fort 1	May Theatres	34,949	348
Fort 2	May Theatres		348
Fort 3	May Theatres		450
McCinema 1	May Theatres		250
McCinema 2	May Theatres		250
McCinema 3	May Theatres		150
McCinema 4	May Theatres		150
McCinema 5	May Theatres		110
McCinema 6	May Theatres		110

FORT SASKATCHEWAN
Gemini 1	Jai Une Lee	13,121	288
SaskatchewanGemini 2	Jai Une Lee		138
Gemini 3	Jai Une Lee		138

G

Grande Prairie
Grand Prairie 1	Cineplex Odeon Corp.	36,735	157
Grand Prairie 2	Cineplex Odeon Corp.		168
Grand Prairie 3	Cineplex Odeon Corp.		166
Grand Prairie 4	Cineplex Odeon Corp.		157
Grand Prairie 5	Cineplex Odeon Corp.		117
Grand Prairie 6	Cineplex Odeon Corp.		117
Grand Prairie 7	Cineplex Odeon Corp.		183
Grand Prairie 8	Cineplex Odeon Corp.		157
Grand Prairie 9	Cineplex Odeon Corp.		157
Grand Prairie 10	Cineplex Odeon Corp.		183
Jan Cinema 1	Landmark Cinemas		348
Jan Cinema 2	Landmark Cinemas		201
Jan Cinema 3	Landmark Cinemas		120
Lyric 1	Landmark Cinemas		325
Lyric 2	Landmark Cinemas		298
Lyric 3	Landmark Cinemas		262

H

HIGH PRAIRIE
Roxy	J. Kachnic	2,737	120

HINTON
Roxy Theatre	Landmark Cinemas	9,405	307

J

JASPER
Chaba 1	Dwain Wacko	3,716	179
Chaba 2	Dwain Wacko		114

L

LAC LA BICHE
Aurora	Fatima Taha	2,776	240

LEDUC
Gaiety 1	Mohammed Fares	15,032	330
Gaiety 2	Mohammed Fares		205
Gaiety 3	Mohammed Fares		150
Gaiety 4	Mohammed Fares		150

LETHBRIDGE
Centre Cinema 1	Famous Players Inc.	67,374	264
Centre Cinema 2	Famous Players Inc.		375
Paramount 1	Famous Players Inc.		703
Paramount 2	Famous Players Inc.		474
Park Place 1	Cineplex Odeon Corp.		202
Park Place 2	Cineplex Odeon Corp.		258
Park Place 3	Cineplex Odeon Corp.		144
Park Place 4	Cineplex Odeon Corp.		144
Park Place 5	Cineplex Odeon Corp.		244
Park Place 6	Cineplex Odeon Corp.		195

M

MANNING
Aurora	Leslie & Paul Snyder	1,293	300

MEDICINE HAT
Medicine Hat 1	Cineplex Odeon Corp.	61,735	140
Medicine Hat 2	Cineplex Odeon Corp.		169
Medicine Hat 3	Cineplex Odeon Corp.		136
Medicine Hat 4	Cineplex Odeon Corp.		120
Medicine Hat 5	Cineplex Odeon Corp.		107

Medicine Hat 6	Cineplex Odeon Corp.		121
Medicine Hat 7	Cineplex Odeon Corp.		220
Medicine Hat 8	Cineplex Odeon Corp.		180
Medicine Hat 9	Cineplex Odeon Corp.		115
Medicine Hat 10	Cineplex Odeon Corp.		145
Monarch Theatre	Landmark Cinemas		451
Towne Cinema Centre 1	Landmark Cinemas		421
Towne Cinema Centre 2	Landmark Cinemas		136
Towne Cinema Centre 3	Landmark Cinemas		130

O

OKOTOKS

Okotok Twin 1	Dan Hunter	11,679	200
Okotok Twin 2	Dan Hunter		180

P

PEACE RIVER

Cinema '72 Twin- 1	Magic Lantern Theatres	6,240	300
Cinema '72 Twin - 2	Magic Lantern Theatres		90

PINCHER CREEK

Fox (2 screens)	Edith Becker	3,666	386

PONOKA

Capitol 1	Jim Kharfan	6,330	260
Capitol 2	Jim Kharfan		88

R

RED DEER

Carnival Cinemas 1	Carnival Cinemas	67,707	119
Carnival Cinemas 2	Carnival Cinemas		140
Carnival Cinemas 3	Carnival Cinemas		204
Carnival Cinemas 4	Carnival Cinemas		160
Carnival Cinemas 5	Carnival Cinemas		160
Carnival Cinemas 6	Carnival Cinemas		155
Carnival Cinemas 7	Carnival Cinemas		140
Carnival Cinemas 8	Carnival Cinemas		116
Park Plaza 1	Famous Players Inc.		605
Park Plaza 2	Famous Players Inc.		152
Park Plaza 3	Famous Players Inc.		152
Park Plaza 4	Famous Players Inc.		152
Park Plaza 5	Famous Players Inc.		218
Park Plaza 6	Famous Players Inc.		230
Uptown Cinema Centre 1	Landmark Cinemas		414
Uptown Cinema Centre 2	Landmark Cinemas		109
Uptown Cinema Centre 3	Landmark Cinemas		143
Uptown Cinema Centre 4	Landmark Cinemas		120

S

ST. ALBERT

Grandin 1	Grandin Theatres	53,081	190
Grandin 2	Grandin Theatres		190
Grandin 3	Grandin Theatres		160
Grandin 4	Grandin Theatres		160
Grandin 5	Grandin Theatres		160
Village Tree 1	Cineplex Odeon Corp.		90
Village Tree 2	Cineplex Odeon Corp.		65
Village Tree 3	Cineplex Odeon Corp.		74
Village Tree 4	Cineplex Odeon Corp.		70
Village Tree 5	Cineplex Odeon Corp.		77
Village Tree 6	Cineplex Odeon Corp.		112
Village Tree 7	Cineplex Odeon Corp.		110
Village Tree 8	Cineplex Odeon Corp.		76
Village Tree 9	Cineplex Odeon Corp.		70
Village Tree 10	Cineplex Odeon Corp.		75
Village Tree 11	Cineplex Odeon Corp.		66
Village Tree 12	Cineplex Odeon Corp.		90

ST. PAUL

Elite 1	Magic Lantern Theatres	5,061	268
Elite 2	Magic Lantern Theatres		116
Elite 3	Magic Lantern Theatres		121

SHERWOOD

Sherwood Park 1	Galaxy Entertainment	47,645	366
ParkSherwood Park 2	Galaxy Entertainment		246
Sherwood Park 3	Galaxy Entertainment		185
Sherwood Park 4	Galaxy Entertainment		137
Sherwood Park 5	Galaxy Entertainment		140
Sherwood Park 6	Galaxy Entertainment		185
Sherwood Park 7	Galaxy Entertainment		236
Sherwood Park 8	Galaxy Entertainment		149
Sherwood Park 9	Galaxy Entertainment		159
Sherwood Park 10	Galaxy Entertainment		254

SLAVE LAKE

Rex	A.C.L. Evans	7,286	355

SPRUCE GROOVE

Magic Lantern Cinema	Magic Lantern Theatres	16,898	253

STETTLER

Jewel Theatre	Landmark Cinemas	5,225	328

STRATHMORE

Joylan	Bill Crispin	7,621	194

W

WAINWRIGHT

Alma 1	May Theatres	5,117	208
Alma 2	May Theatres		83
Alma 3	May Theatres		83

WETASKIWIN

Cinema	Mohammed Fare	11,154	350

WHITECOURT

Vista	Magic Lantern Theatres		260

BRITISH COLUMBIA

A

ABBOTSFORD

Grand 1	Landmark Cinemas	129,475	146
Grand 2	Landmark Cinemas		177
Grand 3	Landmark Cinemas		288
Grand 4	Landmark Cinemas		146
Grand 5	Landmark Cinemas		177
Grand 6	Landmark Cinemas		288
Towne Cinema Centre 1	Landmark Cinemas		304
Towne Cinema Centre 2	Landmark Cinemas		304
Towne Cinema Centre 3	Landmark Cinemas		362
Towne Cinema Centre 4	Landmark Cinemas		321
Towne Cinema Centre 5	Landmark Cinemas		204
Towne Cinema Centre 6	Landmark Cinemas		155
Towne Cinema Centre 7	Landmark Cinemas		244
Towne Cinema Centre 8	Landmark Cinemas		165
Towne Cinema Centre 9	Landmark Cinemas		126

B

BURNABY

Dolphin Cinema 1	A Theatre Near You, Inc.	193,954	350
Dolphin Cinema 2	A Theatre Near You, Inc.		350
SilverCity Metropolis 1	Famous Players Inc.		465
SilverCity Metropolis 2	Famous Players Inc.		465
SilverCity Metropolis 3	Famous Players Inc.		292
SilverCity Metropolis 4	Famous Players Inc.		266
SilverCity Metropolis 5	Famous Players Inc.		158
SilverCity Metropolis 6	Famous Players Inc.		352
SilverCity Metropolis 7	Famous Players Inc.		365
SilverCity Metropolis 8	Famous Players Inc.		268
SilverCity Metropolis 9	Famous Players Inc.		268
SilverCity Metropolis 10	Famous Players Inc.		220
Station Square 1	Famous Players Inc.		492
Station Square 2	Famous Players Inc.		410
Station Square 3	Famous Players Inc.		285
Station Square 4	Famous Players Inc.		202
Station Square 5	Famous Players Inc.		202
Station Square 6	Famous Players Inc.		202
Station Square 7	Famous Players Inc.		196

BURNS LAKE

Beacon	D. Montaldi/G. Anderson	1,942	35

C

CAMPBELL

Galaxy Theatre 1	Landmark Cinemas	33,872	300
RiverGalaxy Theatre 2	Landmark Cinemas		300
Showcase 1	Landmark Cinemas		210
Showcase 2	Landmark Cinemas		192
Showcase 3	Landmark Cinemas		180
Showcase 4	Landmark Cinemas		212
Showcase 5	Landmark Cinemas		293

CASTLEGAR

Castle	R.J. Bennett	8,677	00

CHILLIWACK

Cottonwood 4 - 1	Harris Road Ent. Group Ltd.	69,776	170
Cottonwood 4 - 2	Harris Road Ent. Group Ltd.		135
Cottonwood 4 - 3	Harris Road Ent. Group Ltd.		120
Cottonwood 4 - 4	Harris Road Ent. Group Ltd.		150
Paramount 1	Landmark Cinemas		370
Paramount 2	Landmark Cinemas		236

COQUITLAM

Pinetree 1	George Mah	112,890	60
Pinetree 2	George Mah		260
Pinetree 3	George Mah		260
Pinetree 4	George Mah		439
Pinetree 5	George Mah		283
Pinetree 6	George Mah		232
Eagle Ridge 1	Famous Players Inc.		280
Eagle Ridge 2	Famous Players Inc.		235
Eagle Ridge 3	Famous Players Inc.		234
Eagle Ridge 4	Famous Players Inc.		234
Eagle Ridge 5	Famous Players Inc.		235

Theatre	Company		Seats
Eagle Ridge 6	Famous Players Inc.		273
SilverCity 1	Famous Players Inc.		450
SilverCity 2	Famous Players Inc.		196
SilverCity 3	Famous Players Inc.		196
SilverCity 4	Famous Players Inc.		186
SilverCity 5	Famous Players Inc.		158
SilverCity 6	Famous Players Inc.		158
SilverCity 7	Famous Players Inc.		186
SilverCity 8	Famous Players Inc.		196
SilverCity 9	Famous Players Inc.		345
SilverCity 10	Famous Players Inc.		196
SilverCity 11	Famous Players Inc.		196
SilverCity 12	Famous Players Inc.		345
SilverCity 13	Famous Players Inc.		196
SilverCity 14	Famous Players Inc.		186
SilverCity 15	Famous Players Inc.		158
SilverCity 16	Famous Players Inc.		158
SilverCity 17	Famous Players Inc.		186
SilverCity 18	Famous Players Inc.		137
SilverCity 19	Famous Players Inc.		196
SilverCity 20	Famous Players Inc.		450

COURTENAY

Theatre	Company		Seats
Criterion Twin 1	Criterion Theatres	47,051	300
Criterion Twin 2	Criterion Theatres		90
Palace	Criterion Theatres		500
Rialto Theatre 1	Landmark Cinemas		310
Rialto Theatre 2	Landmark Cinemas		115
Rialto Theatre 3	Landmark Cinemas		125
Rialto Theatre 4	Landmark Cinemas		210

CRANBROOK

Theatre	Company		Seats
Columbia 1	Alta/BC JV Ltd.	24,275	145
Columbia 2	Alta/BC JV Ltd.		210
Columbia 3	Alta/BC JV Ltd.		195
Columbia 4	Alta/BC JV Ltd.		150
Columbia 5	Alta/BC JV Ltd.		130

CRESTON

Theatre	Company		Seats
New Tivoli	Robert Geddes	4,795	250

D

DAWSON CREEK

Theatre	Company		Seats
Center Cinema	Landmark Cinemas	10,754	468

DUNCAN

Theatre	Company		Seats
Duncan Twin	Criterion Theatres	38,813	372
Duncan Twin	Criterion Theatres		293

F

FERNIE

Theatre	Company		Seats
Vogue (2 screens)		4,997	211

FORT NELSON

Theatre	Company		Seats
Phoenix	Doug Roper	4,188	

FORT ST. JAMES

Theatre	Company		Seats
Lido	Kirk Nelson		

FORT ST. JOHN

Theatre	Company		Seats
Aurora Cinema Centre 1	Landmark Cinemas	16,034	245
Aurora Cinema Centre 2	Landmark Cinemas		150
Aurora Cinema Centre 3	Landmark Cinemas		148
Aurora Cinema Centre 4	Landmark Cinemas		124
Aurora Cinema Centre 5	Landmark Cinemas		138
Lido	Landmark Cinemas		375

G

GOLDEN

Theatre	Company		Seats
Golden	R & M Coulter		

GRAND FORKS

Theatre	Company		Seats
Gem	Marius Paquet	4,054	285

H

HAZELTON

Theatre	Company		Seats
Tri-Town	R. Beertema	345	199

HOPE

Theatre	Company		Seats
	Jeff Larson		

I

INVERMERE

Theatre	Company		Seats
Toby	R.W. Peters	2,858	300

K

KAMLOOPS

Theatre	Company		Seats
Aberdeen Mall 1	Cineplex Odeon Corp.	86,491	236
Aberdeen Mall 2	Cineplex Odeon Corp.		215
Aberdeen Mall 3	Cineplex Odeon Corp.		99
Aberdeen Mall 4	Cineplex Odeon Corp.		100
Aberdeen Mall 5	Cineplex Odeon Corp.		100
Aberdeen Mall 6	Cineplex Odeon Corp.		125
Aberdeen Mall 7	Cineplex Odeon Corp.		128
Aberdeen Mall 8	Cineplex Odeon Corp.		330
Northhills	Landmark Cinemas		404
Paramount 1	Landmark Cinemas		632
Paramount 2	Landmark Cinemas		280

KELOWNA

Theatre	Company		Seats
Grand 10 Cinema 1	Landmark Cinemas	108,330	201
Grand 10 Cinema 2	Landmark Cinemas		282
Grand 10 Cinema 3	Landmark Cinemas		269
Grand 10 Cinema 4	Landmark Cinemas		185
Grand 10 Cinema 5	Landmark Cinemas		153
Grand 10 Cinema 6	Landmark Cinemas		153
Grand 10 Cinema 7	Landmark Cinemas		185
Grand 10 Cinema 8	Landmark Cinemas		185
Grand 10 Cinema 9	Landmark Cinemas		247
Grand 10 Cinema 10	Landmark Cinemas		201
Orchard Plaza 1	Famous Players Inc.		362
Orchard Plaza 2	Famous Players Inc.		418
Orchard Plaza 3	Famous Players Inc.		214
Orchard Plaza 4	Famous Players Inc.		147
Orchard Plaza 5	Famous Players Inc.		249
Paramount 1	Landmark Cinemas		427
Paramount 2	Landmark Cinemas		170
Paramount 3	Landmark Cinemas		144

KIMBERLEY

Theatre	Company		Seats
Werner	Karen Franz	6,484	

KITIMAT

Theatre	Company		Seats
Nechako	Bob Corliss	10,285	

L

LANGFORD

Theatre	Company		Seats
Criterion 1	Criterion Theatres	18,840	246
Criterion 2	Criterion Theatres		248
Criterion 3	Criterion Theatres		365

LANGLEY

Theatre	Company		Seats
Colossus 1	Famous Players Inc.	23,643	450
Colossus 2	Famous Players Inc.		241
Colossus 3	Famous Players Inc.		351
Colossus 4	Famous Players Inc.		351
Colossus 5	Famous Players Inc.		227
Colossus 6	Famous Players Inc.		228
Colossus 7	Famous Players Inc.		197
Colossus 8	Famous Players Inc.		241
Colossus 9	Famous Players Inc.		229
Colossus 10	Famous Players Inc.		238
Colossus 11	Famous Players Inc.		450
Colossus 12	Famous Players Inc.		349
Colossus 13	Famous Players Inc.		352
Colossus 14	Famous Players Inc.		229
Colossus 15	Famous Players Inc.		229
Colossus 16	Famous Players Inc.		241
Colossus 17	Famous Players Inc.		197
Colossus 18	Famous Players Inc.		236
Colossus / Imax	Famous Players Inc.		254
Willowbrook 1	Famous Players Inc.		258
Willowbrook 2	Famous Players Inc.		221
Willowbrook 3	Famous Players Inc.		208
Willowbrook 4	Famous Players Inc.		206
Willowbrook 5	Famous Players Inc.		218
Willowbrook 6	Famous Players Inc.		258

M

MISSION

Theatre	Company		Seats
Mission City	Harris Road Ent. Group Ltd.	31,272	210
Silver City 1	Famous Players Inc.		230
Silver City 2	Famous Players Inc.		351
Silver City 3	Famous Players Inc.		197
Silver City 4	Famous Players Inc.		159
Silver City 5	Famous Players Inc.		242
Silver City 6	Famous Players Inc.		197
Silver City 7	Famous Players Inc.		197
Silver City 8	Famous Players Inc.		242
Silver City 9	Famous Players Inc.		159
Silver City 10	Famous Players Inc.		197
Silver City 11	Famous Players Inc.		351
Silver City 12	Famous Players Inc.		230

N

NAKUSP

Theatre	Company		Seats
Arrow Lakes	Bill White	1,698	

NANAIMO

Theatre	Company		Seats
Avalon Cinema Centre 1	Landmark Cinemas	85,664	165
Avalon Cinema Centre 2	Landmark Cinemas		155
Avalon Cinema Centre 3	Landmark Cinemas		185
Avalon Cinema Centre 4	Landmark Cinemas		185
Avalon Cinema Centre 5	Landmark Cinemas		245
Avalon Cinema Centre 6	Landmark Cinemas		280
Avalon Cinema Centre 7	Landmark Cinemas		230
Avalon Cinema Centre 8	Landmark Cinemas		295
The Bay Theatre 1	Landmark Cinemas		500

Theatre	Operator		
The Bay Theatre 2	Landmark Cinemas		240
Rutherford Mall 1	Galaxy Cinemas		287
Rutherford Mall 2	Galaxy Cinemas		300
Rutherford Mall 3	Galaxy Cinemas		177
Rutherford Mall 4	Galaxy Cinemas		177
Rutherford Mall 5	Galaxy Cinemas		292
Rutherford Mall 6	Galaxy Cinemas		181
Rutherford Mall 7	Galaxy Cinemas		176
Rutherford Mall 8	Galaxy Cinemas		176

NELSON
Civic	Karen Franz	9,298	

NEW WESTMINISTER
New Westminster Cinema 1	A Theatre Near You, Inc.	54,656	475
New Westminster Cinema 2	A Theatre Near You, Inc.		292
New Westminster Cinema 3	A Theatre Near You, Inc.		348

N. VANCOUVER
Esplanade 1	Famous Players Inc.	82,310	356
Esplanade 2	Famous Players Inc.		194
Esplanade 3	Famous Players Inc.		257
Esplanade 4	Famous Players Inc.		348
Esplanade 5	Famous Players Inc.		208
Esplanade 6	Famous Players Inc.		253
Park & Tilford 1	Cineplex Odeon Corp.		375
Park & Tilford 2	Cineplex Odeon Corp.		244
Park & Tilford 3	Cineplex Odeon Corp.		231
Park & Tilford 4	Cineplex Odeon Corp.		230
Park & Tilford 5	Cineplex Odeon Corp.		206
Park & Tilford 6	Cineplex Odeon Corp.		386

O

OLIVER
Oliver	David Lesmeister	4,224	444

100 MI. HOUSE
Rangeland	Lyon Appleby	1,692	

P

PENTICTON
Pen-Mar Cinema Centre 1	Landmark Cinemas	41,574	241
Pen-Mar Cinema Centre 2	Landmark Cinemas		171
Pen-Mar Cinema Centre 3	Landmark Cinemas		200
Pen-Mar Cinema Centre 4	Landmark Cinemas		104

PITT MEADOWS
Harris Road - 1	Harris Road Ent. Group Ltd.	14,894	170
Harris Road - 2	Harris Road Ent. Group Ltd.		140
Harris Road - 3	Harris Road Ent. Group Ltd.		130

PORT ALBERNI
Paramount Theatre	Landmark Cinemas	25,396	505

PORT HARDY
Hardy Bay	C. Fitch	4,574	

POWELL RIVER
Patricia	Nokomis Holdings	18,269	449

PRINCE GEORGE
FP 6 - 1	Famous Players Inc.	85,035	157
FP 6 - 2	Famous Players Inc.		157
FP 6 - 3	Famous Players Inc.		255
FP 6 - 4	Famous Players Inc.		251
FP 6 - 5	Famous Players Inc.		253
FP 6 - 6	Famous Players Inc.		253
Magic Shadows	Magic Shadows Theatre Ltd.		322

PRINCE RUPERT
Prince Rupert 1	Famous Players Inc.	15,302	250
Prince Rupert 2	Famous Players Inc.		368
Prince Rupert 3	Famous Players Inc.		312

Q

QUESNEL
Carib Twin 1		24,426	
Carib Twin 2			

R

REVELSTOKE
Roxy	Carl Rankin	7,500	449

RICHMOND
Richmond Centre 1	Famous Players Inc.	164,345	266
Richmond Centre 2	Famous Players Inc.		370
Richmond Centre 3	Famous Players Inc.		359
Richmond Centre 4	Famous Players Inc.		285
Richmond Centre 5	Famous Players Inc.		466
Richmond Centre 6	Famous Players Inc.		238
Silver City Riverport 1	Famous Players Inc.		452
Silver City Riverport 2	Famous Players Inc.		183
Silver City Riverport 3	Famous Players Inc.		226
Silver City Riverport 4	Famous Players Inc.		226
Silver City Riverport 5	Famous Players Inc.		335
Silver City Riverport 6	Famous Players Inc.		193
Silver City Riverport 7	Famous Players Inc.		193
Silver City Riverport 8	Famous Players Inc.		341
Silver City Riverport 9	Famous Players Inc.		226
Silver City Riverport 10	Famous Players Inc.		230
Silver City Riverport 11	Famous Players Inc.		183
Silver City Riverport 12	Famous Players Inc.		449
Silver City Riverport 13	Famous Players Inc.		158
Silver City Riverport 14	Famous Players Inc.		158
Silver City Riverport 15	Famous Players Inc.		158
Silver City Riverport 16	Famous Players Inc.		158
Silver City Riverport 17	Famous Players Inc.		158
Silver City Riverport 18	Famous Players Inc.		158
Silver City Riverport19	Famous Players Inc.		253

S

SALMON ARM
Salmar Grand	Salmon Arm Community Assoc.	15,210	389

SECHELT
Ravens Cry Theatre	D. Proby		274

SMITHERS
Roi 1	A. Buchanan	5,414	
Roi 2	A. Buchanan		

SURREY
Hollywood 1	A Theatre Near You	347,825	202
Hollywood 2	A Theatre Near You		210
Hollywood 3	A Theatre Near You		290
SilverCity Guildford 1	Famous Players Inc.		162
SilverCity Guildford 2	Famous Players Inc.		252
SilverCity Guildford 3	Famous Players Inc.		370
SilverCity Guildford 4	Famous Players Inc.		442
SilverCity Guildford 5	Famous Players Inc.		195
SilverCity Guildford 6	Famous Players Inc.		214
SilverCity Guildford 7	Famous Players Inc.		389
SilverCity Guildford 8	Famous Players Inc.		195
SilverCity Guildford 9	Famous Players Inc.		442
SilverCity Guildford 10	Famous Players Inc.		370
SilverCity Guildford 11	Famous Players Inc.		252
SilverCity Guildford 12	Famous Players Inc.		162
Strawberry Hill 1	Cineplex Odeon Corp.		177
Strawberry Hill 2	Cineplex Odeon Corp.		181
Strawberry Hill 3	Cineplex Odeon Corp.		187
Strawberry Hill 4	Cineplex Odeon Corp.		143
Strawberry Hill 5	Cineplex Odeon Corp.		164
Strawberry Hill 6	Cineplex Odeon Corp.		161
Strawberry Hill 7	Cineplex Odeon Corp.		140
Strawberry Hill 8	Cineplex Odeon Corp.		140
Strawberry Hill 9	Cineplex Odeon Corp.		288
Strawberry Hill 10	Cineplex Odeon Corp.		311
Strawberry Hill 11	Cineplex Odeon Corp.		413
Strawberry Hill 12	Cineplex Odeon Corp.		398

T

TERRACE
Tillicum Twin 1	W. Young	19,980	
Tillicum Twin 2	W. Young		

TRAIL
Royal	John Turcotte	9,119	400

V

VANCOUVER
Capitol 1	Famous Players Inc.	1,986,965	1,030
Capitol 2	Famous Players Inc.		470
Capitol 3	Famous Players Inc.		461
Capitol 4	Famous Players Inc.		251
Capitol 5	Famous Players Inc.		468
Capitol 6	Famous Players Inc.		258
Denman	NewGen Entertainment		
Dunbar	Ken Charko		600
Fifth Avenue - 1	Alliance Atlantis Cinemas		100
Fifth Avenue - 2	Alliance Atlantis Cinemas		214
Fifth Avenue - 3	Alliance Atlantis Cinemas		344
Fifth Avenue - 4	Alliance Atlantis Cinemas		177
Fifth Avenue - 5	Alliance Atlantis Cinemas		151
Granville 1	Cineplex Odeon Corp.		294
Granville 2	Cineplex Odeon Corp.		340
Granville 3	Cineplex Odeon Corp.		329
Granville 4	Cineplex Odeon Corp.		324
Granville 5	Cineplex Odeon Corp.		224
Granville 6	Cineplex Odeon Corp.		230
Granville 7	Cineplex Odeon Corp.		664
Hollywood	D. Fairleigh		752
Oakridge 1	Cineplex Odeon Corp.		648
Oakridge 2	Cineplex Odeon Corp.		255
Oakridge 3	Cineplex Odeon Corp.		255
Park	Alliance Atlantis Cinemas		534
Raja Kingsway	Shafik Rajani		
Raja Commercial	Shafik Rajani		
Ridge	Ingrid Lae		830
Varsity	Ken Charko		468

VANDERHOOF

Reo	K. Niesen	4,390	267

VERNON

FP 1	Famous Players Inc.	51,530	373
FP 2	Famous Players Inc.		178
FP 3	Famous Players Inc.		176
FP 4	Famous Players Inc.		176
FP 5	Famous Players Inc.		176
FP 6	Famous Players Inc.		313
FP 7	Famous Players Inc.		191

VICTORIA

Capitol 1	Famous Players Inc.	288,346	128
Capitol 2	Famous Players Inc.		537
Capitol 3	Famous Players Inc.		219
Capitol 4	Famous Players Inc.		220
Capitol 5	Famous Players Inc.		242
Capitol 6	Famous Players Inc.		323
Roxy Cinegog	Howie Siegel		280
Odeon Victoria 1	Cineplex Odeon Corp.		215
Odeon Victoria 2	Cineplex Odeon Corp.		276
Odeon Victoria 3	Cineplex Odeon Corp.		244
Odeon Victoria 4	Cineplex Odeon Corp.		224
Odeon Victoria 5	Cineplex Odeon Corp.		402
Odeon Victoria 6	Cineplex Odeon Corp.		244
Odeon Victoria 7	Cineplex Odeon Corp.		244
Silver City 1	Famous Players Inc.		230
Silver City 2	Famous Players Inc.		230
Silver City 3	Famous Players Inc.		242
Silver City 4	Famous Players Inc.		242
Silver City 5	Famous Players Inc.		451
Silver City 6	Famous Players Inc.		451
Silver City 7	Famous Players Inc.		351
Silver City 8	Famous Players Inc.		351
Silver City 9	Famous Players Inc.		230
Silver City 10	Famous Players Inc.		230
University 1	Alliance Atlantis Cinemas		266
University 2	Alliance Atlantis Cinemas		177
University 3	Alliance Atlantis Cinemas		184
University 4	Alliance Atlantis Cinemas		219
Vic Theatre	Landmark Clnemas		235

W

WESTBANK

Capitol 1	Landmark Cinemas	15,700	188
Capitol 2	Landmark Cinemas		178
Capitol 3	Landmark Cinemas		188
Capitol 4	Landmark Cinemas		212
Capitol 5	Landmark Cinemas		316

WHISTLER

Rainbow	D. Mathieson	8,891	

WHITE ROCK

Rialto Twin 1	Criterion Theatres	18,250	187
Rialto Twin 2	Criterion Theatres		165
Criterion 1	Criterion Theatres		220
Criterion 2	Criterion Theatres		200
Criterion 3	Criterion Theatres		187
Criterion 4	Criterion Theatres		169

WILLIAMS LAKE

Paradise 1	D. Mathieson.	25,122	392
Paradise 2	D. Mathieson.		300

MANITOBA

B

BEAUSEJOUR

Lyric	M. Baxter	2,772	

BOISSEVAIN

Boissevain	Community Theatre	1,495	350

BRANDON

Capitol Theatre 1	Sask/Man JV Ltd.	39,716	165
Capitol Theatre 2	Sask/Man JV Ltd.		320
Capitol Theatre 3	Sask/Man JV Ltd.		235
Capitol Theatre 4	Sask/Man JV Ltd.		150
Strand	Sask/Man JV Ltd.		430
Univ. of Brandon	Brandon Film Festival		218

C

CHURCHILL

Polar	B. Dingwall	963	200

CLEAR LAKE

Park (Seasonal)	J & B Gowler		492

D

DAUPHIN

Dauphin Theatre	Ron Suchoplas	8,085	200

DELORAINE

Deloraine	Peggy Saunders	1,026	300

F

FLIN FLON

Big Island Theatre	B & M Liefe	6267	

G

GIMLI

Gimli	Larry Minarik	1,930	256

GLENBORO

Gaiety	Don Foster	656	250

H

HARTNEY

Elks	Kieth Evans	446	200

M

MELITA

Strand	B. Holden	1,111	200

N

NEEPAWA

Roxy	Town of Neepawa	3,325	400

R

RESTON

Memorial	Candy Wanless		300

ROBLIN

Roblin	Gordon Andrews	1,818	300

RUSSELL

Avalon	Hank Smith	1,587	348

S

ST.-PIERRE

Cinema Jolys	Lou & Bertell Croteau	912	200

SELKIRK

Garry Theatre	Landmark Cinemas	9,752	483

SOMERSET

Lorne	R & E Raine	459	298

SOURIS

Avalon	Town of Souris	1,683	275

STEINBACH

Keystone	B. Wiebe	9,227	288

STONEWALL

Flicks	Don J. Smith	4,012	290

SWAN RIVER

Star	Brent Scales	4,032	200

T

THE PAS

Lido	G. Rivalin	5,795	350

THOMPSON

Strand	H & G Tsitsos	13,256	480

W

WINKLER

Southland 1	Magic Lantern Theatres	7,943	96
Southland 2	Magic Lantern Theatres		86
Southland 3	Magic Lantern Theatres		106
Southland 4	Magic Lantern Theatres		235
Southland 5	Magic Lantern Theatres		178

WINNIPEG

Cinema City 8 - 1	Cinema City	626,685	220
Cinema City 8 - 2	Cinema City		220
Cinema City 8 - 3	Cinema City		198
Cinema City 8 - 4	Cinema City		198
Cinema City 8 - 5	Cinema City		170
Cinema City 8 - 6	Cinema City		198
Cinema City 8 - 7	Cinema City		171
Cinema City 8 - 8	Cinema City		198
Cinema City Northgate 1	Cinema City		187
Cinema City Northgate 2	Cinema City		187
Cinema City Northgate 3	Cinema City		187
Cinema City Northgate 4	Cinema City		305
Cinema City Northgate 5	Cinema City		305
Cinema City Northgate 6	Cinema City		229
Cinema City Northgate 7	Cinema City		199
Cinema City Northgate 8	Cinema City		321
Garden City 1	Famous Players Inc.		405
Garden City 2	Famous Players Inc.		308
Globe Cinema 1	Landmark Cinemas		490
Globe Cinema 2	Landmark Cinemas		332

Globe Cinema 3	Landmark Cinemas		268
Grant Park 1	Cineplex Odeon Corp.		274
Grant Park 2	Cineplex Odeon Corp.		179
Grant Park 3	Cineplex Odeon Corp.		177
Grant Park 4	Cineplex Odeon Corp.		220
Grant Park 5	Cineplex Odeon Corp.		182
Grant Park 6	Cineplex Odeon Corp.		183
Grant Park 7	Cineplex Odeon Corp.		182
Grant Park 8	Cineplex Odeon Corp.		220
Imax/Portage Place	Manitou Theatre Community Assoc.		283
Kildonan Place 1	Famous Players Inc.		400
Kildonan Place 2	Famous Players Inc.		242
Kildonan Place 3	Famous Players Inc.		228
Kildonan Place 4	Famous Players Inc.		244
Kildonan Place 5	Famous Players Inc.		244
Kildonan Place 6	Famous Players Inc.		248
Silver City Polo Park 1	Famous Players Inc.		365
Silver City Polo Park 2	Famous Players Inc.		159
Silver City Polo Park 3	Famous Players Inc.		229
Silver City Polo Park 4	Famous Players Inc.		229
Silver City Polo Park 5	Famous Players Inc.		159
Silver City Polo Park 6	Famous Players Inc.		452
Silver City Polo Park 7	Famous Players Inc.		452
Silver City Polo Park 8	Famous Players Inc.		159
Silver City Polo Park 9	Famous Players Inc.		229
Silver City Polo Park 10	Famous Players Inc.		229
Silver City Polo Park 11	Famous Players Inc.		159
Silver City Polo Park 12	Famous Players Inc.		159
Silver City Polo Park 13	Famous Players Inc.		159
Silver City Polo Park 14	Famous Players Inc.		365
Silver City St. Vital 1	Famous Players Inc.		456
Silver City St. Vital 2	Famous Players Inc.		237
Silver City St. Vital 3	Famous Players Inc.		347
Silver City St. Vital 4	Famous Players Inc.		225
Silver City St. Vital 5	Famous Players Inc.		450
Silver City St. Vital 6	Famous Players Inc.		238
Silver City St. Vital 7	Famous Players Inc.		347
Silver City St. Vital 8	Famous Players Inc.		226
Silver City St. Vital 9	Famous Players Inc.		226
Silver City St. Vital 10	Famous Players Inc.		268
Towne - 1	Landmark Cinemas		484
Towne - 2	Landmark Cinemas		273
Towne - 3	Landmark Cinemas		96
Towne - 4	Landmark Cinemas		179
Towne - 5	Landmark Cinemas		196
Towne - 6	Landmark Cinemas		182
Towne - 7	Landmark Cinemas		152
Towne - 8	Landmark Cinemas		164

NEW BRUNSWICK

B

BATHURST

Apollo 1	Dean Misener	23,935	230
Apollo 2	Dean Misener		198
Apollo 3	Dean Misener		134
Apollo 4	Dean Misener		135
Apollo 5	Dean Misener		121

BEAVERBANK

Showboat	P. Doucel / M. Purdy		

C

CAMPBELLTON

Cinema North	Cinema North Ltd.	12,463	672
Paramount	V. Anderson Jr.		

CARAQUET

Bellevue	Paul Marcel Albert	4,773	350

CHATHAM

Vogue	George Little	13,784	455

E

EDMUNDSTON

Cinema 1	Gallant Enterprises	22,173	250
Cinema 2	Gallant Enterprises		250

D

DIEPPE

Crystal Palace 1	Empire Theatres Ltd.	14,951	216
Crystal Palace 2	Empire Theatres Ltd.		251
Crystal Palace 3	Empire Theatres Ltd.		326
Crystal Palace 4	Empire Theatres Ltd.		322
Crystal Palace 5	Empire Theatres Ltd.		112
Crystal Palace 6	Empire Theatres Ltd.		133
Crystal Palace 7	Empire Theatres Ltd.		162
Crystal Palace 8	Empire Theatres Ltd.		128

F

FREDERICTON

Regent Mall 1	Empire Theatres Ltd.	75,811	140
Regent Mall 2	Empire Theatres Ltd.		189
Regent Mall 3	Empire Theatres Ltd.		328
Regent Mall 4	Empire Theatres Ltd.		115
Regent Mall 5	Empire Theatres Ltd.		115
Regent Mall 6	Empire Theatres Ltd.		139
Regent Mall 7	Empire Theatres Ltd.		151
Regent Mall 8	Empire Theatres Ltd.		165
Regent Mall 9	Empire Theatres Ltd.		157
Regent -Mall10	Empire Theatres Ltd.		133

M

MIRAMICHI

Studio 1	Empire Theatres Ltd.	18,508	235
Studio 2	Empire Theatres Ltd.		150
Studio 3	Empire Theatres Ltd.		150
Studio 4	Empire Theatres Ltd.		150
Studio 5	Empire Theatres Ltd.		150

MONCTON

FP Moncton 8 - 1	Famous Players Inc.	90,395	364
FP Moncton 8 - 2	Famous Players Inc.		241
FP Moncton 8 - 3	Famous Players Inc.		221
FP Moncton 8 - 4	Famous Players Inc.		190
FP Moncton 8 - 5	Famous Players Inc.		190
FP Moncton 8 - 6	Famous Players Inc.		221
FP Moncton 8 - 7	Famous Players Inc.		244
FP Moncton 8 - 8	Famous Players Inc.		364

O

OROMOCTO

Trio	B. Ritchie	9,114	550

R

ROTHESAY

Show Boat 1	L. Doucet		
Show Boat 2	L. Doucet		
Show Boat 3	L. Doucet		
Show Boat 4	L. Doucet		

S

SACKVILLE

Vogue	Wayne Harper	5,361	400

SAINT ANDREW

James O'Neil Theatre	John Ferguson	1,869	200

SAINT JOHN

Dunn	J. Ferguson / P. Jackson		
Exhibition 1	Empire Theatres Ltd.	122,678	95
Exhibition 2	Empire Theatres Ltd.		95
Exhibition 3	Empire Theatres Ltd.		130
Exhibition 4	Empire Theatres Ltd.		203
Exhibition 5	Empire Theatres Ltd.		294
Exhibition 6	Empire Theatres Ltd.		155
Exhibition 7	Empire Theatres Ltd.		175
Paramount 1	Famous Players Inc.		551
Paramount 2	Famous Players Inc.		407
Showboat 1	Lou Doucette		228
Showboat 2	Lou Doucette		150
Showboat 3	Lou Doucette		150
Showboat 4	Lou Doucette		150

SHIPPAGAN

Acadien	J.D. Gauthier	2,872	450

NEWFOUNDLAND & LABRADOR

B

BONAVISTA

Garrick	Ken Skiffington	4,021	200

BURIN

Burin Theatres	Winston Marshall	2,470	236

C

CARBONEAR

Carbonear	K. Oates	7,465	200

CLARENVILLE

Twin 1	Clarence Russell	5,104	198
Twin 2	Clarence Russell		93

CORNER BROOK

Majestic	N. Kean.	25,742	380
Millbrook 1	Empire Theatres Ltd.		307
Millbrook 2	Empire Theatres Ltd.		291

G

GANDER

Fraser Mall	Vanessa Trask	11,254	513

GOOSE BAY
Arcturus	CFB	7,248	420

GRAND FALLS
Classic	M & L Ivany.	18,981	450

L

LANCE AU CLAIR
Cinema Jean	Town of Lance Au Clair		176

M

MT. PEARL
Sobeys Square 1	Empire Theatres Ltd.	24,964	420
Sobeys Square 2	Empire Theatres Ltd.		235
Sobeys Square 3	Empire Theatres Ltd.		308
Sobeys Square 4	Empire Theatres Ltd.		137
Sobeys Square 5	Empire Theatres Ltd.		149
Sobeys Square 6	Empire Theatres Ltd.		149

P

PORT AUX BASQUES
Grandview	Max Keeping	5,988	250

S

ST. JOHN'S
Studio 1	Empire Theatres Ltd.	172,918	143
Studio 2	Empire Theatres Ltd.		143
Studio 3	Empire Theatres Ltd.		148
Studio 4	Empire Theatres Ltd.		258
Studio 5	Empire Theatres Ltd.		345
Studio 6	Empire Theatres Ltd.		345
Studio 7	Empire Theatres Ltd.		229
Studio 8	Empire Theatres Ltd.		216
Studio 9	Empire Theatres Ltd.		216
Studio 10	Empire Theatres Ltd.		290
Studio 11	Empire Theatres Ltd.		216
Studio 12	Empire Theatres Ltd.		229
Springdale	Twilite		3,381

SPRINGDALE
Twilite	Neil Whitehorn	3,045	200

STEPHENVILLE
Harmon	Max Keeping	7,109	480

NORTHWEST TERRITORIES

F

FORT SMITH
Park	Janine Daniels	2,185	218

H

HAY RIVER
Riverview Cineplex 1	Donna Borchuk		132
Riverview Cineplex 2	Donna Borchuk		

Y

YELLOWKNIFE
Capitol 1	Bellanca Developments Inc.	16,541	250
Capitol 2	Bellanca Developments Inc.		160
Capitol 3	Bellanca Developments Inc.		150

NOVA SCOTIA

A

AMHERST
Paramount 1	Empire Theatres Ltd.	9,502	230
Paramount 2	Empire Theatres Ltd.		98
Paramount 3	Empire Theatres Ltd.		126

ANNAPOLIS
Kings Theatre	Town of Annapolis	530	300

ANTIGONISH
Capitol	D. Younker	4,754	560

B

BEDFORD
Empire 1	Empire Theatres Ltd.		332
Empire 2	Empire Theatres Ltd.		332
Empire 3	Empire Theatres Ltd.		270
Empire 4	Empire Theatres Ltd.		282
Empire 5	Empire Theatres Ltd.		193
Empire 6	Empire Theatres Ltd.		193

D

DARTMOUTH
Empire 1	Empire Theatres Ltd.	82,899	312
Empire 2	Empire Theatres Ltd.		312
Empire 3	Empire Theatres Ltd.		221
Empire 4	Empire Theatres Ltd.		221
Empire 5	Empire Theatres Ltd.		275
Empire 6	Empire Theatres Ltd.		285
Penhorn Mall 1	Famous Players Inc.		237
Penhorn Mall 2	Famous Players Inc.		198
Penhorn Mall 3	Famous Players Inc.		317
Penhorn Mall 4	Famous Players Inc.		411
Penhorn Mall 5	Famous Players Inc.		210

G

GLACE BAY
Savoy	Town of Glace Bay	21,187	877

GREENWOOD
Xedec	C.F.B.		520

H

HALIFAX
Bayers Lake - 1	Empire Theatres Ltd.	359,183	146
Bayers Lake - 2	Empire Theatres Ltd.		167
Bayers Lake - 3	Empire Theatres Ltd.		168
Bayers Lake - 4	Empire Theatres Ltd.		168
Bayers Lake - 5	Empire Theatres Ltd.		167
Bayers Lake - 6	Empire Theatres Ltd.		146
Bayers Lake - 7	Empire Theatres Ltd.		336
Bayers Lake - 8	Empire Theatres Ltd.		336
Bayers Lake - 9	Empire Theatres Ltd.		336
Bayers Lake - 10	Empire Theatres Ltd.		336
Bayers Lake - 11	Empire Theatres Ltd.		183
Bayers Lake - 12	Empire Theatres Ltd.		183
Bayers Lake - 13	Empire Theatres Ltd.		218
Bayers Lake - 14	Empire Theatres Ltd.		218
Bayers Lake - 15	Empire Theatres Ltd.		138
Bayers Lake - 16	Empire Theatres Ltd.		138
Bayers Lake - 17	Empire Theatres Ltd.		138
Bayers Lake - IMAX	Empire Theatres Ltd.		270
Oxford	Empire Theatres Ltd.		442
Park Lane 1	Famous Players Inc.		230
Park Lane 2	Famous Players Inc.		217
Park Lane 3	Famous Players Inc.		255
Park Lane 4	Famous Players Inc.		492
Park Lane 5	Famous Players Inc.		237
Park Lane 6	Famous Players Inc.		202
Park Lane 7	Famous Players Inc.		283
Park Lane 8	Famous Players Inc.		522

K

KINGSTON
Zedex	J. Alexander / K. King		

L

LIVERPOOL
Astor	C. Ball	2,888	625

LOWER SACKVILLE
Studio 1	Empire Theatres Ltd.		253
Studio 2	Empire Theatres Ltd.		126
Studio 3	Empire Theatres Ltd.		146
Studio 4	Empire Theatres Ltd.		146
Studio 5	Empire Theatres Ltd.		146
Studio 6	Empire Theatres Ltd.		146
Studio 7	Empire Theatres Ltd.		146

N

NEW GLASGOW
Studio 1	Empire Theatres Ltd.	9,432	112
Studio 2	Empire Theatres Ltd.		193
Studio 3	Empire Theatres Ltd.		193
Studio 4	Empire Theatres Ltd.		111
Studio 5	Empire Theatres Ltd.		111
Studio 6	Empire Theatres Ltd.		111
Studio 7	Empire Theatres Ltd.		235

NEW MINAS
Empire 1	Empire Theatres Ltd.	4,299	158
Empire 2	Empire Theatres Ltd.		124
Empire 3	Empire Theatres Ltd.		124
Empire 4	Empire Theatres Ltd.		230
Empire 5	Empire Theatres Ltd.		133
Empire 6	Empire Theatres Ltd.		208
Empire 7	Empire Theatres Ltd.		133

S

SHELBURNE
Capitol	Mary Dyokis	7,639	397

SYDNEY
Studio 1	Empire Theatres Ltd.	76,575	177
Studio 2	Empire Theatres Ltd.		177
Studio 3	Empire Theatres Ltd.		149

Studio 4	Empire Theatres Ltd.		149
Studio 5	Empire Theatres Ltd.		149
Studio 6	Empire Theatres Ltd.		165
Studio 7	Empire Theatres Ltd.		128
Studio 8	Empire Theatres Ltd.		106
Studio 9	Empire Theatres Ltd.		263
Studio 10	Empire Theatres Ltd.		305

T

TRURO

Studio 1	Empire Theatres Ltd.	44,276	253
Studio 2	Empire Theatres Ltd.		126
Studio 3	Empire Theatres Ltd.		146
Studio 4	Empire Theatres Ltd.		146
Studio 5	Empire Theatres Ltd.		146
Studio 6	Empire Theatres Ltd.		146
Studio 7	Empire Theatres Ltd.		146

Y

YARMOUTH

Yarmouth 1	Empire Theatres Ltd.	7,561	118
Yarmouth 2	Empire Theatres Ltd.		103
Yarmouth 3	Empire Theatres Ltd.		235

ONTARIO

A

AJAX

Ajax 1	Cineplex Odeon Corp.	73,753	151
Ajax 2	Cineplex Odeon Corp.		231
Ajax 3	Cineplex Odeon Corp.		232
Ajax 4	Cineplex Odeon Corp.		168
Ajax 5	Cineplex Odeon Corp.		110
Ajax 6	Cineplex Odeon Corp.		126
Ajax 7	Cineplex Odeon Corp.		127
Ajax 8	Cineplex Odeon Corp.		127
Ajax 9	Cineplex Odeon Corp.		156
Ajax 10	Cineplex Odeon Corp.		173

ALLISTON

Circle	L & S MacDonald Theatre Ltd.	9,679	340

ANCASTER

Silver City 1	Famous Players Inc.	104,775	218
Silver City 2	Famous Players Inc.		218
Silver City 3	Famous Players Inc.		447
Silver City 4	Famous Players Inc.		238
Silver City 5	Famous Players Inc.		439
Silver City 6	Famous Players Inc.		350
Silver City 7	Famous Players Inc.		218
Silver City 8	Famous Players Inc.		218
Silver City 9	Famous Players Inc.		348
Silver City 10	Famous Players Inc.		226

ARNPRIOR

O'Brien Theatre 1	Kevin D. Marshall	9,095	
O'Brien Theatre 2	Kevin D. Marshall	Total Seats	441

ATIKOKEN

Friendship	Atikoken Native Centre	3,632	134

B

BARRIE

Bayfield 7 - 1	Golden Theatres Ltd.	129,963	260
Bayfield 7 - 2	Golden Theatres Ltd.		210
Bayfield 7 - 3	Golden Theatres Ltd.		150
Bayfield 7 - 4	Golden Theatres Ltd.		130
Bayfield 7 - 5	Golden Theatres Ltd.		140
Bayfield 7 - 6	Golden Theatres Ltd.		130
Bayfield 7 - 7	Golden Theatres Ltd.		130
Grande 1	Cineplex Odeon Corp.		135
Grande 2	Cineplex Odeon Corp.		135
Grande 3	Cineplex Odeon Corp.		135
Grande 4	Cineplex Odeon Corp.		135
Grande 5	Cineplex Odeon Corp.		135
Grande 6	Cineplex Odeon Corp.		135
Grande 7	Cineplex Odeon Corp.		135
Grande 8	Cineplex Odeon Corp.		240
Grande 9	Cineplex Odeon Corp.		247
Grande 10	Cineplex Odeon Corp.		208
Grande 11	Cineplex Odeon Corp.		240
Grande 12	Cineplex Odeon Corp.		336
Imperial 1	Stinson Theatres Ltd.		350
Imperial 2	Stinson Theatres Ltd.		332
Imperial 3	Stinson Theatres Ltd.		200
Imperial 4	Stinson Theatres Ltd.		275
Imperial 5	Stinson Theatres Ltd.		308
Imperial 6	Stinson Theatres Ltd.		308
Imperial 7	Stinson Theatres Ltd.		250
Imperial 8	Stinson Theatres Ltd.		185

BEAVERTON

Strand	Vernon King Flaherty	3,065	300

BELLEVILLE

Empire (Sept. 2003)	Mark Rashotte	61,886	700
FP 1	Famous Players Inc.		224
FP 2	Famous Players Inc.		159
FP 3	Famous Players Inc.		159
FP 4	Famous Players Inc.		354
FP 5	Famous Players Inc.		354
FP 6	Famous Players Inc.		159
FP 7	Famous Players Inc.		159
FP 8	Famous Players Inc.		224

BRACEBRIDGE

Norwood 1	Muskoka Cinemas 3	13,751	
Norwood 2	Muskoka Cinemas 3		
Norwood 3	Muskoka Cinemas	Total Seats	598

BRAMPTON

Gateway 1	Famous Players Inc.	325,428	289
Gateway 2	Famous Players Inc.		289
Gateway 3	Famous Players Inc.		246
Gateway 4	Famous Players Inc.		246
Gateway 5	Famous Players Inc.		200
Gateway 6	Famous Players Inc.		200
Orion Gate Grande 1	Cineplex Odeon Corp.		359
Orion Gate Grande 2	Cineplex Odeon Corp.		359
Orion Gate Grande 3	Cineplex Odeon Corp.		270
Orion Gate Grande 4	Cineplex Odeon Corp.		270
Orion Gate Grande 5	Cineplex Odeon Corp.		121
Orion Gate Grande 6	Cineplex Odeon Corp.		121
Orion Gate Grande 7	Cineplex Odeon Corp.		121
Orion Gate Grande 8	Cineplex Odeon Corp.		121
Orion Gate Grande 9	Cineplex Odeon Corp.		121
Orion Gate Grande 10	Cineplex Odeon Corp.		145
Silver City 1	Famous Players Inc.		469
Silver City 2	Famous Players Inc.		159
Silver City 3	Famous Players Inc.		229
Silver City 4	Famous Players Inc.		159
Silver City 5	Famous Players Inc.		229
Silver City 6	Famous Players Inc.		159
Silver City 7	Famous Players Inc.		159
Silver City 8	Famous Players Inc.		366
Silver City 9	Famous Players Inc.		366
Silver City 10	Famous Players Inc.		159
Silver City 11	Famous Players Inc.		159
Silver City 12	Famous Players Inc.		229
Silver City 13	Famous Players Inc.		159
Silver City 14	Famous Players Inc.		229
Silver City 15	Famous Players Inc.		159
Silver City 16	Famous Players Inc.		469

BRANTFORD

Cinemas 1	Cineplex Odeon Corp.	86,417	216
Cinemas 2	Cineplex Odeon Corp.		285
Cinemas 3	Cineplex Odeon Corp.		489
Cinemas 4	Cineplex Odeon Corp.		235
Cinemas 5	Cineplex Odeon Corp.		165
Cinemas 6	Cineplex Odeon Corp.		220

BROCKVILLE

Brockville Arts Centre	City of Brockville	21,375	759

BURK'S FALLS

Towne	Corp./Burk's Falls	940	246

BURLINGTON

Encore Cinemas 1	Film.CA Inc.	150,836	
Encore Cinemas 2	Film.CA Inc.		
Encore Cinemas 3	Film.CA Inc.		
Encore Cinemas 4	Film.CA Inc.		
Encore Cinemas 5	Film.CA Inc.		
Encore Cinemas 6	Film.CA Inc.	Total Seats	407
Showcase 1	Cineplex Odeon Corp.		330
Showcase 2	Cineplex Odeon Corp.		333
Showcase 3	Cineplex Odeon Corp.		138
Showcase 4	Cineplex Odeon Corp.		138
Showcase 5	Cineplex Odeon Corp.		100
Showcase 6	Cineplex Odeon Corp.		100
Silver City 1	Famous Players Inc.		291
Silver City 2	Famous Players Inc.		189
Silver City 3	Famous Players Inc.		202
Silver City 4	Famous Players Inc.		171
Silver City 5	Famous Players Inc.		202
Silver City 6	Famous Players Inc.		172
Silver City 7	Famous Players Inc.		189
Silver City 8	Famous Players Inc.		291
Silver City 9	Famous Players Inc.		210
Silver City 10	Famous Players Inc.		366
Silver City 11	Famous Players Inc.		159
Silver City 12	Famous Players Inc.		366

C

CAMBRIDGE

Cambridge Centre 1	Galaxy Cinemas	125,952	249
Cambridge Centre 2	Galaxy Cinemas		319
Cambridge Centre 3	Galaxy Cinemas		292
Cambridge Centre 4	Galaxy Cinemas		299
Cambridge Centre 5	Galaxy Cinemas		240
Cambridge Centre 6	Galaxy Cinemas		226
Cambridge Centre 7	Galaxy Cinemas		95
Cambridge Centre 8	Galaxy Cinemas		225
Cambridge Centre 9	Galaxy Cinemas		280

CAMPBELLFORD
| Aron | Aron Cinema Ltd. | 3,675 | 168 |

CARLETON PLACE
| Carleton Place (2 Screens) | Malik Zekry | 9,083 | 150 |

CHATHAM
Chatham Cinema 1	Stinson Theatres Ltd.	44,156	
Chatham Cinema 2	Stinson Theatres Ltd.		
Chatham Cinema 3	Stinson Theatres Ltd.		
Chatham Cinema 4	Stinson Theatres Ltd.		
Chatham Cinema 5	Stinson Theatres Ltd.		
Chatham Cinema 6	Stinson Theatres Ltd.	Total Seats	1344

CLARINGTON
Clarington Place 1	Cineplex Odeon Corp.	69,834	172
Clarington Place 2	Cineplex Odeon Corp.		172
Clarington Place 3	Cineplex Odeon Corp.		172
Clarington Place 4	Cineplex Odeon Corp.		224
Clarington Place 5	Cineplex Odeon Corp.		234
Clarington Place 6	Cineplex Odeon Corp.		234
Clarington Place 7	Cineplex Odeon Corp.		174
Clarington Place 8	Cineplex Odeon Corp.		191
Clarington Place 9	Cineplex Odeon Corp.		149
Clarington Place 10	Cineplex Odeon Corp.		149
Clarington Place 11	Cineplex Odeon Corp.		191

COBURG
Northumberland Mall 1	Northumberland Mall Theatres		
Northumberland Mall 2	Northumberland Mall Theatres		
Northumberland Mall 3	Northumberland Mall Theatres	Total	795

COCHRANE
| Empire | 493251 Ontario Inc. | 4172 | 415 |

COLLINGWOOD
Cinema Four 1	Stinson Theatres Ltd.	16,039	190
Cinema Four 2	Stinson Theatres Ltd.		190
Cinema Four 3	Stinson Theatres Ltd.		225
Cinema Four 4	Stinson Theatres Ltd.		300
Gayety	Dean Hollin		421

CORNWALL
Cornwall 1	Galaxy Cinemas	48,287	346
Cornwall 2	Galaxy Cinemas		224
Cornwall 3	Galaxy Cinemas		163
Cornwall 4	Galaxy Cinemas		129
Cornwall 5	Galaxy Cinemas		202
Cornwall 6	Galaxy Cinemas		202
Cornwall 7	Galaxy Cinemas		212
Port Theatre	Glenn McGillvray		527

D

DRYDEN
| Cinema 86 | Z. Tavares | 6555 | 300 |

E

ELLIOT LAKE
| Lake (2 screens) | 705841 Ontario Inc. | 11,956 | 483 |

ELORA
| Gorge | The Gorge Cinema Inc. | | 136 |

ERIN
| Centre 2000 | Town of Erin | 11,052 | 212 |

F

FOREST
| Kineto Kiwanis Theatre | Kiwanis Club | | 199 |

G

GANANOQUE
| 1000 Islands Cinema 1 | Boulevard Cinema Ltd. | 5,167 | 110 |
| 1000 Islands Cinema 2 | Boulevard Cinema Ltd. | | 110 |

GLOUCESTER
Silver City 1	Famous Players Inc.	104,022	352
Silver City 2	Famous Players Inc.		159
Silver City 3	Famous Players Inc.		230
Silver City 4	Famous Players Inc.		159
Silver City 5	Famous Players Inc.		230
Silver City 6	Famous Players Inc.		159
Silver City 7	Famous Players Inc.		159
Silver City 8	Famous Players Inc.		443
Silver City 9	Famous Players Inc.		443
Silver City 10	Famous Players Inc.		159
Silver City 11	Famous Players Inc.		159
Silver City 12	Famous Players Inc.		230
Silver City 13	Famous Players Inc.		159
Silver City 14	Famous Players Inc.		230
Silver City 15	Famous Players Inc.		159
Silver City 16	Famous Players Inc.		352

GODERICH
| Park | | 7,604 | 413 |

GUELPH
Bookshelf	Bookshelf of Guelph Ltd.	106,920	140
Stone Road Mall 1	Cineplex Odeon Corp.		206
Stone Road Mall 2	Cineplex Odeon Corp.		225
Stone Road Mall 3	Cineplex Odeon Corp.		246
Stone Road Mall 4	Cineplex Odeon Corp.		190
Stone Road Mall 5	Cineplex Odeon Corp.		333
Woodlawn 1	Ed Bauman		299
Woodlawn 2	Ed Bauman		203
Woodlawn 3	Ed Bauman		138
Woodlawn 4	Ed Bauman		249
Woodlawn 5	Ed Bauman		305
Woodlawn 6	Ed Bauman		156

H

HAMILTON
Jackson Square 1	Famous Players Inc.	662,401	505
Jackson Square 2	Famous Players Inc.		366
Jackson Square 3	Famous Players Inc.		282
Jackson Square 4	Famous Players Inc.		282
Jackson Square 5	Famous Players Inc.		218
Jackson Square 6	Famous Players Inc.		202
Upper James 1	Cineplex Odeon Corp.		257
Upper James 2	Cineplex Odeon Corp.		292
Upper James 3	Cineplex Odeon Corp.		189
Upper James 4	Cineplex Odeon Corp.		189
Upper James 5	Cineplex Odeon Corp.		189
Upper James 6	Cineplex Odeon Corp.		240
Upper James 7	Cineplex Odeon Corp.		228
Westdale	Peter Sorok		495

HALIBURTON
| Moulou | Consky Theatres | | |

HANOVER
| Paramount | J.D. Lyons Corp. | 6,869 | 265 |

HEARST
| Cartier | Daniel La Rochelle | 5,825 | |

HARRISTON
| Norgan | Town of Minto | | 250 |

HUNTSVILLE
| Capitol 1 | Stinson Theatres Ltd. | 17,338 | 300 |
| Capitol 2 | Stinson Theatres Ltd. | | 300 |

K

KANATA
Kanata 1	AMC Theatres of Canada	70,320	111
Kanata 2	AMC Theatres of Canada		141
Kanata 3	AMC Theatres of Canada		125
Kanata 4	AMC Theatres of Canada		243
Kanata 5	AMC Theatres of Canada		243
Kanata 6	AMC Theatres of Canada		125
Kanata 7	AMC Theatres of Canada		90
Kanata 8	AMC Theatres of Canada		90
Kanata 9	AMC Theatres of Canada		141
Kanata 10	AMC Theatres of Canada		111
Kanata 11	AMC Theatres of Canada		430
Kanata 12	AMC Theatres of Canada		536
Kanata 13	AMC Theatres of Canada		536
Kanata 14	AMC Theatres of Canada		430
Kanata 15	AMC Theatres of Canada		111
Kanata 16	AMC Theatres of Canada		141
Kanata 17	AMC Theatres of Canada		90
Kanata 18	AMC Theatres of Canada		90
Kanata 19	AMC Theatres of Canada		125
Kanata 20	AMC Theatres of Canada		243
Kanata 21	AMC Theatres of Canada		243
Kanata 22	AMC Theatres of Canada		125
Kanata 23	AMC Theatres of Canada		141
Kanata 24	AMC Theatres of Canada		111

KAPUSKASING
| Royal | A & M. Lebel | 9,238 | 350 |

KENORA
Century 1	Len Rattal	15,838	209
Century 2	Len Rattal		209
Century 3	Len Rattal		140

KESWICK
| Gem | R.J. Gorman | | |

KINCARDINE

Name	Operator		Seats
Aztec	Mark Lalonde	6,410	281

KINGSTON

Name	Operator		Seats
Capitol 1	Famous Players Inc.	108,158	185
Capitol 2	Famous Players Inc.		170
Capitol 3	Famous Players Inc.		209
Capitol 4	Famous Players Inc.		171
Capitol 5	Famous Players Inc.		240
Capitol 6	Famous Players Inc.		218
Capitol 7	Famous Players Inc.		150
Gardiner's Rd. 1	Cineplex Odeon Corp.		479
Gardiner's Rd. 2	Cineplex Odeon Corp.		161
Gardiner's Rd. 3	Cineplex Odeon Corp.		161
Gardiner's Rd. 4	Cineplex Odeon Corp.		161
Gardiner's Rd. 5	Cineplex Odeon Corp.		161
Gardiner's Rd. 6	Cineplex Odeon Corp.		302
Gardiner's Rd. 7	Cineplex Odeon Corp.		209
Gardiner's Rd. 8	Cineplex Odeon Corp.		209
Gardiner's Rd. 9	Cineplex Odeon Corp.		209
Gardiner's Rd. 10	Cineplex Odeon Corp.		432
The Screening Room 1	Terry Laffier		
The Screening Room 2	Terry Laffier	Total Seats	148

KINMOUNT

Name	Operator		Seats
Highlands Cinemas - 1	Keith Stata		71
Highlands Cinemas - 2	Keith Stata		140
Highlands Cinemas - 3	Keith Stata		98
Highlands Cinemas - 4	Keith Stata		172
Highlands Cinemas - 5	Keith Stata		69

KIRKLAND LAKE

Name	Operator		Seats
La Salle			299

KITCHENER

Name	Operator		Seats
Fairway Centre 1	Cineplex Odeon Corp.	387,319	237
Fairway Centre 2	Cineplex Odeon Corp.		203
Fairway Centre 3	Cineplex Odeon Corp.		290
Fairway Centre 4	Cineplex Odeon Corp.		252
Fairway Centre 5	Cineplex Odeon Corp.		183
Fairway Centre 6	Cineplex Odeon Corp.		151
Fairway Centre 7	Cineplex Odeon Corp.		213
Frederick Twin 1	Frederick Twins Cinema Ltd.		269
Frederick Twin 2	Frederick Twins Cinema Ltd.		388
Kings College 1	Famous Players Inc.		357
Kings College 2	Famous Players Inc.		272
Kings College 3	Famous Players Inc.		271
Kings College 4	Famous Players Inc.		407
SilverCity 1	Famous Players Inc.		227
SilverCity 2	Famous Players Inc.		346
SilverCity 3	Famous Players Inc.		198
SilverCity 4	Famous Players Inc.		156
SilverCity 5	Famous Players Inc.		239
SilverCity 6	Famous Players Inc.		198
SilverCity 7	Famous Players Inc.		198
SilverCity 8	Famous Players Inc.		239
SilverCity 9	Famous Players Inc.		156
SilverCity 10	Famous Players Inc.		198
SilverCity 11	Famous Players Inc.		346
SilverCity 12	Famous Players Inc.		227

L

LEAMINGTON

Name	Operator		Seats
Star 1	1066445 Ontario Inc.	28,807	
Star 2	1066445 Ontario Inc.		
Star 3	1066445 Ontario Inc.	Total Screens	420

LINDSAY

Name	Operator		Seats
Century (3 screens)	Ontario Cinemas	17,757	513

LISTOWEL

Name	Operator		Seats
Capitol	Kevin Brown	5,905	137
Capitol	Kevin Brown		108

LONDON

Name	Operator		Seats
Capitol 1	Famous Players Inc.	337,318	401
Capitol 2	Famous Players Inc.		493
Huron Market Place 1	Cineplex Odeon Corp.		205
Huron Market Place 2	Cineplex Odeon Corp.		225
Huron Market Place 3	Cineplex Odeon Corp.		231
Huron Market Place 4	Cineplex Odeon Corp.		280
Huron Market Place 5	Cineplex Odeon Corp.		267
Huron Market Place 6	Cineplex Odeon Corp.		280
Rainbow Galleria 1	Magic Lantern Theatres		141
Rainbow Galleria 2	Magic Lantern Theatres		292
Rainbow Galleria 3	Magic Lantern Theatres		314
Rainbow Galleria 4	Magic Lantern Theatres		261
Rainbow Galleria 5	Magic Lantern Theatres		138
Rainbow Galleria 6	Magic Lantern Theatres		146
Rainbow Galleria 7	Magic Lantern Theatres		325
Silver City 1	Famous Players Inc.		199
Silver City 2	Famous Players Inc.		349
Silver City 3	Famous Players Inc.		221
Silver City 4	Famous Players Inc.		199
Silver City 5	Famous Players Inc.		141
Silver City 6	Famous Players Inc.		210
Silver City 7	Famous Players Inc.		321
Silver City 8	Famous Players Inc.		210
Silver City 9	Famous Players Inc.		141
Silver City 10	Famous Players Inc.		199
Silver City 11	Famous Players Inc.		221
Silver City 12	Famous Players Inc.		345
Wellington-1	Famous Players Inc.		185
Wellington-2	Famous Players Inc.		227
Wellington-3	Famous Players Inc.		175
Wellington-4	Famous Players Inc.		231
Wellington-5	Famous Players Inc.		235
Wellington-6	Famous Players Inc.		309
Wellington-7	Famous Players Inc.		224
Wellington-8	Famous Players Inc.		197
Western Fair Imax Theatre	Western Fair Assn.		300
Western / McKellar Theatre	Univ. Student Council		375
Westmount 1	Cineplex Odeon Corp.		218
Westmount 2	Cineplex Odeon Corp.		157
Westmount 3	Cineplex Odeon Corp.		158
Westmount 4	Cineplex Odeon Corp.		197
Westmount 5	Cineplex Odeon Corp.		160
Westmount 6	Cineplex Odeon Corp.		225

M

MARATHON

Name	Operator		Seats
Marathon	Aaron Schelp	4,381	184

MARKHAM

Name	Operator		Seats
First Markham Place 1	Cineplex Odeon Corp.	208,615	218
First Markham Place 2	Cineplex Odeon Corp.		237
First Markham Place 3	Cineplex Odeon Corp.		179
First Markham Place 4	Cineplex Odeon Corp.		251
First Markham Place 5	Cineplex Odeon Corp.		215
First Markham Place 6	Cineplex Odeon Corp.		198
First Markham Place 7	Cineplex Odeon Corp.		179
First Markham Place 8	Cineplex Odeon Corp.		201
First Markham Place 9	Cineplex Odeon Corp.		235
First Markham Place 10	Cineplex Odeon Corp.		252

MATTAWA

Name	Operator		Seats
Champlain	Remi Gravelle	2,270	250

MIDLAND

Name	Operator		Seats
Mountainview 1	Galaxy Cinemas	29,824	241
Mountainview 2	Galaxy Cinemas		199
Mountainview 3	Galaxy Cinemas		166
Mountainview 4	Galaxy Cinemas		148
Mountainview 5	Galaxy Cinemas		202
Mountainview 6	Galaxy Cinemas		202
Mountainview 7	Galaxy Cinemas		202

MINDEN

Name	Operator		Seats
Beaver	Conskey Theatres	5,312	290

MISSISSAUGA

Name	Operator		Seats
Central Parkway 1	Central Parkway Cinemas	612,925	
Central Parkway 2	Central Parkway Cinemas		
Central Parkway 3	Central Parkway Cinemas		
Central Parkway 4	Central Parkway Cinemas		
Coliseum 1	Famous Players Inc.		155
Coliseum 2	Famous Players Inc.		179
Coliseum 3	Famous Players Inc.		200
Coliseum 4	Famous Players Inc.		214
Coliseum 5	Famous Players Inc.		214
Coliseum 6	Famous Players Inc.		214
Coliseum 7	Famous Players Inc.		288
Coliseum 8	Famous Players Inc.		288
Coliseum 9	Famous Players Inc.		399
Coliseum 10	Famous Players Inc.		403
Coliseum 11	Famous Players Inc.		323
Coliseum 12	Famous Players Inc.		325
Coliseum / Imax	Famous Players Inc.		251
Courtenay Park 1	AMC Theatres Canada Inc.		268
Courtenay Park 2	AMC Theatres Canada Inc.		206
Courtenay Park 3	AMC Theatres Canada Inc.		206
Courtenay Park 4	AMC Theatres Canada Inc.		138
Courtenay Park 5	AMC Theatres Canada Inc.		115
Courtenay Park 6	AMC Theatres Canada Inc.		114
Courtenay Park 7	AMC Theatres Canada Inc.		398
Courtenay Park 8	AMC Theatres Canada Inc.		450
Courtenay Park 9	AMC Theatres Canada Inc.		450
Courtenay Park 10	AMC Theatres Canada Inc.		398
Courtenay Park 11	AMC Theatres Canada Inc.		114
Courtenay Park 12	AMC Theatres Canada Inc.		115
Courtenay Park 13	AMC Theatres Canada Inc.		138
Courtenay Park 14	AMC Theatres Canada Inc.		206
Courtenay Park 15	AMC Theatres Canada Inc.		206
Courtenay Park 16	AMC Theatres Canada Inc.		268
Silver City - 1	Famous Players Inc.		339
Silver City - 2	Famous Players Inc.		246
Silver City - 3	Famous Players Inc.		246
Silver City - 4	Famous Players Inc.		440
Silver City - 5	Famous Players Inc.		440
Silver City - 6	Famous Players Inc.		242
Silver City - 7	Famous Players Inc.		242

Silver City - 8	Famous Players Inc.		218
Silver City - 9	Famous Players Inc.		218
Silver City - 10	Famous Players Inc.		339
Square One 1	Cineplex Odeon Corp.		291
Square One 2	Cineplex Odeon Corp.		239
Square One 3	Cineplex Odeon Corp.		195
Square One 4	Cineplex Odeon Corp.		130
Square One 5	Cineplex Odeon Corp.		419
Square One 6	Cineplex Odeon Corp.		419
Square One 7	Cineplex Odeon Corp.		124
Square One 8	Cineplex Odeon Corp.		188
Square One 9	Cineplex Odeon Corp.		239
Square One 10	Cineplex Odeon Corp.		285

MOUNT FOREST
Roxy Revue	A. Sharpe Contract Ltd.	4306	372

N

NAPANEE
Boulevard 1	Boulevard Cinema Ltd.	7,760	110
Boulevard 2	Boulevard Cinema Ltd.		110
Boulevard 3	Boulevard Cinema Ltd.		70

NEW LISKEARD
Empire	David B. Dymond	4,906	415

NEWMARKET
Silver City 1	Famous Players Inc.	65,778	364
Silver City 2	Famous Players Inc.		157
Silver City 3	Famous Players Inc.		228
Silver City 4	Famous Players Inc.		157
Silver City 5	Famous Players Inc.		228
Silver City 6	Famous Players Inc.		157
Silver City 7	Famous Players Inc.		157
Silver City 8	Famous Players Inc.		467
Silver City 9	Famous Players Inc.		467
Silver City 10	Famous Players Inc.		157
Silver City 11	Famous Players Inc.		157
Silver City 12	Famous Players Inc.		228
Silver City 13	Famous Players Inc.		157
Silver City 14	Famous Players Inc.		228
Silver City 15	Famous Players Inc.		157
Silver City 16	Famous Players Inc.		364

NIAGARA FALLS
Imax Theatre	Niagara Falls Theatre Venture	78,815	620
Niagara Square 1	Cineplex Odeon Corp.		488
Niagara Square 2	Cineplex Odeon Corp.		165
Niagara Square 3	Cineplex Odeon Corp.		165
Niagara Square 4	Cineplex Odeon Corp.		165
Niagara Square 5	Cineplex Odeon Corp.		165
Niagara Square 6	Cineplex Odeon Corp.		303
Niagara Square 7	Cineplex Odeon Corp.		214
Niagara Square 8	Cineplex Odeon Corp.		214
Niagara Square 9	Cineplex Odeon Corp.		214
Niagara Square 10	Cineplex Odeon Corp.		433

NORTH BAY
\North Bay Mall 1	Galaxy Cinemas	52,771	135
North Bay Mall 2	Galaxy Cinemas		135
North Bay Mall 3	Galaxy Cinemas		160
North Bay Mall 4	Galaxy Cinemas		170
North Bay Mall 5	Galaxy Cinemas		200
North Bay Mall 6	Galaxy Cinemas		302
North Bay	Theatre & Arts Community		994

O

OAKVILLE
Winston Churchill 1	AMC Theatres of Canada	144,738	111
Winston Churchill 2	AMC Theatres of Canada		141
Winston Churchill 3	AMC Theatres of Canada		125
Winston Churchill 4	AMC Theatres of Canada		243
Winston Churchill 5	AMC Theatres of Canada		243
Winston Churchill 6	AMC Theatres of Canada		125
Winston Churchill 7	AMC Theatres of Canada		90
Winston Churchill 8	AMC Theatres of Canada		90
Winston Churchill 9	AMC Theatres of Canada		141
Winston Churchill 10	AMC Theatres of Canada		111
Winston Churchill 11	AMC Theatres of Canada		430
Winston Churchill 12	AMC Theatres of Canada		536
Winston Churchill 13	AMC Theatres of Canada		536
Winston Churchill 14	AMC Theatres of Canada		430
Winston Churchill 15	AMC Theatres of Canada		111
Winston Churchill 16	AMC Theatres of Canada		141
Winston Churchill 17	AMC Theatres of Canada		90
Winston Churchill 18	AMC Theatres of Canada		90
Winston Churchill 19	AMC Theatres of Canada		125
Winston Churchill 20	AMC Theatres of Canada		243
Winston Churchill 21	AMC Theatres of Canada		243
Winston Churchill 22	AMC Theatres of Canada		125
Winston Churchill 23	AMC Theatres of Canada		141
Winston Churchill 24	AMC Theatres of Canada		111
Sheridan College Theatre	S.A.C.		451

ORANGEVILLE

Fairgrounds 1	Galaxy Cinemas	27,284	245
Fairgrounds 2	Galaxy Cinemas		179
Fairgrounds 3	Galaxy Cinemas		145
Fairgrounds 4	Galaxy Cinemas		129
Fairgrounds 5	Galaxy Cinemas		193
Fairgrounds 6	Galaxy Cinemas		193
Fairgrounds 7	Galaxy Cinemas		193

ORILLIA
Orillia Cinema Four 1	Stinson Theatres Ltd.	29,121	300
Orillia Cinema Four 2	Stinson Theatres Ltd.		330
Orillia Cinema Four 3	Stinson Theatres Ltd.		175
Orillia Cinema Four 4	Stinson Theatres Ltd.		175

ORLEANS
Orleans Town Centre 1	Cineplex Odeon Corp.		242
Orleans Town Centre 2	Cineplex Odeon Corp.		303
Orleans Town Centre 3	Cineplex Odeon Corp.		237
Orleans Town Centre 4	Cineplex Odeon Corp.		236
Orleans Town Centre 5	Cineplex Odeon Corp.		294
Orleans Town Centre 6	Cineplex Odeon Corp.		241

OSHAWA
Oshawa Centre 1	Famous Players Ltd.	234,779	422
Oshawa Centre 2	Famous Players Ltd.		266
Oshawa Centre 3	Famous Players Ltd.		242
Oshawa Centre 4	Famous Players Ltd.		256
Oshawa Centre 5	Famous Players Ltd.		245
Oshawa Centre 6	Famous Players Ltd.		286
Oshawa Centre 7	Famous Players Ltd.		346
Oshawa Centre 8	Famous Players Ltd.		422

OTTAWA
Bytowne	C.W. Towne Cinema Inc.	774,072	668
Coliseum 1	Famous Players Inc.		204
Coliseum 2	Famous Players Inc.		204
Coliseum 3	Famous Players Inc.		204
Coliseum 4	Famous Players Inc.		204
Coliseum 5	Famous Players Inc.		204
Coliseum 6	Famous Players Inc.		204
Coliseum 7	Famous Players Inc.		408
Coliseum 8	Famous Players Inc.		408
Coliseum 9	Famous Players Inc.		287
Coliseum 10	Famous Players Inc.		287
Coliseum 11	Famous Players Inc.		408
Coliseum 12	Famous Players Inc.		408
Mayfair	Tawa Investments		468
Rideau Centre 1	Famous Players Inc.		559
Rideau Centre 2	Famous Players Inc.		341
Rideau Centre 3	Famous Players Inc.		222
South Keys 1	Cineplex Odeon Corp.		312
South Keys 2	Cineplex Odeon Corp.		312
South Keys 3	Cineplex Odeon Corp.		107
South Keys 4	Cineplex Odeon Corp.		107
South Keys 5	Cineplex Odeon Corp.		134
South Keys 6	Cineplex Odeon Corp.		107
South Keys 7	Cineplex Odeon Corp.		162
South Keys 8	Cineplex Odeon Corp.		133
South Keys 9	Cineplex Odeon Corp.		133
South Keys 10	Cineplex Odeon Corp.		133
South Keys 11	Cineplex Odeon Corp.		133
South Keys 12	Cineplex Odeon Corp.		133
World Exchange 1	Cineplex Odeon Corp.		315
World Exchange 2	Cineplex Odeon Corp.		389
World Exchange 3	Cineplex Odeon Corp.		197
World Exchange 4	Cineplex Odeon Corp.		127
World Exchange 5	Cineplex Odeon Corp.		107
World Exchange 6	Cineplex Odeon Corp.		93
World Exchange 7	Cineplex Odeon Corp.		89

OWEN SOUND
Owen Sound 1	Galaxy Cinemas	31,583	236
Owen Sound 2	Galaxy Cinemas		198
Owen Sound 3	Galaxy Cinemas		146
Owen Sound 4	Galaxy Cinemas		130
Owen Sound 5	Galaxy Cinemas		209
Owen Sound 6	Galaxy Cinemas		202
Owen Sound 7	Galaxy Cinemas		202

P

PARRY SOUND
Strand 1	Gregory Hobson	6,124	
Strand 2	Gregory Hobson	Total Seats	500

PEMBROKE
Algonquin 1	Peter Sorok	23,608	230
Algonquin 2	Peter Sorok		228
Algonquin 3	Peter Sorok		197
Algonquin 4	Peter Sorok		173

PENETAN-GUISHENE
Pen 1	Port Bolster Drive-In Theatres	8,316	535
Pen 2	Port Bolster Drive-In Theatres		192

PETAWAWA
Troyes Theatre	Jeanne Simard	10,656	305

PETERBOROUGH

Cinema 379	Cinema 379 Inc.	102,423	100
Peterborough Square 1	Galaxy Cinemas		405
Peterborough Square 2	Galaxy Cinemas		134
Peterborough Square 3	Galaxy Cinemas		178
Peterborough Square 4	Galaxy Cinemas		178
Peterborough Square 5	Galaxy Cinemas		178
Peterborough Square 6	Galaxy Cinemas		178
Peterborough Square 7	Galaxy Cinemas		196
Peterborough Square 8	Galaxy Cinemas		179
Peterborough Square 9	Galaxy Cinemas		338
Peterborough Square 10	Galaxy Cinemas		222
Peterborough Square 11	Galaxy Cinemas		199

PICKERING

FP 1	Famous Players Inc.	87,139	238
FP 2	Famous Players Inc.		164
FP 3	Famous Players Inc.		129
FP 4	Famous Players Inc.		219
FP 5	Famous Players Inc.		223
FP 6	Famous Players Inc.		219
FP 7	Famous Players Inc.		161
FP 8	Famous Players Inc.		407

PICTON

Regent	The Regent Theatre	377

PORT ELGIN

Port Elgin (3 screens)	106645 Ontario Inc.	6,716	699

PORT HOPE

Capitol	4669	360

R

RENFREW

O'Brien	Murray W. Adolph	8,078	432

RICHMOND HILL

Elgin Mills 1	Cineplex Odeon Corp.	132,030	226
Elgin Mills 2	Cineplex Odeon Corp.		232
Elgin Mills 3	Cineplex Odeon Corp.		259
Elgin Mills 4	Cineplex Odeon Corp.		253
Elgin Mills 5	Cineplex Odeon Corp.		295
Elgin Mills 6	Cineplex Odeon Corp.		253
Elgin Mills 7	Cineplex Odeon Corp.		201
Elgin Mills 8	Cineplex Odeon Corp.		216
Elgin Mills 9	Cineplex Odeon Corp.		207
Elgin Mills 10	Cineplex Odeon Corp.		185
Silver City 1	Famous Players Inc.		447
Silver City 2	Famous Players Inc.		350
Silver City 3	Famous Players Inc.		230
Silver City 4	Famous Players Inc.		230
Silver City 5	Famous Players Inc.		350
Silver City 6	Famous Players Inc.		242
Silver City 7	Famous Players Inc.		242
Silver City 8	Famous Players Inc.		230
Silver City 9	Famous Players Inc.		159
Silver City 10	Famous Players Inc.		230
Silver City 11	Famous Players Inc.		230
Silver City 12	Famous Players Inc.		159
Silver City 13	Famous Players Inc.		230
Silver City 14	Famous Players Inc.		447

S

ST. CATHARINES

Fairview Mall 1	Cineplex Odeon Corp.	129,170	391
Fairview Mall 2	Cineplex Odeon Corp.		297
Fairview Mall 3	Cineplex Odeon Corp.		209
Fairview Mall 4	Cineplex Odeon Corp.		218
Fairview Mall 5	Cineplex Odeon Corp.		254
Fairview Mall 6	Cineplex Odeon Corp.		228
Fairview Mall 7	Cineplex Odeon Corp.		161
Fairview Mall 8	Cineplex Odeon Corp.		161
Fairview Mall 9	Cineplex Odeon Corp.		160
Silver City 1	Famous Players Inc.		238
Silver City 2	Famous Players Inc.		243
Silver City 3	Famous Players Inc.		334
Silver City 4	Famous Players Inc.		304
Silver City 5	Famous Players Inc.		362
Silver City 6	Famous Players Inc.		167
Silver City 7	Famous Players Inc.		178
Silver City 8	Famous Players Inc.		179
Town Twin 1	B. & A. Lestein		521
Town Twin 2	B. & A. Lestein		405

SARNIA

Lambton 1	Famous Players Inc.	88,331	221
Lambton 2	Famous Players Inc.		258
Lambton 3	Famous Players Inc.		305
Lambton 4	Famous Players Inc.		278
Lambton 5	Famous Players Inc.		215
Lambton 6	Famous Players Inc.		208
Lambton 7	Famous Players Inc.		210
Lambton 8	Famous Players Inc.		210
Lambton 9	Famous Players Inc.		210

SAULT STE.MARIE

Station Mall 1	Galaxy Cinemas	78,908	268
Station Mall 2	Galaxy Cinemas		142
Station Mall 3	Galaxy Cinemas		130
Station Mall 4	Galaxy Cinemas		154
Station Mall 5	Galaxy Cinemas		212
Station Mall 6	Galaxy Cinemas		170
Station Mall 7	Galaxy Cinemas		184
Station Mall 8	Galaxy Cinemas		184
Station Mall 9	Galaxy Cinemas		184
Station Mall 10	Galaxy Cinemas		184
Station Mall 11	Galaxy Cinemas		366
Station Mall 12	Galaxy Cinemas		257

SIMCOE

Premier Cinemas 1	Premier Operating Corp.		
Premier Cinemas 2	Premier Operating Corp.Total Seats		356

SIOUX LOOKOUT

Mayfair	572604 Ontario Inc.	3,531	300

SMITHS FALLS

Premier #1	Premier Operating Corp. Ltd.9,977		430
Premier #2	Premier Operating Corp. Ltd.		270

STRATFORD

Stratford Amusement 1	Stratford Amusement Inc.		
Stratford Amusement 2	Stratford Amusement Inc.		
Stratford Amusement 3	Stratford Amusement Inc.		
Stratford Amusement 4	Stratford Amusement Inc.		
Stratford Amusement 5	Stratford Amusement Inc.	Total	560

SUDBURY

Silver City 1	Famous Players Inc.	103,879	231
Silver City 2	Famous Players Inc.		366
Silver City 3	Famous Players Inc.		197
Silver City 4	Famous Players Inc.		159
Silver City 5	Famous Players Inc.		242
Silver City 6	Famous Players Inc.		197
Silver City 7	Famous Players Inc.		197
Silver City 8	Famous Players Inc.		242
Silver City 9	Famous Players Inc.		159
Silver City 10	Famous Players Inc.		197
Silver City 11	Famous Players Inc.		366
Silver City 12	Famous Players Inc.		231
Science North Imax Theatre	Science North		206

T

THORNHILL

Rainbow Promenade 1	Magic Lantern Theatres	116,840	184
Rainbow Promenade 2	Magic Lantern Theatres		243
Rainbow Promenade 3	Magic Lantern Theatres		152
Rainbow Promenade 4	Magic Lantern Theatres		83
Rainbow Promenade 5	Magic Lantern Theatres		206
Rainbow Promenade 6	Magic Lantern Theatres		134

THUNDER BAY

Cumberland 1	May Theatres	103,215	289
Cumberland 2	May Theatres		130
Cumberland 3	May Theatres		190
Cumberland 4	May Theatres		340
Cumberland 5	May Theatres		340
Silver City 1	Famous Players Inc.		230
Silver City 2	Famous Players Inc.		351
Silver City 3	Famous Players Inc.		197
Silver City 4	Famous Players Inc.		159
Silver City 5	Famous Players Inc.		242
Silver City 6	Famous Players Inc.		197
Silver City 7	Famous Players Inc.		197
Silver City 8	Famous Players Inc.		242
Silver City 9	Famous Players Inc.		159
Silver City 10	Famous Players Inc.		197
Silver City 11	Famous Players Inc.		351
Silver City 12	Famous Players Inc.		230

TILLSONBURG

Broadway Cinemas 1	Tillsonburg Broadway Cinemas Inc.	14,052	160
Broadway Cinemas 2	Tillsonburg Broadway Cinemas Inc.		120
Broadway Cinemas 3	Tillsonburg Broadway Cinemas Inc.		120

TIMMINS

Cinema Six 1	Stinson Theatres Ltd.	43,686	
Cinema Six 2	Stinson Theatres Ltd.		
Cinema Six 3	Stinson Theatres Ltd.		
Cinema Six 4	Stinson Theatres Ltd.		
Cinema Six 5	Stinson Theatres Ltd.		
Cinema Six 6	Stinson Theatres Ltd.	Total Seats	1344

TORONTO

Albion Cinemas 1	Golden Theatres Ltd.	4,682,897	700

Name	Operator	Seats	Name	Operator	Seats
Albion Cinemas 2	Golden Theatres Ltd.	400	Interchange 10	AMC Theatres Canada Inc.	87
Abrami		350	Interchange 11	AMC Theatres Canada Inc.	87
Bayview Village-1	Alliance Atlantis Cinemas	222	Interchange 12	AMC Theatres Canada Inc.	168
Bayview Village-2	Alliance Atlantis Cinemas	209	Interchange 13	AMC Theatres Canada Inc.	100
Bayview Village-3	Alliance Atlantis Cinemas	219	Interchange 14	AMC Theatres Canada Inc.	423
Bayview Village-4	Alliance Atlantis Cinemas	230	Interchange 15	AMC Theatres Canada Inc.	581
Beach Cinemas-1	Alliance Atlantis Cinemas	151	Interchange 16	AMC Theatres Canada Inc.	581
Beach Cinemas-2	Alliance Atlantis Cinemas	339	Interchange 17	AMC Theatres Canada Inc.	423
Beach Cinemas-3	Alliance Atlantis Cinemas	151	Interchange 18	AMC Theatres Canada Inc.	100
Beach Cinemas-4	Alliance Atlantis Cinemas	151	Interchange 19	AMC Theatres Canada Inc.	168
Beach Cinemas-5	Alliance Atlantis Cinemas	212	Interchange 20	AMC Theatres Canada Inc.	87
Beach Cinemas-6	Alliance Atlantis Cinemas	212	Interchange 21	AMC Theatres Canada Inc.	87
Canada Square	Famous Players Inc.	257	Interchange 22	AMC Theatres Canada Inc.	87
Canada Square	Famous Players Inc.	281	Interchange 23	AMC Theatres Canada Inc.	189
Canada Square	Famous Players Inc.	264	Interchange 24	AMC Theatres Canada Inc.	295
Canada Square	Famous Players Inc.	125	Interchange 25	AMC Theatres Canada Inc.	253
Canada Square	Famous Players Inc.	125	Interchange 26	AMC Theatres Canada Inc.	189
Canada Square	Famous Players Inc.	125	Interchange 27	AMC Theatres Canada Inc.	100
Canada Square	Famous Players Inc.	217	Interchange 28	AMC Theatres Canada Inc.	100
Canada Square	Famous Players Inc.	171	Interchange 29	AMC Theatres Canada Inc.	168
Carlton 1	Cineplex Odeon Corp.	101	Interchange 30	AMC Theatres Canada Inc.	100
Carlton 2	Cineplex Odeon Corp.	113	Kennedy Commons 1	AMC Theatres Canada Inc.	123
Carlton 3	Cineplex Odeon Corp.	85	Kennedy Commons 2	AMC Theatres Canada Inc.	123
Carlton 4	Cineplex Odeon Corp.	98	Kennedy Commons 3	AMC Theatres Canada Inc.	115
Carlton 5	Cineplex Odeon Corp.	85	Kennedy Commons 4	AMC Theatres Canada Inc.	113
Carlton 6	Cineplex Odeon Corp.	111	Kennedy Commons 5	AMC Theatres Canada Inc.	222
Carlton 7	Cineplex Odeon Corp.	85	Kennedy Commons 6	AMC Theatres Canada Inc.	222
Carlton 8	Cineplex Odeon Corp.	111	Kennedy Commons 7	AMC Theatres Canada Inc.	123
Carlton 9	Cineplex Odeon Corp.	145	Kennedy Commons 8	AMC Theatres Canada Inc.	342
Coliseum Scarborough 1	Famous Players Inc.	228	Kennedy Commons 9	AMC Theatres Canada Inc.	410
Coliseum Scarborough 2	Famous Players Inc.	227	Kennedy Commons 10	AMC Theatres Canada Inc.	410
Coliseum Scarborough 3	Famous Players Inc.	227	Kennedy Commons 11	AMC Theatres Canada Inc.	342
Coliseum Scarborough 4	Famous Players Inc.	228	Kennedy Commons 12	AMC Theatres Canada Inc.	124
Coliseum Scarborough 5	Famous Players Inc.	228	Kennedy Commons 13	AMC Theatres Canada Inc.	124
Coliseum Scarborough 6	Famous Players Inc.	226	Kennedy Commons 14	AMC Theatres Canada Inc.	198
Coliseum Scarborough 7	Famous Players Inc.	414	Kennedy Commons 15	AMC Theatres Canada Inc.	198
Coliseum Scarborough 8	Famous Players Inc.	414	Kennedy Commons 16	AMC Theatres Canada Inc.	123
Coliseum Scarborough 9	Famous Players Inc.	324	Kennedy Commons 17	AMC Theatres Canada Inc.	115
Coliseum Scarborough 10	Famous Players Inc.	324	Kennedy Commons 18	AMC Theatres Canada Inc.	113
Coliseum Scarborough 11	Famous Players Inc.	420	Kennedy Commons 19	AMC Theatres Canada Inc.	123
Coliseum Scarborough 12	Famous Players Inc.	415	Kennedy Commons 20	AMC Theatres Canada Inc.	123
Colossus 1	Famous Players Inc.	449	Kingsway	Festival Cinemas Ltd.	400
Colossus 2	Famous Players Inc.	242	Morningside 1	Cineplex Odeon Corp.	218
Colossus 3	Famous Players Inc.	351	Morningside 2	Cineplex Odeon Corp.	198
Colossus 4	Famous Players Inc.	351	Morningside 3	Cineplex Odeon Corp.	185
Colossus 5	Famous Players Inc.	230	Morningside 4	Cineplex Odeon Corp.	181
Colossus 6	Famous Players Inc.	230	Morningside 5	Cineplex Odeon Corp.	180
Colossus 7	Famous Players Inc.	197	Morningside 6	Cineplex Odeon Corp.	319
Colossus 8	Famous Players Inc.	242	Morningside 7	Cineplex Odeon Corp.	265
Colossus 9	Famous Players Inc.	230	Morningside 8	Cineplex Odeon Corp.	201
Colossus 10	Famous Players Inc.	242	Morningside 9	Cineplex Odeon Corp.	199
Colossus 11	Famous Players Inc.	441	Morningside 10	Cineplex Odeon Corp.	248
Colossus 12	Famous Players Inc.	351	Morningside 11	Cineplex Odeon Corp.	309
Colossus 13	Famous Players Inc.	351	Mt. Pleasant	P. Sorok & P. Stasiuk	386
Colossus 14	Famous Players Inc.	230	Music Hall	Festival Cinemas Ltd.	1200
Colossus 15	Famous Players Inc.	230	Ontario Place Imax	Ontario Place	735
Colossus 16	Famous Players Inc.	230	Ontario Science Centre Imax	Ontario Science Centre	471
Colossus 17	Famous Players Inc.	197	Paradise	Festival Cinemas Ltd.	429
Colossus 18	Famous Players Inc.	230	Paramount 1	Famous Players Inc.	551
Colossus 19 (Imax)	Famous Players Inc.	252	Paramount 2	Famous Players Inc.	549
Cumberland 1	Alliance Cinemas	213	Paramount 3	Famous Players Inc.	387
Cumberland 2	Alliance Cinemas	320	Paramount 4	Famous Players Inc.	387
Cumberland 3	Alliance Cinemas	321	Paramount 5	Famous Players Inc.	134
Cumberland 4	Alliance Cinemas	177	Paramount 6	Famous Players Inc.	136
Eglinton Town Centre 1	Cineplex Odeon Corp.	503	Paramount 7	Famous Players Inc.	182
Eglinton Town Centre 2	Cineplex Odeon Corp.	210	Paramount 8	Famous Players Inc.	182
Eglinton Town Centre 3	Cineplex Odeon Corp.	151	Paramount 9	Famous Players Inc.	192
Eglinton Town Centre 4	Cineplex Odeon Corp.	106	Paramount 10	Famous Players Inc.	228
Eglinton Town Centre 5	Cineplex Odeon Corp.	106	Paramount 11	Famous Players Inc.	227
Eglinton Town Centre 6	Cineplex Odeon Corp.	215	Paramount 12	Famous Players Inc.	316
Eglinton Town Centre 7	Cineplex Odeon Corp.	209	Paramount 13	Famous Players Inc.	306
Eglinton Town Centre 8	Cineplex Odeon Corp.	304	Paramount / Imax 1 2D	Famous Players Inc.	402
Eglinton Town Centre 9	Cineplex Odeon Corp.	305	Paramount / Imax 2	Famous Players Inc.	350
Eglinton Town Centre 10	Cineplex Odeon Corp.	209	Queensway 1	Cineplex Odeon Corp.	487
Eglinton Town Centre 11	Cineplex Odeon Corp.	209	Queensway 2	Cineplex Odeon Corp.	302
Eglinton Town Centre 12	Cineplex Odeon Corp.	105	Queensway 3	Cineplex Odeon Corp.	246
Eglinton Town Centre 13	Cineplex Odeon Corp.	105	Queensway 4	Cineplex Odeon Corp.	209
Eglinton Town Centre 14	Cineplex Odeon Corp.	161	Queensway 5	Cineplex Odeon Corp.	105
Eglinton Town Centre 15	Cineplex Odeon Corp.	209	Queensway 6	Cineplex Odeon Corp.	105
Eglinton Town Centre 16	Cineplex Odeon Corp.	415	Queensway 7	Cineplex Odeon Corp.	246
Fox	Festival Cinemas	251	Queensway 8	Cineplex Odeon Corp.	246
Harbourfront Studio	Harbourfront Corp.	198	Queensway 9	Cineplex Odeon Corp.	302
Humber 1	Cineplex Odeon Corp.	580	Queensway 10	Cineplex Odeon Corp.	302
Humber 2	Cineplex Odeon Corp.	362	Queensway 11	Cineplex Odeon Corp.	246
Interchange 1	AMC Theatres Canada Inc.	100	Queensway 12	Cineplex Odeon Corp.	246
Interchange 2	AMC Theatres Canada Inc.	168	Queensway 13	Cineplex Odeon Corp.	105
Interchange 3	AMC Theatres Canada Inc.	100	Queensway 14	Cineplex Odeon Corp.	105
Interchange 4	AMC Theatres Canada Inc.	100	Queensway 15	Cineplex Odeon Corp.	209
Interchange 5	AMC Theatres Canada Inc.	189	Queensway 16	Cineplex Odeon Corp.	246
Interchange 6	AMC Theatres Canada Inc.	253	Queensway 17	Cineplex Odeon Corp.	302
Interchange 7	AMC Theatres Canada Inc.	295	Queensway 18	Cineplex Odeon Corp.	487
Interchange 8	AMC Theatres Canada Inc.	189	Rainbow Fairview 1	Magic Lantern Theatres	375
Interchange 9	AMC Theatres Canada Inc.	87	Rainbow Fairview 2	Magic Lantern Theatres	235

Rainbow Fairview 3	Magic Lantern Theatres		180
Rainbow Fairview 4	Magic Lantern Theatres		209
Rainbow Fairview 5	Magic Lantern Theatres		172
Rainbow Fairview 6	Magic Lantern Theatres		343
Rainbow Market Square 1	Magic Lantern Theatres		106
Rainbow Market Square2	Magic Lantern Theatres		58
Rainbow Market Square3	Magic Lantern Theatres		186
Rainbow Market Square4	Magic Lantern Theatres		129
Rainbow Market Square5	Magic Lantern Theatres		122
Rainbow Market Square6	Magic Lantern Theatres		154
Rainbow Promenade 1	Magic Lantern Theatres		184
Rainbow Promenade2	Magic Lantern Theatres		243
Rainbow Promenade3	Magic Lantern Theatres		152
Rainbow Promenade4	Magic Lantern Theatres		83
Rainbow Promenade5	Magic Lantern Theatres		206
Rainbow Promenade6	Magic Lantern Theatres		134
Rainbow Woodbine 1	Magic Lantern Theatres		280
Rainbow Woodbine 2	Magic Lantern Theatres		33
Rainbow Woodbine 3	Magic Lantern Theatres		158
Rainbow Woodbine 4	Magic Lantern Theatres		98
Rainbow Woodbine 5	Magic Lantern Theatres		245
Rainbow Woodbine 6	Magic Lantern Theatres		149
Rainbow Woodbine 7	Magic Lantern Theatres		155
Rainbow Woodbine 8	Magic Lantern Theatres		155
Revue	576086 Ontario Ltd.		360
Royal	Princess Royal Cinema Ltd.		440
Sheppard Grande 1	Cineplex Odeon Corp.		347
Sheppard Grande 2	Cineplex Odeon Corp.		428
Sheppard Grande 3	Cineplex Odeon Corp.		428
Sheppard Grande 4	Cineplex Odeon Corp.		343
Sheppard Grande 5	Cineplex Odeon Corp.		429
Sheppard Grande 6	Cineplex Odeon Corp.		437
Sheppard Grande 7	Cineplex Odeon Corp.		275
Sheppard Grande 8	Cineplex Odeon Corp.		265
Sheppard Grande 9	Cineplex Odeon Corp.		275
Sheppard Grande 10	Cineplex Odeon Corp.		275
Silver City Empress Walk 1	Famous Players Inc.		447
Silver City Empress Walk 2	Famous Players Inc.		372
Silver City Empress Walk 3	Famous Players Inc.		242
Silver City Empress Walk 4	Famous Players Inc.		447
Silver City Empress Walk 5	Famous Players Inc.		242
Silver City Empress Walk 6	Famous Players Inc.		242
Silver City Empress Walk 7	Famous Players Inc.		206
Silver City Empress Walk 8	Famous Players Inc.		345
Silver City Empress Walk 9	Famous Players Inc.		242
Silver City Empress Walk 10	Famous Players Inc.		230
Silver City Yonge & Egl. 1	Famous Players Inc.		229
Silver City Yonge & Egl. 2	Famous Players Inc.		230
Silver City Yonge & Egl. 3	Famous Players Inc.		329
Silver City Yonge & Egl. 4	Famous Players Inc.		329
Silver City Yonge & Egl. 5	Famous Players Inc.		330
Silver City Yonge & Egl. 6	Famous Players Inc.		452
Silver City Yonge & Egl. 7	Famous Players Inc.		247
Silver City Yonge & Egl. 8	Famous Players Inc.		401
Silver City Yonge & Egl. 9	Famous Players Inc.		272
Silver City Yorkdale 1	Famous Players Inc.		178
Silver City Yorkdale 2	Famous Players inc.		224
Silver City Yorkdale 3	Famous Players inc.		251
Silver City Yorkdale 4	Famous Players inc.		251
Silver City Yorkdale 5	Famous Players inc.		251
Silver City Yorkdale 6	Famous Players inc.		200
Silver City Yorkdale 7	Famous Players inc.		346
Silver City Yorkdale 8	Famous Players inc.		446
Silver City Yorkdale 9	Famous Players inc.		447
Silver City Yorkdale 10	Famous Players inc.		447
Uptown 1	Famous Players Inc.		921
Uptown 2	Famous Players Inc.		604
Uptown 3	Famous Players Inc.		404
Varsity 1	Cineplex Odeon Corp.		215
Varsity 2	Cineplex Odeon Corp.		226
Varsity 3	Cineplex Odeon Corp.		230
Varsity 4	Cineplex Odeon Corp.		167
Varsity 5	Cineplex Odeon Corp.		131
Varsity 6	Cineplex Odeon Corp.		130
Varsity 7	Cineplex Odeon Corp.		138
Varsity 8	Cineplex Odeon Corp.		579
Varsity 9	Cineplex Odeon Corp.		30
Varsity 10	Cineplex Odeon Corp.		30
Varsity 11	Cineplex Odeon Corp.		36
Varsity 12	Cineplex Odeon Corp.		24
Woodside 1	Golden Theatres Ltd.		424
Woodside 2	Golden Theatres Ltd.		293
Woodside 3	Golden Theatres Ltd.		290

TRENTON

Centre 1	Fratelli Theatres Inc.	2,798	
Centre 2	Fratelli Theatres Inc.		
Centre 3	Fratelli Theatres Inc.	Total seats	639

U

UXBRIDGE

Roxy (2 screens)	Alecait Holdings Inc.	8,540	300

W

WATERLOO

Conestoga Mall 1	Galaxy Cinemas	86,543	315
Conestoga Mall 2	Galaxy Cinemas		228
Conestoga Mall 3	Galaxy Cinemas		134
Conestoga Mall 4	Galaxy Cinemas		169
Conestoga Mall 5	Galaxy Cinemas		234
Conestoga Mall 6	Galaxy Cinemas		234
Conestoga Mall 7	Galaxy Cinemas		169
Conestoga Mall 8	Galaxy Cinemas		134
Conestoga Mall 9	Galaxy Cinemas		228
Conestoga Mall 10	Galaxy Cinemas		315
Princess	The Princess Cinema Inc.		133
Princess Two (Oct. 2003)	The Princess Cinema Inc.		130

WELLAND

Seaway 1	Cineplex Odeon Corp.	48,402	259
Seaway 2	Cineplex Odeon Corp.		360
Seaway 3	Cineplex Odeon Corp.		144
Seaway 4	Cineplex Odeon Corp.		144
Seaway 5	Cineplex Odeon Corp.		144
Seaway 6	Cineplex Odeon Corp.		144
Seaway 7	Cineplex Odeon Corp.		144

WHITBY

Whitby 1	AMC Theatres Canada Inc.	87,413	111
Whitby 2	AMC Theatres Canada Inc.		141
Whitby 3	AMC Theatres Canada Inc.		125
Whitby 4	AMC Theatres Canada Inc.		247
Whitby 5	AMC Theatres Canada Inc.		247
Whitby 6	AMC Theatres Canada Inc.		125
Whitby 7	AMC Theatres Canada Inc.		90
Whitby 8	AMC Theatres Canada Inc.		88
Whitby 9	AMC Theatres Canada Inc.		141
Whitby 10	AMC Theatres Canada Inc.		111
Whitby 11	AMC Theatres Canada Inc.		428
Whitby 12	AMC Theatres Canada Inc.		534
Whitby 13	AMC Theatres Canada Inc.		534
Whitby 14	AMC Theatres Canada Inc.		428
Whitby 15	AMC Theatres Canada Inc.		111
Whitby 16	AMC Theatres Canada Inc.		141
Whitby 17	AMC Theatres Canada Inc.		88
Whitby 18	AMC Theatres Canada Inc.		90
Whitby 19	AMC Theatres Canada Inc.		125
Whitby 20	AMC Theatres Canada Inc.		247
Whitby 21	AMC Theatres Canada Inc.		247
Whitby 22	AMC Theatres Canada Inc.		125
Whitby 23	AMC Theatres Canada Inc.		141
Whitby 24	AMC Theatres Canada Inc.		111

WINDSOR

Devonshire 1	Cineplex Odeon Corp.	263,204	411
Devonshire 2	Cineplex Odeon Corp.		397
Devonshire 3	Cineplex Odeon Corp.		170
Devonshire 4	Cineplex Odeon Corp.		213
Devonshire 5	Cineplex Odeon Corp.		249
Devonshire 6	Cineplex Odeon Corp.		170
Devonshire 7	Cineplex Odeon Corp.		213
Devonshire 8	Cineplex Odeon Corp.		247
Devonshire 9	Cineplex Odeon Corp.		247
Devonshire 10	Cineplex Odeon Corp.		248
Devonshire 11	Cineplex Odeon Corp.		309
Devonshire 12	Cineplex Odeon Corp.		372
Forest Glade 1	Forest Glade Cinemas		334
Forest Glade 2	Forest Glade Cinemas		195
Forest Glade 3	Forest Glade Cinemas		232
Palace 1	2012209 Ontario Inc.		197
Palace 2	2012209 Ontario Inc.		183
Palace 3	2012209 Ontario Inc.		248
Palace 4	2012209 Ontario Inc.		272
Silver City 1	Famous Players Inc.		350
Silver City 2	Famous Players Inc.		192
Silver City 3	Famous Players Inc.		191
Silver City 4	Famous Players Inc.		224
Silver City 5	Famous Players Inc.		229
Silver City 6	Famous Players Inc.		447
Silver City 7	Famous Players Inc.		445
Silver City 8	Famous Players Inc.		229
Silver City 9	Famous Players Inc.		229
Silver City 10	Famous Players Inc.		194
Silver City 11	Famous Players Inc.		194
Silver City 12	Famous Players Inc.		347

WINGHAM

Lyceum	Dale Edger	2,885	177

WOODSTOCK

Gallery 1	Gallery Cinemas (Woodstock) Inc.	33,061	274
Gallery 2	Gallery Cinemas (Woodstock) Inc.		236
Gallery 3	Gallery Cinemas (Woodstock) Inc.		167
Gallery 4	Gallery Cinemas (Woodstock) Inc.		143
Gallery 5	Gallery Cinemas (Woodstock) Inc.		105
Gallery 6	Gallery Cinemas (Woodstock) Inc.		91
Gallery 7	Gallery Cinemas (Woodstock) Inc.		91

PRINCE EDWARD ISLAND

C

CHARLOTTETOWN

City Cinema	Derek Martin	38,114	90

S

SOURIS

Souris	Gary Carter	1,248	250

SUMMERSIDE

Studio 1	Empire Theatres Ltd.	16,200	235
Studio 2	Empire Theatres Ltd.		150
Studio 3	Empire Theatres Ltd.		150
Studio 4	Empire Theatres Ltd.		150
Studio 5	Empire Theatres Ltd.		150

W

WEST ROYALTY

Studio 1	Empire Theatres Ltd.		144
Studio 2	Empire Theatres Ltd.		187
Studio 3	Empire Theatres Ltd.		235
Studio 4	Empire Theatres Ltd.		204
Studio 5	Empire Theatres Ltd.		146
Studio 6	Empire Theatres Ltd.		146
Studio 7	Empire Theatres Ltd.		130
Studio 8	Empire Theatres Ltd.		130

QUÉBEC

A

ALMA

Cinéma Complexe Alma 1	Ghislain Dubois	28,125	350
Cinéma Complexe Alma 2	Ghislain Dubois		152
Cinéma Complexe Alma 3	Ghislain Dubois		135
Cinéma Complexe Alma 4	Ghislain Dubois		59

AMOS

Cinéma Amos	Denis Bédard	10,266	00

AMQUI

Cinéma la Boîte à Films	Martine Soucy	5,034	300

ALYMER

Galeries Aylmer 1	Denis Bédard	36,085	154
Galeries Aylmer 2	Denis Bédard		154
Galeries Aylmer 3	Denis Bédard		154
Galeries Aylmer 4	Denis Bédard		267

B

BAGOTVILLE

BCF Alouette	Alain Benoit	1,064	200

BAIE-COMEAU

Ciné Centre Vidéo 1	Réjean Guy	10,266	194
Ciné Centre Vidéo 2	Réjean Guy		154
Ciné Centre Vidéo 3	Réjean Guy		55

BEAUPORT

Beauport 1	Cinéplex Odéon	72,813	492
Beauport 2	Cinéplex Odéon		249
Beauport 3	Cinéplex Odéon		164
Beauport 4	Cinéplex Odéon		164
Beauport 5	Cinéplex Odéon		164
Beauport 6	Cinéplex Odéon		213
Beauport 7	Cinéplex Odéon		249
Beauport 8	Cinéplex Odéon		308
Beauport 9	Cinéplex Odéon		308
Beauport 10	Cinéplex Odéon		249
Beauport 11	Cinéplex Odéon		213
Beauport 12	Cinéplex Odéon		164
Beauport 13	Cinéplex Odéon		164
Beauport 14	Cinéplex Odéon		164
Beauport 15	Cinéplex Odéon		249
Beauport 16	Cinéplex Odéon		492

BOUCHERVILLE

Boucherville 1	Jean Colbert	36,253	84
Boucherville 2	Jean Colbert		234
Boucherville 3	Jean Colbert		150
Boucherville 4	Jean Colbert		95
Boucherville 5	Jean Colbert		108
Boucherville 6	Jean Colbert		112
Boucherville 7	Jean Colbert		126
Boucherville 8	Jean Colbert		93
Boucherville 9	Jean Colbert		95
Boucherville 10	Jean Colbert		117

C

CAP-DE-LA MADELEINE

Galeries du Cap 1	Ciné-Entreprise	32,534	236
Galeries du Cap 2	Ciné-Entreprise		236
Galeries du Cap 3	Ciné-Entreprise		207
Galeries du Cap 4	Ciné-Entreprise		195
Galeries du Cap 5	Ciné-Entreprise		195
Galeries du Cap 6	Ciné-Entreprise		195
Galeries du Cap 7	Ciné-Entreprise		195

CHANDLER

Paradiso 1	Louis Roy	3,004	325
Paradiso 2	Louis Roy		78

CHAPAIS

L'Aventure	Légie Lalancette	1,795	250

CHÂTEAUGUAY

Carnaval 1	Shiraz Tajdin	41,003	220
Carnaval 2	Shiraz Tajdin		104
Carnaval 3	Shiraz Tajdin		147
Carnaval 4	Shiraz Tajdin		113
Carnaval 5	Shiraz Tajdin		172
Carnaval 6	Shiraz Tajdin		233
Chateauguay Encore 1	Cinéplex Odéon		158
Chateauguay Encore 2	Cinéplex Odéon		188
Chateauguay Encore 3	Cinéplex Odéon		158
Chateauguay Encore 4	Cinéplex Odéon		146
Chateauguay Encore 5	Cinéplex Odéon		92

CHIBOUGAMAU

Cinémax	Roger Pearson	7,922	250

CHICOUTIMI

Odyssée 1	Ciné-Entreprise	60,008	156
Odyssée 2	Ciné-Entreprise		136
Odyssée 3	Ciné-Entreprise		251
Odyssée 4	Ciné-Entreprise		251
Odyssée 5	Ciné-Entreprise		275
Odyssée 6	Ciné-Entreprise		275
Odyssée 7	Ciné-Entreprise		156
Odyssée 8	Ciné-Entreprise		156

COWANSVILLE

Princesse	Réjean Daigle	12,032	300

D

DÉGELIS

Dégelis	Guy Simard	3,317	410

DOLBEAU-MISTASSINI

Chaplin 1	Hugues Morin	14,879	127
Chaplin 2	Hugues Morin		100
Chaplin 3	Hugues Morin		56

DELSON

Delson 1	Cinéplex Odéon		109
Delson 2	Cinéplex Odéon		135
Delson 3	Cinéplex Odéon		216
Delson 4	Cinéplex Odéon		183
Delson 5	Cinéplex Odéon		117
Delson 6	Cinéplex Odéon		154
Delson 7	Cinéplex Odéon		136

DOLLARD DES ORMEAUX

Des sources 1	Cinémas Guzzo		207
Des sources 2	Cinémas Guzzo		228
Des sources 3	Cinémas Guzzo		280
Des sources 4	Cinémas Guzzo		230
Des sources 5	Cinémas Guzzo		234
Des sources 6	Cinémas Guzzo		157
Des sources 7	Cinémas Guzzo		174
Des sources 8	Cinémas Guzzo		164
Des sources 9	Cinémas Guzzo		164
Des sources 10	Cinémas Guzzo		123

DORIAN

Carrefour Dorion 1	Cinéplex Odéon		182
Carrefour Dorion 2	Cinéplex Odéon		182
Carrefour Dorion 3	Cinéplex Odéon		147
Carrefour Dorion 4	Cinéplex Odéon		96
Carrefour Dorion 5	Cinéplex Odéon		124
Carrefour Dorion 6	Cinéplex Odéon		184
Carrefour Dorion 7	Cinéplex Odéon		155
Carrefour Dorion 8	Cinéplex Odéon		124

DORVAL

Dorval Cinema 1	Famous Players Inc.	17,706	276
Dorval Cinema 2	Famous Players Inc.		305
Dorval Cinema 3	Famous Players Inc.		545
Dorval Cinema 4	Famous Players Inc.		218

DRUMMONDVILLE

Capitol 1	Marcel Venne	68,451	304
Capitol 2	Marcel Venne		92
Capitol 3	Marcel Venne		150
Capitol 4	Marcel Venne		51
Capitol 5	Marcel Venne		66
Capitol 6	Marcel Venne		100
Capitol 7	Marcel Venne		108

Capitol 8	Marcel Venne		204

G

GASPÉ

Cinéma Baker	Pascal Dennis	14,932	100

GATINEAU

Cinéma Gatineau 1	Didier Farré	102,898	160
Cinéma Gatineau 2	Didier Farré		245
Cinéma Gatineau 3	Didier Farré		240
Cinéma Gatineau 4	Didier Farré		380
Cinéma Gatineau 5	Didier Farré		164
Cinéma Gatineau 6	Didier Farré		173
Cinéma Gatineau 7	Didier Farré		160
Cinéma Gatineau 8	Didier Farré		135
Cinéma Gatineau 9	Didier Farré		160

GRANBY

Fleur de Lys 1	Ciné-Entreprise	53,106	270
Fleur de Lys 2	Ciné-Entreprise		192
Fleur de Lys 3	Ciné-Entreprise		96
Fleur de Lys 4	Ciné-Entreprise		221
Fleur de Lys 5	Ciné-Entreprise		221
Galeries de Granby 1	André Robert		512
Galeries de Granby 2	André Robert		190
Galeries de Granby 3	André Robert		232

GREENFIELD

Mega-plex Taschereau 1	Cinémas Guzzo	16,978	395
ParkMega-plex Taschereau 2	Cinémas Guzzo		389
Mega-plex Taschereau 3	Cinémas Guzzo		342
Mega-plex Taschereau 4	Cinémas Guzzo		248
Mega-plex Taschereau 5	Cinémas Guzzo		200
Mega-plex Taschereau 6	Cinémas Guzzo		210
Mega-plex Taschereau 7	Cinémas Guzzo		176
Mega-plex Taschereau 8	Cinémas Guzzo		200
Mega-plex Taschereau 9	Cinémas Guzzo		220
Mega-plex Taschereau 10	Cinémas Guzzo		188
Mega-plex Taschereau 11	Cinémas Guzzo		115
Mega-plex Taschereau 12	Cinémas Guzzo		115
Mega-plex Taschereau 13	Cinémas Guzzo		115
Mega-plex Taschereau 14	Cinémas Guzzo		115
Mega-plex Taschereau 15	Cinémas Guzzo		450
Mega-plex Taschereau 16	Cinémas Guzzo		268
Mega-plex Taschereau 17	Cinémas Guzzo		176
Mega-plex Taschereau 18	Cinémas Guzzo		343

GRENVILLE

Laurentien 1	Yvon Myner	1,315	
Laurentien 2	Yvon Myner		

H

HULL

StarCité 1	Famous Players Inc.	66,246	365
StarCité 2	Famous Players Inc.		159
StarCité 3	Famous Players Inc.		230
StarCité 4	Famous Players Inc.		159
StarCité 5	Famous Players Inc.		230
StarCité 6	Famous Players Inc.		159
StarCité 7	Famous Players Inc.		159
StarCité 8	Famous Players Inc.		453
StarCité 9	Famous Players Inc.		453
StarCité 10	Famous Players Inc.		159
StarCité 11	Famous Players Inc.		159
StarCité 12	Famous Players Inc.		230
StarCité 13	Famous Players Inc.		159
StarCité 14	Famous Players Inc.		230
StarCité 15	Famous Players Inc.		159
StarCité 16	Famous Players Inc.		366

I

ILES DE LA MADELEINE

Cinéma Cyrco	Cinémas Cyrco		194

J

JOLIETTE

Carrefour Joliette 1	Marcel Venne	35,821	60
Carrefour Joliette 2	Marcel Venne		129
Carrefour Joliette 3	Marcel Venne		285
Carrefour Joliette 4	Marcel Venne		188
Carrefour Joliette 5	Marcel Venne		142
Carrefour Joliette 6	Marcel Venne		244
Carrefour Joliette 7	Marcel Venne		105
Carrefour Joliette 8	Marcel Venne		264
Carrefour Joliette 9	Marcel Venne		137
Carrefour Joliette 10	Marcel Venne		105

ONQUIÈRE

Jonquière 1	Ciné-Entreprise	54,842	251
Jonquière 2	Ciné-Entreprise		163

K

KIRKLAND

Colisée 1	Famous Players Inc.	20,434	230
Colisée 2	Famous Players Inc.		230
Colisée 3	Famous Players Inc.		230
Colisée 4	Famous Players Inc.		230
Colisée 5	Famous Players Inc.		230
Colisée 6	Famous Players Inc.		230
Colisée 7	Famous Players Inc.		417
Colisée 8	Famous Players Inc.		417
Colisée 9	Famous Players Inc.		325
Colisée 10	Famous Players Inc.		325
Colisée 11	Famous Players Inc.		418
Colisée 12	Famous Players Inc.		418

L

LACHENAIE

Triomphe 1	Ciné-Entreprise	21,709	369
Triomphe 2	Ciné-Entreprise		252
Triomphe 3	Ciné-Entreprise		249
Triomphe 4	Ciné-Entreprise		209
Triomphe 5	Ciné-Entreprise		252
Triomphe 6	Ciné-Entreprise		209
Triomphe 7	Ciné-Entreprise		369
Triomphe 8	Ciné-Entreprise		252
Triomphe 9	Ciné-Entreprise		209
Triomphe 10	Ciné-Entreprise		209

LA MALBAIE

La Malbaie	Ciné-Quilles D.L. Inc.	9,143	210

LA POCATIÈRE

Le Scenario 1	Marie Josée D'Anjou	4,518	108
Le Scenario 2	Marie Josée D'Anjou		155
Le Scenario 3	Marie Josée D'Anjou		226

LASALLE

Angrignon 1	Famous Players Inc.	73,983	146
Angrignon 2	Famous Players Inc.		160
Angrignon 3	Famous Players Inc.		159
Angrignon 4	Famous Players Inc.		159
Angrignon 5	Famous Players Inc.		123
Angrignon 6	Famous Players Inc.		91
Angrignon 7	Famous Players Inc.		271
Angrignon 8	Famous Players Inc.		141
Angrignon 9	Famous Players Inc.		165
Angrignon 10	Famous Players Inc.		329
Place Lasalle 1	Cinéplex Odéon		130
Place Lasalle 2	Cinéplex Odéon		249
Place Lasalle 3	Cinéplex Odéon		251
Place Lasalle 4	Cinéplex Odéon		100
Place Lasalle 5	Cinéplex Odéon		132
Place Lasalle 6	Cinéplex Odéon		226
Place Lasalle 7	Cinéplex Odéon		184
Place Lasalle 8	Cinéplex Odéon		84
Place Lasalle 9	Cinéplex Odéon		90
Place Lasalle 10	Cinéplex Odéon		249
Place Lasalle 11	Cinéplex Odéon		249
Place Lasalle 12	Cinéplex Odéon		131

LAVAL

Colossus 1	Famous Players Inc.	343,005	455
Colossus 2	Famous Players Inc.		225
Colossus 3	Famous Players Inc.		368
Colossus 4	Famous Players Inc.		368
Colossus 5	Famous Players Inc.		225
Colossus 6	Famous Players Inc.		225
Colossus 7	Famous Players Inc.		145
Colossus 8	Famous Players Inc.		194
Colossus 9	Famous Players Inc.		145
Colossus 10	Famous Players Inc.		225
Colossus 11	Famous Players Inc.		457
Colossus 12	Famous Players Inc.		368
Colossus 13	Famous Players Inc.		365
Colossus 14	Famous Players Inc.		225
Colossus 15	Famous Players Inc.		225
Colossus 16	Famous Players Inc.		194
Colossus 17	Famous Players Inc.		146
Colossus 18	Famous Players Inc.		145
Pont-Viau 1	Cinémas Guzzo		230
Pont-Viau 2	Cinémas Guzzo		230
Pont-Viau 3	Cinémas Guzzo		210
Pont-Viau 4	Cinémas Guzzo		180
Pont-Viau 5	Cinémas Guzzo		230
Pont-Viau 6	Cinémas Guzzo		310
Pont-Viau 7	Cinémas Guzzo		300
Pont-Viau 8	Cinémas Guzzo		240
Pont-Viau 9	Cinémas Guzzo		200
Pont-Viau 10	Cinémas Guzzo		150
Pont-Viau 11	Cinémas Guzzo		150
Pont-Viau 12	Cinémas Guzzo		150
Pont-Viau 13	Cinémas Guzzo		150
Pont-Viau 14	Cinémas Guzzo		220
Pont-Viau 15	Cinémas Guzzo		320
Pont-Viau 16	Cinémas Guzzo		430

LEBEL-SUR-QUEVILLON

Centre Communautaire	Johanne Paradis	3,236	289

LÉVIS

Lido 1	André Gilbert	40,926	308
Lido 2	André Gilbert		141
Lido 3	André Gilbert		120
Lido 4	André Gilbert		111
Lido 5	André Gilbert		144
Lido 6	André Gilbert		116
Lido 7	André Gilbert		142
Lido 8	André Gilbert		93
Lido 9	André Gilbert		136

LONGUEUIL

Mega-Plex Jacques-Cartier 1	Cinémas Guzzo	128,016	205
Mega-Plex Jacques-Cartier 2	Cinémas Guzzo		205
Mega-Plex Jacques-Cartier 3	Cinémas Guzzo		205
Mega-Plex Jacques-Cartier 4	Cinémas Guzzo		250
Mega-Plex Jacques-Cartier 5	Cinémas Guzzo		270
Mega-Plex Jacques-Cartier 6	Cinémas Guzzo		250
Mega-Plex Jacques-Cartier 7	Cinémas Guzzo		270
Mega-Plex Jacques-Cartier 8	Cinémas Guzzo		300
Mega-Plex Jacques-Cartier 9	Cinémas Guzzo		250
Mega-Plex Jacques-Cartier 10	Cinémas Guzzo		50
Mega-Plex Jacques-Cartier 11	Cinémas Guzzo		205
Mega-Plex Jacques-Cartier 12	Cinémas Guzzo		205
Mega-Plex Jacques-Cartier 13	Cinémas Guzzo		270
Mega-Plex Jacques-Cartier 14	Cinémas Guzzo		165

LOUISEVILLE

Pixel 1	Robert Binette	7,622	98
Pixel 2	Robert Binette		131
Pixel 3	Robert Binette		165

M

MACAMIC

Cinemak	Stéphane Labrie		135

MAGOG

Magog 1	Ginette Pradella	14,283	215
Magog 2	Ginette Pradella		122
Magog 3	Ginette Pradella		60

MANIWAKI

Merlin	Anne Jolivette	4,168	250

MATANE

Gaiété	Jacques Desjardins		151

MÉGANTIC

Mégantic 1	Bernard Fortier	5,897	267
Mégantic 2	Bernard Fortier		126

MONT-LAURIER

Laurier	Réjean Martineau	7,365	300

MONT-TREMBLANT

Des Monts 1	Tom Fermanian	8,352	115
Des Monts 2	Tom Fermanian		96

MONTMAGNY

Cinéma Lafontaine	Guy Couillard	11,654	150

MONTRÉAL

Cavendish Mall 1	Cineplex Odéon	3,426,530	143
Cavendish Mall 2	Cineplex Odéon		186
Cavendish Mall 3	Cineplex Odéon		247
Cavendish Mall 4	Cineplex Odéon		161
Cavendish Mall 5	Cineplex Odéon		146
Cavendish Mall 6	Cineplex Odéon		189
Cavendish Mall 7	Cineplex Odéon		189
Cavendish Mall 8	Cineplex Odéon		204
Centre Eaton 1	Famous Players Inc.		447
Centre Eaton 2	Famous Players Inc.		477
Centre Eaton 3	Famous Players Inc.		219
Centre Eaton 4	Famous Players Inc.		274
Centre Eaton 5	Famous Players Inc.		219
Centre Eaton 6	Famous Players Inc.		257
Cinéma Beaubien 1	Corp. de développement e Dauphin		172
Cinéma Beaubien 2	Corp. de développement e Dauphin		219
Cinéma Beaubien 3	Corp. de développement e Dauphin		70
Cinéma ONF	National Film Board		143
Côte de Neiges 1	Cineplex Odéon		294
Côte de Neiges 2	Cineplex Odéon		248
Côte de Neiges 3	Cineplex Odéon		263
Côte de Neiges 4	Cineplex Odéon		250
Côte de Neiges 5	Cineplex Odéon		428
Côte de Neiges 6	Cineplex Odéon		493
Côte de Neiges 7	Cineplex Odéon		255
Du Parc 1	La soc. de cinéma de rép. de Mtl.		250
Du Parc 2	La soc. de cinéma de rép. de Mtl.		199
Du Parc 3	La soc. de cinéma de rép. de Mtl.		179
Ex-Centris 1	Daniel Langlois		300
Ex-Centris 2	Daniel Langlois		200
Ex-Centris 3	Daniel Langlois		100
Le Forum 1	AMC Entertainment Inc.		175
Le Forum 2	AMC Entertainment Inc.		262
Le Forum 3	AMC Entertainment Inc.		587
Le Forum 4	AMC Entertainment Inc.		354
Le Forum 5	AMC Entertainment Inc.		360
Le Forum 6	AMC Entertainment Inc.		175
Le Forum 7	AMC Entertainment Inc.		114
Le Forum 8	AMC Entertainment Inc.		222
Le Forum 9	AMC Entertainment Inc.		222
Le Forum 10	AMC Entertainment Inc.		175
Le Forum 11	AMC Entertainment Inc.		102
Le Forum 12	AMC Entertainment Inc.		114
Le Forum 13	AMC Entertainment Inc.		156
Le Forum 14	AMC Entertainment Inc.		195
Le Forum 15	AMC Entertainment Inc.		134
Le Forum 16	AMC Entertainment Inc.		134
Le Forum 17	AMC Entertainment Inc.		134
Le Forum 18	AMC Entertainment Inc.		134
Le Forum 19	AMC Entertainment Inc.		195
Le Forum 20	AMC Entertainment Inc.		134
Le Forum 21	AMC Entertainment Inc.		114
Le Forum 22	AMC Entertainment Inc.		102
Paradis 1	Cinémas Guzzo		402
Paradis 2	Cinémas Guzzo		278
Paradis 3	Cinémas Guzzo		208
Paramount 1	Famous Players Inc.		381
Paramount 2	Famous Players Inc.		312
Paramount 3	Famous Players Inc.		158
Paramount 4	Famous Players Inc.		222
Paramount 5	Famous Players Inc.		310
Paramount 6	Famous Players Inc.		389
Paramount 7	Famous Players Inc.		405
Paramount 8	Famous Players Inc.		312
Paramount 9	Famous Players Inc.		158
Paramount 10	Famous Players Inc.		222
Paramount 11	Famous Players Inc.		308
Paramount 12	Famous Players Inc.		389
Paramount Imax	Famous Players Inc.		340
Parisien 1	Famous Players Inc.		154
Parisien 2	Famous Players Inc.		212
Parisien 3	Famous Players Inc.		197
Parisien 4	Famous Players Inc.		480
Parisien 5	Famous Players Inc.		312
Parisien 6	Famous Players Inc.		509
Parisien 7	Famous Players Inc.		299
Quartier Latin 1	Cineplex Odéon		257
Quartier Latin 2	Cineplex Odéon		114
Quartier Latin 3	Cineplex Odéon		153
Quartier Latin 4	Cineplex Odéon		134
Quartier Latin 5	Cineplex Odéon		146
Quartier Latin 6	Cineplex Odéon		150
Quartier Latin 7	Cineplex Odéon		106
Quartier Latin 8	Cineplex Odéon		257
Quartier Latin 9	Cineplex Odéon		354
Quartier Latin 10	Cineplex Odéon		258
Quartier Latin 11	Cineplex Odéon		115
Quartier Latin 12	Cineplex Odéon		154
Quartier Latin 13	Cineplex Odéon		135
Quartier Latin 14	Cineplex Odéon		151
Quartier Latin 15	Cineplex Odéon		153
Quartier Latin 16	Cineplex Odéon		170
Quartier Latin 17	Cineplex Odéon		224
Star Cité 1	Famous Players Inc.		478
Star Cité 2	Famous Players Inc.		369
Star Cité 3	Famous Players Inc.		230
Star Cité 4	Famous Players Inc.		230
Star Cité 5	Famous Players Inc.		230
Star Cité 6	Famous Players Inc.		158
Star Cité 7	Famous Players Inc.		159
Star Cité 8	Famous Players Inc.		159
Star Cité 9	Famous Players Inc.		159
Star Cité 10	Famous Players Inc.		160
Star Cité 11	Famous Players Inc.		159
Star Cité 12	Famous Players Inc.		478
Star Cité 13	Famous Players Inc.		371
Star Cité 14	Famous Players Inc.		231
Star Cité 15	Famous Players Inc.		159
Star Cité 16	Famous Players Inc.		159
Star Cité 17	Famous Players Inc.		159
Versailles 1	Famous Players Inc.		485
Versailles 2	Famous Players Inc.		482
Versailles 3	Famous Players Inc.		299
Versailles 4	Famous Players Inc.		319
Versailles 5	Famous Players Inc.		341
Versailles 6	Famous Players Inc.		324

N

NEW RICHMOND

Baie des Chaleurs	Louis Morin	3,760	660

NEW CARLISLE

Cinéma Royal	Louis Roy	1,431	191

P

POINTE-CLAIRE

Famous 1	Famous Players	29,268	169
Famous 2	Famous Players		233
Famous 3	Famous Players		201
Famous 4	Famous Players		469
Famous 5	Famous Players		268
Famous 6	Famous Players		187
Famous 7	Famous Players		248
Famous 8	Famous Players		232

Q

QUÉBEC CITY

Galeries de la Capitale 1	Famous Players Inc.	682,757	158
Galeries de la Capitale 2	Famous Players Inc.		332
Galeries de la Capitale 3	Famous Players Inc.		319
Galeries de la Capitale 4	Famous Players Inc.		235
Galeries de la Capitale 5	Famous Players Inc.		304
Galeries de la Capitale 6	Famous Players Inc.		304
Galeries de la Capitale 7	Famous Players Inc.		505
Galeries de la Capitale 8	Famous Players Inc.		182
Galeries de la Capitale 9	Famous Players Inc.		401
Galeries de la Capitale 10	Famous Players Inc.		369
Galeries de la Capitale 11	Famous Players Inc.		317
Galeries de la Capitale 12	Famous Players Inc.		103
Place Charest 1	Cineplex Odéon		599
Place Charest 2	Cineplex Odéon		145
Place Charest 3	Cineplex Odéon		123
Place Charest 4	Cineplex Odéon		206
Place Charest 5	Cineplex Odéon		158
Place Charest 6	Cineplex Odéon		235
Place Charest 7	Cineplex Odéon.		320
Place Charest 8	Cineplex Odéon		238

R

REPENTIGNY

Plaza Repentigny 1	Ciné-Entreprise	54,550	346
Plaza Repentigny 2	Ciné-Entreprise		322
Plaza Repentigny 3	Ciné-Entreprise		197
Plaza Repentigny 4	Ciné-Entreprise		182
Plaza Repentigny 5	Ciné-Entreprise		138
Plaza Repentigny 6	Ciné-Entreprise		120

RIMOUSKI

Auditorium 1	Claude Pearson	47,688	
Auditorium 2	Claude Pearson		
Auditorium 3	Claude Pearson		
Lido 1	Aldéric Racine		282
Lido 2	Aldéric Racine		157
Lido 3	Aldéric Racine		154
Lido 4	Aldéric Racine		153
Lido 5	Aldéric Racine		111

RIVIÈRE-DU LOUP

Princesse 1	Guy Simard	22,339	257
Princesse 2	Guy Simard		156
Princesse 3	Guy Simard		98
Princesse 4	Guy Simard		98

ROBERVAL

Chaplin 1	Hugues Morin	10,906	129
Chaplin 2	Hugues Morin		81
Chaplin 3	Hugues Morin		52

ROCK FOREST

Rock Forest 1	Galaxy Entertainment .	21,562	146
Rock Forest 2	Galaxy Entertainment		194
Rock Forest 3	Galaxy Entertainment		88
Rock Forest 4	Galaxy Entertainment		157
Rock Forest 5	Galaxy Entertainment		166
Rock Forest 6	Galaxy Entertainment		164
Rock Forest 7	Galaxy Entertainment		124
Rock Forest 8	Galaxy Entertainment		282
Rock Forest 9	Galaxy Entertainment		102

ROUYN-NORANDA

Paramount 1	Pierre Gaudreault	36,308	155
Paramount 2	Pierre Gaudreault		167
Paramount 3	Pierre Gaudreault		87
Paramount 4	Pierre Gaudreault		107
Paramount 5	Pierre Gaudreault		52

S

SAINTE-ADÈLE

Cinéma Pine 1	Tom Fermanian		250
Cinéma Pine 2	Tom Fermanian		51
Cinéma Pine 3	Tom Fermanian		112
Cinéma Pine 4	Tom Fermanian		104
Cinéma Pine 5	Tom Fermanian		45
Cinéma Pine 6	Tom Fermanian		138
Cinéma Pine 7	Tom Fermanian		135
Cinéma Pine 8	Tom Fermanian		93

SAINTE-FOY

Le Clap 1	Michel Aubé		202
Le Clap 2	Michel Aubé		184
Le Clap 3	Michel Aubé		104
Le Clap 4	Michel Aubé		129
Le Clap 5	Michel Aubé		58
Le Clap 6	Michel Aubé		58
Odeon Ste-Foy 1	Cineplex Odéon		446
Odeon Ste-Foy 2	Cineplex Odéon		249
Odeon Ste-Foy 3	Cineplex Odéon		164
Odeon Ste-Foy 4	Cineplex Odéon		164
Odeon Ste-Foy 5	Cineplex Odéon		164
Odeon Ste-Foy 6	Cineplex Odéon		213
Odeon Ste-Foy 7	Cineplex Odéon		306
Odeon Ste-Foy 8	Cineplex Odéon		306
Odeon Ste-Foy 9	Cineplex Odéon		213
Odeon Ste-Foy 10	Cineplex Odéon		164
Odeon Ste-Foy 11	Cineplex Odéon		164
Odeon Ste-Foy 12	Cineplex Odéon		164
Odeon Ste-Foy 13	Cineplex Odéon		249
Odeon Ste-Foy 14	Cineplex Odéon		446
Star Cité 1	Famous Players Inc.		371
Star Cité 2	Famous Players Inc.		162
Star Cité 3	Famous Players Inc.		234
Star Cité 4	Famous Players Inc.		162
Star Cité 5	Famous Players Inc.		162
Star Cité 6	Famous Players Inc.		234
Star Cité 7	Famous Players Inc.		162
Star Cité 8	Famous Players Inc.		162
Star Cité 9	Famous Players Inc.		162
Star Cité 10	Famous Players Inc.		476
Star Cité 11	Famous Players Inc.		476
Star Cité 12	Famous Players Inc.		162
Star Cité 13	Famous Players Inc.		162
Star Cité 14	Famous Players Inc.		234
Star Cité 15	Famous Players Inc.		162
Star Cité 16	Famous Players Inc.		234
Star Cité 17	Famous Players Inc.		162
Star Cité 18	Famous Players Inc.		361

SEPT-ILES

Ciné-Centre Vidéo 1	Réjean Guy	26,952	166
Ciné-Centre Vidéo 2	Réjean Guy		108
Ciné-Centre Vidéo 3	Réjean Guy		60

SHAWINIGAN

Biermans 1	Claude Bellerive	57,304	246
Biermans 2	Claude Bellerive		150
Biermans 3	Claude Bellerive		159
Biermans 4	Claude Bellerive		155
Biermans 5	Claude Bellerive		141
Biermans 6	Claude Bellerive		97
Biermans 7	Claude Bellerive		102
Biermans 8	Claude Bellerive		139

SHERBROOKE

Maison du Cinema 1	Jacques Foisy	153,811	125
Maison du Cinema 2	Jacques Foisy		146
Maison du Cinema 3	Jacques Foisy		300
Maison du Cinema 4	Jacques Foisy		86
Maison du Cinema 5	Jacques Foisy		80
Maison du Cinema 6	Jacques Foisy		75
Maison du Cinema 7	Jacques Foisy		124
Maison du Cinema 8	Jacques Foisy		162
Maison du Cinema 9	Jacques Foisy		207
Maison du Cinema 10	Jacques Foisy		132
Maison du Cinema 11	Jacques Foisy		130

ST-ANDRÉ AVELIN

Théâtre des Quatre soeurs	Yvan Tanguay		350

ST-BASILE

St-Basile 1	Ciné-Entreprise		325
St-Basile 2	Ciné-Entreprise		325
St-Basile 3	Ciné-Entreprise		155
St-Basile 4	Ciné-Entreprise		175
St-Basile 5	Ciné-Entreprise		275
St-Basile 6	Ciné-Entreprise		150
St-Basile 7	Ciné-Entreprise		150

ST-BRUNO

St-Bruno 1	Cineplex Odéon		199
St-Bruno 2	Cineplex Odéon		199
St-Bruno 3	Cineplex Odéon		198
St-Bruno 4	Cineplex Odéon		97
St-Bruno 5	Cineplex Odéon		107
St-Bruno 6	Cineplex Odéon		107
St-Bruno 7	Cineplex Odéon		107
St-Bruno 8	Cineplex Odéon		107
St-Bruno 9	Cineplex Odéon		107
St-Bruno 10	Cineplex Odéon		182
St-Bruno 11	Cineplex Odéon		298

ST-EUSTACHE

Cinema St-Eustache 1	Brigitte Mathers		183
Cinema St-Eustache 2	Brigitte Mathers		170
Cinema St-Eustache 3	Brigitte Mathers		170

Cinema St-Eustache 4	Brigitte Mathers		183
Cinema St-Eustache 5	Brigitte Mathers		291
Cinema St-Eustache 6	Brigitte Mathers		154
Cinema St-Eustache 7	Brigitte Mathers		150
Cinema St-Eustache 8	Brigitte Mathers		223
Cinema St-Eustache 9	Brigitte Mathers		185
Cinema St-Eustache 10	Brigitte Mathers		185
Cinema St-Eustache 11	Brigitte Mathers		185
Cinema St-Eustache 12	Brigitte Mathers		167
Cinema St-Eustache 13	Brigitte Mathers		167
Cinema St-Eustache 14	Brigitte Mathers		195
Cinema St-Eustache 15	Brigitte Mathers		195
Cinema St-Eustache 16	Brigitte Mathers		399

ST-GEORGES DE BEAUCE

Centre-Ville 1	Michel Busque	221
Centre-Ville 2	Michel Busque	110
Centre-Ville 3	Michel Busque	91
Centre-Ville 4	Michel Busque	170
Centre-Ville 5	Michel Busque	130
Centre-Ville 6	Michel Busque	110

ST-HYACINTHE

Galeries St-Hyacinthe 1	Jean Colbert	89
Galeries St-Hycainthe 2	Jean Colbert	110
Galeries St-Hyacinthe 3	Jean Colbert	130
Galeries St-Hyacinthe 4	Jean Colbert	186
Galeries St-Hyacinthe 5	Jean Colbert	156
Galeries St-Hyacinthe 6	Jean Colbert	117
Galeries St-Hyacinthe 7	Jean Colbert	99
Galeries St-Hycainthe 8	Jean Colbert	99

ST-JEAN

BCF St-Jean	Denyse Dumont	238
Cinecapitol 1	GalaxyEntertainment	133
Cinecapitol 2	Galaxy Entertainment	184
Cinecapitol 3	Galaxy Entertainment	127
Cinecapitol 4	Galaxy Entertainment	127
Cineapitol 5	Galaxy Entertainment	162
Cineapitol 6	Galaxy Entertainment	73

ST-JÉRÔME

Carrefour du Nord 1	Guy Gagnon	120
Carrefour du Nord 2	Guy Gagnon	160
Carrefour du Nord 3	Guy Gagnon	120
Carrefour du Nord 4	Guy Gagnon	178
Carrefour du Nord 5	Guy Gagnon	58
Carrefour du Nord 6	Guy Gagnon	118
Carrefour du Nord 7	Guy Gagnon	120
Carrefour du Nord 8	Guy Gagnon	100
Carrefour du Nord 9	Guy Gagnon	160

ST-LAURENT

Spheretech 1	Cinémas Guzzo	140
Spheretech 2	Cinémas Guzzo	154
Spheretech 3	Cinémas Guzzo	323
Spheretech 4	Cinémas Guzzo	323
Spheretech 5	Cinémas Guzzo	246
Spheretech 6	Cinémas Guzzo	110
Spheretech 7	Cinémas Guzzo	110
Spheretech 8	Cinémas Guzzo	110
Spheretech 9	Cinémas Guzzo	214
Spheretech 10	Cinémas Guzzo	220
Spheretech 11	Cinémas Guzzo	216
Spheretech 12	Cinémas Guzzo	323
Spheretech 13	Cinémas Guzzo	154
Spheretech 14	Cinémas Guzzo	140

ST-LÉONARD

Langelier 1	Cinémas Guzzo	218
Langelier 2	Cinémas Guzzo	216
Langelier 3	Cinémas Guzzo	240
Langelier 4	Cinémas Guzzo	265
Langelier 5	Cinémas Guzzo	265
Langelier 6	Cinémas Guzzo	386
Mega-Plex Lacordaire 1	Cinémas Guzzo	239
Mega-Plex Lacordaire 2	Cinémas Guzzo	148
Mega-Plex Lacordaire 3	Cinémas Guzzo	173
Mega-Plex Lacordaire 4	Cinémas Guzzo	109
Mega-Plex Lacordaire 5	Cinémas Guzzo	150
Mega-Plex Lacordaire 6	Cinémas Guzzo	128
Mega-Plex Lacordaire 7	Cinémas Guzzo	182
Mega-Plex Lacordaire 8	Cinémas Guzzo	106
Mega-Plex Lacordaire 9	Cinémas Guzzo	119
Mega-Plex Lacordaire 10	Cinémas Guzzo	125
Mega-Plex Lacordaire 11	Cinémas Guzzo	245
Mega-Plex Lacordaire 12	Cinémas Guzzo	259
Mega-Plex Lacordaire 13	Cinémas Guzzo	257
Mega-Plex Lacordaire 14	Cinémas Guzzo	275
Mega-Plex Lacordaire 15	Cinémas Guzzo	328
Mega-Plex Lacordaire 16	Cinémas Guzzo	305
St-Leonard 1	Dominic Piccolo	
St-Leonard 2	Dominic Piccolo	
St-Leonard 3	Dominic Piccolo	
St-Leonard 4	Dominic Piccolo	

ST-NICOLAS

Cinéma des Chutes 1	André Gilbert	210
Cinéma des Chutes 2	André Gilbert	145
Cinéma des Chutes 3	André Gilbert	110
Cinéma des Chutes 4	André Gilbert	110
Cinéma des Chutes 5	André Gilbert	77
Cinéma des Chutes 6	André Gilbert	83
Cinéma des Chutes 7	André Gilbert	160
Cinéma des Chutes 8	André Gilbert	80

ST-PÂCOME

Louise 1	Alain Chamberland	189
Louise 2	Alain Chamberland	76

ST-RAYMOND

Alouette 1	Nady Moisan	234
Alouette 2	Nady Moisan	93

STE-ANNE-DES-MONTS

Haute Gaspésie	Jean-Paul Gaumond	150

STE-MARIE-DE-BEAUCE

Lumiere 1	Michel Busque	187
Lumiere 2	Michel Busque	108
Lumiere 3	Michel Busque	144

STE-THÉRÈSE

Plaza Sainte-Thérèse 1	Cinémas Guzzo	187
Plaza Sainte-Thérèse 2	Cinémas Guzzo	281
Plaza Sainte-Thérèse 3	Cinémas Guzzo	320
Plaza Sainte-Thérèse 4	Cinémas Guzzo	171
Plaza Sainte-Thérèse 5	Cinémas Guzzo	173
Plaza Sainte-Thérèse 6	Cinémas Guzzo	180
Plaza Sainte-Thérèse 7	Cinémas Guzzo	154
Plaza Sainte-Thérèse 8	Cinémas Guzzo	195

T

TERREBONNE

Megaplex Terrebonne 1	Cinémas Guzzo	43,149	202
Megaplex Terrebonne 2	Cinémas Guzzo		250
Megaplex Terrebonne 3	Cinémas Guzzo		314
Megaplex Terrebonne 4	Cinémas Guzzo		295
Megaplex Terrebonne 5	Cinémas Guzzo		295
Megaplex Terrebonne 6	Cinémas Guzzo		345
Megaplex Terrebonne 7	Cinémas Guzzo		347
Megaplex Terrebonne 8	Cinémas Guzzo		345
Megaplex Terrebonne 9	Cinémas Guzzo		347
Megaplex Terrebonne 10	Cinémas Guzzo		295
Megaplex Terrebonne 11	Cinémas Guzzo		295
Megaplex Terrebonne 12	Cinémas Guzzo		314
Megaplex Terrebonne 13	Cinémas Guzzo		250
Megaplex Terrebonne 14	Cinémas Guzzo		202

THETFORD MINES

Pigalle 1	Julie Bernier	26,323	250
Pigalle 2	Julie Bernier		106

TRACY

Cinéma St-Laurent 1	Marcel Venne	55
Cinéma St-Laurent 2	Marcel Venne	93
Cinéma St-Laurent 3	Marcel Venne	119
Cinéma St-Laurent 4	Marcel Venne	153
Cinéma St-Laurent 5	Marcel Venne	202
Cinéma St-Laurent 6	Marcel Venne	76
Cinéma St-Laurent 7	Marcel Venne	277

TROIS-PISTOLES

CinéPlus	Jacquelin Théberge	3,635	225

TROIS-RIVIÈRES

Fleur de Lys 1	Galaxy Entertainment	137,507	170
Fleur de Lys 2	Galaxy Entertainment		394
Fleur de Lys 3	Galaxy Entertainment		93
Fleur de Lys 4	Galaxy Entertainment		218
Fleur de Lys 5	Galaxy Entertainment		188
Fleur de Lys 6	Galaxy Entertainment		88
Fleur de Lys 7	Galaxy Entertainment		88
Fleur de Lys 8	Galaxy Entertainment		154
Fleur de Lys 9	Galaxy Entertainment		100

V

VAL D'OR

Capitol 1	Louiselle Blais	32,423	220
Capitol 2	Louiselle Blais		92
Capitol 3	Louiselle Blais		110
Capitol 4	Louiselle Blais		85
Capitol 5	Louiselle Blais		130

VALLEYFIELD

Le Paris 1	Jacques Patry	39,491	484
Le Paris 2	Jacques Patry		116
Le Paris 3	Jacques Patry		134
Le Paris 4	Jacques Patry		145
Le Paris 5	Jacques Patry		85
Le Paris 6	Jacques Patry		87
Le Paris 7	Jacques Patry		50

VICTORIAVILLE

Galaxy Victoriaville 1	Galaxy Entertainment	41,233	270
Galaxy Victoriaville 2	Galaxy Entertainment		200
Galaxy Victoriaville 3	Galaxy Entertainment		150
Galaxy Victoriaville 4	Galaxy Entertainment		120
Galaxy Victoriaville 5	Galaxy Entertainment		124
Galaxy Victoriaville 6	Galaxy Entertainment		124
Galaxy Victoriaville 7	Galaxy Entertainment		133
Laurier 1	Robert Carrier		680
Laurier 2	Robert Carrier		182
Laurier 3	Robert Carrier		140
Laurier 4	Robert Carrier		192

VILLE-MARIE

Ville-Marie	Denis Bédard	2,770	300

(Source: Alex Films Inc.)

SASKATCHEWAN

A

ARCOLA

MacMurray Theatre	Danny Showers	532	517

B

BIGGAR

Majestic	Town of Biggar	2,243	313

C

CARNDUFF

Community Theatre	Community Theatre Assoc.	1,017	280

CUTKNIFE

Elks	Elks Club	556	532

E

ESTERHAZY

Maple Leaf	Doug Larson	2,348	300

ESTEVAN

Orpheum		13,083	570

F

FLIN FLON

Big Island Theatre	B & M Liefe		

G

GRAVELBOURG

Gaiety Renaissance	Jack Walon	1,187	300

GULL LAKE

Lyceum	W. Laberge	1,016	240

H

HUDSON BAY

Community Theatre	Town of Hudson Bay	1,778	100

I

INDIAN HEAD

Nitehawk	G & H Stewart Holdings	1,758	370

ITUNA

Ituna	Paul Butchko	709	240

K

KERROBERT

Lux	Kevin Ackerland	1,111	

KINDERSLEY

Capitol	Magic Lantern Theatres	4,548	274

L

LANGENBURG

Community Theatre	Community Association	1,107	300

LLOYDMINSTER

May Cinema Centre 1	May Theatres	7,840	352
May Cinema Centre 2	May Theatres		156
May Cinema Centre 3	May Theatres		210
May Cinema Centre 4	May Theatres		225
May Cinema Centre 5	May Theatres		127

M

MEADOW LAKE

Dynasty Twin 1	Dynasty Theatres		
Dynasty Twin 2	Dynasty Theatres		

MELFORT

Dynasty Twin 1	Dynasty Theatres	5,559	198
Dynasty Twin 2	Dynasty Theatres		149

MELVILLE

Melville Theatre	F. Cox	4,453	153

MOOSE JAW

Town 'N Country 1	Galaxy Cinemas	32,631	166
Town 'N Country 2	Galaxy Cinemas		190
Town 'N Country 3	Galaxy Cinemas		223
Town 'N Country 4	Galaxy Cinemas		117
Town 'N Country 5	Galaxy Cinemas		224
Town 'N Country 6	Galaxy Cinemas		190

MOOSOMIN

Community Theatre	B. Fisch	2,361	200

N

NIPAWIN

Roxy	D. McGirr	4,275	239

NORTH BATTLEFORD

Capitol	Dynasty Theatres	17,512	353
Frontier Twin Cinema 1	Dynasty Theatres		183
Frontier Twin Cinema 2	Dynasty Theatres		133

P

PORCUPINE PLAIN

Community Theatre	Town of Porcupine Plains	820	180

PRINCE ALBERT

South Hill Mall 1	Galaxy Cinemas	41,460	300
South Hill Mall 2	Galaxy Cinemas		175
South Hill Mall 3	Galaxy Cinemas		110
South Hill Mall 4	Galaxy Cinemas		125
South Hill Mall 5	Galaxy Cinemas		155
South Hill Mall 6	Galaxy Cinemas		200

R

REGINA

Coronet 1	Cineplex Odeon Corp.	192,800	211
Coronet 2	Cineplex Odeon Corp.		253
Coronet 3	Cineplex Odeon Corp.		168
Coronet 4	Cineplex Odeon Corp.		324
Coronet 5	Cineplex Odeon Corp.		235
Coronet 6	Cineplex Odeon Corp.		330
Normanview 1	Galaxy Cinemas		250
Normanview 2	Galaxy Cinemas		215
Normanview 3	Galaxy Cinemas		138
Normanview 4	Galaxy Cinemas		189
Normanview 5	Galaxy Cinemas		335
Normanview 6	Galaxy Cinemas		335
Normanview 7	Galaxy Cinemas		189
Normanview 8	Galaxy Cinemas		122
Normanview 9	Galaxy Cinemas		215
Normanview 10	Galaxy Cinemas		250
Rainbow 1	Magic Lantern Theatres		184
Rainbow 2	Magic Lantern Theatres		184
Rainbow 3	Magic Lantern Theatres		154
Rainbow 4	Magic Lantern Theatres		150
Rainbow 5	Magic Lantern Theatres		150
Rainbow 6	Magic Lantern Theatres		150
Rainbow 7	Magic Lantern Theatres		140
Rainbow 8	Magic Lantern Theatres		107
Rainbow 9	Magic Lantern Theatres		127
RPL Film Theatre	Regina Public Library		124
Sask. Centre of the Arts	Sask. Centre of the Arts Bd.		
Southland Mall 1	Cineplex Odeon Corp.		238
Southland Mall 2	Cineplex Odeon Corp.		256
Southland Mall 3	Cineplex Odeon Corp.		362
Southland Mall 4	Cineplex Odeon Corp.		199
Southland Mall 5	Cineplex Odeon Corp.		199
Southland Mall 6	Cineplex Odeon Corp.		198
Southland Mall 7	Cineplex Odeon Corp.		145
Southland Mall 8	Cineplex Odeon Corp.		145
Southland Mall 9	Cineplex Odeon Corp.		145
Southland Mall 10	Cineplex Odeon Corp.		146

ROCK GLEN

Dreamland	T. Pyle		300

S

ST. BRIEUX

Midway	Town of St. Brieux	505	287

SASKATOON

Broadway	Friends of the Broadway	225,927	600
Capitol 1	Famous Players Inc.		324
Capitol 2	Famous Players Inc.		326
Capitol 3	Famous Players Inc.		358
Capitol 4	Famous Players Inc.		361
Centre 1	Cineplex Odeon Corp.		141
Centre 2	Cineplex Odeon Corp.		141
Centre 3	Cineplex Odeon Corp.		137
Centre 4	Cineplex Odeon Corp.		117
Centre 5	Cineplex Odeon Corp.		109
Centre 6	Cineplex Odeon Corp.		260
Centre 7	Cineplex Odeon Corp.		164

Pacific 1	Cineplex Odeon Corp.		338
Pacific 2	Cineplex Odeon Corp.		332
Pacific 3	Cineplex Odeon Corp.		313
Pacific 4	Cineplex Odeon Corp.		405
Rainbow 8 - 1	Magic Lantern Theatres		213
Rainbow 8 - 2	Magic Lantern Theatres		173
Rainbow 8 - 3	Magic Lantern Theatres		147
Rainbow 8 - 4	Magic Lantern Theatres		108
Rainbow 8 - 5	Magic Lantern Theatres		143
Rainbow 8 - 6	Magic Lantern Theatres		185
Rainbow 8 - 7	Magic Lantern Theatres		185
Rainbow 8 - 8	Magic Lantern Theatres		133

SHAUNAVON

Plaza Theatre	H. Goldstein	1,775	

SWIFT CURRENT

Cinemas 1 & 2	Kathy Pratt	14,821	476

T

TISDALE

Falkon	D. Falkner	3,063	336

V

VAL MARIE

Palais Royale	Town of Val Marie	134	

W

WATSON

Towne	M. Weinrauch		

WASKESIU

Twin Pine 1 (Seasonal)	M. Weinrauch		300
Twin Pine 2 (Seasonal)	M. Weinrauch		180

WEYBURN

Soo Theatre	Landmark Cinemas	9,534	308

Y

YORKTON

Tower Theatre	Landmark Cinemas	17,554	510

YUKON

W

WHITEHORSE

Qwanlin Centre 1	Landmark Cinemas	21,405	196
Qwanlin Centre 2	Landmark Cinemas		196
Yukon Cinema Centre 1	Landmark Cinemas		212
Yukon Cinema Centre 2	Landmark Cinemas		212

DRIVE-IN THEATRES

Theatres are listed by province, then by the cities within each province. Listings include the theatre name, the licensee/owner, the city's population and the car capacity.

ALBERTA

REDCLIFF

Gemini	Landmark Cinemas	4,372	473

BRITISH COLUMBIA

CRESTON

Valley	Gerald Chugg	4,795	323

SURREY

Hillcrest	Bob Cowan	347,825	

TRAIL

Auto-Vue	Martinelli Ltd.	9,119	199

MANITOBA

FLIN FLON

Big Island	B. & M. Liefe	6,267	250

WINNIPEG

Odeon	Cineplex Odeon Corp.	626,685	996

NEW BRUNSWICK

BATHURST

Bayview	J.C. Mourant	23,935	400

BOIS BLANC

Satellite	Paul Marcel Albert		400

CARAQUET

Ciné Parc Satellite	Paul Marcel Albert	4,773	500

LE MEQUE

Venus	Paul Marcel Albert		300

SHEDIAC

Neptune	Sheila LeBlanc	15,430	400

SUSSEX

Sussex	Sussex Drive In Theatre Ltd.	8,063	300

TRACADIE

Neguac		4,723	325

NOVA SCOTIA

CAMBRIDGE

Cambridge D.I.	Kirk Longmeyer		723

CAPE BRETON
A. Sitnakis

NEW GLASGOW

Empire	Empire Theatres Ltd.	9,432	504

SYDNEY

Cape Breton	J. Sifnakis	76,575	300

ONTARIO

BARRIE

Barrie Triple 1	Stinson Theatres Ltd.	129,963	475
Barrie Triple 2	Stinson Theatres Ltd.		340
Barrie Triple 3	Stinson Theatres Ltd.		300

DRYDEN

Sunset	Z. Tavares	6,555	250

ELMVALE

Elmvale	Samuel Russ		300

FONTHILL

Can-View 1	1066455 Ontario Inc.		420
Can-View 2	1066455 Ontario Inc.		595
Can-View 3	1066455 Ontario Inc.		574
Can-View 4	1066455 Ontario Inc.		462

GRAND BEND

Starlite	766280 Ontario Ltd.		

GRAVENHURST

Muskoka D.I.	Muskoka D.I. Theatres Ltd.		300

GUELPH

Mustang	John Dadetta	106,920	

HAMILTON

Starlite	766280 Ontario Ltd.	662,401	

HANOVER

Hanover	J.D. Lyons Corp.	6,869	300

KINGSTON

Family Fun World (3 screens)	Dan Wanamacher	108,168	600

LINDSAY

Lindsay Twin (2 screens)	Larry Baxter	17,757	

LONDON

Mustang 1	Premier Operating Corp. Ltd. 337,318	
Mustang 2	Premier Operating Corp. Ltd. ......Total	806

MIDLAND

Midland	Port Bolster Drive-In Theatres.....29,824	400

OAKVILLE

Five Twin 1	Premier Operating Corp. Ltd. 144,738	
Five Twin 2	Premier Operating Corp. Ltd. ......Total	943

ORILLIA

Orillia	Lorna Burrows 29,121	424

OWEN SOUND

Twin 1	Stinson Theatres Ltd. 31,583	416
Twin 2	Stinson Theatres Ltd.	300

PEFFERLAW

Cinedrive	Cinedrive Movie Theatre Inc..	200

PEMBROKE

Skylight	Matt McLaughlin Motors.............23,608	200

PETERBOROUGH

Mustang	Geraldo Parente 107,423	

PICTON

Mustang	Boulevard Cinemas	

PORT BOLSTER

Cinedrive (1 screen)	

PORT HOPE

Port Hope D.I.	Century Theatre Services	346

SHARON

North York (3 screens)	N. York DI Theatre Ltd.	900

STONEY CREEK

Starlite	1520878 Ontario Inc...................	400

TORONTO

The Docks	Docks Entertainment 4,682,897	408

WOODSTOCK

Oxford	532552 Ontario Ltd. 33,061	200

QUEBEC

ALMA

Jeannois	Jacques Bernier 28,125	375

BONAVENTURE

Gaspesien	Louis Roy	225

BOUCHERVILLE

Odeon 1	Cineplex Odéon (Québec) Inc.....36,253	988
Odeon 2	Cineplex Odéon (Québec) Inc.....	990

CHÂTEAUGUAY

Chateauguay 1	Cineplex Odéon (Québec) Inc.....41,003	703
Chateauguay 2	Cineplex Odéon (Québec) Inc.....	564
Chateauguay 3	Cineplex Odéon (Québec) Inc.....	448

DRUMMONDVILLE

Drummond 1	Marcel Venne.............................68,451	490
Drummond 2	Marcel Venne.............................	415

GRANDE-RIVIÈRE

René François	Louis Roy	325

JOLIETTE

Joliette 1	Marcel Venne.............................35,821	530
Joliette 2	Marcel Venne.............................	405
Joliette 3	Marcel Venne.............................	287

LAVAL

Laval 1	Cinéplex Odéon 343,005	500
Laval 2	Cinéplex Odéon	384
Laval 3	Cinéplex Odéon	281
Laval 4	Cinéplex Odéon	711

ORFORD

Orford 1	André Monette............................	500
Orford 2	André Monette............................	550

RIMOUSKI

Rimouski 1	Claude Pearson.........................47,688	
Rimouski 2	Claude Pearson	

RIVIÈRE AU RENAUD

Cartier	Guy & Yves Côté	390

SEPT-ILES

Des Iles	Yvan Beaulieu 26,952	800

ST-EUSTACHE

St-Eustache 1	Brigitte Mathers 32,226	1,050
St-Eustache 2	Brigitte Mathers	850
St-Eustache 3	Brigitte Mathers	350
St-Eustache 4	Brigitte Mathers	550
St-Eustache 5	Brigitte Mathers	500

ST-GEORGES DE BEAUCE

St-Georges 1	Richard Busque
St-Georges 2	Richard Busque

ST-HILAIRE

St-Hilaire 1	André Monette............................	750
St-Hilaire 2	André Monette............................	550

ST-NICOLAS

De la Colline 1	Cinéplex Odéon...........................	698
De la Colline 2	Cinéplex Odéon...........................	550

TEMPLETON

Templeton 1	Paul Touchet...............................	230
Templeton 2	Paul Touchet...............................	300

TROIS-RIVIÈRES

Trois Rivières 1	Ciné-Entreprise. 137,507	750
Trois Rivières 2	Ciné-Entreprise.	650
(Source: Alex Films Inc.)		

PRINCE EDWARD ISLAND

ALBERTON

Princess Pat	Anna White.................................1,115	500

WINSLOE

Brackley Beach	Linda & George Boyle 240	500

SASKATCHEWAN

CARLYLE

Prairie Dog Park	Ray Boutin

KYLE

Clear Water	Ken Kelk 478	304

PRINCE ALBERT

Pine	Wm. Mahon 41,460

REGINA

Cinema 6	Wilf Runge.................................192,800

SASKATOON

Sundown 1 & 2	D. Besenski...............................225,927

WATROUS

Jubilee	B. Crawford 1,808	200

Editor's note:
Population figures from Statistics Canada 2001 Census (Geosuite).

ASSOCIATIONS & GUILDS

ACADEMY OF CANADIAN CINEMA & TELEVISION /ACADEMIE CANADIENNE DU CINEMA ET DE LA TELEVISION
National Office, 172 King St. E., Toronto, ON M5A 1J3
(416) 366-2227 / (800) 644-5194, FAX (416) 366-8454
www.academy.ca
PRESIDENT & CEO
Maria Topalovich
MANAGING DIRECTOR
Jeanette Slinger
DIRECTOR OF FINANCE & DEVELOPMENT
Cynthia Dron
AWARDS DIRECTOR
Carmen Celestini
MEMBERSHIP MANAGER
Francis Domingue
PUBLICATIONS & ARCHIVE MANAGER
Christine Maloney
SENIOR CO-ORDINATOR, GEMINIS
Jennifer Enright
SPECIAL EVENTS ASSISTANT
Dionne Francis
COMMUNICATIONS MANAGER
Joanne Kovich Robinson
SENIOR CO-ORDINATOR, GENIES
Erin McLeod

Annual Genie, Gemini, and Gémeaux Awards, as well as year-round educational, professional development and promotional services and programs, publications, information and research.

BRITISH COLUMBIA
1385 Homer St., Vancouver, BC V6B 5M9
(604) 684-4528, FAX: (604) 684-4574
MANAGER, WESTERN DIVISION
Judy Jackson-Rink

QUÉBEC
225 rue Roy est, bur. 106, Montréal, QC H2W 1M5
(514) 849-7448, FAX: (514) 849-5069
DIRECTOR
Patrice Lachance
AWARDS CO-ORDINATOR
Jocelyne Dorris
ADMINISTRATION & SPECIAL PROJECTS QUEBEC
Danièle Gauthier

NATIONAL BOARD OF DIRECTORS
CHAIRMAN
Rudy Buttignol
PRESIDENT & CEO
Maria Topalovich
IMMEDIATE PAST CHAIR
Ann Medina
VICE-CHAIR CINEMA
Paul Gratton
VICE-CHAIR WEST
Brigitte Prochaska
VICE-CHAIR EAST
Bill Niven
VICE-CHAIR ONTARIO
Ed Robinson
VICE-CHAIR QUÉBEC
Michel Poulette
TREASURER
John Vandervelde
ADVISOR TO THE BOARD
Ron Cohen

REPRESENTATIVES
EXECUTIVES
Michael Donovan
ART DEPARTMENT
Andrew Deskin
BROADCAST JOURNALIST
Peter Kent
CINEMATOGRAPHY
Bob Brooks
CREATIVE SUPPORT
Joanne Smale
DIRECTORS
Giles Walker
EDITORS
Richard Wells
MUSIC
Amin Bhatia

PERFORMERS
MacKenzie Gray
PRODUCERS
Jay Firestone
SCREENWRITERS
Robert Geoffrion
SOUND
Stephen Barden
THEATRICAL SHORT & DOCUMENTARY
Barbara Doran
VISUAL EFFECTS & ANIMATION
Bernie Melanson

ACFC WEST, LOCAL 2020 CEP
108 – 3993 Henning Dr., Burnaby, BC V5C 6P7
(604) 299-2232 (ACFC), FAX: (604) 299-2243
E-mail: info@acfcwest.com, www.acfcwest.com
BUSINESS MANAGER
Greg Chambers

ACFC West – The Association of Canadian Film Craftspeople, Local 2020 Communications, Energy & Paperworkers Union of Canada, is a technical film union representing craftspeople in 23 departments from Accounting through to Transportation.

THE ACTORS' FUND OF CANADA
10 St. Mary St., Ste. 860, Toronto, ON M4Y 1P9
(416) 975-0304 / (877) 399-8392, FAX: (416) 975-0306
E-mail: contact@actorsfund.ca, www.actorsfund.ca
PRESIDENT
Bruce Clayton
VICE-PRESIDENT
William Webster
TREASURER
Kenneth Wickes
DIRECTORS
Penelope Doob
Alison MacLeod
Kenneth Wickes
William Webster
Vanessa Harwood
Judy Richardson,
Bruce Clayton
Avery Saltzman
EXEC. DIRECTOR
David Hope

Charitable organization providing emergency financial assistance for entertainment industry professionals who are in crisis.

ACTRA (ALLIANCE OF CANADIAN CINEMA, TELEVISION & RADIO ARTISTS)
NATIONAL OFFICE
625 Church St., Ste. 300, Toronto, ON M4Y 2G1
(416) 489-1311 / (800) 387-3516, FAX: (416) 489-8076
E-mail: national@actra.ca, www.actra.ca
NATIONAL EXEC. DIRECTOR
Stephen Waddell
DIRECTOR, FINANCE & ADMINISTRATION
Anna Bucci
NATIONAL PRESIDENT
Thor Bishopric

ALBERTA
ACTRA CALGARY (WESTERN REGIONAL OFFICE)
Mount Royal Place
1414 – 8th St. S.W., Ste. 260, Calgary, AB T2R 1J6
(403) 228-3123, FAX: (403) 228-3299
E-mail: westernregion@actra.ca / calgary@actra.ca
www.actracalgary.com

ACTRA EDMONTON
10324 – 82nd Ave., Suite 302, Edmonton, AB T6E 1Z8
(780) 433-4090, FAX: (780) 433-4099
E-mail: edmonton@actra.ca

BRITISH COLUMBIA
Union of B.C. Performers
400 – 856 Homer St., Vancouver, BC V6B 2W5
(604) 689-0727, FAX: (604) 689-1145
E-mail: info@ubcp.com, www.ubcp.com

MANITOBA
ACTRA Manitoba
203 – 245 McDermot Ave., Winnipeg, MB R3B 0S7
(204) 339-9750, FAX: (204) 947-5664
E-mail: manitoba@actra.ca

NEWFOUNDLAND
ACTRA NEWFOUNDLAND / LABRADOR
354 Water St., Ste. 324, St. John's, NF A1C 5H3
(709) 722-0430, FAX: (709) 722-2113
E-mail: newfoundland@actra.ca

NOVA SCOTIA
ACTRA MARITIMES
103 –1660 Hollis St., Halifax, NS B3J 1V7
(902) 420-1404, FAX: (902) 422-0589
E-mail: maritimes@actra.ca

ONTARIO
ACTRA FRATERNAL BENEFIT SOCIETY
1000 Yonge St., Toronto, ON M4W 2K2
(416) 967-6600 / (800) 387-8897, FAX: (416) 967-4744 / (888) 804-8929. E-mail: benefits@actrafrat.com

ACTRA PERFORMERS' RIGHTS SOCIETY (PRS)
625 Church St., 3rd Fl., Toronto, ON M4Y 2G1
(416) 489-1311 / (800) 387-3516, FAX: (416) 489-1040
E-mail: prs@actra.ca

ACTRA OTTAWA
The Arts Court
2 Daly Ave., Rm. 170, Ottawa, ON K1N 6E2
(613) 565-2168, FAX: (613) 565-4367
E-mail: ottawa@actra.ca

ACTRA TORONTO
625 Church St., 1st & 2nd Fl., Toronto, ON M4Y 2G1
(416) 928-2278 / (877) 913-2278, FAX: (416) 928-0429
E-mail: info@actratoronto.com, www.actratoronto.com

QUÉBEC
ACTRA MONTRÉAL (EASTERN REGIONAL OFFICE)
530 – 1450 City Councillors St., Montréal, QC H3A 2E6
(514) 844-3318, FAX: (514) 844-2068
E-mail: easternregion@actra.ca / montreal@actra.ca

SASKATCHEWAN
ACTRA SASKATCHEWAN
212 – 1808 Smith St., Regina, SK S4P 2N4
(306) 757-0885, FAX: (306) 359-0044
E-mail: saskatchewan@actra.ca

ALBERTA MOTION PICTURE INDUSTRIES ASSOCIATION
11456 Jasper Ave., Ste. 401, Jasper Centre, Edmonton, AB
T5J 0M1. (780) 944-0707, FAX: (780) 426-3057
E-mail: info@ampia.org, www.ampia.org
EXEC. DIRECTOR
Alan Brooks

The Alberta Motion Picture Industries Association (AMPIA) is a non-profit professional service association serving the independent motion picture production community in the province of Alberta. AMPIA was founded in 1973 with the single aim of furthering the independent motion picture industry as a viable economic and cultural force within the province. Historically, AMPIA has been recognized and called upon to serve as a voice for the Alberta film and video industries. In 1994 the Association strengthened this voice by expanding its membership to include a broader base of industry professionals within its voting membership. Likewise, the organization expanded the size and scope of the AMPIA Board of Directors to reflect the various sectors of this dynamic industry. A monthly newsletter, Keep It Rolling, goes out to more than 500 people in the film industry, both members and non-members of AMPIA. Other Association activities include industry advocacy, professional development and information services.

ALBERTA RECORDING INDUSTRIES ASSOCIATION (ARIA)
10109 – 106 St., Ste. 1205, Edmonton, AB T5J 3L7
(780) 428-3372 / (800) 465-3117, FAX: (780) 426-0188
www.aria.ab.ca
EXEC. DIRECTOR
Maryanne Gibson
PROGRAM & EVENT CO-ORDINATOR
Nathalie Clarke
MEMBERSHIP CO-ORDINATOR
Melanie Sinclair

The 400-member professional association conducts workshops and seminars. Provincial music industry association comprises studios, record labels, distributors, musicians, songwriters and other music industry professionals.

ALLIANCE FOR CHILDREN & TELEVISION (ACT)
1400 boul. René Levesque est, bur. 713, Montréal, QC H2L
2M2. (514) 597-5417, FAX: (514) 597-5205
E-mail: caroline_fortier@radio-canada.ca
NATIONAL DIRECTOR
Caroline Fortier

A national, non-profit organization dedicated to enhancing the television experience of Canadian children. Projects and services include workshops, awards of excellence, a specialized resource library, publications and Prime Time Parent (a media workshop kit).

AMERICAN FEDERATION OF MUSICIANS OF THE UNITED STATES & CANADA (AFM)
75 The Donway West, Ste. 1010, Don Mills, ON M3C 2E9
(416) 391-5161, FAX: (416) 391-5165
E-mail: afm.can@afm.org, www.afm.org
VICE-PRESIDENT, CANADA
David J. Jandrisch
DIRECTOR OF POLICIES & PROCEDURES
Len Lytwyn

ASIFA-CANADA /
ASSOCIATION INTERNATIONALE DU FILM D'ANIMATION
CP 5226, St-Laurent, QC H4L 4Z8
Fax: (514) 283-4443
PRESIDENT
Benard Boulad
CONTACT
Diane Martindale, (514) 283-9332

ASSOCIATION DES PRODUCTEURS DE FILMS ET DE TELEVISION DU QUEBEC (APFTQ)
1450 City Councillors, bur. 1030, Montréal, QC H3A 2E6
(514) 397-8600, FAX: (514) 392-0232
www.quebec.audiovisuel.com/engl/ core.asp
PRÉSIDENTE/DIRECTRICE-GÉNÉRALE
Claire Samson

L'association des producteurs de films et de télévision du Québec (APFTQ) regroupe plus de 130 entreprises indépendantes de production cinématographique et télévisuelle, oeuvrant en dramatique, documentaire, variété, animation et film publicitaire. L'APFTQ représente ses membres auprès des gouvernements et négocie les ententes collectives avec les associations d'artistes et syndicats de techniciens.

ASSOCIATION DES REALISATEURS ET REALISATRICES DU QUEBEC (ARRQ)
3480 rue Saint-Denis, Montréal, QC H2X 3L3
(514) 842-7373, FAX: (514) 842-6789
E-mail: realiser@arrq.qc.ca, www.arrq.qc.ca
DIRECTRICE GÉNÉRALE
Lise Lachapelle
ADJOINT À L'ADMINISTRATION
Jacques Langlois
ADJOINTE AUX COMMUNICATIONS
Patricia Lavoie

ASSOCIATION OF BRITISH COLUMBIA ANIMATION PRODUCERS (ABCAP)
548 Beatty St., Vancouver, BC V6B 2L3
(604) 734-2866, FAX: (604) 734-2869. www.abcap.org
CONTACT
Rob Davies, rob@atomiccartoons.com

ASSOCIATION QUEBECOISE DES CRITIQUES DE CINEMA (AQCC)
C.P. 1134, Succ. Place d'Armes
435 rue Saint-Antoine ouest, Montréal, QC H2Z 1H0
(514) 847-0178. E-mail: cast49@hotmail.com
PRESIDENT
Élie Castiel

Association affiliée à la Fédération internationale de la presse cinématographique (FIPRESCI).

CANADIAN ACTORS' EQUITY ASSOCIATION
44 Victoria St., 12th Fl., Toronto, ON M5C 3C4
(416) 867-9165, FAX: (416) 867-9246
E-mail: mail@caea.com, www.caea.com
EXEC. DIRECTOR
Susan Wallace

CANADIAN ASSOCIATION OF BROADCASTERS (CAB)
Box 627, Stn. B, 306 – 350 Sparks, Ottawa, ON K1P 5S2
(613) 233-4035, FAX: (613) 233-6961. www.cab-acr.ca
PRESIDENT & CEO
Glenn O'Farrell

CANADIAN ASSOCIATION OF FILM DISTRIBUTORS AND EXPORTERS /
L'ASSOCIATION CANADIENNE DES DISTRIBUTEURS ET EXPORTATEURS DE FILMS
30 Chemin des Trilles, Laval, QC H7Y 1K2
(450) 689-9950, FAX: (450) 689-9822
E-mail: CAFDE@ça.inter.net
CHAIRMAN / PRÉSIDENT
André Link
PRESIDENT / CEO
Richard J. Paradis
TREASURER
Michel Mosca

CANADIAN BROADCASTERS RIGHTS AGENCY INC.
176 Bronson Ave., Ottawa, ON K1R 6H4
(613) 232-4370, FAX: (613) 236-9241
E-mail: patm@cbra.ca, www.cbra.ca
PRESIDENT
Grant Buchanan

Represents claims to Canadian retransmission royalties on behalf of privately owned Canadian broadcasters.

CANADIAN BROADCAST STANDARDS COUNCIL (CBSC)
Box 3265, Stn. D, Ottawa, ON K1P 6H8
(613) 233-4607, FAX: (613) 233-4826
Email: info@cbsc.ca, www.cbsc.ca
NATIONAL CHAIR
Ron Cohen
EXEC. DIRECTOR
Ann Mainville-Neeson

CANADIAN CABLE TELEVISION ASSOCIATION
360 Albert St., Ste. 1010, Ottawa, ON K1R 7X7
(613) 232-2631, FAX: (613) 232-2137. www.ccta.ca
PRESIDENT & CEO
Janet Yale

ONTARIO
8 Talbot St., Ste 224, Picton, ON K0K 2T0
(613) 476-0268, FAX: (613) 476-0270
E-mail: robrien@sprint.ca
EXEC. DIRECTOR, ENGLISH SYSTEMS
Roy O'Brien

QUÉBEC
745 St. André, Montréal, QC H2L 5C2
(514) 844-9308, FAX: (514) 849-7326
E-mail: parenteau@ccta.com
EXEC. DIRECTOR, FRENCH SYSTEMS
Lysline Parenteau

THE CANADIAN CONFERENCE OF THE ARTS
130 Albert St., Ste 804, Ottawa, ON K1P 5G4
(613) 238-3561, FAX: (613) 238-4849
E-mail: info@ccarts.ca, www.ccarts.ca
PRESIDENT
Denise Roy
NATIONAL DIRECTOR
Megan Williams
CONTACT/COMMUNICATIONS & PUBLIC RELATIONS MGR.
Kevin Desjardins

The CCA is Canada's oldest and largest arts advocacy organization and artists' network. A national, non-governmental, non-profit association, it endeavours to strengthen public and private support to the arts and enhance the awareness of the role and value of the arts through communication, information, research, promotion and consultation activities. As part of its information program, the CCA publishes various bilingual policy papers and reports on the arts, as well as a handbook – The Directory of the Arts – a selective guide to federal and provincial departments, agencies and people with responsibility for arts and culture and a guide to more than 150 national associations, service organizations and unions in the fields of broadcasting, copyright, crafts, dance, education, film, heritage, music, publishing, recording, theatre, visual arts and writing. The Directory, which is updated bi-annually, also features a listing of provincial arts associations across Canada.
The CCA also publishes BLIZZART, a quarterly newsletter on current arts issues.

CANADIAN FILM AND TELEVISION PRODUCTION ASSOCIATION (CFTPA) /

ASSOCIATION CANADIENNE DE PRODUCTION DE FILM ET DE TELEVISION (ACPFT)
151 Slater St., Ste. 605, Ottawa, ON K1P 5H3
(613) 233-1444 / (800) 656-7440, FAX: (613) 233-0073
E-mail: ottawa@cftpa.ca
PRESIDENT & CEO
Elizabeth McDonald
EXEC. VICE-PRESIDENT
Guy Mayson
V.P. OF COMMUNICATIONS & MEDIA
Jane L. Thompson
GOVERNMENT ADVISOR
Beatrice Raffoul
NATIONAL DIRECTOR, EXTERNAL RELATIONS & MEMBER SERVICES
Margot Hallam
NATIONAL DIRECTOR, MENTORSHIP PROGRAM
Deborah Andrews

The CFTPA / ACPFT is a non-profit association promoting the general interest of independent Canadian film, television and new media industry by lobbying government on policy matters, negotiating labour agreements on behalf of independent producers, offering mentorship programs, seminars, an annual conference, and producing industry publications such as The Guide, a concise and complete picture of the Canadian film and television industry.

BRITISH COLUMBIA
1140 Homer St., Ste. 301, Vancouver, BC V6B 2X6
(604) 682-8619 / (866) 390-7639, FAX: (604) 684-9294
E-mail: vancouver.@cftpa.ca
V.P.
Neil Haggquist
DIRECTOR, INDUSTRIAL AND EXTERNAL RELATIONS
Andrew Williamson

ONTARIO
20 Toronto St., Ste. 830, Toronto, ON M5C 2B8
(416) 304-0280 / (800) 267-8208, FAX: (416) 304-0499
E-mail: toronto@cftpa.ca
NATIONAL V.P., INDUSTRIAL RELATIONS AND COUNSEL
John Barrack
NATIONAL DIRECTOR, INDUSTRIAL RELATIONS
Cara Martin
NATIONAL INDUSTRIAL RELATIONS MANAGER
Jayson Mosek

CANADIAN INDEPENDENT RECORD PRODUCTION ASSOCIATION (CIRPA)
150 Eglinton Ave. E., Ste. 403, Toronto, ON M4P 1E8
(416) 485-3152, FAX: (416) 485-4373
E-mail: cirpa@cirpa.ca, www.cirpa.ca
PRESIDENT
Brian Chater
MEMBERSHIP SERVICES & COMMUNICATIONS
Sharon Hookway
POLICY & GOVERNMENT RELATIONS
Donna Murphy
INTERNATIONAL TRADE SHOWS
Mary Vrantsidis

CANADIAN MEDIA GUILD
144 Front St. W., Ste. 300, Toronto, ON M5J 2L7
(416) 591-5333, FAX: (416) 591-7278
E-mail: guild@interlog.com, www.cmg.ca
PRESIDENT
Lise Lareau
STAFF REPRESENTATIVES
Dan Oldfield
Kathy Viner
Keith Maskell
Bruce May
Glenn Gray
Gabi Durocher
Gerry Whelan

CANADIAN MOTION PICTURE DISTRIBUTORS ASSOCIATION (CMPDA)
22 St. Clair Ave. E., Ste. 1603, Toronto, ON M4T 2S4
(416) 961-1888, FAX: (416) 968-1016
PRESIDENT
Hon. D.C. Frith, P.C.
VICE-PRESIDENT
Susan Peacock

The Canadian Motion Picture Distributors Association is one of the country's senior film industry trade associations. It is the Canadian affiliate of the Motion Picture Association Inc. (MPA) and serves as the voice and advocate of the major U.S. studios whose distribution divisions market feature films, entertainment programming for TV, and pre-recorded videocassettes/DVDs in Canada. CMPDA protects copyright owners and directs an anti-piracy program to protect films, videos and television shows.

MEMBER COMPANIES
Buena Vista International Inc., Columbia Pictures Industries Inc., Metro-Goldwyn-Mayer Studio Inc., Paramount Pictures Corporation, Twentieth Century Fox International Corporation, Universal International Films Inc., Warner Bros. Entertainment Inc.

CANADIAN FILM AND VIDEO SECURITY OFFICES (FVSO)
7900 Taschereau, Ste. C210, Brossard, QC J4X 1C2
(450) 672-1990, FAX: (450) 672-1660
NATIONAL DIRECTOR
Serge Corriveau
INVESTIGATOR
Jim Sweeney (416) 686-8854

CANADIAN MUSICAL REPRODUCTION RIGHTS AGENCY (CMRRA)
56 Wellesley St. W., Ste. 320, Toronto, ON M5S 2S3
(416) 926-1966, FAX: (416) 926-7521
E-mail: inquiries@cmrra.ca, www.cmrra.ca
PRESIDENT
David A. Basskin

CANADIAN PICTURE PIONEERS
21 Dundas Sq., Ste. 906, Toronto, ON M5B 1B7
(416) 368-1139, FAX: (416) 368-1130

The Canadian Picture Pioneers was formed in 1940 as an organization dedicated to the welfare of all men and women of the motion picture industry. It has grown to its present-day strength of over 900 members in six branches across the country.

Original membership requirements called for 25 years of service in the industry. This period of service has now been reduced to 15 years. Anyone qualifies for membership – doorman, cashier, caretaker, manager, projectionist, booker, etc. Its Trust Fund helps members of the film industry by, for example, frequently paying additional costs not covered by a health insurance plan and providing for wheelchairs and special treatments.

AIMS & OBJECTIVES
To create and promote friendly relations among those who have been or are engaged in or connected with the motion picture industry.

To create and promote friendly relations and understanding between the public and those engaged in or connected with the motion picture industry.

To aid those in need who were formerly in the motion picture industry without requiring repayment of any kind from the recipient.

NATIONAL EXECUTIVE
PRESIDENT
Phil May
VICE-PRESIDENT
Denise James
SECRETARY-TREASURER
John Freeborn
DIRECTORS
Harriet Bernstein
Colin Davis
Karen Davis
Michael Goldberg
Jennifer Hofley
Michael Kennedy
Robert Wales
Sandra Stewart
Paul Wroe

BRANCH PRESIDENTS
ALBERTA
Neil Campbell
BRITISH COLUMBIA
Dene Joyal
QUÉBEC
Denis Hurtubise
MARITIMES
Greg MacNeil

TRUST FUND
CHAIRMAN
Michael Taylor
TREASURER
Paul Wroe
TRUSTEES
Phil Carlton
Barry Myers
Phil May

Pioneer of the Year Award – In 1952 the Canadian Picture Pioneers marked the Golden Anniversary of the Silver Screen in Canada, dating it from the establishment of the first successful motion picture theatre – the Electric of John Schulberg on Cordova Street, Vancouver, which he opened in the fall of 1902. At the celebration banquet, held in the Royal York Hotel, Toronto, Schulberg, Jule Allen of Toronto, George Ganetakos of Montréal, A.J. Mason of Springhill, Nova Scotia, Léo-Ernest Ouimet of Montréal and Fred G. Spencer of Saint John, New Brunswick, were honoured as pre-1910 pioneers who had done the most to advance the motion picture as a popular form of entertainment in its early days.

The next year, the Pioneer of the Year Award was inaugurated. The most recent appointees were:
2000 - John Bailey
2001 - Doug Isman
2002 - Cathy Watson

CANADIAN RETRANSMISSION COLLECTIVE (CRC) / SOCIETE COLLECTIVE DE RETRANSMISSION DU CANADA (SRC)
20 Toronto St., Ste. 830, Toronto, ON M5C 2B8
(416) 304-0290, FAX: (416) 304-0496
E-mail: info@crc-scrc.ca, www.crc-scrc.ca
EXEC. DIRECTOR
Carol J. Cooper

Represents claims to Canadian retransmission royalties on behalf of owners of independently produced Canadian content, programs carried on PBS signals, programs owned by non-North Americans and TVOntario.

CANADIAN SCREENWRITERS COLLECTION SOCIETY
366 Adelaide St. W., Ste. 401, Toronto, ON M5V 1R9
(416) 979-7907, FAX: (416) 979- 9273
E-mail: d.tay@wgc.ca
EXEC. DIRECTOR
Maureen Parker
DIRECTOR OF OPERATIONS
Doris Tay

Establishes claims, and will collect and distribute, on behalf of members, royalty and levy payments arising from secondary uses made in Europe and other jurisdictions.

CANADIAN SOCIETY OF CINEMATOGRAPHERS (CSC)
3007 Kingston Rd., Ste. 131, Toronto, ON M1M 1P1
(416) 266-0591, FAX: (416) 266-3996
E-mail: admin@csc.ca, www.csc.ca
PRESIDENT
Joan Hutton, csc
VICE-PRESIDENT
Richard Stringer, csc
SECRETARY
Ernie Kestler
TREASURER
Joseph Sunday, PhD
MEMBERSHIP
Philip Earnshaw, csc
EDUCATION
Harry Lake, csc
PUBLICITY
Robert Brooks, csc
ADMINISTRATOR
Susan Saranchuk
CSC EDITOR
Don Angus, editor@csc.ca

Promotes the art and craft of cinematography. The CSC publishes an annual directory listing its members and their credits. The Society also publishes a newsletter ten times a year. Subscriptions are available for non-members at $75/yr.

CANADIAN WOMEN IN COMMUNICATIONS (CWC) / ASSOCIATION CANADIENNE DES FEMMES EN COMMUNICATIONS (AFC)
67 Yonge St., Ste. 804, Toronto, ON M5E 1J8
(416) 363-1880, (800) 361-2978, FAX: (416) 363-1882
E-mail: cwcafc@cwc-afc.com
PRESIDENT
Stephanie MacKendrick

CWC is a national, bilingual, not-for-profit association dedicated to promoting the advancement of women in the communications industry including radio, television and specialty broadcasting, telecommunications, cable, print, film & video, the Internet, new media and allied fields. CWC has over 1,500 members in 12 chapters across the country.

L'AFC est un organisme national bilingue sans but lucratif ayant pour mandat de favoriser et de promouvoir l'avancement des femmes au sein du secteur des communications dont la radio, la télévision, les télécommunications, la câblodistribution, l'imprimé, le film, la vidéo, les nouveaux médias, Internet et les domaines connexes. Plus de 1500 membres répartis dans 12 sections à travers le Canada font partie de l'AFC.

CASTING DIRECTORS OF CANADA (CDC)
119 Oakwood Ave., Toronto, ON M6H 2W1
(416) 658-8455, FAX: (416) 658-8572
CO-CHAIRS
Tina Gerussi
Diane Kerbel

Established 1982, CDC is a self-governing body of independent casting directors who strive to maintain the highest standards of business practices within the casting community across Canada.

CINEVIC, SOCIETY OF INDEPENDENT FILMMAKERS
2022 Douglas St., Victoria, BC V8T 4L1
(250) 389-1590, FAX: (250) 380-1547
E-mail: director@cinevic.ca, www.cinevic.ca
PRESIDENT
Jim Knox
EXEC. DIRECTOR
Elaine Dowling

COMMERCIAL PRODUCTION ASSOCIATION OF TORONTO (CPAT)
Box 1204, Stn. A, Toronto, ON M5W 1G6
(416) 729-3265, FAX: (416) 729-0019
E-mail: info@cpat.ca, www.cpat.ca
CONTACT
Michelle D'Ercole

COMMUNICATIONS, ENERGY AND PAPERWORKERS UNION (CEP)
350 Albert St., Ste. 1900, Ottawa, ON K1R 1A4
(613) 230-5200, FAX: (613) 230-5801
V.P., MEDIA
Peter Murdoch

ATLANTIC REGIONAL OFFICE
1077 St. George Blvd., Ste. 440, Moncton, NB E1E 4C9
(506) 857-8647, FAX: (506) 858-8313

ONTARIO REGIONAL OFFICE
701 Evans Ave., Ste. 200, Etobicoke, ON M9C 1A3
(416) 622-2740, FAX: (416) 620-0781

QUÉBEC REGIONAL OFFICE
9100 – 565, boul. Crémazie est, Montréal, QC H2M 2V6
(514) 384-9000, FAX: (514) 384-9988

WESTERN REGIONAL OFFICE
1199 W. Pender St., Ste. 540, Vancouver, BC V6E 2R1
(604) 682-6501, FAX: (604) 685-5078

COPYRIGHT COLLECTIVE OF CANADA (CCC)
22 St. Clair Ave. E., Ste. 1603, Toronto, ON M4T 2S4
(416) 961-1888, FAX: (416) 968-1016
PRESIDENT
Douglas C. Frith
VICE-PRESIDENT
Susan Peacock

Represents claims to Canadian retransmission royalties on behalf of U.S. entertainment program suppliers.

**DIRECTORS GUILD OF CANADA / LA GUILDE CANADI-
ENNE DES REALISATEURS**
NATIONAL OFFICE:
1 Eglinton Ave. E., Ste. 604, Toronto, ON M4P 3A1
(416) 482-6640 / (888) 972-0098, FAX: (416) 486-6639
E-mail: mail@dgc.ca, www.dgc.ca
PRESIDENT
Alan Goluboff
EXEC. DIRECTOR
Pamela Brand
ASSOCIATE EXEC. DIRECTOR
Leah Bazian
COMMUNICATIONS MANAGER
Andrew Mitchell
MEMBERSHIP
Christina Choe

ALBERTA DISTRICT COUNCIL
2526 Battleford Ave. S.W., Ste. 133, Bldg. B8, Currie Barracks, Calgary, AB T3E 7J4
(403) 217-8672, FAX: (403) 217-8678
E-mail: dgc@dgcadc.ca, www.dgcadc.ca

ATLANTIC REGION DISTRICT COUNCIL
1657 Barrington St., Ste. 333, Halifax, NS B3J 2A1
(902) 492-3424 / (888) 342-6151, FAX: (902) 492-2678
E-mail: inquiries@dgcatlantic.ca, www.dgcatlantic.ca

BRITISH COLUMBIA DISTRICT COUNCIL
1152 Mainland St., Ste. 430, Vancouver, BC V6B 4X2
(604) 688-2976, FAX: (604) 688-2610
E-mail: info@dgcbc.com, www.dgcbc.com

MANITOBA DISTRICT COUNCIL
138 Portage Ave. E., Ste. 507, Winnipeg, MB R3C 0A1
(204) 940-4300, FAX: (204) 942-2610
E-mail: dgc.mdc@shawcable.com, www.dgcmanitoba.ca

ONTARIO DISTRICT COUNCIL
890 Yonge St., 9th Fl., Toronto, ON M4W 3P4
(416) 925-8200, FAX: (416) 925-8400
E-mail: odc@dgcodc.ca, www.dgcodc.ca

QUÉBEC DISTRICT COUNCIL
4067 boul. St-Laurent, Ste. 200, Montréal, QC H2W 1Y7
(514) 844-4084, FAX: (514) 844-1067
E-mail: cqgcr@cam.org

SASKATCHEWAN DISTRICT COUNCIL
2440 Broad St., Ste. W213B, Regina, SK S4P 4A1
(306) 757-8000, FAX: (306) 757-8001
E-mail: sk.dgc@sk.sympatico.ca, www.dgcsask.com

**DOCUMENTARY ORGANIZATION OF CANADA / DOCU-
MENTARISTES DU CANADA (DOC)**
NATIONAL OFFICE / TORONTO CHAPTER
517 College St., Ste. 325, Toronto, ON M6G 4A2
(416) 599-3844. E-mail: info@cifc.ca, www.cifc.ca
EXEC. DIRECTOR
Sandy Crawley

BRITISH COLUMBIA
2906 West Broadway, Ste. 137, Vancouver, BC V6K 2G8
(604) 253-2432 (CIFC). E-mail: cifcvancouver@canada.com
www.cifcvancouver.com

NOVA SCOTIA
2103 Bauer St., Halifax, NS B3K 3W4
(902) 422-1337. E-mail: clapp@istar.ca
CONTACT
Chuck Lapp

QUÉBEC
4067 St. Laurent, Ste. 201, Montréal, QC H2W 1Y2
(514) 484-1145. E-mail: cifcquebec@sympatico.ca
CO-ORDINATOR
Dan Emery

The DOC is a national professional association with close to 500 members. Its mandate is to develop, promote and support the production and distribution of independent Canadian film and video (primarily documentary). An independent production is the creative work of the film or video maker where the maker has control over the production in every phase. The DOC is a not-for-profit organization.

Membership fee: Varies by chapter. $133.75 (includes GST), Full membership, Toronto chapter
POV Magazine: Individual: $18/4 issues / Institution: $24/4 issues

FEMA – FILM & ELECTRONIC MEDIA ASSOCIATION
Box 308, London, ON N6P 1P9
(519) 850-3000 / (519) 652-9960, FAX: (519) 652-1541
E-mail: info@fema.on.ca, www.fema.on.ca
PRESIDENT
Wendy Nesseth
Cooperative of individuals and companies involved with film and electronic media production in S.W. Ontario. Call for locations, crews and resources. Contact association for resource guide.

FILMCAN
P.O. Box 1602, Stn. C, St. John's, NF A1C 3P5
(709) 726-1501, FAX: (709) 726-4338
E-mail: filmcrew@seascape.com
www.newcomm.net/filmcan/
The Film Crew Association of Newfoundland (Film CAN) represents the majority of film technicians and production workers in Newfoundland

**THE GUILD OF CANADIAN FILM COMPOSERS / LA
GUILDE DE COMPOSITEURS DE CANADIENS DE
MUSIQUE DE FILM**
275 King St. E., Box 291, Toronto, ON M5A 1K2
(416) 410-5076 / (866) 657-1117, FAX: (416) 410-4516
E-mail: gcfc@gcfc.ca, www.gcfc.ca
EXEC. DIRECTOR
Lori Davies
The Guild of Canadian Film Composers is a professional association of composers who specialize in film and TV scoring. Membership encompasses composers from across the country and includes people who work in all aspects of the music industry. The Guild represents the interests of film composers to such bodies as the CRTC, the performing rights society SOCAN, and various trade associations in the industry.

**IATSE - INTERNATIONAL ALLIANCE OF THEATRICAL
STAGE EMPLOYEES, MOVING PICTURE TECHNICIANS,
ARTISTS AND ALLIED CRAFTS OF THE UNITED STATES,
ITS TERRITORIES AND CANADA**
CANADIAN OFFICE
258 Adelaide St. E., Ste. 403, Toronto, ON M5A 1N1
(416) 362-3569, FAX: (416) 362-3483
www.iatse.lm.com
DIRECTOR OF CANADIAN AFFAIRS
John M. Lewis

IATSE, DISTRICT 11
(Ontario / Quebec / Atlantic Canada)
83 – 2111 Montreal Rd., Gloucester, ON K1J 8M8
(613) 748-7622, FAX: (613) 748-1901
SECRETARY-TREASURER
Sean McGuire

IATSE, LOCAL 63
Theatrical Stage Employees / Motion Picture Projectionists
Box 394, Winnipeg, MB R3C 2N6
(204) 944-0511, FAX: (204) 944-0528
BUSINESS AGENT
Bert Oja

IATSE, LOCAL 118
Theatrical Stage Employees
601 Cambie St., Ste. 202, Vancouver, BC V6B 2P1
(604) 685-9553, FAX: (604) 685- 9554

PRESIDENT
Mike Phelan
BUSINESS AGENT
Martin Elfert

IATSE, LOCAL 173
Toronto Motion Picture Projectionists
603A – 15 Gervais Dr., North York, ON M3C 1Y8
(416) 444-0776, FAX: (416) 444-0846
BUSINESS AGENT
Rob McPherson

IATSE, LOCAL 210
Stage and Film Production Members
10428 123rd St., Edmonton, AB T5N 1N7
(780) 423-1863, FAX: (780) 426-0307
PRESIDENT
Peter Gerrie
BUSINESS AGENT
Malcolm Kerr

IATSE, LOCAL 212
Building B8
141 – 2526 Battleford Ave. S.W., Calgary, AB T3E 7J4
(403) 250-2199, FAX: (403) 250-9769
E-mail: ia212@iatse212.com
PRESIDENT
Damian Petti
BUSINESS AGENT, PRODUCTION
Tom MacRae

IATSE, LOCAL 262
Montreal Motion Picture Projectionists & Employees Cinemas
3177 rue St-Jacques ouest, bur. 201, Montréal, QC H4C 1G7
(514) 937-6855, FAX: (514) 846-0165
PRESIDENT
Alain Beaudoin
BUSINESS AGENT
Nabil Hanna
BUSINESS AGENT, SUBCONSTRUCTION DEPT.
Eric LaFrance

IATSE, LOCAL 295
Film, Stage and Projection
1808 Smith St., Ste. 201, Regina, SK S4P 2N4
(306) 545-6733, FAX: (306) 545-8440
BUSINESS AGENT, FILM
Rob Parrell
BUSINESS AGENT, STAGE
Wayne Gaillard
BUSINESS AGENT, PROJECTION
Bill Abel

IATSE, LOCAL 300
Box 1361, Saskatoon, SK S7K 3N9
(306) 343-8900, FAX: (306) 343-8423
E-mail: ia300@sk.sympatico.ca
PRESIDENT
Jim Arthur
SECRETARY
Greg McKinnon
BUSINESS AGENT, STAGE AND FILM
Greg McKinnon
BUSINESS AGENT, PROJECTION
Clay Brander

IATSE, LOCAL 302
Alberta Projectionists and Video Technicians
Bldg. B8, Ste. 251, 2526 Battleford Ave. S.W., Calgary, AB T3E 7J4. Tel. & FAX: (403) 282-8267
CALGARY BUSINESS MANAGER
Douglas Harkness, (403) 217-2588
BUSINESS AGENT
Malcolm Cahoon

IATSE, LOCAL 303
Hamilton Motion Picture Projectionists Union
897 Cloverleaf Dr., Burlington, ON L7T 3Y8
(905) 639-6178 / 522-9566, FAX: (905) 639-6178
BUSINESS AGENT
Domenico Marcone

IATSE, LOCAL 348
B.C. Projectionists & Video Technicians
601 Cambie St., Ste. 203, Vancouver, BC V7C 4B7
(604) 685-0007, FAX: (604) 685-9554
BUSINESS AGENT
Steve Tohill

IATSE, LOCAL 411
Production Coordinators
629 Eastern Ave., Bldg. A, Ste. 201, Toronto, ON M4M 1E4
(416) 645-8025, FAX: (416) 645-8026

E-mail: iatse@411.bidcon.net
BUSINESS AGENT
Ken Leslie-Smith

IATSE, LOCAL 667
International Photographers – International Cinematographers Guild
9 Gloucester St., Toronto, ON M4Y 1L8
(416) 368-0072, FAX: (416) 368-6932
E-mail: camera@iatse667.com, www.iatse667.com
PRESIDENT
Ciaran Copelin
BUSINESS AGENT:
Rick Perotto

IATSE, LOCAL 669
International Photographers Guild
555 Brooksbank Ave., 5/210, N. Vancouver, BC V7J 3S5
(604) 983-5580, FAX: (604) 983-5579
BUSINESS AGENT
Gerald Paglaro

IATSE LOCAL 680
Box 711, Halifax, NS B3J 2T3
(902) 455-5016, Pager: (902) 458-9552, FAX: (902) 455-0398
PRESIDENT
Michael Davis
BUSINESS AGENT
Colin Richardson

IATSE LOCAL 849
Motion Picture Studio Production Technicians
c/o West End Mall
6960 Mumford Rd., Ste. S4, Halifax, NS B3L 4P1
(902) 425-2739, FAX: (902) 425-7696
E-mail: info@iatse849.com
PRESIDENT
Ruth Leggett
BUSINESS AGENT
Charlotte Shurko

IATSE, LOCAL 873
Motion Picture Studio Production Technicians
474 Adelaide St. E., Toronto, ON M5A 1N6
(416) 368-1873, FAX: (416) 368-8457
PRESIDENT
Matthew Pill
BUSINESS AGENT
Mimi Wolch

IATSE, LOCAL 891
Motion Picture Studio Production Technicians
1640 Boundary Rd., Burnaby, BC V5K 4V4
(604) 664-8910, FAX: (604) 298-3456
E-mail: elmart@iatse.com, www.iatse.com
PRESIDENT
Don Ramsden
BUSINESS AGENT
Elmar Theissen

INDEPENDENT FILM AND VIDEO ALLIANCE / ALLIANCE DE LA VIDEO ET DU CINEMA INDEPENDANT
4550 Garnier, Montréal, QC H2J 3S7
(514) 522-8240, Fax: (514) 522-8011
E-mail: ifva@cam.org, www.ifva.ca / www.avci.ca
NATIONAL DIRECTOR / DIRECTEUR NATIONAL
Peter Sandmark

The Independent Film and Video / Alliance de la vidéo et du cinéma indépendant (IFVA/AVCI) was formed in 1980 to provide a forum for the exchange of information and ideas, and for the purpose of lobbying around issues of common interest to independent film and video makers, exhibitors, and distributors across Canada. With 50 member-groups, the Alliance represents over 7,000 film and video makers. The Alliance holds its Annual General Meeting and its Showcase in a different province each year. It is a unique opportunity for the public to screen the films and videos from the Alliance membership.

Independent Film and Video / Alliance de la vidéo et du cinéma indépendant (IFVA/AVCI) a été fondée en 1980 dans le but de fournir une structure permettant des échanges d'idées et d'informations et ayant des activités de lobbying sur les sujets qui touchent les différents domaines du secteur de la vidéo et du cinéma indépendants. L'Alliance est une association nationale réunissant 50 groupes impliqués dans la production, la distribution et la présentation de vidéos et de films indépendants. Elle représente plus de 7000 personnes.

L'Alliance tient son assemblée générale ainsi que ses Rencontres annuelles dans une province différente à chaque année. À cette occasion, la production des groupes membres de l'Alliance est mise à l'honneur dans le cadre de projections publiques.

INSTITUTE OF COMMUNICATIONS & ADVERTISING

2300 Yonge St., Ste. 500, Box 2350, Toronto, ON M4P 1E4
(416) 482-1396 / (800) 567-7422, FAX: (416) 482-1856
E-mail: ica@ica-ad.com, www.ica-ad.com

Represents advertising agencies in a wide variety of beneficial activities. The diversity of ICA member agencies, when combined, account for over 90% of national media billings in Canada.

MANITOBA MOTION PICTURE INDUSTRY ASSOCIATION

Main Floor, 376 Donald St., Winnipeg, MB R3B 2J2
(204) 949-8869, FAX: (204) 947-9290
E-mail: info@mmpia.mb.ca, www.mmpia.mb.ca
CHAIR
Phyllis Laing / Buffalo Gal Pictures
CO-CHAIR
Jamie Brown / Frantic Films
EXEC. DIRECTOR
RoseAnna Schick
FILM PROGRAMS MANAGER
Tara Walker
ASSOCIATION CO-ORDINATOR
Susan Conrad

MMPIA represents the interests of motion picture professionals in Manitoba. Through its programs and initiatives, MMPIA creates opportunities for the production, promotion and appreciation of film and video in Manitoba.

MCA-I MEDIA COMMUNICATIONS ASSOCIATION - INTERNATIONAL

(Formerly ITVA)
HEADQUARTERS
1000 Executive Parkway, Ste. 220
St. Louis, MO 63141 U.S.A.
(314) 514-9995, FAX: (314) 576-7989
E-mail: info@mca-i.org, www.mca-i.org
EXEC. DIRECTOR / CONTACT
Ernie Stewart

BRITISH COLUMBIA
Box 47101, 19 – 555 West 12th Ave., Vancouver, BC V5Z 4L6
(604) 528-2116
CONTACT
Wayne Carlow

ONTARIO
Box 154, Stn. F, 50 Charles St. E., Toronto, ON M4Y 2L5
(905) 845-0359. E-mail: itvatorontochapter@hotmail.com
PRESIDENT, TORONTO CHAPTER
Erin Carey

QUÉBEC
(514) 895-6090. E-mail: chettel@videotron.ca
PRESIDENT, QUEBEC CHAPTER
Christopher Hettel

MOTION PICTURE THEATRE ASSOCIATIONS OF CANADA

146 Bloor St. W., Toronto, ON M5S 1P3
(416) 969-7057, FAX: (416) 964-6007
E-mail: mptac.ca@ca.inter.net, www.mptac.ca
PRESIDENT
Robb Chase
EXEC. DIRECTOR
Adina Lebo
SECRETARY
Dean Leland
TREASURER
Dan McGrath

A national non-profit association for theatre owners whose purpose is to:
a) maintain a national trade association of motion picture theatre exhibitors, consisting of owners, operators, executives and managers;
b) forward and promote the general welfare and prosperity of motion picture exhibitors;
c) gather, receive and disseminate such information as may seem helpful to members and associated organizations; to interchange ideas in rendering mutual assistance and to provide helpful vocational advice and guidance, and in general to act as a group representing national interests. The Association's head office is in Toronto, and each province has its own organization.

SHOWCANADA
The Association's annual convention and trade show is held at a different location in Canada each year, and member provinces take turns hosting the three-day event. Four hundred delegates participate in the seminars and social activities, which include screenings of new products. In 2004 the convention will be held at the The Westin Bayshore in Vancouver.

SHOWCANADA SHOWMANSHIP AWARDS
The Showmanship Awards, presented at a ceremony during each convention, were devised to encourage managers to create promotions around film product and special showings. The current five categories for theatre-level personnel are:

THE BLOCKBUSTER FILM AWARD
– for studio-initiated films with massive merchandising and promotional components
SHOWMANSHIP AWARD
– for a film-specific campaign which has been developed by a theatre manager or circuit
AUDIENCE DEVELOPMENT AWARD
– for programs focusing on community service and audience development
CONCESSIONS AWARD
– for the best snack promotion
PROMOTIONS OF CANADIAN FILM, FRENCH AND ENGLISH

MUSIC & ENTERTAINMENT INDUSTRY EDUCATORS ASSOCIATION

451 St-Jean St., Montréal, QC H2Y 2R5
(514) 845-4141
CONTACT
David Leonard

MUSIC INDUSTRY ASSOCIATION OF NEWFOUNDLAND AND LABRADOR (MIANL)

155 Water St., Ste. 102, St. John's, NF A1C 1B3
(709) 754-2574, FAX: (709) 754-5758
E-mail: dparker@nfld.com, www.mia.nf.ca
PRESIDENT
John Hutton
EXEC. DIRECTOR
Denis Parker
VICE-PRESIDENT
Johnny Graham
Full music industry information.

MUSIC INDUSTRY ASSOCIATION OF NOVA SCOTIA (MIANS)

Box 36119, Halifax, NS B3J 3S9
(902) 423-6271, FAX: (902) 423-8841
E-mail: info@mians.ca, www.mians.ca
CONTACT
Kasia Morrison

An association of musicians and industry professionals and amateurs intent on creating a healthier music industry through providing educational activities, initiating programs, lobbying regulatory bodies, advising government, and maintaining information on various organizations, programs and projects that relate to the industry.

NABET LOCAL 700 CEP

100 Lombard St., Ste. 203, Toronto, ON M5C 1M3
(416) 536-4827, FAX: (416) 536-0859
E-mail: info@nabet700.com, www.nabet700.com
BUSINESS AGENT
David Hardy
MEMBERSHIP STEWARD
Greg Caley
MEMBERSHIP SERVICES
Katherine Doyle

NEW BRUNSWICK PRODUCERS' ASSOCIATION (APNBPA)

140 Botsford St., Ste. 20, Moncton, NB E1C 4X4
(506) 854-0334, FAX: (506) 857-1806
E-mail: gllosier@nbnet.nb.ca
PRESIDENT
Gilles Losier

A professional organization of film producers in the province of New Brunswick / Une organization professionnelle des producteurs de film de la province du Nouveau Brunswick.

NORTH AMERICAN BROADCASTERS ASSOCIATION (NABA)

Box 500, Stn. A, Toronto, ON M5W 1E6
(416) 598-9877, FAX: (416) 598-9774
E-mail: info@nabanet.com, www.nabanet.com
SECRETARY GENERAL
Michael McEwan

ONTARIO FILM & TELEVISION STUDIO OWNERS ASSOCIATION (OFTSOA)

c/o Wallace Studios
258 Wallace Ave., Ste. 100, Toronto, ON M5P 3M9
(416) 537-3471, FAX: (416) 532-3132
www.oftsoa.com
CONTACT
Lillyann Goldstein

PRODUCERS ASSOCIATION OF NEWFOUNDLAND (PAN)

155 Water St., Box 72, Ste. 301, St. John's, NF A1C 5H5
(709) 579-2308, FAX: (709) 579-2386
E-mail: pan@nfld.com, www.pan.nf.ca

QUEBEC PICTURE PIONEERS
2396 Beaubien E., Montréal, QC H2G 1N2
(514) 722-6682, FAX: (514) 721-6684
GENERAL MANAGER
Mario Fortin

QUICKDRAW ANIMATION SOCIETY
201 – 351 11th Ave. S.W., Calgary, AB T2R 0C7
(403) 261-5767, FAX: (403) 261-5644
E-mail: qas@shaw.ca, www.quickdrawanimation.com
The Quickdraw Animation Society (QAS) is a non-profit, artist-run film co-op in Calgary. It is the only animation resource centre in Alberta, offering the use of production equipment, personnel, film, video and text resources. Its first objective is the production of new and innovative personal animation by independent filmmakers. QAS offers beginner animation classes as well as workshops and seminars on specific aspects of frame-by-frame filmmaking so that artists can adapt their previous discipline to animation.

The second objective is to build appreciation for all types of animation. QAS provides a variety of activities for the general public, including presentations, lectures and children's animation classes.

QAS also serves as a unique source of information and resources, including videotapes, books, magazines, newsletters and personnel. QAS is there for both members and non-members to promote and encourage this unique type of filmmaking.

LES RENDEZ-VOUS DE CINÉMA QUÉBÉCOIS (RVCQ)
2160 Logan St., Montréal, QC H2K 4P2
(514) 526-9635, FAX: (514) 526-1955

The Rendez-vous du cinéma québécois offer a yearly review of Quebec audiovisual production: all film production as well as a selection of videos and documentaries intended for television. The event, which gathers filmgoers, Quebec professionals and foreign partners, ensures the promotion of Quebec production.

SASKATCHEWAN MOTION PICTURE ASSOCIATION (SMPIA)
2425 – 13th Ave., Ste. 200, Regina, SK S4P 0W1
(306) 525-9899, FAX: (306) 569-1818
E-mail: smpia@smpia.sk.ca, www.smpia.sk.ca
CEO / EXEC. DIRECTOR
Barry Taman

SOCAN / SOCIETY OF COMPOSERS, AUTHORS AND MUSIC PUBLISHERS OF CANADA / SOCIETE CANADIENNE DES AUTEURS, COMPOSITEURS ET EDITEURS DE MUSIQUE
41 Valleybrook Dr., Don Mills, ON M3B 2S6
(416) 445-8700 / (800) 55-SOCAN, FAX: (416) 445-7108
www.socan.ca
CEO
André LeBel
V.P., CFO
Joel Grad
V.P., LEGAL SERVICES & GENERAL COUNSEL
C. Paul Spurgeon
V.P., BUSINESS DEVELOPMENT
Tom Flannery
V.P., BUSINESS CHANGE
Doreen Cable
V.P., INFORMATION TECHNOLOGY
Marian Wilson
V.P., HUMAN RESOURCES
Randy Wark
DIRECTOR, LICENSING, CENTRAL CANADA & NATIONAL POLICIES
Gina Pollock
DIRECTOR, MEMBER SERVICES, CENTRAL CANADA & NATIONAL POLICIES
Lynne Foster
QUEBEC DIVISION: V.P., LICENSING & GENERAL MANAGER, QUÉBEC & ATLANTIC DIVISION
France Lafleur
WEST COAST DIVISION: V.P., MEMBER SERVICES & GENERAL MANAGER, WEST COAST DIVISION
Kent Sturgeon
DARTMOUTH MANAGER
Gini Cornell
EDMONTON OFFICE MANAGER
Bruce Wilde

SOCAN is the Canadian copyright collective for the public performance of musical works. SOCAN administersthe performing rights of its members (composers, lyricists, songwriters and their publishers) and those affiliated international societies by licensing the use of their music in Canada. The fees collected are distributed as royalties to our members and to affiliated performing rights societies throughout the world. We also distribute royalties received from those societies to our members for the use of their music worldwide. SOCAN has offices in Toronto, Montreal, Vancouver, Edmonton and Dartmouth.

ALBERTA
1145 Weber Centre, 5555 Calgary Trail
Edmonton, AB T6H 5P9
(780) 439-9049 / (800) 51-SOCAN, FAX: (780) 432-1555

BRITISH COLUMBIA
1201 West Pender St., Ste. 400, Vancouver, BC V6E 2V2
(604) 669-5569 / (800) 93-SOCAN, FAX: (604) 688-1142

NOVA SCOTIA
45 Alderney Dr., Ste. 802, Queen Sq.
Dartmouth, NS B2Y 2N6
(902) 464-7000 / (800) 70-SOCAN, FAX: (902) 464-9696

QUÉBEC
600 boul. de Maisonneuve ouest, bur. 500, Montréal, QC H3A 3J2. (514) 844-8377 / (800) 79-SOCAN, FAX: (514) 849-8446

SOCIÉTÉ DES AUTEURS DE RADIO, TÉLÉVISION ET CINEMA (SARTeC)
1229 rue Panet, Montréal, QC H2L 2Y6
(514) 526-9196, FAX: (514) 526-4124. www.sartec.qc.ca
PRESIDENT
Marc Grégoire
Professional association representing French writers for film, television and radio in Canada.

SOCIETY OF TELEVISION LIGHTING DIRECTORS (CANADA)
c/o 2310 Mohawk Trail , Campbellville, ON L0P 1B0
(905) 854-4028
CONTACT
Bruce Whitehead, P.Eng.

SYNDICAT DES TECHNICIENNES ET TECHNICIENS DU CINEMA ET DE LA VIDEO DU QUEBEC (S.T.C.V.Q.)
630 Sherbrooke ouest, bur. 710, Montréal, QC H3A 1E4
(514) 985-5751, FAX: (514) 985-2227
E-mail: info@stcvq.qc.ca, www.stcvq.qc.ca
UNION REPRESENTATIVE
Michel Desvosiers
ON LOCATION PRODUCTION LIAISON
Arden R. Ryshpan

TEAMSTERS LOCAL 155
490 E. Broadway, Vancouver, BC V5T 1X3
(604) 876-8898, FAX: (604) 873-1595
E-mail: team155@teamsters155.org
www.teamsters155.org
BUSINESS AGENT
Jack C. Vlahovic
FIELD STEWARD
Brad Swannie

TELEVISION BUREAU OF CANADA
160 Bloor St. E., Ste. 1005, Toronto, ON M4W 1B9
(416) 923-8813, FAX: (416) 413-3879
E-mail: tvb@tvb.ca, www.tvb.ca
TELECASTER COMMERCIAL ANALYSTS
Rhonda-Lynn Bagnall
Nathalie Simard
Katherine Harper
RESEARCH ANALYSTS
Kirk Donaldson
Debra Rughoo
A resource centre for members — television stations, networks and their sales representatives. TVB markets the benefits, values and effectiveness of television as an advertising medium to advertisers and agencies.

TORONTO FILM CRITICS ASSOCIATION
c/o Angela Baldassarre
133 Northcliffe Blvd., Toronto, ON M6E 3K5
(416) 652-2696, FAX: (416) 652-3454
PRESIDENT
Bruce Kirkland
CONTACT & VICE-PRESIDENT
Angela Baldassarre
TREASURER
Ingrid Randoja
FOUNDING MEMBERS
Cameron Bailey
Angela Baldassarre
Marc Glassman
Peter Howell
Brian D. Johnson
Bruce Kirkland
Liam Lacey
Ingrid Randoja
Denis Seguin.
The Toronto Film Critics Association (TFCA) was formed in August 1997 to promote excellence in both filmmaking and in the criticism of film. At the end of each year the TFCA hosts an award ceremony honouring the best films released in Toronto

that year, including awards for Best Film, Best Actor – male & female, Best Director and Best Canadian Film. The first annual TFCA Awards took place in January 1998.

UNION DES ARTISTES (UDA)
Siége Social
3433 rue Stanley, Montréal, QC H3A 1S2
(514) 288-6682, FAX: (514) 288-1807
www.uniondesartistes.com
COMITÉ EXÉCUTIF
PRÉSIDENT
Pierre Curzi
PREMIER VICE-PRÉSIDENT
Raymond Legault
DEUXIÈME VICE-PRÉSIDENT
Vincent Champoux
SECRÉTAIRE GÉNÉRALE
Lise Le Bel
TRÉSORIER
Katerine Mousseau

SECTION DE QUÉBEC CITY
580 av. Grande-Allée E., bur. 350, Quebec, QC G1R 2K2
(418) 523-4241, FAX: (418) 523-0168
CONTACTS
Nathalie Magnan
Jacques Verret

SECTION DE TORONTO
625 Church St., Ste 103, Toronto, ON M4Y 2J1
(416) 485-7670, FAX: (416) 485-9063
CONTACT
Marco Defour

VIDEO SOFTWARE DEALERS ASSOCIATION
(A division of Retail Council of Canada)
1255 Bay St., Ste. 800, Toronto, ON M5R 2A9
(416) 922-6678. E-mail: membership@retailcouncil.org
www.retailcouncil.org

The trade organization that represents the home video entertainment industry — includes the home video divisions of all major and independent motion picture studios, major distributors and other related businesses.

U.S.A.
16530 Ventura Blvd., Ste. 400, Encino, CA 91436-4551
(800) 955-8732, FAX: (818) 385-0567
E-mail: vsdaoffice@vsda.org, www.vsda.org

WOMEN IN FILM AND TELEVISION – TORONTO (WIFT-T)
2300 Yonge St., Ste. 405, Box 2386, Toronto, ON M4P 1E4
(416) 322-3430, FAX: (416) 322-3703
Executive 2002/2003:
PRESIDENT
Kate Hanley
CHAIR
Emily Morgan

Women in Film and Television – Toronto is a leading internationally affiliated industry organization that recognizes, trains and advances women in screen-based media. WIFT-T offers a year-round slate of skills development, networking events and industry awards, providing the tools to succeed in Canada's global entertainment industry. In operation for 19 years, WIFT-T serves over 700 women and men in Canadian screen-based media, connecting them to close to 10,000 leading film, television and new media professionals worldwide.
Membership fees:
Full $187.25
Associate $133.75
Friend $181.90
Students & Seniors . . . .$ 53.50
Fees include a one-time administration fee and GST.

WOMEN IN FILM & VIDEO – VANCOUVER
1269 Howe St., Vancouver, BC V6Z 1R3
(604) 685-1152, FAX: (604) 685-1124
E-mail: info@womeninfilmcca, www.womeninfilm.ca
PRESIDENT
Jacqueline Samuda
CO-ORDINATOR
Jessie Kergan

A non-profit organization of professional women founded to support, advance, promote and celebrate the professional development and achievements of women involved in the B.C. film, video, TV and multimedia industry through education, training, networking and advocacy.

Full membership: open to all women working in the creative, technical, administrative and service fields. Also: Associate; Friends (men and women); Geographically Distant; Seniors; Students.

Activities: workshops, speakers, screenings, industry initiatives
Publications: Producers Workbook III; Newsletter
Membership fees:
Full $107.00
Associate . . . .$ 93.00
Friend . . . .$ 93.00
Students, Seniors &
Geographically Distant . . . .$ 40.13

WRITERS GUILD OF CANADA (WGC)
366 Adelaide St. W., Ste. 401, Toronto, ON M5V 1R9
(416) 979-7907 / (800) 567-9974, FAX: (416) 979-9273
E-mail: info@wgc.ca, www.wgc.ca
EXEC. DIRECTOR
Maureen Parker
DIRECTOR, POLICY & COMMUNICATIONS
Gail Martiri
DIRECTOR OF INDUSTRIAL RELATIONS
Laurie Channer
MANAGER, MEMBER AND INFORMATION SERVICES
Doris Tay
The WGC is the guild representing over 1,700 writers working in film, TV, radio, animation, corporate video and multimedia. The WGC belongs to the North American Council of Writers Guilds, to the International Affiliation of Writers Guilds and is a member of the Coalition of Creators and Copyright Owners.

CANADIAN DIGITAL TELEVISION ASSOCIATION (CDTV)
c/o 2727 Russland Rd., Vars, ON K0A 3H0
(613) 835-1555, FAX: (613) 835-1556. www.cdtv.ca
PRESIDENT
Michael McEwen, mmcewen@cdtv.ca
E.A. & OFFICE MANAGER
Christine Jack, cjack@cdtv.ca

THE CALGARY SOCIETY OF INDEPENDENT FILMMAKERS (CSIF)
Building J2
2711 Battleford Ave. S.W., Calgary, AB T3E 7L4
(403) 205-4747 / (403) 205-4748, FAX: (403) 237-5838
E-mail: info@csif.org, www.csif.org
COORDINATOR OF OPERATIONS
Melody Jacobson
EXHIBITIONS COORDINATOR
Pete Harris
COORDINATOR OF PRODUCTION
David Jones

MEDIA AWARENESS NETWORK
1500 Merivale Rd., 3rd Fl., Ottawa, ON K2E 6Z5
(613) 224-7221, FAX: (613) 224-1958
E-mail: info@media-awareness.ca, www.media-awareness.ca
MEDIA CONTACT
Bill Allen (613) 224-7120, ballen@media-awareness.ca

Media and Internet education resources for teachers and parents

GOVERNMENT AGENCIES

FEDERAL GOVERNMENT

CANADA COUNCIL FOR THE ARTS
Arts Services Unit
350 Albert St., Box 1047, Ottawa, ON K1P 5V8
(613) 566-4414 / (800) 263-5588, FAX: (613) 566-4409
www.canadacouncil.ca TTY: (613) 565-5194
GRANTS AVAILABLE FOR MEDIA ARTISTS AND ORGANIZATIONS

THE CANADA COUNCIL FOR THE ARTS OFFERS A VARIETY OF GRANTS AND SERVICES TO PROFESSIONAL CANADIAN MEDIA ARTISTS AND ORGANIZATIONS. ALL CANADA COUNCIL PROGRAMS ARE ACCESSIBLE TO ABORIGINAL ARTISTS OR ARTS ORGANIZATIONS AND ARTISTS OR ARTS ORGANIZATIONS FROM DIVERSE CULTURAL AND REGIONAL COMMUNITIES OF CANADA.

For more information on any of the programs described below, call toll-free at 1-800-263-5588 or (613) 566-4414 and choose the appropriate extension number.

GRANTS FOR MEDIA ARTISTS
GRANTS TO FILM AND VIDEO ARTISTS:
Research/Creation Grants provide film and video artists with opportunities for creative renewal, experimentation, professional development and research. Production Grants cover the direct costs of production and post-production of independent film or video artworks by film and video artists. Scriptwriting Grants cover the direct costs of scriptwriting (which includes research for artists' documentaries) for independent film and video artworks.

Deadlines: 1 March and 1 October

Anglophone established artists and all francophone artists: Josette Bélanger, ext. 4252

Anglophone mid-career and emerging artists: Ian Reid, ext. 4264

GRANTS TO NEW MEDIA AND AUDIO ARTISTS AND NEW MEDIA RESIDENCIES:
Research Grants provide time where established artists may research and develop ideas, concepts and projects, experiment with tools and technologies, work with specialists to develop knowledge and skills, and pursue other activities related to their personal, professional and/or creative development. Production Grants cover the direct costs of production leading to finished works of art for emerging and established artists. New Media Residencies encourage creative collaboration and knowledge exchange for established artists through Research Residencies and Production Residencies.

Deadlines: 1 March and 1 October
Nichola Feldman-Kiss, ext. 4262

ABORIGINAL MEDIA ARTS PROGRAM:
This program offers grants to emerging and established Aboriginal artists to help them develop their career as media artists and produce independent media artworks. The program offers two components: Creative Development Grants and Production Grants.

DEADLINE: 1 APRIL
Ian Reid, ext. 4264

TRAVEL GRANTS TO MEDIA ARTS PROFESSIONALS:
Grants assist independent media artists and media arts critics and curators to travel on occasions important to the development of their artistic practice or career. Examples are to present their work at recognized festivals or exhibition venues, or to participate in workshops, residencies or other professional development opportunities.

APPLICATION DEADLINE: ANY TIME
Joanne Desroches, ext. 4088

MEDIA ARTS COMMISSIONING PROGRAM:
This program supports organizations commissioning Canadian artists to produce media artworks for presentation to local, national or international audiences. Grants contribute to costs related to the production and presentation of commissioned works.
Deadline: 1 December
Program Officer, ext. 4262

CANADA COUNCIL FOR THE ARTS/NATURAL SCIENCES AND ENGINEERING RESEARCH COUNCIL OF CANADA NEW MEDIA INITIATIVE:
The Canada Council for the Arts (Canada Council) and the Natural Sciences and Engineering Research Council of Canada (NSERC) New Media Initiative is intended to promote collaboration linking artists, scientists and/or engineers to combine creativity with the development and application of new technologies and knowledge.
Deadline: 1 March.
Nichola Feldman-Kiss, ext. 4262

GRANTS FOR MEDIA ARTS DISSEMINATION
ANNUAL ASSISTANCE TO DISTRIBUTION ORGANIZATIONS:
Assistance is available to Canadian, non-profit artist-run organizations that demonstrate a serious, ongoing commitment to the distribution of independent Canadian film, video, audio or new media artworks.

Application deadline: 1 November
Zainub Verjee, ext. 4253

ANNUAL ASSISTANCE FOR PROGRAMMING:
Assistance is available to Canadian, non-profit artist-run organizations for a one-year period. Grants contribute to the ongoing presentation and dissemination of innovative, independent media artworks produced by Canadian artists.

Deadline: 1 May
Zainub Verjee, ext. 4253

ANNUAL ASSISTANCE TO MEDIA ARTS FESTIVALS:
This program supports festivals that advance the development, understanding and appreciation of Canadian, independent media artworks by publicly presenting these works within a critical context, with a view to developing committed audiences.

Deadline: 1 November
Zainub Verjee, ext. 4253

ANNUAL ASSISTANCE TO CINEMATHEQUES:
This program supports work undertaken by cinematheques to advance the development, understanding, and appreciation of Canadian independent media artworks. Support is provided to organizations whose principal mandate is to present, collect, document, interpret and publish critical writing on independent media artworks by Canadian media artists.

Deadline: 1 November
Zainub Verjee, ext. 4253

DISSEMINATION PROJECT GRANTS:
Grants assist Canadian non-profit arts organizations/groups to undertake innovative, short-term projects. Eligible projects include curated exhibitions/ events, touring exhibitions, broadcasting initiatives, and special marketing and audience development activities.

Deadlines: 1 May and 1 November
Zainub Verjee, ext. 4253

GRANTS TO MEDIA ARTS PRODUCTION ORGANIZATIONS
ANNUAL ASSISTANCE TO MEDIA ARTS PRODUCTION ORGANIZATIONS:
This program offers operating and equipment acquisition assistance to Canadian non-profit, artist-run media arts production organizations. Grants assist organizations that provide ongoing support for the creation and production of independent film, video, new media and audio projects by Canadian media artists.

Deadline: 1 October
Josette Bélanger, ext. 4252

DEVELOPMENT PROJECT GRANTS:
Grants support time-limited projects initiated by Canadian non-profit, artist-run organizations, groups or collectives. Eligible projects must provide enhanced opportunities for the production of independent media artworks by Canadian artists.
1 May
David Poole, ext. 4250

The following are other Canada Council for the Arts programs which may be of interest to media artists and organizations.

OUTREACH PROGRAM
NEW AUDIENCE AND MARKET DEVELOPMENT TRAVEL ASSISTANCE:
The purpose of this program is to increase and enhance programming options for presenters, programmers and curators of professional Canadian artists and to assist Canadian professional artists and their managers to develop and reach new audiences and markets in Canada and internationally. This program is divided into three components: Audience and Market Development Within Canada, International Marketing and Promotions, and Travel Assistance for International Buyers (Pilot).
Deadline: Any time
Sandra Bender, ext. 5272

VISUAL ARTS SECTION
GRANTS TO PROFESSIONAL ARTISTS:
The Visual Arts Section provides a range of grants in recognition and support of the independent creative work of professional Canadian artists of all cultures. These grants are intended for professional artists working in architecture, the visual arts, independent criticism and curating, fine craft and photography.

Architecture, Prix de Rome and Ronald J. Thom Award
Deadline: 1 March
Brigitte Desrochers, ext. 5109

Fine Craft
Deadline: 1 March
Marianne Heggtveit, ext. 5269

Independent Critics and Curators
Deadline: 1 February
Melinda Mollineaux, ext. 5094

Visual Arts (including Photography)
Deadline: 1 April, 1 September and 1 December
Michel Gaboury, ext. 5265 and Program Officer, ext. 4030

Travel Grants
Deadline: Any time
Joanne Desroches, ext. 4088

ABORIGINAL ARTS SECRETARIAT
ABORIGINAL PEOPLES COLLABORATIVE EXCHANGE:
This program assists individual artists or artistic groups from Aboriginal communities to travel to other Aboriginal communities to share traditional and/or contemporary knowledge or practices that will foster the development of their artistic practice. The program also supports projects that develop an appreciation, understanding or awareness of an artist's or artistic group's discipline within the communities visited.
Deadline: Any time (for grants of $2,500 or less)
Deadline: 1 February (for grants over $2,500)
Louise Profeit-LeBlanc, ext. 5212

INTER-ARTS OFFICE
INTER-ARTS PROGRAM:
Supports creation, production, dissemination and professional development by Canadian inter-arts professional artists and arts organizations in one of three inter-arts practices: performance art, interdisciplinary work and new artistic practices (including artists and community collaboration activities in one of these three artistic practices).

Travel Grants
Deadline: Any time

Creation/Production Grants, Dissemination Grants and Annual Funding Grants:
Deadline: 15 November

Off the Radar – Initiatives in Critical Thinking:
Deadline: Any time. (for 2004 only)
Claude Schryer, ext. 4062

MULTIDISCIPLINARY FESTIVALS PROJECT GRANTS:
This program supports Canadian non-profit organizations for the production and presentation of programming at multidisciplinary festivals. It encourages festivals to develop new programming initiatives, enhance existing programs, and introduce Canadian artists from diverse regional and cultural backgrounds to new audiences.
Deadline: 1 May
Claude Schryer, ext. 4062

Canada Council for the Arts and National Research Council:
Artist-in-Residence for Research (AIRes) Pilot Program: The AIRes program supports research by established independent artists within specific Institutes of the NRC. The personal research grants are intended to encourage creativity, collaboration and knowledge transfer between artists and scientific or engineering researchers.

Deadline: 15 April (Investigative Stage)
Deadline: 2 September (Residency)
Katherine Watson, ext. 4510

Visit the web site at www.canadacouncil.ca

Hearing-impaired callers with a TTY machine can contact the Canada Council for the Arts at (613) 565-5194.

CANADIAN AUDIO-VISUAL CERTIFICATION OFFICE (CAVCO)
Department of Canadian Heritage
100 Sparks St., 4th Fl., Ottawa, ON K1A 0M5. (613) 946-7600 / (888) 433-2200. FAX: (613) 946-7602
www.pch.gc.ca/cavco
DIRECTOR
Robert Soucy
Film Industry Services, International Tax Directorate / Canada Customs and Revenue Agency
344 Slater St., 6th Fl., Ottawa, ON K1A 0L5
(613) 941-1503, FAX: (613) 941-9674
www.ccra-adrc.gc.ca
MANAGER
Natalie Stibernik

The Canadian Audio-Visual Certification Office (CAVCO) and the Canada Customs and Revenue Agency (CCRA) jointly administer the Canadian Film or Video Production Tax Credit (CPTC) and the Film or Video Production Services Tax Credit (PSTC).

Canadian Film or Video Production Tax Credit Program (CPTC)
Under the Canadian Film or Video Production Tax Credit program, CAVCO performs two distinct functions: (1) Canadian content recognition, and (2) estimation of the eligible expenses of production. The responsibilities of the CCRA are to provide assistance to claimants; to interpret and apply section 125.4 and all other provisions of the Income Tax Act and the Income Tax Regulations that may have an impact on the CPTC; review or audit the film tax credit claims within a reasonable time frame; and provide timely refund cheques.

The CPTC is available at a rate of 25% of eligible salaries and wages expended after 1994. Eligible salaries and wages qualifying for the credit may not exceed 48% of the cost of the production, net of assistance, as certified by the Minister of Canadian Heritage. Therefore, the tax credit could provide assistance of up to 12% of the cost of production, net of assistance. However, the tax credit may not be claimed in respect of a Canadian production if any part of the cost is financed by flowing-out capital cost allowance or other deductions to investors.

Film or Video Production Services Tax Credit Program (PSTC)
CAVCO's role under the Film or Video Production Services Tax Credit is to determine the eligibility of the production and to issue an Accredited Film or Video Production Certificate on behalf of the Minister of Canadian Heritage. The CCRA's role is to provide assistance to claimants; interpret and apply section 125.5 and all other provisions of the Income Tax Act and the Income Tax Regulations that may have an impact on the PSTC; review or audit the film tax credit claims within a reasonable time frame; and provide timely refund cheques.

The PSTC is a tax credit equal to 11% of salary and wages paid to Canadian residents or taxable Canadian corporations (for amounts paid to employees who are Canadian residents) for services provided to the production in Canada. This refundable tax credit has no cap on the amount that can be claimed, and it is available to taxable Canadian corporations or foreign-owned taxable corporations with a permanent establishment in Canada.

CANADIAN HERITAGE / LES TERRASSES DE LA CHAUDIÈRE
Film, Video and Sound Recording Branch
15 Eddy St., 6th Fl., Hull, QC K1A 0M5. (819) 997-5918. FAX: (819) 997-5709. www.pch.gc.ca
DIRECTOR GENERAL
Jean-François Bernier
ADMIN. ASSISTANT
Tina Giguere
POLICY & PROGRAM ANALYSTS, FILM & VIDEO
Lynn Foran
Karyn Wichers
MANAGER, FILM & VIDEO
Nathalie Chamberland
SOUND RECORDING POLICY & PROGRAM ANALYSTS
Charlene LaRose
Lynn Buffone
ECONOMIC ANALYST FOR POLICY MONITORING
Kevin MacDougall
POLICY ANALYST FOR POLICY MONITORING
Suzanne Grundy

The Film, Video and Sound Recording Policy and Program Section provides advice and assistance to the Minister of Canadian Heritage in the formulation and development of policies and programs for the achievement of cultural objectives in the area of film, video and sound recording.

CANADIAN INTERNATIONAL DEVELOPMENT AGENCY (CIDA)
200 Promenade du Portage, Hull, QC K1A 0G4
(819) 997-1663 / (800) 230-6349, FAX: (819) 953-4933
E-mail: mmi_imm@acdi-cida.gc.ca / www.acdi-cida.gc.ca/mmi

Through its Mass Media Initiative (MMI), CIDA's Development Information Program financially supports communication projects aimed at increasing Canadian public awareness and understanding of international development. MMI supports a wide variety of Canadian activities such as television and radio productions, magazine features, newspaper articles and exhibits. MMI issues at least one formal request for proposals every year. International organizations must be part of a Canadian-led consortium or partnership to apply.

CANADIAN RADIO-TELEVISION AND TELECOMMUNICATIONS COMMISSION / CONSEIL DE LA RADIODIFFUSION ET DES TELECOMMUNICATIONS CANADIENNES (CRTC)
CENTRAL OFFICE LES TERRASSES DE LA CHAUDIÈRE
Central Bldg.
1 Promenade du Portage, Hull, QC. (819) 997-0313 / (877) 249-2782 (CRTC). FAX: (819) 994-0218
Client Services: (819) 997-0313, Media Services: (819) 997-9403. www.crtc.gc.ca

COMMISSIONERS
CHAIRMAN / VICE-CHAIRMAN, TELECOMMUNICATIONS / COMMISSIONER, ATLANTIC REGION
David Colville
VICE-CHAIRMAN, BROADCASTING
Andrée P. Wylie
COMMISSIONER, BRITISH COLUMBIA & YUKON REGIONS
Cindy Grauer
COMMISSIONER, ALBERTA & NORTHWEST TERRITORIES REGIONS
Ronald D. Williams
COMMISSIONER, MANITOBA & SASKATCHEWAN REGIONS
Barbara Cram
COMMISSIONER, ONTARIO REGION
Martha Wilson
COMMISSIONER, QUÉBEC REGION
Andrée Noël
COMMISSIONERS
Andrew Cardozo
David McKendry
Joan Pennefather
Jean-Marc Demers
James Stuart Langford

An independent public authority that regulates and supervises broadcasting and telecommunications in Canada.

REGIONAL OFFICES
ALBERTA
10405 Jasper Ave., Ste. 520, Edmonton, AB T5J 3R8
(780) 495-3224

BRITISH COLUMBIA
530 – 580 Hornby St., Vancouver, BC V6C 3B6
(604) 666-2111, FAX: (604) 666-8322

MANITOBA
275 Portage Ave., Ste. 1810, Winnipeg, MB R3B 2B3
(204) 983-6306, FAX: (204) 983-6317

NOVA SCOTIA
Metropolitan Place
99 Wyse Rd., Ste. 1410, Dartmouth, NS B3A 4S5
(902) 426-7997, FAX (902) 426-2721

ONTARIO
55 St. Clair Ave. E., Ste. 624, Toronto, ON M4T 1L8
(416) 952-9096

QUÉBEC
405 de Maisonneuve Boul. est, Ste. B 2300, Montréal, QC H2L 4J5. (514) 283-6607, FAX: (514) 283-3689

SASKATCHEWAN
Cornwall Professional Bldg.
2125 –11th Ave., Ste. 103, Regina, SK S4P 3X3
(306) 780-3422

FOREIGN AFFAIRS AND INTERNATIONAL TRADE
Arts and Cultural Industries Promotion Division (ACA)
125 Sussex Dr., Ottawa, ON K1A 0G2
(613) 944-ARTS / (888) 757--7752, FAX: (613) 992-5965
www.dfait-maeci.gc.ca/arts
DEPUTY DIRECTOR (CULTURAL INDUSTRIES)
Albert Galpin
FILM & TELEVISION OFFICER
Sonya Thissen

Sources of funding for film & television companies and for Canadian festivals

GRANTS & LOANS
TRAVEL GRANTS FOR INTL. MARKET DEVELOPMENT:
DFAIT provides grants for producers and/or directors to travel to international festivals, selected pitching sessions and premiere screenings outside of Canada.
www.dfait-maeci.gc.ca/arts/film-en.asp

CANADIAN FESTIVAL GRANTS:
DFAIT/ACA provides grants for Canadian festivals to invite foreign buyers to their events.
www.dfait-maeci.gc.ca/arts/film-en.asp

PROGRAM FOR EXPORT MARKET DEVELOPMENT (PEMD):
Under this program, DFAIT provides up to 50% forgivable loans in order for companies to develop new export markets.
www.dfait-maeci.gc.ca/pemd

PROGRAMS & SERVICES
EXPORTUSA
(NEBS, EXTUS & Reverse NEBS): DFAIT provides funds in support of the government's initiative to increase the number of active Canadian exporters to the United States. NEXOS is a similar program for Europe.
www.dfait-maeci.gc.ca/nebs

TEAM CANADA MISSIONS:
These missions help familiarize Canadian companies with new markets, facilitate access to foreign political and business leaders, enhance visibility in foreign markets and strengthen relationships with Canadian and foreign business partners and clients.
www.tcm-mec.gc.ca

EXPORT SOURCE:
This is Team Canada's online resource for export information.
www.exportsource.gc.ca

VIRTUAL TRADE COMMISSIONER:
Provides Canadian companies with a network of trade commissioners abroad, geographic and industry market reports as well as personalized core services to help export-ready companies prepare for the challenges of international business.
www.infoexport.gc.ca

CULTURAL ATTACHÉS ABROAD:
DFAIT puts companies in contact with Canadian cultural representatives abroad who have detailed market knowledge & contacts.
www.dfait-maeci.gc.ca/arts/abroad-en.asp
For further information visit the website.

LIBRARY & ARCHIVES OF CANADA / ARCHIVES NATIONALES DU CANADA
Audio-Visual Sector / Secteur audio-visuel
395 Wellington St., Ottawa, ON KIA 0N3. www.archives.ca
CHIEF, AV ACQUISITION
Richard Lochead
(613) 996-2282. FAX: (613) 995-6575
CHIEF, AV PRESERVATION
Andris Kesteris. (819) 994-5241

Public Service requests: (866) 578-7777
Reference Service: (613) 992-3884

A division of National Archives of Canada with authority to aquire, describe and provide specialized reference services to archivally significant Canadian film, TV and sound documents produced both publicly and privately. Initiated as a project of the Public Archives of Canada in 1969. The Audio-Visual Sector was formally established by Cabinet in January 1976 with a mandate to acquire all film, video and sound collections of national significance. At present, the Audio-Visual Sector holds over 300,000 hours of moving image and sound recordings.

THE NATIONAL FILM BOARD OF CANADA
Box 6100, Stn. Centre-Ville, Montréal, QC H3C 3H5
HEAD OFFICE
Constitution Sq., 360 Albert St., Ste. 1560, Ottawa, ON K1A 0M9. (613) 992-3615, Sales: (514) 283-9000 / (800) 267-7710
www.nfb.ca
GOVERNMENT FILM COMMISSIONER & CHAIRPERSON
Jacques Bensimon
DIRECTOR GENERAL, ENGLISH PROGRAM
Tom Perlmutter
ASSISTANT DIRECTOR GENERAL
Ravida Din
EXEC. PRODUCER, ANIMATION STUDIO
David Verrall
EXEC. PRODUCER, ATLANTIC CENTRE
Kent Martin
EXEC. PRODUCER, QUEBEC CENTRE
Sally Bochner
EXEC. PRODUCER, ONTARIO CENTRE
Sylvia Sweeney
EXEC. PRODUCER, WESTERN CANADA
Graydon McCrea
EXEC. PRODUCER, PACIFIC CENTRE
Rina Fraticelli
EXEC. PRODUCER, INTL. CO-PRODUCTION UNIT
Éric Michel
DIRECTOR GENERAL, FRENCH PROGRAM
André Picard
ASSISTANT DIRECTOR GENERAL
Martin Dubé
EXEC. PRODUCER, ANIMATION & YOUTH STUDIO
Marcel Jean
EXEC. PRODUCER, DOCUMENTARY STUDIO/MONTREAL (SOCIETY & SCIENCE)
Colette Loumède
PRODUCER, DOCUMENTARY STUDIO/MONTREAL (REALITIES.DOC)
Yves Bisaillon
PRODUCER, ACADIA DOCUMENTARY STUDIO/MONCTON
Jacques Turgeon
PRODUCER, QUEBEC REGIONS
Jacques Turgeon

The National Film Board of Canada (NFB) was founded by an act of Parliament on May 2, 1939. Its mandate is "to produce and distribute films designed to interpret Canada to Canadians and other nations. The NFB operates a national toll-free sales and information telephone system and maintains partnerships with over 35 libraries, as well as relationships with over 400 other distribution points across Canada to ensure that Canadians have direct access to NFB productions. The NFB catalogue is available on the website. The NFB also has offices in New York, Paris and London, arranging the commercial distribution of NFB titles through private sector distributors, promoting the direct sales of films and videos, and negotiating sales to broadcasters.

REGIONAL PRODUCTION CENTRES
ALBERTA & NORTHWEST TERRITORIES
10815 – 104 Ave., Ste. 100, Edmonton, AB T5J 4N6
(780) 495-3013, FAX: (780) 495-6412
PRODUCER, DOCUMENTARY
Jerry Krepakevich

BRITISH COLUMBIA & YUKON
200 — 1385 W. 8th Ave., Vancouver, BC V6H 3V9
(604) 666-3838, FAX: (604) 666-1569
PRODUCER, DOCUMENTARY
Gillian Darling Kovanic
PRODUCER, SPECIAL MANDATE
Selwyn Jacob
PRODUCER, ANIMATION, CHILDREN, INTERACTIVE
George Johnson

ATLANTIC PROVINCES
Queen's Court, 2nd Fl., 5475 Spring Garden Rd., Halifax, NS
B3J 1G2. (902) 426-7351, FAX: (902) 426-8901
PRODUCER, DOCUMENTARY
Kent Martin

MANITOBA & SASKATCHEWAN
300 — 136 Market Ave., Winnipeg, MB R3B 0P4
(204) 983-7996, FAX: (204) 983-0742
PRODUCER, DOCUMENTARY
Joseph MacDonald
PRODUCER, ANIMATION, CHILDREN, INTERACTIVE
Jennifer Torrance, (204) 983-7985

NEW BRUNSWICK — ACADIA
95 Foundry St., Moncton, NB E1C 5H7
(506) 851-6104, FAX: (506) 851-2246
PRODUCER, DOCUMENTARY (FRENCH PROGRAM)
Jacques Turgeon

ONTARIO
150 John St., Toronto, ON M5V 3C3
(416) 973-6856, FAX: (416) 973-7007
PRODUCERS, DOCUMENTARY
Silva Basmajian
Peter Starr
Gerry Flahive
PRODUCER, SPECIAL MANDATE
Karen King

325 Dalhousie St., Rm. 800, Ottawa, ON K1N 7G2
(613) 995-3659, FAX: (613) 995-3738
PRODUCER, ONTARIO / WEST REGIONS DOCUMENTARY
(FRENCH PROGRAM)
Jacques Ménard
PRODUCER, QUÉBEC REGION DOCUMENTARY
(FRENCH PROGRAM)
Jacques Turgeon

QUÉBEC
3155 Côte de Liesse Rd., St-Laurent, QC H4N 2N4
(514) 283-9285, FAX: (514) 496-4424
DIRECTOR-GENERAL (FRENCH PROGRAM)
Vacant
ASSISTANT DIRECTOR-GENERAL (FRENCH PROGRAM)
Martin Dubé
EXEC. PRODUCER, ANIMATION / YOUTH STUDIO
(FRENCH PROGRAM)
Marcel Jean
PRODUCER, YOUTH (FRENCH PROGRAM)
Jean-Jacques Leduc

(514) 283-9316, FAX: (514) 283-4300
EXEC. PRODUCER, DOCUMENTARY (FRENCH PROGRAM) /
MONTRÉAL (SOCIETY & SCIENCE)
Éric Michel

(514) 496-1171, FAX: (514) 283-7914
EXEC. PRODUCER, DOCUMENTARY (FRENCH PROGRAM) /
MONTRÉAL (RÉALITÉS.DOC)
Yves Bisaillon

(514) 496-2216. Fax: (514) 283-5487
PRODUCER, DOCUMENTARY
Adam Symansky
PRODUCER, SPECIAL MANDATE
Germaine Wong

(514) 283-9571. FAX: (514) 283-3211
PRODUCERS, ANIMATION
Michael Fukushima
Marcy Page
PRODUCERS, CHILDREN'S PROGRAM
Tamara Lynch
Pierre Lapointe

STATISTICS CANADA / STATISTIQUE CANADA
Statistical Reference Centre
R.H. Coats Building, Ottawa, ON K1A 0T6
(613) 951-8116 / (800) 263-1136 (Main), FAX: (613) 951-0581
E-mail: infostats@statcan.ca, www.statcan.ca

CULTURE, TOURISM & THE CENTRE FOR
EDUCATION STATISTICS
DIRECTOR
Maryanne Webber
MANAGER, RADIO (LISTENING) & TV (VIEWING)
Lofti Chahdi, (613) 951-3136
MANAGER, FILM & VIDEO (PRODUCTION & DISTRIBUTION)
Fidel Ifedi, (613) 951-1569

Established in 1972 within the Institutional Statistics Program of
Statistics Canada, the Culture Statistics Program has the man-
date to collect, analyze and publish statistical information on the
state of culture in Canada and the cultural activities of
Canadians. The CSP includes ten major project areas: Book
Publishing, Periodicals, Film (4 surveys), Radio and Television,
Sound Recording, Performing Arts, Heritage Institutions, Cultural
Labour Force, Participation of Canadians in Cultural Activities
and Government Expenditures in Culture.

Results of surveys are presented in annual publications and in
a quarterly newsletter "Focus on Culture". Customized tabula-
tions are also available for specific research purposes.

TELEFILM CANADA / TÉLÉFILM CANADA
360 St. Jacques St., Ste. 700, Montréal, QC H2Y 4A9
(514) 283-6363/1 (800) 567-0890, FAX: (514) 283-8212
www.telefilm.gc.ca

TELEFILM OFFICES IN CANADA / BUREAUX AU CANADA
310 — 440 Cambie St., Vancouver, BC V6B 2Z5
(604) 666-1566/1 (800) 663-7771, FAX: (604) 666-7754

1684 Barrington St., 3rd Fl., Halifax, NS B3J 2A2
(902) 426-8425/1 (800) 565-1773, FAX: (902) 426-4445

474 Bathurst St., Suite 100, Toronto, ON M5T 2S6
(416) 973-6436/1 (800) 463-4607, FAX: (416) 973-8606

EUROPEAN OFFICE / BUREAU EUROPÉEN
5 rue de Constantine, 75007 Paris, France
(011) 33-1-44-18-35-30, FAX: (011) 33-1-47-05-72-76

BOARD OF DIRECTORS / CONSEIL D'ADMINISTRATION
CHAIR/PRÉSIDENT
Charles Bélanger (Montréal)
VICE-CHAIR/VICE-PRÉSIDENTE
Jeanine C. Beaubien, O.C. (Montréal)
CHAIR, AUDIT AND FINANCE COMMITTEE / PRÉSIDENT,
COMITÉ DE VÉRIFICATION ET DES FINANCES
Ronald S. Bremner (Calgary)
MEMBERS
Jacques Bensimon (Government Film Commissioner /
Commissaire du gouvernement à la cinématographie,
Montréal), Bluma Appel (Toronto)
Elvira Sánchez De Malicki (Etobicoke)
Louise Pelletier (Montréal)

MANAGEMENT / DIRECTION
EXECUTIVE DIRECTOR / DIRECTEUR GÉNÉRAL
Richard Stursberg
DIRECTOR, FINANCE AND ADMINISTRATION /
DIRECTEUR, FINANCES ET ADMINISTRATION
Danny Chalifour
DIRECTOR, COMMUNICATIONS AND CORPORATE AFFAIRS
/ DIRECTRICE, COMMUNICATIONS ET AFFAIRES
PUBLIQUES
Danielle Dansereau
DIRECTOR, INTERNATIONAL DEVELOPMENT AND
PROMOTION / DIRECTRICE, PROMOTION ET
DÉVELOPPEMENT À L'INTERNATIONAL
Sheila de La Varende
DIRECTOR, POLICY, PLANNING AND RESEARCH /
DIRECTEUR, POLITIQUES, PLANIFICATION ET RECHERCH-
ES
Guy DeRepentigny
HEAD OF DEVELOPMENT AND IMPLEMANTATION OF
NATIONAL STANDARDS AND SECTOR HEAD - FEATURE
FILM / RESPONSABLE DE L'ELAORATION ET DE L'IMPLAN-
TATION DES STANDARDS NATIONAUX ET RESPONSABLE
SECTEUR - LONGS METRAGES
Karen Franklin
DIRECTOR, MEDIA / DIRECTRICE, MEDIAS
Elizabeth Friesen
INTERIM DIRECTOR, ONTARIO AND NUNAVUT OFFICE /
DIRECTEUR PAR INTÉRIM, BUREAU DE L'ONTARIO ET DU
NUNAVUT
John Galway
DIRECTOR, ATLANTIC REGION OFFICE AND SECTOR
HEAD – PROFESSIONAL AND SECTORAL TRAINING /
DIRECTEUR, BUREAU DE LA RÉGION DE L'ATLANTIQUE ET
RESPONSABLE DES PROGRAMMES DE FORMATION
PROFESSIONNELLE ET SECTORIELLE
Ralph Holt
DIRECTOR, WESTERN REGION OFFICE AND SECTOR
HEAD – NEW MEDIA / DIRECTEUR, BUREAU DE LA
RÉGION DE L'OUEST ET RESPONSABLE SECTEUR –
NOUVEAUX MÉDIAS
Earl Hong Tai

GENERAL COUNSEL AND ACCESS TO INFORMATION COORDINATOR / CHEF DU CONTENTIEUX ET COORDONNATEUR DE L'ACCÈS À L'INFORMATION
Stéphane Odesse
DIRECTOR, QUEBEC OFFICE AND SECTOR HEAD – TELEVISION / DIRECTEUR, BUREAU DU QUÉBEC ET RESPONSABLE SECTEUR – TÉLÉVISION
Michel Pradier
DIRECTOR, HUMAN RESOURCES / DIRECTRICE, RESSOURCES HUMAINES
Stella Riggi
DIRECTOR, MUSIC ENTREPRENEUR PROGRAM / DIRECTEUR DU PROGRAMME DES ENTREPRENEURS DE LA MUSIQUE
Shelley Stein-Sacks

Telefilm Canada is a federal cultural agency created in 1967 and reporting to the Department of Canadian Heritage.

As a cultural investor in film, television, new media and music, Telefilm Canada encourages the creation and distribution of stories and images that touch Canadians and foster connection and understanding from coast to coast.

Building audiences for Canadian productions is central to Telefilm's concerns and initiatives. With its financial, promotional and strategic support, the Canadian cultural industries are capturing ever-growing favour both at home and around the globe.

The main funds are : Canada Feature Film Fund, Canadian Television Fund – Equity Investment Program, Canada New Media Fund and Canada Music Fund – Music Entrepreneur Program.

Please consult the website for additional information concerning regional offices, funds and programs, coproduction, festivals, markets, catalogues and news.

Téléfilm Canada est un organisme culturel fédéral créé en 1967, qui relève du ministère du Patrimoine canadien. En tant qu'investisseur culturel en cinéma, télévision, nouveaux médias et musique, Téléfilm Canada encourage la création et la diffusion d'histoires et d'images qui touchent les Canadiens et leur permettent de mieux se connaître et de mieux se comprendre.

Accroître le public des œuvres canadiennes est au centre des préoccupations et des initiatives de Téléfilm Canada. Notre appui financier, promotionnel et stratégique permet aux industries culturelles canadiennes de se tailler une meilleure place ici et ailleurs dans le monde.

Les principaux fonds sont: Fonds du long métrage du Canada, Fonds canadien de télévision – Programme de participation au capital, Fonds des nouveaux médias du Canada, Fonds de la musique du Canada – Programme des entrepreneurs de musique. Veuillez consulter site web pour avoir toutes les informations concernant nos bureaux régionaux, les divers fonds et programmes, la coproduction, les festivals et marchés, les catalogues et les actualités.

U.K. EXHIBITION CIRCUITS

ABBEY FILMS LTD.
35 Upper Abbey Street, Dublin 1. Tel: (353 1) 8044520.
FAX: (353 1) 8783069
MANAGING DIRECTOR
Leo Ward

ABC CINEMAS LTD OWNED BY ODEON CINEMAS
54 Whitcomb Street, London WC2H 7DN. Tel: (020) 7321 0404
www.odeon.co.uk

APOLLO LEISURE (UK) LTD. - CINEMA DIVISION
60 Hamilton Street, Saltcoats, Ayrshire, KA21 5DS Tel: (01294)
472772. FAX: (01294) 467 930.
CONTACTS
Celina Kelly

ARTIFICIAL EYE COMPANY
14 King Street, London WC2E 8HN Tel: (0207) 240 5353.
FAX: (0207) 240 5252.

BELLEVUE CINEMA
General Enquires, Northfield Avenue, London, W13 9RH
Tel: (020) 8830 0822.

BLOOM THEATRES
37 Museum Street, London WC1A 1LP
Tel: (0207) 242 5523. FAX: (020) 7430 0107.

BROADWAY CINEMAS
Eastcheap, Letchworth. Tel: (0146) 268 1223.

CALEDONIAN CINEMAS
28, Allan Park, Stirling, Stirlingshire, FK8 2LT.
Tel: (01786) 451622 FAX: (01786) 446915.

CARLTON CLUBS
Box 21, 23-25 Huntley St., Inverness, Scotland 1VI 1LA.
Tel: (01463) 237611.
CONTACTS
Mr. P. Perrins

CINE-UK LTD.
Chapter House, 22 Chapter St., London SW1P 4NP.
Tel: (020) 7932 2200. FAX: (020) 7932 2222. www.cine-uk.com
CONTACTS
Steve Wiener

CIRCLE CINEMAS
Thornbury House, Thornbury Close, Rhiwbina, Cardiff, South
Glamorgan CF14 1UT. Tel: (029) 2052 2606

CITY SCREEN
16-18 Beak Street, London W1F 9RD Tel: (0207) 734 4342
FAX: (0207) 734 4027.
CONTACTS
Tony Jones Tel: 01223 328383

COSMO LEISURE GROUP
Central Hall, 62-66 Market St., Stalybridge, Cheshire SK15
2AB.

CORONET CINEMAS
103 Notting Hill Gate, London W11 3LB. Tel: (020) 7727 6705.

CURZON CINEMAS,
Wingate House, 93-107, Shaftsbury Avenue, London W1D 5DA
Tel: (020) 7734 9209. Fax: (020) 7734 1977
CONTACTS
Rob Kenny
Nicki Tucker

DOMINION CINEMA
18, Newbattle Terrace, Edinburgh, Midlothian EH10 4RT. Tel:
(0131) 447 2660.

DUBLIN CINEMA GROUP LTD
Savoy Building Upper O'Connell Street, Dublin 1 Tel: 353 1
8044500

MAINLINE PICTURES
37 Museum Street, London WC1A 1LP. Tel:(0207) 242
5523. FAX: (0207) 430 0170.

LONDON IMAX THEATRE
1 Charlie Chaplin Walk, South Bank, Waterloo, London SE1
8XR. Tel: (020) 7960 3110.

CONTACTS
Mr. Jason Bainbridge

THE METRO CINEMA
19, Rupert Street, London W1D 7PA Tel: (0207) 437 0747.

METRO TARTAN DISTRIBUTION LTD
5 Wardour Street, London W1D 6PB. Tel: (0207) 494 1400.
FAX: (0207) 4391922.
CONTACT
Camilla Summers

NATIONAL AMUSEMENTS SHOWCASE CINEMAS
Jenkins Lane, Barking, Essex, IG11 OAD.
Tel: (020) 8477 4520.
USA: 200 Elms Street, Dedham, Massachusettes, 02026
Tel: (001) 781 461 1600 UK (01159) 862 508 FAX: (001) 781
329 4831 UK (01159) 862 392

OASIS CINEMAS AND FILM DISTRIBUTION LTD
8, Kensington Park Road, Nottinghill Gate, London W11. Tel:
(0207)733 8989.
CONTACTS
John McGrawry

ODEON CINEMAS
54 Whitcomb Street, London WC2H 7DN. Tel: (020) 7321 0404
www.odeon.co.uk

PICTUREDROME THEATRES LTD
5, D'Abernon Close, Esher, Surrey, KT10 8PT.
Tel: (01372) 460108

REELTIME CINEMAS
Townhall Buildings, St Mildred's Road, Westgate on Sea, Kent
CT8 8RE. Tel: (01843) 834 609. www.realtime –cinemas.co.uk
CONTACTS
Michaels Vickers

ROBINS CINEMAS
St. Johns Place, Bath, Avon, BA1 1ET
Tel: (01225) 461506.

SCOTT CINEMAS
Market Street, Newton Abbot, Devon, TQ12 2RB.
Tel: (01626) 335432

SHOWCASE CINEMAS
Redfield Way, Lenton, Nottingham NG7 2UW. Tel: (0115)
986 6766.www.showcasecinemas.com

TAYLOR CLARK LEISURE PLC
Inverness Ice Centre, Bught Drive, Inverness, Inverness-Shire,
IV3 5SR. Tel: (01463) 717050

TYNESIDE FILM CINEMA
10 Pilgrim Street, Newcastle-Upon-Tyne NE1 6QG.
Tel: (0191) 232 8289.

UCI-UNITED CINEMAS INTERNATIONAL UK
Lee House, 90 Great Bridgewater Street, Manchester M1
5JW. Tel: (0161) 455 4000. FAX: (0161) 455 4079.
www.uci-cinemas.co.uk
MANAGING DIRECTOR
Roger Harris

UGC UK LTD.
In UK have 42 cinemas and 396 screens
Power Road Studios, Power Road, Chiswick, London, W4 5PY.
Tel: (020) 8987 5000.
MANAGING DIRECTOR
Margaret Taylor
Lisa Hynes (PA)

VIRGIN CINEMAS LTD. OWNED BY UGC
Power Road Studios, Power Road., Chiswick, London W4 5RY.
Tel: (0208) 987 5000. FAX: (0208) 742 2998.

WARD-ANDERSON CINEMA GROUP
Film House, 35 Upper Abbey Street, Dublin 1, Ireland. Tel:
(353 1) 872 3422/3922. FAX: (353 1) 872 3687.
www.warnervillage.com
MANAGING DIRECTOR
Leo Ward
98 Theobalds Road, London WC1X 8WB.
Tel: (020) 7984 6790

CIRCUIT MULTIPLEXES

Theatre Name	City	Circuit	Screens
ABC	Bath, Avon	Odeon	3
ABC	Bournemouth, Dorset	Odeon	8
ABC	Plymouth	Odeon	3
Apollo	Bangor	Apollo	2
Apollo	Blackburn	Apollo	5
Apollo	Barrow, Cumbria	Apollo	6
Apollo	Crewe	Apollo	3
Apollo	Burnley	Apollo	9
Apollo	Paignton, Torbay	Apollo	9
Apollo	Leamington Spa	Apollo	4
Apollo	Morecombe	Apollo	4
Apollo	Port Talbot	Apollo	6
Apollo	Rhyl	Apollo	5
Apollo	Stafford	Apollo	3
Cineworld, The Movies	Ashford	Cine UK	9
Cineworld, The Movies	Bishop's Strotford	Cine UK	6
Cineworld, The Movies	Bexleyheath	Cine UK	7
Cineworld	Bradford	Cine UK	10
Cineworld	Braintree	Cine UK	10
Cineworld, The Movies	Bristol	Cine UK	10
Cineworld	Burton on Trent	Cine UK	8
Cineworld	Castleford	Cine UK	14
Cineworld, The Movies	Chesterfield	Cine UK	7
Cineworld	Chichester	Cine UK	9
Cineworld	Falkirk	Cine UK	11
Cineworld, The Movies	Feltham	Cine UK	8
Cineworld	Huntingdon	Cine UK	8
Cineworld	Ilford	Cine UK	8
Cineworld	Jersey	Cine UK	9
Cineworld	landudno	Cine UK	8
Cineworld, The Movies	Luton	Cine UK	9
Cineworld	Milton Keynes	Cine UK	8
Cineworld	Newport	Cine UK	9
Cineworld	Rugby	Cine UK	7
Cineworld	Runcorn	Cine UK	8
Cineworld, The Movies	Shrewsbury	Cine UK	8
Cineworld	Solihull	Cine UK	8
Cineworld, The Movies	Stevenage	Cine UK	13
Cineworld	St. Helens	Cine UK	9
Cineworld	St. Helier	Cine UK	10
Cineworld, The Movies	Swindon	Cine UK	10
Cineworld, The Movies	Wakefield	Cine UK	9
Cineworld	Weymouth	Cine UK	8
Cineworld	Wolverhampton	Cine UK	10
Cineworld, The Movies	Wood Green	Cine UK	7
Cineworld	Yeovil	Cine UK	8
Deluxe	Bradford	Cine UK	4
Deluxe	Huntingdon	Cine UK	4
Deluxe	Isle Of Wight	Cine UK	3
Movie House	Yorkgate, Belfast	Movie House	14
Movie House	Maghera	Movie House	3
Movie House	Glengormley	Movie House	6
Odeon	Aberdeen	Odeon	3
Odeon	Allerton	Odeon	1
Odeon	Ayr, Strathclyde	Odeon	4
Odeon	Aylesbury	Odeon	6
Odeon	Banbury	Odeon	2
Odeon	Barnet	Odeon	5
Odeon	Barnsley	Odeon	2
Odeon	Bath	Odeon	1
Odeon	Beckenham	Odeon	6
Odeon	Birmingham	Odeon	8
Odeon	Blackpool	Odeon	10
Odeon	Westover Road, Bournemouth	Odeon	6
Odeon	27 Westover Road, Bournemouth	Odeon	3
Odeon	Bridgend	Odeon	9
Odeon	Brighton	Odeon	8
Odeon	Briston	Odeon	1
Odeon	Bromborough	Odeon	11
Odeon	Bromley	Odeon	4
Odeon	Bury St Edmunds	Odeon	2
Odeon	Canterbury	Odeon	2
Odeon	Chelmsford	Odeon	8
Odeon	Cheltenham	Odeon	7
Odeon	Chester	Odeon	5
Odeon	Colchester	Odeon	8
Odeon	Coventry	Odeon	9
Odeon	Darlington	Odeon	3
Odeon	Doncaster	Odeon	3

Theatre Name	City	Circuit	Screens
Odeon	Dumfries	Odeon	1
Odeon	Dundee	Odeon	10
Odeon	Dunfermline	Odeon	10
Odeon	Lothian Road, Edinburgh	Odeon	4
Odeon	Wester Hailes, Edinburgh	Odeon	8
Odeon	Epsom	Odeon	8
Odeon	Esher	Odeon	4
Odeon	Exeter	Odeon	4
Odeon	Gerrards Cross	Odeon	2
Odeon	Renfield Street, Glasgow	Odeon	9
Odeon	Springfield Quay, Glasgow	Odeon	12
Odeon	Grimsby	Odeon	3
Odeon	Guildford	Odeon	9
Odeon	Harlow	Odeon	3
Odeon	Harrogate	Odeon	5
Odeon	Hastings	Odeon	4
Odeon	Hemel Hempstead	Odeon	8
Odeon	Hereford	Odeon	1
Odeon	Hull	Odeon	10
Odeon	Ipswich	Odeon	5
Odeon	St.Helier Jersey	Odeon	4
Odeon	Kettering	Odeon	8
Odeon	Kilmarnock	Odeon	8
Odeon	Kingston Upon Thames	Odeon	14
Odeon	Leicester	Odeon	12
Odeon	Lincoln	Odeon	9
Odeon	Leeds Bradford	Odeon	13
Odeon	Liverpool	Odeon	12
Odeon	Camden Town, London	Odeon	5
Odeon	Covent Garden, London	Odeon	4
Odeon	Holloway, London	Odeon	8
Odeon	Kensington, London	Odeon	6
Odeon	Leicester Square, London	Odeon	6
Odeon	Marble Arch, London	Odeon	5
Odeon	Muswell Hill, London	Odeon	3
Odeon	Panton Street, London	Odeon	4
Odeon	Putney, London	Odeon	3
Odeon	Streatham, London	Odeon	8
Odeon	Swiss Cottage, London	Odeon	6
Odeon	Wardour Street, London	Odeon	4
Odeon	West End, London	Odeon	2
Odeon	Wimbledon, London	Odeon	12
Odeon	London Road, Liverpool	Odeon	10
Odeon	Switch Island, Liverpool	Odeon	12
Odeon	Maidstone	Odeon	8
Odeon	Manchester	Odeon	7
Odeon	Mansfield	Odeon	8
Odeon	Newcastle Upon Tyne	Odeon	12
Odeon	Nuneaton	Odeon	8
Odeon	George Street, Oxford	Odeon	6
Odeon	Magdalene Street, Oxford	Odeon	2
Odeon	Portsmouth	Odeon	4
Odeon	Plymouth	Odeon	3
Odeon	Quinton	Odeon	4
Odeon	Rochadale	Odeon	
Odeon	Salisbury	Odeon	5
Odeon	Sheffield	Odeon	10
Odeon	Southampton	Odeon	13
Odeon	Southend	Odeon	8
Odeon	Stoke on Trent	Odeon	10
Odeon	Sutton Cold Field	Odeon	4
Odeon	Richmond, Surrey	Odeon	3
Odeon	Taunton	Odeon	5
Odeon	Tunbridge Wells	Odeon	9
Odeon	Uxbridge	Odeon	9
Odeon	Weston-Super-Mare	Odeon	4
Odeon	South Woodford	Odeon	7
Odeon	Worcester	Odeon	7
Odeon	Wexham	Odeon	7
Odeon	York	Odeon	3
Omniplex	Borehamwood	Ward Anderson	5
Omniplex	Carrickfergus	Ward Anderson	6
Omniplex	Enniskillen	Ward Anderson	7
Omniplex	Lisburn	Ward Anderson	14
Piccadilly	Birmingham	Ind. Avtar Singh	1
Piccadilly	City Centre, Leicester	Ind. Avtar Singh	1
Piccadilly	Evington, Leicester	Ind. Avtar Singh	1
Showcase	Birmingham	National Amusements	10
Showcase	Bluewater	National Amusements	10
Showcase	Bristol	National Amusements	12
Showcase	Glasgow East Coatbridge	National Amusements	11
Showcase	Coventry	National Amusements	12
Showcase	Derby	National Amusements	9
Showcase	Dudley	National Amusements	10
Showcase	Leeds	National Amusements	13
Showcase	Liverpool	National Amusements	10
Showcase	Wood Green, London	National Amusements	6
Showcase	Manchester	National Amusements	12

Theatre Name	City	Circuit	Screens
Showcase	Nantgarw	National Amusements	11
Showcase	Newham	National Amusements	11
Showcase	Nottingham	National Amusements	10
Showcase	Phoenix Retail Park, Paisley	National Amusements	11
Showcase	Peterborough	National Amusements	10
Showcase	Reading	National Amusements	10
Showcase	Stockton on Teeside	National Amusements	10
Showcase	Walsall	National Amusements	10
Ster Century	Basinstoke	Ster Century	10
Ster Century	Cardiff	Ster Century	14
Ster Century	Edinburgh	Ster Century	12
Ster Century	Leeds	Ster Century	13
Ster Century	Norwich	Ster Century	8
Ster Century	Romford	Ster Century	16

UCI =JV between Paramount and Universal

Theatre Name	City	Circuit	Screens
UCI	Basildon	UCI	12
UCI	Bracknell	UCI	10
UCI	Brierley Hill,Dudley	UCI	10
UCI	Cardiff	UCI	12
UCI	Warrington, Cheshire	UCI	10
UCI	Clydebank	UCI	12
UCI	Meteor Centre, Derby	UCI	10
UCI	East Kilbride	UCI	9
UCI	Kinnaird Park , Edinburgh	UCI	12
UCI	Hatfield	UCI	10
UCI	High Wycombe	UCI	6
UCI	Huddersfield	UCI	9
UCI	Hull	UCI	8
UCI	Lee Valley	UCI	12
UCI	Whiteleys, London	UCI	8
UCI	Greenwich, London	UCI	14
UCI	Empire Cinema Leicester Square, London	UCI	3
UCI	Surrey Quays, London	UCI	9
UCI	Dantzic Street, Machester	UCI	20
UCI	Trafford Centre, Manchester	UCI	20
UCI	Maidenhead	UCI	8
UCI	North Shields	UCI	9
UCI	Northampton	UCI	10
UCI	Norwich	UCI	14
UCI	Poole	UCI	10
UCI	Port Solent Portsmouth	UCI	6
UCI	Preston	UCI	10
UCI	Scunthorpe	UCI	7
UCI	Sheffield	UCI	10
UCI	Solihull	UCI	8
UCI	Sutton, Surrey	UCI	6
UCI	Swansea	UCI	10
UCI	Tamworth	UCI	10
UCI	Telford	UCI	10
UCI	Metro Centre, Gateshead,Tyne and Wear	UCI	11
UCI	Warrington	UCI	10
UCI	West Thurrock	UCI	10
UGC	Aberdeen	UGC	9
UGC	Bedford	UGC	7
UGC	Belfast	UGC	10
UGC	Arcadian, Birmingham	UGC	8
UGC	Broad Street, Birmingham	UGC	12
UGC	Rubery, Birmingham	UGC	11
UGC	Boldon	UGC	10
UGC	Bolton	UGC	14
UGC	Brighton	UGC	9
UGC	Cardiff	UGC	14
UGC	Chester	UGC	6
UGC	Crawley	UGC	13
UGC	Didsbury	UGC	10
UGC	Dundee	UGC	9
UGC	Eastbourne	UGC	7
UGC	Edinburgh	UGC	13
UGC	Renfrew Street, Glasgow	UGC	16
UGC	Parkhead, Glasgow	UGC	7
UGC	Gloucester	UGC	6
UGC	Harlow	UGC	6
UGC	Hull	UGC	8
UGC	Ipswich	UGC	13
UGC	Liverpool	UGC	8
UGC	Chelsea, London	UGC	4
UGC	Ealing, London	UGC	3
UGC	Enfield, London	UGC	14
UGC	Fulham, London	UGC	6
UGC	Hammersmith, London	UGC	4
UGC	Haymarket, London	UGC	3
UGC	Shaftsbury Avenue, London	UGC	6
UGC	Staples Corner, London	UGC	7
UGC	West India Quay, London	UGC	11
UGC	Middlesborough	UGC	10
UGC	Newport	UGC	12
UGC	Northampton	UGC	9
UGC	Rochester	UGC	9

Theatre Name	City	Circuit	Screens
UGC	Sheffield	UGC	18
UGC	Slough	UGC	10
UGC	Southampton	UGC	6
UGC	Stockport	UGC	10
UGC	Swindon	UGC	7
UGC	Wigan, Greater Manchester	UGC	11
Warner Village	Bury	Vue Entertainment	12
Warner Village	Basingstoke	Vue Entertainment	10
Warner Village	Belfast	Vue Entertainment	12
Warner Village	Birkenhead	Vue Entertainment	7
Warner Village	Birmingham	Vue Entertainment	30
Warner Village	Bolton	Vue Entertainment	12
Warner Village	Cribbs, Bristol	Vue Entertainment	12
Warner Village	Longwell, Bristol	Vue Entertainment	10
Warner Village	Bury	Vue Entertainment	1
Warner Village	Cambridge	Vue Entertainment	8
Warner Village	Carlisle	Vue Entertainment	7
Warner Village	Cheshire Oaks	Vue Entertainment	11
Warner Village	Oaks, Croydon	Vue Entertainment	8
Warner Village	Grants, Croydon	Vue Entertainment	10
Warner Village	Dagenham	Vue Entertainment	9
Warner Village	Doncaster	Vue Entertainment	7
Warner Village	Edinburgh	Vue Entertainment	12
Warner Village	Harrow	Vue Entertainment	9
Warner Village	Hartlepool	Vue Entertainment	7
Warner Village	Inverness	Vue Entertainment	7
Warner Village	Islington	Vue Entertainment	9
Warner Village	Leeds	Vue Entertainment	9
Warner Village	Leiceste	Vue Entertainment	9
Warner Village	Finchley Rd., London	Vue Entertainment	8
Warner Village	Lido. Finchley Road, London	Vue Entertainment	8
Warner Village	Acton, London	Vue Entertainment	9
Warner Village	Fulham, London	Vue Entertainment	9
Warner Village	Shepherds Bush, London	Vue Entertainment	12
Warner Village	West End, London	Vue Entertainment	9
Warner Village	Newcastle-Under-Lyme	Vue Entertainment	8
Warner Village	Newcastle Upon Tyne	Vue Entertainment	9
Warner Village	Nottingham	Vue Entertainment	12
Warner Village	Plymouth	Vue Entertainment	15
Warner Village	Portsmouth	Vue Entertainment	11
Warner Village	Preston	Vue Entertainment	7
Warner Village	Reading	Vue Entertainment	10
Warner Village	Salford Quays	Vue Entertainment	7
Warner Village	Sheffield	Vue Entertainment	11
Warner Village	Staines	Vue Entertainment	10
Warner Village	Thurrock	Vue Entertainment	7
Warner Village	Watford	Vue Entertainment	8
Warner Village	Worcester	Vue Entertainment	6
Warner Village	York	Vue Entertainment	12

Producers & Distributors

AARDMAN ANIMATIONS
Gas Ferry Road, Bristol, BS1 6UN. Tel: (0117) 984 8485.
FAX:(0117) 984 8486. www.aardman.com
CONTACT
Paul Deane

ABSOLUTELY PRODUCTIONS LTD
226, Craven House, 121 Kingsway, London, WC2B 6PA.
Tel: (020) 7930 3113. FAX: (0207) 934 4114
email: info@absolutely-uk.com
www.absolutely-uk.com
MANAGING DIRECTOR
Miles Bullough

ABBEY FILMS LIMITED
Film House, 35 Upper Abbey Street, Dublin 1, Ireland.
Tel:(353 1) 872 3922. FAX: (353 1) 872 3687.
DIRECTORS
K. Anderson
L. Ward
A. Ryan

ACTIV MEDIA (PRODUCTIONS) LTD
Georgian Court, 39-41, Stockport Road, Romily, Stockport,
Cheshire, SK6 3AA
Tel: 0161 285 2244

ADDICTIVE TELEVISION LTD
39a, North Road, London N7 9DP Tel: (020) 7700 0333
email: mail@addictive.com
www.addictive.com
PRODUCER
Nick Clarke

ADN ASSOCIATES/HOLLYWOOD CLASSICS
8 Cleveland Gardens, London, W2 6HA. Tel: (020) 7262 4646.
FAX: (020) 7262 3242. www.hollywoodclassics.com
email: joe@ hollywoodclassics.com
CONTACTS
Pano AlaFouzo
Joe Dreier
John Flynn (USA)

ADVENTURE PICTURES
6 Blackbird Yard, Ravenscroft St., London E2 7RP.
Tel: (0207) 613 2233. FAX: (0207) 256 0842.
CONTACT
Sally Potter

AGFA GEVAERT LTD. (MOTION PICTURE DIVISION)
27 Great West Road, Brentford, Middlesex, TW8 9AX. Tel:
(020) 8231 4985. FAX: (020) 8231 4951.
www.agfa.co.uk

ALL FILMS
2nd Floor, 21, Little Portland Street, London W1W 8BT Floor,
Tel: (020) 7612 0190. FAX: (020) 7612 0199
email: all@allfilms.co.uk

AMARANTH FILM PARTNERS LTD
162-168 Regent Street, London
W1R 5TB. Tel: (0207) 439 3734. FAX: (0207) 734 6839.
CONTACTS
Paul Hill

AMY INTERNATIONAL PRODUCTIONS
Higher Eastcott Farm, PO Box 55, Minehead, Somerset, TA24
7WA Tel:(01398) 371270. FAX: (01398) 371428.
DIRECTORS
Simon MacCorkindale
Susan George

ANGLO-FORTUNATO FILMS
170 Popes Lane, London W5 4NJ. Tel: (0208) 932 7676
FAX: (0208) 932 7491.
CONTACT
Luciano Celentino

ANTELOPE
Drounces, White Chimney Row, Westbourne, Emsworth, PO10
8RS, UK Tel: (1243) 370 806. FAX: (1243) 376 985
email: mick.csaky@antelope.co.uk
www.antelope.co.uk
CONTACT
Mick Csaky

ANVIL POST PRODUCTION LTD
Denham Studios, North Orbital Road, Denham, Uxbridge,
Middlesex, UB9 5HLH Tel: (01895) 83 3522.

ARROW FILM DISTRIBUTORS
18 Walford Road, Radlett, Hertfordshire, WD7 8LE.
Tel: (1923) 85 8306. FAX: (1923) 85 9673.
email: info@arrowfilms.co.uk. www.arrowfilms.co.uk

ARTIFICIAL EYE FILM CO
14, King Street, London WC2E 8HR. Tel: (020) 7240 5353

ASIAN PICTURES UK LTD
1st Floor, 787 High Road, London E11 4QS.
Tel: (0208) 539 6529. FAX: (0208) 558 9891.

RICHARD ATTENBOROUGH PRODUCTIONS LIMITED
Beaver Lodge, Richmond Green, Richmond, Surrey, TW9 1NQ.
Tel: (0208) 940 7234. FAX: (0208) 940 4741.
DIRECTORS
Lord Richard Attenborough, CBE
The Lady Attenborough
Richard Blake
Claude Fielding

AUTOCUE LTD.
265 Merton Road, London, SW18 5JS.
Tel: (0208) 8870 0104. FAX: (0208) 874 3726

AVS ROTHMAR
Common Farm, London Road, Milton Common, Thames,
Oxfordshire OX92NU.
Tel: (01844) 27 9291. FAX: (01844) 27 9192
www.avsrothmar.co.uk

JANE BALFOUR SERVICES LTD.
Flat 2 Cresecent Mansions, 122 Elgin Crescent, London W11
2JN. Tel: (0207) 267 5392.

BASILISK COMMUNICATIONS LTD.
Registered offices: Suite 323 Kemp House, 152-160, City
Road,London, EC1V 2NX

BEAMBRIGHT LTD
Registered offices: 109a Bell Street, London, NW1 6TL

BLACK DOG FILMS
42-44. Beak Street, London, W1F 9RH. Tel: (020) 7434 0787
MANAGING DIRECTOR
Kai-Lu Hsiung

BOOM
27/29 Berwick Street, London, W1V 3RF.
Tel: (0207) 437 0136. FAX: (020) 7447 88601.

BRITISH FILM INSTITUTE
21 Stephen Street, London, W1P 1PL. Tel: (020) 7255 1444.
FAX: (020) 7436 7950.

BLUE DOLPHIN FILM DISTRIBUTORS LTD
40 Langham Street, London, W1N 5RG. Tel: (020) 7255 2494.
FAX: (020) 7580 7670. email: info@bluebdolphinfilms.com
www.bluedolphinfilms .com

REUTERS VIDEO NEWS
85 Fleet Street, London, EC4P 4AJ
Tel: (020) 7250 1122.

BRITISH LION
Working from Los Angeles office 001 818 789-9112.

BRIGHT MOVIETONEWS LTD.
Denham Media Park, Denham Nr. Uxbridge, UB9 5HQ.
Tel: (01895) 833071. FAX: (01895) 834893.
e-mail: programsales@mtone.co.uk, www.movietone.com

BRITISH SKY BROADCASTING LTD
Grant Way, Isleworth, Middx. TW7 5QD. Tel: (0207) 705 3000.
FAX: (0207) 705 3030. www.sky.com
CHIEF EXECUTIVE & MANAGING DIRECTOR
Tony Ball

BRITISH SCREEN FINANCE LTD.
10 Little Portland Street, London, W1W 7JG.

BRITISH UNIVERSITIES FILM AND VIDEO COUNCIL
77 Wells Street, London, W1T 3QH. Tel: (020) 7734 3687.
FAX: (0207) 287 3914.

BUENA VISTA PRODUCTIONS LIMITED.
3 Queen Caroline Street, Hammersmith, London, W6 9PE
Tel: (020) 8222 1000.

CALLISTER COMMUNICATIONS LTD
88 Causeway End Road, Lisburn, Co, Antrim BT28 3ED.
Tel: (028) 9267 3717.
MANAGING DIRECTOR
John Callister
The Barley Mow Centre, London, W4 4PH.
Tel: (0870) 241 6350. FAX: (02870) 241 6550.
www.cancommunicate.com
DIRECTORS
David Wooster

CAPITOL FILMS LTD.
21-23, Queensdale Place, London, W11 4SQ.
Tel: (020) 7471 6000, FAX: (020) 7471 6012

CARLTON COMMUNICATIONS PLC
Part of ITC Entertainment Group Ltd
25 Knightsbridge, London, SW1X 7R2. Tel: (0207) 663 6363.
FAX: (0207) 7663 6300

CARLTON FILM DISTRIBUTORS LTD.
35-38 Portman Square, London W1H 6NU. Tel: (020) 7224
3339. FAX: (020) 7612 7244.

CASTLE ROCK INTERNATIONAL
Registered offices: Warner House, 98, Theobalds Road,
London, WC1X 8WB.

CASTLE ROCK PRODUCTIONS LTD
Beaufort House, Tenth Floor, London EC3A 7EE.
Tel: (001) 310 285 2300

CASTLE TARGETING INTERNATIONAL
A29 Barwell Business Park, Leatherhead Road, Chessington,
Surrey KT9 2NY. Tel: (0208) 974 1021. FAX: (0208) 974 2674.

CHRYSALIS VISUAL ENTERTAINMENT
13 Bramley Road, London W10 6SP. Tel: 0207 465 6208.
FAX: (0207) 465 6159.

CINE UK LTD.
22 Chapter House, London SW1P 4NP.

CINEMA SEVEN PRODUCTIONS LTD.
C/O Pinewood Studios, Iver Heath, Bucks, SL0 0NH.
Tel: (0175) 365 1700.

CINEMA VERITY PRODUCTIONS LTD.
The Mill House, Millers Way, 1a Shepherds Bush Road,
London, W6 7NA. Tel: (020) 7460 2777.

CINTEL INTERNATIONAL LTD.
(Manufacturer of equipment for broadcast and film/tape transfer.)
Watton Road, Ware, Hertfordshire SG12 OAE.
Tel: (01920) 463 939. FAX: (01920) 460 803. www.cintel.co.uk
MANAGING DIRECTOR
Adam Welsh

CLARENDON FILM PRODUCTIONS LTD.
7 Trinity Crescent, London SW17 7AG Tel: (0208) 488 9208.
FAX: (0208) 488 3959. email: nrgmmi@aol.com

BRIAN CLEMENS ENTERPRISES LTD.
Park Farm Cottage, Ampthill, Beds. Tel: (01525) 402 215.
FAX: (01525) 402 954.

BRIMAR LTD.
Greenside Way, Middleton, Manchester M24 1SN.
Tel: (0161) 681 7072. FAX: (0161) 682 3818.
MANAGING DIRECTOR
John Heaton

COLSTAR INTERNATIONAL TELEVISION LTD
78, York Street, London W1H iDP. Tel: (020) 7625 6200.

COLUMBIA PICTURES CORPORATION LTD.
Europe House, 25 Golden Square, London W1F 9LU.
Tel: (020) 7533 1001. FAX: (020) 7533 1015.

COLUMBIA TRI STAR FILMS (IRELAND)
Segrave House, 20, Earlsfort Terrace, Dublin 2, Ireland. Tel:
(353 1) 6163200. Fax: (353 1) 6163210
MANAGING DIRECTOR
Jerry Flynn

COLUMBIA TRI STAR FILMS (UK)
Europe House, 25 Golden Square, London W1F 9LU.
Tel: (020) 7533 1001. FAX: (020) 7533 1015.

CONTEMPORARY FILMS
24 Southwood Lawn Road, Highgate, London, N6 5SF.
Tel:(0208) 340 5715.

CORI FILM DISTRIBUTORS
19 Albemarle Street, Mayfair, London, W1S 4HL.
Tel: (020) 7493 7920. FAX: (0207) 493 8088.

CURZON FILM DISTRIBUTORS LTD.
2nd Floor, 20-22 Stukely Street, London, WC2B 5LR.
Tel: (020) 7438 9502 FAX: (020) 7242 3552

DECENT EXPOSURE (TELEVISION) LTD.
The Gardens, Watchet, Somerset, Tel: (01494) 862667

DE LANE LEA SOUND CENTRE: BOOM
75 Dean Street, London, W1D 3SQ.
Tel: (020) 7439 1721, FAX: (020) 7437 0913.

DELUXE FILM SERVICES RANK/FILM SERVICES LTD
(A subsidiary of the Rank Organisation PLC. Operation of
video and broadcast facilities and video cassette duplication.)
17, Wadsworth Road, Greenford, Middlesex, UB6 7JD.
Tel: (020) 8997 8161. FAX: (020) 8991 9457.

DE WARRENNE PICTURES LTD.
2 Queen Victoria Terrace, Sovereign Court, London E19HA
Tel: (020) 7734 7648

DIGITAL FILM LAB LONDON LTD
52, St John's Street, London, EC1M 4HF. Tel: (020) 7490 4050.

DIPLOMAT FILMS LTD.
Oakdene House, Parkfield Road, Altrincham, Cheshire
WA14 2BT. Tel: (0161) 929 1603.

WALT DISNEY COMPANY LTD
3, Queen Caroline Street, Hammersmith, London W6 9PE.
Tel: (020) 8222 1000. FAX: (020) 8222 2116

DISTANT HORIZON LTD.
36-42 Whitfield Street, London, W1T 2RH.
Tel: (020) 7813 3133.

DOGSTAR UK LTD.
Registered Offices: 11, Trinity Rise, London, SW2 2QP

DOLBY LABORATORIES INC.
Interface Park, Wootton Bassett, Wiltshire, SN4 8QJ.
Tel:(01793) 842100. FAX: (01793) 842101.

DUCK LANE FILM PRODUCTIONS LTD.
8 Duck Lane, London, W1V 0HZ. Tel: (020) 7439 3912.
FAX:(020) 7437 2260.

EAST WIND FILMS
The Old Rectory, Rosary Road, Norwich, Norfolk NR1 1TA.
Tel: (01603) 628 728.

EATON FILMS
10 Holbein Mews, Lower Sloane Street, London SW1W 8NN.
Tel: (020) 7823 6173. FAX: (020) 7823 6017.

EDUCATIONAL AND TELEVISIONAL FILMS LTD.
Contact The British Film Institute, 21, Stephen Street, London,
W1T 1LN Tel: (020) 7255 1444 www.bfi.org.uk

ELECTRIC PICTURES
404 Montrose Avenue, Slouth, Berkshire, SL1 4TJ.
Tel: (01753) 568220. www.colorific.co.uk

ENGLISH FILM COMPANY LIMITED.
71 Mainridge Road, Chislehurst, Kent, BR7 6DN

ENIGMA PRODUCTIONS LTD.
29a, Tufton Street, London, SW1 3PL.
Tel: (020) 7222 5757. Fax: (020) 7222 5858

ENTERTAINMENT FILM DISTRIBUTORS LTD
Eagle House, Jermyn Street, London, SW1Y 6HB. Tel: (020)
7930 7744. FAX: (020) 7930 9399
DIRECTORS
Trevor H. Green
Nigel G. Green

EON PRODUCTIONS LTD.
138 Piccadilly, London, W1V 9FH. Tel: (0207) 493 7953.
FAX: (0207) 408 1236.
DIRECTORS
M. G. Wilson

EUROPA FILMS LTD.
Registered Office: Park House 158/160, Arthur Road,
Wimbledon Park, London, SW19.

EUSTON FILMS LTD.
Broom Road, Teddington Lock, Teddington, Middlesex, TW11
9NT. Tel:(020) 7691 6692.

EYE FILM AND TELEVISION LTD.
9-11a, Dove Street, Norwich, Norfolk NR2 1DE. Tel: (01603)
762551.

EYELINE PRODUCTIONS
10 Park View, Swillington, Leeds, West Yorkshire, LS26 8UJ.
Tel: (0113) 287 0303

F.I.L.M.S. LTD.
Registered Offices: The Courtyard, High Street, Chobam,
Surrey, GU24 8AF

FTS BONDED LIMITED
Heston Industrial Estate, Aerodrome Way, Cranford Lane,
Hounslow, Middlesex, TW5 9QN. Tel: (0208) 897 7973.
FAX:(0208) 897 7979.
SALES DIRECTOR
Kim Cowley

FILM AND GENERAL PRODUCTIONS LTD.
4 Bradbrook House, Studio Place, Kinnerton Street, London,
SW1X 8EL. Tel: (020) 7235 4495

FILM FINANCES LTD.
14-15, Conduit Street, London, W1S 2XD. Tel: (020)
7629 6557.

FILM FOUR INTERNATIONAL
124 Horseferry Road, London, SW1P 2TX. Tel: (020) 7306
8602. FAX: (020) 7306 8691
www.channel4.com

FILMARKETEERS LTD.
PO Box 31511, London, W11 3TH. Tel: (020) 7792 5531.
FAX: (020) 7229 2524.

FILM VERHUURKANTOOR DE DAM B. V.
4, Red Lion Yard, London, W1J 5JR. Tel: (0207) 233
6034. FAX: (0207) 233 6036.

THE FIRST FILM COMPANY LTD.
38 Great Windmill St, London W1D 7LU. Tel: (020) 7439 1640

FIRST INDEPENDENT FILMS LTD.
Registered Offices: The London Television Centre, Upper
Ground, London, SE1 9LT

FLASHLIGHT FILMS
10 Golden Square, London W1F 9JA. Tel: (020) 7287 4252.
FAX: (020) 7287 4232. www.flashflightfilms.com

FOCUS FILM PRODUCTIONS LTD.
The Rotunda Studio, Rear of 116-118 Finchley Road, London
NW3, 5HT. Tel: (020) 7435 9004.

FORGED FILMS
Third Floor, 8 West Newington Place, Edinburgh EH9 1QT. Tel:
(0131) 667 0230. FAX: (0131) 667 0230.

MARK FORSTATER PRODUCTIONS LTD.
27, Lonsdale Road, London NW6 6RA. Tel: (020) 7624 1123.
DIRECTOR
Mark Forstater

FOUR STAR FILMS LTD.
52 Queen Anne Street, London, W1M 9LA. Tel: (0207) 935
1186. Fax: (020) 7487 2900
DIRECTORS
N. Butt
G. Golledge

FREEDOM PICTURES
10 Rylett Crescent, Shepherd's Bush, London W12 9RL.
Tel: (0208) 743 5330.
CONTACTS
Tim White

FREEWAY FILMS LTD. RING BACK HAVE MAILED
67 George Street, Edinburgh, Midlothian EH2 2JG.
Tel: (0131) 225 3200, FAX: (0131) 225 3667. email:
100012.3206@compuserve.com
DIRECTOR
John McGrath

FRONTROOM FILMS LTD.
Registered Offices: 62, New Cavendish Street, London, W1G
8TA

JANE FULLER ASSOCIATES
10 Golden Square, London W1F 9JA. Tel: (020) 7949 2067
Fax: (020) 7734 9147

GFD COMMUNICATIONS LTD.
Unit 15a, Parkmore Industrial Estate, Long Mile Road,
Dublin 12, Ireland. Tel: (353 1) 4569500.
DIRECTORS
C. M. Anderson
R. J. Whitty

GAINSBOROUGH (FILM & TV) PICTURES LTD.
Registered Offices: 10, College Road, Harrow,
Middlesex, HA1 1DA.

GALA FILM DISTRIBUTORS LTD.
26 Danbury St., Islington, London, N1 8JU.
Tel: (020) 7226 5085.

GANNET FILMS LTD.
45, Great Peter Street, London, SW1P 3LT.
Tel: (020) 7222 7272

GENERAL SCREEN ENTERPRISES LTD.
Denham Media Park, North Orbital Road, Denham, Uxbridge,
Middlesex, UB9 5HG. Tel: (01895) 831931.
FAX: (01895) 835338.

WILLIAM GILBERT ASSOCIATES LTD.
Mulberry, Cottage, Duffield Lane, Stoke Poges, Slough,
Berkshire, SL2 4AA. Tel: (01753) 669440.

GINGER FILM PRODUCTIONS LTD.
39 41 Hanover Steps, St. Georges Fields, Albion Street,
London, W2 2YG. Tel: (0207) 402 7543.
FAX: (0207) 262 5736.
CONTACT
Brian Jackson

GLOBAL ENTERTAINMENT MANAGEMENT LTD.
22 Wadsworth Road, Perivale, Middx. NB6 7JD.
Tel: (0208) 991 5051. FAX: (0208) 998 3521.

GOLDCREST FILM AND TELEVISION LTD.
65 66 Dean Street, London, W1V 6PL.
Tel: (020) 7437 8696, FAX: (020) 7437 4448.
CHIEF EXECUTIVE
John Quested

ROBERT GOLDEN PICTURES
Registered Offices: 843 Finchley Road London NW11 8NA

GRADE COMPANY
8 Queen Street, London, W1X 7PH. Tel: (0207) 409 1925.
FAX: (0207) 408 2042.

GRANADA GROUP PLC.
London Television Centre, Upper Ground, London, SE1 9LT.
Tel: (020) 7620 1620, FAX: (020) 7451 3008.

GREEN UMBRELLA LTD.
The Production House, 147A St Michael's Hill, Bristol Co.,
Bristol, Avon BS2 8DB. Tel: (0117) 973 1729.
FAX: (0117) 946 7432. www.umbrella.co.uk
email: postmaster@umbrella.co.uk
CONTACT
Gina Shepherd
MANAGING DIRECTOR
Nigel Ashcroft

HAMMER FILM PRODUCTIONS LTD.
92, New Cavendish Street, London, W1W 6XN.
Tel: (020) 7637 2322.

HAMMER FILMS LTD
Elstree Studios, Borehamwood, Hertfordshire, WD6 1JG.
Tel: (020) 8953 1600

HAMMERWOOD FILMS
110 Trafalgar Rd. Portslade, Brighton,
East Sussex BN41 1GS.
Tel: (01273) 277333. FAX: (01273) 705451.

HANDMADE FILMS (DISTRIBUTORS) LTD.
Registered Offices: 930 High Road, London, N12 9RT

HARKNESS HALL LTD.
Gate Studios, Station Road, Borehamwood, Herts., WD6
1DQ. Tel: (0208) 953 3611. Cables: Screens, London.
Tel: (0208) 207 3657. FAX: (0208) 207 3657.

HEMDALE COMMUNICATIONS INCORPORATED UK.
10 Avenue Atudios, Sydney Close, London, SW3 6HW.
Tel: (020) 7581 9734.

JIM HENSON PRODUCTIONS
30 Oval Road, Campden, London, NW1 7DE.
Tel:(020) 7428 4000.

HERO FILMS
Alma Studios, Stratford Road, London W8 6QF.
Tel:(020) 7938 4848,

HERO FILM PRODUCTIONS LTD
23-24, Greek Street, London, W1D 4DZ. Tel (020) 7287 4060

HIGH POINT FILMS AND TELEVISION LTD.
25 Elizabeth Mews, London, NW3 4UH. Tel: (0207) 586 3686.
FAX: (0207) 586 3117.

HIT AND RUN PRODUCTIONS
3rd Floor, Alfred House, 23-24 Cromwell Road, London SW7
2LD. Tel: (020) 7590 2600, FAX: (020) 7584 5774.

HIT ENTERTAINMENT PLC
5th Floor, Maple House, 141-150 Tottenham Court Road,
London, W1T 7NF. Tel: (020) 7554 2500. FAX: (020) 7388 9321
www.hitentertainment.co.uk
CONTACTS
David King

HOLDINGS ECOSSE LTD.
2 Tweeddale Court, 14 High Street, Edinburgh, Midlothian
EH1 1TE. Tel: (0131) 557 2678. FAX: (0131) 557 4954.

HOLMES ASSOCIATES LTD
37, Redington Road, London, NW3 7QY. Tel: (020) 7813 4333.

HOT PROPERTY FILMS
27 Newman Street, London W1P 3PE. Tel: (020) 7323 9466.
FAX: (0207) 323 9467.

HOURGLASS PICTURES LTD.
117 Merton Road, Wimbledon, London SE19 1ED. Tel: (020)
8850 8786. FAX:

HUDSON FILM LTD.
24 St Leonards Terrace, London SW3 4QG.
Tel: (0207) 730 0002. FAX: (0207) 730 8033.
email: hudsonfilm@aol.com
DIRECTOR
Hugh Hudson

IDEAL WORLD PRODUCTIONS LTD.
St Georges Studios, 93-97 St Georges Road, Glasgow, G3 6JA.
Tel: (0141) 353 3222. FAX: (0141) 353 3221.

IMAGE DYNAMIC PRODUCTIONS LTD.
10A Belmont Street, London NW1 8HH.
Tel: (020) 7267 0066. FAX: (020) 7485 4255.

INDEPENDENT IMAGE FILM AND TV CO.
Teddington Studios
Broom Road, Teddington, Middlesex TW11 9NT.
Tel: (0208) 943 3555. FAX: (0208) 943 3646.
email: info@kilroy.co.uk
CHAIRMAN
Robert Kilroy-Silk

INTERNATIONAL BROADCASTING TRUST
3-7, Euston Centre, London NW1 3JG. Tel: (020) 7874 7650.

BRIAN JACKSON FILMS AND TELEVISION LTD
39 41 Hanover Steps, St. Georges Fields,
London, W2 2YG. Tel: (020) 7402 7543.

KENILWORTH FILM PRODUCTIONS LTD.
Newhouse, Mersham, Ashford, Kent TN25 6NQ.
Tel: (01233) 503 636. FAX: (01233) 502 244.
DIRECTORS
Lord Brabourne
Richard Goodwin

KENSINGTON TELEVISION LTD
Epirus Mews, London, SW6 7UP. Tel: (020) 7467 1700.

LIBERTY FILMS
Registered Offices: 3rd Floor 18, Meadonbank Terrace,
Edinburgh, EH8 7AS.

LION'S DEN COMMUNICATION MANAGEMENT LTD.
75 Valetta Road, London W3 7TG.
Tel: (020) 85766500.

LONDON FILM PRODUCTIONS LTD.
71, South Audley Street, London, W1K 1JD.
Tel: (020) 7499 7800.

LONDON INDEPENDENT PRODUCERS LTD.
52 Queen Anne Street, London, W1G 9LA.
Tel: (020) 7935 1186.

LUCIDA PRODUCTIONS LTD.
Registered Offices: Risebridge Barn Ranters Lane, Goudhurst
Cranbrook, Kent, TN17 1HN

MAINLINE PICTURES
37 Museum Street, London, WC1A 1LP. Tel: (020) 7242 5523.
FAX: (020) 7430 0170.

MAJESTIC FILMS AND TELEVISION INTERNATIONAL
Registered Offices: 12, Great James Street, London WC1N
3DR.

MAYA VISION INTERNATIONAL LTD
43 New Oxford Street, London WC1A 1BH.
Tel: (020) 7836 1113 FAX: (020) 7836 5169

MEDIA RELEASING DISTRIBUTORS LTD.
27 Soho Square, London, W1D 3QR. Tel: (0161) 9534045

MEDUSA COMMUNICATIONS LTD.
Regal Chambers, 51 Bancroft, Hitchin, Herts., SG5 1LL. Tel:
(01462) 421 818. FAX: (01462) 420 393.

CHAIRMAN
David Hodgins

MERCHANT IVORY PRODUCTIONS
46 Lexington Street, London W1P 0LP. Tel: (020) 7437 1200.
FAX: (020) 7734 1579.
CONTACTS
Ismail Merchant
James Ivory

MERSHAM PRODUCTIONS LTD.
39, Montpelier Walk, London, SW7 1JH. Tel: (020) 7589 8829.
FAX: (01233) 502 244.
DIRECTORS
Lord Brabourne
Michael John Knatchbull
Richard Goodwin

METRO TARTAN LTD.
79 Wardour Street, London, WID 6QB. Tel: (020) 7851 7042
FAX: (020) 7287 2112

METROCOLOR LONDON LTD.
91 95 Gillespie Road, Highbury, London, N5 1LS.
Tel: (020) 7326 4422, FAX: (020)7359 2353

MW ENTERTAINMENTS
48 Dean Street, London W1D 5BF. Tel: (020) 7734 7707
FAX:(020) 7734 7727. email: contact@michaelwhite.co.uk

MIRACLE COMMUNICATIONS LTD.
18, Fallowfield, Stanmore, Middlesex, HA7 3DF.
Tel: (020) 8958 8512. FAX: (020) 8958 5112

MIRAMAX FILMS (UK)
Esley House, 24-30 Great Titchfield Street, Swansea
Enterprise Park, London, W1W 8BF. Tel: (001) 2129413800.

MOVING PICTURE COMPANY LTD
127 Wardour Street, London, W1F 0NL. Tel: (020) 7434 3100.
FAX: (020) 7287 5187

MTM ARDMORE STUDIOS LTD.
Herbert Road, Bray, Co. Wicklow, Ireland. Tel: (353 1) 862971.
FAX: (353 1) 861 894.

MTV NETWORK EUROPE
United Kingdom House, 180, Oxford Street, London W1D 1DS.
Tel: (020) 7478 6000.
37 Ovington Square, London, SW3 1LJ.
www.mtveurope.com

NAMARA LTD.
27 Goodge Street, London, W1T 2LD. Tel: (020) 7636 3992.
FAX: (020) 7637 1866.

NATIONAL FILM BOARD OF CANADA
Canada House, Trafalgar Square, London, SW1Y 5BJ.
Tel: (020) 7258 6480. FAX: (0207) 258 6532.

NATIONAL SCREEN SERVICE LTD
Unit 1, Phoenix Trading Estate, Bilton Road, Greenford,
Middlesex, UB6 7DZ. Tel: (020) 8992 3210.

NATIONAL SCREEN
2 Wedgwood, Mews, 12 13 Greek Street, London, W1D 4BH.
Tel: (020) 7437 4116.
DIRECTORS
John Mahony
Brian Mcmail
Norman Darkins

OASIS FILM DISTRIBUTION
20, Rushcroft Road, London, SW2 1LA. Tel: (020) 7733 8989.
FAX: (020) 7733 8790.
MANAGING DIRECTOR
Peter Buckingham

ODEON CINEMAS LTD.
(54 Whitcomb Street, London WC2H 7DN.
Tel: (020) 7321 0404. www.odeon.co.uk

OIL FACTORY LTD.
26, Little Portland Street, London W1W 8BT.
Tel: (020) 7255 6255., FAX: (020) 7255 6277.
MANAGING DIRECTOR
John Stewart

OPEN EYE PRODUCTIONS
Registered offices: Palladium House, 1-4 Argyll Street,
London W1V 2LD.
www.openeye.co.uk

OXFORD SCIENTIFIC FILMS
Lower Road, Long Hanborough, Oxon OX29 8LL.
Tel: (01993) 881 881. FAX: (01993) 882 808.
45-49, Mortimer Street, London, W1W 8HJ.
Tel: (020) 7323 0061.

DAVID PARADINE PRODUCTIONS LTD.
First Floor, 5, St. Mary Abbots Place, Kensington, London, W8 6LS.
Tel: (020) 7371 3111. FAX: (020) 7602 0411.

PARADOGS LTD.
206 Panther House, 38 Mount Pleasant, London WC1X 0AP.
Tel: (020) 7833 1009. Fax: (020) 7486 7397

PARALLAX PICTURES
7, Denmark Street, London, WC2H 8LS.
Tel: (020) 7836 1478, FAX: (020) 7497 8062.
DIRECTOR
Ken Loach

PARAMOUNT BRITISH PICTURES LTD.
UIP House, 45 Beadon Road, Hammersmith, London, W6 0EG.
Tel: (020) 8741 9041. FAX: (020) 8563 4266.

PARAMOUNT PICTURES (UK) LTD.
UIP House, 45 Beadon Road, Hammersmith, London, W6 0EG.
Tel: (020) 8741 9041. FAX: (020) 8563 4266.

PARK ENTERTAINMENT LTD.
51, Conduit Street, London, W1S 2YZ. Tel: (020) 7434 4176.

PATHE ENTERTAINMENT LTD.
Kent House, 14-17 Market Place, Great Titchfield, London,
W1N 8AR. Tel: (020) 7323-5151. FAX: (020) 7631-3568.
www.pathe.co.uk

PBF MOTION PICTURES
The Little Pickenhanger, Tuckey Grove, Ripley, Woking,
Surrey, GU23 6JG. Tel: (01483) 225179. FAX: (01483) 224118.
www.pbf.co.uk email: image@pbf.co.uk

PEARL & DEAN CINEMAS LTD.
3, Waterhouse Square, 138-142 Holborn, London EC1N 2NY
Tel: (020) 7882 1100. FAX: (020) 7882 1111

PHOENIX FILM & TELEVISION PRODUCTIONS LTD.
Three Mills Fim Studios, Unit D2, Sugar House Lane, Stratford,
London E15 2QS. Tel: (020) 8536 3690.
email: info@phoenixmedia.co.uk

PICTURE PALACE FILMS
13, Egbert Street, London NW1 8LJ. Tel: (020) 7586 8763.
FAX: (020) 7586 9048. www.picturepalace.com

PINEWOOD STUDIOS LTD.
(A subsidiary of the Rank Organisation PLC. Film and
TV studios; goods and services.)
Pinewood Road, Iver, Buckinghamshire SL0 0NH. Tel: (01753)
651 700. Telex: 847505. FAX: (01753) 656 844.

THE PINK FILM COMPANY LTD.
8-18 Smith's Court off Great Windmill Street, London W1D
7DN. Tel: (020) 7287 5502. FAX: (020) 7287 5503.

POLYGRAM VIDEO/ UNIVERSAL PICTURES
1 Sussex House, Hammersmith, London, W6 9XS.
Tel: (020) 8910 5000
www.universalpictures.com

PORTOBELLO PICTURES LTD
42 Tavistock Road, London W11 1AW. Tel: (020) 7221 5307.

PORTOBELLO PICTURES
14-15 D'Arblay Street, London, W1F 8DZ.
Tel: (020) 72229 7420

POSH PICTURES LTD.
420 Sauchiehall Street, Glasgow, Lanarkshire G2 3JD.
Tel: (0141) 353 0456. FAX: (0141) 353 1012

POST OFFICE FILM AND VIDEO UNIT
(Archival Material) Education House, Castle Road, Stoney
Middleton,Sittingbourne, Kent, ME10 3RL. Tel: (01795) 426465.

THE PRODUCERS LIMITED
8 Berners Mews, London W1T 3AW. Tel: (0207) 636 4226.
FAX: (0207) 636 4099.
PRODUCERS
Jeanna Polley
Jenny Edwards

PROMINENT FEATURES LTD.
34, Tavistock Street, London, WC2E 7PB.
Tel: (020) 7497 1100. FAX: (020) 7497 1133.
DIRECTORS
Steve Abbott
Terry Gilliam
Eric Idle
Anne James
Terry Jones
Michael Palin

PYTHON (MONTY) PICTURES LTD.
34, Thistlewaite Road, London, E5 0QQ. Tel: (020) 8510 0348.
DIRECTORS
John Cleese
Terry Gilliam
Eric Idle
Terry Jones

PTV LIMITED
The Studios, Hornton Place, London W8 4LZ. Tel: (0207) 937
9819. FAX: (0207) 937 4326. email: production@ptvltd.com
MANAGING DIRECTOR
Trevor Rogers

QUAD PRODUCTIONS LTD.
26 Kingly Court, London W1B 5PW. Tel: (020) 7494 9191.
FAX:(020) 7494 9192.

THE RANK ORGANISATION PLC
6 Connaught Place, London, W2 2EZ. Tel: (020) 7706 1111.
FAX: (020) 7262 9886.
CHAIRMAN
Alan Cathcart
MANAGING DIRECTOR & CHIEF EXECUTIVE
Mike Smith

TAYLOR HOBSON LTD.
(Manufacturer of precision measurement equipment,
professional cine lenses.)
P.O. Box 36, Leicester, Leicestershire, LE4 9JQ.
Tel: (0116) 276 3771. FAX: (0116) 274 1350.
MANAGING DIRECTOR
Bruce Wilson

RANK FILM SERVICES LTD/DELUXE FILM SERVICES
(A subsidiary of the Rank Organisation PLC. Operation of
video and broadcast facilities and video cassette duplication.)
17, Wadsworth Road, Greenford, Middlesex, UB6 7JD.
Tel: (020) 8997 8161. FAX: (020) 8991 9457.

RECORDED PICTURE COMPANY LTD.
24, Hanway Street, London, W1T 1UH. Tel: (020) 7636 2251.
FAX: (020) 7636 2261
CHAIRMAN
Jeremy Thomas,
CHIEF EXECUTIVE
Peter Watson
www. Recordedpicture.com

REDIFFUSION FILMS LTD.
Registered offices: 124-130, Seymore Place, London, W1H
1BG

REUTERS VIDEO NEWS
85 Fleet Street, London, EC4P 4AJ
Tel: (020) 7250 1122.

ROBOT PRODUCTIONS LTD.
2-3, Duck Lane, London, W1F 0HT. Tel: (020) 7734 7773.

PETER ROGERS PRODUCTIONS LTD.
Pinewood Studios, Iver Heath, Bucks. SL0 0NH. Tel: (01753)
651 700. FAX: (01753) 656 844.
DIRECTORS
Peter Rogers
D. E. Malyon

ROMULUS COMPUTER AND VIDEO SYSTEMS.
84, Temple Chambers, Temple Avenue, London, EC4Y 0HP.
Tel: (0145) 528 5000. FAX: (0207) 352 7457.

ROMULUS FILMS LTD
Registered Offices: 214, The Chambers, Chelsea Harbour,
London, SW10 0XF

ROYAL SOCIETY FOR THE PROTECTION OF BIRDS
Film and Video Unit, The Lodge, Sandy, Beds. SG19 2DL.
Tel: (01767) 680 551. FAX: (01767) 683 262.
www.rspb.org.uk
FILM PRODUCER/MANAGER
Mark Percival

SAFIR FILMS LTD.
49 Littleton Road, Harrow, Middlesex HA1 3SY.
Tel: (020) 8423 0763. FAX: (020) 8423 7963.

SALAMANDER FILM PRODUCTIONS LTD.
Seven Pines, Lake Road, Virginia Water, Surrey, GU25 4QP.
Tel: (0134) 484 2349 FAX: (01344) 845 174.
DIRECTORS
Bryan Forbes
Nanette Newman

SAMUELSON FILMS LTD
13, Manette Street, London W1D 4AW. Tel (020) 7439 4900

SAMUELSON PRODUCTIONS LTD
23 West Smithfield, London EC1A 9HY.

SANDS FILMS STUDIO
119 Rotherhithe Street, London SE16 4NF. Tel:(0207) 231 2209. FAX: (0207) 231 2119.
www.sandsfilms.co.uk
CONTACT
Olivier Stockman

SCALA PRODUCTIONS
15, Frith Street, London W1D 4RF. Tel: (020) 7734 7060.
FAX:(020) 7437 3248. email: scalaprods@aol.com
CONTACTS
Nick Powell

SCIMITAR FILMS LTD.
219, Kensington High Street, London, W8 6BD.
Tel: (020) 7734 8385., FAX: (020) 7602 9217.
DIRECTORS
Michael Winner M.A. (Cantab)
John Fraser, M.A. (Oxon), M.Phil

SCOTT FREE ENTERPRISES LTD.
42-44. Beak Street, London, W1F 9RH. Tel: (020) 7437 3163.
FAX: (020) 7439 2478
DIRECTOR
Ridley Scott

SCREEN SCENE
Unit 2, St. Andrews Square, Bolton-Upon-Dearne, Rotherham, South Yorkshire S63 8BA. Tel: (01709) 893752

SCREEN SCENE PRODUCTIONS LTD.
41, Upper Mount Street, Dublin 2, Ireland.
Tel: (353 1) 661 1501, FAX: (353 1) 661 0491
Email: info@screenscene.ie

SEPTEMBER FILMS LTD.
Glen House, Glenthorne Road, London W6 0PP.
Tel: (020) 8563 9393. FAX: (020) 8741 7214.
email: september@septemberfilms.com
MANAGING DIRECTOR
David Green

SEVENTH HEAVEN PRODUCTIONS LTD.
Registered offices: 18, Upper Grosvenor Street, London, W1X 9PB.

HASAN SHAH FILMS LTD.
153 Burnham Towers, Adelaide Road, London NW3 3JN.
Tel: (020) 7722 2419. FAX: (020) 7483 0662.
PRODUCER AND DIRECTOR
Hasan Shah

SHART BROS LTD.
52 Lancaster Road, London N4 4PR. Tel: (0207) 263 4435.
FAX: (0207) 436 9233.
PRODUCER
Patrick Shart

SHEPPERTON FILM STUDIOS
Studios Road, Shepperton, Middx. TW17 0QD.
Tel: (01932) 562 611. FAX: (01932) 568 989.

SILVER LIGHT (SCI-FI) LTD
72, Staunton Raod, Oxford, Oxfordshire, OX3 7TP
Tel: (01865) 744451

SILVER PRODUCTION (LONDON) LTD.
29 Castle Street, Salisbury, Wiltshire SP1 1TT.
Tel: (01722) 336221. FAX: (01722) 336 227.
email: info@silver.co.uk. www.silver-productions.co.uk

SKREBA FILMS LTD.
2nd Floor. 7, Denmark Street, London, WC2H 8LZ.
Tel: (020) 7240 7149.

SKYLINE FILMS
P.O. Box 8210, London W4 1WH. Tel: (0208) 354 2236. FAX: (0208) 354 2219. email: sky@easynet.co.uk
MANAGING DIRECTOR
Steve Clark-Hall

SMART EGG PICTURE SERVICES
11-12, Barnard Mews, Barnard Road, London, SW11 1QU.
Tel: (020) 7350 4554.

SPECIFIC FILMS
25 Rathbone Street, London W1T 1NG. Tel: (020) 7580 7476.
FAX: (020) 7434 2676. email: info@specificfilms.com
PRODUCERS
Michael Hamlyn
Christian Routh

STARFIELD PRODUCTIONS
50 Chiswick High Road, London W4 1SZ.
Tel: (020) 8995 8060. FAX: (020) 8994 1113.

STERLING PICTURES LTD.
Registered Offices: 8, Great James Street, London WC1N 3DA
STERLING PRODUCTIONS
1, Steadham Place, London WC1A 1HU. Tel: (07768) 551532

SYNDICATE PICTURES LTD.
Registered Offices: 62, Wilson Street, London, EC2A 2BU

TALISMAN FILMS LTD.
5 Addison Place, London W11 4RJ. Tel: (020) 7603 7474.
FAX: (020) 7602 7422. email: email@talismanfilms.com
PRODUCERS
Richard Jackson Andrew Lawton

TKO COMMUNICATIONS LTD.
P.O. Box 130, Hove, East Sussex, BN3 6QU.
Tel: (01273) 550 088. FAX: (01273) 540 969.
DIRECTORS
J. S. Kruger
R. Kruger

TARGET INTERNATIONAL LTD.
A 29 Barwell Business Pk., Leatherhead Road, Chessington Castle, Surrey KT9 2NY. Tel: (0208) 974 1021.
FAX: (0208) 974 2674.
CHAIRMAN
Terry Shand
MANAGING DIRECTOR
Geoffrey Kerpin

TARTAN VIDEO LTD.
5, Wardour Street, London, WCD 6PB. Tel: (020) 7494 1400
FAX: (020) 7439 1922.
www.tartanvideo.com
CONTACT
Hamish McAlpine

TECHNICOLOR LTD.
(Subsidiary of Thompson Multimedia.)
Bath Road, West Drayton, Middlesex, UB7 0DB.
Tel: (020) 8759 5432. FAX: (0208) 897 2666.
www.technicolor.com
MANAGING DIRECTOR & CEO
Ashley Hopkins

THIN MAN FILMS
9 Greek Street, London W1D 4DQ. Tel: (020) 7734 7372.
FAX:(020) 7287 5228.
PRODUCER
Simon Channing-Williams
DIRECTOR
Mike Leigh

THE 39 PRODUCTION COMPANY LTD.
The Estate Offices, Knebworth House, Knebworth, Hertfordshire SG3 6PY. Tel: (01438) 814150. FAX: (01438) 816909.

TOTEM PRODUCTIONS
8 York Mansions, Prince of Wales Drive, London SW11 4DN.
email: 101505.2156@compuserve.com
CONTACT
Francis Gerard

TRING ENTERTAINMENTS
Registered Offices: 10, College Road, Harrow, Middx, HA1 1DA

TWENTIETH CENTURY FOX PRODUCTIONS LTD.
20th Century House, 31 32 Soho Square, London, W1D 3AP.
Tel: (020) 7437 7766. FAX: (020) 7434 2170.
www.fox.co.uk
DIRECTORS
S. Moore (LA Based)

TWICKENHAM FILM STUDIOS LTD.
The Barons, St. Margarets, Twickenham, Middlesex, TW1 2AW.
Tel: (020) 8607 8888. FAX: (020) 8607 8889.
www.twickenhamstudio
CONTACT
G. Humphreys

TYRO PRODUCTIONS
The Coach House, 20 A Park Road, Teddington, Middlesex TW11 0AQ. Tel: (0208) 943 4697.

UGC UK LTD.
Power Road Studios, Power Road, Chiswick, London, W4 5PY
Tel: (020) 8987 5000. FAX: (020) 8987 2301.
www.ugccinemas.co.uk
MANAGING DIRECTOR
Margaret Taylor

UNITED ARTISTS CORPORATION LTD.
UIP House, 45 Beadon Road, London, W6 0EG.
Tel: (020) 8741 9041, FAX: (0208) 748 8990
www.uip.com and www.uipcorp.com
PRESIDENT & CEO
Stewart Till
SENIOR V.P., GENERAL COUNSEL
Andrew Cripps

UNITED CINEMAS INTERNATIONAL UK LTD.
Lee House, 90 Great Bridgewater Street, Manchester, MI 5JW.
Tel: (0161) 455 4000. FAX: (0161) 455 4079.
MANAGING DIRECTOR
Steve Knibbs

UNITED INTERNATIONAL PICTURES UK
12, Golden Square, Soho, London, W1F 9JA
Tel: (020) 7534 5200. FAX: (020) 7534 5201

UNITED VISUAL ARTIST LTD
Unit 309, The Bon Marche Centre, 241-251, Fernadale Road,
London SW9 8BJ. Tel: (020) 7978 8405

UNIVERSAL PICTURES INTERNATIONAL
76, Oxford Street, London, W1D 1BS. Tel: (020) 7307 1300
Fax: (020) 7307 1301. www.universalpictures.com

UNIVERSAL PICTURES VISUAL PROGRAMMING
1 Sussex Place, Hammersmith, London, W6 9EA. Tel: (020)
8910 5000 Fax: (020) 8742 5579. www.universalpictures.com

VICTOR MITCHELL FILM & TELEVISION SERVICES
9, Hindes Road, Harrow, HA1 1SH. Tel: (01553) 774745.

VIRGIN CINEMAS GROUP LTD.
120, Camden Hill Road, London, W8 7AR.
Tel: (020) 7229 1282.

VIVA FILMS LIMITED
C/O NLPAC, 76 St James Lane, London N10 3DF.
Tel: (0208) 444 5064. FAX: (020) 8444 1074.
email: vivafilms@dial.pipex.com
CONTACT
John Goldshmidt

WALPORT INTERNATIONAL LTD.
Registered Offices: Unit 2, Aerodrome Way, Cranford Lane,
Hounslow, Middx, TW5 9QB

WANDERING STAR LIMITED
Strode Manor Farm, Netherbury, Blandford Forum, Dorset
DT11. Tel: (01258) 881178. FAX: (01258) 881170.

WARNER BROS DISTRIBUTORS LTD.
98, Theobald's Road, Holborn, London, WC1X 8WB.
Tel: (020) 7984 5000.FAX: (020) 7984 5201.
www.warnerbros.co.uk
DIRECTORS
R. Fox
C. Young
E. Savat
W. Duband
C. Lima

**WARNER BROS OPERATIONAL DIVISION
(TELEVISION AND VIDEO)**
98, Theobald's Road, Holborn, London, WC1X 8WB. Tel: (020)
7984 5000,, FAX: (020) 7984 5201. www.warnerbros.co.uk

WARNER BROS PRODUCTION LTD.
Warner Suite, Pinewood Studios, Iver Heath, Bucks., SL0
0NH. Tel: (01753) 654 545. FAX: (01753) 55703
MANAGING DIRECTOR
R. D. Button
DIRECTORS
E. H. Senat
A. R. Parsons

WELBECK FILM DISTRIBUTORS LTD.
52 Queen Anne Street, London, W1G 9LA.
Tel: (020) 7935 1186. FAX: (020)7 487 2900
DIRECTORS
Mrs. J.E. Thomas

WORKING TITLE FILMS LTD.
76, Oxford Street, London, W1 1BS. Tel:(020) 7307 3000.
FAX: (020) 7307 3002. www.workingtitlefilms.co.uk
DIRECTORS
Tim Bevan
Eric Fellner

WORLD FILM SERVICES LTD.
Eagle House, 50 Marshall Street, Palmers Green, London,
W1F 9BQ. Tel: (020) 7493 3045, Fax: 758 7000.

**WORLDMARK PRODUCTION COMPANY LTD.
OPERATING AS CAN COMMUNICATE**
The Barley Mow Centre, London, W4 4PH.
Tel: (0870) 241 6350. Fax: (02870) 241 6550.
www.cancommunicate.com
DIRECTORS
David Wooster

WORLD PRODUCTIONS LTD.
Eagle House, 50, Marshall Street, London W1F 9BQ.
Tel: (0207) 734 3536, FAX: :(020) 758 7000. www.world-
productions.com

WORLD WIDE GROUP LTD.
21 25 St. Anne's Court, London, W1V 3AW.
Tel: (020) 7434 1121. FAX: (020) 7734 0619.
CONTACTS
R. King
R. Townsend
C. Courtenay Taylor

CHRISTOPHER YOUNG FILMS LTD.
56, Palmerston Place, Edinburgh, Midlothian, London, EH12 5AY.

ZENITH GROUP
43 45 Dorset Street, London W1H 4AB.
Tel: (020) 7224 2440, FAX: (020) 7224 3194.
www.zenith-entertainment.co.uk
DIRECTOR OF PRODUCTION
Scott Meek.

ZEPHYR FILMS LTD.
33, Percy Street, London W1T 2DF. Tel: (020) 7255 3555.
FAX: (020) 7255 3777. email: user@zephyrfilms.co.uk
PRODUCER
Philip Robertson
MANAGING DIRECTOR
Chris Curleng

ANIMATION

A FOR ANIMATION LTD.
Registered Offices: 52, Old Market Street, Bristol, Avon, BS2 0ER

AARDMAN ANIMATIONS
Gas Ferry Rd., Bristol, Avon BS1 6UN. Tel: (0117) 984
8485. FAX: (0117) 984-8486. www.aardman.com
MANAGING DIRECTOR
Sonia Davies

THE ANIMATION PARTNERSHIP LTD.
13-14, Golden Square, London W1F 9JF. Tel: (020) 7636 3300.
FAX: (020) 7580 9153
CONTACT
Carl Gover

THE ANIMATION PEOPLE LTD.
22, Churchmead Close, East Barnet, Barnet Hertfordshire,
EN4 8UY. Tel/Fax: (020) 8449 1601.
www.animationpeople.co.uk
CONTACT
Brian Larkin

ANTICS WORKSHOP
42 Champion Hill, Camberwell, London SE5 8BS.
Tel/FAX: (0207) 274 0135.

BERMUDA SHORTS LTD.
1 Lower John St., London W1F 9DT. Tel: (020) 7437
7335. FAX: (0207) 437 7334.
www.bermudashorts.com
CONTACT
Julie Pye

BOLEXBROTHERS LTD.
3 Brunel Lock Development, Cumberland Basin, Bristol
BS1 6SE. Tel: (0117) 985 8000. FAX: (0117) 985 8899.
www.bolexbrothers.co.uk mail@bolexbrothers.co.uk
CONTACT
Andy Leighton

BROOKE EDWARDS ANIMATION
13, Risborough Street, London SE1 OHF. Tel: (020) 7620 2595.
FAX: (020) 7620 2596. email:
www.banimation.com
CONTACT
Chris Forrester

THE CANNING FACTORY
11b Albert Place, London W8 5PD. Tel: (020) 7937 1136.
FAX: (0207) 938 1896. email:
canningfactory@online.rednet.co.uk
DIRECTOR
Kate Canning - Check

CARTWN CYMRU
Ben Jenkins Court, 19a High Street, Llandaf, Cardiff, South
Glamorgan CF52. Tel: (0129) 2057 5999.

CELL LTD.
Registered offices: Hallsteads, Dove Holes, Derbyhshire, SK17 8BL

THE COMPUTER FILM COMPANY
NOW TRADING AS FRAME STORE CFC
19-23 Wells St., London W1P 3PQ . Tel: (020) 7344 8000.
FAX: (020) 7344 8001.
www.framestore-cfc.com
MANAGING DIRECTOR
William Sargent

CONCEPT MEDIA LTD.
Orwell Place, 172, Tunbridge Rd, Wateringbury Kent ME18
5NS., Tel: (01622) 817 177. Fax: (01622) 817 178
Email: enquiries@concept-media.co.uk
CONTACT
Denise Peckham

TONY CUTHBERT PRODUCTIONS
7A Langley St., London WC2H 9JA. Tel: (020) 7437 8884.
FAX: (020) 7734 6579.
www.tonycuthbert.com
CONTACT
Saunder Satterlee

WALT DISNEY PRODUCTIONS LTD.
3, Queen Caroline Street. Hammersmith, London W6 9PE.
Tel: (020) 8222 1000. FAX: (020) 8222 2795

EALING ANIMATION
90, Brandon Street, London SE17 1AL. Tel: (020) 7358 4820.
CONTACT
Richard Randolf

EAST ANGLIAN PRODUCTIONS
POBox 7336 Frinton-on-Sea, Essex CO13 0WZ
Tel: (01255) 676 252.
CONTACT
Ray Anderson

EDITPOINT VIDEO SERVICES
Medway Centre, Enterprise Close, Rochester, Kent, ME2 4LY
Tel: (01634) 720321.

FAIRWATER FILMS LTD.
Registered offices: 17, St Andrews Crescent, Cardiff, South
Glamorgan, CF1 3DB.

ESPRESSO ANIMATION
100, Oxford Street, London W1D 1LN. Tel: (020) 7637 9090 /
(020) 7637 9339. www.expressoanimation.com
DIRECTOR
Philip Vallentin

FLICKS FILMS LTD.
101 Wardour St., London W1F OUN. Tel: (020) 7734 4892.
FAX: (0207) 287 2307. www.flicksfilms.com
CONTACT
Mirella Barrow

FAMOUS FLYING FILMS LTD
4, Haven Green, London W5 2UU. Tel:
(020) 8998 9970. FAX: (020) 89989970.
CONTACT
David Johnson

FRAMELINE
33-34 Rathbone Pl., London W1T 1JQ. Tel: (020) 7636 1303.
FAX: (020) 7436 8878.

FRAME STORE CFC
19-23 Wells St., London W1P 3PQ . Tel: (020) 7344 8000.
FAX: (020) 7344 8001. www.framestore-cfc.com
MANAGING DIRECTOR
William Sargent

BOB GODFREY FILMS
199 Kings Cross Rd., London WC1X 9DB. Tel: (020) 7278
5711. FAX: (020) 7278 6809.
CONTACT
Bob Godfrey

COG
27, Beethoven Street, London W10 4LG. Tel: (0208) 964
0234. FAX: (0208) 968 7710. www.cogonline.co.uk
CONTACT
Julian Roberts

GRIFFILMS LTD
Gronant Buildings, 14, South Penralt, Caernarfon, Gwynedd
LL55 1NS. Tel: (01286) 676678. FAX: (01286) 676577.
email: mail@grissilms.com
DIRECTOR
Hywel Griffith

HIBBERT RALPH ANIMATION LTD.
10 D'Arblay St., London W1F 8DZ. Tel: (020) 7494 3011.
FAX: (020) 7494 0383. www.hibbert-ralph.co.uk
email: info@hra-online.com
CONTACTS
Claire Tredgett

HELLZAPOPPIN PICTURES LTD
2 Eaton Crescent, Clifton, Bristol, Co Bristol BS8 2EJ. Tel:
(0117) 923 7581. FAX: (0117) 923 7810.

HONEYCOMB ANIMATION STUDIOS
Berkeley House, 27, High Street, Cullompton, Devon EX15
1AB, Tel: (01884) 839202., FAX: (01884) 839212
CONTACT
Gareth Conway

ICE PICS
111A Wardour St., London W1F OUN. Tel: (020) 7437 3505.
FAX: (020) 7287 0393.
CONTACT
Mike Davis

KING ROLLO FILMS
Dolphin Court, High Street, Honiton Devon EX14 1HT.
Tel: (01404) 45218 FAX: (01404) 45328.
CONTACT
Jeanette Archer

KLACTOVEESEDSTEENE ANIMATIONS
NOW OPERATING AS OSCAR GRILLOT & TED ROCKLEY ANIMATIONS
11, Gordon Road, London W5, 2AD.
Tel: (020) 8991 6978
CONTACTS
Oscar Grillot
Ted Rockley

LEEDS ANIMATION WORKSHOP
45 Bayswater Row, Leeds LS8 5LF. Tel: (0113) 248 4997.
FAX: (0113) 248 4997.
www.leedsanimation.demon.co.uk
CONTACT
Jane Bradshaw

LIQUID TELEVISION GRAPHICS LTD
1-2 Portland Mews, Soho, London W1F 8JF.
Tel: (020) 7437 2623. FAX: (020) 7437 2618. www.liquid.co.uk
email: info@liquid.co.uk

MATTES AND MINIATURES
Bray Studios, Water Oakley, Windsor, Berks SL4 5UG. Tel:
(01628) 506626, FAX: (01628) 506702.
www.mattesandminatures.com
CONTACT
Leigh Took
Ben Hall

MELENDEZ FILMS
44, Newman Street, London W1T 1QD.
Tel: (020) 7323 5273.
CONTACT
Stephen Melendez

THE MILL
40-41 Great Marlborough St., London W1V 1DA.
Tel: (020) 7287 4041. FAX: (020) 7287 8393.
CONTACTS
Dave Levy
Will Cohen

ONE
71 Dean St., London W1D 3FF. Tel: (020).7439 2730.
FAX: (020) 7734 3331

HILL ROBERTS FILMS OPERATING AS COG
27, Beethoven Street, London W10 4LG. Tel: (0208) 964
0234. FAX: (0208) 968 7710. www.cogonline.co.uk
CONTACT
Julian Roberts

RAY MOORE ANIMATION LTD.
Animation Centre, 113 Humber Rd., London SE3 7LW.
Tel: (020)8 853 1164. FAX: (020) 8853 3043.
CONTACT
Ray Moore

NISSELL LTD.
Maxted Close, Hemel Hempstead, Herts HP2 7BS.
Tel: (01422) 69101.

OSCAR GRILLOT & TED ROCKLEY ANIMATIONS
11, Gordon Road, London W5, 2AD. Tel: (020) 8991 6978
CONTACTS
Oscar Grillot
Ted Rockley

PASSION PICTURES LTD.
33 Rathbone Place, London, W1T 1JN. Tel: (020) 7323
9933. FAX: (020) 7323 9030, www.passion-pictures.com
CONTACT
Sian Rees

PEARCE STUDIOS LTD
NOW OPERATING AS ROD LORD
Old Lodge Farm, Coningsby Lane, Fifield, Maidenhead, Berks
SL6 2PF. Tel: (01628) 627032. www.rodlord.com
CONTACT
Rod Lord

PICASSO PICTURES LTD.
9-11, Broadwick Street., London W1F 0DB. Tel: (020) 7437
9888. FAX: (020) 7437 9040. www.picassopictures.com
CONTACT
Jane Bolton

PIZAZZ PICTURES NOW OPERATING AS STUDIO AKA
30 Berwick St., London W1S 8RH. Tel: (0207) 434 3581. FAX:
(0207) 437 2309.
www.studioaka,co.uk

CONTACT
Pam Dennis

PUPPET VISUALS
60 Catton Chase, Old Catton, Norwich, Norfolk NR6 7AS.
Tel: (01603) 482513.
CONTACT
Jan King

RAGDOLL PRODUCTIONS
11 Chapel Street, Stratford upon Avon, Warwickshire CV 37
6EP. Tel: (01789) 262 772 FAX: (01789) 262 773

ROCKY ROAD PRODUCTIONS LTD.
9 Wellington Road, Wimbledon Park London SW19 8EQ.
Tel: (020) 8947 2404. FAX: (020) 8947 2404.
CONTACT
John Lee

ROD LORD
Old Lodge Farm, Coningsby Lane, Fifield, Maidenhead, Berks
SL6 2PF. Tel: (01628) 627032. www.rodlord.com
CONTACT
Rod Lord

SIMONETTI PRODUCTIONS LTD.
18 Leighton Crescent, Kentish Town London NW5 2QY. Tel:
(0207) 284 1164. FAX: (0207) 284 1392.
MANAGER
Gina Heffler

SIRIOL PRODUCTIONS
3, Mountstuart Square, Cardiff, South Glamorgan, CF10 5EE.
Tel: (029) 2048 8400

SOHO 601 OPERATING AS ONE
71 Dean St., London W1D 3FF. Tel: (020) 7439 2730.
FAX: (020) 7734 3331.

SOHO 601 DIGITAL PRODUCTIONS
142, Wardour Street, London W1F 8ZR. Tel: (020) 7791 2492

STARDUST PICTURES LIMITED
Registered offices: 335, City Road, London, EC1V 1LJ

BRIAN STEVENS ANIMATED FILMS LTD.
11 Charlotte Mews, London W1P 1LN. Tel: (020) 7637 0535.
CONTACT
Brian Stevens

STUDIO AKA
30 Berwick St., London W1F 8RH. Tel: (0207) 434 3581. FAX:
(0207) 437 2309. www.studioaka,co.uk
CONTACT
Pam Dennis

RICHARD TAYLOR CARTOON FILMS
76 Dukes Ave., London N10 2QA. Tel: (0208) 444 7547.
FAX: (0208) 444 7218.
CONTACT
Richard Taylor

TJFX DEPARTMENT
NOW OPERATING AS THE MILL DONE
40-41 Great Marlborough St., London W1V 1DA. Tel: (0207)
287 4041. FAX: (0207) 287 8393.
CONTACTS
Dave Levy
Will Cohen

TRIFFIC FILMS
6, St Pauls Court, St., Stony Stratford, Milton Keynes, Bucks
MK11 1LAJ. Tel: (01908) 261 234. FAX: (01908) 263 050.
www.trifficfilms.co.uk
CONTACT
Tim Searle

TV CARTOONS
39 Grafton Way, London W1T 5DA. Tel: (020) 7388 2222.
FAX: (020) 7383 4192.
CONTACTS
John Coastes

WARDOUR MOTION PICTURES LTD.
Flint Studios Knatts Valley Nr Brands Hatch, Sevenoaks, Kent
TN15 6XY. Tel & FAX: (0147) 485 3538
CONTACT
Mike Sutton

WOODLAND ANIMATIONS LTD
(NOW OPERATING AS ENTERTAINMENT RIGHTS)
Colet Court, 100 Hammersmith Road, London W6 7JP.
Tel: (020) 8762 6200. FAX: (020) 762 6299
www.entertaimentrights.com
CONTACT
Jane Smtih

Costume Suppliers

ACADEMY COSTUMES
50 Rushworth Street, London SE1 0RB. Tel: (020) 7620 0771
FAX: (0207) 928 6287. www.academycostumes.com
PRODUCTION INFORMATION
Adrian Gwillym
EMPLOYMENT INFORMATION
Andrew Allen

ANGELS & BERMANS
119, Shaftsbury Avenue, London, WC2H 8AE.
Tel: (020) 7836 5678.FAX: (020) 7240 9527.
email: fun@fancydress.com, www.fancydress.com
HEAD OFFICE:
Garrick Road, London NW9 6AA. Tel: (020) 8202 2244
CONTACTS
Tim Angel
Jonathan Lipman

THE ANTIQUE CLOTHING SHOP
282 Portobello Rd., London W10 5TE. Tel: (020) 8964 4830.
CONTACT
Sandy Stagg

ARMS & ARCHERY
The Coach House, Thrift Lane, London Road, Ware, Herts,
SG12 9QU. Tel: (01920) 460 335. FAX: (01920) 461 044.
email: tgou104885@aol.com
CONTACT
Terry Goulden

BBC COSTUME & WIGS
172-178 Victoria Road, London W3 6UL. Tel: (020) 8576 1761
FAX: (020) 8993 7040. www.bbcresources.com/costumewig
Email: or wigs@bbc.co.uk
CONTACTS
Hilary Swift
Philippa Devon

THE BUSINESS
Unit F36, The Acton Business Centre, School Road, London
NW10 6DT. Tel: (0208) 963 0668. FAX: (0208) 838 0867.
email: bronwen@costume-rental.com
CONTACT
Bronwen Nolan

CARLO MANZI RENTALS
32 33 Liddell Road, London, NW6 2EW. Tel: (0207) 625 6391.
FAX: (0207) 625 5386.
CONTACT
Carlo Manzi

CLANCAST CONTRACTS LTD
48, Shaw Street, Govan, Glasgow,
Lanarkshire G51 3BL. Tel: (0141) 440 2345
FAX: 0141 445 5599.
www.grp.co.uk
CONTACT
Karen Hogg

COSPROP LTD.
26-28 Rochester Place, London, NW1 9JR. Tel: (020) 7485
6731. FAX: (020) 7485 5942. www.cosprop.co.uk
email: enquires@cospop.co.uk
CONTACT
Bernie Chapman

THE COSTUME STUDIO
Montgomery House, 159-161 Balls Pond Rd., Islington N1
4BG Tel: (020) 7275 9614/7388 4481. FAX: (020) 837 6576
www.thecostumestudioltd.co.uk
email: costume.studio@easynet.co.uk
DIRECTORS
R A Griffiths
R C Griffiths

M.B.A. COSTUMES
Good Year House, 52-56 Osnaburgh St., London NW1 3ND.
Tel: (020) 7388 4994. FAX: (0207) 383 2038.
www.handembroidery.com
CONTACTS
Alistair McCloed
Pearce McCloed

PULLONS PM PRODUCTIONS
St. Georges Studio
Wood End Lane, Coventry, West Midlands, CV7 8DF.
Tel: (01676) 541 390. FAX: (01676) 542 438.

ROYAL NATIONAL THEATRE COSTUME HIRE
Chichester House, Kennington Park Estate, London, SW9 6DE.
Tel: (020) 7587 0404

ROYAL NATIONAL THEATRE PROPS & FURNITURE HIRE
Salisbury House, kennington Park Estate, London SW9 6DE.
Tel: (020) 7820 1358. FAX: (020) 7820 9324.

ROYAL SHAKEPEARE COMPANY
Royal Shakespeare Theatre, Waterside, Sratford Upon Avon,
Warks CV37 6BB. Tel: (01789) 296655. FAX: (01789) 205920.
 email: info@rsc.org.uk
COSTUME HIRE
Alison Mitchell
TORBAY COSTUME HIRE
31-35 Market St., Torquay, Devon TQ1 3AW. Tel: (01803) 211
930. FAX: (01803) 293 554.
CONTACT
Lionel Digby

EDITING SERVICES

124 FACILITIES
124-126, Horseferry Rd, London SW1P 2TX.
Tel: (020) 7306 8040. FAX: (020) 7306 8041. www.124.co.uk
CONTACTS
Tony Chamberlain

ASCENT-MEDIA CAMDEN
13, Hawley Crescent, Camden Town, London, NW1 8NP.
Tel: (0207) 284 7900. FAX: (020) 7284 1018.
www.ascent-media.co.uk
CONTACTS
Sam Web
Michael Ashley
Rachel Bernard

BBC RESOURCES SCOTLAND
Broadcasting House, Glasgow G12 8DG.
Tel: (08700) 100 222/ 100 123.
Email: www.bbc.co.uk/scotland

BLUE POST PRODUCTION
58 Old Compton St., London W1D 4NU. Tel: (020) 7437 2626.
FAX: (020) 7439 2477.
CONTACT
Samantha Greenwood

CAPTIAL FX
Denham Media Park, North Orbital Road, Denham, Uxbridge,
Middlesex UB9 5HG. Tel: (01895) 831 931.
FAX: (01895) 835 338. www.capital-fx.co.uk
CONTACT
Rick Corne

CAPITAL TELEVISION
13 Wandsworth Plain, London SW18 1ET. Tel: (020) 8874
0131. FAX: (020) 8877 0234. www.capitalstudios.com
CONTACT
Clare Phillips

CHRYSALIS TODD-AO EUROPE
NOW OPERATING AS ASCENT-MEDIA CAMDEN
13, Hawley Crescent, Camden Town, London, NW1 8NP. Tel:
(0207) 284 7900. FAX: (020) 7284 1018.
www.ascent-media.co.uk
CONTACTS
Sam Web
Michael Ashley
Rachel Bernard

CLIPPER PICTURES
65, Valiant, Vicarage Crescent, London SW11 31X. Tel:
(020) 7228 2657. email: info@clipperpictures.co.uk
www.clipperpictures.co.uk

CLOCKHOUSE
34 Hanway Street, London W1T 1UW. Tel: (0207) 436 7702
FAX: (0207) 436 7679. www.clockhouse.co.uk
CONTACT
Graham Hobbs
Tony Fox

CUT & RUN LTD
93, Wardour Street, London W1F OUD. Tel: (020) 7432 9696.
FAX: (020) 7434 2277. email: info@cutandrun.co.uk
CONTACT
Steve Gandolfi

EDIT HIRE POST PRODUCTION SERVICES
11, Wardour Mews. London W1F 8AN, Tel: (020) 7529 9900.

EDV PRODUCTIONS
Canlot Studios, 222 Kensal Road, London W10 5BN
Tel: (020) 8968 70000 www.edv.com

THE FILM EDITORS
6-10 Lexington St., London W1F OLB. Tel: (020) 7439 8655.
FAX: (020) 7437 0409, www.thefilmeditors.co.uk
CONTACT
Pam Power

FILM MEDIA SERVICES LTD.
Unit 8, Space Waye, North Feltham Trading Est., Feltham,
Middlesex TW14 0TH. Tel: (0208) 890 8780. 020 87517222
www.ids-fms.co.uk
CONTACT
Brian Gilmore

FINAL CUT LTD
55-57 Great Marlbourough St., London W1F
7JX. Tel: (0207) 556 6300. FAX: (0207) 287 2824.
CONTACT
Rick Russell

FOUNTAIN TELEVISION PROPERTIES
Venture House, Davis Road, Chessington, Surrey KT9 1TT.
Tel: (020)8794 1234. FAX: (020) 8974 1622.

400 COMPANY
Unit B3, Askew Crescent Workshops, 2a Askew Crescent,
Shepherd's Bush, London W12 9DP. Tel: (020) 8746 1400.
FAX: (0208) 746 0847. www.the400.co.uk
email: info@the400.co.uk
CONTACT
Mark Sloper

FRONTIER POST
66-67 Wells Street, London W1T 3PY. Tel: (020) 7291 9191.
FAX: (020) 7291 9199. www.frontierpost.co.uk

FACILITY DIRECTOR
Beth Jefferyes

GENERAL SCREEN ENTERPRISES
NOW OPERATING AS CAPTIAL FX
Denham Media Park, North Orbital Road, Denham, Uxbridge,
Middlesex UB9 5HG. Tel: (01895) 831 931.
FAX: (01895) 835 338. www.capital-fx.co.uk
CONTACT
Rick Corne

GOLDCREST POST PRODUCTION FACILITIES
36-44 Brewer Street, London W1F 9TA. Tel: (020) 7437 7972.
FAX: (020) 7437 5402. www.goldcrest.org
CONTACTS
Peter McCrae
Susie Edmunds

HOLLOWAY FILM & TELEVISION LTD
68-70 Wardour St., London W1F 0TB. Tel: (020) 7494 0777.
FAX: (020) 7494 0309.
CONTACT
David Holloway

LONDON POST
34-35 Dean St., London W1D 4PR. Tel: (020) 7439 9080. FAX:
(020) 7434 0714. www.londonpost.co.uk
CONTACT
Verity Laing

THE LONDON STUDIOS
The London Television Centre, Upper Ground, London SE1
9LT. Tel: (020) 7261 3473. FAX: (020) 7261 3815.
CONTACT
Charlotte Bernard

THE MILL
40-41 Great Marlborough St., London W1V 1DA. Tel: (020)
7287 4041. FAX: (020) 7287 8393. www.mill.co.uk
HEAD OF PRODUCTION
Derryn Clarke

MOLINARE
34 Fouberts Pl., London W1F 7PX. Tel: (020) 7478 7000.
FAX: (0207) 734 6813. www.molinare.co.uk
CONTACTS
Kate George

NATS POST PRODUCTION
10 Soho Square, London W1D 3NT. Tel: (020) 7287 9900.
FAX: (0207) 287 8636. www.nats.ltd.uk
CONTACT
Gary Williams

PANTHER POST PRODUCTION
Unit 13-14, Barley Shots Business Park, London W10
5YG. Tel: (0208) 962 9780. FAX: (0208) 962 9781.
CONTACTS
Craig Golding

PARALLAX INDEPENDENT LTD.
7 Denmark St, London WC2H 8LS. Tel: (020) 7836 1478.
FAX: (0207) 497 8062.
CONTACT
Sally Hibbin

PINEWOOD STUDIOS LTD.
Pinewood Road., Iver, Bucks SL0 0NH. Tel: (01753) 651 700.
FAX: (01753) 656 844. www.pinewood-studios.co.uk
CONTACT
David Whight

QUANTEL LTD.
31, Turnpike Road, Newbury, Berks RG14 2NX. Tel: (01635)
48222. FAX: (01635) 815815.www.quantel.com
CONTACT
Roger Thornton

THE QUARRY
26-28 Brewer St., London W1R 3FW Tel: (0207) 437 4961.
FAX: (0207) 437 1491. www.the-quarry.co.uk
CONTACT
Tor Allen

RED POST PRODUCTION
Hammersly House, 5-8 Warwick Street, London W1B 5LX.
Tel: (020) 7439 1449. FAX: (020) 7439 1339.
email: production@red.co.uk
PRODUCER
Annika Ahl
MANAGING DIRECTOR
Stephen Luther

SHEARS POST PRODUCTION SERVICES NOW OPERAT
Warwick House, Shapone Pl., Dean St., London W1D 3BF.
Tel: (020) 7437 8182. FAX: (020) 7437 8183. www.xpression.tv
CONTACT
Richard Meadowcroft
Simon Adams
Gavin Watney

SNG BROADCAST SERVICES
The London Broadcast Centre, 11-13 Point Pleasant, London
SW18 1NN. Tel: (020) 8433 8080 FAX: (020) 8433 8081
email: info@sng.co.uk

TANGRAM POST PRODUCTIONS
1, Charlotte Street., London W1T 1RB. Tel: (020) 7637 2727.

TV MEDIA SERVICES LTD.
3rd floor, 420 Suchiehall St., Glasgow G2 3JD. Tel: (0141) 331
1993. FAX: (0141) 332 9040.
www.tvms.com
CONTACT
Charles Chalmers

THE WHITEHOUSE POST PRODUCTION
12-13 Kingly St., London W1B 5PP. Tel: (020) 7287 3404.
FAX: (0207) 287 9670.

FILM & VIDEO LABORATORIES

BUCKS LABORATORIES LTD.
714 Banbury Avenue, Slough, Berks., SL1 4LH. Tel: (01753)
576 611. FAX: (01753) 691 762.
www.bucks.co.uk
CONTACTS
Harry Rushton
Mike Bianchi.

COLOUR FILM SERVICES LTD.
26, Berwick Street, London, W1F 8RG. Tel: (020) 7734 4543.
10 Wadsworth Road, Perivale, Greenford, Middx., UB6 7JX.
Tel: (0208) 998 2731. FAX: (0208) 997 8738.

COLOUR VIDEO SERVICES LTD.
10 Wadsworth Rd., Perivale, Greenford, Middlesex UB6 7JX.
Tel: (0208) 998 2731. FAX: (0208) 997 8738.
CONTACT
Jess Morgan

DELUXE LONDON
Denham, Uxbridge, Middlesex, UB9 5HQ.
Tel: (01895) 832 323. Telex: 934704. FAX: (01895) 833 617.
MANAGING DIRECTOR
Ken Biggins
DIRECTOR OF SALES
Terry Landsbury

HALLIFORD STUDIOS
Manygate Lane, Shepperton, Middlesex, TW17 9EG.
Tel: (01932) 226 341. FAX: (01932) 246 336.
www.hallifordfilmstudios.co.uk
STUDIO MANAGER
Callam Andrews

METROCOLOR LONDON LTD.
91/95 Gillespie Road, Highbury, London, N5 1LS

PORTLAND FILMS LTD.
Unit 7, Wyrefield Industrial Estate, Poulton-le-Fylde,
Lancashire, FY6 8JF. Tel: (01253) 890825
FAX: (01253) 894815

RANK FILM LABORATORIES LTD
NOW OPERATING AS DELUXE LONDON
Denham, Uxbridge, Middlesex, UB9 5HQ.
Tel: (01895) 832 323. Telex: 934704. FAX: (01895) 833 617.
MANAGING DIRECTOR
Ken Biggins
DIRECTOR OF SALES
Terry Landsbury

SOHO IMAGES GROUP LTD.
8-14 Mead Street, London, W1D 3SG. Tel: (020) 7437 0831.

TECHNICOLOR LTD.
Bath Road, West Drayton, Middx., UB7 0DB.
Tel: (020) 8759 5432. FAX: (020) 8897 2666.
MANAGING DIRECTOR
Ashley Hopkins

TWICKENHAM FILM STUDIOS, LTD.
The Barons Street, St. Margarets, Twickenham, Middlesex,
TW1 2AW. Tel: (020) 8607 8888.

WORLD WIDE GROUP
21-25, St. Anne's Court, London, W1F OBJ. Tel: (020) 7434
1121. FAX: (020) 7734 0619.

Financial Services

AUDIO VISUAL ASSET MANAGEMENT
Little Orchard House, Bears Den, Kingswood, Surrey KT20
6PL. Tel: (01737) 830084. FAX: (01737) 830063.
CONTACT
Duncan Rushmer

BAIN HOGG GROUP LTD
Lloyds Chambers, 1 Portsoken Street, Wealdstone, London, E1 DF.
Tel: (020) 726 3843 FAX: (020) 7216 3826

BARCLAYS BANK PLC
54, Lombard Street, London, EC3P 3AH. Tel: (020) 7626 1567.
FAX: (020) 8699 2693.
www.barclays.com

FINELINE MEDIA FINANCE
Heron House, Heron Square, South West Denton, Richmond
Surrey, TW9 1EL. Tel: (020) 88334 4182

GENERAL ENTERTAINMENT INVESTMENTS
Market House, Church Street, Harleston, Norfolk, IP20 9BB.
Tel: (01603) 723711. FAX: (020) 7792 9005.

GUINNESS MAHON & CO. LTD.
2,Gresham Street, London, EC2 7QP. Te: (020) 7597 4510.
FAX: (020) 7783 4811

GUINNESS MAHON INTERNATIONAL LTD.
32 St. Mary at Hill, London, EC3P 3AJ. Tel: (020) 7597 4000.

INTERNATIONAL COMPLETION INC.
Pinewood Studios, Pinewood Road, Iver Heath, Bucks SL0 0NH.
Tel: (01753) 651 700. FAX: (01753) 656 564.

INTERNATIONAL FILM GUARANTORS INC.
9, hanover Street, London, W1S 1YF. Tel: (020) 7493 4686

KPMG
8, Salisbury Square, London, EC4Y 8BB. Tel: (020) 7311 1000.
Fax: (020) 7311 3311
www.kpmg.co.uk

MEDIA ADVISORY GROUP
5 Elstree Gate, Elstree Way, Borehamwood, Hertfordshire
WD6 1JD Tel: (0208) 207 0602 FAX: (0208) 207 6758.

MOVING IMAGE DEVELOPMENT AGENCY
109 Mount Pleasant, Liverpool, Merseyside L3 5TF Tel: (0151)
708 9858 FAX: 0151 708 9859.

ROLLINS BURDICK HUNTER (INTERNATIONAL) LTD.
Braintree House, Braintree Road, Ruislip, Middx., HA4 0YA.
Tel: (0208) 841 4461. FAX: (0208) 842 2124.

RUBEN SEDGWICK INSURANCE SERVICES
Pinewood Studios, Pinewood Road, Iver, Bucks., SL0 0NH.
Tel: (01753) 651 700. FAX: (01753) 656 564.

SAMUEL MONTAGU & CO. LTD.
NOW OPERATING AS HSBC
8, Canada Square, London E14 5HQ Tel: (020) 7260 9000.

SARGENT-DISC LTD.
Pinewood Studios, Pinewood Road, Iver, Bucks. Tel: (01753)
630300. FAX: (01753) 655 881.
www.sargent-disc.co.uk

SCOTTISH SCREEN
249 West George Street, Glasgow, Lanarkshire G2 4QE Tel:
(0141) 302 1700 FAX: (0141) 302 1714.
www.scottishscreen.com
email: info@scottishscreen.com
CHAIRMAN
Ray MacFarlane

STAFFORD KNIGHT
ENTERTAINMENT INSURANCE BROKERS
18 London Street, London EC3R 7JP. Tel: (020) 7716 2700

UNITED MEDIA ENTERTAINMENT PARTNERS LTD.
15, Golden Square., London, W1F 9JG
Tel: (020) 7434 3604.

WILLIS GROUP LIMITED
10, Trinity Square, London, EC3P 3AX.
Tel: (020) 7488 81111.

PRODUCTION EQUIPMENT
AND SUPPLIES

ADVENT COMMUNICATIONS LTD.
Watermeadow House, Watermeadow Chesham, Bucks. HP5
1LF. Tel: (01494) 774 400.

AGFA-GEVAERT (MOTION PICTURE DIVISION)
27 Great West Road, Brentford, Middlesex, TW8 9AX.
Tel: (020) 8231 4301. FAX: (020) 8231 4315. www.agfa.co.uk

AMPEX GREAT BRITAIN
Ampex House, Beechwood, Chineham Business Park,
Basingstoke, Hampshire, RG24 8WA
Tel: (01256) 814410.

AMSTRAD PLC
Brentwood House, 169 Kings Road, Brentwood, Essex, CM14
4EF. Tel:(01277) 228888.

ASTON COMMUNICATIONS.
2, St Johns Buildings, Friern Barnet Road, London, N11 3DP.
Tel: (010) 8361 8711

AUTOCUE LTD.
265 Merton Road, London, SW18 5JS. Tel: (020) 8870 0104.
FAX: (0208) 874 3726.
www.autocue.co.uk

BETTER SOUND LTD.
31, Cathcart Street, London, NW5 3BJ. Tel: (020) 7482 0177.
Fax (020) 7497 9285.

CAMERON VIDEO SYSTEMS LTD.
Burnfield Road, Glasgow G46 7TH, Scotland. Tel: (0141) 638
5529. FAX: (0141) 763 1765.

CANON (UK) LTD.
TV Products Dept., Canon House, 2 Manor Rd., Wallington,
Surrey, SM6 0AJ. Tel: (01737) 220000.

CINESOUND INTERNATIONAL LTD.
Registered offices: Howard House 121-123 Norton Way South
Letchworth, Herts SG6 1NZ

CINEVIDEO LTD.
Unit 2, Hertsmere Industrial Park, Warwick Road,
Borehamwood, Hertfordshire. WD6 1GT.
Tel: (020) 8381 5000. FAX: (020) 8207 1100.

DESISTI LIGHTING (UK) LTD.
15 Old Market Street, Thetford, Norfolk IP24 2EQ.
Tel: (01842) 752 909. FAX: (01842) 753 746.

DOLBY LABORATORIES INC.
Interface Park, Wootton Bassett, Swindon, Wiltshire, SN4 8QJ.
Tel: (01793) 842 100. FAX: (01793) 842 101.
www.dolby.co.uk

JOE DUNTON CAMERAS LTD.
Wickham Road, Wembley, Middlesex, TW17 0DQ. Tel: (020)
8902 8835. FAX: (020) 8902 3273

E2V TECHNOLOGIES
Waterhouse Lane, Chelmsford, CM1 2QU Essex.
Tel: (01245) 493493, FAX: (01245) 492492.
www.e2vtechnologies.com

EDRIC AUDIO VISUAL LTD.
24, Newton Road, London, W2 5LT. Tel: (0800) 9802853

ENGLISH ELECTRIC VALVE COMPANY LTD
NOW OPERATING AS E2V TECHNOLOGIES
Waterhouse Lane, Chelmsford, CM1 2QU Essex.
Tel: (01245) 493493, FAX: (01245) 492492.
www.e2vtechnologies.com

ELECTRA FILM & TV LTD
Wharf House, Brentwaters Business Park, The Ham, Brentford,
Middlesex, TW8 8HQ Tel: (020) 82328899
FAX: (020) 8232 8877.

EXTREME FACILITIES
15-17 Este Rd, London SW11 2TL Tel: (020) 7801 9111.
FAX: (0207) 801 9222.

FUJI PHOTO FILM (UK) LTD.
Fuji Film House, 125 Finchley Road, London, NW3 6JH. Tel:
(0207) 586 5900. FAX: (0207) 722 4259, Telex: 8812995.
www.fujifilm.co.uk
DIVISIONAL MANAGER
E. J. Mould

GE LIGHTING LTD
153 Lincoln Road, Enfield, Middlesex EN1 1SB.
Tel: (0208) 640 1221. FAX: (020) 8727 4400.
www.gelighting.com

HARKNESS HALL LTD.
Gate Studios, Station Road, Boreham Wood, Herts., WD6
1DQ. Tel: (020) 8953 3611. FAX: (020) 8207 3657.

HAYDEN LABORATORIES LTD.
Hayden House, Chiltem Hill, Chalfont St. Peter, Gerrards
Cross, Bucks., SL9 9UG. Tel: (01753) 888 447. FAX: (01753)
880 109.

HENDON FILM STUDIOS
Goldsmith Avenue, London, NW9 7EU. Tel: (020) 205 2240.
FAX: (0208) 203 7377.

HITACHI DENSHI (UK) LTD.
Unit 14 Garrick Industrial Centre, Irving Way, Hendon, London,
NW9 6AQ. Tel. (020) 8202 4311. FAX: (020) 8202 2451.

I.C. FILM EQUIPMENT LTD.
Unit 1 Bridge Wharf, 156 Caledonia Road, London, NW1 9UU.
Tel: (020) 7278 0908

ITN ARCHIVE LTD.
200 Gray's Inn Road, London, WC1X 8XZ.
Tel: (020) 7430 4197.
Enquires about factual and documentary production:
itn.factual@itn.co.uk

JVC PROFESSIONAL EUROPE LTD.
Ullswater House, Kendall Avenue, London, W3 0XA. Tel: (020)
8896 6000. FAX: (020) 8896 6060.

KEM ELECTRONIC LTD
Registered offices: 25, Forestdrive West Leyton, London, E11 1JZ

THE MAIDSTONE STUDIOS
Vinters Park, Maidstone, ME14 5NZ. Tel: (01622) 691 111.
FAX: (01622) 684 456.

SIEMENS GEC COMMUNICATIONS SYSTEMS LTD
Hillgate House, 26 Old Bailey, London, EC4M 7HW.
Tel: (020) 7457 4000

KODAK LTD.
Professional Motion Imaging, P.O. Box 66, Kodak House,
Station Road, Hemel Hempstead, Herts., HP1 1JU. Tel:
(01442) 61122. FAX: (01442) 844458. www.kodak.co.uk
CHAIRMAN AND MANAGING DIRECTOR
Peter Blackwell

LEE COLORTRAN LTD.
Ladbroke Hall, Barlby Rd., London, W10 5HH. Tel: (0208) 968
7000.

LEE FILTERS LTD.
Central Way, Walworth Industrial Estate, Andover, Hants.,
SP10 5AN. Tel: (01264) 66245.

LEE LIGHTING
Wycombe Road, Wembley, Middlesex, HA0 1QD.
Tel: (020) 8900 2900. FAX: (020) 8902 5500. www.lee.co.uk
email: info@lee.co.uk

LEITCH EUROPE LTED CORPORATION
Leitch Europe, Holland Park House, Oldbury, Bracknell,
BerkshireRG12 8TQ Tel: (01344) 446000. (01344) 446100
www.leitch.com

MGB FACILITIES
Capital House, Sheepscar Court, Meanwood Rd, Leeds, West
Yorkshire LS7 2BB. Tel: (0113) 243 6868 FAX: (0113) 243
8886. www.mgb.tv.co.uk/mgb

THE MINIATURE CAMERA COMPANY
7 Portland Mews, London W1V 3FL Tel:
(020) 7734 7776. FAX: (020) 7734 1360. www.skarda.net
CONTACTS
Martin Davidson

OPTEX (OPTICAL AND TEXTILE) LTD
22 26 Victoria Road, New Barnet, Herts. EN4 9PF. Tel: (020)
8441 2199. FAX: (020) 8449 3646.

OSRAM LTD.
Bold Industrial Park, Niells Road, St. Helens, Merseyside, WA9
4XG. Tel: (01744) 812221.

PANASONIC BROADCAST EUROPE
West Forest Gate, Wellington Road, Wokingham, Berkshire,
Berks, RG40 2AQ. Tel: (0118) 902 9200.

PANAVISION (UK)
The Metropolitan Centre, Bristol Road, Greenford, Middx. UB6
8GD Tel: (020) 8839 7333. www.panavision.co.uk

PHILIPS LIGHTING LTD.
The Philips Centre, 420-430, London Road, Croydon, Surrey
CR0 9YB. Tel: (020) 8665 6655.

PHOENIX VIDEO LTD
Global House, Denham Media Park, North Orbital Road,
Uxbridge, Middlesex UB9 5HL Tel: (01895) 837000

PHOTOMEC (LONDON) LTD.
Valley Road Industrial Estate 16, Porters Wood, St. Albans,
Herts, AL3 6NU. Tel: (01727) 8501 711. FAX: (01727) 843991.

RADAMEC BRAODCAST SYSTEMS LTD.
Bridge Road, Chertsey, Surrey, KT16 8LJ. Tel: (01932) 561
181. FAX: (01932) 568 775.

CINTEL INTERNATIONAL LTD.
(Manufacturer of equipment for broadcast and film/tape
transfer.) Watton Road, Ware, Hertfordshire SG12 OAE.
Tel: (01920) 463 939. FAX: (01920) 460 803.
www.cintel.co.uk
MANAGING DIRECTOR
Adam Welsh

PHILIP RIGBY & SONS LTD.
14 Creighton Avenue, Muswell Hill, London, N10 1NU. Tel:
(020) 8883 3703. FAX: (020) 8444 3620.

RONFORD-BAKER
Oxhey Lane, Oxhey, Watford, Herts., WD19 5RJ. Tel: (020)
8428 5941. FAX: (020) 8428 4743.

SAMUELSON FILMS LTD.
13, Manette Street, London, W1D 4AW, Tel: (020) 7439 4900.

MICHAEL SAMUELSON LIGHTING LTD.
Pinewood Studios, Iver Heath, Bucks. SL0 0NH. Tel: (01753)
631133. FAX: (01753) 630485.

SHURE ELECTRONICS LTD.
Registered Offices: 20, Reform Street, Dundee, Angus, DD1
1RG

S & H TECHNICAL SUPPORT GROUP
Unitit 3, Artesian Close, London, NW10 8RW.
Tel: (020) 8451 580

SIGMA FILMS
840-860 Govan Road, Glasgow, Lanarkshire, G51 3UU
Tel: (0141) 445 0400

SONY BROADCAST & COMMUNICATIONS LTD.
Jay Close, Viables, Basingstoke, Hants, RG22 4SB.
Tel: (01256) 355011.

SOHO IMAGES GROUP LTD.
71, Dean Street, London, W1D 3SG. Tel: (020) 7437 0831.
FAX: (020) 7734 1823.

STRAND LIGHTING
Unit 3, Hammersmith Studios, Yeldham Road, Hammersmith,
London, W6 8JF. Tel: (020) 8735 9790..

TECHNOVISION UK LTD.
Unit 4, St. Margaret's Business Centre, Drummond Place,
Twickenham, Middlesex, TW1 1JN. Tel: (020) 8891 5961.
FAX: (020) 8744 1154.

VIEWPLANE
13a, Lamb Street, London, E1 6EA., Tel: (020) 7247 3561.

VINTEN BROADCAST
Western Way, Bury St. Edmunds, Suffolk, IP33 3TB. Tel:
(01284) 752 121. FAX: (01284) 750 560.

PRODUCTION FACILITIES
AND SERVICES

CARLTON TELEVISION BIRMINGHAM
Gas Street, Birmingham, B1 JT. Tel: (0121) 643
9898. FAX: (0121) 633 4473.
www.calton.com

CINEBUILD EUROPE LTD.
Studio House, Rita Road, Vauxhall, London SW8 1JU. Tel:
(020) 7582 8750.

CINEVIDEO LTD.
Unit 4, Elstree Distribution Park, Elstree Way, Borehamwood,
Hertfordshire,WD6 1RU. Tel: (020) 8381 5000. FAX: (020) 8207
1100, www.cinevideo.co.uk

NIKKI CLAPP
18 Cresswell Rd., East Twickenham, Middx., TW1 2DZ.
Tel: (0208) 891 0054.

COMPLETE VIDEO SERVICES
51, Cardy Road, Hemel Hempstead, Hertforshire, London, HP1
1SQ. Tel: (01442) 217896

COMPONENT GROUP
(now operating as SUITE LIMITED)
28,Newman St, London, W1T 1PR. Tel: (020) 7631 4400.
FAX: (020) 7636 0444. www.suitetv.co.uk

DIGITAL FILM LAB LONDON LTD
52, St., John Street, London, EC1M 4HF. Tel: (020) 7490 4050.

FRONTLINE TELEVISION SERVICES
35, Bedfordbury, London, WC2N 4DU. Tel:
(020) 7836 0411./ 7759 7100 FAX: (020) 7379 5210.
www.frontlinetv.co.uk

FOUNTAIN TELEVISION
128, Wembley Park Drive, Wembley, Middlesex, HA9 8HP.
Tel: (020) 8900 1188.

CHARLES H. FOX LTD.
22 Tavistock Street, Covent Garden, London WC2E 7PY.
Tel. (020) 7240 3111. Fax (020) 7379 3410

GENERAL SCREEN ENTERPRISES
Denham Media Park, North Orbital Road, Denham, Uxbridge,
Middlesex, UB8 5HX. Tel: (01895) 831 931.
FAX: (01895) 835 338.

INFOVISION LTD.
Registered offices: 23, Robins Way, Staines, Middlesex, TW18
4RL

LWT PRODUCTION FACILITIES
South Bank TV Centre, London, SE1 9LT.
Tel: (0207) 261 3683. FAX: (020) 7737 8840
www.londonstudios.co.uk

MOLINARE
34 Fouberts Place, London, W1F 7PX. Tel: (020) 7478 7000.
FAX: (020) 7478 7299.
SALES & MARKETING
Mark Foligno, email mark@molinare.co.uk

OASIS TELEVISION LTD.
6-7, Great Pulteney Street., London, W1F 9LX. Tel: (020) 7434
4133. FAX: (020) 7494 2843.

ONE POST TV
71, Dean Street, London, W1D 3SF. Tel: (020) 7734 1600.
FAX: (020) 7734 3331. www.onepost.tv

PEERLESS CAMERA CO.
Unit A, 32, Bedfordbury, London, WC2N 4DU.
Tel: (020) 7836 1195.
CONTACT
John Paul Docherty, email: Paul@peerless.co.uk

PRATER AUDIO VISUAL LTD.
35, Coleraine Road, London, SE3 7PF. Tel: (020) 8269 0609.

RANK VIDEO SERVICES LTD.
Phoenix Park, Great West Rd., Brentford, Middlesex, TW8
9PL. Tel: (020) 8232 7600. FAX: (020) 8232 7601.

REUTERS TELEVISION LTD.
200, Grays Inn Road, London, WC1X 8XZ.
Tel: (020) 7250 1122. , www.reuters.com

RUSHES POSTPRODUCTIONS LTD
Old Compton Street, London, W1D 4UH. Tel: (020) 7437 8676.
FAX: (020) 7734 2519.
MANAGING DIRECTOR
Joce Capper, email: Joce@rushes.co.uk

SUITE LIMITED
28,Newman st, London, W1T 1PR. Tel: (020) 7631 4400. Fax:
(020) 7636 0444, www.suitetv.co.uk

SVC TELEVISION NOW OPERATING AS ONE POST TV
71, Dean Street, London, W1D 3SF. Tel: (020) 7734 1600.
FAX: (020) 7734 3331. www.onepost.tv

THAMES TELEVISION LIMITED
1, Stephen Street, London, W1T 1AL. Tel: (020) 7691 6000.
Fax: (020) 7691 6100, www.thamestv.co.uk

VIDEO EUROPE
8, Golden Square, London, W1 9JA. Tel: (020) 7494 1818.

WEST ONE TELEVISION
20, St. Anne's Court, London, W14 OBH. Tel: (020) 7437 5533.

PUBLICITY AND MARKETING

THE ASSOCIATES LIMITED
Registered offices: 51, Greenhill Road, Altrincham, Cheshire, WA15 7BG

AVALON PUBLIC RELATIONS LIMITED
4a Exmoor Street, London W10 6BD. Tel: (020) 7598 7222. FAX: (020) 7598 7223.

BLUE DOLPHIN FILMS
40, Langham Street, London, W1W 7AS. Tel: (020) 7255 2494. FAX: (020) 7580 7670.

BYRON ADVERTISING LTD
Byron House, Wallingford Road, Uxbridge, Middlesex UB8 2RW. Tel: (01895) 252131. FAX: (01895) 252 137.

BYRON PUBLICITY LTD
Byron House, Wallingford Road, Uxbridge, Middlesex UB8 2RW. Tel: (01895) 252131. FAX: (01895) 252 137.

MAX CLIFFORD ASSOCIATES
45-50 New Bond Street, London W1S 1RD. Tel: (020) 7408 2350 FAX: (020) 7409 2294.
CONTACT
Max Clifford

CONSOLIDATED COMMUNICATIONS MANAGEMENT
15 Poland Street, London, W1F 8PR. Tel: (020) 7287 2087. FAX: (020) 7734 0772.

CORBETT & KEENE
Registered offices: 19-20, Poland Street, London, W1F 8QF

THE CREATIVE PARTNERSHIP
13, Bateman Street, London W1D 3AH. Tel: (020) 7439 7762. FAX: (020) 7437 1467. www.creativepartnership.co.uk

DENNIS DAVIDSON ASSOCIATES LTD.
Royalty House, 72 74 Dean Street, London, W1V 5HB. Tel: (020) 7534 6000. FAX: (020) 7437 6358.

EDELMAN PUBLIC RELATIONS
Haymarket House, 28-29, Haymarket, London, SW1 4SP. Tel: (020) 7344 1200, www.edelman.com

FEREF ASSOCIATES LTD.
14 17 Wells Mews, London, W1A 1ET. Tel: (020) 7580 6546. FAX: (020) 7631 3156, www.feref.co.uk
CONTACTS
Peter Andrews
Robin Behling

LYNNE FRANKS PR
Tower House, 8-14 Southampton Street, London WC2E 7HA. Tel: (020) 7379 3234., FAX: (020) 7465 8241

HPS-PR LTD.
Park House, Desborough Park Road, High Wycombe, Buckinghamshire HP123 DJ. Tel: (01494) 684 353. FAX: (01494) 440952.
Email: r.hodges@hps-pr.co.uk
CONTACT
Ms Ray Hodges, Mcam MIPR

SUE HYMAN ASSOCIATES LTD.
Suite 1, Waldorf Chambers, Aldwich, London, WC2B 4DG. Tel: (020) 7379 84420.

RICHARD LAVER PUBLICITY
3 Troy Court, High Street Kensington, London, W8 7RA. Tel: (020) 7937 2788.

MCDONALD AND RUTTER
34, Bloomsbury Street, London WC1B 3QJ. Tel: (020) 7637 2600 FAX: (020) 7637 3690. email: info@mcdonaldrutter.com
CONTACTS
Charles McDonald
Jonathan Rutter

ROGERS & COWAN INTERNATIONAL
14, Grey's Inn Road, London, WC1X 8WS. Tel: (0870) 9905465. FAX: (0870) 9905422.

PETER THOMPSON ASSOCIATES
12, Bourchier Street, London, W1D 4HZ. Tel: (020) 7439 1210.

TOWN HOUSE PUBLICITY
45 Islington Park Street, London, N1 1QB. Tel: (020) 7226 7450. FAX: (020) 7359 6026.

Sound Services

APS LTD.
The Old Town Hall, Lapwing Lane, West Didsbury, Manchester M20 2WR. Tel: (0161) 448 9990. FAX: (0161) 448 2023.
www.aps-av.com

ABBEY ROAD STUDIOS
3, Abbey Road, St. John's Wood, London NW8 9AY. Tel: (020) 7266 7000. FAX: (020) 7266 7250.

ANVIL POST PRODUCTION.
Denham Media Park, North Orbital Road., Denham, Nr. Uxbridge,
Mdsx UB9 5HL. Tel: (01895) 833 522. FAX: (01895) 835 006.
STUDIO MANAGER
Mike Anscombe

ASCENT MEDIA
Film House, 142 Wardour, London W1F 8DD. Tel: (020) 7878 0000., FAX: (020) 7878 7800.
MANAGING DIRECTOR
Simon Kaye

BACKYARD RECORDING STUDIOS
West Penyllan Churchstoke, Montgomery Powys, SY15 6HT.
Tel: (01588) 6200129.

BOUNDARY ROW STUDIOS
1-7 Boundary Row, London SE1 8HP. Tel: (020) 7633 9629.
FAX: (020) 7928 6082.

CTS STUDIOS LTD.
Suite 1a, Lansdowne House, Lansdowne Road, Holland Park, W11 3LP0 (020) 7467 0099. FAX: (020) 7467 0098.
CONTACT
Sharon Rose

D B POST PRODUCTIONS LTD.
1-8 Batemans Buildings, South Soho Square, London W1D 3EN. Tel: (020) 7434 0097. FAX: (020) 7287 9143.

DE LANE LEA SOUND CENTRE LTD.
75 Dean St., London W1D 3SQ. Tel: (020) 7439 1721.

THE DIGITAL AUDIO COMPANY
3 Carleton Business Park, Carleton New Rd., Skipton, North Yorkshire BD23 2AA. Tel: (01756) 797 100. FAX: (01756) 797 101. www.the-digital-audio.co.uk

FOUNTAIN TELEVISION LTD.
128, Wembley Park Drive, Wembley, Middlesex, HA9 8HP. Tel: (020) 8900 1188.

GRAND CENTRAL SOUND STUDIOS
25-32 Marshall St., London W1F 7ES.
Tel: (020) 7306 5600 FAX: (020) 7306 5616.

HULABALOO STUDIOS
8 Albany Road, Manchester, Lancashire M21 0AW.
Tel: (0161) 882 0007 FAX: (0161) 882 0774.

IBF
15 Monmouth Street, London WC2H 9DA. Tel: (0207) 497 1515. FAX: (0207) 379 8562
CONTACT
Martin Reekie

INDUSTRIAL ACOUSTICS CO. LTD. (STUDIO DIVISION)
IAC House, Moorside Road, Winchester SO23 7US. Tel: (01962) 873 000. FAX: (01962) 873 111.

INHOUSE PRODUCTIONS LTD.
10th Floor, Astley House, Quay Street, Manchester M3 4AE.
Tel: (0161) 832 4504.

INTERACT SOUND LTD
160 Barlby Rd, London W10 6BS. Tel: (0208) 960 3115 FAX: (020) 8964 3022.
CONTACT
Tony Martin

LANSDOWNE MUSIC PUBLISHING LTD.
1, Lansdowne House, Lansdowne Rd., London W11 3LP. Tel: (020) 7727 0041. FAX: (020) 7792 8904.

MAGMASTERS SOUND
NOW OPERATING AS ASCENT MEDIA
Film House, 142 Wardour, London W1F 8DD. Tel: (020) 7878 0000, FAX: (020) 7878 7800.
MANAGING DIRECTOR
Simon Kaye

MATINEE SOUND & VISION
132-134 Oxford Road, Reading, Berks RG1 7NL. Tel: (0118) 958 4934. FAX: (0118) 959 4936.

MAYFAIR RECORDING STUDIOS
11a Sharpleshall St. London NW1 8YN. Tel: (020) 7586 7746.
FAX: (020) 7586 9721.

NINTH WAVE AUDIO
PO Box 5517, Birmingham B13 8QW. Tel: (0121) 442 2276.
FAX: (0121) 689 1902.

OASIS TELEVISION LTD.
6-7 Great Pluteney St, London W1F 9LX. Tel: (020) 7434 4133. FAX: (020) 7494 2843.

ORANGE TREE MUSIC PRODUCTION STUDIO & SOUND DESIGN
33, Lauderdale Road, Hunton Bridge, Kings Langley, Hertfordshire, WD4 8QA Tel: (01923) 440550

PERFECT PITCH LIMITED
Registered offices: 30, Mattock Lane, London, W5 5BH

PINEWOOD SOUND DEPARTMENT
Pinewood Studios, Pinewood Rd., Iver, Bucks SL0 0NH.
Tel: (01753) 656 301. FAX: (01753) 656 014.

RED BUS RECORDING & VIDEO STUDIOS LTD
Broadley House, 48 Broadley Terrace, London NW1 6LG.
Tel: (0207) 258 0324. FAX: (0207) 724 2361.
CONTACT
Mark French

THE SOUNDHOUSE LTD.
Unit 11, Goldhawk Industrial Estate, 2A Brackenbury Rd., Shepherds Bush, London W6 0BA. Tel: (0208) 743 2677.

STUDIO SOUND NOW OPERATING AS IBF
15 Monmouth Street, London WC2H 9DA. Tel: (0207) 497 1515. FAX: (0207) 379 8562
CONTACT
Martin Reekie

TRIANGLE TELEVISION
81 Whitfield Street, London W1T 4HG. Tel: (0207) 255 5215.
FAX: (0207) 255 5216.

TRIDENT SOUND STUDIO LTD.
17 St. Annes Court., London W1F 0BQ.
Tel/FAX: (020) 7734 6198
CONTACT
Peter Hughes
Stephen O'Toole

UNIVERSAL SOUND
134a, North End Road, West Kensington, London, w14 9PP.
Tel: (020) 7385 6437. FAX: (0208) 991 9461.

VIDEOLONDON SOUNDSTUDIOS
16-18 Ramillies St., London W1V 1DL. Tel: (0207) 734 4811.
FAX: (020) 7494 2553.

VIDEOSONICS LTD.
13 Hawley Crescent, London NW1 8NP. Tel: (020) 7209 0209.
FAX: (020) 7419 4460.
DUBBING MIXER
Howard Bargroff
SOUND EDITOR
Terry Brown

WARWICK SOUND STUDIOS
111 A Wardour St., London W1F 0UJ. Tel: (020) 7437 5532.
FAX: (020) 7439 0372.

WILD TRACKS AUDIO STUDIOS LTD
2nd Floor, 55 Greek Street, London W1D 3DX. Tel: (020) 7734 6331 FAX: (020) 7734 6195.

SPECIAL EFFECTS

AARDMAN ANIMATIONS LTD.
Gas Ferry Rd., Bristol, Avon BS1 6UN. Tel: (0117) 984 8485.
FAX: (0117) 984 8486. www.aardman.com

ALBATROSS MODELS, SETS, EFFECTS
Unit 2, Beckett's Wharf, Lower Teddington Rd., Hampton Wick,
Kingston-upon-Thames, Surrey KT1 4ER.
Tel: (020) 8943 4720. FAX: (020) 8977 0854.

ANIMATED EXTRAS
Shepperton Film Studios, Studios Rd.,
Shepperton, Middlesex TW17 0QD. Tel: (01932) 572342.

ANY EFFECTS
64 Weir Rd., London SW19 8UG. Tel :(020) 8944 0099,
FAX: (020) 8944 6989. www.anyeffects.com
email: jules@anyeffects

ARTEM VISUAL EFFECTS
Perivale Industrial Park, Horsenden Lane, South Perivale,
Middlesex UB6 7RH. Tel: (020) 8997 7771. FAX: (020) 8997
1503. www.artem.com email: info@artem.com

CHRIS CORBOULD
Fir Tree Farm, 101 Woodlands Road, Little Bookham, Surrey
KT 23 4HN
Tel/FAX: (01372) 454088
CONTACT
Chris Corbould

CINE IMAGE FILM OPTICALS
7A Langley St., Covent Garden, London WC2H 9JA. Tel:
(020) 240 6222. FAX: (0207) 7240 6242.
CONTACTS
Steve Boag, email: steve@cineimage.co.uk
Martin Bullard, email: martin@cineimage.co.uk

CRAWLEY CREATURES
Unit 22-23, Rabans Close, Needham Market, Aylesbury,
Buckinghamshire, HP19 3RS.
Tel: (01296) 336315. FAX: (01296) 339590.
 Email: jez@gibsonharris.freeserve.co.uk

THE DEFINITIVE SPECIAL PROJECTS LTD
P. O. Box 169 Wood End Ardeley, Stevenage, Hertfordshire,
SG2 7BB Tel: (01438) 869 005
FAX: (01438) 869 006. www.definitivespecialprojects.co.uk
CONTACT
Steve Hitchins

EFFECTS ASSOCIATES LTD.
Pinewood Studios, Pinewood Rd., Iver Heath, Bucks SL0 0NH.
Tel: (01753) 652 007. FAX: (01753) 630 127.
www.cinesite.com email:ea@effectsassociates.co.uk
GENERAL MANAGER, PRODUCTION
Janine Modder
CONTACTS
Carmila Gittens
Elaine Wishart

ENTERPRISES UNLIMITED SPECIAL EFFECTS
Unit 9, Cowbridge Business Park, Cowbridge, Boston, Lincs
PE22 7DJ. Tel: (01205) 310 440. FAX: (01205) 310 450.
www.snowboy.co.uk

GENERAL SCREEN ENTERPRISES
Denham Media Park North Orbital Road Denham, Middlesex
UB9 5HG. Tel: (01895) 831931. FAX: (01895) 835338.

HALCYON DESIGNS
25 Cortayne Road, London SW6 3QA. Tel: (020) 7736 8744
FAX: (020) 7736 8407. email: fleroux@btclick.com
CONTACT
Fabrice Le Roux

IMAGE ANIMATION
Pinewood Studios, Pinewood Rd., Iver, Bucks SL0 0NH. Tel:
(01753) 651 700.

JOHN MILLS FILMS AND TELEVISION
4, Effingham Road, Surbiton Surrey, KT6 5JY.
Tel: (020) 8398 8084

LASER CREATIONS INTERNATIONAL LTD.
55 Merthyr Terrace, Barnes, London SW13 8DL.
Tel: (0208) 741 5747. FAX: (020) 9748 9879.
www.lci-uk.com

LIQUID IMAGE
4a, Sheet Stroes Industrial Estate, Long Eaton, Nottingham,
Nottinghamshire, NG10 1AU
Tel: (0115) 946 1555

MILL FILM SHEPPERTON
Shepperton Studios, Studios Rd., Shepperton, Mdsx
TW17 0QD. Tel: (01932) 572 424. FAX: (01932) 568 944.
www.millfilms.co.uk

OTTER EFFECTS
Registered offices: Kingsway House, 123, Goldsworth Road,
Woking, Surrey, GU21 6LR

OXFORD SCIENTIFIC FILMS LTD.
Lower Rd, Long Hanborough, Oxford OX29 8LL. Tel: (01993)
881 881. FAX: (01993) 882 808.

PERDIX FIREARMS LTD.
P.O. Box 1670 Salisbury SP4 6QL, Tel: (01722) 782402.
FAX: (01722) 782 790.
Email: perdix@eclipse.co.uk

QUANTEL LTD.
31, Turnpike Rd., Newbury, Berkshire RG14 2NE. Tel: (01635)
48222. FAX: (01635) 31776.

BRYAN SMITHIES SPECIAL EFFECTS
No 1Lyne Close Cottages, Lyne Close, Virginia Water Surrey
GU25 4EA. Tel: (01344) 843 251. FAX: (01344) 843 337.
CONTACT
Bryan Smithies

SNOW BUSINESS (UK) LTD
The Snow Mill, Bridge Road, Ebley, Stroud, Gloucestershire,
GL5 4TR Tel/FAX: (01453) 840077.
Email: snow@snowbusiness.com

Studio Facilities

ARDMORE STUDIOS LTD.
Herbert Road, Bray, Co. Wicklow, Ireland. Tel: (353 1) 2862971

BRAY FILM STUDIOS
Down Place, Windsor Road, Water Oakley, Windsor, Berks SL4
5UG. Tel: (01628) 622111. FAX: (01628) 770 381.
STUDIO MANAGER
Beryl Earl

CAPITAL GROUP STUDIOS
13 Wandsworth Plain, London, SW18 1ET.
Tel: (020) 8877 1234. FAX: (020) 8877 0234.

EALING STUDIOS
Ealing Green, Ealing, London, W5 5EP. Tel: (020) 8567 6655.
Email: info@ealingstudios.com

FOUNTAIN TELEVISION
128, Wembley Park Drive, Wembley, Middlesex, HA9 8HP.
Tel: (020) 8900 1188.

GUERILLA FILMS
35 Thornbury Road, Isleworth, TW7 4LQ England.
Tel: (0208) 758 1716. FAX: (0208) 758 9364

HILLSIDE STUDIOS
Hillside, Merry Hill Road, Bushey, Watford WD23 1DR.
Tel: (020) 8950 7919. FAX: (020) 8421 8085.
HEAD OF FACILITES
Dave Hillier, email: dave.hillier@hillside-studios.co.uk

BRIAN JACKSON LTD.
39/41 Hanover Steps, St. George's Fields, Albion Street,
London, W2 2YG. Tel: (0207) 402 7543. FAX: (0207) 262 5736.
CONTACT
Brian Jackson

LEAVESDEN STUDIOS
Hill Farm Avenue, Leavesden, Watford, Hertfordshire. WD25
7LT. Tel: (01923) 685 060. FAX (01923) 685061.
www.leavesdenstudios.com

THE LONDON TELEVISION CENTRE
Upper Ground, London SE1
9LT. Tel: (0207) 737 8888. FAX: (0207) 928 8405.
www.londonstudios.co.uk

PINEWOOD STUDIOS
Pinewood Rd., Iver Bucks., SL0 0NH. Tel: (01753) 651 700.
FAX: (01753) 656 844.

SHEPPERTON STUDIOS
Studios Road, Shepperton, Middlesex, TW17 0QD.
Tel: (01932) 562 611. FAX: (01932) 568 989.
www.sheppertonstudios.co.uk.
MANAGING DIRECTOR
Steve Jaggs
STUDIO MANAGER
David Godfrey

TEDDINGTON STUDIOS
Broom Road, Teddington Lock, Middx., TW11 9NT.
Tel: (020) 8977 3252. FAX: (0208) 943 4050.
Email: sales@teddington.tv

TWICKENHAM STUDIOS
St. Margaret's, Twickenham, Middlesex, TW1 2AW. Tel: (020)
8806 8888. FAX: (020) 8607 8889
www.twickenhamstudios.com

WORLD WIDE GROUP
21-25 St. Anne's Court, London, W1F 0BJ. Tel: (020) 7434
1121. FAX: (020) 7734 0619.

British Trade Organizations And Government Units

ADVERTISING ASSOCIATION
Abford House, 15 Wilton Road, London, SW1V 4NJ. Tel: (020)
7828 2771. FAX: (020) 7931 0376.
DIRECTOR GENERAL
Andrew Brown
SECRETARY
Debbie Harber

**ADVERTISING FILM AND VIDEOTAPE PRODUCERS'
ASSOCIATION**
26 Noel Street, London W1F 8GY D Tel: (020) 7434-2651.
FAX: (020) 74349002. email: INFO@a-p-a.net.
www.A-P-A.NET
CHIEF EXECUTIVE
Stephen Davies

AGENTS ASSOCIATION
54 Keys House, Dolphin Square, London SW1V 3NA Tel:
(020) 7834 0515 FAX: (020) 7821 0261. www.agents-uk.com
email: association@agent-uk.com

**AMALGAMATED ENGINEERING & ELECTRICAL
UNION.AMICUS/AEEU**
Hayes Court, West Common Road, Bromley, BR2 7AU.
Tel: (0208) 462 7755. FAX: (020) 8315 8234.
www.aeeu.org.uk
GENERAL SECRETARY
Derek Simpson

THE AGENTS ASSOCIATION (GREAT BRITAIN)
54 Keyes House, Dolphin Square, London, SW1V 3NA.
Tel: (0207) 834 0515. FAX: (0207) 821 0261.
www.agents-uk.com
PRESIDENT
Jenny Dunster
SECRETARY
Chris Lynn

ASSOCIATION OF MOTION PICTURE SOUND
28 Knox Street, London W1H 1FS. Tel: (0207) 723 6727.
www.amps.net

**ASSOCIATION OF PROFESSIONAL RECORDING
SERVICES LTD.**
PO Box 22, Totnes, Devon, TQ9 7YZ. Tel: (01803)
868600. FAX: (01803) 868444, www.aprs.co.uk
CHIEF EXECUTIVE
Peter Filleul

BRITISH ACADEMY OF COMPOSERS & SONGWRITERS
British Music House, 26, Berners Street, London
W1T 3LR. Tel: (020) 7636 2929.
www.britishacademy.com
email: info@britishacademy.com

BRITISH ACADEMY OF FILM AND TELEVISION ARTS
195 Piccadilly, London, W1J 9LN. Tel: (020) 7734 0022.
FAX: (020) 7734 1792.,
www.bafta.org
PRESIDENT
Lord Attenborough
VICE PRESIDENT
David Puttnam, C.B.E.
CHAIRMAN
Michael Attwell
CHIEF EXECUTIVE
Amanda Berry

BRITISH ACTORS' EQUITY ASSOCIATION
Guild House, Upper St. Martin's Lane, London, WC2 9EG.
Tel: (020) 7379 6000. FAX: (020) 7379 7001. www.equity.org.uk
COMMITTEE SECRETARY
Diane Fisk (020) 7670 0257

BRITISH BOARD OF FILM CLASSIFICATION
3, Soho Square, London, W1D 3HD. Tel: (020) 7440 1570.
FAX: (0207) 287 0141. www.bbfc.co.uk
email: webmaster@bbfc.co.uk
DIRECTOR
Robin Duval

BRITISH FEDERATION OF FILM SOCIETIES
The Ritz Building Mount Pleasant Campus, Swansea, West
Glamorgan, SA1 6ED
Tel: (01792) 481170.

BRITISH FILM DESIGNERS GUILD
78, Loudon Road, London, NW8 0NA
Tel/Fax: (020) 7722 0754. www.Filmdesigners.co.uk
CHAIRMAN
Austin Spriggs
SECRETARY
Giles Masters

BRITISH KINEMATOGRAPH, SOUND AND TELEVISION SOCIETY (BKSTS)
The Moving Image Society
Pinewood Studios, Iver Heath, Bucks, SL0 0NH.
Tel: (01753) 656656. FAX: (01753) 657016.
www.bksts..com, Email: bksts@bksts.demon.co.uk
PRESIDENT
Martyn Hurd
DIRECTOR
Wendy Laybourn

BRITISH MUSIC INFORMATION CENTRE
(Reference library of works by 20th Century British Composers.)
10 Stratford Place, London, W1C 1BA.
Tel: (020) 7499 8567. FAX: (020) 7499 4795.

BRITISH SOCIETY OF CINEMATOGRAPHERS LTD.
PO BOX 2587, Windsor Road, Gerrards
Cross, Bucks., SL9 7WZ. Tel: (01753) 888 052.
FAX: (01753) 891 486. www.bscine.com
email: britcinematographers@compuserve.com
SECRETARY & TREASURER
Frances Russell

BRITISH VIDEO ASSOCIATION LTD.
167 Great Portland Street, London, W1M 5FD.
Tel: (020) 7436 0041. FAX: (020) 7436 0043.
email: general@bva.org.uk
DIRECTOR GENERAL
Mrs. Lavinia Carey

BROADCASTING ENTERTAINMENT CINEMATOGRAPH
AND THEATRE UNION
373-377, Clapham Road, London SW9 9BT. Tel: (020) 7346
0900. FAX: (020) 7436 0901. www.bectu.org.u

CASTING DIRECTORS' GUILD
PO BOX 34403, London N6 0YG. Te/FAX:
(020) 8741 1951. www.castingdirectorsguild.co.uk
email: casting@directorsguild.1in2home.co.uk

CHILDREN'S FILM & TELEVISION FOUNDATION LTD.
Elstree Studios, Boreham Wood, Herts., WD6 1JG. Tel:
(020) 8953 0844. FAX: (020) 8207 0860.

CINEMA ADVERTISING ASSOCIATION LTD.
The Advertising Association
Abford House, 15 Wilton Road, London, SW1V 4NJ. Tel: (020)
7828 2771. FAX: (020) 7931 0376.
DIRECTOR GENERAL
Andrew Brown
SECRETARY
Debbie Harber

BRITISH CINEMA AND TELEVISION VETERANS
22 Golden Square, London, W1F 9AD.
Tel: (020) 7437 6567. FAX: (020) 7437 7186
SECRETARY
Valerie Haywood

CINEMA AND TELEVISION BENEVOLENT FUND
22 Golden Square, London, W1F 9AD. Tel: (020) 7437
6567. FAX: (020) 7437 7186.

CINEMA EXHIBITORS' ASSOCIATION
22 Golden Square, London, W1F 9JW.
Tel: (020) 7734 9551. FAX: (020) 7734 6147.
CHIEF EXECUTIVE
John Wilkinson, c/o CEA.
CHARMAN
Barry Jenkins
SECRETARY
Annette Bradford

APOLLO LEISURE (UK) LTD. - CINEMA DIVISION
Houston House, 12 Sceptre Court, Sceptre Point, Preston,
PR5 6AW Tel: (01772) 323544.
FAX: (01772) 323545.
MANAGING DIRECTOR
James Whittell

CINE-UK LTD.
2nd Floor , Chapter House, 22 Chapter Street, London, SW1P.
Tel: (020) 7932 2212.
CHIEF EXECUTIVE OFFICER
Steve Wiener

NATIONAL AMUSEMENTS (UK)
200 Elm St., Dedham, Massachuetts 02026. Tel: (001 781) 461
1600. UK (01159) 862 508
SENIOR VICE PRESIDENT INTERNATIONAL OPERATIONS
Duncan Short
Michelle Connor PA (UK),

ODEON CINEMAS LTD.
54 Whitcomb St., London WC2H 7DN. Tel: (020) 7321 0404.
CHIEF EXECUTIVE
Ian Pluthero
Debbie Mitchell (PA)

REELTIME CINEMAS
Carlton Cinema, St Mildred's Road, Westgate on Sea, Kent
CT8 8RE
Tel: (0845) 166 2370
MANAGING DIRECTOR
Mike Vickers

STER CENTURY
3rd Floor, St George's House, Knoll Road, Camberley, Surrey,
GU15 3SY
Tel: (01276) 605 605
CHIEF EXECUTIVE OFFICER
Mike Ross

UNITED CINEMAS INTERNATIONAL (UK)
Lee House, 90 Great Bridgewater St., Manchester M1 5JW.
Tel: (0161) 455 4000.
VICE PRESIDENT AND GENERAL MANAGER
Lorraine Johnson

UGC
Power Road Studios, Power Road, Chiswick, London, W4 5PY.
Tel: (020) 8987 5000
MANAGING DIRECTOR
Margaret Taylor

VUE ENTERTAINMENT
10, Chiswick Park, 566 Chiswick High Road, London W4 5XS
Tel: (0208) 396 0110.
CHIEF EXECUTIVE OFFICER
Tim Richards
Clare Wilkinson (PA)

BRITISH ACADEMY OF COMPOSERS AND SONGWRITERS
British Music House, 26 Berners Street, London W1T 3LR. Tel:
(020) 7636 2929. FAX: (020) 7636 2212
Eamil: info@britishacadmy.com
PRESIDENT
Sir Tim Rice
FELLOWS
Sir Malcolm Arnold
John Barry
Sir Paul McCartney
CHARMAN
David Ferguson

BRITISH FILM COMMISSION
10, Little Portland Street, London, W1W 7JG.
Tel: (020) 7861 7860 FAX: (020) 7861 7864.
Email: internationalinfo@ukfilmcouncil.org.uk
www.britfilmcom.co.uk

CRITICS' CIRCLE
51, Vartry Road, London N15 6PS.
Email: info@criticscircle.org.uk www.criticscircle.org.uk
CHAIRMAN
Charles Osbourne
HON. SECRETARY
Charles Hedges

DIRECTORS GUILD OF GREAT BRITAIN
Acorn House, 314-320, Gray's inn Road, London, WC1X 8DP.
Tel: (020) 7278 4343. FAX: (020) 7278 4742.
Email: guild@dggb.co.uk
CHIEF EXECUTIVE
Malcom Moore
ADMINISTRATIVE DIRECTOR
Jane V. Grater

EDINBURGH AND LOTHIAN SCREEN INDUSTRIES OFFICE
Filmhouse, 88 Lothian Road, Edinburgh EH3 9BZ, Scotland.
Tel: (0131) 228 5960. FAX: (0131) 228 5967.

FEDERATION AGAINST COPYRIGHT THEFT (FACT)
7 Victory Business Centre, Worton Road, Isleworth, Middx.,
TW7 6DB. Tel: (020) 8568 6646. FAX: (020) 8560 6364.
Email: contact@fact-uk.org.uk
DIRECTOR GENERAL
Brian Conlon

FILM ARTISTES' ASSOCIATION
c/o 111, Wardour Street, London W1V 4AY. Tel: (0207) 437
8506. FAX: (020) 7434 1221. Email: smacdonald@bectu.org.uk
NATIONAL OFFICIAL
Spencer MacDonald

FILM CENSOR'S OFFICE
16 Harcourt Terrace, Dublin 2, Republic of Ireland.
Tel: (353 1) 676 1985. FAX: (353 1) 676 1898.

FILM DISTRIBTUTORS ASSCIATION LTD
22 Golden Square, London, W1RF 9JW. Tel: (020) 7437
4383. FAX: (020) 7734 0912.
www.launchingfilms.com
CHIEF EXECUTIVE
Mark Batey

FILM INSTITUTE OF IRELAND
Irish Film Centre, 6 Eustace Street, Dublin 2, Republic of
Ireland. Tel: (353 1) 679 5744. FAX: (353 1) 677 8755.

GUILD OF BRITISH CAMERA TECHNICIANS
c/o Panavision UK, Metropolitan Centre, Bristol Road,
Greenford, Middx., UB6 8GD. Tel: (020) 8813 1999.
www.gbct.org

GUILD OF BRITISH FILM EDITORS
Travair, Spurlands End Road, Great Kingshill, High Wycombe,
Bucks, HP15 6HY. Tel: (01494) 712 313. FAX: (01494) 712313
email: cox.gbfe@btinternet.com
CONTACT
Alfred E. Cox

GUILD OF FILM PRODUCTION EXECUTIVES
(now operating as THE PRODUCTION GUILD OF GREAT BRITAIN)
Pinewood Studios, Iver Heath, Buckinghamshire, SL0 0NH.
Tel: (01753) 651767, FAX:(01753) 652803.
Email: admin@productionguild.com
CHIEF EXECUTIVE
David Martin

**GUILD OF FILM PRODUCTION ACCOUNTANTS AND
FINANCIAL ADMINISTRATORS
NOW OPERATING AS
THE PRODUCTION GUILD OF GREAT BRITAIN**
Pinewood Studios, Iver Heath, Buckinghamshire, SL0 0NH.
Tel: (01753) 651767. FAX:(01753) 652803.
Email: admin@productionguild.com
CHIEF EXECUTIVE
David Martin

INTERNATIONAL ANIMATED FILM CENTRE
Cica c/o Conservatoire d'art et D'histoire, 18 Avenue du
Tresum, BP 399, 74013 Annecy – France
Tel: (33 0) 4 50 10 90 00. Fax: (33 0) 4 50 10 90 70.
Email: www.annecy.org

**INTERNATIONAL VISUAL COMMUNICATION
ASSOCIATION (IVCA)**
IVCA Business Communication Centre,
19 Pepper Street, Glengall Bridge, London, E14 9RP.
Tel: (020) 7512 0571. FAX: (020) 7512 0591.
www.ivca.org
INFORMATION OFFICER
Howard Ely

IRISH ACTORS EQUITY GROUP
Liberty Hall, Dublin 1, Republic of Ireland.
Tel: (353 1) 8586401.

MECHANICAL COPYRIGHT PROTECTION SOCIETY LTD.
(MCPS)
29-33, Berners Street, London, W1T 3AB.
Tel: (020) 7580 5544. FAX: (020) 7306 4350.
www.mcps.co.uk
ADMISSIONS
Tel: (020) 7306 4805

MUSICIANS' UNION
60 62 Clapham Road, London, SW9 0JJ. Tel: (020) 7582
5566. FAX: (020) 7582 9805. email: webmasters@musicu-
nion.org.uk, www.musiciansunion.org.uk

PACT LTD.
(Producers Alliance for Cinema and Television)
45 Mortimer Street, London W1W 8HJ.
Tel: (020) 7331 6000. FAX: (020) 7331 6700.

SECOND LOCATION:
249, West George Street, Glasgow, G2 4QE.
Tel: (0141) 222 4800. FAX: (0141) 111 4881.
www.pact.co.uk
CHIEF EXECUTIVE
John McVay
OFFICE ADMINISTRATOR
Omar Bedja

THE PERFORMING RIGHT SOCIETY LTD. (PRS)
29-33, Berners Street, London, W1T 3AB.
Tel: (020) 7580 5544. FAX: (020) 7306 4350.
www.prs.co.uk
ADMISSIONS
Tel: (020) 7306 4805

THE PERSONAL MANAGERS' ASSN. LTD.
Rivercroft, One Summer Road, East Molesey, Surrey KT8
9LX. Tel: (020) 8398 9796. FAX: (020) 8398 9796.

**SOCIETY OF FILM DISTRIBUTORS LTD I
NOW OPERATING AS
FILM DISTRIBTUTORS ASSOCIATION LTD**
22 Golden Square, London, W1RF 9JW. Tel: (020) 7437
4383. FAX: (020) 7734 0912.
www.launchingfilms.com
CHIEF EXECUTIVE
Mark Batey

VARIETY CLUB OF GREAT BRITAIN
93, Bayham Street, London NW1 0AG. www.varietyclub.org.uk

WOMEN IN FILM AND TELEVISION
6, Langley Street, London, WC2H 9JA.
Tel: (020) 7240 4875. Email: info@wftv.org.uk
CHIEF EXECUTIVE
Jane Cussons, Email: jane@wftv.org.uk

THE WRITERS' GUILD OF GREAT BRITAIN
15, Britannia Street, London, WC1X 9EN. Tel: (020) 7833
0777, FAX: (020) 7833 4777.
email: admin@writersguild.org.uk
GENERAL SECRETARY
Bernie Corbett. Email: Corbett@wrtiersguild.org.uk

GOVERNMENT DIVISIONS
ON FILM & TELEVISION AFFAIRS

BRITISH COUNCIL
Film, TV and Video Department, 10, Spring Gardens, London,
SW1A 2BN. Tel: (020) 7930 8466. FAX: (020) 7389 6347.
www.britishcouncil.org

THE BRITISH DEFENCE FILM LIBRARY
Chalfont Grove, Chalfont St. Peter, Gerrards
Cross, Bucks, SL9 8TN. Tel: (01494) 878 278. FAX: (01494)
878 007. www.ssvc.co.uk

MILITARY FOOTAGE
Robert Dungate. Email: Robert.dungate@ssvc.com

BRITISH FILM INSTITUTE (BFI)
(The BFI's divisions and departments include: BFI on the
South Bank (National Film Theatre, BFI National Library Land
London Film Festival); Research (Research and
Theatre,Education, Book Publishing and "Sight and Sound"
magazine); BFI IMAX; the National Film and Television Archive;
Exhibition and Distribution; Library and Information Services;
Planning Unit; BFI Production.),
British Film Institute, British National Library
21 Stephen Street, London, W1P 1PL.
Main Switchboard Tel: (020) 255 1444.. www.bfi.org.uk

BRITISH FILM COMMISSION
10, Little Portland Street, London W1W 7JG.
Tel: (020) 7861 7860. FAX (020) 7861 7864.
Email: internationalinfo@ukfilmcouncil.org.uk
BRITISH FILM COMMISSIONER
Steve Norris
HEAD OF MARKETING AND EVENTS
Sarah McKenzie
HEAD OF INFORMATION
Alison Sawkill

BRITISH SCREEN ADVISORY COUNCIL

13, Manette Street, London W1D 4AW. Tel: (020) 7287 1111 FAX: (020) 7287 1123. www.bsac.uk.com
CHAIRMAN
David Elstein
HONORARY PRESIDENT
Lord Attenborogh of Richmond Upon Thames

CENTRAL OFFICE OF INFORMATION (COI COMMUNICATIONS)

Hercules House, Hercules Road, London, SE1 7DU. Tel: (020) 7928 2345. FAX: (020) 7928 5037. www.coi.gov.uk

DEPARTMENT FOR CULTURE, MEDIA AND SPORT

2-4 Cockspur Street, London, SWIY 5DH. Tel: (020) 7211 2000. Email: enquires@culture.gov.uk

FILM LONDON

20 Euston Centre, Regent's Place, London NW1 3JH. Tel: (0207) 387 8787. FAX: (0207) 387 8788.

www.filmlondon.org.uk
CONTACT
Anna Faithful

NATIONAL FILM AND TELEVISION SCHOOL

Beaconsfield Studios, Station Road, Beaconsfield, Bucks., HP9 1LG. Tel: (01494) 671 234. FAX: (01494) 674 042. www.nftsfilm-tv.ac.uk
DIRECTOR OF FULL TIME PROGRAMME
Roger Crittenden

THE SERVICES SOUND & VISION CORPORATION

Chalfont Grove, Narcot lane, Chalfont St. Peter, Gerrards Cross, Buckinghamshire., SL9 8TN. Tel: (01494) 874461. FAX: (01494) 872982. www.ssvc.co.uk
CHAIRMAN
David Hatch
MANAGING DIRECTOR
David Crwys Williams, CB FIPM, FIMGT, RAR

ALBANIA

Population: 3.5 million.

EXHIBITORS

CINEMA PARIS
'Ish Pallati Kultures "All Kelmendi", Tirana, Albania

ARGENTINA

Population: 37 million.
Average Ticket Price: $7.00.
Domestic Production: 35 films.

ORGANIZATIONS

INCAA (INSTITUTO NACIONAL DE CINE Y ARTES AUDIOVISUALES)
Lima 319, 1073 Buenos Aires. FAX: (54 11) 4383 0029. email: info@incaa.gov.ar

DISTRIBUTORS

ALFA FILMS
Av. Corrientes 2025, 2 Piso A, 1045 Buenos Aires. Tel: (54 11) 4957 9901. email: alfafilms@ssdnet.com.ar

ARTISTAS ARGENTINOS ASOCIADOS
Lavalle 1977/79, 1051 Buenos Aires. (54 11) 4811 5016. email: artasoc@infovia.comar

CINE3 S.A.
Lavalle 1527, PB 2, 1048 Buenos Aires. Tel: (54 11) 4374 4327. email: cine3sa@cotelco.com.ar

COLUMBIA TRISTAR FILMS OF ARGENTINA, INC.
Ayacucho 533/37, 1026 Buenos Aires. Tel: (54 11) 954 3820. FAX: (54 11) 4375 0133.
GENERAL MANAGER
Oscar Scarinci

DISTRIBUTION COMPANY S.A.
Ayacucho 595, 1026 Buenos Aires. Tel: (54 11) 4372 9945. email: dcazupnik@artnet.com.ar

DISTRIFILMS S. A.
Lavalle 1860, 1051 Capital Federal, Buenos Aires. Tel: (54 11) 371 3438. FAX: (54 11) 374 9250.
PRESIDENT
Luis Albert Scalella

EUROCINE
Tucuman 1980, PB, 1050 Buenos Aires. FAX: (54 11) 4373 0547. email: eurocine@navigo.com.ar

IFA ARGENTINA
Riobamba 329, 2 Piso A, 1025 Buenos Aires. FAX: (54 11) 4373 7967. email: ifa@cine3.com.ar

PRIMER PLANO FILM GROUP S.A.
Riobamba 477, 1025 Buenos Aires. FAX: (54 11) 4374 0648. email: orlersa@comnet.com.ar

UNITED INTERNATIONAL PICTURES
Ayacucho 520, 1026 Buenos Aires. Tel: (54 11) 4373 0261. FAX: (54 11) 4373 5098.
MANAGER
Juan Manuel Fascetto

WARNER BROS.
Tucuman 1938, 1050 Buenos Aires. Tel: (54 11) 4372 6094. FAX: (54 11) 4372 6097. email: maicat@ssdnet.com.ar
GENERAL MANAGER
Anibal Codebo

EXHIBITORS

HOYTS ARGENTINA
Avda Corriertes 447, 5 Piso, 1043 Buenos Aires.

Number of Theatres: 5
Number of Screens: 52

VILLAGE CINEMAS
Tucuman 2133, Planta 2, 1050 Buenos Aires. Tel: (54) 1 954-6245.

Number of Screens: 47

VILLAGE ROADSHOW, LTD.
(For complete listing see Australian branch.)
206 Bourke St., Melbourne, VIC 3000 Australia. Tel: (613) 96 67 66 66. FAX: (613) 96 39 15 40.

Number of Theatres: 7
Number of Screens: 69

PRODUCERS

ALEPH PRODUCIONES S.A.
Constitucion 3156, Buenos Aires. FAX: (54 11) 4374 6448.

ATOMIC FILMS
Castillo 1366, 1414 Buenos Aires. FAX: (54 11) 4771 6003. email: www.fiehnerfilms.com

BD CINE
Cabello 3650, 1D, 1425 Buenos Aires. FAX: (54 11) 4802 4218. email: bdcine@movi.com.ar

FILM SUEZ S.A.
Florida 681, 2 Piso, 1375 Buenos Aires. FAX: (54 11) 4314 7800. email: suez@interprov.com

KOMPEL PRODUCCIONES S.A.
Avenida Corrientes 1660, 1042 Buenos Aires. FAX: (54 11) 4814 2657.

OSCAR KRAMER PRODUCCIONES
Figueroa Alcorta 3351, Piso 1, Officina 104, 1425 Buenos Aires. FAX: (54 11) 4807 3254. email: okafilms@overnet.com.ar

UGC PRODUCCIONES S.A.
Lavalle 1619, 3 Piso E, 1048 Buenos Aires. FAX: (54 11) 4373 8208. email: cineojo@interlink.co.ar

AUSTRALIA

Population: 19.2 million.
Number of Screens: 1,600.
Domestic Production: 30-40 films.

FILM COMMISSIONS

AUSTRALIAN FILM COMMISSION
Level 4, 150 William Street, Woolloomooloo NSW 2011. Tel: (61 2) 9321 6444. FAX: (61 2) 9357 3737. email: info@afc.gov.au
www.afc.gov.au

Level 15, 111 George St., Brisbane QLD 4000. Tel: (61 7) 3224 4114. FAX: (61 7) 3224 6717. email: ojohnston@pftc.com.au

Level 2, 120 Clarendon St., Southbank, VIC 3006. Tel: (61 3) 8646 4300. FAX: (61 3) 9696 1476. email: infomelb@afc.gov.au

AUSTRALIAN FILM FINANCE CORP.
Bob Campbell, G. P.O. Box 3886, Sydney NSW 2001
130 Elizabeth St., Sydney NSW 2001. Tel: (61 2) 9268 2555. FAX: (61 2) 9264 8551. www.ffc.gov.au

AUSTRALIAN FILM, TELEVISION & RADIO SCHOOL
P.O. Box 126, North Ryde, NSW 2113. Tel: (61 2) 9805 6611. FAX: (61 2) 9887 1030. email: direct.sales@syd.aftrs.edu.au

FILM AUSTRALIA
101 Eton Road, Lindfield NSW 2070, Level 12. Tel: (61 2) 9413 8777. FAX: (61 2) 9416 5672.

N.S.W. FILM & TELEVISION
P.O. Box 1744, Sydney, NSW 2000. Tel: (61 2) 9380 5599. FAX: (61 2) 9360 1090.

NEW SOUTH WALES FILM & TV OFFICE
Level 6, 1 Francis St., East Sydney, NSW 2000. Tel: (61 2) 9380 5599. FAX: (61 2) 9360 1090, 9360 1095.

PACIFIC FILM & TELEVISION COMMISSION
Level 16, 111 George St., Brisbane, QLD 4000. Tel: (61 7) 3224 4114. FAX: (61 7) 3224 4077.

SCREEN WEST
Western Australian Film & TV, Office 4 Catherine Court, 420 Hay St., Subiaco, WA 6008. Tel: (61 9) 9382 2500. FAX: (61 9) 9381 2848.

GOVERNMENT OFFICES

AUSTRALIAN TAXATION OFFICE
GPO Box 4197, Sydney, NSW 2001. Tel: (61 2) 9374 2111. FAX: (61 2) 9374 8150.

DEPARTMENT OF ARTS, SPORTS, ENVIRONMENT, TOURISM & TERRITORIES
GPO Box 1920, Canberra City, ACT 2601. Tel: (61 6) 9275 3000. FAX: (61 6) 9275 3819.

FILM AUSTRALIA PTY., LTD.
101 Eton Road, Lindfield, NSW 2070. Tel: (61 2) 9413 8777. FAX: (61 2) 9416 9401.

FILM AND LITERATURE BOARD OF REVIEW
Level 1, 255 Elizabeth St., Sydney, NSW 2000. Tel: (61 2) 9581 7000. FAX: (61 2) 9581 7001.

NATIONAL FILM & SOUND ARCHIVE
McCoy Circuit, Acton, ACT 2601. Tel: (61 6) 9267 1711. FAX: (61 6) 9247 4651.

SOUTH AUSTRALIAN FILM CORPORATION
3 Butler Dr., Hendon, SA 5014. Tel: (61 8) 8348 9300. FAX: (61 8) 8347 0385.

STATE FILM CENTRE OF VICTORIA
17 St. Andrew's Place, East Melbourne, VIC. 3002. Tel: (61 3) 9651 1301. FAX: (61 3) 9651 1502.

STATE FILM LIBRARY OF NEW SOUTH WALES
Macquarie St., Sydney, NSW 2000. Tel: (61 2) 9230 1414. FAX: (61 2) 9223 3369.

DISTRIBUTORS AND PRODUCERS

ACORN FILM PRODUCTIONS PTY. LTD.
354 Highett St., Richmond, VIC 3121. Tel: (61 3) 9429 4531. Mobile: (018) 329 646. FAX: (61 3) 9428 4116.

A COUPLE A COWBOYS
38 Atchinson St., Crows Nest, NSW 2065. Tel: (61 2) 9438 2044. FAX: (61 2) 9438 4859.

THE AIREDALE FILM CO. PTY., LTD.
Ste. 4/6 Gurrigal St., Mosmon, NSW 2088. Tel: (61 2) 9968 4180.

ALCHEMY FILMS
2nd Flr., The Metro Building, 109 Edward St., Brisbane, QLD 4000. Tel: (61 7) 3221 1487. FAX: (61 7) 3221 4375.

ALFRED ROAD FILMS
25a Billyard Ave., Elizabeth Bay, NSW 2011. Tel: (61 2) 9356 3344. FAX: (61 2) 9358 1613.

ALMOST MANAGING CO. P/L
192 Elgin St., Carlton, VIC 3053. Tel: (61 3) 9347 1800. FAX: (61 3) 9347 0235.

ANJOHN INTERNATIONAL
19/151 Bayswater Rd., Rushcutters Bay 2011, NSW. Tel: (61 2) 9361 6536. FAX: (612) 9361 6521.

APOCALYPSE
111-114 Chandos St., Crows Nest, NSW 2065. Tel: (61 2) 9439 5044. FAX: (61 2) 9438 2647.

APPALOOSA FILMS
P.O. Box 552, Elsternwick, VIC 3185. Tel: (61 3) 9699 9722. FAX: (61 3) 9690 1764.

ARANDA FILM PRODUCTIONS PTY., LTD.
40 Bay St., Brighton, VIC 3186. Tel: (61 3) 9596 4847. FAX: (61 3) 596 3580.

ARENAFILM
270 Devonshire St,. Surry Hills, NSW 2010. Tel: (61 2) 9319 7011. FAX: (61 2) 9319 6906.
CONTACTS
Robert Connolly
John Maynard

ARCHIVE GENERATION FLMS PTY., LTD.
111 Nott St., Port Melbourne, VIC 3207. Tel: (61 3) 9646 1033. FAX: (61 3) 9646 2158.

ARTIST SERVICES
33 Nott St., Port Melbourne, VIC 3207. Tel: (61 3) 9646 3388. FAX: (61 3) 9646 7644.
CONTACTS
Andrew Knight
Steve Vizzard

AUSTRALIAN FILM THEATRE
114 Glenmore Rd., Paddington, NSW 2021. Tel: (61 2) 9368 5739. FAX: (61 2) 9360 1051.

AUSTRALIAN FILM INSTITUTE
49 Eastern Rd., South Melbourne, VIC 3205. Tel: (61 2) 9332 2111. FAX: (61 2) 9331 7145. www.afi.org.au
email: afi@vicnet.net.au
CEO
Ruth Jones

AUSTRAL VISION
52 Victoria St., North Sydney, NSW 2060. Tel: (61 2) 9922 4311. FAX: (61 2) 9922 6956.

AVALON FILMS CORPORATION
9 Albert St., Narranbeen, NSW 2101. Tel/FAX: (61 2) 9913 1175.

BANSKIA FILM & TV DISTRIBUTION
202 Tynte St., North Adelaide, SA 5006. Tel: (61 8) 8267 0290. FAX: (61 8) 8267 3383.

BARRON FILMS
Ste. 7, 85 Forrest St., Cottesloe, WA 6011. Tel: (61 8) 9385 1551. FAX: (61 8) 9385 2299.
OWNER
Paul Barron

BBC ENTERPRISES
11th Fl. 50 Berry St., North Sydney, NSW 2060. Tel: (61 2) 9957 3777. FAX: (61 2) 9957 6448.

BAZMARK
P.O. Box 430, Kings Cross, NSW 1340. Tel: (61 2) 9361 6668. FAX: (61 2) 9361 6667.
PRESIDENT
Baz Luhrmann

RICHARD BENCE PRODUCTIONS
299 Moray St., South Melbourne, VIC 3205. Tel: (61 3) 9690 9922. FAX: (6 13) 9699 1288.

BENDIGO STREET PRODUCTIONS
22 Bendigo St., Richmond, VIC 3121. Tel: (61 3) 9420 3377. FAX: (61 3) 9420 3654.

BEYOND INTERNATIONAL
1st Flr., 53 55 Brisbane St., Surry Hills 2010, NSW. Tel: (61 2) 9281 1266. FAX: (612) 9281 1261. www.beyond.com.au
CONTACT
Mikael Borglund

BIG BEAR PICTURE COMPANY PTD., LTD.
1 Simmons Lane, South Belgrave, VIC 3160. Tel: (61 3) 9754 5548. FAX: (61 3) 9754 8834.

BILCOCK & COPPING FILM PRODUCTIONS
183 Rouse St., Port Melbourne, VIC 3205. Tel: (61 3) 9646 0466. FAX: (61 3) 9646 0282.

BILL BENNETT PRODUCTIONS PTY., LTD.
P.O. Box 4117, Castlecrag, NSW 2068. Tel: (61 2) 9417 7744. FAX: (61 2) 9417 7601. email: billbenprods@aol.com

BINNABURA FILM CO. PTY., LTD.
P.O. Box 2124, Clovelly, NSW 2031. Tel: (61 2) 9665 6135. FAX: (61 2) 9665 4378. email: glenysmerle@one.act.au
CONTACT
Glenys Rowe

BLACK
80 Campbell St., Surry Hills, NSW 2010. Tel: (61 2) 9281 0088. FAX: (61 2) 9281 4616.

RICHARD BRADLEY PRODUCTIONS
Ste. 8 / 1st Flr., Sydney, Theatrical Centre, 2-8 Ennis Rd., Milson's Point, NSW 2061. Tel: (61 2) 9959 3588. FAX: (61 2) 9955 3808.

BRAY & HAYES
1/1 Ridge St., North Sydney, NSW 2060. Tel: (61 2) 9957 1559. FAX: (61 2) 9922 1931.

BRILLIANT FILMS
11/39 Rockley Rd., South Yarra, VIC 3141. Tel: (61 3) 9826 9682. FAX: (61 3) 9827 7419.

ROBERT BRUNING
P.O. Box 105, Cremorne Junction, NSW 2090. Tel: (61 2) 9906 6144, 9953 5867. FAX: (61 2) 9906 5402, 9953 3184.

BUCKINGHAM PICTURE PRODUCTIONS PTY., LTD.
98 Queens Parade, Newport Beach, NSW 2106. Tel: (61 2) 9979 9977. FAX: (61 2) 9979 9279, 9973 1341.

ANTHONY BUCKLEY PRODUCTIONS
P.O. Box 124, Willoughby, NSW 2068. Tel: (61 2) 9428 2344. FAX: (61 2) 9427 0247.

BURROWES FILM GROUP
1st Fl., 407 Coventry St., South Melbourne, VIC 3205. Tel: (61 3) 9690 0388. FAX: (61 3) 9696 1543.

CALIFORNIA CONNECTION PTY., LTD.
8 Stella Close, East Killara, NSW 2071. Tel: (61 2) 9498 7697. FAX: (61 2) 9499 2559.

CASCADE FILMS & MELBOURNE FILM STUDIOS
117 Rouse St,. Port Melbourne, VIC 3207. Tel: (61 3) 9646 4022. FAX: (61 3) 9646 6336. www.cascadefilms.com.au
email: info@cascadefilms.com.au
CONTACTS
David Parker
Nadia Tass

C B FILMS
Level 10, 8 West St., North Sydney, NSW 2060. Tel: (61 2) 9957 2788. FAX: (61 2) 9955 5759.

CENTAUR ENTERPRISES PTY., LTD.
89 Eddy Rd. Chatswood, NSW 2067. Tel: (61 2) 9411 5885. FAX: (61 2) 9411 1458.

CHRISTIAN TELEVISION ASSOCIATION OF QUEENSLAND
16 Hasp St., Seventeen Mile Rocks, QLD 4073. Tel: (61 7) 3279 0600. FAX: (61 7) 3279 0699.

CINEMATIC SERVICES PTY., LTD.
Lvl 1/116 Prince Albert St., Mosman, NSW 2088. Tel: (61 2) 9960 3811.

CINE SERVICE
233-235 Moray St., South Melbourne, VIC 3205. Tel: (61 3) 9699 6999.

COLOSIMO FILM PRODUCTIONS
22 Hanover St., Fitzroy, VIC 3065. Tel: (61 3) 9417 1241. FAX: (61 3) 9416 1779.

COLUMBIA TRISTAR FILM DISTRIBUTORS INTERNATIONAL
GPO Box 3342, ydney, NSW 2001. Tel: (61 2) 9272 2900. FAX: (61 2) 9272 2991.

CONTINENTAL MOUNTS AUSTRALIA
45 Grafton St., Naremburn, Sydney, NSW 2065. Tel: (61 2) 9906 4777. FAX: (61 2) 9436 3553.

CO-PRODUCTIONS AUSTRALIA PTY., LTD.
104 Longwood Rd., Heathfield, North Adelaide, SA 5153. Tel/FAX: (61 8) 8370 9062.

JANINA CRAIG SCREEN SERVICES PTY., LTD.
16 Bridport St., South Melbourne, VIC 3205. Tel: (61 3) 9690 1229. FAX: (61 3) 9699 6986.

PAUL DAVIES FILM AND TELEVISION ENTERPRISES
62 South Road, Brighton, VIC 3186. Tel: (613) 9597 0596. FAX: (613) 9598 6853.

DENDY FILMS
34 Louisa Rd., Birchgrove 2041, NSW. Tel: (612) 810 8733. FAX: (612) 810 3228.

DIGITAL ARTS FILM & TELEVISION
1 Ledger Rd., Beverly, SA 5009. Tel: (618) 8347 4691. FAX: (618) 8347 4692.

DISCOVERY INTERNATIONAL
P.O. Box 550, Malvern 3144, Victoria. Tel: (613) 563 9344. FAX: (613) 563 9885.

EASTWAY COMMUNICATIONS
Ste. 109, 6/8 Clarke St., Crows Nest, NSW 2065. Tel: (612) 9437 6155. FAX: (612) 9439 4387.

EDGECLIFF FILMS
25 Suffolk St., Paddington, NSW 2021. Tel: (612) 9331 6277. FAX: (612) 9331 2588.

EMPRESS ROAD PRODUCTIONS PTY., LTD.
1-126 Brighton Rd., Bondi, NSW 2026. Tel: (612) 9365 4073. FAX: (612) 9365 4529.

EN CUE PRODUCTIONS PTY., LTD.
P.O. Box 5291, West End, QLD 4101. Tel: (617) 3844 6242. FAX: (617) 3844 6285.

ENTERTAINMENT MEDIA PTY., LTD.
157 Eastern Rd., South Melbourne, VIC 3205. Tel: (613) 9690 1044. FAX: (613) 9690 1764.

ENTREG PTY., LTD.
1075 High St., Armdale, VIC 3143. Tel: (613) 9822 6999. FAX: (613) 9822 0957.

FAST FORWARD PTY., LTD.
Innovation Hse., Technology Park, The Levels, SA 5095. Tel/FAX: (618) 8260 8139.

FILM & TELEVISION INSTITUTE (WA) INC
92 Adelaide St., Fremantle, WA 6160. Tel: (619) 335 1055. FAX: (619) 335 1283.

FILM ASSOCIATES
22 Lindsay Ave., Murrumbeena, VIC 3163. Tel: (613) 9568 3741.

FILM AUSTRALIA
Eaton Rd., Linfield 2070, NSW. Tel: (612) 413 8777. FAX: (612) 416 5672.

THE FILM BUSINESS & PARTNERS
91 Reservoir St., Surry Hills, NSW 2010. Tel: (612) 9281 8380. FAX: (612) 9281 8155.

FILM CENTRE AUSTRALIA
E270 The Esplanade, Swan Point, TAS 7275. Tel/FAX: (613) 6399 4903.

FILMPARTNERSHIP & ASSOCIATES
12 Fifth St., Black Rock, VIC 3193. Tel: (613) 9589 3622. FAX: (613) 9534 3502.

FILM TAGGS
52a Anzac Ave., West Ryde, NSW 2114. Tel/FAX: (612) 9807 4914.

FIRST CLASS FILMS
40 Osgathorpe Rd., Gladesville, NSW 2111. Tel: (612) 9816 1813. FAX: (612) 9816 5402.

FONTANA FILMS PTY., LTD.
360 Pacific Highway, Crows Nest, NSW 2068. Tel: (612) 9906 2188. FAX: (612) 9906 2337.

FOX TELEVISION
Level 25, 44 Market St., Sydney, NSW 2000. Tel: (612) 9299 2941. FAX: (612) 9290 2623.

FRONTIER FILMS
P.O. Box 294, Harbord, NSW 2096. Tel: (612) 9938 5762.

FUNNY FARM
68 Cecil St., South Melbourne, VIC 3205. Tel: (613) 9690 4466. FAX: (613) 9696 7977.

GARNER MACLENNAN DESIGN
P.O. Box 1418, Crows Nest, NSW 2065. Tel: (612) 9438 1002. FAX: (612) 9439 6710.

GENESIS FILMS PTY., LTD.
82 Eton Rd., Somerton Park, SA 5044. Tel: (618) 8295 5353. FAX: (618) 8295 6898. email: genesisfilm@msn.com

GOLDEN DOLPHIN PRODUCTIONS
P.O. Box 398, Spit Junction, NSW 2088. Tel: (612) 9971 1783. FAX: (612) 9971 2261.

GREAT SOUTHERN FILMS PTY., LTD.
5 Haig St., South Melbourne, VIC 3205. Tel: (613) 9699 6466. FAX: (613) 9699 6400.

GREAT SOUTHERN FILMS (SA) PTY., LTD.
16 Conyngham St., Glenside, SA 5065. Tel: (618) 8388 2811. FAX: (618) 8388 3090.

GREAT SOUTHERN FILMS (SYD) PTY., LTD.
Studio 18, 37 Nicholson St., Balmain East., Sydney 2041. Tel: (612) 9818 3377. FAX: (612) 9818 3378.

GREATER UNION ORGANISATION PTY., LTD.
State Theatre Building, 49 Market St., Sydney, NSW 2000. Tel: (612) 9373 6600. FAX: (612) 9267 5277.

HANNA-BARBERA AUSTRALIA
c/o Southern Star Group, 8 West St., North Sydney, NSW 2060. Tel: (612) 9202 8555. FAX: (612) 9925 0849.

DAVID HANNAY PRODUCTIONS
2 Buckland St. Amend, Broadway, NSW 2007. Tel: (612) 9211 2022. FAX: (612) 9212 2350.

THE HAYDEN GROUP OF COMPANIES
380 Military Rd., Cremorne, NSW 2090. Tel: (612) 9908 1799. FAX: (612) 9908 4238.

HAYDON PRODUCTIONS
P.O. Box 185, Rose Bay, NSW 2029. Tel: (612) 9388 1990. FAX: (612) 9388 1991.

HELICAM
P.O. Box 310, Yandina, QLD 4561. Tel/FAX: (6174) 46 8482.

HOUSE AND MOORHOUSE FILMS PTY.
117 Rouse St., Port Melbourne, VIC 3207. Tel: (613) 9646 4025. FAX: (613) 9646 6336.

HOYTS FOX COLUMBIA TRI-STAR FILMS
490 Kent St., Sydney 2000, NSW. Tel: (612) 261 7800. FAX: (612) 283 2191.

ILLUMINATION FILMS
1 Victoria Ave., Albert Park, VIC 3206. Tel: (613) 9690 5266. FAX: (613) 9696 5625.

INLAND FILMS PTY., LTD.
27 Surfside Ave., Clovelly, NSW 2031. Tel: (612) 9665 2977. Mobile: (018) 259 936. FAX: (612) 9665 7773.

JD PRODUCTIONS
116 Crescent Rd., Newport, NSW 2106. Tel: (612) 9997 1601. FAX: (612) 9979 5083.

J'ELLY BALLANTYNE PRODUCTIONS
119B Old Mt. Barker Rd., Stirling, SA 5152. Tel: (618) 8370 9458 FAX: (618) 8370 9487.

JNP FILMS
87 Alexander St., Crows Nest, NSW 2065. Tel: (612) 9439 5855. FAX: (613) 9436 0583.

JSA PRODUCTIONS PTY., LTD.
16/16 Lyall St., Leichhardt, NSW 2040. Tel/FAX: (612) 9564 1957.

KALEIDOSCOPE PRODUCTIONS
22 Hewlett St., Waverley, NSW 2024. Tel: (612) 9387 7117. FAX: (612) 9387 7156.

KANANGRA FILMS
56 Carranya Road, Lane Cove, NSW 2066. Tel: (612) 9428 4268.

KAVANAGH PRODUCTIONS PTY., LTD.
7/15 South Terrace, Clifton Hill, VIC 3068. Tel: (613) 9481 4312. (613) 9481 4695.

KENNEDY MILLER
Metro Theatre, 30 Orwell St., Kings Cross, NSW 2011. Tel: (612) 9357 2322. FAX: (612) 9356 3162.

KESTREL FILM & VIDEO
367 Bridge Road, Richmond, VIC 3121. Tel: (613) 9429 1688. FAX: (613) 9428 6202.

KOOKABURRA PRODUCTIONS PTY. LTD.
P.O. Box 555, Artarmon, NSW 2064. Tel: (612) 9438 4344. FAX: (612) 9906 1701.

LATENT IMAGE PRODUCTIONS PTY. LTD.
82 Glenmore Rd., Paddingfton, NSW 2021. Tel: (612) 9331 4155. FAX: (612) 9331 4135.

LEA FILMS
P.O. Box 93, North Carlton, VIC 3084. Tel: (613) 9646 9455. FAX: (613) 9646 0220.

LOOK PRODUCTIONS
83 Willoughby Road, Crows Nest, NSW 2065. Tel: (612) 9436 1647. FAX: (612) 9438 3660.

LORI DALE PRODUCTIONS PTY., LTD.
120 Bridport St., Albert Park, VIC 3206. Tel: (613) 9699 8400. FAX: (613) 9699 3048.

LOVELL FILMS
P.O. Box 701, Avalon Beach, NSW 2107. Tel: (612) 9918 2999. FAX: (612) 9918 0883.

PETER LUCK PRODUCTIONS
19 Edward St., East Balmain, NSW 2041. Tel: (612) 9810 2458. FAX: (612) 9818 5325.

LUCKY COUNTRY PRODUCTIONS
Tagallant House, Scotland Island, NSW 2105. Tel: (612) 9977 3405. FAX: (612) 9977 8953.

LUMIERE PRODUCTIONS PTY. LTD.
51 Farnell St., Hunters Hill, NSW 2110. Tel: (612) 9879 6140.

LYONS-SINCLAIR PRODUCTIONS
P.O. Box 83, Toorak, VIC 3142. Tel/FAX: (613) 9827 4641.

MACAU LIGHT CORPORATION LTD.
16 Lang Road, Centennial Park, NSW 2021. Tel: (612) 9361 3961. FAX: (612) 9360 3346.

MARLO AUDIO VISUAL
P.O. Box 50, Belgian Gardens, Townsville, QLD 4810. Tel: (61018) 777 709. FAX: (61018) 180 927.

MASON PICTURE COMPANY
Ste. 3/239 Pacific Hwy., North Sydney, NSW 2060. Tel: (612) 9959 3500. FAX: (612) 9959 3679.

MAX STUDIOS
19-25 Birmingham St., Alexandria, NSW 2015. Tel: (612) 9317 2999. FAX: (612) 9667 4528.

MCA
1st Flr., MCA Universal House, 23 Pelican Street, Sydney 2010, NSW. Tel: (612) 267 9844. FAX: (612) 264 1742.

M. C. STUART AND ASSOCIATES
88 Highett St., Richmond 3121, Victoria. Tel: (613) 429 8666. FAX: (613) 429 1839.

MEANINGFUL EYE CONTACT
18 Moor Ave., West Lindfield, NSW 2071. Tel/FAX: (612) 9416 9662.

MEDIACAST PTY., LTD.
P.O. Box 67, Round Corner, Dural, NSW 2158. Tel: (612) 9651 4219. FAX: (612) 9482 1298.

MEDIA WORLD
278 Gore St., Fitzroy, VIC 3065. Tel: (613) 9417 4888. FAX: (613) 9417 5383.

METRO TELEVISION, LTD.
249 Oxford St. (Cnr Oatley Rd.), Paddington, NSW 2021. Tel: (612) 9361 5318, 9361 3048. FAX: (612) 9361 5320.

MGM/UA
P.O. Box 6125, Shopping World, North Sydney, NSW 2060. Tel: (612) 9966 1711. FAX: (612) 9966 1969.

HARRY MICHAEL PRODUCTIONS
7 McCabe Place, Willoughby, NSW 2068. Tel: (612) 9417 5700. FAX: (612) 9417 5879.

HARRY M. MILLER AND COMPANY MANAGEMENT PTY., LTD.
174 Cathedral St., Woolloomooloo, NSW 2011. Tel: (612) 9357 3077. FAX: (612) 9356 2880.

MILTON INGERSON PRODUCTIONS
2a Torrens St., Linden Park, SA 5065. Tel: (618) 8338 1666. FAX: (618) 8338 2510.

MODERN TIMES PTY., LTD.
P.O. Box 908, Bondi Junction, NSW 2022. Tel: (612) 9365 2416. FAX: (612) 9365 2454.

MURRAY MANCHA PTY., LTD.
199 Richardson St., Middle Park, VIC 3206. Tel: (613) 9690 2510. FAX: (613) 9690 6981.

NALUSA PTY., LTD.
1st Fl., 34 Burton St., Kirribilli, NSW 2061. Tel: (612) 9925 0716. FAX: (612) 9922 3063.

NEW BLOOD & OLD MONEY
28-30 Surrey St., Darlinghurst, NSW 2010. Tel: (612) 9361 5002. FAX: (612) 9361 4701.

NEW VISION FILM DISTRIBUTORS
2nd Flr., 254 Bay St., Port Melbourne 3207, Victoria. Tel: (613) 646 5555. FAX: (613) 646 2411.

N.S.W. FILM & TELEVISION
GPO Box 1744, Sydney, NSW 2000. Tel: (612) 9380 5599. FAX: (612) 9360 1090.

ORACLE PICTURES
St. Dugham St., Level 12, 15/19 Boundary St., Rushcutters Bay, NSW 2011. Tel: (612) 9358 3788. FAX: (612) 9357 1723.

ORANA FILMS PTY. LTD.
133 Dowling St., Woolloomooloo, NSW 2011. Tel: (612) 9356 2266. FAX: (612) 9356 2629.

OPEN EYE (FILM & TV)
1/87 Bent St., North Sydney 2060, NSW. Tel: (612) 954 3626. FAX: (612) 959 3253.

OXFORD FILM SERVICES
Ste. 1, 372 Anzac Pde., Kingsford, NSW 2032. Tel: (612) 9662 8842. FAX: (612) 9662 7663.

PACIFIC LINK COMMUNICATIONS
2A Eltham St., Gladesville 2111, NSW. Tel: (612) 817 5055. FAX: (612) 879 7297.

PALACE ENTERTAINMENT
1/101 Union St., North Sydney 2060, NSW. Tel: (612) 954 3323. FAX: (612) 954 3306.

PARAMOUNT PICTURES
Ste. 3209, Australia Square, Sydney 2000, NSW. Tel: (612) 247 9367. FAX: (612) 251 3251.

DAMIEN PARER PRODUCTIONS
5 Longfellow St., Norman Park, QLD 4170. Tel: (317) 3899 1555. FAX:(317) 3899 1936.

PAVILLION FILM PTY., LTD.
P.O. Box 701, Avalon Beach, NSW 2107. Tel: (312) 9918 2999. FAX: (312) 9918 0883.

PICTURE START
4 Glen St., Milsons Point, NSW 2061. Tel: (612) 9959 5550. Mobile: (0181) 961 013. FAX: (612) 9929 5961.

POLYGON PICTURES
19 Forest Knoll Ave., Bondi, NSW 2026. Tel: (612) 9365 2955. FAX: (612) 9365 2711.

POLYGRAM FILMED ENTERTAINMENT
3 Munn Reserve, Sydney 2000. Tel: (612) 207 0500. FAX: (612) 241 1497.
CONTACT
Richard Sheffield MacClure

PREMIUM FILMS
92 Bay St., Port Melbourne 3207, Victoria. Tel: (613) 645 1612. FAX: (613) 645 1591.

PRO FILMS
Level 2/486 Pacific Highway, St. Leonards, NSW 2065. Tel: (612) 9438 3377. FAX: (612) 9439 1827.

QUANTAS
14 Bourke Rd., Mascot 2020, NSW. Tel: (612) 691 1069. FAX: (612) 691 1865.

QUEST FILMS
4 Marshall Ave., St. Leonards, NSW 2065. Tel: (612) 9436 1970. Mobile: (18) 967 336. FAX: (612) 9436 1970.

REEPRODUCTIONS PTY., LTD.
56 Gipps St., Birchgrove, NSW 2041. Tel: (612) 9818 4908. Mobile: (18) 416 704. FAX: (612) 9810 3086.

REID AND PUSKAR
44 Moruben Rd., Mosman 2088, NSW. Tel: (612) 969 2077. FAX: (612) 960 4971.

R I P PRODUCTIONS
5 Little Chapel St., Prahan, VIC 3181. Tel: (613) 9529 2144. FAX: (613) 9529 6953.

RKA THE ANIMATION STUDIO
21 Harris St., Paddington, NSW 2021. Tel: (612) 9362 4669. FAX: (612) 9362 3711.

ROADSHOW COOTE AND CARROLL PTY.
1st Flr., 608 Harris St., Ultimo, NSW 2009. Tel: (612) 9211 2211. FAX: (612) 9211 2144.

ROGUE PRODUCTIONS
30 South St., Fremantle, WA 6160. Tel: (619) 335 2426.

ROSEN HARPER ENTERTAINMENT
5/2 New McLean St., Edgecliff, NSW 2027. Tel: (612) 9363 5658.

ROSS WOOD PRODUCTIONS
36 Gosbell St., Paddington, NSW 2021. Tel: (612) 9331 5154. FAX: (612) 9360 1583.

SAGITTA FILM PRODUCTIONS
32 Barcoo St., East Roseville, NSW 2069. Tel: (612) 9417 5643. FAX: (612) 9417 6443.

SAMSON PRODUCTIONS
119 Pyrmont St., Pyrmont, NSW 2009. Tel: (612) 9660 3244. FAX: (612) 9692 8926.

SEA FILMS PTY., LTD.
7 Woodsmans Copse, Hallett Cove, SA 5158. Tel/FAX: (618) 8322 3127.

SERIOUS ENTERTAINMENT
P.O. Box 600, North Sydney, NSW 2060. Tel: (612) 9957 5375. FAX: (612) 9955 8600.

SEVEN DIMENSIONS PTY., LTD.
8 Daly St., South Yarra, VIC 3141. Tel: (613) 9826 2277. FAX: (613) 9826 4477.

SHARMILL FILMS
Ste. 4, 200 Toorak Rd., South Yarra 3141, Victoria. Tel: (613) 826 9077. FAX: (613) 826 1935.

SHOT PRODUCTIONS
P.O. Box 305, Darlinghurst, NSW 2010. Tel: (612) 9360 5733. FAX: (612) 9360 5535.

SIMPLE STORIES
RMB 1117A, Wodonga, VIC 3691. Tel: (6157) 545 262. FAX: (613) 699 3123.

SMILEY FILMS
33 Riley St., Woolloomooloo, NSW 2011. Tel: (612) 9361 4164. FAX: (612) 9692 8387.

SOERABAIA PICTURES PTY., LTD.
6 David St., Forest Lodge, NSW 2037. Tel: (612) 9552 2634. FAX: (612) 9692 8387.

SOKOL FILM PRODUCTIONS
P.O. Box 1599, North Sydney, NSW 2059. Tel: (612) 9959 5526. Mobile: (018) 678 792. FAX: (612) 9959 5714.

SORENA
P.O. Box 215, French Forest, NSW 2086. Tel: (612) 9417 8112, 9417 8138.

SOUTH AUSTRALIAN FILM CORPORATION
3 Butler Dr., Hendon, SA 5014. Tel: (618) 8348 9300. FAX: (618) 8347 0385.

SOUTHERN CROSS NETWORK
1-3 Bowen Rd., Moonah, TAS 7009. Tel: (613) 6344 0202. FAX: (613) 6343 0340.

SOUTHERN STAR ENTERTAINMENT
10th Flr., 8 West St., North Sydney, NSW 2060. Tel: (612) 9202 8555. FAX: (612) 9925 0849.

SOUTHERN STAR INTERNATIONAL
10th fl., 8 West St., North Sydney, NSW 2060. Tel: (612) 9202 8555. FAX: (612) 9925 0849.

WILL SPENCER PRODUCTIONS PTY., LTD.
22 Hanover St., Fitzroy, VIC 3065. Tel: (613) 9417 1241. FAX: (613) 9416 1779.

SPOTZ CASTING AGENCIES
10/a 31-37 Thompson St., Bowen Hill, QLD 4006. Tel: (617) 3854 1949. FAX: (617) 3252 7237.

SPROWLES OFF BROADWAY FILMS
8-14 Nelson St., Annandale, Sydney, NSW 2038. Tel: (612) 9550 5599. FAX: (612) 9550 5742.

STRAUSS PRODUCTIONS
P.O. Box 167, Round Corner, NSW 2158. Tel: (612) 9899 1691. Mobile: (018) 222 886. FAX: (612) 9680 2871.

STUART, M C & ASSOCIATES PTY., LTD.
88 Highett St., Richmond, VIC 3121. Tel: (613) 9429 8666. Telex: AA 33147 MCSAA. FAX: (613) 9429 1839.

D. L. TAFFNER AUSTRALIA
Unit 20, Greenwich Square, 130-134 Pacific Highway, Greenwich 2065, NSW. Tel: (612) 439 5699. FAX: (612) 439 4501.

TAFFNER RAMSEY PRODUCTIONS
Ste. 303, 156 Pacific Hwy., Greenwich, NSW 2065. Tel: (612) 9437 5433. FAX: (612) 9437 4501.

WILLIAM THOMAS FILM PRODUCTIONS
10 Carlton Rd., Camden Park, SA 5038. Tel: (618) 8294 4468. FAX: (618) 8294 9434.

TMS DISTRIBUTION
Level 1, 50 King St., Sydney, NSW 2000. Tel: (612) 9299 5788. FAX: (612) 9299 5704.

TROUT FILMS PTY., LTD.
189 St. Georges Rd., North Fitzroy, VIC 3068. Tel: (613) 9489 3127. FAX: (612) 9486 3618. email: troutfilms@ibm.net
DIRECTOR
Chris Warner

ULLADULLA PICTURE COMPANY
Ste. 5, 600 Military Rd., Mosman, NSW 2088. Tel: (612) 9969 7599. FAX: (612) 9969 5011.

UNITED INTERNATIONAL PICTURES
Unit 1, 11 Parkview St., Milton, QLD 4064. Tel: (617) 367 0633. FAX: (617) 367 0688.
208 Clarence St., Sydney 2000, NSW. Tel: (612) 264 7444. FAX: (612) 264 3203.
Unit 4, 113 Adderley St., West Melbourne, VIC 3003. Tel: (613) 9326 6966. FAX: (613) 9329 6247.
MANAGER
Michael Selwyn

VALKYRIE FILMS
166 Glebe Point Rd., Glebe 2037, NSW. Tel: (612) 552 2456. FAX: (612) 552 2457.

VIACOM INTERNATIONAL
Ste. 3501, Level 35s Tower, North Point, 100 Miller St., North Sydney, NSW 2060. Tel: (612) 9922 2322. FAX: (612) 9955 6808.

VICTORIAN COUNCIL FOR CHILDREN'S FILM & TV
41 St. Andrews Place, East Melbourne, VIC 3002. Tel: (613) 9651 1919. FAX: (613) 9651 1238.

VICTORIAN INTERNATIONAL PICTURES
Melbourne Film Studios, 117 Rouse St., Port Melbourne, VIC 3207. Tel: (613) 9646 4777. FAX: (613) 9646 4946.

VIEW FILMS PTY., LTD.
2nd fl., 41 Oxford St., Darlinghurst, NSW 2010. Tel: (612) 283 3066.

VILLAGE ROADSHOW PICTURES
Warner Roadshow Movie World, Studios, Pacific Way, Oxenford, Gold Coast, QLD 4210. Tel: (7) 5588 6666. FAX: (7) 5573 3698.

VILLAGE ROADSHOW PICTURES
4th Flr., 235 Pyrmont St., Pyrmont 2009, NSW. Tel: (612) 552 8600. FAX: (612) 552 2510.

VIRGIN VISION AUSTRALIA
99 Victoria St., Potts Point 2011, NSW. Tel: (612) 368 1700.

VISIONLINK & CULT PRODUCTIONS
44 Sailors Bay Road, Northbridge, NSW 2063. Tel: (612) 9958 2077. FAX: (612) 9958 2974.

WALKER CLANCY
Unit 16, 2 Greenkowne Ave., Potts Point, NSW 2021. Tel: (612) 9358 1163. FAX: (612) 9368 1064.

THE WALT DISNEY COMPANY
149 Castlereagh St., Sydney 2000, NSW. Tel: (612) 268 942. FAX: (612) 264 1289.

WARNER BROTHERS AUSTRALIA
Level 22, 8-20 Napier St., North Sydney, NSW. Tel: (612) 957 3899. FAX: (612) 956 7788.
CONTACT
Fiona Curtis

WESTBRIDGE PRODUCTIONS PTY., LTD.
P.O. Box 219, Port Douglas, QLD 4871. Tel: (6170) 985 577. FAX: (6170) 994 295.

WILD VISUALS PTY., LTD.
133 Dowling St., Woolloomooloo, NSW 2011. Tel: (612) 9331 0877. FAX: (612) 9357 4126. email: info@wildvisuals.com.au

WORLD VISION ENTERPRISES
2nd Flr., 5-13 Northcliff St., Milsons Point 2061, NSW. Tel: (612) 922 4722. FAX: (612) 955 8207.

ZAP PRODUCTIONS PTY., LTD.
24 Calotta St., Artamon, NSW 2064. Tel: (612) 9438 4333. FAX: (612) 9439 5172.

THEATRE EQUIPMENT

AUS-WIDE CINEMA & THEATRE SUPPLY
P.O. Box 205, Geebung, QLD 4030. Tel: (617) 3216 2566. FAX: (617) 3216 2588.
CONTACT
John Coleman

CAMATIC SEATING
93 Lewis Rd., Wantirna South, VIC 3152. Tel: (613) 9837 7777. FAX: (613) 9887 3485.
CONTACT
Horst Arton

COMPUTONICS
P.O. Box 276, Rockdal, NSW 2216. Tel: (612) 9559 4555. FAX: (612) 9559 4455.
CONTACT
Ossie Cesaro

ENTERTAINMENT SERVICES
Unit 7, 24 Deakin St., Drendale, QLD 4500. Tel: (617) 3881 3233. FAX: (617) 3881 3122.
CONTACT
Margaret Robbins

FERCO SEATING
No. 7m Jalan Sungau Besar 26/27, Section 2G, Shah Alam Selangor, Malaysia 40400. Tel: (603) 511 3233. FAX: (603) 512 9303.
CONTACT
Nadia Gourievidis

GOLD MEDAL
P.O. Box 2274, Mansfield, QLD 4122. Tel: (617) 3829 6228. FAX: (617) 3343 2998.
CONTACTS
Adrian Laugher
Pat Laugher

ICON SOFTWARE
Suite 3, 271 Alfred St. N., North Sydney, NSW 2060. (612) 9922 1400. FAX: (612) 9957 2459.
CONTACT
Matthew Ezra

IP FOODSERVICE
P.O. Box 81, Kingston, QLD 4114. Tel: (617) 9922 1400. FAX: (617) 3808 3133.
CONTACT
Andrew Fletcher

KODAK ENTERTAINMENT IMAGING
P.O. Box 90, Coburg, VIC 3058. Tel: (613) 9353 3784. FAX: (613) 9353 2962.
CONTACT
Karen Eastmure

MARS CONFECTIONARY OF AUSTRALIA
P.O. Box 633, Ballarat, VIC 3055. Tel: (613) 5337 7092. FAX: (613) 5337 7096.
CONTACT
Steve Porter

NESTLE AUSTRALIA & DISTRIBUTORS
P.O. Box 4320, Sydney, NSW 2000. Tel: (612) 9931 2628. FAX: (612) 9931 2926.
CONTACTS
Brenton Cornell
Nick Johnson

SUPERPOP
P.O. Box 153, Mt. Waverly, VIC 3149. Tel: (613) 9558 8000. FAX: (613) 9558 8288.
CONTACT
Janis Kondarovkis

TASCOT TEMPLETON CARPETS
119 Church St., Richmond, VIC 3121. Tel: (613) 9428 4925. FAX: (613) 9429 6234.
CONTACT
Anna M. Pulvirenti

TICKET SYSTEMS
26/380 Eastern Valley Way, Chatswood, NSW 2067. Tel: (612) 9417 6644. FAX: (612) 9417 6488.
CONTACT
Rowan Morrison

VAL MORGAN CINEMA ADVERTISING
P.O. Box 538, North Sydney, NSW 2095. Tel: (612) 9929 0388. FAX: (612) 9929 7297.
CONTACT
Angela Grozos

EXHIBITORS

AUSTRALIAN MULTIPLEX CINEMAS (AMC)
P.O. Box 2152, Brookside Centre, QLD 4520. Tel: (617) 33 55 33 53. FAX: (617) 33 54 47 00. www.a-m-c.com.au
email: amc@powerup.com.au
CHAIRMAN
James C. Sourris
CEO
Michael Hawkins

Number of Theatres: 6
Number of Screens: 39
QLD (5); NSW (1).

BIRCH CARROLL & COYLE
(owned by Greater Union)
418 Adelaide St., Brisbane, QLD 4000. Tel: (617) 33 35 02 22. FAX: (617) 38 32 11 01.

Number of Theatres: 29
Number of Screens: 214

DENDY CINEMAS
19 Martin Pl., Sydney, NSW 2000. Tel: (612) 92 33 85 58. FAX: (612) 92 32 38 41. www.dendy.com.au
email: dendy@dendy.com.au
HEAD OF DENDY CINEMAS
Mark Sarfaty

Number of Theatres: 5
Number of Screens: 11
NSW, QLD, VIC.

GRAND CINEMAS
P.O. Box 2137, Warwick, WA 6024. Tel: (618) 94 48 31 88. FAX: (618) 92 46 17 55. www.moviemasters.com.au
email: grandcin@wanet.com.au.
CHAIRMAN
Colin Stiles
MANAGING DIRECTOR
Alan Stiles

Number of Theatres: 3
Number of Screens: 19

THE GREATER UNION ORGANISATION
(Including BIRCH CARROLL & COYLE)
49 Market St., Sydney, NSW 2000. Tel: (612) 93 73 66 00. FAX: (612) 93 73 65 32. www.greaterunion.com.au
email: info@greaterunion.com.au
EXECUTIVE DIRECTOR
David Sergeant
GENERAL MANAGER
Richard Parton
MANAGER & FILM BUYER
Peter Cody
NATIONAL MARKETING MANAGER
Chris McGlinn
NATIONAL OPERATIONS MANAGER
Meil Merrin

Number of Theatres: 28 (Australia)
Number of Screens: 216 (Australia)

Theatres outside Australia: United Arab Emirates, Poland, The Netherlands, Germany.

HAYDEN THEATRES
380 Military Rd., Cremorne, NSW 2090. Tel: (612) 99 53 56 99. FAX: (612) 99 53 88 63. www.orpheum.com.au
CHAIRMAN
Mike Walsh
GENERAL MANAGER
Paul Dravet

Number of Theatres: 1
Number of Screens: 6

HOYTS CINEMAS PTY., LTD.
GPO Box 110, Sydney, NSW 2001. Tel: (612) 92 73 73 73. FAX: (612) 92 73 7356. www.hoyts.com.au
CEO
Paul Johnson
CFO
Wilfred Steiner
GENERAL MANAGER, PROGRAMMING
Noel Collier
GENERAL MANAGER, FINANCIAL & COMMERCIAL
Tony Murray
GENERAL MANAGER, NSW, VIC & QLD
David Maclagen
GENERAL MANAGER, SA & WA
Paul Colreavy

Number of Theatres: 46 (Australia)
Number of Screens: 361 (Australia)
NSW (18), ACT (1), VIC (9), SA (4), WA (5), QLD (4).
Number of Screens outside Australia: 1443

Hoyts Argentina
Avda Corriertes 447, 5 Piso, Buenos Aires, Argentina

Hoyts Chile
Roger de Flores #2736, Piso 6, Las Condes, Santiago, Chile

Hoyts Europe
St. Andrews House
22-28 High St., Epsom Surrey, KT19 89H

Hoyts New Zealand
44, 47 Wakefield St., Auckland.

NOVA CINEMAS
Lygon Court Shopping Centre, 380 Lygon St., Carlton, VIC. Tel: (613) 93 47 53 31. FAX: (613) 93 47 26 95.
EXECUTIVES
Natalie Miller
Barry Peake

OWNERS
Natalie Miller
Barry Peake
Palace Cinemas

Number of Theatres: 2
Number of Screens: 15

PACIFIC CINEMAS
P.O. Box 3018, Loganholme, QLD 4129. Tel: (617) 38 01 17 88. FAX: (617) 38 01 39 86. email: eatont@tq.com.au
CHAIRMAN
Terri Jackman
GENERAL MANAGER
Kirrily Nichols

Number of Theatres: 5
Number of Screens: 56

PALACE CINEMAS
P.O. Box 191, Balwyn, VIC 3103. Tel: (613) 98 17 64 21. FAX: (613) 98 17 49 21. www.apalce.net.au
MANAGING DIRECTOR
Antonio Zeccola
DIRECTOR
Benjamin M. Zeccola
GENERAL MANAGER
Sam Di Pietro
NATIONAL PROGRAMMING MANAGER
Kim Petalas
NATIONAL MARKETING MANAGER
Lynda Watts

Number of Theatres: 16
Number of Screens: 66

READING ENTERTAINMENT AUSTRALIA
6 Bay St., Port Melbourne, VIC 3207. Tel: (613) 69 44 19 00. FAX: (613) 96 46 11 85. www.readingcinemas.com.au
COO
Neil Pentecost
DIRECTOR, DEVELOPMENT
David Lawson
CFO
Eugene Cheah

Number of Theatres: 13
Number of Screens: 93

REGENT CINEMA–SOUTH COAST THEATRES PTY., LTD.
197 Keira St., Wollongong, NSW 2500. Tel: (612) 42 29-51 30.
MANAGING DIRECTOR
Rowena Milgrove

RONIN FILMS
P.O. Box 1005, Civic Square, ACT 2608. Tel: (612) 62 48 08 51. FAX: (612) 62 49 16 40. www.roninfilms.com.au
EXECUTIVES
Andrew Pike
Merrilyn Pike
OWNER
Pike-Fitzpatrick Nominees Pty., Ltd.

Number of Screens: 3

ROSEVILLE TWIN CINEMAS
112 Pacific Hwy., Roseville 2069. Tel: (612) 9416-5988. FAX: (612) 9416-3473.
MANAGER, DIRECTOR & OWNER
Emma van Pinxteren
MANAGER, DIRECTOR & OWNER
Lisa van Pinxteren
MANAGER, DIRECTOR & OWNER
Sue van Pinxteren

VILLAGE ANDERSON MANAGEMENT
P.O. Box 277, Ballarat, VIC 3353. (613) 53 31 13 39. FAX: (613) 53 33 43 68. email: glabc@vam.com.au
DIRECTOR
Marie Anderson
GENERAL MANAGER
Chris Glab

Number of Theatres: 2
Number of Screens: 17

VILLAGE ROADSHOW, LTD.
206 Bourke St., Melbourne, VIC 3000. Tel: (613) 96 67 66 66. FAX: (613) 96 39 15 40.
CHAIR
John Kirby
MANAGING DIRECTOR
Graham W. Burke
FINANCE DIRECTOR
P.E. Foo
GROUP COMPANY SECRETARY
P. Leggo
CO-CEO (VILLAGE CINEMAS INTL.)
J. Anderson
EXECUTIVE CHAIR & CO-CEO, EXHIBITION
J. Crawford

Number of Theatres: 79 (Australia)
Number of Screens: 574 (Australia)

Number of Theatres Worldwide: 192
Number of Screens Worldwide: 1538
Worldwide locations: Austria, Argentina, Czech Republic, Fiji, France, Greece, India, Italy, Korea, Malaysia, New Zealand, Singapore, Taiwan, Thailand, U.K.

WALLIS THEATRES
139 Richmond Rd., Richmond, SA 5033. Tel: (618) 8352 1377. FAX: (618) 8352 1865. email: wallis@wallis.com.au
CHAIRMAN
Bob Wallis
PROGRAM MANAGER
Bob Parr

Number of Theatres: 8
Number of Screens: 20

WARNER BROS. INTERNATIONAL THEATRES
4000 Warner Blvd., Building 160, 2nd flr., Burbank, CA 91522. Tel: (818) 977-6278. FAX: (818) 977-6040.
PRESIDENT
Millard L. Ochs
V.P., OPERATIONAL FINANCE, INFORMATION SERVICES & ADMINISTRATION
David Bent
S.V.P., WORLDWIDE OPERATIONS
Dave Pearson
V.P., FINANCE
Paul Miller
V.P., BUSINESS AFFAIRS & GENERAL COUNSEL
James Birch
V.P., INTERNATIONAL FILM RELATIONS
Peter Dobson
S.V.P., ARCHITECTURE & CONSTRUCTION
Ira Stiegler

Level 6, 116 Military Rd., Neutral Bay, NSW 2089. Tel: (612) 94 95 30 70. FAX: (612) 94 95 30 67.
VICE PRESIDENT, AUSTRALIA
William S. Prentice
MANAGER, FINANCE, AUSTRALIA
Matt Turner

Number of Theatres (Australia): 30
Number of Screens (Australia): 318

WESTSIDE CINEMAS
P.O. Box 77, Indooroopilly, QLD 4068. Tel: (617) 33 78 15 66. FAX: (617) 33 78 15 04. www.eldorado8.com.au
EXECUTIVES
Ray Roobottom
Judy Roobottom
Paul Roobottom

Number of Theatres: 2
Number of Screens: 10

AUSTRIA

Population: 8.1 million.
Ticket Price: $6.24.
Theatre grosses: $80.9 million.

ASSOCIATIONS & ORGANIZATIONS

AKTION FILM
(Austrian Section of the International Center of Films for Children and Young Children), Neubaugasse 25, Vienna A-1070. Tel: (431) 523 2437. FAX: (431) 523 3971.

ARGE OSTERREICHISCHES DREHBUCHAUTOREN-DREHBUCHFORUM WIEN
Stiftgasse 6, Vienna A-1070. (431) 526 8503 500. FAX: (431) 526 8503 550.

ART DIRECTORS & COSTUME DESIGNERS ASSOCIATION
Siegelgasse 1/16, Vienna A-1030. (431) 523 6085. FAX: (431) 523 6085.

ASIFA-AUSTRIA (INTERNATIONAL ANIMATED FILM ASSOCIATION)
Huttelberggasse 75/1, Vienna A-1140. (431) 914 7797. FAX: (431) 712 0392.

ASSOCIATION OF AUSTRIAN FILM DIRECTORS
Spittelberggasse 3, Vienna A-1070. Tel: (431) 526 0006. FAX: (431) 426 0006 16.

ASSOCIATION OF AUSTRIAN FILM JOURNALISTS
Speisinger Strasse 4, Vienna A-1130. Tel: (431) 804 3561. FAX: (431) 804 1720.

ASSOCIATION OF AUSTRIAN FILM PRODUCERS
Speisinger Strasse 121-127, Vienna A-1230. Tel: (431) 888 9622.

ASSOCIATION OF DISTRIBUTORS
Wiener Hauptstrasse 63, P.O. Box 327, Vienna A-1045. Tel.: (431) 50105 3011. FAX: (431) 50206 376.

AUSTRIA FILMMAKERS CO-OPERATIVE
Wahringer Str. 59, Vienna A-1090. Tel: (431) 408 7627. FAX: (431) 408 7627.

AUSTRIAN ASSOCIATION OF CINEMATOGRAPHERS (AAC)
Karlsplatz 5, Künstlerhaus, Vienna A-1010. Tel: (431) 713 6611. FAX: (431) 587 9665.

AUSTRIAN FILM COMMISSION–AFC
Stiftgasse 6, Vienna A-1070. Tel: (431) 526 3323 200. FAX: (431) 526 6801.

AUSTRIAN FILM FUND
Stiftgasse 6, Vienna A-1070. Tel: (431) 526 9730 406. FAX: (431) 526 9730 440.

AUSTRIAN FILM INSTITUTE
Stiftgasse 6, Vienna A-1070. Tel: (431) 523 9730 400. FAX: (431) 526 9730 440.

AUSTRIAN SOCIETY OF SOUND ENGINEERS
Natteregasse 4, Laxenburg A-2361. Tel: (43) 2236 71307. FAX: (43) 2236 71307.

FEDERATION OF AUSTRIAN FILM PRODUCERS
Neubaugasse 25, Vienna A-1070. Tel: (431) 523 7437. FAX: (431) 526 4302/3.

NATIONAL TOURIST OFFICE
Margaretenstrasse 1, Vienna A-1040. Tel: (431) 588 660. FAX: (431) 588 660.

AUDIENCE RESEARCH

AUSTRIAN SOCIETY FOR FILM SCIENCES, COMMUNICATION & MEDIA STUDIES
Rauhensteingasse 6, Vienna A-1010. Tel: (431) 512 9936. FAX: (431) 513 5330. email: oegfkm@cybertron.at

DISTRIBUTORS

AKTION FILM (AUSTRIAN SECTION OF THE INTERNATIONAL CENTER OF FILMS FOR CHILDREN AND YOUNG PEOPLE)
Neubaugasse 25, Vienna A-1070. Tel: (431) 523 2437. FAX: (431) 523 3971.

ALPHA FILM
Neubaugasse 4, Vienna A-1070. Tel: (431) 523 7660. FAX: (431) 523 7660.

AUSTRIA FILMMAKERS CO-OPERATIVE
Wahringer Strasse 59, Vienna A-1090. Tel: (431) 408 7627. FAX: (431) 408 3871.

BUENA VISTA INTERNATIONAL (BVI)
Hermannagasse 18, Vienna A-1071. Tel: (431) 526 9467. FAX: (431) 526 9468 5.

CENTFOX FILM GMBH
Neubaugasse 35, Vienna A-1070. Tel: (431) 932 2629. FAX: (431) 526 7297.

CINESTAR
Opernring 19, Vienna A-1010. Tel: (431) 587 8406. FAX: (431) 587 5711.

CLASSIC-FILM
Magaretenstrasse 24, Vienna A-1040. Tel: (431) 319 6386.

COLUMBIA TRISTAR
Wallgasse 21, Vienna A-1060. Tel: (431) 597 1515. FAX: (431) 597 1516.

CONSTANTIN FILM
Siebensterngasse 37, Vienna A-1070. Tel: (431) 521 2850. FAX: (431) 521 2860.

CZERNY FILM
Lorgasse 17, Vienna A-1150. Tel: (431) 982 0249. FAX: (431) 982 4081.

EINHORN FILM
Unterfeld Strasse 29, P.O. Box 158, Bludenz A-6700. Tel: (4355) 526 7034. FAX: (4355) 526 3674.

EPO FILM PRODUCTIONS
Edelsinn Strasse 58, Vienna A-1120. Tel: (431) 812 3718. FAX: (431) 812 3718 9.

FILMHAUS STOBERGASSE
Stobergasse 11-15, Vienna A-1050. Tel: (431) 545 3244. FAX: (431) 545 3244.

FILMLADEN
Mariahilferstrasse 58, Vienna A-1070. Tel: (431) 523 4362. FAX: (431) 526 4749.

FLEUR FILM
Stadlgasse 2, Enns A-4470. Tel: (431) 7223 2670. FAX: (431) 7223 2406.

INDEPENDENT MOVIES
Paracelsusgasse 19-21, Gablitz A-3003. Tel: (432) 231 4629.

JUPITER FILM
Neubaugasse 36, Vienna A-1070. Tel: (431) 521 270. FAX: (431) 523 8253.

OEFRAM FILM
Neubaugasse 36, Vienna A-1070. Tel: (431) 523 7611. FAX: (431) 523 3709.

POLYFILM VERLEIH
Margaretenstrasse 78, Vienna A-1050. Tel: (431) 581 3900 20. FAX: (431) 581 3900 39.

SMILE FILM
Lange Gasse 52/2/20, Vienna A-1080. Tel: (431) 408 9843. FAX: (431) 408 9843.

STADTKINO FILMVERLEIH
Spittelberggasse 3, Vienna A-1070. Tel: (431) 522 4814. FAX: (431) 522 4815.

TOP FILM
Lindengasse 56, Vienna A-1070. Tel: (431) 526 1919. FAX: (431) 526 1918.

UNITED INTERNATIONAL PICTURES
Neubaugasse 1, P.O. Box 280, Vienna A-1071. Tel: (431) 523 4631. FAX: (431) 526 7548.

WARNER BROS.
Zieglergasse 10, Vienna A-1072. Tel: (431) 523 8626. FAX: (431) 523 8626 31.

WEGA FILM
Hagelingasse 13, Vienna A-1140. Tel: (431) 982 5742 0. FAX: (431) 982 5833.

PRODUCERS

AICHHOLZER FILM PRODUCTION
Mariahilferstrasse 58, Vienna A-1070. Tel: (4310) 523 4081. FAX: (431) 526 4749.

ALLEGRO FILM PRODUCTIONS
Krummgasse 1A, Stg. 1, Vienna A-1030. Tel: (431) 712 5036. FAX: (431) 712 5036 20.

ARION FILM
Wuerzburgergasse 11, Vienna A-1130. Tel: (431) 804 2000.

CINE CARTOON
Haydngasse 5, Vienna A-1060. Tel: (431) 597 4162 12. FAX: (431) 597 4162 20.

CINECOOP FILM PRODUCTIONS
Mariahilferstrasse 1B, Vienna A-1060. Tel: (431) 587 6735. FAX: (431) 587 6735 20.

CINEDOC FILM PRODUCTION
Hauslabgasse 6-10/1, Vienna A-1050. Tel: (431) 545 6645 90. FAX: (431) 545 6645 90.

CINE-FILM PRODUCTION
Speisingerstrasse 234, Vienna A-1238. Tel: (431) 889 3366. FAX: (431) 889 2831.

CINEMERCURY
Hietzinger Kai 169, Vienna A-1130. Tel: (431) 876 3066. FAX: (431) 876 3099.

DEGN FILM
Konstanze Webergasse 3, Salzburg A-5020. Tel: (43662) 831 992. FAX: (43662) 822 688.

DOR FILM PRODUCTION
Neulerchenfelderstrasse 12, Vienna A-1160. Tel: (431) 403 2138. FAX: (431) 402 2139.

EXTRA FILM
Grosse Neugasse 44/24, Vienna A-1040. Tel: (431) 581 7896. FAX: (431) 587 2743.

FILM & CO.
Lainzerstrasse 71, Vienna A-1170. Tel: (431) 877 7875. FAX: (431) 877 7876.

GOESS FILM & MEDIA
Metternichgasse 2/8, Vienna A-1090. Tel: (431) 713 3905. FAX: (431) 713 2827.

INTERSPOT
Lainzerstrasse 121, Vienna A-1130. Tel: (431) 804 8363. FAX: (431) 804 8363 10.

LOTUS FILM
Sechshauserstrasse 83, Vienna A-1150. Tel: (431) 892 8808. FAX: (431) 892 8809 11.

ADI MAYER FILM
Lindengasse 65, Vienna A-1070, Tel: (431) 523 4788. FAX: (431) 526 6673.

MUNGO FILM
Munichreiterstrasse 18, Vienna A-1130. Tel: (431) 876 3600. FAX: (431) 876 3646.

NEUE STUDIO FILM
Hietzinger Hauptstrasse 11, Vienna A-1130. Tel: (431) 877 6253. FAX: (431) 877 3564.

ODELGA FILM PRODUCTIONS
Landhausgasse 2.37, Vienna A-1010. Tel: (431) 535 0433. FAX:
(431) 532 8496.

PAMMER FILM
Neubaugasse 1, Vienna A-1070. Tel: (431) 523 9191. FAX: (431) 523
9192.

PAN FILM
Obkirchergasse 41, Vienna A-1070. Tel: (431) 321 4033. FAX: (431)
325 7169.

MICHAEL PILZ FILM
Teschnergasse 37, Vienna A-1180. Tel: (431) 402 3392. FAX: (431)
408 4649.

PPM FILMPRODUCTIONS
Lerchenfelderstrasse 136, Vienna A-1080. Tel: (431) 408 1630 0.
FAX: (431) 408 9243.

SATEL FILM
Computerstrasse 6, Vienna A-1101. Tel: (431) 661 1090. FAX: (431)
667 5650.

SCHOENBRUNN FILM
Neubaugasse 1, Vienna A-1070. Tel: (431) 523 2265. FAX: (431) 523
9568.

SK FILM
Salzachstrasse 15A, Salzburg A-5026. Tel: (43662) 625 969. FAX:
(43662) 625 969 22.

STAR FILM
Konstanze Webergasse 3, Salzburg A-5020. Tel: (43662) 831 992.
FAX: (43662) 822 688.

TEAM FILM PRODUCTION
Waaggasse 5, Vienna A-1040. Tel: (431) 587 2542 0. FAX: (431) 587
2542 27.

TERRA FILM
Lienfeldergasse 39, Vienna A-1160. Tel: (431) 484 1101 0. FAX:
(431) 484 1101 27.

WEGA FILM
Hagelingasse 13, Vienna A-1140. Tel: (431) 982 5742 0. FAX: (431)
982 5833.

EXHIBITORS

VILLAGE ROADSHOW, LTD.
(For complete listing see Australian branch.)
206 Bourke St., Melbourne, VIC, 3000. Tel: (613) 96 67 66 66.
FAX: (613) 96 39 15 40.

Number of Theatres: 1
Number of Screens: 8

BAHAMAS

EXHIBITORS

RND CINEMAS LIMITED
P.O. Box EE-17203, Nassau, Bahamas. Tel: (242) 394-6456. FAX:
(242) 394-6457.
PRESIDENT
A. Brent Dean
VICE PRESIDENT
Jerome K. Fitzgerald.

BELGIUM

Population: 10.1 million.
Screens: 434.
Admissions: 21 million.
Average Ticket Price: $5.52.

ASSOCIATIONS & ORGANIZATIONS

APEC
Association for the Promotion of Belgian Cinema in Education, 73
Ave. de Coccinelles, Brussels B-1170. Tel: (322) 672 9459.

ASSOCIATION OF DIRECTORS AND PRODUCERS
109 Rue du Fort, Brussels B-1060. Tel: (322) 534 3152. FAX: (322)
534 7637.

CINEMATHEQUE ROYALE DE BELGIQUE
23 Rue Ravenstein, Brussels B-1000. Tel: (322) 507 8370. FAX:
(322) 513 1272.

EUROPEAN ACADEMY FOR FILM & TELEVISION
69 Rue Verte, Brussels B-1210. Tel: (322) 218 6607. FAX: (322) 217
5572.

FEDERATION DES CINEMAS DE BELGIQUE
10-12 Ave. L'Montmarts, Brussels B-1140. Tel: (322) 705-0670. FAX:
(322) 705-0664.

**MINISTERIE VAN DE VLAAMSE GEMEENSCHAP
ADMINISTRATIE KUNST BESTUUR MEDIA**
29-31 Kolonienstraat, Brussels B-1000. Tel: (322) 510 3565. FAX:
(322) 510 3651.

MUSEE DU CINEMA/FILMMUSEUM
9 Baron Horta St., Brussels B-1000. Tel: (322) 507 8370. FAX: (322)
513 1272.

POUR LE CINEMA BELGE
12 Rue Paul-Emile Janson, Brussels B-1050. Tel: (322) 649 5969.
FAX: (322) 649 3340.

DISTRIBUTORS AND PRODUCERS

ALAIN KEYTSMAN PRODUCTION
159 Berkendaelstraat, Brussels B-1060. Tel: (322) 347 5710. FAX:
(322) 347 2462.

ALCYON FILMS
89 Rue de Lorrian, Brussels B-1210. Tel: (322) 426 7981. FAX: (322)
426 7981.

ALTERNATIVE FILMS
10 Place Colignon, Brussels B-1030. Tel: (322) 242 1930. FAX: (322)
242 0180.

BEECK TURTLE
27F Van Den Bosschestraat, Lennik B-1750. Tel: (322) 582 8318.
FAX: (322) 582 8318.

BUENA VISTA INTERNATIONAL
Chausee Romaine, 468 Romeinsesteenweg, 1853 Grimbergen,
Brussels. Tel: (322) 263 1700. FAX: (322) 263 1797.

CINELIBRE
270 Chaussee de Haecht, Brussels B-1030. Tel: (322) 245 8700.
FAX: (322) 216 2575.

CONCORDE FILM
Terhulpsesteenweg 130, Brussels B-1050. Tel: (322) 675 2050. FAX:
(322) 675 3076.

IMAGE CREATION
92 Rue Colonel Bourg, Brussels B-1040. Tel: (322) 733 3451. FAX:
(322) 732 6666.

INDEPENDENT FILMS
1 Doornveld, Box 42, Zellik-Asse B-1731. Tel: (322) 463 1130. FAX:
(322) 466 9460.

KINEPOLIS FILMS DISTRIBUTION
89 Boulevard du Centenaire, B 1020 Brussels. Tel: (322) 474 2600.
FAX: (322) 474 2606. www.kinepolis.com

PROGRES FILMS
243 Rue Royale, Brussels B-1210. Tel: (322) 218 0960. FAX: (322)
218 4354.

UNITED INTERNATIONAL PICTURES
288 Rue Royale, Brussels B-1210. Tel: (322) 218 5206. FAX: (322)
218 7933.

WARNER BROS. BELGIUM
42 Boulevard Brand Whitlock, Brussels B-1200. Tel: (322) 735 4242.
FAX: (322) 735 4919.

EXHIBITORS

FED DES CINEMAS DE BELGIQUE
Av. L. Mommaertslaan 10-12, B-1140, Brussels. Tel: (322) 218-1455.
FAX: (322) 217-2372.
PRESIDENT
Mrs. Claeys-Vereecke
SECRETARY/GENERAL
Guy Morlion

GAUMONT CINEMAS
(For complete listing see French branch.)
Gaumont NV
Brussels, Belgium

Number of Theatres: 2
Number of Screens: 20

KINOPOLIS GROUP H.V.
Eeuwfeestlaan 20, Brussels, 1020. Tel: (32) 2 47 4 26 00. FAX: (32)
247 22 606.
CEO
Joost Bert
CEO
Florent Gilbels
CFO
Jan Staelens
RESEARCH & DEVELOPMENT OFFICER
Luc Van de Casseye
CORPORATE DIRECTOR, MARKETING & OPERATIONS
Gilbert Deley

Number of Theatres: 16
Number of Screens: 212
Belgium (10), France (5), Spain (1).

UGC BELGIQUE
Av. De La Toison D'or 8, Brussels, B-1050. Tel: (32) 22 89 71 00.
FAX: (32) 22 89 71 01.
GENERAL MANAGER
Andre Harvie
SALES & MARKETING MANAGER
Jean-Philippe Van Nyen
PROGRAMMING DIRECTOR
Eric Carvels
Number of Theatres: 2
Number of Screens: 26

BERMUDA

Population: 64 thousand.

EXHIBITORS

THE LIBERTY THEATRE
49 Union Square, Hamilton, HM 12, Bermuda. Tel: (809) 292-7296.
FAX: (809) 295-5667.
OWNER
Bermuda Industrial Union
CHAIRMAN & PRESIDENT
Derrick Burgess
GENERAL SECRETARY
Helena Burgess
TREASURER
Cecil Durham
MANAGER & FILM BUYER
Nelda L. Simons

BOLIVIA

Population: 8.2 million.

DISTRIBUTORS

MANFER FILMS S.R.L.
Ave. Montes 768, 4th Flr., Box 4709, La Paz. Tel: (5912) 376 834.
FAX: (5912) 391 158.

WAZA FILMS
(Agent for UIP), Edificio Caraas-2do. piso, Avenida 16 de Julio No.
1456, Casilla 2613, La Paz. Tel: (5912) 354 635. FAX: (5912) 354
054.

MARKET RESEARCH

REN
Guachalla, Casilla 9773, La Paz. Tel/FAX: (5912)376 992. Telex:
3317 guatec BV.

BRAZIL

Population: 172.8 million.
Number of Screens: 1,600.
Average Ticket Price: $8.00 (max. $10.00).

DISTRIBUTORS & PRODUCERS

C.E.F. REPRESENTACOES
(Agent for Columbia Tristar)
Rua Aarao Reis 538, S/206 Centro, 3012000-000 Belo Horizonte,
Mias Gerais. Tel: (5531) 273 2093.

COLUMBIA TRISTAR
Av. Rio Branco, 277-Sobrejola 101-Centro, 20040-009 Rio de
Janeiro. Tel: (5521) 262 0722. FAX: (5521) 262 0675.

DISTRIBUIDORA DE FILMES WERMAR
Rua General Bento Martins 268, 90010-080 Porto Alegre, Rio
Grande de Sul. Tel: (5551) 228 6275.

FOX/WARNER BROS. FILM DO BRASIL
Calcada dos Cravos 141, Centro Commercial Alphaville, 06453-000
Barueri, Sao Paulo. Tel: (5511) 725 5999. FAX: (5511) 725 0767.

SETIMA ARTE SERVICOS
Av. Barbosa Lima, 149 S/102, Centro, 50030-330 Recife-
Pernambuco. Tel: (5581) 224 3732.

UNITED INTERNATIONAL PICTURES
Rue Desmbargado, Viriato 16, CEP 20030-090, Rio de Janeiro. Tel:
(5521) 210 2400. FAX: (5521) 220 9491.
MANAGER
Jorge Peregrino

WARNER BROS. (SOUTH)
Rua Senador Dantas 19-10 Andar, 20031-200 Rio de Janeiro. Tel:
(5521) 282 1322. FAX: (5521) 262 0195.

EXHIBITORS

PLAYARTE CINEMAS
Avenida Republica do Libano, 2155-04501-003 Sao Paulo SP, Brazil.
Tel: (55) 11 575-6996.
Number of Screens: 40

UCI BRAZIL
Rue Mexito, 51-3 Andar, Cinelandia CEP 20031, Rio de Janeiro 144,
Brazil. Tel: (55) 21 262-6404.

CHILE

Population: 15.2 million.

DISTRIBUTORS AND PRODUCERS

SILVIO CAIOZZI PRODUCTIONS
Federico Froebel 1755, Santiago. Tel: (562) 209 9031. FAX: (562)
204 8988.
PRESIDENT
Silvio Caiozzi

CHILE INC./WARNER BROS. (SOUTH), INC.
(Columbia Pictures, Tri-Star, Hollywood Pictures, Touchstone
Pictures, Orion), Chilefilms, La Capitania 1200, Las Condes,
Santiago. Tel: (562) 220 3086

CINE CHILE S. A.
(Umbrella organization of the Association of Producers)
Huerfanos 878, Ste. 918, Santiago. Tel: (562) 633 3948. FAX: (562)
632 5342

ARTHUR EHRLICH
Huerfanos 786, Ste. 210, Santiago. Tel: (562) 633 2503 FAX: (562)
639 7921. Rep. for: Twentieth Century Fox

FILMOCENTRO
Gerona 3450, Santiago. Tel: (562) 225 2203. FAX: (562) 209 1671.
PRODUCER
Eduardo Larrain

UNITED INTERNATIONAL PICTURES
Huerfanos 786, Office 808, Casilla 3462, Santiago. Tel: (562) 639
5005. FAX: (562) 633 0562.
MANAGER
Mario Cuevas

EXHIBITORS

CONATE
La capitania No. 1200, Las Condes, Santiago, Chile. Tel: (562) 212-
5071.
Number of Screens: 39

HOYTS CHILE
Roger de Flores #2736, Piso 6
Las Condes, Santiago, Chile

CHINA

Please see Hong Kong in a separate section below.
Population: 1.26 billion.
Number of Screens: 3,300 fixed screens, 180,000 factory-based
screens and outdoor theatres.
Admissions: 6 billion.

ASSOCIATIONS & ORGANIZATIONS

CHINA FILM EXPORT & IMPORT CORPORATION
25 Xin Wai St., Beijing 100088. Tel: (861) 225-4488. FAX: (861) 225-
1044.

CHINA FILMMAKERS' ASSOCIATION
22 Beisanhuan Donglu, Beijing 100013. Tel: (861) 421-9977. FAX:
(861) 421-1870.

DISTRIBUTOR

SONY PICTURES ENTERTAINMENT BEIJING
Ste. 1819, Beijing Asia Jinjiang Hotel, 8 Xinzhong Xi Je, Gongti Bei
Lu, Beijing 100027. Tel: (861) 508 9869. FAX: (861) 500 7335.

EXHIBITORS

VILLAGE ROADSHOW, LTD.
(For complete listing see Australian branch.)
206 Bourke St., Melbourne, VIC 3000, Australia. Tel: (613) 96 67
66 66. FAX: (613) 96 39 15 40.

COLOMBIA

Population: 39.7 million.
Admissions: 21 million.

DISTRIBUTORS

AMERICAN FILMS
Av. 2C Norte No, 24 N 40, Cali. Tel: (5723) 685 792.

COLUMBIA TRISTAR FILMS OF COLOMBIA
Carrera 13A, No. 97-23, Bogota. Tel: (571) 610 0149. FAX: (571) 610
0125.

ELEPHANT JOSEPH & CIA
(Agent for Warner Bros.), Calle 96 No. 12-10, Santafe de Bogota,
D.C. Tel: (571) 610 2142. FAX: (571) 610 2060.

L.D. FILMS
Calle 23 No. 5-85 Interior 201, Bogota. Tel: (571) 341 7285. FAX: (571) 286 5960.

PROGRAFILMS
Carrera 53 No. 59-77, Edificio Royal Films, Barranquilla. Tel: (5753) 318 520.

UNITED INTERNATIONAL PICTURES
Calle 77 No. 15-09 Paratado Aereo 3450, Bogota. Tel: (571) 256 2139. FAX: (571) 218 6089. Manager: Maitland Pritchett.

EXHIBITORS

CINE COLUMBIA S.A.
Carrera 13, No. 38-85, Santa Fe De Bogota, Columbia, South America. Tel: (57) 1 28 58 431. FAX: (57) 1 28 75 160.
OWNER
Mayaguez Organization
CHAIRMAN
Alvaro Correa Holguin
CEO & FILM BUYER
Munir Falah
MANAGER, DISTRIBUTION
Maria Jose Iragorri
V.P., ADMINISTRATION
Alvaro Beltran
V.P., OPERATIONS
Gilberto Gallego
V.P., FINANCE
Eduardo Medrano

CROATIA

Population: 4.3 million.

DISTRIBUTORS AND PRODUCERS

BLITZ FILM & VIDEO
Sv Mateja 121-04, Zagreb 10000. Tel: (3851) 687 541. FAX: (3851) 692 814.

CONTINENTAL FILM
Sostariceva 10, Zagreb 10000. Tel: (3851) 421 312. FAX: (3851) 428 247.

JADRAN FILM DD
Oporovecka 12, Zagreb 10000. Tel: (3851) 298 7222. FAX: (3851) 251 394.

KINEMATOGRAFI
(UIP), Tuskanac 1, Zagreb 41000. Tel: (3851) 426 305. FAX: (3851) 426 531.
CONTACT
Davor Koracevic

ORLANDO FILM
Nasicka 14, Zagreb 10000. Tel: (2851) 334 587. FAX: (3851) 170 167.

ZAUDER FILM
Jablanicka 1, Zagreb 10040. Tel: (3851) 245 724. FAX: (3851) 245 973.

CZECH REPUBLIC

Population: 10.3 million (1.5 million in Prague).
Number of Screens: 920.

ASSOCIATIONS & ORGANIZATIONS

AUTHORS' PRODUCTION AND DISTRIBUTION
P.O. Box 60, Prague 10 10100. Tel: (422) 729 204. FAX: (422) 725 453.

CZECH FILM SOCIETY
Novotneho Lavka 5, Prague 1 11000. Tel: (422) 298 138.

FILMOVY PODNIK HL. M. PRAHY
Vodickova 30, Prague 1 11000. Tel: (422) 242 16010. FAX: (422) 242 26497.

FILMOVY PRUMYSL (EQUIPMENT)
Krizeneckeho Nam. 322, Prague 5. Tel: (422) 294 510. FAX: (422) 542 539.

FITES-UNION OF TV AND FILM
Pod Nuselskymi Schody 3, Prague 2 12000. Tel: (422) 691 0310. FAX: (422) 691 1375.

MINISTRY OF CULTURE
Valdstejnske Nam 4, Prague 1 11000. Tel: (422) 513 1111. FAX: (422) 536 322.

SLOVENSKA POZICOVNA FILMOV
Priemyselna 1, Bratislava 82460. Tel: (427) 211 301. FAX: (427) 215 685.

DISTRIBUTORS AND PRODUCERS

AVED
Wenzigova 15, Prague 12000. Tel: (422) 299 290. FAX: (422) 297 137.

BONTONFILM
Nardoni Trida 28, Prague 1 11000. Tel: (422) 2422 7644. FAX: (422) 2422 5263.
DIRECTOR
Ales Danielis

CINEMART
Nardoni Trida 28, Prague 1 11121. Tel: (422) 2422 7202. FAX: (422) 2110 5234.

FALCON FILM
Stroupenznickeho 6, Prague 5 15000. Tel: (422) 538 085. FAX: (422) 533 194.
GENERAL MANAGER
Michael Malek

FILMEXPORT PRAGUE
Na Moranhi 5, Prague 5 12800. Tel: (422) 293 275. FAX: (422) 293 312.

GAUMONT CINEMAS
(For complete listing see French branch.)
Bonton Gaumont AS
Prague, Czech Rep.

GEMINI FILMS
V Jame 1, Prague 1 11000. Tel: (422) 2416 2142. FAX: (422) 2422 6562.

GUILD ENTERTAINMENT FILM AND VIDEO
Krliprovo Nam-3, Prague 6. Tel: (422) 328 094. FAX: (422) 311 8852.

GUILD ENTERTAINMENT (FILM DISTRIBUTION)
V Jame 5, Prague 1 11000. Tel: (422) 2421 5738. FAX: (422) 2422 6385.

HEUREKA
Litevska 8, Prague 10 11174. Tel: (422) 6731 5219. FAX: (422) 6731 5221.

LUCERNA FILM
Narodni Trida 28, Prague 111 21. Tel: (422) 2422 7644. FAX: (422) 422 2563.

NATIONAL PRODUCTION
Krizeneckeho Nam 322, Prague 5 15252. Tel: (422) 692 7291. FAX: (422) 2451 0628.

SPACE FILM
Karlovo Namesti 19, 12000 Prague 2. Tel: (422) 249 12937. FAX: (422) 249 11370.

EXHIBITORS

INTERSONIC TAUNUS PROD., LTD.
Stare Grunty 36, 842 25 Bratislava, Slovakia. Tel: (421) 772 2070. FAX: (421) 772 1017.

MULTIKINO 93
Plackeho 8, Prague 1. Tel: (422) 261 134. FAX: (422) 261 134.

DENMARK

Population: 5.3 million.
Screens: 346
Admissions: 10.9 million.

ASSOCIATIONS & ORGANIZATIONS

DANISH FILM DISTRIBUTORS ASSOCIATION
Bulowsvej 50A, Fredericksberg DK-1870. Tel: (45) 3536 5616. FAX: (45) 3135 5758.
DIRECTOR
Anne-Grete Wezelenburg

DANISH FILM INSTITUTE
Miels Hemmingsensgade 20, Bh3, Copenhagen K DK-1153. (45) 3315 6760. FAX: (45) 3391 5242.

DANISH FILM MUSEUM
Store Sondervoldstraede 4, Copenhagen DK-1419. Tel: (45) 3157 6500. FAX: (45) 3154 1312.

DANISH FILM WORKSHOP
Versterbrogade 24, Copenhagen DK-1620. Tel: (45) 3124 1624. FAX: (45) 3124 4419.

DANISH PRODUCERS' ASSOCIATION
Kroprinsensgade (B 3, Copenhagen K DK-1114. Tel: (45) 3314 0311. FAX: (45) 3314 0365.

FILM KONTAKT NORD
Skindergade 29 A, Copenhagen DK-1159. Tel: (45) 3311 5152. FAX: (45) 3311 2152.

NORDIC FILM/TV SOCIETY
c/o MGM Nordisk Film Biografer, Axeltorv 9, Copenhagen DK-1609. Tel: (45) 3314 76906. FAX: (45) 3314 7979.

DISTRIBUTORS AND PRODUCERS

AB COLLECTION
Hirsemarken 3, Farum DK-3520. Tel: (45) 4499 6200. FAX: (45) 4295 1786.

ALL RIGHT FILM DISTRIBUTION
Indiakaj 12, Copenhagen DK-2100. Tel: (45) 3544 1100. FAX: (45) 3543 4008. www.allright-film.dk
CEO
Jesper Boas Smith

BUENA VISTA INTERNATIONAL
Ostergade 24B, 3rd Flr., Copenhagen K DK-1100. Tel: (45) 3312 0800. FAX: (45) 3312 4332.

CAMERA FILM
Mikkel Bryggergade 8, Copenhagen K DK-1460. Tel: (5) 3313 6112. FAX: (45) 3315 0882.

CINNAMON FILM
Brandts Passage 15, Odense C DK-5000. Tel: (45) 6612 1716. FAX: (45) 6612 8082.

CONSTANTIN APS
Skelbaekgade 1, Copenhagen V DK-1717. Tel: (45) 3325 2424. FAX: (45) 3325 0707.

DAN INA FILM
Huset, Radhusstraede 13, 2. Flr., Copenhagen DK-1466. Tel: (45) 33 324077. FAX: (45) 33 325077.

EGMONT AUDIO VISUAL
Skelbaekgade 1, Copenhagen V DK-1717. Tel: (45) 3325 4000. FAX: (45) 3123 0488.

FOX FILM
Skelbaekgade 1, 3, Copenhagen V DK-1717. Tel: (45) 3325 4000. FAX: (45) 3123 0488.

HUSETS BIOGRAF
Huset, Radhusstraede 13, 2nd Flr., Copenhagen K DK-1466. Tel: (45) 3315 2002. FAX: (45) 3332 5077.

KRAK VIDEO
Virumsgardvej 21, Virum DK-2830. Tel: (45) 4583 6600. FAX: (45) 4583 1011.

NORDSIK FILM ACQUISITION
Skelbaekgade 1, Copenhagen DK-1717. Tel: (45) 3123 2488. FAX: (45) 3123 0488. email: nikki@inet.uni-c.dk

PATHE-NORDISK
Skelbaekgade 1, Copenhagen DK-1717. Tel: (45) 3123 2488.

REGINA FILM IMPORT
Bregnegaardsvej 7, Charlottenlund DK-2920. Tel: (45) 3962 9640.

SAGA FILM INTERNATIONAL
Soendergada 5, Hjorring DK-9800. Tel: (45) 9892 2199. FAX: (45) 9890 0439.

SCALA FILM
Centrumpladsen, P.O. Box 215, Svendborg DK-5700. Tel: (45) 6221 8866. FAX: (45) 6221 0821.

SCANBOX DANMARK A/S
Hirsemarken 3, Farum DK-3520. Tel: (45) 4499 6200. FAX: (45) 4295 1786.

SFC
Vestergade 27, Copenhagen P DK-1456. Tel: (45) 3313 2686. FAX: (45) 3313 0243.

SIRIUS FILM
Gammel Kongevej 10, Copenhagen, DK 2200. Tel: (45) 33 117060. FAX: (45) 33 1428 88. URL: www.siriusfilm.dk
CONTACT
Steen Iversen

UNITED INTERNATIONAL PICTURES
Haunchvej 13, Frederiksberg C DK-1825. Tel: (45) 3131 2330. FAX: (45) 3123 3420.

WARNER & METRONOME FILM
Sondermarksvej 16, Copenhagen, Valby DK-2500. Tel: (45) 3646 8822. FAX: (45) 3644 0604.

ZENTROPA PRODUCTION
Ryesdage 106A, Copenhagen DK-2100. Tel: (45) 3542 4233. FAX: (45) 3542 4299. email: zentrop@zentropa-film.com.
URL:http://www.zentropa-film.com

EXHIBITORS

NORDISK FILM BIOGRAFER A/S
Axeltorv 9, Copenhagen 1609. Tel: (45) 33 14 76 06. FAX: (45) 33 14 76 06.
CEO
Morten Anker Nielsen
V.P. & CFO
Henrik Pallesen
V.P., FILM & ADVERTISING
Helle Smith
V.P., CONSTRUCTION & EQUIPMENT
Steen Laesen

SANDREW METRONOME FILM AB
Sondermarksve 16, 2500 Valby.

DOMINICAN REPUBLIC

Population: 8.4 million.

EXHIBITORS

REGENCY CARIBBEAN ENTERPRISES, INC.
(d.b.a. Caribbean Cinemas)
Cinema Centro, Avenida George Washington, Santo Domingo, Dominican Repupblic. Tel: (809) 688-8710. FAX: (809) 686-2642.
PRESIDENT
Victor Carrady

CARIBBEAN CINEMAS OF THE VIRGIN ISLANDS, INC.
Centro del Cibao SA, Estrella Sadala No. 20, Santiago, Dominican Republic. Tel: (809) 686-2642. FAX: (809) 971-5991.
ADMINISTRATOR
Amado Perez

ECUADOR

Population: 12.9 million.

EXHIBITORS

MULTICINES
Amazonas y N.N.U.U., C.C.I., Piso 3, Quito, Ecuador. (593) 2265-061. FAX: (593) 225-503.
DIRECTOR, PROGRAMMING
Rafael Barriga
MANAGER
Guillermo Dahik

EGYPT

Population: 68.4 million.

FREE FILM CENTERS

THE AMERICAN CENTER
Part of the American Embassy, Cairo.

THE BRITISH CENTER
Part of the British Embassy, Cairo.
Both the American and British Centers have film libraries.

THE CATHOLIC FILM CENTER
9, Adly St., Cairo.

CENTER CULTURAL FRANCE
One at Al Mounira, Cairo, and at Hiliopolice.

PRINCIPAL PRODUCTION COMPANIES & DISTRIBUTORS

AFLAM FARID SHAWKI
Farid Shawki 36, Sherif St., Cairo.

AFLAM GALAL
Nader Galal 85, Ramses St., Cairo.

ALAMIA T. V. & CINEMA
Hussein Kalla-41, Guizira Elwosta, Zamalek, Cairo.

AFLAM MISR ALAMIA
Yousef Shahin 35, Champion St., Cairo.

ARTIST UNITY
Farid Shawki 16, Adly St., Cairo

BADIE SOBHI
Badie Sobhi 12, Soliman Elhalabi St., Cairo.

CENTRAL FILM
Nagib Spiro, 85, Ramses St., Cairo.

EL-LEITHY FILMS
Ihab El-Leithy 37, Kasr El-Nil St., Cairo.

GAMAL EL-LEITHY
Gamal El-Leithy 11, Saray El-Azbakia St., Cairo.

HANY FILM
Zaki Guirges 4, Soliman Elhalabi St., Cairo.

KASR EL-NIL INTERNATIONAL AHMED SAMI
(Ahmed Sami & Co.) 4, Hussein Almimar St., Kasr El Nil, Cairo, Tel. (202) 574 5416. FAX: (202) 291 8059.

MANAR FILM
Atef Ibrahim, 11, Saray El-Azbakia St., Cairo.

MASR EL-GUIDIDA
Salah Kharma, 36, Orabi St., Cairo.

MISR EL-ARABIA
Wasef Faiez 12, Soliman Elhalabi St., Cairo.

NASR FILM
Mohamed Hassan 33, Orabi St., Cairo.

OSIRIS FILM
Omran Ali 87, Ramses St., Cairo.

SOAT EL-FANN
D. Abdel Wahab 16, Adly St., Cairo.

TAMIDO FILM
Medhat Sherif 4, Zaki St., Orabi, Cairo.

DISTRIBUTORS AND PRODUCERS

MGM
35 Talaat Harb St., Cairo. Tel: (202) 393 3897. FAX: (202) 392 7998.
MANAGER
Fouad Nader

TWENTIETH CENTURY FOX IMPORT CORP.
11 Saray el Ezbekieh, Box 693, Cairo. Tel: (202) 591 2477. FAX:
(202) 591 2829.
MANAGER
Zagloul Gad El Karim Salama

UNITED MOTION PICTURES
(Licensee for Warner Bros.)
7 26th of July St., P.O. Box 923, Cairo. Tel: (202) 591 2477. FAX:
(202) 591 2829.
MANAGER
Antoine Zeind

FIJI

Population: 832 thousand.

EXHIBITORS

VILLAGE ROADSHOW, LTD.
(For complete listing see Australian branch.)
206 Bourke St., Melbourne, VIC, 3000, Australia. Tel: (613) 96 67
66 66. FAX: (613) 96 39 15 40.

Number of Theatres: 2
Number of Screens: 10

FINLAND

Population: 5.2 million.

ASSOCIATIONS & ORGANIZATIONS

ASSOCIATION OF FINNISH FILM DIRECTORS
Suomen Elokuva Ohjaajalitto SELO, PI 116, Helsinki 00171. Tel:
(3580) 632 108.

ASSOCIATION OF FINNISH FILM WORKERS
Soumen Elokuvaja Videotyontekijain, Litto Set, Metritullinkatu 33,
Helsinki 00170. Tel: (3580) 135 6370. FAX: (3580) 135 6658.

ASSOCIATION OF INDEPENDENT PRODUCERS
Suomen Audiovisuaalisen Alan Tuottajatm SATU, Kanavaranta 3 D
31, Helsinki 00160. Tel: (3580) 622 1690. FAX: (3580) 622 1860.

**AVEK—THE PROMOTION CENTRE FOR AUDIOVISUAL CUL-
TURE IN FINLAND**
Hietaniemenkatu 2, Helsinki 00100. Tel: (3580) 446 411. FAX: (3580)
446 414.

CENTRAL ORGANISATION OF FINNISH FILM PRODUCERS
Kaisaniemenkatu 3 B 29, Helsinki 00100. Tel: (3580) 636 305. FAX:
(3580) 176 689.

FINNISH FILM CHAMBER
Kaisaniemenkatu 3 B 29, Helsinki 00100. (3580) 636 305.

FINNISH FILM CONTACT
Annakatu 13 B 11, Helsinki 00120. Tel: (3580) 645 126. FAX: (3580)
641 736.

FINNISH FILM FOUNDATION
Kanavakatu 12, Helsinki 00160. Tel: (3580) 622 0300. FAX: (3580)
6220 3050.

STATE COMMITTEE FOR CINEMA
Valion elokuvataidetoimikunta PL 293, Helsinki 00171. Tel: (3580)
134 171. FAX: (3580) 624 313.

DISTRIBUTORS AND PRODUCERS

ALFA PANORAMA FILM & VIDEO
Laipattie 5, Helsinki 00880. Tel: (3580) 759 2600. FAX: (3580) 755
5460.

ARISTA FILM
Pohjoisranta 11, Box 24, Pori 28100. Tel: (35839) 633 4433. FAX:
(35839) 633 4433.

AXEL FILM
Maneesikatu 1-3 J, Helsinki 00170. Tel: (3580) 278 1996.

BUENORAMA PICTURES
Purimiehenkatu 27, Helsinki 00150. Tel: (3580) 2709 0490. FAX:
(3580) 622 3855.

CINEMA MONDO
Unioninkatu 10, Helsinki 00130. Tel: (3580) 629 528. FAX: (3580)
631 450.

DADA-FILMI
Kolmas Linja 5, Helsinki 00530. Tel: (3580) 737 788. FAX: (3580) 730
734. email: rile@dada.pp.fi

EL-KO FILMS
Kavallvagen 23A, Grankulla 02700. Tel: (3580) 505 2600.

EUROPA VISION
Koivuvaarankuja 2, Vantaa 01641. Tel: (3580) 852 711. FAX: (3580)
853 2183.

FINNKINO OY
Koivuvaarankuja 2, Vantaa 01641. Tel: (3580) 131 191. FAX: (3580)
1311 9300.

KINOFINLANDIA
Maunnkatuoiu 2, Helsinki 00170. Tel: (3580) 278 1783. FAX: (3580)
278 1763.

KINOSCREEN/KINOPRODUCTION
Katajanokantuu 6, Helsinki 00160. Tel: (3580) 663 217. FAX: (3580)
662 048.

KOSMOFILMI
Steinbackinkatu 8A, Helsinki 00250. Tel: (3580) 477 3587. FAX:
(3580) 477 3583.

MIO-FILM
Hiidentie 1 A 7, Oulu 90550. Tel: (35881) 314 1732. FAX: (35881)
314 1730.

OULUN ELEKUVAKESKUS
Torikatu 8, Oulu 90100. Tel: (35881) 881 1292. FAX: (358) 81 881
1290.

SENSO FILMS
Uudenmaankatu 13D, Helsinki 00120. Tel: (358) 0602 810. FAX:
(358) 0602 292.

TALENT HOUSE
Tallberginkatu 1 A, loc. 141, Helsinki 00180. Tel: (358) 0685 2227.
FAX: (3580) 685 2229.

UNITED INTERNATIONAL PICTURES OY
Kaisaniemenkatu 1C 98, Helsinki 00100. Tel: (358) 0662 166. FAX:
(3580) 665 005.

URANIA FILM
Hiidentie 1 A 7, Oulu 90550. Tel: (358) 81 881 1291. FAX: (358) 81
881 1290.

WALHALLA
P.O. Box 1134, Helsinki 00101. Tel: (358) 01311 9365. FAX: (358)
0637 023.

WARNER BROTHERS FINLAND OY
Kaisaniemenkatu 1B A 69, Helsinki 00100. Tel: (358) 0638 953. FAX:
(358) 0638 161.

EXHIBITORS

SANDREW METRONOME FILM AB
Kaisaniemenkatu 2B, 00100 Helsinki, Finland

FRANCE
Population: 59.3 million.
Screens: 4,900

ASSOCIATIONS & ORGANIZATIONS

ACADEMIE DES ARTS ET TECHNIQUES DU CINEMA
19 Ave. du President Wilson, Paris 75116. Tel: (331) 4723 7233.
FAX: (331) 4070 0291.

ATELIERS DU CINEMA EUROPEEN
(European Film Studio), 68 Rue de Rivoli, Paris 75004. Tel: (331)
4461 8830. FAX: (331) 4461 8840.

AUXITEC (SOCIETE AUXILIAIRE POUR LE CINEMA ET LA TV)
Ibis Ave. du Roi Albert, Cannes 06400. Tel: (3393) 940777. FAX:
(339) 3438 8895.

BUREAU DE LIAISON EUROPEEN DU CINEMA
c/o FIADF, 43 Blvd. Malesherbes, Paris 75008. Tel: (331) 4266 0532.
FAX: (331) 4266 9692.

CENTRE FRANCAIS DU COMMERCE EXTERIEUR
10 Ave. d'Iena, Paris Cedex 16 75783. Tel: (331) 4073 3000. FAX:
(331) 4073 3979.

CENTRE NATIONAL DE LA CINEMATOGRAPHIE
12 Rue Lubeck, Paris 75016. Tel: (331) 4434 3440. FAX: (331) 4755
0491.

**CHAMBRE SYNDICALE DES PRODUCTEURS &
EXPORTATEURS DE FILMS FRANCAIS**
5 Rue de Cirque, Paris 75008. Tel: (331) 4225 7063. FAX: Tel: (331)
4225 9427.

CICCE
(European Committee Film Industries Commission)
5 Rue du Cirque, Paris 75008. Tel: (331) 4225 7063. FAX: (331)
4225 9427.

CONSEIL SUPERIEUR DE L'AUDIOVISUEL (CSA)
39-43 Quai Andre-Citroen, Paris Cedex 15 75015. Tel: (331) 4058
3800. FAX: (331) 4579 0006.

EUROPA CINEMAS
54 Rue Beaubourg. Paris 3 75003. Tel: (331) 4271 5370. FAX: (331) 4271 4755.

FEDERATION INTERNATIONALE DES ASSOCIATIONS DE DISTRIBUTEURS DE FILMS
43 Blvd. Malesherbes, Paris 75008. Tel: (331) 4266 0532. FAX: (331) 4266 9692.

FEDERATION NATIONALE DES CINEMAS FRANCAIS (FNCF)
10 Rue de Marignan, Paris 75008. Tel: (331) 4359 1676. FAX: (331) 4074 0864.

FEDERATION NATIONALE DES DISTRIBUTEURS DE FILMS
43 Blvd. Malesherbes, Paris 75008. Tel: (331) 4266 0532. FAX: (331) 4266 9692.

FEDERATION OF THEATRE, CINEMA & AUDIOVISUAL UNIONS
14-16 Rue des Lilas, Paris 75015. Tel: (331) 4240 1495. FAX: (331) 4240 9020.

INSTITUT NATIONAL DE L'AUDIOVISUEL
4 Ave. de l'Europe, Bry-Sur-Marne 94366. Tel: (331) 4983 2000. FAX: (331) 4983 3195.

INTERNATIONAL FEDERATION OF FILM PRODUCERS
33 Champs Elysées, Paris 75008. Tel: (331) 4225 6214. FAX: (331) 4256 1652.

INTERNATIONAL UNION OF CINEMAS
10 Rue de Marignan, Paris 75008. Tel: (331) 4359 1676. FAX: (331) 4074 0864.

MINISTERE DES AFFAIRES ETRANGERES
244 Blvd. St. Germaine, Paris 75007. Tel: (331) 4317 9662. FAX: (331) 4317 9242.

SESAM
16 Place de la Fontaine, Aux Lions, Paris 19 75920. Tel: (331) 4715 4905. FAX: (331) 4715 4974.

SOCIETE DES REALISATEURS DE FILMS (SRF)
215 Rue de Faubourg-Honoré, Paris 75008. Tel: (331) 4563 9630. FAX: (331) 4074 0796.

UNIFRANCE FILM INTERNATIONAL
4 Villa Bosquet, Paris 75007. Tel: (331) 4753 9580. FAX: (331) 4705 9655.

UNION DES PRODUCTEURS DE FILMS
1 Place des Deux Ecus, Paris 75001. Tel: (331) 4028 0138. FAX: (331) 4221 1700.

DISTRIBUTORS AND PRODUCERS

AAA DISTRIBUTION
12bis Rue Keppler, Paris 75011. Tel: (331) 4475 7070. FAX: (331) 4705 4554.

AGENCE DU COURT METRAGE
2 Rue de Toqueville, Paris 75017. Tel: (331) 4380 0365. FAX: (331) 4267 5971.

A.I.L.O. PRODUCTIONS
9 Rue Fontaine, St. Denis 93200. Tel: (331) 4813 0666. FAX: (331) 4813 0632.

AMLF
10 Rue Lincoln, Paris 75008. Tel: (331) 4076 9100. FAX: (331) 4225 1289.

ARCHEO PICTURES
9 Rue René Boulanger, Paris 75010. Tel: (331) 4240 4899. FAX: (331) 4239 9413.

FARIANE FILMS
15 Rue de Colonel Pierre Avia, Paris 75015. Tel: (331) 4662 1777. FAX: (331) 4662 1797.

ARP
75 Ave. des Champs Elysées, Paris 75008. Tel: (331) 4359 4330. FAX: (331) 4563 8337.

ARTEDIS CINEMA ARTS ENTERTAINMENT
44 Rue du Colisee, Paris 75008. Tel: (331) 4256 2275. FAX: 33 1 4256 1087.

A.S.P.
23 Rue Raynouard, Paris 75016. Tel: (331) 4224 5050. FAX: (331) 4224 6642.

BAC FILMS
5 Rue Pelouze, Paris 75008. Tel: (331) 4470 9230. FAX: (331) 4470 9070.

CELLULOID DREAMS
24 Rue Lamartine, 75009 Paris. Tel: (331) 4970 0370. FAX:(331) 4970 0371.

CIBY DISTRIBUTION
90 Ave. des Champs Elysées, Paris 75008. Tel: (331) 4421 6417. FAX: (331) 4421 6435.

CINEMADIS FILMS
78 Ave. des Champs Elysées, Paris 75008. Tel: (331) 4562 8287. FAX: (331) 4289 2198.

COLUMBIA TRISTAR FILMS
131 Ave. de Wagram, Paris 75017. Tel: (331) 4440 6220. FAX: (331) 4440 6201.

CONNAISSANCE DU CINEMA
22 Rue du Pont Neuf, Paris 75001. Tel: (331) 4013 0722. FAX: (331) 4026 2544.

CYTHERE FILMS
34 Ave. des Champs Elysées, Paris 75008. Tel: (331) 4289 0767. FAX: (331) 4256 0773.

EUROCINE
33 Ave. des Champs Elysées, 75008 Paris. Tel: (331) 4225 6492. FAX: (331) 4225 7338.

FILMS SANS FRONTIERES
70 Blvd. de Sebastopol, Paris 75003. Tel: (331) 4277 2184. FAX: (331) 4277 4266.

GAUMONT
30 Ave. Charles de Gaulle, Neuilly-sur-Seine 92200. Tel: (331) 46 43 20 00. FAX: (331) 46 43 21 68.

GAUMONT/BUENA VISTA INTERNATIONAL
5 Rue du Clisée, Paris 75008. Tel: (331) 4643 2000. FAX: (331) 4643 2047.

HAUT ET COURT
5 Passage Piver, Paris 75011. Tel: (331) 4338 5300. FAX: (331) 4338 3872.

JECK FILM
5 Rue Rene Boulanger, Paris 75010. Tel: (331) 42 40 78 00. FAX: (331) 48 03 02 64.

K—FILMS
15 Rue Saintonge, Paris 75003. Tel: (331) 4274 7016. FAX: (331) 4274 7024.

LES ACACIAS CINE AUDIENCE
33 Rue Berger, Paris 75008. Tel: (331) 4256 4903. FAX: (331) 4256 0865.

LES FILM DE L'ATALANTE
100 Rue Monfletard, Paris 75005. Tel: (331) 4287 0202. FAX: (331) 4287 0189.

LES FILMS DU LOSANGE
26 Ave. Pierre 1er de Serfie, Paris 75116. Tel: (331) 4720 5412/ 4443 8715. FAX: (331) 4952 0640.

LES FILMS NUMBER ONE
16 Ave. Hoche, Paris 75008. Tel: (331) 4563 4402. FAX: (331) 4289 1921.

LES FILMS SINGULIER
20 Rue Michelet, Montreuil 93100. Tel: (331) 4287 5908. FAX: (331) 4287 0189.

LES GRANDS FILMS CLASSIQUES
49 Ave. Theophile Gautier, Paris 75016. Tel: (331) 45 24 43 24. FAX: (331) 45 25 49 73.

LE STUDIO—CANAL PLUS
17 Rue Dumont D'urville, Paris 75116. Tel: (331) 4443 9800.
COO
Brahin Chioua
HEAD OF INTERNATIONAL SALES
Daniel Marquet

LOGOS
24 Ave. du Recteur Poincare, Paris 75016. Tel: (331) 46 47 97 48. FAX: (331) 46 47 97 58.

METROPOLITAN FILMEXPORT
1 Rue Lord Byron, Paris 75008. Tel: (331) 4563 4560. FAX: (331) 4563 7731.

MK2
55 Rue Traversiere, Paris 75012. Tel: (331) 4467 3000. FAX: (331) 4341 3230.

OUTSIDER DIFFUSION
63 Rue Pascal, Paris 75013. Tel: (331) 43 35 81 74. FAX: (331) 47 07 10 49.

POINT DU JOUR
38 Rue Croix des Petits Champs, Paris 75001. Tel: (331) 47 03 40 00. FAX: (331) 47 03 39 48.

POLYGRAM FILM DISTRIBUTION
107 Blvd. Periere, Paris 75017. Tel: (331) 4415 6666. FAX: (331) 4764 3638.

PRETTY PICTURES
9 Rue Charlot, Paris 75003. Tel: (331) 4029 0044. FAX: (331) 4029 0121.

PYRAMIDE DISTRIBUTION
6 Rue Catulle Mendes, Paris 75017. Tel: (331) 42 67 44 66. FAX: (331) 42 67 80 28.

QUINTA COMMUNICATIONS
16 Ave. Hoche, Paris 75008. Tel: (331) 4076 04540. FAX: (331) 4256 6921.

REVCOM INTERNATIONAL/LES FILMS ARIANE
15 Rue du Colonel Pierre Avia, Paris 75015. Tel: (331) 4662 1777. FAX: (331) 4662 1797.

REZO FILMS
52 Rue Charlot, Paris 75003. Tel: (331) 4027 8525. FAX: (331) 4027 0887.

TWENTIETH CENTURY FOX
8 Rue Bellini, Paris 75116. Tel: (331) 4434 6000. FAX: (331) 4434 6105.

U.F.D.
2 Ave. de Montaigne, Paris 75008. Tel: (331) 5367 1717. FAX: (331) 5367 1700.

UNITED INTERNATIONAL PICTURES
1 Rue Meyerbeer, Paris 75009. Tel: (331) 4007 3838. FAX: (331) 47472 5716.

WARNER BROS.
67 Ave. de Wagram, Paris 75017. Tel: (331) 4401 4999. FAX: (331) 4763 4515.

EXHIBITORS

CINE-ALPES
150, rue Haute Tarentaise, 73700 Bourg Saint Maurice. Tel: (33) 04 79 07 61 40. FAX: (33) 04 79 07 61 41.
PRESIDENT
Gerard Davoine

Number of Theatres: 53
Number of Screens: 110

CINEMA LES ECRANS
9-11, place Denis Dussoubs, 87000 Limoges. Tel: (33) 05 55 77 40 79. FAX: (33) 05 55 79 49 91.
PRESIDENT
Michel Fridemann

Number of Screens: 30

CINEMAS 14 JUILLET
M.K. 2, 55, rue Traversiere, 75012, Paris. Tel: (33) 44 67 30 00. FAX: (33) 43 41 32 30.
PRESIDENT
Marin Karmitz

Number of Theatres: 9
Number of Screens: 44

CIRCUIT GEORGES RAYMOND (CGR)
8, rue Blaise Pascal, Z.I. de Perigny, 17039 La Rochelle Cedex. Tel: (33) 05 46 44 01 76. FAX: (33) 05 46 44 55 85.

Number of Screens: 330

GAUMONT CINEMAS
30, Av. Charles de Gaulle, Neuilly, Sur Seine 92200. Tel: (33) 1 46 43 20 00. FAX: (33) 1 46 43 24 28.
CHAIRMAN, CEO, & PRESIDENT
Nicolas Seydoux
EXECUTIVE V.P. & COO
Patrice Ledoux
V.P., EXHIBITION
Jean-Louis Renoux
DIRECTOR OF DEVELOPMENT
Jean-Yves Rabet.

Number of Theatres: 47
Number of Screens: 365
Foreign Screens: 20
France (40), Belgium (2)

GROUPE AUBERT
5, place de Gaulle, 06400 Cannes. Tel: (33) 4 93 39 38 20. FAX: (33) 4 93 38 01 90.
PRESIDENT
Raoul Aubert

Number of Theatres: 9
Number of Screens: 49

LES IMAGES MEGARAMA
62, rue Grande Rue, 25000 Besancon. Tel: (33) 45 00 01 22. FAX: (33) 45 00 01 99.
GENERAL DIRECTOR
Jean-Pierre Lemoine

Number of Screens: 37

M.K.2
55, rue Traversiere, 75012, Paris. Tel: (33) 44 67 30 00. FAX: (33) 43 41 32 30.
PRESIDENT
Marin Karmitz

Number of Theatres: 9
Number of Screens: 44

PATHE PALACE
21 Rue Francois 1er, 75008 Paris. Tel: (33) 49 24 40 03. FAX: (33) 49 24 45 10.

PRESIDENT, PATHE GROUP
Jerome Seydoux
GENERAL DIRECTOR, CINEMAGRAPHIC EXHIBITION
Thierry Marques

Number of Theatres: 46
Number of Screens: 300

SOCOGEX
7, rue Rameau, 78000 Versailles. Tel: (33) 39 50 78 78. FAX: (33) 39 49 09 67.
ADMINISTRATORS
Francois Dupuy
Jean-Francois Edeline

SOREDIC
3E, rue de Paris - BP 135, 35513 Cesson-Sevigne. Tel: (33) 2 99 83 78 00. FAX: (33) 2 99 83 29 37.
PRESIDENT
Philippe Paumelle

Number of Theatres: 150
Number of Screens: 200

UGC FRANCE
24 ave Charles de Gaulle, 92200 Nuyilly-sur-Seine. Tel: (33) 46 40 44 30. FAX: (33) 46 24 37 28.

VILLAGE ROADSHOW FRANCE
4-6, Rond Point Champs Elysees, 75008, Paris. Tel: (33) 53 93 92 00. FAX: (33) 42 89 20 43.
MANAGING DIRECTOR
Didier Bedin

Number of Theatres: 2
Number of Screens: 11

STUDIOS

ACME FILMS
14 Rue Sthrau, Paris 75013. Tel: (331) 5394 5151. FAX: (331) 4570 7004. www.acme-films.fr

BOULOGNE-BILLANCOURT
2 Rue de Silly, Boulogne 92100. Tel: (331) 4605 6569. FAX: (331) 4825 2347.

CAIMAN
30 Blvd. de la Bastille, Paris 75012. Tel: (331) 4344 1122. FAX: (331) 4344 7930.

PARIS STUDIO BILLANCOURT
50 Quai du Point-du-Jour, Boulogne-Billancourt 9200. Tel: (331) 4609 9324. FAX: (331) 4620 2471.

STUDIOS LA VICTORINE COTE D'AZUR
16 Ave. Edouard Grinda, Nice 06200. Tel: (3393) 725 454. FAX: (3393) 719 173.

GERMANY

Population: 82.8 million.
Screens: 4,760.

ASSOCIATIONS & ORGANIZATIONS

BERLIN PROVINCIAL FILM SERVICE
Bismarckstrasse 80, 1000 Berlin 12. Tel: (4930) 313 80 55.

GERMAN INSTITUTE FOR FILM INFORMATION
Schaumainkai 41, Frankfurt am Main 60596. Tel: (4969) 617 045. FAX: (4969) 620 060.

GERMAN INSTITUTE FOR FILM INFORMATION/FILM ARCHIVE
Kreuzbergerring 56, Wiesbaden 65205. Tel: (49611) 723 310. FAX: (49611) 723 318.

INSTITUTE FOR FILM AND THE VISUAL ARTS IN EDUCATION
Bavariafilmplatz 3, Geiselgaskig 82031. Tel: (4989) 64971. FAX: (4989) 649 7300.

DISTRIBUTORS AND PRODUCERS

ALHAMBRA FILMVERLEIH
Friedrich Ebertstrasse 12, Dusseldorf 40120. Tel: (49211) 352 972.

ARSENAL FILMVERLEIH STEFAN PAUL KG
Neue Strasse 2, Tuebingen 72012. Tel: (497071) 92960. FAX: (497071) 929611.

ATLAS FILM UND AV GMBH & CO. KG
Ludgeristrasse 14-16, Duisburg 47057. Tel: (49203) 378 6222. FAX: (49203) 362 482.

ATLAS INTERNATIONAL
Rumfordstrasse 29-31, Munich D-80469. Tel: (4989) 227 525. FAX: (4889) 224 332.

BAUER FILMVERLEIH-KINO UND GASTRONOMIE
Schmiedingstrasse 19, Postfach 100329, Dortmund 4600. Tel: (49231) 148 078.

BAVARIA FILM GMBH
Bavariafilmplatz 7, Geiselgasteig, Munich D-82031. Tel: (4989) 6499 2681. FAX: (4989) 6499 2240.

BEATE UHSE FILMVERLEIH
Gutenbergstrasse 12, Flensburg 24941. Tel: (49461) 996 6221.

BOJE BUCK PRODS./DELPHI FILM
Kantstrasse 12a, Berlin 10623. Tel: (4930) 313 2200, (4930) 312 6070. FAX: (4930) 312 9996.

BUENA VISTA INTERNATIONAL
P.O. Box 800329, Munich D-81603. Tel: (4989) 9934 0270. FAX: (4989) 9934 0139.

CENTRAL FILMVERTRIEB
(Represents Senator Filmverleih & Jugendfilm), Uhlandstrasse 179/180, Berlin 10263. Tel: (4930) 8842 8570. FAX: (4930) 8842 8512.

CINE INTERNATIONAL
Leopoldstrasse 18, Munich D-80802. Tel: (4989) 391 025. FAX: (4989) 331 089.

CINEMA FILMVERLEIH
Braystrasse 20, Munich D-811677. Tel: (4989) 472 061. FAX: (4989) 474 736.

CINEPOOL
Sonnenstrasse 21, Munich D-80331. Tel: (4989) 5587 6188. FAX: (4989) 5587 6188.

CINEVOX
Bavariafilmplatz 7, Gruenwald 82031. Tel: (4989) 641 8000. FAX: (4989) 649 3288.

COLUMBIA TRISTAR FILM
8 Ickstattstrasse 1, Munich D-80469. Tel: (4989) 230 370. FAX: (4989) 264 380. Sales: Gerd Bender.

CONCORDE—CASTLE ROCK/TURNER FILMVERLEIH
Rosenheimer Strasse 143b, Munich D-81671. Tel: (4989) 450 6100. FAX: (4989) 4506 1010.

CONNEXION FILM VETRIEBS & PRODUKTIONS GMBH
Rothembaumchaussee 80c, Hamburg 20148. Tel: (4940) 419 9750. FAX: (4940) 419 9799.

CONSTANTIN FILM
Kaiserstrasse 39, Munich D-80801. Tel: (4989) 386 090. FAX: (4989) 386 9242.

CONTACT FILMVERLEIH
Huttenstrasse 40, Dusseldorf 40215. Tel: (49211) 374 024. FAX: (49211) 374 025.

DAZU FILM BONN
c/o Daniel Zuta Filmproduktion, Kaiserstrasse 39, Frankfurt am Main D-60329. Tel: (4869) 253 735. FAX: (4989) 239 058.

ENDFILM
Am Vogelherd 4, Bach D-93090. Tel: (4994) 823 377. FAX: (4994) 823 378.

FILMWELT—PROKINO VERLEIHGEMEINSCHAFT
Ismaninger Strasse 51, Munich D-81675. Tel: (4989) 418 0010. FAX: (4989) 4180 0143.

FUTURA/FILMVERLAG DER AUTOREN
Rambergstrasse 5, Munich 80799. Tel: (4989) 381 7000. FAX: (4989) 381 70020.

GERMANIA FILMVERLEIH
Blissestrasse 38-40, Berlin 10713. Tel: (4930) 821 3072.

HIGHLIGHT FILMVERLEIH
Herkomerplatz 2, Munich D-80000. Tel: (4989) 9269 6602. FAX: (4989) 981 543.

HVW FOCUS FILMVERTRIEB
Wurmtalstrasse 125, Munich D-81375. Tel: (4989) 740 9411. FAX: (4989) 740 9319.

JUGENDFILM VERLEIH GMBH
Reichstrasse. 15, Berlin D-14052. Tel: (4930) 300 6970. FAX: (4930) 3006 9711.

KERYX FILM
Immenried 97, Kisslegg D-88353. Tel: (497563) 8372 8147. FAX: (497563) 8372 8217.

KINOWELT FILMVERLEIH
Pfisterstrasse 11, Munich 80331. Tel: (4989) 296 963. FAX: (4989) 221 491.

KIRCHGROUP
Robert-Burklestrasse 2, Ismaning W-8045. Tel: (4989) 9508 8323. FAX: (4989) 9508 8330.

KLASING
Siekerwass 21, Bielefeld 33602. Tel: (49521) 5590. FAX: (49521) 559 113.

KORA FILMVERLEIH
Leopoldstrasse 65, 8000 Munich 40. Tel: (4989) 334 409.

KUCHENREUTHER FILM GMBH
Film Theater Verleih Produktion, Leopoldstrasse 80, Munich 80802. Tel: (4989) 332 224. FAX: (4989) 333 742.

MERCATOR FILMVERLEIH
Postfach 101950, Bielefeld 33519. Tel: (49521) 124 061. FAX: (49521) 131 010.

NEUE CONSTANTIN FILM
Kaiserstrasse 39, Munich 80801. Tel: (4989) 386 090. FAX: (4989) 3860 9242.

PANDORA FILM
Hamburger Allee 45, Frankfurt 60486. Tel: (4969) 779 094. FAX: (4969) 707 4033.

PROGRESS FILMVERLEIH
Burgstrasse 27, Berlin 10178. Tel: (4930) 280 5110. FAX: (4930) 282 9157.

SCOTIA INTERNATIONAL
Possartstrasse 14, Munich 81679. Tel: (4989) 413 0900. FAX: (4989) 470 6320.

SELLENG FILMAGENTUR
Lietzenburgerstrasse 51, Berlin 1000. Tel: (4930) 213 6788.

TIME MEDIENVERTRIEBS
Nymphenburgerstrasse 158, Munich D-80634. Tel: (4989) 160 923. FAX: (4989) 162 056. Distribution: Annette Niehues.

TOBIS FILMKUNST GMBH & CO.
Pacelliallee 47, Berlin 14175. Tel: (4930) 839 0070. FAX: (4930) 890 0765.

TWENTIETH CENTURY FOX OF GERMANY
Hainer Weg 37-53, 70 Frankfurt am Main D-60599. Tel: (4969) 609 020. FAX: (4969) 627 715.

UNITED INTERNATIONAL PICTURES
Hahnstrasse 31-35, Frankfurt am Main D-60528, Tel: (4969) 669 8190. FAX: (4969) 666 6509. Manager: Paul Steinshulte.
Lietzenburger Strasse 51, Berlin 10789. Tel: (4930) 211 2063. FAX: (4930) 213 3148.

WARNER BROS. FILM
Hans-Henny-Jahn-Weg 35, Hamburg D-22085. Tel: (4940) 227 1250. FAX: (4940) 2271 2519. Sales: Hans Hermann Schopen.

WILD OKAPI FILM VERLEIH VERTRIEB
Kreuzbergstrasse 43, Berlin 10965. Tel: (4930) 785 0376. FAX: (4930) 785 9620.

EXHIBITORS

BLUE MOVIE
Gutenbert 12, Flensburg 24941. Tel: (49461) 996 6247. FAX: (49461) 96265.

BROADWAY ENTERTAINMENT GMBH
Merkurstr 9-11, 66849, Landstuhl. Tel: (49) 63 71 93 70 00. FAX: (49) 63 71 93 71 11.
MANAGING DIRECTORS
Renate Goldhammer
Ernst Pletsch

BROADWAY FILMTHEATER, GMBH
Im Feld 53, 51427 Bergisch-Gladbach. Tel: (49) 22 04 65 595. FAX: (49) 22 04 62 450.
MANAGING DIRECTORS
Helmut Brunotte
Claudia Hebbel

BROADWAY FTB GMBH
Paulinstr. 18, 54292 Trier. Tel: (49) 65 1 246 05. FAX: (49) 65 1 261 11.

BROADWAY KINO
Ehrenstrasse 11, Cologne 50672. Tel: (49221) 925 6570. FAX: (49221) 9257 5714.

CADILLAC
Rosenkavalierplatz 12, Munich 81925. Tel: (4989) 912 000. FAX: (4989) 916 390.

CASABLANCA GASTST, KULTUR & KINO GMBH
Johannisstr. 17, 26121 Oldenburg. Tel: (49) 4 41 88 47 57. FAX: (49) 4 41 88 80 72.
MANAGING DIRECTOR
Dr. Detlef Rossman

CINEMAXX H.J. FLEBBE FILMTHEATERBETRIEBE
Mittelweg 176, 20148 Hanburg. Tel: (49) 40450 680. FAX: (49) 40 450 68201.
PRESIDENT & GENERAL MANAGER
Hans-Joachim Flebbe
GENERAL MANAGER & CFO
Michael Pawlowski
DIRECTOR, MARKETING
Jens Thomsen

Number of Theatres: 49
Germany (47), Turkey (1), Switzerland (1).

CITY KINO
Schwanthalerstrasse 7, Munich 80331. Tel: (4989) 598 749. FAX: (4989) 550 2171.

COLM ENTERTAINMENT AG
Alte Poststr 3, 701 73 Stuttgart. Tel: (49) 7 11 29 22 45. FAX: (49) 7
11 2 26 3411.
MANAGING DIRECTOR
Roman Colm

COLM FILMTHEATERBETRIEBE
Alte Poststrasse 3, Stuttgart 70197. Tel: (49711) 650 400. FAX:
(49711) 657 2530.

COMET FTB-GMBH
Konigstr 20, 41236 Moenchengladbach. Tel: (49) 21 66 94 4050.
FAX: (49) 21 66 94 6067.
MANAGING DIRECTOR
H.J. Brandtner

CONSTANTIN KINOTRIEBE GMBH
Cinedom Im Mediapark, 50670 Koln. Tel: (49) 2 21 95 19 51 07. FAX:
(49) 2 21 95 51 08.

DELPHI FILMVERLEIH
Kantstrasse 12a, Berlin 10623. Tel: (4930) 313 2200. FAX: (4930)
313 9996.

ECKART AND WOLFRAM WEBER-FTB
Gewerbemuseumpsl 3, 90403 Nurnberg. Tel: (49) 11 20 66 60. FAX:
(49) 11 20 66 612.

ERASMUS KINOVERWALTUNG
Grimmstrasse 30A, Stuttgart 70197. Tel: (49711) 650 400. FAX:
(49711) 657 2530.

FILMTHEATERBETRIEBE BERLIN
Schuchardtweg 9B, Berlin 14109. Tel: (4930) 805 4829. FAX:
(4930) 805 5258.

FILMTHEATERBETRIEBE GEORGE REISS
Sophienstrasse 1, Munich 803333. Tel: (4989) 552 1650. FAX:
(4989) 5521 6525.

FILMTHEATER-VERWVLTUNG REHS
44787 Bochum, Viktoriastr. 29. Tel: (49) 34 96 1710. FAX: (49) 34
96 17199.

FREYMUTH SCHULTZ VEREINGTE LICHTSPIELE
Jann-Berghaus-Str. 9, 26757 Borkum. Tel: (49) 22 91 810. FAX:
(49) 22 91 8141.

FTB ADRIAN KUTTER
88400 Biberach. Tel: (49) 73 51 7 23 31. FAX: (49) 73 51 1 37
64.

FTB BERLIN
Schuchardtweg 9, 14109 Berlin. Tel: (49) 30 805 48 29. FAX: (49)
30 805 52 58.
MANAGING DIRECTOR
Peter H. Vollman

FTB W. BURTH
88212 Marienpl. 4, Ravensurg. Tel: (49) 7 51 36 14 436. FAX:
(49) 7 51 36 14 459.
MANAGING DIRECTOR
Axel Burth

FTB DR. HERIBERT SCHLINKER
34414 Warburg, Johanaistorstr 35. Tel: (49) 56 41 23 63. FAX:
(49) 56 41 54 40.

FTB GEORG REISS GMBH
Sophienstr. 1, 80333 Munchen. Tel: (49) 89 55 21 650. FAX: (49)
89 55 21 6525.

FTB HANS-GEORGE SAWATZKI
55543 Bad Kreuznach, Kreuzstr. 57-63. Tel: (49) 06 71 28883.

FTB MANFRED EWERT KG
Moritzstr. 6, 65185 Wiesbaden. Tel: (49) 6 11 30 00 35.

FTB MARTIN OHG
Vogelgesang 1, 36251 Bad Hersfeld. Tel: (49) 66 21 7 70 44.
FAX: (49) 66 21 5 14 29.

FTB SPICKERT
Lichtenberger Str. 10, 67059 Ludwigshafen. Tel: (49) 6 21 59
1090. FAX: (49) 66 21 5 14 29.

FUTURA KINOBETRIEBS GMBH
80799 Munchen, Rambergstr. 5. Tel: (49) 89 38 17 000. FAX: (49)
8938 17 0020.

FWU FILM INSTITUTE
Bavaria Film Platz 3, Gruenwald 82131. Tel: (4989) 64970. FAX:
(4989) 647 7360.

GILDE DEUTSCHES FILMKUNSTTHEATER
Waldseerstrasse 3, Biberach/Riss 884000. Tel: (4973) 517 2331.
FAX: (4973) 511 3764.

THE GREATER UNION ORGANISATION
(including BIRCH CARROLL & COYLE)
49 Market St., Sydney, NSW 2000, Australia. Tel: (612) 93 73 66 00.
FAX: (612) 93 73 65 32.
MANAGING DIRECTOR
Robert Manson
Number of Theatres: 30 (Germany)
Number of Screens: 246 (Germany)

HANSEATER FILMTHEATERBETRIEBE
Kurfuerstendamm 33, Berlin 10719. Tel: (4930) 883 6086. FAX:
(4930) 883 6520.

HERMANN-CLOSMANN ERBEN D.G. FTB
Biegenstr. 8, 35037 Marburg. Tel: (49) 64 21 17 300. FAX: (49)
64 21 17 30 40.
MANAGING DIRECTOR
Gerhard Closmann

WALTER H. JANN WERBE & FILMBETR. GMBH
Hauptstr. 16, 82319 Starnberg. Tel: (49) 81 51 1 37 92. FAX: (49)
81 51 2 83 20.

KIEFT & KIEFT FILMTHEATER GMBH
Muehlenbruecke 9-11, 23552 Luebeck. Tel: (4517) 030 200. FAX:
(4517) 030 222.
MANAGERS
Marlis Kieft
Heiner Kieft

Number of Theatres: 37
Number of Screens: 179

KINEMATOGRAPH FILM GMBH
Biedersteiner Str. 11, 80802 Munchen. (49) 89 55 71 60. FAX:
(49) 89 59 45 59.
PRESIDENT & OWNER
Dr. Dieter Buchwald
EXECUTIVE V.P.
Klans Ungerer

KINOCENTER OTTOBRUNN
Ottostrasse 72, Ottobrunn 85521. Tel: (4989) 609 4141. FAX:
(4989) 609 9696.

KINOPOLIS MAIN–TAUNUS GMBH & CO.
Main-Taunus-Zentrum, Sulzbach/Hossen, 65843. Tel: (49) 6 39
14 03 80. FAX: (49) 6 93 14 03 899.
MANAGING DIRECTOR
Wolfgang Theile
MANAGER
Hans-Jurgen Jochum

KRUGMANN & WEISCHERMUNDSBURGER
Hamburgerstrasse 152, Hamburg 22083. Tel: (4940) 291 111.
FAX: (4940) 291 117.

KUCHENREUTHER FILM
Sonnenstrasse 22, Munich 80331. Tel: (4989) 596 717. FAX:
(4989) 596 286.

LISELOTTE JAEGER FILMTHEATERBETRIEBE
Holzgraben 26, Frankfurt 60313. Tel: (4969) 285 205. FAX: (4969)
281 957. Second Address: Zeil 125, 60313 Frankfurt. Tel: (49) 69 28
52 05. FAX: (49) 69 28 19 57.

LUDWIG SCHEER & CO. KG-FTB
Juliuspromenade 68, 97070 Wurzburg. Tel: (49) 93 15 31 31. FAX:
(49) 93 15 51 01.

MEGA EXTREM CINEMA GMBH
August-Horch-Str. 2a, 56070 Koblenz. Tel: (49) 2 61 8 09 05 15. FAX:
(49) 2 61 8 09 05 30.
MANAGING DIRECTOR
Dieter Tobolik

MUENSTERSCHE FILMTHEATER
Bahnhofstr. 20-22, 48143 Muenster. Tel: (49) 2 515 60 07. FAX: (49)
2 515 60 08.

NEUE CONSTANTIN KINOBETRIEBE
Kaiserstrasse 39, Munich 80801. Tel: (4989) 386 090. FAX: (4989)
3860 9166.

OLYMPIC/HEINZ RIECH & SON
Graf Adolfstrasse 96, Dusseldorf 40210. Tel: (49211) 169 060. FAX:
(49211) 169 0633.

OMNIPLEX FILMTHEATERBETRIEBE
30159 Hannover. Luisenstr. 10-11. FAX: (49) 51 132 27 11.

PALAST/SCHMID & THEILE
Lautenschlagerstrasse 3, Stuttgart 70173. Tel: (49711) 225 750.
FAX: (49711) 225 7599.

PEP FILMTHEATER GMBH
35757 Driedorf, P.O. Box 1221. Tel: (49) 27 75 95 05 03. FAX: (49)
27 75 95 05 04. email: Plass@gloria.dill.de
MANAGING DIRECTOR
Peter Plass

GERD POLITT FILMTHEATERBETRIEBE
Konigswall 4, 45657 Recklinghausen. Tel: (49) 23 61 93 350. FAX:
(49) 23 61 22 287.

POTSDAM FILM MUSEUM
Martsall, Potsdam 14467. Tel: (49331) 271 810. FAX: (49331) 271 8126.

ROLF THEILE FILMTHEATERBETRIEBE
Holdgestrasse 12, Darmstadt 6100. Tel: (49615) 129 780. FAX: (49615) 129 7832.

ROSSLENBROICH-FTB GMBH
Dusseldorfer Str. 2, 40822 Mettman. Tel: (49) 21 04 7 43 66. FAX: (49) 21 04 7 46 34.
MANAGING DIRECTORS
M. Papenhoff
G. Rosslenbroich

ROYAL PALAST
Goetheplatz 2, Munich 80337. Tel: (4989) 533 956. FAX: (4989) 530 9618.

SCALA: FTB GMBH
78462 Konstanz Rosgartenstr. 9. Tel: (75) 31 2 45 22. FAX: (75) 31 1 63 23.
MANAGING DIRECTOR
Kurt Rabe

UFA THEATER AG
Graf-Adolf-Strasse 96, 40210 Dusseldorf. Tel: (49) 211 169 060. FAX: (49) 211 169 0633.
DIRECTOR
Volker Riech
Number of Screens: 500

UNION KG KRUGMANN & WEISCHER
Hamburger St., 152, 22083 Hamburg. Tel: (49) 40 2 07 05. FAX: (49) 40 29 90 71 77.

UNITED CINEMAS INTERNATIONAL MULTIPLEX GMBH
Oskar-Hoffman-Strasse 156, 44789 Bochum. (49) 234 937 190.

Number of Screens: 123

VEREINIGTE LICHTSPIELE
72016 Pf. 2609 Tubingen. Tel: (49) 70 71 2 36 61. FAX: (49) 70 71 2 14 21.

VILLAGE ROADSHOW, LTD.
(For complete listing see Australian branch.)
206 Bourke St., Melbourne, VIC, 3000, Australia. Tel: (613) 96 67 66 66. FAX: (613) 96 39 15 40.

Number of Theatres: 8 (Germany)
Number of Screens: 74 (Germany)

WETTLAUFER KINOBETRIEBS-GESELLSCHAFT MBJ
82456 Garmisch- Partenkirchen, Postfach. 1624. Tel: (49) 88 21 23 70. FAX: (49) 88 21 95 01 44.
EXECUTIVES
Georg Wettlaufer
Nora Wettlaufer

YORK–KINO GMBH-FTB
10789 Rankestrasse 31, Berlin . Tel: (49) 30 2 12 98 00. FAX: (49) 30 21 29 80 99.

GREECE

Population: 10.6 million.
Screens: 200 plus an equal number of open air cinemas open during summer months.

ASSOCIATIONS & ORGANIZATIONS

ASSOCIATION OF TECHINICIANS (ETEKT)
25 Veltetsiou St., Athens 106 80. Tel: (301) 360 2379. FAX: (301) 361 6442.

GREEK ACTORS GUILD
83 Kaningos St., Athens 10677.

GREEK FILM & TV PRODUCERS UNION
1A Egyptou St., Athens. Tel: (301) 883 8460. FAX: (301) 883 8410.

GREEK FILM CENTER
19 Paneoistimiou St., Athens 10671. Tel: (301) 363 4586. FAX: (301) 351 4336.

GREEK FILM DIRECTORS UNION
11 Tositsa St., Athens 10683. Tel: (301) 822 3205. FAX: (301) 821 1390.

MOTION PICTURE DIRECTORATE BY THE MINISTRY OF CULTURE
12 Aristidou St., Athens 105 59.

PANHELLENIC FEDERATION OF FILM EXHIBITORS
96 Academias St., Athens 10677. Tel: (301) 801 1045.

TENIOTHIKI TIS HELLADOS
Greek Film Archives, 1 Kanari St., Athens 10671. Tel: (301) 361 2046. FAX: (301) 362 8468.

THESSALONIKI FILM FESTIVAL
153 Egratias St., Thessaloniki, 36 Sina St., Athens 10672. FAX: (301) 362 1023.

DISTRIBUTORS AND PRODUCERS

AMA FILMS
22 Tositsa St., Athens 10583. Tel: (301) 381 2640. FAX: (301) 384 2559.
GENERAL MANAGER
George Stergiakis

HELLINIKI KINIMSTROGRAFIKI ENOSSI (ELKE)
(Distributes films of Warner Bros, Goldcrest, Carolco, Lorimar, Globe, Rank, Thames International, etc.) 96-98 Academias St., Athens 10677. Tel: (301) 382 3801. FAX: (301) 380 301.
GENERAL MANAGER
George V. Michaelides

NEA KINISSI
9-13 Gravias St., Athens, 10677. Tel: (301) 382 4545. FAX: (301) 383 9008.
GENERAL MANAGER
Antonis Karatzopoulos

ODEON FILMS (ELKE)
96-98 Academias St., Athens 10677. Tel: (301) 382 3801. FAX: (301) 382 3801.

OVO FILMS
27 Themistokleous St., Athens 10677. Tel: (301) 330 4521. FAX: (301) 330 4523.

PROOPTIKI S. A.
(Distributes films of Columbia Pictures, Orion, Touchstone, Walt Disney, Tri Star, Cannon.)
40-42 Koleti St., Athens 10682. Tel: (301) 383 3541. FAX: (301) 381 3762.
GENERAL MANAGER
Pantelis Metropoulos

ROSEBUD MOTION PICTURES ENTERPRISES
(Distributes independent American, European & international films)
96 Academias St., Athens 10677. Tel: (301) 384 4293. FAX: (301) 383 9208.
GENERAL MANAGER
Zenos Panayotides

SPENTZOS FILMS S. A.
(Distributes films of Twentieth Century Fox, New Line Cinema, independent and European films.)
9-13 Gravias St., Athens 10678. Tel: (301) 362 0297. FAX: (301) 382 1438.
GENERAL MANAGER
George Spentzos

UNITED INTERNATIONAL PICTURES (UIP)
(Distributes films of MGM, Paramount, Universal, United Artists.)
4 Gamveta St., Athens 10678. Tel: (301) 381 1472. FAX: (301) 383 5396.
GENERAL MANAGER
John Takaziadis

EXHIBITORS

APOSTOLOS FOUKIS
Messoguion St., Athens 11522.
Theaters: Galaxias, Metropolitan.

ATTICA CINEPLEX
12 Messoguion St., Athens 16231.,
Theaters: Opera I, Opera.

K. GEORGOPOULOS S.A.
109 Kifissias St., Athens 11524.
Theaters: Danos.

HOME VIDEO HELLAS
325 Messoguion St., Athens 15231.
Theaters: Opera I, Opera II, Radio City, Assos Odcon I, Assos Odcon II, Tropical, Havana, Anessis, Assos Odeon Maroussi, Olympion I and Olympion II, Assos Odeon.

IONAIDES FILMS EPE
12 Nikiforou Lytra St., Athens 11474.
Theaters: Astron.

STAVROS ISAAKIDES
26 Velvendous St., Athens 11364.
Theaters: Ilyssia.

KAPSIS HEIRS
14 Kifissias St., Athens.
Theaters: Anessis.

CHRISTOS KARAVIAS & COMPANY
12 Alexandras Ave., Athens.
Theaters: Nirvana.

A KARAVOYKYROS – K. FRANTZIS, S.A.
122 Patrission St., Athens 11257.
Theaters: Athena.

KONTOULIS
152 EL. Venizelos St., Callithea, Athens.

Theatres: Etoile.

FOTIS KOSMIDES
Korae St., Athens 10566.

Theaters: Asty, Hellinis.

VICTOR MICHAELIDES
Theatre Palac, 4 Voukoutestiou St., Athens 10565.

PANAYOTOPOULOS
3 Patriarchou Ioakem, Athens 1-673.

Theaters: Embassy.

D.P. SKOURAS FILMS
19 Stadium St., Athens 10561.

Theaters: Attikon, Apollon.

SPENTZOS FILMS S. A.
9-13 Gravias St., Athens 10678. Tel: (301) 382 0957. FAX: (301) 382 1438.

Theaters: Ideal, Aliki, ABC, Oscar, Ideal Maroussi.

STERIAKIS BROTHERS/AMA FILMS
122 Patrission St., Athens 11257.

Theaters: Athena.

VILLAGE ROADSHOW, GREECE
(For complete listing see Australian branch.)
11 Mistral St., Neo Psyhiko, Athen 15451. Tel: (301) 685 6833. FAX: (301) 685 6830

Number of Theatres: 4 (Greece)
Number of Screens: 44 (Greece)

HONG KONG
Population: 6.3 million.

ASSOCIATIONS & ORGANIZATIONS

EAST ASIA FILM AND VIDEO SECURITY
13/F, Rm B, Lockhart Centre, 301 Lockhart Rd., Wanchai. Tel: (852) 575 7842. FAX: (852) 838 0937.

HONG KONG AND KOWLOON CINEMA AND THEATRICAL ENTERPRISE FREE GENERAL ASSOCIATION
Flat A-B, 9/F, 88 Nathan Rd., Kowloon. Tel: (852) 376 3833. FAX: (852) 721 9225.

KOWLOON & NEW TERRITORIES MOTION PICTURE INDUSTRY ASSOCIATION
319 Beverley Commercial Centre, 87-105 Chatham Rd., Tsimshatsui, Kowloon. Tel: (852) 311 2692. FAX: (852) 311 1178.

FILM DISTRIBUTORS AND PRODUCERS

ATLAS FILM
Rm. 905-6, Winning Commercial Bldg., 46-48 Hillwood Rd., Tsimshatsui, Kowloon. Tel: (852) 367 1057. FAX: (852) 369 0855.

CAPITAL ARTISTS
No. 1, Leighton Rd., Causeway Bay. Tel: (852) 833 9192. FAX: (852) 832 5055.

CITY ENTERTAINMENT
Flat E, 14/F, Tung Nam Bldg., 475 Hennessy Rd., Wanchai. Tel: (852) 892 0155. FAX: (852) 838 4930.

CHINA STAR ENTERTAINMENT, LTD.
Unit 503C, Miramar Tower, 1-23 Kimberley Rd., TST, Kowloon. Tel: (852) 2323 1888. FAX: (852) 2191 9888. email: mal@chinastar.com.hk

CLEVELAND FILM
Imperial Cinema, 29 Burrows St., Wanchai. Tel: (852) 572 0002. FAX: (852) 834 0723.

CONTINENTAL FILM DISTRIBUTORS
Unit 1922, Star House, 3 Salisbury Rd., Tsimshatsui, Kowloon. Tel: (852) 730 4373. FAX: (852) 730 2977.

CRYSTAL CORPORATION
10/F, Lee Kar Bldg., 4-4A Carnarvon Rd., Tsimshatsui, Kowloon. Tel: (852) 367 4077. FAX: (852) 723 3054.

DELON INTERNATIONAL FILM
7B Astoria Bldg., 24-30 Ashley Rd., Tsimshatsui, Kowloon. Tel: (852) 376 1168. FAX: (852) 376 2569.

EKDO FILMS
19/F Fung Hse, 19-20 Connaught Rd., Central. Tel: (852) 523 1152. FAX: (852) 810 6670.

ERA COMMUNICATIONS
Unit 604, Taikoktsui Centre, 11-15 Kok Cheung St., Kowloon. Tel: (852) 787 3612. FAX: (852) 787 4367.

FILM CITY DISTRIBUTION
Flat A-F, 16/F, Marvel Bldg., 25-31 Kwai Fung Cres, Kwai Chung, New Territories. Tel: (852) 423 4272. FAX: (852) 420 0352.

FILM CONSORTIUM
Rm. 1302, 1 Hysan Av., Causeway Bay. Tel: (852) 5760321. FAX: (852) 895 5471.

FOX COLUMBIA TRISTAR
Rm. 1014, World Commerce Centre, 11 Canton Rd., Tsimshatsui, Kowloon. Tel: (852) 736 6277. FAX: (852) 736 3872.

GOLDEN COMMUNICATIONS
8 Hammer Hill Rd., Kowloon. Tel: (852) 726 5541. FAX: (852) 351 1683.

GOLDEN GLOBE FILM
1203 Tak Woo Hse, 17-19 D'Aguilar St., Central. Tel: (852) 576 0321.

GOLDEN HARVEST ENTERTAINMENT CO. LTD.
8 King Tung Street, Hammer Hill Rd., Kowloon. Tel: (852) 2352 8222. FAX: (852) 2351 1683.

GOLDEN PRINCESS AMUSEMENT
6th Flr., 742-744 Nathan Rd., Kowloon. Tel: (852) 391 9988. FAX: (852) 789 1365.

HAPPY INTERNATIONAL ENTERTAINMENT
Rm. 1205, Shun Tak Centre, 200 Connaught Rd., Central. Tel: (852) 559 1051. FAX: (852) 858 2657.

WILLIAM HAY & CO.
5th Flr. Rear, 234 Nathan Road. Central. Tel: (852) 368 8319. FAX: (852) 311 6727.

IMPACT FILMS PRODUCTION
22/F Waterloo Plaza, 53-55 Waterloo Rd., Kowloon. Tel: (852) 332 1762. FAX: (852) 783 8225.

IN-GEAR FILM DISTRIBUTION INTERNATIONAL
14th Flr., 206-208 Prince Edward Rd., Kowloon. Tel: (852) 397 1452. FAX: (852) 380 5216.

INTERCONTINENTAL GROUP HOLDINGS LTD.
(Subsidiaries: Intercontinental Film Distributors, Mini Cinema Ltd., Intercontinental Video, Jesu International Entertainment, Lauro Films, Intercontinental Communications and Perfect Advertising & Production Co.)
27/F Wyler Centre, Phase 2, 200 Tai Lin Pai Rd., Kwai Chung, New Territories. Tel: (852) 2481 6693. FAX: (852) 2481 6377.

JOY SALES FILM & VIDEO DISTRIBUTORS
2/F Hang On Mansion, 239-249 Portland St., Mongkok, Kowloon. Tel: (852) 771 6161. FAX: (852) 770 6218.

KOREAN MOTION PICTURE PROMOTION (HK)
Ste. B1, 14/F, Golden Crown Ct, 68 Nathan Rd., Tsimshatsui, Kowloon. Tel: (852) 369 2789. FAX: (852) 311 3425.

NEWPORT ENTERTAINMENT
19/F, Southland Bldg., 47 Connaught Rd., Central. Tel: (852) 543 6973. FAX: (852) 544 9574.

PARSONS INTERNATIONAL
11J Far East Mansion, 5-6 Middle Rd., Tsimshatsui, Kowloon. Tel: (852) 721 8647. FAX: (852) 311 5383.

SALON FILMS LTD.
6 Devon Rd., Kowloon Tong, Kowloon. Tel: (852) 2338 0505. FAX: (852) 2338 2539.

SAM LOON INTERNATIONAL
12/F, Vincent Commercial Centre, 21 Hillwood Rd., Tsimshatsui, Kowloon. Tel: (852) 723 6239. FAX: (852) 721 4954.

SOUTHERN FILM
1902 Dominion Centre, 37-59 Queens Rd. East, Wanchai. Tel: (852) 527 7282. FAX: (852) 865 1449.

UIP INTERNATIONAL SERVICES
Ste. 1501, Dina Hse., 11 Duddell St., Central. Tel: (852) 526 6841. FAX: (852) 845 9581.

THE WALT DISNEY STUDIOS HONG KONG
15th Flr., Citibank Tower, Citibank Plaza, 3 Garden Rd., Central. FAX: (852) 2536 2453.

WARNER BROS. (FAR EAST)
12/F Siberian Fur Bldg., 38-40 Haiphong R., Tsimshatsui, Kowloon. Tel: (852) 376 3963. FAX: (852) 376 1302.

EXHIBITORS

EDKO FILMS LIMITED
1212 Tower II, Admiralty Centre, 18 Harcourt Rd., Hong Kong. Tel: (85) 2 25 29 3898. FAX: (85) 2 25 29 5277.
EXECUTIVE DIRECTOR
William Kong
THEATRE OPERATIONS
Eric Li
DISTRIBUTION DEPT.
Audrey Lee
ADVERTISING DEPT.
Leung Yuet Ngor
ACCOUNTS DEPT.
Angela Fung

Number of Theatres: 9
Number of Screens: 29

Mongkok (3), Kernhill (3), Tgnen Wan (3), Kwai Fong (5), Kowloon Bay (3), Ynen Long (4), Silvercord (2), Windsor (2), Cinematheque (4).

GOLDEN HARVEST ENTERTAINMENT CO., LTD.
16/F Peninsula Office Tower, 18 Middle Rd., Kowloon. Tel: (852) 2352 8222. FAX: (852) 2353 5989.
EXECUTIVE DIRECTORS
Mr. Chow Ting Hsing
Raymond
Mr. Graham Burke
Mr. C.K. Phoon
Mr. Albert Lee
Mr. Stephen Chu
Mr. Richard Potter

Number of Theatres: 58
Number of Screens: 251
Hong Kong (7), Malaysia (33), PRC (2), Singapore (9), Thailand (7).

GOLDEN VILLAGE
8 Hammer Hill Rd., Kowloon. Tel: (852) 352-8222.

Number of Screens: 14

STUDIO CITY CINEMA HOLDINGS, LTD.
Rm. 409-411, 4/F, World Commerce Centre, 11 Canton Rd., Kowloon. Tel: (85) 27 35 4633. FAX: (85) 23 75 8869.
GENERAL MANAGERS
Bob Vallone
Maureen Koh
Ben Keung
EXECUTIVE DIRECTORS
James Kralik
Hamilton Tang
CHAIRMAN
Ira D. Kaye

UNITED ARTISTS CINEMA CIRCUIT, LTD.
Room 409-410/F, World Commerce Centre, 11 Canton Rd., Kowloon. Tel: (852) 2736-4633.

Number of Screens: 30.

VILLAGE ROADSHOW, LTD.
(For complete listing see Australian branch.)
206 Bourke St., Melbourne, VIC, 3000, Australia. Tel: (613) 96 67 66 66. FAX: (613) 96 39 15 40.

Number of Theatres: 8
Number of Screens: 29

HUNGARY

Population: 10.1 million.

ASSOCIATIONS & ORGANIZATIONS

ASSOCIATION OF CINEMAS OF HUNGARY
Maria u 19, Szolnok H-5000. Tel. (3656) 420 612.

GUILD OF HUNGARY
Varosligeti Fasor 38, Budapest H-1068. Tel: (361) 342 4760. FAX: (361) 342 4760.

HUNGARIAN FILM INSTITUTE & ARCHIVE
Budakeszi u 51B, Budapest H-1021. Tel: (361) 176 0205. FAX: (361) 176 7106.

MOTION PICTURE FOUNDATION OF HUNGARY
Szalaiu 10, Budapest H-1054. Tel. (361) 1126417.

DISTRIBUTORS AND PRODUCERS

BUDAPEST FILM
Batori u 10, Budapest H-1054. (361) 111 6650. FAX: (361) 131 5946.

CINEMAGYAR KFT (HUNGAROFILM EX)
Batori u 10, Budapest H-1054. (361) 111 4614. FAX: (361) 153 1317.

DUNA/UIP DANUBE
Tarogato u 24, Budapest H-1021. Tel: (361) 174 7291. FAX: (361) 176 7291.

EUROFILM STUDIO
Rona u 174, Budapest H-1145. Tel: (361) 252 5069. FAX: (361) 251 3986. email: eurofilm@hungary.net

FLAMEX
Labanc u 22B, Budapest H-1021. Tel: (361) 176 1543. FAX: (361) 176 0596.

FOCUSFILM LTD.
Pasareti ut 122, Budapest H-1026. Tel: (361) 200 6857, (361) 275 2312 . FAX: (200) 200 6858. email: focusflm@mail.matav.hu
MANAGING DIRECTORS
Aron Sipos
Denes Skeres

HUNNIA FILMSTUDIO
Rona u 174, Budapest H-1145. Tel: (361) 252 3170. FAX: (361) 251 6269.

INTERCOM
Karolina ut. 65, Budapest H-1113. Tel: (361) 209 0933. FAX: (361) 209 0930.

MOKEP
Bathori u 10, Budapest H-1054. Tel: (361) 111 2097. FAX: (361) 153 1613.

UIP—DANUBE INTERNATIONAL PICTURES
Tarogato u 2-4/2nd Flr., Budapest H-1021. Tel: (361) 176 7291. FAX: (361) 274 2177.
MANAGER
Peter Balint.

EXHIBITORS

BUDAPEST FILM
Bathori u 10, Budapest H-1054. Tel: (361) 111 2494. FAX: (361) 111 2687.

CORVIN BUDAPEST FILMPALACE
Corvin koz 12, Budapest H-1082. Tel: (361) 303 1500. FAX: (361) 303 2526.

CINEPLEX ODEON INTERNATIONAL MOZI
Polus Centre, Szentmihalyi ut 131, 1153 Budapest. Tel: (361) 419 4223. FAX: (361) 419 4228.

CONTACT
Ana LeRoux

Number of Theatres: 1
Number of Screens: 6

HUNGARIAN FILM INSTITUTE & FILM ARCHIVE
Budakeszi u 51B, Budapest H-1021. Tel: (361) 176 0205. FAX: (361) 176 7106.

VILLAGE ROADSHOW, LTD.
206 Bourke St., Melbourne, VIC, 3000, Australia. Tel: (613) 96 67 66 66. FAX: (613) 96 39 15 40.
(For complete listing see Australian branch.)

Number of Theatres: 4 (Hungary)
Number of Screens: 26 (Hungary)

ICELAND

Population: 276 thousand.
Average Ticket Price: $7.18

ASSOCIATIONS & ORGANIZATIONS

ASSOCIATION OF FILM DISTRIBUTORS IN ICELAND
Stjornubio, Laugaveg 94, Reykjavik 101. Tel: (3541) 551 6500. FAX: (3541) 554 4630.

ASSOCIATION OF ICELANDIC FILM DIRECTORS
Hverfisgata 46, Reykjavik 121. (3541) 562 1850. FAX: (3541) 552 5154.

ASSOCIATION OF ICELANDIC FILM PRODUCERS
Posthusstraeti 13, Reykjavik 101. (3541) 152 8188. FAX: (3541) 162 3424.

DIRECTORS GUILD OF ICELAND
Hverfisgata 46, Reykjavij 101. (3541) 551 2260. FAX: (3541) 552 5154.

ICELANDIC FILM FUND
Laugavegur 24, Reykjavik 101. (3541) 562 3580. FAX: (3541) 562 7171.

ICELANDIC FILMMAKERS ASSOCIATION
Laugavegur 24, P.O. Box 320, Reykjavik 101. (3541) 562 3225. FAX: (3541) 562 7171.

MINISTRY OF CULTURE & EDUCATION
Solvholsgotu 4, Reykjavik 105. Tel: (3541) 560 9500. FAX: (3541) 562 3068.

DISTRIBUTORS AND PRODUCERS

BERGVIK
Armula 44, Reykjavik. Tel: (3541) 588 7966. FAX: (3541) 588 0288.

HASKOLABIO UNIVERSITY CINEMA
Hagatorg, Reykjavik 107. Tel: (3541) 561 1212. FAX: (3541) 562 7135. email: cinema@centrum.is

ICELANDIC FILM COMPANY
Hverfisgata 46, Reykjavik 101. Tel: (3541) 551 2260. FAX: (3541) 552 5154.

LAUGARASBIO
Laugaras, Reykjavik 104. Tel: (3541) 563 8150. FAX: (3541) 568 0910.

MYNDFORM
Holshraun 2, Hafnarfirdi 220. (354) 565 1288. FAX: (354) 565 0188.

SAM FILM
Alfabakki 8, Reykjavik 109. Tel: (3541) 587 8900. FAX: (3541) 587 8930.

SKIFAN
Skeifan 17, Reykjavik 108. Tel: (354) 525 5000. FAX: (3541) 525 5001.

STJOERNUBIO
Laugavegi 94, Reykjavik 101. Tel: (3541) 551 6500. FAX: (3541) 554 4630.

EXHIBITORS

BORGARBIO
Akuyeri. Tel: (354) 462 3500. FAX: (354) 461 2796.

HASKOLABIO-UNIVERSITY CINEMA
Hagatorg, Reykjavik 107. Tel: (3541) 561 1212. FAX: (3541) 562 7135. email: cinema@centrum.is
DIRECTOR
Fridbert Palsson

LAUGARASBIO
Laugaras, Reykjavik 104. Tel: (3541) 563 8150. FAX: (3541) 568 0910.

REGNBOGINN
Hverfisgata 54, Reykjavik 101. Tel: (3541) 462 3500. FAX: (3541) 461 2796.

SAM FILM
Alfabakka 8, Reykjavik 109. Tel: (3541) 587 8900. FAX: (3541) 587 8930.

STJOERNUBIO
Laugavegi 94, Reykjavik 101. Tel: (3541) 551 6500. FAX: (3541) 554 4630.

INDIA
Population: 1 billion/
Theatres: 13,000.

ASSOCIATIONS & ORGANIZATIONS

CINEMATOGRAPH EXHIBITOR'S ASSOCIATION OF INDIA
Flat 22/23B, 1st Flr., Vellard View, Tardeo Rd., Bombay 400034.

EASTERN INDIA MOTION PICTURE ASSOCIATION
98E Chowringhee Square, Calcutta.

FILM FEDERATION OF INDIA
91 Walkeshwar Rd, Bombay 400006.

INDIAN DOCUMENTARY PRODUCERS ASSOCIATION
305 Famous Cine Bldg., Mahalaxmi, Bombay 400018.

INDIAN FILM EXPORTERS ASSOCIATION
305 Famous Cine Bldg., Mahalaxmi, Bombay 400018.

THE INDIAN MOTION PICTURE DISTRIBUTORS' ASSOCIATION
33 Vijay Chamber, Tribhuvan Rd, Bombay 400004.

INDIAN MOTION PICTURE PRODUCERS' ASSOCIATION
Dr. Ambedkar Road, Bandra (W), Bombay 400050.

SOUTH INDIA'S FILM CHAMBER OF COMMERCE
122 Mount Road, Madras 60002.

PRINCIPAL EXPORTERS

ANAND EXPORTS
730 Chandra Niwas, Annex Shop 2, 11th Rd., Khar, Bombay 400052. Tel: (9122) 646 2755.

CITIZEN INTERNATIONAL
B/6 3rd Flr., Everest, Tardeo Road, Bombay 400034. Tel: (9122) 495 1688.

FAIRDEAL EXPORTS LTD.
10 Kashi Kunj, 2nd Flr., Waterfield Road, Bandra, Bombay 400050. FAX: (9122) 604 2429.

NATIONAL FILM DEVELOPMENT CORP., LTD.
Nehru Centre, Dr. A. Besant Road, Worli, Bombay 400018. Tel: (9122) 495 2662.

NEPTUNE ENTERPRISES
C 8/9 Everest, 4th Flr., Tardeo Rd., Bombay 400034. FAX: (9122) 492 0890.

RAJSHRI PRODUCTIONS LTD.-BHAVNA
1st Flr., Opp Kismat Cinema, Prabhadevi, Bombay 400025. FAX: (9122) 422 9181.

TRIMURTI EXPORTS
B/11 Commerce Centre, Tardeo Road, Bombay 400034. FAX: (9122) 811 667.

PRINCIPAL IMPORTERS

ALLIED ARTS OF INDIA INC.
Metro House, M. G. Road, Bombay 400020.

COLUMBIA TRISTAR FILMS OF INDIA LTD.
Metro House, 1st Flr., M. G. Road, Bombay 400020. Tel: (9122) 201 4264. FAX: (9122) 201 4321.

METRO-GOLDYN-MAYER FILMS OF INDIA LTD.
Metro House, M. G. Road, Bombay 400020.

PARAMOUNT FILMS OF INDIA, LTD.
(Also representing Universal)
Hague Building, Sprott Rd., Bombay 400020. Tel: (9122) 261 3877.

FAX: (9122) 261 2856.
MANAGER
Sarabjit Singh

TWENTIETH CENTURY FOX CORP. (INDIA), LTD.
Metro House, 3rd Flr., M. G. Road, Bombay 400020. Tel: (9122) 205 4290. FAX: (9122) 208 9388. Calcutta: Tel: (9133) 249 5623. New Delhi: (9111) 332 0351. Madras: Tel: (9144) 852 0078.
GENERAL MANAGER
Sunder Kimatrai

UNITED ARTISTS CORP.
Metro House, M. G. Road, Bombay 400020.

UNIVERSAL PICTURES INDIA P LTD.
Hague Bldg, Sprott Road, Bombay 400020. Tel: (9122) 266 6146. FAX: (9122) 261 2856.

WARNER BROS (F. D.) INDIA
Eros Theatre Bldg., 42 M. Karve Road, Bombay 400020. Tel: (9122) 285 6557. FAX: (9122) 285 0984.
Leslie House, 19A Jawarharlal Nehru Rd., Calcutta 700087. Tel: (9133) 249 5613.
Dinroze Estate, 69 Mount Rd., Madras 600002. Tel: (9144) 852 5964.
Plaza Thatre Bldg., Connaught Circus, New Delhi 110001. Tel: (9111) 332 1544.
MANAGING DIRECTOR
J. Fernandes

EXHIBITORS

THE BALJI GROUP
8 Thiru-V-Ka Rd., Chennai 600014. Tel: (91) 44 85 24 875, (91) 44 852 3813. FAX: (91) 44 85 21 972.
CONTACT
KR Subramaniam
MANAGING PARTNER
Mr. Vijaykumar

CHAPHALKAR GROUP OF CINEMAS
Mangala Cinema, 111 Shivajinagar, Pune 411005. Tel: (91) 21 2 323468, 323519. FAX: (91) 21 2 323973.
MANAGING DIRECTOR
Ajay Bijlee
CONTACT
D.D. Prakash Chaphalkar

MARIS THEATRES PVT, LTD.
Fort Station Rd., Tiruchirapally 62 0002.

MODI U.A.T.C. (PVT) LTD.
4 Lands End, 54 Byramji Jeetibhoy Rd., Bandra, Bombay 400050. Tel: (9122) 645 0000. FAX: (9122) 645 8282.
CHIEF EXECUTIVE
Rajiv Sahai

PRIYA VILLAGE ROADSHOW LIMITED
Priya Cinema and Anupam Cineplex, 50 W. Regal Bldg., Connaught Pl., New Delhi 110001. Tel: (91) 11 37 32 089 and 334 0605. FAX: (91) 11 374 71 39.

RAJSHRI PICTURES
42 Virsavarkar Rd., Post Box No. 9103, Prabha Devi, Bombay 400025, India. Tel: (912) 422 7705 and 430 7688. FAX: (912) 242 9181.

SHRINGAR CINEMAS PVT., LTD.
B-103, Kailash, Juhu Church Rd., Juhu, Mumbai, 400 049, Maharashtra State. Tel: (91) 22 625-5900. FAX: (91) 22 625-5272. email: Shrigar001@vsnl.com
DIRECTOR
Shravan Shroff

VILLAGE ROADSHOW, LTD.
(For complete listing see Australian branch.)
206 Bourke St., Melbourne, VIC, 3000, Australia. Tel: (613) 96 67 66 66. FAX: (613) 96 39 15 40.

Number of Theatres: 2 (India)
Number of Screens: 5 (India)

WESTERN INDIA THEATRES LIMITED
Liberty Bldg., 41-42 New Marine Lines, Bombay 400020. Tel: (91) 22 20 1 42 17, (91) 22 20 1 43 18. FAX: (91) 22 20 57 939.
CONTACTS
Roosi K. Modi
Kamal Barjatiya

INDONESIA

Population: 224.7 million.

DISTRIBUTORS

UNITED INTERNATIONAL PICTURES (UIP)
c/o PT Camila Internuse Film, Subentra Bank Building, Ste. 716, Jl. Jend, Gatot Subroto Kaz 21, Jakarta 12930, Indonesia. Tel: (6221) 522 0063. FAX: (6221) 522 0064.
REPRESENTATIVE
Douglas Lee

EXHIBITORS

SUBENTRA GROUP
Subentra Bank Building, 21 Jl. Send, Gatot Subroto, Jakarta 12930. Tel: (6221) 522 0122. FAX: (6221) 522 0078.
MANAGING DIRECTOR, EXHIBITION & DISTRIBUTION
Harris Lasmana
Number of Screens: 500

ISRAEL

Population: 5.8 million.

ASSOCIATIONS & ORGANIZATIONS

ISRAEL FILM CENTRE
Ministry of Industry & Trade, 30 Gershon Agron St., P.O. Box 299, Jerusalem 94190. Tel: (9722) 750 433. FAX: (9722) 245 110.

ISRAEL FILM SERVICE
Ministry of Education & Culture, P.O. Box 13240, Hakirya Romema, Jerusalem 91130. Tel: (9722) 512 248. FAX: (9722) 526 818.

DISTRIBUTORS AND PRODUCERS

ALBERT D. MATALON & CO.
(Agency for Columbia TriStar & Twentieth Century Fox), 13 Yona Hanavi St., Tel Aviv 63302. Tel: (9723) 516 2020. FAX: (9723) 516 1888.
CONTACT
Amnon Matalon

FORUM FILM LTD.
P.O. Box 12598, Herzlia Pituah, Industrial Zone 46766. Tel: (9729) 562 111. FAX: (9729) 561 581.

NACHSHON FILMS
22 Harakeuel St., Tel Aviv 66183. Tel: (9723) 356 40015. FAX: (9723) 350 05112.

NOAH FILMS/UNITED INTERNATIONAL PICTURES (UIP)
10 Glickson St., Tel Aviv 63567. Tel: (9723) 200 221. FAX: (9723) 202 071.
CONTACT
Jonathan Chissick

SHAPIRA FILMS
34 Allenby Rd., P.O. Box 4842, Tel Aviv 63325.

SHOVAL-FILM PRODUCTION
32 Allenby Rd., Tel Aviv. Tel: (9723) 659 288. FAX: (9723) 659 289.

TAMUZ FILMS
5 Pinsker St., Tel Aviv. Tel: (9723) 201 512. FAX: (9723) 528 1564.

EXHIBITORS

TAMUZ FILMS
5 Pinsker St., Tel Aviv. Tel: (9723) 201 512. FAX: (9723) 528 1564.

STUDIOS

G. G. ISRAEL STUDIOS
Communications Centre, Neve Ilan, D. N. Harei, Yehuda 90850. Tel: (9722) 349 111. FAX: (9722) 349 9000.

JERUSALEM CAPITAL STUDIOS
P.O. Box 13172, 206 Jaffa Rd., Jerusalem 91131. Tel: (9722) 701 711. FAX: (9722) 381 658.

ORION FILMS
4 Shamgar St., Jerusalem 90058. Tel: (9722) 238 0221. FAX: (9722) 238 0925.

TEL AD JERUSALEM STUDIOS
20 Marcus St., P.O. Box 4111, Jerusalem Theatre Building, Jerusalem 91040. Tel: (9722) 619 988. FAX: (9722) 611 451.

ITALY

Population: 57.6 million.

ASSOCIATIONS & ORGANIZATIONS

ANICA
Viale Regina Margherita 286, Rome 00198. Tel: (396) 4423 1480. FAX: (396) 440 4128.

CINECITTA INTERNATIONAL
Via Tuscolana 1055, Rome 00173. Tel: (396) 722 2824. FAX: (396) 722 3131.

ENTE AUTONOMO GESTIONE CINEMA
Via Tuscolana 1055, Rome 00173. Tel: (396) 722 861. FAX: (396) 722 1883.

PRESIDENZA DEL CONSIGLIO DEI MINISTRI
Via Della Ferracella in Laterano 51, Rome 00184. Tel: (396) 77321. FAX: (396) 759 2602.

DISTRIBUTORS AND PRODUCERS

AB FILM DISTRIBUTORS
Via Monte Zebio 28, Rome 00195. Tel: (396) 321 9554. FAX: (396) 361 3641.

ACADEMY PICTURES
Via F. Ruspoli 8, Rome 00198. Tel: (396) 884 0424. FAX: (396) 841 7043.

ADRIAN CHIESA ENTERPRISES
Via Barnaba Oriani 24A, Rome 00197. Tel: (306) 807 0400. FAX: (306) 8068 7855.

ARTISTI ASSOCIATI INTERNAZIONALE
Via Degli Scipioni 281-283, Rome 00192. Tel: (396) 321 0367. FAX: (396) 321 7245.

BIM DISTRIBUZIONE
Via G. Antonelli 47, Rome 00196. Tel: (396) 323 1057. FAX: (396) 321 1984.

BUENA VISTA INTERNATIONAL ITALIA
Via Palestro 24, Rome 00185. Tel: (396) 445 2269. FAX: (396) 445 1202.

CDI (COMPAGNIA DISTRIBUZIONE INTERNAZIONALE)
Via Saleria 292, Rome 00199. Tel: (309) 854 8821. FAX: (396) 854 1691.

CECCHI GORI GROUP
Via Valadier 42, Rome 00193. Tel: (306) 324 721. FAX: (306) 3247 2300.

CHALLENGE FILM INTERNATIONAL
Via Lazio 9, Rome 00187. Tel: (396) 481 8117. FAX: (396) 482 4890.

CHANCE FILM
Via G. Mercalli 19, Rome 00197. Tel: (396) 808 5041. FAX: (396) 807 0506.

CIDIF
Via Vicenza 5a, Rome 00185. Tel: (396) 446 9636. FAX: (396) 446 9636.

CLEMI CINEMATOGRAFICA
Via Salaria 292, Rome 00199. Tel: (396) 854 8821. FAX: (396) 841 9749.

COLUMBIA TRISTAR FILMS ITALIA
Via Palestro N. 24, Rome 00185. Tel: (396) 494 1196. FAX: (396) 446 9936.

DELTA
Via Elenora Duse 37, Rome 00197. Tel: (396) 808 4458. FAX: (396) 807 9331.

EAGLE PICTURES
Via M. Buonarroti 5, Milan 20149. Tel: (392) 481 4169. FAX: (392) 481 3389.

EDIZIONI EDEN
Via A. Grandi 1, Mazzo Di Rho, Milan 20017. Tel: (392) 9350 9822.

ENRICO GAMBI
Via C. Sul Clitunno 20, Rome 00181. Tel: (396) 788 7746. FAX: (396) 780 6803.

EUPHON TECHNICOLOUR
Via Po 13-15, San Giuliano Milanes 20098. Tel: (392) 9828 0406.

FILMAURO
Via Della Vasca Navale 58, Rome 00146. Tel: (396) 556 0788. FAX: (396) 559 0670.

FULVIA FILM
Via Bruno Nuozzi 36, Rome 00197. Tel: (396) 808 1575. FAX: (396) 808 1510.

GRANATO PRESS
Via Marconi 47, Bologna 40122. Tel: (3951) 237 737.

GRUPPO BEMA
Via N. Martelli 3, Rome 00197. Tel: (396) 808 8551. FAX: (396) 807 5454.

GRUPPO CURTI COMMUNICAZIONE
Via Domenico Cimarosa 18, Rome 00198. Tel: (396) 854 3382. FAX: (396) 855 8105.

IMPERIAL BULLDOG PRODUCTIONS
Via B. Eustachi 12, Milan 20129. Tel: (392) 2952 2363.

INTERNATIONAL MOVIE COMPANY
Lungotevere Flaminio 66, Rome 00196. Tel: (396) 361 0344. FAX: (396) 361 2676.

ISTITUTO LUCE
Via Tuscolana 1055, Rome 00173. Tel: (396) 722 2492. FAX: (396) 722 2493.

ITALIAN INTERNATIONAL FILM
Via Gian Domenico Romagnosi 20, Rome 00196. Tel: (396) 361 1377. FAX: (396) 322 5965.

KINA
Piazza Duomo 16, Milan 20122. Tel: (392) 8646 4102. FAX: (392) 7200 1817.

LIFE INTERNATIONAL
Via Monte Zebio 43, Rome 00195. Tel: (396) 321 5972. FAX: (396) 361 0036.

LUCKY RED
Via Antonio Baiamonti 10, Rome 00195. Tel: (396) 3735 2296. FAX: (396) 3735 2310.

MARGY FILM
Via Orti 2, Milan 20122. Tel: (392) 551 7545. FAX: (392) 545 9918.

MEDUSA FILM
Via Aurelia Antica 422-424, Rome 00165. Tel: (396) 66301. FAX: (396) 663 960.

MFD
Largo A., Ponchielli 6, Rome 00198. Tel: (396) 854 0542. FAX: (396) 854 1691.

MIKADO FILM
Via Victor Pisani 12, Milan 20124. Tel: (392) 6671 1476. FAX: (392) 6671 1488.

MIMA FILMS
Largo V. Alpini 12, Milan 20145. Tel: (392) 349 2860.

MOVIETIME
Via Nicola Ricciotti 11, Rome 00195. Tel: (396) 322 6709. FAX: (396) 3600 0950.

MULTIMEDIA FILM DISTRIBUTION
Via L. Ximenes 21, Florence 50125. Tel: (3955) 225 622. FAX: (3955) 233 6726.

NEMO DISTRIBUZIONE CINEMATOGRAFICA
Via Livigno 50, Rome 00188. Tel: (396) 331 851. FAX: (396) 3367 9491.

NINI GRASSIA COMMUNICATIONS
Via Velletri 49, Rome 00198. Tel: (396) 855 1745. FAX: (396) 844 3572.

NUOVE INIZIATIVE COMMERCIALI SRL
Via Flaminia 872, Rome 00191. Tel: (396) 333 9416. FAX: (396) 333 6367.

PEGASO INTER-COMMUNICATION
L. Gen. Gonzaga del Vodice 4, Rome 00195. Tel: (396) 360 0830. FAX: (396) 3611 13251.

PENTA DISTRIBUZIONE
Via Aurelia Antica 422, Rome 00165. Tel: (396) 663 901. FAX: (396) 663 9040.

ROYAL FILM ENTERPRISES
Via A. Caroncini 47. Rome 00197. Tel: (396) 808 3506.

SACIS
Via Teulada 66, Rome 00195. Tel: (396) 374 981. FAX: (396) 372 3492.

SIRIO FILM
Viale Parioli 28 Int. 1, Rome 00197. Tel: (396) 808 2144. FAX: (396) 808 8748.

SKORPION
Via L. Caro 12-A, Rome 00193. Tel: (396) 324 2223. FAX: (396) 321 0890.

SO CINEMATOGRAFICA
Lungotevere Delle Navi 19, Rome 00196. Tel: (396) 321 5114. FAX: (396) 361 2852.

STARLIGHT
Via Bellerio 30, Milan 20161. Tel: (392) 646 6441. FAX: (392) 646 6444.

SURF FILM
Via Padre Filippini 130, Rome 00144. Tel: (396) 529 3811. FAX: (396) 529 3816

TWENTIETH CENTURY FOX
Largo Amilcare Ponchielli 6, Rome 00198. Tel: (396) 8530 1060. FAX: (396) 8530 0971.
MANAGING DIRECTOR
Osvaldo De Santis

UNITED INTERNATIONAL PICTURES
Via Bissolati 20, Rome 00187. Tel: (396) 482 0626. FAX: (396) 482 0628.
MANAGER
Richard Borg

VARIETY FILMS COMMUNICATIONS
Via Nomentana 257, Rome 00161. Tel: (396) 3600 1409. FAX: (396) 3600 1022.

VISTARAMA
Via Savoia 72, Italy 00198. Tel: (396) 854 6646. FAX: (396) 8535 0050.

WARNER BROS. ITALIA
Via Varesse 16B, Rome 00185. Tel: (396) 446 3191. FAX: (396) 675 1022.

ZENITH DISTRIBUZIONE
Via Soperga 30, Milan 20127. Tel: (392) 261 3207. FAX: (392) 261 0768.

EXHIBITORS

CECCHI GORI GROUP
Via Valadier 42, Rome 00193. Tel: (396) 3247 2236. FAX: (396) 3247 2300.
Number of Screens: 61

CINEMA 5
Via Aurelia Antica 422, Rome 00165. Tel: (396) 663 901. FAX: (396) 6639 0440.

CIRCUITO GERMANI
Piazza Strozzi 2, Florence 50123. Tel: (3955) 295 051.

ERNESTO DI SARRO
Via Soperga 36, Milan 20127. Tel: (392) 260 3207.

ISTITUTO LUCE
Via Tuscolana 1055, Rome 00173. Tel: (396) 722 2492. FAX: (396) 722 2493.

LORENZO VENTAVOLI
Via Pomba 18, Turin 10123. Tel: (3911) 544 083.

LUIGI DE PEDYS
Via Sorpega 43, Milan 20127. Tel: (392) 284 6756.

DAVID QUILLERI
Via Ville Patrizi 10, Rome. Tel: (396) 884 4731.

RAFFAELE GAUDAGNO
Cinema President, Largo Augusto 1, Milan 20122. Tel: (392) 7602 1410. FAX: (392) 7602 2223.

UCI ITALIA SRL
Via Giarezzo No. 4, Milan 20145. Tel: (392) 4855 9029. FAX: (392) 469 4998.
DIRECTOR
Donna Roberts

UGO POGGI
Via Fiume 11, Florence 50123. Tel: (3955) 218 682.

VILLAGE ROADSHOW, LTD.
(For complete listing see Australian branch.)
206 Bourke St., Melbourne, VIC, 3000, Australia. Tel: (613) 96 67 66 66. FAX: (613) 96 39 15 40.
Number of Theatres: 6 (Italy)
Number of Screens: 60 (Italy)

JAPAN

Population: 125.5 million.

ASSOCIATIONS & ORGANIZATIONS

HI-VISION PROMOTION ASSOCIATION
1-9-6 Sendagaya, Shibuya-ku 151, Tokyo. Tel: (813) 3746 1125. FAX: (813) 3746 1138.

HI-VISION PROMOTION CENTER
Kowa Kawasaki Nishiguchi Bldg. 4F, 66-2, Horikawa-Cho, Saiwai-ku 210, Kanagawa-Ken. Tel: (8144) 541 6331. FAX: (8144) 541 6335.

UNI JAPAN FILM(ASSOCIATION FOR THE DIFFUSION OF JAPANESE FILMS ABROAD)
Nakamura Bldg., 9-13 Ginza 5, Chuo-Ku, Tokyo 104. Tel: (813) 3572 5106. FAX: (813) 3572 8876.

DISTRIBUTORS AND PRODUCERS

ASCII PICTURES
12 Mori Bldg SF. 1-17-3 Toranomon, Minato-ku, Tokyo 105. Tel: (813) 3581 9501. FAX: (813) 3581 9510.

ASIA COORDINATION
505 Premier Nakano, 2-5-4 Chuou, Nakano-Ku, Tokyo 164. Tel: (813) 3360 0704. FAX: (813) 3360 5956.

BUENA VISTA INTERNATIONAL JAPAN
Roppongi DK Bldg., 7-18-23 Roppongi 106, Minato-ku. Tel: (813) 3746 5009. FAX: (813) 3746 0009.

CHANNEL COMMUNICATIONS, INC.
303 Mitsuai Bldg., Take-Kanta, Minato-Ku, Tokyo 108. Tel: (813) 3280 0971. FAX: (813) 3280 0555.

COMMUNICA FILM CORP.
401, 5-1-25 Minami-Aoyama, Minato-Ku, Tokyo 107. Tel: (813) 3409 0431. Telex: 2423210 EVRGRN J. FAX: (813) 3498 1086.

CREATIVE ENTERPRISE INTERNATIONAL INC. (TOKYO)
Villa Bianca 205, 33-12-2 Cho-Me, Jingu-Mae, Shibuya-Ku, Tokyo 150. Tel: (813) 3403 4893. FAX: (813) 3404 3766.

DAIEI
1-1-16 Higashi Shimbashi, Minato-ku 105-8671, Tokyo. Tel: (813) 3573-8717. FAX: (813) 3573 8720.

DELA CORPORATION
Rozan Bldg. 813, 7-15-13, Roppongi, Minato-ku, 106, Tokyo. Tel: (813) 479 0591. FAX: (813) 479 0602.

EURO SPACE
24-8-601 Sakuragaoka-Cho, Shibuya-ku 150, Tokyo. Tel: (813) 3461 0212. FAX: (813) 3770 1179.

GAGA COMMUNICATIONS
East Roppongi Bldg., 3-16-35 Roppongi, Minato-ku, Tokyo 106. Tel: (813) 5410 3507. FAX: (813) 5410 3558.

IWANAMI PRODUCTIONS INC.
3-19-11 Yushima, Bunkyo-Ku, Tokyo 113. Tel: (813) 5688 3551. FAX: (813) 5688 3566.

KAJIMAVISION PRODUCTION CO. LTD.
6-5-13 Akasaka, Minato-Ku, Tokyo 107. Tel: (813) 3582 6661. FAX: (813) 3588 0883.

KIROKU EIGASHA PRODUCTIONS INC.
2-12-1 Yoyogi, Shibuya-Ku, Tokyo 151. Tel: (813) 3370 3386. FAX: (813) 3370 3469.

MARUBENI CORPORATION
4-2, Ohtemachi 1-Chome, Chiyoda-u, Tokyo. Tel: (813) 282 4136. FAX: (813) 3282 4835.

MEDIA INTERNATIONAL CO., LTD.
Koyo Bldg 2F, 1-37-8 Yoyogi, Shibuya-Ku, Tokyo 151. Tel: (3) 3370 6577. FAX: (3) 3370 0243.

MEDIA INTERNATIONAL CORPORATION
2-14-5 Akasaka, Minato-ku, Tokyo 107. Tel: (813) 5561 9571. FAX: (813) 5561 9550/49.

MITSUBISHI CORPORATION
3-1, Marunouchi 2-Chome, Chiyoda-ku, Tokyo 100-86. Tel: (813) 3210 7795. FAX: (813) 3210 7397.

MOTION PICTURE PRODUCERS ASSOCIATION OF JAPAN INC.
Sankei Bldg., Bekkan, 1-7-2 Otemachi, Chiyoda-Ku, Tokyo 100. Tel: (813) 3231 6417. FAX: (813) 3231 6420.

NEXUS (JAPAN), LTD.
47 Poland St., London W1V 3DF. Tel: (0171) 434 9243. FAX: (0171) 437 3720.

NHK INTERNATIONAL, INC.
Daini Kyodo Bldg., 7-13 Udagawacho, Shibuya-Ku, Tokyo 150. Tel: (813) 3464 1823. Telex: 29518 NHKINT J. FAX: (813) 3770 1829.

OPTO-ELECTRONICS MEDIA DEPT.
New Select, Nakamura Bldg., 7th Flr., 5-9-13 Ginza, Chuo-ku. Tel: (813) 3573 7571. FAX: (813) 3572 0139.

ORIENT FILM ASSOCIATES, INC.
Naoki Bldg., 2-11-14 Minami Aoyama, Minato-Ku, Tokyo 107. Tel: (813) 334 792 340. Telex: 26193. FAX: (813) 334 792 319.

SHIBATA ORGANIZATION
2-10-8 Ginza, Chuo-ku, Tokyo. Tel: (813) 3545 3411. FAX: (813) 3545 3519.

SHOCHIKU COMPANY
13-5, Tsukiji, 1-Chome, Chuo-ku 104, Tokyo. Tel: (813) 3542 5551. FAX: (813) 3545 0703.

SONY PICTURES ENTERTAINMENT, JAPAN
Hamamatsucho-TS Bldg. 5F, 8-14, Chome, Hamamatsucho Minato-ku, Tokyo 105. Tel: (813) 5476 8361. FAX: (813) 5473 8369.

TELECOM JAPAN INTERNATIONAL INC.
80 St. Marks Place, New York, NY 10003. Tel: (212) 254 2845. FAX: (212) 254 7845.

TKK ASSOCIATES INC.
Tokyo Bldg., 2-17-3 Takanawa, Minato-ku, Tokyo 108. Tel: (813) 3447 5241. FAX: (813) 3441 7826.

TOEI COMPANY
2-17, 3-Chome, GinzaJapan, Chuo-ku 104, Tokyo. Tel: (813) 535 7621. FAX: (813) 535 7622.
CHARIMAN & CEO
Shigeru Okada
PRESIDENT & COO
Tan Takaiwa

TOHO INTERNATIONAL (A DIVISION OF TOHO CO., LTD.)
1-8-1, Yurakucho, Chiyoda-ku, Tokyo 100-0006. Tel: (813) 3213 6821. FAX: (813) 3213 6825.

TOHO SEISAKU CO. LTD.
7-7-4 Akasaka, Minato-ku, Tokyo 107. Tel: (813) 3505 7350. FAX: (813) 3505 7357.

TOHO TOWA COMPANY
6-4, Ginza 2-Chome, Chuo-ku, Tokyo 104. Tel: (813) 3562 0109. FAX: (813) 3535 3656.

TV MAN UNION
30-13 Motoyoyogi-Cho, Shibuya-ku, Tokyo. Tel: (813) 5478 1611. FAX: (813) 5478 8141.

TWENTIETH CENTURY FOX (FAR EAST)
Fukide Bldg. 4-1-13 Toranomon, Minato-ku, Tokyo. Tel: (813) 3436 3421. FAX: (813) 3433 5322.

WARNER BROS. THEATRICAL DISTRIBUTION JAPAN
1-2-4 Hamamatsu-Cho, Minato-ku 105, Tokyo. Tel: (813) 5472 8000. FAX: (813) 5472 8029.

WORLD TELEVISION CORPORATION
6F 8-10 Ban Bldg., 8-10-8 Ginza, Chuo-ku, Tokyo 104. Tel: (813) 3571 8047. FAX: (813) 3572 2307.

EXHIBITORS

SHOCHIKU COMPANY
13-5, Tsukiji, 1-Chome, Chuo-ku 104, Tokyo. Tel: (813) 3542 5551. FAX: (813) 3545 0703.

TOEI COMPANY
2-17, 3-Chome, GinzaJapan, Chuo-ku 104, Tokyo. Tel: (813) 535 4641.

TOHO INTERNATIONAL (A DIVISION OF TOHO CO., LTD)
1-8-1, Yurakucho, Chiyoda-ku, Tokyo 100-0006. Tel: (813) 3213 6821. FAX: (813) 3213 6825.

TOHO TOWA COMPANY
6-4, Ginza 2-Chome, Chuo-ku, Tokyo 104. Tel: (813) 3562 0109. FAX: (813) 3535 3656.

UCI JAPAN KK
4F Izumi Akasaka Building, 2-22-24 Akasak, Minato-ku, Tokyo 107. Tel: (813) 3224 3200. FAX: (813) 3224 3212.
DIRECTOR
Adam Gover

Number of Screens: 27

WARNER MYCAL CORP.
2nd Flr., Izumikan Sanban-cho, Bldg. 3-8, Sanban-cho, Chiyoda-ku, Tokyo 102-0075. Tel: (81) 33 26 20 096. FAX: (81) 35 21 02 552.
CONTACT
Yoji Ikushima

Number of Theatres: 31
Number of Screens: 232

Akashi (7), Chigasaki (60, Ebetsu (8), Ebina (7), Fukushima (7), Higahikishiwada (8), Hirosaki (6), Hiroshima (7), Hofu (7), Ichikawamyoden (9), Ishinomaki (7), Itabashi (12), Kamimine (7), Kanazawa (8), Kenoh (7), Kitakami (7), Kuwana (8), Minatomirai (8), Ohi (7), Ohnojo (8), Okyouzuka (8), Otaru (7), Shinyurigaoka (9), Suzuka (7), Takamatsu (7), Takaoka (6), Tobata (8), Toyokawa (7), Utazu (7), Yonezawa (7), Yukarigaoka (8).

LUXEMBOURG

Population: 437 thousand.

EXHIBITORS

KINEPOLIS GROUP
89 Boulevard du Centenaire, B 1020, Brussels. Tel: (322) 474 2600. FAX: (322) 474 2606.www.kinepolis.com

UTOPIA S.A.
45 avenue J.F. Kennedy, L-1855 Luxembourg. Tel: (352) 42 95 111. FAX: (352) 42 95 1191.
CHAIRMAN & MANAGER
Nico Simon
MANAGER
Luc Nothum
FINANCES
Didier Briere

Number of Theatres: 7
Number of Screens: 48

Luxembourg (3), Belgium (3), France (1).

MALAYSIA

Population: 21.8 million.

STATE ASSOCIATIONS

MALAYSIAN MINISTRY OF INFORMATION
Angkasapuri, 50610 Kuala Lumpur. Tel: (603) 282 5333. FAX: (603) 282 1255.

MINISTRY OF INTERNATIONAL TRADE & INDUSTRY
Block 10, Government Offices Complex, Jalan Duta 50622, Kuala Lumpur. Tel: (603) 254 0033. FAX: (603) 255 0827.

EXHIBITORS & DISTRIBUTORS
(Local addresses and telephone numbers are listed where available, otherwise please contact the corporate headquarters below.)

CATHAY ORGANISATION (M) SDN BHD
1 Jalan SS22/19 Damansara Jaya, 47400 Petaling Jaya, Selangor, Malaysia 47400. Tel: (603) 71 95 666. FAX: (603) 71 92 179. (A branch of Plantations Berhad, 17th Flr., Wisma Jerneh, 38 Jalan Sultan Ismail, 50250 Kuala Lumpur, Malaysia.)
CHAIRMAN
Jen (R) Tan Sri Dato Mohd Ghazali Seth
CHIEF EXECUTIVE
Ong Te Cheong
EXECUTIVE DIRECTOR
Chuah Teong Tor

Number of Theatres: 34
Number of Screens: 47

GOLDEN COMMUNICATIONS
8 Hammer Hill Rd., Kowloon, Hong Kong. Tel: (852) 726 5541. FAX: (852) 351 1683.

TANJONG GOLDEN VILLAGE
Level 1, Bukit Raja Shopping Centre, Persiaran Bukit Raja 2, Bandar Baru Klang, 41150 Klang, Malaysia. Tel: (603) 344-1688.
Number of Screens: 47

TANJONG PLC
17th Flr., Menara Boustead, Jln Raja Chulan, 50200 Kuala Lumpur. Tel: (603) 244 3388. FAX: (603) 244 3388.

TWENTIETH CENTURY FOX FILM
Sendirian Berhad, 22 Jalan Padang Walter Grenier off Jalan Imbi, 55100 Kuala Lumpur. Tel: (603) 242 4396. FAX: (603) 248 3129.

UNITED INTERNATIONAL PICTURES
No. 22 Jalan SS26/6, Taman Mayang Jaya, 47301 Petaling Jaya, Selangor, Malaysia. Tel: (603) 704 4899. FAX: (603) 703 7833.
MANAGER
Nicholas Yong.

VILLAGE ROADSHOW, LTD.
(For complete listing see Australian branch.)
206 Bourke St., Melbourne, VIC, 3000, Australia. Tel: (613) 96 67 66 66. FAX: (613) 96 39 15 40.
Number of Theatres: 40 (Malaysia)
Number of Screens: 145 (Malaysia)

WARNER BROS.
24 Jalan Padang Walter Grenier off Jalan Imbi, 55100 Kuala Lumpur. Tel: (603) 242 3669. FAX: (603) 248 9670.

MEXICO

Population: 100.4 million.
Average Ticket Price: $0.30–$3.95.

DISTRIBUTORS

COLUMBIA TRISTAR FILMS DE MEXICO
Av. Ejercito Nacional, 343-3er Piso, Col. Granada, Delegacion Miguel Hidalgo, Mexico D.F. 11520. Tel: (525) 531 1428. FAX: (525) 545 1986.

UNITED INTERNATIONAL PICTURES
Apartado Postal No. 70 bis, Mexico D.F. 06000. Tel: (525) 255 5727. FAX: (525) 255 5657.

EXHIBITORS

CINEMASTAR LUXURY THEATRES, INC.
12230 El Camino Real, Ste. 320, San Diego, Calif., U.S. 92130. Tel: (619) 509-2777. FAX: (619) 509-9425.
CHAIRMAN & CEO
Jack Crosby
PRESIDENT & COO
Frank Moreno
CFO
Norman Dowling
EXECUTIVE V.P.
Neal Austrian Jr.
Number of Screens: 10

CINEMARK USA, INC.
Lateral Del Rio Churubusco, Esq. Canal De Miramontes, Col. Country Club, Mexico D.F. 0422 011.
7502 Greenville Ave., Ste. 800, Dallas, TX 75231. (214) 860-0823. FAX: (214) 696-3946. International: FAX: (214) 860-0792.
CHAIRMAN & CEO
Lee Roy Mitchell
PRESIDENT
Alan Stock
PRESIDENT, CINEMARK INTERNATIONAL
Tim Warner
DIRECTOR, MEXICO
Enrique Benhumea
Number of Theatres: 14
Number of Screens: 151
Breakdown of screens: Acapulco: Oceanic 2000 (8); Aguascalientes: Expo Plaza (10); Chihuahua: Plaza Hollywood (12); Guadalajara: Plaza Sol (12); Hermosillo: Metro Centro (10); Irapuato: Movies (10); Juarez: Cinemark (10); Mexico City: Centro Cultural (12), Pedregal Plaza Cinemark (10), Rojo Gomez, Villacoapa (15); Monterey: Plaza Le Fe (10); Quertaro: Cinemark (12); Reynosa: Cinemark (10); Tijuana: Minarete (10).

CINEMEX/CADENA MEXICANA DE EXHIBICION S.A. DE C.V.
CINEMEX
Blvd. Manuel Avila Camacho No. 40 Piso 16, Col. Lomas de Chapultepec, Mexico 11000 DF. Tel: (525) 201-5800. FAX: (525) 201-5813.
CO-DIRECTOR GENERAL
Matthew Heyman
CO-DIRECTOR GENERAL
Adolfo Fastlicht
CO-DIRECTOR GENERAL
Miguel Angel Davila

COMPANIA OPERADORA DE TEATROS S.A. DE C.V. COTSA
Insurgentes Sur 453, Col. Condesa, Mexico D.F.C.P. 06140. Tel: (525) 264-6010.
GENERAL DIRECTOR
Pablo Hernandez
Number of Theatres: 13
Number of Screens: 64
Mexico City (9), Colima (1), Cordova, Veracruz (1), Jalapa, Vercruz (1), Orizaba, Veracruz (1).

COTSA
Insurgentes Sur #453, 2nd Piso, Mexico DF. Tel: (525) 264-6010.
Number of Screens: 64

ORGANIZACION RAMIREZ S.A. DE C.V. MULTICINEMAS & CINEPOLIS
Avenida Enrique Ramirez Miguel #701, Fraccionamiento Las Americas, Morelia, Michoacan 58270. (524) 3220 526 229, (524) 3220 505. FAX: (524) 3220 511.
PRESIDENT
Enrique Ramirez Villalon
Number of Screens: 670

NETHERLANDS

Population: 15.9 million.

ASSOCIATIONS & ORGANIZATIONS

AMSTERDAMSE ARTS COUNCIL
Kloveniersburgwal 47, Amsterdam 1011 JX. Tel: (3120) 626 4315. FAX: (3120) 626 7584.

AMSTERDAM FUND FOR THE ARTS
Keizerstraat 223, Amsterdam 1016 DV. Tel: (3120) 624 2443. FAX: (3120) 624 6053.

ASSOCIATION FOR FILM & TELEVISION PROGRAMME MAKERS (NBF)
Jan Luykenstraat 2, Amsterdam 1071 CM. Tel: (3120) 664 6588. FAX: (3120) 664 3707.

ASSOCIATION OF DUTCH FILM THEATRES
2e der Helstraat 38, 1072 PE Amsterdam. Tel: (3120) 671 67 76. FAX: (3120) 673 08 04.

AUDIOVISUAL PLATFORM/MEDIA DESK NETHERLANDS
Postbus 256, Sumatralaan 45, Hilversum 1200 AG. Tel: (3135) 623 8641. FAX: (3135) 621 8541.

CARTOON
E Hoogt 4, Utrecht 3512 GW. Tel: (3130) 233 1733. FAX: (3130) 233 1079.

CIRCLE OF DUTCH FILM CRITICS (KNF)
Snelliuslaasn 78, Hilversum 1222 TG. Tel: (3135) 685 6115.

COMMISSARIAAT VOOR DE MEDIA
Emmastraat 51-53, P.O. Box 1426, Hilversum 1200 BK. Tel: (3135) 672 1721. FAX: (3135) 672 1722.

DUTCH ARTS COUNCIL
RJ Schimmelpennincklaan 3, The Hague 2517 JN. Tel: (3170) 346 9619. FAX: (3170) 361 4727.

DUTCH CULTURAL BROADCASTING PROMOTION FUND
Korte Leidsedwarsstraat 12, Amsterdam 1017 RC. Tel: (3120) 623 3901. FAX: (3120) 625 7456.

DUTCH FILM & TELEVISION ACADEMY
Ite Boeremastratt 1, Amsterdam 1054. Tel: (3120) 683 0206. FAX: (3120) 612 6266.

DUTCH FILM MUSEUM
Vondelpark 3, Amsterdam 1071 AA. Tel: (3120) 589 1400. FAX: (3120) 683 3401.

DUTCH FOUNDATION FOR AUDIOVISUAL CONGRESSES (SAM)
Honongstraat 14B, P.O. Box 262, Hilversum 1200 AG. Tel: (3135) 624 5589. FAX: (3135) 623 8208.

FILM INFORMATION & DOCUMENTATION SERVICE (FID)
Postbus 805, Utrecht 3500 AV. Tel: (3130) 332 328. FAX: (3130) 334 018.

FILM MAKERS SOCIETY OF THE NETHERLANDS (GNS)
P.O. Box 581, Amsterdam 1000. Tel: (3120) 676 5088. FAX: (3120) 676 5837.

HOLLAND FILM PROMOTION
Jan Luykenstraat 2, Amsterdam 1071 CM. Tel: (3120) 664 4649. FAX: (3120) 664 9171.

NEDERLANDS FEDERATION FOR CINEMTOGRAPHY
Jan Luykenstraat 2, P.O. Box 75048, Amsterdam 1070 AA. Tel: (3120) 619 9261. FAX: (3120) 675 0398.

NEDERLANDS INSTITUTE FOR AUDIOVISUAL MEDIA
Neuyskade 94, P.O. Box 97734, The Hague 2509 GC. Tel: (3170) 356 4107. FAX: (3170) 364 7756

THE PRODUCERS WORKSHOP (RBS)
Aalbrechtskade 129, Rotterdam 3023 JE. Tel: (3110) 425 7477. FAX: (3110) 425 7193.

SOURCES
Jan Luykenstraat 92, Amsterdam 1071 CT. Tel: (3120) 672 0801. FAX: (3120) 672 0399.

STICHTING FUURLAND/FILMKRANT
Prinsengracht 770-IV, Amsterdam. Tel: (3120) 623 0121. FAX: (3120) 627 5923.

UNITED AUDIOVISUAL PRODUCTION COMPANIES (UAP)
c/o H. Wennink, Mozartlaan 27, Hilversum 1217 CM. Tel: (3135) 623 8677. FAX: (3135) 623 8674.

VEVAM
P.O. Box 581, Amsterdam 1000 AN. Tel: (3120) 676 5088. FAX: (3120) 676 5837.

DISTRIBUTORS AND PRODUCERS

ARGUS FILM
P.O. Box 18269, Amsterdam 1001 ZD. Tel: (3120) 625 4585. FAX: (3120) 626 8978. email: argusfilm@xs4all.nl

BIOSCOOP EXPLOITATIE MINERVA BV
P.O. Box 7220, Amsterdam 1007 JE. Tel: (3120) 644 6823. FAX: (3120) 644 8946.

BUENA VISTA INTERNATIONAL (NETHERLANDS)
P.O. Box 349, Badhoevedorp 1170 AH. (3120) 658 0300. FAX: (3120) 659 3349.

CINEMA INTERNATIONAL
P.O. Box 9228, Amsterdam 1006 AE. Tel: (3120) 617 7575. FAX: (3120) 617 7434.

CINEMIEN FILM AND VIDEO DISTRIBUTORS
Entrepotdok 66, Amsterdam 1018 AD. Tel: (3120) 625 8857. FAX: (3120) 620 9857.

CNR FILM RELEASING
Amstellandlaan 78, Weesp 1382 CH. Tel: (3129) 446 1800.

COLUMBIA TRISTAR FILMS
Van Eeghenst 70, Amsterdam 1071 GK. Tel: (3120) 673 6611. FAX: (3120) 573 7656.

CONCORDE FILM BENELUX
Lange Voorhout 35, Den Haag 2514 EC. Tel: (3170) 3605810. FAX: (3170) 360 4925.

THE FILM COMPANY AMSTERDAM
Entrepotdok 66, Amsterdam 1018 AD. Tel: (3120) 620 9504. FAX: (3120) 620 9857.

HUNGRY EYE PICTURES
Duivendrechtsekade 82, Amsterdam 1096. Tel: (3120) 668 6126. FAX: (3120) 668 3452.

INTERNATIONAL ART FILM
Vodelpark 3, Amsterdam 1071 AA. Tel: (3120) 589 1418. FAX: (3120) 683 3401.

KINEPOLIS GROUP
89 Boulevard dy Centenaire, B 1020 Brussels. (322) 474 2600. FAX: (322) 474 2606. www.kinepolis.com
DIRECTOR OPERATIONS, NETHERLANDS
Boudewijn Muts

LAVA FILM DISTRIBUTION & SALES
Korte Leidsedwarstraat 12, Amsterdam 1017 RC. Tel: (3120) 625 5442. FAX: (3120) 620 2426.

MELIOR FILMS
Steynlaan 8, Hilversum 1217 JS. Tel: (3135) 624 5542. FAX: (3135) 623 5906.

METEOR/POLYGRAM FILM
P.O. Box 432, Hilversum 1217 JS. Tel: (3135) 626 1500. FAX: (3135) 624 8418.

MOONLIGHT FILMS
Geerdinkhof 236, Amsterdam 1103 PZ. Tel: (3120) 695 3811. FAX: (3120) 588 4343.

THE MOVIES ARTHOUSES & FILM DISTRIBUTION
Haarlemmerdjik 161, Amsterdam 1013 KH. Tel: (3120) 624 5790. FAX: (3120) 620 6758.

NETHERLANDS INSTITUTE FOR ANIMATION FILM
P.O. Box 9358, Tillburg 5000 HJ. Tel: (3113) 535 4555. FAX: (3113) 535 0953.

NFM/IAF
Vondelpark 3, Amsterdam 1071 AM. Tel: (3120) 589 1418. FAX: (3120) 683 3401.

NIS FILM DISTRIBUTION HOLLAND
Abba Paulownastraat 76, The Hague 2518 BJ. Tel: (3170) 356 4208. FAX: (3170) 356 4681.

POLYGRAM FILMED ENTERTAINMENT
P.O. Box 432, Hilversum 1200 AK. Tel: (3135) 626 1700. FAX: (3135) 624 8418.

SHOOTING STAR FILM COMPANY
Prinsengracht 546, Amsterdam 1017 KK. Tel: (3120) 624 7272. FAX: (3120) 626 8533.

STICHTING STEMRA
Prof. E. M. Meijerslaan 3, 1183 AV Amstelveen. Tel: (3120) 5407911. FAX: (3120) 5407496.

THREE LINES PICTURES
Laapersveld 68, Hilversum 1213 VB. Tel: (3135) 623 0555. FAX: (3135) 623 9966.

TWENTIETH CENTURY FOX
Mozartlaan 27, Hilversum 1217 CM. Tel: (3135) 622 2111. FAX: (3135) 623 9966.

TWIN FILM
Sarphatistraat 183, Amsterdam 1018 GG. Tel: (3120) 6228206. FAX: (3120) 6248729.

UNITED DUTCH FILM COMPANY
Jan Luykenstraat 5-7, Amsterdam 1071 CJ. Tel: (3120) 675 7774. FAX: (3120) 675 7754.

UNITED INTERNATIONAL PICTURES
Willemsparkweg 112, Amsterdam 1071 HN. Tel: (3120) 662 2991. FAX: (3120) 662 3240. Manager: Max van Praag.

WARNER BROS.
De Boelelaan 16 3H, Amsterdam 1083 HJ. Tel: (3120) 541 1211. FAX: (3120) 644 9001.

EXHIBITORS

ACTUEEL BIOSCOOPEXPLOITATIE B.V.
Potterstraat 30 - 4611 NJ Bergen, op Zoom, Netherlands. Tel: (31) 16 42 54 886.
Number of Screens: 5

A.E.M.M. KOOPAL-WASKOWSKY
P.O. Box 1194 - 4801 BD Breda.
Number of Screens: 5

ASSOCIATION OF DUTCH FILM THEATRES
2E Der Helstraat 38, Amsterdam 1072 PE. Tel: (3120) 671 6776. FAX: (3120) 673 0804.

A.TH. ABELN
P.O. Box 82 -7890 AB, Klazienaveen. Tel: (31) 59 13 12798. FAX: (31) 59 13 18426.
Number of Screens: 5

BIOSCOOPEXPLOITATIE J.M. PUNT HEERHUGOWAARD B.V.
P.O. Box 2071 - 7500 CB ,Heerhugowaard. Tel: (31) 72 57 43 344. FAX: (31) 72 57 42 437.
Number of Screens: 7

BIOSCOOPEXPLOITATIEMAATSCHAP-PIJ CINEX B.V.
P.O. Box 2071 - 7500 CB, Enschede. Tel: (31) 53 43 23 552. FAX: (31) 53 43 23 562.
Number of Screens: 5

BIOSCOOPONDERNEMING AF WOLFF B.V.
Postbus 777, 3500 AT Utrecht. Tel: (31) 30 233-1312
Number of Screens: 27

B.V. BIOSCOOP EXPLOITATIE MINERVA
Kromme Mijdrechtstraat 110 - 1079 LD, Amsterdam. Tel: (31) 20 64 46 823. FAX: (31) 20 64 48 946. email: info@minervagroup.nl
Number of Screens: 43
Arnhem, Alkmaar, Breda, Eindhoven, Deventer,Venlo, Zwolle, Zaandam, Tilburg, Haarlem, Maastricht.

B.V. 'DE NIEUWE BUITENSOCIETEIT'
Stationsplein 1 - 8011 CW Zwolle. Tel: (31) 38 42 60 260. FAX: (31) 38 43 60.
Number of Screens: 7

B.V. UTRECHTSE FILMONDERNEMING UFIO
Postbus 777 - 3500 AT Utrecht. Tel: (31) 30 23 1312. FAX: (31) 30 23 15 2276.
Number of Screens: 12

DE HEER R. VAN STEEN
Binnenwatersloot 1 - 2611 BJ Delft. Tel: (31) 15 21 43 426. FAX: (31) 1521 44 922.
Number of Screens: 5

JOGCHEM'S THEATERS BV
Veenestraat 31, 3751 GE Bunschoten, P.O. Box 127, 3750 GC Bunschoten. Tel: (31) 33 29 84 884. FAX: (31) 33 29 84 908.
MANAGING DIRECTOR & OWNER
J. Van Dommelen
MANAGING DIRECTOR & OWNER
W. Van Dommelen
Number of Screens: 46
Alphen a/d Rijn, Amerefoort, Apeldoorn, Arnhem, Dordrecht, Eindhove, Hilversum, Hertogenbosch, Nijmegen.

THE MOVIES ARTHOUSES & FILM DISTRIBUTION
Haarlemmerdjik 161, Amsterdam 1013 KH. Tel: (3120) 624 5790.
FAX: (3120) 620 6758.

NEW GALAXY CINEMAS
P.O. Box 128, Walter Nisbeth Rd., 37, Philipsburg, St. Maarten,
Dutch Antilles. Tel: (599) 525 871. FAX: (599) 523 425.
CONTACTS
G. Pelgrum
M. Hodge
T. Heyliger

PATHE CINEMAS
P.O. Box 75948, 1070 AX, Amsterdam. Tel: (31) 20 57 51 751. FAX:
(31) 20 57 51 777.
MANAGING DIRECTOR
Lauge Nielsen

Number of Theatres: 12
Number of Screens: 66
Amsterdam (4), Eindhoven (1), Groningen (1), Rotterdam (2), The
Hague (3), Utrecht (1).

POLYFILM ALMERE B.V.
P.O. Box 5 - Lelystad 8200 AA. Tel: (31) 320.24 6506. FAX: (31) 320
28 0488.

Number of Screens: 17

UNITED DUTCH FILM COMPANY
Jan Luykenstraat 5-7, Amsterdam 1071 CJ. Tel: (3120) 675 7774.
FAX: (3120) 675 7754.

WARNER–MORGAN CREEK–CHARGEURS CINEMAS
De Boelelaan 16, Amsterdam 1083. Tel: (4620) 541 1211. FAX:
(4620) 644 9001.

WOLFF CINEMA GROEP
P.O. Box 777 - 3500 AT Utrecht. Tel: (31) 23 32312. FAX: (31) 30 23
15227. email: woff@bioswolff.nl

Number of Screens: 37.
Haarlem, Enschede, Huizen, Tilburg, Groningen, Utrecht,
Nieuwegein.

NEW ZEALAND

Population: 3.8 million.
Screens: 265.

ASSOCIATIONS AND ORGANIZATIONS

MANU AUTE
P.O. Box 38-141, Petone, Wellington. Tel: (644) 385 9387. FAX: (644)
384 2580.

NEW ZEALAND FEDERATION OF FILM SOCIETIES INC.
P.O. Box 9544, Te Aro, Wellington. Tel: (644) 385 0162. FAX: (644)
801 7304.

NEW ZEALAND FILM ARCHIVE
Corner Cable St. and Jervois Quay, P.O. Box 9544, Wellington. Tel:
(644) 384 7647. FAX: (644) 384 9719.

NEW ZEALAND FILM COMMISSION
Flr. 2, Film Centre, Corner Cable St. and Jervois Quay, Wellington.
Tel: (644) 385 9754. FAX: (644) 384 9719.

QE II ARTS COUNCIL OF NZ
Old Public Trust Bldg., P.O. Box 3806, Wellington. Tel: (644) 473
0880. FAX: (644) 471 2865.

DISTRIBUTORS AND PRODUCERS

ENDEAVOUR ENTERTAINMENT
P.O. Box 68-445, Auckland. Tel: (649) 378 1900. FAX: (649) 378
1905.

EVERARD FILMS
P.O. Box 3664, Auckland 1. Tel: (649) 302 1193. FAX: (649) 302
1192.

FIRST TRAINING
P.O. Box 17096, Auckland. Tel: (649) 579 1332. FAX: (649) 579 5113.

FOOTPRINT FILMS
P.O. Box 1852, Auckland. Tel: (649) 309 8388. FAX: Tel: (649) 373
4722.

UNITED INTERNATIONAL PICTURES
P.O. Box 105263, Auckland. Tel: (649) 379 6269. FAX: (649) 379
6271.

WARNER BROS (NZ)
P.O. Box 8687, Mt. Eden, Auckland. Tel: (649) 377 5223. FAX: (649)
309 2795.

EXHIBITORS

EVERARD FILMS
P.O. Box 3664, Auckland 1. Tel: (649) 302 1193. FAX: (649) 302
1192.

HOYTS CINEMAS
(For additional listings, please see Australia, Chile & Belgium)
44, 47 Wakefield St., Auckland. Tel: (649) 303 2736. FAX: (649) 307
0011.
GENERAL MANAGER
Wilfred Steiner

Number of Theatres: 15
Number of Screens: 106

VILLAGE FORCE CINEMAS
82 Symonds St., Auckland. Tel: (649) 309-9137. FAX: (649) 307
2522. email: joe_moodabe@village.co.nz
CEO
Joe Moodabe
COO
Joanne Watt
CFO & TREASURER
Jane Carr
MARKETING
Victoria Hoffman
EQUIPMENT BUYER
Roger Cox

Number of Theatres: 15
Number of Screens: 89

VILLAGE ROADSHOW, LTD.
(For complete listing see Australian branch.)
206 Bourke St., Melbourne, VIC, 3000, Australia. Tel: (613) 96 67
66 66. FAX: (613) 96 39 15 40.

Number of Theatres: 40 (New Zealand)
Number of Screens: 139 (New Zealand)

WELLINGTON FILM SOCIETY
P.O. Box 1584, Wellington. Tel: (644) 384 6817. FAX: (644) 384 6248.

NORWAY

Population: 4.5 million.
Screens: 630.
Average Ticket Price: $5.62.

ASSOCIATIONS & ORGANIZATIONS

NORSK FILMFORBUND
Storengvn 8 B, Jar N-1342. Tel: (47) 2259 1000. FAX: (47) 2212
4865.

NORSK FILMINSTITUTT
Grev Wedelsplass 1, P.O. Box 482 Sentrum, Oslo N-0105. Tel: (47)
2242 8740. FAX: (47) 2233 2277.

NORSK FILMKLUBBFORBUND
Teatergata 3, Oslo N-0180. Tel: (47) 2211 4217.

NORSK FILMKRITIKERLAG
Norwegian Society of Film Critics, Radhusgata 7, N-0151 Oslo 1. Tel:
(47) 2241 9409. FAX: (47) 2242 0356.

DISTRIBUTORS AND PRODUCERS

ACTION FILM
Valerenggata 47, P.O. Box 9343, Valerenga, Oslo N-0610. Tel: (47)
2267 3131. FAX: (47) 2267 3005.

ARTHAUS
Teatergaten 3, Oslo N-0180. Tel: (47) 2211 2612. FAX: (47) 2220
7981.

BV-FILM INTERNATIONAL
N-4262, Avaldnsnes. Tel: (47) 5284 3544. FAX: (47) 5284 3575.

EGMONT FILM
P.O. Box 417, Asker N-1370. Tel: (47) 6690 4121. FAX: (47) 6690
4175.

EUROPAFILM
Stortingsgt 30, Oslo N-0161. Tel: (47) 2283 4290. FAX: (47) 2283
4151, Mobile: 9202 1017.

FIDALGO
P.O. Box 2054 Posebyen, Kristiansand N-4602. Tel: (47) 3802 4004.
FAX: (47) 3802 2354.

HOLLYWOOD FILM
Baneviksgt 7, Stavanger N-4014. Tel: (47) 5153 4045. FAX: (47)
5152 7398.

KIKU VISUAL PRODUCTIONS
Gange Rolvsgt 1, Oslo N-0273. Tel: (47) 2244 9650. FAX: (47) 2244
5098, Mobile: 9424 5294.

KOMMUNENES FILM-CENTRAL
Nedre Voligt 9, Oslo N-0158. Tel: (47) 2241 4325. FAX: (47) 2242
1469

NORSK FILM DISTRIBUTION
Stortingsgt 12, Oslo N-0161. Tel: (47) 2242 3600. FAX: (47) 2242
2313.

ROYAL FILM
Hedmarksgt 15, Oslo N-0658. Tel: (47) 2268 5140. FAX: (47) 2219
7393.

SF NORGE
P.O. Box 6868 St Olavs Plass, Grensen 3, Oslo N-0130. Tel: (47) 2233 4750. FAX: (47) 2242 7293.

UNITED INTERNATIONAL PICTURES
Hegdehaugsvn 27, P.O. Box 7134, Homansbyen, Oslo N-0307. Tel: (47) 2256 6115. FAX: (47) 2256 7181.

WARNER BROS (NORWAY)
Oscarsgt 55, P.O. Box 7053, Homansbyen, Oslo N-0258. Tel: (47) 2243 1800. FAX: (47) 2255 4683.

EXHIBITOR ASSOCIATION

NATIONAL ASSOCIATION OF MUNICIPAL CINEMAS
Kongensgt. 23 0153, Oslo 1. Tel: (47) 2233 0530. FAX: (47) 2242 8949.

EXHIBITORS

FREDERIKSTAD KINEMATOGRAFER
Boks 383, 1601 Frederikstad. FAX: (47) 6931 0615.
Number of Theatres: 3

HAUGESUND KINEMATOGRAFER
Boks 488, 5501 Haugesund. FAX: (47) 5271 3986.
Number of Theatres: 5

KRISTIANSAND KINO
Boks 356, 4601 Kristiansand. FAX: (47) 3802 0390.
Number of Theatres: 6

OSLO KINEMATOGRAPHER
P.O. Box 1584, Stortingsgt 16, 0161, Oslo N-0118. Tel: (47) 2242 7154. FAX: (47) 2282 4368.
Number of Screens: 29

SANDNES KINEMATOGRAFER
Boks 14, 4301 Sandnes. FAX: (47) 5566 8872.
Number of Theatres: 3

SANDREW METRONOME FILM AB
P.O. Box 1178, N-0107, Oslo, Norway.

STRAVANGER KINEMATOGRAPHER
Boks 194, 4001 Stravanger. FAX: (47) 5150 7016.
Number of Theatres: 8

TROMSO KINO
Boks 285, 9001 Tromso. FAX: (47) 7768 3570.
Number of Theatres: 2

TRONDHEIM KINO
Prinsensgt. 2B, Trondheim N-7013. Tel: (47) 7254 7369. FAX: (47) 7352 2550.
Number of Theatres: 13

PAKISTAN

Population: 141.5 million.
Average Ticket Price: varies widely between Rs .10—Rs. 50.

ASSOCIATION & ORGANIZATIONS

THE CENTRAL BOARD OF FILM CENSORS
Street No. 55-F, Blue Area, Islamabad. Tel: (9251) 920-4387. FAX: (9251) 920-4338.

THE NATIONAL FILM DEVELOPMENT CORPORATION LTD.
NAFDEC Complex, Blue Area, Islamabad. Tel: (9251) 821 154. FAX: (9251) 221 863.

PAKISTAN FILM DISTRIBUTORS' ASSOCIATION
Geeta Bhawan, Lakshmi Chowk, Lahore. Tel: (9242) 58785.

PAKISTAN FILM EXHIBITORS' ASSOCIATION
National Auto Plaza, C Block, 3rd Flr., Marston Road, Karachi. Tel.: (9221) 772-7764.

PAKISTAN FILM PRODUCERS' ASSOCIATION
Regal Cinema Building, The Mall, Lahore. Tel.: (9242) 322 904.

PAKISTAN MOTION PICTURE INVESTORS' ASSOC.
National Auto Plaza, 3rd Flr., C-Block, Marston Road, Karachi. Tel: (9221) 772 7764.

IMPORTERS

AJRAK ENTERTAINMENT
357 Hotel Metropole, Karachi. Tel: (9221) 567-0313, 567-1046. FAX: (9221) 568 4377.

AL HAVIZ CORPORATION
Al Hafiz Mansion, 11 Royal Park, Lahore. (9242) 636-3484.

CARRY-ON FILMS
Moon Bldg., 4 Royal Park, Lahore. Tel: (9242) 722 2543.

CLASSIC PICTURES
Ismail Building, 5 Royal Park, Lahore. Tel: (9242) 637-3018.

CONTINENTAL TRADERS
Ex-Rally Bros. Bldg., Talpur Rd., Karachi. Tel: (9221) 241 3254. FAX: (9221) 243 7451.

EVERLAST PICTURES
Haroon Mansion, Royal Park, Lahore. (9242) 636-3148.

GOLDEN BIRD PICTURES
1, Abbot Road, Lahore. (9242) 722-2138.

GOLDEN EAGLE PICTURES
Shaikh Building, Royal Park, Lahore. (9242) 722-2279.

HEENA FILMS
Dar Chambers, Royal Park, Lahore. (9242) 631-1964.

JAVED PICTURES
Gaba Building, Royal Park, Lahore. (9242) 722-3051.

MANDVIWALA ENTERTAINMENT
Nishat Cinema Bldg., M.A. Jinnah Rd., Karachi. Tel: (9221) 721 9505, 722-3535/6. FAX: (9221) 722 7259.

PAKISTAN INTERNATIONAL CORPORATION
Lyric Cinema Bldg., Garden Rd., Karachi. Tel: (9221) 772 7273.

PARAMOUNT COMMUNICATIONS
Marston Road, Karachi. Tel: (9221) 777 8165. FAX: (9221) 568 0981.

PULSE GLOBAL COMMUNICATION
Plot 12, Block 7 & 8, Tipu Sultan Rd., Karachi. Tel: (9221) 453 5001.

STERLING INTERNATIONAL
Paradise Building, Near Passport Office, Saddar, Karachi. (9221) 566-1412, 526 280.

TEE JEES ENTERPRISES
367 Hotel Metropole, Karachi. Tel: (9221) 522 540.

ZEE RAY ENTERPRISES
209 Hotel Metropole, Karachi. Tel: (9221) 414 089. FAX: (9221) 568 0671.

EXHIBITORS

AFSHAN CINEMA
Marston Rd., Karachi. Tel: (9221) 772 4344.

ALFALAH CINEMA
The Mall, Lahore. Tel: (9242) 630 1551.

ANMOL CINEMA
Lahore. Tel: (242) 511-0615.

BAMBINO CINEMA
Garden Rd., Karachi Tel: (9221) 772 9656.

CAPRI CINEMA
M.A. Jinnah Rd., Karachi. Tel: (9221) 721 9904.

GULISTAN CINEMA
Abbot Rd., Lahore. Tel: (9242) 631 3110.

LYRIC CINEMA
Garden Rd., Karachi. Tel: (9221) 772 7274.

MUBARAK CINEMA
Lahore. Tel: (9242) 630-2308.

NAFDEC CINEMA
Blue Area, Islamabad.

NAGINA CINEMA
Lahore. Tel: (9242) 722-6220.

NISHAT CINEMA
M.A. Jinnah Rd., Karachi. Tel: (9221) 721 9505.

ODEON CINEMA
The Mall, Lahore.

PLAZA CINEMA
Queens Rd., Lahore. Tel: (9242) 630 3122.

RATTAN CINEMA
McLeod Rd., Lahore. Tel: (9242) 724-3383.

REGAL CINEMA
The Mall, Lahore. Tel: (9242) 724 9477.

SANGEET CINEMA
Shadra, Lahore. Tel: (9242) 274-4290/

SHABISTAN CINEMA
Lahore. (9242) 636-0731.

SHABISTAN CINEMA
Muree Road, Rawalpindi. Tel: 70 625.

STAR CINEMA
Garden Rd., Karachi. Tel: (9221) 772 8787.

PANAMA

Population: 2.8 million.

EXHIBITORS

SAVOY LANE FILMS, INC.
Via Espana, Edificio Domino, 1er Piso, Oficina 26, P.O. Box 6-4911, Zona 6, Panama. Tel: (507) 262-6585. FAX: (507) 264-1805.
DIRECTOR
Enrique Martin
GENERAL MANAGER
Lucio Marcon
MANAGER (PANAMA)
Victor Chizmar

PHILIPPINES

Population: 81.2 million.

DISTRIBUTORS & PRODUCERS

COLUMBIA PICTURES INDUSTRIES, INC.
Rooms 306-308, Philippine President Lines Bldg., 1000 United Nations Ave., Ermita, Metro Manila 1000. Tel: (632) 521 1381. FAX: (632) 521 3684. Manager: Victor R. Cabrera

MEVER FILMS, INC.
9th Flr., Ave. Theatre Bldg., Rizal Ave., Manila.

UNITED INTERNATIONAL PICTURES
Room 310, Philippine Presidential Lines Bldg., 1000 United Nations Ave., Ermita Metro Manila 1000. Tel: (632) 509304. FAX: (632) 521 6133.
MANAGER
Tristan Leveriza

WARNER BROS.
Room 311, Philippine Presidential Lines Bldg., 1000 United Nations Ave., Ermita Metro Manila 1000. Tel: (632) 596 991. FAX: (632) 521 2673.
MANAGER
Lucas Pasiliao.

EXHIBITORS

MEDEIA FILMES
Rua Tomas Ribeiro 8-20, 1150 Lisboa, Portugal. Tel: (351) 1317-2029.

Number of Screens: 37

WARNER LUSOMUNDO
Rua Luciano Cordeiro 113, 1150 Lisboa, Portugal. Tel: (351) 1315-0860.

Number of Screens: 80

WEST AVENUE THEATER CORPORATION
The SM City, North Ave. cor. EDSA, Quezon City. Tel: (632) 975 452. FAX: (632) 924 4274.
EXECUTIVE V.P.
Engr. Hans T. Sy
OPERATIONS MANAGER
Ricardo B. David

Number of Screens: 56

POLAND

Population: 38.6 million.

ASSOCIATIONS & ORGANIZATIONS

ASSOCIATION OF POLISH FILM PRODUCERS AND PRODUCTION MANAGERS
Pulawska 61, Warsaw 02595. Tel: (4822) 245 5586.

ASSOCIATION OF POLISH FILMMAKERS
Krakowskie Przedmiescie, Warsaw 00071. Tel: (4822) 227 6785. FAX: Tel: (4822) 263 51927.

COMMITTEE OF CINEMATOGRAPHY
Tel: (4822) 263 449. FAX: (4822) 276 233.
PRESIDENT
Tadeusz Sciborylski

FEDERATION OF FILM TRADE GUILDS
Pulawska 61, Warsaw 02595. Tel: (4822) 628 4855. FAX: (4822) 245 5586.

FEDERATION OF NON-PROFESSIONAL FILM CLUBS
Pulawska 61, Warsaw 02595. Tel: (4822) 245 5382.

FILM ART FOUNDATION
Krakowskie Przedmiescie 21/23, Warsaw 00071. Tel: (4822) 226 1409. FAX: (4822) 635 2001.

POLISH FEDERATION OF FILM SOCIETIES
Plocka 16/34, Warsaw 01138. Tel: (4822) 232 1187.

POLISH FILM AND TV DIRECTOR'S GUILD
Pulawska 67, Warsaw 02595. Tel: (4822) 245 5316. FAX: (4822) 245 5316.

POLISH SCREENWRITERS GUILD
Al. Jerozolimskie 49m 41, Warsaw 00697. Tel: (4822) 262 81158.

PRIVATE FILM PRODUCERS CLUB
Walbrzyska 14/11, Warsaw 02738. Tel: (4822) 243 2861.

SOCIETY OF AUTHORS-ZAIKS
Hipoteczna 21, P.O. Box P-16, Warsaw 00092. Tel: (4822) 227 7950. FAX: (4822) 635 1347.

DISTRIBUTORS AND PRODUCERS

ANWA FILM INTERNATIONAL
Str. Smolensk 27/3, Krakow 31-12. Tel: (4812) 215 634.

BEST FILM
Ul. Twarda 16a, Warsaw 00105. Tel: (4822) 220 1201. FAX: (4822) 220 1201.

BLACK CAT
Magnoliowa 2, Lublin. Tel: (4881) 774 654. FAX: (4881) 774 654.

EUROKADR
Potocka Str. 14, Warsaw 01639.Tel: (4822) 233 2491. FAX: (4822) 233 2491.

FILM ART FOUNDATION
Krakowskie Przedmiescie 21/23, Warsaw 00071. Tel: (4822) 261 409. FAX: (4822) 635 2001.

FILM DISTRIBUTION AGENCY
Trebacka 3, Warsaw 00074. Tel: (4822) 635 2038. FAX: (4822) 635 1543.

FILM STUDIO HELIOS
Przybyszewskiego 167, Lodz 93120. Tel: (4842) 812 196. FAX: (4842) 812 481.

GRAFFITI
Ul, SW. Gertrudy 5, Krakow 31306. Tel: (4812) 214 294. FAX: (4812) 211 402.

IMP
Ul. Hoza 66, Warsaw 00950. Tel: (4822) 6287081. FAX: (4822) 628 7691.

ITI CINEMA POLAND
Marszalkowska 138, Warsaw 00004. Tel: (4822) 640 4447. FAX: (4822) 642 5001.
Wernyhory 14, Warsaw 02727. Tel: (4822) 243 3488. FAX: (4822) 243 4532.

KRAKATAU
Ul, Kaminskiego 29/12, Lodz. Tel: (4842) 788 536.

NEPTUN FILM
Piwna 22, Gdansk 80831. Tel: (4858) 314 876. FAX: (4858) 313 744.

NEPTUN VIDEO CENTRE
Grzybowska Str. 6-10, Warsaw 00131. Tel: (4822) 224 0395. FAX: (4822) 224 5969.

ODRA FILM
Ul. Boguslawskiego 14, Wroclaw 50023. Tel: (4871) 33487. FAX: (4871) 441 088.

SILESIA-FILM
Head Office: Plebiscytowa 46, Katowice 40041. Tel: (483) 251 2284. FAX: (483) 251 2245.

STARCUT FILM-POLAND
6 Wybickiego St, Rumia 84230. Tel: (4858) 219 769.

SYRENA ENTERTAINMENT GROUP
Marsz al kowska 115, Warsaw 00102. Tel: (4822) 827 3500. FAX: (4822) 827 5204.
PRESIDENT
Jerzy Jednorowski
MANAGING DIRECTOR
Levis Minford

VISION
Rydygiera 7, Warsaw 01793. Tel: (4822) 239 0753. FAX: (4822) 239 2575.

WARNER BROS. POLAND
Ul. Palawska 37/39, Warsaw 02508. Tel: (4822) 249 5959. FAX: (4822) 249 3598.

EXHIBITORS

APOLLO-FILM STATE FILM DISTRIBUTOR
Pychowicka 7, Krakow 30960. Tel: (4812) 671 355. FAX: (4812) 671 552.

FILM STUDIO HELIOS
Przybyszewskiego 167, Lodz 93120. Tel (4842) 812 196. FAX: (4842) 812 481.

THE GREATER UNION ORGANISATION

(Including Birch, Carroll & Coyle)
49 Market St., Sydney, NSW 2000, Australia. Tel: (612) 93 73 66 00.
FAX: (612) 93 73 65 32.
MANAGING DIRECTOR
Robert Manson

Number of Theatres: 1 (Poland)
Number of Screens: 4 (Poland)

IFDF MAX
Jagiellonska Str 26, Warsaw 03719. Tel: (4822) 219 0481. FAX:
(4822) 218 1783.

ITI CINEMA POLAND
Marszalkowska 138, Warsaw 00004. Tel: (4822) 640 4447. FAX:
(4822) 642 5001.

MULTIKINO
(A joint venture of ITI and United Cinemas International), Tel: (4822)
640 4416. FAX: (4822) 640 4413.
MANAGING DIRECTOR
Aldona Szostakowska

NEPTUN FILM
Piwna 22, Gdansk 80831. Tel: (4858) 313 744. FAX: (4858) 313 744.

SILVER SCREEN/PORTICO DEVELOPMENT
Tel: (4822) 630 7076. FAX: (4822) 630 7077.
MANAGING DIRECTOR
Frank Stork

UCI JOINT VENTURE CO., POLAND
Multiurino Spa, Powsinska 4, Warsaw 02910. Tel: (4822) 2640 4416.
FAX: (4822) 2640 4413.
DIRECTOR
Aldona Szostakowsk

PORTUGAL

Population: 10 million.

ASSOCIATIONS & ORGANIZATIONS

CINEMA, TELEVISION & VIDEO TRADE UNION
Rua D Pedro V 60, 1 Esq., Lisbon 1200. Tel: (3511) 342 2660. FAX:
(3511) 342 6943.

CINEMATICA PORTUGUESA
Rua Barata Salgueiro 39, Lisbon 1200. Tel: (3511) 354 6279. FAX:
(3511) 352 3180.

PORTUGUESE FILM INSTITUTE
Rua Sao Pedro de Alcantara 45, 1st Flr., Lisbon 1250. Tel: (3511)
345 6634. FAX: (3511) 347 2777.

SECRETARY OF STATE FOR CULTURE
Palacio Nacional da Ajuda, Lisbon 1300. Tel: (3511) 364 9867. FAX:
(3511) 364 9872.

DISTRIBUTORS AND PRODUCERS

COLUMBIA TRISTAR & WARNER FILMES DE PORTUGAL
Av Duque De Loule 90 3 Esq., Lisbon 1000. Tel: (3511) 572 007.
FAX: (3511) 315 5389.

FILMES CASTELLO LOPES
Rua de St. Amaro Estrelo 17-A, 5955. Tel: (3511) 395 5955. FAX:
(3511) 395 5924.

FILMES LUSOMUNDO S.A.
Praca de Aleguia 22, Apartado 1063, Lisbon 1294. Tel: (3511) 347
4561. FAX: (3511) 346 5349.

MEDIA
Avenida Joao Crisostomo, 38 C-1, Escr. 3, Lisbon 1050. Tel: (3511)
353 1616. FAX: (3511) 353 1636.

UNITED INTERNATIONAL PICTURES
(See Filmes Lusomundo.)

VITORIA FILME
Avenida Duquer de Loul, 75, 3 Dt, Lisbon 1000. Tel: (3511) 546 195.
FAX: (3511) 546 195.

EXHIBITORS

AMERICAN MULTI-CINEMA
106 West 14th St., Ste. 1700, Kansas City, Missouri, U.S. 64105.
(816) 221 4000.
CHAIRMAN & CEO
Stanley H. Durwood
PRESIDENT & COO
Philip M. Singleton

Number of Theaters: 1 (Porto: Arrabida 20)
Number of Screens: 20

ATALANTA FILMES
Avenida D. Carlos I, 72 D-3, Lisbon 1200. Tel: (3511) 397 0680.
FAX: (3511) 397 4723.

FILMES CASTELO LOPES
Rua de St Amaro Estrelo 17-A, 5955. FAX: (3511) 395 5924.

LUSOMUNDO
Praca da Alegria 22, Lisbon 1294. Tel: (3511) 347 4561. FAX: (3511)
346 5349.

PAULO MARTINS
Avenida Duque de Loul, 75, 3 Dt, Lisbon 1000. Tel: (3511) 546 195.
FAX: (3511) 546 195.

WARNER LUSOMUNDO CINEMAS
(Time Warner Co. and Lusomundo Audiovisuals S.A.)
Rua Luciano Cordeiro 113, 10 Lisbon 1150. Tel: (3511) 315 0860.
FAX: (3511) 355 7784.
400 Warner Blvd., Bridge Bldg. South, 5th Flr., Burbank, Calif., U.S.
91522. Tel: (818) 954 6014. FAX: (818) 954 6655.
PRESIDENT
Millard Ochs
VICE PRESIDENT
Luis da Silva
MANAGING DIRECTOR
Miguel Tecedeiro

Number of Theaters: 4
Number of Screens: 30
Breakdown of screens: Cascais (7); Colombo (10); Gaia (9); Olivais
(4).

RUSSIAN FEDERATION

Population: 146 million.

ASSOCIATIONS & ORGANIZATIONS

COMMITTEE OF CINEMATOGRAPHY OF THE RUSSIAN FEDERATION (ROSKOMKINO)
7 Mal Gnezdnikovsky Ln., Moscow 103877. Tel: (7095) 229 8224.
FAX: (7095) 229 4522.

CONFEDERATION OF FILMMAKERS UNIONS
Maly Kozikhinsky Per 11, Moscow 103001. Tel: (7095) 299 7020.
FAX: (7095) 299 3880.

FEDERATION OF CINEMA CLUBS
Konstantin Simonov St. 5, Cor 3, Apt. 41, Moscow 125167. Tel:
(7095) 255 9105. FAX: (7095) 393 4896.

FILMMAKERS UNION OF REPUBLIC OF BELARUS
5 Karl Marx St., Minsk, Belarus 220050. Tel: (70172) 271 002. FAX:
(70172) 271 451.

KAZAKHINO
Abylai Khana St. 93/95, Alma-Ata 480091, Kazakhstan. Tel: (7327)
269 2418.

STATE FILM CONCERN GRUZIA-FILM
Akhmedeli St. 10a, Tbilisi 308059, Georgia. Tel: (99532) 510 627.
FAX: (99532) 510 010.

STATE FILM CONCERN MOLDOVA FILM
Enunesku St. 10, Kishinev 277012, Moldova. Tel: (3732) 234 405.
FAX: (3732) 234 405.

ST. PETERSBURG CULTURE FUND
Nevsky Prosp. 31, St. Petersburg 191011. Tel: (7812) 311 8349. FAX:
(7812) 315 1701.

DISTRIBUTORS AND PRODUCERS

ARGUS
Olypissicis Prospect 16, Moscow 129090. Tel: (7095) 288 4027. FAX:
(7095) 288 9147.

ATLANT CO
Kirovogradskaya St. 9A, Moscow 113587. Tel: (7095) 312 5203. FAX:
(7095) 312 8127.

EAST WEST CREATIVE ASSOCIATES
Bldg. 4, Stankevich St., Moscow 113587. Tel: (7095) 229 7100. FAX:
(7095) 200 4249.

EKATERINBURG ART
Chebyshev St., 5th Flr., Ekaterinburg 620062. Tel: (73432) 442 1120.
FAX: (73432) 442 343.

GEMINI FILM
Bldg. 6, Myansnitskaya St. 40, Moscow 101000. Tel: (7095) 921
0854. FAX: (7095) 921 2394.

GORKY FILM STUDIOS
8 Einstein St., Moscow 129226. Tel: (7095) 181 0183. FAX: (7095)
188 9871.

KINOTON
Okruzhnoy Proyezd 16, Moscow 105058. Tel: (7095) 290 3412. FAX:
(7095) 200 5612.

KREDO-ASPEK
Novy Arbat St. 11, Moscow 121019. Tel: (7095) 291 7269. FAX:
(7095) 219 6880.

MOST MEDIA
Maly Gnezdnikovsky 7, Moscow 103877. Tel: (7095) 229 1172. FAX:
(7095) 229 1274.

PARADISE LTD. AGENCY
12a Christoprudny Blvd., Ste. 601, Moscow 101000. FAX: (7095) 924
1331.

RUSSKOYE VIDEO
Malaya Nevka 4, St. Petersburg 191035. Tel: (7812) 234 4207.

SKIP CENTRE
2 Flievskaya St. 7/19, Moscow 121096. Tel: (7095) 145 2459. FAX: (7095) 145 3355.

SOVENTURE
Bolshiye Kamenshchiki 17, Lorpus 1, Moscow 109172. Tel: (7095) 912 3065. FAX: (7095) 911 0665.

SOVEXPORTFILM
14 Kalashny Pereulok St., Moscow 103009. Tel: (7095) 290 2053. FAX: (7095) 200 1256.

TRETYAKOVKA
8 Maly Tolmachevsky per, Moscow 109017. Tel: (7095) 231 0183. FAX: (7095) 231 4857.

SINGAPORE

Population: 4.2 million.

ORGANIZATIONS

MINISTRY OF INFORMATION & THE ARTS
#36-00 PSA Bldg., 460 Alexandra Rd., Singapore. Tel: (65) 279 9707. FAX: (65) 279 9784.

SINGAPORE FILM SOCIETY
Robinson Rd., P.O. Box 3714, Singapore. Tel: (65) 235 2088.

DISTRIBUTORS AND PRODUCERS

ALLSTAR FILM
Block 136, Alexandra Rd., 01-161, Singapore 0315. Tel: (65) 472 7554. FAX: (65) 474 2676.

CATHAY ASIA FILMS
11 Dhoby Ghant #05-00, Cathay Building, Singapore 0922. Tel: (65) 337 6855. FAX: (65) 339 5609.

CINEMA VISION
2 Leng Kee Rd., Singapore 0315. Tel: (65) 472 2233. FAX: (65) 475 3346.

ENG WAH FILM
400 Orchard Rd., 16-06 Orchard Towers, Singapore 0923. Tel: (65) 734 0028.

FAIRMOUNT INTERNATIONAL
200 Jalan Sultan, 08-02 Textile Centre, Singapore 0719. Tel: (65) 296 5904. FAX: (65) 293 4742.

GLOBE FILM DISTRIBUTORS
Block 1, Rochor Rd., Singapore 0718. Tel: (65) 296 6324. FAX: (65) 296 6742.

GOLDEN VILLAGE MULTIPLEX PTE., LTD
2 Handy Rd., #15-04, Singapore 229233. Tel: (65) 334 3766. FAX: (65) 334 8397. email: webmaster@golden-village.com.sg. www.goldenvillage.com.sg
EXECUTIVE DIRECTOR & GENERAL MANAGER
Gerald Dibbayawan

KIM FONG FILM
05-03, Block 8, Lorong Bakur Batu, Singapore 1334. Tel: (65) 7480265. FAX: (65) 7470939.

OVERSEAS MOVIE
#04-21 People's Park Complex, Singapore 0106. Tel: (65) 535 0555. FAX: (65) 535 0783.

SHAW ORGANISATION
Shaw Centre, 1 Scotts Rd., Singapore 0922. Tel: (65) 235 2077. FAX: (65) 235 2860.

TWENTIETH CENTURY FOX FILM (EAST)
400 Orchard Rd., 17-064 Orchard Towers, Singapore 0923. Tel: (65) 723 0952. FAX: (65) 235 4957.

UNITED INTERNATIONAL PICTURES
15-04 Shaw Centre, 1 Scotts Rd., Singapore 0922. Tel: (65) 737 2484. FAX: (65) 235 3667.

WARNER BROS. SINGAPORE
04-02 Midlands House, 122 Middle Rd., Singapore 0718. Tel: (65) 337 5060. FAX: (65) 339 1709.

EXHIBITORS

CATHAY CINEPLEXES PTE, LTD.
11 Unity St., #02-01, Robertson Walk, Singapore 237995. FAX: (65) 732-1944.
CHAIRPERSON
Meileen Choo
Number of Screens: 20

CATHAY THEATRE MANAGEMENT PTE LTD.
2 Handy Rd., Cathay BLDG., #05-00, Singapore 229233. Tel: (65) 337 8181. FAX: (65) 338 2153.
MANAGING DIRECTOR
Choo Meileen
Number of Theatres: 6
Number of Screens: 24

GOLDEN HARVEST ENTERTAINMENT CO., LTD.
(For additional listings see Hong Kong, Thailand & Malaysia.)
8 King Tung St., Hammer Hill Rd., Kowloon. Tel: (852) 2352 8222. FAX: (852) 2351 1683.
EXECUTIVES
Raymond Chow
Leonard Ho
Anthony Chow
Peter Chung
S.Y. Ho
Number of Theatres: 11
Number of Screens: 50

GOLDEN VILLAGE ENTERTAINMENT
68 Orchard Rd., #07-10/14 Plaza Singapura, Singapore 238839. Tel: (65) 334-3766. FAX: (65) 334-8397.
GENERAL MANAGER
Gerald Dibbayawan
OPERATIONS DIRECTOR, ASIA
Marcus Khaw
MARKETING MANAGER
Connie Lai
Number of Theatres: 9
Number of Screens: 64

SHAW ORGANISATION GROUP OF COMPANIES
Shaw Centre, 13th & 14th Storeys, 1 Scotts Rd., Singapore 228208. Tel: (65) 235 2077. FAX: (65) 235 2860.
DIRECTOR, ADMINISTRATION
Vee-Meng Shaw
DIRECTOR, DISTRIBUTION
Harold Shaw
DIRECTOR, OPERATIONS
Vee King Shaw
GENERAL MANAGER
S.Y. Liok
GROUP FINANCIAL CONTROLLER
SAJ Jesuthasan
GROUP SECRETARY
B.S. Yap
MANAGER, CHINESES DISTRIBUTION
Tan Chua
MANAGERS, BOOKING
KS Mak
YT Kwan
MANAGER, CONCESSIONS
Brian Tam
Number of Screens: 41

STUDIO CITY CINEMA HOLDINGS, LTD.
5 Magazine Rd., #03-02, Singapore 059571.
CONTACT
Maureen Koh
Number of Screens: 13

VILLAGE ROADSHOW, LTD.
(For complete listing see Australian branch.)
206 Bourke St., Melbourne, VIC, 3000, Australia. Tel: (613) 96 67 66 66. FAX: (613) 96 39 15 40.
Number of Theatres: 9 (Singapore)
Number of Screens: 64 (Singapore)

SOUTH AFRICA

Population: 43.4 million.

ASSOCIATIONS & ORGANIZATIONS

AFRICAN FILM AND TELEVISION COLLECTIVE
P.O. Box 42723, Fordsbury 2033. Tel: (2711) 804 5186. FAX: (2711) 838 3034.

CINEMA THEATRE AND VIDEO UNION
P.O. Box 81338, Parkhurst 2120. Tel: (2711) 782 4273. FAX: (2711) 492 1221.

DEPARTMENT OF HOME AFFAIRS-FILM DEPARTMENT
Private Bag X114, Pretoria 0001. Tel: (2712) 314 3328.

FILM AND ALLIED WORKERS ORGANISATION
P.O. Box 16939, Doornfontein 2028. Tel: (2711) 402 4570. FAX: (2711) 402 0777.

PROFESSIONAL PHOTOGRAPHERS OF SOUTHERN AFRICA
P.O. Box 47044, Parklands, Johannesburg 2121. Tel: (2711) 880 9110. FAX: (2711) 880 1648.

SOUTH AFRICAN SOCIETY OF CINEMATOGRAPHERS
P.O. Box 17465, Sunward Park 1470. Tel: (2711) 902 2826.

SOUTH AFRICAN FILM AND TELEVISION INSTITUTE

P.O. Box 3512, Halfway House 1685. Tel: (2711) 315 0140. FAX: (2711) 315 0146.

DISTRIBUTORS AND PRODUCERS

ATLAS MOTION PICTURE CORPORATION
P.O. Box 87385, Houghton 2041. Tel: (2711) 728 4912. FAX: (2711) 728 5287.

CONCORD FILMS
P.O. Box 8112, Johannesburg 2000. Tel: (2711) 337 5581. FAX: (2711) 337 3913.

EMS
24 Napier Road, Richmond, Johannesburg. Tel: (2711) 482 4470. FAX: (2711) 482 2552.

ENTERTAINMENT WORKERS' UNION
P.O. Box 81338, Parkhurst 2120. Tel: (2711) 782 4273.

FILM FARE INTERNATIONAL
P.O. Box 24, Crawford 7770. Tel: (2721) 637 8028. FAX: (2721) 637 3138.

GENESIS RELEASING
Charter House, 3 Robertson St. Observatory Ext 2198, Johannesburg. Tel: (2711) 487 1060. FAX: (2711) 487 1040.

JAGUAR FILM DISTRIBUTORS
P.O. Box 53126, Yellowood Park 4011. Tel: (2731) 420 610.

MIMOSA FILM DISTRIBUTORS
P.O. Box 50019, Randburg 2125. Tel: (2711) 787 1075.

SAVAGE EYE FILMWORKS
6A Glade Rd., Rondebosch, Cape Town 7700. Tel: (2721) 686 3858. FAX: (2721) 244 313.

STER-KINEKOR (PTY.) LIMITED
Interleisure Park, 185 Katherine St., Eastgate, Sandton. Tel: (2711) 4457 7300. FAX: (2711) 444 1003.

UNITED INTERNATIONAL PICTURES
Castrol House, 7 Junction Ave., Parktown, Johannesburg 2193. Tel: (2711) 484 4215. FAX: (2711) 484 3339.

STUDIOS

FRAMEWORK TELEVISION
P.O. Box 5200, Horizon 1730. Tel: (2711) 475 4220. FAX: (2711) 475 5333.

SONNEBLOM FILM PRODUCTIONS
P.O. Box 3940, Honeydew 2040. Tel: (2711) 794 2100. FAX: (2711) 794 2061.

SONOVISION STUDIOS
P.O. Box 783133, Sandton 2146. Tel: (2711) 783 1100. FAX: (2711) 883 3834.

TORON INTERNATIONAL
P.O. Box 89271, Lyndhurst 2106. Tel: (2711) 786 2360. FAX: (2711) 440 5132.

SOUTH KOREA

Population: 45.5 million.

DISTRIBUTORS

COLUMBIA TRISTAR FILMS OF KOREA
Songpa Bldg., 505 Shinsa-Dong, Kangnam-Gu, Seoul. Tel: (9822) 545 0101. FAX: (822) 546 0020.

DAEWOO
(Agency for New Line International), 12th Flr., Daewoo Foundation Bldg., 526 5 Ga Namdaemoon Ro, Jung Gu 100-095, Seoul.

TWENTIETH CENTURY FOX KOREA
Asia Cement Bldg., 8th Flr., 726 Yeok Sam-dong, Kangnam-ku, Seoul. Tel: (822) 3452 5980. FAX: (822) 3452 7223.

UIP—CIC FILM & VIDEO DISTRIBUTION
Jang Choong Bldg., 2nd Flr., 120-1, 1Ka, Jang Choong-Dong, Jung-ku, Seoul. Tel: (822) 276 0077. FAX: (822) 273 8208. Manager: H.K. Lee.

WALT DISNEY KOREA
4th Flr., Samboo Bldg., 676 Yeok Sam-dong, Kangam-ku, Seoul. Tel: (822) 527 0400. FAX: (822) 527 0399.

WARNER BROS KOREA
M Bldg., 6th Flr., 221-5 Nonhyun-dong, Kangnam-ku, Seoul. Tel: (822) 547 0181. FAX: (822) 547 8396.

EXHIBITOR

VILLAGE ROADSHOW, LTD.
206 Bourke St., Melbourne, VIC, 3000, Australia. Tel: (613) 96 67 66 66. FAX: (613) 96 39 15 40.
(For complete listing see Australian branch.)
Number of Theatres: 2 (Korea)
Number of Screens: 25 (Korea)

SPAIN

Population: 40 million.

ASSOCIATIONS & ORGANIZATIONS

ASSEMBLY OF SPANISH DIRECTORS & PRODUCERS
San Lorenzo 11, Madrid 28004. Tel: (341) 319 6844.

ASSOCIATION OF NATIONAL FILM DISTRIBUTORS & PRO-DUCERS
Blanca de Navarra 7, Madrid 28010. Tel: (341) 308 0120. FAX: (341) 319 0036.

FEDERACION ESPANOLA DE PRODUCTORAS DE CINE PUBLICITARIO Y CORTOMETRAJE
Sanchez Pacheco 64 Entreplanta, Madrid 28002. Tel.: (341) 413 2454. FAX: 34 1 519 2019.

FEDERATION OF SPANISH FILM COMPANIES
Velazquez 10 3 deha., Madrid 28001. Tel: (341) 576 9913. FAX: (341) 576 2774.

FEDERATION OF THEATRICAL DISTRIBUTORS
Velazquez 10, 3 deha., Madrid 28001. Tel: (341) 576 0820. FAX: (341) 578 0028.

MINISTRY OF CULTURE
Plaza del Rey 1, Madrid 28071. Tel: (341) 532 0093. FAX: (341) 522 9377.

PROCINE FOUNDATION
Ayala 20-5 B, Madrid 28001. Tel.: (341) 576 6066. FAX: (341) 578 1915.

DISTRIBUTORS AND PRODUCERS

ALAS FILMS
Maestro Guerrero 4, Madrid 28015. Tel.: (341) 547 6664. FAX: (341) 542 7887.

JOSE ESTEBAN ALENDA
Trujillos 7, Madrid 28013. Tel: (341) 541 1838. FAX: (341) 548 3791.

ALTA FILMS
Martin de los Heros 12, Madrid 28008. Tel: (341) 542 2702. FAX: (341) 542 8777.

ARABA FILMS
Dr. Arce 1b, Madrid 28002. Tel: (341) 564 9498. FAX: (341) 564 5738.

BARTON FILMS S.I.
Iturribide 68, Lonja, Bolbao. Tel: (344) 433 7103. FAX: (344) 433 5086.

BRB INTERNATIONAL
Autovia Fuencarral Alcobendas, Km. 12 220 Edificio Auge 1, Madrid 28049. Tel: (341) 358 9596. FAX: (341) 358 9818.

BREPI FILMS
Corredera Baja de San Pablo, 2-30, Madrid 28004. (341) 522 3108. FAX: (341) 522 5721.

BUENA VISTA INTERNATIONAL SPAIN
Jose Bardasano Baos 9-11, Edificio Gorbea 3, Madrid 28016. Tel: (341) 383 0732. FAX: (341) 766 9241.

CINE COMPANY
Zurbano 74, Madriid 28010. Tel: (341) 442 2944. FAX: (341) 441 0098.

CINEMUSSY
Quintana No. 1, 2 B, Madrid 28029. Tel: (341) 542 0036. FAX: (341) 559 9069.

COLUMBIA TRI-STAR FILMS DE ESPANA
c/o Hernandez de Tejada 3, Madrid 28027. Tel: (341) 377 7100. FAX: (341) 377 7128.
Edificio Piovera Azul, Peonias 2, Madrid 28042. Tel: (341) 320 0744. FAX: (341) 320 6105.

DISTRIBUIDORA COQUILLAT
Denia 43, Valencia 46006. Tel: (346) 341 7000. FAX: (346) 380 4270.

ESICMA
Maestro Lasalle 15, 28016 Madrid. Tel: (341) 345 8708. FAX: (341) 355 7991.

FILMAX GROUP
P. San Gervasio 16-20, Barcelona 08022. Tel: (343) 453 0303. FAX: (343) 453 0608.

FILMAYER INTERNATIONAL
Arda Brugos, 8-A Planta 10-1, Madrid 28036. Tel: (341) 383 0265. FAX: (341) 383 0845.

GOLEM DISTRIBUCION
Corezonde Maria 56-9A, Madrid 28002. Tel: (341) 519 1737. FAX: (341) 416 3626.

HISPANO FOXFILM S.A.E.
Avenida de Bourgos 8-A, Planta 18, Madrid 28036. Tel: (341) 343 4640. FAX: (341) 343 4646.

IBEROAMERICANA FILMS INTERNACIONAL
Velazquez 12, 7 & 8, Madrid 28001. Tel: (341) 4314246. FAX: (341) 435 5994.
CONTACT
Andres Vicente Gomez

IMPALA MONTILLA
Manuel Motilla 1, Madrid 28016. Tel: (341) 350 6200. FAX: (341) 345 1948.
CONTACT
Jose Antonio Sainz de Vicuna

KALEKIA
Comino del Obispo 25, Mostoles, Madrid 28935. Tel: (341) 616 3710. FAX: (341) 616 3710.

LAUREN FILM
Tetuan 29-2, Madrid 28013. Tel: (341) 521 8284. FAX: (341) 522 0616.

LECAS FILM DISTRIBUCION
Galileo 82, Madrid 28015. Tel: (341) 447 4657. FAX: (341) 448 8978.

LIDER FILMS
Isla de Fuenteventura No, 21-10, San Sebastian de los Reyes, Madrid 28700. Tel: (341) 663 9000. FAX: (341) 663 9320.

MOVIERECORD
Martires de Alcala 4, Madrid 28015. Tel: (341) 559 9205. FAX: (341) 547 5985.
CONTACT
Jesus Martin Sanz

MULTIVIDEO
La Luna 15, Madrid 28004. Tel: (341) 522 9347. FAX: (341) 532 8695.

MUSIDORA FILMS
Calle Princesa 17, Madrid 28008. Tel: (341) 541 6869. FAX: (341) 541 5482. Contact: Javier de Garcillan.

NEPTUNO FILMS
Cardaire 36-38, Terassa, Barcelona 08221. Tel: (341) 784 1622. FAX: (341) 784 2938.

POLYGRAM FILM ESPANA
Manuel Montilla 1, Madrid 28016. Tel: (341) 350 6200. FAX: (341) 350 1371.

PRIME FILMS
Padre Xitre 5-7C, Madrid 28002. Tel: (341) 519 0181. FAX: (341) 413 0772.

REX FILMS
Provenza 197-199. Barcelona 08008. Tel: (343) 451 3315. FAX: (343) 453 5391.

SOGEPAQ DISTRIBUCION
Manual Montilla 1, Madrid 28016. Tel: (341) 350 6200. FAX: (341) 345 1948.
PRESIDENT
Jose Vicuna

SUCESORES DES JESUS RODRIGUEZ DORESTA
Triana 68-1, Las Palmas de Gran Canaria 35002. Tel: (3428) 371 560. FAX: (3428) 371 560.

SUPER FILMS S.A.
Provenza 197/199, Barcelona 08008. Tel: (343) 451 3315. FAX: (343) 453 5391.

SURF FILMS
Zurbano 74, Madrid 28010. Tel: (341) 442 2944. FAX: (341) 0441 0098.

TRIPICTURES
Doce De Octubre 28, Madrid 28009. Tel: (341) 574 9008. FAX: (341) 574 9005.

U FILMS/UNION FILMS
Maestro Guerrero 4, Madrid 28015. Tel: (341) 547 6664. FAX: (341) 542 7887.

UNITED INTERNATIONAL PICTURES
Plaza del Callao 4-6, Madrid 28013. Tel: (341) 522 7261. FAX: (341) 532 2384.
MANAGER
Gaulberto Bana

VICTORY FILMS
Cuesta de Santo Domingo 11, Madrid 28013. Tel: (341) 541 8734. FAX: (341) 541 4612.

WANDA FILMS
Avenida de Europa 9, Pozuelo, Madrid 28224. Tel: (341) 352 8376. FAX: (341) 345 1948.

WARNER ESPANOLA
Manual Montilla 1, Madrid 28016. Tel: (341) 350 6200. FAX: (341) 345 1948.

EXHIBITORS

ALPHAVILLE
Martin de Los Heros 14, Madrid 28008. Tel: (341) 559 3836. FAX: (341) 541 5482.

ALTA FILMS S.A.
Cuesta de San Vicente 4, 28008, Madrid. Tel: (349) 1542-2702.
Number of Screens: 108

AREA CATALANA D'EXHIBICIO CINEMATOGRAFICA, S.A.
221 Mallorca St., 6th Flr., Barcelona 08008. Tel: (3493) 323 6426. FAX: (3493) 323 7223.
PRESIDENT
Jaime Tarrazon Badia
VICE PRESIDENT
Jaume Camprecios
MANAGER
Francisco Garcia Bascunana
Number of Theatres: 41
Number of Screens: 112
Badalona (2); Cerdanyola (1); Cornella (2); Granollers (4); Igualada (2); Hospitalet (2); Mataro (4); Manresa (2); Mollet (1); Reus (1); Sabadell (5); Tarragona (2); Terrassa (1).

BAUTISTA SOLER
Abada 14, Madrid 28013. Tel: (341) 531 6107. FAX: (341) 522 2202.

CASABLANCA CINEMA
Paseo de Gracia 115, Barcelona 08008. Tel: (343) 218 4345.

CINESA
Floridablanca 135, Barcelona 08011. Tel: (34) 93 228 96 00. FAX: (34) 93 424 38 05.
SENIOR V.P., SOUTHERN EUROPE & BRAZIL
Jose Batle
GENERAL MANAGER & V.P., OPERATIONS
Javier Fernandez
V.P., CONSTRUCTION, SOUTHERN EUROPE
Eduardo Fontcuberta
MARKETING DIRECTOR
Ricardo Gil
FINANCIAL DIRECTOR
Jose Lopez
LEGAL, SOUTHERN EUROPE
Agustoin Sanchez
MIS DIRECTOR
Juan Luis Bernabe
HEAD FILM BUYER, SOUTHERN EUROPE
Juan Antonio Gomez
Number of Theatres: 29
Number of Screens: 167

COLISEO ALBIA
Alameda de Urquijo 13, Bilbao 48008. Tel: (344) 423 2148. FAX: (344) 423 1001.

COMPANIA DE INICIATIVAS Y ESPECTACULOS
Floridablanca 135, 08011 Barcelona. Tel: (349) 3423-2455
Number of Screens: 149

DIFUSARA CULTURAL CINEMATOGRAFICA
Cines Golem, Avenida de Bayona 52, Pamplona 31008. Tel: (3448) 174 141. FAX: (3448) 171 058.

DIFUSORA BURGOS
Avenida Sanjurjo 36, Cines Can Golem, Burgos 09004. Tel: (3448) 174 141. FAX: (3448) 171 058.

DIFUSORA LOGRONO
Cines Golem, Parque de San Adrian s/n, Logrono 26006. Tel: (3448) 174 141. FAX: (3448) 171 058.

EMPRESA BALANA
Provenza 266, 5, Barcelona 08008. Tel: (343) 215 9570. FAX: (343) 215 6740.

FRANCISCO HERAS
Van Dyke Cinema, Van Dyke 59-61, Salamanca 37005. Tel: (3423) 243 538.

IZARO FILMS
Raimundo Fernandez Villaverde 65, Madrid 28003. Tel: (341) 555 8041. FAX: (341) 555 8292.

KINEPOLIS GROUP
89 Boulevard dy Centenaire, B 1020 Brussels. (322) 474 2600. FAX: (322) 474 2606. www.kinepolis.com

LAUREN FILMS VIDEO HAGAR
Balmes 87, Barcelona 08008. Tel: (343) 451 7189. FAX: (343) 323 6155.

PALAFOX CINEMA
Luchana 15, Madrid 28010. Tel: (341) 446 1887. FAX: (341) 447 3441.

PEDRO BALANA
Provenza 266, Barcelona 08008. Tel: (343) 215 9570. FAX: (343) 215 6740.

REAL CINEMA
Plaza de Isabel II 7, Madrid 28013. Tel: (341) 547 4577. FAX: (341) 547 4650.

TABEXSA CINE
Albatros Minicines, Plaza Fray Luis Colomer 4, Valencia 46021. Tel: (346) 369 4530. FAX: (346) 360 1469.

UNION CINE CIUDAD
Alameda de Hercules 9 y 10, Edifico Alameda Multicines, 41002
Sevilla, Spain. Tel: (349) 5437-5900.

Number of Screens: 204

WARNER LUSOMUNDO CINES DE ESPANA, S.A.
(Warner Bros. International Theaters in partnership with Lusomundo
SGPS, S.A.)
Miniparc, 1 c/Azalea, No.1, Edificip B, Primera planta, El Soto de la
Moraleja Alcobendas, 28109, Madrid.
EXECUTIVE DIRECTORS
Millard Ochs
Luis Silva
Ele Juarez
MANAGING DIRECTOR
Tomas Naranjo

YELMO CINEPLEX DE ESPANA
Princesa 31, 3rd Flr., 28008 Madrid, Spain. Tel: (349) 1758-9600.

Number of Screens: 190

YELMO FILMS
Jacometrezo 4 7 Piso, Madrid 28013. Tel: (341) 523 1560. FAX:
(341) 523 1658.

SWEDEN

Population: 8.8 million.

ASSOCIATIONS & ORGANIZATIONS

PRODUCERS CONTROL BUREAU
Box 1147, Solna S-171 23. Tel: (468) 735 9780. FAX: (468) 730
2560.

SVENSKA TEATERFORBUNDET
Hantverkargatan 4, Stockholm S-112 21. Tel: (468) 785 0330. FAX:
(468) 653 9507.

SWEDISH DISTRIBUTORS ASSOCIATION
P.O. Box 49084, Stockholm S-100 28. Tel: (468) 785 0400. FAX:
(468) 730 2560.

DISTRIBUTORS AND PRODUCERS

BUENA VISTA INTERNATIONAL
Box 5631, Stockholm S-114 86. Tel: (468) 679 1550. FAX: (468) 678
01728.
GENERAL MANAGER
Eric Broberg.

CAPITOL FILM DISTRIBUTION
Sodravagen 12, Kalmar S-392 33. Tel: (46480) 12215. FAX: (46480)
24085.

CINEMA SWEDEN
P.O. Box 20105, Bromma S-161 02. Tel: (468) 280 738. FAX: (268)
299 091.

COLUMBIA TRISTAR FILMS (SWEDEN)
Hornsbruksgatan 19, 1 Tr, P.O. Box 9501, Stockholm S-102 74. Tel:
(468) 658 1140. FAX: (468) 841 204.
GENERAL MANAGER
Peter Jansson.

EGMONT FILM
P.O. Box 507, Taby S-183 25. Tel: (468) 5101 0050. FAX: (468) 5101
2046.

FOLKETS BIO
P.O. Box 2068, Stockholm S-103 12. Tel: (468) 203059. FAX: (468)
204023.

FOX FILM
Box 9501, Stockholm S-102 74. Tel: (468) 658 1144. FAX: (468) 841 204.

NORDISK FILM TV DISTRIBUTION
P.O. Box 9011, Soder Malarstrand 27, Stockholm S-10271. Tel: (468)
440 9070. FAX: (468) 440 9080.

PLANBORG FILM
Granhallsvagen 23, Stocksund S-182 75. Tel: (468) 655 80 70. FAX:
(468) 655 03 40.

SANDREW FILM & TEATR
P.O. Box 5612, Stockholm S-114 86. Tel: (468) 234 700. FAX: (468)
103 850.

SONET FILM
Tappvagen 24, P.O. Box 20105, Bromma S-161 02. Tel: (468) 799
7700. FAX: (468) 285 834.

SVENSK FILMINDUSTRI
Dialoggatan 6, Stockholm S-12783. Tel: (468) 680 3500. FAX: (468)
710 4460.
email: stefan.klockby@sf.se
PRESIDENT
Jan Edholm

SVENSKA FILMINSTITUTET
Filmhuset, Borgvagen 1-5, P.O. Box 27126, Stockholm S-102 52. Tel:
(468) 665 1100. FAX: (468) 661 1820.

UNITED INTERNATIONAL PICTURES (SWEDEN)
P.O. Box 9502, Stockholm S-102 74. Tel: (468) 616 7400. FAX: (468)
843 870.

WARNER BROS. SWEDEN
Hornsbruksgatan 19, 4th Flr., Stockholm S-117 34. Tel: (468) 658
1050. FAX: (468) 658 6482.

EXHIBITORS

FILMOVID R REISS
Ralangsvegen 6, Enskede S-120 42. Tel: (468) 910 316. FAX: (468)
910 316.

FOLKETS BIO
P.O. Box 2068, Stockholm S-103 12. Tel: (468) 402 0820. FAX: (468)
402 0827.

SANDREW METRONOME FILM AB
P.O. Box 5612, Stockholm S-114 86. Tel: (468) 762 1700. FAX: (468)
103 850.
PRESIDENT & CEO
Klas Olofsson
HEAD OF EXIBITION
Bo Nilsson
HEAD OF ACQUISITION
Bertil Sandgren
Number of Theatres: 31
Number of Screens: 104

SF BIO AB
S-12783 Stockholm. Tel: (468) 680 3500. FAX: (468) 680 3748.
PRESIDENT & CEO
Jan Bernhardsson
SENIOR V.P., DEVELOPMENT
Johan Wrangel
SENIOR V.P., PROMGRAMMING
Sture Johansson
SENIOR V.P., CONCESSIONS
Steve Sodergren
MEDIA/MARKETING DIRECTOR
Per Rustner

Number of Theatres: 33
Number of Screens: 176

SVENSK FILMINDUSTRI
Dialoggatan 6, Stockholm S-12783. Tel: (468) 680 3500. FAX: (468)
710 4460.
PRESIDENT
Jan Edholm

STUDIOS

EUROPA STUDIOS
Tappvagen 24, P.O. Box 20105, Stockholm S-16102. Tel: (468) 764
7700.

FILM HOUSE STUDIOS
P.O. Box 27 066, Stockholm S-102 51. Tel: (468) 665 1200. FAX:
(468) 661 1053.

MEXFILM
P.O. Box 17607, Stockholm S-11892. Tel: (468) 642 0035. FAX: (468)
642 9850.

STUDIO 24
Sibyllegatan 24, Stockholm S-114 42. Tel: (468) 662 5700. FAX:
(468) 662 9240.

SWITZERLAND

Population: 7.3 million.
Average Ticket Price: $9.20.

ASSOCIATIONS AND ORGANIZATIONS

CINELIBRE
Swiss Associations of Film Societies and Non-Commercial
Screening Organisations, Postfach, CH-4005 Basel. Tel: (4161) 681
3844. FAX: (4161) 691 1040.

FEDERAL DEPARTMENT OF FOREIGN AFFAIRS
Sektion fur internationale kulturelle und UNESCO-Angelegenheiten,
Schwarztorstrasse 59, CH-3003 Bern. Tel: (4131) 325 9267. FAX:
(4131) 325 9358.

FEDERAL OFFICE OF CULTURE
Sektion Film, Hallwylstrasse 15, CH-3003 Bern. Tel: (4131) 322
9271. FAX: (4131) 322 9273.

SUISSIMAGE
Neuengasse 23, CH-3001 Bern. Tel: (4131) 312 1106. FAX: (4131)
311 2104.

SWISS CINEMATHEQUE
Case Postale 2512, CH-1002 Lausanne. Tel: (4121) 331 0101. FAX:
(4121) 320 4888.

SWISS FILM DISTRIBUTORS ASSOCIATION
Effingerstrasse 11. P.O. Box 8175. CH-3001 Bern. Tel: (4131) 381
5077. FAX: (4131) 382 0373.

SWISS FILM THEATRES ASSOCIATION

Effingerstrasse 11. P.O. Box 8175. CH-3001 Bern. Tel: (4131) 381 5077. FAX: (4131) 382 0373.

DISTRIBUTORS AND PRODUCERS

ALEXANDER FILM
Lagernstrasse 6, CH-8037 Zurich. Tel: (411) 362 8443. FAX: (411) 361 1603.

ALPHA FILMS S. A.
4 Place du Cirque, Case Postale 5311, CH-1211 Geneve 11. (4122) 328 0204. FAX: (4122) 781 0676.

BERNARD LANG AG
Dorf Strasse 14D, Freienstein, CH-8427 Zurich. Tel: (411) 865 6627. FAX: (411) 865 6629.

BUENA VISTA INTERNATIONAL (SWITZERLAND) LTD.
Am Schanzengraben 27, CH-8002 Zurich. Tel: (411) 201 6655. FAX: (411) 201 7770. .

COLUMBUS FILM AG
Steinstrasse 21, CH-8036 Zurich. Tel: (411) 462 7377. FAX: (411) 462 0112.

CONDOR FILMS
Restelbergstrasse 107, CH-8044 Zurich. Tel: (411) 361 9612.

FAMA-FILM AG
Balthasarstrasse 11, CH-3027 Bern. Tel: (4131) 992 9280. FAX: (4131) 992 6404.

FILMCOOPERATIVE ZURICH
Fabrikstrasse 21, Postfach 172, CH-8031 Zurich. Tel: (411) 271 8800. FAX: (411) 271 8038. Contact: Wolfgang Blosche.

KINEPOLIS GROUP
89 Boulevard du Centenaire, B 1020 Brussels. (322) 474 2600. FAX: (322) 474 2606. www.kinepolis.com

IMPERIAL FILMS S. A.
Ave. de la Gare 17, CH-1002 Lausanne. Tel.: (4121) 732 1830. FAX: (4121) 738 7882.

MASCOTTE-FILM AG
Dienerstrasse 16-18, CH-8026 Zurich. Tel: (411) 296 9070. FAX: (411) 296 9089.

MONOPOLE PATHE FILMS S. A.
Neugasse 6, CH-8005 Zurich. Tel: (4311) 271 1003. FAX: (411) 271 5643.

REGINA FILM S. A.
4 Rue de Rive, CH-1204 Geneve. Tel: (4122) 310 8136. FAX: (4122) 310 9476.

RIALTO FILM AG
Neugasse 6, CH-8021 Zurich. Tel: (411) 271 4200. FAX: (411) 2714203.

SPIEGEL FILM AG
Ebelstrasse 25, Postfach 179, CH-8030 Zurich. Tel: (411) 252 7406. FAX: (411) 251 1354.

STAMM-FILM AG
Lowenstrasse 20, CH-8023 Zurich. Tel: (411) 211 6615.

TWENTIETH CENTURY-FOX FILM CORPORATION
P.O. Box 1049, CH-1211 Geneva 26. Tel: (4122) 343 3315. FAX: (4122) 343 9255.
MANAGER
Peter Danner.

UNITED INTERNATIONAL PICTURES (SCHWEIZ)
Signaustrasse 6, CH-8032 Zurich. Tel: (411) 383 8550. FAX: (411) 383 6112.
MANAGER
Hans Ulrich Daetwyler.

WARNER BROS. (TRANSATLANTIC)
Studerweg 3, Postfach, CH-8802 Kilchberg. Tel: (411) 715 5911. FAX: (411) 715 3451.
SALES
Richard Broccon.

EXHIBITORS

CINEMAX
Tel: (411) 273 2222. FAX: (411) 273 3354.

CINEMAXX H.J. FLEBBE FILMTHEATERBETRIEBE
Mittelweg 176, 20148 Hanburg. Tel: (49) 40450 680. FAX: (49) 40 450 68201.
PRESIDENT & GENERAL MANAGER
Hans-Joachim Flebbe
GENERAL MANAGER & CFO
Michael Pawlowski
DIRECTOR, MARKETING
Jens Thomsen
Number of Theatres: 1 (Switzerland)
Number of Screens: 8 (Switzerland)

CINEMOBIL OPEN AIR CINEMA
Dorfstrasse 77, CH-8105 Regensdorf. Tel: (411) 840 5342.

CINETYP
Obergrundstrasse 101, CH-6005 Lucerne. Tel: (4141) 422 257. FAX: (4141) 422 746.

ERNO INTERNATIONAL
Niedergaslistrasse 12, CH-8157 Dielsdorf. Tel: (411) 855 5353. FAX: (411) 855 5350.

FILMCOOPERATIVE ZURICH
Fabrikstrasse 21, Postfach 172, CH-8031 Zurich. Tel: (411) 271 8800. FAX: (411) 271 8038.

KITAG KINO THEATER AG
Laupenstrasse 8, 3008 Bern. Tel: (413) 1390-110.
Number of Screens: 29

LIAG CAPITOL
Bergstrasse 42, CH-8032 Zurich. Tel: (411) 251 5228. FAX: (411) 251 4444.

METROCINE
Ch. de Rosenack 6, CH-1000 Lausanne 13. Tel: (4121) 614 3333. FAX: (4121) 614 3399.

QUINNIE CINEMA FILMS, LTD.
Seilestrasse 4, 3011 Bern (Schweiz), Switzerland. Tel: (413) 1381-1721. FAX: (413) 1398-1272.
OWNER
Roland Probst

V ESPOSITO
4 Rue de Reve, CH-1204 Geneva. Tel: (4122) 782 1417. FAX: (4122) 310 9476.

VILLAGE ROADSHOW, LTD.
(For complete listing see Australian branch.)
206 Bourke St., Melbourne, VIC, 3000, Australia. Tel: (613) 96 67 66 66. FAX: (613) 96 39 15 40.
Number of Theatres: 1 (Switzerland)
Number of Screens: 10 (Switzerland)

WALCH KINOBETRIEBS
Steinentorstrasse 8, CH-4051 Basel. Tel: (4161) 281 0908. FAX: (4161) 281 6564.

TAIWAN

Population: 22.2 million.

ORGANIZATION

MOTION PICTURE DEVELOPMENT FOUNDATION
2 Tien-Tsin St., Taipei. 866 2 3516625. FAX: (8862) 341 6252.

DISTRIBUTORS

BUENA VISTA FILM CO. LTD.
4th Flr., No. 1, Hsiang Yang Rd., Taipei. Tel: (8862) 383 6309. FAX: (8862) 382 5348.

COLUMBIA TRISTAR FILMS OF CHINA, LTD.
City Hero Plaza, 8F-A No. 59, Chung-hua Rd., Section 1, Taipei 100. Tel: (8862) 331 9456. FAX: (8862) 381 4492.

PARAMOUNT FILMS OF CHINA, INC.
(Also: MGM of China, Inc., United Artists of China, Inc, Universal Picture Corp of China, Inc.), 2nd Flr., 18 Kwei Yang St., Section 2, Taipei. Tel: (8862) 331 4929. FAX: (8862) 331 1967.

TWENTIETH CENTURY FOX
City Hero Plaza, 8F-A No. 59, Chung-hwa Rd., Section 1, Taipei 100. Tel: (8862) 315 3773. FAX: (8862) 381 4492.

WARNER BROS. VILLAGE CINEMAS
(Warner Bros. International Theatres in association with Village Roadshow International)
P.O. Box 167, Taipei 100. Tel: (8862) 389 0159. FAX: (8862) 311 8526.
4000 Warner Blvd., Bridge Bldg. South, 5th Flr., Burbank, Calif., U.S. 91522. Tel: (818) 954 6014. FAX: (818) 954 6655.
PRESIDENT
Millard Ochs

EXHIBITORS

STUDIO CITY CINEMA HOLDINGS, LTD.
No. 226-1 Cheng Kung, 1st Rd., B1 B2 Flrs., Kaohslung, Taiwan.
CONTACT
Ben Leung

VILLAGE ROADSHOW, LTD.
(For complete listing see Australian branch.)
206 Bourke St., Melbourne, VIC, 3000, Australia. Tel: (613) 96 67 66 66. FAX: (613) 96 39 15 40.
Number of Theatres: 1 (Taiwan)
Number of Screens: 17 (Taiwan)

WARNER VILLAGE CINEMAS
No. 18 Sung Shou Rd., B1 Flr., Taipai. Tel: (886) 287 80 1166.
Number of Screens: 17.

THAILAND

Population: 61.2 million.
Screens: approx. 250.

ASSOCIATIONS & ORGANIZATIONS

AMERICAN MOTION PICTURE ASSOCIATION
Rm. 602, Akane Bldg., 315 Silom Rd., Bangkok 10500. Tel: (662) 234 0240.

MOTION PICTURE EXHIBITORS ASSOC. OF THAILAND
352 Siam Theatre, Tama 1 Rd., Pathumwan, Bangkok 10500.

THAILAND FILM PROMOTION CENTRE
599 Bumrung Muang Rd., Bangkok 10100. Tel: (662) 223 4690. FAX: (662) 253 1817.

THAI MOTION PICTURES PRODUCERS ASSOCIATION
15/79 Soi Chokchairuammit, Viphavadee-Rangsit Rd., Bangkhen, Bangkok 10900. Tel: (662) 275 8833. FAX: (662) 281 8460.

DISTRIBUTORS AND PRODUCERS

APEX INTERNATIONAL CORP.
215 1 6 Rama 1 Rd., Siam Sq., Pathumwa, Bangkok 10500. Tel: (662) 251 8476. FAX: (662) 255 3131.

CINEAD GROUP
40 19 Sol Amonphannivas 4, Vipavadee Rangsit Road, Bangkok 10900. Tel: (662) 561 1965. FAX: (662) 561 1887.

CO BROTHERS ORGANISATION
117/2 Phayathai Rd., Rajthevi, Bangkok 10400. Tel: (662) 251 7163. FAX: (662) 254 7714.

FIVE STARS
31 345 Petchburi Rd., Phayathai, Bangkok 10400. Tel: (662) 215 0704.

GOLDEN TOWN FILM
69/55 Phayathai Atehn Theater Rd., Bangkok 10400. Tel: (662) 251 9168. FAX: (662) 259 3117.

HOLLYWOOD FILM DISTRIBUTION
420 Petchburi Rd., Phayathai, Bangkog 10400. Tel: (662) 251 5211.

MOVIELINK
40/19 Soi Amorn Pannives 4, Vipavadee-Rangsit Rd., Bangkok. Tel: (662) 561 1915.

NONTANUND ENTERTAINMENT
113/10 Suriwong Centre, Suriwong Rd., Bangkok 10500. Tel: (662) 236 7504. FAX: (662) 253 4830.

PYRAMID ENTERTAINMENT
216/1-6 Rama Rd., Siam Square, Bangkok 10500. Tel: (662) 252 7416.

SAHA MONGKOL FILM
1081/5 Phaholyothin Rd., Bangkok 10400. Tel: (662) 279 8456.

TWENTIETH CENTURY FOX/WARNER BROS.
Rm. 603, South East Insurance Bld., 315 Silom Road, Bangkok 10500. Tel: (662) 233 0920. FAX: (662) 236 4384.

UNITED INTERNATIONAL PICTURES (UIP)
Rm. 605, South East Insurance Bldg., 315 Silom Road, Bangkok 10500. Tel: (662) 233 4225. FAX: (662) 236 7597.

EXHIBITORS

ENTERTAIN GOLDEN VILLAGE
110 Moo 9 Petchkasem Rd., Bang Wa, Pasricharowen, Bangkok 10160. Tel: (662) 455-0150.

Number of Screens: 73

GOLDEN HARVEST ENTERTAINMENT CO., LTD.
(For additional listings, see Hong Kong, Singapore & Malaysia)
8 King Tung St., Hammer Hill Rd., Kowloon. Tel: (852) 2352 8222. FAX: (852) 2351 1683.
EXECUTIVES
Raymond Chow
Leonard Ho
Anthony Chow
Peter Chung
S.Y. Ho

Number of Theatres: 13
Number of Screens: 75

VILLAGE ROADSHOW, LTD.
(For complete listing see Australian branch.)
206 Bourke St., Melbourne, VIC, 3000, Australia. Tel: (613) 96 67 66 66. FAX: (613) 96 39 15 40.

Number of Theatres: 17 (Thailand)
Number of Screens: 93 (Thailand)

TURKEY

Population: 65.6 million.

ASSOCIATIONS & ORGANIZATIONS

ISTANBUL FOUNDATION FOR CULTURE & ARTS
Besiktas, Istanbul 80700. Tel: (90216) 259 1738. FAX: (90216) 261 8823.

SOCIETY OF IMPORTERS AND DISTRIBUTORS
Yesilcam Sok 7/1, Beyoglu, Istanbul. Tel: (90216) 249 0986.

SODER, THE SOCIETY OF ACTORS
Mete Cad Yani Prefabrik Binasi, Taksim, Istanbul. Tel: (90216) 252 6566.

DISTRIBUTORS AND PRODUCERS

BARLIK FILM
Ahududu Cad 32/3, Beyoglu, Istanbul 80060. Tel: (90216) 244 1542. FAX: (90216) 251 0386.

KILIC FILM
Yesilcam SK 26/2, Beyoglu, Istanbul 80070. Tel: (90216) 249 5804. FAX: (90216) 244 1612.

UNITED INTERNATIONAL PICTURES
Filmcilik ve Ticaret Ltd. Sti, Spor Cad. Acisu Sok. 1/7-8, Macka, Istanbul 80200. Tel: (90216) 227 8205. FAX: (90216) 227 8207.

WARNER BROS. A.S. TURKEY
Bronz Sokak, Bronz Apt. 3/6, Macka, Istanbul 80200. Tel: (90216) 231 2569. FAX: (90216) 231 7070.

EXHIBITORS

AFM CINEMA GROUP
416 Akmerkez Etiler, Istanbul, 80600. Tel: (90) 212 282 0508. FAX: (90) 212 282 0507. www.afm.com.tr
PRESIDENT
Sedat Akdemir
VICE PRESIDENT
Adnan Akdemir
CHAIRMAN
Yalcin Selgur
GENERAL MANAGER
Agah Tansev
GENERAL COORDINATOR
Gediz Tetik
V.P., FINANCE
Berent Akdemir

Number of Theatres: 19
Number of Screens: 63
Dr.-Ins: 1
Istanbul, Izmir, Bursa, Denizli, Isparta, Corlu.

CINEMAXX H.J. FLEBBE FILMTHEATERBETRIEBE
Mittelweg 176, 20148 Hanburg. Tel: (49) 40450 680. FAX: (49) 40 450 68201.
PRESIDENT & GENERAL MANAGER
Hans-Joachim Flebbe
GENERAL MANAGER & CFO
Michael Pawlowski
DIRECTOR, MARKETING
Jens Thomsen

Number of Theatres 1 (Turkey)
Number of Screens 5 (Turkey)

UNITED ARAB EMERATES (UAE)

Population: 2.4 million.

EXHIBITOR

THE GREATER UNION ORGANISATION
(Including BIRCH CARROLL & COYLE)
49 Market St., Sydney, NSW 2000, Australia. Tel: (612) 93 73 66 00. FAX: (612) 93 73 65 32.
MANAGING DIRECTOR
Robert Manson

Number of Theatres: 1 (UAE)
Number of Screens: 6 (UAE)

U.S. TERRITORIES

PUERTO RICO

Population: 3.8 million.

EXHIBITORS

REGENCY CARIBBEAN ENTERPRISES, INC.
(d.b.a.: Caribbean Cinemas)
1512 Fernandez Juncos, Stop 22-1/2, Santurce. Tel: (809) 727-7137. FAX: (809) 728-2274.

U.S. VIRGIN ISLANDS

Population: 120 thousand..

EXHIBITORS

CARIBBEAN CINEMAS OF THE VIRGIN ISLANDS, INC.
P.O. Box 9700, St. Thomas 00801. Tel: (809) 775-2244. FAX: (809)
724-2274.
ADMINISTRATOR
Jeff McLaughlin
PRESIDENT, CEO & CFO
Victor Carrady
V.P., COO & FILM BUYER
Robert Carrady
THEATRE OPERATIONS
Joe Ramos
Alfredo Morales
EQUIPMENT BUYER
Joel Matos

WEBSITE GUIDE

EXHIBITION CIRCUITS

Ajay Theatres, LLC	www.moviepage.com
Allen Theatres, Inc.	www.allentheaters.com
AMC Entertainment, Inc.	www.amctheatres.com
AmStar Entertainment	www.amstarcinemas.com
Brenden Theatres	www.brendentheatres.com
Camera Cinemas	www.cameracinemas.com
Carmike Cinemas	www.carmike.com
Century Theatres	www.centurytheatres.com
Campbell Plaza Theatres, Inc.	www.cineluxtheatres.com
Cinema Center	www.cinemacenter.com
Cinemagic Theatres	www.cinemagictheatres.com
Cinemark USA, Inc.	www.cinemark.com
Cinemastar Luxury Theatres, Inc.	www.cinemastar.com
Cinema West Theatres	www.cinemawest.com
City Cinemas	www.city-cinemas.com
Classic Cinemas	www.classiccinemas.com
Clearview Cinema Corp.	www.clearviewcinemas.com
Cleveland Cinemas	www.clevelandcinemas.com
Cobb Theatres	www.cobbtheatres.com
Consolidated Theatres	www.consolidatedmovies.com
Crown Theatres	www.crowntheatres.com
Destinta Theatres	www.destinta.com
Dickinson Theatres, Inc.	www.dtmovies.com
Dipson Theatres, Inc.	www.dipsontheatres.com
Douglas Theatre Co.	www.douglastheatres.com
Eastern Federal Corp.	www.easternfederal.com
Edwards Theatres (Now with Regal Entertainment Group)	www.regalcinemas.com
Entertainment Cinemas	www.entertainmentcinemas.com
Flagship Cinemas	www.flagcinemas.com
Fridley Theatres	www.fridleytheatres.com
Galaxy Theatre Corp.	www.galaxy-movie-theatre.com
Galaxy Theatre LLC	www.galaxytheatres.com
General Cinema Theatres (Now part of AMC Theatres)	www.moviewatcher.com
GKC (George Kerasotes Corp.)	www.gkctheatres.com
Goodrich Quality Theatres, Inc.	www.gqti.com
Greater Huntington Theatre Corp.	www.ourshowtimes.com
Harkins Theatres	www.harkinstheatres.com
Kerasotes Theatres	www.kerasotes.com
Krikorian Premiere Theatres	www.krikoriantheatres.com
Laemmle Theatres	www.laemmle.com
Landmark Theatres	www.landmarktheatres.com
Jack Loeks Theatres	www.bigscreenmovies.com
Loews Cineplex Entertainment Corp.	www.enjoytheshow.com
Logan Theatres	www.loganmovie.com
Malco Theatres, Inc.	www.malco.com
Marcus Theatres Corporation	www.marcustheatres.com
Marquee Cinemas	www.marqueecinemas.com
MegaStar Cinemas	www.megastarcinemas.com
M.E. Theatres	www.metheatres.com
Metropolitan Theatres Corp.	www.metrotheatres.com
The Movie Experience	www.movieexperience.com
Muller Family Theatres	www.mullerfamilytheatres.com
Muvico Theaters	www.muvico.com
National Amusements, Inc.	www.nationalamusements.com
NCG (Neighborhood Cinema Group)	www.ncgmovies.com
Nova Cinetech, Inc.	www.novacinemas.com
O'Neil Theatres, Inc.	www.movie-info.com
The Patriot Cinemas, Inc.	www.patriotcinemas.com
R/C Theatres	www.rctheatres.com
Regal Cinemas, Inc.	www.regalcinemas.com
Reynolds Theatres Entertainment, Inc.	www.reynoldstheatres.com
Ritz Theatre Group	www.ritzfilmbill.com
Rogers Cinema, Inc.	www.rogerscinema.com
Santikos Theatres	www.santikos.com
Signature Theatres	www.signaturetheatres.com
Silver Cinemas, Inc.	http://silver.hollywood.com
Star Cinema	www.starcinema.com
Starnet Cinemas	www.starnetcinemas.com
Starplex Cinemas	www.starplexcinemas.com
Trans-Lux	www.transluxmovies.com
UltraStar Cinemas	www.ultrastarmovies.com
United Artists Theatre Circuit, Inc. (Now with Regal Entertainment Group)	www.regalcinemas.com
Wallace Theatre Corporation	www.wallacetheatres.com
Wehrenberg Theatres, Inc.	www.wehrenberg.com
Westates Theatres	www.westatestheatres.com
W.F. Cinema Holdings (Mann Theatres)	www.manntheatres.com
Wildwood Theatres	www.wildwoodtheatres.com

MOTION PICTURE PRODUCERS & DISTRIBUTORS

Abandon Entertainment ... www.abandonent.com
Ace Storyboard on Demand ... www.markpacella.com
Affinity Films International Ltd. ... www.affinityfilms.com
Alliance Atlantis Communications Inc. ... www.allianceatlantis.com
Amazing Movies ... www.amazingpix.com
AMC Entertainment Inc. ... www.amctheatres.com
American Zoetrope ... www.zoetrope.com
Arrow Entertainment ... www.arrowfeatures.com
Artisan Entertainment ... www.artisanent.com
Artistic License Films ... www.artlic.com
The Artists' Colony ... www.theartisitscolony.com
Avenue Pictures ... www.avepix.com
The Badham Co. ... www.badhamcompany.com
Baltimore/Spring Creek Pictures, LLC ... www.Levinson.com
Benderspink ... www.benderspink.com
Brickman Marketing ... www.brickmanmarketing.com
Jerry Bruckheimer Films ... www.jbfilms.com
Burrud Productions ... www.burrud.com
Castle Rock Entertainment ... www.castle-rock.warnerbros.com
Cecchi Gori Pictures ... www.cecchigori.com
The Cinema Guild ... www.cinemaguild.com
Cinevista, Inc. ... www.cinevistavideo.com
Cine Excel Entertainment ... www.cineexcel.com
Coliseum Pictures Corporation ... www.coliseumpictures.com
CPC Entertainment ... www.cpcentertainment.com
Crown International Pictures, Inc. ... www.crownintlpictures.com
Crystal Pyramid Productions ... www.crystalpyramid.com
Curb Entertainment ... www.curbentertainment.com
Digital Domain ... www.d2.com
The Walt Disney Company ... www.disney.com
Disney Channel ... www.disneychannel.com
Distant Horizon ... www.distant-horizon.com
The Drive-By Film Shooting Company ... www.michaeladdis.com
Eastman Kodak Company ... www.kodak.com
Entertainment Ventures International ... www.smart90.com/evi
First Look Pictures/Overseas Film Group ... www.firstlookmedia.com
First Run Features ... www.firstrunfeatures.com
Fox, Inc. ... www.newscorp.com; www.fox.com
Full Moon Universe ... www.fullmoonpictures.com
Gotham Metro Studios, Inc. ... www.GothamMetro.com
Gotham Pictures ... www.resolutionprod.com
Grainy Pictures ... www.grainypictures.com
Greenestreet Films, Inc. ... www.greenestreetfilms.com
Hargrove Entertainment, Inc. ... www.HargroveTV.com
Jim Henson Pictures ... www.henson.com
Home Box Office, Inc. ... www.hbo.com
IFM World Releasing ... www.ifmfilm.com
Imagine Entertainment ... www.imagine-entertainment.com
International Film Circuit ... www.winstarcinema.com
Italtoons Corp. ... www.italtoons.com
Iwerks Entertainment ... www.iwerks.com
Killer Films, Inc. ... www.killerfilms.com
Kino International Corp. ... www.kino.com
Leisure Time Features ... www.leisurefeat.com
Lions Gate Films Production ... www.lionsgate-ent.com
Liveplanet ... www.liveplanet.com
Longbow Productions, LLC ... www.longbowfilms.com
Lucasarts Entertainment Company ... www.lucasarts.com
Lucas Digital Ltd. ... www.ilm.com
Lucasfilm, Ltd. ... www.lucasfilm.com
Lucid Media ... www.marinocolmano.com
Malibu Bay Films ... www.adnysidaris.com
Manhattan Pictures International ... www.manhattanpics.com
Marvel Characters, Inc. ... www.marvel.com
Matrixx Entertainment ... www.mecfilms.com
Merchant-Ivory ... www.merchantivory.com
Metro-Goldwyn-Mayer ... www.mgm.com
Miramax Films Corp. ... www.miramax.com
Moving Pictures, Ltd. ... www.movingpics.net
MTV Films ... www.mtv.com
Muse Productions, Inc. ... www.musefilm.com
National Geographic ... www.nationalgeographic.com/main.html
National Lampoon ... www.nationallampoon.com
New Cannon, Inc. ... www.newcannoninc.com
New Concorde Corp. ... www.concorde-newhorizons.com
New Line Cinema Corporation ... www.newline.com
New Regency Productions ... www.newregency.com
New Yorker Films ... www.newyorkerfilms.com
Octograph Inc. ... www.octograph.com
Omega Entertainment, Ltd. ... www.omegapic.com
100% Entertainment ... www.100percentent.com
Outlaw Productions ... www.outlawfilm.com
Oxygen Media ... www.oxygen.com
Picture This Entertainment ... www.picturethisent.com
Platinum Studios, LLC ... www.platinumstudios.com
Porchlight Entertainment ... www.porchlight.com

Edward R. Pressman Film Corp. . . . . .www.pressman.com
Rainbow Film Co./Rainbow Releasing . . . . .www.rainbowfilms.com
Redeemable Features . . . . .www.redeemable.com
Regent Entertainment, Inc. . . . . .www.regententertainment.com
Revelations Entertainment . . . . .www.revelationsent.com
RGH/Lions Share Pictures, Inc. . . . . .www.lionsharepictures.com
RKO Pictures . . . . .www.rko.co
Roxie Releasing . . . . .www.roxie.com
Samuelson Productions Limited . . . . .www.oscarwilde.com
Saturn Films . . . . .www.saturnfilms.com
Seventh Art Releasing www.7thart.com
Shonkyte Productions, Inc. . . . . .www.seanyoung.org
Sony Pictures Entertainment, Inc. . . . . .www.spe.sony.com
Strand Releasing/New Oz Productions . . . . .www.strandreleasing.com
Swartwout Enterprises, Inc. . . . . .www.supervue.com
Taurus Entertainment Co. . . . . .www.taurus-entertainment.com
Telling Pictures . . . . .www.tellingpix.com
Bob Thomas Productions, Inc. . . . . .www.bobthomasprods.com
Tribeca Productions . . . . .www.tribecafilm.com
Troma Entertainment, Inc. . . . . .www.troma.com
Vanguard Documentaries . . . . .www.vanguarddocumentaries.com
Viacom, Inc. . . . . .www.viacom.com
View Askew Productions, Inc. . . . . .www.viewaskew.com
Vivendi Universal Entertainment . . . . .www.universalstudios.com
West Glen Communicatons, Inc. . . . . .www.popcornreport.com
Wellspring Media . . . . .www.wellspring.com
Saul Zaentz Film Center . . . . .www.zaentz.com
Zeitgeist Films Ltd. . . . . .www.zeitgeistfilm.com
Zide/Perry Entertainment . . . . .www.inzide.com
Zollo Productions, Inc. . . . . .www.members.aol.com/zpi/index.html

THEATRE EQUIPMENT & SERVICES

2POP www.2pop.com
Ace Communications . . . . .www.aceav.com
Acorto, Inc. . . . . .www.acorto.com
Action Lighting . . . . .www.actionlighting.com
Adaptive Micro Systems . . . . .www.adaptivedisplays.com
Admit One Products . . . . .www.admitoneproducts.com
Advanced Strobe . . . . .www.strobelamps.com
Alcops Incorporated . . . . .www.alcops.com
Allen Products Co., Inc. . . . . .www.allenproducts.com
All-Star Carts and Vehicles, Inc. . . . . .www.allstarcarts.com
Alvarado Manufacturing . . . . .www.alvaradomfg.com
Aly Construction, Inc. . . . . .www.birtcherconst.com
American Cinema Equipment Inc. . . . . .www.cinequip.com
American Concession Supply, Inc. .www.americanconcessionsupply.com
American Seating Company . . . . .www.americanseating.com
AOL Entertainment . . . . .www.mars-tms.com
Arrowstreet, Inc. . . . . .www.arrowstreet.com
Ashly Audio, Inc. . . . . .www.ashley.com
Atlas Specialty Lighting . . . . .www.asltg.com
Audex, Assistive Listening Systems . . . . .www.audex.com
Automatic Bar Controls/Wunder-Bar . . . . .www.wunderbar.com
Automatic Devices Company . . . . .www.automaticdevices.com
Avica Technology Corp. . . . . .www.avicatech.com
AVL Systems, Inc. . . . . .www.avlonline.com
Bagcraft . . . . .www.bagcraft.com
Ballantyne of Omaha/Strong International . . . . .www.ballantyne-omaha.com
Barco Projection Systems America . . . . .www.barco.com
Bass Industries . . . . .www.bassind.com
Beaver Machine Corp. . . . . .www.beavervending.com
Behr Browers Architects Inc. . . . . .www.behrbrowers.com
Benchmark Design Group . . . . .www.benchmark.com
Berry Plastics . . . . .www.berryplastics.com
BGW Systems . . . . .www.bgw.com
Big Sky Industries . . . . .www.bigskyindustries.net
Boston Light & Sound . . . . .www.blsi.com/kinoton
Bradley Fixtures Corp. . . . . .www.bradleycorp.com
Brass Smith, Inc. . . . . .www.brasssmith.com
Brejtfus Theatrical Interiors . . . . .www.brejtfus.com
Braun Brush Company . . . . .www.brush.com
Brintons U.S. Axminster . . . . .www.brintons.net
Bux-Mont Signs . . . . .www.buxmontflagpoles.com
C & A Advertising . . . . .www.onscreenads.com
C. Cretors & Company . . . . .www.cretors.com
Caddy Cupholder . . . . .www.mediatechsrc.com
California Seating & Repair Company, Inc. .www.californiaseating.com
California Stage & Lighting . . . . .www.calstage.com
Camatic Seating . . . . .www.camatic.com
Cardinal Sound & Motion Picture Systems, Inc. . . . . .www.cardinalsound.com
Cardlogix . . . . .www.cardlogix.com
Carrier Corporation . . . . .www.carrier.utc.com
Cawley Company . . . . .www.thecawleycompany.com
Celestial Lighting Products . . . . .www.celestiallighting.com
Cerwin-Vega . . . . .www.cerwin-vega.com
Chart Industries/MVE . . . . .www.chart-inc.com

Christie Digital Systems U.S.A., Inc.	www.christiedigital.com
Cincom–The Megaplex Cinema Specialists	www.cincom.net
Cinema Equipment, Inc.	www.cinemaequip.com
Cinema Lighting Corporation	www.cinemalighting.com
Cinema Products International	www.cinprod.com
Cinema Supply Co.	www.cinemasupply.com
Cinemeccanica U.S., Inc.	www.cinemeccanica-us.com
Cinemedia Systems, LLC	www.cinemediasystems.com
Cinetech, Inc.	www.cinetech.net
Cintas Corporation	www.cintas-corp.com
Claco Equipment And Service, Inc.	www.clacoequipment.com
Classic Industries	www.classicusa.com
Cleannet USA	www.cleannetusa.com
Colgate-Palmolive Company	www.colpalipd.com
Commerical Block Systems	www.commericalblocksystems.com
Community Professional Loudspeakers	www.loudspeakers.net
Component Engineering	www.componentengineering.com
Credit Card Center	www.ccc-atm.com
Crest Audio, Inc.	www.crestaudio.com
Crown Audio, Inc.	www.crownaudio.com
Crown Industries, Inc.	www.gocrown.com
Custom Color Corp.	www.customcolor.com
Cy Young Industries, Inc.	www.cyyoungind.com
Daktronics, Inc.	www.daktronics.com
Data Display U.S.A.	www.data-display.com
Data Quest Investigations, Ltd.	www.dataquestonline.com
David Tyson Lighting, Inc.	www.davidtyson.com
Decoustics Cine-Line	www.decoustics.com
Digital Projection	www.digitalprojection.com
Digital Sparks	www.digitalsparx.com
Digital Theater Systems	www.dtsonline.com
Dillingham Ticket Company	www.dillinghamticket.com
Dimensional Innovations	www.dimin.com
DLP Cinema	www.dlpcinema.com
Dolby Laboratories	www.dolby.com
Dolch Touch Controls, Inc.	www.touchcontrol.com
Duraform	www.duraformcpi.com
Durkan Patterned Carpet	www.durkan.com
EAW, Inc. (Eastern Acoustic Works)	www.eaw.com
ECI–www.Ticketing Systems	www.ticketingsystems.com
Edward H. Wolk Inc.	www.edwolk.com
Eims, Inc.	www.eims-inc.com
EOMAC	www.eomac.com
Eprad, Inc.	www.eprad.com
Fandango	www.fandango.com
Fantasy Entertainment	www.fantasyent.com
Fashion Seal Uniforms	www.superioruniformgroup.com
Fawn Vendors	www.fawnvendors.com
Field Container Co., LP	www.southfieldcarton.com
Figueras International Seating	www.figueras.com
Flavor Wear	www.flavorwear.com
Fryworks	www.fryworks.com
G&S Acoustics (Golterman & SABO), Inc.	www.golterman.com
Gabriella Imports	www.gabimports.com
Gamma Technologies	www.gamma-tech.com
Gemini, Inc.	www.signletters.com
General Theatrical Supply	www.getgts.com
Glassform	www.Glassform.net
Globe Ticket & Label Co.	www.globeticket.com
Gold Medal Products	www.gmpopcorn.com
Goldberg Brothers, Inc.	www.goldbergbrothers.bizhosting.com
Great Western Products Co.	www.theatreequipment.net
Grosh Scenic Rentals, Inc	www.grosh.com
Hafler Professional	www.hafler.com
Hanover Uniform Company	www.hanoveruniform.com
Harkness Hall	www.harknesshall.com
High End Systems, Inc	www.highend.com
High Performance Stereo	www.hps4000.com
Hollywood Software, Inc.	www.hollywoodsoftware.com; www.theatricaldistribution.com; www.rightsmart.com
Hoshizaki North Eastern	www.hoshizak.com
Hurley Screen Corp. /(Cemcorp)	www.hurleyscreen.com
Hussey Seating Company	www.husseyseating.com
Image National	www.imagenational.com
IMI Cornelius Inc.	www.cornelius.com
Indiana Cash Drawer Company	www.icdpos.com
Integrated Food Systems	www.ifs.com
International Cinema Equipment	www.iceco.com
Ira Tec/Pro Audio	www.iratec.50megs.com
Irwin Seating Company	www.irwinseating.com
ISCO-Optic GMBH	www.iscooptic.de
Iwerks Entertainment	www.iwerks.com
Jarco Industries	www.concessionstands.com
JBL Professional	www.jblpro.com
Johnson/McKibben Architects	www.johnsonmckibben.com
JVC Professional	www.jvc.com
Kelmar Systems, Inc.	www.kelmarsystems.com
Kinetics Noise Control	www.kineticsnoise.com

Kinetronics ... www.kinetronics.com
Kinoton America ... www.kinotonamerica.com
Klipsch Audio Technologies ... www.klipsch.com
KMD Architects ... www.kmd-arch.com
Koala Corp. ... www.koalabear.com
Krispy Kist Machine Company (C. Cretors) ... www.cretors.com
Krix ... www.krix.com.au
Lancer Corp., Inc. ... www.lancercorp.com
Lavi Industries ... www.lavi.com
Lawrence Metal Products, Inc. ... www.lawrencemetal.com
Lehigh Electric Products ... www.lehighdim.com
Lennox Industries ... www.davelennox.com
Lighting & Electronic Design (LED) ... www.ledlinc.com
Lino Sonego & C.S.R.L. ... www.linosonego.it
Lowell Manufacturing Co. ... www.lowellmfg.com
Lucasfilm/THX ... www.thx.com
Lutron Electronics ... www.lutron.com
Mackie Designs, Inc. ... www.mackie.com
Mainstreet Menu Systems ... www.mainstreetmenus.com
Manutech Company ... www.manutech.com
Marcel Desrochers, Inc. (MDI) ... www.mdicinema.com
Maroevich, Oshea & Coghlan ... www.maroevich.com
Marquee Technical Services ... www.marqueetech.com
Mars Sequel Theater Management System/AOL Moviefone ... www.mars-tms.com
Martek Contracts, Ltd. ... www.martek.co.uk
Martek CRS, Inc. ... www.martek-us.com
Martin Audio Limited ... www.martin-audio.com
Masland Carpets, Inc. ... www.maslandcarpets.com
Maxpanel (Div. of Brejtfus Enterprises, Inc.) ... www.maxpanel.com
MBI Products ... www.mbiproducts.com
MDC Wallcoverings ... www.mdcwallcoverings.com
Megasystems ... www.megasystem.com
Melded Fabrics, Inc. ... www.meldedfabrics.com
Mesbur & Smith Architects ... www.mesbursmith.com
MHB/Paradigm Design ... www.mhbparadigm.com
Mica Lighting Company, Inc. ... www.micalighting.com
Michaelo Espresso, Inc. ... www.michaelo.com
Microlite Lighting Control ... www.microlite.net
Miller & Kreisel Sound Corp. ... www.mksound.com
Milliken Carpet ... www.millikencarpet.com
Miracle Recreation Equipment Company ... www.miraclerecreation.com
Misco/Minneapolis Speaker Co., Inc. ... www.miscospeakers.com
Modular Hardware ... www.modularhardware.com
Monster Cable Products, Inc. ... www.monstercable.com
Moviead Corp. ... www.moviead.com
Movie Ad Media ... www.movieadmedia.com
MPO Videotronics ... www.mpo-video.com
Multimedia, Inc. ... www.multimedialed.com
Multiplex Company ... www.multiplex-beverage.com
Namco Cybertainment ... www.namcoarcade.com
Nation Glass & Gate Services, Inc. (N.G.&G. Facility Services) ... www.nationalglass.com
National Cinema Network, Inc. ... www.ncninc.com
National Cinema Service ... www.ncservice.com
National Cinema Supply Corporation ... www.ncsco.com
National Ticket Company ... www.nationalticket.com
Nec Solutions ... www.nectech.com
Neumade Products Corp./Xetron Division ... www.Neumade.com
Norcon Communications, Inc. ... www.norcon.org
Novar Controls Corp. ... www.novar.com
Oakview Construction, Inc. ... www.oakviewconst.com
Odyssey Products, Inc. ... www.odyssey-products.com
Omega Pattern Works, Inc./Artisans, Inc. ... www.omegaflooring.com; www.artisanscarpet.com
Omniterm Data Technology Ltd. ... www.omniterm.com
Osram Sylvania, Inc. ... www.sylvania.com
P & O Nedlloyd ... www.ponl.com
Pacer/Cats ... www.pacercats.com
Pacific Concessions, Inc. ... www.pacificconcessions.com
Packaging Concepts ... www.packagingconceptsinc.com
Panasonic ... www.panasonic.com/broadcast
Panastereo, Inc. ... www.panastereo.com
Paskal Lighting ... www.paskal.com
Peavey Architectural Acoustics ... www.peavey.com; aa.peavey.com
Perkin Elmer Optoelectronics ... www.perkinelmer.com
Permlight Theatre Products ... www.Permlight.com
Pescor Plastics ... www.pescor.com
Phonic Ear ... www.phonicear.com
PNC West Inc. ... www.pncwest.com
Poblocki And Sons ... www.poblocki.com
Practical Automation ... www.practicalautomation.com
Premier Chemical Products ... www.premierchemical.com
Premier Southern Ticket Company ... www.premiersouthern.com
Priority Manufacturing, Inc. ... www.customuniforms.com
Pro Star Industries ... www.prostarindustries.com
Proctor Companies ... www.proctorco.com
Protocol ... www.air-serb.com
Quality Installations ... www.qualityinstallations.org
QSC Audio ... www.qscaudio.com

Quinette Gallay . . . . www.quinette.fr
R.S. Engineering & Mfg. . . . . www.rsem.com; www.cinemaparts.com
Radiant Systems, Inc. . . . . www.radiantsystems.com
Ranack Constructors . . . . www.ranack.com
Raxxess . . . . www.raxxess.com
RDS Data Group . . . . www.rdsdata.com
Retriever Software . . . . www.venue-pos.com
Roundup Food Equipment . . . . www.ajantunes.com
Rtas LLC . . . . www.commericalblocksystems.com
S & K Theatrical Draperies . . . . www.sktheatricaldraperies.com
Sani-Serv . . . . www.saniserv.com
Saul Zaentz Film Center, The . . . . www.zaentz.com
Schneider Optics, Inc. . . . . www.schneideroptics.com
Schult Design And Display . . . . www.schult.com
Seating Concepts, LLC . . . . www.seatingconcepts.com
Sennheiser Electronic Corp. . . . . www.sennheiserusa.com
Sensible Cinema Software . . . . www.sensiblecinema.com
Server Products, Inc. . . . . www.serverproducts.com
Smart Devices, Inc. . . . . www.smartdev.com
Smart Products . . . . www.smartproducts.com
Sony Cinema Products Corporation . . . . www.sdds.com
Sound Associates, Inc. . . . . www.soundassociates.com
Sound Related Technologies . . . . www.soundrelatedtech.com
Soundcraft USA . . . . www.soundcraft.com
Soundfold . . . . www.soundfold.com
Source One . . . . www.source-one-now.com
Special Optics . . . . www.specialoptics.com
Spectra Cine, Inc. . . . . www.spectracine.com
Stadium Savers, Ltd. . . . . www.stadiumsavers.com
Stadium Seating Enterprises/Andrew L. Youngquist Construction . . . . www.alyconstruction.com
Stage Accompany USA . . . . www.StageAccompany.com
Star Manufacturing International . . . . www.star-mfg.com
Stewart Filmscreen Corp. . . . . www.stewartfilm.com
Strong International . . . . www.strong-cinema.com; www.ballantyne-omaha.com
Sunnywell Display Systems . . . . www.sunnywell.com
Superior Quartz Products, Inc. . . . . www.sqpuv.com
System Operating Solutions, Inc. . . . . www.sosticketing.com
Targetti North America . . . . www.tivolilighting.com
Taylor Company . . . . www.taylor-company.com
Technicolor Digital Services . . . . www.technicolordigital.com
Techni-Brite, Inc. . . . . www.techni-brite.com
Technology International . . . . www.techintl.com
Telex Communication, Inc. . . . . www.electrovoice.com
Tempo Industries, Inc. . . . . www.tempoindustries.com
Theatre Services Intl. . . . . www.theatre-services.com
Theatre Support Services, Inc. . . . . www.theatresupport.com
THX . . . . www.thx.com
Ticket.International . . . . www.ticket-international.com
Ticketing Systems.Com . . . . www.ticketingsystems.com
Ticketpro Systems . . . . www.ticketpro.org
TK Architects . . . . www.tkarch.com
Trans-Lux Corp. . . . . www.trans-lux.com
Tri State Theatre Supply Co. . . . . www.tristatetheatre.com
Triangle Scenery Drapery & Lighting . . . . www.tridrape.com
Trimotion . . . . www.trimotion.com
Troy Sound Wall Systems . . . . www.troysoundwalls.com
Tube Lighting Products . . . . www.tubelightingproducts.com
Turbochef Technologies . . . . www.turbochef.com
Ultra Stereo Labs . . . . www.uslinc.com
Uniforms To You . . . . www.uty.com
United Receptacle, Inc. . . . . www.unitedrecept.com
Universal Seating/Bass Industries . . . . www.bassind.com
Vantage Lighting, Inc. . . . . www.vanltg.com
VCS Timeless . . . . www.vcstimeless.com
Vista Manufacturing, Inc. . . . . www.vistamfg.com
Visteon . . . . www.visteon.com
Wagner Zip Change, Inc. . . . . www.wagnerzip.com
Weldon, Williams & Lick, Inc. . . . . www.wwlinc.com
Wesnic (Sales Representatives For Hines III) . . . . www.wesnic.com
Whisper Walls . . . . www.whisperwalls.com
Williams Sound Corp. . . . . www.williamssound.com
Wing Enterprises . . . . www.ladders.com
Winpak Technologies, Inc. . . . . www.winpak.com
Winters Theatre Cleaning . . . . www.theatrecleaning.com
Wolfe Merchandising . . . . www.wolfe-intl.com
Worldwide Safe & Vault . . . . www.worldwidesafe.com
WPH Architecture . . . . www.wphinc.com
Wulf Installations . . . . www.wulfinstallations.com
Xenonbulbs.Com . . . . www.XenonBulbs.Com

ALPHABETICAL INDEX OF SUBJECTS

This index lists selected companies, agencies and organizations from major sections of the book. If the company you are looking for is not in the index, please find the company in alphabetical order within the relevant section.

C

D

E

M

N

O

P

U

X

Y

Z